CDX Learning Systems™

FUNDAMENTALS OF

Medium/Heavy Duty Commercial Vehicle Systems SECOND EDITION

Gus Wright
Professor, Centennial College

Owen C. Duffy

JONES & BARTLETT
LEARNING

World Headquarters
Jones & Bartlett Learning
25 Mall Road
Burlington, MA 01803
978-443-5000
info@jblearning.com
www.jblearning.com

Jones & Bartlett Learning books and products are available through most bookstores and online booksellers. To contact Jones & Bartlett Learning directly, call 800–832-0034, fax 978–443-8000, or visit our website, www.jblearning.com.

Substantial discounts on bulk quantities of Jones & Bartlett Learning publications are available to corporations, professional associations, and other qualified organizations. For details and specific discount information, contact the special sales department at Jones & Bartlett Learning via the above contact information or send an email to specialsales@jblearning.com.

Production Credits

General Manager: Kimberly Brophy
VP, Product Development: Christine Emerton
Product Manager: Chris Benson
Senior Managing Editor: Donna Gridley
Senior Content Development Editor: Amanda Brandt
Project Manager: Kristen Rogers
Project Specialist: Brooke Haley
Digital Project Specialist: Angela Dooley
Marketing Manager: Amanda Banner

Manufacturing and Inventory Control Supervisor: Amy Bacus
Composition: Integra Software Services Pvt. Ltd.
Project Management: Integra Software Services Pvt. Ltd.
Cover Design: Scott Moden
Text Design: Integra Software Services Pvt. Ltd.
Cover Image: © Tetra images RF/Getty Images
Printing and Binding: LSC Communications
Cover Printing: LSC Communications

Library of Congress Cataloging-in-Publication Data unavailable at time of printing.

6048

Printed in the United States of America
25 24 23 22 21   10 9 8 7 6 5 4 3

BRIEF CONTENTS

SECTION 1   Foundation and Safety 3

CHAPTER 1   Introduction to Heavy-Duty Commercial Vehicles 4
CHAPTER 2   Careers, Employability Skills, and Workplace Practices 29
CHAPTER 3   Safety, Personal Protective Equipment, and First Aid 54
CHAPTER 4   Tools and Fasteners 93
CHAPTER 5   Hand Tools 115
CHAPTER 6   Lifting and Hoisting Equipment 136
CHAPTER 7   Bearings, Lubricants, and Seals 159

SECTION 2   Electrical and Electronic Systems 189

CHAPTER 8   Principles of Electricity 191
CHAPTER 9   Generating Electricity 212
CHAPTER 10   Basic Electrical Circuits 230
CHAPTER 11   Circuit Control Devices 251
CHAPTER 12   Semiconductor Devices and Digital Electronics 274
CHAPTER 13   Electrical Test Equipment 299
CHAPTER 14   Commercial Vehicle Batteries 318
CHAPTER 15   Advanced Battery Technologies 337
CHAPTER 16   Servicing Commercial Vehicle Batteries 355
CHAPTER 17   Heavy-Duty Starting Systems and Circuits 376
CHAPTER 18   Charging Systems and Service 409
CHAPTER 19   Electrical Wiring and Circuit Diagrams 449
CHAPTER 20   Body Electrical Systems—Lighting Systems 474
CHAPTER 21   Body Electrical Systems—Instrumentation 493
CHAPTER 22   Body Electrical Systems—Accessory Electrical Circuits and Systems 512
CHAPTER 23   Principles of Electronic Signal Processing 533
CHAPTER 24   Sensors and Input Circuit Devices 556
CHAPTER 25   Understanding and Servicing Electronic Control Systems 595
CHAPTER 26   Onboard Vehicle Networks and Electronic Service Tools 639

SECTION 3   Suspension, Steering, and Brakes 675

CHAPTER 27   Commercial Vehicle Tires 676
CHAPTER 28   Wheel Rims and Hubs 716
CHAPTER 29   Front Axles and Vehicle Alignment Factors 744
CHAPTER 30   Truck Frames 771
CHAPTER 31   Suspension Systems 795
CHAPTER 32   Steering Systems and Integral Steering Gears 832
CHAPTER 33   Braking Fundamentals and Air Brake Foundations 867

CHAPTER 34   Air Brake Circuits and Valves 907
CHAPTER 35   Servicing Air Brake Air Systems 952
CHAPTER 36   Servicing Air Brake Foundation and Parking Brake Systems 977
CHAPTER 37   Antilock Braking, Vehicle Stability, and Collision Avoidance Systems 1012
CHAPTER 38   Fundamentals of Hydraulic and Air-Over-Hydraulic Braking Systems . . . 1046
CHAPTER 39   Fifth Wheels and Hitching Devices 1100

SECTION 4   Drivetrains 1133
CHAPTER 40   Heavy-Duty Clutches 1135
CHAPTER 41   Servicing Heavy-Duty Clutches 1163
CHAPTER 42   Basic Gearing Concepts 1188
CHAPTER 43   Standard Transmissions 1202
CHAPTER 44   Servicing Standard Transmissions 1244
CHAPTER 45   Automated Manual Transmissions 1274
CHAPTER 46   Torque Converters 1314
CHAPTER 47   Planetary Gear Concepts 1338
CHAPTER 48   Hydraulically Controlled Automatic Transmissions 1355
CHAPTER 49   Electronically Controlled Automatic Transmissions 1379
CHAPTER 50   Maintaining Automatic Transmissions 1453
CHAPTER 51   Heavy-Duty Drive Shaft Systems 1471
CHAPTER 52   Heavy-Duty Drive Axles 1503
CHAPTER 53   Servicing and Maintaining Drive Axles 1534
CHAPTER 54   Electric Drive Vehicles and AC Traction Motors 1563
CHAPTER 55   Autonomous Driving and Advanced Driver Assistance Systems for
              Commercial Vehicles 1600
CHAPTER 56   Hybrid Drive Systems and Series-Type Hybrid Drives 1621
CHAPTER 57   Allison EV Drive and Series-Parallel Hybrid Systems 1643

SECTION 5   Heating, Ventilation, and Air Conditioning 1661
CHAPTER 58   Principles of Heating and Air Conditioning Systems 1662
CHAPTER 59   Servicing Heating and Air Conditioning Systems 1700
CHAPTER 60   Trailer Refrigeration 1731

SECTION 6   Hydraulics 1753
CHAPTER 61   Principles of Hydraulic Systems 1754

SECTION 7   Preventative Maintenance and Inspection 1801
CHAPTER 62   Developing a PM Inspection System 1802

Appendix A   2018 ASE Medium/Heavy Truck Master Service Technology (MTST)
              Task List Correlation Guide 1838

              Glossary 1850

              Index 1884

CONTENTS

SECTION I   Foundation and Safety

CHAPTER 1 Introduction to Heavy-Duty
Commercial Vehicles. 4
Introduction. 5
Classification by Operating Environment 5
Vocational Applications of Commercial Vehicles 6
Design Factors for Vocational Applications 11
Powertrains 13
Cabs. 15
Suspensions 16
Classification of Heavy Vehicles by Weight
    and Length 17
Classification of Heavy Vehicles by Combination . . .20
Hitching Devices 21
Common Terms and Conventions. 22
Ready for Review. 26
Key Terms. 26
Review Questions 27
ASE Technician A/Technician B Style Questions 27

CHAPTER 2 Careers, Employability Skills,
and Workplace Practices 29
Introduction. 30
Careers in the Commercial Vehicle Industry. 30
Workplace Habits and Employability Skills 33
Legal Requirements of Repair Facilities. 42
Vehicle Identification Labels. 43
Service Information Resources 45
Ready for Review. 50
Key Terms. 51
Review Questions 51
ASE Technician A/Technician B Style Questions 52

CHAPTER 3 Safety, Personal Protective
Equipment, and First Aid 54
Introduction. 55
Safety Overview. 55
Legal Requirements in the Workplace. 57
Safety and Emergency Procedures in the
    Workplace 58
Personal Protective Equipment 63
Fire Suppression Systems 69
Legal Responsibilities of Hazardous Materials. 73

Principles of First Aid. .86
Ready for Review. 90
Key Terms. 90
Review Questions 91
ASE Technician A/Technician B Style Questions 92

CHAPTER 4 Tools and Fasteners. 93
Introduction. 94
Threaded Fasteners. 94
Threaded Fastener Specifications 97
Mechanical Strength. 99
Threaded Nuts. 102
Tightening Fasteners 103
Self-Locking Hardware. 105
Thread Repair 107
Ready for Review. 111
Key Terms. 112
Review Questions 112
ASE Technician A/Technician B Style Questions . . .113

CHAPTER 5 Hand Tools 115
Introduction. 116
Tool Storage. 116
Wrenches 117
Sockets and Ratchets. 120
Torque Wrenches 123
Screwdrivers 124
Types of Pliers 125
Metal Cutting. 128
Hammers 129
Pullers 130
Measuring Tools 131
Impact Wrenches. 132
Ready for Review. 133
Key Terms. 134
Review Questions 134
ASE Technician A/Technician B Style Questions . . .134

CHAPTER 6 Lifting and Hoisting Equipment. . 136
Introduction. 137
Proper Manual Lifting Techniques 137
Lifting in the Shop 139
Vehicle Hoists 142
Selecting Appropriate Hoisting Equipment 144

Wire Rope Application and Use 152
Ready for Review. 156
Key Terms. 156
Review Questions 157
ASE Technician A/Technician B Style Questions . . .157

CHAPTER 7 Bearings, Lubricants,
and Seals **159**
Introduction. 160
Bearing Functions 160
Classification of Bearings. 162
Antifriction Bearings 163
Bearing Fit 166
Bearing Maintenance 169
Functions of Seals 174
Radial Lip Seal Construction 177
Gaskets and Sealants 181
Gasket Installation Guidelines 183
Seal Service and Maintenance 184
Ready for Review. 185
Key Terms. 186
Review Questions 186
ASE Technician A/Technician B Style Questions . . .187

SECTION 2   Electrical and Electronic
Systems

CHAPTER 8 Principles of Electricity. 191
Introduction. 192
Trends and Market Forces Influencing Design. 192
Understanding the Behavior of Electricity. 194
Basic Electricity 197
Understanding Electrical Current 199
Electrical Versus Electronic Circuits 208
Ready for Review. 208
Key Terms. 209
Review Questions 209
ASE Technician A/Technician B Style Questions . . .210

CHAPTER 9 Generating Electricity 212
Introduction. 213
Sources of Electricity. 213
Electricity from Magnetism 216
Electrochemisty—Electricity from
Chemistry. 225
Ready for Review. 226
Key Terms. 227
Review Questions 227
ASE Technician A/Technician B Style Questions . . .228

CHAPTER 10 Basic Electrical Circuits 230
Introduction. 231
Current Flow in Circuits .231
Ohm's Law and Power. 235
Circuit Malfunctions. 239
Circuit Protection Devices 242
Inspecting and Testing Circuit Protection Devices. . .246
Ready for Review. 248
Key Terms. 248
Review Questions 249
ASE Technician A/Technician B Style Questions . . .249

CHAPTER 11 Circuit Control Devices 251
Introduction. 252
Switches. 252
Automatic Type Switches. 255
Smart Switches 258
Resistors 260
Electromechanical Relays. 262
Solenoids 265
Servicing Circuit Control Devices. 267
Ready for Review. 271
Key Terms. 272
Review Questions 272
ASE Technician A/Technician B Style Questions . . .272

CHAPTER 12 Semiconductor Devices
and Digital Electronics **274**
Introduction. 275
Differences Between Electrical and Electronic
Devices. 275
What Are Semiconductors?. 275
Diodes 276
Bipolar Junction Transistors. 284
Field Effect Semiconductors: Unipolar
Semiconductors 287
Metal Oxide Semiconductor Field Effect
Transistors (MOSFETs) 290
Integrated Circuits (IC) 291
Capacitors 293
Ready for Review. 296
Key Terms. 296
Review Questions 297
ASE Technician A/Technician B Style Questions . . .298

CHAPTER 13 Electrical Test Equipment. . . . 299
Introduction. 300
Test Lights 300
Multimeters 302

Electrical Measurement with Multimeters. 304
Circuit Tracers 312
Graphing Meters and Oscilloscopes 312
Vibration Analyzers 313
Electronic Service Tools—Scanners. 314
Ready for Review. 315
Key Terms. 316
Review Questions 316
ASE Technician A/Technician B Style Questions . . .317

CHAPTER 14 Commercial Vehicle
  Batteries 318
Introduction. 319
Battery Operation and Functions 320
Types and Classification of Batteries. 322
Battery Construction and Operation 323
Battery Ratings. 328
Low- and No-Maintenance Batteries 332
Ready for Review. 334
Key Terms. 334
Review Questions 335
ASE Technician A/Technician B Style Questions . . .335

CHAPTER 15 Advanced Battery
  Technologies 337
Introduction. 338
Nickel–Metal Hydride Battery (NiMH). 338
Lithium-Ion Battery Applications. 339
Valve-Regulated Lead-Acid Batteries (VRLA) 343
Ultra-Capacitors 346
Battery-Management Systems 347
Hybrid Battery-Management Systems. 350
Ready for Review. 352
Key Terms. 353
Review Questions 353
ASE Technician A/Technician B Style Questions . . .354

CHAPTER 16 Servicing Commercial
  Vehicle Batteries .355
Introduction. 356
Battery Service Precautions 357
Causes of Battery Failure. 357
Battery Inspection, Testing, and Maintenance. 360
Charging Batteries. 366
Measuring Parasitic Draw 369
Ready for Review. 372
Key Terms. 373
Review Questions 373
ASE Technician A/Technician B Style Questions . . .374

CHAPTER 17 Heavy-Duty Starting
  Systems and Circuits. 376
Introduction. 377
Fundamentals of Starting Systems and Circuits. . .377
DC Motor Principles 379
Series Motors 381
Components of Starters .384
Starter Control Circuits .390
Starting System Testing .394
Repairing a Starter Motor 404
Ready for Review. 406
Key Terms. 406
Review Questions 406
ASE Technician A/Technician B Style Questions . . .407

CHAPTER 18 Charging Systems and
  Service 409
Introduction. 410
Overview of Charging System Construction and
    Features 412
Principles of Alternating Current Generation. 415
Alternator Components .417
Voltage Regulation 427
Charging System Service 434
Removing, Inspecting, and Replacing an
    Alternator 442
Ready for Review. 445
Key Terms. 446
Review Questions 446
ASE Technician A/Technician B Style Questions . . .447

CHAPTER 19 Electrical Wiring and Circuit
  Diagrams 449
Introduction. 450
Electrical System Wiring .450
Wiring Connectors 454
Wiring Failure and Repair 459
Wiring Diagrams 460
Ready for Review. 471
Key Terms. 472
Review Questions 472
ASE Technician A/Technician B Style Questions . . .472

CHAPTER 20 Body Electrical Systems—
  Lighting Systems. .474
Introduction. 475
Fundamentals of the Body Electrical System. 475
Lighting Systems. 476
Lighting Technologies 476

Trailer Cords and Plugs 485
Ready for Review. 490
Key Terms. 490
Review Questions 490
ASE Technician A/Technician B Style Questions . . .491

**CHAPTER 21 Body Electrical Systems—
Instrumentation** **493**
Introduction. 494
Warning Lights. 494
Gauge Operating Systems 495
Sending Units. 500
Speedometers 504
Driver Information Screens. 505
Troubleshooting Instrument Gauge Problems 507
Ready for Review. 509
Key Terms. 509
Review Questions 509
ASE Technician A/Technician B Style Questions . . .510

**CHAPTER 22   Body Electrical Systems—
Accessory Electrical Circuits and Systems. . . 512**
Introduction. 513
Connecting and Programming Electrical
    Accessories 513
Windshield Wiper and Cleaning Systems 515
Power Windows. 521
Power Door Locks 524
Mirrors. 526
Ready for Review. 529
Key Terms. 530
Review Questions 530
ASE Technician A/Technician B Style Questions . . .531

**CHAPTER 23   Principles of Electronic
Signal Processing.** **533**
Introduction. 534
Benefits of Electronic Signal Processing 534
Elements of Electronic Signal Processing
    Systems. 537
Classification of Electrical Signals 538
Serial Data 542
Pulse Width Modulation 543
Ladder Logic 546
Radio Signals 549
Electromagnetic Interference (EMI). 550
Ready for Review. 552
Key Terms. 553

Review Questions 553
ASE Technician A/Technician B Style Questions . . .554

**CHAPTER 24 Sensors and Input Circuit
Devices.** **556**
Introduction. 557
Applications of Sensor's Technology 557
Switches as Sensors. .558
Resistive Sensors 561
Pressure Sensors 569
Voltage Generating Sensors. 571
Mass Airflow Sensors. 574
Exhaust Gas Sensors .576
Diesel Exhaust Fluid (DEF) Sensors. 580
Sensor Fault Detection Principles 580
Pinpoint Testing of Sensors 588
Ready for Review. 591
Key Terms. 592
Review Questions 593
ASE Technician A/Technician B Style Questions . . .593

**CHAPTER 25 Understanding and Servicing
Electronic Control Systems** **595**
Introduction. 596
Electronic Control Systems. 597
Areas of Electronic Control 604
Principles of Electronic Control Loops 606
Multiple-Input Multiple-Output (MIMO)
    Control Systems. .612
Principles of Model Predictive Control 615
Construction and Operation of
    Microcontrollers .623
Microcontroller Functions. 625
Microcontroller Versus Microprocessor
    Architecture. 628
Field Replacement and Programming of
    Electronic Control Units (ECUs). 632
Ready for Review. 634
Key Terms. 636
Review Questions 637
ASE Technician A/Technician B Style Questions . . .637

**CHAPTER 26 Onboard Vehicle
Networks and Electronic Service Tools** **639**
Introduction. 640
Early Network Concept 642
Network Electrical System Control Advantages. . .643
Network Construction 648

Controlled Area Networks (CANs) 653
Unified Diagnostic Service (UDS) 660
Common Data Bus Problems 661
Freightliner Smartplex Network Overview 662
Navistar's Diamond Logic Electrical System 666
Wireless Network Communication 667
Power Line Carrier (PLC) Communication
     SAE J2497 669
Electronic Service Tool 669
Ready for Review 670
Key Terms 671
Review Questions 671
ASE Technician A/Technician B Style Questions . . .672

SECTION 3   Suspension, Steering, and Brakes

CHAPTER 27 Commercial Vehicle Tires 676
Introduction 677
Fundamentals of Commercial Vehicle Tires 677
Tire Service Safety 679
Classifications of Commercial Vehicle Tires 680
Tire Identification and Sizing 682
Construction of Commercial Vehicle Tires 686
Tire Inflation Factors 693
Tire Pressure Monitoring Systems 696
Maintenance and Service of Commercial Tires 701
Inspecting the Wheel Assembly for Air Loss 710
Ready for Review 712
Key Terms 712
Review Questions 713
ASE Technician A/Technician B Style Questions . . .714

CHAPTER 28 Wheel Rims and Hubs 716
Introduction 717
Fundamentals of Wheels and Rims 717
Wheel Types 717
Wheel Dimensions 719
Hub and Stud Piloted Disc Wheels 721
Hub Piloted Wheel Retention 723
Wheel Nut Torque Versus Clamping Force 726
Wheel Service 728
Hub System Fundamentals 731
Standard Hubs 733
Preset Hubs 735
Cast Spoke Hubs 737
Hub Seals and Lubricant .738
Ready for Review 740

Key Terms 741
Review Questions 742
ASE Technician A/Technician B Style Questions . . .742

**CHAPTER 29 Front Axles and Vehicle
Alignment Factors 744**
Introduction 745
Types and Functions of Non-Drive Axles 745
Lift, Tag, and Pusher Axles 750
Fundamentals of Vehicle Alignment 750
Toe 756
King Pin and Steering Axis Inclination Angles 757
Basic Steering Geometry .758
Types of Wheel Alignment 760
Performing Vehicle Alignments: In-Service
     Wheel Alignment 761
Front Axle Inspection 765
Ready for Review 767
Key Terms 767
Review Questions 768
ASE Technician A/Technician B Style Questions . . .769

CHAPTER 30 Truck Frames 771
Introduction 772
Fundamentals of Frame Design 772
Construction of Frames 776
Frame-Supported Attachments 779
Inspection, Service, and Maintenance of
     Truck Frames 782
Frame Alignment 784
Welding Frames 787
Ready for Review 791
Key Terms 792
Review Questions 793
ASE Technician A/Technician B Style Questions . . .793

CHAPTER 31 Suspension Systems 795
Introduction 796
Fundamentals of Suspension Systems 796
Components of a Suspension System 799
Leaf-Spring Systems 802
Equalizing Beam Suspensions 808
Air-Spring Suspension Systems 811
Electronically Controlled Air-Suspension
     Systems 815
Suspension System Inspection and
     Maintenance 817
Ready for Review 827

Key Terms.................................829
Review Questions 830
ASE Technician A/Technician B Style Questions . . .831

CHAPTER 32 Steering Systems and Integral Steering Gears 832
Introduction...............................833
Fundamentals of Steering Systems.............833
Steering System Classifications 833
Components of Basic Steering Systems 835
Steering Gears.............................838
Power Recirculating-Ball Steering Gears........840
Rack-and-Pinion Steering....................844
Steering Linkage...........................845
Hydraulic Components of Power Steering
    Systems..............................848
Maintenance and Service of the Steering
    System 854
Maintenance and Service of the Hydraulic
    System 857
Ready for Review...........................862
Key Terms.................................863
Review Questions 864
ASE Technician A/Technician B Style Questions . . .865

CHAPTER 33 Braking Fundamentals and Air Brake Foundations............. 867
Introduction...............................868
How Brakes Work..........................868
Types of Braking Systems....................873
Air Brake Foundation Systems 875
Cam Brake System Operation.................876
Brake Fade...............................883
Brake Torque and Balance 886
Brake Drums 886
Brake Chambers and Actuators...............888
Slack Adjusters............................894
Air Disc Brakes (ADB) 900
Wedge Brakes 903
Ready for Review...........................904
Key Terms.................................904
Review Questions 905
ASE Technician A/Technician B Style Questions . . .906

CHAPTER 34 Air Brake Circuits and Valves.................................. 907
Introduction...............................908
Advantages of Air Systems...................908

Air Brake Subsystems and Control Circuits 909
Components of the Air Supply System 911
Components of Air Delivery and Control
    Systems...............................926
Pneumatic Brake Balance....................934
Park/Emergency Brake Circuit................939
Trailer Air Circuits.........................943
Ready for Review...........................947
Key Terms.................................948
Review Questions 949
ASE Technician A/Technician Style Questions 950

CHAPTER 35 Servicing Air Brake Air Systems 952
Introduction...............................953
Safety During Brake System Service...........953
Diagnosing Brake System Malfunctions.........955
Troubleshooting Air Braking Problems 956
Conducting Preliminary Inspections on
    Brake Systems 956
Testing the Automatic Emergency Brake System. . .963
Conducting Advanced Brake Balance Testing 964
Servicing the Air Supply System Components 969
Ready for Review...........................974
Key Terms.................................975
Review Questions 975
ASE Technician A/Technician B Style Questions . . .976

CHAPTER 36 Servicing Air Brake Foundation and Parking Brake Systems 977
Introduction...............................978
Vehicle Preparation and Safety During Brake
    System Service 978
Preliminary Brake Inspection.................978
Inspecting and Adjusting Air Brakes............979
Testing Parking Brake Function 984
Brake Drum Service 986
Brake Shoe Service 989
Camshafts 994
Slack Adjuster Inspection and Maintenance.......996
Servicing Air Disc Brakes....................1000
Inspecting and Measuring Brake Pad-Rotor
    Running Clearance......................1005
Disc Brake Pad Replacement.................1007
Ready for Review..........................1009
Key Terms................................1009
Review Questions 1009
ASE Technician A/Technician B Style Questions . .1010

CHAPTER 37 Antilock Braking, Vehicle Stability, and Collision Avoidance Systems . . 1012
Introduction. 1013
Fundamentals of Antilock Braking Systems 1014
Antilock Braking System Requirements 1016
Antilock Braking System Components 1018
ABS Configurations 1029
Vehicle Dynamic Control Systems. 1031
Rollover Stability Control (RSC). 1034
Directional Stability Control (DSC) 1036
Collision Avoidance Systems 1037
Maintenance and Service Procedures 1040
Ready for Review. 1042
Key Terms. 1043
Review Questions 1044
ASE Technician A/Technician B Style Questions. . .1044

CHAPTER 38 Fundamentals of Hydraulic and Air-Over-Hydraulic Braking Systems 1046
Introduction. 1047
Features and Advantages of Hydraulic Power Brakes. 1047
Hydraulic Braking System Configurations. 1048
Brake-by-Wire Braking Systems 1053
Conventional Hydraulic Braking Systems 1055
Hydraulic Brake Fluid. 1058
Foundation Components of Hydraulic Braking Systems. 1061
Wheel Cylinders 1065
Advantages of Disc Brakes 1069
Hydraulic Brake Power Assist Systems 1076
Hydraulic Brake Antilock Braking System (HABS) 1082
Full Power Hydraulic Brake System. 1087
Parking Brake and Emergency Braking Systems . .1092
Hydraulic Brake System Inspection. 1094
Ready for Review. 1097
Key Terms. 1097
Review Questions 1098
ASE Technician A/Technician B Style Questions. . .1099

CHAPTER 39 Fifth Wheels and Hitching Devices. 1100
Introduction. 1101
Common Configurations for Combination Vehicles. 1101
Vehicle Weight Ratings and Capacity. 1106
Types of Fifth Wheels and Coupling Devices. 1107

Fifth Wheels are Plate-Type Coupling Devices . . .1110
Fifth Wheel Ratings and Capacity 1112
Construction of Fifth Wheels 1114
Mounting Fifth Wheels. 1116
Troubleshooting Fifth Wheel Locking Complaints. 1119
Maintenance and Service of Fifth Wheels and Upper Couplers 1119
Landing Gear 1126
Ready for Review. 1127
Key Terms. 1128
Review Question 1129
ASE Technician A/Technician B Style Questions. . .1129

SECTION 4   Drivetrains

CHAPTER 40 Heavy-Duty Clutches 1135
Introduction. 1136
Fundamentals of Heavy-Duty Clutches. 1136
Types and Design of Clutches 1139
Components of Clutches 1144
Clutch Brakes. 1152
Clutch Actuation Systems 1154
Ready for Review. 1159
Key Terms. 1159
Review Questions 1160
ASE Technician A/Technician B Style Questions. . .1161

CHAPTER 41 Servicing Heavy-Duty Clutches. 1163
Introduction. 1164
Preventative Maintenance of Clutches 1164
Troubleshooting Clutch Problems. 1171
Clutch Repair and Replacement Procedures. 1173
Component Inspection with Clutch Removed . . .1176
Clutch Installation Procedures 1179
Self-Adjusting Clutch Repair and Replacement. . .1183
Ready for Review. 1184
Key Terms. 1185
Review Questions 1186
ASE Technician A/Technician B Style Questions. . .1186

CHAPTER 42 Basic Gearing Concepts 1188
Introduction. 1189
Fundamentals of Gears .1189
Gear Ratio Calculations. 1192
Types of Gears. 1196
Ready for Review. 1198

Key Terms.................................1199
Review Questions 1200
ASE Technician A/Technician B Style Questions. . .1200

CHAPTER 43 Standard Transmissions 1202
Introduction...............................1203
Fundamentals of Transmissions..............1203
Types of Sliding-Gear and Constant-Mesh
    Transmissions..........................1207
Single-Countershaft Transmission Operation
    and Power Flows 1211
Multiple Countershaft Transmissions..........1217
Auxiliary Sections 1220
Auxiliary Section Air Control 1231
FR Model Transmission Shift Controls.........1236
Transfer Cases and Power Take Offs 1238
Ready for Review...........................1240
Key Terms.................................1241
Review Questions 1242
ASE Technician A/Technician B Style Questions. . .1243

CHAPTER 44 Servicing Standard
Transmissions 1244
Introduction...............................1245
Fundamentals of Standard Transmission
    Lubrication............................1245
Preventative Maintenance of Transmissions 1248
Troubleshooting Common Transmission
    System Problems 1249
Diagnose and Repair Air Shift System Problems ..1255
Common Transmission Inspection Procedures...1258
Common Repair Procedures for Standard
    Transmissions..........................1259
Analysis of Transmission Failure 1270
Ready for Review...........................1271
Key Terms.................................1271
Review Questions 1272
ASE Technician A/Technician B Style Questions. . .1272

CHAPTER 45 Automated Manual
Transmissions 1274
Introduction...............................1275
Benefits of Automated Transmissions 1275
Operation of Automated Manual
    Transmissions..........................1279
Eaton Procision Dual-Clutch Automated
    Transmission...........................1288
Three Module Transmissions.................1296

Troubleshooting Automated Manual
    Transmissions..........................1306
Ready for Review...........................1310
Key Terms.................................1311
Review Questions 1312
ASE Technician A/Technician B Style Questions. . .1312

CHAPTER 46 Torque Converters 1314
Introduction...............................1315
Functions of Torque Converters..............1315
Components of Torque Converters 1316
Operation of Torque Converters 1318
Torque Converter Hydraulic Circuits.........1324
Troubleshooting Torque Converter
    Failure................................1326
Servicing Torque Converters................1331
Ready for Review...........................1334
Key Terms.................................1335
Review Questions 1335
ASE Technician A/Technician B Style Questions. . .1336

CHAPTER 47 Planetary Gear Concepts. . . 1338
Introduction...............................1339
Fundamentals of Planetary Gearing............1339
Planetary Gear Power Flows.................1340
Ratio Calculations for Planetary Gears.........1343
Powertrain Control Devices 1344
Compound Planetary Gear Set
    Combinations...........................1346
Ready for Review...........................1351
Key Terms.................................1352
Review Questions 1353
ASE Technician A/Technician B Style Questions. . .1353

CHAPTER 48 Hydraulically Controlled
Automatic Transmissions 1355
Introduction...............................1356
The History of Transmissions in the North
    American Truck and Coach Market..........1356
Components of Allison Hydraulically Controlled
    Automatic Transmissions 1356
Allison Transmission Power Flows............1358
Allison Transmission Hydraulic Control
    System Components 1363
Operation of Allison Hydraulically Controlled
    Automatic Transmissions 1372
Ready for Review...........................1375
Key Terms.................................1376

Review Questions 1377
ASE Technician A/Technician B Style Questions. . .1377

CHAPTER 49 Electronically Controlled
Automatic Transmissions 1379
Introduction. 1380
Basics of Electronic Control—Allison
    Transmission Electronic Control (ATEC)
    and Commercial Electronic Control (CEC) . . .1380
World Transmission 1393
Electrohydraulic Control—WTEC II and
    WTEC III 1401
Allison Fourth- and Fifth Generation
    Electrohydraulic Control Valve Body 1416
TC-10-TS. 1430
Voith DIWA Transmissions 1440
ZF Friedrichshafen AG EcoMat and EcoLife
    Transmissions. 1447
Ready for Review. 1449
Key Terms. 1450
Review Questions 1451
ASE Technician A/Technician B Style Questions. . .1452

CHAPTER 50 Maintaining Automatic
Transmissions 1453
Introduction. 1454
Fundamentals of Transmission Fluids. 1454
Basic Troubleshooting Procedures for
    Automatic Transmissions 1458
Maintenance of Automatic Transmissions 1459
Transmission Replacement Procedures. 1464
Ready for Review. 1468
Key Terms. 1469
Review Questions 1469
ASE Technician A/Technician B Style Questions. . .1470

CHAPTER 51 Heavy-Duty Drive Shaft
Systems 1471
Introduction. 1472
Fundamentals of Driveshaft Systems. 1472
Operation of Driveshafts. 1478
Driveshaft Angle Cancellation 1480
Checking and Adjusting Driveline
    Angularity. 1483
Troubleshooting Driveshaft Vibrations and
    Failures. 1488
Inspection and Maintenance of
    Driveshafts 1492

Ready for Review. 1499
Key Terms. 1500
Review Questions 1501
ASE Technician A/Technician B Style Quiz 1501

CHAPTER 52 Heavy-Duty Drive Axles 1503
Introduction. 1504
Fundamentals of Axles. 1504
Functions of Differential Gear Sets 1509
Types of Differential Gear Sets 1512
Double Reduction and Multi-Speed Drive
    Axles. 1515
Inter-Axle Differentials (Power Dividers) 1521
Role of Drive Axles and Drivelines in
    Greenhouse Gas Reduction Strategies 1527
Ready for Review. 1530
Key Terms. 1531
Review Questions 1532
ASE Technician A/Technician B Style Questions. . .1532

CHAPTER 53 Servicing and Maintaining
Drive Axles 1534
Introduction. 1535
Fundamentals of Drive Axle Service 1535
Drive Axle Overhaul, Removal, and
    Inspection. 1537
Setting Gear Set Contact Patterns 1549
Overhauling the Inter-Axle Differential
    (Power Divider) 1552
Diagnosing Component Failures in Drive Axle
    Systems. 1555
Ready for Review. 1559
Key Terms. 1560
Review Questions 1560
ASE Technician A/Technician B Style Questions. . .1561

CHAPTER 54 Electric Drive Vehicles and
AC Traction Motors 1563
Introduction. 1564
Factors Influencing Adoption of CBEV
    and ADAS. 1564
Classification of Medium and Heavy Duty
    (MHD) Electric Vehicles. 1564
Evolution to CBEVs. 1567
Commercial Battery Electric Vehicle
    Architecture. 1570
Traction Motor Propulsion System 1572
Types of Traction Motors 1572

Permanent-Magnet Motors 1578
Switched Reluctance Motors (SRMs) 1581
Generator Mode 1582
Electric Motor (EM) Mechanical Transmission. . . .1582
Energy Storage System (ESS) 1583
Battery Charging 1588
High-Voltage Hazards and Safety 1592
Ready for Review 1596
Key Terms. 1597
Review Questions 1597
ASE Technician A/Technician B Style Questions. . .1598

**CHAPTER 55 Autonomous Driving and
Advanced Driver Assistance Systems for
Commercial Vehicles. 1600**
Introduction. 1601
What Is Autonomous Driving Capability?. 1603
Autonomous Control Enabling Technologies 1610
GPS Navigation 1614
Autonomous Communication Technology 1616
Ready for Review. 1618
Key Terms. 1618
Review Questions 1618
ASE Technician A/Technician B Style Questions. . .1619

**CHAPTER 56 Hybrid Drive Systems
and Series-Type Hybrid Drives. 1621**
Introduction. 1622
Fundamentals of Hybrid Drives. 1622
Types of Hybrid Drives 1623
Hybrid Drive Electrical Safety 1626
Series-Type Hybrid Drive Systems 1628
Maintenance and Service. 1639
Ready for Review. 1639
Key Terms. 1640
Review Questions 1640
ASE Technician A/Technician B Style Questions. . .1641

**CHAPTER 57 Allison EV Drive and
Series-Parallel Hybrid Systems 1643**
Introduction. 1644
Overview of Allison EV Drive Hybrid
    System 1644
System Components 1645
Energy Storage System 1650
Operating Modes. 1654
EP System Maintenance .1655
Ready for Review. 1656

Key Terms. 1657
Review Questions 1657
ASE Technician A/Technician B Style Questions. . .1658

**SECTION 5   Heating, Ventilation,
and Air Conditioning**

**CHAPTER 58 Principles of Heating and Air
    Conditioning Systems. 1662**
Introduction. 1663
Development of Air Conditioning Systems 1663
Air Conditioning Benefits 1664
Air Conditioning Operating Principles 1666
Basic Refrigeration Cycle. 1670
Refrigeration System Components 1671
Thermostatic Expansion Valve (TXV) 1675
Evaporators 1682
Receiver-Dryers. 1684
Refrigerant and Oil 1684
Air Conditioning Controls 1688
Air Conditioning Protection and Diagnostic
    System (APADS). 1690
Air Distribution System. .1693
Ready for Review. 1696
Key Terms. 1697
Review Questions 1698
ASE Technician A/Technician B Style Questions. . .1698

**CHAPTER 59 Servicing Heating and
    Air Conditioning Systems 1700**
Introduction. 1701
The Air Conditioning Service Process. 1701
Leak Testing 1708
Reclaiming and Recharging Refrigerant. 1711
Inspecting the Condenser for Airflow
    Restrictions 1715
Inspecting the Evaporator Housing. 1715
Maintenance and Repair .1716
Ready for Review. 1728
Key Terms. 1728
Review Questions 1729
ASE Technician A/Technician B Style Questions. . .1729

CHAPTER 60 Trailer Refrigeration 1731
Introduction. 1732
Fundamentals of Transport Refrigeration 1732
Heating Principles 1734
Types of Transport Refrigeration Systems 1735

Overview of Heating, Cooling, and Defrost
  Cycles................................1737
Components of Trailer Refrigeration Systems ...1741
Alarm Codes 1747
Refrigeration System Maintenance 1748
Ready for Review..........................1748
Key Terms................................1748
Review Questions 1749
ASE Technician A/Technician B Style Questions...1749

SECTION 6 Hydraulics

CHAPTER 61 Principles of Hydraulic
Systems 1754
Introduction..............................1755
Fundamentals of Hydraulic Systems 1755
Work and Power in a Hydraulic Circuit 1759
Hydraulic System Components...............1760
Hydraulic Pumps 1763
Hydraulic Fluids 1768
Hydraulic Fluid Reservoirs 1772
Hydraulic Lines and Hoses 1773
Hydraulic Actuators........................1782
Control Valves 1785
Pressure-Relief Valves......................1790
Hydraulic Accumulators 1791
Hydraulic System Preventative Maintenance.....1793
Ready for Review..........................1796
Key Terms................................1797
Review Questions 1798
ASE Technician A/Technician B Style Questions...1798

SECTION 7 Preventative Maintenance and Inspection

CHAPTER 62 Developing a PM Inspection
System 1802
Introduction..............................1803
Categories of Preventative Maintenance and
  Inspection (PMI).........................1803
Why Perform PM? 1804
Who Performs PM?........................1808
PM Service Intervals 1808
Commercial Vehicle Safety Alliance Inspections...1811
Administration of Safety Inspection Programs ...1812
Lubricants Used in PMI 1813
Finding Information on Recalls 1815
Preparation for PM and PMI 1815
PMI Process 1816
Inspecting the Braking System................1821
Inspecting Tires and Wheels 1826
Inspecting Wheel Alignment 1828
Performing Under-Vehicle Inspections 1828
Inspecting Cargo-Handling Devices............1832
Ready for Review..........................1834
Key Terms................................1835
Review Questions 1835
ASE Technician A/Technician B Style Questions...1836

Appendix A   2018 ASE Medium/Heavy Truck
  Master Service Technology (MTST) Task
  List Correlation Guide....................1838
Glossary.................................1850
Index 1884

ACKNOWLEDGMENTS

Writing a textbook to put the best possible information in the hands of technicians about the latest technology in commercial vehicle chassis systems could not take place without the practical support, critical feedback, and assistance of many individuals. We're grateful for those who have allowed us to gain knowledge and skills from their vast experiences and expertise. As industry contacts patiently fielded our questions during the preparation of this textbook, it's been a privilege to meet many remarkable people working in this industry who have an infectious excitement for education in skilled trades and a genuine passion for service excellence. Our colleagues at Centennial College in Toronto, Canada, have been extremely helpful and supportive. To Professors David Morgan and Gino Tamburro, whose insights helped us at many stages of the project, we extend our heartfelt thanks. We also want to thank Ian Andrew, whose input was essential.

In addition, along with the CDX editorial team, we'd like to thank the following individuals for their contributions to and feedback about this textbook:

Abraham P. Arispe
Tidewater Community College

Robert Arney
Washburn Institute of Technology

Jim Baird
Jones Technical Institute

Larry Baker
Aims Community College

Ron Beaumont
Brisbane, Queensland, Australia

Westin A. Blidy
Orleans Niagara BOCES

Gary Bronson
Laurel Oaks Career Development Campus

Les Brown
UAW LETC

Pete Carpentier Jr.
Delmar College

Jerry Clemons
Elizabethtown Community and Technical College

Tim Dunn
Sydney, New South Wales, Australia

Casey Eglinton, M.Ed.
Western Technical College

Mike Erny
Ivy Tech Community College

Mike Hagan
Cherokee High School

Curtis Happe
Richland Community College

Scott Heard
Fleming College

Kevin Heimbach
Berks Career and Technology Center

Doyle Howard
West Kentucky Community and Technical College

Jim Hunnicutt
Jacksonville, Florida

Ron Iocandro
Chisholm Institute

Jack Ireland
Johnson County Community College

Edward Jackson
ASE Certified Instructor

Kevin Jesser
Member of Institute of Automotive Mechanical Engineers

Bob Johnson
Fred W. Eberle Technical Center

Dr. John F. Kershaw
Harrisburg Area Community College

Brian King
Boone County Area Technology Center

Kevin Knaebel
Ivy Tech Community College

Aaron A. Lemoine
South Louisiana Community College T.H. Harris Campus

Robbie Lindhorst
Southeastern Illinois College

Stefan Liszka
Chisholm Institute

Paul Losh
Lincoln Technical Institute (retired)

James Mack
Berks Career and Technology Center

Hugh M. Mann
Houston Community College

Michael Mauntel
Ivy Tech Community College

Jim McEwen
UAW-LETC

Jonathon Merritt
James Sprunt Community College

Jed Metzler
South Branch Career and Technical Center

John Miller
Valley Career and Technical Center

James Mitchell
Tampa Bay Technical High School

John Murphy
Centennial College

Brent Newville
Dakota County Technical College

Chad M. Parsons
Wyotech

Brian L. Particka
Huron Area Technology Center

Billy Phillips
Johnston Community College

Adam Prusakiewicz
University of Northwestern Ohio

Christopher Scharrer
Washburn Institute of Technology

James D. Scott
Crowder College

Larry Seibel
Miami Valley Career Technology Center

Tyler Slettedahl
North Dakota State College of Science

David Stone
High Plains Technology Center

Chris Thompson
Alexandria Technical & Community College

Claude Townsend
Oakland Schools

J. W. Turnpaugh
Mid America Technology Center

Larry Wehunt
Gwinnett Technical College

John Yinger
Ozarks Technical Community College

Lamar Zorn
Florida Panhandle Technical College

We've also been challenged by the exceptional students who have attended Centennial College. They are an extraordinary class of technicians who daily compel us to pursue teaching excellence and keep us from succumbing to the occupational hazard of falling behind in our comprehension of the industry's technological advancements.

We particularly want to thank Vern Anthony who saw the potential of this project, gave it a home at CDX, and pushed hard to see this work reach fruition.

And finally for our families—thank you Vivian and Ingrid for the immeasurable and unconditional support that you offered and the countless week-ends, evenings, and vacations you gave up to allow us to finish this work. Without your steadfast patience and inspiration, the task would have been impossible.

SECTION I
Foundation and Safety

CHAPTER 1   **Introduction to Heavy-Duty Commercial Vehicles**

CHAPTER 2   **Careers, Employability Skills, and Workplace Practices**

CHAPTER 3   **Safety, Personal Protective Equipment, and First Aid**

CHAPTER 4   **Tools and Fasteners**

CHAPTER 5   **Hand Tools**

CHAPTER 6   **Lifting and Hoisting Equipment**

CHAPTER 7   **Bearings, Lubricants, and Seals**

CHAPTER 1

Introduction to Heavy-Duty Commercial Vehicles

Learning Objectives

After reading this chapter, you will be able to:

- **LO 1-1** Define and describe the classification of medium- and heavy-duty vehicles according to operating environment.
- **LO 1-2** Identify and explain the classifications of vehicles according to type of vocation.
- **LO 1-3** Identify and explain how vehicle application determines design factors for major chassis systems.
- **LO 1-4** Identify and explain the design of powertrains according to vocational application.
- **LO 1-5** Identify cabs according to application.
- **LO 1-6** Explain the functions of suspension systems.
- **LO 1-7** Identify and explain the terminology associated with the measurements of vehicle dimensions, lengths, weight, and axle configuration.
- **LO 1-8** Identify and explain the classification of combination vehicles.
- **LO 1-9** Identify and describe hitching devices.
- **LO 1-10** Explain common terminology associated with classification of commercial vehicles.

You Are the Technician

A tractor-trailer combination vehicle has arrived at your repair shop. The vehicle requires a mandatory safety inspection and a determination made for which inspection sheets and other documentation are required to be completed and submitted to government regulators, as well as filed for the shop records. The vehicle is a tractor combined with two trailers. Part of your job is to determine what set of inspection regulations apply—whether to inspect the vehicle as a complete unit or separately for the tractor and trailers. To begin generating the correct documentation, you have recorded the serial numbers of each unit and examined the vehicle information decals. Your observations also include:

- The tractor has three axles with a single front axle and tandem rear drive axles. Information decals indicate a gross vehicle weight rating (GVWR) of 12,000 lb (5454 kg) for the front axle, and 20,000 lb (9090 kg) for each of the tandem axles.
- The lead trailer is approximately 45' (13.72 m) and has two axles at the rear.
- The lead trailer has a frame connected to the back of the trailer supporting a fifth wheel.
- The second trailer, approximately 28' (8.53 m) in length, is coupled to the fifth wheel connected to the front trailer.

As you prepare to research what regulations must be met for inspection procedures, which inspection stickers should be attached after any repairs are completed, reporting, and other documentation requirements, consider the following questions to guide your determination:

1. What class of vehicle is the tractor?
2. What type of trailer combination is this: A, B, or C?
3. What is the general allowable GCVW for this combination vehicle?

Introduction

Globally, commercial vehicles perform an endless variety of revenue-generating tasks having unique, and even unusual, functions. Each of these unique jobs, functions, or purposes is called a vehicle vocation. When thinking about the types of commercial vehicles seen every day, one begins to understand how vast the categories and configurations are—medium-sized delivery vehicles used almost exclusively in cities, ambulances, fire and rescue vehicles, highway semi-trailers, gravel haulers, fuel tankers, utility trucks, highway coaches, urban transit buses, etc. **FIGURE 1-1** illustrates several different commercial vehicles separated into their classifications. This chapter examines the range of commercial vehicles from different parts of the globe and their application. The one common observation in these examples is that, no matter where a technician works, the same set of fundamental skills are required for working on them. In this chapter, predominantly North American classifications are used as examples. If a technician is in another country, please refer to the regulations for the correct classifications specific to that region.

No matter where you are in the world, within each of those various larger vehicle classification categories, there are an enormous number of subtypes based on the vehicle's application. For example, buses transporting children to school every day are very different from the ones moving people on urban transit systems or intercity travel by highway coaches. Each application is built according to its own specialized requirements, such as carrying people or products, or performing specific tasks and services. Those specialized requirements can include factors, such as whether they operate specialized equipment and accessories, where they travel, what they carry, how much they carry, how far they travel, maneuverability, safety, capacity, stability, and speed. These are just a few design considerations determining the unique ways a vehicle is built and operates according to its vocation.

To properly maintain and service commercial vehicles, it is important to understand the variety of ways commercial vehicles are classified and configured. The reason for this is that a vehicle's application, operating conditions, and design determines service practices and recommendations for scheduling its maintenance.

Classification by Operating Environment

LO 1-1 Define and describe the classification of medium- and heavy-duty vehicles according to operating environment.

One of the most fundamental ways to classify commercial vehicles is by considering where a commercial vehicle performs its primary job or vocation. Whether a vehicle operates only inside a city with its frequent slow speed, stop and start conditions, off-road, or at steady high speeds encountered during on-highway operation, or in a combination of several operating environments, it has a major influence on vehicle design, operation, and maintenance. The choice of its engine, how well it needs to maneuver, its requirements for traction on various road or off-road surfaces, and service and inspection intervals are just a few variables affected by a vehicle's operating environment. Each of these environments can also have further subcategories. For example, truck delivery, or even bus operations, can be classified as regional or long haul. Regional operations return more than 90% of vehicles back to a terminal in a single day. Long-haul operations dispatch vehicles on trips lasting days—and even weeks—before they return to a dispatch, loading, or maintenance facility.

As already mentioned, road surface conditions also shape the classification of vehicles. That is, vehicles can be classified according to their suitability for travel on various road surfaces or grades. As shown in **FIGURE 1-2**, road grade is expressed as

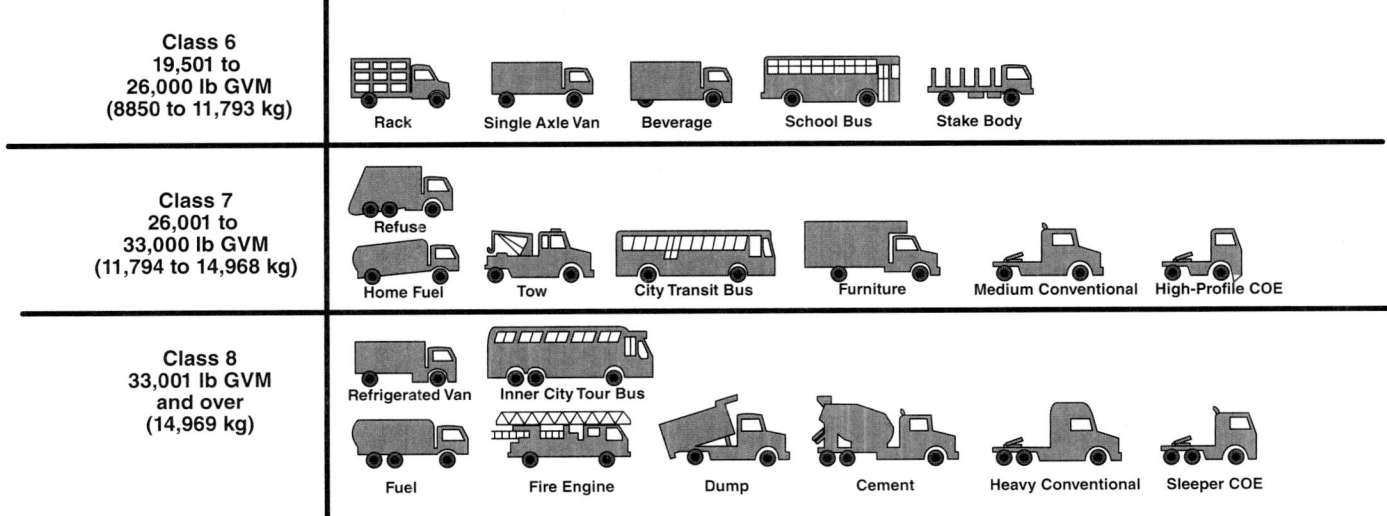

FIGURE 1-1 One of many ways to classify the various configurations of commercial vehicles is by gross vehicle weight rating (i.e., the maximum load carried by the vehicle).

FIGURE I-2 Road grade indicates steepness.

a percentage and refers to the steepness of a hill. For example, a 15% grade means the road drops or increases 15' (4.6 m) for every 100' (30.5 m) traveled.

Similarly, heavy-duty commercial vehicles can be classified according to how frequently they start and stop, or even by their speed of travel. When classifying commercial vehicles by operating conditions, five broad categories are used: Turnpike or interstate; on-highway; on-off-highway or mountainous highway; off-highway; and urban.

Turnpike or Interstate

Major highways are constructed differently than secondary highways. The road materials, vehicle speeds, amount of stop-and-go driving, and slope of the road crown are all factors that determine a vehicle's suitability for turnpike or interstate applications. Those factors also influence the design, equipment, and accessories an interstate vehicle uses. Vehicles classified for operation on interstates, highways, or turnpikes are designed to run on limited-access, well-maintained, multi-lane highways made of excellent concrete or asphalt with maximum adverse grades not in excess of 3%.

On-Highway

Vehicles classified for use in on-highway operating conditions operate exclusively on well-maintained major highways of excellent concrete or asphalt construction. Roads are typically level to rolling with occasional maximum grades to 8%. These vehicles must operate within legal weight and dimensional limitations and be capable to handle the steeper grades that may be encountered.

On-/Off-Highway or Mountainous Highway

Vehicles classified for on-/off-highway or mountainous highway operating conditions should expect to spend 20% of their total operating time on secondary roads. These roads are normally made from good concrete or asphalt. Intermittent grades of up to 12% may be encountered. The remaining time is traveled on off-highway roadways that are based on well-maintained crushed rock or similar material. Road grades in this class are more severe than on-highway operation. Operations are subject to legal weight and dimensional limitations.

Off-Highway

In this classification, vehicles spend more than 20% of their travel time on gravel roads or roads with a maintained crushed rock surface. The maximum grade can be as much as 12%, and grades of 8% are frequently encountered. This operation is not generally subject to legal weight or dimensional limitations.

Urban

Vehicles in this classification face operating conditions that are primarily within cities and suburban areas. That means these vehicles are subject to frequent stops and starts. Operation occurs on concrete, asphalt, and maintained gravel road surfaces. Because of the urban environment, vehicles in this class must have greater levels of maneuverability than is required of other classes. Vehicles in this class often use engines with a lower power output and transmissions with more steps.

Vocational Applications of Commercial Vehicles

LO I-2 Identify and explain the classifications of vehicles according to type of vocation.

A second major way to classify commercial vehicles is by the job (vocation) the vehicle performs. Common vocational applications include:

- Pick-up and delivery
- Construction
- Fire service
- Heavy haul
- Intercity coach
- Line haul
- Logging
- Mining
- Refuse collection
- Rescue vehicles
- School bus
- Urban transit coach

The following sections discuss these classifications in greater detail.

Pick-Up and Delivery

Vehicles classified primarily for picking-up and delivering goods and services operate mostly within cities and/or suburban areas. A delivery vehicle typically travels three miles (4.8 km) between starts/stops with a 100% load capacity going and 40% load on return. Common vehicles included in this category are:

- Drop-bed auto haulers, as shown in **FIGURE 1-3**
- Moving vans
- Refrigerated delivery trucks
- Beverage trucks
- Municipal work trucks
- Flatbed trucks
- Parcel delivery trucks
- Tow trucks and wreckers

A common configuration of vehicle in North America for pick-up and delivery operations is the straight or conventional truck configuration, such as the one shown in **FIGURE 1-4**. A straight truck used in the city typically has a single axle because weight limits on city streets are much lower than those on major highways. In addition, a single axle helps the vehicle to be more maneuverable. A cab-over-engine (COE) design, which places the cab over the front axle and engine, is exclusively used in Europe where shorter vehicle length regulations prevail and roads are often narrow and twisty with sharp turns. While less comfortable to operate, COE designs provide exceptional maneuverability because the vehicle is shorter and visibility is improved (**FIGURE 1-5**).

These vehicles use mid-bore diesel engines ranging from 3 to 7 L in displacement because of their superior fuel economy and superior low speed torque. This category of vehicle is the most adaptable vehicle for hybrid electric or battery electric operation since they do not travel far and return to a yard every day.

Construction

Vehicles used in construction are primarily engaged in moving material to and from a job site. Operating conditions are generally 90% of loaded operation on road surfaces made of concrete, asphalt, gravel, crushed rock, or hard-packed dirt, and up to 10% of loaded operation in loose sand or on muddy job sites. Maximum grades encountered are 12%. As a result, construction vehicles tend to use short-step, deep-reduction transmissions combined with low-torque-rise engines providing more consistent torque over a wider engine speed range torque. Loads are distributed equally from side to side.

Common vehicles included in this category are:

- Asphalt and gravel trucks, frequently referred to as dump trucks, as shown in **FIGURE 1-6**
- Flatbed trucks hauling lumber and building supplies
- Tank trucks, as shown in **FIGURE 1-7**
- Landscape trucks, often referred to as tipper trucks outside North America, as shown in **FIGURE 1-8**
- Concrete mixers
- Snowplows

Fire Service

These vehicles are used to transport people and equipment to extinguish fires, paramedics, or for ambulance services. Annual distances traveled are typically less than 20,000 miles

FIGURE 1-3 Drop-bed auto hauler.

FIGURE 1-4 A straight truck.

FIGURE 1-5 This COE tandem-axle tractor used in Europe provides exceptional maneuverability for urban operation.

(32,187 km) per year. Typical vehicle routes are three miles (4.8 km) between start and stop. High deceleration stops are frequent.

Common vehicles in this category are:

- Aerial ladders and fire trucks, as shown in **FIGURE 1-9**
- Pumpers tankers
- Aerial platforms and special applications, as shown in **FIGURE 1-10**
- Ambulance/paramedic

Heavy Haul

Vehicles in the heavy-haul category move heavy equipment or materials at legal maximums for length, width, and weight. They may exceed those limits with special loading permits. Operation is mostly on road surfaces made of concrete, asphalt, and maintained gravel. Load weights are 100% of vehicle capacity going and empty on return. Vehicles in this classification require high horsepower, high-torque-rise engines with the ability to pull the heaviest loads. **FIGURE 1-11** illustrates a typical heavy-haul configuration.

FIGURE 1-9 A fire truck (also known as a fire appliance or fire apparatus).

FIGURE 1-6 Dump truck.

FIGURE 1-10 Specialist applications.

FIGURE 1-7 Tanker.

FIGURE 1-8 Tipper truck.

FIGURE 1-11 A heavy-haul configuration.

Typical vehicle types in this category are:

- Equipment-hauling flatbed trailers
- Steel haulers using high or low trailers

Intercity Coach

This category of vehicle transports people, and occasionally light freight, between cities and/or suburban areas. Intercity coaches travel on highway and in urban conditions accumulating high mileage on routes exceeding 30 miles (48.3 km) between start and stop.

Typical vehicle types in this category are:

- Tour coaches
- Cross-country coaches

Line Haul

Line-haul trucks move freight over long distances—generally over 60,000 miles/year (96,561 km/year). More than 30 miles (48.3 km) of distance between starting and stopping are typical for line-haul service. Straight trucks (trucks with only a box) use either single or tandem axles. Tractor-trailer combinations are most common.

FIGURE 1-12 General freight truck.

FIGURE 1-13 Flatbed truck.

Typical line-haul vehicles include:

- General freight trucks in either straight or tractor-trailer configurations, such as shown in **FIGURE 1-12**
- Refrigerated food trucks
- Livestock tractor trailers
- Flatbed trailers, such as the one in **FIGURE 1-13**
- Side curtains, as shown in **FIGURE 1-14**, that enable fast pallet unloading and loading with forklift trucks

Line-haul trucks travel long distances with heavy loads and at high speeds. As a result, line-haul trucks have unique vehicle requirements for their engines, tires, suspensions, cab configurations, etc.

Logging

Logging trucks move shipments of wood logs, chips, and pulp between logging sites or to and from logging or paper mills. Logging trucks travel distances of 3 to 30 miles (4.8 to 48.3 km) between starts and stops. Mostly, they travel on road surfaces of concrete, asphalt, maintained gravel, crushed rock, or hard-packed dirt, but up to 10% of their loaded operation can occur on sandy or muddy job sites. Trucks are loaded to 100% capacity when delivering loads and empty when returning.

Typical logging vehicles are:

- Wood-chip haulers—either a straight truck or tractor and trailer
- Log-hauling tractor-trailer combinations, as shown in **FIGURE 1-15**

FIGURE 1-14 Side curtains.

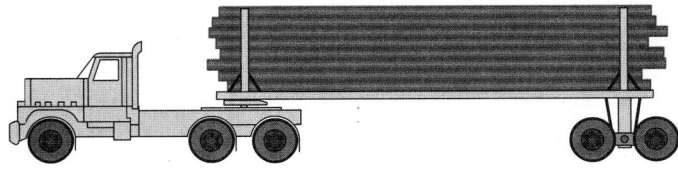

FIGURE 1-15 A logging truck.

Logging trucks that operate in off-road conditions have unique requirements for specialized traction capabilities provided by tires and drive axles. Heavy frames are also needed to resist damage from twisting and bending. Suspensions are designed to better handle severe off-road terrains while carrying the heaviest possible loads.

Mining

Mining operation trucks move rock, ore, gravel, and other minerals. Average trip distances are 30 miles (48.3 km) between starting and stopping. While most operations are on-highway, up to 10% of distances traveled are over sandy or muddy job sites. The trucks are typically 100% loaded while delivering and empty on return trips.

Typical mining vehicle types are:

- Belly dump trailers
- Semi-end dump hopper trailer combinations

The gravel hauler in **FIGURE 1-16** is an example of a mining application. The tilting dump box requires a power take-off to operate a hydraulic pump called a wet-line.

Refuse Collection

Refuse vehicles, better known as garbage trucks, are used for pick-up and transportation of residential garbage or recycling materials. These vehicles encounter steep grades of up to 20% when they travel into landfill, transfer, or recycling sites. Refuse trucks typically have a high proportion of starts and stops for every mile traveled.

Typical refuse vehicles are:

- Front-/rear-/side-loading garbage trucks, as shown in **FIGURE 1-17**
- Sewer/septic/vacuum trucks
- Liquid waste haulers

To enable the greatest level of maneuverability and highest load capacity, refuse vehicles are typically built on low-entry, COE chassis.

Rescue Vehicles

Rescue vehicles are specialized vehicles designed for rapid acceleration to crash sites on highways or airport tarmacs away from hydrant hookups. They are low mileage operation vehicles with high horsepower engines and automatic transmissions.

Typical rescue vehicle types are:

- Airport Rescue Fire (ARF)
- Crash Rescue Fire (CRF)
- Rapid Intervention Vehicle (RIV) Emergency Service

Some of the most powerful trucks with the fastest acceleration rates are crash-and-rescue trucks, as shown in **FIGURE 1-18**. These trucks are used to quickly extinguish fires at airports or on the highway because of accidents. As a result, crash-and-rescue trucks require high-speed capabilities while carrying heavy loads.

School Bus

School buses are familiar people haulers that transport students to and from school or school-related events. Two stops per mile over mixed road surfaces are typical. School buses frequently operate under fully loaded capacity.

Typical school bus configurations are:

- Front-engine commercial chassis
- Front- or rear-engine integral coach, as shown in **FIGURE 1-19**

Urban Transit Coach

As the name indicates, urban transit coaches are the city buses that transport people in and around cities or suburban areas. City buses operate on well-maintained highways and

FIGURE 1-17 Garbage truck.

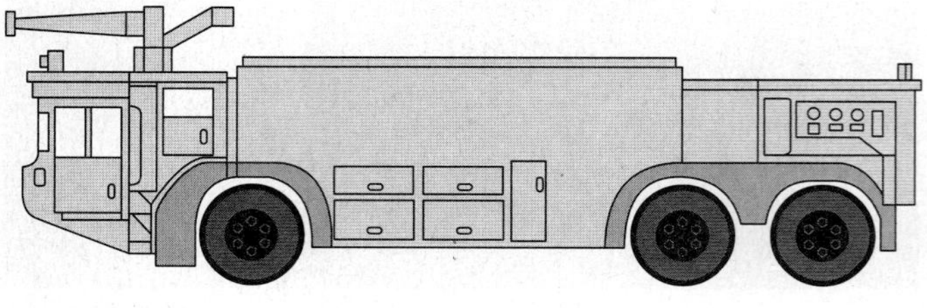

FIGURE 1-16 A gravel hauler.

FIGURE 1-18 Crash-and-rescue truck.

residential streets made of asphalt or concrete. These units have a high frequency of starts and stops per mile—nine is considered typical.

Typical urban transit vehicles are:

- Airport shuttle buses
- City transit buses, such as the one in **FIGURE 1-20**

These can come in a range of configurations, as shown in **FIGURE 1-21A** and **FIGURE 1-21B**, including double deckers and articulated or "bendy buses," as they are known in some countries.

Design Factors for Vocational Applications

LO 1-3 Identify and explain how vehicle application determines design factors for major chassis systems.

A commercial vehicle's design features are strongly influenced by its application. Depending on the operating conditions and job performed by the vehicle, a commercial vehicle has a particular chassis, engine, powertrain, cab, suspension, and other specific chassis equipment, as discussed in the following sections.

Chassis Frames

The frame of a truck or bus are the vehicle's backbone, supporting the vehicle loads of freight, equipment, and passengers. All equipment, such as engines, suspension systems, and the cab, ultimately must mount or attach to the frame. A frame must be sized and built appropriately to be capable of supporting the loads applied to it while adapting to the forces that bend and twist the frame, such as when the wheels hit bumps or potholes or the load shifts. Two main frame designs are:

1. Ladder
2. Tubular-type frames

Ladder frames are the most common type of frame. They use two main large cross-sectional area side rails that are arranged longitudinally in the vehicle. Side rails are made from box or C-channel cold rolled alloyed steel. Smaller cross members join each of the side rails together using high-strength bolts or rivets to form a sub frame, providing good torsional strength to resist twisting and bending. The passenger compartment of the cab is attached to the frame after the frame is built. It does not require as much strength or rigidity since the frame provides the primary structural strength. Many trucks, trailers, and buses are built on a ladder-type frame, such as the one shown

FIGURE 1-19 School bus with rear engine.

FIGURE 1-20 City transit bus.

FIGURE 1-21 A. Double decker bus. **B.** Articulated bus.

in **FIGURE 1-22**. When used in semi-trailers, the floor members use dozens of small I-beams attached across two smaller main frame rails with each end attached to the trailer side plate. The king-pin area of the trailer frame usually has steel plate reinforcement.

Tubular frames do not use heavy side rails but, instead, as the name suggests, uses tubular steel to construct a ribbed structure of many lighter pieces of box sections. Attachment points for the engine and suspension system are present, but there is no separate passenger compartment cell like a ladder frame because the tubes integrate the compartment into a single frame structure. Structural integrity is provided by metal tubes, bulkheads, and box sections. Tubular frames are much more complex to build but are substantially lighter than ladder frames and provide much more room for passengers and freight (**FIGURE 1-23**). The passenger compartment area is safer since the frame cell is less likely to deform in an event, such as a vehicle roll-over.

Engines

Engines must have enough power to move heavy loads and accelerate up grades while providing good fuel economy. Diesel engines are primarily used for the following reasons:

1. Superior fuel economy compared to any other internal combustion engine
2. Higher torque output, especially at low speeds
3. Durability—lasting three or more times longer than spark-ignition engines
4. Fewer maintenance requirements due to the absence of a spark-ignition system

Battery-powered electric vehicles (BEVs) are rapidly becoming popular since they produce no noxious emissions at street levels. Very little maintenance is required by the electric motors too. Torque output is comparable or even greater than a diesel, but only at low speeds. Given the low cost of electricity to charge the batteries compared to the cost to purchase diesel fuel, BEVs are perceived to have low operating costs.

Torque is the most important factor in choosing an engine for commercial vehicles since it is torque that ultimately moves a load. Torque is the twisting force applied to the crank-shaft and then, finally, to the wheels. Torque is a function of cylinder pressure and it is the force that accelerates or moves a vehicle and its load.

Horsepower is a function of engine speed and torque. **Horsepower** describes how fast the engine can turn while producing torque. A high-horsepower, high-torque engine can produce lots of power at high engine speeds. In contrast, a high-torque, low-horsepower engine cannot turn as fast while it produces torque. The following is an equation for horsepower:

$$\text{Horsepower} = \text{RPM} \times \frac{\text{Torque}}{5252}$$

Torque rise is the difference between engine torque produced at rated speed (maximum engine rpm under load) and **peak torque**, or maximum torque an engine can produce. Torque rise is expressed as a percentage of torque at the rated speed.

To calculate torque rise, use the following equation:

$$\% \text{ Torque} = \frac{\text{Peak torque} - \text{Rated torque}}{\text{Rated torque}} \times 100$$

For example, consider a vehicle with a peak torque rise of 1800 ft-lb (2440.5 N-m) and a torque at rated speed of 1200 ft-lb (1627 N-m). The percent torque rise is calculated as follows:

$$\% \text{ Torque rise} = \frac{1800 - 1200}{1200} \times 100$$

$$\text{Torque rise} = 20\%$$

High-torque-rise engines are used for line-haul applications and require a steep increase in torque, such as when climbing hills or steep grades. Vocational vehicles and those used in urban environments, such as transit buses or pick-up and delivery vehicles,

FIGURE 1-22 A ladder-type frame/chassis.

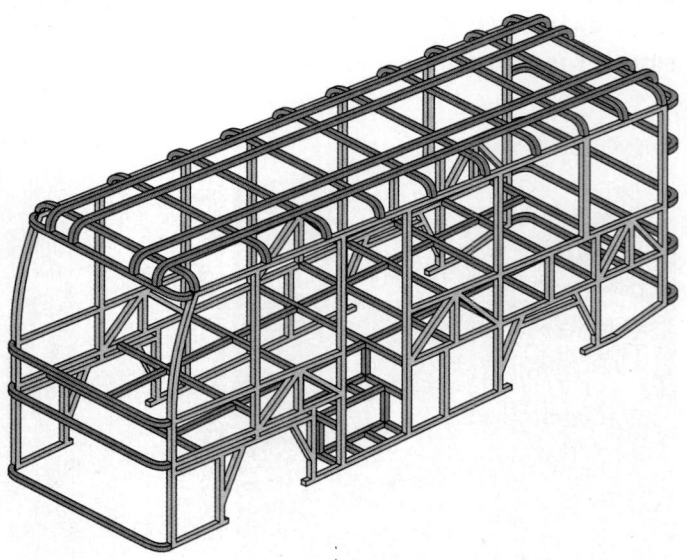

FIGURE 1-23 Buses and some trailers are constructed from tubular frames.

use low-torque-rise engines, which have less peak torque but more torque is available over a wider engine operating range. **FIGURE 1-24** graphically illustrates the difference between low torque rise and high torque rise.

High-torque-rise engines allow the vehicle's driver to keep the vehicle in a higher gear range longer under load. This explains why high-torque-rise engines are only used in line-haul, on-highway trucks and buses. Torque is available in high-torque-rise engines only over a narrow speed range. At low speeds, little torque is available. However, its peak torque occurs at 10 to 15 mph (16.1 to 24.1 kph) or so below its cruising speed. This corresponds to about two-thirds of its maximum engine speed when the vehicle is correctly geared.

Low-torque-rise engines produce more consistent torque output over a wider engine rpm operating range. That makes them ideal for stop-start traffic and varying speed/load conditions. Torque output is not as high but more widely available.

Another difference between high-torque-rise and low-torque-rise engines is in their gearing. High-torque-rise vehicles generally use transmissions with fewer gears and wider ratio steps between gears. Low-torque-rise engines use transmissions with smaller ratio steps but need more gears.

Electric Powered Vehicles

Electric vehicles use traction motors to supply propulsion power to commercial vehicles. Two major types are BEVs, which are only powered by on-board batteries that must be recharged, and hybrid-electric vehicles (HEVs). Hybrids combine engines and electric traction motors to propel the vehicle. BEVs are rapidly becoming popular since they are less expensive than hybrids and produce no noxious emissions at street levels. Very little maintenance is required by the electric motors either. Torque output is comparable, or even greater, than a diesel, but only at low speeds. Given the low cost of electricity to charge the batteries compared to the cost to purchase diesel fuel, battery-powered vehicles are perceived to have low operating costs. Currently, the cost of batteries and the operating range of

BEVs means there is limited demand for these types of propulsion systems relative to diesel-powered or even HEVs in North America (**FIGURE 1-25**).

Powertrains

LO 1-4 Identify and explain the design of powertrains according to vocational application.

Commercial vehicles require powertrains designed specifically for their particular vocations. **FIGURE 1-26** illustrates the powertrain in a conventional configuration of a heavy truck. Transmissions and rear axles provide the mechanical advantage through gear ratios to efficiently use engine power while moving the vehicle at the road speeds and grades required by its operation. Gear ratios should be numerically fast enough to achieve desired highway speeds for the particular operation. In addition, gears must be available that are also numerically slow enough to provide the mechanical advantage for maximum hill-climbing ability with the lowest gear combinations and maximum startability under all operating conditions.

Startability is an important feature or specification factor for some trucks. **Startability** refers to the capability to begin moving forward on a specified grade. An engine's torque

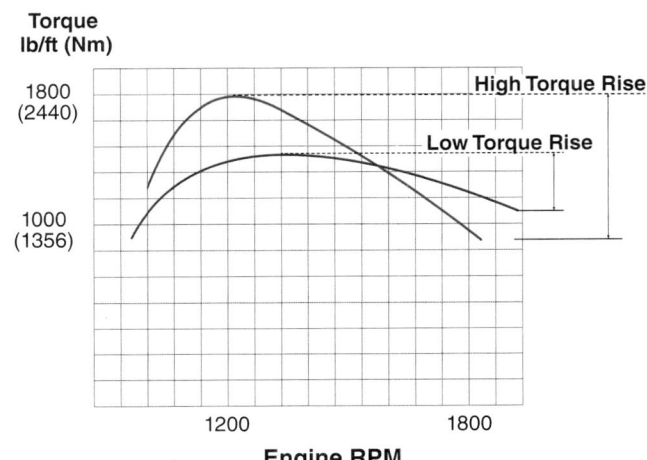

FIGURE 1-25 This BEV chassis uses electric traction motors to propel the vehicle. Batteries are placed outside each frame rail behind the cab.

FIGURE 1-24 The relationship between torque and engine rpm.

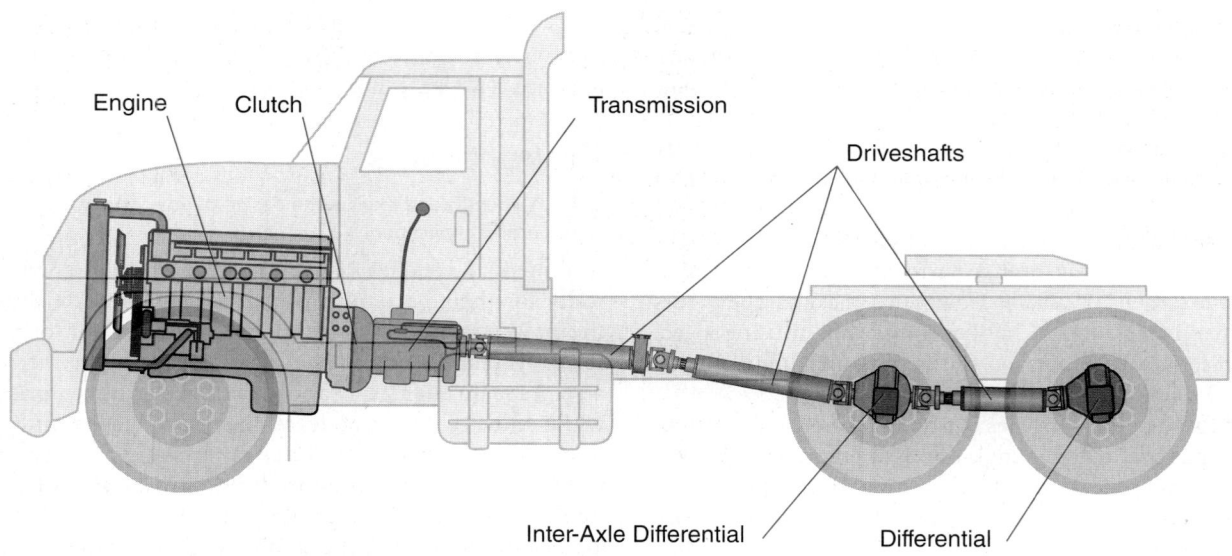

FIGURE 1-26 The power train and engine locations in a conventional heavy truck.

output and powertrain gear ratios determine the steepest grade a truck can begin to climb from a standing stop. A similar term, **gradability**, refers to the capability to maintain forward motion on specified grade while maintaining a minimum speed.

Tractors and trucks can also be classified according to their drive and non-drive axle configurations. Trailers may be classified according to the number of axles, but by non-drive axle configurations. Single-unit, or straight, trucks can have two, three, four, or sometimes more axles. Typically these include closed (van-type) trailers, dump trucks, tankers, and heavy concrete mixers.

Another element of the powertrain that varies, depending on vehicle vocation, is the rear axle. Factors influencing rear axle selection include:

- Gross combination weight rating (GCWR)
- Type of terrain
- Road speed
- Tire size
- Axle ratio required
- Transmission ratios
- Engine torque
- Engine speed

Trucks are categorized by the number of wheel positions and drive axles they have. **TABLE 1-1** charts classification by wheel ends and drive axles. For example, a 4 × 2 vehicle has four wheel positions with one drive axle having two wheels driven. This is a single rear axle truck or bus. **FIGURE 1-27** illustrates a typical tire-and-wheel configuration of an 18-wheeler. Tires 1 and 2 and 11 to 18 are on non-driving axles. Tires 3 to 10 are drive tires, which are a part of a tandem drive axle configuration. **FIGURE 1-28A** depicts an 8 × 4 configuration, and **FIGURE 1-28B** depicts a 6 × 4 configuration.

A common configuration is the tandem axle combination. It uses two drive axles and has the following advantages:

- Greater ability to carry legal loads
- Better traction
- Better weight distribution over road surfaces
- Better braking capability for improved safety
- Improved load distribution over axles, tires, and frame
- Reduced road shock to chassis components

FIGURE 1-29A and **FIGURE 1-29B** show different configurations using tandem axles.

Two other types of axles used on heavy-duty commercial vehicles are the pusher axle and tag axle. A pusher axle is

TABLE 1-1 Truck Classification by Drive Wheels

Chassis Type	Total Wheel Ends	Driven Wheels	Driven Axles	Total Axles
4×2	4	2	1	2
4×4	4	4	2	2
6×2	6	2	1	3
6×4	6	4	2	3
6×6	6	6	3	3
8×8	8	4	2	4
8×8	8	8	4	4

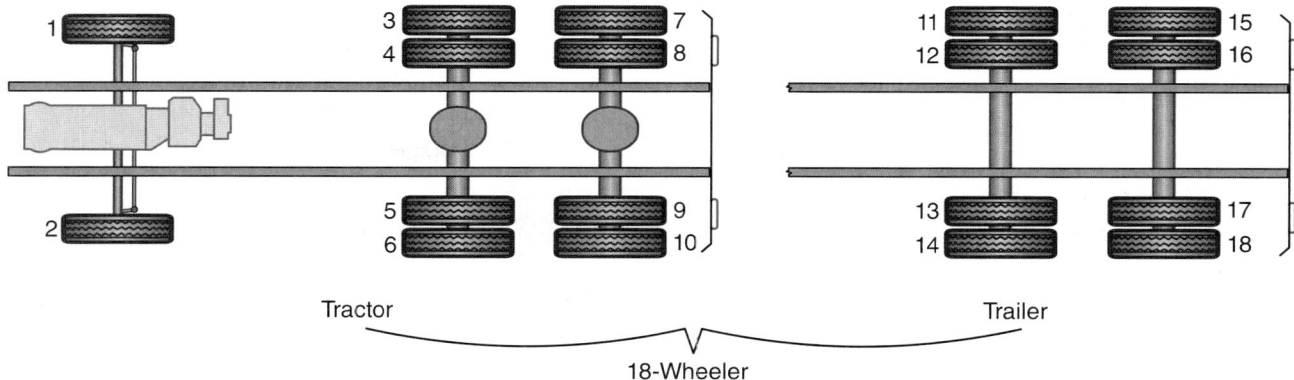

FIGURE 1-27 The tire and wheel configuration of an 18-wheeler.

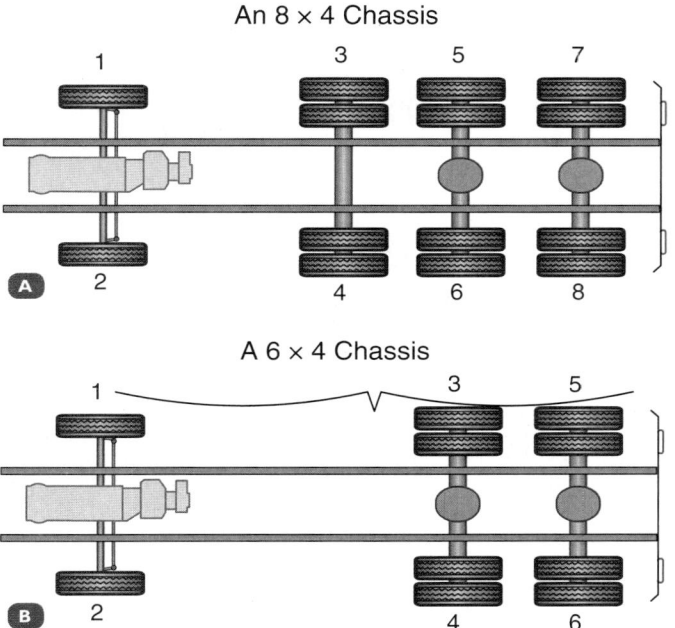

FIGURE 1-28 A. An 8 × 4 chassis configuration. **B.** A 6 × 4 chassis configuration.

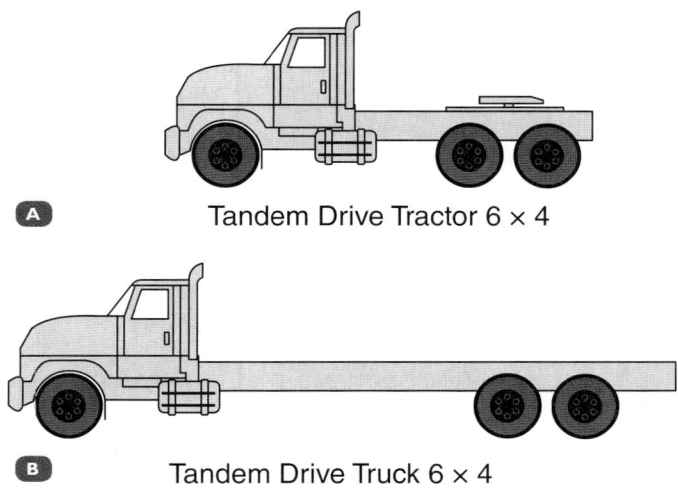

FIGURE 1-29 A. A tractor with tandem drive axle and a fifth wheel to haul a semi-trailer. **B.** A straight truck with a tandem axle.

non-driving and is located in front of a drive axle. A tag axle is located behind the drive axles. Both pusher and tag axles help increase maximum GVWRs. **FIGURE 1-30A–D** shows various axle configurations using pusher and tag axles.

Cabs

LO 1-5 Identify cabs according to application.

Just as different vocations of trucks use specific engines and powertrains, they also use cabs designed for specific types of usage. **FIGURE 1-31** shows three conventional tractors, each using an identical engine and powertrain. The cabs, however, are different and bring different enhancements to the vehicle. The cab shown in **FIGURE 1-31A** has a high-rise bunk integrated into the cab and also has aerodynamic fairings or skirts around the chassis. The cab shown in

FIGURE 1-31B has no bunk and for that reason is sometimes called a "day cab." The cab shown in **FIGURE 1-31C** has an integral bunk with grab handles for improved access to the back of the cab.

Regardless of design, most cabs include some type of aerodynamic fairings and wind deflectors to improve fuel economy. Aerodynamic enhancements are, therefore, another consideration when developing vehicle specifications. **FIGURE 1-32** shows how various aerodynamic enhancements are integrated into a cab's design.

A common configuration of cab is the conventional cab in which the engine is placed in front of the cab. The ride in a conventional cab is smoother than in the common COE configuration, which is illustrated in **FIGURE 1-33**. The COE configuration enables the use of a longer trailer, however, and the design also allows for greater maneuverability than a conventional cab when a small turning radius is needed.

The location of the front axle can also influence the turning radius of a vehicle and affect ride quality. A set-back axle moves the axle closer to the cab to shorten the vehicle's turning radius. **FIGURE 1-34** illustrates how set-back and

6 × 6

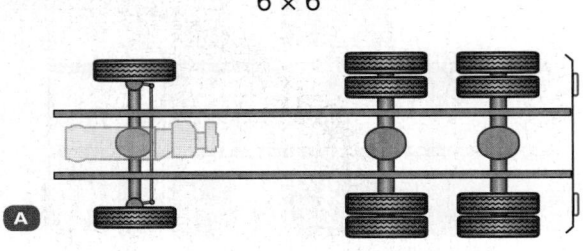

12 × 4 Dual Drive with Pusher & Tag Axles

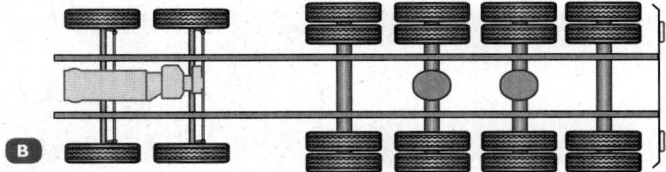

6 × 4 Tandem Axle Dual Drive

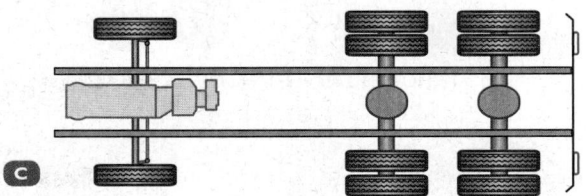

8 × 4 Tandem Axle with Pusher Axle

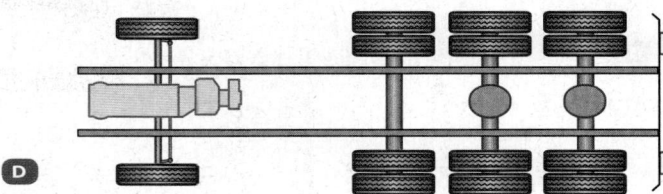

FIGURE 1-30 A. A 6 × 6 configuration. **B.** A 12 × 4 dual drive with pusher and tag axles. **C.** A 6 × 4 tandem axle with dual drive. **D.** An 8 × 4 tandem configuration with a pusher axle.

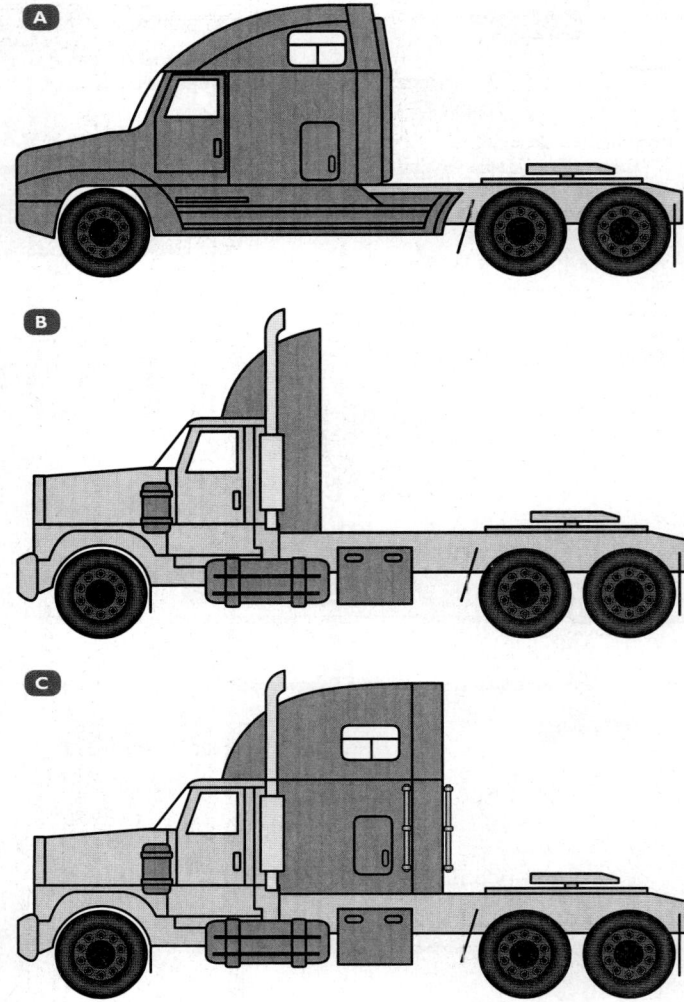

FIGURE 1-31 A. A cab with antegral bunk anc aerodynamic fairings. **B.** A day cab. **C.** A cab with a high rise bunk and grab handles.

set-forward axles work in COE vehicles and in conventional vehicles. **FIGURE 1-34A** shows a higher truck with a higher COE entry and a set-forward axle. **FIGURE 1-34B** shows a lower entry truck with a set-back front axle.

Suspensions

LO 1-6 Explain the functions of suspension systems.

While it is evident that a vehicle suspension is needed to support the load on the chassis and absorb road shock, it serves some other basic functions. The suspension:

- Transmits braking and drive forces to the chassis
- Enables **articulation** or movement of axles to adapt to road conditions
- Promotes proper vehicle tracking while enabling safe steering and minimization of tire wear

Many different types of suspensions systems are made to best adapt the vehicle's function to operating conditions and load support. Suspension systems commonly use the following materials for springs:

- Air
- Solid rubber
- Steel leaf spring

Other Chassis Equipment

Specialized chassis equipment used on a vehicle largely depends on what the vehicle does and where and how far the vehicle travels. The following is a list of special equipment options that vary by application:

- Fuel tanks—number and size
- Exhaust—vertical or horizontal
- Hitching devices and fifth wheels
- Batteries—type and number
- Auxiliary power supplies

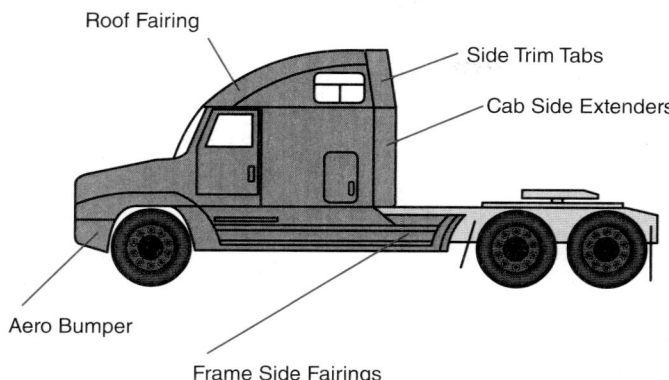

FIGURE I-32 Aerodynamic features of cabs.

FIGURE I-33 Cab-over-engine (COE) configuration.

- Auxiliary heaters
- Back of cab access
- Day cab or sleeper cab
- Seating—air ride, bench, or fixed seat
- Power take-off's
- Steps
- Lighting and conspicuity markings
- Deck plates
- Braking systems—hydraulic or air; disc or drum brakes
- Auxiliary braking devices—engine compression, exhaust-based, or driveline retarders
- Aerodynamic fairings
- Tires—designed for off-road traction, fuel economy, longevity, or maneuverability

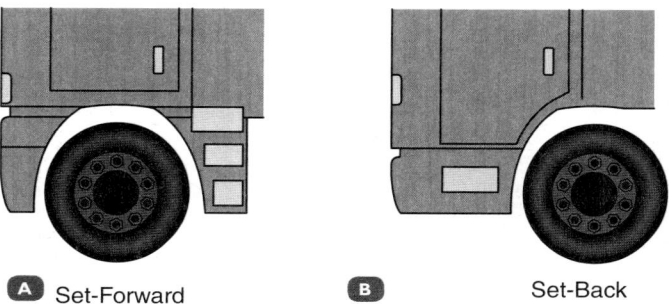

A Set-Forward   **B** Set-Back

FIGURE I-34 A. Front axle set-forward in a COE vehicle. **B.** Front axle set-back in a COE vehicle.

Classification of Heavy Vehicles by Weight and Length

LO I-7 Identify and explain the terminology associated with the measurements of vehicle dimensions, lengths, weight, and axle configuration.

Design and vocation are not the only considerations in the classification of heavy vehicles. Considerations must also be given to their configurations based on weight and length regulations. Combination vehicles that use hitching devices, for example, are configurations that have specific characteristics.

Federal Bridge Gross Weight Formula

In the early 20th century, vehicle weight limits were legislated to protect dirt and gravel roads from damage caused by the heavy wheel weights of commercial vehicles. As truck traffic and load weights increased truck weight limits began to focus primarily on gross weight limits to protect bridges from damaging loads. **Gross weight limits** are the maximum legal weight of a vehicle that can travel on roads and bridges.

By the mid-1970s, regulations were established to limit the weight-to-length ratio of heavy trucks to protect roads and bridges from the damage caused by the concentrated weight of shorter trucks. The regulation created is called the **Federal Bridge Gross Weight Formula** (also known as **Bridge Formula B** and the **Federal Bridge Formula**). Those formulas established the maximum weights for a

Bending Moment

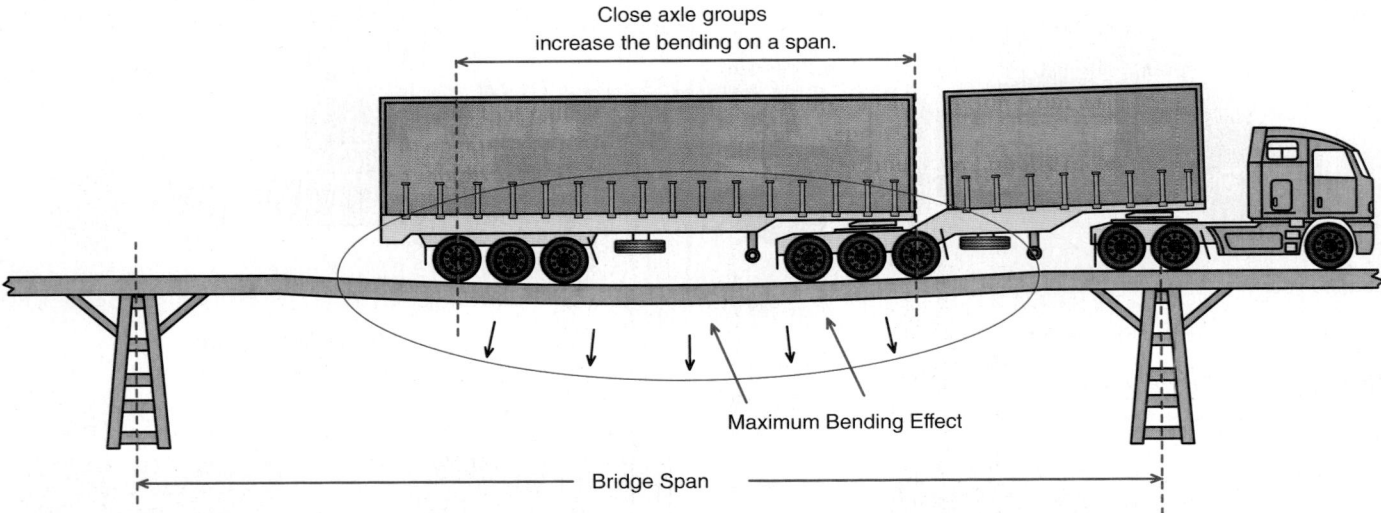

FIGURE I-35 The bridge formula was developed to calculate the maximum weight allowed on axles for any given distance between axle centers.

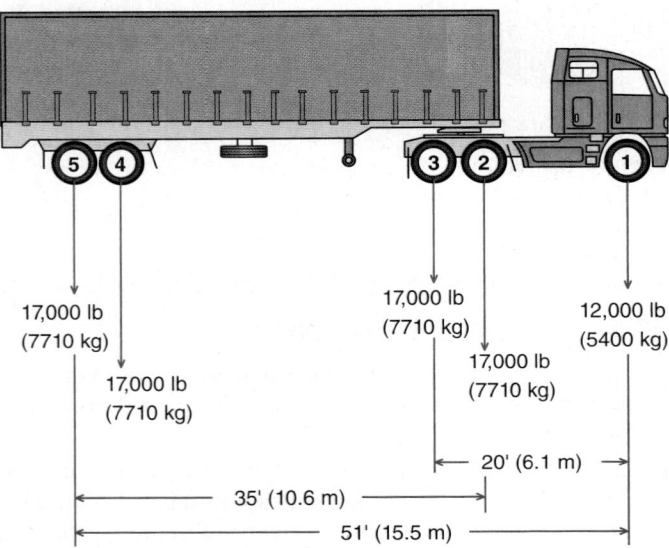

FIGURE I-36 Gross vehicle weight per axle.

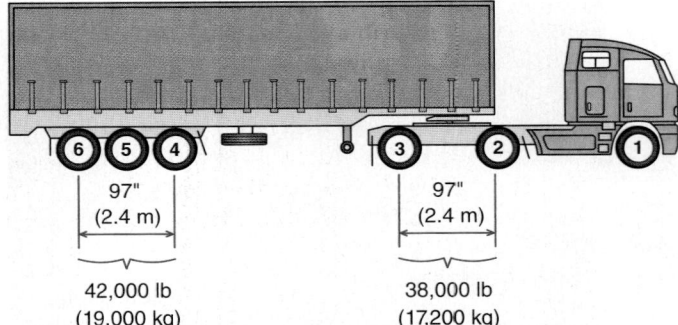

FIGURE I-37 Identical axle spacings with different weights.

commercial motor vehicle (CMV) based on the number of axles the vehicle had and the spacing between those axles.

The formula is part of North American weight and length regulations regarding interstate/interprovincial commercial traffic. Axle spacing is as important as axle weight in bridge design. Consider a vehicle with two axles carrying significant weight. If not spaced far enough apart, those two axles act like a single axle in terms of loading road surfaces. The longer the axle spread—a distance measured from axle center to axle center—a better weight distribution is achieved to prevent road and bridge damage. **FIGURE I-35** illustrates the impact of vehicle weight on bridges.

The bridge formula, therefore, allows motor vehicles to be loaded to maximum weight only if each group of axles and their spacing also satisfy the requirements of the formula. In North America, the weight limit is typically 20,000 lb (9072 kg) per

axle for a single-axle vehicle or, the total weight on one or more axles that are more than 40" (101.6 cm) apart. For tandem axles, the total weight limit is typically 34,000 lb (15,422 kg) for a vehicle with its full weight on two or more consecutive axles that are between 40" and 96" (101.6 cm and 243.8 cm) apart. Because the bridge formula defines the maximum weight allowed on each axle according to the distances between each axle, the vehicle illustrated in **FIGURE I-36** is allowed a gross vehicle weight (GVW) of 80,000 lb (36,287 kg).

Axle spacing is, therefore, a critical consideration. The vehicle illustrated in **FIGURE I-37** has two axle groups. The distance between each group is identical, but there is a critical difference. The three-axle group carries only minimal amount of extra load compared to the tandem group since the axles are close together.

To increase a vehicle's potential load rating, vehicle designers may specify certain features. For example, according to the Federal Bridge Formula, no more than 600 lb psi (42.18 kg/cm²) is allowed on a tire's contact patch. Designers may specify super-single tires, as shown in **FIGURE I-38**, as a way to reduce a vehicle's overall weight (by using fewer tires), but still be in compliance with the regulation.

FIGURE 1-38 Super-single tires reduce vehicle weight.

Vehicle Weight Ratings

Numerous configurations of trucks, tractor trailers, and even buses can be classified by length, weight, number of axles, and number of wheels. In North America, one of the most common ways trucks are categorized is by **gross vehicle weight (GVW)**. GVW refers to the maximum design weight of a vehicle including a full tank of fuel, fully loaded to its capacity, and with all passengers. **TABLE 1-2** shows the classifications of vehicles by GVW. The heaviest classification using this method is GVW class 8 vehicles. Class 8 includes vehicles weighing more than 33,001 lb (14,969 kg) and are usually considered heavy trucks.

Gross Vehicle Weight Rating

A similar classification system based on weight is **gross vehicle weight rating (GVWR)**. GVWR is the design rating specified by a manufacturer as the recommended maximum weight of a vehicle when fully loaded. Trucks or power units (tractors) are classified primarily into a class between 4 and 8 based on their GVWR.

General legislation in North America limits the gross vehicle weight of a vehicle, or a combination of vehicles, according to the number of axles and the distance between the axles. Those limits are listed in **TABLE 1-3**.

Many exceptions and variations are made to the general rule. As an example of how axle spacing affects maximum load, consider that vehicles with multiple axles whose centers are less than 4' (1.2 m) apart are classified as a single-axle unit. The situation is even more complex for triaxle combinations. When a vehicle has a single axle with center-to-center distances closer than 10' (3.0 m) (or a steering axle closer than 9' (2.7 m) to a triaxle unit, the single axle is considered part of that triaxle. The presence of the additional axle does not increase the allowable legal load capacity of that triaxle unit.

FIGURE 1-39A shows a manufacturer's decal with GVWR for a tandem-axle tractor; **FIGURE 1-39B** shows a decal with GVWR of a single-axle straight truck.

FIGURE 1-39 A. Manufacturer's GVWR decal for a tandem-axle tractor. **B.** Manufacturer's GVWR decal for a single-axle tractor.

TABLE 1-2 Classification of Chassis by Gross Vehicle Weight (GVW)

Class	Gross Vehicle Weight (GVW) lb (kg)
1	6000 lb (2721.6 kg) or less
2	6001–10,000 lb (2722–4535.9 kg)
3	10,001–14,000 lb (4536.4–6350.3 kg)
4	14,001–16,000 lb (6350.7–7257.5 kg)
5	16,001–19,500 lb (7257.9–8845.1 kg)
6	19,501–26,000 lb (8845.5–11,793.4 kg)
7	26,001–33,000 lb (11,793.9 kg–14,968.5 kg)
8	33,001 lb (14,969 kg) or more

TABLE 1-3 General Law Gross Weight Limits

Number of Axles	Weight Limit
2 Axles	34,000 pounds (15,422.1 kg)
3 Axles	54,000 pounds (24,494 kg)
4 Axles	69,000 pounds (31,297.9 kg)
5 Axles	80,000 pounds (36,287.4 kg)
6 or More Axles	100,000 pounds (45,359.2 kg)

Gross Combined Weight Rating

The **gross combined weight rating (GCWR)** is a specific maximum weight limit determined by the vehicle manufacturer. Unlike other weight ratings, the GCWR takes into account two individual (yet attached) vehicles—the tow vehicle, or tractor, and the trailer.

Classification of Heavy Vehicles by Combination

LO 1-8 Identify and explain the classification of combination vehicles.

Combination vehicles are two or more combined or coupled vehicle units. Combined vehicles can be divided into tractor/semi-trailers, truck/full trailers, and truck/pole trailers. A **full trailer** is a trailer that is supported at both ends with an axle and does not rest on a fifth wheel of a lead vehicle. The name **semi-trailer** comes from the coupling method where some of the trailer's load is carried by the tractor through a connection known as a fifth wheel, which is a hitching device located above its drive axles. Hitching devices are covered in greater detail in the chapter Fifth Wheels and Hitching Devices.

In contrast to a semi-trailer, a full trailer has axles at the front and rear of the trailer, which carry the entire load. That allows the trailer to be pulled by any vehicle with an appropriate hitching system. Combination vehicles may also have multiple trailers, referred to as A-trains, B-trains, and C-trains, which are categorized by the hitching method connecting the trailers.

A-Trains

An **A-train's** second trailer is a full trailer unit connected by a draw bar to a single hitch point on the lead (first) trailer. An A-train consists of a tractor pulling a semi-trailer and a second, full trailer, behind the semitrailer. The shape of the articulation point—the "A" shape of the draw bar on the converter dolly—lends the name to the tractor-trailer combination. **FIGURE 1-40A** shows an A-train configuration, and **FIGURE 1-40B** shows how the dolly connects the trailer to the semitrailer.

B-Trains

A **B-train** consists of a tractor pulling a semi-trailer and a second semi-trailer behind the first semi-trailer. This combination gets its name from the shape of the articulation points that connect the trailers, which are shaped like a letter "B," as shown in **FIGURE 1-41A**. The B-train does not use a converter dolly. Instead, the lead trailer has a sliding section of frame to which a fifth wheel is attached. A B-train's second trailer is simply another semi-trailer connected to a fifth wheel on the rear of the first trailer. In some locations, this is referred to as a "B Double" or an "Interlink" arrangement. The B-train is the most stable of the three combinations (A, B, C) because it uses a fifth-wheel connection between trailers. The fifth-wheel connection is the best at resisting the rollover of the second trailer. **FIGURE 1-41B** shows the articulation points of a B-train configuration.

C-Trains

A **C-train** is like the A-train except that it has two drawbars and is, therefore, somewhat more stable. The different dolly types are shown in **FIGURE 1-42**. Depending on the location where C-trains are used, they often have different names. Western doubles, Rocky Mountain doubles, or Road Trains (if more than two trailers are used) are names given to combination vehicles with multiple trailers of different lengths and hitching mechanisms. **FIGURE 1-43** shows a road train.

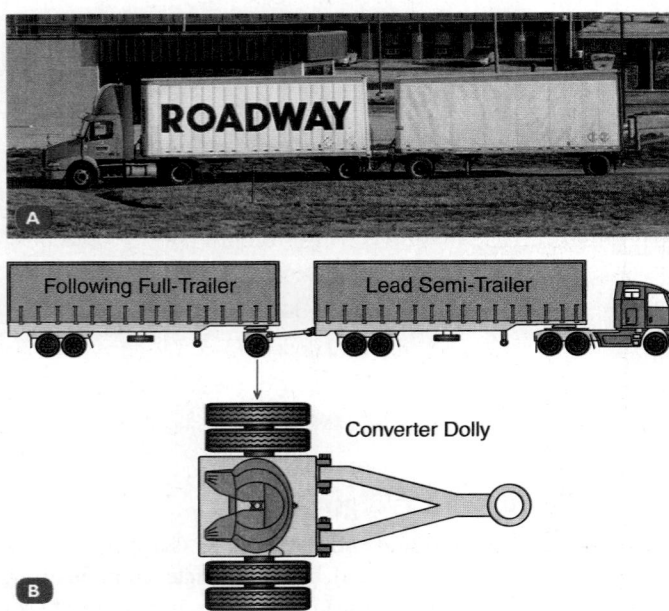

Following Full-Trailer   Lead Semi-Trailer

Converter Dolly

FIGURE 1-40 A. An A-train combination. **B.** The hitching dolly in an A-train combination.

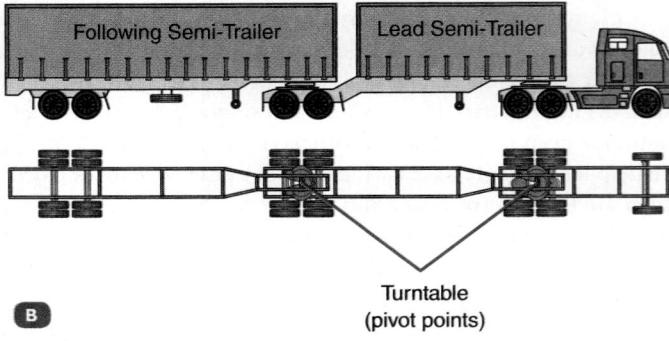

Following Semi-Trailer   Lead Semi-Trailer

Turntable (pivot points)

FIGURE 1-41 A. A B-train combination. **B.** The articulation points on a typical B-train configuration.

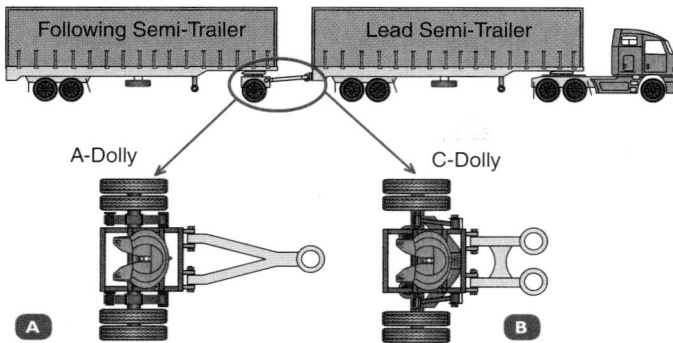

FIGURE 1-42 A. An A-train uses a converter with a single bar shaped like an A. **B.** A C-train uses a converter with two parallel drawbars.

FIGURE 1-43 A road train.

Hitching Devices

LO 1-9 Identify and describe hitching devices.

While a variety of vehicle factors and operating conditions can change the general rules for maximum axle weight, the best solution to enable transportation of heavier and larger loads is to add more axles to the vehicle configuration in order to minimize damage to road surfaces. However, adding more axles to a rigid chassis makes steering and maneuvering a vehicle almost impossible—particularly with the addition of tens of thousands of pounds of cargo. Therefore, trailers must be attached in such a way to enable improved steering and maneuverability and to allow the vehicle to articulate or bend when turning, yet maintain directional stability at road speed.

A variety of coupling devices are used to connect or hitch trailers to tractors while allowing articulation between tractor and towed units. Which type of device is used in each situation depends on the size and type of trailer and the product being transported. Fifth wheels, pintle hooks, couplers, and ball hitches are some of the hitching devices that have been developed to tow trailers and specialized equipment. These are described in greater detail in the following sections.

Fifth Wheels

Fifth wheels are a plate-type coupling device designed to support the weight of a semi-trailer. As illustrated in **FIGURE 1-44**,

FIGURE 1-44 A fifth wheel is the point of articulation for a semi-trailer. The semi-trailer rests and couples to the fifth wheel.

the fifth wheel is mounted on the rear frame of a tractor and has locking jaws that fasten the trailer king pin to the plate. The fifth wheel is the point of articulation between the trailer and the tractor. That means the fifth wheel enables the trailer and tractor to turn effectively, for example, when cornering or changing direction. The flat plate provides directional stability since it resists trailer twisting around its horizontal axis, which can lead to trailer sway.

Resting on the fifth wheel is the upper coupler. As illustrated in **FIGURE 1-45A** and **FIGURE 1-45B**, upper couplers consist of a steel plate and a king pin fastened to the underside of the forward portion of a semi-trailer frame. The upper coupler is designed to tow and support the weight of the trailer. The upper coupler is attached to the underside of the trailer frame. The coupler contains a king pin that latches to the tractor's fifth wheel.

Pintle Hooks and Couplers

Draw bars are used to connect tow vehicles to a tractor or lead towing unit. A lunette, or drawbar eye is the round section of a drawbar that attaches to a pintle hook or coupler. **Pintle hooks** are trailer hitching devices that use a fixed towing horn that connects with a drawbar eye attached to the towed vehicle. As illustrated in **FIGURE 1-46**, pintle hooks are coupled by raising the drawbar eye over the pintle horn and locking it closed with a pivoting latch. An air-cushioned pintle hook is a rigid pintle hook equipped with an air chamber connected to a plunger, which removes the slack between the pintle horn and the drawbar.

Couplers are hitching devices that look similar to pintle hooks with one exception. As illustrated in **FIGURE 1-47**, the towing horn pivots and is not fixed. Since the wider-opening coupler connects easier than a pintle hook, couplers are especially useful in applications with frequent trailer coupling and uncoupling.

Pintle hooks and couplers are selected by towing and vertical weight. To minimize shock loads when initially moving a trailer

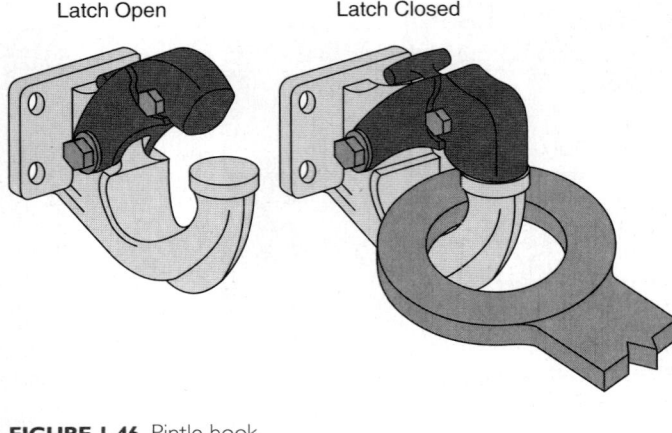

FIGURE 1-46 Pintle hook.

FIGURE 1-45 A. The top plate (lower coupler) of a fifth wheel. **B.** The upper coupler of a fifth wheel with the king pin showing.

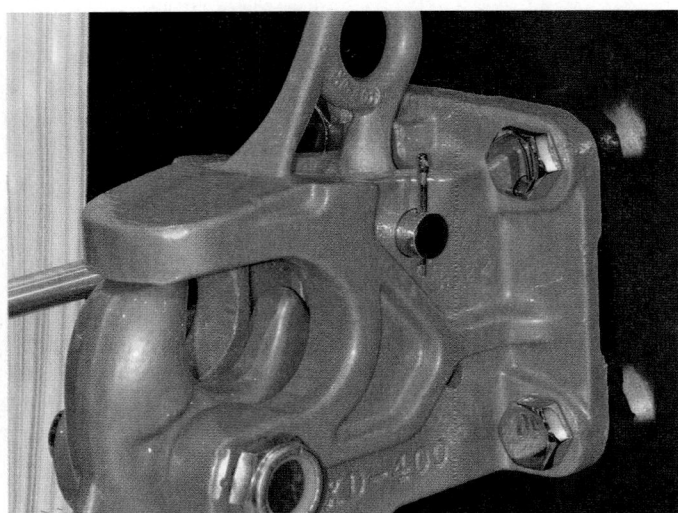

FIGURE 1-47 Coupler.

or during braking, a snubber or load dampener can be used. Rubber cushions or heavy springs are integrated into the device to permit some movement along the centerline to minimize shock loading of the coupler and some side-to-side strain relief.

Ball Hitches

Ball hitches are used with tongue-trailer draw bars. Ball hitches are used on light- and medium and heavy-duty vehicles using a tongue-type tow bar, which loops over a ball. The tow-ball allows swiveling and articulation of a trailer with a trailer tongue. Ball hitches have the advantage of providing a positive no-slack fit.

Ball hitches are classified in two ways. They are classified by the weight supported by the ball or **tongue weight (TW)** and by the **gross trailer weight (GTW)**, which is the weight of the trailer and cargo. Different sizes of balls are used, depending on the category of hitch. A 2-5/16" (5.9 cm) diameter ball coupler is the largest size for a Class 4 hitch. Gooseneck trailers, such as those used for hauling large motor homes, can use ball hitches mounted to a pick-up truck bed. The ball is fastened to the vehicle at a frame section called a receiver. A specialized

3" (76.2 mm) trailer ball is also commonly used for gooseneck towing applications. These are bolted or welded onto a gooseneck hitch and can tow up to 30,000 lb (13,608 kg).

As a rule, the vertical load on the trailer tongue should be at least 10% of the GTW. When loaded properly, the weight of the load assists in stabilizing the drawbar for improved directional control when cornering, and reduces the wear caused by surging speed changes. Excessive vertical load results in accelerated wear on the tongue and tow bar.

Trailer hitches are classified according to the weights listed in **TABLE 1-4**.

Common Terms and Conventions

LO 1-10 Explain common terminology associated with classification of commercial vehicles.

Becoming a successful heavy-duty commercial vehicle technician requires an understanding of common terminology and acronyms. **TABLE 1-5** lists common truck terms, their definitions, and their abbreviations, along with some illustrations to clarify exactly what each term and abbreviation refers to on a heavy-duty vehicle.

TABLE 1-4 Trailer Hitch Classifications

Class	Weight-Carrying Rating in Gross Trailer Weight (GTW)	Weight-Carrying Rating in Tongue Weight (TW)
Class 1	Up to 2000 lb (907.2 kg) GTW	Up to 200 lb (90.7 kg) TW
Class 2	Up to 3500 lb (1587.6 kg) GTW	300–350 lb (136.1–158.8 kg) TW
Class 3*	Up to 5000 lb (2268 kg) GTW	Up to 500 lb (226.8 kg) TW
Class 4	Up to 10,000 lb (4,535.9 kg) GTW	1000–1200 lb (453.6 kg–544.3 kg) TW

* Also sometimes used to refer to a hitch with any 2" (5.1 cm) receiver, regardless of rating.

TABLE 1-5 Common Truck Terms and Abbreviations

Abbr. / Term	Definition
A	Distance from centerline of rear axle to centerline of body and/or payload; centerline of body (at half body length)
AF	Center of rear axle, or tandem, to end of frame
BA	Bumper to centerline of front axle
BBC	Bumper to back of cab
BL	Body length
CA	Back of cab to centerline or rear axle or tandem suspension
CE	Back of cab to end of frame
CFW	Back of cab to center point of king pin hole in fifth wheel
CT	Back of cab to front of semi-trailer in straight-ahead relationship
FH	Frame height
FW	Centerline of rear axle or tandem to center point of fifth wheel
KP	King pin setting—front of semi-trailer to center point of king pins on semi-trailer
LGC	Landing gear clearance—center point of king pin to nearest interface point of landing gear assembly
OAL	Overall length
OWB	Overall wheelbase of tractor and trailer
TL	Semi-trailer length
WB	Wheelbase—distance between centerline of front and rear axle or tandem suspension
Chassis	Basic vehicle—cab, frame, and running gear
Body	Container in which the load is carried
Payload	Commodity to be carried
Curb weight	Weight of chassis only
Body weight	Weight of complete body to be installed on chassis
Payload weight	Weight of commodity to be carried
GVW	Gross Vehicle Weight—total of curb, body, and payload weights

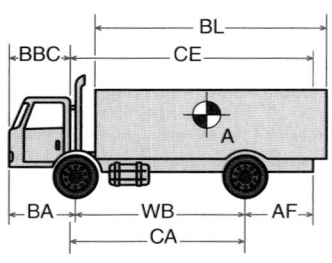
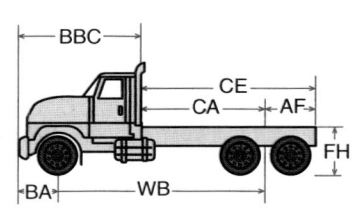
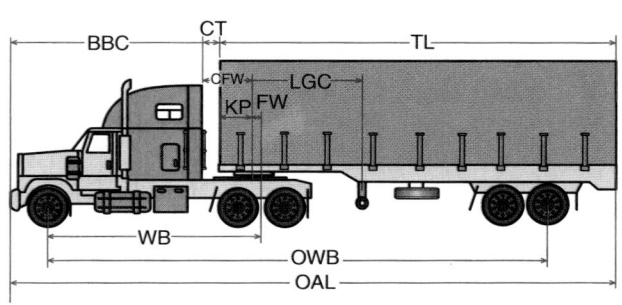

Vehicle Identification Numbers

Large numbers of vehicles with many variations of makes and models with different types of chassis equipment are produced every day across the world. Vehicle information labels have become very important because they help to uniquely identify the vehicle. Those labels contain a vehicle identification number (VIN) that is a unique serial number composed of 17 characters—letters and digits—that is assigned to each vehicle produced. This means that no two vehicles have the same VIN.

As with other vehicle types, every heavy-duty vehicle has a unique identification number. These VINs allow the equipment on a truck or bus to be clearly identified. **FIGURE 1-48** shows how the number and letter positions convey information about the manufacturer, make, vehicle type, chassis, front-axle position, brakes, and more.

Since 1981, the VIN has been made up of 17 characters. The VIN is designed to identify motor vehicles of all types: cars, trucks, buses, motorcycles, etc. It was originally defined in the International Organization for Standardization (ISO) Standard 3779 in 1977 and was revised in 1983. The first digit identifies the country where the product was manufactured. For example, VINs starting with 1, 4, or 5 indicate vehicles made in the US. VINs that begin with 2 are manufactured in Canada, 3, in Mexico.

The second digit designates the original equipment manufacturer (OEM). For example, an "H" in the second position indicates the vehicle was manufactured by Navistar. A "V" is Volvo and "F" is a Freightliner vehicle.

VINs can be used to check the service history of a vehicle and also are used to identify the vehicle for ordering components. Labeling the vehicle and vehicle parts with VINs also deters theft because it provides an easy way of uniquely identifying and tracing the vehicle and its major parts.

Production date codes and vehicle information labels also add to the identification information available on vehicles. The production date is the date of manufacture by year and month. Other information labels are affixed to the vehicle to provide ready access to information—for example, tire inflation pressures, vehicle weight, and load-carrying capacity. All of these information labels are used regularly by technicians to identify vehicles, order parts, and check service history.

Locating the VIN and Production Date Code

In order to locate a VIN and production date code, it is important to understand the principles of VINs and correctly identify the components that make up the 17-character VIN.

The VIN is usually located on the frame, engine, inside the driver's door on an information sticker, and even on some components and in the vehicle's electronic control modules. The VIN is unique worldwide, identifying the country of manufacture, manufacturer's name, division name, model, and other important information. Since 1981, all worldwide vehicle manufacturers use this numbering system. By learning to interpret the system, the identity of a vehicle or a components it uses can be determined and verified.

Whenever a vehicle is registered or a registered vehicle is sold, a record of the is kept. From this registry, information about the vehicle can be accessed, including the title history, which indicates has owned the vehicle. The registry may reveal a salvage title, which indicates that the vehicle has been wrecked and suffered irreparable damage. The registry can also indicate if the vehicle has had an odometer rollback (mileage reduction), which is evidence of odometer tampering.

Decoding a VIN

There are two different, but essentially compatible, 17-character VIN standards shown in Figure 1-48: The North American VIN system and the ISO Standard 3779, which is used in most of the rest of the world. **FIGURE 1-49** shows how the numbers are structured.

To decode a North American VIN, follow the steps in **SKILL DRILL 1-1**.

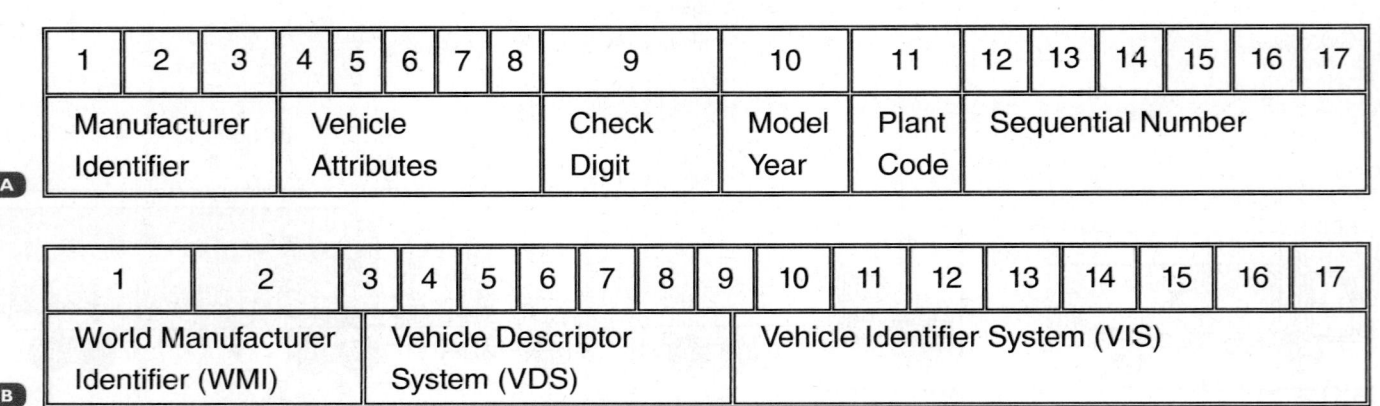

FIGURE 1-48 A. North American VIN system. **B.** ISO standard 3779.

Seventeen-Character Vehicle Identification Number (VIN)									
Typical VIN	1HT	M	K	AA	N	1	7	H	397874
Character Position	1, 2, 3	4	5	6, 7	8	9	10	11	12 thru 17
Code Description									
Manufacturer, Make, Vehicle Type									
Chassis, Front Axle Position, Brakes									
Vehicle Model Series, Cab									
Engine Model, Horsepower Range									
Gross Vehicle Weight Rating (GVWR)									
Check Digit									
Vehicle Model Year									
Plant of Manufacture									
Production Number									

FIGURE 1-49 Vehicle Identification Number and what each digit or character indicates.

SKILL DRILL 1-1 Decoding the VIN

Seventeen-Character Vehicle Identification Number (VIN)									
Typical VIN	1HT	M	K	AA	N	1	7	H	397874
Character Position	1, 2, 3	4	5	6, 7	8	9	10	11	12 thru 17
Code Description									

1. The VIN is 1HTMKAAN17H397874. The first character is the country of origin. This number or letter indicates the company that manufactured the vehicle and the country of origin.
2. The second character is usually a letter; it tells you the name of the manufacturer, which is International in this case.
3. The third character tells you the vehicle type; in this case, "truck."
4. The fourth character indicates the type of chassis.
5. The fifth character describes the model series and cab. This is a Durastar 4400.
6. The sixth and seventh characters tell you the engine model and horsepower range. In this case, it's a DT 466.
7. The eighth character provides details, such as vehicle recommended GVWR, which is in this case is 26,001 to 33,000 lb (11,818 to 15,000 kg).
8. The ninth character is the check character. It is used internally by the manufacturer.
9. The tenth character tells you the year of manufacture. You can decode this character according to a model year identification chart, which in this example shows us that the vehicle was assembled for the 2007 model year.
10. The eleventh character tells you the assembly plant or factory where the vehicle was put together.
11. The final six numbers make up the sequential number of the vehicle as it comes off the assembly line, starting at a base number, which is usually one hundred thousand (100000). So the first vehicle to be produced usually, but not always, has the number 100001.

Wrap-Up

Ready for Review

- Commercial vehicles perform an endless variety of revenue-generating tasks having unique, and even unusual, functions.
- To properly maintain and service commercial vehicles, it is important to understand the variety of ways commercial vehicles are classified and configured.
- A helpful way to classify commercial vehicles is by considering where a commercial vehicle performs its primary job.
- When classifying commercial vehicles by operating conditions, five broad categories are used: turnpike or interstate, on-highway, on-off-highway or mountainous highway, off-highway, and urban.
- Vehicles are also classified by their vocation, or the work they perform, such as transit, hauling, delivery, fire service, and rescue.
- Depending on the operating conditions and job performed by the vehicle, a commercial vehicle adapts using a particular chassis, engine, powertrain, cab, and suspension.
- The frame of every heavy vehicle must be sized and built appropriately to be capable of supporting the loads applied to it while adapting to the forces that bend and twist the frame.
- Heavy-vehicle engines must have enough power to move heavy loads and accelerate up grades while providing good fuel economy.
- Commercial vehicles require powertrains designed specifically for their particular vocations.
- Tractors and trucks can also be classified according to their drive and non-drive axle configurations. Trailers may be according to the number of axles, but are non-drive axle configurations.
- A common tractor configuration is the tandem drive axle combination, which uses two driving axles. Pusher and tag axles are other common types of non-driving axles on heavy-duty vehicles.
- Commercial vehicles are commonly classified by their weight and length.
- The Federal Bridge Gross Weight Formula is a legal calculation that establishes the maximum allowable weight of a commercial vehicle traveling on roads and bridges. Axle spacing is a critical consideration in this calculation.
- A common classification system for heavy vehicles uses their gross vehicle weight (GVW). There are eight classes in this system, with the heaviest vehicles having GVW of 33,000 lb (1360.8 kg) or more.
- In addition to regulating the overall weight of vehicle, in North America, a vehicle's maximum load weight per axle is also regulated.
- Heavy vehicles can also be classified by combination, such as tractor/semi-trailer, truck/full trailer, and truck/pole trailer.

- Combinations may also have multiple trailers, referred to as A-trains, B-trains, and C-trains, which are classified by the hitching mechanism connecting the trailers.
- The best solution to enable transportation of heavier and larger loads is to add more axles to the vehicle configuration in order to minimize damage to road surfaces. Trailers must also be attached in such a way to enable improved steering and maneuverability and to allow the vehicle to articulate or bend when turning.
- The fifth wheel is the point of articulation between the trailer and the tractor, and as such, enables the trailer and tractor to turn effectively, for example, when cornering or changing direction.
- Vehicle classifications by hitching device rely on the gross trailer weight (GTW) and the tongue weight.

Key Terms

articulation The movement of the suspension system in reaction to road bumps or terrain.

A-train A combination vehicle in which the second trailer is a full trailer unit connected by a draw bar to a single hitch point on the lead (first) trailer.

ball hitch A single-point connection configuration for a hitch that uses a tongue-shaped draw bar, which loops over a ball connected to the tow vehicle.

Bridge Formula B *See* Federal Bridge Gross Weight Formula.

B-train A combination vehicle in which the tractor pulls a semi-trailer and a third, full trailer behind the semi-trailer.

combination vehicles Two or more combined or coupled vehicle units.

coupler Trailer hitching device, similar to pintle hooks, but in which the towing horn pivots and is not fixed.

C-train A combination vehicle similar to an A-train but using a convertor dolly that has two parallel drawbars.

draw bars Bars used to connect tow vehicles to a tractor or lead towing unit.

Federal Bridge Formula *See* Federal Bridge Gross Weight Formula.

Federal Bridge Gross Weight Formula Laws that limit the weight-to-length ratio of heavy trucks with the goal of protecting roads and bridges from the damage caused by the concentrated weight of shorter trucks. Also known as *Bridge Formula B* or *Federal Bridge Formula*.

fifth wheel A plate-type coupling device designed to support the weight of a semi-trailer.

full trailer A trailer that is supported at both ends with an axle and does not rest on a fifth wheel of a lead vehicle.

gradability The capability of a vehicle to maintain forward motion on a specified grade while sustaining a minimum speed.

gross combined weight rating (GCWR) A specific maximum weight limit determined by the vehicle manufacturer that takes into account two individual (yet attached) vehicles—the tow vehicle or tractor, and the trailer.

gross trailer weight (GTW) The maximum carrying capacity of a trailer calculated by measuring the trailer weight and load.

gross vehicle weight (GVW) The maximum design weight of a vehicle including a full tank of fuel, fully loaded to its capacity, and with all passengers.

gross vehicle weight rating (GVWR) The design rating specified by a manufacturer as the recommended maximum weight of a vehicle when fully loaded to capacity, including all passengers and a full tank of fuel.

gross weight limit The maximum legal weight of a vehicle that can travel on roads and bridges.

horsepower A unit of measure of power that conveys how fast the engine can turn while producing torque.

peak torque The maximum torque an engine can produce.

pintle hook Trailer hitching device that uses a fixed towing horn that connects with a drawbar eye attached to the towed vehicle.

semi-trailer A trailer that has some of its load carried by the tractor through a hitching device.

startability The capability of a vehicle to commence moving forward on a specified grade.

tongue weight (TW) The weight supported by the ball (tongue) in a ball hitch.

torque rise The difference between engine torque produced at rated speed (maximum engine rpm under load) and peak torque. Torque rise is expressed as a percentage of torque at the rated speed.

Review Questions

1. An example of an operating environment for commercial vehicles includes:
   a. The engine it uses
   b. The steepness of a road grade
   c. The number of steps between transmission gears
   d. The regulations in the region it operates
2. Commercial vehicles operating in on-highway conditions, where the roads are typically level to rolling, encounter occasional maximum road grades up to:
   a. 3%
   b. 8%
   c. 12%
   d. 14%
3. Which of the following operating conditions do vehicles in the pick-up and delivery application most commonly encounter?
   a. Long distances between stops
   b. Most often operating on highways
   c. Low-speed, frequent stop-start operation in cities
   d. High-speed operation

4. Which of the following features is most important to rescue vehicles?
   a. Having specialized equipment, such as aerial ladders
   b. High driving speed capabilities while heavily loaded
   c. Ability to travel long distances without refueling
   d. Equipped with manual transmissions
5. Which of the following statements best describes engine torque?
   a. A measure of power output at maximum engine speed
   b. The speed range where an engine pulls the heaviest load
   c. The twisting force at the flywheel of an engine
   d. A calculation of engine speed multiplied by cylinder pressure
6. Which application requires the use of a high-torque-rise engine?
   a. A transit bus
   b. A line-haul tractor
   c. A pick-up and delivery vehicle
   d. A truck hauling lumber or gravel
7. Which numbers or letters in the VIN typically indicates the type of engine a vehicle uses?
   a. The sixth and seventh characters
   b. The last five digits
   c. The fourth character
   d. The ninth character
8. Which type of combination vehicle pulls a trailer with a tow-bar connected to a single hitch point?
   a. Semi-trailer
   b. A-train
   c. B-train
   d. C-train
9. For tandem axles spreads of more than 48" the total weight on two consecutive axles is typically:
   a. 20,000 lb (9072 kg)
   b. 34,000 lb (15,422 kg)
   c. 36,000 lb (16,329 kg)
   d. 40,000 lb (18,144 kg)
10. What is the General Law Gross Weight Limit for a vehicle with four axles?
    a. 54,000 lb (24,494 kg)
    b. 69,000 lb (31,298 kg)
    c. 75,000 lb (34,019 kg)
    d. 80,000 lb (36,287 kg)

ASE Technician A/Technician B Style Questions

1. Technician A says commercial vehicles are purpose-built according to their own specialized operating requirements. Technician B says each vehicle application is purpose-built to match requirements to carry people, products, or perform services. Who is correct?
   a. Technician A
   b. Technician B
   c. Both Technician A and Technician B
   d. Neither Technician A nor Technician B

2. Technician A says the operating conditions for off-highway includes 20% of the total operating time on secondary roads made from good concrete or asphalt. Technician B says the operating condition of off-highway includes intermittent grades of up to 12%. Who is correct?
   a. Technician A
   b. Technician B
   c. Both Technician A and Technician B
   d. Neither Technician A nor Technician B

3. While discussing construction vehicles, technician A says their operation is primarily movement of material to and from a job site. Technician B says operating conditions are 90% of loaded operation on road surfaces made of concrete, asphalt, gravel, crushed rock, or hard-packed dirt. Who is correct?
   a. Technician A
   b. Technician B
   c. Both Technician A and Technician B
   d. Neither Technician A nor Technician B

4. Technician A says the intercity coach is a category of vehicles that transports people and occasionally light freight between cities and/or suburban areas. Technician B says typical vehicle types in this category are tour buses and cross-country coaches. Who is correct?
   a. Technician A
   b. Technician B
   c. Both Technician A and Technician B
   d. Neither Technician A nor Technician B

5. Technician A says refuse vehicles encounter steep grades of up to 20% when traveling into landfill, transfer, or recycling sites. Technician B says refuse vehicles typically have a high frequency of accelerations and stops for every mile traveled. Who is correct?
   a. Technician A
   b. Technician B
   c. Both Technician A and Technician B
   d. Neither Technician A nor Technician B

6. Technician A says a frame must be sized and built appropriately to be capable of supporting the loads applied to it. Technician B says the frame has the additional task of adapting to the forces that bend and twist the frame. Who is correct?
   a. Technician A
   b. Technician B
   c. Both Technician A and Technician B
   d. Neither Technician A nor Technician B

7. Technician A says startability refers to the capability to begin forward motion on a specified grade. Technician B says an engine's torque output and powertrain gear ratios determine the steepest grade a truck can begin to climb from a standing stop. Who is correct?
   a. Technician A
   b. Technician B
   c. Both Technician A and Technician B
   d. Neither Technician A nor Technician B

8. Technician A says auxiliary braking devices, e.g., compression release, exhaust-based, or driveline retarders, are not considered to be in the category of special equipment. Technician B says aerodynamic fairings are considered special equipment. Who is correct?
   a. Technician A
   b. Technician B
   c. Both Technician A and Technician B
   d. Neither Technician A nor Technician B

9. Technician A says GVW class 8 vehicles are usually considered heavy trucks. Technician B says trucks or power units (tractors) are classified primarily into classes numbered between 2 and 8 based on their GVW. Who is correct?
   a. Technician A
   b. Technician B
   c. Both Technician A and Technician B
   d. Neither Technician A nor Technician B

10. Technician A says the gross combination weight rating (GCWR) is a specific maximum weight limit of a single unconnected vehicle, determined by the manufacturer. Technician B says combinations of tractors and trailers can also be classified according to their GCWR. Who is correct?
    a. Technician A
    b. Technician B
    c. Both Technician A and Technician B
    d. Neither Technician A nor Technician B

CHAPTER 2

Careers, Employability Skills, and Workplace Practices

Learning Objectives

After reading this chapter, you will be able to:

- LO 2-1 Identify career paths in the commercial vehicle industry.
- LO 2-2 Explain the elements of effective workplace habits and employability skills.
- LO 2-3 Describe general legal requirements of repair facilities.

- LO 2-4 Explain the purpose and types of vehicle identification labels.
- LO 2-5 Describe the purpose and use of service information resources.

You Are the Technician

You have been employed as one of 23 technicians at the Torrey Pines Truck Shop for the past six months. You start work at 6 AM. This morning you were ten minutes late for work (the reason you were late was that you were at a party on Sunday night and got to bed very late and had trouble waking up on Monday morning), but you tell your boss that your alarm clock didn't go off and think no more about it. At 10 AM your boss calls you into his office and hands you a disciplinary letter because of tardiness. Your boss explains that he values you as an employee, but that this is the fifth time you have been late in your six months of employment and that further tardiness will lead to further progressive discipline. You accept the letter, but you think your boss over reacted, as it was only ten minutes. After work, you have time to contemplate what happened that day and ask yourself some serious questions.

1. Do you think your boss was right to discipline you?
2. What can you do to prevent repeat tardiness?
3. Did you behave ethically today?
4. Do you owe your boss an apology?
5. Is there really an excuse for being late or are your own actions responsible?

Introduction

The saying "if you've got it, a truck brought it" is a catchy phrase emphasizing the importance of the trucking industry. Whether it is moving groups of people from place to place, transporting raw materials to factories, or delivering manufactured goods to retail centers, commercial vehicles perform a wide variety of essential functions to keep people and economies operating productively and efficiently. In North America alone, on any given day, there are over 12 million commercial vehicles operating on the highways and byways. Skilled technicians are needed to ensure commercial vehicles stay on the road and operate efficiently, safely, and reliably. For a person who values results-oriented work and a vocational pathway requiring hands-on technical abilities, a career as a heavy-duty commercial vehicle technician offers meaningful and satisfying work.

Careers in the Commercial Vehicle Industry

LO 2-1 Identify career paths in the commercial vehicle industry.

Some career possibilities in the commercial vehicle industry include service manager, parts person, sales person, and technician. **FIGURE 2-1** shows a parts department in a commercial vehicle dealership. The following section discusses the role and responsibilities of the commercial vehicle technician and describes the working conditions and educational requirements of this position. Typically, a person starts as an entry-level technician or apprentice and from there, through experience and increased knowledge, he or she progresses to a highly skilled specialist in the field.

Technician Duties

Commercial vehicle technicians are the people who inspect, repair, and diagnose mechanical, electrical, and electronic control systems in heavy-duty trucks, buses, trailers, and medium duty commercial transportation trucks. They are employed by new truck and trailer dealerships, garages of commercial fleets,

specialty repair shops, transit and bus companies, plus other service centers which may include automotive service shops. Technicians are also employed by vehicle manufacturers to perform diagnostic work and major repairs or the installation of components on new vehicles. **FIGURE 2-2** shows a technician at work.

On any typical workday, commercial vehicle technicians are involved in any of the following:

- Road-testing vehicles
- Performing diagnostic testing of vehicle systems and components using specialized equipment and diagnostic software to identify and pinpoint faults or validate their proper operation
- Adjusting, repairing, or replacing parts and components of engine and chassis systems, including the frame, cab, body, air brakes, steering, transmissions, drive axles, fuel injection systems, hydraulics, exhaust after treatment, air conditioning, electrical, and electronic systems
- Testing and adjusting repaired systems to manufacturer's performance specifications
- Performing inspections and preventative maintenance service, such as chassis lubrication, oil changes, and tire repairs
- Making operating and service recommendations to customers about vehicle repairs
- Completing reports, reviewing work orders, and discussing work with supervisors

While many technicians become skilled in diagnosing, servicing, and repairing most vehicle systems, specialization of skills can be achieved in the areas of engine and fuel systems, transmission and driveline, air conditioning, refrigeration and heating systems, brakes, steering, and vehicle alignment, trailer repair, or diagnostic services. **FIGURE 2-3** shows a well-equipped transit bus facility.

FIGURE 2-1 Parts department in a commercial vehicle dealership.

FIGURE 2-2 A technician at work in a specialty shop.

Job Classifications

The commercial vehicle industry offers a range of employment opportunities and a variety of entry-level jobs in service facilities provide a helpful starting point. Cleaning vehicles; picking up and delivering vehicles, equipment and/or parts; assisting with chassis lubrication and oil change services; and washing parts provide useful experience when deciding whether to begin a career in the industry. The training and exposure provided by working and learning in a service facility or vocational college can also lead to positions in management, sales, technical support, or teaching. Service managers, service writers, and technical advisors are typically recruited after they have demonstrated skill and expertise in the trade as technicians. **FIGURE 2-4** shows students learning to service a school bus in a vocational college.

Service Technicians

Starting as a technician in the repair and service sector is a common career starting point. This position allows for maximum exposure to the most recent technological developments and advancements in the industry. Becoming a service technician may require completion of a college program. Many of these programs are run in partnership with truck manufacturers that provide prospective technicians with an in-depth education and some practical experience in the operation and service of all commercial vehicle systems. The experience gained on the job along with the classroom instruction provided by the vocational school or manufacturer provides the student with the skills necessary to handle troubleshooting in a service facility. Technicians are expected to be knowledgeable in machine shop processes, pneumatics, hydraulics, and electronics, as well as have the computer skills required to perform many diagnostic and service procedures. **FIGURE 2-5** shows the hydraulics lab in a typical vocational college.

Job opportunities in almost every field, including commercial vehicle or heavy-duty technicians, are currently predicted to grow at rate of 9% between the years 2016 to 2026. Many older workers from the "baby boomer" generation will be at or reaching retirement age during this time, which is also expected to increase demand for more technicians. Today's technician must be equipped with information about the latest technologically advanced equipment. Entry-level positions in the industry include tire service, service maintenance, or as a trainee or apprentice with an experienced technician. With experience and ongoing training from manufacturers and other sources, technicians can progress to highly skilled professional positions with expertise in electrical, fuel system, and engine diagnoses. **FIGURE 2-6** shows an engine in a test cell attached to an **engine dynamometer**, a machine that tests and evaluates engine operation under load. Highly skilled professional technicians are required to operate a dynamometer.

FIGURE 2-4 Students diagnosing a school bus electrical system under supervision at a vocational college.

FIGURE 2-3 A well-equipped transit bus facility.

FIGURE 2-5 A typical hydraulics lab in a vocational college where students receive hands-on training.

Educational Requirements

In addition to a high-school diploma, service technicians may be required to successfully complete trade-related courses or a program at a college or vocational school. Although it is possible in some jurisdictions to become a technician without formal training, employers prefer technicians who have completed an apprenticeship or received certification from a college vocational-training program. Most employers only recruit technicians with accredited educational qualifications from certificate or associate-degree programs. In Canada, trade qualifications are mandatory to work on motor vehicles operated on public roads. A formal apprenticeship period must be served with an employer before receiving a final general certificate of qualification. After registering the apprenticeship contract with the provincial governing body, apprentices are required to meet performance-based learning outcomes and complete trade-related classes before passing the final exam for a certificate of qualification. An interprovincial red seal is granted to technicians with qualifying exam results to work in all provinces in Canada.

The technology used in the commercial vehicle field, both in the vehicles themselves and the systems used to service and diagnose them, is becoming more sophisticated every day. Continuing education is required to keep up with new developments and expand knowledge as a technician. Courses are offered by the vehicle or component OEMs and by aftermarket suppliers. Never turn down the chance to attend these courses because they are necessary for career advancement. **FIGURE 2-7** shows a typical vocational college shop with the instructor setting up an alignment lab for his students.

ASE Certification

While certification is not a mandatory requirement to work in the trade in the US, the National Institute for Automotive Service Excellence (ASE) offers credentialing to heavy-duty truck, medium-duty truck, and bus/coach technicians. Possessing ASE certification leads to better employment opportunities. To gain the ASE qualifications, candidates need a minimum of two years of work experience before passing an exam for each area of specialization. The National Institute for ASE administers certification procedures throughout the US. Certification tests are given twice a year: in the spring and in the fall. The certification areas needed for technicians in these fields are:

- T-series for medium/heavy-duty truck technicians
- S-series for school bus technicians
- H-series for transit bus technicians

Master Technicians

In the US, several years of experience and proper educational qualifications can fast-track a technician's career to that of a master technician. To be certified as a T-, H-, or S-series ASE Master Technician, the following certification tests must be passed:

- T-Series Master Tech: T2 through T8 inclusive
- S-Series Master Tech: S1 through S6 inclusive
- H-Series Master Tech: H1 or H2 and H3 through H8 inclusive

Specialty Technicians

Electronics, engines, brakes, hybrid vehicles, and alternative fuels are just a few of the specialty areas in commercial vehicle service and repair. A specialized technician engages in in-depth, continuous education to develop and refine skills to diagnose, service, and maintain the latest vehicle technologies.

S- and H-Series Certification

Two certification series were recently added in the categories of qualifications under ASE: the S-series (school bus) and the H-series (transit bus) certification. All ASE's heavy-duty

FIGURE 2-6 An engine being evaluated in a dynamometer test cell.

FIGURE 2-7 A vocational college instructor prepares a lab project for his students.

certifications are designed in such a way that the number represents the subject matter and the letter represents the classification of the vehicle type. Examples of specific S- and H-tests are the following:

- H1 certification for compressed natural gas (CNG)–fueled bus engines
- H8 certification for preventive maintenance
- S1 certification for school bus body systems

Working Conditions

Bus and truck technicians work in well-lit, well-ventilated shops. Shop cleanliness, organization, and care and protection of customer/fleet vehicles are important to a successful and respected business. A well-organized shop is shown in **FIGURE 2-8**. Health and safety legislation demand strict adherence to regulations regarding the use of certified personnel, shop safety, and personal protective equipment for all workers. Today, working conditions minimize exposure to harmful working conditions. Professional-looking uniforms and/or coveralls are always worn to protect clothing from grime, oil, and dirt. Work is occasionally performed outside a shop environment if a vehicle cannot be towed or moved inside for repairs. Some businesses specialize in mobile service work in which technicians perform minor repair work on-site. **FIGURE 2-9** shows a mobile repair truck.

Workplace Habits and Employability Skills

LO 2-2 Explain the elements of effective workplace habits and employability skills.

One of the main requests from employers is that prospective employees demonstrate good workplace ethics and communication skills, including face-to-face communication (both verbal and non-verbal), reading, writing, and interpersonal skills.

These attributes are commonly known as **soft skills**. Employers say that they can train an employee to do the job required of them, but it is difficult to correct bad workplace habits or improve poor communication skills. This section identifies and discusses these important soft skills.

Communication

Communication is one of the most important soft skills and it involves not only being able to express yourself, but also understanding what others are saying or asking of you. Communication can be verbal or non-verbal; body language is an important part of communication.

Think about a time when you were talking to someone and he or she rolled his or her eyes—that is a non-verbal response, and a very strong signal that he or she didn't believe or like what you were saying. Non-verbal communication can be effective and supportive, or it can be dismissive and harmful. Effective communication has three aspects: understanding what is being said, processing or analyzing the message to formulate a response, and effectively delivering a response.

Listening

Listening effectively is essential to good communication and requires complete concentration on what the person is saying, ignoring any distractions. Eye contact is important, even while taking notes. Head nods and/or giving small responses like "I see" helps to encourage the speaker to continue and indicates active listening. Listen to the entire message without jumping to conclusions or thinking you have answer to a situation before you have heard the complete message.

For example, when listening to a customer's concern with his or her truck you may, from your experience, think that you

FIGURE 2-8 A well-organized and well-lit workshop.

FIGURE 2-9 Technicians may become mobile service techs; these positions require a great deal of experience to be able to diagnose the vehicle quickly.

know what is wrong before the customer is finished speaking. This is known as **unconscious bias**, meaning that you are predisposed to think a certain way about a subject or a person. Letting a customer express his or her concern without interruption is essential from both a professional and politeness point of view. Otherwise, an important piece of information could be missed. Listening effectively and understanding the message is more difficult than it seems. Unconscious biases or preconceptions can go beyond work experience and book knowledge; they can greatly affect understanding a message. Unconscious bias is the way we perceive people based on gender, race, age, social class, place of origin, and even the way a person speaks.

This type of bias is formulated by deep-seated environmental and social situations in a person's development. Everyone has some unconscious bias. To be an effective listener, unconscious biases must be recognized and then kept from affecting perception of the problem or situation. So, listening effectively means being willing to listen, being able to understand what is being said, and being able to put aside all conscious and unconscious bias to fully grasp the conversation. **FIGURE 2-10** shows an intent listener.

Empathy

Empathy means to view something from the other person's perspective, to "put yourself in their shoes." Empathy is showing concern for the person's position. For example, a customer explains his or her concern and you realize that the repair will be several thousands of dollars. If the customer is an owner operator, this amount may be a significant blow to his or her bottom line. You can simply tell him or her that is the price and that's it, or you can work with the customer to go through various options. Even if the result is the same, showing empathy for the customer's position lets the customer feel that you care about him or her. Empathy means understanding not only the problem, but the customer's point of view as well. This leads to better customer relationships and builds trust.

Verbal and Non-Verbal Feedback

When someone is speaking, verbal and non-verbal feedback can be a powerful tool both to fully understand the message and to prove that you are interested and concerned about the situation being discussed. Verbal feedback can encourage the speaker to continue or even expand on the message. Simple feedback, such as "I understand" or "I see," gives the speaker reinforcement that you are listening to his or her concern. If the speaker is a customer describing an issue with his or her vehicle, feedback, such as "go ahead" or "go on," urges the customer to give more detail. This can provide extra details to understand the complaint.

Non-verbal feedback is very important when someone is speaking. The way the listener stands, sits, makes eye contact, positions his or her arms (folded arms indicate resistance or defiance and may make the speaker think

FIGURE 2-10 Effective listening requires your full attention.

the listener doesn't believe the speaker, or isn't interested), fidgets, and/or looks bored. All these non-verbal cues can greatly affect the conversation. Try to make eye contact as much as possible and appear intent on hearing what the person is saying. Watch for the non-verbal communication coming from the speaker's body position and/or facial expressions.

Effective verbal and non-verbal communication can be learned and improved with practice. Simply talking to the people is the best way to hone this skill. We all have some knowledge of verbal and non-verbal communications. Think of a time when your father or mother or other authority figure gave you the "look" when you were misbehaving as a child. With a simple look they could speak volumes! Practice verbal and non-verbal communication skills as much as possible. To improve your verbal and non-verbal communication skills, use the guidelines in **SKILL DRILL 2-1**.

Use the above guidelines in all conversations and workplace communications to become an effective communicator.

Speaking

After hearing what a speaker has said and fully understanding the concern or situation, knowledge is analyzed, and a response is formulated. Before actually speaking, an effective communicator thinks about the message he is about to deliver, delivers the message clearly, and then ensures that the message is understood.

When speaking, it is important to consider your tone of voice, the speed at which you are delivering the message, who you are delivering the message to, and that your non-verbal communications are in sync with the message. This is easy when there is time to formulate a message, but sometimes a quick response is needed. Responding quickly requires being able to process information quickly and delivering the response immediately.

SKILL DRILL 2-1 Improving Verbal and Non-Verbal Communication Skills

1. Start a communication with a coworker during a break.
2. Try to remain completely open-minded to what the coworker is saying.
3. Listen intently to what is being said.
4. Watch and interpret the speaker's non-verbal communication; facial expressions, posture, interest level, etc.

5. Encourage the coworker to continue what they are saying by using open-ended questions and listening to the answers.
6. Try to understand the coworker's motivation for the opinions they express. Do not jump to conclusions as to his/her beliefs and/or values.
7. Use your non-verbal communication skills to encourage the coworker to speak or continue to speak—making eye contact, looking interested, and no slouching or fidgeting.
8. If the conversation includes criticism of you or another person, try not to be defensive, listen to the criticism calmly and objectively.
9. Listen to the coworker's opinions and positions, even if they differ from your own. Diversity can help you grow as a person and improve your interpersonal skills.
10. When you are speaking, remember that your tone and emotion can convey a positive or a negative message and act accordingly.
11. Always try to be honest and direct when speaking, say what you mean, and don't expect the listener to figure it out on their own.
12. Seek and take opportunities to converse with your coworkers in social settings, as well as professional ones.

Answering quickly can lead to rushed judgments and errors, so think before giving a measured logical response. Stay calm and take a breath before responding. Ask questions to be sure you fully understand the situation/problem, then organize your response.

After delivering the response, be sure that the information is received and perceived correctly. That is, that the person or persons that you responded to fully understood what you said. Ask questions, such as "Do you know what I mean?" or simply "Did you understand?" If the message was not clear to the listener, reiterate or reword the message to help them understand. In high-energy, stressful situations, it may be harder for people to take in and understand the message. Do not send non-verbal or verbal cues of frustration or irritation. Reformulate the message as necessary and deliver it calmly to ensure understanding.

Questioning

Another important component of effective communication is questioning. Asking questions to either gather more information about a situation, or to clarify a statement or concern, can be a very useful tool. Questions can be open-ended such as "Tell me what happened next," "How did it start?" and so on. These types of questions invite the person to talk about the concern as much as or as little as they like.

Closed-ended questions are designed to solidify the facts of a situation or concern. Closed-ended questions typically start with when, where, how much, how many times, etc. These questions would be used when you are trying to get to the root of the situation, such as "When did you first hear the noise?" when a customer has a noise complaint. These types of questions help to narrow down the concern.

Yes and no questions are used to confirm directions or the essence of the concern. There are only two responses possible. These questions are used to verify things, such as "Do you want us to replace the worn tire?" When the customer responds yes, there can be no mistake about the course of action.

Telephone Communication

Although telephone communication is not used as much as in the past, good telephone skills are still important.

In a small shop, the telephone can be the first contact with a customer. Speaking on the telephone is very different than speaking face to face, as neither person can see the other's non-verbal communication or cues. On the telephone, verbal feedback, such as tone of voice, types of greeting, and general attitude, becomes much more important. The telephone is likely the first impression of the workplace, so it is important to make it a good one.

Receiving Phone Calls

The first part of a telephone conversation is the greeting; this is the most important moment in the call. Hearing a greeting that is mumbled and unintelligible, short and terse, or simply just "hello" is very frustrating to the customer. With any of these three greetings, the customer is annoyed, possibly enough to not call back, or, at the very least, has a bad first impression.

The telephone greeting should be light, cheerful, personal, and informative. "Good afternoon, this is Kevin from ACME Transmission Repair, how may I help you." A greeting such as this greets the customer properly (good afternoon), is personal (this is Kevin) and informative (ACME Transmission Repair), and asks to be of assistance (how may I help you). But even this greeting could be a bad one if it is delivered in a bored and

FIGURE 2-11 Smiling while answering the telephone will come across as friendly and cheerful in the tone of your voice.

depressive voice. Tone, whether depressive or flippant, greatly affects the customer experience. Smiling when you deliver your greeting gives a friendly and helpful tone. **FIGURE 2-11** depicts the correct way to answer the telephone.

Deliver the greeting the same way no matter what your actual situation is at the time; whether you are run off your feet, bored, tired, or frustrated by something else, do not let it come across in your telephone manner. While conversing with the customer on the phone, be concise and receptive, listen to the customer's needs, ask pertinent questions when required, and take notes of your conversation, when required. If you need to put the caller on hold, tell him or her the reason and give him or her the option of you calling him or her back, and be sure to do so.

When concluding a call, be sure that you have all the necessary information, date and time, message, caller's name, number, organization, and a call-back time, if necessary. Always thank the customer for their patronage and end the call with a smile. When making a telephone call, use the same strategies for friendly and effective communication.

Interpersonal Communications

In most workplaces today, employees work as part of a team. A team is simply a set of workers with a common goal, usually the success of a project or of a workplace. Team work can be a rewarding and fulfilling experience where every member of the team benefits, but it requires commitment from every member of the team to be successful. This requires strong interpersonal communication skills. Recall from the section on listening earlier in this chapter that we all have unconscious bias. These biases must be recognized and minimized.

Team work requires working with many diverse people to achieve a common goal and clear, concise communication is required between team members. That means listening intently to each member's input, clearly stating your own input and views to the rest of the team, and using all of the team members' inputs to accomplish the tasks at hand. A good team can be much greater than the sum of its parts as long as the lines of communication remain open and, when used effectively, lead to increased knowledge, productivity, and valuable experience for each team member.

Reading

A commercial vehicle technician must be able to read and process information from service manuals, technical service bulletins, emails, written instructions, etc. Reading the information is much different than having someone verbally explain the information and requires good reading comprehension skills.

Reading Comprehension

The technical manuals that technicians must access, whether online or in written form, are usually extremely large volumes or publications. No technician can remember all the information, but, with experience, may be able to complete some tasks without accessing a service manual. But for most jobs, a technician needs to consult some form of manual for the details of the repair or the specifications.

Finding specifications usually requires skimming through the manual until the data is found and then writing it down. However, a repair requires replacement of a component they have not replaced before, they must find the instructions and understand the task before it can be completed. To determine what repair needs to be done, the technician may need to follow an elaborate trouble tree, which is a sequential troubleshooting chart or set of instructions to determine that parts must be replaced. Both of these scenarios require excellent reading comprehension to ensure the correct component is replaced and replaced properly.

The technician must read the information and instruction very carefully and ensure that they understand the task at hand and the steps and order of steps required. If he or she has questions, he or she should consult with a more experienced technician or management before attempting the repair. Even when a technician has done the same job repeatedly, he or she should review the information on the repair, in case the procedure has changed since the last time that repair was completed.

When reading technical manuals, the technician will find that a lot of terms are abbreviated, such as **EGR** for **exhaust gas recirculation**—a system that uses exhaust gas to reduce combustion temperatures, **DPF** for **diesel particulate filter**—a piece of the exhaust system that filters the soot from diesel exhaust. These abbreviations are agreed to by industry and the Society of Automotive Engineers (SAE). The technician should familiarize himself or herself with the various terms.

▶ TECHNICIAN TIP

The Society of Automotive Engineers (SAE) uses a list of common abbreviations agreed to by industry to name certain commercial vehicle components. Some manufacturers in North America and other parts of the world may use different abbreviations for the same component, which sometimes leads to confusion. It is important for the technician to familiarize himself with these abbreviated terms, as they are used as the common vernacular when discussing problems.

Writing

Writing is another important form of communication for any technician. Technicians are required to document the work they did and report on what they encountered while performing the work and/or inspection. The technician records these

FIGURE 2-12 A wall organizer.

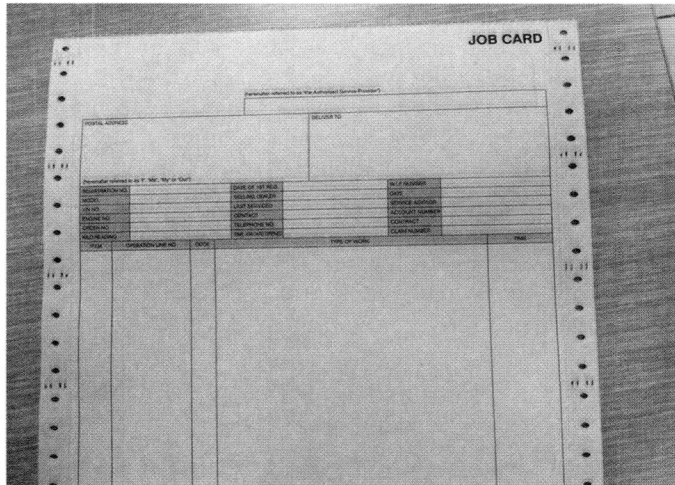

FIGURE 2-13 A typical repair work order or job card.

items on the **repair order**. Repair orders are legal documents, and if required, can be used to settle disputes about the work performed or the suitability of the repair, so it is important that the work order is correct, concise, and accurate as to all the work performed and all the technician's findings. For example, a technician finds that one of the front leaf springs on the truck has a broken leaf. The technician reports this on the work order and recommends replacement of the leaf spring, but the owner refuses the work. The leaf spring eventually fails later and the owner complains that his truck was "just in for service", but the repair order clearly shows that the problem was discovered, and the owner refused to have it fixed. By documenting the broken leaf and the owner's refusal, the technician protects both himself or herself and his or her repair facility from possible legal issues.

The work or repair order is also the way that the company, and, therefore, the technician, gets paid. Every item on a work order usually represents a procedure that the repair facility can charge for. So complete, concise, and accurate listing of the repairs performed is essential. Most shops have a wall organizer for the current repair orders showing who is working on which vehicle and repair. **FIGURE 2-12** shows a typical wall organizer.

Completing a Work or Repair Order

When preparing a repair order, it should contain **the three Cs**, the concern, the cause, and the correction.

- The Concern, or customer's problem, should be clearly stated and includes a report on how the concern was verified before proceeding with the repair.
- The root Cause of the problem should be clearly indicated.
- Finally, the Correction, or how the problem was repaired, should be clearly detailed.

These three Cs must be written clearly and concisely, and in a language that the customer can understand. Do not use technical jargon to explain the Concern, Cause, and Correction. Use laymen's terms, wherever possible.

For example, a customer complains of a clunking sound from the driveline. He says the noise is most prevalent when he first engages the clutch to start off, but he hears it sometimes as he shifts gears.

> CONCERN: Customer reports a clunking sound from the driveline on initial clutch engagement and while shifting. A road test confirms the clunking sound and further investigation points to a worn universal joint. The joint is lacking grease and displays signs of rust. The other joints in the driveline also require greasing but are otherwise OK.

> CAUSE: The root cause of the problem is a failed u-joint because of lack of maintenance.

> CORRECTION: Replace the failed joint, lubricate the driveline, and recommend timely lubrication service for the driveline in the future.

This information clearly states what is wrong, the CONCERN, why it happened, the CAUSE, and how it was fixed, the CORRECTION, and how to prevent reoccurrence. **FIGURE 2-13** shows a typical repair order, also known as a job card.

Any official repair order should always contain the three Cs, but should also contain the following;

- Name and address of customer and repair company
- Make, model, year, vehicle identification number (VIN), license of vehicle
- Date when work started/completed
- Odometer reading upon completion
- Description of work
- Parts installed, specifying whether new, used, or reconditioned
- Price of parts
- Hours billed and cost of labor
- Warranty terms
- Billed shop supplies
- Customer's signature authorizing the repair

While creating a work order, it may be necessary to consult a labor guide. A **labor guide** is a physical or online guide that tells you the amount of time a specific job should take. Labor guides are based on information gathered from many shops and technicians who have completed the specific repair many times before and base the time estimate on their findings. Mitchell provides an online labor guide that covers heavy trucks. The time to complete a specific job, however, can vary depending on several factors, including the age and condition of the vehicle.

As you go through the guide, be sure to read it carefully. Times can vary greatly, depending on the vehicle configuration. For example, the time required to remove a flywheel can be very different, depending on whether the vehicle is equipped with a standard or an automatic transmission, or whether it has a mechanical PTO (power take off unit) that must be removed. The guide typically allows more time for such differences and any add-on devices that must be removed to complete the task. Sometimes the technician or service writer may need to add several times together to arrive at an accurate estimate if the guide does not allow for the add-on equipment. In some shops, these guides are not available or not used and the labor is based on how long the job actually takes to complete.

Most technicians are not responsible for preparing a work order. That job falls to the service writer or the shop manager, but it is important that you understand how it is done and the information required. Technicians may also have to write their conclusions and work procedures that they performed on the work order. Most work orders today are completed on the computer. To prepare a work order, follow the steps in **SKILL DRILL 2-2**.

Other Common Shop Forms

There are several other forms that a technician may be required to complete. These include incident/accident reports, shop safety reports, and broken or defective equipment reports. Most of these types of reports will be made on standardized forms that the company will supply.

An incident/accident report must be filled out whenever there has been a dangerous situation that could have caused an accident (an incident), or an accident when someone has been injured or sickened on the job. A standard incident/accident report form will ask the following:

- Name and address and sometimes other details of the person reporting the incident/accident
- Date and time the incident/accident occurred
- Date and time the incident/accident was reported if different from above
- Location where the incident/accident occurred
- What happened to cause the incident/accident (here you must describe the accident, equipment/tools involved, and the activity that led to the incident/accident)
- Nature of the injury/illness caused by the accident (describe the injury, body parts involved, left side, right side, etc.)
- Who the incident/accident was first reported to and their job title and contact information (if not reported immediately, explain why)

The incident/accident report must be completed clearly and legibly. A properly completed incident/accident report can be a learning tool and help prevent future incidents or accidents from occurring. The report also protects both workers and employers from erroneous or denied claims for compensation because of the incident/accident.

Shop Safety Reports

Most workplaces have a safety committee that is made up jointly of workers and management. In fact, in many jurisdictions, a joint health and safety committee is mandatory. The purpose of these committees is to regularly inspect and report on any deficiencies in the workplace that have the potential to cause injury or illness. The committee conducts scheduled shop safety reports that list any areas of concern so that they can be dealt with before they cause an incident. The committee typically has a standard form that is filled out as the inspection is made. With this type of report, again clarity and conciseness are the

SKILL DRILL 2-2 Preparing a Work Order

1. Access a computerized blank shop work order for your workplace.
2. Fill in the date and your name in the provided space.

3. Ask the customer for the following information and complete the relevant sections of the work order:
  a. The customer's name, address, and phone number
  b. The vehicle information: make and model, year, color, odometer reading, VIN
  c. The concerns the customer wants addressed. Get as much detail as possible to narrow it down.
4. Determine which job is to be completed first, if there is more than one.
5. Print out and assign the work order to the technician who will perform the repair.
6. Carry out the repair, making sure to show your conclusions as to the cause of the original concern and what work was done to correct it in detail, but be concise.
7. List all the parts and supplies you used for the repair in the location provided.
8. Deliver the completed work order to the person responsible for creating the invoice for the customer.

key. You must explain the situation and the cause for concern in a manner that the people who must correct the situation can understand the concern.

Vehicle Inspection Forms

There are many different vehicle inspection forms that are used throughout the heavy-duty vehicle service industry. These are somewhat standardized; however, slight differences are noted from one workplace to the next. Drivers are required to fill out pre-trip inspection reports. This is a walk-around visual inspection of the vehicle the driver completes before driving the vehicle and includes fluid level checks, tire checks, lights, mirrors, and any other visible defects that the driver can see.

Drivers employed by motor carriers also fill out a daily report after their day is done where they can list any problems or unusual operating conditions of the vehicle. These reports are known as **DVIRs** or **Driver Vehicle Inspection Reports**. DVIRs are required by federal law in the United States and, up until recently, had to be filed with the company the driver works for, whether a defect was found or not. Since 2014, a no-defect DVIR (meaning that the driver did not find or was not made aware of any defects) no longer needs to be submitted. The DVIR can be an important tool for the servicing technician. The DVIR form is not standardized and there will be differences, depending on the fleet or vehicle type in the fleet. A sample DVIR is shown in **FIGURE 2-14**.

Technicians usually use inspection forms during preventative maintenance (PM) service. Shops normally have two or three different forms used for this purpose, an "A" inspection, a "B" inspection, and sometimes a "C" inspection.

- An "A" inspection usually involves an oil and filter change and lubrication service and a visual inspection of several key items on the vehicle, including brake adjustment.
- A "B" inspection typically covers everything in an "A" inspection and involves a more in-depth examination of the brakes and other items.
- A "C" inspection typically covers everything in a "B" inspection, but contains other instructions, such as transmission oil change, drive axle oil change, and more.

Careful documentation and recording of PM inspections can help a large or small fleet plan for scheduled preemptive maintenance, rather than waiting for failure to occur. PM inspections are covered in more detail in the last chapter of this book.

Defective Equipment Reports

Many shops have a form that can be used to report equipment that is deficient or defective. This form provides a way to ensure that the equipment is repaired and/or replaced in a timely manner. When a piece of equipment can no longer be used, remove it from normal operating use, fill out the report, and give it to the person responsible for arranging the repair or replacement. This could be a supervisor or another designated person.

Although employees may be reluctant to report defective equipment for fear that they will be blamed for the failure of the piece of equipment or tool, it is more frustrating to attempt to use a piece of equipment or tool only to find it is defective and it

has not been reported. This leads to work delays and time overruns. A tool or piece of equipment may fail for several reasons; it is much better that the problem is reported so that the equipment or tool can be replaced or repaired as soon as possible.

Lock-Out Tag-Out

In a lot of shops, the **Lock-Out Tag-Out (LOTO)** system is used to make sure that defective equipment is not used until it has been properly repaired. The LOTO system places a lock on the defective equipment or machine so that it cannot be unlocked except by the person who locked it out. The person also tags the equipment with a do-not-operate tag that lists the date of lock out and the person who locked out the equipment. The LOTO system can be also used by technicians to prevent the vehicle or component they are working on from being moved or started.

Larger equipment and/or machines lend themselves easier to LOTO procedures. Typically, a machine has an electrical box that supplies power to the machine; if so, the switch is turned off and locked in the off position and tagged with the date, the person's name, and the reason for the LOTO. **FIGURE 2-15** shows a locked-out control panel.

DRIVER'S INSPECTION REPORT

Date: _____
TRACTOR/TRUCK NO.:_____   TRAILER(S) NO.(S):_____

TRACTOR/TRUCK	Defective?	Remarks	TRACTOR/TRUCK	Defective?	Remarks
Air compressor			Brake connections		
Air lines			Brakes		
Battery			Coupling chains		
Brake accessories			Coupling (king Pin)		
Brakes			Doors		
Carburetor			Hitch		
Clutch			Landing gear		
Defroster			Lights—all		
Driveline			Roof		
Engine			Springs		
Fifth wheel			Tarpaulin		
Front axle			Tires		
Fuel tank			Wheels		
Heater			OTHER		
Horn			Condition of vehicle is satisfactory? ○ Yes ○ No		
Lights					
Mirrors			Defects corrected? ○ Yes ○ No		
Muffler					
Oil pressure			Defects need not be corrected for vehicle safety. ○ Yes ○ No		
Onboard recorder					
Radiator			DRIVER'S Signature:		
Reflectors					
Safety equipment			MECHANIC Signature:		
Springs					
Starter					
Steering					
Tachograph					
Tires					
Transmission					
Wheels					
Windows					
Windshield wipers					
OTHER					

FIGURE 2-14 A Driver Vehicle Inspection Report.

FIGURE 2-15 A locked-out control panel for a machine.

FIGURE 2-16 Small defective shop equipment should be removed from the general shop and sent out for repair as soon as possible.

Vehicles can be locked out by removing the ignition key and placing a tag on the vehicle—either on the driver's door handle or on the steering wheel. The key should be stored in a proper key cabinet for that purpose. Smaller equipment that is defective, however, may require only tag-out procedures. Tag-out procedures place a tag on the equipment stating the date, the cause of the tag out, and the person who tagged it.

Smaller tagged-out equipment should be removed from circulation, when possible, and stored in a secure location where it will wait for repair. It is important that after the equipment is LOTO, a report is submitted to initiate the repair procedure, unless the equipment is to be repaired by the person who locked it out.

LOTO procedures are relatively straight forward; however, procedures and steps to follow vary slightly from shop to shop. Make sure you know the correct procedure to follow in your workplace. If you are uncertain of the procedure, have your supervisor work through the system with you. **FIGURE 2-16** shows an impact gun tagged as defective.

Workplace Habits

As seen in the previous section, good communication skills are very important to ensure the success of both the worker and the company they work for. However, the workplace habits of the employee are also crucial to this success. This means behaving in a

FIGURE 2-17 A professional appearance shows you respect your job and take it seriously.

professional, ethical, and courteous manner at work. Good workplace habits and ethics are simply a matter of respect for yourself, your fellow employees, your supervisors, and your workplace.

Appearance and House Keeping

As stated earlier, first impressions are hard to change, and the first impression an employer has of you is how you present yourself at your employment interview. Most people understand and dress-up a bit for an interview, but it doesn't end there. In the workplace, you are constantly giving first impressions to new coworkers, customers, new supervisors, or visiting bosses from outside your workplace. Maintaining a professional look is very important to be taken seriously and respected. Take the job seriously and dress properly for it, including a clean uniform or coveralls, and having good personal hygiene and appearance. **FIGURE 2-17** shows an employee who demonstrates a professional appearance.

Many things can lead to a bad impression: slouching, a shuffling walk, clothes not tucked in, boots not laced up—these bad personal habits indicate disrespect for the job, including a customer's vehicle. A dirty, disorganized work area also shows disrespect for the job. Keeping the work space organized and clean takes less work and time than searching for things that are misplaced. Also, less trips, slips, and falls lead to more productive work.

When a company looks well organized, that is the impression that a potential customer gets, and it makes him or her feel comfortable having his or her vehicle serviced there. Whether it is a personal workspace or the general office, cleanliness and organization inspire confidence in the customer. **FIGURE 2-18** shows a well-organized company.

Time Management

Be on time for your job. It is a simple statement, but it is so important. We all know someone who is constantly late for work or rushing in at the last minute to "beat the clock." This kind of behavior is very frustrating to an employer (**FIGURE 2-19**).

FIGURE 2-18 Good organization inspires confidence in the customer.

FIGURE 2-19 Punctuality is extremely important and shows you care for and respect your job.

There are many excuses: missed the bus, the alarm didn't go off, I had to get the kids to school. Whatever the excuse, there is usually NO real reason to be late for work. Punctuality doesn't start at 6 AM when your alarm goes off and you rush around with your eyes half closed trying to get ready, it starts the night before. You know you must be at work at 7 AM. You know how long it takes for you to get ready and get there, so plan for it properly. Before you go to bed, take care of stuff like getting your lunch ready, getting the garbage out, or whatever tasks you can accomplish now, rather than rushing in the morning. Plan to get to bed at a reasonable hour so you aren't overtired when you wake. Set your alarm to wake you with extra time factored in to allow for traffic anomalies, etc. Plan to arrive at work at least 10 minutes before your specified start time so you are not rushed.

Doing all these things will get you to work on time 99% of the time. There are always circumstances beyond our control that can make us late; car accident, sudden illness, etc., but these things happen very rarely, and you will find your supervisor much more forgiving when it is not just another in a long line of excuses.

Punctuality extends to the work at hand, as well as arriving on time. You should complete your work in a timely fashion. If a certain job takes "X" amount of time, it should be done in that time. Each job will have certain quirks that could delay it, but the amount of time to complete it should average out. Avoid distractions like answering the phone, texting, etc. These can rob enormous amounts of time—not just for the actual event, but the time it takes to refocus on the task after being distracted. If you promise that a job will be finished at a certain time, try to stick to it. Likely your supervisor has told the customer when to expect the vehicle's return. If something goes awry, make sure you let your supervisor know immediately so he can advise the customer of the delay.

Ethics

Being ethical in all you do is another desirable trait in an employee. Ethics basically means treating everyone fairly or treating others as you would have them treat you. Being ethical means being respectful and kind to the people you interact with and knowing the difference between right and wrong. Ethical behavior should be extended to your employer, the business itself, your supervisors, your coworkers, and perhaps most of all, to the customers. This means you respect them and their property. Being ethical is not always easy if people you must deal with do not have the same ethics; however, it is the best way to become a well-respected and admired employee and person.

Customer Service

The customer is the reason that we exist, whether the customer is an owner-operator or a large fleet being serviced. The customer is how we get paid. It is easy sometimes in a fleet shop to lose sight of the fact that the vehicles we service represent customers, but in the fleet shop each vehicle represents several "customers." The driver or operator of the fleet truck is one customer we must satisfy so that he can continue to earn a living. The dispatcher is another; the vehicle must be fixed so that he can assign the vehicle to a run or route, and the company owners are also customers, as each vehicle that is down for service is not earning them money.

It is important that we treat all our customers and their vehicles with respect. Mahatma Gandhi perhaps said it best in his words about the importance of the customer. These words are shown in **FIGURE 2-20**.

The owner-operator who has a bad experience with a shop will not return, losing potential business for the shop. However,

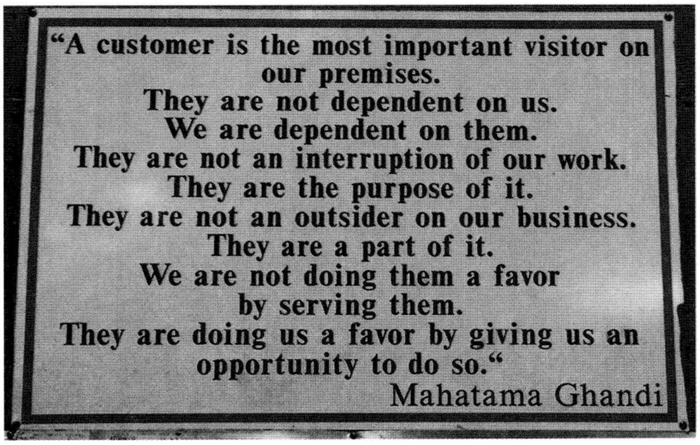

"A customer is the most important visitor on our premises.
They are not dependent on us.
We are dependent on them.
They are not an interruption of our work.
They are the purpose of it.
They are not an outsider on our business.
They are a part of it.
We are not doing them a favor by serving them.
They are doing us a favor by giving us an opportunity to do so."
Mahatama Ghandi

FIGURE 2-20 The importance of the customer cannot be overstated, they are simply the reason we are in the business.

FIGURE 2-21 The interior of a modern class 8 truck; the owner has spent a lot of money on the vehicle, so keep it clean and tidy while working on it.

when a customer leaves, he or she often shares his or her negative experience with many other potential customers. So, one unsatisfied customer can lose multiple customers for the shop. Eventually, jobs are lost if enough business leaves or is deterred by a bad shop reputation.

A fleet shop that has too many errors or costs the company too much money, when compared to other shops, ceases to be, and the work is shipped elsewhere, again likely costing you your job. So, as you can see, taking care of customers is actually taking care of us. When looked at in that respect, it is easy to see that everything we do to help the customer benefits us too. Dealings and relationships with management, coworkers, parts personnel, lube techs, and wash bay attendants all contribute to a good customer experience and help the shop overall and, therefore, help ensure that jobs are retained.

Protect the Customer's Vehicle

Always ensure that the customer's vehicle is kept clean and safe from harm while it is in the shop. Use seat covers, floor covers, and if necessary, body covers, while working on the vehicle to protect the interior and exterior from damage and or dirt. Heavy-duty vehicles today can be appointed with even more features than the highest-end luxury cars and they cost hundreds of thousands of dollars, so protect the customer's investment. **FIGURE 2-21** shows the interior of a modern class 8 truck.

When moving the customer's vehicle or road-testing, be careful not to cause any damage. If damage does occur by accident, be sure to inform the supervisor as soon as possible so the customer can be notified, and repairs can be initiated. Accidents happen, and when they do, it is very important to be honest and explain what happened, rather than ignore the damage and have an irate customer when the truck is picked up. In all, treat the vehicle as if it was your own and care for it in the same fashion.

Preparing the Vehicle for Return to the Customer

Always adhere to shop/company policies when readying a vehicle for return to the customer.

- Review the shop policy for vehicle return from time to time to ensure you are following it correctly.
- Check the cleanliness of the vehicle.

- Remove any protective cover used during service.
- Some shop policies require that the vehicle be washed before return; if so, wash or have the vehicle washed.
- Clean any seat covers or body panel covers and return them to their storage location.

Inspect the vehicle carefully before it is returned to the customer. Small things, such as greasy finger prints on the door handle, a candy wrapper left inside the cab, finger prints on the windows or windshield, packaging from a part used during the repair, and dirty paper floor mat covers, are an irritant to the customer and make them reconsider any repeat business for your company. Making sure that the vehicle is clean and free of any finger prints shows the customer that you respect his or her property and creates a satisfied customer who will return for his or her next service. Remember, an unhappy customer loses not only one client, but likely all those potential clients he or she complains to after he or she has left. The small amount of work involved in making sure the vehicle is clean and tidy helps to ensure that your company is successful, which is an investment in your future.

Legal Requirements of Repair Facilities

LO 2-3 Describe general legal requirements of repair facilities.

As with any business, repair facilities operate under certain legal requirements. For the most part these are not of concern to the technician, but it is important that they are aware that all the forms and sheets technicians are required to complete can be used in a legal context, if needed. All of the inspection sheets, estimates, repair orders, and invoices are documents that could be subpoenaed in a lawsuit or other legal action.

For example, there have been several instances of truck wheels coming off while the vehicle is in motion. The wheel becomes a projectile weighing several hundred pounds and traveling at 30 to 70 miles per hour; it can cause extreme damage, injury, and even death, if it contacts another vehicle. When such an incident occurs, every person that has worked on that vehicle becomes suspect as the investigation looks for the root cause of the failure. While trying to find out what happened, investigators look for the driver's pre-trip inspection form and demand copies of all the documents in the vehicle's service record. These documents are scrutinized by the investigators as they search for the cause of the failure.

Technicians must realize that their names are likely associated with these records and, therefore, they should be accurate and complete when filled out. Imagine that you were the last person that installed the failed wheel; you will likely be called to testify in court as to why the wheel failed. Of course, there are many variables in such a situation, such as "Did the wheel come off because the mounting studs failed? Was it because of wheel end bearing failure? Did the wheel rim itself fail?" You must be able to tell investigators or the court what you did and the way you did it. And because of this, all documents you fill out or complete must be treated as if they were legal documents, because one day they may be. Complete the documents neatly, clearly, and completely so that if you are called to explain them in the future, you can do so.

General Legal Requirements

Legal requirements and responsibilities of repair facilities vary according to the jurisdiction; however, most will be similar to the following.

All repair facilities must be registered with the responsible agency in their area to conduct business and pay a license or registration fee on a regular basis. This license can be suspended if the facility is found to be conducting illegal business practices.

The facility must offer the opportunity for the customer to receive a written estimate prior to work being performed on their vehicle. The customer can waive the right to a written estimate, but if an estimate is given it must include at least the following:

- The repair facility's name, address, phone number, and registration or license number
- The customer's name, address, and phone number
- The vehicle information, make, model, year, mileage, VIN, license plate
- The concern, the proposed repair, and the completion date
- The estimated cost of the parts and time of the labor to complete the repair
- The labor rate, whether hourly or flat rate
- The cost of any shop supplies that may be charged
- The details of any warranty offered with the work (in some jurisdictions there is no legal requirement to offer any warranty; in others, a three-month or 3,000-mile warranty may be required)
- There should also be a place for the customer to authorize the work with his or her signature.
- There should be a provision for the customer to request the replaced components, if he or she wishes.

Once the written estimate is given and accepted by the customer, it becomes a legally binding contract in that the facility contracts to do the work by a set time and at a set price. The cost of the repair cannot exceed the estimate by more than a set amount, typically 10% or $50, whichever is greater, without the customer's express consent. The contract also binds the customer to pay for the work when it is completed. If the final cost is more than the agreed amount, the customer is entitled to legal recourse, and may refuse to pay any extra. If during the repair the facility discovers more repairs are necessary, the customer must be contacted to authorize the extra work and cost.

Once the customer agrees to and signs off on the estimate, a repair order is created, or the estimate becomes the repair order. The customer is required to authorize the work by signing the repair order. The work then proceeds, and the customer is presented with the invoice. Any invoice must include the same information as the estimate above and again becomes a legal document. The customer pays the invoice and the vehicle is released to the customer.

► TECHNICIAN TIP

Quite often when servicing a vehicle, the technician will discover other components that need replacing and/or other service that should be performed. Make sure that these items are recorded on the work order

and that they are brought to the customer's attention. If the customer does not want to proceed with the suggested extra service required, have them initial the work order to acknowledge they were notified of the defects. If anything were to happen to the vehicle because of the refused repair, the shop cannot be held liable.

If the customer refuses to pay the bill, the repair facility can hold the vehicle until payment is made using what is known as a **mechanic's lien**. If the customer defaults on payment, the repair facility can repossess the vehicle to guarantee the bill is paid. The customer can utilize various legal methods to try to retrieve the vehicle, but typically, once a lien is exercised, the only recourse for the customer is to pay the money to the facility.

In some jurisdictions where there is a dispute over the invoice and the facility has exercised its right to withhold the vehicle's release under a lien, the customer can apply to the court and pay a bond in the amount of the invoice and retrieve his or her vehicle. If the customer goes this route, the facility can apply to have the bond money turned over to the facility. The facility must make this request within a certain time limit—usually six months. A lien is usually used as a last resort when all other methods of trying to receive payment for the work have been exhausted.

The repair facility has a legal responsibility to retain records of estimates, work orders, and invoices for a period typically not less than 12 months. Technicians should be aware that their work and documents could be examined by the courts at a later date and behave accordingly; take your work and the documents you fill out seriously.

Vehicle Identification Labels

LO 2-4 Explain the purpose and types of vehicle identification labels.

There are many ways that technicians can access service information for the vehicle they are required to service. These include: written manufacturer's service manuals, online manufacturer's service information systems, technical service bulletins (TSBs), generic or aftermarket service information systems, and more. When a technician is diagnosing a concern on a vehicle, he or she may consult many different information sources before the solution is found. The problem must be researched to make sure the correct course of action is taken. To begin the research, the technician needs information that can be found on the various vehicle information plates and labels.

Vehicle Information Labels

There are many labels attached to a vehicle that can provide the technician with valuable information. These include: The Vehicle Identification number (VIN), the Vehicle Emission Control Information (VECI) label, the Vehicle Safety Certification (VSC) label, the **refrigerant label** showing the refrigerant and capacity used, a belt routing label, and more. From the technician's standpoint, the most important of these is the VIN, which provides important details about the vehicle, such as year of manufacture, model, engine, chassis configuration **FIGURE 2-22** shows a typical VIN label.

FIGURE 2-22 The VIN contains valuable information about the vehicle.

Vehicle Identification Number

The **VIN**, or **vehicle identification number**, identifies the vehicle make, model, year, configuration, and the individual serial number of a vehicle. There are four standards for VINs. Originally, the Federal Motor Vehicle Safety Standards (FMVSS) and then the SAE J853 standards were used in North America until 1980–1981. The International Standards Organization (ISO) standard 3779 and 3780 were used in most of the rest of the world. Both standards use 17 digits. In 1980–1981, North America adopted a compatible, but slightly different, version of the ISO standards. The VIN is a 17-digit alpha-numeric code that contains information about the vehicle.

To avoid confusion, the VIN does not contain the letters I, O, or Q, as these could be mistaken for ones or zeros. The VIN is used by the technician to identify the vehicle. The VIN gives the technician the make and model of the vehicle, the year of manufacture, the engine, the gross vehicle weight rating (GVWR), and the vehicle configuration. Although manufacturers all use the 17-digit standard, there are slight differences to the coding used.

The VIN breaks down as follows: the first three alpha-numeric characters are the World Manufacturer Identification (WMI), a code identifying the manufacturer, and the country of manufacture. The next five or six characters are where the North American and the rest of the world differ. In North America, the five characters following the WMI describe the vehicle type, configuration, engine, GVRW, etc. The next character in North America, the ninth, is called the check digit. This digit allows the VIN to be verified as a valid number. The rest of the world does not use the ninth character as a check digit, so the fourth through ninth characters are all vehicle descriptors. The tenth character is the vehicle year of manufacture. The eleventh character is the manufacturing plant identifier and the digits 12 through 17 are the sequential serial number identifying the individual vehicle.

In the VIN, the characters from 4 through 10 are the ones most important to the technician. This is the part of the VIN that tells him/her the information he or she needs to start to service the vehicle. It is important to note that the codes and digits used in the five or six characters after the WMI that describe the vehicle configuration are not universal and can vary by manufacturer. There are several VIN decoders on the Internet that can be used to get the required information, but it is always advisable to decode the VIN using the manufacturer's information to avoid any errors. The sequential serial number is also important as manufacturers may base a recall or TSB on units prior to or after a certain serial number. **FIGURE 2-23** shows the basic decoding of a VIN.

Seventeen-Character Vehicle Identification Number (VIN)								
Typical VIN	1HT	M	K	AA	N	1	7	H	397874
Character Position	1, 2, 3	4	5	6, 7	8	9	10	11	12 thru 17
Code Description									
Manufacturer, Make, Vehicle Type									
Chassis, Front Axle Position, Brakes									
Vehicle Model Series, Cab									
Engine Model, Horsepower Range									
Gross Vehicle Weight Rating (GVWR)									
Check Digit									
Vehicle Model Year									
Plant of Manufacture									
Production Number									

FIGURE 2-23 Basic VIN breakdown.

Vehicle Emission Control Information Label

The **vehicle emission control information label**, or VECI, is a label that indicates that the vehicle conforms to the emission control regulations for the year it was built. A typical VECI is also known as the emission declaration label. On light- and medium-duty vehicles, these labels are usually found under the hood or in some other conspicuous location. On heavy-duty vehicles, the emission control information/declaration is on the engine as part of or near the engine identification label. A medium-duty VECI label is shown in **FIGURE 2-24**.

Engine Identification Label/Information Plate

The **engine identification label** or **information plate** on a heavy-duty diesel truck is an extremely valuable source of information for the technician. This label contains the engine, serial number, date of manufacture, engine family, model number, size, horsepower rating, rated revolutions per minute (rpm), idle rpm, fuel rate, timing, and valve lash settings. This information is important to the technician as he or she services the engine. As mentioned above, the emission conformation declaration is usually part of or near this label. The engine information label or plate is usually on the engine valve cover or on the front timing gear cover. It makes sense to have the label on the engine for heavy vehicles, as the vehicle can have several engine options with various horsepower ratings, and the engine may be supplied by several different manufacturers. A typical heavy-duty engine information label is shown in **FIGURE 2-25**.

Vehicle Safety Certification Label

The **Vehicle Safety Certification label**, or VSC, certifies that the vehicle conforms to the safety standards required by FMVSS at the date of manufacture. Typically, this label contains information, such as the axles gross axle weight rating (GAWR), the GVWR of the vehicle, the recommended tire sizes for each axle, and the inflation pressures. A typical VSC label is shown in **FIGURE 2-26**.

Other Labels

There may be many other labels on a vehicle, including a **coolant label** that lists the type of coolant used; oil type used in the engine, transmission, and/or drive axles; a **belt routing label** that shows the correct drive belt positions and routing; and more. These labels offer information to the technician and should not be overlooked. There may also be information tags and/or serial number tags attached to major components of the vehicle driveline on the transmission, power divider, and drive axles.

Other systems have information labels, such as air valves and modules. These tags and/or labels should be recorded when work is required on these components. The information they provide is valuable when sourcing parts and/or service information. **FIGURE 2-27** shows a typical coolant label.

Service Information Resources

LO 2-5 Describe the purpose and use of service information resources.

When a vehicle requires service, the technician must make use of various sources of information to diagnose, isolate, and repair the concern so that the problem is fixed correctly the first time. One of the most annoying things in servicing vehicles is the

FIGURE 2-25 The engine information label has important details and specifications for the technician.

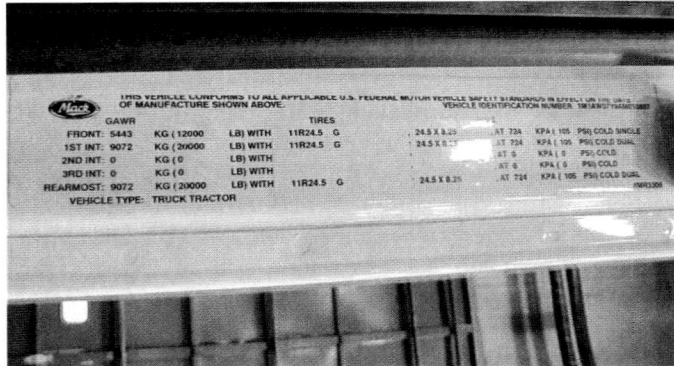

FIGURE 2-26 A typical Vehicle Safety Certification label.

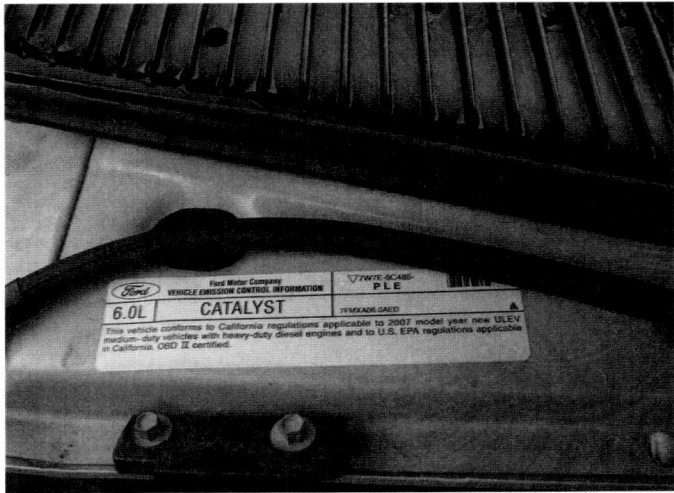

FIGURE 2-24 On medium- and light-duty vehicles, the emission control information label is typically under the hood.

FIGURE 2-27 Labels are used to inform the technician of the type of fluids used in a system.

dreaded **comeback**. That is when a vehicle has been in for service for a complaint and has been purportedly fixed; however, the same problem reoccurs within a short time. This is frustrating to the owner/operator or driver and the service manager, and damaging to the technician's reputation.

To avoid comebacks and repair the problem right the first time, careful research is required to ascertain the actual problem; it is like conducting an investigation. The technician follows a step-by-step process to determine the root cause of the problem. The number one cause of comebacks is jumping to conclusions. That is, thinking you know the cause before you investigate.

First, the technician must understand exactly what the problem is. Let's say the complaint is the engine does not start. Find out more information by asking questions, such as Does the engine turn over (crank), at all or not? Do you hear any noise while cranking? Does the engine attempt to fire? Do you see any smoke when cranking?, until the essence of the problem is understood.

Then, use the available resources to determine why the problem is occurring. Utilize manufacturer's repair manuals, TSBs, manufacturer's service information systems, aftermarket service information systems, educational resources, Internet service assistance programs from manufacturers, and more. When working on heavy trucks, the service manual for the truck does not contain information on the engine and vice versa. You may need service information for a Peterbilt truck and service information for a Cummins engine in order to find a solution. All of today's manufacturers have troubleshooting manuals or sections that list common problems and provide step-by-step diagnostic procedures to reach a solution. These are helpful, but only when used correctly. The following section discusses the various information sources available and explains their use.

Manufacturer's Manuals

Manufacturers prepare several manuals for the vehicles they produce, including the operator's manual, maintenance manual,

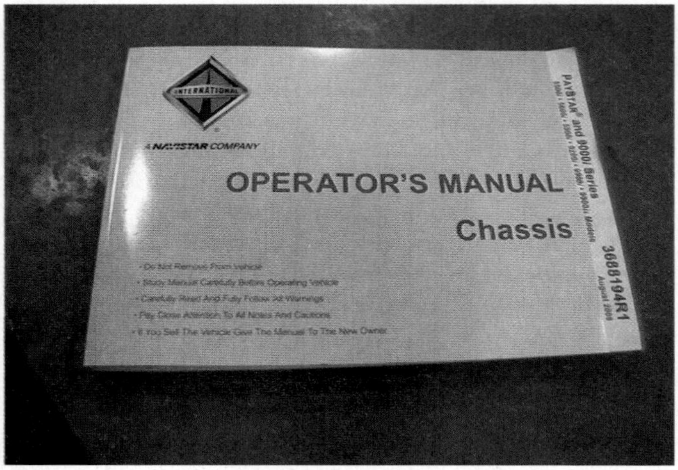

FIGURE 2-28 The operator's manual contains valuable information and should not be overlooked.

service manuals, troubleshooting manuals, etc. The maintenance manual is covered in the "Developing a PM inspection system" chapter, Chapter 63. This section discusses each of the manuals a technician is likely to use when investigating a concern with a particular vehicle.

Operator's Manual

The **operator's manual** is a booklet designed to inform the driver of how to correctly operate the vehicle. This manual shows the driver where all the vehicle controls are located, the positions of switches and fuses, fill points, and capacities for various fluids, etc. The manual contains other elements, such as vehicle security information and who to call for service. The manual also explains the proper operation of vehicle subsystems, such as antilock brakes, traction control, power windows, air-conditioning, wipers-washers. This manual is valuable to the technician and includes the location of fuse panels and the fuse allocations. It also explains the different warning lights associated with the vehicle and what can cause them to illuminate.

The operator's manual explains how a component, such as the power divider or axle lock, should operate so that the technician can determine when it is not functioning correctly. The technician or operator can consult the index when looking for information in the operator's manual. **FIGURE 2-28** shows a typical operator's manual.

Service History

The vehicle **service history** may be recorded at your shop if the vehicle is a fleet or repeat customer. The vehicle service history is a valuable source of information; it can tell you if the current concern is a repeat of past problems or not and list other work that may have been done that could possibly affect or cause the present concern. In most shops, the vehicle service history is available electronically, allowing the technician quick access to the prior work performed. Fleet shops have a detailed vehicle tracking program that can tell everything about the vehicle from the first day it was put in to service to the present, all the work performed, every oil change, etc., and can be analyzed to determine failure trends. **FIGURE 2-29** shows a typical online service history screen.

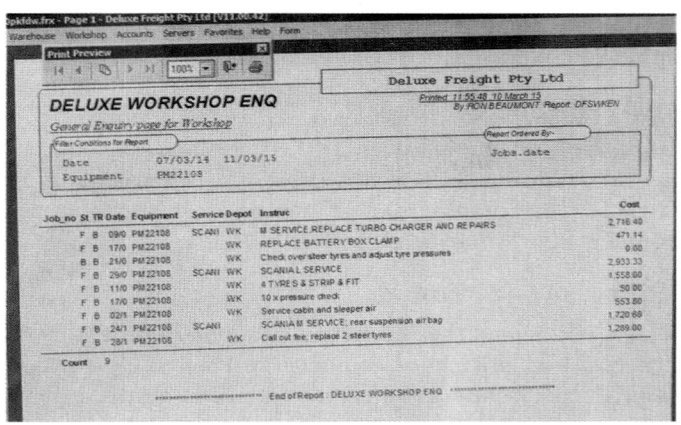

FIGURE 2-29 Service history can be used to identify trends or repeat repairs.

Technical Service Bulletins

When a heavy truck is produced, the manufacturer prepares a service manual, either physical or online, that covers all aspects of the vehicle, excluding the engine. Much of the information in the manual is recycled from year to year, unless the system on the vehicle has changed. The manual contains the required updated information; however, during the life of the vehicle, certain problems may arise. If these problems occur in many of those particular vehicles, the manufacturer produces a **Technical Service Bulletin (TSB)** to alert the technician to the problem and the repair procedure.

Manufacturers are constantly testing their vehicles and systems, and this may lead to a TSB being sent out to correct a mechanical issue, a software issue, or a non-compliance issue with the vehicle. TSBs can be simple, such as a hose rubbing against a shock absorber that needs to be secured, or complex, such as a failing camshaft bearing that must be replaced. TSBs are constantly being produced and updated. In an online environment, the older TSB is automatically overwritten with the new one. If the TSBs are kept in a manual in the shop, the old TSB is discarded when a new one is sent out, so only the latest information is available.

▶ TECHNICIAN TIP

When working on a problem that seems to have you stumped, don't be afraid to seek input from other technicians or your supervisor. Quite often you will find that, by talking out the problem with others, they may have experienced the same problem before, or they may have valuable suggestions. Sometimes, just verbalizing the concern can lead you to realize the solution.

▶ TECHNICIAN TIP

A heavy-truck vehicle service manual typically does not have information on the engine. For engine information, you need to consult a specific engine service manual or the engine manufacturer's online Service Information System (SIS), such as Cummins QuickServe Online (QSOL) or Detroit Diesels' Power Literature.

Service Manuals

A **service manual** is an indexed book produced by the manufacturer or the aftermarket to describe the service and repair procedures required on a vehicle. Although many manufacturers are moving toward a strictly online or digital service manual, the technician may have to consult a paper service manual occasionally. Depending on the manufacturer, these manuals can be one single volume or several volumes that cover specific systems of the vehicle.

If a manufacturer uses a single volume, the book may encompass several thousand pages. If separate system volumes are used, the books are more manageable. As mentioned previously, vehicle manufacturer's manuals typically do not contain engine information, so more than one manual may be needed to do a repair.

TSBs are commonly retained in a separate manual in the shop and should be consulted first for new information about the concern.

When investigating a problem using the service manual, first look in the general index (typically at the front of the book), to see if there is a section on troubleshooting. Note that a multi-volume manual may have the troubleshooting section in a separate volume. Find the troubleshooting reference that covers the concern and go to it; there will be a series of questions designed to ensure you are troubleshooting the correct problem. Again, let's use the no-start problem. The troubleshooting section for no-start asks questions like the ones we asked previously in the service information resources section. In the troubleshooting section on no-start it asks, "Does the engine crank? Yes? No?" and depending on the answer, you are sent to a series of other questions or steps.

Trouble trees are designed to logically bring you to the solution of your problem, so do not skip any steps. After the problem is pinpointed, go to the text reference to obtain the repair procedure instructions and follow the steps to make the repair.

After the repair is completed, test (or road test) the vehicle, to be sure that the problem is corrected. Many comebacks are caused by technicians rushing and overlooking this vital step. **FIGURE 2-30** shows a truck leaving for a road test.

Online Service Resources

As mentioned in the previous section, many manufacturers are switching or have switched to a totally online **Service Information System**, or **SIS**, to replace written service manuals. Some still provide a written version of the manual, if requested. A SIS

FIGURE 2-30 A road test can confirm that the original concern has been rectified.

is an online version of the printed service manual and usually includes access to all the other manuals produced for the vehicle.

Online SISs are extremely helpful to a technician because they can access all the information needed during a diagnosis and repair through the one interface—the personal computer (PC). This interface can take the form of a desktop computer, a laptop computer, a handheld tablet, or a cell phone to access service information. Each manufacturer has their own proprietary SIS. Cummins, for example, has QuickServe OnLine, or QSOL, Caterpillar has their CAT-SIS, Freightliner, Detroit Diesel, and Western Star also have their own systems under the umbrella of their parent company's system, Daimler Trucks North America (DTNA). These resources originally were developed as software-based systems where the user would buy and install the software, and then pay for upgrades as they became available. Today, these systems are almost all subscription-based systems that the user pays a yearly fee to access. The earlier systems were large software programs that required significant space on the computer to operate, but the new subscription-based systems operate by accessing the company's mainframe where the actual software is stored. The system is constantly updated at the source and requires a small amount of software. This allows it to be very portable. As mentioned above, some versions can even be accessed using a cell phone as the interface, although some of the functionality may not be available. These systems all involve connecting the interface device, typically a laptop computer, to the vehicle through the **DDL**, or **Diagnostic Data Link**, a special five- or nine-pin connector on the truck. **FIGURE 2-31** shows a typical DDL location.

Using this connection, any trouble codes present are read and diagnosed using the SIS. The SIS also provides a means to troubleshoot without a code being present. Just as with the physical manual, the SIS includes a trouble tree, asks basic questions to isolate the concern, and gives certain steps to follow to first diagnose, and then complete, the repair. **FIGURE 2-32** shows a technician using an SIS to research a problem.

The Internet is useful for looking up information about a particular concern using various websites. The Internet is also used to interact and converse with other technicians and share information about different problems they have come across and their solutions. Vehicle and component manufacturers have an online presence that is accessed for service information, TSBs, and/or parts information. The steps in **SKILL DRILL 2-3** are researching the information specific to an Eaton transmission using their available online information, but other manufacturers have similar online portals.

Component Manuals

When working on specific components on a vehicle, such as transmissions, drive axles, and other systems, access the component manufacturer's manual for specific information about the component. Component manufacturers, such as Eaton, Meritor, Bendix, Wabco, and others, have an extensive online presence and can be a valuable source of information. These can offer individual specification and overhaul instructions for the components that go into more depth than the vehicle manufacturer's manual. These manuals are available online or in print form.

Other Online Resources

There are other online resources available to the technician, such as aftermarket service information systems. Alldata and Snap-On both have aftermarket service information systems available for subscription. Some manufacturers offer limited access to service information free of charge. For example, Mack and Volvo trucks offer access to TSBs. There are also many organizations online that can offer information and general specifications, such as the American Society of Engineers (ASE); Dieselnet.com, an online technical data base specifically for diesel engines and emissions; government agencies; trucking associations; and other avenues to connect with other technicians. Online resources are increasing and all technicians should try and stay abreast of the resources available to them.

Parts Manuals

Manufacturers publish **parts manuals** for identifying and finding needed vehicle parts. Parts manuals are available either in

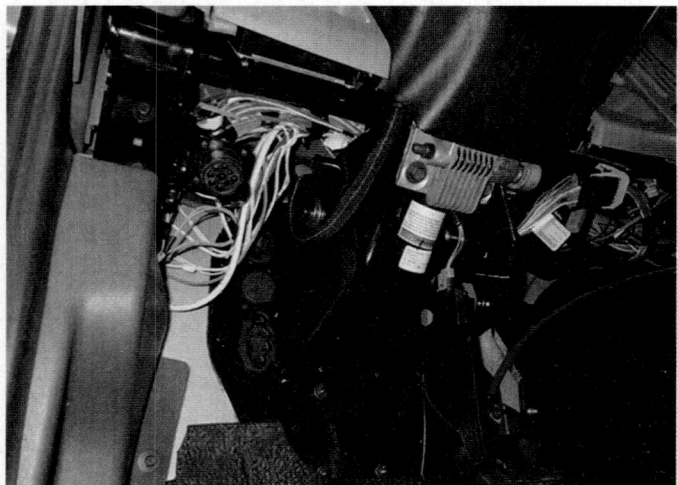

FIGURE 2-31 The DDL is used to connect the truck to the Service Information System.

FIGURE 2-32 A Service Information System in use.

SKILL DRILL 2-3 Using Online Resources

During a clutch repair, you see that the transmission rear yoke seal is leaking, and your boss tells you to look up the part number so that he can order a new one. To do so, follow these steps.

1. Find the transmission model number on the plate on the transmission right lower rear side. In this case, it is RTLOF-14613B.
2. Go to the Eaton website at www.Roadranger.com.
3. Find the hyperlink for the literature section and click on it.
4. On the right-hand side of the literature page, find and select your transmission model number and click go.
5. Search the list of literature that comes up for the illustrated parts list and click on it.
6. Look in the index of the parts list for the "case."
7. Write down the part number for the oil seal or oil seal kit.
8. Give the number to your boss so he can order the correct seal.

written or electronic form, or both. These manuals are used by the technician or the parts professional to order the correct part. The parts manual is divided by systems and includes detailed exploded-view diagrams so that the correct part can be first identified, and then the correct part number found.

Many manufacturers have the parts manual as part of their SIS so that the technician can find the problem and look up the part number of the component to be replaced. Component manufacturers also produce parts manuals. For example, Eaton produces Illustrated Parts Lists for all their components, as do other manufacturers, and are available online. Technicians in an OEM shop have an advantage over those in other shops, as they have access to a parts department and parts professionals onsite to help them decide on the correct replacement parts, and order them, if necessary.

Parts manuals, whether online or in print form, are divided into sections; brakes, chassis, driveline, etc. To select the correct manual and section, basic information from the VIN and possibly the identification tag from a specific component, such as a drive axle, are needed. Parts manuals show detailed exploded-view diagrams of the components being worked on and list the parts numbers of the pieces. It is important to note that each part in each diagram will not look exactly the same as the part you are trying to find. The manual diagrams are somewhat generic so that one manual may cover several models or sizes of components. When a piece is slightly generic like this, the manual qualifies the components by vehicle model year or some other method, such as: (Model years 2002 to 2010 use part number XXXXX, 2011 to present use part number YYYYY).

Technicians should be careful about looking up a part and ordering it by number directly from the supplier because, in many cases, parts are upgraded or (superseded) by newer versions, so use caution ordering parts directly from a supplier by number. Professional parts people are highly experienced and invaluable in making sure that the part number is correct for your model year and configuration. **FIGURE 2-33** shows a professional parts person looking up a component.

FIGURE 2-33 Professional parts people have the experience to make sure the right part is ordered.

Vehicle Recalls/Service Campaigns

Manufacturers recall a vehicle if a problem occurs that is likely to cause a safety issue or is so common in the model that the manufacturer's reputation could be damaged. These **Recalls are also known as Service Campaigns** by certain manufacturers. Recalls can be mandatory by law, meaning that a government agency has forced a company to initiate a recall (if the item is deemed unsafe), or voluntary, if it is something that can affect the reputation of the company or the satisfaction of their customers.

Customers are notified of the recall by mail and email and are told what they must do to have it corrected. Recall repairs are done at no cost to the customer and, therefore, can be quite expensive for the manufacturer. When a recall repair is performed, the repair must be recorded properly, and the vehicle information and the date and nature of the repair is sent to the manufacturer. This allows the manufacturer to keep track and avoids duplication of the repair. A repair tag or information tag is placed on the vehicle to indicate that the particular repair has been performed.

Wrap-Up

Ready for Review

- Over 12 million commercial vehicles operate on US highways every day, and they all require service.
- There are many career possibilities a person can pursue in the commercial vehicle field.
- Most employers hire heavy-duty technicians that have completed a vocational college course.
- Job opportunities in the field are expected to grow by 9% between the years 2016 and 2026.
- Technicians can become highly trained specialists with ongoing training and experience.
- Technicians can become ASE certified, leading to better employment opportunities.
- In different jurisdictions, technicians can become a licensed tradesperson.
- In-demand technicians have many choices of work opportunities, giving them great mobility to move around the country or the world.
- Soft skills are a sought-after quality in an employee.
- Communication is one of the most important soft skills.
- Non-verbal communication is important when speaking or listening to a person.
- Tone of voice, posture, eye contact, hand position, and gestures all enhance or diminish the quality of a conversation.
- Effectively listening is essential to good communication skills.
- Effective listening requires that you give the speaker your full attention.
- Unconscious bias can cloud your understanding during a conversation; try to clear any bias from your mind while listening or speaking.
- It is important to empathize with the speaker to properly understand their conversation.
- When responding in a conversation, take time to digest the information you have received, so that your response is valid to the conversation; don't be rushed.
- When you are rushed, use breathing and pauses to allow yourself more time to respond.
- Use questions, when necessary, to encourage the speaker (open-ended questions), and to solidify data (closed-ended questions).
- A potential customer gets his or her first impression of the business via the telephone; always greet the caller professionally and smile, it reflects as cheerful.
- Record all pertinent data during a phone call.
- Work hard to build your interpersonal relationships with your coworkers and your boss; try to put aside any unconscious biases you may have.
- Reading comprehension is critical when researching problems or verifying specifications.
- Familiarize yourself with the commonly used SAE and OEM abbreviations.
- Use clear and concise writing when recording information or preparing a work order.
- Use the three Cs when preparing a work order: Concern, Cause, and Correction.
- Make sure all work orders contain the required information regarding the company, the customer, and the vehicle.
- Labor guides help estimate the time required to complete a job.
- Many other forms are used in the shop, such as accident incident reports, shop safety reports.
- Many types of vehicle inspection forms are used to evaluate a vehicle's condition.
- Lock Out Tag Out is a system designed to prevent the operation of dangerous or defective equipment, and to prevent the starting or moving of a vehicle undergoing a repair.
- Professional employees should maintain a professional look and keep themselves and their workspace clean and organized.
- Punctuality is a respected quality in an employee, it tells your boss that you are serious about your job.
- Ethical behavior is another well-respected quality in an employee.
- Remember that without customers your company is out of business and you are out of work; the customer is the most important person you deal with.
- Always protect the customer's vehicle as if it was your own and return it in a clean and tidy condition.
- Documents used in the shop, such as work orders and estimates, become legal documents and must be treated that way.
- A mechanic's lien allows the shop to retain or repossess a customer's vehicle until an outstanding bill is paid.
- There are many identification labels on the vehicle that can give the technician vital information, such as the VIN label or plate, the VECI, the engine information label, the VSC.
- Labels also tell the technician what types of fluids are used in the vehicle systems.
- Manufacturers produce several manuals for their vehicles.
- Operator manuals provide the correct way to operate the vehicle and explain how systems should function.
- TSBs are information bulletins that give information about common problems, system revisions, and/or part upgrades.
- Service manuals are used by the technician to research and diagnose problems and to find correct repair procedures; manuals can be in print form and/or electronic.
- There can be several volumes to a service manual that are divided by systems, such as brakes, driveline, troubleshooting.
- Online service information systems (SIS) combine several manuals, including troubleshooting, service, and parts, in one resource.
- SISs are typically subscription-based, meaning that the information exists at the OEMs mainframe computer and you must pay an annual fee to access them.

- ▶ SISs are somewhat better than printed manuals as they are constantly being updated at the source.
- ▶ Component manufacturers also publish repair manuals for the various components on heavy trucks, such as drive axles, transmissions, and antilock brake systems.
- ▶ Component manufacturers manuals are usually available to the technician for free online download.
- ▶ In OEM dealerships, technicians have access to a well-stocked parts room and professional parts people who can look up the correct part.
- ▶ Component manufacturers produce illustrated parts guides that technicians can use to find the correct part number for a component.
- ▶ It is advisable that technicians rely on the service of a professional parts person or department to ensure that the part numbers they locate are correct for the vehicle they are working on.

Key Terms

belt routing label   A label that shows the correct position and routing of the drive belts.

comeback   A colloquial term for repair work that returns with the original complaint.

coolant label   A label that lists the type of coolant installed in the cooling system.

diagnostic data link (DDL)   A special five- or nine-pin connector to connect the vehicle to a computer.

diesel particulate filter (DPF)   A component of the diesel exhaust aftertreatment system that filters soot from diesel exhaust.

Drivers Vehicle Inspection Report (DVIR)   A daily report the driver of a commercial vehicle must complete.

exhaust gas recirculation (EGR)   A system that recycles exhaust gas to reduce combustion temperatures.

engine dynamometer   A machine that measures engine or brake system output. Horsepower, torque and speed are measured by an engine dynamometer.

engine identification label or **information plate** A label that contains the engine, serial number, date of manufacture, engine family, model number, size, horsepower rating, rated RPM, idle RPM, fuel rate, timing, and valve lash settings.

labor guide   A guide that provides information to make estimates for repairs.

lock out tag out (LOTO)   A system used to make sure that defective equipment is not used until it has been properly repaired.

mechanics lien   A mechanics lien allows the repair facility to withhold a vehicle until the bill is paid.

operator's manual   A document that contains the correct operating procedures for the vehicle and systems and how the systems should function.

parts manual   A written or electronic manual for identifying and finding needed vehicle parts.

recall or service campaign   A corrective measure conducted by manufacturers when a safety issue or recurring problem is found with a vehicle.

refrigerant label   A label that lists the type and total capacity of refrigerant that is installed in the A/C system.

repair order   A form used by shops to collect information regarding a vehicle coming in for repair, also referred to as a work order or job sheet.

service history   A complete list of all the servicing and repairs that have been performed on a vehicle.

service information system (SIS)   An online version of the printed service manual that usually includes access to all the other manuals produced for the vehicle.

service manual   An indexed book produced by the manufacturer or by the after-market to describe the service and repair procedures required on a vehicle.

soft skills   Communication and other skills that are very important to employers.

technical service bulletin (TSB)   Information issued by manufacturers to alert technicians of unexpected problems or changes to repair procedures.

three Cs   Concern (the concern, or problem, with the vehicle); cause (the cause of the concern); and correction (fixing the problem).

unconscious bias   Means that you are predisposed to think a certain way about a subject or a person.

vehicle emission control information (VECI) label   Indicates that the vehicle conforms to the emission control regulations for the year it was built.

vehicle identification number (VIN)   A number that identifies the vehicle make, model, year, configuration, and the individual serial number of a vehicle.

vehicle safety certification (VSC) label   A label certifying that the vehicle meets the Federal Motor Vehicle Safety standards at date of manufacturer.

Review Questions

1. Which of the following would not be a responsibility of a commercial vehicle technician?
   a. Repairing the brakes on a semi-trailer
   b. Diagnosing a diesel fuel system
   c. Inspecting a truck driveline
   d. Repairing the shop air compressor
2. Employers are more likely to hire technicians who have completed an apprenticeship or received certification from which of the following?
   a. private college
   b. vocational college
   c. secondary school
   d. business college
3. To achieve ASE certifications, candidates need a minimum of how many years of experience in the field before taking an exam for each area of specialization?
   a. 2
   b. 3
   c. 4
   d. 5

4. The three Cs refer to which of the following?
   a. Care, Cause, and Concentration
   b. Concern, Cause, and Correction
   c. Cause, Cost, and Correction
   d. Concern, Cause, and Cost
5. Which of the following is not recommended to be an effective listener?
   a. Stop what you are doing and give your attention to the speaker.
   b. Smile at the speaker periodically.
   c. Maintain eye contact as much as possible.
   d. Continue listening to the speaker while answering the phone.
6. The lockout/tagout tag system is used to indicate that a tool or component is which of the following?
   a. Is in working order.
   b. Is dangerous to use or defective.
   c. Should be lubricated.
   d. Has been recently repaired.
7. The first three characters of a VIN are known as which of the following?
   a. The world manufacturer identification
   b. The engine manufacturer
   c. The vehicle configuration
   d. The vehicle serial number
8. Which of the following would be an example of effective listening?
   a. Crossing your arms and making a concentrated face to show you care
   b. Talking to the customer while flipping through the manufacturer's manual
   c. Interrupting often to make sure you understand
   d. Maintaining eye contact with the customer in between taking notes
9. Which of the following ASE test series would have to be completed to become certified as a master technician in medium- and heavy-duty trucks?
   a. H-series; H1 or H2 and H3 through H8
   b. M-series
   c. T-series; T2 through T8
   d. H-, M-, and T-series
10. In a typical VIN, which character indicates the vehicle model year?
    a. 4th character
    b. 7th character
    c. 8th character
    d. 10th character

ASE Technician A/Technician B Style Questions

1. Technician A says that keeping a neat and clean workspace shows professionalism. Technician B says that a dirty and cluttered shop indicates that the shop is busy and, therefore, makes the customer think they must be good. Who is correct?
   a. Technician A
   b. Technician B
   c. Both Technician A and Technician B
   d. Neither Technician A nor Technician B
2. Technician A says researching the service record of a vehicle is important before starting the repair. Technician B says that compiling information from TSBs and the service manual helps to ensure the repair is done correctly. Who is correct?
   a. Technician A
   b. Technician B
   c. Both Technician A and Technician B
   d. Neither Technician A nor Technician B
3. Technician A says that an example of an open question is: "What happened after the noise started?" Technician B says that an example of an open question is: "How many times has this happened?" Who is correct?
   a. Technician A
   b. Technician B
   c. Both Technician A and Technician B
   d. Neither Technician A nor Technician B
4. Technician A says that labor guides can help the service writer quote the cost of the repair for a customer. Technician B says that labor guides are not always available for all jobs. Who is correct?
   a. Technician A
   b. Technician B
   c. Both Technician A and Technician B
   d. Neither Technician A nor Technician B
5. Technician A says the most popular career pathway in the commercial vehicle service industry is becoming a technician. Technician B says that most commercial vehicle technicians have no formal education. Who is correct?
   a. Technician A
   b. Technician B
   c. Both Technician A and Technician B
   d. Neither Technician A nor Technician B
6. Technician A says that a mobile commercial vehicle technician requires a lot of experience. Technician B says that evaluating an engine on a dynamometer would require a highly skilled technician. Who is correct?
   a. Technician A
   b. Technician B
   c. Both Technician A and Technician B
   d. Neither Technician A nor Technician B
7. Technician A states that to be successful as a technician, you must adopt a lifelong learning regime to constantly upgrade and advance your skills and experience. Technician B says that he can take a break from learning as soon as he gets his ASE master technician certification. Who is correct?
   a. Technician A
   b. Technician B
   c. Both Technician A and Technician B
   d. Neither Technician A nor Technician B
8. While discussing writing work orders, technician A says a repair order would not be considered a legal document. Technician B says writing work orders clearly and concisely is very important. Who is correct?
   a. Technician A
   b. Technician B

c. Both Technician A and Technician B
d. Neither Technician A nor Technician B

9. Technician A says drivers of commercial vehicles are required to complete a DVIR daily. Technician B says that technicians must complete daily shop safety inspections. Who is correct?
a. Technician A
b. Technician B
c. Both Technician A and Technician B
d. Neither Technician A nor Technician B

10. Technician A says that the customer is the most important person you interact with. Technician B says one of the biggest annoyances of service managers is the comeback; the vehicle should be fixed correctly the first time. Who is correct?
a. Technician A
b. Technician B
c. Both Technician A and Technician B
d. Neither Technician A nor Technician B

CHAPTER 3

Safety, Personal Protective Equipment, and First Aid

Learning Objectives

After reading this chapter, you will be able to:

- **LO 3-1** Explain the fundamentals of safe practices in the workplace.
- **LO 3-2** Describe the legal responsibilities of employees and employers relating to safe working practices.
- **LO 3-3** Describe proper safety and emergency procedures for the workplace and identify workplace hazards.

- **LO 3-4** Describe the various types of personal protective equipment (PPE) used in the workplace.
- **LO 3-5** Describe the various types of fire suppression systems and explain their use.
- **LO 3-6** Explain the legal responsibilities of employees and employers regarding hazardous material in the workplace and interpret hazard information.
- **LO 3-7** Explain the basic principles of first aid and cardiopulmonary resuscitation (CPR) practices.

You Are the Technician

You are emptying the mobile engine oil drain pan into the waste oil tank in the lubrication bay. You roll the drain pan into position and run its hose into the waste oil tank. You hook up the air connection and open the valve so the air pushes the used oil into the waste oil tank. The correct procedure is to stay with the oil drain pan until it is empty, close the valve, and remove the air line and store it correctly, then clean up any mess that occurs if there is a spill. You are momentarily distracted by a coworker who calls you over. When you return to your task, you see that the mobile drain pan has rolled away from the waste oil tank and has spilled a large puddle of waste oil onto the floor.

1. What was the cause of this accident?
2. What PPE should you wear to perform the cleanup?
3. Are there any potential health hazards in coming into contact with waste engine oil?

Introduction

No matter whether you are management or one of the front-line workers, a safe and healthy workplace should be everyone's number one priority. Nobody wants to see someone injured on the job, and most jurisdictions have legislation to make sure that workplaces remain safe. The penalties for failing to maintain a safe workplace can be quite severe and can be imposed on individual workers, supervisors, and on the company itself.

A **hazard** is something that can cause an accident, a sickness, or an injury. A typical heavy-duty repair shop is full of potential hazards. When a vehicle is hoisted in the air or jacked up for service, it becomes a hazard, as it could possibly fall. A bench grinder is a simple tool, but it can be a significant hazard with pieces of metal flying off the grind wheel. Other hazards can be long-time exposure to dangerous fumes or long-term contact with chemicals, which can be absorbed through the skin. Even a carelessly stored piece of equipment, such as an air hose, can be a tripping hazard.

Every worker should be aware of these potential hazards and do everything possible to mitigate their potential to cause harm. Occupational Health and Safety legislation puts the responsibility for keeping a workplace safe on every person in the company: owners, managers, supervisors, and workers. Safety is simply everyone's responsibility. Owners and managers are required to provide training to supervisors and workers as to how to work safely with the products and equipment used in their workplace. Supervisors are responsible to ensure that all workers follow the training and procedures to work safely. You, as a worker, have the responsibility to speak up and inform your supervisor about any work practice or equipment that you feel is unsafe. If you are not sure how to perform a task safely or have not been trained on a piece of equipment, you must stop and ask for a supervisor for help. Do not attempt to learn as you go. Get the instruction or training you need before you start.

All employees must possess and use the correct **PPE (personal protective equipment)**: boots, gloves, eye protection, and hearing protection, when required (**FIGURE 3-1**). In most heavy-vehicle repair shops, green patch safety boots and safety glasses must be worn at all times.

FIGURE 3-1 Personal protective equipment (PPE) are items of wearable safety equipment; safety footwear, clothing, protective eyewear, gloves, and hearing protection are all examples of PPE.

great potential for accidents to occur, but it is important to note that accidents don't just happen—there is always a cause for an accident and it usually comes down to people. Carelessness is probably the number one cause, haste is usually the next. These causes are the simplest to correct, accidents caused by carelessness and haste can be avoided by always paying attention to the work at hand and taking your time to be sure it is done safely and correctly.

▶ TECHNICIAN TIP

After performing the same task over and over, it is quite easy to overlook the potential for danger. The danger that existed the first time you performed a particular job is still there. You must not become complacent and overlook the procedures that keep you safe. Always pay attention to what you are doing. Go through the steps in your mind and remember what the potential problems with the task are. It is quite natural and common when you have done a job over and over that you become quicker at it, but be very wary of taking short cuts. Trying to cut even more time from a job usually leads to improper procedures and increased risks of accidents. Be careful and take your time. Any time you may lose on the job is nothing compared to the time lost due to an accident.

Safety Overview

General Safety

LO 3-1 Explain the fundamentals of safe practices in the workplace.

There are over 12 million registered heavy-duty commercial vehicles operating on the roads in the United States alone, and millions more in the rest of North America and the world. Hundreds of thousands of heavy-duty vehicle servicing facilities keep those vehicles running. Inside those facilities are hard-working technicians providing the day-to-day service those vehicles require. With all this work going on, there is a

There Is No Safe Time When Accidents Can't Occur

You need to be vigilant all the time you are working because accidents don't take time off! In the heavy-duty vehicle servicing industry, you work with many things that could potentially cause accidents leading to injury or worse. Flammable liquids are ever present and are an explosion or fire risk. Electricity can cause fires or electrocution. Commercial vehicle technicians deal with heavy components that can cause crush injuries to body parts, such as fingers. Hundreds of chemicals are used in shops and each one represents its own hazard, ranging from explosion risk, chemical burns, and/or

FIGURE 3-2 Poor lifting techniques can strain your back.

toxicity. A disorganized shop with tools and/or equipment lying around or oil spills can lead to slip or trip injuries. Working at height on trailers or refrigeration units can lead to falls. Poor lifting or carrying techniques can lead to strain injuries—particularly back strain—which can turn into chronic injuries (**FIGURE 3-2**). You should never lift objects by bending your back. Keep your back straight and bend at the knees to pick up the object. Lift using your legs and keep the object as close to your body as possible. Avoid twisting your back to place the object on the bench or table. Instead, turn with your feet. Always ask for assistance if the object is too heavy.

Accidents Don't Happen, They Are Caused and Avoidable

Think about any accident you have been involved in or witnessed. You will find it very hard to recall one that did not have a clear cause. Almost all accidents have an identifiable cause and that means, with proper procedure, the accident could have been prevented. Prevention is simple—remove the cause of the accident and it cannot occur! This, however, is easier said than done.

Most workplaces have strict policies and procedures designed to minimize the potential for accidents. These policies and procedures have been developed through experience and in consultation with accident prevention specialists who likely have studied the risks associated with a certain job and have created the procedure specifically to eliminate or minimize the risks associated with the job. You must do your part too, by following those procedures and having an attitude of safety first. If there is anything about a job that you think presents a hazard, or something that you think makes the job safer to perform, bring it to your supervisor's attention promptly, and likely your observation will become part of a revised procedure for that job. If an accident does occur, report it to your supervisor immediately and document everything about the accident as soon as possible so that it is fresh in your mind. The

information gathered from accident reports typically form the basis for the procedure that is designed or modified to prevent a reoccurrence.

Evacuation Plans

An evacuation plan is a pre-thought-out escape plan designed to get personnel quickly and safely away from danger areas and to a place where they can all be accounted for. Depending on the workplace, the evacuation plan could be very simple. For example, in a single-bay shop, it could be to leave by the nearest exit and meet in the front parking lot; however, in large organized workplaces the plan is usually more sophisticated.

The evacuation plan should be part of initial employee training and, in many workplaces, it is practiced periodically. Evacuation plans normally include preplanned evacuation routes laid out in the workplace and are typically marked with painted lines and arrows indicating the route and the direction. These routes must be kept clear of obstruction at all times and lead to an exit to a safe area. All evacuation routes should lead to clearly marked exits. In some workplaces, the evacuation route has special lighting to lead you out. Typically, there is more than one evacuation route available. You should always identify the best evacuation route from your particular work area.

The second and equally important part of an evacuation plan is the meeting or marshalling places. The plan includes designated meeting places where supervisors or appointed safety marshals make sure all personnel are present and accounted for after the evacuation. It is extremely important that all personnel are identified so that emergency responders can be told whether or not there is anyone still in the building. **FIGURE 3-3** shows a typical evacuation plan route diagram.

> ▶ TECHNICIAN TIP

It is essential that evacuation routes are kept clear of any obstruction of any kind. Never place or store anything on the evacuation route. During an emergency, power may be out, and people are scared and/or nervous. Running into an obstacle while evacuating can greatly slow the process and could be deadly.

Work Area

Safe working conditions start with a safe work environment. That is, that your workspace is clean and well organized. Sloppy habits and disorganization are an accident waiting to happen. Keep hoses and cords coiled properly to prevent trip hazards. Clean spills promptly to avoid slips. Store equipment safely and out of the way. Always use safety stands when raising vehicles—never rely solely on a jack. Poor ventilation in your work area can lead to long-term illnesses. Exhaust extraction systems should be working and the connecting hoses should be in good shape. Vent hoods should be used when welding and/or dealing with chemicals. Keeping a safe work area should be part of initial employee training and should become a good habit for

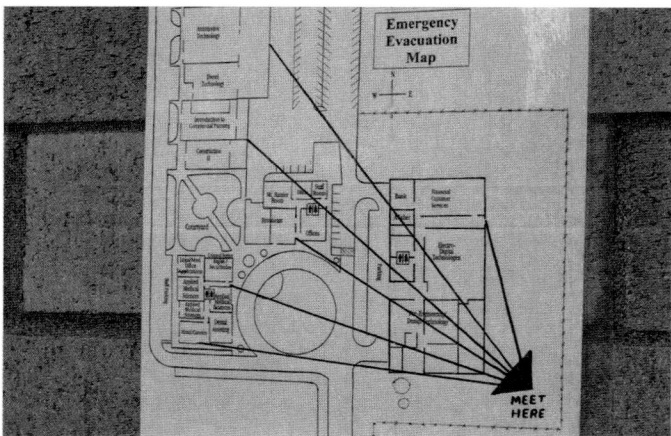

FIGURE 3-3 This sign shows the evacuation routes and the designated meeting place.

the employee. Supervisors should check from time to time that the employee is adhering to the training and maintaining a safe work area.

Legal Requirements in the Workplace

LO 3-2 Describe the legal responsibilities of employees and employers relating to safe working practices.

All workplaces must conform to regulations and legislation designed to protect workers and to protect the environment. Depending on where you are in the world, the legislation may have different names and/or enforcing agencies; however, they are all similar in scope and purpose. In this section, we concentrate on the legislation used in the United States and Canada, but we touch on other jurisdictions, as well.

Occupation Safety and Health Regulations

The United States and Canada, and most countries around the world, have legislation in place designed to protect workers from workplace injury or illness. In the United States, the responsible agency is the Occupational Safety and Health Administration (OSHA), an agency of the Department of Labor. In Canada, the equivalent agency is the Canadian Center for Occupational Safety and Health (CCOSH). In the US, OSHA regulations cover nearly all private-sector workers and some public-sector workers.

Public-sector workers not covered under OSHA directly are covered under similar state or federal legislation. In Canada, there are ten provinces and three territories, each with their own occupational safety and health standards. There are also differences in the legislation, depending on whether a worker is classified as a federal employee or a provincial employee. The CCOSH is actually an umbrella agency that brings all of the varying regulations together for easy access. Even though

there are differences between the occupational safety and health regulations, they are, for the most part, very similar. Whether in the US or Canada, the root of the legislation is to protect the worker from harm.

It is not possible here to list all of the OSHA and/or CCOSH regulations, but the general intent of the regulations is that it is everyone's responsibility to keep the workplace and the workers safe. Typical occupational health and safety legislation does the following:

- Categorizes jobs as to their level of safety
- Sets the rules that workers and employers must follow in the workplace
- Sets out the fines or punishments imposed for non-compliance
- Requires reporting of various injuries in the workplace
- May require the employer to establish a workplace health and safety committee

Employees have the following rights under the legislation under OSHA legislation:

- The right to have their workplace inspected by OSHA in confidence
- The right to receive training and information about hazards, harm reduction methods, and OSHA standards relating to their workplace
- The right to receive copies of work-related injuries in their workplace
- The right to receive copies of any test results done to measure hazards in their workplace
- The right to receive copies of their medical records relating to the workplace
- The right to participate in an OSHA inspection and discuss the results with the inspector
- The right to file a complaint if they have been retaliated against by the employer relating to OSHA
- The right to file a complaint if punished for acting as a "whistleblower" under the OSHA-related federal laws

Employee responsibilities under OSHA legislation:

- Wear required Personal Protective Equipment (PPE): hard hat, gloves, clothing, boots, and safety glasses
- Do not operate equipment in an unsafe way that endangers you or others
- Must inform the supervisor or employer about any device or equipment that is defective and could injure someone
- Abstain from horseplay and/or games in the workplace
- An employee can be held personally responsible if he or she does not fulfill his or her responsibilities.

Employer responsibilities under OSHA legislation:

- Employer must provide a safe workplace.
- Employers must do everything possible to reduce hazards, rather than rely on workers' PPE or safety equipment.
- Prominently display the applicable legislation covering their workplace

- Inform workers of any known hazards or dangerous chemicals through rigorous training, in a language the worker can understand, and other information sources
- Keep accurate workplace injury or illness records
- Provide workplace environmental testing, such as air quality, when required by OSHA standards
- Provide workers with all the required PPE
- Provide any medical testing required by OSHA standards
- Post any OSHA citations and injury/illness records where they are accessible to the employees
- Notify OSHA within 8 hours of a workplace fatality or within 24 hours of any other critical injury

The responsibilities and rights above are relative to the occupational safety and health legislations of the US and Canada; however, most countries that have legislation in place have similar rights and responsibilities.

Environmental Protection

The EPA is the **Environmental Protection Agency (EPA)**, a federal government agency in the United States that deals with all aspects of environmental protection and safety. The EPA investigates and researches environmental issues and formulates standards and rules, and can prosecute employees, supervisors, and/or companies that refuse to follow or ignore the regulations. The EPA can conduct site inspections to ensure compliance with its regulations. Most countries in the world have a similar agency in place to protect the environment.

Many shop activities deal with substances and waste materials that are carefully regulated by the EPA. Diesel fuel, gasoline, engine coolant, engine oil, brake fluid, other lubricants, waste oils, and almost every other chemical or substance you work with in the shop are likely potentially damaging to the environment and subject to EPA rules. Everyone in the workplace is required to deal with these substances according to EPA regulations. Typically, accidental spills or releases of a controlled substance requires prompt reporting to the EPA or other regulating authority. All controlled substances must be properly stored to prevent accidental release. All controlled wastes must be disposed of in a way that conforms to EPA regulations. Penalties for non-compliance with EPA regulations both in the US and around the world can be very stiff, depending on the severity of the incident. Fines can be in the hundreds of thousands, even millions, of dollars and serious or repeat perpetrators can receive multi-year jail sentences.

It is incumbent on you and your employer to be certain that you are aware of the EPA regulations involving proper storage, handling, and disposal of any and all substances you are required to work with. It is also essential that, if you see any leakage, spillage, or improper disposal of these substances, you report it immediately.

Policies and Procedures in the Workplace

Policies and procedures are company designed and serve as guidelines for how shop functions and work tasks are carried out.

While shop policies are not in themselves legal documents, not following the policy or procedure can lead to legal trouble for a worker.

For example, if an accident occurs and the worker responsible has not followed the shop policy, he or she could be open to a lawsuit from an injured party for negligent behavior. If, on the other hand, he or she were following shop policy when the accident occurred, the responsibility likely falls on the shop itself, rather than the worker.

Shop policies and procedures are also formulated around the legislation that governs the workplace under OSHA and the EPA, and following policy means that the worker is complying with OSHA and EPA regulations while conducting the task. A **policy** is an overriding way of acting or behaving, a statement saying that "This workplace complies with all OSHA regulations" is a policy; whereas a **procedure** is a step-by-step process to complete a task in the proper and safe manner, such as the steps required to properly dispose of waste oil. All workplaces undoubtedly have their own set of policies and procedures, depending on the work they conduct and other factors. Your shop's policies and procedures should be explained to you during your initial training for the job. If you have forgotten or are unsure of a policy or procedure, ask your supervisor for clarification. Policies and procedures are revised and updated occasionally, based on new rules and/or methods. Make sure that you are familiar and current in your knowledge of the policies and procedures in your workplace.

Safety and Emergency Procedures in the Workplace

LO 3-3 Describe proper safety and emergency procedures for the workplace and identify workplace hazards.

As mentioned previously, safety in the workplace is paramount, and it is the responsibility of everyone in the workplace. The potential for injury is always present and it only takes a momentary lapse in judgment for an accident to happen and for someone to get hurt. A workplace injury could change your life forever, limiting your future earning potential, or that of someone else. Workplaces have systems set up to try and lessen the possibility of injury, but the responsibility is still on the individual worker to protect him or herself and his or her coworkers. Don't be a victim. Always be aware of the potential for danger. In the following section, we discuss the potential for danger in the workplace and the common steps to mitigate that danger.

Hazardous Environments

Hazardous environments are everywhere—when you cross a busy street or parking lot, you are in a hazardous environment; a **hazardous environment** is simply a place where there are hazards, and a **hazard** is anything that can cause you or others harm. You would be hard-pressed to find any workplace that does not have any hazards; even an office building has hazards.

Think of slips and falls on wet floors, paper guillotines, electrical hazards, and more. A commercial vehicle technician workshop is full of hazards. In a typical shop, you have the basic hazards mentioned above, but you also have many technicians performing numerous different tasks, all of which are, or could be, potential hazards. Welding, cutting, grinding, working with power tools, working with dangerous chemicals—all these activities represent hazards. It is impossible to conduct work without some hazards being present, but the key is to be aware of the hazards and take steps to minimize their potential to cause harm.

Shops install information signs in hazardous areas warning of the potential danger. The information signs contain **signal words**; words that explain the severity of the potential danger. The three common signal words for signs are Danger, Warning, and Caution (more on these signs later). When dealing with hazards in the workplace, it is important to follow these steps.

1. Remove the hazard, if possible, e.g., something is sticking out from under a bench causing a tripping hazard, remove it immediately. Unfortunately, some hazards cannot be removed.
2. Prevent non-essential people from contact with the hazard, e.g., your company uses a dynamometer to test rebuilt engines that causes a noise hazard. Installing the dynamometer in a soundproof room protects the hearing of non-essential personnel.
3. Prevent the hazard from causing harm by using steps or barriers to mitigate the danger, e.g., your company has a

lubrication pit that represents a fall hazard. Paint lines around the hazard as a visible reminder that it is there and erect a physical barrier to prevent people from actually reaching the pit area.
4. Use proper PPE for the person who is working where the hazard exists and anyone that could potentially be harmed, e.g., a worker is grinding on a truck frame preparing for a welding job. The worker should be wearing protective clothing, including heavy leather gloves, safety glasses, and a full-face shield. There should be a shield set up to stop the flying particles from the grinding from traveling into nearby work areas. Ensure that there is no chance of the flying sparks igniting any flammable material. Make sure that fire suppression equipment is close at hand. The worker should also inform anyone who is in the vicinity of the nature of work he or she is about to perform so that they too wear the necessary PPE or remove themselves from the danger area.

Take some time to make yourself aware of the non-removable hazards in your workplace and the procedures used to mitigate their potential for injury.

To identify workplace hazards, follow the steps in **SKILL DRILL 3-1**.

Workplace Safety Measures

All commercial vehicle workplaces are, by nature, hazardous environments. Therefore, several measures are taken to ensure employee safety. These measures can be visual, using signs, flashing lights, or painted lines to indicate the location of a

SKILL DRILL 3-1 Identifying Workplace Hazards

1. Look at the way your shop is laid out or organized. Be aware of where potentially hazardous work is carried out. Look for and read all the information signs and whether they are danger, warning, or caution. Locate and memorize the designated escape routes and marshaling points.

2. Investigate and understand the proper functioning of the exhaust extraction system in your shop and be sure you know how to operate it. Look for any other issues that could cause poor air quality.

3. Check for and locate all the fire suppression equipment in your shop. All fire extinguisher locations should have a highly visible sign. Each extinguisher should have an inspection tag on it showing the date of the last time the fire extinguisher was checked by a registered inspector, and it should be within the last year. Read and understand the operating instructions for each of the extinguisher types.

SKILL DRILL 3-1 Identifying Workplace Hazards (Continued)

4. Locate the storage area for all flammable liquids and be aware of the proper storage requirements. Report any issues to your supervisor.

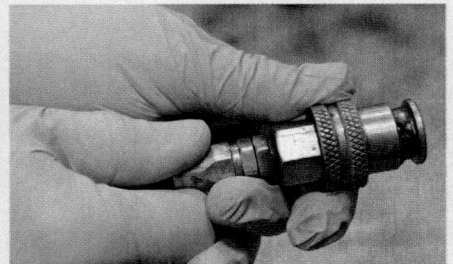

5. Before use, inspect all air line connections. A broken connection can lead to a whipping air line and potential injury from flying particles.

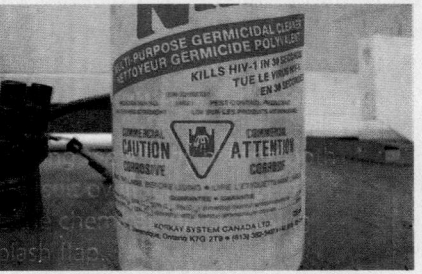

6. Identify any and all caustic or potentially dangerous chemicals that you may be required to work with. Find out where the chemicals are stored and proper storage procedures. Read the safety data sheets (SDSs) for the various materials and identify their hazards and the PPE required for their use. Make yourself aware of the proper disposal procedures for the material or its container.

hazard; physical, such as barriers to separate the worker from the hazard; or audible, such as warning buzzers (when a hazard is not constant, a warning buzzer or siren may be used to indicate when the hazard exists). Make sure that you know the measures used in your workplace.

Workshop Organization

A workshop should be laid out efficiently with clearly defined work and pedestrian areas. The layout should be sequential, for example, if a vehicle needs an inspection and then brake work, the bays should be arranged to complement each other in terms of location, e.g., inspection pit bay, brake bay, cleanup bay. The tire replacement bay should be close to the area where the tires are stored, and so on. Careful shop organization allows the work to flow easily. Parts areas, material storage areas, and common equipment storage areas should be clearly defined and properly laid out. Customer waiting areas should be kept clear of all shop activities, and customers should never be permitted in the shop without being escorted by a designated person—usually the shop foreman or service manager. A well-organized shop is more efficient and is a safer place to work.

Workplace Signs

In a workplace, signs are a common way to indicate many things: exits, restrooms, lunch room, and more, but special hazard signs have been developed over the years by regulatory agencies to describe various levels or seriousness of hazards. These hazard signs are now almost universally accepted; they contain a signal word (danger, warning, or caution) and have specific coloring and designs. The sign may also contain explanatory wording.

- Danger: a danger sign indicates a hazard that can cause immediate serious injury or death, if not avoided. A danger sign has the word "danger" spelled in white letters on a red background and usually has a black border. The message wording on a danger sign is usually black on a white background (**FIGURE 3-4A**).
- Warning: a warning sign indicates a hazard that has the potential of causing serious injury or death, if not avoided. A warning sign normally has the word "warning" printed in black lettering on an orange or yellow background. The sign may have further wording in the same format or in black text on a white background (**FIGURE 3-4B**).
- Caution: a caution sign indicates a hazard that could cause moderate injuries, if not avoided. A caution sign usually has the word "caution" in black letters on a yellow background (**FIGURE 3-4C**).

Shop Safety Equipment

Shop safety equipment usually includes, but is not limited to, the following:

- Painted lines, like hazard signs, are visual indicators of hazards or safe routes to follow. Dangerous equipment or areas in the shop may be surrounded by painted lines to indicate the potential hazard. Painted lines may simply be rectangles, or they may have hash marks to indicate the proximity of the hazard. Painted lines are usually yellow or yellow with black hash marks or white with red hash marks.
- Equipment guards are physical barriers that prevent personnel from accidentally approaching or walking into hazardous equipment.

- Railings or handrails that separate walking personnel from hazardous work areas.
- Soundproofing; certain areas of the shop may be extremely noisy, creating a noise hazard for workers nearby, such as a trailer repair area where bucking rivets is a common

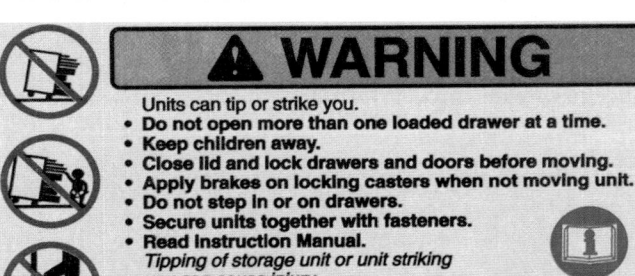

FIGURE 3-4 Signs. **A.** Danger is usually indicated by white text on a red background. **B.** Warning is usually in black text with an orange background. **C.** Caution is usually in black text with a yellow background.

activity. Enclosing and soundproofing these areas protects the rest of the workforce.

- Exhaust extraction system; a system must be in place that can extract the vehicle exhaust to the outside. Running engines produce several dangerous elements in their exhaust. Gasoline and, to a lesser extent, diesel, engines produce carbon monoxide, a lethal odorless, tasteless gas. Many other dangerous fumes are produced, as well. Today's diesel engines with Selective Catalytic Reduction (SCR) systems that are malfunctioning can also produce unused ammonia, iso-cyanic acid, and other dangerous fumes. The extraction system should be robust enough to remove the gas faster than it is produced and should also have a fresh air makeup system to ensure that fresh air is brought back into the shop. **FIGURE 3-5** shows an exhaust extraction system.
- Ventilation; proper exhaust gas extraction equipment is essential, but there should also be an adequate general ventilation system to remove fumes caused by activities, such as bringing vehicles into and out of the shop, welding, working with chemicals, and others.
- Barriers should be used to separate workers from potentially hazardous activities, such as welding, grinding, and more. These temporary barriers contain the hazard to one area.
- Physical doors can be locked to separate customers and/or office workers from hazardous work environments.

▶ TECHNICIAN TIP

Carbon monoxide (CO) is known as the silent killer, although today's engines are designed to produce less CO than ever before, even a small amount of this deadly gas can kill. Fifty parts per million per 8 hours is the OSHA permissible exposure limit or (PEL). Other agencies are calling for an exposure limit of 35 parts per million (ppm) per 8 hours PEL. Any exposure to CO is dangerous, however, because this gas easily attaches itself to the hemoglobin in your blood that normally carries oxygen to your body. With enough CO, a person does not have enough

FIGURE 3-5 The exhaust extraction system should be robust.

oxygen and can asphyxiate. Once the CO attaches to the hemoglobin, it is very difficult to remove. In cases of large exposure, patients are placed in a hyperbaric chamber (increased-pressure chamber) breathing pure oxygen to try and dislodge the CO. Because of this, the effects of CO poisoning can be cumulative, meaning that a worker who is exposed to CO on an ongoing basis can become more and more saturated with the gas. Vehicle technicians, and anyone who works near running engines, need to be very aware cf the immediate and cumulative dangers of this deadly gas.

Shop Safety Inspections

Formal shop safety inspections should be carried out on a monthly basis. These inspections are generally conducted by the workplace joint health and safety committee. During a formal safety inspection, the members of the committee physically walk through the workplace looking for potential hazards or anything that is out of compliance with the workplace's safety policies. The committee checks items, such as exits (to make sure they are clear and accessible and signed), fire extinguishers (to see that the pressures are correct, the seals have not been tampered with, and the tags are in date), general equipment (to look for any wear or tear that could lead to a potential hazard), general cleanliness and shop organization (looking for trip, slip, or fall hazards), and other items deemed necessary by the particular workplace or committee.

An inspection report is prepared and items that are out of compliance are to be remedied as soon as possible. Besides formal safety inspections, all workers have the responsibility to be on the look-out for unsafe or potentially unsafe operations or situations in the shop daily and fix the problem or report it to their supervisor right away. Remember that safety in the workplace is everyone's responsibility.

Electrical Equipment Safety

Electrical equipment always presents a potential hazard. In North America, a shop's basic electrical system today operates at 120 volts. At that voltage, a person can be electrocuted with a current of less than one-half ampere, and most circuits that we deal with are fused at 15 amps. Therefore, electrocution is a definite and deadly hazard. Many systems in your shop may operate at 240, or even higher, voltages, and electrical delivery equipment operates at much higher voltages and amperages. Always respect electrical equipment and recognize its hazards.

Electrical Panels

Make yourself aware of the locations of the electrical panels that control the power in your workplace. The panels should be clearly labeled as to the circuits each circuit breaker or fuse controls. Large equipment normally has its own panel and control switch—locate these panels, as well. If an emergency occurs and a person is being or in danger of being electrocuted, never try to reach or pull the person away until you have shut off the power. Panels need to be accessible. Always keep the space around them clear. In most jurisdictions, there must be 3 feet

(0.9 m) of clear, unobstructed space around any electrical panel. **FIGURE 3-6** shows a typical electrical panel.

Overloaded Circuits

Most receptacles in your shop are fused at 15 amps, meaning that anything over that current blows the circuit breaker. It is important, however, to not overload circuits, as they can become heated and burn leading to fire hazards. Do not use unfused plug multipliers to increase the available number of outlets. If your work area does not have sufficient receptacles, ask your supervisor to arrange for extras to be installed. If you must use several electrical tools for the same job, use a fused extension and only use one tool at a time.

Trouble Lights and Extension Cords

Trouble lights, or drop lights, and extension cords are essential tools for technicians to illuminate a work area on a vehicle or bring power to where it is needed. In the past, trouble lights used incandescent bulbs that could break and cause potential fire hazards if there are flammable vapors or liquids nearby. It is not advisable to use a trouble light with an incandescent bulb. Today's trouble lights are typically made with solid-state circuitry and fluorescent bulbs or light-emitting diode (LED) lights that are much safer (**FIGURE 3-7**).

FIGURE 3-6 A clearly labeled electrical panel.

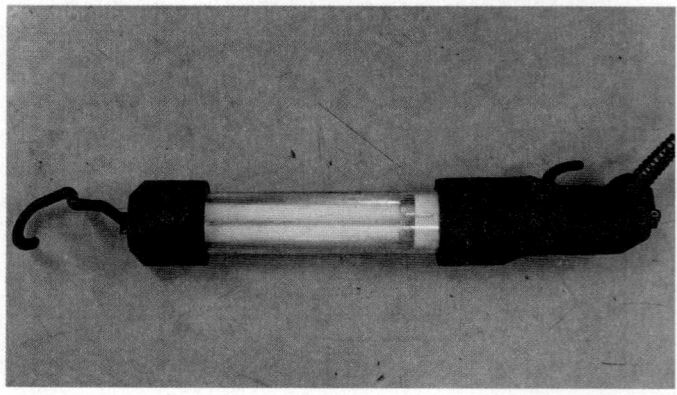

FIGURE 3-7 Fluorescent or LED lights are much safer than incandescent.

Still, a technician must exercise caution when using these lamps and/or extension cords. The cord can be pinched in lifting equipment or snagged in a spot that could cut the cord if you tug on it (if the cord is snagged, always loosen the snag, don't pull the cord through it). Even though you may try hard to avoid it, the cords on trouble lamps and extension cords are constantly being stood on and quite often inadvertently run over with rolling jacks, vehicles, or other equipment. Inspect the cord of the trouble lamp, or the extension cord, every time you use it. Check for worn insulation and/or breaks. Never use a damaged cord. Avoid having the cord come in contact with water (electricity can travel through water). The cords should be neoprene-covered and flexible, as shown in **FIGURE 3-8**.

Electrical Tools and Portable Equipment

A commercial vehicle technician is required to use several electrical tools and/or pieces of equipment; electric drills, grinders, and the like, and/or portable pumps, testing equipment, battery chargers, air-conditioning equipment, and more. With all of these tools and equipment, the potential for electrical burns or electrocution exists. The tool or piece of equipment should be kept in good operating condition and be inspected regularly for any deficiencies. Inspect the cords for fraying or exposed insulation. Be aware of any changes in the operation of the equipment. Noises or overheating are some signs of potential problems. If you notice anything unusual, report it to your supervisor immediately.

> ▶ **TECHNICIAN TIP**
>
> Always inspect the wiring for damage and check the security of the attached plug before connecting a droplight to the power supply. Always switch off and unplug a droplight before changing the bulb.

Personal Protective Equipment

LO 3-4 Describe the various types of personal protective equipment (PPE) used in the workplace.

Before a technician enters a workplace, he or she should be trained in the various types, purpose, and correct way to wear PPE. PPE protects the worker from bodily harm by preventing **hazardous material,** a material that can cause damage or injury to a person, or particles from entering the worker's body or physically injuring the worker. There are all types of PPE available. Depending on the work place or activity, you may need some or all of them. Boots, gloves, shirts, pants, and coveralls fall under the category of PPE clothing. Safety glasses, full-face shields, welding goggles, or masks are to protect the eyes. Soft hats and caps, bump caps, and hard hats are used to protect the hair and/or head. Dust masks, respirators, and supplied air respirators are for breathing protection. Ear-muffs or ear plugs protect your hearing. Fall protection or fall arrest systems are used while working at heights. **FIGURE 3-9** shows a fall prevention system. Here we cover each of the PPE types in detail.

Protective Clothing

Work clothes, whether shirts and pants or coveralls, are typically made from fire-resistant (not fire-proof) material, but not always. Look at the label on the clothes and see if it is listed as fire resistant. If not, check with the supplier to ensure that it is.

- Work clothes should fit properly and not sag or drag on the floor.
- Clothing should be kept clean; greasy or oily coveralls can become a fire hazard.
- Clothing should be maintained—if they become worn or torn, they should be replaced.

Gloves

Gloves come in many types: heavy leather welding gloves; acid- or chemical-resistant gloves for working with caustic or

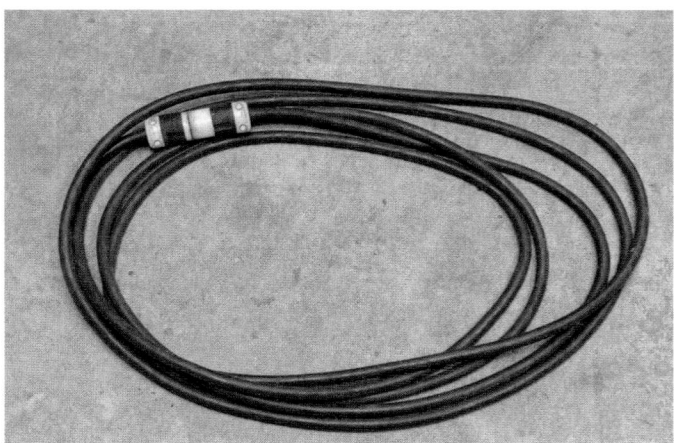

FIGURE 3-8 Extension cords should be flexible and neoprene-covered.

FIGURE 3-9 A fall protection system.

FIGURE 3-10 Heavy leather welding gloves.

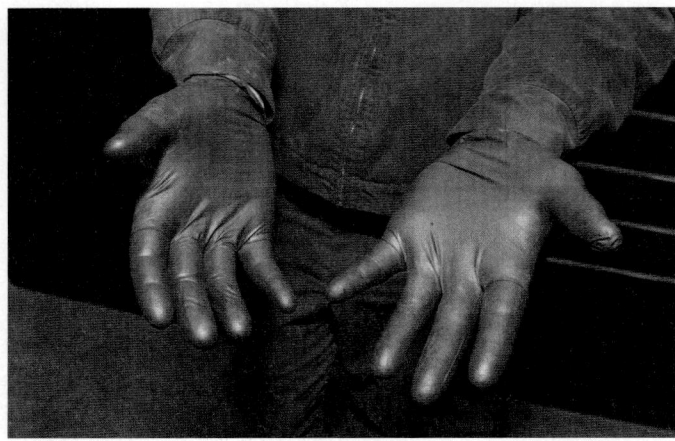

FIGURE 3-12 General-purpose nitrile work gloves.

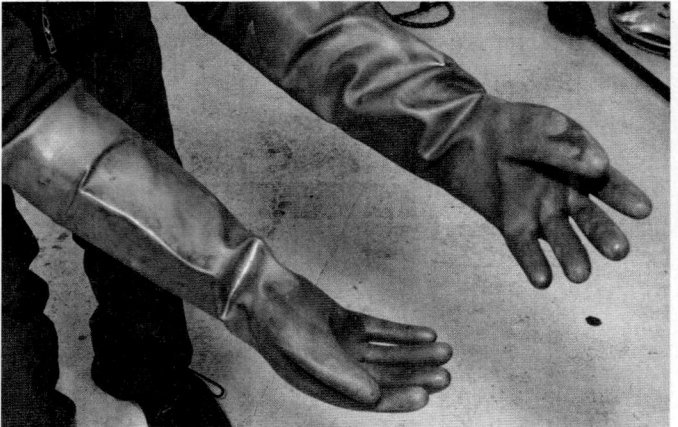

FIGURE 3-11 Chemical-resistant gloves that cover the forearm for increased protection.

FIGURE 3-13 Work boots.

dangerous materials; latex, vinyl, or nitrile work gloves to protect the skin for general work; light cloth gloves for handling sharp objects; and/or insulating gloves for high-voltage work. You should always protect the skin on your hands from exposure to chemicals or solvents. Long-term exposure to these hazards can cause long-term health effects. Welding gloves protect your hands from heat and sparks common during welding procedures. These gloves should have long cuffs to protect the wrists. **FIGURE 3-10** shows welding gloves. **FIGURE 3-11** shows a pair of chemical-resistant gloves and **FIGURE 3-12** shows a pair of general-purpose nitrile gloves that protect the skin.

- Gloves should fit your hand snugly but allow you to flex your knuckles.
- Oil- or water-soaked gloves do not provide the normal level of protection and may become a hazard.
- Vinyl and latex work gloves do not stand up to use in solvents.
- Nitrile gloves protect against solvents, but it is recommended to use heavier chemical-resistant gloves when working with solvents.
- Always check your gloves for holes and/or wear and replace, as necessary.

Work Boots or Shoes

Work boots and/or shoes should always be worn by everyone in a work shop. These specially designed shoes and/or boots have grease-resistant non-slip soles, steel toes to protect the feet from falling objects or equipment, and contain plates in the soles to prevent puncture injuries. Commercial vehicle technician's footwear should also have at least 8-inch-high uppers to protect the ankles from injury. Insulated, rather than uninsulated, work boots are recommended, as they keep your feet warm in cold conditions and cool in warm conditions (**FIGURE 3-13**).

- Boots should fit comfortably and snugly for stability.
- Boots should be kept clean and maintained.
- Replace worn boots (soles or uppers) promptly.
- Insulated work boots keep your feet warm in cold weather and cool in warm weather.
- Keep the laces on your work boots in good condition and always have your boots laced properly.
- Never tuck your pant legs into your work boot, as foreign material could fall into the top of the boot.

Headgear

Several different types of **headgear** can be worn in the shop. Simple cloth caps (without peaks) can be worn to keep debris and grease out of your hair. Bump caps can be used while working under a vehicle in a pit to prevent bumping your head on the underside of the vehicle. (Bump caps are commonly worn by lubrication and inspection personnel.) Hard hats may be worn when working where falling objects are possible.

- All headgear should fit comfortably so you are more likely to wear it.
- A bump cap that is too big or has too much peak can interfere with your vision under a vehicle. Use one that fits and has a small rim, rather than a peak.
- Keep bump caps and hard hats in good condition (a loose adjusting mechanism can be very frustrating, as you have to keep retightening your hat).

Eye Protection

Depending on the work in progress, many different eye protection equipment may be worn. Safety glasses are the basic protection and most workplaces require you to wear safety glasses at all times in the shop. Goggles may need to be worn when working with pressurized equipment, full-face shields may be required if there are dangerous chemicals involved.

Safety Glasses

Safety glasses come in all shapes, designs, and sizes. Various lens tints are also available. Any safety glasses used in the workplace should meet the **ANSI (American National Standards Institute)** standard. ANSI is a non-profit organization that produces quality standards that companies must meet for their products to be ANSI accredited. The current ANSI standard for safety glasses and face protection devices is Z87.1-2015. This standard was introduced in 2015. Standards are revisited every 5 years for upgrading, if necessary. Eye protection that meets this standard is high-impact resistance tested and is marked with Z87+ on the lens and on the frame of the glasses (the frames are part of the impact resistance). **FIGURE 3-14** shows a typical pair of safety glasses.

Safety glasses manufactured prior to 2010 were marked Z87. It is recommended that glasses marked Z87 be replaced, as they are subject to lower impact resistance than the new standard. All new glasses should meet the higher impact-resistant new standard. Safety glasses that meet the ANSI standard have attached side protectors on the frames or formed as part of the lenses. Safety glasses are available with prescription lenses. These should be marked Z87-2+. Always use approved safety glasses.

Safety Goggles

Safety goggles are recommended when working with pressurized systems and/or when there is a chance of liquids getting behind your safety glasses. **FIGURE 3-15** shows a pair of safety goggles. Goggles provide slightly more protection than safety glasses in these working conditions by forming a complete shield around your eyes. Safety goggles must also carry the ANSI Z87+ designation.

Full-Face Shields

A full-face shield in combination with safety glasses is recommended when working with chemicals, such as battery acid, or when grinding. A full-face shield protects the skin on your face if there is a chemical spill or hot particles flying around. Most full-face shields are not impact resistant, so it is essential that you still wear your safety glasses while using one. **FIGURE 3-16** shows a full-face shield.

Welding and Cutting Eye Protection

Oxy-acetylene welding goggles, or **gas welding goggles**, are close-fitting safety goggles with a dark tinted lens. These are worn when cutting or welding metal with gas welding equipment. The lens tint is known as the shade and can range from 3 to 6, depending on how thick the metal being welded or cut is. The higher the number, the darker the shade. Welding goggles protect from harmful infrared radiation given off in most welding and cutting operations. Picking the correct shade is a

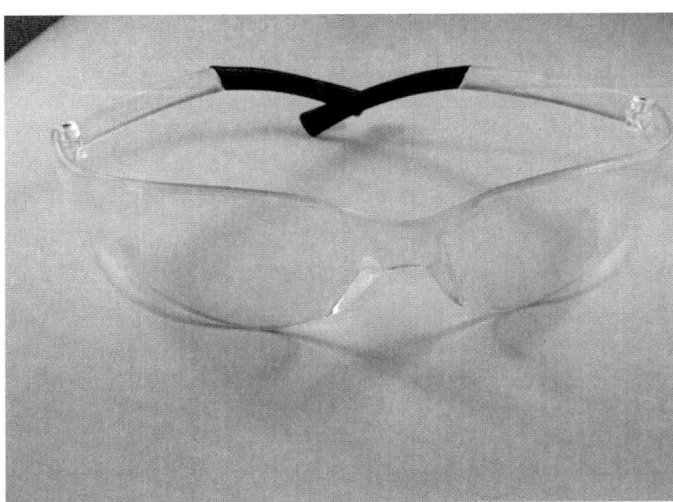

FIGURE 3-14 Safety glass lenses and frames are impact resistant.

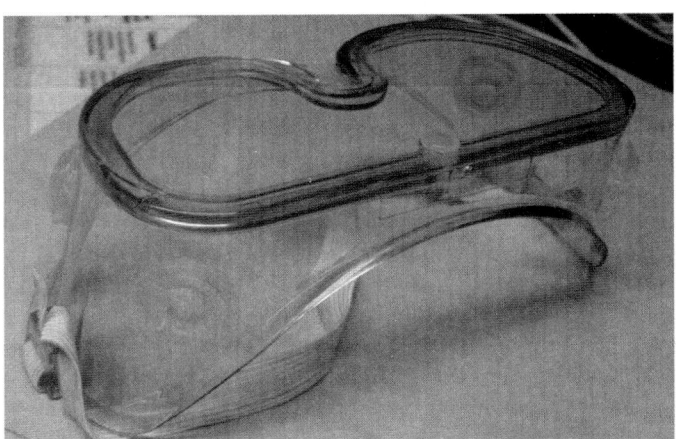

FIGURE 3-15 Goggles provide more protection than glasses when dealing with pressurized systems.

Source: Image © Picsfive/ShutterStock, Inc.

FIGURE 3-16 Full-face shields must be used in combination with safety glasses.

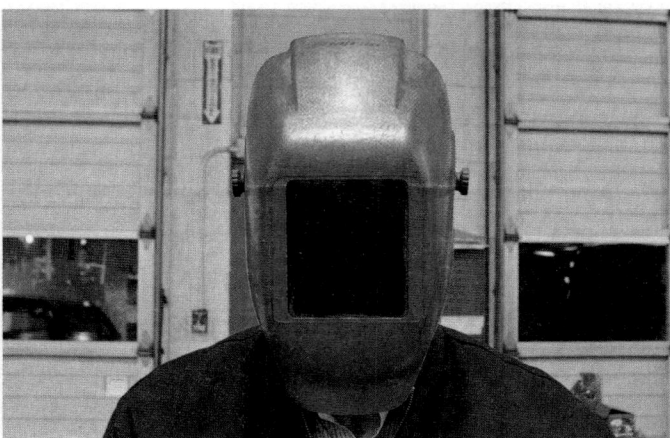

FIGURE 3-18 A welding helmet.

FIGURE 3-17 Gas welding goggles.

matter of choice, but the rule of thumb is to start with the darkest shade, or one that is too dark to see the weld zone, and then use successively lighter shades until you can see the weld zone comfortably. **FIGURE 3-17** shows gas welding goggles.

Arc Welding Protection

Arc welding protection has much darker shading than gas welding. Arc welding shade numbers range from 7 to as high as 14 for carbon arc welding. Arc welding also produces high levels of ultraviolet (UV) light and requires UV, as well as infrared, radiation protection. The UV radiation produced by arc welding is similar to the sun's radiation and can burn your skin just like the sun can. A full **welding helmet** is used for arc welding, as it protects your eyes and your face from the UV radiation and flying sparks or particles. When arc welding, you should also have no exposed skin, as it can burn in a relatively short period of time due to the UV radiation. Welding operations should be behind a shield or barrier to protect workers who may be close by from the radiation. You must always wear your PPE, whether you are actually welding or just assisting the welder. Never look at a welding arc with the naked eye. Severe eye damage can occur almost instantly. Welding helmet shading is so dark that

it is nearly impossible to see the work before the arc is started or struck. Auto-tint welding helmets can be purchased that are much safer and more convenient for the welder. Auto-tint helmets have a clear lens that allows the welder to see the work and then they shade automatically the instant the arc is struck. Auto-tint helmets avoid the need for the welder to lift the helmet to see the work and then lower it quickly when the arc is struck. **FIGURE 3-18** shows an arc weld helmet.

Breathing Protection

In a workshop, you are likely exposed to many different airborne dusts and/or fumes. Some of these may be harmless and others can cause immediate or long-term effects. Dust masks, respirators, and fresh air supplies are systems that are designed to prevent you from aspirating (breathing in) these contaminants. You should always wear the required breathing protection for the job you are doing to protect yourself.

Dust Masks

A dust mask is a disposable paper filtering device that is held against your mouth and nose with elastic straps. The dust mask typically has a metal strip around the nose area, so you can conform it to the shape of your face. There are numerous manufacturers of these masks and they come with many different claims of effectiveness, but dust masks are only to be used in dusty conditions—not when there are known hazards and/or solvent or chemical fumes. Dust masks are single-use disposable breathing protection and should be replaced daily. **FIGURE 3-19** shows a typical disposable dust mask.

Respirators

A **respirator** is a breathing protection device that has removable filter cartridges that can be selected for the task at hand. Respirators can be used to protect against hazardous dust or particles, such as asbestos and/or other recognized carcinogenic dusts. Respirator cartridges can also be selected to protect against solvent and/or chemical fumes. Respirators should be approved by NIOSH (National Institute for Occupational Safety and Health) or a similar regulatory agency.

FIGURE 3-19 Dust masks should be replaced daily.

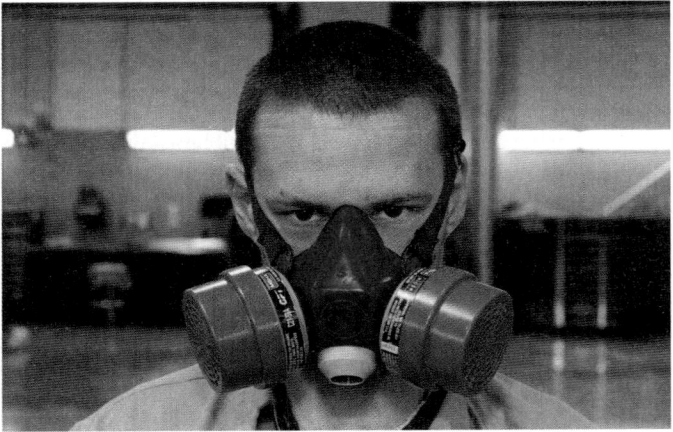

FIGURE 3-20 A respirator must seal against the face to work properly. Facial hair may require the use of a full-face-style respirator.

Respirators must fit snugly to the face to seal and it is important to note that facial hair lessens the effectiveness. People with facial hair should wear a full-face respirator. The cartridges used should be replaced based on the recommendations of the manufacturer of the respirator. The cartridges come in a sealed container and certain types can be affected by moisture in the air, requiring their replacement, so read the manufacturer's instructions carefully. **FIGURE 3-20** shows a typical respirator.

Fresh-Air-Supply Respirator

Technicians working in environments with high levels of solvents or other chemicals may require fresh air-supplied respirators. A fresh-air-supplied respirator has a full-face mask cover and a pump that pumps ambient air into a face shield, and the person breathes this air only. The respirator is equipped with a one-way valving system that allows exhalation to pass out through the respirator.

Most commercial vehicle technicians do not work in conditions where they need this type of respirator, but they may be required when called on to clean and/or inspect the inside of chemical transport trailers. In some cases, the fresh air-supplied respirator has its own portable tank to supply the air.

The Dangers of Dust

In the workshop, there are many different types of dust that you encounter. None of them are good for you. They all have the potential for physical harm. These are known as **toxic dust** and include any dust that can cause physical harm. General dust found, let's say in an unused storeroom, contains many things from dirt to pollen to microscopic pollens, dander from rodents, and more—some of which can be toxic. Protect yourself from these dangers by using a dust mask. Other dust in the shop can be toxic, most with long-term, rather than immediate effects.

In the past, friction material was made from asbestos, which is a carcinogen (meaning it can cause cancer). In the 1970s, manufacturers in North America agreed to no longer use asbestos in friction material, and a change was made to ceramic manmade material or organic materials that did not contain asbestos. The dangers of dust created by these newer materials are still not fully understood. Long-term studies are underway; however, the best rule of thumb for any technician is to avoid all the dust encountered by using a NIOSH-approved respirator, eye protection, and gloves when dealing with friction material dust. When working with dust, it is also critical that you do everything in your power to prevent the dust from becoming airborne. Wash station systems are available that wet and wash the dust into a receptacle so that it can be disposed of correctly. Vacuum systems are also available, but these are only as good as the filtration system at the exit of the vacuum. Never use compressed air to blow dust from a component. Even brushing the component with a whisk or broom can put large amounts of particles in the air, putting everyone in the shop in danger. Asbestos is still sold worldwide and is used by some overseas manufacturers in friction material. To clean brake dust, follow the steps in **SKILL DRILL 3-2**.

Hearing Protection

The shop environment can be a very noisy place. Cutting, grinding, bucking rivets, air tools, and compressors all make significant noise and can cause damage to the hearing if the decibel (dB) level rises above 85. At 85 dB, you must raise your voice to be heard from 2 feet away. **Ear protection** is required at this decibel level or damage to hearing occurs. There are two types of hearing protection commonly available to technicians: ear plugs and ear muffs. Ear plugs can be soft and flexible foam protectors that are first compressed between your fingers, then inserted into the ear canal, and there they expand to fill the canal and block out sound. Ear plugs can also be soft silicone plugs that are inserted into the ear. Ear muffs are large muffs that cover the ear entirely. Of the two systems, the collapsible foam ear plugs are best capable of reducing noise levels. In some situations, ear plugs are used in combination with ear muffs for maximum protection. Be aware that even though the decibel limit is listed at 85, long-term exposure to loud noise has a cumulative detrimental effect on your hearing. Use hearing

SKILL DRILL 3-2 Cleaning Toxic Dust safely

1. Always use a NIOSH-approved respirator, safety glasses, and gloves when cleaning brake or clutch dust. If available, a full-face shield should be used.
2. Prepare the wash station. Make sure it has the correct amount of washing fluid. The fluid is normally a mix of soap and water.
3. Position the wash station so that it catches the fluid running off the component. It may be necessary to use a stand to support the station so that it is close enough to prevent splashing.
4. Turn on the wash station pump and gently wet all the dust thoroughly.
5. Continue to wash the dust from the components until it is clean and all the wet dust has fallen into the wash station.
6. When necessary, dispose of the accumulated dust in the wash station in an approved manner.

FIGURE 3-21 Ear plugs are slightly better at protecting your hearing.

protection, where practical, if you are exposed to loud noises for long periods, to avoid these long-term effects. **FIGURE 3-21** shows the two common types of hearing protection.

▶ TECHNICIAN TIP

Long-term exposure to loud noises at much lower decibel ratings than 85 dB can cause cumulative and permanent hearing loss. Never take a chance with your hearing—always use hearing protection if you have the opportunity. Ask any older rock musician what he would do different, and it will likely be wearing earplugs during his career, as 90% have substantial hearing loss, if they didn't wear protection.

Protecting Your Person

We have discussed PPE in the last few paragraphs, but there are more things that you can do to protect yourself in the workplace. Many personal items, jewelry, long hair, and loose clothing can cause accidents in the shop. Here are some tips to avoid the danger.

Jewelry

Jewelry has no place in the workshop. Rings, watches, necklaces—wearing any jewelry can cause a problem. Wearing a ring on your finger may seem fine, but it can pose several dangers. There are several recorded instances of people losing a finger because of rings. The number one way that this happens is when the ring becomes caught on a protruding screw or bolt as the person is descending from a vehicle and the person's weight causes the stuck ring to amputate the finger. A ring is also an electrical hazard. It can cause a short between a wire and ground on a vehicle and superheat and burn the finger. A ring overheated like this can usually not be removed until it cools back down (very painful).

A watch can cause the same types of problems; it can get caught, leading to broken wrists or severe abrasions. A watch with a metal band can cause electrical shorts and painful burns. Necklaces have the same issues, and they can also become caught in rotating machines, causing the wearer to be pulled into the machine and injured. Never wear jewelry in the workplace.

Long Hair or Loose Clothing

Some people, men or women, prefer to keep their hair long and that is a personal choice, but in a shop, long hair can be deadly. There are many reports of people having the scalp torn from their heads and/or receiving more severe injuries when hair becomes entangled in rotating equipment. Long hair should be secured in such a way that it does not dangle (tying it in a ponytail does not cut it). Hair nets or hats that secure the hair should be worn so that the hair cannot become tangled. The same goes for loose clothing, scarfs, and the like. A particularly dangerous one these days is the hoodie sweatshirt. Many sweatshirt-style hoodies have drawstrings attached to the hood that can be caught up in equipment. These should never be worn in the shop, but many mobile technicians choose them for warmth on road calls. Drawstrings can be deadly and should be removed or cut. Anything on the body that is worn loosely or dangles can become entangled and lead to injury. So tuck in your shirt, tie up or cover your hair, tie your shoelaces, and protect yourself.

Eyewash Stations

Most workplaces have emergency eyewash stations in the event that debris or chemicals gets into your eyes. Using proper PPE should prevent you from injuring your eyes, but accidents can still occur. An eyewash station is designed to flush the eyes with clean water to dislodge and remove debris. The eyewash station is also used if chemicals are splashed into the eye. Flushing the eyes immediately after the entrance of debris or chemicals is considered the best local treatment for eye injury. Eyewash stations can be as simple as a squeeze bottle containing a sterile saline solution, or a more elaborate system that uses fresh water to flood and clean the eyes. **FIGURE 3-22** shows a fresh water-type eyewash station.

If a chemical has been splashed in a coworker's eyes, he or she may need you to assist him or her in finding the eyewash station. When chemicals are involved, it is important that the eyes are flushed for a considerable amount of time. The recommended flushing time varies, depending on the chemical involved, but is seldom less than 15 minutes. In some workplaces, large amounts of chemicals are used, which can lead to chemical exposure of the body. These workplaces may have emergency showers to deal with this kind of exposure. If you or a coworker has been splashed with chemicals, enter the shower immediately, remove contaminated clothing while under the shower, and flush the skin for at least 15 minutes, then seek medical attention.

Fire Suppression Systems

LO 3-5 Describe the various types of fire suppression systems and explain their use.

Because of the activities and materials used in a commercial vehicle shop, fires are a constant threat. There are many types of flammable liquids used. There are typically several ignition sources; sparks from grinding or welding, oxy-acetylene torches, electrical work, and more. Make sure you know where fire suppression equipment is in your workplace and how to use it. The following section discusses fire prevention, and the types and use of fire suppression devices.

Fire Prevention

The safest way to deal with fire is to prevent it from happening in the first place. Many of the components and supplies you will be working with are flammable. Gasoline, diesel fuel, solvents, brake cleaner, and many of the fluids used in commercial vehicles can all, to varying degrees, start or contribute to fires. Gasoline is a very *volatile* fuel (meaning it vaporizes easily) and can very quickly form an explosive mixture in the air. Diesel fuel is not as volatile as gasoline, but it can also easily form an explosive mixture with air if it is atomized under pressure.

When working with flammable fuels or gasses, it is essential to take all the necessary precautions to prevent fires. Always notify those around you that you are working with flammable materials and have the correct type of fire suppression equipment close at hand. Use LED or fluorescent trouble lights that are battery powered to lessen the risk of them becoming an ignition source. **FIGURE 3-23** shows a LED trouble light. When working with any type of flammable material, make sure spills are cleaned up immediately and that there are no potential ignition sources or activities nearby that could ignite flammable liquids.

> ▶ **TECHNICIAN TIP**

Fuel vapor is impossible to see and different fuels can vaporize at varying temperatures. Gasoline, for example, easily vaporizes at room temperature and very quickly forms an ignitable mixture in ambient air. Within minutes of a fuel spill, this ignitable mixture can spread far from the original spill area and ignition sources 40 or 50 feet, or more, away could ignite the mixture, causing an explosive burn.

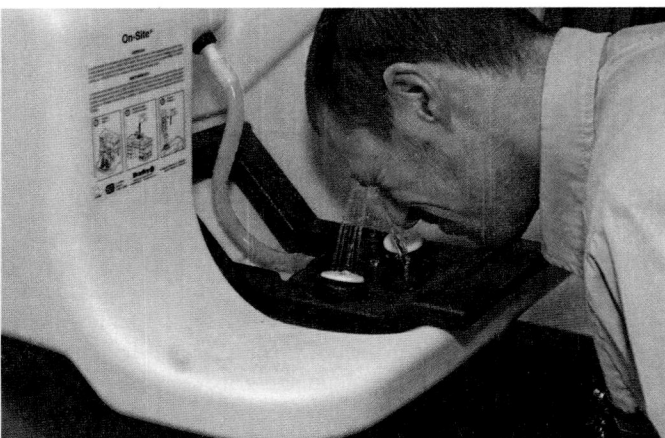

FIGURE 3-22 Flushing the eye immediately is the recommended treatment after the entrance of debris or chemicals.

FIGURE 3-23 LED trouble lights are safer to use than incandescent bulb types.

Although diesel fuel is less volatile than gasoline, it ignites under the correct conditions. When diesel fuel is atomized (meaning it is broken into very small particles), it can ignite easily. Air pressure used to clean filter mounts and high-pressure leaks can atomize diesel fuel, making it ignitable. Diesel fuel also ignites easily if its temperature rises sufficiently.

Spills

Fuel is spilled in most shops on a regular basis. Draining tanks, changing fuel filters or water separators, repairing fuel lines, and more are all activities where a fuel spill is possible. Use extreme care to avoid spills in the first place, but, if they do occur, clean them up immediately. Always keep spill-containment materials close at hand when there is a possibility of a fuel spill. Only use approved techniques and containers when draining or transferring fuel. If you are likely to cause a spill during the job you are performing, such as removing a fuel tank, drain the fuel tank before you begin. Make sure that the container you are draining the fuel into has sufficient capacity to hold the fuel. On-highway class 8 truck fuel tanks can hold 200 or 250 gallons and some can hold even more. Most heavy truck tanks have an easily accessible drain to assist in removing the fuel, or you can use an external pump to pump the fuel from the tank.

Fuel Tank Repair

Heavy truck fuel tanks are made from a variety of materials and can be very expensive to replace; therefore, a common activity is tank repair. Tanks can be damaged by abrasion, rust if they are steel, and/or have collision damage. Usually, the repair includes welding the tank. It is never safe to weld a fuel tank, full or empty, when it is on the vehicle. Full tanks can explode and empty tanks are full of vapors and can represent an even greater explosion risk. Fuel tank repair should be left to the experts. The tank should be drained, washed thoroughly inside and out, and filled with an inert gas before a welding repair is attempted. This is not a job for a commercial vehicle technician.

Never weld on or near a fuel tank, gasoline or diesel. The tank likely will explode if the fuel heats sufficiently. An empty tank can represent an even greater risk of explosion, as it is full of fuel vapor. Tank repair is a specialized job and should only be attempted by experts in the field.

Fire Suppression

A fire requires three elements to exist: something burnable (fuel), sufficient oxygen (the reactant), and a source of heat (or ignition). If you remove any of the three elements, the fire stops. In fire suppression, the idea is to remove one or more of the elements, usually the oxygen. When dealing with fires, always remember you are not a trained fire fighter, you are a service technician. If the fire is significant, the first thing to do is remove yourself from the situation and call emergency services to extinguish the fire. With that said, quite often there are small fires that can be quickly dealt with in a workshop using a fire

FIGURE 3-24 Fire extinguisher locations should be signed and easily visible.

extinguisher or a fire blanket to remove the oxygen from the blaze, but again, do not hesitate to call emergency services if you are concerned that you may not be able to handle the fire or it seems to be getting out of control. Fire extinguisher locations should be well signed as in **FIGURE 3-24**.

Classification of Fires

In North America, fires are classified into five different types by letter:

- Class A fires: These are fires in which normal combustibles are burning, such as paper, wood, or cloth.
- Class B fires: These are fires that involve flammable liquids or gasses.
- Class C fires: These fires involve electrical equipment.
- Class D fires: These fires involve combustible metal such as magnesium, lithium, sodium, or titanium.
- Class K fires: These are fires in which cooking oil or fat is burning.

Fire Extinguisher Types

Fire extinguishers are rated as to which type of fire they are suitable for: A, B, C, D, or K. There are pictograms (a small image depicting the type of burning material the fire extinguisher is recommended for) on the fire extinguisher. A letter in the pictogram also indicates the class of fire the extinguisher is suitable for. Fire extinguishers can contain carbon dioxide, water, dry chemical, or foam. Most types of fire extinguishers are combination extinguishers capable of fighting or suppressing more than one class of fire. The most common fire extinguisher found in a commercial vehicle service facility is a combination ABC fire extinguisher. **FIGURE 3-25** shows an ABC combination fire extinguisher.

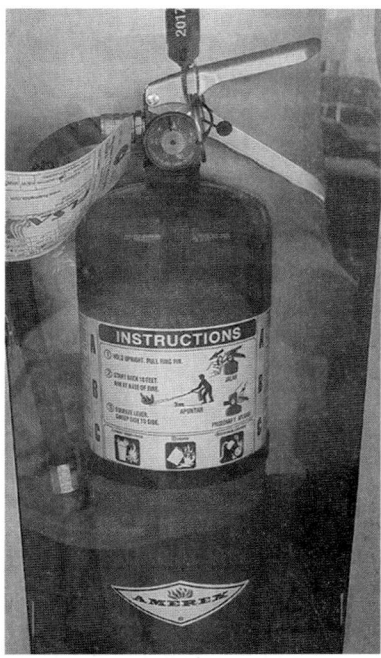

FIGURE 3-25 The most common type of fire extinguisher a technician will use is a combination ABC fire extinguisher.

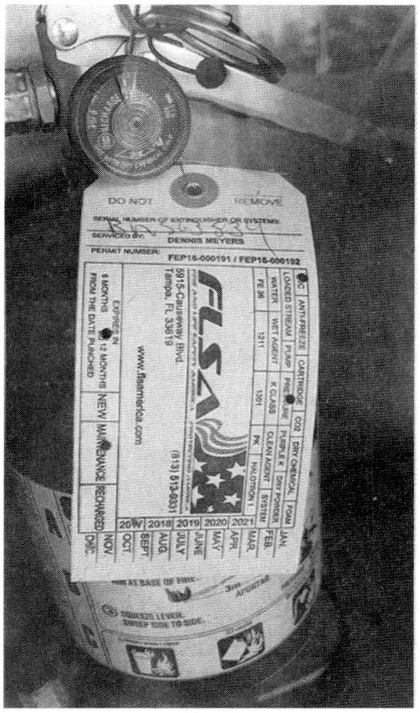

FIGURE 3-26 Fire extinguishers need to be certified on a yearly basis.

An ABC fire extinguisher is capable of fighting A, B, and C class fires. An ABC fire extinguisher has three pictograms side-by-side showing the type of material it is used for. An ABC fire extinguisher is a dry chemical extinguisher that works by starving the fire of oxygen. There are specialized fire extinguishers for certain workplaces where other types of fires are possible or likely. These fire extinguishers may contain foam, water, wet chemicals, or inert gases.

Fire extinguishers must be inspected and certified by a registered specialist, usually on a yearly basis. The inspector tags the fire extinguisher with the name of the inspector, the company he or she works for, and the date of the last inspection. **FIGURE 3-26** shows an inspection tag. The fire extinguishers should also be checked by the joint health and safety committee during each shop safety inspection, making sure the seal is intact and the pressure reading is in the normal range. **FIGURE 3-27** shows the seal and the pressure gauge on a fire extinguisher.

Operation of a Fire Extinguisher

Always remember, you are not a firefighting professional! Before attempting to use a fire extinguisher on a fire, alert your supervisor or a coworker to the fire and the fact that you are trying to extinguish it. Position yourself between the fire and an easy exit. Do not let the fire block your escape! Assess the fire and be sure you have the correct fire extinguisher for the fire class (using a water-based class A fire extinguisher on a flammable liquid fire causes the fire to spread or even explode). A fire extinguisher typically has instructions for proper use displayed on the fire extinguisher, as shown in **FIGURE 3-28**.

Most fire extinguishers have a hose attached. If so, hold the fire extinguisher in one hand by the handle. Pull the pin and

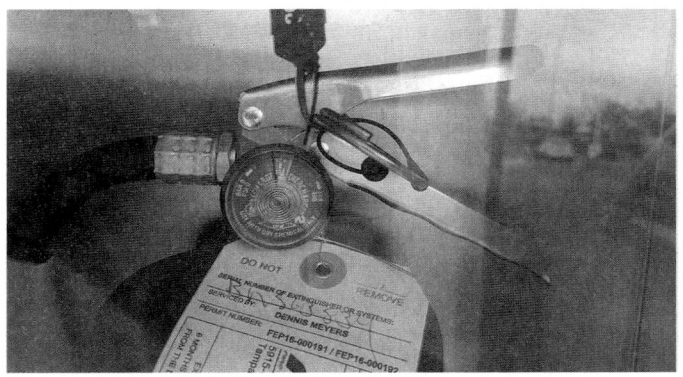

FIGURE 3-27 Ensure the seal on the fire extinguisher is intact and the pressure is correct during each shop safety inspection.

FIGURE 3-28 Take a minute to familiarize yourself with the instructions on the fire extinguishers in your shop.

grasp the hose with the other hand. Squeeze the handle while aiming the hose and nozzle at the base of the fire, not at the flames. Use a sweeping motion from side to side and, if your efforts are having little or no effect, cease immediately and evacuate. When you are safely away from the fire, call emergency services. If you are successful and put the fire out, be very careful that it does not start again. Remove the fuel and/or the source of ignition and monitor the area to be sure the fire is out. To correctly use a fire extinguisher, follow the steps in **SKILL DRILL 3-3**.

Fire Blankets

A **fire blanket** is a blanket made with fire retardant material. It is very useful for putting out small fires. The blanket suffocates the fire by cutting off the oxygen required to keep the fire burning. Fire blankets are also especially good at putting out a fire that has started on a person's clothing. By wrapping the person tightly in the blanket, the fire is suffocated.

Fire blankets are usually contained in a special case or pack and the case or pack is printed with instructions on how to use the fire blanket properly. Remember that the fire blanket works by starving the fire of oxygen, so it is important that when you use the blanket, it covers the entire fire. To use a fire blanket, remove it from the case or pack and completely unfold the blanket. Hold the blanket as a shield between you and the fire being careful to wrap your hands in the blanket to protect them. Place the blanket completely over the fire and leave it in place for sufficient time to extinguish the fire. If, after the fire is extinguished, the blanket shows any type of damage, replace the blanket. If not, return the blanket to its case or pack for the next use.

SKILL DRILL 3-3 Using a Fire Extinguisher

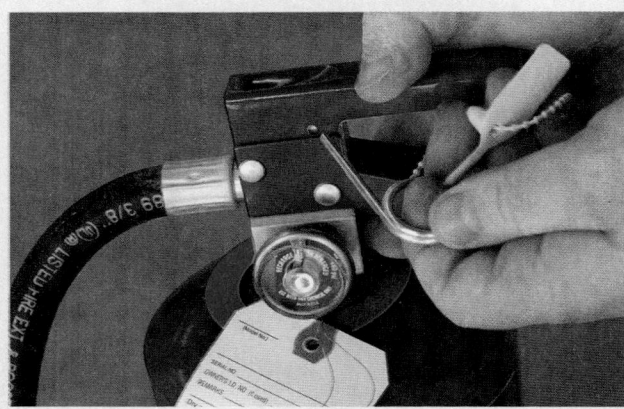

1. Assess the fire to ensure you have the correct fire extinguisher for the fire class. Stand 10 feet (3 m) back from the fire. Grasp the fire extinguisher by the handle, and pull the pin.

2. Grasp the hose (if equipped) in your other hand, and point the hose or the nozzle of the fire extinguisher at the base of the fire—not at the flames.

3. Squeeze the handle to discharge the fire extinguisher.
4. Use a side-to-side sweeping motion as you discharge the fire extinguisher at the fire.

5. If your efforts are unsuccessful, immediately evacuate the area. Only when you are safely clear of the danger area, call emergency services. If you are successful, continue to monitor the fire to ensure it does not restart.

Legal Responsibilities of Hazardous Materials

LO 3-6 Explain the legal responsibilities of employees and employers regarding hazardous material in the workplace and interpret hazard information.

Hazardous materials are materials that can cause harm to a person or the environment when not contained and/or handled or used properly. Governments around the world have instituted hazardous material legislation so that these materials are clearly labeled and that information on their hazardous nature is readily available to the worker that must use the material. Hazardous materials come in all forms—solid, liquids, and gases—and every shop that you work in has several hazardous materials that you likely use daily. This section covers the relevant rules and regulations surrounding hazardous materials in the workplace.

Global Harmonized System (GHS)

For many years, each government had its own regulations on hazardous materials, citing the way the material must be labeled, the information about the product that must be given by the manufacturer, the handling of the material, and the education of the workers required to use the material. This led to some confusion as manufacturers had to meet the standards applicable to the countries where they were shipping their product. The United Nations has since established the Global Harmonized System (GHS) of Classification and Labeling of Chemicals to combat this confusion and uncertainty. The GHS standardizes the classification of hazards, the symbols that are used to represent the hazards, and the information required on what are now known as or **SDSs (safety data sheets)**. Under the older system, these sheets were known as MSDS (Material Safety Data Sheets). The GHS also standardizes the SDSs themselves so that the required information can be obtained quickly without confusion. SDSs are discussed further later.

The United States agencies involved in hazardous material legislation, primarily OSHA, the EPA, and the WHMIS (Workplace Hazardous Material Information System) in Canada have aligned themselves with the GHS, although some elements of the Canadian system still differ slightly from the GHS. But, for the most part, the symbols used, the categories of hazards, and the information on the SDSs are the same in both countries, as well as in all of the countries that have adopted the GHS. The intent behind the GHS and all hazardous material information systems is the same, no matter which country you are in. That is, the protection of the worker and the environment from exposure to or release of hazardous materials. The four main elements of all hazardous material systems are as follows:

- Classification of hazards
- Labels and symbols to identify the hazard
- SDSs that identify the hazardous properties of the chemical
- Training for workers in the safe use and handling of the material

Classification of Hazards

The GHS identifies hazards in three broad groups: Physical hazards, Health Hazards, and Environmental hazards.

Physical hazards are broken into the following categories:

- Explosives
- Flammable Gases
- Flammable Aerosols
- Oxidizing Gases
- Gases Under Pressure
- Flammable Liquids
- Flammable Solids
- Self-Heating Substances
- Substances that, in contact with water, emit flammable gases
- Oxidizing Liquids
- Oxidizing Solids
- Organic Peroxides
- Corrosive to Metals
- Self-Reactive Substances (a substance that can ignite or decompose without the presence of oxygen)
- Pyrophoric Liquids (liquids that can spontaneously combust in air at temperatures of 130° F or below)
- Pyrophoric Solids (solids that can spontaneously combust in air at temperatures of 130° F or below)

Health hazards are broken into the following categories:

- Acute Toxicity
- Skin Corrosion/Irritation
- Serious Eye Damage/Eye Irritation
- Carcinogenicity (can cause cancer)
- Reproductive Toxicology (can interfere with human reproduction and/or off-spring)
- Target Organ Systemic Toxicity (toxic to a specific human organ, can be single or repeat exposure)
- Aspiration Toxicity (can cause pulmonary damage and/or illnesses)
- Respiratory or Skin Sensitization
- Germ Cell Mutagenicity (known to cause heritable mutations in human cells)

Environmental hazards are broken into the following categories:

- Hazardous to the Aquatic Environment
- Acute Aquatic Toxicity (causing death immediately in aquatic organisms)
- Chronic Aquatic Toxicity (causing death over a period of time in aquatic organisms)
- Bioaccumulation Potential (can build up in aquatic organisms)

Most of the categories above have sub-categories that rank the severity of the hazard. Hazards are ranked from 5 to 1, with 1 being the most severe.

Symbols and Labels

GHS hazard symbols are pictograms in a red bordered triangle. There are nine symbols to identify the hazards. **FIGURE 3-29** shows the nine hazard pictograms used with the GHS.

GHS01 Explosive

GHS04 Compressed Gas

GHS07 Harmful

GHS02 Flammable

GHS05 Corrosive

GHS08 Health Hazard

GHS03 Oxidizing

GHS06 Toxic

GHS09 Environmental Hazard

FIGURE 3-29 The nine GHS hazardous material symbols.

Labels complying with GHS have the following elements:

1. Product name should match the name used in the SDSs.
2. A hazard pictogram or symbol identifying the hazard class (can be more than one).
3. A signal word; either "Danger" for more-severe hazards, or "Warning" for less-severe hazards.
4. A standardized hazard statement describing the hazard, e.g., Highly Flammable Liquid and Vapor.
5. Precautionary statements: Measures to use to minimize or prevent hazardous effects, e.g., keep away from heat/hot surfaces/sparks/open flames and other ignition sources and no smoking. These elements are not standardized by the GHS, but should be generally followed.
6. The supplier identification: Name, address, and telephone number of the supplier should be provided on the label.

The label may also contain supplemental information (not required under GHS, but may be required by specific agencies). **FIGURE 3-30** shows a typical GHS label with the six elements numbered.

In the past, different hazardous material information systems used slightly different versions of material data sheets. The information required and its location of the sheet differed from country to country making compliance difficult for manufacturers and information gathering difficult for users of the material. The Globally Harmonized System standardizes the SDSs for hazardous materials so that all SDSs carry the same information about the product and it is in the same location on the SDSs. The GHS SDSs has 16 components and is laid out as follows:

1. Identification of the substance or mixture and of the supplier
   - Recommended use of the chemical and restrictions on use.
   - Emergency phone number.
2. Hazards identification
   - GHS classification of the substance/mixture and any national or regional information.
   - GHS label elements, including precautionary statements.
3. Composition of and information on ingredients and the substance, its chemical identity, common names, synonyms, etc. Any additives that are part of the substance that are themselves classified as hazards.
4. First aid measures, according to exposure routes, symptoms, and effects of exposure and medical treatment required.

Components of a GHS-Compliant Label

PRODUCT XYZ

DANGER

Fatal if swallowed,
Causes Skin irritation.

Wear protective gloves, Wash hands
thoroughly after handling. Do not eat,
drink or smoke while using this product.
If swallowed immediately contact a
poison center or doctor. If on hands
wash with plenty of water and seek
medical attention

See Safety Data Sheet (SDSs)
for further details regarding
safe use of this product.

Any company 1685 Any road, Any town, Pennsylvania, USA 45193 (555)-666-3333

FIGURE 3-30 A typical GHS product label.

5. Firefighting measure hazards caused by the combustion of the product, and special precautions for firefighters.
6. Accidental release measures, personal and environmental, containment method, and cleanup.
7. Handling and storage precautions for safe handling.
8. Exposure controls PPE, occupational exposure limit values, or biological limit values.
9. Physical and chemical properties.
10. Stability and reactivity
    • Chemical stability.
    • Possibility of hazardous reactions.
11. Toxicological information.
12. Ecological information.
13. Disposal.
14. Transport information.
    • UN Number.
    • UN Proper shipping name.
    • Transportation precautions.
15. Regulatory information
    • Safety, health, and environmental regulations specific for the product in question.
16. Other information, including the preparation and revision dates of the SDSs.

All workers should have quick and easy access to the SDSs for each and every hazardous product used in the shop. Timely access to the information required to treat and/or limit the effects of exposure to the product is paramount to protect the workers from injury or illness. Most shops maintain an SDSs binder in which all the SDSs are kept in alphabetical order or have a dedicated computer to access the SDSs. Workers must be able to access the SDSs without having to leave their general work area and, if a computer is used, there must be a back-up system in place in the event of a power outage or other emergency.

In the United States, SDSs are required to be updated only if there is a change to the formulation of the product or to its effects. In other countries, SDSs may expire. Canada, for example, requires revised SDSs every three years.

You should familiarize yourself with all the hazardous materials in your workplace, even if you don't personally use the material, as you may be exposed to the material by accident. Take time to read the labels and then read the SDSs for the materials to learn what can happen and how to avoid adverse effects (**FIGURE 3-31**). Knowing the products that you are working with and their potential ill effects helps keep you safe in the workplace. To interpret an SDSs, follow the steps in **SKILL DRILL 3-4**.

Education

All hazardous material information systems contain an educational component. Proper training is essential for the system to operate and, in most countries, employee hazardous material training is mandatory. Employees should be trained in the safe handling and storage of materials. Improper use and storage are the worst culprits in exposures. Employees decanting small amounts of material into other containers that are improperly labeled can lead to accidental exposure of another worker. Improper care while transporting a hazardous material in the shop can also lead to accidental exposure. Employees need to know what is hazardous in their workplace, how to protect themselves from the hazard using PPE, how to safely handle the hazardous product, and how to find the correct first aid or medical treatment, if exposure occurs. Proper hazardous material training is typically conducted in an ongoing basis in the workplace, with initial training when the employee is hired and timely follow up courses. If you have not had hazardous material training at your workplace, ask your supervisor to arrange it for you. Without proper training, you are a danger to yourself and to your coworkers.

SAFETY DATA SHEET

---

1. Identification

Product identifier	**Brakleen® Non-Chlorinated Brake Parts Cleaner**
Other means of identification	
Product code	05051 (Item #1003666)
Recommended use	Brake parts cleaner
Recommended restrictions	None known.

Manufacturer/Importer/Supplier/Distributor information

Manufactured or sold by:

Company name	CRC Industries, Inc.
Address	885 Louis Dr.
	Warminster, PA 18974 US
Telephone	
General Information	215-674-4300
Technical Assistance	800-521-3168
Customer Service	800-272-4620
24-Hour Emergency	800-424-9300 (US)
(CHEMTREC)	703-527-3887 (International)
Website	www.crcindustries.com

---

2. Hazard(s) identification

Physical hazards	Flammable liquids	Category 2
Health hazards	Skin corrosion/irritation	Category 2
	Serious eye damage/eye irritation	Category 2A
	Specific target organ toxicity, single exposure	Category 3 narcotic effects
	Aspiration hazard	Category 1
Environmental hazards	Hazardous to the aquatic environment, acute hazard	Category 2
	Hazardous to the aquatic environment, long-term hazard	Category 2
OSHA defined hazards	Not classified	

Label elements

Signal word	Danger
Hazard statement	Highly flammable liquid and vapor. May be fatal if swallowed and enters airways. Causes skin irritation. Causes serious eye irritation. May cause drowsiness or dizziness. Toxic to aquatic life with long lasting effects.
Precautionary statement	
Prevention	Keep away from heat/sparks/open flames/hot surfaces. No smoking. Keep container tightly closed. Use explosion-proof electrical/ventilating/lighting equipment. Use only non-sparking tools. Take precautionary measures against static discharge. Use only with adequate ventilation; maintain ventilation during use and until all vapors are gone. Open doors and windows or use other means to ensure a fresh air supply during use and while product is drying. If you experience any symptoms listed on this label, increase ventilation or leave the area. Avoid breathing mist or vapor. Wash thoroughly after handling. Wear protective gloves/eye protection/face protection. Avoid release to the environment.

Response	If swallowed: Immediately call a poison center/doctor. Do NOT induce vomiting. If on skin (or hair): Take off immediately all contaminated clothing. Rinse skin with water/shower. If skin irritation occurs: Get medical advice/attention. Wash contaminated clothing before reuse. If inhaled: Remove person to fresh air and keep comfortable for breathing. Call a poison center/doctor if you feel unwell. If in eyes: Rinse cautiously with water for several minutes. Remove contact lenses, if present and easy to do. Continue rinsing. If eye irritation persists: Get medical advice/attention. In case of fire: Do not use water jet as an extinguisher, as this will spread the fire. Collect spillage.
Storage	Keep cool. Store in a well-ventilated place. Keep container tightly closed. Store locked up.
Disposal	Dispose of contents/container in accordance with local/regional/national regulations.
Hazard(s) not otherwise classified (HNOC)	Static accumulating flammable liquid can become electrostatically charged even in bonded and grounded equipment. Sparks may ignite liquid and vapor. May cause flash fire or explosion.

3. Composition/information on ingredients

Mixtures

Chemical name	Common name and synonyms	CAS number	%
acetone		67-64-1	90 - 100
n-heptane		142-82-5	3 - 5
3-methylhexane		589-34-4	1 - 3
methylcyclohexane		108-87-2	1 - 3
2-methylhexane		591-76-4	< 1
3-ethylpentane		617-78-7	< 1
3,3-dimethylpentane		562-49-2	< 0.2

Specific chemical identity and/or percentage of composition has been withheld as a trade secret.

4. First-aid measures

Inhalation	Remove victim to fresh air and keep at rest in a position comfortable for breathing. Call a POISON CENTER or doctor/physician if you feel unwell.
Skin contact	Take off immediately all contaminated clothing. Wash with plenty of soap and water. If skin irritation occurs: Get medical advice/attention. Wash contaminated clothing before reuse.
Eye contact	Immediately flush eyes with plenty of water for at least 15 minutes. Remove contact lenses, if present and easy to do. Continue rinsing. If eye irritation persists: Get medical advice/attention.
Ingestion	Call a physician or poison control center immediately. Rinse mouth. Do not induce vomiting. If vomiting occurs, keep head low so that stomach content doesn't get into the lungs.
Most important symptoms/effects, acute and delayed	Aspiration may cause pulmonary edema and pneumonitis. May cause drowsiness and dizziness. Headache. Nausea, vomiting. Severe eye irritation. Symptoms may include stinging, tearing, redness, swelling, and blurred vision. Skin irritation. May cause redness and pain.
Indication of immediate medical attention and special treatment needed	Provide general supportive measures and treat symptomatically. Thermal burns: Flush with water immediately. While flushing, remove clothes which do not adhere to affected area. Call an ambulance. Continue flushing during transport to hospital. Keep victim under observation. Symptoms may be delayed.
General information	Take off all contaminated clothing immediately. Ensure that medical personnel are aware of the material(s) involved, and take precautions to protect themselves. Wash contaminated clothing before reuse.

5. Fire-fighting measures

Suitable extinguishing media	Water fog. Alcohol resistant foam. Carbon dioxide (CO_2). Dry chemical powder, carbon dioxide, sand or earth may be used for small fires only.
Unsuitable extinguishing media	Do not use water jet as an extinguisher, as this will spread the fire.
Specific hazards arising from the chemical	Vapors may form explosive mixtures with air. Vapors may travel considerable distance to a source of ignition and flash back. This product is a poor conductor of electricity and can become electrostatically charged. If sufficient charge is accumulated, ignition of flammable mixtures can occur. Static electricity accumulation may be significantly increased by the presence of small quantities of water or other contaminants. Material will float and may ignite on surface of water. During fire, gases hazardous to health may be formed.
Special protective equipment and precautions for firefighters	Self-contained breathing apparatus and full protective clothing must be worn in case of fire.
Fire-fighting equipment/instructions	In case of fire and/or explosion do not breathe fumes. Move containers from fire area if you can do so without risk.
General fire hazards	Highly flammable liquid and vapor.

Material name: Brakleen® Non-Chlorinated Brake Parts Cleaner
05051 (Item #1003666)   Version #: 01   Issue date: 06-20-2017

FIGURE 3-31 (Continued)

6. Accidental release measures

Personal precautions, protective equipment and emergency procedures	Keep unnecessary personnel away. Keep people away from and upwind of spill/leak. Eliminate all ignition sources (no smoking, flares, sparks, or flames in immediate area). Wear appropriate protective equipment and clothing during clean-up. Avoid breathing mist or vapor. Do not touch damaged containers or spilled material unless wearing appropriate protective clothing. Ventilate closed spaces before entering them. Use appropriate containment to avoid environmental contamination. Local authorities should be advised if significant spillages cannot be contained. For personal protection, see section 8 of the SDS.
Methods and materials for containment and cleaning up	Eliminate all ignition sources (no smoking, flares, sparks, or flames in immediate area). Keep combustibles (wood, paper, oil, etc.) away from spilled material. Take precautionary measures against static discharge. Use only non-sparking tools. This product is miscible in water. Prevent product from entering drains.
	Small Spills: Absorb with earth, sand or other non-combustible material and transfer to containers for later disposal. Wipe up with absorbent material (e.g. cloth, fleece). Clean surface thoroughly to remove residual contamination.
	Never return spills to original containers for re-use. For waste disposal, see section 13 of the SDS.
Environmental precautions	Avoid release to the environment. Inform appropriate managerial or supervisory personnel of all environmental releases. Prevent further leakage or spillage if safe to do so. Avoid discharge into drains, water courses or onto the ground. Use appropriate containment to avoid environmental contamination.

7. Handling and storage

Precautions for safe handling	Do not handle, store or open near an open flame, sources of heat or sources of ignition. Protect material from direct sunlight. When using do not smoke. Explosion-proof general and local exhaust ventilation. Minimize fire risks from flammable and combustible materials (including combustible dust and static accumulating liquids) or dangerous reactions with incompatible materials. Handling operations that can promote accumulation of static charges include but are not limited to: mixing, filtering, pumping at high flow rates, splash filling, creating mists or sprays, tank and container filling, tank cleaning, sampling, gauging, switch loading, vacuum truck operations. Take precautionary measures against static discharges. Use non-sparking tools and explosion-proof equipment. Avoid breathing mist or vapor. Avoid contact with eyes, skin, and clothing. Avoid prolonged exposure. Wear appropriate personal protective equipment. Wash hands thoroughly after handling. Avoid release to the environment. Observe good industrial hygiene practices. For product usage instructions, see the product label.
Conditions for safe storage, including any incompatibilities	Keep away from heat, sparks and open flame. Eliminate sources of ignition. Avoid spark promoters. Store in a cool, dry place out of direct sunlight. Store in original tightly closed container. Store in a well-ventilated place. Keep in an area equipped with sprinklers. Store away from incompatible materials (see Section 10 of the SDS).

8. Exposure controls/personal protection

Occupational exposure limits

The following constituents are the only constituents of the product which have a PEL, TLV or other recommended exposure limit. At this time, the other constituents have no known exposure limits.

US. OSHA Table Z-1 Limits for Air Contaminants (29 CFR 1910.1000)

Components	Type	Value
acetone (CAS 67-64-1)	PEL	2400 mg/m^3
		1000 ppm
methylcyclohexane (CAS 108-87-2)	PEL	2000 mg/m^3
		500 ppm
n-heptane (CAS 142-82-5)	PEL	2000 mg/m^3
		500 ppm

US. ACGIH Threshold Limit Values

Components	Type	Value
2-methylhexane (CAS 591-76-4)	STEL	500 ppm
	TWA	400 ppm
3,3-dimethylpentane (CAS 562-49-2)	STEL	500 ppm
	TWA	400 ppm

US. ACGIH Threshold Limit Values

Components	Type	Value
3-ethylpentane (CAS 617-78-7)	STEL	500 ppm
	TWA	400 ppm
3-methylhexane (CAS 589-34-4)	STEL	500 ppm
	TWA	400 ppm
acetone (CAS 67-64-1)	STEL	500 ppm
	TWA	250 ppm
methylcyclohexane (CAS 108-87-2)	STEL	500 ppm
	TWA	400 ppm
n-heptane (CAS 142-82-5)	STEL	500 ppm
	TWA	400 ppm

US. NIOSH: Pocket Guide to Chemical Hazards

Components	Type	Value
acetone (CAS 67-64-1)	TWA	590 mg/m³
		250 ppm
methylcyclohexane (CAS 108-87-2)	TWA	1600 mg/m³
		400 ppm
n-heptane (CAS 142-82-5)	Ceiling	1800 mg/m³
		440 ppm
	TWA	350 mg/m³
		85 ppm

Biological limit values

ACGIH Biological Exposure Indices

Components	Value	Determinant	Specimen	Sampling Time
acetone (CAS 67-64-1)	25 mg/l	Acetone	Urine	*

* - For sampling details, please see the source document.

Appropriate engineering controls Explosion-proof general and local exhaust ventilation. Good general ventilation (typically 10 air changes per hour) should be used. Ventilation rates should be matched to conditions. If applicable, use process enclosures, local exhaust ventilation, or other engineering controls to maintain airborne levels below recommended exposure limits. If exposure limits have not been established, maintain airborne levels to an acceptable level. Provide eyewash station. Eye wash fountain and emergency showers are recommended.

Individual protection measures, such as personal protective equipment

Eye/face protection Wear safety glasses with side shields (or goggles).

Skin protection

Hand protection Wear protective gloves such as: Nitrile. Polyvinyl alcohol (PVA). Viton/butyl.

Other Wear appropriate chemical resistant clothing.

Respiratory protection If engineering controls are not feasible or if exposure exceeds the applicable exposure limits, use a NIOSH-approved cartridge respirator with an organic vapor cartridge. Use a self-contained breathing apparatus in confined spaces and for emergencies. Air monitoring is needed to determine actual employee exposure levels.

Thermal hazards Wear appropriate thermal protective clothing, when necessary.

General hygiene considerations When using, do not eat, drink or smoke. Always observe good personal hygiene measures, such as washing after handling the material and before eating, drinking, and/or smoking. Routinely wash work clothing and protective equipment to remove contaminants.

9. Physical and chemical properties

Appearance

Physical state Liquid.

Form Liquid.

Color Colorless.

Odor Solvent.

Material name: Brakleen® Non-Chlorinated Brake Parts Cleaner SDS US

05051 (Item #1003666) Version #: 01 Issue date: 06-20-2017 4 / 10

FIGURE 3-31 (Continued)

Odor threshold	Not available.
pH	Not available.
Melting point/freezing point	-195.9 °F (-126.6 °C) estimated
Initial boiling point and boiling range	132.9 °F (56.1 °C) estimated
Flash point	< 32 °F (< 0 °C) Tag Closed Cup
Evaporation rate	Fast.
Flammability (solid, gas)	Not available.
Upper/lower flammability or explosive limits	
Flammability limit - lower (%)	1.1 % estimated
Flammability limit - upper (%)	12.8 % estimated
Vapor pressure	223.1 hPa estimated
Vapor density	> 2 (air = 1)
Relative density	0.78
Solubility (water)	Slight.
Partition coefficient (n-octanol/water)	Not available.
Auto-ignition temperature	539.6 °F (282 °C) estimated
Decomposition temperature	Not available.
Viscosity (kinematic)	Not available.
Percent volatile	99.9 % estimated

10. Stability and reactivity

Reactivity	The product is stable and non-reactive under normal conditions of use, storage and transport.
Chemical stability	Material is stable under normal conditions.
Possibility of hazardous reactions	No dangerous reaction known under conditions of normal use.
Conditions to avoid	Avoid heat, sparks, open flames and other ignition sources. Contact with incompatible materials.
Incompatible materials	Strong acids. Acids. Strong oxidizing agents. Halogens. Ammonia. Amines. Peroxides. Strong bases. Aldehydes. Alkalies.
Hazardous decomposition products	Carbon oxides.

11. Toxicological information

Information on likely routes of exposure

Inhalation	May cause drowsiness and dizziness. Headache. Nausea, vomiting. Prolonged inhalation may be harmful.
Skin contact	Causes skin irritation.
Eye contact	Causes serious eye irritation.
Ingestion	Droplets of the product aspirated into the lungs through ingestion or vomiting may cause a serious chemical pneumonia.
Symptoms related to the physical, chemical and toxicological characteristics	Aspiration may cause pulmonary edema and pneumonitis. May cause drowsiness and dizziness. Headache. Nausea, vomiting. Severe eye irritation. Symptoms may include stinging, tearing, redness, swelling, and blurred vision. Skin irritation. May cause redness and pain.

Information on toxicological effects

Acute toxicity	May be fatal if swallowed and enters airways.

Components	Species	Test Results
3-methylhexane (CAS 589-34-4)		
Acute		
Dermal		
LD50	Rabbit	> 2000 mg/kg

Components	Species	Test Results
Oral		
LD50	Rat	> 2000 mg/kg
acetone (CAS 67-64-1)		
<u>**Acute**</u>		
Dermal		
LD50	Rabbit	20000 mg/kg
Oral		
LD50	Rat	5800 mg/kg
methylcyclohexane (CAS 108-87-2)		
<u>**Acute**</u>		
Dermal		
LD50	Rabbit	> 2000 mg/kg
n-heptane (CAS 142-82-5)		
<u>**Acute**</u>		
Dermal		
LD50	Rabbit	3000 mg/kg

* Estimates for product may be based on additional component data not shown.

Skin corrosion/irritation	Causes skin irritation.
Serious eye damage/eye irritation	Causes serious eye irritation.
Respiratory sensitization	Not a respiratory sensitizer.
Skin sensitization	This product is not expected to cause skin sensitization.
Germ cell mutagenicity	No data available to indicate product or any components present at greater than 0.1% are mutagenic or genotoxic.
Carcinogenicity	Not classifiable as to carcinogenicity to humans.

IARC Monographs. Overall Evaluation of Carcinogenicity

Not listed.

OSHA Specifically Regulated Substances (29 CFR 1910.1001-1050)

Not regulated.

US. National Toxicology Program (NTP) Report on Carcinogens

Not listed.

Reproductive toxicity	This product is not expected to cause reproductive or developmental effects.
Specific target organ toxicity - single exposure	May cause drowsiness and dizziness.
Specific target organ toxicity - repeated exposure	Not classified.
Aspiration hazard	May be fatal if swallowed and enters airways. If aspirated into lungs during swallowing or vomiting, may cause chemical pneumonia, pulmonary injury or death.
Chronic effects	Prolonged inhalation may be harmful.

12. Ecological information

Ecotoxicity   Toxic to aquatic life with long lasting effects.

Components		Species	Test Results
acetone (CAS 67-64-1)			
Aquatic			
Crustacea	EC50	Water flea (Daphnia magna)	10294 - 17704 mg/l, 48 hours
Fish	LC50	Rainbow trout,donaldson trout (Oncorhynchus mykiss)	4740 - 6330 mg/l, 96 hours
methylcyclohexane (CAS 108-87-2)			
Aquatic			
Fish	LC50	Striped bass (Morone saxatilis)	5.8 mg/l, 96 hours

FIGURE 3-31 (Continued)

Components		Species	Test Results
n-heptane (CAS 142-82-5)			
Aquatic			
Acute			
Crustacea	EC50	Water flea (Daphnia magna)	1.5 mg/l, 48 hours
Fish	LC50	Fathead minnow (Pimephales promelas)	2.1 - 2.98 mg/l, 96 hours

* Estimates for product may be based on additional component data not shown.

Persistence and degradability

Bioaccumulative potential

Partition coefficient n-octanol / water (log Kow)

acetone	-0.24
methylcyclohexane	3.61
n-heptane	4.66

Mobility in soil   No data available.

Other adverse effects   The product contains volatile organic compounds which have a photochemical ozone creation potential.

13. Disposal considerations

Disposal of waste from residues / unused products   This material and its container must be disposed of as hazardous waste. Collect and reclaim or dispose in sealed containers at licensed waste disposal site. Do not allow this material to drain into sewers/water supplies. Do not contaminate ponds, waterways or ditches with chemical or used container. Dispose in accordance with all applicable regulations.

Hazardous waste code   D001: Waste Flammable material with a flash point <140 F
F003: Waste Non-halogenated Solvent - Spent Non-halogenated Solvent

US RCRA Hazardous Waste U List: Reference

acetone (CAS 67-64-1)	U002

Contaminated packaging   Since emptied containers may retain product residue, follow label warnings even after container is emptied. Empty containers should be taken to an approved waste handling site for recycling or disposal.

14. Transport information

DOT

UN number	UN1993
UN proper shipping name	Flammable liquids, n.o.s. (acetone RQ = 5556 LBS, heptanes)
Transport hazard class(es)	
Class	3
Subsidiary risk	-
Label(s)	3
Packing group	II
Special precautions for user	Read safety instructions, SDS and emergency procedures before handling.
Special provisions	IB2, T7, TP1, TP8, TP28
Packaging exceptions	150
Packaging non bulk	202
Packaging bulk	242

IATA

UN number	UN1993
UN proper shipping name	Flammable liquid, n.o.s. (acetone, heptanes)
Transport hazard class(es)	
Class	3
Subsidiary risk	-
Packing group	II
ERG Code	3H
Special precautions for user	Read safety instructions, SDS and emergency procedures before handling.
Other information	
Passenger and cargo aircraft	Allowed with restrictions.
Cargo aircraft only	Allowed with restrictions.

IMDG

UN number	UN1993
UN proper shipping name	FLAMMABLE LIQUID, N.O.S. (acetone, heptanes)
Transport hazard class(es)	
Class	3
Subsidiary risk	-
Packing group	II
Environmental hazards	
Marine pollutant	No.
EmS	F-E, S-E
Special precautions for user	Read safety instructions, SDS and emergency procedures before handling.

15. Regulatory information

US federal regulations   This product is a "Hazardous Chemical" as defined by the OSHA Hazard Communication Standard, 29 CFR 1910.1200.

TSCA Section 12(b) Export Notification (40 CFR 707, Subpt. D)

Not regulated.

SARA 304 Emergency release notification

Not regulated.

OSHA Specifically Regulated Substances (29 CFR 1910.1001-1050)

Not regulated.

US EPCRA (SARA Title III) Section 313 - Toxic Chemical: Listed substance

Not listed.

CERCLA Hazardous Substance List (40 CFR 302.4)

3,3-dimethylpentane (CAS 562-49-2)	Listed.
acetone (CAS 67-64-1)	Listed.

CERCLA Hazardous Substances: Reportable quantity

3,3-dimethylpentane (CAS 562-49-2)	100 LBS
acetone (CAS 67-64-1)	5000 LBS

Spills or releases resulting in the loss of any ingredient at or above its RQ require immediate notification to the National Response Center (800-424-8802) and to your Local Emergency Planning Committee.

Clean Air Act (CAA) Section 112 Hazardous Air Pollutants (HAPs) List

Not regulated.

Clean Air Act (CAA) Section 112(r) Accidental Release Prevention (40 CFR 68.130)

Not regulated.

Safe Drinking Water Act (SDWA)   Not regulated.

Drug Enforcement Administration (DEA). List 2, Essential Chemicals (21 CFR 1310.02(b) and 1310.04(f)(2) and Chemical Code Number

acetone (CAS 67-64-1)	6532

Drug Enforcement Administration (DEA). List 1 & 2 Exempt Chemical Mixtures (21 CFR 1310.12(c))

acetone (CAS 67-64-1)	35 %WV

DEA Exempt Chemical Mixtures Code Number

acetone (CAS 67-64-1)	6532

FEMA Priority Substances Respiratory Health and Safety in the Flavor Manufacturing Workplace

acetone (CAS 67-64-1)	Low priority

Food and Drug Administration (FDA)   Not regulated.

Superfund Amendments and Reauthorization Act of 1986 (SARA)

Section 311/312 Hazard categories	Immediate Hazard - Yes Delayed Hazard - No Fire Hazard - Yes Pressure Hazard - No Reactivity Hazard - No
SARA 302 Extremely hazardous substance	No

FIGURE 3-31 (Continued)

US state regulations

US. California. Candidate Chemicals List. Safer Consumer Products Regulations (Cal. Code Regs, tit. 22, 69502.3, subd. (a))

acetone (CAS 67-64-1)

US. New Jersey Worker and Community Right-to-Know Act

3-methylhexane (CAS 589-34-4)
acetone (CAS 67-64-1)
methylcyclohexane (CAS 108-87-2)
n-heptane (CAS 142-82-5)

US. Massachusetts RTK - Substance List

2-methylhexane (CAS 591-76-4)
3-methylhexane (CAS 589-34-4)
acetone (CAS 67-64-1)
methylcyclohexane (CAS 108-87-2)
n-heptane (CAS 142-82-5)

US. Pennsylvania Worker and Community Right-to-Know Law

3,3-dimethylpentane (CAS 562-49-2)
3-methylhexane (CAS 589-34-4)
acetone (CAS 67-64-1)
methylcyclohexane (CAS 108-87-2)
n-heptane (CAS 142-82-5)

US. Rhode Island RTK

acetone (CAS 67-64-1)
methylcyclohexane (CAS 108-87-2)
n-heptane (CAS 142-82-5)

US. California Proposition 65

WARNING: This product contains a chemical known to the State of California to cause cancer and birth defects or other reproductive harm.

US - California Proposition 65 - CRT: Listed date/Carcinogenic substance

acetaldehyde (CAS 75-07-0)	Listed: April 1, 1988
benzene (CAS 71-43-2)	Listed: February 27, 1987
cumene (CAS 98-82-8)	Listed: April 6, 2010
ethylbenzene (CAS 100-41-4)	Listed: June 11, 2004
naphthalene (CAS 91-20-3)	Listed: April 19, 2002

US - California Proposition 65 - CRT: Listed date/Developmental toxin

benzene (CAS 71-43-2)	Listed: December 26, 1997
toluene (CAS 108-88-3)	Listed: January 1, 1991

US - California Proposition 65 - CRT: Listed date/Male reproductive toxin

benzene (CAS 71-43-2)	Listed: December 26, 1997

Volatile organic compounds (VOC) regulations

EPA

VOC content (40 CFR 51.100(s))	10 %
Consumer products (40 CFR 59, Subpt. C)	Not regulated

State

Consumer products	This product is regulated as a Brake Cleaner. This product is compliant for use in all 50 states.
VOC content (CA)	10 %
VOC content (OTC)	10 %

International Inventories

Country(s) or region	Inventory name	On inventory (yes/no)*
Australia	Australian Inventory of Chemical Substances (AICS)	No
Canada	Domestic Substances List (DSL)	No
Canada	Non-Domestic Substances List (NDSL)	Yes
China	Inventory of Existing Chemical Substances in China (IECSC)	No
Europe	European Inventory of Existing Commercial Chemical Substances (EINECS)	No
Europe	European List of Notified Chemical Substances (ELINCS)	No

Country(s) or region	Inventory name	On inventory (yes/no)*
Japan	Inventory of Existing and New Chemical Substances (ENCS)	No
Korea	Existing Chemicals List (ECL)	Yes
New Zealand	New Zealand Inventory	No
Philippines	Philippine Inventory of Chemicals and Chemical Substances (PICCS)	Yes
United States & Puerto Rico	Toxic Substances Control Act (TSCA) Inventory	Yes

*A "Yes" indicates that all components of this product comply with the inventory requirements administered by the governing country(s)
A "No" indicates that one or more components of the product are not listed or exempt from listing on the inventory administered by the governing country(s).

16. Other information, including date of preparation or last revision

Issue date	06-20-2017
Prepared by	Allison Yoon
Version #	01
Further information	CRC # 920B
HMIS® ratings	Health: 2 Flammability: 3 Physical hazard: 0 Personal protection: B
NFPA ratings	Health: 2 Flammability: 3 Instability: 0

NFPA ratings

Disclaimer   The information contained in this document applies to this specific material as supplied. It may not be valid for this material if it is used in combination with any other materials. This information is accurate to the best of CRC's knowledge or obtained from sources believed by CRC to be accurate. Before using any product, read all warnings and directions on the label. For further clarification of any information contained on this (M)SDS consult your supervisor, a health & safety professional, or CRC Industries, Inc..

Revision Information   This document has undergone significant changes and should be reviewed in its entirety.

Material name: Brakleen® Non-Chlorinated Brake Parts Cleaner
05051 (Item #1003666)   Version #: 01   Issue date: 06-20-2017

FIGURE 3-31 An example of an SDSs.

SKILL DRILL 3-4 Interpreting a Safety Data Sheet

1. Look up the SDSs for one of the hazardous materials found in your shop in the SDSs binder or computerized database. You may also find the SDSs for your product online, if necessary.
2. Check the revision date in Section 16 of the SDSs so you know that you have the latest revision.
3. In Section 1, check the correct name and any synonyms for the material.
4. In Section 2 of the SDSs, identify the specific hazards posed by this material and the precautions you can take to avoid exposure.
5. In Section 4, identify the symptoms of exposure and the proper first aid measures for each exposure route, if exposure occurs.
6. In Section 5, read the flammability risks and precautions of the material and the firefighting equipment used to extinguish a fire, if flammable.
7. In Section 6, familiarize yourself with the precautions to take to avoid accidental exposure.
8. In Section 7, read the proper storage and handling techniques associated with the material.
9. In Section 8, Read the upper and lower exposure limits and how to prevent exposure in the workplace.
10. In Section 10, read the reactivity of the material and how to prevent it from reacting with other materials.
11. In Section 11, read the symptoms to be expected by varying exposure routes.
12. Section 12 tells you if the product is harmful to aquatic life.
13. Section 13 describes the proper disposal of the product or its container.

Principles of First Aid

LO 3-7 Explain the basic principles of first aid and cardiopulmonary resuscitation (CPR) practices.

In most workplaces, several designated people—usually the members of the joint health and safety committee—receive formal first aid training and, in fact, in many workplaces it is mandatory to have first aid-certified employees on hand. Make it your duty to know who these people are. These are the people to turn to when first aid is required. With that said, there are times when a situation presents itself when these people are not available, and you may be called on to perform first aid for an injured person. This section is a very brief outline of the principles of first aid and in no way is it designed to replace formal first aid training.

What Is First Aid?

First aid is the care given by the first person to come to the aid of an injured party at the scene of the injury before formal medical care can be given. First aid can be as simple as helping to remove debris from someone's eye to applying a bandage or dressing to a cut. Ideally, the person giving the first aid has first aid training and certification, but this is not always possible. First aid training is a very valuable skill to have in any workplace and it can extend beyond the workplace, as well. First aid training can allow you to help your family, friends, or even strangers in case of an emergency. If you have the opportunity to receive first aid training, you should take it. First aid training is available from many agencies, such as the American Red Cross and others, and in some cases, the training is free. Courses are available in a classroom setting and are even available online.

First Aid Basics

There are three overriding principles when it comes to first aid. These principles should guide anything you do when you come across a situation where you are called on to provide first aid.

1. You must do all in your power to preserve life and minimize the threat of the person dying.
2. You must cause no further injury. If the person has a broken arm, you may further the injury by moving the person. However, if the person is in a burning vehicle or other danger, further injury is likely and you may have to move the person.
3. Promote healing. This may be by applying a bandage or stabilizing an injury.

There are several other considerations when it comes to first aid, but the three overriding principles should always be followed.

When an accident occurs or someone requires first aid, you must first determine what happened and whether it is safe for you to perform first aid. If the person is conscious and alert, ask him or her what happened and if you can be of assistance. If the person is not conscious, have someone immediately call for medical assistance while you survey the situation. The cause of the person's injury may still be present and put you at risk.

- Is there a gas or fume leak that could cause unconsciousness?
- Are there electrical wires around that could have caused electrocution? If so, make sure the power is switched off before you attempt to assist the person.

Once you have determined the likely cause, and it is safe to do so, approach the injured person and begin your first aid. Remove the injured person from a dangerous area only if it is safe for you to do so. It is important that you start first aid as soon as it is safe and/or possible. Delay could cause the person's life to be in danger. If the person is not breathing, for example, brain damage can occur in 6 minutes, and further delay of first aid can lead to brain death.

► TECHNICIAN TIP

Three principles of first aid are:

1. Preserve life.
2. Cause no further injury and allow no further injury to occur.
3. Promote and speed the healing process.

First Aid Steps

Timely first aid can mean the difference between life and death for an injured party, but there are a number of steps that you should take before and while administering first aid. Always send someone else for assistance, if possible, and make sure the person with the most first aid training assists the victim.

1. Make sure that your actions are not going to put you or the injured party in danger. Assess the situation carefully.
2. Check the victim for consciousness. Call out to him or her to see if he or she responds. If he or she does not reply, the victim is non-responsive, and you should continue as if he or she is unconscious.
3. If the victim is non-responsive, have a person nearby call emergency services at once. If you are alone, call as soon as possible, but do not leave the victim.
4. Check the non-responsive victim's breathing. If he or she is not breathing, start chest compressions at once. The latest recommendations from the American Heart Association for cardio-pulmonary resuscitation are as follows:
   • To apply chest compressions, put the victim on a solid surface, kneel beside the victim. Put the heel of one hand on the victim's chest between the nipples. Put your other hand over your first hand and with your shoulders directly above the victim's chest, push down with your upper body (not with your arms). The victim's chest should compress at least 2 inches (5 cm), but not more than 2.4 inches (6 cm). See **FIGURE 3-32**. [*Note:* Chest compressions can be very strenuous, make sure you position yourself correctly so you can continue until help arrives.]
5. If you are not trained in CPR, then apply chest compressions only at a rate of 100 to 120 compressions per minute and continue until help arrives or the victim becomes responsive.
6. If you are trained in CPR, follow your training and deliver 30 chest compressions at a rate of 100 to 120 per minute followed by two rescue breaths. Continue the CPR until help arrives or the victim becomes responsive.

7. If you have access to an AED (Automated External Defibrillator), attach the machine to the victim according to the instructions and give one shock, if directed by the machine. After the first shock, continue with chest compressions as above for 2 minutes or until the AED directs another shock to be administered. Continue following the machine prompts and chest compressions until the victim is responsive or help arrives.

Severe Bleeding

Some injuries cause severe bleeding. Bleeding can be internal or external. **External bleeding** is readily visible and is dealt with by applying a clean gauze bandage to the wound and applying direct pressure until the bleeding stops (**FIGURE 3-33**). If a wound is pumping blood, it indicates an injured vein or artery. Such a wound is catastrophic and can lead to death if not treated quickly. Apply as much pressure to the area as possible to try and stem the bleeding while waiting for assistance. If blood soaks through the applied bandage, do not remove the bandage. Apply another directly over the first and again apply pressure (**FIGURE 3-34**).

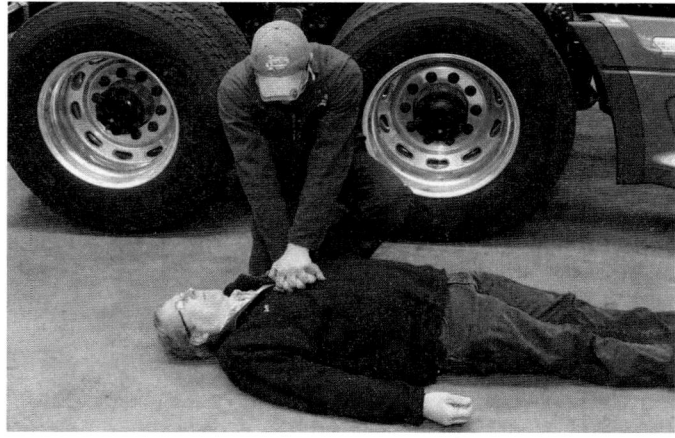

FIGURE 3-32 Make sure you position yourself properly, or you may quickly tire while doing chest compressions.

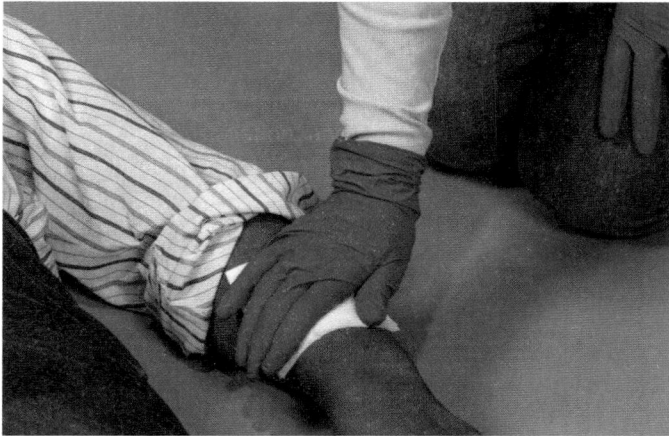

FIGURE 3-33 Apply a gauze bandage and direct pressure to the wound.

Never try to remove an object that has punctured a victim's skin—doing so can lead to increased risk of severe bleeding and infection. Stabilize the object with bandages so that it cannot cause more injury and seek medical assistance.

Internal bleeding, bleeding that occurs inside the body and cannot be seen externally, is difficult for an untrained person to spot. Severe bruising, swelling, and/or coughing or spitting blood can be signs of internal bleeding. Seek emergency medical assistance as soon as possible.

Eye Injuries

Eye injuries are usually caused by foreign objects becoming embedded or chemicals being splashed in the eye. For chemical exposure, flush the eye immediately for at least 15 minutes using an eyewash station. If a piece of debris is in the eye, you may be able to assist the person and remove it with a clean sterile cloth or gauze. You may have to carefully fold the eyelids back to gain access to the object. A cotton swab can assist when folding the upper eyelid (**FIGURE 3-35**).

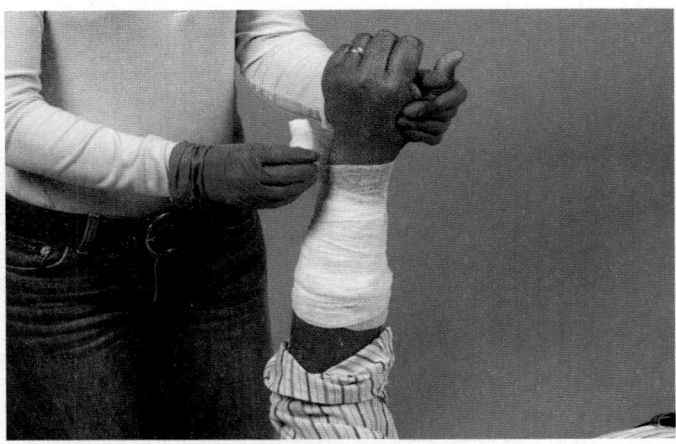

FIGURE 3-34 If blood soaks through the bandage, do not remove the first bandage. Apply another bandage and increase the pressure on the wound.

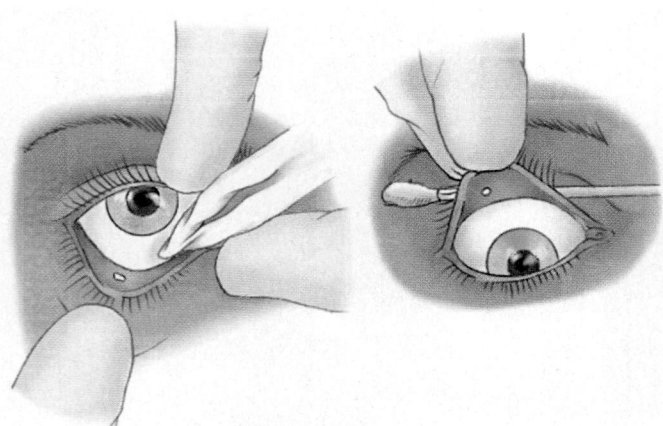

FIGURE 3-35 Assist the person in removing foreign objects from the eye.

As with the skin, never try to remove an object that is embedded in the eye. Doing so can cause severe damage to the eye and increase the risk of infection. Always stabilize the object with a bulky dressing so that it cannot move (**FIGURE 3-36**) and seek immediate emergency medical assistance.

Broken Bones

Broken bones, or fractures, often occur as the result of a slip or fall. Fracture can cause damage internally and can lead to shock. The victim may feel groggy or cold—these are indicators of **shock**, a condition where the rate of blood flow to a person's extremities is diminished. Broken bones must always be treated by medical professionals, as there can be many complications associated with bone fractures.

There are several different types of fractures that can occur: a **hairline fracture** is a cracked bone that has not separated; a **greenstick fracture** is a bone broken on one side only; a **stable or simple fracture** is a complete break, but the bone has not moved out of place; a **comminuted fracture** is one where the bone is broken into three or more pieces; and a **compound or open fracture** is one where the bone pierces the skin, causing bleeding and damage to the surrounding tissue. Recognizing a fracture where the bone has moved or displaced is fairly straightforward, but a simple fracture with no bone movement can be more difficult to spot. There may be localized bruising and or swelling around the fracture. It is likely difficult for the victim to move the affected arm or leg, and there is likely substantial pain in the area surrounding the break.

In all cases of suspected or identified bone fractures, first try to position the victim in a way that minimizes their pain. If the pain increases, the patient may pass out and further injure himself or herself. Have someone call emergency medical services immediately, or call yourself if you are alone and have close access to a phone. Stabilize the suspected break with a splint and bandages and wait for medical assistance. Never attempt to reposition the bones. If there is bleeding, cover the entire area with a sterile gauze bandage before stabilizing the arm or leg. Ice packs can be used to try to ease the pain. Observe the victim

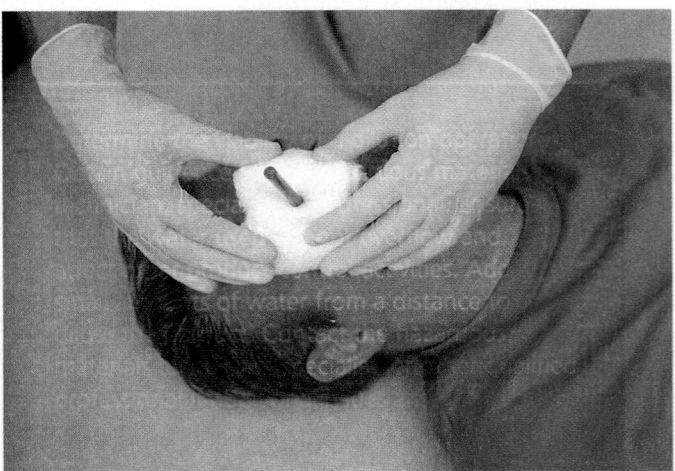

FIGURE 3-36 A bulky dressing is used to stabilize an embedded object.

closely for signs of shock: feeling faint, dizziness, cold extremities, or vomiting. If these symptoms exist, position the person where he or she cannot fall and reinjure him or herself and use a blanket to keep him or her warm until help arrives. Do not try to move the victim unless he or she is in imminent danger.

Overextensions and Dislocations

When a joint is **overextended**, meaning that it has been moved past its normal range of motion, the result is a sprain, or even a dislocation, of the joint. A **sprain** is the stretching or tearing of ligaments that connect our bones and hold our joints together. A sprain can be very painful, and the pain can last for only a few minutes or up to several months, depending on the severity of the strain. Sprains are most common in the ankles, wrists, and knees. When a sprain occurs, try to get the person to keep their weight off the affected limb or foot. Support the injured limb in a raised position and let the person rest. If the pain continues more than a few minutes, seek medical attention to investigate whether the ligaments may be torn, rather than just stretched.

Strained muscles can occur when a muscle is pushed beyond its limit. A **strain** is a stretching or tearing of the muscle tissue itself, or the tendons that attach the muscle to the bone. A strain can be recognized by a sharp pain during, or immediately following, the activity that caused the strain. Strains are treated using immobility. Tell the victim not to use the affected limb, elevate the limb, and use ice packs to control the pain.

Dislocations can occur if a joint is severely overextended. A **dislocation** is when the ligaments no longer hold the joint together and the moveable part of the joint is displaced from its normal location. The shoulder is the most common joint where dislocation occurs. Do not, under any circumstances, try to relocate the joint yourself. Seek medical attention for the victim immediately. If the person is imminent danger, try to stabilize the joint and move the person to a safe location and wait for emergency services.

Burns

Burns to the body's tissues can occur due to exposure to heat, chemicals, or extreme radiation. Burns are rated or classified into three categories:

- **First-degree burns** (**FIGURE 3-37**): These burns are superficial in nature and involve only the top layer of skin, usually accompanied by a slight reddening of the skin and damage to the top layer of skin only.
- **Second-degree burns** (**FIGURE 3-38**): These burns involve two or more layers of skin, usually indicated by blistering and clear damage to the outer layer of skin and below.
- **Third-degree burns** (**FIGURE 3-39**): These burns involve the entire thickness of the skin and are indicated by white or blackened areas and damage to the tissue beneath the skin.

Burns can be caused by exposure to high heat either in the surrounding area, such as a fire or by contacting something hot, or by friction, as is the case with "rope burn." Burns can also be caused by chemical exposure to acids and many other chemicals

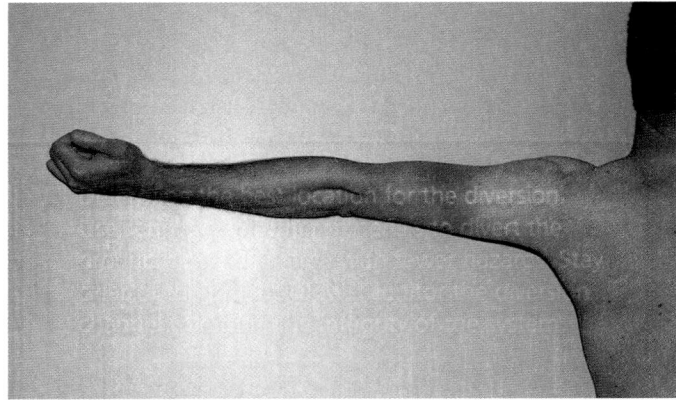

FIGURE 3-37 First-degree burn.

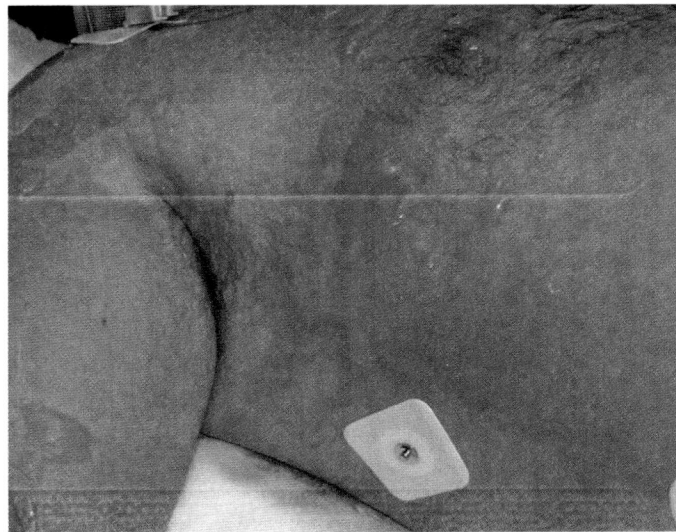

FIGURE 3-38 Second-degree burn.

Source: Image © E. M. Singletary, MD. Used with permission.

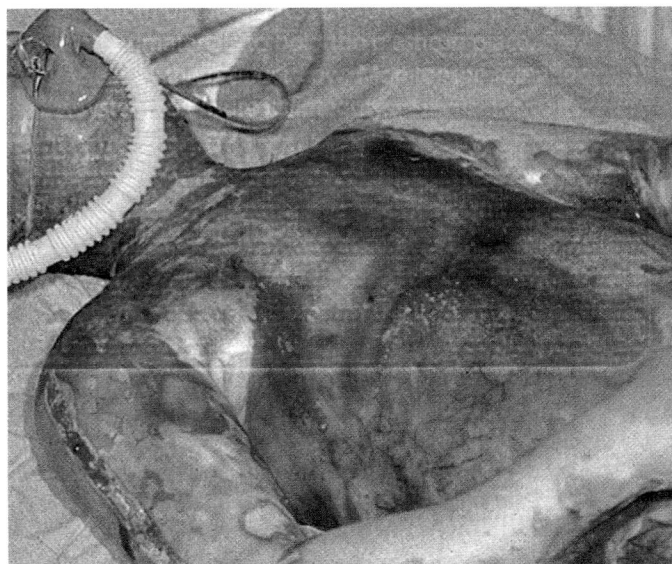

FIGURE 3-39 Third-degree burn.

Source: Image Courtesy of AAOS.

capable of burning the skin and other tissues. Electricity can also cause severe burns. Scalds are burns that occur by coming into contact with hot liquids or steam. All burns can cause severe tissue damage and, if bad enough, can lead to death.

In case of burns, remove the danger or remove the victim from the danger first. If the victim is on fire, use a fire blanket to douse the flames or have the victim drop to the floor and roll until the flames are out. Do not apply any topical lotions to the burn site. These have been shown to increase the tissue damage from burns, rather than decrease it. If the burn is first-degree, have the victim hold the burn under cool running water immediately and for as long as possible. If there is blistering or skin damage, second-degree burns, loosely cover the area with sterile gauze and seek medical attention immediately. If the burn is third-degree, do not attempt to treat the burn. Wait for medical assistance or advice.

Wrap-Up

Ready for Review

▶ Your employer is responsible for maintaining a safe workplace environment; you are responsible for working in a safe and professional manner.
▶ Always wear the correct PPE (personal protective equipment) for the job at hand. PPE protects you from injury but is only be effective if it fits correctly.
▶ Accidents are caused and, therefore, can be prevented.
▶ Shops usually have marked evacuation routes. Make it a point to know the routes in your shop.
▶ OSHA, the Occupation Health and Safety Administration, is the federal agency that oversees workplace safety.
▶ The EPA, Environmental Protection Agency, creates regulations ensuring environmental safety and protection.
▶ Shop policies and procedures ensure compliance with the laws and regulations that relate to a workplace and promote safety in the workplace.
▶ Know the hazards and hazardous materials used in your workplace.
▶ Safety signs include a signal word, such as danger, warning, or caution, along with a specific background color, text, and a pictorial message.
▶ Shop safety equipment is designed to protect the worker from injury.
▶ Air quality must be maintained in the workplace by proper ventilation.
▶ All shops require proper ventilation.
▶ Carbon monoxide from running engines can create a hazardous work environment. Always use exhaust extraction systems.
▶ Be aware of where the electrical panels are in your shop so you are ready in the event of an electrical emergency.
▶ Portable electrical equipment should be kept in good working order.
▶ The shop should be well organized to maximize safety.
▶ Liquid fuels and vapors are potential fire hazards in most shops.
▶ Always ensure your container is of sufficient size when draining fuel tanks.

▶ Types of fires are classified as A, B, C, D, or K.
▶ Most fire extinguishers in a commercial vehicle shop are combination ABC fire extinguishers.
▶ Do not fight a fire unless it is safe for you to do so.
▶ Eyewash stations and emergency showers should be used in the event of chemical splashes or to flush irritants from the eyes.
▶ The Globally Harmonized System (GHS) classifies hazardous material in a standardized format.
▶ Safety data sheets (SDSs) have 16 components under the GHS.
▶ Use a vacuum or water wash station to remove brake or clutch dust safely. Brake and clutch dust may be toxic.
▶ Always ensure that you follow your shop's safety policies and procedures.
▶ Breathing PPE includes disposable dust masks, respirators, and supplied air respirators.
▶ Safety glasses should meet the ANSI Z87+ standard.
▶ Jewelry, watches, and loose hair are all dangerous in the workplace. Remove jewelry and tie up loose hair before entering the shop.
▶ Lifting correctly or seeking assistance prevents back injuries.
▶ First aid means providing immediate care to an ill or injured person.
▶ First aid training is very valuable, and you should try to get proper training, if it is available at your workplace.

Key Terms

comminuted fracture A fracture where the bone is broken into three or more pieces.

compound or open fracture A fracture where the bone pierces the skin, causing bleeding and damage to the surrounding tissue.

dislocation The displacement of a joint from its normal position; it is caused by overextending the ligaments beyond their elastic limit.

ear protection Protective gear worn when the sound levels exceed 85 decibels, when working around operating machinery for any period of time, or when the equipment you are using produces loud noise.

Environmental Protection Agency (EPA) A US Federal government agency that deals with issues related to environmental safety.

external bleeding The loss of blood from an external wound; blood can be seen escaping.

first aid The care given by the first person to come to the aid of an injured party at the scene of the injury before formal medical care can be given.

first-degree burns Burns that show reddening of the skin and damage to the outer layer of skin only.

gas welding goggles Close-fitting safety goggles with a dark tinted lens.

greenstick fracture A bone broken on one side only.

hairline fracture A cracked bone that has not separated.

hazard Something that can cause an accident, a sickness, or an injury.

hazardous environment A place where hazards exist.

hazardous material A material that can cause damage or injury to a person.

headgear Protective gear that includes items like soft caps, bump caps, or hard hats.

internal bleeding Bleeding that cannot be seen externally.

PPE (personal protective equipment) Safety equipment designed to protect the wearer; boots, gloves, eye protection, and hearing protection, when required.

policy An overriding way of acting or behaving.

procedure A step-by-step process to complete a task.

respirator PPE used to protect the wearer from inhaling harmful dusts or gases.

second-degree burns Burns that involve blistering and damage to more than the outer layer of skin.

SDSs (safety data sheet) A sheet standardized by the GHS that provides information about handling, use, and storage of a material that is hazardous.

shock A condition where the rate of blood flow to a person's extremities is diminished.

sprain An injury in which a joint is overextended beyond its natural movement limit.

stable or simple fracture A complete break, but the bone has not moved out of place.

strain An injury caused by the overextension of muscles and tendons.

third-degree burns Burns that involve white or blackened areas and damage to all skin layers and underlying structures and tissues.

toxic dust Any dust that can cause physical harm.

welding helmet A helmet that protects your eyes and your face from the UV radiation and flying sparks or particles during arc welding operations.

Review Questions

1. Safety in the workplace is whose responsibility?
   a. The supervisors and managers
   b. The workers and supervisors
   c. The employer, the supervisors, and the workers
   d. The employer and the managers

2. Your shop should have a(n)_____that clearly identifies the evacuation routes.
   a. safety procedure
   b. safety-first manual
   c. emergency manual
   d. evacuation plan

3. Disposal of controlled wastes must be done according to whose regulations?
   a. EPA
   b. ANSI
   c. OSHA
   d. NATEF

4. A_____is a step-by-step process to complete a task in a proper and safe manner.
   a. theory
   b. measure
   c. policy
   d. procedure

5. Which hazard sign is used if the hazard could cause immediate serious injury or death?
   a. "Danger" sign
   b. "Careful" sign
   c. "Skull and cross bones" sign
   d. "Warning" sign

6. Which of the following are the three signal words used in hazard signs?
   a. stop; warning; danger
   b. warning; general; danger
   c. danger; warning; caution
   d. caution; stop; danger

7. Which of the following is the OSHA PEL for carbon monoxide?
   a. 20
   b. 30
   c. 40
   d. 50

8. Typically, there should be_____of unobstructed space around an electrical panel.
   a. 1 foot
   b. 2 feet
   c. 3 feet
   d. 4 feet

9. Which of the following bulb types presents an extreme fire hazard if broken in the presence of flammable vapors or liquids?
   a. Incandescent
   b. LED
   c. Fluorescent
   d. Solid state

10. Class C fires involve:
   a. electrical equipment.
   b. paper and wood.
   c. flammable liquids.
   d. Burning metals.

ASE Technician A/Technician B Style Questions

1. Technician A says that exposure to solvents may have long-term health effects. Technician B says that accidents are always avoidable. Who is correct?
   a. Technician A
   b. Technician B
   c. Both Technician A and Technician B
   d. Neither Technician A nor Technician B

2. Technician A says that both OSHA and the EPA can inspect facilities for violations. Technician B says that a shop policy does not have to be reviewed once put in place. Who is correct?
   a. Technician A
   b. Technician B
   c. Both Technician A and Technician B
   d. Neither Technician A nor Technician B

3. Technician A says that caution indicates a potentially hazardous situation. Technician B says that an exhaust extraction hose is not needed if the vehicle is only going to run for a few minutes. Who is correct?
   a. Technician A
   b. Technician B
   c. Both Technician A and Technician B
   d. Neither Technician A nor Technician B

4. Technician A says that firefighting equipment includes fire blankets. Technician B says that a class A fire extinguisher can be used to fight an electrical fire only. Who is correct?
   a. Technician A
   b. Technician B
   c. Both Technician A and Technician B
   d. Neither Technician A nor Technician B

5. Technician A says that a good way to clean dust from brake parts is with compressed air. Technician B says the dust from current friction material is not hazardous. Who is correct?
   a. Technician A
   b. Technician B
   c. Both Technician A and Technician B
   d. Neither Technician A nor Technician B

6. Technician A says that personal protective equipment (PPE) does not include clothing. Technician B says that the PPE used should be based on the task you are performing. Who is correct?
   a. Technician A
   b. Technician B
   c. Both Technician A and Technician B
   d. Neither Technician A nor Technician B

7. Technician A says that appropriate work clothes include loose-fitting clothing. Technician B says that you should always tie long hair in a ponytail while working in the shop. Who is correct?
   a. Technician A
   b. Technician B
   c. Both Technician A and Technician B
   d. Neither Technician A nor Technician B

8. Technician A says that a hat can help keep your hair clean when working on a vehicle. Technician B says that chemical gloves may be used when working with solvent. Who is correct?
   a. Technician A
   b. Technician B
   c. Both Technician A and Technician B
   d. Neither Technician A nor Technician B

9. Technician A says that you should wear protective gloves at all times while working in the shop. Technician B says that hearing protection only needs to be worn by people operating loud equipment. Who is correct?
   a. Technician A
   b. Technician B
   c. Both Technician A and Technician B
   d. Neither Technician A nor Technician B

10. Technician A says that safety glasses must meet the ANSI Z87+ standard. Technician B says that arc welding can cause a sunburn. Who is correct?
   a. Technician A
   b. Technician B
   c. Both Technician A and Technician B
   d. Neither Technician A nor Technician B

CHAPTER 4

Tools and Fasteners

Learning Objectives

- **LO 4-1** Explain the importance of selecting and installing the correct type, size, and quality of threaded fasteners.
- **LO 4-2** Describe and explain specification standards for threaded fasteners.
- **LO 4-3** Identify and describe fastener classifications according to mechanical strengths.
- **LO 4-4** Describe the classification of threaded nuts according to grade strength.
- **LO 4-5** Describe and explain principles and methods of tightening fasteners.
- **LO 4-6** Identify and explain the purpose and functions of self-locking hardware.
- **LO 4-7** Identify and explain methods used to repair damaged threads.

You Are the Technician

A major city transit system is extending the service life of its buses and saving substantial replacement costs using a program to completely rebuild chassis and engine systems. At seven-year intervals, buses are pulled off the road and completely disassembled, inspected, and refurbished for another seven-year operating cycle. Specific components are rebuilt and replaced during the refurbishing process. Aluminum and steel body panels, frame components, suspension, and steering and electrical systems undergo rigorous inspection and reconditioning processes. Because the transit authority has invited its technicians to provide feedback and recommendations to improve the rebuild program, you are particularly interested in making recommendations about the uses, repair, and replacement practices for threaded fasteners. As you prepare your written recommendations, include the following information in your outline:

1. What types of fasteners are recommended for reassembling the buses after a major rebuild program? Identify the grade, class, thread type, protective finishes, and other important criteria for your choices.
2. What procedures would you recommend for tightening fasteners for the frame, suspension, steering, and engine components?
3. Outline what types of thread repair methods are best applied to engines and major chassis and systems.

Introduction

Commercial vehicles, like any machinery, are fabricated from parts assembled using fasteners. Some parts are joined using methods creating a permanent joint. Welding, soldering, riveting, crimping, and even the use of specialized high-strength adhesives are examples of permanent fastening methods and material. Non-permanent methods of fastening parts can include the use of clips, keys, wire or plastic ties, snap-rings, heat-shrink tubes, buttons, and various pins, such as cotter, clevis, or spring pins. But, because disassembly and reassembly is necessary to perform maintenance and repair, more components use threaded fasteners. This is significant for commercial vehicle technicians because it highlights the importance for developing skill sets related to working with threaded fasteners. Foundational to any technician's competency is the ability to ensure equipment is assembled with the correct type, size, and quality of fasteners. And, those fasteners must also be reinstalled using the recommended tools and procedures. When learning the trade, adopting recommended practices associated with working with tools and fasteners as personal habits enables a technician to work confidently and develop a reputation for reliable, quality work. Failure to properly assemble components using recommended practices, tools, and equipment will inevitably result in costly mistakes, if not catastrophic failure. A simple, inexpensive cotter pin missing from a nut holding together steering linkage, or a loose bolted joint inside an engine or on a drive shaft can have major economic, if not life-changing, consequences. Identifying fastener types, sizes, and features, and understanding proper installation techniques using the prescribed tools, not only limits potentially negative consequences, but is an essential step toward developing the skills to be a successful technician. This chapter examines the types, features, and applications of various fasteners to enable technicians to make proper recommendations for fastener selection and repair.

Threaded Fasteners

LO 4-1 Explain the importance of selecting and installing the correct type, size, and quality of threaded fasteners.

It is possible to weld, rivet, or glue and, in some instances, tie components and parts of a vehicle together. However, most of a vehicle and its components are assembled using various types of threaded fasteners. Threaded fasteners allow relatively easy assembly and disassembly of components with a minimum of specialized tools whenever maintenance or repairs are necessary. This ease and economy of use explains why they make-up most locking devices holding parts together on a vehicle. Threaded fastener threads are the "V" shaped ridges that wraps around the outside or inside of a threaded device. If the thread is formed on the outside, it is an external thread. When threads are formed inside a fastener, they are internal. Threads function to convert the rotational movement of a nut or screw into a linear or stretching movement of a fastener when it is tightened. A mechanical advantage is achieved by fastener threads to tightly clamp a joint by converting and amplifying the rotational or twisting force used to tighten fasteners into clamping force. V-shaped threads winding inside or outside a fastener act like an inclined plane or ramp. The ramped shape of threads trades off the turning force and rotational movement to magnify joint clamping force holding parts together when fasteners are properly tightened. The rows' and ridges' of the "V" or wedge-shape threads secondary purpose is to help each thread to slide over one another with less friction (**FIGURE 4-1**). Threads used on mechanical screw-type lifting jacks demonstrate the effectiveness of the mechanical advantage supplied by threads of a fastener.

Types of Threaded Fasteners: Screws, Bolts, Nuts, and Studs

The most common types of threaded fasteners are screws, bolts, and nuts (**FIGURE 4-2**). **Bolts** are a broad category of fastener with external threads inserted into a hole passing between two or more parts. The use of a threaded nut on the bolt clamps a joint together when the two parts are tightened. **Nuts** are an internally threaded fastener having thread dimensions that match those on a bolt enabling the two pieces to tighten together to apply a clamping force on a joint.

In contrast to a bolt, a **screw** is an externally threaded fastener that does not use a nut but instead is turned into an internal hole, which may or may not be threaded. For example, a hex head **cap screw**, which is identical to a bolt in a bolt and nut combination, is often incorrectly called a bolt. Hex head cap screws are different from bolts because they turn in and out of a threaded hole to clamp a joint, but a cap screw does not use a nut. Screws may rotate in and out of preformed internal threads of a hole or form their own thread. Sheet metal, self-tapping screws are examples of a screw category forming their own threads. A greater variety of screws than bolts are made because screws

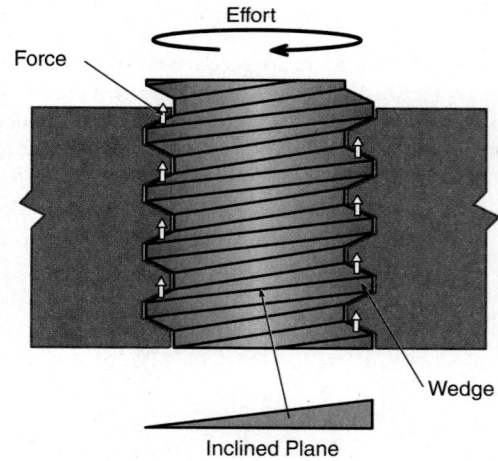

FIGURE 4-1 The angle of threads creates an incline plane that supplies a mechanical advantage by multiplying turning force and rotational movement into clamping force. A wedge-shape thread profile reduces friction.

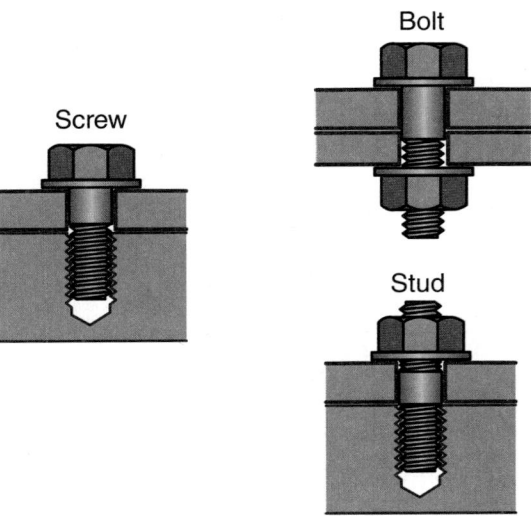

FIGURE 4-2 Example of a bolt-, screw-, and stud-type threaded fastener.

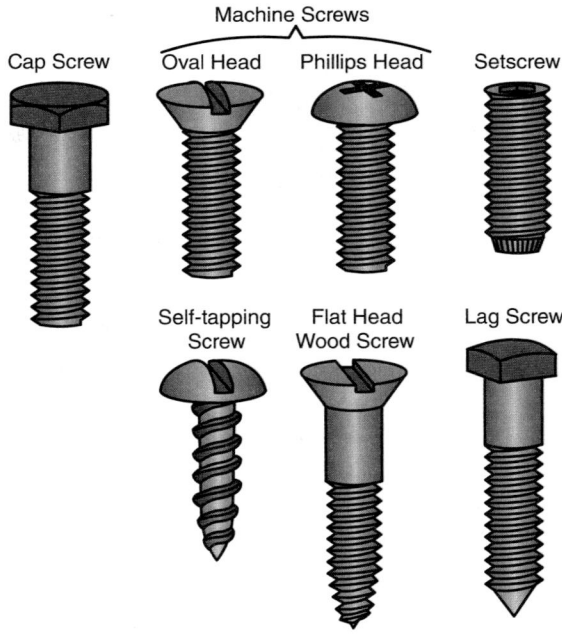

FIGURE 4-3 Screws are threaded fasteners with a wide variety of head shapes. They do not clamp a joint using nuts.

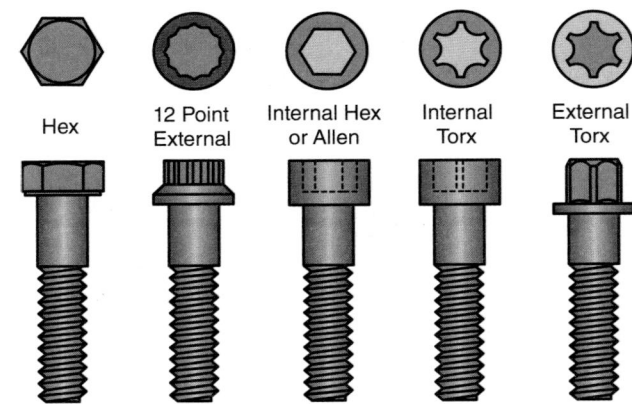

FIGURE 4-4 Specialized applications of fasteners use unique head shapes and require specialized tools to loosen and tighten.

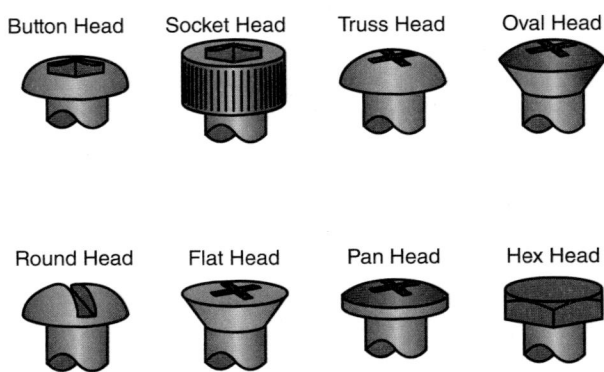

FIGURE 4-5 The shape or profile of a screw is determined by its application.

have more specialized functions and applications (**FIGURE 4-3**). Both screws and bolts are also made using a wide variety of head shapes best suited for a particular use. For example, to tighten or loosen a cap screw, it commonly has a six-sided or hex-shaped head for a socket or wrench to easily turn it. In very tight areas where access is limited, the head shape must be compact. Some screws require a very high degree of tension, such as clamping a cylinder head, so a hex head is replaced with an internal hex head, internal or external Torx, or 12-point head (**FIGURE 4-4**).

Some applications require a fastener head to be flush with a surface, distribute force well, and maintain a smooth low profile so it does not snag clothing or skin. A head that is strong enough to withstand twisting forces when tightened or loosened, or has decorative appeal, also determines the shape of a fastener head (**FIGURE 4-5**).

A **stud** is an externally threaded fastener that has no head. Instead, it is threaded at each end of its shank. A stud can operate like a screw, threading into a hole with internal threads, or it can use a nut on one or both ends. If a stud uses a nut on both ends to create clamping force, it is called a **stud bolt**.

Machining Threads

Threaded fasteners are made by either rolling an external thread onto a blank shank or are cut using a machine **die** (**FIGURE 4-6**). Nuts and threaded holes can only be machined with a tool called a **tap**, which removes metal from material. Rolled threads are much stronger than machine-cut threads for a couple of reasons. First, machine cut threads reduce the minimum thread root-to-root diameter of a bolt or screw. Cutting the material also disrupts the metal grain structure and creates stress risers, which are places where cracks can form. Rolled threaded fasteners have larger root diameters and the metal is compressed — not removed, by the threading die (**FIGURE 4-7**). Because no metal is cut away when threads are rolled, so the metal grain flows smoothly around unbroken curves forming the thread profiles.

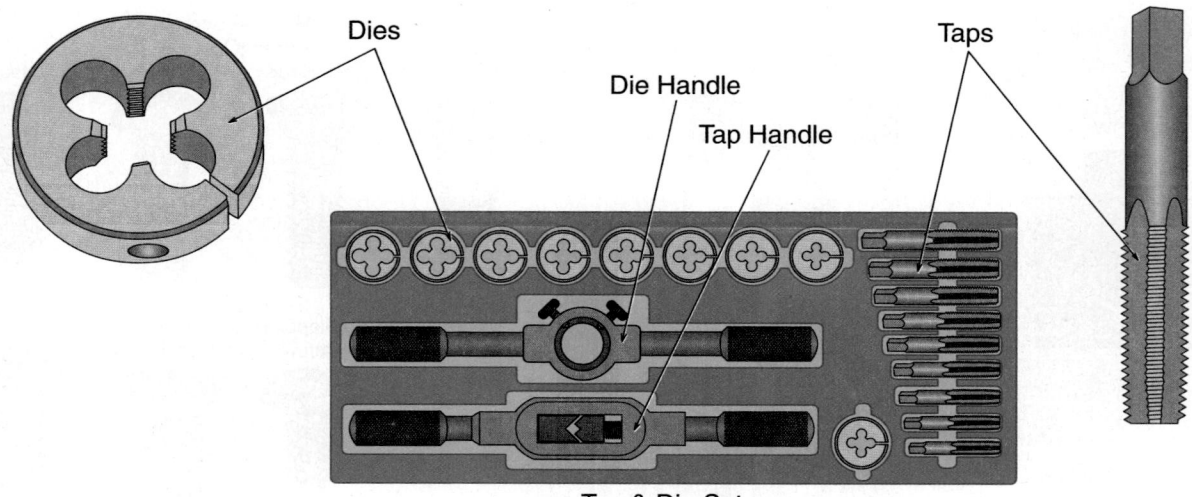

FIGURE 4-6 Dies are used to cut external threads, taps cut internal threads.

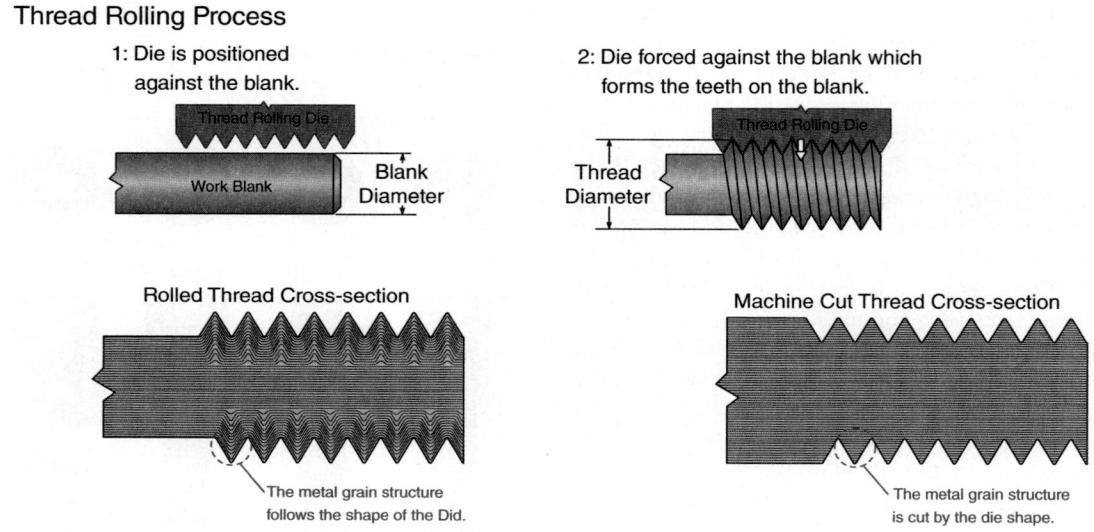

FIGURE 4-7 To create rolled threads, a die presses thread onto a blank cap screw.

A finished fastener has a dark carbon steel appearance that may be oiled to give the threads some corrosion protection. However, to better protect fastener threads from corrosion, the most common and economical method is to apply a zinc coating, giving it a bright, shiny appearance. Zinc formulas can be clear, or have a bluish tint, or a yellow color called zinc plate gold, depending on the zinc formulation. Yellow zinc plating, which is thicker, provides better corrosion protection. Chromates, which had similar colors, are toxic and are no longer used to plate fasteners.

Threaded Fastener Preload

Its important to understand that threaded fasteners behave like elastic bands to tightly clamp a joint, and the threads essentially apply the clamping force. As mentioned above, the shape of the threads operates like an incline plane or ramp. Rotating the fastener in a direction to tighten the joint causes the threads to apply a linear tension or straight-line load through the shank to the head of the cap screw or bolt. This means tightening a threaded bolt or screw lengthens it. A fastener stretches when it is tightened because the fastener head keeps the bolt or cap screw from sinking into the joint. Stretching the bolt while it passes through an elastic state establishes an important fastener clamping force called preload (**FIGURE 4-8**). Preload force is measured in either units of pounds per square inch (psi) or megapascals (MPa). To increase the clamping force holding parts together, the fastener is tightened further, which stretches a bolt or screw, increasing preload force. It's important to have an adequate amount of preload to not only properly clamp a joint, but also to prevent the fastener from loosening. Friction between the threads increases proportionally to preload force, which means the more the fastener is tightened, the less chance

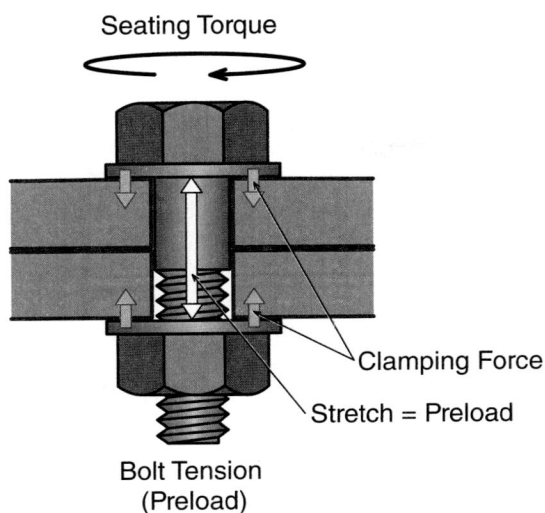

Seating Torque

Clamping Force

Stretch = Preload

Bolt Tension
(Preload)

FIGURE 4-8 Tightening a threaded fastener stretches it, which preloads the bolt. Preload creates clamping force and thread friction.

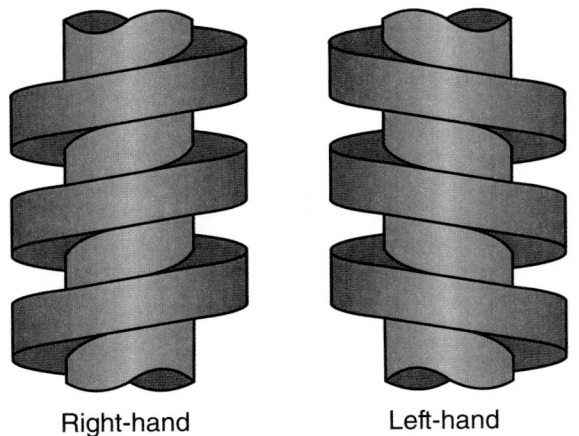

Right-hand   Left-hand

FIGURE 4-9 These left- and right-handed threads are viewed with the hex head cap on top. Note: Right-handed threads slope downwards to the left.

threads will back-off and loosen the joint. Note that there is a limit to the preload force threads can tolerate before the thread ridges break. Excessively tightening a screw or bolt breaks the threads, creating a condition called stripped or pulled threads.

Left- and Right-Handed Threads

Threads are also classified by whether they are right- or left-handed. Right-hand threads are tightened when turned clockwise and left-hand threads are tightened when turned counterclockwise. When examining a thread on a hex head cap screw placed with its head or cap up, right-hand threads slope downwards to the left. Holding the same fastener by the head with the threaded shank pointed up, right-hand threads slope downwards to the right (**FIGURE 4-9**). Internal right-hand threads slope downwards to the right as well when examined from above the thread. Various ideas are used to help visually identify these threads, but it is not necessary because

right-handed threads are universally used with one notable exception. Left-handed threads are often used in situations where rotating loads beneath a fastener could cause right-hand threads to loosen during service. For example, the wheel fasteners on stud-piloted wheels are left-handed to prevent the wheel from quickly separating in operation.

Threaded Fastener Specifications

LO 4-2 Describe and explain specification standards for threaded fasteners.

Screws and bolts are classified in several ways, which include:

- The shape of the fastener head
- Size
- Type of thread
- Plating material
- Tensile and yield strength

To bring uniformity to threaded fastener properties and dimensions allowing interchangeability between different manufacturers, recognized industry standards are established for threaded fasteners. Regulating organizations set standards for materials, mechanical properties, dimensions, and thread tolerances. For metric threads, only International Organization for Standardization (ISO) establishes specifications using millimeters as the unit of measurement. Metric fasteners have the letter M on the head to designate them as metric. For fasteners used in North America, specifications for **Unified Thread Standard (UTS)** use fractions of an inch or imperial measurements. UTS specifications are set by two separate regulators. The American Society for Testing and Materials (ASTM) publishes standards for UTS fasteners according to grades of material and mechanical properties, such as strength and hardness. Overlapping standards set by the ASTM are also published by the Automotive Engineers (SAE). UTS fastener dimensions and thread tolerance standards are set by the American National Standards Institute (ANSI). While metric and imperial fasteners standards are established by separate governing bodies, ISO and UTS standards both use a common 60-degree thread angle for general-purpose fasteners (**FIGURE 4-10**). Tools used to work with these two major classifications of threaded fasteners must adapt to the dimensional differences, resulting in technicians requiring metric and imperial sets of tools.

Unified Thread Standards

UTS are a dimensional standard for threaded fasteners first adopted in the late 1940s at the same time as ISO metric standards. Specifications for UTS cover fastener dimensions and thread features.

Unified National Coarse Thread

UTS threads are specified as either course, fine, or extra-fine thread. Coarse-thread specifications are designated by the abbreviation UNC for Unified National Coarse series fasteners. UNC threads are suited to applications where fast disassembly and assembly are important, where there is potential for stripping threads because the material is soft, or potential for corrosion.

Because the course thread screw has fewer threads per inch, the thread root diameter is smaller and deeper, so there is more internal thread material held between each thread (**FIGURE 4-11**). In soft materials, such as aluminum or cast iron, a coarse thread should be used since it is less likely to pull or strip threads if over tightened. UNC thread fasteners require longer engagement length in thicker-walled materials to compensate for soft internal thread material strength. Bolts, studs, and screws made from softer grades of steel should use coarse and not fine threads for the same reasons. An UNC bolt dimension is expressed like:

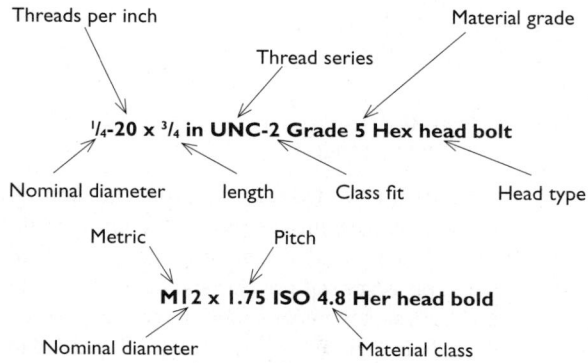

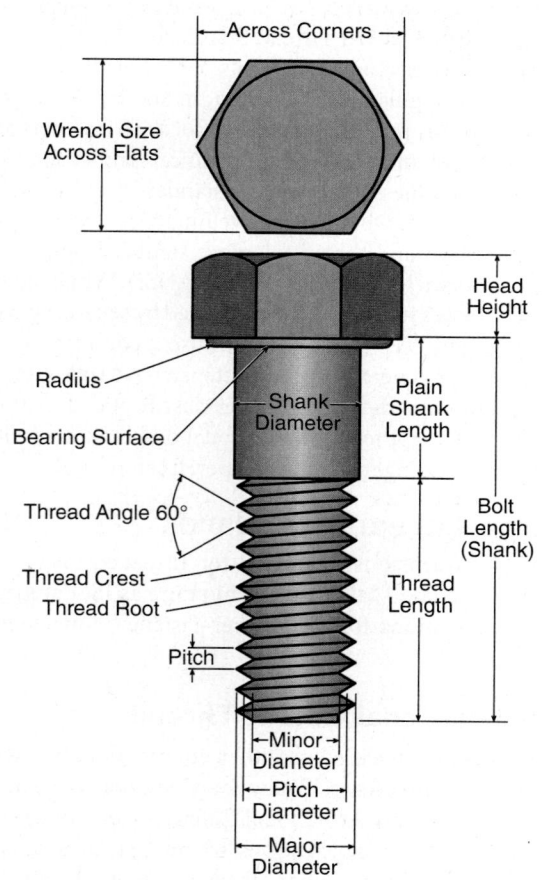

FIGURE 4-10 Terminology used for dimensions of a cap screw.

Unified National Fine Thread

Fine-thread fasteners are designated by the symbol UNF, which are called the Unified National Fine series fasteners. Fine threads are best used where high clamping force is required, fastener engagement length is shorter, and internal thread wall material is thinner. Having more threads per inch and threads with a smaller profile (the difference between the thread crest and root is shorter) means the threads are not only less likely to break but can support higher tensile loading. The number of threads per inch is measured with a thread pitch gauge or counted over the distance of an inch (**FIGURE 4-12**). With more threads per inch, the strength of UNF threads is commonly used in steel, rather than cast iron or softer aluminum materials (**TABLE 4-1**). UNF bolts can be tightened with greater torque and clamp with higher force using the identical amount of torque as a UNC fastener (**FIGURE 4-13**). UNF are best used where clamping forces are higher and require greater precision. Machined parts and many internal engine fasteners often use UNF.

Extra-Fine Thread Series

The rarely used extra-fine thread series is designated by the abbreviation UNEF and is called the Unified National Extra-Fine series. UNEF is used where even finer pitches of threads

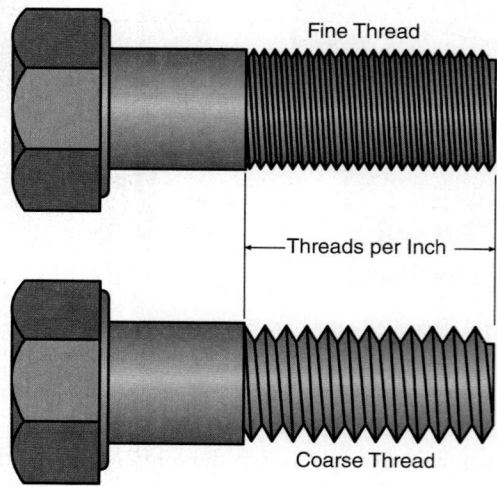

FIGURE 4-11 Comparing UNC and UNF cap screws. UNF threads are stronger because there are more threads per inch and the root is not as deep.

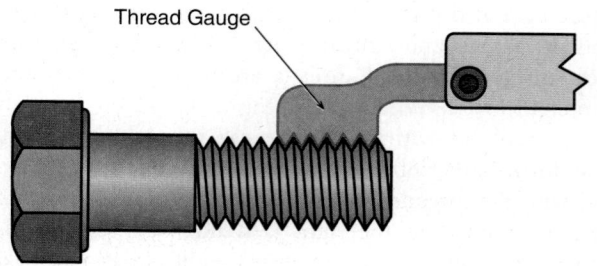

FIGURE 4-12 A thread pitch gauge can quickly determine the number of threads per inch.

TABLE 4-1 ANSI UTS Cap Screw and Bolt Dimensions

Cap Screw Diameter Size (inches)	Hex Head Wrench Size	Threads per Inch (TPI)	
		Coarse Thread UNC	Fine Thread UNF
1/4"	3/8" or 7/16"	20	28
5/16"	1/2"	18	24
3/8"	9/16"	16	24
7/16"	5/8"	14	20
1/2"	3/4"	13	20
9/16"	13/16"	12	18
5/8"	15/16"	11	18
3/4"	1-1/8"	10	16
7/8"	1-5/16"	9	14
1"	1-1/2"	8	12

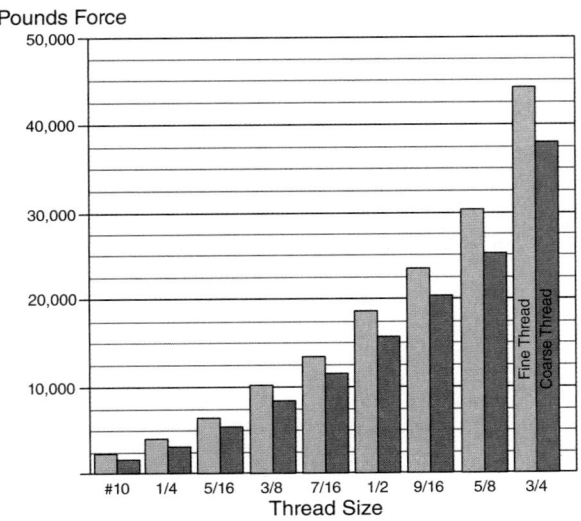

FIGURE 4-13 Comparing the tensile strength of UNF and UNC fasteners. UNF threads are stronger with higher tensile strength.

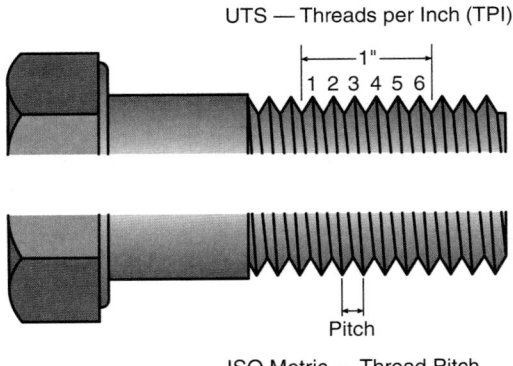

FIGURE 4-14 Comparing the thread of an UTS and metric fastener. Thread pitch, rather than threads per inch, is used to classify coarse and fine threads.

are desirable for short lengths of engagement and when used in thin-walled tubes, nuts, ferrules, or couplings. With the strongest thread designs, these screws, nuts and bolts can best handle shock loads when threads are made from high tensile strength materials. Aerospace industry most commonly uses this thread and only rarely are they used on commercial vehicles. One exception is for threads on some glow-plugs, which must withstand high combustion chamber pressures while maintaining a reliable gas-type seal.

M-Series Fasteners

ISO standards that outline specifications for metric fasteners parallel UTS standards in some familiar ways. For example, there are three kinds of ISO metric threads: coarse, fine, and extra fine. The angle of threads is 60 degrees. Because metric fasteners do not use an inch to indicate thread count per inch, thread pitch is instead measured in millimeters from the crest of

one thread to the next (**FIGURE 4-14**). Because fine threads are not strong in small diameter fasteners, fine thread fasteners are uncommon below 8 mm diameter (**TABLE 4-2**). In fact, in small diameter bolts, fine threads are not available or practical since they do not have adequate engagement with threaded mating surfaces. Metric size fasteners are indicated as M (major diameter) x pitch. An M10 X 1.5 bolt specification means the major or largest diameter of the bolt is 10 mm and the thread pitch is 1.5 mm, which indicates it is a fine-thread fastener.

Mechanical Strength

LO 4-3 Identify and describe fastener classifications according to mechanical strengths.

In addition to dimensional information, technicians need to be familiar with classifications of fasteners according to mechanical strengths. Properties of fasteners mechanical strength predict the response of a fastener to applied loads. One of the most important mechanical properties of threaded fasteners is tensile strength. Tensile strength refers to the breaking point of a fastener when it is stretched. Depending on the diameter and materials it is made from, a bolt or screw will stretch and eventually break when enough tensile load is applied to tighten it. Bolts having larger diameters and high carbon alloyed steel are naturally stronger because the material provides higher tensile strength. Tensile strength indicates the ability of the fastener to carry or transfer load, with higher tensile strength fasteners capable of applying more joint clamping force. Tensile strengths are normally expressed in terms of stress-pounds or tensile load per square inch (psi) for UTS fasteners and megapascals (MPa) for metric fasteners.

Fastener strength for UTS fasteners is graded on an SAE scale of one to eight with eight being the highest strength (**TABLE 4-3**). Raised hash marks or lines on the head of a UTS bolt or cap screw designates the grade. If no marking is present on an UTS fastener, it indicates it is a grade one or two. A grade five fastener has three raised hash marks that the number two is added to, designating the grade of strength. Likewise, grade eight fasteners have only six raised hash marks. Metric fasteners are commonly classified by strength classes from 4.6 to 10.9 with 10.9 the strongest (**TABLE 4-4**). Number markings on the head of each fastener indicate the strength class of an externally

threaded fastener. SAE grade five bolts are equivalent to an 8.8 M series bolt.

Manufacturers produce custom bolt grades for specialized applications, such as the engine cylinder head and crankcase fasteners, such as main bearing and connecting rod caps. These fasteners have unique original equipment manufacturers (OEM) markings designating proprietary strength grades.

▶ TECHNICIAN TIP

The strength grade of a bolt or cap screw is important to technicians because it determines where and how a fastener is used. Frames, steering gears, and hitching devices, such as fifth wheels and tow bar attachment points bolts, require a minimum of SAE grade eight bolts or 10.9 M-series. Bolts are under high tensile and shear loads in these applications require the greatest strength. Grade SAE 8 or 10.9 ISO bolts are costly to make because alloys, such as boron, and special heat-treating processes are used to manufacture the steel used in these fasteners. Less costly fasteners are SAE Grade 5 or 8.8 ISO, which are the most common types used to manufacture and repair most other chassis and engine systems.

TABLE 4-2 ISO Specifications for Cap Screw Dimensions

Cap Screw Diameter Size (mm)	Hex Head Wrench Size	Coarse	Thread Pitch (mm) Fine	Extra Fine
M4	7	0.7	–	–
M5	8	0.8	–	–
M6	10	1.0	–	–
M7	11	1.0	–	–
M8	13	1.25	1	
M10	16 or 17	1.5	1.25	1
M12	18 or 19	1.75	1.5	1.25
M14	21 or 22	2	1.5	–
M16	24	2	–	–
M18	27	2.5	–	–
M20	30	2.5	–	–

TABLE 4-3 SAE Markings and ASTM Strength for UTS External Threaded Fasteners

Grade	Marking	Diameter	Composition	Yield Strength Kips/square inch (KSI)	Tensile Strength KSI	Proof Load KSI
1	None	1/4" to 3/4"	Low or Medium Carbon Steel	36	60	33
2	None	3/4" to 1-1/2"	Low or Medium Carbon Steel	57	74	55
5	|/	1/4" to 1"	Medium Carbon Steel	92	120	85
8	|/ /|\	1/4" to 1-1/2"	Medium Carbon Steel	130	150	120
A325	A325	1/2" to 1-1/2"	Stainless Steel	85	120	92

TABLE 4-4 ISO Designation and Markings for External Threaded Metric Fastener Strength

Grade	Marking	Dimension	Composition	Yield Strength MPa	Tensile Strength MPa	Proof Load MPa
4.6	4.6	M5 – M100	Low or Medium Carbon Steel	240	400	225
4.8	4.6	M1.6 – M16	Low or Medium Carbon Steel	340	420	310
5.8	5.8	M5 – M24	Low or Medium Carbon Steel	420	520	380
8.8	8.8	M16 – M36	Medium Carbon Steel	660	830	600
9.8	9.8	M1.6 – M16	Medium Carbon Steel	650	900	720
10.9	10.9	M5 – M100	Alloyed Medium Carbon Steel	940	1040	830

Shear Strength

Tensile strength is related to several other measurements of a fastener strength. When a force operates to bend a bolt or screw, it is called **shear stress**. Shear strength is the maximum stress applied at a right angle to a fastener before it breaks. Shear strengths of fasteners generally are 60% of their tensile strength. For example, an SAE Grade 5 hex head cap screw has a specified minimum tensile strength of 120,000 psi. Its shear strength is approximately 60% of this value, or 70,000 psi. To have maximum engagement strength, a cap screw must be threaded into a hole at least to a depth equivalent to its diameter.

Yield Strength

Also related to tensile strength is yield strength. Like tensile strength, yield strength is a measurement of the fasteners ability to withstand tensile forces stretching a bolt, but refers instead to the point the fastener is irreversibly distorted but not broken. As mentioned above, fasteners are elastic so tightening a bolt or screw stretches it. When tension is released, it should return to its normal, pre-stretched dimension. However, if it is stretched too far, a bolt or screw is permanently distorted and doesn't return to its normal shape. The threshold where irreversible distortion takes place is called the yield strength. Yield strength is also measured in psi, or MPa for metric fasteners. Yield strength is always less than tensile strength (**FIGURE 4-15**).

Measuring bolt or cap screw length is one method to determine whether tightening has exceeded its yield strength and permanently distorted a fastener. Gauges measuring bolt length are available and a bolt length can be compared with a new bolt of known quality. A condition called "necking" also takes place where a fastener's major diameter is narrowed (**FIGURE 4-16**). A necked bolt should never be reused.

Proof Load

One of the most practical measurements of strength is called proof load. This factor represents the maximum useable load limit of the fastener. **Proof load** is tension-applied load

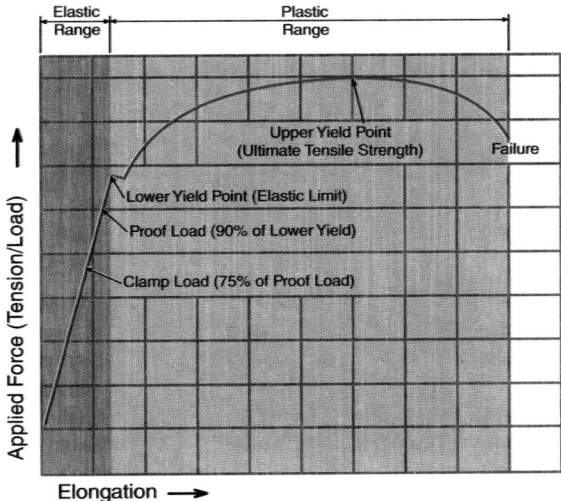

FIGURE 4-15 Yield strength is less than tensile strength. Proof load is less than yield strength.

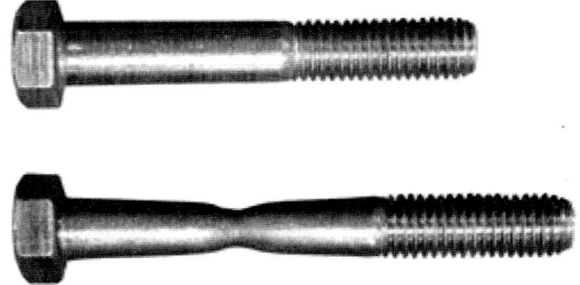

FIGURE 4-16 An example of a cap screw tightened beyond its yield strength.

a fastener can support without measurably deforming or its threads stripping. Proof load and yield strength are not the same, though. Proof load measurements are determined by repeatedly applying and releasing a specified load and then remeasuring a bolt or cap screw's length. A specification for maximum proof load is the tensile load it can repeatedly tolerate yet maintain its original length. Force measurement units for proof load are in pounds or Newton's. This contrasts with yield strength measurement units that are reported in psi or MPa. Maximum proof load is typically 80% to 90% of the yield strength.

Threaded Nuts

LO 4-4 Describe the classification of threaded nuts according to grade strength.

Nuts are block or sleeve-like fasteners with internally threaded holes with thread-mating surfaces that match a bolt. Nuts and bolts are twisted together to clamp a joint. The equivalent of a nut for a cap screw is a threaded hole. The threaded start of a nut is chamfered to allow easier threading of a bolt from a slightly offset angle of entry. Dozens of nut shapes are made, such as square, acorn, jam, closed, castellated, wing, etc. (**FIGURE 4-17**). Hex head nuts with six sides or flats are most common because six sides provide angles small enough for a tool to fit over the head and twist it with enough force while accessing the nut in small areas with limited tool access. More sides of a nut with smaller angles can provide even better access in limited space, but the corners are more easily rounded off.

Nut Grades and Classes

The grade of nuts strength is patterned according to the same standards for SAE grades and ISO classes of externally threaded fasteners. Markings or number markers on the nut's flat sides or on the bearing side, which is the top and bottom nut surface, designate nut grades and classes (**FIGURE 4-18**). However, the material strength of nuts is slightly less than bolts. The intent of this practice is to create nut threads that are more pliable, having higher yield strength and being less brittle than a bolt. Higher nut yield strength is more important than tensile strength because 73% of the tensile load is carried by only the first three threads of a nut (**FIGURE 4-19**). Nut threads with greater yield strength are less likely to strip when paired with an externally threaded bolt, compared to a nut-and-bolt combination with identical yield strength. In other words, a nut-and-bolt combination with a slightly softer nut strength can be tightened to a higher proof load (**TABLE 4-5**). Higher classes for strength property of nuts may replace lower property class nuts in a nut-and-bolt combination.

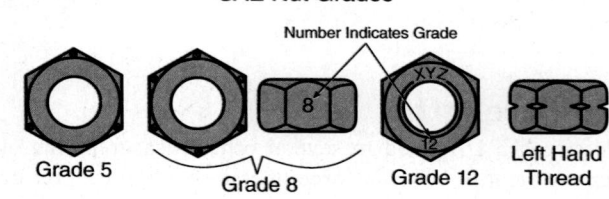

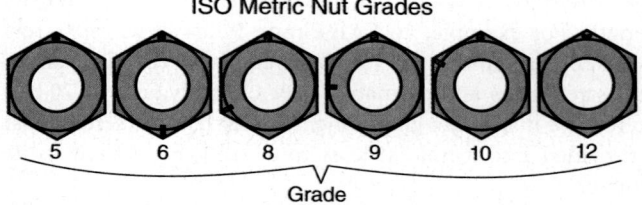

FIGURE 4-18 Hex nuts are marked by an indentation on the bearing surface or by a number on the flat of the hex nut. Metric nut classes are read like a clock face. Class 8.9 has markings indicating 8 o'clock.

FIGURE 4-17 Nuts are made in a wide variety of shapes and have additional functions beyond just clamping a joint.

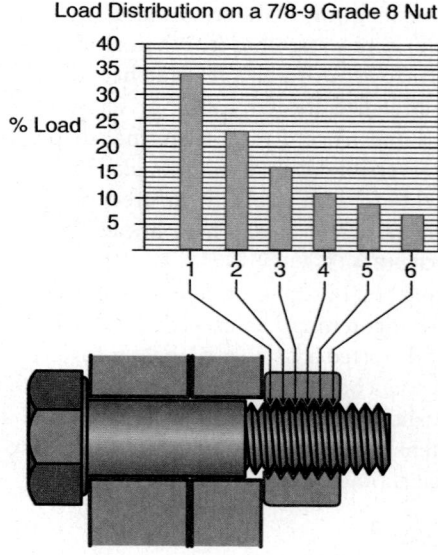

FIGURE 4-19 The first three threads of a nut carry 73% of the tensile load of a nut-and-bolt joint.

TABLE 4-5 Strength Properties of Metric Class Fasteners

Nut Property Class	5	6	8	9	10	12
Mating Bolt Property Class	5.8	6.8	8.8	9.8	10.9	12.9

▶ **TECHNICIAN TIP**

While the first three threads of a nut carry 73% of the tensile load of a bolted joint, a bolt or cap screw must engage at a minimum depth equal to or greater than its diameter into any nut. If not, the strength or clamping force of the fasteners is much less than its shear or tensile load strength specifications.

Tightening Fasteners

LO 4-5 Describe and explain principles and methods of tightening fasteners.

Fatigue-related failures make up most fastener problems. It may seem counter-intuitive, but broken bolts are the likeliest indication of fatigue-related failures caused by under tightening and the absence of correct preload or clamping force. Overtightening can break a fastener; however, more frequently, under tightening is the cause of failure. This observation may appear unexpected until one understands, that cyclic stress causes fatigue failure leading to broken fasteners. A bolted joint with loosely tensioned fasteners repeatedly stretches and relaxes. Cyclic stress like this causes fatigue failure, which has an effect similar to bending or flexing stress. For example, consider a bolted joint with a normal preload of 60,000 lb. If it is only loosely tightened to have a preload of 5000 lb, but stretched under load from 5000 to 50,000 lb, the stress is identical to having 45,000 lb of tensional loading cyclically applied and released. If it is correctly preloaded, no cyclic stretching and relaxation takes place at all since the bolt is already under 60,000 lb of tensile load. When tensioned, the bolt does not stretch any further unless it has more than 60,000 lb of load applied. Fatigue failure does not take place in this situation because there is no cyclic loading and unloading of the fastener.

Unless a bolt is correctly tensioned, joint movement can also cause bending back and forth or cyclic stressing of the fastener from shear loads. Eventually, stress cracks develop and quickly cause a fracture failure when tensile loading is not within normal limits. However, if the bolt is correctly tensioned, it resists both bending and stretching up to the point of its preloaded force. To prevent premature fastener failure, proper preload must be established to not only adequately clamp a joint, but to prevent fastener failure, elongation, and loosening of the joint. Even a slightly over-tightened fastener is less likely to break than an under-tightened fastener.

Tightening Methods

For a joint to achieve and maintain the proper clamping force and prevent premature fastener failure, a designated amount of

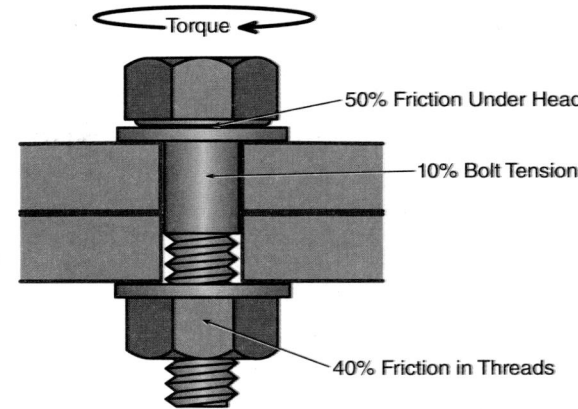

FIGURE 4-20 Most of the rotational force of torque is consumed by friction. It is important to clean and lightly oil a fastener to increase the preload tension.

tension or preload is applied to a screw, nut, or bolt. Properly tightening a joints fastener to its optimal preload force increases thread friction, which, in turn, minimizes the possibility of the fastener loosening while in service. Correct preload places a fastener in its elastic range with the recommended proof load. This is typically done by applying a rotational twisting force—called torque—to a fastener that ideally is close its correct preload force. However, achieving the correct preload by tightening the fastener with a prescribed amount of torque is only an estimate or prediction that the correct tensile load is applied to the fastener. Reliably and accurately establishing correct preload is difficult since a large percentage of force applied to turn the fastener during tightening is used to overcome thread friction. In fact, after initial tightening, engaged threads have increasing pressure applied against one another, causing friction to increase exponentially. More force is needed to overcome friction than is used to stretch or tension the fastener. Estimates are that 50% of rotational force of torque applied to a bolt is used to overcome a bolt or cap screw's head-bearing friction, 40% is to overcome thread friction, and only 10% is directed into producing tensile preload (**FIGURE 4-20**). This explains why a standard practice is to always clean rusty thread holes and clean them with a thread chaser before assembling oil-lubricated nuts, bolts and cap screws. Specialty greases containing molybdenum, an ideal dry lubricant, are available to coat threads and the bearing surfaces beneath the head of a cap screw or nut (**FIGURE 4-21**). If bolts and cap screws are corroded, pitted, nicked, or damaged in any way, they should be replaced since they cannot be properly tightened and the damage can create stress risers.

Several techniques are used to apply the preload tension to a fastener. These include:

1. Technician judgement — Tightening by feel is the most common fastener tensioning method. This method is satisfactory when the clamping force is not critical — needed only to hold parts together, enable the fastener to maintain clamping load

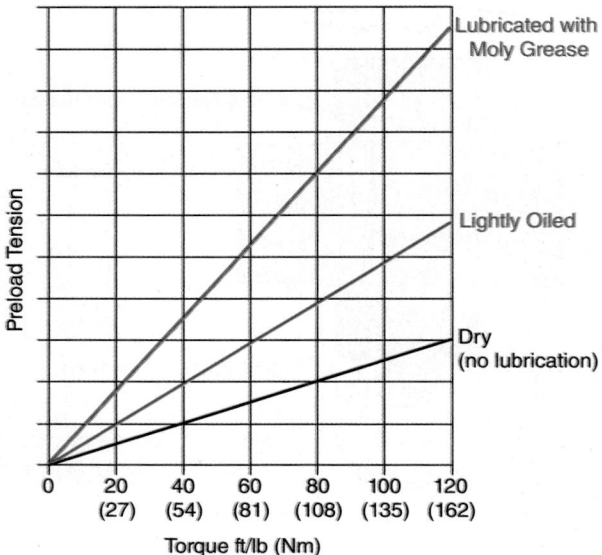

FIGURE 4-21 Applying light oil to fasteners lowers thread friction and resistance to rotation. More turning torque converts to clamping force.

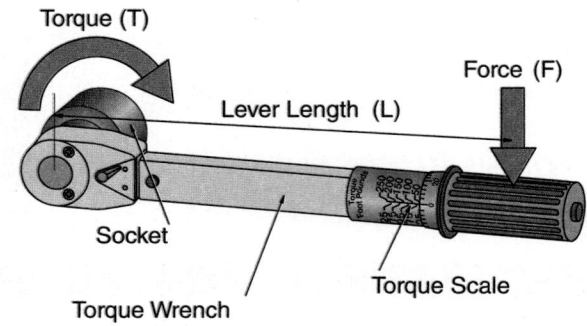

FIGURE 4-22 Torque is a function of the force applied to a lever times its length.

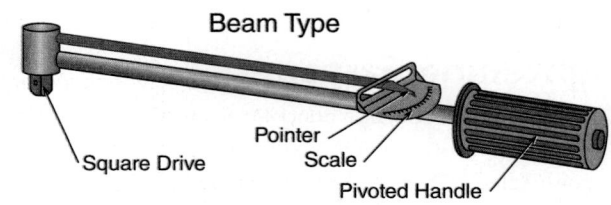

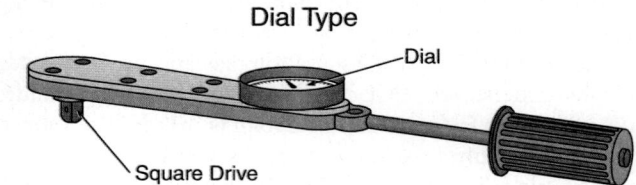

FIGURE 4-23 Two types of torque wrench.

(stay tight), and when it is not expected to encounter vibration. Technician experience and skill is critical to achieve accurate or even adequate preload force.

2. Torque wrench — Tightening with a torque wrench method is a preferred tensioning method for precision-engineered joints. Torque is a function of the length of a lever multiplied by its length. A torque wrench with a calibrated setting indicates when the correct amount of twisting force or torque is applied to the fastener (**FIGURE 4-22**). Variations from the correct preload vary + or - 25% using a torque wrench (**FIGURE 4-23**).

3. Torque Turn Method — The most accurate method to preload a fastener is time-consuming but provides the best results for important joints, such as cylinder head gaskets, crankcase fasteners, or precision-machined joints, using thin, lightweight metals. An initial preload force is applied by tightening a fastener to a torque value using a torque wrench. Next, the cap screw or nut is turned a specific number of degrees or "flats" on the cap screw head. This may be anywhere from 180 degrees or three flats to two complete turns requiring the use of an impact gun (**FIGURE 4-24**). Because the fastener is turned additional number of degrees after initial tightening, the factor friction plays in producing wide variations in preload force, is ignored and more precise preload force is achieved.

Other techniques, such as using an air-regulated impact gun or ratchet until it stalls, can produce consistent clamping forces. **Torque sticks**, which are steel rods used as extensions on impact guns, are effective when lighter tensioning is needed, giving up to 150 ft-lb of force. A calibrated cross-sectional dimension of the stick transmits torque up to a specific torsional force and then coils like a spring when any further torque is applied. Tire shops use color-coded torque sticks, designating

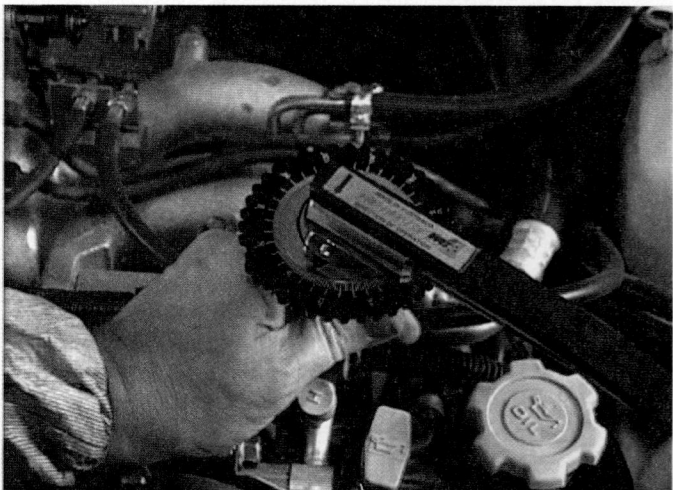

FIGURE 4-24 A turn-angle gauge is used to accurately measure how far to turn a fastener after its initial torque tightened position.

a maximum twisting force. The sticks with forged hex head sockets are used like extensions on impact guns when tightening wheel fasteners.

Self-Locking Hardware

LO 4-6 Identify and explain the purpose and functions of self-locking hardware.

Self-locking hardware is used to help prevent fastener loosening after preload force is lost or to prevent loss of preload tension. It is designed to increase what is called **prevailing torque**, a term used to describe the friction needed to loosen a fastener. Any joint movement or vibration tends to cause a fastener to lose tension, but high prevailing torque resists loosening.

Methods to prevent loosening include:

- Jam nuts — the addition of a thinner nut tightened against a regular nut.
- Castellated nuts with cotter pins or spring pins. The tops of these nuts have several machined cut-outs allowing a cotter pin to pass through the nut and into a hole in the threaded fastener beneath the nut. The pin locks the nut in position on the fastener thread (**FIGURE 4-25**).
- Wire ties — Fastener heads are drilled, and a wire is threaded through and tied to prevent loosening.
- Chemical thread locker — A chemical-based metal glue that is applied to clean threads prior to installation. The chemical cures anaerobically, which means it hardens in the absence of air, which can take place only after tightening the threaded fastener. Thread locker is especially useful in areas where oil can enter around threads, which can cause a fastener to loosen more quickly (**FIGURE 4-26**).
- Lock washers and similar devices to prevent loosening of a fastener by increasing friction between a bolt and nut or between screw and joint material.
- Locking nuts.

Locking Washers

Lock washers are used to resist loosening of bolted joints. There are basically two types:

- Spring-action lock washers
- Tooth lock washers

Spring-action lock washers are also called split-spring washers and are placed beneath a nut or screw head (**FIGURE 4-27**). When tightened, they compress, and the washer's spring tension can help compensate for some wear between parts. Because the split-spring washer flattens when tightened, its locking action can't take place until the fastener has slightly loosened. Two sharp edges at the washer end dig into the underside of a bolt head and nut to prevent further rotation.

Tooth lock washers are available with internal and external teeth. Movement in the fastener head causes the teeth to dig into the head and surface of the joint to prevent loosening. Keps nuts or K-lock nuts are a nut with a captive free-spinning tooth washer. These washers are easier to work with because the washer is attached or captive to the nut. One

FIGURE 4-25 A castellated nut is locked to the axle spindle with a cotter pin.

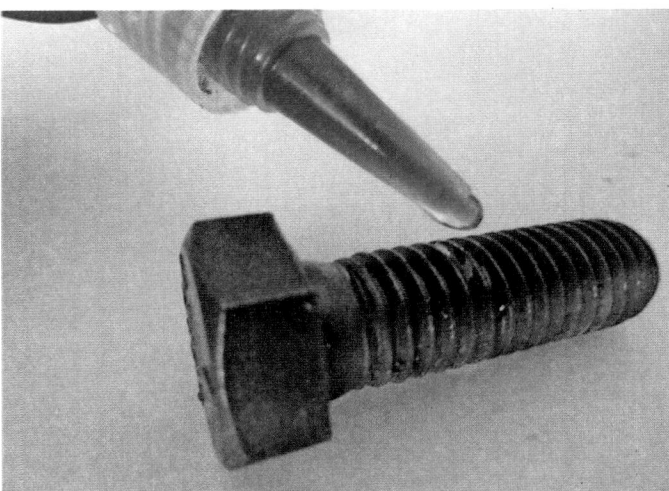

FIGURE 4-26 A chemical adhesive can seal and lock threads of a fastener to increase prevailing torque.

disadvantage is a tooth lock washer can scratch joint mating surfaces.

Lock Nuts

Another name for lock nuts are prevailing torque hex lock nuts. When made from only metal, the device is a one-piece self-locking nut that is crimped to create distorted threads near their top threads. The top surface is cone-shaped, and the bottom is flat to easily identify the nut and assist orientating it for correct installation. Commonly used on frame bolts or as a flange nut, these devices resist loosening caused by shock, vibration, and other joint movement. Because these nuts are all-metal, they can better resist temperature changes and chemical erosion that contributes to loosening in non-metallic lock nuts using nylon inserts. Prevailing torque lock nuts have limited repeated

FIGURE 4-27 A spring washer **(A)** and a serrated-edge toothed washer **(B)** prevent fasteners from loosening.

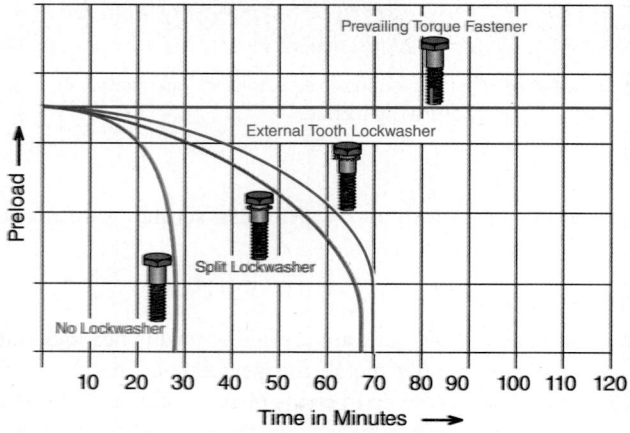

FIGURE 4-28 Prevailing torque bolts are one of the most effective methods to prevent loss of fastener preload.

use because the thread resistance is lost when the threads are straightened the first time the nut is used. However, they are one of the most effective methods to prevent loss of preload force (**FIGURE 4-28**). These nuts create more resistance when tightened so additional torque is needed achieve correct clamping force.

FIGURE 4-29 Flange bolts and nuts are often used on frames. The bottom of the nut and bolt have a wide area to distribute clamping force to make the joint more rigid.

FIGURE 4-30 A nylon insert at the top of this nylock self-locking nut helps prevent loosening.

Another similar nut design is a flange nut that is like a prevailing torque lock nut, but has a wide, flat underside to distribute clamping force over a wider area. This nut is used with an SAE Grade 8 or class 10.9 flange-type bolt on high tensile strength frames and frame-mounted components that have holes that are slightly larger than the bolt (**FIGURE 4-29**). The wider area beneath the bolt head and nut help stiffen the joint to make it more resistant to movement in this high-stress application. Optional serrated edges beneath the nut and bolt head dig into metal surfaces, which provides further resistance to loosening.

Nylon-inserts at the top of a conical-shaped nut are called nylocks. These self-locking nuts are prevailing torque nuts, but use a band of nylon that is smaller than the fastener diameter to increase resistance required to loosen the nut (**FIGURE 4-30**).

Flat Washers

Flat washers are used to increase the bearing surface of a nut or fastener's head, thus spreading the clamping force over a larger area. They are useful when working with soft materials and oversized or irregular shaped holes because the washer can protect a surface and support a nut or bolt head. Washer size refers to its nominal hole size, which is based on the size of fastener it accompanies.

Hardened and high-strength alloy washers are used with grade eight fasteners. Large outside diameter flat washers are called fender washers, which are often used to clamp soft materials, such as mud flaps or inner fender panels.

Thread Repair

LO 4-7 Identify and explain methods used to repair damaged threads.

Thread damage can take place under several common circumstances including:

- Excessive tightening of bolts, nuts, and screws
- Cross-threading caused by starting and continuing the installation of a fastener at an incorrect angle
- Using the wrong size of fastener or one that has a mismatched thread pitch
- Corrosion caused by rusting or galvanic action when dissimilar, incompatible metals are used together. Aluminum and steel combined with the presence of water and road salt is a frequent cause of galvanic corrosion.
- Fretting, which is a condition caused by heavy vibration of loose threads
- Worn threads caused by over use
- Broken fasteners, such as a cap screw or stud broken in a casting

Determining the best repair method for a damaged or broken thread depends on several criteria. The time, cost, and availability of replacing a component with damaged threads are the first considerations. If the value of the part compared with the labor time to repair it is less, the option to replace is clear. Safety of a repair should be considered too. Severely damaged or stripped threads on safety-related items, such as steering linkage, hitching devices, wheels, and hubs should generally never be repaired and re-used, they should be replaced instead. The design of a component and accessibility to the damaged threads are important factors for choosing the type of repair. For example, one repair technique involves drilling out damaged internal threads and tapping the threads to a larger thread diameter. Alternatively, following the step of drilling out damaged internal threads, a threaded sleeve is installed. However, if the part is weakened by drilling and installation of larger diameter fasteners or a threaded sleeve, other techniques must be considered, such as the use of liquid epoxy or metal putty thread repair kits. Welding new material into a hole with an MIG welder (Metal Inert Gas Welding with a wire feed) and machining new threads is one such alternative.

Drilling and Tapping

A basic thread repair technique involves drilling out damaged threads to an oversize diameter and machining new threads. This repair is performed on internal threads and requires the replacement of an original-sized fastener with a larger diameter. A tap-drill chart is used to determine the size of drill to use for a particular size of fastener (TABLE 4-6). Usually, one step in major diameter size is used to repair damaged threads. This means a stripped 5/16" fastener is replaced with a 3/8" or an M8 with an M10. Note that smaller tolerances between thread clearances require a slightly smaller diameter drill to before machining new threads with a tap. Fine and coarse threaded fasteners require slightly different drill sizes too (TABLE 4-7). Typically, the hole or drill diameter equals nominal fastener diameter minus thread pitch. Once the hole is drilled and cleaned, a tap is selected to cut new threads.

TABLE 4-6 Metric Tap-Drill Sizes

Tap Size	Major Diameter (mm)	Thread Pitch	Drill Size (mm)
M4 × 0.7	4	0.7	3.3
M5 × 0.8	5	0.8	4.2
M6 × 1.0	6	1.0	5.0
M8 × 1.25	8	1.25	6.8
M8 × 1.0	8	1.0	7.0
M10 × 1.5	10	1.5	8.5
M10 × 1.25	10	1.25	8.8
M12 × 1.75	12	1.75	10.2
M12 × 1.25	12	1.25	10.8
M14 × 2	14	2.0	12
M14 × 1.5	14	1.5	12.5
M16 × 2.0	16	2.0	14.0
M16 × 1.5	16	1.5	14.5
M18 × 2.5	18	2.5	15.5
M18 × 1.5	18	1.5	16.5

TABLE 4-7 UTS Tap-Drill Sizes

UTS — UNC/UNF Threads				
Tap Size	UNF/UNC	Threads per Inch	Major Diameter (Inches)	Drill Size
1/4-20	UNC	20	1/4 (0.2500)	13/64
1/4-28	UNF	28	1/4 (0.2500)	3/16
5/16-18	UNC	18	5/16 (0.3125)	1/4
5/16-24	UNF	24	5/16 (0.3125)	9/32
3/8-16	UNC	16	3/8 (0.3750)	5/16
3/8-24	UNF	24	3/8 (0.3750)	21/64
7/16-14	UNC	14	7/16 (0.4375)	23/64
7/16-20	UNF	20	7/16 (0.4375)	25/64
1/2-13	UNC	13	1/2 (0.5000)	27/64
1/2-20	UNF	20	1/2 (0.5000)	29/64
9/16-12	UNC	12	9/16 (0.5625)	31/64
9/16-18	UNF	18	9/16 (0.5625)	33/64
5/8-11	UNC	11	5/8 (0.6250)	17/32
5/8-18	UNF	18	5/8 (0.6250)	37/64
3/4-10	UNC	10	3/4 (0.7500)	21/32
3/4-16	UNF	16	3/4 (0.7500)	11/16
7/8-9	UNC	9	7/8 (0.8750)	49/64
7/8-14	UNF	14	7/8 (0.8750)	13/16

Using Taps

A tap is a metal machining tool used to cut new internal threads. Dies are used to cut external threads (**FIGURE 4-31**). Three types of taps are used; taper, plug, and bottoming. A taper tap is the most common tap design for creating new threads. It's identified by tapered end where the first 8 to 10 cutting edges of the tap are as wide as the full tap diameter. Instead, the tapered cutters enable the tap to easily center in a hole and gradually begin cutting. A plug tap tapers only the first three to five cutting edges. If a hole is closed (called a blind hole), a bottoming tap is required to finish cutting threads after using a taper- or plug-type tap. Cutting edges of a bottoming tap are not tapered, allowing it to cut threads to the bottom of the hole.

When cutting threads, the tap or die is turned three or four rotations and then reversed for a single turn before cutting again. This practice prevents metal cuttings from clogging the flutes of the tap or die. Cutting oil or a lubricant, like WD-40, is used when cutting to ensure a clean and smooth thread finish.

Cutting dies are built with a split and an adjustable set screw. This screw is tightened or loosened to adjust the fitting clearance or tolerance of threads. Looser thread fits cuts external threads deeper into a material.

Thread Chasers

If external or internal threads are not severely damaged, or have only light to moderate corrosion, rather than drilling out an oversized hole and using a cutting tap to install new threads, a thread chaser is used. **Thread chasers** resemble cutting taps and dies without deep flutes to catch metal cuttings.

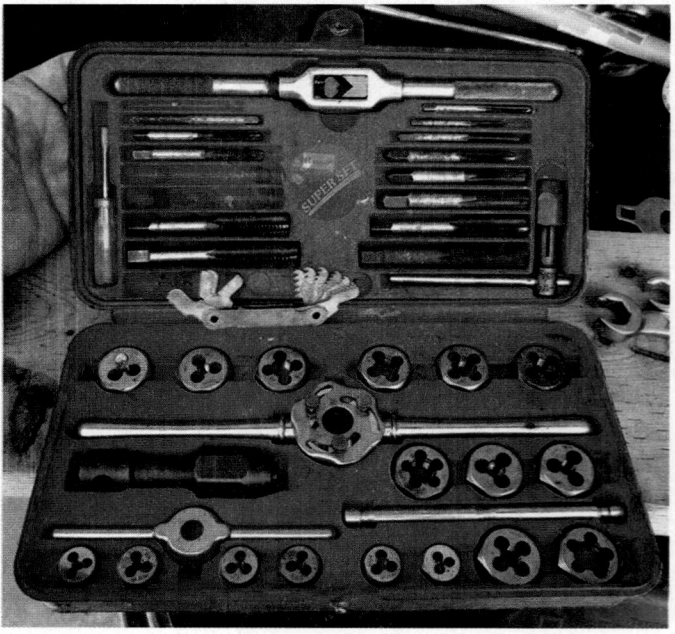

FIGURE 4-31 A set of taps and dies. Note the thread pitch gauge.

Chasers are designed to remove debris and rust and straighten bent threads. A thread file can be used on external threads, such as an axle spindle. An internal thread chaser or external thread file is used by first determining the thread count or pitch. Eight different thread pitches are used on one of several available rectangular-shaped thread files for repairing external threads (**FIGURE 4-32**). After selecting the correct thread on the file for external threads, the part is secured, and the file moved over damaged sections of thread to clean and straighten them. Remember that chasers have limited use and should only be used on moderately damaged threads; they cannot restore a thread to its original strength. Good practice for engine block bolts holes for cylinder heads is to chase threads before installing fasteners.

Epoxy Thread Repairs

In the instance where drilling is not possible, and access to a damaged thread is limited, a variety of two-part epoxy materials and high strength and temperature metal putty are available. This repair method is not intended for applications requiring high clamping force accompanied by high tensile stress and vibration. In both applications, the synthetic materials form the replacement threads (**FIGURE 4-33**). Repair kits are used several ways, depending on the extent of thread damage. The damaged or stripped hole can be drilled out and partly filled with an epoxy or putty. Next, the bolt or screw is installed, centered, and left there until the material hardens. Excess epoxy flows around and out the threaded hole, which must be immediately cleaned away. A release agent can be applied to the fastener to allow its removal after the thread epoxy or putty has cured. Another optional use chemical applied to the fastener can help it bond to the epoxy if removal is not anticipated.

A similar technique used to clean stripped internal threads in material, such as aluminum, is to clean with acetone cleaner. Epoxy or putty is applied to the fastener and the bolt or screw is threaded into place and left until the repair material cures.

FIGURE 4-32 A thread file is used to repair lightly damaged or corroded external threads.

Welding Thread Repair

If drilling an oversize hole is not possible, and the pull-out strength of threads must remain high, replacing damaged thread material can be done with metal filler applied by welding. In this technique, the threads are thoroughly cleaned to enable a metal inert gas (MIG) welder to apply contaminant-free metal to the walls of a hole with damaged threads. Ideally, the damaged thread is drilled out before welding. The MIG welder is used to run beads of new metal onto the walls of the damaged thread hole. Next, the hole is drilled, and a new thread is tapped. This technique can restore threads to almost original condition (**FIGURE 4-34**).

Threaded Inserts

When thread repairs require a high degree of pull-out strength, threaded inserts are a permanent repair option. Threaded inserts are high-quality internal thread repair kits that involve drilling damaged threads and installing an insert having the original thread dimensions. A common method to install the replacement insert is to tap the drilled hole with a thread that mates with an external thread on the insert. Two popular inserts use either a wire coil or solid inserts.

A wire coil thread repair insert, commonly known as a heli-coil, is made from wire with a diamond-shaped thread cross section (**FIGURE 4-35**). The heli-coil kit has a drill and non-standard tap for cutting threads in a drilled hole for the wire insert. Once the hole is drilled and tapped, the wire is threaded in the hole with thread-locking compound applied to the outside thread. Because it is coiled, the wire is installed with a tool that threads the insert by gripping it along a drive tang at the end of the coil. Twisting the coil into a threaded hole using the drive tang tightens the coil, making it smaller to ease installation. After the wire is completely threaded, a punch is used to break off the drive tang, which is removed before installing the fastener (**FIGURE 4-36**).

Solid inserts are installed into tapped threads or, in some cases, driven into the material. A slot for a screwdriver or drive

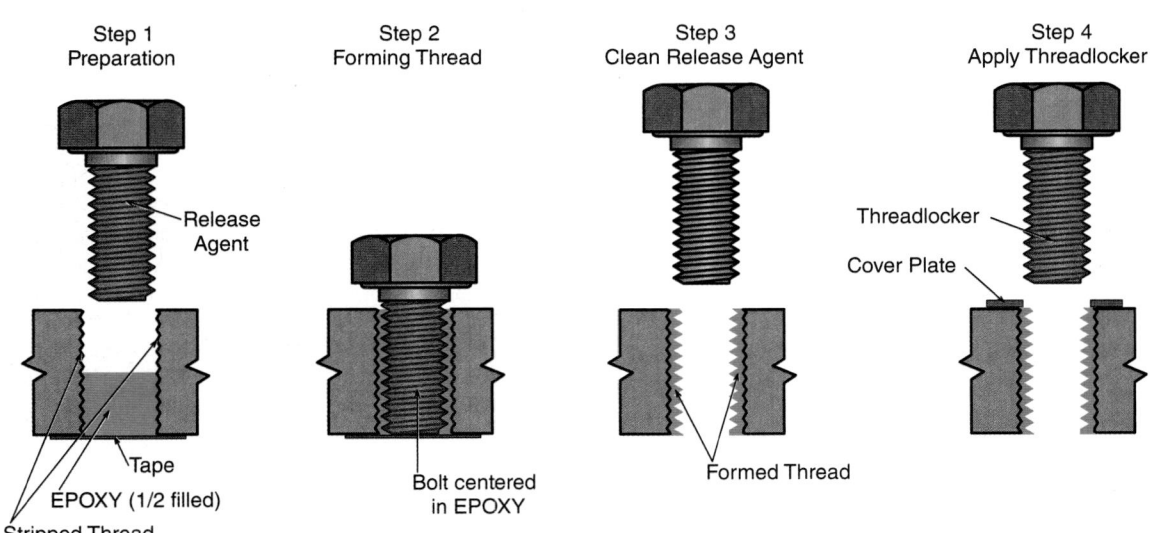

FIGURE 4-33 Steps to perform a thread repair using high temperature and strength epoxy.

tangs at the top of the insert are used to wind the insert into the threaded hole. Wedges or a thread locker are used to lock the insert in place (**FIGURE 4-37**).

Extracting Broken Fasteners

Eventually technicians will encounter broken and seized fasteners that potentially require labor-intensive steps to remove and repair any damaged threads. For every circumstance, there are a multitude of techniques and practices developed in the trade to extract fasteners. Internally threaded nuts that are seized can often be removed by heating with a torch to loosen the mating threads. Heat expands the inside diameter of the nut and creates clearance between mating surfaces. If the nut is simply corroded, thin petroleum solvents with lubricating properties can be applied that wick into the thread joint, separating parts enabling its removal. Another mechanical means is to use a nut splitter. This

is a metal clamp that surrounds the nut, but contains a threaded wedge. Tightening a screw behind the wedge forces the hardened V-shaped wedge into the nut, causing it to split (**FIGURE 4-38**). A variety of nut splitter sizes are made to best suit the diameter of the nut. In addition to splitters, specialized nut removal tools with internal eccentric cams engaged when rotated against a nut are used to provide a better grip on the surface of nut flats if it has its corners rounded over (**FIGURE 4-39**).

Thread Extractors

More commonly, technicians will need to remove a stud or cap screw broken below the surface of a part. The most dependable technique is to drill a pilot hole in its center and install one of many types of thread-extracting tools (**FIGURE 4-40**). These tools are called by numerous names. The general idea is these extractors use a left-hand thread or other cutting feature that grips the inside of the pilot hole. When turned to remove a

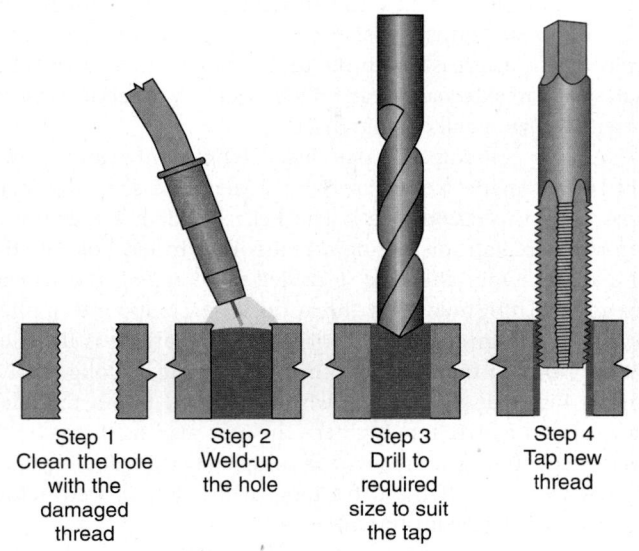

FIGURE 4-34 Steps involved in performing a welded thread repair.

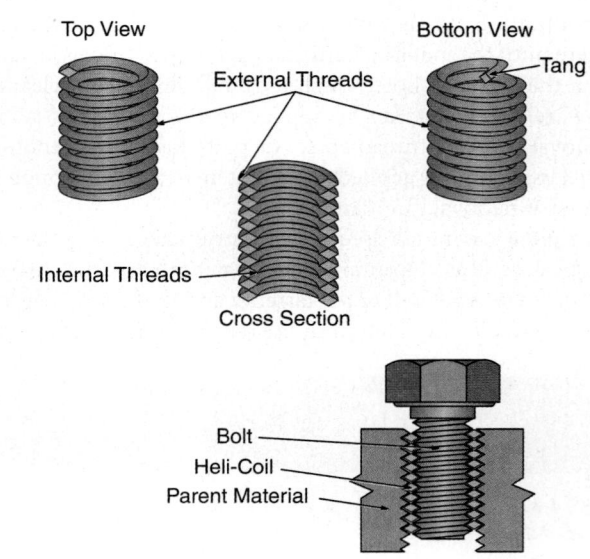

FIGURE 4-35 Features of a coiled wire heli-coil thread repair insert.

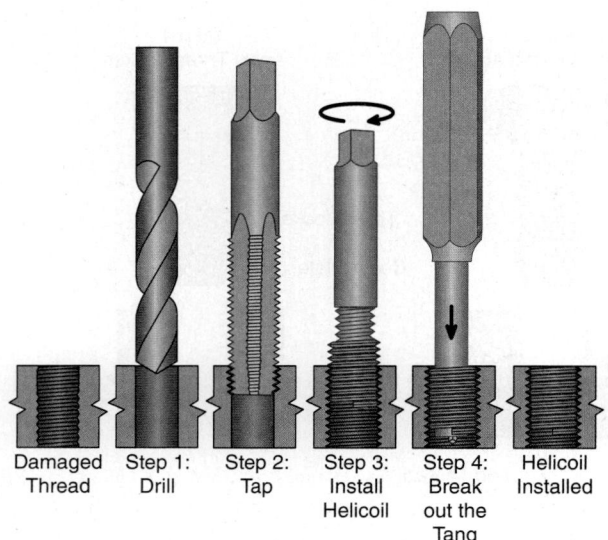

FIGURE 4-36 Steps involved in using a heli-coil thread repair method.

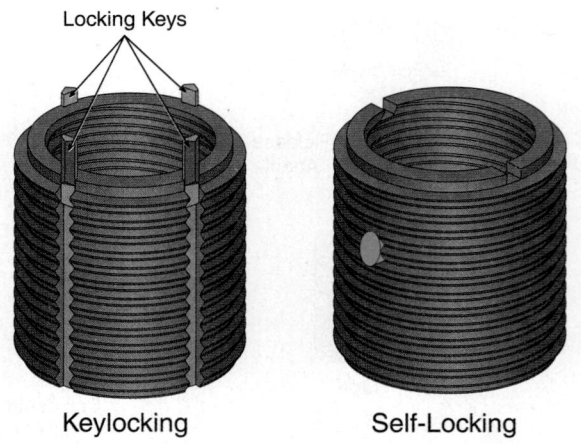

FIGURE 4-37 Solid thread insert repair kits can use locking tabs that are driven into the workpiece to fix its position.

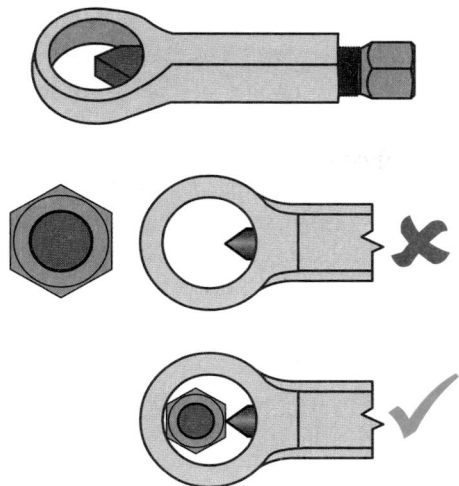

FIGURE 4-38 Operation of a nut splitter.

right-handed threaded fastener, the extractor digs further into the drilled pilot hole to ensure it grips the fastener with enough contact force to remove it. Heating the outside edges of a part helps expand and loosen mating threads, making release easier. Alternatively, left-hand drill bits can be used to drill pilot holes. Often, the rotation of the bit exerts enough torque to remove the broken fastener.

▶ TECHNICIAN TIP

The first step in removing seized and broken bolts is to flatten the surface at the end of the broken bolt. Where bolts have broken, the surface is often jagged and sloped, which causes the drill bit to wander off-center when attempting to drill the hole. A grinder is used to flatten the surface of a broken fastener broken above the work surface. When a cap screw is broken off below the surface of a threaded hole, a jagged break often can be flattened with punches to obtain a flatter surface for drilling.

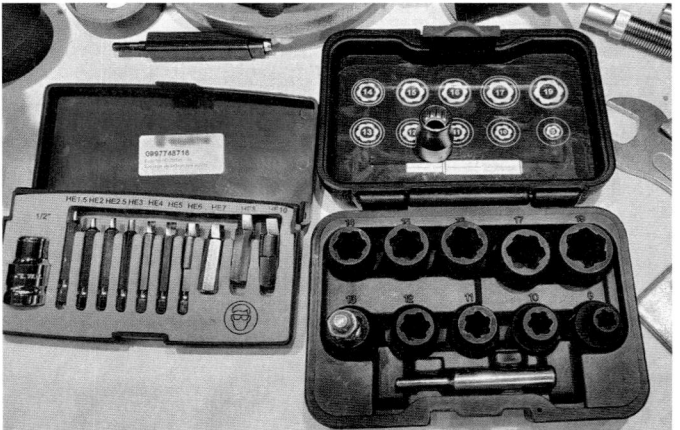

FIGURE 4-39 These sockets to the right of the other thread extractors are used to dig into the rounded flats of stripped nuts.

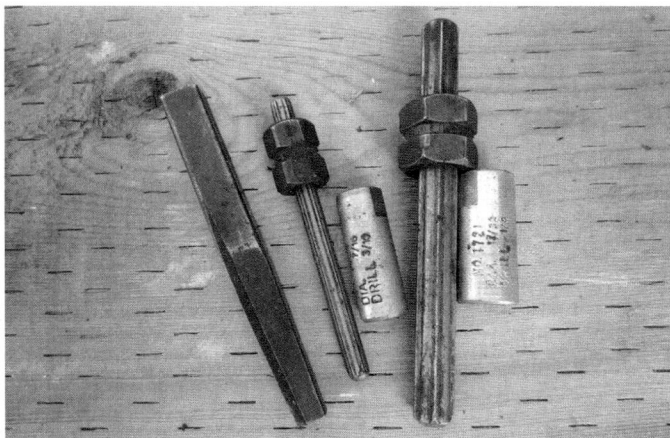

FIGURE 4-40 An E-Z out on the left, extractors with barrel type guides for centering of pilot drilled holes.

Wrap-Up

Ready for Review

▶ Threaded fasteners are a non-permanent method of fastening parts.

▶ Threads both convert and amplify the rotational or twisting force used to tighten fasteners into clamping force.

▶ The most common types of threaded fasteners are screws, bolts, and nuts.

▶ An externally threaded fastener is a screw. A screw becomes a bolt when it is used with a nut.

▶ Threaded fasteners are made by either rolling an external thread onto a blank shank or cut using a machine die.

▶ Rolled threads are much stronger than machine-cut threads.

▶ A finished fastener has a dark carbon steel appearance that may be oiled to give the threads some corrosion protection. A zinc coating gives fasteners a bright, shiny appearance and is the most common and economical method to protect fasteners from corrosion.

▶ Threads are also classified by whether they are right- or left-handed.

▶ Unified Thread Standard (UTS) use fractions of an inch or imperial measurements to establish fastener standards.

▶ UNC Coarse Thread and UNF fine thread are two common categories for UTS fasteners.

▶ Extra-fine thread series UTS fasteners are designated by the abbreviation UNEF and are called the Unified National Extra-Fine series.

▶ UTS fasteners are designated as major dimension X threads per inch.

▶ International Organization for Standardization (ISO) establishes standards for metric fasteners.

- Metric size fasteners are indicated as M (major diameter) x pitch. An M10 X 1.5 bolt specification means the major or largest diameter of the bolt is 10 mm and the thread pitch is 1.5 mm, which means it is a fine thread fastener.
- One of the most important mechanical properties of threaded fasteners is tensile strength, which indicates how strong the fastener is.
- Tensile strength refers to the breaking point of a fastener when it is stretched.
- UTS fastener strength is graded on an SAE scale of one to eight, with eight being the highest strength.
- Metric fasteners are classified by strength classes from 4.6 to 10.9, with 10.9 the strongest.
- Frames, steering gears, and hitching devices, such as fifth wheels and tow bar attachment points bolts, require a minimum of grade eight bolts or 10.9 M-series.
- Markings on the bearing side, which is the top and bottom nut surfaces, or number markers on the flat side designate nut grades and classes.
- Yield strength is a measurement of the fastener's ability to withstand tensile forces stretching a bolt and refers to the point the fastener is irreversibly distorted but not broken.
- Proof load is a factor that represents the maximum useable load limit of the fastener without measurably deforming it or its threads stripping.
- Broken bolts are the likeliest indication of fatigue-related failures caused by under tightening and the absence of correct preload or clamping force.
- Self-locking hardware is used to help prevent fastener loosening after preload force is lost or to prevent loss of preload tension.
- A spring washer and a serrated-edge toothed washer prevent fasteners from loosening.
- Threads can be repaired using thread chasers, drilling and tapping, using epoxy or metal putty, welding, or by using coiled wire or solid thread inserts.

Key Terms

bolts An externally threaded fastener used in combination with a nut to clamp a joint.

cap screw An externally threaded fastener that turns into a threaded hole.

die A metal machining tool used to cut external threads.

nuts An internally threaded fastener used in combination with a bolt to clamp a joint.

prevailing torque The amount of frictional torque possessed by a fastener that is used to resist loosening.

proof load A factor representing the maximum useable load limit of a fastener before deforming or its threads stripping.

screw An externally threaded fastener that turns into a hole that may or may not be threaded.

shear stress The force applied against a material along two different planes that acts on the material at a 90-degree angle.

stud An externally threaded fastener that does not have a head.

tap A metal machining tool used to cut internal threads.

thread chaser Metal working tool used to clean dirty, corroded, or damaged threads.

torque sticks A steel rod used as an extension on an impact gun used to limit maximum torque applied to a fastener.

Unified Thread Standard (UTS) A standard outlining the properties and characteristics of fasteners using imperial units of measurement.

Review Questions

1. Which of the following methods is used by threads to multiply rotational force into clamping force?
   a. Threads act as wedges to produce a mechanical advantage
   b. Threads act as a lever to produce a mechanical advantage
   c. Threads use an incline plane to produce a mechanical advantage
   d. Threads reduce friction between rotating parts
2. Which of the following combinations of fasteners contains a bolt?
   a. An externally threaded fastener with a nut on one end and the other end threaded into an iron casting
   b. An externally threaded fastener that threads into a hole on a transmission
   c. An externally threaded fastener clamping a frame cross-member using a nut
   d. An externally threaded fastener that forms its own threads when inserted into a hole
3. Which of the following types of heads will a cap screw use if there is adequate access and space for a wrench or socket?
   a. Internal hex head
   b. External Torx head
   c. A twelve-point head
   d. Hex head
4. Which of the following combinations of threads are strongest and most resistant to stripping?
   a. Rolled coarse threads
   b. Machine-cut fine threads
   c. Machine-cut coarse threads
   d. Rolled fine threads
5. Which of the following forces acting on a fastener is greatest when it is correctly preloaded?
   a. Tensile load
   b. Shear load
   c. Proof load
   d. Elastic load
6. Consider a bolt with a tensile strength of 120,000 psi. Which of the following situations will most likely cause a fatigue failure resulting in a fractured bolt?
   a. A preload force of 3000 psi
   b. A preload force of 30,000 psi

c. A preload force of 75,000 psi

d. A preload force of 90,000 psi

7. Which of the following tightening methods produces the most accurate preload force on a threaded fastener?

a. Using a torque stick

b. Using an accurately calibrated torque wrench

c. Technician judgement

d. Torque-turn method

8. Which of the following fasteners will support the most load?

a. 3/8" UNC SAE Grade 2

b. M10 X 1.5 Class 10.9

c. M8 x 1.5 Class 8.8

d. 7/16" UNF SAE Grade 5

9. Consider a bolt that is distorted and necked. Which of the bolt's following strength properties has been exceeded by the damaging force?

a. Its yield strength

b. Its tensile strength

c. Its prevailing torque

d. Its shear strength

10. Which thread repair method will have the least capacity to prevent threads from stripping again or has the lowest thread pull-out strength?

a. Welding and tapping threads

b. Drilling an oversize hole and tapping

c. Using a threaded insert

d. Using an epoxy as a thread repair technique

ASE Technician A/Technician B Style Questions

1. Technician A and B were discussing the size and type of cap screws to use to attach a PTO mounting bracket to a cast iron transmission case. Technician A says that fine-threaded cap screws should be used because they have stronger threads than coarse-threaded ones. Technician B says coarse-threaded fastener threads should be used in soft cast material. Who is correct?

a. Technician A

b. Technician B

c. Both Technician A and Technician B

d. Neither Technician A nor Technician B

2. Technician A and B were discussing which grade of bolts to use to attach a pintle tow hook to a tractor frame. Technician A says that Metric class 10.9 would be acceptable. Technician B says that Grade 8s are required. Who is correct?

a. Technician A

b. Technician B

c. Both Technician A and Technician B

d. Neither Technician A nor Technician B

3. After taking over a brake job from another technician, Technician A and B found a box of wheel studs and nuts with both right- and left-hand threads. Technician A said that the left-hand threaded fasteners should be installed on the left-side wheels. Technician B said the left-handed threads should go on the right side to prevent a wheel separation. Who is correct?

a. Technician A

b. Technician B

c. Both Technician A and Technician B

d. Neither Technician A nor Technician B

4. Technician A said that a class 9 nut should not be matched with a class 9.8 bolt because its threads are not as strong as the bolt. Technician B said that a softer nut strength will help prevent threads from pulling or stripping when tightened. Who is correct?

a. Technician A

b. Technician B

c. Both Technician A and Technician B

d. Neither Technician A nor Technician B

5. Technician A says that lubricating fastener threads enables more rotational force to convert to preload and clamping force. Technician B says that zinc-plated fasteners do not require lubrication to reduce thread resistance. Who is correct?

a. Technician A

b. Technician B

c. Both Technician A and Technician B

d. Neither Technician A nor Technician B

6. Technician A says that a fastener that's tightened even a small amount above its maximum torque is more likely to break than one properly tightened. Technician B says that a fastener that is under tightened is much more likely to break than one that's tightened slightly too much. Who is correct?

a. Technician A

b. Technician B

c. Both Technician A and Technician B

d. Neither Technician A nor Technician B

7. Technician A says that tightening a fastener using a torque wrench is the most accurate method to ensure preload tension on a fastener is correct. Technician B says that thread friction can cause wide variations in preload tension after tightening a fastener. Who is correct?

a. Technician A

b. Technician B

c. Both Technician A and Technician B

d. Neither Technician A nor Technician B

8. Technician A says that using prevailing torque flange nuts and flange bolts are the best fasteners to use on truck frames. Technician B says that SAE grade 8 or class 9.8 M series fasteners with flat washers and lock washers are just as effective. Who is correct?

a. Technician A

b. Technician B

c. Both Technician A and Technician B

d. Neither Technician A nor Technician B

9. Technician A says that to repair stripped threads in a bell housing used to attach a transmission, it is best to drill out the damaged thread and install a larger diameter fastener after tapping new threads. Technician B says that the

thickness of the bell housing face is too narrow to drill and install an oversize fastener, and the hole threads should be welded and tapped instead. Who is correct?

a. Technician A
b. Technician B
c. Both Technician A and Technician B
d. Neither Technician A nor Technician B

10. Technician A says that a taper tap is used to cut new threads in a blind hole. Technician B says that a bottoming tap is needed to cut threads to the bottom of the hole. Who is correct?

a. Technician A
b. Technician B
c. Both Technician A and Technician B
d. Neither Technician A nor Technician B

CHAPTER 5

Hand Tools

Learning Objectives

- **LO 5-1** Identify basic hand and air tools and storage practices.
- **LO 5-2** Identify and describe the types, features, and proper use of wrenches.
- **LO 5-3** Identify and describe the types, features, and proper use of sockets and ratchets.
- **LO 5-4** Identify and describe the types, features, and proper use of torque wrenches.
- **LO 5-5** Identify and describe the types, features, and proper use of screwdrivers.
- **LO 5-6** Identify and describe the types, features, and proper use of pliers.
- **LO 5-7** Identify and describe the features and proper use of hacksaws, punches, and chisels.
- **LO 5-8** Identify and describe the types, features, and proper use of hammers.
- **LO 5-9** Identify and describe the types, features, and proper use of pullers.
- **LO 5-10** Identify and describe the types and applications of measuring tools.
- **LO 5-11** Identify and describe the use of impact wrenches.

You Are the Technician

As an experienced technician in your shop, you are often tasked with orientating and mentoring new workers. Many of these new hires have minimal experience working in a medium-heavy duty commercial vehicle repair facility and are new graduates of truck and coach repair programs. A new graduate of a commercial vehicle program is assigned to work alongside you for the next three months to learn practical shop safety, the use of hand tools and service practices in your major skill sets. This means the apprentice will frequently assist in performing work on engines, brakes and steering systems. To ensure consistency in what you are teaching each apprentice and because performance evaluations are based on skill competencies (the ability to successfully perform specific tasks) you are preparing a checklist of topics and items you want to review with each new technician. As you prepare these lists and topical outlines include the following points in your list.

1. If the apprentice has few tools to begin working with, identify which tools and the type of tool box they should prioritize acquiring in the first year.
2. What are the important features the apprentice should look for when selecting socket sets for air tools and hand-operated ratchets?
3. What is the range of wrench sizes and socket types and sizes the apprentice should acquire?

Introduction

Commercial vehicle technicians will purchase and use a large number and types of tools throughout their career that are indispensable to the tasks they perform every day, so the importance of properly selecting and working with hand tools cannot be overestimated. Choosing the correct tool and using it properly is critical to performing work efficiently, accurately, and safely. Damage to vehicles and components is also avoided with the proper selection and use of tools for a specific job. Since a technician's efficiency is directly related to his or her skill and selection of his or her tools, understanding the function and use of each tool — knowing the best tool to do the job — is important. This chapter examines commonly used hand tools, including air-powered tools, to help new technicians to not only correctly identify them, but also to properly select and use tools.

Tool Storage

LO 5-1 Identify basic hand and air tools and storage practices.

Safe, secure storage of tools in an organized manner is the reason technicians purchase a tool box to store their personal tools and equipment. Boxes are made of heavy-gauge sheet metal with a variety of different sizes and depth of drawers to neatly arrange tools. Most drawers are shallow to increase the number of drawers in a cabinet and provide ready access to tools without needing to dig and sort through other tools to find the necessary tool. Good quality tool boxes use ball bearing slides on the drawers and double walled, thick-gauge sheet metal to increase durability. Technicians working on commercial vehicles typically purchase a top tool chest and a lower roll cabinet with casters to enable easy movement of their tools around a shop, while enabling close proximity of tools to the service area on a vehicle. Roll cabinets are often the first storage cabinet purchased until a technician acquires more tools and needs the additional storage capacity of a top chest placed on a roll cabinet. Additional side cabinets are used to store larger bulkier items, and supplies, such as aerosols, lubricants, and other disposable shop items (**FIGURE 5-1**).

Specialty tools are often kept in blow-molded tool cases with cut-outs to organize individual pieces. Misplaced or missing tools are quickly identified with this arrangement (**FIGURE 5-2**). Roll cabinets generally have larger deeper drawers for storing heavier bulkier tools, such as impact guns, 3/4" drive socket sets, seat covers, and trouble lights. The top chest stores frequently used socket sets, and wrenches just under the lid where they are easily accessed without pulling out drawers. Magnetic or mechanical clips position tools to keep them organized. Other frequently used tools, such as pliers, combination wrenches, screwdrivers, hammers, and small air tools, such as ratchets, are stored in the top chest.

Good Tool Storage Habits

The toolbox is often an overlooked element of a technician's tool assets, but it is a focal point for efficient safe work practices and organization. Professional technicians working in truck shops where tools must be rolled to different work areas choose to store tools in a rolling cabinet or mobile workstation.

FIGURE 5-1 A roll cabinet with a top and bottom storage chest.

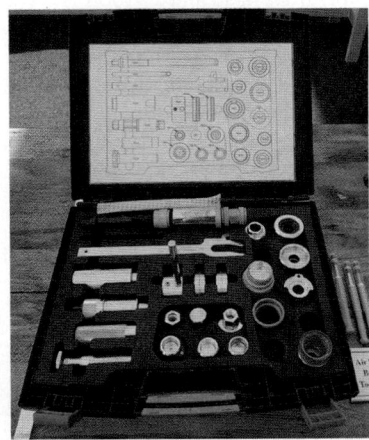

FIGURE 5-2 Specialty tools, like these for servicing air disc brakes, are best stored in blow-molded cases.

A rolling cabinet is a toolbox on wheels that provides storage for all a technician's personal hand and air-operated tools. It consists of a metal frame that contains a variety of drawers of different widths and depths to accommodate large and small tools. Good quality, wide, ball bearing caster wheels on at least each corner of the frame are essential for easy maneuvering around equipment in shops. For boxes that are frequently moved, rigidity is built into them using double- or even triple-walled construction reinforcements with many closely spaced spot welds holding drawers and frames together. While metal gauge for tool box is between 14 and 22 gauge, with the smaller number being thicker metal, a good quality stronger box is typically made from 16 gauge sheet metal. Ball bearing drawer slides on the most frequently used drawers containing the heaviest tools are essential.

Points to remember about tool storage include:

- Organize and store tools in a proper storage place. A tool is useless if it cannot be easily found. Frequently used tools are generally stored at eye level in top chests. Categories of tools are best grouped in specific areas. For example, all sockets, screwdrivers, or wrenches are located together in a drawer, storage tray, or in rails with clips to hold sockets. If each tool is returned to its proper place after use, there will be no trouble or time lost locating it again.

- Keep tools in good condition. Clean tools after use to keep them free from dirt and grease. Cracked, nicked, burred, or rusted tools can become safety hazards. Quickly replace any missing or damaged tools to keep tool sets complete.
- Before storing or using any tool with a handle, make certain tool handles are securely attached.
- When storing and handling edged tools, be aware of the injuries they can inflict while retrieving or handling them.
- Never store or carry pointed tools, such as screwdrivers, or edged tools in pockets or coverall. The tools can not only injure with one wrong movement, but can scrape paint and damage or puncture items such as seats and upholstery, when moving around inside a vehicle.
- Grind away burrs and repair any tool damage before storing a tool. Do not use punches with improperly sharpened points or mushroomed striking heads. Chips and pieces of the tools can fly away and injure users or those working around them.

Wrenches

LO 5-2 Identify and describe the types, features, and proper use of wrenches.

Wrenches are used to tighten or loosen nuts, bolts, couplings, pipe plugs, and line fittings. Specialized wrenches, such as pipe wrenches, are designed to grip round stock, such as pipes, tie rods, and large studs. Several types of wrenches are frequently used during repair and maintenance (**FIGURE 5-3**).

Open-End Wrenches

As the name suggests, the wrench has an end that slides over a bolt or nut on at least two sides, leaving one side open. To enable the wrench to slip over a fastener, its opening is typically from 0.005" to 0.015" larger than the dimension stamped into the wrench (**FIGURE 5-4**). Open-end wrenches' size range in steps beginning with 5/32" upward in steps of 1/32", up to 1-3/4" or 5 mm to 45 mm in one-millimeter increments. Wrench length is proportional to the open end with wider wrenches being increasingly thicker and longer to add more leverage and strength to use with larger fasteners. Open ends of the wrench are formed at an angle between 10 degrees and 23 degrees to the body of the wrench for close quarter work. The offset angle of the wrench allows it to flip over and turn a fastener head where movement is limited (**FIGURE 5-5**).

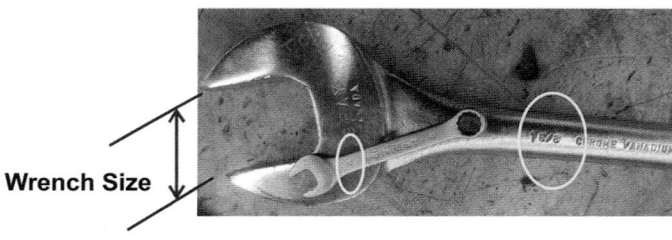

Wrench Size

FIGURE 5-3 The size of a wrench is stamped into the body and refers to the width of the opening or diameter of the boxed end.

Box-End Wrenches

Box-end wrenches are called by this name because they completely surround, or box, a capscrew head or nut (**FIGURE 5-6**). The advantage of a box-end wrench is it has more points to grip the hex shaped head of a fastener and does not slip as easily as an open-end wrench. Rather than grip the corners of a fastener head, it grips its flats. Using straight or offset handles, these wrenches have 6 or 12 points forming a circle around a fastener. This means as little as one sixth or a

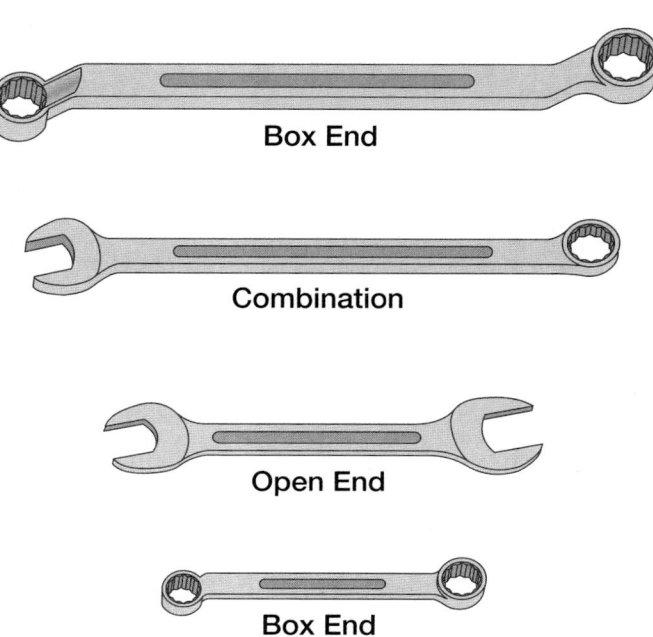

Box End

Combination

Open End

Box End

FIGURE 5-4 Boxed, combination, and open-end wrenches. The wrench size refers to the width of the head of the fastener the wrench is used to loosen or tighten.

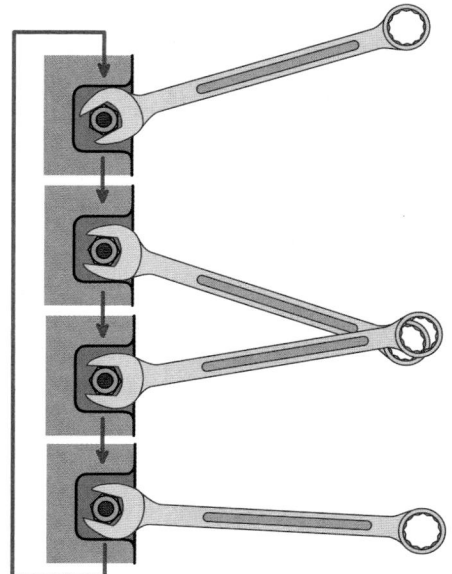

FIGURE 5-5 The offset angle of an open-end wrench enables it to easily remove a fastener where access is limited.

FIGURE 5-6 A combination wrench with one end open and the other boxed compared with a box-end wrench.

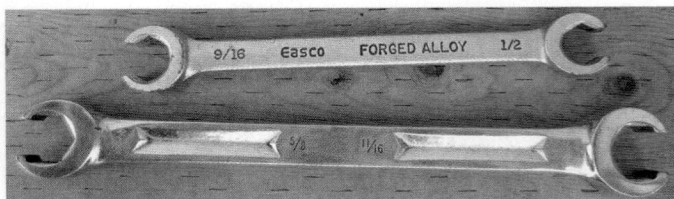

FIGURE 5-8 A line wrench has five sides to resist slippage.

FIGURE 5-7 These electrically insulated box-end ratchet wrenches are used for electrical work on electric and hybrid drive vehicles.

twelfth of a turn is needed to rotate a fastener in an enclosed space. Box-end wrench sizes refer to the diameter of the fastener head and are available in the same sizes as open-end wrenches stepping-up in increments of 1/32" or 1 mm. They usually have two different size openings on each end. Ratchet box wrenches are also used where access is limited, where their thin size is an advantage in tight spaces (**FIGURE 5-7**).

Line Wrenches

The slip-resistant grip of a box-end wrench cannot be duplicated when a wrench is needed to fit over a line nut, but a line wrench attempts to provide greater slip resistance than an open-end wrench. Line wrenches have five sides and are used to loosen line nuts, such as those on hydraulic brake lines, injector lines, or air brake hoses. With the additional sides, line wrenches do not bend open or slip as easily as a regular open-end wrench (**FIGURE 5-8**).

Combination Wrenches

Combination open and box wrenches are the most commonly used wrenches due to their versatility, having one open end and one box end on the same wrench. These combination wrenches are generally used on any fastener where a socket and ratchet cannot be used. The open end will be on either a 15-degree or 22 1/2-degree angle to the handle. The box end is offset 15 degrees to the handle. A popular type of combination wrench is a stubby handle wrench. Again, where access to fasteners is limited or there is interference with a wrench having a longer handle, a stubby is an efficient choice. Unlike open or box-end-only

FIGURE 5-9 A stubby wrench is a combination wrench with a short handle.

wrenches, combination wrenches have fewer step-up increment sizes. Generally, they increase in size in increments of 1/16" for Society of Automotive Engineers (SAE) fasteners and 1 mm for metric fasteners with several metric sizes above 15 mm infrequently used. New technicians require a set of combination wrenches ranging from 5/16" up to 1-5/16" and 8 mm to 24 or 32 mm for work on commercial vehicles. Larger, specialized wrench sizes are generally supplied by the shop. These larger Boxed-end and open-end-only wrenches larger than 1-5/16th" or 32 mm are not commonly purchased by technicians. (**FIGURE 5-9**).

Crowfoot Wrenches

A crowfoot wrench is a short open-end wrench containing a square drive opening that fits a 3/8" or 1/2" drive ratchet extensions. These wrenches are commonly used on brass or hydraulic fittings in deep, limited access areas where a normal wrench or socket cannot be used (**FIGURE 5-10**).

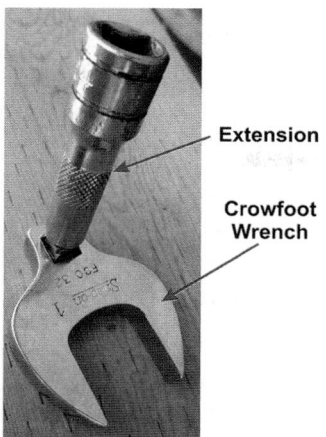

FIGURE 5-10 A crowfoot wrench is a short open-end wrench containing a square drive.

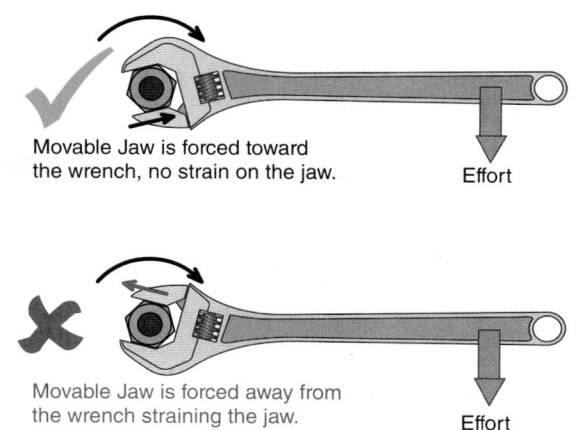

FIGURE 5-11 An adjustable wrench is an open-end wrench with an opening that can be varied to fit a wide size range of bolts, nuts, or pipe plugs. When using an adjustable wrench, the fix jaw should be orientated over the fastener to receive the most pressure.

Adjustable Wrenches

Adjustable wrenches have a movable jaw to change the size of opening needed to fit the head of a fastener (**FIGURE 5-11**). A serrated jaw adjusting screw helps hold the adjustment in position. One jaw is movable and fits into a sliding guide, while the other is fixed. Because the fixed jaw is part of the wrench body, it can handle bending stress better than the movable jaw. This means the tool should be orientated over a fastener and pushed to loosen fasteners with the moving jaw farther away from the user than the fixed jaw. Operating the wrench like this puts more pressure on the fixed jaw and less on the movable jaw. The movable jaw also tends to pry open when more pressure is placed on it. When tightening fasteners, the movable jaw should be closer to the user than the fixed jaw. Because the jaws have some loose operating clearances, the wrench is not intended for use on tight fasteners. This wrench is best adapted for use on pipe fittings of soft brass or large steel hydraulic or air system fittings.

> ► **TECHNICIAN TIP**
>
> Push or pull? If a wrench or ratchet slips when pushing against it, knuckles can be skinned and forward balance may be lost. A worse situation could potentially happen if balance is lost while pulling a wrench. Arms cannot break a fall and one cannot see objects to avoid while stumbling or falling backwards. This means it's generally safer to push rather than pull a tool. When strenuously pushing a wrench or ratchet to loosen a tight fastener, it is also helpful to push with an open hand to minimize damage to knuckles if a slip does take place.

Pipe Wrenches

Pipe wrenches are designed for use on pipes or other round materials, such as tie rods or adjustable suspension arms. The wrench has an adjusting nut, rather than an adjusting screw, and its jaws are at a 90-degree angle to the handle (**FIGURE 5-12**). The adjusting nut is tightened so the jaws of the wrench securely grip the round pipe stock before applying pressure on the wrench

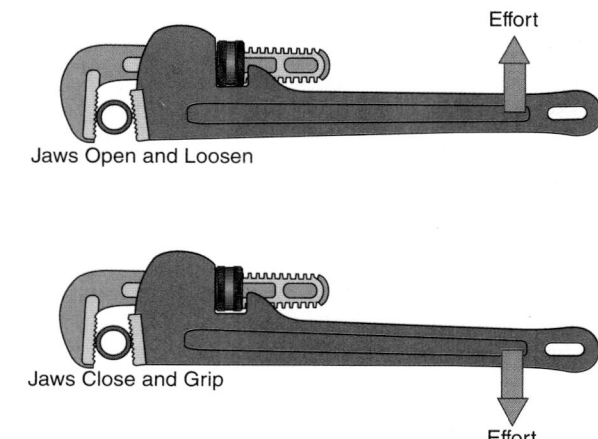

FIGURE 5-12 The pipe wrench must be turned to place the most pressure on the fixed jaw in order to grip pipe stock.

handle. Teeth on the jaw grip a pipe or tube well because the adjustable jaw pieces are slightly loose when first slipped over the work piece. Next, when force is applied to the handle, the slightly loose and adjustable jaw is designed to move slightly and tighten on the material, gripping it more firmly with increasing force applied to the handle. Like the adjustable wrench, one jaw is fixed while the other is movable. Like the adjustable wrench, the fixed lower jaw should have the greatest pressure applied to it to tighten the jaw grip. This means when either tightening or loosening a threaded device, the jaw opening must be facing the user when pulling on the wrench and away from the user when pushing.

Chain and Filter Wrenches

The chain wrench is a length of chain connected at each end by a piece of square stock steel with an insert for a 1/2" drive. These devices are very useful when removing large, oversized,

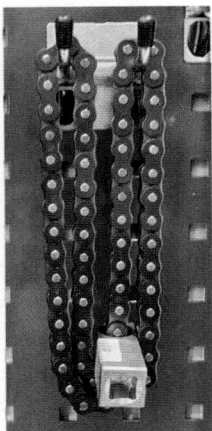

FIGURE 5-13 A chain wrench is used with a long-handled ratchet, wrench or breaker bar to remove filters or hold materials.

FIGURE 5-14 A set of 3/8" drive sockets with a ratchet, socket extensions, and universal joint.

but tightly seized, filters when combined with a long-handled ratchet wrench. Round or irregularly shaped materials, such as hydraulic cylinders or shafts, are gripped using chain wrenches. Some chains have small pins through an end link that allow adjustments to the chain length. A long steel 1/2" extension can also insert into the chain to provide better maneuverability around a component. When using a chain wrench, it should always adjust to the tightest possible position when initially gripping materials, while ensuring the ratchet, wrench, or extension turning the chain is at a 90-degree angle to the work when snugged and before applying heavy force. A 90-degree angle to the work provides the greatest leverage (**FIGURE 5-13**). Filter wrenches are made of metal or heavy fabric bands used to slip over and remove tight filters. Various sizes are available to accommodate small, medium, and large filter diameters.

Sockets and Ratchets

LO 5-3 Identify and describe the types, features, and proper use of sockets and ratchets.

Sockets, sometimes called socket wrenches, are the most commonly used tools to remove and install nuts and bolts. Attached to a ratchet handle, they are the fastest hand-operated tools to tighten and loosen fasteners (**FIGURE 5-14**). The ratchet head contains a reversible one-way clutch that freewheels or slips in one direction and applies torque in another. A small lever or dial at the back of the ratchet head is moved to change the direction the ratchet freewheels, and the direction torque is applied (**FIGURE 5-15**). Because the socket stays on the fastener head and the ratchet handle is swung back and forth, no time is wasted lifting the socket from the work piece. This enables the combined ratchet and socket to remove and install fasteners much faster than using a wrench. The common socket is a metal cylinder-shaped tool with 6 or 12 points to fit over fastener heads and a square hole at the other end used to connect with a square ratchet drive. Ratchet size is determined by the width of its drive and are

FIGURE 5-15 A lever on this ratchet switches the direction that torque is applied.

available as either 1/4", 3/8", 1/2", 3/4", or 1" (**FIGURE 5-16**). Technicians should initially require a 1/4", 3/8", and 1/2" drive ratchet and socket sets with deep and shallow sockets ranging from 1/4" to 1-5/16" or 5 mm to 32 mm. Sockets are available in steps of 32nds, 16ths, or 8ths of an inch. Metric sizes increment in 1 mm steps. The ratchet handles are available in various lengths, with the 1/2" drive ratchet available in several longer handles to provide additional leverage. Breaker bars have a square socket drive, but without a ratchet head, for applying very high amounts of force. Breaker bars are substituted for ratchets to prevent damage to a ratchet mechanism that is not designed to handle very high

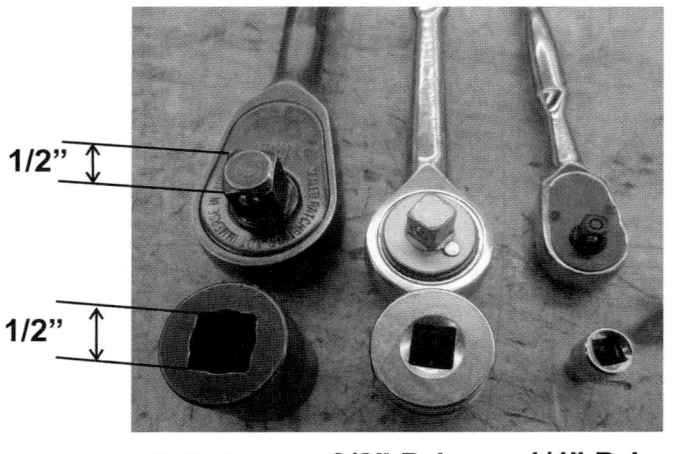

FIGURE 5-16 The size of a ratchet is determined by the width of the drive. The handle is much longer though.

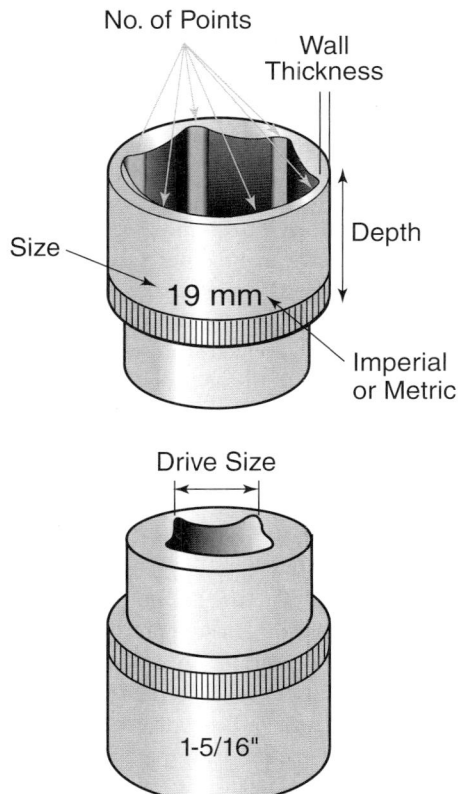

FIGURE 5-17 Features of a socket used with a ratchet wrench.

FIGURE 5-18 Stamped steel sockets for hub nuts.

FIGURE 5-19 Examples of deep 6-point and deep 12-point shallow impact and shallow 12-point chrome sockets.

Sockets

Quality sockets are made from forged alloyed steel. Corrosion-resistant chrome, smooth, thin-walled sockets are used with hand-operated ratchets to fit around nuts and bolts with tight clearances. Twelve-point sockets are thinner walled than 6-point sockets but can crack easier under high torque and slip more easily since 12-point gaps are not as deep as gaps in 6-point sockets (**FIGURE 5-19**). Thicker-walled sockets are used with air impact tools and are not chromed since the hammering action flakes thin chrome into razor-sharp pieces (**FIGURE 5-20**). Impact sockets are recognizable by their flat black color and thick socket walls. Larger sized 3/4" and 1" drive sockets have a locking pin on the ratchet at the drive end that is used to help prevent impact sockets from spinning off high-speed impact guns (**FIGURE 5-21**). Smaller sockets use a spring and detent ball that fits into an indentation in the internal socket drive area to hold the socket onto the drive.

Sockets are available in deep and shallow types and selected depending on the length of stud or bolt the socket must fit over. Universal swivel adapters or flexible sockets enable sockets to be used in difficult-to-access places with an extension driving the socket at an angle (**FIGURE 5-22**).

break-away force required to loosen tight fasteners. Three-quarter-inch drive ratchets can be as long as four to six feet and are usually supplied by the shop. Sockets are typically sized from up to 3-1/8" in steps of 32nds, 16ths, or 8ths of an inch or up to 85 mm in increments of 1 mm (**FIGURE 5-17**). Larger stamped steel 3/4" drive hub nut sockets are also available (**FIGURE 5-18**).

FIGURE 5-20 The flat black socket on the right has a thicker wall that is stronger and intended for use on impact guns, as well as air ratchets. Society of Automotive Engineers.

FIGURE 5-21 A 1" drive ratchet head and a socket with a locking pin.

FIGURE 5-22 A universal flex ½" impact socket.

FIGURE 5-23 A set of internal and external Torx sockets. Security Torx are along the bottom row.

While sockets are commonly driven with hand ratchets, air ratchets, and impact guns, a variety of other drivers can increase torque or speed up operations. Breaker bars are non-ratcheting handles with additional handle length to multiply torque. Speed handles and T bars are also sometimes used when air tools are not available or practical to use.

Torx Sockets

Invented in the 1960s, Torx head screws were designed to resist slipping better than hex head or other types of fastener heads (**FIGURE 5-23**). The unique six-lobed shape of a Torx head is best able to resist a condition called cam-out where a socket or screw driver slips when pressure is applied against fastener corners. Contact pressure of the socket with the walls of the fastener is at 90 degrees, which is the best contact for transmitting torque. This means higher torque can be applied through a Torx fastener than a conventional internal or external hex head socket, without damaging the fastener or tool (**FIGURE 5-24**). Torx sockets are available for internal and external types of screw fasteners. For internal sockets, Torx head sizes use the prefix "T" followed by a number ranging from T1 to T100. The smaller number size corresponds to a smaller socket dimension and the number corresponds to a specific distance across the socket lobes. Security Torx, or Tamper-Resistant Torx, uses a pin in the center of the head that prevents a standard Torx driver or screwdriver from being inserted into a fastener head and used to turn the fastener. External Torx sockets are used primarily on transmissions and engines. A prefix "E" designates external Torx that range from E4 to E44, with the lower number corresponding to the smaller socket dimension.

Hex Head or Allen Sockets

To enable the use of smaller bolt heads, internal hex sockets, commonly called Allen sockets or Allen wrenches, are used. Hex sockets and hex keys, dimensions are measured between two opposite and parallel flat sides of the socket. Imperial and metric sizes are available (**FIGURE 5-25**). When constructed with a ball socket on the end of a hex key, the ball end enables turning the screw with the tool at an angle (**FIGURE 5-26**).

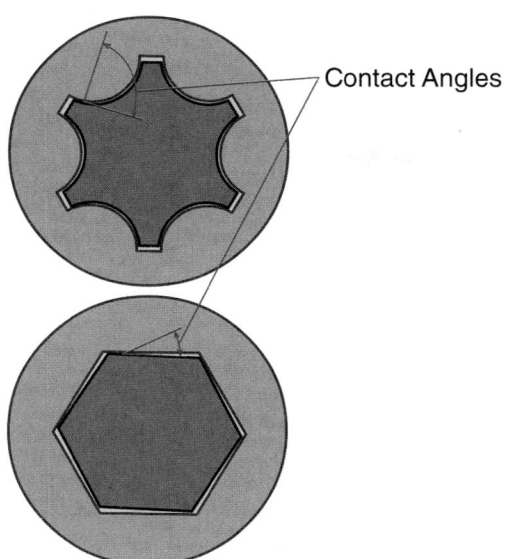

FIGURE 5-24 Torx head screws resist cam-out or tool slippage better than other types of fastener heads.

FIGURE 5-25 Hex head sockets are used to enable the use of more compact bolt heads.

FIGURE 5-26 A set of ball socket hex keys.

Torque Wrenches

LO 5-4 Identify and describe the types, features, and proper use of torque wrenches.

Torque wrenches are precision tools used to apply and measure a twisting force to fasteners. Chapter 4 explained the importance of establishing correct preload on fasteners to prevent breakage and loosening. Correctly clamping

FIGURE 5-27 Torque wrenches are used to apply a precise amount of force to a fastener to obtain the correct fastener preload or stretch.

joints, such as a cylinder head to engine block or delicate transmission valve bodies, need uniform clamping force to prevent warpage and leakage between the joint surfaces. Wheel ends also require correct clamping force to prevent fastener damage and wheel separation. When selecting a torque wrench, the correct capacity must be chosen to prevent overloading the wrench. The desired torque setting should be approximately in the middle two quarters of the wrenches working range. For example, a torque wrench with a maximum capacity of 400 ft-lb (542 N m) supplies the best accuracy when tightening fasteners in the 200 to 300 ft-lb (271 to 407 Nm) range.

Torque is calculated by multiplying the force applied to a lever by its length (Torque = Force X Length).

Three basic types of torque wrenches are commonly used:

- Beam-Type Torque Wrenches
- Dial-Type Torque Wrenches
- Indicating Torque Wrenches (**FIGURE 5-27**)

Beam-Type Torque Wrenches

Beam-type torque wrenches have a calibrated length lever with an additional long rod or beam indicator attached at only the drive end of the wrench. The beam bends in response to the twisting force applied to the drive end. At the other end of the beam is a scale that is calibrated to measure the torque applied to the drive end. Because the beam bending, or deflection, is proportional to applied torque, the scale provides a reliable indication of the twisting force applied.

Dial-Type Torque Wrenches

Dial-type torque wrenches use a mechanical linkage assembly that converts the twisting force at the socket drive end to rotary dial movement on a gauge located near the handle end. These wrenches are a preferred device for measuring rotating torque, such as bearing preloads or making an over-center adjustment on a steering gear.

Signaling-Type Torque Wrenches

As the name suggests, signaling-type torque wrenches provide some audible or mechanical feedback felt in the handle when a preselected torque is reached. Typically, a click is heard as a tensioning spring inside the wrench breaks-over or reaches its torque setting. The signal-type wrench is used when adjusting torque to a specific setting and where watching an indicator is

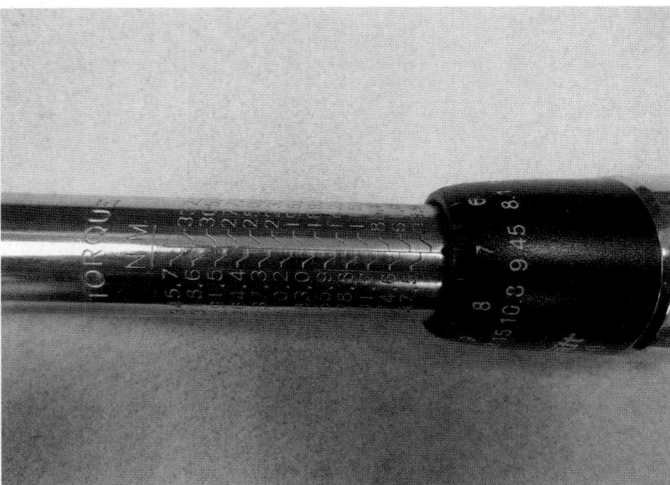

FIGURE 5-28 To adjust the torque wrench signal, an adjustable knob over an indicator scale is turned to increase or decrease the point signaled for a specified torque.

not practical. This type of torque wrench has a ratchet end built into the drive, unlike dial- or beam-type torque wrenches. A torque-adjustment mechanism is usually located in the handle where an internal spring is tensioned by turning a knob at the end of the handle. After adjusting fastener preload using a desired torque setting, the tensioning spring should always be positioned in a relaxed position before storing the wrench (**FIGURE 5-28**).

▶ TECHNICIAN TIP

When tightening fasteners with torque wrenches, a smooth continuous movement is required to obtain precise torque measurement. Slowing or momentarily stopping the wrench motion results in an incorrect measurement since torque increases when speeding up. Break-away torque from a stationary fastener is always higher than applied torque too. When using socket extensions, torque is lost through the spring action of the extension. A general rule of thumb is 5 ft-lb (6.8 Nm) of torque is lost through a 6" (15.2 cm) extension. When using extensions, the loss of torque must be added to the original setting.

▶ TECHNICIAN TIP

In International Organization for Standardization (ISO)-certified shops, torque wrenches must be regularly tested and calibrated at the 20% range and the 100% range of operation. Torque setting must be within 2% accuracy. Calibration or overhaul is required if these tolerances are exceeded. A minimum yearly calibration is required unless the wrench is more frequently used, which requires a monthly calibration in an ISO-certified shop.

Screwdrivers

LO 5-5 Identify and describe the types, features, and proper use of screwdrivers.

Screwdrivers are used for driving or removing screws or bolts using special tips made in a variety of shapes and lengths to perform specific jobs. The shape of the blade tips categorizes the

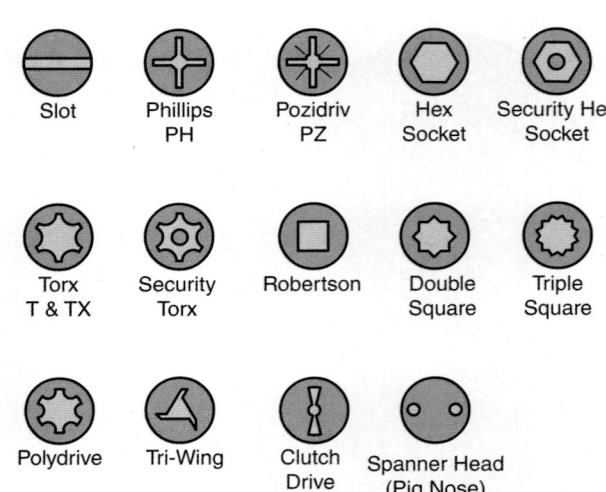

FIGURE 5-29 A wide range of screwdriver tips and bits are made to reduce slippage and provide additional security to prevent unauthorized removal of screws.

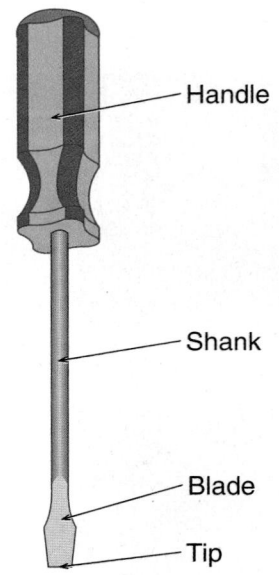

FIGURE 5-30 Parts of a screwdriver.

type of screwdriver (**FIGURE 5-29**). Flat-blade screwdrivers are called slotted screwdrivers, star-shaped tips, also called cross tip, are Phillips. Square-shaped tips are Robertson. Even more screwdriver tips and bits are available, all designed to reduce tip slippage or provide security from tampering by screw removal.

The width a of a flat-blade screwdriver identifies its size. A frequently used flat blade is a 1/4" flat tip that used to be called a "Tune-up" screwdriver since it was frequently used to adjust ignition system parts. A screwdriver size is also designated by the length of the blade (**FIGURE 5-30**). For example, a 6" shank corresponds to a 6" long screwdriver. The width and shape of flat-blade tips vary from a narrow parallel-sided tip to a wide tapered tip. Specialized screwdrivers have tips for cross-slotted recessed screws or bolts and clutch-bit screws used to minimize tampering or add a level of security to the component. When using a screwdriver, the tip is stabilized on a fastener

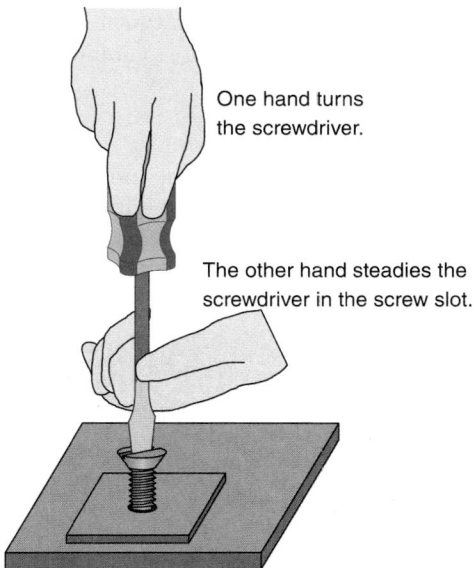

One hand turns the screwdriver.

The other hand steadies the screwdriver in the screw slot.

FIGURE 5-31 Correct technique for using a screwdriver.

FIGURE 5-32 A larger red and smaller green Robertson screwdriver tips.

head with one hand while the handle is turned with the other (**FIGURE 5-31**).

A Phillips screwdriver is made with four different-sized tips numbered 1 through 4, with 1 being the smallest size. Size 1 fits Phillips screws identified as #4 and smaller-size screws. Number 2 Phillips fits #5 to #9 size screws, number 3 fits screw numbers 10 to 16, and number 4 fits 18 and larger. A Posidriv® tip, which resembles a Phillips, was developed with tip edges that are parallel and not tapered like a Phillips. Robertson screwdrivers tip sizes are identified by the color of its handle. Black is the largest of the Robertson square tips, red is the next size smaller, followed by green and yellow, which is the smallest (**FIGURE 5-32**).

An impact driver is used to break loose seized screws. This tool, which uses interchangeable bits, is struck with a hammer after placing the tip on the fastener head. Striking the impact driver simultaneously turns the screw head while preventing tip slippage (**FIGURE 5-33**).

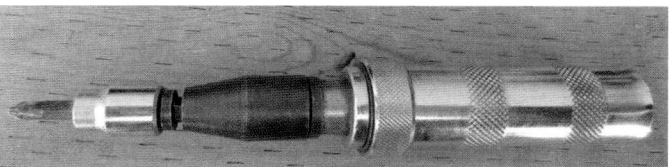

FIGURE 5-33 An impact driver used to remove seized screws. When struck with a hammer, it rotates the screwdriver bit.

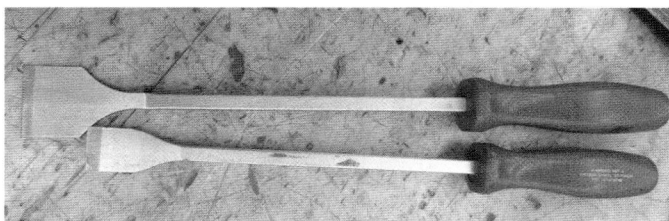

FIGURE 5-34 Gasket scrapers used to clean sealing surfaces.

Gasket Scrapers

A gasket scraper is generally the size and shape of a screwdriver but has a hardened, sharpened flat blade used to scrape gasket surfaces clean. The gasket scraper is occasionally sharpened to make it easier to remove old gasket and sealing compound. Various blade widths are available (**FIGURE 5-34**).

> ▶ TECHNICIAN TIP

When a screw cannot be easily turned, it is sometimes helpful to try tightening it first and trying once more to remove it. Alternately tightening and loosening a screw until it is completely removed prevents the screw from breaking or stripping the head. An impact driver can also be used to remove seized screws.

Types of Pliers

LO 5-6 Identify and describe the types, features, and proper use of pliers.

Pliers are tools used to grip objects. They consist of a pair of hinged or pivoting jaws designed for a specific purpose, such as stripping wire, cutting, shaping, twisting, or holding work. Needle-nose pliers with long narrow jaws and general-purpose pliers are essential pliers for technicians. A large variety of specialty pliers are made.

Specialty Pliers

Other purpose-made pliers include brake spring pliers, filter pliers, wheel nut cover pliers, and snap ring pliers (**FIGURE 5-35**). Snap ring pliers either open outwardly to remove and install external snap rings located on the outside of hubs and shafts or, if the snap ring is an internal type, the snap ring pliers close when the handle is squeezed (**FIGURE 5-36**).

Specialty pliers are also used to cut bolts or sheet metal. Bolt cutters are used in shops to cut heavy battery cable, bolts, rods, chain, and wire cable. Bolt cutters are like giant shears with short blades and long handles to provide tremendous mechanical advantage for cutting heavy materials (**FIGURE 5-37**). Three types of sheet metal pliers are used, making either straight cuts, right-hand circles, or left-hand circles. Yellow-colored, soft-grip, sheet metal pliers, also called aviation snips, cut in a straight line and wide curves. For designating tin snips cutting curves or circles to the left, red handles are used. Green handles cut straight and in a tight curve to the right.

Slip Joint Pliers

These pliers have a moveable pivoting joint that enables the jaw size to increase to hold a wide size range of objects. One of a series of large grooves in the plier's pivot point is selected to determine how far the plier jaw opens. Serrated jaws are used for gripping work (**FIGURE 5-38**). Adjustment of front wheel bearing nuts, such as castellated nuts, are a common use for slip joint pliers wrench.

Diagonal Side Cutters

These are pliers with a fixed pivot point and two sharp jaws, with both edges ground at an angle, to perform flush cuts on electrical wire (**FIGURE 5-39**). They can also make short cuts in light material, plus cut and remove cotter pins. Electrically

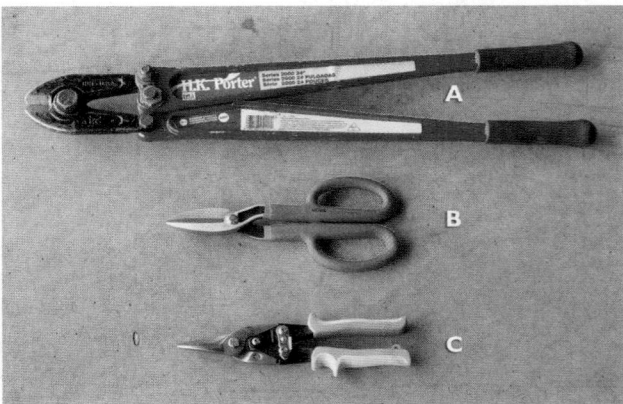

FIGURE 5-37 Bolt cutters and sheet metal snips.

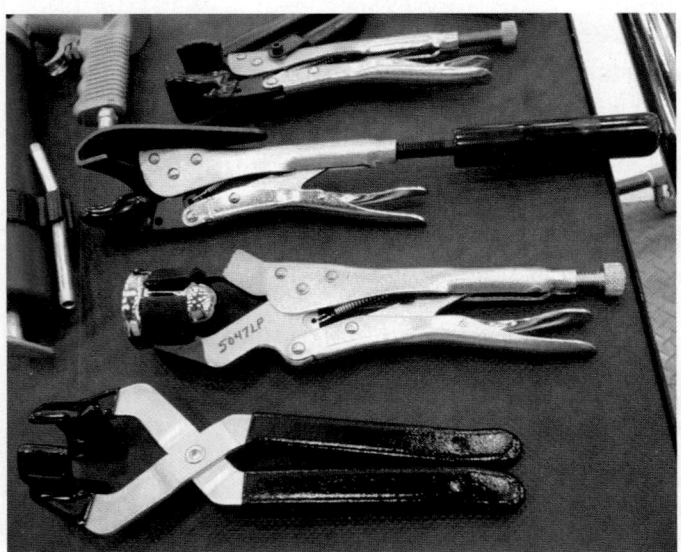

FIGURE 5-35 A pair of specialty pliers used to grip and remove wheel nut covers.

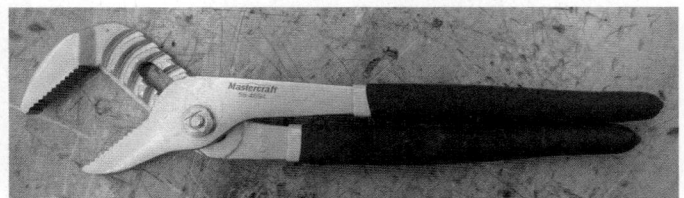

FIGURE 5-38 Slip joint pliers used to grip a variety of objects with varying diameters.

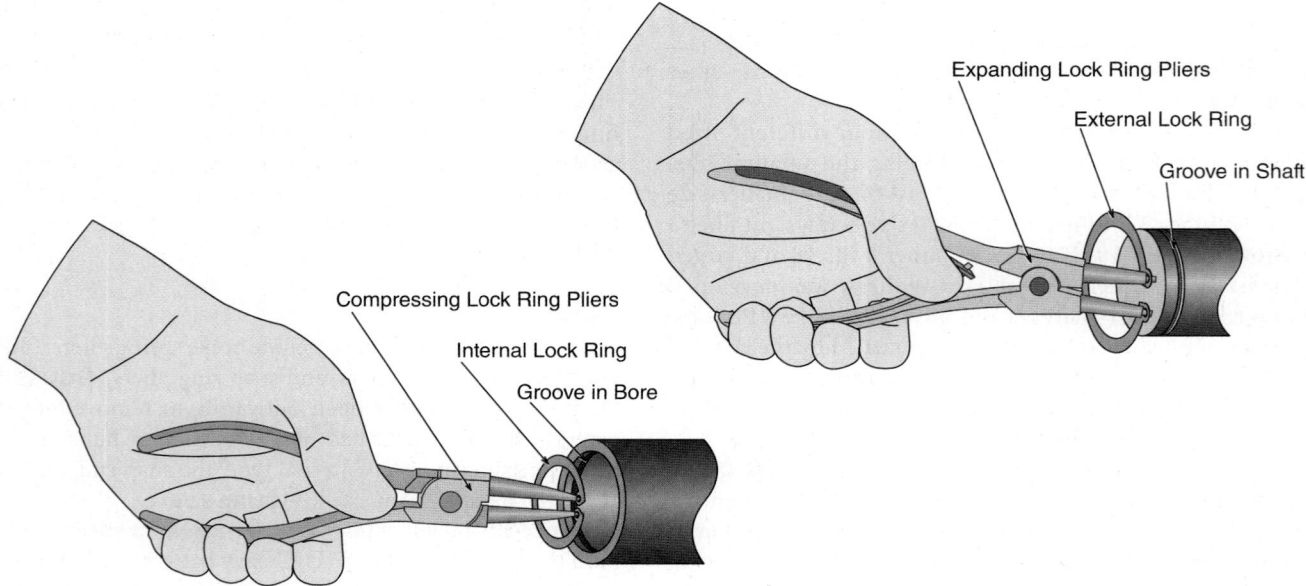

FIGURE 5-36 Internal and external snap ring pliers.

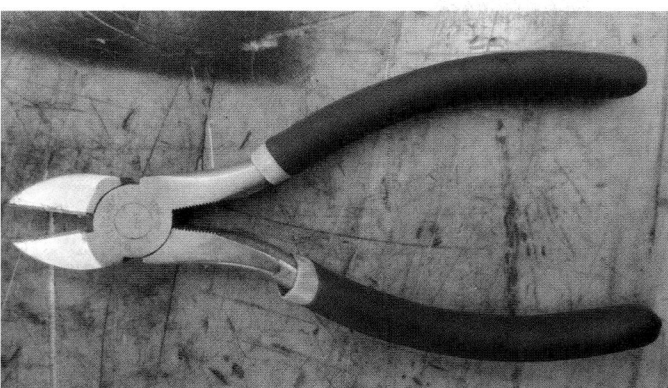

FIGURE 5-39 Diagonal side cutting pliers.

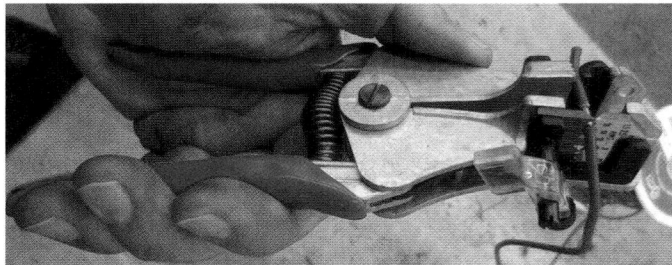

FIGURE 5-40 A wire stripper.

FIGURE 5-41 A wire cutting feature is incorporated into crimping pliers used to assemble crimp connections.

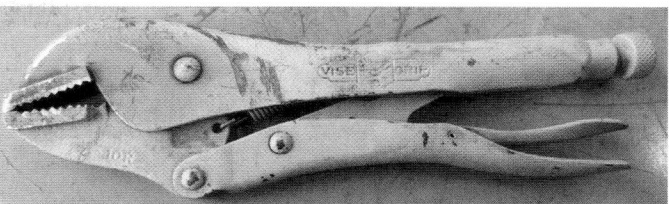

FIGURE 5-42 A common parallel jaw locking type pliers with a spring-type locking mechanism.

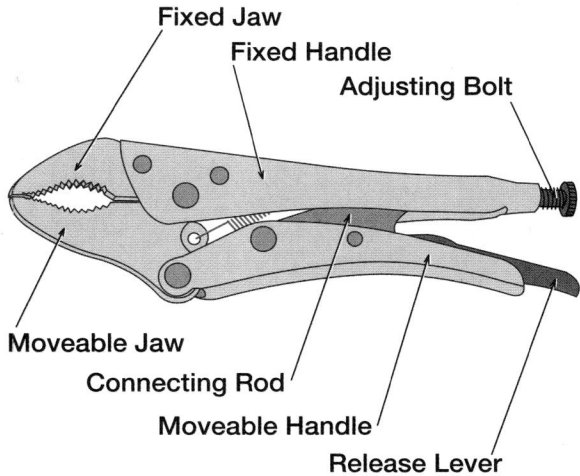

Fixed Jaw
Fixed Handle
Adjusting Bolt
Moveable Jaw
Connecting Rod
Moveable Handle
Release Lever

FIGURE 5-43 Parts of a locking jaw plier.

insulated sleeves over the handle reduce the possibility of electrical shocks if accidentally used in live circuits. Jaws are angled approximately 15 to 30 degrees to allow adequate clearance for knuckles when performing flush cuts. Lineman's pliers are similarly used to shear larger wires, but also have wide jaw gripping tongs used to twist wires.

Wire Strippers Combined Crimping Tool

Wire strippers are used to strip insulation from electrical wire. Several calibrated diameter cutting teeth match various wire gauge size (**FIGURE 5-40**). When closed around wire, only the insulation is cut and the wire core remains intact. Pulling the pliers sideways strips the insulation away from the wire. The combination wire stripper has a cutting edge for cutting wire and a blunt jaw for crimping electrical crimp connectors (**FIGURE 5-41**).

Locking Jaw Pliers

These are more commonly called "vice-grip" after the popular brand name given by one manufacturer. The jaws are constructed to remain almost parallel throughout the range of jaw opening travel (**FIGURE 5-42**). What is more recognized is the adjustable tension spring in the curved handle that limits how far the jaws close and open when they are pulled to unlock the jaws. An over-center spring arrangement of a locking lever gives the pliers its spring lock capability. Jaws that are curved, straight-sided, or flat that are designed to clamp two pieces of metal together are common versions of these pliers needed by most technicians. The first step when using these pliers is to adjust the distance between the two jaws according to the size of the piece to be gripped. Next, the clamping handles are squeezed together to secure the work piece (**FIGURE 5-43**). Technicians commonly use 5", 7", and 10" (12.7, 17.8, and 25.4 cm) locking pliers in curved jaws and long nose design.

Flat Nose Pliers

Sometimes called general-purpose pliers, or linesmen pliers, these curved handle pliers are used to hold or grip small objects with serrated jaws and to twist wire. An edge built into the jaw is useful for shearing wire (**FIGURE 5-44**).

Needle-Nose Pliers

These long-jaw, or needle-nose, pliers are used to grip small objects. A common application is to hold electrical wires when soldering. Extended needle-nose pliers are popular for retrieving objects and access individual wires in wiring harnesses (**FIGURE 5-45**).

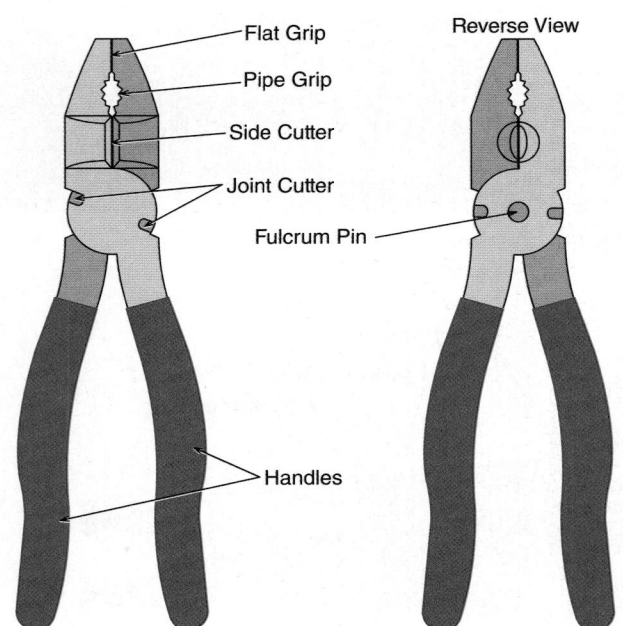

FIGURE 5-44 Features of flat nose pliers.

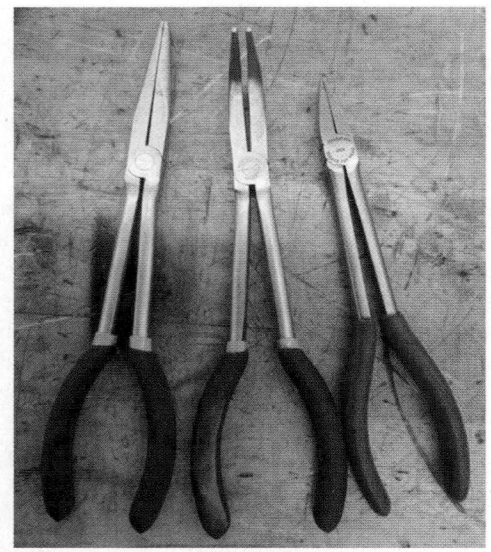

FIGURE 5-45 Long-nosed pliers used to extend reach. Right to left; needle-nose, angled needle-nose, and blunt-nose pliers.

Metal Cutting

LO 5-7 Identify and describe the features and proper use of hacksaws, punches, and chisels.

Hacksaws

Hacksaws are saws designed for cutting metal. Using an adjustable frame that can hold changeable blades from 8" to 16" (20 to 41 cm) long, a variety of blades can be installed to best suit the material to be cut (**FIGURE 5-46**). Blades can be

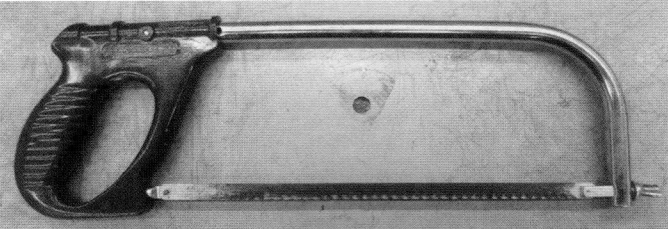

FIGURE 5-46 A hacksaw has a hardened, fine-tooth blade used to cut metal.

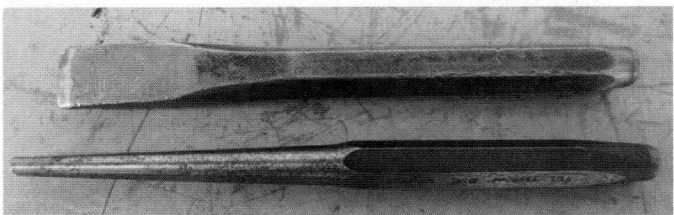

FIGURE 5-47 A cold chisel (top) and pin punch (below).

inserted at two or three different angles. Teeth on the blades point in only one direction, which is forward, when the blade is installed correctly. This means when using a hacksaw, pressure on the blade is applied only on the forward stroke and released on the back stroke. Pressure applied to the blade on the back stroke will quickly dull the blade. Hacksaw blades are made of high-grade tool steel, which is hardened and tempered. Blades range between 7/16" to 9/16" wide, having 14 to 32 teeth per inch (TPI).

A general-use blade with 14 teeth per inch is used on machine steel. This coarse pitch enables fast cutting of steel and cast iron. A blade with 32 teeth per inch is best used on thin-walled tubing. Blades with 24 teeth per inch are best used when cutting tubing, tin, brass, copper, and other soft metals. If fewer teeth are used, the thin, soft stock tends to make it difficult to push the saw. Two or more teeth should be in contact with the work.

Chisels

Chisels are hand tools struck with a hammer that are used to chip or cut metal. Made from a high-grade steel, chisels will cut any metal that is softer than materials of which they are made. The type of chisel most commonly used is the flat cold chisel which is used to cut rivets heads, split nuts, and crack bearing races. It is called a cold chisel because it is used on cold metal as opposed to hot metal (**FIGURE 5-47**).

Punches

Punches are a large category of hand tools struck on one end with a hammer and used to push pins or bearings races. Drift punches have a long, narrow tapered shape and are used to knockout rivets after the heads have been chiseled. Pin punches are made to follow through a hole where a pin was installed to finish driving it out. A center punch is another type of punch used for marking the center of a hole to be drilled.

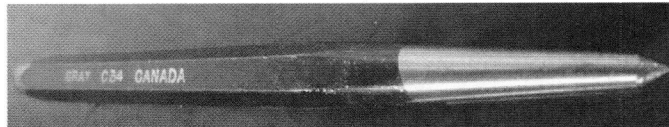

FIGURE 5-48 A pin punch is used to mark a metal surface to enable a drill bit to center over the spot and begin cutting the metal.

FIGURE 5-49 Long-handled pry levers.

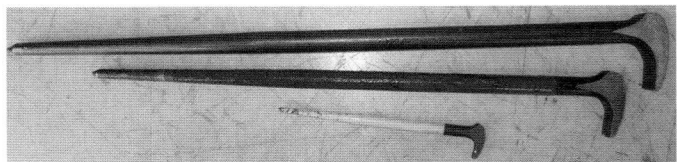

FIGURE 5-50 Roll bars used for high leverage prying or separating parts.

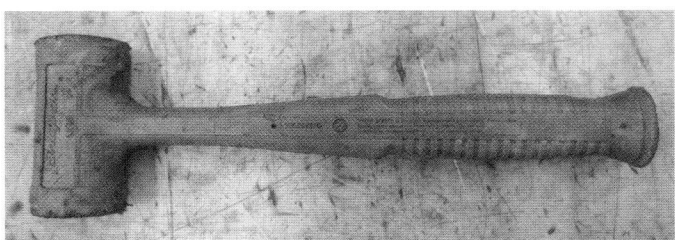

FIGURE 5-51 A soft-faced dead blow hammer.

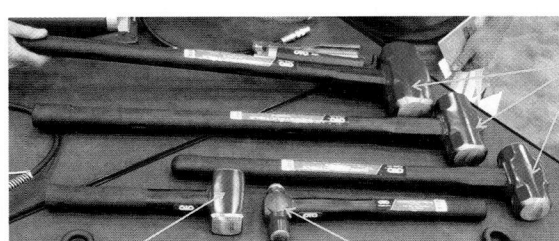

10, 7 and 5-lb Sledge Hammers

3-lb Club Hammer   Ball Pein

FIGURE 5-52 Common hammer types. Note the different sizes and weights of sledge hammer heads and the use of fiberglass handles.

Punching the center or the hole provides an indentation in the metal surface to center a drill bit long enough to begin cutting and prevent the bit from wandering or spinning away from the desired location (**FIGURE 5-48**).

Pry Bars

Pry bars are made from strong, forged, medium-carbon, spring-like steel. They are commonly used as levers to move, adjust, or pry apart heavy components. Pry bars are available in a variety of shapes and sizes. Many have a tapered wedge end with an offset angle to conveniently position the lever for prying (**FIGURE 5-49**). This design works well for applying force to tension belts or for moving parts into alignment. Another type of pry bar is the roll bar, also called a heel bar. One end is sharply curved for prying and the other is tapered. The tapered end has a dull point used to align larger holes, such as transmission bell housings or engine motor mounts (**FIGURE 5-50**). Pry bars are made of hardened steel, and caution is needed to prevent the bar from damaging or bending soft materials, such as aluminum.

Hammers

LO 5-8 Identify and describe the types, features, and proper use of hammers.

Pins, press fit, and seized parts often require additional force to service. Several other service tools require the striking force of hammers to operate. Servicing commercial vehicles accumulating long distance and using heavier parts means technicians will require more than a couple of hammer types. Hammers are classified according to weight, construction material, and the shape of the head. Most hammer heads are made from forged, or malleable steel with an annealed metal surface. **Annealing** is a metal softening process that allows the metal hammer face to slightly dent when struck, rather than fracture or chip. **Forging** is intended to cause the metal to mushroom when striking hard materials. Materials other than steel are used for soft-faced hammers. These hammers are made from rubber or plastic heads or soft brass. Soft-faced plastic or brass heads are used for tapping on precision parts, such as small seals, metal alignment keys between shafts and gears, or heavy cotter pins. Rubber mallets are used on thin metal parts, such as body panels, chrome wheel caps, and nut covers, that are easily dented by a metal hammer. A **dead blow hammer** is another type of soft-face hammer made from a nylon or polypropylene case and filled with lead shot (**FIGURE 5-51**). The head absorbs the blow when the hammer makes contact with heavy parts and lead shot reduces any rebound. The nylon-like face material means these hammers cannot be used to drive steel punches and chisels, but are ideal for hitting heavier metal parts to align them, such as main bearing caps or installing gears onto tapered shafts.

Hammer weight determines the amount of force transferred when a hammer strikes a blow. Heavier hammers can transfer more force than a lighter hammer. A club hammer is the smallest of heavy hammers truck technicians will store in a tool box (**FIGURE 5-52**). Usually around three- or four-pounds head weight, with a rectangular-shaped head, the club hammer is designed for heavy striking force on larger chisels or punches. Sledge hammers are heavy hammers for high-force operations, such as removing kingpins or fifth wheel pivot pins, or loosening steering linkage. Longer hammer handles

FIGURE 5-53 A ball peen hammer is gently tapped on the edge of a casting to form a new gasket.

FIGURE 5-54 This seal installer uses a forcing screw to push the seal into a bore with an interference fit.

are designed to multiply striking force. These hammers range from 5, 7, 10, and 12-lb heads up to 20 or 25 lbs. Hammer handles were traditionally made from vibration-absorbing wood, but lighter fiberglass handles that resist chipping and damage are much more common.

Ball peen hammers are still commonly found in many tool sets, but their original purpose has fallen out of use. The round end was commonly used to peen-over or flatten rivets. The round end was also used to form gaskets by tapping the edge of a metal part with the hammer to cut out the gasket material (**FIGURE 5-53**).

Pullers

LO 5-9 Identify and describe the types, features, and proper use of pullers.

Some parts are assembled using what is called an **interference or press fit**. This assembly method connects and holds parts together with friction and pressure produced between two components of different sizes; one being either slightly larger or smaller than the other. Pushing a gear hub over a tapered shaft with a slightly larger diameter than the center of the gear hub is an example of an interference fit. Taper splined steering wheels are pressed onto steering shafts with an interference fit as well. Most wheel bearing races or cups are interference fit to hold them securely inside a hub. To separate parts having an interference fit, pullers are used. Pullers are devices used to separate parts either assembled with an interference fit or parts that are seized together. Push-pullers are tools frequently used to not only separate parts, but also to press parts together (**FIGURE 5-54**).

The sizes and configurations of pullers are as varied as the parts they are used with. In common is the use of a mechanism to apply pressure to pull or press against a component to separate it from another component. A hardened fine-thread screw

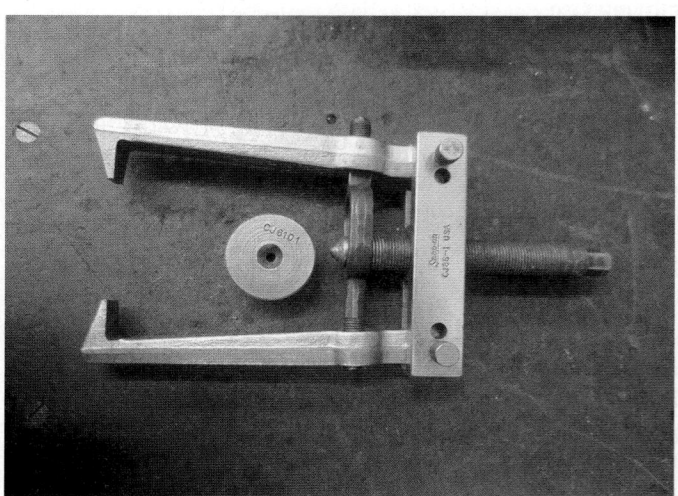

FIGURE 5-55 A two-jaw puller with a T-bar frame and cross arms.

that can apply a mechanical advantage is most common, but a sliding hammer is also used to apply high impact force necessary to separate parts.

One universal puller is a T-bar, which can attach two pulling legs to grip the part to be removed. A center bolt, called a forcing screw or jacking bolt, is turned to produce the mechanical advantage and multiply rotational force on the screw into a linear pulling force. The arms of these pullers are hooked to grip parts from either the outside or inside. A cross-arm prevents the jaws from spreading apart or slipping inward when under high tension loads (**FIGURE 5-55**).

A hub or tripod puller has a forcing screw in a frame with three slots to install bolts. The bolts thread into a component for removal while the forcing screw acts against a shaft. This puller works well removing a steering wheel or gears on an engine drivetrain (**FIGURE 5-56**).

FIGURE 5-56 A tripod puller for removing gear hubs and steering wheels.

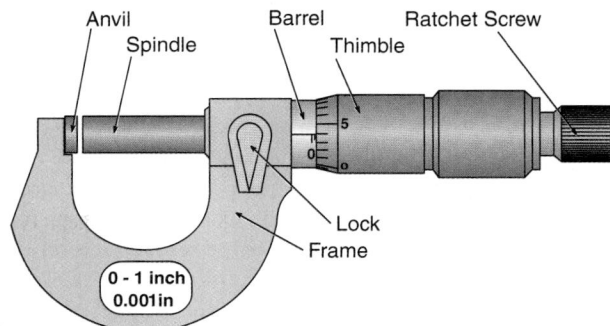

FIGURE 5-57 Micrometers are used to precisely measure the thickness of various objects, such as brake rotors or machine parts.

Measuring Tools

LO 5-10 Identify and describe the types and applications of measuring tools.

Measuring tools are designed to accurately measure distances, clearances, thicknesses, depth, and movement. Common measuring tools used by technicians include Vernier calipers, tape measures, micrometers, dial indicators, and thickness gauges.

Micrometers are made to measure inside or outside a particular dimension. An anvil for an outside micrometer wraps around a part for measurement while a precision threaded spindle is tightened over the part. Graduation markings on the barrel surrounding the spindle precise measure down to an accuracy of 1/1,000th inch. Metric micrometers measure down to 1/100th millimeter. Inside micrometers are used to measure internal dimensions or bore diameters. Outside micrometers measure width or diameters of work pieces (**FIGURE 5-57**).

Similar to a micrometer is a Vernier caliper. This device measures the thickness or distance between two points using a set of jaws that are slid back and forth along a frame. Verniers can measure both the inside and outside diameter of a work piece (**FIGURE 5-58**).

Thickness (feeler) gauges are made in a variety of shapes and sizes. Packaged blades are grouped into one tool and graduated in thousandths of an inch or tenth of a millimeter. Blades are made in various lengths that can be straight, stepped, or bent at 45-degree and 90-degree angles. A package of gauges is typically held together with a locking screw to hold a blade in an extended position (**FIGURE 5-59**).

Dial indicators are gauges used to precisely measure movement or distances in as little as 0.0005" or 0.001 mm

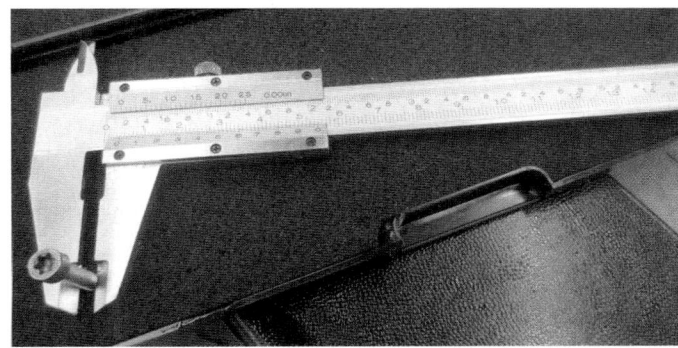

FIGURE 5-58 A Vernier gauge is used to measure inside and outside diameters of objects.

FIGURE 5-59 Thickness gauges or feeler blades are available in a variety of sizes and shapes to suit the measuring purpose.

graduations. A needle-type movement moves around in a dial gauge to indicate distance travelled by a spring-loaded plunger (**FIGURE 5-60**).

Impact Wrenches

LO 5-11 Identify and describe the use of impact wrenches.

Impact wrenches or air guns are air-operated tools with a drive mechanism that couple with impact sockets. Air vanes inside the motor operate a hammer and anvil mechanism, which repeatedly hammers the square drive, applying a high degree of pulsing torque to a socket. The impact wrench to use for a job is based on the torque and speed required to remove and reinstall fasteners. Commonly used impact guns have 4 drive sizes: 3/8", 1/2", 3/4", and 1" drives. Extra-heavy-duty impact wrenches are required in shops servicing commercial vehicles due to the high torque required to remove and reinstall large fasteners on wheel ends, transmissions, and drive axles. For example, wheel nuts on hub piloted wheel ends typically require 500 ft-lb or more of torque to install require at least a 3/4" drive impact gun to remove. (**FIGURE 5-61**). The maximum output torque of the gun is varied by rotating a sliding valve located on the outside of the motor housing. The valve also controls the direction of gun rotation.

Air-operated ratchets and drills are indispensable to technicians and must be well maintained to prevent premature wear. Moisture in the air supply will corrode internal parts and should be removed before entering the tool (**FIGURE 5-62**).

FIGURE 5-60 Dial indicators are a precision measuring gauge used to measure very small movement.

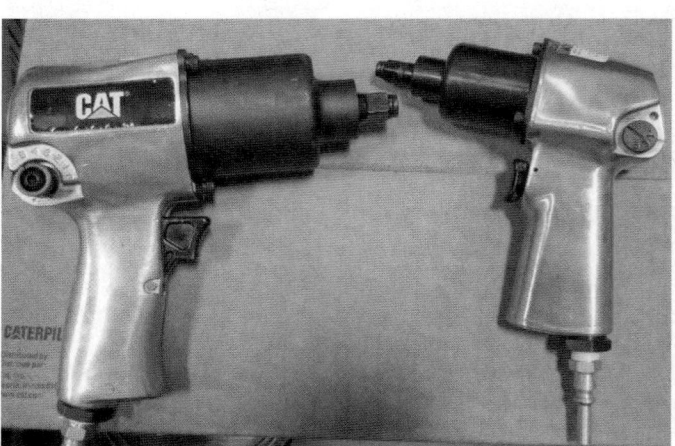

FIGURE 5-61 A 1/2" and a 3/4" impact air gun.

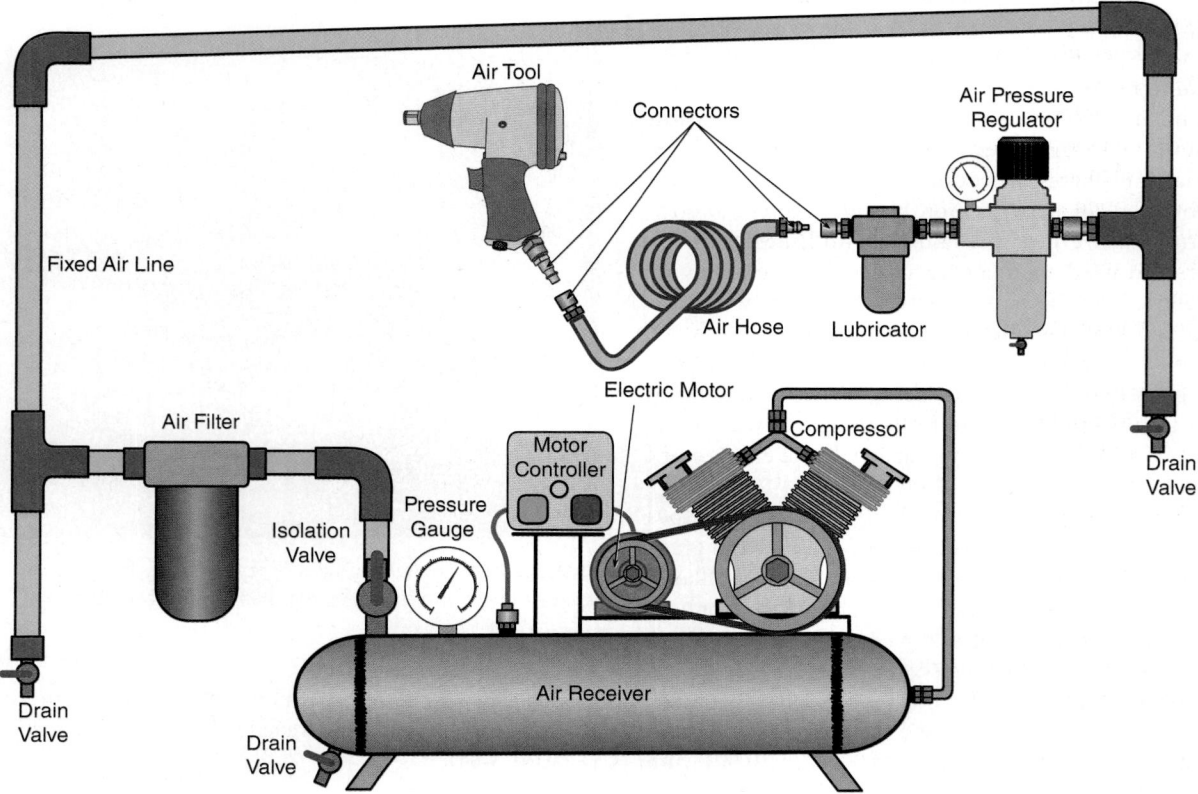

FIGURE 5-62 An arrangement of air controls to properly condition air supply for air-operated tools.

► TECHNICIAN TIP

Air tools need daily oiling to minimize wear of air vanes and help seal the vane tips inside the motor housing for maximum efficiency. To improve operation and increase the tools durability, depending on the size of the tool, about six to eight drops of oil are injected into the tool airline inlet and run freely for 30 seconds to lubricate the motor. Inline oil injectors automatically add oil into the air supply and separate water from the oil.

► TECHNICIAN TIP

Vibration from impact guns can cause an unpleasant, painful tingling sensation in the hands and fingers due to nerve compression. Stop using the impact gun if this occurs. It is recommended an energy-absorbing glove be used when operating guns. Guns should not be tightly gripped by the palms of one's hand but held with a relaxed grip to minimize the transfer of vibration. Never carry an impact gun by the air hose. Impact guns can easily over-torque fasteners. Avoid over-torqueing torque bolts and nuts by using a torque wrench instead to apply the final correct torque to a fastener.

Wrap-Up

Ready for Review

► Choosing the correct tool and using it properly is critical to performing work efficiently, accurately, and safely. A technician's efficiency is directly related to the selection of tools and understanding the function and use of each tool — knowing the best tool to do the job.

► Good quality tool boxes use ball bearing slides on the drawers and double-walled, thick-gauge sheet metal to increase durability. Technicians working on commercial vehicles typically purchase a top tool chest and a lower roll cabinet with casters to enable easy movement of their tools around a shop and bring tools close to the service area on a vehicle.

► A rolling cabinet is a toolbox on wheels that provides storage for all a technician's personal hand and air-operated tools. It consists of a metal frame that contains a variety of drawers of different widths and depths to accommodate large and small tools.

► Wrenches are used to tighten or loosen nuts, bolts, couplings, pipe plugs, and line fittings. Specialized wrenches, such as pipe wrenches, are designed to grip round stock, such as pipes, tie rods, and studs.

► Combination open and box wrenches are the most commonly used wrenches due to their versatility, having one open end and one box end on the same wrench.

► The advantage of a box-end wrench is it has more points to grip the head of a fastener and does not slip as easily as an open-end wrench.

► A wrench size refers to the diameter of the fastener head it is used to tighten or loosen.

► When using adjustable wrenches or pipe wrenches, the movable jaw should be farther away from the user than the fixed jaw when pushing and closer to the user when pulling to put more pressure on the fixed jaw.

► It's generally safer to push rather than pull a tool. When strenuously pushing a wrench or ratchet to loosen a tight fastener, it is also helpful to push with an open hand to minimize damage to knuckles if a slip does take place.

► A ratchet wrench is the fastest hand-operated tool to tighten and loosen fasteners. The ratchet head contains a reversible one-way clutch that freewheels or slips in one direction and applies torque in another.

► Ratchet size is determined by the width of its drive, available as either 1/4", 3/8", 1/2", 3/4", or 1". Sockets are available in steps of 32nds, 16ths, or 8ths of an inch. Metric sizes increment in 1 mm steps.

► Corrosion-resistant chrome, smooth, thin-walled sockets are used with hand-operated ratchets to fit around nuts and bolts with tight clearances.

► Thicker-walled sockets are used with air impact tools and are not chromed since the hammering action flakes thin chrome into razor-sharp pieces.

► 1" drive sockets have a locking pin on the ratchet at the drive end of the socket that is used to help prevent impact sockets from spinning off high-speed impact guns.

► Torx-head screws were designed to resist slipping better than hex-head or other types of fastener heads. Internal Torx-head sizes use the prefix "T" followed by a number ranging from T1 to T100.

► A prefix "E" designates external Torx that range from E4 to E44, with the lower number corresponding to the smaller socket dimension.

► Hex sockets' and hex keys' dimensions are measured between two opposite and parallel flat sides of the socket.

► Three basic types of torque wrenches commonly used are beam-type, dial-type, and indicating torque wrenches.

► A general rule of thumb is 5 ft-lb (6.8 Nm) of torque is lost through a 6" (15.2 cm) extension. When using extensions, the loss of torque must be added to the original setting.

► Teeth on a hacksaw blade point in only one direction, which is forward, when the blade is installed correctly. Pressure on the blade is applied only on the forward stroke and released on the back stroke.

► A dead-blow hammer is a soft-face hammer made from a nylon or polypropylene case and filled with lead shot to reduce rebound.

► Sledge hammers are heavy hammers for high-force operations, such as removing kingpins or fifth-wheel pivot pins, or loosening steering linkage. Longer hammer handles are designed to multiply striking force.

► Parts assembled using an interference or press fit are held together with friction and pressure produced between two components of different sizes. Pullers are used to separate or assemble interference fit parts.

▶ A universal puller is a T-bar, which can attach two pulling legs to grip the part to be removed. A center bolt, called a forcing screw or jacking bolt, is turned to produce the mechanical advantage and multiply rotational force on the screw into a linear pulling force.

▶ Common measuring tools used by technicians include Vernier calipers, tape measures, micrometers, dial indicators, and thickness gauges.

▶ Impact wrenches or air guns are air-operated tools with a drive mechanism that couple with impact sockets. Air vanes inside the motor operate a hammer and anvil mechanism, which repeatedly hammers a square drive, applying a high degree of pulsing torque to a socket.

▶ The impact wrench to use for a job is based on the torque and speed required to remove and reinstall fasteners. Commonly used impact guns have four drive sizes: 3/8", 1/2", 3/4", and 1" drives.

▶ Extra-heavy-duty impact wrenches are required in shops servicing commercial vehicles due to the high torque required to remove and reinstall large fasteners on wheel ends, transmissions, and drive axles.

Key Terms

annealing A metal working process where the outer surface of hardened metal parts is made softer and more pliable. Metal is heated and cooled slowly, often with oil, to anneal a metal surface.

forging A metal stamping process where metal parts softened by heat are repeatedly struck with a forging die to shape a metal part.

Review Questions

1. Where should the most frequently used tools be stored in a tool box?
   a. At eye level in the top storage box
   b. In a drawer with ball bearing-type slides
   c. In a lower drawer chest below eye level
   d. In a portable tool tray

2. What feature of a line wrench gives it an advantage that other wrenches do not have?
   a. Greater turning torque
   b. An angled end to reach difficult fastener heads
   c. A curved handle
   d. Five sides at each open end

3. Which of the following tools is best used to loosen a recessed and seized nut on a stud 1.5" long?
   a. A deep 6-pt socket
   b. A shallow 12-pt socket
   c. A combination wrench
   d. An open-end wrench

4. Which tool is best used to remove a brass hydraulic fitting closely surrounded by other hydraulic fittings?
   a. A crowfoot wrench
   b. A deep 6-pt socket
   c. A line wrench
   d. A box-end wrench

5. Which jaw face of an adjustable wrench should have the most pressure applied when tightening or loosening a fastener?
   a. The fixed jaw
   b. The movable jaw
   c. The serrated jaw
   d. The smooth jaw

6. Which type of socket would be used by a half-inch drive impact gun?
   a. A 6-pt flat black-colored socket
   b. A 12-pt chrome socket
   c. A 6-pt chrome socket
   d. A socket with a locking pin release

7. Which type of fastener drive head is less likely to slip or cam-out?
   a. Internal Torx
   b. Internal hex head
   c. A ball-type Allen socket
   d. An external hex head

8. Which of the following Robertson screw driver tips is the largest?
   a. Yellow
   b. Red
   c. Green
   d. Black

9. When should the most pressure be applied to a hack saw blade when cutting?
   a. On the back stroke when cutting steel and cast iron
   b. On the forward stroke when cutting steel and iron
   c. On the back stroke when two or more teeth contact the work
   d. On the back stroke when cutting thin-walled tubing

10. Sledge hammer handles are typically made from:
    a. Plastic
    b. Polypropylene
    c. Wood
    d. Fiberglass

ASE Technician A/Technician B Style Questions

1. Technician A says that a dead-blow hammer is best used to hit a steel punch because it will not bounce back. Technician B says a club-type steel hammer is used to drive steel punches. Who is correct?
   a. Technician A
   b. Technician B
   c. Both Technician A and Technician B
   d. Neither Technician A nor Technician B

2. Technician A says that pullers can also use a forcing screw to push on components to either install or remove them. Technician B says that a forcing screw is a common feature of pullers. Who is correct?
   a. Technician A
   b. Technician B
   c. Both Technician A and Technician B
   d. Neither Technician A nor Technician B

3. After completing brake jobs on two trailers, Technician A and B were discussing the painful tingling sensation in their hands after installing the wheels nuts and bolts on the brake drums using impact guns. Technician A says that the pain is due to nerve compression. Technician B says that it is muscle soreness. Who is correct?
   a. Technician A
   b. Technician B
   c. Both Technician A and Technician B
   d. Neither Technician A nor Technician B

4. To adjust the bearing preload on a steering gear, the torque required to rotate the input shaft must be correctly measured. Technician A said that an indicating-type torque wrench should be used because it will click when the correct torque is reached. Technician B said that only a dial-type torque wrench should be used. Who is correct?
   a. Technician A
   b. Technician B
   c. Both Technician A and Technician B
   d. Neither Technician A nor Technician B

5. Technician A and B were discussing why they could not remove what looked like cover plate screws to retain an in-dash GPS display unit. A pin was in the center of what looked like a regular Torx screw head. Technician A said it was a secure Torx screw. Technician B said it was not a Torx screw, but a rivet. Who is correct?
   a. Technician A
   b. Technician B
   c. Both Technician A and Technician B
   d. Neither Technician A nor Technician B

6. Technician A says that to make straight cuts in sheet metal to create patches, green-handled aviation's pliers can be used. Technician B says yellow-handled sheet metal snips should be used. Who is correct?
   a. Technician A
   b. Technician B
   c. Both Technician A and Technician B
   d. Neither Technician A nor Technician B

7. Technician A says that to adjust a tie rod using a pipe wrench, the lower jaw should be installed around the tie rod so that its lower jaw will have the most pressure applied to it when attempting to turn the rod. Technician B says that the fixed jaw that is not part of the adjustment mechanism should have the most pressure applied when turning. Who is correct?
   a. Technician A
   b. Technician B
   c. Both Technician A and Technician B
   d. Neither Technician A nor Technician B

8. Technician A says that to loosen a nut that has had its corners rounded, it is best to try a 6-pt socket. Technician B says that a 12-pt socket with more corners is the best choice. Who is correct?
   a. Technician A
   b. Technician B
   c. Both Technician A and Technician B
   d. Neither Technician A nor Technician B

9. Technician A says that the flaking and peeling chrome on a set of sockets is likely caused by using the sockets on an impact wrench. Technician B says that the cause of socket deterioration is corrosion. Who is correct?
   a. Technician A
   b. Technician B
   c. Both Technician A and Technician B
   d. Neither Technician A nor Technician B

10. Technician A says that the loose fit of a small Phillips screwdriver in a fastener head could be improved by changing from a #2 to a #1 screwdriver. Technician B says that changing from a #2 to a #3 Phillips screw driver is the correct choice for a better-fitting screwdriver. Who is correct?
   a. Technician A
   b. Technician B
   c. Both Technician A and Technician B
   d. Neither Technician A nor Technician B

CHAPTER 6

Lifting and Hoisting Equipment

Learning Objectives

After reading this chapter, you will be able to:

- **LO 6-1** Describe proper manual lifting techniques according to occupational health and safety standards.
- **LO 6-2** Describe the types and proper use of jacks, stands, and chocks.
- **LO 6-3** Describe the types and uses of vehicle hoists and their certification criteria.
- **LO 6-4** Describe the different types of and uses of cranes and rigging equipment.
- **LO 6-5** Explain the types, uses, and inspection of wire rope.

You Are the Technician

You are attempting to remove the engine from a Freightliner Cascadia and you have attached your engine crane to a two-chain sling that is bolted to the front and back of the engine. Each time you try to raise the engine, it tilts sharply to the rear and cannot be removed. What should you do to remedy your problem?

1. Should you attach both sides of the chain sling to the rear of the engine?
2. Should you check to ensure that there is nothing still attached at the rear of the engine?
3. Should you use a spreader or a load leveler bar?

Introduction

This chapter introduces the commercial vehicle technician to the principles of lifting, hoisting, and supporting loads and the rigging required to attach the load to the lifting device. We also review the types of equipment used in hoisting. Technicians are required to raise or lift heavy objects constantly throughout their workday. Some of this involves manual lifting of heavy parts or components by hand. Other lifting and hoisting methods involve the use of equipment specifically designed to accomplish the task. This chapter consists of a brief overview of the equipment, techniques, procedures, and safety-related information on these topics. All technicians should receive training in the proper use of any hoisting or lifting equipment prior to using it. If you have not received the required training to use a piece of hoisting or lifting equipment, ask for it from your supervisor.

FIGURE 6-1 An ancient Roman lifting device (replica).

SAFETY TIP

Lifting heavy objects is no joke! The larger and heavier an item is, the more inherent danger there is when undertaking a lifting operation. Always take the time to ensure you are properly trained and qualified and follow safe practices when operating lifting and hoisting equipment and devices.

History of Lifting

The simplest lifting device is the lever. Some of the earliest written accounts and drawings of a mechanical lever were from Archimedes in the 3rd century **BCE** (Before Common Era or before year 1). Although it is certain that levers and lifting devices have been in use for thousands of years prior to Archimedes, his writings and drawings are the earliest proof still existing of the mathematic principles of the lever. Although the actual devices and equipment used for lifting from ancient times may not survive today, signs of their use are clear (**FIGURE 6-1**). The laws of physics have not changed from ancient times; heavy items still require mechanical lifting devices and proper equipment to support their weight.

Proper Manual Lifting Techniques

LO 6-1 Describe proper manual lifting techniques according to occupational health and safety standards.

Many different types of lifting devices are used in the commercial vehicle field. In automotive use, lifting devices are used to raise vehicles and/or remove heavier components, but in the commercial field even something as simple as removing a cylinder head or a set of dual wheels requires a device to raise or lift the components because they are so heavy. The commercial vehicle technician must be able to use a variety of **lifting equipment** throughout the workday, from simple muscle power to operating large overhead gantry cranes capable of lifting several tons. He or she must do so safely and with confidence. In this chapter, we discuss lifting, hoisting, and rigging in the commercial vehicle shop.

FIGURE 6-2 Prevent back injuries when lifting heavy objects by crouching, standing close to the object, and proper positioning.

Manual Lifting

Muscles are the simplest tools for lifting and we all know how to use our muscles; however, using your muscles incorrectly in the shop, or anywhere for that matter, can lead to instant and excruciating pain and to permanent or chronic reoccurring injury. Many new employees, especially young ones, are eager to show how willing they are to get the job done, but rush into lifting something that is too heavy, or try to lift without the proper procedure. This can lead to long-term injury. Older employees also fail to realize sometimes that even the smallest mistake during lifting can lead to injury. It is not the weight that causes injury, but the technique. Poor lifting can cause serious injury. **FIGURE 6-2** shows proper lifting technique.

▶ TECHNICIAN TIP

Many objects are too heavy for one person. If an object is heavy, ask for assistance. Injuries caused by lifting an object that is too heavy can last for years, or even a lifetime.

When bending down to lift an object, for example, always bend at the knees before attempting to lift. Never bend from the waist, which is the surest way to strain your back or, in a worst-case scenario, rupture a disc in your back. Place your feet on either side of the object you want to lift and point them in the direction you wish to travel. If an item is too awkward or large for you to lift on your own, ask someone to help you lift it. To use correct manual lifting techniques, follow the steps outlined in **SKILL DRILL 6-1**.

The Occupational Health and Safety Administration (OSHA) has guidelines for manual lifting. Always follow the guidelines when it comes to manual lifting.

OSHA Standards for Proper Lifting Techniques and Equipment

As discussed previously, in the United States, the government entity that sets rules for occupational health and safety is the **Occupational Safety and Health Administration (OSHA)**. Because the operation of lifting devices can result in serious injuries and death, OSHA has many general and specific rules governing lifting and lifting devices. If you are working outside of the United States, consult your supervisor to determine what rules and standards must be followed for lifting and lifting devices in your country. For the purposes of this chapter, we discuss OSHA and industry rules that apply in the United States.

First, let's set the proper attitude toward safety standards. Safety rules/regulations, OSHA, and other industry safety organizations are not your enemy or an impediment to getting the job done. They are your partner in ensuring the job gets done safely and correctly. Furthermore, you should take the rules, regulations, and advice of these entities seriously. Most of the safety rules and regulations exist because of a serious accident that caused damage to equipment or because someone was seriously injured or died. It would be accurate to say that safety regulations were "written in blood." Therefore, not following safety regulations puts yourself, your coworkers, and your equipment in danger.

Depending on what industry you are working in, as a technician you may have to comply with additional industry regulations set by other government or industry entities. Consult with your supervisor to see what rules and regulations apply for lifting in the shop.

OSHA usually only sets general rules and regulations. It often defers the specifics of how to perform a task or operate a piece of equipment, or what technique or equipment to use, to the equipment manufacturer or another industry body more familiar with the exact situations a worker may encounter. Basically, following OSHA rules is not a substitute for following the equipment manufacturer's recommendations. OSHA often refers to the general duty clause listed in Section 5(a)(1) of the OSHA act, which states:

> Each employer shall furnish to each of his employees, employment and a place of employment which are free from recognized hazards that are causing or are likely to cause death or serious physical harm to his employees.

Now, let's review the OSHA guidelines for manual lifting.

OSHA Guidelines for Manual Lifting

OSHA has some published training material and guidelines for manual lifting. OSHA does not have specific rules, though, for the maximum weight a single person should lift. According to training material for manual lifting on the OSHA website (https://www.osha.gov/SLTC/etools/electricalcontractors/

SKILL DRILL 6-1 Correct Manual Lifting Techniques

1. Plan your movement; what your path of travel will be while carrying the object.
2. Decide whether your item requires one person or two to carry.

3. Determine where the center of gravity of the object is; place the center of gravity closest to your body when lifting.
4. Check to see whether the item has handles; handles are usually properly placed to make it easier to lift an item.
5. Place your feet shoulder-width apart standing directly in front of the item.
6. Squat down, bending at the knees and hips only, to grasp the item.
7. Look straight ahead, keep your back straight, chest out, and shoulders back.
8. Slowly lift by straightening your hips and knees. Keep your back straight and don't twist.
9. Hold the object as close as possible to your body and carry at belly button level.
10. If you must turn while carrying the object, turn with your feet, not with your body.
11. Set the load down carefully, squatting with your knees and hips while keeping your back as straight as possible.

supplemental/principles.html#lifting), the following are some basic techniques for manual lifting:

- The person's head is kept upright, looking straight ahead.
- When standing, the torso should not be bent more than 10–20 degrees from vertical.
- The natural curve of the spine is maintained.
- Pelvis and shoulders face straight ahead.
- Shoulders are relaxed, and knees slightly bent.
- Do not leave items lying on the floor where they may cause a tripping hazard.
- Plan the route of travel and ensure it is clear *before* performing the lift.
- Lift within your *power zone*. The *power zone* is between mid-thigh and mid-chest height. This allows lifting with the least amount of effort.
- Use proper handholds on the items being lifted.
- Pushing is generally preferred to pulling and has a lower chance of injury.
- Rotation of tasks. Employees should rotate repetitive tasks that use different muscles to lower the chance of injury.

OSHA published to its website a letter to clarify rules dealing how much weight a person can safely lift (https://www.osha.gov/pls/oshaweb/owadisp.show_document?p_table=INTERPRE-TATIONS&p_id=29936). OSHA defers to the National Institute for Occupational Safety and Health (NIOSH) for manual lifting information. NIOSH has a model that helps to determine the risk of injury based on the weight being lifted and several other factors (http://www.cdc.gov/niosh/docs/94-110/). These are only voluntary guidelines, though. The lifting equation establishes a maximum load of 51 lb (23 kg). For a manual lift of weights above 51 lb (23 kg), OSHA recommends using other means, such as:

- A two-person lift
- A mechanical lifting device
- Breaking down items into smaller pieces

Although it may seem embarrassing or unnecessary to ask another person for help or to use a mechanical lifting device, it is preferable to being injured and in pain, and possibly out of work.

Lifting in the Shop

LO 6-2 Describe the types and proper use of jacks, stands, and chocks.

Raising a vehicle for access to the underside is probably the most common mechanical lifting procedure in most shops and typically is accomplished with a jack or a hoist, and it seems like a simple process. However, not knowing the correct usage of the equipment, where to put the equipment to accomplish the lift, and not using proper supports to hold the vehicle can lead to catastrophic damage to the vehicle, the equipment, and to the technician or coworkers. A professional shop strives to ensure that all work is done safely, and lifting and hoisting are no different. All lifting equipment should be maintained in proper working order and, in most jurisdictions, annual inspection and certification of hoisting and lifting devices is mandatory.

Mechanical Lifting Devices

Mechanical lifting devices include jacks (hydraulic, pneumatic, and mechanical), vehicle hoists (both permanent and portable), and support systems used to hold the raised component in place. The proper term for raising a vehicle is **lifting**, whether the vehicle is being lifted by a hoist or a jack; if we are raising the vehicle from underneath we are *lifting* the vehicle. **Hoisting** is the action of lifting a load using cables or ropes, i.e., an engine is hoisted from a truck, not lifted. A load is "hoisted" when it is lifted vertically using cables or ropes and is "lifted" when it is pushed up vertically using hydraulic jacks. For the purposes of this chapter, **rigging** or **rigging gear** are all the components used to attach the mechanical hoisting equipment to the load being lifted. This can include rope, wire rope/cables, slings, shackles, eyebolts, eye nuts, links, rings, turnbuckles, etc.

Jacks and Jack Stands

Jacks and jack stands are used every day in commercial vehicle shops to safely lift and support trucks of all shapes and sizes. Although a **jack** is a lifting device, and a **jack stand** is a supporting device, we speak about both here as they are usually used and spoken about together. As with other shop equipment, before use it is important to check jacks and jack stands for safety reasons. If you suspect that they are faulty, *do not use them*. Take them out of service, and have them tested and serviced.

Jacks

A jack, or floor jack, is a lifting tool that can raise part of an object or vehicle from the ground prior to removing or replacing components or raise heavy components into position. Jacks used for lifting commercial vehicles operate the same as automotive jacks. The only difference is that jacks used to lift commercial vehicles are larger and have a greater lifting capacity (**FIGURE 6-3**).

A jack is used to raise a vehicle, but it should never be used to support the vehicle weight during any task that requires you

FIGURE 6-3 Jacks used for commercial vehicles have capacities of several tons.

to get underneath any part of the vehicle. Jack stands, which are metal stands with adjustable heights, are used to support a raised vehicle. NEVER place any part of your body under or crawl under a raised vehicle not properly supported by jack stands. Jacks can fail without warning and you can be crushed. **FIGURE 6-4** shows matched pairs of jack stands.

The three main types of jacks are the **hydraulic jack**, **pneumatic jack** (also known as an **air jack**), and **mechanical jack**. Hydraulic and pneumatic jacks are the most common types. They can be mounted on slides or on a wheeled platform. Hydraulic jacks use pressurized oil acting on a piston to provide the lifting action. The hydraulic pressure can be supplied by a manual pump or can be air over hydraulic, or electric over hydraulic action, meaning that air or electricity operates the hydraulic pump. Pneumatic or air jacks use compressed air acting on a large piston to lift the vehicle. Usually these are connected to shop air. Mechanical jacks use gears or screws to gain mechanical advantage to lift the vehicle or component; mechanical jacks are not typically found in commercial vehicle shops.

Different jacks are available for different purposes:

- **Floor jacks** are a common type of hydraulic jack that is mounted on four wheels, two of which swivel to provide a steering mechanism. The floor jack has a long handle that is used both to operate the jacking mechanism and to move and position the jack. Floor jacks have a low profile, making them suitable to position under vehicles. **FIGURE 6-3** shows a typical floor jack.
- **Bottle jacks** are portable jacks that usually have a hydraulic ram mechanism that rises vertically from the jack's center as the handle is operated. Bottle jacks are commonly used in commercial vehicles to raise a component of the vehicle, rather than the vehicle itself.
- **Pneumatic** or **air jacks** use compressed air to operate a large ram to lift the vehicle. Often the air jack is fitted to a moveable platform with a long handle. Air jacks are used to lift vehicles as an alternative to floor jacks. Because they require a compressed air supply, air jacks are usually used in the shop rather than for mobile operations. An air bag-type jack is another type of air jack that can be especially useful in situations where a very low-profile jack is

needed; the airbag jack must sit on an uneven surface; or the load to be lifted must be spread out over a larger area of jacking surface. **FIGURE 6-5** shows a typical air jack used to raise a vehicle by its wheel.

- **Sliding-bridge jacks** are typically found on hoist mechanisms. The hoist lifts the vehicle and then the sliding-bridge jack is positioned to further raise a portion of the vehicle to lift it off the hoist runway. Although more common in lighter-duty shops, you may come across these jacks in commercial vehicle facilities. Sliding-bridge jacks are typically air over or electric over hydraulic in their operation.
- **Transmission jacks** are specialized jacks that are fitted with several sets of mounting brackets, allowing them to fit to the shape of many different transmissions, so that the transmission can be lowered and raised safely. These jacks also have a method of securing the transmission to the jack's platform, usually a chain or chains, so it cannot fall. Transmission jacks are hydraulically or air operated. **FIGURE 6-6** shows a typical hydraulic transmission jack.

FIGURE 6-5 This jack uses air operating on a large ram to raise the vehicle.

FIGURE 6-4 Jack stands should only be used as matched pairs.

FIGURE 6-6 Transmission jacks have replaceable mounting brackets to adapt to many transmissions.

- **Clutch jacks** are a hydraulic jack equipped with exchangeable transmission input shafts that are used to align a clutch assembly, and then raise it into place, while it is being installed or removed. A clutch assembly for a class 8 tractor can weigh more than 175 pounds. The use of a clutch jack is highly recommended when working with these clutches. **FIGURE 6-7** shows a clutch jack.

Jack Stands

Jack stands, also known as *just stands*, are adjustable supports used with jacks. They are designed to support a vehicle's weight once it has been raised by a jack. The capacity of the stand is stamped on the stand or on a label affixed to the stand. They normally come in matched pairs and should always be used as a pair (**FIGURE 6-8**).

Jack stands are mechanical devices, meaning they mechanically lock in place at the height selected. Always use stands that have a rating capacity higher than the weight of the vehicle they are going to support. They are very dependable when used properly.

Always grip jack stands by the side to move them. The top portion is moveable to adjust the height and can pull out, causing the stand support to fall and/or pinching your fingers.

Lighter-duty stands have a handle on the side that can be used to move them, but be aware that the extendable part of the stand retracts when the handle is lifted and can pinch fingers. Ensure that the stand's base is on a level surface before lowering the vehicle onto the stand or the stand could tip over, causing the truck to slip off. Make sure that the stands are positioned under a part of the vehicle that will support the weight, and then lower the vehicle onto the stands. Then the jack can be removed.

SAFETY TIP

Never use jack stands without the lock pin (height-adjusting pin) in place and ensure that the pin goes fully through both sides of the stand.

Jack stands provide a stable support for a raised truck. A jack does not provide a stable support—the jack could fail or be mistakenly lowered, as mentioned previously. Never work under a vehicle that is supported by a jack alone. To lower the vehicle, raise the vehicle once more with the jack to clear the jack stands, remove the stands carefully, and then lower the vehicle. Remember to always use jack stands that are the correct capacity for the job.

SAFETY TIP

Never use non-conventional items to support a vehicle. Do not use concrete blocks or wood blocks for support; they can crumble. Only use jack stands that are approved and rated for the weight of the vehicle.

Chocking

Chocks are blocks of material placed against a wheel to prevent undesired rolling movement. They should be constructed of a material that does not crush easily and of a size that the tire cannot roll over easily. Prior to lifting any wheeled piece of equipment, always chock in front and behind one of the tires to prevent unwanted rolling (**FIGURE 6-9**). Chocks should be placed on the downhill side of the vehicle. When possible, use two chocking points due to the weight shifting when the item is lifted. Also, ensure the item is locked out, to prevent anyone else from accidentally attempting to start or move the vehicle.

FIGURE 6-7 Clutch jacks have a series of replaceable input shafts to hold and align various clutches for installation.

FIGURE 6-8 Always use jack stands in matched pairs that have enough capacity for the job.

FIGURE 6-9 Chocking on both sides of the tire before lifting prevents unintended movement of the equipment during the lift.

SKILL DRILL 6-2 Lifting and Securing a Vehicle with a Floor Jack and Stands

1. Position the vehicle on a level, solid surface. Depending on the operation, place the vehicle in neutral or park and apply the parking brake. Chock the wheels to prevent movement.
2. Select a pair of jack stands that are identical and of large enough capacity to support the vehicle (using two different stands, even if the capacity is the same, can lead to the vehicle being off level when supported).
3. Position the jack in a suitable position under the vehicle, typically under the front I-beam or the rear axle banjo housing. Tighten

the valve in the handle of the jack, usually clockwise. Use the handle with a pumping action to raise the jack just to contact the lifting point. Look carefully at the contact area to ensure the jack is properly and securely positioned. Note: if you are jacking the vehicle up by the frame, use a piece of hardwood between the jack and the frame to protect the frame.
4. Continue pumping the handle until the wheels lift from the floor. Again, check the position and security of the jack.
5. Continue lifting it until the vehicle is at the required height for you to work on it safely.
6. Position the two jack stands under the vehicle at the same height and in the same location on opposite sides. Ensure the stands are in contact with a part of the vehicle that can support its weight. Slowly turn the valve in the jack handle counterclockwise to lower the vehicle just until it contacts the stands on both sides.
7. Check the positioning of the stands once more and when you are confident that the contact is correct, push the vehicle side to side to check it is secure. Again, slowly turn the handle valve counterclockwise and lower the jack, then remove the jack.
8. When you are finished working under the vehicle, use the jack to raise the vehicle just enough to clear the jack stands and carefully remove the stands.
9. Slowly turn the jack handle valve counterclockwise and lower the truck to the ground. Return the jack and the jack stands to their proper storage location.

SAFETY TIP

Before working underneath any equipment, make sure it is properly supported. Inspect the jack stands or supports, and check that wheels are chocked. If something does not seem right, *stop* and check with your supervisor or another competent person. Don't risk your life trusting someone else's improper work.

Using Vehicle Jacks and Jack Stands

The weight of the vehicle being lifted determines the type of jack needed. Remember that the jack is rated for a certain load, so do not try to lift a vehicle that exceeds that load rating. Lifting a dump truck that is empty is much different than lifting one that is full of wet sand! Be aware of circumstances that can make a vehicle heavier than you expect and use a jack with the correct capacity. This is true for jack stands as well. Make sure their capacity exceeds the weight of the vehicle and/or vehicle and combined load. To lift a vehicle with a floor jack and support it on stands, follow the steps in **SKILL DRILL 6-2**.

Vehicle Hoists

LO 6-3 Describe the types and uses of vehicle hoists and their certification criteria.

A **vehicle hoist** raises the entire vehicle off the ground so that a technician can work underneath the vehicle easily. Hoists can also be used to raise the vehicle to the correct height so that work can be done at the side of the vehicle in a standing position. There are several different designs of vehicle hoists:

- Platform hoists, where a vehicle is driven onto two parallel platforms that are then raised
- Single post hoist, this type of hoist has a single central hydraulic ram fitted with four moveable arms that lift the vehicle
- Two post hoists, these have one post on either side of the vehicle with two moveable arms that lift the vehicle
- Scissor-lift hoists

Hoists also come in varying capacities, depending on the type of vehicle that needs to be lifted. Hoists can also be portable and can be moved around the shop to where they are needed. Hoists are typically electric over hydraulic powered, meaning that an electric motor supplies hydraulic pressure, which is then used to raise the vehicle on the hoist.

Stability on a Hoist

The platform hoist is a very stable hoist as the vehicle is lifted on its wheels (**FIGURE 6-10**). You merely drive the vehicle onto the platform and then raise it. A drawback to this type of hoist is that the wheels of the vehicle cannot be removed unless a sliding-bridge-type jack is used to lift the wheels off the hoist platform. Single-post and two-post hoists are typically used for lighter vehicles and both can be unstable if the arms of the hoist and the vehicle are not arranged correctly. It is very important to try and center the vehicle and the lifting points in a way that spreads the vehicle weight out evenly, so it does not tip forward or backward when being lifted. As with all lifting and hoisting equipment, hoists should be inspected and certified on a regular basis, usually annually.

FIGURE 6-10 A platform hoist is very stable as it raises the vehicle on its wheels.

FIGURE 6-12 Using four posts together, the entire vehicle can be raised.

FIGURE 6-11 Portable lifting hoist posts can be used in pairs or four can be used at once.

Portable Lifting Hoists

Portable lifting hoists are the most versatile type of hoist for a commercial vehicle facility that works on different types of vehicles. These hoists are usually made up of four or more individual posts and each one is used to lift one wheel of a vehicle. This allows the hoist to be moved to the place in the shop where it is required and to be stored away when it is not required. The hoist can adapt to any size vehicle (if it does not exceed the hoist's capacity) simply by repositioning the posts. The hoist posts are connected electrically so they work as one unit. The posts can be used as a two-post hoist to lift only one end of a vehicle or four or six posts to lift the entire vehicle. **FIGURE 6-11** shows the four posts of a portable lifting hoist.

Portable lifting hoists have thick cables that are used to connect the posts together. These cables must always be securely stored on the provided cable hangers on the posts, so they do not become damaged. Most portable lifting hoists have a master control panel on one of the posts; therefore, this post

must be used as one of the posts in any of the configurations. Some systems come with a remote control, so the technician can operate the hoist system from any location. The posts of the portable lifting hoist have an interlock system, so that if one post is not operating correctly, the entire hoist stops working. Portable lifting hoists typically have a system that allows a hydraulic maneuvering wheel to be pumped into place to move the hoist posts around. It is essential that these wheels are raised out of contact with the floor before you raise the vehicle, or the wheels will break! **FIGURE 6-12** shows a portable hoist in action.

Safety Locks

All hoists have safety locking systems that lock into place as the vehicle is raised. These are usually large ratchet-like structures that are part of the posts and can typically be heard clacking as the post rises by each ratchet tooth. Once the vehicle has been raised to the correct height, it is lowered onto the last ratchet tooth to lock the hoist in position. To lower the hoist, the hoist is raised slightly to lift it off the safety locks, then the locks are released, and the vehicle is lowered. **FIGURE 6-13** shows the detail of a safety lock on a portable hoist post.

Ratings and Inspections

All hoists are rated for a certain capacity and vehicle type. Never use a hoist for anything other than the job it was intended for. Never try to lift a vehicle that exceeds the hoist capacity. As mentioned previously, all hoists must be inspected and certified, typically on an annual basis. Before using any hoist, check the certification tag to ensure it is in compliance. **FIGURE 6-14** shows a typical certification tag. Always use care when operating a hoist. Look above before and during lifting and look below during lowering. Always check for items that can be snagged while raising or lowering, such as exhaust hoses, lights, or extension cords, and the like. Be particularly careful when using interconnected portable hoist posts that their cables do not become pinched or stretched.

Safety Lock
Ratchet System

FIGURE 6-13 All hoists have a safety lock system that must be disengaged to lower the hoist.

FIGURE 6-14 Compliance testing tags contain details of when the last test was done and when the next test is due.

► **TECHNICIAN TIP**

Before using a hoist, make sure the most recent inspection recorded on the test certificate is up to date. If it is not, the test certificate has expired, and you should notify your supervisor and not use the equipment.

Inspection Pits

As an alternative to lifting a vehicle on a hoist, an inspection pit can be used as a safe and easy way to view the vehicle from the underside. Inspection pits are commonly used in commercial vehicle shops for lubrication service and are usually equipped with draining systems for used oils and other fluids. Inspection pits are usually highly visibly outlined with painted caution lines (**FIGURE 6-15**) or barriers to prevent people from accidentally falling into the pit. Inspection pits by their nature can accumulate fumes and become an explosion hazard. To prevent this, they are commonly equipped with an extraction fan system and explosion-proof fully sealed lighting systems.

FIGURE 6-15 Inspection pits are commonly used for lubrication service. They should be clearly marked for safety.

Selecting Appropriate Hoisting Equipment

LO 6-4 Describe the different types of and uses of cranes and rigging equipment.

Even though we use vehicle hoists to lift vehicles, hoisting means raising or lifting something from above, rather than below. Hoisting uses cranes, mobile gantries, and overhead cranes to vertically raise a load. For example, we hoist an engine out of a truck with an engine crane. **FIGURE 6-16** shows a typical overhead crane in a commercial vehicle shop.

FIGURE 6-16 This overhead crane can lift several tons.

The equipment used to attach the hoisting device, i.e., the crane, to the load is also known as **rigging**. The term rigging covers all the ropes, chains, cables, slings, shackles, eye hooks, and any other equipment used for attachment to the load. Each piece of hoisting equipment and rigging has a maximum weight it can support. The maximum operating capacity is usually expressed as the **safe working load (SWL)**. For example, if the SWL is 1 ton, the equipment can safely lift up to 2000 pounds (907 kg).

When using hoisting equipment, never exceed its capacity, and always maintain some reserve capacity as an extra safety margin. In addition, you should use each piece of lifting equipment for its designed purpose only. When hoisting, the piece of rigging equipment that has the lowest capacity is the maximum lift that can be undertaken. Using lifting equipment incorrectly may lead to equipment failure that can cause serious injury and damage.

The Safe Use of Hoisting Equipment

In addition to double-checking safe working loads and using equipment only for its intended purpose, technicians can take several other steps to ensure a safe operating environment. These include testing and test certification. Requirements can vary by country and your local area, so be sure to check with your supervisor if you have any questions.

SAFETY TIP

Know which hoisting equipment in your shop requires special training and/or certification. If you do not have the special training and certification to operate a piece of hoisting equipment, *do not* operate it. Find a qualified person to operate the equipment and perform the task you need to have completed. These items require special training and certification for a reason; they can be extremely complex to operate and present a huge potential safety hazard.

▶ TECHNICIAN TIP

When using multiple pieces of lifting or hoisting equipment, the SWL (safe working load) is limited to the lowest-rated piece of equipment. Remember, "A chain is only as strong as its weakest link." Consider the rigging, such as the chains, cables, ropes, fittings, and rings; the equipment tie-down points; and the lifting equipment, such as the hoist or crane you are using on a lift. The lifting equipment's capacity is limited by the strength of the weakest single component. For example, a 5-ton chain with a 3-ton D-shackle has a maximum lifting capacity of 3 tons or less.

Hoisting Equipment Certification

Hoisting equipment, like other lifting equipment, is tested and certified on a regular basis. The certification should be on a tag on the piece of equipment. Rigging usually has the SWL stamped on the piece, such as on a shackle or a d-ring, or on a tag that is attached to the piece of rigging, e.g., a tag on a wire rope sling. Inspections should look for any damage, such as cracks, dents, marks, cuts, and abrasions, which could lessen SWL of the piece. Rigging should be recertified from time to time. Any piece of rigging that shows signs of damage or fatigue should be discarded or sent for recertification. **FIGURE 6-17** shows the inspection/certification tag on a piece of rigging.

FIGURE 6-17 Rigging must be inspected and certified from time to time. Check your rigging before use.

Selecting Appropriate Lift Points

When dealing with lifting heavy objects, it is critical to lift the object using solid and secure lift points with enough capacity to lift the item without damage. Most engines, for example, have specified lifting hooks or plates that should be used when hoisting. Check the manufacturer's information for the correct attachment points (**FIGURE 6-18**).

SAFETY TIP

Failure to utilize proper lift points may result in equipment damage or injury. Ensure you use designated and proper lift points when available. Lifting a heavy item can place a lot of strain into a very small area, possibly resulting in failure of the lifting point. In the absence of a manufacturer's designated lifting point, utilize the strongest area available.

FIGURE 6-18 Make sure that the attachment points are correct and secure before lifting a load.

Center of Gravity

Just as important as ensuring that the lifting points are strong enough to support the lift is making sure that the correct lifting point positioning is used. In explaining this, we need to define a few terms. The **center of gravity (CG)**, also called the center of balance, of an object is the point, or position, at which the item's weight is evenly dispersed, and all sides are in balance. If the item were to be supported in a direct vertical axis from the center of gravity, it would balance perfectly. As the center of gravity is a position, it has units of length: inches, feet, meters, centimeters. The center of gravity of an object can be described as the distance from an arbitrary reference point on the item to the center of gravity. The arbitrary reference point from where the center of gravity is measured is called the **reference datum line (RDL)**. For instance, the manufacturer of a certain vehicle may describe the vehicle's center of gravity as being 200" (508 cm) from the front end of the vehicle at a height of 24" (61 cm) above ground level. Where the RDL is on an item does not matter, so long as it is specifically defined and does not change. The further away the item is supported from the vertical axis of the center of gravity, the more it tends to rotate. The tendency of an item to rotate about a pivot is called **torque**.

Take the case in which you are hoisting a heavy item from above. If the crane is attached at a lifting point not in the same vertical axis as the center of gravity, the item tends to rotate as it is being lifted. In many cases, this is not desirable and creates an unstable condition. The load rotates until the center of gravity of the load is in the same vertical axis as the lifting hook. **FIGURE 6-19** shows the effects of the object's center of gravity during a lifting or hoisting operation.

However, if the crane is attached at a lifting point that is in the same vertical axis of the item's center of gravity, it lifts straight up and does not rotate. Therefore, it is important to determine the item's center of gravity, before lifting. An item that is hoisted by utilizing a poorly positioned attachment point can become unstable and fall.

Unfortunately, the technician who is required to hoist a heavy engine from a truck does not know the engine's center

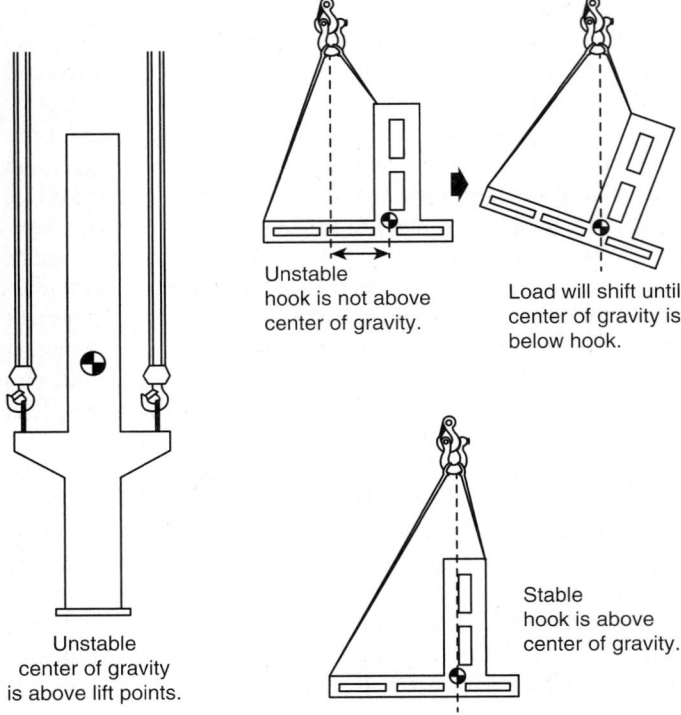

Effect of Center of Gravity on Lift

FIGURE 6-19 The position of the lifted item's center of gravity with respect to the lifting hook and lifting points is critical. Poor positioning causes the load to shift and may result in equipment damage and injury.

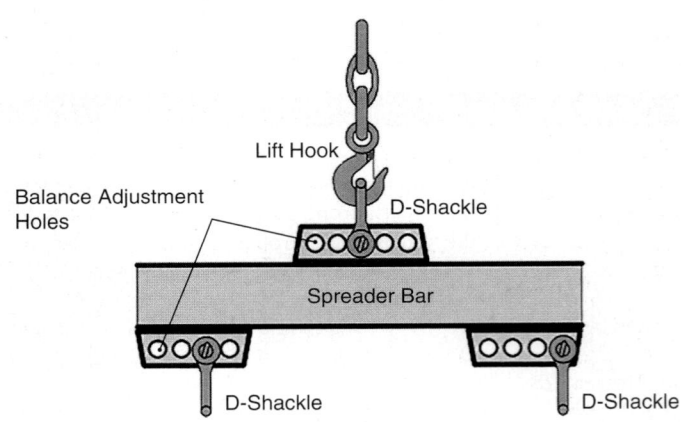

FIGURE 6-20 Spreader bars or load levelers are used to change the attachment points to level a load.

of gravity, so requires the use of a **load leveler**. A load leveler or a **spreader bar** is a bar with moveable attachment points (**FIGURE 6-20**). The bar is attached to the load at two or more points and the crane is attached to the hook eye of the bar. To level the load, the attachment points are then changed by trial and error to level the load. Some spreader bars are adjustable using a long-threaded rod, which is turned to position the hook in the best spot to level the load as it is raised.

When available, use the manufacturer's dedicated lift points. When lifting a load follow these guidelines:

- Ensure that the lifting points capacity is known and is not exceeded.
- When lifting an item from above by hoisting, use a lift point that is directly *above* the item's center of gravity, if possible.
- When lifting using a single lift point, use a lift point in the same vertical axis as the item's center of gravity.
- When hoisting using two lift points, place them symmetrically the same distance apart from the item's center of gravity.
- When lifting an item by hoisting, keep the lifting hook in the same vertical axis as the item's center of gravity.

Using Various Types of Lifting Equipment

Lifting equipment is used not only to raise heavy components, but also to move and lower pieces into place. The equipment used depends on a part's size, weight, and type, as well as the job being performed. This section looks at several different types of lifting and moving equipment.

Chain Blocks and Mobile Gantry Cranes

Chain blocks and mobile gantry cranes are often used together to lift larger components inside commercial vehicle shops. **Chain blocks (block and tackle)** use mechanical advantage to raise or hoist components. The typical block, also known as chain falls, consists of two grooved wheels with a chain wound around them in the same fashion as a block and tackle. The chain wound around the two wheels creates a simple machine that uses the leverage and the increased lifting ability created by the two wheels to lift heavy weights. Chain blocks can be attached to, and hang from, a mobile gantry crane. A **mobile gantry crane** is simply an A-frame on wheels that can be moved around the shop to provide an attachment point for a chain block.

Chain blocks have a safety latch and hook fittings that attach to lifting points on a component (**FIGURE 6-21**). Once attached to a load, the chain block can lift heavy components with little effort by the technician. Mobile gantries are usually wheeled to the place where the hoisting must be done.

FIGURE 6-21 A chain block's hook should have a safety latch to prevent the rigging from coming out of the hook.

Overhead Gantry Cranes

Shops where heavy lifting is done on regularly may have overhead gantry cranes. An **overhead gantry crane** is a moveable framework with a chain block or other hoisting mechanism attached. The chain block can be positioned directly above the point where hoisting must occur in the shop. Typically, the crane has electric hand controls to position the chain block and to raise and lower the hook (**FIGURE 6-22**). You should be trained in the overhead crane's correct operation before you attempt to use it.

Chain blocks and gantry cranes both relieve the technician of having to exert a lot of effort to remove heavy components and lower them into an area where they can be serviced. Carefully check the lifting hooks on these devices before use,

FIGURE 6-22 Overhead gantry crane with electric controls used for heavy lifting.

to make sure the end of the hook hasn't opened beyond the standard limit. Inspect chains for any mud or grit and examine safety latches to be sure they are working properly. Overhead gantry cranes can easily be positioned to remove items, such as transmissions (**FIGURE 6-23**).

OSHA Rules for Lifting Equipment

OSHA sets standards for inspection and certification of lifting and hoisting devices, such as cranes and vehicle hoists. Several OSHA regulations deal with lifting equipment, depending on the type. We review some basic OSHA rules for several types of lifting equipment here. Remember, it is your responsibility to research and know the applicable OSHA, industry standards, and equipment manufacturer specific rules and regulations.

The following is an excerpt of the OSHA standards:

- Overhead and Gantry Cranes (OSHA Standard 1910.179, 1926.1438)
  - The rated load of the crane shall be plainly marked and visible.
  - Equipment and all rigging devices must comply with the manufacturer's recommendations.
  - Crane movement shall be clear of obstructions.
  - Functional inspection should be performed daily.
  - Full inspection performed should be monthly to every 12 months, depending on frequency of use.
  - Employee training is required.
- Hoisting/Lifting Equipment with a Capacity of 2,000 lb or Less (OSHA Standard 1926.1441)
  - The rated load should be marked on the lifting device.
  - Equipment and all rigging devices must comply with the manufacturer's recommendations.
  - Post-assembly (after being attached to the load) inspection is required to verify that equipment and connections meet the manufacturer's specifications.
  - Employee training is required.

Notice that the common rules from OSHA are that the personnel operating lifting equipment must be trained to use the equipment; the lifting capacity must be clearly marked; the equipment manufacturer's recommendations must be followed; the equipment and load (once connected) must be inspected; and the maximum working load capacities of any devices and equipment must not be exceeded.

When guidance is needed about specific lifting procedures, rigging equipment, and best practices, consult a certified **rigger** (a person who has been trained in lifting, hoisting, and rigging). For further details, refer to the OSHA standards for the specific equipment you are using, any applicable industry standards, and the lifting equipment manufacturer's information. **FIGURE 6-24** shows the certification tag for an overhead gantry crane.

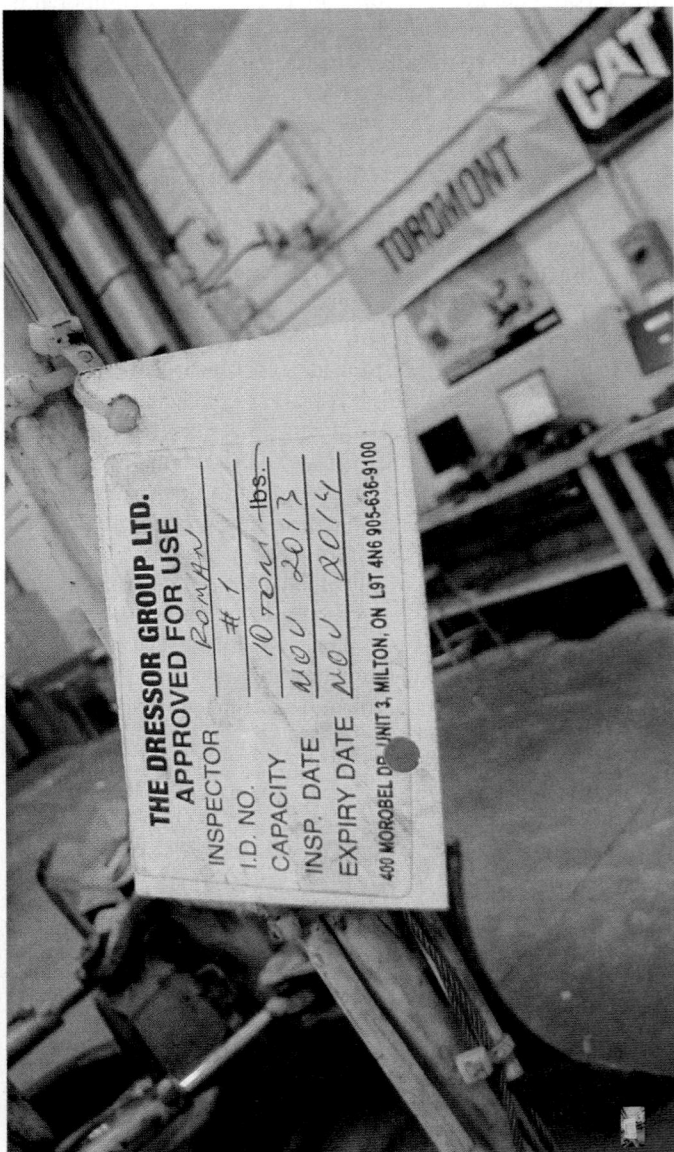

FIGURE 6-24 Overhead cranes need recertification on an annual basis.

FIGURE 6-23 An overhead gantry crane makes removing this transmission easier.

Slings and Shackles

Slings are one type of rigging equipment technicians use to lift and lower many things in the shop. For example, a transmission, engine, or differential can be lifted using slings (**FIGURE 6-25**). Slings are made from strong webbing material, wire rope, or chain. Webbed slings have an eye at each end for the connection of shackles (discussed later in this section) to attach loads. **FIGURE 6-26** shows a web sling.

Wire rope and chain slings may have any number of different fittings for different applications. Regardless of the sling type and its fittings, each has a maximum working load that cannot be exceeded. As with all lifting equipment, slings must be tested regularly to ensure they are safe to use. If you suspect that any piece of lifting equipment is damaged, do not use it; replace it or have it recertified.

- *Webbed slings* are usually flat in appearance and made from strong synthetic materials, such as polyester. Webbed slings are available in a variety of lifting capacities for different lifting tasks.
- *Synthetic slings* can be more susceptible to cutting or abrasive damage than harder materials, such as chains or wire, and should be checked before each use to ensure they are not damaged. When using synthetic slings, always ensure they are protected from sharp corners, which may damage the slings and reduce lifting capacity.
- *Wire rope slings* are made from many strands of fine wire and a core. The size, number, and arrangement of the wires determine the sling's lifting capacity. Wire rope slings are less susceptible to abrasion and cutting than synthetic slings, but should be checked for any damage, such as kinks and broken or cut wires, as these reduce the lifting capacity. See the section on wire rope near the end of the chapter to view the out-of-service criteria for wire rope.
- *Chain slings* are made from hardened steel and are not as susceptible to damage as synthetic or wire rope slings. Cracks, excessive corrosion and gouges can reduce the capacity of chain. Before using chain or chain slings for lifting, check

for these and other defects. Chains can have several different types of fittings attached to the ends, such as eyes, shackles, and hooks (**FIGURE 6-27**). Always check the capacity of the hooks and end fittings and check them for spreading or other defects. Remember that the lowest SWL-rated piece in a lifting setup is the maximum lift that the rigging can be used for, and always leave extra capacity for safety. Chains, like all lifting equipment, should be checked for damage before being used and regularly tested and tagged.

Shackles are attached to slings and chains to use as connectors between a component and various applications, such as lifting equipment. **FIGURE 6-28** shows an anchor-type shackle. Note that the lifting capacity is stamped on the shackle, in this case ¾ ton or 1500 pounds (680 kg); do not use shackles with an unknown lifting capacity/rating.

Shackles should be stamped with their SWL. If they are not stamped, do not use the shackle. In lifting equipment, shackles are secured with a pin through the bottom of the shackle. Secure D-shackles, a common type of shackle, has a piece of wire through the shackle's eye to lock the pin and prevent it from working loose. The same applies to bow shackles. As with all lifting equipment, inspect shackles to make sure they are in good condition and free from dirt and grime.

Sling and Chain Capacity

When using slings, the capacity of the rigging must be carefully monitored. Take for example, a lift where you are using four chains with a 500 pound (227 kg) capacity to lift an object by

FIGURE 6-25 Slings and other heavy lifting components in a shop.

FIGURE 6-26 A webbed sling.

Single-leg Kuplink and hook   Single-leg master link and hook   Two-leg master link and hooks   Collar align with Kuplink each end   Collar align with egg link each end

FIGURE 6-27 Chains can have many different types of fittings at either end.

FIGURE 6-28 Anchor-type shackles can be used to connect pieces of lifting equipment.

its four corners. You may think that the total capacity for the chains used is 2000 pounds (907 kg). However, when lifting an object in this fashion, usually only two of the chains carry the total weight at any given time during the lift, the two other chains are merely stabilizing the object. Therefore, the capacity of the slings for this lift is only 1000 pounds (454 kg).

The sling angle is another important consideration. When the slings are attached to an object so they are vertical or 90 degrees to the object during the lift, the sling capacity is the rated capacity on the sling. However, if the sling is at an angle, the capacity is reduced. If the sling is at 60 degrees, the load on the sling is increased by approximately 15%. As the angle gets smaller, the load on the sling increases dramatically to where at a 5-degree angle, the load on the sling has increased to over 500%. Always take sling angle into account when checking capacity for the lift. **FIGURE 6-29** depicts the load change on slings as the angle changes.

Engine Hoists/Cranes

Engine hoists, or **mobile floor cranes**, can lift very heavy objects, such as engines, while the engines are being removed from a vehicle or refitted. The engine hoist's lifting arm is moved by a

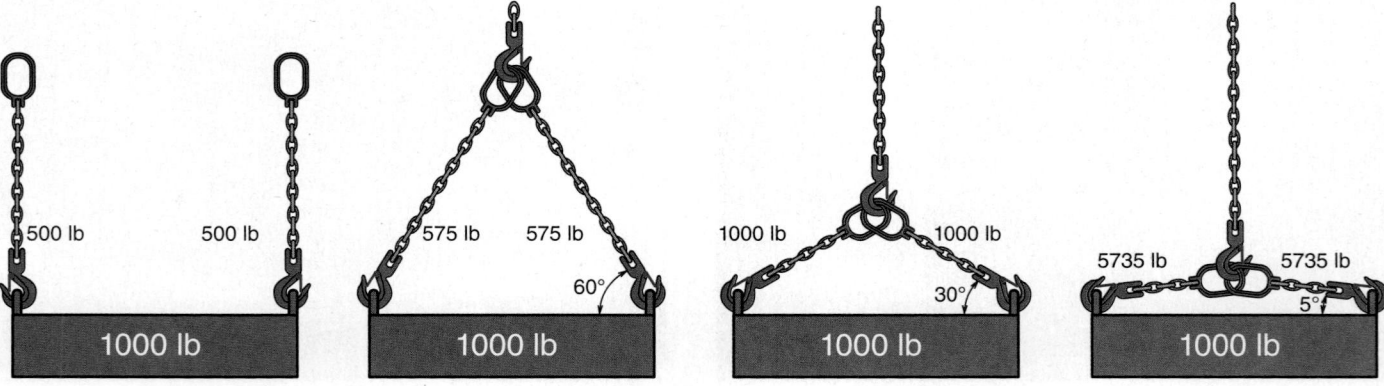

| 500 lb | 500 lb | 575 lb | 575 lb 60° | 1000 lb | 1000 lb 30° | 5735 lb | 5735 lb 5° |

1000 lb   1000 lb   1000 lb   1000 lb

FIGURE 6-29 Sling angle greatly affects the load on a sling during a lift. Try to keep the angle greater than 60 degrees.

hydraulic cylinder and is adjustable for length. However, extending the lifting arm reduces its lifting capacity because it moves the load farther away from the supporting frame. The hoist is stamped with the varying capacities as the arm is extended. You can sometimes extend the supporting legs for stability, but the more you extend the arm and the legs, the lower the engine hoist's total lift capacity. The engine or component to be lifted is attached to the lifting arm by a sling or a lifting chain. Make sure the lifting attachment at the end of the lifting arm is strong enough to lift the engine and is not damaged or cracked. When attaching the lifting chain or sling to an engine, make sure it is firmly attached and that the engine hoist is configured to lift that weight. Make sure the fasteners attaching the lifting chain, or sling, have a tensile strength that is more than the engine's weight. In areas where space is limited for lifting, you should use a spreader bar or load leveler to aid the lifting operation. A spreader bar allows you to move the attachment points so that the engine's center of gravity is below the hook while lifting. When the engine or other component has been lifted and slowly and carefully moved away from the truck, it should be lowered onto an engine stand suitable for its weight. Do not lower the engine directly to the floor. The weight of the engine may be enough to crush the oil pan or other engine components. **FIGURE 6-30** shows an engine hoist or crane folded for storage.

Engine Hoist Stability

The farther off the ground an engine is lifted, the less stable the engine hoist becomes. As the center of gravity of the engine and the hoist combined is changing, keep the engine as close to the ground as possible. When moving a suspended engine, move the engine hoist slowly. Do not change direction quickly because the engine will swing and may cause the whole apparatus to tumble. When using these types of hoists or cranes, always make sure that the slings and rope, cables, and chains that are used are compliant with relevant regulations and do not exceed the load ratings. Remember, the capacity during the lift is the capacity of the lowest-rated part of the rigging (**FIGURE 6-31**).

SAFETY TIP

Never use a hoist to lift any weight greater than the lifting capacity, which is the lowest SWL of the rigging or the hoist.

Safety While Using Lifting Equipment

Like many shop activities, using lifting equipment involves managing risks. Think carefully about what you are going to do, plan your activities, and check the equipment to make sure it is safe to use. To use engine hoists and stands, follow the steps in **SKILL DRILL 6-3**.

▶ TECHNICIAN TIP

- The engine hoist's load rating must be greater than the weight of the object to be lifted.
- Never leave an unsupported engine hanging on an engine hoist. Secure the engine on an engine stand before starting to work on it.
- If using an engine stand, make sure it is designed to support the weight of the engine and that you have the correct number of bolts to hold the engine to the stand.
- Always extend the engine hoist's legs in relation to the lifting arm to ensure adequate stability.

FIGURE 6-30 A folded engine hoist. Note how the capacity changes as the hoist arm is extended. Engine hoists come in many sizes and lifting capacities.

FIGURE 6-31 Inspect to make sure all chains, hooks, fixtures, and riggings are in good condition and of the correct capacity for the lift.

SKILL DRILL 6-3 Using Engine Hoists and Stands

1. Prepare to use the engine hoist. Lower the lifting arm and position the lifting end and chain over the center of the engine.
2. Wear appropriate personal protective equipment (PPE), such as leather gloves, during the entire operation, beginning with inspecting the chain, steel cable, sling, and bolts to make sure they are in good condition. Before you use the crane, make sure the chain or sling is rated higher than the weight of the item to be lifted. Also, ensure that the lifting arm is only extended to the length of its lifting capacity applicable to the weight of the item to be lifted. Only use

approved lifting equipment—nothing homemade. Look carefully around the component that is about to be lifted, to determine whether it has lifting eyes or other anchor points.

3. If the engine or component has lifting eyes, attach the sling with D-shackles or chain hooks. If you need to screw in bolts and spacer washers to lift the engine, make sure you use the correct bolt and spacer size for the chain or cable. Screw the bolts until the sling is held tight against the component.
4. Attach the hoist's hook under the center of the sling and raise the engine hoist just enough to lift the engine to take the slack up on the cable, chain, or sling. Double-check the sling and attachment points for safety. The engine's or component's center of gravity should be directly under the engine hoist's hook, and there should be no twists or kinks in the chain or sling.
5. Raise the engine hoist until the engine is clear of the ground and any obstacles. Slowly and gently move the engine hoist and lifted component to the new location with minimum ground clearance to prevent swinging and potential tilting of the whole crane.
6. Make sure the engine is positioned correctly. You need to place blocking under the engine to stabilize it or mount the engine to a suitable stand. Once you are sure the engine is stable, lower the engine hoist, and remove the sling and any securing fasteners.
7. Return the equipment to its storage area.

Lifting heavy items is inherently dangerous. It is important for the technician to know the basic principles of lifting items safely and properly. It is also important to know the different types of lifting devices in your shop, which ones require special certification or training, how to inspect them for proper operation and safety inspection certifications, and how to operate them properly and safely.

▶ TECHNICIAN TIP

When involved with a lift, never place yourself or a body part underneath the item being lifted or jacked during the lift. When overhead cranes are in use, stand well outside the danger area, and never stand underneath an unsupported load. Only begin work underneath an item after it has been properly supported and all safety precautions have been inspected and followed. Always have an escape route planned when involved in a lift. Plan the fastest and most direct route to get out of danger should the equipment collapse, including a route that is clear of any additional rolling or falling equipment, should something go wrong.

Wire Rope Application and Use

LO 6-5 Explain the types, uses, and inspection of wire rope.

Because wire rope is found in many applications in a commercial vehicle shop, we discuss the basics of wire rope and its uses and inspection. Wire rope can be found in slings, in other rigging, winch cables, and more. Wire rope is simply rope made from wire. A wire rope consists of three basic components; individual wires that are twisted together to form a **strand** and then

several strands are twisted together around the core of the rope. The core of the rope can be made of fiber or it can be a wire strand core, where the strands of the rope are twisted around a multiwire strand, or it can be an independent wire rope core (IWRC) in which the strands are twisted around a separate wire rope at the core. Wire rope has many different constructions, as shown in **FIGURE 6-32**.

Wire rope is designated by the number of strands in the rope and the number of wires in each strand. The different construction designs give the rope different qualities, such as increased strength, flexibility, heat resistance, and more, for varying applications. Take, for example, a ½" (1.3 cm) diameter wire rope called a 6 × 19; it is made from six strands each containing 19 wires. A ½" (1.3 cm) rope made of 6 strands, each containing 37 thinner wires, is called a 6 × 37. The first rope is the strongest and less susceptible to abrasion, but the second rope is more flexible. Because of its usefulness, wire rope is used for many purposes, such as for this sling in **FIGURE 6-33**. Wire rope is also called *cable*.

Advantages of Wire Rope

Wire rope was initially developed as an alternative to metal chains. In a metal chain, a single failure in one chain link causes a catastrophic failure. A single failure of a wire in a wire rope does not lead to a catastrophic failure, as it has many other wires and wire strands to share the load, should one fail. In addition, because of the twisted wire, internal friction between the wires also prevents a catastrophic failure, should a single wire break. The most common material for wire rope is steel. Wire rope is

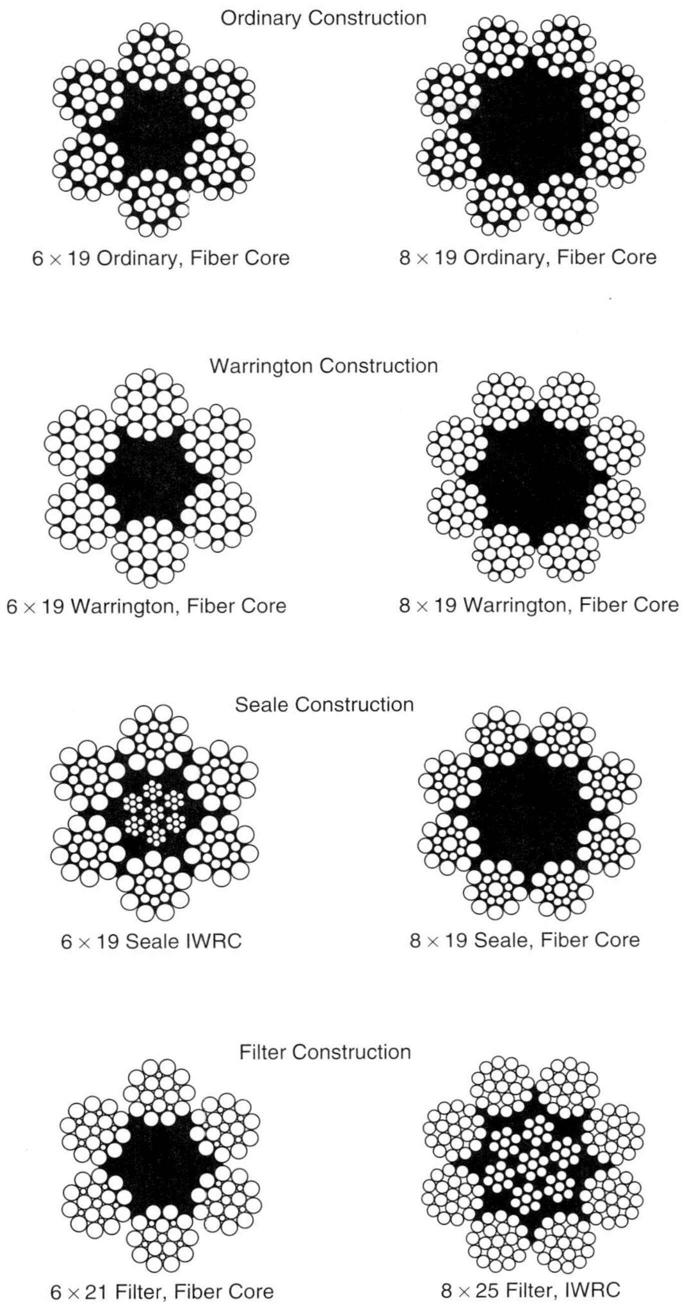

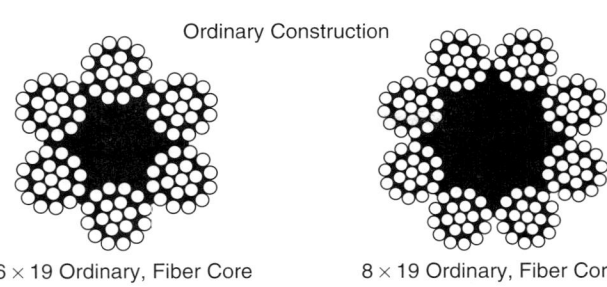

Ordinary Construction

6 × 19 Ordinary, Fiber Core

8 × 19 Ordinary, Fiber Core

Warrington Construction

6 × 19 Warrington, Fiber Core

8 × 19 Warrington, Fiber Core

Seale Construction

6 × 19 Seale IWRC

8 × 19 Seale, Fiber Core

Filter Construction

6 × 21 Filter, Fiber Core

8 × 25 Filter, IWRC

FIGURE 6-32 Wire rope comes in many designs.

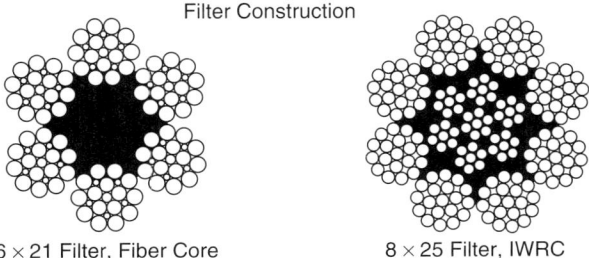

FIGURE 6-33 Wire rope is used all around us in many devices and equipment, from a window regulator in a passenger car to the supporting cables in massive suspension bridges.

used in many applications, such as guy wires to support large towers, in suspension bridges, and for lifting and hoisting in cranes and elevators. Wire rope is quite strong, comes in many sizes, can come in very long applications, and is resistant to abrasion and crushing. Some important limitations to wire rope are listed here:

- It must be kept from bending, twisting, or kinking—all of which can decrease its SWL.
- Sharp bends and contact with sharp edges can cause damage.

- Wire rope conducts electricity.
- It must be inspected periodically (prior to use in critical applications, such as lifting and rigging).

Wire Rope End Terminations

A wire rope **end termination** is the treatment at the end or ends of a length of wire rope, usually made by forming an eye or attaching a fitting, and designed to be the permanent end termination on the wire rope that connects it to the load. Without the end terminations, the wire rope is not able to connect to a load to perform a lift. The end terminations are just as important as the wire rope itself. An entire sling or rigging assembly is only as strong as the weakest part. Because of this, the end terminations and associated hardware can be a limiting factor on the SWL of an entire sling or lifting assembly. One wire rope termination that a commercial vehicle technician normally uses is the **speltered socket end**, where the wire rope is run through a cone-shaped socket and spread out, then molten zinc is poured into the socket to attach the wire rope. The second type is the **swaged end** where the rope is formed into an eye around a thimble (**FIGURE 6-34**) and the two pieces are swaged together using a steel sleeve that is compressed hydraulically. These two types of end terminations have 100% of the SWL of the rope when done correctly.

Wire rope clips (**FIGURE 6-35**) can be used to form an end termination, but the SWL end termination is reduced to 80% of the rope itself. When an end termination is made with wire rope clips, the number of clips and their orientation is critical. The formula for the number of clips required is 3 × the rope diameter in inches plus 1, so for a ½" rope × 3 equals 1½ +1 or three

clips (always round up). A thimble must be used in the eye and the clips should be spaced at 6 × the rope diameter in inches, or 3" (7.6 cm) apart for a ½" (1.3 cm) rope.

The saddles of the wire rope clips must be on the active side of the rope and the U-bolt on the **bitter end**, or dead end, of the rope, as the U-bolt crushes the rope, reducing its capacity. **FIGURE 6-36** shows the three wire rope terminations discussed here. There are other end terminations, but the commercial vehicle technician is not likely to come across them. It is recommended that technicians only use wire rope and slings that have end terminations that are swaged or speltered, and those should have the correct certification tags attached.

FIGURE 6-34 A thimble protects the wire rope in the eye from abrasion.

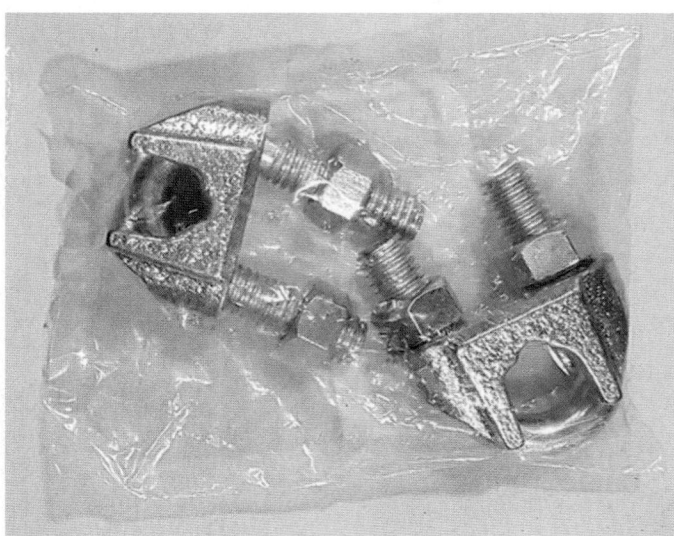

FIGURE 6-35 Wire rope clips can be used to form an end termination, but the SWL is reduced to 80% of the rope's SWL.

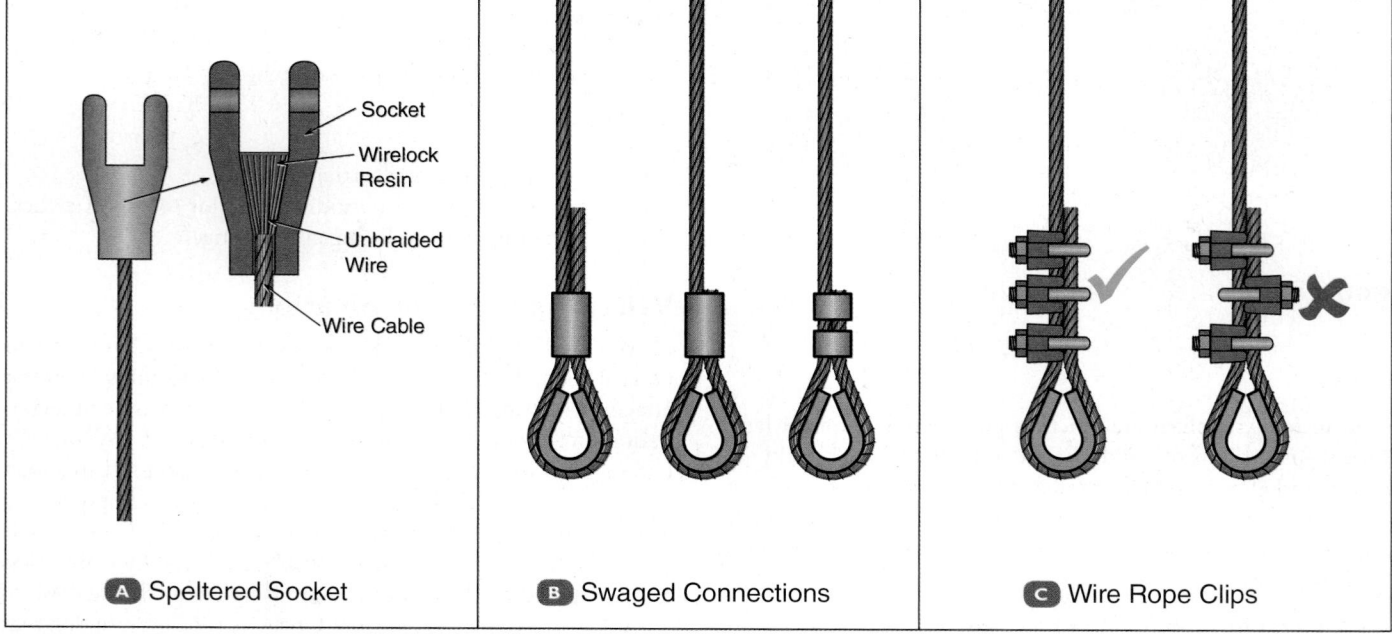

A Speltered Socket — Socket, Wirelock Resin, Unbraided Wire, Wire Cable

B Swaged Connections

C Wire Rope Clips

FIGURE 6-36 Wire rope end terminations. **A.** Speltered socket. **B.** Swaged connections. **C.** Wire rope clips.

Personnel that assemble end terminations to wire rope and slings have specific knowledge and training to ensure they are done properly. Many shop accidents have been caused by lifting-sling failures due to end terminations assembled improperly and/or not proof tested. If in doubt as to whether a wire rope end termination was done properly, consult a rigging manual from a reputable industry authority or a wire rope manufacturer. A good general rule of thumb is, if the wire rope and/or sling does not have the manufacturer's tag, it should be suspect.

Wire Rope Inspection

Because wire rope has a finite lifespan and is susceptible to wear and failure, regular inspections, and the frequency and type of inspection, are mandated by government and industry safety agencies for continued proper and safe operation. Failure to follow government and industry regulations regarding inspection may result in civil or criminal penalties. Consult your country and industry regulations about inspection of wire rope

and lifting equipment. Typically, wire rope should be inspected daily, before it is used, for visual deficiencies. See **SKILL DRILL 6-4** for general information that can be used as a rough guide for inspecting wire rope used for horizontal pulling/towing and vertical lifting. It is not the intention here to give comprehensive inspection guidelines for wire rope. Always consult the manufacturers for specific inspection criteria. Always err on the side of caution—if you are not fully confident that the wire rope is up to the job, do not use it.

As you service vehicles, you are tasked to lift, tow, and move heavy equipment and parts. This carries inherent safety risks that can damage equipment, property, and result in injury to yourself and others. Ensure that you know the proper regulations, rules, equipment, and procedures to use. If you don't know, find out from a competent person or an authoritative source. Don't place yourself and others at risk by not knowing the correct way to perform a lifting or towing operation. Conversely, don't place your life in someone else's hands without verifying everything has been done correctly.

SKILL DRILL 6-4 Inspecting Wire Rope Applications Prior to Use (General External Physical Inspection)

1. Check wire rope for manufacturer's specification tag with name of manufacturer, date of manufacture, load capacity, and date of last inspection by a certified individual or authority. Do not use wire ropes or cables with an unknown load capacity.
2. If available, look up and utilize the specific inspection instructions from the cable manufacturer's website or technical data.
3. Visually inspect the end terminations and hardware for excessive corrosion and wear, as well as for proper placement, tightness, breakage, or deformation. Repair or replace any end attachments showing signs of failure.
4. Ensure one end of the wire rope remains stationary. While wearing thick gloves, wrap a thick towel around the wire rope. Gripping around the towel and wire rope tightly, run the towel down the entire length of the wire rope to the end attachments. You can feel any wires that have separated on the outside of the wire rope. Now, repeat the same thing, running the towel the other direction on the wire rope to the end. Note and mark any broken wires found. Although replacement guidelines for

wire rope vary slightly with the design of the rope, common replacement or out-of-service criteria is if there are six or more random broken wires in any one rope **lay** (the distance it takes for a strand to complete one revolution of the rope), three or more broken wires in one strand in one rope lay, or any broken wires at an end termination.

5. While performing the above step, visually inspect the outside of the wire rope, paying attention to the following failure conditions:
   • Kinks
   • Birdcages (wires pushed out to form a cage)
   • Core protrusions
   • Broken or frayed wires
   • Changes in wire rope diameter, indicating an internal core failure
   • Excessive wear and abrasion

The above failures and/or rope conditions are not repairable and, depending on severity, requires rope replacement.

6. Ensure the entire length of the wire rope/cable is inspected. If any failures or damage are found, consult the wire rope manufacturer's inspection criteria to determine whether replacement is needed.
7. Check the diameter of the wire rope at several locations. If its diameter has decreased by more than 5%, the rope should be replaced (note: always check the largest outside diameter across the outside of the strands, not the flat area between the strands).
8. *Important notes:* Some critical applications may require further inspection of the wire rope/cable, such as magnetic or other nondestructive inspection techniques. Consult the wire rope manufacturer's manual, as well as applicable government and industry standards, for more information.

Wrap-Up

Ready for Review

▶ Always use the proper lifting techniques when moving heavy objects.

▶ The safe working load indicates the operating capacity for lifting equipment.

▶ Lifting equipment includes vehicle hoists, floor jacks, jack stands, engine and component hoists, chains, slings, and shackles.

▶ Periodically check and test lifting equipment; consult the test certificate if available.

▶ Jacks can be classified by the type of lifting mechanism they use: hydraulic, pneumatic, or mechanical.

▶ Jack types include floor jacks, bottle jacks, air jacks, scissor jacks, sliding-bridge jacks, and transmission jacks.

▶ Choose jacks according to size and lifting capacity.

▶ Jack stands support a vehicle's weight when it has been raised; always use jack stands in pairs.

▶ Vehicle hoists raise the vehicle to allow technicians underside access.

▶ Never use a vehicle hoist without activating the safety lock, or for lifting a vehicle heavier than the rated limit.

▶ Make sure a vehicle has enough clearance over the lifting mechanism.

▶ Engine hoists can lift heavy objects out of a vehicle and onto an engine stand.

▶ Check for damage before using an engine hoist, and make sure all components have the lifting capacity needed for the task.

▶ Always have a safe attitude when using tools and equipment and wear necessary personal protection equipment.

▶ Always inspect lifting, rigging, and blocking equipment and devices prior to use.

▶ Never stand underneath an item being lifted.

▶ Always have an escape route planned should something go wrong during a lifting, towing, or coasting operation.

▶ Never sacrifice your body to save a piece of equipment from damage or falling.

▶ Don't exceed the rated capacity of a lifting or towing device.

Key Terms

BCE Before Common Era or before year 1.

bitter end The dead end of the wire rope.

bottle jacks Portable jacks that usually have a hydraulic ram mechanism to raise a component.

center of gravity (CG) Also called the center of balance. The center of gravity, or CG, of an object is the point, or position, at which the item's weight is evenly dispersed, and all sides are in balance. If the item were to be supported in a direct vertical axis from the center of gravity, it would balance perfectly.

chain blocks A chain block is a piece of equipment used to lift heavy items. The typical block, also known as chain falls, consists of two grooved wheels with a chain wound around them in the same fashion as a block and tackle. The chain wound around the two wheels creates a simple machine that uses the leverage and the increased lifting ability created by the two wheels to lift heavy weights.

chocks Blocks of material placed against a wheel to prevent undesired rolling movement.

clutch jacks A hydraulic jack equipped with exchangeable transmission input shafts that are used to align a clutch assembly and then raise it into place while it is being installed or removed.

end termination The way the end of a wire rope is treated, usually by forming an eye that becomes the attachment for the wire rope.

engine hoist A crane used to lift engines.

floor jack A type of hydraulic jack mounted on four wheels that can be rolled into position.

hoisting The action of lifting a load using cables or ropes.

hydraulic jack A type of vehicle jack that uses oil under pressure to lift vehicles.

jack stands Metal stands with adjustable height to hold a vehicle once it has been jacked up.

lay The distance it takes for one strand to complete one revolution of the wire rope.

lifting Raising the vehicle from underneath.

lifting equipment Also known as lifting gear, any equipment or devices used to lift a load vertically. This can include jacks, a block and tackle, hydraulic lift, hoist, gantries, cranes, slings or rigging, wire rope/cables, and any other items used to lift a load vertically.

load leveler A bar with moveable attachment points also known as a spreader bar.

mechanical jack A type of jack that utilizes mechanical power to provide lifting. A screw jack is a type of mechanical jack.

mobile gantry crane An A-frame on wheels that can be moved around the shop to provide an attachment point for a chain block.

Occupational Safety and Health Administration (OSHA) The agency that assures safe and healthy working conditions by setting and enforcing standards and by providing training, outreach, education, and assistance.

overhead gantry crane A moveable crane with a chain block or other hoisting mechanism attached.

pneumatic or **air jacks** A type of vehicle jack that uses compressed gas or air to lift a vehicle.

portable lifting hoists A type of vehicle hoist that is portable and can be moved from one location to another.

Reference Datum Line (RDL) The arbitrary reference point from where the center of gravity is measured. Determined by the equipment manufacturer.

rigger A person who specializes in lifting and moving heavy objects.

rigging or **rigging gear** All the components used to attach the mechanical hoisting equipment to the load being lifted. This can include rope, wire rope/cables, slings, shackles, eyebolts, eye nuts, links, rings, turnbuckles, rigging hooks, and rigging.

safe working load (SWL) The maximum safe lifting load for lifting equipment.

sliding-bridge jacks Jacks that are typically found on hoist mechanisms that can be slid into position to raise a portion of a vehicle.

spreader bar This is a bar with moveable attachment points, also known as a *load leveler*.

strand A part of a wire rope consisting of several wires twisted together.

transmission jacks Are specialized jacks that are fitted with several sets of mounting brackets, allowing them to fit to the shape of many different transmissions.

vehicle hoist A type of vehicle lifting tool designed to lift the entire vehicle.

Review Questions

1. When using four chains instead of two to lift an object, the weight you can lift is which of the following?
   a. The same as with two chains
   b. Twice as much as with two chains
   c. Half as much as with two chains
   d. Four times as much as with two chains
2. When lifting an object using a hoist from above, the lifting devices should be attached _____ the item's center of gravity.
   a. above
   b. below
   c. on either side of
   d. with no reference to
3. When an item is lifted from above using a two-chain hoist, with the chains at a 30-degree angle from the horizontal axis, the actual lifting capacity of the chains is _____ than if they were placed vertically.
   a. less
   b. more
   c. the same
4. The actual lifting capacity of an overhead crane is limited by _____.
   a. the crane's capacity/rating
   b. the rigging device(s) capacity/rating
   c. the attachment points on the item being lifted
   d. the lowest capacity/rating between the crane, rigging, and attachment points
5. When lifting an object using a jack from below, the jacking points are best if they are _____ the item's center of gravity.

   a. above
   b. below the level of
   c. on either side of
   d. below and on the vertical axis of
6. True/False. It is acceptable to mix types and materials of lifting and rigging equipment attached to the same load, if their capacity is not exceeded.
   a. True
   b. False
7. True/False. A lifting device with a capacity less than 2000 lb (907 kg) does not require operator training.
   a. True
   b. False
8. Which of the following is the maximum weight for a manual lift by a single person?
   a. 31 pounds (14 kg)
   b. 41 pounds (19 kg)
   c. 51 pounds (23 kg)
   d. 61 pounds (28 kg)
9. Which of the following should you *not* do while performing a manual lift?
   a. Rotate your back to place the load on the nearest bench
   b. Lift with your legs
   c. Keep the load as close to your body as possible
   d. Try to keep the center of gravity of the load as close to your body as possible
10. Which of the following is the most stable type of hoist?
    a. portable hoist
    b. single post hoist
    c. two post hoist
    d. platform hoist

ASE Technician A/Technician B Style Questions

1. Technician A says that wire rope must be inspected before each use. Technician B says that wire rope must be inspected before use and as often as the wire rope manufacturer, government, or industry standard requires. Who is correct?
   a. Technician A
   b. Technician B
   c. Both Technician A and Technician B
   d. Neither Technician A nor Technician B
2. Technician A says the parking brake must be applied before jacking a vehicle. Technician B says chocks must be installed in front of and behind a wheel before jacking a vehicle. Who is correct?
   a. Technician A
   b. Technician B
   c. Both Technician A and Technician B
   d. Neither Technician A nor Technician B
3. Technician A says that a wire rope can have broken wires along its length and still be useable. Technician B says that if there are broken wires at an end termination, the rope should be replaced. Who is correct?
   a. Technician A
   b. Technician B

c. Both Technician A and Technician B
d. Neither Technician A nor Technician B

4. Technician A says that anything that weighs more than 51 pounds (23 kg) should be lifted by two people or with a mechanical device. Technician B says that if you are comfortable with the weight, you can lift anything. Who is correct?
   a. Technician A
   b. Technician B
   c. Both Technician A and Technician B
   d. Neither Technician A nor Technician B

5. Technician A says that a wire rope sling with swaged end terminations has the same SWL capacity of the rope it is made from. Technician B says that if the correct number and orientation of wire rope clips are used when forming an end termination, the termination has the same SWL capacity as the rope. Who is correct?
   a. Technician A
   b. Technician B
   c. Both Technician A and Technician B
   d. Neither Technician A nor Technician B

6. Technician A says that OSHA rules require training for employees before they operate a lifting device. Technician B says that training is only required if the lifting device is heavier than 2000 pounds (907 kg). Who is correct?
   a. Technician A
   b. Technician B
   c. Both Technician A and Technician B
   d. Neither Technician A nor Technician B

7. Technician A says that a 5% change in the diameter of a length of wire rope may indicate internal failure and require replacement. Technician B says a length of wire rope that has a birdcage in it can be repaired by straightening and then wrapping the area in steel wire. Who is correct?
   a. Technician A
   b. Technician B
   c. Both Technician A and Technician B
   d. Neither Technician A nor Technician B

8. Technician A says that a wire rope that has six or more random broken wires in one rope lay must be replaced. Technician B says that a wire rope that has six broken wires in one strand over a length of two rope lays is still ok to use. Who is correct?
   a. Technician A
   b. Technician B
   c. Both Technician A and Technician B
   d. Neither Technician A nor Technician B

9. Technician A says that you should not use a piece of lifting or jacking equipment with an expired test certificate. Technician B says that you should perform an inspection of all lifting and jacking equipment prior to use. Who is correct?
   a. Technician A
   b. Technician B
   c. Both Technician A and Technician B
   d. Neither Technician A nor Technician B

10. Technician A says that a wire rope can have an independent wire rope core. Technician B says that wire ropes only have fiber cores so they can hold lubrication. Who is correct?
    a. Technician A
    b. Technician B
    c. Both Technician A and Technician B
    d. Neither Technician A nor Technician B

CHAPTER 7

Bearings, Lubricants, and Seals

Learning Objectives

After reading this chapter, you will be able to:

- LO 7-1 Identify and describe the purpose and functions of bearings.
- LO 7-2 Identify and describe the classification of bearings.
- LO 7-3 Identify and describe the types of construction and operating principles of antifriction bearings.
- LO 7-4 Describe the purpose, methods, and service practices for retaining bearings in place on shafts and in bearing housings.
- LO 7-5 Outline methods to inspect and maintain bearings and identify defective bearings.

- LO 7-6 Identify and describe the types and function of seals.
- LO 7-7 Describe the construction features, inspection, and service techniques associated with radial lip-type seals.
- LO 7-8 Identify and describe the purpose, types, and function of gaskets and sealants.
- LO 7-9 Outline gasket installation guidelines.
- LO 7-10 Describe seal service and maintenance.

You Are the Technician

At the commercial vehicle dealership where you work, used vehicles are regularly taken in as trades on new trucks and buses. As part of an inspection procedure to determine the equipment's value and subsequent decision to keep, scrap, or resell the vehicles at auction, the traded units are given a thorough inspection. The condition of safety-related parts, major components, and any excessive wear or defects found on the chassis are documented during the inspection process. Of the more than two hundred inspection points and items listed on the inspection inventory, the condition of bearings, bushings, gaskets, and seals in each of the major chassis systems is required. As you work through the inspection checklist for a tandem axle highway tractor, consider the following criteria:

1. Identify and describe a method to determine whether any bearings or bushings are excessively worn or noisy in the drive axles and wheel ends.
2. What steps or procedure would you follow if you discovered many of the engine's gaskets and seals were leaking?
3. What items should be inspected if it is discovered that wheel seals and both drive shaft seals for the power divider were leaking?

Introduction

Seals, bearings, and gaskets are not a formal chassis system, but these components are essential to the operation of many commercial vehicle systems (**FIGURE 7-1**). Without these often overlooked, but critical, elements to component operation, the life of important chassis parts is dramatically shortened. Bearings reduce friction and supply replaceable wear surfaces. Seals and gaskets often work to complement bearing functions by sealing lubricant inside a bearing while keeping dirt and contaminants from entering lubricant or a bearing cavity. Seals and gaskets also provide barriers to block the movement of fuel, oil, coolant, brake fluid, gases, and other substances to prevent leakage or cross contamination.

Seals, bearings, and gaskets tend to be ignored when thinking about maintenance and service because they are generally low-cost, disposable items. Failing to correctly understand the purpose, construction, and operation of these parts, which is foundational to service practices, can result in catastrophic failures. To provide the necessary background for maintaining bearings, gaskets, and seals, to correctly identify potential failures, and to develop proper maintenance and service practices, this chapter examines the

Oiler Cap Gasket   Tapered Roller Bearings   Rubber Case Wheel Seal

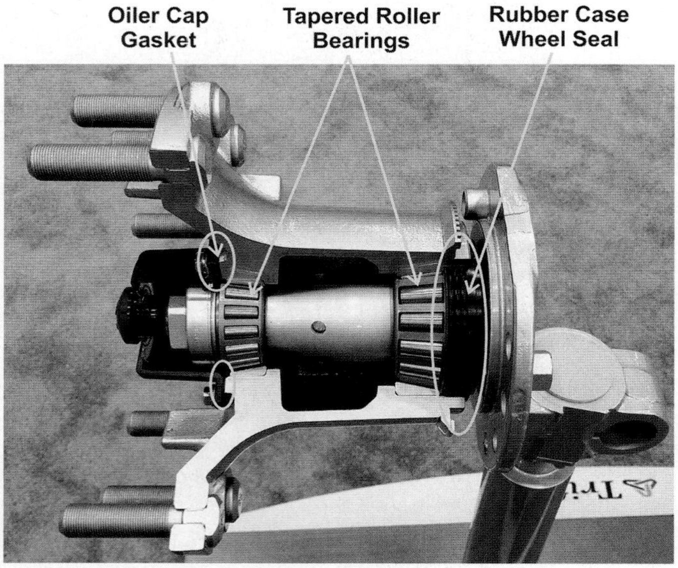

FIGURE 7-1 Seals, bearings, and gaskets are used by many vehicle systems and components, such as this wheel hub.

types, operation, and construction of each. Various service techniques and tools associated with bearing gasket and seals are also covered.

Bearing Functions

LO 7-1 Identify and describe the purpose and functions of bearings.

A function common to all bearings is to minimize friction between moving parts. Friction produces heat and wear that can quickly destroy components. The destructive process happens even more quickly when moving parts are supporting heavy loads. Friction reduction is also important because more energy or effort is required to operate devices with high friction. Lubricants can reduce friction, but not as effectively as a bearing can, particularly when its operation is combined with a lubricating film (**FIGURE 7-2**). This friction-reducing capability of bearings helps explain why precision parts in major components, such as transmissions, engines, differentials, power dividers, and steering gears, use various types of bearings (**FIGURE 7-3**). Even some body parts, such as door and hood hinges, are examples of a wide range of vehicle systems using bearings to extend the lifecycle of commercial vehicles.

A second important function of bearings is to operate as replaceable wear surfaces. Because bearings are placed between moving parts, some wear always takes place and requires bearing replacement when excessive wear is present. A third function of bearings is to support loads while aligning components, such as shafts, pins, armatures, or spindles, with other components, such as flanges, hubs, drums, and wheel ends. To precisely align moving parts while supporting heavy weights, bearings loads are either applied radially, axially, or angularly using a combination of both angular and radial forces (**FIGURE 7-4**). When a load is applied toward the centerline of a shaft, it is considered a radial load. The loads imposed by two meshed gears toward a shaft or cylinder combustion pressure on a crankshaft are examples of radial loads. Axially loading takes place along a shaft centerline and is also called a thrust load (**FIGURE 7-5**). Meshed helical cut gears (gear teeth cut at an angle), which push away from one another, or the force of a turbocharger compressor wheel driving air flow are examples of axial loads.

Friction and Bearings

Various types of friction result in resistance to mechanical movement (**FIGURE 7-6**). However, bearings can reduce friction and wear caused by two common types of friction: sliding and

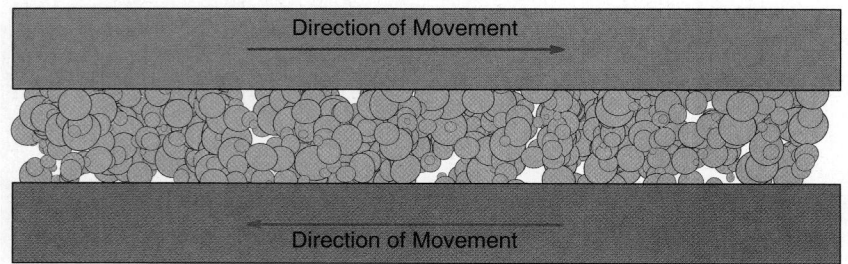

Direction of Movement

Direction of Movement

FIGURE 7-2 Oil lubrication behaves like ball bearings, enabling metal surfaces to slide over one another without metal-to-metal contact.

rolling contact. Sliding contact friction is demonstrated when an object is dragged across a surface, such as a book across a desk or a trailer's upper coupler plate across a fifth wheel. The amount of sliding friction depends primarily on the weight of the book or downward force, the type of materials on the book and desk surfaces, and the area of the book in contact with the desk. Rough surfaces may increase friction but putting marbles beneath the book allows the book to move with much less effort, partly because the area in contact with the desk is much smaller. But even with the marbles between the book and desk there is still some resistance to movement. Sliding friction, which is a stronger friction force, is replaced with rolling friction when marbles are placed between the book and desk surface. Rolling friction generates less resistance than sliding friction. This same conversion from sliding to rolling friction takes place when a sled that is dragged is placed on wheels (**FIGURE 7-7**). Rolling friction is the force or resistance that slows down the movement of a rolling ball or wheel. The primary source of rolling friction is the energy used to deform the rolling objects and the surfaces they move across. Even if the marble is rolling on a flat surface, the marble distorts or dents the surface below it, and the marble itself may even be deformed. How much friction is present is

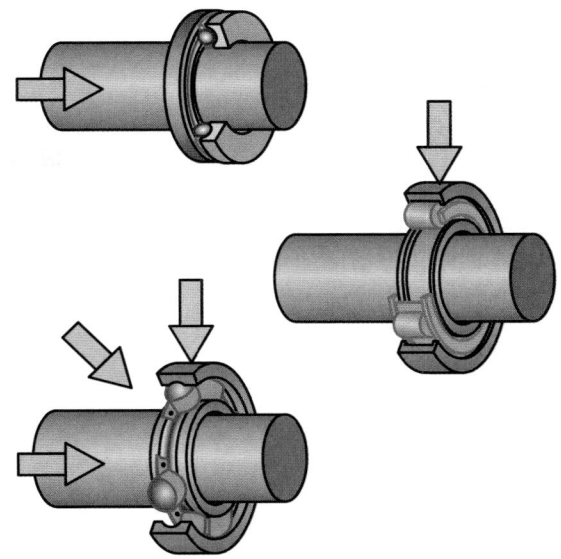

FIGURE 7-5 Thrust loads are applied along the axis of a shaft, hub, housing, or spindle. Different bearing designs are used to handle each type of load.

FIGURE 7-3 Major components, such as this transmission, use numerous bearings, seals, and gaskets.

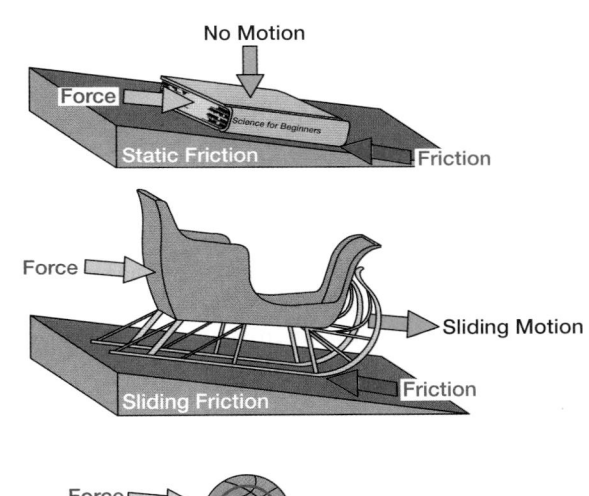

FIGURE 7-6 Different types of friction that resist movement.

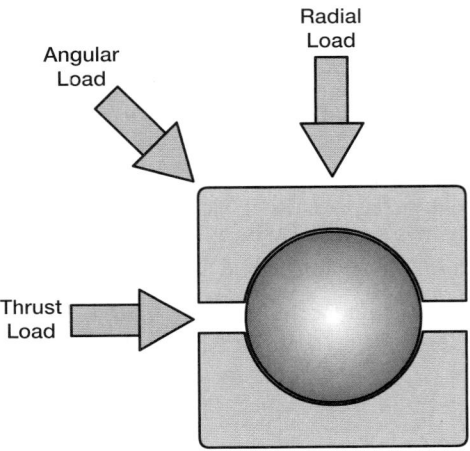

FIGURE 7-4 Bearings, such as this deeply grooved ball bearing, can align forces applied radially, axially, or from a combination of forces.

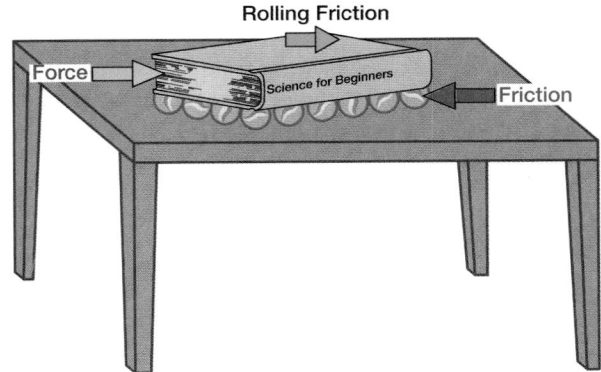

FIGURE 7-7 Marbles replace sliding friction with less resistive rolling friction.

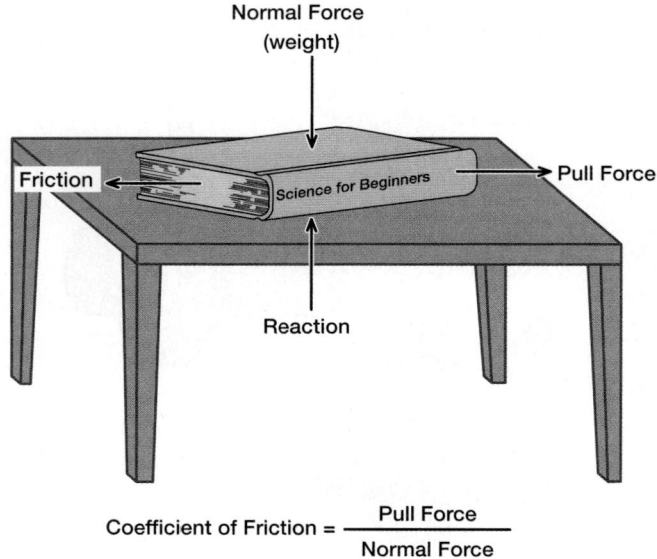

$$\text{Coefficient of Friction} = \frac{\text{Pull Force}}{\text{Normal Force}}$$

FIGURE 7-8 Coefficient of friction is expressed as the force required to move a load divided by the weight of the load.

FIGURE 7-9 This plain bushing and two thrust washers are examples of plain friction-type bearings.

measured using a factor called the coefficient of friction (CoF). The coefficient of friction is expressed as the Force/Load. This means a book having a CoF of 0.5 requires a force equal to half the weight of the book to overcome the friction between the desk to move the book (**FIGURE 7-8**). Better known examples of frictional coefficients are a steel train wheel on a steel track having a CoF of 0.001 or a truck tire on dry pavement having between 0.006 and 0.01. The marvelous feature of wheels and rolling objects is they can be used to reduce sliding CoFs by hundreds or even thousands of times.

Classification of Bearings

LO 7-2 Identify and describe the classification of bearings.

Concepts of sliding and rolling friction are used to help categorize the two major types of bearings:

1. Friction bearings, which often use an oil film to reduce friction and slide over moving parts
2. Antifriction bearings, which use rolling balls, barrels, or cylinders to reduce friction and use lubricant to reduce friction

Friction bearings are recognized by solid and simple construction, which lends them the name plain bearings (**FIGURE 7-9**). Plain bearings slide over moving parts and frequently, but not always, use a lubricating film or low CoF material on contact surfaces. Large surface areas of the bearing support loads and reduce resistance from sliding friction. Bushings, also called sleeve bearings, are a common type of plain friction bearing. These bearings can have direct surface contact and minimize wear caused by sliding friction when positioned in areas such as the ends of electric motor or alternator shafts, around king pins in steering knuckles, and leaf suspension spring bushings (**FIGURE 7-10**). Using bushings made of softer materials, such as

FIGURE 7-10 A set of king pin bushings with bronze-backed, dimpled nylon bushings are friction-type bearings. Lubricant is retained in the bushing dimples. Roller-type antifriction bearings are used as thrust bearings.

bronze, Teflon (polytetrafluoroethylene; PTFE), or even nylon, ensures the replaceable bushing wears first. When the bushing metal is dissimilar to the metal it is supporting, rather than using the same metals to slide against one another, the friction between them is less due to a property called **compatibility**. The advantages of plain bearings include:

- Simple to manufacture
- Smaller diameter than antifriction bearings
- Often faster to assemble and disassemble
- Quiet, smooth operation

To assist assembly and disassembly, plain bearings can be split, such as those used by engine crankshaft bearings

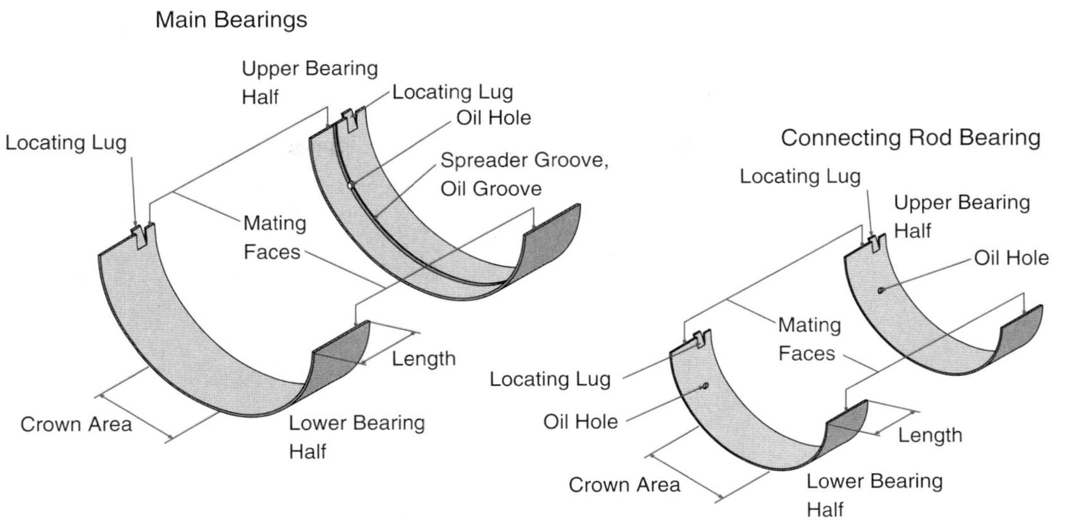

Main Bearings

Connecting Rod Bearing

FIGURE 7-11 Split bearing inserts are used by the crankshaft main and connecting rod bearings.

(**FIGURE 7-11**). Split plain bearings are typically multilayered to provide important bearing characteristics. For example, a bearing with a lead-tin or bronze alloy friction surface uses a steel backing layer to provide additional strength to the softer bearing material (**FIGURE 7-12**). Thrust washers, such as those used behind camshaft gears, are another example of a plain-type friction bearing.

At high speeds, too much friction and heat are generated, so plain bearings often use lubricant to reduce friction between the sliding surfaces. Indentations or grooves are often made in the bearing surface and retain lubricant to distribute over the sliding bearing surface. When a fluid lubricant forms a film between the sliding surfaces to prevent direct contact between moving parts, the bearing is also known as fluid film bearings.

Antifriction Bearings

LO 7-3 Identify and describe the types of construction and operating principles of antifriction bearings.

Rather than using wide areas of sliding contact like friction bearings and bushings, antifriction bearings use rolling contact to reduce friction (**FIGURE 7-13**). As the name suggests,

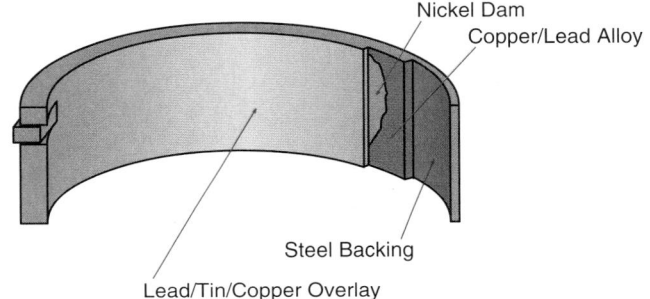

FIGURE 7-12 Split bearings have laminated construction to provide uniquely formulated bearing properties.

friction is minimized by replacing sliding friction contact with rolling point contact. Rolling balls or cylinder-shaped rolling elements have either a point- or line-type contact that rolls, rather than slides, over bearing surfaces (**FIGURE 7-14**). While antifriction bearing construction is more complex, these bearings are generally capable of supporting heavier, complex loads originating from multiple angles, and can operate effectively at high speeds. Smaller operating clearances between elements

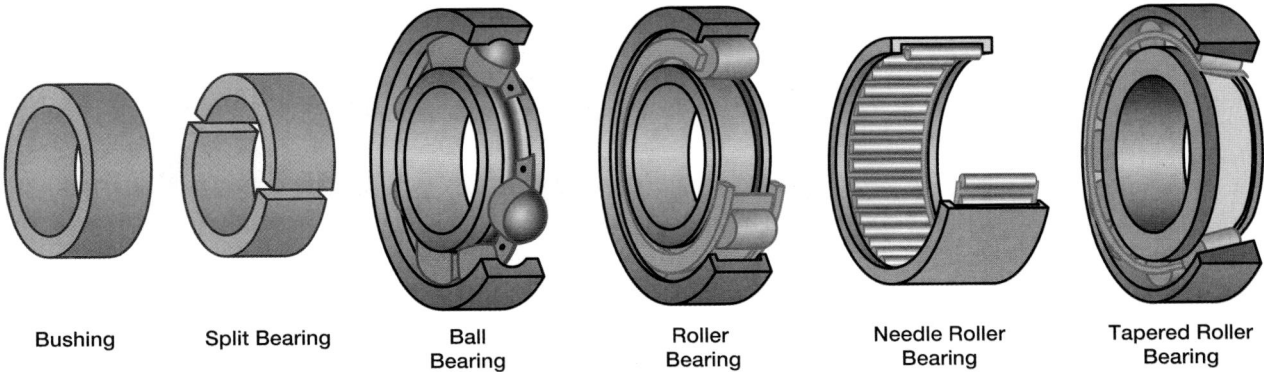

Bushing   Split Bearing   Ball Bearing   Roller Bearing   Needle Roller Bearing   Tapered Roller Bearing

FIGURE 7-13 Common bearing configurations.

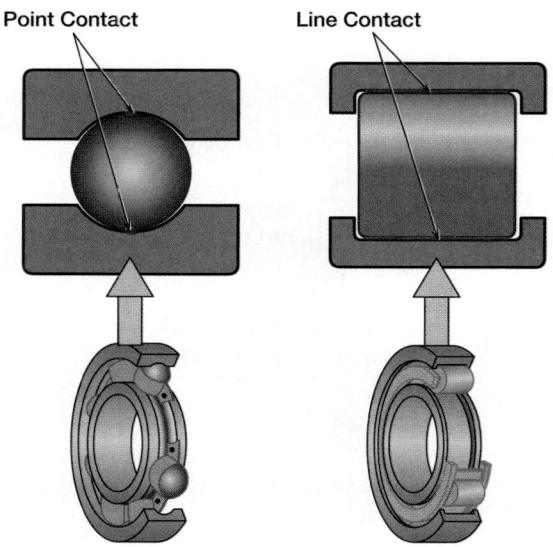

FIGURE 7-14 Line or point rolling contact reduces bearing friction.

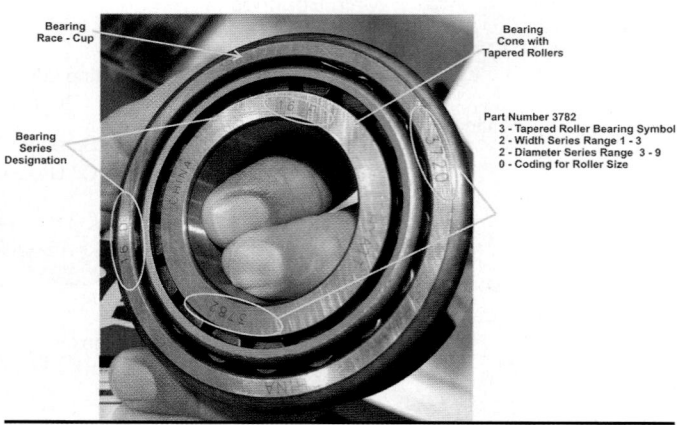

FIGURE 7-16 A tapered roller bearing using a standardized ISO part number designation system indicating bearing type and dimensions. The letter prefix designation is used by the original equipment manufacturers (OEM) to identify unique manufacturing features.

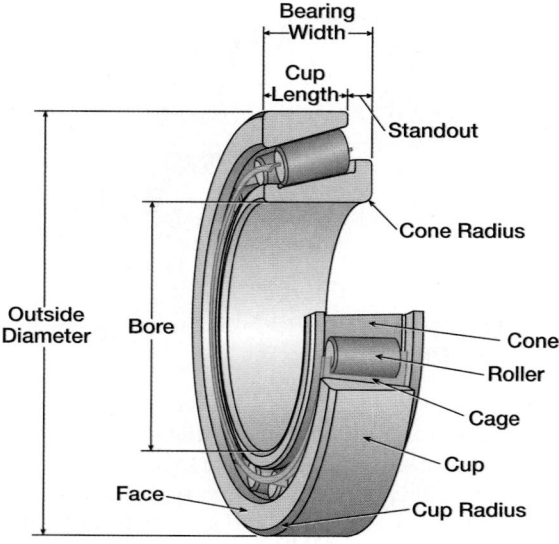

FIGURE 7-15 Dimensions of a tapered roller bearing. Bearing numbers reference angles and diameters of the cup and cone.

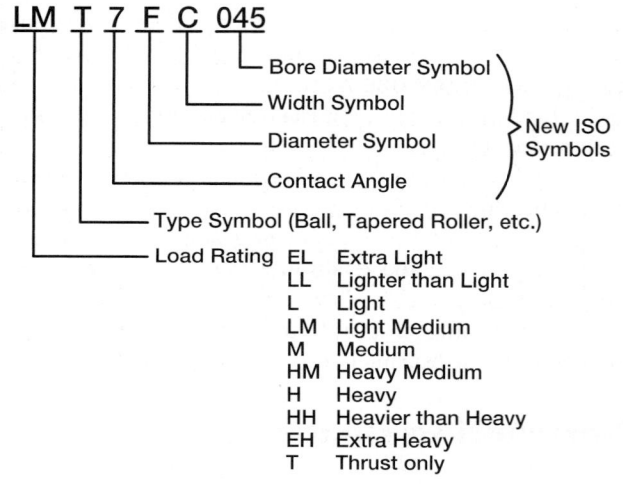

FIGURE 7-17 An example of a standardized ISO bearing numbering system using prefixes to designate the weight rating or service duty.

of the antifriction bearings provide more precise alignment of components. Bearing diameters, however, are larger than plain bearings, but bearing length is shorter than comparable plain bearings. Antifriction bearings also have a standardized identification system used among bearing manufacturers. There is no standardized bearing numbering system for imperial or inch bearing dimensions. Instead, bearing manufacturers use their own system or share popular bearing numbering systems for imperial or inch bearing sizes. However, most bearings manufactured today use metric dimensions and follow an International Organization for Standardization (ISO) system for bearings numbering using metric measurement dimensions. ISO bearing numbering designates bearing numbers using four or five fields plus a suffix or prefix. The numbering fields include, but are not limited to:

1. Bearing Type Code
2. Series—Bearing width
3. Bore—Bearing diameter
4. Suffix—Unique characteristics for a bearing (**FIGURES 7-15**, **7-16**, and **7-17**).

Construction of Antifriction Rollers

Several different shapes of antifriction bearing rollers are used. The five most commonly encountered are: ball, cylindrical roller, tapered roller, barrel roller, and needle roller bearings (**FIGURE 7-18**). Three essential elements of an antifriction bearing needed to function are its hardened steel alloy outer ring, inner ring, and rolling elements (**FIGURE 7-19**). The rolling elements turn freely between the inner and outer rings, which are called races. Inner and outer races,

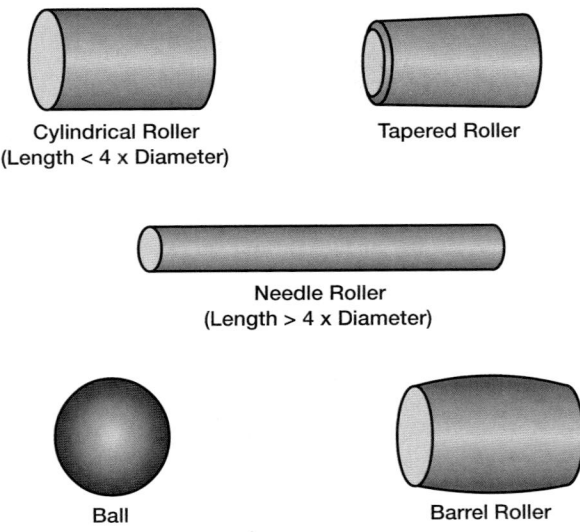

Cylindrical Roller
(Length < 4 x Diameter)

Tapered Roller

Needle Roller
(Length > 4 x Diameter)

Ball

Barrel Roller

FIGURE 7-18 Types of rolling contact made by common antifriction bearings.

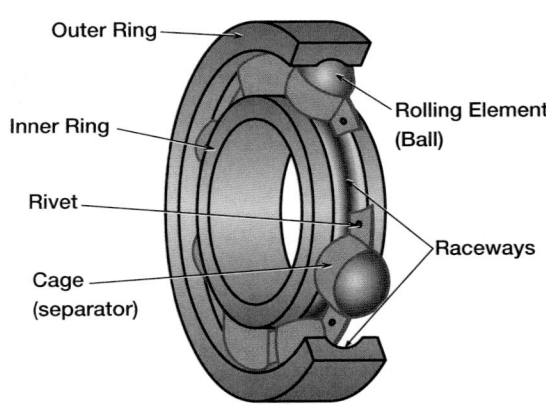

Outer Ring

Inner Ring

Rivet

Cage
(separator)

Rolling Element
(Ball)

Raceways

FIGURE 7-19 Elements of a roller-type antifriction bearing.

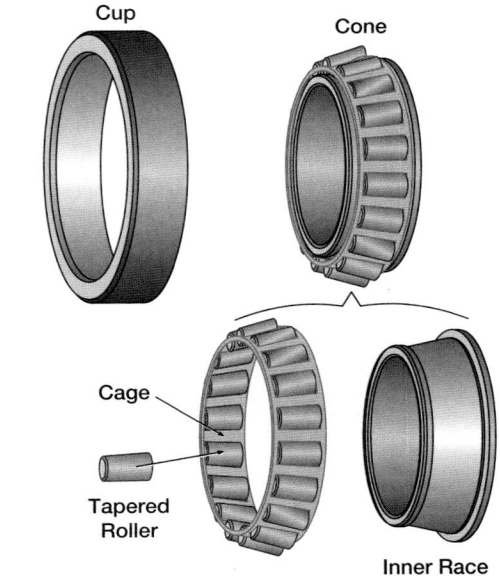

Cup

Cone

Cage

Tapered
Roller

Inner Race

FIGURE 7-20 A tapered roller bearing separates the bearing into two halves. The outer race is called the cup. The inner race, rollers, and cage form the cone.

the cage, and rolling elements are inseparable parts in ball-type bearings. A tapered roller bearing separates the outer race, called a cup, from rollers integrated into the inner race, called the cone (**FIGURE 7-20**). A bearing cage made of metal or plastic is added to maintain a clearance between each rolling element to evenly space rollers, to prevent contact with one another, and equally distribute loads. When a bearing is permanently lubricated during the manufacturing process, a rubber-like seal on each side of the rollers retains lubrication between the inner and outer rings and prolongs bearing life by keeping contaminants out (**FIGURE 7-21**). A second metal shield installed on the outside of the seal prevents the rubber-like seal from external damage.

Shape and Operation of Rolling Elements

Ball bearings can support radial loads, but if the ball operates in a deep groove within the inner and out race, it can support high angular, in addition to axial-type, loads. Straight or

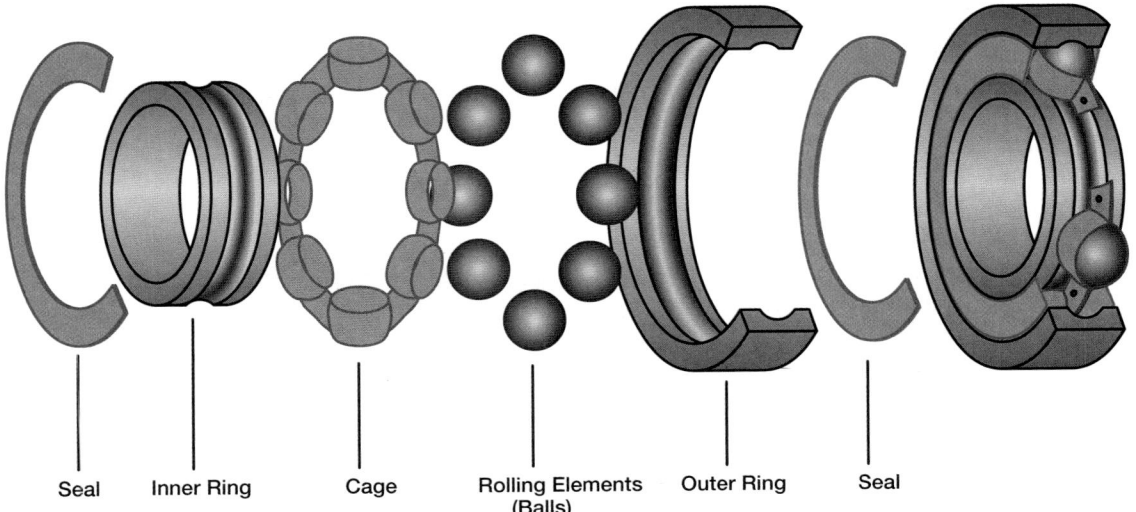

Seal

Inner Ring

Cage

Rolling Elements
(Balls)

Outer Ring

Seal

FIGURE 7-21 A sealed roller bearing with seals to retain lubricant and exclude contamination.

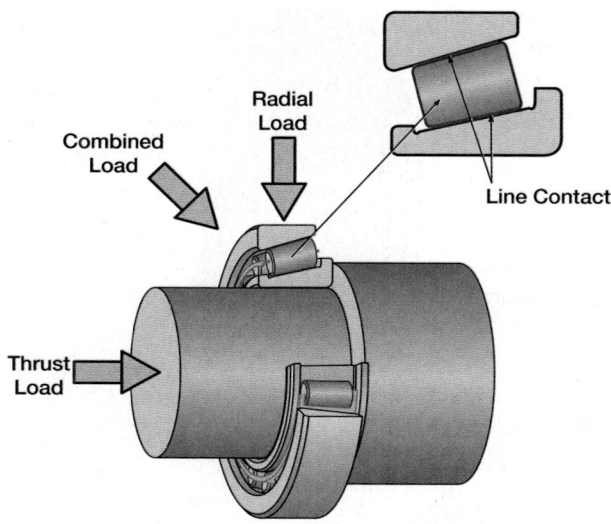

FIGURE 7-22 A tapered roller bearing separates the bearing into two halves. The outer race is called the cup. The inner race, rollers, and cage form the cone.

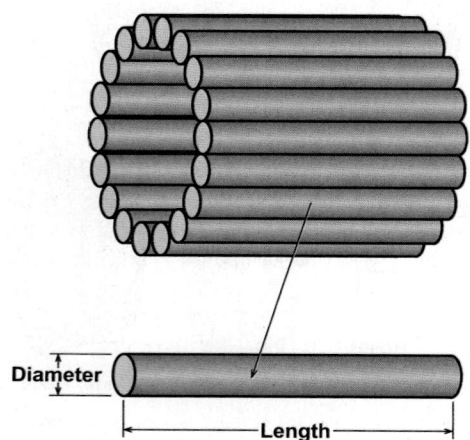

FIGURE 7-23 Needle bearings are used where bearing size must be kept small but support high radial loads.

cylindrical shaped rollers have a wider line contact area than ball bearings to primarily support heavier radial loads. When thrust and radial loads are high, a tapered roller bearing is used (**FIGURE 7-22**). In wheel ends where thrust loads originate from two opposite directions, two tapered roller bearings are used. Needle bearings have very long rollers compared to their diameter, which is best used to distribute high radial loads in a very compact-sized bearing (**FIGURE 7-23**). Driveshaft universal joint bearing caps are a common place where needle bearings are used. Thrust washers can be made from needle- or cylinder-type roller-shaped bearings.

Barrel-shaped rollers are used in applications where the bearing must self-align, such as on shafts that deflect and move slightly around its centerline. Driveshaft hanger bearings are one application where barrel-shaped rollers are installed in a bearing enclosed in a rubber cushion. Double rows of barrel-shaped rollers allow the bearing to absorb radial and axial

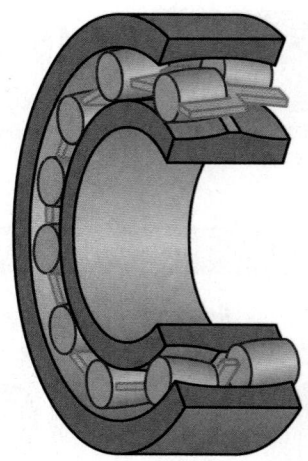

FIGURE 7-24 A double set of barrel-shaped rollers allow some shaft deflection and help realign the shaft if it moves off center.

loads but, more importantly, allow some small change in shaft angle because the bearings can shift from side to side within the race (**FIGURE 7-24**).

Roller Bearings

Roller bearings are designed to support only radial loads. Transmission shafts or shafts in the differential and power diver often use roller bearings. When balls are used as rolling elements, a very small point contact is established that has the least amount of friction. When heavier radial loads are used, wider cylinder-shaped rollers create a line contact capable of distributing weight over a wider area.

Tapered Roller Bearings

Another common bearing design used is tapered roller bearings. Tapered roller bearings consist of four parts:

1. Taper-shaped rolling elements
2. An outer bearing race, more commonly called a cup
3. An inner bearing race, more commonly called a cone
4. A bearing cage

Tapered bearings are designed for combination loads, such as in wheel hubs supporting the weight of the vehicle and axial loads from side-to-side movement of the tires when maneuvering. These bearings can typically support axial or side-to-side loads, which are 60% of the maximum radial load. The angle of the bearing may be steep or shallow, depending on the combined axial radial loads.

Bearing Fit

LO 7-4 Describe the purpose, methods, and service practices for retaining bearings in place on shafts and in bearing housings.

For antifriction bearings, the inner and outer races are locked onto a shaft or spindle supported by the bearing or a hub or housing so that no movement takes place between bearing races and the housings or shafts during operation (**FIGURE 7-25**). This arrangement ensures only the rolling elements will move. Some bearings, often tapered roller bearings, may allow the inner race or cone to snugly fit on an axle spindle for easily removing the hub during service, but the outer race is tightly pressed into the hub. Loose bearings can potentially allow a bearing race to spin and damage a shaft or housing. Noise and vibration are also generated by loose fitted bearings. The most effective method to lock the bearing races into place is to use an **interference fit** between a bearing's race and the shaft or housing the race fits into. An interference fit means the bearings inner or outer race is either slightly larger or smaller by a few thousandths of an inch or millimeters than the shaft or housing it locks to. Friction holds the bearing race and prevents one or both races from moving. However, when an interference fit is used to lock bearings in place, the downside is ease of installation and disassembly is lost. Special service tools and techniques are required to install and remove

the bearing races (**FIGURE 7-26**). Hydraulic presses and bearing drivers hit with heavy hammers are often used to install these bearings (**FIGURE 7-27**). Specialized bearing separators or pullers are used to disassemble bearings from housings and shafts. Various other destructive and non-destructive techniques are used to replace bearings.

Bearing Removal

If a housing, shaft, or spindle supporting a bearing race does not use an interference fit, but instead uses a clearance fit where both the race and opening diameter are identical, the bearing bore, shaft, or spindle should be lightly lubricated to ease installation.

If a bearing is installed in a hub, housing, or on a shaft using an interference fit, friction strongly holds the bearing in place and a large amount of force is required to remove it. If the bearing is replaced because it is defective, several destructive removal methods are frequently used. One technique is to split or cut the outer race of cylindrical or ball-type roller bearings. A bearing's outer race can be cut with an abrasive saw, grinder, or cutting torch. After removing the outer race and cage, the remaining inner race can be removed with a drift punch and hammer or heated to expand the inner race for easier removal. The inner race may also be carefully cut (**FIGURE 7-28**). Threaded studs may be welded to a bearing and used in a T-Bar puller to remove a bearing.

Non-destructive removal techniques are used if a bearing requires inspection or reuse but are also used when the bearing is simply discarded. Tapping a bearing on the outside of a sturdy race with a soft iron or brass drift punch may be all that is necessary to remove a bearing from the bore of a transmission or differential case. External jaw-type pullers, commonly using three or four legs, are placed around the outside edge of a race and the puller uses a forcing screw to pull the bearing from the shaft or housing (**FIGURES 7-29** and **7-30**). Bearing pullers with

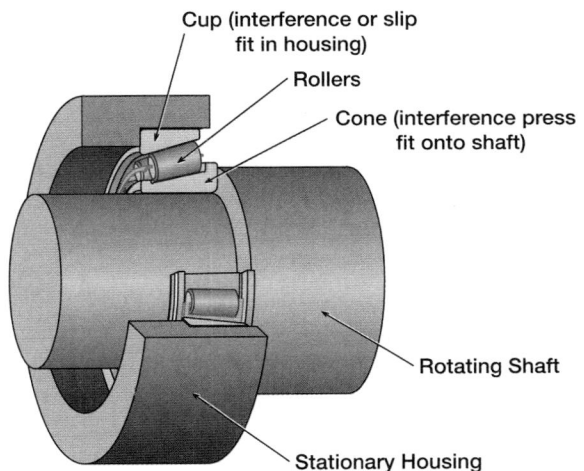

Cup (interference or slip fit in housing)
Rollers
Cone (interference press fit onto shaft)
Rotating Shaft
Stationary Housing

FIGURE 7-25 Three types of fits. A clearance fit has space between parts. A transition fit has no space. An interference fit makes either the hole or shaft 0.002" smaller so the parts must be forced together.

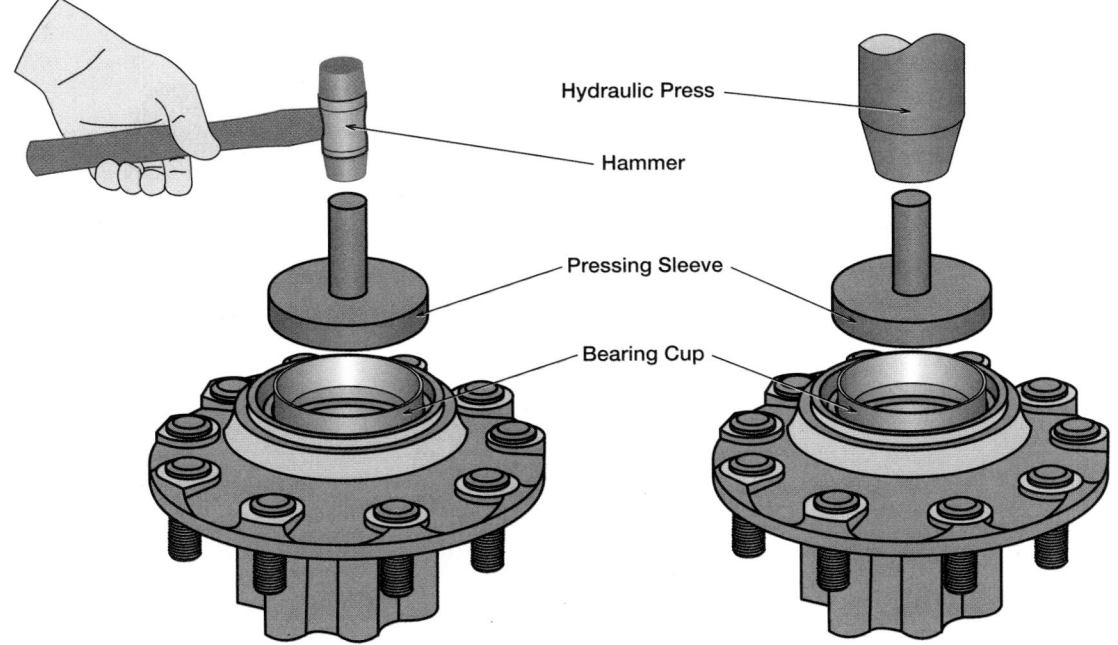

Hydraulic Press
Hammer
Pressing Sleeve
Bearing Cup

FIGURE 7-26 A driver squarely seats a bearing by applying pressure to the race using either a hammer or hydraulic press.

a forcing screw or a slide hammer attached to a set of expanding jaws called a collet, can grasp the inside of a race and be pulled with a slide hammer or forcing screw.

The most common type of bearing removal tool is a bearing splitter or separator, also called a strong back puller (**FIGURE 7-31**). Strong back pullers help with bearing removal when the use of traditional jaw pullers is restricted due to limited space or a long reach is needed (**FIGURE 7-32**). Thin wedges of a splitter, which is a part of the puller, slide in behind a bearing and the shoulder on

the shaft is tightened there. Firmly gripping behind the bearing's inner race minimizes the force required to remove the bearing. Separators are then connected to a puller with extension pieces, if needed, to remove the bearing with a forcing screw or a hydraulic cylinder. Extension pieces can thread into the separator to adapt the pulling length of the device.

Good work practice is to remove any metal burrs or ridges from a shaft or spindle that the bearing must cross when pulled. A metal file is used to smoothen the shaft. Bearings that are installed over a shaft or spindle can be heated to help remove it. Generally, a heated bearing should never be reused.

When installing bearings having an interference fit, the bearing is usually driven onto a shaft or into a hub or housing with a bearing driver or specifically sized sleeves (**FIGURE 7-33**). The drivers are used with a hammer or hydraulic press to seat the bearing components. Presses can smoothly install a bearing and its race and are preferable to avoid denting or brinelling of bearings, which can happen with hammers. Only the inner race of a bearing is hit or pressed with any large amount of force to prevent the bearing from breaking and falling apart.

If a bearing is not heated to help install it, it is cold-driven or cold-mounted. In most cold-mounting methods, force must be applied to the bearing. Never apply hammer blows directly to a bearing. Always use a clean bearing driver or sleeve of the correct size. To install a bearing, follow the steps in **SKILL DRILL 7-1**.

SAFETY TIP

Never hit an outer race with a hammer to break it apart. Very often, rolling elements will fly out of the broken bearing at very high velocity and severely injure technicians or anyone near the work area.

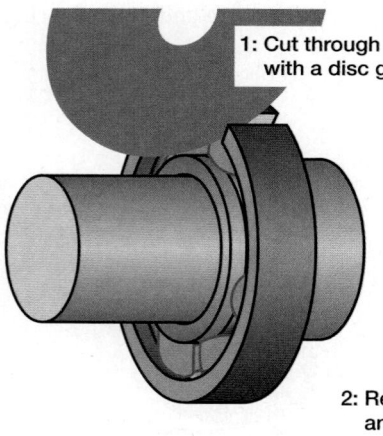

FIGURE 7-27 A 25-ton hydraulic press used to press bearing and races on or off shafts or housings.

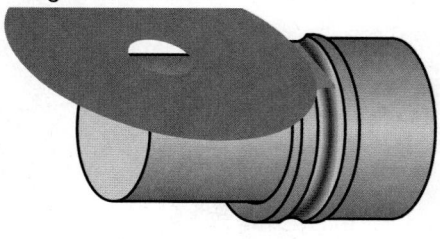
1: Cut through the outer ring with a disc grinder.

3: Grind the inner ring at a tangent to the shaft.

2: Remove the rolling elements and their cage.

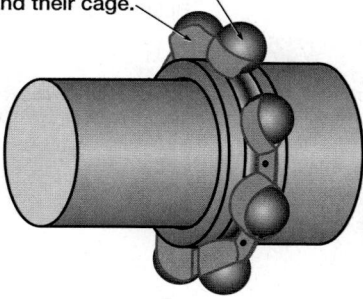

4: Slide the inner ring off the shaft.

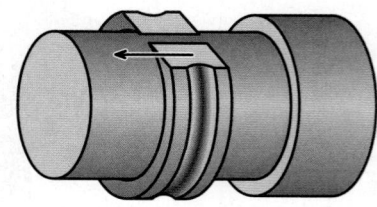

FIGURE 7-28 Steps involved in cutting a bearing for removal.

FIGURE 7-29 A three-leg jaw puller gripping the inner bearing race to remove the bearing from a shaft.

Bearing Maintenance

LO 7-5 Outline methods to inspect and maintain bearings and identify defective bearings.

One of the most critical factors for extending bearing life and reliability is cleanliness. Abrasive dirt between the bearing surfaces not only prematurely wears the bearing but increases bearing temperatures, which further accelerates wear and potentially leads to other types of bearing failures. Lubricant contamination taking place after installation is one way dirt enters and shortens bearing life, but poor installation practices can contaminate lubricant too. To minimize bearing lubricant contamination during service of antifriction-type bearings, the following precautions should be taken when bearings are removed for cleaning and inspection.

FIGURE 7-30 A three leg jaw puller gripping the inner bearing race to remove the bearing from a shaft using a spacer.

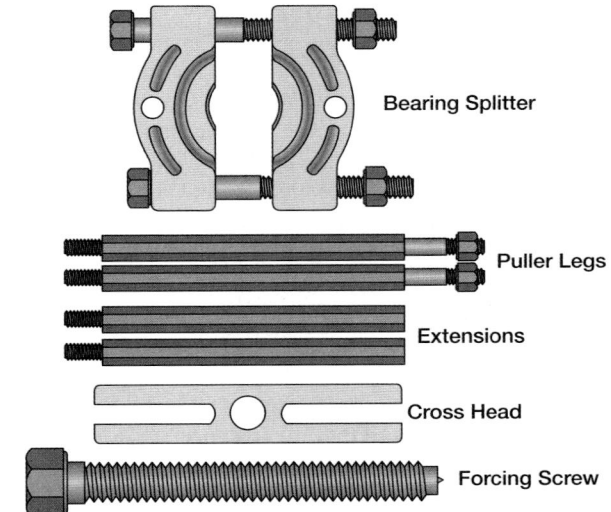

Bearing Splitter

Puller Legs

Extensions

Cross Head

Forcing Screw

FIGURE 7-31 A bearing splitter uses narrow tapered edges to fit behind a bearing and shaft to assist bearing removal.

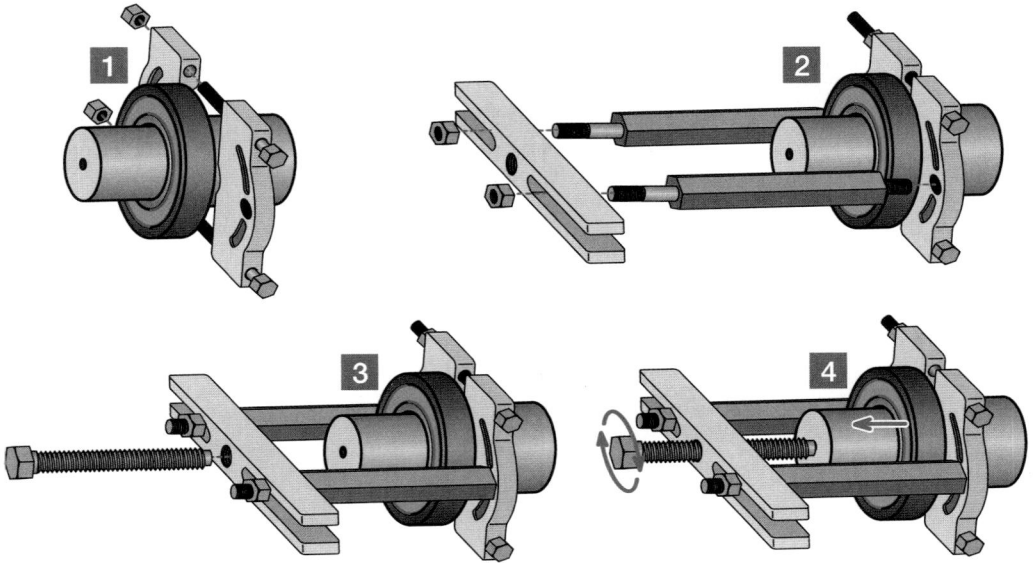

FIGURE 7-32 Steps to removing a bearing using a splitter combined with a strong back puller.

FIGURE 7-33 A bearing driver set contains plates the width of bearing races that are used to drive bearings in or out of position.

- Use clean nitrile gloves when handling bearings. Water and natural substances on hands can etch and corrode bearings.
- Clean bearings in nonflammable solvents. Exxsol hexane is an example of one of the newest low-odor, low-toxicity hydrocarbon cleaning solvents that has replaced Varsol.
- Allow the bearings to dry and never spin a bearing at high speed with compressed air. Solvent can be removed using compressed air, but spinning a bearing at high speeds can cause the cage to separate, turning rolling elements into shrapnel. Moisture in a compressed air supply can also cause bearing corrosion. Lightly oil the bearing if they are to be stored for very long and wrap the bearings in lint-free shop towels until they are installed.

- Inspect the bearing races, cups, and cones of tapered bearings under a bright light. Examine the inner race areas by turning the cage and verifying the race surfaces are smooth and bright.
- If bearings are lubricated, verify the lubricant is compatible with the bearing and correct for the application. Oil used for non-preloaded bearings may not be suitable for preloaded bearings.
- If a bearing is greased, the bearing must be packed with grease before installation. A mechanical grease gun can be used, or the bearing can be packed by hand. Push grease between the rollers from between one-third and two-thirds of the total free volume. Work grease in between the rollers by hand using grease placed on one's hand. *Note*: overlubricating a bearing with too much grease or oil will cause a bearing to overheat since they are insulators and prevent heat from properly dissipating form a bearing (**FIGURE 7-34**).
- If a hub or component uses oil, spin by hand or rotate the device without a load first to ensure the bearing is properly lubricated. Prelube all bearings before installation. Soaking a bearing in oil, especially sintered bronze bushings, just prior to installation adequately prelubes a bearing.
- Carefully follow manufacturer service procedures to establish correct bearing preload. This is often done using selective shims or adjusting nuts. Preload, which is typically an axial load placed against the bearing through an adjustment procedure, applies a light force to cause the bearing rollers to rotate (**FIGURE 7-35**). Without roller rotation, either due to a loose or an excessively tight bearing adjustment, means the bearings will not pick up lubricant and overheat.

SKILL DRILL 7-1 Bearing Installation

1. Clean the shaft where the bearing is to be installed and lightly oil the bearing seat. Remove any burs or ridges on the shaft or mounting should with a metal file.

2. Verify that the bearing driver sleeve or cup is very clean on all surfaces to prevent bearing contamination during installation.
3. Use a clean dead blow hammer or a hammer that will not cause the sleeve or driver mandrel to flake or splinter.
4. If it is practical, use a hydraulic press to install the bearing and push on the sleeve to eliminate any impact force.
5. Verify the housing and bearing correctly match in size for a clearance or interference fit. A small chamfer on the bearing bore should be visible, smooth, and free of burrs or ridges.
6. Clean and lightly oil the bearing bore and slide the bearing assembly into place.
7. Start the bearing into the bore as squarely as possible using the hammer and correct driver sleeve or cup.
8. If the bearing becomes crooked when driving it, tap it only on its high side to straighten it. If misalignment persists, do not drive it any further, which can damage the bore or shaft. Remove the bearing or cup to inspect for damage or burrs or metal particles then restart the driving process.
9. Bearing cups should be driven until the sound of the hammer blows indicate the bearing piece is solidly seated in its bore or against an abutment on a shaft.

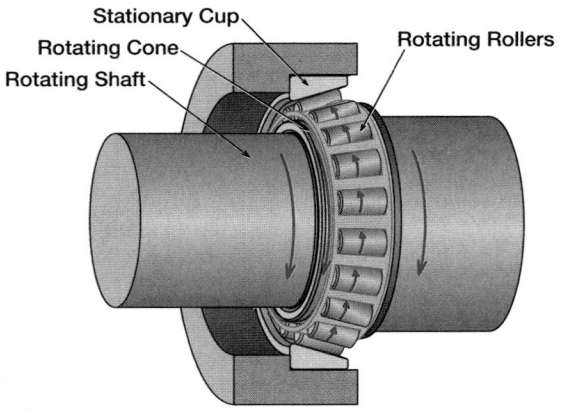

FIGURE 7-34 To rotate, rolling elements must have some slight pressure applied to them through preload.

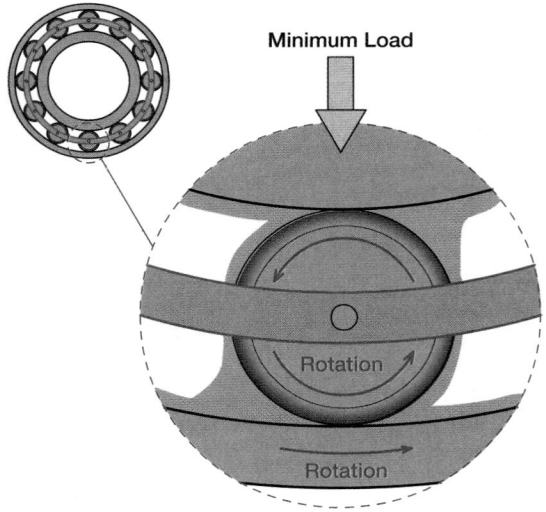

FIGURE 7-35 When a bearing's rolling elements roll due to adequate preload, lubricant is picked up and lubricates the rollers.

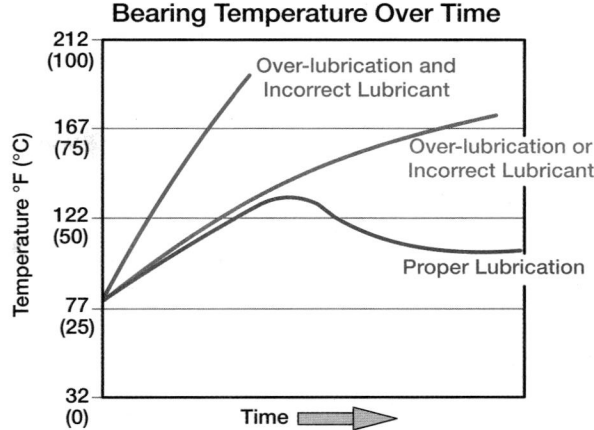

Proper Lubrication (do not overgrease)
- Fill roller bearings between 1/3 and 2/3 of their free volume.

FIGURE 7-36 Over-lubricating and under-lubricating a bearing can lead to premature failure.

▶ **TECHNICIAN TIP**

Over-greasing or immersion of a bearing completely in oil causes heat buildup in the bearing, which can potentially lead to premature bearing failure. When grease or oil completely surrounds the bearing, heat cannot be dissipated because there is nowhere for the heat to go because the lubricant behaves like an insulator. An over-greased or over-lubricated bearing retains more heat than one that's properly filled with grease or oil. Heat combined with bearing movement can also force the grease to the outside of the bearing rolling elements where it can break down and harden, preventing any further lubrication (**FIGURE 7-36**).

Antifriction bearings may be packed with grease by hand or using a hand-operated or grease gun-operated bearing packer. For a general guideline when packing bearings, follow the steps in **SKILL DRILL 7-2**.

SKILL DRILL 7-2 Packing a Bearing with Grease

1. Wear nitrile or suitable gloves to prevent absorption through the skid of hydrocarbons and other substances in grease.
2. Place an amount of grease in one hand that fits onto the palm. Grasping the bearing with the other hand, point the larger open end of the bearing roller cage end toward the palm grease and at the edge of the grease.
3. Pull the bearing toward yourself into the palm to force the grease into the bearing rollers. Repeat this process while observing the movement of grease along the rollers and outwards onto the cage.
4. When grease has begun to push through the bearing and appear on the opposite side or the roller, turn the bearing slightly and repeat this process of pushing grease through the bearing rollers.
5. Turn the bearing and push grease through the rollers until all the rollers have had grease only beginning to push through to the opposite side of the bearing. Smear grease around the outer circumference.

SKILL DRILL 7-2 Packing a Bearing with Grease (Continued)

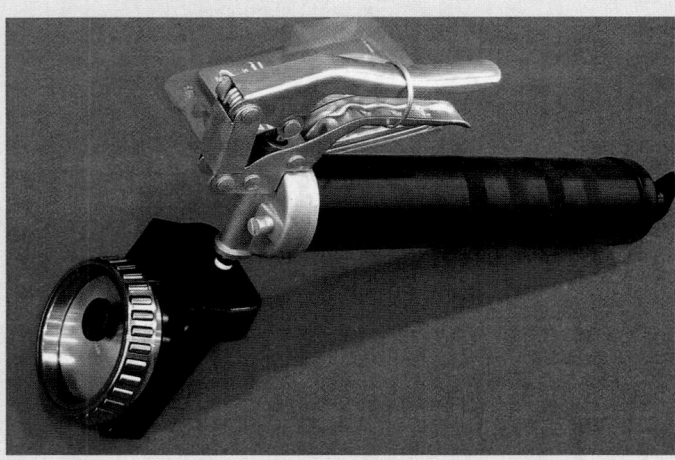

6. When using a mechanical grease packer, verify that the bearing is installed with the correct side down. For tapered bearings, the wider side faces down and has greased pushed up past the rollers to exit the opposite side. Verify grease pushes up through the bearing rather than around the outside of the bearing.

Bearing Inspection

Only after properly cleaning a bearing with solvent and drying it, can the bearing be properly inspected. Using a bright work light, visually examine the entire bearing, cups, and cones for indications of excessive wear or damage. Examine the inner race surfaces by inspecting the race between the rolling elements. A dull but light reflective finish is expected on a bearing rolling elements and races with moderate wear. Also:

- Verify that races or cup surfaces have no gouges or grooves indicating that the bearing was not moving and consequently turned in the support housing or hub, bearing bore, on a spindle or shaft. Dirt or large pieces of foreign material, excessive preload, or overheating will prevent the bearing from turning, creating a condition called a spun bearing.
- Inspect for corrosion or pitting on the rolling elements and races.
- Inspect the races and rolling elements for cracks, flaking, peeling, or pitting.
- Inspect the cage and rolling elements for damage from corrosion.
- Inspect the rolling elements and races for dents caused by shock loads.
- Inspect for arc tracks caused by electric arcing inside the bearing. Look for discoloration from overheating.
- Inspect for overheating, which is evident by congealed hardened grease, a heavy varnish-like film discoloring the bearing rolling elements. Varnish is created by oil oxidation, and is indicated by metal that is darkened and no longer reflects light.

Troubleshooting Antifriction Bearing Failures

The major cause of bearing failure is lubricant contamination with dirt or liquids, such as water. Other factors contributing to bearing failure include using incorrect lubricant, such as using non-synthetic oils when high operating temperature requires synthetic oil; misadjustment; misalignment; vibration; or shock loading of parts. Triboelectric currents generated by rubber tires continuously separating from dry road pavement is conducted through bearings and damages bearings by electrical arcing.

When a bearing first begins to fail, it generally becomes noisy and operates hot. Contamination increases bearing friction, which in turn increases a bearing's operating temperature. A wheel hub is hot to touch or hotter than other hubs. To accurately verify this observation, an infra-red thermometer can measure hub or housing temperatures to identify potentially defective bearings. Bearing vibrations that are transmitted through housings, hubs, and shafts can amplify the noise and vibration, so it is important to listen for sounds. Note that sounds a transmission can make or a noise or squeal from the front of the vehicle or beneath the vehicle can sound like it is originating the rear or at a higher level on the vehicle. Good practice is to identify or eliminate common areas where bearing failures are likely to happen while the vehicle is stationary—before performing road tests. An example is a transmission bearing that becomes noisy when the vehicle is in neutral gear with the clutch engaged but the sound disappears when the clutch is released.

Placing a vehicle on safety stands or on a hoist and operating it enables faster and more accurate identification of bearing noises than a road test. Vibration analyzers with sensors detecting vibration frequencies are also used to pinpoint bearing problems. The sensors are placed in strategic locations on the chassis, including beneath the driver's seat to pinpoint unusual mechanical conditions sometimes created by defective or failing bearings. Knowing the frequency of the vibration—whether it is speed or load dependent—helps identify the bearing location.

▶ TECHNICIAN TIP

When welding a chassis with any type of electric welding equipment, it is possible to damage bearings with electric arc tracks. Electric arc tracks are pits or marks that appear like pencil lines on bearing races and rolling elements caused by current flow through the bearings. This same failure can be caused by triboelectric charges. The bearing becomes noisy and can eventually fail if arc tracks are made. To prevent damage from welding, always attach the welding equipment ground as close as possible to where the welding is performed. Never position the ground with a bearing between the ground and the surface or component where the electrode is welding.

Types of Bearing Failures

Peeling of bearing metal surface is caused by an insufficient lubricating film and can produce a frosted appearance on the bearing race surfaces (**TABLE 7-1**). Spalling is a condition where chunks from the surface of the bearing rollers or races break or flak away. This condition is caused by excessive bearing loads,

TABLE 7-1 Bearing Failure Modes

Term	Description	Image
Galling	Bearing surface is smeared with metal from metal-to-metal transfer. Wear of the bearing caused by inadequate lubrication.	
Spalling	Pitting and flaking of the bearing surface caused by fatigue from excessive loads and contaminated lubrication.	
Brinelling	Dents in the bearing caused by high impact loads, such as from hammering on the bearing or shock loads.	
Peeling or Flaking	Smaller patches of metal flakes and fine line cracks caused by lubricant contamination.	

such as an incorrect preload setting or poor lubricant quality. Brinelling is a condition that appears as dents on race surfaces from the impact of balls or cylindrical rollers. These bearings are very noisy during operation. Hitting bearings improperly with hammers during installation, using impact guns to tighten pinion nuts, or shock loading of a bearing cause brinelling.

SAFETY TIP

When separating bearings with interference fits using a hydraulic press, very high mechanical forces under tension are produced while separating a bearing. If there is defect in the bearing, it could explosively disintegrate under pressure and pieces of the bearing and separating mechanisms can fly apart. To minimize the likelihood of personal injury, always use a safety cage around the hydraulic press. As with other bearing-separating mechanisms, stand at the end of the any housing or shaft opposite to the end that the puller is on. Also, stand to the side of any hydraulic press when parts are under tension.

Functions of Seals

LO 7-6 Identify and describe the types and function of seals.

Seals are barriers used to either control or prevent movement of liquids, gases, or contaminants that may or may not be under pressure (**FIGURE 7-37**). A seal typically may separate different types of fluids and gases from leaking from one area to another. Seal construction must also take into account that movement of various substances may be influenced by pressure or vacuum sources. Commercial vehicles use a variety of types of seals classified according to function and construction or whether they are sealing moving or stationary parts. A seal required to function on moving components is a dynamic seal, while a stationary sealing barrier is a static seal. Common examples of static seals include O-rings and gaskets. In either application, a seal's functions are to provide a barrier to fluids, such as fuels, oil, or coolant and semifluid grease. Seals commonly prevent leakage of these substances out of a component or system while preventing potentially destructive contamination. Air, exhaust, and refrigerant gases may also require sealing. Given the wide range of operations where seals are used, a large variety of seal classifications are described in the following sections.

O-Rings

O-rings are round-shaped elastomer seals and the most common type of seal used on commercial vehicle equipment. The term **elastomer** simply refers to the seal's elastic, rubber-like stretchable properties. The cross section of O-rings is also round and are made in a wide variety of thicknesses and diameters. O-rings are sorted according to internal and external diameter, as well as thickness measured in mm or inches. An O-ring's shape allows them to effectively fit and seal round-shaped tubing or shafts. Typically, they are made from materials that resist deterioration from fuels, oils, solvents, other liquids, and gases. The color of the O-ring frequently, but not always, indicates the ring's construction material, which is matched to an application according to its physical properties and compatibility with particular substances (**TABLE 7-2**). For example, light-green-colored O-rings are used to seal the ends of air conditioning lines and prevent leakage of very small refrigerant molecules through the material. These O-rings are made from Highly Saturated Nitrile (HSN) also known as Hydrogenated Nitrile. Other colored air conditioning O-rings are used that may be red or yellow and made of different materials. When multiple O-rings are used to seal high- and low-pressure fuel or oil on a component, such as an injector, the color may not only indicate compatibility with fluids, but also designate its position (**FIGURE 7-38**).

Because O-rings are compressible and flexible, they can take up clearances and compensate for surface imperfections to make excellent face seals or gaskets. This same property allows

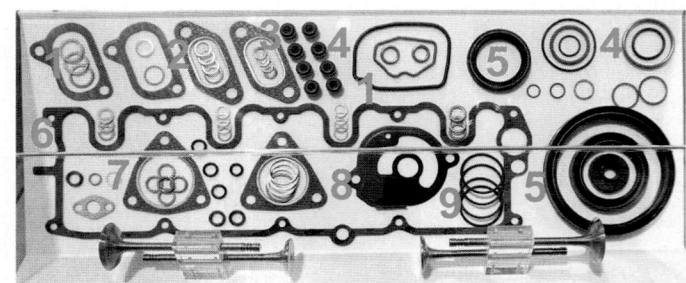

FIGURE 7-37 An upper engine gasket and seal kit. 1. Copper sealing washers. 2. Metallic exhaust manifold gasket. 3. Umbrella valve stem seals. 4. O-Rings. 5. Radial lip seal. 6. Neoprene valve cover gasket. 7. Cellulose gasket. 8. Plastic polymer gasket. 9. Square-Lathe cut O-ring.

TABLE 7-2 O-Ring Materials and Property

Property	Nitrile (Buna-N)	Ethylene-Propylene (EP)	Fluoro-elastomer (Viton)	PTFE
Common Color	Black	Multi-colored: blue, red, yellow	Black, green, grey	Primarily white but multi-colored
Tensile Strength	Fair - Good	Good - Excellent	Good - Excellent	Excellent
Heat Resistance	Good (225° F; 107° C)	Excellent (275° F; 135° C)	Excellent (400° F; 204° C)	Excellent (450° F; 232° C)
Cold Resistance	Fair - Good (−40° F; −40° C)	Good - Excellent (−55° F; −48° C)	Good (−20° F; −29° C)	Best (−110° F; −79° C)
Tear Resistance	Good	Good	Fair	Excellent
Petroleum Oil	Excellent	Poor	Excellent	Excellent
Cost	$	$	$$$$	$$$

(Source: Some cells excerpted from https://www.sterlitech.com/oring-compatibility-chart)

FIGURE 7-38 O-rings on this injector seal low-pressure fuel supply and oil. Seal color designates, size, position, and material compatibility.

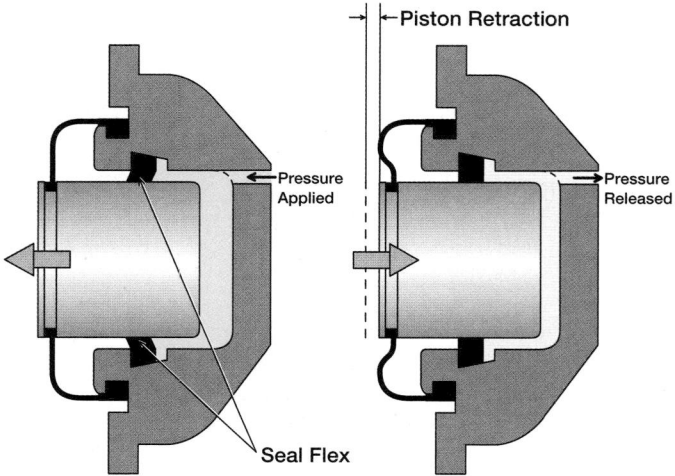

FIGURE 7-39 The square cut O-ring used to seal brake fluid pressure helps retract the caliper piston away from the rotor when the brakes are released.

them to seal a wide range of fluid and gas substances under pressure. Pump housings and fluid leakage around sleeves, pistons, and cylinders are blocked by O-rings. Abrasion-resistant, tough O-rings are also used in dynamic applications. Air brake valves commonly use O-rings to seal valve pistons. To help extend seal reliability, a lubricant, such as silicone, is used on the O-ring sealing surfaces.

Lathe Cut O-Rings

Lathe cut rings are an inexpensive and close relative of O-rings. These round diameter rings have a square, X-shaped or rectangular cross section instead of a round shape. Lathe cut rings are made from elastomer tubing that is cut to a specific length. Unlike O-rings with round cross-sectional profiles, lathe-cut seals provide wider surface edge for sealing, improving its ability to seal high-pressure air or hydraulic fluids. Lathe cut O-rings commonly have an additional mechanical function when relative motion takes place between parts. For example, a lathe cut O-ring is used to seal a hydraulic piston of a disc brake caliper. The ring can seal extreme hydraulic brake pressure without leaking and prevent air from entering the brake system fluid when negative pressure is present, such as when the brakes are released. What is unique is the assistance the ring provides the brake caliper to help it retract when brakes are released. Small movement of the caliper stretches one edge of the ring, lifting it from its retaining groove in the caliper. The elastic tension

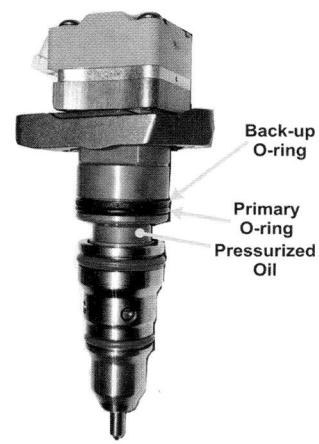

FIGURE 7-40 The back-up O-ring on this hydraulically actuated electronically controlled unit injector (HEUI) prevents the primary O-ring from distorting and flattening against pressure exerted by high-pressure oil.

created by piston movement across the ring helps retract the piston when brake pressure is released (**FIGURE 7-39**).

Back-Up Rings

When O-rings are used in high-pressure applications, a thin metal back-up ring or another thinner O-ring is placed next to the ring opposite the pressure side of the primary O-ring. The use of a back-up ring can extend the life of an O-ring and assist in sealing the primary O-ring. If pressure applied to an O-ring is variable on both sides of the ring, two back-up O-rings may be used (**FIGURE 7-40**).

Mechanical Wedge Seals

Hydraulic rams with sliding piston movement require high-pressure sealing capable of repetitive sliding movement. A common type of sealing mechanism is a wide-dimension chevron-shaped mechanical seal. Mechanical seals are different from packing seals, which use rope-like materials embedded with wax that wrap around the shaft of a pump or hydraulic piston to minimize leakage. A nut may be combined with the seal to tighten the packing and maintain pressure on the shaft. However, the most popular mechanical seals for hydraulic rams or pistons use multiple chevron-shaped seals placed side by side with sealing lips that overlap one another to block fluid movement (**FIGURE 7-41**). The lips of the seals are designed to trap any pressurized fluid and force the lip edge against the cylinder and piston surfaces. The effect of forcing sealing lips against these surfaces is to form a tighter seal using pressurized hydraulic fluid. Fluid leakage is essentially stopped by either a wedge or V-ring-shaped seal. When the piston retracts under low or negative pressure, the seal lips fold and squeeze fluid back into the cylinder cavity.

Radial Lip Seals

Radial lip seals are dynamic-type seals used to prevent fluid, gas, or contaminant leakage around rotating shafts and hubs. The lip provides a low-friction, narrow contact point on the rotating component to seal either liquids, oils, or grease in a cavity while preventing contaminants from entering the liquid

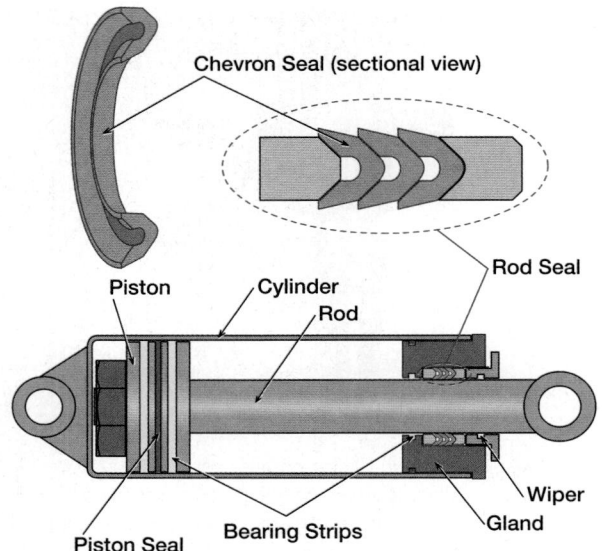

FIGURE 7-41 Mechanical seals in hydraulic cylinders commonly use multiple chevron-shaped seals.

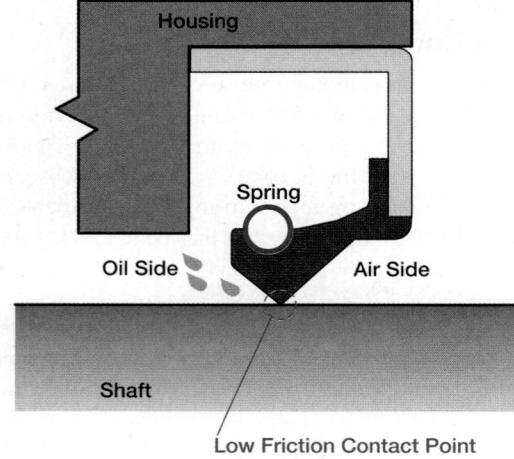

FIGURE 7-42 Radial lip seals form a barrier to contaminants and to prevent lubricant or other leaks past the seal.

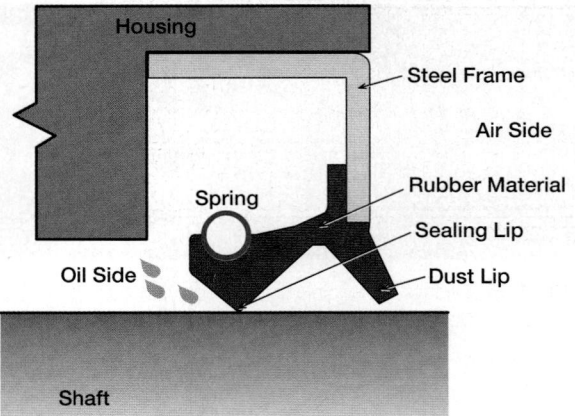

FIGURE 7-43 A garter spring tightens the seal lips around the shaft of a radial lip seal. A dust lip provides an additional barrier to dirt and contaminants from entering a seal cavity.

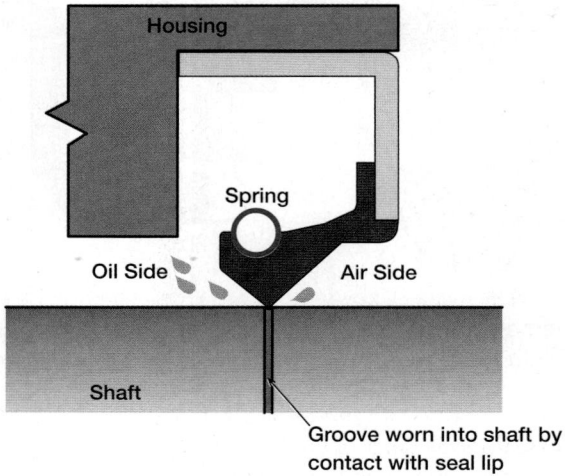

FIGURE 7-44 A groove is worn into a shaft by the seal lip. A wear ring with a groove can be replaced or a new wear ring installed to restore the seal surface.

or lubricant cavity (**FIGURE 7-42**). The narrow contact point where the seal lip contacts the rotating component is designed to maintain a barrier that holds liquids or greases in on one side and excludes contaminants on the opposite side. Because dirt and contaminants dramatically shorten bearing life, seals often function to keep contaminants out of a cavity where a greased or oil-lubricated bearing operates. A seal that functions as a barrier to dirt and contaminants is called an **exclusion seal** but may commonly be called a dust lip (**FIGURE 7-43**).

To establish a consistent contact force between the sealing lip and rotating component to form an efficient barrier, the seal's lip has a smaller diameter than the diameter of the rotating shaft or spindle. When there is a difference between the seal lip and the shaft diameter, the difference is known as the interference dimension. Interference is the primary factor that enables the seal to function effectively as a barrier to leakage and contaminants. To further enhance the sealing lip capabilities, a garter spring is placed in a groove behind the lip. This metal spring is a helically wound

coil formed into a ring that applies more force to the seal lip. If the seal only retains grease, a garter spring may not be present because grease does not move easily. A second reason is that a spring can also shorten seal life by increasing friction and wear at both the seal and the surface it rotates around (**FIGURE 7-44**). This explains why it is important to lubricate a seal surface during installation— the lubricant reduces seal friction. A replaceable thin metal wear ring may be installed on a shaft, which is replaced during seal service or a new ring can be installed over the original shaft.

▶ TECHNICIAN TIP

When installing most seals, it is important to lubricate the seal's lip to prevent damage caused by a dry start rotation. Without some oil or slight weepage of lubricant past the seal, the dry rotating surfaces can rapidly tear or wear the lip, leading to premature leakage and cavity contamination. Always wipe a small amount of grease or heavy oil on the seal lip and surface the seal will rotate over. Teflon or PTFE seals and urethane seals used in places like the crankshaft rear main and preset wheel bearing hubs should not be lubricated during installation.

FIGURE 7-45 Dual-lip radial seal used at the rear of the crankshaft. Note the replaceable wear ring below the seal lip.

Radial Lip Seal Construction

LO 7-7 Describe the construction features, inspection, and service techniques associated with radial lip-type seals.

In the 1950s, when technology enabled the chemical bonding of rubber to metal, composite seals were created. Composite construction means the rubber-like seal lip and metal case are one piece. Five basic parts of a composite seal are the outer and inner shell or case, the primary lip, a secondary lip also called the auxiliary or exclusion lip, and the garter spring. The edge of a primary lip always points to the liquid or lubricant side of the seal. An exclusion seal lip always points directly downward or to the air or contaminant side (**FIGURE 7-45**). When installing a seal, the direction of the primary lip should be verified to ensure the seal is not installed backward. Markings on the seal case should point outwards, away from the lubricating or liquid cavity.

The length and direction of the primary lip seal orientation also lend the seal the capability to not only rotate but allow some oscillating and reciprocating movement. Oscillating movement takes place if there is some axial endplay in a support bearing, such as a wheel bearing. However, too much bearing endplay causes the seal to operate in an elliptical-shaped rotation and quickly wears out the seal. Some deflection of the seal lip is always possible but short lips create a firmer seal which wears more quickly (**FIGURE 7-46**).

In addition to the primary sealing lip, seals may include secondary sealing lips to exclude dirt, liquids, and other contaminants from a cavity protected by a seal. Unlike the primary lip, the exclusion lip faces the outside or air side to block contaminants that can also rapidly wear the primary lip when they are trapped between the sealing surface and rotating lip. In fact, some seal designs use a sealing surface that locks onto the rotating shaft or spindle and the sealing surfaces. No movement takes place at the seal lip and spindle surface. Another rotating sealing lip is internal to the seal case and creates a more difficult pathway for contaminants to reach and cause abrasive wear damage to the sealing lips. It's also important to note the primary seal lip benefits from any increased pressure inside a sealed cavity because it uses cavity pressure to apply more force against the primary seal lip. Up to a point, the lip flattens out, improving

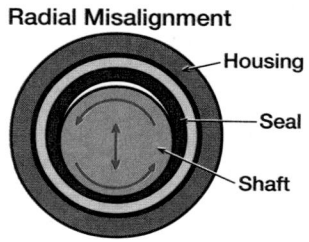

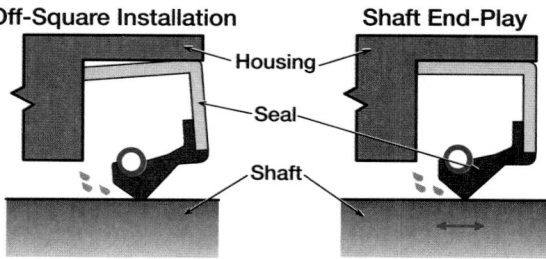

FIGURE 7-46 Flexing of the seal lip deflects slightly to accommodate a limited amount of shaft or spindle run-out called eccentricity.

seal performance. Wear is also distributed over a larger surface area, potentially extending service life. However, excessive pressure causes the seal to leak and prematurely wears the seal lips.

Replaceable wear rings are frequently used on seal surfaces either from the factory or as a service item. Because a seal lip can wear a groove on the rotating shaft, a new wear ring is installed when the seal is replaced. If a different style or manufacturer of seal is used, the seal lip will rotate on a slightly different area of a rotating shaft surface, which may be pitted or have scratches. Installation of a new wear ring accompanying a seal replacement restores the sealing surface to like-new condition and provides a slightly different interference diameter. An application of a thin film of sealant is generally used beneath the wear ring to prevent leakage between the wear ring and shaft during the ring's installation.

> ▶ TECHNICIAN TIP

To prevent installing a seal in the wrong direction, always verify the direction of the angle of the primary seal lip. A primary lip always points toward the direction of the liquid or substance that it forms a barrier with. An exclusion seal lip points toward the air or contaminant side of the seal.

Seal Cases

The seal case is pressed snugly into a seal bore and has two functions. The first is to provide a support structure to the sealing lip that is bonded to the case. The second is to prevent damage to the seal during installation. During installation, the case accurately aligns the centerline of the bore and seal to provide concentric seal rotation on a shaft or spindle. Cocking and uncontrolled movement during installation is minimized by the sturdy case construction along with the use of a seal driver. A seal driver helps to evenly press a seal into its bore, which has a slight interference fit with the outside diameter of the seal case (**FIGURES 7-47** and **7-48**). The shape of the case can vary to accommodate different seal lip designs; however, there are three basic categories: metal, rubber, and a combination. The outside diameter of metal cases is typically coated with paint or sealant to prevent corrosion and to assist in retaining the case in the seal bore. Small scratches and nicks in the bore can create leak paths for lubricating oil, so applying a thin coat of room temperature vulcanizing (RTV) silicone or gasket sealer to the outer diameter (OD) of the seal case is good practice and may be required for some lightly damaged seal bores.

A rubber case enables a tighter elastic fit in the bore than with metal alone to minimize leak paths. These seals often do not require specialized sets of seal drivers to install in the seal bore, unlike metal cases, which must be driven into position (**FIGURE 7-49**). Seals featuring both metal and rubber OD are selected for damaged seal bores and wear surfaces because the seal lip area is often shifted with this type of construction.

▶ TECHNICIAN TIP

Two common causes of seal failure are related to damage to the seal lip. If lubricating oil becomes contaminated with dirt or metal filings, such as during an engine, transmission, or wheel bearing failure, the metal particles tear up the seal. A second failure that quickly takes place is when a seal operates on a shaft with an elliptical-shaped rotation. Worn, loose or misadjusted bearings do this and cause the seal lip to rapidly wear. Torque converter seals for the transmission quickly leak if a bell housing centerline is not concentric with the crankshaft. Always replace seals anytime bearing lubricant is contaminated and verify that excessive radial run-out is not present when a seal fails prematurely.

▶ TECHNICIAN TIP

Wheel seals on drive axles may appear to have failed if pressure in the housing is excessive. Pressure caused by a plugged axle vent or a leaking power divider shift cylinder O-ring can push oil past a good wheel-and-pinion seal creating the impression of a failed seal. Engine oil seals and gaskets can leak and appear to have failed in a similar way if engine blow-by is excessive. Before replacing multiple seals and gaskets, inspect for air leakage into axle housings and whether the axle vent is plugged. Confirm that crankcase pressure is not excessive due to a worn-out engine or caused by other potential causes for high crankcase pressure.

▶ TECHNICIAN TIP

Radial lip seals cannot provide a perfect liquid-tight or gas-tight barrier. If an axle housing, wheel hub, or engine crankcase is overfilled with oil, the seal will leak. Always check lubricant levels before identifying a radial lip seal as the cause of a leak.

Composite PTFE Seals

The selection of seal lip materials typically requires a compromise between advantages and disadvantages, such as cost, durability, installation methods, and material compatibility with liquids or lubricants. Traditional sealing lips are made from a variety of materials, such as leather, polyurethane, and common elastomer compounds, such as nitrile rubber, N-Buna, silicone, polyacrylate, Viton, and propylene (**FIGURE 7-50**). The most recent seal technology uses PTFE or Teflon as a seal lip material. Because PTFE is often bonded to another elastomer material, the seals are sometimes called composite seals (**FIGURE 7-51**). PTFE seal material is used because it has a low CoF. This means it can withstand more abrasive operating conditions, such as high temperatures, high pressures, and dry rotation, that destroy elastomeric sealing lip materials. Preset bearings in wheel hubs, crankshaft rear main, and steering gear shafts are a few examples where PTFE seals are now commonly used. With operating temperatures ranging from –300° F to +550° F (–184° C to 288° C), high resistance to chemical degradation, and very low CoFs, the seal lasts much longer than conventional seals. However, PTFE seal lips do not have the same elastic properties as elastomer seals, which makes them more

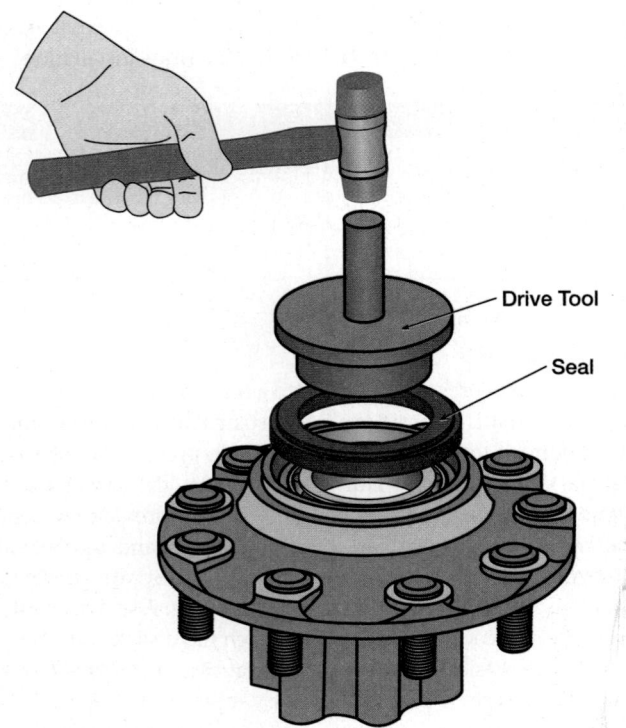

FIGURE 7-47 A seal may be installed in a wheel hub using a seal driver.

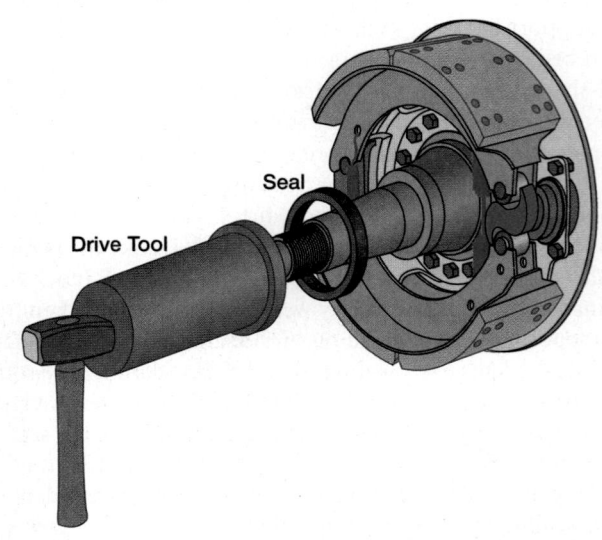

FIGURE 7-48 A seal driver used to install a seal or wear ring over the shoulder or seal surface of a spindle. The driver is hollow like a pipe with a flange on one end and a cap on the other.

FIGURE 7-49 A seal driver used to press a rear main bearing seal into place. Two bolts entering the bolt holes for the flywheel center the driver and a pressure screw pushes the seal, which may include a wear ring, into its bore.

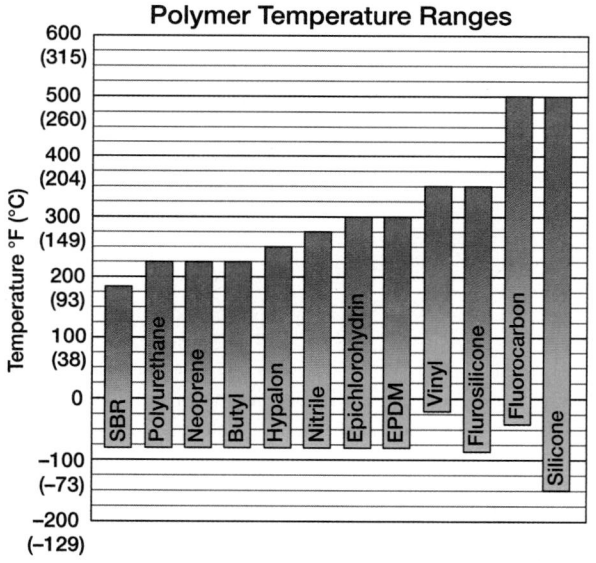

FIGURE 7-50 Many different elastomer polymers are used to make O-rings and other types of seals. Each has temperature-unique resistant properties.

FIGURE 7-51 A Teflon or PTFE radial lip seal with a protective plastic sleeve to prevent lip damage during installation.

▶ **TECHNICIAN TIP**

Radial lip seals are not perfect liquid- or gas-tight seals. Some calibrated amount of lubricant can pass beneath the seal lip to lubricate the seal and extend its service life. A problem for technicians is deciding whether a seal is excessively worn or damaged and requires replacement if there is oil leaking past the seal. Generally, a slight amount of wetting on the sealing surfaces is acceptable. If liquid accumulates to the point where a droplet has formed, the seal should be replaced and the component checked for other possible causes for seal wear and damage.

vulnerable to damage. The absence of good elastic properties explains why special care must be taken to prevent damage during installation and handling and help ensure proper operation and function. To prevent seal distortion during storage and damage during installation, PTFE seals are often packaged and installed using a thin-walled plastic or metal sleeve to protect the seal material from sharp edges on splines, drilled holes, and sharp-edged shaft ridges that can easily damage PTFE lips. Whenever possible, potentially damaging features can be covered by using tape or thin-walled installation tools made from plastic or metal. Because PTFE seals have a low CoF, pre-lubrication is not necessary.

Unitized Seals

Often a sealing surface or seal bore is damaged after a seal or bearing failure. One method to repair the damage is to use a unitized seal (**FIGURE 7-52**). These seals are one piece—meaning they generally do not have a wear ring. However, the entire seal is made from two separate pieces—one that locks into the seal bore and the other that locks onto the shaft or spindle. The sealing surfaces are inside the seal, eliminating the problem encountered by damaged sealing surfaces that could shred seal lips. If the case is rubberized, the seal is commonly driven over a wheel spindle shoulder where the sealing surface is normally located. The inner seal ring locks onto the shaft with an

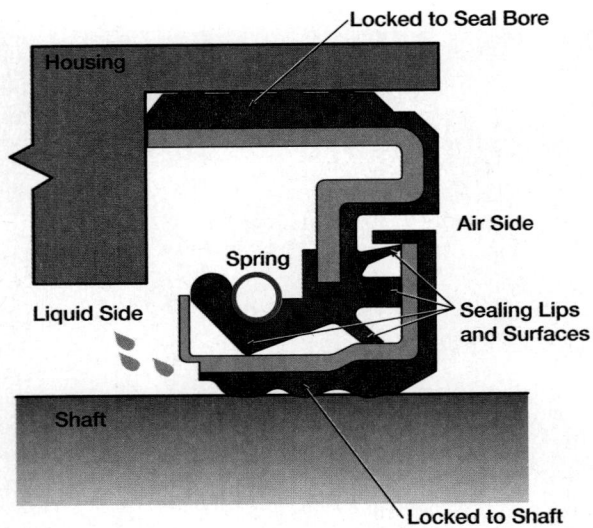

FIGURE 7-52 A unitized seal has the sealing surfaces located inside a two-part, one-piece seal.

interference fit that also eliminates leak paths. The hub is drawn over the seal when the wheel bearing is tightened.

Dual Seals

Two seals are often used when gear-driven accessories, such as power steering, coolant, or fuel pumps, are installed on engines. The outside seal exposed to engine crankcase and lubricating oil is installed with the seal lip pointed toward the engine oil to exclude oil from the pump. The second inner seal lip points to the liquid side of the pump to block oil or fuel from leaking out of the pump. A weep hole located between the two seals is used to allow coolant or fuel to leak externally rather than contaminate engine lubricating oil if the inner seal leaks. Engine oil leaking from the weep hole indicates the outer seal is leaking and likely damaged. However, if the outer seal lip for a power steering pump is damaged, in some applications the power steering can pull engine oil past the damaged exclusion seal and into the pump. The result is a power steering oil reservoir that overflows with engine oil. For a wheel seal installation, follow the steps in **SKILL DRILL 7-3**.

SKILL DRILL 7-3 Installing Wheel Seals

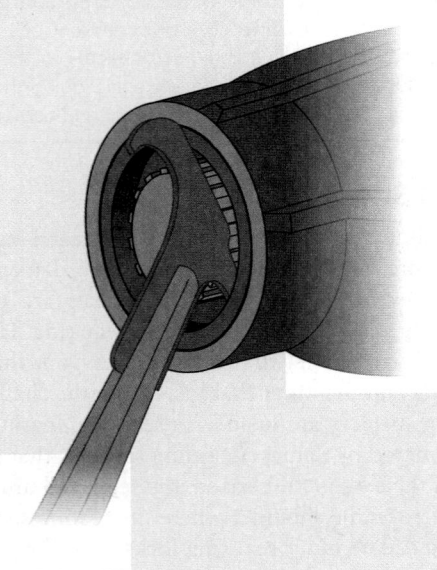

1. Remove the hub from the spindle per manufacturer's instructions. Remove the wheel seal from the hub using a roll bar or purpose-made seal removing tool. Pry the seal from the seal bore by placing the curved end of seal remover tool between the inner wheel bearing and seal. A tool to remove a seal is placed between the bearing and seal to pry the seal from its bore. Various shapes of purpose-made seal removers pry the seal from its bore by using the bearing or bearing bore as a fulcrum point.

2. Clean and inspect wheel bearings and seal bore areas.

3. Inspect the spindle for a wear ring. If a wear sleeve is present, remove it by tapping the sleeve with the round end of a ball-peen hammer. This expands the thin ring far enough to easily remove it. NEVER chisel or use a sharp tool to remove a wear ring.

4. Wipe the sealing area on shaft or spindle with a soft cloth to allow visual inspection. Remove any small nicks, pitting, ridges, or roughness with abrasive emery cloth or a file. Clean oil or grease from the hub and spindle. Clean and inspect spindle threads and any hub surfaces in contact with lubricant.

5. Install a new wear ring onto the spindle if the replacement seal requires a wear ring. If a wear ring is used, wipe a thin film of gasket eliminator or silicone lubricant beneath the wear ring to prevent leakage between the ring and spindle. Use the appropriate driver to press the wear ring onto the spindle.

6. Lightly lubricate the wear ring if it uses an elastomer wheel seal. Generally, PTFE seals should not be lubricated. Verify the correct seal fit by placing the seal over the spindle sealing surface and check for an interference fit.

7. After any required bearing or hub service, pre-lube the inner bearing with the same lubricant the bearing uses.

8. Place the hub or wheel and hub wheel flat or lean it at a 45-degree angle. Place the inner bearing inside hub in the bearing cup. If the seal has a metal case, select the appropriate seal driver tool and place the seal on the installation tool with the primary seal lip facing toward the hub. If the seal case is rubber, it may require installation by hand only or a flat plate-type driver.

SKILL DRILL 7-3 Installing Wheel Seals (Continued)

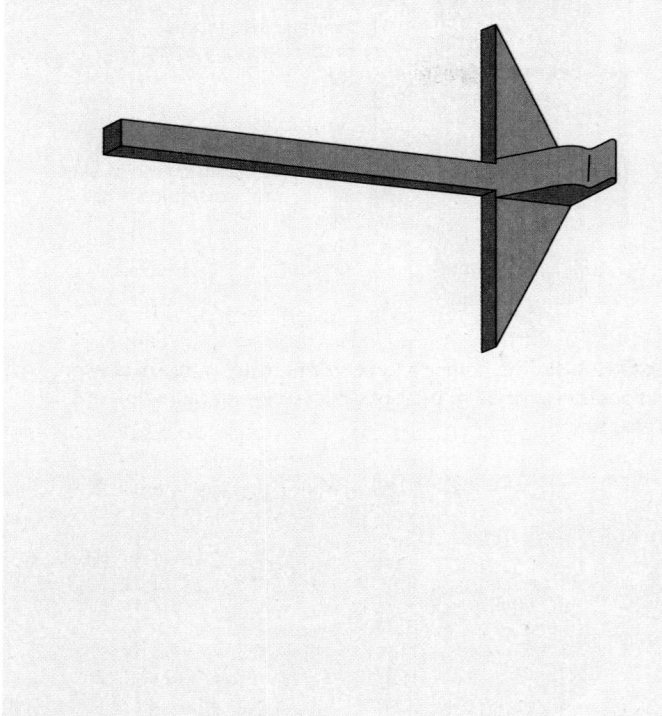

9a. Lightly lubricate the seal lip with clean oil and drive the seal straight into the hub using a three to five-pound hammer. The seal is driven until it bottoms out in the hub and the sound of the hammer blows become sharper and louder when the seal is driven completely into the hub.

9b. If the seal is a spindle-mounted-type bearing, the seal is first installed onto the spindle and then the hub is pulled over the seal using the force of a tightening spindle nut. Place the seal as far onto the spindle by hand as possible. Select the appropriate seal driver to fully drive and seat the seal onto the shoulder of the spindle. Lube the rubber case exterior and install the wheel bearing onto the spindle. Align the hub with the spindle and draw the hub over the seal by tightening the spindle nut according to the OEM procedures.

10. Place the wheel or hub assembly onto the appropriate lifting device, such as a wheel dolly, to install the hub onto the spindle. Fill the hub cavity with clean oil or grease, being careful not to overfill the hub or pack the hub completely with grease.

11. Install the hub over the spindle and install the adjusting nut. Adjust the wheel bearing according to the Technology and Maintenance Council (TMC) method or other recommended method appropriate for the style of adjusting nut.

12. Install the hub oiler cap cover or reinstall the drive axle. Top-up the oil level of the oiler cap, if equipped. On drive axles, tilt the axle housing to completely fill the hub by lifting the axle on the opposite side.

13. Recheck and top-up, if necessary, the axle housing oil level when the axle housing is level again. If equipped, inspect the vent plug on the axle housing to verify it is open and free of dirt.

Gaskets and Sealants

LO 7-8 Identify and describe the purpose, types, and function of gaskets and sealants.

Another category of seals used to prevent leakage of fluids and gases between two stationary surfaces is gaskets and sealants. Gaskets are thin preformed seals made from solid materials combining various materials, such as paper, cork, rubber, fiber, metal, silicone, and an assortment of other materials. Gaskets are needed to seal potential leak paths between irregular surfaces of bolted components. Perfectly smooth and aligned surfaces do not require gaskets. But due to the limits of machining capabilities and the cost of producing precisely machined parts without any potential for distortion, a gasket is used instead to compensate for surface distortions and limits to finish smoothness (**FIGURE 7-53**). A gasket, however, is only effective when it is properly compressed between bolted surfaces. Gasket material sinks into uneven and rough surface finishes when clamped in place and its thickness takes up space between gaps of machined mating of surfaces.

In contrast to gaskets, sealants are thick viscous liquids that are a "formed in place gasket" and in fact replace gaskets in many places (**FIGURE 7-54**). Sealants are also used to prevent gas and leakage of liquids past threaded connections, such as pipe fittings for air system fittings or bolts entering liquid passageways for oil, fuel, or coolant. After the sealant is applied to the surfaces of parts, it cures or stiffens to various degrees of rigidity to prevent leakage across gasket surfaces. The major difference between sealants and gaskets is sealants typically have lower cohesive strength but higher elasticity.

Gaskets are either metallic or non-metallic material, such as cork, rubber, plastic, or a combination of various materials. Metallic gaskets, such as metal washers, which can withstand high temperatures and pressure, are formed from metal of various thicknesses. Thin pieces of metal can also sandwich a

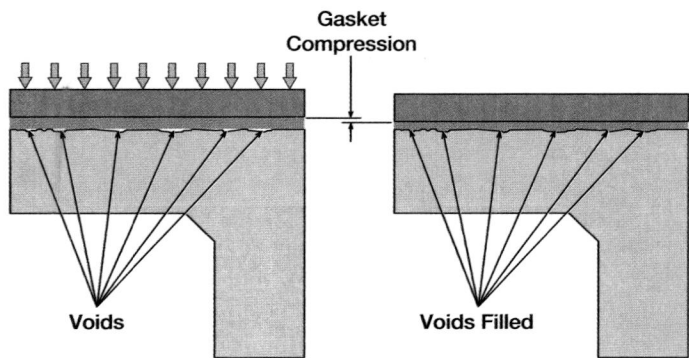

FIGURE 7-53 Gaskets seal potential leak paths by filling up the voids and irregular surface finish on mating halves of parts.

FIGURE 7-54 Room temperature vulcanizing rubber or silicone is one of the most commonly used sealants.

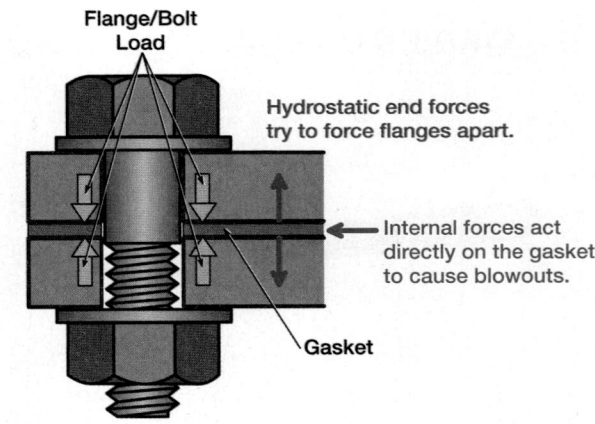

FIGURE 7-55 The clamping force, gasket material thickness, and composition function to prevent gasket blow-out caused by internal pressure.

corrugated metal gasket, giving it the ability to withstand higher pressures and temperatures. Combining non-asbestos fibers, such as fiberglass with rubber, can further improve the temperature and pressure performance capabilities of a gasket.

Gasket Clamping Force

It is important that a gasket is adequately compressed to compensate for irregularities in the mating surfaces. Clamping force applied by a bolted joint must be applied consistently to the gasket materials because temperature or pressure cycles can cause a gasket to relax or weaken and leak. Without a strong clamping force, the surface irregularities cannot be filled, and the pressure applied to the gasket can push out the gasket and create a leak path (**FIGURE 7-55**). The number, size, and tension applied to the bolts used in the joint determine the clamping force on the gasket. Greater clamping force translates into improved gasket performance and resistance to blow-out.

Surface Finish

The surface finish of the mating parts has strong influence on the sealing capabilities of a gasket. If surfaces are polished to a mirror-like finish, side pressure from gases and liquids acting on the gasket cross-sectional area allows the gasket to slip and blow-out. Some roughness, then, is required to give the gasket material some grip or traction to resist movement. Surface smoothness or roughness is measured in microinches—a millionth of an inch. There is no metric equivalent to the term, but a microinch is equivalent to 25.4 nanometers (nm). Machinists recommend that metal surfaces be machined to a finish roughness of 125 to 500 microinches depth, with 250 microinches as the optimum depth for non-metallic gaskets. Surface finish is an an important factor when materials with dissimilar properties are clamped together because of a factor called creep. **Creep** is the movement of components across another component, such as a cylinder head across an engine block, caused by thermal expansion and contraction. If machined surfaces expand at different rates, the grip one surface has on a gasket tend to allow one surface to slide and another to grip, potentially tearing or wearing away a gasket material (**FIGURE 7-56**).

To achieve a clean gasket surface finish, wire wheels installed on air drills or die grinders are commonly used to clean

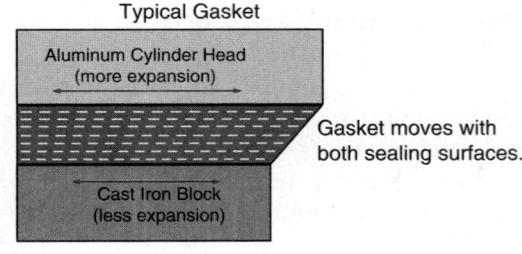

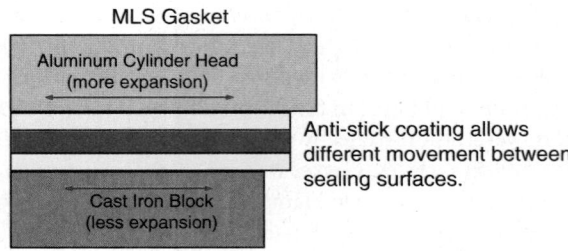

FIGURE 7-56 The cylinder head gasket is a critical and precision-made gasket that accommodates two different rates of expansion.

gasket surfaces after they are scraped with a sharp gasket scraper (**FIGURE 7-57**). Steel brass and composite fiber wire wheels are available, but care must be given to ensure excessive material is

FIGURE 7-57 These abrasive fiber discs are made from varying degrees of abrasiveness from fine to coarse. Different sizes and adapters are used to mount the abrasive wheels on die grinders and air drills used to clean gasket surfaces.

not removed from a surface when cleaning old gasket material. Flat sanding blocks with emery cloth sandpaper can be used on flat surfaces to prevent uneven removal of steel or iron metal surfaces. Aluminum is soft and should not be scraped with a sharp hardened blade of a gasket scraper. Instead, a hard-plastic scraper should be used on soft aluminum surfaces to prevent gouging and damaging the aluminum.

Gasket Installation Guidelines

LO 7-9 Outline gasket installation guidelines.

A gasket joint leak is often caused by improperly installed gaskets. Basic guidelines to follow when installing a gasket include:

- When replacing gaskets, properly clean all gasket surfaces with a sharp gasket scraper and use a semi-abrasive pad or wire wheel on an air tool to clean gasket material from steel or iron surfaces. Never use a sharp hardened scraper, sandpaper, or abrasive discs on aluminum. Instead, use a plastic scraper blade and aluminum cleaner.
- Verify satisfactory surface finish and flatness. Inspect all gasket surfaces for warpage, surface imperfection, gouges, or deep scratches that can form leak paths. A straight edge placed on top of the surface helps detect areas of warpage if a thin feeler blade—usually 0.006" (0.15 mm) thickness or less, is slid beneath the straight edge at various spots (**FIGURE 7-58**).
- Tighten bolts to specification to uniformly compress and clamp a gasket.
- When assembling components with gaskets, ensure all bolt holes are clean and free of damaged threads. Use a thread chaser to clean threads. Lightly lubricate fasteners before tightening fasteners to specification.
- Use a torque wrench to tighten lightly lubricated fasteners with clean threads.
- Tighten joints in progressive stages of typically one-third of final torque
- Follow an OEM recommended sequence when tightening multiple bolts in a gasketed joint to apply a consistent clamping force. Tightening bolts by moving in a star

FIGURE 7-58 Inspecting a head gasket with a feeler blade and straight edge to check for warpage.

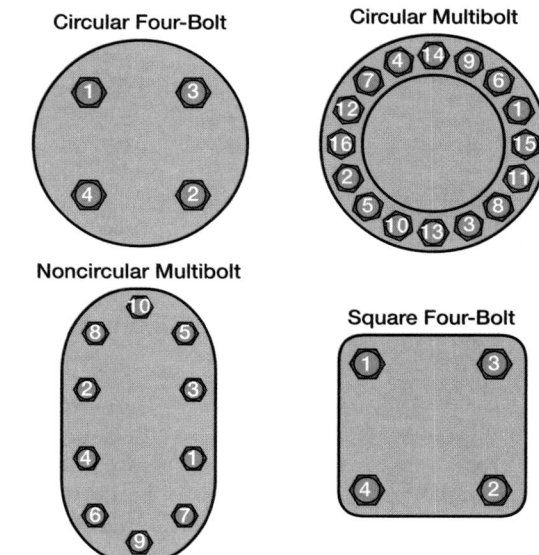

FIGURE 7-59 The tightening pattern used to clamp a gasket should allow the gasket to spread out evenly, not bunch-up, and have consistent clamping force.

pattern, spiral, or moving from side-to-side and outward from the center are common bolt-tightening patterns for gasketed joints (**FIGURE 7-59**).
- Use hardened flat washers and lock washers to ensure consistent fastener preload force.
- Make a final check pass at the target torque value, moving consecutively from bolt to bolt.

▶ TECHNICIAN TIP

Applying slippery silicone sealant to a gasket material, such as cork or paper fiber, may cause the gasket to slip or easily blow out after it is tightened. This happens because the rough mating surface finish is filled with silicone, making the surfaces too smooth for a gasket to have any grip or traction. When compressed, the gasket will squeeze out of place or easily blow out.

Classification and Application of Sealants

Gasket-replacing sealants are categorized into three large classes.

1. Fast-drying, fast-hardening sealants. These are epoxy-like sealants that are used in applications not likely to be disassembled. This sealant is used to seal expansion plugs in an engine block or lock bearing races or seal high-pressure bolt threads.
2. Slow-drying, non-hardening sealants. These are the most familiar sealants using rubber or silicone bases that after curing have different amounts of flexibility. **RTV Silicone** is one of the most recognizable sealants used by technicians and is a two-part rubber compound. When exposed to air, a chemical cures or hardens the rubber, a process called vulcanization, causing the rubber to stiffen to various degrees of hardness required for specific applications (**FIGURE 7-60**).
3. Brush-applied, slow-drying, non-hardening sealants. These gaskets that are more like tacky adhesives (Figure 7-60). A thin or thick coat to layer is brushed on metal flanges or machined surfaces to form a non-hardening finish that can be easily resealed. Copper gasket sealant is an example of fast-drying adhesive with metal content suspended in the sealant to help dissipate heat and improve heat transfer between the mating surfaces (**FIGURE 7-61**). Because it can withstand temperatures of up to 500° F (260° C), copper gasket sealant is used to help seal some cylinder head and exhaust manifold gaskets.

RTV Silicone Sealers

RTV silicone is available in applicators, such as squeezable tubes or caulking guns. The material is often color-coded to identify particular properties. For example, a grey color is used to designate high-torque and high-vibration applications requiring stiffer hardened rigidity. Oil pans, valve covers, and bell housing to transmission sealing are typical applications. Blue- or black-colored RTV may be used for more general-purpose high-temperature applications. Operating temperature ranges for RTV are between –65°F to 700°F (–54°C to 371°C). Copper is added to some formulations to provide additional heat resistance and transfer capabilities. RTV is usually an aerobically cured material, which means it requires initial exposure to oxygen to begin to vulcanize or harden. Once begun, the vulcanizing process continues. The strong vinegar-like smell is acetic acid that is often released during the curing processes. Additional chemical additives are packaged into other formulations to make the RTV more resistant to deterioration from oil, fuel, and antifreeze. One important additive used to seal oil pans and valve cover gaskets is oil dispersants, which enable the silicone to stick to metal crankcase rails of cylinder blocks, even though a film of oil is present.

Anaerobic Sealers

Anaerobic sealers are designed to be used when air is not available to assist the curing process. Thread-locking compounds often use an anaerobic-type sealant to cure only after the bolt is tightened and no air can reach the thread.

Seal Service and Maintenance

LO 7-10 Describe seal service and maintenance.

- Most gaskets, O-rings, radial lip seals, and packings must be discarded and replaced when removed, even if the seal has not failed. Once compressed, a static seal cannot be compressed a second time in order to conform to surface irregularities. Reusing gaskets, O-rings, and seals usually results in an almost immediate failure. When seals, such as gaskets, O-rings, or radial lip seals have leaked, it is important to investigate the root cause to prevent a repeat failure. Inspection items include:
- Check for whether the cause of a radial lip seal failure is due to consequential damage from metal originating from a bearing failure.
- When disassembling components, carefully note whether bolts and nuts fasteners were correctly tightened and have

FIGURE 7-60 This color coded RTV is for gasket applications requiring high stiffness.

FIGURE 7-61 Copper metal in this silicone gasket eliminator is used for high-temperature sealing applications.

consistent tension. Inspect bolt holes and fasteners for corrosion and pitting.

- Examine gaskets and O-rings for cuts and damage due to excessive pressure or heat.
- Examine O-rings to determine if they rolled and twisted during installation. For example, O-rings sealing cylinder liners should have a small pick rotated around the O-ring, lifting and stretching it out while smoothing it after its installed. If it is twisted, the procedure will unroll any tight spots that form leak paths.
- Examine seal rotating surfaces. The mark left by a radial lip seal should be perfectly vertical or concentric around a shaft or spindle. Areas where seal wear is deep, such as on the bottom of an axle spindle, and non-concentric indicate bearing looseness. A misaligned seal leaves a wide wear mark.

- Inspect radial sealing lips for tears, wear, cracks, distortion, or indications of misalignment on the seal case.
- When reassembling, tighten fasteners in the correct sequence and in stages to achieve the correct clamping force.
- Verify that gaskets and O-rings are the correct dimension as the originals.
- When using pipe or thread sealants, do not use excessive amounts that could contaminate a system or cause malfunctioning of sensitive components.
- Verify a seal lip is installed in the correct direction—a primary seal points to the liquid.

Wrap-Up

Ready for Review

- Seals and gaskets operate as barriers to block the movement of fuel, oil, coolant, brake fluid, gases, and other substances to prevent loss or cross-contamination.
- Bearings function to minimize friction between moving parts, are replaceable wear surfaces, and support and align loads.
- Bearings loads are either applied radially, axially, or angularly using a combination of both forces.
- Bearings can reduce friction and wear caused by two common types of friction: Sliding and rolling contact.
- When two dissimilar metals slide across one another, friction is reduced compared to the situation when the metals are the same. This property is called compatibility.
- When a fluid lubricant forms a film between the sliding surfaces to prevent direct contact between moving parts, the bearing is known as fluid film bearings.
- Antifriction bearings use rolling contact to reduce friction. Friction bearings use sliding contact to reduce friction.
- Antifriction bearings use rolling balls, barrels, or cylinders to reduce friction by changing sliding to rolling friction.
- The coefficient of friction is expressed as the Force/Load. If the force required to move an object is equal to half the object's weight, it has a coefficient of friction of 0.5.
- The five most commonly encountered rolling element shapes are: Ball, cylindrical roller, tapered roller, barrel roller, and needle roller bearings.
- A tapered roller bearing separates the outer race, called a cup, from rollers integrated into the inner race, called the cone.
- Straight or cylindrical-shaped rollers have a wider line contact area than ball bearings to primarily support heavier radial loads.
- The most effective method to lock the bearing races into place is to use an interference fit between a bearing's race and the shaft or housing the race fits into. An interference fit means the bearings inner or outer race is either slightly larger or smaller by a few thousandths of an inch or millimeters than the shaft or housing it locks to.

- Specialized bearing separators, splitters, or pullers are used to dissemble bearings from housings and shafts. Various other destructive and non-destructive techniques are used to replace bearings.
- The most common type of bearing removal tool is a bearing splitter or separator, also called a strong back puller. Strong back pullers help with bearing removal when the use of traditional jaw pullers is restricted due to limited space or a long reach is needed.
- When installing bearings having an interference fit, the bearing is usually driven onto a shaft, into a hub or housing with a bearing driver, or specifically sized sleeves.
- Overlubricating and under-lubricating a bearing can lead to premature failure.
- Preload, which is typically an axial load placed on the bearing through an adjustment procedure, applies a light force to cause the bearing rollers to rotate.
- To rotate, rolling elements must have some slight pressure applied to them through preload. Only when a bearing rotates is lubricant picked-up by the rollers.
- The major cause of bearing failure is lubricant contamination with dirt or liquids, such as water. Contamination increases bearing friction, which in turn increases a bearing's operating temperature.
- When a bearing first begins to fail, it generally becomes noisy and operates hot.
- O-rings are round-shaped elastomer seals and the most common type of seal used on commercial vehicle equipment.
- When O-rings are used in high-pressure applications, a thin metal back-up ring or another thinner O-ring is placed next to the ring opposite the pressure side of the primary O-ring.
- Radial lip seals are dynamic-type seals used to prevent fluid, gas, or contaminant leakage around rotating shafts and hubs.
- A common type of mechanical seal sealing mechanism used on hydraulic rams is a wide-dimension chevron-shaped mechanical seal.

- When installing most seals, it is important to lubricate the seal's lip to prevent damage caused by a dry start rotation.
- In addition to the primary sealing lip, radial lip seals may include secondary sealing lips to exclude dirt.
- PTFE seal material is used because it can withstand more abrasive operating conditions, such as high temperatures, high pressures, and dry rotation that destroy elastomeric sealing lip materials.
- PTFE seals are often packaged and installed using thin-walled plastic or metal sleeves to protect the seal material from sharp edges on splines, drilled holes, and sharp-edged shaft ridges that can easily damage PTFE lips.
- The sealing surfaces of a unitized-type seal are inside the seal, eliminating the problem encountered by damaged sealing surfaces that could shred seal lips.
- A gasket is used to compensate for surface distortions and limits to finish smoothness to prevent gas and liquid leaks between parts.
- Sealants are thick viscous liquids that are a "formed in place gasket" and replace gaskets in many places.
- The major difference between sealants and gaskets is sealants typically have lower cohesive strength but high elasticity.
- Gaskets are either metallic or non-metallic material, such as cork, rubber, plastic, or a combination of various materials.
- Without a strong clamping force, the surface irregularities cannot be filled and the pressure applied to the gasket can push out the gasket and create a leak path.
- RTV (Room-Temperature-Vulcanizing) Silicone is one of the most recognizable sealants used by technicians and is a two-part rubber compound. When exposed to air, a chemical begins to cure or harden the rubber, a process called vulcanization. Vulcanization causes the rubber to stiffen to various degrees of hardness required for specific applications.

Key Terms

anaerobic sealers A category of sealant that cures or hardens in the absence of oxygen or air.

compatibility A friction-reducing property obtained when dissimilar metals are used to slide across one another rather than using the same materials, which increases friction.

creep The type of movement of components across another component caused by thermal expansion and contraction. Creep takes place when a cylinder head expands and contracts across the engine block.

elastomer A rubber-like material that stretches and has elastic properties. Elastomer materials are often used to make seals and gaskets.

exclusion seal A part of a seal or type of seal that functions as a barrier to dirt and contaminants.

RTV (Room-Temperature-Vulcanizing) Silicone A sealer that begins to harden or chemically cure when exposed to air at room temperature. The curing process is called vulcanization, and causes the rubber to stiffen to various degrees of hardness required for specific applications.

Review Questions

1. What type of load is applied when a force is applied through the centerline of a shaft?
   a. Radial load
   b. Axial load
   c. Thrust load
   d. Combination load
2. Which of the following bearings reduce friction produced by sliding contact?
   a. Ball bearing
   b. Roller bearing
   c. Tapered roller bearing
   d. Plain bushing
3. Which of the following types of bearings can best support a combined load?
   a. Ball bearing
   b. Roller bearing
   c. Tapered roller bearing
   d. Plain bushing
4. Which of the following bearing fits have a slightly larger shaft diameter than the internal diameter of a bearing that fits over the shaft?
   a. Clearance fit
   b. Interference fit
   c. Tolerant fit
   d. Exact fit
5. Which reason best explains why some bearing preload is required by most bearings?
   a. It prevents the rollers from spinning and damaging the race.
   b. It enables the bearings to roll and pick up lubricant.
   c. It eliminates axial movement.
   d. It eliminates radial movement.
6. When packing a wheel bearing with grease, what portion of grease should cover the bearing rollers?
   a. 1/3 covering
   b. 1/3–2/3 covering
   c. 3/4 covering
   d. Completely covered
7. Which of the following statements correctly describes the fit between a seal lip diameter and a shaft diameter?
   a. The seal lip is slightly larger than the shaft.
   b. The seal lip is slightly smaller than the shaft.
   c. The seal lip is the same size as the shaft diameter.
   d. The seal lip has a clearance-type fit with the shaft.
8. Where is a back-up O-ring installed?
   a. On the pressure side of the primary O-ring
   b. On the opposite side of the pressurized size of the primary O-ring
   c. One back-up O-ring on each side of a primary O-ring in low-pressure applications
   d. On the pressurized side of the primary O-ring in low-pressure applications
9. Which property of PTFE radial lip seals makes it a seal of choice for harsh condition applications?
   a. It can withstand low temperatures.
   b. It is more elastic than other seal materials.

c. It can withstand cutting and resist damage from sharp surfaces, such as splines and keyways.

d. It has a low coefficient of friction.

10. Which of the following is the likely cause of a power steering reservoir overfilling with engine oil?

a. An outer seal lip failure on a dual-seal input shaft for an engine-driven PS pump

b. An inner seal lip failure on a dual-seal input shaft for an engine-driven PS pump

c. A defective PS pump O-ring

d. A failed PS pump input shaft bearing

ASE Technician A/Technician B Style Questions

1. While cleaning and preparing an engine gasket surface during reassembly, Technician A said that it was important to polish the engine block and cylinder head surfaces to mirror-like smoothness. Technician B said that preparing surfaces to a mirror-like smoothness could result in a leak and some surface roughness is needed. Who is correct?

a. Technician A

b. Technician B

c. Both Technician A and Technician B

d. Neither Technician A nor Technician B

2. To prepare the aluminum front cover of an engine for a gasket replacement, Technician A recommended scraping old gasket material away using a sharpened steel scraper and smoothing the surface with emery sandpaper as this is critical to quickly and properly preparing the surface for a new gasket. Technician B recommended a hard-plastic scraper and cleaning the surface with a non-metallic fiber disc. Who is correct?

a. Technician A

b. Technician B

c. Both Technician A and Technician B

d. Neither Technician A nor Technician B

3. While examining a cork-rubber gasket valve cover gasket that had blown out, Technician A said it likely prematurely failed because the technician had installed it with a film of silicone RTV. Technician B said it likely prematurely failed due to improper fastener tightening method. Who is correct?

a. Technician A

b. Technician B

c. Both Technician A and Technician B

d. Neither Technician A nor Technician B

4. Technician A says that RTV silicone does not require air or oxygen to cure and harden, which makes it an anaerobic sealant. Technician B says that RTV silicone requires exposure to air to begin the process of vulcanization. Who is correct?

a. Technician A

b. Technician B

c. Both Technician A and Technician B

d. Neither Technician A nor Technician B

5. While examining a prematurely leaking wheel seal, Technician A says that a loose wheel bearing likely caused the seal to leak. Technician B says that wheel seals can leak if an axle housing or wheel hub is overfilled with lubricant. Who is correct?

a. Technician A

b. Technician B

c. Both Technician A and Technician B

d. Neither Technician A nor Technician B

6. Technician A says that a tapered bearing part number stamped onto the cup and cone is interchangeable with other bearing manufacturers using the same numbers. Technician B says that bearing numbers are unique to each OEM and are not interchangeable. Who is correct?

a. Technician A

b. Technician B

c. Both Technician A and Technician B

d. Neither Technician A nor Technician B

7. While packing a bearing with grease, Technician A said that filling between the bearing rollers with as much grease as possible and filling the bearing cavity with grease will minimize the likelihood of a bearing failure. Technician B says that overfilling a hub and packing a bearing with excessive grease will cause the bearing to overheat and potentially fail. Who is correct?

a. Technician A

b. Technician B

c. Both Technician A and Technician B

d. Neither Technician A nor Technician B

8. While attempting to identify the source for a potential bearing noise in the driveline, Technician A suggested running the vehicle while on safety stands to try and pinpoint the origin of the noise. Technician B said that a road test is a better method to identify the source of the vibration. Who is correct?

a. Technician A

b. Technician B

c. Both Technician A and Technician B

d. Neither Technician A nor Technician B

9. Technician A says that copper added to sealants causes them to cure at room temperature. Technician B says adding copper to sealants helps prevent corrosion. Who is correct?

a. Technician A

b. Technician B

c. Both Technician A and Technician B

d. Neither Technician A nor Technician B

10. Technician A says that thread-locking sealants never completely harden because threads are not exposed to air after they are tightened. Technician B says that thread-locking sealants are anaerobic and can cure or harden in the absence of air. Who is correct?

a. Technician A

b. Technician B

c. Both Technician A and Technician B

d. Neither Technician A nor Technician B

SECTION 2
Electrical and Electronic Systems

CHAPTER 8   **Principles of Electricity**

CHAPTER 9   **Generating Electricity**

CHAPTER 10   **Basic Electrical Circuits**

CHAPTER 11   **Circuit Control Devices**

CHAPTER 12   **Semiconductor Devices and Digital Electronics**

CHAPTER 13   **Electrical Test Equipment**

CHAPTER 14   **Commercial Vehicle Batteries**

CHAPTER 15   **Advanced Battery Technologies**

CHAPTER 16   **Servicing Commercial Vehicle Batteries**

CHAPTER 17   **Heavy-Duty Starting Systems and Circuits**

CHAPTER 18   **Charging Systems and Service**

CHAPTER 19   **Electrical Wiring and Circuit Diagrams**

CHAPTER 20   **Body Electrical Systems—Lighting Systems**

CHAPTER 21 Body Electrical Systems—Instrumentation

CHAPTER 22 Body Electrical Systems—Accessory Electrical Circuits and Systems

CHAPTER 23 Principles of Electronic Signal Processing

CHAPTER 24 Sensors and Input Circuit Devices

CHAPTER 25 Understanding and Servicing Electronic Control Systems

CHAPTER 26 Onboard Vehicle Networks and Electronic Service Tools

CHAPTER 8

Principles of Electricity

Learning Objectives

After reading this chapter, you will be able to:

- **LO 8-1** Identify and describe trends and market forces influencing electrical system design for current commercial vehicles.
- **LO 8-2** Describe fundamental behaviors of electricity.
- **LO 8-3** Identify and explain a model for describing the movement of electricity.

- **LO 8-4** Define and explain concepts of electrical polarity, voltage, amperage, and resistance.
- **LO 8-5** Identify and explain the differences between electrical and electronic circuits.

You Are the Technician

When measuring the amount of amperage drawn by a starting motor cranking a 15L Detroit Diesel DD15 engine, a technician observed close to 900 amps of current was needed. The engine cranking speed sounded normal but slower than an expected 225 rpm. The technician also observed light smoke rising from some of the battery cable connections. After replacing all three batteries and making sure all batteries were fully charged, only 500 amps of current was needed to crank and start the engine and the engine cranking speed increased to normal cranking rpm.

1. Explain why more amperage was used by the starting motor before replacing the truck's batteries than after replacing the batteries.
2. If it were possible for the 12-volt starting motor to be used in a 24-volt circuit, what would you predict would happen to the amount of amperage drawn by the starting motor?
3. Explain why smoke was rising from the battery cable connections when the cranking amperage was high. Include the name of the applicable electrical law in your explanation.

Introduction

Not long ago, technicians serviced a typical heavy-duty (HD) truck having fewer than 200 electrical circuits. Lighting, starting, and charging were the most significant electrical systems, along with a few other electrical accessories, like the horn, radio, and windshield wipers. Complete electrical system wiring diagrams could fit into a booklet of less than six pages. Today, the number of electrical circuits has increased into the thousands, and hardly a single truck and bus system is without electronic control. Where the radio was once the most sophisticated electrical device, electronic control unit (ECU) using microcontrollers not only coordinate the operation of the traditional electrical systems, such as lighting, starting, charging, and other electrical accessories, but run software that now operates braking, transmissions, air operated accessories, and engine systems. Even more advanced network connected electronic control units ECU's control chassis systems to support semi-autonomous or advanced driver assistance systems, integrating navigation, steering, and braking systems into autonomous vehicle control (**FIGURE 8-1**). Studying a printed wiring diagram found in a booklet is no longer practical. Tracing circuits and locating electrical system components or connectors is best done using software to navigate thousands of potential connections and components.

Trends and Market Forces Influencing Design

LO 8-1 Identify and describe trends and market forces influencing electrical system design for current commercial vehicles.

Legislation has applied significant pressure to develop increasingly sophisticated HD electrical systems. One example is the National Highway Traffic Safety Administration (NHTSA) regulations directed at class 7 and 8 tractors requires stability control systems for all of these vehicles, beginning in 2017. A mandate for radar-based collision-avoidance systems, which is standard on European vehicles, is also under consideration for North America. Already, Greenhouse Gas (GHG) legislation phased in beginning in 2016 is intended to reduce carbon dioxide emission by reducing fuel consumption. More sophisticated electrical systems are part of the efforts to minimize fuel consumption and GHG regulations have accelerated commercial vehicle design in an entirely new direction, with electric and hybrid electric powertrains now under development or being offered by almost every truck and bus manufacturers. GHG legislation follows emission regulations, which have not only reduced emissions from HD commercial vehicles to almost undetectable levels, but simultaneously increased engine efficiency, power output, added performance-enhancing features, and durability. Much of the advance in reducing exhaust emissions has been achieved by applying electronic controls to regulate

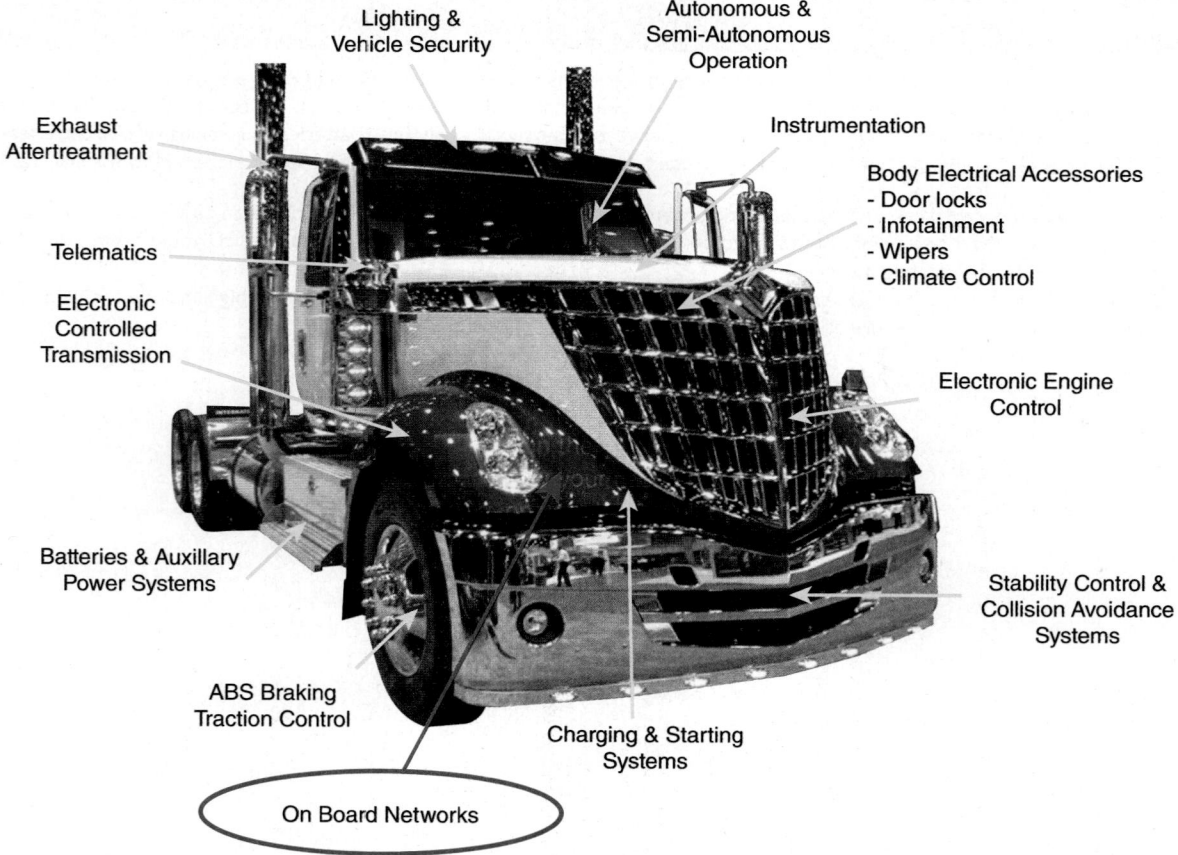

FIGURE 8-1 A few of the many major sections of electrical system control in today's HD vehicles.

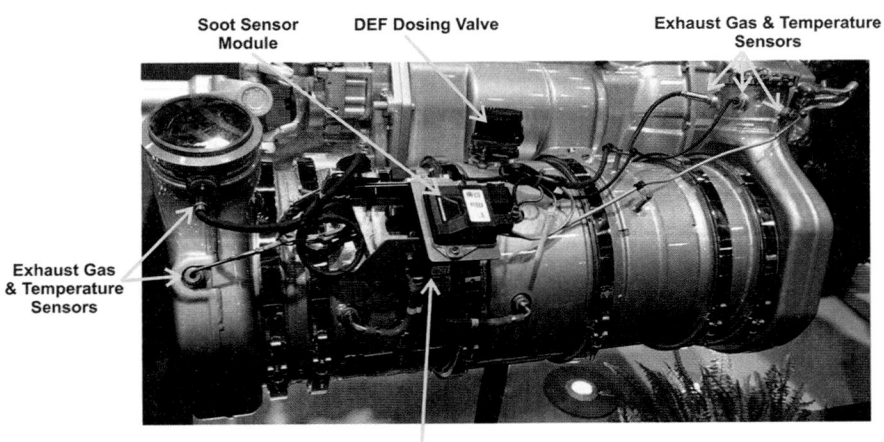

FIGURE 8-2 The after-treatment system for a 2018 diesel engine uses multiple solid-state exhaust gas sensors, temperature and pressure sensors, plus ammonia and soot sensors to detect excess emissions.

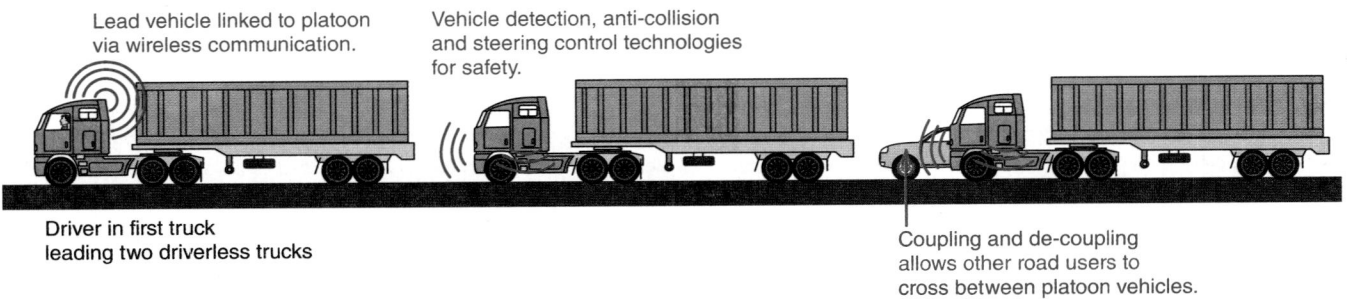

FIGURE 8-3 Platooning uses telematics, which includes vehicle-to-vehicle communication, to enable a single driver to lead multiple driverless vehicles.

and monitor the exhaust system. Advanced solid-state exhaust gas sensors, combined with temperature and pressure sensors introduced only a decade ago, are essential to emission control operation and part of the fast-paced trend to more sophisticated vehicle electrical systems (**FIGURE 8-2**).

Telematics is another rapidly developing commercial vehicle technology changing the way electrical systems are designed and operated, while adding new features and benefits to owners and operators. Telematics, which is vehicle-to-vehicle communication or vehicle communication with a remote location using internet-, satellite-, or cell phone-based communication technology, has now connected trucks and buses to not only the dispatch office but also to the internet. Information from the low-fuel warning is integrated with intelligent vehicle controls, which can inform the driver through the on-board navigation system of nearby fueling stations. A GPS tracking system used to locate goods or people in a truck, trailer, or bus reroutes—without prompting—a vehicle around traffic jams based on information automatically transmitted to the vehicle. Platooning of trucks is undergoing trials in various jurisdictions. **Platooning,** which uses a single driver in a lead truck followed by multiple driverless trucks is enabled

by vehicle-to-vehicle communication. A communication bridge is formed between the trucks to allow the lead vehicle to maintain close, but safe, driving distance between the following trucks. The lead vehicle's direction, speed, and braking are duplicated by the following trucks through the communication bridge (**FIGURE 8-3**).

Distributed Networked Electrical System Controls

One of the most significant modern trends in the evolution of HD electrical systems is the use of distributed network control. Electrical system components, from simple switches, horns, wipers, and lights to starting motors and vehicles sensors, are no longer separated into distinct systems. Connections are made between components through electronic control units (ECUs), that collect and process enormous amounts of data. The ECU, in turn, provides electrical signals to operate electrical system output devices using rules coded into software. ECUs responsible for the operation of major sections of the electrical system are connected together to form on-board networks enabling control of the electrical system to be distributed over many ECUs (**FIGURE 8-4**).

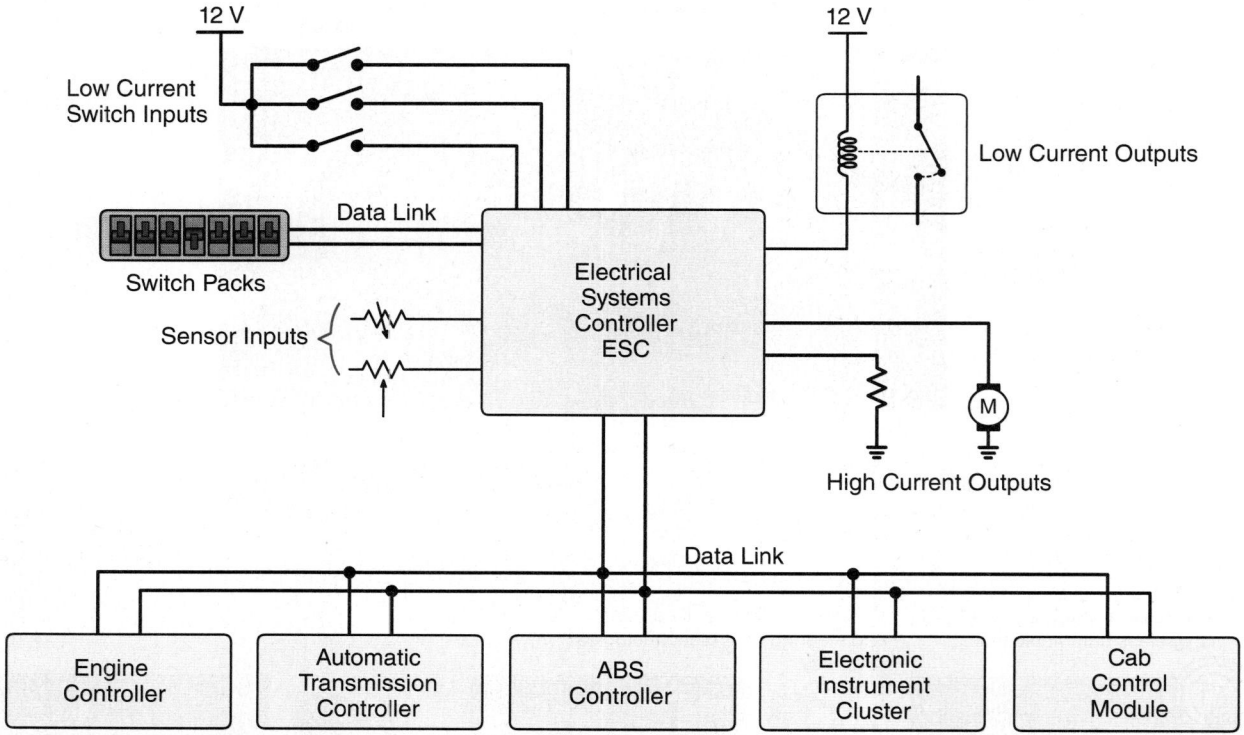

FIGURE 8-4 Contemporary truck electrical system architecture. All electronic control modules are connected to an on-board vehicle network, which provides distributed control of the electrical system.

Networking electrical system components adds new vehicle features that can enhance safety, performance, and passenger comfort simply by adding only software and a twisted pair of wires to allow connected modules to communicate and share electrical system information and control. Some common examples of the advantages offered by network control are observed when the transmission is shifted into reverse or when the power take-off (PTO) automatically mutes the radio volume to prevent driver distraction and allows the driver to hear warnings while backing up. The radio is muted because communication takes place between the transmission and an infotainment control module. Intermittent wiper speeds default to the slowest sweep frequency when the parking brake is set, regardless of wiper switch position. This feature, enabled by communication between the body electrical control and antilock braking (ABS) module reduces wiper blade replacement and wear on the wiper mechanism.

To prevent a vehicle roll-away situation, the horn honks if the driver's door is opened and the park brake is not set; a wheel slip event detected by the ABS module sends a message to the engine ECU to disable engine brakes or reduce engine power while the ABS module lightly applies the brakes to the slipping wheel, enabling torque transfer to non-slipping wheels. Countless examples of interoperability between electrical system inputs and outputs provide enhanced safety for passengers and operators, to prevent vehicle damage, and reduce wear and

maintenance requirements. Tremendous gains in operating efficiency, vehicle design, and reduced construction costs are also enabled by networking modules that distribute electrical system control over multiple ECMs.

The purpose of highlighting some of the electrical system features in today's commercial vehicles is not to intimidate or discourage new technicians from learning and working on this system. Instead, noting the sophisticated reach of electrical technology into every vehicle system emphasizes how much the overall success and value of a technician rests on skills developed from having a sound understanding of electrical principles underlying HD vehicle electrical systems. Arguably, a technician's most essential skills are to understand principles of electrical current movement, analyze electrical problems, comprehend electrical system and component operation, plus know how to properly select and use test equipment to diagnose electrical problems.

Understanding the Behavior of Electricity

LO 8-2 Describe fundamental behaviors of electricity.

Understanding the behavior of electricity can potentially be more difficult than understanding mechanical concepts, such as four-stroke cycle engine operation or braking fundamentals, since electricity itself cannot be directly observed, but only its

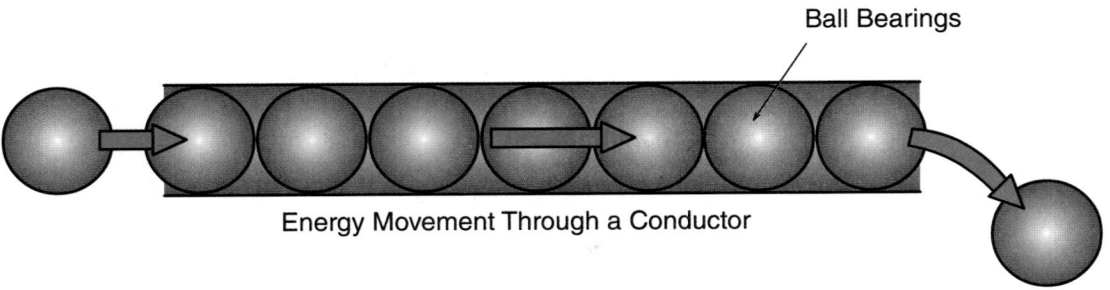

Ball Bearings

Energy Movement Through a Conductor

FIGURE 8-5 To visualize electricity using the particle model of electricity, ball bearings moving through a tube can represent the movement of electrical energy.

effects. At the same time, electrical principles underlying the electrical system operation are governed by straightforward laws of physics, so learning how electricity behaves can be approached in a logical manner. Taking the time to understand simple electrical laws and principles enables one to make sense of electrical system operation in order to effectively diagnose and repair these complex and sophisticated systems.

To help technicians develop these essential skills, this chapter explores basic principles about the nature of electricity and how it behaves. Explaining the characteristics of electricity using both a hydraulic model and a particle model assists a technician to visualize the behavior of electricity and apply the models to help solve electrical problems occurring on a daily basis.

Hydraulic and Particle Models

Hydraulic and particle models of electricity are good comparisons to help visualize electrical behavior. Both models are useful in understanding different aspects of electricity's properties. Visualizing electrical concepts using these comparisons helps many learners to more easily understand electrical principles. In the particle model analogy, electricity can be thought of as the movement of steel ball bearings from one point to another (**FIGURE 8-5**).

Conductors, such as wires and electrical components, provide a pathway for the bearings to roll. Energy contained by the speed and number of rolling bearings are converted into other forms of energy, such as magnetism, heat, light, or sound. Electrical devices, such as a lightbulb, starting motor, or injector solenoid, extract energy from the force of rolling bearings. While the particle model is useful for understanding principles about electric charges and the operation of many electronic devices, such as capacitors and **semiconductors**, there are times when it falls short in helping to visualize other types of electrical behavior (**FIGURE 8-6**).

Electrical concepts of voltage, amperage, and resistance describing the flow of electricity are better explained by comparing electricity to the flow of water in tubes. In the hydraulic model, pumps move the fluid-like characteristics of electricity through pipes or tubes and electrical devices convert the force of flowing electrical current into a variety of other forms of energy, such as light, heat, sound, or magnetic

FIGURE 8-6 Electrical devices, such as this ECM, extract or convert energy from moving electrons.

fields. In both models, electricity is a source of energy that can be harnessed and made to perform work or some specialized function (**FIGURE 8-7**).

Electrostatic Charges

Electrical energy can be converted into a variety of other forms, such as light, heat, sound, electrical signals, or magnetic fields, which are then used to operate motors, lights, solenoids, touch screens, radios, instruments, or microcontrollers. To explain some of the mystery of how electricity does this, the particle model is especially useful. Remembering that electricity can be likened to uncompressible ball bearings pressed against one another and rolling along inside a pipe, it's reasonable to suppose some force is necessary to start the balls rolling and keep them moving.

That force is **electrostatic force**, which is a term describing a property of electrical particles that either repels or attracts other electrical particles. Electrostatic forces are essential to produce the flow of electrical current and operate all electrical devices. Electrostatic forces of repulsion and attraction are incredibly powerful and the energy they emit can be harnessed by electrical devices to perform work. Two fundamental categories of electrostatic force are positive (+) and negative (-) charges. Lines of force move either in or out of these two

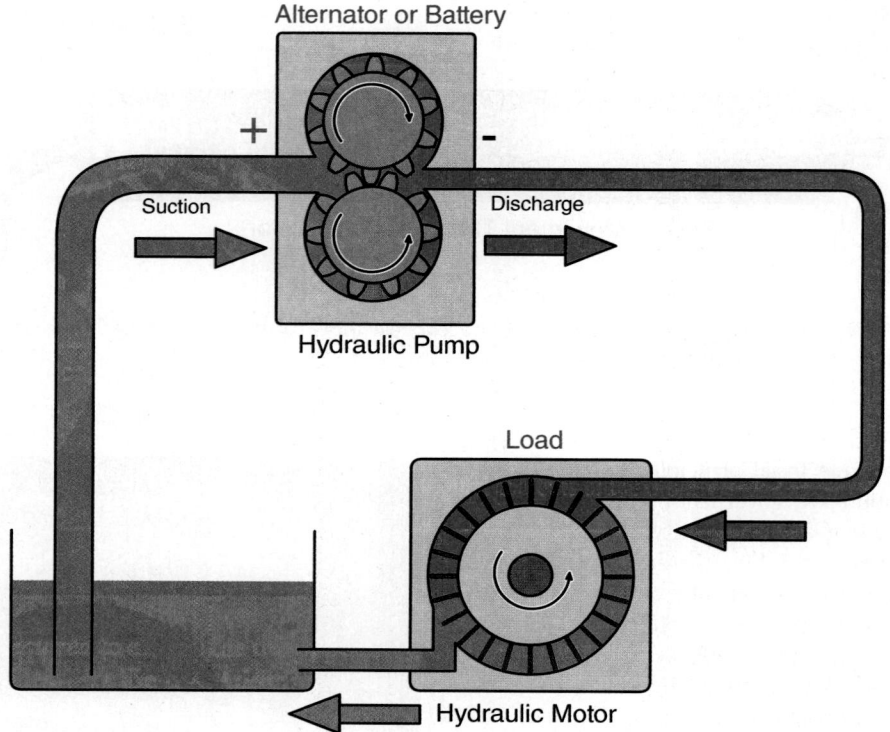

FIGURE 8-7 The hydraulic model of electricity compares electrical current flow to the movement of fluid through pipes or tubes. Electrical devices convert electron movement into another form energy.

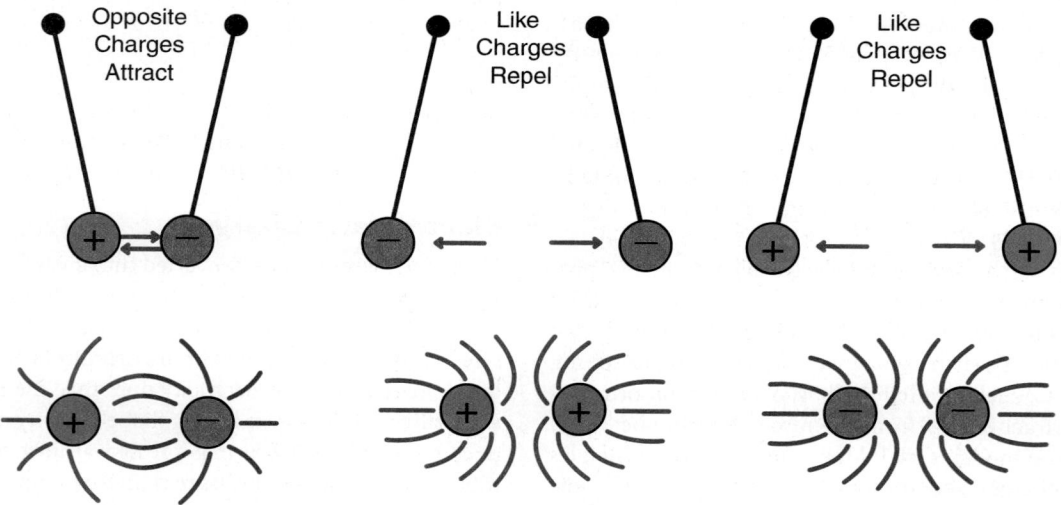

FIGURE 8-8 Summary of electrostatic laws.

charges, almost the same way a magnet's North and South poles have directional lines of force.

Moving electrical particles in a circuit involves using positive and negative charges that are governed by basic **electrostatic theory**. The theory, which is really an observable fact, states that negative and positive charges are attracted to one another and like charges—negative and negative, positive and positive—are repelled by one another (**FIGURE 8-8**). These

forces of charge repulsion and attraction are called electrostatic laws and govern all electrical behavior.

Electrostatic Law Summary:

■ A proton (+) charge repels another proton's (+) charge.
■ An electron's (−) charge repels another electron's (−) charge.
■ A proton (+) charge attracts an electron (−) charge.

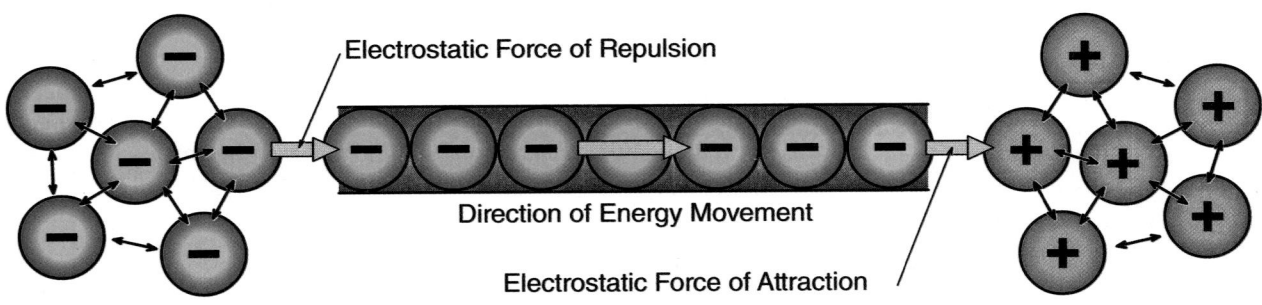

FIGURE 8-9 Electrostatic forces pushing and pulling charged particles through a conductor create electrical energy.

In an electric circuit or any electrical device, the push and pull producing the movement of electricity is supplied by electrostatic forces. A concentration of negative charges at one end of a conductor pushes negatively charged ball bearings through the pipe using the force of electrostatic repulsion (**FIGURE 8-9**). Movement of negative charges can be accelerated by supplying the attractive force of a positive charge at the opposite end of the conductor. It's important to note though, the electrical energy is carried by the movement of electrons and not positive charges alone.

Basic Electricity

LO 8-3 Identify and explain a model for describing the movement of electricity.

All questions about the nature of electricity lead to the composition of matter. All matter is made up of atoms, as shown in **FIGURE 8-10**. For convenience, the model of the atom used to teach technicians is known as the Rutherford model of the atom. Rutherford's concept was proposed around 1910 and is traditionally used to teach electrical concepts. The model constructs the atom; electrons, protons, and neutrons, into a solar system-like arrangement. It does not reflect a contemporary understanding of the atom, but it does satisfactorily convey information necessary to understand electrical phenomenon. Rutherford's model of the atom pictures it as composed of electrons orbiting a nucleus made of protons and neutrons. Positive electrical charges are found on protons, negative charges on electrons, and no electrical charge on neutrons. Both neutrons and protons are necessary to form the nucleus of an atom. Neutrons are needed to prevent the nucleus from bursting apart from the electrostatic repulsion of protons. In a sense, neutrons are the electrical glue that holds the nucleus together. Moving around the nucleus are one or more negatively charged electrons. Electrons travel in different layers, or shells, around the nucleus. Each shell is limited to holding only a specific maximum number of electrons.

With equal numbers of protons and electrons, the positive and negative electrical charges within an atom cancel out or balance each other, leaving the atom with no overall charge. Electrostatic laws make the goal of every atom to achieve this state of neutral balance by holding equal numbers of electrical charges. It is important to remember that only electrons can be

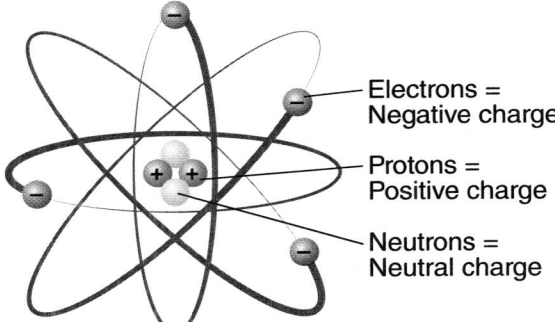

FIGURE 8-10 A model of the atom based on a 1910 understanding. The model, while not accurate, is useful to explain electrical principles.

removed or added to an atom and not protons. The addition or loss of a proton from the nucleus would change the very nature of the atomic element. If an atom loses or gains an electron, it is called an **ion**. An atom with more electrons than protons has an overall negative charge and is called a **negative ion**. The term ion simply means the atom has an imbalance of electrical charges due to the gain or loss of electrons. Ions are unstable, and the atom wants to return to a state where the electrical charges are balanced or neutral. In the case of a negatively charged ion, the presence of an extra electron causes the forces of repulsion to try to push the electron away from the atom, as illustrated in **FIGURE 8-11**.

A deficiency of electrons gives the atom an overall positive charge and is called a **positive ion**. The atom's electrical charges are not balanced, and it tries to achieve a state of balance between the positive and negative charges to become neutral. In this case, the positively charged protons pull on any available electron surrounding the atom to return the atom to a state of balance between electrical charges.

If a negative ion and positive ion are close enough, the negative charge on the negative ion exerts a repelling force on the extra electron, causing it to be pushed away from its atom. At the same time, the positive ion exerts an attracting force on the extra electron. These forces of repulsion and attraction cause the electron to be pushed from one atom and pulled toward the positive atom, balancing the charges on both atoms. It is this movement of electrons from one atom to another that is called **electricity**.

Electrical Conductivity

Not all atoms can give up or accept electrons easily. Materials that hold electrons loosely enable electrons in its outer shell to easily move. These materials are categorized as **conductors**, while materials that hold electrons tightly and prevent electron movement are called **insulators**. Electrons are held by an atom according to the strength of the positive charges exerted by the protons in the nucleus. When another force that is strong enough to overcome the forces binding an electron to the atom, the electron can be moved. These other forces are examined in more detail later, but the forces are typically magnetic, chemical, heat, light and kinetic energy.

Another fact about conductors is that electrons in the outer shell of an atom are furthest away from the nucleus and more loosely held. Atoms with fewer than the maximum number of electrons in the outer shell, and particularly atoms with the fewest electrons in its outer shell, are the best conductors. Copper (Cu) is an example of a metal with only one electron in the atom's outer shell (**FIGURE 8-12A**). Because a single electron is held loosely by the nucleus, copper makes an excellent conductor. By contrast, argon (Ar) is an atom with an outer shell filled with a maximum number of electrons.

This explains why argon is an inert gas, meaning that it generally does not share electrons to form molecules, and so is an excellent insulator (see **FIGURE 8-12B**). Semiconductors, such as silicon (Si), can be made into an insulator or a conductor by alloying or mixing it with other materials having either loosely or tightly held electrons. Because of their importance to electrical systems and electronic devices, semiconductor materials, which are essential to create electronic circuits, are discussed in greater detail in the chapter on semiconductors (see **FIGURE 8-12C**). **TABLE 8-1** shows how the conductivity of other metals compares to the conductivity of copper. A number higher than 1 indicates the material conducts electrons better than copper.

Metals typically have easily moved electrons, which make them good conductors. But it's not just metals that conduct electricity; liquids can too. "Electrolytes" is a term for liquids that conduct electric current. The liquid inside a lead-acid battery is an example of the use of an electrolyte. Under some circumstances, air and other gases can conduct electricity, which is seen when a spark crosses an air gap. When a gas conducts electricity, it is in a plasma state, and can also be influenced by magnetic fields. Neon and fluorescent lighting are examples of

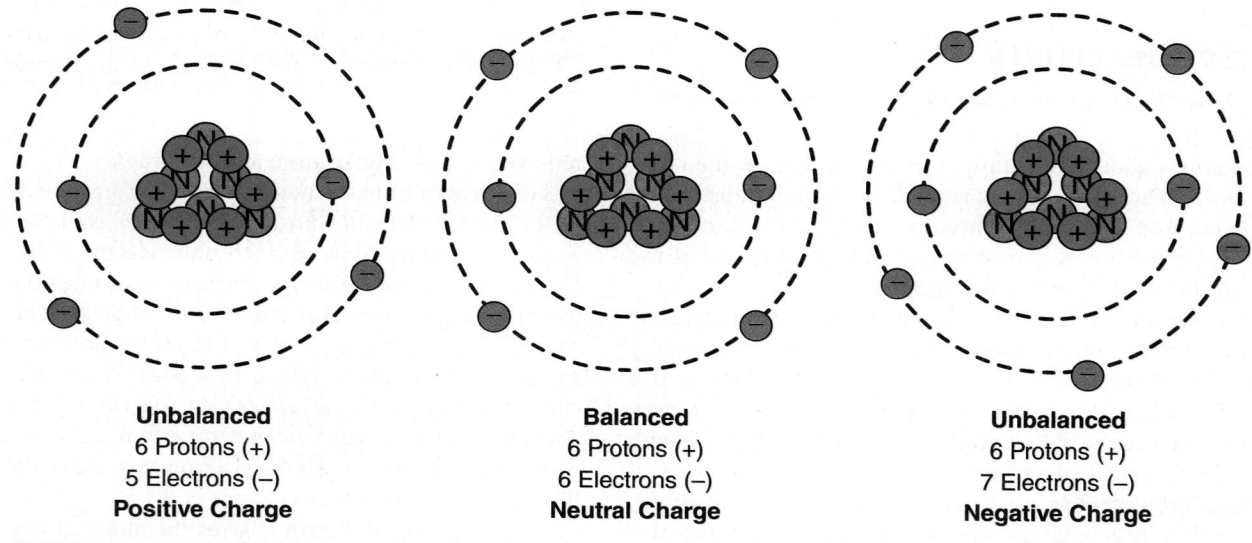

Unbalanced	Balanced	Unbalanced
6 Protons (+)	6 Protons (+)	6 Protons (+)
5 Electrons (−)	6 Electrons (−)	7 Electrons (−)
Positive Charge	**Neutral Charge**	**Negative Charge**

FIGURE 8-11 Imbalances between the number of electrons and protons produces an electrical charge.

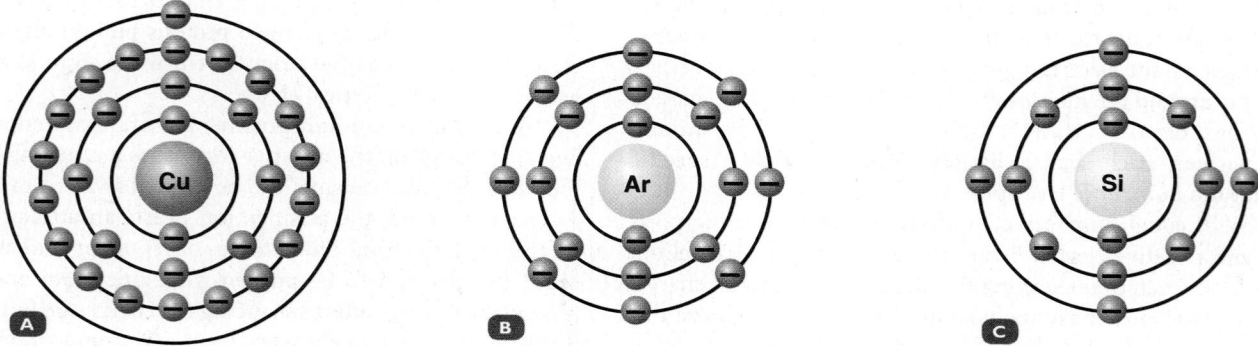

FIGURE 8-12 A. Conductor. **B.** Insulator. **C.** Semiconductor.

the use of electrically conductive gases in a plasma state. Plasma displays used in some instrument clusters contain small cells of electrically excited gases to produce different colors, depending on the gas contained in the cells.

Understanding Electrical Current

LO 8-4 Define and explain concepts of electrical polarity, voltage, amperage, and resistance.

Understanding electrical conduction is the foundation of understanding electric current. This section discusses the basics of current movement, how quickly electrical currents move, and in what direction.

TABLE 8-1 Conductivity of Different Metals Compared to Copper

Conductor	Conductivity Compared to Copper
Silver	1.064
Copper	1.000
Gold	0.707
Aluminum	0.659
Zinc	0.288
Brass	0.243
Iron	0.178

Movement of Electric Current

The forces that can move electrons on or off an atom include:

- light
- heat
- pressure
- friction
- magnetic fields
- chemical energy

The force applied by each of these energy sources against an electron determines how fast an electron is moved from one atom to the next. The idea of putting electrons into motion can be compared to hitting a baseball (**FIGURE 8-13**). The harder the ball is hit, the faster it travels and the greater force it can transmit. As an electrical concept, voltage is the speed of electron travel through a conductor from atom to atom (**FIGURE 8-14**). Increasingly higher electron **voltage** means the electrostatic forces pushing or pulling an electron are progressively stronger. When using an analogy of electricity represented as water in a pipe, the concept of voltage is like pressure (**FIGURE 8-15**). Just as higher pressure in a pipe moves water faster, high voltage means electrons move with greater speed through a conductor.

Amperage is another electrical term used to describe or measure the number of electrons moving in an electrical circuit. The unit of measurement for amperage is the **ampere**. While

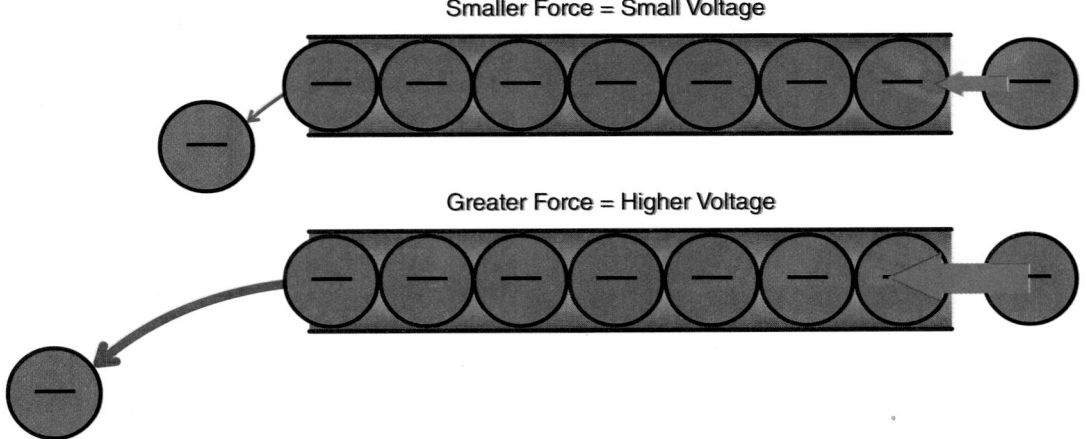

Smaller Force = Small Voltage

Greater Force = Higher Voltage

FIGURE 8-13 The force moving electrons through a circuit is voltage. The greater the force pushing the electrons, the higher the voltage.

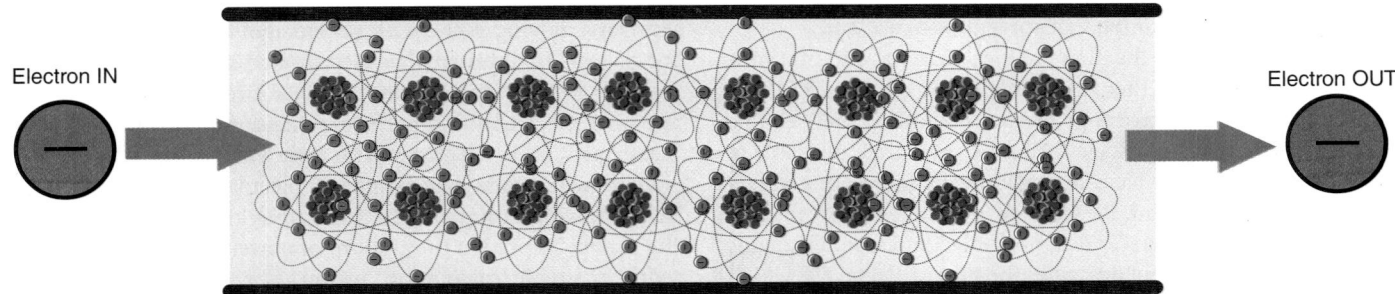

Electron IN

Electron OUT

FIGURE 8-14 Electricity is the movement of electrons from atom to atom. The force or pressure moving electrons through a circuit is voltage.

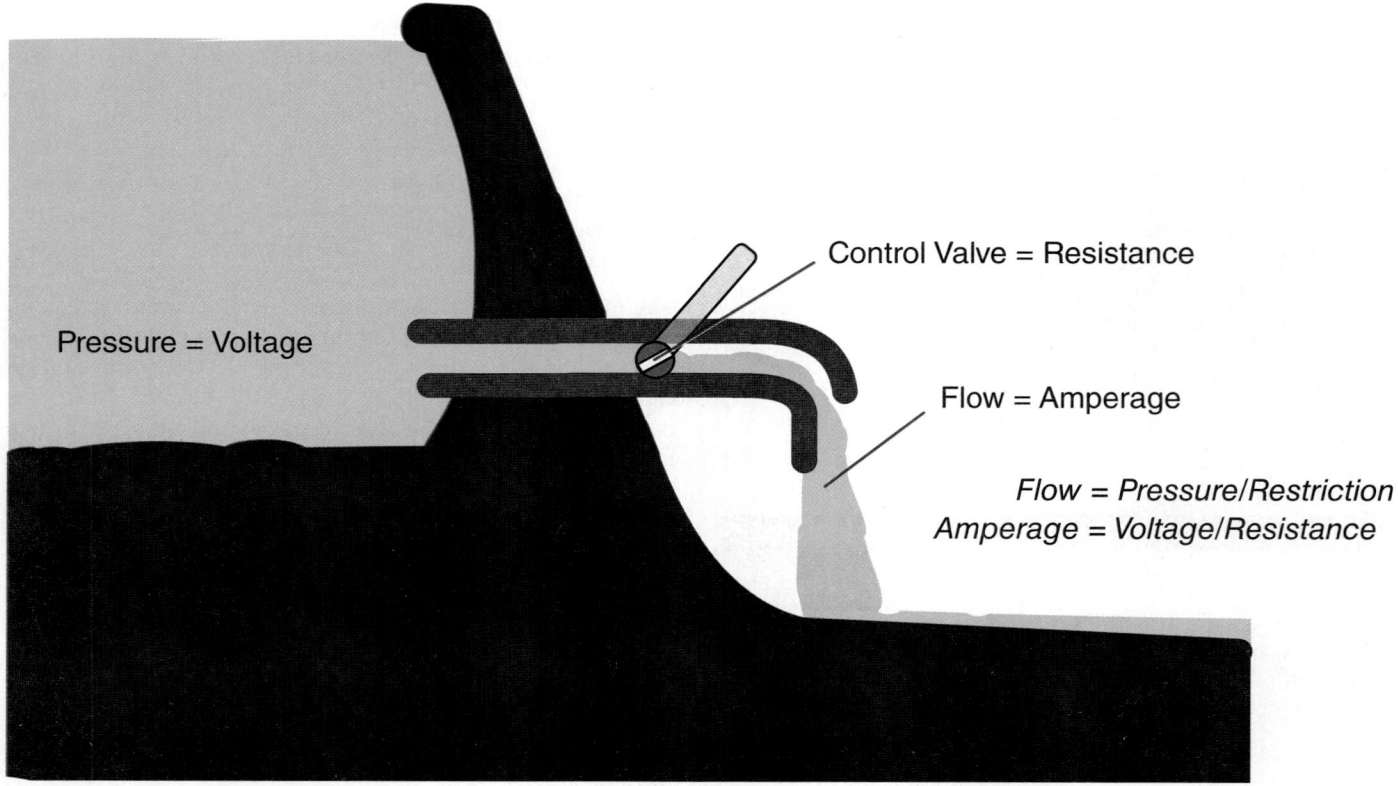

FIGURE 8-15 The concepts of electrical current flow using a hydraulic model: voltage, amperage, and resistance.

voltage describes the average speed of one or many electrons, amperage measures the quantity or how many electrons are passing through a circuit at any given moment in time. When using the analogy of water in a pipe to describe the movement of electrons, amperage can be compared to the number of gallons or liters moving past a point in the pipe per second of time. Stated another way, amperage describes the volume of electron flow per second of time.

The particle model further helps explain the concept of amperage. Because an ampere of electron flow refers to the number of electrons passing through a single point in a circuit at any moment of time, a unit of electron quantity and time is used to estimate circuit amperage. The term **coulomb**, which is a measuring unit of electric charge describing a large but specific number of electrons, measures the quantity of electrons. If one coulomb of electrons passes through a single point in a circuit per second of time, that measurement of electron flow per second equals one ampere of current (**FIGURE 8-16**).

When describing the flow of electricity, a circuit's voltage and amperage together is called **electric current**. Without either of these two electrical properties operating, there can be no electric current. No voltage means no pressure is available to push or pull electrons. No amperage means there are no electrons moving in a circuit. Please note, often the term "current" is used in some textbooks to describe only amperage. Throughout this textbook, current describes the flow of electricity, which needs both voltage and amperage.

In many textbooks and in industry, the use of the electrical term "current" has traditionally been used to describe only the amperage flowing through a circuit. The substitution of the term amperage with current, or referring to the concept of amperage using only the term current can be confusing to learners. A more precise definition of electric current that more accurately describes the flow of electric current includes voltage and amperage since current flow requires both to be present. In other words, without voltage and amperage no electrical current can flow. Be careful when reading service literature to distinguish whether the writer's intention is to describe just amperage or the concept of electrical current flow, which requires both amperage and voltage to take place.

Calculating Electric Power

Together, the force of the electric current (**volts**) and volume of electrons moving in a circuit (amperage) are harnessed to perform work. It's intuitive that the number of electrons in motion and the average speed they travel is directly proportional to the work electricity can perform. One hundred slower-moving electrons, that is, electrons with little voltage, have less power than one hundred faster-moving electrons. This means the faster-moving group can do more work than the slower-moving group. To predict the amount of power available to perform work, a simple calculation answers the question about how much work can be done per second of time. Watts or wattage

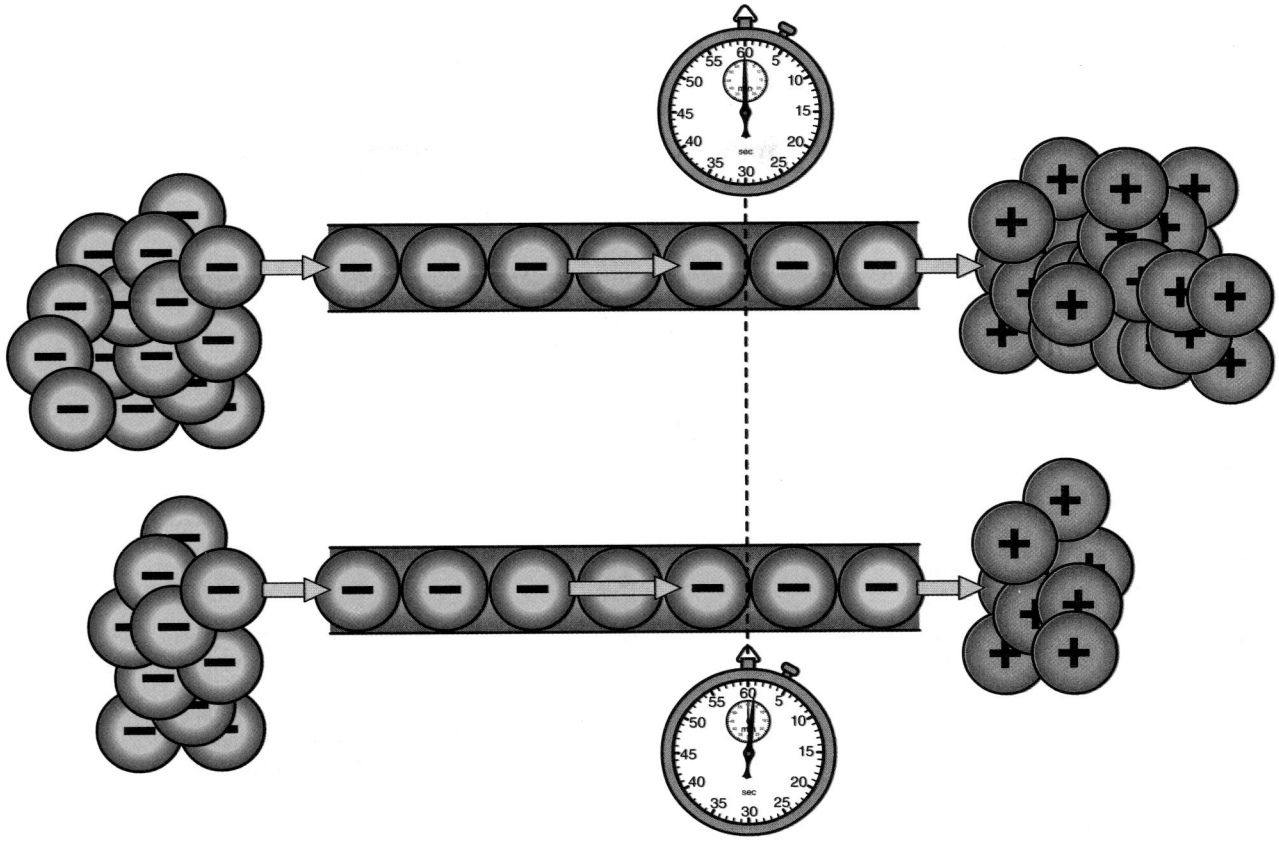

FIGURE 8-16 Amperage is an electrical term that describes the number of electrons moving past a point in the circuit in 1 second of time: 1 coulomb of electron flow per second equals 1 ampere of current.

is the unit for measuring electrical power. Wattage is a function of Voltage × Amperage, or Power = Volts × Amps. For example, if one wanted to find out how many amps are required to crank an engine with a 10-horsepower (hp) starting motor, the calculation would be this: Since 746 watts is defined as being equal to 1 hp; 10 hp × 746 watts = 7460 watts. If the available voltage is 12 volts, the equation would be 7460 = 12 × amps and 7460/12 = 621.6 amps.

Now this calculation does not take into consideration energy losses due to friction, heat, circuit resistance, the magnetic efficiency of the starting motor, and so on. More current is in fact required to produce starter motor cranking torque. However, to illustrate the difference changing voltage has on the work electrons can perform, consider the situation if 24 volts were available rather than 12 volts. In this case, the same power calculated in the previous scenario could be produced with half the amperage, or 311 amps. Alternatively, 1243 amps would be needed if only 6 volts were powering the starting motor.

Resistance

Another important electrical concept is resistance. **Electrical resistance** is a material's property that impedes or slows down the movement of electrical current. In other words,

resistance reduces voltage and amperage in an electrical current. Electrical resistance is similar to the concept of friction (**FIGURE 8-17**). Like friction, which can slow objects down, anything that slows down the speed of electron movement is considered a **resistor**.

Factors that determine the amount of resistance in a circuit include:

1. Type of material: Conductors vary in the strength with which they hold electrons. If more energy is required to dislodge and move an electron, resistance increases.
2. Length of the conductor: As the length of a circuit or conductor increases, electrons travel farther and lose some energy moving from atom to atom.
3. Diameter of the conductor: The larger the cross section of a conductor, the greater its capacity to carry current (see **FIGURE 8-18**).
4. Temperature of the conductor: Electrons require more energy to move through a conductor as its temperature increases.

Ohm's Law

In a general sense, resistors convert the energy in current flow to other forms of energy. Often resistance produces only heat. But electrical devices can also harness and convert electrical energy

Diameter

Smaller Diameter (More Resistance)   Larger Diameter (Less Resistance)

 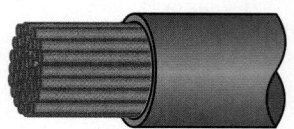

Length

Longer Length (More Resistance)

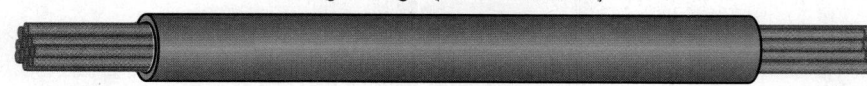

Shorter Length (Less Resistance)

Temperature   **Physical Condition**

Temperature Increase   Broken Wires (More Resistance)
(More Resistance)

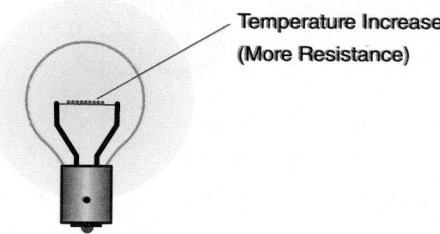   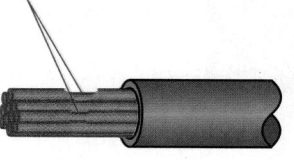

FIGURE 8-17 Factors affecting resistance in a circuit.

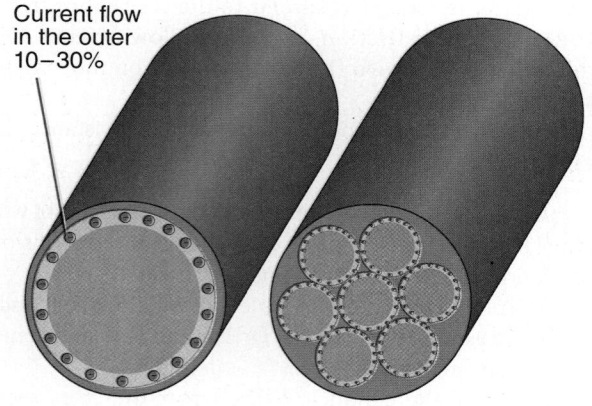

Current flow
in the outer
10–30%

FIGURE 8-18 The forces of repulsion cause electrons to move to the outer surface of a conductor. Current flows on the outer surface to only a depth of 10% to 30% of its cross-sectional diameter. Larger-diameter wire and stranded wire with more surface area conducts current with less resistance.

into other forms, such as light, sound, movement, magnetism, and electrical signals carrying information, which means every electrical device has some resistance. Electrical devices using electrical energy are called loads and always have some measurable resistance (**FIGURE 8-19**).

The electrical unit for measuring the amount of resistance in a direct current (DC) circuit is **ohms**. The term is named after the person who discovered that one volt of electrical pressure is required to push one amp of current through a circuit, if the circuit has a resistance of one ohm (**FIGURE 8-20**).

This relationship is known as **Ohm's law**. Stated mathematically, Ohm's law is:

$$\text{Voltage} = \text{Resistance} \times \text{Amperage}$$

Restating Ohm's law using a hydraulic analogy, one psi of water pressure is needed to push one gallon of water through a pipe in one second having a diameter (resistance) of one inch.

Although the hydraulic analogy is not perfect, it provides a good visual image for remembering that, according to Ohm's law, increasing voltage in a circuit is like increasing water pressure. Just as more water flows through a pipe when water pressure is higher, more amperage flows through a circuit with higher voltage if the resistance or restrictions remain the same. Likewise, making a pipe smaller in diameter, which restricts the flow of water through the pipe, is like increasing a circuit's

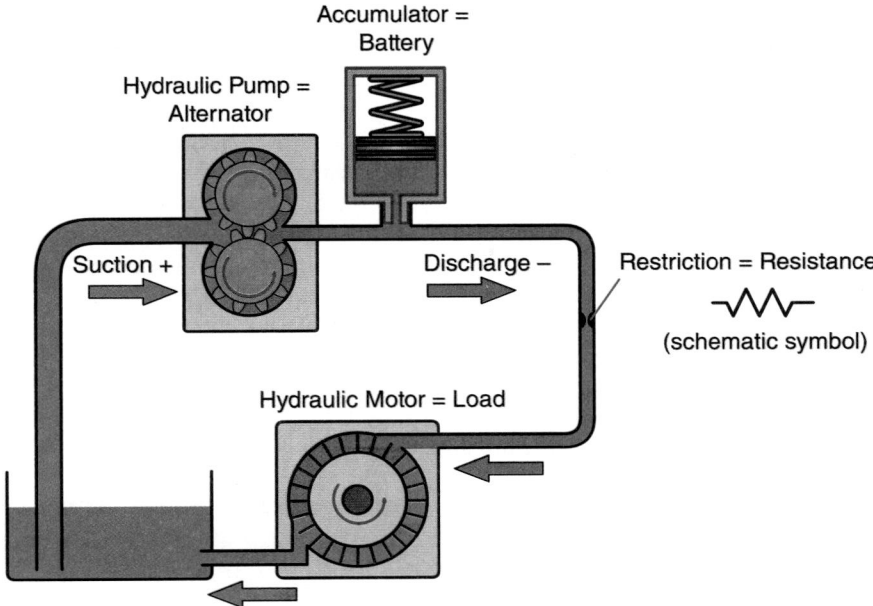

FIGURE 8-19 The analogy to resistance in the hydraulic model of current flow is a restriction in a pipe.

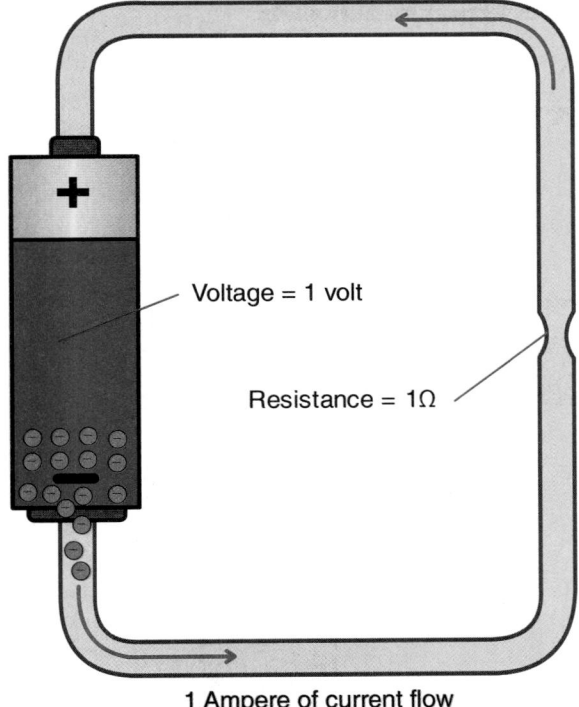

FIGURE 8-20 An ohm is the measuring unit for resistance. One volt of pressure is required to push one amp through one ohm of resistance.

resistance. Just as water pressure and volume drop in a narrower or restricted pipe, voltage and amperage or current flow are both reduced with increased circuit resistance. The Greek letter omega (Ω) is the symbol representing Ohms as the unit for electrical resistance.

Observing the relationship between the three factors of Ohm's law leads to the following conclusions:

- *If voltage is held constant in a circuit:*
  - Amperage increases if resistance decreases.
  - Amperage decreases if resistance increases.
- *If resistance is held constant in a circuit:*
  - Amperage increases if voltage increases.
  - Amperage decreases if voltage decreases.
- *If amperage is to remain the same in a circuit:*
  - Voltage must increase if resistance increases.
  - Voltage must decrease if resistance decreases.

Resistance produces a decrease or drop in voltage. The concept of voltage drop is a very important electrical concept to apply when troubleshooting problems in electrical circuits. An ohmmeter can be used to measure resistance, and learning how to measure voltage drop in a circuit with a voltmeter is one of the most essential electrical diagnostic skills, and a helpful method to identify unwanted resistance in an electric circuit. Understanding how to measure voltage drops is covered in the chapter, "Electrical Test Instruments."

Polarity—Direction of Current Flow

To recap what was explained earlier, it is important to remember that only electrons can be moved on and off an atom to create either a negative or positive electric charge. An electric charge is created when a source of energy, such as a moving magnetic field, adds or removes electrons from the outer shell of an atom. Electron movement changes the charge balance on an atom. Movement of electrons through a conductor continues to take place by using the electrostatic forces of repulsion and attraction.

When areas of positive or negative charges are created, a pole or polarity is established. **Polarity** is simply the state of charge in an area. In **FIGURE 8-21**, areas of unbalanced electrical charges create positive or negative poles. Polarity in this instance not only determines the direction of electron flow but the relative concentration of charges creates a pressure difference that is described as a potential difference. This means that the greater the difference between the magnitude or size of positive and negative charges in an area, the higher the force there is to move electrons. Voltage is another term used interchangeably with potential difference (**FIGURE 8-22**).

The movement of negatively charged electrons to a positive charge pole is called the **electron theory of current movement**. It is actually not a theory, but a fact. The idea that electric current movement takes place when positive charges move to a negative pole is called **conventional current theory**. Conventional current theory of electric charge movement was based on Rutherford's 1910 model of the atom, which was incomplete. Later investigation found this idea was incorrect and only negatively charged electrons moved in a circuit—in a negative to positive direction.

There are still many textbooks and training aids used to teach conventional theory to explain electrical behavior. Trying to separate electron and conventional theory in practice can become confusing. However, in practice, the acceptance and use of either idea is generally not important for the technician. It is only important to remember that current flow is described by both concepts.

Technicians should be aware that some test instruments, such as Amp/Volt/Resistance (AVR) machines are designed presuming current flow is conventional (**FIGURE 8-23**). By contrast, a **digital multimeter,** as shown in **FIGURE 8-24**, uses electron theory, and the direction of current flow is generally indicated

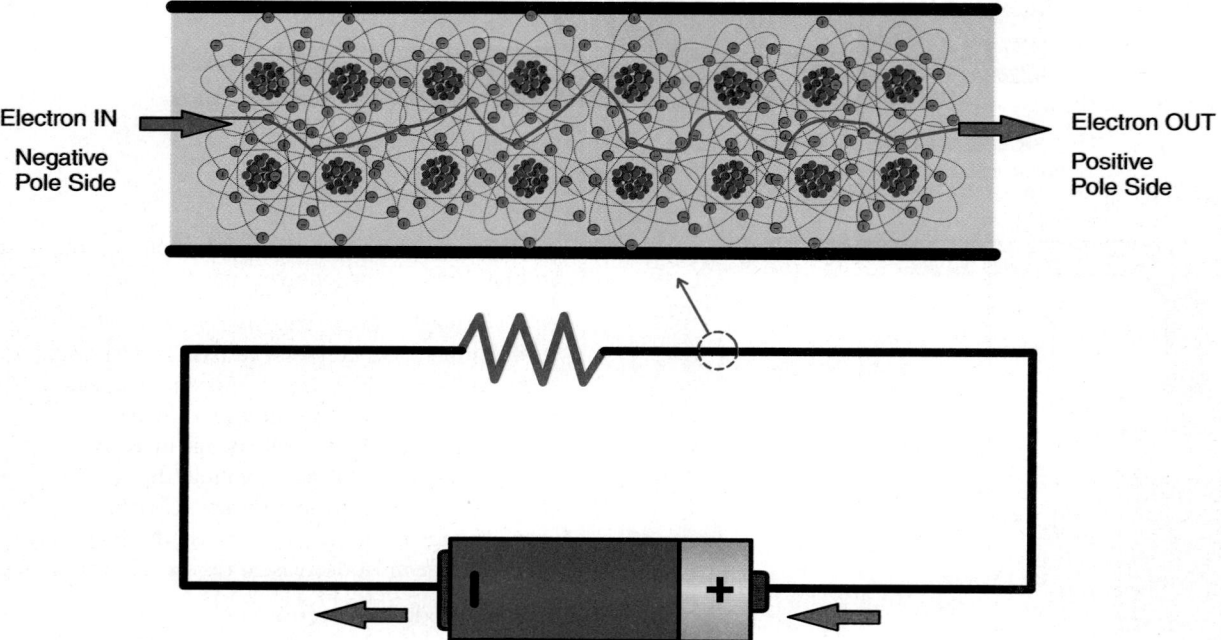

FIGURE 8-21 Polarity and electrostatic forces produce current flow.

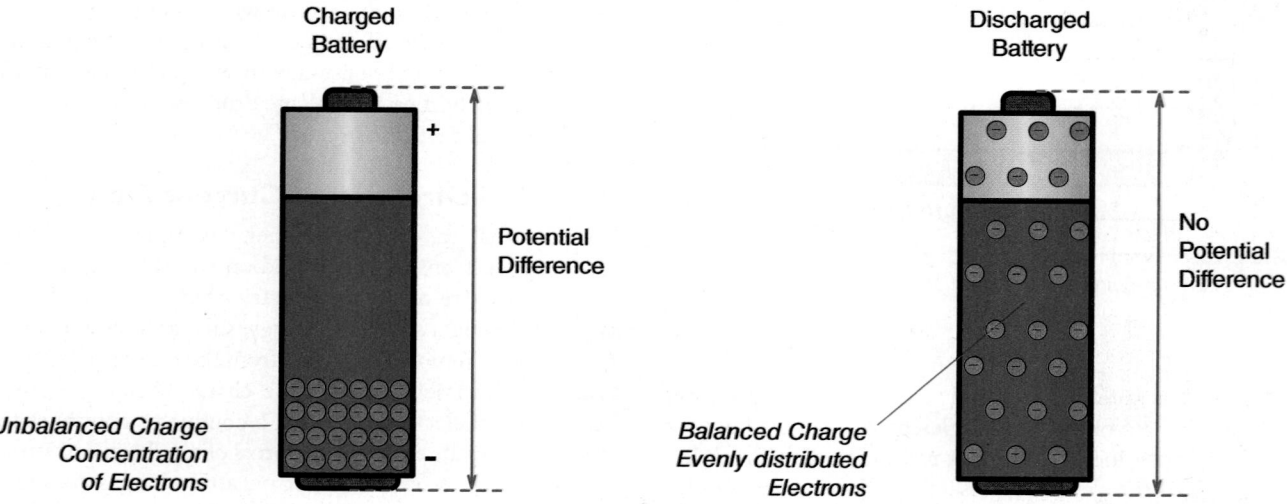

FIGURE 8-22 The pressure difference between poles produces current flow. The pressure or potential difference is measured in volts.

by polarity indicators. Connecting the black or common lead of a meter to a positive current source and the positive meter lead to a negative current source causes the meter to display a negative symbol beside the number in the digital display. Diagnosing an unintended key-off current draw or parasitic current loss is one place where the direction of current flow is important to note by asking the question whether current is leaving or entering the more negatively charged negative battery post? Electron theory should prevail when trying to understand these types of problems. Some electrical faults and catastrophic electrical fires caused by a grounded alternator cable are best understood using electron theory. For example, whether an engine was running and an alternator was charging when a battery to alternator cable grounded out is determined by which end of the cable was burned at the point of the grounding fault. Was it between the ground and the alternator or the ground and the battery?

Electron theory is also best used to describe the operation of semiconductors and more advanced electronic devices. Tracing current flow in wiring diagrams, however, is often easier using conventional theory.

Direct Current and Alternating Current

When electrons move only in one direction in a circuit, the current is **direct current (DC)**. In a DC circuit, electrons move continuously from negative to positive poles (**FIGURE 8-25**). When electrons are alternately pulled and pushed in a conductor by a rapidly switching polarity, it rhythmically changes the direction of current flow. That type of current flow is

FIGURE 8-24 A digital multimeter displays electrical measurements in digits rather than using a sweeping needle.

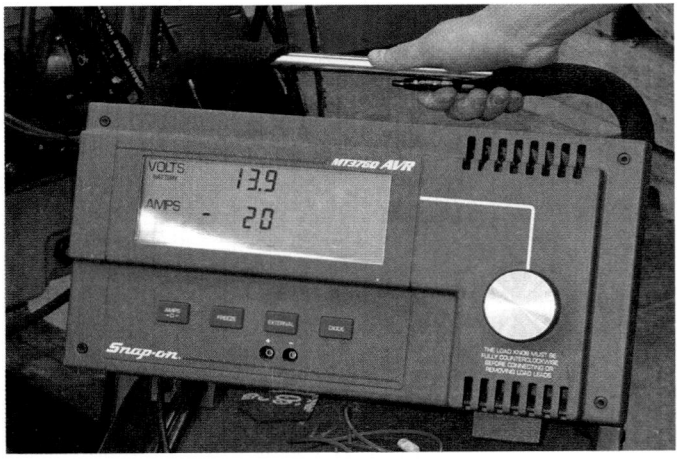

FIGURE 8-23 An amps-volts and resistance (AVR) test instrument.

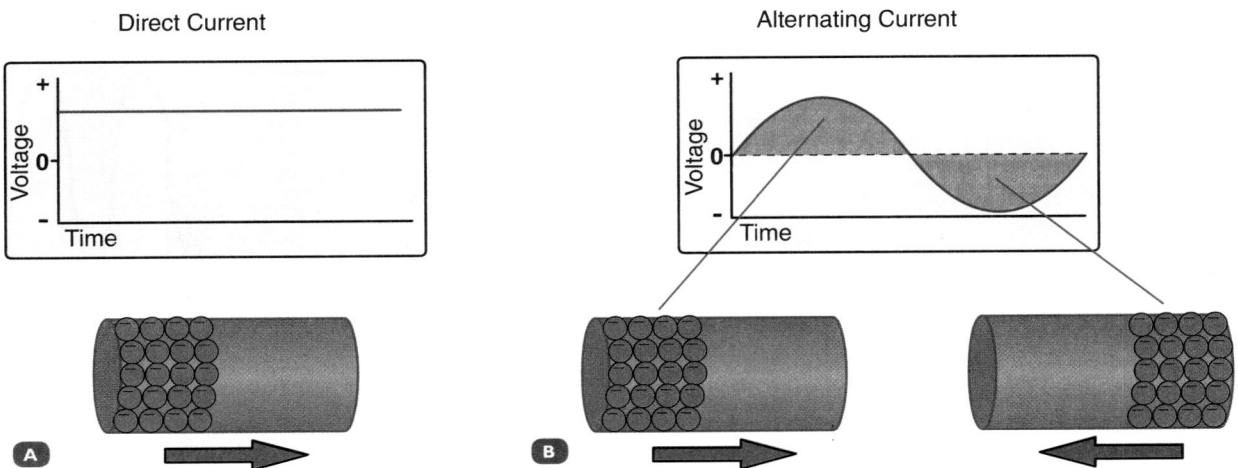

FIGURE 8-25 A. Current flow in one direction only is called direct current. **B.** Current flow that continuously changes direction is alternating current.

described as **alternating current (AC)** (**FIGURE 8-26**). In addition to describing AC in terms of voltage and amperage, AC is measured by how frequently the current polarity changes the direction of current flow each second. Units for AC frequency (direction changes per second) is called Hertz (Hz), which is another term for cycles per second. Plotting DC voltage on a graph produces a straight line, as shown in **FIGURE 8-27**. Plotting AC voltage on a graph produces what is called a **sine wave** shape.

Polarity and Chassis Ground

DC flows only in one direction—from a negative to a positive pole. A truck or bus chassis are an example where DC flow takes place through the chassis's metal frame, which makes up half the circuit pathway of a vehicle. High concentrations of extra electrons at the negative polarity battery post are connected to the frame with a ground strap. When electrons travel through the metal frame, forming the vehicle's **ground** circuits, before passing through electrical devices to reach the positive polarity battery post, the vehicle is considered to have a negative ground system. A few specialized vehicles use a positive ground chassis.

Battery voltage is determined by the potential difference between the over-concentration of electrons at the negative post and electron deficiency at the positive post. The greater the difference in electron concentration between the two battery poles, the higher the battery voltage or electrostatic forces of attraction and repulsion. How much resistance is present in the circuits separating the positive and negative posts determines the volume or amperage of electrons that can flow between the battery poles.

> ### ▶ TECHNICIAN TIP
>
> During the first half of the twentieth century, many vehicle chassis used a positive-ground metal frame. The insulated wiring had a negative polarity. The idea for this arrangement was based on conventional theory of current flow. The problem, though, is that a positively charged "chassis ground" attracted electrons from other substances to fill the outer valances, or shells, of positively charged chassis metals. This meant that positive-ground systems caused rapid body corrosion as road salt and oxygen filled the positively charged, electron-deficient chassis metal atoms. Electron theory also explains why the battery positive post corrodes much more than a negative post. The positive post's electron deficiency attracts other atoms with electrons to share and balance its positive charge. Positive-ground chassis are still used by some European off-road equipment manufacturers and a few military applications to increase the electrical system's reliability. Insulated wire connections with negative charges do not corrode as easily compared to positive insulated wiring. Fewer electrical problems is the advantage since corrosion takes place on heavier chassis frame and metal plate body panels. To prevent chassis corrosion and improve the operation of radios, negative-ground chassis are standard today. While corrosion caused by exposed positive voltage potentials is a problem, it is better managed on the positive insulated wires.

DC circuits are used in virtually all chassis circuits because a battery can easily store and supply DC. But DC has one major disadvantage: The farther it travels, the more resistance is present in the circuit. If circuit amperage is high and the correct size of wiring is not used, battery voltage can drop from 12.6 volts at a truck battery to just over 9 volts at the rear of a trailer.

AC is used to power electric motors used by electric- and hybrid-drive vehicles. AC is a more efficient type of current to power electric motors, and using it simplifies motor construction. The speed of AC electric motors is also regulated by the frequency of AC with higher frequency AC translating into faster motor speed.

Alternating Current Flow

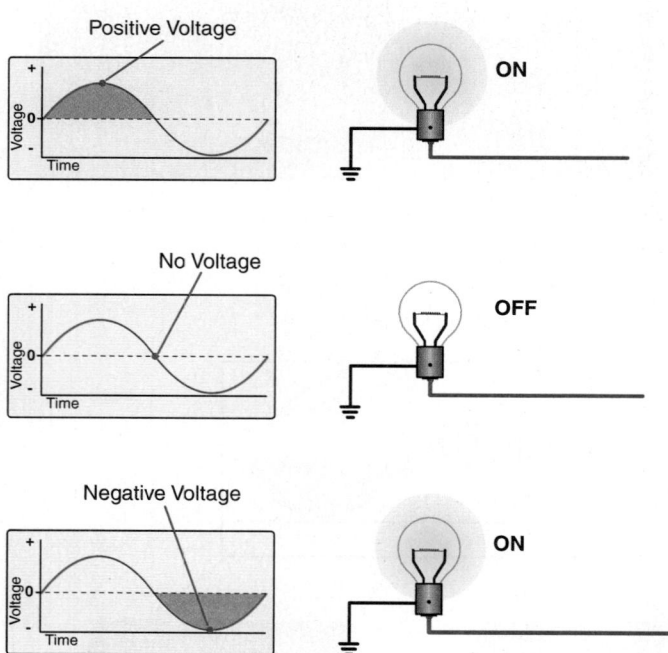

FIGURE 8-26 AC changes direction. The number of times it changes per second is measured in Hertz (HZ). Note where zero volts is on the graphing meter.

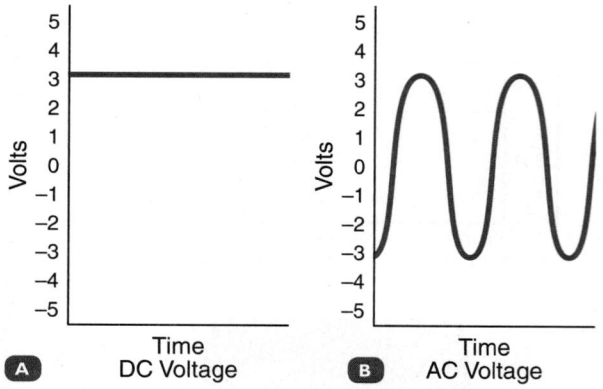

FIGURE 8-27 Waveforms. **A.** Direct current. **B.** Alternating current. Voltage is plotted over time.

AC's main advantage is that it can be transmitted farther distances with less resistance and little voltage drop compared to DC. Resistance in an AC circuit is proportional to the frequency of AC polarity change. That is, the higher AC's frequency, the less resistance AC has in a circuit.

This low transmission resistance property of AC explains why it is used to supply electricity to homes and industry over long distances with little power loss. The application of Ohm's Law formula for DC circuits predicting amperage and voltage does not apply to AC flow except to calculate voltage drop through resistors. The term impedance and different mathematical formulas are used instead to describe the relationship between voltage, amperage, and resistance in AC circuits.

Alternators produce AC, which is then changed to DC inside the alternator using diodes. To change DC to AC, a device known as a wave inverter, shortened to just **inverter**, is used. A variable reluctance-type sensor, such as the one shown in **FIGURE 8-28**, is used to measure wheel or engine speed, and it also can produce AC.

Heating Effect of Electric Current

When an electric current travels through a bulb filament or electric heating element, the filament or element converts current into heat energy. Resistance in these loads changes electrical energy into heat. This observation is referred to as the "heating effect of current." As amperage and resistance increase in a circuit, so does the amount of heat produced from conversion of electrical energy, as shown in **FIGURE 8-29**.

The heating effect can be understood by answering this question: Why does the bulb filament heat and glow, but the wires connecting the bulb do not? The simple answer is that the narrowing of the circuit conductor at the filament causes collisions to take place between the electrons as they funnel into the narrower filament pathway or the electrically restrictive resistance of a heating element. Electrons, which are three times the size of protons, release kinetic energy present in electric current. When collisions between moving electrons takes place, the electrical energy converts to heat and even light.

To visualize this effect, think of a busy highway as traffic merges from six lanes to a single lane. The single lane cannot accommodate all the vehicles, so traffic must slow. Applying brakes reduces vehicle speed, much like voltage drop, and

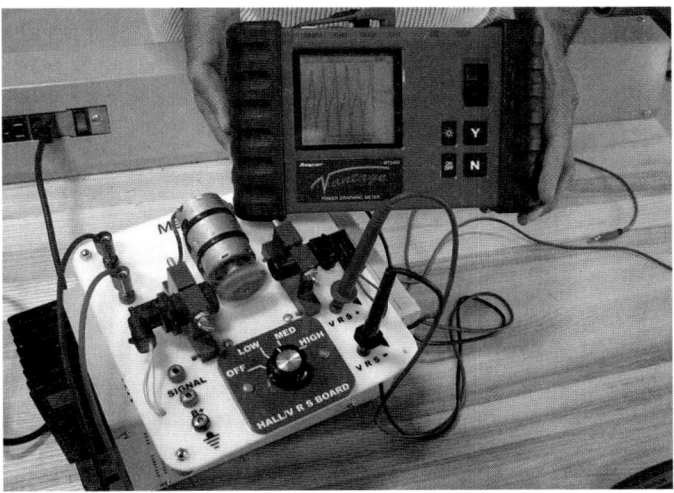

FIGURE 8-28 This variable reluctance sensor (VR) produces AC voltage. The waveform is displayed on a graphing meter.

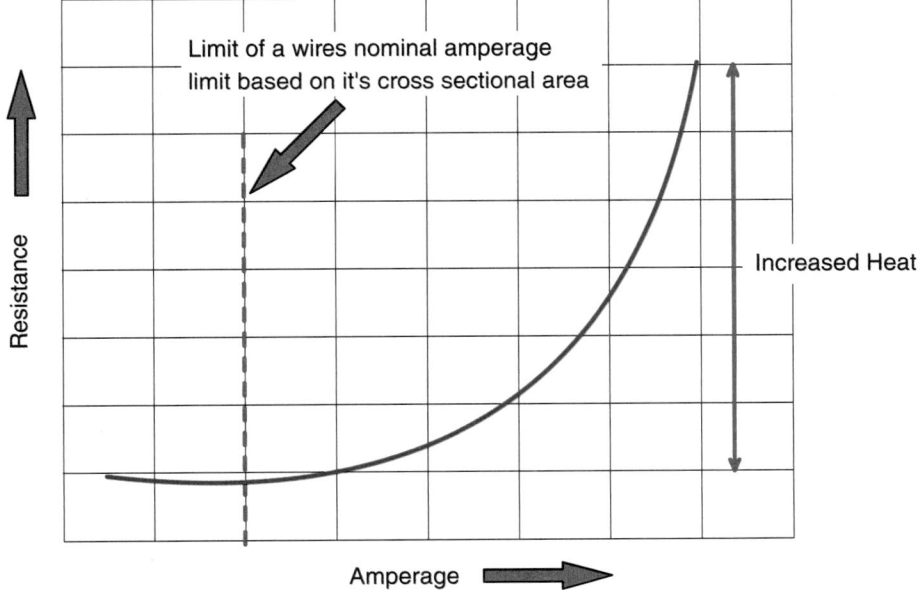

FIGURE 8-29 Exceeding the nominal amperage limit for a conductor causes it to heat, and its temperature increases exponentially.

kinetic energy of a moving vehicle converts to heat due to friction between the brake drums, rotors, and friction material.

Electrical circuit fuses take advantage of this heating effect by using a narrow metal strip made of highly conductive material. When the amount of amperage passing through the fuse exceeds the temperature of the wire's melting threshold, the strip melts first to protect circuit wiring from heating and burning caused by excessive amperage. The amount of heat produced is directly proportional to the fuse's resistance, the time current flows, and the amount of amperage in the current. The transformation of current into heat is measured in Joules. Mathematically, the relationship is described as:

$$H = I2Rt$$

where H is the heat output, I is the current amperage, R is the resistance in the circuit (ohms), and t is the time (seconds). So, if 2 amps pass through a wire with 25 ohms of resistance over the course of one minute (60 seconds), then the heat output is 6,000 Joules:

$$H = (22) \times (25) \times (60)$$

$$H = 6,000 \text{ Joules}$$

6,000 joules of heat may heat quickly and burn a small-gauge wire, but not a larger wire. A larger wire can absorb more heat and radiate excess heat better than a small-diameter wire. Rapid heating of the small wire also increases its resistance faster compared to a larger-diameter cable conducting the same amount of amperage. Rapid heating, in turn, increases a conductor's resistance, which converts more electrical energy into heat.

The heating effect of electric current accounted for by Joule's law helps explain why larger-diameter conductors are required to conduct current with higher amperage. It's important for technicians to understand that increasing amperage in a circuit increases resistance, an effect not predicted by Ohm's Law, but only by Joule's Law of heating. The effect of Joule's Law is also amplified when even a minimal amount of resistance in a conductor or connector is present. Two conductors with seemingly small resistance exponentially increase in resistance as circuit amperage also rises. The smaller conductor or connector also heats faster than the larger one. Likewise, two conductors or connectors with slightly different resistances heat at dramatically different rates when amperage increases. The higher-resistance pathway more rapidly heats and becomes more resistive as amperage increases. This important concept is examined more thoroughly in the chapter on starting motors, since the effect of Joule's heating is an important diagnostic tool for high current flow circuits. Electrical connections, such as battery cable terminals, with no apparent resistance when measured with an ohmmeter become warm or too hot to touch when current flow is high when there is already some resistance in the circuit. The suspect component or connector's resistance can be identified using a voltmeter to measure voltage drop when the circuit is under load and conducting large amounts of electric current.

Electrical Versus Electronic Circuits

LO 8-5 Identify and explain the differences between electrical and electronic circuits.

Even though electricity is used to operate electrical and electronic circuits, the two types of circuits are not identical. What are the differences between electrical and electronic circuits? Electrical circuits usually conduct higher amounts of current through heavier conductors and commonly operate high current flow devices, such as solenoids, relays, motors, lights, and more. Electronic circuits use electricity flowing through low current flow semiconductors, such as transistors, integrated circuits, or microcontrollers. Electronic circuits use less amperage and often process electrical signals rather than perform the work of lighting, heating, and mechanical movement.

Wrap-Up

Ready for Review

▶ Today, the number of electrical circuits has increased into the thousands, and hardly a single truck and bus system is without electronic control.

▶ Control of electrical system components on heavy-duty vehicles are no longer separated into distinct subsystems. Electrical control is distributed over multiple electronic control modules (ECMs) often with more than one ECM influencing the operation of an electrical component. ECMs are connected to form on-board networks.

▶ It may be helpful to think of electricity as the movement of charged particles from one point to another. The analogy of electric current flow to hydraulic flow is helpful to understand concepts of voltage, amperage, and resistance.

▶ The concept of voltage describes the speed of electron movement from atom to atom. It is equivalent to the measurement of pressure in a pipe in pounds per square inch (psi).

▶ Amperage is a measurement of the number of electrons flowing past one point in a circuit during one second. It is equivalent to the concept of flow or volume in a pipe measured in gallons or liters of flow per second.

▶ Electrical resistance is like the idea of friction. Resistance slows down electron speed, which in turn lowers voltage and amperage.

▶ Forces of repulsion and attraction between electrons and protons are termed electrostatic force and are the primary type of energy contained in electricity used to perform work.

- Atoms are made of three fundamental particles: electrons, protons, and neutrons. Positive electrical charges are found on protons, negative charges on electrons, and no charge on neutrons.

- Poles are areas of concentrated positive and negative electrical charges. Polarity is needed to produce electron flow.

- Ions are atoms with an imbalance of electrical charges due to the gain or loss of electrons.

- The flow of electrons from atom to atom describes the basic concept of electricity.

- Current can be described as a function of voltage and amperage in a circuit—in other words, the speed and quantity of electron flow through a conductor. Without either voltage and amperage, there is no flow of electricity in a circuit.

- The number of free electrons in an atom's outer valence shell determines how conductive the atom is. Fewer outer shell electrons are associated with greater conductivity.

- Electron theory states that electrons move from negative to positive. Conventional theory states that electrons move from positive to negative. Both theories convey the idea of current flow and each may be helpful when performing electrical diagnostic work.

- Electrical circuits usually conduct higher amounts of current through heavier conductors, and electronic circuits use electricity to operate semiconductors using lower voltages.

- The two fundamental types of current flow are direct current (DC) and alternating current (AC).

- Direct current has a constant polarity; alternating current has continuously changing polarity that produces a sine wave.

- Resistance is measured in ohms and depends on the type of material and the length, diameter, and temperature of the conductor.

- Good conductors have low resistance, and insulators have high resistance. Electrical energy lost through resistance is converted into heat.

- Increasing amperage in a circuit increases the resistance of an undersized conductor. When a conductor's resistance increases, its temperature increase produced by current flow and resistance is predicted using Joules law of heating.

Key Terms

alternating current (AC) A type of current flow that continuously changes direction and polarity.

amperage A unit of measurement for the quantity of electrons moving through a circuit per second of time.

ampere (amp) The unit for measuring the quantity of electrons flowing past one point in a circuit per unit of time.

conductor A material that easily allows electricity to flow through it. It is made up of atoms with very few outer shell electrons, which are loosely held by the nucleus.

conventional current theory The theory that the direction of current flow is positive to negative.

direct current (DC) Movement of current that flows in one direction only.

electrical resistance A material's property that reduces voltage and amperage in an electrical current.

electron theory of current movement The movement of negatively charged electrons to a positive charge pole.

electrostatic theory The idea that like charges repel one another and unlike electrical charges attract.

ground The name given to their negative current pathway through a vehicle chassis.

insulator A material that holds electrons tightly and prevents electron movement.

inverter A device that changes direct current into alternating current. Also called a *wave inverter*.

ohm The unit for measuring electrical resistance.

Ohm's law An electrical law that defines the relationship between amperage, resistance, and voltage.

polarity The state of charge, positive or negative.

resistor A component designed to produce electrical resistance.

semiconductor A material that can have properties of both conductors and insulators and that can switch back and forth between either state using small electrostatic charges.

sine wave A mathematical function that describes a repetitive waveform, such as an alternating current signal.

volt The electrical unit used to measure potential difference or electrical pressure.

voltage The speed at which electrons travel from atom to atom.

Review Questions

1. Consider an atom with 28 protons and 29 electrons. It could be accurately described as:
   a. Aluminum
   b. Negatively charged
   c. Positively charged
   d. Anion

2. According to conventional electrical theory, which way does electricity move in most commercial vehicle chassis?
   a. From the negative ground, through the load, then back to the battery
   b. From the "hot" insulated wire, through the load, then back to the battery
   c. From negative charge potentials to positive charge potentials
   d. Electrons leave the negative terminal of the battery and return through the positive post

3. The concept of amperage refers best to the following:
   a. The speed of electrical impulse
   b. The force of electrical impulse
   c. The quantity of electron movement
   d. The pressure of the electrical impulse

4. Which of the following terms best describes the electrical pressure that causes current to flow in a circuit?
   a. Resistance
   b. Amperage
   c. Voltage
   d. Current
5. Consider two objects with electrical charges. Objects A and B both repel one another. What is the polarity of the charges found on the objects?
   a. A is positive, B is negative.
   b. A and B are both positive.
   c. A is negative, B is positive.
   d. A is negative, B is neutral.
6. Which of the following types of matter are expected to have the fewest electrons in the outer valence orbital?
   a. Conductors
   b. Insulators
   c. Semi-conductors
   d. Resisters
7. Which of the following electrical terms is most closely associated with "electrical friction"?
   a. Amperage
   b. Current
   c. Voltage
   d. Resistance
8. Which of the following descriptions best describes the electrical term, polarity?
   a. The electrical pressure in a circuit
   b. The direction of electron movement
   c. The force of electrostatic attraction
   d. The direction of electrostatic repulsion
9. Which measurement of electrical flow measures electron movement in number of electrons past a single point in a circuit per second of time?
   a. Coulomb
   b. Voltage
   c. Resistance
   d. Amperage
10. Consider the principle of Joules heating. Which of the following units of electrical measurement changes when amperage increases through a circuit?
    a. Resistance
    b. Voltage
    c. Farads
    d. Capacitance

ASE Technician A/Technician B Style Questions

1. Technician A says there are two theories of current flow: the electron theory and the conventional theory. Technician B says it is only important to remember that current flow is described by both concepts. Who is correct?
   a. Technician A
   b. Technician B
   c. Both Technician A and Technician B
   d. Neither Technician A nor Technician B

2. Technician A says AC circuits are used in virtually all chassis circuits because a battery can easily store and supply AC current. Technician B says DC current is used to power hybrid drive electric motors. Who is correct?
   a. Technician A
   b. Technician B
   c. Both Technician A and Technician B
   d. Neither Technician A nor Technician B
3. Technician A says AC's main advantage is that it can be transmitted farther distances with less resistance and little voltage drop. Technician B says the term resistance is used with AC circuits as well as DC circuits. Who is correct?
   a. Technician A
   b. Technician B
   c. Both Technician A and Technician B
   d. Neither Technician A nor Technician B
4. Technician A says that the resistance of a circuit or load determines the amount of amperage flowing through it. Technician B says that the voltage in a circuit determines its resistance. Who is correct?
   a. Technician A
   b. Technician B
   c. Both Technician A and Technician B
   d. Neither Technician A nor Technician B
5. Technician A says electronic circuits use less amperage and often process electrical signals rather than perform the work of lighting, heating, and mechanical movement. Technician B says electrical circuits usually conduct higher amounts of current through heavier conductors and commonly operate high current flow devices, such as solenoids, relays, motors, lights, and more. Who is correct?
   a. Technician A
   b. Technician B
   c. Both Technician A and Technician B
   d. Neither Technician A nor Technician B
6. Technician A says that Ohm's Law predicts that a conductor's resistance increases when amperage increases. Technician B says that Joule's Law predicts a small amount of resistance in a circuit becomes much greater when amperage increases. Who is correct?
   a. Technician A
   b. Technician B
   c. Both Technician A and Technician B
   d. Neither Technician A nor Technician B
7. Technician A says that Ohm's Law predicts increased circuit resistance as voltage increases. Technician B says Ohm's Law predicts both amperage and voltage in a circuit vary depending on circuit resistance. Who is correct?
   a. Technician A
   b. Technician B
   c. Both Technician A and Technician B
   d. Neither Technician A nor Technician B
8. Technician A says today's electrical system components are no longer separated into distinct systems. Technician B says

networking electrical system components add new vehicle features that can enhance safety, performance, and passenger comfort. Who is correct?

a. Technician A
b. Technician B
c. Both Technician A and Technician B
d. Neither Technician A nor Technician B

9. Technician A says the forces of electrostatic repulsion and attraction move electrons through a circuit. Technician B says the movement of electrons and protons from one atom to another is called electricity. Who is correct?

a. Technician A
b. Technician B
c. Both Technician A and Technician B
d. Neither Technician A nor Technician B

10. Technician A says metals typically have lots of easily moved electrons, which make them good conductors. Technician B says liquids cannot function as a conductor. Who is correct?

a. Technician A
b. Technician B
c. Both Technician A and Technician B
d. Neither Technician A nor Technician B

CHAPTER 9

Generating Electricity

Learning Objectives

After reading this chapter, you will be able to:

- **LO 9-1** Identify and describe methods to produce electricity.

- **LO 9-2** Identify and explain principles of electromagnetic induction.
- **LO 9-3** Identify and describe principles of electrochemistry.

You Are the Technician

While performing brake service on several tractors with dual wheels, the hub-piloted outer aluminum disc wheels were very hard to separate and remove from the inner steel rims. After the first few wheel rims were removed using a purpose-built puller, it was discovered that the aluminum rims were very badly corroded around the wheel studs, and likely all needed to be discarded. The inner steel disc wheels were unaffected by the corrosion, but needed to be cleaned and repainted. The wheel nuts were in acceptable condition for reuse, but all the contact points on the aluminum rims beneath the nuts were corroded as well.

1. What was the likely cause of the aluminum wheel disc corrosion?
2. What service practice would have prevented the destruction of the aluminum rims?
3. What service recommendations would you make to prevent this situation from happening again, either to these tractors or others in the fleet?

Introduction

The extensive use of electrical devices, and the reach of electronic controls into almost every commercial vehicle system, makes understanding electrical principles and developing skills related to servicing electrical systems indispensable to technicians. Foundational knowledge for understanding the electrical system operation is identifying the various ways electricity is produced on a bus, truck, or trailer chassis. The use of batteries and alternators relying on chemical reactions and magnetism to quickly move electrons are familiar methods of generating electricity. But there are a surprising number of electrical effects technicians should be aware of that involve creating electricity, and have significant implications for safety, maintenance practices, and making decisions about choosing proper service procedures. The importance of other methods of generating electricity is easily overlooked and can leave not only gaps in knowledge, but also in background information needed to build skills related to servicing new electrical components and technology as it is introduced. Building on the introductory electrical content in the previous chapter, this chapter examines various methods used to produce electrical charges and electrical current and apply them to commercial vehicle chassis.

Sources of Electricity

LO 9-1 Identify and describe methods to produce electricity.

Seven methods to produce electron flow are generally recognized. These include:

- Friction
- Light
- Heat
- Pressure
- Magnetism
- Chemical reactions
- Fuel cells

Electricity from Friction

Electric charges can be produced when two materials rub together or separate. Electron transfer producing static or stationary electrical charges, in both instances, uses friction that leaves one material with more electrons than the other. Producing electricity using friction is known as **triboelectricity** (tribo means friction). The zap of an electric shock after walking across a carpet and then touching a metal handle is a common way to experience triboelectricity. Static electricity is another name given to triboelectricity, but more accurately refers to objects with stationary high-voltage charges. By either adding or removing electrons from an object, stationary or static positive and negative charges are established.

Triboelectricity is produced because different materials have varying capacities to retain electrons. Interactions between different materials resulting in electrically charged materials are predicted using a chart called the triboelectric series. The triboelectric series identifies which materials easily give up electrons, and which materials attract or retain electrons removed from materials surrendering electrons. It is important to note that the triboelectric effect is observed when materials in close contact are separated vertically or horizontally or through sliding contact. Consider separating plastic wrap from paper, as in **FIGURE 9-1**. The large difference in positive and negative charges between the materials after they are separated causes them to cling to one another to rebalance the charges. Another important example of an instance where strong electrical charges are established through material separation takes place when liquid fuels are drained from a fuel tank. Unless proper grounding protocols are followed, fires can result when draining fuel tanks or filling fuel containers while draining fuel from another container.

The triboelectric series is a name for the list that indicates the tendency of materials to become either positively or negatively charged when separated, or during frictional contact with one another (**TABLE 9-1**).

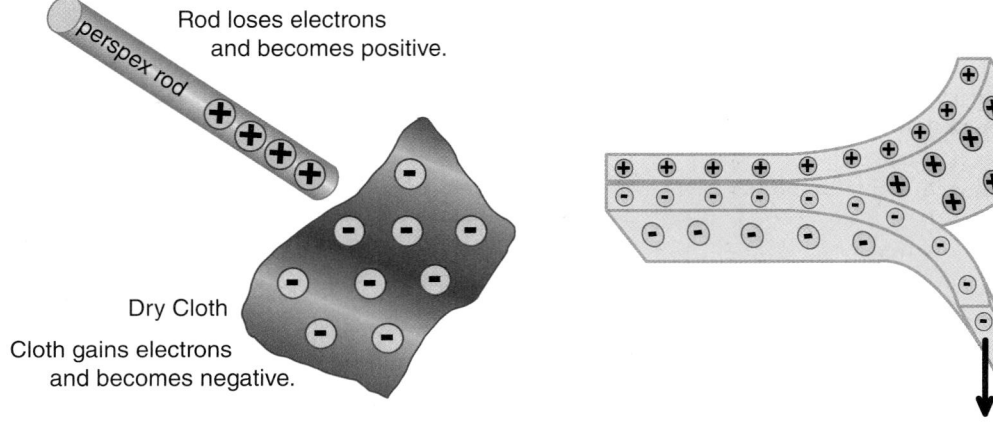

FIGURE 9-1 Triboelectric current is electricity produced through friction or material separation.

TABLE 9-1 Triboelectric Series

Charge	Material
Positive + More likely to lose electrons	• Acetate • Leather • Glass • Hair • Nylon • Wool • Lead • Aluminum • Paper • Cotton • Steel – Neutral • Wood • Nickel – Copper • Rubber • Platinum
Negative – More likely to gain electrons	• Saran Wrap • Polyester • Polyethylene • Polyvinyl Chloride (PVC) • Silicon • Teflon

ATTENTION
OBSERVE PRECAUTIONS
FOR HANDLING
ELECTROSTATIC
SENSITIVE DEVICES

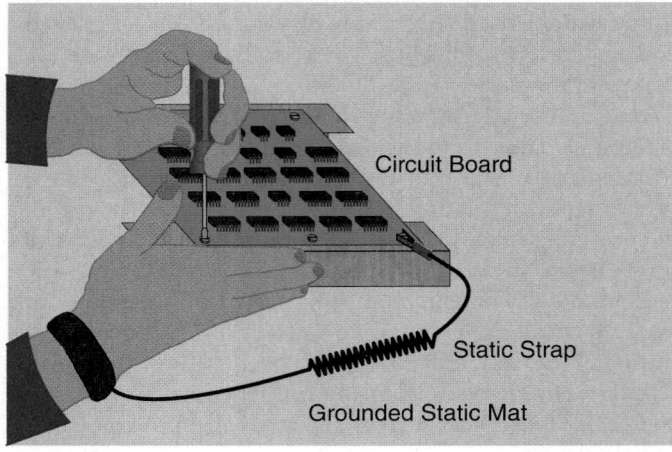

Circuit Board

Static Strap

Grounded Static Mat

FIGURE 9-2 A grounded bracelet is one means of preventing static charges from damaging sensitive electronic components.

Understanding that electricity is produced through friction is important to the technician trying to solve, or even prevent, electrical problems. For example, grounding protocol must be observed when handling components with sensitive microelectronic circuits, as they may be damaged by electrostatic discharge (ESD) (**FIGURE 9-2**). It is important to remember that after moving around in polyester coveralls over seats made of nylon or leather materials, static electric charges are created. To prevent damage to electronic components, charges can be drawn off one's clothing and body by touching a metal door handle or a metal workbench. Using a special bracelet or anklet is a standard practice while handling unconnected integrated circuits. Sensitive electronic components are usually wrapped in electrically conductive Mylar packaging for protection against high-voltage static electricity and should be left wrapped in the packaging until they are installed.

Electrons are also removed from the bodies of trucks, buses, and trailers by wind friction. Sliding friction between plastic pipe on an open trailer with wind continually passing around the pipe can build tremendous static electric charges. Even some buses are equipped with static wicks, which are conductive cables that drag along the road to prevent small electric shocks to exiting passengers. When fuel and powdered products, such as flour or cement, are removed from a tanker trailer, the separation of the materials produces a build-up of high-voltage static charges. To minimize the likelihood of an explosion caused by a high-voltage spark, a grounding clamp is connected between the chassis and an earth ground. Earth grounds attached to a truck or trailer body before a product is loaded or unloaded can absorb or release the electrons needed to balance electrical charges before a build-up of electrical charges produces a spark that can cause an explosion or ignite a product (**FIGURE 9-3**). Radiators, heater cores, and body panels often have ground straps connected to the frame to prevent charge build-up. It is important these straps are always reconnected after servicing any of the components.

Electrostatic charging through separation occurs when rubber-based airbags for air suspension systems move up and down over aluminum pedestals. Ground straps must be properly connected to the suspension system to remove the charge build-up.

▶ TECHNICIAN TIP

Electrostatic discharge (ESD) caused by the build-up of static charges on a technician's clothing can damage sensitive electronic components. It is estimated that 30% to 70% of all failures in these components are caused by ESD. Handling sensitive components during service is one occasion where damage is done. Always remove charges by wearing a ground bracelet or making contact with a metal part of the chassis, such as the door handle. Leave components in conductive foam packing until installation.

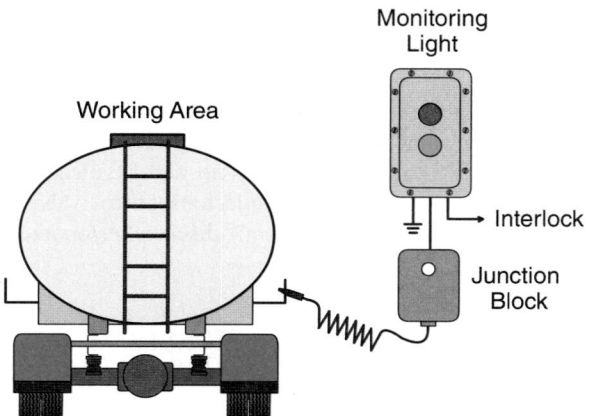

FIGURE 9-3 A bonded ground system neutralizes static electrical charges accumulated on the chassis of a tanker hauling fuel or powdered products, such as flour or cement dust. Without the bonded ground system in place during loading or off-loading, a spark caused by moving charges can lead to a catastrophic explosion.

Electricity from Light

Approximately 1,000 watts of sunlight energy per square meter strike the planet's surface daily. The most efficient photovoltaic cells, more commonly known as solar cells, can convert less than half this energy into electricity. Converting light into electricity uses a process called the called the **photovoltaic (PV) effect**. A PV cell made from silicon crystals can produce approximately 0.60-volts DC when bright sunlight is reflected at the correct angle on the cell. Photovoltaic cells are connected in series to form higher voltage outputs that can be used to trickle-charge batteries. Connecting cells together to form a panel that's four feet × two feet can produce approximately 100 watts or 7–8 amps of current at 12 volts (**FIGURE 9-4**). Beyond use as a trickle charger for batteries, the dependency on sunlight, cost, and inefficiency of solar cells means they have limited current use in commercial vehicles. However, trailers equipped with solar panel roofs, such as Shell Fuels proof of Starship concept, uses 5,000 watts of solar panels to charge a 48-volt lithium battery to power accessory electronic components, such as LED lights, wipers, and blower motors.

Electricity from Heat

Electricity produced by heat is a phenomenon known as thermoelectricity (**FIGURE 9-5**). When two dissimilar metals are brought together and heated, electricity is produced at the junction points. Coupling and heating two dissimilar metals to produce electricity is called thermocoupling, and forms a device that is called a **thermocouple**. The exhaust pyrometer used to measure exhaust temperature is an example of an application for a thermocouple (**FIGURE 9-6**). Exhaust aftertreatment temperature sensors typically use thermocouples because of their ability to withstand high temperatures. The wires of the most commonly used thermocouple, a K type with wires made from nickel and aluminum alloys, produce close to 50 millivolts at 2,732°F (1,500°C). This device works to measure

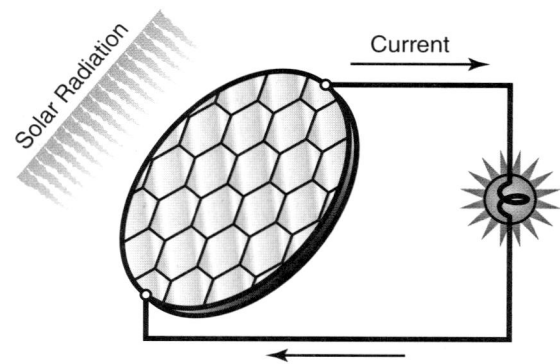

FIGURE 9-4 Photovoltaic cells convert light energy into electricity. One common application is use as a trickle charger.

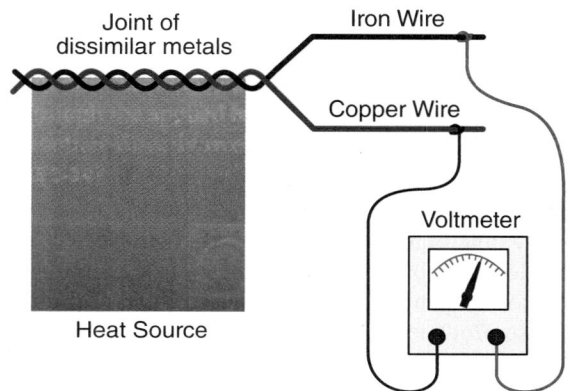

FIGURE 9-5 Electricity from a thermocouple is produced when two dissimilar metals are heated.

FIGURE 9-6 A thermocouple pyrometer in the exhaust pipe measures exhaust temperature. Increased cylinder temperatures correspond to higher voltages from the thermocouple device.

the exhaust temperature through voltage signals produced by the pyrometer. The hotter the device becomes, the greater the output voltage.

Thermoelectric Device (TED)

Opposite the effect of heating a thermocouple junction is a cooling effect that is observed when electricity passes through the thermocouple's junction. A temperature differential results as one of the metals becomes hot and the other cold. When semiconductors are used instead of metal wires, heat can be transferred across the device. An application for this effect is in thermoelectric devices (TEDs). TEDs are solid-state heat pumps formed from several layers of semiconductor materials (**FIGURE 9-7**). When voltage is applied in one direction through the material, heat is created on one side and a cooling effect is observed on the opposite side. Changing polarity reverses the direction of heating and cooling. TEDs are used for cooling or heating small areas in vehicles, including cooled seats, steering wheels, cup holders, or beverage storage compartments.

Electricity from Pressure

When certain types of mineral crystals are squeezed or bent, electron flow is created according to the **Piezoelectric effect**. Piezoelectric crystals are commonly used to generate the electric current in a variety of devices, ranging from pressure sensors to microphones (**FIGURE 9-8**). Piezoelectric crystals are even found in barbecue grill lighters. Just as squeezing the crystal produces current, passing electric current through the crystal also produces movement. Natural piezoelectric crystals are also manufactured as piezoceramic discs that can change shape when current is passed through the material. This feature has application in some common rail injectors. When energized with electric current, the ceramic material expands instantly to

switch fuel flow on and off through the injector to produce a much faster injector response than electromagnetic actuators. Reversing the polarity of current through the actuators contracts the actuator to provide even faster injector response times and more injection events during a combustion cycle (**FIGURE 9-9**). No magnetic fields are produced or needed by piezoceramic actuators to open and close an injector control valve; only the mechanical forces of piezoceramic disc expansion and contraction are used.

Electricity from Magnetism

LO 9-2 Identify and explain principles of electromagnetic induction.

One of the most common ways electricity is produced on a heavy-duty vehicle is through the use of the energy found in magnetic fields. **Magnetism** is a force that can pull or push electrons to produce electric charges, depending on whether the south or north pole is influencing the electrons. When a conductor is moved through a magnetic field—or a magnetic field moves across a conductor—the magnetic lines of force move electrons. When electron movement is caused by the influence of magnetic fields the effect is known as magnetic induction. Many devices also use magnetic and electromagnetic principles to operate, so it is important to understand basic principles of magnetism and induction. Important principles to remember about magnetism include:

1. A bar magnet has a north and south pole. Magnetic lines of force move directionally and leave the north pole then reenter the south pole.

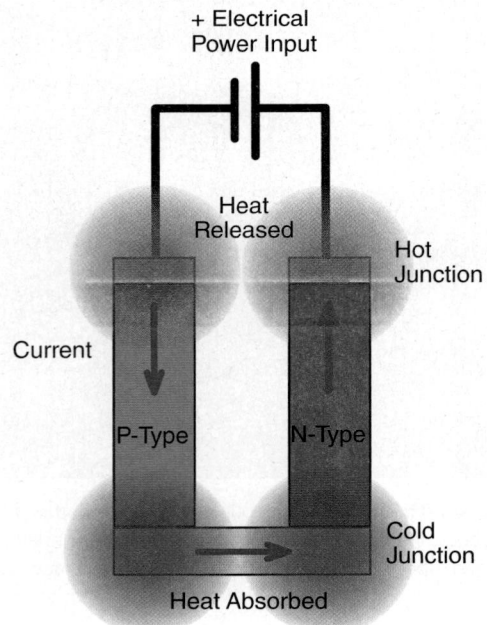

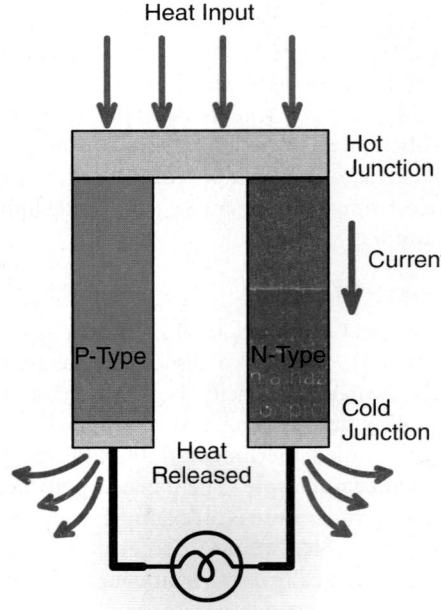

FIGURE 9-7 As electricity passes through the thermoelectric cooler (left), the cold junction gets colder. Conversely, the thermocouple on the right creates an electric current as heat is applied to the hot junction.

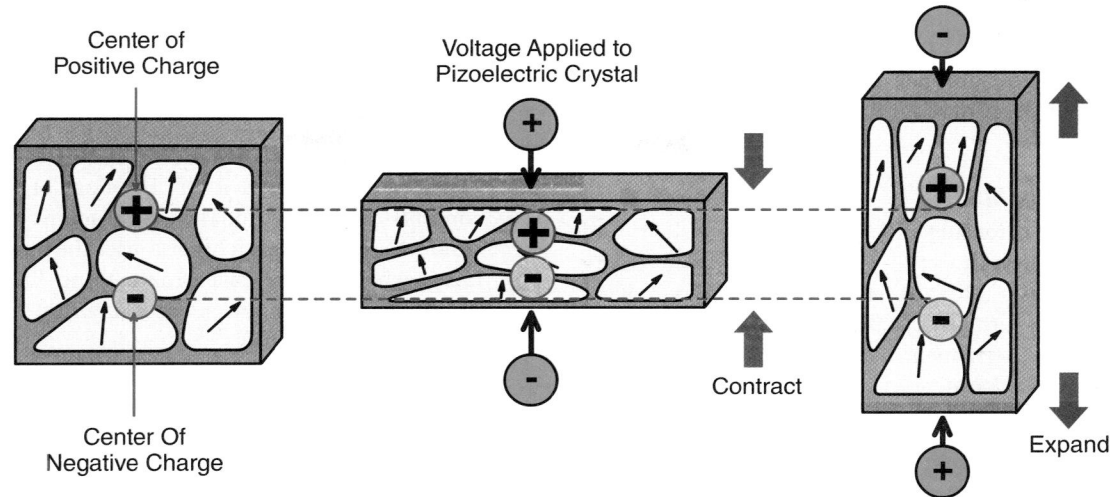

Center of
Positive Charge

Voltage Applied to
Pizoelectric Crystal

Center Of
Negative Charge

Contract

Expand

FIGURE 9-8 Current is generated when ceramic piezoelectric crystals are compressed. Applying current to either of the crystal's poles changes the crystal's shape.

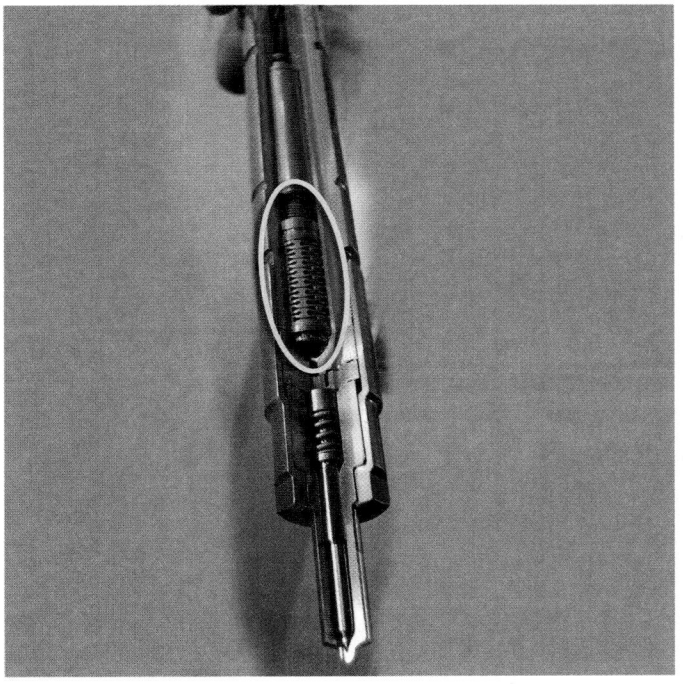

FIGURE 9-9 The newest application for piezo crystals is in common rail injectors. Current passing through the piezoceramic actuators open and close an injector control valve. Reversing polarity contracts the actuator.

FIGURE 9-10 A soft iron laminated core used by starter motor field coils to intensify magnetic field strength.

2. Like poles repel each other, and unlike poles attract each other.
3. If you divide a permanent magnet, the result is two shorter magnets, each with its own north and south poles.
4. There is no known insulation against magnetic lines of force. However, magnetic lines of force can be redirected through more permeable materials. Soft iron material is one of the most permeable materials to magnetic fields.

Laminated soft iron, which is made from thin layers of iron, is the best conductor of magnetic lines of force (**FIGURE 9-10**).

Important terms associated with magnetism include:

- **reluctance**—opposition or resistance to magnetic lines of force. Reluctance is to magnetism as resistance is to electricity (**FIGURE 9-11**).

- **flux**—the number of lines of magnetic force. Stronger magnets have more flux (**FIGURE 9-12**).
- **flux density**—the number of magnetic lines of force per square inch. More lines of force mean a stronger magnetic field.

Electromagnetism

A corresponding relationship exists between electricity and magnetism—magnetism can produce electricity, and electricity can produce magnetism (**FIGURE 9-13**). Electric current moving through a conductor produces a magnetic field that behaves nearly the same as a permanent magnet. As electrical current flows from negative to positive, magnetic lines of force travel north to south. Unlike a permanent magnet, the polarity of an electromagnet can change. This is done by changing the direction of current flow or reversing the polarity of the current supply.

The following are some important facts about electromagnetism.

1. A straight wire that carries current creates an endless magnetic field around itself. The lines of force rotate in concentric circles around the wire. Placing current-carrying conductors near to each other causes the magnetic fields to merge when current travels in the same direction. Placing conductors closer to one another intensifies magnetic field strength (**FIGURE 9-14**).
2. An **electromagnet** is produced when a straight current-carrying conductor is formed into a single loop. Lines of force turn from the inside of the loop to the outside.
3. Increasing the number of wire loops increases the magnetic field strength.
4. Air has a high reluctance to magnetic lines of force. For example, the smaller the air gap between a variable reluctance sensor containing a permanent magnet and the iron reluctor wheel, the greater the number of lines of force between them (**FIGURE 9-15**).
5. When a soft iron core is inserted into the coil of an electromagnet, lines of force easily travel through it because it has low reluctance. The magnetic field flux (lines of force) increases as much as several hundred times because the permeability of soft iron which is close to 2,500 times that of air (**FIGURE 9-16**).
6. Amperage through a coil or conductor and the strength of its magnetic field are directly proportional. This means that increasing amperage increases magnetic

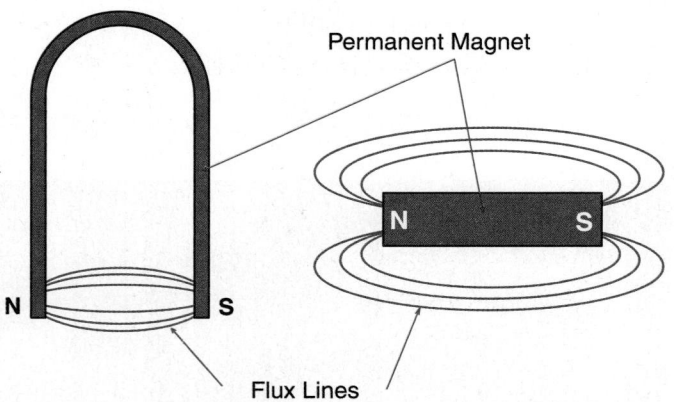

FIGURE 9-11 Reluctance refers to the resistance to magnetic lines of force. Materials with low reluctance conduct and intensify magnetic flux.

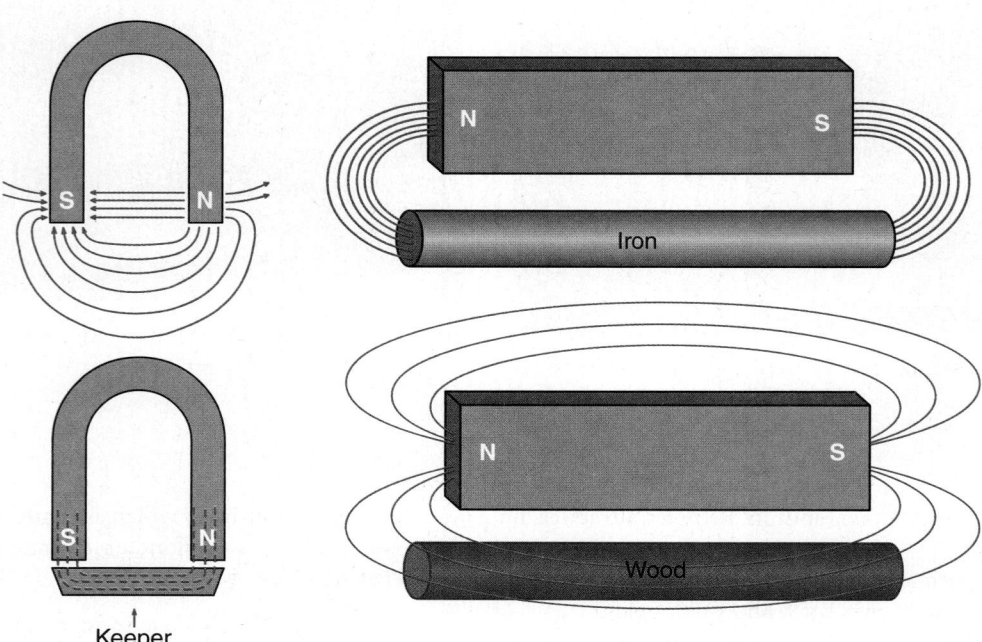

FIGURE 9-12 Magnetic lines of force have direction and are referred to as flux lines. Magnetic force is proportional to the number or density of flux lines.

field strength. For example, if amperage is increased five times from 10 to 50 amps, the magnetic lines of force also increase in the ratio of five times, or 1:5 (**FIGURE 9-17**).

7. Magnetic field strength of an electromagnet is calculated by multiplying Amperage × Number of Wire Turns. For example, the same magnetic force is produced by an electromagnet having 1,000 turns of wire carrying 10 A as that of an electromagnet having 200 turns of wire carrying 50 A. In either case, the number of turns times the amperes equals 10,000 ampere-turns (**FIGURE 9-18**).

8. The left-hand rule is used to determine the direction of magnetic lines of force when the electron theory is applied. When your left hand is wrapped around a conductor with the thumb pointed in the direction of current flow, magnetic lines of force follow the direction of your fingers.

9. The magnetic field of a current-carrying conductor behaves in the same manner as the magnetic field of a permanent magnet as long as current is flowing through it. When the direction of current flow is changed, the direction of the lines of force also changes.

▶ TECHNICIAN TIP

Relays that switch high-amperage circuits, such as those supplying starter motors, have thicker, less resistive windings and are only for intermittent use. When available battery voltage drops during cranking, the low-resistance, high-amperage flow windings in the relay produce a stronger magnetic field to hold switch contacts together longer. However, since these relays use more amperage, they burn out after several hours if continuously energized. Continuous-duty relays operating devices, such as lights, blower motors, or electric fuel pumps, use thinner, more resistive windings, enabling them to stay energized longer with less heat. These relays should never be interchanged since the intermittent-duty relay fails quickly and the continuous duty relay chatters in low-voltage operating conditions (**FIGURE 9-19**).

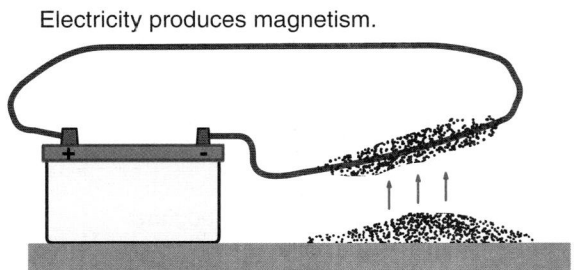

Electricity produces magnetism.

Iron filings are attracted to the magnetic field around the current carrying wire.

FIGURE 9-13 Passing current through a conductor produces magnetic lines or force.

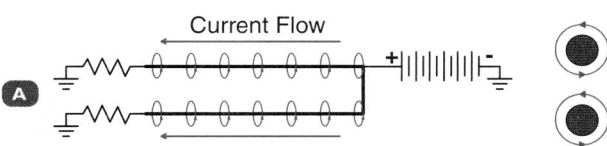
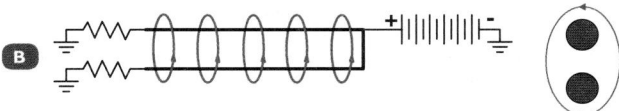
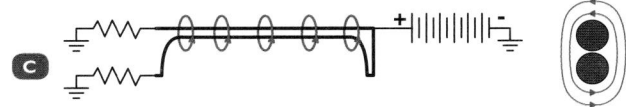

Current Flow

FIGURE 9-14 Magnetic lines have a specific direction and interact with one another. Lines of force rotate around a conductor carrying current. **A.** Normal magnetic fields. **B.** Magnetic fields merge. **C.** Magnetic fields merge and intensify.

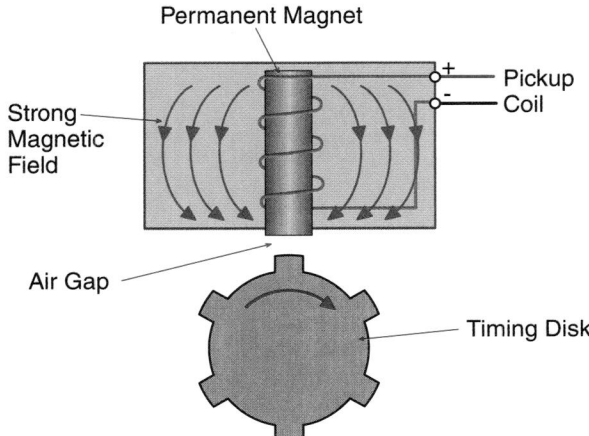
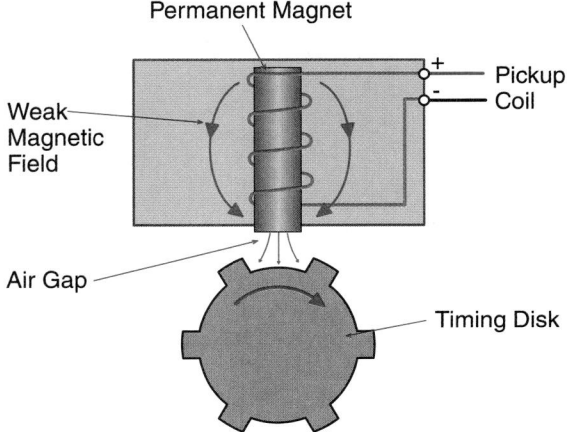

FIGURE 9-15 Variable reluctance sensors generate current by winding a wire around a permanent magnet. When the tooth of the reluctor wheel approaches the sensor's magnet, its magnetic field intensifies due to the lower reluctance of iron compared with air. When the reluctor tooth moves away from the sensor, magnetic field strength drops and its size contracts.

FIGURE 9-16 The pole pieces of this rotor found inside an alternator intensifies the magnetic field created by the electromagnet. **A.** Iron pole pieces. **B.** Electromagnetic coil.

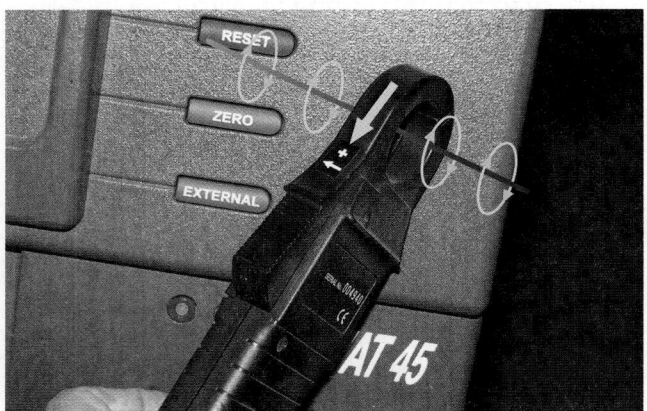

FIGURE 9-17 An inductive-type pick-up measures amperage by sensing the magnetic field flux density. Magnetic field strength is directly proportional to amperage. A Hall effect sensor, which is influenced by magnetic flux, is used to sense the field strength.

10. When two conductors carrying equal currents flowing in opposite directions are placed side by side, the lines of force turn in opposite directions and are more concentrated between the conductors than on the outside of the two conductors. The current-carrying conductors repel one another and are pushed apart until the fields are concentric.

11. If there is an equal current flow in the same direction through two or more parallel conductors, each conductor alone creates a circular field of magnetic force that joins with the other to move in the same direction.

Electron flow can be created using magnetic fields in one of three ways:

1. Magnetic induction or electromagnetic induction
2. Self-induction
3. Mutual induction

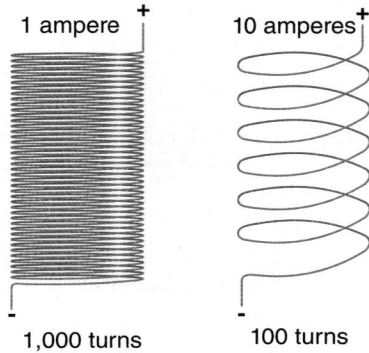

FIGURE 9-18 Two windings both exert the same magnetic field of strength. The less resistive thicker winding conducts higher amperage and is not sensitive to voltage drops as much as the more resistive thinner winding.

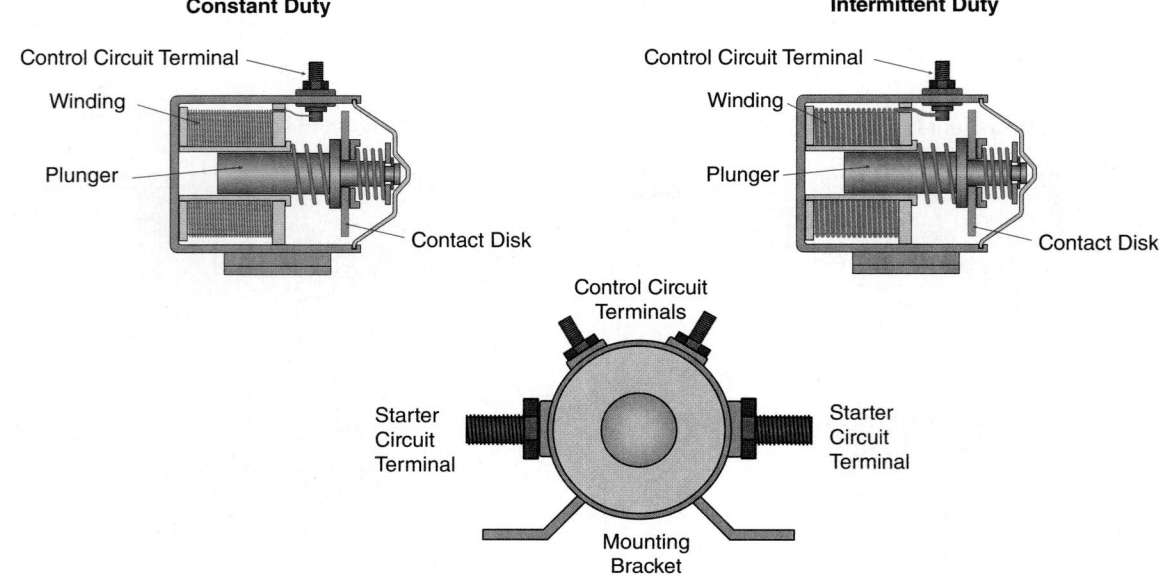

FIGURE 9-19 Thicker windings conduct more current, but maintain a strong magnetic field when the voltage drops. Thinner windings can be used for continuous operation, but lose magnetic field strength when voltage drops.

Electromagnetic Induction

The principle of producing electrical current flow using electromagnets is known as **electromagnetic induction**. Alternators, generators, and speed sensors use this electrical principle to produce electrical current. Lines of force leaving the north pole of the magnet push electrons. The south pole, with lines of force moving inward, pulls electrons (**FIGURE 9-20**). For example, a magnetic field cutting across a wire moves electrons, producing a positive and negative charge at each end of the wire. Charge polarity depends upon the angle of wire movement relative to the magnetic field poles and the direction of conductor movement relative to the magnetic field (**FIGURE 9-21**).

Some important facts to remember about electromagnetic induction are:

1. *The strength of the magnetic field changes induced voltage.* If the magnetic field is made stronger—for example, by using a more powerful magnet—the conductor cuts more lines of force and induces higher voltage. Increasing current flow through an electromagnet increases its magnetic field strength.

2. *The speed at which lines of force are cutting across the conductor changes induced voltage.* If the relative motion between the conductor and magnetic field is increased, more magnetic force is applied to move electrons, so the induced voltage is higher.

3. *The number of conductors that are cutting across the lines of force changes induced amperage.* If a straight wire conductor is wound into a coil that is then moved across the magnetic field, more conductor electrons are influenced by lines of force since all the loops of wire are merged. The amperage induced in each loop are added together to produce higher amperage (**FIGURE 9-22**).

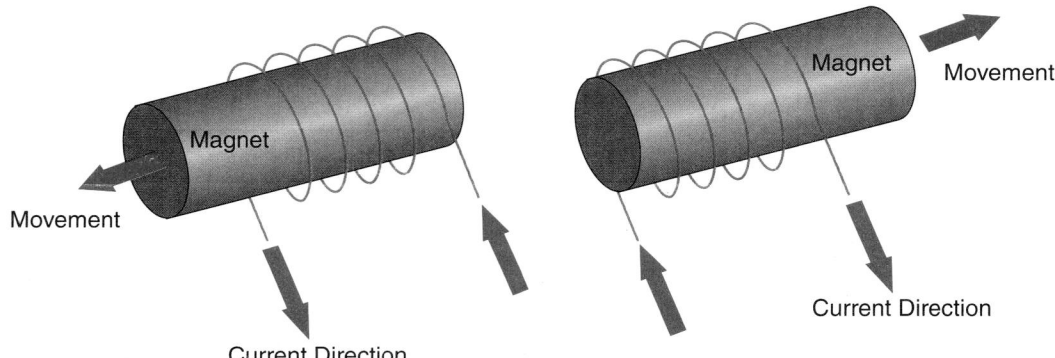

FIGURE 9-20 The direction of the magnetic field or conductor movement determines the polarity of induced current.

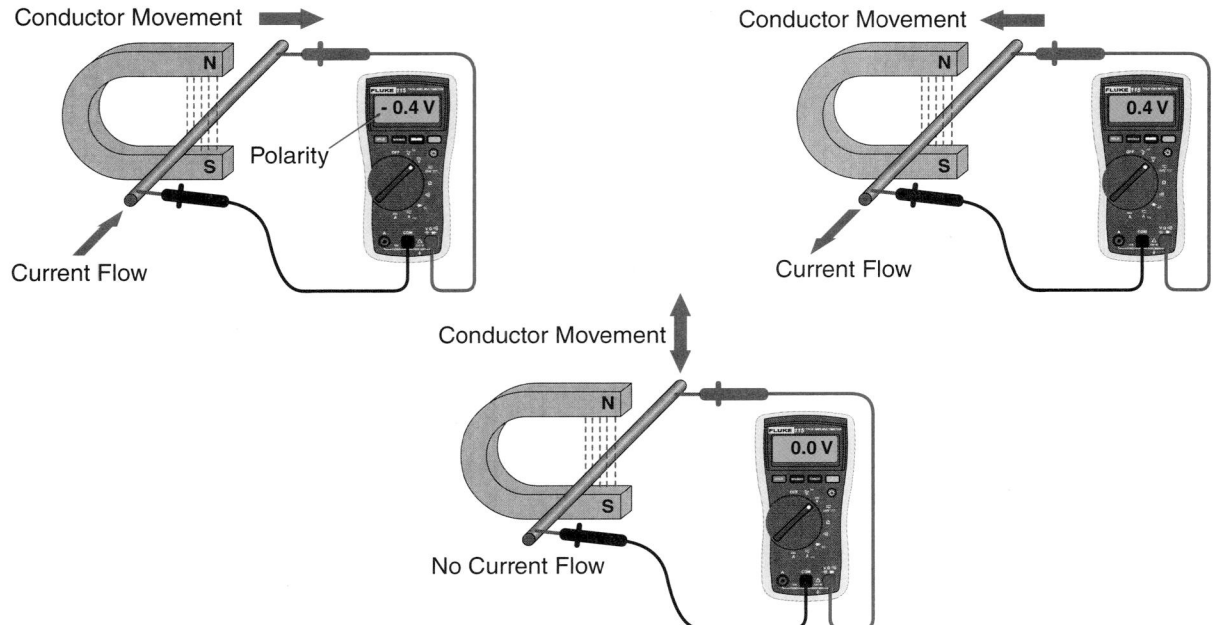

FIGURE 9-21 Direction of movement, angle, and speed determine the amount of induced current. Cutting the lines of force at 90 degrees induces the greatest amount of electrical current.

Self-Induction

Self-induction is observed in a current-carrying wire when the current in the wire is changing. In self-induction, no separate magnetic field, such as a permanent magnet or separate electromagnet, is used (**FIGURE 9-23**). Instead, the changing magnetic field strength created by an increasing or decreasing current through the wire itself induces current in the opposite direction in the wire (**FIGURE 9-24**). The difference between the former and new magnetic field strength represents a moving magnetic field. Hence, the current is self-induced. The cause of self-induction is the changing size and strength of the magnetic field. Changing current flow expands or contracts the magnetic field. Because there is relative motion between the size of the magnetic field and the conductor producing the field, the conditions necessary for inducing current are met.

It is important for technicians to know that the polarity of the self-induced current flow is the opposite of that of the current that induced the original magnetic field. This means the polarity of an induced current opposes a change in the current that produced it. Another term describing this effect is inductive reactance or inductive resistance (**FIGURE 9-25**). This explains why there is a delay between the time when current is applied to a coil and the instant when electromagnetic coils reach full magnetic field strength. Full magnetic field strength needs maximum current flow. In a coil, current flow inducing a magnetic field is opposed or resisted by reactive inductance or resistance produced by self-induction.

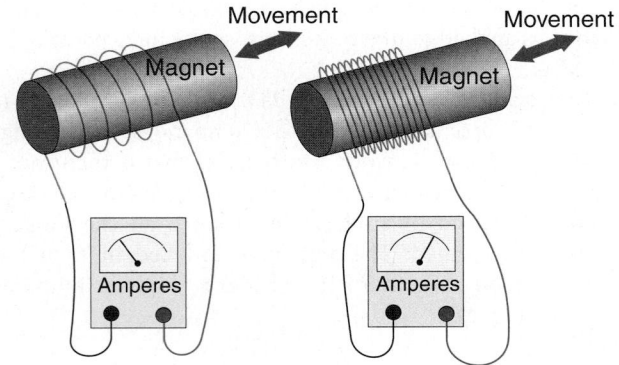

FIGURE 9-22 The number and size of conductors cut by magnetic lines of force changes the amount of current induced in the conductors.

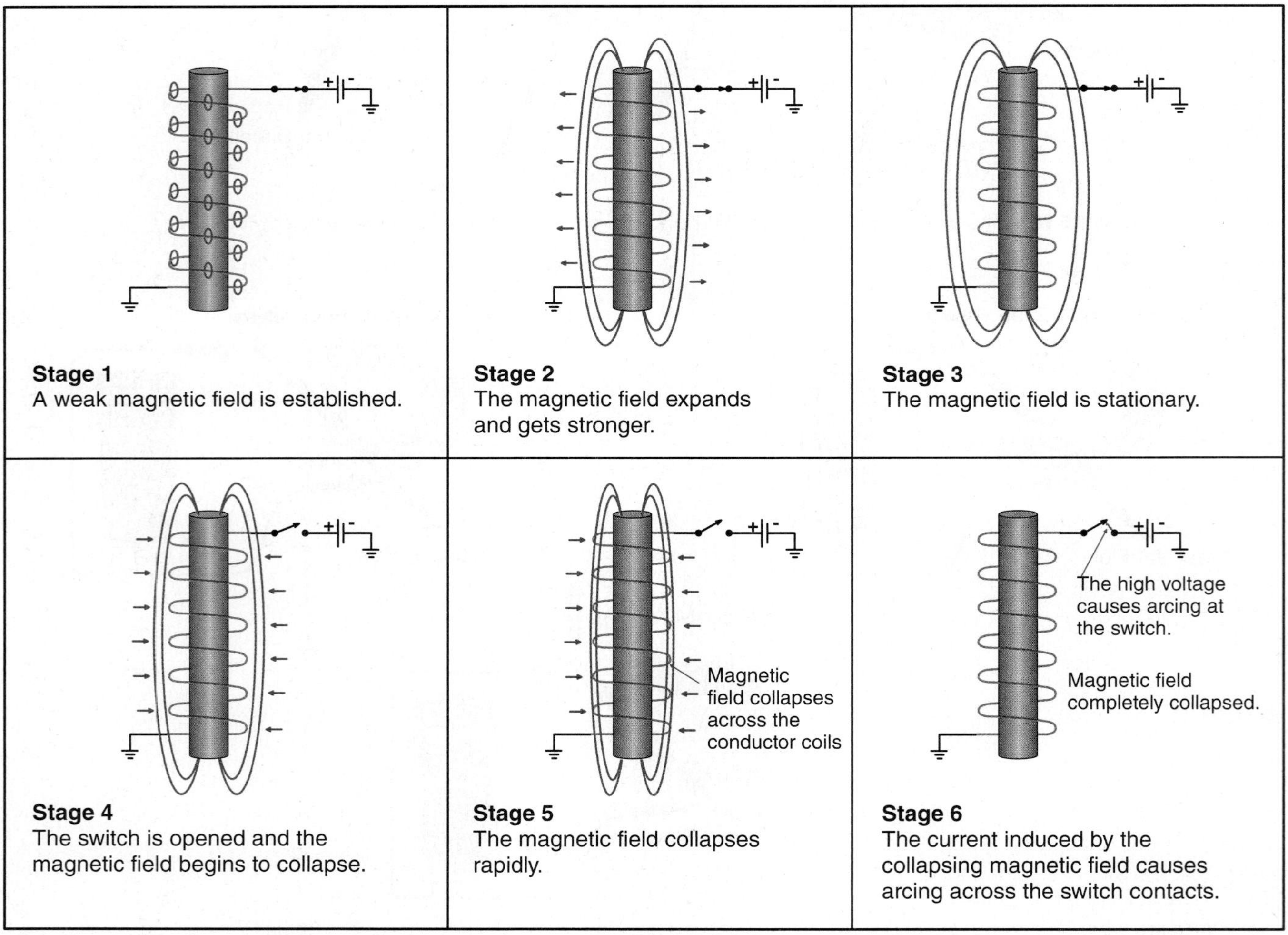

Stage 1
A weak magnetic field is established.

Stage 2
The magnetic field expands and gets stronger.

Stage 3
The magnetic field is stationary.

Stage 4
The switch is opened and the magnetic field begins to collapse.

Stage 5
The magnetic field collapses rapidly.

Magnetic field collapses across the conductor coils

Stage 6
The current induced by the collapsing magnetic field causes arcing across the switch contacts.

The high voltage causes arcing at the switch.

Magnetic field completely collapsed.

FIGURE 9-23 Self-induction is caused by the changing size of magnetic field in a coil of wire. Lines of force from a contracting magnetic field move rapidly across the conductors. When current to a coil is turned-off, a large spark is observed at the switch due to self-induced voltage.

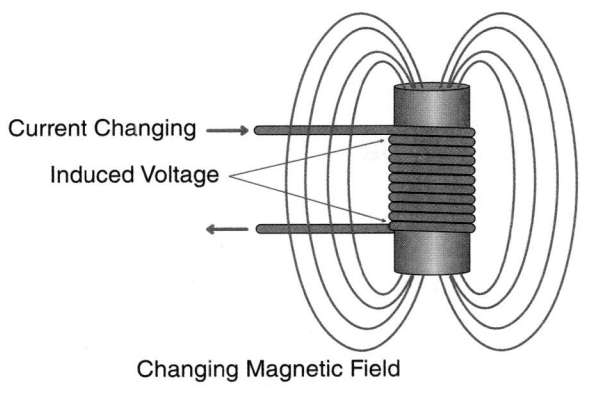

FIGURE 9-24 The speed of magnetic field collapse and the number or mass of conductors determine self-induced voltage. Induced voltage is always much higher than the voltage initially producing the magnetic field.

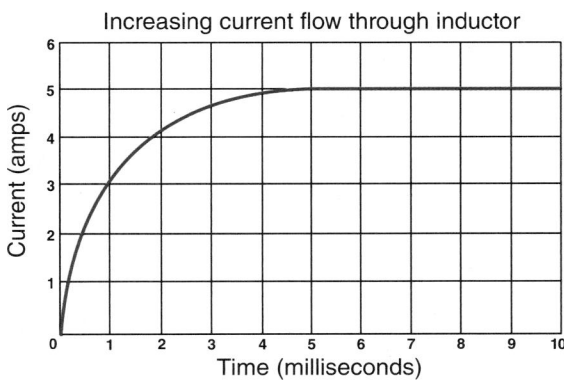

FIGURE 9-25 Increasing current flow through an inductor. Initially, the current rises dramatically, but over time levels off.

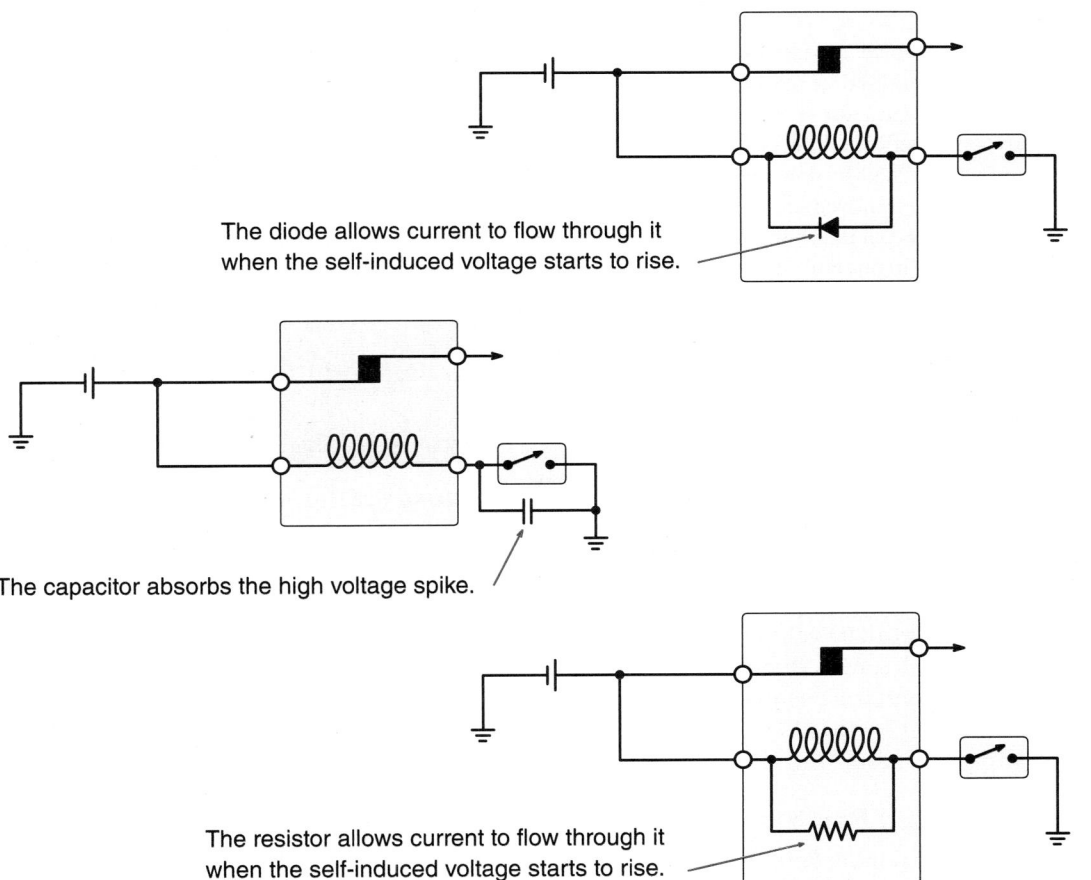

FIGURE 9-26 Self-induction produces a voltage spike, which can damage sensitive electrical components connected to the same circuit. Resistors, diodes, and capacitors are commonly used to suppress voltage spikes.

The current that is induced when the magnetic field collapses after a circuit is opened can have much higher voltage than the voltage in the closed circuit. The level of induced current depends on the number of conductors that are cut by the collapsing magnetic field, and the speed at which the field collapses, which is faster than the speed the magnetic field is first established due to inductive resistance.

Any coil of wire in an electrical system can produce hundreds, if not thousands, of volts when it is de-energized.

The degree of self-induction of any coil is determined primarily by the number of turns of wire, their spacing, and the type of material used in the core of the coil. Suppression of the destructive voltage spikes from any magnetic coil on a vehicle is very important. This can be accomplished using diodes, capacitors, resistors, or induction coils. Without suppression, the voltage spike can travel back in a circuit to its source and damage any sensitive electronic component (**FIGURE 9-26**).

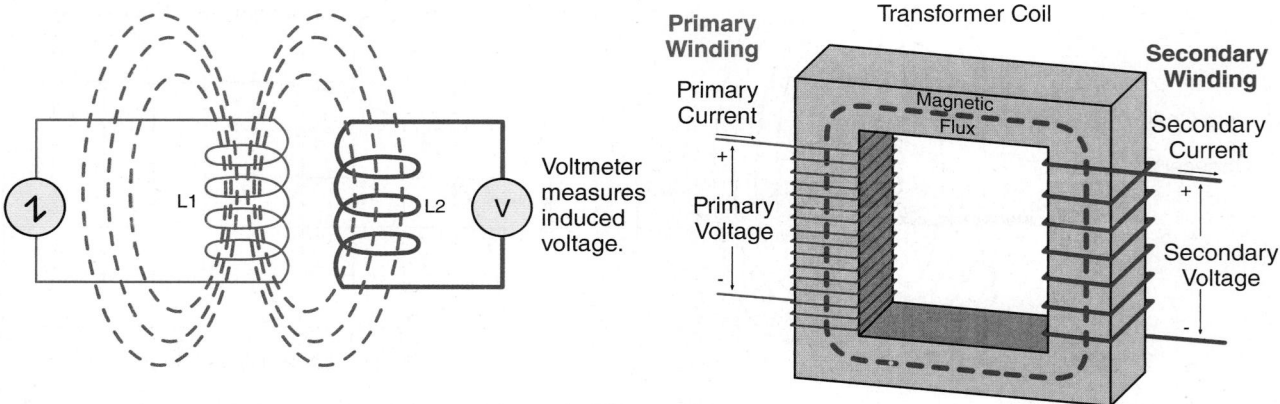

FIGURE 9-27 Mutual induction takes place when a magnetic field induces current in another conductor.

Mutual Induction

Whereas self-induction involves producing current flow in a single coil of wire, mutual induction involves two or more coils or conductors. Only one conductor or coil with current flow is required to produce a magnetic field necessary for mutual induction. A changing magnetic field in one energized conductor or coil is then used to produce a movement of electrons in another conductor or coil (**FIGURE 9-27**). If a changing magnetic flux created by varying current flow in one coil cuts across the windings of a second coil, current is induced in the second coil. For example, if two conductors are adjacent to one another and one conductor has either current switched on or off, the expanding or collapsing magnetic field induces current in the adjacent conductor.

Step-up transformers and **step-down transformers** use principles of mutual induction to increase or decrease voltage through one of two coils. The ratio of turns between a **primary winding,** which is supplied current, and the **secondary winding,** where current is induced, determines what voltage is induced in the secondary winding or coil. For example, a coil with a 100:1 turn ratio supplying 12 volts in the primary coil increases that voltage to 1,200 volts in the secondary coil. Injector drive modules and circuits driving injectors in older ECU's often use step-up transformers to increase the voltage in a 12-volt system to between 75 and 110 volts to energize injectors (**FIGURE 9-28**).

Induction and Twisted Pair Wires

The phenomenon of mutual induction explains why onboard network data bus wires use a twisted pair of wires to carry low-voltage serial data. Twisting the wires helps to reduce the signal noise caused primarily by mutual induction with other current-carrying conductors. Signal noise, which is also called cross talk, interferes with the transfer of serial data in network data bus wiring. Serial data is the digital language electronic modules use to talk and listen to one another. The wire pair is like the telephone line carrying the information. Any voltage induced in these wires can interfere with communication and potentially be erroneously processed as valid data or cause increased signal errors, leading to longer communication time.

FIGURE 9-28 The injector drive module powering **H**ydraulically **A**ctuated **E**lectronically controlled, **U**nit **I**njector (HEUI) fuel system uses step-up transformers to energize injectors. **A.** Injector current storage capacitor (2). **B.** Inductors—step-up transformers (2).

By twisting the wires, any current induced by a magnetic field is canceled in every loop or twist of the next. When under the influence of a magnetic field creating mutual inductance, every twist in a wire pair is induced with either a positive or negative voltage signal, which interferes with the transmission of an otherwise steady induced voltage to cancel it out at the end of the conductor. Twisting the wires one to two times per cm (approximately five turns per inch) effectively cancels the induced current by using the voltage induced in each loop or twist in front or behind it.

Enclosing the twisted wire pair in a metal foil further helps reduce signal interference. Magnetic fields and low-frequency radio waves that can also induce current in conductors are stopped by the low magnetic reluctance of the metal foil. The magnetic field instead conducts and travels along the foil or shielding layer, inducing current flow in the foil much easier than in a signal wire beneath the foil. If the shielding foil is connected to a chassis ground at one end, the electrical charge can easily be absorbed by the ground, allowing it to drain from

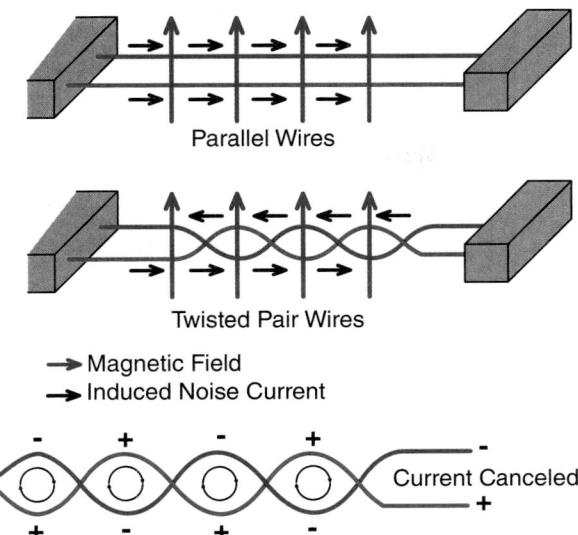

FIGURE 9-29 Twisting voltage-sensitive wiring helps cancel electromagnetic interference caused by mutual induction. A magnetic field induces current flow in the opposite direction of each loop of twisted pairs and cancels the induced signal.

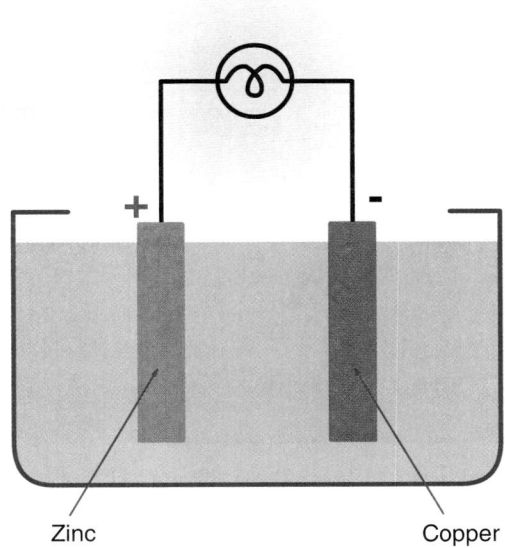

FIGURE 9-30 A galvanic reaction is produced when two dissimilar metals are immersed in an electrolyte.

the foil. Induction happens in the metal foil because magnetic lines of force and electromagnetic waves find an easier pathway through the low-reluctance foil than penetrating through high-reluctance air. It is important to remember when servicing shielded conductors that the ground wire connected to the foil is connected at only one end and not both. If a ground wire is connected to both ends, the foil can conduct more current and actually cause mutual induction in the wires it is insulating. Current flow through a shielding foil is especially high if the voltage difference between two ground points is large due to the distance spanned by the shielded wire (**FIGURE 9-29**).

Electrochemisty—Electricity from Chemistry

LO 9-3 Identify and describe principles of electrochemistry.

Producing electricity from chemical reactions is commonly done with galvanic reactions. Galvanic reactions take place when two dissimilar metals are placed in an electrolyte (**FIGURE 9-30**). An electrolyte is any liquid that conducts electric current. For example, pure water does not conduct current. Tap water, however, often contains various minerals and chlorine, and those impurities enable the conduction of current. Water-containing salt, acids, or alkaline (soapy) solutions are even better conductors of electricity.

Dissimilar metals form electrodes, which become elements of a galvanic cell forming the positive and negative poles. Chemical action between the electrolyte and electrodes strips or pushes electrons from one metal electrode and adds electrons to another electrode, which produces galvanic cell polarity.

Galvanic reactions are observed in many places. Corrosion is one of the most common examples of a galvanic reaction. For

example, the cooling system of an engine contains water, an electrolyte, and dissimilar metals, such as copper injector tubes, cast iron blocks, aluminum water pump housings, etc., forming potential electrodes. Some metals losing electrons disintegrate (corrode); other metals can remain unaffected. To prevent engine corrosion, additives in antifreeze minimize the transfer of electrons through the coolant between metals. When an aluminum disc wheel is installed against a steel disc one, an electrically insulating Mylar or nylon gasket is placed between them to minimize corrosion from galvanic reactions. If no electrical insulator is used, corrosion caused by galvanic reaction accelerates the disintegration of aluminum. Similarly, aluminum side rails on trailer bodies must be insulated from steel cross members to prevent premature corrosion. Dielectric grease, which is an electrical insulator, protects metals, such as exposed electrical terminals, from exposure to electrolytes, such as road spray or rain water.

Modern batteries use a variety of chemistries to produce electrical power from chemical reactions. Inside the lead-acid battery is the most recognizable of all galvanic reactions. The material from which the electrodes are made and the type of electrolyte determine the voltage potential of a battery. The area of electrodes determines the capacity or amperage of a battery (**FIGURE 9-31**).

Fuel Cells

Another type of electrochemical device producing electricity is a **fuel cell**, which combines hydrogen and oxygen to produce electricity and water. Unlike a battery, a fuel cell does not require recharging, but produces energy in the form of electricity and heat as long as the electrodes are supplied a steady amount of hydrogen and oxygen (**FIGURE 9-32**).

Dozens of varieties of fuel cells exist, but they all fundamentally work in the same manner. Like batteries, fuel cells consist of

FIGURE 9-31 The area of electrodes determines the capacity of a battery.

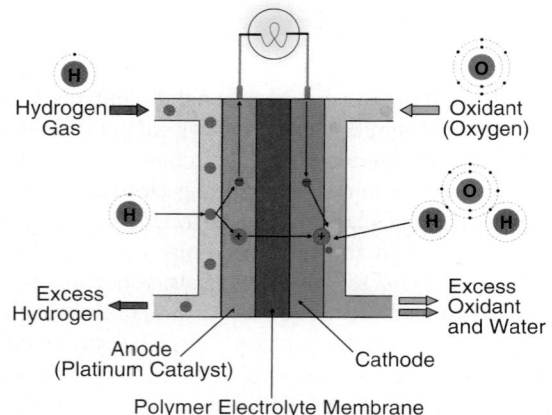

FIGURE 9-32 Process of converting hydrogen and oxygen in a fuel cell into electricity, heat, CO_2, heat, and water.

three sections—the positive and negative plates and a plate separator called the electrolytic membrane. Two chemical reactions occur between three different sections—the negative, positive, and fuel cell membrane—creating water, heat, and electricity.

As hydrogen and oxygen combine, an electron transfer must take place between the gases to combine the elements that form water. An electron from the hydrogen gas at the negative plate essentially travels through the electrical load connected to

FIGURE 9-33 A specialized grease for electrical terminals used to coat terminals exposed to outside elements.

the fuel cell to reach the positive plate, where oxygen is. Because oxygen is deficient in electrons in its outer valance shell, it readily attracts the electron donated by the hydrogen atom.

To supply oxygen and hydrogen to a fuel cell, the raw gases must be supplied or it must operate with a fuel reformer. A reformer generates the necessary gases by removing hydrogen from diesel fuel, natural gas, methanol, or gasoline. Oxygen is sourced from the atmosphere. The appeal of fuel cells lies in their use of chemistry, and not combustion, to produce electrical energy. Therefore, fuel cells themselves emit zero noxious emissions.

Voltage from a single cell is approximately 0.7 volts, so fuel cells are connected in a series to increase output voltage. More than a dozen prototype electric trucks powered by hydrogen fuel cells are available from Nikola and a Toyota-Paccar partnership. Electric traction motors are supplied current from fuel cells enabling travel ranges and fueling time equal to diesels.

▶ **TECHNICIAN TIP**

Galvanic reactions can quickly corrode exposed wiring. When repairing wire terminals and conductors exposed to outside elements, it is not a good practice to use terminals made of different materials, or even join wiring made from different metals. To minimize contact with electrolytes, always solder connections and use shrink tube to protect the joint from water intrusion. Covering a wiring splice with shrink tube and then wrapping it with tape after soldering helps protect the connection from abrasion and mechanical strain. Exposed wire terminals should always be covered with a dielectric grease (electrically non-conduction silicone grease) or suitable corrosion inhibitor, such as rust-proofing corrosion inhibitors (**FIGURE 9-33**). Sealing exposed connections prevents galvanic reactions from quickly corroding connections.

Wrap-Up

Ready for Review

▶ Friction, heat, chemicals, light, pressure, and magnetic induction are all sources of electricity. Each of these types of energy can move electrons so they can do work.

▶ Static electricity can be induced by rubbing or separating two materials on opposite sides of the triboelectric series. During this process, one material loses electrons to the other to create positive and negative static (stationary) charges.

- If two different metals are joined and heated, a small electrical current can be generated. This system is a thermoelectric source of energy.
- Galvanic reactions producing electricity are the result of two dissimilar metals being immersed in an electrical conductive liquid called an electrolyte.
- Fuel cells are a type of electrochemical device that combines hydrogen and oxygen to produce water and, in the process, it produces electricity and heat.
- The three basic elements to a fuel cell are the anode, the cathode, and the electrolytic membrane.
- Photovoltaic energy is produced from converting light to electricity. Solar cells are an example of photovoltaic energy.
- The Piezoelectric effect creates electricity when crystals of certain materials, such as quartz, are subjected to mechanical stress, such as bending or squeezing.
- Piezoelectric materials have a polarity and can expand or contract when current passes through them.
- Electricity can also create magnetic effects, referred to as electromagnetism. These magnetic forces can be used to create mechanical movement, such as in a relay or electric motor.
- Magnetic induction involves moving a conductor across a magnetic field to induce current flow. Similarly, magnetic induction can take place by moving a magnetic field across a conductor, such as a stationary coil of wire.
- Magnetic field strength of an electromagnet is calculated by multiplying the amperage times the number of turns in the wire. The units of magnetic field strength are Amp-turns.
- Magnetic fields made from coils of wire having thicker wire but fewer turns conduct more amperage, remain stronger, and are less sensitive to voltage drop than coils made from thinner wire with more turns having the same amp-turn strength.
- Continuous duty relays use magnetic coils made from thinner wire with more turns than intermittent duty relays with fewer turns and thicker wire.
- If continuous duty relays are used in place of intermittent duty relays, they will chatter when voltage drops such as when the starter motor cranks an engine. Intermittent duty relays will overheat and quickly burn-out when used in place of continuous duty relays.
- Mutual induction involves two coils or conductors with a changing magnetic field in one producing a movement of electrons in the other. Step-up and step-down transformers use mutual induction, plus a turn ratio difference between the primary and secondary coil windings.
- Self-induction is observed in a current-carrying coil when the current in the wire is changing. Expanding or collapsing a magnetic field self-induces current flow in the coil. In self-induction, no separate magnetic field, such as a permanent magnet or separate electromagnet, is used.
- Self-induction in electromagnetic coils produces potentially damaging high voltage spikes and must be suppressed with diodes, resistors, capacitors, and induction coils.
- Twisting the data bus wire lines helps to reduce the signal noise from electromagnetic interference produced from mutual induction. Electromagnetic interference, is cancelled by loops in front or behind the loop with induced current.

Key Terms

electromagnet A conductor wound into a coil that produces a magnetic field when current flows through it.

electromagnetic induction The production of an electrical current in a conductor when it moves through a magnetic field or a magnetic field moves past it.

fuel cell An electrochemical device that combines hydrogen and oxygen to produce electricity, heat, and water.

magnetism A fundamental force that can be used push or pull electrons.

photovoltaic (PV) effect The conversion of light into electricity.

Piezoelectric effect A type of electricity produced by bending or squeezing a unique type of quartz crystal.

primary winding The electromagnetic coil of wire which creates the magnetic field in a step-up or step-down transformer.

secondary winding The coil of wire in which voltage is induced through mutual induction in a step-up or step-down transformer.

step-down transformer A transformer used to reduce primary coil voltage in the secondary coil. A battery charger would use a step-down transformer to change 120 volts (AC) into 12 volts (AC).

step-up transformer A transformer used to increase the voltage from a primary coils lower input voltage.

thermocouple A thermoelectric device consisting of two dissimilar metals that produce voltage when heated.

Review Questions

1. Which one of the following energy sources is used by a "pyrometer" to move electrons?
   a. Friction
   b. Heat
   c. Magnetism
   d. Induction
2. Which of the following energy sources moves the electrons in the conductors of an alternator?
   a. Rotational
   b. Friction
   c. Magnetic
   d. Dynamic
3. Which of the following types of induction can cause a large spark after a coil of wire is disconnected from a power source?
   a. Self-induction
   b. Mutual induction
   c. Cross-talk induction
   d. Magnetic reluctance

4. Which of the following electromagnets has a stronger magnetic field?
   a. One wound with 100 turns of wire and 1 amp of current
   b. One wound with 750 turns of wire and 0.1 amp of current
   c. One wound with 500 turns of wire and 0.1 amps of current
   d. One wound with 75 turns of wire with 1.5 amps of current

5. Which of the following sources of energy is used to produce static electrical charge?
   a. Heat
   b. Light
   c. Friction
   d. Pressure

6. Which of the following devices uses galvanic reactions to produce electric current?
   a. Alternators
   b. Batteries
   c. Solar cells
   d. Piezoelectric crystals

7. Why should fuel tankers and tankers carrying powders (e.g., cement, flour) be grounded before removing product?
   a. To add missing electrons to the tanker body
   b. To remove excess electrons from a tanker body
   c. To minimize the likelihood of a spark when the product is transferred
   d. To prevent generating electric current from mutual induction

8. When handling sensitive electronic parts, which is the best practice a technician should follow to prevent electrostatic damage?
   a. Ground the truck-bus chassis
   b. Remove electronic parts wrapped in mylar packaging as soon as possible
   c. Wear a copper wrist bracelet
   d. Momentarily touch a metal door-handle or chassis part before handling parts

9. Which of the following best describes what a material with high "reluctance" is most capable of doing?
   a. Passing electric current
   b. Conducting magnetic fields
   c. Resisting conduction by magnetic fields
   d. Resisting electric current

10. Which induction principle does a transformer use to change voltage?
    a. Self-induction
    b. Electromagnetic induction
    c. Mutual induction
    d. Reactive inductance

ASE Technician A/Technician B Style Questions

1. Technician A says electric charges are produced when two different materials are separated. Technician B says static electricity is another name given to triboelectricity because objects can develop stationary high voltage charges from friction. Who is correct?
   a. Technician A
   b. Technician B
   c. Both Technician A and Technician B
   d. Neither Technician A nor Technician B

2. Technician A says solar cells that can produce electricity are widely used in commercial vehicle applications. Technician B says commercially available cells are used as trickle chargers for batteries. Who is correct?
   a. Technician A
   b. Technician B
   c. Both Technician A and Technician B
   d. Neither Technician A nor Technician B

3. Technician A says thermoelectric devices (TEDs) are solid-state heat pumps formed from several layers of semiconductor materials. Technician B says TEDs are used for cooling or heating small areas, including seats, steering wheels, cup-holders, or beverage storage compartments. Who is correct?
   a. Technician A
   b. Technician B
   c. Both Technician A and Technician B
   d. Neither Technician A nor Technician B

4. Technician A says one of the most common ways electricity is produced in a heavy-duty vehicle is through the use of the energy found in magnetic fields. Technician B says magnetism is the force that attracts or repels electric charges. Who is correct?
   a. Technician A
   b. Technician B
   c. Both Technician A and Technician B
   d. Neither Technician A nor Technician B

5. Technician A says that piezoceramic injectors can often operate faster than injectors with electromagnetic actuators. Technician B says magnetic fields can build up faster in a piezoceramic actuator. Who is correct?
   a. Technician A
   b. Technician B
   c. Both Technician A and Technician B
   d. Neither Technician A nor Technician B

6. Technician A says the principle of producing electrical current flow using electromagnets is known as electromagnetic induction. Technician B says alternators, generators, and speed sensors use this electrical principle to produce electrical current. Who is correct?
   a. Technician A
   b. Technician B
   c. Both Technician A and Technician B
   d. Neither Technician A nor Technician B

7. Technician A says the current that is induced when the magnetic field of a wire coil collapses after a circuit is opened has a much lower voltage than the voltage in the closed circuit. Technician B says any coil of wire in an electrical system can produce hundreds of volts when it is de-energized. Who is correct?

a. Technician A
b. Technician B
c. Both Technician A and Technician B
d. Neither Technician A nor Technician B

8. Technician A says suppression of the voltage spike from magnetic coils is accomplished using diodes, capacitors, resistors, or induction coils. Technician B says without suppression, the voltage spike can travel to other circuits connected to the coil damaging sensitive electronic components. Who is correct?
a. Technician A
b. Technician B
c. Both Technician A and Technician B
d. Neither Technician A nor Technician B

9. Technician A says the primary winding is where current is induced in a step-up transformer. Technician B says the secondary winding is supplied current to step-down voltage. Who is correct?
a. Technician A
b. Technician B
c. Both Technician A and Technician B
d. Neither Technician A nor Technician B

10. Technician A says dozens of varieties of fuel cells exist, but they all fundamentally work in the same manner. Technician B says like a battery, a fuel cell requires recharging. Who is correct?
a. Technician A
b. Technician B
c. Both Technician A and Technician B
d. Neither Technician A nor Technician B

Basic Electrical Circuits

Learning Objectives

After reading this chapter, you will be able to:

- **LO 10-1** Define, describe, and classify circuits according to arrangement of current paths.
- **LO 10-2** Describe and mathematically predict the relationship between voltage amperage, power, and resistance in electrical circuits.

- **LO 10-3** Describe and classify circuits according to common failure modes.
- **LO 10-4** Identify the purpose and types of circuit protection devices used in commercial vehicle electrical systems.
- **LO 10-5** Identify and explain the methods used to test the operation of circuit protection devices.

You Are the Technician

An intercity bus has arrived at your shop with the request to install several wave inverters to enable bus passengers to charge cell phones and tablets and use laptop computers. To do this, the bus company wants you to supply 120-volts AC to a receptacle with one receptacle for each of the 36 rows of seats. Upon inspection, you find that the bus is equipped with a split-voltage electrical system with the electrical system accessories, such as lighting, windshield wipers, and horn, using 12 volts, but a 24-volt alternator is used to charge the batteries for the 24-volt starter motor. An isolated ground is used to separate the bus, which uses 12 volts for all lights and accessories outside the engine compartment. When you ask the bus company representative what amount of amperage the company wants to supply for each receptacle, the representative asks you to make a recommendation.

After researching the problem, you learn that the heaviest power users would be laptops consuming 3–5 amps to charge a dead battery. As you prepare quotes and recommendations for supplying DC-AC converters, wiring them, and providing circuit protection to the inverters, you need to consider the following:

1. What would be the maximum wattage required for the inverter if one inverter is supplying power to two rows of seats? Assume there is no resistive voltage drop in circuits, resistive heating, or other losses of electrical energy.
2. What would be the minimum fuse rating for each of the inverters using a single positive conductor if they were supplied with either 12 or 24 volts?
3. What would be the minimum size of the conductors required if the inverters were connected to either 12- or 24-volt power supply?

Introduction

Circuits are pathways made by electrical conductors that enable the flow of electrons. A variety of classifications are used to identify circuit configurations and failures. It is very important for technicians to understand how circuits are identified according to the way they are constructed. With that knowledge, a technician can properly analyze electrical problems, use correct diagnostic procedures with test instruments, and, of course, make accurate recommendations for repair, rather than guess at what may be wrong.

As shown in **FIGURE 10-1**, circuits consist of the following basic parts:

- Power source—in the form of a battery or alternator
- Conductors—paths for electricity (e.g., wiring, printed circuits, chassis frame, etc.)
- Loads—the working devices that convert electrical energy into some other form of energy. Examples of loads are lights, motors, radio, electronic control units, and more.
- Control—a device, such as a switch, that directs the flow of electrons though the circuit

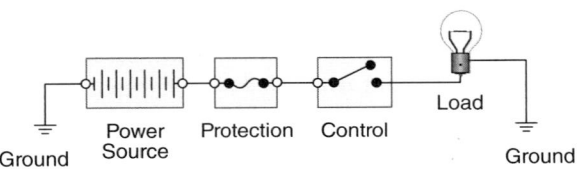

FIGURE 10-1 Minimum elements of a circuit include a power supply, circuit protection, circuit control, and a resistive load.

- Safety/circuit protection devices—fuses, circuit breakers, and virtual fuses, which protect the electrical system components and wiring by interrupting the flow of current if the current flow becomes excessive

Current Flow in Circuits

LO 10-1 Define, describe, and classify circuits according to arrangement of current paths.

Electrons making up current flow are not magically created by the circuit or power source. Only the electrons found in the conductors of a circuit move in a circuit. That means only the electrons already present in conductors, electrolyte, or current-carrying devices of the circuit are put in motion. An analogy for an electrical circuit is a closed hydraulic system using a water pump shows that only electrons already present in the circuit are flowing (**FIGURE 10-2**). Consider water that is pulled from the reservoir and put into motion by a pump. Water pressure and volume determine how much power or wattage the system has. A motor converts the energy of moving water into mechanical energy. Eventually, the water pushed out of the water pump outlet returns to its inlet to maintain the flow. In the same way, electrons are pulled and pushed though conductors and the loads in electrical circuits The negative terminal pushes electrons using electrostatic forces of repulsion, and the positive terminal pulls electrons by forces of electrostatic attraction. For example, the alternator is a device corresponding to the water pump. The battery is represented as a hydraulic accumulator that stores water under pressure by compressing a spring-loaded diaphragm. When the water pump, or in the case of an

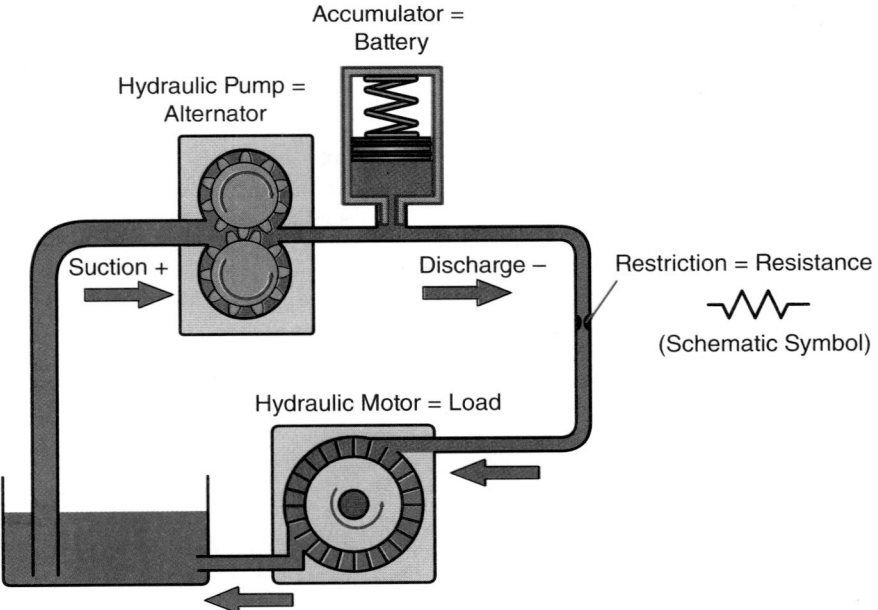

FIGURE 10-2 Current flow in a circuit is like a closed hydraulic system. Just as no new water is added in this hydraulic system, the conductors in any circuit are the only source of electrons. Loads use the energy in the flowing water and convert it to another form, such as motion, sound, light, or heat.

electrical system—the alternator, is not driven, stored energy in the accumulator temporarily supplies energy.

Resistance

Resistance refers to the force in a circuit that impedes or slows the transfer of electrons from one atom to the next. Explained another way, resistance is like electrical friction. Resistance lowers both voltage and amperage in a circuit in proportion to the amount of resistance. Electrical loads appear resistive because they convert energy in moving electrons into another form of energy. Ohm's law mathematically describes the electrical relationship between voltage amperage and resistance. Ohm's law is discussed in greater detail in the section Ohm's Law.

> ▶ TECHNICIAN TIP
>
> Technicians rarely need to use an electrical formula to diagnose and repair a problem on the shop floor. And most instructors would agree that mathematical calculations are rarely used in the average repair facility. So, the question that naturally follows this observation is: What is the point of learning formulas or performing calculations while learning about electrical systems? It is simply this—mathematics is another language that is effective in describing the behavior of electricity. Many learners who have struggled to understand electrical concepts have quickly grasped important insights while performing calculations using formulas based on electrical laws. Math is often a shortcut to better comprehension of electrical subject matter.

Circuit Classification

Circuits found in commercial vehicles are classified in three ways:

1. Operational state—open or closed (also sleeping or hibernating in onboard networks)
2. Arrangement of current pathways—simple, parallel, series, combination
3. Failure mode—grounded, shorted, open, resistive, and intermittent circuit malfunctions

Operational State

Open and closed are the terms used to describe whether current is flowing through a circuit. An open circuit's electrical pathway is broken or unconnected (**FIGURE 10-3A**). This means current cannot flow because there is an open gap preventing flow between two points of the circuit. Current cannot move across the opening and continue flowing along its intended path until the opening is closed.

A closed circuit has a complete electrical pathway for current to flow between the negative and positive terminal, as shown in **FIGURE 10-3B**. Sleep or hibernation mode is a related term given to electronic control modules to describe a state where current flow is reduced after the ignition key is switched off or after a predetermined length of time has elapsed. Sleep mode reduces unnecessary and prolonged high current drains from the battery.

Circuit Arrangement

Electric circuits are also classified according to the way electric components and loads are connected. Circuits on commercial vehicles are made from these types of arrangements:

- Simple
- Series
- Parallel
- Series-parallel, also called combination circuits

Simple circuits are circuits that have only two parts: a power supply and a load. These are not used in commercial vehicles. This section, therefore, concentrates on series, parallel, and combination circuit arrangements.

Series Circuits

Series circuits are the most common type of circuit used in commercial vehicles. In a **series circuit**, there are multiple loads and other devices, but only one path for current to flow (**FIGURE 10-4**). Each device is connected like a chain, with all current flowing through one device or load after another. Again, the defining characteristic of a series circuit is that only one single pathway exists for current to flow. The conductors, circuit protection device, loads, and source current are connected, one after the other, allowing current to move through a single pathway. If any part of the circuit is opened, such as when a light bulb burns out in a lighting circuit, all current flow through the circuit stops.

The following features characterize series circuits:

- Only one single pathway exists for current to flow.
- The resistance of each load or device may vary, but the amount of current flowing through each is the same.

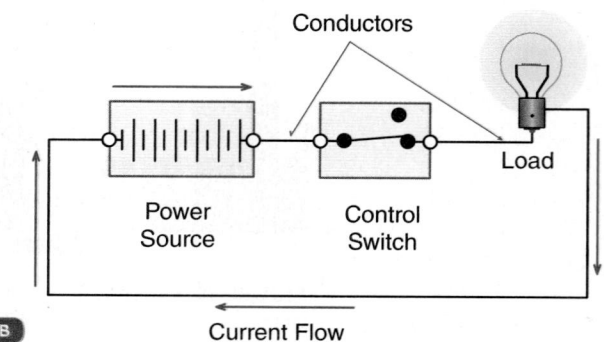

FIGURE 10-3 A. An open circuit has a broken electrical pathway. **B.** Closing the switch completes the electrical pathway.

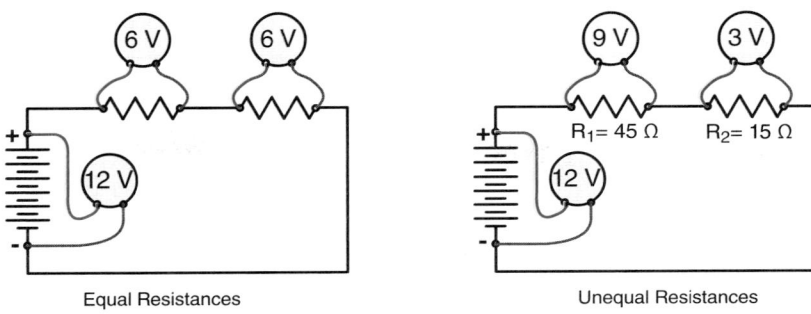

Equal Resistances

Unequal Resistances

FIGURE 10-4 Observations for series circuits.

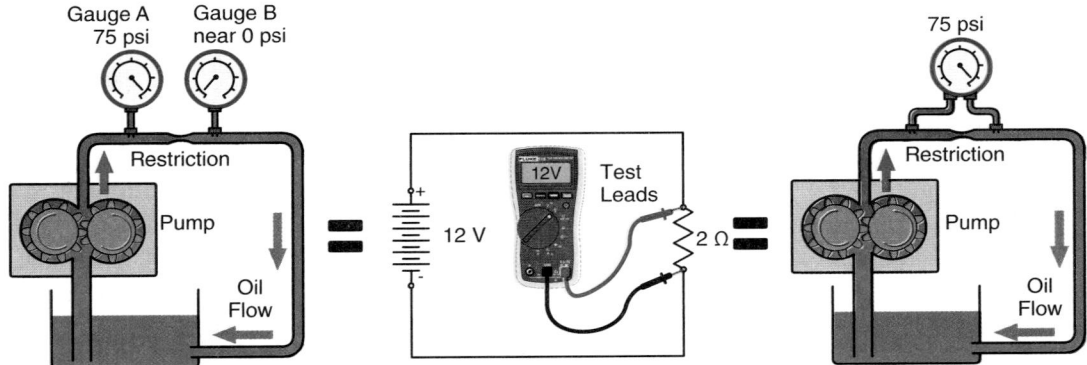

FIGURE 10-5 Voltage drop is the loss or lowering of voltage or electron pressure as current passes through each circuit load. A voltmeter is used to measure the drop. In a sense, voltmeters measure a circuit's electron pressure differential. Note that adding all voltage drops together equals the supply or source voltage.

The sum of the voltage drop across all loads is equal to the source voltage. This means all the voltage is used up pushing electrons through the loads. Understanding this simple idea is vital to understanding and solving the most commonly encountered electrical problems. The relationship between source voltage and the total voltage drops is referred to as **Kirchhoff's law** and is illustrated in **FIGURE 10-5**. Naturally, the amount of voltage dropped across each of the loads changes, according to the resistance of each device. However, when the amount of each voltage drop in a circuit is added together, it equals the voltage supplying a circuit.

- At any given point in the circuit, the amperage is the same in a series circuit.
- The total circuit resistance is equal to the sum of each individual resistance.

Most vehicle circuits are series circuits because switches, terminals, circuit protection, loads, cables, etc., are common circuit components that operate when connected in series (**FIGURE 10-6**). It is useful to remember this because identifying problems in series circuits is a matter of identifying unexpected voltage drops to locate poor connections and deteriorated or defective components (**FIGURE 10-7**). Connections should have little or no measurable voltage drop if they are properly working. Only the loads in the circuit should be observed to drop the most voltage when a voltmeter is connected on either side of the

load. That means when a device is operating, a positive lead of the voltmeter connected to the most positive side of the load, or the + side, and the negative lead to the opposite, the meter displays a voltage reading corresponding to the voltage drop. Ground connections, switches, and circuit protection devices have almost no measurable voltage drop in a correctly functioning and properly constructed circuit.

A starter cable voltage-loss test is one example of a test procedure using series circuit electrical principles to locate problems causing hard starting. A starter motor circuit is an example of a series circuit. Current passes from chassis ground, through the brushes, and field coils of the motor before entering the solenoid and then back to the battery through the starter positive cable. An open brush or coil prevents the starter motor from turning and so will a loose or corroded cable because it is a series circuit. By carefully selecting the correct points in a circuit to measure voltage drop, excessively resistive points in a circuit are identified. This test is always performed when the starter is cranking or high current flow is present in the circuit.

Parallel Circuits

A more complex circuit than a series circuit arrangement is a **parallel circuit**. In a parallel circuit, there are multiple pathways for current flow, and all components are connected directly to the voltage supply. On paper, the schematic diagram

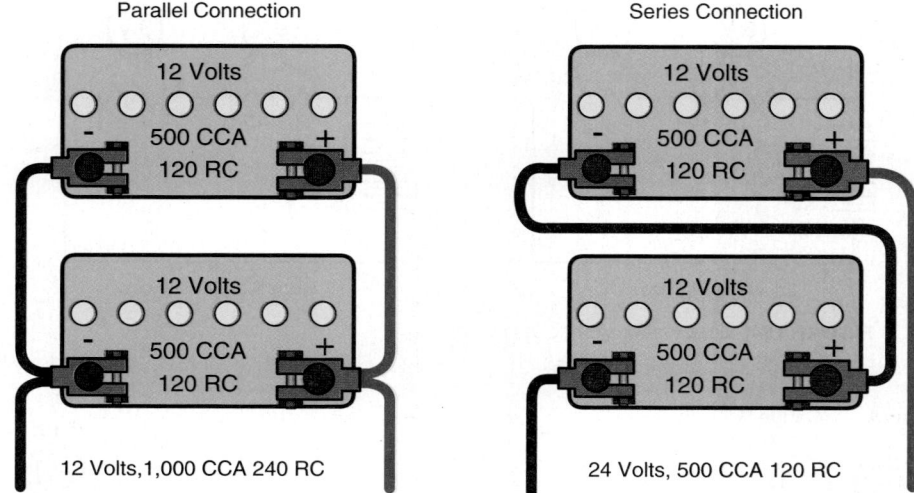

Parallel Connection

Series Connection

FIGURE 10-6 Connecting batteries in series increases voltage by addition. Available amperage or capacity remains the same.

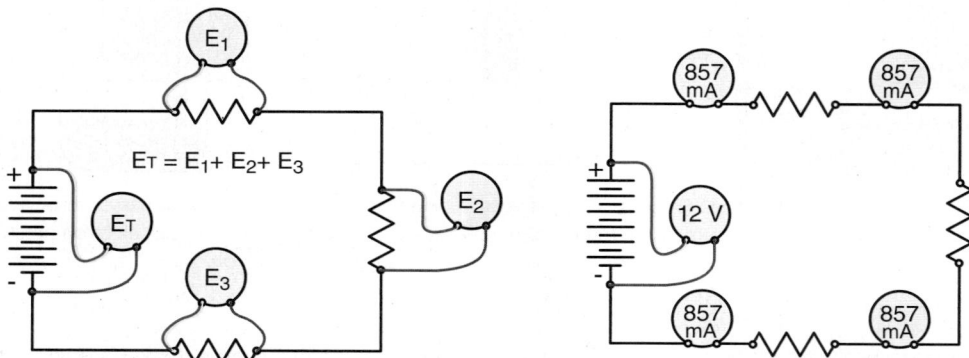

$$E_T = E_1 + E_2 + E_3$$

FIGURE 10-7 Understanding the behavior of voltage, amperage, and resistance in a series circuit. With each resistance, the voltage (electron pressure) drops. The voltage drop is cumulative and distributed across all the loads. Amperage (volume of electron flow) in the circuit is dependent on the total of circuit resistances. The amperage remains constant anywhere it is measured in the circuit.

of a parallel circuit resembles a ladder placed on its side. The ladder sides are sources of voltage—the top is positive, and the bottom is negative. The ladder rungs are called circuit branches. Because all branches connect to the same positive and negative current source, amperage in each branch can be different, depending on the branches' resistance. Adding the amperage flowing through each branch determines total amperage in the circuit (**FIGURE 10-8**). Adding loads increases the number of current pathways, which lowers circuit resistance; the total circuit resistance is always less than the smallest resistance in any branch.

In summary, a parallel circuit is characterized by:

- Two or more pathways for the current (**FIGURE 10-9**)
- The voltage supplied to each branch is the same throughout the circuit (**FIGURE 10-10**).
- Amperage flow through each branch depends on the branch resistance; if the resistances in each branch are the same, the amperage is the same in each branch.

FIGURE 10-8 Connecting batteries together in parallel adds available cranking amperage, but voltage stays the same.

- If one branch of the circuit is broken, current continues to flow in the other branches.
- Total circuit resistance is always less than the resistance of the smallest resistor (**FIGURE 10-11**).

Lighting circuits are common examples of parallel circuits. Clearance light or taillight circuits are all connected in parallel with same battery voltage applied to each bulb. Adding more lights creates more pathways for current to flow. This explains why amperage consumed in a parallel circuit increases with every additional load. More pathways reduce circuit resistance and, because resistance determines the amount of amperage passing through a circuit, adding branches increases total circuit amperage (**FIGURE 10-12**).

Combination Circuits

Combination circuits, also called **series-parallel circuits**, use elements of both parallel and series circuits. Typically, the power supply, circuit protection, and control device are in series, but the loads are in parallel. A wiper motor circuit is a common example of this series-parallel or combination circuit. When calculating or measuring voltage, amperage, and resistance, the rules for parallel and series circuits apply to each part of the circuit. That means the circuit must be operationally subdivided into series and parallel circuits, and then calculations can be performed for each type of circuit.

Ohm's Law and Power

LO 10-2 Describe and mathematically predict the relationship between voltage amperage, power, and resistance in electrical circuits.

Ohm's law defines the relationship between current, resistance, and voltage. Ohm's law calculations are seldom used by a technician, but comprehending and applying its

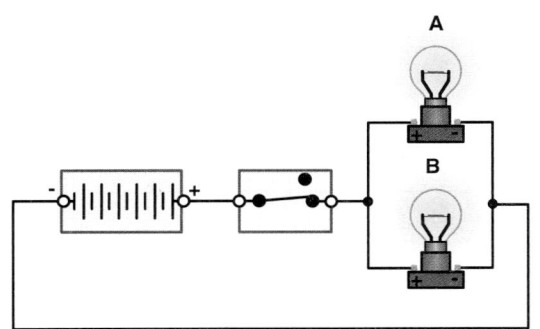

FIGURE 10-9 An example of a parallel circuit. Bulbs **A** and **B** are branches of the circuit.

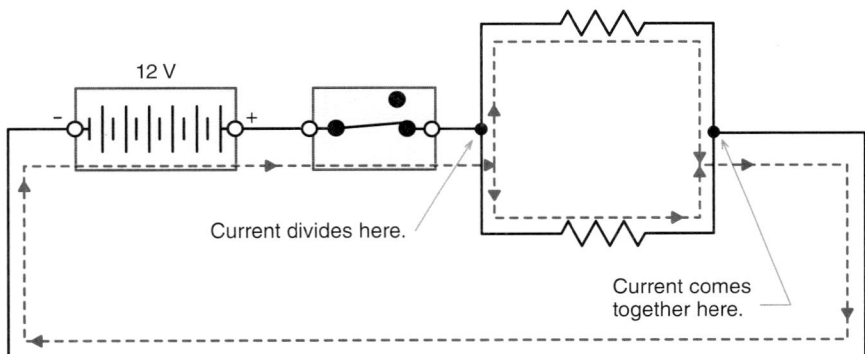

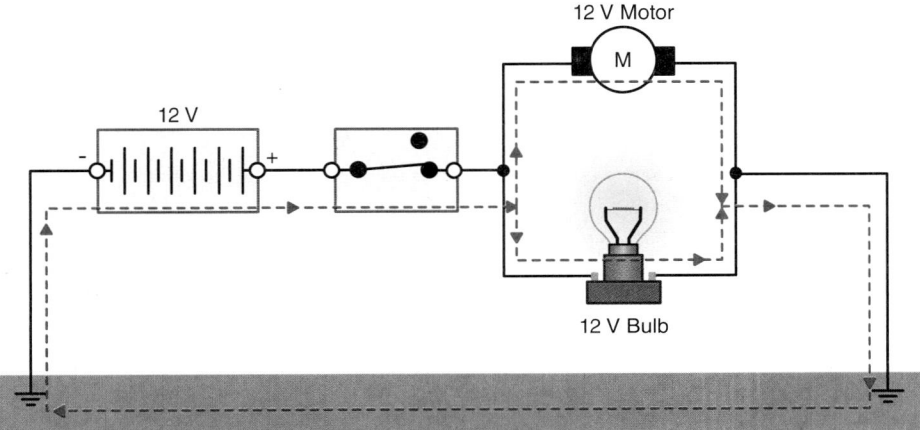

FIGURE 10-10 All loads in a parallel circuit receive the same voltage. The amperage used by each branch varies with the resistance in each branch.

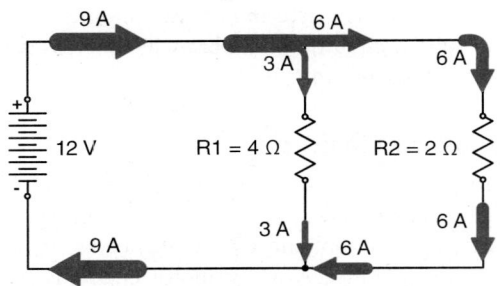

The highest current flow is through the branch with the lowest resistance.

FIGURE 10-11 Amperage passing through each branch of a parallel circuit varies with the resistance.

principles can help a technician better understand how electricity behaves. Working through calculations using Ohm's formula also enhances your intuitive understanding of electricity, which is invaluable when troubleshooting electrical circuits. The tradesperson's triangle in **FIGURE 10-13** is used to help calculate the values of either voltage, amperage, or power. Covering (e.g., with a finger) the unknown value helps determine whether the other two values should be multiplied or divided.

Ohm's law explains in mathematical language the relationship between amperage, voltage, and resistance in a circuit.

$$\text{Voltage} = \text{Amps} \times \text{Resistance}$$

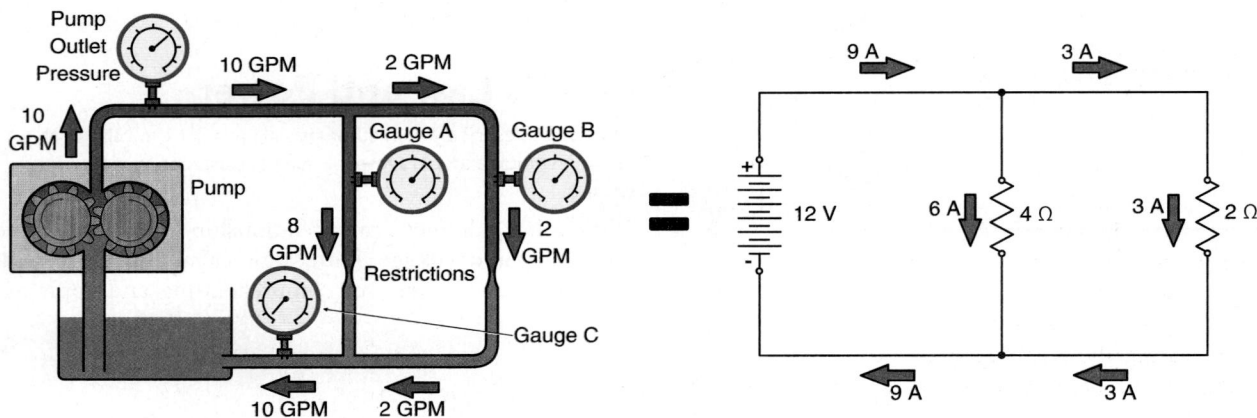

FIGURE 10-12 Comparing a hydraulic model of a parallel circuit with a schematic version. Note the same pressure is applied to all circuit branches and the voltage drops to zero after passing through the loads.

Ohm's Law states: Voltage = Amperage x Resistance

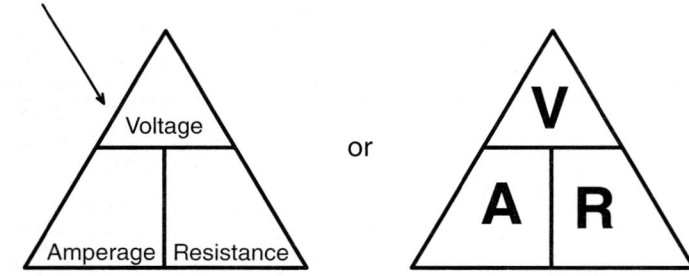

Arrange the variables into a "Tradeperson Triangle"

or

By covering up the unknown it is easy to transpose the formula.

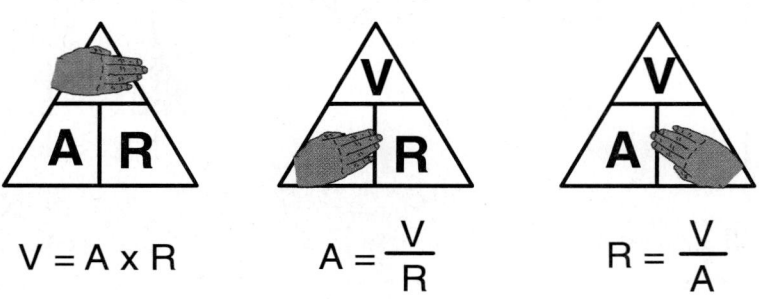

$$V = A \times R \qquad A = \frac{V}{R} \qquad R = \frac{V}{A}$$

FIGURE 10-13 The tradesperson's triangle for calculating power.

Simply stated, one volt is required to push one amp of current through a circuit that has a resistance of one ohm. Ohms (Ω) is the unit used to measure resistance (**FIGURE 10-14**).

One application for Ohm's law is to estimate the voltage drop in a conductor for trailer wiring. All conductors, particularly long ones, have some resistance, so there is a voltage drop between the battery and the lights at the rear of the trailer. The amount of the drop depends on the amperage carried by the circuit and the resistance of the wiring. By plugging in the resistance values for the length and diameter of a conductor along with the amperage consumed by a circuit, the expected voltage drop is estimated. **TABLE 10-1** summarizes recommended wire gauge size required to minimize voltage drop.

Watt's Law

Watt's law, which is related to Ohm's law, explains the relationship between resistance and amperage (**FIGURE 10-15**). Mathematically described, Watt's law is

$$\text{Power (Watts)} = \text{Voltage} \times \text{Amperage}$$

Remember from Joules Law, outlined in Chapter 9, that increasing amperage through a circuit produces proportionally more resistance. Heat is generally an unwanted by-product of resistance. Heat is produced as electron energy is lost due to resistance. Collisions occurring between electrons as they converge at "choke points" or resistive parts of a circuit produce heat. Increasing the amperage in a circuit is something like increasing the number of cars on the highway during rush hour—the greater the number of cars, the slower the traffic. More collisions between electrons take place in a crowded conductor, and electron energy is converted to heat.

This relationship between amperage and resistance explains why a thin wire can carry low amperage current but would burn-up (or at least overheat) if it were carrying excessive amperage. Excessive amperage through terminals and connectors produces heat because they always have a slight amount of resistance that increases as more amperage passes through the conductors. Increased resistance and heating in turn loosens electrical connections due to temperature cycling. Very small amounts of resistance in connections at the battery or in a starter motor circuit, which are undetectable with an ohmmeter, show up as heat when a starter is cranking or when heavy loads are switched on in a vehicle. The most effective way to measure resistances in these circuits is to perform a voltage drop test when the high amperage circuits are operating. Resistance is observed as voltage loss or drop is measured across resistive connections and components.

Advantages of the 24-Volt System

The 24-volt electrical systems used by transit buses, military vehicles, and off-road heavy equipment have several advantages. First, by using higher voltage, less amperage passes through a

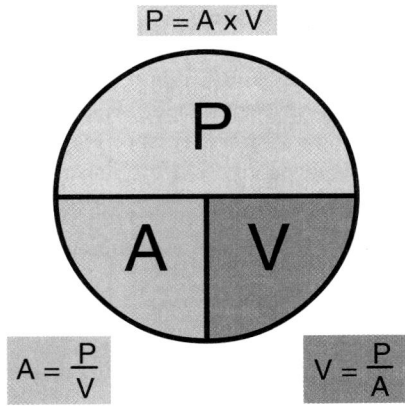

P = A x V

P = Power measured in WATTS
A = Amperes measured in AMPS
V = Electromotive force measured in VOLTS

FIGURE 10-15 The relationship of power, voltage, and amperage according to Watt's law.

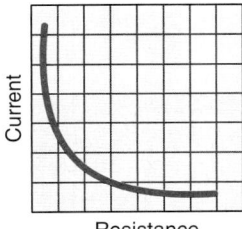 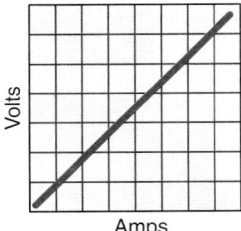

FIGURE 10-14 The relationship between volts, ohms, and amperage in Ohm's law.

TABLE 10-1 Recommended Wire Gauges to Minimize Voltage Drop

Amperage	10-Feet Gauge	20-Feet Gauge	30-Feet Gauge	50-Feet Gauge	100-Feet Gauge
1	18	18	18	18	18
2	18	18	18	18	16
3	18	18	18	16	16
5	18	18	18	14	12
10	18	16	14	12	10
25	16	12	10	8	6
50	12	10	8	6	2

circuit to produce the same amount of power as a 12-volt circuit. For example, a device needing 120 watts of power would use 10 amps at 12 volts (Power = Amperage × Voltage). Electric motors are examples of constant power devices (**FIGURE 10-16**). This means the number of watts they use to maintain speed is the same if circuit voltage and amperage change. For example, a 96-watt blower motor can consume 12 volts and 8 amps (power = volts × amperage). Alternatively, it could also use 9.6 amps at 10 volts or 16 amps at 6 volts. At 24 volts, only 5 amps is required.

Reducing amperage through a circuit not only reduces resistance, but also the diameter needed for conductors. This means voltage drops in the system are reduced as well. More importantly, operating at 24 volts, in comparison to using 12 volts, gives an electrical system greater reliability. That is because heating and loosening of electrical connections are minimized since amperage is lower. Finally, the size of components and the diameter and weight of wiring harnesses can be reduced with increased power supplied by 24 volts (**FIGURE 10-17**).

Power Calculations for 12- and 24-Volt DC Systems

It can be useful for a technician to be able to perform quick estimates of the DC amps required to operate a DC-AC inverter. The following examples use a "rule of thumb" guideline for estimating. A safety factor should be included when selecting wire sizes, inverter capabilities, and circuit protection.

Consider supplying current to a small bunk refrigerator that is rated for 5 amps of power consumption at 120 volts AC. One needs to know how many watts of power is needed 12-volt DC-AC inverter to supply:

$$Power = Voltage \times Amperage$$

$$Wattage = 120 \times 5 \ amps = 600 \ watts$$

A 600-watt minimum inverter rating is required.

The same formula can be used to make basic calculations, such as determining how many DC amps a 12-volt inverter requires to operate a 600-watt electrical load.

$$Power = Voltage \times Amperage$$

$$12 \ watts = 12 \ volts \times 1 \ amp$$

$$600 \ watts/12 \ watts \ per \ amp = 50\text{-}amps \ DC \ at \ 12\text{-}volts.$$

50-amps DC per hour is needed to operate a 120-volt, 600-watt appliance using an inverter.

OR

$$5 \ amps \ at \ 120 \ volts = 10 \times 5 \ amps \ at \ 12 \ volts.$$

$$\frac{5\text{-}amps}{120\text{-}volts \ AC} = \frac{X\text{-}amps}{12\text{-}volts} \qquad X = 50\text{-}amps$$

Finally, depending on the voltage of the system, one may need a completely different circuit amperage. To determine the difference between circuit amperage of a 60-watt light operating at 12 or 24 volts, use this formula:

$$Amperage = \frac{Watts}{Volts}$$

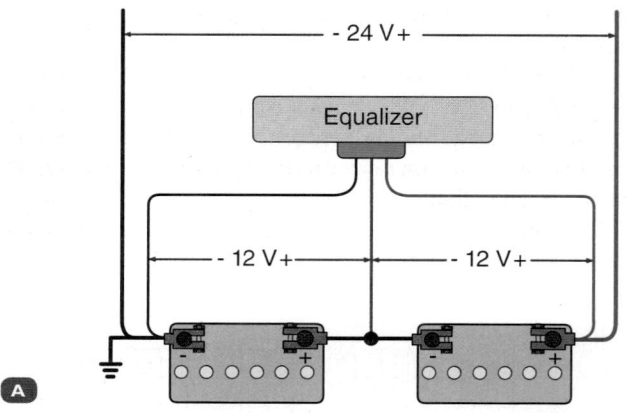

FIGURE 10-17 Transit buses and highway coaches typically use 24-volt systems due to longer runs of wire and the greater use of electrical accessories, such as lighting and ventilation. Voltage drops and electrical system problems due to high current flow are minimized. **A.** A battery equalizer allows voltage to split between 24-volt and 12-volt devices. **B.** A battery equalizer.

FIGURE 10-16 Electric motors are examples of constant power devices.

At 12 volts, the calculation looks like this:

$$\frac{60}{12} = 5 \text{ amps}$$

At 24 volts, the calculation looks like this:

$$\frac{60}{24} = 2.5 \text{ amps}$$

The 24-volt system uses half the amperage required by a 12-volt system.

Ohm's and Watt's laws can be combined to calculate wattage, voltage, and amperage if two circuit variables are known. Combining Watt's and Ohm's laws provides these equations:

$$\text{Power} = \text{Voltage}^2/\text{Resistance}$$

$$\text{Resistance} = \text{Power}/\text{Amperage}^2$$

$$\text{Power} = \text{Amperage}^2 \times \text{Resistance}$$

Circuit Malfunctions

LO 10-3 Describe and classify circuits according to common failure modes.

Just as there are categories for operational circuits, defective circuits have names based on failure mode. Classification of circuit malfunction can include:

- Opened
- Shorted
- Grounded
- High resistance
- Intermittent

Open Circuit Faults

When a circuit defect is caused by an opening in the electrical pathway, no current can flow. Opened circuits can be caused by a variety of problems, including poor ground or terminal connections, defective switches, and broken wiring (**FIGURE 10-18**). An open circuit does not burn the fuse, but the fuse is opened if the circuit is overloaded by a grounded circuit, resulting in excess amperage passing through the fuse. Where the opening in the circuit occurs determines how the failure presents itself. For example, a broken wire to a single clearance light is only a branch in a parallel circuit and has a different effect than a blown fuse.

Depending on the type of fault, open circuits are typically detected using test lights and multimeters (**FIGURE 10-19**). Radio waves are also used to identify faults in bundles of wiring or in long runs of wiring hidden behind panels. A radio transmitter (**FIGURE 10-20**) installed in the fuse of an open or shorted circuit emits short bursts of high-frequency radio signals at low-voltage current into the defective circuit. The energy creating the signal is not powerful enough to damage wiring, but it allows open circuits and shorts to be located using a hand held

radio receiver. A schematic diagram is useful when identifying open circuits to locate strategic points where circuit voltage can be measured using a test light or multimeter. An ohmmeter can be used to find points where circuit continuity is lost only if the circuit is not powered.

In on-board diagnostic (OBD) system circuits, the continuous component monitor constantly checks for open circuits by analyzing voltage drops through a circuit. This strategy is fully explained in the Electrical Signal Processing chapter.

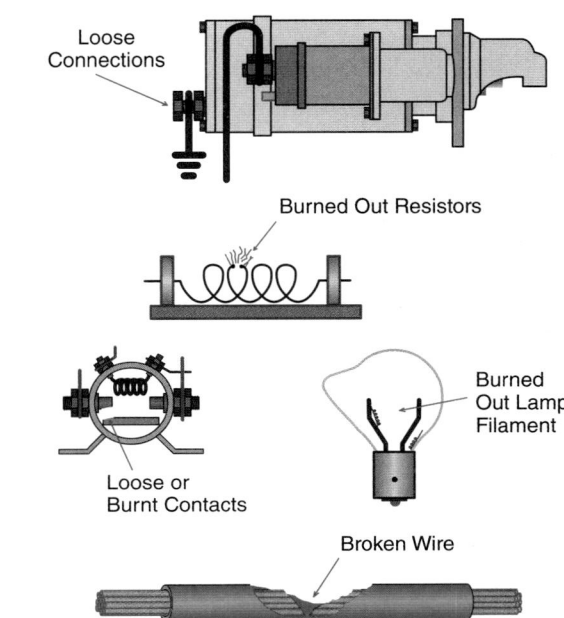

FIGURE 10-18 Causes of open and intermittent circuits.

FIGURE 10-19 Conventional test light and a more advanced light. More advanced test lights are battery-powered. Single probe tip can be used to determine polarity and detect ground, power, shorts, and breaks. Red LED indicates power; green LED indicates ground.

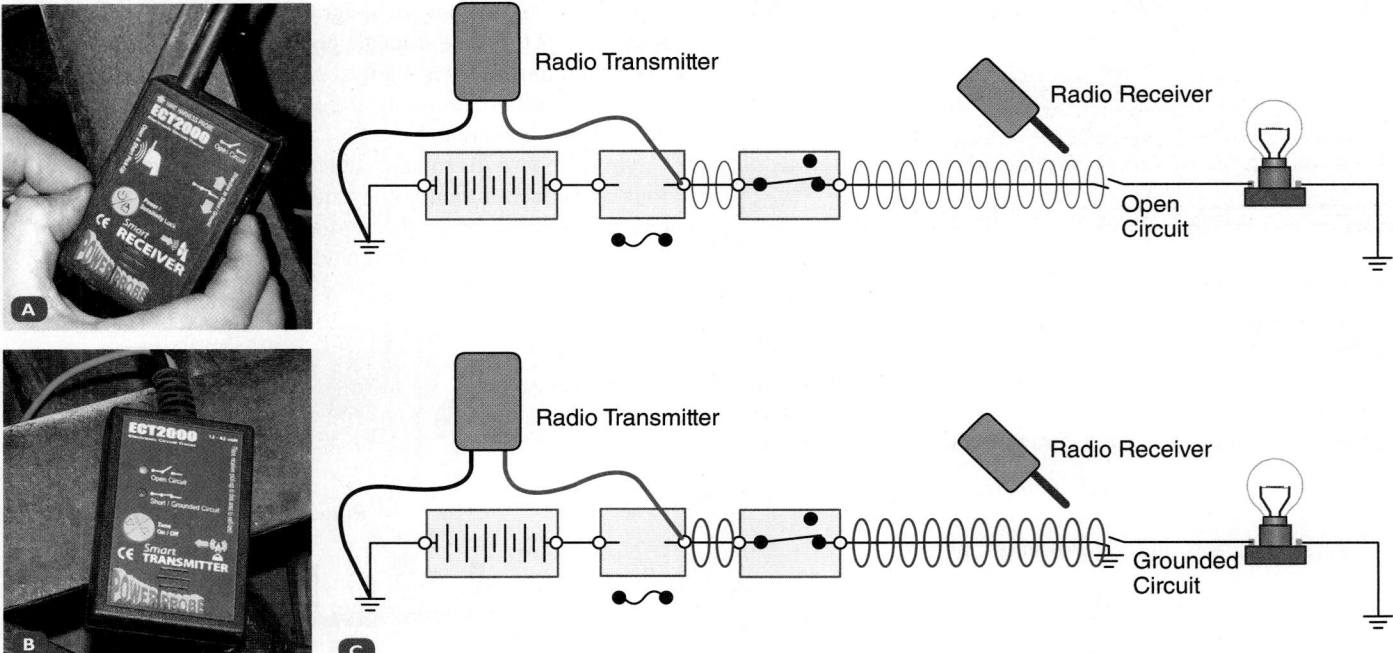

FIGURE 10-20 A. Radio receiver. **B.** Radio transmitter. **C.** This radio signal generator is designed to find opens, shorts, or grounded circuits without damaging the wire. A radio signal is injected into the circuit by connecting a transmitter. Moving the receiver in the vicinity of the wire locates the break, unintentional ground or short, as well as the direction of the ground in the circuit, according to the direction of magnetic lines of force.

Short Circuits

Short circuits are commonly, but incorrectly, thought of as the unwanted, high amperage flow between battery power and negative ground. However, that type of fault is better described as a grounded circuit. As its name suggests, a short is an electrical circuit that is formed between two points, allowing current to flow through an unintended pathway (**FIGURE 10-21**). A short may draw a higher or lower than normal amperage and simply be an unintended connection between two wires or circuits. A coil of wire is considered shorted if current does not pass through all the intended loops, but instead takes a shorter path. Another simple example of a short circuit is a short to power malfunction. A short to power could be an unintended connection in a taillight assembly between the brake light 12 V+ and 12 V+ conductors to park or clearance lights circuits. Stepping on the brakes would cause the clearance lights to illuminate and vice versa.

OBD systems that continuously monitor electrical signals from sensors and output devices detect shorted conditions, too. For example, if a three-wire sensor signal circuit is shorted to +12 volts, it meets conditions required to generate the fault code "Sensor Input Voltage High" (**FIGURE 10-22**). The fault description "Sensor Input Voltage Low" is produced if either the sensor +5-volt supply to a two-wire sensor is shorted to a negative voltage source, such as a chassis ground, or the sensor signal wire or a three-wire sensor is shorted to a negative ground.

Grounded Circuits

A **grounded circuit**, sometimes called "dead short," is characterized by an unwanted low resistance connection between

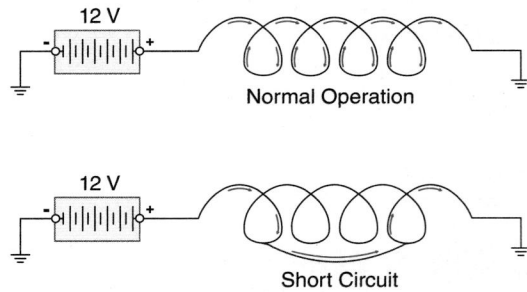

FIGURE 10-21 When current bypasses its intended load, it is referred to as a short circuit.

battery positive power and chassis ground. High current flow generally accompanies a grounded circuit fault. Unlike the short-to-power malfunction, the short-to-ground is an unintended battery + connection that draws higher than expected current. A common example of a grounded circuit would be a battery or power cable insulation rubbing through and connecting to the negative-ground chassis frame (**FIGURE 10-23**). The direct, low-resistance connection would cause high current flow, resulting in blown fuses, fusible links, or activation of other circuit protection devices.

High-Resistance Circuits

When grounds or power connections in circuits become resistive, circuits cannot properly function because insufficient current is supplied to the loads. Neither can they operate properly if components become excessively resistive. Dirty, corroded, or

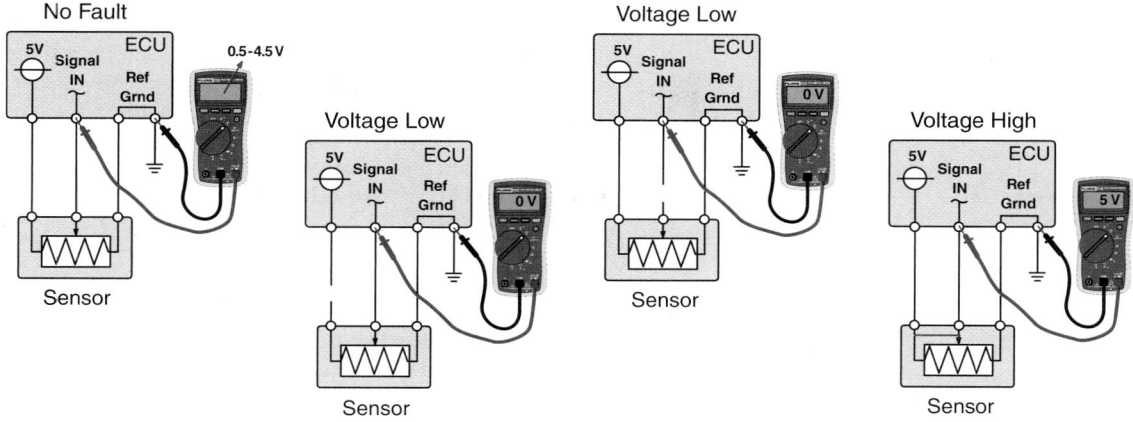

FIGURE 10-22 Sensor signal circuits are monitored by the on-board diagnostic system, which continually evaluates electrical system operation. Short circuits generate fault codes, such as shorted high or low, or input voltage high or low.

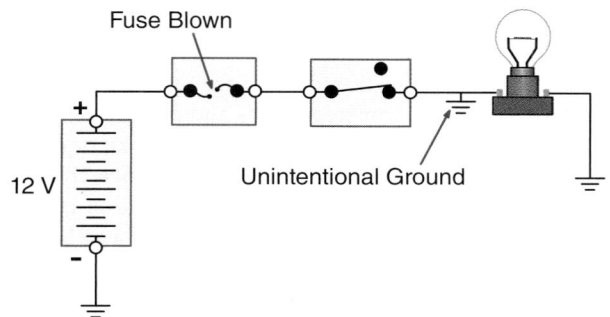

FIGURE 10-23 A grounded circuit fault occurring at a point after the protection device, but before the circuit load, results in an unintended low-resistance path to chassis ground. If the fuse or circuit breaker quickly opens when the control switch is closed, a grounded circuit is likely the cause.

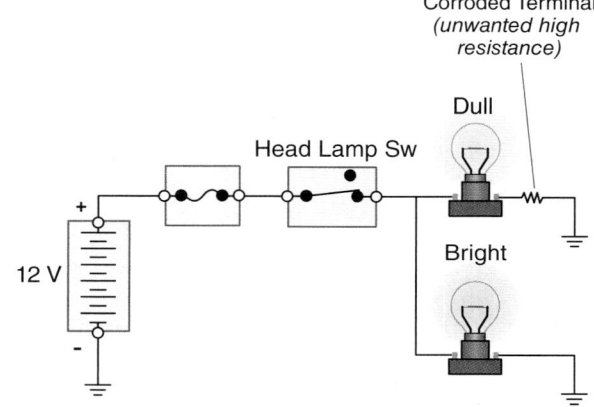

FIGURE 10-24 A poor ground is one cause of a resistive circuit.

loose connections result in **resistive circuits** that do not allow components to properly operate. Battery terminals, light bulb sockets, and connector sockets are common points for resistances to develop.

High current flow through a connection or circuit that has almost no resistance can turn highly resistive if high amperage passes through the connection. Resistive ground connections can often be difficult to troubleshoot because circuits find alternate grounds or components operate in very unusual ways that may not indicate low current flow. Double filament combined stop/tail bulbs are one common example of what is sometimes called a "back-feed" due to resistive grounds (**FIGURE 10-24**). A poor ground in the bulb socket of one tail lamp causes the current to find a ground through the bulb on the opposite side of a vehicle. For example, current flows though the stop/turn filament and then flows through the common ground it shares inside the bulb with the taillight filament to form a series circuit inside the bulb. Current in the taillight circuit is still seeking a ground pathway. Since the left and right taillight filaments share a common positive conductor, a pathway to ground is made through the taillight filament on the opposite side of the vehicle in a taillight with a good ground connection. When

that happens, both taillights will flash when the turn signal is switched on to the bulb with the resistive ground. Both taillight and stop/turn bulb filaments glow dimly in the tail lamp with the resistive bulb ground when the brake lights are switched on (**FIGURE 10-25**).

Intermittent Circuits

Intermittent circuits are characterized by uneven current flow. Intermittent current flow through circuits is often caused by loose connections and vibration from a moving vehicle. An example is the connectors on the engine electronic control module (ECM), which receive a lot of engine vibration and have the added strain of heavy wiring harnesses. Heat at terminal connections can cause continuous thermal cycling of terminal pins, which eventually loosen contact. Combined with engine vibration, the ECM pins and terminal connections can have a momentary loss of continuity. The result is the report of hundreds, if not thousands, of fault counts or occurrences for one or more circuits connected to the ECM plug. ECM connections that are packed with dielectric grease can dampen vibration and transfer away some heat to prevent this condition from taking place (**FIGURE 10-26**).

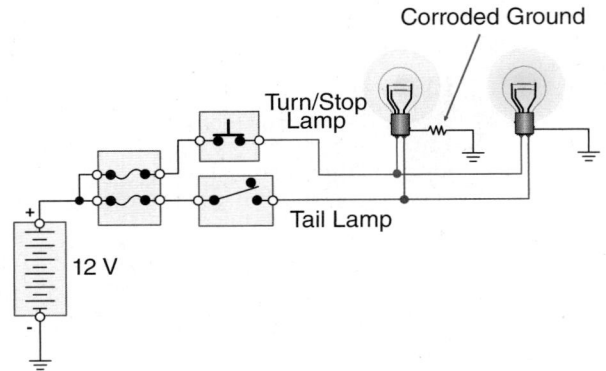

FIGURE 10-25 A resistive ground at the left 3157 stop/taillight bulb causes a current to flow through the right taillight bulb filament when the tail or left turn signal is switched on. The left-side bulb seeks a ground in the right side. Both left-side bulb filaments glow dimly when the brake lights are switched on because the ground is in series with the right-side bulb.

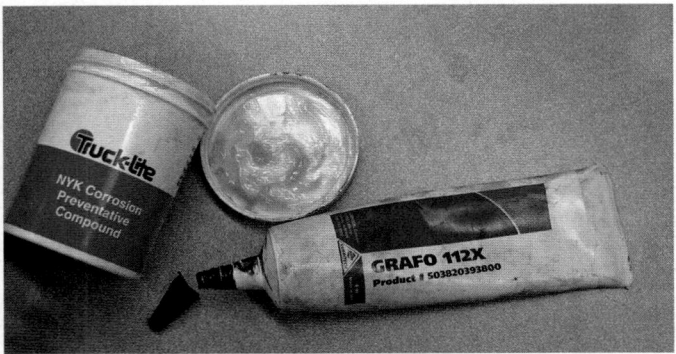

FIGURE 10-26 The use of dielectric or electrically non-conductive grease helps prevent corrosion and absorbs vibration leading to intermittent connections.

Pins on ECM and other wiring harnesses are intentionally kept small to minimize thermal expansion and contraction that leads to loose connections. Terminals on the J-560 trailer cord have split pins to help prevent loosening of the electrical pin connection from heat and vibration. The split pin possesses spring-like capabilities to keep the trailer cord connectors in contact with the receptacle pins, regardless of the temperature.

Overheated modules and coils are often another source of intermittent circuit problems. Heat causes resistance to climb in some semiconductor devices, as well as electromagnetic coils in solenoids or relays. If, after allowing modules or coils to cool, the devices or circuits return to normal operation, it is an indication that these heat-sensitive, components should be replaced.

Electrical connectors should be packed with dielectric grease wherever possible during assembly. Unlike chassis grease, dielectric grease is electrically non-conductive and prevents corrosion of terminal pins. The grease transfers away some heat and also helps absorb mechanical vibration to prevent terminal pins from loosening or breaking electrical contact for a split second.

Despite the advanced electrical technology today, the J-560 trailer cord plug used in North America has the same configuration it did 50 years ago. Split pins in the receptacle are used to help maintain a good electrical connection using the pin's spring-like capabilities. Over time, the pin's diameter becomes smaller. To maintain a good connection, the pins occasionally need to be spread open again using a flat-blade screwdriver.

Circuit Protection Devices

LO 10-4 Identify the purpose and types of circuit protection devices used in commercial vehicle electrical systems.

High amperage flow through circuits produces resistance induced heat. If excess amperage is allowed to pass through conductors, they can become overheated to the point where the insulation melts, and a fire can result. Circuits overloaded with high current-demanding components or grounded circuits can quickly cause damage to wiring, and even start fires. So, to protect wiring harnesses and the safety of vehicle occupants, circuit protection devices are used. This also helps explain why only low amperage loads and conductors are now used in the cab interior. The likelihood of smoke or electrical fires is reduced if only low voltage and amperage circuits are inside a cab. A second reason for circuit protection is because damage to sensitive electronic components can also be caused by unintended reversal of battery polarity, such as when jump-starting a dead battery using booster cables. Third, excessive charging system voltage can push more electrical current through these devices and destroy them. Circuit protection devices can be designed to open a circuit when charging systems voltages exceed a maximum threshold.

The lack of proper circuit protection Circuit protection can have enormous costs and fatal consequences. In a study commissioned by the Federal Motor Carrier Safety Administration (FMCSA) in the years between 2003 and 2008, the study found 2.6% of commercial vehicles were involved in fires, with 28% of those fires involving defective insulation around electrical wiring. An Australian Insurance bureau report elaborates further, noting in a 2015 report covering its 2013 insurance claims, it found truck fires accounted for 10.7% of large loss incidents with electrical failures accounting for 68.5% of cabin/engine compartment fires.

Traditional fuses, fuse links, and circuit breakers are connected in series between a load and supply current. The devices typically use heat, produced from excessive current flow in overloaded circuits, to open the circuits. Fuses and circuit breakers blow and open overloaded circuits when amperage exceeds 10% to 15% of the fuse rating. This means a 20-amp fuse opens at 22 to 23 amps of current. Recently, network control of the electrical system in late-model equipment has enabled software control of current flow through circuits, introducing what is called the virtual fuse—circuit protection without a fuse. Technicians and the manufacturer of electrical systems set rules to choose how much current is excessive and what an appropriate response to excessive current should be, based on the type of circuit load.

Thermal Fuses

Thermal fuses are fuses opened by heat and are available in several configurations (**FIGURE 10-27**). Three basic types of fuses currently in use that are opened by heat produced from resistance produced by high amperage flow:

- Cartridge type
- Blade type
- Inline type

Cartridge fuses use strips of metal made in various thicknesses that are enclosed in a glass tube. The metal is manufactured to melt at a low temperature. If excessive current flows through the circuit, the fuse element melts at specific amperage due to the calibrated thickness of the metal strip. When inspecting the fuse to see whether it is blown, a break in the metal strip is observed in open fuse. A test light should also light up when both sides of an intact fuse are probed, and the ignition switch is on. To reduce the size of power distribution boxes and fuse panels, cartridge fuses are seldom used on newer equipment.

Blade or spade-type fuses have blade-like metal lugs connected by a fusible metal wire. The compact, transparent, plastic body allows more fuses to be inserted into a fuse carrier in today's vehicles, with ever increasing numbers of circuits. The fuses, which can handle up to 32 volts, are built using a standard industry color code to indicate the maximum amperage rating. Smaller and larger versions of the blade-type fuses have been introduced since the first ones, designated ATC/ATO, were made in the 1970s. Micro and mini versions designated ATM are built in several sizes while larger maxi fuses commonly designated APX handle heavier amperage circuits, of up to 80 amps (**TABLE 10-2**). Even larger OEM-specific blade fuses for alternators are made but are not designed according to an industry standard. The difference between ATC and the less common ATO is whether the metal fuse wire is completely sealed in the plastic body or not. If the fuse is in an application where it is exposed to road spray or combustible materials, the sealed ATO is used since it is both corrosion and spark resistant. It is easy to check the continuity of the metal ATC fuse wire using a test

light probe of the metal spade ends. These are accessed from the outside of the fuse. Breaks in the fuse wire or smoke residue of melted plastic are also visible through the transparent plastic body. An additional feature of some of the latest replacement fuses is a tiny LED light that is illuminated when the fuse is open. The indicator is helpful when searching for open fuses in dark and difficult-to-access fuse panels containing many fuses (**FIGURE 10-28**).

Inline fuses are connected in series with the electrical devices needing additional circuit protection. These fuses are located outside a fuse panel or power distribution box. Inline fuses are used to protect a device that may already be connected in a protected circuit but may have a lower tolerance for over-current or reverse polarity conditions. ECMs are a common example of devices with inline fuses protecting the constant battery voltage supply line and supply of current from the ignition switch (**FIGURE 10-29**). When the fuse is placed closer to the device, it blows more quickly, which can reduce consequential damage caused by over-current of reverse polarity conditions.

Low-amperage fuses are easily blown in over-current and reverse polarity conditions due to internal circuits using Zener diodes. These arrangements of voltage-sensitive diodes allow battery-positive supply current to go to ground under abuse conditions when a threshold voltage is exceeded or the polarity of current is reversed. Inline fuses are also used when adding electrical accessories to a circuit. Locating the fuses as close to the devices as possible shortens the time needed to blow the fuse. **TABLE 10-3** provides the recommended maximum fuse ratings for the corresponding wire size (per the American Wire Gauge system).

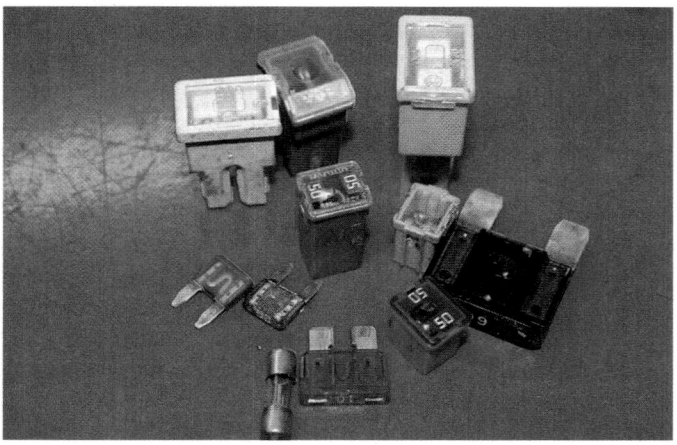

FIGURE 10-27 Thermal fuses come in many configurations.

TABLE 10-2 Color Coding of Blade fuses

Color	Amps	ATM (Mini)	ATC/ATO	APX Maxi
Black	1		X	
Gray	2	X	X	
Violet	3	X	X	
Pink	4	X	X	
Tan	5	X	X	
Brown	7.5	X	X	
Red	10	X	X	
Blue	15	X	X	
Yellow	20	X	X	X
Clear	25	X	X	Gray
Green	30	X	X	X
Blue-Green	35	X	X	Brown
Orange	40	X	X	X
Red	50			X
Blue	60			X
Amber/Tan	70			X
Clear	80			X
Violet	100	.	.	X
Purple	120	.	.	X

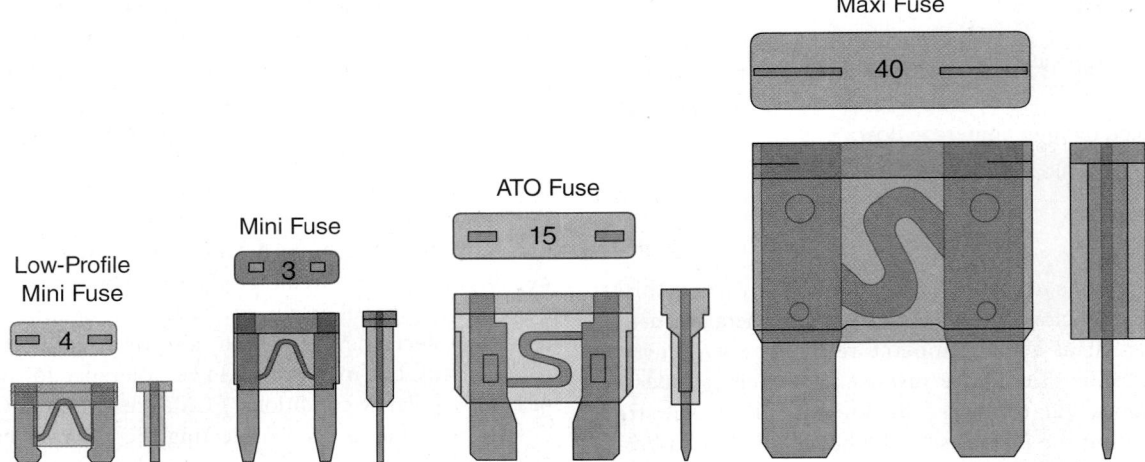

FIGURE 10-28 Blade fuse types—Mini, ATC, Maxi, and AMG. Fuses are color coded to designate the maximum current.

FIGURE 10-29 Fuses at the battery box are usually protecting the power circuits to the engine ECM.

TABLE 10-3 Recommended Maximum Fuse Ratings by Wire Gauge

Wire Gauge (AWG)	Recommended Maximum Fuse Rating
00	400 amps
0	325 amps
1	250 amps
2	200 amps
4	125 amps
6	80 amps
8	50 amps
10	30 amps
12	20 amps
14	15 amps
16	7.5 amps

▶ **TECHNICIAN TIP**

Gone are the days when adding a 12-volt electrical accessory, such as a dash camera, cab beacon light, or GPS system, could be done by splicing into a 12 V+ wire beneath the dash or fuse panel. Today's cabs, using networked control of all electrical devices and accessories, potentially disconnects any circuit that doesn't have an anticipated current load. Adding electrical accessories commonly requires programming electrical circuit protection and switch functions with dealer level software.

Major Harness Protection

Fuses are used to protect individual circuits, but not necessarily major wiring harnesses. For those, fusible links can be used. Fuse links are short sections of wire installed in series with larger diameter conductors. At one quarter of the gauge of the main conductor, the fuse link overheats and melts, instead of the larger conductor, when excessive amperage passes through the wire. This means brief overloads are possible with fuse links without causing current disruptions. Special plastic covers the link and bubbles when the link melts. Fuse links are effective protection in major harnesses because limiting amperage in harnesses is not as critical as protecting them from overheating and burning.

Glow plug circuits, alternator battery cables, and major cab harness cables are a few examples where fuse links were once used. Fuse links are checked with test lights or by simply pulling the conductor where it usually attaches to a major battery terminal or starter cable connection. A link that stretches excessively like a rubber band is likely internally melted. Current should be found on both sides of an intact link if checked with a test light.

Maxi fuses have replaced fuse links as circuit protection devices. The use of power distribution boxes, usually located under the hood and out of the cab, has broken down commercial vehicle electrical system harnesses into smaller and more numerous sections using shorter runs of wiring (**FIGURE 10-30**). Easier to replace maxi fuses found inside distribution boxes, typically in sizes from 20 to 80 amps, protects several circuits. Larger specialized ratings are available from OEMs.

When replacing blown fuses and circuit breakers, never install one with a higher amp rating. This could cause a wire or component to overheat and possibly cause an electrical fire. If a breaker or fuse is operating in an overloaded circuit, replace the wiring with a larger diameter and then increase the rating of the circuit protection device.

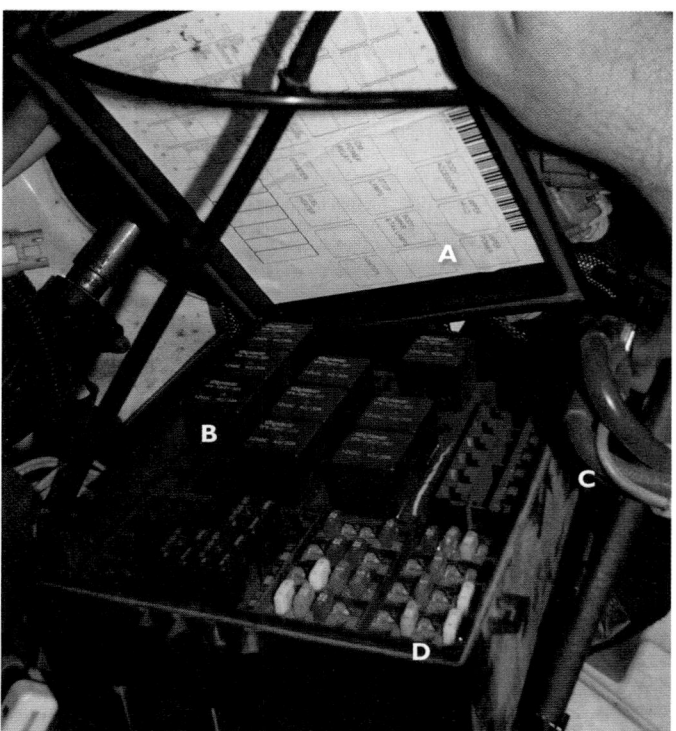

FIGURE 10-30 Power distribution boxes are the main location for circuit protection. The boxes break the electrical system into smaller and more numerous sections. Large electrical conductors do not pass through the occupant compartment, where potential fires can occur. **A.** Cover with component locator. **B.** Relays. **C.** Insulated positive cables. **D.** Blade-type fuses.

Circuit Breakers

Circuit breakers are used in circuits where intermittent current overloads are common and where power must be rapidly restored, such as with wipers, headlights, and other lighting circuits. Unlike fuses, circuit breakers do not require replacement when they trip. Instead, they may either automatically reset or require a manual reset.

Typically, circuit breakers are made from bimetallic contacts connected in series with a circuit. These are strips of metal made from two different materials with different rates of expansion. When heated, the bimetallic strip bends and opens the contacts, disconnecting current flow from the circuit. Heat is produced when too much current flows through the bimetallic strip in the circuit breaker. In **Type 1 circuit breakers**, are automatically resetting breakers, current is restored when the bimetallic strip cools (**FIGURE 10-31**).

A circuit breaker can be a non-cycling type too. Typically, those are **Type 2 circuit breakers**. One type is reset by removing the power from the circuit. A heating coil connected in parallel with the contacts is wrapped around a bimetal arm, keeping the arm hot and contacts disconnected after it has tripped. This current is not enough to operate a load, but heats the bimetal arm until power is removed. Another non-cycling breaker is the **Type 3 circuit breaker**, which must be reset by depressing a reset button. The reset button pushes an over-center spring-back mechanism back into position. That spring force holds the bimetal contacts open after the breaker has tripped. **TABLE 10-4** shows this classification for circuit breakers.

TABLE 10-4 Classification of Circuit Breakers

Type 1	Automatically resetting—Cycles the circuit breaker on and off until the overload condition is removed.
Type 2	Modified Type 1—Keeps the circuit breaker open until the overload condition is removed.
Type 3	A manual resetting thermal non-cycling circuit breaker—Remains tripped until the operator manually resets it by pushing a button located on the breaker.

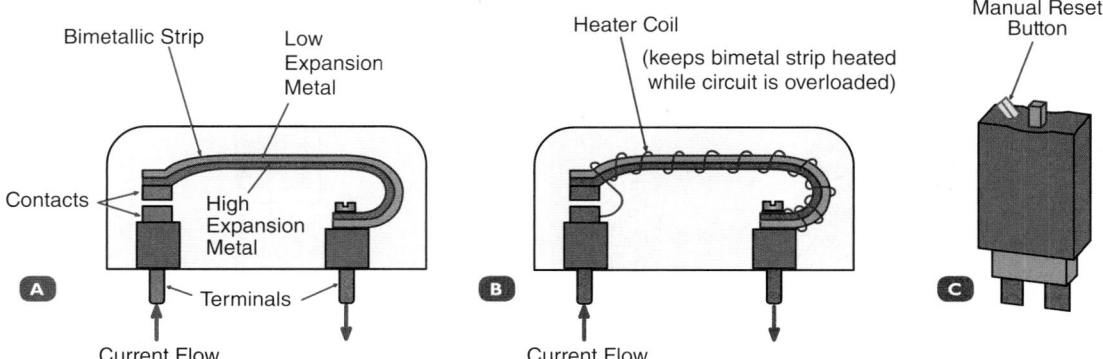

FIGURE 10-31 Three types of circuit breakers: **A.** Cycling. **B.** Non-cycling. **C.** Manual reset. Bimetal strips of metal with different expansion rates bend when heated. Heat produced during high current flow causes contacts inside the breaker to open to protect the circuit wiring from overheating.

PPT Coefficient Fuses

A **polymeric positive temperature coefficient (PPTC) device**, commonly known as a **resettable fuse**, is a thermistor-like electronic device used to protect against circuit overloads. These devices are like non-linear positive temperature coefficient (PTC) thermistors used as temperature sensors. When heated while conducting excessive current, they quickly cycle between a conductive and non-conductive state until after the current is removed or the device has cooled (**FIGURE 10-32**). Resistance in the device suddenly increases to thousands of ohms.

Current trip ratings for PPTC devices range from 20 mA to 100 mA. Dozens of these devices are used in a single electrical control module to harden them against damage from shorts to power or ground, as well as other electrical faults in the external circuits they control. Electric motors used for window regulators typically use larger PPTC circuit protection capable of opening at much higher current loads to prevent motor overheating when a window is jammed.

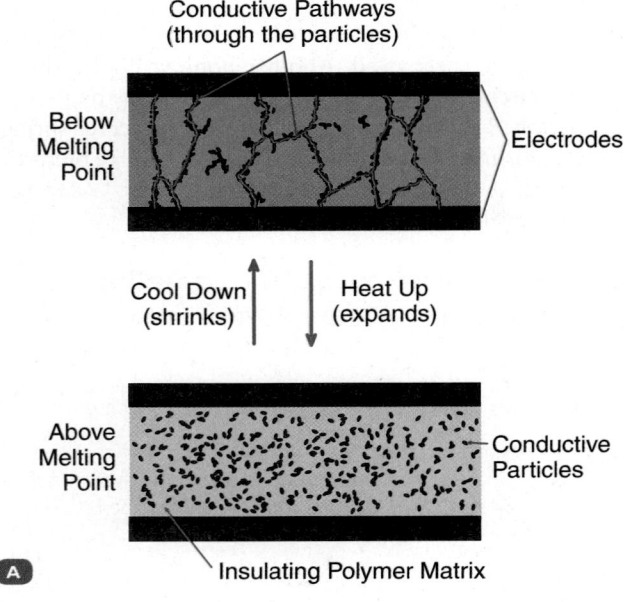

FIGURE 10-32 A. When heated while conducting excessive current, PPTC devices quickly cycle between a conductive and non-conductive state until after the current is removed or the device has cooled.
B. Surface-mount resettable PTC devices are used in this injector drive module. The fuses protect the sensitive microcontrollers against grounded circuits, reverse polarity, and electromagnetic interference.

Virtual Fuses

E-fuses are a more recent innovation in circuit protection. **E-fuses**, or **virtual fuses** as they are sometimes called, are software-controlled fuses that use field effect transistors (FET) for the circuit control device. The development of virtual fuses is important because it saves not only the cost of the fuse, but the fuse holder, and the largest cost associated with using a traditional fuse—the wiring to and from the fuse. Relays and most other fuses are expected to be replaced by virtual fuses as body electrical control modules evolve and gain a proven track record for reliability.

Virtual fuses are now used in most power distribution modules in multiplexed electrical systems to enable programmable limits of amperage to body-builder-installed circuits, and any other vehicle circuits. Combinations of two FETs are used, along with a signal from a microcontroller, is used to establish a maximum current threshold before a circuit is opened (**FIGURE 10-33**). These fuses are reset when the ignition switch is either turned off or when the FETs have sensed the overcurrent condition has ended.

Inspecting and Testing Circuit Protection Devices

LO 10-5 Identify and explain the methods used to test the operation of circuit protection devices.

Protection devices are designed to prevent excessive current from flowing in the circuit. Protection devices, such as fuses and fusible links, are sacrificial, meaning that if excessive current flows, they blow or trip and must be replaced. Circuit breakers can be reset. Once they trip, they either reset automatically or require a manual reset by pushing a button or moving a lever.

Fuses, fusible links, and circuit breakers are available in various ratings, types, and sizes, and must always be replaced with the same rating and type. In most vehicles, protection devices are in the power distribution box in series with the

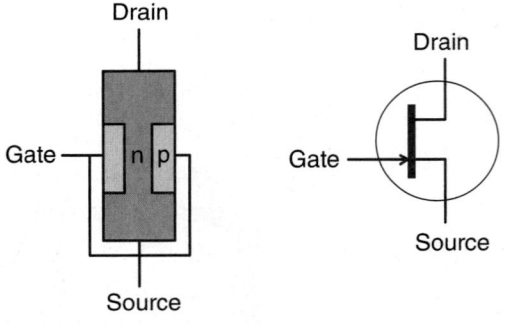

N-channel Fet

FIGURE 10-33 One of many types of FET that can conduct high current flow with very little heating. By regulating the current applied to the gate, the amperage through the FET is controlled. Software enables programming of FET capabilities to act as virtual fuses or e-fuses.

battery positive side of the circuit. A blown or faulty fuse can be tested using a voltmeter, but a test lamp that draws some current in the rare case of high circuit resistance is preferable because it still displays 12-volts availability when using a high impedance voltmeter. A good fuse has the same voltage on both sides when the lead of the test light or common lead of the voltmeter is connected to chassis ground. A blown fuse has battery voltage on only one side of the fuse and 0 volts on the other side. They can also sometimes be visually inspected. This may require the removal of the fuse from the fuse holder. The fusible metal strip should be intact and, if measured by an ohmmeter, should have no, or very low, resistance. The contacts on both the fuse and the fuse holder should be clean and free of corrosion and should fit snugly together. To inspect and test circuit protection devices, follow the steps in **SKILL DRILL 10-1**. To identify a resistive ground connection, follow the steps in **SKILL DRILL 10-2**.

SKILL DRILL 10-1 Inspecting and Testing Circuit Protection Devices

1. Identify the protection device to be inspected and tested. A fuse or circuit breaker is most commonly checked at a power distribution box or fuse panel.
2. Turn the ignition switch to the run or on position to supply power to the fuse.
3. Using a test light, probe the fuse or circuit breaker on each side (to battery supply and load) to determine whether current is supplied to the device and whether current is available to the loads in the circuit.
4. If there is only power available to the circuit protection device and not to the load, the fuse is open. This requires replacement, if it is a fuse, or resetting the circuit breaker, if possible. Fuse replacement is performed after identifying the cause for the overloaded circuit.

SKILL DRILL 10-2 Identifying a Resistive Ground Connection

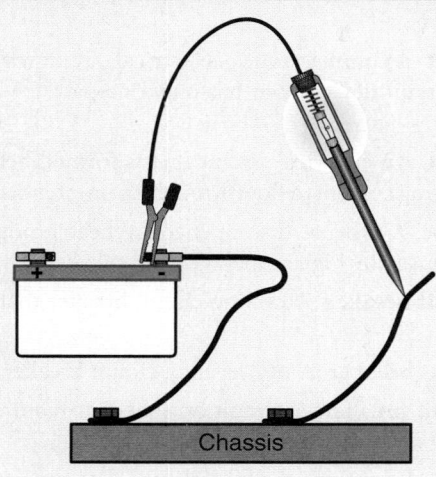

1. Locate a suspected ground connection. This is usually a bolt on a chassis or terminal on a wire lead attached to a stud.
2. Using a voltmeter, place the common lead of the voltmeter onto the chassis ground.
3. Place the other lead on the ground connection at the device that is not operating correctly.
4. Energize the device or operate the circuit.
5. Analyze the voltmeter readings. No voltage should be measured if the ground is good, i.e., having no resistance. Any measurable voltage indicates a resistive ground that requires cleaning or repair.

Wrap-Up

Ready for Review

- A basic electrical circuit includes a power supply, a fuse, a switch, a load, and wires connecting them all together. More complex circuits also include circuit protection devices, control device, and load and connecting wires.
- According to conventional theory of current flow, the positive pole is the supply side of the circuit, and the ground pole is the return side of the circuit.
- Many vehicles connect the chassis and body to the negative battery terminal, which means most of the metal components on the vehicle are grounded.
- A component with no ground connection results in an open circuit and no current flow.
- There are three types of short circuit: short to ground, short to power, and unintended high resistance.
- An open circuit has infinite resistance.
- Unintended high resistance in a circuit causes a reduction in amperage in the circuit, as well as a drop in voltage at the resistance.
- Volts, amps, and ohms are three basic units of electrical measurement.
- Circuit resistance determines the amperage drawn by any electrical circuit. The higher the circuits resistance, the less amperage flows in the circuit for any voltage.
- The lower the circuits resistance, the higher the amperage flow in the circuit.
- Ohm's law is a mathematical formula that expresses the relationship among volts (V), amps (A), and ohms (R): $A = V \times R$.
- Voltage drop that is the result of resistance is calculated using Ohm's Law (Voltage Drop = Amperage/Resistance).
- Most of the time, when circuits fail, it is because the current flow is too low or non-existent.
- Circuits come in two basic configurations—series circuits and parallel circuits. The two types can also be combined into what is called a series-parallel circuit.
- In a series circuit, the loads and devices that have resistance are connected one after the other; thus, the total resistance is calculated by adding all the resistances together.
- Kirchhoff's Law states all the voltage drops in a series circuit added together always equal source voltage.
- Excessively high current flow through circuits produces heat that has the potential to overheat conductors or components to the point where the insulation melts, and a fire can result.
- Traditional fuses, fuse links, and circuit breakers are connected in series and use heat produced from excessive current flow in overloaded circuits to open the circuits.
- Circuit protection devices are designed to prevent excessive current from flowing in the circuit.

- Circuit protection devices, such as fuses and fusible links, are sacrificial, meaning that if excessive current flows, they burn out and need replacement.
- Circuit breakers are resettable. A fuse or circuit breaker should be overrated by about 10%–15% to prevent accidental tripping.
- Virtual fuses save not only the cost of the fuse, but also the fuse holder and the largest cost associated with using a traditional fuse—the wiring to and from the fuse.

Key Terms

circuit breaker A device that trips and opens a circuit, preventing excessive current flow in a circuit. It is resettable to allow for reuse.

combination (series-parallel) circuit A circuit that uses elements both of series and parallel circuits.

e-fuse A software-controlled fuse that uses field effect transistors for the circuit control device. Also called *virtual fuses.*

grounded circuit A circuit characterized by an unwanted low resistance connection between battery positive power and chassis ground.

intermittent circuit A circuit characterized by uneven current flow.

Kirchhoff's law A law that states that the sum of the voltage drops in a series circuit equals source voltage.

parallel circuit A circuit in which all branch components are connected directly to the voltage supply.

Polymeric Positive Temperature Coefficient (PPTC) device (resettable fuse) A thermistor-like electronic device used to protect against circuit overloads. Also called *resettable fuse.*

resistive circuit A circuit in which current has excessive unwanted resistance and cannot properly function due to excessive resistance.

series circuit A common type of electrical circuit with multiple loads and circuit devices, but has only one path for current to flow.

short circuit An electrical circuit that is formed between two points, allowing current to flow through an unintended pathway.

thermal fuse A type of fuse opened by heat produced from resistance caused by high amperage flow.

type 1 circuit breaker A cycling circuit breaker that automatically resets.

type 2 circuit breaker A non-cycling circuit breaker.

type 3 circuit breaker A circuit breaker that requires manual reset.

virtual fuse A software-controlled fuse that monitors circuit amperage and shuts off the circuit when amperage exceeds a predetermined threshold. Also called *e-fuses.*

Watt's law An electrical law that defines the relationship between power, amperage, and voltage.

combined Watts and Ohm's laws Mathematical equations predicting the relationship between power, amperage, resistance, and voltage.

Review Questions

1. When electrical current begins to move in a basic electrical circuit, where does electron flow take place?
   a. In the battery
   b. In the load
   c. In all circuit conductors
   d. In the circuit protection device
2. Which of the following takes place in a series circuit when more loads are added to the circuit?
   a. Resistance goes down
   b. Voltage goes up
   c. Circuit amperage decreases when measured after each load
   d. Resistance increases
3. Consider a series circuit supplied with 12 volts. It has three loads. The voltage drop across the first two loads is 3 and 4 volts, respectively. What is the voltage drop across the third load?
   a. 3.5 volts
   b. 12 volts
   c. 7 volts
   d. 5 volts
4. Consider again the series circuit described in question 3. The amperage in the circuit after the first two loads was measured as 1 amp. What is the amperage between the first and second load?
   a. 1 amp
   b. 2 amps
   c. 3 amps
   d. 4 amps
5. Consider a parallel circuit supplied with 12 volts that has three loads. The first load has a resistance of 3 ohms, the second has 4 ohms, and the third has 5 ohms. How much voltage drop will take place across the 4-ohm load?
   a. 3 volts
   b. 4 volts
   c. 8 volts
   d. 12 volts
6. Consider a 12-volt system with a load of 30 amps. How much amperage will the same load require if the supply voltage is 24 volts instead of 12?
   a. Not enough information
   b. 60 amps
   c. 8 amps
   d. 15 amps
7. Which of the following conditions exists when a grounded circuit malfunction is present?
   a. Current returns to the positive side of the battery through an electrical accessory.
   b. High circuit resistance is present.
   c. Current returns to the positive side of the battery before reaching the intended load, resulting in a heavy current draw.
   d. Current bypasses the normal electrical circuit through a pathway with lower resistance than the intended pathway.
8. Consider a double contact stop/turn/taillight bulb. It has a dirty and corroded lamp socket. Which type of circuit problem will most likely be created by the corrosion?
   a. A parallel circuit is created.
   b. A resistive circuit is created.
   c. A grounded circuit is created.
   d. A closed circuit is created.
9. Which type of circuit breaker must be reset by depressing a reset button?
   a. Type 1
   b. Type 2
   c. Type 3
   d. Type 4
10. Consider a conductor required to carry a maximum of 10 amps of load. The circuit is 20 feet in length. What is the recommended minimum thickness of wire required to prevent excessive voltage drop?
    a. 18 gauge
    b. 16 gauge
    c. 12 gauge
    d. 10 gauge

ASE Technician A/Technician B Style Questions

1. Technician A says that adding more loads to a series circuit increases the amperage used by the circuit. Technician B says adding more loads to a parallel circuit increases the amperage flowing through a circuit. Who is correct?
   a. Technician A
   b. Technician B
   c. Both Technician A and Technician B
   d. Neither Technician A nor Technician B
2. Technician A says resistance is like electrical friction. Technician B says resistance in a circuit produces heat, just like friction. Who is correct?
   a. Technician A
   b. Technician B
   c. Both Technician A and Technician B
   d. Neither Technician A nor Technician B
3. Technician A says continual cycling of a circuit breaker (opening and closing) is usually an indication of high circuit resistance. Technician B says that excessive cycling of a circuit breaker can indicate excessive amperage is drawn through a circuit. Who is correct?
   a. Technician A
   b. Technician B
   c. Both Technician A and Technician B
   d. Neither Technician A nor Technician B

4. Technician A says a series circuit is a circuit with multiple loads and only one path for current to flow. Technician B says in a series circuit, total circuit resistance is equal to the sum of the individual resistances. Who is correct?
   a. Technician A
   b. Technician B
   c. Both Technician A and Technician B
   d. Neither Technician A nor Technician B
5. Technician A says Watt's law, which is related to Ohm's law, explains the relationship between resistance and amperage. Technician B says Watt's law is used to calculate electrical power. Who is correct?
   a. Technician A
   b. Technician B
   c. Both Technician A and Technician B
   d. Neither Technician A nor Technician B
6. Technician A says a grounded circuit malfunction is a type of short circuit. Technician B says a common example of a grounded circuit would be a battery or power cable insulation rubbing against the negative ground chassis frame. Who is correct?
   a. Technician A
   b. Technician B
   c. Both Technician A and Technician B
   d. Neither Technician A nor Technician B
7. Technician A says circuit protection is required to prevent damage to wiring, or even start fires. Technician B says a fuse or circuit breaker can prevent damage caused by reverse polarity. Who is correct?
   a. Technician A
   b. Technician B
   c. Both Technician A and Technician B
   d. Neither Technician A nor Technician B
8. Technician A says fuse links are short sections of wire installed in series with larger diameter conductors. Technician B says fusible links have been replaced by maxi fuses. Who is correct?
   a. Technician A
   b. Technician B
   c. Both Technician A and Technician B
   d. Neither Technician A nor Technician B
9. Technician A says a polymeric positive temperature coefficient (PPTC) device is a thermistor-like electronic device used to protect against circuit overloads by window regulator motors. Technician B says PPTC devices are self-resetting fuses. Who is correct?
   a. Technician A
   b. Technician B
   c. Both Technician A and Technician B
   d. Neither Technician A nor Technician B
10. Technician A says virtual fuses, or e-fuses, are a recent innovation in circuit protection. Technician B says virtual fuses are software-controlled fuses that use Field Effect Transistors (FET) as the circuit control device. Who is correct?
   a. Technician A
   b. Technician B
   c. Both Technician A and Technician B
   d. Neither Technician A nor Technician B

CHAPTER 11

Circuit Control Devices

Learning Objectives

After reading this chapter, you will be able to:

- **LO 11-1** Identify and describe the construction, operation, and applications of switches.
- **LO 11-2** Identify and describe the construction, operation, and applications of automatic switches.
- **LO 11-3** Identify and describe the construction, operation, and applications of switched inputs to electronic control modules.
- **LO 11-4** Identify and describe the types, functions, and applications of resistive-type circuit control devices.

- **LO 11-5** Identify and describe the construction, operation, and applications of common types of electromagnetic relays.
- **LO 11-6** Identify and describe the construction and operation of electromagnetic solenoids.
- **LO 11-7** Outline service and test procedures for circuit control devices.

You Are the Technician

A 26' straight truck arrives at your shop with the request to install 20 additional clearance lights on the box, five additional lights on the top and bottom of each side in addition to the six lights already on each side. After calculating the current load for the additional lights using 0.6 amps/light, you find that an additional load is 12 amps plus 8 amps for the other lights in place. Deciding the truck's original headlamp switch cannot handle the additional current, you wire a relay to the clearance light circuit to switch the higher amperage. The headlight switch opens and closes the relay's control circuit. After successfully installing the lights and relay, the customer returns the next day complaining the clearance lights no longer work. When investigating, you discover the relay has developed an internal open circuit and smells burned. After replacing the relay with a different one, you discover the relay "buzzes" and the lights flicker unless the engine is running.

1. What is a likely cause for the first relay to have burned-up so quickly?
2. What is a likely cause for the second relay to buzz and cause the lights to flicker unless the charging system is supplying current?
3. Suggest a practical solution for correcting the problem of buzzing, chattering relays, and flickering lights.

Introduction

Electric circuits use control devices to supply, remove, change, or redirect the flow of current energizing a circuit. Circuit control devices are a fundamental building block for any circuit. The simplest type of circuit control switches electric current either on or off by opening or closing a set of electrical contacts. If the control devices are operated by a person, it is a manual control. More complex circuits provide an option for sending current through more than one electrical pathway, or establish a condition for opening and closing a circuit or switching current flow to a different pathway. A common option for switching and redirecting the path of electric current is dependency on a physical state, such as pressure, temperature, position, fluid level, or mechanical movement. These later types of switches are considered automatic types because they are operated by mechanical forces—or another electric circuit—rather than a person.

It's important to remember that circuit control generally involves switching or changing the supply of current flow powering a circuit, and does not include the circuit stage, where current flow is processed electronically to produce an electrical signal. For example, in contrast to circuit control devices, current can be converted into an electrical signal using electronic components, such as capacitors, diodes, transistors, or microcontrollers. Signal processing changes some characteristics of the current, such as its voltage, amperage, and frequency, or alters some fundamental property of current, such as converting it to digital signals, radio waves, or light. Once processed, the signal can then transmit information in either digital or analog form or perform work of a different nature, such as make decisions (computing) or locate objects (radar). Current can also be used to produce an output, such as sound, light, or movement of an electric motor. Circuit control, however, involves simply the use of switches, electromagnetic relays, solenoids, and resistors to switch current flow on and off or vary the supply of current to power a circuit. Given that each of the thousands of electrical circuits used in contemporary commercial vehicle chassis has at least one circuit control device, this chapter covers the most common types encountered by technicians. It's important for any competent technician to correctly understand the construction and operation of circuit control devices to diagnose circuit problems; develop test strategies; confirm the normal operation of circuit controls; and replace, properly select, and use circuit controls when installing auxiliary electrical devices.

Switches

LO 11-1 Identify and describe the construction, operation, and applications of switches.

Switches are the simplest circuit control device (**FIGURE 11-1**). Opening and closing switches either completes or breaks a circuit's electrical pathway. Simple switches are categorized by the number of input and output circuits they switch. Switch input connections are called poles, and output connections are called throws, as described in **TABLE 11-1**. The simplest switch is a single pole single throw (SPST) that connects the switch pole and throw to either open or close an electric circuit pathway.

A double pole double throw switch is called DPDT. A SPDT connects the input pole to one of two output throws when it is operated. An example of where this switch is used is the headlight dimmer switch to supply power to either the low- or high-beam light circuit. Other switches are DPST, and multi-pole multi-throw (MPMT). The MPMT is used in applications such as a rotary-style dash headlight switch selecting between park lights, automatic operation, low-beam, high-beam, fog light, and simultaneous operation of more than one light circuit. More than one source of current supplies the switches poles. Another MPMT is for a transmission range selector switch moving the transmission between park, several possible forward drive positions, and reverse.

Switches are also categorized by operation. If the switch closes a circuit while it is in its resting position (without any energizing or human input), or when it is switched to its off position, it is called normally closed (NC). If the switch opens a circuit in its resting or off position, it is called normally open (NO). Pushbutton momentary contact switches are an example of a switch classified as either NC or NO. And of course, switches can latch in either a NO or NC state.

Types of Switches

Switches can be manually or automatically operated. When a person operates a switch by moving its position, the switch is considered a manual type. Automatic switches rely on another circuit or are state-dependent in operation, meaning some outside force, such as the influence of a magnetic field, pressure, temperature, position, fluid level, or mechanical movement, operates the switch (**FIGURE 11-2**). Common manually operated

FIGURE 11-1 There are more switches than ever in today's trucks and buses.

switches are push button, toggle, and rotary type. These manually operated switches can be momentary contact, or latch in or out of the switch positions. A momentary contact switch remains in position as long as a person is pressing or holding the switch in position. When released, the switch returns to a resting position as either normally closed or open. A starter button or the horn button are examples of momentary contact switches. To prevent accidental operation, switches latch or lock in and out of position.

Because automatic and manual switches may be toggled slowly, resulting in damage to internal switch contacts from resistive heating, an over-center mechanism is used to ensure quick operation of the contacts. An over-center mechanism is designed to produce a rapid "snap-acting" type of operation that rapidly latches the switch into an on or off, open or closed position (**FIGURE 11-3**). The over-center mechanism typically uses a spring operated switching mechanism to ensure the switch latches into position, regardless of the operator speed, so that it is never between positions. **Rotary switches**, which are turned to operate, use a spring-loaded detent ball to provide turning resistance to prevent accidental movement or inaccurately positioning the switch poles and throws (**FIGURE 11-4**). **TABLE 11-2** shows and describes several types of manually operated switches.

TABLE 11-1 Common Contact Arrangements

Term	Abbreviation	Description	Contact Diagram
Single Pole Single Throw	SPST	Simple on/off set of contacts	
Single Pole Double Throw	SPDT	A switch with a single input that supplies two output terminals controlled by a single mechanism	
Double Pole Single Throw	DPST	A switch with two input circuits that switches an output either on or off using a single throw mechanism	
Double Pole Double Throw	DPDT	Equivalent to two SPST sets of contacts controlled by a single mechanism	

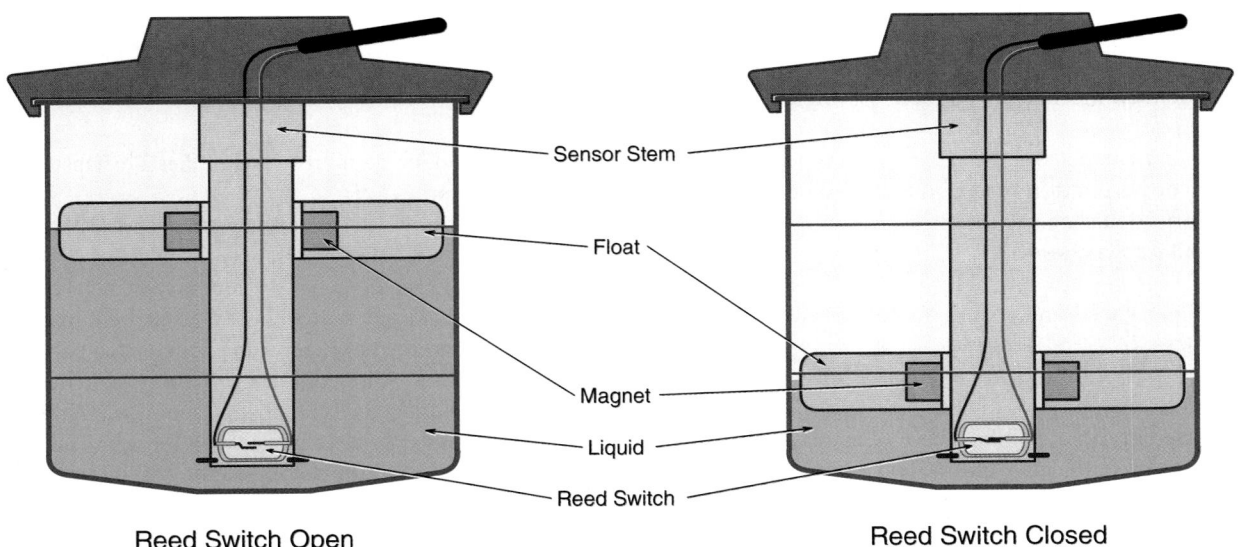

Reed Switch Open   Reed Switch Closed

FIGURE 11-2 A magnetic reed-type switch is an automatic switch that either opens or closes a set of electrical contacts when under the influence of a magnetic field. Fluid level sensors are common applications.

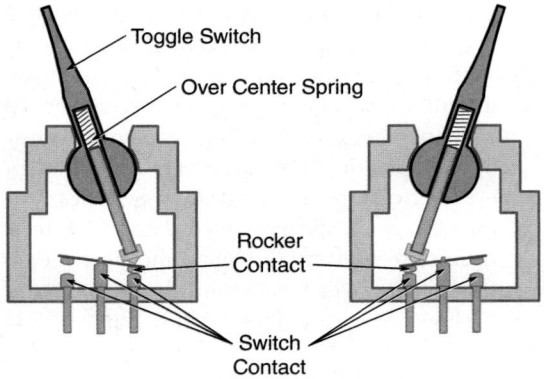

FIGURE 11-3 An over-center mechanism in a switch ensures the switch latches quickly and the contact is firm to prevent consequential damage caused by a loose resistive connection.

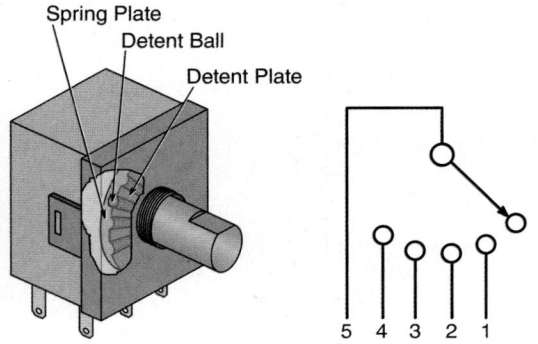

FIGURE 11-4 A rotary-type single pole multiple throw switch used to regulate wiper or blower motor speed.

Summary of Common Switch Types

1. *Toggle switches* use an angled lever having an internal spring-loaded mechanism to rapidly switch into its latch position.
2. *Momentary contact* switches are manual types that may be toggled or pushbutton type, and may also be either NC or NO. Horn contact or starter button are examples of momentary contact switches.
3. *Rotary switches* are manually rotated to select an output. Wiper speed and blower motor speed are common examples.
4. *Pressure-sensitive switches* are used for gas or liquids. Pressure is applied to a piston, diaphragm, or bellows to close or open contacts. Low-pressure oil, air, or the refrigerant sensors in the air-conditioning systems are examples of pressure-sensitive switches (**FIGURE 11-5**).
5. *Magnetic switches* contain thin reed-type switch contacts that are opened and closed by magnetic fields. Magnetic reed switches can be used to sense the level of engine coolant,

TABLE 11-2 Assorted Switches

Type	Application	Image
Toggle on/off SPST	Common switch used to turn on and off lights and many other accessories.	
Rocker switch on/off SPST Has built in warning light that comes on when the switch is on.	Common switch used where a warning light is required, for example, a spotlight or power divider switch.	
Toggle switch DPDT	Double pole double throw switch used to control two circuits with one switch.	
Toggle switch momentary action center off	Can be used to control a electric motor, such as for a window regulator.	
Push button momentary action	Can be used as starter, windshield washer, or horn switch.	

brake fluid level, and the level of diesel exhaust fluid (DEF) in reservoirs.
6. *Temperature-sensitive switches* use a bimetal arm that bends when heated. Internal contacts complete or open a circuit.
7. *Proximity switches* sense the approach of metal components. Simple-proximity switches use a permanent magnet to toggle a sealed reed switch mechanism as two parts approach one another. More complex proximity switches use a coil of wire energized with high-frequency AC. As the strength of the magnetic field changes with the approach of another metal part, induced current in the coil intensifies due to a change in magnetic reluctance. Proximity sensors are used in bus passenger door mechanisms, hydraulic systems using lifting rams, and other power components to sense position (**FIGURE 11-6**).

Switch Current Ratings

Switches are further categorized by the maximum amount of amperage and voltage they can safely handle. If voltage through the switch is more than it is designed to handle, current can internally bypass the contacts and arc. Excess amperage through a switch creates resistance heating of switch contacts, potentially melting and eventually burning the switch. To prevent these types of failures and unsafe conditions, switches are labeled with information indicating the maximum voltage and amperage the switch can tolerate on continuous duty. Selecting the appropriate switch depends, then, on the maximum anticipated amperage and voltage a circuit uses.

Automatic Type Switches

LO 11-2 Identify and describe the construction, operation, and applications of automatic switches.

In many applications, switches are designed to sense a physical state and automatically switch its position to open and close. Low coolant or brake fluid level, too high or low temperatures, low engine oil pressure, or low air brake reservoir air pressure require automatic switches to alert an operator to potentially dangerous conditions. Automatic switch operation sensing pressure, liquid level, or temperature switches on instrument cluster warning lights when predetermined thresholds are crossed. Automatic switches are different from sensors that supply a wide range of physical data in the form of electrical signals. Switches supply only binary data, which means they have only two states—open or closed. Even though switches are binary, on/off open/closed type switches can also be used as sensor inputs for electronic control modules, indicating whether a door is open, a pedal is pushed, or whether there is enough gas or fluid pressure to allow a system to safely operate. This next section examines the construction and operation of several common types of automatic switches.

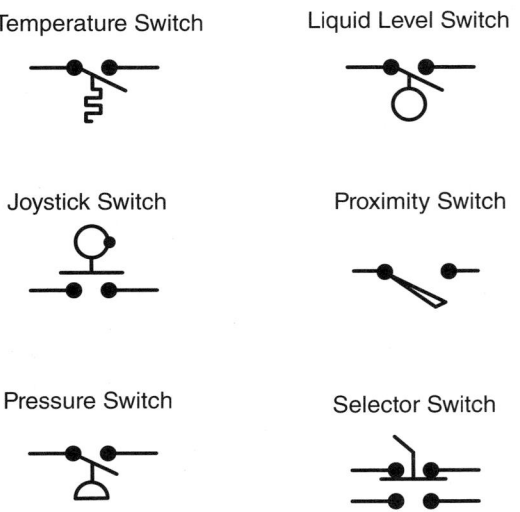

FIGURE 11-5 Schematic symbols for switch types organized by function.

Magnetic Reed Switches

Magnetic reed switches are automatic circuit control devices because they can switch current flow on and off when influenced by an external magnetic field (**FIGURE 11-7**). Various liquid level sensors operate with magnets attached to floats that are used to open and close switch contacts. Measuring fluid levels are popular applications for several reasons:

- Without mechanical operating force, there is little to no wear in the switch
- Non-corroding contacts because the switch contacts are enclosed in a sealed vacuum tube, which makes them ideal for use in corrosive environments

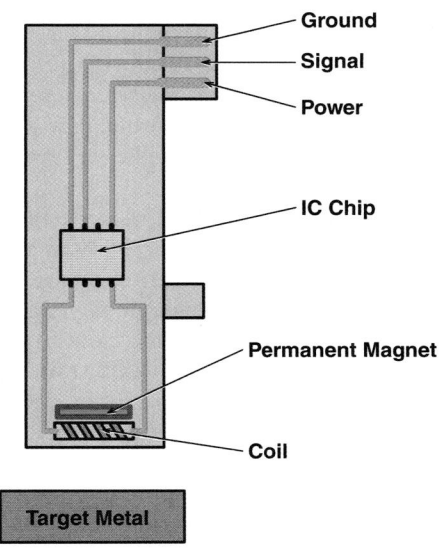

FIGURE 11-6 A proximity sensor has switch-like characteristics when used to indicate whether or not a metal target is correctly positioned.

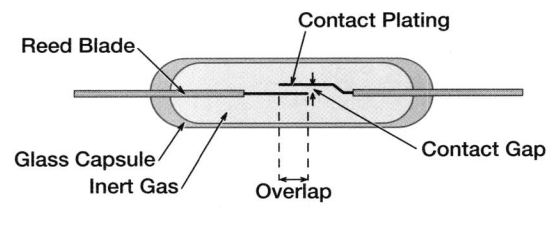

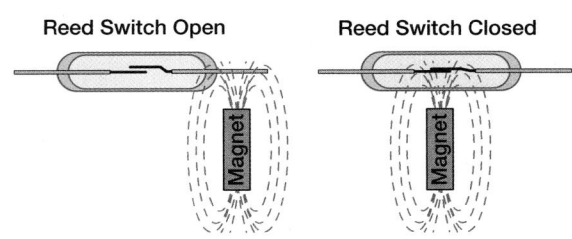

FIGURE 11-7 Reed switches can be either opened or closed when under the influence of magnetic fields. If one reed contact is magnetized, the polarity determines whether it opens or closes.

- High sensitivity to magnetic fields through thick non-magnetic materials translates into reliable, accurate switch operation
- Very low voltage can flow through contacts and no external voltage source is required to open or close the switch in potentially hazardous environments
- More compact size compared to mechanical switches

Magnetic reed sensors are also used in collision sensors, or as proximity sensors for doors and mechanical linkage. A cover, mechanical lever, or door with a magnet embedded in its surface can open and close reed switch contacts. Even the lid of a laptop or cover of a tablet uses reed switches to shut off a display.

Magnetic reed switches are **momentary contact switches** deriving their name from two or more thin, flat, ferrous metal strips encased in a glass envelope filled with nitrogen gas. The two spring-like strips can either be connected or separated when not influenced by a magnetic field. Bringing a strong magnet near the iron reeds pulls the reeds together or separates them, if one of the reeds is also magnetized.

Diesel exhaust fluid (DEF) level sensors, and even some fuel gauge level sensors, are constructed from multiple reed switches. Resistors connected in series change total circuit resistance through the level sending unit, depending on which point in the series circuit a reed switch closes, to form a current pathway through the resistors (**FIGURE 11-8**). A strong permanent magnet embedded in a float opens or closes the sealed switch contacts, depending on the fluid level. Changing the relative position of the float's magnet with the reed switches, in turn, sends circuit current through more or fewer resistors and vary the current supplied to a voltmeter-type instrument gauge. Smooth gauge operation using magnetic reed switches

as inputs is achieved by conditioning the switch signals or the use of software to estimate fluid consumption between stages of switch opening and closing.

Pressure-Sensitive Switches

Another common switch type encountered on commercial vehicles are pressure-sensitive switches. These switches open or close a set of electrical contacts when a specific pressure is reached. Pressure switches are calibrated to open or close in response to either fluid or gas pressure, depending on the application where they are used. For example, pressure switches found in air conditioning systems to sense low refrigerant pressure switch at between 10 and 20 psi to prevent system operation when refrigerant charge is low. Excessive refrigerant pressure, which could burst hoses, is prevented by the use of high refrigerant pressure switches that switch at pressures rising above 250 psi and shut off the air conditioning system compressor. Low air pressure in air brake reservoirs switch on mandatory warning buzzers and warning lamps in the instrument cluster. Pressure switches are also used to sense low oil pressure, or filter restrictions. Two or more pressure settings can also be incorporated into a single switch body. A binary switch contains two different pressure settings and switch contacts. A trinary switch contains three pressure switches with different pressure settings. Trinary switches for AC systems contain a high-and-low pressure switches for refrigerant pressure.

Pressure-sensitive switches are constructed to respond to a specific fluid or gas pressure using two types of designs: spring-loaded diaphragms and pistons. An elastic diaphragm opposed by spring pressure is best used for low pressure gas switching (**FIGURE 11-9**). The rubber-like diaphragm, which moves a switch contact, can respond well to small changes in pressure, but can be easily damaged by pressure surges, and the diaphragm material may be incompatible with certain fluids, such as fuel or oil. Constant cycling may weaken and break the diaphragm over time.

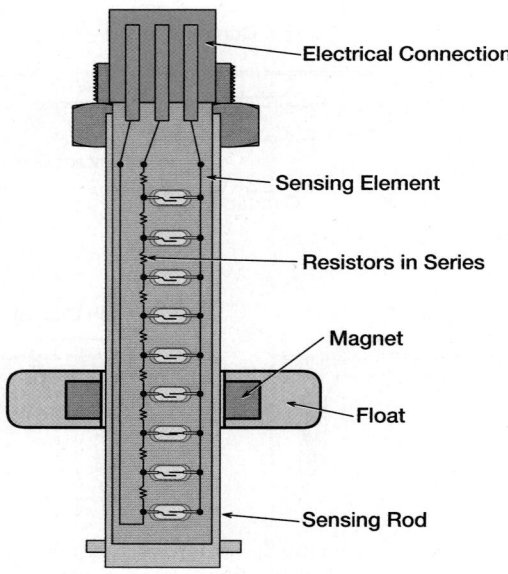

FIGURE 11-8 Magnetic reed switches are commonly used to sense fluid levels using magnetized floats to open and close contacts.

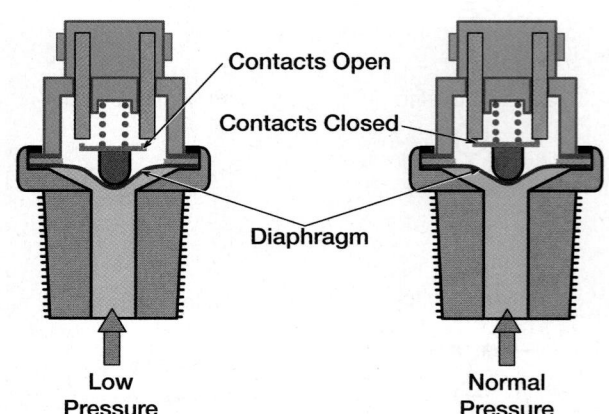

FIGURE 11-9 Construction details of a diaphragm-type pressure switch.

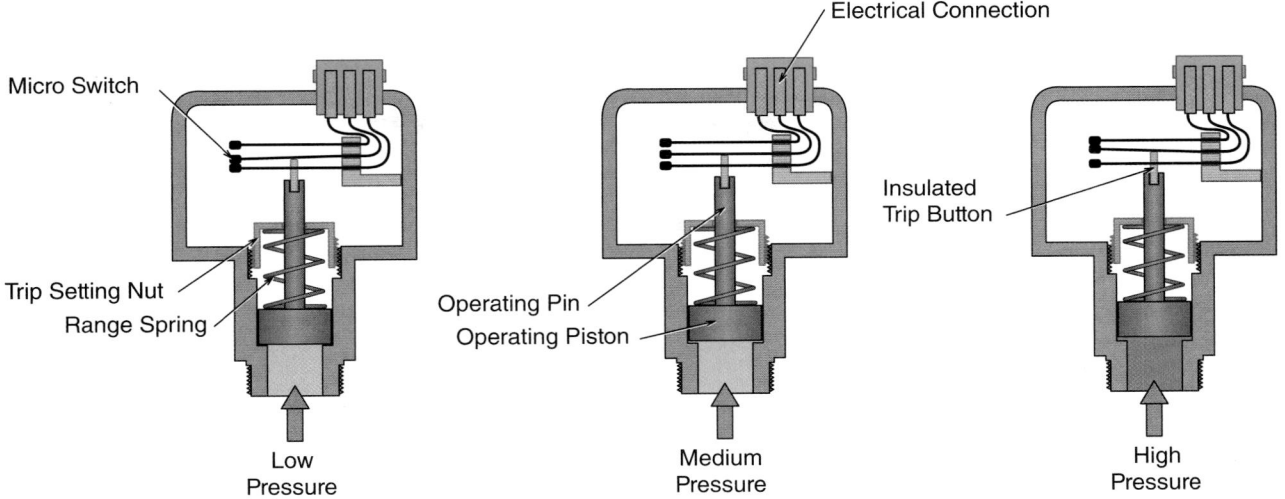

FIGURE 11-10 Construction details of a piston pressure-sensitive switch. An internal adjusting nut sets the pressure threshold for switch closing.

To overcome the problems with diaphragm-type pressure switches, a spring-loaded metal piston can be used to move an electrical contact. This design is best used for high-pressure hydraulic pressure switching and can best resist pressure spikes and fatigue caused by frequent pressure cycling (**FIGURE 11-10**).

Because pressures can change slowly and lead to a switch remaining in an in-between condition that is neither open nor closed, an over-center spring mechanism quickly latches the switch contacts with high contact force. Latching contacts with high spring force prevents contact damage from resistive heating caused by loose contact.

Temperature-Sensitive Switches

As the name suggests, temperature switches toggle or switch between an open and closed position when a predetermined temperature is reached. Thermostats and warning systems for excessive fluid temperatures or component temperatures, such as starting motor frames, are common applications for temperature-sensitive switches. Oil or coolant temperatures, which could result in catastrophic engine damage, can switch on instrument cluster warning lights to avoid damage. Low-temperature switches can activate electric intake heaters. Excess temperatures from over-current conditions in electric motors operating window regulators use temperature-sensitive switches, too.

Temperature-sensitive switches are similar in construction to automatic-type circuit breakers that use two types of temperature-sensitive mechanisms: **Bimetal and Positive Temperature Coefficient (PTC) devices**. Bimetal devices bond two different strips of metals together that have different expansion rates when heated or cooled (**FIGURE 11-11**). When heated or cooled, the metal strip bends. A set of electrical contacts can open and close in response to the deflection of a metal strip. The

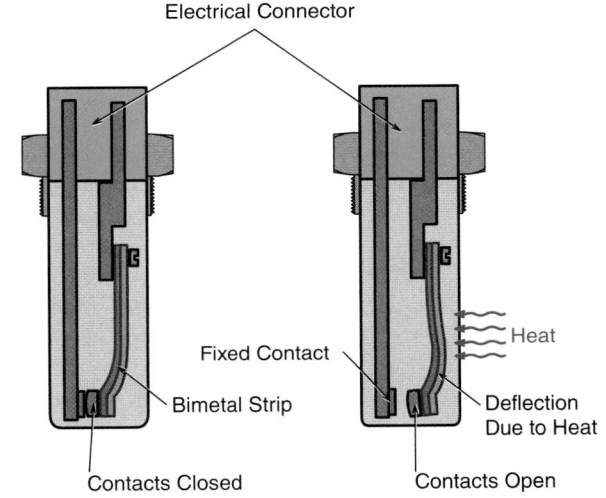

FIGURE 11-11 A metal strip made from binding two dissimilar metals with different expansion rates bends in response to temperature changes.

temperature set point of the bimetal strip is calibrated by spring tension, the types of metals used, and length of the bimetal material. Once again, a spring-loaded over-center device latches the switch into position to prevent damage from electrical resistance created by loose contacts.

PTCs are another type of temperature switch made from high-density polyethylene combined with graphite. Electric current flowing through a PTC switch heats the unique polymer material and causes the conducting particles to suddenly and sharply increase in resistance (**FIGURE 11-12**). In a heated, open state, the PTC switches off almost all current flow. Only a small amount of leakage current can pass through the PTC switch. Once cooled, the PTCs reset to a closed state and conduct current.

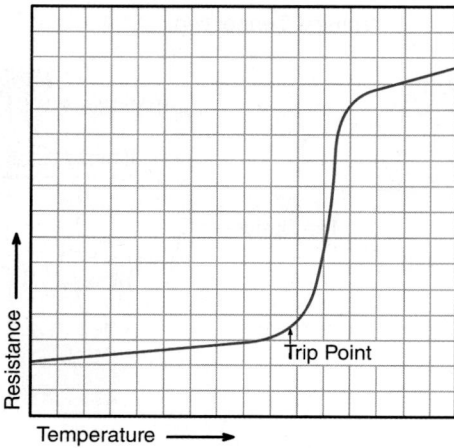

FIGURE 11-12 At a calibrated temperature, the PTC material properties change, resulting in a sharp increase in resistance.

Smart Switches

LO 11-3 Identify and describe the construction, operation, and applications of switched inputs to electronic control modules.

The complexity of today's commercial vehicles requires the capacity of on-board diagnostic systems to quickly identify faults. Switches controlling current flow in circuits can be defective, unintentionally disconnected, have wires broken or short circuited. Not only do faults and the nature of the faults in a complex system need to be quickly identified, but even performing pinpoint diagnostic tests to identify the problem—differentiating between defective switches and broken components or disconnected wiring in tightly wrapped harnesses with long runs of wiring passing through multiple connection points—can be time-consuming. To solve this problem, smart switches with some self-diagnostic capabilities are more frequently used.

A second purpose for evolving switch design is to supply control circuit current to electronic control modules. Circuit control switches do not carry all the current to energize a device, but instead supply only an input signal to an electronic control unit (ECU), which in turn energizes a device. Operating with an ECU, **smart switches** function only as digital inputs to electronic control systems. One of the problems this arrangement presents is that because switches can be in only one of two states, switch input information can only be binary. This means a switch can provide data, such as whether a device or system is on or off, high or low, open or closed, up or down, etc.—but gives no diagnostic information if a fault exists. A broken, shorted, or disconnected switch supplies data, but it is wrong and supplies potentially dangerous reports about switch state. To prevent this, information about the switches location and function can be added to the smart switch capabilities.

Pull-Up and Pull-Down Switches

Understanding smart switches should begin by first understanding how an ECU interprets switch information. The most basic switch input to an ECU provides current flow to a

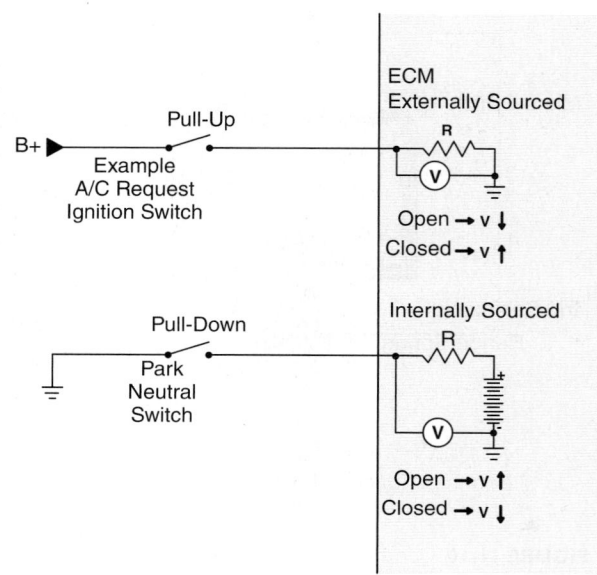

FIGURE 11-13 Depending on the polarity of input voltage to an ECM, switches are categorized as pull-up or pull-down.

designated pin on an ECU. Because it is connected to a specific pin, its function is understood by ECU programming by assigning a meaning to the pin data. Such switches with inputs to an ECU are categorized as either pull-up or pull-down, depending on the polarity of voltage supplied to an ECU. A switch connecting a positive voltage source to the ECU is a pull-up; switching a negative voltage or ground input on or off is considered a pull-down switch (**FIGURE 11-13**) (Down generally means toward ground).

One of the first types of smart switches is used not only to supply a pull-up or pull-down voltage input to the ECU, but also to incorporate one or two resistors to differentiate a closed or open switch from a circuit problem (**FIGURE 11-14**). For example, a high- or low-pressure refrigerant switch used by the air-conditioning system could become disconnected, shorted, or grounded, causing the system to malfunction and become severely damaged.

By installing a resistor in parallel across the switch contacts, the control module could detect one of several conditions. If the switch is open, only the resistance value of the resistor is measured (**FIGURE 11-15**). If the wire to the switch is disconnected or broken, the ECM measures infinite resistance and identifies a fault in the circuit. A closed switch has no resistance. Two resistors are used to differentiate between a shorted, grounded, or open circuit. One resistor is connected in parallel across the switch contacts and another is in series with the switch (**FIGURE 11-16**). An open switch supplies a voltage proportional to the voltage drop across the parallel and series resistor. A closed switch provides a voltage drop across only the series resistor.

In either the open or closed state, then, some resistance is always measured by the ECM across the switch when the circuit is properly functioning. A wire shorted to ground, to

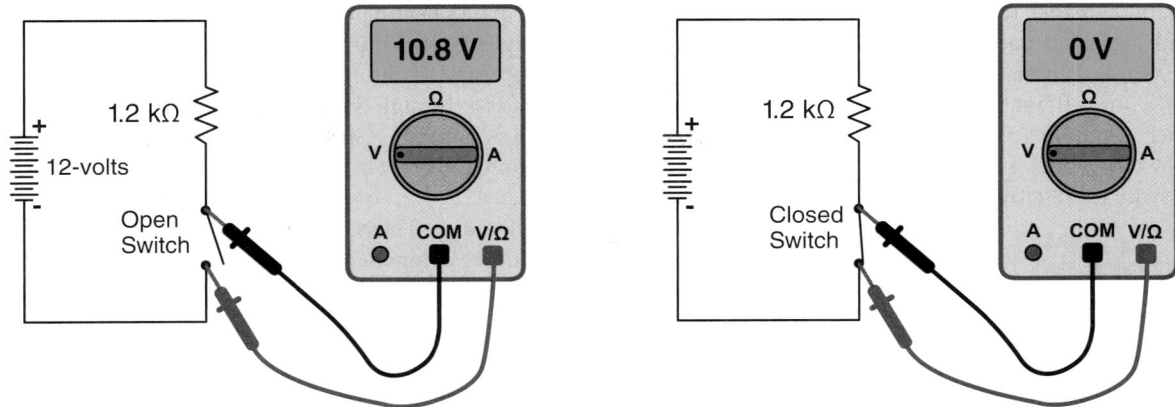

FIGURE 11-14 Voltage drop is measured here to illustrate the idea that a resistor connected in series with a switch can help the ECM detect whether a switch is open, closed, or has a broken circuit.

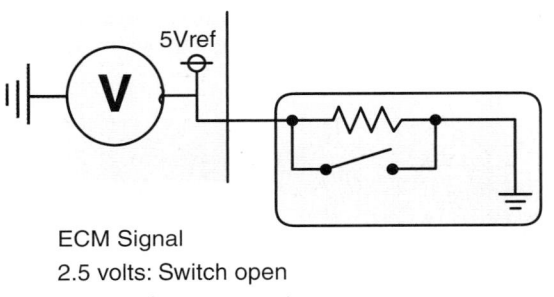

ECM Signal

2.5 volts: Switch open

0 volts : Switch closed

0 volts : Broken wire

FIGURE 11-15 A resistor connected in series across a switch can help differentiate a closed voltage signal from an open switch or open circuit.

a positive voltage source, or simply disconnected, supplies an out-of-expected-range voltage to the ECU and a fault would be identified.

Multiplex Switches

To minimize the amount of wiring required for switch circuits and provide identification of a switch function to the ECU, switch circuits can be designed with multiplex capabilities. Multiplexing is simply a system or signal involving simultaneous transmission of several messages or electrical signals along a single communication channel. In the case of **multiplex switches**, two or more switches can share a single wire for a switch pole and throw circuit, but transmit unique circuit control information from each switch. To help understand

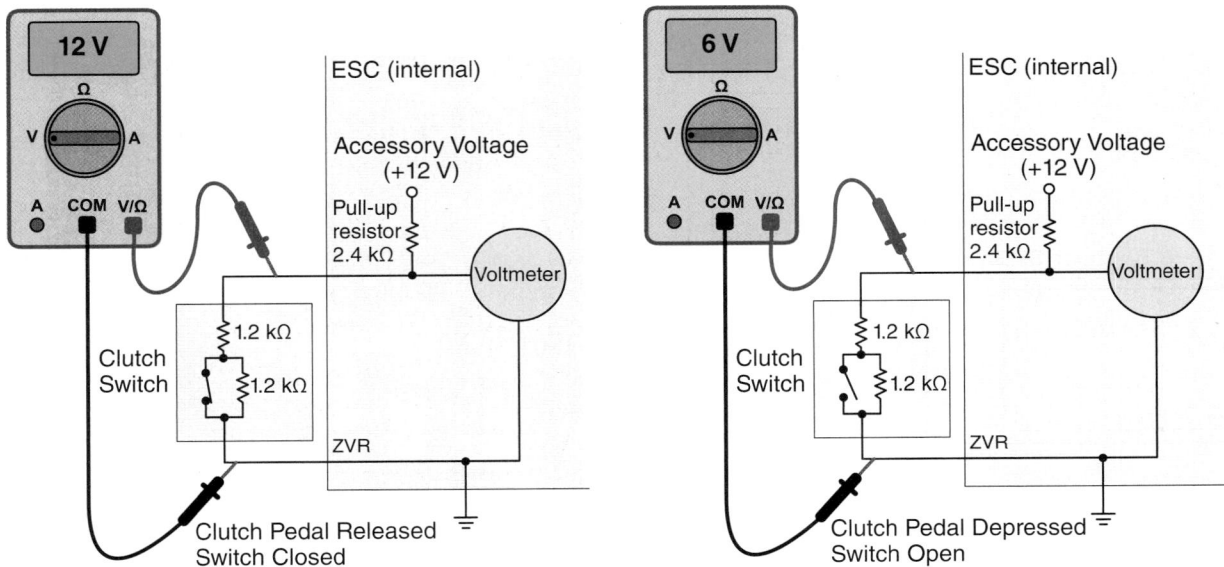

FIGURE 11-16 Diagnosable smart switches can integrate a resistor in parallel and in series with the switch.

this concept, consider the situation when several switches are connected in switch packs, such as those used by the cruise control or in dash-mounted switch clusters. The switches can use resistors of different values placed in either a series, parallel, or series-parallel to transmit a unique voltage value for a specific switch, while using a single wire input to the ECM for multiple switches (**FIGURE 11-17**).

Resistors

LO 11-4 Identify and describe the types, functions, and applications of resistive-type circuit control devices.

Another major category of electric circuit control devices used to change the flow of current are resistors. Changing circuit resistance alters the voltage and amperage passing through a circuit. Three types of resistors are commonly found in commercial vehicles:

1. Fixed
2. Stepped
3. Variable

Fixed Resistors

Fixed-type resistors are designed to conduct either heavy or light amounts of current. Wire-wound (power) resistors are made from resistive nickel/chrome wire. These function as current limiters because they become more resistive when connected in series with another electrical device and when amperage increases. Current limiters are often used to protect components from over-current abuse conditions and prevent burnout from overheating caused by resistive heating. For example, fast-start glow-plugs, which heat to incandescent temperatures within a couple of seconds, have a current-limiting resistor in series with the plug's heating element. As the heating element draws more amperage, the current-limiting resistor increases circuit resistance and limits the maximum amount of heating amperage passing through the heating element, thus extending its service life. Axial-type resistors once made from carbon, or more commonly today from more reliable metal oxides, are another type of current-limiting resistor commonly found in electronic circuit boards. These resistors change or limit the supply of current to other components on circuit boards. Colored bands around the axial-type resistor identify its numerical resistance in ohms (**FIGURE 11-18**).

Stepped Resistors

Stepped resistors are made from two or more wire-wound resistors. A common application for this type of resistor is in a blower motor speed control circuit (**FIGURE 11-19**). Each of these resistors connected in series is also connected to a terminal on the blower switch. The output of the resistor is connected to a blower motor. Varying the switch position changes the current available to the blower motor. Locating

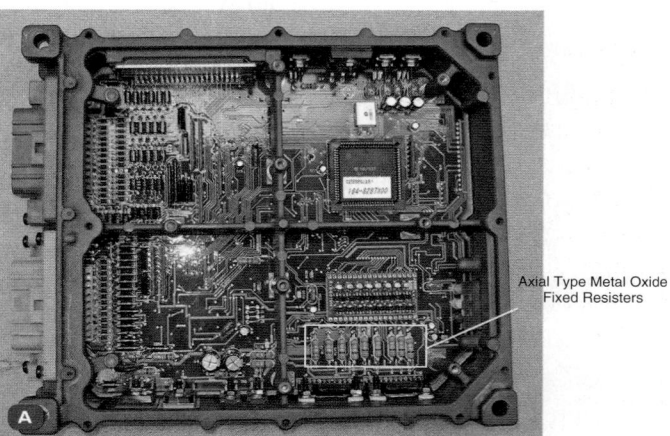

Axial Type Metal Oxide Fixed Resisters

Surface Mount Fixed Resisters

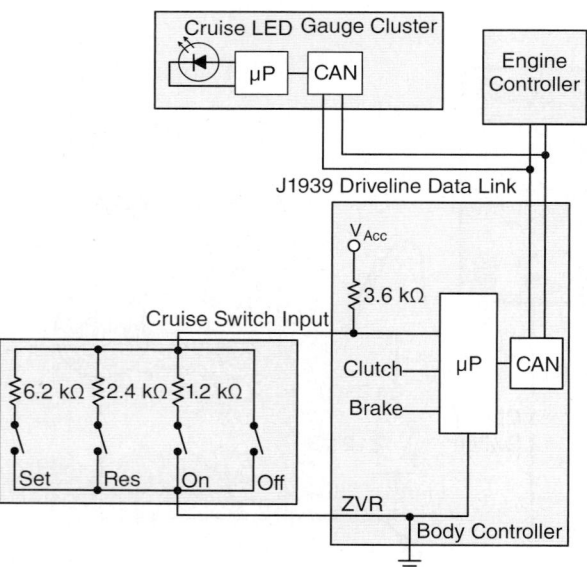

FIGURE 11-17 A unique voltage drop across a switch pack is measured by the ECM. The voltage drop corresponds to a specific switch in the open or closed state when a resistor is connected in series with the switch.

FIGURE 11-18 Two types of fixed resistors are used in these engine ECMs. **A.** Metal oxide axial-type. **B.** Surface mount. Axial resistors use color bands to identify resistance value. Newer circuit boards use surface mount resistors.

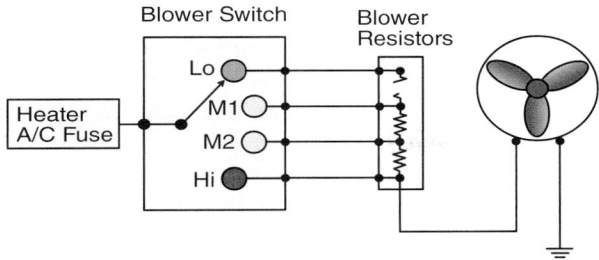

FIGURE 11-19 A stepped resistor arrangement for a blower motor circuit. One resistor is open, which prevents low-speed operation.

the resistor in the blower motor housing where it is cooled helps prevent premature burn-out of the resistor.

Variable Resistors

Variable resistors are a type of resistor with an adjustable resistance. A variety of variable resistors exist that are made from materials ranging from wound nickel/chrome wire to resistive carbon tracks to resistors made from semiconductors, and are digitally, rather than mechanically, adjusted. For this chapter on circuit control devices, the two most important types of variable resistors are:

1. Rheostat
2. Potentiometer

Rheostats

Rheostats vary current flow by passing current through a long, resistive, tightly coiled wire (**FIGURE 11-20**). A wiper-like contact sliding over the coil supplies a variable current output. The change in current output is produced as the wiper contact sliding over the resistive wire winding changes the length of the resistive pathway between the resistor input and the wiper output. Moving the wiper closer to the powered input end of the resistive wire reduces resistance. Moving the wiper farther from the input increases resistance. Instrument cluster dimmer switches and fuel tank sending units are examples of applications where rheostats were once commonly used. Rheostats have only two terminals—a fixed input and a variable output.

Potentiometers

Like the rheostat, **potentiometers** are variable resistors, but with three connections—one at each end of a resistive path. A third connection is a sliding wiper contact that moves along the resistive pathway (**FIGURE 11-21**). Unlike rheostats, which limit current flow, potentiometers perform a voltage-dividing function. This means the third sliding wiper terminal is usually supplied current to divide or portion the current between the other two terminals along a resistive pathway. Voltage at the two other terminal connections changes because there may be a little or a lot of resistance between the wiper terminals, depending on the wiper's position along the resistive track. A radio speaker balance control supplying an audio signal to the wiper terminal distributes the signal with more or less volume to two other speakers connected to the other two terminals, connected to each end of the resistive track. A throttle pedal position sensor is another common application for potentiometers. In this application, voltage output of the wiper terminal varies according to its position relative to a reference

FIGURE 11-20 This fuel tank sending unit uses a rheostat to vary current flow through a ground path. A position change in the tank float, which is connected to the rheostat, varies current flow through the fuel level gauge in the instrument cluster. **A.** 5-volt input. **B.** Resistive film strip. **C.** Signal return. **D.** Wiper whisker. **E.** Float arm.

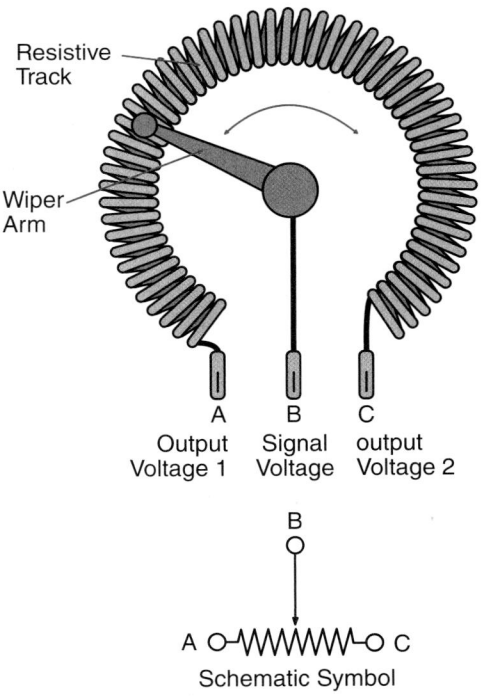

FIGURE 11-21 A potentiometer has three leads and is a variable resistor. Changing the wiper position increases or decreases voltage at either of the output signal pins.

voltage input supplied to another pin of the potentiometer. When configured this way, the third pin is also connected to the ECM, which measures the voltage drop across the potentiometer's entire resistive track to check whether the resistive circuit has worn out, is open, or is shorted.

Electromechanical Relays

LO 11-5 Identify and describe the construction, operation, and applications of common types of electromagnetic relays.

A relay is an automatic switch that uses a small amount of current to switch a larger amount of current. Relays are useful devices for switching higher amperage current to heavy electrical loads using low-current output circuits from an ECU or manually operated cab switch. Relays can eliminate the need for heavy current to pass through cab switches, which can potentially catch fire. Another reason for using relays is the ability to reduce voltage drops in circuits with manual or automatic switches. Locating a relay closer to a load requiring large amounts of current eliminates voltage drop caused by resistance from long runs of wires to manual or automatic switches in the cab.

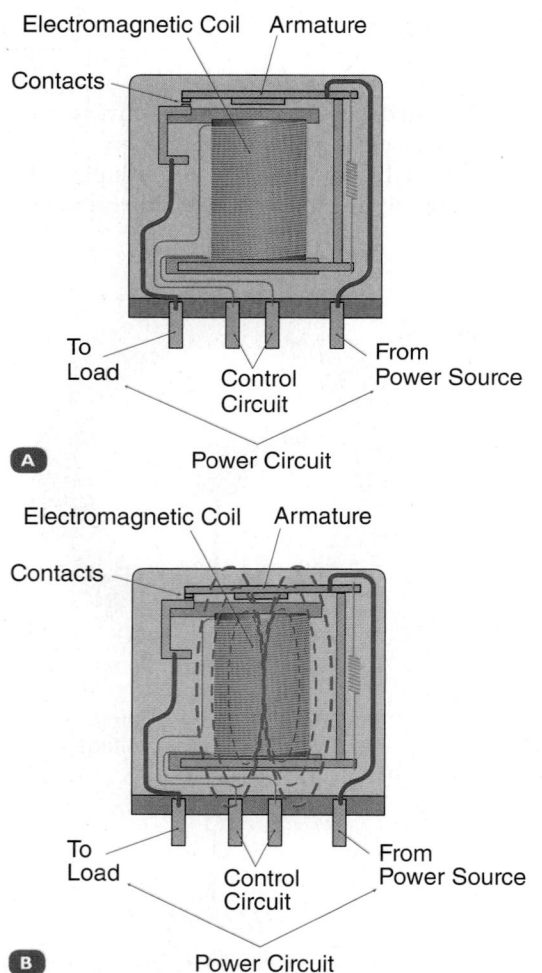

FIGURE 11-22 Operation of a relay with a single contact. **A.** Non-energized with contacts open. **B.** Energizing the electromagnet with a small amount of electrical current closes the contacts, which can switch high-amperage current flow.

The simplest relay has a control circuit and a load circuit. The control circuit is supplied current through a switch, which often is opened or closed by an electronic control unit or the vehicle operator. Inside the relay, an electromagnetic coil pulls a set of contacts closed. It is across these electromechanically operated contacts that a larger amount of current is switched. The relay's control circuit can be switched on or off by using either a battery positive or negative ground to the relay. If an ECU supplies a positive voltage to switch the control circuit, it is termed a pull-up circuit. If it supplies a ground, it is called a pull-down circuit. The other terminal of the control circuit must receive a continuous supply of either negative- or positive-polarity current to complete the electrical pathway through the control circuit.

International Standards Organization (ISO) relays, also called cube relays, are the most common relays used in commercial vehicle chassis today. Two of the most popular sizes are an ISO Mini and Micro. The mini is approximately 1" (~25 mm) in length, width, and height. The micro relay is the same size except it is only half as wide as a mini relay to enable more relays to fit in a power distribution or fuse box. Both four- and five-pin designs are used by the mini and micro relay, but different pin numbering is used (**FIGURES 11-22** and **11-23**). The relay is standardized to be used across all vehicle manufacturers, having standard pin numbers, functions, and dimensions to fit into a power distribution box. These relays can switch as much as 35 amps in a 12-volt system. ISO standards designate current supply polarity to each terminal (**TABLES 11-3** and **11-4**). See New Chart ISO standards. The control circuit coil should be supplied with +12 V to terminal 86 and grounded by terminal 85. This is especially important since most relays use a diode to suppress voltage spikes induced through self-induction when power is disconnected from the coil. The relay does not operate at all if the control circuit is supplied an incorrect polarity

FIGURE 11-23 Mini ISO relays in a power distribution box. Current suppressed relays use a diode, resistor, and sometimes a capacitor, to minimize a voltage spike produced through self-induction.

TABLE 11-3 Terminal Designation Standards for ISO Mini Relays

Terminal Number	Current Supply	Circuit Designation
85	12 or 24 +	Control circuit coil
86	12 or 24 −	Control circuit coil
87	Either + or −	Normally Open (NO) contact
87a	Either + or −	Normally Closed (NC) contact not present on four-pin relays
30	Either + or −	Common pole connection to NO & NC terminals

TABLE 11-4 Terminal Designation Standards for ISO Micro Relays

Terminal Number	Current Supply	Circuit Designation
1	12 or 24 +	Control circuit coil
2	12 or 24 −	Control circuit coil
3	Either + or −	Normally Open (NO) contact
4	Either + or −	Normally Closed (NC) contact not present on four-pin relays
5	Either + or −	Common pole connection to NO & NC terminals

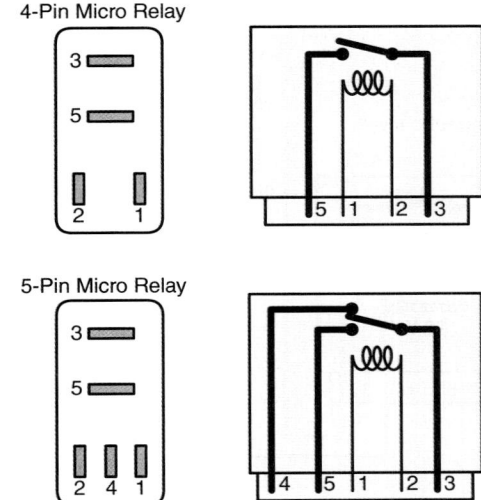

FIGURE 11-24 The pin-out configuration for four- and five-pin ISO micro relays.

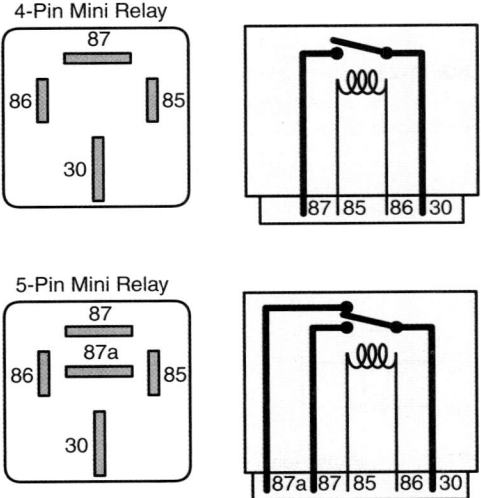

FIGURE 11-25 The pin-out configuration for four- and five-pin ISO mini relays.

and a diode is used. Polarity of other terminals can be either positive or negative to form correctly functioning circuits.

The simplest four-pin relays are known as make or break relays since there is only a single pole and throw opened and closed by the magnetic field of the control circuit coil (**FIGURE 11-24**). The circuit between relay terminals 30 and 87 is closed when the control circuit is energized in a normally open relay. Five-pin relays are called change-over because they contain a single pole double throw switch (**FIGURE 11-25**). One throw is normally open and the other throw is normally closed until the control circuit is energized.

Because relays use electromagnetic coils, a large voltage spike is produced when the coils are de-energized (**FIGURES 11-26** and **11-27**). The rapidly collapsing magnetic field moves across the coil conductors, inducing over 200 volts in the control circuit when power is switched off. If the relay control circuit shares a voltage supply with the ignition switch or sensitive electronic component, electrical damage can occur. To prevent this, a diode or resistor connected in parallel across the coil provides an alternate pathway for the voltage spike to dissipate though the coil when the magnetic field collapses. At least in the aftermarket repair and modification industry, newer inexpensive solid-state relays are replacing electromechanical relays. The silent operation of these relays and the extremely low triggering current

make them practical for upfitters installing audio equipment, security alarms, lighting, and other power accessories (**FIGURE 11-28**).

▶ TECHNICIAN TIP

Relays that buzz during operation indicate insufficient voltage to the control circuit due to causes, such as excessive current flow through a relay load, which drops available voltage to the control circuit when the pole and throw are closed; low battery voltage; resistive control circuit connections; or a resistive circuit of another relay or component sharing the same ground or battery positive circuit. This last condition is commonly called an electrical back-feed, but is an unintentional electrical pathway forming though the relay control circuit supplied by another ground or power source attempting to find an electrical pathway through the relay.

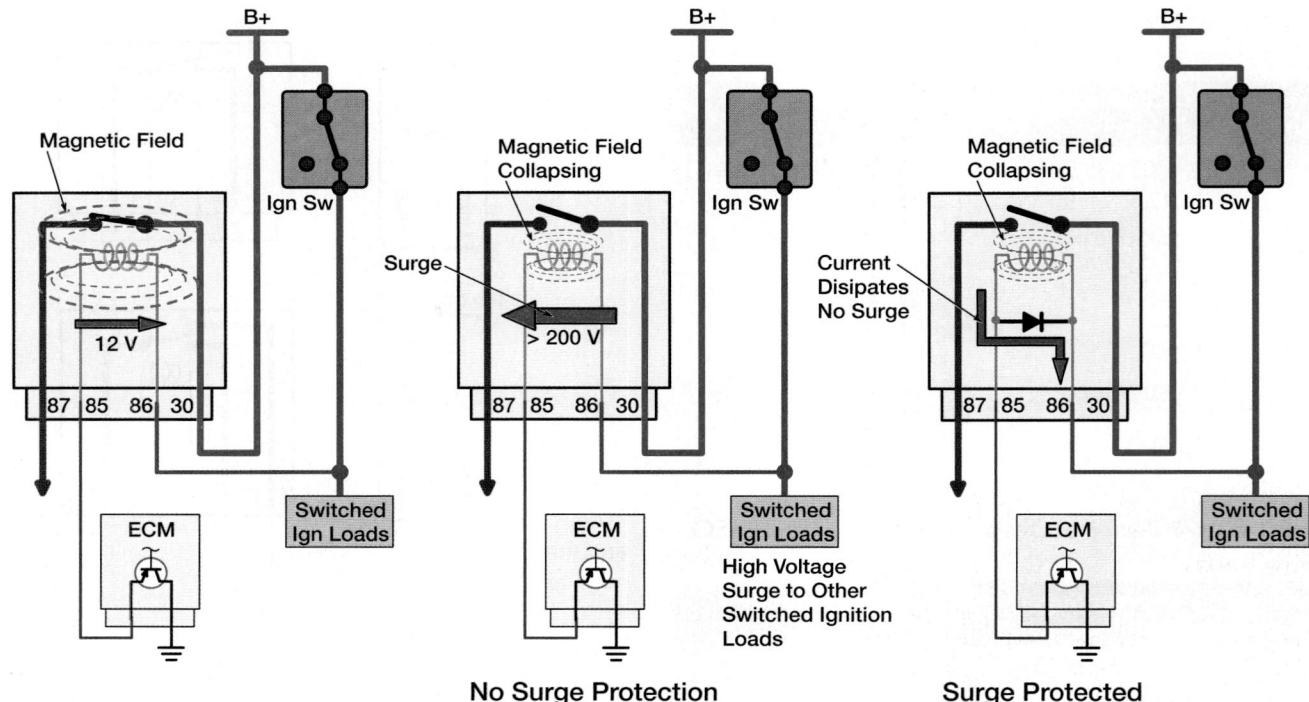

FIGURE 11-26 Self-induction inside a relay can supply a large voltage spike, which can damage sensitive electronic components. No conduction takes place through the diode during normal operation. High-voltage current moving in the opposite direction of the original current forward biases the diode, and current dissipates through resistance in the circuit.

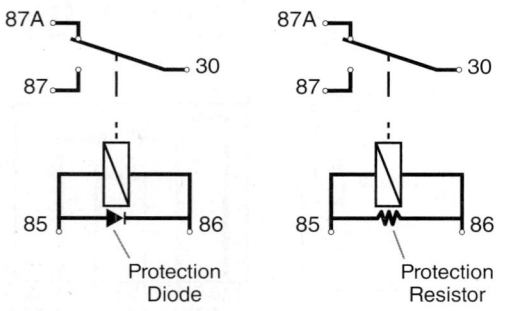

FIGURE 11-27 A resistor or a diode is used to suppress voltage spike produced through self-induction.

FIGURE 11-28 An ISO-style solid-state relay with a heat sink operates silently in DC circuits and requires low triggering current, yet delivers 40 amps of current.

Magnetic Switches

Magnetic or **"mag" switches** are identical in function to relays except that they switch even larger amounts of current and have different dimensions compared to ISO cube relays (**FIGURE 11-29**). Magnetic switches are also classified as continuous- or intermittent-duty service. When switching heavy amounts of current, such as to the starter motor solenoid, available battery voltage can drop as the starting motor cranks (**FIGURE 11-30**). Low available voltage reduces the magnetic field strength in the switch, causing the mag-switch to "chatter" as it rapidly engages and disengages when the electrical system voltage cycles between low voltage (when cranking) and increased voltage when the starting motor is momentarily disconnected by the mag switch.

To counter this chattering effect caused by excessive voltage drop in the electrical system, the electromagnetic coil windings can be wound from heavier-gauge wire. The result is fewer coils, but more amperage through the low-resistance coil, which helps build and maintain a stronger magnetic field (**FIGURE 11-31**). A problem with this arrangement is high amperage flow through the winding causes the coil to quickly burn out after just a few minutes or hours of continuous operation. To prevent that, continuous-duty relays are made from thinner wire with higher resistance. The number of amp-turns strength of the magnetic field is adequate and they can remain energized for longer periods of time. However, a continuous-duty relay with thinner gauge wiring in the control circuit coils is sensitive to voltage drop, leading to relay chatter.

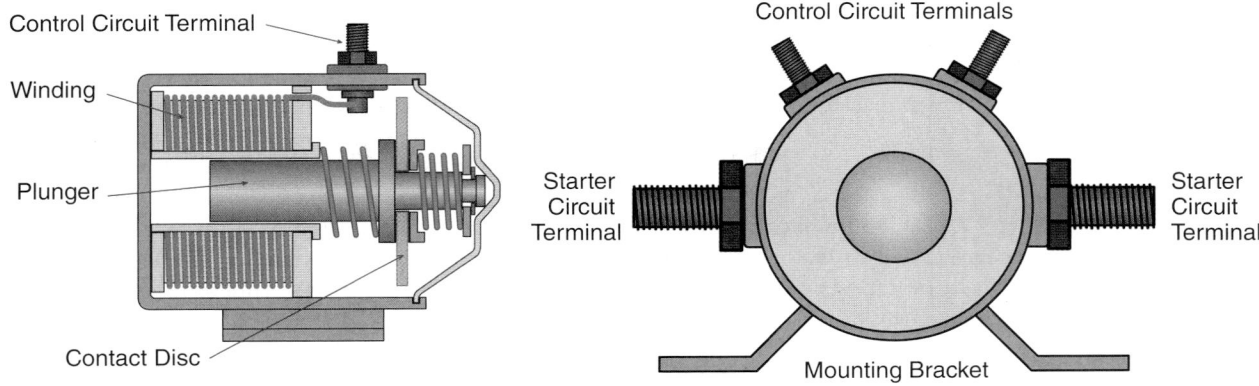

FIGURE 11-29 Construction of a larger magnetic switch used for switching large amounts of electrical current.

FIGURE 11-30 A. A magnetic switch used to switch high current flow to the **B.** starter solenoid. The chassis ECM supplies a ground to energize the control circuit.

▶ **TECHNICIAN TIP**

Continuous- and intermittent-duty magnetic switches can look identical but cause problems if not used in the correct application. Continuous-duty relays, when used to operate glow plugs or starter motor solenoids, chatter during cranking and prevent the engine from starting. Intermittent-duty relays burn out if left energized for a few hours. Always verify the mag switch is meant for its intended applications if encountering frequent mag-switch failures or starter and mag-switch chatter.

Solenoids

LO 11-6 Identify and describe the construction and operation of electromagnetic solenoids.

Solenoids are devices with a movable core that converts current flow into mechanical movement (**FIGURE 11-32**). A familiar application of solenoids is in starter motors. When energized, the solenoid moves a mechanical lever to engage the drive

FIGURE 11-31 A. Continuous-duty relays use thinner, more resistive winding, which does not burn-out due to high current flow. **B.** The windings of intermittent-duty mag switches are thicker. Thicker windings use more amperage, but stay engaged longer, when available battery voltage drops during cranking.

mechanism while switching heavy current into the motor. Solenoids are also used to actuate door-lock mechanisms, control air and hydraulic flow, move shut-off levers on fuel systems, and any other place where electric control of mechanical movement is needed (**FIGURE 11-33**).

Solenoid Operation

Solenoids can be either pull-type or push-and-pull type. In pull-in-type solenoids, an electromagnet pulls a soft iron core into the coil. The strength of the magnetic field must be stronger than spring force, which opposes the movement of the soft iron core and returns the core to its resting deenergized position. When

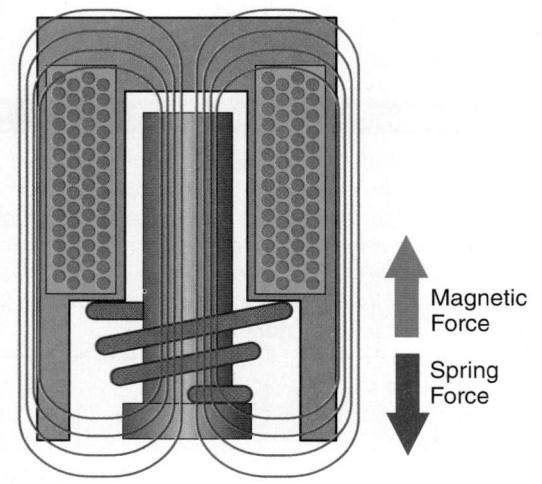

FIGURE 11-32 Solenoids may use a spring to return the actuator to a resting position.

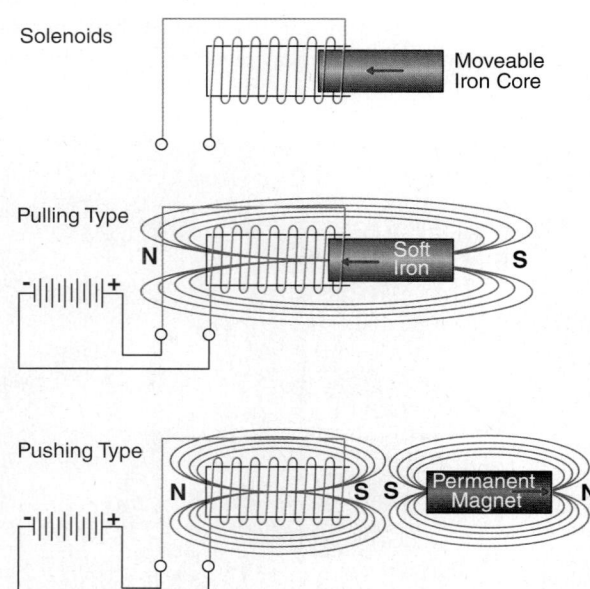

FIGURE 11-33 Push- and pull-type solenoids. Reversing the direction of current flow through the winding changes its polarity. If the actuator is magnetized, the actuator is either pulled or pushed by the magnetic field.

a high amount of force is required for moving such devices as a starter drive mechanism or fuel-injection pump shut-off lever, two electromagnetic coils are used. Two coils prevent the solenoid from continuously drawing a high amount of current and potentially burning out, or unnecessarily drawing power from the electrical system. The first coil initially energized is a pull-in winding, which uses thick wire windings developing high amp times turns equals magnetic field strength. (Recall Magnetic field strength = amperage × number of turns) A second hold-in coil "holds" the solenoid's iron core in place, taking over from the work done by the pull-in winding. The hold-in winding has more turns made of narrower diameter, but more resistive wire, drawing less amperage, yet having strong magnetic field amp X turn strength. Once the high amperage pull-in winding has done its job, it is electrically disconnected. An internal switching mechanism inside the solenoid is responsible for the change-over from high amperage pull-in to lower amperage hold-in winding.

Push-pull type solenoids use a permanent magnet instead of an iron core to produce bidirectional movement. By changing the polarity of the coil, the magnetic field around the permanent magnet core can either repel or attract the coil. Push-pull solenoids are commonly used to actuate electric door locks.

▶ **TECHNICIAN TIP**

It is important for the pull-in winding of a solenoid to be electrically disconnected after a solenoid is initially engaged. The thinner, more resistive windings of the hold-in winding take over from the pull-in windings and hold the core in place, which is attached to a lever. If the solenoid remained engaged, the pull-in windings would burn out due to excessive current flow. Adjustment of solenoid travel is crucial to enable an internal change-over switch to operate and prevent this from happening. Adjustable linkage on the solenoid plunger should be checked against manufacturer's specifications if a solenoid has frequent failures (**FIGURE 11-34**). This adjustment is especially critical on fuel shut-off lever solenoids for injection pumps.

FIGURE 11-34 This injection pump shut-off solenoid has a high-amperage pull-in and low-amperage hold-in winding to move the control rack from no-fuel position.

Servicing Circuit Control Devices

LO 11-7 Outline service and test procedures for circuit control devices.

Switches and relays are reliable electrical components if they are operated within specified voltage and amperage ratings. Loose wiring and terminal connectors caused by vibration, overheating, or mis-assembly can cause resistive connections and even further damage from resistive heating. If terminals and socket pins are exposed to elements, corrosion can take place at pins and terminals. More rapid terminal loosening and corrosion takes place if pins and terminals are not sealed with a purpose-made corrosion-inhibiting grease, such as dielectric grease, which also can dampen vibration, leading to loose connections. One of the biggest challenges for technicians is to correctly identify defective switches and relays when encountering inoperative or intermittently operative circuits. Without a clear understanding of how a circuit is constructed using a switch or how a relay functions, these components are often unnecessarily replaced during trial and error diagnosis, or simply overlooked after other parts are unnecessarily replaced. This next section briefly describes techniques for identifying control circuit components.

▶ **TECHNICIAN TIP**

When diagnosing problems with relays and switches, non-powered test lights using incandescent bulbs are the best instruments to check for the presence of switched power at terminal throws. High-impedance multimeters may display a correct voltage of 12 or 24 V DC, but does not draw enough power from a live circuit to identify highly resistive, corroded, or burnt electrical contacts. The small amount of amperage drawn by a test light bulb produces a significant voltage drop across resistive contacts to identify a resistive set of contacts. This practice of using a non-powered test light is especially important when checking switches exposed to any type of fluid that can enter a switch and increase contact resistance.

Servicing Switches

When a circuit is not functioning correctly, the first check made should be to verify the fuse and any circuit protection device is intact. If the circuit is powered with the ignition on, the fuse or circuit breaker should be probed on both sides—battery supply and circuit out—with a test light. During a visual inspection of a switch, no severe discoloration, evidence of burning, or loose connections should be observed. The switch should consistently operate smoothly and lock into the correct position. Apart from manufacturer recommended troubleshooting steps, switches can be checked with test lights, voltmeters, and ohmmeters. Defective smart switches are identified by fault codes and, in most cases, pinpoint testing of switches and circuits takes place using an ohmmeter after a fault code has identified the proper diagnostic troubleshooting sequence recommended by the manufacturer.

There are two basic methods used to perform pinpoint tests of a switch. One method is to disconnect a switch from its circuit and test for continuity between the poles and throws. In a closed position, there should be no resistance between a pole and throw. When open, infinite resistance should be measured between open poles and throws. These checks apply to single- or double-pole switches with one or more throws.

With a 12-volt or 24-volt switch that is powered on, probing the switch pins or terminals with a non-powered test light is a best practice. The light should appear to be the same brightness at the powered pole and throw. Internal resistance caused by corroded or burnt switch contacts dim the light's intensity and a switch replacement is recommended. To verify resistive internal contacts, a voltmeter connected between a switch pole and throw should indicate no more than 1/10th of a volt drop across switch terminals when the circuit is powered, and the switch is closed.

Replacing Switches

When a switch is defective, it should be replaced. If an exact replacement is unavailable, switches can be substituted using a different style, such as replacing a push button on/off with a toggle switch or a rocker lever. However, the switch should be physically compatible with the original mounting location and easily usable for the operator. It's important, when selecting a substitute, that the replacement have the following features:

- At least the same number of poles and throw
- The same number of positions, to avoid user confusion
- Identical in whether the switch is momentary or locked contact
- At least the same or greater current ratings than the original switch

Servicing Solenoids

When a solenoid is suspected of operating incorrectly, intermittently or not at all, a visual inspection of the solenoid should indicate the solenoid's linkage is operating smoothly and not binding. If rubber boots sealing the linkage mechanism are used, they should be present and intact (**FIGURE 11-35**). When energized for a long period, the solenoid should be warm to touch, but not so hot that it cannot be firmly held. Resistive connections or low-voltage supplied to the solenoid causes it

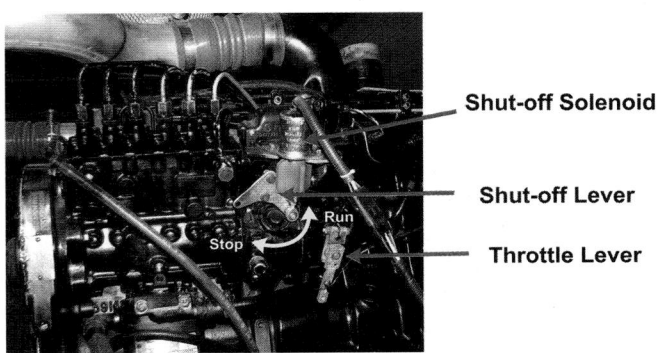

FIGURE 11-35 The electric shut-off solenoid used for an inline pump-line-nozzle-type injection pump.

to disengage after some time. Terminals should be insulated and tight without corrosion present.

When operating the solenoid on and off, movement should be rapid and consistent. On solenoids with separate hold-in and pull-in windings, the linkage moves to its farthest extended during cranking, or when the ignition key is initially switched on. Current flow is highest at this point. In a run position, or after a moment when the key is switched on, it is normal to observe a solenoid retract to a hold-in position. Misadjusted solenoid linkage causes the solenoid to prematurely fail or to engage and quickly drop out. Correctly adjusted linkage prevents both conditions, especially rapid burn-out of solenoid windings. This explains why it is important to compare solenoid adjustment against specifications.

Next, measure the supply voltage to the solenoid. It should be the same as chassis voltage. When the solenoid is disconnected, check the resistance of the windings. The ohmmeter can be connected to the winding lead and an isolated ground terminal on the solenoid, or the case, if the ground is not insulated or isolated from chassis ground. Again, there should be some resistance in the windings with no open windings and a

difference in measurements of resistance between the hold in and pull-in winding.

Servicing Mag Switches and Relays

Relays and magnetic switches should be visually inspected and any circuit protection device, such as fuses and breakers, properly validated prior to any pinpoint testing. Visual inspection of the switch should show no evidence of physical damage, overheating, or loose connections. Some switches ground through a metal case and the contact point between the case, and cab or frame should be both tight and clean. Verify the ground is connected to the control circuit and chassis using a test light clipped to a positive battery source. The light should illuminate brightly when the ground terminal on the mag-switch is probed. On a mag-switch for a push-button starter, the push button should be pressed while the lead to the starter solenoid is disconnected to perform a voltage drop check of the control circuit. To perform these tests, follow the steps in **SKILL DRILL 11-1**.

Available voltage can be checked using a test light and voltmeter, but the voltage drop between the battery positive of the starter and the control circuit should be measured with a digital

SKILL DRILL 11-1 Performing a Magnetic Switch Test

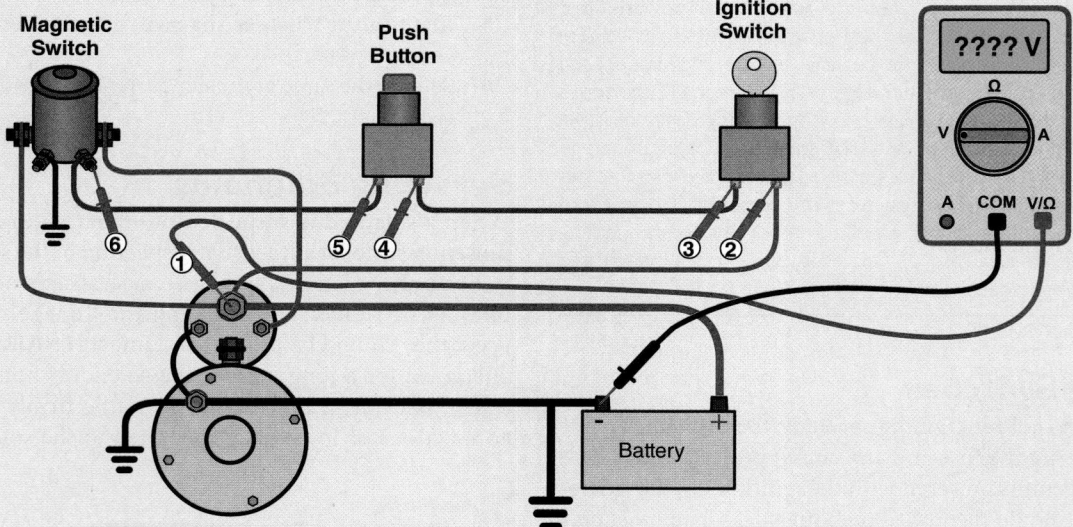

1. Verify all circuit protection devices, such as fuses and circuit breakers, are intact and supplying power to appropriate circuits.
2. Verify the battery is in a charge state of at least 75% or more.
3. Visually inspect the switch and connected wiring for physical damage, looseness, or overheating. Clean and repair any corroded or damaged terminals and recommend replacement of a switch with melted connections or burned terminals.
4. Using a voltmeter, measure the voltage available to the mag-switch at the battery terminal by placing one lead on a good frame connection and the other on the stud of the mag-switch terminal. If the voltage is not the same as battery voltage, inspect, clean, and repair battery cable connections and check for an open circuit in the cable. Use the ohmmeter function on

the multimeter to inspect for loose or open connections in the cable after disconnecting it from the switch and battery supply.
5. Verify whether the mag-switch is operating correctly by activating the control circuit. Cycle the starter button or switch for an electric motor lift gate on and off while listening for a sharp clicking sound from the switch as it closes and opens. Use a test light to verify current flow is at the load terminal of the relay when the switch is activated.
6. If the switch clicks, when cycled, measure the voltage drop across the switch contacts. Connect the voltmeter leads to the battery and load terminals of the switch using a digital multimeter ranged to measure battery voltage. Cycle the switch on and off to observe and record voltage drop. If more

SKILL DRILL 11-1 Performing a Magnetic Switch Test (Continued)

than 0.5 volts is measured on a 12-volt chassis (two volts in a 24-volt system), replace the switch. The contacts have become excessively resistive.

7. If the switch does not operate correctly or operate at all, high resistance in the control circuit prevents switch closing and causes the switch to disconnect or drop-out. To check for resistances and open circuits, perform voltage tests of the control and load circuit.

8. Disconnect the lead wire of the mag-switch to load. On a starting motor, this is the "S" terminal.

9. Connect a voltmeter ranged to measure less than 20-V DC to the two small control circuit terminals on the mag-switch. If the mag-switch has only one control circuit terminal, use the switch case or its bracket for the ground connection.

10. Press or toggle the button for the mag-switch control circuit. (i.e., starter button or key). Measure and record the voltage reading. If the mag-switch operates, indicated by a click, and the voltage is within one-volt of actual battery voltage for

a 12-volt system (two volts in a 24-volt system), the control circuit is ok.

11. If the mag-switch does not "click" closed, and voltage is within specification, the control circuit is open, and the mag-switch requires replacement.

12. If the control circuit voltage drops are outside specification, more than either specified one- or two-volts below battery, check for a poor control circuit ground. Do this by moving the test lead from the positive terminal to a good frame or battery-ground connection while leaving the other lead on the switch case or bracket. Cycle the switch on and off. If the voltage drop is more than either one or two volts, depending on chassis voltage of 12- or 24-volts battery, clean and repair the resistive switch case ground or ground lead.

13. If no control circuit voltage is measured, a voltage drop measurement must be performed for the battery supply. Perform the voltage drop test in step 10 for each of any additional control circuit switches shown in the figure.

voltmeter. When a voltage drop test is performed between the battery positive and the control circuit positive or ground connections, Delco Remy suggests there should be no more than a one-volt (two volts in 24-volts systems) difference between available voltage and battery voltage when the switch is energized (**FIGURE 11-36**).

ISO Relay Testing

Diagnosing problems or confirming ISO relays are operating correctly perplexes inexperienced technicians who have not taken the time to understand relay operation. However, the relays can be easily checked several ways. Removed from the relay socket and tested on a bench, continuity testing between poles and throws and the resistance of the control circuit coil can

be performed using an ohmmeter. When the relay is in place, its in-use operation can be checked to verify correct current flow is present at each terminal by back-probing wiring to the relay using a voltmeter. But, when checking for in-use current flow, a non-powered test light is preferably used, which better identifies resistive contacts and connections with dimmer bulb lighting compared to a brighter bulb light when connected to battery voltage. Each of these methods is described in **SKILL DRILL 11-2**.

To simplify relay testing, and provide enhanced diagnostic tests, several aftermarket models of relay test equipment are available to check relay operation. One popular piece of test equipment is described in **SKILL DRILL 11-3**. Another aftermarket test equipment item provides a breakout harness to check the function of each pin using a digital multimeter, while following

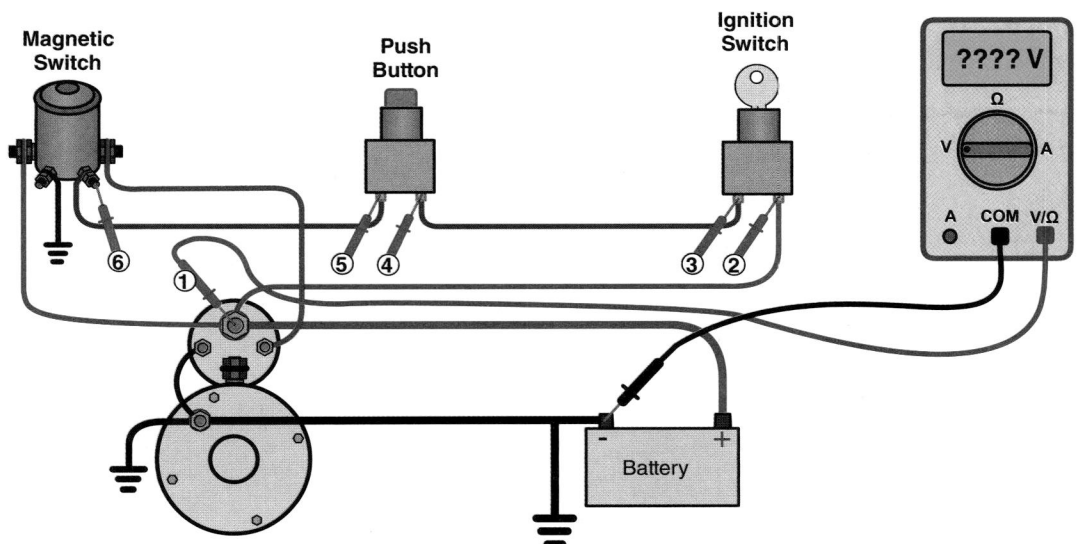

FIGURE 11-36 The available voltage test compares battery voltage and voltage available to the starting motor during cranking. The difference should be no more than one volt in a 12-volt system, with no more than 0.5-volt drop allowable in each cable to the starter.

SKILL DRILL 11-2 Testing an ISO Relay

Simple Relay Circuit

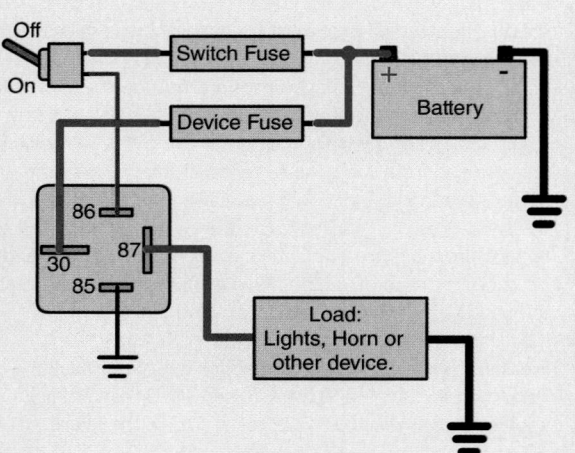

A slight clicking noise can be heard when an ISO-type electromagnetic relay is energized. If a relay does not click or activate a circuit it is intended to operate, it can be comprehensively tested using a voltmeter, test light, or ohmmeter. Carefully examine any diagram, symbols, and terminal number markings on the relay.

1. Control circuit continuity check: Remove the relay from its socket and, using an ohmmeter, measure the resistance of the control circuit coil. The circuit should draw between 150–200 mA in a 12-volt system, which means the coil has between 12- and 16-ohms resistance. If the circuit appears open because its polarity is diode-protected, reverse the meter leads to measure and record. Replace the relay if the control circuit is open.

2. To check the diode-suppression operation that protects against high-voltage current induction, in control circuit, range the meter to the diode-testing mode. Place the digital multimeter positive and negative leads across the control circuit terminals (#85 and #86 in ISO Mini, #1 and #2 in ISO micro). A functioning diode has two different readings for the control circuit. A faulty diode has the same readings in both directions of the control circuit. The diode should block current flow from the meter in one direction and allow current flow when the lead positions are switched. Replace any diode-protected relay that does not block current in one direction only.

3. Relay contact-testing method #1: Using an ohmmeter, measure the resistance or continuity between the relay pole (#30 on a mini, #5 on a micro) and each throw. On a five-terminal ISO mini relay, continuity exists between the NC pin #87 (#4 on a mini) when the control circuit is not energized. No continuity should exist between pin #87a (#5 micro). Energize the control circuit terminals using 12-volts applied with the correct polarity to the correct control circuit pins (+85, −86, or +1, −2). Measure and confirm continuity between pins #30 and 87a (#5 on a micro). Confirm continuity does not exist to pin #87 (#4 on a micro). Replace any relay that does not demonstrate correct pole-to-throw continuity.

4. Relay contact-testing method #2: Repeat the same steps as step 3 above, only this time use a non-powered test light. Remember that high-impedance digital voltmeters draw almost no current from the circuit. This means that resistance at contacts are not easily detected using a voltmeter or ohmmeter, unless some significant current flow takes place. To overcome this problem, supply either battery positive or negative to pin #30 (#5 on a micro relay) and check for continuity through each pole to throw. If a ground is supplied to pin #30, be sure to clip the test light lead to the positive terminal of the same power source, supplying pin a ground to pin #30. Verify the test light brightness is the same at both the throw and pole. Discard any relay that does not demonstrate the correct pattern for pole-to-throw continuity or has a dimmer test light bulb at the throw in comparison to the pole.

SKILL DRILL 11-3 Testing a Relay with an Electronic Relay Tester

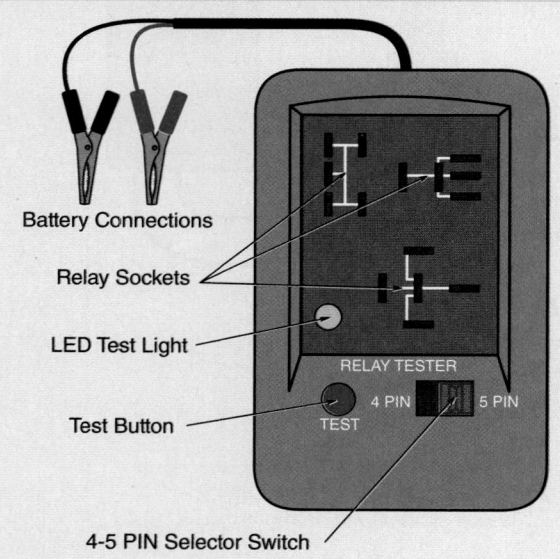

A common type of electronic relay tester compressively evaluates several types of relays by cycling the relay several times and comparing the consistency of the relay's electrical characteristics during each cycle.

1. Insert the relay to be tested into one of the instrument's sockets.
2. If the relay is an atypical style, use a relay adapter to connect the relay to an appropriate relay socket on the equipment.
3. Position the selector switch to choose between testing either a four- or five-pin relay.
4. Press the test button and then observe the color of the LED test light. If the light is red, the relay has failed.
5. Count the number of times the red LED test light flashes and record the result after completing the test. One, two, or three flashes indicates the relay's failure mode.

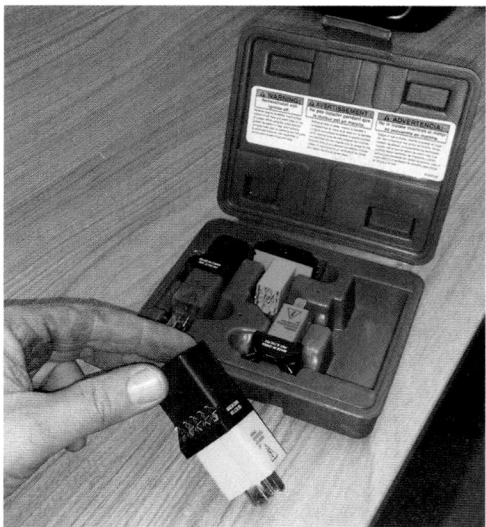

FIGURE 11-37 These relay adapters can be used to check pin functions of a relay to verify that the current flow is supplied to each relay pin for correct relay and circuit operation.

instructions included in the kit (**FIGURE 11-37**). While aftermarket equipment is potentially an asset, when the operation of a relay is properly understood by a technician, it becomes intuitive to perform tests with a test light or ohmmeter to quickly identify whether an intermittently operating circuit or one that is not operating at all is caused by a relay or another problem in either the circuit or component the relay is energizing.

Solid-state relays are also checked with an ohmmeter when the relay is de-energized. Using a digital multimeter, the resistance or continuity between each pole and the corresponding NC and NO throw terminals for that pole are checked and should provide the same meter readings as an electromagnetic relay. In other words, NC contacts should have 0 ohms resistance to the corresponding pole and any NO contacts should measure infinite resistance to the corresponding pole. When the relay control circuit is energized, the NC and NO throws should switch reading measurements between 0 and infinite ohms compared with its unenergized state.

To check the control circuit of a solid-state relay, it is checked the same way a diode-protected electromagnetic relay is tested by using the diode-test range of a multimeter. In the diode-test range, the meter leads are placed across the control circuit terminals. The voltage level of the small amount of current supplied by the meter in diode-test range enables the semiconductor to conduct in one direction and indicates 0.7 VDC if it is a common silicon-type diode or semiconductor. When the meter leads are reversed while still in the diode-test range, the meter measurement is 0 or outside limit (OL) or out of range, meaning there is no continuity between the control circuit terminals. Any readings not falling into normally anticipated ranges indicate a defective relay.

Wrap-Up

Ready for Review

▶ Electric circuits use control devices to direct the flow of current. Controls can be electrical switches, resistors, or electromagnetic relays.
▶ Switches are the simplest circuit control device. Opening and closing switches completes or breaks a circuit's electrical pathway.
▶ Simple switches are categorized by the number of input and output terminals they have and by their operation.
▶ Smart switches can function as digital inputs to electronic control systems.
▶ Resistors in commercial vehicles are typically fixed, stepped, or variable.
▶ Fixed-type resistors are designed to conduct either heavy or light amounts of current.
▶ Stepped resistors are made from two or more wire-wound resistors.
▶ Common variable resistors used as circuit control devices include rheostats and potentiometers.
▶ Relays use a small amount of current to switch a larger amount of current. As such, they eliminate voltage drop caused by long lengths of wire and eliminate the use of heavy conductors inside the cab.
▶ A typical relay has a control circuit and a load circuit.
▶ ISO relays have standardized terminal location, numbering, and dimensions.

▶ ISO mini and micro are the two most common types of relays used by commercial vehicles.
▶ Solid-state relays perform the same function as electromagnetic relays, but can switch without noise and use less control circuit current.
▶ Magnetic switches are identical in function to relays, except that they switch even larger amounts of current and have different dimensions from relays.
▶ Magnetic switches are available as intermittent-duty or continuous-duty relays. The two types of mag-switches are not interchangeable.
▶ An intermittent-duty relay quickly burns out when it is used in a continuous-duty application. A continuous-duty relay chatters when used in place of an intermittent-duty relay.
▶ Solenoids are devices with a movable core that converts current flow into mechanical movement.
▶ Solenoids can be either pull-type or push-and-pull type. In pull-type solenoids, an electromagnet pulls a soft iron core into the coil. Push-pull-type solenoids use a permanent magnet, instead of an iron core, to produce bidirectional movement.
▶ It is important to check the linkage adjustment of a solenoid with a pull-in and hold-in winding during service to ensure it doesn't drop out and to prevent premature burning out of pull-in windings.

Key Terms

magnetic reed switch Automatic-type switch with contacts opened or closed by magnetic fields.

magnetic switch A magnetic relay-type switch designed to handle higher current flow than smaller ISO relays.

momentary contact switches Manual-type switch that may be toggled or pushed, but does not latch into position. Horn contact or starter button are examples of momentary contact switches.

multiplex switch A switch arrangement using two or more switches that can share a single wire for a switch pole and throw circuit, but transmit unique circuit control information from each switch.

positive temperature coefficient (PTC) thermistor A thermistor in which resistance increases as the temperature increases.

potentiometer A variable resistor with three connections— one at each end of a resistive path, and a third sliding contact that moves along the resistive pathway.

pressure-sensitive switches Automatic-type switches that are activated by gas or liquid pressure.

proximity switches Switches designed to sense the approach of metal components.

rotary switches Manual-type switch rotated to select an output. Wiper speed and blower motor speed are common examples.

smart switches Automatic-type switches with self-diagnostic capabilities. These switches usually have at least a resister connected in parallel with switch contacts.

toggle switches Manual-type switch featuring the use an angled lever having an internal spring-loaded mechanism to rapidly switch into its latched or closed position.

Review Questions

1. Which of the following activates a manual control switch?
   a. Oil pressure
   b. An analog electrical signal
   c. A human finger
   d. A digital electrical signal
2. Which of the following switches has a single throw?
   a. SPDT
   b. SPST
   c. DPDT
   d. SPMT
3. Which of the following switch types is most likely an automatic switch?
   a. Toggle
   b. Slider
   c. Momentary contact
   d. Coolant level
4. Which of the following types of switches has contacts opened and closed by a permanent magnet?
   a. A pressure-sensitive switch
   b. An air-pressure switch
   c. An ISO mini or micro relay
   d. A reed switch
5. What type of resistor most likely controls current flow through a heater/AC blower motor?
   a. Fixed
   b. Stepped
   c. Variable
   d. Analog
6. Which type of circuit control device most likely indicates whether the linkage of a bus door has properly closed?
   a. A variable resistor
   b. A toggle switch
   c. An ISO relay
   d. A proximity sensor
7. Which type of circuit control device is most likely used to indicate the level of coolant, brake, or DEF fluid?
   a. A stepped resistor made from two or more wire-wound resistors
   b. A diaphragm-type automatic switch
   c. A bimetal-type switch
   d. A reed switch
8. What type of switch would most likely supply a negative-polarity current signal to the pin of an ECU?
   a. A pull-down switch
   b. A smart switch
   c. A switch with two resistors driving circuit voltage
   d. A pull-up switch
9. What is most likely to result from replacing a continuous-duty relay with an intermittent-duty relay?
   a. The relay burns out
   b. The relay chatters
   c. A high-voltage inductive spike can damage connected circuits
   d. The relay control circuit is excessively resistive and does not operate correctly
10. Which of the following combinations are the correct terminal numbers for the throws of an ISO mini and micro relay?
    a. 85 and 86
    b. 5 and 30
    c. 87a and 87
    d. 86 and 2

ASE Technician A/Technician B Style Questions

1. Technician A says simple switches are categorized by the number of input terminals they have. Technician B says input terminals are called throws, and output terminals are called poles. Who is correct?
   a. Technician A
   b. Technician B
   c. Both Technician A and Technician B
   d. Neither Technician A nor Technician B

2. Technician A says smart switches can function as digital inputs to electronic control systems. Technician B says because smart switches can be in only one of two states, smart switch inputs are binary inputs. Who is correct?
   a. Technician A
   b. Technician B
   c. Both Technician A and Technician B
   d. Neither Technician A nor Technician B

3. Technician A says fixed-type resistors are designed to limit circuit current. Technician B says colored bands around the body of an axial-type resistor identify its resistance. Who is correct?
   a. Technician A
   b. Technician B
   c. Both Technician A and Technician B
   d. Neither Technician A nor Technician B

4. Technician A says a relay is a switch that uses a small amount of current to switch a larger amount of current. Technician B says locating a relay closer to a load requiring large amounts of current minimizes voltage drop caused by resistance from long runs of wires. Who is correct?
   a. Technician A
   b. Technician B
   c. Both Technician A and Technician B
   d. Neither Technician A nor Technician B

5. Technician A says magnetic switches do not function as electrical relays. Technician B says magnetic switches can be classified as continuous- or intermittent-duty service. Who is correct?
   a. Technician A
   b. Technician B
   c. Both Technician A and Technician B
   d. Neither Technician A nor Technician B

6. Technician A says that the terminals and pins of an ISO relay have standardized functions. Technician B says an ISO relay control circuit has standardized polarity. Who is correct?
   a. Technician A
   b. Technician B
   c. Both Technician A and Technician B
   d. Neither Technician A nor Technician B

7. Technician A says a SPST toggle switch rated for 12-volts and 20-amps of current can be replaced with a similar size and style rated for 100-volts 20-amps. Technician B says a switch rated for 12-volt 10-amp would be a better choice for replacement. Who is correct?
   a. Technician A
   b. Technician B
   c. Both Technician A and Technician B
   d. Neither Technician A nor Technician B

8. Technician A says that ISO mini relays with diode protection need to have the control circuit connected with the correct polarity of current to operate. Technician B says that current supplied to pins #30, 87, and 87a of an ISO mini relay can switch current of either positive or negative polarity. Who is correct?
   a. Technician A
   b. Technician B
   c. Both Technician A and Technician B
   d. Neither Technician A nor Technician B

9. Technician A says that a frequent cause of failure of a pull-in winding of a solenoid is misadjusted linkage. Technician B says solenoid failure is most often caused by incorrectly connected pull-in and hold-in windings. Who is correct?
   a. Technician A
   b. Technician B
   c. Both Technician A and Technician B
   d. Neither Technician A nor Technician B

10. Technician A says that resistive contacts in a magnetic switch or relay are easily detected using a high-impedance voltmeter or ohmmeter. Technician B says resistive contacts are best checked when current flows through contacts and current flow is checked with a test light, or by measuring voltage drop. Who is correct?
    a. Technician A
    b. Technician B
    c. Both Technician A and Technician B
    d. Neither Technician A nor Technician B

CHAPTER 12

Semiconductor Devices and Digital Electronics

Learning Objectives

- LO 12-1 Differentiate between electrical and electronic circuit control components.
- LO 12-2 Identify and explain the construction and operating characteristics of bipolar semiconductor materials.
- LO 12-3 Identify and classify diode types and explain the construction, operation, application, and characteristics of diodes.
- LO 12-4 Identify the characteristics, construction, and operation applications of bipolar junction transistors.

- LO 12-5 Identify and explain the construction and operating characteristics of field effect type, unipolar semiconductor's materials, and transistors.
- LO 12-6 Identify and explain the construction, operation, and characteristics of metal oxide field effect semiconductors.
- LO 12-7 Identify, describe, and differentiate between the construction and operation of microprocessors and microcontrollers.
- LO 12-8 Describe the construction, operation, applications, and testing of capacitors.

You Are the Technician

Several sander-salting trucks in your fleet that you help maintain use a specialized electronic control module to regulate the speed of an auger according to the road speed. The module is connected to the vehicle's electrical system to power the module and receive road speed signals to change the quantity of salt and sand spread over the road by the auger. Unfortunately, the vehicle often operates in severe weather, causing snow and salt to enter the battery box and corrode battery cables, or quickly discharge the batteries from surface leakage of current over the battery cases. On numerous occasions, while attempts were made to jump start the truck, the booster cables were connected incorrectly, or the alternator began overcharging the batteries with voltage above 15.5 volts. The incorrect polarity and over-voltage conditions have frequently caused module failures. Not only has the problem caused the trucks to be out of service during emergency conditions, the modules, which are custom produced by the truck-body builder, have cost thousands of dollars to replace. You've been tasked to develop solutions to prevent any future module failures and increase trucks uptime. As you prepare to present several solutions, consider the following questions:

1. What simple electronic components could be used to prevent damage to the module from reverse polarity conditions during jump starting or battery replacement? Sketch out the proposed circuit.
2. What simple electronic components could be used to prevent the modules from failing during an over-voltage charging condition? Sketch out the proposed circuit.
3. What industry standards could you ask the supplier of the electronic control modules to meet when supplying replacement control modules?

Introduction

Not long ago, the only electronic component in a commercial vehicle was a radio. In fact, commercial vehicles have historically adopted electronic components more cautiously than automotive counterparts. Integrating electronic components and control systems did not begin to rapidly take place until the technology matured to the degree where control modules and other electronic devices didn't jeopardize a vehicle's mission-critical performance. Dependability was the overarching concern that had greater priority than the efficiencies, features, and benefits of using electronic components. Apprehensions about the use of potentially unreliable electronics and wiring over proven mechanical systems were captured by a '1980's advertisement from a major OEM truck maker showing a tractor-trailer combination being lifted upward with only a single piece of thin electrical wiring. Next to the odd image was the by-line: "Would you let one wire hold up 80,000 lb?"

Since those earlier days, concern for dependability and long-term reliability of electronic devices in the harsh, competitive operating environment of a commercial vehicle has stimulated the development of more rugged electronic products. So much integration of electronic and mechanical systems has taken place that a new term—mechatronics, combining the term mechanical and electronics, is now needed to describe this extensive category of devices. **Mechatronics** refers to the integration of mechanical components, electronic devices, and microcontrollers into a single component or system. A considerable portion of a vehicle's value and service work is now tied to the mechatronics technology in items as simple as seating and cab controls to vehicle stability and engine control systems integrating electronics with hydraulic, pneumatic, and other mechanical systems. Foundational to understanding the operation of electronic devices used so extensively in vehicles is the construction and operating principles of semiconductors and other electronic devices covered by this chapter. Semiconductors are examined because they are the basic building block of almost all electronic components.

Technicians are not expected to understand their detailed operation but should have a basic idea of how they work and where they are used, with a goal of developing service practices based on a proper understanding of how semiconductors and electronic devices work. An understanding of basic electronic principles is used in later chapters of this book to explain the operation of other engine and chassis systems' operations ranging from simple LED lighting to more sophisticated electronic control systems and on-board network communication.

Differences Between Electrical and Electronic Devices

LO 12-1 Differentiate between electrical and electronic circuit control components.

The purpose of circuit control components examined in the previous chapter is to supply, remove, change, or redirect the flow of current energizing a circuit. Devices in this category of

FIGURE 12-1 Electronic control modules like this use a variety of semiconductor-type electronic components. As much as 20% of the production cost of late-model vehicles is related to the use of electronic components.

electrical components include various types of switches, electromechanical relays, solenoids, and resistors capable of changing the direction and quantity of electric current energizing a circuit. Electrical devices, in general, conduct large amounts of current to produce heat, magnetism, motion, light, or sound. Electronic control devices can also control current flow, like electrical devices, but operate using different principles. One major distinction is electronic devices generally operate at lower current levels because they manipulate current flow at an electron level using semiconductors operating according to principles of electrostatics—the attraction and repulsion of electrons using electric fields or charges. Semiconductor materials used by electronic devices can behave as either an insulator or conductor, can be operated to control current flow, and produce electrical effects. Compared to simpler electrical devices, lower-voltage electric current and electrical signals pass through electronic circuits. Low-voltage signals can also be amplified, modulated (modified), or digitized in electronic circuits. In more sophisticated electronic devices, electrical signals can be modified to produce light and radio waves or conditioned to carry complex information in either digital or analog form. Common electronic semiconductor circuit-controlled devices include wide varieties of diodes, transistors, integrated circuits, microprocessors, and microcontrollers used in electronic control modules (**FIGURE 12-1**).

What Are Semiconductors?

LO 12-2 Identify and explain the construction and operating characteristics of bipolar semiconductor materials.

Semiconductors are the most important material used to construct electronic devices. Diodes, transistors, and integrated circuits, which are essential components in electronic devices, are constructed from semiconductors. This material can have properties of both conductors and insulators and can switch back and forth between either electrical state when influenced by small electrostatic charges. By themselves, the changeable conductor and insulator properties of semiconductors are not much use. But after combining them, semiconductors form some of the most useful electronic components created to build electronic devices.

Two types of semiconductors are used in commercial vehicles today: unipolar and bipolar. Differentiating between either category depends on whether circuit current passes through only one semiconductor's (unipolar) or two (bipolar) semiconductors' materials making up the device. Both types are used to form a wide variety of diodes, transistors, and integrated circuits. The earliest developed and widely used semiconductor is the **bipolar semiconductor**, which is examined first. The second type, unipolar semiconductors, while invented around the same time, were only developed later and use electrostatic fields to either block or enable conduction through semiconductors. Unipolar-type semiconductors are more widely used to build field effect devices, such as Field Effect Transistors (FET) and almost all contemporary integrated circuits.

Bipolar Semiconductor Construction

Silicon, one of the most abundant elements on earth, is a material commonly transformed into a semiconductor. In its pure state, there are no free or easily moved electrons in silicon, making it an effective insulator. Electrons in silicon are all arranged in tight bonds with adjacent atoms, resulting in the formation of a hard-crystalline lattice structure. However, by adding a small amount of metal and nonmetal impurities to the crystal when it is heated into a liquid state, electrical properties of silicon are changed, allowing it to become a conductor under the right circumstances—but at times behave as an insulator, which is why it is called a semiconductor.

Various types of impurities are added to silicon through a process called **doping**. In one type of doping process, metals, such as boron, aluminum, germanium, indium, or gallium, are alloyed with silicon. Nonmetals, such as phosphorous and arsenic, plus a few others, are used to dope silicon, too. Depending on the doping material used, it combines with the silicon atom to create one of two conditions. In the first condition, an electron in the silicon atom is left over after doping that cannot find a place in any of the other silicon's electron shells. This means the electron is only loosely held and the overall charge in the material is still neutral. With all the valence shell spots for electrons in the silicon atom filled or bound, the free, unbound electron is easily moved. Because the silicon alloy material has unbound electrons, it now has a movable negative charge, which explains why it is called **N material**—N representing the idea its net charge is still neutral but has a moveable electron, which can be used to create negatively charged regions in the semiconductor material.

In the second doping process using another type of impurity, doped silicon can have an electron deficit, rather than a surplus. In this condition, the valence shell of the silicon atom requires an electron to complete its outer shell. This deficiency or absence of electrons creates what is commonly referred to as a hole in the doped material. Without having all the electrons the material prefers to have, it has a positive charge potential, which makes the silicon alloy receptive to electrons. The net

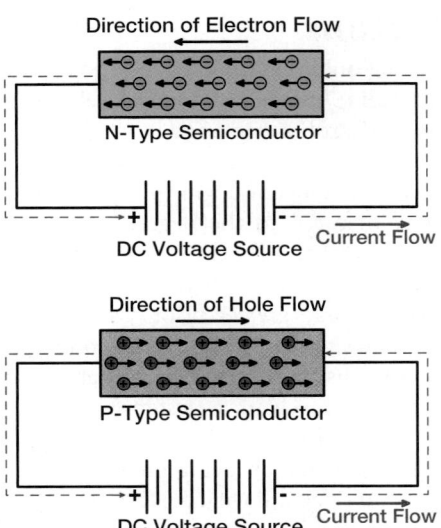

FIGURE 12-2 In P-type semiconductors, electrons are pulled from the negative side of the power supply into the positively charged holes. The positive terminal of the power supply pulls electrons out of the P channel. The opposite situation takes place in N-type channel conductors.

charge is neutral, but the material has spaces for electrons. Using doping impurities to create holes or spaces for electrons in the silicon lattice creates a movable positive charge or a **P material** P- and N-type semiconductor materials have no valuable purpose by themselves, but can both conduct current when either of them is connected to a power supply (**FIGURE 12-2**). If P and N materials are joined together in various arrangements and share a junction point, they can be manipulated to perform a long list of important tasks in electronic circuits (**FIGURE 12-3**).

Diodes

LO 12-3 Identify and classify diode types and explain the construction, operation, application, and characteristics of diodes.

Sandwiching a P and N semiconductor material produces a diode. Diodes are electronic devices that operate as one-way electrical check valves. Current can flow in only one direction through a diode but is blocked when the direction of flow is reversed. Diodes have this ability because of the way P and N materials behave. When the N material is connected to a positive potential of a battery and the P material to the negative terminal, the extra negative electrons in the N material are attracted to the positive terminal of the battery. Likewise, the positive holes in the P material are attracted to the negative terminal of the battery. Under these conditions, an area forms at the junction or boundary between the P and N materials, commonly called the depletion zone. It is called the depletion zone because there are no electrical charges at the boundary between the N and P materials. Free negative electron charges in the N material are pulled toward the positive battery terminal and away from the junction point of the P and N materials.

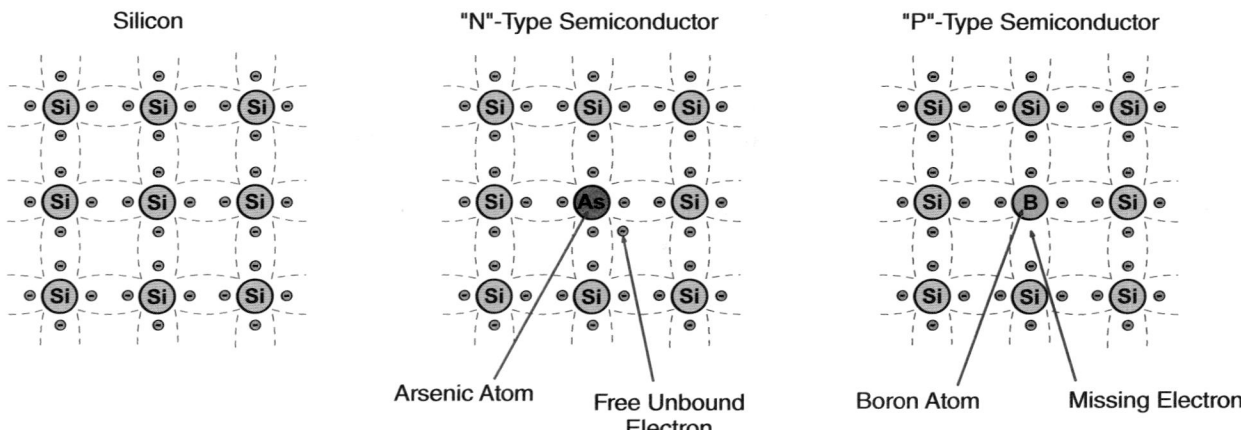

FIGURE 12-3 Two of the most basic semiconductor materials are classified as either "P" or "N"-type. Pure silicon crystal lattice has four bond connections and all electrons are tightly held. Free electrons characterize the "N" material; missing electrons create holes for electrons that characterize the "P"-type material.

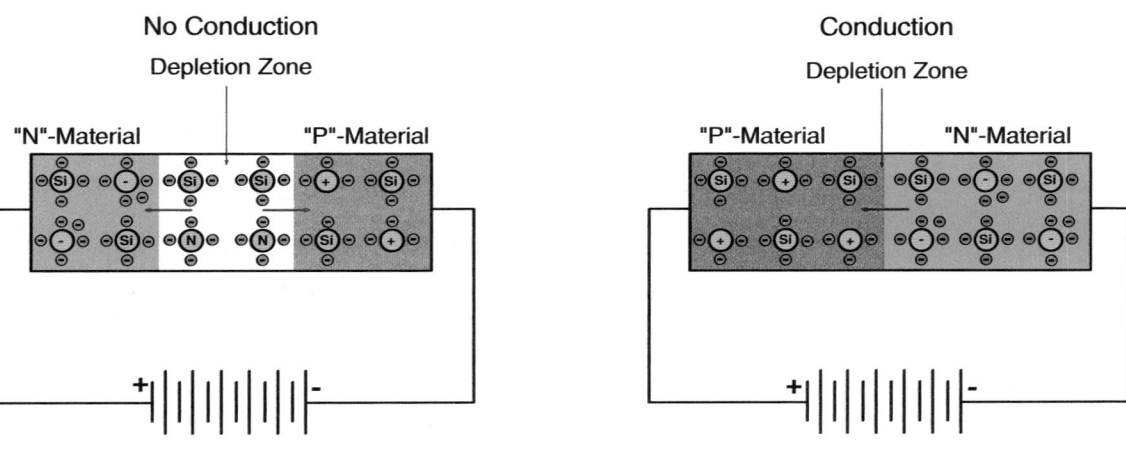

Charges are drawn to the ends of material by battery polarity creating a depletion zone that has no electrical charge. The depletion zone acts as an insulator.

Charges are drawn into the depletion zone causing it to shrink to almost nothing. The depletion zone acts as a conductor.

FIGURE 12-4 A depletion zone is created at the junction between N and P materials. Electrical charges in the zone determine whether the diode blocks or conducts current flow.

Likewise, the negative battery terminal pulls positively charged holes away from the junction to form the depletion zone. At the junction point between the N and P materials, no current can cross the depletion zone, which means the diode is blocking current flow from the negative to the positive terminal of the battery. That is because only insulating material remains in the junction or depletion zone area—there are no holes or electrons (FIGURE 12-4). Once again, because at the P-N junction, the positive holes and the free electrons are each moving away from one another.

Forward and Reverse Bias in Diodes

If the battery polarity is reversed, connecting the positive terminal with P material and negative with N material, the diode

readily conducts current across the junction and through the former depletion zone (FIGURE 12-5). That is because free electrons in the N material are driven toward the junction area by the excess electrons at the negative terminal of the battery (FIGURE 12-6). The electron holes in the P material are also repelled by the positively charged battery terminal, pushing the holes into the junction area. At the junction between the N and P materials, holes and free electrons join, and all the material at the junction and in the P and N materials becomes conductive. Movement of the electrons takes place in the material, through the junction, and into the P materials because electrons enter the junction's positive holes. At the same time, electrons that have entered the P material are transported through holes and travel onto the battery positive terminal. As electrons are drawn into the battery's positive plates, depleting the P material of electrons, more electrons are drawn into the N material by the positive charge in the P material. Movement of electrons from the N material through the junction and into the P material causes current to continuously flow through the diode.

When a diode conducts current, it is said to be in **forward bias**. When the diode blocks flow, it is in **reverse bias**. Diodes block current in reverse bias until the voltage reaches the diodes' Zener point. The Zener point for a silicon diode typically ranges from 20 to 70 volts. If the circuit voltage exceeds diodes' Zener point, the diode is destroyed by either permanently opening or shorting it closed. Note, however, there is a purpose-made diode that conducts current in both directions when a predetermined threshold is reached. This type of diode is called a Zener diode. Zener diodes are not damaged when the diode exceeds its Zener point and conducts current in reverse bias.

Barrier Voltage

While electron flow takes place easily when the correct polarity of current is connected to the diode (and through a load), some force is required for electrons to cross the bipolar diode's P-N junction. In fact, electron pressure drops crossing the P-N junction. The pressure drop is more accurately described as a voltage drop, and takes place only in a bipolar diode as electrons overcome a natural resistance to crossing the P-N junction. The voltage drop, or pressure differential, measured across the junction, is called the **barrier voltage** (or threshold voltage), and is typically between 0.3 and 0.7 volts in bipolar diodes. A minimum voltage at this level and above is required to forward bias a diode, or get it to conduct current (**FIGURE 12-7**). Like any resistance in an electrical circuit, heat accompanies the voltage drop across the diode. A circuit with 12.6 volts falls to 11.9 volts due to the 0.7-volt barrier voltage. Heat sinks, which are like radiators, help cool diodes, converting the drop

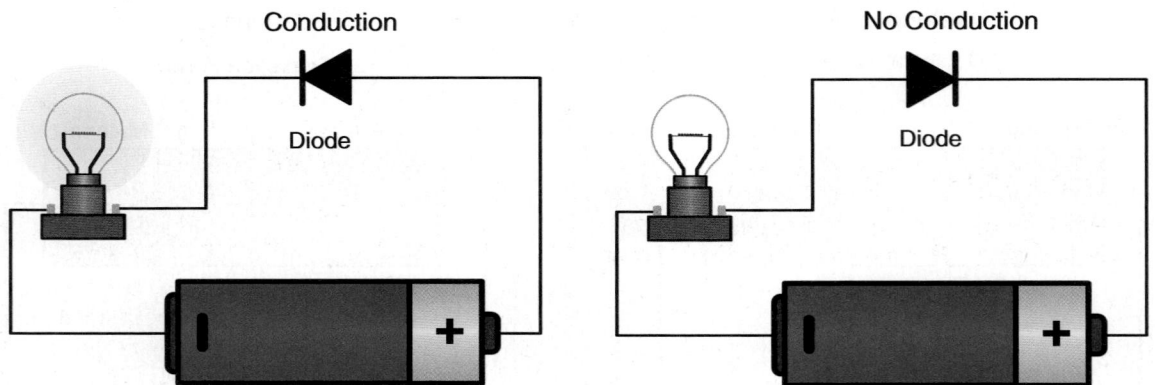

FIGURE 12-5 The correct polarity must be applied to a diode for conduction to take place.

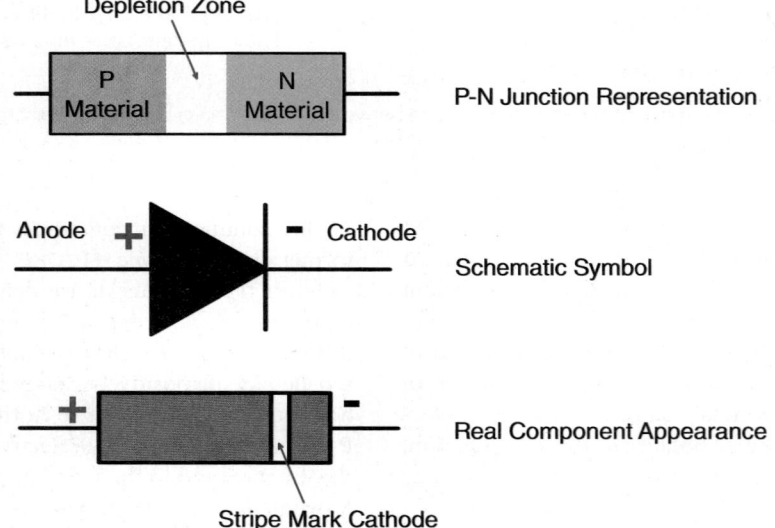

FIGURE 12-6 Symbol for a diode. Remember the negative side has a negative line turned 90 degrees. The arrow points out the direction of flow using conventional theory of current flow. Electron flow actually takes place in the opposite direction of the arrow. The arrowhead can also be thought of as a loudspeaker indicating the direction of current flow. A line on a diode body designates the (N-material) negative or cathode side.

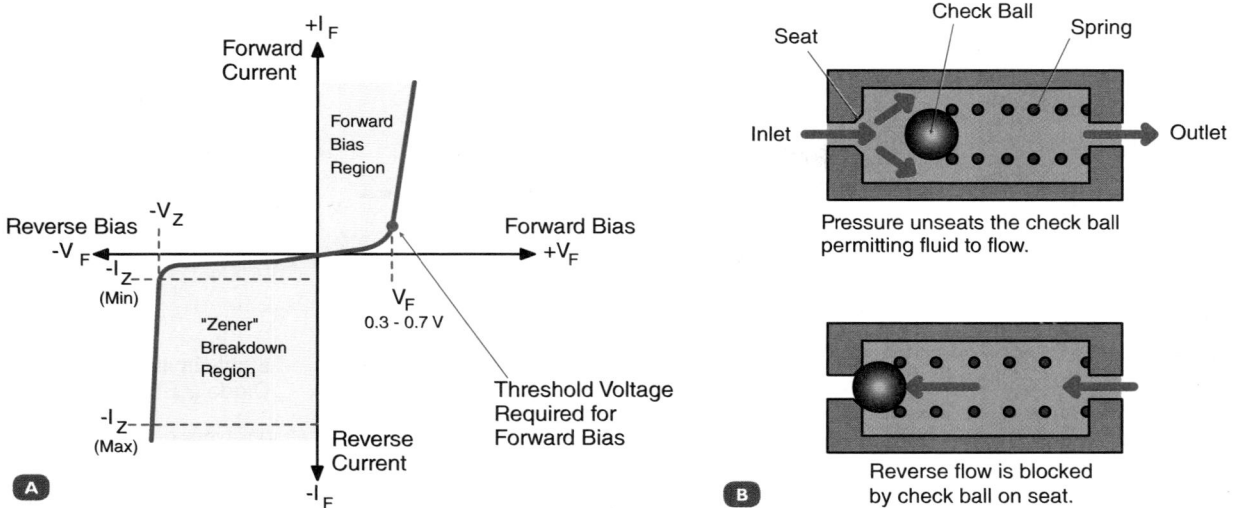

FIGURE 12-7 **A.** A minimum amount of voltage is needed to push electrons across the junction barrier between the P and N materials. Threshold voltage required to cross the barrier depends on the type of materials used, which can range from as little as 0.3 volts to 0.7 volts. **B.** Barrier or threshold voltage required for forward bias can be thought of as a one-way check valve requiring a minimum pressure to open.

in barrier current voltage across the diodes junction into heat (**FIGURE 12-8**). Note, because current flows through both the P and N materials, this type of diode semiconductor is called a bipolar diode. Diodes like this are typically made from silicon and germanium crystals using various types of doping impurities, which results in slightly different measurements of barrier voltage.

> ▶ TECHNICIAN TIP
>
> Electronic control modules must meet a rigorous set of standards to be approved for use in a commercial vehicle chassis. Expensive failures are potentially caused by battery-related mishaps, such as incorrectly connecting a battery, jump starting, and brief high-voltage spikes caused by connecting and disconnecting inductive loads (electrical devices with wire coils). One common specification is the reverse-polarity test outlined in the ISO 16750-2 standard. For 12-V systems, the control module must properly operate after a reverse polarity voltage of 14 volts is supplied to its input for one minute, and 24-volt systems require a survival after 28 volts is applied for a minute. Other similar tests involve momentarily supplying a reverse polarity of 100 to 150 volts. High-voltage spikes like this are caused whenever self-induction takes place in devices, such as AC compressor clutches or electromagnetic relays. The use of diodes and other semiconductor devices is critical to prevent failures caused by these abuse conditions.

Zener Point Voltage

When a diode conducts current, it is said to be in **forward bias**. When the diode blocks flow, it is in **reverse bias**. Diodes block current in reverse bias until the voltage reaches the diodes' **Zener point**. As mentioned earlier, the Zener point for a silicon diode typically ranges from 20 to 70 volts. At that point, the diode is destroyed by either permanently opening or shorting closed. These purpose-made diodes have a much lower Zener point and are often used for circuit protection—opening

a pathway to ground to intentionally blow a fuse if alternator voltage is too high or there is a reverse polarity condition sensed. Zener diodes also establish the set-point of voltage regulators.

Types of Diodes

A variety of diodes exist including: rectifying, Zener, light-emitting, and organic light-emitting diodes (**FIGURE 12-9**). *Rectifying diodes* or power diodes are commonly silicon diodes, because of their more rugged ability to withstand heat and abuse, are used inside an alternator to convert alternating current (AC) to direct current (DC) output. These diodes are also used as a simple device to protect against reverse polarity. By installing the diode in the correct direction in series with the power

FIGURE 12-8 Diodes rectifying AC to DC are placed in heat sinks to help remove heat from the diodes, which is created by the voltage dropped across the P-N junction barrier.

supply to a module or other device, the diode blocks the flow of current if the polarity is reversed, such as when incorrectly jumpstarting a battery. Silicon power diodes are frequently used to minimize self-induction in electromagnets made from wire coils found in magnetic switches, relays, or air conditioning compressor clutches. To test a clamping diode, follow the steps in **SKILL DRILL 12-1**.

Zener Diodes

Zener diodes are a type of diode that behaves like a conventional bipolar silicon-type diode up to a calibrated voltage-blocking current in one direction and conducting it in the other. After reaching the calibrated voltage, called the Zener point, the uniquely constructed Zener diode is purposely designed to no longer block current in one direction.

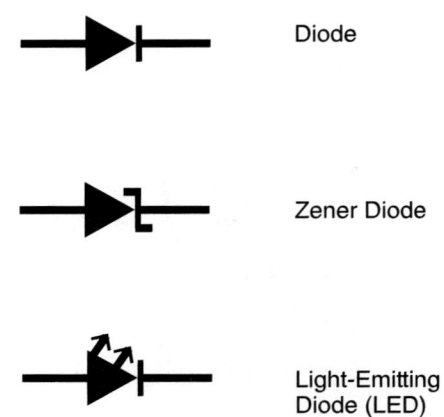

FIGURE 12-9 Schematic symbols for various types of diodes.

SKILL DRILL 12-1 Testing a Clamping Diode

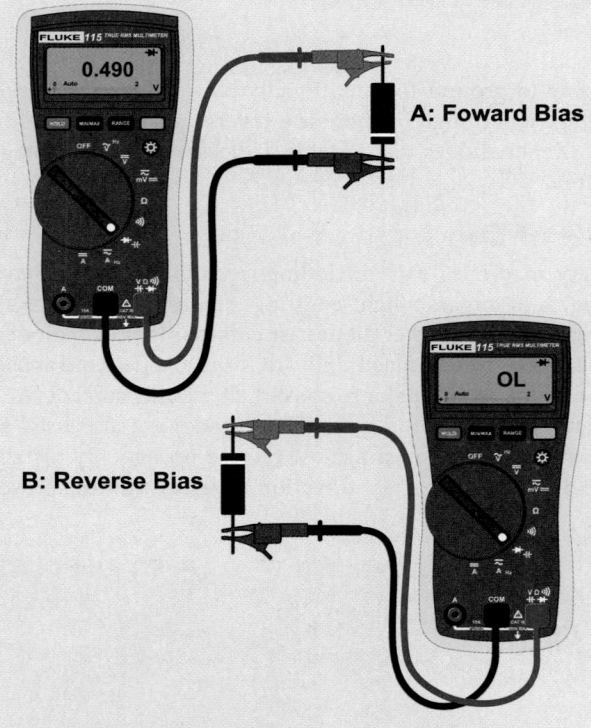

A: Foward Bias

B: Reverse Bias

Two methods can be used to test diodes in applications, such as alternators, or in clamp circuits used to suppress voltage spikes. One method is to use a multimeter. The second method is to use a test light with a low-voltage power supply (12-volts DC).

Method A: Testing a Silicon Diode with a Multimeter

1. Connect the – negative black lead to the COM terminal on the multimeter.
2. Connect the + positive red lead to the volt-ohm terminal of the multimeter.
3. Range the multimeter by turning the range dial to the diode symbol on the multimeter. This increases the voltage supplied to the probe leads above 0.7 volts or barrier voltage. It also

supplies the correct polarity to current supplied by the test leads. Do not use an ohmmeter to test the diode since the meter may not supply enough voltage to bias the diode.

4. Switch on the multimeter if it is not already switched on or has an auto shut-off. The display window should indicate infinite resistance with either 0 L (out of range) or OPEN.
5. To test for forward bias operation, select the positive red lead and connect it to the P material end of the diode opposite the end with the bar indicating the negative or N material.
6. Connect the black negative probe to the negative or N end of the diode, which has a bar designating the N material end. The multimeter either beeps, which indicates the diode is conducting voltage, and/or displays a voltage reading for the barrier voltage. The silicon diode should be approximately 0.7 volts.
7. The diode is defective if the voltage reading is above 0.7 volts or the display indicates the diode is open.
8. To test for reverse bias operation, reverse the test leads by connecting the red lead to the N material and black lead to the P material.
9. The meter should not beep, and the circuit should display an open circuit if the diode is operating correctly.

Method B: Testing Diodes with a Test Light

Defective diodes may pass a test using a multimeter but break down when any significant amount of current passes through the diode. Testing a diode with a power supply and test light is a recommended method to check diodes used in rectifier bridges or clamping circuits.

1. Connect a test light ground clip to a battery positive terminal.
2. Place the negative or N material end of the diode against the negative terminal of a battery or clip it to the negative terminal of the same 12-volt power supply. (This is the end with the bar designating the negative end of the diode.)
3. Touch the test light lead to the positive end of the diode. The test light should light up brightly.
4. Reverse the orientation of the diode with the positive (P) end touching the negative terminal of the battery or power supply and the test light clipped to the negative or N end of the diode. There should be no light observed at all since the diode should block the current flow.

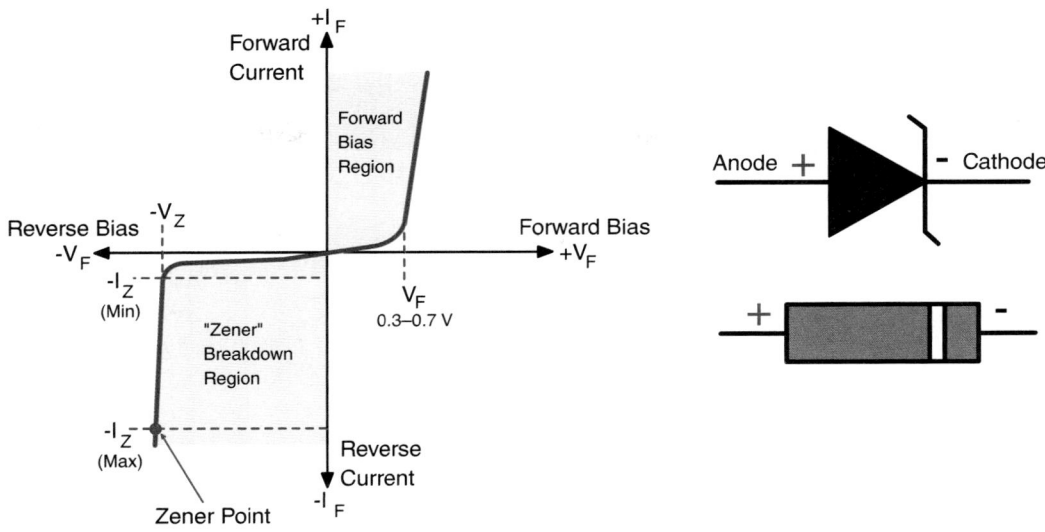

FIGURE 12-10 The Zener point refers to the voltage a diode conducts current in reverse bias or in both directions. Normally the Zener voltage is very high—50-volts or more in regular PN diodes, but the Zener point is intentionally lowered for a Zener diode application.

It does not become damaged, either, like a conventional diode does under over-voltage conditions exceeding its Zener point. Instead, a Zener diode conducts current in either direction without being damaged (**FIGURE 12-10**). By using specialized doping material, a conventional diode can take on the characteristics of a Zener. One common application of a Zener diode is for circuit protection. For example, a diode with a Zener point of 15 volts can be connected across the positive and negative inputs of a power supply to an ECM to protect against over-voltage conditions. At 15 volts, that same diode immediately conducts current in either direction, drawing large amounts of current and blowing a protective fuse if it is connected in series with the Zener diode (**FIGURE 12-11**). Zeners are also used in voltage regulators to function as voltage-sensitive switches that determine the charging system's voltage set point. The Zener diode symbol has a Z-shaped line on the negative N material side of the diode.

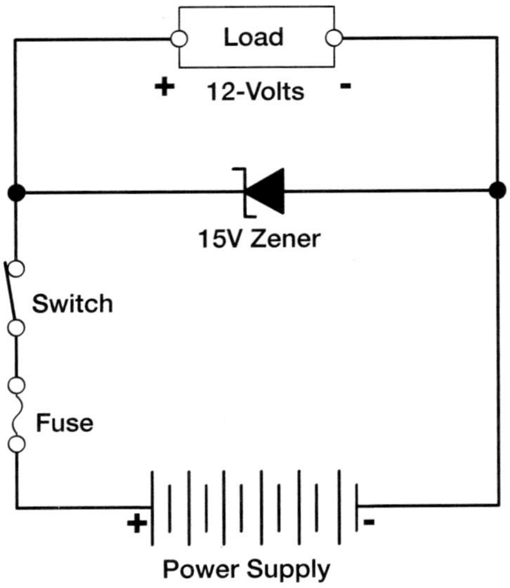

Light-Emitting Diodes (LEDs)

Light-emitting diodes (LEDs) are used in a large variety of digital displays and lighting applications and are replacing incandescent bulbs in most applications (**FIGURE 12-12**). In the last decade, the development of super bright white LEDs has enabled headlights to now operate with LED lights. The rapid growth in use of LED for all lighting applications is not due only to technical developments offering lower cost and a white light, but LED reduces power consumption by lighting to between 50% and 75%, which reduces fuel consumption by the alternator. Unlike incandescent lighting, LED shock resistance properties combined with a lifecycle as long as 100,000 hours of

FIGURE 12-11 This 15-volt Zener blocks current flow between battery positive and negative up to 15 volts. After 15 volts, the diode conducts current in either direction.

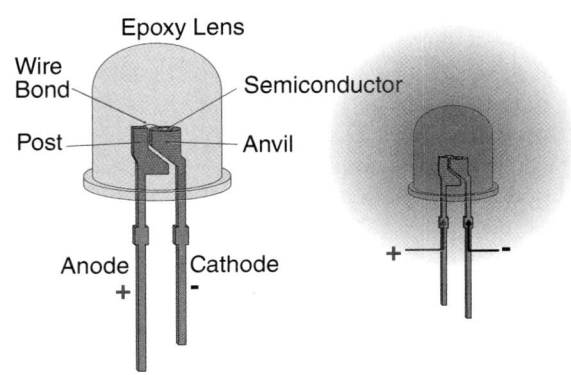

FIGURE 12-12 Construction of a light-emitting diode.

operation means they do not need replacement or require labor hours to service during a vehicle's normal service life.

The LED is made from P and N materials like other diodes. The shape of the LED case and leads helps identify the cathode and anode terminals. When the correct polarity of current is supplied to the LED, current flows easily from the P-side, or anode, when connected to a positive current source, and then through the N-side, or cathode, if connected to a negative current source. However, an LED blocks current flow like a conventional diode if the polarity is reversed or in reverse bias. Unlike silicon and germanium diodes, which release heat when electrons cross the P-N junction, electrons passing through LED diodes dissipate energy by emitting photons when electrons combine with positive holes at the P-N junction. Light is emitted from the P-N junction when the diode is forward biased, but not in reverse bias. Photons are released because the electron loses energy during the process, which is primarily converted to light instead of heat.

To create LED's emitting having different colors, other manufacturing materials can be used. The elements gallium, indium, or germanium are used as a base instead of silicon. The materials are commonly doped with aluminum, arsenic, nitrogen, or phosphorous. Gallium arsenide phosphide (GaAsP) and gallium phosphide (GaP) are two common semiconductor doping materials used to create LEDs. Red, orange, and yellow colored LEDs are made from GaAsP. GaP semiconductors produce red, orange, and green light. White LEDs can be made from combining several colors or from more exotic materials, such as yttrium, aluminum, and garnet. Varying the voltage supplied to some LEDs can change the color from red to green, which is a useful feature to show a device is ready (green) or on standby, not ready (red). Others combine two bulbs in a single package and use three power supply leads to individually control the light.

Three different sizes of LEDs are commonly used. Miniature bulbs used in indicator lamps require 1 V to 3 V and forward bias current ranging from 200 mA to 100 mA. Larger LEDs used in lamps and visible in direct sunlight require current between 2 and 4.5 volts at 20 mA. LEDs have low electrical resistance and do not behave according to Ohm's law. LEDs draw as much current as possible, but at the same time are sensitive to over-voltage conditions. Unless a current-limiting resistor is placed in series with the bulbs, they quickly burn up if excessive voltage is supplied.

High-output LED headlight bulbs consume almost as much power as incandescent bulbs at 12 volts on low-beams and require additional cooling to prevent them from being destroyed. The latest LED headlights for aftermarket replacement bulbs can use about 40 watts less power than incandescent bulbs, where both high and low beams consume 110 watts (**TABLE 12-1**).

Organic Light-Emitting Diodes (OLEDs)

Organic light-emitting diodes (OLEDs) are the latest flat screen display technology. The OLED displays operate along similar principles of conventional LEDs—emitting light when positive holes combine with electrons. Rather than using

TABLE 12-1 Comparing LED and Incandescent Bulb Power Consumption

Function	Power Consumption Per Lamp - Watts	
	Incandescent	High Output LED
Low beam	56.2	54.0
High beam	63.9	34.4
Marker lamp	7.4	1.7
Front turn signal	26.8	6.9
Stop lamp	26.5	5.6
Tail lamp	7.2	1.4

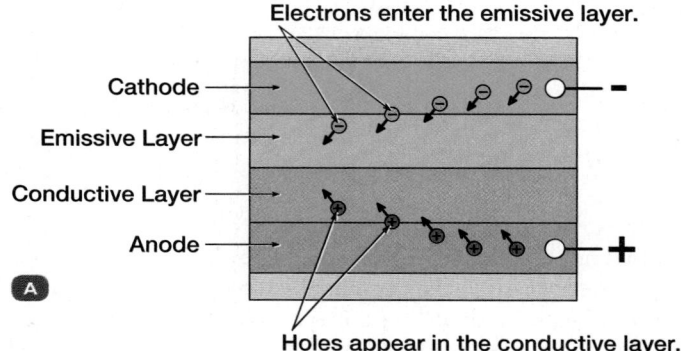

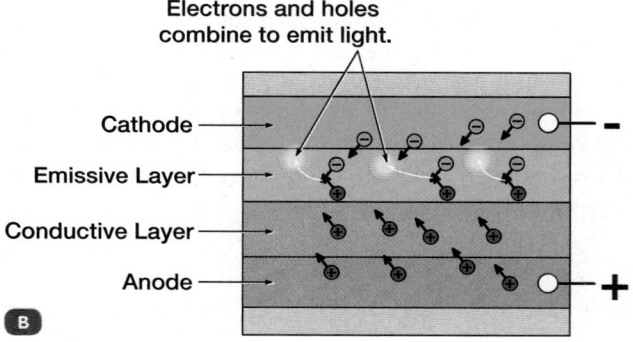

FIGURE 12-13 A. OLEDs are multilayered and have a conductive layer for electrons and positive charges. **B.** Light is emitted from OLEDs when the electrons combine with positive holes in a light emitting or emissive layer of an OLED.

mineral crystals or metals for a diode base, the silicon, gallium, or germanium material is replaced with carbon-based semiconductor material, which lends the term *organic* to the diodes. However, these devices do not simply join P and N materials. Instead, OLED have four or more layers that have colored filters to enable the displays to emit light with different color wavelengths. Despite having multiple layers, OLEDs are much thinner and brighter than LED displays. They also consume much less power while responding 200 times faster to electrical signals. These features make them desirable for instrument cluster or driver information display centers (**FIGURE 12-13**).

Photodiodes

Photodiodes are a unique category of diodes that are also made from P-N semiconductors but produce current when light strikes the diode (**FIGURE 12-14**). Because they convert light into electrical energy, they are also referred to as photo-detectors, photo-sensors, or light detectors. Solar cells that convert bright light energy into electricity are a category of large-area photo diode. The device produces current flow when a photon strikes the P and N material, knocking out an electron in each to create an electron-hole pair. Current flows in a reverse bias direction with electrons leaving the P material and entering the N material. This means that to charge a battery, the P-side of the photo-diode is connected to the negative terminal of the battery and the N-side is connected to the positive terminal of the battery. Until light strikes the diode, no current can flow in either direction. A **phototransistor** is a light-sensitive transistor that allows emitter-collector current flow when a photon strikes the transistor base. Photodiodes and transistors are often used by rain sensors and automatically dimming lights. In auxiliary coolant heaters powered by diesel fuel, the small furnaces use

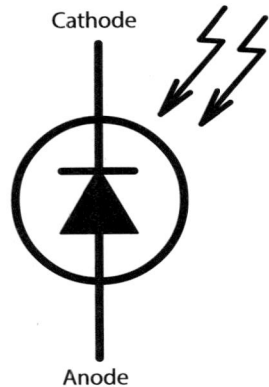

FIGURE 12-14 Photodiodes forward bias only when light strikes the diodes.

photodiodes and transistors to detect combustion light through a quartz crystal lens to enable a fail-safe operation of the furnace. That means if no light from the diesel combustion is detected inside the furnace, the furnace operation shuts down.

Suppression of Voltage Spikes with Diodes

One important application of diodes is to suppress high-voltage spikes caused by self-induction in coils. The rapid collapse of a coil's magnetic field induces high-voltage current in the opposite direction of the current flow that originally produced the magnetic field. Induced voltage can be hundreds of volts and can damage any sensitive components connected to the circuit. Arcing of switch contacts also take place.

To prevent this from occurring, a diode can be connected in parallel with an inductive load, such as a coil, found in a magnetic switch or AC clutch. When the coil is energized, the diode is connected to be in reverse bias, so all current flows through the coil. When the circuit is open, however, the direction of current flow through the coil changes. The diode is now in a forward bias position and induced current flows through the diode, forming a current loop through the coil. The inductive voltage spike is quickly dissipated through coil resistance (**FIGURE 12-15**). The use of an electronic circuit to suppress voltage spikes is called a **clamp circuit**.

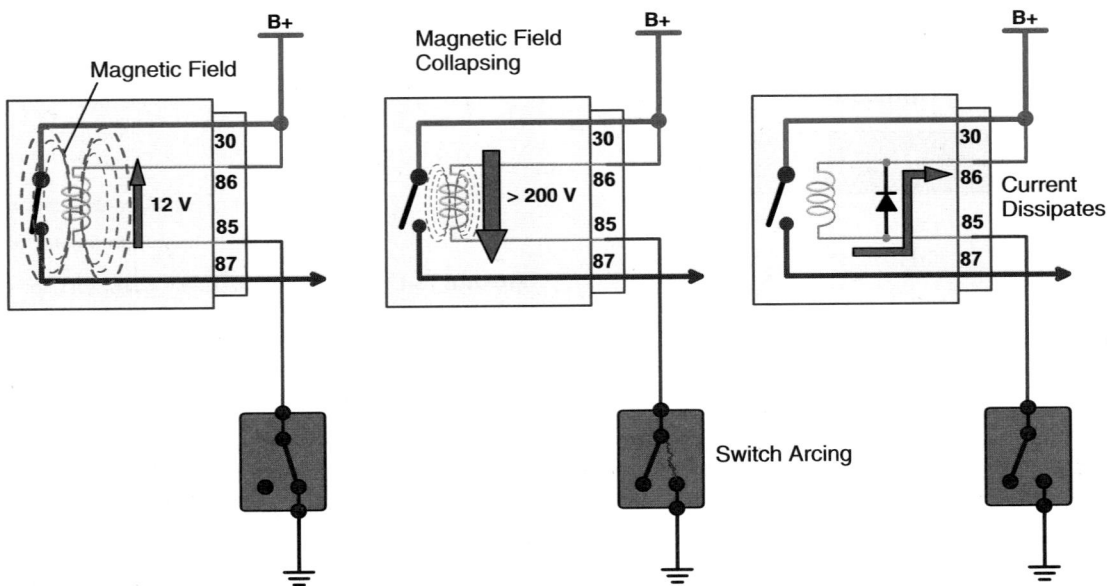

FIGURE 12-15 Diodes are used to surpass voltage spikes caused by self-induction in wire coils.

Bipolar Junction Transistors

LO 12-4 Identify the characteristics, construction, and operation applications of bipolar junction transistors.

Bipolar junction transistors (BJTs) are semiconductor devices composed of three blocks of a P and N material (**FIGURE 12-16**). They primarily function as electronic switches, amplifiers, and voltage-controlled resistors. In fact, the name *transistor* communicates its function by combining the words resistor and transformer.

There is an enormous variety of transistors developed since their first appearance in the 1950s, but a representative type, the **bipolar transistor**, combines either two P or N materials with a single P- or N-type material, forming **PNP or NPN transistors**. The fact that current flows through both P and N materials during transistor operation gives the transistor its classification as a BJT. The two predominant materials, made from either two P or N materials, form what is called an emitter-collector circuit. The emitter-collector path through the diode conducts the bulk of current in and out of the transistor. The middle semiconductor material made from either an N or P forms what is known as the base. Current cannot flow through the emitter-collector circuit unless a small amount of current of the correct polarity is applied to the base. In a sense, the transistor is like a solid-state relay with a small amount of current applied to the base, switching a larger amount of current through the larger emitter-collector circuit (**FIGURE 12-17**). Just as the diode needed charges on each end to send free electrons and positive holes through the junction, the BJT transistor does too. In the transistor though, two junctions are formed between the base and the emitter-collector circuit. **TABLE 12-2** compares NPN to PNP transistors.

Transistor Bias

To conduct current, the NPN transistor requires the base to have a positive voltage applied to it to allow current to pass across the emitter-collector circuit. When current flows through the emitter-collector circuit, the transistor is said to forward bias. In a PNP transistor, the base must be negative to forward bias the transistor.

To achieve the greatest current flow across the emitter-collector circuit (rather than the emitter base or collector base), the P and N semiconductor materials are doped differently than the base material (**FIGURE 12-18**). The emitter semiconductor of a transistor is the most heavily doped, producing the greatest number of free electrons or holes depending on the material. Slightly less doping is used in the collector circuit; the base is relatively thin and has the least amount of doping with impurities.

In the transistor symbols, the arrow that designates the emitter points in the direction of current flow (according to conventional theory). The collector is opposite the emitter, and the base is located at the bottom of the "T." Electron flow takes place in the opposite direction of the arrows in both transistors.

Transistor Applications

A small amount of current applied to the base produces a much larger flow of current through the emitter-collector circuit. The increase in current flow through the emitter-collector

NPN Transistor

| C — | N | P | N | — E |

B

PNP Transistor

| C — | P | N | P | — E |

B

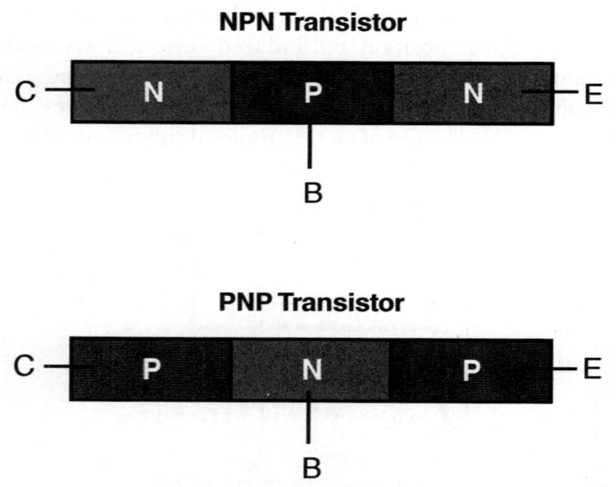

FIGURE 12-16 Arrangement of P and N materials comprising the PNP and NPN bipolar transistors.

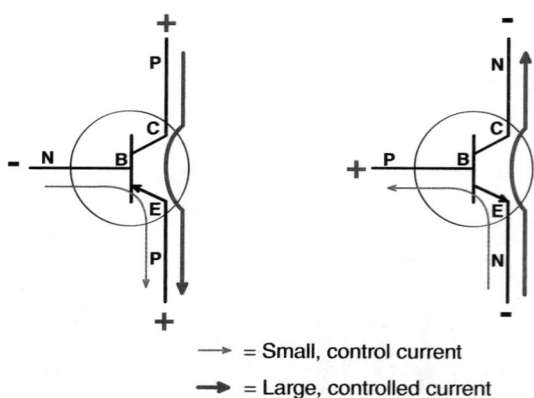

⟶ = Small, control current

➡ = Large, controlled current

FIGURE 12-17 In conventional bipolar transistors, the emitter is designated by the arrow. Current flows opposite the direction of the arrow when using electron theory.

TABLE 12-2 NPN-Type and PNP-Type Transistors

NPN Type	Forward Bias—Conduction	PNP Type	Forward Bias—Conduction Polarity
Emitter–N	Negative polarity	Emitter–P	Positive polarity
Base–P	Positive polarity	Base–N	Negative polarity
Collector–N	Positive polarity	Collector–P	Positive polarity

circuit compared to the base current is referred to as gain (**FIGURE 12-19**). When a transistor has the characteristic where its gain can be controlled in a way that is directly proportional to the base current, it can be used as an amplifier. Alternatively, a transistor can be used as a relay or switch in applications where a small amount of base current can switch a larger amount of current either on or off. Injector drivers in an ECM are a common application for switching transistors, which are called output drivers. To observe these characteristics and test a BJT transistor, follow the steps in **SKILL DRILL 12-2**.

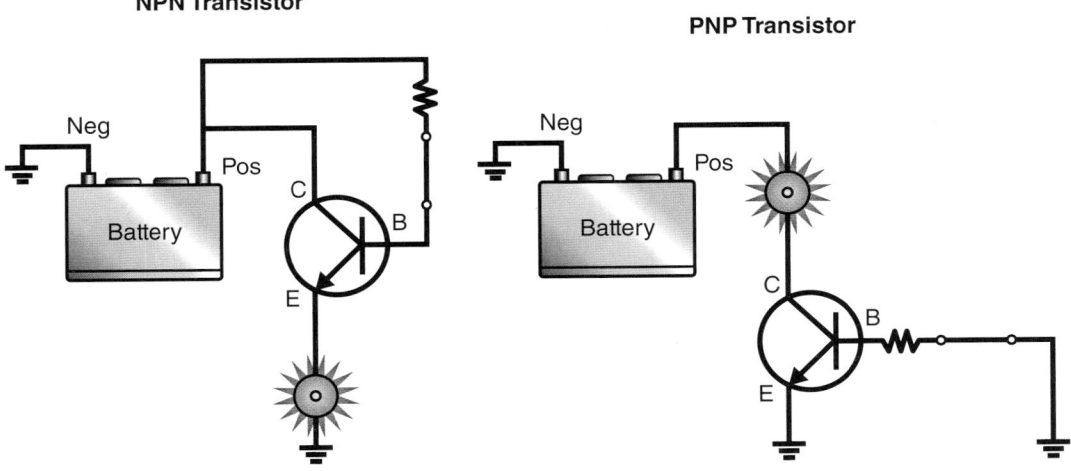

FIGURE 12-18 Applying small amounts of current to the base allows a larger current to flow through the emitter-collector circuit.

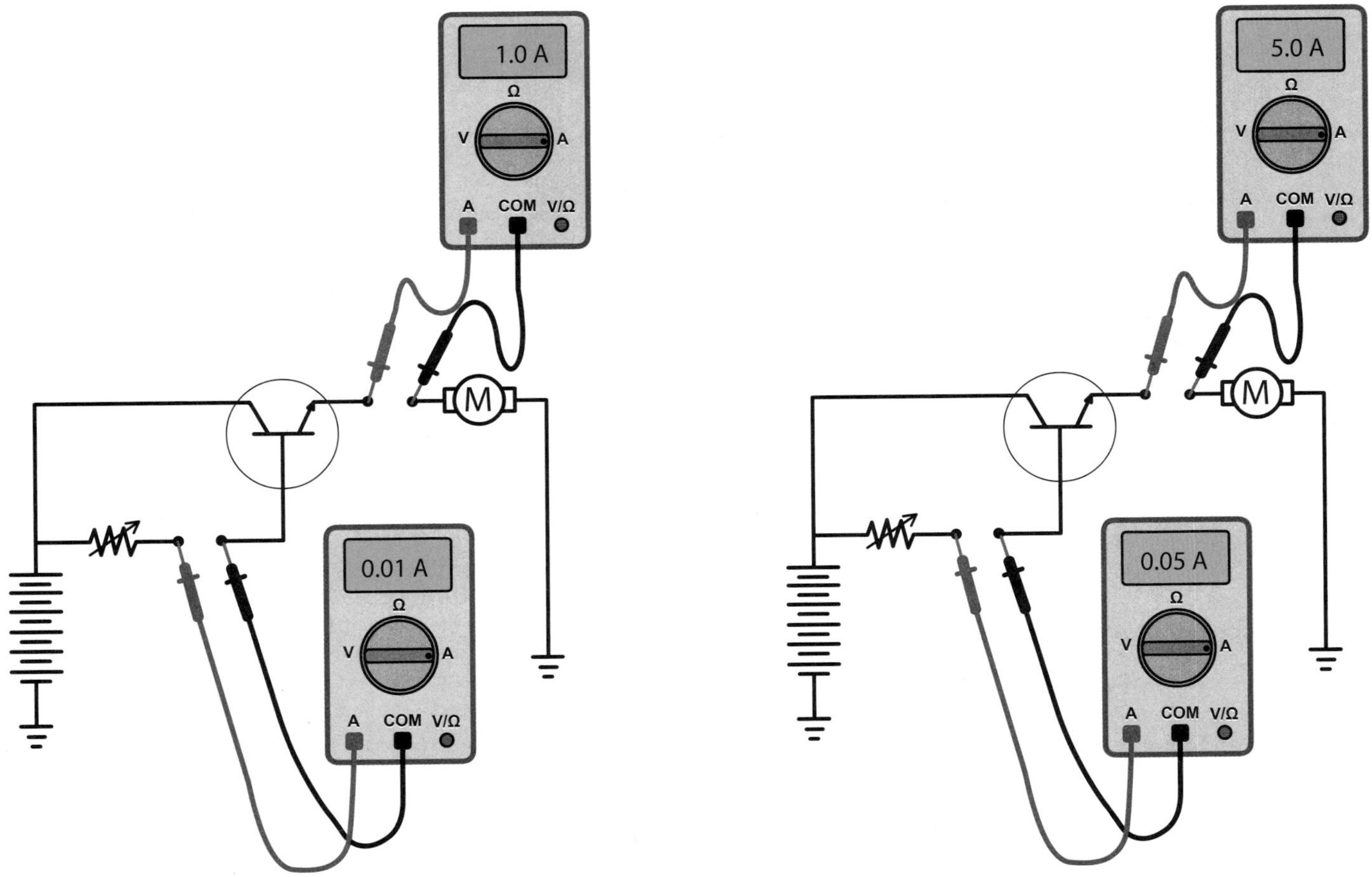

FIGURE 12-19 Transistor gain is observed by observing the ratio between the current applied to the base and flow across the emitter-collector circuit.

SKILL DRILL 12-2 Testing a Bipolar Transistor

NPN Transistor Testing

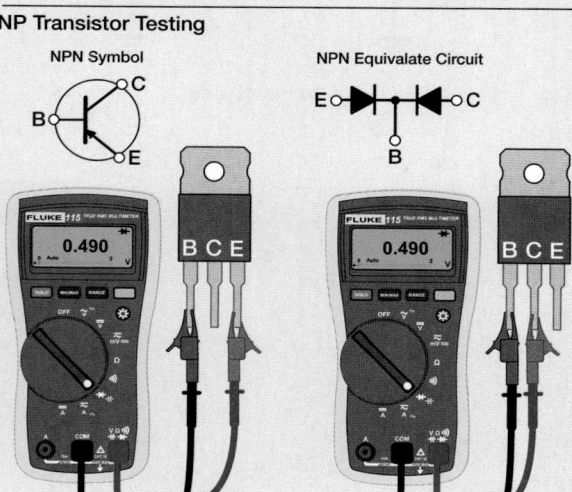

PNP Transistor Testing

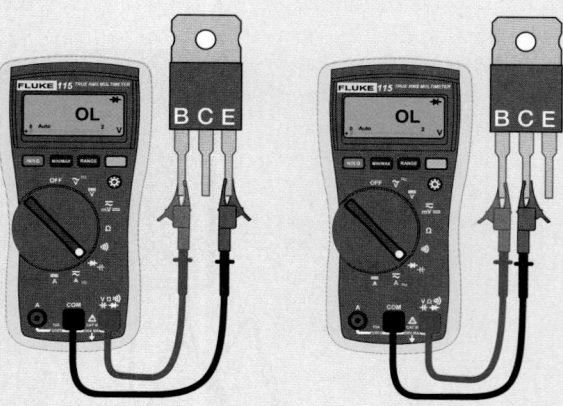

A transistor behaves as two diodes when testing with a multimeter. Testing a transistor with a multimeter must be done on the diode setting since it supplies adequate voltage with the correct polarity to exceed the junction threshold voltage needed to bias the transistor. A multimeter does not supply enough voltage through the probes on the resistance range.

1. Connect the – negative black lead to the COM terminal on the multimeter.
2. Connect the + positive red lead to the volt-ohm terminal of the multimeter.
3. Range the multimeter by turning the range dial to the diode symbol on the multimeter. This increases the voltage supplied to the probe leads above 0.7 volts or barrier voltage. It also supplies the correct polarity to the test leads. Do not use an ohmmeter to test the diode since the meter may not supply enough voltage to bias the diode.
4. Switch on the multimeter if it is not already switched on or has an auto shut-off. The display window should indicate infinite resistance with either 0 L (out of range) or OPEN.

5. To test an NPN transistor for forward bias operation, connect the positive red lead to the base terminal. On a PNP type transistor, connect the negative black lead to the base terminal.
6. Connect the black negative probe to the emitter of an NPN. The multimeter either beeps, which indicates the base to emitter circuit is conducting voltage, and/or displays a voltage reading for the barrier voltage. The transistor should have a barrier voltage between 0.3 and 0.8 volts. For a PNP transistor, the negative lead should be connected to the base and the positive to the emitter.
7. The transistor is defective if the voltage reading is above 0.8 volts or indicates the diode is open.
8. Repeat the procedure for the base to collector circuit using either the negative lead on the base for PNP transistors and the positive lead on the base for a NPN transistor.
9. To test for reverse bias operation, reverse the test leads by connecting the red lead to the base for a PNP transistor and the positive lead to the base on a NPN transistor.
10. The meter should not beep and the circuit should display an open circuit if the transistor is operating correctly.

Field Effect Semiconductors: Unipolar Semiconductors

LO 12-5 Identify and explain the construction and operating characteristics of field effect type, unipolar semiconductor's materials, and transistors.

In most electronic devices today, bipolar semiconductors have been displaced by unipolar semiconductors, which are more commonly called field effect devices. Given that 90% of all semiconductors produced today are field effect type, it is important to understand some details about the operation and unique characteristics of field effect semiconductors.

The term **unipolar semiconductor** is given to field effect devices because they can conduct current through just one doped semiconductor of either P or N material (**FIGURE 12-20**). The necessity of joining a P and N semiconductor together to form a junction to enable switching or blocking of current flow in bipolar devices is not necessary in unipolar devices operating according to field effect principles. Instead, either a P or N material is influenced by an electric field created by a positive or negatively charged metal plate placed next to the semiconductor. The positively or negatively charged metal plate can create an electrostatic field capable of penetrating silicon crystals enabling a semiconductor to conduct or block the flow through channels built for either negative to positive direction of current flow or vice versa. Conduction depends on a difference in charge potentials at each end of the channel—each end must be connected to a more or less positive or negative potential than the other end.

The operating principles of field effect semiconductors have been understood and demonstrated for almost as long as bipolar semiconductors, but field effect devices did not become common until the 1970s. The introduction of integrated circuits requiring the use of field effect devices to construct low-cost,

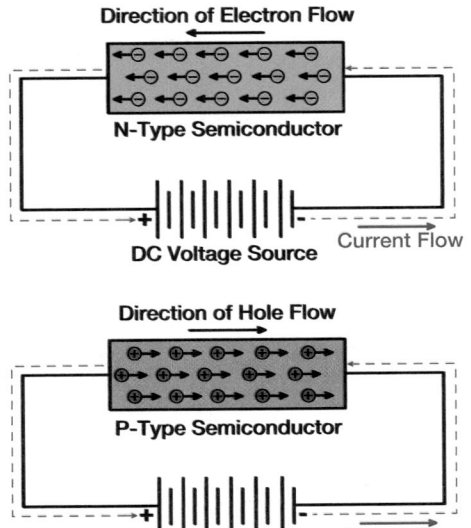

FIGURE 12-20 In P-type semiconductors, electrons are pulled from the negative side of the power supply into the positively charged holes. The positive terminal of the power supply pulls electrons out of the P channel. The opposite situation takes place in N-type channel conductors.

low-energy-consuming microprocessors and microcontrollers and other integrated circuits primarily drove the adoption of field effect devices.

Field Effect Principles

Like bipolar-type semiconductors, unipolar or field effect devices also use P and N materials commonly made from doped silicon to conduct current. However, when discussing field effect devices, the P and N materials are simply channels or charge carriers. Regardless of the terminology, semiconductor material in field effect devices are doped to possess either unbounded or loosely bound electrons (N) or materials seeking electrons to fill incomplete valances. The latter creates positive holes or P materials. Doped material enables channels to conduct current when a charge potential, a difference in the strength of the negative or positive charges, exists at each engine of the channel. By themselves, the P and N materials cannot accomplish much. This situation can change when an electric field is brought near the silicon crystals. For example, in one scenario, a positively charged metal plate placed close to the surface of an N-type semiconductor attracts and aligns the N material electrons randomly located inside the semiconductor material. As these electrons stream to the channel surface near the plate, there is an abundance of free electrons brought together that form a highly conductive current pathway for the normally blocked current. Only a very small amount of electric charge applied to the metal is required to create a channel for electron flow (**FIGURE 12-21**).

Because the device depends on an electric field to operate and can create current flow between the source and drain, it is known as a field effect transistor (FET). This device uses three leads like a bipolar transistor. Labelling of the leads, however, is different. Instead of an emitter-collector circuit, the P- and N-type equivalents in a FET are labelled gate, source, and drain with the source supplying current, with the drain being the terminal where current leaves the FET conductive channel. The FET gate is equivalent to the bipolar transistor's base since the voltage signal applied to the metal gate opens or closes the channel. Using an analogy of a water valve, the gate opens and closes the source-drain circuit, just as a water tap controls the flow of water. Compared to bipolar devices, FETs have the advantage of operating much cooler, using less power, switching faster, and being much more sensitive to input signals that can open or close the gate. Cooler operation is possible because there is no voltage dropped across a P-N junction point as in a bipolar transistor. Instead, current flows through only a single current-carrying channel that is opened and closed by the electrostatic field produced by the gate. FETs are much less expensive to make and are very reliable.

Enhancement and Depletion Mode

Consider again the example of a FET described in the previous paragraph. Because the charge on the plate compared to its effect on current flow through the source-drain channel is many times greater, amplification of gate signal takes place. When the electric charge on the gate's metal plate creates conduction in the P or N channel, the field effect is termed to operate in **enhancement mode**. Enhancement mode produces a disproportionately greater current flow through the source-drain channel compared

1: With no gate voltage the electrons are distributed randomly through the N-Material, channel is closed.

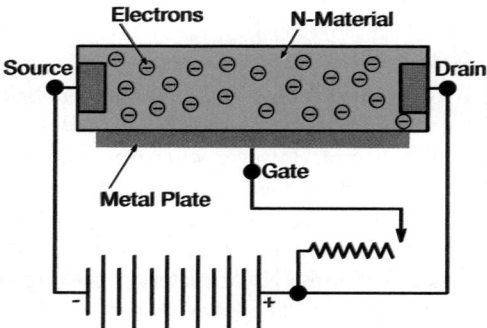

2: Applying gate voltage creates positive electrostatic field around the metal plate.

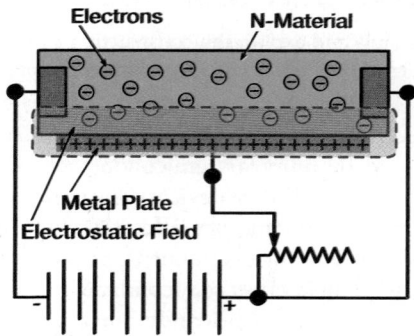

3: The electrons are attracted by the electrostatic field and move toward the metal plate, the channel is opening.

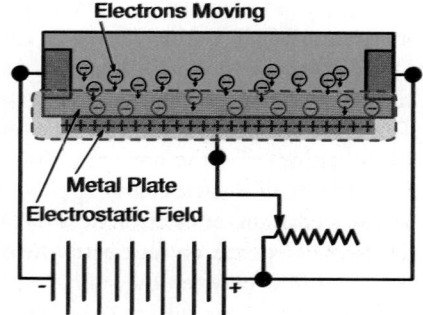

4: When the electrons are aligned along the metal plate the channel is open and will conduct current.

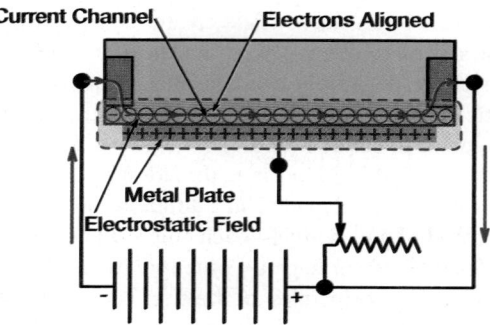

FIGURE 12-21 Field effect devices commonly use a small voltage signal applied to a metal plate to create an electrostatic field. The field creates a pathway for current to flow through a channel next to the plate in the semiconductor.

to the charge on the gate. By changing the voltage applied to the metal plate, more or less current can pass through the charge-carrying channel. The FET device constructed like this can operate like a bipolar transistor, allowing the device to switch, amplify, or even resist current flow through the semiconductor channel.

The use of an electric field can also be used to close a current-conducting channel in an FET. If a semiconductor device is doped in such a way to *normally* enable it to easily conduct positive or negative electric charges through P or N channels, a metal plate with a charge can be used to misalign a current pathway through the channel. Increasing gate voltage creates a non-conductive, ion-depleted zone in a normally conductive channel (**FIGURE 12-22**). This means increasing or decreasing the charge on the metal plate acting as a channel gate can disrupt the electrostatic field to pinch off a source-drain conductive channel. Progressively increasing the voltage applied to the gate reduces or resists current flow through the source-drain channel by narrowing the size of the conductive pathway. This happens because field disrupts the arrangement of free electrons or positive holes necessary to easily conduct charges through P- or N-type materials. When the field effect operates to constrict or pinch a channel this way, the device is said to operate in **depletion mode**. This effect is like the depletion zone

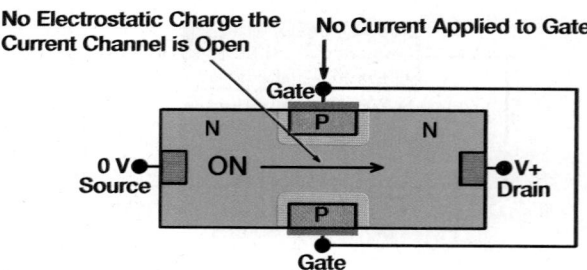

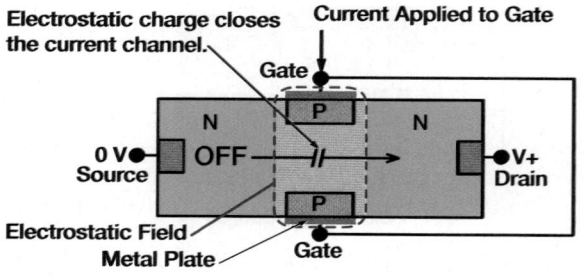

FIGURE 12-22 A JFET is normally conductive until a voltage is applied to the gate. The voltage applied to the gate disrupts the conductive pathway through a P- or N-type semiconductor by creating a depletion zone where free electrons or holes for conduction do not exist.

No Gate Voltage = No Resistance

Minimal Gate Voltage = Increased Resistance

Moderate Gate Voltage = More Resistance

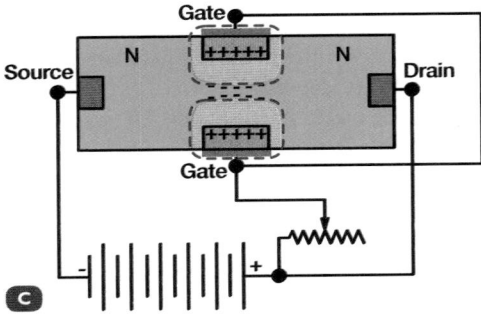

High Gate Voltage = High Resistance

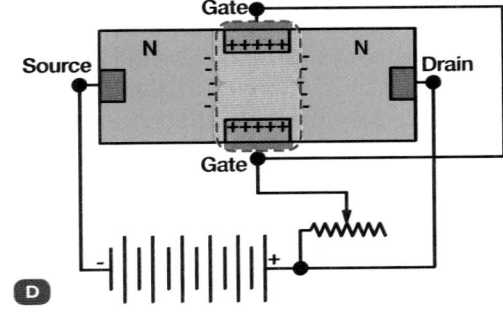

FIGURE 12-23 A. A JFET is normally conductive until a voltage is applied to the gate. **B.** A voltage applied to the gate disrupts the conductive pathway through a P- or N-type semiconductor. **C.** Increasing voltage creates a larger depletion zone where there are free electrons or holes for conduction. **D.** High gate voltage blocks current flow through the JFET.

at the junction of a bipolar diode or transistor in reverse bias (**FIGURE 12-23**). Another more common name given to FETs operating according to principles of depletion mode is **junction field effect transistor** or **JFET**.

To switch off an N-channel JFET device operating in depletion mode requires a negative gate-source voltage. Conversely, to switch off a P-channel JFET requires a positive gate voltage signal. The operation of the depletion mode FET is seen in the schematic symbols representing the transistor (**FIGURE 12-24**). The arrow head on the schematic shows the polarity of the P-N junction formed between the channel and the gate.

Biasing Field Effect Devices

Unlike bipolar transistors, the signal used to open and close the FET channel is only voltage-controlled. That is, the voltage applied to the gate is only a signal, which, in turn, varies the strength of the field and hence the amount of current flow from the source to the drain. No significant amount of amperage is needed to produce the gate charge. This is unlike bipolar transistors that have a base that is current-dependent, meaning a larger amount of amperage than a field effect device is necessary to bias the transistor to switch it on or off. Operating a voltage, rather than current-dependent, FET gate is an important observation, since it is key to understanding several of the unique characteristics of FET devices. The first is that FETs have what is known as high-input impedance gate. (You may recall that impedance refers to the resistance a device has to current of an

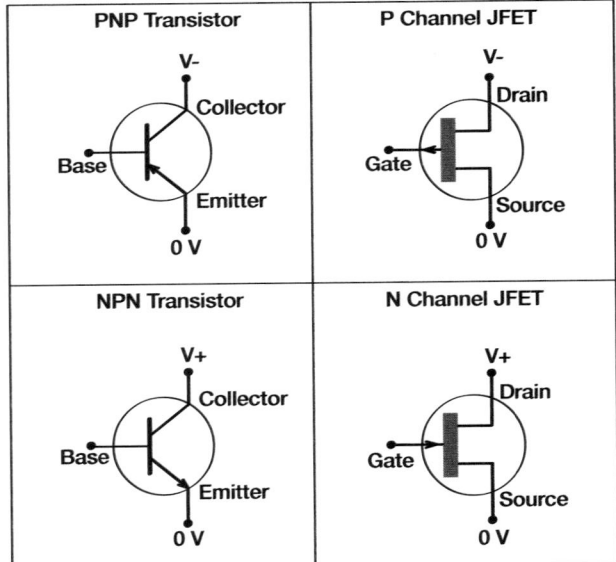

FIGURE 12-24 Comparing bipolar transistors to JFETs. Note the polarity of the P- or N-channel gate is indicated by the direction of the arrow, which is identical to a bipolar transistor.

electrical load.) An FET device with high impedance means that only the smallest amount of current is required to open, close, or modulate current flow from source-drain. Little to no electrical load is imposed or power is continuously absorbed, triggering the gate. Any current used to operate the gate is not dragged low due to power absorption by the gate. When only a high-impedance gate is used to bias an FET, the devices can be extremely sensitive to any gate signals. In fact, simply touching the gate lead of some JFETs with a finger supplies enough of an electrical charge to open or close the gate.

Voltage-only sensitive gates used to bias FETs, which either blocks or conducts current, not only translates into very low power consumption but much cooler operation. Unlike bipolar devices that have a barrier voltage of as much as 0.7 volts between P and N materials encountered when current crosses P and N junction points, FETs do not use P and N junctions, which continuously consume power. FETs only require enough current to initially create a field at the gate and, without P-N junctions, there is little to no voltage drop across the channels. The advantage of using unipolar field effect devices is they operate much cooler and consume much less power than bipolar devices. Also, remember that enhancement-mode FETs normally block or conduct current through channels without the need to apply any voltage to the gate. In this state, the devices consume or absorb almost no energy at all during operation.

FETs and Electrostatic Discharge

The downside to a high-impedance, voltage-sensitive gate is electrostatic discharge (ESD) can easily damage the field effect device. When a technician carries a "static" electrical charge, touching the terminals or leads of modules or other components containing FET semiconductors can easily damage and destroy the FET gate. Thinner channels and gates than bipolar semiconductors allow the FET gate material to literally be blown apart by ESD. Field effect devices can easily be damaged when jump starting a vehicle and inductive loads generate brief high-voltage spikes. Circuits require additional "hardening" through the use of other devices, such as positive temperature coefficient resistors.

Metal Oxide Semiconductor Field Effect Transistors (MOSFETs)

LO 12-6 Identify and explain the construction, operation, and characteristics of metal oxide field effect semiconductors.

Field effect transistors (**FIGURE 12-25**) are built and operate differently for a wide range of applications, including switching, amplification, and variable resistance. To build conductor channels capable of transferring more current with less resistance and switching faster using even less gate voltage, metal plate gates are replaced with metal oxides. By placing a layer of metal oxide insulating material between the gate and conductor channel, a different dielectric field strength is obtained that enhances the effectiveness of the electrostatic field. These new devices insulating the gate from the conductor body with metal oxide are also given the name insulated gate bipolar transistors (IGBT). IGBTs are important devices used in electric and hybrid vehicle inverter modules to convert DC to AC and regulate the speed of variable frequency drive motors.

Like using plastic or paper insulation between plates of a capacitor, rather than air, the dielectric strength and behavior of the electrostatic charges enables the field to improve channel conduction and transfer higher voltages. The newest field effect devices do not even use metal oxide insulators; however, the term MOSFET is still used and is by far the most common transistor used in digital circuits. Millions of these transistors may be included in a memory chip, microcontroller, or microprocessor.

MOSFETs, like other FETs, use voltage applied to the gate terminal to increase conductivity of the P or N channels. In depletion mode, voltage applied to the gate reduces the conductivity. As already mentioned, what is distinct is that MOSFETs are universally recognized to have an insulated gate separate from the body of the transistor. Additionally, the MOSFET body generally has an additional terminal that provides another input to operate the gate. That means two separate circuits can connect to a MOSFET and open the gate. In a sense, the gate is like a fourth terminal on the FET, and electric charges applied to the body can influence electrical conduction between the source and drain (**FIGURE 12-26**).

■ *Increase current flow exponentially through the source and drain circuit compared with the gate voltage.*

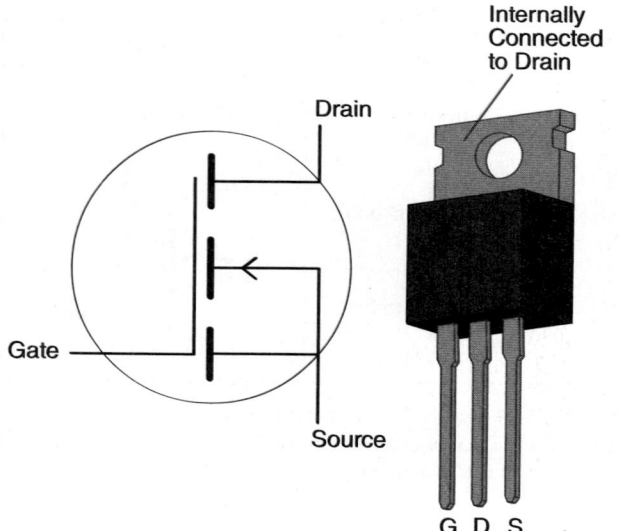

FIGURE 12-25 Construction of a FET with an insulated gate. FETs can be designed to operate as variable resistors and capacitors by controlling the charges applied to the various terminals.

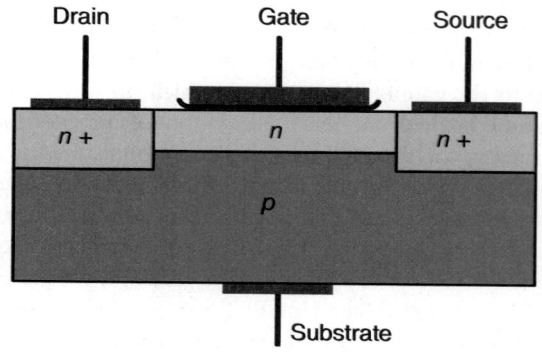

FIGURE 12-26 The gate of a FET controls current flow through the drain and source. The body of a MOSFET is like a fourth terminal, creating two connections to the gate on many FETs.

- *Operate as voltage-controlled resistors.* Varying the voltage between the gate and body changes the conductivity between the drain and source. This feature, called the body effect or body-gate, allows FETs to be programmed to operate as virtual fuses and cut current flow to output devices drawing excessive current. Only voltage is affected, not amperage.
- *Have voltage-blocking capabilities superior to bipolar transistors.* FETs can, therefore, operate as switches, blocking voltage of 120 volts in the OFF state. IGBTs that combine a MOSFET and bipolar transistor can conduct hundreds of amps and block voltages up to 6,500 volts.
- *Conduct large amounts of current without damage.* A single FET found as an output driver in an ECM can continuously conduct 30 amps in its ON state (**FIGURE 12-27**). While controlling over 2,000 watts (12.5 volts at 160 amps) of power, they emit only 100 watts or less of heat. This happens because there is virtually no voltage drop through an FET across a channel (bipolar transistors have that drop across P and N junction points). The output circuits of all multiplexed electrical devices—whether they are lighting, body accessories, or auxiliary electrical devices—use MOSFETs.

Virtual Fusing

Specialized FETs, called MOSFETs, can be configured into pairs that are capable of measuring the amount of current being conducted by the FET. This information is sent back to the microcontroller enabling the FET to be switched off if the FET is conducting too much current for a circuit's current rating. Grounded circuits or simply circuits with too many loads trigger this event.

Virtual fusing is the description given to the use of FETs that replace a fuse or circuit breaker in the individual high-side controlled circuits. Virtual fusing is also designed to imitate the characteristics of SAE Type I and II circuit breakers. SAE

Type I circuit breakers reset automatically, typically trying to reset every ½ second. If the current flow is still excessive, the cycle time becomes even longer with every successive reset. SAE Type II circuit breakers reset when the load is disconnected and reapplied or, in this case, the key is cycled on and off. Software instructions are used to calculate a combination of time amperage flows through the circuit to determine whether the load is excessive. A diagnostic fault code can be set and stored even after the FET is cycled back on. Virtual fusing is also discussed in the Electric Circuits and Circuit Protection chapter.

Integrated Circuits (IC)

LO 12-7 Identify, describe, and differentiate between the construction and operation of microprocessors and microcontrollers.

An integrated circuit miniaturizes a set of electronic circuits onto one small flat piece of semiconductor material, typically made from silicon. Anywhere from a hundred to over a billion transistors can be embedded into a single silicon chip, called a wafer. Naturally, massive electronic capabilities can be built into the chips, incorporating so many components built at a microscopic scale. Because integrated circuits are not constructed one transistor at a time, the cost to produce electronic devices is lower. Field effect devices are formed on the wafer to duplicate the operation of common electronic circuit components, including diodes, transistors, resistors, and capacitors (**FIGURE 12-28**). The silicon wafer is packaged in a ceramic or plastic body with multiple metal pins forming input and output connection points.

To create these complex devices having enormous capabilities, a process called photolithography is used to etch the circuits into layers of the silicon wafer. To do this, circuits are first drawn on large display boards before they are photographically reduced from dozens of square feet to nanometer sized images.

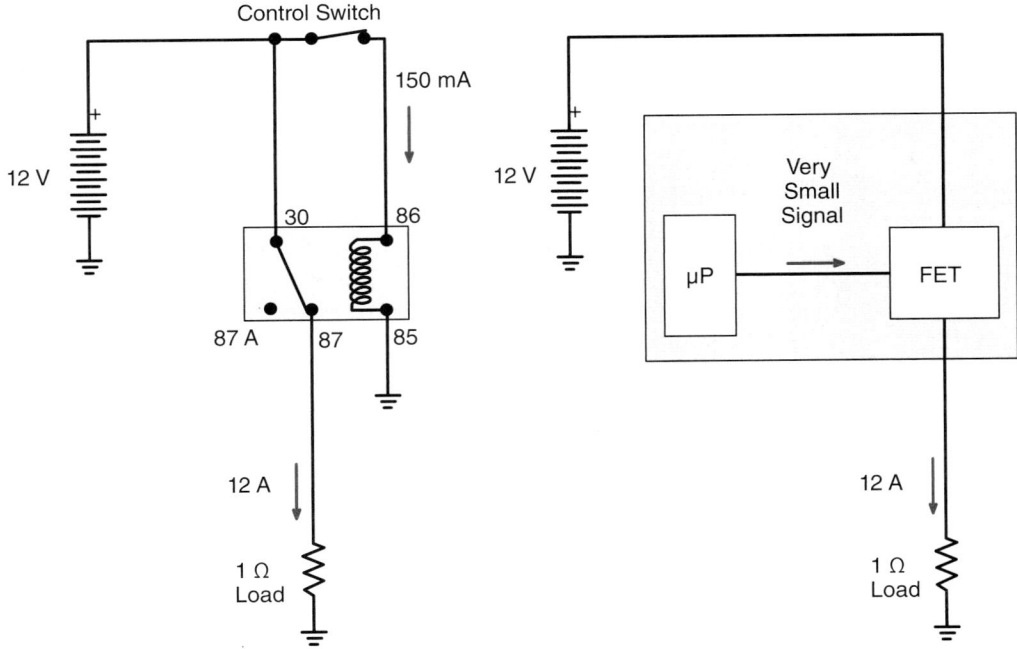

FIGURE 12-27 Comparing high current flow FET to a relay.

Circuit images are then transferred onto silicon wafers using light-sensitive chemical treatments that either deposit materials onto, or etch, the silicon. Miniaturization of ICs makes devices smaller and faster while consuming less power. Without the low power consumption and cooler operating capabilities of FETs, the sophisticated functions of today's integrated circuits are not possible. Two common applications of integrated circuits are microprocessors and microcontrollers (**FIGURE 12-29**).

Microprocessors

Microprocessors use integrated circuitry formed from vast numbers of transistors, resistors, and capacitors in multiple layers. They contain memory, arithmetic, and logic circuits that enable them to operate using sophisticated programmed sets of instructions. The biggest difference between a microprocessor and other integrated circuits, like microcontrollers, is microprocessors require an external operating system. One can think of Linux, Windows, or Android when referring to an operating system controlling the performance of a microprocessor. Microprocessors also require external interface devices to operate, such as keyboards, touchscreens, different types of memory, a serial data bus to connect it with memory, and ports, plus other input and output devices. Microprocessors using operating system software supply electronic signals to operate or coordinate multiple other control systems. Sophisticated on board entertainment systems and autonomous vehicle control systems use microprocessor-based operating systems to interface with navigational, object detection, and control systems. Currently, only a few microprocessor-based control systems are used by some OEMs. AUTOSAR (Automotive Open System Architecture) is one example of a standardized operating system used to reduce the hardware complexity of today's vehicles.

Microcontrollers

Microprocessors and microcontroller are both sophisticated integrated circuits built to perform specific operations by following a set of programmed instructions. Microcontrollers retrieve instructions from the memory and execute using arithmetic or logic processing capabilities. Sensors data stored temporarily in memory also supplies processors with data, and an arithmetic unit performs calculations using algorithms based on programmed instructions. (Algorithms are simply mathematical formulas used to solve problems, such as when to fire an injector or how long to energize an injector coil based on driver demand and operating conditions.) The results of these operations are used to provide an output signal or power an output device. What distinguishes a microcontroller from a microprocessor is all the hardware needed to operate it, such as memory, and the programmed set of instructions located on the chip itself and not in an external operating system (**FIGURE 12-30**).

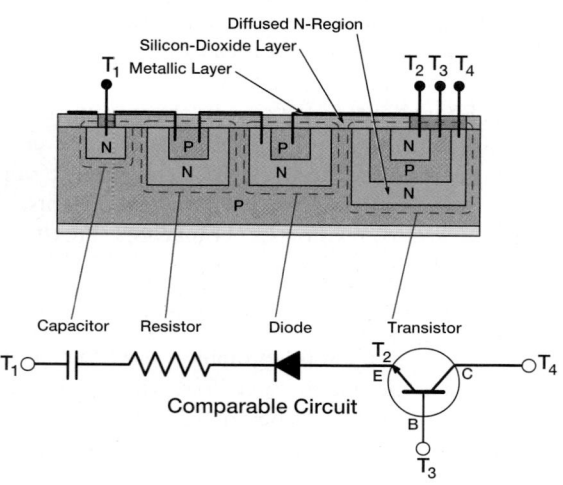

FIGURE 12-28 One of the first integrated circuits. An integrated circuit can miniaturize the operation of transistors, diodes, and capacitors.

FIGURE 12-29 Both microprocessors and microcontrollers execute programmable instructions. The operation of smaller microcontrollers on this board are coordinated by the larger 16-bit microcontroller. FETs used to conduct high current to output devices are called drivers. **A.** FET drivers. **B.** 2-bit microcontrollers. **C.** 16-bit microcontroller.

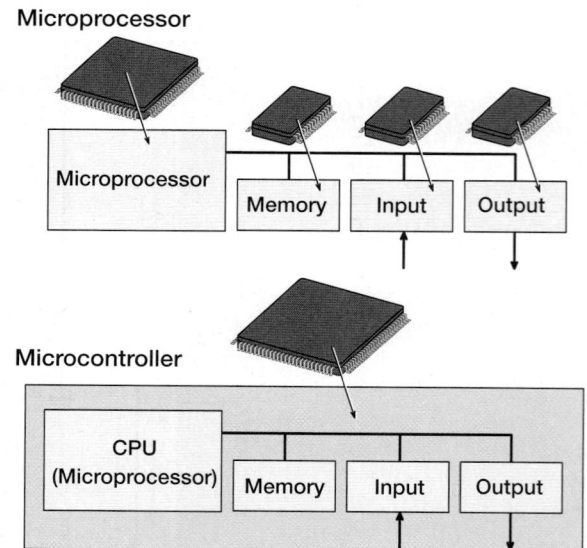

FIGURE 12-30 What differentiates a microprocessor from a microcontroller? A microprocessor uses an operating system and requires several external support systems and components to operate. A microcontroller contains all the hardware necessary to perform its job.

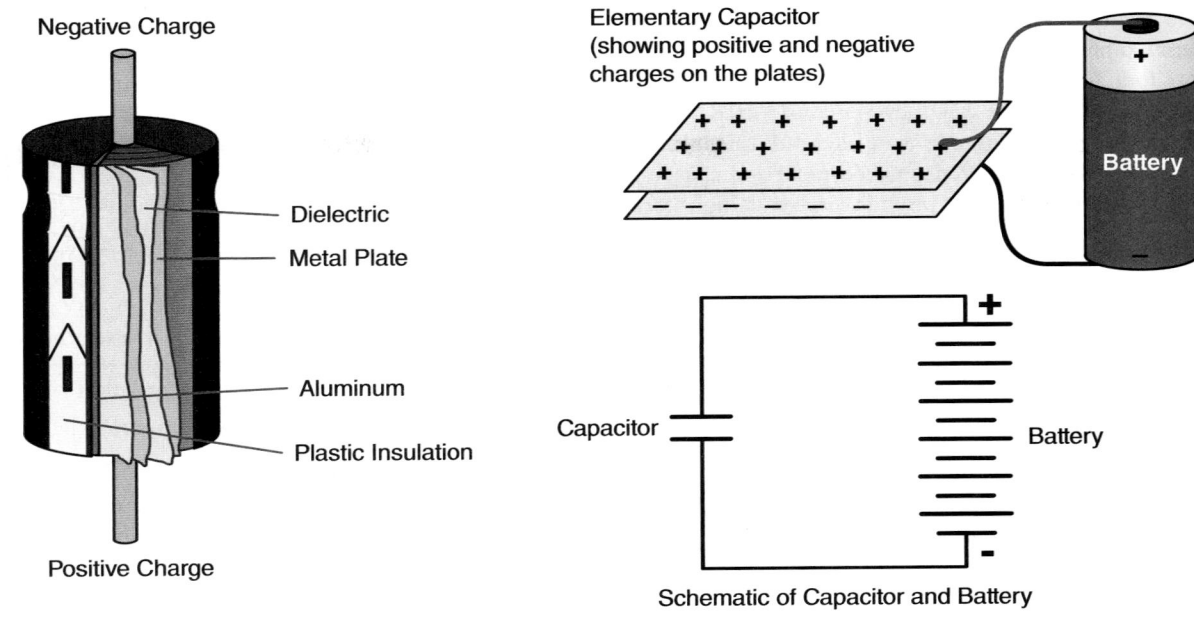

FIGURE 12-31 A typical capacitor showing construction and schematic representation.

Microcontrollers differ from microprocessors in that they have minimal requirements for memory and software and use no operating system. Typical input and output devices operated by microcontrollers include sensors and stepper motors. Microcontrollers often operate more like digital signal processors (DSPs). For example, a microcontroller's output may be a pulse-width-modulated electrical signal, making it possible for it to control resistive loads, motors, ABS solenoids, and engine controls. Microcontrollers having different degrees of sophistication are found on circuit boards or inside sensors, used as controllers for electric motors and stepper motors, drive instrument clusters, body controls, and other vehicle systems.

Capacitors

LO 12-8 Describe the construction, operation, applications, and testing of capacitors.

Capacitors are another type of electronic control device that act like electric shock absorbers and can store and discharge current, much like a battery or hydraulic accumulator. Ordinary fixed capacitors can store a calibrated amount of electric charge in electrostatic fields. These capacitors are simple devices made up of three components—two metal plates and an insulating material separating the plates (**FIGURE 12-31**). The insulation is called a dielectric. The plates are not connected, but each has a lead (**FIGURE 12-32**). The dielectric material, another name for an electrical insulator, separates the plates from making contact and is made from a variety of materials, such as air, paper, plastic, ceramic, mica, and so on.

When the lead of either plate is connected to a positive or negative of a power source, electrostatic induction occurs. This involves the positive lead of the power supply removing electrons from one plate, thereby creating a positive charge. The positively charged plate now can attract electrons to another closely placed metal plate. If the other plate is connected to a negative terminal of the power supply, electrons are attracted to the positive electrostatic charge of the opposite plate and due to electron pressure at the negative terminal of the power supply (**FIGURE 12-33**). Alternatively, when an electron is added to one plate, an electron is driven away from the opposite plate due to electrostatic forces of repulsion.

The capacitor can hold the charge almost indefinitely because of the electrostatic attraction of the charges located on opposite plates. The area of the plates and properties of the dielectric determine the charge-holding capacity of the capacitor, which is measured in Farads. Maximum charge voltage is the same as the power supply connected to the capacitor.

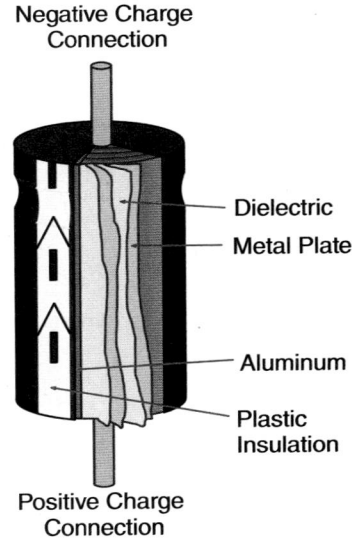

FIGURE 12-32 Construction of an electrolytic capacitor.

A capacitor's voltage rating is based on the ability of the dielectric material to prevent internal arcing.

Capacitors are categorized by their capacity, the type of dielectric material, and the way they are constructed. Variable capacitors are used by radios to tune or filter radio signals. Electrolytic capacitors, which are also called polarized capacitors, have metal oxide dielectrics that provide them with high storage capacity. Super capacitors, also called ultra-capacitors, have carbon plate material that has enormous storage capacity and these capacitors are currently used to assist starting batteries.

> ▶ **TECHNICIAN TIP**
>
> When checking for parasitic draws, remember that a capacitor pulls current until it is charged, and then stops. Test lights and meter connected between the battery and vehicle electrical system lights up momentarily until any on-board capacitors are charged. The alternator is one point where a large capacitor draws current until charged. Connecting battery cables often produce some sparking due to current draw from capacitors.

Capacitor Applications

Capacitors can be discharged more rapidly than batteries, making them ideal for energizing injectors operating above battery voltage. Injector drive modules use electrolytic capacitors to store and supply voltage for piezoelectric-type injector actuators, which require as much as 200 volts to open an injector nozzle (**FIGURE 12-34**). They are also useful for smoothing out or "stiffening" voltage fluctuations that interfere with the operation of sensitive electronic components (**FIGURE 12-35**). Connected across a power supply positive and negative terminal, the capacitor absorbs momentary increases in voltage and discharges the current when voltage drops for devices, such as alternators and radios.

Capacitors can also absorb voltage spikes caused by inductive reactance when a magnetic field of a coil collapses. Ignition systems need capacitors connected in parallel to ignition coil switching devices to prevent damage that is caused during the induction of magnetic fields.

Capacitors are also used as timers in circuits, such as wiper delay modules or dimming of dome lights. When connected to the base of a transistor, a charged capacitor can forward bias the transistor to modulate or vary current flow through the emitter-collector circuit for a short amount of time. By using a fixed- or

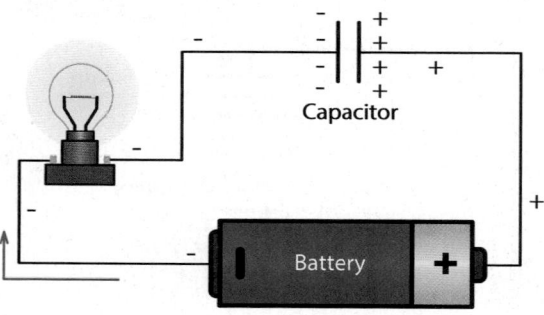

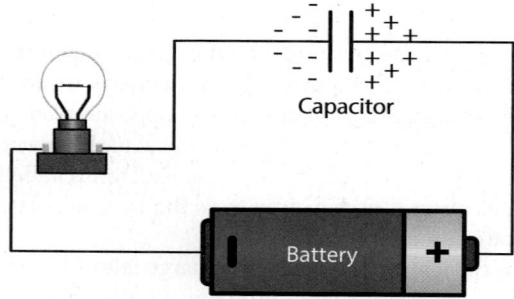

FIGURE 12-33 While positive charges are pulling electrons to the opposite plate of the capacitors, electrons move through the filament to light the bulb. After the capacitor is charged, no more electron movement takes place and the light goes out. Reversing the battery polarity causes the process to start all over as the capacitor discharges and recharges again.

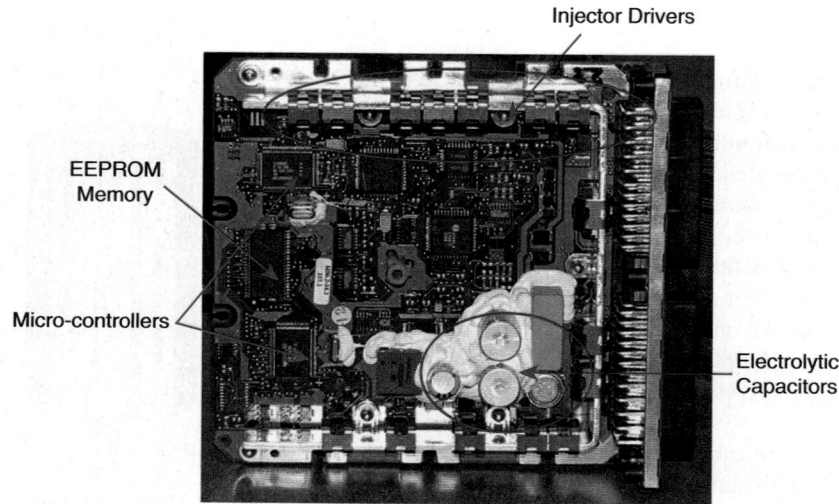

FIGURE 12-34 The electrolytic capacitors in this injector drive module are used to energize piezoelectric actuators with more than 200 volts for common rail injectors.

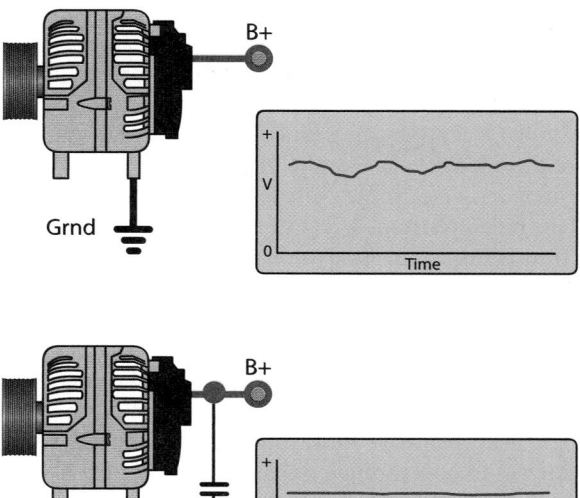

FIGURE 12-35 Connecting a smoothing capacitor in parallel across the alternator's output helps reduce small current fluctuations called AC ripple.

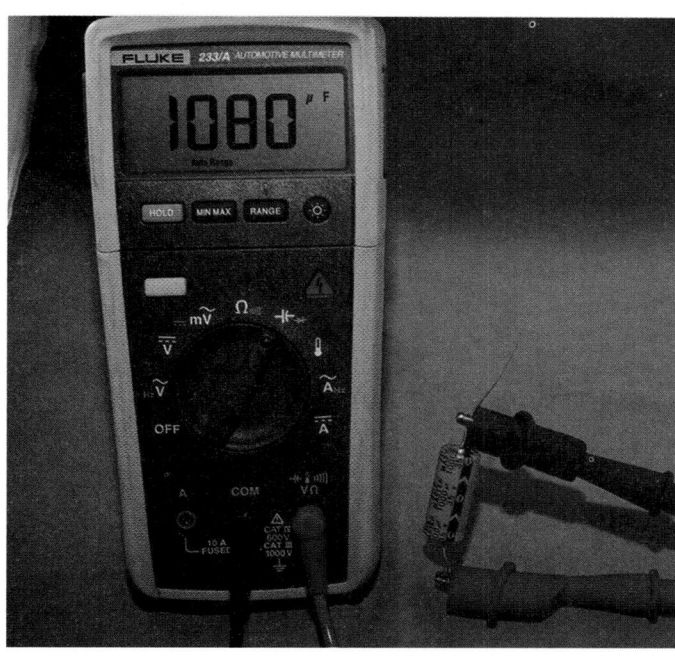

FIGURE 12-36 Testing a capacitor with the meter ranged for measuring capacitance.

variable-type resistor connected in series with the capacitor, the speed of the capacitor's charge rate is controlled, which in turn controls how much current passes through the emitter-collector circuit, and for how long a timer circuit operates.

▶ TECHNICIAN TIP

A clamping circuit is an electronic circuit that prevents or minimizes voltage spike caused by self-induction. Diodes and capacitors are often installed in parallel across the power supply to a circuit containing wire coils that can create voltage spikes whenever power is initially supplied, but more often and much higher when current is removed or disconnected.

Testing Capacitors

Capacitors never wear out, but they can short out. See **SKILL DRILL 12-3** for a procedure to evaluate whether a capacitor is shorted. An ohmmeter connected to each lead of the capacitor should show no continuity. It may briefly show some continuity as current from the meter charges the capacitor, but that should quickly diminish. Shorted plates allow continuity. A meter measures the time it takes to charge a capacitor with a small amount of voltage (**FIGURE 12-36**). The voltage applied to charge the capacitor and time required to charge it are used to calculate its capacitance.

SKILL DRILL 12-3 Testing Capacitors

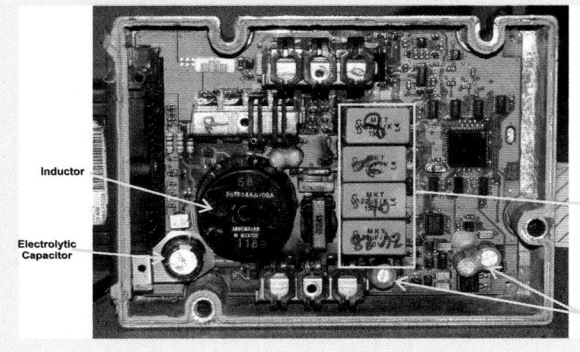

Capacitors can be tested for short circuits using a multimeter.

1. Range the multimeter to measure resistance or continuity.
2. Place the meter leads on each terminal pin. If there is only one lead, the capacitor case is the other terminal.
3. The capacitor charges while connected to the multimeter and its resistance increases, as long as the meter is connected to the capacitor, until it has reached the same voltage level as the current leaving the meter.
4. The capacitor is shorted or defective if the meter reads 0 ohms.

Wrap-Up

Ready for Review

- Commercial vehicles were slow to adopt electronic components because dependability was an overarching concern that had greater priority than achieving the efficiencies, features, and benefits of using electronic components.
- In contrast to electrical and electromechanical devices, which conduct large amounts of current, electronic circuits exert control of electrons using principles of electrostatics—the attraction and repulsion of electrons using electric fields or charges.
- Common electronic semiconductor circuit-controlled devices include wide varieties of diodes, transistors, integrated circuits, microprocessors, and microcontrollers used in electronic control modules.
- Semiconductors are the most important material used to construct electronic devices. This material can have properties of both conductors and insulators and can switch back and forth between either state using small electrostatic charges.
- Two types of semiconductors are used today: unipolar and bipolar. The difference is whether circuit current passes through one (unipolar) or two (bipolar) parts of the two common semiconductor materials making up the device.
- Unipolar devices operate according to field effect principles.
- Semiconductors are created by introducing impurities into silicon through a process called doping. The impurities introduced can be of several materials, and the material used creates a movable positive P or negative N charge.
- Sandwiching a P- and N-semiconductor material produces a bipolar diode, which is an electronic device through which current can flow in only one direction.
- When a diode conducts current, it is said to be in forward bias. When the diode blocks flow, it is in reverse bias. Diodes block current in reverse bias until the voltage reaches the diode's Zener point, where it is damaged.
- Types of diodes include: rectifying, Zener, light-emitting, and organic light-emitting.
- Zener diodes are purposely made to stop blocking current after reaching its Zener point.
- Light is emitted from the P-N junction of a light-emitting diode when the diode is forward biased, but not in reverse bias. Photons are released at the junction because the electron loses energy during the process, which is primarily converted to light instead of heat.
- LEDs have low electrical resistance and do not behave according to Ohm's law. LEDs draw as much current as possible, but at the same time are sensitive to over-voltage conditions.
- A critical function of diodes is to suppress high-voltage spikes caused by self-induction in coils.
- Bipolar transistors are semiconductor devices composed of three blocks of a P and N material. They primarily function as electronic switches, amplifiers, and voltage-controlled resistors.
- Transistors can be used as relays and current amplifiers.
- Field effect transistors (FETs) are the most common transistors used in digital and analog circuits today. FETs can also be configured to perform as virtual fuses.
- Field effect devices commonly use a small voltage signal applied to a metal plate to create an electrostatic field. The field creates a pathway for either positive or negative current to flow through a channel created next to the plate in the semiconductor.
- Field effect transistor (FET) leads are labeled gate, source, and drain, with the source supplying current and the drain being the terminal where current leaves the FET conductive channel. The FET gate is equivalent to the bipolar transistor's base, since the voltage signal applied to the metal gate opens or closes the channel.
- When the field effect produced by the charge on the gate's metal plate produces conduction in the source-drain circuit, the FET is termed to operate in enhancement mode.
- When the field effect operates to constrict or pinch a channel by increasing the size of the depletion area, the device is said to operate in depletion mode.
- MOSFETs are universally recognized to have an insulated gate separate from the body of the transistor. The MOSFET body generally has an additional terminal that provides another input to operate the gate.
- Integrated circuits (IC) are semiconductor devices having anywhere from a hundred to over a billion transistors embedded into a single silicon wafer.
- Two common applications of integrated circuits are microprocessors and microcontrollers.
- Microprocessors contain memory and logic circuits that enable them to operate using sophisticated programmed sets of stored instructions. By contrast, microcontrollers have minimal requirements for memory and software and contain no operating system.
- Capacitors act like electric shock absorbers and can store and discharge current. Capacitors are made up of three components—two plates and an insulating material separating the plates.

Key Terms

bipolar semiconductor   A semiconductor having a junction between P and N material that conducts current through both the semiconductor materials and junction.

bipolar transistor   A transistor that combines either two P or N materials with a single P or N-type material forming PNP or NPN transistors.

capacitor   A circuit-control device made up of two plates separated by an insulating material.

depletion mode   A condition in a unipolar-type semiconductor when either a P or N channel current carrying pathway is disrupted by the polarity of voltage applied to the gate.

enhancement mode   A condition in a unipolar-type semiconductor when either a P- or N-channel current-carrying pathway is made conductive by the polarity of voltage applied to the gate.

forward bias   A condition in which a diode or transistor conducts current.

mechatronics   The integration of mechanical systems, electronic devices, and microcontroller-based systems.

N material   A material with a movable negative charge.

NPN transistor   A type of bipolar transistor with two blocks of N material and one block of P material.

organic light-emitting diode (OLED)   A light-emitting diode that uses carbon-based semiconductor material.

P material   A material with a movable positive charge.

photodiode   A diode that forwards bias only when light strikes it.

phototransistor   A transistor that is forward biased when light strikes its base, which is made from a photo-sensitive semiconductor.

PNP transistor   A type of bipolar transistor with two blocks of P material and one block of N material.

reverse bias   A situation in which a diode blocks current flow.

unipolar semiconductor   A semiconductor device made of either P or N material that conducts current through only one channel.

Zener diode   A type of diode that behaves like a typical silicon diode up to a precise voltage threshold, called the Zener point. After it reaches the Zener point voltage, the diode conducts in both directions.

Zener point   The voltage at which a diode conducts current in both directions instead of just one.

Review Questions

1. Which of the following statements is the best explanation to describe the term mechatronics?
   a. The use of electrical force to power mechanical movement.
   b. The use of circuit controls, such as simple switches, resistors, electromagnetic relays, and solenoids, to control mechanical devices.
   c. The use of more reliable mechanical devices to replace an electronic device.
   d. The integration of mechanical, electronic, and microcontrollers into a component or system.

2. Which of the following is the major difference between electrical and electronic components?
   a. Electronic components use more current to produce heat, light, magnetic fields, and sound.
   b. Electronic components use semiconductors.
   c. Electrical components can amplify, digitize, or modify electrical signals.
   d. Electronic components tend to be more reliable than electrical components.

3. Which of the following devices is a unipolar-type semiconductor?
   a. A NPN-type transistor
   b. A rectifying diode used in an alternator
   c. A PNP-type transistor
   d. A junction-type field effect transistor (JFET)

4. Which of the following are parts or elements used by a bipolar-type electronic component?
   a. A gate, source, and drain
   b. Two P-type semiconductors
   c. An emitter and collector current pathway
   d. A metal oxide insulated gate

5. Which of the following materials does not conduct electric current?
   a. P-type semiconductor material
   b. N-type semiconductor material
   c. Silicon
   d. The junction of a P and N semiconductor

6. Which of the following generates the greatest amount of heat in an electronic component?
   a. The junction of a bipolar semiconductor made from doped silicon
   b. The junction of a unipolar semiconductor made from metal oxide
   c. The insulated gate of an IGBT
   d. Either P- or N-type semiconductor materials

7. What happens when the voltage in a circuit supplied to a 15-volt Zener diode rises above 15-volts DC?
   a. The diode either shorts out or burns.
   b. The diode blocks current flow in only one direction.
   c. The diode blocks current flow in both directions.
   d. The diode opens and allows current to flow in either direction.

8. What happens at the junction of an LED when it is in reverse bias state?
   a. It emits light.
   b. It blocks current flow.
   c. It releases light and heat.
   d. A voltage drop takes place.

9. Which of the following can take place when a negative current signal is applied to the base of a bipolar PNP transistor?
   a. Current flow through the emitter-collector circuit is blocked.
   b. Current flow through the emitter collect circuit can take place.
   c. The transistor is in a reverse bias condition.
   d. Current flows through the base-collector circuit.

10. Which of the following can take place when a negative voltage signal is applied to the gate of a MOSFET with an N-channel conductor?
    a. Current flow through the channel is resisted or blocked.
    b. Current flow through the channel is switched on or amplified.
    c. Current flow is enabled in a P-channel conductor.
    d. Current flow takes place between the source and gate terminals.

ASE Technician A/Technician B Style Questions

1. Technician A says that accidentally attempting to jump start a vehicle by connecting jumper cables using incorrect polarity blows all the electronic control modules on a vehicle. Technician B says that only fuses in circuits that are powering a control module are likely to blow. Who is correct?
   a. Technician A
   b. Technician B
   c. Both Technician A and Technician
   d. Neither Technician A nor Technician B

2. Technician A says MOSFETs, a type of unipolar transistor, can be used as a fuse to shut off current to circuits drawing too much current. Technician B says only a Zener diode can shut off current in a circuit drawing too much amperage. Who is correct?
   a. Technician A
   b. Technician B
   c. Both Technician A and Technician B
   d. Neither Technician A nor Technician B

3. Technicians A and B are discussing what they learned in a training class regarding semiconductors. Technician A says that FETs operating in depletion mode can block current flow through N- and P-type channels. Technician B says that an FET operating in enhancement mode allows conduction through P and N channels if a voltage signal of the opposite polarity to the channel is applied to the gate. Who is correct?
   a. Technician A
   b. Technician B
   c. Both Technician A and Technician B
   d. Neither Technician A nor Technician B

4. Technician A says that current flow in a bipolar transistor takes place from source to drain terminals. Technician B says that most current flow takes place between the emitter and collector terminals. Who is correct?
   a. Technician A
   b. Technician B
   c. Both Technician A and Technician B
   d. Neither Technician A nor Technician B

5. Technician A says that a MOSFET unipolar conductor operates much cooler than a bipolar transistor because there is no voltage drop across a junction. Technician B says MOSFETs operate cooler than bipolar transistors since the gate and insulating material is made from metals, such as aluminum, which better radiate heat. Who is correct?
   a. Technician A
   b. Technician B
   c. Both Technician A and Technician B
   d. Neither Technician A nor Technician B

6. Technician A says capacitors are devices that act like electric shock absorbers and can store and discharge current, much like a battery or hydraulic accumulator. Technician B says capacitors are simple devices made up of three components—two plates and an insulating material. Who is correct?
   a. Technician A
   b. Technician B
   c. Both Technician A and Technician B
   d. Neither Technician A nor Technician B

7. Technician A says capacitors can be used to absorb current produced by self-induction of wire coils. Technician B says that diodes help minimize any voltage spike produced by self-induction of wire coils. Who is correct?
   a. Technician A
   b. Technician B
   c. Both Technician A and Technician B
   d. Neither Technician A nor Technician B

8. Technician A says that microcontrollers are far more commonly used in electronic control modules than microprocessors. Technician B says that each electronic control module on a vehicle uses at least one microprocessor. Who is correct?
   a. Technician A
   b. Technician B
   c. Both Technician A and Technician B
   d. Neither Technician A nor Technician B

9. Technician A says that a bipolar transistor or diode operating in reverse bias is conducting electric current. Technician B says that when a diode or transistor is in a reverse bias state, it is blocking current. Who is correct?
   a. Technician A
   b. Technician B
   c. Both Technician A and Technician B
   d. Neither Technician A nor Technician B

10. While testing a set of diodes in the rectifier bridge of an alternator, Technicians A and B observe a 0.7-volt drop across each diode when testing the diodes with a 12-volt battery, voltmeter, and lightbulb. Technician A says that the observation about the voltage drop was normal. Technician B says that the diodes are likely defective, and the rectifier bridge requires replacement. Who is correct?
    a. Technician A
    b. Technician B
    c. Both Technician A and Technician B
    d. Neither Technician A nor Technician B

CHAPTER 13

Electrical Test Equipment

Learning Objectives

After reading this chapter, you will be able to:

- **LO 13-1** Identify and describe the types of test lights and explain how they are used to test electrical circuits.
- **LO 13-2** Identify and describe the purpose of digital multimeters (DMM) and explain safe work practices when using multimeters during measurement and testing of electrical circuits.
- **LO 13-3** Describe the set-up of a DMM and procedures for performing basic electrical measurements.
- **LO 13-4** Identify and describe the operation of circuit tracers and explain how they are used to perform tests of electrical circuits.

- **LO 13-5** Identify and describe the operation of graphing meters and oscilloscopes and explain how they are used to test and perform measurements of electrical circuits.
- **LO 13-6** Identify the purpose of vibration analyzers and explain how they are used to pinpoint sources of vibration.
- **LO 13-7** Identify the purpose of vehicle network interface devices and explain how they are used to communicate with on-board networks.

You Are the Technician

In the school bus fleet that you help maintain, quite a high number of buses are developing electrical short circuits, grounded circuits, and open circuits in the wiring connecting the driver's console to the rear lights. Many of the problems are likely the result of wiring being improperly secured, insulated, and tied at the factory. Repairing the wiring problem has become very time-consuming, as several wiring circuits pass through the cavity between the inner and outer sheet metal. Often, the panels need removing to replace or repair the wiring. Even after replacing large sections of wiring between the body panels, many of these same buses need further repairs. Later repairs need to be made to the wiring that connects the signal and clearance lights, as corrosion has taken place due to punctures from test lights. While reviewing maintenance strategies and procedures, consider the following:

1. What electrical test instrument would you recommend using to find shorts, grounded circuits, and open circuits behind the bus body panels?
2. What electrical test instrument would you recommend for finding grounded circuits in the wiring between the lights and the grounded wire that is routed through an open channel beneath the bus?
3. What maintenance recommendations would you make to prevent further repeat repairs of wiring after technicians have performed initial repairs?

Introduction

Diagnosing and repairing electrical problems requires not only logic and deductive reasoning, but electrical test tools, too. A variety of electrical test instruments are needed, which range from the simple test lights and electrical multimeters to more elaborate instrumentation for checking fault codes and viewing electrical signal wave forms.

Test Lights

LO 13-1 Identify and describe the types of test lights and explain how they are used to test electrical circuits.

A **test light** is the simplest piece of electrical test equipment used to determine the presence or absence of current. It consists of either a 12- or 24-volt incandescent light bulb connected to an insulated lead and a sharpened metal probe. The insulated lead is a long wire with an alligator clip used to connect to chassis ground or insulated positive. The sharpened metal probe is used to pierce insulation and surface corrosion at test points. Taking the shape of a screwdriver, the internal lamp inside the handle lights whenever current can flow between the lead and test light probe. Test lights are used by connecting the alligator clip to chassis ground or current at the insulated positive side of a circuit. A blown fuse, for example, lights up a test light when probed on only one side with the key-on. Both sides should light up if the fuse is good. Electrical connections to switches, motors, relays, and power distribution blocks are easily checked with test lights. Current in insulated positive wire is traced by probing the wire with the sharpened metal end (**FIGURE 13-1**).

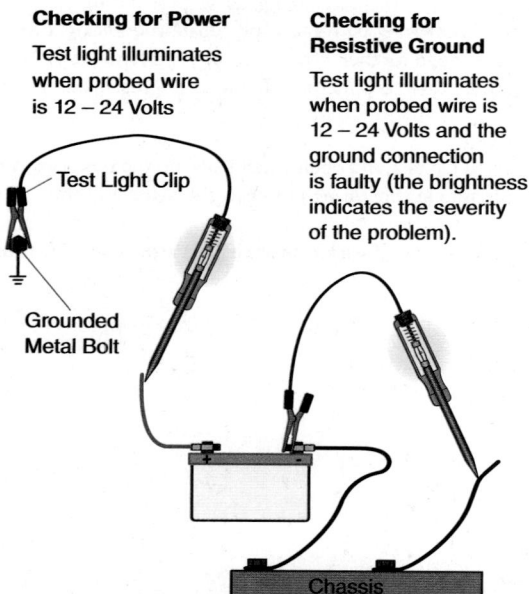

Checking for Power

Test light illuminates when probed wire is 12 – 24 Volts

Test Light Clip

Grounded Metal Bolt

Checking for Resistive Ground

Test light illuminates when probed wire is 12 – 24 Volts and the ground connection is faulty (the brightness indicates the severity of the problem).

Chassis

FIGURE 13-1 A test light is commonly used to check for current. To check for a resistive ground, an illuminated test light glows when connected in series between the component ground and chassis ground.

The metal probe of a test light is designed to pierce electrical insulation and penetrate the surface of lightly corroded terminals and metal surfaces. Piercing wire can allow water and oxygen into the wiring, causing corrosion and oxidation. Avoid piercing a wire with a test light probe. In instances where this is not practical, always reseal pierced points on an electrical wire with adhesive sealant (**FIGURE 13-2**). This is especially necessary with conductors outside the cab/body, where wiring is exposed to the elements.

When connected in series with a circuit, test lights can indicate bad grounds or parasitic current drawn from a battery (**FIGURE 13-3**). If the test light illuminates when connected between chassis ground and component ground, it indicates a resistive or missing ground connection.

High voltage from hybrid drives, the latest common rail injectors, and other electric systems can easily kill or cause serious physical harm if pierced by a technician. Always ensure appropriate power disconnect switches are removed when working around these circuits. Also, never pierce wiring covered in heavy protective loom or brightly colored insulation without first determining what voltage the conductors are carrying. The bright color and insulation often designate high-voltage or sensitive circuits, such as a circuit deploying airbags for supplemental restraint systems (**FIGURE 13-4**).

Self-Powered Test Light

Self-powered test lights are like regular test lights except that they contain a 1.5-volt battery (**FIGURE 13-5**). Self-powered lights can be used to check for both open circuits and grounded circuits when either chassis power or ground is removed from the circuit (**FIGURE 13-6**). The internal battery can supply current needed to illuminate the light. To check for an opening in a circuit, the vehicle battery is first disconnected. The light's alligator clip is connected to ground and the circuit is probed sequentially from the switch or power supply to the load. Where

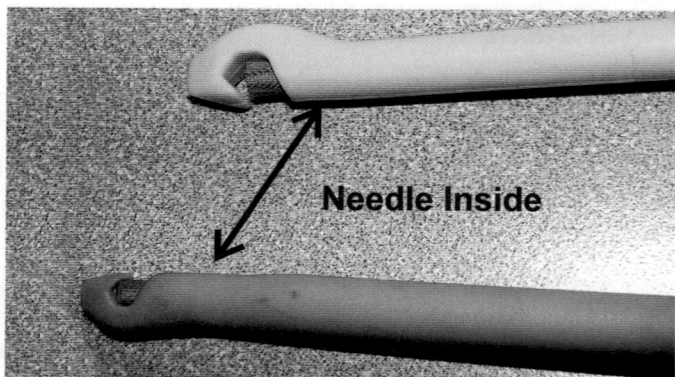

Needle Inside

FIGURE 13-2 A "wrap-around probe" is used to probe a wire where it is difficult to support. After placing the wire in wrap-around support, a trigger is pulled and the wire is pierced.

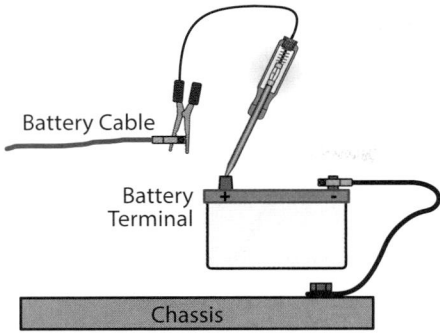

FIGURE 13-3 Using a test light to check for parasitic draw. Parasitic current drawing more than 0.3 amps easily lights the bulb in the lamp. A brightly burning bulb with the key off indicates too much current is being used by a component in the equipment, leading to a dead battery. A darkened or dimly glowing light is normal.

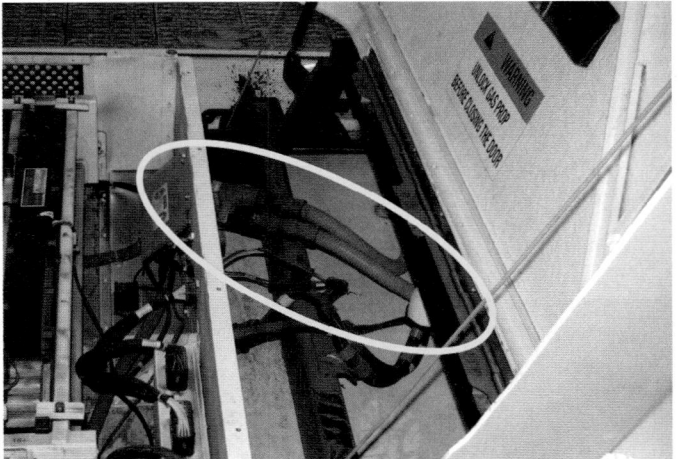

FIGURE 13-4 High-voltage cables, such as those on hybrid vehicles have heavy protective insulation, which is brightly colored.

FIGURE 13-5 A self-powered electrical probe.

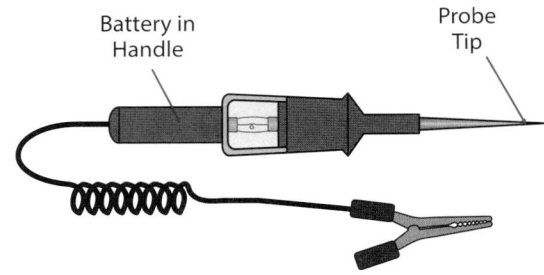

FIGURE 13-6 A self-powered test light can be used to find open, shorted, and grounded circuits after disconnecting the circuit from vehicle power and ground. The battery supplies the ground connection through the alligator clip.

the test light glows, the circuit is closed from chassis ground to power. An open circuit prevents current from traveling from the ground to an insulated positive. For example, a broken wire between a heater blower motor and fuse illuminates between the blower motor and break in the wire, but not after the break and before the fuse.

Grounded circuits are checked in a similar manner. While probing the circuit, its switches and connectors are opened. The light stays illuminated in the section that is grounded. However, the light goes out after the section of circuit with an unintentional ground is disconnected. Self-powered voltmeters with probes are also useful for close-quarter probing of electrical circuits.

► TECHNICIAN TIP

A 12- or 24-volt battery current easily blows the bulb out of self-powered test lights, so battery current should always be removed when using these lights. Although 1.5 volts is relatively low, it is still enough to damage computer circuits. They should never be used in electronic circuits using semiconductors—that includes sensors.

Self-Powered LED Test lights

One of the disadvantages of incandescent test lights is that they can draw excessive current from a circuit to operate the bulb. In some cases, adding the additional load of a test light may damage a circuit. Using light-emitting diodes (LEDs) instead of a bulb overcomes this difficulty and adds capabilities to a test light. A popular type of LED test light is battery powered and has two LEDs—one red and the other green. A third white LED may be used by some models to indicate the light is connected properly to an external power source rather than internal batteries. With two LEDs, the technician can find out what

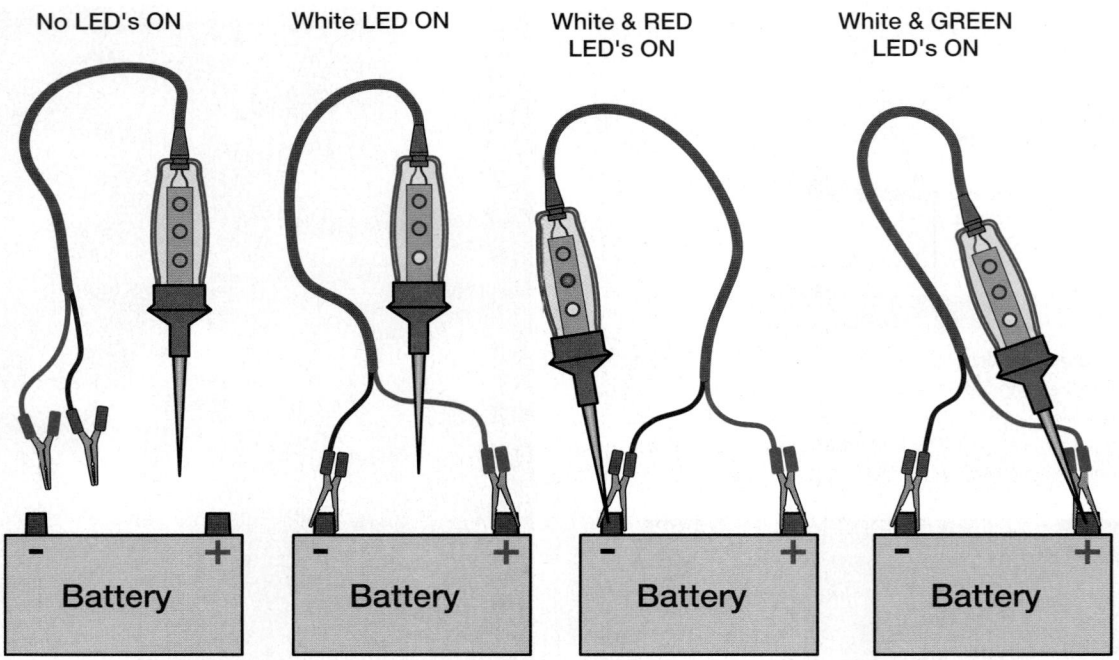

No LED's ON   White LED ON   White & RED LED's ON   White & GREEN LED's ON

FIGURE 13-7 Three LED lights are used by this self-powered test light. The red lights up when the probe touches battery +. The green lights up when probing battery negative or ground. White indicates the light is properly connected to an external power supply.

polarity or electrical charge is present in a circuit as it's being tested. For example, once powered up, the probe first contacts test points in an energized circuit. If the probe is connected to a positive polarity current source, the red LED comes on. Touching a point in the circuit that's connected to battery negative or ground produces a green LED light (**FIGURE 13-7**). One disadvantage of LED lights is they provide no indication of the level of circuit voltage and become relatively bright when voltage is between 1.5 to 3 volts. An incandescent light changes brightness, depending on the circuit's voltage.

Multimeters

LO 13-2 Identify and describe the purpose of digital multimeters (DMM) and explain safe work practices when using multimeters during measurement and testing of electrical circuits.

Multimeters are electrical measuring instruments combining functions of at least voltage, resistance, and amperage measurement into a single compact instrument. **Digital multimeters** are the most common category of multimeters and provide numerical displays of electrical data (**FIGURE 13-8**). **Analog meters** use a sweeping needle that continuously measures electrical values (**FIGURE 13-9**). Digital multimeters are almost exclusively used today because they are easiest to use and draw the least amount of current from circuits being measured. Sampling very little of a circuit's own current to take a measurement is a characteristic of **high-impedance multimeters**. High impedance refers to a meter's internal resistance to current flowing from a live circuit into the meter when measuring voltage and amperage. In sensitive

FIGURE 13-8 A digital multimeter with typical basic features.

electronic circuits, a test light or digital meter can act like a load and use too much current. The result is an overloaded or damaged circuit. Specifications for a multimeter indicate its impedance or resistance to electric current when measuring circuit electrical values.

Basic Multimeter Electrical Measurements

Before using a multimeter, it is important to understand the basic measurements that it can produce. A multimeter typically measures resistance, continuity, voltage, and amperage:

FIGURE 13-9 An analog meter uses a needle and sweeping scale to measure properties of electrical current.

1. **Resistance** – Measures circuit resistance and report it in units of ohms to determine whether it is within specifications. Wire coils and heating elements are examples of common devices where a measure of resistance determines service condition. Open and short circuits are easily detected using the ohmmeter to measure resistance to unintended electrical pathways (**FIGURE 13-10**).
2. Continuity – Determines whether two points are electrically connected. Continuity is also valuable when checking for opens and shorts.
3. Voltage – Measurements are used to determine whether a component or circuit has the correct amount of available power. Measuring voltage drops in a circuit can help identify resistance in high-amperage circuits, such as the starting circuit. A voltmeter behaves like a pressure differential gauge by measuring the difference in electron pressure between two points in a circuit.
4. Amperage – Most measurements of amperage are performed at levels higher than multimeters can typically handle, so an inductance amp clamp is used instead. However, meters are usually capable of measuring up to 10 amps of current flow. Starter draw and alternator output are two common measurements of amperage regularly made using multimeters with an inductance clamp meter accessory.

Multimeters may also perform additional electrical measures including:

- Diode testing
- Frequency
- Capacitance
- Temperature using external thermocouples, such as a K-type thermocouple
- Duty cycle
- Transistor testing
- Continuity tester with beeper
- Waveform display

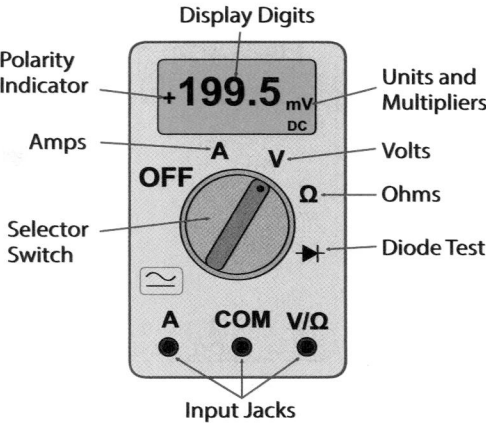

FIGURE 13-10 Features of a basic DMM.

- Accessories, such as handheld inductive amp-clamps, pressure sensors, and rpm sensors are connected to the standardized multimeter port location and size for positive voltage and common. The devices produce a voltage signal proportional to the state of the condition measured and display it on the multimeter

Manual and Auto-Ranging Meters

Multimeters are available as auto- or manual-ranging types. An **auto-ranging multimeter** has fewer positions on its range selection knob. When set to amps, volts, or ohms, the meter automatically selects the correct range when meter test leads are connected to a circuit.

This feature contrasts with **manual-ranging multimeters** that must be set to the correct range first, based on anticipated values measured. For example, the DC-volts range of a manual meter may include a setting of 200 mV, 2 V, 20 V, 200 V, and 500 V. To measure 12-volt battery voltage, the range value just above the anticipated voltage is the 20-volt scale (**FIGURE 13-11**). An auto-ranging meter would only require selecting DC volts and the meter would do the rest. Auto-ranging meters can be slower to measure electrical values because they need time to adjust the operating range. As an alternative, auto-ranging meters can usually be set to operate as manual-ranging units.

With either automatic or manual-ranging meters, it is important to learn the electrical symbols and units of measurement listed in **TABLE 13-1**.

▶ **TECHNICIAN TIP**

When making measurements and performing diagnostic tests with auto-ranging meters, the display may change continuously for some time until the correct range is established. Even moving test leads in a shop with many radio waves transmitted by cell phones and WiFi induces current flow in leads that distort readings. If the measured value changes or test lead probes move too much, the meter may begin to auto-range once again. The process can lead to incorrect results if measurements are taken too quickly. Using the peak and hold feature or auto-hold helps produce more accurate values. Otherwise, more patience and care is required when using these meters.

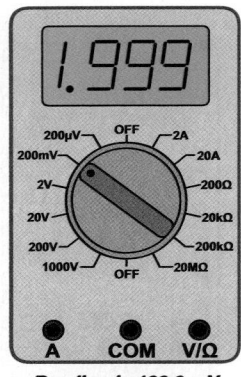
Reading is 199.9 mV

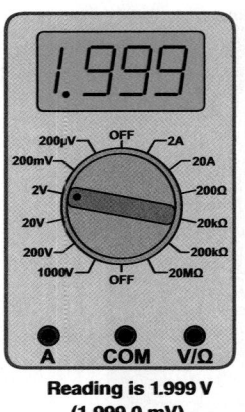
Reading is 1.999 V
(1,999.0 mV).

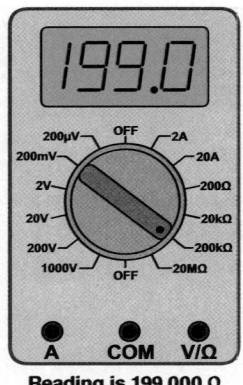
Reading is 199,000 Ω
(199 kΩ).

FIGURE 13-11 A manual-ranging meter moves the decimal point for many electrical measurements.

TABLE 13-1 Symbols and Meanings for Electrical Units of Measurement

Symbol	Meaning
M	Mega or million
K	Kilo or thousand
m	Milli or one thousandth
μ	Micro or one millionth
$\overline{V}$	Volts direct current
$\tilde{V}$	Volts alternating current
mV	Millivolts (0.001 V or 1/1000 V)
A	Amperage (amps)
mA	Milliamps (0.001 A or 1/1000 A)
μA	Microamps (0.000001 A or 1/1,000,000 A)
Ω	Resistance (ohms)
kΩ	Kilo-ohms (1000 ohms)
MΩ	Megaohms (1,000,000 ohms)
)))	Continuity beeper
Diode ▸�	Diode testing
Hz	Frequency (hertz, which is cycles/sec)
dB	Sound (decibels)
F	Capacitance (farad)
μF	Microfarads
nF	Nanofarads
Touch Hold & Auto HOLD	The last recorded stable reading
MIN MAX	Highest, lowest recorded readings
OL	Out of range or over limit

Meter Shunts

Before using a digital meter, one of the first things to check is whether its shunts or fuses are in place and functioning. Shunts are internal conductors with a small calibrated resistance, which directs some current flow into the meter when measuring amperage (**FIGURE 13-12**). Almost all circuit current passes through the meter shunt, but some resistance is needed to send current into the measuring circuits of the meter. Shunts operate like fuses and have a maximum rating. A shunt should blow in an extremely short time if current exceeds the meter's capacity. If an ordinary fuse is used to replace a fast-blowing shunt, current enters and damages the meter in the time it takes to open the ordinary fuse.

Shunts are checked by connecting one end of the positive lead probe while it is inserted in the volt/ohm port, and the other end into the amperage probe port (**FIGURE 13-13**). A meter set to check continuity or resistance should display continuity and some resistance. If two amperage ports are used on a meter, the larger amperage shunt has a higher resistance than the low amperage shunt. To check meter shunts, follow the steps in **SKILL DRILL 13-1**.

Electrical Measurement with Multimeters

LO 13-3 Describe the set-up of a DMM and procedures for performing basic electrical measurements.

Multimeters are versatile instruments that allow the technician to take a variety of measurements. Three types of measurements—voltage, resistance, and amperage—can be taken from circuits in three different ways. Understanding them is necessary to prevent meter damage and produce the correct measurement.

Measuring Resistance—Ohmmeters

Ohmmeters are one of the most commonly used functions of a multimeter, and many electrical diagnoses are made using an ohmmeter. By checking the resistance or circuit continuity with an ohmmeter, a circuit can be evaluated for shorts, opens, or high resistance. An ohmmeter uses a small amount of electrical current from an internal battery and sends it through a circuit or component.

The amount of voltage that flows through the component or circuit depends on the circuit's resistance (**FIGURE 13-14**). If the return voltage is high, the circuit resistance is low, and if the return voltage is low, the circuit resistance is high. Ranging the meter is done by using internal resistors to change the amount of current

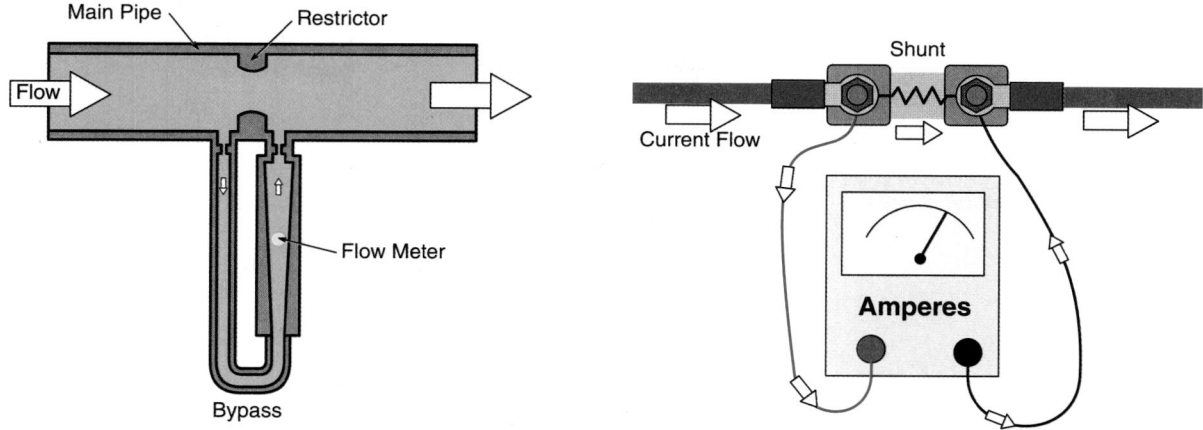

FIGURE 13-12 An ammeter shunt allows most of the current to pass through the shunt while allowing some small amount of current into the meter's measurement mechanism.

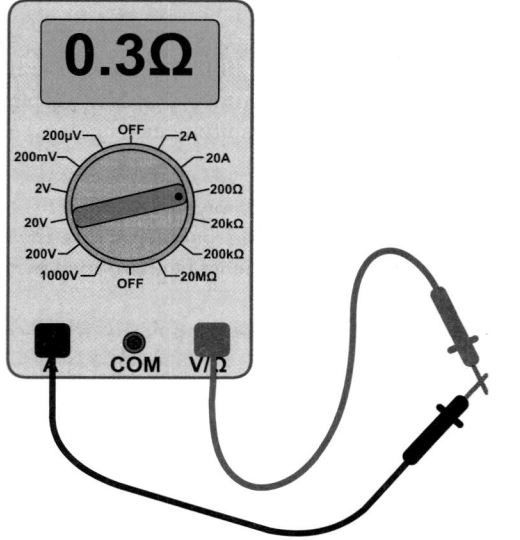

FIGURE 13-13 Checking the ammeter shunts should show continuity between the Volts/Ohm/Amp red and amperage lead ports.

voltage entering the circuit. This means that when selecting a meter range of higher resistance—for instance, 100 megaohms rather than a 10-ohm scale—higher voltage must leave the meter to pass thorough the highly resistive circuit (**FIGURE 13-15**).

Because ohmmeters are self-powered, it is critically important to remember that ohmmeters should never be connected to a powered circuit. Connecting an ohmmeter into a powered circuit blows the fuse or battery in the meter or otherwise damages the meter. Semiconductor circuits and some sensors should not be checked with an ohmmeter because the meter current may damage the device (**FIGURE 13-16**).

Ohmmeters are ineffective when checking for resistances in high-amperage, very low-resistance circuits, such as when measuring battery cable voltage loss. Measuring voltage drop with a voltmeter when a circuit is operating is a more effective way of measuring resistances (**FIGURE 13-17**).

When measuring with an ohmmeter, it is important to observe how a meter displays infinite resistance or an open circuit. Some meters display either a 1 or 0 to indicate an open circuit (**FIGURE 13-18**). It is important to understand also the range

SKILL DRILL 13-1 Checking Meter Shunts

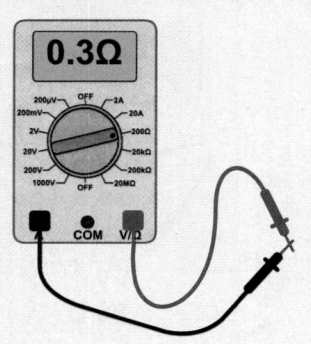

1. Plug the test lead in volts/ohms input.
2. Select ohms range.
3. Insert the other end of the probe tip into mA input and read the value. A small amount of resistance should be noted when probing the amperage inputs with the positive volt/ohm probe.
4. Insert probe tip into any second amp input and read the value. It should have a larger amount of resistance than the mA input.

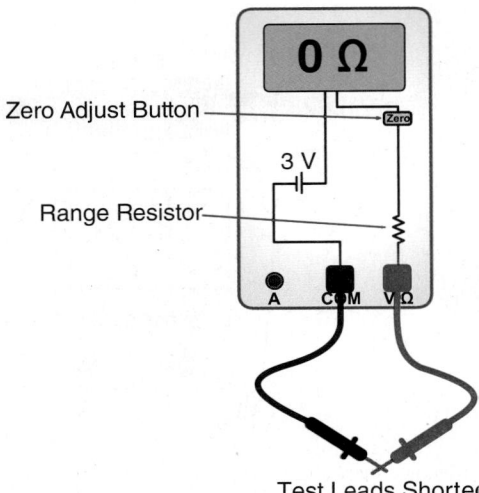
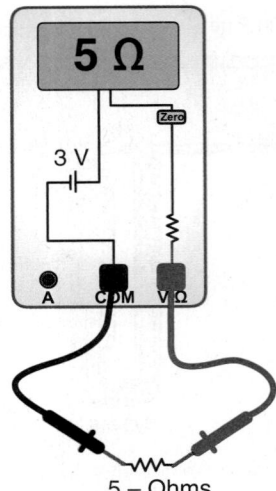

FIGURE 13-14 Ohmmeters use a small amount of current supplied by a battery to measure resistance. Voltage through the circuit is measured by the meter, which is reported in ohms. Voltage is proportional to circuit resistance.

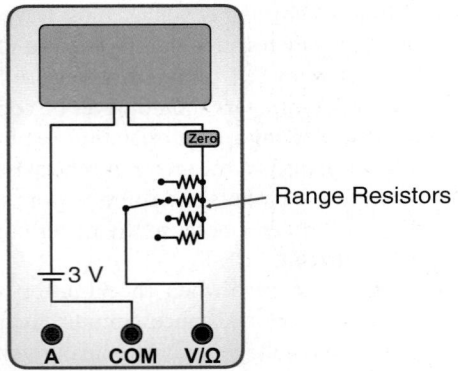

FIGURE 13-15 Manual or auto-ranging meters extend the range of the ohmmeter by substituting different resistances in series with the internal power source.

that the display is reporting. Million, thousand, and hundred are common ranges for an ohmmeter, and the displayed value may need to be multiplied by multimeter range.

When using an ohmmeter:

- The circuit must never be powered.
- The meter is connected in parallel across the circuit or component to measure the voltage dropped by the circuit resistance.
- It is not necessary to observe polarity when connecting test leads.
- The positive test lead is connected to the ohms port and the negative lead to the common port of the meter.
- The meter needs to be properly ranged if not using an auto-ranging meter. Start at the highest range values and work down if the resistance is unknown.

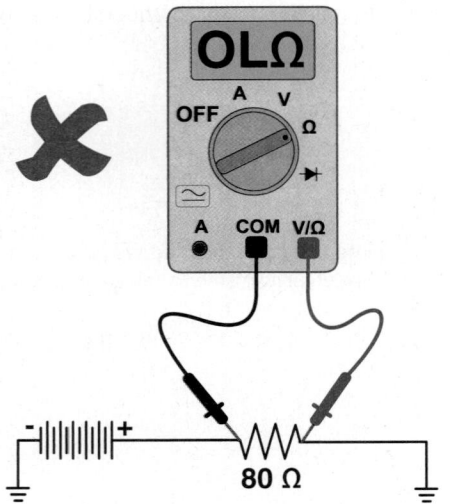
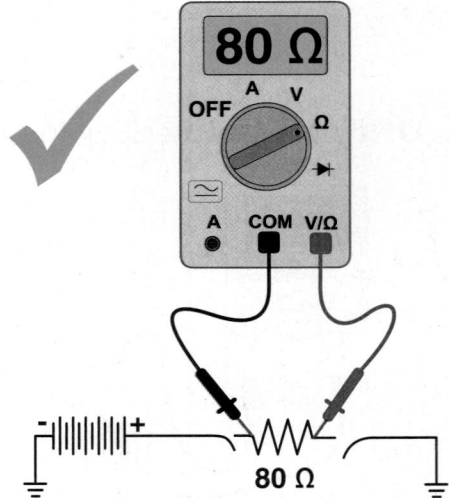

FIGURE 13-16 Because ohmmeters indirectly measure voltage, it is critical to remove power from a circuit before connecting the meter. Meter damage occurs, otherwise.

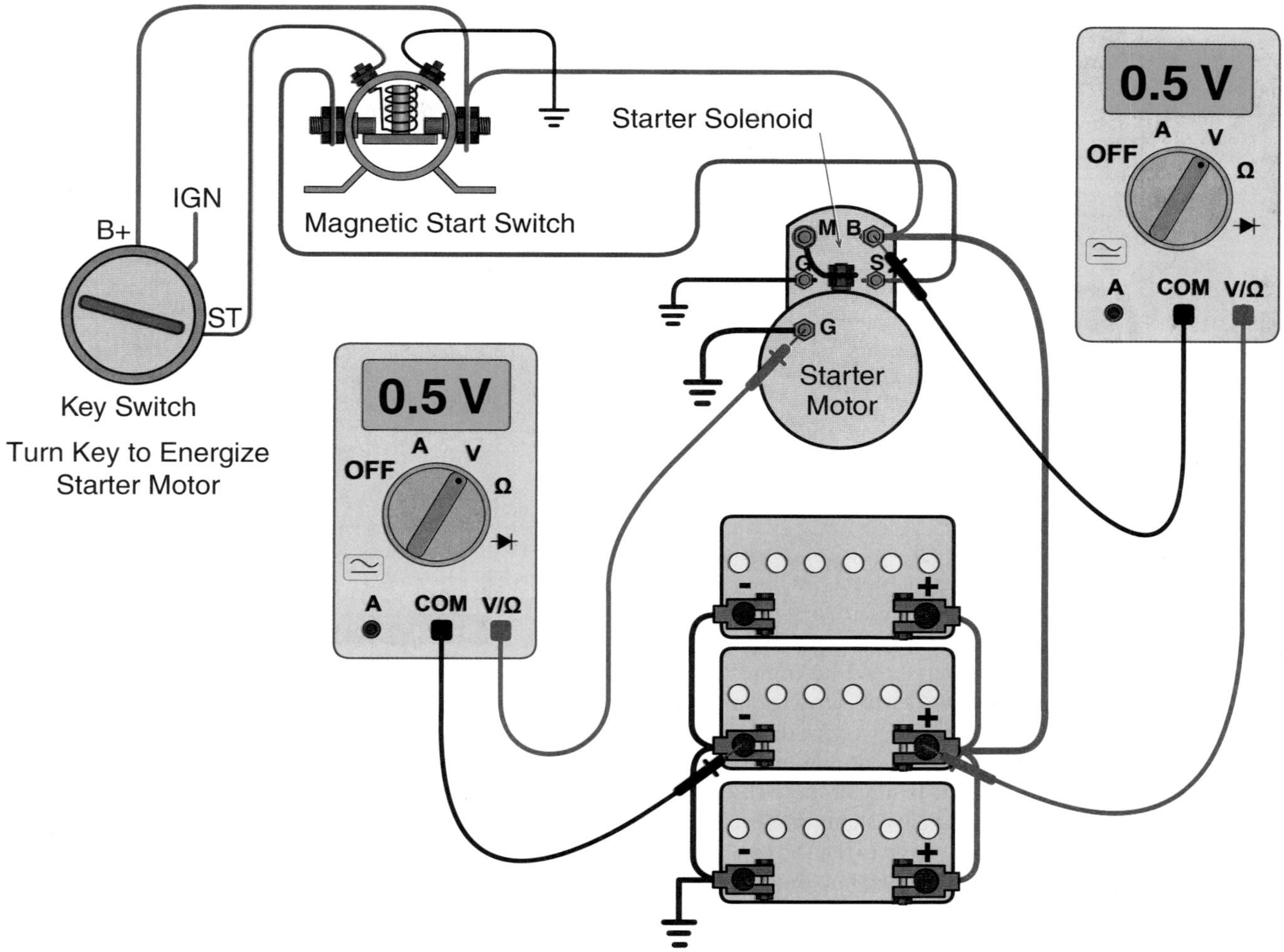

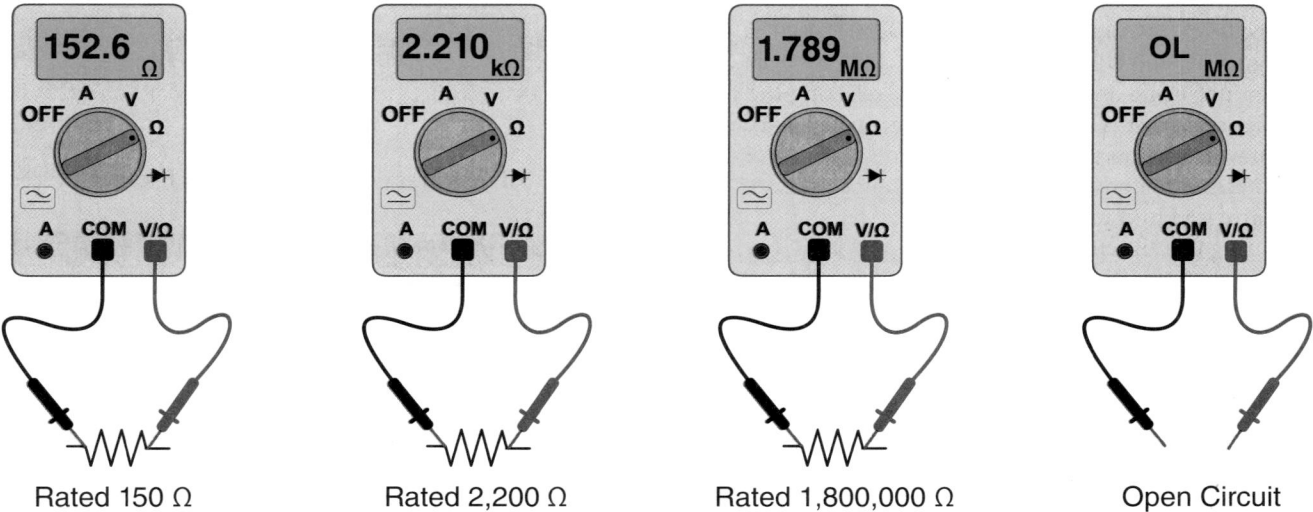

FIGURE 13-17 A voltmeter is best used to check for resistance in high amperage circuits. Voltage drop means the circuit has resistance.

Rated 150 Ω   Rated 2,200 Ω   Rated 1,800,000 Ω   Open Circuit

FIGURE 13-18 The ohmmeter display may need multiplying to observe the correct resistance value. On a 10 k scale the number "1" would indicate a value multiplied by 10,000, meaning the actual value is 10,000 ohms.

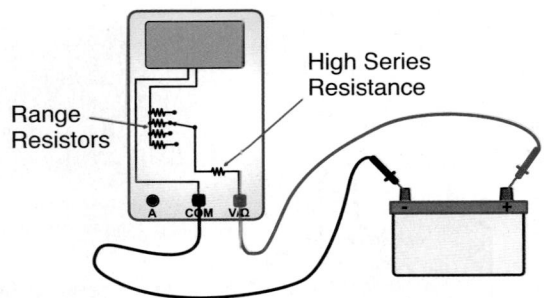

FIGURE 13-19 Only a small amount of current enters the voltmeter. Voltmeters with high internal resistance are called high-impedance meters.

- Not to be used with semiconductors and potentially inaccurate when testing diodes.

Measuring Voltage—Voltmeters

Voltmeters measure the difference in electrical pressure or electron velocity between two different points in the circuit (**FIGURE 13-19**). Using a voltmeter is similar to measuring a pressure differential or speed drop between two points.

When measuring volts, the meter should be connected in parallel with the voltage source (**FIGURE 13-20**). On a commercial vehicle, one would commonly be measuring voltage drops across loads, determining whether there is sufficient power to a component, or measuring sensor voltages. In any of these cases, the meter would be set to 20 volts for 12-volt systems or 40 volts for 24-volt systems. Auto-ranging meters are set to the DC volts scale.

The positive meter lead probe is inserted into the volt-ohms port and the negative to the common port (**FIGURE 13-21**). If the circuit polarity is not correctly observed (i.e., the negative probe is connected to the positive side of the circuit and vice versa), digital meters show a negative volts symbol.

Practices to observe when measuring voltage include:

- Connecting the voltmeter in parallel with the circuit
- Observing polarity when measuring DC volts, (but not AC voltage) (**FIGURE 13-22**)
- Ranging AC and DC volts separately
- When not using an auto-range meter, selecting the first voltage scale that is higher than the anticipated voltage; if unknown, starting at the highest scale
- Connecting the positive lead to volts/ohms port and the negative lead to common port
- Ensuring that the circuit is powered

Voltmeters commonly include several protections against damage and safety risks **TABLE 13-2**.

SAFETY TIP

Multimeters can and do blow up, causing personal injury and equipment damage. Safety features—such as using positive temperature coefficient (PTC) thermistors in the ohmmeter, which become highly resistive when heated—are built into meters to limit damage to the meter. Voltage circuits are capacitive coupled eliminating a direct connection to meter circuits. Low-impedance ammeters use shunts that blow when overloaded. Double insulation of meters, shrouded connectors, and the use of finger guards on probe tips are other safety features. Check meters before

using to see that insulation is not melted, cut, or cracked. Connectors and leads should not show any damage, such as insulation pulled away from end connectors. Probe tips should not be loose or broken off. Make sure the meter is safe for the application in which it is being used. IEC 61010 is a safety standard that establishes safety limits for meters. A Cat I meter in this standard, which is satisfactory for most technicians, should not be used to check voltages above 600 volts continuous, or 2,500 volts at momentary peaks. The top-rated CAT III meter can operate with 1,000 volts continuous and 8,000 volts transient peak (**FIGURE 13-23**).

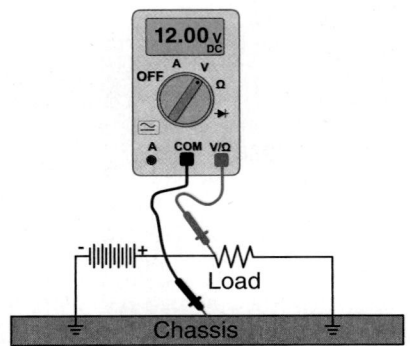

FIGURE 13-20 Voltmeters are connected in parallel in a circuit.

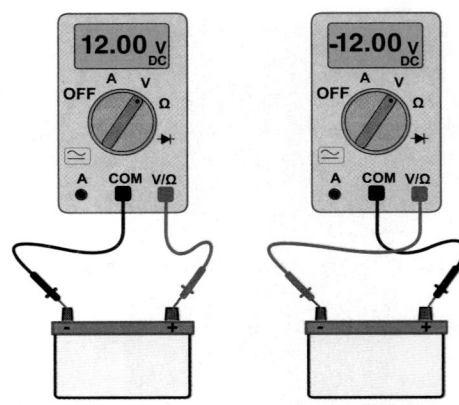

FIGURE 13-21 When connecting a voltmeter, the polarity of the meter and circuit should match. A polarity indicator uses electron theory and shows a meter is connected incorrectly to a circuit.

TABLE 13-2 Multimeter Features to Protect Meter and User

Risk	Protection
Electrical arcing from transient high-voltage sources (lightning, load switching)	Independent certification to meet CAT III-1000 V and CAT IV-600 V or higher
Voltage damage to meter while in continuity or resistance ranges	Overload protection in ohms up to the meter's volt rating
Measuring voltage with test leads in amperage inputs	Fast-blowing, high-energy fuses rated to the meter's voltage rating. Use induction clamps to measure amperage
Shock from accidental contact with live components	Double-insulated test leads, recessed and/or shrouded with finger guards

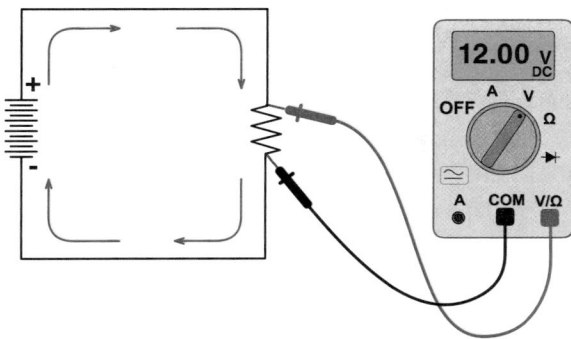

When measuring DC volts, the meter must be connected to the circuit with the correct polarity or the meter reading will be incorrect.

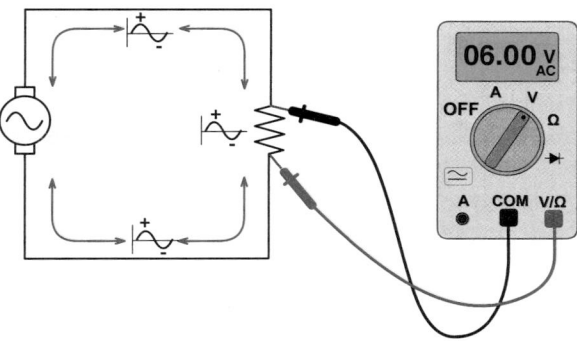

When measuring AC volts, the polarity of the meter to the circuit is unimportant and will not affect the meter reading.

FIGURE 13-22 Polarity does not need to be observed when measuring AC voltage.

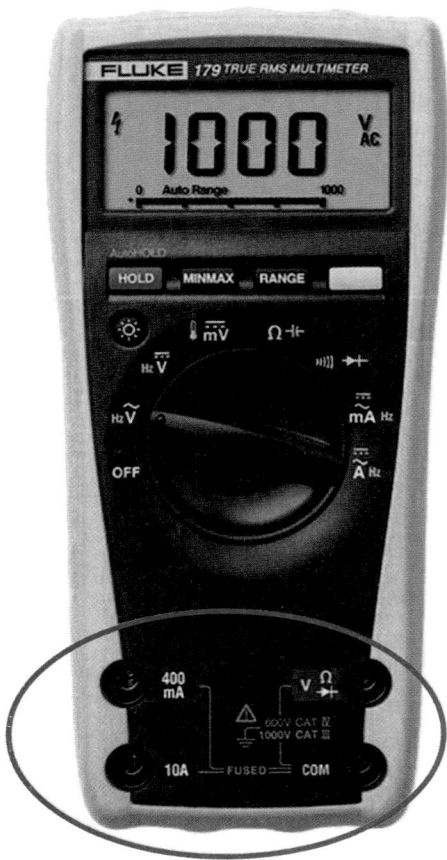

FIGURE 13-23 This meter has a safety rating of CAT III at 600 volts and CAT IV at 1,000 volts.

Measuring Amperage—Ammeters

Ammeters measure the quantity of electrons flowing through a circuit per second of time. Amperage is the volume aspect of current flow, and voltage is the speed or pressure of

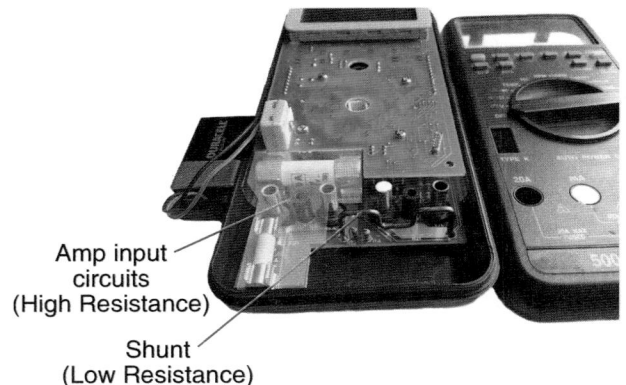

FIGURE 13-24 Ammeters use shunts that allow most circuit current to pass through the shunt, rather than the meter.

electrical flow. Measuring amperage requires that the circuit be broken, and the meter placed in series with the circuit, so that all the current flows through the meter shunts. See **FIGURES 13-24** and **13-25**. Because all circuit current flows through the meter, the meter should never be connected to a current source in parallel, as it is the equivalent of shorting out a circuit. Two ports for the positive leads are commonly used to measure low amperage—milliamps, and amperage above one amp. Failure to move meter leads from low- to high-amperage ports blows the meter shunt and may even damage the meter.

Practices to observe when measuring amperage include:

- Ensuring that the circuit is powered
- Ensuring that the ammeter is connected in series, causing all the current in the circuit to flow through the meter shunts
- Observing polarity when measuring DC volts but not AC voltage (**FIGURE 13-26**)
- Choosing the correct shunt or port in the meter for connecting leads based on anticipated amperage. The common port is used for the negative lead, and A, mA, and uA are used for the positive lead (**FIGURE 13-27**)

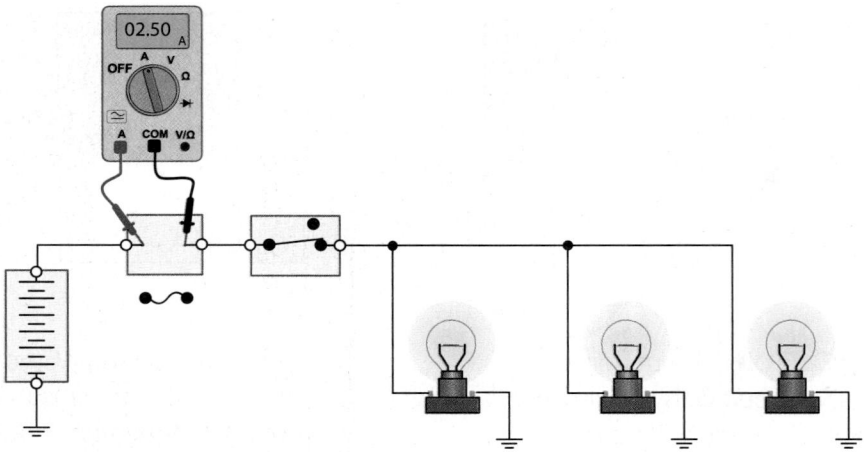

FIGURE 13-25 Connecting an ammeter in series to measure amperage.

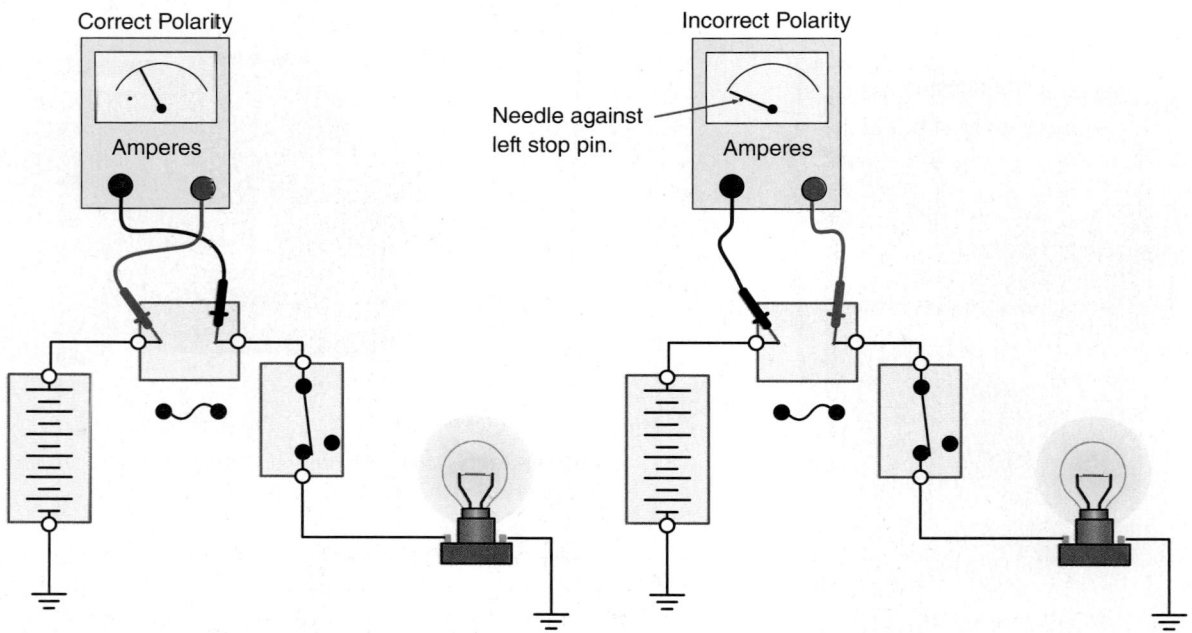

FIGURE 13-26 Ammeters require connection using correct polarity, as noted, using this analog ammeter. Digital meters indicate when the polarity is incorrect.

- When not using an auto-range meter, selecting the first amperage scale that is higher than the anticipated amperage; if unknown, starting at the highest scale
- When measuring more than 10 amps of current, using an inductive-type probe or dedicated amp clamp

Inductive Amp Clamps

In powered circuits, **inductive amp clamps** placed around a conductor are used to measure amperage. These devices work by measuring a conductor's magnetic field strength, which is proportional to amperage (**FIGURE 13-28**). While using an amp

clamp, an electrical circuit does not need to be disturbed by opening the circuit to connect a meter in series.

Two types of amp or inductive clamps are used, which are connected to the voltage/common ports of a multimeter.

- Measuring AC only
- Measuring both DC and AC (**TABLE 13-3**)

Clamps that measure only AC use a current transformer built into the pick-up. The AC passing through a conductor produces a magnetic field, which induces voltage through mutual induction into transformer windings located inside the pick-up clamp. Using a specific turn ratio in the transformer,

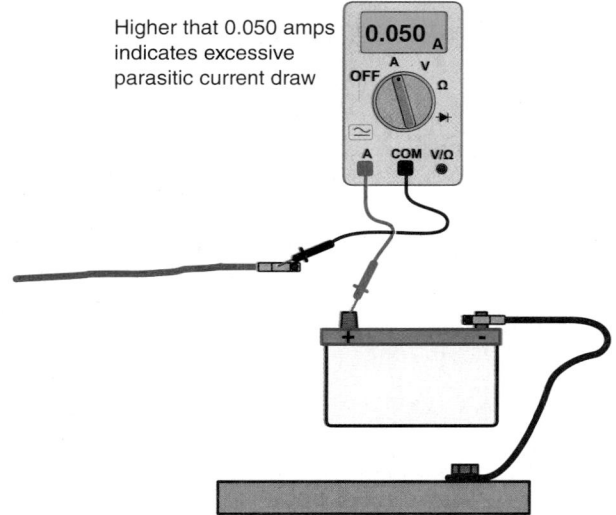

Higher that 0.050 amps indicates excessive parasitic current draw

FIGURE 13-27 Connecting an ammeter in series to measure parasitic current draw that can drain a battery.

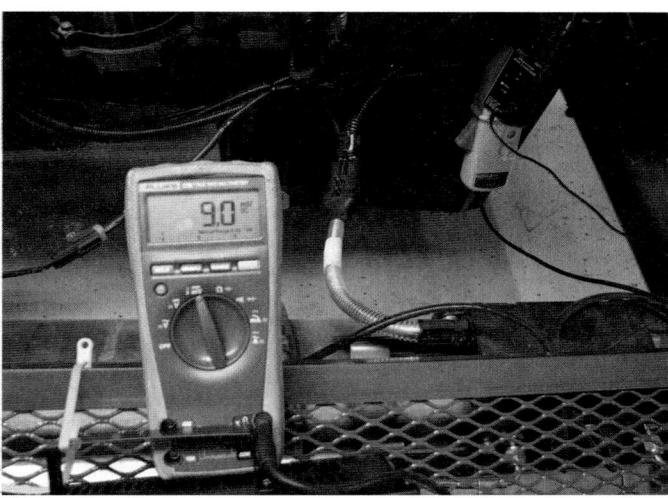

FIGURE 13-28 An inductive amp clamp measures the strength of the magnetic field around a conductor using a Hall Effect sensor. Magnetic field strength is proportional to amperage.

TABLE 13-3 Differences between Features of an AC and an AC/DC Self-Contained Induction Clamp

Feature	AC	AC/DC
Output current	Current	Voltage
Scale factor	1 milliAmp per Amp	1 milliVolt per Amp
Sensor	Current transfer	Hall effect
Battery	No	Yes

such as 1000:1, voltage induced inside the transformer is calculated as a value for amperage. These clamps generate typically 1 millivolt per measured amp, which can be measured by a multimeter, or is self-contained in a clamp-on meter. DC clamps use Hall Effect technology. Hall Effect material found in these sensors changes their electrical resistance based on the strength of a magnetic field (**FIGURE 13-29**). This clamp also produces 1 millivolt per measured amp, which is measured by a voltmeter. Batteries in either the clamp or test instrument are needed to power inductive clamps using Hall Effect sensors.

Measuring Temperature

Multimeters use a thermocouple accessory to measure temperature by contact. Heating the thermocouple produces voltage proportional to temperature. **Type K thermocouples** are low-cost, general-purpose, temperature-sensing elements, and are connected to the same meter terminals for measuring DC millivolts. Internal meter circuits convert the voltage measurements into a temperature reading.

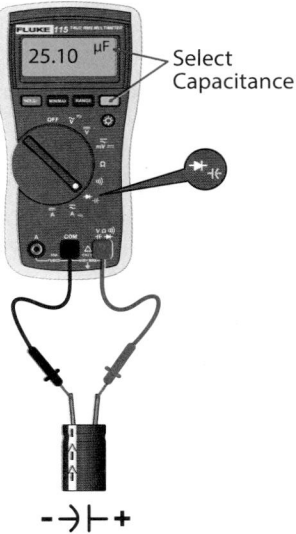

Select Capacitance

FIGURE 13-29 Using the capacitor-testing function of a multimeter. Current supplied by the meter charges the diode and the time to charge the capacitor is measured. The meter calculates the capacitor's capacity in farads.

Diode Scale

The low-voltage settings of an ohmmeter may not properly evaluate a diode, as a good silicon diode requires approximately 0.5–0.7 volts to forward bias or conduct current. Below this voltage, the diode may appear to block current in both directions. When placed in the diode range, a meter puts out higher voltage than barrier voltage of 0.7 volts to cause the diode to reverse and forward bias (**FIGURE 13-30**). This voltage is usually above the voltage supplied when measuring ordinary resistance, so it is important to select this scale, rather than use an ohmmeter.

FIGURE 13-30 A polarity indicator on a DC amp clamp points to the most positive side of the circuit indicated by the direction magnetic fields rotate around a conductor.

FIGURE 13-31 Using the circuit tracers after connecting the signal generator to a defective circuit.

Circuit Tracers

LO 13-4 Identify and describe the operation of circuit tracers and explain how they are used to perform tests of electrical circuits.

Circuit tracers, also called **wire tracers**, are electronic service tools used to trace a single wire over a distance where multiple wires are bundled, shorted, or open. Telephone companies once commonly used these to help field technicians locate problematic phone circuits. These units can identify wires deeply buried behind walls or in tightly bundled harnesses.

Several methods are used to identify circuit problems. Commonly though, one part of the signal tracing unit is clipped to a suspect wire and ground. When switched on, the unit injects a strong, two-tone square-wave radio signal into the wire. The receivers consist of a sensitive radio with an audio amplifier and speaker. Slowly waving this device over a group of wires detects where a conductor is located and ends. See **FIGURES 13-31** and **13-32**. The intensity of the sound produced by the signal or the flickering of an LED light varies with proximity to the wire. The probe's tip is insulated for safety purposes.

Graphing Meters and Oscilloscopes

LO 13-5 Identify and describe the operation of graphing meters and oscilloscopes and explain how they are used to test and perform measurements of electrical circuits.

One of the latest diagnostic tools is a digital **graphing meter** used to analyze electrical waveforms produced by sensors, motors, actuators, and alternators. These test instruments plot an electrical value of a signal over time, displaying an easy-to-read graph with time on the *x*-axis and the signal value on the *y*-axis (**FIGURE 13-33**).

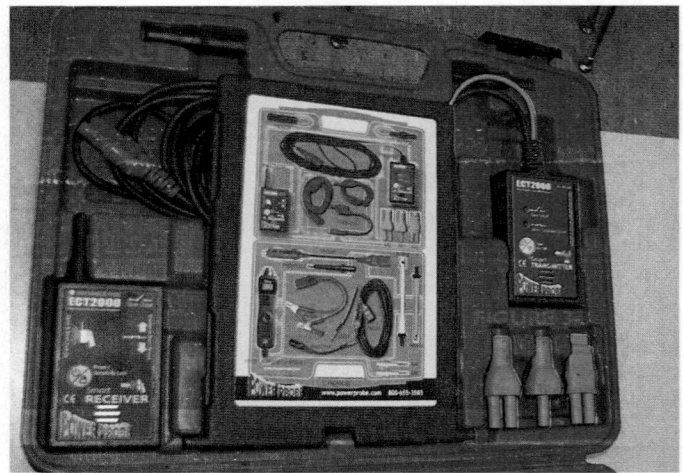

FIGURE 13-32 The transmitter and receiver of a circuit tracer used to trace electrical wires for open and short circuits.

Component serviceability can be determined by analyzing the waveform or comparing it to known signals of good quality (**FIGURE 13-34**). Prior to failure, many electrical devices have waveforms containing telltale signs that failure is imminent. Waveforms generated by components can be analyzed and service recommendations made for component replacement based on the wave form data. For example, a Hall Effect sensor may have intermittent problems or generate a defective waveform that may not be identified by the vehicle's on-board diagnostic system. A faster-sampling graphing meter is better suited to detect a problem like this.

The life expectancy of an electric motor is another example of a component that can be evaluated by examining the small changes in current and voltage spikes caused by worn brushes. Scanners and original equipment manufacturer (OEM) diagnostic software can also graph values captured by the ECM associated with a vehicle system, such as engine, antilock brake system (ABS), or body

FIGURE 13-33 A graph of a pulse-width-modulated signal waveform obtained using a graphing meter.

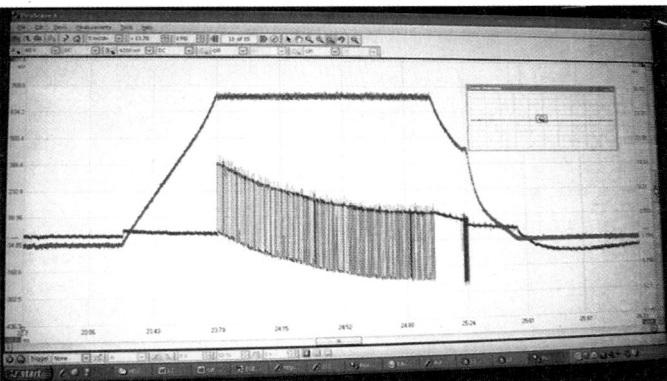

FIGURE 13-34 A graphical display of the electrical signal supplied to an injector using a Picoscope. Two channels measure voltage–blue trace, and amperage–red trace.

FIGURE 13-35 Purpose-made jumper wires with terminal ends matching specific types of connector terminals are used to perform pinpoint tests of volts, amperage, and resistance.

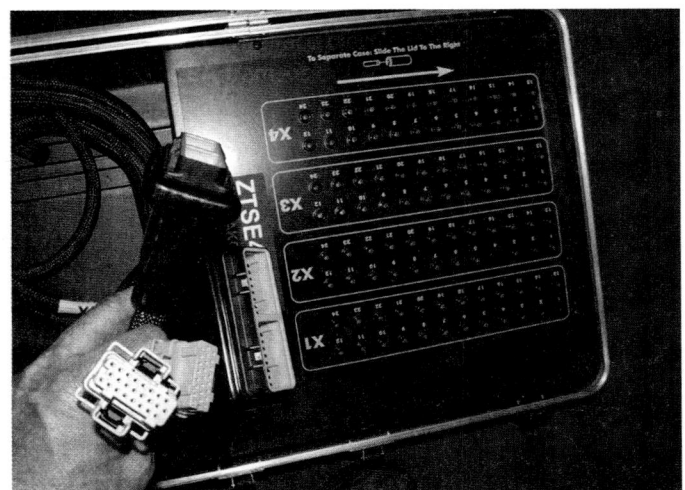

FIGURE 13-36 A break-out box with two matched connectors, female and male, connect in series to major wiring harnesses to perform pinpoint diagnostic tests.

control, through the diagnostic connector. Dedicated graphing meters connect directly to a sensor, circuit, or component needing testing. Whereas a single-channel graphing meter has only one input, two-, three-, and four-channel units have as many inputs and can graph the values together or on separate screens for comparative purposes. Oscilloscopes have more elaborate display modes to capture one-off signal glitches or jitter. Selectable signal triggers, sources, display rulers, slope measurement, and a wider variety of display options are also used by oscilloscopes.

When performing electrical circuit diagnostics, purpose-made jumper wires, fused jumper wires, and break-out boxes are helpful for quickly and effectively diagnosing problems without damaging wiring or connectors by back-probing or piercing wires (**FIGURE 13-35**). A break-out box is connected in series with a major component or wiring harness to an ECM. Signals on each wire in the harness correspond to a pin on the break-out box (**FIGURE 13-36**). OEM templates, which are thin plastic sheets with printed numbers or letters, can be obtained to lay over the pins, helping to identify specific pin functions or circuit numbers. Smaller break-out harnesses, which connect to sensors or special wiring harnesses, are also useful to make pinpoint tests of circuits required by diagnostic procedures (**FIGURE 13-37**).

Vibration Analyzers

LO 13-6 Identify the purpose of vibration analyzers and explain how they are used to pinpoint sources of vibration.

Vibration analyzers are used to identify the root cause of vehicle vibration. Typically, flywheel speed and road speed sensors are used, along with data collected from a

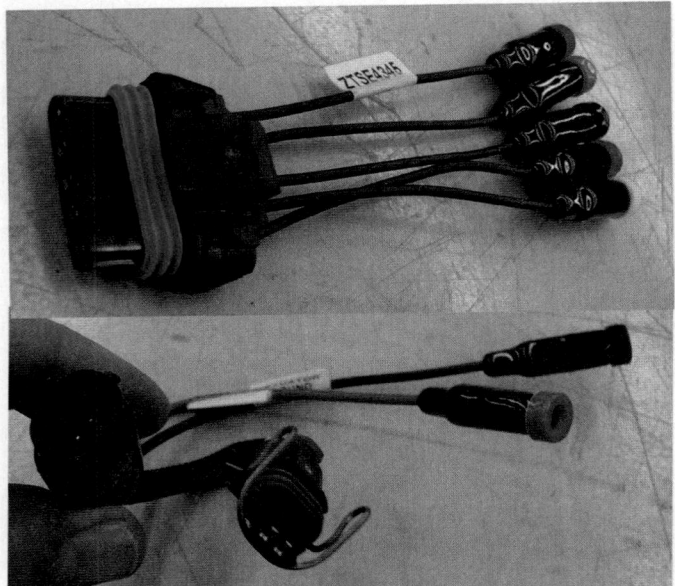

FIGURE 13-37 Break-out harnesses are used to connect to sensors, smaller wiring harnesses, and other components to perform pinpoint tests.

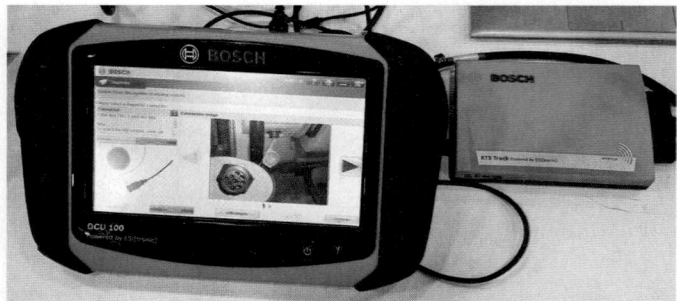

FIGURE 13-38 The Bosch ESI system is a popular series of generic scanners used to troubleshoot problems with electronic control systems of heavy-duty (HD) commercial vehicle systems.

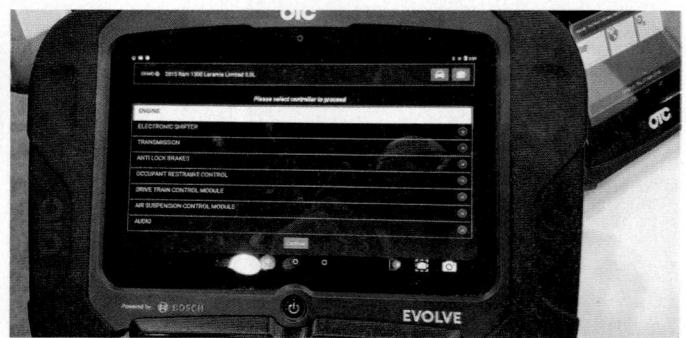

FIGURE 13-39 This Bosch EVO bidirectional scanner can perform many diagnostic functions related to retrieving fault codes or sensor data, and performing diagnostic routines on multiple vehicle systems, such as engine, antilock braking, transmission, or even climate control.

three-axis accelerometer placed under the driver's seat using a magnet. Data is collected from the sensors into a signal-conditioning module that stores the information for analysis by a computer.

Electronic Service Tools— Scanners

LO 13-7 Identify the purpose of vehicle network interface devices and explain how they are used to communication with on-board networks.

A variety of scanner types are used to read serial data from a vehicle data link connector. The hand held scanner uses software or application-specific microcontrollers to translate the serial data, transmitted by the onboard network through the 6- or 9-pin data link connector, into a format that can be read by the technician. See **FIGURES 13-38** and **13-39**. More sophisticated scanners use bidirectional serial communication between the tool and the ECM to send commands that can actuate output devices, or cause an ECU to enter a wide range of diagnostic routines, such as performing cylinder cut-out tests or actuating ABS modulator valves.

Additional Scan Tool Functions

Scan tools are versatile instruments that can perform a variety of additional functions:

- *Bidirectional control* – Scan tools can control selected vehicle components or initiate systems actuator or diagnostic tests on command.

- *Graphical display* – Scan tools can display real-time engine parameters or recorded data in a graphing format.
- *Help menu/trouble code library* – Scan tools can guide a technician through certain procedures or has a built-in library of all the SAE generic trouble codes.
- *Printer/computer output* – Scan tools connect to a printer or computer and prints or displays information from the vehicle.
- *Record/playback or snapshot mode* – Scan tools can record a block of real-time engine data and replay that information to find the root cause of a malfunction.
- *Reprogramming of vehicle ECU* – Scan tools can perform off-board or on-board reprogramming of a vehicle's major control modules.
- *Scopes and meters* – Scan tools can operate as a multimeter (measuring voltage, resistance, amperage, etc.).

Code Readers

The most basic diagnostic scanner is a code reader. Code readers can access, interpret, and display on-board diagnostic (OBD) codes from the vehicle's ECU. Inexpensive models may only display a numerical OBD code. Enhanced readers may provide an alphabetic explanation of the code. Code readers may also clear codes, turn off the malfunction indicator lamp (MIL), and display the "ready" status of various HD-OBD monitors. However, a code reader does not display any sensor data or other operating information needed for advanced diagnostic work.

Code readers can become outdated as new OBD codes are added every year. Updating a code reader's capabilities is usually not possible.

Vehicle Communication Interface Adapters

Vehicle Communication Interface Adapters also commonly referred to as **data link adapters** are used to translate serial data from the diagnostic link connector (DLC) into a format readable by a desktop or laptop computer. The adapter may connect to the PC or laptop using a cable connected to a serial port, USB port, or wirelessly over the internet or Bluetooth communication (**FIGURE 13-40**). To enable universal access of communication interface devices to on-board networks for trucks and coaches, the PC requires adapters be compliant with a "Recommended Practice" of the Maintenance Council called RP1210 a/b or c. RP1210 is a protocol or communication standard used to form a bridge with the onboard network and translate serial data from the data bus. Further information about handheld scanners and vehicle communication adapters is found in the chapter "On-Board Vehicle Networks."

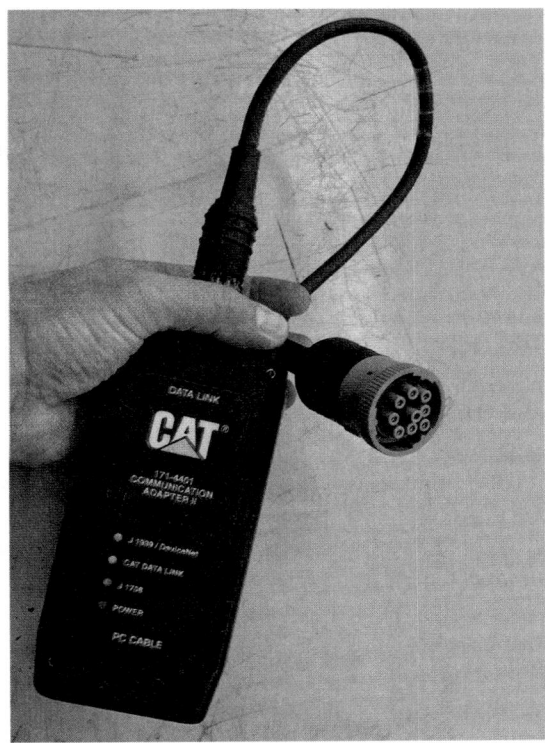

FIGURE 13-40 This data link adapter connected to the vehicle data link can translate DLC serial data into a format readable by PCs or laptops. The adapter can communicate using a cable, with another adapter wirelessly over the same radio frequency as wireless internet, or by using Bluetooth radio frequencies.

Wrap-Up

Ready for Review

▶ A variety of electrical test instruments are needed to diagnose and repair electrical problems.

▶ The simplest piece of electrical test equipment used to determine the presence or absence of current is a test light.

▶ Self-powered test lights are like regular test lights except that they contain a 1.5-volt battery.

▶ Multimeters are electrical measuring instruments combining functions of at least voltage, resistance, and amperage measurement into a single compact instrument.

▶ Multimeters can be analog, digital, or high-impedance, and come in auto-ranging and manual-ranging types.

▶ Before using a digital meter, one of the first things to check is whether its shunts or fuses are in place and functioning. Shunts are internal conductors with a small calibrated resistance, which directs some current flow into the meter when measuring amperage.

▶ By checking the resistance or circuit continuity with an ohmmeter, a circuit can be evaluated for shorts, opens, or high resistance.

▶ Ohmmeters are ineffective when checking for resistances in high-amperage, low-resistance circuits, such as when measuring battery cable voltage loss.

▶ Voltmeters measure the difference in electrical pressure or electron velocity between two different points in the circuit.

▶ Measuring amperage requires that the powered circuit is opened, and the meter placed in series with the circuit, so that all the current flows through the meter shunts.

▶ Inductive amp clamps are useful tools for measuring amperage without opening the circuit.

▶ Multimeters use a thermocouple accessory to measure temperature by contact. Heating the thermocouple produces voltage proportional to temperature.

▶ Circuit tracers are useful for identifying circuit problems in wires deeply buried behind walls or in tightly bundled harnesses.

▶ Graphing meters allow technicians to assess component serviceability by analyzing the waveforms.

▶ When performing electrical circuit diagnostics, purpose-made jumper wires, fused jumper wires, and break-out boxes are helpful for quickly and effectively diagnosing problems without damaging wiring or connectors by back-probing or piercing wires.

▶ A variety of scanner types are used to read serial data from a vehicle data link connector.

▶ The most basic diagnostic scanner is a code reader. Code readers can access, interpret, and display on-board diagnostic (OBD) codes from the vehicle's ECM.

Key Terms

analog meter A meter that uses a sweeping needle that continuously measures electrical values.

auto-ranging multimeter A multimeter that has fewer positions on its range selection knob and automatically selects the correct range when meter test leads are connected to a circuit.

circuit (wire) tracer An electronic service tool used to trace a single wire over a distance where multiple wires are bundled, shorted, or open.

data link adapter A device used to translate serial data from the DLC into a format readable by a desktop or laptop computer.

digital multimeter A type of multimeter that provides numerical displays of electrical data.

graphing meter An electrical test instrument used to analyze waveforms and graphically plot an electrical value of a signal over time.

high-impedance multimeter A meter that samples very little of a circuit's own current to take a measurement.

inductive amp clamp A device that measures amperage by measuring a conductor's magnetic field strength, which is proportional to amperage.

manual-ranging multimeter A multimeter that must be set to the correct range first based on anticipated values measured.

shunts Internal conductors with small calibrated resistance that direct current flow into the meter while measuring amperage.

test light The simplest piece of electrical test equipment, which consists of either a 12- or 24-volt incandescent light bulb connected to an insulated lead and a sharpened metal probe.

Type K thermocouple A low-cost, general-purpose, temperature-sensing element connected to the same meter terminals for measuring DC millivolts.

vibration analyzer A device used to identify the root cause of vehicle vibration.

Review Questions

1. Under which of the following conditions will the test light lamp illuminate when the lead wire is clipped and connected to a good chassis ground?
   a. When the test light probe is touching the battery negative post
   b. When the test light probe is touching the grounded metal case of a starting motor
   c. When the test light probe is touching the circuit, but not the battery-ignition, side of a blown fuse
   d. When the test light probe is touching the battery-ignition supply side of a blown fuse

2. A test light illuminates when connected between a chassis ground and the grounded metal case of a blower motor that is switched on. Which of the following best describes the circuit's condition?
   a. The motor has a parasitic draw
   b. The motor has a short to ground
   c. The motor has an open ground circuit
   d. The motor has a defective switch

3. Which of the following multimeter arrangements is best used to check for an open circuit inside an ~3' long (1 m) ground cable connecting the frame to the engine block?
   a. Disconnect the cable and check its continuity
   b. Measure the available voltage at each end of the connected cable with the key on
   c. Measure the amperage passing through the cable with the key off
   d. With the key on, measure the cable resistance

4. An ohmmeter display indicates the resistance of a circuit is 3.2 kΩ. How many ohms of resistance does this equal?
   a. 3,200 ohms
   b. 32,000 ohms
   c. 320,000 ohms
   d. 3,200,000 ohms

5. An auto-ranging meter is set to measure resistance and the positive test lead is placed in the meters only amp probe port. There is infinite resistance displayed by the meter. What does it indicate?
   a. The meter is functioning correctly.
   b. There is current at the amp probe port.
   c. The meter shunt is open.
   d. The meter shunt is intact.

6. What is the correct procedure to measure amperage in a DC circuit?
   a. Open the circuit and place the meter in series with an energized circuit
   b. Connect the ammeter in parallel and observe polarity
   c. Disconnect the battery and connect the meter in parallel
   d. Open the circuit and connect the meter series with a current-limiting resister

7. How is the strength of a magnetic field sensed when measuring DC amperage?
   a. Measuring the number of lines of force in a rotating magnetic field
   b. Using a Hall Effect sensor
   c. Using an inductor
   d. Using a K-type thermocouple

8. Which of the following test instruments is the best to measure electrical signals from multiple wires connecting to an ECU?
   a. An ammeter
   b. A voltmeter

c. A signal tracer

d. A break-out box

9. Which electrical service tool is best used to locate a broken wire behind a body panel?

a. A voltmeter

b. A signal tracer

c. A graphing meter

d. An inductive-type clamp

10. Which is the best reason for using a vehicle communication interface adapter?

a. To obtain engine-related fault codes

b. To enable a PC or laptop to communicate with a vehicle network

c. To enable bidirectional communication between a PC and ABS module

d. To actuate network-connected output devices on the vehicle

ASE Technician A/Technician B Style Questions

1. Technician A says that a test light is the simplest piece of electrical test equipment used to determine the presence or absence of current. Technician B says that a test light consists of either an 18- or 36-volt incandescent light bulb connected to an insulated lead and a sharpened metal probe. Who is correct?

a. Technician A

b. Technician B

c. Both Technician A and Technician B

d. Neither Technician A nor Technician B

2. Technician A says that a popular type of LED test light is battery powered and has two LEDs—one red and the other green. Technician B says that the LED light changes brightness depending on the circuit's voltage. Who is correct?

a. Technician A

b. Technician B

c. Both Technician A and Technician B

d. Neither Technician A nor Technician B

3. Technician A says that multimeters are electrical measuring instruments combining functions of at least voltage, resistance, and amperage measurement into a single compact instrument. Technician B says that digital multimeters are the most common category of multimeters and provide numerical displays of electrical data. Who is correct?

a. Technician A

b. Technician B

c. Both Technician A and Technician B

d. Neither Technician A nor Technician B

4. Technician A says that a multimeter measures resistance, continuity, voltage, and amperage. Technician B says that the multimeter can be used to measure circuit resistance in amps to determine whether amperage is within specifications. Who is correct?

a. Technician A

b. Technician B

c. Both Technician A and Technician B

d. Neither Technician A nor Technician B

5. Technician A says that before using a digital multimeter, the first task is to check that its shunts and fuses are in place and functioning. Technician B says that shunts do not operate like fuses and do not have a maximum rating. Who is correct?

a. Technician A

b. Technician B

c. Both Technician A and Technician B

d. Neither Technician A nor Technician B

6. Technician A says that the multimeter is connected in series with the circuit or component to measure the voltage dropped by the circuit resistance. Technician B says that the ohmmeter works well in testing semiconductors. Who is correct?

a. Technician A

b. Technician B

c. Both Technician A and Technician B

d. Neither Technician A nor Technician B

7. Technician A says that ammeters measure the quantity of electrons flowing through a circuit per second of time. Technician B says that measuring amperage requires that the circuit be broken, and the meter placed in series with the circuit, so that all the current flows through the meter shunts. Who is correct?

a. Technician A

b. Technician B

c. Both Technician A and Technician B

d. Neither Technician A nor Technician B

8. Technician A says that multimeters use a thermocouple accessory to measure temperature by contact. Technician B says that heating the thermocouple produces amperage proportional to temperature. Who is correct?

a. Technician A

b. Technician B

c. Both Technician A and Technician B

d. Neither Technician A nor Technician B

9. Technician A says that circuit tracers, also called wire tracers, are electronic service tools used to trace a single wire over a distance to check for shorts, or open circuits. Technician B says that circuit tracers can identify broken wires deeply buried behind walls or in tightly bundled harnesses. Who is correct?

a. Technician A

b. Technician B

c. Both Technician A and Technician B

d. Neither Technician A nor Technician B

10. Technician A says that vibration analyzers are used to identify the root cause of vehicle vibration. Technician B says that, typically, flywheel speed and road speed sensors are used along with data collected from a three-axis accelerometer placed under the driver's seat using a magnet. Who is correct?

a. Technician A

b. Technician B

c. Both Technician A and Technician B

d. Neither Technician A nor Technician B

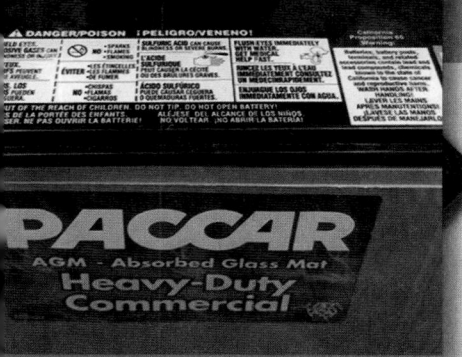

CHAPTER 14

Commercial Vehicle Batteries

Learning Objectives

After reading this chapter, you will be able to:

- **LO 14-1** Identify and describe the construction, operating principles, and functions of lead-acid batteries used in commercial vehicles.
- **LO 14-2** Identify and describe the classification and applications of lead-acid batteries.
- **LO 14-3** Identify and describe the construction features and operation of valve-regulated lead-acid batteries.

- **LO 14-4** Identify and define battery terminology and explain battery ratings.
- **LO 14-5** Identify and describe the construction details and operating characteristics of low- and no-maintenance batteries.

You Are the Technician

As a technician with many years of service in your truck and heavy equipment dealership, you've been asked to join the health and safety committee. Your experience working in a shop environment has made you conscious of the importance of using safe working practices and making workplace safety a top priority. One of the initiatives of the health and safety committee is implementing the best safety practices to use while working with batteries. In fact, in addition to Occupational Safety and Health Administration (OSHA) workplace requirements, development of a more comprehensive in-house policy originates from a recent incident where one worker was injured by an exploding battery while jump-starting a vehicle. As you are considering the various procedures that should be rigorously followed in the shop to avoid any accidents, injuries, or damage to customer vehicles and property, include answers to the following questions:

1. List the major safety issues related to working with batteries.
2. What protective equipment should you use when filling batteries or checking cell electrolyte with a hydrometer?
3. Outline a sequence of actions a technician should follow while jump-starting a vehicle.

Introduction

Batteries are the most essential component in a vehicle's electrical system (**FIGURE 14-1**). Not only do batteries provide starting power for engines and operating electrical accessories when the alternator does not supply enough current, batteries play a critical role in proper operation and longevity of many other electrical components (**FIGURE 14-2**). The recent development of medium- and heavy-duty engine start-stop systems and hybrid drive vehicles has added to the battery's list of jobs. In addition to their traditional functions, batteries must now supply energy to electric drive motors and help recover energy during braking. More frequent battery discharge and charge cycles accompany the use of start-stop systems. These systems automatically shut the engine off when stopped at a traffic light, and then immediately restarts the engine when the accelerator is depressed. Electrical current to power accessories, including

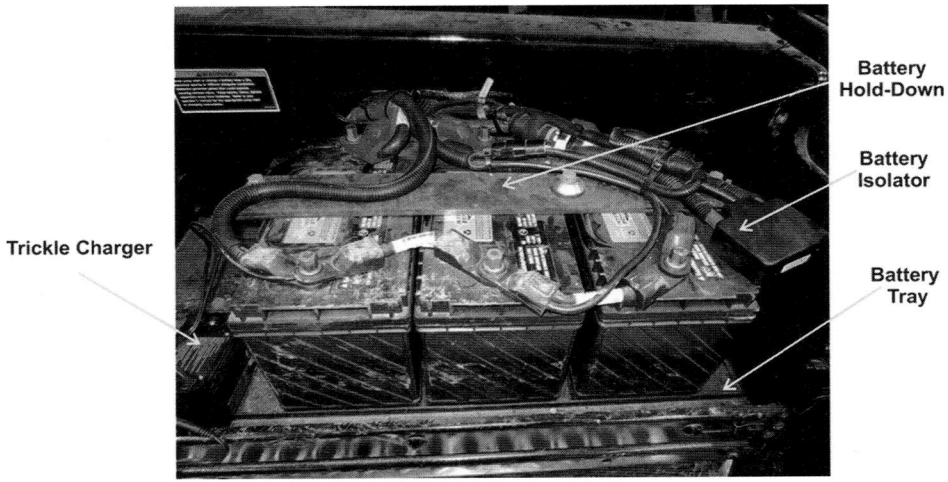

FIGURE 14-1 Multiple batteries are connected in parallel to supply higher cranking amperage and adequate current flow for starting motors and electrical accessories in a commercial vehicle chassis.

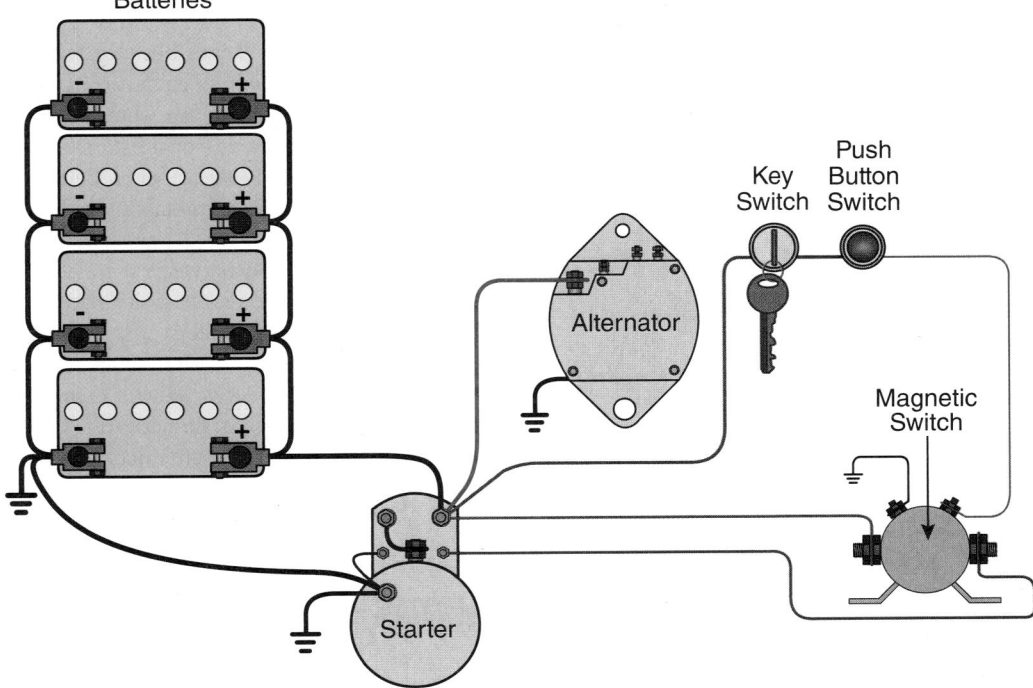

FIGURE 14-2 Batteries traditionally supply starter current and power to run electrical accessories when the engine is not running.

the air conditioning system and pumps for a variety of devices not powered by the engine during short shut down periods, must now be supplied by the batteries. Today's technicians need to know a lot more about the various types of batteries they encounter, how those batteries work, make recommendations for battery replacement, and know what should be done to maintain, test, and work safely with them.

Battery Operation and Functions

LO 14-1 Identify and describe the construction, operating principles, and functions of lead-acid batteries used in commercial vehicles.

Batteries are not devices that store electricity. They just convert chemical energy into electrical energy and vice versa. When connected to an electrical load, such as a light or electric motor, chemical reactions taking place inside the battery force extra electrons from the negative battery terminal and pull them to the positive terminal of the battery though the load. Flow of electricity ends when the chemical energy of the battery is depleted by the electrical loads in the circuit. Movement of electrons in a single direction during the discharge period means a battery is a source of direct current (DC).

Battery Classifications

Batteries can be classified into two basic categories: primary and secondary. In a **primary battery**, chemical reactions are not reversible, and the battery cannot be recharged. In contrast, **secondary batteries** are rechargeable (**FIGURE 14-3**). By reversing the direction of current and pushing electricity back into the battery, the chemical reactions that originally produced electrical current are reversed. Renewing the state of charge allows the secondary battery to be used repeatedly. For this reason, secondary batteries are the most practical for use in commercial vehicle applications. Secondary batteries for commercial vehicles are commonly constructed from lead and acid, which

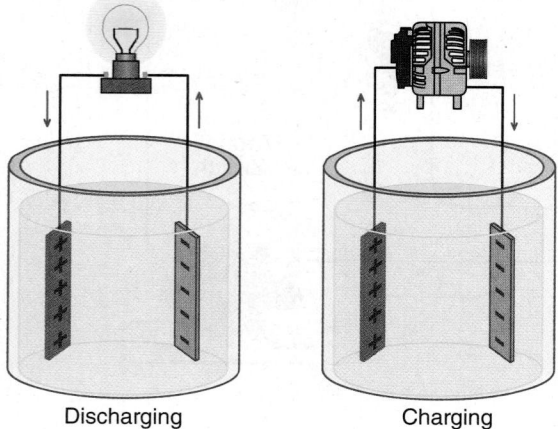

FIGURE 14-3 Secondary batteries can be repeatedly charged and discharged.

convert chemical energy into electric current using **galvanic reactions**. A galvanic reaction is a chemical process which produces electricity when two dissimilar metals are placed in an electrolyte. Electrolytes are liquids that conduct electricity, and electric poles are created at each metal electrode as electrons are stripped from one electrode and move through the electrolyte to create a surplus at the opposite metal electrode. Charge potentials are created at the positive and negative battery posts when the positive post is stripped of electrons and forced onto the negative post. The battery charge is depleted when the movement of electrons is reversed by allowing the electrons at the negative post to return to the positive posts through the vehicle loads connected to the battery posts.

Various types of lead-acid batteries make up most of the secondary batteries found in commercial vehicles, but more advanced battery technologies are also used: lithium-ion, nickel metal hydride (NiMH), and battery-like devices called electrolytic capacitors that store charges. This chapter covers fundamental information about basic lead-acid batteries. Technology associated with advanced lead-acid batteries and other battery types, such as lithium, nickel metal hydride, and electrolytic capacitors, are covered in the next chapter on Advanced Battery Technology.

Galvanic Batteries

The term *battery* more accurately refers to a collection of electrochemical cells that are connected. A discovery made more than two hundred years ago by a medical experimenter named Galvani found that electricity is produced when two dissimilar metals are placed in an electrolyte. **Electrolyte**, in an electrochemical cell, refers to any liquid that conducts electric current. Not all liquids conduct electricity, though. For example, pure water does not conduct current and is not an electrolyte. Tap water, however, does. That's because tap water often contains traces of minerals, such as calcium, iron, and elements, such as chlorine, which enables tap water to become an electrolyte. Water containing salt, acids, or substances creating alkaline solutions (soap-like solutions) are even better conductors of electricity. The two dissimilar metals placed in an electrolyte form electrodes, which produce the positive and negative electrical poles. Chemical action between the electrolyte and electrodes strips electrons from one metal electrode and adds electrons to another electrode. That electron transfer process between the two electrodes determines the voltage and amperage available at the battery's poles. After Galvani created an electrochemical cell, another experimenter named Volta built the first battery by connecting multiple electrochemical cells together using copper and zinc plates alternately stacked next to one another and separated with a piece of saltwater-soaked cardboard. Volta named it a "voltaic pile" after demonstrating its electrical properties.

▶ TECHNICIAN TIP

The information about the development of batteries isn't just dull history. The application of these same, commonplace observations is relevant to work practices since galvanic reactions and voltaic piles are observed in many areas on commercial vehicles. Corrosion is one example of a galvanic reaction. The cooling system of an engine contains water (an electrolyte) in contact with dissimilar metals like copper injector tubes, cast iron blocks, aluminum water pump housings, and so on. Metals losing electrons disintegrate while other metals remain unaffected. However, the electron transfer between the metals through coolant is easily observed by placing a voltmeter with one lead in the coolant and the other on the engine block or other metal part. (Corrosion inhibitors in the cooling system work by minimizing the loss of electrons from metals, which lowers the observed voltage levels.) To minimize corrosion caused by galvanic reactions, dissimilar metals are separated by electrical insulators. On trailers, aluminum side plates are separated with a piece of non-conductive Mylar or insulating tape to electrically isolate the aluminum plate from steel I-beams supporting the floor. For the same reason, when aluminum and steel disc wheels are placed together on the same wheel end, they must be separated with a plastic or nylon gasket.

A single battery cell consists of two dissimilar metals: an insulator material separating the metals and an electrolyte, which is an electrically conductive solution. The material from which the electrodes are made and the type of electrolyte determine the voltage potential of a battery. The area of the plates making up each positive and negative electrode determines the capacity or available amperage the battery can deliver.

The traditional commercial vehicle battery type is the lead-acid battery. It is available in a variety of sizes and designs to reliably meet the unique electrical requirements for various applications. For example, the construction of a lead-acid battery used for starting a vehicle's engine is different from the battery construction used for a boat, golf cart, or bulldozer. Each requires unique design characteristics based on its applications. Batteries for commercial vehicles using diesel engines are designed to supply high amperage to the starting motor for only short periods of time. After starting, the alternator charges the battery and supplies current to the vehicle electrical loads, such as lighting, and supplies the electrical loads connected to the ignition circuit. The application for primarily supplying starting, lighting, and ignition electrical loads lends the name to this type of battery construction; starting, lighting, and ignition (SLI) battery. Another lead-acid battery less commonly used by commercial vehicles is a deep-cycle battery. Deep-cycle batteries are intended for use where its current is continuously used up until its charge is almost completely depleted. Compared to the brief peak loads required by an SLI battery during starting, a deep-cycle battery has less amperage drawn by the constant electrical loads and is infrequently charged before its charge is depleted.

▶ TECHNICIAN TIP

Maintaining a strong negative ground on a vehicle minimizes chassis corrosion caused by galvanic reaction. You may notice most corrosion takes place at positive battery posts and at the end of non-insulated, positively charged wires. This happens because positively charged wire ends and battery posts are deficient of electrons. Oxygen and molecules in road salt are examples of substances that easily provide those electrons to electron-depleted metal and then are electrically bound to positive terminals and wire ends. Some military equipment and off-road heavy equipment from Europe use a positive ground system to protect

the exposed wiring on starters, alternators, and wiring harnesses from the effects of corrosion. Electrical system reliability is enhanced at the expense of chassis corrosion, which instead attacks large, heavy, steel chassis components.

Battery Functions

Batteries have traditionally been used in heavy vehicles to provide starting current and operate electrical accessories if the engine is not running. And, although supplying electric current for starting is the most obvious function for a battery, it's important to explain further the other jobs the battery performs that are critical to proper electrical system operation. Battery functions on medium- and heavy-duty commercial vehicles include:

1. Providing electrical energy to the vehicle whenever the engine is not running. When the engine is running, a properly designed and operational charging system supplies electrical current to meet most electrical demands and charge the battery. For today's heavy vehicles and equipment, the limitation on or, even elimination of, engine idle means batteries need to supply electrical current for prolonged periods to devices, such as electrohydraulic pumps for hydraulic brakes, power steering, coolant pumps, and air conditioning compressors. Hybrid electric vehicles are now commonplace in urban transit. Hybrid electric transit buses are dependent on battery-supplied electrical current to operate all electrical devices, including electric drive motors and all electrical accessories, for much longer periods than conventional vehicles using accessories driven by an internal combustion engine.
2. Providing electrical energy to operate the starter motor, ignition, and other electrical systems during cranking. Other devices, such as hydraulic or air starter motors, could be used to start engines. However, even electronically controlled diesel injection systems require current to operate during cranking. When electric starter motors are used, batteries must be capable of delivering high current flow for short periods of time. Batteries used for cranking purposes have unique construction features and are commonly termed **starting, lighting, and ignition (SLI) batteries**. Commercial equipment, particularly diesel-powered equipment, use multiple batteries, called a bank of batteries, connected in series or parallel to produce adequate starting current.
3. Providing extra electrical power whenever power requirements exceed the output of the charging system. High current demands are occasionally placed on the electrical system. For example, when an engine is idling, the charging system current output is low. Current flow to blower motors operating at high speed for heating or air conditioning systems, lighting circuits, and other electrical devices can exceed the output of the charging system. To maintain proper operation of these circuits, the batteries should be sized to provide adequate current.
4. Storing energy over long periods of time. Even when vehicles are not in use for extended periods of time, the battery is still

expected to deliver current to start a vehicle. Today, heavy vehicles and equipment have numerous **key-off electrical loads**. These are current draws on the battery when the ignition is switched off. Also called **parasitic draw**, this battery current is required to continually operate vehicle security systems, GPS devices, and computer memory for multiple electronic control modules, entertainment systems, and other electrical accessories requiring constant power.

5. Acting as an electric shock absorber for the vehicle's electrical systems. The use of microprocessors and microcontrollers in almost every vehicle system makes today's heavy equipment sensitive to fluctuations in voltage. Operating on current in the millivolt range, stray and uneven electrical current can interfere with, and even damage, the operation of these sensitive electronic devices. The operation of common components, such as alternators, switches, and electrical devices, with inductive coils regularly produce this type of electrical interference. Batteries help minimize fluctuations in a vehicle electrical system by absorbing and smoothing variations in electrical current.

6. Operating electric drive traction motors. The development of battery and hybrid electric vehicles (HEVs) has created new functions, in addition to the traditional purposes of batteries. In HEVs, batteries must provide even higher amounts of current for longer periods of time to operate electric traction motors used to propel the vehicle, as illustrated in (**FIGURE 14-4**). The same battery is used to store energy recovered by the drive motors during braking. HEVs require new battery chemistry and construction to extend battery life, reduce weight, increase energy density, charge more quickly, and discharge and charge more frequently, while delivering higher amounts of current flow for extended periods of time. Batteries must accomplish these goals in the harsh operating environment and duty cycle of commercial

vehicles. At the same time, batteries must perform with greater and more consistent reliability than ever before. New types of batteries and battery-management systems are used to help meet these operational demands.

▶ TECHNICIAN TIP

When batteries wear out due to frequent charge and discharge cycles, they lose their ability to properly function. Some chassis may be equipped with electrical equipment, in particular, electronic control modules that are sensitive to electrical interference from high-frequency voltage fluctuations produced by an alternator. When the battery cannot absorb and smooth these voltage fluctuations, strange and apparently unrelated electrical system complaints are produced. Engines run rough, instrument gauges operate erratically, the ABS system can have numerous fault codes, the cruise control may not work, and the transmission may shift poorly. Even communication over the data link connector slows down. To avoid unnecessary waste of time and resources investigating these complaints and any electrical system problems, always qualify the working condition of the battery first. Replace or substitute a known good set of batteries during diagnostic testing to determine whether batteries have lost the ability to absorb high-frequency voltage fluctuations.

Types and Classification of Batteries

LO 14-2 Identify and describe the classification and applications of lead-acid batteries.

Batteries are generally classified by the type of construction and application. In other words, batteries are classified according to what they are used for and how they are made. Batteries are also classified according to the type of plate materials and chemistry used to produce current. Until recently, lead-acid batteries have

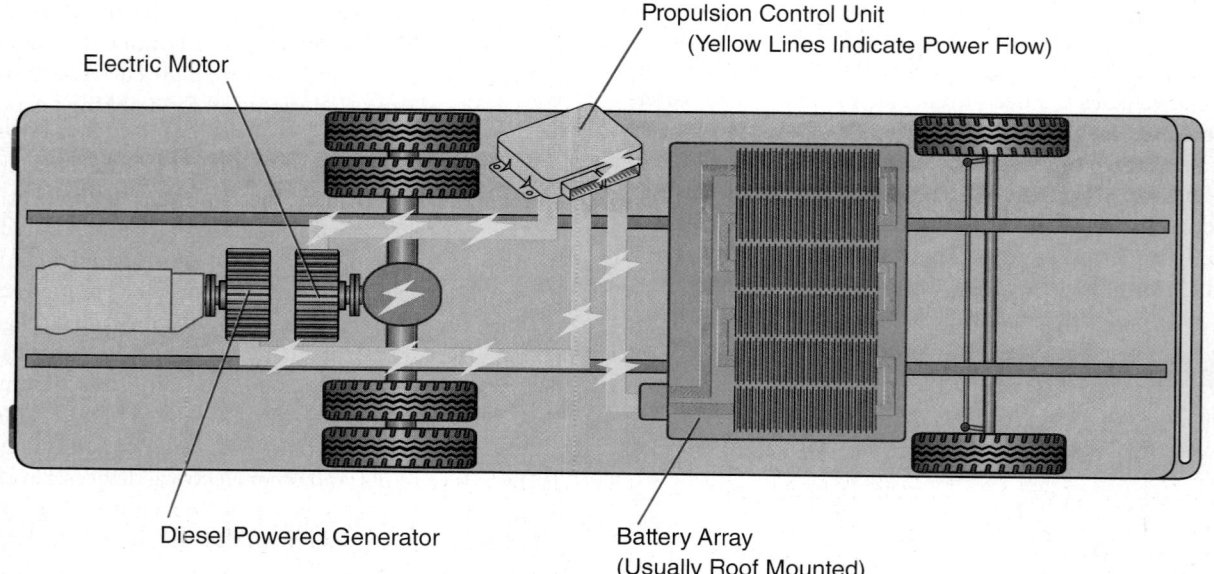

FIGURE 14-4 Batteries are now required to provide current to electric traction motors and store current produced during regenerative braking.

been the only battery technology used in commercial vehicles. While the search for more durable and reliable lead-acid batteries has brought innovation to that category of batteries, the development of battery electric vehicles (BEV's) and hybrid drive vehicles has resulted in the introductions of different types of battery technology, such as nickel-metal hydride and lithium batteries. These and other battery chemistries are further discussed in the Advanced Battery Technologies chapter.

Lead-Acid Battery Classification

Lead-acid batteries have been developed commercially for over 130 years and are a mature, reliable, and well-understood technology. They are also the most common battery used in the transportation industry. Lead-acid batteries deliver high rates of current with a higher tolerance for physical and electrical abuse compared to other battery technology. These batteries hold a charge well and when stored dry—without electrolyte—the shelf life is indefinite. Relatively simple compared to other battery technologies, lead-acid batteries are also the least expensive to manufacture in terms of cost per watt of power.

Contributing to the popularity of lead-acid batteries is the fact that they are available in a wide range of sizes and capacities from many suppliers worldwide. Six types of lead-acid battery construction are found in on-highway commercial vehicles, but the basic chemical action is identical in all, including:

- Flooded cell, including low maintenance (like that shown in (**FIGURE 14-5**) or maintenance free.
- Deep-cycle flooded cell.

Valve-regulated lead-acid (VRLA) battery, also called absorbed glass mat (AGM) battery, **sealed lead-acid (SLA) battery**, or recombinant battery, like that shown in (**FIGURE 14-6**), is a category that includes:

- Flooded
- Gel cell
- Absorbed glass mat (AGM)
- Spiral cell (Optima batteries)

Starting, Lighting, and Ignition (SLI) Batteries

Among the categories of lead-acid batteries, the most common use is for SLI. SLI batteries are designed for one short-duration deep discharge of up to 50% depth of discharge (DOD) during engine cranking. Discharging is quickly followed by a charging period, and a full charge is maintained. The operating requirements of an SLI battery are very different from traction batteries used in hybrid electric vehicles. **Traction batteries** are rechargeable batteries used for propulsion systems with electric motors in electric powered vehicles. Though identical in appearance, SLI batteries are also constructed differently than deep-cycle batteries.

Deep Cycle—Deep Discharge

A **deep-cycle battery** is used to deliver a lower, steady level of power for a much longer period of time than an SLI-type battery. Furthermore, battery plate construction and charging and discharging characteristics of deep-cycle batteries are different from SLI-type batteries. In heavy vehicles, deep-cycle batteries are used to supply current to constantly powered accessories, like driver and vehicle communication devices. Deep-cycle batteries also supply power to wave inverters, which in turn supply alternating current (AC) to on-board appliances, such as refrigerators, TVs, or laptop chargers. In addition, deep-cycle, batteries are used to power accessory lighting, electric winches, and tailgates. This type of battery typically uses a battery isolator system that separates the main vehicle electrical system from the deep-cycled battery circuit. The charging system replenishes the deep-cycle battery charge, but the deep-cycle battery cannot be accessed by the main vehicle electrical circuits.

Battery Construction and Operation

LO 14-3 Identify and describe the construction features and operation of valve-regulated lead-acid batteries.

The basic components of a battery are its case, terminals, plates, and electrolyte. Even though the construction of batteries can

FIGURE 14-5 A typical low- or no-maintenance SLI battery.

FIGURE 14-6 A tubular-type VRLA sealed battery from Optima.

vary depending on their type and application, these basic components remain the same. It is important that the correct size, type, and construction are selected for the application. Before selecting a battery for an application, the technician needs to answer several questions. For example, is the requirement for a starting battery or a deep-cycle battery used to supply electrical accessories? Is the battery working in extremes of temperature? Is it a high vibration environment? What electrical load does the battery need to supply and for how long? What case and terminal configuration is required?

This section examines battery construction and discusses how those questions and their answers aid in the selection of the correct battery for an application. This section also explains the charge and discharge cycle of a battery.

Flooded Lead-Acid Batteries

A **flooded lead-acid battery** refers to battery cell construction where the electrodes are made from thin lead (Pb) alloy plates submersed in liquid electrolyte. Two dissimilar compositions of lead form the positive and negative electrodes (**FIGURE 14-7**). Sponge lead, which is lead made porous with air bubbles, forms the negative plate. Lead dioxide (PbO_2) is the active material of the positive plate.

The electrodes and electrolyte of a lead-acid battery cell produce approximately 2.1 volts. Connecting the internal cells together in series allows batteries to be produced in a variety of output voltage. This means a fully charged 12-volt battery, produces 12.6 volts with no electrical loads by connecting in series six cells with 2.1-volts output. 24-volt electrical systems are commonly used in heavy-duty off-road equipment, urban transit buses, highway coaches, and by the military. 24-volt electrical systems are most commonly made from combinations of 12-volt batteries connected in series to produce 24 volts.

Adding Amperage and Voltage

The amount of amperage a battery supplies is a function of the surface area of the plates. To increase the amperage deliverable from a battery, the surface area or number of plates needs to increase. Plates are connected in parallel within each cell increasing the amperage or capacity of a battery. Positive plates are connected only to other positive plates within each cell and likewise with negative plates. Plate straps for each cell set of positive and negative plates are joined through a connector to another strap in adjacent cells. There are two rows of these inter-cell straps and connectors: one terminating at the negative post and the other at the positive post. In a 12-volt battery, three positive plate straps are linked in series to three negative plate straps, alternating a positive strap to negative strap as each cell is connected (**FIGURE 14-8**). The last cell in the series circuit connects to one of the battery posts, either positive or negative. Strap connections between the cells are made either through the cell partitions in the case or over the top of the partition.

Separator Plates

To prevent the battery positive and negative plate from touching and short circuiting, separator plates are placed between each plate in every cell. Separator plates are very thin, porous, but dense glass-fiber materials allowing electrolyte to diffuse freely throughout the cell and at the same time prevent plate contact.

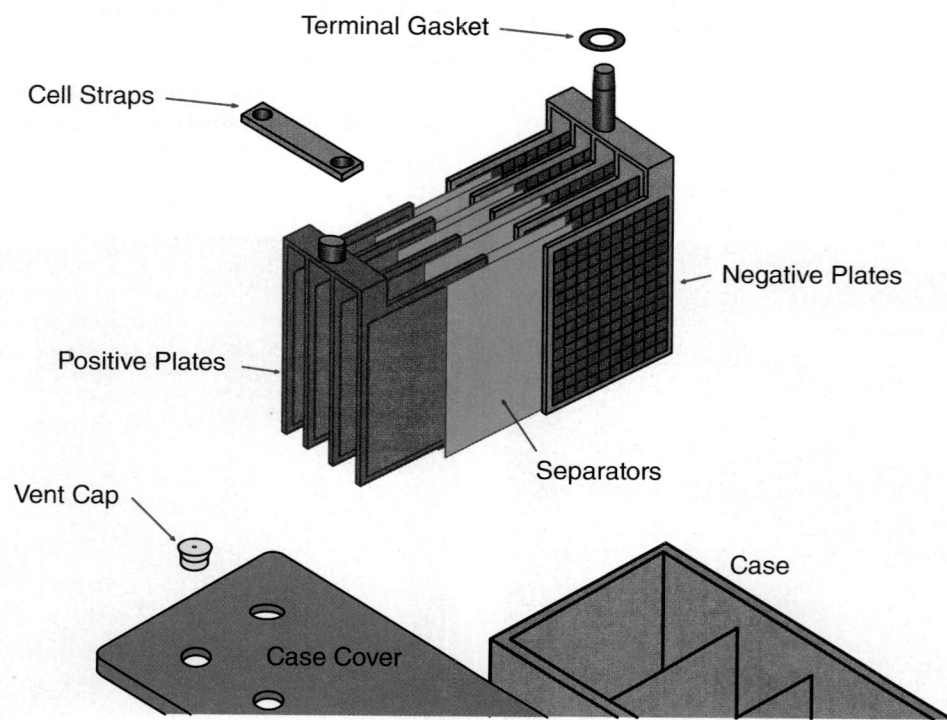

FIGURE 14-7 Typical plate arrangement in a wet cell battery.

FIGURE 14-8 Interconnections between all six cells in a battery, are made through two sets of plate straps terminating at either the positive and negative battery posts.

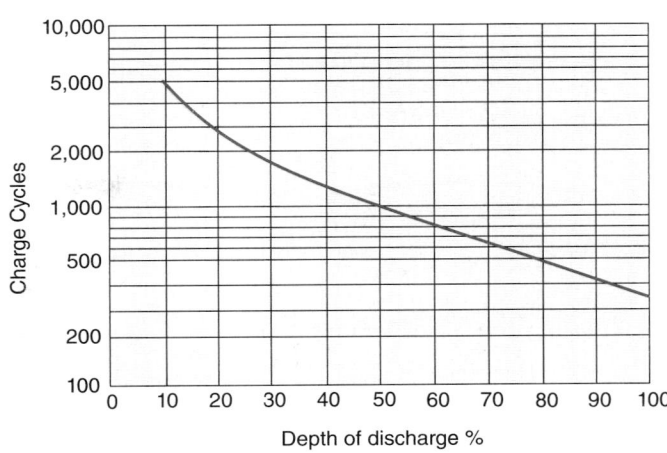

FIGURE 14-9 Deeply discharging a battery shortens battery life.

▶ TECHNICIAN TIP

SLI batteries are designed and constructed to deliver a short, high-amperage burst of current for starting. Using a deep-cycle battery to replace a SLI battery can cause damage to starting motors and conductors through a condition known as low-voltage burn-out. This happens when battery voltage drops very low while supplying high cranking amperage to the starting motor. Because the deep-cycle battery cannot maintain as high an output voltage, the excessive amperage drawn by the starter circuit produces resistance and heat in motors, cables, and connection windings, leading to burn-out. (See the Heavy-Duty Starting Systems and Circuits chapter for a complete explanation of low-voltage burn-out.)

Deep-Cycle Versus SLI Battery Construction

SLI batteries are designed to produce a quick burst of energy for starting and should not be discharged less than 50% before recharging. Deeply discharging SLI batteries dramatically shortens their service life. Ideally, the longest service life is achieved when this battery is discharged no more than 5% and quickly recharged (**FIGURE 14-9**).

In contrast, deep-cycle batteries are made for deep discharging by continuous, but light, electrical loads until completely discharged. To optimize SLI battery characteristics, plates are made thin to fit more plates in each cell. More plates per cell that are made thinner to fit inside the cell translates into higher available amperage due to increased plate surface area. However, continuous discharge of SLI batteries for prolonged periods of time causes the current flow to overheat, distort, and warp the thin plates. Similarly, charging SLI batteries with high current flow from a deeply discharged state can cause plates to overheat, dramatically shortening battery life. To minimize the likelihood of either condition, the primary physical difference between deep-cycle batteries and SLI is the thickness of the plates (**FIGURE 14-10**). Deep-cycle plates are thicker to resist distortion during a discharge/charge cycle. However,

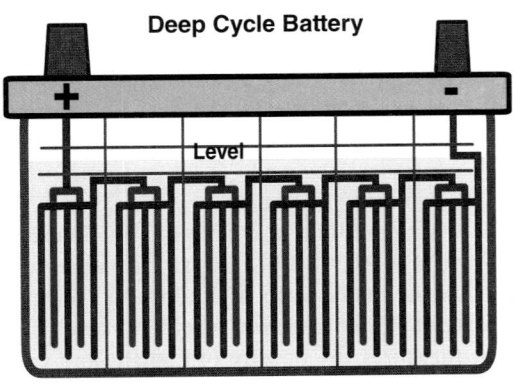

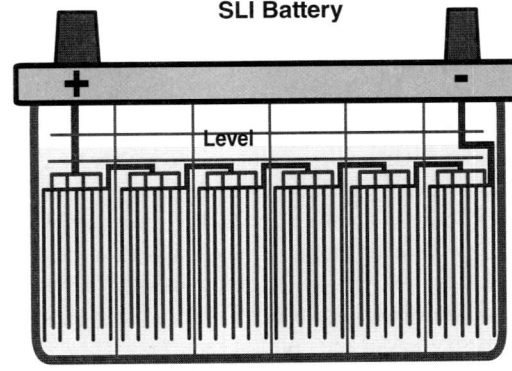

Deep Cycle Battery

- Fewer, Thicker Plates
- Less Plate Surface Area
- Heavier

SLI Battery

- More, Thinner Plates
- More Plate Surface Area
- Lighter

Comparison Deep Cycle to SLI Battery of the Same Dimension

FIGURE 14-10 An SLI battery uses thinner plates.

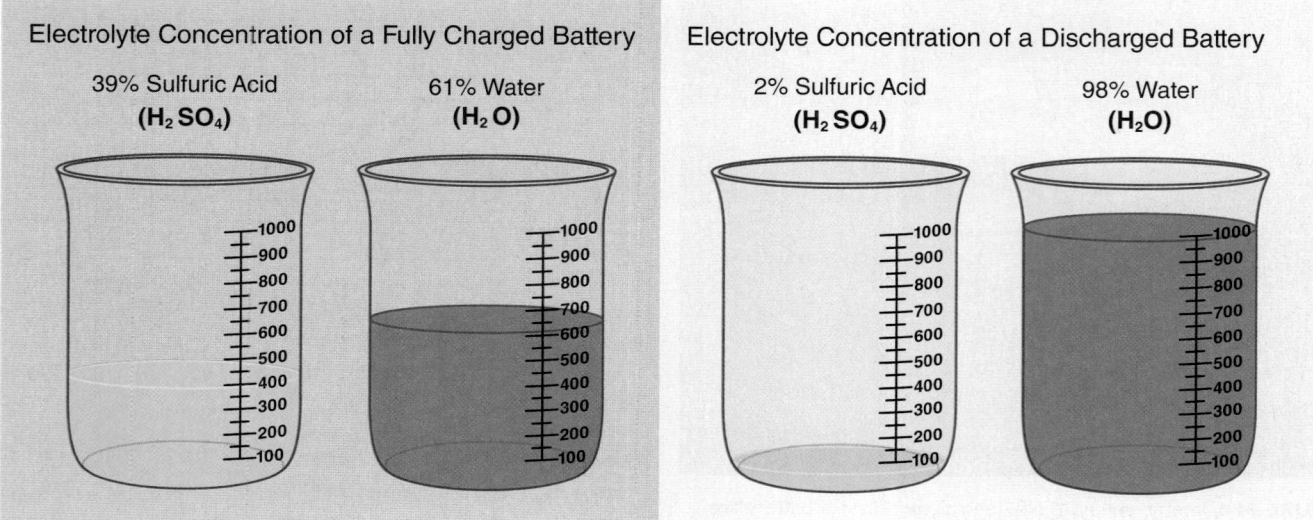

FIGURE 14-11 Electrolyte water and acid mixture for charged and discharged batteries.

thicker plates mean fewer plates compared to a SLI battery with identical dimensions. Thicker plate batteries also have higher resistance during high amperage charging and discharging in comparison to SLI batteries.

Electrolyte

Lead-acid battery electrolyte is a mixture of 36% sulfuric acid and 64% water. The specific gravity of water is 1.000. **Specific gravity (SpGr)** is a measure of a liquid's density compared to water with a SpGr of 1.00. Sulfuric acid has a specific gravity of 1.835, which means it is much heavier than water. Combined, the sulfuric acid and water solution has a specific gravity of 1.265. This makes the electrolyte 1.265 times heavier than plain water. During charging and discharging, the SpGr of the electrolyte changes. When discharging occurs, sulfate from the sulfuric acid leaves the electrolyte to enter both positive and negative plates. Oxygen also leaves the positive plate and combines with hydrogen left in the electrolyte by the departing sulfate. This means the electrolyte has increasingly more water content and less acid during discharge, as illustrated in (**FIGURE 14-11**). The process reverses during charging, when sulfate is electrically driven from the plates and re-enters the electrolyte. Understanding this process helps explain why measuring the SpGr or density of an electrolyte is a good measurement of a battery's state of charge (SOC).

Flooded cell batteries can be manufactured with or without an electrolyte. Dry batteries (without electrolyte) can be stored on the shelf for extended periods without the fear of sulfation and are lighter to transport. For this reason, electrolyte is often only added to the battery at the point of sale.

When the SpGr of battery acid is too low, such as when a battery is discharged, it may freeze in colder climates. An electrolyte that has lost water and is, therefore, over concentrated with acid, can accelerate corrosion of battery grids which binds lead plate material.

It is important to note that sodium bicarbonate (baking soda, not baking powder) is an effective way to neutralize

FIGURE 14-12 Typical hydrometer.

electrolyte spills. Using a power washer, for example, reduces the concentration of acid, but does not neutralize it. Squirting a mixed solution of ammonia and water on spilled battery acid also neutralizes the acid. Water and ammonia also evaporate, leaving no mess to clean up.

A squeeze bulb and float type **hydrometer**, like the one shown in (**FIGURE 14-12**), is an instrument used to measure the density or the SpGr of liquids. It also can be used to measure the SpGr of batteries. A refractometer is an optical device that measures the density of coolant and battery electrolyte. When a drop of liquid is placed beneath the lens of the device, and then held up against a bright light source, a graduated scale in the viewfinder indicates the battery's SpGr. A refractometer is shown in (**FIGURE 14-13**). **TABLE 14-1** indicates the various SpGr and voltage readings for flooded lead-acid batteries. Electronic hydrometers enable faster, temperature-compensated measurement of the battery's state of charge.

FIGURE 14-13 Refractometer.

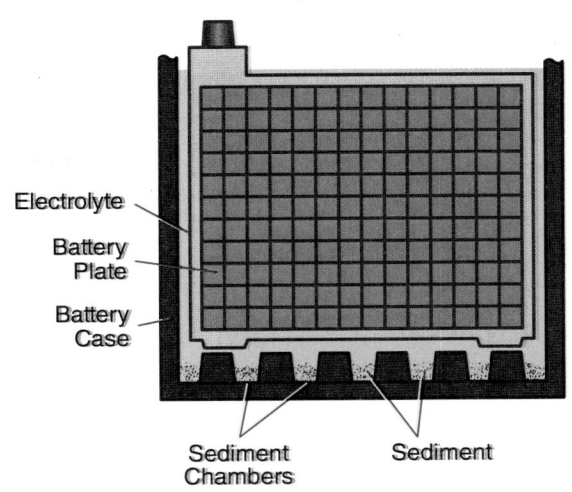

FIGURE 14-14 A typical sediment chamber in a flooded cell battery.

TABLE 14-1 State of Charge as Indicated by Specific Gravity and Voltage Reading for Flooded Cell Batteries*

Open Circuit Voltage	Specific Gravity	Percentage of Charge
12.65 or greater	1.265 (minimum)	100%
12.45	1.225	75%
12.24	1.190	50 %
12.06	1.155	25%
11.89	1.120	0%

*AGM voltages differ. AGM 100% SOC = 12.7 – 12.9 volts

Remember that battery acid is highly corrosive, so when using these devices, properly protect yourself by wearing eye protection, a rubber apron, and acid-resistant gloves, particularly when handling electrolyte.

Battery Cases

The battery case is usually made of polypropylene. Ribbing and irregular features on the outside of the case are designed to increase the length of resistive electrical conductive pathways made when dirt and water accumulate on the case. These accumulations can allow current to drain from the battery posts. Each of the six cells in a 12-volt battery is sealed and electrolytes cannot move between cells. A gap between the plates and the bottom of each cell forms a sediment trap, as illustrated in (**FIGURE 14-14**). The trap collects battery plate material that sheds during operation. Vibration and deeply discharging a battery accelerate the loss of plate material and reduce the battery's capacity. Without the trap, plate material would accumulate and potentially short circuit the plates, leading to rapid self-discharge of the battery.

During charging and discharging, batteries produce hydrogen and oxygen gas caused by the breakdown of water through a process called hydrolysis. These gases require venting and are an explosion hazard. In older flooded batteries, each cell used a cap to vent gases, add water to the electrolyte

level, and permit inspection of the electrolyte with a hydrometer. Low-maintenance batteries use a small, single vent near the top of the battery. Extra electrolyte is added to these batteries to compensate for water loss over the expected lifetime of the battery. Low-maintenance batteries have advanced plate material that result in less water loss than conventional flooded batteries. Nonetheless, a removable plug located at the top of the cell is often still used to allow access to the electrolyte during testing and servicing.

Sizing and Terminal Configuration

Batteries for commercial vehicles are available in a wide variety of sizes. Manufacturers build their batteries to an internationally adopted Battery Council International (BCI) group number. BCI group numbers are established according to the physical case size, terminal placement, terminal type, and polarity. For example, battery terminals used in medium- and heavy-duty commercial applications use a top post, threaded stud, or "L" terminal, with combinations of each of these types. **TABLE 14-2** classifies various heavy-duty commercial battery groups.

Other designations relate to the battery terminal configuration, which refers to the shape and location of the positive and negative terminals on the battery, as illustrated in **FIGURE 14-15**. Different types of battery posts are also available for batteries, including top post, threaded stud, side terminal, or "L" terminal, as well as combinations of each of these types.

▶ TECHNICIAN TIP

To help identification and prevent incorrect connection to post-type batteries, the positive terminal is 1/16" (1.6 mm) larger than the negative terminal (11/16" vs 5/8" [17.5 mm vs 15.9 mm]). Because terminals are only soldered to the cell straps and anchored by the polyethylene case, they are vulnerable to damage if abused. Prying and hammering on posts are common types of abuse that break the seal between the post and case and damage the connection to the plate strap.

TABLE 14-2 Heavy-Duty Commercial Batteries Groups (12-Volt)

BCI Group Size	Length (mm)	Width (mm)	Height (mm)	Length (inches)	Width (inches)	Height (inches)
4D	527	222	250	20 ¾	8 ¾	9 ⅞
6D	527	254	260	20 ¾	10	10 ¼
8D	527	283	250	20 ¾	11 ⅛	9 ⅞
28	261	173	240	10 ⁵⁄₁₆	6 ¹³⁄₁₆	9 ⁷⁄₁₆
29H	334	171	232	13 ⅛	6 ¾	9 ⅛ 10
30H	343	173	235	13 ½	6 ¹³⁄₁₆	9 ¼ 10
31	330	173	240	13	6 ¹³⁄₁₈	9 ⁷⁄₁₆

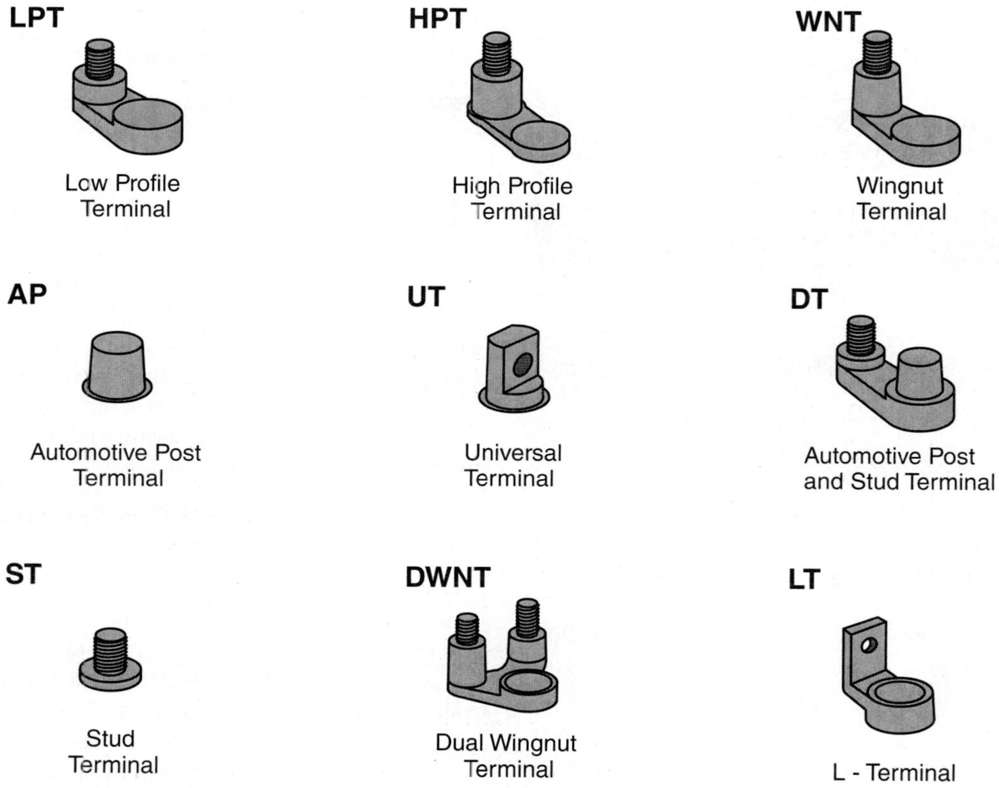

LPT

Low Profile
Terminal

HPT

High Profile
Terminal

WNT

Wingnut
Terminal

AP

Automotive Post
Terminal

UT

Universal
Terminal

DT

Automotive Post
and Stud Terminal

ST

Stud
Terminal

DWNT

Dual Wingnut
Terminal

LT

L - Terminal

FIGURE 14-15 Typical types of layouts that use a lettering system for identification purposes.

Battery Ratings

LO 14-4 Identify and define battery terminology and explain battery ratings.

The **electrical capacity** of a battery is the amount of electrical current a lead-acid battery can supply. Common battery capacity ratings used by North American manufacturers are established by the BCI and the Society of Automotive Engineers (SAE). Technicians encounter other rating systems, depending on the origin of the vehicle and while using some testing equipment, including:

- Japanese Industrial Standard (JIS)
- EN (European Norms) Standard

- DIN (Deutsches Institut für Normung)
- IEC (International Electrotechnical Commission) Standard

There are several methods used to rate lead-acid battery capacity. The three most common are cold-cranking amps (CCA), cranking amps (CA), and reserve capacity (RC). **Cold-cranking amps (CCA)** is a measurement of battery capacity, in amps, that a battery can deliver for 30 seconds while maintaining a voltage of 1.2 volts per cell (7.2 volts for a 12-volt battery) or higher at 0°F (−18°C) (**FIGURE 14-16**). **Cranking amps (CA)** measure the same thing, but at a higher temperature: 32°F (0°C). A 500-CCA battery has about 20% more capacity than a 500-CA battery.

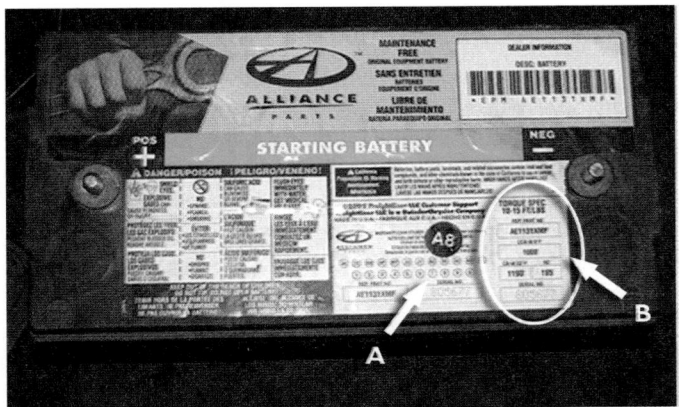

FIGURE 14-16 Battery ratings are indicated on battery label. **A.** Date code. **B.** Battery ratings CCA, CA, and RC.

Reserve capacity (RC) is the length of time, in minutes, a battery can be discharged under a specified load of 25 amps at 80°F (26.6°C) before battery cell voltage drops below 1.75 volts per cell (10.5 volts for a 12-volt battery). This measure is modeled on estimates of how long an automobile could be driven after an alternator fails, with electrical loads from headlights and other loads, before the ignition system fails.

Amp-hour is a measure of a battery's capacity. Specifically, it is a measure of how much amperage a battery can continually supply over a 20-hour period without the battery voltage falling below 10.5 volts. Amp-hour is measured at 80°F (26.6°C)—the temperature at which lead-acid batteries perform best. A battery with a 200 amp-hour rating delivers 10 amps continually for 20 hours (20 hours × 10 amps). This is an important rating when selecting a deep-cycle battery.

Early commercial vehicles with minimal electrical loads used 6-volt batteries for a 6-volt electrical system. In the 1950s, 12-volt systems and batteries became widely used. Systems using 24-volts are made from combinations of 12-volt batteries connected in series to produce 24 volts. Operating with higher voltages means less amperage flows through electrical circuits and connections, yet maintains the same power levels (Remember Power (Watts) = Volts × Amperage). With less amperage travelling through conductors, the reliability of the vehicle's electrical system improves because connections and cables do not heat nearly as much from high amperage flow. The size of components and wire diameters are reduced as well.

Multiple-Battery Configurations

Batteries can be connected to supply either more amperage or more voltage. Diesel engines, which require more cranking torque, either connect batteries in parallel, like those illustrated in **FIGURE 14-17** to supply more cranking amperage, or in series to supply higher voltage. For example, if two 600-CCA 12-volt batteries were connected in parallel, the batteries' potential output would be 1,200 CCA at 12 volts. If the batteries are connected in series, the batteries' voltage output is added together, even though the cranking amperage remains the same. That means, if two 600-CCA 12-volt batteries are connected in series, the batteries' potential output is 600 CCA at 24 volts.

Multiple Battery Selection

Factors that determine the battery rating required for a vehicle include the current needed for key-off loads, operating electrical accessories, the engine type (diesel or spark ignited), the engine size, and climate conditions under which equipment must operate.

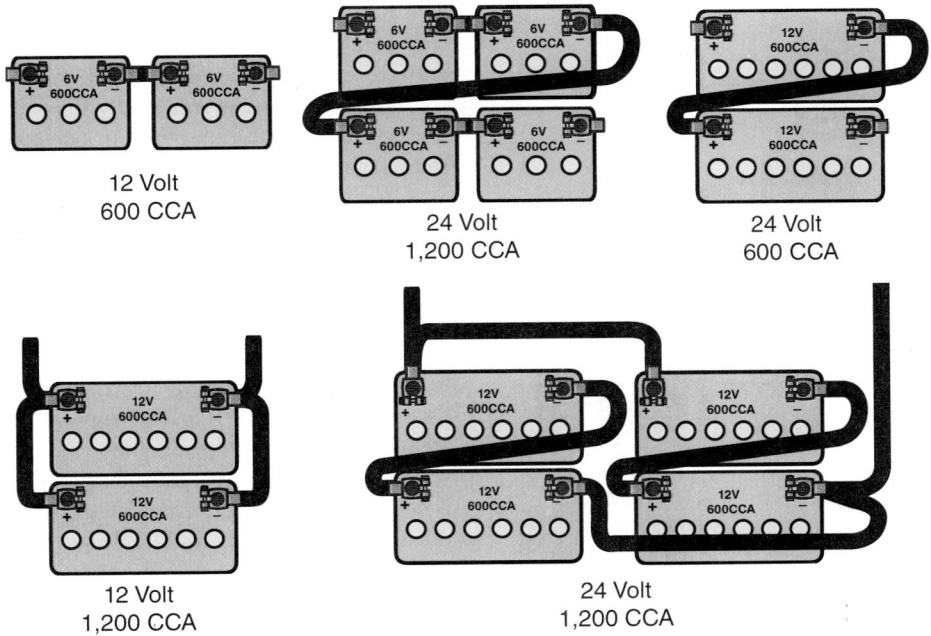

FIGURE 14-17 Typical battery bank configurations.

In cold weather, battery power drops drastically because the electrolyte thickens and cold temperatures slow chemical activity inside the battery. In colder weather, engines are also harder to crank due to increased resistance from oil thickening. It is calculated that engine resistance increases between 50% to 250% in the winter compared to the summer, as illustrated in **FIGURE 14-18**. Simultaneously, cold weather slows chemical reactions inside the battery, and output current can drop as much as 75%. As batteries age, their capacity drops too.

▶ TECHNICIAN TIP

Equipment with excessive battery capacity (too many CCAs) can lead to premature failure of the starter motor and starter drive due to excessively high torque. Excessive battery CCA increases the amperage through cables, connections, and starter circuit components, causing damage from resistance heating. However, inadequate battery capacity shortens battery life from deep discharging. Equipment may even fail to start in cold weather or as batteries age. Starter motors, cables, and circuits can be damaged from low-voltage, high-amperage burn-out caused by undersized batteries.

BCI estimates diesel engines require 220% to 300% more battery power than a similar gasoline engine. A typical 15L diesel engine today uses approximately 10,000 watts of current (or close to 12 horsepower) during cranking, and initially needs 15,000 watts, or approximately 20 horsepower. Vehicle manufacturers make recommendations about the capacity of batteries. The CCA rating of the battery is the most important rating considered when selecting batteries. Although selecting a battery with excessive current capacity might seem like a good idea, it is not. Extra capacity is expensive and high amperage capacity available from batteries can lead to premature starter

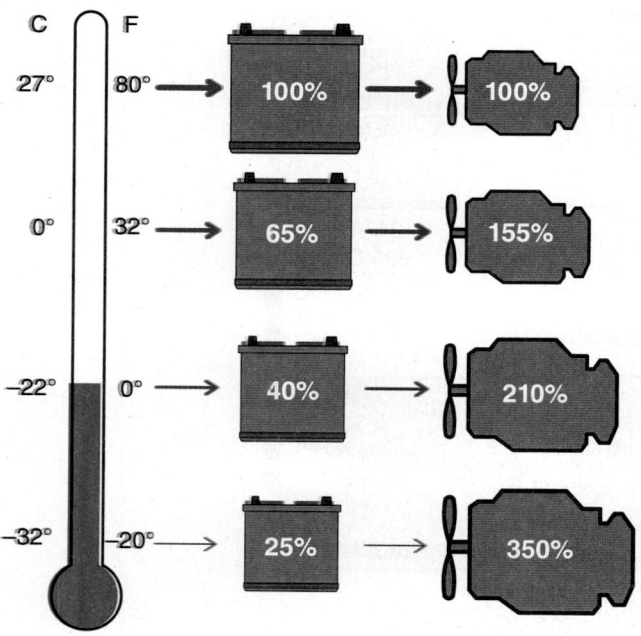

FIGURE 14-18 As temperature drops, engine rotation resistance increases, and battery chemical reactions slow.

drive failure from excessive torque and damage from excessive amperage through starting circuit connections.

Equipment manufacturers use several variables when calculating battery capacity, but the most significant one is battery voltage at the end of engine cranking. Generally, batteries are sized to ensure a minimum cranking voltage of no less than 10.5 volts after three consecutive cranking periods of 30 seconds with a two-minute cool-down period between each cranking period.

Internal Resistance of Batteries

All electrical devices have internal resistance—even batteries. Not all battery types have the same internal resistance, however. A battery's internal resistance depends on the types of materials used to make the plates and the chemical composition of the electrolyte. A battery's internal resistance determines how quickly a battery can be charged or discharged.

Batteries with a relatively low internal resistance, such as a standard lead-acid battery, can be charged quickly, and they can also be discharged quickly to supply a lot of current over a short period of time. This makes them ideal for use in vehicles as starter batteries because they can supply the high discharge current required by the starter motor to start the vehicle. Batteries are available with a lower internal resistance than that of a lead-acid battery. These include newer lithium batteries now being used in battery banks for electric and hybrid vehicles. These types of batteries are more expensive than the standard lead-acid battery, and their lower internal resistance is generally not needed for everyday starter motor applications.

Battery Charging and Discharging Cycle

Battery plates are made of two different compositions of lead fabricated from paste bonded to lead alloy grids (**FIGURE 14-19**). The negative plate uses lead (Pb) and the positive plate uses lead peroxide (PbO_2). Antimony, calcium, or other metals are alloyed with the lead grid material to minimize corrosion of the lead by acidic electrolyte. Because the plates are made of dissimilar metals, the addition of electrolyte causes galvanic reactions in each cell.

In a fully charged condition, the positive plate material is predominantly lead peroxide, and the negative plate is sponge lead. The composition of the electrolyte is 64% water and 36% sulfuric acid. Chemical interactions between the plates and electrolyte strip electrons from the positive plate and add electrons to the negative plate. That produces a 12.6-volt difference between the battery terminals. A lead-acid battery remains in this condition without a load applied. However, due to activity of chemical reactions, a slow rate of self-discharge occurs, which eventually discharges the battery. This self-discharge rate is dependent on temperature and the selection of materials used during manufacturing. In hot climates, complete self-discharge is measured in weeks. Cold slows down chemical reactions, so the self-discharge rate can take almost two years in colder climates.

When a load is applied across the battery, electrons moving from the negative to the positive terminal accelerate galvanic

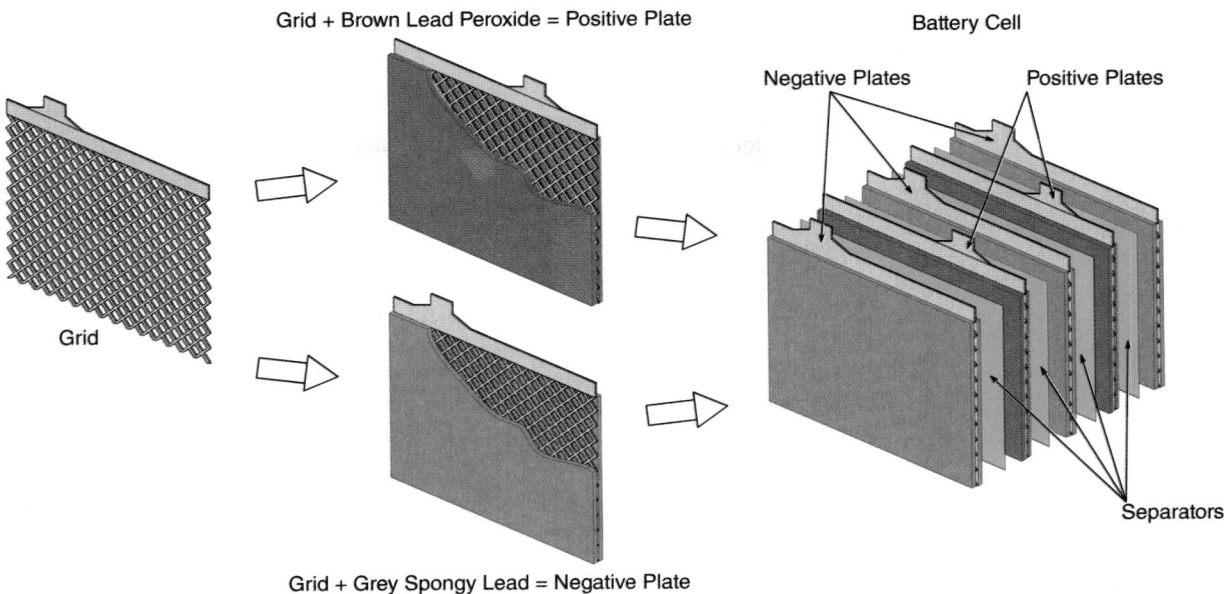

Grid + Brown Lead Peroxide = Positive Plate

Battery Cell

Negative Plates   Positive Plates

Grid

Separators

Grid + Grey Spongy Lead = Negative Plate

FIGURE 14-19 Battery grids made of lead alloys are the foundation for the battery cell. Grids have a lead paste baked onto the support mesh to form a positive or negative plate.

reactions. This process is illustrated in **FIGURE 14-20A**. Both plates and the electrolyte composition change because of electron movement. Oxygen atoms in the positive plate move into the electrolyte, while the sulfate part of the acid moves into the positive plate, changing the cell from lead peroxide (PbO_2) to lead sulfate ($PbSO_4$). On the negative plate, sulfate also moves into the plate material, forming lead sulfate. The electrolyte becomes less acidic and turns to water as sulfate leaves and hydrogen in the electrolyte combines with oxygen driven from the positive plate.

Galvanic reaction in a battery stops under two circumstances. One is if the battery has the electrical load removed. Opening circuits connected to the battery halts chemical reactions producing movement of electrons from one battery terminal to the other. Electron movement also stops when the positive and negative plates become saturated with sulfate when the battery is fully discharged, in a process called **sulfation**. Because the plates are made of identical material when the charge is depleted, no further electron movement takes place.

When charging a lead-acid battery, the chemical reactions used to produce current are reversed, restoring the plate and electrolyte to its charged condition (**FIGURE 14-20B**). While charging, sulfate is driven from both plates back into the electrolyte. Oxygen in the electrolyte recombines with the lead in the positive plate.

The chemical action to reverse plate sulfation is accomplished by connecting a charger or an alternator (DC current), stripping the positive post of electrons and forcing

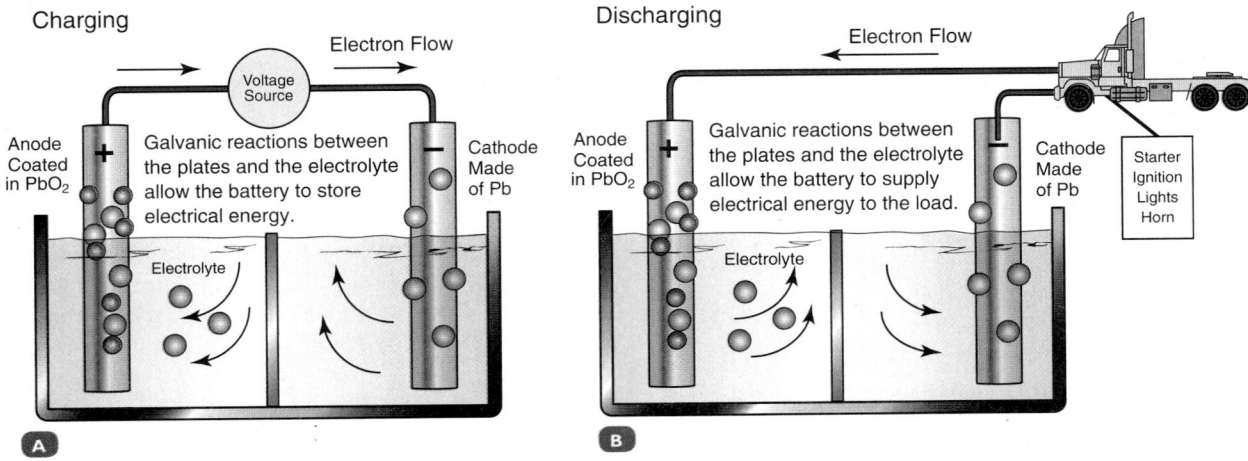

Charging

Electron Flow

Anode Coated in PbO_2

Voltage Source

Galvanic reactions between the plates and the electrolyte allow the battery to store electrical energy.

Cathode Made of Pb

Electrolyte

Discharging

Electron Flow

Anode Coated in PbO_2

Galvanic reactions between the plates and the electrolyte allow the battery to supply electrical energy to the load.

Cathode Made of Pb

Starter Ignition Lights Horn

Electrolyte

A

B

FIGURE 14-20 A. Charging cycle. **B.** Discharge cycle.

them back into the negative terminal. This means the positive terminal is made more positively charged and the negative terminal more negatively charged. Charging voltage needs to be sufficiently high enough to overcome a battery's natural resistance to current flow. Most charging systems maintain a maximum charging voltage of approximately 0.5 volts above battery voltage. This explains why the charging system set point for most 12.6-volt batteries is approximately 14.1 volts. Higher charging voltages used by battery chargers are able to push more current into the battery at a higher amperage.

Plate Sulfation

Sulfate is driven off battery plates when charging, as shown in (**FIGURE 14-21**). However, if a battery is left in a discharged state for a long period of time, continually undercharged, or left partially charged, the soft sulfate turns to a hardened crystalline form, as shown in (**FIGURE 14-22**). Hard sulfate cannot be driven from the plates.

This means the battery cannot be recharged and the remaining active plate material develops a high resistance to charging. The latest innovation to lead-acid battery technology incorporates black-carbon graphite foam into the plate paste to prevent sulfation damage. Graphite-foam carbon increases plate strength and surface area, which translates into greater power density and durability.

Battery Gassing

During charging and discharging, water (H_2O) in the electrolyte is broken apart into its constituent hydrogen and oxygen. This process, called **electrolysis**, releases both gases. Note: Hydrogen gas released during charging and discharging is explosive, and even higher explosive forces are possible when mixed with oxygen. Battery electrolyte is depleted through the loss of water by electrolysis. If battery electrolyte is too low, the plates dry out, and the increased acid concentration of electrolyte permanently damages the grids. Severe **gassing** occurs when cell charging voltage is

pushed beyond 2.4 volts or severe discharge takes place, such as when a wrench or piece of metal is laid across battery terminals.

Low- and No-Maintenance Batteries

LO 14-5 Identify and describe the construction details and operating characteristics of low- and no-maintenance batteries.

The use of antimony alloy in the plate grids of conventional flooded battery technology minimizes grid corrosion and allows these batteries to accept up to 10 times more overcharging current than newer low- or no-maintenance batteries. Unfortunately, antimony-alloyed grids cause excessive gassing, resulting in substantial water loss. No- or low-maintenance battery technology solves that problem.

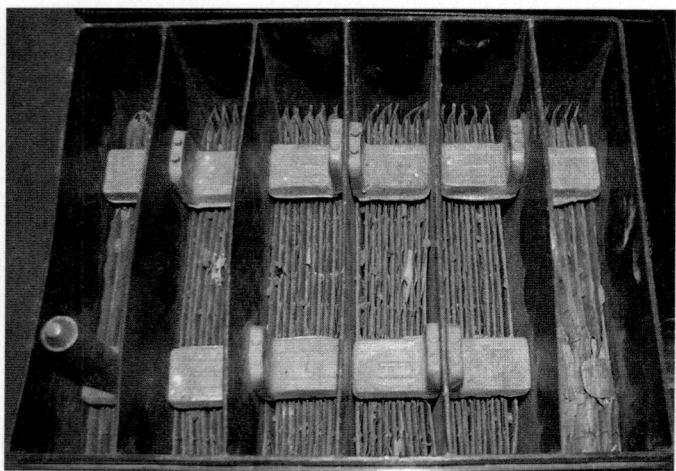

FIGURE 14-21 Normal plate condition.

FIGURE 14-22 Sulfated plates.

FIGURE 14-23 The caps on the top of this conventional lead-acid low-maintenance battery are removable to check the condition of electrolyte.

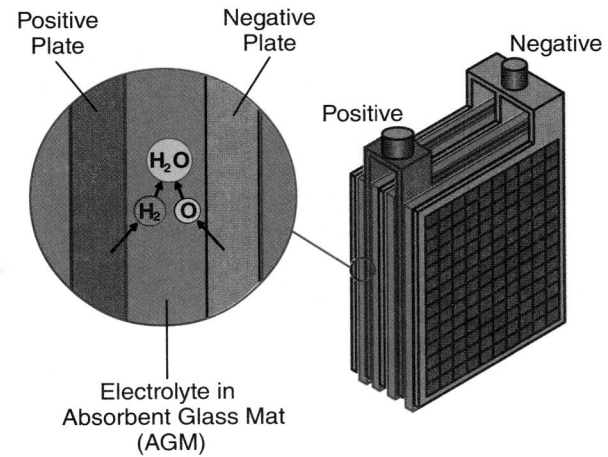

FIGURE 14-24 AGM batteries trap and recombine oxygen and hydrogen gases inside the glass mat next to the plates.

Introduced in the middle 1970s, no- and low-maintenance batteries reduce or eliminate the antimony content in grids. Calcium is used primarily now to replace antimony, but barium, cadmium, or strontium are also used. No-maintenance batteries eliminate all the antimony, whereas low-maintenance batteries contain a reduced level of antimony content (approximately 2%). No- and low-maintenance batteries still require venting and need a large electrolyte reserve area above the plates to compensate for some water loss.

Another recent advance in grid composition involves the addition of silver into the calcium-lead alloy. Silver alloy has demonstrated a very high resistance to grid growth and corrosion. Thus, silver alloy significantly lengthens battery life in high heat and severe service conditions.

The advantages of low- or no-maintenance batteries include:

- Less water usage
- Less grid corrosion
- Less gassing
- Lower self-discharge rate
- Less terminal corrosion because less corrosive gas is emitted from the vents

The disadvantages of low- and no-maintenance batteries include:

- A lower electrical reserve capacity
- Often a shorter life expectancy
- Grid growth/expansion when exposed to high temperatures
- More quickly discharged by parasitic losses
- Difficulty accepting a boost when completely discharged

Although no-maintenance batteries contain a vent located beneath the top cover, the battery tops are completely sealed. Delco, which introduced the first no-maintenance battery, uses a built-in hydrometer that has colored balls. These balls rise or fall in the electrolyte, depending on the electrolyte density, thereby providing an indication of the state of charge. Due to the unique plate-grid composition, some oxygen and hydrogen

ions are needed in the cell electrolyte before they can be charged. To boost these batteries from a completely discharged state, a small charge rate of just a few amps is recommended for about 10 minutes to begin the hydrolytic process of breaking water into hydrogen and oxygen. After that, the batteries can receive a higher rate of charge.

Low-maintenance batteries may look completely sealed, but they usually have a means of adding water, if required. Often, the caps are concealed under a plastic cover that is removed to reveal cell caps that can be unscrewed (**FIGURE 14-23**).

The latest and most advanced commercial vehicle battery technology are **absorbed glass mat (AGM) batteries**. AGM's, also called Valve Regulated Lead Acid batteries (VRLA's), provide improved safety, efficiency, and durability over existing battery types. The electrolyte is absorbed into a fine glass mat, as shown in **FIGURE 14-24**, preventing it from sloshing or separating into layers of heavier acid and water. The fiber first helps by enhancing gas recombination, rather than simply venting gas to the atmosphere and lowering electrolyte levels. AGM material also possesses low electrical resistance. As a result, AGM-type batteries can deliver more cranking amperage and absorb up to 40% more charging current than conventional lead-acid batteries, leading to faster charging.

Higher open-circuit cell voltage in a battery with a 100% charge state is between 12.7 and 12.9 volts. Because there is little ability for the cells to accommodate extra gas volume when charging, these batteries are very sensitive to damage from overcharging by higher charging voltage accompanying excessive charging amperage. Microcontroller operated or "smart-type" chargers are mandatory for AGM batteries to prevent damage. Service topics associated with VRLA or AGM batteries are covered in the Advanced Battery Technologies and Servicing Commercial Vehicle Batteries chapters.

Wrap-Up

Ready for Review

▶ There are two types of batteries. Primary batteries cannot be recharged; secondary batteries are rechargeable.

▶ Secondary batteries operate using the principles of galvanic reaction and are the most practical for use in commercial vehicle applications.

▶ Through a galvanic reaction, electricity is produced when two dissimilar metals are placed in an electrolyte.

▶ Batteries have traditionally been used in heavy vehicles to provide starting current and operate electrical accessories if the engine is not running.

▶ Batteries are classified by use, application, and chemistry used within the battery. Although lead-acid batteries are most prevalent, hybrid-drive vehicles also make use of nickel-metal hydride and lithium batteries.

▶ Lead-acid batteries deliver high rates of current with a higher tolerance for physical and electrical abuse compared to other battery technology. These batteries hold a charge well and when stored dry—without electrolyte—the shelf life is indefinite.

▶ Regardless of battery construction, all batteries have the same basic components: case, terminals, plates, cell straps, and electrolyte.

▶ A starting-lighting-ignition battery can supply very high discharge currents while maintaining a high voltage, which is useful when cold starting. A lead-acid battery gives high power output for its compact size, and it is rechargeable.

▶ Starting, lighting, and ignition batteries (SLI) are designed for a single short-duration deep discharge during engine cranking. Deep-cycle batteries provide lower amperage current continually for electrical devices and accessories.

▶ Lead-acid batteries can be manufactured with electrolyte or dry. Dry batteries can be stored on the shelf for extended periods without the fear of sulfation and are lighter to transport.

▶ During charging and discharging, batteries produce hydrogen and oxygen gas caused by the breakdown of water through a process called hydrolysis. These gases require venting and are an explosion hazard.

▶ Batteries can be configured into battery banks in cases where higher cranking amperage or higher-voltage batteries are required.

▶ Battery temperature plays an important role in the performance of a battery and lead-acid batteries have ideal operating temperature range. A battery's internal resistance depends on the types of materials used to make the plates and the chemical composition of the electrolyte. A battery's internal resistance determines how quickly a battery can be charged or discharged.

▶ Sulfation takes place when a battery is left in a discharged or only partially charged condition long enough for sulfate to permanently bond to the plates.

▶ Sulfate originates from the sulfuric acid in electrolyte that enters the plates when the battery is discharging. Sulfate is originally soft but becomes a hardened crystal over time.

Key Terms

Absorbed Glass Mat (AGM) battery A battery in which electrolyte is absorbed in a fine glass mat that prevents the solution from sloshing or separating into layers of heavier acid and water.

amp-hour A measure of how much amperage a battery can continually supply over a 20-hour period before the battery voltage falling below 10.5 volts.

Cold-Cranking Amps (CCA) A measurement of the load, in amps, that a battery can deliver for 30 seconds while maintaining a voltage of 1.2 volts per cell (7.2 volts for a 12-volt battery) or higher at 0°F (−18°C).

Cranking Amps (CA) A measurement of the load, in amps, that a battery can deliver for 30 seconds while maintaining a voltage of 1.2 volts per cell (7.2 volts for a 12-volt battery) or higher at 32°F (0°C).

deep-cycle battery A battery used to deliver a lower, steady level of power for a much longer time.

electrical capacity The amount of electrical current a lead-acid battery can supply measured in cranking amps or cold cranking amp capacity.

electrolysis The use of electricity to break down water into hydrogen and oxygen gases.

electrolyte An electrically conductive solution.

flooded lead-acid battery A lead-acid battery in which the plates are immersed in a water–acid electrolyte solution.

galvanic reaction A chemical reaction that produces electricity when two dissimilar metals are placed in an electrolyte.

gassing A situation that occurs when overcharging or rapid charging causes some gas to escape from the battery.

hydrometer An instrument used to measure the specific gravity of liquids.

key-off electrical loads Unwanted drain on the vehicle battery when the vehicle is off; also called *parasitic draw*.

parasitic draw Unwanted drain on the vehicle battery when the vehicle is off; also called *key-off electrical load*.

primary battery A battery in which chemical reactions are not reversible and the battery cannot be recharged.

reserve capacity The time, in minutes, that a new, fully charged battery at 80°F (26.6°C) supplies a constant load of 25 amps without its voltage dropping below 10.5 volts for a 12-volt battery.

sealed lead-acid (SLA) battery A battery that does not have a liquid electrolyte nor requires the addition of water; also called a *valve-regulated lead-acid battery (VRLA)* or *recombinant battery*.

secondary battery A rechargeable battery.

Specific Gravity (SpGr) A measurement of the density of a substance.

Starting, Lighting, and Ignition (SLI) battery A battery designed for one, short-duration, deep discharge of up to 50% depth of discharge (DOD) during engine cranking.

sulfation A chemical reaction that results in the soft sulfate turning to a hardened crystalline form that cannot be driven from the plates in the battery.

traction battery A rechargeable battery used for propulsion in hybrid electric vehicles.

Valve-Regulated Lead–Acid (VRLA) battery A type of sealed lead-acid battery used in heavy-duty equipment; it does not require the addition of water; also called a *sealed lead-acid battery (SLA) or recombinant battery*.

Review Questions

1. Battery electrolyte is a mixture of water and:
   a. Sulfate
   b. Lead sulfate
   c. Sulfuric acid
   d. Ammonia
2. What is the positive plate material made of in a discharged battery?
   a. Lead peroxide
   b. Lead sulfate
   c. Sponge lead
   d. Hydrogen dioxide
3. Consider three 12-volt 500 CCA batteries connected in series. What is the available voltage and amperage of the combined batteries?
   a. 12 volts 1,500 amps
   b. 36 volts 500 amps
   c. 12 volts 500 amps
   d. 24 volts 1,000 amps
4. Which of the following is the open-circuit voltage (when no electrical loads are connected) of a battery between 50% to 75% charge?
   a. 12 volts
   b. 12.6 volts
   c. 7.3 volts
   d. 12.4 volts
5. Which of the following procedures can best neutralize battery acid?
   a. Applying baking soda to the acid
   b. Applying baking powder to the acid
   c. Power washing the acid
   d. Diluting the acid with kerosene or diesel fuel
6. The two gases produced by a battery during charging and discharging are:
   a. Carbon dioxide and hydrogen
   b. Carbon monoxide and hydrogen
   c. Oxygen and hydrogen
   d. Nitrogen and hydrogen
7. A maintenance-free or VRLA battery contains almost none of the following alloy in its plate grid material:
   a. Calcium
   b. Barium
   c. Antimony
   d. Strontium
8. A battery that is left in a discharged state for a long period of time becomes:
   a. Cycled
   b. Shorted
   c. Sulfated
   d. Overheated
9. What battery measurement is performed when measuring the electrolyte's specific gravity?
   a. The open-circuit voltage
   b. The battery capacity
   c. The battery's state of charge
   d. The battery's potential cranking amperage
10. Which method of plate construction is used in a SLI-type battery?
    a. Cells with many thin, highly resistive plates
    b. Cells with thicker, low-resistance plates
    c. Cells with thinner, low-resistance plates
    d. Cells with thicker, high-resistance plate

ASE Technician A/Technician B Style Questions

1. While observing a truck with an alternator cable that is burnt and has many fuses and fusible links blown, Technician A says that the battery was connected in reverse polarity. Technician B says that batteries were likely deeply discharged and charged at a high current rate. Who is correct?
   a. Technician A
   b. Technician B
   c. Both Technician A and Technician B
   d. Neither Technician A nor Technician B
2. Technician A says that a spiral cell (Optima battery) is not considered a sealed lead-acid (SLA) battery. Technician B says that an absorbed glass mat (AGM) battery is not considered a SLA battery. Who is correct?
   a. Technician A
   b. Technician B
   c. Both Technician A and Technician B
   d. Neither Technician A nor Technician B
3. Technician A says that a fully charged 12-volt battery is 12 volts. Technician B says that a battery with a 50% state of charge has close to 6 volts when no electrical loads are connected. Who is correct?
   a. Technician A
   b. Technician B
   c. Both Technician A and Technician B
   d. Neither Technician A nor Technician B

4. Technician A says that the primary difference between deep-cycle batteries and SLI is the thickness of the plates. Technician B says that deeply discharging SLI batteries dramatically shortens their service life. Who is correct?
   a. Technician A
   b. Technician B
   c. Both Technician A and Technician B
   d. Neither Technician A nor Technician B
5. Technician A says that lead-acid battery electrolyte is a mixture of 64% sulfuric acid and 36% water. Technician B says that sulfuric acid has a specific gravity of 1.835, which means it is much heavier than water. Who is correct?
   a. Technician A
   b. Technician B
   c. Both Technician A and Technician B
   d. Neither Technician A nor Technician B
6. Technician A says that the battery case is usually made of polypropylene with ribbing and irregular features to reduce the amount of current leakage across the battery surface. Technician B says that ribbing and irregular features on the outside of the case add to the strength of the battery and make it sturdier. Who is correct?
   a. Technician A
   b. Technician B
   c. Both Technician A and Technician B
   d. Neither Technician A nor Technician B
7. Technician A says that battery plates are made of two different compositions of lead that are fabricated from paste and bonded to lead-alloy grids. Technician B says that the negative plate uses lead peroxide (PbO_2) and the positive plate uses lead (Pb). Who is correct?
   a. Technician A
   b. Technician B

   c. Both Technician A and Technician B
   d. Neither Technician A nor Technician B
8. Technician A says that both soft and hard sulfate can be driven from the plates, bringing the battery back into service. Technician B says that leaving a battery in a state of discharge for a long time hardens and prevents sulfate from being driven from the plates. Who is correct?
   a. Technician A
   b. Technician B
   c. Both Technician A and Technician B
   d. Neither Technician A nor Technician B
9. Technician A says that during charging and discharging, water in the electrolyte is broken apart into its constituent hydrogen and oxygen through a process called electrolysis. Technician B says if battery electrolyte is too low, the plates dry out, and the increased acid concentration of electrolyte permanently damages the grids. Who is correct?
   a. Technician A
   b. Technician B
   c. Both Technician A and Technician B
   d. Neither Technician A nor Technician B
10. Technician A says that hydrogen and oxygen gasses produced when charging and discharging AGM batteries can cause an explosion if a spark is produced at the battery terminal when boosting. Technician B says that the AGM battery can deliver more cranking amperage and absorb more charging current than conventional lead-acid batteries. Who is correct?
    a. Technician A
    b. Technician B
    c. Both Technician A and Technician B
    d. Neither Technician A nor Technician B

CHAPTER 15

Advanced Battery Technologies

Learning Objectives

After reading this chapter, you will be able to:

- **LO 15-1** Identify and describe the features of nickel-metal hydride batteries.
- **LO 15-2** Identify and describe the types, construction, operation, and safety practices associated with lithium-ion batteries.
- **LO 15-3** Describe the types, advantages, construction features, and electrical characteristics of valve-regulated lead-acid batteries.

- **LO 15-4** Describe the operation and applications of ultra-capacitors for medium- and heavy-duty commercial vehicles.
- **LO 15-5** Identify and explain the operation of battery isolators, low voltage disconnect, charge equalizers, and battery-management systems.
- **LO 15-6** Identify the functions of a battery-management system used by a hybrid-electric drive system.

You Are the Technician

Maintaining a fleet of trucks, buses, and other diesel-powered machinery in an extreme winter climate has its own unique challenges. One of the problems you are encountering is hard starting of engines on cold winter mornings and nights, when even hot engines drop to ambient temperature in just a couple of hours. A significant amount of downtime, labor, and associated expense is lost to jump-starting vehicles and equipment—not to mention the cost of battery replacements.

One solution you've tried is the use of electric battery warmers. You have also insulated battery boxes with high-density polyurethane foam to try and keep battery temperature warmer during the shutdown periods. Your reasoning is that since battery temperatures increase when batteries are charging, retaining some of that heat improves starting capabilities after several hours. Consider the following questions as you investigate other strategies to reduce the aggravation level and cost of service for no-start conditions due to cold.

1. What is the purpose of keeping batteries warm?
2. List and explain several ways an ultra-capacitor battery helps promote faster starter start-up.
3. Which battery technology is least affected by cold temperatures?

Introduction

The demand for advanced battery technology in commercial vehicles is growing. Fuel economy and emission legislation are driving the change to electric and hybrid powertrains, while the economics of operating electric and hybrid vehicles is becoming more appealing with technological advancements, particularly in reducing the cost and increasing the efficiency of batteries. One example where efficiency gains promise significant return on investment is with the start-stop nature of refuse/garbage truck operations. These vehicles are some of the least energy-efficient but fit an operating pattern that is ideal for using electric traction motors capable of regenerative braking. Not only do the increasingly popular battery electric vehicles (BEV's) and hybrid-electric vehicles (HEV's) require advanced batteries, heavy-duty commercial vehicles also have a greater need for electrical storage capacity to run accessories. Several key factors are at play in determining which application of a variety of battery technologies to use on commercial vehicles, including:

- Energy density—expressed in Watt-hour per kilogram (Wh/kg) and Watt-hour per liter (Wh/l) (**FIGURE 15-1**)
- Energy efficiency—the ability to convert charging current into storage capacity

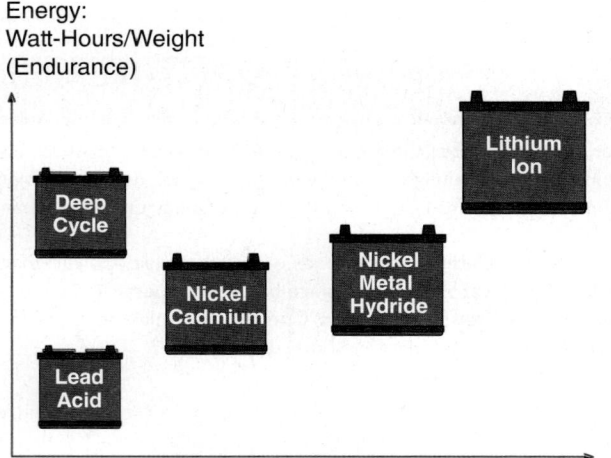

FIGURE 15-1 Comparing the energy density of various battery technologies. Lithium-ion produces the greatest amount of energy for the longest time per kilogram of weight.

- Life span—measured by the number of charge/discharge cycles as a function of depth of discharge (DOD)
- The state of charge window—the availability of usable battery voltage
- Cost in dollars per kilowatt-hour (kWh)

The major advanced battery technologies used in heavy-duty commercial vehicles are nickel–metal hydride (NiMH), lithium-ion, and lead-acid. Each technology has distinct capabilities, which is discussed in this section. **TABLE 15-1** compares the capacities of different battery types.

Nickel–Metal Hydride Battery (NiMH)

LO 15-1 Identify and describe the features of nickel-metal hydride batteries.

Nickel–metal hydride (NiMH) batteries are used not only in consumer electronics, but are also a preferred battery chemistry for hybrid-drive vehicles. That is because NiMH batteries are relatively lightweight and have high power output and long life expectancy. Because they approach the weight of lithium batteries, but are much less expensive than lithium batteries, the greatest number of hybrid vehicles have used NiMH batteries. For example, Allison Ev heavy-duty hybrid buses use these, as well as many older automotive electric-hybrid systems from Ford and Toyota. Toyota began switching to lighter lithium batteries only in 2016 in some of its heavier car models to help reduce overall weight. NiMH batteries provide twice the energy storage of lead-acid by weight, but only a little more than half the power density and an output voltage of 1.2 volts/cell, compared to 2.1 volts/cell for lead-acid batteries. As illustrated in (**FIGURE 15-2**), NiMH uses electrodes made from two different alloys of nickel metal. The negative electrode is formed from a nickel metal hydroxide ($NiOH_2$), which is an unusual alloy belonging to the chemical family of rare earth metals. This important electrochemical material has a unique ability to absorb hydrogen. The positive electrode is made of nickel oxide (NiO). The electrolyte is composed of potassium hydroxide (KOH), which is a strong alkaline substance when mixed with water. Potassium hydroxide is used because it can produce more pure hydrogen than other types of electrolytes. The liquid electrolyte produces no sediment and lowers the battery's freezing temperature. It also allows the nickel alloy plates to remain clean.

TABLE 15-1 Comparison of Properties for Different Battery Chemistries

Range			Energy Density		
Battery Type	Voltage/cell	Cost Watt/hour	Watt-hour/kg	Joules/kg	Watt-hour/liter
Lead–acid	2.1 volts	Lowest = 1	41	146,000	100
NiMH	1.2 volts	6 times lead-acid	95	340,000	300
Li–ion	~ 4.0 volts	25 times lead-acid	128	460,000	230
Ultra-capacitors	~ 2-3 volts	4–5 times lead-acid	30–60	–	–
Diesel Fuel	–	–	–	–	10,942

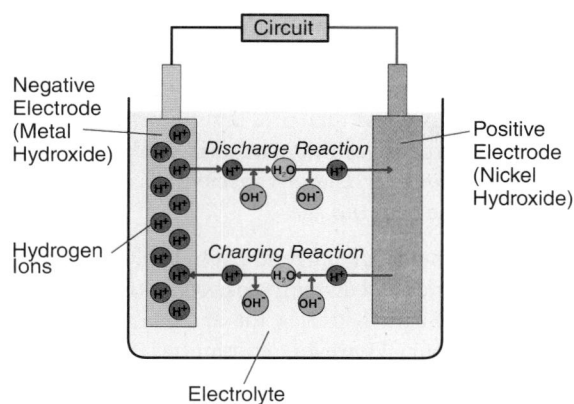

FIGURE 15-2 Chemical reactions in a NiMH-type battery.

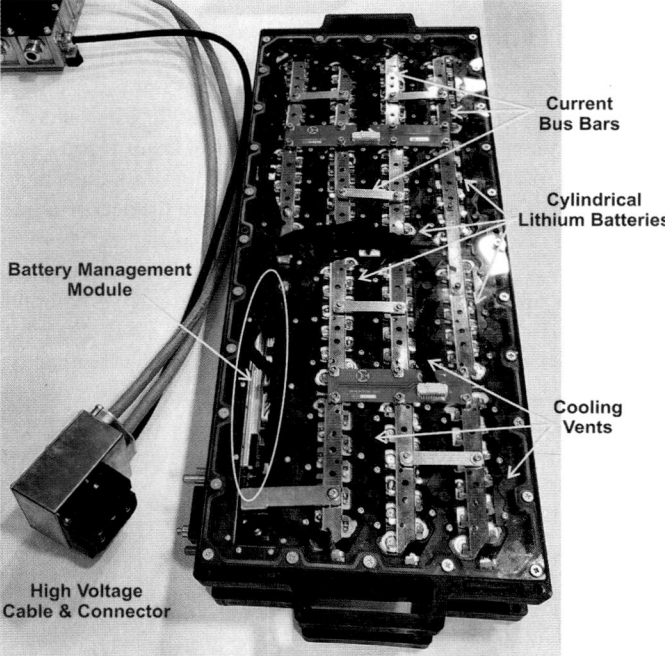

FIGURE 15-3 A water cooled lithium-ion battery module with a battery management control module.

Lithium-Ion Battery Applications

LO 15-2 Identify and describe the types, construction, operation, and safety practices associated with lithium-ion batteries.

Lithium-ion (Li-ion) batteries were developed for commercial use in the early 1990s. Since then, they have been used in laptops, cell phones, and other consumer electronic devices. Lithium-ion batteries used in commercial hybrid vehicles are secondary batteries and are not the same as small disposable, primary-type lithium batteries, which contain metallic lithium. Lithium batteries are best adapted to store energy recovered by regenerative vehicle braking and power traction motors in hybrid-electric and electric vehicles because they can absorb, store, and discharge current more efficiently than any other type of battery. Recently available third-generation lithium batteries can also supply more cold-cranking amperage than lead-acid batteries. The transition to 48-volt electrical systems by mild-hybrid

systems with electric stop-start capabilities are expected to make 48-volt lithium batteries even more common (**FIGURE 15-3**). A 48-volt electrical system architecture and batteries is needed to supply energy to smaller electric motors integrated into the alternator or in series with the engines. Newly developed electrically heated catalysts for diesel engines enables hybridization of smaller diesels for stop and go urban driving cycles. Smaller diameter electrical conductors and the capacity to supply current to electric motors powering air conditioning compressors or power-steering pumps without expensive power inverters is another distinct advantage the 48-volt system offers. The primary reason for adoption of 48-volt electrical systems and batteries for mild-hybrid systems is to help meet fuel economy and emission standards by combining internal-combustion engines with inexpensive electric motor-assisted stop-start capabilities.

> ▶ **TECHNICIAN TIP**
>
> The choice of 48-volt current is chosen by many OEMs because Federal Motor Vehicle Safety Standards (FMVSS) classifies an electrical system operating at 60 volts direct current (DC) and higher as high-voltage systems. Using higher-voltage systems requires costlier electrical conductor insulation and shielding, plus identification of high-voltage conductors by bright orange shielding insulation. Whenever encountering highly shielded wiring colored bright orange, always consult OEM service literature to learn which safety precautions must be followed when servicing these vehicles.

Lithium-Ion Battery Advantages

While Li-ion technology appears to have every advantage over other battery technology, use of Li-ion technology is restricted by a number of limitations. Extensive investment and research is currently aimed at reducing cost and correcting serious limitations to the use of Li-ion technology in hybrid and battery electric-propulsion systems. As a result, a variety of Li-ion chemistry systems are now competing for widespread use, each with unique advantages and disadvantages. Advantages to using lithium-ion batteries in commercial vehicles, include:

1. The best power-to-weight ratio compared to other battery technology. For example, the replacement of lead-acid batteries on a BAE-Orion Hybrid transit bus with equivalent lithium-ion reduces battery pack weight from 4100 lb (1865 kg) to 1000 lb (455 kg). Li-ion batteries have twice the power density per kilogram of weight compared to NiMH chemistry (Bulletin from the Toronto Transit Commission).

2. Li-ion batteries have higher cell voltages—with as much as 5 volts in some designs. A typical cell voltage averages between 3.7 and 3.9 volts, which means fewer Li-ion cells are required to form high-voltage batteries. It also translates into fewer vulnerable and resistive cell connections and reduced electronics in the battery-management system. One lithium cell can replace three nickel–cadmium (NiCad) or NiMH cells, which have a little more than half the energy density and a cell voltage of only 1.2 volts.

3. Li-ion cells maintain a constant voltage for over 80% of their discharge curve. In comparison, conventional lead-acid batteries maintain a fully charged voltage until only 50%

discharged. Therefore, in a Li-ion battery, more stored energy is usable over longer periods to supply electrical accessories or to power a traction motor before becoming effectively discharged. It also means that a smaller-capacity battery can be used to supply a vehicle's power needs.

4. Li-ion batteries operate well over wide temperature ranges –60°F (–51°C) to 167°F (75°C). Cold slows down chemical reactions in other battery technology. However, cold temperatures do not slow the non-galvanic reactions in Li-ion batteries.

5. Charging characteristics of Li-ion batteries are superior to other batteries. In consumer electronic devices, Li-ion batteries have demonstrated the capacity to re-charge as much as 90% within five minutes when charged at between 4.2 and 4.3 volts. That speed is a distinct advantage for the efficiency of regenerative braking used by electric and hybrid-electric vehicles. Once charged, Li-ion batteries self-discharge at a very low rate. A lithium battery's usable capacity falls approximately 10% for every 70 milli-volt drop in open-circuit voltage, which is fully charged at between 3.7 and 3.9 volts, depending on the battery chemistry.

6. Li-ion batteries have low internal resistance and can discharge their current four times faster when compared to lead-acid batteries. In addition, high discharge and charge rates do not wear out a Li-ion battery to the extent that charge and discharge cycles reduce the lifespan of other types of batteries. The latest Li-ion iron phosphate ($LiFePO_4$) or LFP batteries can withstand 2000–7000 charging cycles at 100% DOD cycle, yet remain at 80% of original capacity. This compares to 500–800 cycles for lead-acid and 1500 for NiMH, as illustrated in (**FIGURE 15-4**). Li-ion batteries can last for up

to 10,000–15,000 micro-discharge cycles. A micro-discharge cycle occurs when the charge is maintained between 40% and 80%. In contrast, lead-acid batteries last the longest only when discharged less than 5%. Eight years is the expected lifecycle for expensive lithium batteries replacement in HEV and BEV's. However, charge capacity falls and charge time increase as the batteries age.

One disadvantage of current Li-ion battery technology is cost. Li-ion batteries currently cost eight times more than conventional lead-acid batteries for each kilowatt of power produced per hour. However, continuous innovation and increasing production efficiencies are steadily dropping the price differential.

Lithium-Ion Battery Construction and Operation

Naturally, a major component making-up lithium-ion batteries used by hybrid and electric vehicle-propulsion systems is lithium. It's interesting to note that in one of the latest 70 kWh 454 kg (1000 lb) battery packs made from hundreds of lithium-ion cells, the amount of lithium is only 63 kg (138.6 lb), or less than 14%. Dozens of different compositions of lithium are used to produce batteries. But to supply the energy demands of electric motors, about four of six different, but popular, lithium-ion battery chemistries are commonly used with energy densities ranging between 110–170 watts per kilogram (**TABLE 15-2**). Each of the different chemistries trades off production cost, capacity, cell voltage, charging and discharging characteristics, cooling requirements, durability, weight, and safety.

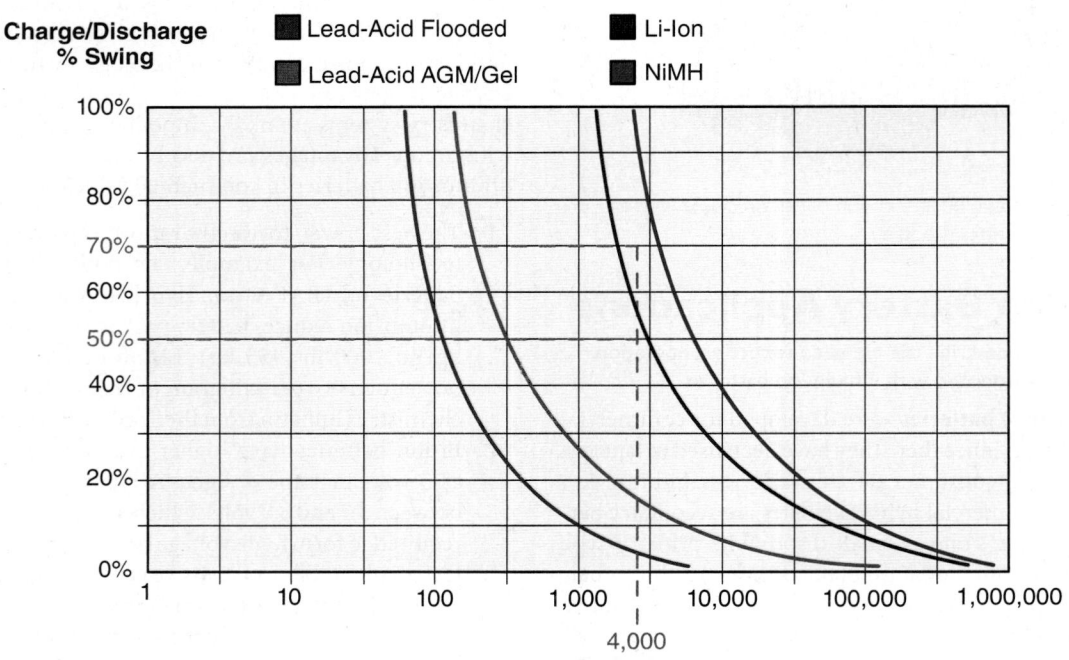

FIGURE 15-4 The extent to which a battery is discharged has a significant impact on battery life. The graph compares the service life compared to the DOD for four common commercial vehicle battery technologies. Minimizing the DOD dramatically improves battery life.

LFP batteries have been preferred for electric vehicles because they have a favorable trade-off between cost and the high discharge rates needed for acceleration, low weight, and longer life. For example, (**FIGURE 15-5**) shows a transit bus with battery tubs containing lithium batteries. The tubs and the battery-management system are both located on the roof of the vehicle. Note that the stairs used to access the rooftop battery tubs have been specially designed for this purpose. A123 Systems produces LFP batteries for use in heavy-duty hybrid and electric vehicles produced by BAE Systems, Navistar, Eaton, and Magna Steyr. Lithium-manganese (LMO) batteries follow-up closely for automotive applications and Tesla's current battery for electric propulsion is NCA (nickel, cobalt, aluminum), which has the heaviest battery construction, but delivers high capacity for the longest driving ranges.

Regardless of their specific chemistry, lithium batteries have a higher energy density for their weight than other battery types, such as lead-acid, nickel–cadmium, and NiMH, as shown in (**FIGURE 15-6**). Unlike conventional batteries, the chemical reactions in Li-ion batteries are not galvanic, and depending on the type of lithium battery, the material separating the electrodes is not a liquid, but a gel, salt, or plastic-like solid material. With no liquid electrolyte, these types of Li-ion batteries are immune to leaking. Like conventional batteries, all Li-ion batteries have electrodes and use lithium in the electrolyte between the electrodes. During charging and discharging, a lithium battery simply relocates lithium ions at each electrode leaving the battery chemically unaltered. The greatest differences between the batteries is found in the composition of the negative and positive electrodes.

TABLE 15-2 Lithium Battery Chemistries and Applications

Lithium Battery Type	Negative Electrode Material - Abbreviation	Primary Application
Lithium Cobalt Oxide	$LiCoO_2$ (LCO)	Consumer electronics – laptops, cellphones,
Lithium Manganese Oxide	$LiMn_2O_4$ (LMO)	Power tools, Electric Vehicles
Lithium Iron Phosphate	$LiFePO_4$ (LFP)	Power tools, Electric Vehicles
Lithium Nickel Cobalt Aluminum Oxide	$LiNiCoAlO_2$ (NCA)	Electric grid storage (house batteries), Electric Vehicles
Lithium Titanite Oxide	$Li_4Ti_5O_{12}$ (LTO)	Electric grid storage (house batteries), Electric Vehicles

FIGURE 15-5 Transit bus with rooftop battery tubs and battery-management system.

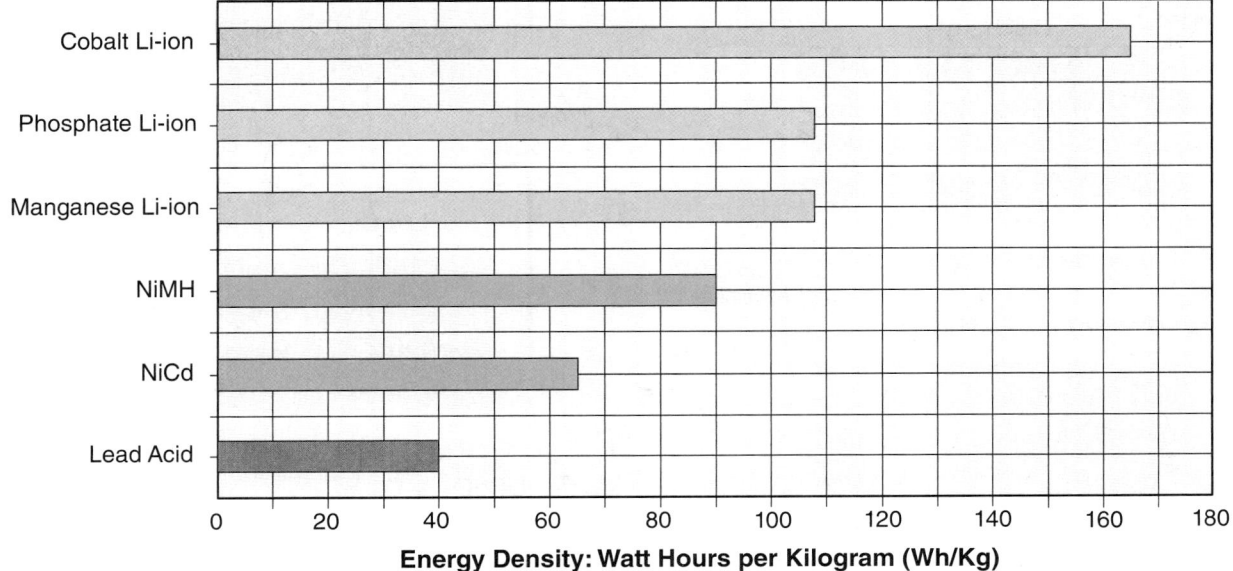

FIGURE 15-6 Comparing different lithium-ion battery energy densities with other battery types.

Lithium Iron Phosphate Batteries

Because the LFP battery is the most commonly used configuration, it's important to examine its construction and operation to understand lithium battery safety and service practices, in general. The positive electrode of a $LiFePO_4$ cell is made of a thin conductive copper sheet deposited with porous graphite on its surface. The negative electrode is made of aluminum covered with LFP material, which is a type of ceramic alloy (**FIGURE 15-7**). Porous insulating separators prevents cells from shorting out, and an electrolyte surrounds them. In this battery, the electrolyte is commonly made of lithium salt composed of lithium phosphate material dissolved in a solvent. Unfortunately, the solvent is flammable and can ignite and burn when exposed to heat and air. There is no free liquid in a LFP cell since the solvent is fully absorbed into the porous plates and cell separators, so no leakage occurs from these batteries.

During charging, negatively charged lithium ions with extra electrons are moved to the negative electrode (**FIGURE 15-8**). During discharge, the electrons are removed from the lithium ions and relocated to the positive electrode to power electrical loads (**FIGURE 15-9**). LFP batteries are the most chemically stable of lithium batteries. However, a condition called plating can occur, if the charge rate becomes too high. If the charge rate exceeds the negative electrode's ability to absorb negative lithium ions, lithium metal is instead deposited onto the electrode surface. That results in irreversible damage to the electrode and loss of capacity. If the cell voltage rises to 4.3 volts or above, due to overcharging, the solvent in the electrolyte breaks down into gas and can over-pressurize the cell, causing it to explode and potentially ignite.

Undercharging creates another problem. If a LFP battery is discharged below 2.0 volts, the electrode polarity can suddenly reverse. The result is the copper in the positive plate begins to dissolve and it forms hard, sharp crystals capable of piercing the thin insulating separator between positive and negative

electrodes. If this happens, the cell shorts out after it begins to be recharged. Rapid heating takes place and an explosion of gas combined with the high electrical discharge rate occurs.

These two types of failures explain why catastrophic failures of LFP batteries are always associated with recharging and

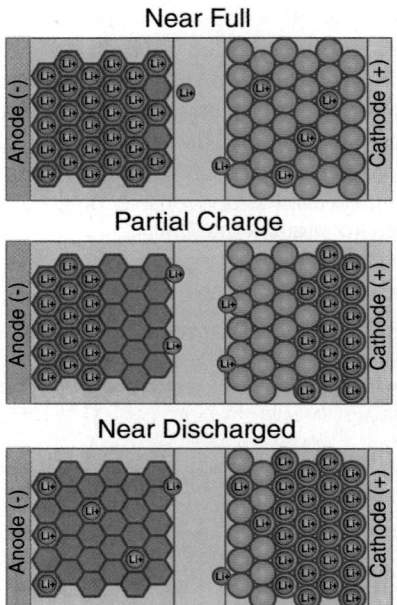

FIGURE 15-8 Movement of lithium ions inside a lithium battery during various states of charge.

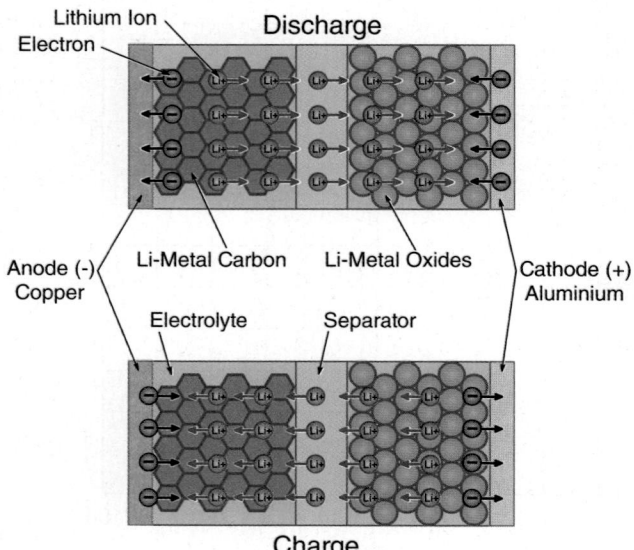

FIGURE 15-7 Construction details of a LFP battery.

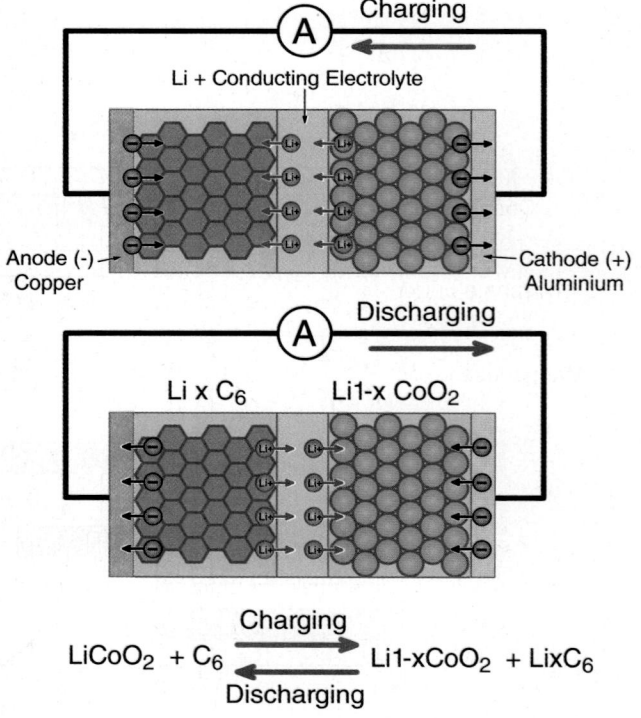

$$LiCoO_2 + C_6 \xrightarrow[\text{Discharging}]{\text{Charging}} Li_{1-x}CoO_2 + Li_xC_6$$

FIGURE 15-9 Electrochemistry of a LFP battery when charging and discharging.

overcharging with excessive voltages. When transported, safety regulations require that batteries are charged to no more than 30%, to prevent battery damage and potential explosions.

Battery Temperature Regulation

Chemical processes increase internal resistance in lithium-ion batteries which prevents fast charging of cells when their temperature is less than 41°F (5°C), and cannot be charged at all when the temperature is below 32°F (0°C). Lithium cells also deteriorate when their temperature exceeds 113°F (45°C). To avoid either problem, batteries require cooling when charging, or if ambient temperatures are hot. Heating battery cells may also be required when battery temperatures are low to prevent damage during fast charging. A separate temperature control system is used to regulate battery temperatures. Air cooling using fans or circulating liquid coolant around the batteries is another common method.

Lithium-Ion Battery Safety

The highly reactive chemistry of any Li-ion cell requires special safety precautions to prevent physical or electrical abuse of the battery. To maintain the cells within design operating limits, a microcontroller-operated battery-management system is required for Li-ion batteries to prevent damage and extend life cycle. Chemical stability of Li-ion batteries is also a concern. Charging and discharging generates heat, and without thermal management systems, which cool the batteries with circulating liquids, batteries are destroyed at high temperatures. Lithium batteries are notoriously known to even catch fire when overcharged or damaged. When heated above a critical 266°F (130°C), the separator film between electrodes melts, resulting in an electrode short circuit and an explosive release of electric energy. Cell electrolyte materials burn for up to one minute, releasing heat and driving the cell to over 932°F (500°C). Damage does not remain isolated in a single cell. Neighboring cells can also overheat, causing an electrical short with the same catastrophic result. Impact damage results in internal short circuits and the same thermal runaway conditions. However, propulsion batteries used in electric and hybrid vehicles use reinforced and self-healing separators. Safety is enhanced, but making separators less prone to abuse or damage makes the batteries larger and even more expensive.

Most Li-ion batteries are ruined if completely discharged. Below a cell voltage of 3.0 volts, the battery's typically use and external circuit protection often disconnects loads. Discharged below 1.5 volts for more than a week, and the battery can begin to form internal copper shunts, which are the crystals that cause internal short circuits, and can trigger thermal runaway conditions. Specifications depend on the manufacturer, but this phenomenon explains why internal circuit protection of Li-ion batteries cuts off any current from cells after cell voltage falls to between 2.2 and 2.9 volts/cell and does not reset until the battery is recharged. Electronic controls and specialized circuit protection add costs to battery production.

When working with Li-ion batteries, extra caution is needed when handling and testing lithium-ion batteries, since the electrolyte is highly flammable, and the battery can explosively rupture, causing physical injury or death. Use only a foam-type, CO_2, or dry chemical fire extinguisher. If a burning lithium-ion battery cannot be extinguished, allow the battery to burn out on its own. Only pour water around a burning battery to prevent the fire from spreading.

The following safety precautions should be observed to prevent thermal runaway conditions:

- Never allow a battery to be overcharged, crushed, dropped, or punctured
- Remove any battery from service if its temperature rises more than 18°F (7° C) during a normal charging cycle
- Never connect or charge a battery in reverse polarity
- Never expose a lithium battery to high temperatures
- Never attempt to disassemble battery packs and cells
- Use battery chargers specifically designed for use with lithium-ion batteries, which have correct charging rate algorithms
- Use lithium-ion cells with a purpose-built circuit protection

Valve-Regulated Lead-Acid Batteries (VRLA)

LO 15-3 Describe the types, advantages, construction features, and electrical characteristics of valve-regulated lead-acid batteries.

Recall from the Commercial Vehicle Batteries chapter that valve-regulated lead-acid (VRLA) batteries are sealed lead-acid batteries that have a liquid electrolyte absorbed in a gel or glass mat but does not require the addition of water. That design has numerous advantages. Plate and electrolyte technology used in VRLAs result in lower self-discharge rates because VRLAs typically lose only 1% to 3% of their charge per month. This compares to lead antimony grid batteries having a self-discharge rate of 2% to 10% per week and 1% to 5% per month for batteries using lead calcium grids.

Since VRLA batteries are completely sealed, they can be installed in any position without leaking—even under water. Sealing the battery eliminates the need to replenish the electrolyte or to check specific gravity. Battery state of charge is determined through voltage checks. A typical AGM battery has a minimum open-circuit voltage of 12.8 volts and may reach as much as 12.9–13.0 volts.

Other advantages of VRLA batteries include:

- No required specific gravity readings or adjustments
- No need to add distilled water
- No acid or lead to deal with in wash water
- No cable corrosion from corrosive gases
- No tray corrosion from corrosive gases
- No corrosive gas in battery compartment to damage electronics
- The longest service life of all lead acid battery types
- The highest cranking amps, even at low temperature
- The fastest recharge rate possible for a lead-acid battery
- The highest vibration resistance

- 400 full recharge cycles (80% DOD)
- Triple the life of traditional lead-acid batteries

There are two common types of VRLA battery—absorbed glass mat (AGM) and gel. Additionally, a spiral cell battery, which is a variation of AGM technology, has actually become the most recognizable of the AGM-type batteries. Each of these VRLA batteries is discussed in greater detail in the following sections.

Absorbed Glass Mat (AGM) Battery

Absorbed glass mat (AGM) batteries, as illustrated in (**FIGURE 15-10**), feature a unique and highly absorbent, thin glass fiber plate separator that absorbs the electrolyte like a sponge. The fiberglass-like plate separator, or mat, material gives the battery its AGM name. These batteries eliminate water loss through a process called oxygen recombination. No vents are used. Instead, the battery case is pressurized constantly to between 1–4 psi (6.9–27.6 kPa). Because of the special properties of the glass mat, pressurizing the battery causes over 99% of the hydrogen and oxygen gases to recombine back into water when recharging. A piece of foil in place of a traditional vent cap allows the battery gases to vent only under severe conditions, such as during overcharging when voltage is greater than 15 volts at room temperature. If venting occurs, the battery is likely damaged, and the cell dries out like any other cell. Charging voltage should be no more than approximately 2.48 volts per cell at room temperature. This means that in a 12-volt battery, charging voltage should not exceed 15.3 volts. When charging above 2.7 volts per cell, the battery is severely and irreparably damaged. A float voltage, which is the voltage a trickle charger should be temperature corrected and set at to maintain a full state of charge, is 2.32 volts per cell at normal room temperature.

Advantages to AGM Batteries

AGM batteries have several advantages. AGM cell design places plates and separator mats closer together, which lowers the battery's internal resistance. A more efficient and faster chemical reaction between battery electrolyte and the plates can take place using the unique boron–silicate glass mat separator plate. Lower resistance and faster chemical reactions means AGM batteries can charge up to five times faster than the rate of conventional lead-acid batteries. AGM cells produce slightly more voltage: generally, 12.80–12.90 volts open-circuit voltage, compared to 12.65 volts for conventional flooded lead-acid. As a result, AGMs deliver more amperage at higher voltage when cranking. **TABLE 15-3** compares the state of charge and open-circuit voltage of flooded, gel, and AGM batteries.

Glass mat plate separators used in AGMs absorb mechanical shock better than other batteries. The vibration-resistant battery can, therefore, be used in operating conditions where other battery plates are quickly destroyed. In one study, a fleet of 68 trucks with conventional flooded batteries was compared to a fleet of 69 trucks with AGM batteries. Thirty-four months later, 113 of the flooded batteries had been replaced, compared to eight of the AGM designs.

Service Precautions with AGM Batteries

AGM cells are extremely sensitive to damage from overcharging and require chargers that limit charging voltage to between 14.4 and 14.6 volts maximum at 68°F (20°C). Using conventional shop taper chargers, which can charge at up to 18 volts, destroys an AGM battery. Sustained charging of a 12-volt battery above 15 volts at room temperature also causes the battery to overheat and gas excessively due to electrolysis. Instead, a smart charger, such as the one shown in (**FIGURE 15-11**) should be used. A **smart charger** is a battery charger with an internal microcontroller used to regulate charging rates and times. It uses algorithms to calculate the optimal charging based on its state of charge when a temperature-compensated charger measuring ambient temperature is set to "AGM." Because cell voltage is slightly higher for AGM batteries, a vehicle's charging system voltage may need adjustment to keep it in range between 13.8 and 14.4 volts maximum at 68°F (20°C) for optimum performance and service life.

Voltage-regulator settings on some vehicles are too high for AGM batteries and may require adjustment. The higher open-circuit voltage also means that AGM batteries cannot be mixed with other battery types to prevent unequal charging and shortened battery life. Without access to the electrolyte, AGM state of charge can only be determined by measuring battery voltage.

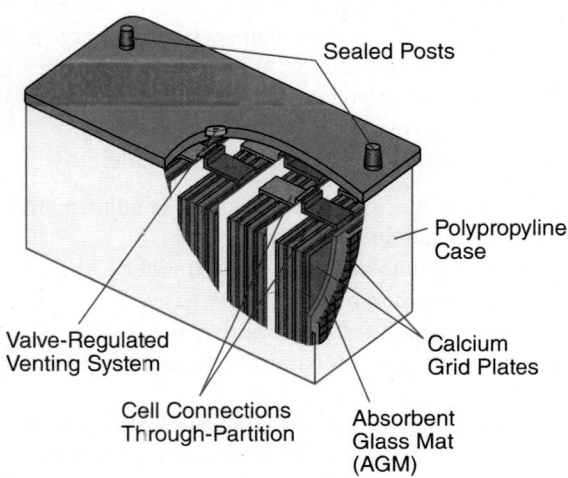

FIGURE 15-10 Construction details of a flooded AGM battery.

Sealed Posts

Polypropyline Case

Valve-Regulated Venting System

Calcium Grid Plates

Cell Connections Through-Partition

Absorbent Glass Mat (AGM)

TABLE 15-3 State of Charge versus Open-Circuit Voltage

Charge	Open-Circuit Voltage		
	Flooded	Gel	AGM
100%	12.65	12.85	12.80+
75%	12.40	12.65	12.60
50%	12.20	12.35	12.30
25%	12.00	12.00	12.00
0%	11.80	11.80	11.80

The DOD also affects the life cycle of AGM batteries. In general, the deeper the discharge between charges, the shorter the life cycle of batteries. **TABLE 15-4** compares the DOD against the number of charge/discharge cycles that can be expected from different battery chemistry types.

AGM batteries are very sensitive to overcharging, as they produce gas excessively and burst cell vents. Intelligent, microcontroller operated chargers that limit maximum charging voltage to below 15 volts are required. Traditional taper chargers (used by most shops) have an adjustable charging amperage setting that should never be used to charge AGM batteries. This is because taper chargers increase charging amperage to batteries by raising charging voltage to over 15 volts—and as much as 18 volts under some conditions.

Spiral Cell Optima Batteries

In the late 1980s, AGM battery technology advanced further with the introduction of spiral-wound plate technology. A typical spiral-wound cell battery is shown in (**FIGURE 15-12**). **Spiral-wound cell batteries** are AGM batteries in every way except that the electrodes for each cell are not made of rectangular plates. Instead, two long, thin, lead plates—the positive and negative electrodes—are coiled into a tight spiral cell with an absorbent micro-glass mat placed between the plates absorbing the electrolytes, as illustrated in (**FIGURE 15-13**). Replacing multiple plates with two coiled electrodes reduces internal battery resistance even further, thus enabling higher charging absorption rates for faster charging and higher discharge rates. These batteries also use higher internal gas pressures than other AGM batteries.

▶ TECHNICIAN TIP

Many commercial vehicles use several batteries connected in parallel, or series and parallel, to supply adequate current for starting and operating electrical accessories. It is not a good practice to mix battery types or old and new batteries within battery banks for several reasons. First, slight open-circuit voltage differences exist between battery types caused by variations in plate and electrolyte composition. Similarly, variations exist in the internal resistances of different types of batteries. All these changes produce different discharge and charging characteristics. In a mixed set of batteries, some batteries discharge quicker at higher rates of current. Others do not accept a charge easily. Those differences quickly lead to shorter battery life, undercharging, and eventually, one or more dead batteries in a set of batteries.

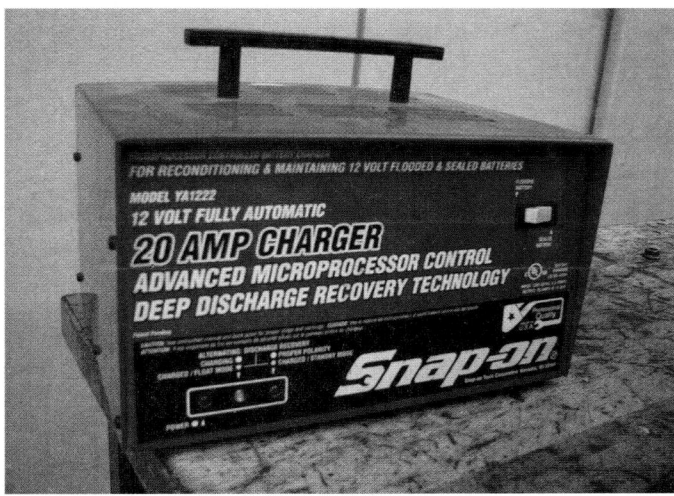

FIGURE 15-11 Only microcontroller-controlled, or "smart," chargers using algorithms to calculate optimal charging rates should be used to charge AGM batteries.

FIGURE 15-12 A typical spiral-wound cell battery. Note the cylindrical cells.

TABLE 15-4 Comparison of Depth of Discharge Cycle to Battery Life for Different Battery Chemistries

Depth of Discharge	Gel: Cycle Life	AGM: Cycle Life	Flooded Lead-acid: Cycle Life	Li-ion	NiMH
100%	450	200	30–150	Potentially ruined/damaged with some Li-ion chemistries	500–3000 (demonstrated only)
80%	600	250			
50%	1000	500	500	2000	
25%	2100	1200			
10%	5700	3200	2000	Millions+	300,000+ (demonstrated only)

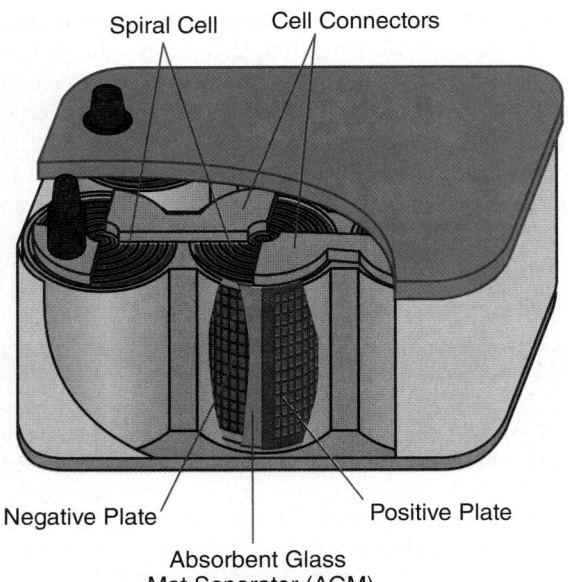

FIGURE 15-13 Spiral-cell batteries are the more recognizable type of AGM battery technology.

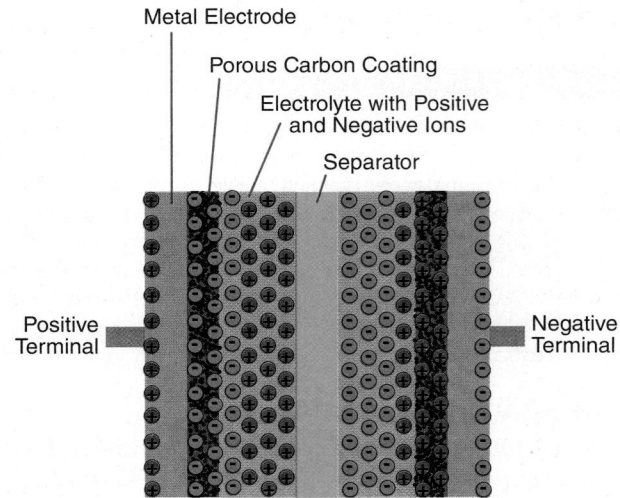

FIGURE 15-14 Construction of an ultra-capacitor.

Spiral cell batteries are produced in three categories, designated by the color of the battery's top cover.

- Red top—a 12-volt SLI battery
- Blue top—a deep cycle battery
- Yellow top—a combination deep cycle and SLI or leisure battery

Gel Cell

Just as battery plate and grid materials technologies have advanced to allow more powerful, lighter, and longer-lasting lead-acid batteries, electrolyte technology has also evolved. In the mid-1960s, spill-proof batteries were introduced using gel cells. **Gel-cell batteries** are created by adding silica powder to the electrolyte, which turns the liquid into the consistency of petroleum jelly, hence the name "gel cells." A fully charged gel-cell battery has an open-circuit voltage of at least 12.85 volts and, like AGM cells, gel batteries are sensitive to overcharging and can be ruined by overcharging.

Ultra-Capacitors

LO 15-4 Describe the operation and applications of ultra-capacitors for medium- and heavy-duty commercial vehicles.

Compared to more traditional capacitors, **ultra-capacitors** are a new generation of high-capacity and high-energy density capacitors. Capacitors are electrical devices well known for their ability to temporarily store and rapidly discharge bursts of electrical energy. For example, capacitors suppress and smooth voltage fluctuations, or ripple, from alternators. Capacitors also suppress electromagnetic interference (EMI) caused by electrical system voltage fluctuations when connected across the 12-volt power line-in on sensitive electrical devices. Ultra-capacitors

can supply much larger bursts of energy and quickly recharge themselves, which make them ideal for use for energy storage in the latest commercial vehicles. Ultra-capacitors are particularly advantageous in situations requiring regenerative braking, and in frequent stop-start systems, such as those in electric and hybrid vehicles.

Ultra-capacitors have a very low internal resistance when compared to lead-acid batteries. Consequently, ultra-capacitors deliver and absorb high-energy currents much more readily. In electric vehicles, using regenerative braking applications, batteries are slow to absorb a charge, thus limiting the maximum recovery of energy. Ultra-capacitors do not have this problem and are quickly recharged when depleted. This also makes them ideal for electric vehicle technology because they allow vehicles to recharge in seconds—not hours. Furthermore, unlike other battery technologies, ultra-capacitors are not worn out by continuous charge and discharge cycles. Whereas other battery technologies can only be cycled between 200 and several thousand times, ultra-capacitors can be cycled literally millions of times.

An ultra-capacitor is constructed using two electrodes (plates), an organic or carbon-based electrolyte, and a separator plate, as illustrated in (**FIGURE 15-14**). The dielectric material is double-layered—not single-layered, as in conventional capacitors—and is made from a porous carbon. While the construction features are similar to a cell of a galvanic-type battery, the method by which it stores electrical energy is different. Ultra-capacitors store electrical energy within electrostatic fields (electrostatically) and do not produce electricity through electrochemical reactions. This means plates in a capacitor are created with strong positive and negative charges. Like any capacitor, the main factors that determine how much electrical energy an ultra-capacitor can store are as follows:

- Plate/electrode surface area—the greater the plate area, the higher the capacity.
- Distance between the plates—the closer the plates are, the higher the capacity.
- Electrical properties of the dielectric insulating layer separating the electrodes—some dielectric materials create capacitors with better storage properties than others, or better than just allowing air to separate the plates.

A popular ultra-capacitor-type battery is the Maxwell ESM Ultra series (**FIGURE 15-15**). Having the same dimensions as a group 31 battery, one model can also produce 1800 CCA for 3 seconds and is unaffected by the cold. Three terminals are used. Two are for charging the battery, and a third connects directly to the starter motor. An internal control module regulates the charging rate to each cell and performs diagnostic tests (**FIGURE 15-16**).

FIGURE 15-15 Maxwell ESM Ultra series battery.

Ultra-capacitors are currently used to assist batteries for the first 1.5 seconds during cranking, where they can supply an additional 2000 amps of current to supplement the starter batteries, as illustrated in (**FIGURE 15-17**). That supplement increases starter torque and speed when cranking amperage draw is highest during the initial starter engagement.

Battery-Management Systems

LO 15-5 Identify and explain the operation of battery isolators, low voltage disconnect, charge equalizers, and battery-management systems.

Battery failure is a costly service issue for commercial vehicles. Weak batteries can lead to premature failure of starting and charging system components and loss of service caused by no-start conditions. The severe operating conditions and use of multiple batteries in many commercial vehicles contributes to shortened battery life. To minimize the expense and disruption due to battery failures, various electrical devices and systems are used to manage battery performance. **Battery-management systems (BMS)** are designed to perform the following functions:

- Protect the cells or the battery from damage
- Prolong the life of the battery
- Maintain the battery in a state of charge to perform the work for which it was specified

The development of commercial electric and hybrid-vehicle applications places more demands on batteries and requires sophisticated BMS for sensitive battery technology. Components of the BMS include battery isolators, low-voltage

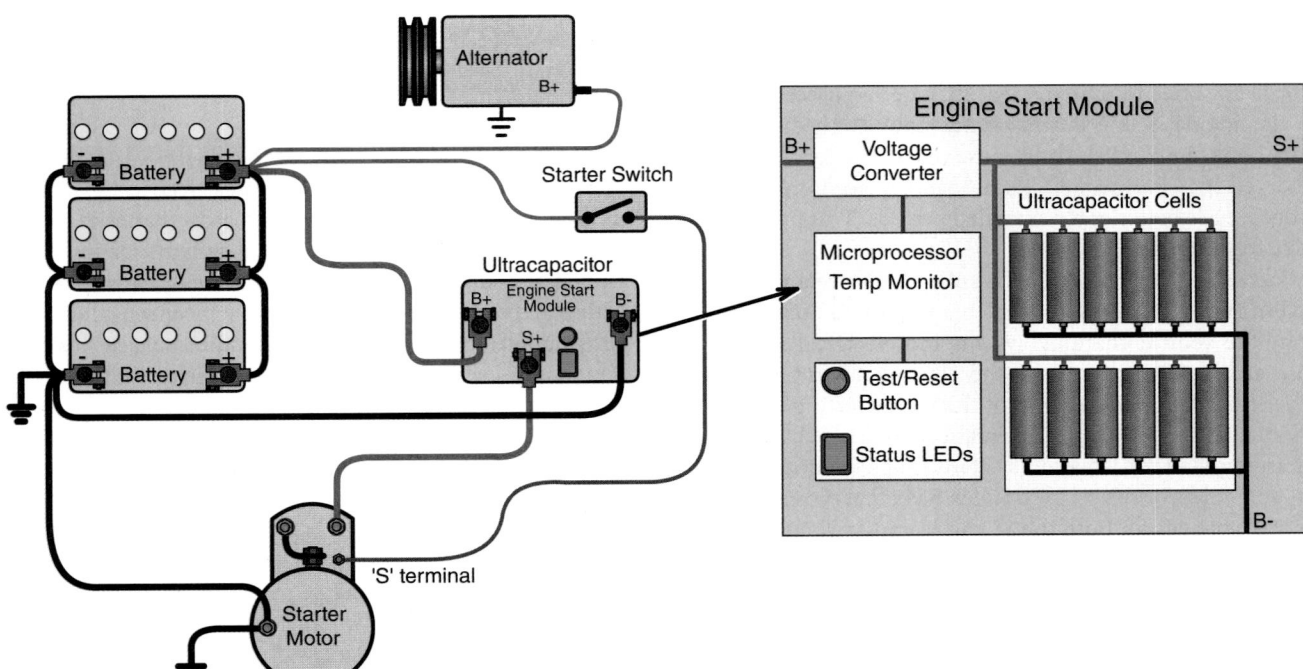

FIGURE 15-16 Construction of a Maxwell ultra-capacitor battery.

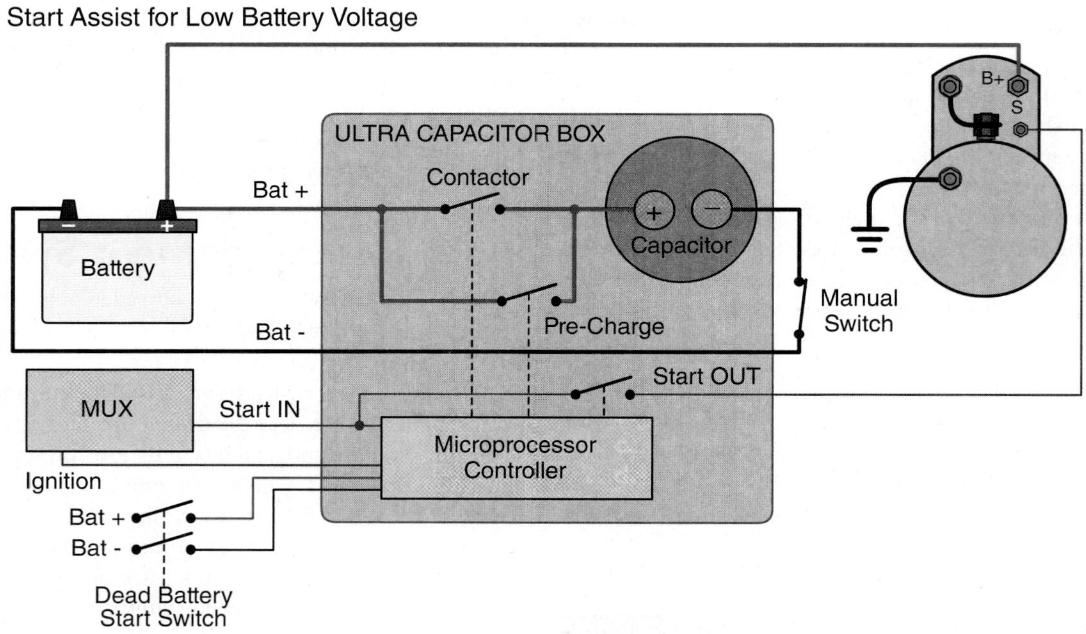

Start Assist for Low Battery Voltage

FIGURE 15-17 This ultra-capacitor is used to supplement the cranking current for a 24-volt bus battery, which reduces starting time.

disconnects, battery balancers and equalizers, and battery monitors. Each of these components is discussed in the following sections.

Battery Isolators

Many commercial vehicles use multiple batteries that can be separated according to function. For example, consider a vehicle with one battery bank of starting, lighting, and ignition (SLI) batteries for the starting and main vehicle-operating system and another set of batteries for auxiliary deep cycle batteries for accessories or systems that may be required to operate after the engine is shut down. Permanently connecting all the battery banks in parallel could cause the SLI battery to become discharged if a continual electrical load is placed on the auxiliary deep-cycle batteries for extended periods. This prevents the vehicle from starting.

Battery-isolator systems, or split-charge relays, as illustrated in (FIGURE 15-18), enable charging of an auxiliary battery by the vehicle charging system and electrical separation of the auxiliary battery from the starting circuit when the engine shuts down. Separation of the main starting and auxiliary batteries can take place automatically during charging and discharging. Battery-isolation systems range from simple, isolating solenoids, or relays, to complex BMS that monitor charge rates and voltages for both the SLI and auxiliary batteries.

Low-Voltage Disconnect (LVD)

Low-voltage disconnects (LVD) are devices that monitor battery voltage and disconnect non-critical electrical loads when the battery voltage level falls below a preset threshold value. LVD devices preserve battery current to a level adequate to start the

vehicle's engine when key-off loads or other parasitic draws are draining the battery. LVD devices then reconnect the electrical loads when the battery level is restored to a high-enough voltage—for example, when the alternator begins charging above 12.6 volts. No intervention is required by the vehicle operator to protect the batteries, as the LVD automatically disconnects and reconnects the load. An audible warning typically alerts the operator before a disconnect event occurs, which is generally between 12.0 and 12.2-volts. LVDs can be integrated with the vehicle's power distribution system and progressively shed loads as battery voltage drops.

Battery Balancers and Equalizers

Higher cranking amperage and greater electrical loads in commercial equipment require two or more batteries connected either in series, for 24-volt electrical systems, or in parallel, in 12-volt systems. Charging and discharging resistance changes with battery use and the electrical distance from the alternator. For example, longer battery cables and more electrical connections are almost unavoidable in many vehicles. This means one or more batteries in a bank gets undercharged, which in turn leads to undercharging and progressive plate sulfation. Sulfation, in turn, increases battery resistance, causing the battery to become harder to charge, and reduces effective plate area (FIGURE 15-19).

Balancers (sometimes called battery equalizers), illustrated in (FIGURE 15-20), attempt to adjust battery voltage to compensate for unequal charge resistances in multiple batteries. Equalizers are found in many commercial applications using 24-volt charging systems, including transit and tour buses, private coaches, off-highway equipment, yachts, and alternative energy systems.

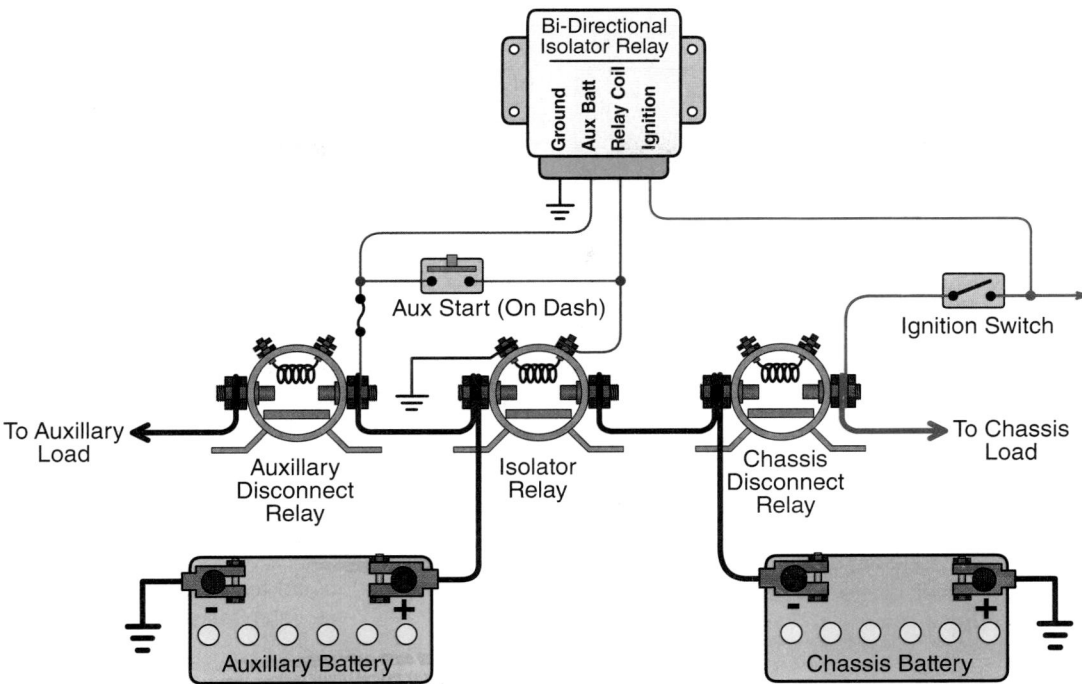

FIGURE 15-18 An isolator circuit ensures the chassis battery used for starting is not drained by auxiliary loads when the charging system is not operating. When the engine starts, both batteries are charged by the alternator with the control module switching the isolator relay on and off under the appropriate conditions.

In multiple battery configurations, whether connected in series or in parallel, batteries eventually charge and discharge unevenly, shortening battery life. For example, you may often discover that while testing two 12-volt batteries connected in parallel, one battery becomes completely dead, while the other stays in good condition. When testing three batteries, one is good, another fair, and the third defective. The defective battery is always the farthest from the alternator in terms of electrical distance.

There are two methods of correcting this common condition of unequal charge and discharge rates. One is to regularly rotate the batteries and exchange their positions in the configuration. Another method is to use a battery equalizer. Also, remember to check the equipment manufacturer's recommendation for connecting battery cables. Properly connecting cables is one way to minimize the charge and discharge imbalances between batteries.

Various configurations of charge equalizers enable:

- Charging 12-volt batteries from a 24-volt charging system
- Charging 24-volt batteries from a 12-volt charging system
- Charging series-connected 12-volt batteries at 24 volts and providing a 12-volt output for 12-volt chassis electrical loads
- Balanced battery charging of 12-volt batteries from 24 volts to within a difference of 0.1 volts
- Balanced draining of batteries to supply a 12-volt load so that each battery is depleted to within a difference of 0.1 volts

A common bus-coach configuration has 12-volt batteries connected to the equalizer that interfaces the batteries with the 24-volt alternators, as illustrated in (**FIGURE 15-21**). The equalizer senses battery voltage and drives a higher charge rate into weaker batteries and less current into stronger batteries. The voltage balance and charge acceptance rate of each battery is kept to within 0.1 volts under light charging loads and within 0.5 volts at full charging loads. When the voltage of Battery A is higher than that of Battery B, the battery equalizer switches to standby mode. This means no power is transferred from its 24-volt alternator input to its 12-volt output. If a 12-volt load is present, and Battery A's voltage decreases to just below the voltage of Battery B, the battery equalizer activates and transfers sufficient current from Battery B to Battery A, satisfying the load and maintaining an equal voltage and charge in both batteries.

More complex systems, like that illustrated in (**FIGURE 15-22**), can have both battery isolation and battery equalization across multiple banks. For example, auxiliary or house batteries used in motor homes and chassis batteries are isolated from each other when the alternator is not charging, but are connected together so both banks charge when the alternator is charging—along with battery equalization for each bank.

Charge equalization is critical for series-connected battery cells in hybrid-vehicle applications. The higher voltage in hybrid-drive systems requires very long, series strings of batteries pushing battery performance to extremes. Without battery-management systems incorporating charge equalization, battery banks quickly fail.

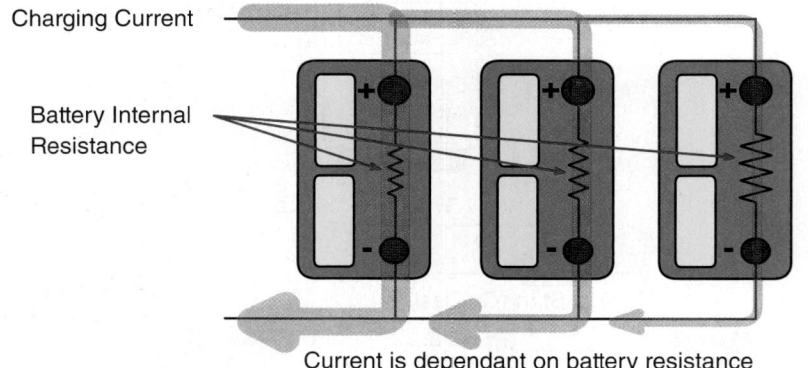

Current is dependant on battery resistance

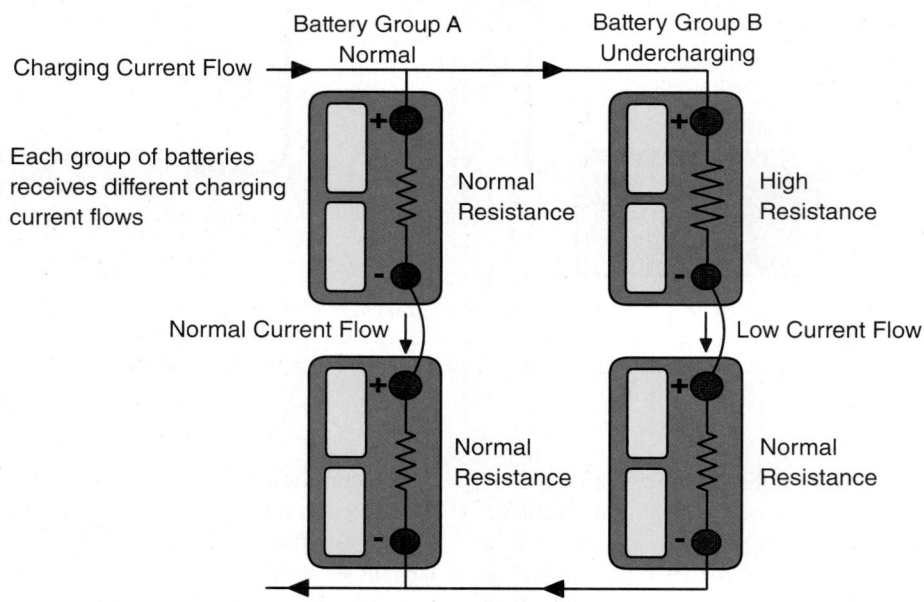

FIGURE 15-19 Batteries can develop unequal resistances with use.

Hybrid Battery-Management Systems

LO 15-6 Identify the functions of a battery-management system used by a hybrid-electric drive system.

Hybrid-drive battery management is much more demanding than the previously described battery-management devices. Batteries in these applications work in a demanding and harsh environment because of rapidly changing charging and discharging conditions, such as when the vehicle accelerates using electric motors and charges during regenerative braking. Li-ion and NiMH batteries are best charged to between 40% and 70% of full capacity to allow absorption of current generated during braking and to extend their lifecycle. An on-board BMS performs some, but not necessarily all, of the following functions (**FIGURE 15-23**):

■ Monitoring the state of charge (SOC) of the battery and battery cells that compose the battery banks; this function is often the equivalent of a fuel gauge distance-to-empty reading

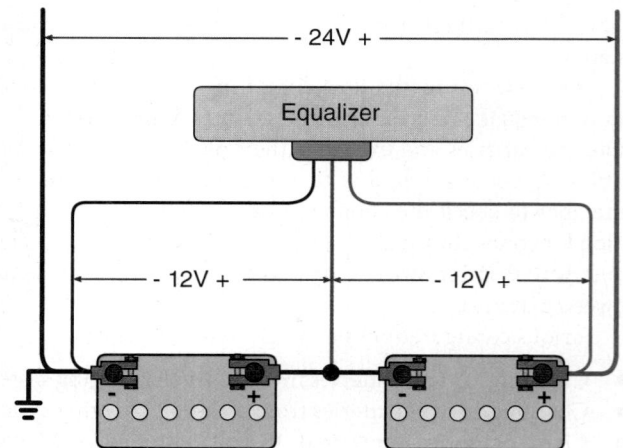

FIGURE 15-20 The equalizer controls the charging rate of two 12-volt batteries, as well as evenly balancing the current drawn from each.

■ Maintaining the SOC of all the cells with both voltage and amperage protection against overcharging and undercharge conditions

- Providing service and diagnostic information on the condition of the batteries and cells; this includes recording battery service and diagnostic data (battery voltage readings, temperature, hours, faults, out-of-tolerance conditions)
- Providing information for driver displays and alarms
- Providing an emergency protection mechanism in the event of damage, uncontrolled overheating, or other abuse condition

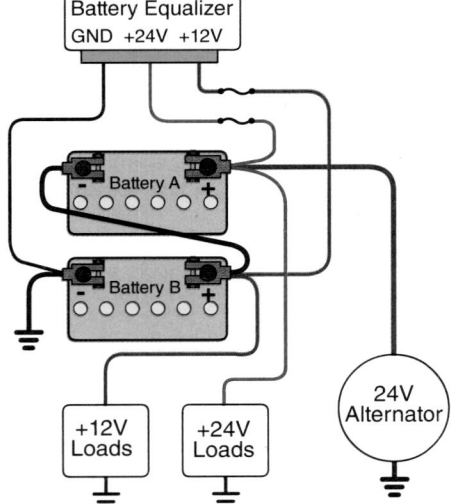

FIGURE 15-21 Battery equalizer used to ensure batteries within the bank remain charged with 12- and 24-volt mixed loads.

- Isolating the batteries or cells
- Charge equalization within the battery bank
- Adjusting the battery SOC to enable regenerative braking charges to be absorbed without overcharging the battery
- Communicating with the on-board vehicle network to receive information and instructions from other electronic vehicle-control units and responding to changes in the vehicle operating mode
- Calculating the optimum charging rate to each battery and or cell
- Enabling adaptive strategies or emergency "limp-home" mode in case of battery failure
- Provide reverse-polarity protection
- Control temperature-dependent charging; some batteries can be damaged by charging when temperatures are lower than 32°F (0°C) or above 100°F (45°C)
- Discharge current protection to prevent damage to cell due to short circuits
- DOD cut-off

Battery Monitors

Hybrid commercial vehicles use battery monitors to collect battery data for display to the operator and service technician. The data that is typically collected includes:

- Temperature of each battery or pack
- Voltage of the pack
- Rate of charge or discharge

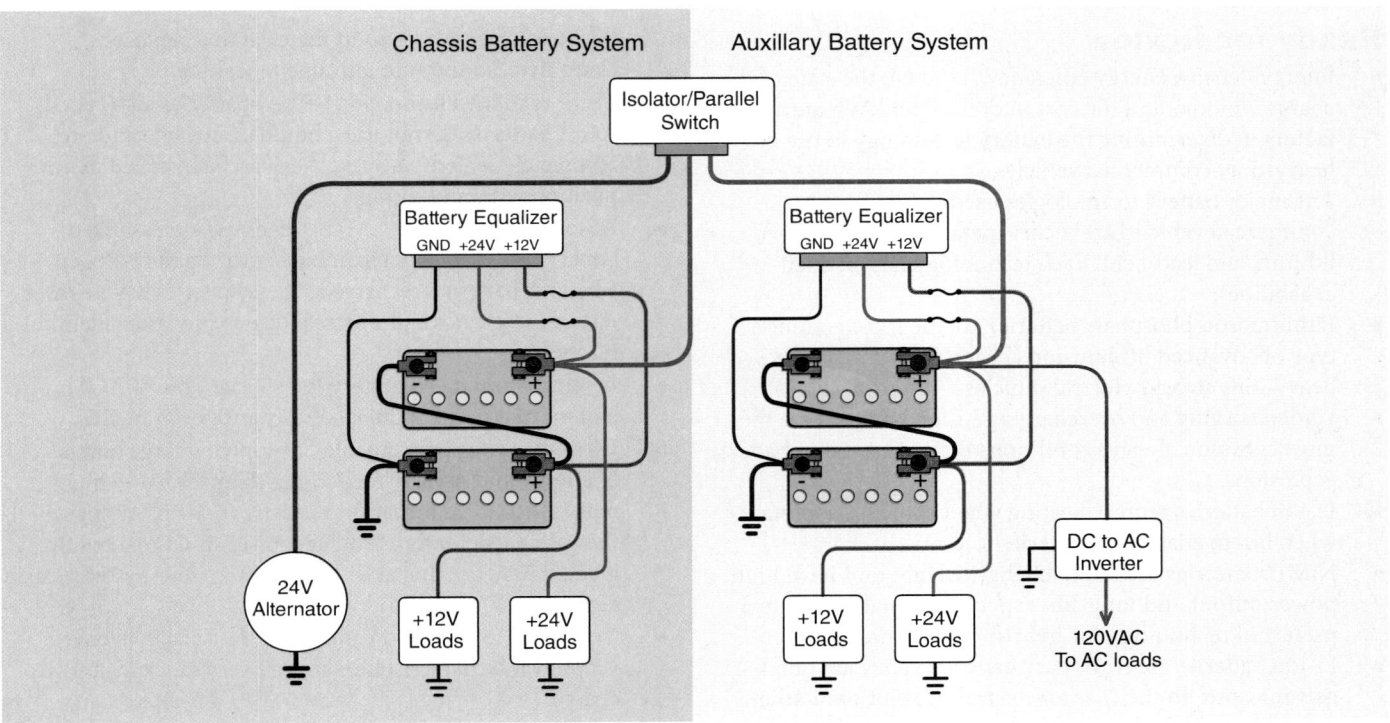

FIGURE 15-22 Representative diagram of a battery equalizer combined with a battery isolator. The chassis system provides current to supply the starting motor batteries.

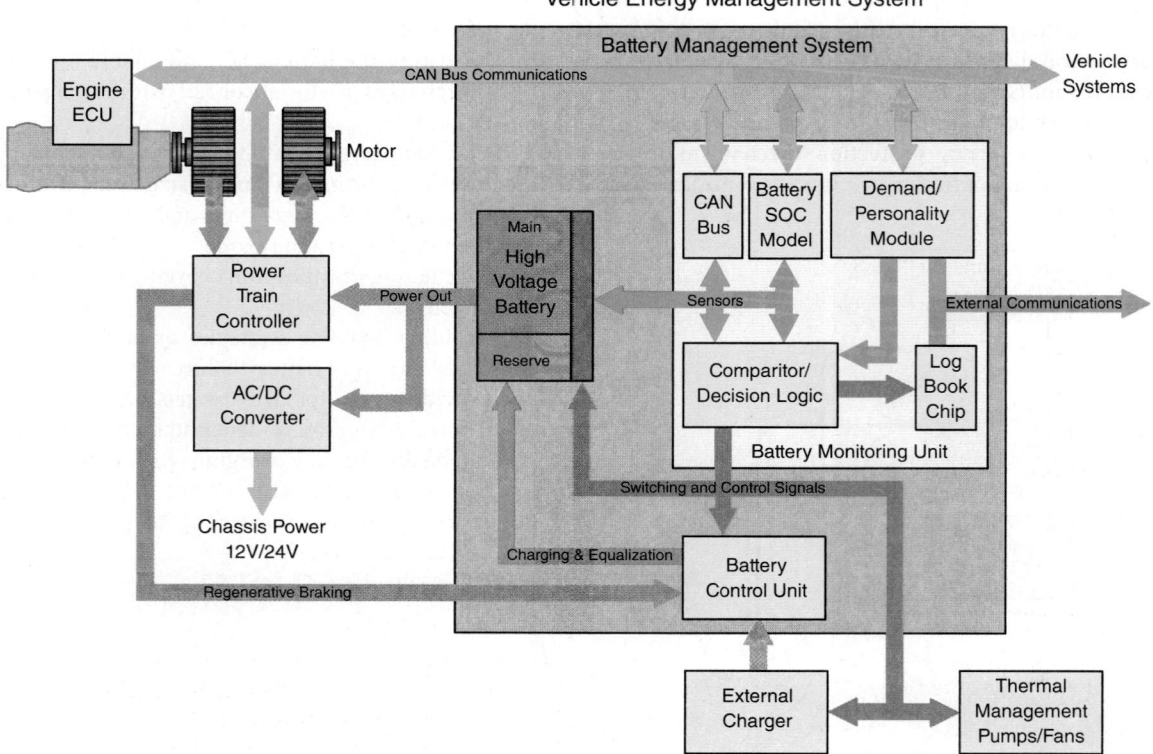

FIGURE 15-23 Diagram of the operation of a battery-management system used in a hybrid-vehicle chassis.

Wrap-Up

Ready for Review

▶ Energy density, energy efficiency, life span, the state of the charge window, and the cost in dollars per kWh are all factors in determining the battery technology to use on heavy-duty commercial vehicles.

▶ The major battery technologies used in heavy-duty commercial vehicles are nickel-metal hydride (NiMH), lithium, and lead-acid. Each technology has distinct capabilities.

▶ Lithium iron phosphate batteries are the most common type of advanced lithium-ion (Li-ion) battery used by heavy-duty hybrid-electric vehicles.

▶ Undercharging and overcharging Li-ion batteries are the most common abusive conditions that can result in battery explosions.

▶ Li-ion batteries require heating when cold and cooling when hot to enable the batteries to properly charge.

▶ NiMH batteries are relatively lightweight and have high power output and long-life expectancy, making them a preferred technology for hybrid-drive vehicles.

▶ Li-ion batteries are secondary batteries. They are not galvanic, nor do they use an electrolyte solution. Rather,

they use a gel, salt, or solid material that replaces electrolyte, so they are immune to leaking.

▶ Valve-regulated lead-acid (VRLA) batteries also called AGM batteries do not use a liquid electrolyte and are completely sealed. As such, they can be installed in any position without leaking.

▶ Absorbed glass mat (AGM) batteries use a pressurized battery case that helps recombine oxygen and hydrogen when the battery is recharged. These batteries have a lower internal resistance and a more efficient and faster chemical reaction.

▶ A spiral-wound cell battery is a special type of AGM battery that reduces internal resistance even further.

▶ Ultra-capacitors are capable of supplying large bursts of energy and quickly recharging themselves—which make them ideal for use in modern vehicles. As such, they are particularly advantageous in situations requiring regenerative braking and frequent stop-start systems, such as in electric and hybrid vehicles.

▶ Compared to lead-acid batteries, ultra-capacitors have very low internal resistance and are very quick to absorb a charge.

▶ To minimize and prevent battery failure, many vehicles incorporate a battery-management system to protect the cells, prolong battery life, and maintain the battery in a state of charge.

▶ Battery-isolation systems allow the multiple batteries in a battery bank to be separated according to function.

▶ When multiple batteries are connected in parallel, batteries eventually charge and discharge, unevenly shortening battery life. Batteries should, therefore, be rotated through the different positions in the battery compartment or a balancer (equalizer) should be used to compensate for unequal charges in multiple batteries.

▶ Hybrid-drive battery management is much more demanding than the conventional battery-management devices due to the harsher environment in which hybrid-drive batteries operate (e.g., rapidly changing charging and discharging conditions).

Key Terms

balancers A device designed to adjust battery voltage to compensate for unequal charges in multiple batteries. Also called *battery equalizers*.

battery equalizers A device designed to adjust battery voltage to compensate for unequal charges in multiple batteries. Also called *balancers*.

battery-isolator systems A system designed to separate the main starting battery and the auxiliary battery. Also called a *split-charge relay*.

Battery-Management System (BMS) A system of electrical devices used to manage battery performance.

gel-cell battery A type of battery to which silica has been added to the electrolyte solution to turn the solution to a gel-like consistency.

lithium-ion (Li-ion) battery A type of battery that uses lithium in the battery electrodes.

Low-Voltage Disconnect (LVD) A device that monitors battery voltage and disconnects non-critical electrical loads when battery voltage level falls below a preset threshold value.

Nickel–Metal Hydride (NiMH) battery A battery in which metal hydroxide forms the negative electrode and nickel oxide forms the positive electrode.

smart charger A battery charger with a microcontroller regulating charging rates.

spiral-wound cell battery A type of AGM battery in which the positive and negative electrodes are coiled into a tight spiral cell with an absorbent micro-glass mat placed between the plates.

split-charge relay A system designed to separate the main starting battery and the auxiliary battery. Also called a *battery-isolator system*.

ultra-capacitor A type of high-capacity and high-energy density capacitors.

Review Questions

1. Which of the following statements is most correct concerning the nickel–metal hydride battery?
   a. NiMH batteries are lighter than lithium-ion batteries.
   b. NiMH batteries have two times more power density than lead-acid batteries.
   c. NiMH batteries have a liquid electrolyte-containing potassium hydroxide.
   d. Nickel alloy is used in only one electrode of a NiMH battery.

2. Which of the following lithium-ion batteries is most commonly used in medium- and heavy-duty electric and hybrid vehicles?
   a. Lithium nickel cobalt aluminum (NCA)
   b. Lithium iron phosphate (LFP)
   c. Lithium manganese oxide (LMO)
   d. Lithium titanite oxide (LTO)

3. When is bright orange insulation and cable shielding required for electrical conductors on medium- and heavy-duty commercial vehicles?
   a. When electrical system voltage exceeds 60-volts DC
   b. When conductors potentially carry more than 50 amps
   c. For cables not protected by specialized circuit-protection devices
   d. On any hybrid or electric-powered chassis

4. Which battery technology has the best energy density for its weight?
   a. Lithium-ion batteries
   b. Lead-acid batteries
   c. Absorbed Glass Mat (AGM) batteries
   d. Nickel metal hydride (NiMH) batteries

5. What problem is encountered by lithium batteries when temperatures fall below 41°F (5°C)?
   a. The available battery voltage falls to close to half its voltage at room temperature.
   b. The battery becomes excessively resistive and cannot be charged.
   c. The battery can potentially develop a short circuit.
   d. A fully charged battery capacity falls to less than 50%.

6. When depleted of 100% of its charge over 8000 times, which electrical storage technology can operate near its fullest capacity when fully recharged?
   a. Ultra-capacitors
   b. Lithium phosphate batteries
   c. Lithium manganese oxide batteries
   d. Nickel metal hydride batteries

7. Which of the following reasons best explains the low internal resistance of AGM batteries?
   a. The composition of the plate material
   b. The composition of the cell electrolyte
   c. The use of glass mat plate separators
   d. The use of gel rather than liquid electrolyte

8. Which of the following features of a capacitor will increase its storage capacity?
   a. Placing plates further apart
   b. Using a dielectric material to separate the plate

   c. Increasing the plate area
   d. Using air to separate plates
9. Which of the following devices is used to protect the battery from completely discharging when electrical loads are accidentally left on?
   a. A battery isolator
   b. A low-voltage disconnect
   c. A battery balancer and equalizers
   d. A battery-management system
10. Which of the following procedures is required to restore the operation of all electrical system components after a low-voltage disconnect event?
   a. Clear electrical system fault codes with a hand-held scanner
   b. Disconnect and reconnect the batteries
   c. Charge the batteries and clear fault codes with a scanner
   d. Start the engine and run it until the alternator begins to charge the batteries

ASE Technician A/Technician B Style Questions

1. Technician A says that the demand for advanced battery technology in commercial vehicles is growing. Technician B says that not only do the increasingly popular hybrid-electric vehicles require advanced batteries, heavy-duty commercial vehicles also have a greater need for electrical storage capacity to run accessories. Who is correct?
   a. Technician A
   b. Technician B
   c. Both Technician A and Technician B
   d. Neither Technician A nor Technician B
2. Technician A says that nickel–metal hydride (NiMH) is a popular battery used to crank starting motors in diesel-powered commercial vehicles. Technician B says that absorbed glass mat batteries, along with ultra-capacitors, are the best possible combinations of advanced battery technology for powering electric propulsion motors. Who is correct?
   a. Technician A
   b. Technician B
   c. Both Technician A and Technician B
   d. Neither Technician A nor Technician B
3. Technician A says that Li-ion cells maintain a constant voltage for over 90% of their discharge curve as compared to conventional lead–acid batteries maintaining voltage until only 60% discharged. Technician B says that once charged, Li-ion batteries self-discharge at very low rate. Who is correct?
   a. Technician A
   b. Technician B
   c. Both Technician A and Technician B
   d. Neither Technician A nor Technician B
4. Technician A says that one disadvantage of current Li-ion battery technology is cost. Technician B says that Li-ion batteries cost double the amount of conventional lead–acid batteries for each kilowatt of power produced per hour. Who is correct?
   a. Technician A
   b. Technician B
   c. Both Technician A and Technician B
   d. Neither Technician A nor Technician B
5. Technician A says that a VRLA battery has the highest cranking amps—even at low temperature. Technician B says that a VRLA battery should not be charged with a taper-type charger. Who is correct?
   a. Technician A
   b. Technician B
   c. Both Technician A and Technician B
   d. Neither Technician A nor Technician B
6. Technician A says that no vents are used on AGM batteries. Technician B says that AGM batteries are damaged if charged at greater than 13.2 volts. Who is correct?
   a. Technician A
   b. Technician B
   c. Both Technician A and Technician B
   d. Neither Technician A nor Technician B
7. Technician A says that a smart charger is a battery charger that uses algorithms to control charging rates and times. Technician B says that AGM state of charge can be tested with a battery hydrometer. Who is correct?
   a. Technician A
   b. Technician B
   c. Both Technician A and Technician B
   d. Neither Technician A nor Technician B
8. Technician A says that ultra-capacitors supplement increases to starter torque and speed. Technician B says that ultra-capacitors are currently used to assist batteries for the first 3.5 seconds during cranking, during which time they can supply up to an additional 1000 amps of current to supplement the starter batteries. Who is correct?
   a. Technician A
   b. Technician B
   c. Both Technician A and Technician B
   d. Neither Technician A nor Technician B
9. Technician A says that a low-voltage disconnect system simply requires a scanner to clear fault codes in order to restore disconnected electrical loads. Technician B says that charging batteries automatically reconnect the disconnected electrical loads. Who is correct?
   a. Technician A
   b. Technician B
   c. Both Technician A and Technician B
   d. Neither Technician A nor Technician B
10. Technician A says that battery balancers attempt to adjust battery voltage to compensate for unequal charges in multiple batteries. Technician B says that equalizers are found in many commercial applications using 24-volt charging systems, including transit and tour buses, private coaches, and off-highway equipment. Who is correct?
   a. Technician A
   b. Technician B
   c. Both Technician A and Technician B
   d. Neither Technician A nor Technician B

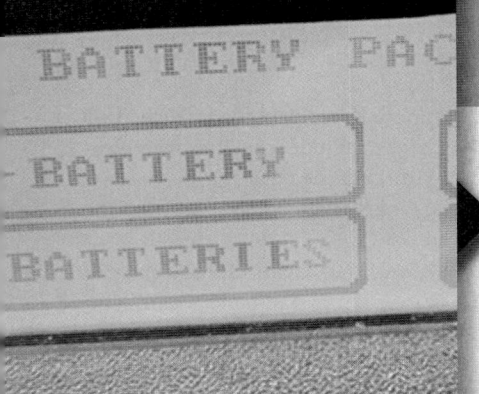

CHAPTER 16

Servicing Commercial Vehicle Batteries

Learning Objectives

After reading this chapter, you will be able to:

- **LO 16-1** Identify safety equipment and safe work practices for servicing batteries.
- **LO 16-2** Identify and describe failure modes of batteries and their causes.
- **LO 16-3** Identify and describe service procedures used to analyze the condition of batteries.
- **LO 16-4** Identify and describe the stages of battery charging and the types of battery chargers used to restore a battery to a full state of charge.
- **LO 16-5** Define and explain a parasitic load condition and identify procedures used to pinpoint a parasitic load.

You Are the Technician

Maintaining a fleet of trucks, buses, and other diesel-powered machinery in hot climates presents unique challenges. One of the problems you may frequently encounter is hard starting of engines due to dead batteries. Within a few months, many of the vehicle batteries become defective, usually just one out of two batteries or two out of three batteries in a multiple-battery configuration. One battery usually remains in good condition. A significant amount of downtime, labor, and associated expenses is lost to jump-starting vehicles and equipment in addition to the cost of battery replacements. From your experience working in other areas, and even during cooler months, you have learned to associate hot weather with more frequent battery failures. Even if the batteries do not fail during hot weather, the first cold morning after a long season of heat often produces many no-start conditions. To avoid these problems outline strategies to reduce the aggravation level and cost of service for no-start conditions due to the effects of high temperatures on batteries. IN your outline, include answers to the following questions:

1. Why do batteries fail more quickly in hot climates?
2. How can you determine if batteries are sulfated?
3. Identify several maintenance procedures used to minimize battery failure due to sulfation.

Introduction

Batteries are the logical starting point when diagnosing starting system complaints, such as hard starting, slow cranking, or no-start conditions (**FIGURE 16-1**). Battery testing is also recommended when many other electrical system problems are reported. For example, because batteries are required to supply adequate current flow to the electrical system when the charging system output cannot match electrical system loads, battery testing is indicated when headlights excessively dim at idle, or when instrument cluster voltmeters displays only a nominal open circuit voltage below 12.6 volts when the engine is running. Battery testing is also recommended whenever an alternator or starting motor is replaced because it is defective. Batteries in poor condition can stress these components, either through excessive charging system demands or low-voltage motor burn-out leading to premature failure of starting system replacement parts. Often overlooked is the job of the battery to smoothen voltage fluctuations and reduce electromagnetic interference in the electrical system. As batteries age and approach the end of their service life, they lose this vital ability to stabilize electrical system voltage, which can result in very unusual electrical system complaints. A variety of instruments and tools are used to evaluate the condition of vehicle batteries, and several unique procedures are commonly used to service batteries during maintenance checks. These diagnostic techniques and service methods are described in this chapter.

Traditional comprehensive maintenance and testing of batteries includes the following evaluation methods:

- Visual inspection, cleaning, filling, and battery replacement
- State of charge testing using a voltmeter
- Cell voltage checks
- Load or capacity testing
- Conductance or impedance testing
- Charging batteries
- Jump-starting vehicles
- Measuring parasitic draw

Batteries should be evaluated visually before proceeding with any other tests. Visual checks include checking the electrolyte level, if it is possible. However, because most batteries today are sealed or a low- or no-maintenance type, checking the electrolyte level is not practical.

Another basic maintenance task is to make sure the exterior case is dry and free of dirt. Dirt on top of the battery can actually cause premature self-discharge of the battery as current "leaks" across the path of dirt or grime. Grime mixed with electrolyte vapors originating from a battery can deposit onto the battery case. When this happens, the case becomes conductive and allows current to drain from the battery terminals over time. To tell if the surface of the battery is leaking current, use a voltmeter like the one shown in **FIGURE 16-2**, set to "DC volts" to measure the voltage on the top surface of the battery. A meter lead is placed on either the positive or negative battery terminal, while the other lead is moved around the top of the battery, measuring the voltage present there. Any surface voltage leakage measurement exceeding 0.5 volts means the battery should be washed down with water. Do not use mixtures of diluted ammonia or baking soda in this area because they can enter the battery cells and contaminate electrolyte.

Batteries should be maintained fully charged to perform properly and prolong their service life. A weakened battery causes the alternator to work harder charging batteries and shortening its life. Lower current level available to the starter leads to low-voltage burn-out of the starter too.

> ▶ **TECHNICIAN TIP**
>
> Insulating paste or lacquers designed to cover battery terminals should be applied to both positive and negative battery terminals to prevent corrosion and accompanying resistance from developing at battery connections. These chemicals are not electrically conductive and typically do not damage cable-insulating materials. Do not use chassis grease since chassis grease contains electrically conductive minerals, such as molybdenum or lithium, and causes the battery to self-discharge and potentially corrode battery terminals.

FIGURE 16-1 Regular battery maintenance reduces downtime.

FIGURE 16-2 Measure voltage between points on the surface of the battery top to determine if there is any leakage current.

Battery Service Precautions

LO 16-1 Identify safety equipment and safe work practices for servicing batteries.

Nearly 6,000 people in the United States are reported to have suffered eye injuries from batteries, according to the Prevent Blindness America organization. Safety should be the first priority when working around and servicing batteries. Batteries are dangerous for a couple of reasons. First, electrolyte inside lead-acid batteries is corrosive. Acid on skin, in eyes, on clothing, or on paint burns, causing bodily harm and vehicle damage. Also, an explosive gas mixture consisting of hydrogen and oxygen is produced during charging and discharging of the battery. Ensure the following precautions are followed to reduce the risk when working with batteries:

- Always wear protective clothing, such as rubber gloves and goggles or full-face shields, when handling batteries. When handling a battery or checking electrolyte levels, wear a rubber apron to protect clothing from splashed battery acid. If acid contacts your skin or eyes, flush with water immediately.
- Never wear any conductive jewelry (neck chains, watches, or rings) when working on or near batteries, as they may provide an accidental short-circuit path for high currents.
- Do not smoke, weld, or grind metal near batteries because sparks may ignite the explosive gas mixture.
- Never create a low-resistance connection, or short, across the battery terminals. A battery can quickly gas, overheat, and explode if an object, such as a wrench, accidently connects to the battery posts.
- Never disconnect a battery charger, jumper cables, or power booster from a battery when charging or jump-starting. Sparks occur when disconnected and can result in battery explosions. Shut the power booster off. Disconnect the chassis ground clamp that is away from the battery first. Connect the ground clamp last when boosting.
- Charge batteries in a well-ventilated area.
- Always remove the negative or ground terminal first when disconnecting battery cables, because this procedure reduces the possibility of a wrench creating a short circuit between any positive voltage wiring and the chassis ground.
- All battery cable connections to the battery terminals need to be properly tightened and sealed with a dielectric or non-conductive paste or sealer. Loose connections are resistive and may cause sparks (**FIGURE 16-3**).
- Never set a wrench or other tool on a battery, as doing so can cause short battery terminals, leading to gassing, overheating, and an explosion in an alarmingly short period.

Always connect and disconnect the main chassis battery ground cable first when servicing battery banks. If there are other ground cables connected to the battery for the engine and other electronic control modules, connect those grounds last. When additional

FIGURE 16-3 Dielectric grease, paint, or sealers should be applied to clean battery terminals after cleaning and tightening connections. Caps and terminal sealing paint prevent corrosion of battery terminals.

grounds are either connected or disconnected and the main battery chassis ground is NOT connected, inductive voltage spikes produced from relays, step-up transformers, or other coils internal or external to modules can be generated and may damage electronic control modules without a large battery to absorb and lower the momentary high-voltage current.

Never allow a spark or flame around a battery, and never try to jump-start a frozen, faulty, or open-circuit battery. Excessive battery gassing that can potentially take place under these conditions could cause the battery to explode, causing serious injury.

Causes of Battery Failure

LO 16-2 Identify and describe failure modes of batteries and their causes.

According to several industry studies, over half of vehicle breakdowns or maintenance-related failures to provide service are caused by batteries. Tires are the next most common reason for breakdowns (15%), followed by engines (8%). The two most common complaints concerning batteries are that they either do not charge or do not hold a charge. Internal short circuits allow a battery to lose its charge as good cells discharge into a defective cell with lower cell voltage. Batteries may also suddenly fail through the loss of a cell or open circuits within the internal connections. Parasitic key-off electrical loads on a battery that drain the battery and prevent starting are not caused by defective batteries. It is important to pinpoint the cause of excessive key-off loads, rather than replace a battery that is discharged every night.

Batteries slowly fail over time and self-discharge more quickly through the gradual loss of capacity caused by plate deterioration. Capacity is another term describing the battery's ability to supply electrical power, which is a function of voltage and amperage. Battery capacity is said to increase if it can supply an increasing amount of amperage for any given voltage level of, for example, 12 volts. That means a battery capable of supplying 500 amps of current at 12 volts has more capacity than one only able to supply 400 amps at the same voltage. Battery failure due to a loss of capacity means the battery cannot supply enough amperage at a specific voltage level during a standardized industry test. The test procedure compares the battery's actual capability to to deliver current and compares it to its rated capacity. A battery losing more than 20% of its capacity is considered defective and should be replaced. Standardized load testing or conductance testing procedures reveals a battery's in-service current storage capacity.

Battery Internal Resistance

The internal resistance of a battery is an important concept to understand and apply when servicing and testing batteries. The most significant influence of internal resistance is the effect on charging and discharging electrical current. Batteries with high internal resistance do not easily absorb an electrical charge, charge more slowly, produce excessive gas, and become hot when charging. Similarly, high internal resistance limits maximum discharge current. The notion that batteries delivering electrical current have internal resistance is not an obvious concept, but a new battery may have as little as 10 milli-ohms, which can increase to over three ohms by the end of its service life. However, a battery's actual internal resistance varies according to its size, construction, age, chemical composition, temperature, and the amount of current charging or discharging through the battery (**FIGURE 16-4**). High charging and discharge current make the battery more resistive and generates heat. The state of charge also has an effect on internal resistance, with a fully charged battery having much higher resistance than a discharged battery. Batteries connected in parallel charge and discharge unevenly if internal resistances are different. This situation accelerates battery failure in one or more batteries connected to a battery bank.

Sulfation

According to an independent industry study, of all lead-acid batteries returned to the manufacturer under warranty, close to half were found to have no defect. Of those found defective, close to 80% were caused by sulfation. Sulfation can be observed as a powdery white colored substance that embeds into and swells battery plates and cells, as shown in **FIGURE 16-5**. Removing cell caps to reveal cell plates can often enable direct observation of plates to identify a severe sulfation condition. Sulfation occurs when batteries are subjected to prolonged undercharge conditions. During normal use, soft sulfate crystals derived from sulfuric acid in the electrolyte form on the plates but then dissipate when charged, which is part of the normal charge and discharge cycle. During periods of a prolonged undercharged condition, the sulfate converts to hard crystals and deposits on both the positive and negative plates. During subsequent

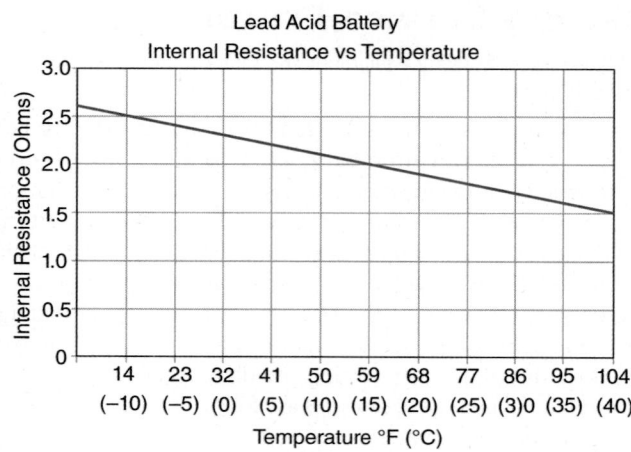

FIGURE 16-4 Battery resistance increases as its temperature decreases. Less cranking amperage is supplied at low temperature.

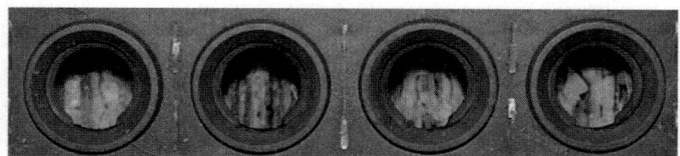

FIGURE 16-5 Sulfate on the top of the plates of a lead acid battery.

charging, the hardened sulfate cannot be driven from the plate and reduces the active area of plate material. Consequently, battery capacity is reduced by sulfation. Sulfation also increases the internal resistance of a battery. This means the amount of electrical current leaving the active battery plate area is reduced by resistance. Higher charging voltage is also needed to regenerate moderately sulfated plate material into active plate material. Understanding the relationship between battery resistance and sulfation explains why charging time increases and the maximum charging amperage or rate is lower in sulfated batteries. While not commonly used, some pulse-type battery chargers have a setting for potentially recovering sulfated batteries or batteries that have been stored for long periods of time in an undercharged state. These chargers rectify only half an alternating current (AC) sine wave, producing a 0.5–60 HZ on/off direct current (DC) charging pulse.

Common reasons for sulfation include:

1. *Leaving batteries too long in a state of discharge*—Soft sulfation occurring during normal discharge turns to hard sulfate crystals over time. Batteries should be recharged as soon as possible after discharging. Key-off loads, also called parasitic drains, contribute to sulfation caused by prolonged discharge.
2. *Undercharging of a battery*—High resistance at battery connections, particularly in batteries connected in parallel with uneven resistance at terminal connections or unequal cable lengths to each battery, leads to undercharging of cells. Incorrect charging system voltage can also cause undercharging.

3. *High ambient temperatures*—Temperatures more than 100°F (39°C) speed-up chemical activity inside a battery, accelerating the self-discharge of a battery. It is calculated that a new, fully charged, flooded battery would self discharge and most likely not start an engine if continuously exposed to 110°F (47°C) in as little as 30 days. Significantly higher rates of battery failures occur in warm regions of North America than in cold areas. To minimize self-discharge, batteries are best stored in cool, dry places. Part departments storing charged batteries in unheated sheds in winter is, in fact, good practice to lengthen battery storage life and maintain their state of charge.

4. *Low electrolyte level*—Battery plates exposed to air dry out and prevent transfer of sulfate from the plate material back into electrolyte during charging. Adding acid to a battery does not recover a dead battery. Instead, it increases the concentration of sulfate in the battery.

> ▶ TECHNICIAN TIP
>
> Regularly scheduled battery rotation is a good service practice to prevent sulfation damage in battery banks of two or more batteries. Batteries that are electrically more distant from the alternator due to resistance from factors, such as unequal cable length or more electrical connections between the alternator and battery, do not charge as quickly as those closer to higher alternator voltage. Hard sulfation can set into a battery, making it even more resistive to fully charging. To minimize this condition and extend battery life, battery positions can be rotated to move a battery that is electrically furthest from the alternator to a position closest to having the least resistive pathway to the alternator.

Performing a Sulfation (Three-Minute Charge) Test

Sulfation is indicated using a three-minute battery charge test. This test is not performed as part of a regular battery evaluation, but only to verify a diagnosis of sulfation. This battery test requires an automatic or taper-type battery charger adjusted to charge the battery at 30–40 amps for three minutes. With a separate voltmeter, battery charging voltage is measured with the charger set to this fast charge rate. If the voltage rises above 15.5 volts before the end of the three-minute period, it demonstrates the battery is excessively resistive and is likely sulfated.

Vibration

Excessive vibration can cause open circuits in the internal battery connections and "shed" or shake loose plate material, which settles to the bottom of the battery case. **Shedding** reduces the plate surface area and, therefore, reduces capacity. Shedding may also produce short circuits between the bottom of positive and negative plates. Sediment chambers at the bottom of cell plates are designed to trap (shed plate material) to prevent short circuits between plates. Securely holding batteries in place minimizes shedding. Battery trays should ideally have some ability to dampen shock and vibration. Some shops install a shock-absorbing piece of mud-flap beneath the batteries with the aim to further reduce transmission of vibration into batteries.

Electrolyte Level and Condition

Low electrolyte level exposes the plates to air, preventing the transfer of sulfate from the plate material back into the electrolyte during charging. It is critical to maintain the correct acid-water mix of electrolyte. If electrolyte level is lost through electrolysis (a process where water is split into hydrogen and oxygen gases), then distilled water should be added. If electrolyte is lost due to spillage, then the battery should be topped up with electrolyte.

Plates and grids that are damaged are often detected by examining the electrolyte. Gray or dirty electrolyte observed in any cell qualifies a battery as defective. Batteries self-discharge in as little as a few hours if a single cell is shorted by shed plate material suspended in the electrolyte. Although voltage and electrolyte readings may be satisfactory, contaminants cause the battery to self-discharge quickly to 0 volts because series connections between cells cause even one dead or defective cell to discharge all other cells into the dead cell. Electrolyte condition is checked at the same time specific gravity is evaluated.

Grid Corrosion

Grid corrosion, like that illustrated in **FIGURE 16-6**, takes place primarily in the positive grid and is accelerated by overcharging and high temperatures. Alloys in the lead grid are intended to minimize grid corrosion but battery acid can disintegrate this plate material used to conduct plate electrical current. When corrosion begins to take place, often during sulfation conditions, grid resistance increases during charging and discharging. Grids are the foundation and the electrical conducting layer for the battery plate. Although grids are alloyed with antimony, calcium, or sometimes barium, to minimize the corrosive effects of the electrolyte, grids do disintegrate. The mud-like lead paste attached to grids also disintegrates when grids corrode.

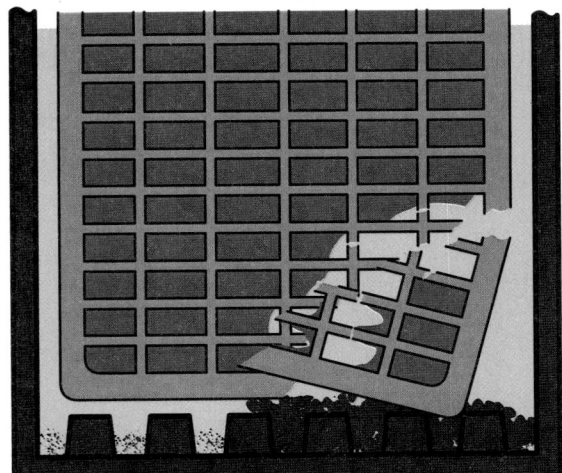

FIGURE 16-6 Corroded grids increase battery resistance, making the battery harder to charge and causing low supply voltage when cranking.

Battery Inspection, Testing, and Maintenance

LO 16-3 Identify and describe service procedures used to analyze the condition of batteries.

As noted earlier, batteries last longer if they are properly maintained by keeping the case cleaned and the batteries in a full state of charge. In addition to the battery condition, one of the most common causes of vehicle no-starts is dirty, loose, or corroded battery cables. Inspecting, cleaning, and topping off electrolyte (if not maintenance-free) are common tasks that should be performed every six months to one year on top-post batteries, and one to two years on side-post batteries. During periodic maintenance, battery compartments should be checked for proper ventilation. All slide mechanisms on battery trays should work properly. Battery cables should be inspected for rubbing or binding. Battery terminals should be tight and show no evidence of overheating. Always coat battery terminals with a dielectric sealer to prevent corrosion made worse by battery gases and heating caused by high current flows.

Batteries should be evaluated visually first before proceeding with any other significant tests. Visual checks include:

- Cracks
- Bulges—Indicate batteries are severely sulfated and have either overheated, excessively gassed, or been frozen
- Cable connections—Connections should be clean, tight, acid-resistant, and show no signs of heat damage
- Battery hold-downs—Loose or missing hold-downs cause plate shedding
- Dirty case—Causes current to leak out of batteries
- Leaks
- Electrolyte level—Level should be above the plates
- Electrolyte appearance—Liquid should be clear; a brownish or grey-colored contamination indicates the plates may be damaged or the electrolyte contaminated

To inspect, clean, fill, or replace the battery, battery cables, clamps, connectors, and hold-downs, follow the steps in **SKILL DRILL 16-1**.

SKILL DRILL 16-1 Inspecting, Cleaning, Filling, or Replacing the Battery, Battery Cables, Clamps, Connectors, Hold-Downs, and Battery Boxes

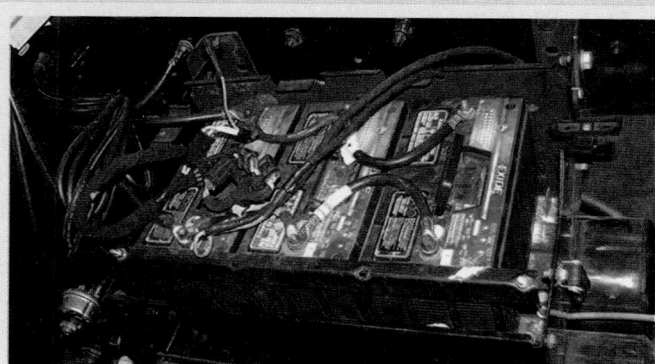

1. In battery banks, which consist of multiple batteries connected in parallel and series combinations, always disconnect the negative battery cables from the battery negative terminals first. Then remove the positive terminal cables. While they are disconnected, bend the cables back or if necessary, tie them out of the way, so that they cannot fall back and accidently reconnect the battery terminals.

2. Disconnect and remove the battery-battery jumper cables or buss bars, which are thin, flat, metal conductor plates connecting battery terminals of the same polarity.

3. Remove the battery hold-downs or other hardware securing the batteries. Battery hold-downs are commonly made of ¼" (6.35 mm) to 3/8" (9.53 mm) diameter threaded rod tightened to pieces of angle iron securely clamping the edges of a battery case.

4. Keeping each upright, remove each battery from its tray and place it on a clean, level work surface. Visually inspect the batteries for damage, cracks, bulges, loose or leaking posts, and so on. If any are found, the battery needs to be replaced. Wash dirty batteries, if necessary, to prevent current leakage over the battery cases from the terminals.

5. A few minutes after the batteries are disconnected and inspected, measure and record the open circuit voltage (OCV)

for each battery. (OCV is the voltage reading with no electrical loads connected to the battery.) Battery voltages should all be within 1/10th of a volt (+ or – 0.1 volts). All batteries drain to voltage of the lowest OCV.

6. Remove cell caps, if the electrolyte is serviceable. Check the electrolyte level and its appearance. Electrolyte should not only cover all the plates but have additional fill volume within the battery cells. Top up any cell that is low, but discard any battery that has had plates not covered in electrolyte.

7. Clean the battery compartment, hold-downs, the battery tray and box either by (a) power washing them, or by (b) wiping them with damp rags if the battery box is not excessively dirty. Wear protective rubber gloves while wiping the case to minimize exposure to any corrosive electrolyte leaked from the battery.

8. Clean the battery posts or screw terminals with a battery terminal tool. On lead post-type terminals, the preferred tool is a scraper style, since it is designed to produce smooth surfaces that are more airtight when clamped together. Wire brush threaded terminals.

9. Clean the cable terminals with the same battery terminal tool or wire brush. Inspect the battery cables to terminal connections for fraying or corrosion. Replace any terminals that appear loose or burned.

10. Reinstall the cleaned and serviced battery. Reinstall the hold-downs and make sure the battery is securely held in position. Note the location and polarity of terminals prior to battery installation to ensure proper cable routing and connection polarity is maintained. Reconnect the positive battery terminal and tighten it in place. Once the positive terminal is finished, reconnect the negative terminal and tighten it.

11. Coat the terminal connections with anti-corrosive paste or spray to keep oxygen and corrosive battery gasses from the terminal connections. Verify that a proper electrical connection is made by cranking and starting the vehicle several times.

► TECHNICIAN TIP

To prevent batteries from unevenly charging and discharging, it is critical to connect starter and other heavy-gauge battery cables to battery banks in a pattern that enables the most equal current rates to enter and leave each battery. Most heavy-duty cranking systems use at least two positive and ground battery cables when three or four batteries are used. Those cables should be arranged to provide the shortest and most equal length of current pathway from each battery. For example, if only two batteries are used, a positive cable is connected to one battery while the negative ground cable connects to the other battery (**FIGURE 16-7**).

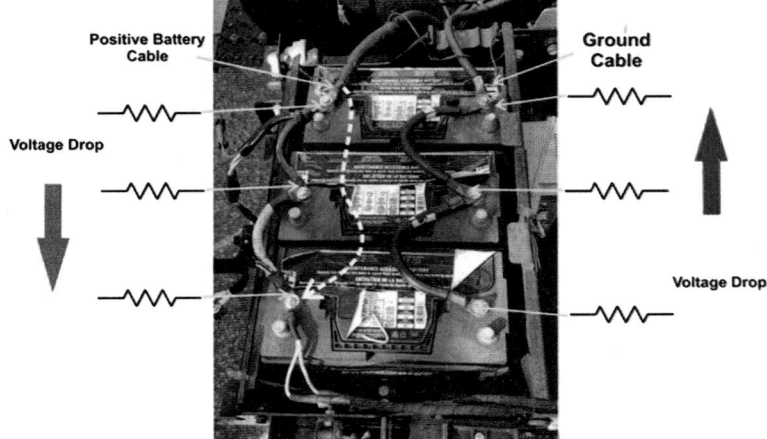

FIGURE 16-7 Some of the worst practices for connecting battery cables are represented here. The battery opposite the end where both cables are connected does not receive the same charging current as the first battery. Additional jumper cables and connections create resistance in positive and negative current pathways, as do other wire terminals sandwiched between battery terminals. The dotted arrow shows where the positive cable should connect.

Testing Battery State of Charge and Specific Gravity

Although the capacitance test is the industry standard to evaluate battery condition, other tests are used alongside capacity testing. One of those tests is the state of charge test. A **State of charge (SOC) test** tells you how charged or discharged a battery is, but not how much capacity it has.

A fully charged battery should have an open-circuit voltage of 12.65 volts. If the battery has been recently charged, it has a slightly higher open-circuit voltage, but a light load applied to the battery, such as switching on all vehicle lights for a minute, removes a surface charge on the plates that does not correctly indicate the battery's SOC. OCV is proportional to the battery electrolyte's specific gravity (SpGr). The SOC is also affected by temperature. About 1/10-volt change occurs for every 10°F (–12°C) below 80°F (27°C). **TABLE 16-1** shows SOC, as indicated by SpGr and voltage reading. The table compares SOC according to voltage measurement and

SpGr for two common types of lead-acid batteries used for starting, lighting, and igniting (SLI) purposes.

Voltage reading can also identify defective cells. Using a multi-meter, place one meter lead on either terminal of the battery, and dip the other lead into battery electrolyte (if accessible). The meter should record a change of 2.1 volts increase for each cell when moving across the battery and away from the terminal post. The exception is the first cell where the battery terminal post and cell share the same electrolyte. To measure the incremental voltage change of this cell, the same procedure is performed starting from the opposite terminal post. By touching one voltmeter lead to the terminal post and dipping the other lead in each cell's electrolyte, a successive increase of 2.1 volts should be observed in each cell after the first cell, allowing measurement of the cell voltage for the entire battery when the procedure is done starting from each terminal post.

TABLE 16-1 State of Charge Indicated by Specific Gravity and Voltage Reading

Open Circuit Voltage		Specific Gravity	Percentage State of Charge
Absorbed Glass Mat (AGM)	Flooded Lead Acid	Flooded Lead Acid	
12.90	12.65 or greater	1.265 (minimum)	100%
12.60	12.45	1.225	75%
12.30	12.24	1.190	50%
12.20	12.1	1.170	40%
12.0	12.06	1.155	25%
11.80	11.89	1.120	0%

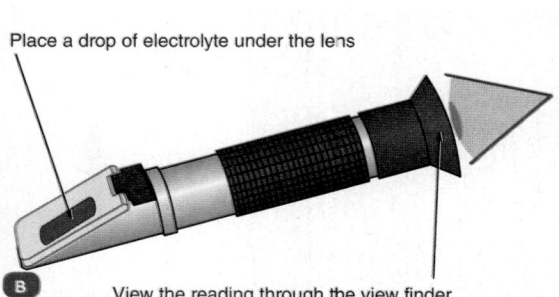

Place a drop of electrolyte under the lens

View the reading through the view finder

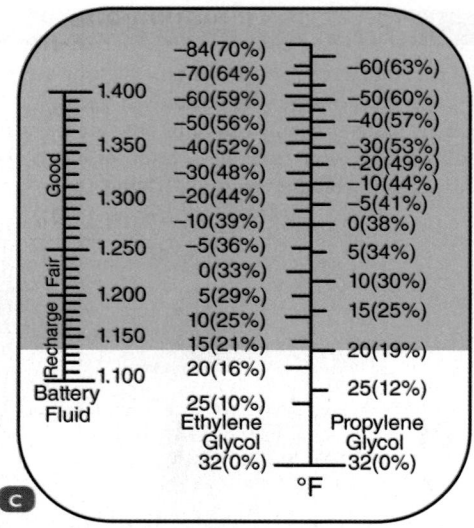

°F

FIGURE 16-8 A. A hydrometer. **B.** A refractometer. Either can be used to check the specific gravity (SpGr) of battery electrolyte in flooded cell batteries. **C.** The viewfinder of a refractometer displays a boundary between light and dark measurements for several fluids. Note the scale for battery electrolyte. The boundary line indicates the SpGr for the electrolyte.

Voltage readings in each cell can quickly determine the SOC in each cell, which can identify weak or defective cells. However, the SOC is best evaluated by measuring the density of electrolyte in each cell using either a bulb-type hydrometer or refractometer. Electronic refractometers are also available that can display electrolyte density readings in digital format. SpGr is a measurement of a liquid's density relative to water with a specific gravity of 1.0. The SpGr of electrolyte increases proportionally with the state of cell charge, with a fully charged cell having a density or SpGr of 1.265 greater than water. Cells should not have wide variations. If the SpGr reading between the highest and lowest cell is more than 0.050 points, the battery is defective. For example, if the highest SpGr is 1.265 points in one cell and only 1.210 in the lowest, the battery is scrap. **FIGURE 16-8** shows two different tools used to measure battery SpGr. An example of the type of scale for reading battery electrolyte is in Figure 16-8c.

Unlike the reading from a refractometer, the hydrometer's reading must be corrected for electrolyte temperature. The density of battery electrolyte changes with temperature and 1.265 SpGr is only the density of electrolyte at 80°F (27°C). To correct for temperature effects on SpGr, add or subtract 4 points to the reading either above or below 80°F (27°C) for every 10°F (6°C) temperature change. (For example, add 0.004 for temperatures at 70°F [21°C].) While electrolyte temperature changes with temperature, battery voltage readings change very little, with typically less than 1/10th of a volt reduction in open circuit voltage at 80°F (27°C) compared with 0°F (−18°C). Because the hydrometer draws electrolyte into it to raise a float, the electrolyte level must be at least slightly above the top of the plates to measure SpGr. If it is not, then distilled water needs to be added and the battery fully charged. To perform a battery SOC test, follow the steps in **SKILL DRILL 16-2**.

▶ **TECHNICIAN TIP**

When performing a state of charge test using battery electrolyte, keep these tips in mind:

- When filling a battery that is not fully charged, never fill it to the top of the full line, because charging the battery raises the electrolyte level.
- Only use distilled water, not tap water, since tap water with high minerals content can cause unintended chemical reactions and discharge the battery.
- Small amounts of electrolyte in the hydrometer may leak out, potentially damaging and corroding parts and battery terminals. Rinse the battery with water to remove corrosive electrolyte.
- Do not inadvertently remove electrolyte from one cell or add it to another cell when testing; doing so causes incorrect readings.
- Do not top up discharged batteries with an electrolyte solution, since the electrolyte acid content is overconcentrated when charged.

▶ **TECHNICIAN TIP**

A growing number of vehicle manufacturers require a scan tool connected to the on-board diagnostics (OBD) port to indicate to the battery management system or electrical system control module that a new battery is installed. Whenever a battery is replaced, a battery reset procedure commands the charging system to perform a re-adaption of charging system voltages to the new battery. Settings for threshold voltages for low-voltage disconnect system may also change during the reset procedure. Inputs during the reset procedure may include identifying the battery manufacturer, the type of battery technology, and battery capacity rating. Failure to perform a battery reset may cause an over- or undercharging condition, shorten the battery life, and even set fault codes resulting in power derates. Currently, the reset feature applies to only light-duty vehicles and some light trucks from Ford. However, the increasing reach of the battery management systems and electrical system controls on heavy-duty vehicles will likely soon result in the introduction of similar battery-reset procedures.

SKILL DRILL 16-2 Performing a Battery State of Charge Test

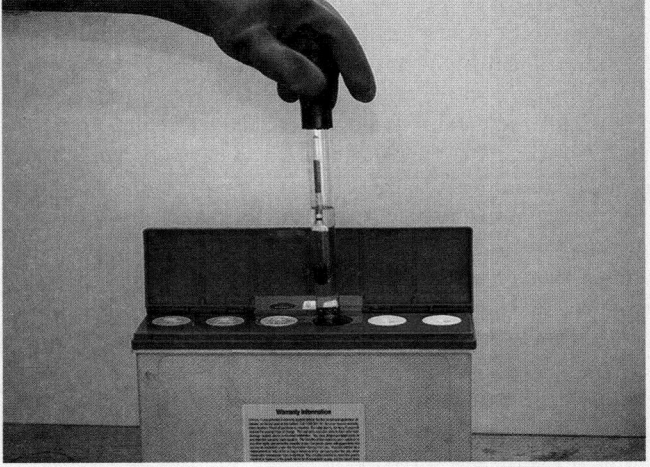

1. If the battery is not a sealed unit, it has individual or combined removable caps on top. Remove them and look inside to check the level of the electrolyte. If the level is below the tops of the plates and their separators inside, add distilled water or water with a low mineral content until it covers them. Be careful not to overfill the cells; they could "boil" over when charging. If water is added, the battery needs to be charged to ensure the newly added water mixes with the electrolyte before measuring the SpGr.

2. Using a hydrometer designed for battery testing, draw some of the electrolyte into the tester and look at the float inside it. A scale indicates the battery's relative SOC by measuring how high the float sits in relation to the fluid level. A very low overall reading (1.150 or below) indicates a low SOC. A high overall reading (about 1.280) indicates a high SOC. The reading from each cell should be the same. If the variation between the highest and lowest cell exceeds 0.050, the battery is defective and should be replaced. Be sure to consult temperature correction tables if the battery electrolyte temperature is not at or around 80°F (27°C).

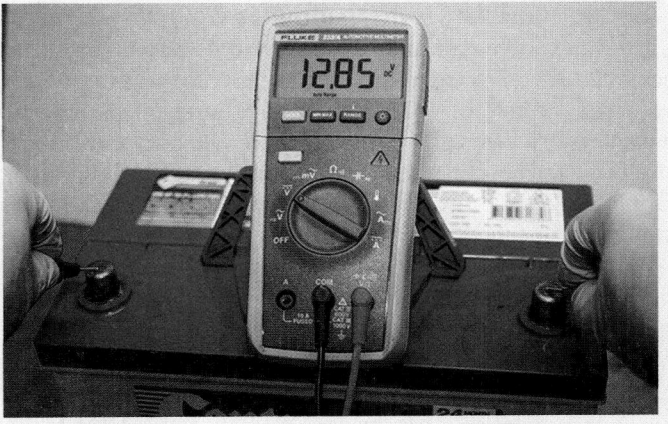

3. Using the refractometer, place one or two drops of electrolyte on the specimen window and lower the cover plate. Make sure the liquid covers the specimen window. If not, add another drop of electrolyte:
- Look into the eyepiece with the refractometer under a bright light.
- Read the scale for battery acid. The point where the dark area meets the light area is the reading. Compare the readings with the values given in step 2.

4. For open circuit voltage testing with a voltmeter, perform the following procedure: (a) With the engine off, select the "volts DC" range on the voltmeter and attach the positive and negative leads to the battery terminals. (b) With all electrical loads switched off and the battery near 80°F (27°C), the voltage reading should be at least 12.65 volts if the battery is fully charged. This reading does not drop more than 0.10 volts at 0°F (–18°C).

Testing Battery Capacity

Generally speaking, battery capacity refers to the amount of electrical current or power a battery is capable of delivering. How powerful a battery is directly relates to its capacity. This means the capacity of a battery is a measurement of the amperage supplied for a given voltage. Another way to think of a load test is it tests the battery's ability to produce the high cranking amperage, while maintaining enough voltage to operate the engine's electronic control systems.

Traditionally, a battery's capacity is measured using a high amperage discharge load test. The **load test** determines the ability of a battery to deliver cranking amperage at a specific voltage and is based on the battery's Cold-Cranking Amps (CCA) rating. According to the Battery Council International (BCI) standards, a 1,000 CCA battery is expected to deliver at least 1,000 amps at 0°F (–18°C) for 30 seconds, while supplying a voltage of no less than 7.2 volts during the test. When performing a load test, only half the CCA rating is applied as an electrical load, discharging battery current for 15 seconds.

Before performing a load test, the battery's state of charge must be evaluated and determined to be at least 75% to accurately measure its capacity. A carbon pile is used to simulate a high amperage electrical load on the battery. The carbon pile is a large-capacity variable resister made from stacks of thin carbon discs. Squeezing carbon discs together to increase disc-to-disc pressure lowers the resistance between the discs, increasing the amperage discharged by the battery. At the end of 15 seconds, after one-half the CCA rating has been applied, battery voltage must not fall below 9.6 volts. If it does, the battery is scrap. Because temperature affects battery resistance, 0.1 volts is subtracted from the failure threshold voltage level of 9.6 volts for every 10°F below 70°F (21°C) (**FIGURE 16-9**).

An inductive-type amp clamp is placed around one of the heavy test leads of the carbon pile load tester to measure amperage when the load is applied. This amp clamp has a directional indicator for current flow polarity since DC amp clamps use Hall Effect-type sensors measuring magnetic field strength. To properly sense the strength of the magnetic field rotating around the conductor, the clamp must be correctly orientated (**FIGURE 16-10**).

If the battery fails the load test after it has had its SOC properly qualified, the battery should be discarded. No attempt should be made to recharge and re-load test a marginally performing battery after it has failed the first time. To load test a battery, follow the steps in **SKILL DRILL 16-3**.

Testing Battery Conductance

A **conductance test**, like a load test, determines the battery's capacity, which refers to its ability to produce current. Conductance testing has displaced high amperage load testing because of a number of problems with conventional load testing. Evaluating a battery's condition using hydrometers, refractometers, and load testers provides reasonably accurate results if the instruments are used correctly and the battery is tested under proper conditions. In the field, however, batteries often need charging for as much as a day before they can be load tested, and preliminary SOC testing is time-consuming.

In cold weather, testing batteries in equipment operated outside presents other problems, too. Battery capacity drops with temperature and the likelihood of false failures increases if outdoor test results are not properly temperature-corrected. To avoid the problem of falsely failing batteries because they are simply cold or in a poor SOC when tested, several types of rapid-test battery analyzers have emerged. These battery analyzers eliminate the need for preliminary SOC testing and validation before performing a high amperage discharge-type battery load test. These newer types of battery analyzers are called conductance-, impedance-, or ohmic-type testers and measure the amount of active plate surface area available for chemical reaction (**FIGURE 16-11**). Active plate surface area, measured according to how well it conducts alternating current, is a reliable indication of a healthy battery because it corresponds directly to battery capacity (**FIGURE 16-12**). The terms ohmic, impedance, and conductance tester refer to the same principle used by all these analyzers in that they measure the battery's resistance to

BATTERY LOAD TEST TEMPERATURE/VOLTAGE CHART								
Temperature in degrees Fahrenheit								
70°	60°	50°	40°	30°	20°	10°	0°
9.6	9.5	9.4	9.3	9.1	9.0	8.7	8.5
Minimum battery voltage at end of test								

FIGURE 16-9 A load tester has a chart to correct for battery temperature at the 15-second voltage cut-off point. Lower cut-off voltage is allowed when the battery is cold.

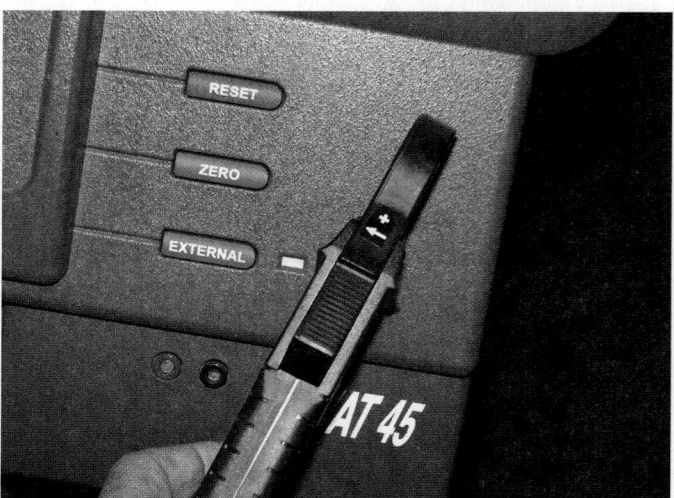

FIGURE 16-10 An amp clamp, which measures amperage by sensing the strength of a magnetic field around a conductor uses a Hall Effect sensor. The clamp must be properly oriented according to the direction of current flow to correctly measure amperage.

SKILL DRILL 16-3 Load Testing a Battery

1. With the carbon pile controls in the off position, connect the heavy positive and negative cable leads to each terminal post of a single battery. Observe the correct polarity when connecting leads and be sure the lead clamps fully contact the battery terminals to enable high amperage to pass through the clamps.

2. Place the inductive-type amp clamp around either the positive or negative leads for the carbon pile. Note, the amp clamp must be correctly oriented, according to the direction of current flow. A directional indicator for current flow is always used on an amp clamp containing a Hall Effect sensor.

3. Verify that the battery's state of charge is more than 75% before beginning the test. Also, measure the battery's temperature to make any correction to the cut-off voltage threshold.

4. If an automatic load tester is used, enter the battery's CCA and select "test" or "start." If you are using a manual load tester, calculate the test load, which is half of the CCA. Rotate the control knob on the carbon pile to increase the rate of discharge amperage or press the "start" button on an automatic load tester.

5. Maintain calculated load of one-half the CCA rating for 15 seconds while observing the load test unit's voltmeter. At the end of the 15-second test load, observe and record both the cut-off voltage and amperage then immediately turn the carbon pile control knob off. At room temperature, the voltage must be 9.6 volts or higher at the end of the 15-second load. If the battery is colder than room temperature, correct the battery failure threshold voltage against temperature. This correction chart is usually located on the load tester. Close to 1/10 volt lower is allowed for every 10°F below 70°F (21°C). Using the results from the test, determine any necessary action.

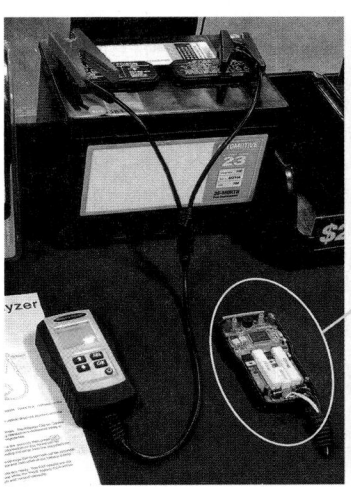
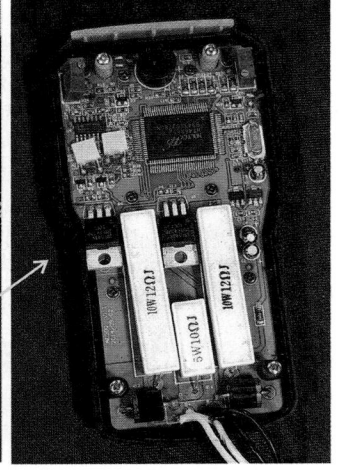

FIGURE 16-11 Conductance testers calculate battery resistance typically by sending several AC waves of different frequency, amperage, and voltage through the battery to calculate resistance.

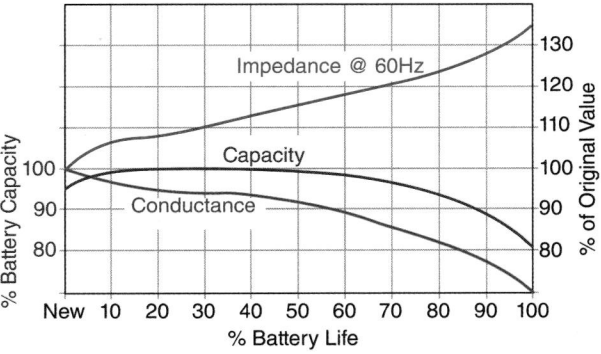

FIGURE 16-12 A battery's resistance is directly correlated with conductance to AC current which is measured by impedance. Battery capacity or life is inversely proportional to its resistance or impedance.

a low-amperage, low-voltage AC sent through the battery. By measuring various features of the 50 HZ to 1 kHZ AC signal leaving the battery after it passes through cell plates, connectors, and terminal straps, the battery's resistance to the signal is calculated (**FIGURE 16-13**). Good quality or premium featured conductance testers can also consider the SOC of a battery and apply a correction factor to measurements taken from even partially charged batteries having as little as 2 volts during the test, adjusting measurements to a fully charged state. Also referred to as impedance testing, the AC equivalent term for resistance,

battery plate conductance declines as the battery deteriorates. Several signals with different frequencies and current levels may be sent through the battery, depending on the sophistication of the analyzer. Varying voltage and amperage along with different frequencies of the AC signal enables calculation of battery resistance using Ohm's Law (resistance = voltage/amperage), which applies to AC for only resistive-type loads).

The widespread acceptance of conductance testing is underlined by the practice of all manufacturers now requiring the use of a conductance test, instead of a high-amperage load test, before warranty claims are considered. Many of the testers have integrated printers and, for the battery to be warranted, a printout of the test result has to accompany the returned battery (**FIGURE 16-14**). Advantages of conductance testing are as follows:

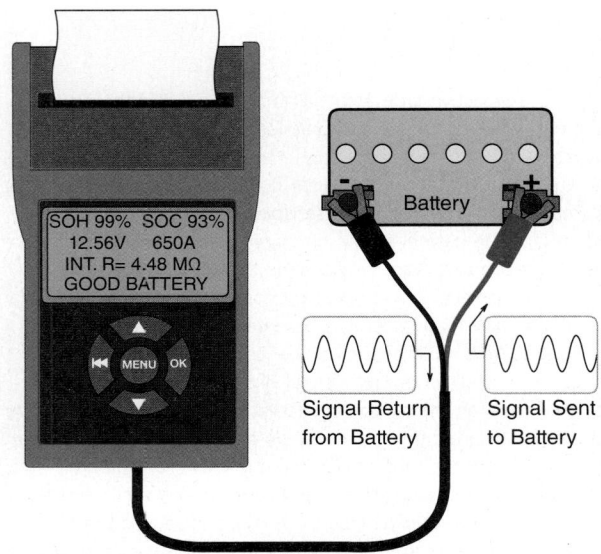

FIGURE 16-13 A conductance tester analyzes an AC waveform transmitted through a battery as a factor used to calculate battery resistance.

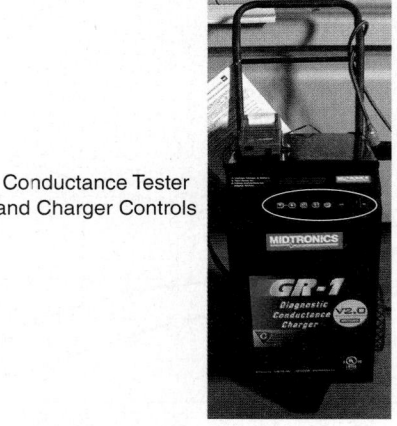

Conductance Tester and Charger Controls

FIGURE 16-14 A conductance-type battery analyzer integrated with an intelligent battery charger for absorbed glass mat (AGM) valve-regulated lead-acid (VRLA)-type batteries.

- It does not require any high-amperage battery discharge activity.
- It requires only minimal technician involvement, because only two clip-on connectors are attached to the battery terminals during the test.
- It is fast—the testing can usually be performed in under two minutes.
- Low-amperage, low-frequency AC waves current do not affect battery.
- Conductance testing does not prematurely age the battery
- It is safe—no heat or gassing is produced.
- Conductance testing can be repeated immediately to verify result.
- Batteries can be evaluated in a state of discharge; some testers only require as little as 2 volts of battery voltage to accurately qualify the condition of the battery.

FIGURE 16-15 Printouts from a conductance tester.

- The testing method is endorsed by all electrical standards testing organizations, including BCI.
- Printed read-outs can be supplied to the customer or accompany warranty claims (**FIGURE 16-15**).

The most common type of conductance tester works by applying an AC voltage of a known frequency and amplitude across the battery. The battery's response to the signal is interpreted by a microcontroller inside the test unit. Conductance, or acceptance of the AC voltage, is measured by comparing the shape of the AC waveform exiting the battery to the waveform sent into the battery. The closer the waveforms match, the better the conductivity of the battery.

The most sophisticated testers today analyze lead acid, Li-ion, and NiMH batteries using a microcontroller storing models of waveforms that match known good battery configurations. These analyzers can identify not only the type and condition of a battery, but more sophisticated models identify the manufacturer and other battery details.

To conductance test a battery, follow the steps in **SKILL DRILL 16-4**.

> ▶ **TECHNICIAN TIP**

Never use steel bolts, nuts, washers, etc. on battery terminals when using conductance testers Instead, only use the lead adapters supplied with the conductance tester. The materials and any coatings on other hardware interfere with the signals sent through the battery and affect the tester's accuracy. Conductance testing is best suited for starting, lighting, and ignition (SLI) batteries and may not provide accurate results for deep-cycle batteries using thicker plates.

Charging Batteries

LO 16-4 Identify and describe the stages of battery charging and the types of battery chargers used to restore a battery to a full state of charge.

Battery chargers are used not only to charge partial or fully discharged batteries, but to maintain a battery in a full state of charge. A flooded lead-acid battery should not be charged when charging voltage exceeds cell voltage of 2.15 volts, or 12.9 volts for a 12-volt battery at room temperature. Increasing charging

SKILL DRILL 16-4 Conductance Testing a Battery

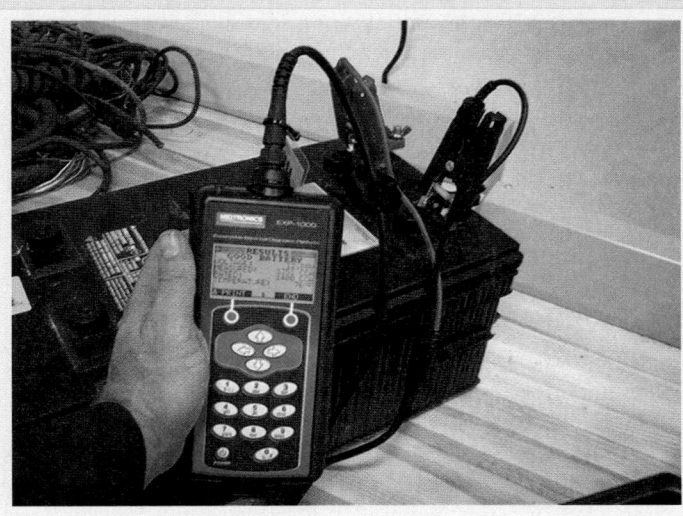

1. Consult manufacturers' procedures and guidelines for the battery being tested and tester being used.
2. Isolate batteries, if they are connected in a bank, so they can be individually tested.
3. Identify the type of battery, CCA rating, and voltage for input into the test unit. Some units also require a temperature input, since battery capacity and resistance vary with temperature.
4. Save information and input, as required, into the test unit.
5. Install lead terminals on threaded stud-type battery posts. The battery post material affects the conduction of wave forms and false failures result if lead terminals are not used.
6. Run the test.
7. Analyze the result by comparing them to manufacturer specifications.
8. Print or record results of the battery test. Repeat steps if multiple batteries are to be tested.

voltage increases the charging rate, enabling more amperage to flow into a battery. As the battery charges, its resistance increases and limits the charging rate, even though the charging voltage remains the same. Battery resistance also increases when it is cold, which requires higher charging voltage to achieve the same charge rate at room temperature. For example, battery resistance at –4°F (–20°C) requires close to 16.5 volts to achieve an acceptable charging rate. Similarly, less voltage is needed to charge a battery when temperatures exceed 80°F (27°C).

When charging above 2.35 volts per cell or 14.1 volts for a 12-volt, flooded lead-acid battery, it begins to gas, which means water in the electrolyte is broken down into hydrogen and oxygen gas through electrolysis. A battery can be charged at this rate, and even higher, but the plates and electrolyte begin to overheat during prolonged charging above gassing voltage. Depending on its size and the charging voltage, water loss, grid corrosion, and even plate buckling, can take place when a battery is charged for a long time, usually measured in days, when continuously charged above its gassing voltage. However, during an initial charge-absorption stage, it is acceptable to charge at a higher charge rate until the battery temperature becomes excessive or the battery begins to gas. An initial fast charge lasting for a few minutes uses a charging voltage that is typically between 14.58 to 15.18 volts. Once an initial charge is absorbed by the battery, a longer charge-absorption stage can take place where the battery reaches its full charge level using a charge voltage of no more than approximately 2.4 volts per cell, or 14.6 volts for a 12-volt battery. After a battery is 100% charged, it can remain connected to a charger to maintain its capacity by compensating for the self-discharge rate of the battery. Charging voltage during the maintenance period after a battery is charged is called the float voltage and is 2.25 volts per cell, or 13.5 volts for a 12-volt battery.

Batteries go dead for a variety of reasons. Parasitic drains, self-discharge, or battery leakage are common reasons a battery may quickly lose its charge. A number of different chargers are available to recharge dead batteries, each with its own advantages and disadvantages.

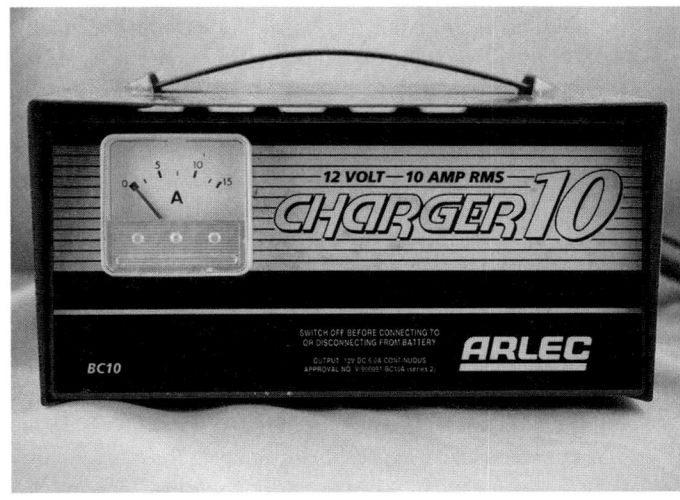

FIGURE 16-16 Care should be taken with this type of basic constant-voltage charger to ensure overcharging does not occur.

Battery Charger Types

Differentiating between the types of battery chargers is useful for determining the best method for recharging a battery, given its condition and other operating variables. The most common types of chargers include constant-voltage chargers, constant-current chargers, taper-current chargers, pulse chargers, and intelligent chargers.

■ **Constant-voltage chargers**, like the one shown in **FIGURE 16-16**, are DC power supplies that use a step-down transformer and a rectifier to convert AC voltage to DC voltage for charging. As the name suggest, output voltage is constant between 13 and 14 volts. A manual switch may allow the voltage setting to increase or decrease to change the charge rate or amperage the battery is charged with. These designs are found in inexpensive chargers and must be used with care because they can cause overcharging of batteries. **Trickle chargers**, which charge a battery at a low-amperage rate, are made following this design. Slow charging or trickle charging a battery with less than an amp of current is less hazardous to a battery than fast charging because a low-amperage charge does not excessively heat and gas a battery.

■ **Constant-current chargers** automatically vary the voltage applied to the battery to maintain a constant amperage flow into the battery. Voltage is automatically varied to maintain the constant current into the battery as its resistance changes. Also called series chargers, several batteries can be connected together in series and charged together. These are premium, high-end chargers not commonly found in service facilities.

■ **Taper-current chargers**, like that shown in **FIGURE 16-17**, are the most common found in repair shops. Either constant voltage or constant amperage is applied to the battery through a manually adjusted current-selection switch. Charger current only diminishes as the cell voltage increases. These chargers can cause serious damage to batteries through overcharging if the charge current (amperage) is adjusted too high. Timers can automatically shut off the charger to prevent overcharging causing excessive electrolyte gassing and plate damage.

■ **Pulse chargers** are recommended to recover sulfated batteries and send current into the battery in pulses of one-half to one-second cycles. Varying the voltage and length of time a DC pulse is applied to the battery controls the charging rate. During the charging process, a short rest period between pulses improves the quality of chemical reactions in the battery.

■ An **intelligent charger's** output varies with the sensed condition of a battery. This means the charger, like the one shown in **FIGURE 16-18**, monitors battery voltage and temperature and varies its output based on these variables. The charger also calculates the optimal charge current and varies it over the charging period, depending on the type of battery connected to it. Charging terminates when the voltage, temperature, or charge time indicates a full charge. VRLA batteries are best suited to these types of chargers. These chargers can be left connected indefinitely without

overcharging since they can maintain a float charge. This means the charging voltage floats at just above a cell voltage of 2.15 volts until it senses that the battery voltage has fallen and then resumes charging.

> ▶ **TECHNICIAN TIP**
>
> Removing the negative battery terminal while charging a battery reduces the risk of an inductive type high voltage spike damaging any electronic devices on the vehicle if the ignition key is switched on.

Charging Battery Banks: Series or Parallel

Manufacturers install multiple batteries in most heavy-duty commercial vehicles to provide additional cranking amperage. Knowing how the batteries are connected determines how to properly connect a battery charger. Batteries can be connected in series or parallel. Batteries connected in series have terminal polarities connected in line or in series with each other, with the positive of one connected to the negative of the other, and so on. Connecting batteries in series increases battery voltage by addition. For example, two 12-volt batteries with 500 CCA capacity connected in series deliver 24 volts with 500 CCA capacity. Batteries connected in parallel have terminal polarities connected with positive to positive and negative to negative. Connecting batteries in parallel adds capacity but does not change battery voltage. Two 12-volt 500 CCA batteries connected in parallel can deliver 12 volts with 1,000 CCA capacity.

To charge a 24-volt set of batteries, a 24-volt charger is needed to charge all the batteries at the same time. If only a 12-volt charger is available, there are two options: either charge one battery at a time, or reconnect the batteries so they are connected in parallel. To charge batteries, follow the steps in **SKILL DRILL 16-5**.

FIGURE 16-18 This intelligent charger automatically controls the charge going to the battery. Different battery types can also be selected to ensure the correct charge rate for the battery type.

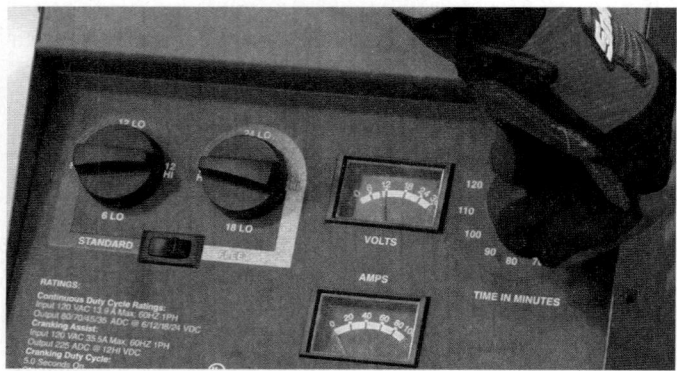

FIGURE 16-17 Note the timer on the right-hand side of this taper-current charger to reduce the risk of overcharging.

SKILL DRILL 16-5 Charging Commercial Batteries

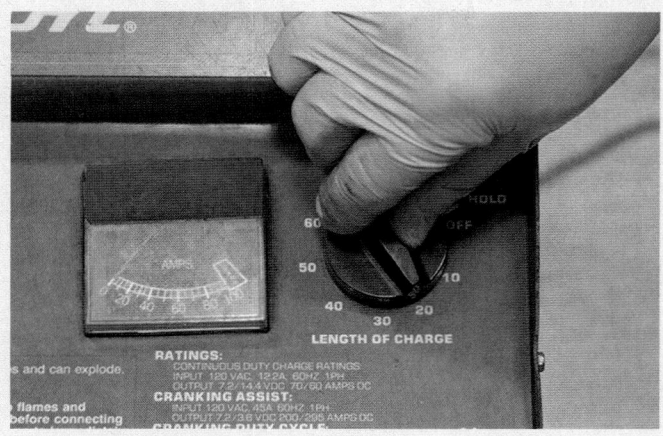

1. Determine the voltage of the system that needs charging. If you are charging a 12-volt battery, use the 12-volt setting on the charger. If you are charging a 24-volt battery, or two 12-volt batteries connected in series, use the 24-volt setting on the charger, if it has one.
2. Identify the positive and negative terminals. Never simply use only the color of the cables to determine the positive or negative terminals; use the + and − or the Pos and Neg terminal-post markings.

3. Visually inspect the battery to ensure there are no cracks, holes, or damage to the casing.
4. To avoid igniting explosive battery gases by electrical sparks, verify that the charger is unplugged from the wall and turned off. Connect the positive (+) red lead from the charger to the positive (+) battery terminal. Connect the black lead (−) from the charger to the negative battery terminal.
5. Adjust the settings on the charger that best match the battery condition. A partially discharged battery may require a temporary fast charge. Otherwise, select an automatic function.
6. Turn the charger on and select the automatic setting, if equipped. Select the rate of charge. A slow charger usually charges at a rate of less than 5 amperes. A fast-charging rate charges at a much higher ampere rate using higher charging voltage, depending on the original battery state of charge; a fast charge should be carried out only under constant supervision.
7. Verify that the voltage and amperage the charger is putting out is correct.
8. Once the battery is charged, turn the charger off. Disconnect the black lead from the negative battery terminal and then the red lead from the positive battery terminal.
9. Allow the battery to stand for at least five minutes before testing the battery. Using a load tester or hydrometer, test the charged state of the battery.

SAFETY TIP

When connecting jumper cables, a spark almost always occurs on the last connection you make. That is why it is critical that you make the last connection on the chassis away from the battery and any other flammables. A spark also occurs when you disconnect the first jumper cable connection, so that also needs to be the connection somewhere on the chassis.

- Keep your face and body as far back as you can while connecting jumper leads.
- Do not connect the negative cable to the discharged battery because the spark may blow up the battery, if it is heavily gassed.
- Use only specially designed heavy-duty jumper cables to start a vehicle with a dead battery. Do not try to connect the batteries with any other type of cable.
- Always make sure you wear the appropriate personal protective equipment (PPE) before starting the job. Remember, batteries contain sulfuric acid, and exploding batteries not only disintegrate into sharp pieces of plastic battery cases, but also send acid flying in all directions.
- Always follow any manufacturer's personal safety instructions to prevent damage to the vehicle you are servicing.

Jump-Starting Vehicles

Jump-starting a vehicle is the process of using one vehicle with a charged battery to provide electrical energy to start another vehicle that has a discharged battery. Because starting a vehicle requires a high amount of electrical energy, jump-starting a vehicle can stress the alternator on the vehicle supplying current and create the potential for inductive voltage spikes produced when connecting and disconnecting current sources. Voltage spikes can result in unexpected electrical system damage on both vehicles.

To jump-start commercial vehicles, follow the steps in **SKILL DRILL 16-6**.

Measuring Parasitic Draw

LO 16-5 Define and explain a parasitic load condition and identify procedures used to pinpoint a parasitic load.

All modern vehicles consume a small amount of current draw when the ignition is turned off. This current is used to operate some of the vehicle systems, such as security systems, and other modules connected to the onboard vehicle network. The vehicle control systems also require a small amount of power to retain the keep-alive memory while the vehicle is off. Normal key-off electrical loads should only draw a relatively small amount of current, since excessive draw can quickly discharge the battery. When key-off loads are unintentional and quickly drain the battery, they are called parasitic electrical loads.

Key-off current draw does not necessarily immediately drop to its lowest level the instant the ignition is turned off. Load shedding can occur over a period of usually less than a

SKILL DRILL 16-6 Jump-Starting Commercial Vehicles

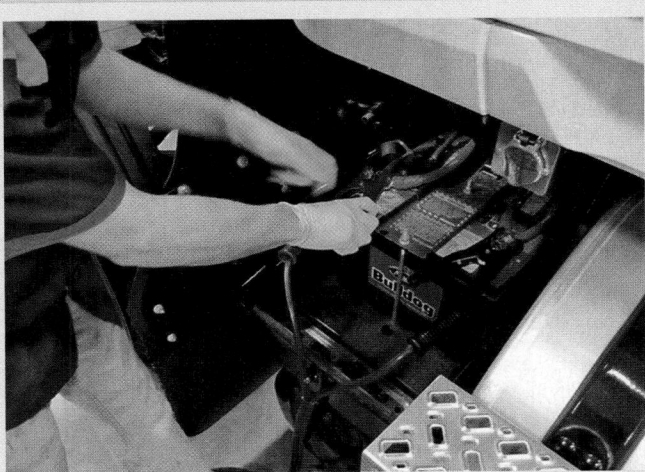

1. Position the charged battery close enough to the discharged battery that it is within comfortable range of your jumper cables. If the charged battery is in another vehicle, make sure the two vehicles are not touching.
2. Always connect the leads in this order:
   • First, connect the red jumper lead to the positive terminal of the discharged battery in the vehicle you are trying to start. The positive terminal is the one with the plus sign. Check for remote-located jumper posts, like the ones in the figure shown below.

Jumper Cable Posts

Battery cable connections like this allow convenient connection points to jump start batteries without creating sparks around batteries, or the need to remove access covers to battery banks.

   • Next, connect the other end of this lead to the positive terminal of the charged battery.
   • Then connect the black jumper lead to the negative terminal of the charged battery. The negative terminal is the one with the minus sign.
   • Connect the other end of the negative lead to a good ground on the chassis of the vehicle with the discharged battery, and as far away as possible from the battery.
   • DO NOT connect the lead to the negative terminal of the discharged battery itself; doing so may cause a dangerous spark.
3. Try to start the vehicle with the discharged battery. If the booster battery does not have enough charge or the jumper cables are too small in diameter to do this, start the engine in the booster vehicle and allow it to partially charge the discharged battery for several minutes. Try starting the first vehicle again with the booster vehicle's engine running.
4. Disconnect the leads in the reverse order of connecting them. Remove the negative lead from the chassis ground away from the battery. Then disconnect the negative lead from the booster battery. Next remove the positive lead from the booster battery, and lastly, disconnect the other positive end from the battery in the vehicle you have just started. If the charging system is working correctly and the battery is in good condition, the battery is recharging while the engine is running. Note, a deeply discharged set of batteries can cause the alternator to charge at an excessively high rate for too long and damage the alternator.

half an hour as various control modules go into hibernation or sleep mode. This explains why it is important to consult the manufacturer's service information to determine the maximum allowable parasitic current draw and the permissible time period for normal key-off loads present after the ignition is initially switched off.

Parasitic current draw can be measured in several ways. The traditional method is using an ammeter capable of measuring milliamps and connecting it in series between the battery post and the battery terminal. A better and more common method is to use an inductive-type amp clamp and place it over a battery cable lead. If more than one battery cable lead is used

SKILL DRILL 16-7 Measuring Parasitic Draw on a Battery

1. Research the parasitic draw specifications in the appropriate service information system for the vehicle with a suspected parasitic, key-off excessive current draw. Typically this maximum is between 0.035 amps and 0.050 amps (35–50 milliamps).
2. Connect the low-current amp clamp around (or insert the ammeter in series with) the negative or positive battery cable and measure the parasitic draw. Compare the parasitic draw with specifications.
3. Disconnect the vehicle circuit fuses one at a time to isolate the source of excessive parasitic current draw. Determine any necessary actions by comparing key-off current draws for the device against original equipment manufacturer (OEM) specifications.

for either the positive or negative cables, a measurement must be made on both cables of either positive or negative polarity. That means both positive or both negative cable amperage is measured, added together, and the total electrical current drawn is recorded. Note that the vehicle's control module sleep timers may reset during the process of disconnecting the battery terminal and connecting the ammeter in series, so a period of waiting for the modules to hibernate is required. If excessive parasitic draw is measured, disconnect fuses or systems one at a time, while monitoring parasitic current draw, to isolate the circuit causing excessive draw. Each major component in that circuit requires isolation with an ammeter to pinpoint the cause of excessive current draw.

Disconnecting the battery can be avoided if a sensitive low-current (that is, milliamps) clamp is available. The low-amp **current clamp** measures the magnetic field generated by a very small current flow through a wire or cable. Placing the low-amp current clamp around the negative or positive battery cable allows you to measure the parasitic draw. To measure parasitic draw with a parasitic load test, follow the steps in **SKILL DRILL 16-7**.

Identify and Test Low-Voltage Disconnect (LVD) Systems

Low-voltage disconnect (LVD) systems disconnect a battery load when the voltage of the battery falls below a preset threshold. By doing this, they protect the battery from being excessively discharged and enable the vehicle to maintain enough battery capacity to start. The voltage threshold is normally set between 12.2 and 12.4 volts. Once the battery voltage rises above the set threshold, as it does when the vehicle starts and the alternator commences charging, the load is reconnected automatically. In many cases, LVDs also incorporates an audible alarm and visual warning light to alert the operator before disconnection occurs.

LVDs are connected in series with the load. They are tested by varying the amount of input voltage around the threshold settings

and checking the switching of the output or load to determine if the device switches on and off at the correct voltages. Testing can be conducted on the vehicle or off the vehicle on a test bench. The LVD is tested on the vehicle by monitoring the input and output, or load voltage, with a voltmeter while placing a load across the battery to lower battery voltage. At the threshold point, the device should turn the power off to the output or load. If a voltmeter is not available, a test lamp may be used to indicate when the output or load voltage drops away as the device switches off, although the output voltage should be measured at some point to ensure the load is receiving full battery voltage when the LVD has the load switched on. Compare the threshold voltages for swtich on and off with the manufacturer's specifications. The units are usually sealed and are not serviceable, although some units may provide a means for adjusting threshold voltages.

The LVD can also be tested off vehicle using a variable-voltage power supply. When using a variable-voltage power supply to test an LVD, duplicate the connections made on the vehicle with the power supply taking the place of the battery. Verify that the power supply is capable of supplying enough current to operate the LVD and any load connected to it on the bench. Once the unit is connected to the power supply and load, as per manufacturer requirements, slowly increase and decrease the power supply voltage to test the threshold voltages at which the LVD switches on and off the output or load. To identify and test a LVD system, follow the steps in **SKILL DRILL 16-8**.

Battery Recycling

Disposal is a critical issue at the end of every battery's service life. Batteries contain many environmentally damaging chemicals and neurotoxic lead. If they find their way into a landfill, the lead can contaminate the soil and groundwater. For this reason, recycling of batteries is mandatory. Many local governments require battery recycling and levy a "core charge" on every new lead-acid battery sold. The core charge is refunded if an old battery is brought in and exchanged for the new one. This process helps prevent batteries from being discarded in landfills. Check local laws and regulations to ensure that batteries are disposed of correctly.

SKILL DRILL 16-8 Identifying and Testing a Low-Voltage Disconnect (LVD)

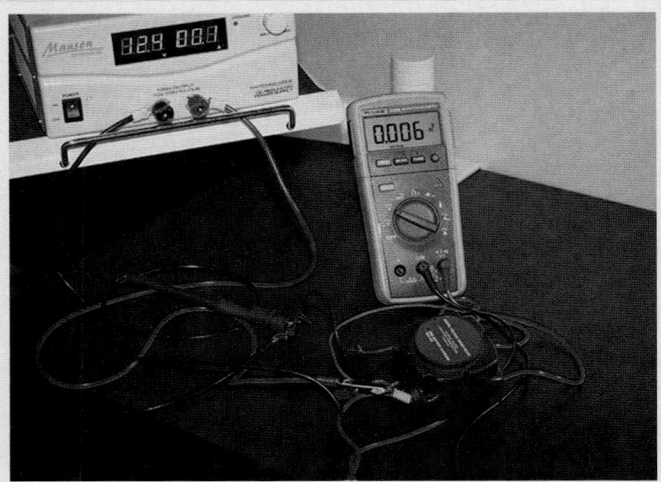
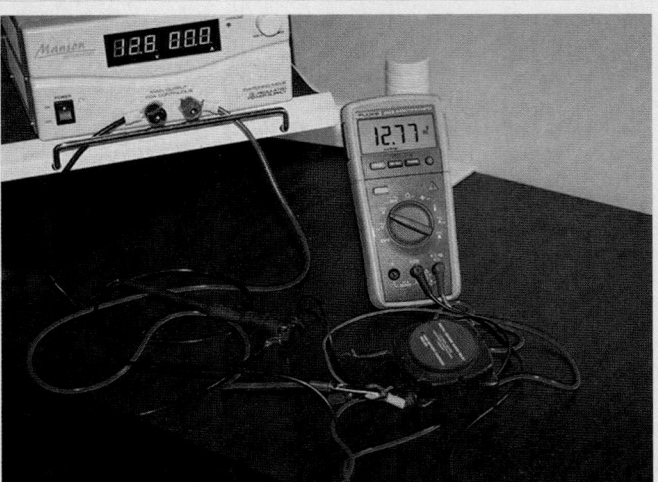

1. Research the LVD specifications, such as the wiring schematic, device operation, and threshold voltages, in the appropriate manufacturer's information.
2. Check the unit on the vehicle for appropriate power and grounds, as per the manufacturer's specifications. If no battery voltage is present on the input side of the LVD, check fuses or circuit breakers for correct operation. Correct any power or ground problems before proceeding to check LVD threshold voltages.
3. If testing the unit on a test bench, remove the unit from the vehicle and connect both power and grounds to the unit, as per manufacturer's specifications.
4. Connect a voltmeter to the input or battery-side connection of the LVD and a second voltmeter or test lamp to the output or load-side connection. Observe and record the voltage readings on both the input and output of the LVD.
5. Vary the battery voltage by connecting a carbon pile load bank, like the one used to load test batteries to the vehicle battery,

if testing in the vehicle, or adjust the voltage supply, if using a variable-voltage power supply for bench testing.
6. Note the voltmeter readings of the threshold voltages from the input of the LVD as the unit turns the load or output on and off. Compare the voltage readings with manufacturer's specifications. If the unit does not meet specifications, adjust the threshold voltage, if adjustment is possible. If the unit is not adjustable or cannot be adjusted to manufacturer's specifications, then the unit needs to be replaced.
7. Connect an appropriate load to the output or load side of the LVD and recheck the threshold voltages to ensure the unit is capable of supplying the current with minimal voltage drop between the input and output or load.
8. Check the operation of any warning lights or bulbs fitted to the unit, ensuring they turn on and off as the output or load of the LVD is turned on and off. Report any recommendations and return the unit to normal operation.

Wrap-Up

Ready for Review

▶ Testing the batteries should be the starting point when diagnosing complaints, such as hard starting, slow cranking, or no start; when lights dim when an engine idles, or other electrical problems occur; and whenever an alternator is replaced.

▶ Keeping the battery and terminals clean is one of the best maintenance practices for batteries.

▶ Safety should be the first priority when working around and servicing batteries. The electrolyte inside lead-acid batteries is corrosive and can cause injury to skin and eyes and can cause damage to clothing and the vehicle's parts.

▶ Batteries also produce an explosive gas mixture of hydrogen and oxygen during charging and discharging of the battery.

▶ Batteries fail suddenly due to the loss of a cell or open circuits within the internal connections. Batteries also fail gradually through loss of capacity caused by age, sulfation, extremes in operating temperature, vibration, low electrolyte levels, and grid corrosion.

▶ Inspecting, cleaning, and filling (if not maintenance-free) are common task°s that should be performed every six months to one year on top-post batteries

▶ The reverse current flow from a battery can damage some or all of the electronic control units (ECUs) throughout the vehicle, so it is critical to connect the battery correctly to prevent sending the current in the reverse direction through the electrical system.

▶ The capacitance test is the preferred test of battery condition.

▶ State-of-charge testing indicates how charged or discharged a battery is. Low-maintenance or no-maintenance-type batteries may not provide access to the electrolyte in the cells for SOC testing.

▶ Technicians use hydrometers and refractometers to measure the specific gravity of the electrolyte in the battery during a SOC test.

▶ Load testing has long been used to test a battery's capacity and internal condition, but is no longer used. Manufacturers now insist on conductance testing for batteries, particularly any battery returned under warranty.

▶ There are a number of different battery charger types available for charging batteries: constant-voltage, constant-current, taper-current, pulsed charger, and intelligent chargers.

▶ Even with the ignition turned off, all modern vehicles have a small amount of current draw used to run some of the vehicle systems, such as the on-board network modules.

▶ The parasitic current draw should be a relatively small amount of current, since excessive draw discharges the battery over a short amount of time.

▶ Correct disposal of batteries by recycling them is good for the environment, and the precious metals can be reclaimed for reuse.

Key Terms

conductance test A type of battery test that measures a battery's capacity using alternating current (AC) voltage.

constant-current charger A battery charger that automatically varies the voltage applied to the battery to maintain a constant amperage flow into the battery.

constant-voltage charger A direct current (DC) power that is a step-down transformer with a rectifier to provide the DC voltage to charge.

current clamp A device that clamps around a conductor to measure current flow. It is often used in conjunction with a digital volt-ohmmeter (DVOM).

intelligent charger A battery charger that varies its output according to the sensed condition of the battery it is charging.

load test A battery capacity test that electrically loads the battery to a high rate of discharge, while measuring final voltage after 15 seconds of electrical load.

pulse charger A battery charger that sends current into the battery in pulses of one-second cycles; used to recover sulfated batteries.

shedding A process that reduces the plate surface area and, therefore, reduces capacity. Shedding may also produce short circuits between the bottom of positive and negative plates.

state of charge (SOC) test A test that indicates how charged or discharged a battery is, not how much capacity it has.

taper-current charger A battery charger that applies a selected amperage to charge a battery through a manually adjusted current-selection switch.

trickle charger A battery charger that charges at a low amperage rate.

Review Questions

1. Which of the following reasons best explains why a battery should be tested or replaced after an alternator or starting motor is replaced?
   a. Battery capacity drops with age, which affects the alternator and starting motor.
   b. Batteries become resistive, which causes the alternator to increase its output voltage.
   c. A defective battery can cause an alternator to increase charging amperage or cause low-voltage burnout of a starting motor.
   d. Battery replacement helps synchronize electrical system performance after a starter or alternator is replaced.

2. Which of the following conditions causes surface voltage leakage from a battery?
   a. Sulfated plates
   b. Plate grid corrosion
   c. Grime and electrolyte deposits
   d. Overcharging

3. Which of the following statements best explains the term battery capacity?
   a. Battery capacity is the combined volume and weight of cell plates.
   b. Capacity is the volume of battery electrolyte.
   c. Capacity is the ability of a battery to hold an electrical charge.
   d. Capacity is the ability of a battery to deliver amperage at an acceptable voltage.

4. At what level is a loss of battery capacity unacceptable?
   a. When a battery loses more than 20% of its electrolyte
   b. A loss of 20% or more of its original supply of electrical power
   c. A loss of 10% or more of plate active material
   d. Whenever the battery becomes sulfated

5. How does battery resistance change?
   a. It decreases as a battery moves from 0% to 100% charged
   b. It drops to as little as 3 ohms as it ages
   c. Resistance drops as the amount of amperage supplied by the battery goes up
   d. Resistance typically increases with age

6. What effect does cold temperatures have on a battery compared to warm temperatures?
   a. Internal resistance and voltage required to charge the battery increases.
   b. Open-circuit battery voltage drops approximately 5% for every 10°F (6°C) drop in temperature.
   c. Increased plate sulfation takes place.
   d. The self-discharge rate of a battery increases as temperature decreases.

7. Which of the following conditions leads to hard sulfation of a battery?
   a. Temporarily leaving a battery in a discharged condition
   b. An incorrect voltage-regulator setting or resistive battery cable, leading to an undercharged condition

c. Storing a battery in a cold room in a fully charged condition

d. Leaving a battery on a low-amperage float charge for weeks at a time

8. What is the correct service recommendation for a battery whose charging voltage increases to 15.8 volts at a 40-amp charge rate after 2 minutes?

a. Charge it at a lower charge rate

b. Scrap the battery

c. Put the battery on a trickle charge

d. Return the battery to service—it is fully charged

9. The electrolyte in the cells of a battery range between 1.190 and 1.170 when measured with a refractometer. What is the correct service recommendation?

a. Charge and retest the battery

b. Scrap the battery

c. Fill the cells with electrolyte

d. Top the electrolyte off with distilled water

10. After a 15-second high-amperage discharge load test, the cut-off voltage of a 12-volt 500 CCA battery was 9.5 volts when loaded with 250 amps. The battery temperature was 80°F (27°C). What is the correct service recommendation?

a. Scrap the battery

b. Charge and retest the battery

c. Return the battery to service

d. Recommend replacing the battery with one having a smaller CCA rating

ASE Technician A/Technician B Style Questions

1. Two technicians were examining the results of a conductance tests on three batteries in a battery bank. One battery had close to 100% of its rated capacity, another 50%, and the other less than 10%. Technician A says that failed batteries were likely sulfated. Technician B said the batteries did not receive the same charging voltage. Who is correct?

a. Technician A

b. Technician B

c. Both Technician A and Technician B

d. Neither Technician A nor Technician B

2. Technician A says that conductance testing measures a battery's internal resistance. Technician B says that all conductance testing must be performed on fully charged batteries since internal resistance changes according to the state of charge. Who is correct?

a. Technician A

b. Technician B

c. Both Technician A and Technician B

d. Neither Technician A nor Technician B

3. Technician A says that conductance testing analyzes an alternating voltage signal after it has passed through a battery to determine its capacity. Technician B says that battery impedance to an AC signal is evaluated during conductance testing. Who is correct?

a. Technician A

b. Technician B

c. Both Technician A and Technician B

d. Neither Technician A nor Technician B

4. Technician A says that batteries may slowly fail over time due to the loss of a cell or open circuits within the internal connections. Technician B says that batteries may slowly fail over time through the gradual loss of capacity caused by plate deterioration. Who is correct?

a. Technician A

b. Technician B

c. Both Technician A and Technician B

d. Neither Technician A nor Technician B

5. Technician A and B are examining the measurements of electrolyte specific gravity from six cells of battery, taken using a refractometer. The highest cell had a SpGr of 1.285, while the lowest SpGr measured was 1.210. Technician A says the battery should be scrapped. Technician B says that the battery should be charged and re-tested. Who is correct?

a. Technician A

b. Technician B

c. Both Technician A and Technician B

d. Neither Technician A nor Technician B

6. Technician A says to always coat battery terminals with chassis grease to prevent corrosion. Technician B says that dielectric-type grease should be used instead because some types of chassis grease are electrically conductive. Who is correct?

a. Technician A

b. Technician B

c. Both Technician A and Technician B

d. Neither Technician A nor Technician B

7. Technician A says that a fully charged battery should have an open-circuit voltage of at least 12.25 volts. Technician B says that, if the battery has been recently charged, a light load applied to the battery for a few minutes removes a surface charge. Who is correct?

a. Technician A

b. Technician B

c. Both Technician A and Technician B

d. Neither Technician A nor Technician B

8. Technician A says that a set of four batteries connected in a series-parallel arrangement that produces 24 volts can be charged while connected using a 12-volt battery charger. Technician B says that to charge the batteries, only a 24-volt charger can be used. Who is correct?

a. Technician A

b. Technician B

c. Both Technician A and Technician B

d. Neither Technician A nor Technician B

9. Technician A says that the high-discharge amperage load test measures the ability of a battery to supply enough power during cranking, and the battery's capacity is tested based on its CCA rating. Technician B says that a battery must be 100% charged to perform a capacity test, so SOC must be first evaluated before proceeding. Who is correct?

a. Technician A

b. Technician B

c. Both Technician A and Technician B
d. Neither Technician A nor Technician B
10. Technician A and B were discussing the 0.2 amps of current drawn from the battery after the ignition was switched off. Technician A says that all late-model commercial vehicles continue to draw a small amount of current from the batteries when the ignition is switched off. Technician B

says that key-off electrical loads are typically produced by control modules before they switch to sleep mode. Who is correct?
a. Technician A
b. Technician B
c. Both Technician A and Technician B
d. Neither Technician A nor Technician B

CHAPTER 17

Heavy-Duty Starting Systems and Circuits

Learning Objectives

After reading this chapter, you will be able to:

- **LO 17-1** Identify and describe the various classifications and construction features of heavy-duty (HD) starting motors and circuits.
- **LO 17-2** Explain the operating principles of DC motors.
- **LO 17-3** Describe the construction and operation of series-type electric-starting motors.
- **LO 17-4** Identify and describe the major components of a starting system.

- **LO 17-5** Identify and explain the purpose and function of starting system control components used in the starting circuits.
- **LO 17-6** Identify and describe the procedures for performing an on-vehicle and off-vehicle starting system tests.
- **LO 17-7** Identify and outline inspection and repair procedures for a starting motor.

You Are the Technician

The cost of a no-start condition in the fleet of diesel-powered equipment you maintain is extraordinarily high. Equipment productivity, labor hours, and driver and operator time are all lost. In addition, an increase in late deliveries caused by out-of-service vehicles increases customer aggravation levels, raising the cost of resolving no-start conditions. At the specific direction from management to end or dramatically reduce the number of no-start complaints, you begin to analyze some of the common root causes of the starting system failures. Reviewing service records for the repaired equipment, you discover that the starting motors are frequently burned-out and cable terminals are loose and often burned as well. You also notice that there doesn't seem to be a specific preventative maintenance schedule in place to evaluate the condition of the starting system. It is only when the equipment does not start that the problems are identified, but that occurs too late to prevent disruption of operations.

As you consider what steps to take to prevent the no-start complaints, answer the following questions.

1. Explain how the conditions that cause low-voltage burn-out actually damage starting motors and starting-motor connections.
2. What maintenance practices would you recommend to prevent low-voltage burn-out of starting motors and connections?
3. What patterns would you observe regarding the voltage and amperage measurements made during a starter draw test if a starter were beginning to fail due to burnt brushes, armature, and field windings?

Introduction

Dozens of electric motors are found in heavy vehicles operating a variety of devices, from electric seats, fuel and coolant pumps, fan blower motors, and even instrument gauges. The largest of all these electric motors is the starter motor, like the one shown in **FIGURE 17-1**. The starting system provides a method of rotating (cranking) the heavy vehicle's internal combustion engine (ICE) to begin the combustion cycle. The starter is designed to work for short periods of time and must crank the engine at sufficient speed for it to start. Modern starting systems are very effective, provided that components are properly selected and they are well-maintained.

Understanding and maintaining starting systems is important since diagnosing "no-start" conditions are costly, in terms of vehicle downtime and component costs, if they are "over-repaired" or haphazardly investigated. In fact, various manufacturers have noted that between 55% and 80% of all starters returned for warranty were not defective. Vehicle and passenger safety are also jeopardized if the starting system is not properly repaired and maintained and the vehicle cannot start in adverse weather or after stalling in congested traffic. Interlocked circuits, which prevent the engine from starting under various operating conditions, and the high current supplied by multiple starting batteries, add to the safety concerns with this system.

Fundamentals of Starting Systems and Circuits

LO 17-1 Identify and describe the various classifications and construction features of heavy-duty (HD) starting motors and circuits.

The starting/cranking system consists of the battery, high- and low-amperage cables, a solenoid, a starter motor assembly, ring gear, and the ignition switch. On electronic control unit (ECU)-controlled starting systems, the ECU enables the operation of a relay to energize the starter circuit. Data supplied by other on-board network modules, along with control algorithms in the module, determine when and for how long the starter cranks. Control system logic determines when and if the cranking circuit functions.

During the cranking process, two actions occur. The pinion of the starter motor engages with the flywheel ring gear, and the starter motor then rotates to turn over, or crank, the engine. In most cases, the starter motor is an electric motor mounted on the engine block or transmission. Air and hydraulic systems are used, and the latest mild-hybrid systems use an electric "motor and generator" (MAG) unit mounted on the accessory drive system to crank the engine. When the starter is mounted on the engine block, it is typically powered by a 12- or 24-volt battery and is designed to have high rotational torque at low speeds. The starter cables are the heaviest conductors in the vehicle because they carry the high current needed by the starter motor. The starter motor causes the engine flywheel and crankshaft to rotate from a resting position and keeps them turning until the engine starts and runs on its own.

High-compression-ratio diesel engines with large displacements require high amounts of electrical current, so multiple batteries are connected to supply more amperage or voltage. To supply more cranking amperage in a 12-volt system, batteries are connected in parallel. Adding more batteries increases the amount of amperage available for cranking, but the system voltage remains the same. Connecting batteries in series increases available voltage, but amperage supplied to the starter remains the same.

Demands on Today's Starting Systems

Today's heavy-vehicle engines demand the most from starter motors, since emission reduction strategies have increased engine cylinder pressures during cranking. Anti-idling laws, which require drivers to reduce the amount of time their engines idle, require modern starter motors to crank when engines are worm and more mechanically resistive, rather than cold. Start-stop energy-reducing drive systems and mild-hybrid drive vehicles place even more strain on starter motors due to high frequency re-start cycles.

Despite the increasing demands, new designs of starter motors and systems controls are enabling starters to last longer and increase output torque while substantially reducing starting motor weight. A typical example of this is the improvements and changes that have occurred to Delco Remy™ starter motors in recent times. The earlier Delco Remy™ 42MT weighed 58 lb (26 kg) (**FIGURE 17-2A**). The 39MT is the latest generation starter using a gear reduction planetary drive system to multiply torque output. The 39MT weighs approximately 30 lb (14 kg) or half the weight of the first generation of starters. Both starters are used on engines with 10 to 15-liter (L) displacement (**FIGURE 17-2B**). Minimum life expectancy for a starter now is 4 years with 7,000 start cycles.

FIGURE 17-1 Typical starter motor cross section.

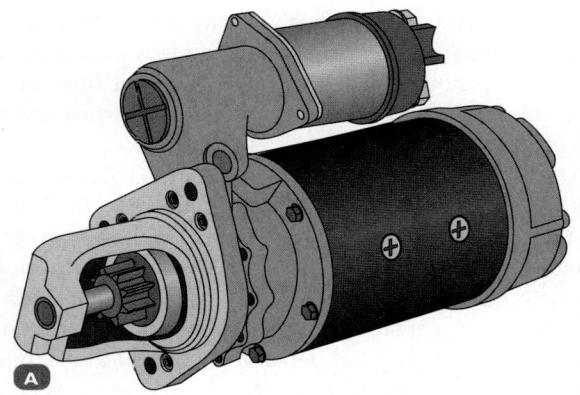

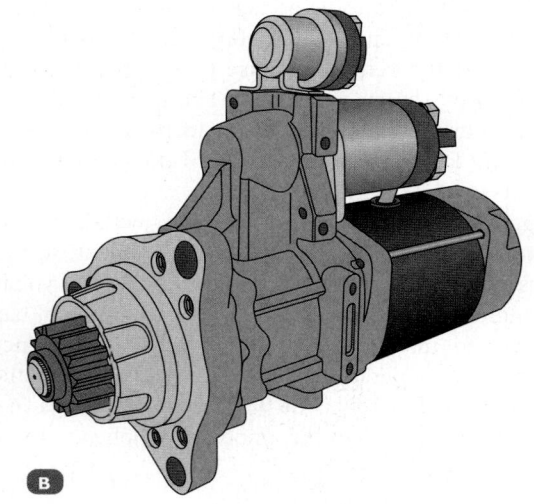

FIGURE 17-2 Two generations of improvements in starters.
A. 42MT Direct Drive. **B.** 39MT Planetary Drive.

Most starting systems have only a single starter motor to crank the engine. In large displacement engines, where the starting demands are higher, two starter motors may be required to crank the engine over.

Starter Motor Classification

Electric starter motors were first installed in the 1912 Cadillac cars to replace hand-operated engine cranks. While electric motors were invented decades before this, the concept that made electric starters practical was the idea of building motors to operate at high amperage levels for a few seconds and not burn out. The Dayton Electric Company, later shortened and called DELCO™, pioneered the use of high-current-draw motors that enabled the starter to develop a tremendous amount of torque. The motors were unlike any compact electric motors of the day, which were all designed for continuous operation.

Using a small-diameter pinion gear, the starter motor rotates the engine through a ring gear attached to the flywheel. When the starter motor begins to turn, the pinion teeth quickly line up with the flywheel teeth and rotate the engine at a minimum of 125 rpm for a four-stroke diesel engine to an average of 200–250 rpm. In gasoline engines, the ratio between the flywheel ring gear and pinion gear is anywhere between 10 and 15:1. In contrast, the higher cranking torque required for diesel engines use 18:1 to 25:1, with 20:1 being most common.

Currently, there are three major categories of electric starters used in heavy vehicles.

- **Direct drive**—The motor armature directly engages the flywheel through a pinion gear. In this arrangement, as illustrated in (**FIGURE 17-3**), the only gear torque multiplication is between the pinion gear and the ring gear.
- **Reduction gear drive**—The motor multiplies torque to the starter pinion gear by using an extra gear between the armature and the starter drive mechanism. The gear reduction allows the starter to spin at a higher speed with lower current, while still creating the required torque through the reduction gear to crank the engine. The reduction drive of this type of starter motor is approximately between 3.3:1 and 5.7:1. These types of starters, like that illustrated in **FIGURE 17-4**, can be identified by an offset drive housing to the motor housing.
- **Planetary gear reduction drive**—Another type of gear reduction system, the planetary gear system, illustrated in **FIGURE 17-5**, reduces the starter profile using a planetary gear set, rather than a spur-type gear design of reduction gear drive starters, to multiply motor torque to the pinion gear. Placing the planetary gear set inline or along the same axis as the armature can reduce the weight of gear reduction-type starters by more than 50%.

Direct drive starters are becoming less common due to their larger size, heavier weight, and higher current requirements. The use of gear reduction and planetary gear reduction starter designs means the motor requires less current, is more compact, and is lighter—while increasing cranking torque. Higher motor speeds used in these units result in potentially less motor damage than direct drive units because less current is needed to produce torque. The disadvantage of the smaller starter profile, in comparison to direct drive starters, is the inability of the smaller starter mass to tolerate high heat loads caused by prolonged engine cranking.

Pneumatic, or air starters, like that shown in **FIGURE 17-6**, are another type of starter motor used on some older diesel engines, particularly two-stroke Detroits, which need a

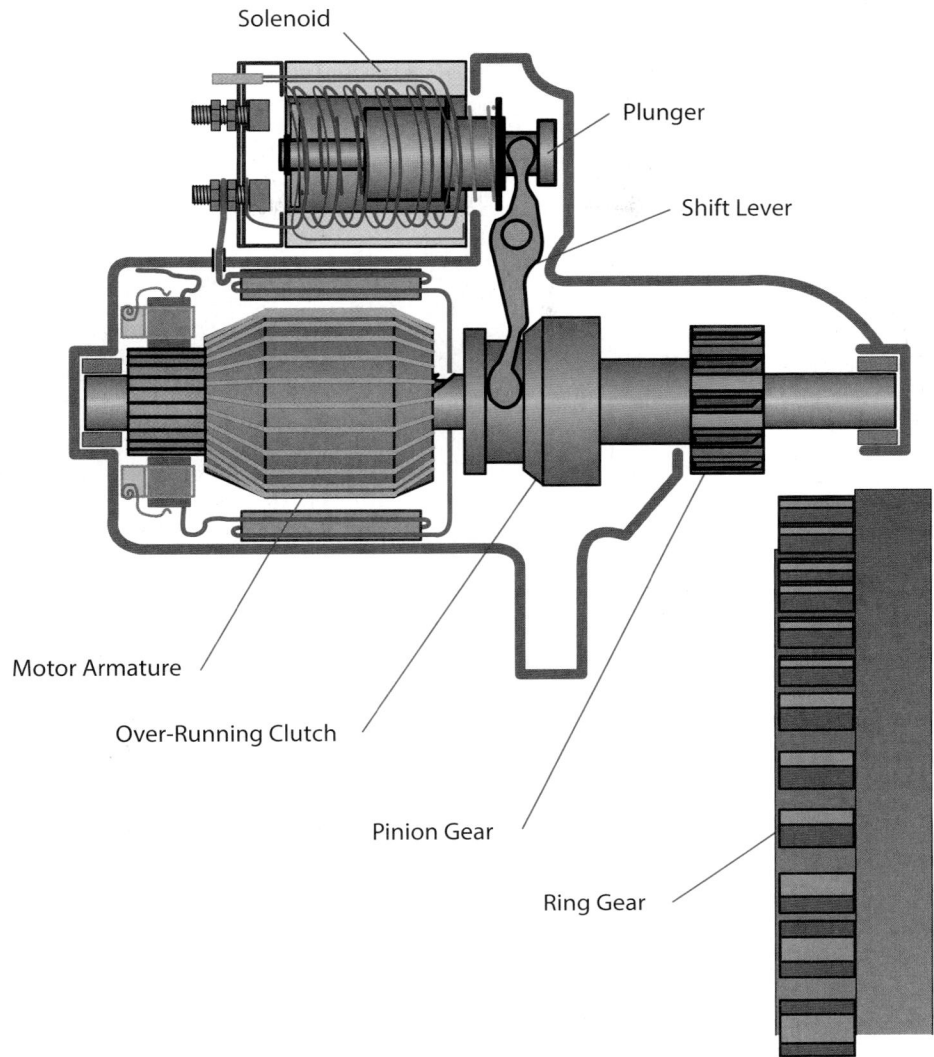

FIGURE 17-3 A typical direct drive starter motor.

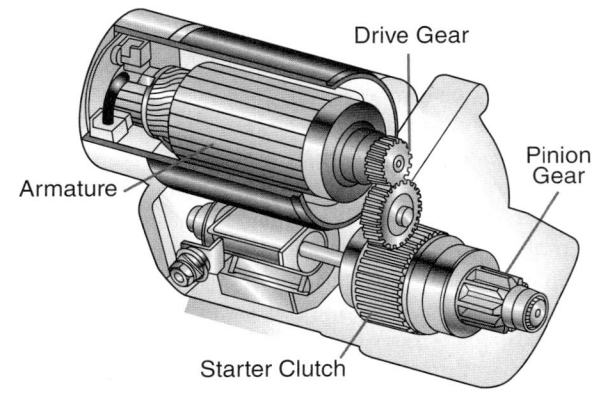

FIGURE 17-4 A typical reduction drive starter motor.

minimum of 200 cranking rpm to start. The system consists of a geared air motor, starting valve, and a pressure tank. Compressed air from a dedicated reservoir tank is used to spin the motor after the operator pushes a spring-loaded dash-mounted air valve. A set of reduction gears between the motor and pinion gears multiplies motor torque while engaging the flywheel ring gear. Once running, the engine recharges the starter reservoir tank.

DC Motor Principles

LO 17-2 Explain the operating principles of DC motors.

All electric motors operate using principles of magnetic attraction and repulsion. Because like magnetic poles repel one another and unlike poles attract, it is possible to arrange magnetic poles within the motor to be continuously in a state of repulsion and attraction. That produces the motor action.

The magnetic fields are produced either by permanent magnets or electromagnets, which use coils or loops of conductors with electric current flowing through them to create magnetic fields. Two magnetic fields are required for motor action: one surrounds the motor armature and is called the field winding, and the other is in the rotating armature, as illustrated

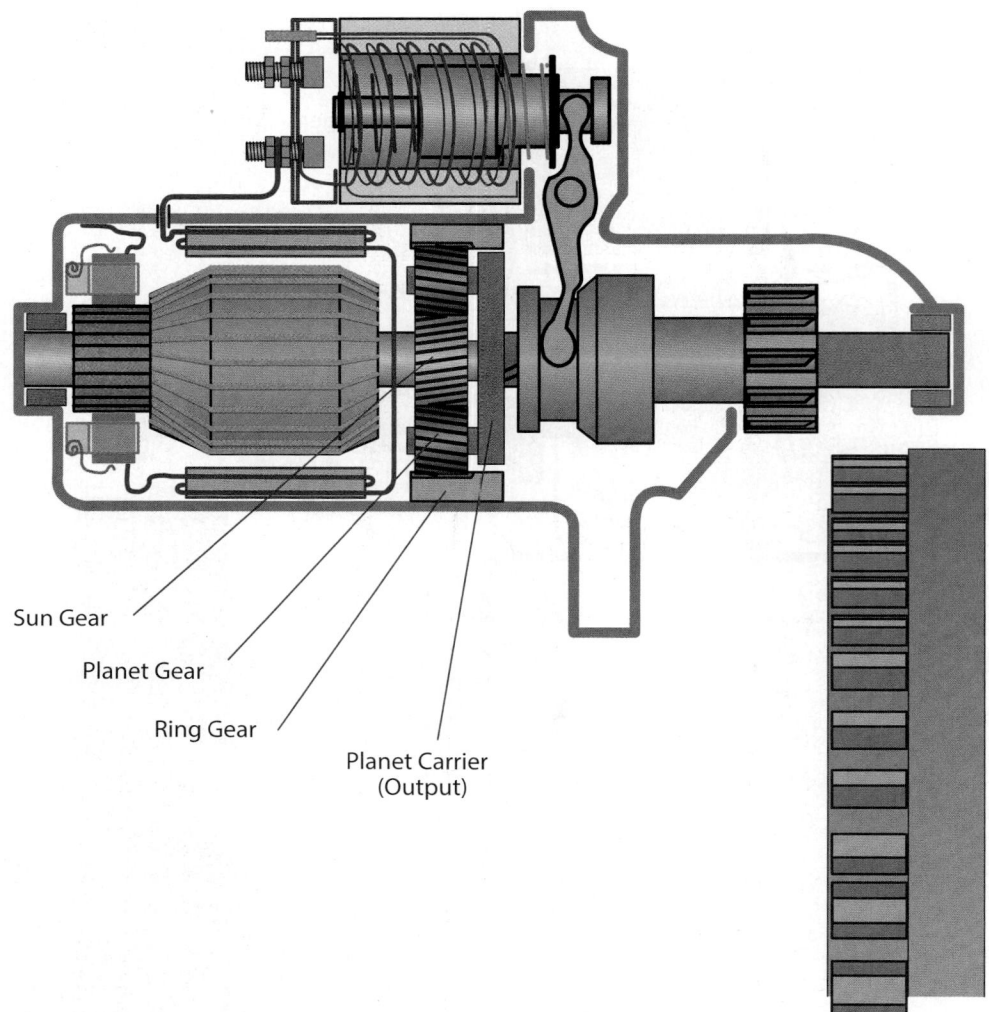

Sun Gear

Planet Gear

Ring Gear

Planet Carrier
(Output)

FIGURE 17-5 A typical planetary gear reduction drive starter motor.

FIGURE 17-6 A typical air-starter.

in **FIGURE 17-7**. The magnetic field acting on the armature is intensified by the starter's iron case. Only electromagnets having much stronger magnetic fields to produce higher motor torque output are used in all heavy-duty starters. The armature's

magnetic field is generated in loops of wire that form the armature windings. Motor action occurs through the interaction of the electromagnetic fields of the field coils and the armature, which causes a rotational force to act on the armature, producing the turning motion.

HD starter motors use electromagnets in the field and armature windings, which are intensified by the low-reluctance laminated-iron armature shaft and soft-iron starter case. Motors used for smaller applications, such as blower and wiper motors, may use permanent magnets for the field and electromagnets for the armature.

Regardless of its design, a starter motor consists of housing or case, field coils, an armature, a commutator and brushes, end frames, and a solenoid-operated shift mechanism. Major variations between starters are in the starter drive mechanism, with most starters now using a gear-reduction drive rather than a direct-drive configuration.

Types of DC Motors

Direct current motors are categorized by the arrangement of electromagnetic circuits producing magnetic forces of repulsion

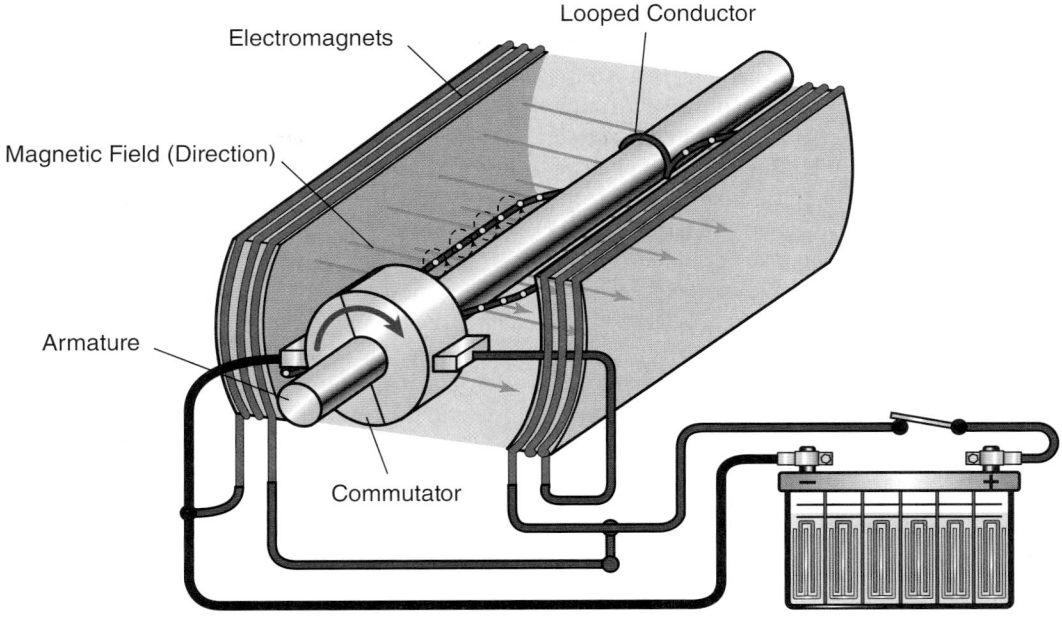

FIGURE 17-7 Basic direct-current electric motor operation. Two magnetic fields are required for motor action, one in the field and the other in the armature.

and attraction. Common electric motor classifications used in heavy vehicles include:

- Series—Field and armature windings are connected in series. These motors develop the highest torque and are used as starting motors.
- Shunt (parallel wound)—Field and armature windings are connected in parallel. These motors develop less torque but maintain a constant speed. They are often used as blower motors.
- Compound—Field and armature windings have both series and parallel connections. The motor has good starting torque and stable operating speed. These motors are commonly used in wipers and power seats.
- Stepper—The field is made from two or more electromagnets that are energized by microcontroller logic circuits. Two or more permanent magnets are used in the armature. These motors are used in instrument cluster's gauges, turbochargers, and EGR actuators where high precision movement is required.

Series Motors

LO 17-3 Describe the construction and operation of series-type electric-starting motors.

The series and shunt motor are the two most common types found in the automotive industry. **FIGURE 17-8** shows the current flow of circuits through a series and a shunt motor. Note the difference in the way the current flows through the fields. Series motors are called "series" because the field and armature

Series Wound Motor

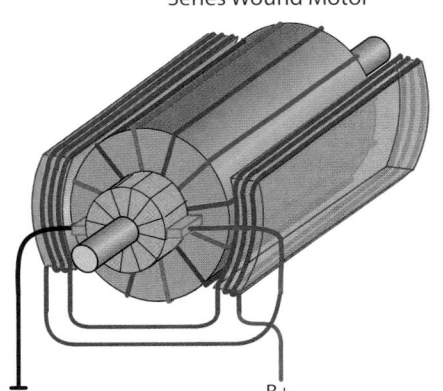

Shunt or Parallel Wound Motor

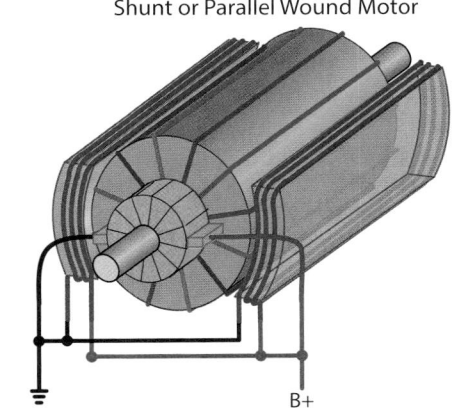

FIGURE 17-8 Typical circuits for basic series and shunt motors.

windings are connected in series. This means current first passes from the negative chassis ground, through a brush, and into the armature. Current leaves from another brush and passes into the field coils, before returning to the battery positive through the motor terminal. Because it is a series circuit, any unwanted resistance inside the motor, whether it is a burnt contact or loose brush, reduces current flow throughout the entire motor circuit.

Series-wound motors are primarily used in starter motors because they develop the greatest amount of torque at stall or 0 rpm, which is ideal for developing break-away torque needed to crank a stopped engine. As magnetic field strength is always proportional to amperage and not voltage, the initial amperage drawn by a series motor produces the most torque. In comparison, as illustrated in **FIGURE 17-9**, shunt motors produce less torque than series motors, but do not drop as much speed as torque diminishes. This makes them ideal for applications like blower motors.

Series Motor Current Flow

The current flow for a series motor, such as the one illustrated in **FIGURE 17-10**, is as follows:

1. Current first enters the motor through the brush connected to negative chassis ground. Current passes through the armature via the commutator and leaves through the second brush

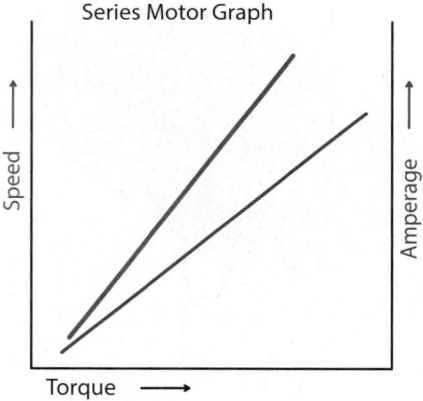

Series Motor Graph

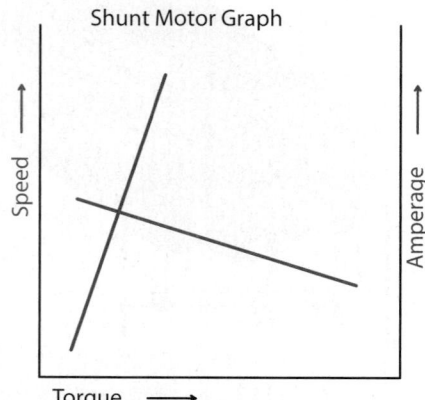

Shunt Motor Graph

FIGURE 17-9 Comparing amperage drawn, speed, and torque of series and shunt motors.

connected to the field winding. A magnetic field is created in the armature.

2. Current passes through the windings of the field coils. The laminated iron making up the pole shoes intensifies the magnetic field strength. The direction the winding is wound around the pole shoe establishes the polarity of the pole shoe. The field windings are wound in directions opposite to one another to produce a like pole to the armatures, which always opposes the magnetic pole produced in the armature.

3. The forces of repulsion between the field coil and armature cause the armature to turn.

4. Each armature winding is connected to a pair of segments on the commutator. The commutator turns with the armature, causing the stationary brushes to continuously connect with a new armature winding as the armature rotates. This arrangement enables the forces of repulsion to constantly reposition as the armature turns to maintain starter motor rotation.

Series Motor Operational Characteristics

Series-wound motors also are self-limiting in speed due to the development of a **counter-electromotive force (CEMF)**. CEMF is produced by the spinning magnetic field of the armature, which induces current in the opposite direction of battery current through the motor. Induced CEMF current behaves like resistance to starter current, which means progressively less current passes through a starting motor as its speed increases. Battery current and CEMF current both flow through a motor at the same time, but in opposite directions. The faster the motor turns, the higher the CEMF, and the less current is drawn from the battery. Higher voltage from cranking batteries produces greater motor speed and more CEMF. **FIGURE 17-11** illustrates the relationship between motor speed, torque, and amperage draw.

Consider the following relationship between armature speed, CEMF, amperage, and torque for a series starter motor:

■ The faster the armature spins, the greater the CEMF current induced in the opposite polarity of battery voltage.

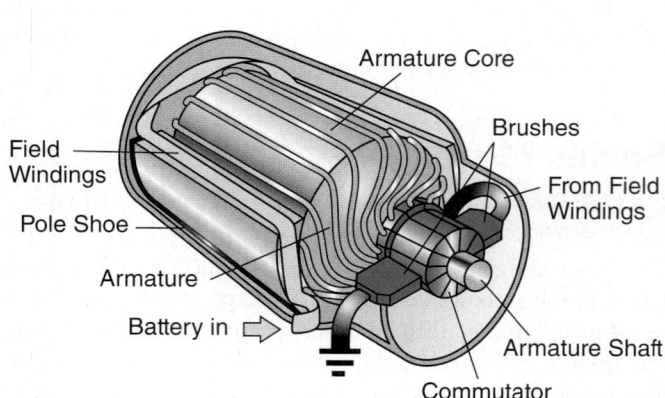

FIGURE 17-10 Current flow in a series motor and through the armature and fields in series.

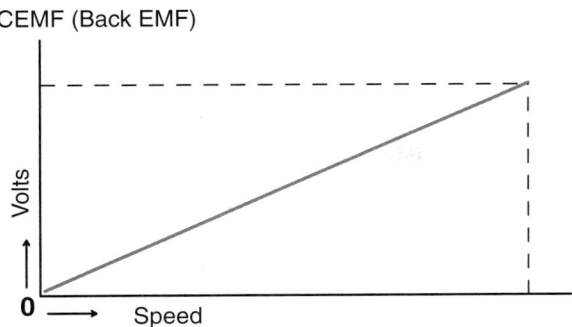

FIGURE 17-11 As motor speed increases, more CEMF is produced.

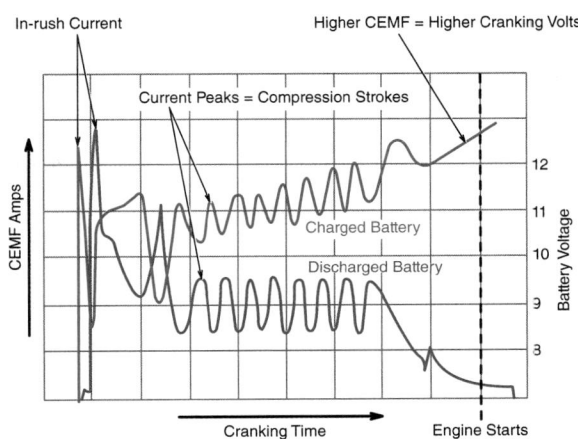

FIGURE 17-12 The amount of amperage drawn by a starting motor is directly proportional to the torque required. Peaks and valleys in amperage reflect the changing torque requirement caused by compression events. Available voltage increases as starter speed increases.

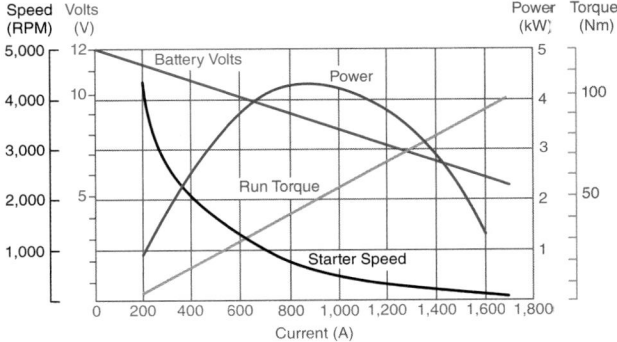

FIGURE 17-13 The relationship between starter motor speed, amperage, and voltage. As the starter slows down, it draws more amperage and lowers CEMF. Available voltage decreases with reduced starting motor speed.

- The starter draws less current from the battery as it spins faster due to CEMF resistance.
- Since less current is used at higher speeds, magnetic fields weaken and starter torque drops off.
- Slower motor speeds mean less CEMF resistance to current flow through the starter and higher battery amperage drawn by the starter.
- Greatest torque is produced at low speed since the motor draws the highest amperage.

▶ TECHNICIAN TIP

Weak and discharged batteries are a starting motor's worst enemy because they can cause low-voltage burn-out. Low battery voltage prevents the starter from spinning as fast as it should, which reduces CEMF—a starter's internal resistance when operating. With lower internal resistance, the starter draws more amperage than it should, which leads to heat damage to starter windings, solenoids, and external circuits.

Amperage drawn by a starter at normal room temperature with a fully charged battery ranges from an average of 350 amps for a 7-liter engine to 800 or 900 amps for a 15-liter engine. Initial starting amperage is much higher because the engine is stopped and needs more torque from the starting motor to accelerate the engine from 0 rpm to cranking speed. Because of the high amperage drawn during cranking, the starter can only operate for short periods of time before it requires cooling. Heat produced by continuous operation for any length of time causes serious damage to the motor. Connections become loose and burnt. Some even melt. Brushes and insulation become burned, as well as motor windings. To prevent heat damage, armature windings are brazed, rather than soldered, to the commutator. The starter must never operate for more than 30 seconds at a time and should rest for 2 minutes between extended crank cycles. This permits the heat to dissipate without damage to the unit (**FIGURE 17-12**).

Low-Voltage Burn-Out

Cranking an engine with low battery voltage causes one of the most damaging conditions for a starter. **Low-voltage burn-out** occurs when excess amperage flows through the starter, causing the motor to burn out prematurely. When battery voltage is low, the starter uses even more amperage to rotate. This

happens because starters are constant power devices. That is, starters use any combination of voltage and amperage to produce the necessary power for cranking torque, which is measured in watts. For example, if 7,200 watts of power is needed to operate a starter at 12 volts, 600 amps is needed. If available battery voltage falls to 10 volts, then 720 amps are needed according to Watt's Law (Power (watts) = Volts × Amperage). Note though, by increasing amperage drawn from batteries, in turn, increases batteries' internal resistance. Increased resistance causes available battery voltage to drop even further, which in turn increases the amperage needed to rotate the starter. Slower starter rotation means less CEMF is developed. Consequently, amperage through the starter climbs even more (**FIGURE 17-13**). To prevent damage to the starter, cables, solenoid, and switches from low voltage, several design and maintenance practices are required.

- Correct battery sizing. Batteries must be sized according to their CCA to maintain a cranking voltage of no less than

10.5 volts after three consecutive cranking periods lasting 30 seconds. The appropriate two-minute cooling period is included in this estimate.

- Correct sizing of battery cables. Dedicated battery negative and positive cables are needed for heavier starting systems. Cable diameters should be sized for maximum amperage capacity using original equipment manufacturers (OEM) recommendations. Double cables are needed when using four or more starting batteries.

- Using overcrank protection (OCP) switches. Thermal protection switches may be in the starter housing and connected in series with the starter solenoid ground circuit. When hot, the switch opens and prevents the starter solenoid from operating until the starter is sufficiently cooled.

- Using voltage-sensitive starter control circuit relays. Starter relays are produced that disengage when battery voltage falls below a predetermined level, thus disconnecting the starter circuit. Alternatively, an ECU, which supplies current to energize the starter, can monitor battery voltage, enabling the ECU to disconnect the starter relay when battery current falls too low during cranking. Disconnect voltage is approximately 7.2 volts.

- Using ultra-capacitors. Ultra-capacitors are a recent application of organic capacitors used to provide cranking assist to HD starters. Up to 1,800 amps of current can rapidly discharge for a moment to provide battery assist to the starting motor. As illustrated in **FIGURE 17-14**, ultra-capacitors connected in parallel to the battery provide a high initial current to the starter to speed up the armature rotation. Supplementing the available amperage to the

starter during the initial cranking period reduces the likelihood of a low-voltage burn-out due to low CEMF when armature speed is reduced. One precaution to note is that excessive battery capacity and amperage can potentially twist an armature shaft and break a starter pinion gear if the engine has abnormal level of resistance.

▶ **TECHNICIAN TIP**

Battery capacity is specifically designed to meet the cranking requirements of the engine. An under-capacity set of batteries is not capable of delivering the required current flow to the starter motor while still maintaining sufficient battery voltage. The batteries may cause low-voltage burn-out of the starter and damage the starter circuit. It may also create a situation where there is insufficient voltage available to operate the engine's ECM during cranking. Although not as common a problem, excessive battery capacity can also damage the starter motor by supplying too much amperage while cranking. This can create a situation in which excessive torque is produced from the starter motor, damaging the starter drive and ring gear.

Components of Starters

LO 17-4 Identify and describe the major components of a starting system.

Regardless of the motor design, a starter motor consists of housing, field coils, an armature, a commutator, brushes, end frames, and a solenoid-operated shift mechanism. Major variations between starters are in the starter drive mechanism. Some starters use a gear-reduction drive, while others use a direct-drive

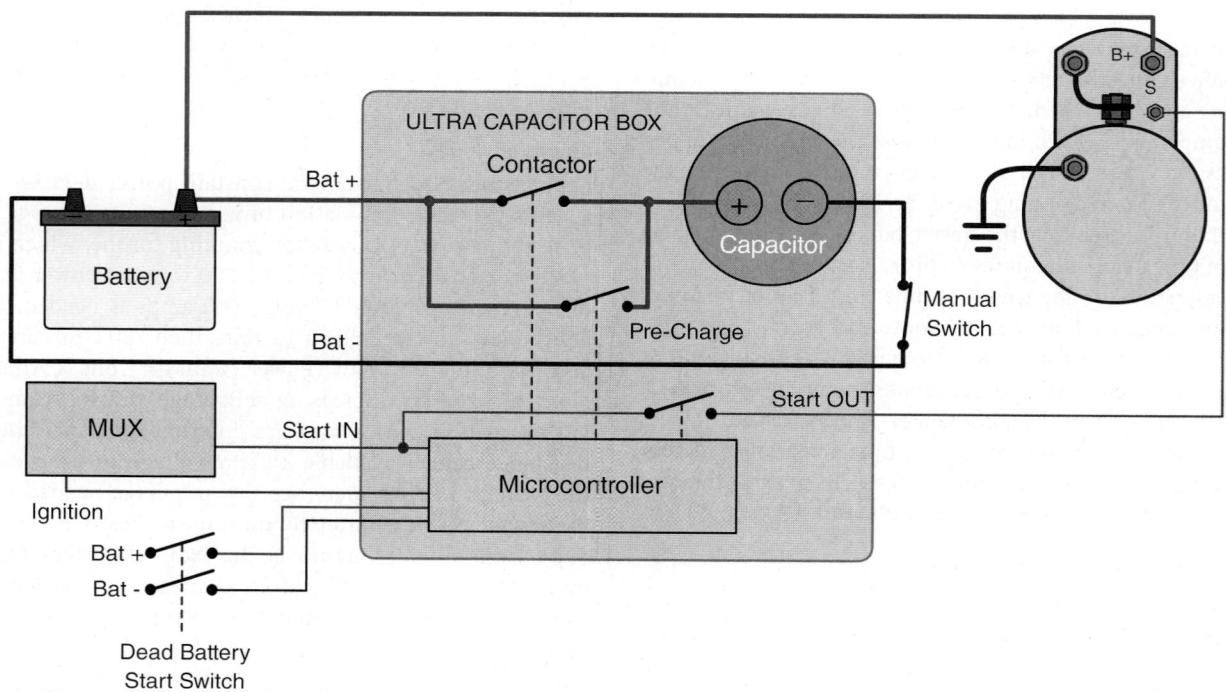

FIGURE 17-14 Power assist from ultra-capacitors reduces the likelihood of low-voltage burn-out.

configuration. Still other starter motors, called axial starter motors, are a type of direct-drive starter. Axial starter motors use an axial sliding armature to engage the pinion with the flywheel. This type of starter is discussed later in this chapter.

Starter Housing and Field Coils

The starter housing, or frame, encloses and supports the internal starter components, protecting them and intensifying the magnetic fields produced in the field coils. Housings and pole shoes are made from soft iron, which conduct magnetic fields with less resistance than air or other materials, which concentrate the magnetic field produced in the fields, making a more powerful magnet. In the starter housing shown in **FIGURE 17-15**, field coils and their pole shoes are securely attached to the inside of the iron housing. The field coils are insulated from the housing and are connected to a terminal, called the motor terminal, which protrudes through to the housing. Fields have a "North" or "South" magnetic polarity facing inward or outward, depending on the direction of current flow. The magnetic flux of the pole shoes is illustrated in **FIGURE 17-16**.

Field coils are connected in series with the armature windings through the starter brushes. In a four-brush starter motor, two brushes are used to connect the field coils to the armature and the other two brushes connect to ground to complete the series circuit.

Armature

The **armature** is the only rotating component of the starter. Armatures, like that shown in **FIGURE 17-17**, have three main components: the shaft, windings, and the commutator.

Armature Shaft and Windings

Different from the thin wire used in shunt motors, armature windings are made of heavy, flat, copper strips that can handle the heavy current flow of the series motor. The windings are made of numerous coils of a single loop each. The sides of these loops fit into slots in the armature core or shaft, but they are insulated from it with insulating strips and varnish applied to the winding before placement. Each slot contains the side of one half of a coil and a commutator segment. In a four-brush motor, each half of a coil is wound at 90 degrees to each other. The coils connect to each other at the commutator so that

FIGURE 17-15 A set of starter motor fields, windings, and housing.

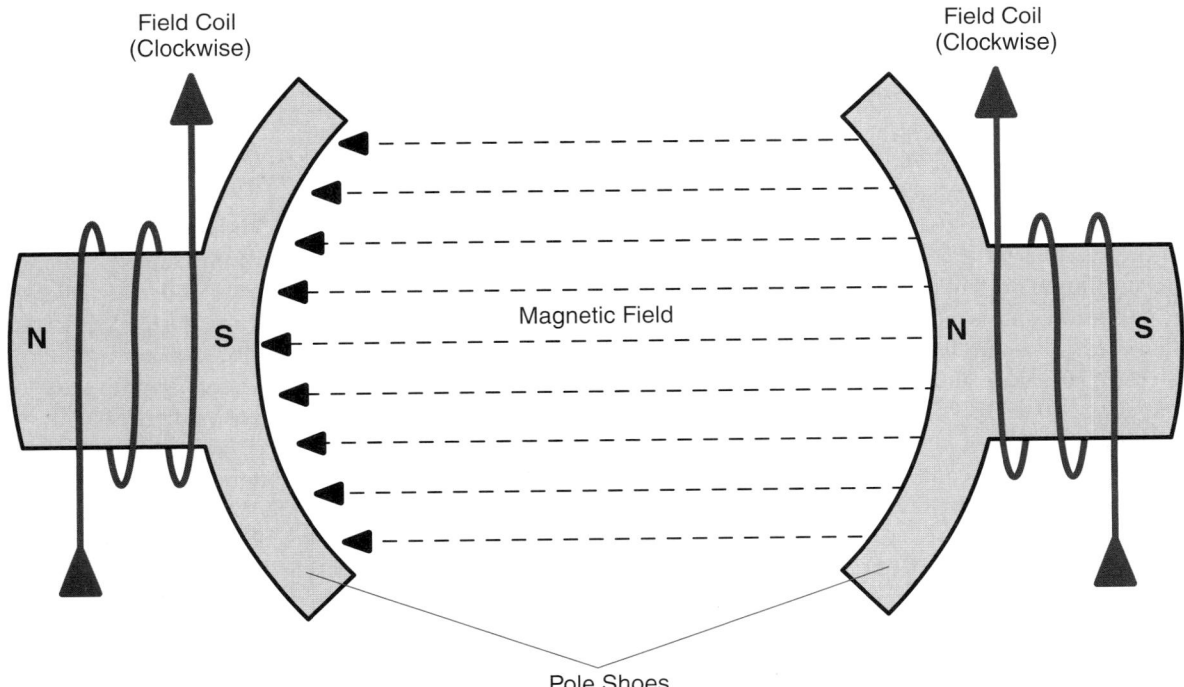

FIGURE 17-16 Field coils are wound around pole shoes producing a north and a south magnetic field.

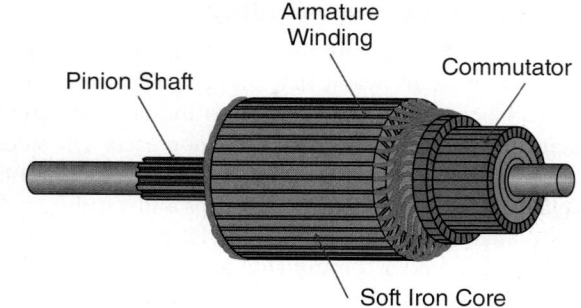

FIGURE 17-17 Features of an armature.

current flows through all the armature windings at the same time. This arrangement generates tremendous magnetic forces of repulsion between the magnetic field around each armature winding and field coil. Current flow through the field and armature windings creates magnetic fields that produce the torque or twisting force that turns the armature.

Commutator and Commutation

The commutator assembly presses onto the armature shaft. It is made up of heavy copper segments separated from each other and the armature shaft by insulation. The commutator segments connect to the ends of the armature windings. Starter motors have four or more brushes that ride on the commutator segments and carry the heavy current flow from the stationary field coils to the rotating armature windings via the commutator segments. A brush holder holds the brushes in position.

The commutator's role is to switch the direction of current flow through each armature coil as the armature rotates, thereby maintaining the rotary movement by ensuring the magnetic pole in the field winding is always the same as the pole in the armature winding opposite it. For a simple explanation of how a commutator works, consider a basic motor with a single loop of wire. When current flows in a conductor, an electromagnetic field is generated around it. If the conductor is placed in a stationary electromagnetic field with current flowing through the field in the opposite direction, the two magnetic fields oppose one another, and the conductor is repelled or pushed away from the stationary field. This means a south-to-south, or north-to-north, pole orientation of two magnetic fields is needed for repulsion and armature movement to take place. The problem is that once the armature turns, the force of repulsion between the armature and field coil prevents the armature from rotating 360 degrees. The same pole orientation that began the movement stops it after the armature makes a half turn. To enable the armature coil to approach the field winding, the polarity of the two magnetic fields needs to change to allow attraction between the armature and field magnetic poles. A north-to-south and south-to-north orientation is needed for a half turn until the rotating armature with a single field and armature coil can complete 360 degrees of rotation. Reversing the direction of current flow in the conductors causes the conductors to attract one another. Once they are lined-up together, the north/south-south/north orientation needs to change once more to cause the armature to turn due to the force of magnetic repulsion. It's the job of the commutator to switch the direction of current flow in the armature to maintain its rotational movement. When the force of magnetic repulsion and attraction are used to rotate an armature, it is known as the motor effect. The force of repulsion and attraction is greatest when the current-carrying conductor and the stationary magnetic field are at right angles to each other.

By switching the direction of current flow through the conductor at the correct time, the conductor can be continuously pushed away from one field winding and pulled toward another, as illustrated in **FIGURE 17-18**. The turning motion produced by the motor effect causes the loop to rotate until it is, in this example, at 90 degrees to the magnetic field. To continue rotation, the direction of current flow in the conductor must be reversed. A commutator is used to continually reverse the current flow to maintain rotation of the loop, as illustrated in **FIGURE 17-19**. A commutator in this example consists of two semicircular segments that are connected to the two ends of the loop and are insulated from each other. Carbon brushes provide a sliding connection to the commutator to complete the circuit and allow current to flow through the loop.

This continuously changing direction of current through the loop maintains a consistent direction of rotation of the loop. To achieve a uniform motion and torque output, the number of loops must be increased. The additional loops smooth out the rotational forces. A starter motor armature uses a corresponding number of conductor loops and commutator segments. A simple multi-loop motor is depicted in **FIGURE 17-20**.

Starter Solenoid and Shift Mechanism

The solenoid on the starter motor performs two main functions:

1. It switches the high current flow required by the starter motor on and off.
2. It engages the starter drive with the ring gear.

The solenoid-operated shift mechanism is mounted in a case that is sealed to keep out oil and road splash, as in **FIGURE 17-21**. In direct-drive starters, the case is flange mounted to the starter motor case and contains two electromagnets around a hollow core. A moveable iron plunger is installed in the hollow core. Energizing the electromagnets pulls the iron plunger, which, in turn, moves a shift lever, engaging the drive pinion gear. This is illustrated in **FIGURE 17-22**. At the same time, moving the iron core also closes a set of contacts to connect battery current with the motor terminal, directing full battery current to the field coils and starter motor armature for cranking power. The starter pinion gear engages the flywheel ring gear before energizing the motor terminal to prevent damage to either gear from spinning teeth, as illustrated in Figure 17-22.

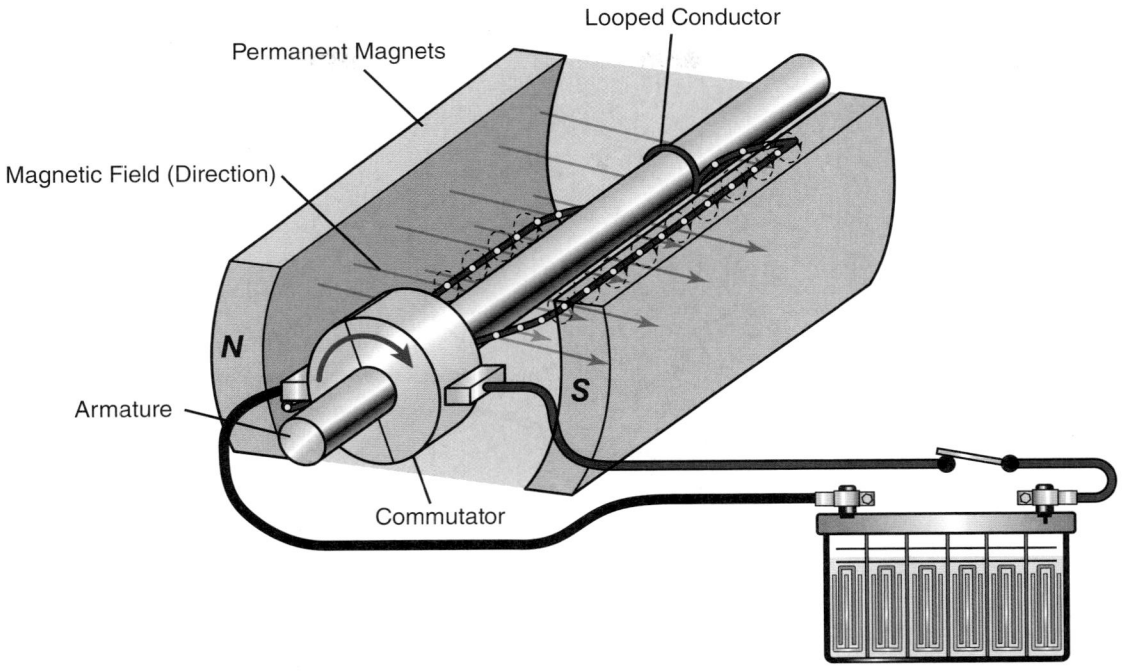

FIGURE 17-18 Simple single-loop motor and electromagnetic fields—with commutator and brushes.

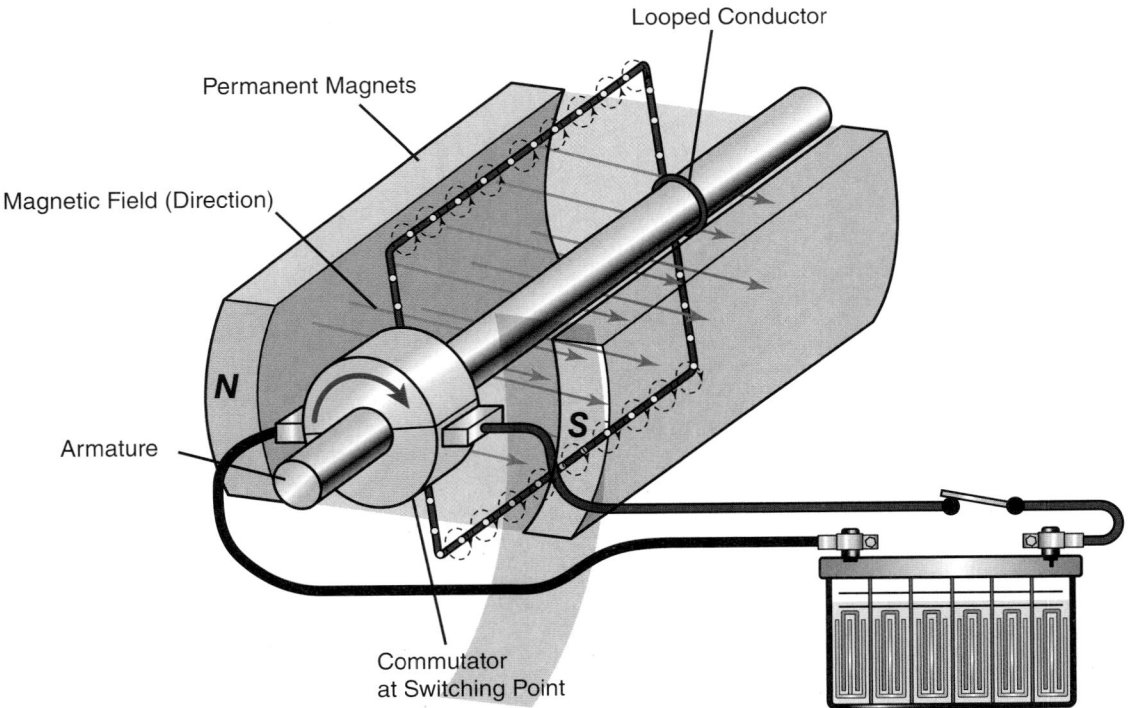

FIGURE 17-19 Simple single-loop motor and electromagnetic fields at the switching point of the commutator.

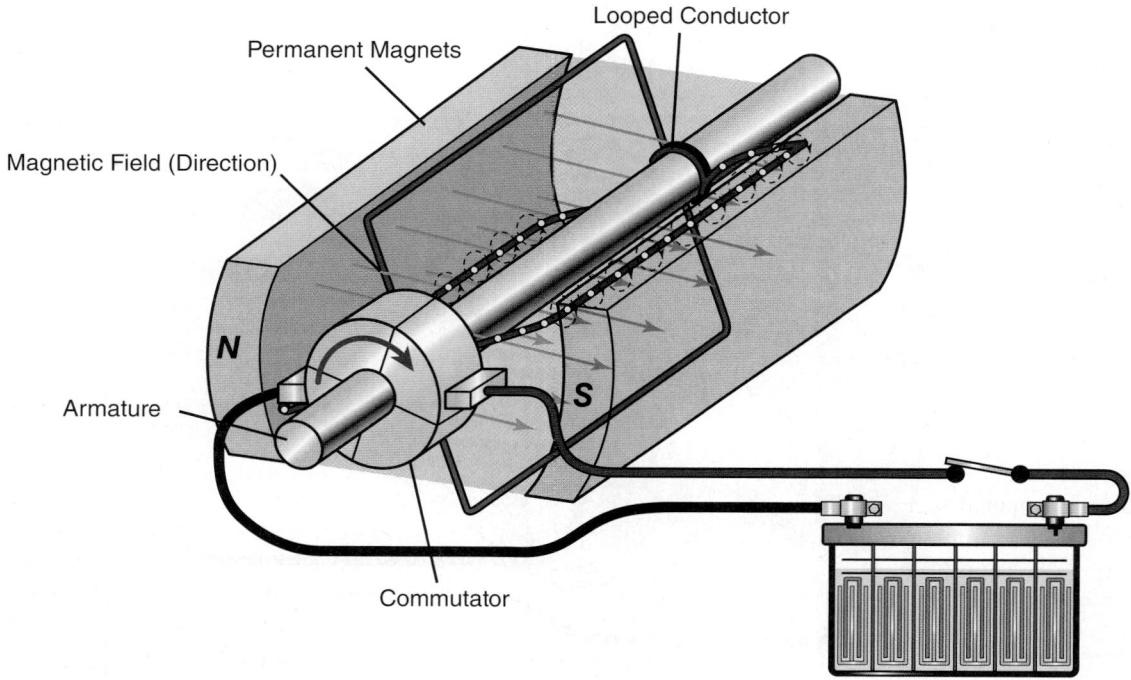

FIGURE 17-20 Simple multi-loop motor and electromagnetic fields—with commutator and brushes.

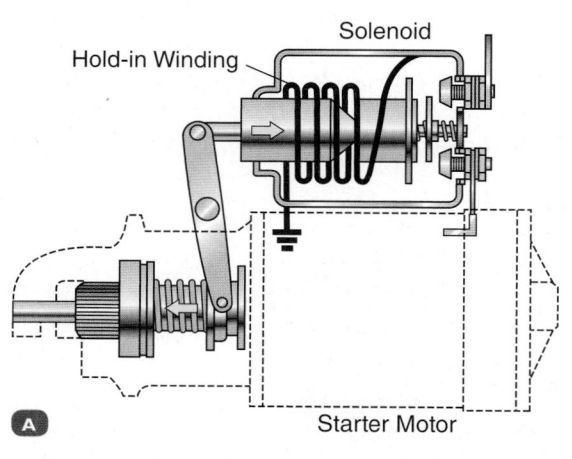

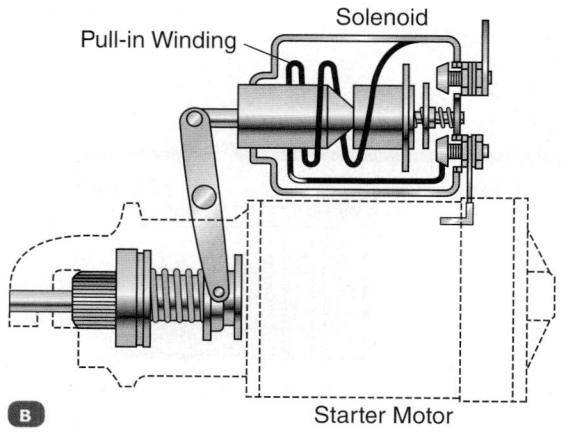

FIGURE 17-21 The solenoid uses two electrical windings. **A.** A hold-in winding. **B.** A pull-in winding.

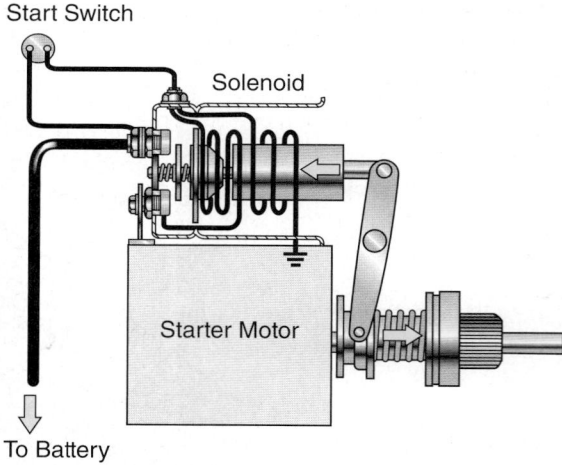

FIGURE 17-22 Solenoid starter contacts and starter drive linkage.

▶ **TECHNICIAN TIP**

A solenoid is an electromagnet that is used to perform work and has mechanical action. A solenoid is made with one or two coil windings wound around an iron tube. When electrical current is passed through the coil windings, it creates electromagnetic force that creates linear action either pushing or pulling an iron core inside the iron tube. When the core is connected to a lever or other mechanical device, the solenoid can put this mechanical movement to practical use. For example, it may: engage the pinion of the starter motor with the flywheel; shift gears in electronically controlled transmissions; shut off air, fuel, or oil supplies; engage engine and exhaust brakes; move the fuel rack in a diesel engine; and so on. Solenoids can also close contacts, such as the solenoid contact in a starter motor solenoid.

Low battery voltage produces starter chatter—the rapid cycling of the solenoid plunger in and out of engagement. This happens because the thinner windings of the hold-in circuit are more sensitive to voltage drop than pull-in windings. When the solenoid closes the connection between the battery and motor terminal, the available voltage also drops due to the increased amperage flow from the battery.

Starter Drive Mechanisms

The starter drive transmits the rotational force from the starter armature to the engine via the ring gear that is mounted on the engine flywheel or torque converter. Armature rotation is transferred to the pinion gear through a variety of mechanisms.

Direct-drive starters, which diesel engines used exclusively for many decades, transferred torque from the armature directly to the pinion gear. Today, gear reduction starters using both planetary and spur-gear mechanisms have replaced direct drives.

With a solenoid-actuated, direct-drive starting system, the pinion gear does not immediately mesh with the flywheel ring gear. If this occurs, a spring located behind the pinion gear is compressed by the solenoid shift fork to help line up the ring gear tooth gaps with the pinion gear teeth so that the solenoid plunger can complete its stroke. Because the grooves along the armature shaft that the pinion gear slides along are helical- or spiral-shaped, the pinion approaches the ring gear while turning about a ¼ turn as it travels toward the ring gear. This slight rotation enables the pinion gear teeth to quickly line up with the flywheel teeth and the spring pressure behind the pinion gear helps them to mesh. Only after the pinion gear engages the ring gear can the starter motor begin to rotate. See **FIGURE 17-23**.

The pinion drive gear is attached to a roller-type, one-way, or overrunning clutch that is splined to the starter armature as in **FIGURE 17-24**. A one-way clutch is in all pinion gears and operates like a ratchet to protect the starter motor. It drives when turned in one direction and slips when turned in the opposite direction.

When the engine starts and runs, the starter motor is damaged if it remains connected to the engine through the flywheel. The ring gear-to-pinion gear ratio, which multiplies starter torque, also multiplies the starter's speed when driven by the engine. At idle, with a 20:1 gear ratio, the starter's armature turns 14,000 rpm or more, which destroys the armature windings through centrifugal force. To prevent this, the one-way overrunning clutch between the armature shaft and pinion gear allows the pinion gear to spin—but not turn the armature if it remains or is accidentally engaged with the flywheel. When the solenoid is deenergized, the shift assembly is pulled away from the flywheel through spring pressure.

Most heavy-vehicle starters have a pinion clearance adjustment to ensure the pinion engages fully with the flywheel while maintaining a clearance from the drive end housing (**FIGURE 17-25**). Proper adjustment of the mechanism is important to prevent two complaints. The first is damage to the ring gear teeth caused by a starting motor that begins to rotate before the starter drive pinion teeth are engaged with the flywheel (**FIGURE 17-26**). Damage to the ring gear is called starter tooth abutment, which occurs if the travel limit for the starter drive pinion gear is too short (**FIGURE 17-27**). The complaint associated with this condition is a loud grinding sound when the starter cranks the engine, since the spinning teeth of the pinion gear are engaged only with the face of the ring gear rather than its teeth. If the travel of the starter drive is adjusted to allow too long a drive gear travel limit, a complaint of "click no crank" is a likely result. This second problem is caused by misadjusted pinion travel happens because the contact disc inside the solenoid does not connect the battery positive and motor terminals together before the pinion gear reaches the end of its travel. Starter motors usually use one of the following four methods for providing pinion clearance adjustment, as illustrated in **FIGURE 17-28**.

1. An eccentric shift fork pin, which is turned until the correct pinion clearance is measured and then locked off by a lock nut

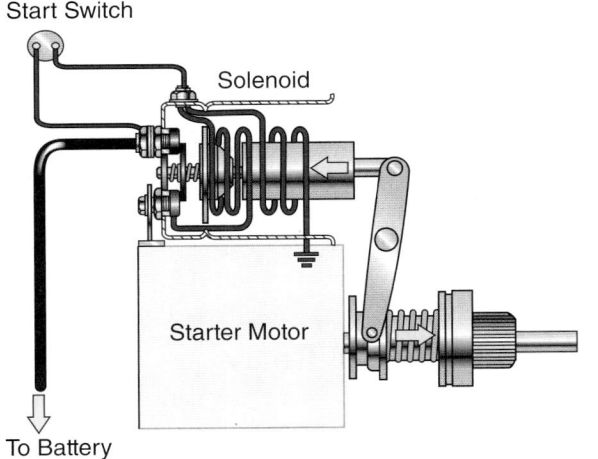

FIGURE 17-23 Both windings are energized, and the solenoid plunger is starting to move toward the cap.

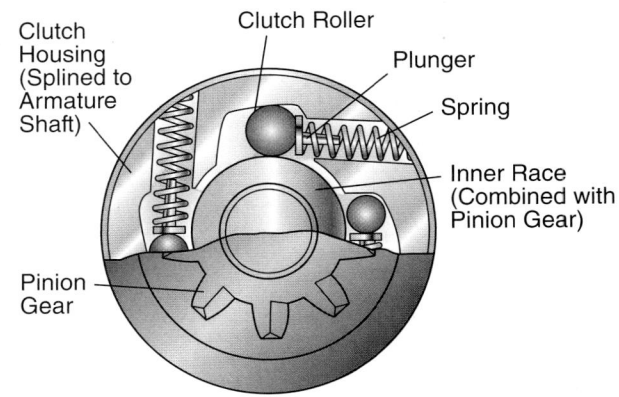

FIGURE 17-24 Starter drive one-way clutch.

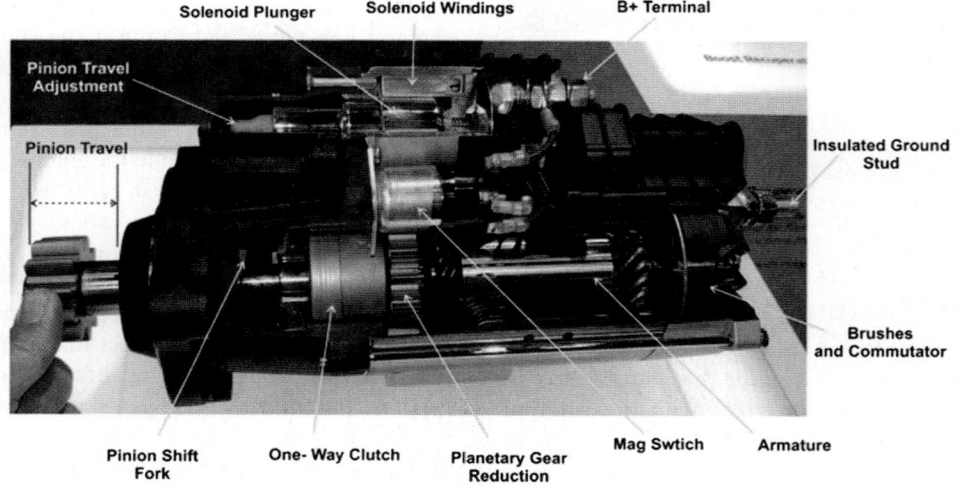

FIGURE 17-25 Location of the pinion shift adjustment mechanism of a gear reduction starter.

FIGURE 17-26 Ring gear damage can result from poorly adjusted pinion clearance or engagement of the pinion while the ring gear is rotating.

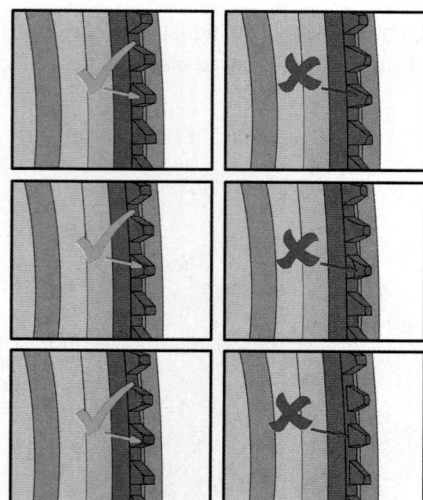

FIGURE 17-27 Incorrect adjustment of the starter drive travel can either cause click and no crank complaints or allow the armature to turn the pinion gear before it engages the flywheel teeth.

2. Shims, which are placed between the solenoid and housing to adjust pinion clearance
3. A screw or nut on the solenoid core where it connects to the shift fork; tightening and loosening the screw or nut adjusts pinion clearance
4. Elongated slots around the solenoid housing mounting bolts that enable a forward and back adjustment of solenoid housing on the starting motor

Starter Control Circuits

LO 17-5 Identify and explain the purpose and function of starting system control components used in the starting circuits.

The starter control circuit, in its most basic form, has an ignition switch directly controlling the starter solenoid to operate the starter motor. In modern heavy vehicles, the circuits are more complex, because relays and control circuits, such as transmission neutral and clutch switches, are added to improve reliability and the safety of vehicles. The latest models of vehicles use an electrical system control module, which communicates with the on-board vehicle network that receives data from various sensors, to control the operation of the starter control circuit. Starting lock-outs prevent the starting motor operation until safe conditions are present to crank and start the engine. The body control module or engine ECM have a set of programmed logic rules to inhibit the starter relay operation until a correct set of conditions for starting are met. Inhibiting starter operation simply means the control module does not supply a ground path or battery + signal to activate the starter relay.

Solenoid Control Relay

Since it is neither practical nor safe to have large battery and starter cables routed in the cab of a vehicle, the starter control circuit allows the operator to use a small amount of battery current provided by the ignition switch to control the flow of a large amount of current in the starting circuit. The control circuit may also have

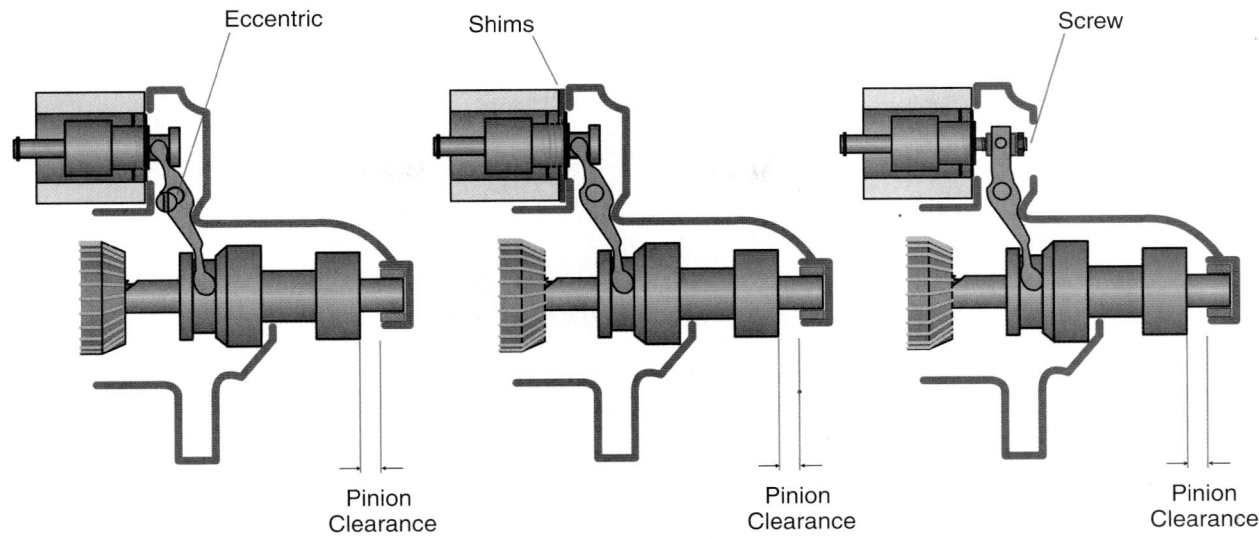

FIGURE 17-28 Typical methods of adjusting pinion clearance.

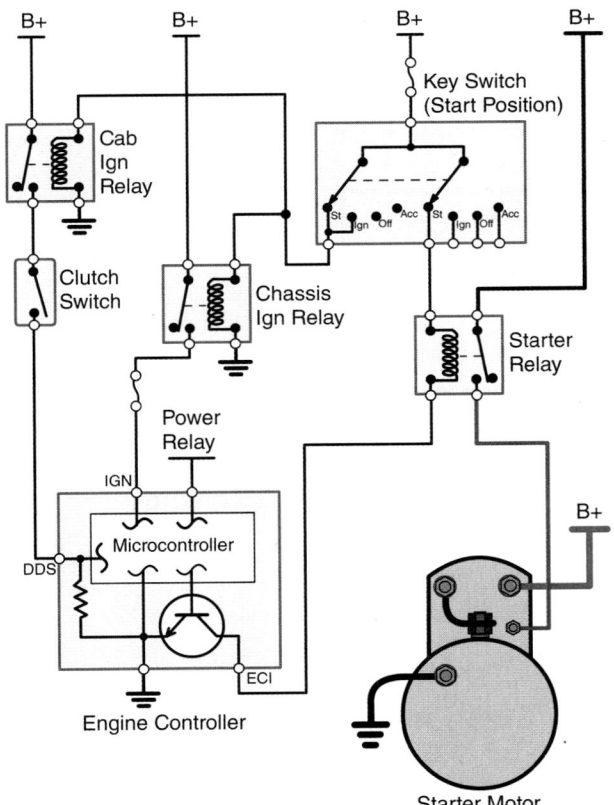

FIGURE 17-29 Electronic control modules take switch and other sensor input into account to determine whether a safe set of conditions is met before activating the starter circuit relay.

a provision for locking out the starter engagement if the engine is running or the starter has overheated. Safety switches, also called neutral safety switches (**FIGURE 17-29**) are in either of two places in the control circuit—interrupting either the ground or battery

positive of the starter relay control circuit. Placing the transmission in PARK or NEUTRAL and/or depressing the clutch closes the starter control circuit so current can flow to the relay switch. A second safety switch can also be connected between the relay switch and its ground so that the switch must be closed before current can flow from the relay switch to ground.

ECU-controlled circuits use the ignition key as an input device and control the starter operation by supplying a ground to the starter relay. The starter relay, also called an integral magnetic switch (IMS) when located on the starter, is the point in the starting system where the control circuit and starter solenoid circuit join (**FIGURE 17-30**). Because starter solenoids can consume between 30 and 60 amps, relays are needed to switch low current from the ignition switch, electronic control module, or starter button to energize the starter solenoid circuit. Starter relays are a type of intermittent-duty relay. This means they are not intended for continuous operation or operation longer than a minute. The intermittent-duty relay has heavy, large-gauge windings in the control circuit capable of producing strong magnetic fields, which are less sensitive to voltage drop during cranking.

As there is a relatively high amount of amperage drawn by the starter solenoid itself, solenoid circuits have a minimum of one relay to switch current flow to the solenoid circuit. The relay may be controlled by a separate push button located in the dash or by an ignition key switch. On electronically controlled engines, it is more common to have the circuit controlled by a start button than the key switch. Having a start button minimizes voltage drops through the ignition switch that can lower current flow to ignition circuits during cranking. Likewise, a start button also prevents voltage spikes from the magnetic field collapse of the relay's coil that could travel back to other ignition circuits through the key (**FIGURE 17-31**).

The ignition switch has other jobs besides controlling the starting circuit. The ignition switch normally has at least four separate positions: Accessory, Off, On (Run), and Start. There

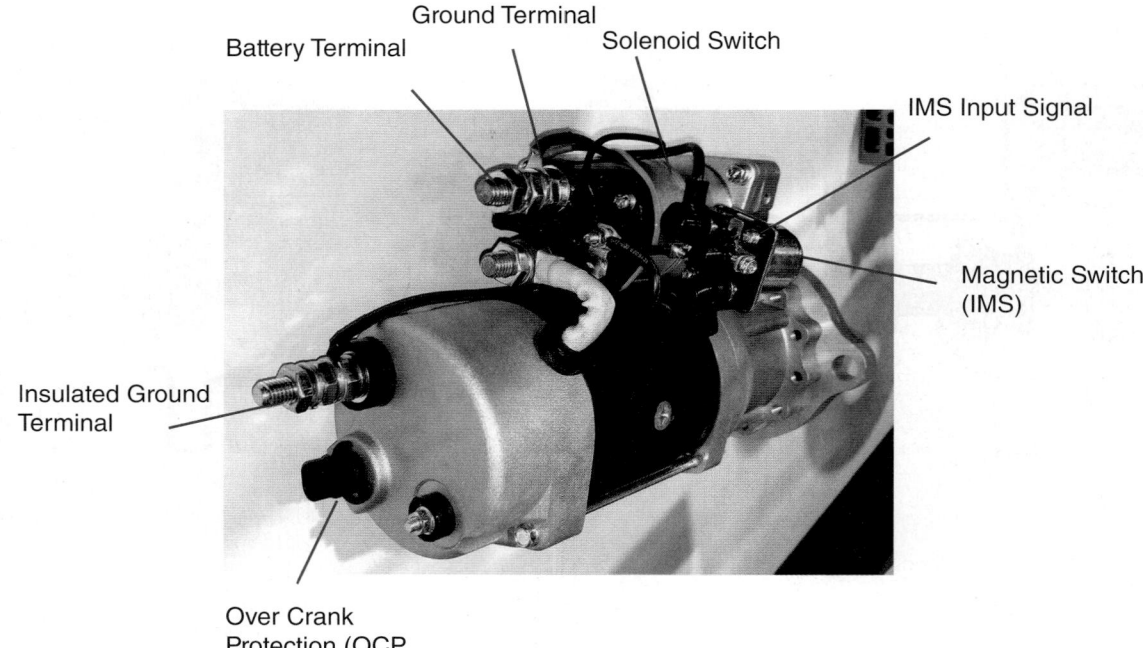

FIGURE 17-30 The use of a mag switch on the starter reduces the voltage drop created by high current flow between the starter solenoid and the relay.

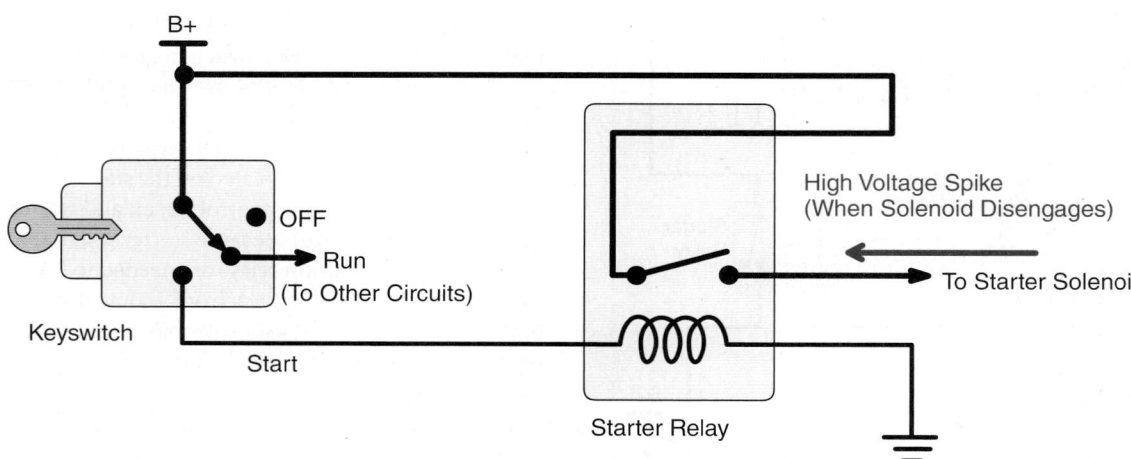

FIGURE 17-31 A relay prevents high voltage spikes produced through self-induction in the solenoid from damaging the electrical system.

may be a separate position for "proving-out," which test illuminates on-dash lights and gauges. When a vehicle has a pushbutton starter switch, battery voltage is available to the button switch only when the ignition switch is in the ON position. When the starter pushbutton is pushed, current flows through the control circuit to the starter relay. Most ignition switches used today are simply low-voltage inputs to the body electrical control module that produces a low-current output signal to the starter mag switch.

Relays use electromagnets to close contacts and act like a switch. Larger relays are sometimes referred to as "mag" switches.

Overcrank Protection (OCP)

Some starter motors are equipped with an **overcrank protection (OCP) thermostat**. The thermostatic switch, illustrated in **FIGURE 17-32**, is sensitive to the temperature of the motor. If prolonged cranking causes the motor temperature to exceed a safe threshold, the thermostatic switch opens and interrupts current flow through the relay-circuit control circuit used to energize the solenoid windings.

ADLO Lockout

Another device that may be used within the starter control circuit is **automatic disengagement lockout (ADLO)**, like that illustrated in **FIGURE 17-33**. The ADLO circuit prevents the starter motor from operating if the engine is running. It does this by using a **frequency-sensing relay** connected to the alternator R terminal, which detects AC only when the alternator is charging. The ADLO relay contacts are connected in series in the starter motor control circuit. If the engine is running, the relay prevents starter engagement and disengages the starter if the key switch is left engaged too long after the engine starts.

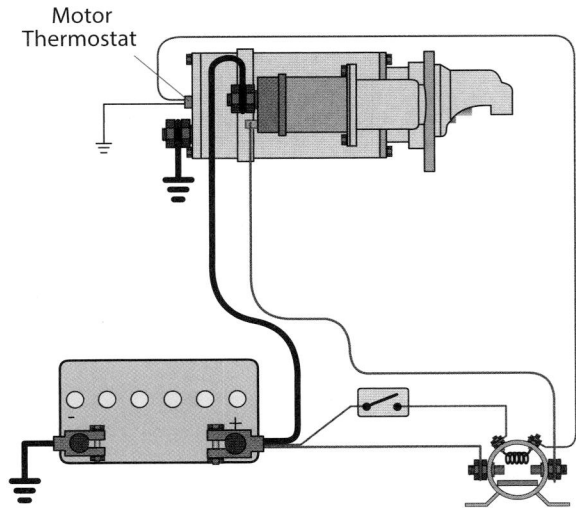

FIGURE 17-32 A thermostat switch is sensitive to starting motor temperature and opens the starter circuit if the starter motor overheats.

Voltage-Sensing Relay

Because starters can be damaged from low battery voltage, some companies find the solution is to prevent the starter from cranking when the battery voltage is too low. This also has the additional benefit of preventing prolonged cranking. The voltage-sensing relay, as illustrated in **FIGURE 17-34**, is connected in series to the solenoid control circuit. When the battery voltage drops below 7.2 volts while cranking, the voltage-sensing relay typically open-circuits the starter relay circuit.

Series-Parallel Electrical Systems—Split Load

Series-Parallel Electrical Systems, or split load as it is generally called, use two, four, or six 12-volt batteries connected in series through an equalizer to supply most of the vehicle's electrical systems. Buses and heavy equipment are common examples of vehicles using split loads for several reasons. Large engines with high starter torque requirements use 24-volt starters. Other electrical devices using large amounts of power benefit from 24 volts, as their size and the gauge of electrical wire supplying current is smaller.

Conducting less amperage also means resistance in circuits is reduced, with less damage and heat related loosening of electrical connections. On buses, the 24-volt supply powers the majority of the vehicle's electrical components, while on other vehicles, 12 volts may supply the exterior lighting or other 12-volt accessories. Batteries are recharged by a 24-volt alternator, and current is redistributed by a battery equalizer to ensure the batteries charge at an equal rate (**FIGURE 17-35**).

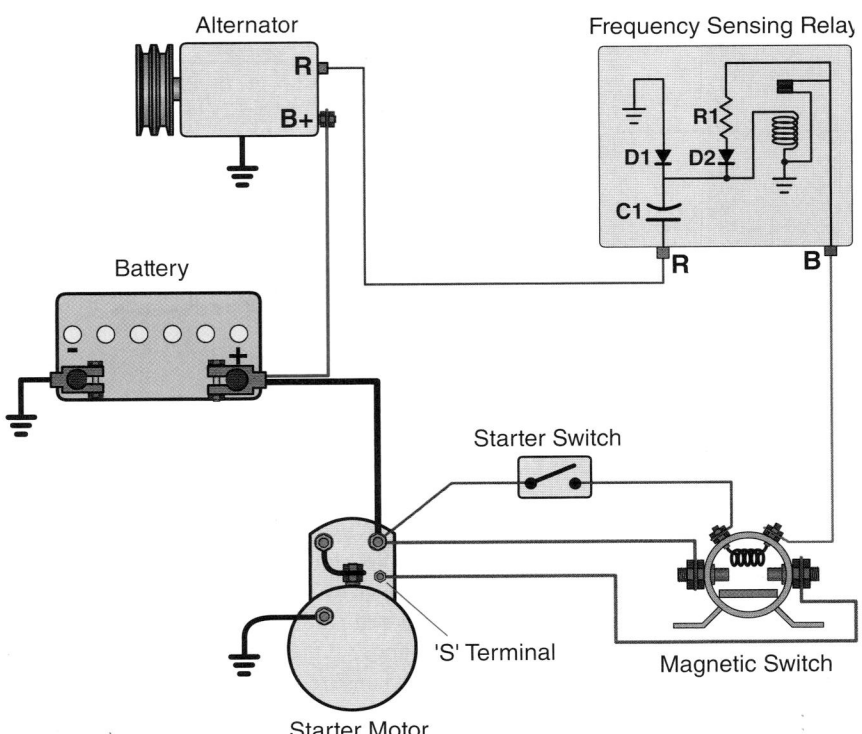

FIGURE 17-33 The ADLO relay senses alternator frequency and prevents the starter motor from operating while the engine is running.

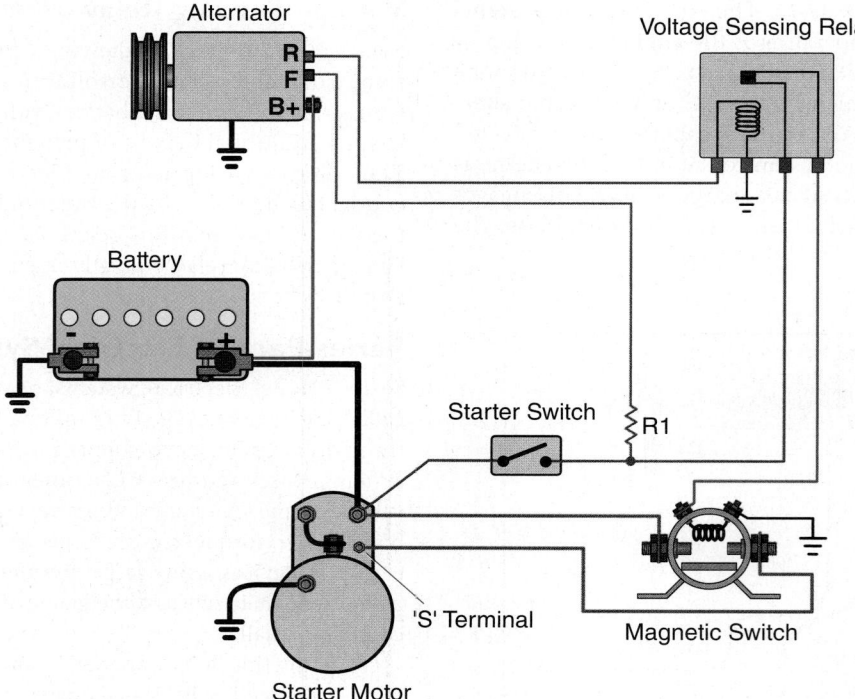

FIGURE 17-34 A low voltage-sensing relay can be connected in series with the starter control circuit to prevent the starter motor from operating if a low battery voltage condition occurs.

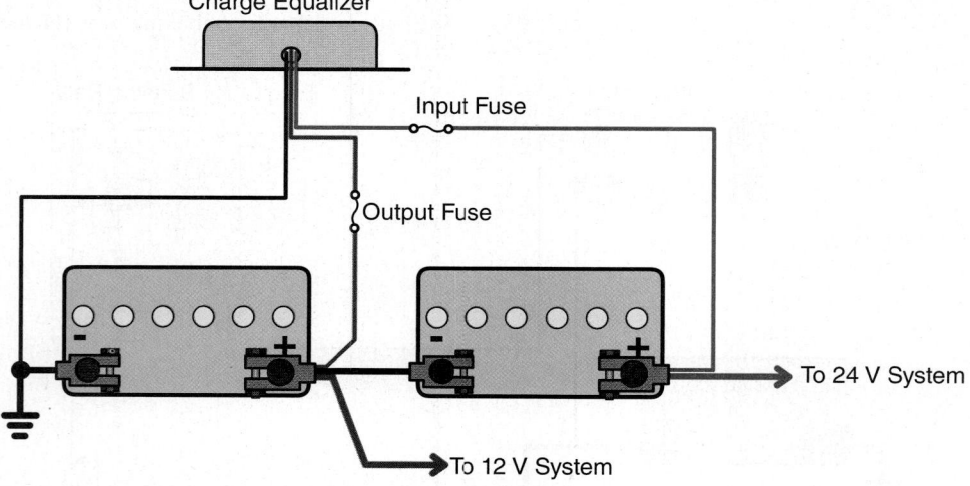

FIGURE 17-35 Circuit diagram showing a 24-volt system with a 12-volt circuit and battery equalizer.

Starting System Testing

LO 17-6 Identify and describe the procedures for performing an on-vehicle and off-vehicle starting system tests.

The starting system requires testing when the engine does not crank, cranks slowly, cranks intermittently, or when the starter motor does not turn. Major manufacturers report that between 55% and 80% of defective starters returned for warranty, work normally when tested. That points to poor or incomplete diagnosis of the starting and related systems and circuits. The starting system is just part of the overall vehicle's electrical and mechanical system. As such, there are areas of overlap between the various electrical and mechanical systems on the vehicle. For example, the starter system makes use of the batteries to supply power for starting, but the charging system needs to provide an adequate charge to ensure there is enough power to start the engine. At the same time, the engine's mechanical condition affects the load on the starter motor. So, when testing the starting system, it is important to remember that other electrical systems and mechanical items may require inspection to ensure a successful repair.

Because cranking torque produced from a starting motor is also affected by the condition and charge of the battery, the condition of the battery needs to be qualified first, before performing starting systems checks. Battery checks include:

- Verifying the battery voltage matches the voltage rating of the starter motor
- Ensuring that cranking amperage (CA or CCA) of the batteries meet or exceed OEM recommendations
- Verifying that the state of charge is not lower than 50% and that open-circuit voltage is not less than 12.4 volts or 24.8 volts
- Measuring the batteries' capacity through load testing or conductance testing

For information on how to undertake battery checks, review the Servicing Commercial Vehicle Batteries chapter.

Differentiating Between Electrical and Mechanical Problems

When diagnosing either a slow-crank or a no-crank condition, failure of the engine to crank over properly can be caused by both electrical and mechanical problems. It's important to remember that slow-crank, prolonged cranking, and no-crank conditions can be caused by problems in the fuel system, electrical system, and/or mechanical faults. To efficiently diagnose starting-related complaints, it's critical to identify the root cause of the fault through comprehensive testing to properly recommend repairs the first time the complaint is investigated. For example, slow cranking could result from an electrical fault, such as high resistance in the solenoid contacts. This problem could be resolved by replacing the starter with a new or remanufactured unit. But the slow-crank condition could also be caused by a mechanical engine fault, such as a spun main bearing that is causing a lot of drag on the crankshaft and preventing the starter from cranking it over at normal speed. In this case, the entire engine needs to be rebuilt. Prolonged cranking before starting is often caused by fuel system-related problems or even worn-out engines.

▶ TECHNICIAN TIP

Low battery voltage and weak batteries are the primary cause of stress to starters and of excessive starter amperage draw. Faulty batteries also stress charging circuits, as an alternator is forced to continually charge a weak battery. Liquid starting aids can also produce engine "kick-back" and apply extreme twisting forces to the motor. Heat from overcranking, low-voltage burn-out, and vibration from loose mountings are other leading causes of starter damage (**FIGURE 17-36**).

Given the large number of possible causes for starting system complaints, it is important to be able to differentiate between the mechanical, electrical, and even fuel system faults. Typical electrical problems that can cause starting system problems include loose, dirty, or corroded terminals and connectors,

FIGURE 17-36 A burned solenoid-contact disc caused by low available voltage.

some discharged or faulty batteries, a defective starter motor, or a faulty control circuit.

Mechanical problems that may cause starting system problems include seized pistons or bearings, hydrostatic lock from liquid in the cylinder(s) (for example, a leaky injector or water ingestion during off-road operation), a clutch that is not releasing, a seized alternator or other belt-driven device, and so on. Before proceeding to diagnose a defective starter, always attempt to bar the engine over at least two revolutions to check for seizure, lock-up, or excessive turning resistance. It's also critical to gather as much customer and vehicle information as possible to assist in pinpointing faults causing slow starting or no-starting complaints. Often, asking when the problem takes place, if the complaint is intermittent, provides important clues.

A slow-crank condition accompanied by a high draw could be due to a fault in the starter or to engine mechanical fault. If a mechanical fault is suspected, check the oil and coolant for signs of contamination. If the coolant and oil are mixing, suspect a head gasket or cracked head/block issue. If the oil and coolant are not contaminated, bar the engine over to check for excessive turning resistance. Remember that a warm diesel engine is usually much harder to turn than a cold engine, due to higher compression pressures when an oil film is present on the cylinder walls. Removing and cutting open the oil filter to check for metal particles or debris indicates whether there is engine bearing damage. If the engine is harder to turn than it should be, disconnect any power take off (PTO) shaft or remove the accessory drive belt, spin each of the accessories, and try to turn the engine over again. If the crankshaft cannot be turned a complete revolution, remove the injectors and see if liquid is ejected out of one or more cylinders. If so, the engine was hydro-locked, and you need to determine the type of liquid to pinpoint the cause.

Starter Motor Tests

The inspection and measurement procedures used to diagnose starting system complaints should be symptom based. That is, a flow chart should be used to begin a proper sequence of pinpoint checks recommended by the OEM. Symptoms include intermittent and no start, slow cranking, prolonged cranking, starter chatter, or starter noise. Any diagnostic procedure should begin with qualifying the condition of the batteries and inspecting all battery cables, grounds, and connections. Information on how to undertake battery checks can be found in the Servicing Commercial Vehicle Batteries chapter.

Faults within the starter motor may include:

- Worn brushes—Intermittent starter operation or starter operation that resumes after it is tapped with a hammer indicates brushes with poor commutator contact. Poor contact could be due to weak spring tension after a brush wears out. Poor brush contact with the commutator can also be caused by loss of brush spring tension due to heating from excessively high amperage flow—often due to prolonged cranking or low battery voltage. It can be evidenced by blue colored or even charred brush springs.
- Damaged field coils—Insulation can break down, causing shorts between coils or shorts to ground. This can be caused by age, by contaminants breaking down the insulation, or by excessive current flow. Excessive heat may also cause connections to be melted, creating additional resistance in the circuit.
- Damaged armature—An armature may have the commutator excessively worn or unevenly worn. The armature may also develop shorts between the windings, shorts to ground, and opens between windings and the commutator. A test instrument called a growler is used to test an armature.

- Worn bushings or bearings—Sintered brass bushings or, in some cases, bearings, are used to suspend the armature in the starter case. Because motor efficiency is dependent on having the smallest clearance between the armature and field coils, any wear of bushing or bearings causes contact between the armature and field coils. Worn bushing or bearings cause excessive current draw that can be observed during a starter draw test.
- Burnt contactor switch plate in the solenoid due to excessive amperage passing through a starter. Again, excessive engine resistance and batteries in poor condition create high starter amperage draws.

Use **TABLE 17-1** below to assist in diagnosing starting system problems. Always consult manufacturers' information before commencing any work.

The tests explained in the following sections include:

- Available voltage test
- Measuring starter current draw
- Measuring starter circuit voltage drop
- Inspecting and testing the starter control circuit
- Inspecting and testing relays and solenoids

Available Voltage Measurement Test

If the starting system complaint is slow cranking, the available voltage test is recommended. This test measures the amount of voltage at the starter battery positive cable and ground stud on the starter, if equipped (**FIGURE 17-37**). Minimum available voltage to the starter must not fall below 10.5 volts after three consecutive cranking periods of 30 seconds, with a 2-minute cooling period between each cranking period. If the voltage falls below 10.5 volts, the electrical system may not have adequate current to energize injectors or operate ECUs, even though cranking speed is adequate.

TABLE 17-1 Starting System Diagnosis Chart

Concern	Possible Cause	Remedy
Engine cranks slowly, does not start	Discharged batteries or batteries with low capacity	Charge; test and replace, if necessary
	Very low temperature	Allow engine and batteries to warm up and then recheck
	Battery cables too small or poor connections	Install correct battery cables or clean and replace connections
	Defective starter motor	Repair or replace, as needed
	High mechanical resistance	Check engine for high mechanical resistance, hydraulic locks, damaged bearings, or seized accessories
Solenoid clicks, chatters	Low battery voltage and excessive starter circuit resistances	Remove, clean and, reinstall all cables and connections Qualify the condition of the batteries
	Batteries discharged or low capacity	Charge; load test and replace, if necessary
	Solenoid incorrectly adjusted	Measure and adjust pinion travel
No cranking	Open circuit in starter or starter control circuit	Test, repair, or replace starter
	Safety-related lock-out enabled	Check solenoid, relays, and neutral start switch or clutch switch; repair or replace if needed; check that any safety lock-outs for outriggers, booms and PTOs are not enabled

TABLE 17-1 Starting System Diagnosis Chart (Continued)

Concern	Possible Cause	Remedy
Slow cranking	Discharged or defective batteries	Charge and test battery; replace, if necessary
	High resistance at battery connections	Clean and tighten terminal connections
	Loose or corroded battery and starting-circuit terminals	Remove, clean, reinstall
	Very low temperature	Allow battery and engine to warm up; check circuits and battery
	Armature contacting and shorting against field winding	Replace starter
	Grounded circuit in starter	
	Engine mechanical defect	Bar engine over to check for high mechanical resistance
	Overrunning clutch defective	Repair or replace, as needed
Starter noise— grinding during starting or whine after disengagement	Incorrect pinion travel	Check and adjust pinion gear travel
	Incorrect pinion travel	Check and adjust pinion gear travel
	Damaged flywheel ring gear teeth	Remove and replace flywheel
	Pinion gear abutment with flywheel	Check pinion alignment with ring gear; check for worn or out-of-round starter opening in bell housing; check for misaligned starter and bell housing
Starter turns, engine does not	Pinion slipping	Replace or repair starter
	Damaged flywheel ring gear teeth	Remove and replace flywheel ring gear
	Solenoid plunger sticking	Repair or replace solenoid
Pinion disengages slowly when engine starts	Overrunning clutch defective	Repair or replace, as needed
	Weak solenoid return spring	Replace solenoid or starting motor
	Pinion gear clearances too tight; starter and flywheel out of alignment	Check pinion alignment with ring gear teeth

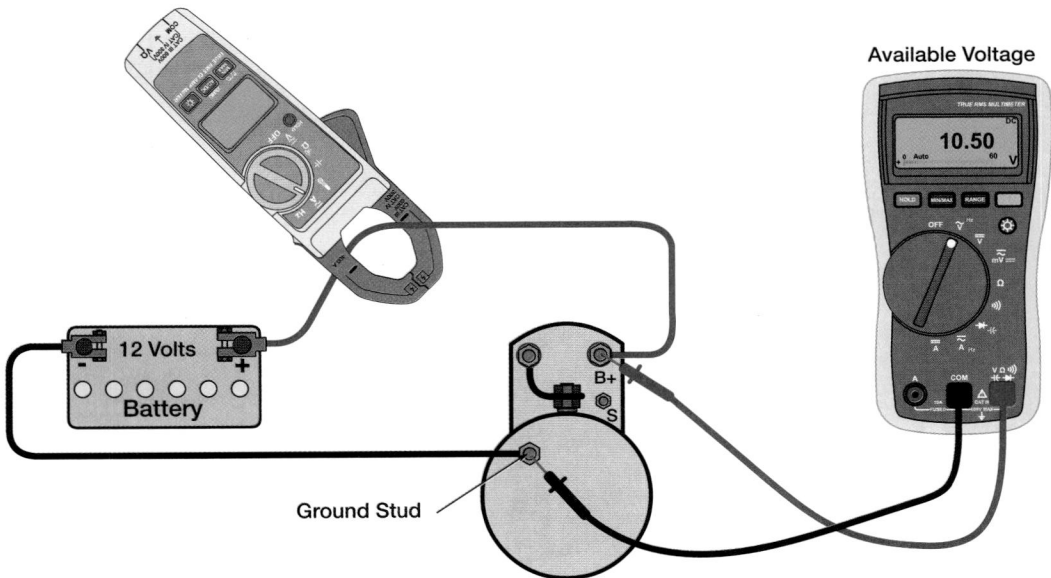

FIGURE 17-37 Measurement points for checking the starter current draw and the available starter voltage, which are important reference point for starter motor circuit testing.

To measure available voltage, first disable the engine from starting by removing a fuse for the ECU, disabling the shut-off solenoid, or alternative method. Then, connect a voltmeter between the starter ground stud and battery positive terminal on the solenoid. While cranking the engine, measure and record the amperage and voltage and evaluate the results.

Starter Current Draw Testing

Testing starter motor current draw is the best indicator of overall cranking system performance. Manufacturers may provide specifications for the current draw for starter motors, and any tests must be performed with a fully charged and correct capacity battery for the vehicle. Starter motors can be tested in two ways: on vehicle or off vehicle. The on-vehicle test is usually called a starter draw test, while the off-vehicle test is called a no-load test. A test graph outlining motor speed, current draw, voltage, and even temperature are provided by the motor manufacturer for no-load testing.

If the starting system complaint is slow cranking, a starter draw and available voltage test is recommended, using the following steps:

1. The engine is disabled from starting by removing a fuse for the ECU or, disconnecting the engine shut-off solenoid, disconnecting engine position sensors, or some alternative method.
2. A voltmeter is connected between the starter ground stud and battery positive terminal on the solenoid.
3. An inductive-type amp clamp is placed over either the positive or negative battery cables to the starter.
4. While cranking, the amperage and voltage are measured and recorded.

Results are compared with the manufacturer's specifications found in a shop manual. Properly charged batteries with adequate capacity should not allow available voltage to fall below 10.5 volts during cranking (**FIGURE 17-38**). Engine-cranking speed and the amperage drawn by the starting motor should fall within an acceptable range when performing the test. When test specifications are not available, the technician can still interpret the results by analyzing the engine-cranking speed and amperage and voltage readings obtained during the test. Engine-cranking speed could be monitored using an optical tachometer or a less reliable method depends on a technician's familiarity with the sound of an engine and starter cranking at normal speed. Depending on the measured observations, replacement of a starting motor is recommended if two conditions are apparent. The first is if the motor appears to be excessively resistive due to defective, burnt, or worn internal components. The starting draw test indicating excessive resistance is followed up with a voltage drop test to verify the starting motor is in fact the source of resistance in the series circuit. The second condition indicating the need for motor replacement is a motor drawing excessive current. In the absence of a mechanical defect that makes the engine resistant to rotation, or inadequate battery capacity, a motor that draws excessive amperage likely has an internally grounded circuit pathway.

Starter Draw Test Analysis

If cranking speed is low, and amperage measured is below normal but available voltage is high, the starting motor or starting circuit has high electrical resistance. Current needed to provide

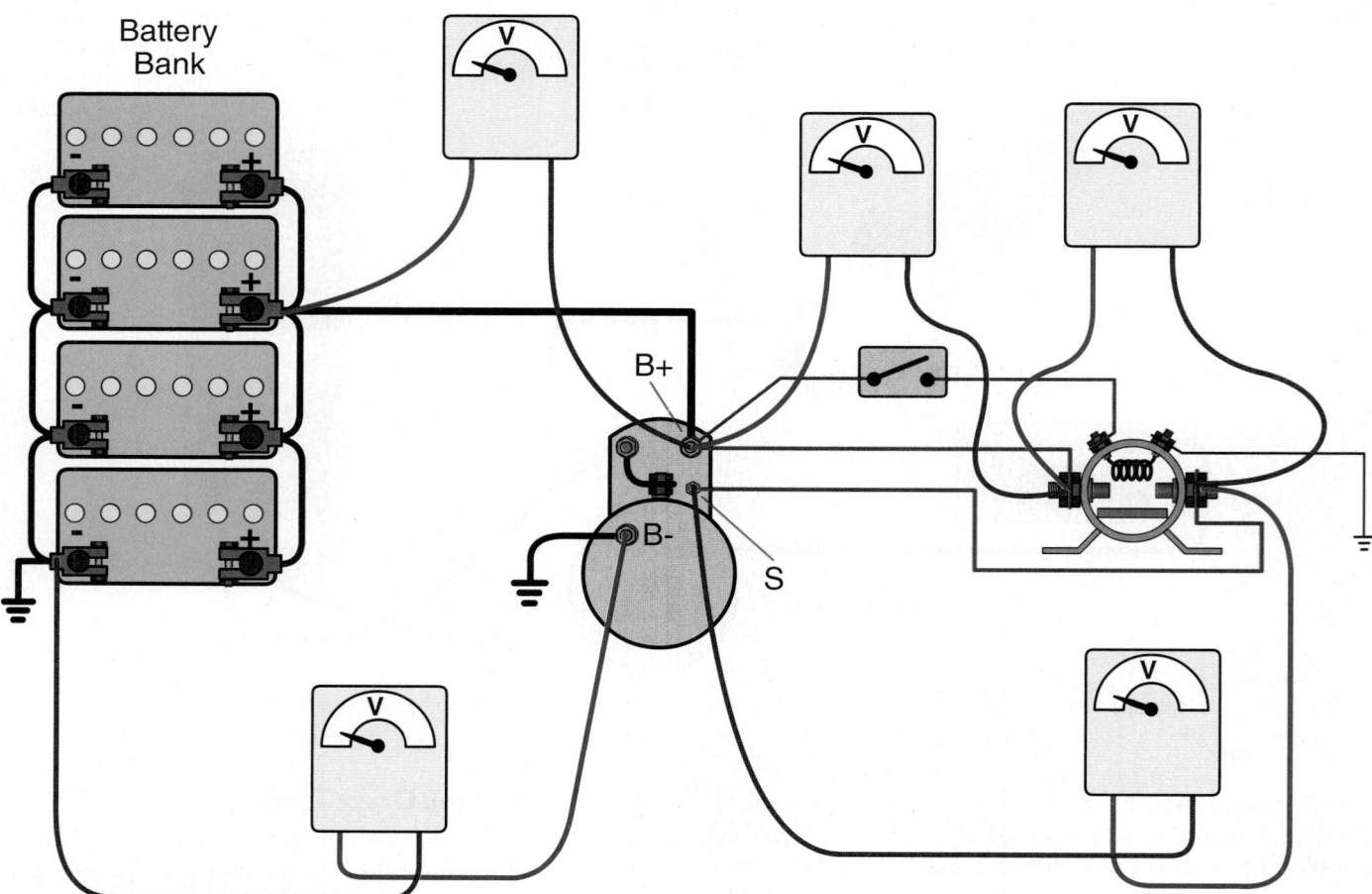

FIGURE 17-38 Positioning of the voltmeter to measure voltage drop across different parts of the starter circuit.

cranking torque is simply not available. Resistive cable connections, worn brushes, or loose or burnt internal connections could cause this condition.

If amperage drawn by the starting motor is excessively high and available voltage low, the starter may be defective internally, the engine seizing or resistive, or the battery voltage low. Shorted field coils caused by the armature contacting the coils is a likely cause of an internal defect. Low available voltage to the starter may also be the cause. Undersized cables, loose connections, or a corroded and highly resistive connection reduces available voltage to the starter, causing excessive amperage draw. Each electrical connection and cable in the starter circuit needs to be measured for voltage loss due to excessive resistance in this situation. Small resistances become larger as amperage increases as predicted by Joule's Heating Law. Resistive wire or connections drop voltage and heat up at the same time. By using a carbon pile to load cables and circuits to 500 amps, voltage loss added from all positive and negative cables should not total more than 5% in a 12-volt circuit (0.5 volts), with no more than 2% loss in any single cable.

It is important to note there is no "fixed" amount of amperage draw for each engine. However, no more than 1 amp per cubic inch of engine displacement should be observed at normal room temperatures. Manufacturers publish some guidelines for an engine or starter configuration. The amount of amperage varies, however, due to the following reasons:

- Engine displacement—larger engines require more torque to turn and, consequently, more cranking amperage.
- The compression ratio may change the amount of cranking torque.
- The type of starter, direct drive or gear reduction, changes the amount of amperage used.
- Mechanical condition of engine—loose or tight due to varying mechanical conditions, such as temperature, amount of lubrication, wear, bearing or piston seizure, ring condition, combustion chamber deposits, and so on
- The starter drive-to-flywheel ratio
- The condition of the battery
- Engine temperature and oil viscosity

To test the starter draw, follow the guidelines in **SKILL DRILL 17-1**.

Testing Starter Circuit Current Draw Test

A starter draw test indicates whether low current draw is the cause of slow cranking speed. High resistance in any part of the starter circuit reduces the available current, which in turn reduces cranking speed. Abnormal starter draw test results can be followed up with a voltage drop test to identify the part or resistive component in the circuit. Two areas of the starter circuit where voltage drop tests are performed are in the control circuit and motor circuit. The high-current motor circuit consists of the battery, main battery cables to the starter motor solenoid, solenoid contacts, and heavy ground cables back to the battery from the engine and chassis. The control circuit activates the solenoid and can be ECU controlled. Voltage drop can occur across both the high-current and control circuits.

A voltmeter is used to measure voltage drop across all sections of the series circuit to identify resistances. Since the starter is a series circuit, Kirchhoff's Law is applied, which states: the sum of the voltage drops in a circuit equals source voltage. A starter that has low available voltage should have a voltage drop test performed to pinpoint excessive circuit resistances that could cause slow cranking speed or no start conditions. Excessive voltage drop located in the starter cables or terminals can be quickly identified and corrected. Excessive drop in the starter solenoid or starter itself indicates internal resistances from burnt or worn electrical connections, which likely requires starter motor replacement. A voltmeter with a

SKILL DRILL 17-1 Testing Starter Draw

1. Research the specifications for the starter draw test.
2. Place an inductive-type amp-clamp over either the positive or negative battery cables connected to the starter. It doesn't matter which starter cable is measured because it is a series circuit, so amperage is the same at any point in the circuit. Note that when two cables are used, the amperage measured in each cable must be added together to determine total amperage drawn.
3. Connect voltmeter leads to the battery positive stud at the starter and the ground stud to measure available voltage. The meter should be ranged to measure less than 20 volts DC.
4. Disable the engine from starting by removing a fuse from the engine ECM or disabling the injection system shut-off solenoid.
5. With the engine disabled, crank the engine and record the amps and volts as soon as the engine rpm and amperage readings stabilize.
6. Compare the readings with the specifications and analyze the results in terms of voltage and amperage measurements.

minimum/maximum range setting is very useful when measuring voltage drop because it records and holds the maximum voltage drop that occurs for a cranking test cycle. Small electrical resistances and poor connections are magnified when high amperage passes through the circuit—resistances that are not observable when low amperage current passes through a circuit.

Starting system voltage drop is tested while the circuit is under load, either by cranking the starter or using a carbon pile load tester. The voltmeter is connected in parallel across the component, cable, or part of the circuit that is to be tested for voltage drop. Stated another way, the voltmeter is simply measuring the voltage or pressure differential between two points. This means the voltmeter is connected on each end of a starter cable's terminals to measure resistance in the cable (**FIGURE 17-39**).

For example, to measure the voltage drop across a starter solenoid, one voltmeter lead touches the battery stud on the solenoid, while the lead touches the motor terminal stud where battery current leaves the solenoid and enters the motor. When the starter is cranked, or a load applied through a carbon pile load tester, any resistance is observed as a voltage reading (**FIGURE 17-40**). The higher the voltage measured, the greater the resistance present in the circuit. To measure voltage, drop in long starter cables. A voltmeter with extra-long leads can be connected to each end of a battery cable. Generally, no more than 0.5 volts is ideally allowed in a 12-volt circuit or 1.0 in a 24-volt circuit. However, in HD starting circuits where starting motors can momentarily draw more than 1,000 amps, allowable voltage drop depends on the amperage used in a circuit. When all circuit voltage drops are added together, as much as

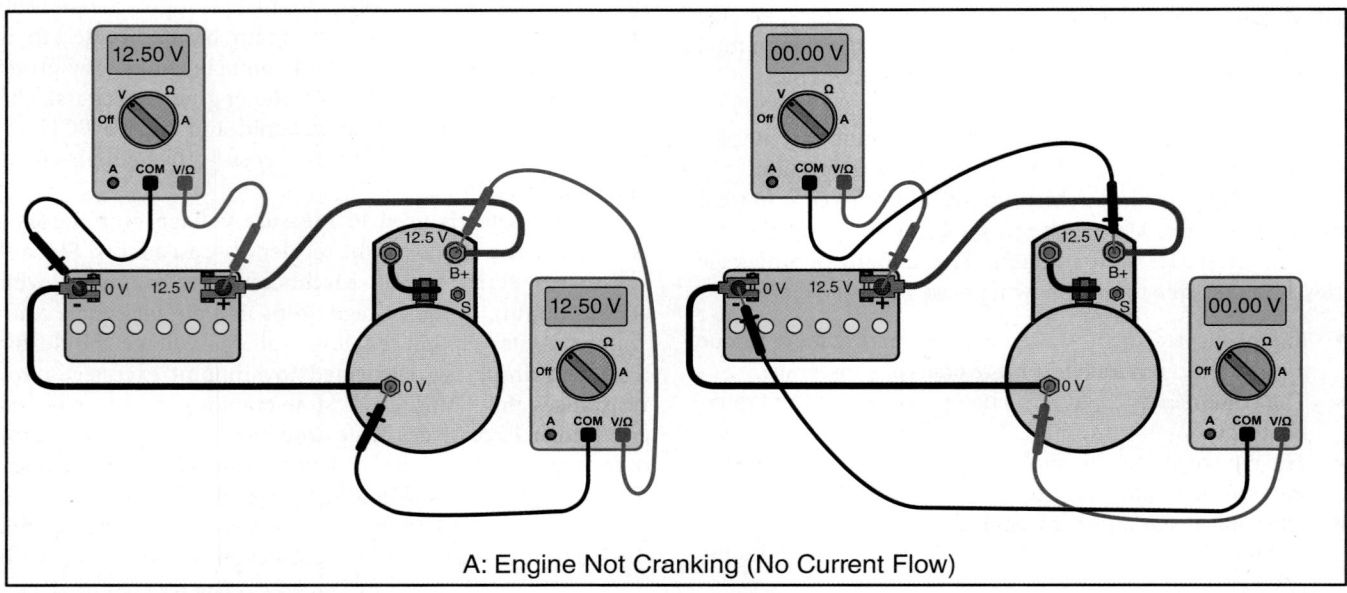

A: Engine Not Cranking (No Current Flow)

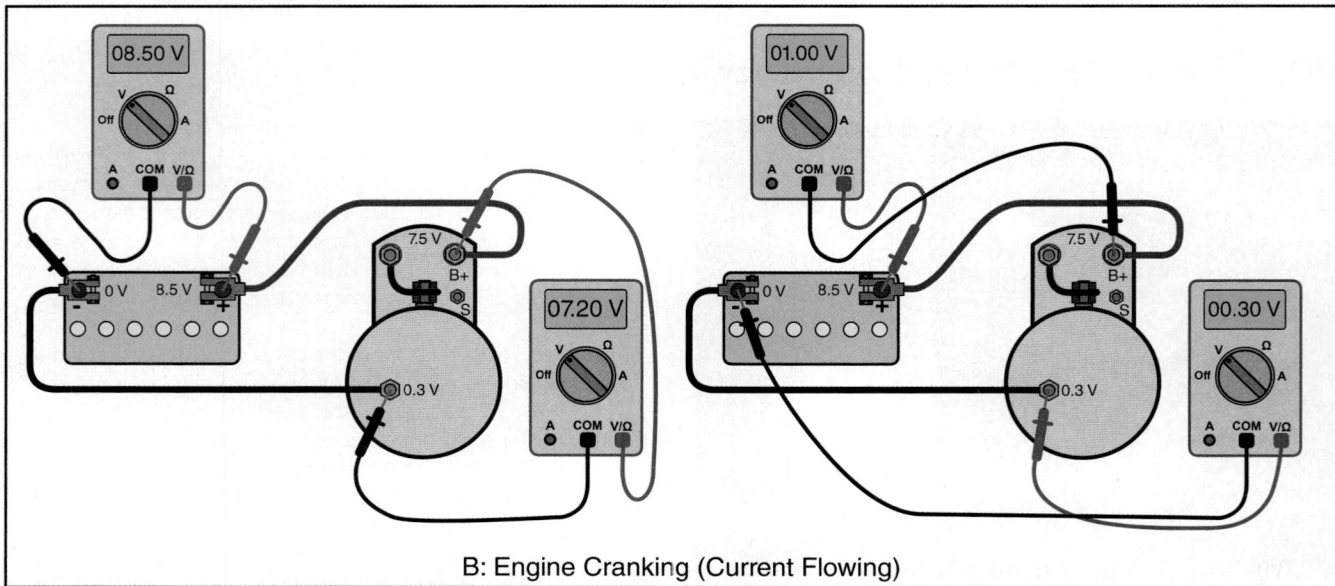

B: Engine Cranking (Current Flowing)

FIGURE 17-39 Carefully examine A and B. Note the placement of the voltmeter, which identified a 1-volt difference between the available voltage measurement at the starter and battery voltage when cranking. Another 0.3 volts was dropped along the ground cable.

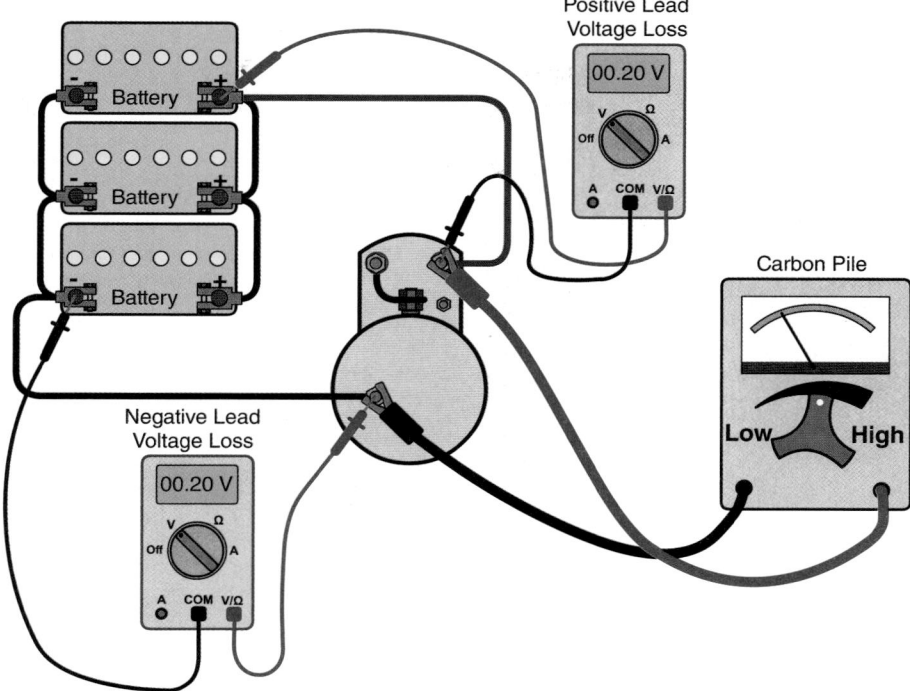

FIGURE 17-40 A carbon pile can apply a load to test starter circuits.

TABLE 17-2 Voltage Drops

Amps	Maximum Acceptable Combined Voltage Drop
375–449	0.6
450–549	0.7
550–624	0.8
625–724	0.9
725–799	1.0
800–874	1.1
875–974	1.2
975–1,025	1.3

1.3 volts is allowed when over 1,000 amps is moving through cables and motors (**TABLE 17-2**).

To test starter circuit voltage drop, follow the steps in **SKILL DRILL 17-2**.

Inspecting and Testing the Starter Control Circuit

The starter control circuit energizes the starter solenoid, and the starter solenoid energizes the starter motor. If there is a problem in the starter control circuit, the vehicle does not crank at all, or maybe intermittently. The control circuit is made up of the battery, ignition switch, neutral safety switch (automatic vehicles), clutch switch (manual vehicles), starter relay, and solenoid windings. If the starter is controlled by an ECU, then potentially other security features could prevent cranking such as an immobilizer or requirement for a correct pass code.

To inspect and test the starter control circuit, follow the steps in **SKILL DRILL 17-3**.

▶ TECHNICIAN TIP

The starter relay bypass test is a quick method of determining if the relay is operational. This test should be performed when the starter motor does not crank when the ignition is in the start position (or when the starter button is depressed). Connect a jumper wire between the battery+ and starter terminal on the relay. This connection bypasses the control circuit of the relay, so the starter should crank the engine. If the engine cranks with the jumper installed, check to see whether current is supplied to the relay when the ignition key or starter button is in the crank position. Use a test light for this step. If current is available to the relay, check the ground circuit supplying the control circuit to determine whether it is properly connected or resistive. If the control circuit is properly energized, and the starter cranks when the battery or ground jumper wire is used, the circuit between the relay and ignition switch or button is defective.

Inspecting and Testing Relays and Solenoids

The starting system typically contains solenoids and relays that activate the control circuit. The solenoid is mounted on the starter motor, while one or more of the starter circuit relays are found on the starter, or firewall.

SKILL DRILL 17-2 Measuring Starter Circuit Voltage Drop

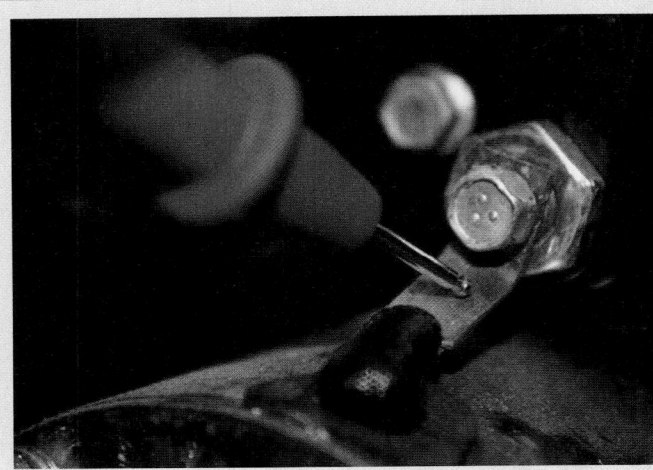

1. Qualify the condition of the batteries before performing a starter draw test. The batteries should be fully charged and have an open-circuit voltage of 12.6-volts. Testing cannot proceed if voltage is less than 12.4 volts for conventional lead-acid batteries. Batteries should have adequate capacity, demonstrated by a load or conductance test, before proceeding with the test. Low battery voltage prevents correct measurement of voltage drops, since current is excessive.

2. Measure and record the available voltage at the starter and the batteries. This is done by connecting a voltmeter's leads at the batteries and another to the starter's battery stud on the solenoid and the ground stud. An alternative method to load circuits, other than by cranking the engine, is to load circuits with a carbon pile load tester set to 500 amps. The load is applied momentarily by a second person while voltage measurements are made.

3. Crank the engine. Observe and record the available voltage. Available voltage should be no less than 10.5 volts and not have more than 0.5-volt drop between the battery and starter voltage. This number depends on the amount of amperage drawn by the starter. If amperage is high due to cranking torque required by a large displacement engine, more drop is allowed. The available voltage figure is used to help identify all the voltage drops in the circuit. Since it is a series circuit, the sum of all voltage drops add up to equal available voltage or source voltage.

4. Measure and record voltage drop in all positive and negative cables connected to the starter while cranking, or when using a carbon pile to load the circuits to approximately 500 amps.

5. If the observed voltage drop is more than 0.5 volts in a 12-volt circuit, measure the voltage drop in smaller sections, such as across terminals and connecting studs or in just the cable.

6. Measure the voltage drops across the solenoid battery and motor terminals, the L-strap connecting the motor terminal to the starter, if equipped, and the voltage drop between the motor terminal and ground stud.

7. Add the voltage drops in all the cables, solenoid, and across the starter motor. The number should equal the available voltage.

8. Analyze the results. If available voltage at the starter is less than 10.5 volts, and the cables have no more than a 0.5 volt drop, the starting motor has excessive mechanical resistance.

9. Isolate the voltage drops across the starter solenoid and L-strap to determine whether excessive resistance is there or in the starting motor.

10. If excessive starting circuit resistance is discovered in the starting motor, recommend starter replacement.

SKILL DRILL 17-3 Inspecting and Testing the Starter Control Circuit

1. Use a DC voltmeter to measure voltage between the solenoid control circuit terminal on the solenoid (R) terminal and the ground stud of the starter while the engine is cranking.

2. If the voltage is less than 10.5 volts, measure the voltage drop between the R terminal and the starting motor relay.

3. If the voltage drop is less than 0.5 volt, measure the voltage drop on the ground side of the relay control circuit.

4. If the voltage drop is higher than 0.5 volt on either side of the circuit, use the wiring diagram to guide you in isolating the voltage drop on that side of the circuit. Continue conducting voltage drop tests across individual components and cables.

5. If the voltage drops are within specifications on both sides of the circuit, the resistance of the solenoid pull-in and hold-in windings needs to be measured. If out of specifications, the solenoid or starter motor and solenoid must be replaced.

Before performing any tests, ensure that the vehicle battery is charged and in good condition. The manufacturer's wiring diagrams should be checked to determine the circuit operation, identification, and location of all components in the starter circuit.

Relays must be tested in two or three ways, depending on the relay. The simplest test is to measure the resistance of the relay control circuit winding. This is performed using an ohmmeter connected across the control circuit terminals of the relay. If it is out of specifications, the relay needs to be replaced. Remember that most relays have a diode suppressing voltage spike caused by self-induction. This means that the meter may not measure resistance the same way if the leads to the control circuit are switched. If energized, the relay clicks and closes when proper polarity of current is applied to the terminals, but not when the polarity is reversed. If the relay control circuit is okay, then the switch contacts need to be tested for an excessive voltage drop. The best way to do this is by measuring voltage drop across the battery+ terminal and the output lead to the starting motor R terminal. Energizing the relay while the starter is cranked allows current flow to flow across the contacts so that a voltage drop measurement can be taken. Any excessive voltage drop across the relay contacts requires the replacement of the relay.

Solenoid voltage drop is tested by measuring the voltage drop between the battery terminal and motor terminal. The first test to perform is a voltage drop test across the solenoid contacts. Place the red lead on the solenoid B+ stud and the black lead on the motor terminal. The voltage drop should be less than 0.5 volt for a 12-volt system and less than 1.0 volt for a 24-volt system. If not, replace the solenoid or starter assembly. Testing of the solenoid hold-in and pull-in windings is done by measuring the resistance between the R terminal and ground for the hold in winding. The pull-in winding resistance is measured between the R terminal and the motor terminal.

Removing and Replacing a Starter, and Inspecting the Ring Gear or Flex Plate

The starter motor needs to be removed to measure no-load speed during a bench test. An optical tachometer is typically used to determine whether the motor reaches rotational speed identified by OEM specification. Whenever a starter motor is removed, it is important to inspect the flywheel ring gear by slowly rotating the engine and observing the condition of the ring gear. To replace a starter motor and inspect the ring gear or flex plate, follow the steps in **SKILL DRILL 17-4**.

SKILL DRILL 17-4 Replacing a Starter Motor and Inspecting the Ring Gear or Flex Plate

1. Disconnect the batteries by removing the ground cables first.
2. At the starter, disconnect the ground cable and electrical connections to the starter motor. Tape together, tag, or label wiring to the battery positive stud on the starter to prevent mixing terminal connections when reconnecting the starter.
3. Loosen and remove the mounting bolts. Often the top bolt should be the last to remove to prevent bending of the starter bolts and aluminum mounting flange.
4. Remove the starter motor while supporting its weight as the last mounting bolts are removed. Some assistance may be needed to support the weight of the starter while it is removed.

5. Inspect the flywheel ring gear teeth for damage. Slowly have someone rotate the engine or use a barring tool to rotate the engine while examining the teeth for damage or excessive wear.
6. Also check the flywheel bolts to ensure none are broken or a no-start condition has not been caused by sheared flywheel bolts. In a six-cylinder engine, there are normally three points of wear on the teeth. These wear points correspond to the engine's stopping position on compression stroke.
7. Count the number of drive teeth on the starter and carefully match up the replacement starter with the old starter. Ensure the direction of starter rotation is the same as the old starter. Check the drive gear locks in one direction and freewheels in the same direction as the old starter. Compare the chamfer on the drive gears' leading edge is also the same.
8. Compare the orientation of the starter solenoid with the nose cone. It may be necessary to rotate the nose cone housing of a replacement starting motor to match the solenoid position of the original starting motor. To change solenoid position, loosen and remove the recessed Allen head bolts from the drive housing bolts.
9. Rotate the drive housing to match the position of the old starter and reinstall the bolts.
10. Reinstall and connect the new starter. Torque all bolts and electrical connector fasteners.
11. Seal electrical connections with dielectric grease to minimize corrosion.
12. Reconnect the battery cables and test starter motor operation.

Repairing a Starter Motor

LO 17-7 Identify and outline inspection and repair procedures for a starting motor.

Inspecting and repairing a starter motor was, at one time, a cost-effective practice, particularly if the motor was new and repairing it could likely be more reliable than installing a rebuilt unit. While this is no longer the case in retail operations, some fleets may still inspect a starter to determine whether it is feasible to clean, adjust, lubricate, and repair small defects.

When disassembling the starter, always mark the position of the nose cone and motor housings in relation to each other. Depending on the engine, many starter nose cones may be rotated at various angles to obtain clearance between the solenoid and other engine or chassis parts. When assembling, lubricate all bushings and linkage with dielectric silicone grease.

Once the starter motor has been disassembled into its component parts, conduct the following tests for each component as follows:

- Solenoid:
  - Measure the resistance and current draw of the pull-in and hold-in windings.
  - Check for the free movement of the iron plunger.
  - Check contacts and terminal end cap for wear and cracks. Make replacements, if necessary.
  - Measure the pinion gear travel and compare with specifications.
- Drive and yoke:
  - Visually inspect the drive engagement yoke for wear and damage. Replace if there is excessive wear.
  - Check the drive clutch for slippage. This is done by attempting to turn the clutch repeatedly in a locked and unlocked direction. If there is any slippage, replace the drive.
- Brushes:
  - Check the length of the brushes with the manufacturer's specifications and replace, if necessary.
  - Check the brush springs for tension, brush movement in the brush holder, and the insulation of the brush holder.
- Field windings:
  - Visually check the insulation for cracks or damage. Check for short circuits through the field insulation and case by connecting a purpose made 110-volt test lamp in series between the field coil and case. During the insulation stress test, the lamp lights if there is a short circuit. If the field insulation fails, the field needs to be replaced or reinsulated.
- Armature:
  - Clean the commutator with crocus-cloth abrasive, and use a sharp tool to clean the insulation between the commutator bars.
  - Inspect the armature on a growler for shorts between windings. Using a thin metal strip, rotate the armature in the growler, which has an alternating-current magnetic field. If the thin metal strip, such as a hacksaw blade, is held over the armature along its axis, it begins to vibrate at 60 times/second if there is a short in the armature windings (**FIGURE 17-41**).

FIGURE 17-41 A starter armature on a growler. No continuity should exist between the armature shaft and commutator.

- Inspect for shorts between the commutator and the armature shaft. Use a lamp-type insulation stress tester with a voltage no higher than 110 volts for a 12- or 24-volt armature. Note that to pass an insulation test, the armature needs to be dry and free of contaminants.
- Inspect the armature shaft for wear or damage to the bearing surfaces. Also check the drive splines for wear or damage. Inspect the shaft to ensure it is not bent. Check the windings to ensure they are not damaged or bent. Any damage to the above items means the armature needs to be replaced.
- Housings:
  - Inspect the housings for damage or wear. Replace if they are cracked, worn or broken.
- Armature Bushings:
  - Check the bushings for wear using the armature shaft surfaces. The bushings should fit snugly around the shaft to prevent contact between the armature and field windings. Replace the bushings if they are worn.

Once the starter motor has been repaired, it should be tested on a starter test bench with a full load, if possible. If a full-load test is not possible, conduct a no-load bench test as per the procedure in this chapter.

Starter No-Load Testing

After a starting motor is repaired, a no-load starting motor test is performed to measure starting motor speed, voltage, and amperage drawn. These numbers are graphed and compared with test specifications established by the OEM (**FIGURE 17-42**). During the test on a proper bench-testing machine, the motor is also gradually loaded from no-load up to its full-load limit under a controlled condition, while all operating parameters are measured and recorded. The armature run-down time test may also be measured, which refers to the time the motor requires to come to a full stop. Temperature of the armature is also checked to evaluate whether any other problem may be present (**FIGURE 17-43**).

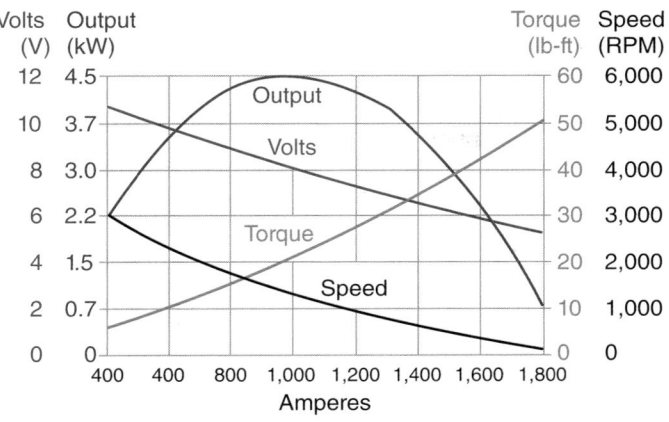

FIGURE 17-42 A starting motor performance curve, which is used to analyze the results of a no-load test of a starting motor. Comparison of no-load test results should be identical.

Engine and Starter Rotation

When observing engine rotation, many technicians often note the front engine pulley/harmonic balancer turns clockwise. However, not all engines are mounted in-line with the driveline (e.g., "V" drives). Some engines are mounted sideways in a vehicle and some are mounted at the rear and sideways. Since there is an abundance of configurations for positioning engines in a chassis, in addition to engine positions used in HD off-road equipment and stationary applications, the Society of Automotive Engineers (SAE) references engine rotation from the flywheel end of the engine. Most automotive engines are LEFT-HAND (or CCW; counter-clockwise) rotation.

The location and position of the starter on the engine can determine which direction the engine is cranked. Starter drive mechanism and the cut of the teeth are changed, along with helix features of the armature that moves the drive.

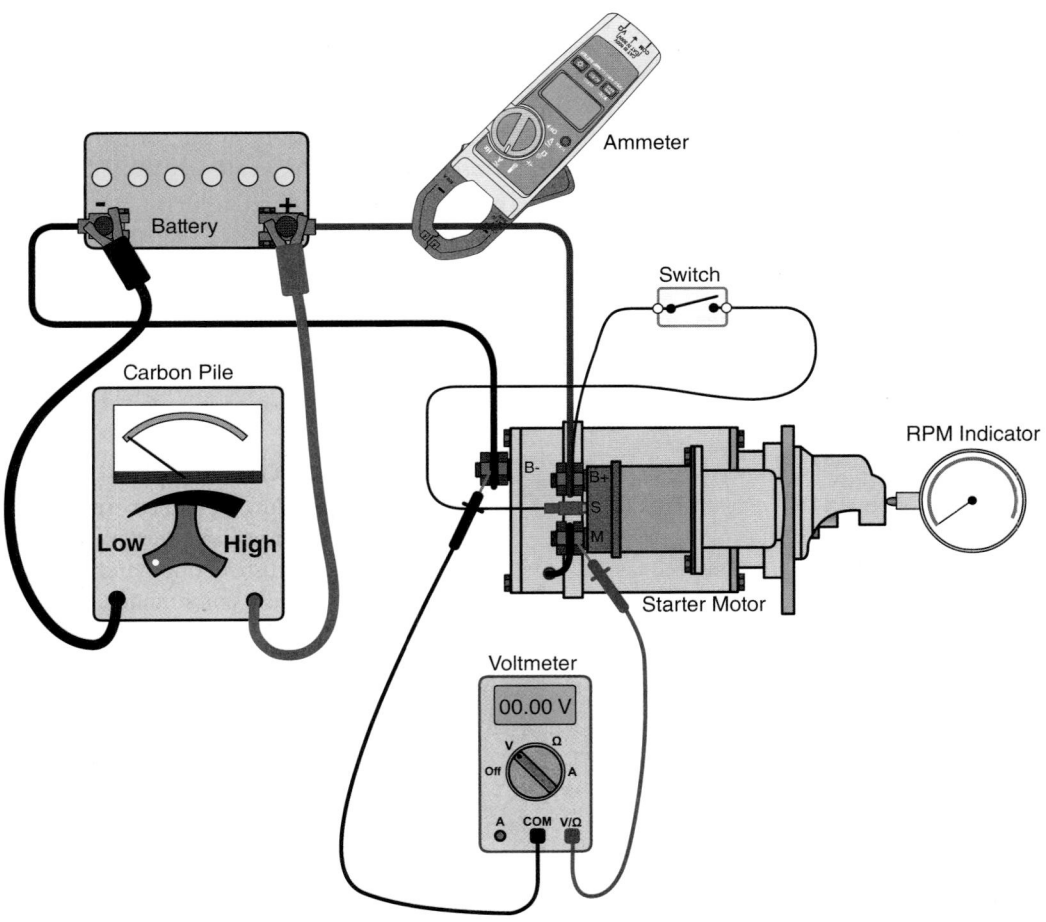

FIGURE 17-43 The set-up for a no-load test of a starter measuring and graphing speed, amperage, and voltage.

Wrap-Up

Ready for Review

▶ The starting system provides a method of rotating (cranking) the vehicle's engine to begin the combustion cycle.

▶ Diesel engines require large starter current draw, so several batteries are often connected in parallel or series to increase available cranking amperage or voltage.

▶ New designs of starter motors and systems controls are enabling starters to last longer and increase output torque, while substantially reducing motor weight.

▶ There are three major categories of electric starters used in heavy vehicles: direct drive, reduction, and planetary gear reduction.

▶ The three most common types of DC motors found in commercial vehicles are series, shunt, and compound motors.

▶ Series motors are called "series" because the current pathway through various components inside the motor is in series. Because it is a series circuit, any unwanted resistance inside the motor, whether it is a burnt contact or loose brush, reduces current flow throughout the entire motor circuit.

▶ Series-wound motors also are self-limiting in speed due to the development of a counter-electromotive force (CEMF) that induces current in the opposite direction of battery current through the motor.

▶ Cranking an engine with low battery voltage is destructive to a starter motor.

▶ Regardless of the motor design, a starter motor consists of housing, fields, an armature, a commutator, brushes, end frames, and a solenoid-operated shift mechanism.

▶ Some starter motors are equipped with overcrank protection thermostats that open the relay circuit and interrupt the current to the solenoid, if prolonged cranking causes the motor temperature to exceed a safe threshold.

▶ Another protection device for the starter control circuit is the automatic disengagement lockout, which prevents the starter motor from operating if the engine is running.

▶ Dual-voltage systems allow the vehicle to be started on 24 volts for improved electrical efficiency, while the other electrical loads operate on the more common 12 volts.

▶ The starting system is just part of the overall vehicle's electrical and mechanical system. As such, there are areas of overlap between the various electrical and mechanical systems on the vehicle.

▶ Whether a slow-crank or a no-crank condition, failure to crank-over properly can be caused by electrical or mechanical problems. It is important to be able to differentiate between the two types of faults, so that a wrong diagnosis can be avoided and the problem fixed appropriately the first time.

Key Terms

armature The only rotating component of the starter; has three main components: the shaft, windings, and the commutator.

automatic disengagement lockout (ADLO) A device that prevents the starter motor from operating if the engine is running.

counter-electromotive force (CEMF) An electromagnetic force produced by the spinning magnetic field of the armature or rotor, which induces current in the opposite direction of battery current through the motor or alternator.

direct drive A starter motor drive system in which the motor armature directly engages the flywheel through a pinion gear.

frequency-sensing relay A relay connected to the alternator that detects alternating current only when the alternator is charging.

low-voltage burn-out A damaging condition for starter motors in which excess current flows through the starter, causing the motor to burn out prematurely.

overcrank protection (OCP) thermostat A thermostat that monitors the temperature of the motor and opens a relay circuit to interrupt the current to the solenoid if prolonged cranking causes the motor temperature to exceed a safe threshold.

planetary gear reduction drive A type of gear reduction system in which a planetary gear set reduces the starter profile to multiply motor torque to the pinion gear.

reduction gear drive A starter motor drive system in which the motor multiplies torque to the starter pinion gear by using an extra gear between the armature and the starter drive mechanism.

Review Questions

1. Which of the following is the correct sequence for current flow through a series-type starter motor?
   a. Field poles, brush, commutator, armature, brush
   b. Armature, brush, commutator, brush, field poles
   c. Brush, armature, commutator, brush, field poles
   d. Field poles, armature, brush, commutator, brush

2. What test instrument is best used to check for resistance in a starter circuit when cranking?
   a. AVR
   b. Ohmmeter
   c. Voltmeter
   d. Test light

3. Consider a starter has a "chattering" solenoid when attempting to crank the engine. If sufficient battery current is available to the solenoid, which of the following is most likely defective?
   a. Hold-in winding
   b. Pull-in winding
   c. Misadjusted pinion clearance
   d. The starter relay

4. A starting motor should not be operated for longer than:
   a. 15 seconds
   b. 30 seconds
   c. 1 minute
   d. 2 minutes
5. Which of the following changes takes place to the electrical properties of a starter circuit as the flow of amperage increases?
   a. Increase in voltage through the circuit
   b. Increase in resistance through the circuit
   c. Decrease in resistance through the circuit
   d. Increased CEMF through the circuit
6. Consider performing three consecutive starter cranking cycles of 30 seconds with two-minute rest intervals between cycles. If batteries are correctly sized and no defects are present in the starter circuit or engine, battery voltage during cranking should not fall below:
   a. 7.5 volts
   b. 9.6 volts
   c. 10.5 volts
   d. 12.4 volts
7. Which of the following reasons best explains why gear reduction starters draw less current than direct-drive starters?
   a. Gear reduction starters produce more torque.
   b. Gear reduction starters have more resistance in armature and field windings.
   c. Gear reduction starters rotate faster.
   d. Gear reduction starters have less capacity to absorb heat from extended cranking periods.
8. When testing the starting system on a vehicle with a six-cylinder 855-cubic inch diesel engine, you find that the engine cranks slowly. The starter current draw is 90 amps, and the battery voltage during cranking is 12.1 volts. What should you do next?
   a. Check the starter circuit for resistances
   b. Load test the battery
   c. Replace the starter
   d. Inspect the engine for seizure
9. What is the maximum voltage drop allowed when performing a starter cable voltage drop test on a 12-volt system?
   a. 0.2 volt–0.8 volt for the entire circuit
   b. 0.5 volt for each connection
   c. 1.0 volt for entire circuit
   d. 0.5 volt–0.8 volt for each cable
10. What is the most likely cause for a failure of an engine to crank, but the starting motor turns?
    a. Bent armature
    b. Defective solenoid
    c. Defective starter drive mechanism
    d. An open hold-in winding on the solenoid

ASE Technician A/Technician B Style Questions

1. Technician A says that dozens of electric motors are found in heavy vehicles operating a variety of devices from electric seats, fuel and coolant pumps, fan blower motors, and even instrument gauges. Technician B says that the largest of all these electric motors is the starter motor. Who is correct?
   a. Technician A
   b. Technician B
   c. Both Technician A and Technician B
   d. Neither Technician A nor Technician B
2. Technician A says that all electric motors operate using principles of magnetic attraction and repulsion. Technician B says that, because like magnetic poles attract one another and unlike poles repel, it is possible to arrange magnetic poles within the motor to be continuously in a state of repulsion and attraction. Who is correct?
   a. Technician A
   b. Technician B
   c. Both Technician A and Technician B
   d. Neither Technician A nor Technician B
3. Technician A and B are analyzing the results of a starter drive test on a starter circuit for a six-cylinder 855-cubic inch diesel engine. The engine cranks slowly and starter current draw is 90 amps. The battery voltage during cranking is 12.1 volts. Technician A says that the starter armature likely has an open winding. Technician B says that the results are likely due to a burnt contactor disc in the starter solenoid. Who is correct?
   a. Technician A
   b. Technician B
   c. Both Technician A and Technician B
   d. Neither Technician A nor Technician B
4. Technician A says that series-wound motors also are self-limiting in speed due to the development of a counter-electromotive force (CEMF). Technician B says that CEMF is produced by the spinning magnetic field of the armature, which induces current in the same direction of battery current through the motor. Who is correct?
   a. Technician A
   b. Technician B
   c. Both Technician A and Technician B
   d. Neither Technician A nor Technician B
5. Technician A says that cranking an engine with low battery voltage causes one of the most damaging conditions for a starter. Technician B says that low-voltage burn-out occurs when excess amperage flows through the starter, causing the motor to burn out prematurely. Who is correct?
   a. Technician A
   b. Technician B
   c. Both Technician A and Technician B
   d. Neither Technician A nor Technician B

6. Technician A and B are analyzing the results of a starter drive test on a starter circuit for a six-cylinder 855-cubic inch diesel engine. The engine cranks slowly and starter current draw is 1,250 amps. The battery voltage during cranking is 7.1 volts. Technician A says that the starter armature likely has an open winding. Technician B says that the results could be caused by a damaged, oil-starved engine bearings. Who is correct?
   a. Technician A
   b. Technician B
   c. Both Technician A and Technician B
   d. Neither Technician A nor Technician B

7. Technician A says that starter chatter can be caused by low battery voltage. Technician B says that the use of an intermittent-duty relay in the starter control circuit can cause a chattering condition. Who is correct?
   a. Technician A
   b. Technician B
   c. Both Technician A and Technician B
   d. Neither Technician A nor Technician B

8. Technician A says that the solenoid on the starter motor switches on and off the high current flow required by the starter motor. Technician B says that the solenoid on the starter motor engages the starter drive with the pinion gear. Who is correct?
   a. Technician A
   b. Technician B
   c. Both Technician A and Technician B
   d. Neither Technician A nor Technician B

9. Technician A says that if available voltage to a starter drops below 10.5 volts, the starter requires replacement. Technician B says that low available voltage requires battery replacement. Who is correct?
   a. Technician A
   b. Technician B
   c. Both Technician A and Technician B
   d. Neither Technician A nor Technician B

10. Technician A says that some starter motors are equipped with an overcrank protection (OCP) thermostat, which opens the control circuit when the starter is overheated. Technician B says that the thermostat monitors the temperature of the motor and the chassis electrical control module inhibits the operation of the starter relay when the motor is overheated. Who is correct?
   a. Technician A
   b. Technician B
   c. Both Technician A and Technician B
   d. Neither Technician A nor Technician B

CHAPTER 18

Charging Systems and Service

Learning Objectives

- **LO 18-1** Identify and describe the construction, operation, and features of the charging system.
- **LO 18-2** Identify and describe the principles of alternating current generation.
- **LO 18-3** Identify and describe the construction, function, and operation of alternator components.

- **LO 18-4** Identify and describe the principles and operating characteristics of alternator voltage regulation.
- **LO 18-5** Identify indicators for charging system service and outline steps involved in inspecting charging system operation.
- **LO 18-6** Outline the steps involved in removing, disassembly, testing repair, and reinstallation of alternators.

You Are the Technician

There is a bus that has had numerous service calls for jump-starting because the batteries often go dead. Service calls are taking place almost every day, causing a high level of aggravation to the customer and at the service center where you work. On previous occasions, the batteries have been replaced. In addition, the charging system output has been measured and found to be OK. Furthermore, the presence of parasitic draws has been checked, and none were found.

The bus drivers have often been blamed for the problems, assuming that they have left lights or other accessories on, draining the battery. Out of frustration, the service manager has asked you to accompany the bus driver for a day to find out when the bus batteries drain and whether electrical loads are left on. After the bus has stopped for a 45-minute break, you find the batteries are dead. Checking the alternator, you discover that the back of the alternator where the rectifier bridge is located has become excessively hot to touch. Finally, the cause has been found. Before explaining the fault to the customer, you'll need to have answers to the following questions.

1. Why has the rectifier bridge of the alternator become hot to touch while the engine was shut down?
2. During previous checks of the charging system, what inspection procedure would have identified that fault?
3. What component has failed in the rectifier bridge? Be specific.

Introduction

Modern heavy-duty commercial vehicles are increasingly dependent on electronic and electrical systems that require a constant and reliable supply of electrical power. As heavy-duty vehicles become more sophisticated and add more comfort and convenience items, alternators are working harder than ever to meet the demands of the electrical system. For example, years ago, a direct current (DC) generator supplying 8 to 45 amps of current was all that was needed to supply the entire electrical system, consisting of just lights, wipers, and the horn. Surplus generator capacity was used to charge the batteries depleted during cranking. Today, the average 12-volt electrical system loads for a late-model highway tractor can add up to 150 amps at peak, with an 84-amp average. School buses have an even higher 102-amp average load, and highway coaches use as much as 160 amps at 24 volts just to power the heating, ventilation, and air conditioning system (**TABLE 18-1**). It is now normal for vehicles to use 200- to 365-amp alternators and larger, like that in **FIGURE 18-1**, to supply adequate electrical system current at idle, plus additional amperage to charge depleted batteries. Lighting, electronic powertrain controls, heating and air conditioning, power accessories, electrically heated catalysts, communication and telematic systems, many new electrical accessories, and control modules with significant key-off loads add to the long list of electrical loads supplied by contemporary alternators.

It's important for technicians, when selecting replacement alternators and servicing the charging system, to realize generating onboard electrical current is not cheap. Charging system-related service practices used by technicians have an unseen, but significant, impact on operating costs, which can be either beneficial or detrimental. Alternators, which can easily consume over five-horsepower when supplying normal electrical loads of an on-highway tractor, can make contributions to fuel savings through more efficient alternator and electrical system designs and when accompanied by proper charging system maintenance practices.

Even small gains in charging system efficiency on vehicles using as much power as an average household have outsized impacts on fuel consumption and operating costs. Outlining the impact of the charging system on operating costs, Delco Remy published a discussion paper where it estimates the annual cost to produce 100 amps of electricity is $3000 for a line haul truck, running 5000 hours per year (using $4/gallon fuel cost). This estimate is based on fuel consumed to generate electricity from an alternator, which typically has approximately only 55% efficiency, but the entire fuel-to-electricity conversion cycle has only approximately 21% efficiency (**FIGURE 18-2**).

TABLE 18-1 Cost of Generating Onboard Electric Current

Application	Average Charging Current	Fuel Cost with Base Efficiency	Fuel Cost with a 20% Improvement in Efficiency	Fuel Savings = Higher Efficiency - Base Efficiency
Line Haul Tractor	84 amps	$4534/500,000 miles (804,000 km)	$3778/500,000 miles (804,000 km)	$756/500,000 miles (804,000 km)
City Tractor	40 amps	$2235/350,000 miles (563,000 km)	$1863/350,000 miles (563,000 km)	$372/350,000 miles (563,000 km)
School Bus	102 amps	$9040/250,000 miles (402,000 km)	$7533/250,000 miles (402,000 km)	$1507/250,000 miles (402,000 km)

Source: From Mike Bradfield, MSME, "Improving Alternator Efficiency Measurably Reduces Fuel Costs" [white paper, page 1] (Copyright 2008). Accessed May 31, 2018: http://www.delcoremy.com/documents/high-efficiency-white-paper.aspx.

FIGURE 18-1 A typical belt-driven heavy-duty alternator used to supply all the electrical system demands for electric current.

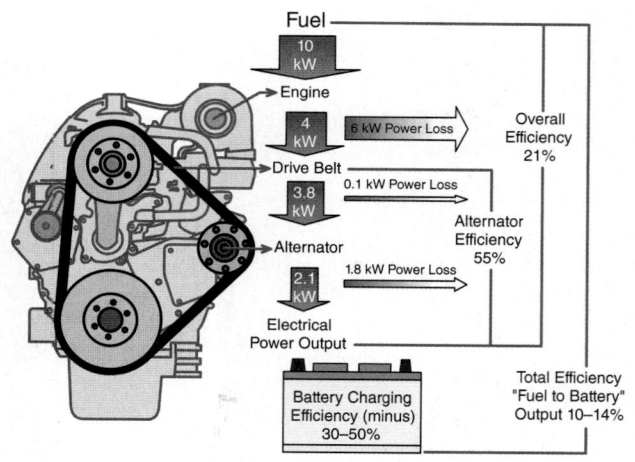

FIGURE 18-2 Producing onboard electricity is expensive, since alternators can convert only 21% of the energy in fuel into electricity.

Power generation costs like this may seem astonishingly high until the various losses in energy efficiency are factored into each stage of a process converting fuel energy into electrical energy. Energy changes state several times before electricity is produced, with most energy lost by the engine extracting mechanical energy from energy stored in fuel. Some energy is lost transmitting the engine's energy to the alternator using belts and pulleys. Even more energy is lost converting mechanical energy into electrical energy inside the alternator, before finally charging the batteries, which further reduces energy efficiency. When comparing the quantity of electrical power used to charge a battery to the quantity of electrical power supplied by the battery, lead-acid batteries are between 50% to 70% efficient. Accounting for this loss of efficiency can further cut the 21% estimate charging system efficiency almost in half.

Because of the high cost of producing on-board electrical current and greenhouse gas (GHG) emissions produced by an engine generating current, more efficient alternator construction designs and operational strategies have not escaped the attention of manufacturers' efforts aimed at reducing vehicle fuel consumption to reach the latest goals of GHG legislation. Increasing alternator capacity to increase overall efficiency is one common method. It's not uncommon for the latest commercial vehicles to be equipped with alternators with maximum amperage output far exceeding the electrical system's normal demands. 235–300-amp alternators are frequently used on vehicles having less than 80 amps continuous electrical loads. Twenty years ago, these same vehicles used only a maximum of an 80–135-amp output alternator.

The primary reason for using alternators that far exceed requirements for normal electrical loads is fuel economy. Alternators become increasingly less efficient when they are required to produce more amperage at higher output speeds (**FIGURE 18-3**). This happens first because producing high amperage current inside an alternator increases the temperature and resistance of stator windings and other components. Thinner stator wire used in low output alternators combined with hotter windings increases electrical resistance at higher output amperage, which further decreases efficiency (**FIGURE 18-4**).

Turning alternators faster also uses more energy, but does not supply a proportional increase in electrical energy output. To reduce fuel consumption, an alternator should operate in an optimal efficiency range, so a good practice is to select an alternator with a much higher amperage output than is normally needed and operate it at a lower, more efficient range of output amperage. Alternators running cooler with lighter loads are not only more efficient, but also last longer. A third reason for increased fuel efficiency from using high output alternators is alternators rated at higher output amperage produce more current at lower speeds. Alternator pulley ratios can also change to slow alternator speed while delivering adequate output current to supply all normal electrical loads at near idle speeds. When more output amperage is needed, less energy is wasted by an alternator trying to generate current at a higher speed operating range where resistance of stator windings is greater and current generation is less efficient.

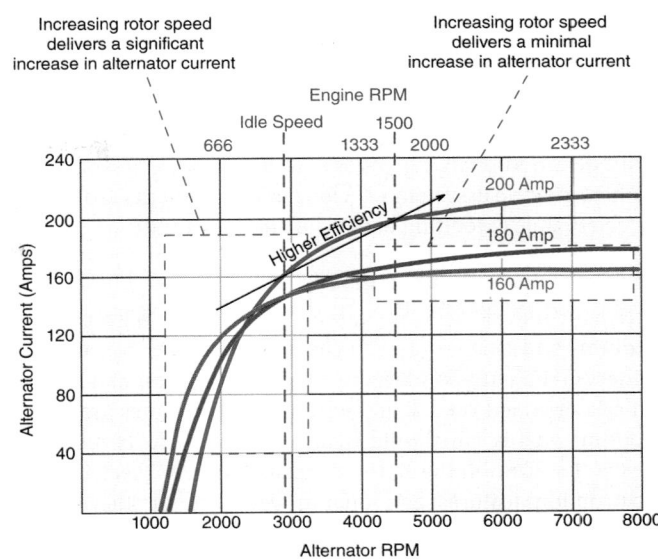

FIGURE 18-3 Note alternator output flattens with increased speed. At a 200-amp output rating, the alternator produces close to 160 amps at idle using a common 3:1 alternator pulley ratio.

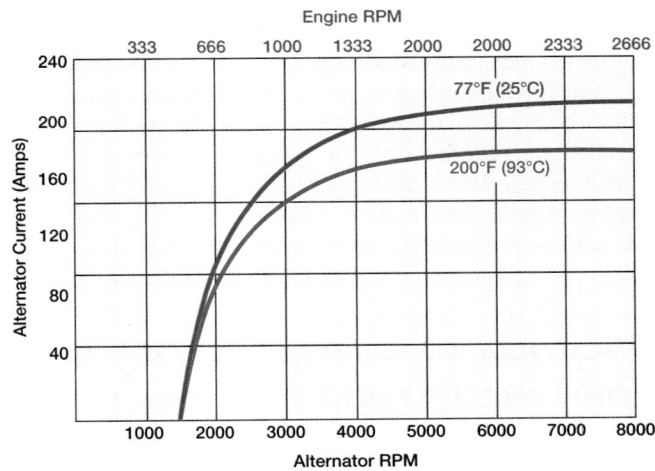

FIGURE 18-4 High alternator temperatures increase resistance. Heat is produced from generation of high amperage current passing through stator windings.

▶ **TECHNICIAN TIP**

When replacing an alternator, a better practice is to maintain or increase alternator charging capacity than to install a less expensive one with lower output amperage—even though it will do the job. Because alternators are more efficient when charging at lower speed, installing a cheaper alternator with lower output capacity uses more fuel than a higher capacity alternator charging at the same output current. Similarly, old batteries with high resistance require the alternator to work harder to charge them and uses more fuel than newer batteries with lower internal resistance.

In addition to the industry demands for more efficient alternator operation, battery technology is also changing alternator construction and operation. For example, OEMs are using more absorbed glass mat (AGM) batteries now because AGMs can absorb an electrical charge up to five times faster than older flooded-type lead-acid batteries. AGM batteries can also provide higher cranking current due to their lower internal resistance. Alternators ideally adapt to different battery technology with optimized charging voltages and charging rates to obtain the best electrical system efficiencies and benefits from these batteries while extending battery life and reliability.

Mild-Hybrid Alternators

Alternator-like devices are taking on an even bigger role in medium- and heavy-duty vehicles to reduce fuel consumption to meet GHG emission targets. The latest pick-up and delivery vehicles operated on urban package delivery routes are rapidly adopting what is called mild-hybrid, 48-volt, belt-driven starter alternators. Combining both alternator and AC electric motor construction features and operating principles, these motor generator units (MGUs) are located on the engine, along with other engine-driven accessories. Because they can function as either an alternator or electric motor, MGUs can either drive the engine and engine-driven accessories or generate electric current used to charge a 48-volt lithium ion battery. The engine start-stop capabilities provided by an MGU allow the engine to shut off when the vehicle is stopped, yet still operate engine-driven accessories, like the air conditioning compressor (**FIGURE 18-5**).

In heavy-duty vehicles, alternator-like devices are available that can be placed in the wheel hubs. These electric hubs, as they are called, can reduce the rate of wear in brake friction materials through regenerative braking. Rather than using brake foundation components to do all the work of converting mechanical force into heat, the electric hubs can convert some braking force into electricity used to charge batteries (**FIGURE 18-6**).

Overview of Charging System Construction and Features

LO 18-1 Identify and describe the construction, operation, and features of the charging system.

The charging system is designed to provide electrical energy for all the normal power demands made by electrical system components on the vehicle after the engine starts. In addition to supplying enough electrical energy to power the vehicle's electrical system, it needs additional capacity to recharge the batteries drained by the starting motor and any additional charge lost to engine-off electrical loads. The main parts of a contemporary charging system, as illustrated in **FIGURE 18-7**, include the battery, the alternator, the voltage regulator (which is almost always integrated into the alternator), a charge warning light or voltmeter, and wiring that completes the circuits.

Either an alternator or a DC generator is used to supply the electricity to power a vehicle's electrical system after the engine starts. The terms *generator* and *alternator* are often used interchangeably, but there are major differences between the construction and operation of both devices. The most significant distinction is that a generator produces only DC electricity, while an alternator produces AC, which is converted

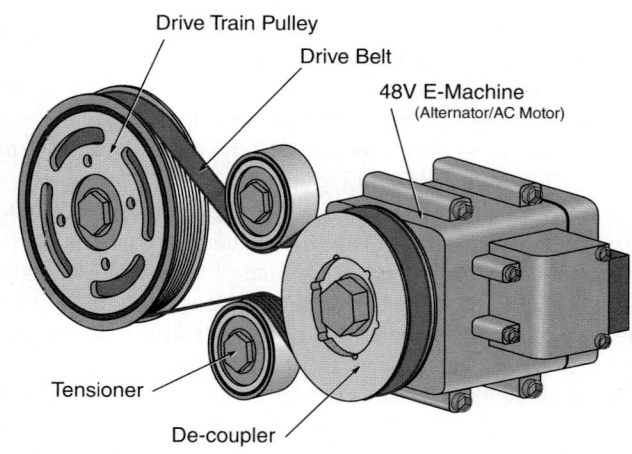

FIGURE 18-5 Combining a starter and alternator to form a motor generator unit is used on mild-hybrid vehicles to increase fuel efficiency.

FIGURE 18-6 Electric hubs for heavy-duty (HD) vehicles are now available that can produce electricity used to charge batteries and perform regenerative braking functions.

to DC before leaving the alternator. Both generators and alternators are mechanically driven by the engine and produce electric current using principles of magnetic induction.

Current flow is induced in wire windings by the movement of magnetic fields relative to the windings. One critical difference between the two devices is whether it is the magnetic field or wire windings that are moved. In a DC generator, the wire conductors, where induction of electric current takes place, are part of the generator shaft turned inside a stationary magnetic field by power extracted from the engine. The rotating wire windings attached to the generator shaft are called the armature and they turn inside a magnetic field formed by multiple electromagnets arranged inside the generator case. Electromagnets making up the generator's stationary magnetic field are called pole shoes. In an alternator, the location of the magnetic field and wire windings

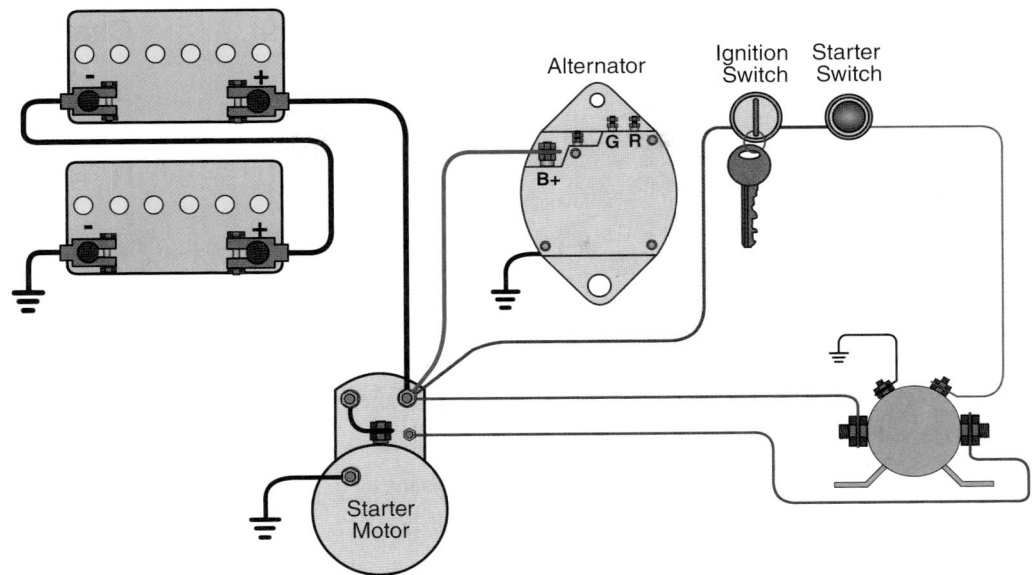

FIGURE 18-7 Typical heavy-vehicle charging system diagram.

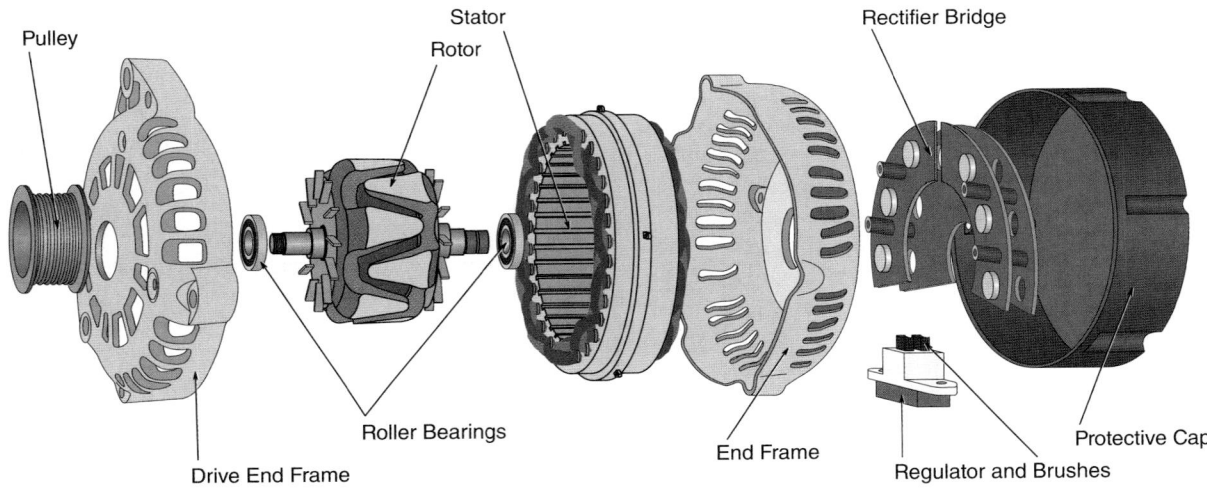

FIGURE 18-8 Construction details and names of basic alternator components.

where current is induced is opposite to a DC generator. In an alternator, the electromagnetic field rotates to induce current flow in a stationary set of wire windings. The spinning magnetic field is attached to the alternator shaft and the assembly is called the rotor (**FIGURE 18-8**). Surrounding the rotor is a stationary set of wire windings, called the stator windings, where AC is induced by the rotation of the rotor.

Alternators can more reliably and efficiently produce many times more electric current than a comparably sized DC generator, which explains why alternators have displaced generators in modern commercial vehicles.

Charging System Operation

The battery stores an electrical charge provided by either a generator or alternator in the form of chemical energy. The battery also acts as a voltage-dampening device to smoothen small variations in electrical system voltage or minimize voltage spikes, which can disrupt the operation of electrical system devices. Most importantly, the battery provides the electrical energy for cranking the engine and key-off or engine-off electrical loads. Once the engine is running, the alternator—which is connected to the engine and driven by a drive belt or a drive gear—converts mechanical energy from the engine into electrical energy, and should be sized to supply all normal power demands of the electrical system. While supplying the electrical system power requirements, the alternator requires additional capacity to charge the battery to replace the energy used up when starting the engine. A voltage regulator circuit controlling the alternator output current maintains the batteries at an optimal state of charge by **sensing** battery voltage and adjusting the charging system output voltage and amperage.

FIGURE 18-9 An external voltage regulator for a 24-volt alternator with voltage regulator adjustment (circled).

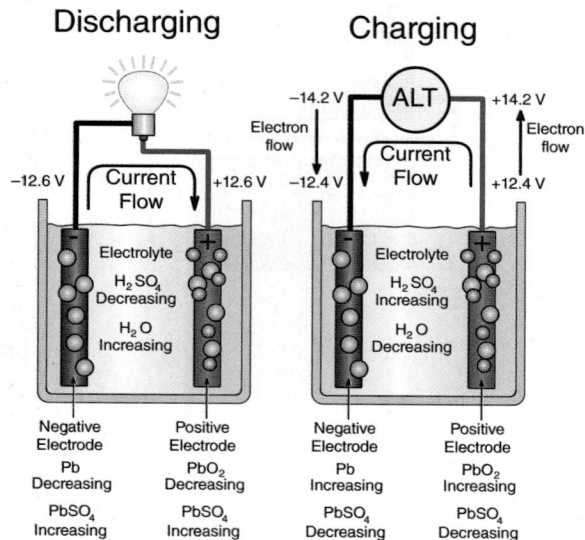

FIGURE 18-10 The alternator reverses chemical reactions in the battery by changing the direction of electron flow. The alternator positive and negative poles each become more negative and positive than the discharged battery.

Older vehicles had separate (discrete) regulators mounted somewhere outside the alternator and were serviced separately from the alternator. Contemporary charging systems now use voltage regulators that are located inside the alternator, which may be adjusted or serviced separately or replaced with the alternator. One exception is heavy-duty bus alternators, which use external voltage regulators (**FIGURE 18-9**).

Even more recently, a vehicle, if equipped with a dedicated electrical system control module, exchanges electrical signals with the alternator to control the charging rate. This configuration where an internal voltage regulator receives inputs from an electrical system control module is called external-field regulation. Electrical signals from the control module simply increase or decrease the alternator charging rate by signaling the alternator's voltage regulator. A more sophisticated exchange of messages between the control module and an internal multifunctional-type voltage regulator takes place inside the alternator. Microcontroller-based regulators like this can provide additional functions other than just voltage regulation. Regardless of which control strategy is used to adjust charging system output through an electrical system control module, distributed network control of the charging system enables the alternator output to be regulated more efficiently based on a wider number of parameters, such as engine load and speed, alternator capacity, battery type, and ambient temperature.

Fuel economy is the primary benefit of network control of alternator charging output, using multifunctional voltage regulators with up to a 2% improvement in fuel economy plus benefits in alternator efficiency claimed by manufacturers using it. New features can also be added to sophisticated microcontroller-type internal voltage regulators, such as the ability to transmit fault codes; share alternator data, such as speed and temperature, with other control modules; protect the alternator and electrical system from electrical damage; and balance output from multiple alternators that can be added to supplement the current supplied to the vehicle's electrical system.

To recharge the battery, the chemical reactions taking place during discharge are reversed by the alternator. Electron flow that had begun at the battery negative post, passing through electrical system loads before ending up at the positive post, is reversed by the alternator. When charging, the B+ terminal of the alternator becomes more positive than the battery positive post. Electrons are pulled from the positive post of the battery, by the alternator B+ terminal, which is 14.0 volts, or more positive than the battery B+. The more positive voltage differential of the alternator pulls electrons from the positive plates and pumps them toward the negative battery post and plates. Excess electrons at higher voltage leave the alternator and are pushed toward the less negatively charged battery post by electrostatic forces (**FIGURE 18-10**).

▶ TECHNICIAN TIP

When investigating electrical fires often caused by grounded alternator cables, whether the engine was likely running can be determined by examining the burned section of alternator cable. More severely burned wiring between the grounded section of cable and the alternator B+ terminal indicates the engine was running and the alternator was charging. Burned wiring between the cable's grounded section and the battery positive post indicates the engine was likely not running.

Alternator Advantages

Alternators have not always been used on commercial vehicles. Until the 1960s, DC generators were used to supply direct current to the electrical system and charge batteries. Adding more electrical accessories and devices to vehicles as designs matured meant that the amount of current produced by DC generators became inadequate with increased electrical loads. Generators were especially inefficient at low speeds, leading to a discharged battery condition if only a few short trips were made. The development of low-cost semiconductor-type rectifiers (devices that convert AC to DC) in the late 1950s made the use of more efficient AC "generators" possible. AC—not DC—is produced inside an alternator. But alternating current cannot charge a battery or operate most of the electrical devices and accessories used on a modern commercial vehicle. To overcome this problem, an arrangement of several pairs of diodes, referred to as the rectifier bridge, has the job of converting AC to usable DC that can charge a battery and properly supply a vehicle's electrical load.

Generators are still used on some equipment, mostly off-road but, because of the availability of semiconductor diodes and electronic voltage regulators, alternators have replaced generators due to their comparatively superior operating characteristics. For example, in comparison to generators:

- Alternators weigh less per ampere of output.
- Alternators have fewer moving parts.
- Alternators can produce power at engine idle speeds; generators cannot.
- Alternators can be operated at much higher speeds because alternators use a lighter weight rotor compared with a heavy armature used in generators.
- Alternators conduct less current through the brushes, if equipped, thus reducing wear.
- Alternators do not require current (amperage) regulators; they have a self-limiting maximum amperage output.
- Alternators produce current when rotated in either direction. Output polarity from generators changes depending on the direction of rotation. Note that cooling fans in alternators can turn only in one direction.
- Alternators allow the reduction of battery capacity due to faster recharging rate.

One advantage that generators have over alternators is their reliance on mechanical voltage and current regulation, which is less sensitive to abuse conditions, such as voltage spikes, and reverse polarity conditions. There are no semiconductor devices, such as diodes or microcontrollers, used in DC generators that can suddenly fail in these circumstances. Because alternators use more sensitive electronic parts, generators are still used in portable engine-powered battery-boosting equipment and other applications needing this feature.

Principles of Alternating Current Generation

LO 18-2 Identify and describe the principles of alternating current generation.

The alternator converts mechanical energy into electrical energy by electromagnetic induction, as illustrated in (**FIGURE 18-11**). In a simplified version, bar magnet rotates inside an iron yoke, which concentrates the magnetic field. A coil of wire is wound around each end of the yoke. As the magnet turns, voltage is induced in each coil, producing current flow. When the north or south pole approaches each coil (Step 1), magnetic fields pull or push on the electrons and current flow is induced in each coil, depending on which pole is influencing the wire coil. Electrons pushed by the north magnetic pole create a conductor with a positive electrical polarity, while the south pole pulls electrons to create a negative charge polarity in a wire conductor under its influence. Note that an angle between the wire conductors and the moving magnetic field is necessary to create electron

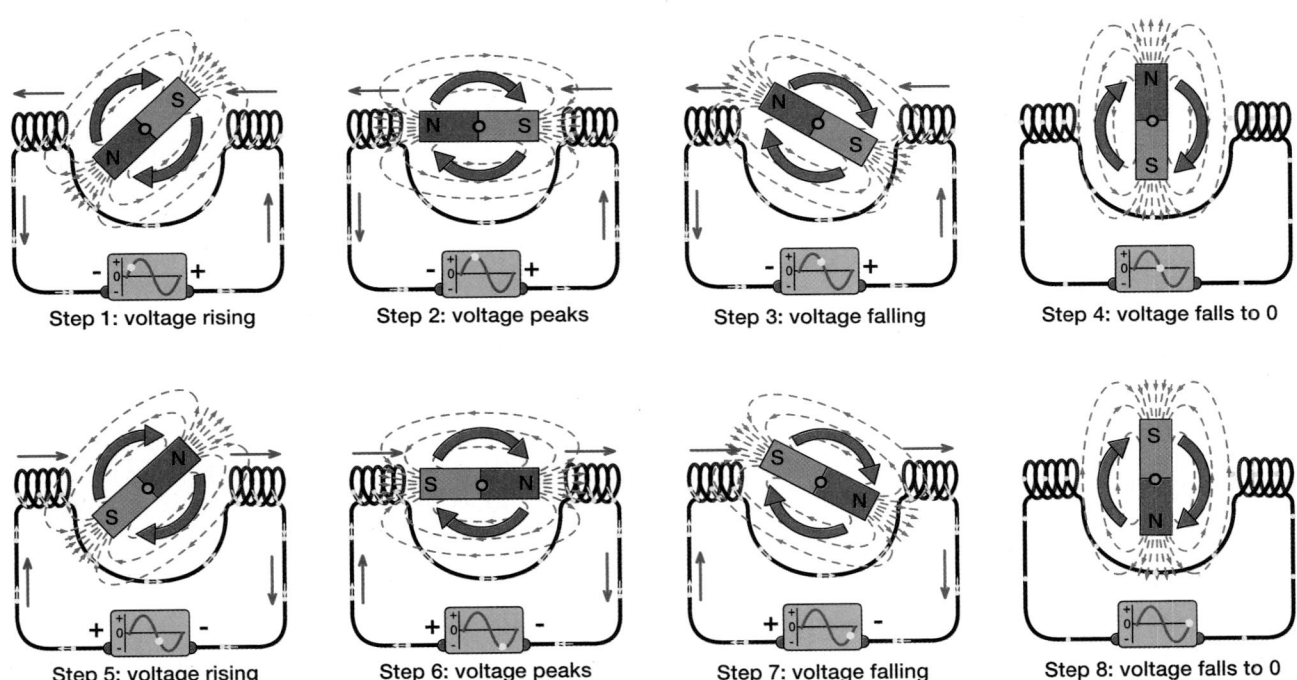

Step 1: voltage rising   Step 2: voltage peaks   Step 3: voltage falling   Step 4: voltage falls to 0

Step 5: voltage rising   Step 6: voltage peaks   Step 7: voltage falling   Step 8: voltage falls to 0

FIGURE 18-11 Electromagnetic induction.

movement. This is a basic principle of magnetic induction. The highest induced voltage takes place when the magnetic field and conductors are at 90 degrees to one another. Electron movement stops when the angle between the magnetic field and conductors is parallel or 0 degrees.

(Step 2). Continued rotation of the bar magnetic produces an increasing angle between the magnetic field and conductors once more. The magnetic fields push and pull electrons again, as in Step 1, but because the magnetic field is moving away from the conductor, rather than approaching it, induced electron movement takes place in the opposite the previous direction. The change in direction of current movement caused by magnetic field movement away from the conductors is illustrated in Step 3. The direction of current flow or polarity in Step 3 is opposite Step 1. Finally, current flow stops again in Step 4 because there is no angle between the magnetic field's lines of force and the direction of the conductor's alignment. As a result, induced voltage falls to 0 volts. Observing current movement as the magnets rotate to begin a second revolution repeats the same pattern of current flow:

- Induced voltage rising as the magnetic poles approach each coil
- Induced voltage falling to 0 volts when aligned with the conductor
- Voltage rising again as the magnet moves away from the conductor
- Voltage falling to 0 volts as the magnetic fields and conductors realign.

Current that cyclically changes direction or polarity in this way is called alternating current (AC). In this example, the change in direction of current through the wire windings occurs two times for every complete revolution of the magnet.

Inducing Alternating Current

The two most important parts in an alternator used to produce electrical current are the rotor and stator winding. The rotor contains a spinning electromagnet that induces current flow in the stator winding, which is made up of numerous coils of wire. These parts of the alternator are illustrated in (**FIGURE 18-12**) and are discussed in more detail in the section on Alternator Components. By varying the amount of current supplied to the rotor's electromagnetic coil, the strength and density of its magnetic field changes. The amount of Electrical Power = (Voltage × Amperage) produced from an alternator is proportional to the following four factors:

1. The strength of the rotor's magnetic field. Increasing the density and strength of the magnetic field increases the force pushing and pulling on electrons in a stator winding. Stronger magnetic fields in the rotor translate directly into higher output voltage and amperage.
2. The speed at which the magnetic field rotates. Like denser magnetic field strength, increasing the speed at which the magnetic fields cut across the conductors increases the energy imparted to move electrons.
3. The angle between the magnetic field and conductors in the stator. An angle is needed between the magnetic lines of force and the conductor to move the electrons. If no angle is present,

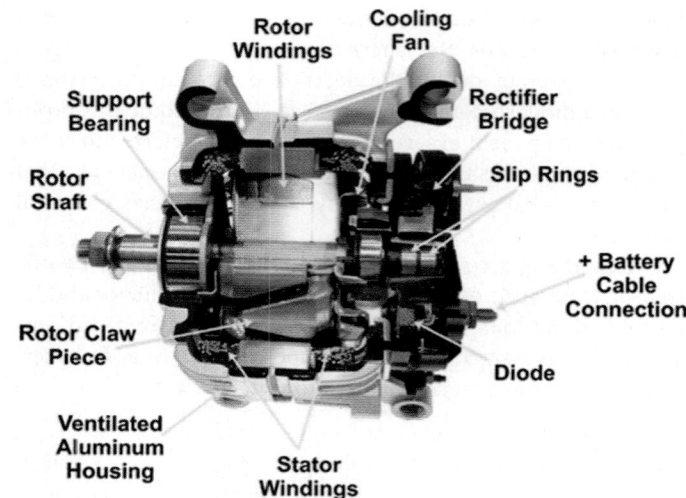

FIGURE 18-12 An alternator.

no moving magnetic force can be imparted to the electrons. A 90-degree angle provides the highest induced voltage.

4. The number and/or size of conductors cutting magnetic lines of force. As the number of conductors, and to some extent the mass of the conductor increase, magnetic lines of force can act on and move a greater number of electrons located near the conductor surface. Denser stator windings, which are shaped more rectangular than round, contribute to more efficient production of electrical energy.

Maximum power output of an alternator is limited by the speed at which an alternator rotates. This maximum current limit is not simply caused by some physical barrier to an alternator rotating faster, but instead is the result of a resistance built-up in the stator windings as rotor speed increases. Resistance to the stator's output current is created by an opposing electrical current self-induced in the stator by the continuously changing polarity of AC. The continuous cycle of building and collapsing magnetic fields induces its own current flow in the stator winding opposing the current flow induced by the rotor's magnetic field. This self-induced current is called counter-electromotive force (CEMF), and it opposes any increase in current induced in the stator by the spinning rotor. At high alternator speeds, the CEMF, with a polarity opposite the direction of output current, begins to increase at a more rapid rate until it equals any increase to induced stator current. The result is CEMF limits or cancels out any increase in the alternator's output. The faster the alternator turns, the higher the CEMF produced in the stator, as shown in (**FIGURE 18-13**). This means that to build an alternator with greater power output, it cannot simply be made to be capable of achieving higher rotational speed. Instead, increasing the number of stator windings, which can also be made thicker, is necessary to produce high power output at lower alternator speeds.

Alternator Classification

Alternators can be categorized by several variables, including whether voltage regulation is internal or external; the diameter of the housing; whether the alternator is sealed, oil-cooled, or externally air-cooled; amperage output; charging voltage;

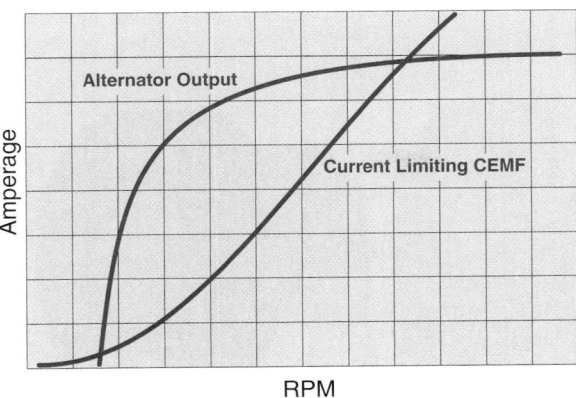

FIGURE 18-13 Chart showing alternator output and current limiting of output caused by CEMF.

manufacturer; and many other factors. The SAE classifies alternator automotive mounting configurations into standards to enable the adaptation of alternators from all manufacturers to fit engines. Two common mounting types for alternators are a pad-mount alternator and a hinge-mount type (**FIGURE 18-14**).

Hinge- or swing-mount alternators use either a short or long hinge where a bolt passes through the alternator end frames. A variation on the pad mount is a T-mount, which is like a pad mount except it is missing one of the four bolt holes used by a pad mount. Another variation on the hinge-type alternator is a spool mount, which has a single hole on the bottom that is 1–3" (25.4–76.2 mm) long. On the top is a foot with three additional threaded holes to attach alternator mounting brackets (**FIGURE 18-15**).

▶ **TECHNICIAN TIP**

Oil-cooled alternators drain oil from internal parts back into the crankcase. Exposure of crankcase oil vapors to alternator conductors carrying high amperage current has the potential to create a small engine explosion if an alternator is defective. Internal alternator parts or windings can short to ground and overheat enough to ignite crankcase oil vapors. If this happens, the oil pan and valve cover both typically blow off the engine, leaving the vehicle immobilized in a pool of engine oil. It's recommended to replace any oil-cooled alternator if the cause of a blown valve cover, oil pan, or gaskets on a diesel cannot be positively identified as having any other cause.

FIGURE 18-14 A. Four bolts are used to secure a pad-mount alternator. **B.** A SAE J-180 hinge-mount style alternator.

Alternator Components

LO 18-3 Identify and describe the construction, function, and operation of alternator components.

Regardless of the alternator's classification, all alternators share common components. Major components of the alternator are illustrated in **FIGURES 18-12** and **18-16**. These include:

- Rotor—A rotating electromagnet that provides the magnetic field to induce voltage and current in the stator.
- Brushes/slip rings—Make an electrical connection to the rotor field coil to supply current from the voltage regulator.

FIGURE 18-15 A spool-mount alternator has a single mounting hole on the bottom and a top foot with three threaded holes on the top.

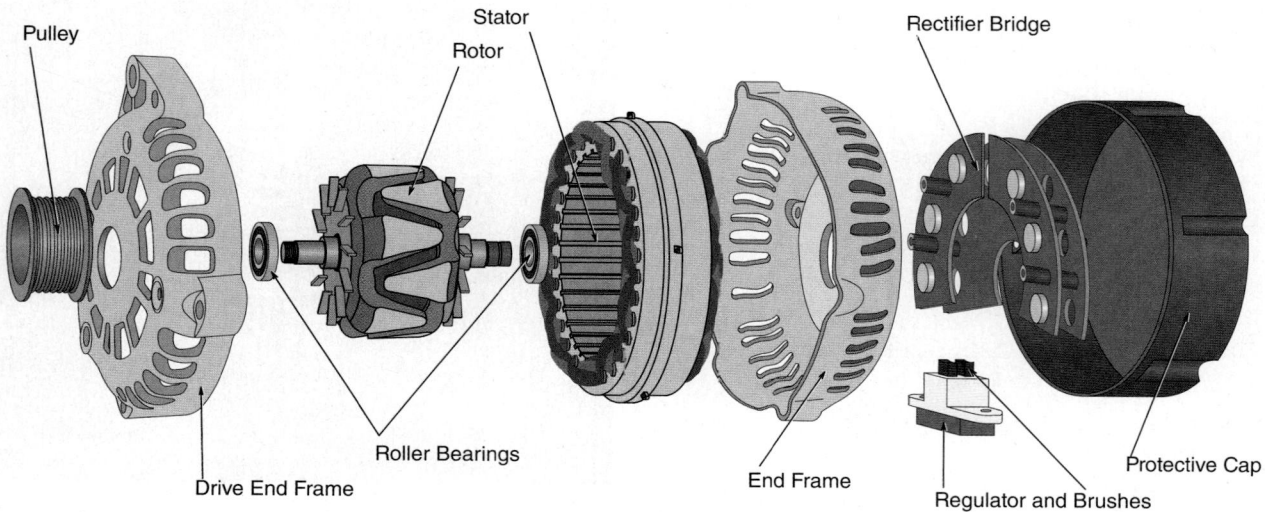

FIGURE 18-16 Alternator components—exploded.

- Stator—Stationary coils of wire in which current and voltage are induced by the magnetic field of the rotor. Wire windings making up the stator are wound onto a separate non-magnetic frame.
- Cooling mechanism (air or oil)—In the case of air cooling, additional airflow is provided using one or two cooling fans.
- End frames and bearings—Alternators have two end frames that fit together to house the components into a single unit. Each end frame contains bearings that support the rotor shaft. A drive mechanism (usually a pulley) is at the front-end frame, while the rear frame contains the rectifier bridge, voltage regulator, and brush assembly. A stator frame with wire windings is located between the two end frames.
- Drive mechanism—In most cases, a pulley drive is used, but gear drive mechanism may also drive the rotor.
- Rectifier—Converts the AC into a DC output.
- Voltage regulator—Controls the maximum output voltage of the alternator by varying the amount of current flowing through the rotor and, therefore, the magnetic field strength.

The Rotor

The rotor provides the rotating magnetic field that cuts the wire coils within the stator to induce the flow of electrical current in the stator. The rotor consists of an iron core that encloses a coil of many turns of wire. Each end of the wire coil is connected to one of two conductive slip rings on the rotor shaft. The wire coil and slip rings are electrically insulated from the rotor shaft. Energizing the rotor's wire coil with two to five amps produces an electromagnetic field beneath two halves of the soft iron core. These two halves are arranged into claws or pole pieces.

The pole pieces have two purposes. One is to intensify the electromagnetic field, and the other is to arrange magnetic field lines of force into magnetic poles on each claw of the rotor. Passing current through the rotor coil magnetizes the two pole pieces and their claws. Each soft iron end of the pole pieces and claws has a stationary north or south pole. Arranging claws from each pole piece into a north to south and back again sequence enables the rotor to sweep across the stator windings with alternating north and south magnetic poles. A heavy, high output alternator has more "claws"—typically between 12 and 16. Fourteen is a common number of claws for most heavy-duty alternators.

The output of the alternator is determined by several of the alternator's physical features. The first is the size and number of windings in the stator that is cut by the magnetic lines of force. The second is the strength of the magnetic field of the rotor. Increasing or decreasing the current flow through the rotor winding changes the magnetic field strength. Usually the maximum possible amperage is five amps or less. Controlling the strength of the magnetic field is the job of the voltage regulator. **FIGURE 18-17** illustrates how the current flows through the rotor.

Brushes and Brushless Alternators

Regulated current to the wire windings in the alternator rotor are supplied through a pair of graphite brushes sliding in contact against slip rings on the rotor shaft. The slip rings and the coil are electrically insulated from the rotor shaft. Lightweight springs help the brushes maintain contact with the slip rings while minimizing wear and extending brush life. Low current flow through the rotor also helps extend brush and slip ring service life. Brushes are designed to have a minimum of 95,000 miles (150,000 km) service life, but eventually wear out. Unless the alternator case is sealed, dirt, fluids, engine blow-by, corrosion, and other substances entering the alternator with cooling air can leave residues on the slip rings or gum up the brush holders, also preventing good contact. Eventually the brushes can wear deep grooves into the slip rings until contact is made

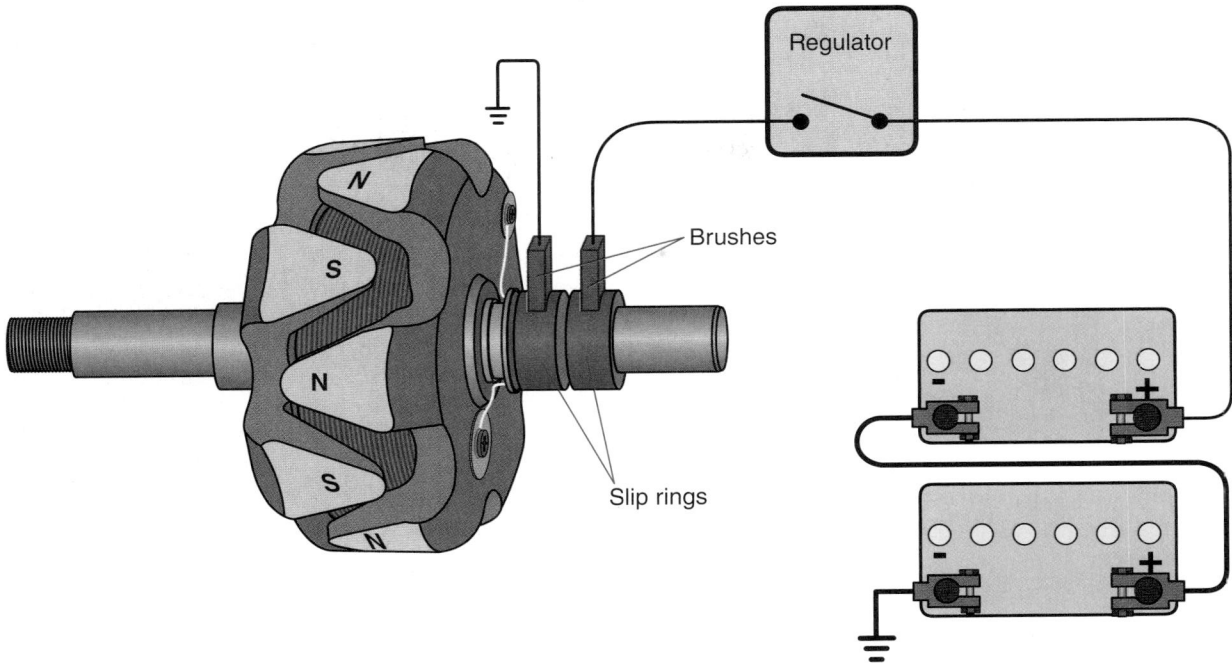

FIGURE 18-17 Current flow through the rotor. Note the two north–south pole pieces and their respective claws.

with the rotor shaft. The brushes themselves can eventually wear out from contact with the slip rings.

Service life of heavy-duty alternators can be extended in chassis accumulating travel distances more than 620,000 miles (1 million kilometers). One way to extend the service life is by using brushless alternator designs, such as the one illustrated in **FIGURE 18-18**, to eliminate the various problems from using brushes. Instead of locating the magnetic field coil inside a rotating rotor, these alternators use a stationary rotor field winding bolted to the alternator end frame. The rotor winding remains directly connected to the voltage regulator and no slip rings or brushes are needed to supply current flow. The rotor's pole pieces continue to rotate, but around the stationary coil. The rotor claws are magnetized into alternating north–south poles through magnetic induction by the stationary electromagnetic coil. Service associated with brushes and slip rings is eliminated with this rotor design.

Exciting the Alternator

To begin charging, the alternator's voltage regulator supplies electric current to the rotor winding (**FIGURE 18-19**). While the voltage regulator supplies current to the rotor, some alternators do not have a voltage regulator supplied with current from the ignition switch. Instead, the voltage regulator is supplied current from a second internal alternator circuit that only generates current after the engine starts. Quickly supplying current to the regulator is vital to efficient operation because the regulator uses this current to energize the rotor circuit. Alternators without an external current source from the ignition switch are identified using only a single wire to the alternator, the main battery + cable (**FIGURE 18-20**).

FIGURE 18-18 A brushless alternator has rotating pole pieces around a stationary field winding. **A.** Rotor. **B.** Pole pieces (2). **C.** Stator windings. **D.** Stationary field coil.

Normally, this arrangement is satisfactory, since a single-wire alternator maintains some residual magnetism on its rotor to generate start-up current. **Residual magnetism** refers to the small amount of magnetism left on the rotor after it is initially magnetized by the coil's magnetic field. Residually magnetized rotors can begin to induce current in the stator windings when the alternator starts rotating without any current passing through the rotor coil. The stator, in turn, supplies current to the voltage regulator through a set of three exciter diodes supplying the

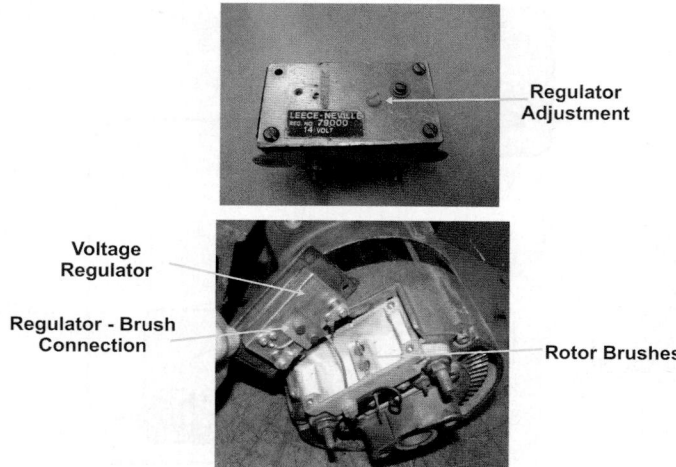

FIGURE 18-19 Electric current for the rotor is supplied to the brushes through spring-loaded contacts of the easily accessible regulator for this Leece Neville alternator.

FIGURE 18-20 Self-exciting alternators typically only have a main battery connection.

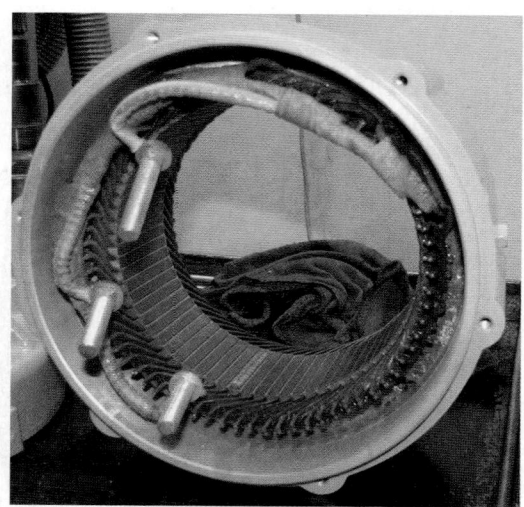

FIGURE 18-21 The stator of this HD bus alternator consists of a cylindrical, laminated iron core, which carries the three separate wire windings in slots on the inside. Sharp hairpin turns of the stator winding enable the use of denser stator windings.

the need for a separate circuit from the key switch to the alternator, which simplifies chassis wiring. And, if the battery voltage has gone to 0 volts, mechanical engines in vehicles with inoperative starters can still be pushed to start and begin charging dead batteries without the need for any battery voltage or jump-starting.

▶ **TECHNICIAN TIP**

Self-exciting alternators do not use a separate circuit connected to the ignition switch to switch on the voltage regulator and supply current to the rotor. Instead, they rely on residual magnetism found in the rotor after it has operated the first time. If the alternator does not charge due to a prolonged shut-down period or after rebuilding, residual magnetism needs to be re-established. The "R" terminal, which supplies current to the alternator exciter diodes, is briefly energized with battery current using a jumper wire connected to the alternators + battery terminal before or after the engine starts. Once the regulator is energized, the alternator begins charging, and the rotor should not need re-magnetizing again. Many alternators are regularly returned as defective because technicians are unaware of the procedure to initially excite the rotor.

regulator with half the alternator's voltage output. These exciter diodes are referred to as the diode trio in Delco-Remy alternators. Normal voltage regulator operation resumes once current is supplied to the regulator by the diode trio.

As mentioned, **self-exciting alternators** do not require the use of a separate circuit from the ignition switch to supply current to the voltage regulator, but the alternator may require a service procedure to magnetize the rotor, leaving residual magnetism on the rotor the first time it is installed. The initial supply of current to the rotor's coil is supplied through the "R", or relay, terminal for the first time after the alternator is installed or when the alternator has been inactive for long periods. Often, vehicles equipped with self-exciting alternators may also require the engine speed to be briefly increased with a snap of the throttle after every start-up to initiate charging at idle speed. While using a self-exciting alternator may seem like a nuisance, these alternators have the advantage of eliminating

The Stator

The stator is made of loops of coiled wire wrapped around a slotted metal alternator frame. The laminated-iron stator frame channels magnetic lines of force through the conductors where current is induced by the rotor's spinning magnetic field. Because the wires are looped and alternating magnetic north–south rotor poles pass beneath the loops, alternating current is induced in the stator (**FIGURE 18-21**). The windings are insulated from each other, and also from the laminated soft iron frame, with one to four layers of a tough polymer or thermoplastic film that resembles wood varnish.

Insulating the windings also protects the stator from corrosion. Individual windings form many conductor loops, which are each swept by the rotating magnetic fields of the rotor. The stator is mounted between two end frame housings, and it holds the stator windings stationary so that the rotating magnetic field cuts through the stator at approximately 90 degrees, inducing electric current in the winding loops. To smoothen the pulsating AC flow, there are three distinct layers of windings each offset 120 degrees from one another. Each of the three sets of windings is referred to as a phase. This arrangement of three winding phases allows an overlapping flow of AC peaks and valleys in the alternator's output current.

The number of loops in each winding corresponds to the number of rotor poles. So, if the rotor has 14 poles, there are 14 loops of wire in each of the three stator windings. Ultimately, the amount of amperage the alternator can produce depends on the wire mass and number of wire loops in the stator. A larger stator having more loops, more turns of wire in each loop, and/or thicker diameter wire has higher maximum output amperage than one with fewer loops, less wire, and thinner wire. **FIGURE 18-22** provides a side-by-side comparison of low- and high-output stators.

Alternators today supply much more power output for their size compared to units built 20 years ago. Increased alternator efficiency is primarily explained by increased stator winding density. By bending windings more sharply and inserting them into slots of the stator frame more tightly, the latest alternators stators are 25% more dense. Denser windings in the latest alternators' designs enable more compact alternator sizes that are 20% lighter, yet increase output by 50%. One of the other changes making alternators more efficient is the shape of the stator wiring, which is often flatter or rectangular, rather than round. Flat or rectangular-type conductors can have more surface area to conduct current than round conductors. With a greater surface area where electrons flow, a flatter stator wire conducts more current flow than a round conductor. Sharp hairpin bends of the rectangular stator winding at each end of the stator frame enable the use of denser windings to increase power output (**FIGURE 18-23**).

Three-Phase Stator Winding Connections

The three sets of windings that commonly make-up the stator must be connected to supply output current. Two methods connecting each of the three phases of winding can be used: the Wye and Delta configurations. Both types of windings produce three-phase alternating current, but voltage and amperage outputs differ, depending on operating conditions. Windings connected in a Wye-type configuration have four connection points. As the name illustrates, **Wye windings** resemble the letter "Y" (**FIGURE 18-24**). Three ends of each of the windings are connected to a point called the neutral junction. The other three free ends are connected to a pair of diodes in the rectifier bridge. The advantage of Wye windings is that they produce higher charging voltage at lower rotor speeds compared to a Delta connected stator. This means the alternator can begin charging a battery at lower engine speeds.

Delta windings, triangularly shaped like the symbol "delta," are more popular in alternators for diesel engines (**FIGURE 18-25**). These windings have only three connection points. The three junction points between the windings are connected to a pair of diodes found in the rectifier bridge. Because each phase of Delta connected stator windings are

FIGURE 18-23 Rectangular-shaped stator winding can be wound more tightly and conducts current with less resistance than round wire.

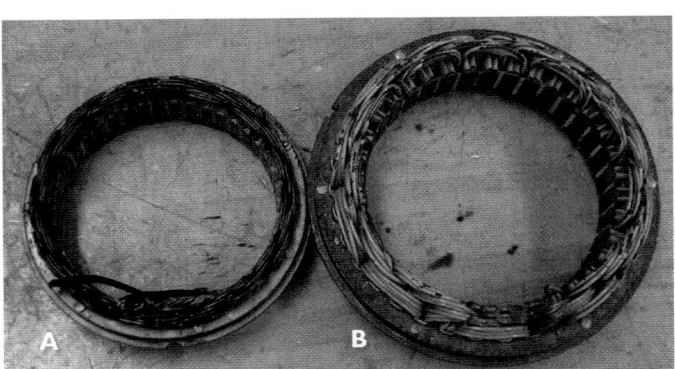

FIGURE 18-22 Comparison between **A.** a low- and **B.** a high-current output stator winding.

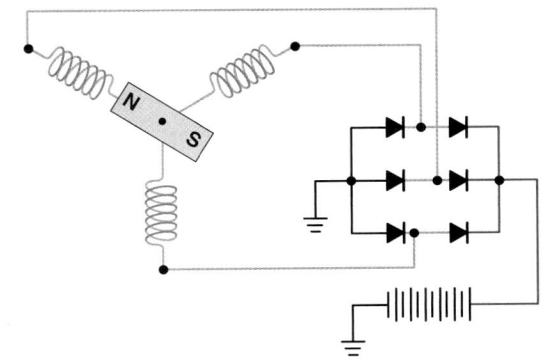

FIGURE 18-24 Wye wound stator configuration.

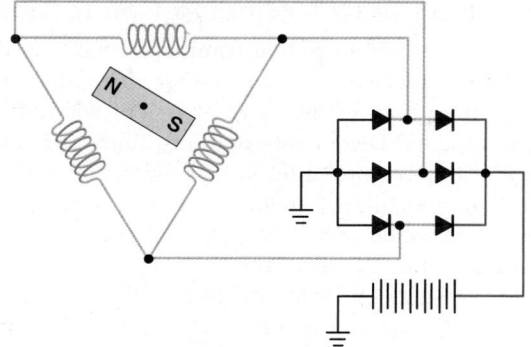

FIGURE 18-25 Delta-wound stator configuration.

FIGURE 18-26 Alternator end frames enclose and support all components and allow for maximum airflow through the alternator to remove excess heat.

connected in parallel, the resistance of Delta windings is one-third less than Wye windings. Wye-winding resistance also increases as alternator charging amperage rises. Although Delta windings produce lower voltage than Wye windings at the same low rotor speeds, they compensate for lower charging voltage by producing substantially higher amperage than the Wye-wound stators at higher rotor speeds. Delta-wound alternators are best adapted to supply higher amperage output to charge multiple batteries and better supply the heavy electrical loads found in trucks and buses. Wye-wound alternators are better adapted to the low speed, stop-and-go driving encountered by automobiles travelling in urban conditions. Combination Wye and Delta stators used in automobiles are rarely, if ever, found in HD alternators.

▶ TECHNICIAN TIP

An alternator needs to be properly sized to generate adequate power for the electrical system. Normal key-on electrical system loads should never exceed an alternator's maximum power output. A general rule is that an alternator should supply at least 1.5 times the normal running loads at approximately 14 volts. Extra capacity is also needed to charge discharged batteries. With all the electrical accessories, such as lights and blower motors, wiper motor, and air conditioning switched on, an electrical system consuming 80 amps of current should have an alternator with no less than 120 amps output. Any less capacity can easily burn out an alternator after just a few hours of operation if loads, such as defective or discharged batteries, are encountered.

▶ TECHNICIAN TIP

Remember, when upgrading an alternator to a higher amperage output, the alternator cable must be increased in diameter to handle higher peak amperage. Excessive voltage drop takes place in an alternator cable that is too narrow to handle a higher amperage alternator. While inspecting the battery + cable connecting the alternator for voltage drops, keep in mind that the cable is frequently undersized, and voltage drops rise dramatically when charging system output current is high. Adding a second cable or upgrading the cable is justified when voltage drop is excessive.

Alternator End Frames and Bearings

The alternator housings support and enclose all the alternator components, and are typically constructed from aluminum, as shown in **FIGURE 18-26**. Vents within the frames provide for a large amount of airflow to assist in dissipating heat. The housings accept the bearing assemblies, which support the rotor at the drive and slip ring ends. A pulley that is driven by a belt is mounted at the end of the rotor shaft. Most end frames enclosing slip ring also house the rectifier bridge assembly. In some cases, the three negative diodes are pressed into holes in the end frame to directly conduct the negative polarity current from each phase of the stator windings directly to ground. The three positive diodes are mounted on insulated plates connected to the B+ output terminal.

Drive Mechanism

A drive gear, rather than a pulley, is used to couple the alternator to the engine. It requires the alternator to be bolted directly to the engine in a location where an engine driving gear is available. This arrangement eliminates maintenance issues around belt tension and replacement, but does require the alternator to be well-sealed to prevent any oil leakage.

The correct gearing or pulley size needs to be selected for the alternator to ensure that the alternator does not over speed at higher engine rpm, but also produces enough output at idle to match electrical system power demand. Since a highway diesel operates typically between 650 rpm and 2100 rpm, a mechanical advantage between the alternator pulley and engine speed is needed to spin the alternator fast enough. Most larger alternators are limited to 8000 rpm, which means the alternator-drive ratio is precisely chosen to produce high output at idle yet stay below maximum speeds. This is particularly true as output curves tend to flatten out, efficiency drops, and brush and bearing wear increase with faster rotational speed.

For large-bore diesel engines found in trucks and buses, the driven ratio is approximately 2.7:1, which means that every engine rpm produces 2.7 rotor shaft revolutions. In recent years,

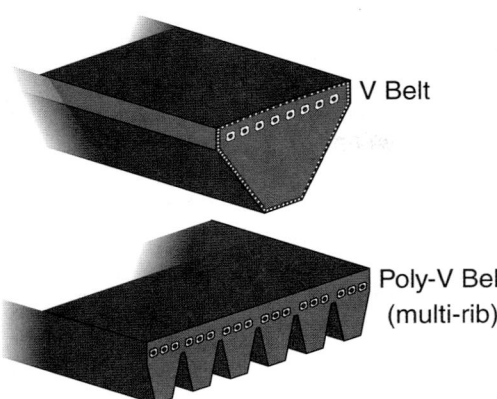

FIGURE 18-27 Comparing V belt and poly-V belt construction.

FIGURE 18-28 A belt tensioner ensures the correct tension s applied to the belt to prevent slippage.

a ratio of 3:1 or even 3.1:1 is becoming common. At 2000 rpm the alternator turns 6000 rpm. Some slow rpm diesels may use a ratio as high as 5:1 in comparison to smaller capacity, higher revving engines that use a ratio as low as 2:1.

V-type belts and pulleys were once the common method for transferring engine rotational force to an alternator. However, for various reasons, including extending belt-maintenance intervals, manufacturers have moved completely away from using V-type pulleys in favor of Poly-V, or otherwise called poly groove, multi-groove, and serpentine belts, like that shown in (**FIGURE 18-27**), equipped with automatic tensioners. A serpentine belt is a type of multi-rib belt that is long enough to drive multiple accessories. Serpentine belts can drive devices on both the back side and V-ribbed side. Due to the length of the serpentine belt and the number of accessories it drives, idler pulleys are required to ensure each pulley has enough belt wrapped around a drive pulley to transmit engine torque from the belt. Serpentine belt systems reduce belt wear while improving the coupling drive torque with multiple accessories. Fewer belts are needed and the width and complexity of the accessory drive system attached to the front of an engine is reduced. In the 1990s, when manufacturers began to use these belts, they were made from nitrile rubber compounds. As nitrile belts encounter stress from repeated torque pulses and high engine heat, the belt ribs crack. More recently, belts are made from ethylene propylene diene monomer (EPDM) rubber. An **EPDM belt** is more elastic and contains fibers that make it far more resistant to engine heat and cracking than older nitrile belts.

Belt tensioners, like that shown in **FIGURE 18-28**, can be spring-loaded or hydraulic, and can absorb some of the torsional vibration found in diesels as the crankshaft speed rhythmically changes with each cylinder compression and combustion event. The alternator drive belt bears the brunt of this damaging force occurring as the crankshaft speed changes, and the alternator's mass resists the speed change. The effect of the torsional engine vibration is the drive belt is snapped, stretched, and slips during each combustion event, before contracting back to its original length, or even loosening its grip on the drive pulley, when the crankshaft slows. This force is magnified by the 3:1 drive ratio between the crankshaft and alternator pulley, creating a

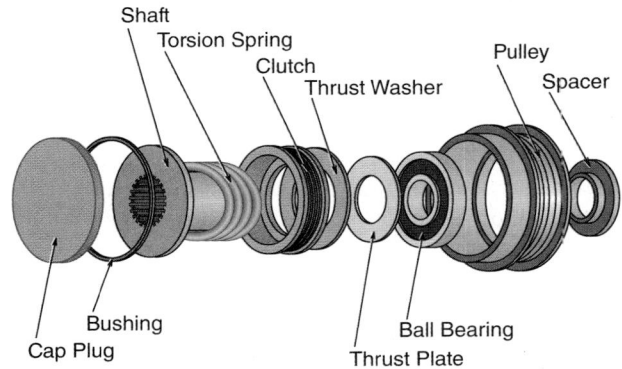

FIGURE 18-29 An overrunning alternator decoupler (OAD) is like a one-way clutch with the ability to absorb some belt shock loading when driving the alternator but freewheel in the opposite direction.

rope-tow effect. To improve belt life and mechanical efficiency, it is becoming common to use **overrunning alternator decoupler (OAD)** pulleys, rather than a conventional solid pulley and belt tensioner (**FIGURE 18-29**). An OAD pulley uses an internal spring and clutch system that allows the pulley to decouple from the rotor shaft to rotate freely in one direction and provide limited, spring-like positive drive in the other direction. The spring inside the coupler's pulley acts like a shock absorber, absorbing the force associated with belt accelerations and speed reversals, enabling the alternator to free-wheel when the belt suddenly decelerates.

▶ TECHNICIAN TIP

A failed OAD pulley does not transmit rotational torque to the alternator's rotor. When inspecting a charging system-related problem using an OAD-coupled alternator, verify the OAD-type drive pulley s locking and driving the alternator rotor. This can be done by placing a tool, such as a screwdriver, through the alternator cooling vent to hold the rotor stationary while the pulley is turned in both directions. Make sure the OAD pulley locks up to rotate the rotor in the correct direction of rotation and freewheels in the other.

Alternator Cooling

Because a significant amount of heat is produced when diodes are blocking or, more correctly, resisting current flow in one direction, the rectifier bridge is designed to absorb and radiate heat to the atmosphere. Stator windings also produce substantial amounts of heat, which can burn the insulation and windings. A quick check of the charging system can involve touching the alternator stator housing while the alternator is charging. A properly functioning alternator is warm, but if it is too hot to touch, it is working too hard and providing above-normal charging current to extra loads, such as weak and defective batteries. Larger 24-volt alternators, such as the Delco 50DN used by buses, circulate oil through the alternator to remove heat from the rectifier and stator windings.

When operating in an atmosphere, such as in a mine or where hydraulic mist in the engine compartment can be present, a spark from an alternator's brush or overheated wiring could trigger an explosion or cause a fire. In these cases, the alternator is sealed, and heat from alternator components is radiated through the housing. Most alternators, however, rely on air to internally cool internal components (**FIGURE 18-30**). If equipped with a cooling fan, the alternator must rotate in a direction that pushes air through the unit. Today, most cooling fans push air through the alternator, regardless of rotational direction. To improve alternator efficiency even more, alternator cases are well-ventilated and use two cooling fans to lower heat-induced electrical resistance (**FIGURE 18-31**). Alternator bearings—particularly the front bearing that is loaded by the accessory drive belt—often use cooling fins to extend bearing life.

Large alternators used by buses, producing as much as 300 amps at 24 volts, require superior cooling. In these situations, oil-cooled alternators, such as the one in **FIGURE 18-32**, may be used. A minimum of 2 gallons (7.6 liters) flow per minute is required. The engine oil cooling system keeps internal engine oil temperatures below 250°F (121°C) and this can be used to cool the alternator. Alternators using oil cooling do need to be sealed well and serviced to prevent any internal shorts or sparks, which may lead to a crankcase explosion caused by ignition of volatile oil vapors inside the alternator case.

Direct Current Rectifiers

Alternators produce alternating current from three phases of stator windings and can be used to operate many electrical devices. However, not all AC-operated devices are cost effective to install in a chassis or efficient to operate in commercial vehicles. AC cannot charge a battery, either. Converting the AC to usable DC is referred to as current **rectification**.

AC is produced in the stator due to the influence of the rotors' magnetic fields. Alternating north–south poles passing in succession over windings cyclically push and pull electrons in each phase. Changing the direction of electron movement back and forth in each phase gives stator current flow its AC characteristic.

Two diodes are connected to an end of each stator phase of either Delta- or Wye-wound stators. The silicon-type diodes behave like a one-way electrical check valve. Using two diodes connected to each of the three junctions of a Delta stator phase separates the positive and negative potentials of an AC sine

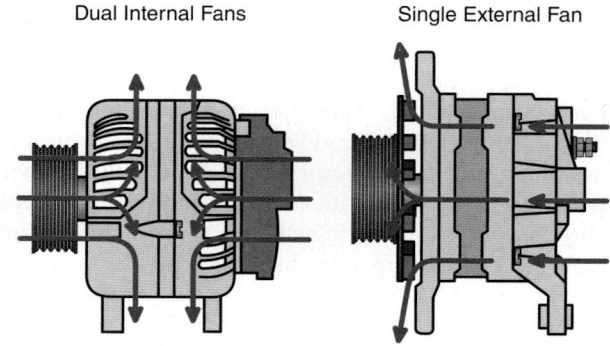

FIGURE 18-31 Cooling helps improve alternator efficiency by reducing heat-related resistance. A single fan pulls cooling air into the alternator over the rectifier bridge first.

FIGURE 18-32 Oil-cooled alternator showing where **A.** the oil goes in and **B.** the oil goes out.

FIGURE 18-30 An internal cooling fan attached to a rotor used to move air through the alternator.

wave. The positive diode connects to the B+ output terminal and the negative diode connects to negative ground. Using two diodes at each of the three connection points for the stator phases enables both the positive and negative portions, or full rectification, of a complete 360-degree AC sine wave to be converted to DC (**FIGURE 18-33**). If only a single diode is used at the end of the windings, only half the AC sine wave is rectified. Because each stator winding produces one of three phases of the alternator's AC (**FIGURE 18-34**), a minimum of six diodes is required to completely rectify current from all three phases of AC into DC (**FIGURE 18-35**).

Diodes are pressed, screwed, or fused to a thin metal plate in the rear section of the alternator and ensure a one-way flow of current out of the alternator. The plate and diodes together are called the rectifier bridge (**FIGURE 18-36**). Heat is released by the diodes resisting current flow and, because of the slight voltage drop, across silicon diodes. Rectifier bridge construction helps dissipate this heat, often by using finned heat sinks that

are air cooled by internal cooling fans. The arrangement of positive and negative diodes in the rectifier bridge ensures that the battery does not discharge through the alternator. Three diodes connected to the B+ terminal and three at the negative terminal have their P and N material arranged to ensure one-way flow of current from the alternator and back to the batteries.

AC Ripple

Overlapping the output phases of each stator winding helps produce a smoother DC output current. But the output current does have some voltage fluctuation as voltage rises and falls between each phase. Small variations in the rectified DC output are caused by the small peaks and valleys between the AC waveforms created by the three overlapping stator phases. The maximum voltage from one peak to minimum voltage

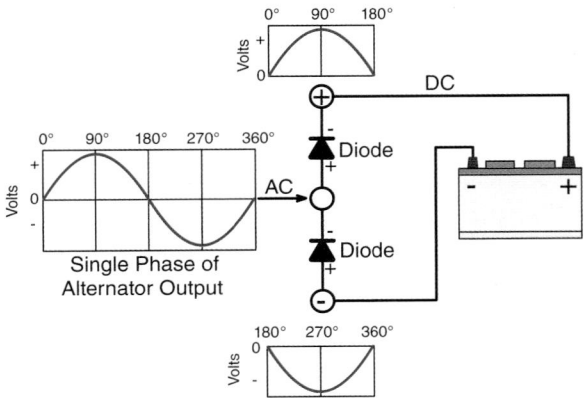

FIGURE 18-33 A pair of diodes separates the positive and negative portion of each AC sine wave. The output of each diode pair is connected to B+ and ground — output terminals of the alternator.

FIGURE 18-35 Diode trio supplies power to the rotor circuit in most alternators. **A.** Ignition terminal. **B.** Voltage regulator. **C.** Diode trio. **D.** Stator connections (3). **E.** Rectifier bridge. **F.** Negative ground connection. **G.** Positive battery terminal. **H.** "R" terminal.

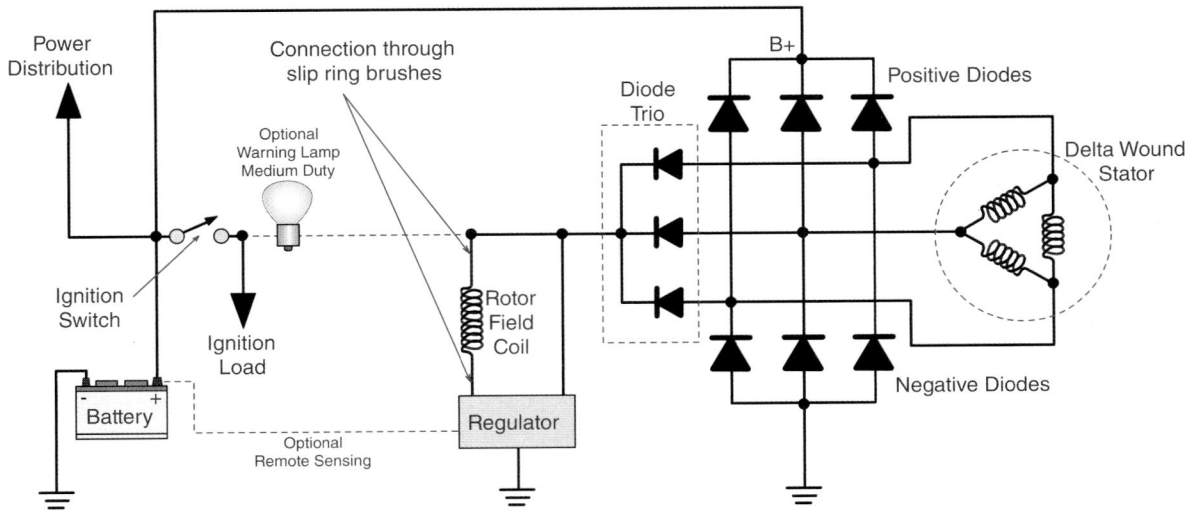

FIGURE 18-34 Current flow through a single phase in the forward direction.

where two phases begin to overlap will typically be less than 0.25 volts. Because the three phase waveforms do not overlap to produce perfectly smooth DC current, the slight variation in DC voltage output is called the alternator ripple. Because normal ripple varies no more than 0.25 volt from peak to valley, it explains why DC voltage fluctuates many times a second between 13.9 and 14.1 volts. This voltage fluctuation is averaged on a DC voltmeter but can be easily detected and measured when an AC voltmeter is ranged to measure low-voltage AC. When graphed, the measured AC waveform voltage looks like a ripple of a wave, hence the term **AC ripple** (**FIGURE 18-37**). AC voltage fluctuations and ripple measurement are important as diagnostic tests to check the condition

of diodes. Defective diodes or defects in the stator are indicated when ripple is excessive (**FIGURE 18-38**). A ripple pattern that is consistent between the output of each windings voltage peak and low indicates that the stator windings and diodes are each consistently generating current flow. A smoothing capacitor inside or outside the alternator connected to the alternator's negative and positive terminals helps minimize AC ripple even further. Irregular ripple patterns indicate a fault in either the diodes or the stator windings. Study the illustrations carefully to understand the job of the rectifier bridge has in providing the relatively smooth DC output required by the vehicle's systems.

▶ **TECHNICIAN TIP**

Alternators can be one of the biggest sources of dangerous electromagnetic interference (EMI). One of the ways alternators produce EMI is through the rapid voltage changes that is a property of alternating current and AC ripple. Electromagnetic waves can be generated from high-speed voltage changes including radio waves, which can penetrate other conductors to induce current flow. EMI like this can be heard on radios and produce an effect called "cross-talk" over controller area network (CAN) communication. EMI can also be conducted by wires through the electrical system. The potential danger of EMI is it can interfere with the operation of signals in sensitive electronic control modules to the point of causing malfunctions and failures. It's important to remember that incorrectly repaired alternators, replacements, or certain types of alternator failures can cause hard to identify, unusual electrical system behaviors.

Smoothing Capacitors

As previously mentioned, capacitors can be used to smooth alternator AC ripple and prevent EMI caused by small, but high-frequency, voltage fluctuations. An electrolytic capacitor, which has an exceptionally high storage capacity, is connected

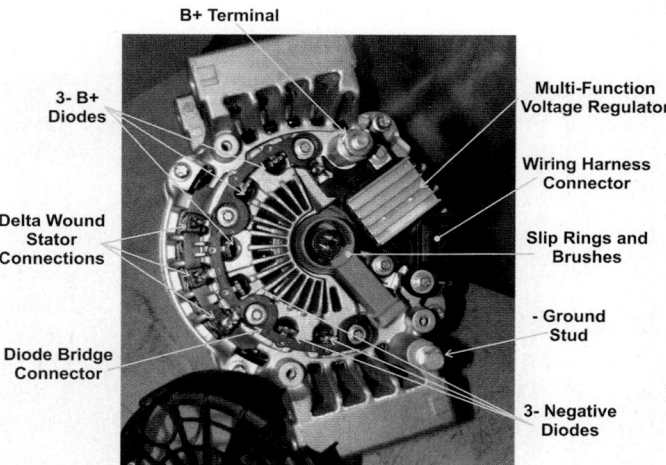

FIGURE 18-36 The rectifier bridge of this late model Delco 24 SI alternator presses 6 diodes into a rectifier bridge. The output of each stator phase is connected to 2 diodes. Through 2 separate conductive layers in the bridge, 3 diodes supply DC output to either the positive or negative output terminals.

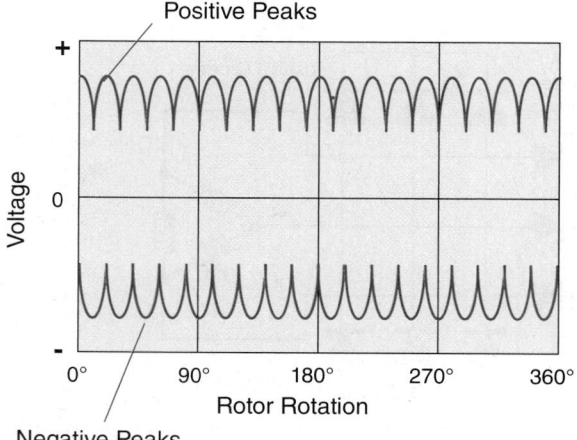

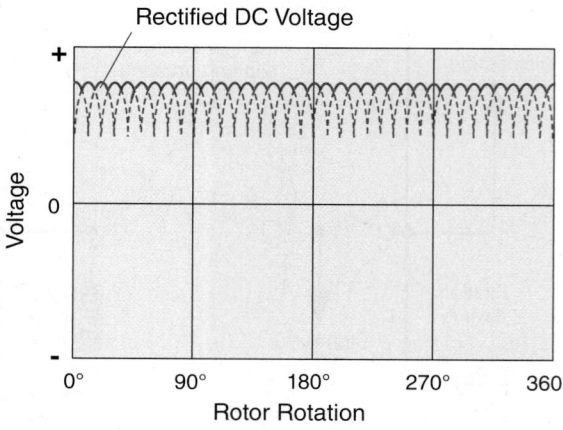

FIGURE 18-37 Typical alternator oscilloscope pattern showing AC ripple.

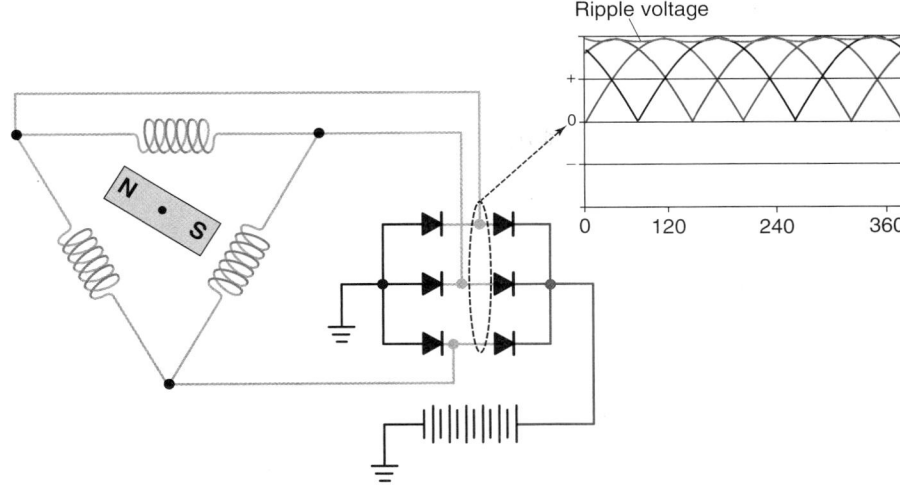

FIGURE 18-38 Three phases rectified.

across the alternator's output terminals to act like an electric shock absorber, to reduce EMI. When the output voltage increases slightly, the capacitor charges and absorb some of the increased current. When voltage drops, the capacitor discharges or drains current back into the lower voltage circuit, topping up the output voltage to smoothen the voltage output.

> ▶ **TECHNICIAN TIP**
>
> A missing or defective alternator capacitor can cause radio noise and EMI interference with chassis electronic modules. When checking for parasitic draws, the capacitor may give a false indication of current draw as it charges for a few seconds after the battery is disconnected and reconnected. If batteries are disconnected for even a short time, the cables will spark when connected as the capacitor charges.

Voltage Regulation

LO 18-4 Identify and describe the principles and operating characteristics of alternator voltage regulation.

Voltage regulators perform several important functions, but its primary job is to maintain the battery in a full state of charge. This means the voltage regulator senses system voltage to limit the alternator's output voltage to between 2.15 and 2.35 volts per cell for lead-acid batteries at room temperature (12.9–14.1 volts for six cell batteries). At this level, the battery can be kept fully charged, yet not cause the conversion of liquid electrolyte to gas, which happens when charging voltage exceeds 14.4–14.7-volt limit for an extended time. Voltage regulators are classified as either external (**FIGURE 18-39**) or internal. Most late-model alternators have internal regulators, which enables them to sense alternator temperature to improve alternator operation. When cold, the alternator charges at higher voltage for several minutes than when warm. Higher initial charging voltage when outside temperatures are cold helps speed up chemical activity in resistive batteries to increase their charge acceptance rate and

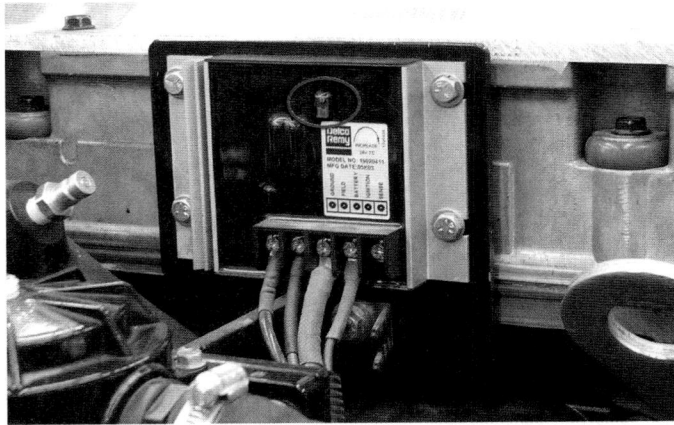

FIGURE 18-39 An external voltage regulator for a 24-volt alternator, with voltage regulator adjustment (circled).

temperature. Regulators can also be categorized by the way circuit connections supply current to the rotor used to induce "field excitation." Knowing the type of field excitation circuit used is helpful to quickly test whether an alternator or voltage regulator is defective. Types of alternator field excitation include:

1. "A" type regulators control the strength of the rotor's magnetic field by changing the resistance to current flow through the rotor on the ground side of the circuit. This means one rotor brush is connected to the ignition switch or the alternator's B+ output and the other brush is connected to ground through the regulator (**FIGURE 18-40**).

2. "B" type regulators control the battery positive current supply to the rotor field. One brush is connected directly to negative ground and the regulator varies battery positive voltage supplied to the other brush. B-type circuits are used only by external regulators. Unfortunately, if the electronic regulator

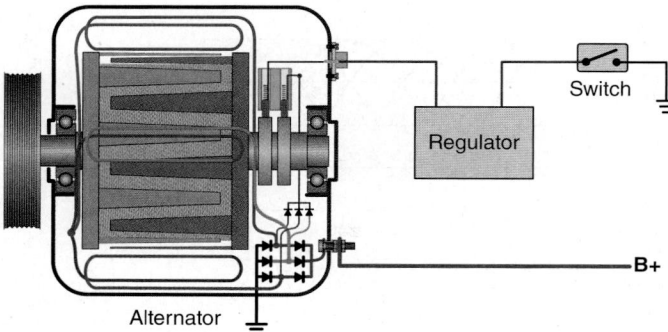

FIGURE 18-40 "A" type regulator connection.

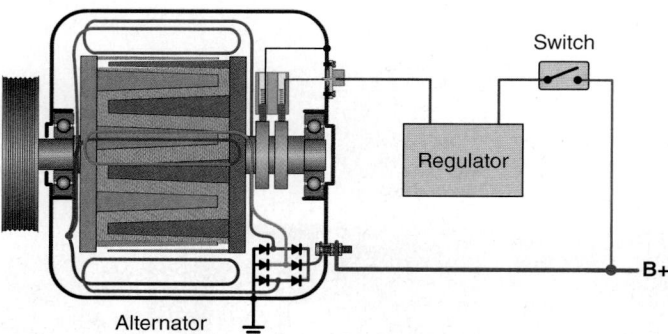

FIGURE 18-41 "B" type regulator connection.

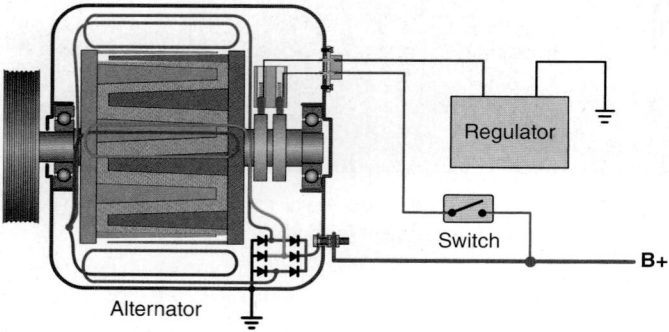

FIGURE 18-42 An isolated field alternator allows connection of either an "A" or "B" type regulator.

fails or develops a resistive ground due to corrosion, it senses low battery voltage, which causes the alternator voltage to increase and overcharge. Overcharging batteries completely gas all electrolyte to dry them out and chassis light bulbs often burn out (**FIGURE 18-41**).

3. Isolated field-type voltage regulators varies current flow through both the negative ground and battery positive current supplied to the rotor field (**FIGURE 18-42**).

In older SI series Delco alternators and several newer models, current supplied to the regulator is provided by the diode trio. These three diodes, also called exciter diodes, perform single-wave rectification of each phase of the alternator's windings. Single-phase rectification means only a

maximum of half the alternator's output voltage is used to excite the rotor.

Most voltage regulators today use digital, pulse-width modulated (PWM) electrical signals to change the strength of the rotor's magnetic field. However, older voltage regulators use transistor-type regulators supplying an analog voltage signal. An analog DC signal continuously varies the strength of the magnetic field to match system demand for current. As the alternator reaches its set point, which is the maximum output voltage, the field current gradually diminishes. A weak magnetic field in the rotor means little charging amperage is produced, but charging voltage is maintained at close to 14.1-volts. Digital regulators using a pulse-width-modulated signal to control the magnetic field strength switch current on and off to the rotor. These alternators have a duty cycle frequency interval of between 10 and 7000 times per second. Within that frequency interval, the voltage regulator changes the length of "on-time" current applied to the rotor. Current is cycled on and off hundreds of times each second, with the length of on-time increasing as higher output is required.

Current or amperage regulation is also a function of voltage regulation. To understand this, consider that an alternator's output amperage depends on two factors. One is the regulator set-point, and the other is the vehicle's electrical system total circuit resistance. An electrical system with a low battery state of charge, and many other electrical loads switched on, has low resistance. Multiple current pathways exist, which lowers the total resistance of the electrical system. Low resistance permits high amounts of amperage to flow out of the alternator. (Remember Ohm's law: Amperage = Voltage/Resistance.) Because the alternator is connected to all these circuits, the voltage regulator supplies the highest possible current flow to the rotor for maximum magnetic field strength. As the batteries charge and some loads are turned off, circuit resistance increases, and less amperage is needed. When the system voltage reaches the alternator's set-point, it reduces, or even turns off, current to the rotor until the voltage falls again.

Charging voltage rises as amperage decreases according to Ohm's power law. This takes place because many electrical system circuits such as the battery are constant power circuits, which means current demands are a function of voltage and amperage. Stated another way, using power law (Power = Volts × Amps)—if 1200 watts of power are needed to supply the electrical system, the voltage-amperage combination could easily be anything between 85 amps at 14.1 volts or 93 amps at 12.9 volts.

A low amperage output alternator supplies circuits at lower voltage longer to maintain high amperage output compared to an alternator with greater capacity. That happens because the regulator of the low output alternator needs to increase the rotor field strength as much as possible to supply adequate power to vehicle circuits. As the demand for current is reduced when circuit resistance increases, the larger capacity alternator supplies more amperage sooner, charging the battery faster and enabling it to reach its voltage set point quickly and reduce rotor field strength.

Charging System Set Point

Alternators must be capable of supplying enough current to adequately charge the batteries, but not so much current that it causes damage to the vehicle's electrical system from excessive current flow pushed by higher voltage. Voltage regulation for 12-volt systems establish a maximum charging voltage, known as the set point. Charging voltage set point averages between 13.5 volts and 14.6 volts. This is 1.5 to 2.0 volts above 12.6-volt open-circuit voltage for a typical 12-volt battery. Twenty-four-volt systems use between 27 and 28.4 volts for a typical set point. Lower charging set point voltages may be encountered, however, particularly on vehicles that are doing long-haul runs or hot climates. Higher voltage set points are used for cold weather operation with extended use of running lights. But before adjusting an alternator charging set-point voltage, it is always advisable to check manufacturer specifications for correct charging voltage ranges for the vehicle and operating conditions. Charging at voltages above 15 volts (12-volt system) and 31 volts (24-volt system) causes:

- Batteries to gas excessively
- Batteries to overheat and lose electrolyte through electrolysis
- Battery plates to shed grid material, buckle, and generally become heat-damaged as the temperature rises above 125°F (52°C)
- Vehicle electrical systems, control modules, and so on can be damaged by high voltage
- Premature and extensive bulb failure and LED light failure

Undercharging leads to battery plate sulfation and grid corrosion. This is a condition where sulfate deposited on the plates during discharge is left too long. If left long enough, sulfate turns to a hard-crystalline structure and cannot be driven off by charging. Multiple battery installations are especially vulnerable to the problems of uneven charge rates causing plate sulfation.

Factors affecting the precise choice of set point voltage include:

- Type of batteries—Flooded batteries (standard lead-acid) charge at lower voltages than no-maintenance or AGM batteries. However, AGM batteries are more easily damaged by overcharging.
  - States of battery charge—Discharged batteries have low resistance to current compared to charged batteries (**FIGURE 18-43**). AGM batteries can absorb 40% higher charge rate than flooded and low-maintenance batteries.
  - Temperature—Battery resistance to charging increases as temperatures decrease. Temperature sensors in voltage regulators can adjust set points. To warm-up the battery, alternators may charge at as high as 16.5 volts for the first few minutes after start-up when the weather is cold.
- Drive cycle—Low-speed engine operation requires higher set points to keep batteries charged.

The vehicle's electrical system can be severely damaged by high-voltage spikes if batteries are disconnected accidentally or intentionally while the alternator is charging. Since the rotor's magnetic fields do not disappear immediately and the battery is unable to absorb current, output voltage can suddenly rise to levels that can damage sensitive electronic devices. Some alternators include a **load-dumping** feature that temporarily suppresses these high voltage spikes. This usually involves using specialized diodes in the rectifier bridges, which become resistive, rather than conductive, at an excessive voltage level. The diodes are called **transient voltage suppression (TVS) diodes**. They temporarily resist high voltage and automatically reset when the overvoltage goes away. Best practice is never to disconnect batteries when the engine is running.

Remote Sensing of Set Point

One of the most critical factors to determine what the alternator's ideal set point should be is the battery state of charge. Accurately sensing battery voltage, which indicates its state of charge, enables the regulator to control the charge rate, preventing under- or overcharging the batteries. In single-wire alternators, the alternator cable is used by the regulator to measure battery voltage. But voltage drop between the alternator and batteries prevents accurate measurement of the batteries' state of charge.

For example, resistance is created at each connection point between the alternator and batteries. Cables connecting the alternator and batteries together also have a connection point at the starting motor, which together adds resistance (**FIGURE 18-44**).

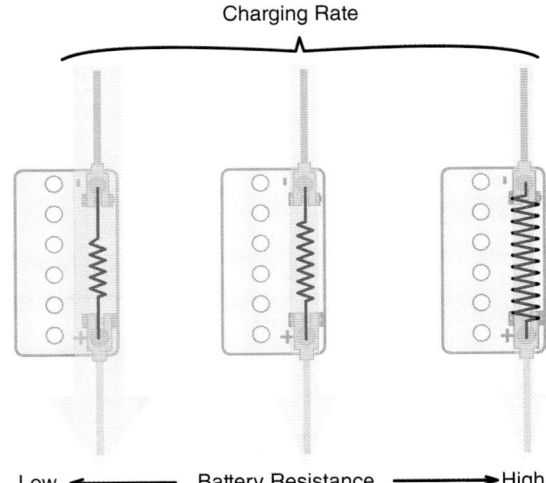

Charging Rate

Low ← Battery Resistance → High

Charging rate is dependent a batteries internal resistance which is inversely proportional to it state of charge.

FIGURE 18-43 Battery resistance determines the charge rate of current supplied by the alternator. The resistance of batteries is highest when fully charged.

Loose or corroded connections, multiple battery connections, plus long cable runs to batteries, prevent the alternator from accurately sensing battery voltage and, consequently, supply a lower voltage and charging rate than is required to keep

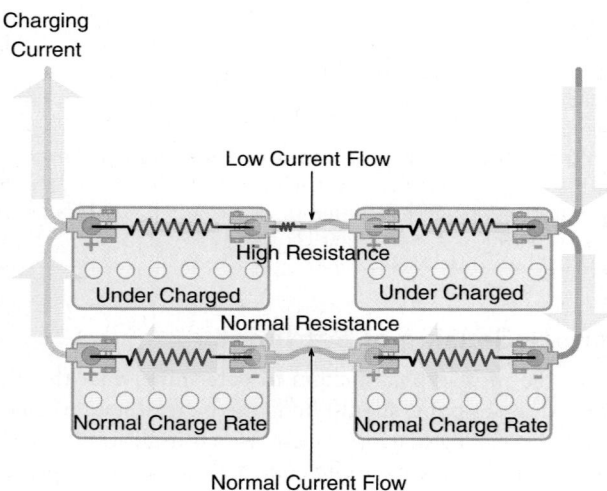

FIGURE 18-44 Resistance in cable connections can cause one or more batteries to remain undercharged and sulfated.

the batteries optimally charged. This is especially problematic on vehicles' operation of short runs or having heavy electrical loads, such as school buses, which may idle with heaters and lights on, or vehicles with power tailgates. It's not uncommon to have 0.5 to 0.75 volt difference between voltage at an alternator's B+ terminal on a single-wire alternator and the batteries. In this case, a 14.1-volt set point at the alternator charges the batteries at only 13.3 to 13.6 volts. Unless the vehicle is operated for a long time, the batteries may not fully charge at all. To prevent shortened battery life and other service issues caused by under-charged batteries, the voltage regulator should have a separate circuit directly connected to the batteries allowing it to properly sense battery voltage. Increasing charging voltage of only ½ volt, from 13.6 to 14.1, reduces the battery charge time by one-half.

Delco Remy uses voltage sensing circuits and refers to this feature as Remote Sense technology. With Remote Sense, a wire circuit connected between the battery and regulator enables the voltage regulator to sense the actual voltage at the battery and automatically change its set-point voltage output to compensate for cable voltage drop. Charging set point voltages can vary between 12.7 volts and as much as 16 volts leaving the alternator (**FIGURE 18-45**). A dedicated terminal on the alternator is used to connect the voltage regulator to a wire connected directly to the batteries (**FIGURE 18-46**). If a vehicle is not equipped with

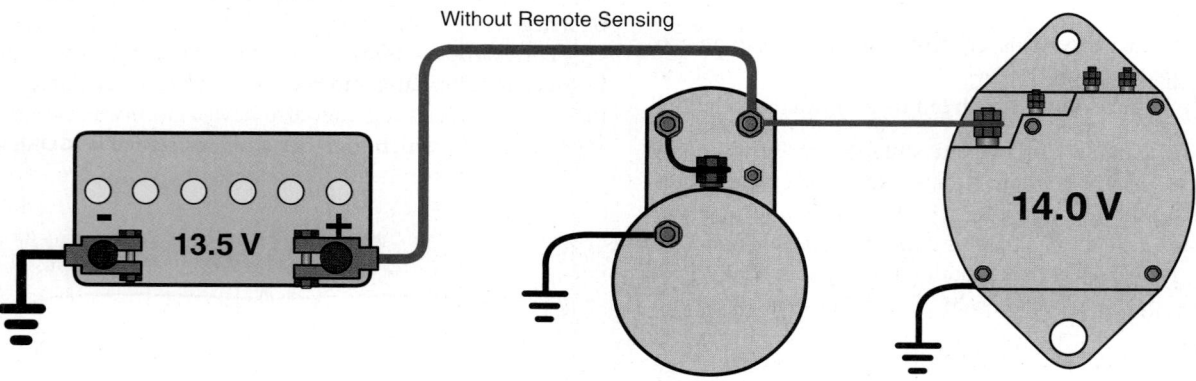

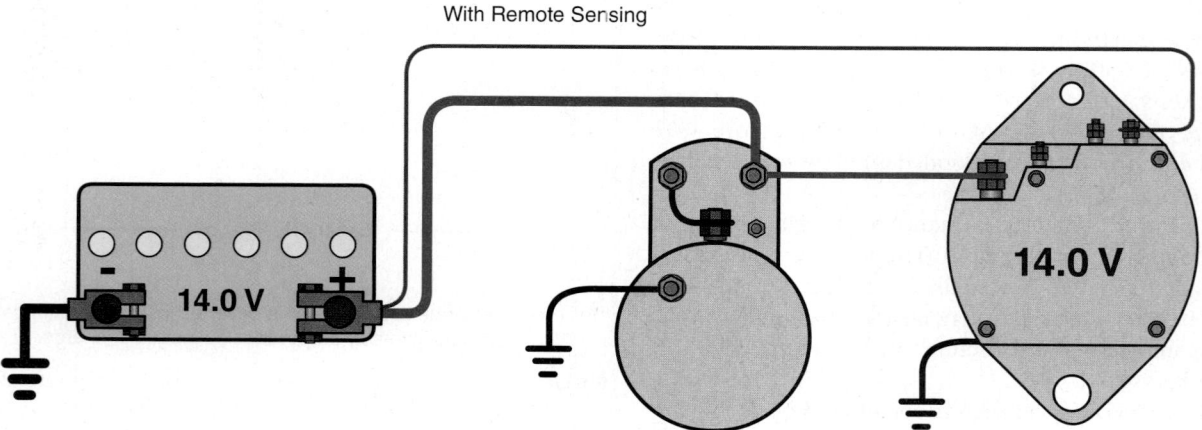

FIGURE 18-45 Remote sensing allows the voltage regulator to use battery voltage as a reference for alternator output voltage.

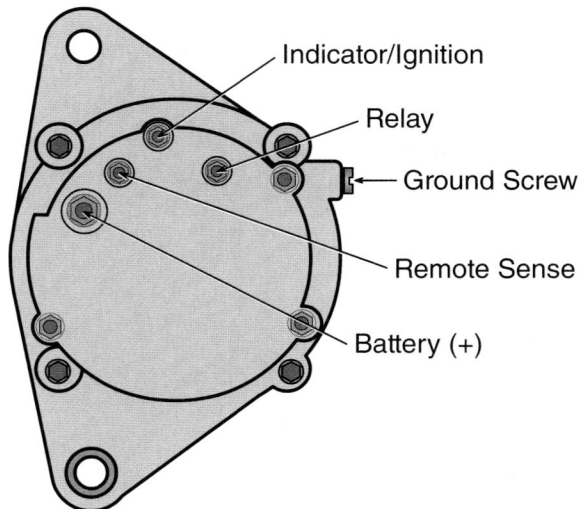

FIGURE 18-46 A dedicated terminal on the alternator is used to connect the remote sensing circuit to the alternator.

the remote sensing circuit, a fused 16-gauge wire can be added to connect the batteries and alternator. Other manufacturers use the ignition circuit connected to the regulator to sense battery voltage.

Networked and ECM-Controlled Voltage Regulation

Voltage regulators controlled by chassis electronic control units (ECU) are multifunctional and now commonplace. Efficiency gains can be provided by networked charging system controls, including:

- Use of higher charging rates for AGM batteries. AGM batteries can absorb higher charging current. Because they charge faster and more efficiently, the alternator uses less fuel and the engine produces fewer GHG emissions.
- Increase engine idle speed if battery voltage is too low.
- Reduce engine load during acceleration, and at idle.
- Adapt charging rates for different battery technology, such as AGM.
- Supply alternator fault codes, which can be accessed through the data link connector.
- Temperature-corrected charging rates of the battery—batteries can be charged at higher voltages to overcome high resistance and increase the charging rate when cold.
- Thermal protection of the alternator—it shuts down or reduces output if current is excessive, and can potentially burn out the alternator, such as when a shorted battery is connected or a grounded circuit on the vehicle draws excessive current.
- Supply alternator speed and, indirectly, engine speed data to other network modules.
- Overvoltage protection.
- Smart or adjustable voltage set point, which can be modified by other network modules, when needed.
- Supply an output signal for a charging system fault lamp.

- Perform alternator diagnostic checks using an electronic service tool, such as a handheld scanner or OEM software for chassis programming.
- Add alternators (six or more possible) and balance the load between the alternators.

Bidirectional communication between an electrical system and the alternator voltage regulator can take place either over a CAN bus, which connects the regulator to all other vehicle modules, or using a single wire operating according to local interconnect network (LIN) connection protocols. In LINs, the electrical system control module or master sends instructions and request information from the voltage regulator, which is the slave module. Because the regulator only does what it's told, it is a cheaper and less sophisticated master-slave network arrangement, compared to a CAN-controlled module. Onboard communication between the vehicle electrical system and voltage regulator takes place over the CAN (**FIGURE 18-47**).

Dual Alternators—Paralleling

Vehicles needing extra high current output at idle, or those with extra electrical loads, can use two or more alternators. Fire trucks, ambulances, RVs, buses, and highway tractors running extra accessories are examples where using **parallel alternators** provides a higher charging voltage at idle with more available amperage. Connecting alternators in parallel requires the output of each to be properly balanced so one does not work harder than the other and prematurely wear out. This can happen unless the alternators are identical and sense the same system voltage. In practice, this is difficult to achieve, because even slight differences using the same regulators and alternators cause one alternator to charge at a slightly higher voltage or amperage than the other. The second alternator does not charge as much, and the first alternator operates inefficiently, wears out, or burns out prematurely.

Several strategies can be used to prevent that from happening:

- Use engineered systems with alternators and regulators designed to work in dual-alternator systems.
- While using an amp-clamp to measure output, the alternators, if equipped with adjustable voltage regulators, are adjusted to produce the same amperage output with the lights and accessories switched-on.
- When using identical alternators matched by model and output and having the same regulators, a shunt or cable is connected between the battery positive terminals on the alternators. This helps both alternators to sense the same output current.
- A single regulator for both alternators can be used so the current supplied to the rotor is identical and should produce similar output amperage and set point.
- ECM-controlled alternators may be configured using OEM software to regulate two or more alternators. In this arrangement, the ECM balances output from each alternator to produce just the right amount of output for the given requirements.

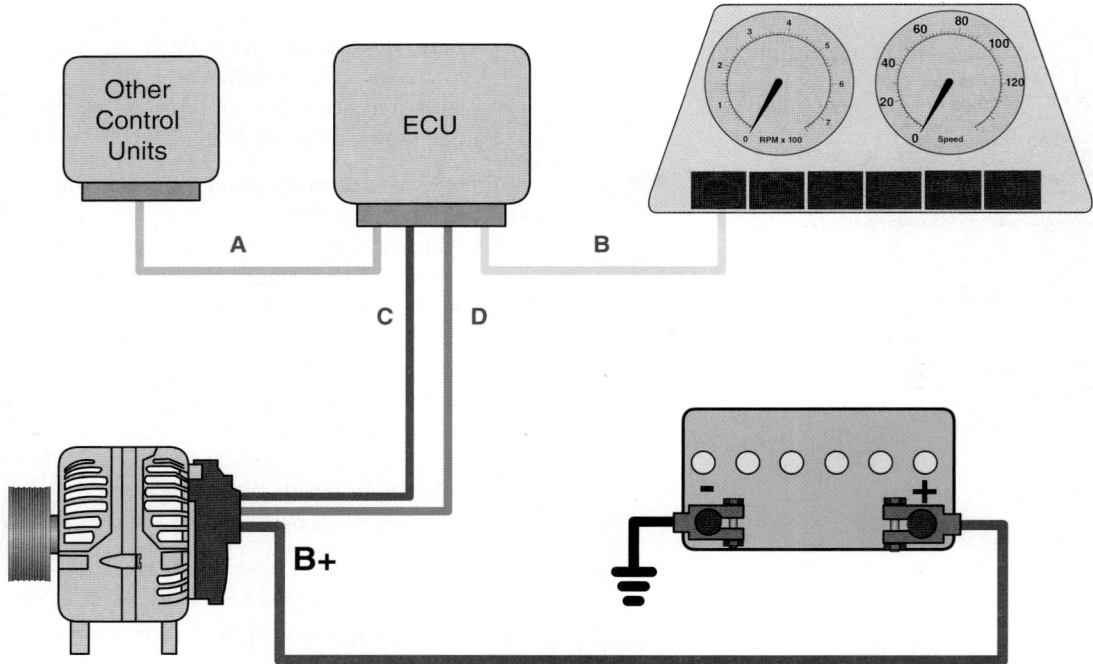

FIGURE 18-47 ECU-controlled alternator. **A.** CANBUS connection. **B.** CANBUS connection to dash for charge lamp. **C.** Monitoring signal. **D.** Control signal.

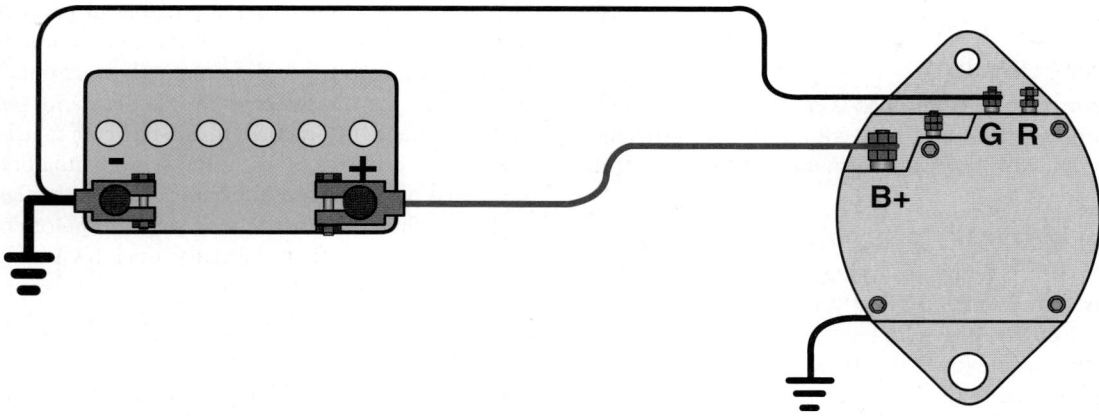

FIGURE 18-48 Circuit diagram for connection of self-exciting alternator.

Alternator Wiring Connections

The terms and connections used in this section are ones commonly used for heavy vehicles. Various manufacturers may use different socket arrangements, color codes, and naming conventions for the various terminals and connectors on alternators, so it is always important to check manufacturer's wiring diagrams and naming conventions for information. The wiring requirements for alternators are relatively simple. This is particularly true for internal regulator self-exciting alternators as they only use a single battery + cable. The battery positive cable is large, gauge wire (4 AWG or larger). It often connects to the battery terminal on the starter and always has voltage present. Some alternators, particularly high-output ones, also have a ground or negative cable.

A large-gauge wire (four AWG or larger) is connected to battery or chassis ground, as illustrated in (**FIGURE 18-48**). This prevents the engine block from conducting hundreds of amps the alternator may produce when grounded only through the engine block and minimizes ground-side voltage drops.

A remote sensing connection, as illustrated in **FIGURE 18-49**, is also used on some alternators and is usually marked on the back of the alternator with an "S." Alternators using **remote sensing** provide a separate wire circuit connected directly to the battery and the alternator sensing terminal that is used to automatically adjust the regulator set point.

External regulator alternators have additional connections to allow for field connections from the regulator to the alternator, as was shown in Figure 18-39. Provision for the connection

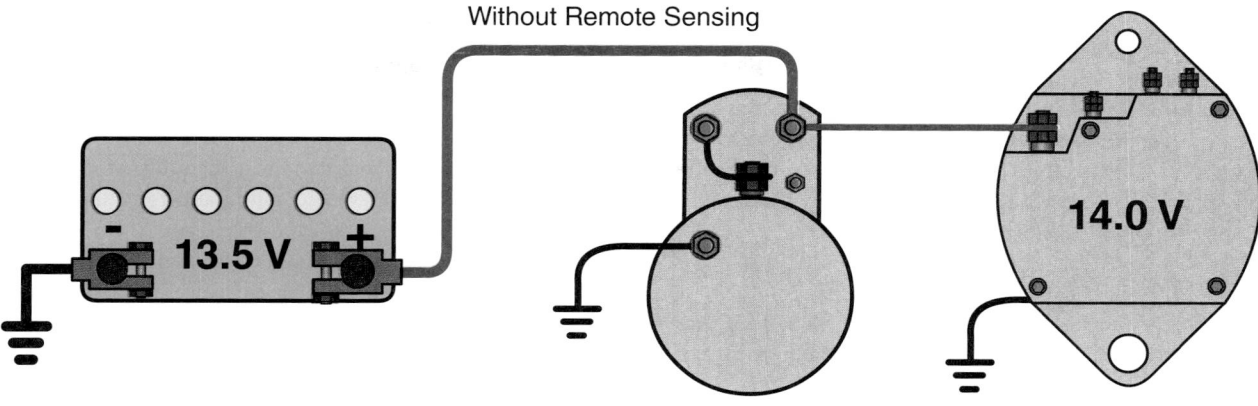

FIGURE 18-49 Remote sensing allows the voltage regulator to use direct battery voltage as a reference for alternator output voltage.

FIGURE 18-50 Charging system warning lights are seldom used in heavy trucks and buses. Instead, voltmeters are used.

of alternator warning lights may also be connected to both internal and external regulator alternators.

Alternators that require external excitation have an ignition excite or "I" connection. This small-gauge wire has voltage present only when the ignition switch is in the run position. Current through this wire switches the voltage regulator on. In heavy-duty vehicles, voltmeters, rather than charge indicator warning lights, are used (**FIGURE 18-50**). In medium-duty vehicles without voltmeters in the dash and equipped with only an instrument cluster charging system warning light, current passes from the ignition switch and to the light before passing to the alternator regulator to provide initial excitation of the rotor's magnetic field. This circuit illuminates the light when the alternator is not charging. When the alternator starts charging, charging voltage appears at the "I" terminal, which provides battery positive to both sides of the light and extinguishes the charging system warning light. In situations where a charge warning light is not required, an ignition feed may be directly connected to the "I" terminal.

Another connection found on many alternators is the relay or "R" terminal. This terminal is connected directly to one phase of the stator winding. Because it is connected directly to the stator, it provides an AC signal whose frequency is related to the speed of the alternator. Because the speed of the alternator is relative to engine speed, this signal can be used to operate a tachometer, hour meter, or a frequency-sensitive starter lock-out relay to disable the cranking circuit when the engine is running. Energizing or flashing this terminal, by temporarily connecting it to battery voltage, is necessary on some self-exciting alternators to magnetize the rotor for initial start-up. Since the rotor is soft iron, the rotor maintains this magnetism once it has been initially excited. However, after rebuilding or through prolonged inactivity, the rotor may lose the residual magnetism. For this reason, the relay terminal is needed on self-exciting single-wire alternators.

Multifunction Regulator Terminals

Newer alternator models with multifunction voltage regulators capable of interfacing with an electrical system control module or CAN have additional terminals and designations. Delco's 24SI with a P-L-I-S or P-L-F-S connector is an example of an alternator with a multifunctional regulator plug. Each terminal letter designates the following functions:

- The "P" terminal refers to phase since it is connected to a single stator winding. This terminal is the equivalent of the Relay or "R" terminal and carries half-system voltage. This means a 14-volt output has seven volts at the terminal, unless there is a defect in the stator or a rectifier diode. The P terminal can be used to control frequency-sensitive relays, such as those for starter motor lock-outs, and for tachometers or similar devices.
- L – Lamp or charge indicator warning light. Current supplied to this terminal switches on the alternator's voltage regulator. Five to 12 volts is all that is necessary to cause the alternator to charge. If the vehicle does not have a charge indicator lamp, the ignition signal must be connected to the I terminal.
- F – Field Monitor. This terminal provides feedback to an external field monitor in a control module, indicating what the alternator load is at any instant. A pulse-width modulated signal is available from this terminal, which changes length proportional to the load.
- I – Ignition. The F and I terminal designations are interchangeable because they have a nearly identical function. The I terminal supplies voltage from 0 to 11 volts, which is proportional to the electrical load on the alternator. If a vehicle does not have a charge indicator lamp, the ignition switch signal must be connected here, rather than the L terminal.
- S – Sensing. As described already, this terminal is used to supply the alternator with battery voltage to enable the regulator to adjust the set point to the optimal charging rate.

Charging System Service

LO 18-5 Identify indicators for charging system service and outline steps involved in inspecting charging system operation.

Complaints about hard starting, slow starting, and not starting often involve inspecting the operation and components of the charging system. Without a proper state of charge maintained in the batteries by the charging system, the cranking circuits

cannot operate correctly and there is inadequate voltage to energize injectors or operate system control modules. Premature battery failures, dead batteries, and defective starting motors indicate the need for a charging system inspection, too, since these components are affected by undercharging and overcharging. During normal maintenance, the alternator drive system, including belts, pulleys, and automatic tensioners, should be inspected and replaced, if excessively worn. Unusual electrical system symptoms or complaints that could be caused by EMI interference should include a measurement of the electrical waveform of an alternators output voltage to eliminate the alternator as a potential source of EMI. Preventative maintenance practices of the charging system typically include:

1. Cleaning cable terminals, wiring, and alternator connection points or corrosion. Alternator surfaces should be cleaned until they are free of accumulations of dirt, grease, and dust. Air passages need to be unobstructed to allow air to easily pass through. All connection points must be clean and free from corrosion, since voltage is sensed from between ground and battery positive.
2. Alternator mounting brackets and belt drive systems should be inspected for loose bolts and to allow correct belt alignment. Broken and loose mounting may indicate damage from engine torsional vibration. If other accessory drive system components are functioning correctly, a sturdier model of alternator may be required.
3. Condition of belts and belt tension. A loose belt slips and causes undercharging. Tensioners must be correctly aligned operating perpendicular to the belt. Multi-grooved belts should be check for cracks, which may extend completely across the belt. The back side of the belt should not be worn and glazed.

Belts can have several issues, as shown in (**FIGURE 18-51**). To replace a serpentine belt, follow the steps in **SKILL DRILL 18-1**.

Charging System Diagnosis

When diagnosing charging system problems, the condition of the batteries must first be validated before proceeding with any other tests. A battery with little capacity, sulfated, shorted or discharged, or having corroded, loose battery cable connections,

FIGURE 18-51 Failure conditions for serpentine belts.

SKILL DRILL 18-1 Replacing a Serpentine Belt

1. For safety reasons, disconnect the battery and set the park brake. Inspect the belt for failure. Repair any condition causing belt contamination or failure due to misalignment.
2. Familiarize yourself with the belt routing. Draw a sketch, take a picture of the belt routing, or locate the belt routing diagram in a shop manual or on the radiator module.

3. Release the belt tension to remove the belt. To release belt tension, the automatic belt tensioner is retracted away from the belt using a wrench, socket wrench, 1/2" drive or 3/8" drive ratchet. Some tensioners, such as those used on Detroit DD series engines, use pins to lock the tensioner in place during belt replacement.
4. Inspect the drive belt pulley system for wear. Make sure the tensioner and the pulleys operate freely, without noise or looseness, and are in good condition. The tensioner pulley should contact the belt squarely; if not, the tensioner should be replaced. The installation of a belt kit containing a new tensioner and drive pulleys is recommended when replacing a belt at high accumulated mileage.
5. Before installing the new belt, inspect the alignment of the pulleys to prevent severe belt wear, damage, and belt noise.
6. Route and install the new belt according to the belt routing diagram. Align the belt ribs with the pulley grooves and ensure that the belt fits squarely on each pulley and all the belt grooves fit into the pulley grooves.
7. Release the belt tensioner once again to install the belt over the tensioner pulley. The automatic tensioner applies the correct tension to the belt. When the installation tension is correct, start the engine and observe if the belt drive and tensioning system is properly functioning.

may cause a no-crank, slow-crank, or other hard starting condition. More comprehensive procedures are outlined in the chapter on battery maintenance, but briefly summarized, the battery should be inspected visually first. Any dirt build-up on the battery cases, a cracked or damaged case, or loose or corroded connections could drain the battery or leave it undercharged. Each battery should have its state of charge evaluated and a capacity test performed on each battery. Batteries validated to be in good condition should be at least 75% charged before proceeding with charging system tests and all cables cleaned and tightened before beginning diagnostic steps. Common charging system complaints and malfunctions are outlined in TABLE 18-2.

Inspecting, Adjusting, and Replacing Drive Components

The second step after validating the condition of the batteries is to perform a visual inspection of the alternator and drive system. The alternator should be securely attached to any brackets or pad. Excessive torsional vibration transmitted through the drive system belts or gears can cause the alternator to loosen and fastener threads to strip. Engine vibration dampeners should be inspected if the alternator is loose and falling off the engine. A heavier alternator having sturdier construction may be needed to replace an alternator that is frequently loosening and becoming misaligned with drive pulleys. All alternator terminals and cable connections should be checked for looseness

and corrosion, and to ensure they are connected to the correct terminals. Belt inspection, pulley alignment, and belt tension should be inspected next.

Belt Inspection and Replacement

Drive belts may be either "V"-type or "poly-V," which is another name for a serpentine belt with multiple grooves. Drive and idler pulleys have either multiple grooves to match the width of the belt, or are smooth to roll over the back side of the belt. The advantages poly-V belts have over older V-type belts has displaced V-type belts in OEM equipment. The older V-type belts are inspected for tension and belt material condition. Pulleys driven by the V-type belts are inspected for wear (FIGURE 18-52). A belt tension gauge or a measurement of belt deflection is commonly used to check the adjustment of V-type belts (FIGURE 18-53). Alternators using V-type belts use a slotted-type top bracket, allowing its bottom hinge to pivot away from the drive pulley to tighten belt tension.

To maintain constant belt tension, and to compensate for wear and belt dimensional changes, automatic belt tensioners are used with serpentine belt-drive systems. These spring-loaded tensioners tighten the belt over a pulley attached to a swing arm. The arm pivots on a bushing or bearing to automatically correct for rhythmic belt stretch and slack caused by changes in crankshaft speed. A hydraulic-like strut or shock absorber is used, along with a heavy spring in some tensioners, to further dampen

TABLE 18-2 Charging System Diagnosis Chart

Concern	Cause	Remedy
Overcharging Condition	Resistive voltage sensing lead connection at alternator or battery	Clean, tighten, or repair
	Open battery voltage sensing circuit	Repair circuit
	Defective voltage regulator or resistive connections to the regulator	Replace regulator
	Incorrectly adjusted voltage regulator	Adjust regulator, if serviceable
	One or more shorted batteries in a battery bank	Replace batteries
Undercharging condition	Loose drive belts	Replace belt tensioner
	Corroded, broken, burnt, or loose wiring connections	Repair connections
	Undersize battery cables	Install proper gauge cables
	Defective batteries	Replace batteries as required
	Batteries too far from sensing lead contact	Reposition
	Open sensing lead contact	Replace fuse or repair wiring
	Defective voltage regulator	Replace regulator
	Incorrectly adjusted voltage regulator	Adjust regulator
	Defective rectifier bridge; shorted or open diodes	Replace or repair alternator
	Open stator windings	Replace alternator or stator
	Defective rectifier diodes	Replace rectifier bridge or replace alternator
	Sulfated or shorted battery	Replace batteries
Alternator Not Charging	Poor contact between brushes and slip rings	Replace alternator or repair brushes
	Damaged or worn brushes/slip rings	Repair or replace alternator/replace brushes
	No residual magnetism present in the rotor	Briefly supply B+ current to "R" terminal
	Defective or improperly adjusted regulator	Adjust or replace regulator as required
	Open, shorted, or grounded rotor winding	Repair or replace alternator/replace rotor
	No ignition or lamp excitation of regulator	Verify correct connection from ignition or charge lamp circuit. Repair connections

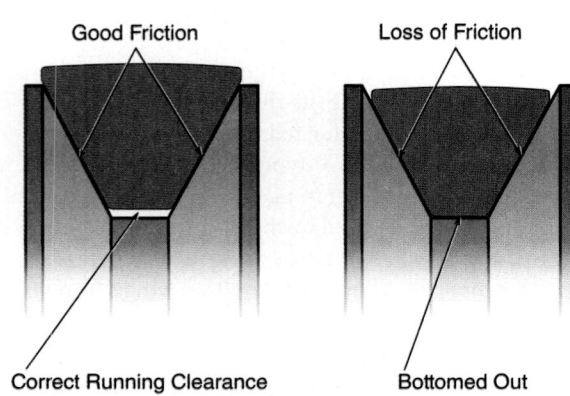

FIGURE 18-52 Worn V belts, incorrect V-belt size selection, or pulleys allow the belt to sit too low in the pulley. The sides of the belt that drive the pulley are not able to develop adequate drive friction when worn.

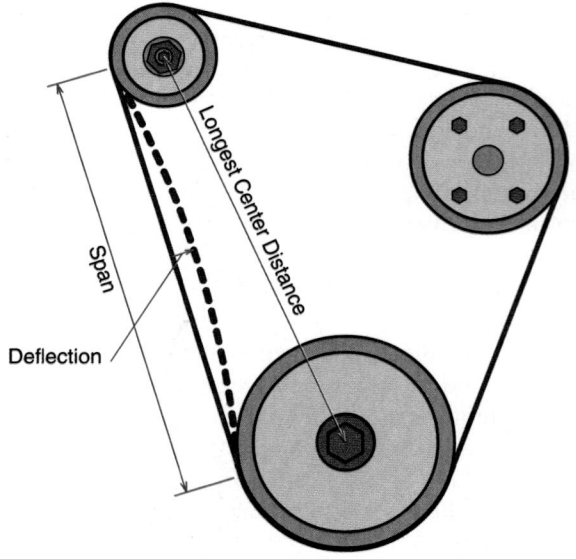

FIGURE 18-53 The adjustment of V-type belt tension is measured using belt deflection.

tensioner oscillation created by engine torsional vibration. These types of belt tensioners should be replaced if any oil leakage from the hydraulic strut is evident during inspection. Idler pulleys loop the drive belt around various other belt-drive accessories, such as the water pump, cooling fan, and AC compressors.

While the engine is running, the belts should be checked for abnormal noise. Belt chirping or squealing is unacceptable. Belt squeal and chirp have distinctly different causes. A squealing noise is usually produced by belt slippage over the drive pulleys. Slippage can be caused by factors, such as low belt tension, a worn belt, a seized pulley, or incorrect belt length. Contamination of the belt or pulley allows the belt to slip as well. Each belt-drive component needs inspection. If belt squeal takes place when electrical loads are switched on, but stops when they are switched off, slippage is taking place between the alternator drive pulley and the belt, which could lead to undercharging.

Unlike squeal, belt chirp is a repetitive, high-pitched noise that is intermittent. Chirping is especially distinct at idle speed and diminishes as the engine speeds up. The noise is typically due to a pattern of intermittent slippage caused by factors related to misalignment of the drive belt. The belt enters and engages pulley grooves, but then is pulled away due to uneven angular stretching, which lengthens only one side of a belt. Intermittent slippage can also be caused by belt contamination, worn belt ribs, and pulley grooves. Defective bearings or particles, like a pebble, embedded in the belt can also cause intermittent noises, but sound different then chirp.

To evaluate the condition of an older nitrile multi-groove belt, a recommended method is to count the number of cracks across a single 3" section of a belt rib. If three or more cracks are observed, the belt is considered to have more than 80% wear and needs replacing. Cracks along the belt, front or back, and missing chunks of belt also justify belt replacement (**FIGURE 18-54**).

With newer EPDM-type belts, visual belt inspection involves the use of a belt inspection tool to estimate remaining service life since EPDM belts do not crack. EPDM belts can appear to be in good condition, but, in fact, can be worn out. EPDM belts are worn out when its raised "V" ribs are worn too narrow and do not wedge into the tapered V pulley grooves. If that happens, the raised edges of the pulley grooves contact only the belt ribs where friction cannot properly transfer adequate drive torque. While the tensioner can compensate for wear, there is less belt surface area engaged with the pulley grooves, causing the belt to slip under load (**FIGURE 18-55**). Two types of tools can check the EPDM multi-groove belt. Both measure the depth of the belt's V grooves by either placing the gauge parallel to or along a groove, or across the groove (**FIGURES 18-56** and **18-57**).

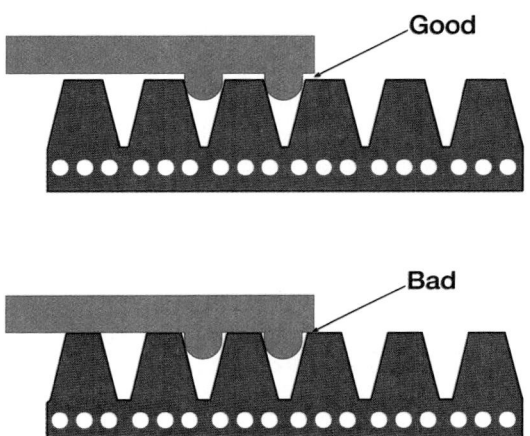

FIGURE 18-55 To transfer drive torque, the edges of the drive pulley grooves must contact the sides of the raised "V" sections of the belt and not the rib.

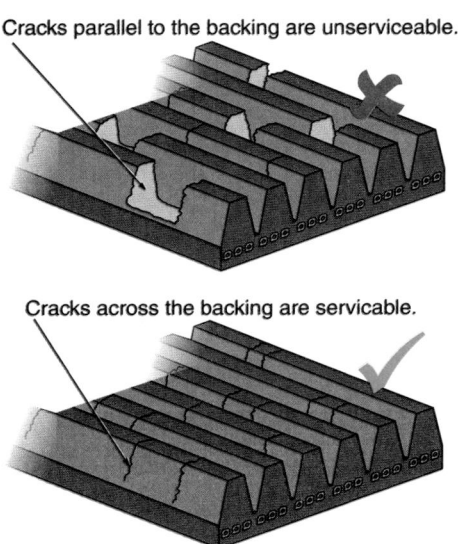

FIGURE 18-54 Older serpentine belts made of nitrile crack from heat and continual stretching.

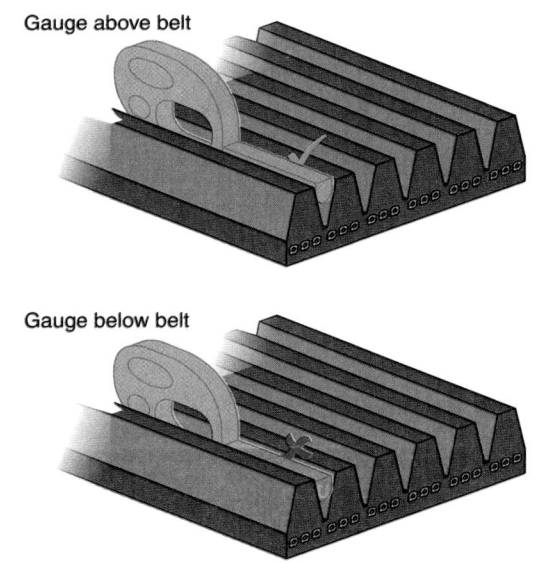

FIGURE 18-56 This tool is placed parallel to or along the belt groove to check for wear. The tool gauge must remain above the level of the belt ribs, or the belt should be replaced.

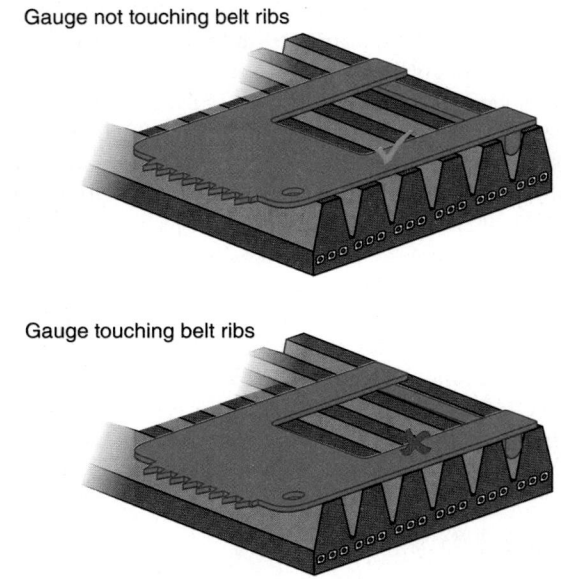

Gauge not touching belt ribs

Gauge touching belt ribs

FIGURE 18-57 This belt tool is used to inspect the belt for excess wear by placing it across the belt. If the tool edge above the belt grooves contacts the top of the belt ribs, the belt is excessively worn.

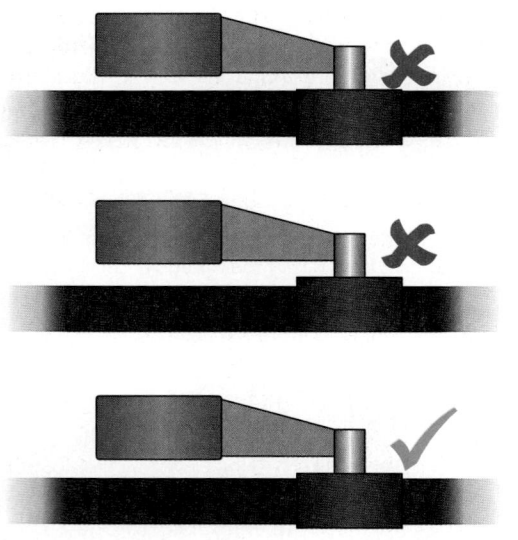

FIGURE 18-58 A correctly aligned and installed belt must be centered over the pulley when the engine is stopped.

Belt and Pulley Alignment

When visually inspecting belts, the belt must have the same number of ribs or projections as the pulley has grooves. So, when replacing belts and verifying the number of ribs a belt should have, count the number of grooves, not V projections, on a pulley. The belt should be installed so that it is centered over a grooved pulley and no edges of the belt should extend beyond the pulley edge (**FIGURE 18-58**). A belt that is not centered indicates it was misaligned when installed or the pulleys are not parallel.

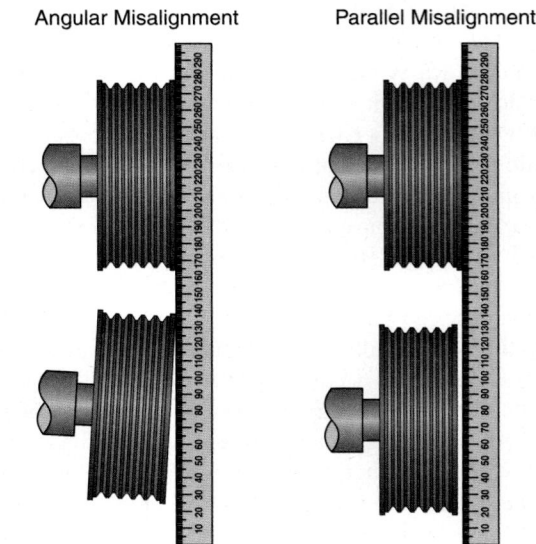

Angular Misalignment   Parallel Misalignment

FIGURE 18-59 Misaligned pulleys cause premature belt wear and noise.

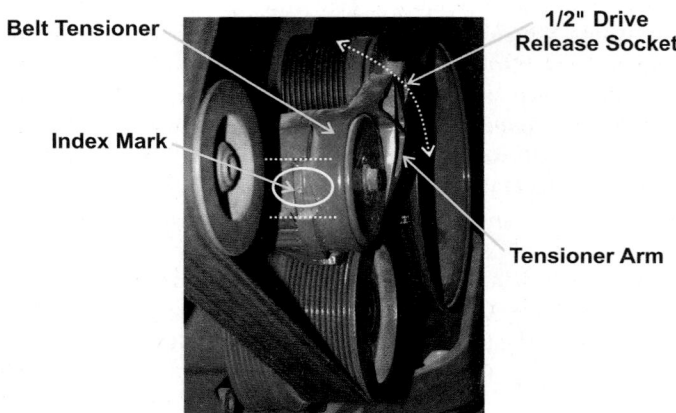

Belt Tensioner   1/2" Drive
                              Release Socket

Index Mark

                              Tensioner Arm

FIGURE 18-60 Location of the index mark on a belt tensioner for a new and correctly installed belt

Pulleys can be misaligned when bearings are worn or if a pulley is not installed correctly. Pulley misalignment can be categorized as a parallel misalignment or an angular misalignment. When worn out or incorrectly installed, a combination of both conditions exists (**FIGURE 18-59**). Alignment can be checked with a straight edge. When the pulleys are spun after a belt is removed, they should spin freely without any roughness and no noise should be detected.

Belt Tensioner Inspection

Excessive belt and/or pulley wear, or the use of an incorrect belt size, can be indicated by the position of the belt tensioner. An index mark of the tensioner should be centered between the maximum and minimum tensioner stops when the belt is correctly installed and is not worn out (**FIGURE 18-60**).

When installed correctly, the belt should allow the index mark on the tensioner arm to be centered between the maximum and minimum bumpers. The tensioner should sit squarely with the belt installed. If it does not, a bushing or bearing is likely defective, and the tensioner must be replaced. A weak tensioner spring allows excessive belt vibration and slippage. If the belts squeal due to a weak tensioner or combined with a worn belt, spraying water over the belts while the engine is running minimizes belt squeal. Both the tensioner and belt should be replaced together (**FIGURE 18-61**).

Charging System Output Test

Vehicle-charging systems are voltage-regulated, which means that the alternator tries to maintain the set-point voltage to maintain a fully charged battery, while also supplying the electrical systems demands. As electrical system loads increase, the alternator voltage begins to drop, which is explained by the electrical power law (Power = Volts × Amps). The voltage regulator senses this voltage drop and increases the magnetic field strength of the rotor, which in turn increases output amperage while trying to maintain the set-point voltage. If the current flow to the rotor is kept below the maximum threshold the regulator can supply, both high amperage output and set-point voltage can be maintained. If current demands by the electrical system increase further, the output voltage eventually drops after the regulator saturates the rotor field with maximum current trying to maintain set-point voltage. If the electrical system's current demands increase even further, the battery supplements the alternator's output current. To test the alternator's capabilities, both its maximum output amperage and set-point voltage are measured separately and compared with specifications.

Set-Point Voltage Measurement

Set-point voltage measurement is the first test performed when testing the alternator's performance. This measurement should be made with a DC voltmeter connected to the alternator B+ terminal and its case. An induction-type amp clamp connected to the alternator output cable can be installed, too, but is not necessary for checking set-point voltage, except to verify the

low current drawn by the electrical system. Before measuring the set point, the batteries should be verified to be fully charged. Electrical loads should be switched off and the engine operated above idle at between 1000 and 1500 rpm. If measured, the alternator output should be 20 amps or less, and the set-point voltage should normally measure between 13.8 and 14.4 volts for a 12-volt system (**FIGURE 18-62**). Most 12-volt systems are ideally close to 14.1, which is 2.35 volts per cell. Twenty-four-volt systems should charge between 27.8 and 28.4 volts. If the voltage of either 12- or 24-volt systems is below this range, and the voltage regulator is not adjustable, the alternator is likely defective. However, if the alternator voltage reads above 15.5 volts, the alternator is overcharging the batteries. Before condemning the alternator, the remote sense circuit should be checked to see whether it is connected to battery voltage. Unless the batteries are deeply discharged, the vehicle headlights should not dim when returning to idle from fast idle if the alternator is operating satisfactorily.

Standard Output Amperage Test

An alternator's output performance is tested under heavy electrical load and measured while the engine is at 1500 rpm and the batteries are ideally in a full state of charge. A standard recommended test uses a carbon-pile variable resister to apply a heavy load to the alternator. A manually operated knob on the carbon pile can vary the electrical load, or automated sequence of loads, applied to the alternator through the resister. While a load is applied, the alternator output amperage and voltage are measured. There are variations of this test that individual

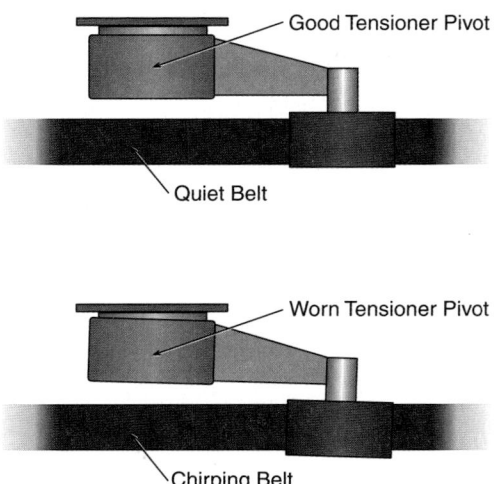

FIGURE 18-61 A good tensioner sits squarely over the drive belt. A worn tensioner bushing or bearing misaligns with the belt and causes belt chirp.

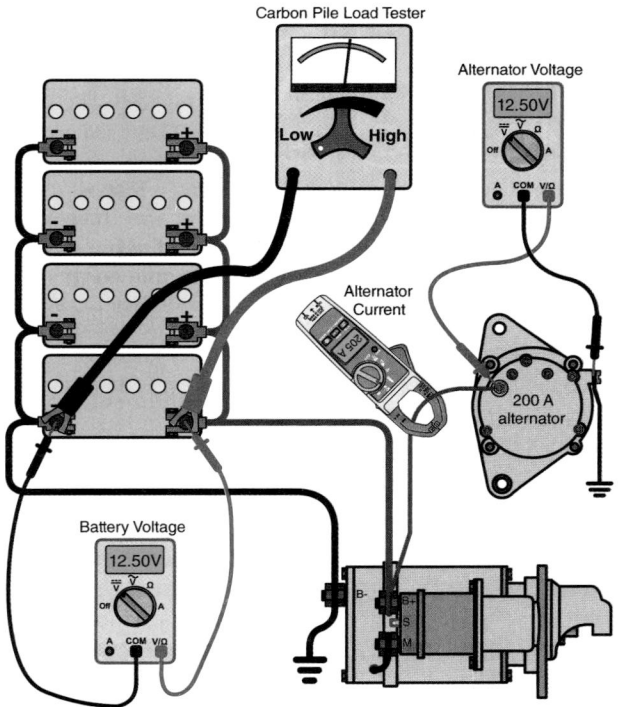

FIGURE 18-62 Connection points on a charging system for testing charging system output, voltage set point, and alternator cable voltage drop.

manufacturers prefer, but the purpose of all of them is essentially to determine how close an alternator's maximum output amperage is to its rated capacity. The most common procedure involves clamping the load tester's heavy cables directly to the alternator B+ terminal and ground, or the batteries. An amp clamp is placed over the alternator output cable to measure amperage during the test, while a voltmeter is connected to measure the alternator's output voltage. With the engine rpm again brought to 1500 for a diesel engine, the electrical system is progressively loaded for a brief time using the carbon pile until it drops to 12.5 volts. At 12.5 volts, the maximum amperage output from the alternator is also measured. Output amperage should generally be within 90% to 110% of the alternator's maximum rating. This means that a 200-amp alternator should deliver at least 180 amps.

External Field-Regulated Output Test

Because externally field-controlled alternators using multifunction voltage regulators may sense the sudden heavy load applied by a load tester as a potential fault in the electrical system, some voltage regulators may stop the alternator from charging to protect the alternator and vehicle from damage or a fire. In this case, another test is commonly performed that measures alternator output at 70% of its maximum output rating. With the engine running at high idle (up to 2000 rpm), the carbon-pile load is progressively increased until the amperage measurement reaches 70% of the alternator rated amperage (e.g., 300 amps x 0.70 = 210 amps). See **TABLE 18-3**.

With this load applied, the battery voltage is again measured. What is different in this test is the battery voltage should not fall more than 1.0 volts below the set-point voltage. If the alternator's output voltage difference between the set point and voltage at 70% load is more than 1.0 volt, the alternator is considered defective and should be replaced.

Voltage Regulator Testing

A failed voltage regulator prevents an alternator from charging or even overcharging. Since most alternators use internal voltage regulators, the entire assembly is replaced, even if only the regulator is defective. However, the high cost of new alternators on late-model vehicles and OEM warranty claim policies may

require testing and replacing the regulator to repair a charging system complaint. To differentiate between a defective regulator and the current-generating section of an alternator, a full-field test of the alternator is performed. This means that the voltage regulator is bypassed, and full-battery voltage is supplied briefly to the rotor slip rings. Before performing this procedure, a good practice is to first determine the type of alternator-regulator circuit.

"A" circuit alternators ground one brush to full-field because the other brush is supplied positive battery voltage. In some Delco alternators, grounding one brush is done by passing a screwdriver through the "D" tab at the back of the alternator (**FIGURE 18-63**). With the screwdriver against the alternator frame and the other end on a tab of the voltage regulator, the regulator is bypassed. A working alternator begins to generate current. A voltmeter connected to the alternator is used to measure output. If voltage rises, the regulator is defective and can be replaced, instead of replacing the entire alternator.

"B" circuits use a jumper wire connected to battery positive to full-field the alternator. Isolated circuits use two jumper wires. Note: a functioning regulator is required for CAN-controlled alternators to provide diagnostic information needed to diagnose alternator problems. If current output does not rise after **full fielding**, it may indicate one of the following conditions:

- A shorted, open, or grounded rotor coil
- Stator windings shorted, open, or grounded
- Rectifier bridge shorted, open, or grounded

To perform a charging system output test, follow the steps in **SKILL DRILL 18-2**.

▶ TECHNICIAN TIP

The battery, or battery terminals, should never be removed when the engine is running. Disconnecting battery terminals on an alternator-equipped vehicle may damage the alternator and sensitive electronic equipment fitted to the vehicle.

TABLE 18-3 Applied Carbon-Pile Load for 70% Output Rating Test

70% Alternator Output Test	
Alternator Rating	70% Applied Load
135	95
160	112
185	130
200	140
240	168
270	189
275	193
300	210

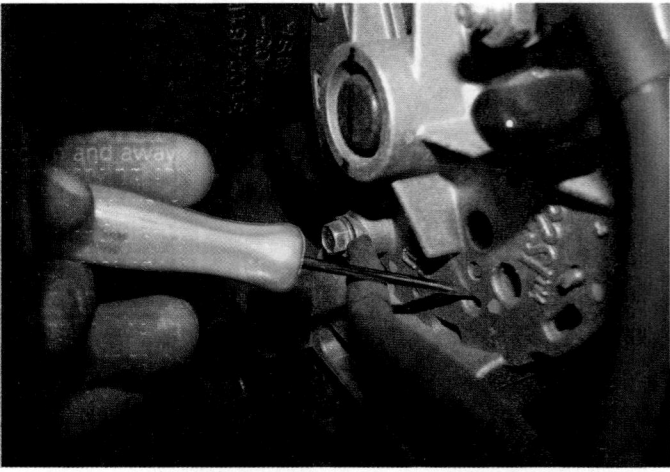

FIGURE 18-63 The D-shaped tab allows access to an internal circuit to bypass the voltage regulator. A tab on the regulator is grounded against the case.

SKILL DRILL 18-2 Performing a Charging System Output Test

1. Connect a charging system load tester to the battery with the red lead to the positive post, the black lead to the negative post, and the amps clamp around the alternator output wire.

2. Start the engine, turn off all accessories, and measure the alternator set-point voltage at around 1500 rpm. The set-point voltage is the highest voltage the system achieves once the battery is charged, which means it places little load on the alternator. An ammeter reading less than about 20–30 amps when the amps clamp is around the alternator output cable indicates the battery is charged. Typical regulated voltage specifications are wider than they used to be due to the ability of the electrical system ECM or remote sensing to adjust the output voltage for a wide range of conditions.

3. Operate the engine at about 1500 rpm and either manually or automatically load down the battery to 12.5 volts or 25 volts for a 24-volt system. Measure the alternator amperage output. This reading should be compared against the alternator's rated output. Normally, the maximum output should be within 10% of the alternator's maximum-rated capacity. A hot alternator may have slightly lower results.

Measuring Charging Circuit Voltage Drop

Undersized alternator cables, resistive connections, and the length of cable carrying high amperage causes a voltage drop between the alternator and the batteries. While remote sense circuits can compensate for most of this drop, undercharging can still result. Alternator output can increase too much, making the alternator work harder if it incorrectly senses battery voltage is too low due to a resistive alternator cable.

Voltage drop between the alternator and batteries can be checked by measuring the battery voltage and alternator output voltage at the alternator. A carbon-pile load tester is connected to the batteries to load the alternator to 75% of its rated output amperage. To avoid a false reading in cable voltage drop, it is important for the current to pass through the cables by connecting the carbon pile to the batteries, rather than the alternator. Depending on the output rating of the alternator, the typical voltage difference should be less than 0.25 volt in a 12-volt circuit or 0.50 volt in a 24-volt circuit. If it is not, all positive and ground wire cable connections should be cleaned and inspected. The cable diameter should also be measured and compared against specifications for the vehicle. If there are no loose or resistive connections and voltage drop is excessive, the cable diameter or routing may need to be changed. The specific area where voltage drop is taking place can be identified through a pinpoint test to check cable voltage drop. To isolate any cable voltage drop, follow the steps in **SKILL DRILLS 18-3** and **18-4**.

SKILL DRILL 18-3 Testing Charging Circuit Voltage Drop

1. The alternator cable voltage drop test is performed to test the alternator's positive cable for excessive resistance between the alternator and the batteries. With the engine running at 1500 rpm and the alternator loaded to 75% of its output capacity, voltage is measured at the alternator and batteries.

2. Set the digital voltmeter to measure DC voltage and select min/max, if available. Connect the positive lead of the meter to the output terminal of the alternator and the negative meter lead to the positive post of the battery. Extra-length leads may be required. The positive lead is connected to the positive battery post because, during the cable voltage drop test, the alternator B+ output terminal voltage is higher voltage than the positive battery terminal. A polarity indicator warning does not appear on the meter during the test if the meter is connected this way.

SKILL DRILL 18-3 Testing Charging Circuit Voltage Drop (Continued)

3. Start the engine and bring the engine to 1500 rpm. Alternatively, switch on as many electrical loads as possible. Observe and record the maximum voltage measured by the voltmeter. This is the measured B+ output cable voltage drop or loss.

4. Move the leads to measure the voltage drop on the ground side of the charging circuit by placing the negative probe on the alternator case and the positive probe on the negative terminal of the battery. With the engine running at 1500 rpm and the circuit still loaded, observe and record the maximum voltage drop for the ground circuit.

5. Add both the B+ cable loss and ground circuit voltage drop together to obtain the total voltage drop for the charging circuit. If the measurements are excessive, measure smaller sections of each part of the circuit with the voltmeter the same way to isolate or pinpoint the resistance.

6. If the voltage drop is over 0.5 volt and the drop occurs over the entire length of the alternator cable, replace the cable with one having a larger diameter recommended according to the amperage carried by the cable and length of the cable, or add a second cable.

SKILL DRILL 18-4 Inspecting, Repairing, or Replacing Connectors and Wires of Charging Circuits

1. Identify the alternator model by examining the tag on the alternator. Locate and follow the appropriate procedure and wiring diagram in the service manual.

2. Move the vehicle into the shop, apply the parking brakes, and chock the vehicle wheels. Observe lock-out tag-out (LOTO) procedures.

3. If the vehicle has a manual transmission, place it in "neutral." If it has an automatic transmission, place it in "park" or "neutral."

4. Trace the wiring harness from the alternator to the battery and around the engine compartment.

5. Check the harness and connectors for wear, damage, or corrosion. Check that it is securely clipped and insulated from rubbing on sharp metal chassis parts and the engine.

6. Compare the alternator terminal designations with the wires that are connected to verify the wiring is connected to the correct designated terminal.

7. Verify current is supplied to the remote sense, ignition terminal, and any warning lamp terminal when the key is switched on.

8. Disconnect the battery negative cable if repairs are necessary.

9. Repair damaged areas with replacement cables or connectors. Ensure all harnesses are secured to prevent abrasion or damage from vibration.

10. Reconnect all harness plugs and secure all connections.

11. Reconnect the battery negative cable.

12. Check repair by visual inspection and running the vehicle.

13. Perform a charging system output test and set-point voltage check to validate any repairs were correctly made.

Removing, Inspecting, and Replacing an Alternator

LO 18-6 Outline the steps involved in removing, disassembly, testing repair, and reinstallation of alternators.

During charging system tests, low voltage and current output problems may indicate a defective alternator. If an alternator is defective, it needs to be replaced. Together the rotors, brushes, stators, rectifier bridges, and cooling fans of the alternator work to create magnetic fields, produce current, and charge the system. When any one of these components fails due to heat damage or wear, other components may fail shortly, too. So, it is more practical to replace the entire alternator than to simply repair it. Replacement alternators must usually have the drive pulley transferred from the defective alternator to the replacement alternator (**FIGURE 18-64**).

To remove, inspect, and replace an alternator, follow the steps in **SKILL DRILL 18-5**.

Testing Stators

Stators, like rotors, are not normally serviced in a repair facility. However, if an alternator is repaired, stators can be visually

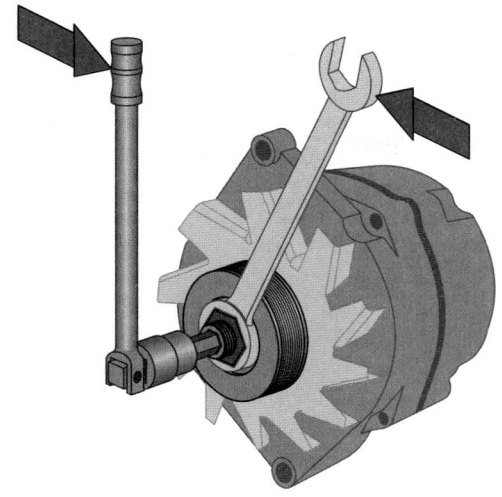

FIGURE 18-64 To remove and transfer an alternator pulley, the rotor shaft is held using a hex head socket while the retaining nut is loosened.

inspected for burnt, cut, or nicked windings and damaged frame laminations. Winding junction points are checked to ensure they are solidly connected. Continuity should exist between all phases of the stator's winding connection points. Uneven resistance between any two phases produces excessive AC ripple and low alternator output. At remanufacturing facilities,

an amperage draw test of each winding is performed to check the resistance and electrical balance between each section of winding. No continuity should exist between the windings and alternator frame. As illustrated in **FIGURE 18-65**, a stator can be tested for short circuits and open circuits. A leakage to ground test evaluates winding insulation and is also known as an insulation stress test. Stress testing involves passing high-voltage, low-amperage current through the windings. Any breakdown in insulation is detected when continuity exists between the windings and frame (**FIGURE 18-66**).

Rectifier Diode Problems

Heat can cause premature failures of diodes (**FIGURE 18-67**). Additional cooling of rectifier bridges can be achieved using heavier diodes attached to heat sinks, or by connecting more diodes in parallel so that six, rather than three, pairs perform the job of current rectification.

Another problem with alternator diodes occurs when the diodes become open or shorted. An internally shorted positive diode causes a parasitic drain of battery current through the alternator when the engine is not running. While only a single diode may fail, a shorted diode causes a disproportionate loss of up to 67% of alternator output because it interferes with the rectification of current from two winding phases. Shorted diodes can be detected with an AC voltmeter measurement of alternator output. Generally, any more than 0.4–0.7 volt of AC superimposed over the DC output indicates that AC current

SKILL DRILL 18-5 Removing, Inspecting, and Replacing an Alternator

1. Locate and follow the appropriate procedure in the service manual.
2. Move the vehicle into the workshop, apply the parking brakes, and chock the vehicle wheels. Observe LOTO procedures.
3. If the vehicle has a manual transmission, place it in "neutral." If it has an automatic transmission, place it in "park" or "neutral."
4. Disconnect the battery from the electrical system and place the batteries on a charger.
5. Release the alternator tensioner by placing either a square drive socket ½" or ¾" drive into the tensioner arm to rotate it. Install a lock pin in the tensioner arm if it uses one.

6. Remove and inspect the alternator belt, idler pulleys, and tensioner.
7. Disconnect the wires at the connector on the alternator. Make a note of the location and any special insulating washers.
8. Loosen and remove the alternator mounting bolts.
9. Lift the alternator out of vehicle.
10. Transfer the alternator drive pulley to the new alternator.
11. Bolt the new alternator onto the engine and reconnect the wiring.
12. Reinstall the belt or its replacement, if needed. Check the alignment of the pulleys and belt over each pulley; verify alignment after running the engine.
13. If required, adjust belt tension using belt tension gauge.
14. Reconnect the batteries and check the state of charge. Deeply discharged batteries can burn out a new alternator.
15. Start the vehicle and verify that the alternator is charging. Recheck belt alignment.
16. If the alternator has only a single wire connecting it to the batteries and does not initially charge, momentarily jump the alternator "R" terminal to battery + to magnetize the rotor.

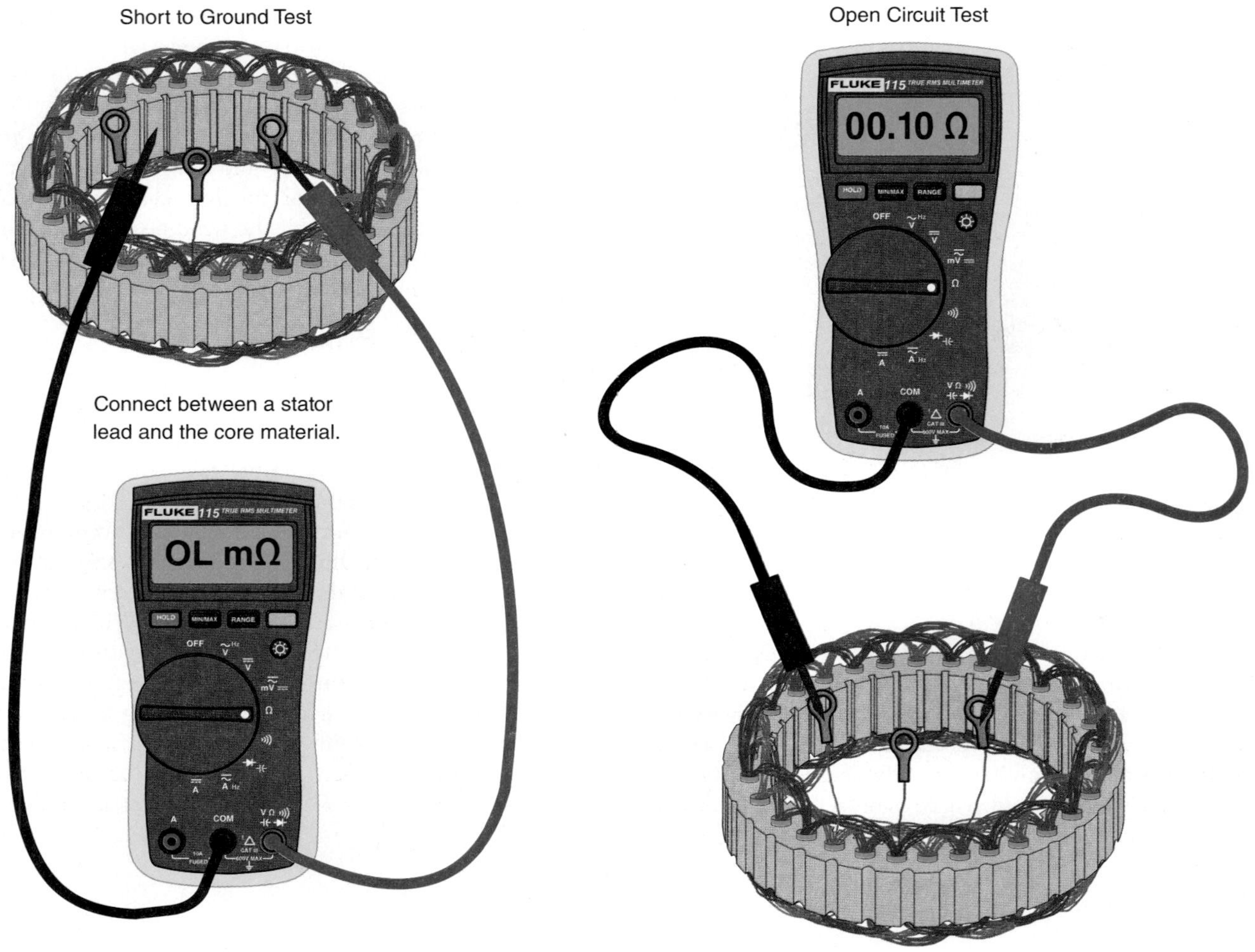

Short to Ground Test

Open Circuit Test

Connect between a stator
lead and the core material.

FIGURE 18-65 A stator can be tested for short and open circuits.

FIGURE 18-66 An insulation stress tester used to inspect stator windings for leakage to the frame caused by a break-down of insulation. High-voltage, low-amperage current passes through the windings while current leakage is checked.

FIGURE 18-67 Rectifier in an alternator housing. Note the fins on the heat sink to remove heat.

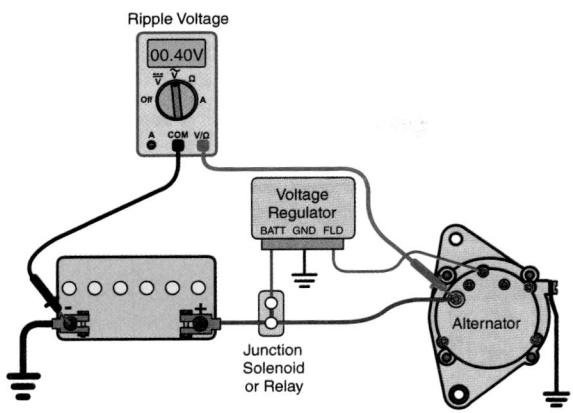

FIGURE 18-68 AC ripple caused by defective diodes or unbalanced stator windings can be detected by measuring alternator output with an AC voltmeter. Ripple is generally less than 0.25 volt.

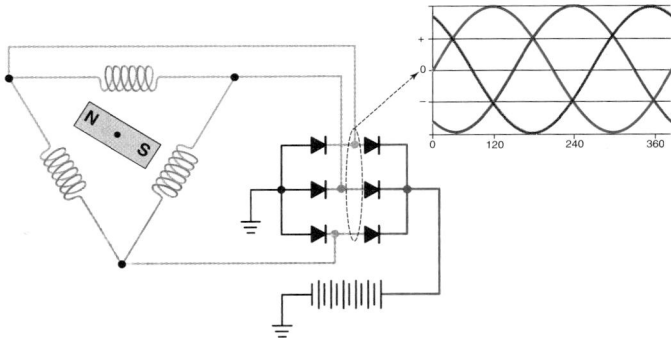

FIGURE 18-69 Three phases—not rectified.

is passing through a shorted, or otherwise defective, diode (**FIGURE 18-68**). Most purpose-built diagnostic equipment for charging systems have a diode ripple feature that detects this large AC waveform and illuminates a diagnostic light on the machine. Graphing the alternator output with a graphing meter or oscilloscope and carefully observing the pattern also can identify defective diodes. An open diode does not cause as much of a loss of output as a shorted diode—only up to 33% of output—but does cause increased fluctuations or pulsing of DC output current.

When measuring alternator output using an AC (not DC) voltmeter, AC can normally be measured. An alternator with output voltage fluctuations—between 13.9 to 14.2 volts DC, for example—produces a 0.3-volt alternating current. AC ripple is suppressed by a capacitor inside the alternator and is also absorbed by the batteries, if they are in good condition and have not become excessively resistive due to age or sulfation. If AC ripple is too great, it leads to radio noise and electromagnetic interference (EMI) in many electronic control devices (**FIGURE 18-69**). For example, an ECM may fail to function correctly, causing the engine to run rough. An antilock brake system (ABS) module may even generate fault codes, while the speedometer, tachometer, and other instrument gauges bounce erratically.

Wrap-Up

Ready for Review

▶ Both DC generators and alternators produce electricity by relative movement of conductors in a magnetic field. The key difference between an alternator and a DC generator is which component rotates or moves to generate electricity.
▶ The charging system provides electrical energy for all the electrical components on the vehicle. The main parts of the charging system include the battery, the alternator, the voltage regulator (which may be integrated into the alternator), a charge warning light or voltmeter, and wiring that completes the circuits.
▶ The alternator converts mechanical energy into electrical energy by electromagnetic induction. The magnetic field in the alternator's rotor can be varied to change the alternator's output current.
▶ A single-phase stator has a single winding, which creates a single sine wave. In a typical alternator, there are three separate coils of wire composing the stator. Each winding is referred to as a phase.

▶ Alternators have a built-in maximum current limitation due to the counter electromotive force (CEMF) in the stator coils. The faster an alternator turns, the more CEMF is generated to resist increased alternator output.
▶ Brushless alternators have greater service life than alternators with brushes.
▶ In single-wire alternators, an initial residual magnetic field in the rotor is needed to initiate the process of generating electricity. Initial rotor field excitation can be either internal or external.
▶ Wye and Delta windings produce three-phase AC, but voltage and amperage outputs differ. The Wye configuration produces higher voltage at lower rotor speeds. Delta-wound stators are more commonly used on diesel engines because they are more efficient and produce higher amperage output than a similarly sized Wye-wound stator at low speed.
▶ Alternators produce more amperage at lower speeds and produce it more efficiently than DC generators.

Alternating current—not direct current—is produced inside an alternator.

► To change AC to DC, alternators use a rectifier assembly consisting of two diodes for every phase of the stator winding. The P and N material of the diodes is arranged so that three diodes connected to the B+ and three to the negative ground. This diode arrangement prevents the battery from discharging through the alternator and ensures one-way flow of current out of the alternator only when it is charging at a higher voltage than the batteries.

► Positive and negative sets of diodes in the rectifier bridge prevent the battery from discharging through the alternator when it is not charging.

► Alternators' maximum voltage output, called the set-point voltage, is controlled by a voltage regulator. The voltage regulator controls current flow through the rotor to change output amperage and charging voltage.

► External field-regulated voltage regulators are controlled by the vehicle's electrical system control module. These regulators have multifunctional capabilities and can supply not only charging system-related fault codes, but additional information about the alternator to the electrical system.

► A significant amount of heat is produced within the alternator from the rectifier, stator, and rotor windings. The two main types of cooling systems used on heavy-duty vehicle alternators are air and oil cooling.

► Alternators can be driven by a pulley or direct drive through a gear.

► Vehicles needing extra high current output at idle, or those with extra electrical loads, can use two or more alternators.

► When diagnosing charging system problems, always start with the battery. A weak or dead battery, corroded battery cable connections, and/or damaged or worn components may cause a no-crank or slow-crank problem.

► Alternators are tested by measuring the maximum set-point voltage and maximum charging amperage when a load applied to it lowers its charging voltage to 12.5 volts.

► On alternators with external field regulation of the internal multifunction voltage regulator, an alternator must supply 70% of its rated output without its set point falling below 1.0 volt.

► An AC ripple test can determine whether the alternator has defective diodes or a defective stator winding, since the DC output current more severely fluctuates or pulses. AC ripple is measured with an AC voltmeter.

► Newer EPDM serpentine belts driving alternators are difficult to visually inspect and require a belt gauge to evaluate for wear.

► Belt tensioners and pulleys must also be inspected for correct alignment, wear, or damage when inspecting and testing the alternator.

► An alternator output cable should be checked for voltage drop if the batteries are undercharged.

Key Terms

AC ripple A pattern produced by DC voltage fluctuations from the alternator that creates differences between the peak voltage and the minimum voltages of overlapping AC sine waves.

Delta windings Stator windings in which the windings are connected in the shape of a triangle or the Greek letter Delta.

EPDM belts A drive-belt material that is resistant to damage from heat and stretching.

full fielding A test procedure that bypasses the voltage regulator to determine whether the alternator can produce output current.

load-dumping A feature that allows temporary suppression of high-voltage spikes when electrical loads are suddenly removed from the alternator.

Overrunning Alternator Decoupler (OAD) A pulley that uses an internal spring and clutch system that allows it to rotate freely in one direction and provide limited, spring-like movement in the other direction.

parallel alternators The practice of connecting alternators in parallel to provide higher charging voltage at idle with more available amperage.

rectification A process of converting alternating current (AC) into direct current (DC).

remote sensing An alternator voltage regulator that has an input circuit with a direct connection to the battery positive terminal. It is used to provide an optimal level for charging voltage.

residual magnetism The small amount of magnetism left on the rotor after it is initially magnetized by the coil windings' magnetic field.

self-exciting alternator An alternator that relies on the residual magnetism found in the rotor to produce current and switch on the voltage regulator to supply additional current to the rotor.

sensing The voltage reference point the alternator uses for regulation of the output.

Transient Voltage Suppression (TVS) diodes Specialized diodes in the rectifier bridge that become resistive, rather than conductive, at a specific voltage level.

Wye windings Stator windings of an induction motor or alternator in which one end of each phase winding is connected together at a single central point.

Review Questions

1. Maximum charging system output amperage an alternator can produce at its highest speed is limited by:
   a. The voltage regulator
   b. Counter Electromotive Force (CEMF)
   c. Magnetic field strength of the rotor
   d. Heat-related electrical resistance in the stator windings

2. How many diodes are required to rectify one complete phase of stator AC output into DC?
   a. One
   b. Two
   c. Four
   d. Six

3. Which of the following components determines the maximum potential output amperage of an alternator?
   a. The stator
   b. The rotor
   c. The rectifier bridge
   d. The voltage regulator

4. What effect does increasing the flow of electric current through the rotor winding have on the charging system?
   a. It increases only output amperage.
   b. It increases only set-point voltage.
   c. It increases the strength of the rotor's magnetic field.
   d. It increases charging system voltage.

5. What effect does heavy electrical loads plus a discharged set of batteries have on the observed measurement of alternator output?
   a. High output amperage, high charging voltage
   b. High output amperage, low charging voltage
   c. Low amperage, high charging voltage
   d. Low amperage, low voltage meter readings

6. What is the purpose of alternators using remote sense technology in HD vehicles?
   a. It changes the alternator set-point voltage to ensure the batteries are charged at an optimal rate.
   b. It increases charging voltage when the alternator and batteries are cold.
   c. It enables a vehicle's electrical control module to change the set-point voltage.
   d. It enables each battery in a battery bank to receive an identical charge voltage.

7. If a voltage regulator can adjust its set-point voltage according to temperature, which of the following is correct?
   a. The charging voltage increases as temperature decreases.
   b. The charging voltage decreases as temperature decreases.
   c. The charging voltage increases as temperature increases.
   d. The charging voltage remains constant, regardless of temperature. changes

8. Consider a 200-amp alternator in a 12-volt system. When tested, its set-point voltage was measured to be 14.1 volts at 20 amps. Its maximum output amperage was 130 amps at 12.5 volts. What is the correct service recommendation?
   a. Charge batteries and retest
   b. Repair a poor ground
   c. Replace the voltage regulator
   d. Replace the alternator

9. Which of the following conditions is caused by a shorted diode in the rectifier bridge of an alternator?
   a. Parasitic drain of battery charge
   b. Overcharging of the batteries
   c. Burned out light bulbs and damaged LED lights
   d. Burned alternator cable wiring

10. Which of the following ratios is the most typical drive-pulley ratio for an alternator used with on-highway heavy-duty diesel engines?
    a. 2:1
    b. 3:1
    c. 5:1
    d. 7:1

ASE Technician A/Technician B Style Questions

1. Technician A says that today, the average 12-volt electrical system loads for a late-model highway tractor with an 84-amp average electrical load uses a 130-amp alternator. Technician B says that a much larger alternator than that is necessary to save fuel, last longer, and supply peak electrical loads at idle. Who is correct?
   a. Technician A
   b. Technician B
   c. Both Technician A and Technician B
   d. Neither Technician A nor Technician B

2. Technician A says that an alternator belt used on today's engines needs to be checked for wear using a belt gauge tool. Technician B says that an alternator belt on a late-model vehicle needs to be checked for cracks and missing chunks. Who is correct?
   a. Technician A
   b. Technician B
   c. Both Technician A and Technician B
   d. Neither Technician A nor Technician B

3. Technicians A and B are inspecting the charging system of a truck and hear a chirping-like belt noise. Technician A says the noise is most likely caused by a worn belt that is slipping. Technician B says that the noise is probably caused by a misaligned belt tensioner with a worn bearing. Who is correct?
   a. Technician A
   b. Technician B
   c. Both Technician A and Technician B
   d. Neither Technician A nor Technician B

4. After switching on all the lights and blower motors of a school bus, a belt squeal is heard. Technician A says that the belt tensioner spring could be broken. Technician B says that the belt is most likely worn. Who is correct?
   a. Technician A
   b. Technician B
   c. Both Technician A and Technician B
   d. Neither Technician A nor Technician B

5. The batteries of a truck are frequently going dead. The rear section of the alternator is also found to be very hot to touch after the batteries are discharged. Technician A says that the voltage regulator has remained energized and discharged the batteries through the rotor winding. Technician B says that one or more diodes in the rectifier bridge is likely shorted. Who is correct?
   a. Technician A
   b. Technician B
   c. Both Technician A and Technician B
   d. Neither Technician A nor Technician B

6. Technician A says that the reason the batteries of a delivery truck with an electric tailgate are undercharged is due to excessive current drawn by the tailgate. Technician B says that the problem could be corrected by adding a remote sense wire to connect the alternator and batteries. Who is correct?
   a. Technician A
   b. Technician B
   c. Both Technician A and Technician B
   d. Neither Technician A nor Technician B

7. Technician A says that a charging voltage of 16.0 volts for a few minutes after an engine starts on cold mornings is normal. Technician B says that a charging voltage of 16.0 volts for a few minutes is likely caused by a poor ground or defective voltage regulator. Who is correct?
   a. Technician A
   b. Technician B
   c. Both Technician A and Technician B
   d. Neither Technician A nor Technician B

8. Technician A found a 300-amp alternator of a late-model truck stopped charging during a charging system output test and said the alternator was defective. After loading the alternator to 225 amps, he said it would no longer charge until the engine was shut off and restarted. Technician B says that was normal and recommended loading the alternator to no more than 210 amps and measuring the charging voltage at that load. Who is correct?
   a. Technician A
   b. Technician B
   c. Both Technician A and Technician B
   d. Neither Technician A nor Technician B

9. After disconnecting the alternator of an engine that was running rough and had low power, normal engine operation was restored. Technician A says that the alternator likely has excessive AC voltage ripple interfering with the operation of the engine's electronic control system. Technician B said the presence of electromagnetic interference (EMI) from voltage ripple could be detected and measured with a DC voltmeter. Who is correct?
   a. Technician A
   b. Technician B
   c. Both Technician A and Technician B
   d. Neither Technician A nor Technician B

10. Technician A says that a voltage drop of 0.75 volt was measured in the positive lead of the alternator cable and requires a cable replacement with a larger diameter cable. Technician B says the voltage drop is acceptable because the alternator charging voltage provided to the batteries is 14.1 volts. Who is correct?
   a. Technician A
   b. Technician B
   c. Both Technician A and Technician B
   d. Neither Technician A nor Technician B

CHAPTER 19

Electrical Wiring and Circuit Diagrams

Learning Objectives

- **LO 19-1** Identify and describe requirements, features, and characteristics of electrical wiring and connectors.
- **LO 19-2** Identify and describe the types, construction, and repair techniques for wiring connectors.

- **LO 19-3** Identify and describe wiring failures and repair techniques.
- **LO 19-4** Identify and describe types and features of electrical system wiring diagrams.

You Are the Technician

After a positive battery cable grounded out near the alternator, high-amperage current melted the cable and burned though several other nearby wiring harnesses, damaging them. Several of the other harnesses also grounded through the battery cable when they were melting. Because the vehicle was relatively new, the insurance adjuster has requested the vehicle be repaired by replacing or repairing the harness, as necessary.

After inspecting the damage, you've determined there are two possible directions for the repairs to take. One approach is to replace the harnesses, as the vehicle has a modular harness system. Several major harnesses would have to be disconnected and removed and a new one reinstalled. The other approach is to replace only damaged sections of the harnesses. This second approach would be less labor-intensive, and the material cost would be substantially lower. There are a few other factors that will also guide your final decisions, but as you weigh them, consider the following:

1. Outline the various factors that will guide the selection of materials for replacing sections of the harnesses. Include information about the features of the wiring, connectors, splices, and so on.
2. Outline in the correct sequence you should take to properly make multiple splices to replace wiring in a major wiring harness.
3. Identify and list the tools and any other resources you will need to make proper repairs of the wiring harness.

Introduction

Wires and wiring harnesses connect components in the vehicle's electrical system, and as such, they need to be kept in good condition, free of any damage or corrosion. They carry the electrical power and signals through the vehicle to control virtually all of the systems on a vehicle. As technology in vehicles has increased, so has the number of wires and cables installed on these vehicles. Although wireless communication is being used in some vehicle security, entertainment, and tire pressure monitoring systems, wires are still the dominant signal carriers in a vehicle. This chapter covers basics about wiring, including wiring requirements, how wires are selected, sized, and coded, basic wiring repair, and types of wiring diagrams.

Electrical System Wiring

LO 19-1 Identify and describe requirements, features, and characteristics of electrical wiring and connectors.

Electrical wiring has numerous requirements specific to heavy-duty vehicles. Wiring is sized and color- and number-coded to ensure the proper wire is used for the specific application.

Wiring Requirements

Because conductors carry electron flow through the electrical system, wiring is a critical component in the electrical system. When selecting wires or cables for applications, consideration needs to be given to the following factors:

- *The amount of amperage flowing through a circuit.* Smaller wires become more resistant and heat up as amperage increases. Larger wiring increases cost and weight.
- *The operating environment.* The type of wire differs, depending on whether it is used in the engine compartment, inside the engine, inside or outside the cab, or along the chassis. Exposure to oil, grease, fuel, abrasion, and the elements changes the requirements for electrical wiring.
- *Circuit identification.* The complexities of chassis wiring require the use of color coding and numbering of circuits for assembling and connecting harnesses, as well as to simplify repairs.

Wire Sizing and Voltage Drop

Increasing amperage through a wire conductor beyond a threshold cross-sectional area increases resistance, as predicted by Joule's Law of Heating. Other names given to this effect, which can be mathematically predicted, are Ohmic or resistive heating. Circuits carrying too much current for a given wire diameter, length, and time can overheat, which, in turn, increases circuit resistance. Anyone who has ever witnessed a circuit with a short to ground knows how quickly a conductor carrying maximum amperage heats, smokes, glows, and burns, to the point where any nearby wiring or flammable materials can catch fire.

This principle of Ohmic heating is also used to identify resistance in circuits because points where current flow is throttled heat up as collisions between electrons take place. Using wires that are too small in diameter may also cause a fire. Ohm's law predicts voltage drop using the formula:

$$V_{drop} = \text{Amperage} \times \text{Resistance}$$

This means a conductor 100' long with 0.5 ohms of resistance required to carry 10 amps of current in a 12-volt circuit sees a voltage drop of five volts (**FIGURE 19-1**). Available voltage at the end of the conductor is:

$$12 - 5 = 7 \text{ volts}$$

> ► **TECHNICIAN TIP**
>
> Using wires that are too small in diameter to carry a given amount of amperage may cause a fire. To prevent damage to wiring, wiring harness, and a catastrophic fire, it is important to correctly calculate and select the correct diameter of wire for the expected amperage a circuit is to carry. Equally important is using the correct amperage rating for the circuit protection device (fuse, circuit breakers, fusible links, and virtual fuses) used to protect the circuit's wiring from excessive current flow. Anytime a new device is added to a circuit, always increase the wire size along with the rating for circuit protection if the device can potentially increase the maximum anticipated amperage carried by the conductors.

The same circuit carrying only five amps of current drops only 2.5 volts, resulting in 9.5 available volts. Therefore, the diameter of wire for a circuit is based on the amount of amperage and the length of the circuit. Longer circuits and higher

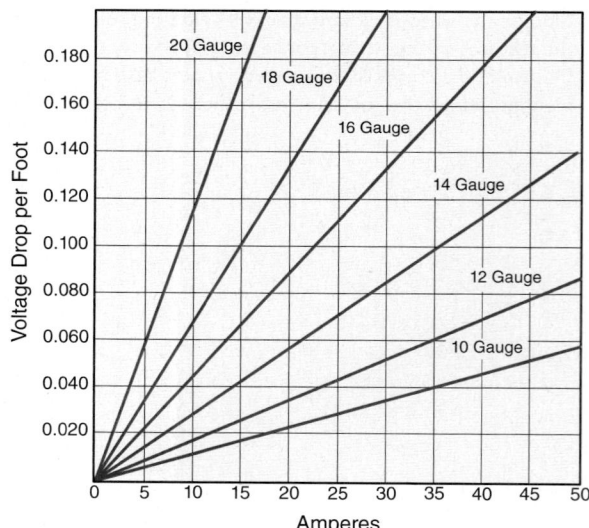

FIGURE 19-1 Wire diameter is dependent on the amount of amperage carried by a circuit and the length of the circuit—both insulated ground and positive. Note that a 24-volt circuit can carry twice the amperage as a 12-volt circuit for the same diameter wire.

TABLE 19-1 Total Footage of Wire from Power Source to the Most Distant Electric Lamp

24 v System	12 v System	10'	20'	30'	40'	50'	60'	70'	80'	90'	100'
2.0	1.0	18	18	18	18	18	18	18	18	18	18
3.0	1.5	18	18	18	18	18	18	18	18	18	18
4.0	2.0	18	18	18	18	18	18	18	16	16	16
6.0	3.0	18	18	18	18	18	16	16	16	14	14
8.0	4.0	18	18	18	16	16	16	14	14	14	12
10.0	5.0	18	18	18	16	14	14	14	12	12	12
12.0	6.0	18	18	16	16	14	14	12	12	12	12
14.0	7.0	18	18	16	14	14	12	12	12	10	10
16.0	8.0	18	18	16	14	12	12	12	10	10	10
20.0	10.0	18	16	14	12	12	12	10	10	10	10
22.0	11.0	18	16	14	12	12	10	10	10	10	8
24.0	12.0	18	16	14	12	12	10	10	10	8	8
30.0	15.0	18	16	12	12	10	10	10	8	8	8
36.0	18.0	16	14	12	10	10	8	8	8	8	8
40.0	20.0	16	14	12	10	10	8	8	8	8	6

(left axis label: Amperage Required)

circuit amperage require larger diameter wires. As shown in **TABLE 19-1**, as wire diameter increases, less voltage is dropped.

Two major classification systems for measuring wire diameter are the American Wire Gauge (AWG) system and the Metric Gauge system (**FIGURE 19-2**). Both systems measure the wire size only and not the wire and insulator. The AWG system is more than 100 years old and measures wire gauge in numbers from 0000 to 50. As the gauge number increases, the diameter of the wire decreases. A 0000 wire is approximately 0.5" diameter, while a 10 gauge is 0.102" in diameter. Using the AWG system, the wire diameter doubles for approximately every 3-gauge change. The gauges 00, 000, and 0000 are often used to measure battery cables and can also be written 2/0, 3/0, and 4/0, respectively.

The Metric Gauge scale measures the cross-sectional surface area of the wire and not its diameter. Sizes are rounded up to provide an even number for the wire size. For example, a 1 mm² wire is 0.823 mm², and a 2.080 mm² wire is 2.5 mm². In most wiring diagrams, metric-sized wire is specified in millimeters, rather than metric gauge diameter. As the diameter of the wire increases in the metric standard, the gauge also increases. This is opposite to the AWG standard, which uses a smaller gauge to indicate a larger diameter wire.

Wire Color Coding

Wire-coding systems are another useful feature of wiring to aid troubleshooting and service of electrical systems. Both colors and numbering systems designate wiring circuits, application, and even the routing of wires. The SAE also recommends color-coding for circuits. For example, the J560 trailer plug connector identifies seven colors used for each lighting circuit.

Wire color codes recommended by the International Organization for Standardization (ISO) are partially listed in **TABLE 19-2**. Note, these are only recommendations and manufacturers often use their own color codes.

A standardized set of abbreviations are used to designate wire colors in wiring diagrams (**FIGURE 19-3**). Wires may also have a second, or even a third, separate color used to help technicians trace a wire through large harnesses with similar colors. A second color is designated after a hyphen for the first color in a numbering scheme. For example, a blue wire with a white tracing stripe is BL-WH abbreviation if it is a solid tracer wire color. If the tracer is separated by hash marks, the designation is followed by an H or BL-WHH. If the tracer color is dotted rather than a hash mark, the designation is BL-WHD.

Wire Insulation: SAE J1128 Standard

The **SAE J1128 standard** and newer ISO 6722 standard specify the dimensions, test methods, and performance requirements for single-core primary wire intended for use in road vehicle applications. Primary wire is the term given to wire used in low-voltage applications under 60 volts. Secondary wire is the term given to wire carrying current higher than 60 volts. The SAE standard outlines the number of strands a wire should have, its temperature rating, and its resistance to chemicals and resistance to oxidation, in addition to many other wire and insulation specifications. Five common types of wire for use in bus, truck, and trailer applications are classified by their insulation. These include:

- **GPT (General Purpose Thermoplastic Wire)**—Has a PVC insulation jacket and is used for general connection wiring inside a cab. Temperature rating is 176°F (80°C).

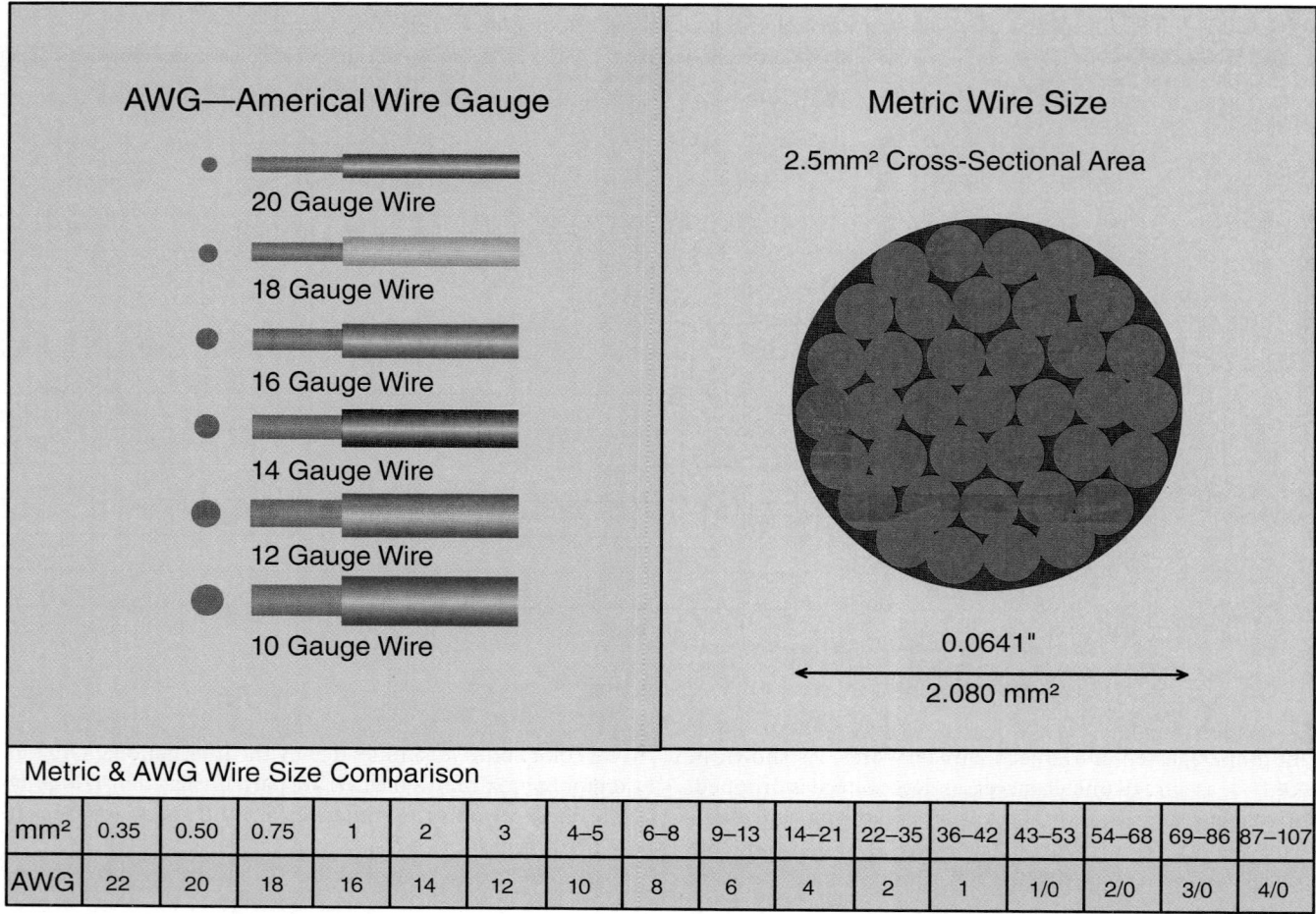

FIGURE 19-2 Comparing American Wire Gauge (AWG) system with the Metric Gauge system. AWG represents the diameter of a wire while Metric measures the cross-sectional area in mm².

- **SXL**—Has extra-thick insulation using cross-linked polyethylene insulation to withstand operating conditions in the engine compartment where the highest heat is possible. Temperature rating is 275°F (135°C). Heat sources cause the wire to blister like popcorn, but insulation does not "melt" off the wire.
- **GXL**—Uses cross-linked polyethylene insulation and, like SXL, is also used where heat, flame, and abrasion resistance is a requirement. The insulation is thinner than SXL and is used typically inside a cab or passenger compartment. Temperature rating is 275°F (130°C).
- **TXL**—Extra-thin primary wire that has a cross-linked polyethylene jacket that is resistant to oil, grease, gasoline, and acids. It is used where small diameter and minimal weight are desirable. Temperature rating is 275°F (130°C).

SGR-type wire refers to starting, ground, and battery cable and is required to meet a different SAE standard than regular primary wiring. These cables use a chlorinated polyethylene (CPE) insulation, which provides the highest heat resistance of any primary wiring. Temperature rating is 194°F (90°C). **Parallel wiring** refers to a type of custom-made wiring harness that encloses multiple conductors into a single vinyl insulator covering. Parallel wiring harness is often used for a rear taillight wiring for trucks, buses, and trailer harness that includes a separate wire for stop, turn, reverse, and tail lights. The harness is typically flat, but can be round with heavy abrasion-resistant insulation. Even though wires are separated and insulated from one another, the wiring insulation in flat conductor harnesses is fused together to form a single harness.

▶ **TECHNICIAN TIP**

Multi-stranded wire is better at conducting higher amounts of current with less resistance because it has more surface area to conduct electron flow. It is also more flexible for routing through a chassis and cab. Multi-stranded wire can break down more quickly, however, with each smaller strand being less resistant to physical damage than a larger single strand. Under the valve cover or inside the harsh operating environment of an engine, single-stranded wire is more durable.

TABLE 19-2 Partial Listing of Wire Color Designations by ISO Wire Color Abbreviation Function

ISO Wire Color	Abbreviation	Function
Black	bk	• Ground and general purpose
Black-red	bk-r	• Battery power • Ignition • Run
Blue-dk	dkbl	• Back-up light • Windshield wipers • Trailer auxiliary
Brown	br	• Tail, marker, and panel lights
Green-dk	dkg	• Right-turn signal • Driver's display • Data recording • J1587 positive • J1939 negative
Orange	o	• ABS or EBS • J1587 negative
Pink	pk	• Starter control • Charging, voltmeter, or ammeter • J1922 negative
Pink-white	pk-w	• Fuel control • Indicators for speed and shut-down
Yellow	y	• Left-turn signal • J1939 positive • GXL insulated wire
White	w	• Transmission • SXL insulated wire

TABLE 19-3 Examples of SAE Circuit Designations to Supplement OEM Wire Identification

Circuit Number	Circuit Description
1	Battery cable, ground
6	Battery cable, 12-volt positive
15	Starter, engine
82	Starter magnetic switch, power supply
117	Speed sensor "+," vehicle, mph (km/h)
118	Speed sensor "−," vehicle, mph (km/h)
295	Radio, AM/FM/CB
305	Ignition switch, accessory
306	Ignition switch, run position
468	Obstacle detection system (ODS), vehicle on-board radar (VORAD)
1102	Ignition buss feed
1504	Cruise control on/off
1515	Air management
1939	Data link, controls, SAE J1939

BK	Black
BN	Brown
RD	Red
OG	Orange
YE	Yellow
GN	Green
BU	Blue
VT	Violet
GY	Gray
WH	White
PK	Pink
TQ	Turquoise

FIGURE 19-3 Abbreviations are used to designate wire colors in wiring diagrams and any tracer used to help further identify the wire.

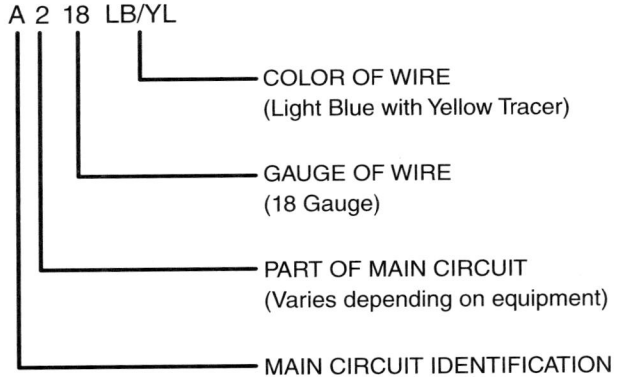

SAE J-2191 wire numbering standard (example)

FIGURE 19-4 An example of a wire code using SAE J-2191 wire numbering standard.

Wire Number Coding

Chassis wiring often uses numerical codes to identify which circuit the wire belongs to, where the wire is in the circuit, which harness it belongs in, and the wire gauge and color.

For North American equipment, the SAE standard J-2191 designates standard numbers for wiring circuits for power and signal distribution systems of Class 8 trucks and tractors. **TABLE 19-3** contains examples of these circuit designations. Vehicles designed and produced by European manufacturers, such as Daimler and Volvo, use "DIN" standards, which is an acronym for Deutsches Institut für Normung or German Institute for Standardization. For North American-designed equipment, a proprietary corporate wire identification number, together with an SAE number, may also be printed on the wire every six to eight inches apart. This means the SAE system more often supplements the manufacturer's system. **FIGURE 19-4** contains an example of SAE wiring code.

Wiring Connectors

LO 19-2 Identify and describe the types, construction, and repair techniques for wiring connectors.

To connect and disconnect electrical wires and harnesses to components or other circuits, terminal connections are used. The simplest type of connector is a terminal block that uses a small stud to which ring- or spade-type connectors are attached and secured with machine screws. Connectors have four basic parts: (1) the metal terminal surrounded, protected, and insulated (2) by its body or housing, (3) a seal that prevents intrusion of liquids, gases, and dirt intrusion into the terminal area, and (4) the latch or lock intended to prevent the connector from separating. The ideal electrical connector offers a low-resistance terminal contact, a body with high insulation value, plus resistance to corrosion, vibration, gases, water, fuel, and oil.

Connectors need to be connected and disconnected easily and repeatedly by hand. Servicing connectors must also require only simple tooling, such as what is shown in **FIGURE 19-5**, that maintains the connectors' shape to preserve the orientation of the connectors with components. Each application requires an emphasis on different connector characteristics, so there are a large variety used. For example, a connector may need to connect to a circuit board, another wiring harness, or a component with a formed connector receptacle. The voltage and amperage carried by the connector, resistance to failures caused by vibration, heating and corrosion, and intrusion of liquids determine connector body and terminal selection. Another important consideration is the security of the connector. Because the terminal contact force and effort required to push terminal bodies together varies, connections are usually designed to produce a slick clicking sound when correctly connected. To maintain the connection, a secondary lock or latch is designed to prevent the mating halves of the connecter or terminal pins from disconnecting. Many connector bodies are keyed or have indexing slots to prevent mis-mating, which damages connectors and pins caused by forcing connectors together at the wrong angle or fitting into incorrectly connected connections.

Connector Terminal Designs

Terminals are gender-differentiated as either male or female. To maintain good terminal contact, female terminals are made with spring-loaded elements that apply pressure to the male pin while allowing for thermal expansion and contraction to take place. Male terminals may have a slight taper shape. Hollow pin shapes minimize the thermal expansion of a pin, but are not as rugged and able to withstand as much vibration or abuse. Both male and female terminals have wings at the end where the wire inserts. These conductor wings are used to crimp and lock the terminal to the wire, wire insulator, or silicone seal (**FIGURE 19-6**). Locking tangs on the terminal help seat the terminal in the connector body and prevent it from backing out when the connector halves are pushed together. These tangs must be released using a purpose-made tool when performing connector repairs (**FIGURE 19-7**).

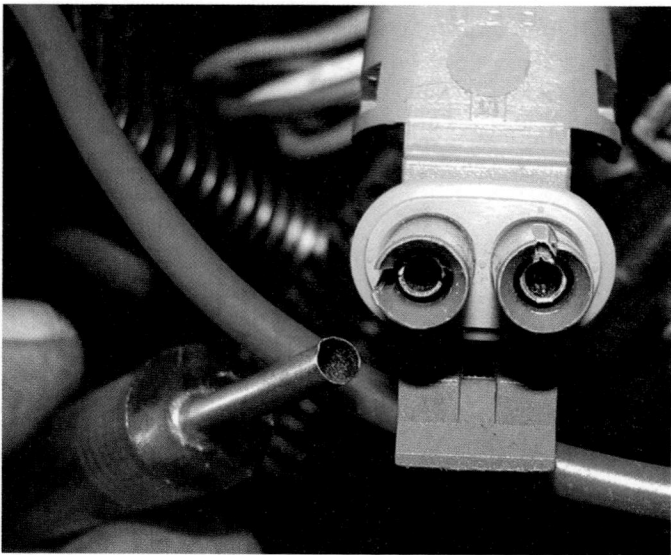

FIGURE 19-5 A variety of release tools are used to remove connectors from the body.

Gold, silver, copper, or tin are metals commonly used to make terminals. Non corroding gold is only used for terminal applications demanding high-reliability conducting with low-resistance and high-frequency electrical signals. Silver is used for high-voltage connectors. Copper-Zinc or Copper-Bronze (e.g., CuSn4) are being replaced by Copper-Nickel-Silicon (CuNiSi) alloys. This last type of terminal material provides

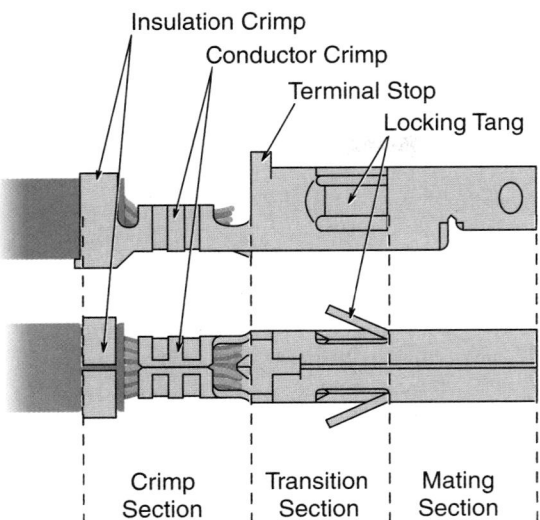

FIGURE 19-6 Profile of male and female terminals. The terminal wings are crimped to the wire insulator to maintain a strong mechanical connection to the wire.

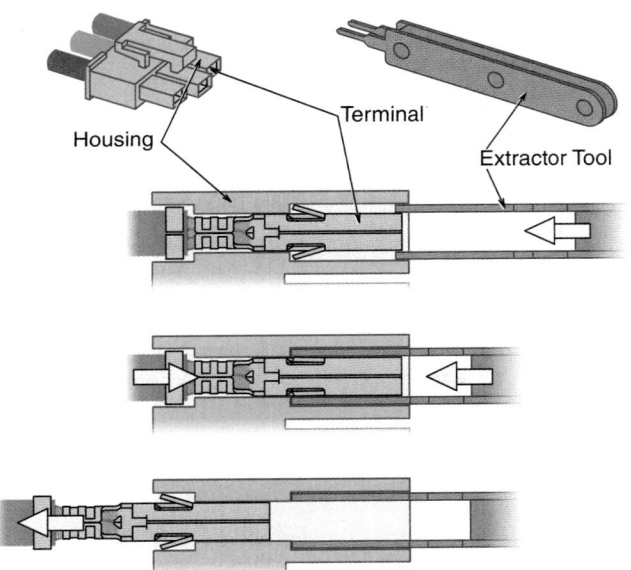

FIGURE 19-7 Terminal release tools are designed to enable the terminal to push in or out of the body by compressing the locking tangs.

more capacity to conduct higher amperage current at a higher temperature limit with superior conductivity—important qualities as connectors become even more compact.

Terminals are generally crimped to the wire rather than soldered (**FIGURE 19-8**). While soldering can increase the mechanical strength of the terminal to wire connector, it can cause more problems than it solves when solder gets into locking tangs or the connector gets hot.

Connector Body Types

The connector housing, or body, generally has three parts: a body or housing, silicone seals to prevent water intrusion, and

the terminal. Terminals are the metal part that is crimped to a wire and housed inside a connector. There are two main types of terminals used in harness connectors—pull-to-seat and push-to-seat terminals. **Pull-to-seat terminals** are terminals that are installed by inserting the wire through the connector cavity, crimping on a terminal, and then pulling the terminal back into the connector cavity to seat it. **Push-to-seat terminals** are inserted into the back of the connector cavity to seat after the terminal is crimped to the wire.

Connector housings have male and female sides and are usually shaped so that they can be connected in only one way. In addition to a secondary lock or latch that holds the connector body together to maintain terminal contact pressure, some connectors also use a connector position assurance (CPA) clip. This is a plastic or metal part of the connector that is manually slid into place or latched over its mating half to add additional assurance that two connector halves

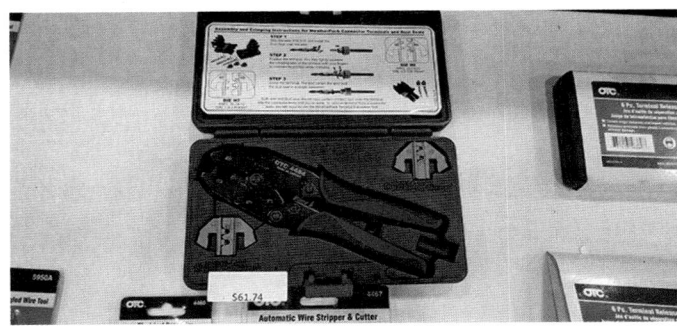

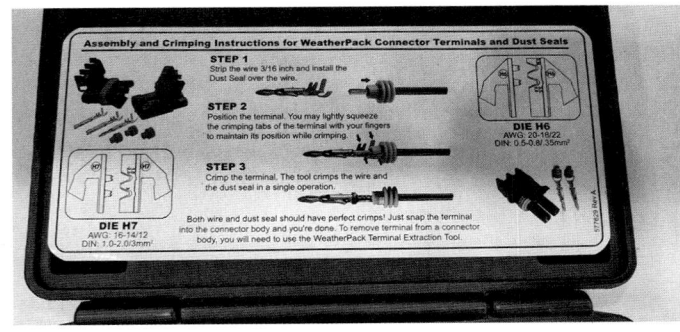

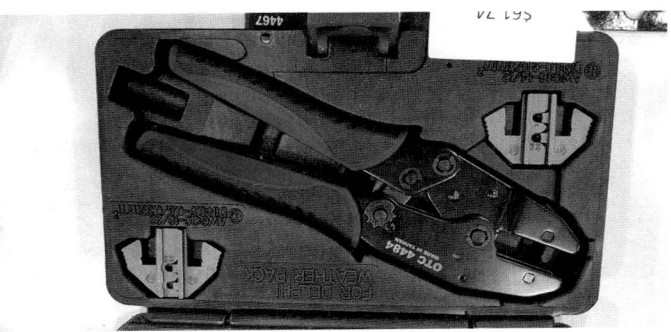

FIGURE 19-8 A purpose-made crimping tool is used to crimp the connector and seal to the terminal wings. Interchangeable dies for the crimper jaws enable a variety of terminals to be crimped.

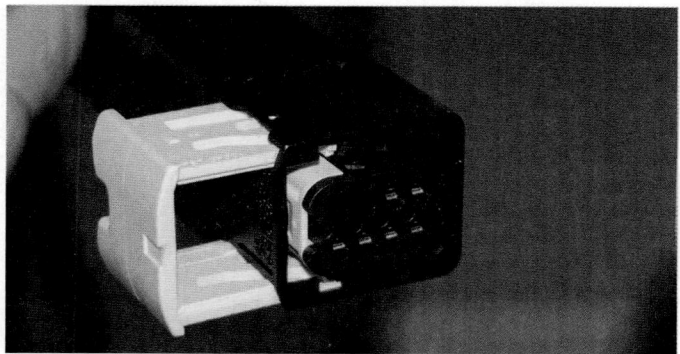

FIGURE 19-9 These two connectors use a latching mechanism to provide additional security to ensure the connector is latched and prevent disconnection.

in critical connections stay locked together and do not work loose. High-vibration connection points on engine sensors or injectors use secondary locks (**FIGURE 19-9**). **FIGURE 19-10** shows typical harness connectors. Most connectors are weatherproofed to keep moisture out. Special tools are usually needed to insert and remove the terminals from the connector housing.

Weather Pack Connectors

A **Weather Pack connector** from Delphi is an environmentally sealed push-to-seat electrical connection system supplied in one- to six-pin configurations. As illustrated in **FIGURE 19-11**, this system uses only round pin terminals and round socket terminals. The male pin end of the connector is called the tower while the female socket end is the shroud. Terminals (pin and sleeve) are tin-plated and have special core wings that allow crimp-only wire attachment, eliminating the need for solder. The self-lubricating silicone connector and cavity seals are triple-ribbed. Connectors are rated at 20 amps per pin at 16 volts DC.

Metri-Pack Connectors

A **Metri-Pack connector** from Delphi is another family of electrical connection systems similar to the Weather Pack connectors, except that the terminals are flat, rather than round, and it is a pull-to-seat connector. **FIGURE 19-12** shows a Metri-Pack connector. Standardized male blade sizes and box-like female terminals designate the five different series of these connectors. Each series has a different

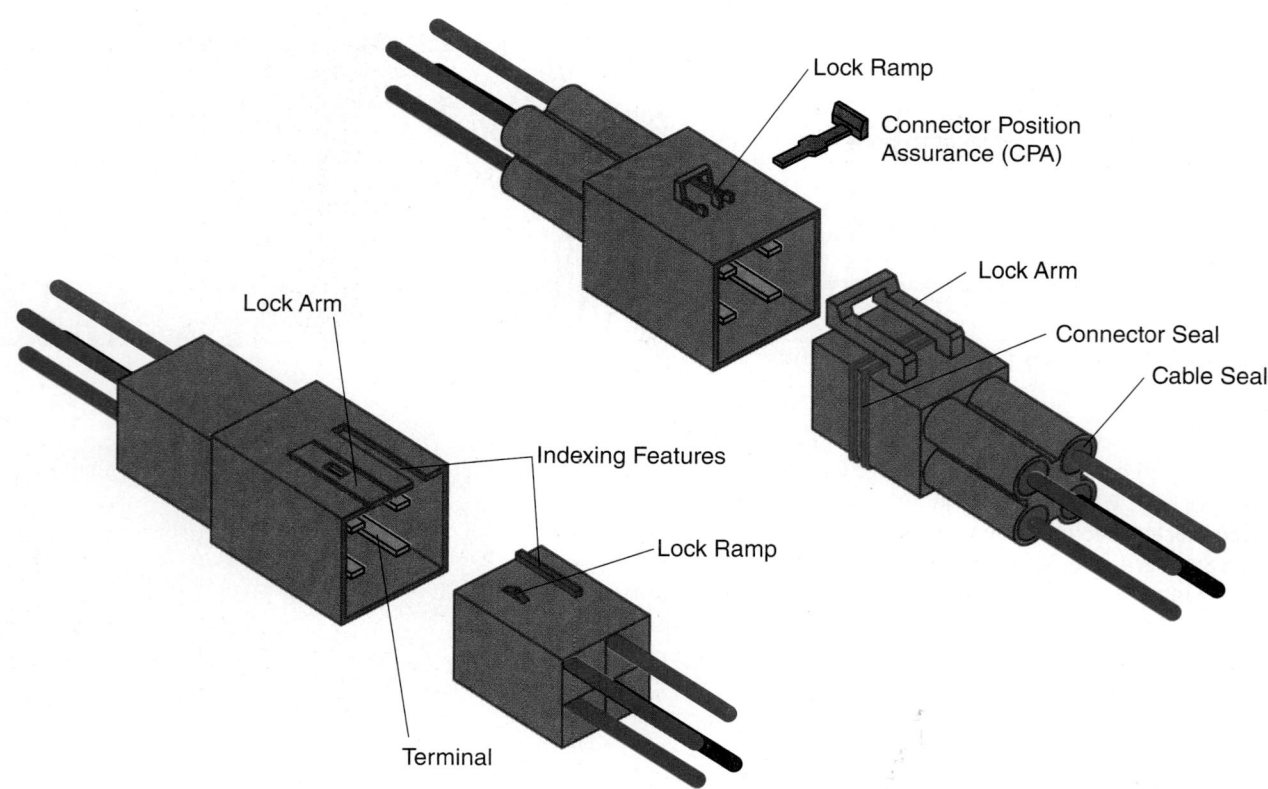

FIGURE 19-10 Typical harness connectors.

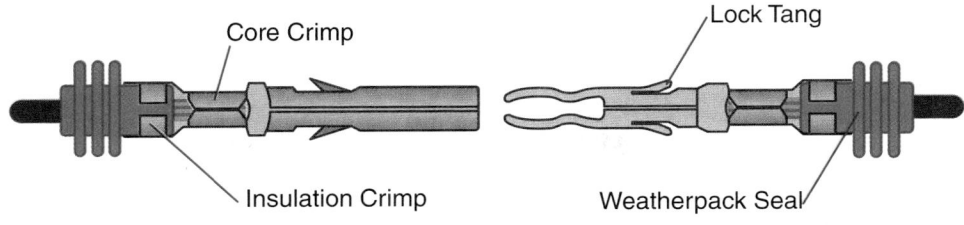

FIGURE 19-11 Weather Pack is a push-to-seat connector.

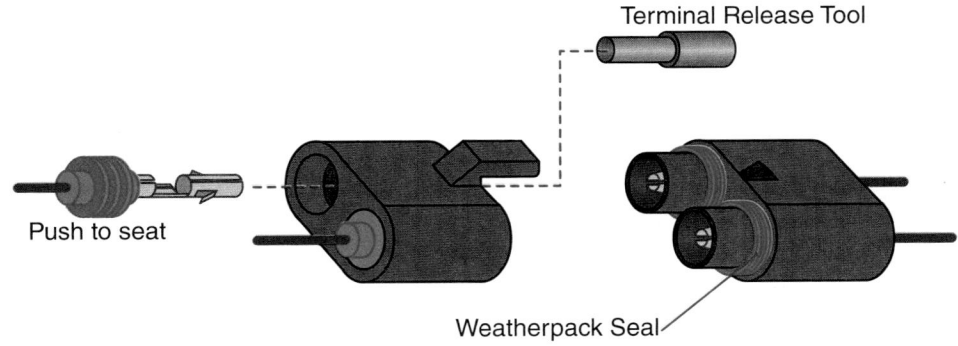

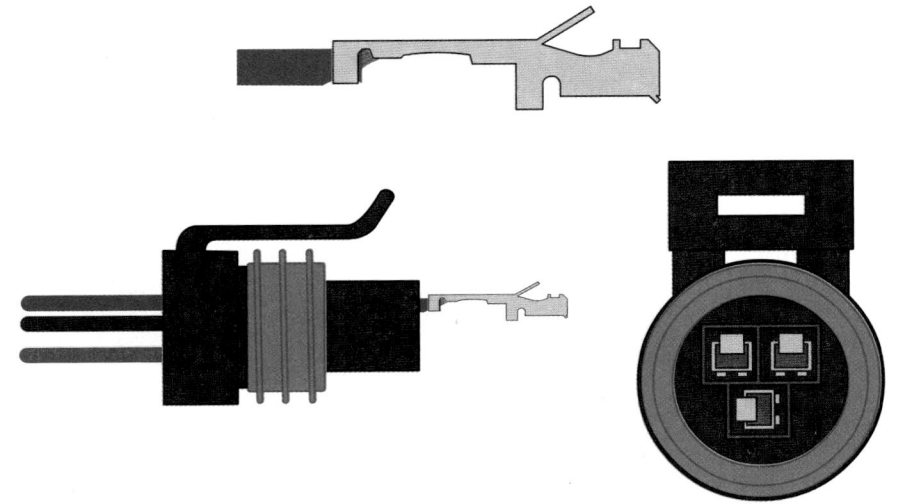

FIGURE 19-12 Metri-Pack is a pull-to-seat connector.

current-carrying capacity. Terminals are tin-plated and have special core wings that allow crimp-only connections, eliminating the need for solder. Silicone seals prevent water intrusion into the connector. To assemble a Metri-Pack connector, follow the steps in **SKILL DRILL 19-1**.

Bosch Connectors

Bosch/AMP connectors use rectangular hollow push-to-seat-type terminals. They are available in two- to six-pin configurations and rated at 9 amps per pin. Like other terminals, they use wings to crimp the wire to terminal. A metal secondary lock on some connector bodies easily helps distinguish this connector from other types.

Deutsch Connectors

Deutsch connectors, such as illustrated in **FIGURE 19-13**, are also an environmentally sealed connector. Terminals often use solid round metal pins and hollow female sockets, Deutsch connectors are much more compact than any other connector. They occupy one quarter of the volume of the **Weather-Pack connectors** and one-half the volume of the Bosch/AMP connectors. Rated at 15 amps per pin, they are considered a premium connector and used when reliability of the connection is of utmost importance. The DT Series of Deutsch connectors is popular on trucks and buses and is available in two- to twelve-pin configurations. To release a Deutsch connector, follow the steps in **SKILL DRILL 19-2**.

SKILL DRILL 19-1 Assembling a Metri-Pack Connector

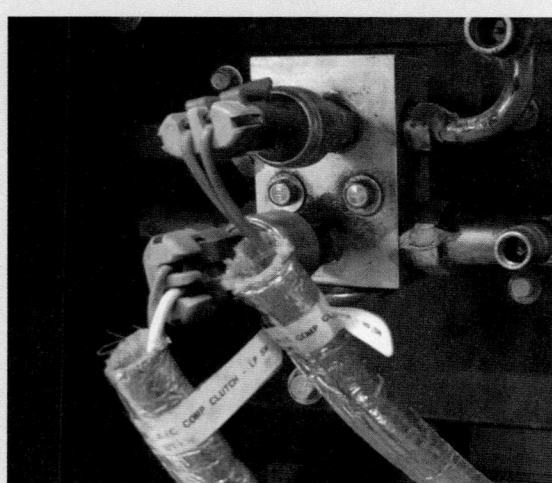

Metri-pack female and male connectors are a pull to seat type connector requiring crimping tool die to properly crimp an open barrel flat or round metal connector. To assemble a Metri-Pack connector, the following are general guidelines for 10 – 22-gauge wires and terminals.

1. Identify and select the appropriate flat or round type open barrel connecter and plastic connector body. Metri-pack connectors are available in a range of sizes grouped in five different series. The 150 series is commonly used connector for low energy environmentally sealed circuits rated for a maximum of 14- 30 amps. Select the connector using the manufacturers past catalog.

2. Blunt cut the end of the wire that will be used for the connector. Thread the wire through the rear of the connector body and push it past the body to provide enough length to assemble the terminal.
3. Select the correct size of silicone environmental seal and slide the seal over the wire end and down wire.
4. Strip approximately 3/16" of the wire end
5. Select the correct metal terminal for the connector and body. Terminals and connector bodies will use charts having part numbers to correctly match the components together
6. Insert the terminal into the correct size and shape of die on the crimper. Two sets of wings are used – smaller ones for the wire and the other for the silicone seal. Hold the terminal using only the wings for the wire to gently hold the terminal in place.
7. Insert the wire into the terminal and verify all wire strands are inside the terminal. Squeeze the crimper to fully crimp the terminal to the wire only using the wings on the terminal for the wire
8. Pull the terminal and wire in opposite directs to verify the connection is secure
9. Slide the seal onto the end of the crimped terminal to fit the leading edge of the seal into the larger terminal wing used to crimp the seal.
10. Use the crimping tool to squeeze the seal wings and secure the seal onto the metal terminal
11. Pull the wire and terminal into the molded connector body. Listen for a clicking noise as the terminal positively locks into the connector body.
12. Close the secondary terminal protector assurance clip cover over the connector body.

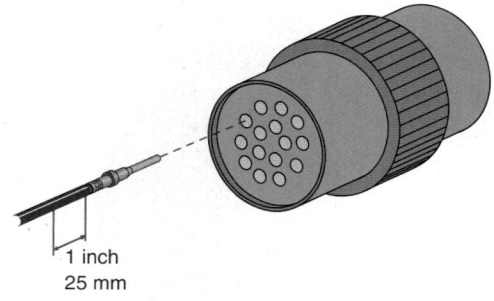

1 inch
25 mm

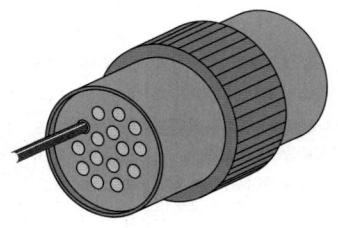

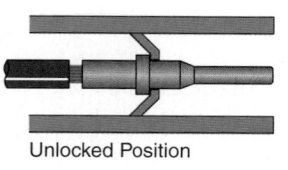

Unlocked Position

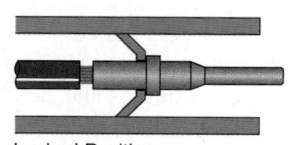

Locked Position

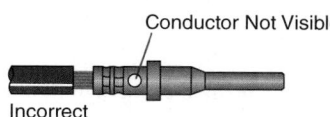

Conductor Not Visible

Incorrect

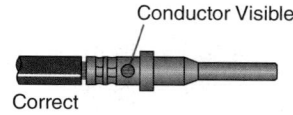

Conductor Visible

Correct

FIGURE 19-13 Deutsch connectors are a push-to-seat-type connector that use a release tool, which is inserted from the rear of the connector.

SKILL DRILL 19-2 Releasing a Deutsch HD Connector

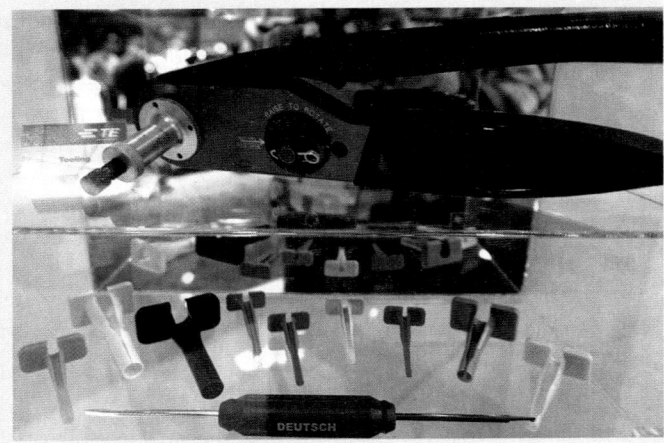

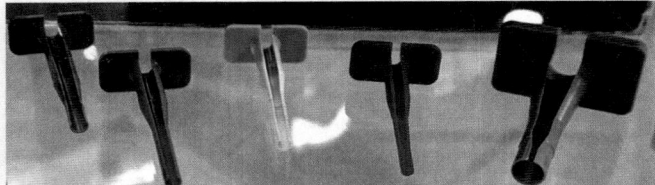

Deutsch female and male connectors are a push-to-seat-type connector requiring specialized crimping tool die to properly crimp a closed round barrel metal connector. To release a Deutsch connector from it's cavity in a plastic housing, the following are general guidelines.

1. Disconnect the connector halves. Determine whether the connector is a DT or HD series. DT series connectors have a terminal wedgelock located on the front face of the connector. The wedgelock is removed by gently pulling with a pair of needle nose pliers. HD series use not wedgelock.

2. Select the appropriate HD terminal release tool. These plastic tools are color coded according to wire size (See New figure Removal Tools). The larger T handle end should face you.
3. Slide the narrow end of the tool towards the connector terminal and gently press the tool into the connector.
4. Wiggle the tool end into the connector and past the terminal until it contacts a point where the terminal stops.
5. With the tool still in the connector and surrounding the terminal, pull on the terminal wire. The terminal and wire should release together and pull away from the connector.
6. Perform any service work necessary. Remember, a specialized crimping tool is used to attach a new terminal to a Deutsch connector.

Wiring Failure and Repair

LO 19-3 Identify and describe wiring failures and repair techniques.

After component failures, wiring and connectors are the leading causes of electrical problems. Wire chaffing; heat, oil and fuel damage; and road debris are common preventable causes for wire and harness failure. Mechanical damage from repeated flexing, probing with test lights, stretching, or bending can break a wire and sometimes leave the insulation intact. Best practices to increase wiring longevity include:

- Covering wiring and harness in a protective loom
- Routing wiring away from heat sources and moving parts
- Securing wire with clips and plastic ties

One of the greatest enemies to wiring is water. Water with dissolved road salt is particularly aggressive at damaging wiring. The tendency of water to "wick" inside insulation is what makes it so destructive. **Water wicking** is the movement of water beneath wiring insulation, due to water's adhesive and cohesive properties. This essentially means water is sticky. It easily attaches itself to copper wire and has a high surface tension. That means water stays together or beads up. Once inside a wire, water moves into the smallest openings and spaces through adhesion. More water gets dragged along inside a wire because the water sticks so well to itself. Because of the effect of wicking, water can travel far along a wire to the point where an entire length of wire is corroded.

Wicking failures often happen close to connectors due to a defective or missing seal. Punctures from test lights also lead to damage of the entire harness. A powder-like substance inside connectors or wire insulation indicates a wicking-related failure. Wiring may actually appear swollen or cracked from corrosion pressure. TABLE 19-4 shows possible remedies for various wiring and terminal faults.

TABLE 19-4 Remedies for Various Wiring Failures

Fault	Remedy
Broken wire conductor	Repair or replace
Corroded wire	Repair or replace
Oil-damaged insulation	Replace
Cracked insulation	Repair if minor; otherwise replace
Melted insulation	Replace
Worn or missing insulation	Replace
Discolored insulation	Replace
Damaged connectors or terminals	Repair or replace with proper tool. Use correct replacement terminals.

Cutting and Stripping Wires

The amount of wire cut out of a damaged portion of wire depends on the amount needed to produce ends that are clean and free of any corrosion. After stripping the insulation from the remaining wire ends, the wires should appear clean and bright. Wire-stripping tools remove only the insulation and do not nick or cut wire. Dull or dirty wiring can be cleaned with fine emery-cloth sandpaper. Tin-plated copper wiring used to add corrosion resistance to wiring in marine applications is commonly used in truck and bus repair too. This wire has a dull gray appearance that cannot be cleaned. The section of wire to replace must be slightly longer than the original section removed to provide some slack.

Splicing and Soldering

Soldering wires together provides a strong-mechanical and lowest-electrical resistance, compared to just twisting. If a connection is not soldered, wiring can move within the connection, leading to arcing and resistance, which ultimately causes connection failure. To enhance the strength of the joint, wires should be joined by bending each into a double-J bend, then twisting to form a Western Union splice (**FIGURE 19-14**). A small amount of solder should be applied to the tip of the soldering iron before touching the tip to the joint surface. Rosin-core solder wire is then applied to the joint but is not brought into contact with the iron. Heat from the joint should melt the solder into the wire. This procedure avoids a cold-solder joint that could cause a poor electrical connection.

> ▶ TECHNICIAN TIP
>
> Solder uses flux to clean the wire surface and enable the solder to stick to the wire. Rosin-core solder is used when soldering electrical wiring. Other solders, such as those used to repair aluminum or plumbing, use different types of flux containing acid for cleaning aluminum surfaces. To make a solid reliable solder connection, only use solder intended for electrical repair.

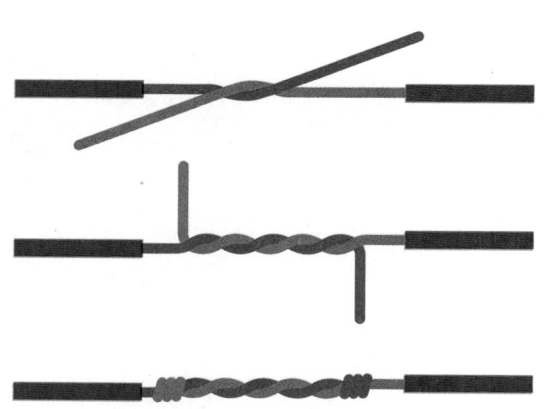

FIGURE 19-14 An alternative to twisting wires together before soldering is to wrap them together using this "Western Union" configuration.

Sealing and Securing

Spliced connections need protection against water wicking. Heat-shrink tubing provides the best seal for a spliced electrical connection. Heat shrink is available in two types—double- and single-wall. Double-walled tubing is recommended because it has an adhesive layer between the tubing and wire. When heated, the inner layer of hot-melt adhesive turns into a water-tight seal when cooled. The outer layer is generally made of flame retardant, cross-linked polyolefin. It shrinks to provide electrical and mechanical protection. Covering the wire with tape provides additional abrasion resistance to the spliced joint. Using nylon ties and insulated clips to secure the wire against movement prevents any further mechanical damage.

> ▶ TECHNICIAN TIP
>
> Heat is required to contract and seal shrink tube. Heat from a hair dryer is not adequate. Rather, a similar-looking heat gun is needed. Heat from the gun provides enough heat to melt the inner adhesive and shrink the outer layer. Propane torches and lighters actually burn, char, and split shrink tube, so they are not recommended tools for activating heat-shrink tubing.

Crimp-Type Connectors

Faster splice repairs are made with crimp-type connectors (**FIGURE 19-15**). Stripped wire ends placed inside aluminum metal tubes are squeezed together with barrel-type crimping pliers.

Crimp connectors can provide mechanical strength like solder but must be used with double-walled shrink tube to make the repair permanent. Color codes are used to designate wire gauge to use for shrink-crimp connectors. An incorrectly sized crimp connector can become loose, leak, and fail.

Wiring Diagrams

LO 19-4 Identify and describe types and features of electrical system wiring diagrams.

A schematic diagram shows current flow and function of an electrical circuit but is not concerned with the physical layout of the wires. Wiring diagrams show the electrical connections between all the electrical system components. This means they contain information about how the wires are connected, which circuits or wires are connected, and where the connections should be located in the actual device.

Unlike a pictorial diagram, a wiring diagram uses abstract or simplified shapes and lines to show components. Pictorial diagrams are often photos with labels or highly detailed drawings of the physical components.

Most symbols used on a wiring diagram look like abstract versions of the real objects they represent. For example, a switch is a break in the line with a line at an angle to the wire, much like a light switch you can flip on and off. A resistor is represented with

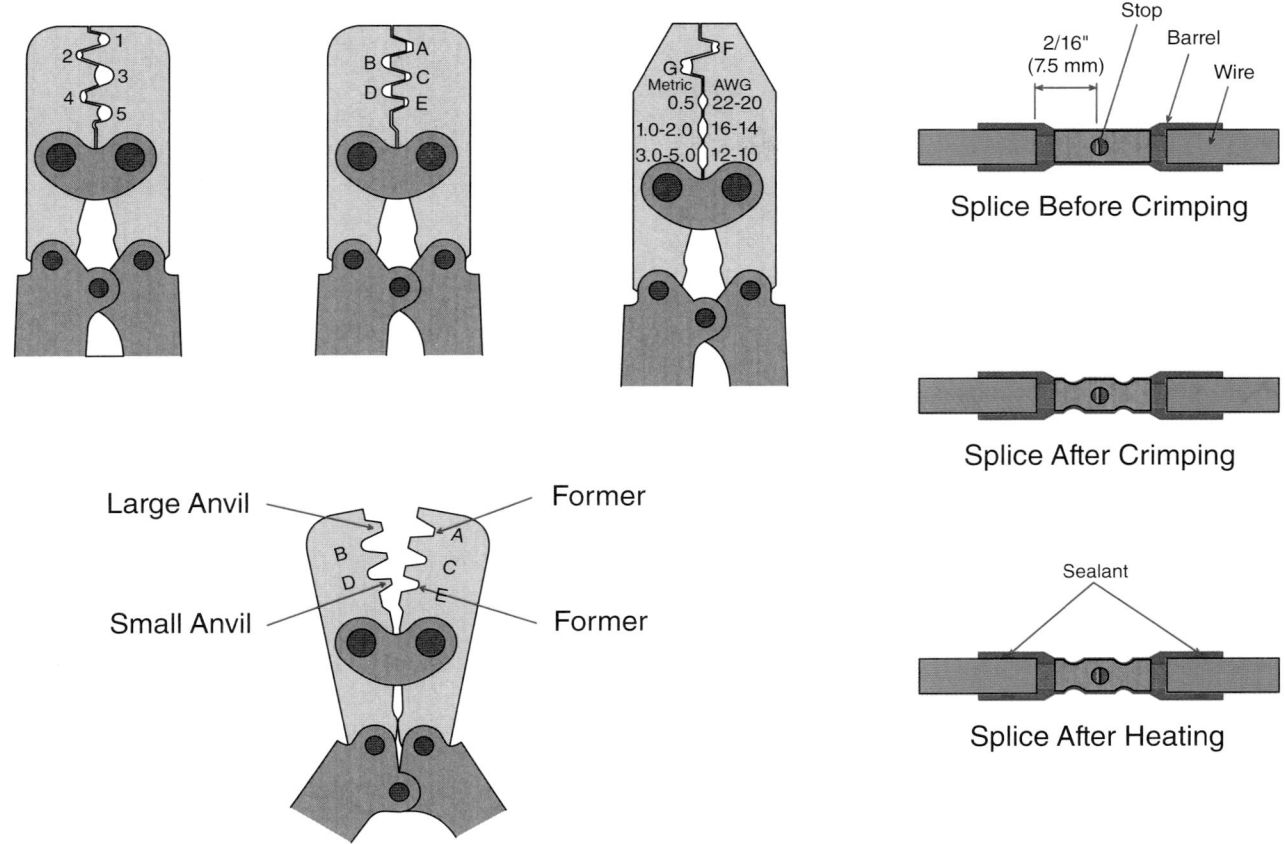

FIGURE 19-15 A variety of crimping pliers are used to join wires with a butt connector. When heated, shrink-type connectors contact and seal the tube ends with an epoxy-like compound.

a series of squiggles symbolizing the restriction of current flow. An antenna is a straight line with three small lines branching off at its end, much like a real antenna.

Magneto ignition systems used at the beginning of the 1900s were the first electrical systems. With only four major components—the high-voltage magnetic, a distributor, spark plugs, and coil—identifying and connecting these components was simple. By 1911, the electrical system expanded to include a DC generator, headlamps, a battery, voltage regulator, and switches. In 1950, the main interests were the starting, ignition, and lighting circuits. Today, the types of electrical components number into the thousands—over 3000 circuits are commonly found in HD commercial vehicles!

Modern electronic controls applied to every vehicle system and networked electrical systems have increased the complexity of today's vehicles. Added to traditional vehicle systems are convenience devices, such as navigational and multimedia devices, vehicle safety and security systems, and custom electrical circuits for body builders.

The complexity of the electrical circuits and their interconnections requires electrical wiring diagrams that allow a technician to trace circuits from power supplies, through switches, components, circuit protection devices, harnesses, splices, junction blocks, connectors, and finally to ground. Technicians must be able to correctly understand and interpret a wiring diagram in order to reduce diagnostic time for electrical problems and eliminate guesswork.

Wiring diagrams are arranged by manufacturers in a number of different styles to show with a high degree of clarity individual circuit components, connections, and their locations. The three main types of wiring diagrams are map, isometric, and schematic diagrams.

Map Diagrams

Map (pictorial) diagrams show the entire vehicle wiring circuit. Symbols for components are usually pictorial (**FIGURE 19-16**). That is, the symbol looks like a component it represents. **FIGURE 19-17** contains a map diagram. Individual components and their spatial relationship to one another are not to scale and do not necessarily represent their location on the vehicle. Linear diagrams are a variation of the map diagram. Linear diagrams use pictorial representations with a mixture of schematic symbols and internal wiring. A linear diagram may start on one page and continue onto several more, mapping out individual circuits with a separate diagram.

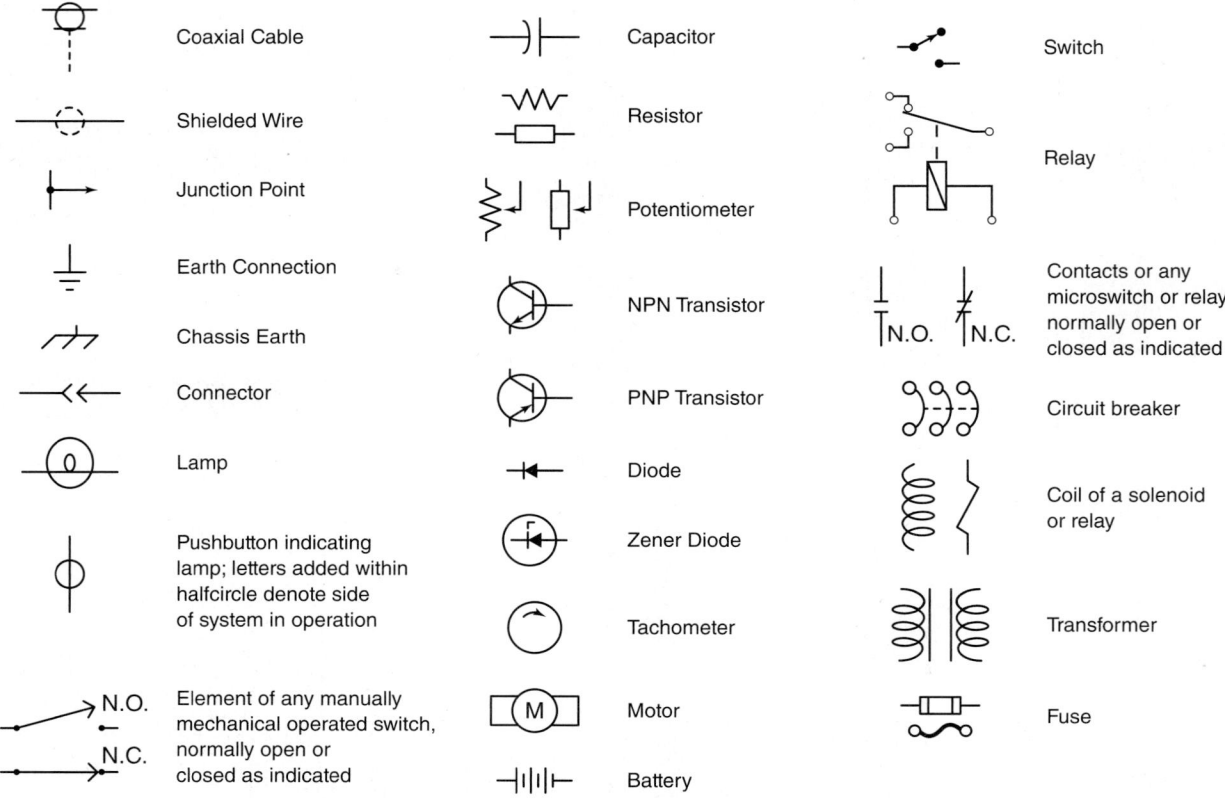

FIGURE 19-16 Every electrical device and component has a corresponding electrical symbol.

Isometric Diagrams

Isometric diagrams are used to locate a component within a system. If the location of a component or wiring harness is unknown, this type of diagram shows the outline of a vehicle or piece of equipment where the component can be found. Various components and wiring harnesses of the electrical system are shown where they are located on the unit (**FIGURE 19-18**).

Schematic Diagrams

Schematic diagrams are line drawings that explain how a system works by using symbols and connecting lines (**FIGURE 19-19**). On schematics, symbols are used to represent devices or components from simple through to complex electrical and electronic systems. There is a great deal of information represented in a small amount of space, and the reading of schematic symbols requires practice. To make them easier to use when diagnosing a problem, the diagrams are divided into sections or represent an individual system. For example, a lighting problem requires reference to the lighting section of the publication.

Schematic circuit diagrams may be supplemented with body diagrams, tables, graphs, and descriptions. Current paths are arranged to show signal or mechanical action from left to right and or top to bottom. Block diagrams are used to represent complex electronic circuitry, such as electronic control modules. On these devices, no internal circuitry is shown and only inputs or outputs are depicted. Dotted lines may represent an area or some mechanical action taking place with a component.

The two most common types of schematic diagrams used today are Deutsche Institute Norm (DIN) and Valley Forge (VF). SAE symbols are used by VF, and DIN symbols are used together with DIN diagrams.

Deutsche Institute Norm (DIN) Diagrams

European-based heavy-vehicle manufacturers use **Deutsches Institut für Normung (DIN) diagrams** (**FIGURE 19-20**). In these diagrams, symbols, terminal connections numbers, line symbols, and operational status of items, such as switches and relays, are defined by a DIN standard. DIN diagrams may be accompanied by illustrations showing the internal circuitry of some devices. Reference coordinates are often supplied to assist in locating components.

DIN schematic diagrams are also called **current track** wiring diagrams because they show the power source at the top of the page and the ground points at the bottom. This format simplifies the wiring diagram and minimizes conductor and symbol overlap where they do not connect. Situated between power and ground are current tracks that contain electrical components and conductors. Symbols are used to represent components and conductors in the wiring diagrams. Arrangement of the components and circuit paths on the diagram do not usually correspond to their physical locations on the vehicle. However, newer DIN standards do indicate on which side of the vehicle a component may be located. For example, an R or L suffix after a component designates a right- or left-side location.

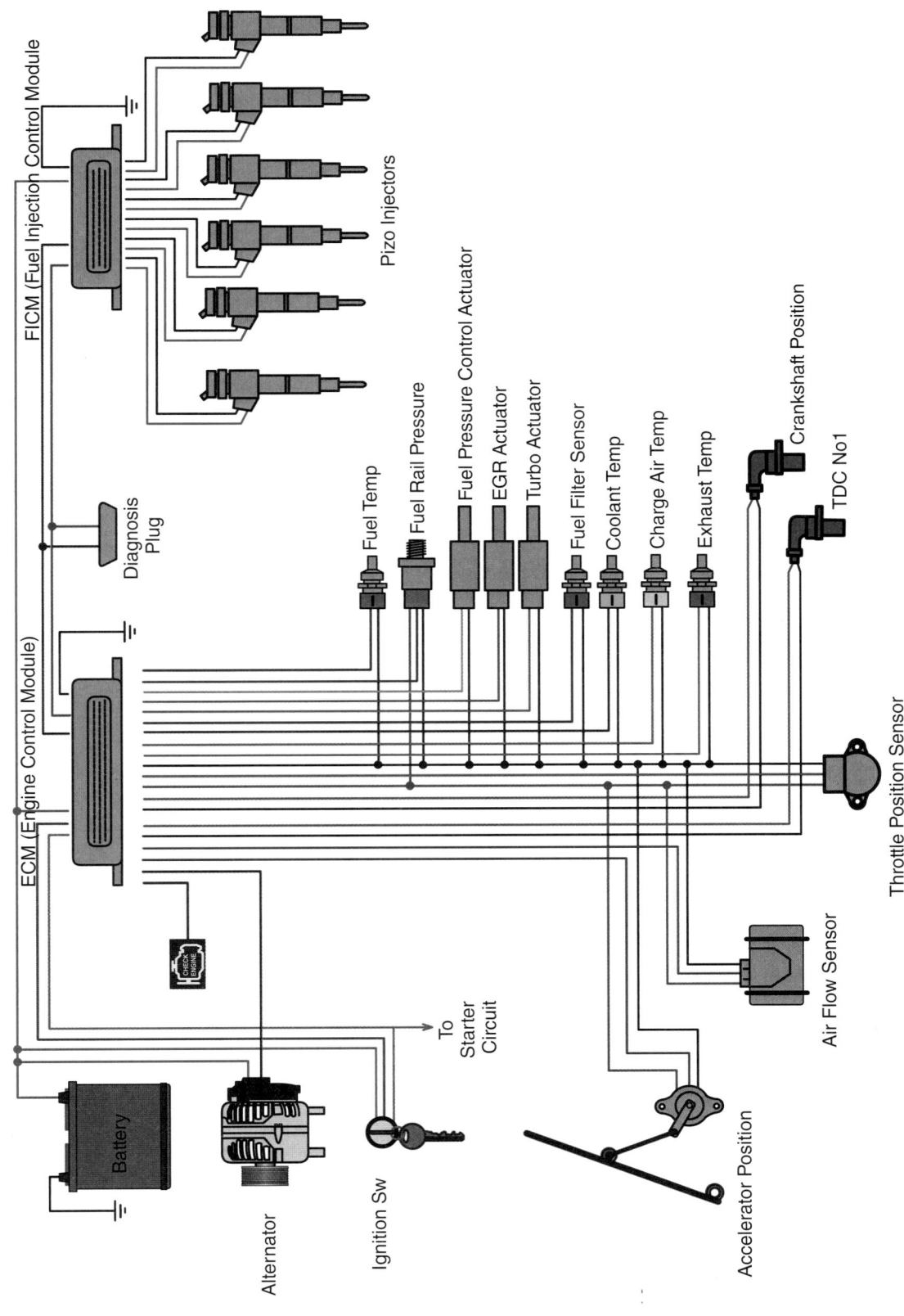

FIGURE 19-17 A pictorial or map diagram of the electrical system.

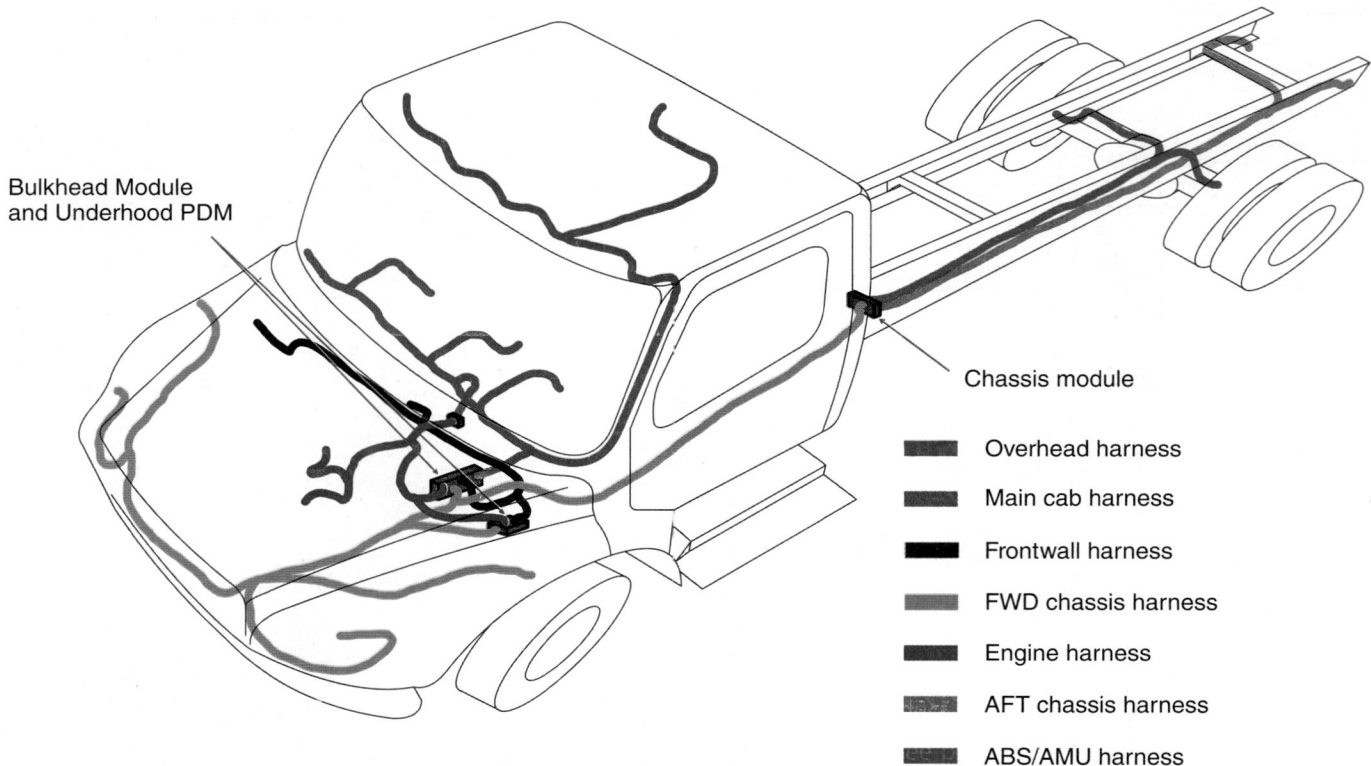

Bulkhead Module
and Underhood PDM

Chassis module

- Overhead harness
- Main cab harness
- Frontwall harness
- FWD chassis harness
- Engine harness
- AFT chassis harness
- ABS/AMU harness

FIGURE 19-18 Modular construction techniques of vehicles today wire vehicles using sections known as looms or harnesses. Harnesses are prewired for sections of a vehicle. The harnesses are enclosed into protective loom and taped, so it is not possible to completely trace a single wire to find a problem. Schematic diagrams are needed to check the circuit at strategic points. Harnesses often use codes to describe location or function.

Elements of a DIN Wiring Diagram

DIN diagrams are representative of all wiring diagrams in use today. They contain elements that every electrical circuit needs, at a minimum, to operate:

- Power supply
- Load
- Ground
- Conductors (usually wire)
- Circuit protection (fuse, virtual fuse)

If any of these are missing, a complete circuit is broken, and the load does not function. The ability to break down a circuit into its individual parts is the key to being able to diagnose failures in the circuit. Wiring diagrams also incorporate many standardized DIN symbols and codes used to illustrate a complete circuit (**FIGURE 19-21**). These DIN unique symbols and codes can include:

- Current track numbers
- Components and devices (DIN standard 40 719 and 42 400)
- Terminal designations (DIN standard 72552)
- Conductors
- Connectors

(**FIGURE 19-22**) identifies many of the features of a DIN schematic diagram:

1. Relay location number on a relay panel.
2. Arrow. Indicates wiring circuit is continued on another page.
3. Connector designation for the relay terminal and connector panel. For example: 17/30 equals terminal 30 of relay connects to terminal 17 of central relay panel.
4. Threaded pin on relay panel. The white circle indicates the connection is threaded.
5. Fuse indicating location and amperage. For example: S228 means fuse 28 is rated for 15 amps.
6. Reference of wire for continuing current track number.
7. Wire connection designation in wiring harness. The locations of wire connections are indicated in the accompanying legend.
8. a. Terminal designation on a multi-point connector.
   b. Terminal designation on a component. This number appears on the component and/or terminal number of a multi-point connector.
9. Ground connection designation in wire harness. The locations of ground connections provided in legend.
10. Component designation, which follows a standardized coding. The legend at bottom of page identifies the component in this diagram.

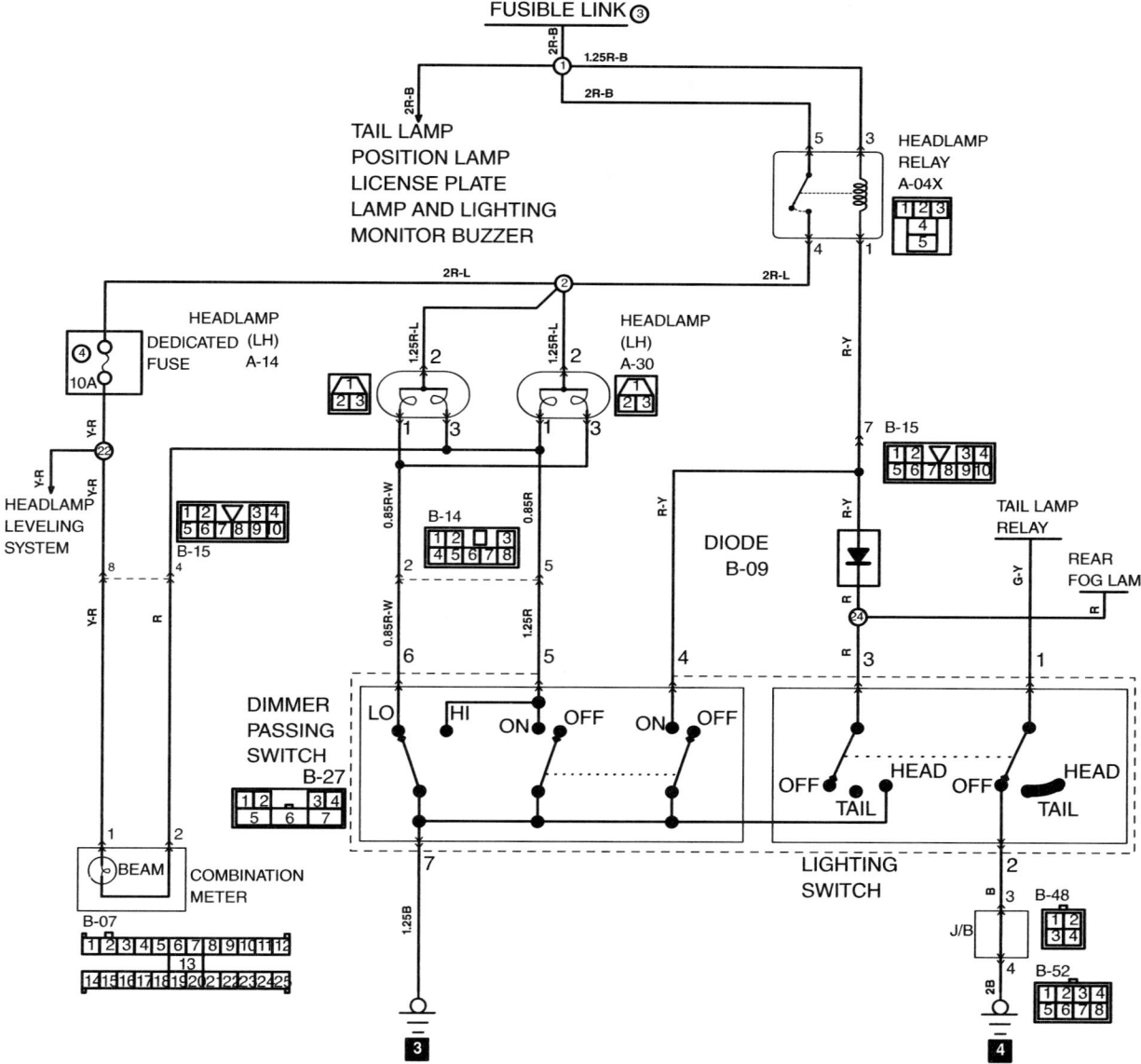

FIGURE 19-19 A schematic wiring diagram. Note the battery in the top right corner begins circuit action, which takes place from left to right, top to bottom.

11. Component symbols. A schematic symbol of component type.
12. Wire cross-section size in mm² and wire colors.
13. Component symbol with an open side indicates the component is continued on another wiring diagram.
14. Internal connections (thin lines) that are not wires. Internal connections allow technicians to trace current flow inside a component or wiring harness.
    a. Internal Harness Splice (Welded connection)
    b. Physical Contact (Mounted to engine)
15. Reference of continuation of wire to component.
16. Central Relay panel connectors, which depicts wiring of multi-point or single connectors on the central relay panel. For example: S3/3 equals Multi-point connector S3, terminal 3.

17. Reference of internal connection continuation. Letters indicate where connection continues on previous and/or next page.
18. Central Relay Panel.
19. Ground Path. In this example, the welded harness connection 135 connects to welded harness connection 81 to welded harness connection 42.

In addition to the above general symbols and codes, individual manufacturers include specialized codes for:

- Harness naming codes
- System identifying codes—Indicates a system to which a circuit belongs. For example, trailer, driveline, or braking electrical circuits have a code associated
- Splice naming standards
- Inline connector naming standards

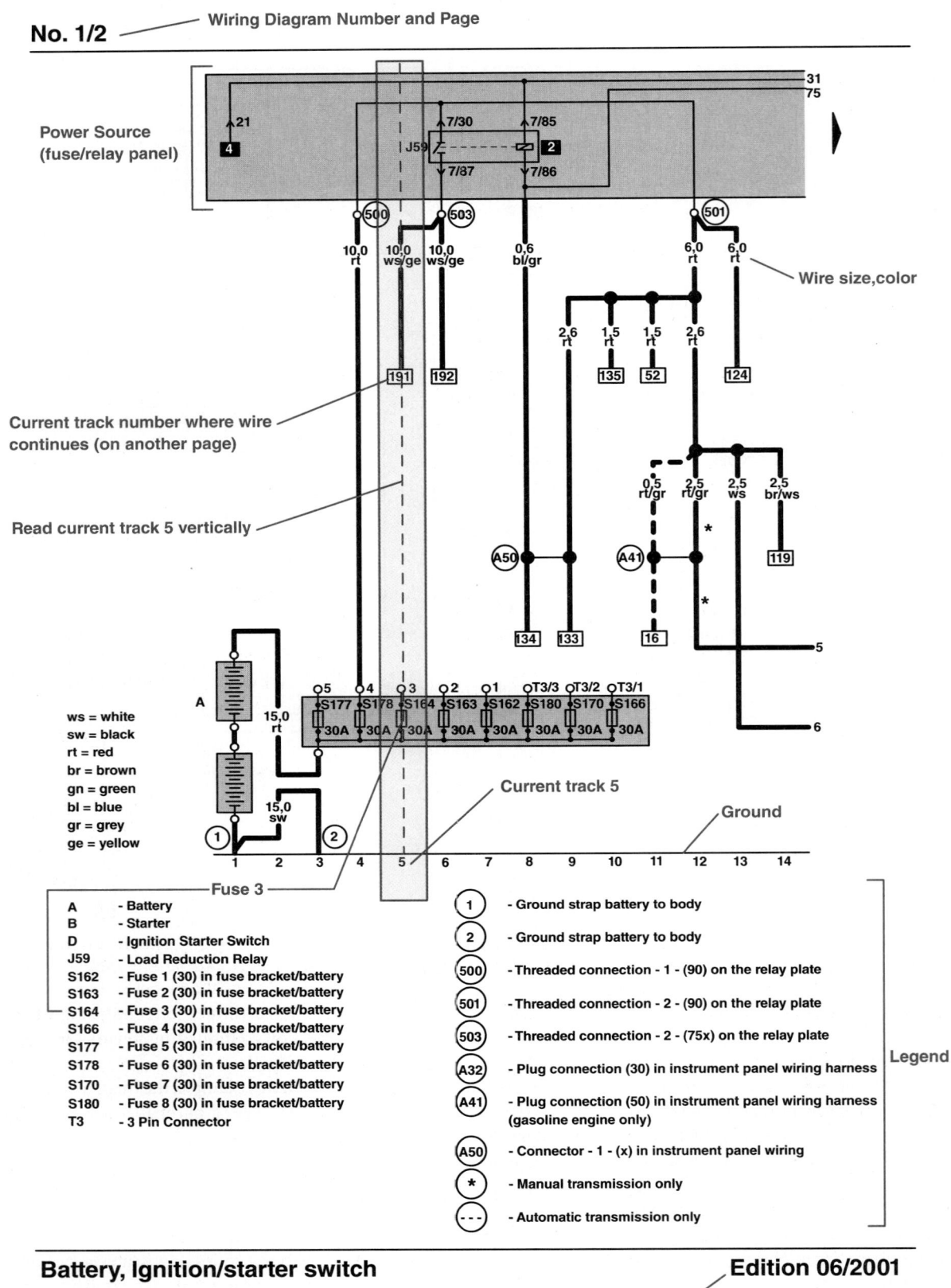

Battery, Ignition/starter switch

Edition 06/2001

Edition number

FIGURE 19-20 A typical Deutsches Institut für Normung (DIN) diagram.

Image Modified from ©2001 Volkswagen of America, Self-Study Program, Course Number 873003

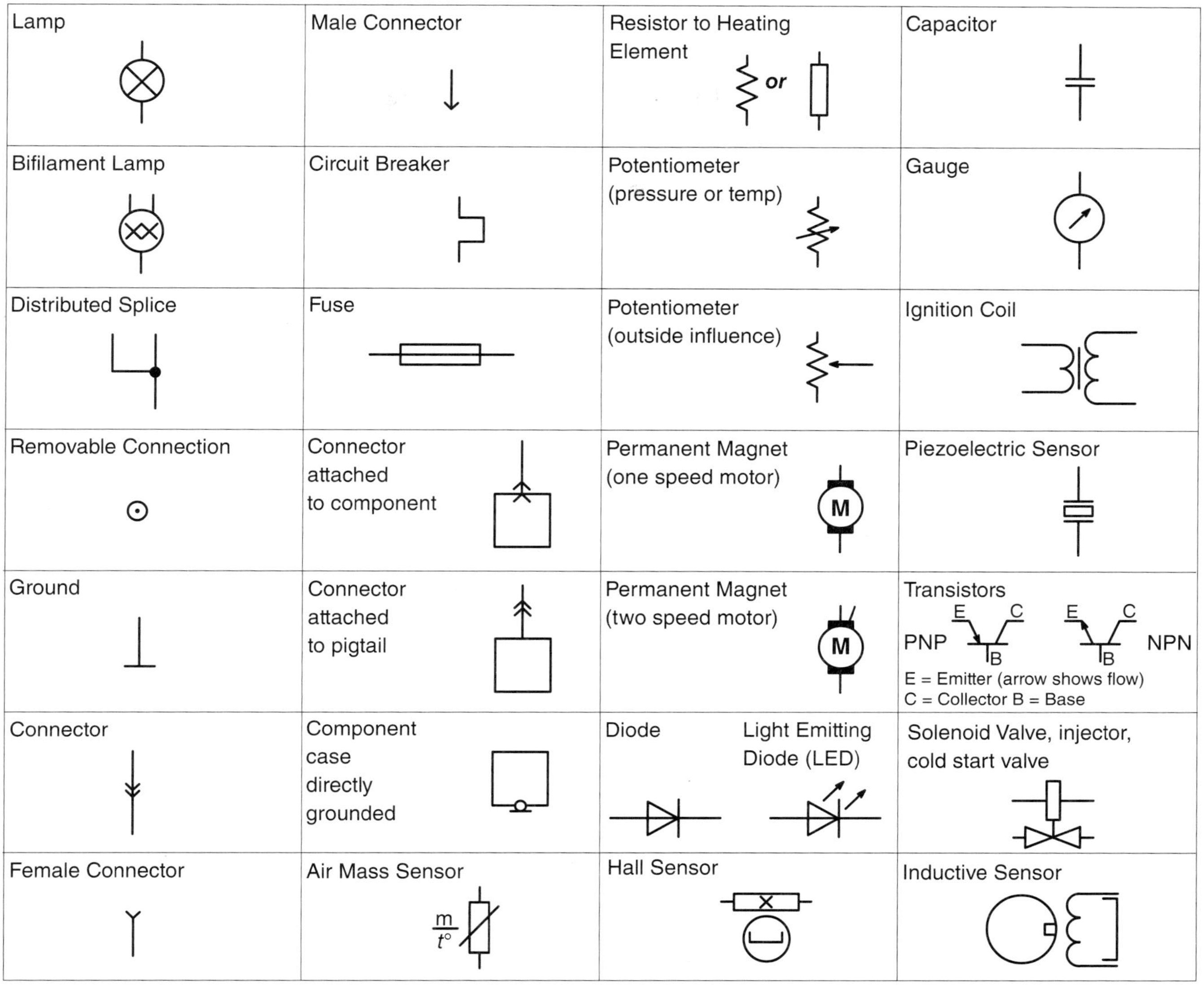

Lamp	Male Connector	Resistor to Heating Element	Capacitor
Bifilament Lamp	Circuit Breaker	Potentiometer (pressure or temp)	Gauge
Distributed Splice	Fuse	Potentiometer (outside influence)	Ignition Coil
Removable Connection	Connector attached to component	Permanent Magnet (one speed motor)	Piezoelectric Sensor
Ground	Connector attached to pigtail	Permanent Magnet (two speed motor)	Transistors PNP NPN E = Emitter (arrow shows flow) C = Collector B = Base
Connector	Component case directly grounded	Diode Light Emitting Diode (LED)	Solenoid Valve, injector, cold start valve
Female Connector	Air Mass Sensor	Hall Sensor	Inductive Sensor

FIGURE 19-21 Some typical DIN symbols.

Together these elements make up a complete and accurate wiring diagram. The key to reading wiring diagrams is in understanding the symbols. These symbols are standardized, allowing quick recognition of various components.

Power Distribution Flow

Since power flow begins at the top of a DIN diagram, a central power, fuse link, or relay panel is typically located at the top of the wiring diagram page. Circuit grounds, ground studs, and splices are located at the bottom of the diagram or the diagram indicates the circuit ground on another page. All ground connections, whether they occur as a splice in a harness or the final ground source, are numbered and identified in the wiring diagram.

Component and Device Codes

Between the central relay panel and the vehicle ground at the bottom of the diagram are located the component symbols and conductors. Components are marked with a component code

listed in the legend. Conductors are marked with wire color and size. Components in wiring diagrams are given a DIN standardized alphanumeric designation for identification (DIN Standard 40717). The first letter portion of the code separates the component into basic groups. The letters A to Z are used with the exception of Q and O. The letter G, for example, designates a device that supplies current that includes alternators, batteries, or even battery chargers. Switches receive an S designation; motors, M.

The next code is a number that differentiates between the various sub-types of electrical devices. A prefix R, for example, is a resistor, which could mean it's a glow-plug, heater element, potentiometer thermistor, and so on. The number 3 in the designation R3 indicates sub-type of resistor. The final number in a DIN code indicates a terminal or designation.

Terminal Designation

DIN Standard 72552 applies to the terminal designations for circuits. The purpose of the terminal designation system is to

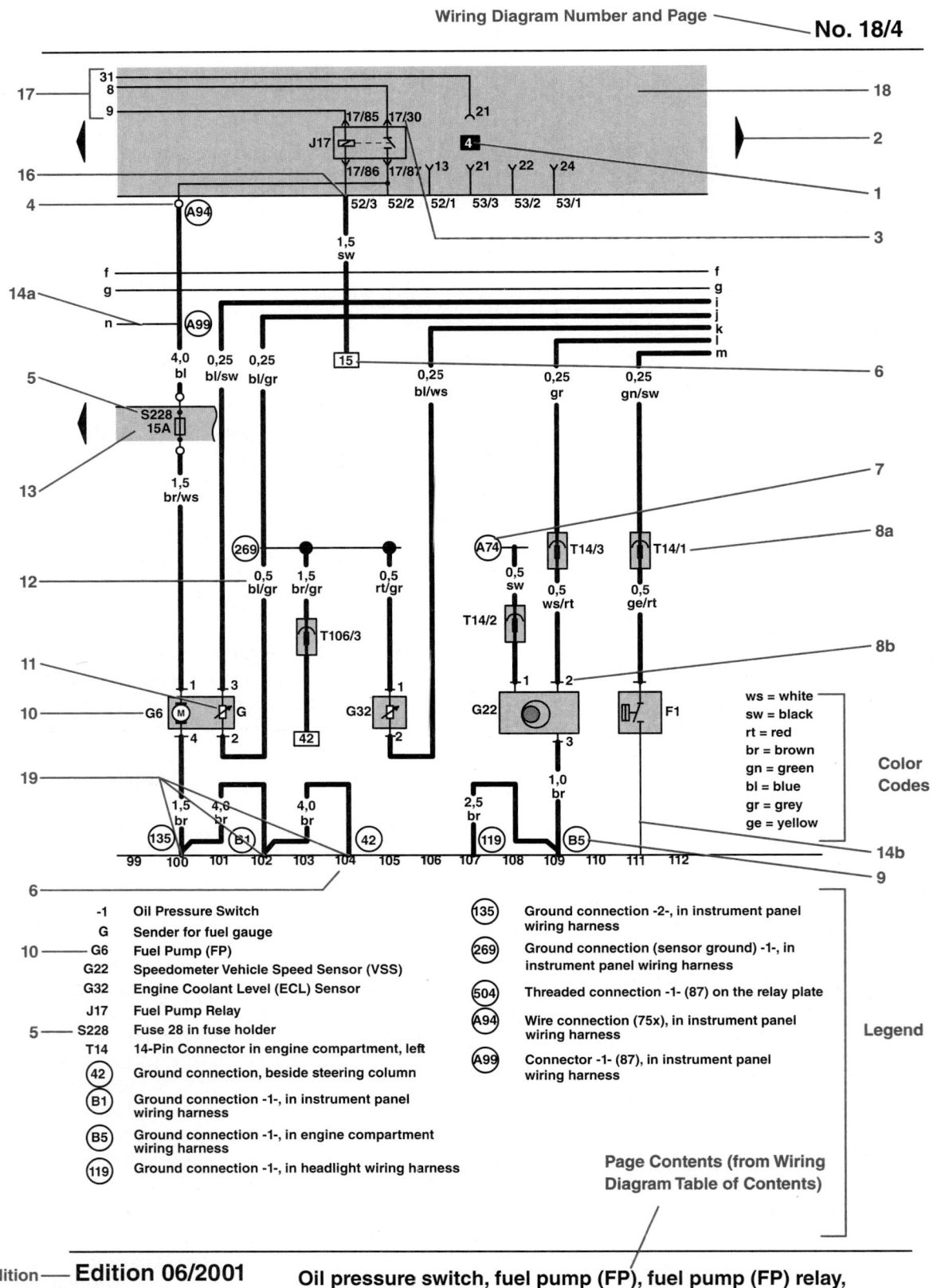

Edition number   **Edition 06/2001**

Oil pressure switch, fuel pump (FP), fuel pump (FP) relay, engine coolant level sensor, speedometer vehicle speed sensor

FIGURE 19-22 Elements of a DIN diagram highlighted.

Image Modified from ©2001 Volkswagen of America, Self-Study Program, Course Number 873003

enable connection verification of wiring to various components when diagnosis and repair is necessary. For example, B+ indicates a battery positive terminal. The number 30 indicates the circuit is a wire conductor to the battery positive terminal. So, the battery positive circuit to a relay has the designation of 30. The relay uses code K and, if it is the fourth of many relays, it has the symbol K4. Some examples of DIN standards for terminal designations are:

- 15 Ignition
- 30 Battery +
- 31 Ground
- 31b Switched ground
- 50 Starter control
- 53 Wiper motor +

Current Tracks

Individual current tracks are identified numerically along the base of the wiring diagram. These numbers are used to find the continuation of a conductor on another page or diagram.

For example, the number 221 inside a small box on one page indicates that the wire is continued on current track 221 on the next page with the same color and size of wire with a small box. Wires are conductors that carry current to components and are usually indicated by a solid line. A wire shown as a dashed line in a wiring diagram indicates that the wire does not apply to all vehicles. That fact is usually noted in the key for the wiring diagram.

Wire Colors

Knowing the standards for wiring colors makes the job of reading and interpreting schematics easier. Some colors and terminal designations for wiring are used across a number of standards, for example:

Red	Battery +
Green	Ignition (1)
Brown	Ground (31)
Yellow	Headlights (58)

In DIN diagrams, wire colors are shown as abbreviations of the German word for the color (DIN standard 47 002) for example:

bl	Blue
br	Brown
ge	Yellow
gn	Green
ro	Red
sw	Black
li	Violet
ws	White

The International Organization for Standardization (ISO) uses different colors to designate circuit functions, as listed in Table 19-2.

Wire Sizes on Diagrams

Wiring diagrams also indicate the wire gauge used (shown in mm^2), designating the cross-sectional area of the wire. Because standards exist for the maximum permissible voltage drop across a circuit, wire gauge is critical. If the voltage drop across the wire is too high, one or more of the following may occur:

- The circuit may overheat
- The load may not operate properly (due to low voltage condition)
- Components may be damaged

Complex Symbols

Often the internal schematic of the component is shown to allow the technician to follow current flow through the component. These internal symbols are a combination of several basic symbols. This allows the technician to take a more complex symbol and break it down into its smaller components. Even the most complex components are nothing more than a combination of smaller basic symbols. More complex components may contain complex control circuitry. In DIN schematics, this is indicated with the symbol of a transistor in the component symbol.

A relay in a DIN schematic is an example of a combination of symbols in a single component. Relays require a signal from an outside source to activate. Relays share the component designator J with control units. The basic five-pin relay in **FIGURE 19-23** contains two separate components: a switch and a solenoid. The coil in the solenoid is energized with low current, creating a magnetic pull that closes or opens the switch. Terminal designation for a standard five-pin relay is:

- 30 Receives + battery current
- 87 Normally closed contact to load
- 86 Control circuit receives a switched battery positive
- 85 Receives a switched ground to activate the solenoid winding in the relay
- 87a Normally open contact to load

Note: All switches and relays are shown in a non-operated state.

Valley Forge Diagrams

The **Valley Forge (VF) diagram** is a type of wiring diagram used by many North American-based OEMs. VF diagrams share many

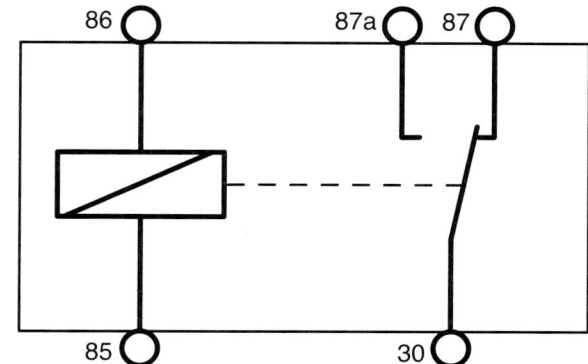

FIGURE 19-23 A typical DIN relay diagram.

commonalities with DIN standards. For example, VF diagrams also show power flow from top to bottom and circuit operation from left to right, with inputs on the left and outputs on the right. VF diagrams use standards for wiring colors, circuit codes, and symbols.

A primary difference between the two types of schematic diagrams is that VF diagrams use SAE-type symbols. Conductor sizes, symbol representations, component, and terminal designations are different from DIN standards. Some of the common features shown in the VF diagram in **FIGURE 19-24** are:

1. Battery positive. Begins at top right of diagram, indicating a location to check for power.
2. Dotted line indicates the fuse location in a fuse block, but the dotted line means the component is not completely shown.
3. Thermal fuse. Circuit protection fuse size, circuit name, and location.
4. Wiring splice number indicates wires are joined. 121 indicates the splice number and "S" designates a splice.
5. Terminal location designated A. It shows a connection point on the horn relay.
6. A diode for suppression of voltage spike produced when the magnetic field of the relays, coil collapses.
7. Control circuit of the relay.
8. Dotted line represents mechanical action.

9. G indicates the wire position in the connector. 201 is the circuit number. C designates it as a connector.
10. Identification of wire color, circuit number, and size. 1 indicates the wires, cross-sectional area is 1 mm². ORN indicates an orange wire. The wire circuit number is 40.
11. A ground symbol indicates the component itself is grounded.
12. G indicates a ground source. 101 indicates the number and location of the ground.

Module Connector Pin Assignments

Wiring diagrams tell the user at which pin numbers the wires terminate. Knowing where the wires terminate simplifies diagnosis. There are four main types of terminal designations:

- Push-on/multi-point connections
- Component/multi-point
- Central/relay panel
- Relay

Generally, pin assignments are labelled on the plastic hard-shell connector housing and/or the corresponding component. On larger connectors, pin assignments are labelled at either end of a row (**FIGURE 19-25**). For example, the Engine Control Module (ECM) plug often has four to ten rows, each with 12 or more terminals. Each row is marked on each end to facilitate diagnosis.

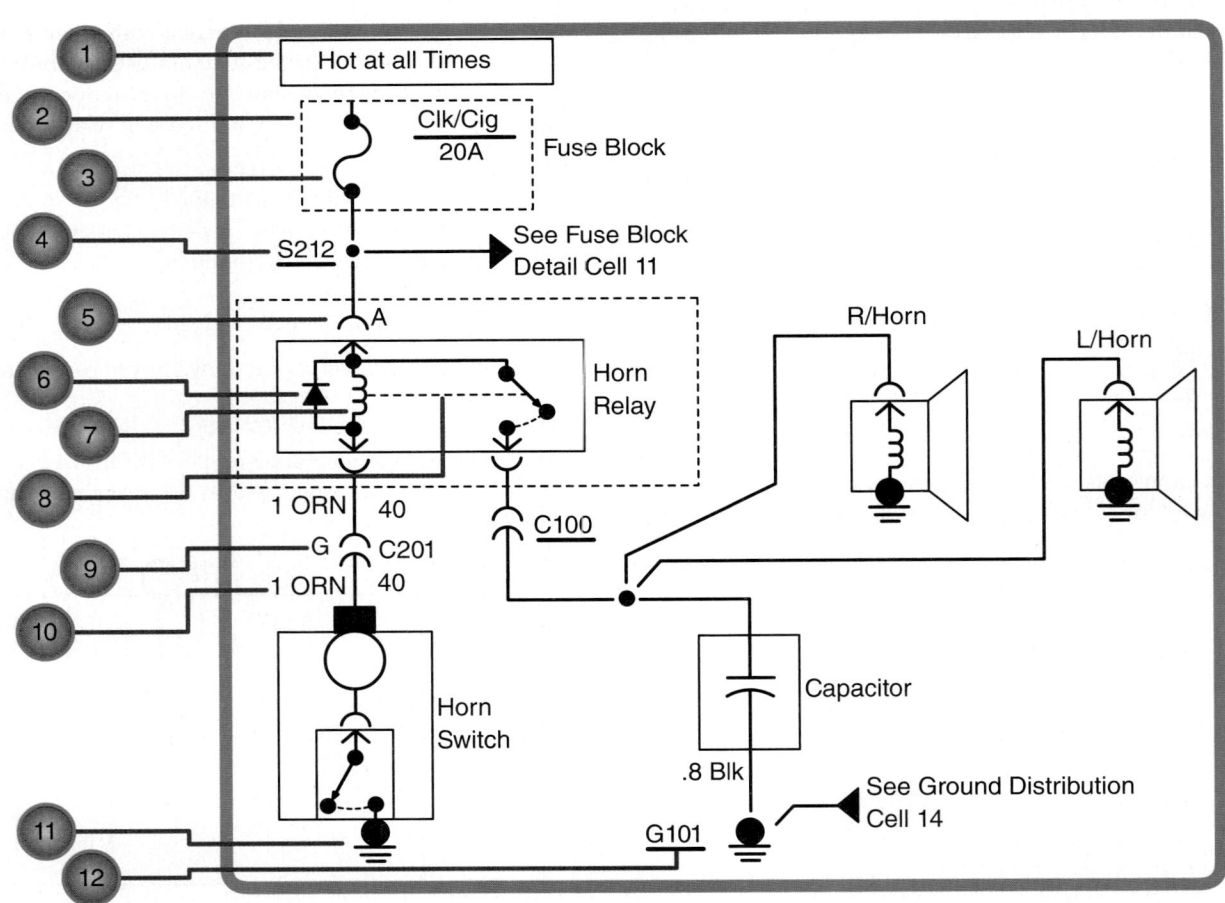

FIGURE 19-24 A typical Valley Forge diagram.

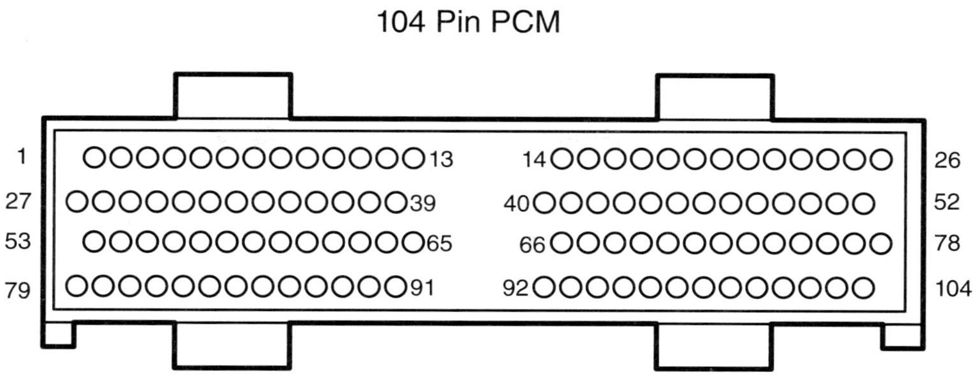

104 Pin PCM

FIGURE 19-25 The engine control module, like other electronic control units, has module pins that are numbered from left to right at either end of the row.

Wrap-Up

Ready for Review

▶ Wires and wiring harnesses carry the electrical power and signals through the vehicle to control virtually all of the systems on a vehicle.

▶ Electrical wires are used to conduct current around the vehicle. Wire can also be referred to as cable, although cable typically refers to large-diameter wire.

▶ Wiring harnesses are subject electrical noise or EMI noise. To prevent noise, some vehicles use shielded wiring harnesses.

▶ Shielded wiring harnesses can be twisted-pair shielding, Mylar tape, or drain lines.

▶ Wire size relates to the correct operation of electrical circuits. Selecting a wire gauge that is too small for an application has an adverse effect on the operation of the circuit. Selecting a wire gauge that is too large increases costs and the weight and size of wiring harnesses.

▶ The resistance of a wire affects how much current it can carry.

▶ There are two scales used to measure the sizes of wires: the metric wire gauge and the American wire gauge (AWG).

▶ Wire-coding systems are another useful feature of wiring to aid troubleshooting and service of electrical systems. Both colors and numbering systems designate wiring circuits, application, and even the routing of wires.

▶ SAE and ISO standards specify the dimensions, test methods, and requirements for single-core primary wire intended for use in road vehicle applications.

▶ Chassis wiring often uses numerical codes to identify which circuit the wire belongs to, where the wire is in the circuit, which harness it belongs in, and the wire gauge and color.

▶ Terminals installed to the wire ends provide low-resistance termination to wires. Terminals allow electricity to be conducted from the end of one wire to the end of another wire.

▶ There are two main types of terminals used in harness connectors—pull-to-seat and push-to-seat terminals. Connector housings have male and female sides and are usually shaped so that they can be connected in only one way.

▶ Wires are generally trouble-free and long-lasting, and any issues with wiring are more likely to be with the terminals than with the wires themselves.

▶ One of the greatest enemies to wiring is water. The tendency of water to "wick" inside insulation is what makes it so destructive.

▶ When electrical wire is joined to other wires or connected to a terminal, the insulation needs to be removed using wire-stripping tools.

▶ Solderless terminals are quick to install and effective at conducting electricity across joints that are designed to be disconnected. Connectors can also be soldered.

▶ Wiring diagrams use abstract graphical symbols to represent electrical circuits and their connection or relationship to other components in the system. They are essentially a map of all of the electrical components and their connections.

▶ Three main types of wiring diagrams are map, isometric, and schematic diagrams.

▶ The two most common types of schematic diagrams are the Deutsches Institut für Normung (DIN) and the Valley Forge (VF).

▶ Schematic wiring diagrams show power supply, load, ground, conductors (wires), and circuit protection.

▶ Schematic wiring diagrams show power flow from top to bottom and circuit operation from left to right, with inputs on the left and outputs on the right.

▶ Reading a wiring diagram is like reading a road map. There are a lot of interconnected circuits, wires, and components to decipher.

Key Terms

current track A numbered block at the end of a wire in a DIN type schematic diagram.

Deutsch connector A compact, environmentally sealed electrical connector that uses solid, round, metal pins and hollow female sockets.

Deutsches Institut für Normung (DIN) diagram A schematic wiring diagram on which symbols, terminal connection numbers, line symbols, and operational status of items, such as switches and relays, are defined by a DIN standard. Also called *current track*.

isometric diagram A wiring diagram used to locate a component within a system that shows the outline of a vehicle or piece of equipment where the component can be found.

map (pictorial) diagram A wiring diagram that shows the entire vehicle wiring circuit using pictorial symbols.

Metri-Pack connector A pull-to-seat electrical connector with flat terminals instead of round.

parallel wiring A type of custom-made wiring harness that encloses multiple conductors into a single vinyl insulator covering.

pull-to-seat terminal A terminal installed by inserting the wire through the connector cavity, crimping on a terminal, and then pulling the terminal back into the connector cavity to seat it.

push-to-seat terminal A terminal inserted into the back of the connector cavity to seat after the terminal is crimped to the wire.

SAE J1128 standard A standard that specifies the dimensions, test methods, and requirements for single-core primary wire intended for use in road vehicle applications.

schematic diagram A line drawing that explains how a system works by using symbols and connecting lines.

Valley Forge (VF) diagram A schematic wiring diagram that uses SAE-type symbols.

water wicking The movement of water through wiring due to its adhesive and cohesive properties.

Weather-Pack connector An environmentally sealed push-to-seat electrical connection system supplied in one- to six-pin configurations.

Review Questions

1. Fuses prevent damage to wiring by:
   a. stopping excessive current flow
   b. reducing wiring length
   c. limiting voltage increases
   d. decreasing circuit resistance
2. The size of a fuse used in an electrical circuit is primarily determined by:
   a. The diameter of the wire
   b. The length of the wire or circuit
   c. The total amperage drawn by the circuit loads
   d. A safety factor
3. What is the major difference between a Metri-Pack and Weather-Pack connector?
   a. Terminal material
   b. Push-to-seat versus pull-to-seat
   c. The current rating
   d. Crimped versus soldered connection to the wire

4. To enhance the strength of the joint, wires should be joined by bending each into a double J bend then twisting to form a:
   a. Butt connection
   b. Crimped connection
   c. Overlapping X shape
   d. Western Union splice
5. Which of the following is a term given to a diagram identifying the location of a component or connection in a chassis?
   a. Schematic
   b. Isometric diagram
   c. Pictorial diagram
   d. DIN-type diagram
6. After a butt-type connecter is crimped, it should be:
   a. Covered with protective loom
   b. Sealed with electrical tape
   c. Sprayed with corrosion-inhibiting paint
   d. Sealed with heat-activated shrink tube
7. Which type of diagram is commonly used by North American manufacturers to locate a wiring connection in the electrical system?
   a. Linear diagram
   b. DIN diagram
   c. Isometric diagram
   d. Valley Forge diagram
8. What is the purpose of current tracks?
   a. To find the continuation of a conductor on another page
   b. To match the wiring to the vehicle
   c. To assist in locating a battery terminal
   d. To trace current flow in the electrical system
9. Wire gauge is a measurement of:
   a. only the wire diameter
   b. diameter of wire plus its insulator
   c. length of wire
   d. wire material
10. What does the letter "G" designate in a DIN-type wiring diagram?
    a. A ground
    b. Green wire color
    c. A switch
    d. A battery or alternator

ASE Technician A/Technician B Style Questions

1. Technician A says that low-voltage wiring carries no more than 60 volts and uses primary-type wire. Technician B says that secondary wire carries 60 volts or less and is used in the wiring harnesses of most commercial vehicles. Who is correct?
   a. Technician A
   b. Technician B
   c. Both Technician A and Technician B
   d. Neither Technician A nor Technician B
2. Technicians A and B were examining wire supplied by the parts department to repair a wiring harness. It had a dull gray appearance that could not be cleaned. Technician A says the wire color is normal because it is tin plating

designed to provide corrosion resistance. Technician B says the wiring is very poor quality and should not be used. Who is correct?

a. Technician A
b. Technician B
c. Both Technician A and Technician B
d. Neither Technician A nor Technician B

3. Technician A says that adding a set of fog lights to the same circuit as the high/low-beam headlights requires increasing the amperage of the circuit protection device to prevent the circuit from being overloaded. Technician B says that the diameter of the wiring likely must increase and the headlight circuit wiring needs replacement. Who is correct?

a. Technician A
b. Technician B
c. Both Technician A and Technician B
d. Neither Technician A nor Technician B

4. Technician A says selecting a wire gauge that is too large increases the amount of current flowing into the wiring harnesses, which also increases resistance. Technician B says the resistance of the circuit decreases if larger-diameter wiring is used. Who is correct?

a. Technician A
b. Technician B
c. Both Technician A and Technician B
d. Neither Technician A nor Technician B

5. Technician A says that terminals attached to wire ends need only to be crimped and not soldered. Technician B says that terminals should be soldered to increase connector reliability. Who is correct?

a. Technician A
b. Technician B
c. Both Technician A and Technician B
d. Neither Technician A nor Technician B

6. Technician A says that regardless of which manufacturer designs and builds a truck, all wiring diagrams now use DIN-type wiring diagrams. Technician B says that only Valley Forge-type diagrams are used in North America. Who is correct?

a. Technician A
b. Technician B
c. Both Technician A and Technician B
d. Neither Technician A nor Technician B

7. Technician A says wiring diagrams generally show current flow from top to bottom. Technician B says circuit operation is shown from left to right. Who is correct?

a. Technician A
b. Technician B
c. Both Technician A and Technician B
d. Neither Technician A nor Technician B

8. Technician A says DIN schematic diagrams are also called power source track wiring diagrams because they show the power source at the top of the page and the ground points at the bottom. Technician B says newer DIN standards use SAE schematic symbols. Who is correct?

a. Technician A
b. Technician B
c. Both Technician A and Technician B
d. Neither Technician A nor Technician B

9. Technician A says knowing the standards for Valley Forge wiring colors makes the job of reading and interpreting schematics easier. Technician B says that only DIN diagrams use standards for wiring color components and circuits. Who is correct?

a. Technician A
b. Technician B
c. Both Technician A and Technician B
d. Neither Technician A nor Technician B

10. Technician A says wiring diagrams also indicate the wire diameter used (shown in mm^2), designating the cross-sectional area of the wire. Technician B says only AWG standards are used for wiring diagrams, so a cross-sectional wire area is not displayed in a diagram. Who is correct?

a. Technician A
b. Technician B
c. Both Technician A and Technician B
d. Neither Technician A nor Technician B

CHAPTER 20

Body Electrical Systems—Lighting Systems

Learning Objectives

After reading this chapter, you will be able to:

- **LO 20-1** Identify a vehicle's optional and accessory electrical systems.
- **LO 20-2** Describe and explain network control of lighting circuits.

- **LO 20-3** Identify and describe various types of lighting technology used in commercial vehicles.
- **LO 20-4** Identify and describe trailer cords and plugs.

You Are the Technician

As a technician working in a fleet operation where you are responsible for safety compliance of hundreds of trucks and trailers crossing many jurisdictional boundaries, so lighting system safety is a major concern. The use of particular lighting configurations in one area is not necessarily tolerated in another area. There have been several high-profile accidents at night in which cars have collided with trucks and trailers parked or broken down on the side of the road. Drivers are often adding additional lights or installing different colored light lenses for decorative reasons on trucks they regularly drive. On top of that, there is a steady amount of maintenance work related to replacing broken lights and burned-out light bulbs, problems with resistance in trailer electrical cords, loose trailer cord electrical pins—not to mention damage to wiring harnesses that often takes place due to improper repair procedures. To enhance vehicle safety and reduce the costs of lighting system maintenance and fines for noncompliance, as well as blemishes on the company's safety record, you are considering a number of strategies. As you contemplate next steps, consider the following:

1. What legal standard or reference can you use to determine the minimum safety requirements for vehicle lighting and reflective markers?
2. List the advantages of using LED lighting for all marker, tail, and clearance lights for vehicles in your fleet.
3. How could a charging system voltage test reduce maintenance costs for vehicle lighting?

Introduction

A traditional body electrical system consists of basic functional electrical systems found in all vehicles. This chapter covers the body electrical systems related to lighting, but before examining those details, it is necessary to discuss how the electrical systems are organized, as well as how they are classified by category according to whether they are conventional or use distributed network control.

Fundamentals of the Body Electrical System

LO 20-1 Identify a vehicle's optional and accessory electrical systems.

A traditional body electrical system consists of two parts. The first section is the mandatory electrical systems found in all vehicles, such as lighting, wipers, horn, directional signal indicators, heater blower motors, and instrumentation. Optional accessories make up the other section of the body electrical system. Power windows, seats, supplemental restraint systems (SRS), on-board entertainment systems, vehicle security, and collision avoidance systems are just a few examples of the hundreds of electrical accessories available today.

Conventional and Network Control

Body electrical systems are now also classified into two major categories. Conventional systems, which are quickly disappearing, use electrical components operating in isolation. Point-to-point wiring connects the dome light, horn, or power windows to a switch operated by the driver. Other devices, such as the wipers, head lights, or power door locks, operate independently of one another. However, most body electrical systems today use a networked or distributed control of the electrical system. Switching on the wipers typically activates the headlights. Locking the doors with a remote transmitter beeps the horn while momentarily switching on the dome and headlights circuits. Adding weight to the rear axles may cause the headlights to automatically level.

Just as an electronic control module is used to operate the engine or antilock brake system (ABS), an electronic control module now controls large sections of the electrical system by switching current on or off to devices. Decisions are based on inputs received from a variety of sources, including the driver and logic circuits, or programmable templates designed by original equipment manufacturers (OEM) software (**FIGURE 20-1**). Electronic control modules not only control electrical circuit operation, but also serve as a power distribution point for the electrical system. Instead of fuses, circuits are protected using electronic switches. Adding accessories more likely involves changing electrical templates for system control software instructions and less likely adding wiring and switches.

Ladder Logic

Body electrical equipment varies by application. For example, the wipers and heating system in a transit bus are very different than those found in an ambulance or highway tractor. So, too, do the

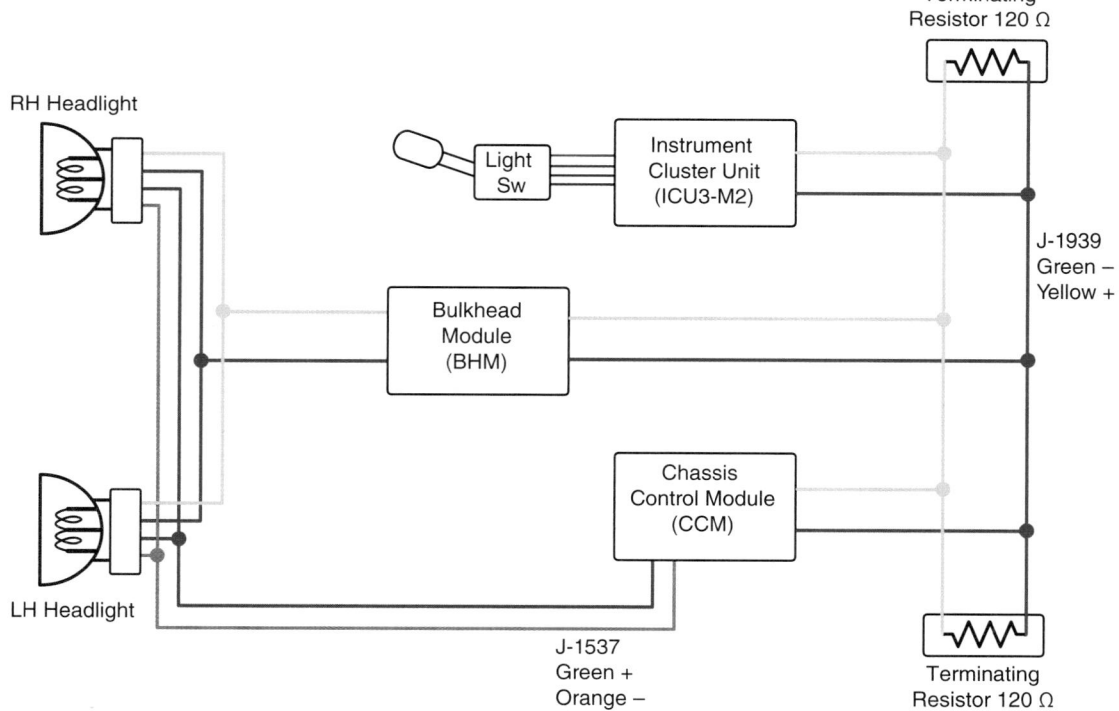

FIGURE 20-1 Distributed control of the electrical system means a variety of modules share control of the electrical system operation rather than the direct point-to-point wiring connections. For example, the headlights in this Freightliner receive current from the chassis control module (CCM). The bulkhead module or master module receives an input from the dash switch and commands the CCM to switch headlights on.

electrical door locking mechanisms. In addition to the variety of electrical accessories, the sophistication of these systems makes it almost impossible to solve electrical problems without the ability to access, read, and interpret electrical schematic diagrams. A few systems even require an understanding of how circuit logic operates. For example, in a networked system, a technician needs to know what conditions are necessary to activate a specific electrical circuit. The simple action of extending a signal arm from a school bus requires a number of other actions to occur before it can take place. In other systems, park brakes may not release if outriggers are still extended, wheel chocks are not stowed away, or a bus door is open. The designed-in logic of a circuit that determines what activates a specific circuit is referred to as **ladder logic**.

Lighting Systems

LO 20-2 Describe and explain network control of lighting circuits.

There are many different styles and types of lights. Each style and type is designed to perform specific roles. For example, warning lamps, indicators, stop lights, taillights, courtesy lamps, and headlamps all perform different roles. In addition, modern vehicles use many different kinds and sizes of bulbs. There are several bulb types available, including standard incandescent bulbs, fluorescent bulbs, halogen bulbs, high-intensity discharge (HID) lamps, daytime running lights, and light-emitting diodes (LEDs). Conventional incandescent bulbs are being replaced in many applications by these other, more durable and efficient types of lights.

Lighting Circuits

Exterior lighting and reflectors are not only part of the vehicle safety systems, but are also designed to identify the length, width, and orientation of a commercial vehicle. Lighting standards are legislated by the Federal/Canadian Motor Vehicle Safety Standard 108 (FMVSS 108). Any light on the exterior of the vehicle must have **photometric certification** for FMVSS 108 standards (**FIGURE 20-2**). This means lamps are submitted to testing labs to evaluate factors, such as light color, brightness, and the angle at which the light is effectively observed. Light lenses carry Society of Automotive Engineers (SAE) or in Europe, and ECE identification numbers indicating the standard they meet. Generally, lamps facing rearward must emit red light, lamps facing sideways must emit amber light, lamps facing front must emit white or yellow light, and no other colors are permitted except on emergency vehicles, which may use blue lights. Bulb numbers indicate they meet standards for durability and light intensity necessary for use in motor vehicles. Major exterior lighting circuits include:

- Headlights
- Clearance identification lights
- Park-taillights
- Turn signals
- Hazard lights (four-way flashers)
- Reverse lights
- Fog lights

Vehicle lighting is depicted in **FIGURE 20-3**.

FIGURE 20-2 The SAE code found on every exterior light indicates the position where it can be used and the photometric standard it meets.

▶ **TECHNICIAN TIP**

FMVSS are legislated regulations written to provide minimum safety performance requirements for motor vehicles and motor vehicle equipment. To protect the public against unreasonable risk of death or injury due to crashes, FMVSS legislates standards for the design, construction, or performance of motor vehicles. The design of commercial vehicle body electrical systems is affected by a number of these standards, including:

- FMVSS 103 Windshield defrosting and defogging systems
- FMVSS 104 Windshield wiping and washing systems
- FMVSS 108 Lamps, reflective devices, and associated equipment
- FMVSS 112 Headlamp concealment devices
- FMVSS 118 Power-operated window, partition, and roof panel systems
- FMVSS 124 Accelerator control systems
- FMVSS 131 School bus pedestrian safety devices
- FMVSS 125 Warning devices
- FMVSS 217 Bus emergency exits and window retention and release

Lighting Technologies

LO 20-3 Identify and describe various types of lighting technology used in commercial vehicles.

What is light? Light is produced by atoms whenever an electron moves from a higher orbital ring (farther from the nucleus) to a lower orbital requiring less energy. Energy given up by the electron is released in the form of a photon. **Photons** are particles of energy and are the basic unit of light (**FIGURE 20-4**).

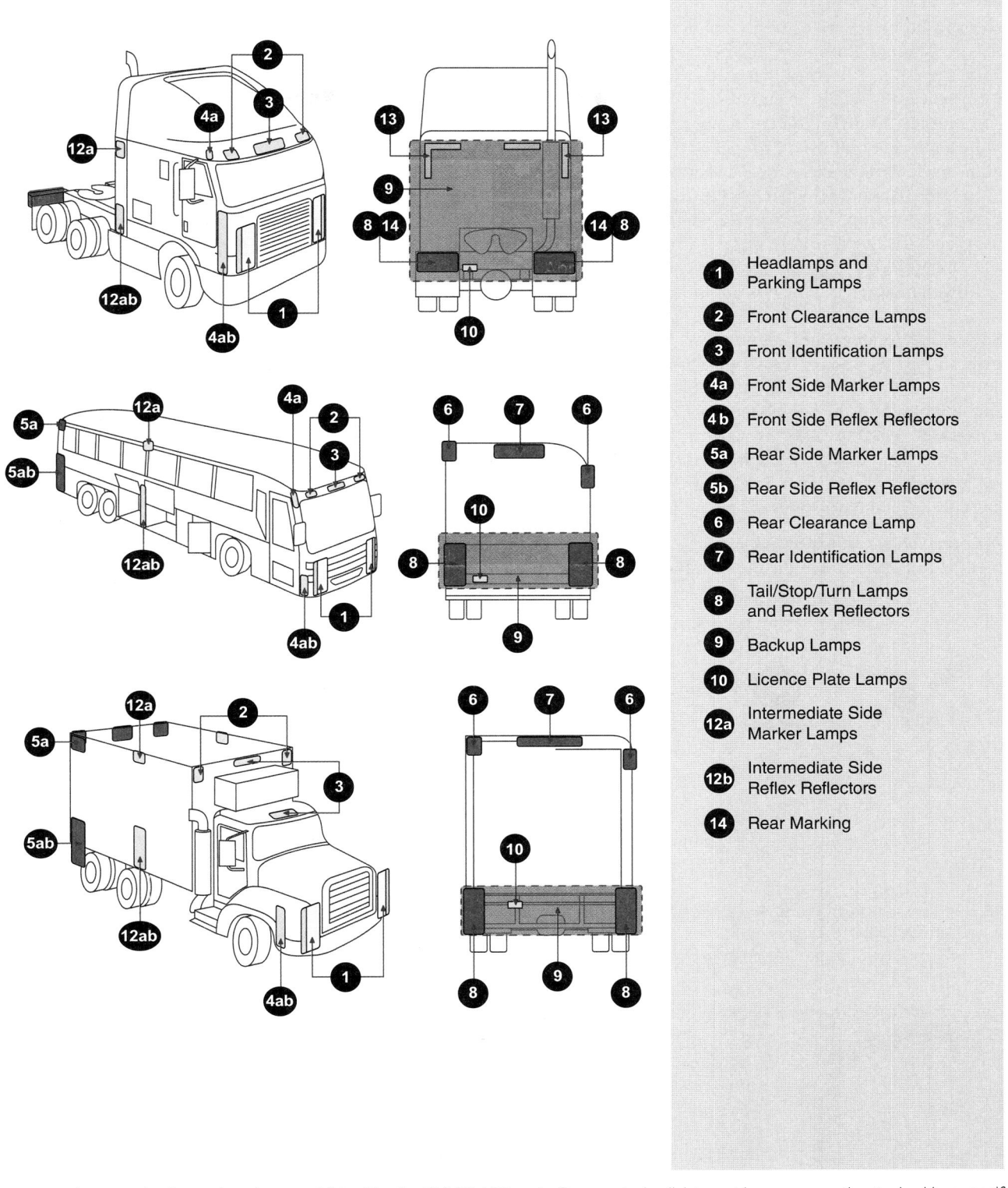

FIGURE 20-3 Lamp and reflector locations established by the FMVSS 108 code. Every exterior light must be permanently attached in a specific location and comply with FMVSS 108 requirements. The face of any device on the front, rear, and sides must be perpendicular and parallel to vehicle centerline unless it is photometrically certified at installation angle.

To produce light and illuminate interiors and instrument clusters, lighting technology has evolved rapidly in recent years beyond the use of incandescent bulbs. These include:

- Fluorescent
- Halogen
- LEDs

Incandescent Bulbs

Incandescent bulbs are the conventional bulb technology first invented by Thomas Edison. A filament of metal, which is essentially a resistor, is electrically heated to the temperature at which it produces light. The energy lost by colliding electrons trying to squeeze through the filament is converted into light energy. Incandescent bulbs were originally manufactured with a vacuum inside a glass enclosure. That was because air rapidly oxidizes the filament at high temperatures, and the filament would quickly burn up. Even inside a vacuum, the filament eventually boils away, depositing metal on the cooler walls of the bulb. Filling the bulb with an inert gas, such as argon or an argon-nitrogen mixture, is done now to slow evaporation of the filament.

Features are designed into automotive bulbs to allow them to operate in harsher environments with greater resistance to vibration that destroys ordinary bulbs. Single- and double-filament supports and thicker filament wires are a couple of unique features (**FIGURE 20-5**). To ensure that lights operate effectively, the SAE establishes standards and numbers for exterior lighting.

There are several types of incandescent light failures:

- An over-voltage failure leaves small blobs of melted filament wire at each end of the filament (**FIGURE 20-6A**).

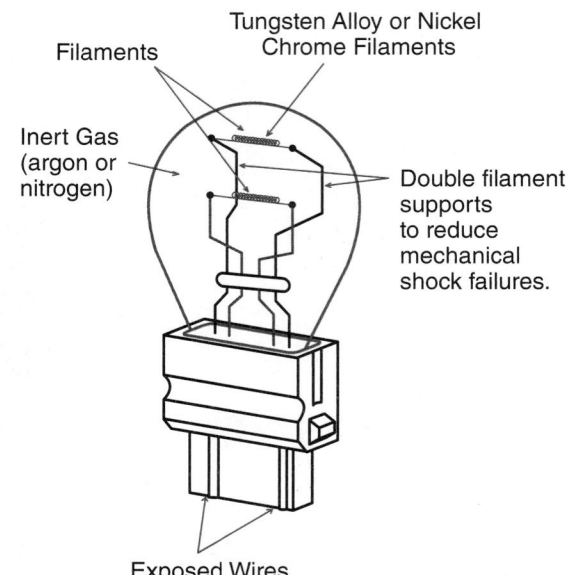

FIGURE 20-5 Construction of a 3157 wedge type automotive-type bulb.

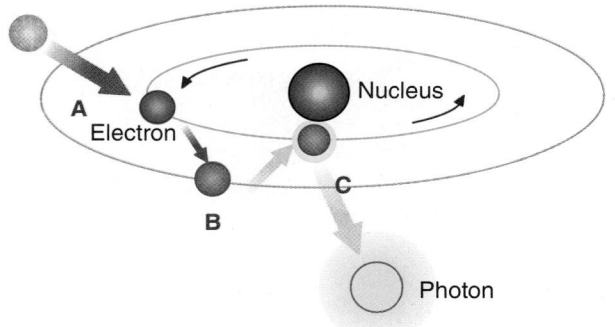

FIGURE 20-4 How light is produced: **A.** A collision excites the atom. **B.** Then, an electron jumps to a higher energy level. **C.** Finally, the electron moves back to its proper ring, emitting a photon.

- Leakage of air into the bulb leaves a smoky residue inside the bulb. Air can leak through the glass channels carrying wire (**FIGURE 20-6B**).
- A broken bulb when the filament is hot causes the filament to absorb oxygen and expand farther than normal.
- A bulb damaged by vibration or shock generally breaks and separates at the filament support (**FIGURE 20-6C**).
- A burnt-out bulb with a chrome filament deposits the chrome evaporated from the filament onto the cooler bulb wall (**FIGURE 20-6D**).
- A burnt-out tungsten bulb has a brown interior bulb coating.

Over-voltage conditions cause 60% of all lighting failures. For every one volt above designed limits, the life expectancy of the bulb drops by 50% (**FIGURE 20-7**).

Bulbs can have different types of contacts. Bulbs with bayonet contacts are inserted with a push and turn (**FIGURE 20-8A**). Edison-types screw into the socket (**FIGURE 20-8B**) and wedge-types push in (**FIGURE 20-8C**). Some wedge bulbs have no plastic base, and the wires turn up toward the sides of the bulb.

FIGURE 20-6 A. Voltage failure melts bulb filaments. **B.** Air leakage. **C.** Mechanical shock breaks filaments. **D.** Condensed chrome vapor on the bulb walls causes filament evaporation.

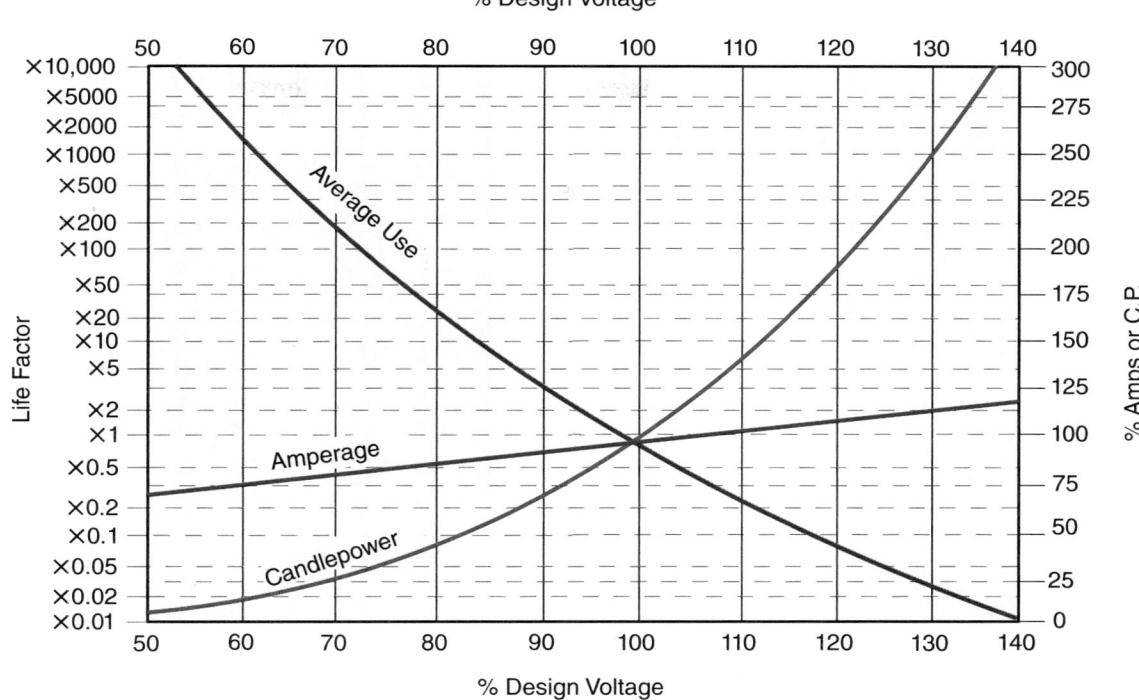

FIGURE 20-7 Increasing voltage supplied to a bulb causes it to become brighter but shortens its service life.

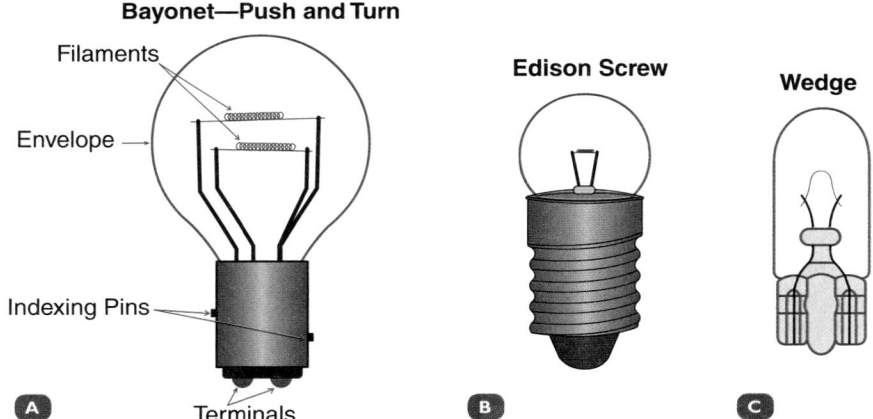

FIGURE 20-8 A. A bayonet mount with two different-sized filaments for a tail and brake light. To prevent the wrong filament from being energized, the base contacts have features allowing installation in only one way. **B.** A single contact is used for the separate park/tail lamp. **C.** A wedge bulb.

Fluorescent Bulbs

Because **fluorescent bulbs** are electrically efficient and distribute light well, they have some use as dome and cargo lights. Like incandescent bulbs, fluorescent light uses electrically heated filaments too. However, the light produced by fluorescent bulbs is created by exciting the phosphor coating on the inside of the bulb with ultraviolet light (UV).

UV light is produced indirectly by the electric filaments, located at each end of a tube filled with a small amount of mercury or a noble gas, such as neon, argon, or xenon. A step-up voltage circuit or transformer causes electrons to be released from the filaments while heating some of the mercury and turning it to a vapor, which in turn enables the gas inside the tube to become ionized. In other words, the gas becomes electrically conductive.

Electrons emitted from the filament move through the gas and hit mercury atoms, which momentarily knocks their electrons into higher orbits. When the electrons fall back to their normal energy levels, the energy lost is converted into photons (**FIGURE 20-9**). A phosphor coating on the inside of the bulb converts the mostly ultraviolet light into visible light. While the bulbs consume less energy than incandescent bulbs and last longer, the disadvantage is fluorescent bulbs and fixtures are much more expensive to produce. In addition, they do not usually work well at low temperatures.

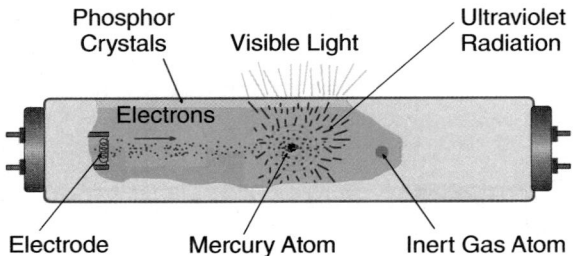

FIGURE 20-9 Operation of fluorescent lights. The high-voltage current at the filament sends electrons through the gas, the vapors of which are excited by the mercury. The energy given up by electrons moving up and down in orbitals produces light energy. The bulb's interior coating absorbs and re-emits the light into a visible spectrum.

Halogen Bulbs

Several disadvantages exist for conventional incandescent technology. As they age, the bulb wall often darkens as evaporating filament metal deposits on the bulb wall. These bulbs also operate at approximately 10% efficiency, converting most of the electrical energy into heat. To eliminate the problem of filament deposition on bulb walls, **halogen bulbs** are an alternative. Halogen bulbs are produced by adding small quantities of gases from the halogen family, such as iodine and bromine, into the bulb envelope to improve the efficiency and extend the life of the bulb. This takes place because halogen gases combine with vapors from the tungsten bulb filament when hot. Instead of depositing material onto the bulb walls, the tungsten recombines with the filament as halogen gas convection currents inside the bulb bring the tungsten back into contact with the filament instead of allowing it to condense on the bulb walls. Pressurizing the gas inside the bulb further diminishes filament evaporation. Quartz silica glass is used to withstand the higher temperatures and pressures inside the bulb, while simultaneously reducing its size (**FIGURE 20-10**). Because the filament can be operated at a higher temperature without burning up, more energy is converted to light, the light is whiter, and the bulb's life is extended (**FIGURE 20-11**). Headlight bulbs are commonly made using halogen gases.

Halogen Infrared Discharge (HID)

Halogen infrared discharge (HID) bulbs should not be confused with high-intensity discharge bulbs. Halogen infrared discharge bulbs use a special coating on an inside portion of the bulb wall. The coating reflects infrared heat back onto the filament, causing it to burn hotter. Increased filament heat produces more light with the same energy. These bulbs are used only in headlight applications (**FIGURE 20-12**).

▶ TECHNICIAN TIP

Any surface contamination, such as from greasy fingerprints, can damage the halogen bulb's quartz glass after it is heated. Hot spots on the bulb surface are created during operation, as the bulb cannot release heat at that point. In extreme cases, the localized heating changes the composition of the quartz, allowing pressurized bulb gases to leak out. A weakened bulb may also explode or form a bubble, distorting the glass envelope. Manufacturers recommend that halogen bulbs be handled

FIGURE 20-10 Halogen bulbs use thicker quartz glass, and contain some halogen gas combined with other gases under pressure.

The Halogen Regenerative Cycle

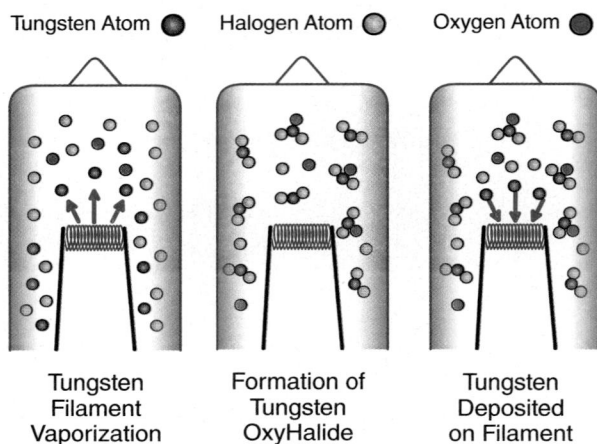

FIGURE 20-11 The halogen cycle recirculates tungsten back onto the filament instead of depositing it onto cooler bulb walls.

without touching the envelope. Using a clean paper towel while handling, or handling the bulb only by its base, lengthens bulb life. If the quartz is contaminated, it can be cleaned with alcohol before use.

SAFETY TIP

Halogen bulbs pose a number of safety hazards. First, halogen bulbs operate hot enough to severely burn anyone touching them while illuminated, and can even cause fires. Touching the bulb walls or contaminating the bulb surfaces in any way leads to bulb walls weakening, and even exploding. Pressurized gas inside the bulbs spreads shards of quartz glass a considerable distance.

High-Intensity Discharge Lamps (HID)

High-intensity discharge (HID) lamps used for headlight systems employ an electric arc to produce the light. Another name for these lamps is xenon lamps, which use the gas to initially activate the bulb's electric arc (**FIGURE 20-13**). Their higher light output of between 2800 and 3800 lumens is brighter than

FIGURE 20-12 Halogen infrared discharge bulbs use a reflective coating inside the bulb, causing it to glow brighter.

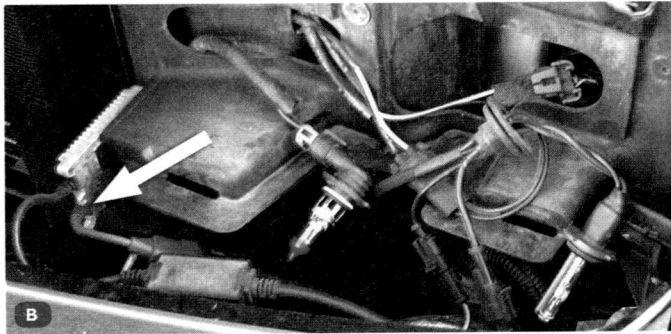

FIGURE 20-13 **A.** High-intensity discharge (HID) bulb that uses xenon gas and an electric arc to produce light. **B.** High-voltage igniter module.

FIGURE 20-14 A high-intensity discharge (HID) lamp xenon headlight uses dangerously high voltage, which can injure technicians if wiring is probed while illuminated.

Courtesy of Philips Lighting Holding B.V.

the 700 to 2100 lumens output of halogen lights. A **lumen** is a measure of light intensity. In general, small automotive lamps produce between 50 and 400 lumens. For reference, a standard 23-watt automotive stop light produces about 400 lumens of light output. The intensity of light from high-intensity discharge bulbs is produced using only half the current consumed by halogen bulbs, and yet the bulbs last twice as long, with a life cycle of 2000 hours.

In high-intensity discharge bulbs, light is produced by using a high-voltage electric arc of between 2000 and 2500 volts inside a chamber containing gasified metal, which requires a ballast to step up battery voltage (**FIGURE 20-14**). Approximately 3 amps of current are used to excite the electrons of the metal atoms into producing a bright white light. When in use, the bright light can produce excessive glare for oncoming drivers. A headlamp lens cleaning system and automatic beam leveling control used in Europe are recommended but not required in North America. A headlamp self-leveling system senses the change in vehicle inclination produced by a cargo load or road grade to automatically adjust the headlamps' vertical aim. The high cost of these systems currently limits their use.

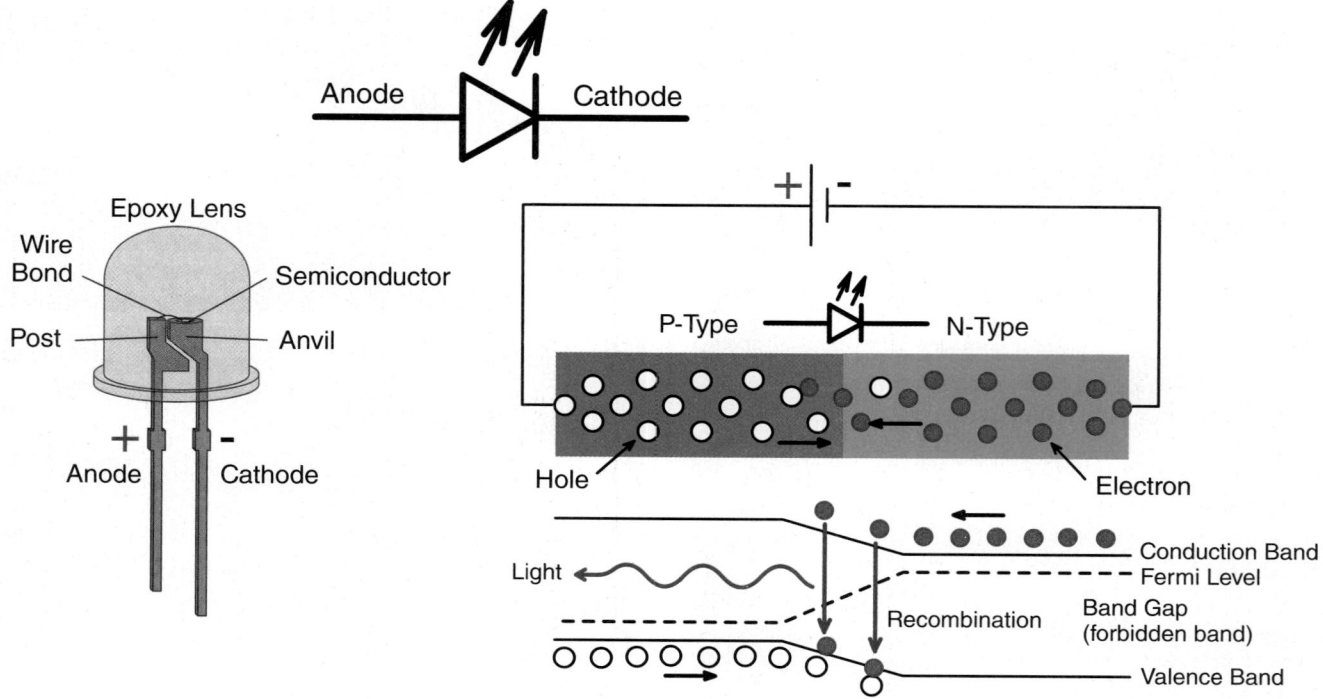

FIGURE 20-15 Construction and operating principles of LED lamps.

HID/Xenon Projector Headlights

Halogen and HID versions of projector headlights use a metal shield in front of the headlight bulb that helps focus the light in a specific direction with the help of a special lens inside the headlight housing. The metal light shield covers the high-beam bulb, even when the high-beam switch is activated.

▶ **TECHNICIAN TIP**

An intensive study by a major manufacturer has estimated the cost of producing power from a truck alternator is four times the cost to power a household. The cost of on-board electricity at 0.13 kW/hour assumes a fuel cost of $4/gallon and an alternator efficiency of approximately 60%. Broken down another way, the cost to produce a single amp per hour is $0.015. Assuming a lights-on only current load of 20 amps, the cost to light a vehicle is $0.31 for a single hour, travelling at 60 miles at highway speed. This also works out to $5.16 for a thousand miles.

FIGURE 20-16 A white light LED bulb combines red, green, and blue LED semiconductors.

Light-Emitting Diodes

A **light-emitting diode (LED)** is another unique type of diode that emits light when forward biased. Each time an electron fills a positively charged hole, some energy is released as a photon (**FIGURE 20-15**). The light frequency that determines the color is related to the semiconductor material used. To provide different colors, diodes use a wide combination of semiconductor materials, such as gallium, indium, arsenic, aluminum, phosphorus, and many others.

The first LED was red and made from a gallium insulator doped with arsenic and phosphorous. Green, yellow, blue, and almost any other color can now be produced from LEDs. To produce the impression of white light, red, green, and blue are mixed (**FIGURE 20-16**). High-intensity white LED lights, such as spotlights and headlights, use a phosphor material to convert a blue or ultraviolet LED to broad-spectrum white light. This is similar to the way a fluorescent lightbulb works (**FIGURE 20-17**).

FIGURE 20-17 Bright white lamps are the latest LED lighting development.

FIGURE 20-18 Look closely. This LED side marker lamp uses a current-limiting resistor and a silicon diode for every LED bulb on the lamp.

Organic LEDs (OLEDs), the latest LED technology, use a carbon material as a semiconductor, rather than inorganic crystal semiconductors. These devices, while using even less current, have shorter life spans, but may have more future use in instrument panels, driver information centers and touch panels, or other sources of low-intensity light.

Because an LED operates like a conventional diode, polarity must be observed when connecting an LED. Like other diodes, LEDs only emit light when connected correctly in a circuit. Individual LEDs operate at relatively low voltages between one and four volts, and draw currents between 10 and 40 milliamperes. Current above these levels can melt an LED chip. The main advantages of LEDs include the following:

- **Long life.** The life of an LED is roughly 100,000 hours, which means it can often last the life of the vehicle. Incandescent bulbs last anywhere between 1000 to 5000 hours. LEDs are shock-resistant, so they dim rather than abruptly fail. This extended durability translates into reduced maintenance expenses for fleets.
- **Safety.** Because LEDs light up instantly—0.5 seconds faster—following vehicles have more time to brake. Incandescent lamps need 0.25 seconds to heat and brighten. This shortened time translates into about 80' (24 m) more stopping distance at 60 mph (98 kph).
- **Low current consumption.** Using LEDs not only reduces power consumption and the need for larger wires, but can also help maintain sufficient voltage for the trailer ABS system to function when all the lights are on. An 85% drop in current takes place when lights are converted to LEDs.

Despite those many advantages, LEDs do have some disadvantages, including:

- LEDs are voltage sensitive—and quickly fail in even moderate over-voltage conditions. Quality lamps connect LEDs in series to limit over-voltage failures and protect the lights against reverse-polarity failures with diodes (**FIGURE 20-18**).
- LEDs have a high initial cost compared to other lighting, but these costs are rapidly falling. Higher initial costs can be offset by reduced electrical loads on the charging system and fuel savings over the vehicle lifecycle.

- Just replacing incandescent headlights with LEDs reduces power consumption by 40 watts to 70 watts. Depending on the assumptions for fuel cost engine efficiency and so on, the savings translate into $0.75 per bulb for every 1000 miles.
- LED output is temperature dependent—meaning that LEDs do not produce enough heat to melt snow and ice covering exterior lighting. Heating circuits are required to maintain unobstructed lighting in snowy weather. However, their light output actually rises at colder temperatures. Their efficiency drops with increased temperature.

Headlamps

A headlamp system is required to produce a low and a high beam, which may be integrated into a single lamp or individual lamps for each function. When used in pairs, the low beam must always be located on the outside when placed side-by-side, or the upper beam when stacked (**FIGURE 20-19**). Composite headlights used on most vehicles today incorporate turn signals, and even fog lamps, into their design (**FIGURE 20-20**). Adjustments of the beam and access to replace the bulbs is from the rear of the lamp housing (**FIGURE 20-21**).

High beams cast most of their light straight ahead, maximizing visibility distance, but produce excessive glare for oncoming drivers. High beams also reduce visibility due to light reflection when driving in fog, snow, or rain. This effect, called back-dazzle, is minimized by the use of lights with bluer spectrum and the use of fog lights. To alert the driver when high beams are operating, a high-beam indicator is placed in the instrument cluster. Low-beam lights direct their light downward and rightward to provide safe forward visibility without causing excessive glare to oncoming drivers or back-dazzle (**FIGURE 20-22**).

Low beams and high beams may operate together only when the high beams are illuminated. A dimmer switch is used to switch current between the two circuits. Composite lamps using nonstandard shapes and an internal reflector enable the use of replaceable bulbs.

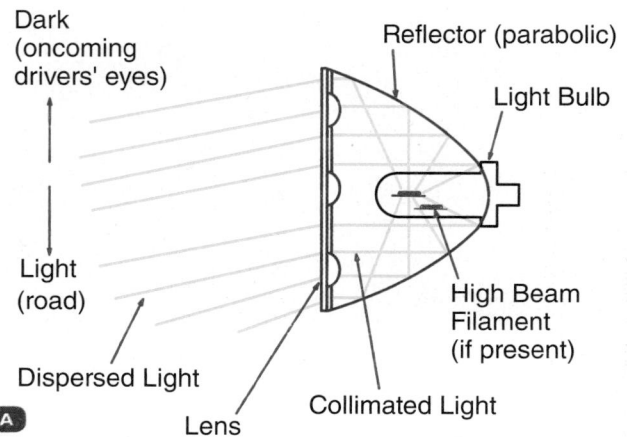

FIGURE 20-19 A. A high beam light filament uses a reflector in a non-standard shaped composite headlight. **B.** Low beams are always located on the outside of the composite headlights. A reflector controls the direction of light.

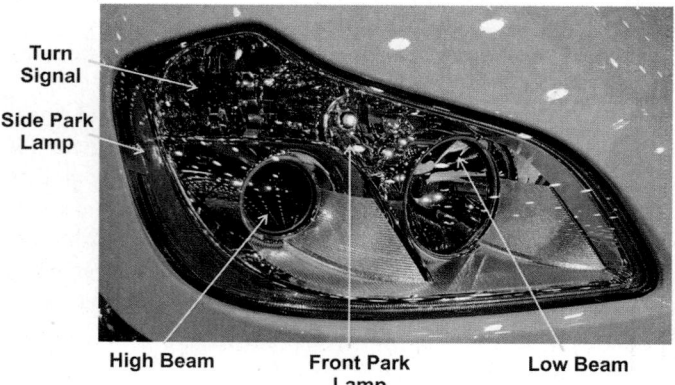

FIGURE 20-20 A composite headlight incorporates more than one light in its housing. This housing has a high, low, turn, and park light.

HID/Xenon Projector Headlights

Halogen and HID versions of projector headlights use a metal shield in front of the headlight bulb that helps focus the light in a specific direction with the help of a special lens

FIGURE 20-21 Bulb replacement and adjustment of the composite headlight is done at the rear.

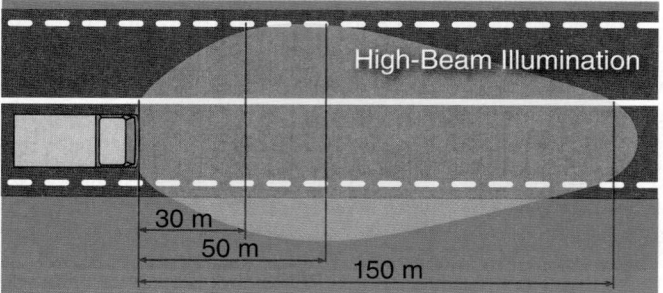

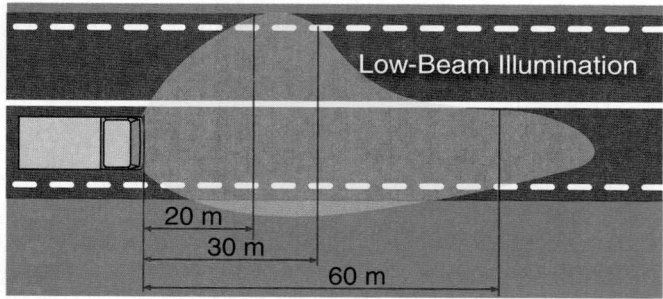

FIGURE 20-22 Low beams and high beams use different illumination patterns.

inside the headlight housing. The metal light shield covers the high beam bulb even when the high beam switch is activated (**FIGURE 20-23**).

▶ **TECHNICIAN TIP**

Because vehicle lighting is photometrically certified and meets FMVSS 108 standards when built, any change to lighting may change conformity to safety standards. Adding additional taillights, for example, might seem like a good idea, but it is frowned upon in some jurisdictions and can earn the driver a ticket. Using blue light lenses, replacing headlight bulbs with all-weather bulbs, adding additional clearance lights, and placing additional lighting around license plates or at the rear of a tractor's cab are also changes that are considered to alter or interfere with FMVSS 108 conformity.

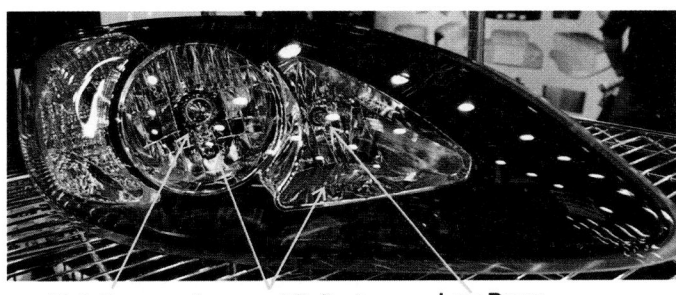

FIGURE 20-23 This projector-type composite head lamp uses a shield and special lens to focus light onto a particular area of the road.

Daytime Running Lights (DRL)

Daytime running lights (DRL) are designed to improve vehicle visibility in the daytime. Either the low- or high-beam circuits are powered at a reduced voltage of approximately 80% system voltage. This is accomplished using a DRL module containing a resistor connected in series with the headlight beam filaments. When the headlamp switch is engaged, the DRL module resistor is disconnected and the light filaments receive 100% system voltage.

Trailer Cords and Plugs

LO 20-4 Identify and describe trailer cords and plugs.

The **J-560 trailer connector** is an SAE standard set for connecting the trailer cord to the tractor and trailer electrical system together and has existed since the late 1950s. This seven-pin connector bears the stamp SAE J560, indicating compliance with physical and performance standards of the SAE. Plugs may be plastic or a die-cast zinc metal material. With the mandatory introduction of trailer ABS in 2001, constant battery power to the module could be supplied through the #7-pin blue color-coded wire of the J-560 plug. However, if auxiliary equipment, such as electrically operated solenoids for lift axles, on the trailer is controlled by a dedicated cab, tractors and trailers connecting two circuits through the #7 pin do not supply enough current. **FIGURE 20-24** shows the color code for a J-560 trailer plug.

A tractor and trailer may also be equipped with either a 13-pin or 15-pin Euro-style connector, which provides room for as many as six additional circuits, or an International Organization for Standardization (ISO) 3731 connector in tandem with the J-560 (**FIGURE 20-25**). The ISO 3731 connector resembles a J-560, with the exception of an inverted female ground terminal to prevent a connection with a J-560 plug. The connecting cable has a recessed male pin for a ground connection. A tractor using a J-560 in combination with an ISO 3731 plug allows it to hook up with older non-ABS trailers, trailers with ABS and no other electrical accessories, or trailers with ABS and other switched circuits (**FIGURE 20-26**).

7-Pin Heavy Duty J-560 Plug and Socket

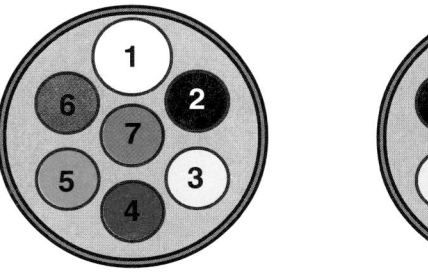
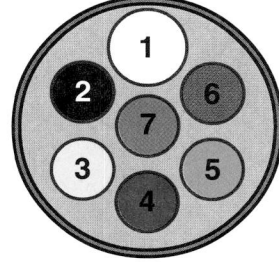

7-Pin Plug   7-Pin Socket

Pin No	Circuit	Color
1 (31)	Ground Return	White
2 (58L)	LHR Clearance & Marker	Black
3 (L)	LH Turn	Yellow
4 (54)	Stop Lamps	Red
5 (R)	RH Turn	Green
6 (58R)	RHR Clearance & Marker	Brown
7 (Center)	Reversing/Auxillary	Blue

FIGURE 20-24 Color code for J-560 trailer plug.

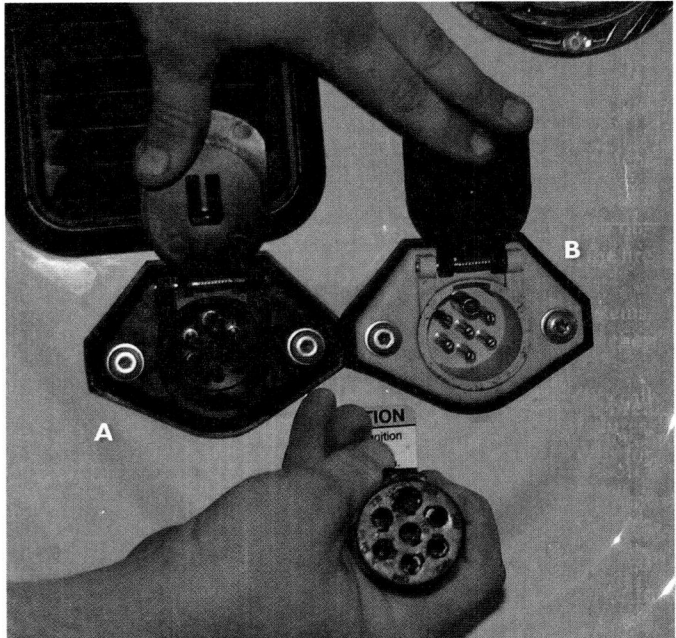

FIGURE 20-25 The **A.** J-560 and **B.** ISO 3731 trailer plugs.

An index lug on the cord and spring-loaded door, plus highly polished surfaces, improve latching force to prevent light flickering. Split pins with radial spring tension ensure a good connection between the plug and cable terminals in spite of regular thermal cycling caused by current flow through the connectors. Solid or split pins are acceptable, and male split pins can be spread with a small screwdriver if the connection becomes loose.

Trailer Cords

Trailer cords connecting the trailer and tractor are coiled and appear between 60" (152.4 cm) and 100" (254 cm) in working length. When uncoiled, the 60" (152.4 cm) cable could be as long as 12' (3.7 m) in length, while the 100" (254 cm) cable could be as long as 20' (6 m). Plugs at the end of each cable may be molded and hard-wired with strain relief to prevent the weight of the cord from disconnecting from the plug. Replacement plug leads are available and commonly used by technicians to repair cables.

15-Pin ISO 12098 Connector

FIGURE 20-26 Alternatives to the J-560 include several ISO standard pin configurations. Some trailers have as many as three or four trailer cord connector sockets.

TABLE 20-1 shows minimum wire sizes and standardized SAE color code used for each circuit. Green-colored cables designate trailer cords containing larger-gauge wire for the ABS circuits. Yellow cables and connectors designate ISO 3731.

Trailer Cord Maintenance

Cable plugs and connectors need periodic inspection for broken, bent, corroded, or collapsed pins. Cords should not have any cuts or abrasions that could penetrate the wiring. When not in use, cords should have a storage place where they will not be easily damaged. Wiring should be checked for pull-out from plugs caused by cable strain (**FIGURE 20-27**).

Turn Signal Circuits

Any vehicle operating on public roads and highways requires a turn signal-brake light system. In North America, the turn and stop light bulb signal are integrated with the major bulb filament of a double-filament bulb. The bulb's brighter element then operates through the red-colored lens covering the stop-turn signal. The smaller, minor filament of a double-filament bulb is the taillight. In European systems, the stop-turn signal is not integrated and uses a separate bulb and circuit for each. In those non-integrated systems, the stop signals are red, while the turn signals are amber.

The directional signal switch in mechanical directional signal systems is supplied current from two sources (**FIGURE 20-28**). One is the service brake light switch; the other is through the turn signal flasher relay. Internal switch contacts within the directional signal switch supply current to the stop-turn bulb filaments. Current is always supplied to the directional signal switch and either stops in the switch or is directed to the left or right turn-signal lights as well as the indicator lights in the instrument cluster. Brake switch power flows through the switch, to the light bulb filaments of the stop-turn lights and then to chassis ground. When the brakes are applied, current is supplied by the brake light switch through the directional switch to the bulb that is not illuminated by current from the flasher relay (**FIGURE 20-29**). If a four-way hazard flasher

TABLE 20-1   Minimum Wire Sizes and Colors Based on Type of Circuit

Plug Pin Number	Circuit Function	Gauge – w/ABS	<52 feet (<15.85 meters)	>52 feet (>15.85 meters)
#1—White	Ground	10	10	10
#2—Black	Clearance ID Lights License Light (circuit balanced with brown #6)	14	14	12
#3—Yellow	Left Turn or Stop	14	14	12
#4—Red	Stop Intermittent ABS Power	12	12	8
#5—Green	Right Turn or Stop	14	14	12
#6—Brown	Taillight Clearance Lights (circuit balanced with black #2)	14	14	12
#7 – Blue	Constant ABS Power or Auxiliary	12	14	12

Conductor No.	Color	Key	Lamp and Signal Circuits
1	White	⏚	Ground return to towing vehicle
2	Black	✖	Side marker and identification lamps
3	Yellow	▦	Left-hand turn signal and hazard signal
4	Red	▲	Stop lamps and antilock devices
5	Green	⬣	Right-hand turn signal and hazard signal
6	Brown	●	Tail, combined rear clearance, and license plate
7	Blue	AUX	Auxiliary, optional lamps, dome, etc.

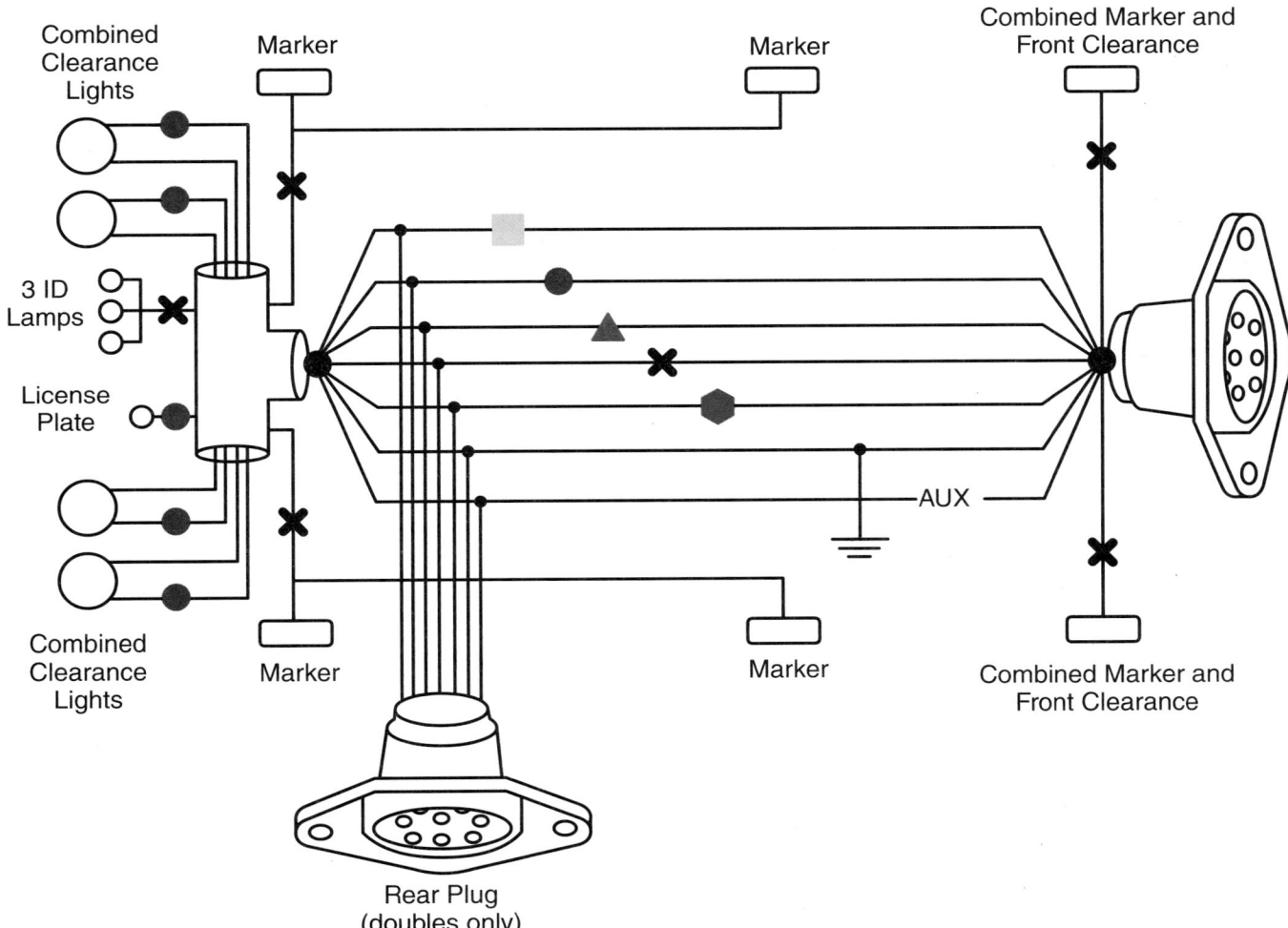

FIGURE 20-27 Wiring connections for a seven-way J-560 trailer plug.

switch is integrated into the directional signal switch, the four-ways supply power to both turn signals. This means applying the brakes causes the brake lights to remain on constantly since power is no longer being supplied by only the flasher relay.

Power for the integrated stop-turn is often constantly supplied in commercial vehicles integrating a four-way hazard signal switch, so leaving the turn signal stalk switched left or right causes the lights to remain flashing with the ignition off. This configuration prevents excessive battery use through other ignition-on loads when the turn signals or the frequently used four-way hazard flashers only are used. The additional number of turns the steering wheel a truck or bus rotates through also means there is no canceling mechanism for many medium and heavy-duty vehicles.

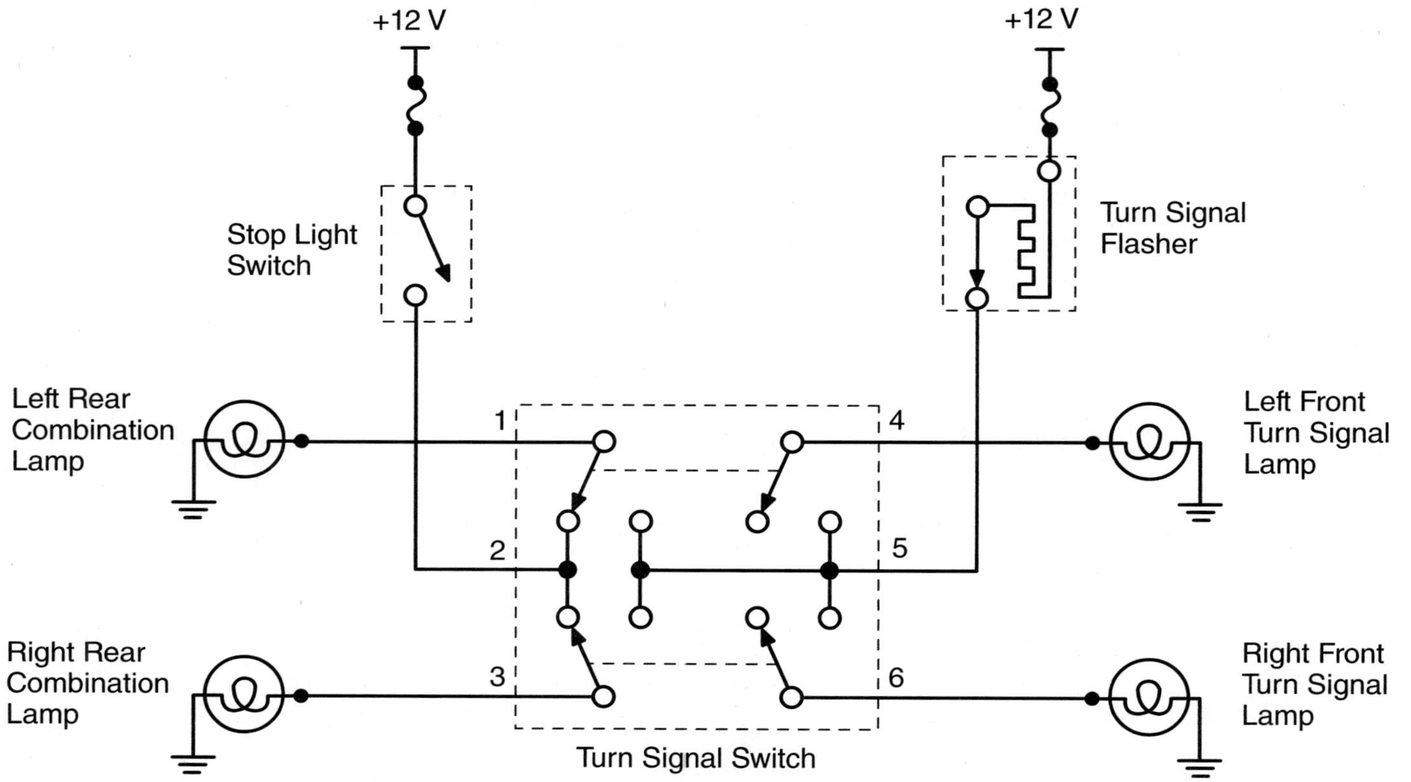

FIGURE 20-28 The circuit for an integrated stop-turn signal lamp system.

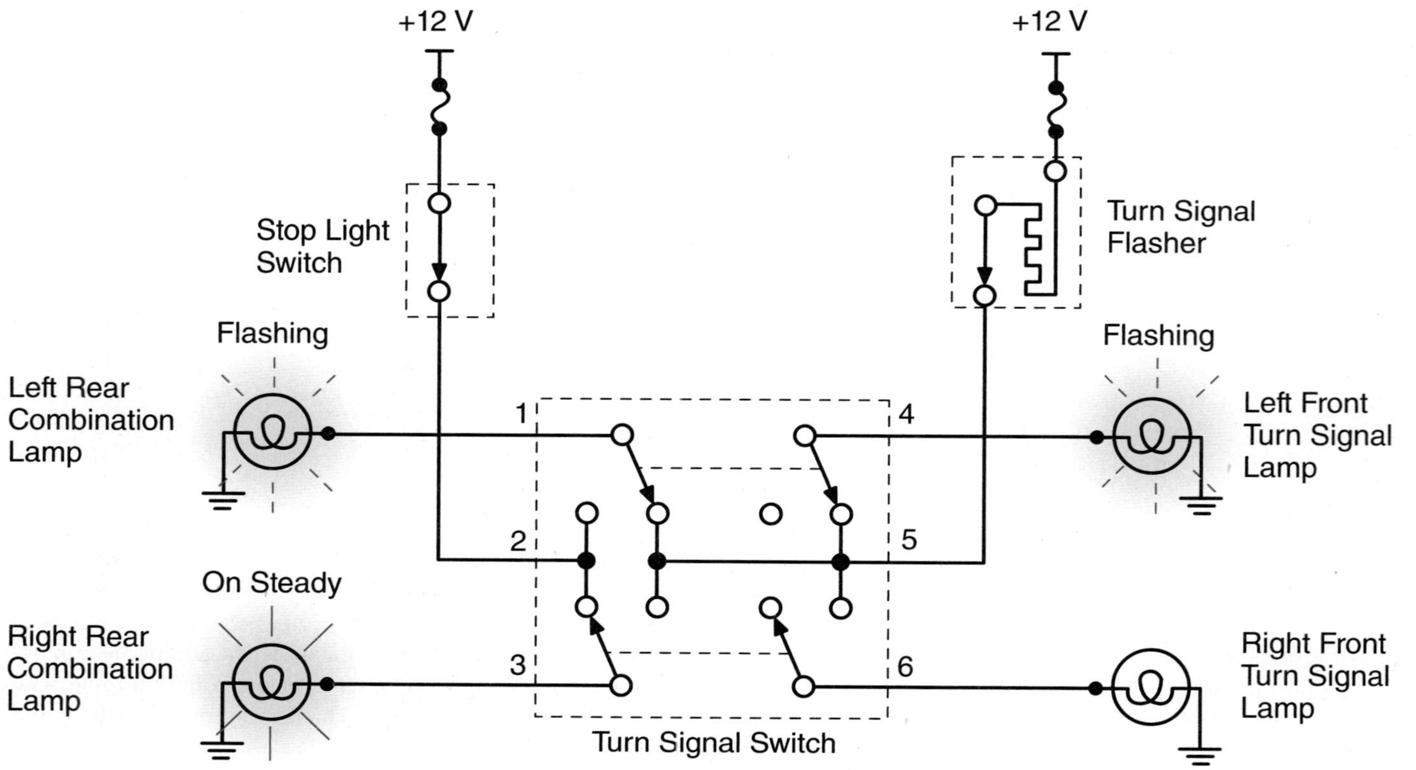

FIGURE 20-29 Current flow through the stop turn-signal light system with the brakes applied.

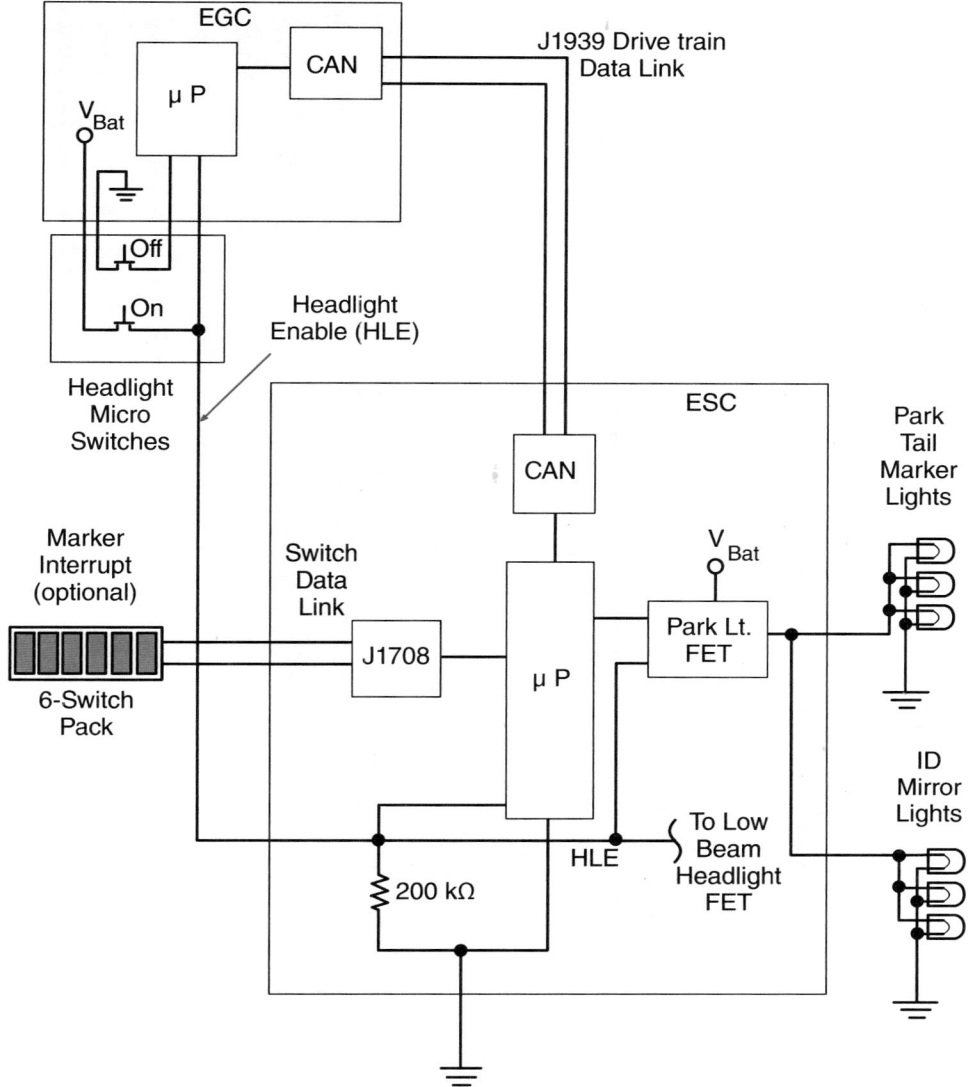

FIGURE 20-30 The lighting control module uses high current flow field effect transistors (FET).

The flasher relay is uniquely designed to interrupt power at a fixed frequency. Older flasher relays with few lamp loads used a bimetallic contact that heated and opened switch contacts when current flowed through the relay. Opening the contacts allowed a bimetal switch to cool and close the light circuit again. More recent flasher relays, which do not control directional signals through an ECM used for body electrical control, use timer circuits with a relay or even completely transistorized designs for high numbers of lamp loads.

Interrupter Switch

Flash to pass or interrupter lights are integrated into most HD tractors. This switch should interrupt only the top clearance light circuit on the tractor and trailer to signal other drivers it is safe to pass (**FIGURE 20-30**). An interrupter switch is generally located in the turn signal switch (**FIGURE 20-31**).

FIGURE 20-31 The directional turn signal switch integrates an interrupter switch.

Wrap-Up

Ready for Review

▶ Electrical systems on modern vehicles are becoming increasingly complex with the addition of a range of electronic and accessory systems. Many of these systems are controlled by electrical system control modules.

▶ Incandescent lamps consist of one or more filaments, which heat up until they glow.

▶ Halogen lamps have a much longer life, are generally brighter, and produce more light per unit of power consumed, but they become very hot during use.

▶ High-intensity discharge (HID) headlamps produce light with an electric arc, rather than a glowing filament.

▶ Lighting regulations should always be consulted before modifying or adding to any of the vehicle lighting systems.

▶ Hazard lights can warn other road users that a hazardous condition exists or that the vehicle is standing or parked in a dangerous position on the side of the road; they normally use the same bulbs as the turn signal indicators.

▶ Park, tail, and marker lamps are all photometric certified lamps used to mark the outline or width of the vehicle.

▶ The low beam is always set to the outside of the front, and the high beams are closer to the front center of the vehicle.

▶ The driving lights are installed on the front of the vehicle and provide higher-intensity illumination over longer distances than standard headlight systems.

▶ Networking or multiplexing light systems eliminate the amount of wire required for the lighting system and are controlled through a central electrical system control module.

Key Terms

daytime running lights (DRL) Forward running lights designed to improve vehicle visibility in the daytime.

fluorescent bulb A light bulb that uses electrically heated filaments located at each end of a tube filled with a small amount of mercury or a noble gas, such as neon, argon, or xenon.

halogen bulb An incadescent light bulb that adds small quantities of gases from the halogen family, such as iodine or bromine.

halogen infrared discharge (HID) bulb A light bulb that has a special coating on an inside portion of the bulb wall that reflects infrared heat back onto the filament, causing it to burn hotter.

high-intensity discharge (HID) lamps Lamps that use an electric arc to produce higher light outputs of between 2800 and 3800 lumens.

incandescent bulb A conventional bulb that electrically heats a filament of metal to the temperature at which it produces light.

J-560 trailer connector An SAE standards for an electrical trailer cord plug and receptacle located at the rear of the tractor.

ladder logic The designed-in logic sequence of a circuit control devices that determines what steps activates a specific output.

light-emitting diode (LED) A diode that produces light in different colors, depending on the doping material used in its manufacture.

lumen The units used to measure light intensity.

photometric certification A certification based on testing lamps to evaluate factors, such as light color, brightness, and the angle at which the light is effectively observed.

photon A particle of energy and the basic unit of light.

Review Questions

1. According to FMVSS standards, which color of lights are allowed for forward-facing body lamps?
   a. White and yellow
   b. Green and yellow
   c. Red and yellow
   d. Green or red

2. Which of the following lighting technologies produces the brightest lighting with the longest life?
   a. Halogen
   b. Incandescent
   c. Fluorescent
   d. OLED

3. Which of the following statements best explains how light is produced?
   a. Light is produced by atoms whenever an electron moves from a lower orbital valence to a higher orbital (farther from the nucleus) requiring less energy.
   b. Energy given up by the electron is released in the form of a photon.
   c. Protons release photons, which are particles of light energy.
   d. Electrons fill a positive charge hole in a material that causes it to heat and glow.

4. A fluorescent bulb works best as a:
   a. marker light.
   b. dome light.
   c. backup light.
   d. license plate lamp.

5. Which of the following applications are best for halogen infrared discharge (HID) bulbs?
   a. Marker lights
   b. Tail lights
   c. Fog lights
   d. Headlights

6. Which of the following explains the operation of daytime running lights?
   a. A headlamp system that uses only the low-beam bulbs and supplies them with 20% of system voltage.
   b. A headlamp system that uses only the high-beam bulbs and supplies them with 80% of system voltage.
   c. A headlamp system that connects the low-beam and high-beam bulbs in series.
   d. A headlamp system that uses either the low- or high-beam bulbs and supplies them with 80% of system voltage.

7. At which of the following voltages do individual LED operate?
   a. 0.5 and 3
   b. 1 and 4
   c. 4 and 6
   d. 7 and 10
8. Which trailer cord plug uses a recessed ground pin?
   a. The 7-pin J-560 plug
   b. The 7-pin ISO 3731 plug
   c. The 15-pin Euro style plug
   d. The 13-pin Euro style plug
9. Where does the supply of battery voltage for the turn signal switch originate from for the integrated rear brake/turn bulbs when the turn signals are not indicating a left or right turn?
   a. There is no current supplied to the switch.
   b. The flasher relay circuit
   c. The brake light switch
   d. A double contact bulb
10. Which of the following best explains the operation of an interrupter switch?
    a. It momentarily interrupts power to the brake light bulbs.
    b. The interrupter switch momentarily opens the circuit to the top clearance light circuit on the tractor and trailer to signal other drivers it is safe to pass.
    c. The push-on push-off switch is generally located on the floor of the cab.
    d. The interrupter switch momentarily opens the circuit supplying all clearance, tail, and park light bulbs.

ASE Technician A/Technician B Style Questions

1. Technician A says that a traditional body electrical system consists of two parts. Technician B says that the first section is the standard electrical systems found in all vehicles and that optional accessories make up the other section of the body electrical system. Who is correct?
   a. Technician A
   b. Technician B
   c. Both Technician A and Technician B
   d. Neither Technician A nor Technician B
2. Technician A says that the designed-in logic of a circuit that determines what activates a specific circuit is referred to as ladder logic. Technician B says that it is not necessary to have the ability to access, read, and interpret electrical schematic diagrams to repair electrical circuits. Who is correct?
   a. Technician A
   b. Technician B
   c. Both Technician A and Technician B
   d. Neither Technician A nor Technician B
3. Technician A says that lighting standards are legislated by the Federal/Canadian Motor Vehicle Standard 105 (FMVSS 105). Technician B says that it is not necessary for light lenses to carry SAE or ECE identification numbers indicating the standard they meet. Who is correct?
   a. Technician A
   b. Technician B
   c. Both Technician A and Technician B
   d. Neither Technician A nor Technician B
4. Technician A says that incandescent bulbs are the conventional bulb technology first invented by Thomas Edison. Technician B says that for every one volt above designed limits, the life expectancy of the bulb drops by 25%. Who is correct?
   a. Technician A
   b. Technician B
   c. Both Technician A and Technician B
   d. Neither Technician A nor Technician B
5. Technician A says that halogen bulbs are produced by adding small quantities of gases from the halogen family, such as iodine and bromine, which extends the efficiency and life of the bulb. Technician B says that because the filament can be operated at a higher temperature without burning up, more energy is converted to light, the light is whiter, and the bulb's life is extended. Who is correct?
   a. Technician A
   b. Technician B
   c. Both Technician A and Technician B
   d. Neither Technician A nor Technician B
6. Technician A says that high-intensity discharge (HID) lamps used for headlight systems employ an electric arc to produce the light. Technician B says that the intensity of light from HID bulbs is produced using close to half the current consumed by halogen bulbs, and the bulbs last half as long. Who is correct?
   a. Technician A
   b. Technician B
   c. Both Technician A and Technician B
   d. Neither Technician A nor Technician B
7. Technician A says that daytime running lights are designed to improve vehicle visibility in the daytime. Technician B says that either the low- or high-beam circuits are powered at a reduced voltage of approximately 50% system voltage. Who is correct?
   a. Technician A
   b. Technician B
   c. Both Technician A and Technician B
   d. Neither Technician A nor Technician B
8. Technician A says that the J-560 electrical connector is an SAE standard set for connecting the trailer cord to the tractor and trailer electrical system together and has existed since the late 1950s. Technician B says that this five-pin connector bears the stamp SAE J560, indicating compliance with physical and performance standards of the SAE. Who is correct?
   a. Technician A
   b. Technician B
   c. Both Technician A and Technician B
   d. Neither Technician A nor Technician B

9. Technician A says that plugs at the end of each cable may be molded and hard-wired with strain relief to prevent the weight of the cord from disconnecting from the plug. Technician B says that replacement plug leads are available and commonly used by technicians to repair cables. Who is correct?
   a. Technician A
   b. Technician B
   c. Both Technician A and Technician B
   d. Neither Technician A nor Technician B

10. Technician A says that the directional signal switch in mechanical directional signal systems is supplied current from two sources. Technician B says that stop-turn lamp power is supplied by the service brake light switch; the other is through the turn signal flasher relay. Who is correct?
   a. Technician A
   b. Technician B
   c. Both Technician A and Technician B
   d. Neither Technician A nor Technician B

CHAPTER 21

Body Electrical Systems— Instrumentation

Learning Objectives

After reading this chapter, you will be able to:

- **LO 21-1** Describe the purpose and operation of warning lights.
- **LO 21-2** Describe the operation of gauge operating systems.
- **LO 21-3** Identity and describe the operation of sending units.
- **LO 21-4** Describe the purpose and operation of speedometers.

- **LO 21-5** Describe the operation of capacitance and resistive type touch driver information screens.
- **LO 21-6** Outline procedures to troubleshoot gauge problems.

You Are the Technician

A late-model truck has arrived at your shop with several complaints related to the electrical system. One complaint is about the yellow check engine light is illuminated. Another is about the instrument gauges going to zero and sweeping from zero to full scale and then back again to a correct reading while driving down the road. Other times the instrument gauge cluster does not move at all when the vehicle is started and running. In addition to asking that the electrical problems are corrected, the driver expresses concern about running out of fuel if the gauges are not reading accurately. Having time-sensitive loads, and an incorrect fuel guage reading for a fuel tank that is actually empty would be financially disastrous to the company.

As you proceed to diagnose the problem, you discover that lightly pulling on the wiring harness going to the gauge cluster duplicates the complaint about the gauges sweeping from zero to full scale and back again to a correct reading again. Consider the following questions to predict what you think the technician will write on the work order.

1. Explain why the gauges complete a full-scale sweep when electrical power is interrupted.
2. What is potentially the simplest procedure the technician could use to identify the problem illuminating the yellow check engine light?
3. Outline a procedure the technician could use to validate the correct gauge readings for the fuel level.

Introduction

Instrument gauges, warning lamps, and driver information centers enable the operator to monitor the vehicle's operating condition, status of equipment, and safety systems. The types of displays, warning lights, and gauges differ widely among vehicles and manufacturers but break down into common gauge groups for safety, maintenance, and sensing systems. For example, monitoring engine operation involves measuring pressures and temperatures in the lubrication, cooling, and air induction system. Charging voltage and amperage of the electrical system, fuel level, air pressure, engine, and vehicle speed are other common gauge systems. Warning lights for systems ranging from supplemental restraint, antilock braking, traction control, low air pressure, body doors, parking brakes, etc. are used in situations where limited, but simplified, safety information is useful. Newer digital instrumentation has superior accuracy plus built-in self-diagnostic capabilities, offering the driver confidence that gauges and warning systems are operational. Driver display and input systems communicating with the vehicle controller area network (CAN) provide information capabilities far beyond previous instrumentation design.

Warning Lights

LO 21-1 Describe the purpose and operation of warning lights.

Warning lights provide easily understood information to alert the equipment operator to potentially dangerous operating conditions (**FIGURE 21-1**). Low air pressure, antilock brake faults, low diesel exhaust fluid, door ajar lights, etc. are activated several ways and include:

- Mechanical ground switches
- Electronic switches
- Voltage drop circuits

The charging system indicator light is an example of a light that may be operated through voltage drop (**FIGURE 21-2**). After the engine starts and the alternator begins charging, positive battery voltage and charging system voltage are applied to both terminals of a bulb. If battery voltage is higher than charging system voltage, the voltage differential causes the light to illuminate.

Mechanical ground switches are used to indicate low fluid levels, low air pressure warning systems, or power divider engagement locks (**FIGURE 21-3**). Normally closed pressure switches opened with air or oil pressure provide a path to ground to illuminate a bulb (**FIGURE 21-4**).

Electronic switches connected to electronic control units (ECU) are the most common method warning lights are illuminated in today's vehicles. If a condition is sensed to which the driver needs to be alerted, the module has control logic to supply a either a ground or battery positive voltage to the light.

Prove-Out Sequence

In order to validate the correct operation of a warning light, the instrument cluster is designed to illuminate a bulb for several brief seconds after the ignition is switched on (**FIGURE 21-5**). If the engine starts, a warning light may remain lit until proper operating conditions are met, such as correct oil pressure is reached, the supplementary restraint system is operational, or coolant level is satisfactory. That sequence is called a **prove-out sequence**.

In older vehicles, the ignition key supplies a circuit to provide a ground and/or positive battery voltage path to illuminate instrument warning lights. ECUs perform the same function during key-on events. The malfunction indicator lamp (MIL) and check engine lamp (CEL) illuminate for approximately three to five seconds during engine start-up and then extinguish. If there are active fault codes, the lights switch back on after start-up (**FIGURE 21-6**). Gauge cluster pointers using stepper motors perform a full sweep of the gauge, from minimum to maximum, back to minimum, and then to received value. This prove-out sequence enables the driver to have confidence in the correct operation of the gauge unit.

Blink codes are often used by some manufacturers to provide fault code data for a specific system. These codes are interpreted by counting the number of flashes from a warning lamp and observing longer pauses between the blinking lights. For example, OEM-specific antilock brake system (ABS) codes, or engine fault codes, may be either two or three digits in length. The fault code of 32 is displayed by the ABS warning light displaying three light blinks in quick succession, followed by a short pause and two more blinks. A longer pause separates multiple codes.

> ▶ **TECHNICIAN TIP**
>
> Urban transit buses may have a brake and accelerator interlock system with a warning light. The interlock applies the rear brakes and holds the throttle in idle position when a passenger door is open. The interlock releases the brakes and throttle after the door is closed. For security reasons, this warning light may remain illuminated even after the ignition is switched off until the door is closed. The exterior rear brake light may even illuminate after the ignition is switched off and the door remains open.

FIGURE 21-1 Warning lights are located in a dedicated light panel and use an light-emitting diode (LED) warning light located at the bottom of each critical gauge.

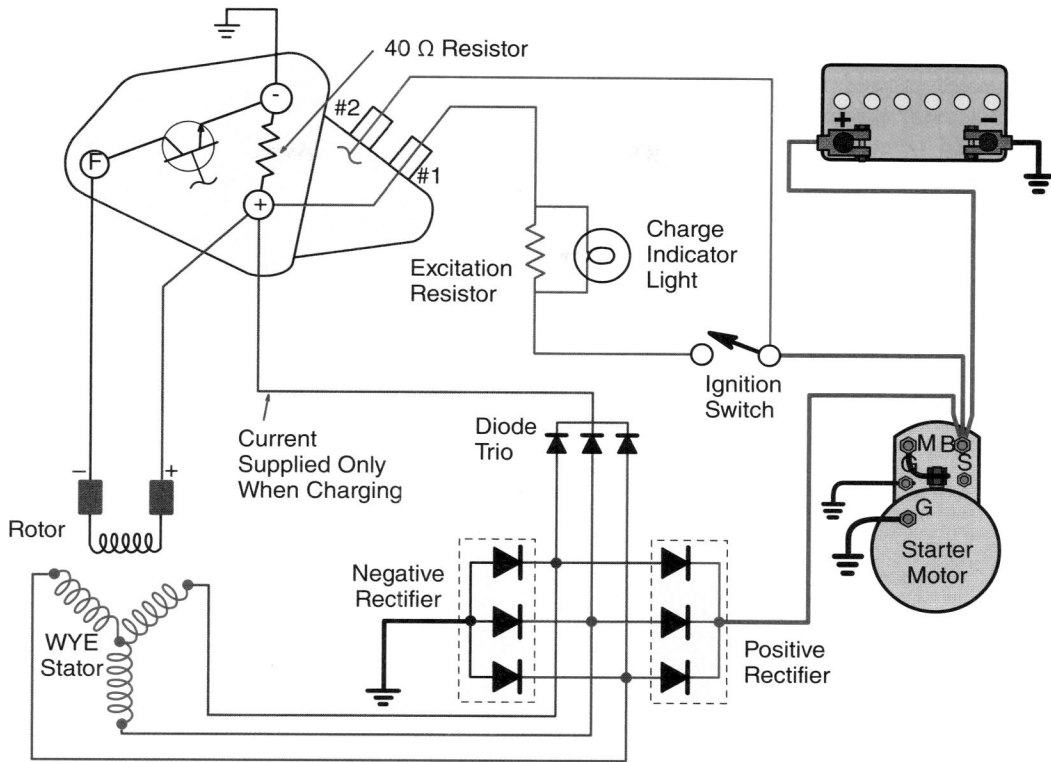

FIGURE 21-2 Some alternator voltage regulators provide a ground path for a bulb when not charging and supply battery + current when charging to the warning light bulb terminal to extinguish the light.

FIGURE 21-3 A water-in-fuel sensor is a mechanical float-type switch in this Duramax diesel fuel filter. Denser water raises the float fluid level sensor and ground the signal wire. **A.** Fuel filter. **B.** Internal electric float. **C.** Water-in-fuel sensor signal wire.

▶ **TECHNICIAN TIP**

In the absence of a readily available electronic service tool used to obtain fault codes, warning lights are often capable of flashing fault codes. Supplemental restraint systems, antilock brakes, and engine fault codes are often provided by blinking warning lamps. Consult the operator or shop manual to determine the procedure for obtaining blink codes. In newer vehicles, the driver's information display system is a CAN node, which means it communicates with the network and is capable of supplying fault codes and CAN data about the vehicle.

Gauge Operating Systems

LO 21-2 Describe the operation of gauge operating systems.

Common gauge systems use the following technologies:

- Mechanical (direct reading)
- Bimetallic
- Electromagnetic
- Stepper motor
- Digital display

Mechanical Gauges

Mechanical direct reading gauges are not electrical since they depend on cables, air, or fluid pressure to operate. Speedometers operated by cables and oil pressure displayed by bourdon tube gauges are examples of direct-reading mechanical gauges.

Pressure Sensors

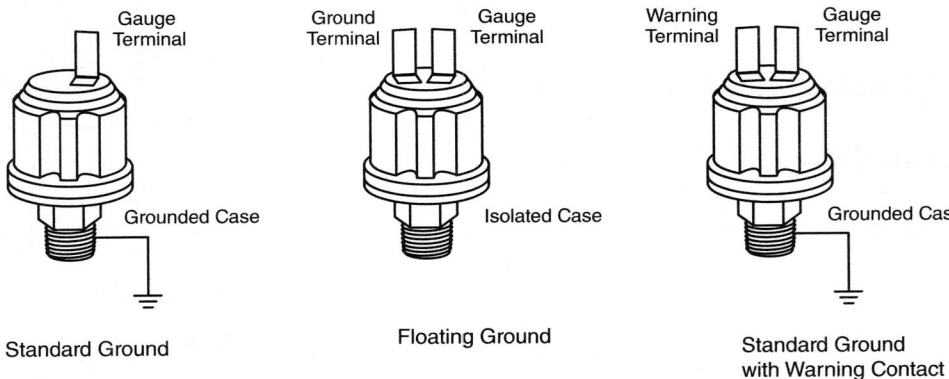

FIGURE 21-4 This normally closed hydraulic or air pressure switch is opened with pressure and closed when pressure is too low. A calibrated internal spring allows the switch to complete a ground circuit when pressure drops below a preset amount.

FIGURE 21-5 All warning lights illuminate during initial key-on period to ensure the bulbs are functioning. The engine warning and stop lamp blink original equipment manufacturers (OEM) flash codes when prompted by a diagnostic switch. **A.** Blink code diagnostic switch. **B.** Stop engine light: red. **C.** Warning light: yellow.

Sending units are used by the electrical instrumentation to convert pressure and temperature measurements into analog electrical signals used by instrument gauges. Sending units differ from sensors in that they are electromechanical devices, whereas sensors are nonmechanical electronic devices. Pressure- and temperature-sensitive switches often operate warning lights.

Bimetallic Gauges

Bimetallic gauges used only in old vehicles work by heating metal strips, which bend and move a gauge pointing needle (**FIGURE 21-7**). Two dissimilar pieces of metal are bonded together into a strip, much like a circuit breaker, and expand at different rates as when heated. Heat produced through resistance of a wire coil wrapped around the bimetal strip is proportional to current flow (**FIGURE 21-8**). Varying current flow supplied by a sending unit changes the position of the pointing needle attached to the bimetal strip. Because vehicle voltage fluctuates with changes to electrical loads and charging system

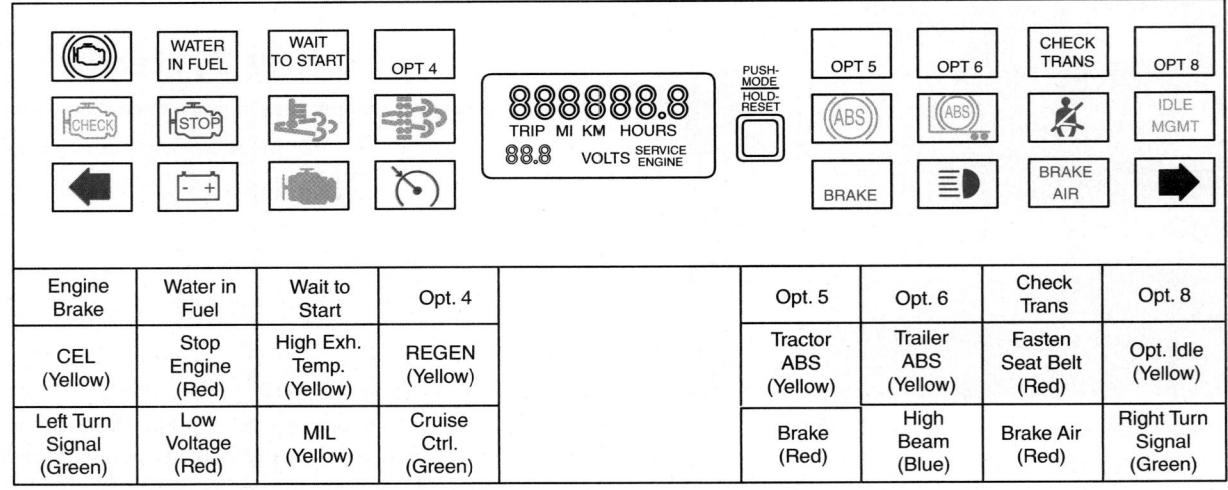

Engine Brake	Water in Fuel	Wait to Start	Opt. 4			Opt. 5	Opt. 6	Check Trans	Opt. 8
CEL (Yellow)	Stop Engine (Red)	High Exh. Temp. (Yellow)	REGEN (Yellow)			Tractor ABS (Yellow)	Trailer ABS (Yellow)	Fasten Seat Belt (Red)	Opt. Idle (Yellow)
Left Turn Signal (Green)	Low Voltage (Red)	MIL (Yellow)	Cruise Ctrl. (Green)			Brake (Red)	High Beam (Blue)	Brake Air (Red)	Right Turn Signal (Green)

FIGURE 21-6 The EPA 2010+ fault lamps warn of emission-related faults.

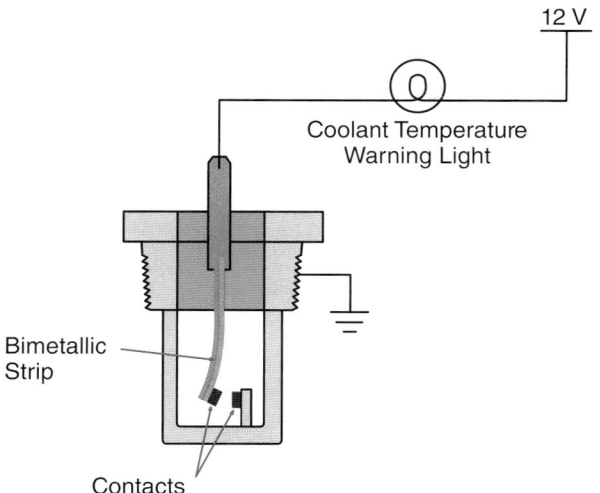

FIGURE 21-7 Bimetallic gauge operation. Bending of the bimetal strip changes the position of the pointer.

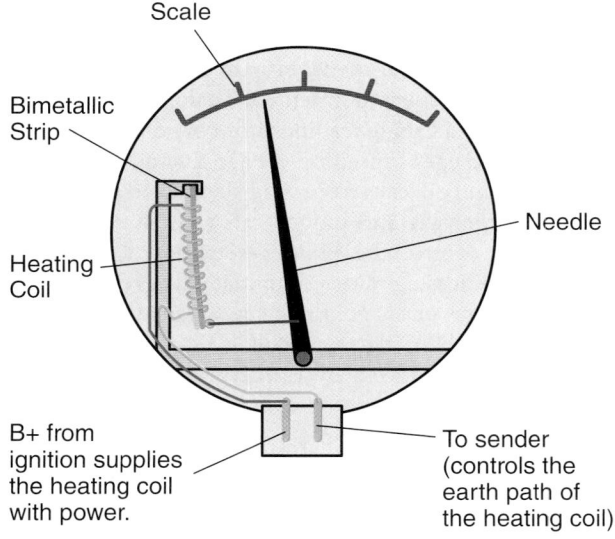

FIGURE 21-8 Construction and operation of a bimetal fuel gauge. Dissimilar metals expand at different rates when heated. The rheostat in the fuel tank controls current flow through the heater element.

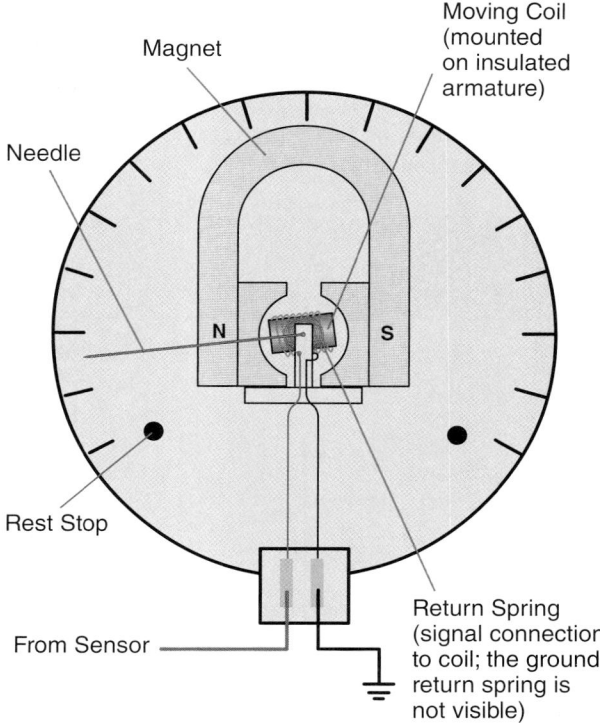

FIGURE 21-9 D'Arsonval movement gauges use a coil mounted between two permanent magnets. Changes in the coil's magnetic field strength pulls it toward one magnet and pushes it away from the other, causing rotation of the needle movement. A small light spring can return the pointer to a rest position.

output, a voltage regulator is required to maintain consistent gauge readings. Commonly, another bimetallic-type device holds voltage supplied to gauges and sending units steady at anywhere between approximately 5 and 10 volts. The instrument voltage regulator (IVR) uses a bimetal arm with a set of breaker points that open and close rapidly when heating and cooling to maintain a consistent supply of voltage to bimetallic instrument gauges.

D'Arsonval Gauges

D'Arsonval gauges are a type of electromagnetic gauge that moves a pointing needle directly proportional to current flow through an electromagnet attached to the pointer (**FIGURE 21-9**). Needle deflection is controlled by current

supplied to the coil, which changes magnetic field strength interacting with the fields of two permanent magnets fixed on either side of the coil. A larger flow of current produces a magnetic field that opposes one of the permanent magnet's fields and is attracted to another. Voltmeters are an example of a gauge that currently use D'Arsonval movement. Other gauges using a D'Arsonval movement require a voltage regulator to maintain consistent readings.

Two- and Three-Coil Movements

Variations of the D'Arsonval movement use a pointer with a permanent magnet rather than an electromagnet. Two or three electromagnetic coils surround the pointer to rotate the gauge. Two-coil designs require a voltage regulator to maintain consistent readings, as charging voltage varies, while three-coil designs generally do not (**FIGURE 21-10**, **FIGURE 21-11**). Both these gauges are more accurate than D'Arsonval movement gauges and are unaffected by temperature. In the two-coil gauge design, the field coils are wound in series but in opposite directions. This places a north and south pole on maximum and minimum reading sides of the pointer's magnet.

Regulated ignition current is supplied to one end of the series coil, and the second ground pathway is through a sending unit. Increasing current flow through the second coil intensifies the forces of magnetic attraction compared to current flow in the first coil. Pointer rotation takes place to the right or left as magnetic field strength increases or decreases proportional to current flow in the coils.

In the **three-coil gauge** design, a coil is placed at the low or minimum and high or maximum reading ends of the pointer's rotation duplicating the effect of permanent magnets in

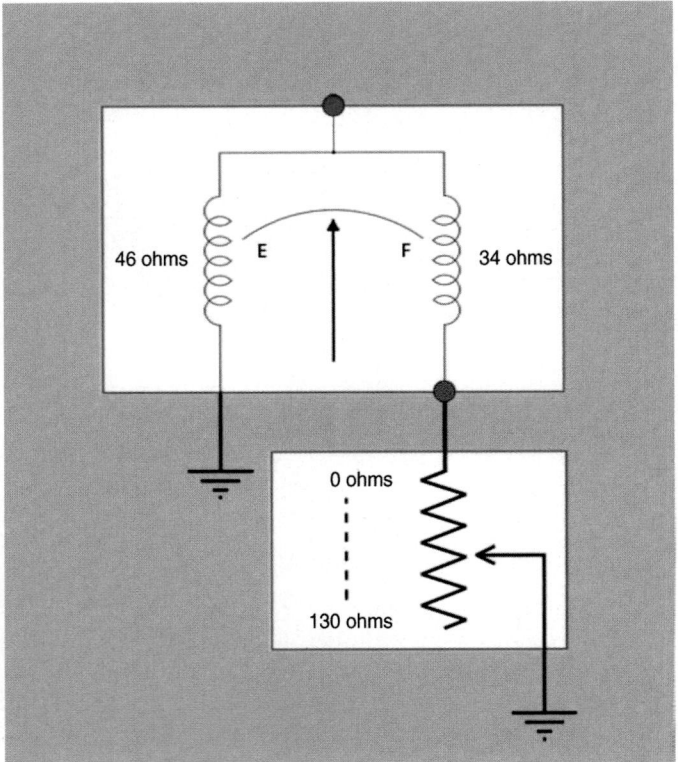

FIGURE 21-10 Two-coil gauges are connected to battery + in parallel but wound in the opposite direction. Both coils share a common resistive ground. However, the ground of a second coil is connected to a rheostat sending unit that varies the current passing through the coil and its magnetic field strength. Depending on whether the sending unit is for oil pressure or fuel level, current flow passes through the sending unit, depending on the level or pressure sensed. The needle is pulled to the coil with the strongest magnetic field strength.

a D'Arsonval gauge (**FIGURE 21-12**). A third coil, called a bucking coil, is placed between the minimum and maximum gauge reading. Ignition current passes through all three coils, which are wound in series. Two ground connections are supplied to the coil. One is at the end of the maximum coil, allowing all current to pass through all three coils. The other is a ground supplied through a sending unit. This ground connects to the gauge at a point between the minimum coil and bucking coil. Current flow passes through all three coils when resistance through the sending unit ground path is high. This pulls the needle towards the stronger magnetic field created by two coils at the minimum position.

The maximum reading coil exerts the greatest force to pull the pointer magnet in that direction, because the low or minimum reading and bucking coil are wound in opposite directions to cancel each other's magnetic field. However, decreasing resistance through the sending unit permits more current to pass through the minimum reading coil, which progressively intensifies the magnetic field in the bucking coil and cancels out the effect of the low coil's magnetic field.

Stepper Motor Gauge Design

By far, **stepper motor gauges** are the most commonly used gauge technology in late-model instrument clusters. The use of stepper motors to rotate pointers for analog displays bypasses the problem of inaccurate readings from bimetallic and electromagnetic coil gauges caused by voltage fluctuations, temperature changes, and oil leaks from fluid-dampened gauge clusters.

This inexpensive and unique category of electric motors can precisely control the pointer rotation by dividing full motor rotation or gauge sweep into many fine resolution steps. A motor shaft has permanent magnets arranged like teeth that rotate inside a set of electromagnetic field coils. These coils are sequentially energized by a microcontroller to align the toothed magnets on the motor shaft to produce gauge rotation or hold the gauge pointer in a specific spot (**FIGURE 21-13**). Most gauges using stepper motors have 3060 possible steps of positions between zero and full-scale deflection. Speedometers, tachometers, pressure, level, and temperature gauges use stepper motors in almost all commercial vehicles to accurately display instrument data. Stepper motors are brushless, direct current

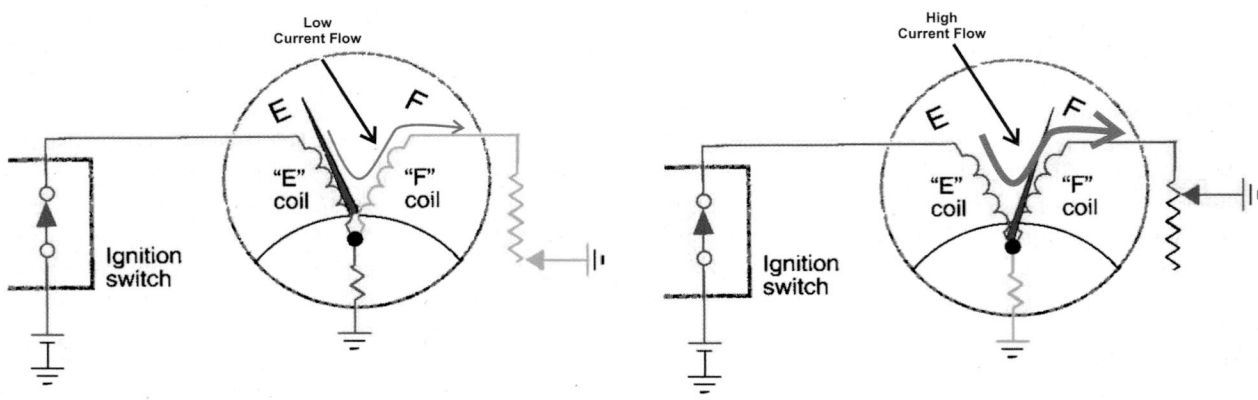

FIGURE 21-11 Current flow through a second coil changes according to the current passing through a sending unit. Note the resistor in the common ground connection.

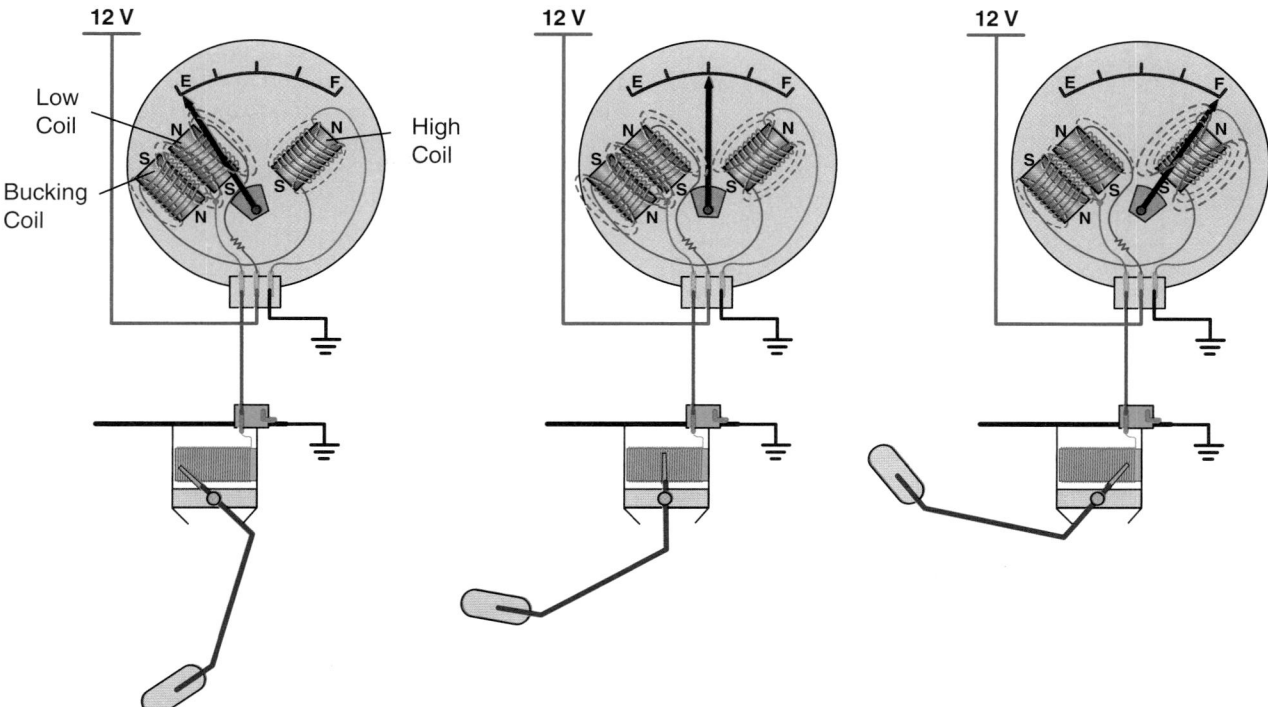

FIGURE 21-12 Operation of a three-coil design gauge. The bucking coil progressively cancels the effect of the minimum reading coil as more current passes through the sending unit.

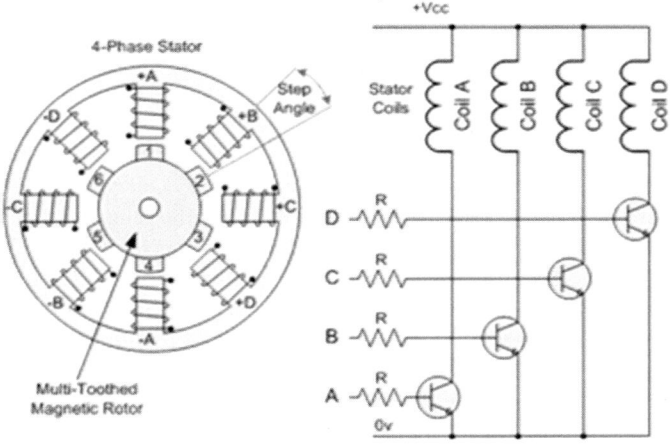

FIGURE 21-13 A stepper motor is a brushless DC motor that uses a microcontroller to electronically commutate the motor.

(DC) electromechanical devices that use a permanent magnet armature shaft with multiple magnetic poles surrounded by two or more pairs of electromagnetic coils. Three, four, and six field coil motors are commonly used with an armature having dozens of magnetic poles. Energizing one or more of these field coils causes the permanent magnet poles on the armature shaft to align with the field coils, pulling and holding the shaft in a stationary position. A needle pointer mounted on the armature shaft indicates a gauge position against a scale printed on the gauge face. When one field coil is energized, the motor shaft begins to rotate by aligning the armature magnet with the coil. To continue rotating the shaft after an initial position is set,

another field coil next to the first is energized, causing the shaft's pole magnets to realign with the energized coil while the first coil is deenergized. Each time the motor armature advances or moves backwards as a field coil is switched on and off, it is called a step. The ability to rotate the armature in incremental steps lends the name stepper motor to this motor design.

Alternately energizing and deenergizing coils in a particular sequence moves the shaft in the desired direction in incremental steps. A large number of fine steps make the gauge appear to move in a smooth motion. The speed of rotation can be precisely controlled by changing the rate at which coils are switched on and off. A sequence of energizing and de-energizing of coils pulls and/or pushes the shaft in a full 360 degrees of rotation, but full rotation is unnecessary because the gauge only sweeps through 270 degrees for its minimum and maximum range. To precisely energize the field coils at the correct time and sequence, a microcontroller is used to switch current on and off to each coil to energize and deenergize the magnetic field coils. The microcontroller receives an input signal commanding a gauge position and translates that signal into output signals supplied to each coil to produce the correct commanded gauge position. Because the motor is brushless and has no commutator like a conventional DC motor, these motors are also called **electronically commutated motors**.

Stepper Motor Position Calibration

To know which field coils to energize and where the gauge needle is pointing, these gauges use a couple of techniques to identify the angle or armature position. The most accurate method is to embed highly sensitive Hall-effect switches

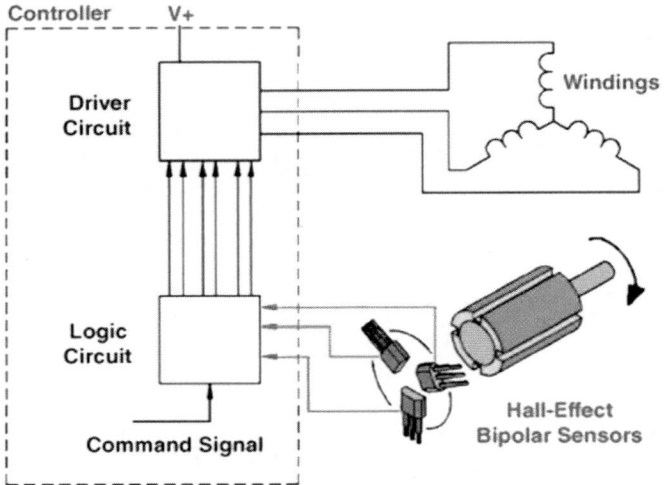

FIGURE 21-14 A microcontroller switches field windings on and off to rotate the motor armature in graduated steps. Hall-effect switches provide feedback about motor shaft position needed to energize field coils at the correct time and sequence.

around armature in the motor stator where the field coils are located (**FIGURE 21-14**). The magnetic field in the armature is sensed by the switches that open and close, sending this information to the microcontroller logic circuits. Using this data, the microcontroller can predict the angle of the gauge armature and synchronize field coil energization to produce the correct output. When Hall-effect switches are used, the microcontroller must learn exactly where the armature is initially positioned and verify how many steps make up a full gauge sweep. This explains why a gauge will move through a full needle sweep when the ignition is switched on and the gauge is powered up. This learning period after powering up also calibrates the gauge to correct for any wear or deterioration in the gauge. Maximum and minimum gauge limits, gauge speed and any resistance to gauge motion are identified during the calibration sweep to prevent under or over driving the field coils with current. Once it has learned the number of steps making up a full sweep, it can easily calculate how many steps are needed to move the gauge back and forth to display a specific pressure, temperature or speed display.

Another method to sense motor angle or position uses a circuit to analyze disturbances in the magnetic field of unenergized coils. The moving permanent magnets in the armature induce current flow that is analyzed by a circuit to predict motor position. This information is supplied to the microcontroller logic circuit to switch motor field coils on and off.

Unipolar Stepper Motor

Two common types of stepper motors are used for instrument gauges: unipolar and bipolar motors. The unipolar stepper motor is identified by its five or six wires that connect four field coils. The ends of all the coils have one common connection that is supplied power, giving the motor the name unipolar stepper because power always is supplied to this single point to form electromagnetic poles in the field coils. The other coil ends are

connected to microcontroller driver circuits switching current flow on and off. Using digital logic and microcontrollers, the field coils are switched on and off to rotate the motor forward or backward, or to hold the shaft (**FIGURE 21-15**).

TABLE 21-1 shows the steps used to rotate a 4-pole unipolar stepper motor. Either a constant battery positive or ground is supplied to the coils while a ground or positive current source is switched on and off to rotate the motor.

Bipolar Stepper Motor

Unlike unipolar steppers, bipolar stepper motors have no common connection between the motor stator. Instead, coils used in the stator are independent sets of coils that enable a change in current polarity (**FIGURE 21-16**). Unlike unipolar motors that cannot reverse current flow through individual coils, bipolar motors are capable of finer steps by reversing current polarity across some coils. Note that directional rotation changes are possible in both unipolar and bipolar stepper motors. The differences in coil windings make it possible to differentiate between bipolar and unipolar stepper motors. By measuring the resistance between the lead wires, bipolar steppers are distinguished from unipolar motors since any two pairs of wires have equal resistance and no continuity between the coils in the stator (**FIGURE 21-17**). Like unipolar motors, digital logic in bipolar stepper motors is programmed into the microcontroller to produce desired motor travel characteristics. Torque is decreased from bipolar motors at the expense of finer steps to produce rotation.

Digital CAN Gauges

Digitally driven, networked gauges, or intelligent gauges, are designed to display information broadcast over CAN using SAE J1939 communications. These gauges, which can use stepper motors or liquid-crystal displays (LCDs)/LEDs, are connected directly to the J1939 CANbus. Circuits inside the gauges that can display alpha-numeric messages eliminate the need for a graphic label, interface module, or other device to drive them. Custom programming of the gauge at the manufacturer level is required to translate the CAN communication messages to properly interpret use user-defined values (**FIGURE 21-18**). Entire instrument clusters rich with data are operated now using CAN-driven data generated by control modules throughout the vehicle. Just two wires connecting the instrument panel gauge clusters to the CAN are all that is necessary to display vehicle data and trip information, provide fault codes, and display warning lamps.

Sending Units

LO 21-3 Identity and describe the operation of sending units.

Sending units are electromechanical devices that convert pressure or fluid level into a variable voltage signal. Sending units are different from sensors, which are low-voltage electronic devices with no moving parts. Most sending units are a variable resistive type (**FIGURE 21-19**).

The fuel tank sending unit, for example, uses a resistive wiper mechanism. An electrical whisker or conductive brush attached to a float moves along a resistive track and positions

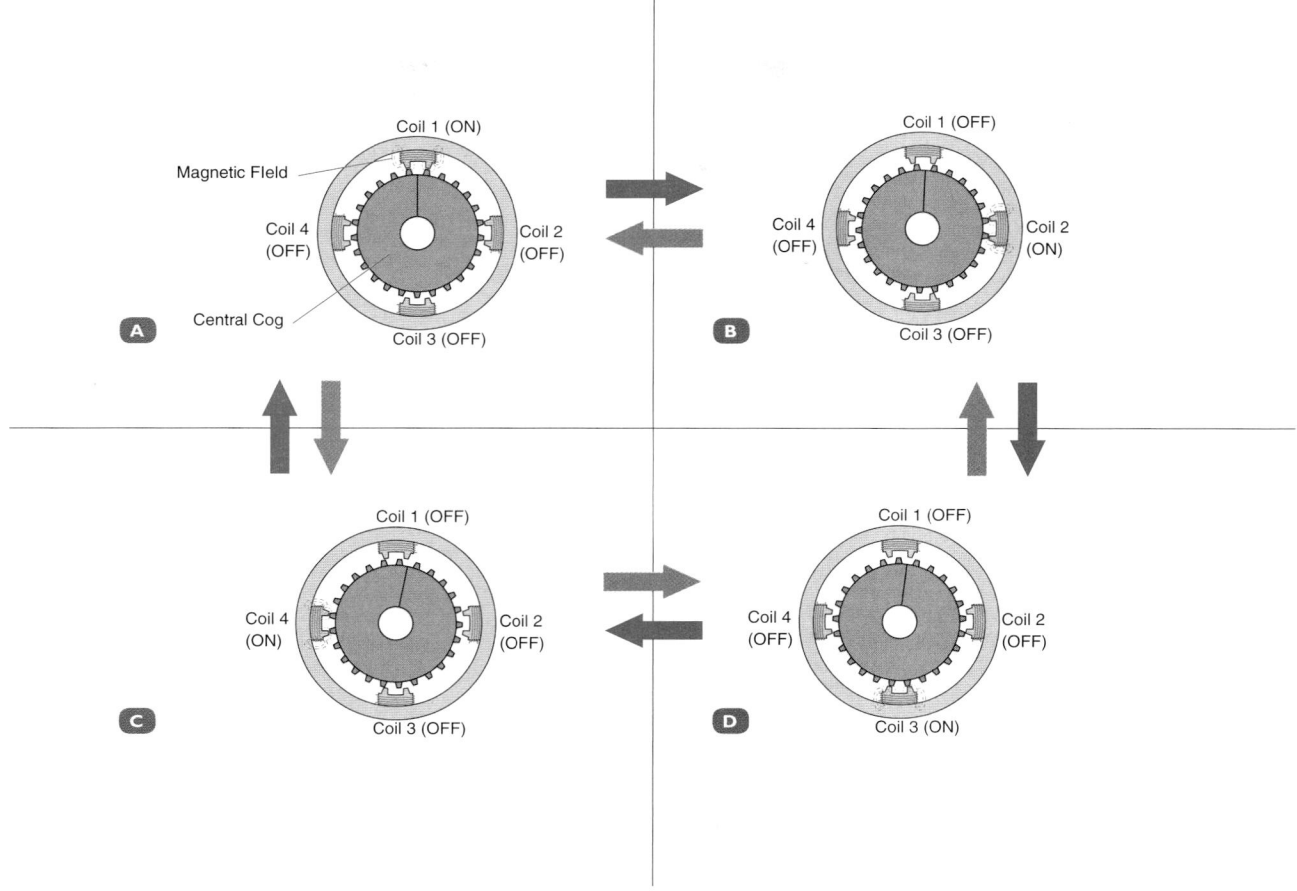

FIGURE 21-15 Unipolar motor operation. **A.** The upper electromagnet (1) is activated and the permanent magnet teeth of the central armature cog line up accordingly. **B.** The upper electromagnet (1) is deactivated and the right one (2) is switched on. The closest armature cog teeth then rotate to line up with this new magnetic field. This causes a step turn of 1.8 degrees if there are 200 step turns. **C.** The right electromagnet (2) is deactivated and the lower one (3) is switched on. The cog teeth then rotate to line up with the bottom electromagnet. This causes another step. **D.** The lower electromagnet (3) is switched off and the left (4) electromagnet is switched on. The cog teeth then jump to line up with the left electromagnet, producing another step.

TABLE 21-1 Steps Used to Rotate a 4-Pole Unipolar Stepper Motor

Step Number	Coil A	Coil B	Coil C	Coil D
1	5 volts	0	0	0
2	0	0	5 volts	0
3	0	5 volts	0	0
4	0	0	0	5 volts
5	5 volts	0	0	0

itself according to fuel level. Low-voltage current originating through the instrument panel fuel gauge passes through the resistor track and then through to ground via the whisker. Depending on where the brush contacts the resistive track, current flow passes through the brush to ground.

Oil pressure sending units use a flexible bellow also containing an electrically conductive whisker that passes along a resistor track. Pressure below the bellows moves the whisker

along the resistive track to before current passes to ground (**FIGURE 21-20**). Current to the sending unit is also supplied by the gauge. With less resistance in the sending unit, more current passes through the gauge to ground to deflect the pointer somewhere between minimum and maximum readings according to the circuit resistance.

Temperature sending units use a wax pellet similar to the design of a coolant thermostat. As temperature changes, the wax pellet expands or contracts. A disc over the wax pellet acts like a whisker to change the resistance of the current pathway through an internal resistive track. Electronic control modules are available to convert variable voltage values into digital signals for use by digital gauges.

Diagnosing Sending Units and Gauges

Resistive-type gauges are quickly checked by opening the circuit to the sending unit or grounding the sending unit lead. When a circuit is opened, circuit resistance becomes infinite and moves a gauge to either its minimum or maximum reading. If that does not happen, the circuit can be grounded to observe the effect

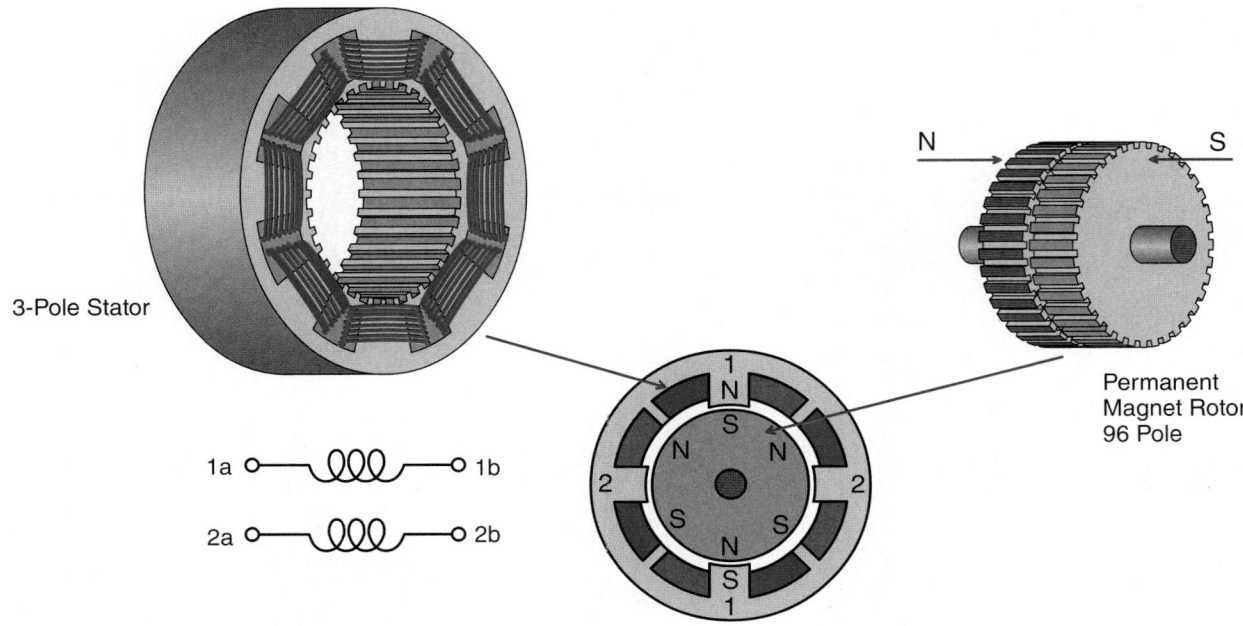

FIGURE 21-16 Bipolar motors are brushless DC motor designs that use permanent magnet mounted on the motor shaft. Bipolar motors can reverse current polarity across their coils, while unipolar motors cannot.

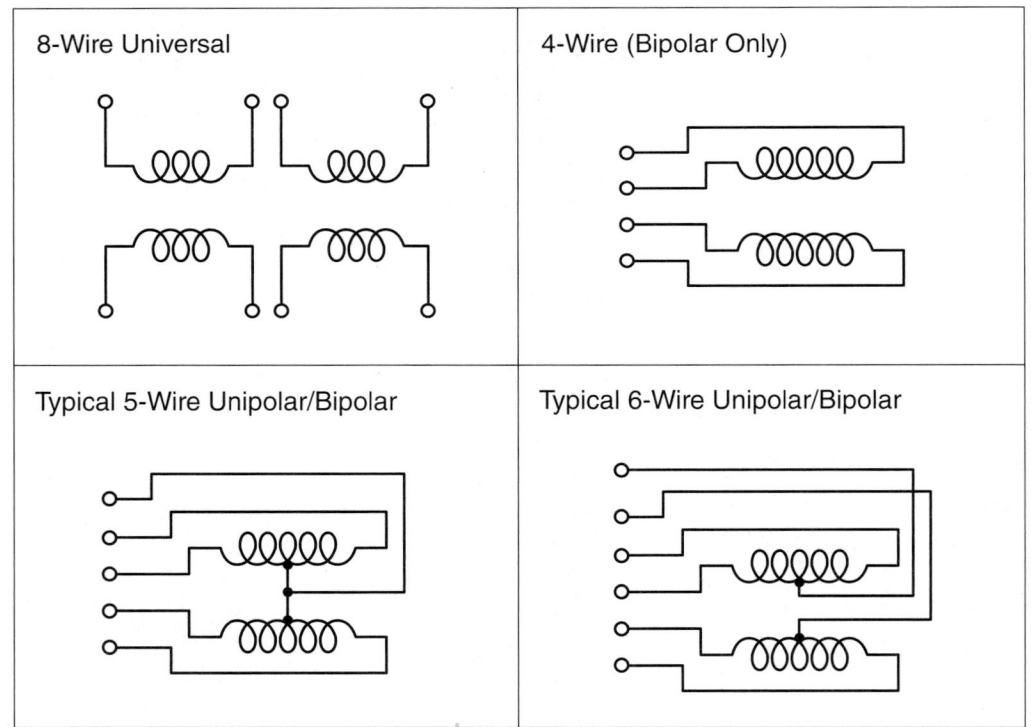

FIGURE 21-17 A variety of wiring combinations exist for various stepper motors. Stepper motor coils are energized one at a time, in pairs or groups to increase torque output.

on the gauge. If the gauge moves very little or does not fully sweep between a minimum and maximum value, the gauge circuit or the gauge itself is defective. The type of gauge construction—D'Arsonval, two-, or three-wire—determines which direction the gauge moves when opened or grounded. A gauge testing unit can evaluate gauge accuracy by supplying a resistance of known value to the circuit and observing whether the gauge pointer is positioned where expected. The accuracy of a

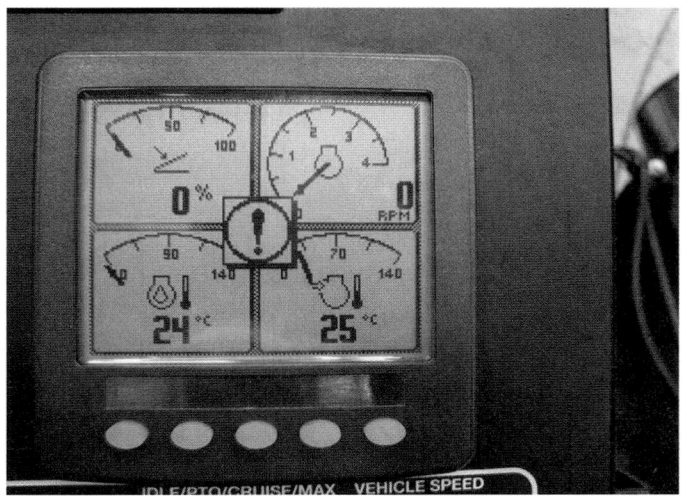

FIGURE 21-18 A CAN-driven gauge displays data available on the vehicle network. CAN displays are both input and output devices. Menu buttons allow the driver or technicians to access a variety of data sets.

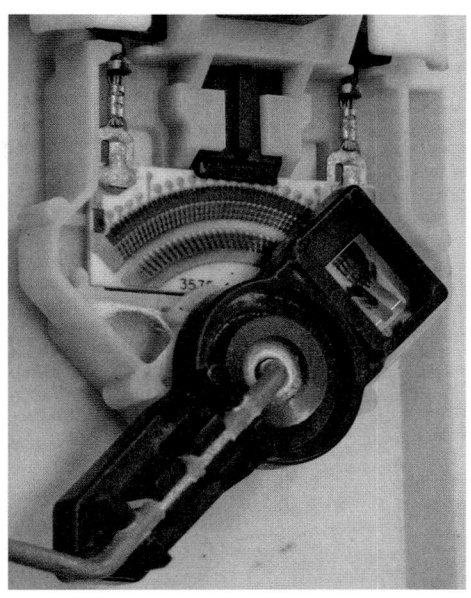

FIGURE 21-19 A rheostat used for the sending unit of a fuel tank.

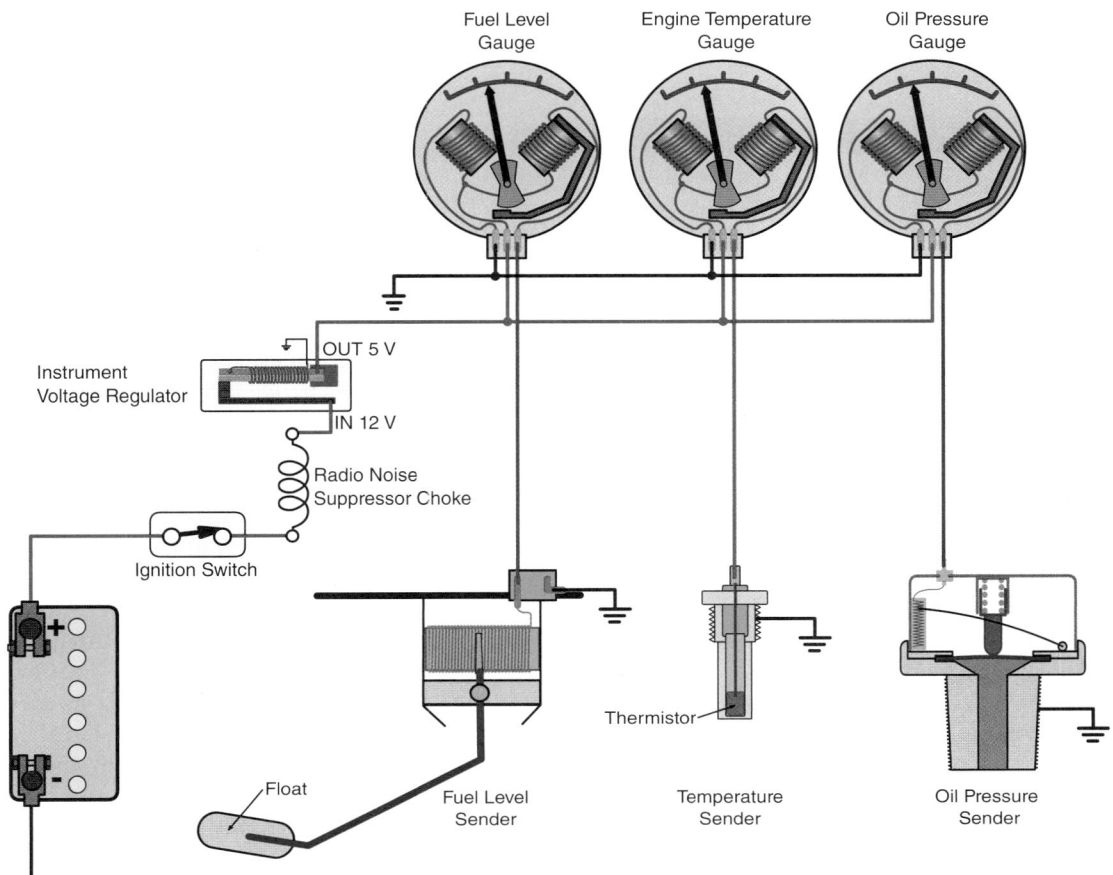

FIGURE 21-20 Construction of a variety of sending units with two-coil gauges. Note the voltage regulator used to maintain consistent gauge readings when charging system voltage varies.

fuel gauge is ideally evaluated using this method. The tank can also be dipped with a stick to verify the gauge readings correspond to the tank level. Resistance of a sending unit measured with an ohmmeter can also determine if its resistance is within the range expected for a given pressure temperature or liquid level (**FIGURE 21-21**). It's important to verify the ground supplied

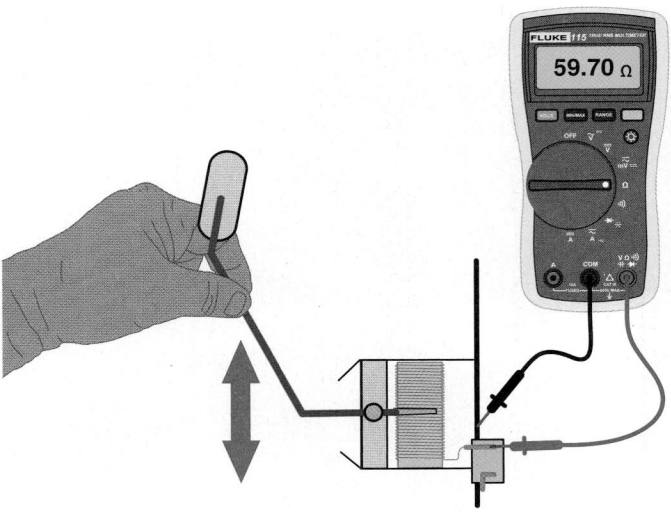

Slowly move the float arm from full to empty

FIGURE 21-21 Measuring the resistance of a fuel sending unit.

to the sending unit is good, because a resistive ground circuit interferes with sending unit resistance values. Some sending units are designed with two terminals, one of which provides a dedicated ground for the gauge circuit.

▶ **TECHNICIAN TIP**

Low or no resistance of a sending unit to ground through the engine block, transmission, or axle case is critical for accurate gauge operation. Undiagnosed resistive grounds can often lead to unnecessary replacement of sending units and gauges. Always check the continuity of a major component case or block-to-chassis ground as part of a diagnostic pinpoint test. The use of Teflon tape can also interfere with sending unit continuity. Use liquid thread sealer rather than tape to prevent thread leakage. Because gauges often operate at low voltage, never touch the sender lead to ignition + 12 volt.

Speedometers

LO 21-4 Describe the purpose and operation of speedometers.

Today's speedometers electronically measure the driveshaft speed by counting a series of electrical pulses produced per mile or kilometer of distance travelled. A variable reluctance sensor uses a toothed metal wheel typically placed at the transmission output shaft to measure driveline speed, which corresponds to road speed. An alternative method uses an average speed of ABS wheel speed sensors to produce a calculated road speed. Accurate tire size must be inputted and stored in the ABS module to correctly calculate vehicle speed. This data is broadcast over the CAN and used by modules, such as the instrument cluster, to report vehicle speed. Because commercial vehicles are sold with customized tire sizes, rear axle ratios, and transmission ratios, a calibration method is also often used to adapt the speedometer to the pulse count from the vehicle driveline speed sensor.

Speedometers have a pulse-per-mile adjustment performed using OEM software. When a new tire is installed, the supplier can typically provide a rolling diameter that translates into

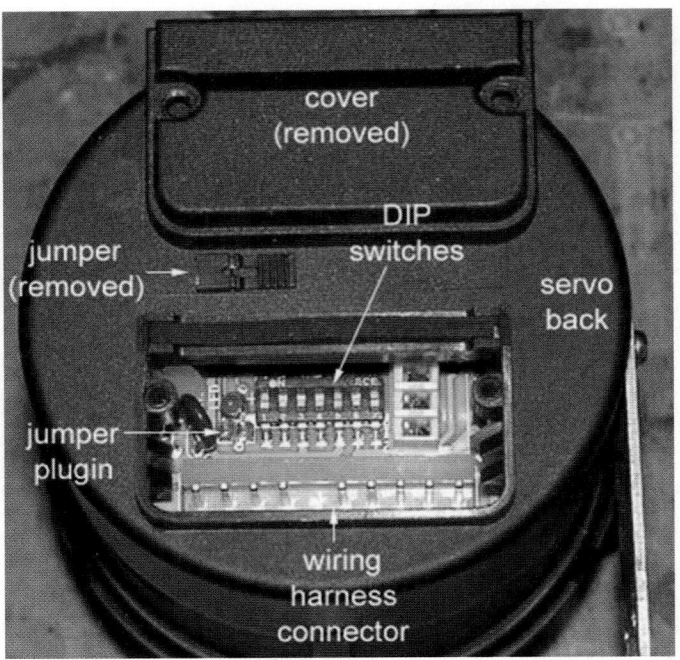

FIGURE 21-22 A speedometer with DIP switches is used to calibrate the display with pulses per mile from the speed sensor. Tire sizes and rear axle ratio require different DIP switch settings.

a specific number of rotations per mile or kilometer. This data is compared to a chart in a service manual that converts the rotations per mile (km) into pulses per mile generated by the transmission speed sensor. Earlier equipment enables customized calibrations for the various chassis pulse counts using **DIP switches**. These are small slide switches located at the rear of the speedometer head, placed in either the on or off (1 or 0) position. Circuits inside the speedometer convert the number of received speed sensor pulses to a pulse count per mile that varies with wheel speed. While dual in-line package (DIP) switches are set at the factory for an original equipment pulse count, switches may need to be reset if the drive line components, such as tire size or rear axle ratios, have changed from those originally installed on the chassis. Procedures to adjust the DIP switches are outlined in service manuals and usually involve plugging variables for tire size or rolling radius and rear axle into a formula to determine the settings (**FIGURE 21-22**). Inaccurate or fluctuating speedometer readings can be caused by other systems associated with the speedometer signal. Interference can originate from the cruise controls, ABS module, engine/transmission signals and controllers, the alternator, and other charging system components. Alternating current ripple from the alternator can also induce electrical interference with speedometer signals. Failures or interference with signals from the variable reluctance speed sensor are best analyzed using a graphing meter or voltmeter set to measure alternating current (AC) voltage. Comparing the observed signal pattern with known good quality wave forms can identify potential problems with the speed signal. Open circuits in the sensor are checked with an ohmmeter.

Most speedometers have tolerances of ±10% due primarily to variations in tire diameter. Sources of error due to tire diameter variations are wear, temperature, pressure, vehicle load, and nominal tire size. Vehicle manufacturers usually calibrate speedometers to read slightly higher than actual road speed by an amount equal to the average error. This practice eliminates potential liability caused by speedometers displaying a lower speed than the actual road speed of the vehicle. Dynamometers and even global positioning systems (GPSs) can be used to validate the calibration of a speedometer.

Manufacturers currently use unique, proprietary software and diagnostic and maintenance tools to enable access to the vehicle speed settings whenever changes in tire size or rear axle ratios are made to adjust the speedometer calibration. Speed limiters required by many jurisdictions are associated with speedometer settings. Typically, access to the speed limit settings and related calibration parameters are protected by a customer password.

Tachometers and Odometers

Tachometers used to report engine speed are constructed and operate almost identically to speedometers. Variable reluctance or Hall-effect sensors are used to generate signals to the tachometer head. The engine electronic control unit counts all the pulses from both the speedometer and tachometer to track overall distance traveled by vehicle and engine. Several times per second in networked vehicles, the ABS also sends out a packet of information consisting of a header with speed-distance data. The header is identifying the packet as a distance or speed data that can be read by the tachometer or odometer. Distance travelled may also be stored in an instrument cluster control module. In networked vehicles, trip values stored in the ECM are compared with an instrument cluster control. This means that if an attempt is made to roll back the odometer, the value stored in the ECM does not match and generates a fault code.

Tachographs

Tachographs are devices used to record a vehicle's speed over time. Data can determine whether the vehicle is stopped or moving and at what speed. Data recorders, which are connected to the CAN, also log time, distance, position, and a variety of other vehicle data for retrieval. Older mechanical tachographs used a pen and ink to plot speed on a rotating paper disk that completed one revolution in 24 hours. As this type was vulnerable to tampering, electronic tachographs are now used to record data on removable smart cards. Trip information and accumulated vehicle totals can also be extracted from the ECM using proprietary software, or even accessed through the driver information center located in the instrument panel (**FIGURE 21-23**).

Compass

Electronic compasses are microcontroller devices constructed to sense and measure any source of magnetic fields. Sources of magnetic fields in commercial vehicles include permanent magnets in audio speakers, motors, electric magnetism produced from current flow through wiring, either AC or DC, and magnetic metals. An algorithm, or mathematical formula,

FIGURE 21-23 This driver's information screen has an alert to indicate when the driver is due for a rest stop. Mandatory rests stops are legislated and tracked by driver logs.

is embedded in the microcontroller that distinguishes the Earth's magnetic field from these sources. This formula essentially subtracts the fields sensed on the vehicle from the Earth's magnetic field. The magnetic sensor itself is made from Hall effect-type sensors. Depending on the sophistication of the microcontroller, two, three, or four sensors are arranged symmetrically around a piece of iron, which concentrates magnetic fields passing through the microcontroller. Slight differences in the strength of the Earth's magnetic field induced in the iron are detected as a differential voltage between the sensors (**FIGURE 21-24**). The signals are then conditioned and converted into a digital output.

Driver Information Screens

LO 21-5 Describe the operation of capacitance and resistive type touch driver information screens.

Most driver information screens offered in commercial vehicles today display vehicle speed, fluid levels, fluid temperatures, warning lights, trip information, and some basic diagnostic information or codes on LCDs (**FIGURE 21-25**). Enormous amounts of other information systems can be added to the list, including tire pressure, fuel consumption, compass headings, outside temperature, telematics, and freight information. To navigate the driver's information display menu, a variety of options are available: odometer buttons, the turn-signal wiper stalk, or a touch screen.

Liquid-Crystal Display (LCD)

LCDs can use a compact passive display technology and consume little current to operate. Passive display means that LCDs do not emit light but instead use ambient light around the display to reflect images. The displays are made of several layers. An important one contains the liquid crystal, which is an organic substance having a liquid form with a crystal molecular structure (**FIGURE 21-26**). The liquid is made of rod-shaped molecules that are arranged in a parallel lattice-like structure—a property that makes crystals transparent. However, an electric field can be used to control arrangement of the molecules to block light.

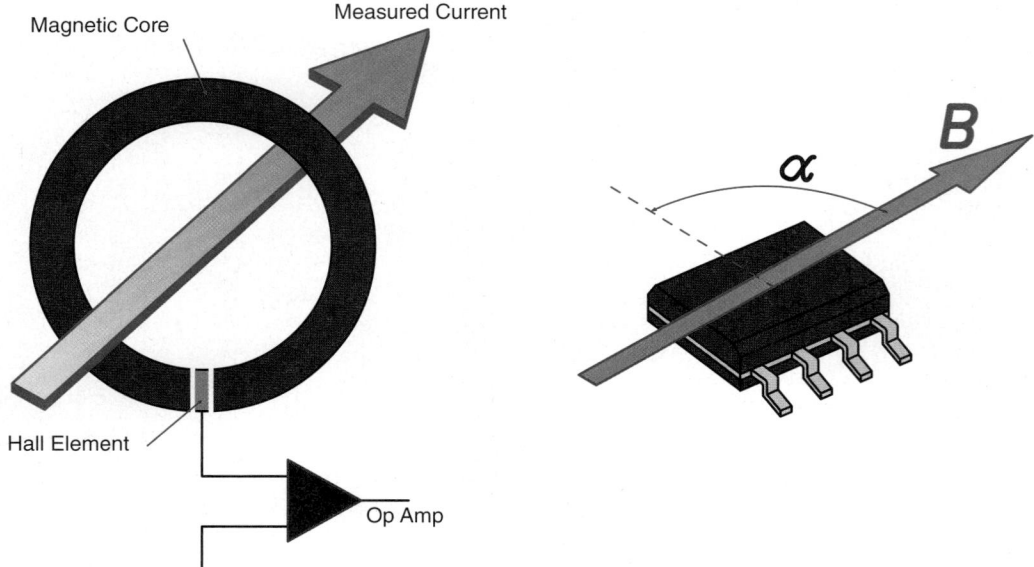

FIGURE 21-24 One type of position sensor uses magneto-resistive complementary metal–oxide–semiconductor (CMOS) technology. The sensor uses two or more magnets fixed perpendicular to one another in separate planes. The Earth's magnetic field influences the strength of the core, which is measured by the Hall-effect sensor. The difference in strength between the two cores is measured, and an output signal of varying voltage is provided, which is relative to the North Pole.

FIGURE 21-25 A driver's information screen uses a navigable set of menu items to obtain vehicle and trip information. This Mercedes transit bus uses an LCD.

To do this, LCD glass has transparent electrical conductors embedded into each side of the glass, which are in contact with the liquid crystal fluid. Made of indium-tin oxide (ITO), the liquid crystal molecules rotate in the direction of the electric current when it passes through the glass. When this happens, incoming light can pass through the glass and is reflected off a silver, gray, or black reflector surface called the rear analyzer. What is observed is a black or gray character on a silver background taking the shape of the LCD cell. When the current is switched off, the molecules revert back to a twisted, light-blocking structure that reflects ambient light back to the observer, resembling a light gray or silvery image. Using multiple selectable current pathways through the glass and selectively applying voltage to the current paths, a variety of patterns can be achieved.

Resistive Touchscreens

All touchscreen devices digitize the input from finger contact using an x/y coordinate. This means that there is a unique input determined by how far the contact is from the horizontal screen bottom or vertical side (**FIGURE 21-27**). Two types of technology used to sense the coordinates are capacitance and resistive touchscreens.

Resistive touchscreens are composed of two flexible transparent sheets lightly coated with an electrically conductive, yet slightly resistive, material. The sheets are separated by an air gap or microdot that closes like a switch when finger, object, or other pressure is applied to the screen. A unique voltage value is sensed by conductors placed at the x and y coordinate edge of the screen. Signal voltage is translated into coordinates and an input command goes to the screen microcontroller. The resistive touchscreen's advantages include its low cost, scratch resistance, durability, and capacity to operate in all climate conditions. Input can be made using either a finger or stylus.

Capacitance Touchscreens

Capacitance touchscreens use two transparent plates as well. However, they use only one electrically charged layer that typically is a glass panel with a transparent coating of indium metal (**FIGURE 21-28**). When a finger is placed on the screen, it draws electrons from a finger at that specific point onto the charged plate because pressing the screen changes the dielectric strength of the air gap electrically separating the plates. A unique voltage signal is sensed by conductors on the x- and y-axis of the screen. The signal varies in strength from left to right and up and down, proportional to where the contact was made. A microcontroller works out the x-y position based on the voltage signal caused by a change of plate capacitance produced by finger contact.

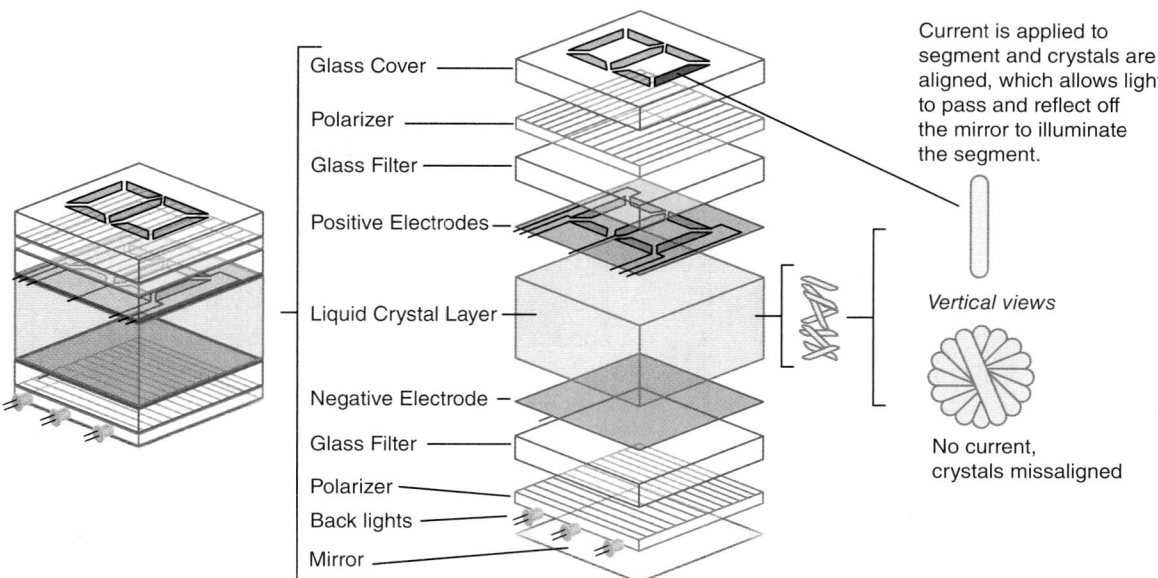

FIGURE 21-26 LCDs do not emit light, but reflect it. Electric current passing through layers of glass distorts liquid crystals, which allows light to either pass through and be reflected from the rear polarizer (on), or block light and reflect light from the top polarizer (off). Light reflected from the rear polarizer hits a dark gray or black surface. Light reflected from the top polarizer layer is silver or light gray.

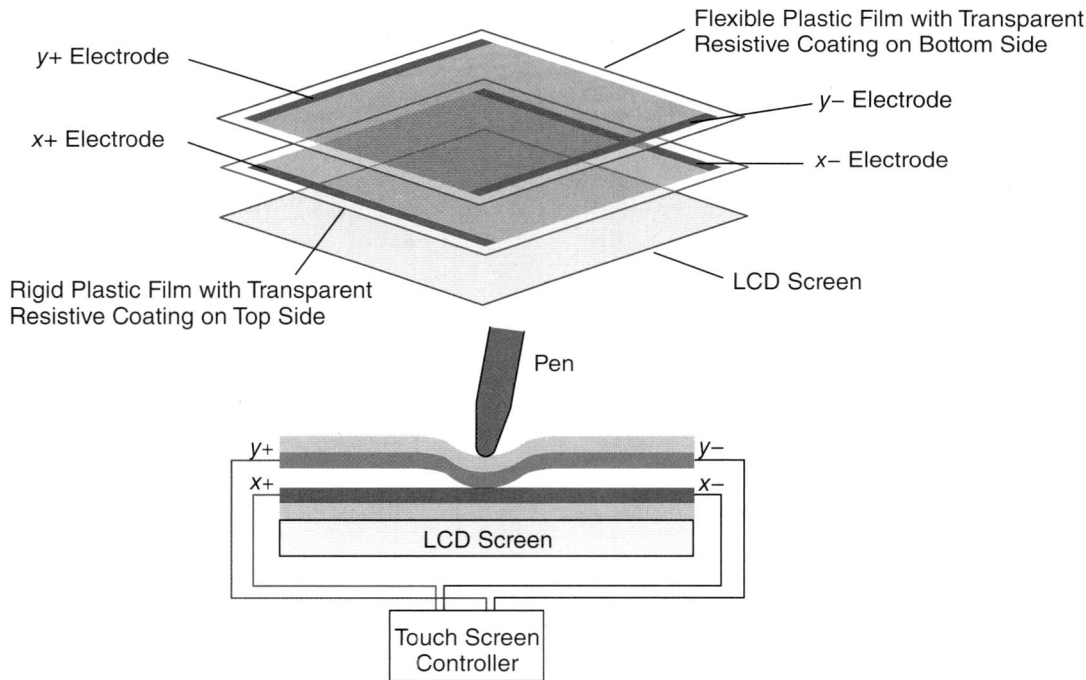

FIGURE 21-27 Resistive-type touchscreens plot the location of a finger or stylus by plotting coordinates using a resistive film screen material. A unique resistance value on a screen is generated by pressing one current carrying resistive film against another.

If gloves, such as thin latex examination gloves, which prevent electron movement, are used, the screen does not operate. Neither does it operate if a stylus is used, and the screen is confused under wet or high humidity conditions. Capacitance-type touchscreens, however, permit dual-finger touch processes and do not require as much pressure as resistive screens.

Troubleshooting Instrument Gauge Problems

LO 21-6 Outline procedures to troubleshoot gauge problems.

Technicians must be able to accurately diagnose gauge problems. A guide to troubleshooting gauge problems is in **TABLE 21-2**.

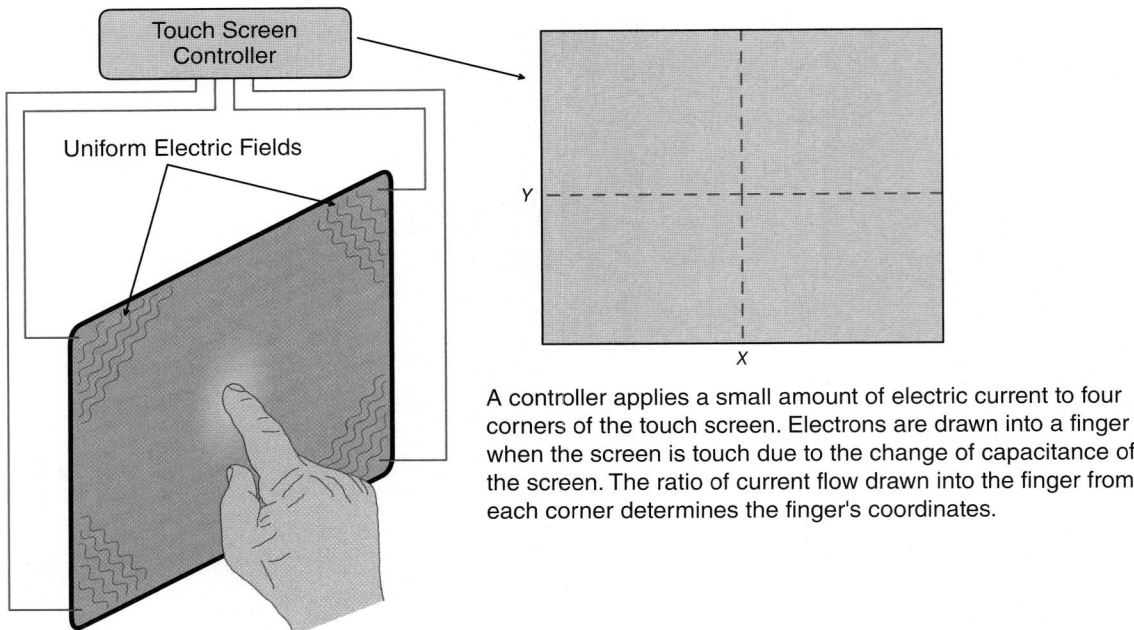

A controller applies a small amount of electric current to four corners of the touch screen. Electrons are drawn into a finger when the screen is touch due to the change of capacitance of the screen. The ratio of current flow drawn into the finger from each corner determines the finger's coordinates.

FIGURE 21-28 Operation of a capacitive touchscreen.

TABLE 21-2 Troubleshooting Instrument Gauge Problems

Symptom	Possible Cause	Diagnostic Strategy
Gauges do not respond with a prove-out sequence when ignition is switched on	Missing or broken ignition or ground wire	Check for power and grounds to instrument cluster
	Blown fuse	Check fuses and breakers
	Defective stepper motor	Continuity checks of stepper motor coils
Erratic gauge readings	Loose connections at sender unit and/or gauge	Verify connections
	Poor, loose, or resistive grounds	Measure resistance of sending unit and compare with specifications
	Defective sending unit or gauge	Evaluate gauge during prove-out Stepper motor gauges should smoothly sweep from min to max values, then to minimum, before moving to sensed value
Gauge stays at minimum or maximum value all the time (i.e., fuel empty, no oil pressure, low coolant temperature)	Sender unit wire disconnected or open-circuited	Verify oil pressure with master mechanical gauge Visually check fuel tank level Verify engine temperature using an infrared thermometer
	Sender unit wires shorted to ground	Remove sender wire Check harness, isolate shorts to ground, and repair
	Sender unit defective (i.e., broken unit, missing or leaking float, internally shorted to ground)	Measure resistance of sending unit over its full range Check float
	Defective gauge	Supply a calibrated resistance to sending unit lead to evaluate gauge Ground out sending unit wire to observe whether gauge moves Disconnect sending unit wire to observe whether gauge moves
No data on CAN instrument gauge display	Pinched, shorted, or open CANbus to instrument cluster	Check CAN signal to clusters using oscilloscope or graphing meter Measure CAN power and ground with voltmeter
	Missing terminating resistors	Measure CAN signals using a voltmeter Measure resistance of CAN line batteries disconnected

Wrap-Up

Ready for Review

- Instrument gauges, warning lamps, and driver information centers enable the driver to monitor the vehicle's operating condition, status of equipment, and safety systems.
- Warning lights provide easily understood information to alert the driver to potentially dangerous operating conditions—low air pressure, antilock brake faults, low diesel exhaust fluid, door ajar, etc.
- Warning lights can be switched on by mechanical ground switches, voltage drop circuits, or electronic modules.
- Mechanical ground switches (sender units) are used to indicate low fluid levels, low air pressure warning systems, or power divider engagement locks.
- Electronic switches found in engine control modules are the most common way warning lights are illuminated in today's vehicles.
- To test the correct operation of a warning light, vehicles use a prove-out sequence in which the instrument cluster illuminates the warning lights for several brief seconds with the key on and engine off or during key-on engine cranking.
- Manufacturers use blink codes to provide fault code data.
- Gauge systems are designed to inform the driver about a developing problem by displaying a representation of a physical measure of system conditions (pressure, temperature, or fluid level).
- Common gauge systems are mechanical, bimetallic strip, electromagnetic, stepper motor, and digital display.
- For gauges to work accurately, they require voltage regulators to supply a steady current and smooth out variations from the alternator and from accessory systems being turned on and off.
- Stepper motors increase the precision of the pointer rotation on a gauge and can be either unipolar or bipolar.
- Most speedometers have tolerances of ±10% due primarily to variations in tire diameter. Sources of error due to tire diameter variations are wear, temperature, pressure, vehicle load, and nominal tire size.
- Today's commercial vehicles include data displays that allow the driver to view information about tire pressure, fuel consumption, compass headings, outside temperature, telematics, freight information, and more. Many of these displays use liquid crystal technology.
- Touchscreens can use resistive or capacitance touch technologies.
- Vehicles use a number of different types of gauge sending units, including thermistors and variable resistors.
- Electrical problems, such as blown fuse or faulty wiring, gauges, or sender units, can result in faulty gauge readings.

Key Terms

electronically commutated motors A method to produce motor rotation using switching transistors to control current flow through a DC motor rather than brushes.

bimetallic gauge A gauge in which two dissimilar pieces of metal are bonded together and expand at different rates when heated, thereby converting the heating effect of electricity into mechanical movement.

capacitance touchscreen A display screen that uses two transparent plates, one of which is electrically charged.

D'Arsonval gauge A type of electromagnetic gauge that moves a pointing needle directly proportional to current flow through an electromagnet attached to the pointer.

DIP switches A small slide switch located at the rear of the speedometer head placed in either an on or off (1 or 0) position.

prove-out sequence A sequence in which the warning lights illuminate for several brief seconds with the key on and engine off or during key-on engine cranking.

resistive touchscreen A display screen composed of two flexible, transparent sheets lightly coated with an electrically conductive, yet slightly resistive, material.

tachograph A logging device fitted to a vehicle to record various pieces of information, such as time, speed, rest periods, and distance traveled by each of the vehicle's drivers.

three-coil gauge A gauge in which three field coils are wound in series, with a coil at minimum reading, one at maximum reading, and one between the two.

Review Questions

1. Which of the following instrument display technologies is most sensitive to touch?
   a. LCD panels
   b. Resistive touch panels
   c. Driver information centers
   d. Capacitance touchscreens
2. Which of the following is the most common method for illuminating warning lights in today's vehicles?
   a. Voltage drop circuits
   b. Pneumatic switches
   c. Mechanical ground switches
   d. Electronic switches
3. Which of the following statements explains the purpose of the warning light prove-out sequence?
   a. The ignition key supplies a circuit to provide a ground and/or positive battery voltage path to illuminate instrument warning lights.
   b. It validates the correct operation of a warning lights.
   c. It provides time for instrument gauge clusters to perform a sweep.
   d. It is the time period used to check that warning buzzers work.

4. Which of the following technologies calibrates the instrument gauges every time the ignition switch is cycled on?
   a. LCD touch panel
   b. Stepper motors
   c. Three-coil gauges
   d. Digital displays

5. How do stepper motors gauges sense the angle or position or angle of the gauge pointer?
   a. Using Hall-effect switches
   b. Measuring the magnetic field strength field coils
   c. Counting steps made by the motor armature
   d. Measuring current flow through field coils

6. Which of the following is the most common type of instrument gauge used in late-model commercial vehicles?
   a. D'Arsonval gauge
   b. Bimetallic gauges
   c. Three coil gauges
   d. Brushless DC stepper motor

7. What is an example of an instrument gauge that can best use D'Arsonval movement?
   a. Ammeter
   b. Voltmeter
   c. Fuel pressure
   d. Water temperature

8. Which of the following methods is used to correct the speedometer readings when tires of a different size than the original are installed?
   a. Changing DIP switch positions
   b. The rolling diameter of the tire is measured and entered into the driver information center.
   c. A gear on the output shaft of the transmission is changed.
   d. A GPS unit is used to recalibrate the settings.

9. Which of the following observations are made when the wire to a resistive-type sending unit is disconnected?
   a. The gauge operation becomes erratic.
   b. The gauge pointer is centered.
   c. The gauge pointer moves to either the maximum or minimum position.
   d. The gauge pointer does not sweep when the ignition is switched on.

10. Which of the following describes a blink code?
    a. A sequence of light flashes from a warning light that represents a numerical fault code
    b. A warning light that flashes on and off to indicate a system is operating correctly
    c. A pulse per mile count from a speed sensor indicating tire size
    d. A warning light in a gauge cluster to alert the driver to a vehicle fault

ASE Technician A/Technician B Style Questions

1. Technician A says warning lights can be built into gauges or mounted in a dedicated panel in the instrument. Technician B says warning lights can blink out fault codes. Who is correct?
   a. Technician A
   b. Technician B
   c. Both Technician A and Technician B
   d. Neither Technician A nor Technician B

2. Technician A says normally closed pressure switches open with air or oil pressure to provide a path to ground to illuminate a bulb. Technician B says normally open pressure switches close with air or oil pressure provide a path to ground to illuminate a bulb. Who is correct?
   a. Technician A
   b. Technician B
   c. Both Technician A and Technician B
   d. Neither Technician A nor Technician B

3. Technician A says after the engine starts and the alternator begins charging, positive charging system voltage is applied to both terminals of a bulb. Technician B says the charging system indicator light is an example of a warning light operated through voltage drop. Who is correct?
   a. Technician A
   b. Technician B
   c. Both Technician A and Technician B
   d. Neither Technician A nor Technician B

4. Technician A says the malfunction indicator lamp (MIL) and check engine lamp (CEL) illuminates for approximately three to five seconds during engine start-up and then extinguish. Technician B says if there are active fault codes, the lights switch back on after extinguishing. Who is correct?
   a. Technician A
   b. Technician B
   c. Both Technician A and Technician B
   d. Neither Technician A nor Technician B

5. Technician A says stepper motor gauges reduce the problems associated with inaccurate readings from bimetallic and electromagnetic coil gauges caused by voltage fluctuations. Technician B says stepper motors are brush-type DC electromechanical devices that generally have a permanent magnet field surrounding an electromagnetic armature. Who is correct?
   a. Technician A
   b. Technician B
   c. Both Technician A and Technician B
   d. Neither Technician A nor Technician B

6. Technician A says speedometers electronically measure the driveshaft speed by counting a series of electrical pulses produced per mile or kilometer of distance traveled. Technician B says two wires connecting the instrument panel gauge clusters to the CAN network are all that is necessary to supply the data needed to display vehicle speed plus trip information, provide fault codes, and display warning lamps. Who is correct?
   a. Technician A
   b. Technician B
   c. Both Technician A and Technician B
   d. Neither Technician A nor Technician B

7. Technician A says that an erratic speedometer reading could be caused by a defective alternator. Technician B says the wrong tire size stored in the ABS module could cause erratic speedometer display. Who is correct?
   a. Technician A
   b. Technician B
   c. Both Technician A and Technician B
   d. Neither Technician A nor Technician B

8. Technician A says that a poor ground between the rear axle and chassis ground could produce incorrect axle oil temperature measurements. Technician B says that a dedicated ground wire from the temperature sending unit in the rear axle housing will minimize the likelihood of a inaccurate temperature measurement. Who is correct?
   a. Technician A
   b. Technician B
   c. Both Technician A and Technician B
   d. Neither Technician A nor Technician B

9. Technician A says that the best way to verify an engine temperature sending unit is inaccurate is to replace the sending unit. Technician B says the engine temperature could be measured with an infrared temperature gun and compared to actual gauge readings. Who is correct?
   a. Technician A
   b. Technician B
   c. Both Technician A and Technician B
   d. Neither Technician A nor Technician B

10. Technician A says an ohmmeter can be used to check the operation of a fuel tank sending unit. Technician B says the fuel sender unit wire can be disconnected and then grounded to check for full-range gauge operation. Who is correct?
    a. Technician A
    b. Technician B
    c. Both Technician A and Technician B
    d. Neither Technician A nor Technician B

CHAPTER 22

Body Electrical Systems—Accessory Electrical Circuits and Systems

Learning Objectives

After reading this chapter, you will be able to:

- **LO 22-1** Describe the purpose and outline service procedures used to connect and program electrical system accessories.
- **LO 22-2** Describe and explain the construction and operation of windshield wiper and cleaning systems.
- **LO 22-3** Describe and explain the construction and operation of power windows.

- **LO 22-4** Describe and explain the construction and operation of power door locks.
- **LO 22-5** Describe and explain the construction, operation, and adjustment of power mirrors.

You Are the Technician

A late-model straight truck has arrived at your original equipment manufacturers (OEM) dealership with several warranty-related complaints. The primary concerns are the vehicle cruise control does not operate, the engine often suddenly quits while driving, and often the engine only idles. When attempting to perform a diagnostic inspection of the vehicle, you find that retrieving stored information, such as fault codes, and accessing live data is very slow. Inside the cab you also notice an aftermarket wireless remote starter and vehicle security system has been installed by a local retail electronics store. Several wiring harnesses for the devices are connected beneath the dash and spliced into the vehicle's instrument cluster and dash wiring harnesses. When asked about when the accessory components were installed, the customer indicated the installation coincided with the appearance of the operating symptoms. While you prepare your service recommendations after following diagnostic procedures, consider answering the following questions.

1. What is likely the root cause of the customers complaints? Explain your answer.
2. What service recommendations would you make to the customer about the installation of the remote starter and security system accessories? Make at least two recommendations.
3. What is the likely cause of the slow communication between the service tool and vehicle while retrieving fault codes?

Introduction

Cab electrical accessories are a subdivision of the electrical system. Unlike major electrical system sub divisions, such as the starting, cranking, or lighting systems, today's commercial vehicles have many more electrical items that could be called electrical accessories. Common cab electrical accessories are generally considered to consist of:

- Windshield wiper and cleaning systems
- Comfort and convenience items, such as power mirrors, door locks, power seats, and windows
- Driver information or entertainment systems, such as the navigation and radios

Comfort and convenience items are a group of essential electrically powered devices that were once manually operated. For example, to raise and lower windows, window regulators required drivers to crank handles. Mirrors were physically adjusted by loosening and moving mirror brackets and arms before locking the adjustment in place by tightening the hardware. Safety regulations and growing sophistication of electrical systems technology have rapidly transformed the older mechanical operation of accessories from seat adjustment and single band radios to information systems integrating global positioning systems (GPS) telematic operations and satellite communication.

Today's systems provide not just a more comfortable workplace for drivers but enhance safety by allowing the operator to give more attention to the essential tasks of driving while reducing fatigue, collision-related injuries, and improved situational awareness regarding location, driving route, weather, and traffic congestion. Integration of the accessory electrical system means new features and functions are enabled through controller area network (CAN) communication (**FIGURE 22-1**). This chapter examines the construction and operation of the basic electrical accessories systems to provide background knowledge necessary to develop proper service and diagnostic practices associated with each system.

Connecting and Programming Electrical Accessories

LO 22-1 Describe the purpose and outline service procedures used to connect and program electrical system accessories.

On almost all late-model chassis, the electrical system uses distributed electronic control of components enabled through an onboard network sharing information processed by a variety of chassis control modules through CAN communication. This arrangement adds new features and increased levels of safety, comfort, and efficiency. For example, doors automatically lock after a vehicle moves to protect occupants from being ejected during a collision. Low-beam headlights switch on when wipers are used to increase visibility in poor weather conditions. Hydraulic or air-operated accessories, such as power take offs (PTOs), lifting booms, or vehicle stabilizers, such as outriggers, do not allow a vehicle to move if they are operational (**FIGURE 22-2**). Sound systems raise and lower the volume when receiving a cell call or mute the sound system when a vehicle is backing up.

Prior to the use of distributed network control and CAN communication, adding any electrically controlled accessory typically involved cutting into chassis wiring to install new circuits with multiple relays and inline fuses. The instrument panel and dashes were drilled to install warning lights, buzzers, cables, and switches, which often appeared unsightly and left permanent damage if removed. Furthermore, this approach created safety hazards without the use of a proper **safety interlock**, which prevents unsafe accessory operation if any number of correct operating conditions are not met. For example, a dump box installed after a vehicle was built could easily remain hoisted in the air without warning while driving down the road at high speeds. Equipment compatibility with new components could be compromised too. For example, installing a radio, remote start, or vehicle security system can cause a vehicle to unexpectedly shut down or interfere with other network communication if connected to an onboard network without verifying the device can correctly communicate, or is not properly paired and introduced to other network components. These devices may simply not work at all because they are not recognized by the onboard network. Splicing into today's wiring

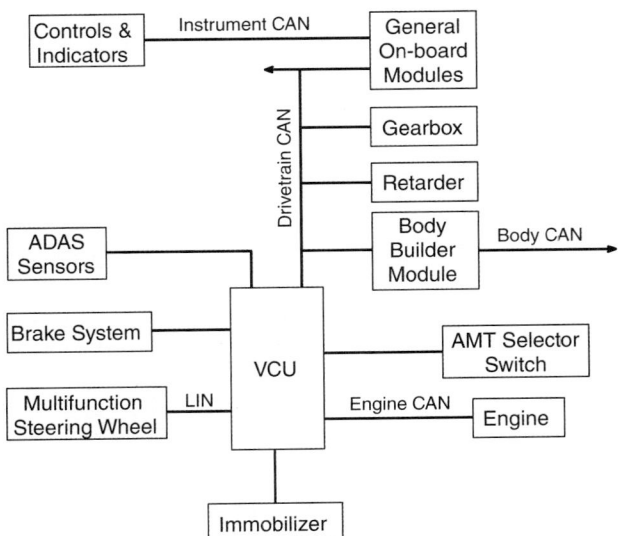

FIGURE 22-1 Switches for cab accessories distribute control through several modules by communicating over one or more CAN networks.

FIGURE 22-2 Air-operated devices and accessories are electronically controlled through a programmable air management unit.

harnesses to install a device is likely to trip a virtual fuse because the out-of-range current levels are sensed by control modules that continuously monitor circuits for faults.

► **TECHNICIAN TIP**

When an incompatible electrical accessory component is connected to the onboard, it can interfere with proper network communication. Common complaints are the engine only idles, the transmission doesn't shift, instrument clusters do not display correct information, and service tools communicate very slowly or not at all. The vehicle may not start at all or suddenly shuts down when operating. When this happens, network diagnostic tests should be performed. When defective or incompatible modules are disconnected, proper network operation is restored.

Electrical System Programming for Accessories

Today every manufacturer requires network control of almost every electrical device and accessory. This includes air and hydraulically operated accessories with electrical controls. The electrical system and its accessories are configurable only using software that allows a set of electrical components to operate and interact with other system components. Accessories and electrical options are managed using programming software and templates developed by the manufacturer or qualified aftermarket installers. Low-voltage "Smart" dash switches allow a customer to customize switch functions and print labels needed for a vehicle accessory and configure the output circuits for specific functions (**FIGURE 22-3**).

Electrical system modules with access points for connecting electrical circuits must be programmed to supply current. Not a single wire is cut or spliced to connect electrical, air, or hydraulic accessories. Whether the accessory is a fifth wheel with an air slide or a device needing to control the throttle, software, such as Navistar's **Diamond Logic** or Paccar's **Electronic Service Analyst (ESA)** and Freightliner's **ServiceLink**, are web-based service tools used to program and properly connect electrically activated accessories (**FIGURE 22-4**). To connect and configure

FIGURE 22-3 Blank switches in this dash can be configured using proprietary OEM to operate accessories.

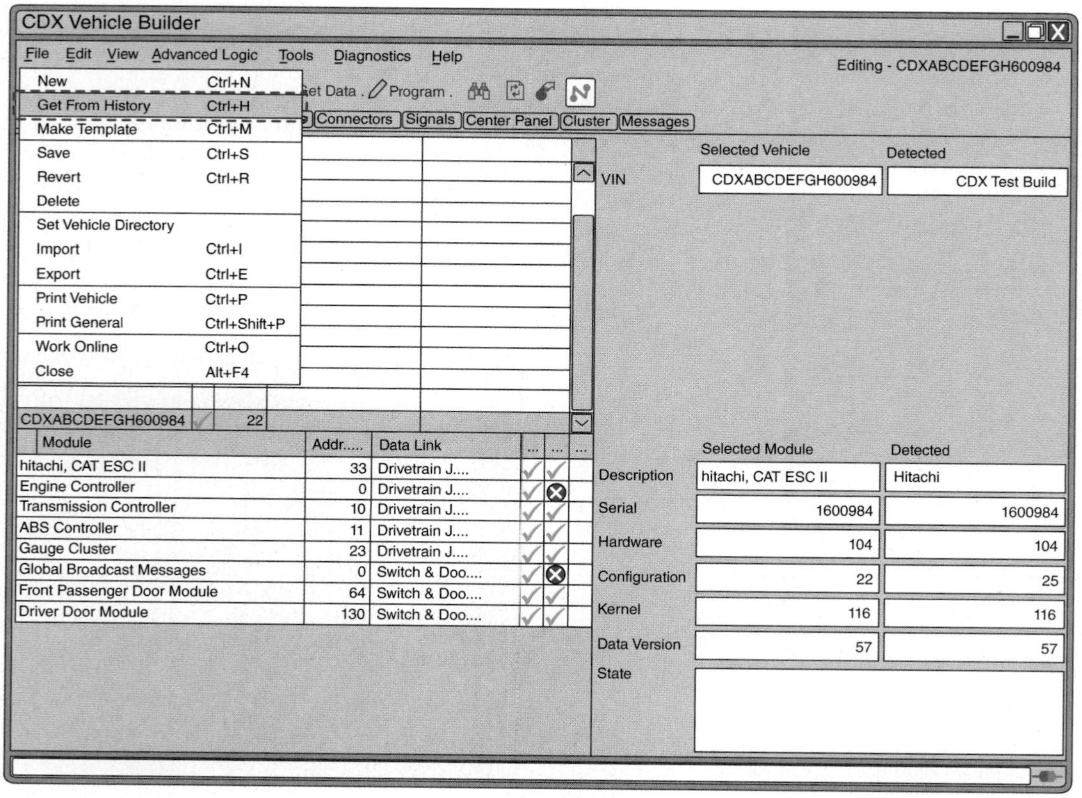

FIGURE 22-4 An example of proprietary OEM software used to retrieve the vehicle electrical system template or configuration.

an accessory, a connection to the vehicle is established first using a laptop and appropriate communication adapter for programming. The vehicle's original programming parameters are saved to an OEM mainframe before any new programming is performed. Next, changes are made to the system configuration and saved to a new file called an **electrical system template** (**FIGURE 22-5**). The template is created for the new electrical configuration capturing any changes to the vehicle configuration. Technicians can also search an OEM data base to find identical templates for common accessories rather than building a new one. After a new template is created or found through a search, it's uploaded to the vehicle.

▶ **TECHNICIAN TIP**

A safety interlock is a type of software programming rule that prevents the operation of an electrical device if several specific conditions are not met. For example, vehicle speed is limited if the PTO is engaged. When diagnosing a complaint about the failure of an electrically operated accessory to work, do not overlook the possibility of an interlock rule interfering with an accessory operation.

Windshield Wiper and Cleaning Systems

LO 22-2 Describe and explain the construction and operation of windshield wiper and cleaning systems.

Because a windshield covered in rain, snow, ice, and dirt can block an operator's visibility, a cleaning system made up of a

windshield wiper combined with a washer pump is essential for safety. Federal Motor Vehicle Safety Standard (FMVSS) safety standards for the device require two speed wipers with a low speed "Speed 1" wiping frequency of 20 wiping movements every 10 seconds in North America. European standards require only ten. A high-speed wiping action at a "Speed 2" setting requires 45 wiping movements. When the wipers are switched off, they move to a park position, which lowers the blades to a position parallel with the bottom edge the windshield or somewhere outside the driver's sight-line.

An intermittent wiping speed allows interruption of the wiping cycle with a variable interval between 2 and 45 seconds between sweeps. Intermittent wiping prevents a wiper from prematurely wearing or distracting the driver when the wiper blades sweep a dry windshield. Integration of the wiper control system with the rest of the electrical system through CAN communication adds several additional features. One is speed-sensitive rain-sensing wipers. A wiper control setting allows a rain sensor to activate the wipers and automatically adjust the wiper speed and sweep frequency according to two factors. One is the intensity of the rain or snow contacting the windshield, the other is vehicle speed. Vehicle speed data is collected, processed, and distributed over the CAN by the antilock brake system (ABS) module. Another feature is that the wipers can be disabled when the vehicle is parked and the park brake is applied. Without the need for visibility while parked, the park brake switch supplies a condition to disable wipers when they are not needed to prevent premature wear. A third feature achieved by distributed control of the electrical system is to switch

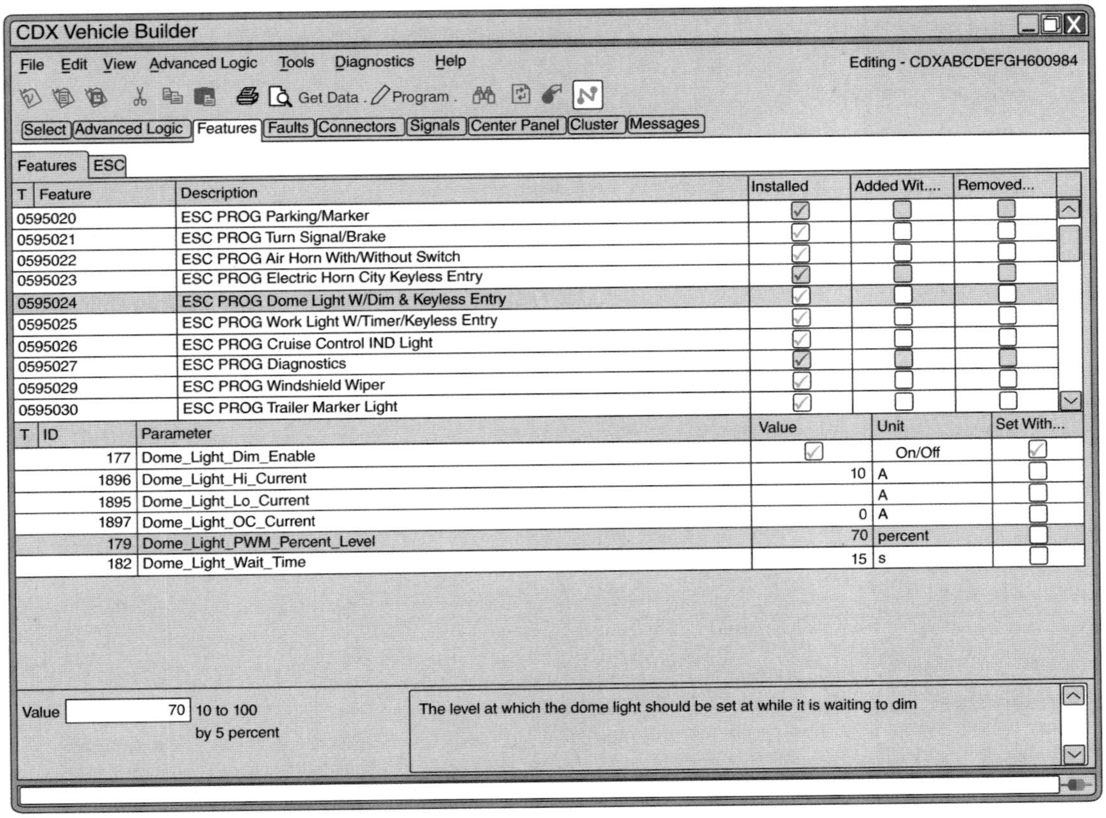

FIGURE 22-5 A screen used to edit an electrical system template.

on headlights when the wipers are in use. Many jurisdictions require the lights to operate whenever the wipers are activated to improve visibility of a vehicle to other road users.

One or two wiper motors are used, depending on the length of the wiper blades and expected drag across the windshield. The wiper motors may be installed above the windshield and activated separately as some coaches do, or below the windshield in the cab cowl (**FIGURE 22-6**). To minimize the transfer of noise and vibration from wiper motors and linkage, heavy aluminum mounting brackets with bolt holes insulated with rubber bushings are used to mount wiper mechanisms (**FIGURE 22-7**).

Splined wiper arms attach to wiper linkage to position the arms maximum range of travel. The arms can be removed to change the lower and maximum sweep position on the windshield. One or two wiper motors can be used or the linkage arranged to produce either a tandem or opposed sweep action (**FIGURE 22-8**).

Wiper Motor Operation

Wiper motors are generally electric **shunt-type motors** (**FIGURE 22-9**). Shunt-type motor is another name for a parallel-wound motor where the armature and field windings are connected in parallel. Lower-current draw, permanent magnet, series-wound motors are also used, but the shunt-type motor is preferred because it can maintain a constant speed, regardless of the load on the motor. Unlike the series-wound motors, field windings of a direct current (DC) shunt motor are constructed from a smaller-gauge wire having more turns. The higher number of winding turns creates a strong magnetic field, but the smaller gauge wires are more resistive and prevent excessive current flow so torque output is not as high as a series-wound motor. Starting torque of a DC shunt motor is low, and increases with speed. This means the load on the motor must be low at start-up to prevent the motor from stalling.

FIGURE 22-6 One or two wiper motors are used in commercial vehicles, depending on the size of windshields and length of wiper blades.

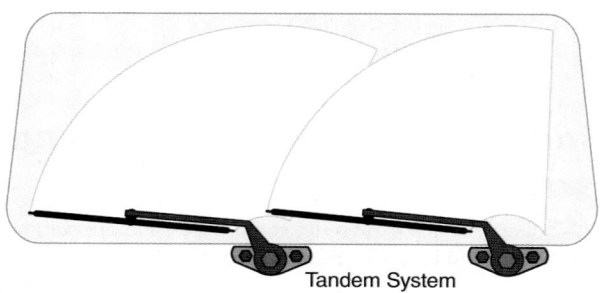

FIGURE 22-8 A tandem or opposed sweep arrangement is produced by the method connecting wiper linkage.

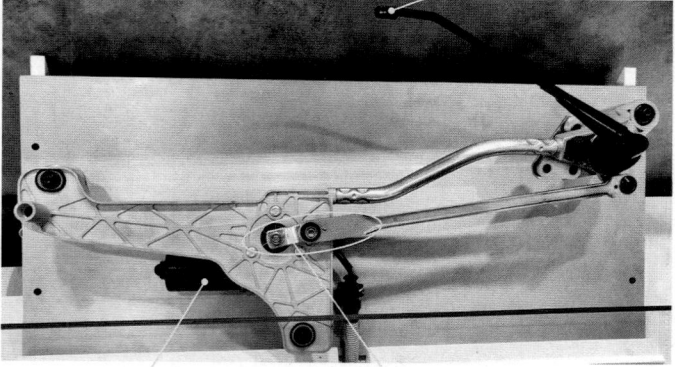

FIGURE 22-7 Heavy aluminum mounting brackets and braces minimize the transfer of noise and vibrations from the wiper mechanism.

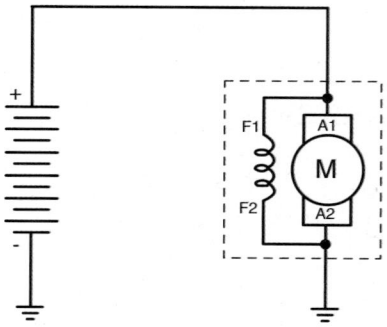

FIGURE 22-9 A shunt-wound motor describes a motor where the armature and field windings are connected in parallel to power and ground.

To create more torque, the motor output shaft has a worm gear that turns a drive gear, together supplying a 50:1 speed reduction but a similar multiplication of torque output. A drive gear connected to the worm gear is, in turn, connected to a simple short arm that rotates at 90 degrees to the motor housing. Linkage for the wiper mechanism connects to a pivoting joint on the short arm. As the wiper motor rotates, the short arm moves in a circular direction, causing the longer wiper linkage to sweep wiper arms back and forth across the windshield for an expected life of 1.5 million sweeps.

To produce the minimum two-speed output required from the motor, three brushes connect to the motor commutator. One brush is connected to negative chassis ground and the high-speed brush is connected to battery positive at 180 degrees opposite to it. When arranged like this, magnetic fields formed in the armature are at the best angle to produce the most torque and speed from the motor. By placing a third brush, connected to the low-speed circuit at an offset angle to the ground brush, magnetic forces of repulsion are not as strong compared to those formed between the ground and high-speed brush. The efficiency loss of the low-speed brush results in lower motor speed when only this circuit is energized. The use of two powered wiper circuits and a ground supplied

to the commutator is indicated by a minimum of three power supply wires connected to the motor (**FIGURE 22-10**). Two additional wires may be used to connect to an isolated park switch circuit that opens and closes a motor circuit connecting the cab wiper switch or the intermittent wiper control. The intermittent wiper circuit momentarily energizes the motor when the park switch has opened the motor circuit. An additional park switch circuit connection to the wiper switch may also be used to provide position feedback to an electronic control module used to stop-start and park the wipers, or even reverse the direction of motor rotation to lower the wipers arms further in the park position (**FIGURE 22-11**).

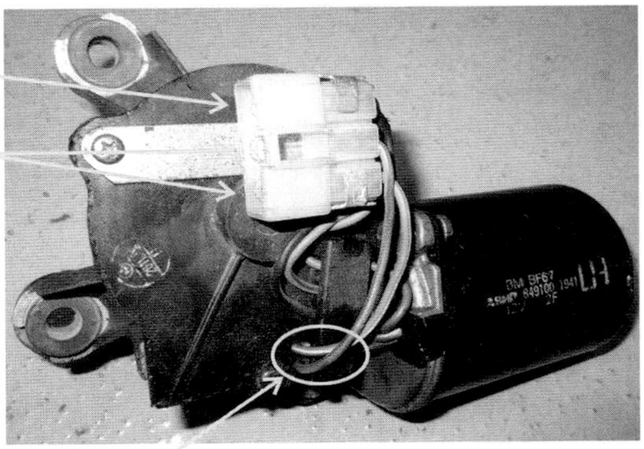

Wiper Motor Park Position

A unique switch is used to place the wipers in a park position after the wiper switch has switched the wipers off. If power to the motor was simply disconnected when switched off, the wipers would remain in the same position where they were when switched off and possibly obstruct the driver's sight-line. However, two sources of switched battery current are supplied by the wiper switch to the wiper motor – power for either the high- or low-speed circuit through the park switch and a second circuit with switched ignition-battery current (**FIGURE 22-12**). When the main Hi-Low wiper control circuit to the wipers is switched off by the driver, battery power to the park circuit continues to supply current to the motor until the wiper arms have moved to a parked position. Only at this point are both sources of motor current disconnected. Again, park position is parallel with the bottom of the windshield or another predetermined location out of the driver's line of sight. The park switch is located in the wiper motor housing along with the drive gear and continues to supply current to the motor until the wiper mechanism has reached the park position. A cam lever on the drive gear opens the normally closed park switch contacts at this precise

![wiper motor photo with labels Negative Ground, Low and High Speed Circuits, From Park Switch]

FIGURE 22-10 Three wires connect to the wiper motor – ground plus a high-speed and a low-speed supply circuit.

FIGURE 22-11 Five wires used on this wiper motor, only two are connected to an isolated park switch.

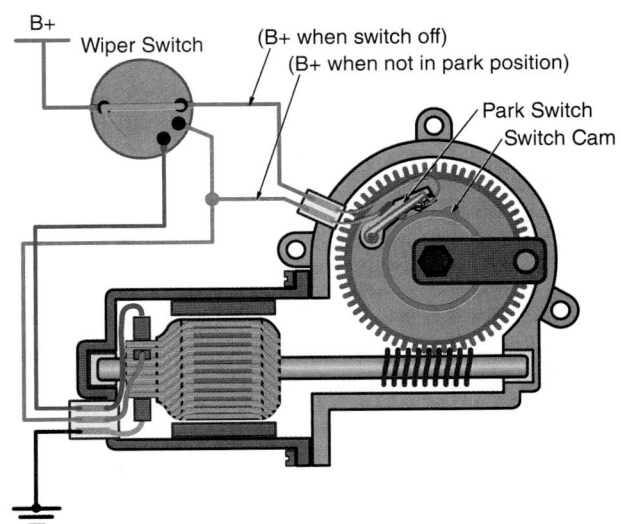

FIGURE 22-12 The park switch circuits supplies a second source of current to the motor until it opens when the wipers are in the parked position.

position, disconnecting the second supply of ignition switched battery current to the motor (**FIGURE 22-13**).

On some motors, the housing covering the park switch can be rotated a few degrees clockwise or counterclockwise to adjust the wiper parked position. This is only done if the wiper arms are not correctly synchronized with the motor park switch-off position. Turning the cover containing the park switch repositions the switch relative to the park position cam on the drive gear. A defective park switch that remains closed will prevent the wipers from stopping until the ignition is switched off.

Washer Pump

A separate washer pump circuit is activated by the same wiper control in the multi function turn signal switch (**FIGURE 22-14**). When the washer switch is pressed, the washer pump circuit is energized and supplies current to a centrifugal-type pump immersed in washer fluid inside the washer fluid reservoir (**FIGURE 22-15**). Washer cleaning fluid is pumped to two spray nozzles attached to the wiper arms on commercial vehicles or a nozzle at the top of the windshield. After a brief moment following the initial washer spray, the wiper mechanism is activated. The windshield wipers sweep the windshield several times before moving to the park position.

The motor is serviceable by pushing or pulling it in or out of a rubber grommet in the fluid reservoir. Another locking method for the washer pump uses a push and turn to lock, bayonet-style attachment.

> ▶ **TECHNICIAN TIP**
>
> When installing bayonet-type washer pumps or a pump with a friction-fit grommet, apply some dielectric grease on the sealing grommet to prevent the grommet from folding and leaking after installation.

Multifunction Wiper Switch

In conventional electrical systems, the wiper circuit is controlled by a single-pole, multiple-throw switch operated by the driver. In late-model vehicles, control of the wipers and washers is distributed over one of more electronic control modules. Park brake status, vehicle speed, and rain sensors combine with driver input signals for the wipers originating from a multifunction turn signal, headlight dimmer switch. Like other input signals from steering wheel mounted sensors, low-voltage signals from the turn signal stalk on most commercial trucks and buses connect to the instrument cluster module (ICU), a major node on the CAN network (**FIGURE 22-16**). Signals from the turn signal stalk are monitored by the ICU and the status of each switch broadcast along the CAN data bus. The ICU identifies which switch is activated by the driver by measuring the voltage signals at the multifunction switch pins. Each switch function has a unique combination of resistors that controls the voltage signal to ICU (**TABLE 22-1**). Because the ICU is programmed to recognize a particular resistance or voltage drop from a multifunction switch, it interprets the voltage measurements and

Parking Cam   Drive Gear   Cam Switch

Worm Gear   To Brushes

FIGURE 22-13 A cam lever on the driver gear opens the park circuit switch only in the parked position.

FIGURE 22-14 The turn signal stalk is a multifunction switch controlling the wipers and washers.

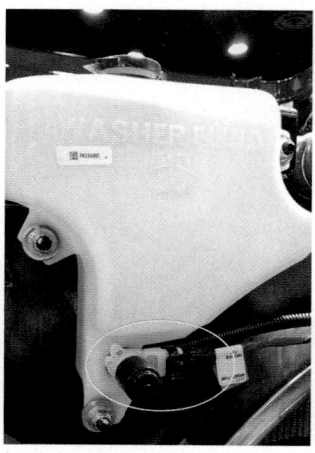

FIGURE 22-15 The washer reservoir with a motor and fluid level switch.

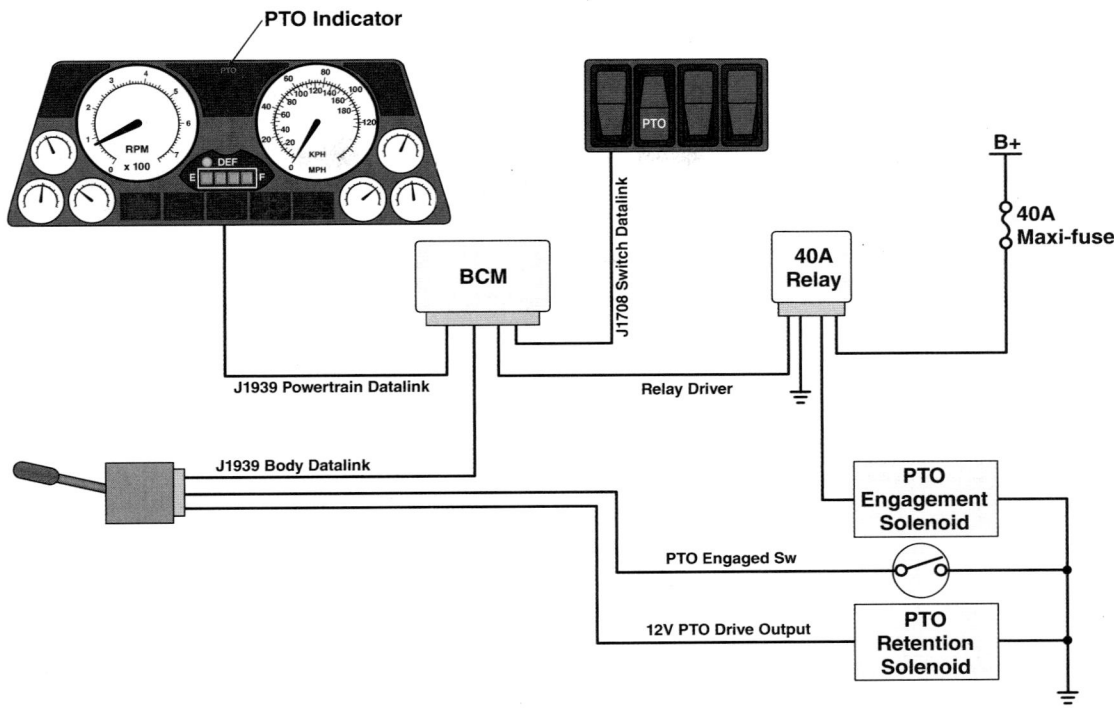

FIGURE 22-16 Switches for cab accessories distribute control through several modules by communicating over one or more CAN networks.

TABLE 22-1   Resistance Values for a Multifunction Switch

Function	Resistor	Resistance Value – Ohms
Washer	R1	1500
Flash to Pass – High beam	R2	300
Low Beam	R3	180
Wiper Off	R4	12.5
Wiper Intermittent 1	R5	56
Wiper Intermittent 2	R6	100
Wiper Intermittent 3	R7	150
Wiper Intermittent 4	R8	250
Wiper Intermittent 5	R9	400
Wiper Low Speed	R10	675
Wiper High Speed	R11	1600
Right Turn	R12	500
Left Turn	R13	825

generates a corresponding CAN message to the module driving the output function. Less wiring is needed with this arrangement because a multifunction switch can have more than a dozen possible switch combinations but only connect 5 wires to the ICU (**FIGURE 22-17**). In the case of wipers, Freightliner's earlier architecture used the Bulkhead Module (BHM) to activate outputs. Navistar's body electrical control module, which resembles a BHM function, also produces the appropriate output current to operate the wipers and washers based on a CAN

message transmitted by the ICU (**FIGURE 22-18**). More recent Freightliner electrical system architecture has replaced the bulkhead module with the Signals Acquisition Module for the cab (SAM cab). And instead of transmitting switch signals to the ICU, a more compact network device, called the **Modular Switch Field (MSF)** control unit, replaces the ICU as a switch signal hub. Signals from the MSF pass to the SAM-cab through a star point connector. The MSF network device processes switch inputs for the entire cab, including inputs from a slave

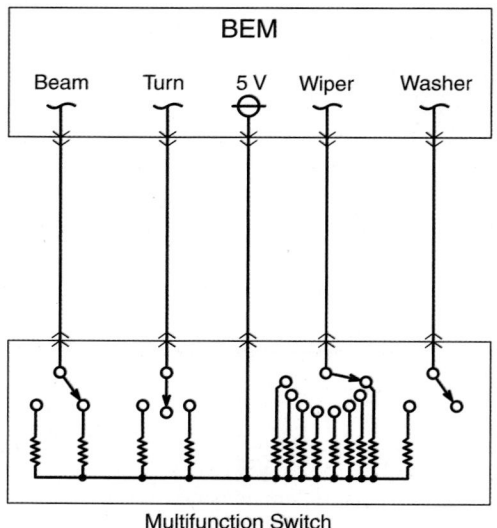

FIGURE 22-17 A unique voltage for each switched position of the turn signal stalk identifies switched inputs signals to the MSF control unit.

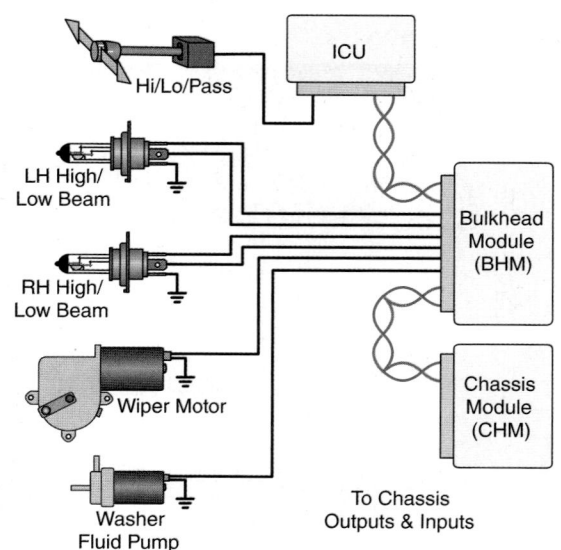

FIGURE 22-18 Switch input signals from the multifunction turn signal stalk are often transmitted to the instrument cluster control unit, which in turn broadcasts CAN messages to the BHM and CHM control units.

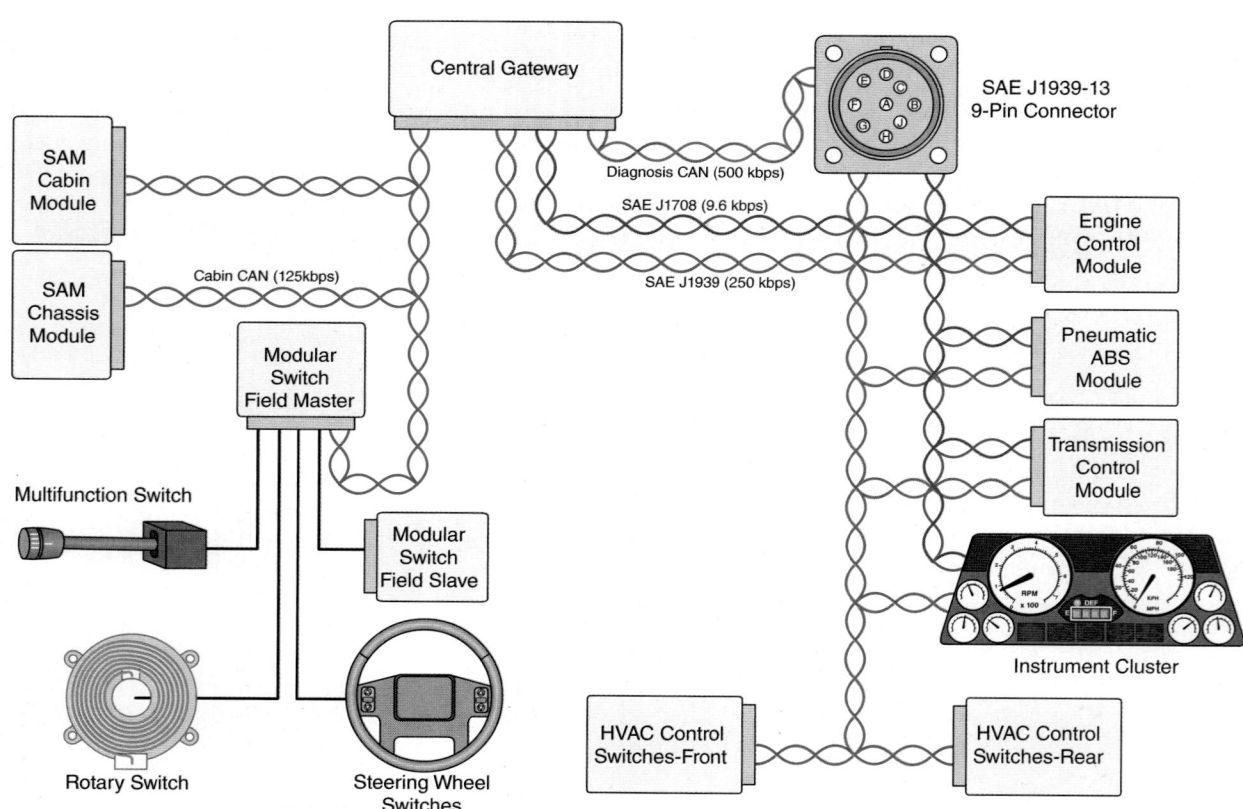

FIGURE 22-19 In the latest Freightliner chassis, the Modular Switch Field (MSF) control unit processes all switch input signals and broadcasts Unified Diagnostic Service control messages over the CAN network.

switch expansion module. It then transmits CAN messages to the SAM cab module, which produces output current for electrical system devices (**FIGURE 22-19**). These CAN messages are now frequently in the format of proprietary **Unified Diagnostic Service (UDS)** protocols, which resemble CAN messages but are encrypted to prevent any hacking of the cab control system.

How long each switch function is toggled can influence the output action or CAN message. Bumping the switch for a moment may not activate an output because a longer press and hold time is necessary. How long a high beam switch is toggled may make the difference between the high beams only momentarily lighting or latching to keep the high beams activated.

Universal Diagnostic Services (UDS) is a secure network protocol described more completely in the chapter covering onboard networks. UDS has many applications but an important one is to prevent remote hacking of onboard networks and taking over control of the vehicle electrical system or electrical accessories. Radio and cell phone communication modules connected to the network is one access point that makes trucks and buses vulnerable to malicious hacking. UDS uses encrypted messages to secure the network from remote intrusions. This explains why proprietary service tools are required to diagnose or communicate interactively with electrical networks controlling electrical accessories.

Rain and Dirt Sensors

Rain and dirt sensors are used as input signals to the wiper-washer system to automatically activate either the wipers or the wipers and washers whenever water droplets and dirt can obscure the driver's vision. Rain sensors are widely used in

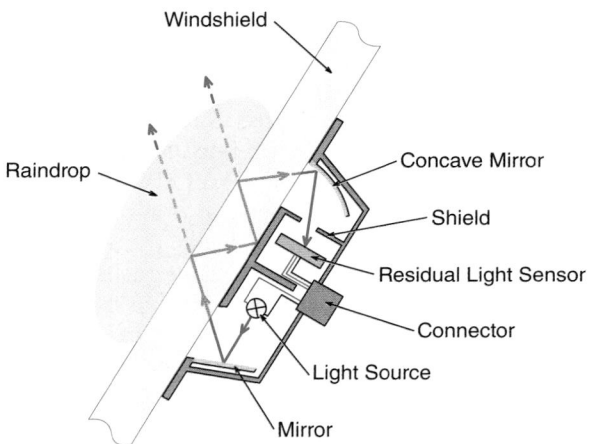

FIGURE 22-20 Rain sensors use two mirrors and an LED light to collect light signals bounced off water droplets on the windshield surface. Rain causes more of the light to reflect back into the sensor.

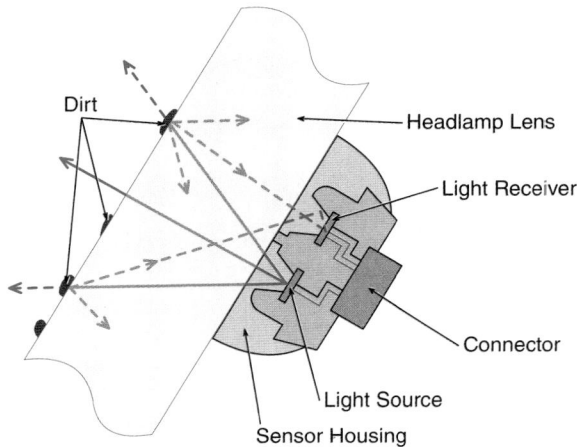

FIGURE 22-21 Dirt on a windshield causes light to be reflected directly back into the sensor. Signal output is proportional to the amount of dirt.

North America and Europe. Both these devices use a light-emitting diode (LED) as a light emitter and a photoreceiver able to detect the infrared light emitted by the LED. In the rain sensor, the LED light is bounced off a mirror at an angle onto the windshield surface. Normally, when no rain is present on the outer surface, light continues to pass through the glass and almost none is reflected back to the receiver. If water droplets are on the surface, light is reflected back onto the photoreceiver using a concave mirror. The signal the device produces is proportional to the amount of light reflected back into the sensor (**FIGURE 22-20**).

Dirt sensors work in a similar way except that light is not directed outward at an angle and no mirrors are used. Instead, dirt tends to reflect light directly back into the sensor where the signal strength of the sensor is proportional to the amount of reflected light (**FIGURE 22-21**).

Power Windows

LO 22-3 Describe and explain the construction and operation of power windows.

The driver and passenger door windows use electric motors driving worm gears to turn either a spur drive gear of a scissor-type regulator or a cable-and-drum mechanism (**FIGURE 22-22**). The drum mechanism is used in doors with little operating clearance between the inside and outside sheet metal. Wrapping or unwrapping a **Bowden cable** around the drum raises or lowers the window. When a gear drive motor is used, the window regulator operates on the scissor principle.

Scissor-Type Window Regulators

In the scissor-type regulator, two lifting arms arranged like scissors raise and lower the window. Both arms slide along two horizontal rails. One rail is fixed near the bottom door area, the other is attached to the lower edge of the window. The motor action causes the lifting arms to open and close. As the arms close together, as if cutting like scissors, the arms move together, and the window is lowered as a gear-driven mechanism pulls the upper arm down and closer to the lower

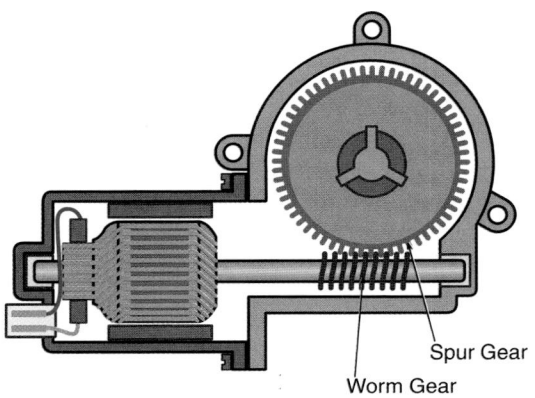

FIGURE 22-22 A worm gear on the motor shaft turns a drive gear attached to either a spur gear like this or a drum to operate a window regulator.

arm fixed in the door. Reversing the direction of the motor to lift the window is done by switching the polarity of current supplied to the motor (**FIGURE 22-23**).

Scissor-type regulators fail when nylon wheels sliding along the arms wear out, become loose, and break. Lack of lubricant on the horizontal rail surfaces where the rollers slide also causes binding and slow window operation. Noisy, slow window operation precedes failure. If the rollers break and one arm is loose, the upper rail allows the glass to tilt and fall at an angle inside the door.

Bowden Cable-Type Regulators

A second type of window regulator mechanism uses wire cables to winch a window up between vertical guides called whiskers (**FIGURE 22-24**). The operation is not unlike using cable to raise or lower a drawbridge. The Bowden cable regulator uses a drum mechanism to either lengthen a cable or shorten it by winding the cable around a drum. The electric motor is fixed in its position inside the door, but one end of each cable is attached to the drum rotated by the motor. The cables generally are crossed like the letter X with the opposite end of each cable fixed to the bottom of the window moveable window clamps or horizontal rail attached to the window.

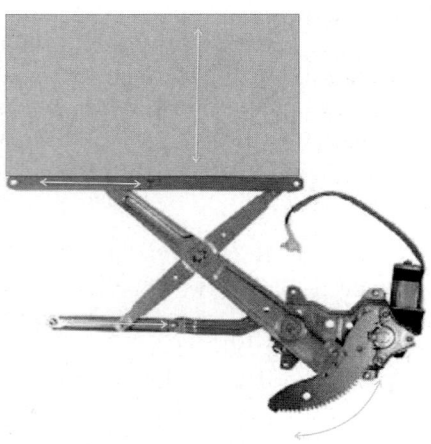

FIGURE 22-23 A scissor-type regulator uses the spur gear driving a geared arm to raise and lower the window by moving an arm up or down.

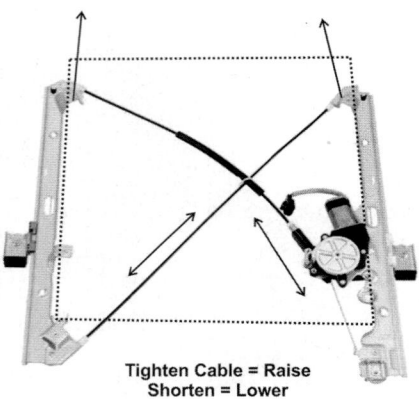

Tighten Cable = Raise
Shorten = Lower

FIGURE 22-24 A Bowden cable is used to winch a window up and down along vertical guides by shortening and lengthening the cable.

When the cables are tightened, they pull upward on the horizontal rail or clamp attached to the bottom corners of the window. Because the cables are also wound around pulleys on each side of the regulator corners, shortening the cable easily raises the window. To lower the window, the weight of the window that is suspended by the cables glides downward as the cables lengthen. Downward movement is permitted when the motor unwinds cables from the drum. As in the scissor mechanism, reversing motor polarity changes the direction the window moves to either open or close.

If a cable breaks, the window glass will fall down the guides. Cables and pulleys can wear, particularly if the vertical guides become sticky with dirt and tree sap.

Power Window Motors and Switches

The use of permanent magnets for fields in these DC motors keeps the unit compact and draws less current than motors with wire field windings. Positive temperature coefficient resettable fuses provide circuit protection at the motor in the event they are jammed or have high mechanical resistance. When the PTC fuses get hot, they become very resistive to current and prevent further operation until they cool. Window operation in non-networked vehicles is controlled by the power window rocker switches mounted in the door switch panel. Double pole, single throw-type switches are used to reverse motor polarity to move the windows up and down (**FIGURE 22-25**). High current draw by motors is handled by a pair of standard ISO single pole, double throw relays. A pair of relays for each motor can also switch current polarity supplied to the window motors without the need to switch polarity at the rocker switches in the door panels. **FIGURE 22-26** shows the relays can be signaled using either positive or negative polarity current supplied by the rocker switches when each is connected to the switched output circuits of the relay. The driver door switch panel has two switches that control the windows on both the driver and passenger doors (**FIGURE 22-27**). The passenger door switch panel has one switch that controls only the passenger window.

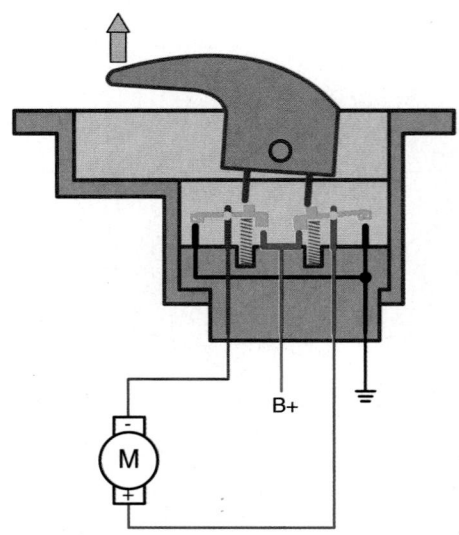

FIGURE 22-25 A single pole, single throw window switch used to reverse the polarity to a window motor.

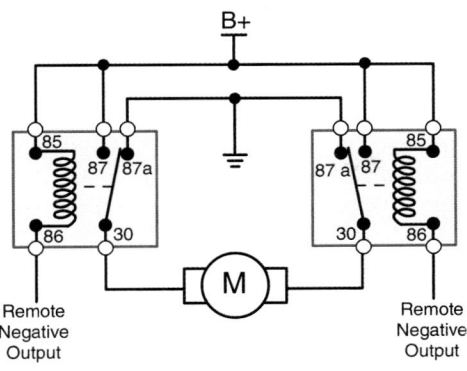

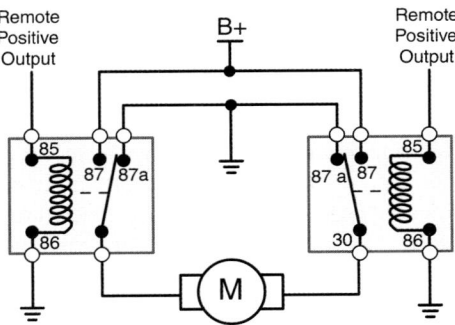

FIGURE 22-26 Two relays supplied for each window motor can switch motor current polarity using single pole, single throw door switches having either negative or positive current output.

Express Up and Down Function

Each power window switch can have two positions for up and down movement with four possible positions on each switch. One position step is used to adjust the window position up or down through the switch movement. A second position step requires only a longer momentary contact in the second of two positions to produce either an express-up or express-down feature. This feature uses a control module connected in series between the window switch and motor (**FIGURE 22-28**).

Current models of commercial vehicles send door window switch inputs to the cab-body electrical control module to handle all window and door lock switch functions. Based on switch input signals and control algorithms, the windows receive control signals from the cab-body control module.

Window Position Sensors

Safety regulations have required power windows to have limiter switches that stop a window from rolling up if an object, such as a person's hand, fingers, or arm, is trapped. One method was to electronically measure the surge in current as motor torque increased when it either reached the end of its travel or encountered resistance from a body part. Expensive and complex electronics were required to sense unusual changes in motor speed and current flow that were expected when this happened. While the systems often worked in normal circumstances, temperature extremes made the current measurements unreliable. A simpler method now used involves sensing motor speed rotation and directional change using magnetic reed sensors (**FIGURE 22-29**). Using two simple switches that are

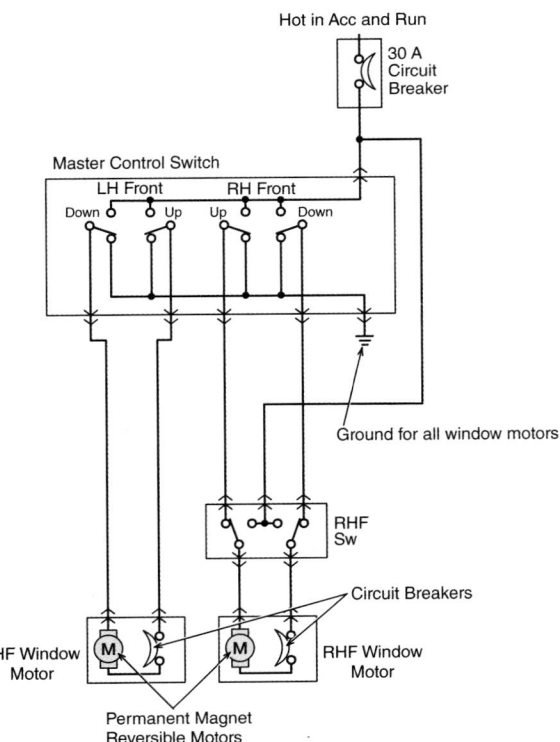

FIGURE 22-27 A schematic for the operation of window rocker switches having double pole, single throw switches to reverse current polarity to each window motor.

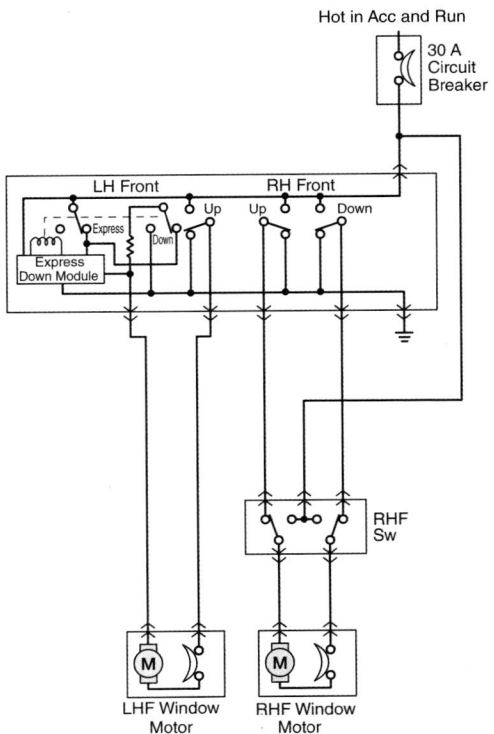

FIGURE 22-28 The window express up and down feature is added using an electronic module that senses current signals from the rocker switch.

opened and closed by a magnet enables manufacturers to control motor operation as the window reaches the end of its travel limits. A permanent magnet is attached to the motor drive gear and at least two or more magnetic reed sensors are placed at 90 degrees to one another. When the motor operates, the time between the sequence of each switch closing and opening is used by a control module to predict speed and window position. If a window does slow, the unusual pattern of reed switch operation measured by the control module stops the motor's supply of current.

Window Recalibration-Reset Programming

The use of magnetic reed sensors and a permanent magnet to sense motor speed and direction is a simple, reliable solution to the problem of power window safety. However, electronic controls monitoring these sensors must learn limits for the end of window travel. It does this by measuring the number of rotations the motor completes and the motor position after it completely sweeps a window up and down. Many vehicles do this automatically the first time the windows are moved up or down, but each manufacturer has a unique adaptive learning strategy to perform this task. One common method is to hold the window switch in the down or up position for a few seconds after the window completes it range of travel. The electronic controls can recognize the sequence of events and circuit electrical conditions to store a new window travel limit. Whenever the battery is disconnected or the vehicle is inspected for predelivery, the control module must learn position limits for each window. Without entering a learning or adaption mode, the window may not move all the way down or up or the express function may not work.

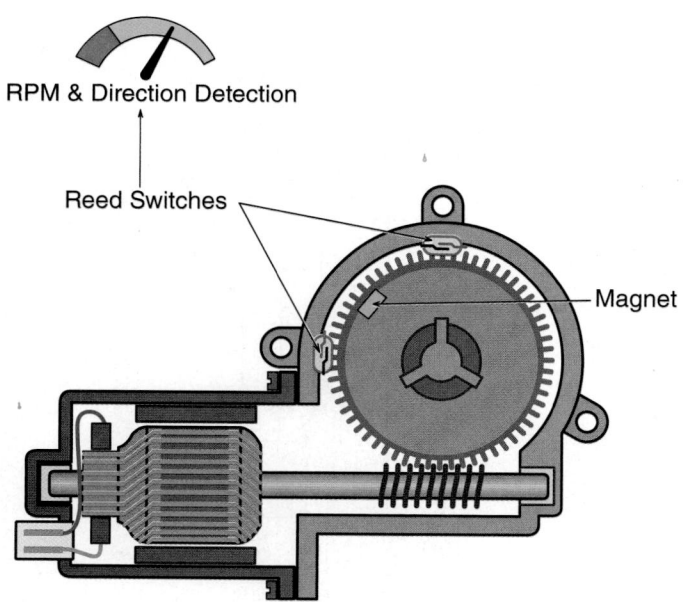

FIGURE 22-29 Window motor rotational speed and direction are learned using a permanent magnet attached to a motor drive gear to open and close magnetic reed sensors.

Window express down or up is often only available for all windows after window limits are learned. By momentarily depressing the window switch completely down to a second step or detent, the express function should work. If it doesn't, the switch may need to be held for several seconds after the window has finished rolling down, and even rolling up, before the function appears. If it still doesn't appear, consult service literature for the product to determine whether the function is available and whether a unique procedure must be followed for teaching window travel limits.

Power Door Locks

LO 22-4 Describe and explain the construction and operation of power door locks.

Some power door actuators use solenoids with permanent magnet cores. This configuration works by moving the actuator in two directions whenever the polarity of current changes as it flows through the solenoid coil. One or two springs help either center the linkage or lightly hold it in one direction. Linkage from the solenoid core or pole piece is connected to linkage for each of the door locks. The electromagnetic magnetic field in the core exerts either a pull or push against the poles on the permanent magnet core to lock or unlock a door lock mechanism. One disadvantage of using a solenoid is that a push-pull solenoid has little or no mechanical resistance to prevent tampering with a door lock mechanism by some means other than a key or electrical signal. Because electrical current no longer flows and holds the solenoid in a latched or locked position, it is relatively easy to open the lock using other mechanical methods. An increasingly common and more secure arrangement for lock actuator mechanisms uses a compact electric motor to turn a set of spur gears driving a worm gear (**FIGURE 22-30**).

A helically cut drive shaft or pinion gear arrangement moves an actuator lever up or down to operate the lock mechanism. The gears not only provide a mechanical advantage to help a small electric motor operate the lock, but increase mechanical resistance in the mechanism to prevent the lock

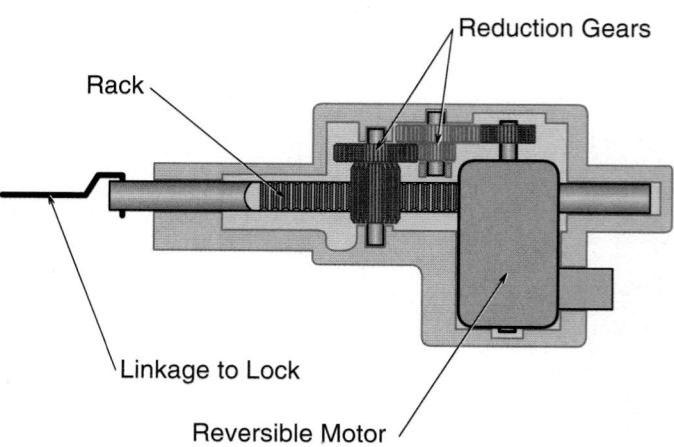

FIGURE 22-30 An electrically driven door actuator with a gear reduction system.

from being easily opened without operating the motor or using a key. A permanent magnet motor combined with a gear reduction system multiplies the permanent magnet motor's natural resistance to external effort to turn the armature.

▶ **TECHNICIAN TIP**

When electric motors combined with a gear reduction system are used for any type of actuator, never try to force the actuator into position when installing it. Connect the actuator to the vehicle circuit and attempt to move it electrically. Alternatively, try to use a small nine-volt battery to energize the actuator. Attempting to move the actuator linkage against the motor resistance multiplies force in the gear reduction system and will damage or even break external linkage a gear reduction system will damage or even break linkage.

Power Door Lock Control

The earliest power locks used a rocker switch to send electric current to the lock actuators. Changing the direction of current polarity using the switch or relays opened or closed the lock actuators. This means that an inoperative power door lock could be caused by the door switch, solenoid, wiring, or mechanical wear of the linkage.

Today, it is common for a door control module control to not just operate the locks, but also operate windows and power mirrors (**FIGURE 22-31**). CAN communication signals send messages based on switched inputs from the driver and other modules (**FIGURE 22-32**). Vehicle speed input to a distributed electrical control system is used to lock doors above a specified speed, such as 5 mph (8 kph). This feature can be programmed to change the activation speed or even disable a feature. In addition to CAN signals, Local Interconnect Network (LIN) communication can operate a door module. In a LIN, the main

body electrical control module containing master programming instructions communicates with the slave module operating the door. Over just a single wire, the master control module sends digital serial communication signals to the slave module. The slave module carries out the commands to send output electrical signals to operate the devices it is connected to. The slave module only responds to instructions from the master, such as open or close a circuit for the electric motor. Another instruction could be: Have you completed X task?

Remote Keyless Entry (RKE)

Keyless remotes contain a short-range radio transmitter capable of transmitting at a range of only up to 50' (20 m). These devices are also called key fobs, which is an acronym for a **frequency-operated button (FOB)**. When a button on the **RKE** is pushed, it transmits a radio signal with coded digital information to a radio receiver usually connected to the vehicle network. When the signals sent by the fob match, the radio receiver incorporated into a control module unlocks the doors. RKE must be programmed while near the vehicle to work with a specific vehicle. A coding procedure using the vehicle as a source for a pass code must be followed when adding or replacing RKE transmitters. Whenever a new RKE is added or replaced, it must be coded to match a vehicle. Blank RKE fobs must be taught what code to transmit only after first receiving a key or code from the vehicle. To perform a programming process commonly used on Navistar vehicles, follow the steps in **SKILL DRILL 22-1** as a general guideline.

Power lock mechanisms also have a key lock-unlock detection switch to electrically activate the door locks to open or close with the ignition switch key turning in the lock cylinder. More recent locking systems with a keyless entry system use a radio signal produced by the vehicle that activates a passive radiofrequency identification (RFID) chip in the key fob. The key fob RFID chip sends a coded signal back using a 40- or 128-bit encrypted digital signal to the radio transmitter in the vehicle. If the encrypted code sent by the key fob matches

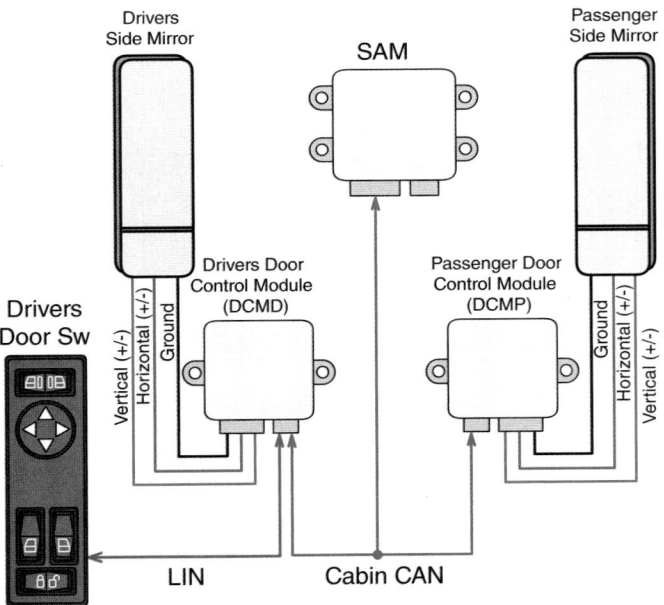

FIGURE 22-31 Freightliner's latest onboard network architecture uses a door module to control all electrical actions for a door.

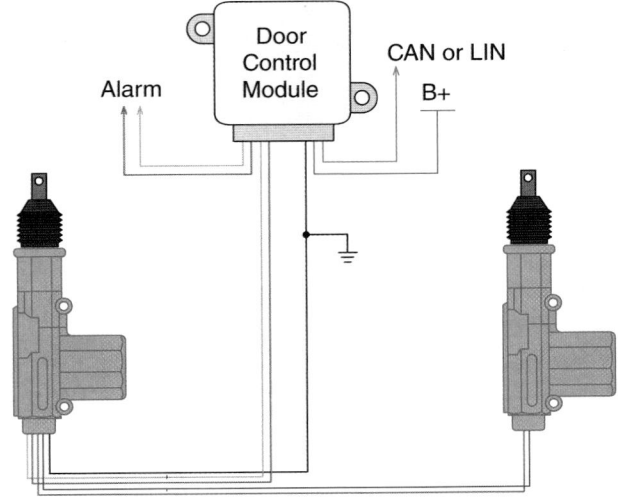

FIGURE 22-32 A pictorial wiring diagram of a power lock system using a door module.

SKILL DRILL 22-1 Coding a Remote Keyless Entry (RKE)

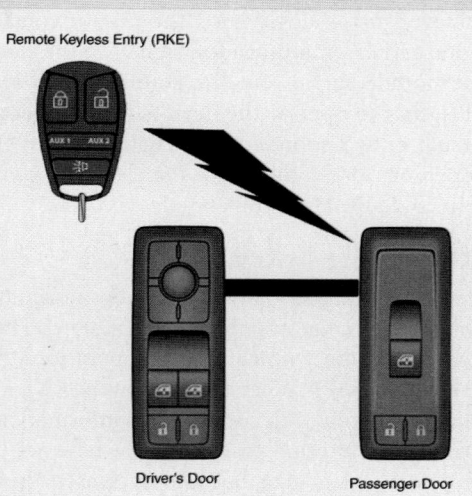

1. Obtain a blank RKE transmitter.
2. To code the new RKE fob, a signal must be transmitted from the vehicle to the RKE. Send the signal by first holding, at the same time, both the door lock and unlock buttons located in the passenger door.
3. With both the lock and unlock buttons pushed, rapidly press down and release the passenger door window control switch at least five times within no more than two seconds. This begins a 30-second interval where transmission of the codes to the RKE takes place.
4. Release both the door lock and unlock buttons.
5. Push any of the five buttons on the RKE transmitter to enable the transmitter to store key codes.
6. The code learning process ends after no further activity of the RKE.

what the control module expects the correct passcode should be, it sends a door open signal to a control module. With RFID technology, a vehicle can be unlocked without the driver needing to physically push a key fob button. The vehicle, rather than the key fob, initiates communication for more secure transactions as the user approaches the vehicle.

Mirrors

LO 22-5 Describe and explain the construction, operation, and adjustment of power mirrors.

Mirrors by themselves are not electrical accessories because they are regulated by the FMVSS 111. However, powered mirrors and new camera systems currently promoted as a replacement for mirrors or an enhancement for visibility are electrical accessories (**FIGURE 22-33**). Mirrors are required by safety standards to reduce the number of accidents, deaths, and injuries that occur when the driver does not have a clear view to the rear of a vehicle. In large trucks, the driver's view around the vehicle is considerably more restricted by the structure of the vehicle and a trailer, if it is towing one. This means more mirrors with larger viewing areas and several placements are needed for commercial vehicles (**FIGURE 22-34**). Safety provided by a clear unobstructed view around a bus is even more critical, with FMVSS 111 setting mirror standards for school buses and heavy vehicles, with details such as:

- The size of the mirror area
- The minimum field of view area on both sides of the vehicle
- The use of horizontal and vertically adjusted mirrors
- Mirror brackets and supports

FIGURE 22-33 This Mercedes has no external mirror. Only cameras provide daytime, nighttime, and all-weather views surrounding the truck. Driver display panels are inside near the front cab pillars.

FIGURE 22-34 Note the use of flat, convex, and cross-over mirrors for improved visibility.

- Visibility requirements, leading to the use of convex, cross-over, and interior mirrors for bus operators to see through windows at the rear of the bus
- Testing procedures to validate school buses meet safety standards

Flat side mirrors on any vehicle class 3 and higher must have a mirror flat surface of 323 cm² or 50 square inches on each side capable of viewing at least 150' (46 m) along each side of the vehicle (**FIGURE 22-35**). Convex mirrors mounted below, and sometimes above, the side flat mirrors enable a wider view beyond each side (**FIGURE 22-36**). Cross-over mirrors mounted on the left and right front corners or in front of the windshield are used to monitor traffic, check overhead clearances, and check for pedestrians at the sides and to the rear of the vehicle. Cross-over mirrors are especially important for buses to see danger zones at the front bumper and front wheel area (**FIGURE 22-37**). Because cross-over mirrors are a convex-type mirror, they distort the driver's view of objects, people, and relative distances.

Power Mirrors

Flat side mirrors are the most common power mirror option. A bracket supporting the mirror head is attached to the cab door or front cab pillar. The bracket may be manually adjusted or electrically operated to fold in. European vehicles use fold-in mirrors extensively for clearances in narrow streets and tunnels. Mirror brackets are designed to break away when hit to avoid further cab or object damage. Power mirrors are operated from the directional control pad next to the driver. They are available in either single- or dual-axis configurations. A single-axis motor allows only one direction of movement – up and down or left to right. Dual-axis mirrors have two electric actuators (**FIGURE 22-38**). An electric motor operates a rotating screw-like device to push or pull against an articulating socket. Turning the screw out and in provides the action to tilt the mirror head in one direction or another.

The mirror control switch knob selects which mirror is controlled (**FIGURE 22-39**). Positioning the L/R switch to the Left or Right position selects which side mirror to adjust. Positioning the up/down or left-right switch changes the polarity to the mirror motors, causing them to rotate in or out and move the mirror glass.

A resistive-type heating element is glued against the back of the mirror glass. Battery current supplied to the resistive element heats the mirror, causing condensation, frost, or ice to melt from the mirror. A thermostatic or manually controlled switch activates the heating element.

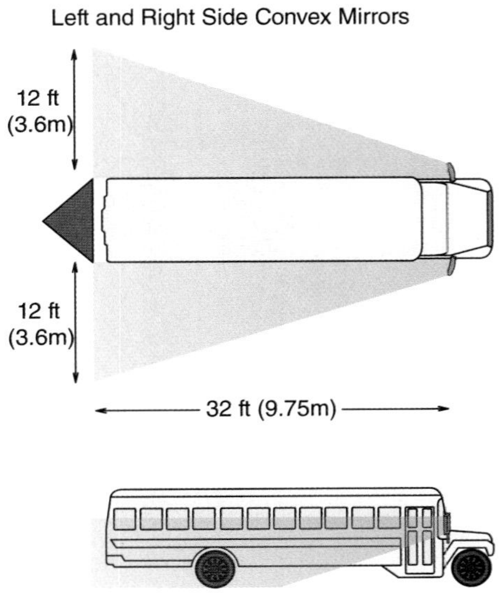

Left and Right Side Flat Mirrors

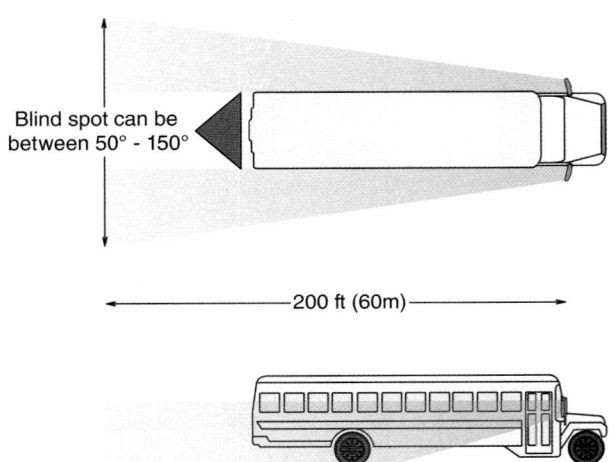

FIGURE 22-35 A flat side mirror provides visibility along each side to a distance of at least 150'.

Left and Right Side Convex Mirrors

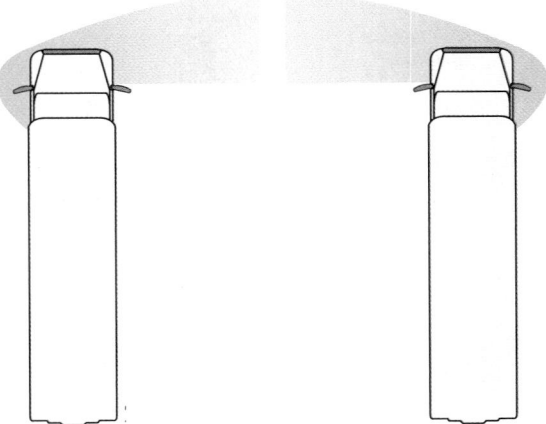

FIGURE 22-36 A convex mirror provides increased lateral visibility along each side of the vehicle.

Left and Right Side Cross-over Mirrors

FIGURE 22-37 Cross-over mirrors provide a view of the danger zone near the front bumper.

Camera Monitor System

The purpose of the new camera-monitor system (CMS) is to ensure that the driver has clear lines of sight around the entire vehicle at all times. These systems are intended to replace exterior mirrors with screen monitors in the cab. High-definition digital cameras and cameras with infrared-light sensors provide color night vision, low light sensitivity, and glare reduction in bright sunlight. Because using cameras to replace two large mirrors reduces wind drag, a 2% to 3% reduction in fuel consumption is reported to be achievable. A camera at the back of the trailer can help when reversing direction and avoiding collisions when making turns (**FIGURE 22-40**).

To verify power mirror adjustments or conventional external mirrors are adjusted correctly on a school bus, follow the steps in **SKILL DRILL 22-2** for the grid that can be laid out and used to confirm correct lines of sight required by FMVSS 111 Field of View Test.

FIGURE 22-38 Construction elements of a heated power mirror. Pin-type actuators with screws are rotated by an electric motor to tilt and turn the mirror.

FIGURE 22-39 A control switch for a truck's 2-axis mirrors. A left- and right-side selection switch and mirror heater switch is present.

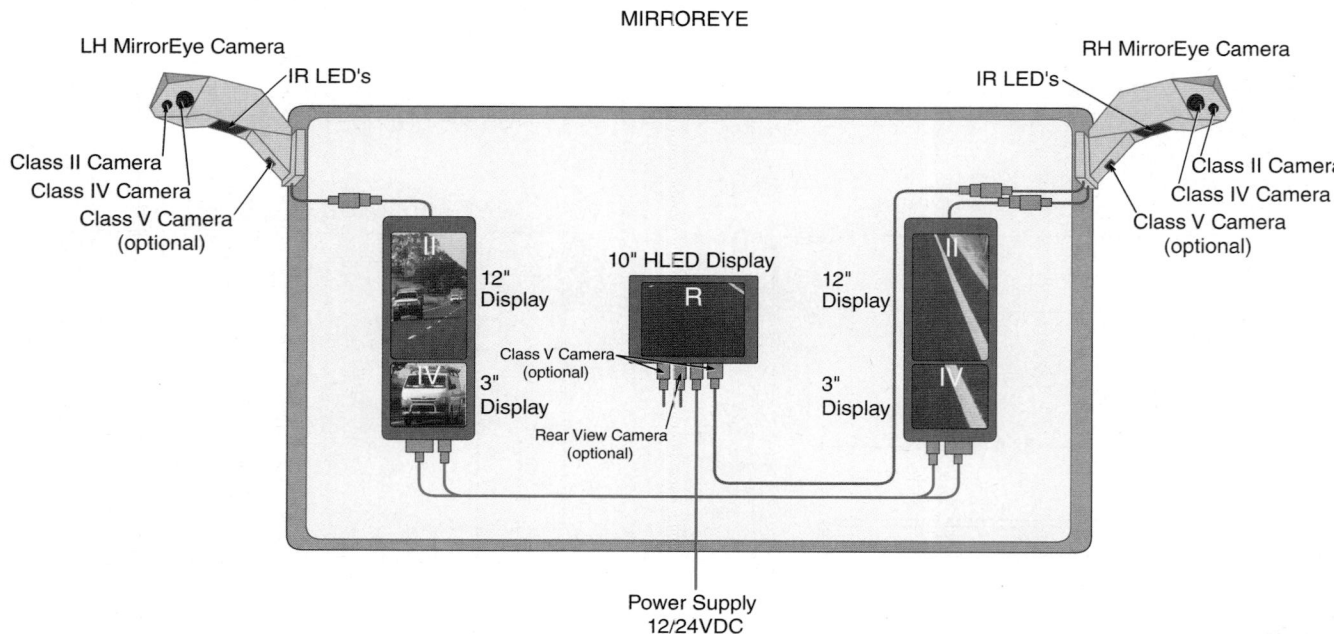

FIGURE 22-40 Flat screen displays inside the cab show a wider field of vision for externally mounted cameras.

SKILL DRILL 22-2 Verifying Power and Exterior Mirror Adjustments

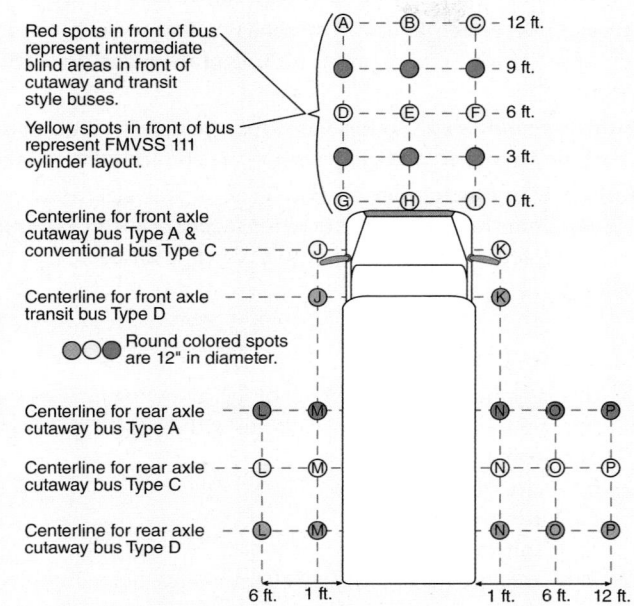

Red spots in front of bus represent intermediate blind areas in front of cutaway and transit style buses.

Yellow spots in front of bus represent FMVSS 111 cylinder layout.

Centerline for front axle cutaway bus Type A & conventional bus Type C

Centerline for front axle transit bus Type D

Round colored spots are 12" in diameter.

Centerline for rear axle cutaway bus Type A

Centerline for rear axle cutaway bus Type C

Centerline for rear axle cutaway bus Type D

1. Using the accompanying diagram, use colored paint, chalk, or small cones to lay out the FMVSS 111 Field of View test grid on a level surface.

2. If more than one type of bus or length is used, add additional spots for transit (Type D) and shorter school bus wheel bases (Type A). A conventional school bus is Type C. Use different colors or cone sizes to distinguish between targets differentiated by the type and length of buses.

3. Drive the bus so the front bumper stops immediately next to the first row of spots or indicators. The sides of the bus must be centered between the outer left and right grid lines.

4. Verify both side-rearview mirrors called System A are correctly adjusted. The driver needs to use both side mirrors in order to see the entire field of vision referred to in FMVSS 111 as System A. To do this, confirm the driver must see the markers or spots labelled L, M, N, and O.

5. Confirm that the driver can see spots or markers 200' behind them using side-rearview mirror System A. The bottom of the rear tires should also be seen at the same time.

6. Verify the front cross-over or cross-view mirror system, called System B in FMVSS 111, is correctly adjusted. The driver must see the markers or spots A through K, and L, O, and P.

7. Both cross-over mirrors must be used together to see the complete field of view.

8. While not a part of the FMVSS 111 test, the interior mirror above the driver's side windshield should be adjusted to see the road surface out the bottom window at the rear of the bus.

9. Adjust mirrors, as necessary, to obtain the correct field of view.

Wrap-Up

Ready for Review

▶ Today's accessory devices in the electrical systems provide not just a pleasanter workplace for drivers but enhance safety and efficiency.

▶ On almost all late-model chassis, the electrical system accessories are operated through distributed electronic control enabled through an onboard network exchanging data through CAN communication.

▶ Universal Diagnostic Services (UDS) is another network communication protocol broadcasting electrical system accessory messages. It is an encrypted network protocol to prevent hacking and take-over of the vehicle electrical system by remote hackers.

▶ Electrical system modules have access points for connecting electrical circuits that must be programmed to supply current. Not a single wire is cut or spliced to connect electrical, air, or hydraulic accessories.

▶ When the wipers are switched off, they move to a park position, which lowers the blades to a parallel position with the bottom edge of the windshield.

▶ Integration of the wiper control system with the rest of the electrical system through CAN communication adds several additional features, such as speed sensitivity, rain-sensing automatic operation, park disable, and interlock with the low-beam headlights.

▶ Wiper motors are generally electric shunt-type motors, which maintain a constant speed regardless of load.

▶ To produce the minimum two-speed output required from the wiper motor, three brushes connect to the motor commutator: One each for high- and low-speed operation plus a ground.

▶ A park switch is used to place the wipers below the windshield after the wipers are switched off.

▶ The park switch supplies current to the wiper motor after the cab switch is shut off. Power continues to be supplied to the motor until the park switch cam opens the park circuit.

▶ On many commercial vehicles, switched low-voltage input signals from steering wheel-mounted sensors and turn signal stalk connect to the instrument cluster module (ICU), a major node on the CAN network.

▶ A body electrical control module receives CAN communication signals from the ICU body and supplies the appropriate output current to operate the wipers and washers.

▶ Rain sensors use a LED light and a photoreceiver that sense rain when infrared light is reflected back into the sensor

▶ Power windows use two types of window regulator mechanisms: Scissor and Bowden cable.

▶ Positive temperature coefficient resettable fuses provide circuit protection at the window regulator motor in the event it is jammed or has high mechanical resistance.

▶ A second position step on a power window switch requires only a momentary contact to produce either a window express-up or express-down feature.

▶ The express up and down window function requires a control module connected in series between the window switch and motor.

▶ Safety regulations have required power windows to have limiter switches that stop a window from rolling up if an object, such as a person's hand, fingers, or arm, is trapped.

▶ A simpler window limiter switch senses motor speed and the direction of rotation using a permanent magnet and at least two magnetic reed sensors.

▶ Windows with limiter switches generally require a window recalibration-reset programming procedure to obtain all window functions, such as express up and down.

▶ Camera mirror systems are intended to replace exterior mirrors with screen monitors in the cab. High-definition digital cameras and cameras with infrared-light sensors provide color night vision, low light sensitivity, and glare reduction in bright sunlight.

Key Terms

Bowden cable A flexible metal cable with an inner and outer cable that is used to transmit mechanical force through the inner cable passing through the stationary hollow outer cable.

Diamond Logic Navistar's proprietary software used to service and perform service programming of the vehicle electrical system.

electrical system template A vehicle-specific software file that contains all the electrical system control logic and operating parameters.

Electronic Service Analyst (ESA) Paccar's proprietary software used to service and perform service programing of the vehicle electrical system.

frequency-operated button (FOB) The user element of the RKE system carried by the driver that transmits radio signals with coded digital information to a network radio receiver to operate the door locks or other electrical accessories.

Modular Switch Field (MSF) A control unit used by Freightliner to process all cab switch signals and broadcast them to the SAM-cab module through a star point connector.

RKE An acronym for a remote keyless entry system. It uses a short-range radio transceiver to remotely operate door locks and other electrical accessories.

safety interlock A safety feature commonly used by electrically operated devices that prevents unsafe operation by locking out its operation unless a set of safe operating conditions are met.

ServiceLink Freightliner's proprietary software used to service and perform service programming of the vehicle electrical system.

shunt-type motors Another name for a parallel-wound motor where the armature and field windings are connected in parallel.

Unified Diagnostic Service (UDS) A global electronic service and communication protocol for mechatronic devices that has encrypted security features to prevent malicious network hacking.

Review Questions

1. In a late-model vehicle, which of the following devices supplies an electrical accessory circuit with operating current?
   a. A control switch
   b. A circuit breaker
   c. A control module
   d. A software program

2. Why are door locks activated after a vehicle begins to move?
   a. To prevent someone from opening a door and exiting
   b. To prevent intruders from opening a door when the vehicle is parked
   c. It is a self-check monitoring procedure to verify door lock operation.
   d. It helps prevent ejection of cab occupants during a collision.

3. When wipers are activated, which other electrical device is often simultaneously activated?
   a. The park switch circuit
   b. The washer circuit
   c. The rain sensor
   d. The low-beam headlights

4. How many motor brushes are used in a typical wiper motor?
   a. Two
   b. Three
   c. Four
   d. They are brushless

5. How many battery + powered connections are there to a wiper motor when it is operating?
   a. One
   b. Two
   c. Four
   d. None

6. When does the wiper parking switch cam open the park switch?
   a. When the wiper arms are below the lower edge of the windshield
   b. When the intermittent wiper circuit removes power from the wiper motor
   c. When the wipers are above the lower edge of the windshield
   d. When the wipers are switched off

7. Which of the following conditions will cause a signal from a rain sensor to indicate water droplets are on the windshield?
   a. When signal voltage is between 0.5 and 2.0 volts
   b. When no infrared light is detected by the photo receiver
   c. When light from an LED is reflected back into the sensor
   d. When light from an LED passes through the windshield

8. What is the purpose of magnetic reed switches in a window regulator motor?
   a. They sense motor direction.
   b. They indicate whether the window glass is up or down.
   c. They function as part of a window limiter system.
   d. They protect the motor from burning out if the motor is jammed.

9. How many wires are typically used to transmit a digital serial message over a LIN?
   a. 1
   b. 2
   c. 3
   d. 4

10. What vehicle features are regulated by FMVSS 111?
    a. Power windows
    b. Wiper systems
    c. Power door locks
    d. Power mirrors

ASE Technician A/Technician B Style Questions

1. Technician A says that on any late-model commercial vehicle, power for an electrically controlled accessory can be sourced from splicing into a power circuit near a fuse block. Technician B says that splicing into an electrical circuit is likely to create an electrical fault sensed by a control module. Who is correct?
   a. Technician A
   b. Technician B
   c. Both Technician A and Technician B
   d. Neither Technician A nor Technician B

2. While investigating the failure of a new RKE fob to operate, Technician A says that the fob must be programmed with an encrypted key to match the vehicle. Technician B says that another fob programmed at the factory should be ordered. Who is correct?
   a. Technician A
   b. Technician B
   c. Both Technician A and Technician B
   d. Neither Technician A nor Technician B

3. Technician A and B are investigating a complaint that the door locks do not lock after the vehicle moves. Technician A says the automatically locking door locks is an option that may need to be properly configured with service software. Technician B says that the locking problem is caused by a problem with a defective ABS module. Who is correct?
   a. Technician A
   b. Technician B
   c. Both Technician A and Technician B
   d. Neither Technician A nor Technician B

4. Technician A and B were investigating a problem with window glass that had completely fallen inside to the bottom of the door. Technician A says that it is likely a scissor-type regulator that has a broken cable. Technician B says the cause is likely a stripped drive gear for a cable and drum-type regulator. Who is correct?
   a. Technician A
   b. Technician B
   c. Both Technician A and Technician B
   d. Neither Technician A nor Technician B

5. Technician A and B were diagnosing a failure of the turn signal switch to operate in a brand-new truck. Technician A says that the problem could be in the Master Switch Field Control Unit. Technician B says that since most vehicles connect the turn signal switch to the instrument cluster, the cluster could be defective. Who is correct?
   a. Technician A
   b. Technician B
   c. Both Technician A and Technician B
   d. Neither Technician A nor Technician B

6. Technician A says that the newest door locks are solenoids with permanent magnet cores. Technician B says that the newest door lock mechanisms use electric motors. Who is correct?
   a. Technician A
   b. Technician B
   c. Both Technician A and Technician B
   d. Neither Technician A nor Technician B

7. Technician A and B were diagnosing a problem with a power window that would roll down but only intermittently roll up. Technician A says that the motor was likely defective. Technician B says that the problem is likely the window switch. Who is correct?
   a. Technician A
   b. Technician B
   c. Both Technician A and Technician B
   d. Neither Technician A nor Technician B

8. Technician A and B were discussing a problem with a bus with windshield wipers that continued to operate after they were switched off. Technician A says that the park switch in the wiper motor is defective. Technician B says that there is likely an open circuit in the wipers' wiring harness. Who is correct?
   a. Technician A
   b. Technician B
   c. Both Technician A and Technician B
   d. Neither Technician A nor Technician B

9. Technician A and B were discussing a problem with a window that would not completely roll up or down. Technician A says that the problem is likely caused by

incorrect programming of the windows limiter switch. Technician B says that the problem is likely the express-down programming function. Who is correct?

a. Technician A
b. Technician B
c. Both Technician A and Technician B
d. Neither Technician A nor Technician B

10. Technician A and B were installing fifth wheels on new tractors with an electrically controlled air slide mechanism.

Technician A said that the air could be supplied by an electronically controlled air manifold but the dash switch needed to be programmed for the switch function. Technician B said that a template for the vehicle's electrical system needed to be changed. Who is correct?

a. Technician A
b. Technician B
c. Both Technician A and Technician B
d. Neither Technician A nor Technician B

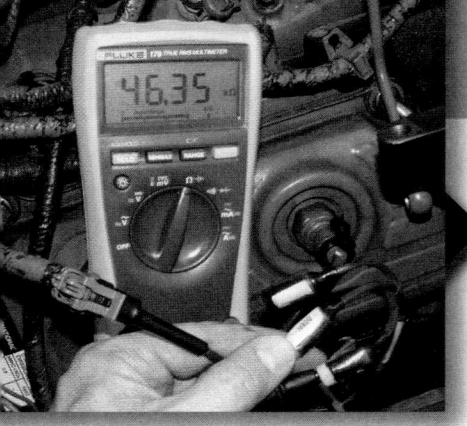

Principles of Electronic Signal Processing

Learning Objectives

After reading this chapter, you will be able to:

- **LO 23-1** Identify and explain the advantages of electronic signal processing over mechanical system control.
- **LO 23-2** Identify and describe the elements of electronic signal processing systems.
- **LO 23-3** Identify and describe the classification of electrical signals.
- **LO 23-4** Identify, describe, and explain the purpose of serial data.

- **LO 23-5** Identify and describe characteristics of pulse-width–modulated electrical signals.
- **LO 23-6** Identify ladder logic diagrams and explain the use of ladder logic.
- **LO 23-7** Outline the applications of radio signals.
- **LO 23-8** Identify the mechanisms for generating, transmitting, and minimizing electromagnetic interference.

You Are the Technician

A number of vehicles have arrived at your shop with a list of apparently unrelated complaints: speedometer needle that begin to bounce at 55 mph (90 kph), cruise controls that do not work or disengage unexpectedly, automatic transmissions that shift erratically, dozens of antilock brake system (ABS) codes for components and circuits that have no faults, and rough running engines. On one of the vehicles, when performing some pinpoint tests with a digital multimeter, you accidentally set the meter to read alternating current (AC) and not direct current (DC) voltage. You are surprised to discover close to four volts of AC are superimposed on the system's 12-volt DC. Realizing that the only component that could produce AC is the alternator, you disconnect the alternator and find the AC voltage has disappeared, along with the unusual electrical system complaints. To repair the problem, the alternator is replaced and so are the vehicle's batteries, which all tested defective. As you prepare to document the diagnosis and justify the parts replacement on the work orders, consider the following questions:

1. What shop equipment could be used to capture and record the AC voltage signal frequency and waveform to document the problem?
2. Could the engine control module (ECM) process the correct data from some sensor inputs if AC voltage accompanies the DC voltage inputs? Explain your answer.
3. After gaining the experience repairing these vehicles, what checks would you recommend in future for diagnosing electrical problems that may be related to electrical signal interference?

Introduction

The tasks technicians regularly perform on late-model equipment involve working with more understanding about electricity than just applying principles of direct current (DC) and alternating current (AC) flow that operates lights, turns electric motors, and charges batteries. Electricity is shaped and manipulated into signals that can communicate information, operate specialized electrical output devices, such as injectors and control valves; be used as a tool to make complex decisions in microcontrollers; and create radio waves capable of detecting objects for collision avoidance systems and advanced driver assistance features. This chapter identifies the various types of electronic signals technicians can encounter on a daily basis, and explains the principles and applications of electronic signal processing on commercial vehicle chassis. Tools used by technicians to analyze these signals are also identified to help technicians develop practical skills related to servicing and maintaining medium- and heavy-duty electrical systems.

Benefits of Electronic Signal Processing

LO 23-1 Identify and explain the advantages of electronic signal processing over mechanical system control.

Electronic control systems made possible using a wide variety of electrical signals offer many benefits to today's commercial vehicles, including increased power and efficiency, enhanced information reporting capabilities, telematics, increased safety, self-diagnostic capabilities, and an increasing number of programmable features. Diesel engines were the first commercial vehicle systems transformed by electronic controls (**FIGURE 23-1**). Diesel engines with only mechanical controls had reached their limit of efficiency, so the next logical step was to apply electronic controls already used on gasoline engines. The immediate benefits of these refinements to engine operation are lower engine emissions, improved fuel economy, increased reliability, and enhanced performance. Smarter engines continue to deliver ever-increasing power from smaller displacements, accompanied by quieter operation, and longer service intervals, in addition to needing less maintenance. The increased costs of some of these features are offset through improved engine efficiency and durability. Many of the electronic control systems have in fact lowered the cost of vehicle production while adding more features with improved operating benefits. In comparison to mechanical controls, electronic controls enable far greater flexibility to adjust fuel injection metering, injection rate control, and timing over a large number of operating conditions. When engine operational problems leading to excess emissions occur, self-monitoring and self-diagnostic capabilities of electronic controls can identify the problem, alert the operator, and revert to operating modes that minimize noxious emission production. The application of electronic controls on engines has moved to almost every vehicle system, including braking, transmissions, climate control, steering, instrumentation, etc.

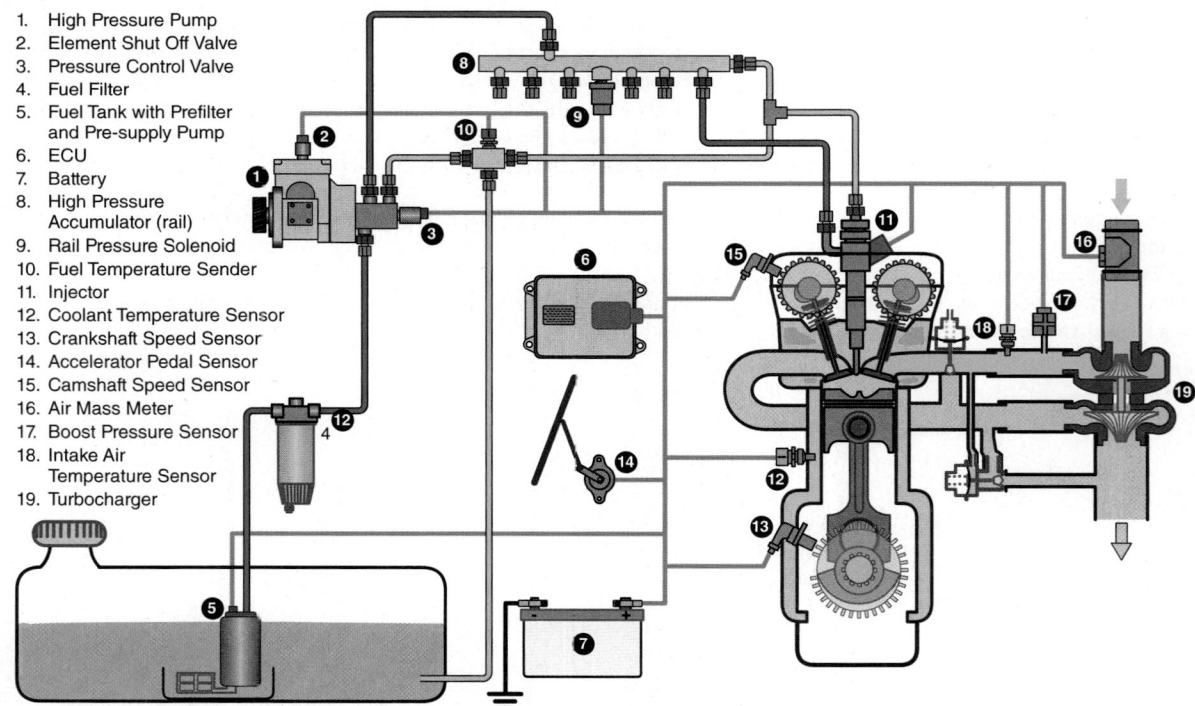

1. High Pressure Pump
2. Element Shut Off Valve
3. Pressure Control Valve
4. Fuel Filter
5. Fuel Tank with Prefilter and Pre-supply Pump
6. ECU
7. Battery
8. High Pressure Accumulator (rail)
9. Rail Pressure Solenoid
10. Fuel Temperature Sender
11. Injector
12. Coolant Temperature Sensor
13. Crankshaft Speed Sensor
14. Accelerator Pedal Sensor
15. Camshaft Speed Sensor
16. Air Mass Meter
17. Boost Pressure Sensor
18. Intake Air Temperature Sensor
19. Turbocharger

FIGURE 23-1 An overview of components used for the engine management system of a common rail diesel engine. Extensive use of electronics translates into precise control of combustion events for low emissions, superior performance, and fuel efficiency.

Increased Power and Efficiency

TABLE 23-1 shows the increase in power output per cubic inch of displacement and lowering of emissions achieved through advanced technology and electronic control of the fuel system.

Enhanced Information Processing Capabilities

Life cycle costs of operating vehicles with electronically controlled rather than mechanical engines is further reduced through the ability of the vehicle control systems to interface wirelessly with cell phones and tablets through Bluetooth communication devices. Repair, maintenance, and other operating costs are reduced because service technicians, particularly in fleet operations, can access a wealth of diagnostic and service data much faster and with more precise detail than before using Windows-based diagnostic and service software (**FIGURE 23-2**). Trip reports from the vehicle ECM (engine control module)

extracted during scheduled maintenance intervals report details, such as diagnostic fault codes, fuel consumption, idle time, emission system performance, and vehicle abuse statistics (**FIGURE 23-3**).

Telematics

In addition to obtaining vehicle and trip information downloaded at scheduled maintenance intervals, ECM data can be collected and modified by other means (**FIGURE 23-4**). When connected to the correct vehicle interface devices, any information available over the onboard network data bus can be transmitted to service departments or telematic service providers. Maintenance and software calibration adjustments affecting vehicle operation can be performed from distant locations (**FIGURE 23-5**). **Telematics**, a branch of information technology, uses specialized telecommunication applications for long-distance transmission of information to and from a vehicle (**FIGURE 23-6**). For example, when vehicles are equipped with radio-satellite or cellular-based vehicle communications, a technician or equipment manager can remotely monitor any

TABLE 23-1 Increase in Power Output per Cubic Feet of Displacement

Engine Model	1988 7.3L IDI Diesel	2019 6.7L Powerstroke
Horsepower	180 hp	450 hp
Torque	338 ft/lb @ 1600 rpm (458 Nm @ 1600 rpm)	935 ft/lb @ 1800 rpm (1268 Nm @ 1600 rpm)
NO_x emissions	2.5 grams/bhp-hr	0.002 grams/bhp-hr (EPA limit)
Intake air flow @ 3330 rpm	360 CFM (10 m³/min)	732 CFM (21 m³/min)
Exhaust flow @ 3300 rpm	1080 CFM (31 m³/min)	1499 CFM (42 m³/min)
Fuel system	Mechanical distributor pump	Bosch piezoelectric injectors CP4.2 Common rail pump electronic

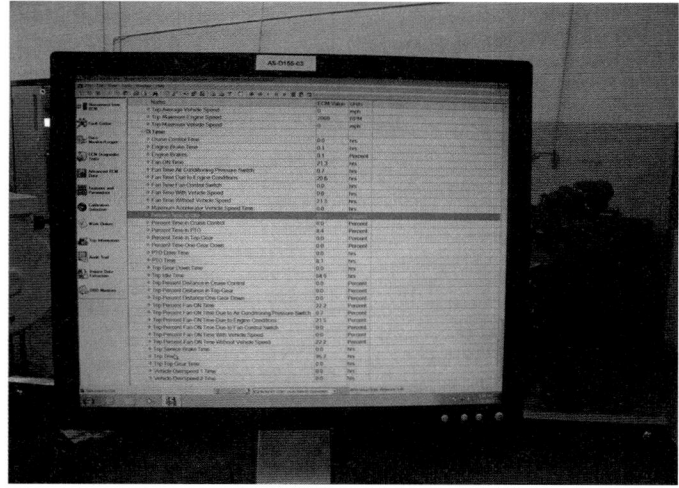

FIGURE 23-3 Trip information is data produced from monitoring vehicle operation, such as engine efficiency, manual transmission shifting patterns, idling characteristics, and hard braking.

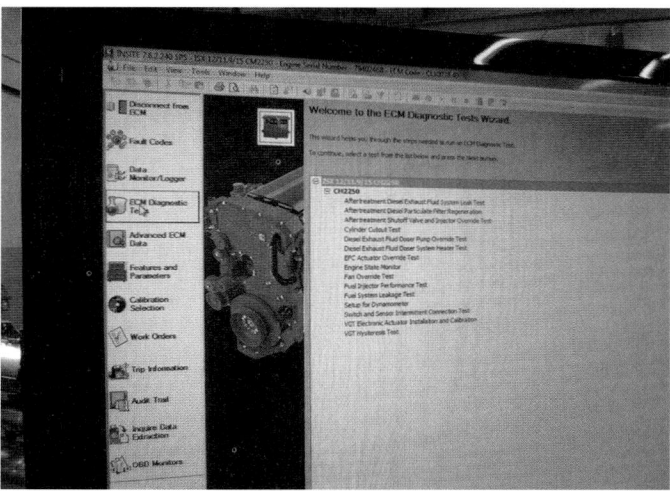

FIGURE 23-2 A screenshot with a menu of the various diagnostic routines available to troubleshoot engine operation.

FIGURE 23-4 The instrument cluster can provide information to the driver about a variety of vehicle operating conditions.

information about the vehicle, engine, or product the vehicle is carrying that is transmitted by the vehicle's controller area network (CAN) communication. Messages can be sent back and forth between the vehicle and a central dispatch location. Integrating the Internet with the vehicle networks provides an even longer list of features and benefits. For example, if low on fuel, a list of nearby fuel stops can be generated with the least interference or delay to a trip. A GPS can report vehicle location to a dispatcher, as well as display fuel stop locations. Topographical maps provided by digital map makers can optimize transmission shift schedules and improve fuel efficiency in hilly terrain

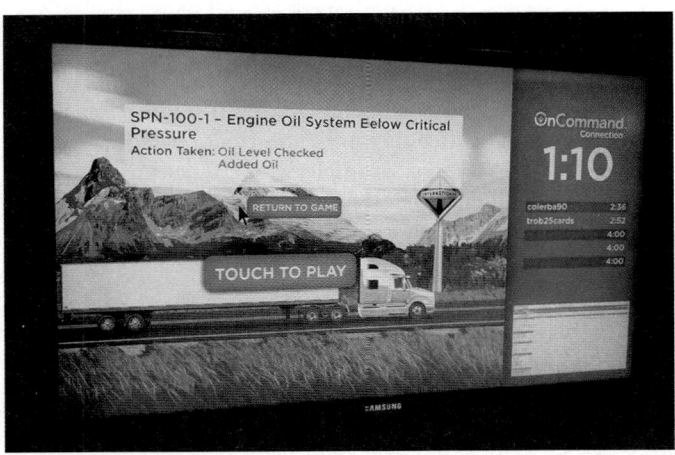

FIGURE 23-5 A screenshot of a diagnostic fault code display seen by a driver and a service technician possibly hundreds of miles or kilometers away from a vehicle.

using predictive cruise control. A fault code can be remotely evaluated to determine if immediate repairs are needed. For large fleet operations, short-range wireless technology allows diagnostics and programming of vehicles when they are in the vicinity of a maintenance or other service facility for increased productivity. A network bridge to adjacent trucks exchanging enormous amounts of data enables the use of truck platooning. The platooning concept uses a single driver in a lead vehicle to guide a series of driverless trucks or trucks operating in semiautonomous mode and accompanied by a qualified driver behind it.

Safety

The use of electronic vehicle control and advanced driver assistance features provides for enhanced vehicle and occupant safety and security. Collison avoidance systems using radar or a camera with object identification capabilities can help a commercial vehicle stay in lane or detect objects at a distance to automatically brake a vehicle. Engine systems can be monitored for operating conditions having destructive potential. Low oil pressure, high intake, or coolant temperatures are commonly monitored conditions that can initiate an adaptive response to prevent catastrophic failure or damage. Dangerous operating conditions can trigger the engine to shut down, de-rate power, or simply warn the operator. The programmable **microcontrollers** in large ECUs make it possible to build in features that protect the power train from damage due to abuse, excessive torque, or speed as well. Hard braking and speeding are other measurable conditions monitored by management systems to improve road safety.

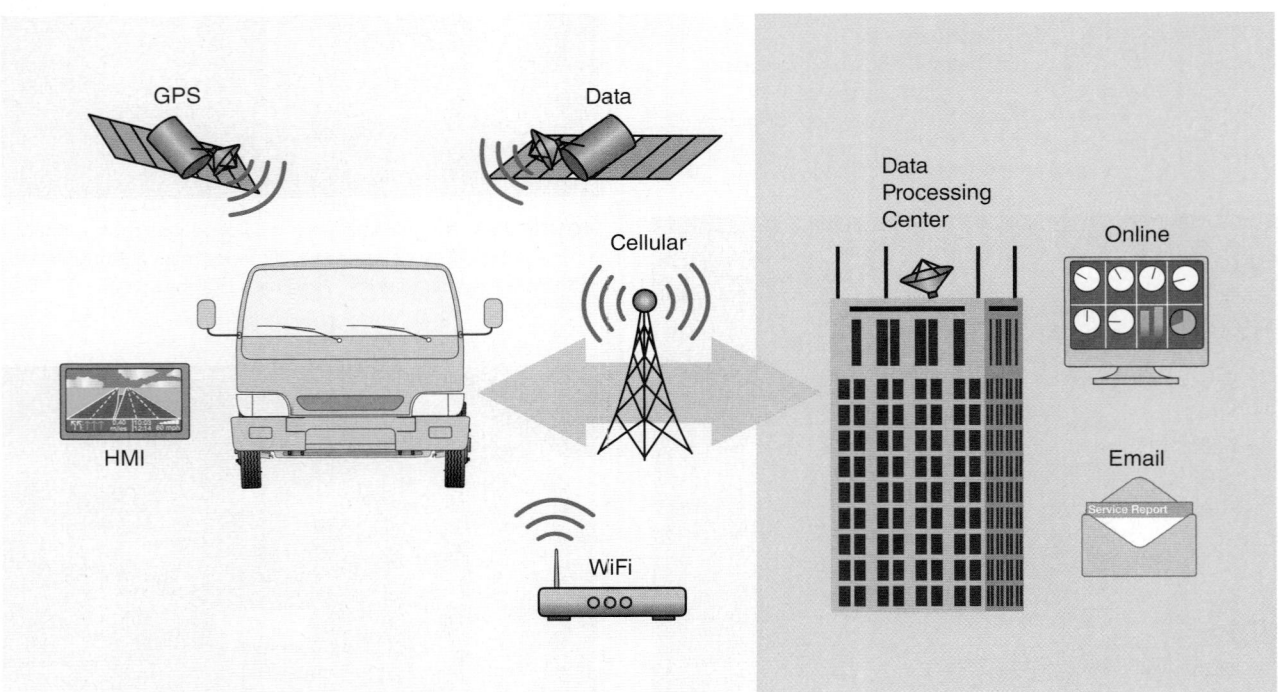

FIGURE 23-6 Telematics uses satellite communication or cell phone technology to interface with the on-board vehicle network. Any network data can be read and sent to a remote monitor, reporting diagnostics and other service-related information.

Programmable Vehicle Features

Service technicians and operators can take advantage of programmable electronic controls. Programmable software provides flexibility to engines, transmissions, ABS, chassis accessories and body accessories for adaptation to specific job applications, enhancing vehicle productivity, safety, longevity, and driver comfort. Programmable changes may include things as simple as idle shut-down timers, cruise control, or maximum vehicle speed limits to adding safety interlocks preventing the vehicle from moving if a door is open, a boom is raised, or outriggers are extended.

Power and torque rise profiles are easily altered electronically. Depending on the application, it is beneficial to performance and fuel economy to have maximum torque appear over different rpm ranges. Instead of replacing an injection pump and turbocharger to change engine power characteristics, electronically controlled engines are recalibrated with new software instructions. In a few minutes with some keystrokes, a stock vehicle chassis can be reprogrammed to operate as an ambulance, an on-highway tractor, dump truck, bus, rental truck, or recreational vehicle.

Self-Diagnostic Capabilities

Electronic systems are potentially more reliable because they do not have many moving parts to wear out, but the systems can be complex. Diagnostics on electronically controlled vehicle systems can be performed easily, often with fewer tools and in less time than on mechanical systems (**FIGURE 23-7**). When something goes wrong with a component or circuit, it can be extremely time consuming and difficult to identify the problem without some built-in self-diagnostic capabilities. Built into electronic control systems are self-monitoring and self-diagnostic capabilities to check operation of circuits and electrical devices, and that evaluate whether voltages are out of range, the rationality of data, and system functionality. Problems are quickly identified as they occur. The presence of faults is communicated through the malfunction indicator lamps. An engine may even lose power or de-rate to prevent excessive emission production, engine damage to provide an incentive to have the condition repaired. Electronic service tools assist the technicians to perform off-board diagnostics, that is, perform pinpoint checks to precisely identify system faults. Software-based diagnostics deliver huge amounts of data about system operation, enabling service technicians to identify problems more quickly than with mechanical systems. Since modules, sensors, and actuators are more compact, they are replaced quickly with minimal training and experience required.

Elements of Electronic Signal Processing Systems

LO 23-2 Identify and describe the elements of electronic signal processing systems.

At first glance, operation of electronic control systems is difficult to understand with its use of a variety of sensors, wires, electrical actuators, and electronic modules operated with invisible electrical signals. Knowing what various electrical signals are needed to operate the electronic hardware and generated to control output devices is a first step to understanding and working with these systems. But before beginning to examine signal processing, it is first helpful to briefly observe that the operation of any control system can be broken down into three major functions:

- Sensing
- Processing
- Output or actuation (**FIGURE 23-8**)

Sensing, Processing, and Output Functions

Sensing functions collect data about operational conditions or the state of a device by measuring some value, such as temperature, position, speed, pressure, flow, and angle. Sensors are devices designed to collect specific data in an electronic format.

Processing refers to the control system element that collects sensor data and determines outputs based on a set of instructions or program software. This is the job of the electronic control unit which uses programmable microcontrollers. Inside the microcontroller are operational algorithms, which are simply mathematical

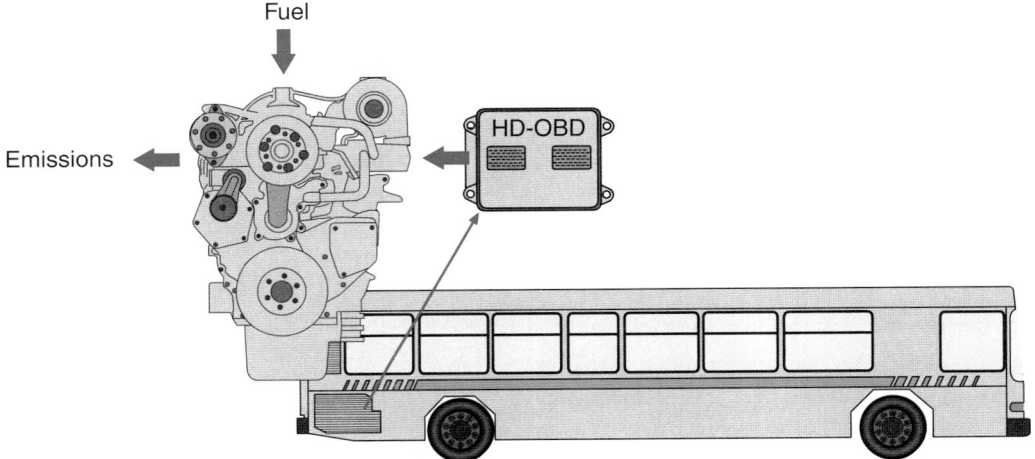

FIGURE 23-7 HD-OBD refers to a legislated standard for on-board diagnostic capabilities to identify conditions potentially causing excess emissions.

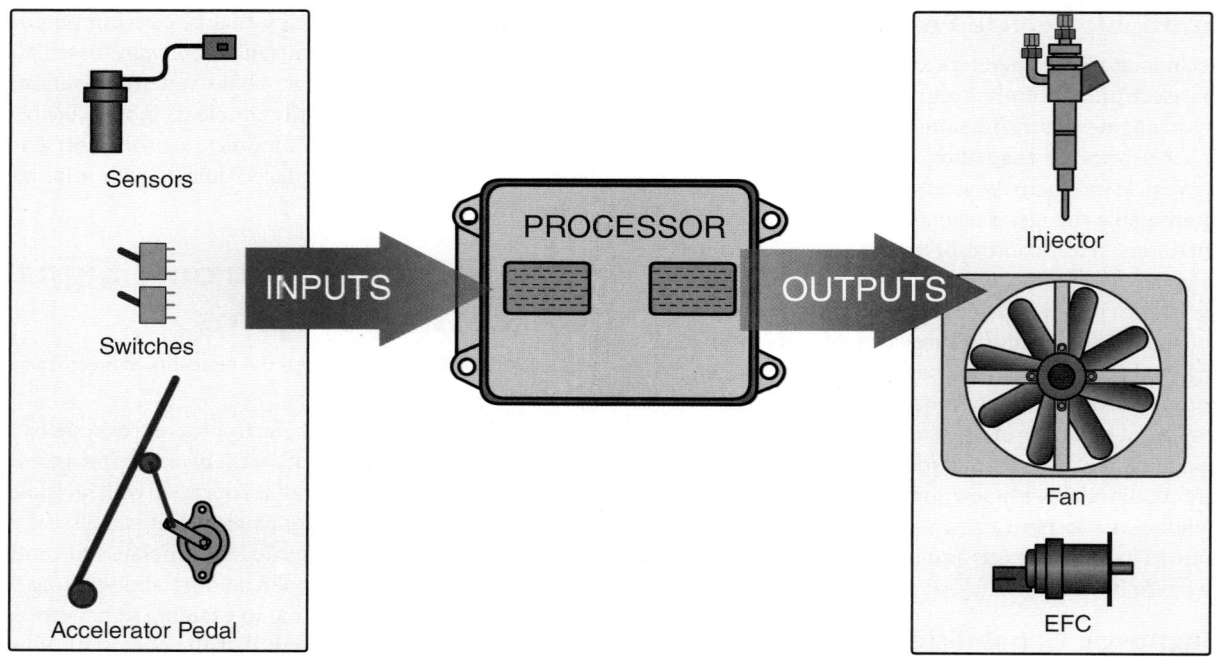

FIGURE 23-8 All engine management systems process electrical signals in three distinct stages: data collection from sensor inputs; data processing inside an electronic control module; and production of output signals, which control electrically operated devices or produce communication signals.

formulas used to solve problems. The algorithms are part of the instructional steps stored in microcontrollers memory of logic unit that directs how data is processed. Calibration information, which is primarily reference data used by algorithms, is stored in memory too. Calibration information is different from the microcontroller programming in that the calibration information contains unique information for a specific application. For example, a vehicle may have an engine made by the same manufacturer but the calibration files for a 10L engine in a bus chassis are different than ones for a line haul tractor or by a 15L engine. How much torque should be produced, where actuator settings should be when operating, what circumstances switch on MIL lights or set fault codes are examples of the calibration data.

Outputs of a control system are essentially the electrical signals produced from the processing stage. Output signals operate actuators, supplying current to operate solenoids, electric motors, injectors, control valves, lights, or other electromechanical devices. Output signals can include information transmitted to other control modules, remote locations, voice commands, data for a digital display of numeric or alphabetic information, or radio waves for collision avoidance radars.

Classification of Electrical Signals

LO 23-3 Identify and describe the classification of electrical signals.

As already mentioned, electricity can supply more than the brute force needed to crank over an engine, light up a roadway, or blow air into a passenger compartment. Electricity can be shaped and manipulated by electronic circuits and specialized electrical devices into unique signals capable of exerting control over electrical components, transmitting complex information,

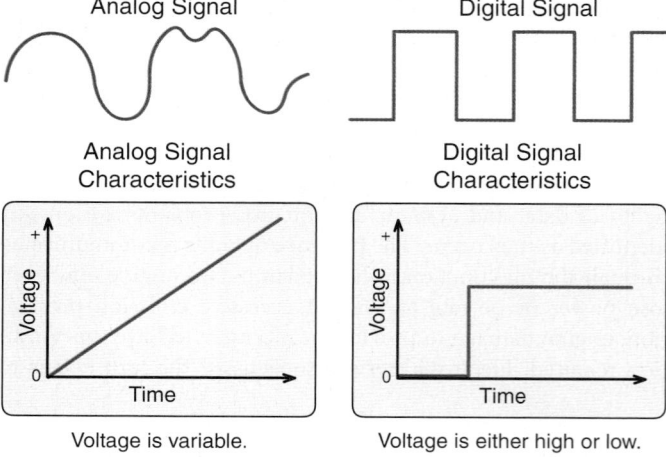

FIGURE 23-9 Electrical signal waveforms for two basic types of electrical signals are digital and analog.

and detecting remote objects while precisely calculating their speed and distance. Electricity can be shaped into language understood by machines, and even used as a tool to make logical decisions. There are three basic types of electrical signals used by the electrical system to process information and control electrical devices. Each of these electrical signals is commonly used as either an input or output signal (**FIGURE 23-9**).

Three types of electrical signals in electronic engine control applications are:

- Analog
- Digital
- Pulse width modulation (PWM)

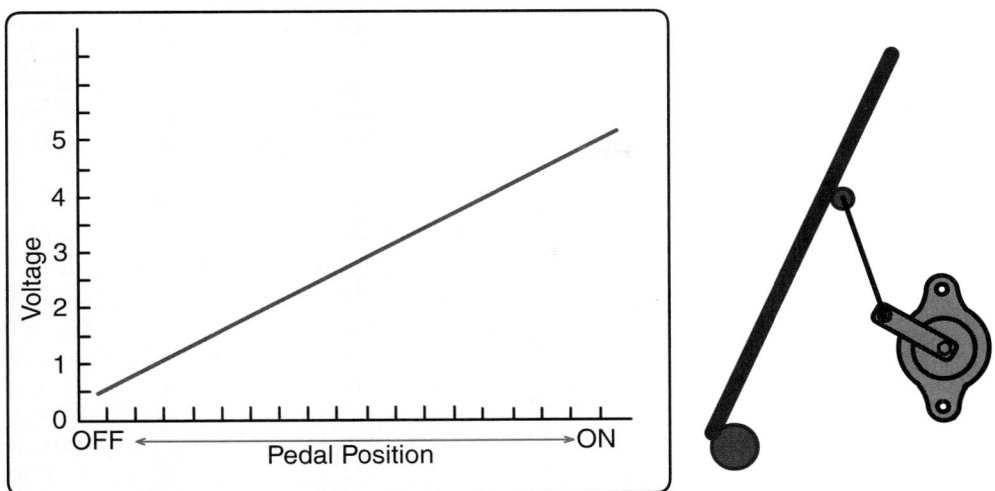

FIGURE 23-10 The signal voltage from this throttle position sensor is a type of analog data. An infinite number of values for voltage exist between idle and wide-open throttle.

Analog Signals

The general meaning of the term analog is "something that is similar to something else." If one thing is similar to another, the two are said to be analogous. Stated another way, an analog is a duplicate of something else. When referring an **analog signal** electrical signal, it is a signal with current that is proportional to, or duplicates another continuously changing variable. The continual variability of the signal can take place over an indefinite amount of time. A liquid mercury thermometer and the pointing needle on the dial of an air pressure gauge are examples of a non-electric analog signal. The mercury column rises and falls proportionally with temperature or the gauge's needle moves back and forth according to air pressure stored in a reservoir.

An example of an analog electrical signal is the audio signal that drives a loudspeaker. The voltage of the audio signal, at any instant of time, controls the pressure of the sound waves produced by a loud speaker. Like other analog electrical signals, the analog audio signal is proportional or similar to its input, which in this case is sound supplied to a microphone.

Over time, analog signals can have a changing value of voltage, amperage, frequency, or amplitude. Because temperature changes continuously, a mercury thermometer measuring temperature can represent every possible temperature change with the movement of liquid in a glass or a needle on a dial. An analog electrical signal also can represent the smallest change in temperature using voltage value that is proportional to temperature.

Measurement of alternating electrical current is another example of an analog signal. Variable reluctance-type sensors, such as wheel speed or some engine position sensors, produce AC electricity. Changing wheel or engine speeds alters the switching frequency of current polarity produced by the sensor, which means wheel speed is proportional to AC frequency. The level of the AC voltage produced by the sensor also varies continuously and in proportion to speed.

A throttle position sensor is another example where analog data can be measured. The varying voltage signal produced

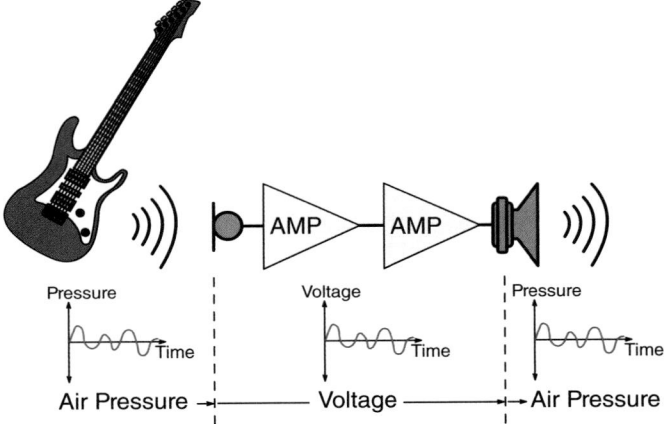

FIGURE 23-11 An analog signal is proportional to or duplicates another continuously changing variable. The analog of the sound waves are the electrical signals created by the guitar pick-up (like a microphone) or transducer. Electrical signals are converted back into sound waves.

by the sensor changes proportionally to pedal angle. Changing voltage output from the sensor varies with the driver pedal position or driver demand (**FIGURE 23-10**).

Outputs can be analog as well. The intensity of a light from an output device, such as a lamp, can be produced by varying voltage and frequency of an electrical signal. An incandescent light is dimmed or brightened by increasing or decreasing current flow through the bulb.

An analog signal can be easily visualized when graphed. Because an analog signal varies over time, when it is plotted with time on the horizontal or x-axis, and the changing voltage, frequency, amplitude, or amperage aspect of the signal on the vertical y-axis, it remains continuously on, but changes over time to form loops or waves with sharp or low peaks and valleys. Looking at a graph of a signal is usually the easiest way to identify if it is analog or digital—a time-versus-voltage graph of an analog signal is typically smooth and continuous (**FIGURE 23-11**).

Frequency

Frequency is the number of events or cycles that occur in a period, usually one second. The units of measure for frequency are **hertz (Hz)**, which is the number of cycles per second. A common application for frequency measurements are units for AC electricity. When AC switches from zero volts to positive, then to negative, then back to zero volts again, one cycle is completed (**FIGURE 23-12**).

Digital Signals

In contrast to analog signals, **digital signals** do not vary in voltage, frequency, or amplitude. Instead, they are electrical signals that represent data in discrete, finite values. This means the data is broken down into separate, limited, or smaller meaningful values. For example, the movement of hands on an analog clock represents countless values for time. However, a digital watch represents time in finite values, such as seconds. A digital multimeter represents data the same way. The numerical display for an electrical measurement is represented as a fixed number or digit (**FIGURE 23-13**). In contrast, an analog meter measures the same electrical value using a sweeping needle on a scale.

Binary Code

A more common understanding of digital signals are as binary representations of information. Binary data means information is found in only one of two states. If digital data is binary, it is expressed using one of two conditions or values. Examples of binary information include on or off, yes or no, 1 or 0, open

or closed, up or down, etc. Binary code is an example of the most widespread use of a digital signal. Every number from 0 to infinity and the letters of the alphabet are represented by a combination of 0s and 1s. Binary code easily lends itself to use in microcontroller circuits where processing large amounts of alphabetic or numerical data is represented in strings of 0s or 1s.

Vehicle control systems process information electronically using digital signals represented by binary code. This means that all information, whether analog or alphabetic, is converted into 1s and 0s (**TABLE 23-2**). Using long strings of 1s and 0s may seem cumbersome, but just as the Morse code tapped out by telegraphs could send information using only dots and dashes, the 1s and 0s of binary code can satisfactorily represent all kinds of information (**FIGURE 23-14**). The difference between digital signal processing and Morse code is in the speed and accuracy achieved using electronic circuits. Processing millions and billions of 1s and 0s per second is something digital electronics can do to compensate for the cumbersomeness of using only long strings of 1s and 0s representing alpha numeric data.

Binary and Hexadecimal Code

Binary code is used by microcontrollers and microprocessors at a machine level to process information. The operation of transistors, logic circuits, and memory storage that efficiently switch to either an on or off state lends itself well to using 1s and 0s of binary machine code. Because the length of a number or word can be very long when represented only in binary code it can be difficult for humans to interpret or understand it. To shorten binary coded information with the purpose to make it more understandable for humans interpreting it, digital hexadecimal

Alternating Current Flow

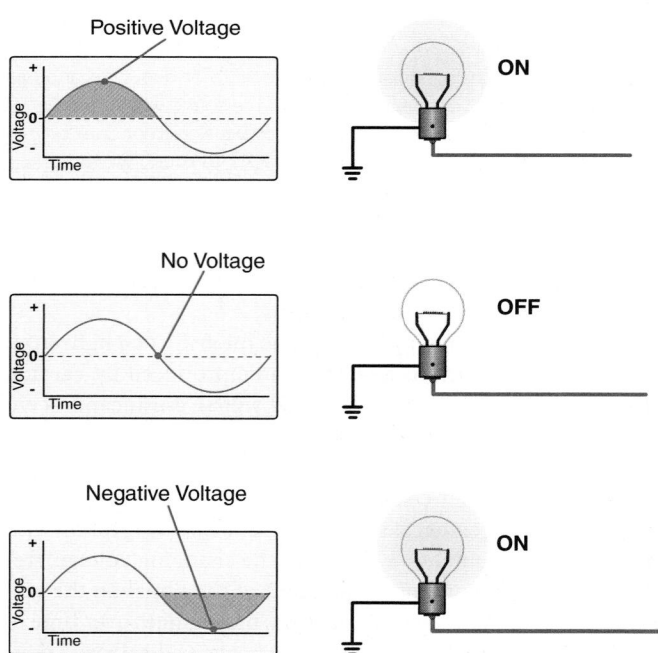

FIGURE 23-12 Frequency refers to the number of times a cycle occurs. Hertz is the unit of measurement that refers to the number of times the cycle occurs in one second.

FIGURE 23-13 This digital multimeter data represents resistance as a fixed precise digit value. Smaller changes in resistance—several places to the right of the decimal—are not measured.

code is used to express pure binary data. **Hexadecimal code** uses a combination of 0s, 1s, and letters to represent data. Technicians often see hexadecimal codes displayed beside fault codes, or network communication, by original equipment manufacturers (OEM) software, and in look-up tables. It is important to note that computers do not use hexadecimal, only humans. Binary code is converted to hexadecimal for human use and the computers that convert binary to hexadecimal code. Hexadecimal code has 16 symbols that can be used to represent any number or letter combination. The symbols are 0, 1, 2, 3, 4, 5, 6, 7, 8, 9, A, B, C, D, E, and F. The letters A–F are used at the 10th–15th digits placeholder (**TABLE 23-3**). To avoid confusing a hexadecimal with a binary and decimal system numbers, a $ symbol or 0x is placed in front of the hexadecimal number (**FIGURE 23-15**).

TABLE 23-2 Binary Alphabet Code

A	1000001	N	1001110
B	1000010	O	1001111
C	1000011	P	1010000
D	1000100	Q	1010001
E	1000101	R	1010010
F	1000110	S	1010011
G	1000111	T	1010100
H	1001000	U	1010101
I	1001001	V	1010110
J	1001010	W	1010111
K	1001011	X	1011000
L	1001100	Y	1011001
M	1001101	Z	1011010

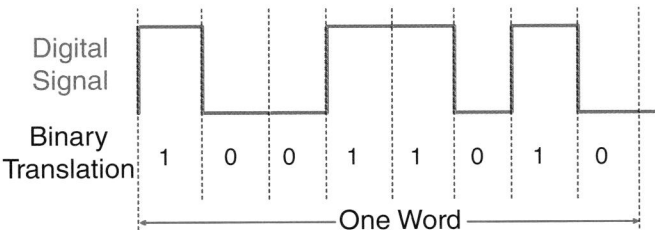

FIGURE 23-14 A bit is the smallest piece of digital information that is either a 1 or a 0. A byte is a unit of 8 bits. Digital binary code represents letters and numbers in strings of 1s and 0s.

When using a voltmeter to measure the signal of a rapidly changing analog signal, such as a wheel speed or engine speed sensor, the voltmeter should be set to AC volts ranged below a 10-volt scale. The voltage display only provides an average voltage reading and may not give a proper indication of whether the signal is acceptable or not, such as whether there are teeth missing, the sensor is loose, or the reluctor wheel is bent. Glitchy signals where the signal is briefly lost or has a problem is not detectable using only a voltmeter. If the analog signal is suspected as potentially corrupted or faulty, the use of a graphing meter or oscilloscope is recommended to visually analyze the signal.

Bits and Bytes

A **bit** is a shortened term for binary digit. This is the smallest piece of digital or binary information and is represented by a single 0 or 1. As illustrated in Figure 23-14, a **byte** is a combination of eight bits. The speed data is processed in an electronic control unit (ECU) module, also called ECM or electronic control module (ECM), is measured in bits. The number of bits it can process during one central processing unit (CPU) clock cycle provides an indication of how powerful the controller is. Desktop or laptop

TABLE 23-3 Hexidecimal Counting

Hexadecimal	Decimal	Binary
0	0	0000
1	1	0001
2	2	0010
3	3	0011
4	4	0100
5	5	0101
6	6	0110
7	7	0111
8	8	1000
9	9	1001
A	10	1010
B	11	1011
C	12	1100
D	13	1101
E	14	1110
F	15	1111

J1939 Calibration Information (DM19)

ECU	ECU Description	Calibration Verification Number (CVN)
0	Engine # 1	0x74A20000
0	A/C Pressure #1 Circuit Range/Performance	0x2D3A8402
0	Outside Air Temp Circuit Low Input	0x03CC91A
0	Inside Air Temp Sensor #1 Circuit Low Input	0xD9BCF13E

FIGURE 23-15 Hexadecimals are used to identify the engine calibration codes and calibration verification number in this diagnostic report.

computers often use 64-bit processors. A Pentium IV processor is 32 bits, whereas a late-model major ECU has a 16-bit or 32-bit capability. A 3.0-MHz processor has three million clock cycles per second, which means a 32-bit processor processes 96 million bits of data per second. While the clock speeds and bit size of the processors in a major ECU are smaller than an average desktop, so is the programming code. The capabilities of an ECU may appear to lag behind a personal computer (PC), but the PC is expected to operate using hundreds of complex software programs and run several at the same time. An engine or powertrain control microprocessor that operates using only one program with much simpler software code to process information and produce output signals has enormous processing capability.

▶ TECHNICIAN TIP

Various terms for electronic components and control units are used by manufacturers and easily recognized by technicians, but do not strictly follow the methodology outlined by standards organizations. Naming of electronic control units is supposed to follow a convention developed by either the Society of Automotive Engineers (SAE) standard J1930 Electrical/Electronic Systems Diagnostic Terms, Definitions, Abbreviations, and Acronyms or its equivalent International Organization for Standardization (ISO)15031—2. Terminology in these documents describes a function, but not a purpose, which is information a technician needs most. Term modifiers provide further meaning, such as the application or system location for a component. However, as the number of electrical and electronic systems has increased, so have the number of terms, abbreviations, and acronyms. For example, at least six different terms alone are used interchangeably by ISO to describe engine control modules. OEMs often use marketing terms unique to their product, which can further add to the confusion about using a single precise term. Because there are a limited number of terms and descriptions or useful letter combinations for acronyms, expect to see interchangeable terms and look for more information that helps identify a component's function, system application, and location.

Serial Data

LO 23-4 Identify, describe, and explain the purpose of serial data.

While discussing binary code and digital signals, it is necessary to understand the important concept of serial data. The term **serial data** originates from the way data is transmitted. It is transmitted in voltage pulses produced in series—one bit after another. Serial data can be transmitted along a single wire or two-wire pair. In both single and paired wires, serial digital data is transmitted by a voltage pulse represented as a square or rectangular digital waveform. In two-wire pairs, the wires have a **differential voltage**, which means the voltage on each of the wires in the pair is a mirror-opposite of voltage of the other when transmitting serial data (**FIGURE 23-16**). This means that during signal transmission, one wire's voltage becomes more positive, and the opposite more negative, at the same time. When it becomes more positive, the signal wire is considered to pull high and the negative wire is said to sink low. Differential voltage helps control modules and service tools distinguish electrical noise from signals. To further help separate noise from signals, both wires often have a resting

voltage that is close, but not exactly, the same. This resting voltage on CAN networks is close to +2.5 volts. Normally, both wires change voltage by close to the same amount. However, under most conditions, a small voltage pulse of either positive or negative polarity on only one wire that is not reflected on the other will not be interpreted as a bit. Neither is a voltage pulse with incorrect positive and negative values — only the overall differential voltage between the two wires is interpreted as a one or zero. A large differential voltage pulse where the positive or CAN-HI wire is pulled more positive while the negative CAN-LO wire sinks to an equal but more negative voltage is interpreted as "0". When the wires have identical voltage, the data is interpreted as "1". The pulses must be triggered within a specific time frame to be recognized as serial data and not just an endless string of zeros or ones.

Serial data is important because it is used to exchange information from one electronic module to another. On-board data networks share information and control vehicle operation by communicating using serial data. The relevance of the network and serial data to technicians is that service tools connected to the diagnostic data link connector read messages and send commands using serial data. The most important network on board commercial vehicles is carrying serial data exchanged by electronic control systems with high-priority messages, such as the ABS, engine, and transmission. This serial data pathway is called the controller area network (CAN), named this since microcontrollers in various ECU communicate over it. Problems with the network serial data transmission interferes with communication between control modules, which could prevent the vehicle from operating and either prevent the engine from starting or only starting and idling.

The rate at which serial data is transmitted over the network is referred to as the baud rate. **Baud rate** is the number of data bits transmitted per second. The latest serial data transmission speeds on commercial vehicles use a protocol called CAN with Flexible Data-Rate (CAN FD), which transmits data twice as fast as the previous protocol. CAN FD capabilities in normal mode are from 500 kb/s to a potential of 2 Mb/s, such as when flashing or programming microcontrollers over the CAN network using the data link connector (**FIGURE 23-17**).

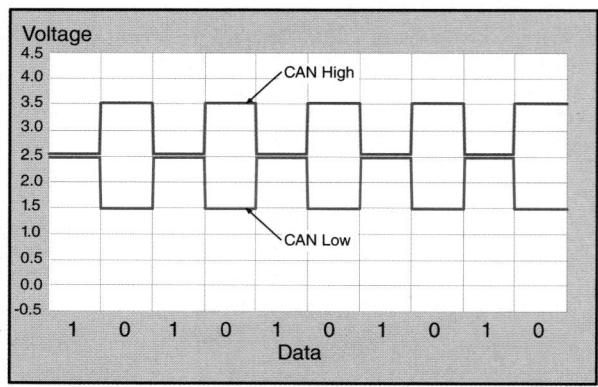

FIGURE 23-16 Serial data transmits a series of 1s and 0s and has a digital format. The wide part of the waveform represents 0 or a string of 0s, while the narrow part of the wave form represents 1 or a string of 1s.

Analog to Digital Conversion

Because electronic processing units can only handle binary digital data, analog signals are converted to digital signals in a process called **analog to digital conversion** (**FIGURE 23-18**). To convert analog signals to digital binary information, special circuits, known as buffers or analog to digital (AD) converters, are used (**FIGURE 23-19**).

To convert an analog signal, the electronics do a couple of things. First, the changing analog signal is sampled or divided up into segments like a loaf of bread. In one second, the varying analog signal could be sampled 10, 100, or even 256,000 times

FIGURE 23-17 This green-colored 9-pin data link connector designates the on-board network as CAN FD. CAN FD transmits serial data at 500 kb/s and higher.

(**FIGURE 23-20**). Each of these segments represent a specific voltage value. The finer or more accurate the processor wants the data to be, the more frequent the sampling rate, resulting in better signal resolution or fidelity. Each of the segments is assigned a digital value translated into a binary number.

Pulse Width Modulation

LO 23-5 Identify and describe characteristics of pulse-width–modulated electrical signals.

An important type of electrical signal that shares similar characteristics to a digital signal is the pulse width modulation (PWM) electrical signal (**FIGURES 23-21**, **23-22**, **23-23**). **Pulse width modulation (PWM)** refers to a signal that switches on and off and varies its time "ON" and "OFF." That means it is digital in one respect because it appears in one of two states only—either on or off, or high or low. However, the ratio between the on or off time is variable. The units for measuring a

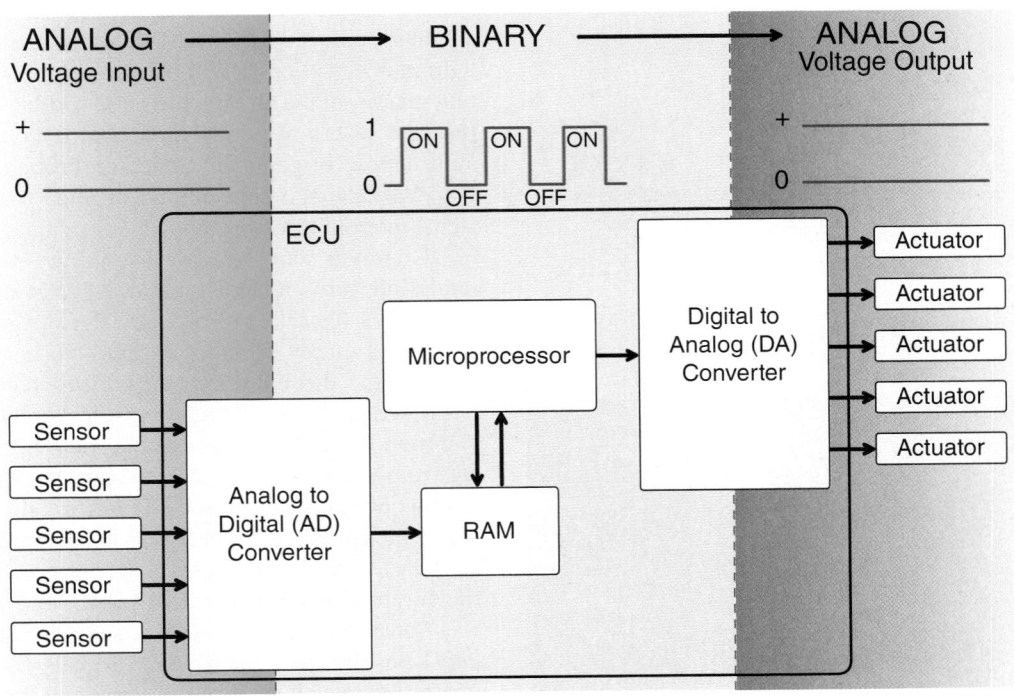

FIGURE 23-18 Analog to digital conversion occurs in both the input circuits of the ECM. Digital to analog signal conversion may also occur in the output circuits of the ECM.

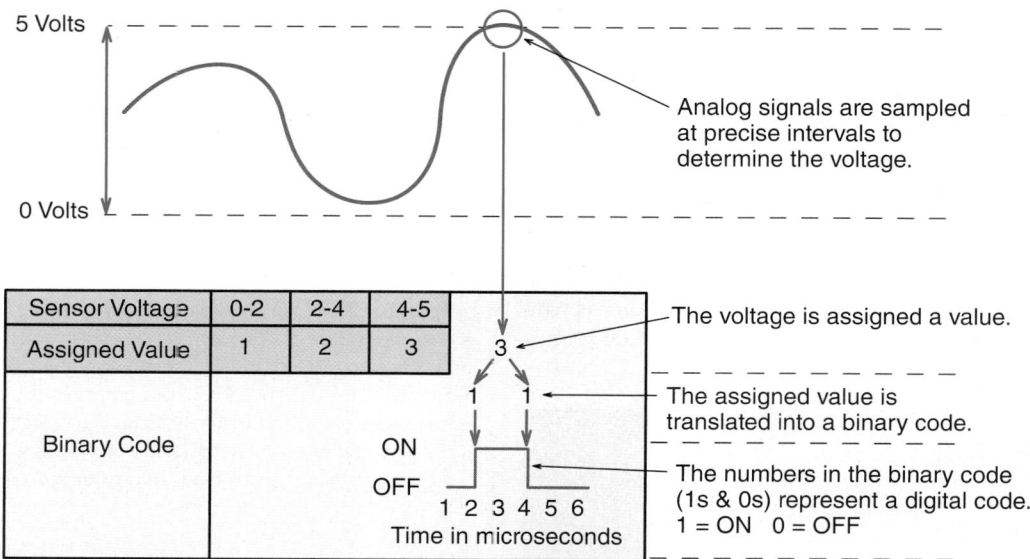

FIGURE 23-19 An analog to digital conversion. An analog waveform is sampled and measured many times a second to generate a digital representation of the waveform. This process is identical to forming MP3 files from an analog sound signal. The more frequently the signal is sampled per second—128K, 256K, or more—the higher the signal quality.

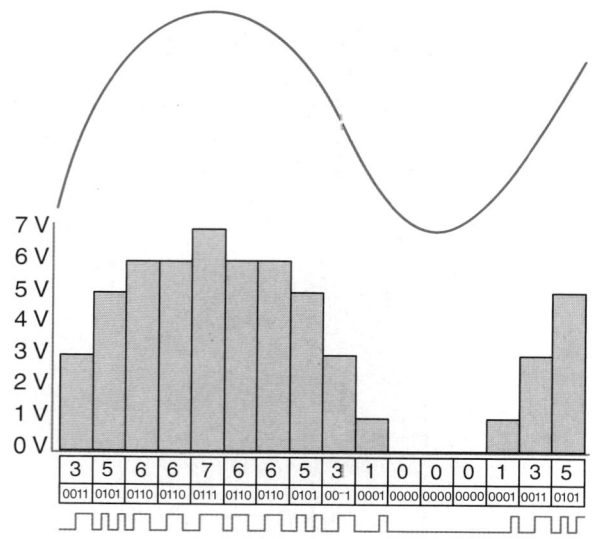

FIGURE 23-20 Analog signals from engine sensors are converted into digital signals for processing by the ECM.

FIGURE 23-21 A pulse width modulation signal displayed on a graphing meter. Notice the width of the pulses is similar.

signal pulse width are always expressed in units of time. Time is the measurement for how long the signal is switched on or high.

Voltage levels for PWM signals are held constant and are commonly between 5- and 12-volts DC, but can be higher. If the ratio between on time versus off time is longer, the current flow consequently increases through a device, such as a coil of wire. A longer pulse width in a coil of wire increases the strength of its magnetic field.

To further understand an application for PWM, consider a light illuminated by a PWM signal. In one second of time the light may be cycled on and off once. If the signal is applied for one-quarter of the second, the pulse width is 0.25 seconds wide (FIGURE 23-24). Naturally, the longer the on versus off time, a lamp appears brighter and amperage through a circuit increases. If a PWM signal is controlling a magnetic field, a longer PWM signal intensifies the magnetic field strength.

Common examples of devices using PWM signals are solenoids, injectors, and light circuits. A PWM signal's unit of measurement is typically milliseconds. PWM signals are commonly used as an output signal of an ECU. For example, the current supplied to a fuel injector or the pressure regulator of a hydraulically actuated electronically controlled unit injector (HEUI) or common rail pump is changed by varying the on time of the electromagnetic control valve (FIGURE 23-25). Output drivers of microcontroller are types of switches, usually switching transistors, which produce PWM signals to operate devices in an "ON" or "OFF" state. The microcontroller device can also easily vary the duration time a driver circuit opens and closes.

Caterpillar uses throttle position sensors that transmit pedal position data using PWM signals. This type of data is unaffected by voltage drops encountered through long runs of wiring harnesses and multiple connectors between the sensor and ECU in the same way as an analog signal.

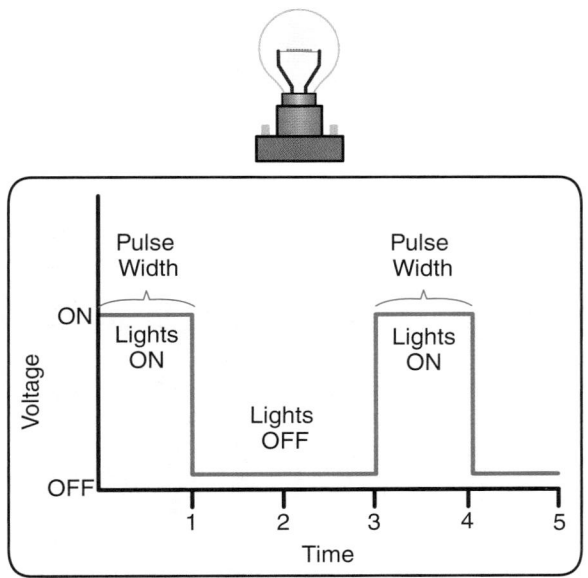

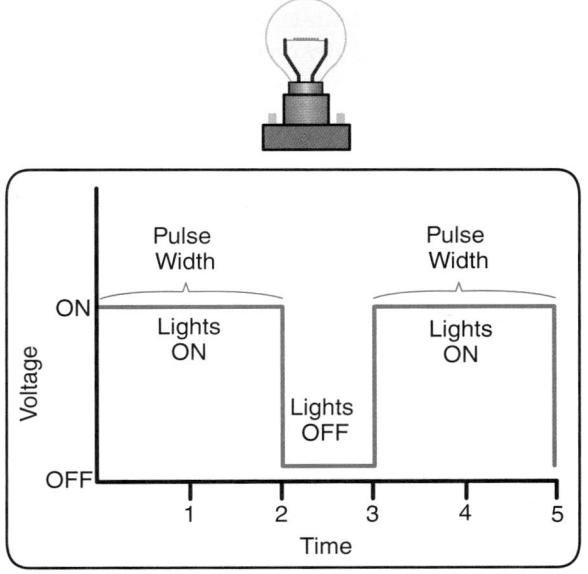

FIGURE 23-22 The longer the pulse width, the brighter the light, since more current flows through the circuit when pulse width on time lengthens.

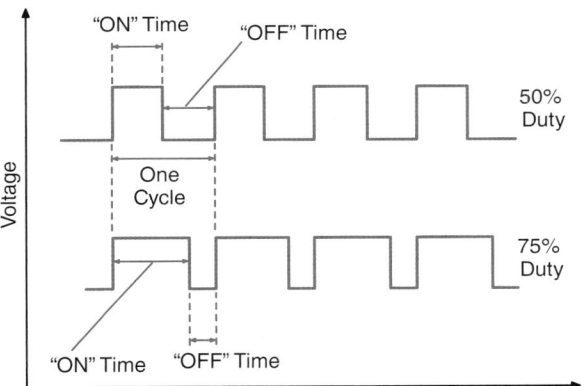

FIGURE 23-23 Duty cycle is a comparison of on time to off time in one cycle. A cycle can be 1 second, 500 msec, or any length of time, but the cycle time is fixed when measuring pulse width.

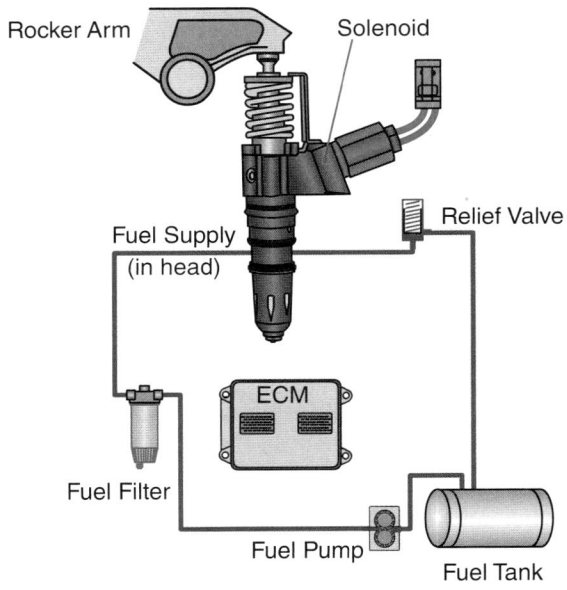

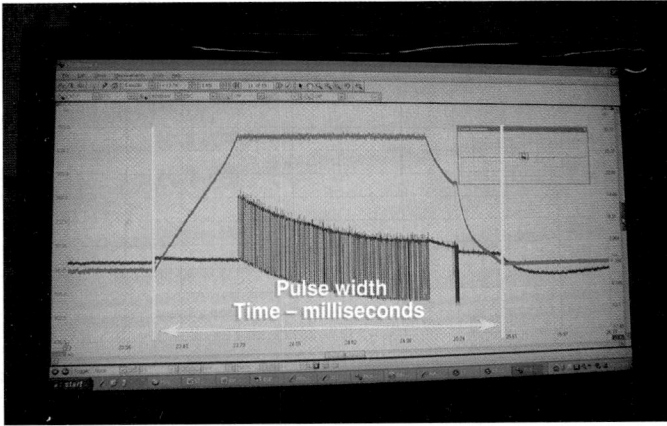

FIGURE 23-24 The pulse width of the energization time of an injector solenoid is measured in milliseconds.

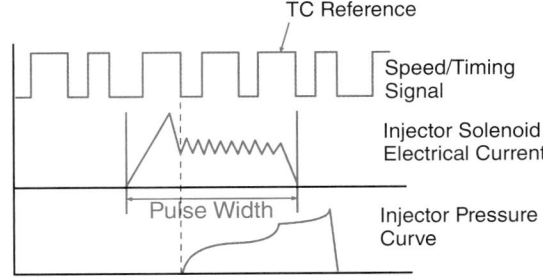

FIGURE 23-25 Varying the length of time electrical current energizes an injector solenoid changes the quantity of fuel injected into a cylinder.

Duty Cycle

Related to the term pulse width length is the term duty cycle, illustrated in Figure 23-23. **Duty cycle** is another unit for measurement for PWM signals. While a pulse width is measured in time units, duty cycle is measured as a percentage—on time versus off time. Duty cycle refers to the percentage of time a PWM signal is high or on, in comparison to off time (**FIGURE 23-26**). One on and off time for a PWM signal represents one duty cycle. For example, if the pulse width is 0.8 seconds and the off time is 0.2 seconds, a cycle is one second in length. This means the duty cycle is 80%. A 100% duty cycle means the signal is on all the time, while a 0% duty cycle is off.

The difference between the application of duty cycle measuring units and PWM time-on depends on how the signal is used. Duty cycle is commonly displayed to indicate the ratio between on and off time when a signal is applied to an output device operating at a fixed frequency. In contrast, a pulse width measures the time a signal is on when operating a device at a varying frequency interval. For example, an engine may speed up and slow down, so the pulse width or time an injector is energized varies with speed. It is practical to measure energization time only, since it is difficult to always know the frequency of a cycle—rpm, in this instance. Depending on engine speed, 10 or 20 injections may take place in one second, and the pulse width is measured in units of time for each injection event—in this case it is measured in milliseconds.

Consider the use of duty cycle to energize an electro-hydraulic pressure regulator. This device has a PWM signal applied to incrementally or gradually close a valve and increase pressure. Gradually reducing the pulse width time causes pressure to decrease. When PWM signal is reported in duty cycle, the time the signal is switched on or applied is broken into fixed time intervals. Therefore, a wire coil energized for this device may be on for 0.20 seconds out of fixed one-second intervals.

This gives it a pulse width of 0.20 seconds but a duty cycle of 20% (**FIGURE 23-27**). To practically interpret system operation, a measurement of duty cycle is more meaningful.

Ladder Logic

LO 23-6 Identify ladder logic diagrams and explain the use of ladder logic.

Understanding detailed operation about how microcontrollers and electronic control systems operate is not relevant to most technician tasks. However, having some background knowledge about digital logic can help technicians diagnose computerized control systems more effectively.

This is especially important for bus and coach technicians where understanding logic circuits and diagrams is essential. Working on electrical systems used by coach and transit buses requires skills related to understanding, interpreting, and diagnosing problems using ladder logic. Ladder logic is a system of symbols used by software programs for **programmable logic controllers (PLCs)**. PLCs are another name for the ECUs used on buses and trucks dedicated to electrical system control. PLCs use inputs from switches and sensors, and evaluate the signals according to a stored logic program. In turn, the program generates output signals to control the chassis electrical systems (**FIGURE 23-28**). The program logic is written with symbols arranged like rungs on a ladder, lending the name *ladder logic* to the visual representation of logic step. Logic moves from left to right on a ladder logic diagram with outputs on the right. If switches and other input devices meet all the required conditions shown on a rung, the logic energizes the circuit activates an output circuit. It should be noted that even on commercial vehicle trucks where the electrical system is programmable using software, ladder logic runs in the background behind the user interface.

Cranking a starting motor or switching on a light uses program logic that is viewed using a ladder logic diagram (**FIGURE 23-29**). Manufacturers use PLC software to perform

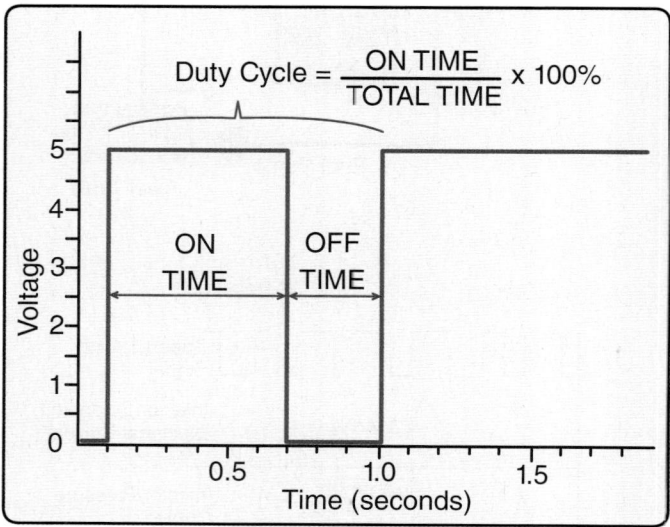

FIGURE 23-26 The measurement units for a PWM signal can also be a duty cycle. Duty cycle is expressed as a percentage of on time versus off time.

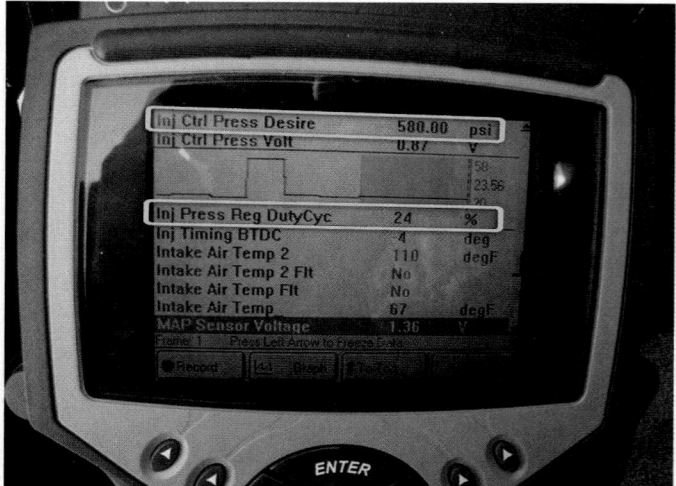

FIGURE 23-27 The duty cycle of this injection control pressure regulator for a HEUI fuel system is graphed and measured in duty cycle.

almost every electrical operation from switching on a light to operating hybrid drive propulsion systems or adding and modifying vehicle features, such as wheelchair lift ramps, ride height controls to stabilize a vehicle with high center of gravity. Behind the program interface of more advanced versions of

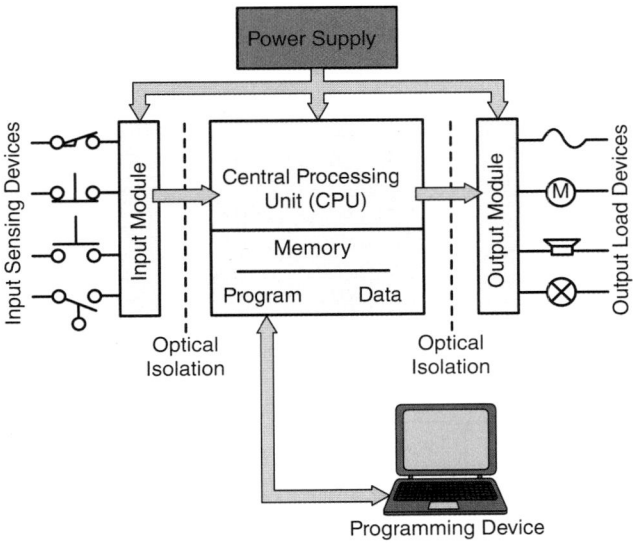

FIGURE 23-28 A PLC system uses inputs from switches and sensors to control output signals using programmed ladder logic.

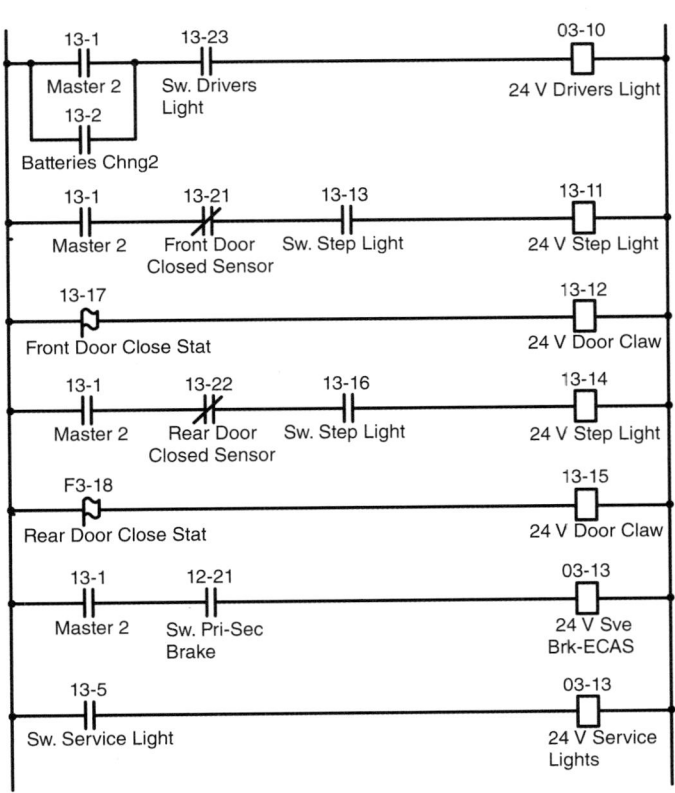

FIGURE 23-29 Ladder logic symbols represent the steps of control logic used to determine the conditions required to operate an output device.

PLC software are ladder logic symbols. Transit technicians often do not have the luxury of using advanced software hiding the changes behind a user-friendly interface. Instead, they rely on ladder logic diagrams supplied by PLC designers, such as Allen-Bradley, Vansco, and DINEX (**FIGURE 23-30**). Understanding the operation of ladder logic resembles the operation of logic gates, which are the basic building blocks or computer circuits in microcontrollers and processors. Diagnostic checks often involve verifying the ladder logic status on the PLC diagram. LED lights illuminate when an electrical signal is received (**FIGURE 23-31**). Using the lights to effectively diagnose a problem requires verifying the status of the circuit's. LED lights and the use of ladder logic diagrams.

Digital Logic Gates

Microcontrollers use digital binary code as a language to process data. Binary data works its way from the processor inputs to output after passing through devices called logic gates. **Logic gates** are the basic digital building blocks for computer circuits. The name is used because the gates are constructed from transistors arranged to process two or more digital signals using a set of rules, or logic. At an operational level, gates are essentially switches with a voltage signal representing "1" as on, and 0 or off represented by the absence of voltage. A combination of different voltage signals at the gate input switches the gates output to

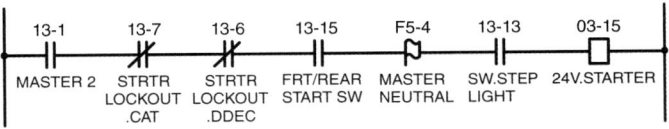

FIGURE 23-30 A rung of ladder logic symbolizing the conditions required to crank a starting motor need caption.

FIGURE 23-31 This transit bus uses five PLC controllers to for five zones of electrical system control. The LED's indicate whether inputs and outputs have signals.

either on or off. Combinations of the gates are then used to perform mathematical operations, such as subtraction and addition or more advanced arithmetic. Control logic for each step of program instruction is contained in machine language, which is essentially program software code translated into electrical signals to operate each of the gates.

There are six common logic gates named after the way they process logic: AND, OR, NOT, NAND, NOR, and XOR. Each gate is represented by a unique symbol and operates according to a set of rules outlined in a truth table. When displayed in a chart form, truth tables contain the various combinations of inputs to produce a specific output when binary data is processed by the gate.

AND Gate

Logic of the AND gate can be represented mechanically by two switches connected in series. An output voltage of 1 is possible only when both switches are closed. If either gate switch is open, the AND circuit does not operate. In other words, the AND gate requires one switch *and* another closed to produce a logic output of 1 (**FIGURE 23-32**).

OR Gate

An OR gate can be represented mechanically as two switches connected in parallel. This means that only if both switches are closed, an output voltage of 1 or on is produced. If either switch is open, there is no voltage output from the gate. In other words, the logic for an OR gate is no output if either switch one *or* switch two is open (**FIGURE 23-33**).

NOT Gate

Logic of the NOT gate can be represented by a switched input of a normally closed relay. This means the NOR gate output voltage is always the opposite of the input voltage. Another description given to this logic is inversion—the input is always the opposite of the output. The logic of this gate could be described as if the control switch is open (0), the relay is NOT energized (0), and the contacts are closed (**FIGURE 23-34**).

NAND Gate

Gates can also be a combination of simpler AND, NOR, and NOT gates. A NAND gate combines the logic of an AND and NOT gate. Its logic functions like an AND but its output is inverted like a NOT gate. The logic rules are that the output is 1 or on for all input conditions except when there is voltage, or a 1, at both inputs (**FIGURE 23-35**).

NOR Gate

NOR gate logic combines the OR gate and the NOT gate, enabling it to function like the OR gate except the output is the opposite or inverted. Logic rules for this gate switches the output on or to 1 only if there is no voltage at both inputs. In other words, no voltage at input 1 *nor* 2 produces a voltage output of 1 (**FIGURE 23-36**).

"OR" Gate

Truth Table

Input		Output
A	B	C
0	0	0
0	1	1
1	0	1
1	1	1

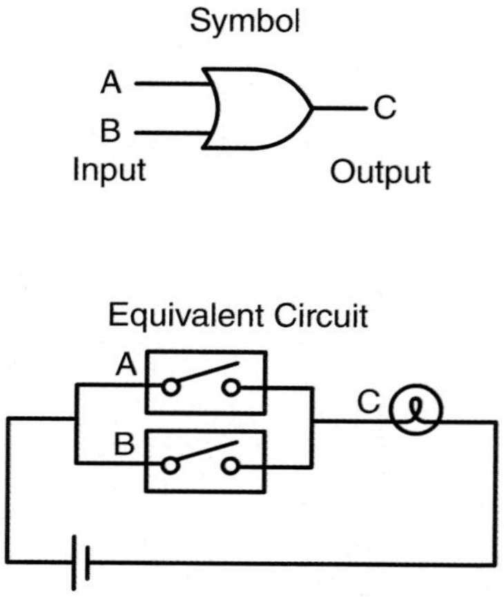

FIGURE 23-33 Control logic and truth table for an OR gate.

"AND" Gate

Truth Table

Input		Output
A	B	C
0	0	0
0	1	0
1	0	0
1	1	1

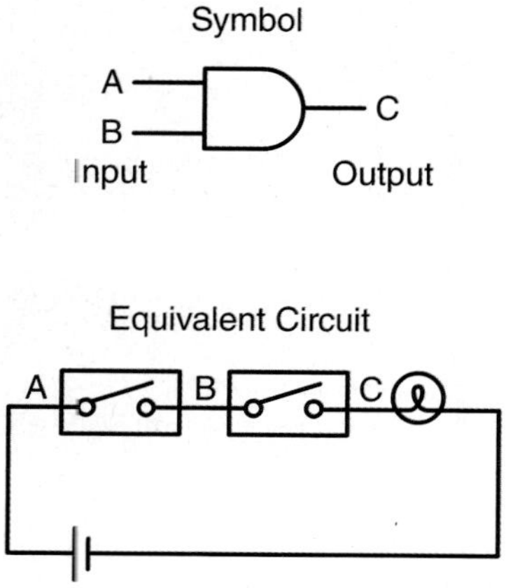

FIGURE 23-32 Control logic and truth table for an AND gate.

"NOT" Gate

Truth Table

Input	Output
A	C
0	0
1	1

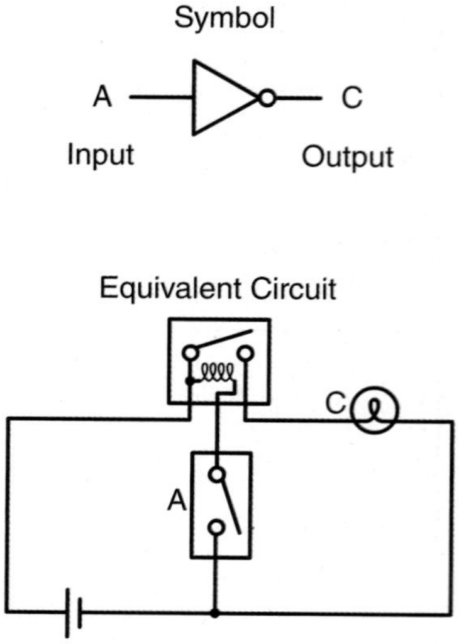

FIGURE 23-34 Control logic and truth table for a NOT gate.

XOR Gate

The XOR gate provides an output voltage of 1 only when both inputs are either 1 or 0. This arrangement means the output compares the combination of inputs to produce an output. Only the same number of 1s *or* 0s produce a 1 or voltage output. The XOR gate symbol is different than the OR gate in that it has an additional curved line at the input to indicate both must be the same to produce an output voltage or 1 (**FIGURE 23-37**).

"NAND" Gate

Truth Table

Input		Output
A	B	C
0	0	1
0	1	1
1	0	1
1	1	0

Symbols

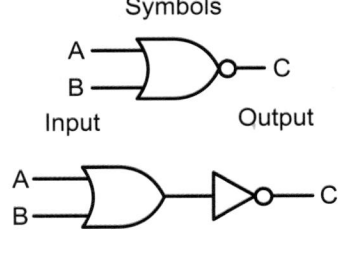

FIGURE 23-35 Control logic and truth table for a NAND gate.

"NOR" Gate

Truth Table

Input		Output
A	B	C
0	0	1
0	1	0
1	0	0
1	1	0

Symbols

FIGURE 23-36 Control logic and truth table for a NOR gate.

"XOR" Gate

Truth Table

Input		Output
A	B	C
0	0	0
0	1	1
1	0	1
1	1	0

Symbol

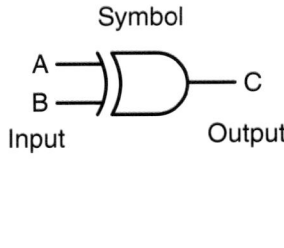

FIGURE 23-37 Control logic and truth table for an XOR gate.

Radio Signals

One other important type of electrical signal used to carry information is a radio wave. Radio waves do not carry current, but are produced by current carrying conductors and can induce current flow in a conductor because they have electromagnetic properties. Signals from radio waves are used by GPS navigation, collision avoidance systems, adaptive cruise control, blind spot detectors, and lane change assistance systems that use **radar** to detect objects. RADAR, an acronym for RAdio Detection And Ranging, is an object-detection system that uses radio waves to estimate the range, angle, and relative speed of objects. The material an object is made from and its shape can also be determined by advanced radar technology.

Radio waves are generated by the changing speed or rapid vibration of the electric charge on an electron. Energy generated by the moving electrons is released in two ways. One is through electromagnetism created by a moving charge. Energy is also released from the electric field, which is distorted by electron movement (**FIGURE 23-38**). Energy is first absorbed and then released as a radio wave from the electrical field surrounding the electron. Just as light is released from electrons moving down from one high-energy valance level of the atom to another, radio wave energy is emitted by simply vibrating or rapidly accelerating and then decelerating the movement of an electron. High voltage combined with a very-high-frequency AC in a wire is an effective way to produce radio waves. Sparks created in the ignition system, or any electrical contact, are a familiar source of radio waves. In these situations, electrons release radio waves as they move across and lose energy jumping the air gap of a spark plug, electrical switch, or commutator of an electric motor. The energy they give up can be heard over a radio or seen as interference of a video signal on a television (**FIGURE 23-39**).

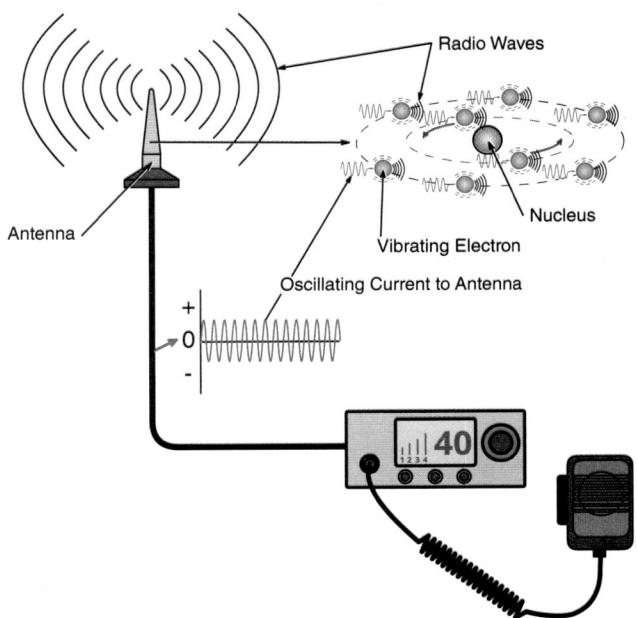

FIGURE 23-38 Electrons can absorb energy and release it as a radio wave.

Radio waves pass easily through air but are reflected by the hard surface of objects. A radar can measure the distance to an object by timing the delay between the start of a pulse of a radio wave and the time it takes to bounce back. If the object is moving, it slightly compresses the reflected radio wave and causes the wave frequency to change. Measuring frequency and reflection time of radio waves are the fundamental principles of radar object and speed detection (**FIGURE 23-40**).

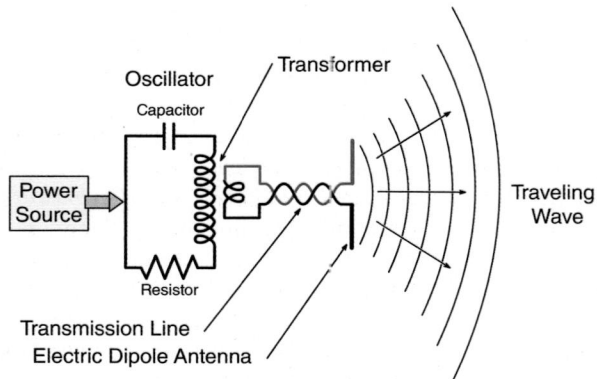

FIGURE 23-39 Radio waves are produced by high-voltage alternating current switching at very high frequency, which rapidly accelerates and decelerates the movement of electrons.

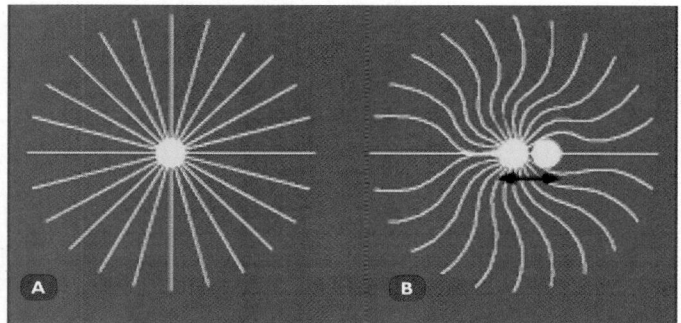

A. Lines of force for the electric charge surround an electron.
B. Moving an electron distorts the charge field. The field emits the absorbed energy as radio waves when the distortion is released.

Electromagnetic Interference (EMI)

LO 23-8 Identify the mechanisms for generating, transmitting, and minimizing electromagnetic interference.

Electromagnetic interference (EMI) is a major electrical system problem caused by the induction of unwanted electrical signals into current-sensitive vehicle circuits. The problem with EMI on commercial vehicles became a mission-critical issue when microcontrollers and on-board networks were added. Low-voltage and low-current circuits used by integrated circuits operating with digital signal-processing techniques are extremely sensitive to EMI signals. Excessive or stray current flow in the wrong circuits at a critical moment can permanently damage the microelectronic circuitry. False electrical signals and excessive current in the onboard network or any ECU can disrupt the control system operation. If a safety critical control signal or information needed to operate a major ECU needs to be retransmitted because it is corrupted or slowed down, it is a potential safety issue. Not surprisingly, safety standards are established for testing and measuring EMI disruption on vehicles to prevent potentially catastrophic failures. During vehicle development, equipment is bombarded with sources of EMI many times beyond what it encounters in the field to ensure equipment and passengers are properly protected.

Electromagnetic Interference Generation and Transmission

EMI is created whenever current flows in a conductor is disrupted by an external force. This broad definition of EMI can be further broken down, classifying it according to sources of EMI. For example, EMI is created when current flow in a circuit suddenly stops and starts, such as when switch or relay contacts open and close. When this takes place, the magnetic field strength around a conductor rapidly changes. Sudden movement of electric charges and moving magnetic fields generate a strong electromagnetic radio wave. As noted in the section on radio waves, if the changing magnetic field strength happens frequently and fast enough, radio signal waves are produced. Radio waves, which are a type of electromagnetism, can induce current flow in conductors the same way they generate electrical signals in radio-receiving antennas. When EMI is induced from radio signals, it is also called radio frequency interference (RFI).

Vehicle Radar Tasks

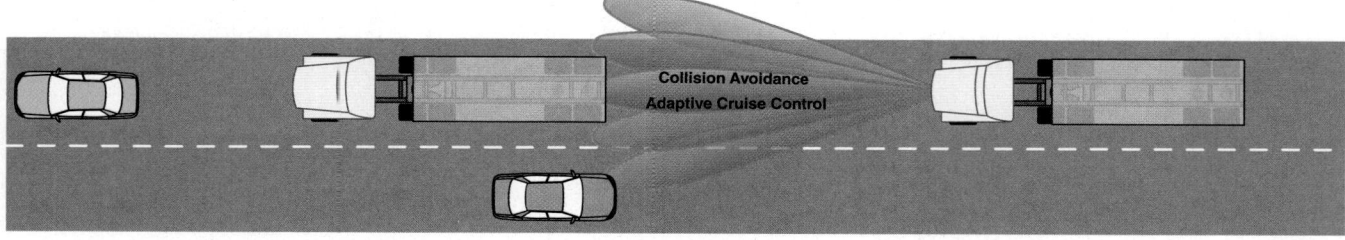

FIGURE 23-40 Radio waves are used by collision avoidance and adaptive cruise systems.

One less well-known source of EMI is caused by friction between dissimilar materials or separating materials resulting in triboelectric effects. Rubber airbags on the aluminum pedestals of air suspension systems moving up and down, separating the rubber and aluminum materials, can build up tremendous static electric charges. Plastic pipe material on open trailers and even the friction-separation effects between tires and road surfaces, or engine drive belts and their pulleys, can create areas of static high-voltage charges. Well-documented failures of engines and other major components are traced to these unexpected sources of EMI current.

EMI is transmitted into a vehicle's electrical system in four common ways:

1. Conductive coupling through circuit conductors
2. Capacitive coupling caused by an electrostatic field between two conductors
3. **Inductive coupling** that takes place through mutual induction between magnetic fields and nearby conductors
4. Radio frequency interference

Conductive Coupling

Conductive-coupling interference is transmitted into a circuit by connecting a sensitive electrical circuit to a source of interference. An example is an alternator with AC voltage ripple that is superimposed over the chassis DC. The AC and frequent change of voltage is transmitted throughout the electrical system connected to the alternator output cable. It's noticeable when the AC ripple causes the speedometer or tachometer to bounce or fluctuate at particular speeds coinciding with the frequency of the AC ripple. Random unexpected fault codes are set in the ABS and other control systems. Ripple can interfere with signals transmitted by the CAN and to the engine sensors or ECU and cause unstable operation (**FIGURE 23-41**).

To minimize conductive coupling, capacitors, resistors, or choking coils can be installed across many circuits, such as alternators, electric motors, and switches with inductive loads. The capacitor absorbs voltage spikes at switching points and discharges the stored current when the circuit voltage lowers.

Induction coils, which are choking coils, are connected to the power supply input to sensitive components can reduce or smoothen current fluctuations resulting from self-induction or mutual induction. They are often combined with capacitors to act as EMI filter circuits for wiper motors and electric fuel pump motors. A common conductive-type coupling problem is indicated by hums and electrical noise through charging cell phones and Bluetooth systems. A condition called a ground loop forms when two points of a circuit have different or changing negative potentials. A radio or Bluetooth device with a different ground voltage than the cell phone it's coupled to amplifies noise because of the potential voltage differences between them. (**FIGURE 23-42**).

Capacitive Coupling

Capacitive-coupling interference is transmitted into wiring harnesses and circuits by strong electrostatic charges on body panels and other large surfaces. A hood or other body panel with wind friction can build up static electric charges that induce current in nearby wiring harnesses by electrostatic field. Installing ground straps between body panels where no electrical circuit for lights or other devices exist only function to drain static electric EMI. Without the ground strap, the panel can function as a large capacitor with the air gap acting like a dielectric for an electrostatic field and then couple with sensitive digital circuits in ECUs and the onboard network data bus routed near the body panel. This explains why it is important to reinstall ground straps on components, such as body panels and heater cores, which can have air friction establish triboelectric static charges (**FIGURE 23-43**).

Radiofrequency Interference

RFI takes place when radio waves induce current in wiring that acts as a receiving antenna. The use of CB radios was at one time a strong source of RFI. Today, cell phones can potentially induce RFI-type interference. RFI transmission is minimized by the use of metal or metalized plastic shielding. The radio signals conduct through the metal circuits to ground. Engine wiring

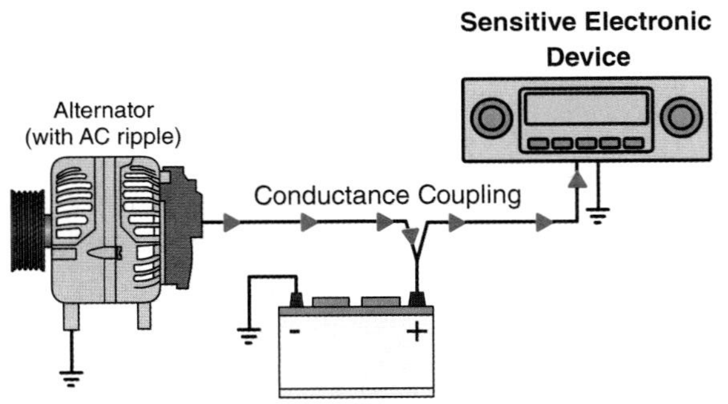

FIGURE 23-41 Conductance coupling is caused by voltage fluctuations from a device connected to the electrical system or sensitive circuit.

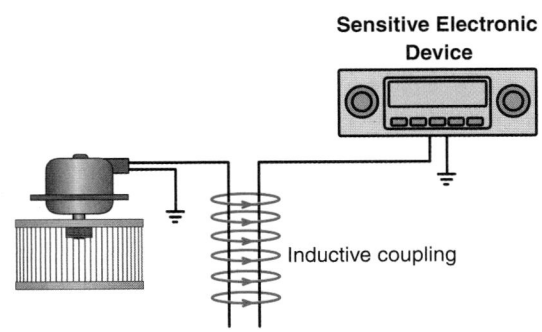

FIGURE 23-42 Inductive coupling takes place when voltage fluctuations create a moving magnetic field that induces current flow in an adjacent conductor.

harnesses using foam-over harness-style with electrically conductive insulation are an example of a newer type of RFI shielding (**FIGURE 23-44**).

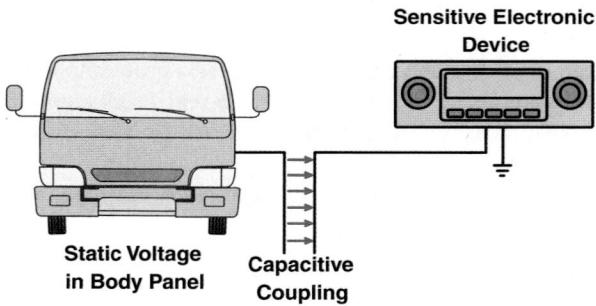

FIGURE 23-43 Capacitive coupling takes place when the electric field of a nearby object pushes or pulls electrons in a wiring harness or sensitive electronic device.

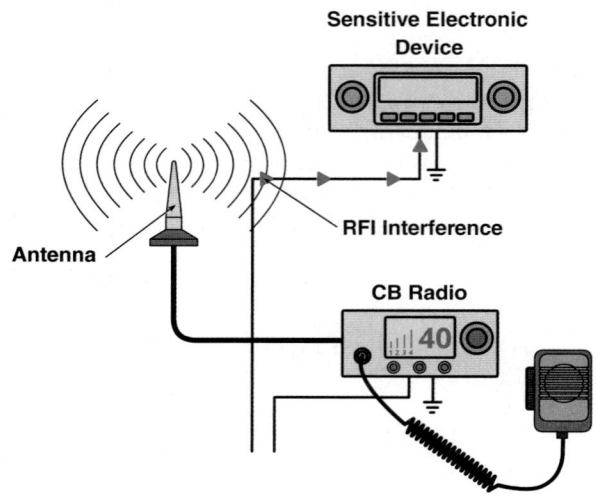

FIGURE 23-44 RFI can induce current flow in sensitive circuits and conductors.

Wrap-Up

Ready for Review

▶ Electronic systems using microcontroller-based controls provide operational capabilities far exceeding any mechanical system. The dominance and sophistication of electronic control makes skill development related to servicing this technology one of the most important priorities for successful technicians.

▶ Diesel engines were the first commercial vehicle systems transformed by electronic controls. The immediate benefits of these refinements to powertrain control include lower engine emissions, improved fuel economy, increased reliability, and enhanced performance.

▶ Service technicians, particularly in fleet operations using medium-heavy-duty engines, can access a wealth of diagnostic and service information much faster and with more precise detail than before.

▶ Telematics, a branch of information technology, uses specialized applications for long-distance transmission of information to and from a vehicle. Messages can be sent back and forth between the vehicle and a central dispatch location.

▶ The use of electronic engine and vehicle control systems provides for enhanced vehicle and occupant safety and security.

▶ Programmable software provides flexibility to engines, transmissions, and body accessories to adapt to specific job applications while providing enhanced vehicle productivity, longevity, and driver comfort. Programmable features include idle shut-down timers, cruise control, maximum vehicle speed limits, and safety interlocks that prevent the vehicle from moving if a door is open, a boom is raised, or outriggers are extended.

▶ Built-in electronic control systems allow vehicles to check the operation of circuits and electrical devices, evaluate the rationality of data, and identify problems as they occur. The presence of faults is communicated through the malfunction indicator lamps, electronic service tools, or Windows-based diagnostic software.

▶ Electronic control systems can be broken down into three major divisions: sensing, processing, and output or actuation.

▶ Sensing functions collect data about operational conditions or the state of a device by measuring some value, such as temperature, position, speed, pressure, or flow.

▶ Processing collects sensor data and determines outputs based on a set of instructions or program software.

▶ The outputs of a system are functions performed in response to electrical signals produced by the processor.

▶ Three types of electrical signals commonly used as either inputs or outputs in electronic engine control applications are analog, digital, and PWM.

▶ An analog signal is an electric current that is proportional to a another continuously changing variable.

▶ In contrast to analog signals, digital signals do not vary in voltage, frequency, or amplitude. Instead, they are electrical signals that represent data as binary values, such as on-off, 0 or 1, yes-no, up-down, open-closed, etc.

▶ Binary code is an example of a digital signal. "Bit" is a shortened term for binary digit. This is the smallest piece of digital or binary information and is represented by a single 0 or 1. A byte is a combination of eight bits.

▶ Serial data is used to transmit information from one electronic module to another. On-board data networks share information and control vehicle operation using serial data.

▶ Because electronic processing units can only handle binary digital data, analog signals are converted to digital signals by special circuits known as buffers or AD converters.

▶ An electrical signal that shares similar characteristics with both a digital and analog signal is the PWM electrical signal. PWM refers to a signal that varies in on and off time. A PWM signal is typically measured in milliseconds.

▶ Duty cycle is another unit of measurement for PWM signals, and it refers to the percentage of time a PWM signal is on versus the time it is off. Duty cycle is commonly used to measure the time a signal is applied to an output device operating at a fixed frequency, whereas pulse width measures a signal applied to devices operating at a varying frequency interval.

▶ Frequency is the number of events or cycles that occur in a period. The unit of measure for frequency is hertz (Hz), which is the number of cycles per second.

▶ Logic gates are the basic building blocks of electronic circuits used in microcontrollers and processors. Logic gates are arranged together to perform mathematical computations and process software logic.

▶ Logic gates process digital signals using binary code. Hexadecimal numbers are converted from binary digits to shorten the length of a binary word or number.

▶ Hexadecimal numbers are not used by logic gates or microcontrollers, but only by humans.

▶ Ladder logic is used by PLC controllers to process output signals according to switch and sensor inputs.

▶ Electromagnetic interference is a major electrical system problem caused by the induction of unwanted electrical signals into current-sensitive vehicle circuits. Four types of methods are used to introduce EMI into a vehicle and a unique method for each type of EMI prevents it from disrupting vehicle operation.

Key Terms

analog signal   An electric current that is proportional to another continuously changing variable.

analog to digital conversion   The process when an analog waveform is sampled and measured many times a second to generate a digital representation of the waveform.

baud rate   The rate at which serial data is transmitted.

bit   The smallest piece of digital information that is either a 1 or 0.

byte   A unit of eight bits.

capacitive coupling   A category of EMI interference transmitted into wiring harnesses and circuits by strong electrostatic charges on body panels and other large surfaces.

conductive-coupling   A category of EMI transmitted into a circuit by wiring connected to a source of interference.

differential voltage   Refers to the voltage difference on a wire pair when one wire's voltage is the mirror-opposite voltage. A wide separation between the voltage pulses represents a 1 and a narrow separation represents a 0.

digital signals   Electrical signals that represent data in discrete, finite values. Digital signals are considered as binary, meaning it is either on or off, yes or no, high or low, 0 or 1.

duty cycle   The percentage of time a PWM signal is ON in comparison to OFF time.

electromagnetic interference (EMI)   An electrical system problem caused by the transmission of unwanted electrical signals into current-sensitive vehicle circuits.

frequency   The number of events or cycles that occur in a period, usually 1 second.

hertz (Hz)   The unit for electrical frequency measurement, in cycles per second.

hexadecimal code   A numbering system using a combination of 0s, 1s, and letters to represent data. It shortens the length of binary words and numbers to make them more readable.

Inductive coupling   A category of EMI transmitted by changing magnetic field strength in a conductor or device inducing current flow in a nearby conductor through mutual induction.

microcontroller   A special-purpose integrated circuit containing control logic with limited capabilities, designed to perform a set of specific tasks.

Programmable Logic Controllers (PLC)   Electronic control modules that use inputs from switches and sensors, and generate output signals according to a stored logic program.

pulse width modulation (PWM)   An electrical signal that varies in on and off time.

RFI   A category of EMI caused by radio waves inducing current in wiring or electrical components that acts as a receiving antenna.

telematics   A branch of information technology that uses specialized applications for long-distance transmission of information to and from a vehicle.

Review Questions

1. Which of the following was the earliest control system to switch from mechanical to electronic control?
   a. Transmissions
   b. Diesel engines
   c. Anti-lock braking
   d. Climate control

2. Which of the following reasons best explain the necessity for self-diagnostic capabilities that are built into electronic control systems?
   a. It enables the use of personal computers, tablets, and cell phones to diagnose problems.
   b. Service technicians can collect more diagnostic and service data than before.

   c. It is too time consuming to trace faults using a multimeter.

   d. Fault codes can be stored for review.

3. Which of the following statements best describes the job of electrical signals?

   a. They provide the electrical force needed to operate components drawing high amounts of electrical current.

   b. They are used to operate low current accessories, such as LED lights and illuminated instrument displays.

   c. They are switched and manipulated using relays, switches, and manual control devices.

   d. They are produced by electronic circuits to transmit information and control electrical devices.

4. Which of the following types of signals are only used by telematics?

   a. Analog signals

   b. Digital signals

   c. Pulse-width–modulated signals

   d. Radio signals

5. Which of the following diagnostic strategies is used by technicians during off-board diagnostics?

   a. Performing pinpoint tests of circuits and components

   b. Retrieving fault codes

   c. Identification of out-of-range voltage codes

   d. Verifying correct system functionality

6. What type of electrical signal is viewed using a sweeping needle of a voltmeter?

   a. Digital

   b. Analog

   c. PWM

   d. Radio wave

7. What type of signal is produced by a toggle switch?

   a. Analog

   b. Digital

   c. PWM

   d. Hybrid analog–digital

8. Which of the following is most likely an example of hexadecimal number?

   a. 58

   b. 00110101 00111000

   c. $003A

   d. 5x0011

9. Which of the following would most likely be the cause of conductive-coupling EMI?

   a. A missing body panel ground strap

   b. A defective alternator

   c. Wires without conductive EMI shielding

   d. Self-induction

10. Consider a electrohydraulic pressure regulator operating with a fixed frequency of 0.5 seconds. The duty cycle is 50%. How long is the pressure regulator energized?

   a. 0.5 seconds

   b. 0.25 seconds

   c. 0.75 seconds

   d. 50 milliseconds

ASE Technician A/Technician B Style Questions

1. Technician A says that most vehicle systems now operate with at least some degree of electronic control. Technician B says that using electronic control systems has increased the cost and time involved diagnosing complaints. Who is correct?

   a. Technician A

   b. Technician B

   c. Both Technician A and Technician B

   d. Neither Technician A nor Technician B

2. Technician A says that electronic signals can transmit information and control electrical devices. Technician B says that only binary information can be processed by microcontrollers built into an electronic control module. Who is correct?

   a. Technician A

   b. Technician B

   c. Both Technician A and Technician B

   d. Neither Technician A nor Technician B

3. Technician A says that telematics uses specialized telecommunication applications for long-distance transmission of information to and from a vehicle. Technician B says that telematics is not capable of transmitting information on fault codes. Who is correct?

   a. Technician A

   b. Technician B

   c. Both Technician A and Technician B

   d. Neither Technician A nor Technician B

4. Technician A says that the units for reporting a pulse-width–modulated signal are measured only in milliseconds. Technician B says that a PWM signal is only reported as a percentage or duty cycle. Who is correct?

   a. Technician A

   b. Technician B

   c. Both Technician A and Technician B

   d. Neither Technician A nor Technician B

5. Technician A says that a PWM signal appears as a continuous wave when displayed on a graphing meter or oscilloscope. Technician B says that a PWM signal appears rectangular or square-shaped when graphed. Who is correct?

   a. Technician A

   b. Technician B

   c. Both Technician A and Technician B

   d. Neither Technician A nor Technician B

6. Technician A says that processing refers to the control system element that collects sensor data and determines outputs based on a set of instructions or program software. Technician B says that calibration data provides the control system with data that is unique or specific to the ECU application. Who is correct?

   a. Technician A

   b. Technician B

   c. Both Technician A and Technician B

   d. Neither Technician A nor Technician B

7. Technician A says that serial data is used by ECUs to communicate information. Technician B says that serial data transmits information using binary code. Who is correct?
   a. Technician A
   b. Technician B
   c. Both Technician A and Technician B
   d. Neither Technician A nor Technician B

8. Technician A says that a missing ground strap on a chassis with air ride suspension could potentially produce a type of EMI interference. Technician B says that EMI is only caused by strong radio signals from a cell phone of CB radio. Who is correct?
   a. Technician A
   b. Technician B
   c. Both Technician A and Technician B
   d. Neither Technician A nor Technician B

9. Technician A says that serial data is used to exchange data between electronic service tools and an ECU. Technician B says that baud rate of serial data refers to the number of data bits transmitted per minute. Who is correct?
   a. Technician A
   b. Technician B
   c. Both Technician A and Technician B
   d. Neither Technician A nor Technician B

10. Technician A says that logic gates can only process binary data. Technician B says that binary, hexadecimal, and alphabetic information are outputs from an ECU. Who is correct?
   a. Technician A
   b. Technician B
   c. Both Technician A and Technician B
   d. Neither Technician A nor Technician B

CHAPTER 24

Sensors and Input Circuit Devices

Learning Objectives

After reading this chapter, you will be able to:

- **LO 24-1** Identify applications of sensor's technology.
- **LO 24-2** Explain the operation of switches as circuit input devices.
- **LO 24-3** Identify and describe the construction and operation of resistive type sensors.
- **LO 24-4** Identify and describe the construction and operation of pressure sensors.
- **LO 24-5** Identify and describe the construction and operation of voltage generating sensors.

- **LO 24-6** Identify and describe the construction and operation of mass airflow sensors.
- **LO 24-7** Identify and describe the construction and operation of exhaust gas sensors.
- **LO 24-8** Identify and describe the operation of diesel exhaust fluid (DEF) sensors.
- **LO 24-9** Recommend and describe diagnostic procedures for sensors used in electronic control systems.
- **LO 24-10** Outline procedures for pinpoint testing of sensors.

You Are the Technician

A customer has brought a truck to your shop complaining that the engine will occasionally not accelerate. Sometimes, after the throttle pedal is pushed multiple times, the engine will only idle. Other times the engine drops to idle while the vehicle is moving in traffic. The problem generally corrects itself after the ignition key is cycled; at other times the throttle pedal starts operating correctly on its own. After checking for fault codes, you learn the truck has recently had codes erased. You suspect the problem is in the accelerator position sensor (APS), but without fault codes or duplicating the problem, you want to make sure the problem is not related to wiring, another electrical system issue, or the fuel system. Limited throttle and power could also indicate a power de-rate condition caused by an emission-related fault. After carefully inspecting the wiring harness and connectors to the APS, you verify they are in good condition. Next you connect a software-based vehicle diagnostic program to the vehicle data link to monitor the APS. There are three APS signals displayed with different voltages on each sensor. Consider the following as you proceed:

1. Does this APS use an idle validation switch?
2. What complaint would the driver have if one, two, or three of the APS voltages were incorrect?
3. How will you determine if the APS has a fault?

Introduction

Sensors are traditionally considered to be devices that convert physical conditions or states into proportional low-voltage electrical signals. A transducer is the active element of a sensor that converts a physical energy into electrical energy. Pressure, temperature, angle, sound, speed, mass, level, gas concentrations, magnetic field, and light are just a few of the changing physical variables about which sensors supply either analog or digital electrical data to electronic control units. Recent developments in control system strategies have introduced a completely new category of sensor called the **virtual sensor**. Virtual means not physically existing but the data reported from the sensor is made to appear real using software. This new sensor uses predictive algorithms to report data, meaning it calculates an estimated value for a physical variable that usually cannot be directly measured. Except for the software code that supports it, key advantages of virtual sensors are that they cost almost nothing and do not break or wear out. Model Predictive Control (MPC) systems, discussed in a later chapter, use virtual sensors.

Given the extreme operating conditions in which sensors function, it is not surprising that sensor failures are routinely encountered when performing electrical diagnostic work. But sensors are also frequently misdiagnosed and unnecessarily replaced. Contributing to this problem are misunderstandings about the operation of on-board diagnostic systems and how it generates fault codes for what appears to be sensor-related defects. Fault codes that most often lead to misdiagnosis are in fact related only to sensor circuits and mechanical performance issues present in systems monitored by sensors. Further pinpoint testing is required to isolate faults in sensor circuits, and move past the diagnostic limitation of sensor monitors to differentiate between a defective sensor, wiring, or mechanical system performance issue. This chapter is intended to not only help technicians understand sensor construction, applications, and operation, but to develop service practices and diagnostic skills related to sensors and other circuit input devices.

Applications of Sensor's Technology

LO 24-1 Identify applications of sensor's technology.

An enormous number of sensor types exist to measure various types of data required by increasingly sophisticated commercial vehicle control systems. To get an idea about the wide variety of sensors used in commercial vehicles, common sensor applications include, but are not limited to:

- Accelerometers for vehicle dynamic control and airbags
- Pressure sensors for engine oil, fuel, crankcase, and intake boost
- Position sensors for wheel speed, camshafts, crankshafts, and pedal position
- Humidity sensors for adjusting air-fuel ratio control and cabin comfort control
- Sunlight and rain/moisture sensors

- Distance sensors for near obstacle detection and collision avoidance (sensors for short-range and long-range RADAR and ultrasonic sound sensors)
- Magnetoresistive (MR) sensors that use the earth's magnetic field to operate vehicle electronic compasses and navigation systems
- Torque sensors
- Fuel level sensors
- Oil quality sensors
- Diesel exhaust fluid level and quality
- Particulate sensors
- Temperature sensors
- Coolant level sensors
- Barometric pressure sensors
- Mass airflow sensors
- Engine knock sensors
- Exhaust gas: NO_X, ammonia, soot and oxygen sensors
- Yaw sensors using the Coriolis effect to sense yaw rates
- Global positioning sensors for radio wave GPS
- Virtual sensors using software algorithms to estimate a physical value that is not practical or possible to directly measure

These applications can be classified according to several core technologies, such as switched inputs; variable capacitance; piezoelectric and strain gauge-type pressure sensors; resistive-type sensors measuring variables, such as temperature, position, and fluid levels; galvanic sensors; and sensors using magnetic fields, light, sound, and even electrostatic fields. In addition to radio and high-frequency sound wave sensors, another newer category of sensors are galvanic voltage generators measuring concentrations of various exhaust gases. In this category are oxygen, NOx, and ammonia sensors.

When examining sensor technology, a distinction is made between sending units and sensors. Sensors provide low-voltage electrical signals to electronic control units, whereas sending units provide analog or switched current electrical information to instrument gauges. Sensors are also different from transducers, which convert one form of energy into electrical energy. Heat, pressure, and light are examples of forms of energy that are converted by transducers into proportional electrical energy signals. Some sensors use transducers as part of their construction, but sensors perform the additional function of conditioning transducer signals and convert them to to proportional electrical signals.

Active Versus Passive Sensors

In addition to the type of application and core sensor technology, sensors are further classified as either active or passive, depending on whether they use power supplied by the electronic control unit (ECU) to operate. **Active sensors** use current supplied by the ECU to operate an internal transducer, signal conditioning circuit while **passive sensors** do not (**FIGURE 24-1**). A sensor, such as a variable resistor-type sensor, may use electrical current, but if the sensing element that generates the signals does not require current to condition the output signal of the sensor in some way, it is a passive sensor.

Switches as Sensors

LO 24-2 Explain the operation of switches as circuit input devices.

Switches are the simplest sensors of all, because they are found in only one of two states—open or closed. Simple switches typically have no resistance in the closed position and infinite resistance in the open position. While they are supplied current, switches do not require power to operate so they are considered passive-type sensors. Switches are categorized as sensors whenever they provide information to an electronic control system. The data may indicate a physical value, such as open or closed, up or down, or high or low (e.g., a coolant level sensor or oil pressure switch), or it may indicate on and off (e.g., a brake light switch).

Switches as Digital Signals

The simplest digital signal is a single pole single throw (SPST) switch. It is found in either an open or closed state. The on/off, open/closed state data provided by this switch can provide input information to an ECU required for decision making. For example, the decision to start an engine based on whether a transmission is in neutral or the clutch is disengaged depends on the signal from a switch (**FIGURE 24-2**). A zero-volt signal typically indicates an open switch, while five or 12 volts is interpreted as a closed switch. Ignition, brake, or door switches provide similar data to ECU to answer simple yes or no, open or closed, or on or off questions posed by control system logic.

Pull-Up and Pull-Down Switches

Switches are further categorized by their connection to a current source and polarity of current switch on or off through the ECU. When the switch is connected between the ECU

and a battery positive, the switch is known as a **pull-up switch** (**FIGURE 24-3**). A circuit inside the control module monitoring the switch status measures the voltage supplied to the ECU pin. When the switch closes, the ECU sees positive ignition switch voltage. When it opens, no current flows or 0 volts is measured

FIGURE 24-1 This opened pressure sensor is an active sensor. Note the integrated circuit inside used to condition the transducers measurement of physical data into an electrical signal used by the electronic control unit (ECU).

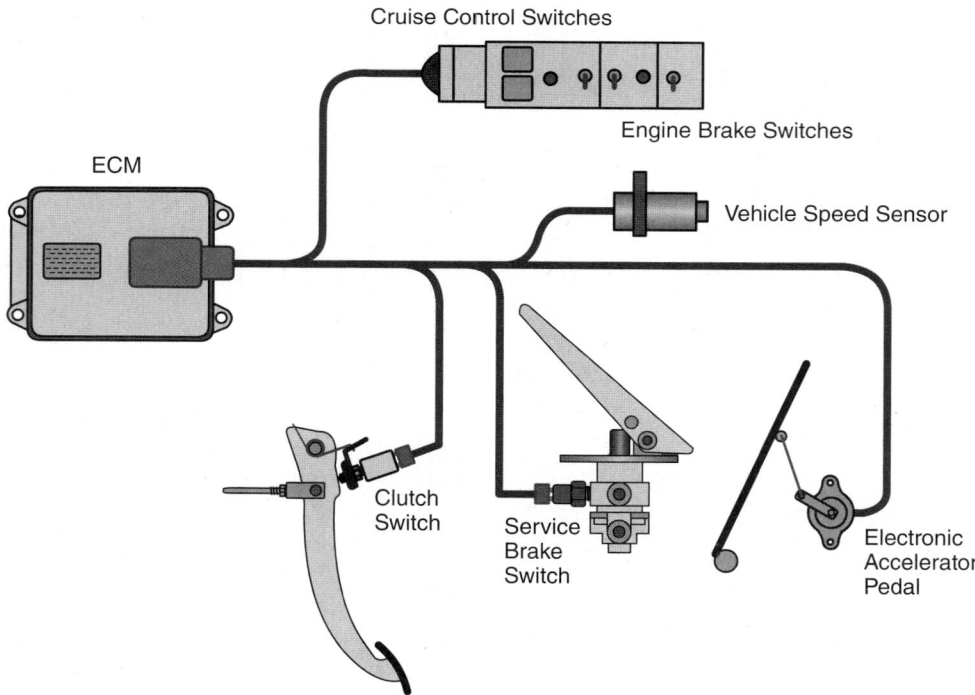

FIGURE 24-2 Examples of some basic switched inputs: clutch, brake, cruise control, and engine brake.

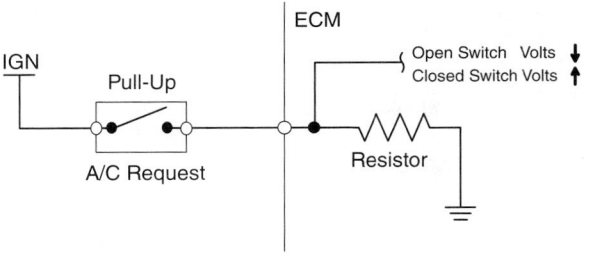

FIGURE 24-3 When a positive polarity is switched and supplied to the ECU, it is referred to as a pull-up switch.

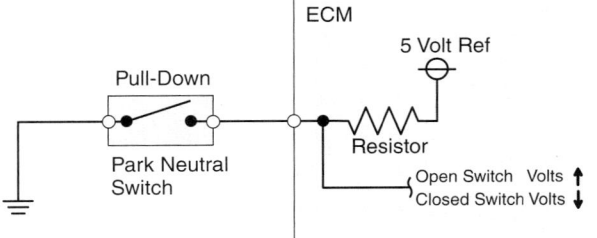

FIGURE 24-4 When a negative polarity is switched and supplied to the ECU, it is known as a pull-down switch.

between the ignition switch and the ECU. A resistor inside the ECU limits current flowing through the pull-up switch. Voltage at the ECU pin monitored inside the ECU determines whether the switch status is opened or closed. This information is then supplied to control logic.

A **pull-down switch** is connected between the ECU and a negative ground current potential (**FIGURE 24-4**). When the switch is closed, negative ground current flows between the ECU and switch to reach the +5 Vref located behind a current-limiting resistor, which prevents excessive current flow through the circuit. Most current flows across the pull-down resistor, but some are diverted to a voltage-sensing circuit inside the ECU.

When this happens, the ECU measures the voltage dropped across the pull-down resistor inside the ECU. When the switch opens, the voltage measured by the ECU voltage-sensing circuit rises to five volts since the less-resistive pathway through the switch is no longer available. Voltage data provides information to control system logic that reports the switch as either opened or closed.

Smart-Diagnosable Switches

Disconnected switches, shorted switch wiring, and resistive switch contacts cannot be diagnosed using open or closed diagnostic logic. For example, if an air conditioning system's high-pressure or low-pressure switches are defective or disconnected, the wrong information is supplied to a control module operating the system and the ability to protect or operate the system is lost. Furthermore, isolating the fault can be time-consuming because the electrical circuit needs to be traced and tested in addition to other diagnostic tests. To differentiate a disconnected switch from an open switch, resistors are placed in series, in parallel, or use two or more resistors installed in both series and parallel resistors with the switch. See **FIGURE 24-5**.

Carefully examine Figure 24-5. Note how the use of resistors arranged with the switches provides a unique voltage signal to the microcontroller. Arrangement of the resistors enables the microcontroller to not only identify problems in the wiring, but where in the circuit the faults are located. Unique voltage readings are produced by either the resistors and switch faults help pinpoint the fault location. Wiring between the switch and ECU can be identified having failures, such as shorted to ground or open-circuited wiring. When properly connected in a functioning circuit, the resistor incorporated into the switch in series has a calibrated resistance sensed by the microcontroller and measured as a specific voltage drop. If a switch has a resistor connected in parallel across its contacts, opening the switch

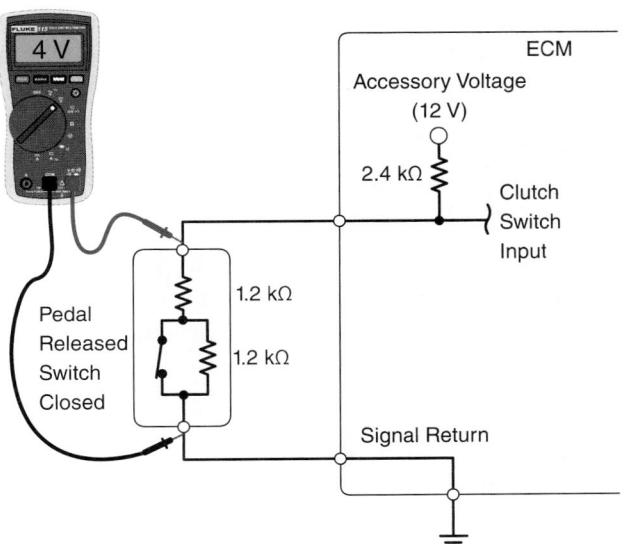

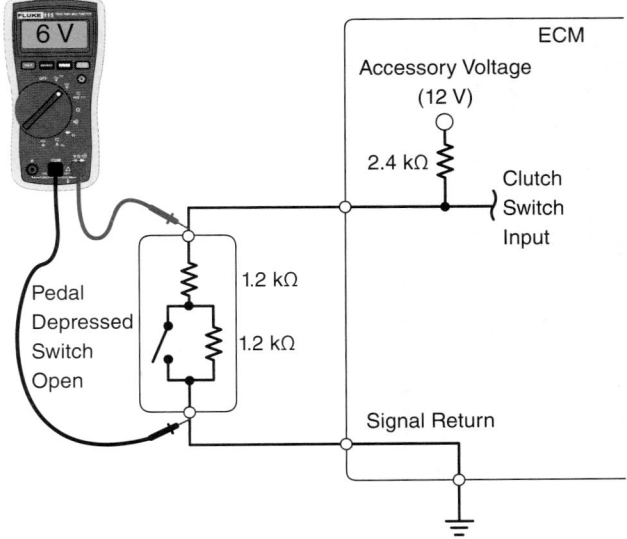

FIGURE 24-5 Placing resistors in series when opening and closing switches with different resistor values identifies switch status for each of these "smart switches."

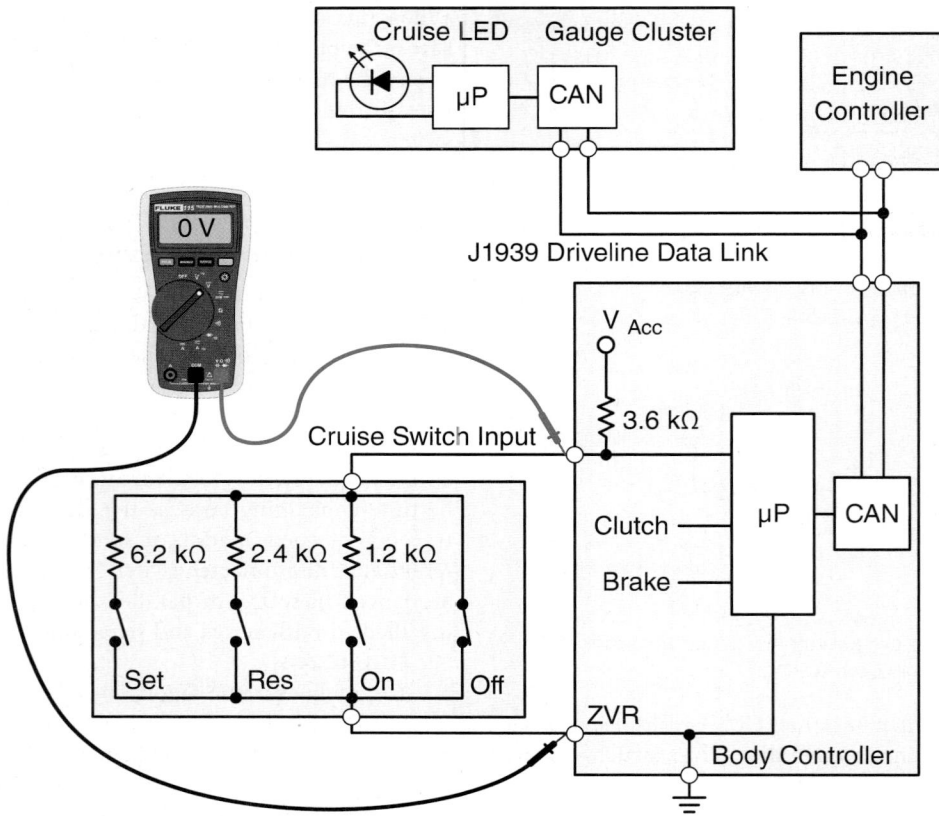

FIGURE 24-6 Resistors internal to the microcontroller are used to identify the status of different switches in a vehicle for proper control logic.

provides a specific voltage drop measured by the microcontroller. If the switch wiring is shorted to ground, to battery positive, or simply disconnected, logic programmed in the microcontroller identifies the much higher or lower circuit voltage as abnormal from the switch's expected resistance. When voltage drop measurements are abnormally high or low when the switch is expected to be either opened or closed, the microcontroller logs the appropriate fault code (**FIGURE 24-6**). Pull-up resistors can be connected in series with the switches to further enhance the diagnostic capabilities of the microcontroller. Clutch, brake light, or air conditioning (A/C) pressure switches often use these arrangements because of their critical operating functions.

Reference Voltage and Zero Volt Return

For active-type sensors requiring power from the ECU to function, positive direct current is supplied by **reference voltage (Vref)**. The use of reference voltage (+Vref) and zero-volt return (ZVR) are important concepts to understand when examining sensors and circuit operation. Vref refers to a precisely regulated positive voltage supplied to sensors. ZVR is the negative polarity or ground side of the sensors supply of current. Both Vref and ZVR current signals originate from inside the ECU and are conditioned or "cleaned-up" to eliminate any electrical interference that could create unwanted signal noise or errors. Vref value is typically +5 volts direct current (VDC), but manufacturers

occasionally use 8 or 12 volts for some sensors. Active sensors use Vref to energize transducers inside the sensor body, which have electrical signals conditioned or further processed by integrated circuits.

Another important use for reference voltage is to help calculate the unit value of the physical variable measured by a voltage drop across the sensor. The value of the sensor signal measurement is reported as a proportional voltage less than Vref, but it is converted by the ECU to report a temperature, position, angle, percentage, or level. During the process when sensor voltage signals are sampled and converted from an analog to digital format, the conversion is sometimes reported as a **sensor count**. A sensor count value refers to the amount of change from a baseline measurement that is detected by the final reported measurement. Detroit Diesel is an example of one manufacturer that duplicates its reports of sensor data measurements in counts to represent a digital value for a conversion from analog to digital measurement.

A very important concept to understand how sensor signal voltages are measured is the microcontroller's use of a voltage-dividing circuit. Voltage dividing circuits are used to discover the unknown resistance or voltage drop through a part of a circuit. By connecting another resistor in series with either the signal voltage of an active sensor or Vref current supplied to a resistive sensor, voltage signals are measured by a microcontroller. Using the concept of voltage dividing means splitting the voltage drop in a circuit across a known and unknown resistance. If in a series circuit the voltage drop across a known resistance can be accurately measured, the unknown is calculated mathematically. Whether it is sensor signal voltage from an active sensor or sensor resistance of a passive sensor, voltage dividing principles are based on Kirchhoff's Law. Kirchhoff's Law states the sum of the voltage drops in a series circuit equals source voltage (**FIGURE 24-7**). Practically applied, the electrical law predicts that if +5 Vref source voltage is returned to the ECU with one volt dropped across either a pull-up or pull-down resistor inside the ECU, the external sensor would have a voltage drop of four volts or a signal voltage of four volts (4 volts drop + 1 volt drop = 5 volts source). Or, if the sensor is supplying an unknown output signal voltage, the voltage drop measured across a resistor of known value indicates what the signal voltage value is (**FIGURE 24-8**). For example, if a 2 volt drop is measured across the internal resistor, the ECU would know a 2.5 volt signal voltage is supplied by the sensor if the maximum voltage it supplies is +4.5 volts. Again, inside the ECU, a voltmeter-like circuit measures the voltage dropped across a known resistance of either a pull-up or pull-down resistor **FIGURE 24-9**. The voltage data is converted to a digital signal to produce a sensor reading with the appropriate units of measurement. **FIGURE 24-10** shows how +5 Vref is connected to sensor circuits and is used in voltage drop calculations performed by an ECU to measure sensor resistance.

Never perform a wiring repair to a sensor circuit by connecting the zero-volt return circuit to chassis ground. The sensor circuit will work, but electrical signal noise from the alternator on the ground circuit and other electrical devices can be amplified by a ground loop inside the ECU. Ground loops are created when there is a difference between chassis and ECU ZVR ground voltage. Because charging system and battery voltage can also vary, electrical signals converted to physical values can have errors and report incorrect data.

Resistive Sensors

LO 24-3 Identify and describe the construction and operation of resistive type sensors.

Resistive sensors are a category of sensors that condition or change a Vref signal through voltage drop across the sensor and supply a signal voltage output proportional to the measured

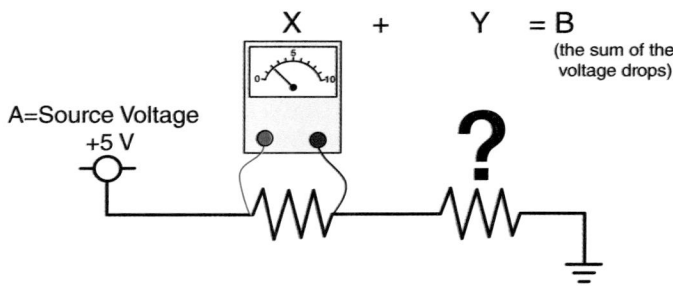

B (the sum of the voltage drops) Always = A

B = X + Y = A
Unknown Value Y = A − X
Y = 5 volts − 2 volts = 3 volts

FIGURE 24-8 Voltage dividing circuits calculate the value of an unknown resistance by placing a resistor of known value in series with an unknown voltage or resistance.

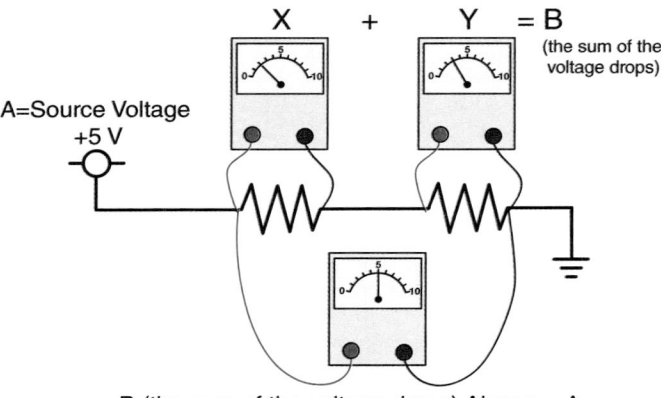

FIGURE 24-7 Kirchhoff's Law states that the sum of the voltage drops in a series circuit should equal source voltage.

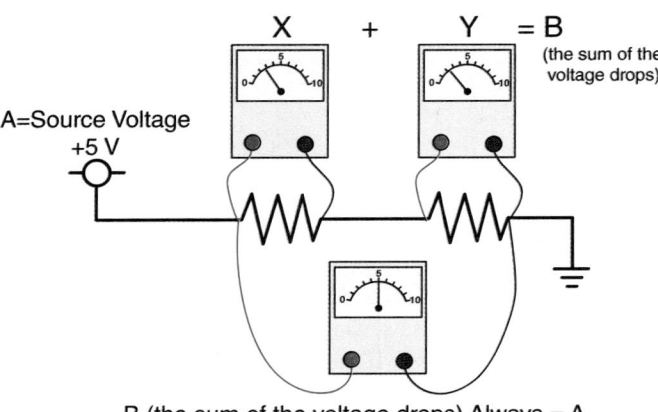

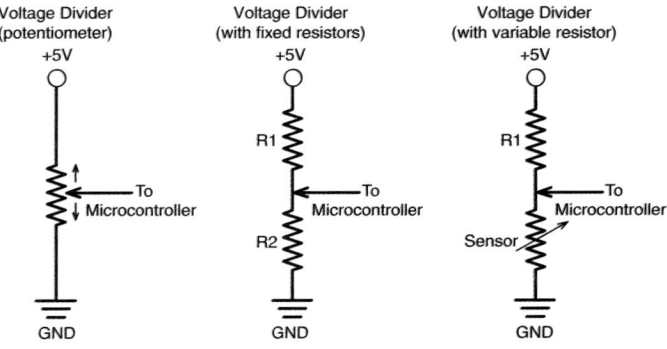

FIGURE 24-9 Depending on whether a sensor has a variable resistance, is a switch with fixed resistance, or is a potentiometer, the microcontroller calculates the resistance or voltage using a voltage dividing circuit.

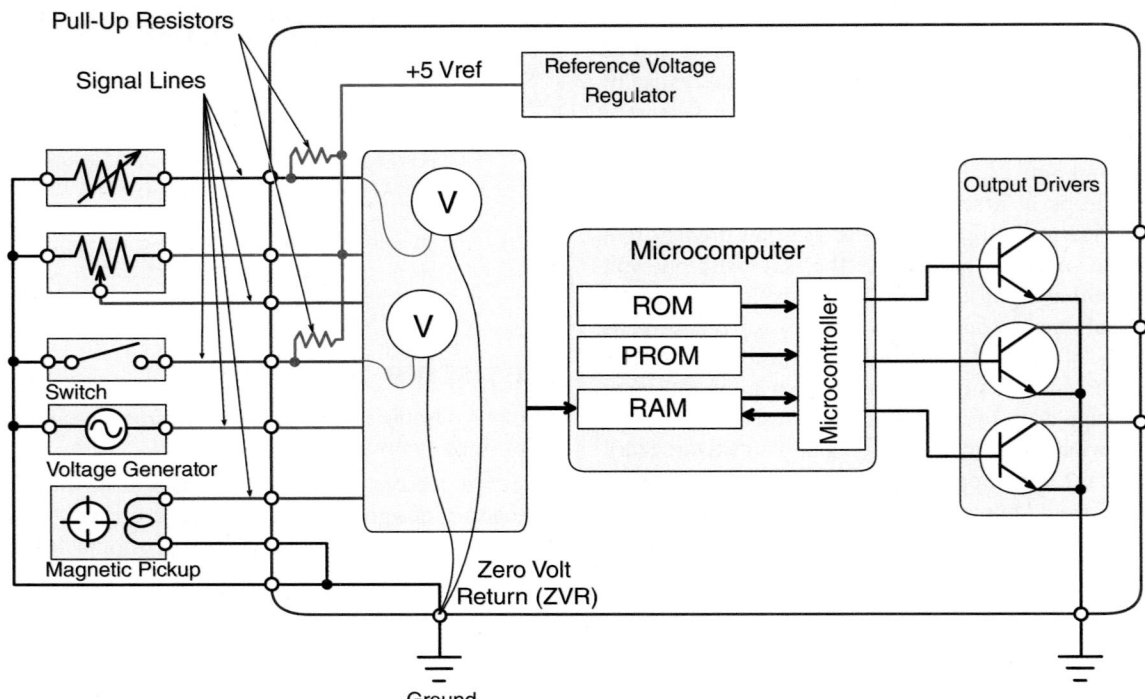

FIGURE 24-10 Reference voltage is supplied to power active sensors or to accurately calculate voltage drop across the resistance of a passive-type sensor. The resistor in series with the reference voltage also limits current to the sensors if it shorts to ground.

physical state. Many variations of resistive sensors are used. Temperature and position sensors are the most common. Resistive-type sensors are either two or three wire with sensors.

Thermistors

A **thermistor** is a temperature-sensitive variable resistor commonly used to measure coolant, oil, fuel, exhaust, and air temperatures. The name itself combines the words thermal and resistor. With the exception of the type used in exhaust systems and other very high temperature areas, thermistors have two-wires connected to a semiconductor-like material that changes resistance according to temperature. When they are supplied Vref they have a variable voltage output, which means thermistors provide analog data to microcontroller circuits. When the sensor is measuring air temperature, such as in an intake manifold, the sensor is often constructed with a plastic body to minimize heat transfer from surrounding metal. When used to measure coolant or oil temperature, the sensor element is enclosed in a brass case to make it more responsive to temperature change (**FIGURE 24-11**).

Two types of thermistors are used in commercial vehicles: negative and positive temperature coefficient. In a negative temperature coefficient (NTC) thermistor, the resistance decreases as the temperature increases (**FIGURE 24-12**). In a positive temperature coefficient (PTC) thermistor, the resistance increases as the temperature increases (**FIGURE 24-13** and **FIGURE 24-14**).

The most common type of thermistor is an NTC, in which the sensor's resistance goes down as the temperature goes up. So, when the sensor is cold and temperature is low, the sensor

FIGURE 24-11 Three thermistor applications. **A.** For intake manifold temperature. **B.** For coolant temperature. **C.** For intake manifold temperature. Note the semiconductor material in the fast-response, air-intake thermistor.

resistance is high, and the microcontroller measures *less* voltage dropped across an internal resistor connected in series compared to the larger voltage dropped across the highly resistive sensor. This voltage drop across the sensor is interpreted as a temperature value. Likewise, when the sensor warms, the internal resistance of the sensor decreases, and less voltage is dropped across the sensor. If less voltage is dropped by the sensor, *more* voltage is dropped across an internal resistor connected in series with Vref. The microcontroller measures this voltage drop across the internal resistor to produce voltage data proportional to temperature.

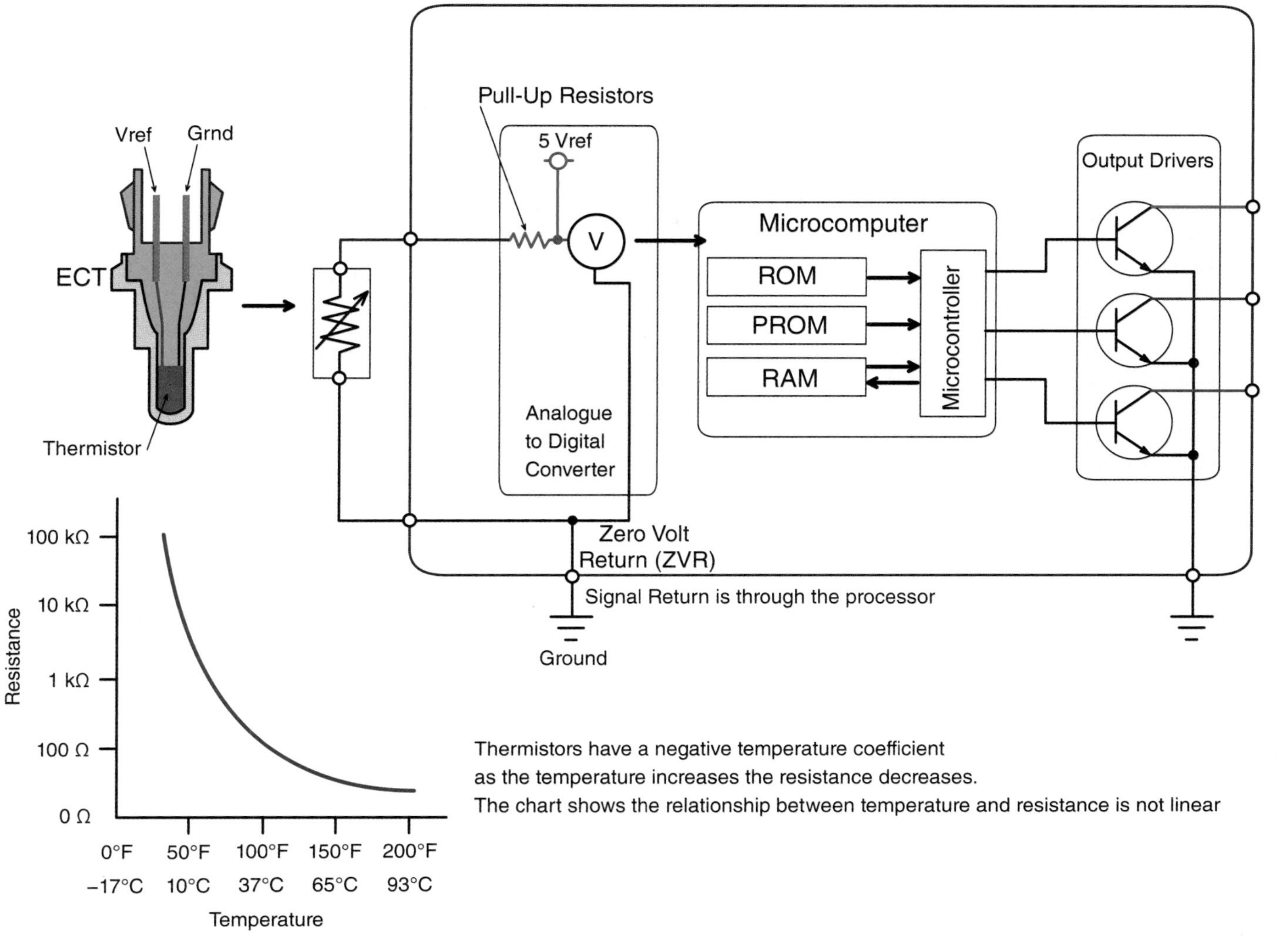

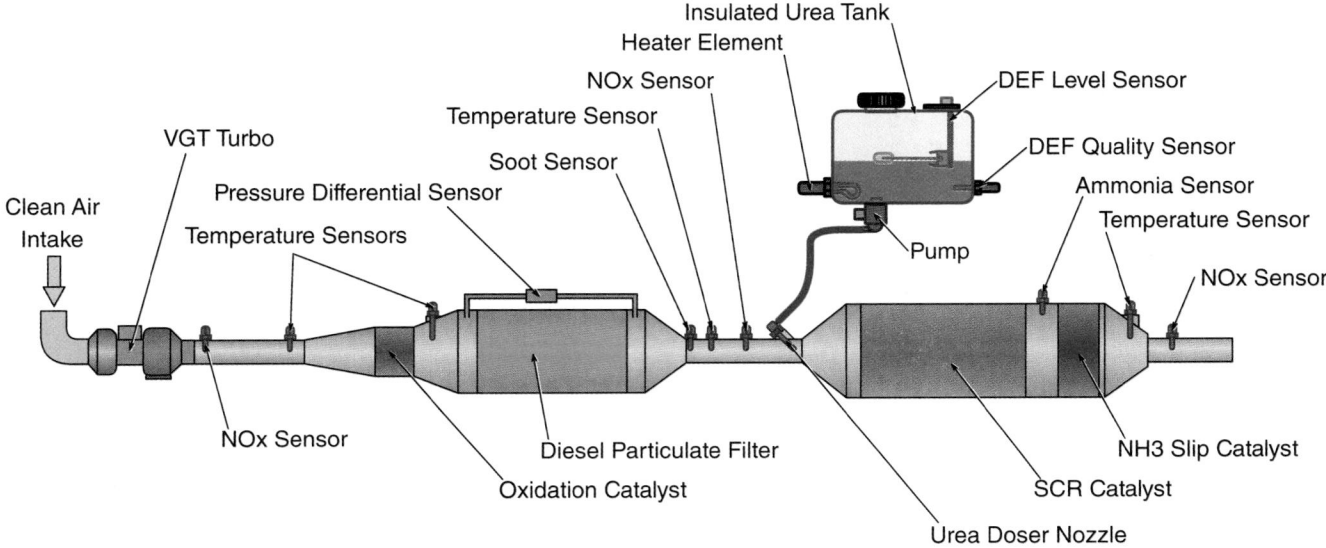

Thermistors have a negative temperature coefficient as the temperature increases the resistance decreases. The chart shows the relationship between temperature and resistance is not linear

FIGURE 24-12 A thermistor circuit. Note the graph that illustrates the relationship between temperature and resistance.

FIGURE 24-13 The diesel exhaust system is rich with sensor data. PTC thermistors are found in the exhaust system and increase their resistance when heated.

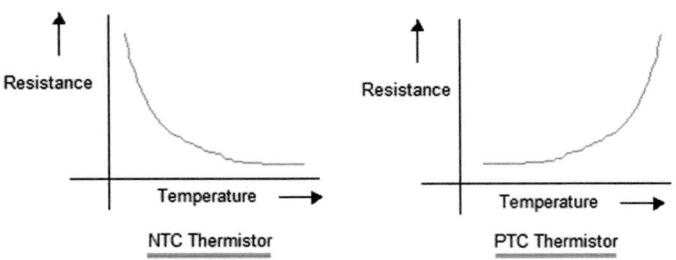

FIGURE 24-14 Comparing an NTC and PTC sensor response to temperature change. As temperature increases, an NTC resistance decreases but a PTC increases.

Positive temperature coefficient thermistors used in the exhaust system change resistance according to temperature. Nickel alloy wires that are commonly used inside these sensors become more resistive when heated. Other PTC thermistors are made from ceramic or polymer plastic mixtures. In the case of PTC thermistors in the exhaust, increased exhaust temperatures produce higher sensor resistance. When sensor voltage drop is measured, its resistance is used by the microcontroller to predict the gas temperature. PTC thermistors in the exhaust are not like other exhaust temperature sensors, such as exhaust pyrometers using thermocouple operating principles. In thermocouples, current is generated when two dissimilar metals are joined and heated. The signal output is measured in millivolts and is proportional to temperature. Note, generally no microcontroller is used to convert a thermocouple signal. Because thermocouples have a more rugged construction, they can withstand high exhaust temperatures.

Soot Sensors

Contemporary diesel engines use two types of soot sensors, depending on where they are regulated — in Europe or North America. Soot sensors, required since 2015 on North American diesels that are heavy-duty onboard diagnostics (HD-OBD) compliant, are another type of simple resistive sensor. If soot, which is primarily made of electrically conductive carbon, accumulates on the sensor, its resistance decreases. Burning soot off the sensor during regeneration events cleans the sensor. If the sensor builds up soot too quickly, compared to the predicted maximum rate of accumulation, the voltage signal is used by the microcontroller to set a fault code for a leaking, cracked, or missing particulate filter (**FIGURE 24-15**).

Rheostats

Rheostats are also two-wire variable resistance sensors. They are not commonly used as input devices to an ECU, but are instead used to signal sending units, such as for fuel level and oil pressure (**FIGURES 24-16, 24-17**). Rheostats use a variable resistance, sliding, electrically conductive contact moving along a resistive wire or carbon track. When current passes through the resistive wire, the sliding contact conducts current flow from the wire. Voltage at the sliding contact varies, depending on its position along the resistive wire. If the sliding contact supplies a variable positive voltage, when it is closer to the positive end of the resistive track, its voltage will be higher than when it is farthest away from the positive end.

Three-Wire Resistive Sensors

Three-wire sensors, regardless of how they appear or what function they perform, have a common wiring configuration: They all have ground, signal return, and positive voltage reference wire leads (**FIGURE 24-18**).

One wire provides reference voltage to the sensor. If it is an active sensor, reference voltage supplies positive current to operate an integrated circuit chip or transducer inside the device. A second wire, the ZVR, is also used to supply negative current to the transducer inside the sensor body. The ZVR negative polarity circuit connects to ground through the ECU. In three-wire analog-type sensors, the ZVR has two purposes. One is to provide a point at the sensor to monitor the resistive element inside the sensor. The diagnostic system checks for the correct voltage drop across the entire resistive element to verify the circuit is complete. The second important purpose is to provide a reference point to measure voltage drop between it and the positive polarity sensor signal circuit. This is an important point to remember when testing sensors supplying analog data, such as a pressure or throttle position sensor: Sensor voltage is always measured between the signal wire and ZVR

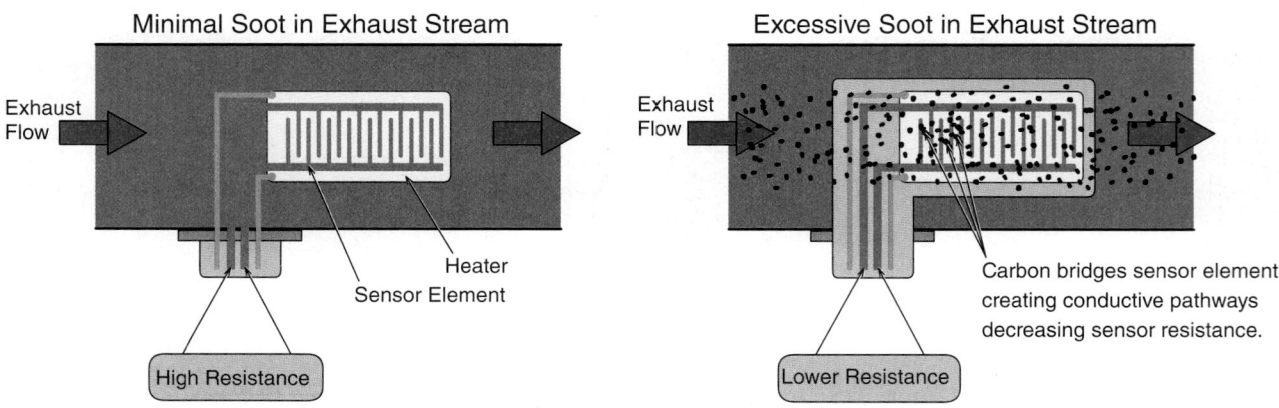

FIGURE 24-15 Soot sensors installed after the exhaust particulate filter accumulate electrically conductive carbon. If the resistance of the carbon path falls below a specific threshold, the filter is likely leaking or missing.

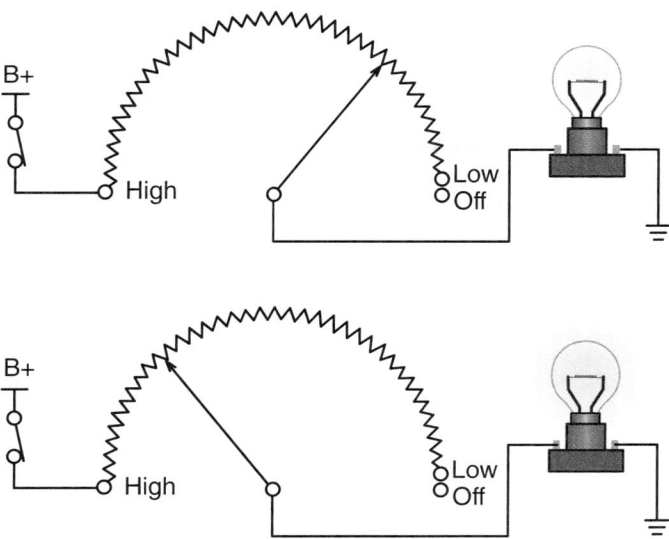

FIGURE 24-16 Operation of a rheostat controlling the intensity of a light bulb.

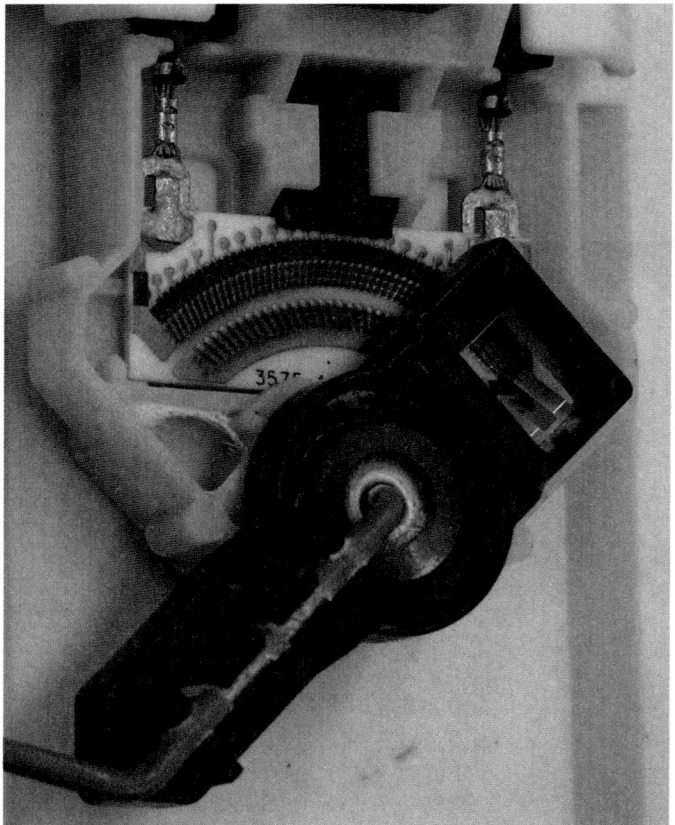

FIGURE 24-17 A rheostat for a fuel level sending unit. The sliding wiper transfers current from one resistive track to another. A varying voltage signal is supplied by the wiper.

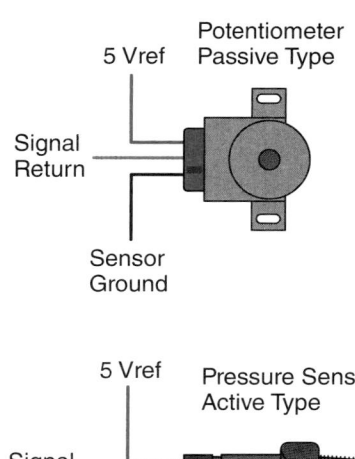

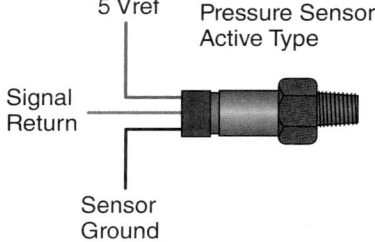

FIGURE 24-18 Three-wire reference voltage sensors have a ground, a positive signal return, and positive voltage reference wire lead.

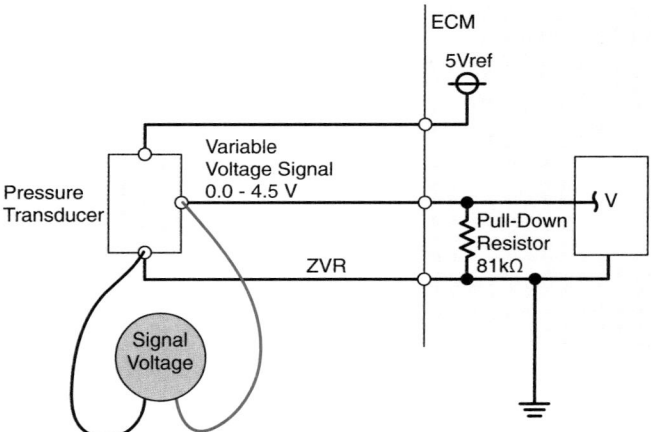

FIGURE 24-19 Sensor pinpoint measurements for two- and three-wire digital and analog sensors are made between ZVR and the signal wire.

ground (**FIGURE 24-19**). Note that on some digital-type three-wire sensors, such as a Hall-effect sensor measuring rotational speed, such as on an engine, camshaft, or even some antilock brakes system (ABS) wheel speed sensors, the digital wave form

is measured between Vref and the signal voltage. A resistor is placed between the signal and Vref to drop the +5 volt signals present on both pins in order for a waveform viewer or graphing meter to display the signal. This procedure is necessary because both the Vref and signal wire leads on a digital three-wire sensor have a very rapidly changing positive polarity voltage operating close to +5 volts. Without the resistor, no measurable voltage change is available, so a resistor is needed between the two points to drop voltage and produce a signal waveform on a graphing meter. (**FIGURE 24-20**).

The third wire of a three-wire sensor is a signal return from the sensor. This sensor circuit provides a positive voltage proportional to the physical value measured by the sensor. If pressure is the physical input measured, the signal wire data carries an analog voltage signal proportional to pressure. Typically, low

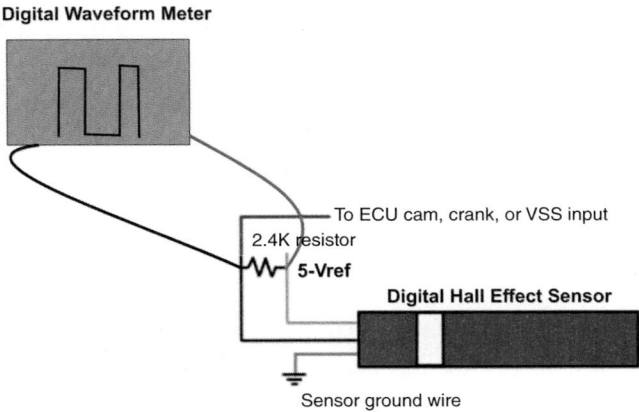

FIGURE 24-20 A resistor needs to be placed between the two positive sensor wires: Signal and Vref to graph measure or occasionally measure a digital signal.

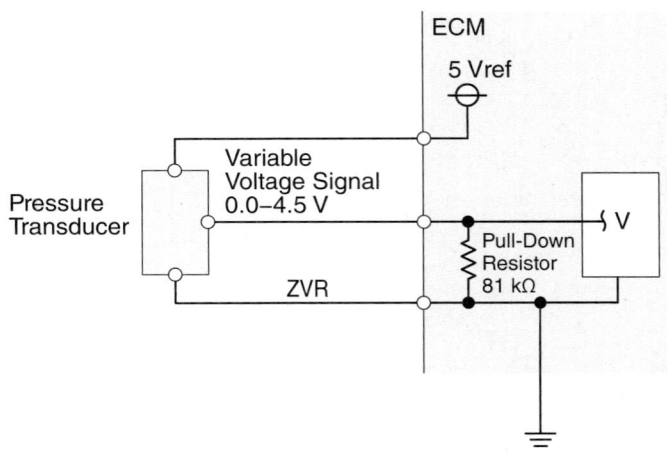

FIGURE 24-21 The ECU supplies the +5 Vref and ZVR ground. In this sensor, the ECU measures signal voltage across a pull-down resistor between the + signal supply and ZVR.

voltage of, for example, 0.8 volts, represents little to no pressure, while 3.9 volts represents high pressure, depending on the range of the sensor.

The advantage of using three-wire sensors is that they provide comprehensive diagnostic information about the sensor and its circuit operation. Sending units can be constructed with reduced complexity and expense and yet still provide the ECU with data to operate an engine, transmission, or other device. However, sending units lack the capability to self-monitor circuit operation. Consider an open or shorted to ground signal wire from a single-wire sensor. In this case, there is no means by which the ECU could accurately detect the fault condition. The signal wire could be broken or rubbed through and, with some fault conditions, such as a short to another positive voltage source, the voltage data received by the ECU is not different from normal. It is very labor-intensive to find an electrical fault based on only an operational symptom—if no fault codes or malfunction indicator lights are available to identify a malfunction.

The ECU has the capability to monitor and diagnose two- and three-wire sensor circuits to an extent not possible with single-wire sensors. By monitoring the voltage range of the Vref to ZVR path, ZVR and signal voltage, and reference voltage, the ECU can determine if the sensor and associated circuits are functioning correctly and within normal voltage ranges (**FIGURE 24-21**). Sensor values can also be compared with expected values to determine if the data is within range or rational. An explanation of how sensors and electronic circuits perform self-diagnostics and generate codes is covered in the service section of this chapter.

Potentiometers

Potentiometers are similar to rheostats in that they vary signal voltage depending on the position of a sliding contact or wiper moving across a resistive material. They are three-wire sensors with the signal wire connected to the internal wiper that moves across a resistive pathway. The Vref and

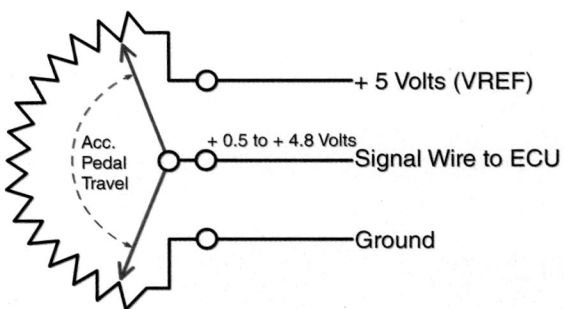

FIGURE 24-22 The throttle position sensor can be a variable resistor-type potentiometer.

ZVR are at each end of the pathway in devices like the throttle position sensors. Another classification name given to a potentiometer is a ratiometric sensor. A **ratiometric** sensor has an unamplified output signal that changes in proportion to Vref. Potentiometers supply analog data to processing circuits (**FIGURE 24-22**).

A common application of a potentiometer is a position sensor, such as the exhaust gas recirculation (EGR) valve position sensor or throttle position sensor (TPS) (**FIGURE 24-23**). This sensor is connected to a throttle pedal and provides data regarding the driver's desired engine speed or power output by measuring pedal angle or travel. The ECU measures the voltage drop between ZVR and the signal pins on the ECU to calculate pedal position. Voltage sensed at the signal wire is proportional to the pedal travel. This means that at idle or part throttle, the voltage at the signal wire is low because the wiper with signal voltage is placed farthest from the +5 Vref, but closest to the ZVR. In the event of a fault, such as a wire to the pedal is broken, or the pedal is disconnected, this arrangement of low voltage signalling idle speed keeps the engine speed at a safe low speed. Pressing on the throttle pedal typically produces increasing voltage from the signal wire as the sensor's internal wiper moves closer to the +5 Vref end of the resistive element.

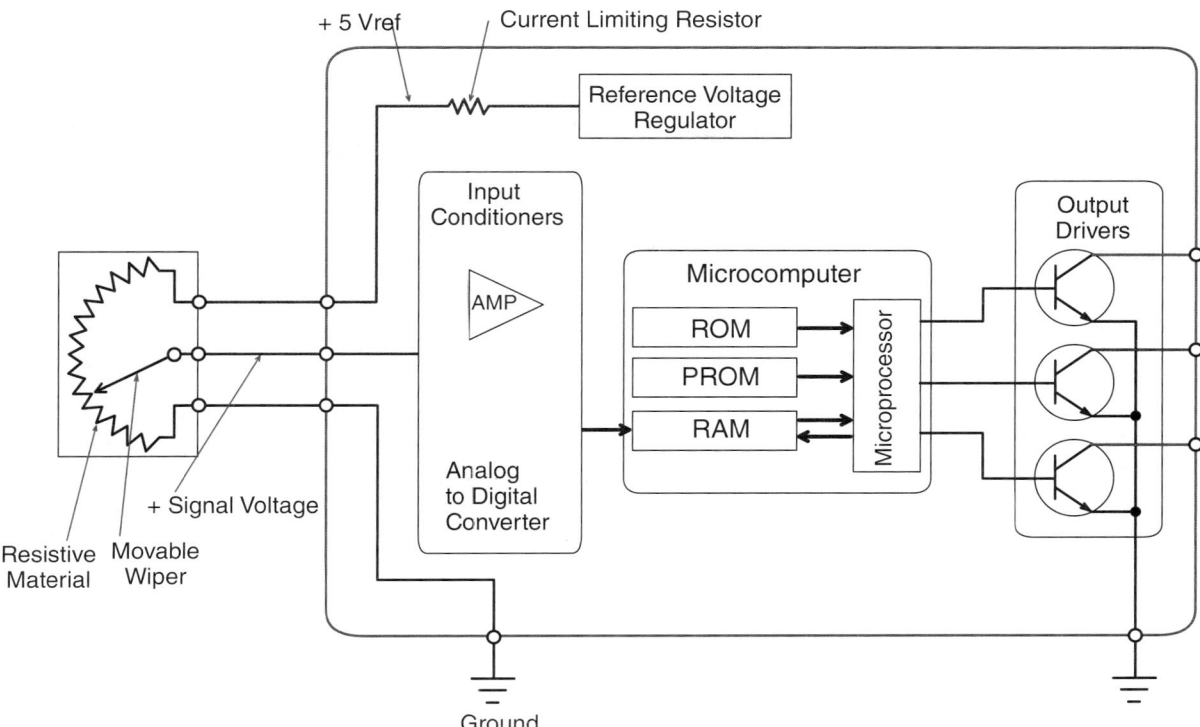

FIGURE 24-23 The TPS circuit commonly uses a potentiometer to measure throttle angle.

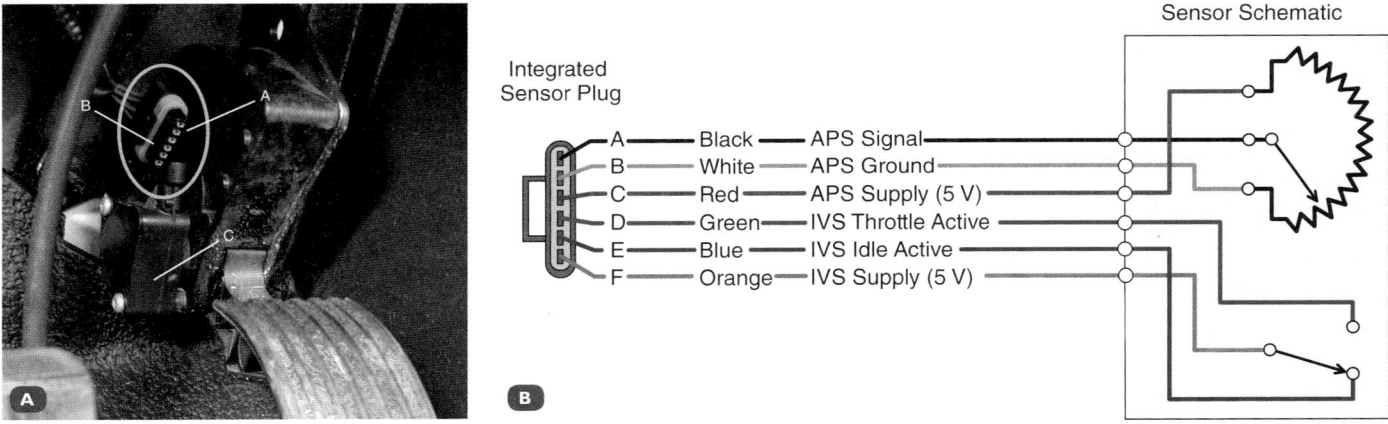

FIGURE 24-24 The IVS is usually integrated with the TPS. The IVS uses reference voltage and switches the state of a normally open and a normally closed switch when moved off idle. **A.** Three sensor wires (A), three IVS wires (B), and the throttle position sensor (C). **B.** Color coding for integrated sensor plug.

Idle Validation Switches and Throttle Position Sensors

A short circuit or incorrect data from the TPS, also called the accelerator position sensor (APS), can potentially cause uncontrolled acceleration of an engine. For safety reasons, manufacturers build an additional safety system to verify commanded throttle position. One common throttle safety system is the **idle validation switch (IVS)**. This circuit uses two switches. At idle, one switch is open and the other closed.

Off idle, the switches change state, which means the normally open switch closes, and the normally closed switch opens (**FIGURE 24-24**). This data is used by the ECU to verify the driver has in fact moved the accelerator pedal and the circuit is not malfunctioning. At idle, the state of the switch must correspond to the TPS voltage sensed by the ECU. If the expected position sensor voltage and IVS position do not match, the ECU reverts engine speed to idle or does not allow the engine rpm to increase beyond idle speed.

Dual, Multiple-Path, and PWM Throttle Position Sensors

To improve reliability of a TPS and validate accelerator position signals, most manufacturers have now replaced the single TPS sensor track with a dual-track, or even three-path, TPS. The voltage of one sensor pathway is compared with another to verify that the sensor is operating at expected values (**FIGURE 24-25**). If there is an unexpected difference between the voltage signals, the engine only operates at idle speed. If one or even two of the resistive tracks wears out, the engine may still accelerate normally, but an APS fault is logged and the yellow fault warning indicator lamp illuminates. Dual-path TPSs are also potentiometers. Hall-effect TPSs are even more reliable, because they have no moving parts. This throttle position sensor uses an alternating current (AC) magnetic field to induce current in a rotor moved by the throttle pedal (**FIGURE 24-26**).

A circuit is used to convert the rotor's voltage into position which is interpreted as pedal position. This type of noncontact TPS sensor has no sliding friction parts to wear out (**FIGURE 24-27**).

A dual ratiometric sensor that uses Hall-effect technology can generate two analog outputs that are proportional to the pedal position. With these sensors, one output signal, called the primary signal, produces a voltage that is two times the voltage of the secondary output. Cummins has required this type of APS for their engines since 2007.

A pulse-width–modulated (PWM) sensor produces a digital-like throttle signal. Because it is PWM, an integrated circuit inside the sensor converts a potentiometer signal for pedal position into a pulse width. This means the width of the voltage pulses are proportional to the pedal position with the shortest on versus off time at idle or low speed demand. Caterpillar requires this type of throttle position sensor for its engines. The digital-like PWM signal makes the commanded

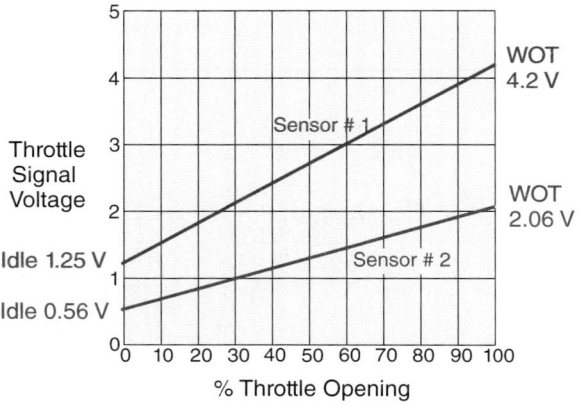

FIGURE 24-25 Voltages of accelerator position for the three-path sensor. Operating voltages are different for any given throttle angle. If one sensor fails, the other can supply a signal to operate the vehicle. If two signals fail, the vehicle typically only idles.

FIGURE 24-26 The position sensor in this VGT actuator uses a Hall-effect, non-contact-type sensor.

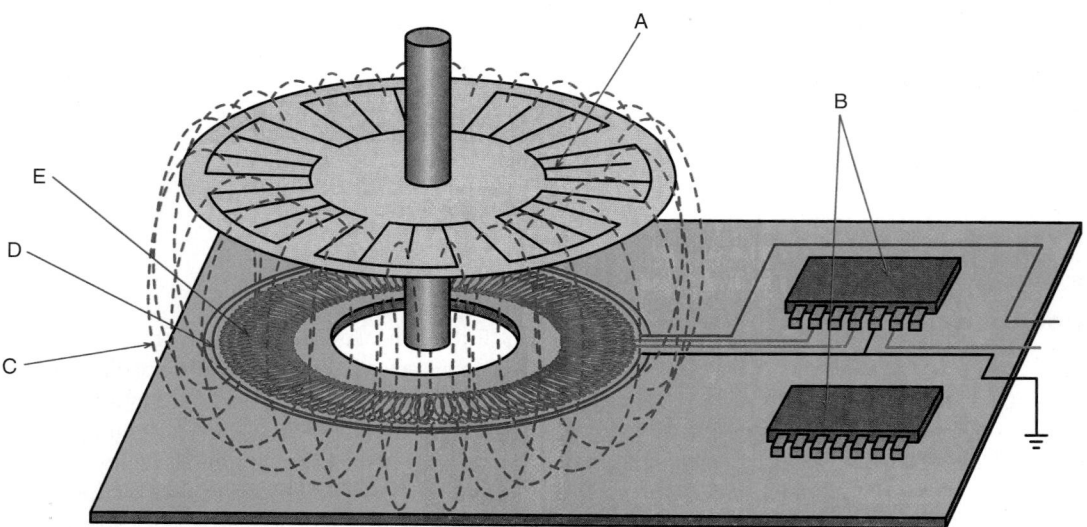

FIGURE 24-27 Hall-effect throttle position sensor. **A.** Conductive loops in rotor. **B.** Integrated circuits, APP1 and APP2. **C.** Electromagnetic field lines of force. **D.** Stator excitation coils. **E.** Stator receiver coils.

throttle position signal less vulnerable to voltage drop over long circuits in marine and off-road equipment (**FIGURE 24-28**).

Pressure Sensors

LO 24-4 Identify and describe the construction and operation of pressure sensors.

Pressure measurements, such as intake manifold boost, barometric pressure, and oil and fuel pressure, use two types of sensor technology: strain gauge resistive-type sensors and variable capacitance sensors. These are both active sensors that produce ratiometric analog output signals.

Strain Gauge Pressure Sensor

A strain gauge measures small changes in the resistance of tiny wires caused by stretching or contraction. Construction of this type of pressure-sensing device uses resistive wires, called strain gauge wires, embedded in a flexible glass block. Behind the block may be a vacuum chamber to provide a reference point of zero for measurement of absolute pressure. If the device measures gauge pressure, the chamber has atmospheric pressure as the reference value for zero pressure.

When the glass plate flexes under pressure, the small resistive wires in it stretch and change resistance slightly. (**FIGURE 24-29**). A Wheatstone bridge electrical circuit, which measures changes in resistance of an unknown variable resistor, is used to measure this small difference in resistance of the strain gauge wires which is used to calculate a signal proportional to pressure (**FIGURE 24-30**).

Piezoresistive Pressure Sensors

Piezoresistive sensors rely on the ability of certain mineral crystals to produce voltage or change resistance when compressed (**FIGURE 24-31**). Rather than using a strain gauge

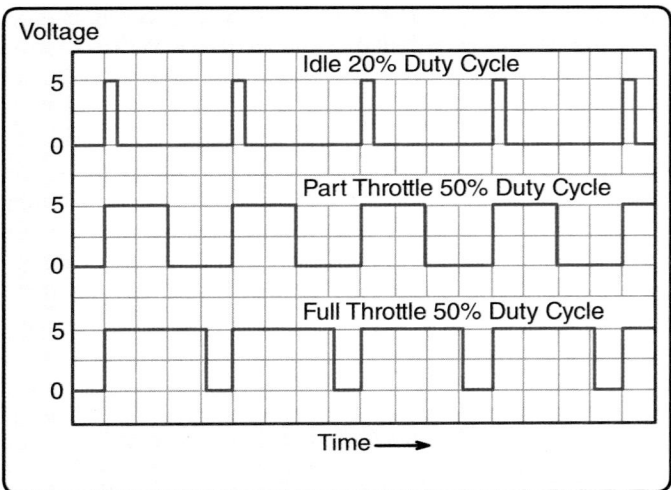

FIGURE 24-28 A varying duty cycle from Caterpillar's TPS is less sensitive to voltage drop over long circuits.

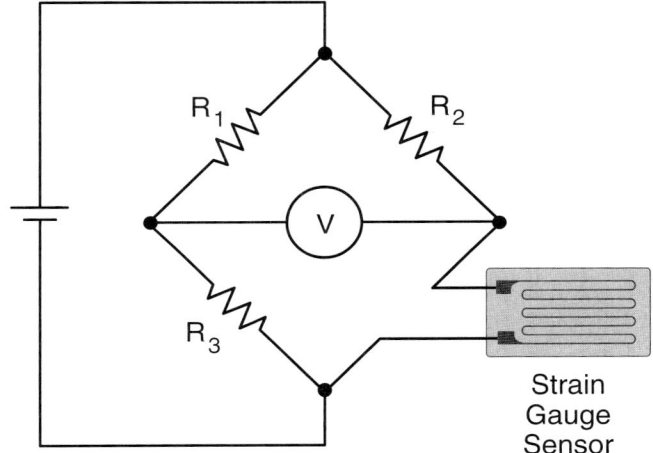

FIGURE 24-29 A strain gauge senses pressure using wires embedded in glass or on a metal film that changes resistance as it is stretched under pressure.

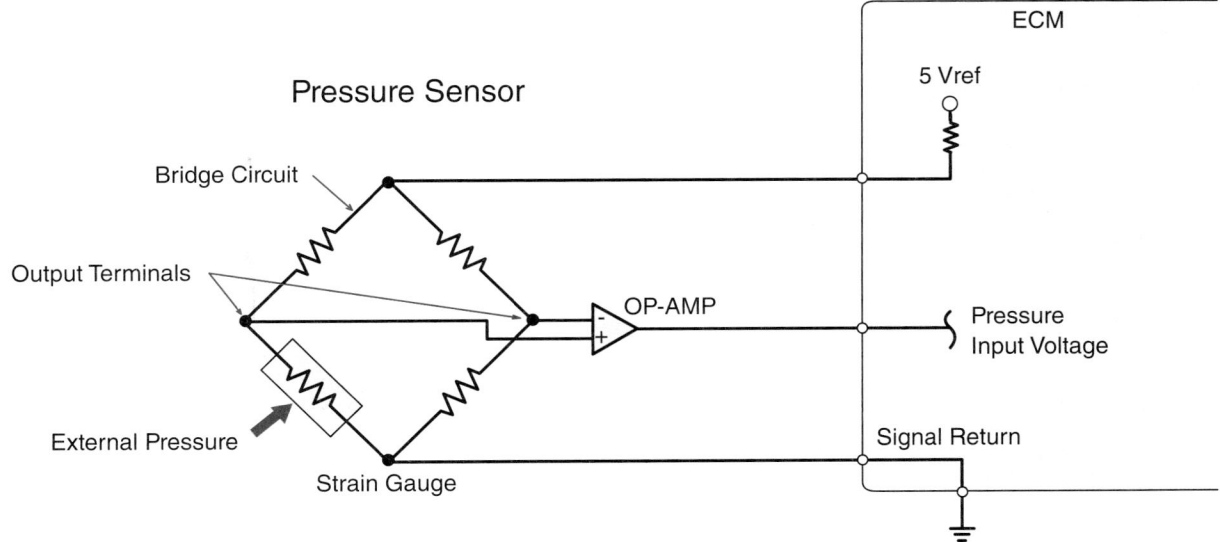

FIGURE 24-30 A Wheatstone bridge calculates the value of an unknown resistor using several other resistors of known fixed value.

wire construction, these sensors have a piezoresistive crystal arranged with a Wheatstone bridge to measure the change in resistance of the piezo crystal. These sensors produce analog electrical signals and are typically ratiometric-type sensors.

The advantage of piezoresistive-type sensors is their ability to measure very high pressures. Because of the sturdiness of the crystal, piezo sensors are better adapted to measuring vibration and dynamic or continuous pressure changes. Knock sensors measuring abnormal combustion signals are a common application of piezoresistive sensors. Another type of piezoresistive sensor uses mineral crystals arranged on a substrate of silicon (**FIGURE 24-32**). The crystals behave like a semiconductor to produce electrical signals

that are amplified and conditioned by internal circuits. Silicon-based piezoresistive sensors are very sensitive to slight pressure changes.

Variable Capacitance Pressure Sensor

A **variable capacitance pressure sensor** is an active sensor that measures both dynamic and static pressure. Though they are more expensive to manufacture than a piezoresistive or strain gauge sensor, the variable capacitance pressure sensor offers a greater range of measurement flexibility and more accurate readings. Because it is an active sensor, the stronger circuit signals to the ECU are not as vulnerable to voltage drop or electromagnetic interference.

Variable capacitance sensors use the distance between two metal plates, inside the sensor to measure pressure. The distance between the two plates is an electrical insulator called the dielectric strength. The time an electric charge takes to build-up on these plates varies with the dielectric strength (**FIGURE 24-33**). Because only one plate diaphragm moves in response to intake manifold, oil, fuel, or some other physical pressure, it changes the sensor's dielectric strength, allowing the sensor to measure pressure. The other plate is fixed and has on one side a reference vacuum or an atmospheric pressure chamber to calibrate it for accurate pressure readings. As pressure increases or decreases, the distance between the two plates changes. An electrical charge is applied to the fixed plate, and the time it takes to fully charge the opposite plate across the dielectric gap is measured. Charging time changes proportionally to the dielectric strength of the electrostatic field between the plates. An electronic circuit in the chip integrated inside the sensor measures the changing voltage/time value produced by the flexing plate and produces an analog output signal with a voltage of less than five volts. Pressure sensor signal voltage generally falls with decreasing pressure, which increases the distance between plates. Signal voltage increases as pressure goes up.

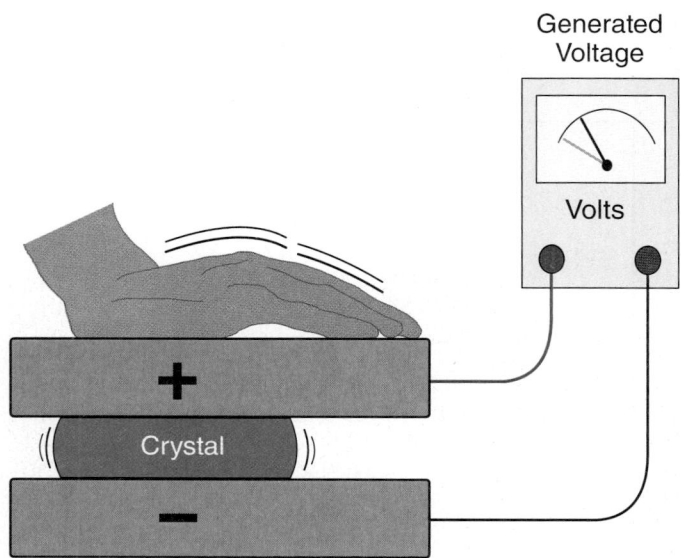

FIGURE 24-31 The piezoresistive principle.

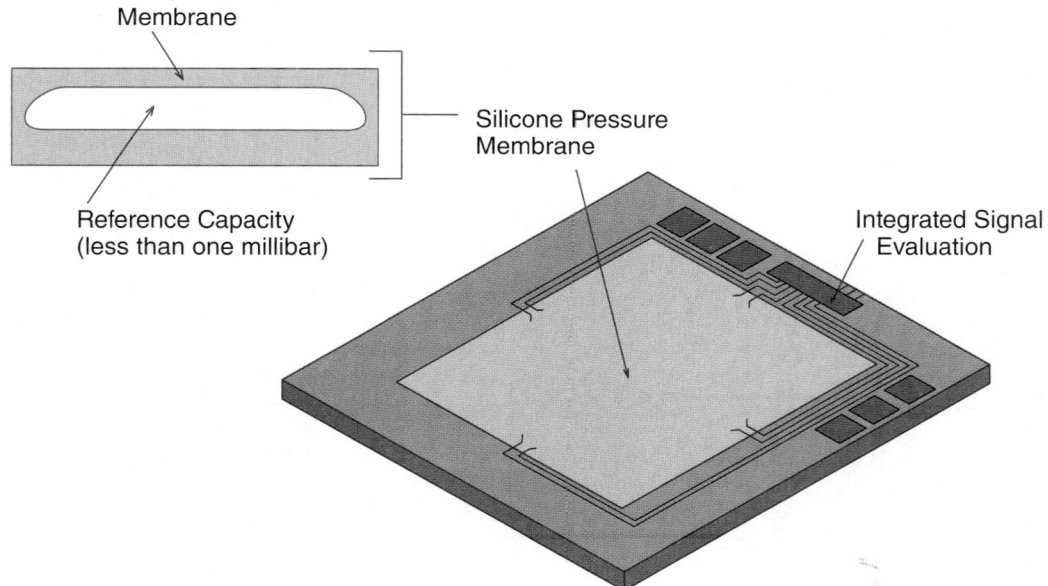

FIGURE 24-32 Construction of a silicon-based piezoresistive sensor. The silicone-ceramic material generates a voltage under pressure that is converted to an analog signal.

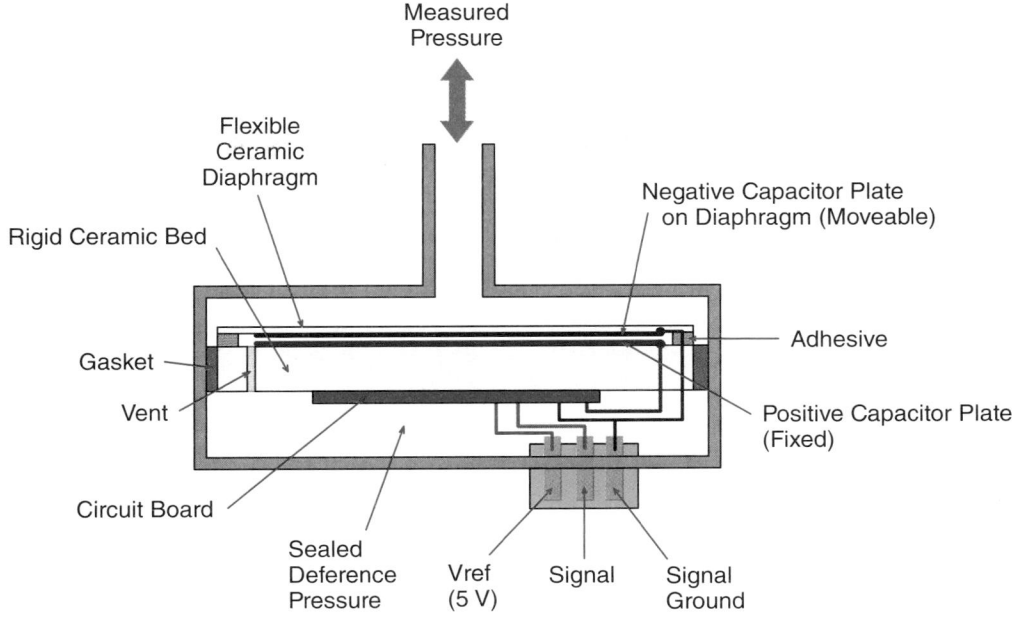

FIGURE 24-33 Cross section of a variable capacitance sensor.

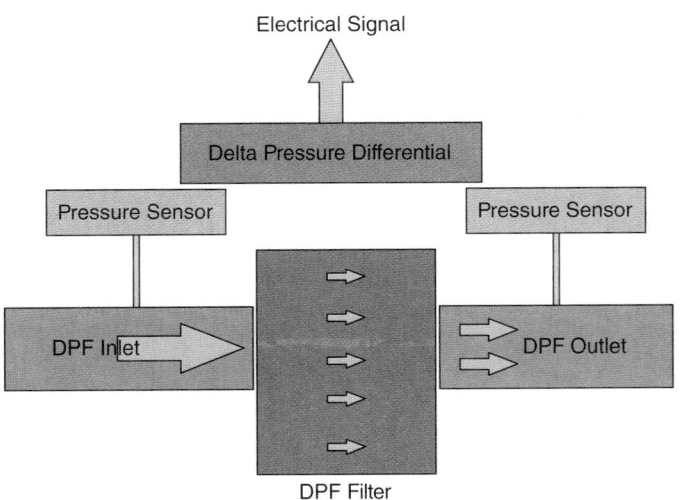

FIGURE 24-34 A pressure differential sensor combines two pressure sensors to generate a single output signal.

FIGURE 24-35 This pressure differential sensor for an EGR system has two ports, one located on each side of a venture.

Pressure Differential Sensors

Pressure differential sensors typically incorporate two pressure sensors with one output signal or two separate sensors with one or two output signals (**FIGURE 24-34**). These sensors are used to measure the soot and ash restriction in the particulate filter. Data from these sensors is also used to by a control module to calculate the mass or weight of EGR and other gases. The sensor is located across a restriction in a tube called a venturi. A pressure reading is taken on each side of the venturi. As the velocity or mass of gas flow increases, so does the pressure drop or differential across the restriction (**FIGURE 24-35**). When pressure data like this is combined with temperature data, the controller can calculate the weight of a gas like EGR gas entering the engine.

Voltage Generating Sensors

LO 24-5 Identify and describe the construction and operation of voltage generating sensors.

Voltage generating sensors include a wide variety of sensors that use operating principles enabling them to measure gas concentrations in the exhaust to measuring the speed of shaft, wheel, or engine. The simplest demonstration of voltage generating sensors is observed in the operation of what are called variable reluctance sensors, which use principles of magnetic induction to produce speed signals. Variable reluctance sensors are passive-type sensors and produce an analog signal of varying voltage and AC frequency. More complex sensors measuring gas concentrations of oxygen, NOx, and ammonia generate voltage in the sensor's transducers using galvanic reactions. A significant amount of signal conditioning is necessary to convert the voltages induced from platinum electrodes exposed to different levels of oxygen, ammonia, or NOx concentrations into a useful electrical signal.

Variable Reluctance Sensors

Variable reluctance (VR) sensors are two-wire sensors typically used to measure rotation of shafts and flywheels. Wheel speed, vehicle speed, engine speed, and camshaft and crankshaft position sensors are their most common applications (**FIGURE 24-36**). Signals from the camshaft and crankshaft VR

position sensors are used to calculate engine position for determining the beginning of engine firing order and injection timing. When graphed against time, the start of a leading and/or trailing edge of the AC waveform produced by the sensor data is used to calculate not only engine speed, but also degrees of crankshaft rotation (**FIGURE 24-37**).

The ability of a material to conduct or resist magnetic lines of force is known as reluctance. Variable reluctance sensors use changing sensor reluctance produced by the raised teeth and gaps of a moving reluctor wheel to induce current flow by changing magnetic field strengths inside the sensor. Voltage is induced in a variable reluctance sensor using two main parts:

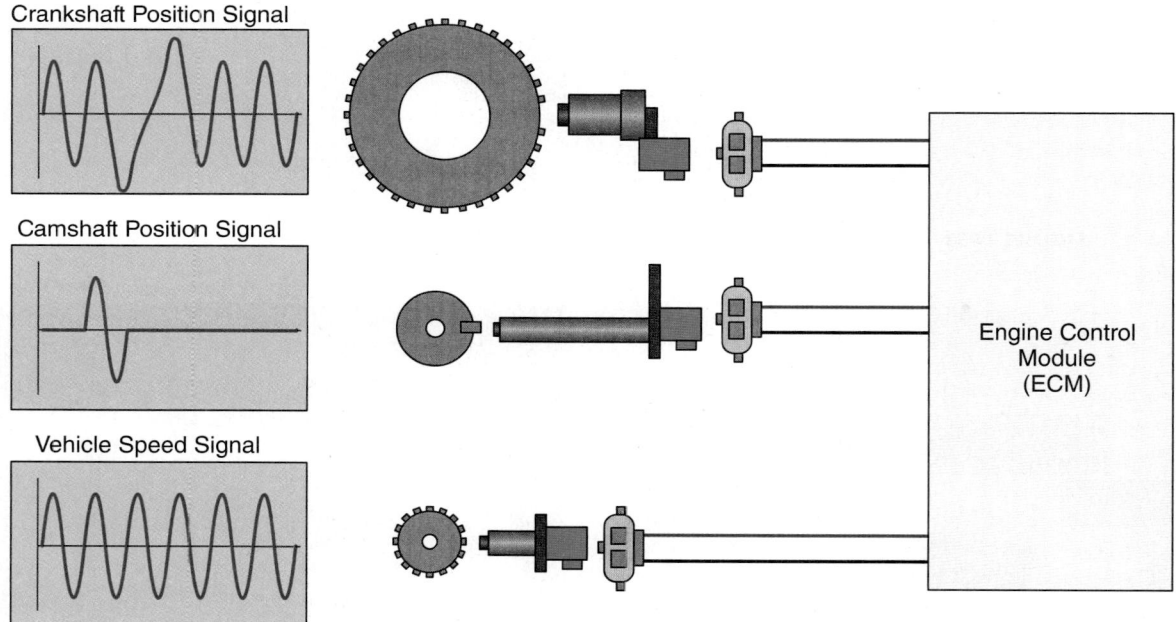

FIGURE 24-36 Common applications of variable reluctance sensors.

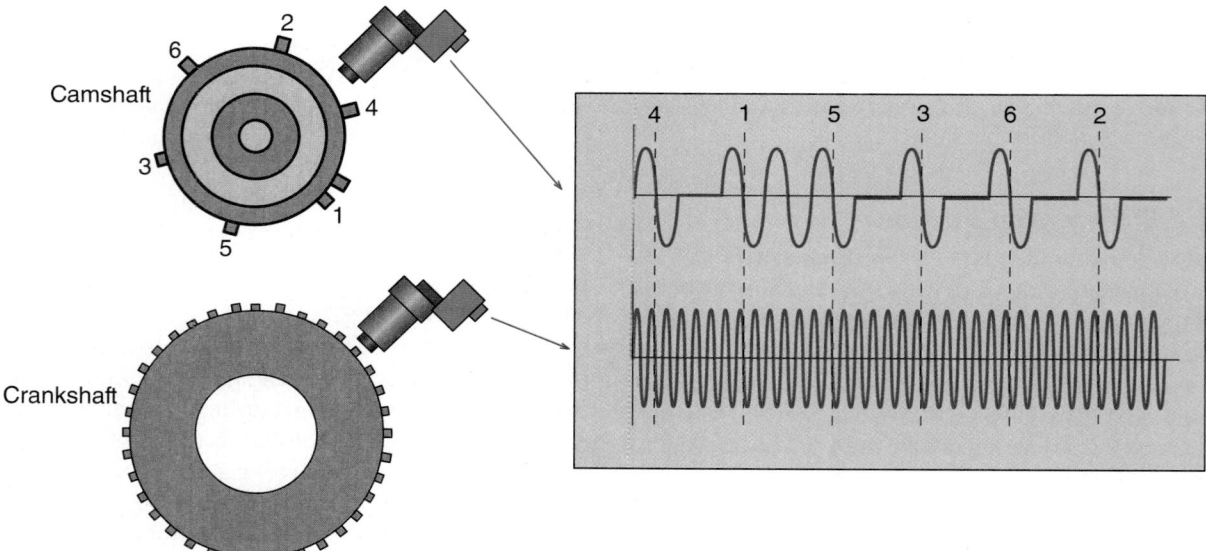

FIGURE 24-37 The raised teeth and gaps of a reluctor wheel of the crankshaft and camshaft sensors generate unique AC waveforms that identify crankshaft and cylinder position, as well as engine speed.

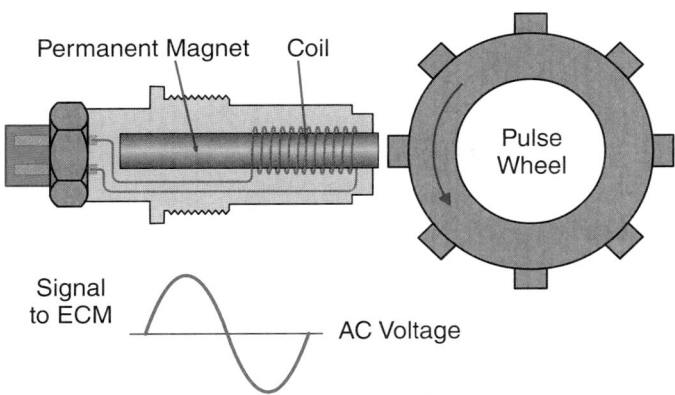

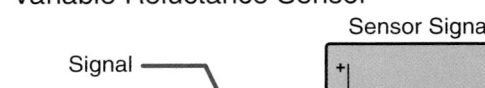

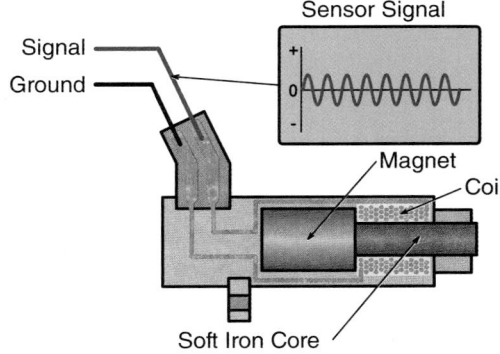

FIGURE 24-38 The reluctor ring helps the variable reluctance sensor generate an AC voltage signal.

a coil of narrow-gauge wire wrapped many times around a permanent magnet, and a reluctor ring (also called the sensor wheel, pulse wheel, or tone wheel), which has soft iron teeth and is locked onto a shaft or hub to rotate with it (**FIGURE 24-38**). Recall that the term reluctance refers to the resistance to magnetic lines of force. Because ferrous metals, particularly soft iron, have low reluctance to magnetic lines of force and air has high reluctance, the strength of the sensor's magnetic field expands and contracts as the reluctor ring's iron teeth pass across the sensor's permanent magnet. Magnetic fields more easily penetrate the iron tooth, which increases the number of lines of force and the sensor's magnetic field strength when a tooth is directly over the magnet. As the tooth approaches, the lines of force making up a magnetic field widens or moves across the wire coil wrapped around the magnet. Moving the tooth away from the magnet weakens the magnetic field and it contracts. By changing the density of magnetic lines of force, and moving the magnetic field by alternately expanding and contracting the field when a gear tooth or gap passes by the sensor, current is induced in the wire coil surrounding the sensor magnet. Increasing reluctor wheel speed increases the voltage induced in the sensor. A small air gap of approximately 0.02–0.03" (0.51–0.76 mm) is maintained between the sensor and the reluctor wheel. Too much or too little air gap prevents the sensor from detecting tooth movement. Software inside the ECU detects and counts the number of teeth passing by the sensor to calculate shaft speed. Other circuits can sense the tooth edge approach and departure, triggering a circuit to convert the analog AC signal into a digital signal.

If the processing circuits containing a clock have memorized how many teeth complete one rotation of the shaft, rpm is easily calculated. If the engine software can divide the number of teeth passing by the sensor per second of time, it can precisely calculate the number of degrees of crankshaft rotation for any moment of engine operation.

Hall-Effect Sensors

While not a voltage generator type of sensor, the Hall-effect sensor also uses changing magnetic field strength of a reluctor wheel to measure shaft speed and position. **Hall-effect sensors** are more complex and expensive to manufacture than variable reluctance sensors, but Hall-effect sensors have the advantage

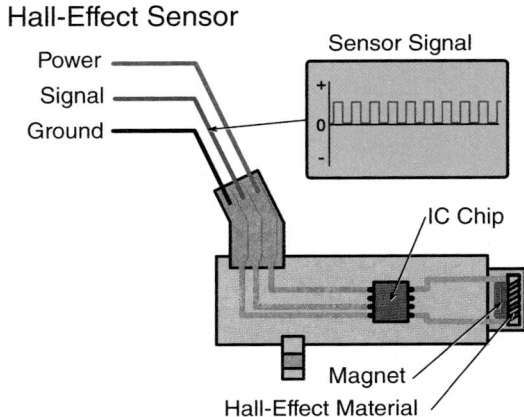

FIGURE 24-39 Comparing the construction of a Hall-effect sensor to a variable reluctance-type speed sensor.

of producing a digital signal with a square waveform and have strong signal strength at low shaft rotational speeds. This is especially useful when cranking an engine when engine rpm is slow. They can even detect the presence of a stationary piece of metal and do not need movement to identify position of a lever or metal object (**FIGURE 24-39**). This allows them to operate as proximity sensors (**FIGURE 24-40**). The durability and accuracy of the digital signal is preferred when more precise position data is needed for injection timing. This explains why most engines today use Hall-effect sensors.

The operating principle of a Hall-effect sensor is simple: current flow through a Hall-effect material changes resistance in the presence of a magnetic field (**FIGURE 24-41**). When current is applied to a Hall-effect material, no conduction occurs. However, in the presence of a magnetic field, the material conducts current. Conductivity of the electric current through the Hall-effect material is proportional to magnetic field strength. As long as the material is under the influence of a magnetic field, it conducts current. The electrical signal output from the sensor material is analog, but circuits within the sensor convert and amplify the rising and falling voltage produced by a reluctor wheel into a square-shaped, digital electrical waveform (**FIGURE 24-42**).

To produce the signal from the Hall-effect sensor, two configurations are used. The most common arrangement is the use of a metal interrupter ring or shutter and a permanent magnet positioned across from the sensor. Because ferrous metals have a lower magnetic reluctance than air, magnetic lines of force from a magnet placed opposite the sensor flows through the metal shield, rather than the sensor. Gaps in the interrupter ring allow magnetism to penetrate the sensor, changing current flow through the Hall-effect material. Attaching the interrupter ring to a moving shaft provides rotational speed information to the control module.

Another configuration for the Hall-effect sensor incorporates the magnet into the sensor itself. When a gear tooth or other ferrous metal trigger is present near the sensor, like the

FIGURE 24-40 This Hall-effect sensor is used to detect the proximity of a dump box when it is lowered onto the frame. The box position is critical to vehicle safety and a safety supplies data to the interlock feature.

variable reluctance sensor, the magnetic field expands. Movement of the ferrous trigger or tooth away from the magnet causes magnetic field contraction. This pulsing magnetic field generates the signal within the sensor (**FIGURE 24-43**).

Mass Airflow Sensors

LO 24-6 Identify and describe the construction and operation of mass airflow sensors.

The mass airflow (MAF) sensor is an active-type sensor device that measures the weight of air entering the engine intake. Its unique design also reports data about air density and, to some extent, the vapor content.

MAF sensors are common on engines operating at stoichiometric air-fuel ratios. However, on the diesel engines operating with an excess air ratio, the MAF is used as part of the HD-OBD component monitor for the EGR, measuring aftertreatment oxygen levels, and detecting problems associated with air flow. Natural gas engines also use sensors operating identically to MAF sensors to measure gas mass mixing with air and entering the engine. A variety of electrical signals originate from MAF sensors, but the most common type works by measuring the voltage drop across a heated wire. Heated platinum wires or a thin film of silicon nitride embedded with several heated platinum wires are located in the intake air stream. A microcontroller-operated heating circuit maintains a fixed voltage drop across the wires, so that a constant resistance and temperature of the wires is maintained, regardless of the quantity of air mass flow in the intake system (**FIGURE 24-44**). Increasing air mass flow tends to cool the wire more, which requires more current flow through the wire to maintain its temperature. The opposite condition is present if air mass flow decreases—the wire requires less current flow.

In a sense, air flow is proportional to current flow through the wire. This means that if a voltage drop of five volts is maintained across the heated wire, more current needs to flow

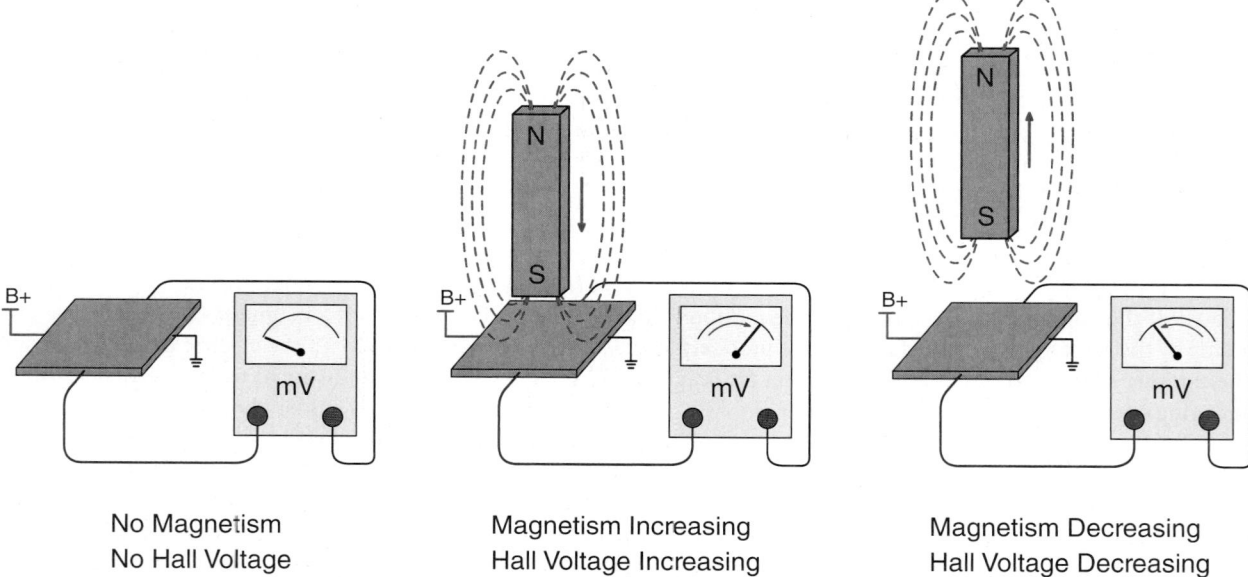

No Magnetism
No Hall Voltage

Magnetism Increasing
Hall Voltage Increasing

Magnetism Decreasing
Hall Voltage Decreasing

FIGURE 24-41 Hall-effect material is semiconductive and its ability to conduct electrical current changes in the presence of a magnetic field.

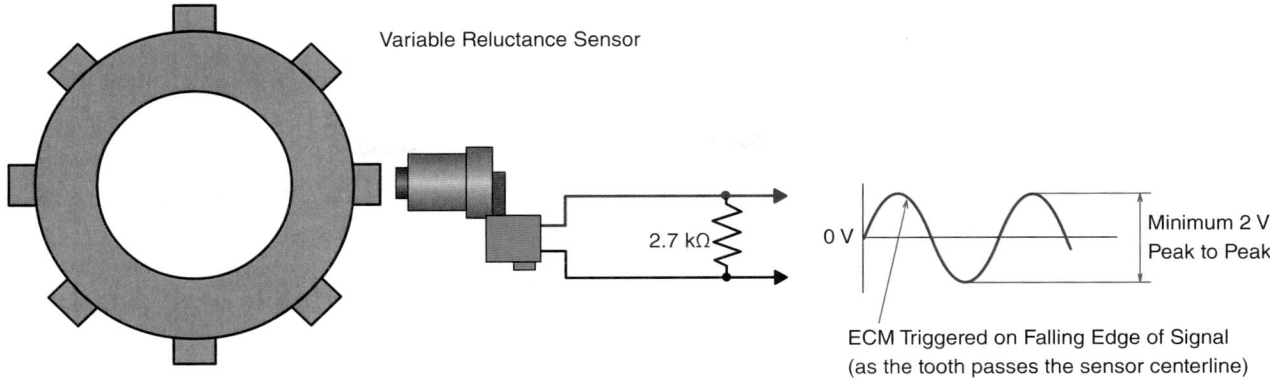

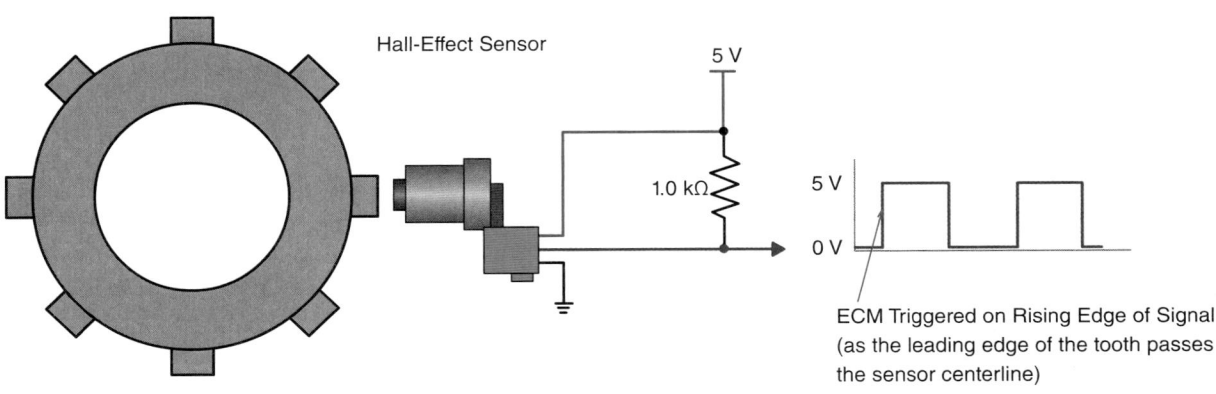

FIGURE 24-42 Comparing the signals of a Hall-effect sensor and variable reluctance sensor.

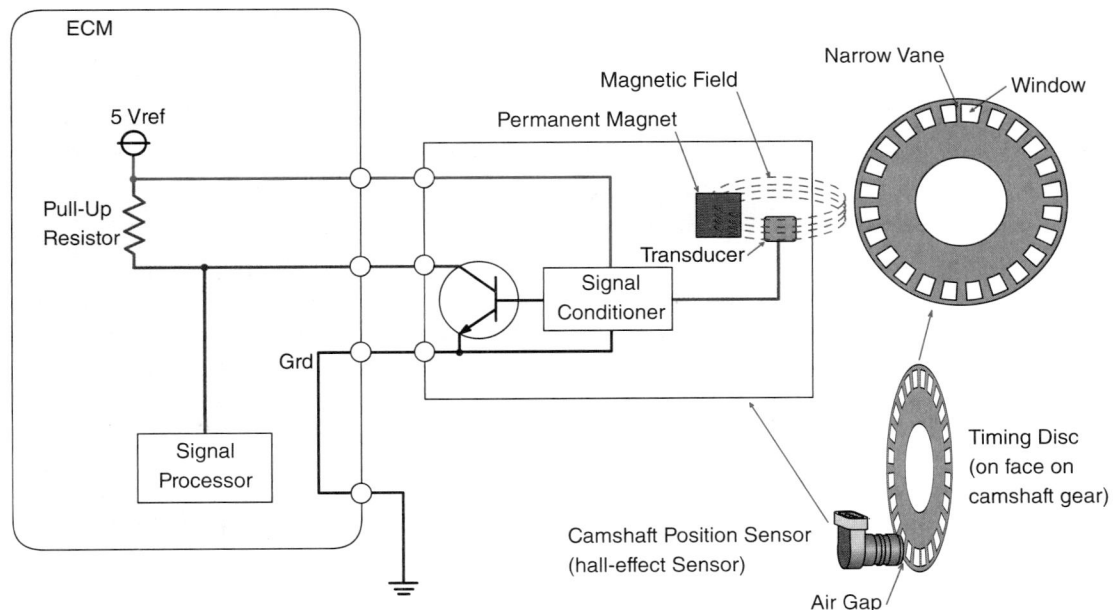

FIGURE 24-43 Operation of a camshaft position Hall-effect sensor using an internal permanent magnet.

through the wire if it cools faster due to increased airflow. Similarly, if airflow drops, less current is needed to maintain the same voltage drop across the wire (**FIGURE 24-45**). Circuits internal to the MAF measure the variation in current flow proportional to the cooling effect of air mass. Due to the large valve overlap characteristic of diesel engines, some intake air

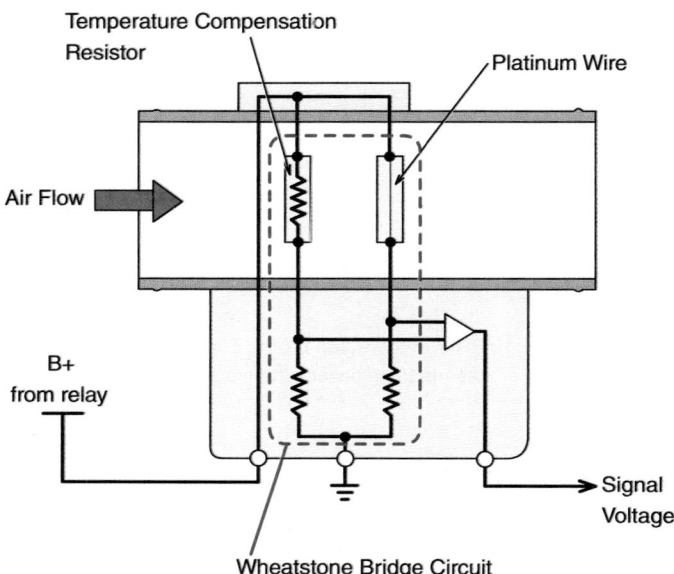

FIGURE 24-44 A Wheatstone Bridge circuit helps determine the resistance change in the heated wire of a MAF sensor.

FIGURE 24-45 Heated wires change resistance as airflow across the sensor increases or decreases. Air mass is calculated based on how much electrical current is required to cancel the cooling effect of airflow across a heated wire.

may be forced back out in pulses from the intake system. MAF sensors on some engines use a reverse airflow detection circuit. Because colder air is denser than warmer air, manufacturers also use an air temperature sensor to provide additional data for calculations to compensate for the change in air mass (FIGURE 24-46).

MAF sensor connector usually have five wires. Two wires with a circuit-protecting fuse supply current to the heating element. Another three wires form the sensor Vref, signal, and ZVR. A sixth terminal on some combination sensors is used to supply a separate signal for the air temperature thermistor in the intake air stream. Data from the thermistor may also be used to apply a correction factor to the signal from the MAF circuit.

FIGURE 24-46 A combination pressure and temperature sensor is used to calculate air mass entering an engine using a speed density algorithm. Note the two white signal wires.

Exhaust Gas Sensors

LO 24-7 Identify and describe the construction and operation of exhaust gas sensors.

Exhaust aftertreatment systems in diesel engines have created demand for sensors capable of measuring exhaust gas levels of oxygen, NOx, and ammonia. These sensors share some operating principles with gasoline engine exhaust sensors, but operate differently to measure gas concentration levels. In diesels, oxygen sensors must be capable of accurately measuring gas concentrations in very lean or oxygen-rich exhaust gases. This data is used to adjust EGR rates and supply an input to a model of engine operation for predicting fuel rates. NOx sensors must detect levels of oxides of nitrogen down to a few parts per million required to achieve the almost undetectable levels of noxious emissions from today's engines. Data from these sensors not only identifies fault conditions, but is used by engine and aftertreatment control systems to adjust operating strategies for positioning a variety of actuators and injection events and to accommodate faults or adapt to normal deterioration of exhaust catalyst efficiencies.

Gas sensor technology essentially compares the electrical signals a gas of a known concentration with electrical signals from an unknown gas concentration. The principle is similar to the use of a voltage-dividing circuit used to measure signal voltage or resistance from sensors. Using principles of galvanic chemistry, the **Nernst cell**, common to oxygen, ammonia, and NOx sensors, is a gas sensor configuration that compares the voltage induced in electrodes surrounded by unknown exhaust gas concentrations to voltage signals of known reference gases (FIGURE 24-47). A microcontroller compares the differences between the electrical signals in the two cells and supplies an electrical signal proportional to the gas concentration of the previously unknown gas measured in the exhaust. A microcontroller in a module associated with the sensor operates sensor circuits and then analyzes and conditions the electrical signals to produce a message reported over the vehicle controller area network (CAN) or an analog output (FIGURE 24-48).

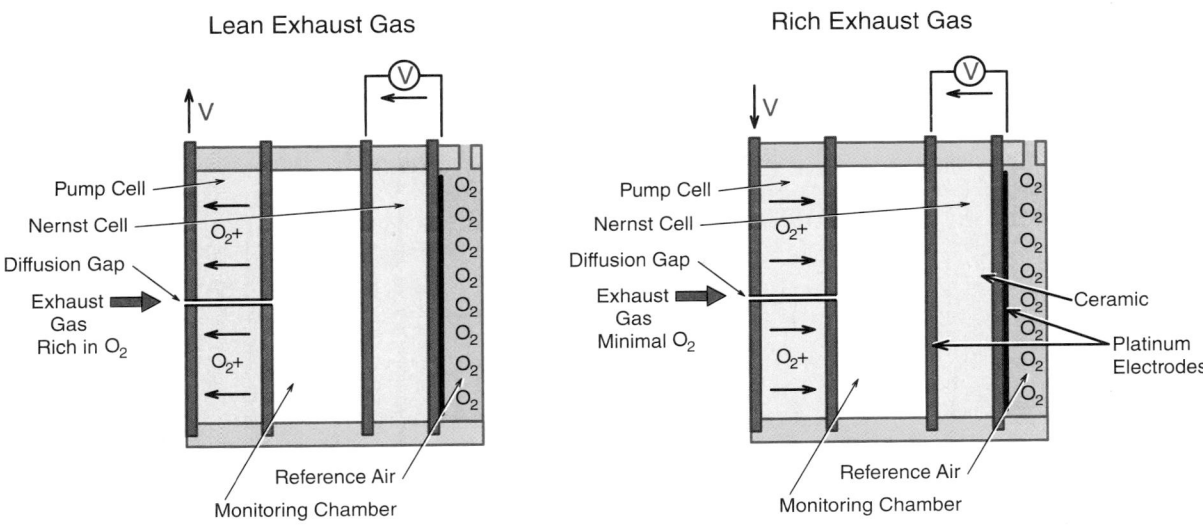

FIGURE 24-47 An electrochemical Nernst cell used in oxygen sensors measures the unknown gas concentration by comparing it to a known gas concentration. Oxygen sensors can use either an internal or external source of reference air to measure unknown exhaust gas concentrations.

FIGURE 24-48 A NOx sensor connected to a control module that drives the sensor analyzes its electrical signals and produces an output signal.

Oxygen Sensors

Oxygen sensors are used to measure air-fuel ratios in the exhaust system in order to calibrate EGR flow rates, regulate the operation of lean NOx traps, and monitor air-fuel ratios for exhaust aftertreatment devices. Diesel engines usually use a heated planar, wide-band, zirconium-dioxide (ZrO_2) dual-cell oxygen sensor (**FIGURE 24-49**). This sensor technology is different from the narrow-band oxygen sensor technology used commonly on gasoline engines operating at stoichiometric air-fuel ratios. Wide-band oxygen sensors are used in diesel engines because they use lean-burn combustion systems, which normally leaves an excess of air in the exhaust. Rather than producing a sharply falling and rising voltage near 0.5 volts, with 2% exhaust oxygen content found in gasoline engines, wide-band

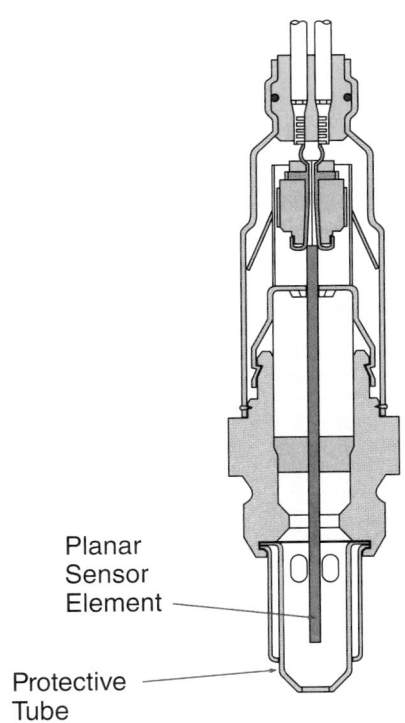

FIGURE 24-49 An internal view of a wide-range planar oxygen sensor for diesel exhaust with the protective shield removed.

sensors produce a voltage proportional to a widely varying oxygen level (**FIGURE 24-50**). The type of ceramic sensing element commonly used by wide-band sensors is a platinum-coated oxide of zirconium (Zr). An important property of this ceramic is that it becomes electrically conductive at high temperatures.

Wide-range planar sensors, means the gas sensor is flat, rather than thimble-shaped like the sensors used on older gasoline-fueled engines (see **FIGURE 24-51**). They are also wide-band, which means they generate a signal with a wide air-fuel

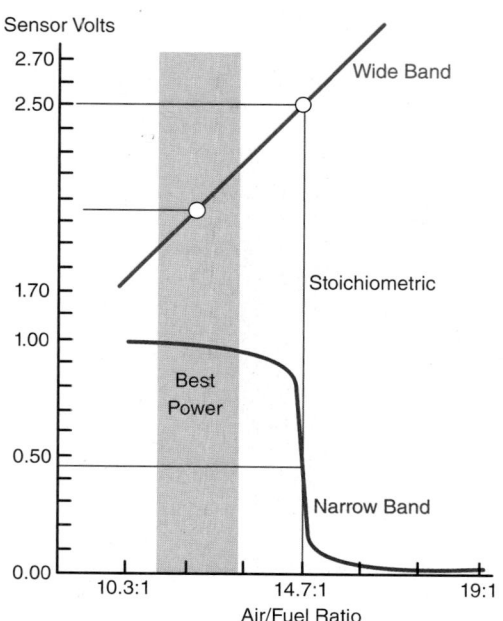

FIGURE 24-50 The voltage signal produced by a wide-band oxygen sensor. Note that unlike gasoline engine O₂ sensors, the current flow continues to increase past the stoichiometric ratio which is about 15:1 to 20:1 for diesel fuel.

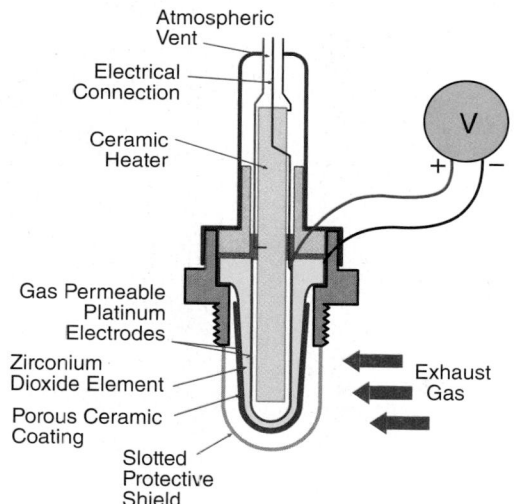

FIGURE 24-51 Voltage is generated when the oxygen composition of the platinum coatings on ZrO₂ is different due to a change in the relative oxygen content of the coatings.

ratio between 0.7:1 and infinity. When heated to over 1200°F (700°C), the sensor becomes electrically conductive to oxygen ions. Because the oxygen content in the exhaust sample chamber is less than the oxygen concentration in the atmosphere, the oxygen content absorbed by the platinum coating on the ZrO₂ ceramic is slightly different (**FIGURE 24-52**). This chemical difference in the oxides of platinum in the ceramic sensor alloy generates a voltage proportional to the oxygen content in the exhaust stream. The greater the difference in oxygen content between the exhaust side and reference oxygen sample, the

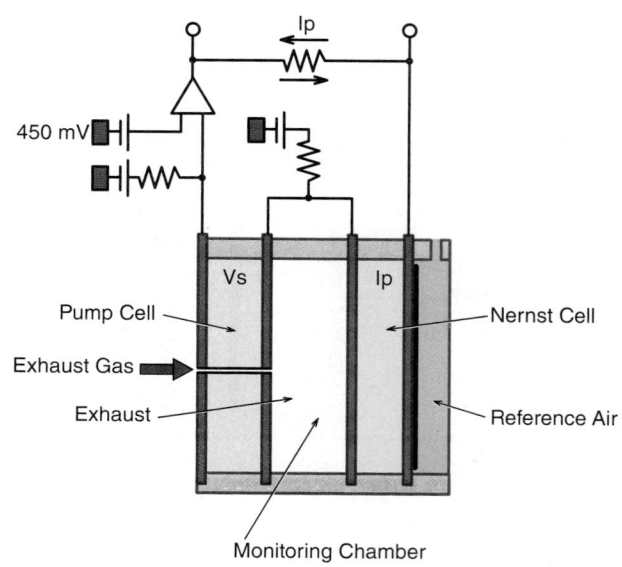

FIGURE 24-52 A wideband oxygen sensor signal is based on the current flow, measured in microamps or nanoamps, required to maintain the same electrical charge or voltage on the pump cell electrodes as the reference cell electrodes.

higher the voltage signal generated by the sensor and is proportional to exhaust gas oxygen content. This voltage is produced because of the galvanic effect where dissimilar metals in the presence of an electrolyte (the conductive ceramic material) produce electric current. In the case of an exhaust gas sensor, the electrolyte is not a liquid but a solid formed by layers of materials in the planar elements. The voltage produced by this cell is compared to another cell exposed to only clean air or oxygen. A microcontroller conditions the signals to produce an output usable to the engine or aftertreatment system controller.

Using the voltage produced across the two platinum-ceramic coatings, an amplifier circuit, called an oxygen pump cell circuit, transfers electrons back and forth between the coating in the exhaust gas chamber to the electrode in the atmospheric reference chamber. The direction the oxygen pump transfers electrons and the number of electrons transferred is proportional to the concentration of oxygen in the exhaust. The amount of current used to transfer these electrons and the direction the transfer takes place is also relative to the stoichiometric ratio of the fuel with no movement of electrons taking place when exhaust and reference chamber oxygen content is the same. Oxygen levels are measured according the amount of current transferred necessary to balance the voltage differential between two cells (Figure 24-52).

NOx Sensors

NOx sensors are exhaust gas sensors used to measure NOx concentrations to evaluate the operation of selective catalyst reduction (SCR) systems. These sensors measure NOx produced from the engine and NOx emitted from the tailpipe after passing through the exhaust system. A pair of NOx sensors should verify

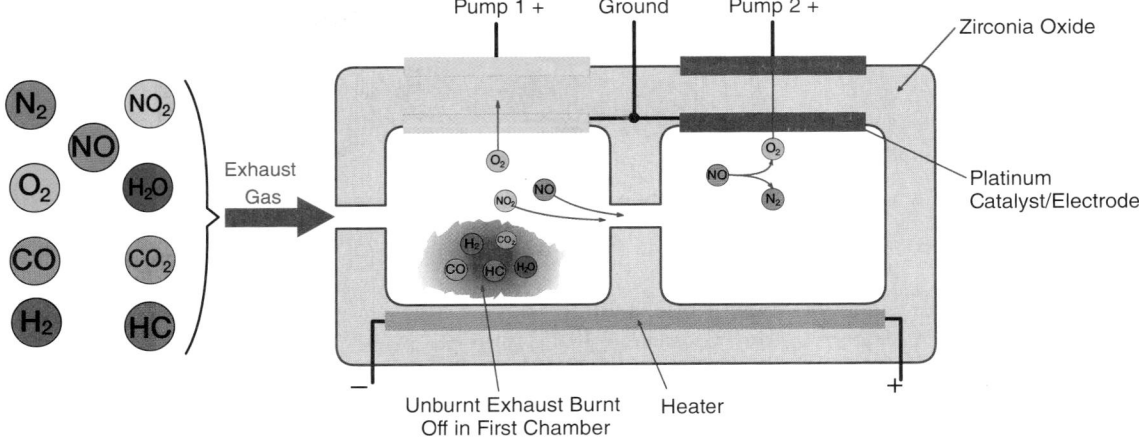

Pump Cell 1
Extracts all oxygen remaining
in the exhaust and burns off
everything else except the NOx.

Pump Cell 2
Breaks down the NOx and
measures the released oxygen.

Pump 1 +   Ground   Pump 2 +

Zirconia Oxide

Platinum
Catalyst/Electrode

Exhaust
Gas

Unburnt Exhaust Burnt
Off in First Chamber   Heater

FIGURE 24-53 Operation of a NO$_x$ sensor. These sensors are also sensitive to any nitrogen in the exhaust stream and can detect ammonia gas as well.

a significant drop in NOx emissions after it passes through the SCR catalyst. NOx sensors are constructed and operate similarly to wide-range planar oxygen sensors using ZrO$_2$ ceramic substrate, except different concentrations of alloys are used in the NOx sensor's platinum sensor walls. Also, NOx sensors include a chamber that first removes excess oxygen, then separates NOx into nitrogen and oxygen, before allowing the remaining oxygen into a sampling chamber. Only oxygen ions separated from NOx are supplied to the sensor sampling chamber and not atmospheric oxygen from the exhaust. The two-chamber shape and multilayered platinum element enable these sensors to differentiate with high precision oxygen ions originating from nitric oxide (NO) from among the oxygen gas present in the exhaust gas.

The NOx sensor's ZrO$_2$ chamber, which is the size of a thumbnail, is heated to 1200°F (700°C). It is housed in a metal can that has a hole for exhaust gas entrance. The metal catalysts in the chamber walls break apart the NO into nitrogen and oxygen components. The amount of oxygen produced at this stage is proportional to the amount of NO. After this stage, the NOx sensor operates like an oxygen sensor, but measuring only the oxygen content of the gas removed from the NO. Because the oxygen in the second sampling chamber originated only from NOx, an accurate measurement for NOx in the exhaust gas is made. A module connected to the sensor conditions the electrical signal to represent a value proportional to the amount of NOx sensed in the exhaust stream (**FIGURE 24-53**). This module often stores calibration information with information about the sensor's characteristics. This explains why each sensor must be matched to a module and both are serviced together (**FIGURE 24-54**).

Because NOx sensors are damaged by water, the sensor is heated for a short time after the engine starts and before the

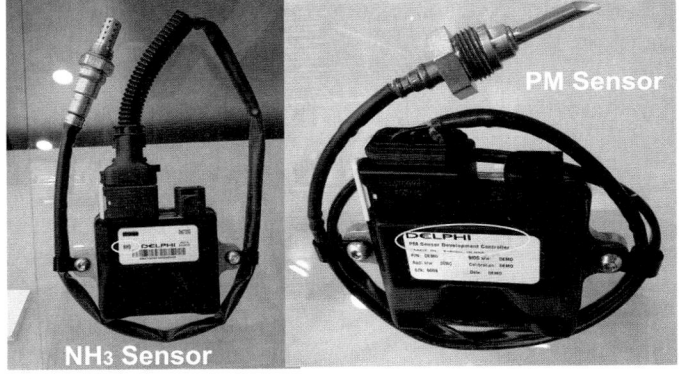

FIGURE 24-54 NOx and ammonia sensors contain calibration information that helps the control system adapt to manufacturing tolerances between sensors. Sensors must be paired with modules and are serviced together.

module operates the sensor. The temperature of the sensor must exceed the dew point of water for the operating conditions it is working under.

Ammonia Sensors

An NOx SCR system used on late-model diesel engines involves injecting urea, a colorless and odorless liquid, into the exhaust stream. Exposed to exhaust heat, the urea quickly breaks down to form ammonia, which reacts with NO$_x$ and renders it into harmless nitrogen, water, and oxygen molecules. However, ammonia is a noxious substance and should not escape into the atmosphere. The potential for ammonia to be released or slip into the atmosphere requires the use of an ammonia sensor for most engine exhaust systems produced since 2015. The **ammonia sensor** provides data to the ECU that is used to determine whether the amount of exhaust ammonia detected is out of an anticipated range. The most commonly used ammonia sensor is constructed like a wide-range planar NOx or oxygen sensor, but an ammonia sensor uses an aluminum oxide substrate, rather than a ZrO_2 planar element, to detect and generate a voltage for ammonia in a range from 0 to 100 ppm. This substrate makes it sensitive to just ammonia in proportion to the concentrations in the exhaust stream.

Diesel Exhaust Fluid (DEF) Sensors

LO 24-8 Identify and describe the operation of diesel exhaust fluid (DEF) sensors.

DEF is technically called reductant, lending the name **reductant quality (RDQ) sensor** to the mandatory sensor used on late-model vehicles with SCR systems. RDQ sensors can identify poor quality in less than 30 seconds and when concentration changes by more than 1% to 5%. The new sensors do not require dosing to take place to detect problematic DEF quality. The ability for RDQ sensors to identify poor-quality DEF and eliminate other nuisance, high NOx faults also helps minimize troubleshooting time and the complexity of diagnostic procedures.

The most common type of RDQ sensors use ultrasonic sound waves to measure fluid density (**FIGURE 24-55**). Like other fluids, DEF has a specific density. When the ultrasound waves generated by the RDQ sensor penetrate the fluid, they travel at speeds proportional to DEF density. If DEF density does not match an expected value, the ECU connected to the sensor sets a fault code that eventually leads to an engine de-rate or even failure to start. Ultrasonic-type sensors are the favored technology because they can operate to also measure DEF level.

Another common sensor technology measures the fluid's capacitance or dielectric properties. When fluid is placed between two plates of a capacitor, the dielectric properties of the fluid are changed and the capacitor charge plates charge time is measured by a circuit.

Sensor Fault Detection Principles

LO 24-9 Recommend and describe diagnostic procedures for sensors used in electronic control systems.

Diagnostic trouble codes (DTCs) are the most common go-to data supplied by the onboard diagnostic (OBD) system to identify system-related faults. It is important to realize that fault codes only locate the smallest identifiable and repairable subsystem or component that the ECU can determine has failed. More pinpoint testing is almost always required to isolate and confirm a failed part or circuit. Codes narrow down the location of a fault or abnormal system condition, but require further testing to differentiate between several possible root causes or to verify the root cause. Understanding how sensor-related faults are detected by a control system and the diagnostic strategies used by an ECU are critically important diagnostic skills.

Sensor Faults and Onboard Diagnostics

Electronic control systems have self-diagnostic capabilities to identify faults in circuits and sensors. Without the ability of an ECU to monitor circuit operation, diagnosing faults would become an extraordinarily difficult task, requiring the technician to manually perform voltage, resistance, and current measurements for every circuit with the potential to produce a particular symptom for a system malfunction. Analyzing waveforms from sensors producing varying frequencies, pulse width modulation, digital, or sine wave would also require a staggering amount of time and resources to analyze.

Because all vehicles are required by emission legislation to monitor engine and other system operations for faults that could produce excessive emissions, evaluating sensor operation is a critical function of the HD-OBD system. Three major categories of fault codes identified by engine manufacturer diagnostics (EMD) and HD-OBD are:

1. *Out-of-range faults*. These faults primarily check sensor voltages, and in a few cases, they also check current draw to determine whether the sensor or associated circuits are open or have shorts. Signal voltage should normally be within 85% of reference voltage. That means for most sensors operating with a 5 Vref, signal voltages should not fall below 0.5 volts or above 4.5 volts (**FIGURE 24-56**).
2. *Rationality, plausibility, or logical faults*. Manufacturers use different terms to describe the same fault detection strategy whereby the validity or accuracy of sensor data is evaluated by comparing sensor signal voltages with expected values. Most often, sensor data from several more sensors or measurement systems is compared with data from a particular sensor to see if the data makes sense (that it's logical or rational). Another name given to these types of faults is in-range faults, because the sensor could produce signal voltages that are not above or below an out-of-range fault threshold voltage, but the sensor may have failed and is supplying incorrect data.

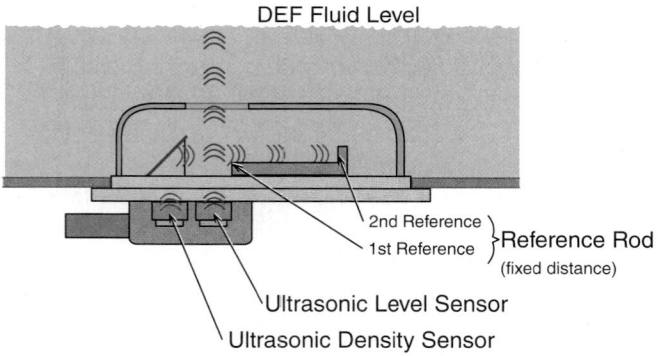

DEF Fluid Level

2nd Reference
1st Reference
} Reference Rod (fixed distance)

Ultrasonic Level Sensor
Ultrasonic Density Sensor

Level Sensing
- To determine the DEF level the ultrasonic signal is reflected back from the surface once.

Density Sensing
- To determine the DEF density the ultrasonic signal is reflected back twice from the first and second reference points.

FIGURE 24-55 An RDQ or DEF-quality sensor is now required for SCR systems. An ultrasonic-type sensor measures fluid density and DEF level.

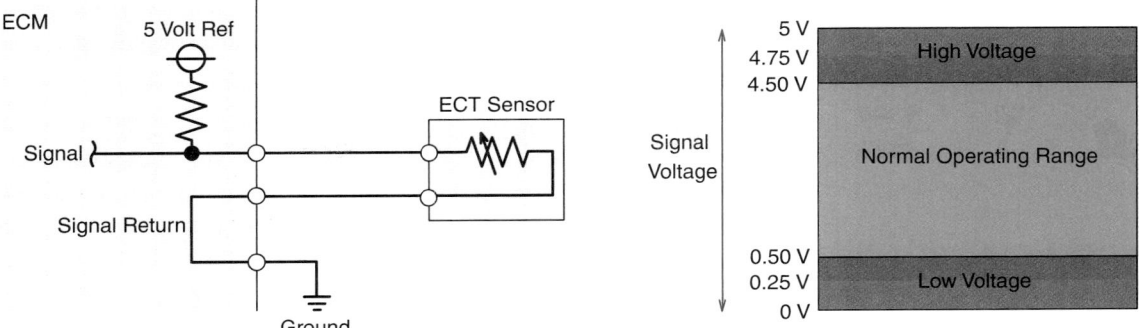

FIGURE 24-56 Out-of-range voltage codes on sensors are produced when the signal voltage falls outside 85% of reference voltage. This means signal voltages below 0.5 and above 4.5 typically trigger out-of-range voltage codes.

3. *Functionality faults.* HD-OBD systems are required to evaluate the operation of at least 12 to 14 other major emission systems, such as the exhaust aftertreatment, boost pressure, and EGR. Simple or elaborate fault detection strategies are used to check whether a particular emission system is functioning correctly. The major system monitors, as they are called, depend on sensor data to function, but they do not specifically check the sensor except to analyze the significance of sensor data for a system. For example, if a system could not enter closed loop operation because the sensor data was out of range, irrational, or had some problem with its operation, such as abnormal operating frequency or switching time or a defective waveform, the sensor would be identified as having a fault. However, NOx sensor faults are a common example in which the sensor is working properly but, due to some other incorrect system function, the sensor fault code set points to an out-of-range NOx sensor reading. In many cases, the NOx sensor is identified as being faulty, but a problem is often with a catalytic converter, EGR valve, SCR dosing valve, DEF quality, or restricted air intake systems causing what appears to be an in-range fault. This means the problem lies outside the sensor.

Comprehensive Component Monitor

The comprehensive component monitor (CCM) is one of the system monitors required for EMD and HD-OBD systems. It is a monitor that constantly checks for malfunctions in any engine or emission-related electrical circuit or component providing input or output signals to an ECU. Electrical inputs and outputs are evaluated for circuit continuity and shorts by measuring voltage drops in a circuit. The monitor is also responsible for performing rationality checks of sensors. For example, if an oil pressure sensor indicates the engine has 40 psi (276 kPa) of oil pressure and the engine is stopped, the data does not make sense and, therefore, a rationality fault is stored. Another example is that of a coolant temperature sensor that indicates the coolant is warm at 140°F (60°C), but all other sensors, such as oil, fuel, air inlet, and transmission, temperatures are at −20°F (−29°C) and the engine has just started after cold soaking for 20 hours. Such

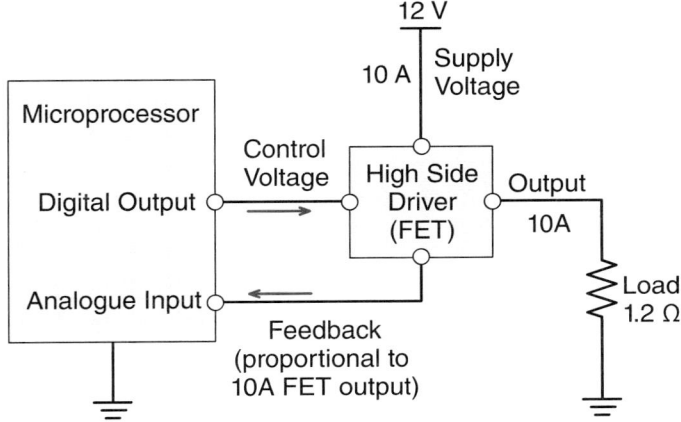

FIGURE 24-57 Smart FETs can provide feedback to the ECU about amperage moving through the transistor gate.

a code could be triggered by plugging in a block heater, or it might indicate a defective sensor. Rationality codes need careful pinpoint diagnostic tests to determine if a sensor is defective or some external or mechanical factor is affecting sensor data.

Outputs, such as injector solenoids, relays, and dosing valves, are evaluated by the CCM for opens and shorts by monitoring a feedback circuit from the field effect transistor (FET) or "smart driver" associated with the output circuit. Smart FETs, as they are called, are FETs designed to supply data about the amount of amperage passing through the transistor gate (**FIGURE 24-57**). These same gates can operate as virtual fuses that can disconnect power to the circuit if current flow is excessive. CCM codes use fault mode indicators (FMIs) developed by the Society of Automotive Engineers (SAE) that indicate how an electrical circuit has failed (**TABLE 24-1**). Out-of-range voltage codes that are the most common when sensors and circuits are open or shorted report FMI 3 and 4 after identifying the circuit name. J1587 and J1939 SAE rationality codes are 0, 1, and 2. J1939 also adds FMI codes 15–18, 20, and 21 for rationality-related faults. FMI codes 8–10 are used to report problems with waveforms from sensors or systems. FMI codes 5 and

TABLE 24-1 Society of Automotive Engineers (SAE) J1939 Failure Mode Identifier (FMI)

FMI	SAE Text
0	Data valid but above normal operational range—most severe level
1	Data valid but below normal operational range—most severe level
2	Data erratic, intermittent, or incorrect
3	Voltage above normal or shorted to high source
4	Voltage below normal or shorted to low source
5	Current below normal or open circuit
6	Current above normal or grounded circuit
7	Mechanical system not responding or out of adjustment
8	Abnormal frequency, pulse width, or period
9	Abnormal update rate
10	Abnormal rate of change
11	Root cause not known
12	Bad intelligent device or component
13	Out of calibration
14	Special instructions
15	Data valid but above normal operating range—least severe level
16	Data valid but above normal operating range—moderately severe level
17	Data valid but below normal operating range—least severe level
18	Data valid but below normal operating range—moderately severe level
19	Received network data in error
20–30	Reserved for SAE assignment
31	Condition exists

6 are used by smart drivers detecting excessive or insufficient amperage in a circuit. Only FMI codes 11–14, 19, and 31 are not used by the CCM.

Circuit Monitoring—Voltage Drop Measurement

The method in which switches are monitored helps provide a foundation to understand how other sensor circuits are monitored using voltage dividers. Two basic types of switch inputs to the ECU are pull-up and pull-down switches. The terms pull-up and pull-down are used to describe whether current through a circuit is supplied by either the positive or negative current polarity. Pull-up means current is originating from a positive voltage source, and pull down from a negative source. In the case of switches, pull-up switches supply a positive battery voltage input, while pull-down supply a ground or negative voltage input (**FIGURE 24-58**). Inside the ECU, a current-limiting resistor is connected in series with either of the switch types. This current-limiting resistor splits the voltage drop across the

resistor and switch contacts. The microcontroller connects to the voltage dividing circuit after the pull-up or pull-down resistor to measure the voltage drop across a known resistance. This allows the microcontroller to accurately calculate the value of the unknown sensor resistance using Kirchhoff's Law. Voltage drops across the current-limiting resistor change when switch contacts are opened or closed. A high-impedance microcontroller capable of measuring voltage between an internal ECU ground and an internal resistor that is connected in series with the external switch changes resistance when the switch is opened or closed. This means that voltage drop across the current-limiting resistor, whether it is a pull-up or pull-down switch, is measured by an internal voltmeter to indicate switch status (i.e., whether open or closed).

Diagnostics with Pull-Up Resistors

When two resistors are connected in series, the greatest voltage drop takes place across the resistor with the highest resistance. The remaining resistor drops the remaining voltage in a circuit. This is predicted by Kirchhoff's law, which states the sum of the voltage drops in a circuit equals source voltage (**FIGURE 24-59**). Because the microcontroller inside the ECU that measures voltage has very high impedance, it behaves like the largest of the resistors in a circuit. A pull-up resistor has the most voltage drop measured after the resistor when the switch is open, because it places the microcontroller in series with the resistor. In this case, only a small amount of voltage is dropped by the current-limiting resistor and the most voltage through the highly resistive microcontroller measuring voltage. When the switch is closed, the very low resistance across the contacts causes the most current to flow through the switch contacts and the series-connected current-limiting resistor. Almost no current flows through the highly resistive microcontroller, because the microcontroller has much higher resistance compared to the pull-up resistor and switch, and current takes the path of least resistance through the switch circuit, rather than through the microcontroller.

Smart-Diagnosable Switches

Disconnected switches, shorted switch wiring, and resistive switch contacts cannot be diagnosed using open or closed diagnostic logic. To differentiate a disconnected switch from an open switch, resistors are placed in series or in parallel with the switch (**FIGURE 24-60**). This enables the microcontroller to identify problems in the wiring between the switch and ECU for failures, such as shorted to ground or open circuited wiring. When properly connected in a functioning circuit, the resistor incorporated into the switch in series has a calibrated resistance sensed by the microcontroller and measured as a specific voltage drop. If a switch has a resistor connected in parallel across its contacts, opening the switch provides a specific voltage drop that matches the switch status as open, which is measured by the microcontroller. If the switch wiring is shorted to ground, to battery positive, or simply disconnected, programmed logic within the microcontroller identifies the

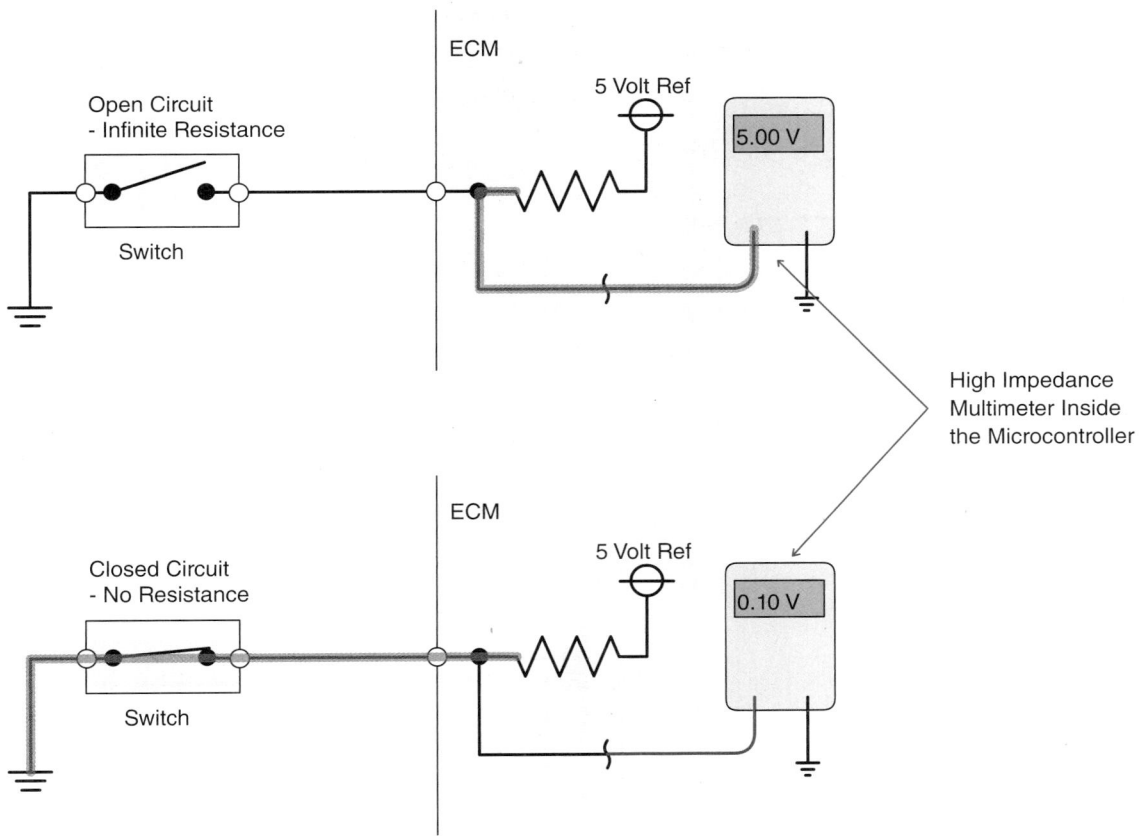

FIGURE 24-58 Pull-up switches supply a positive voltage to the ECU, while pull-down switches supply negative or ground.

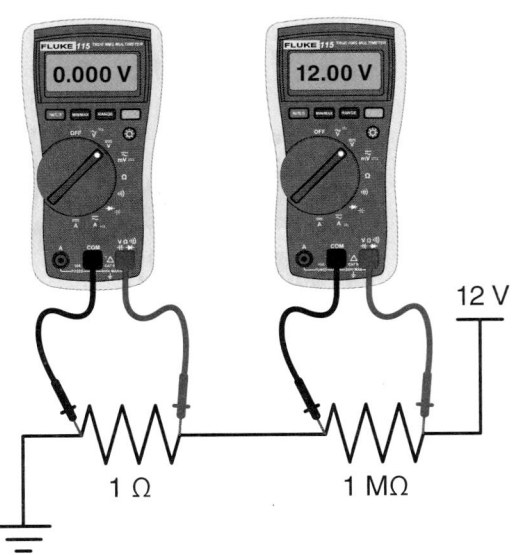

FIGURE 24-59 With two resistors connected in series, most voltage drops across the resistor with the highest resistance, which is predicted by Kirchoff's Law.

voltage reading as different from the normally expected switch resistance when opened or closed and logs the appropriate fault code (**FIGURE 24-61**). Pull-up resistors can be connected in series with the switches to further enhance the diagnostic

capabilities of the microcontroller. Clutch, brake light, or A/C pressure switches often use these arrangements because of their critical functions.

► **TECHNICIAN TIP**

It is a very important and fundamental principle of electrical troubleshooting that when an ECU stores a diagnostic code, the code generally points to a problem somewhere in the circuit and not necessarily to the device connected to the circuit. If a code for a sensor is logged, further pinpoint testing using a diagnostic flowchart is required to properly diagnose the circuit.

► **TECHNICIAN TIP**

+5 Vref to sensors and switch circuits and a regulated zero volt return ground circuit is shared by multiple sensors and switches. The electronic control module has only two or three circuits to supply all the sensors and switches on an engine. Sometimes an active sensor can short internally and supply +5 volts to the ground circuit that is shared with other sensors. If this happens, a proper ground return and even a +5 Vref signal is not supplied to the remaining sensors and switches. The result is multiple fault codes in a sensor circuit or switch unrelated to the actual fault. When performing pinpoint tests, it is critical to eliminate the possibility of what is commonly called a "back-feed" current supply from another sensor to pinpoint the root cause for a code. A quick test is to use an LED to identify any back-fed current from a sensor failure. A diode placed in series with the ZVR after each sensor should light up in only one direction.

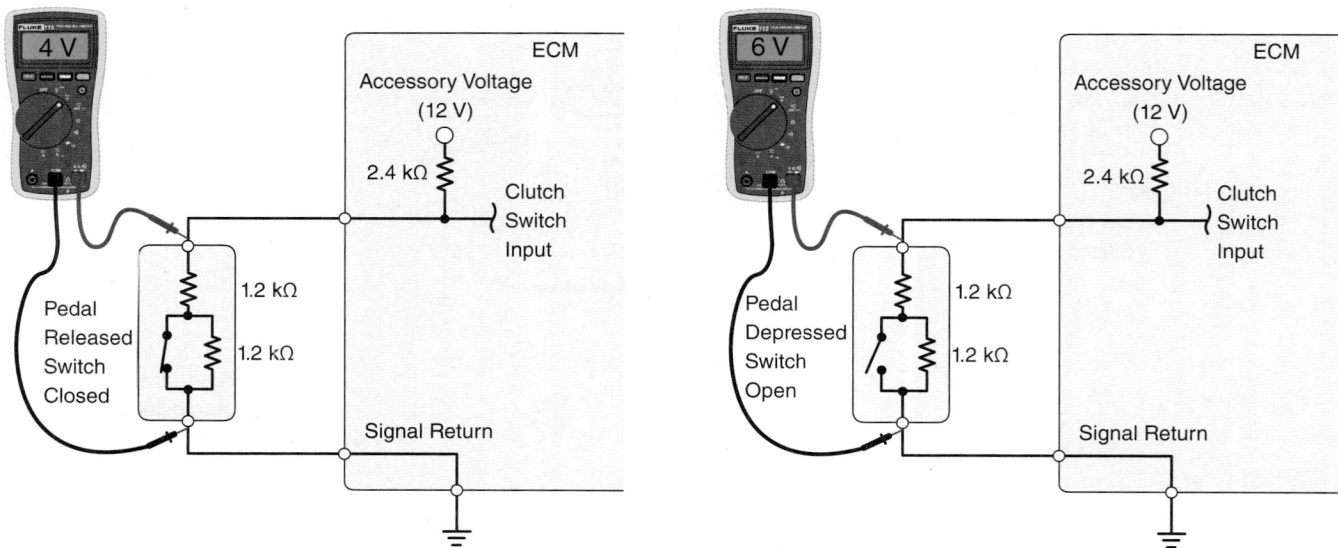

FIGURE 24-60 Placing resistors in series with opening and closing switches with different resistor values distinguishes switch status for each of these "smart switches."

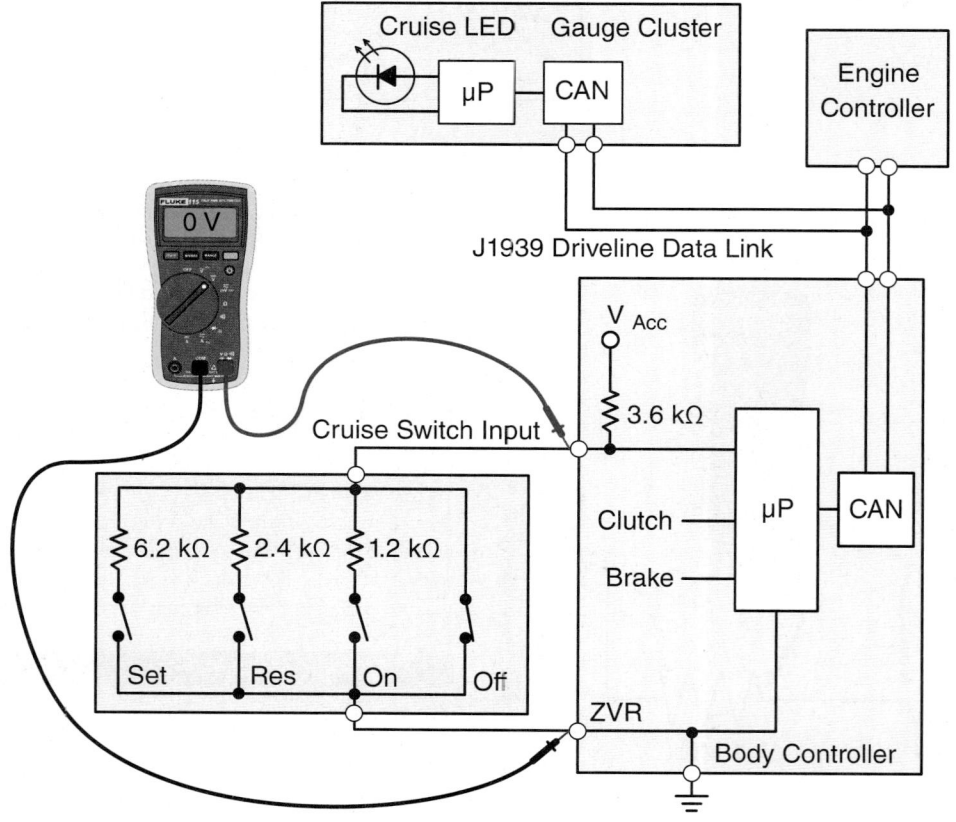

FIGURE 24-61 Resistors internal to the microcontroller are used to identify the different switches in a vehicle for proper control logic.

Two-Wire Pull-Up Circuit Monitoring

To identify faults and measure correct signal voltage, thermistors are often connected to internal pull-up resistors (**FIGURE 24-62**). Thermistors are variable resistors that change resistance with temperature. These temperature-sensing devices are monitored for:

- Resistance to validate normal signal voltage and detect out-of-range faults
- Open circuits, either internal or in the circuit wiring
- Shorts to power
- Shorts to ground

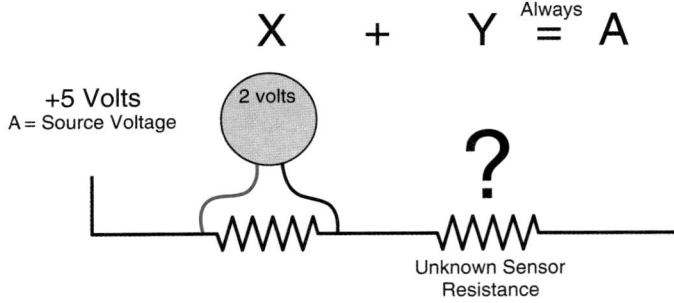

Sum of Voltage Drops Always = A
(Unknown Value = 5 volts - 2 volts = 3 volts)

FIGURE 24-62 The voltage drop across a known sensor value inside the ECU changes according to the resistance of an external sensor resistance.

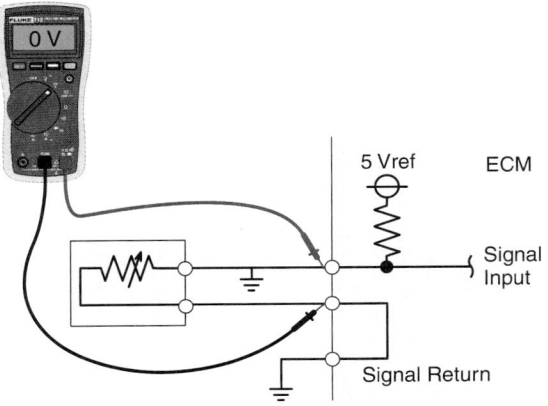

FIGURE 24-63 Circuit monitoring of thermistors involves measuring the voltage drop after a pull-up resistor. This circuit will have an FMI 4 code which is voltage low or shorted low.

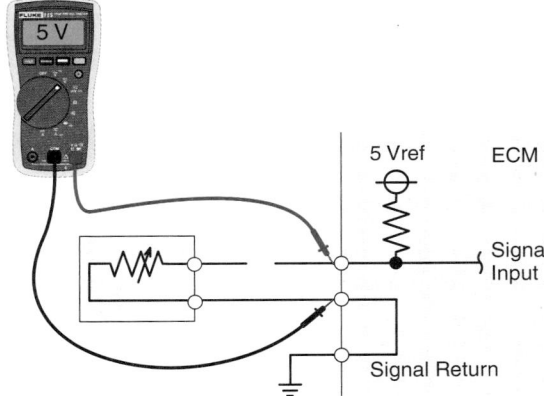

FIGURE 24-64 A thermistor with an open signal wire, generating an SAE fault code of FMI 3: voltage high or shorted high.

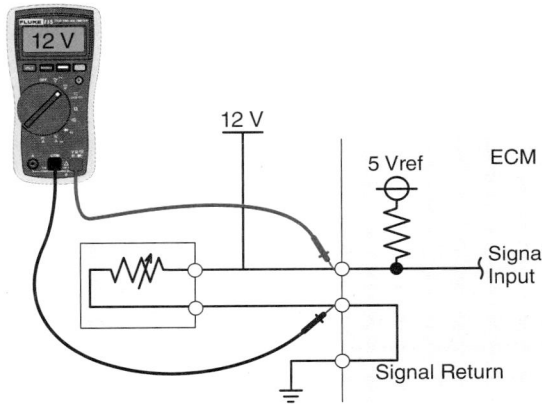

FIGURE 24-65 A thermistor with an SAE fault code of FMI 3: Shorted high or voltage high.

Like switches, the control module measures voltage drop across an internal current-limiting resistor to estimate the voltage drop across a thermistor. NTC thermistors increase resistance when they become colder and decrease resistance when they become warmer. As the resistance of the thermistor increases, less voltage is dropped across the pull-up resistor and more across the thermistor. The microcontroller measures more voltage drop across the pull-up resistor when the thermistor becomes less resistive. Unwanted extra resistance in the circuit, such as a loose or open circuit, produces a higher voltage drop across the sensor, generating colder temperature readings. An open circuit (high resistance) reads the coldest temperature possible. Circuit-monitoring fault detection is typically designed to recognize sensor resistance values within approximately 85% of Vref voltage supplied from the pull-up resistor to be within normal range, and voltage readings outside of that range are recognized as abnormal (**FIGURE 24-63**). Normal signal voltage range used to diagnose most sensor circuits covers the entire operating range of the sensor signal, and the circuit should always have some resistance, whether hot or cold. A disconnected sensor has infinite resistance, and no voltage is dropped across the thermistor. In these circumstances, the voltage reading by the circuit's microcontroller sees maximum Vref voltage between its internal ground and the current-limiting resistor. An open sensor or disconnected open wiring produces an SAE fault code description of "out-of-range high or shorted high" (FMI 3) (**FIGURE 24-64**).

The SAE FMI code FMI 3 description points to the higher voltage sensed by the microcontroller because no voltage is dropped by the disconnected or open thermistor circuit and all voltage is now dropped by the microcontroller. Note that the sensor signal wire that is shorted to positive battery voltage or another +5 volt supply generates an identical fault code (**FIGURE 24-65**). The logic used by the microcontroller that senses no or little voltage drop across the pull-up resistor could be caused by a positive voltage supply shorted to the signal wire. The ZVR could also be open and produce the same voltage readings by the microcontroller. Both conditions require appropriate pinpoint testing to isolate the fault.

If a thermistor signal wire is rubbed through and making contact to chassis ground, more current flows through the signal circuit and the fault code description typically includes:

- Out-of-range low or shorted low (FMI 4)
- Signal wire shorted to sensor return or battery negative (OEM code)
- Signal source shorted to ground (OEM code)

Excessive current flow across the pull-up resistor connected in series with the grounded circuit means low or no voltage is dropped across the pull-up resistor and the signal wire. This happens because most current flows through the short to ground, and little current flows through the highly resistive microcontroller. A code is set typically when the voltage drop is less than 0.5 volts. This explains why the code description given is out-of-range low or shorted low (FMI 4). Under these conditions, diagnostic logic programmed into the microcontroller points to a short to ground, causing excessive voltage drop across the current-limiting resistor of more than 85% of the voltage supplied to the resistor **TABLE 24-2**.

Manufacturers can go beyond SAE minimum standards for reporting faults using J1939 protocols and add additional fault code descriptions using their own coding system. In the case of the disconnected thermistor, an enhanced code could carry a code description such as "signal wire shorted to sensor supply" or "short to battery voltage," "signal source shorted to voltage source," "open return," or "signal circuit."

Pressure, temperature, position, and other sensors can share a +5 Vref or ZVR wire. ZVR is the equivalent to chassis ground through the control module, which is free of electromagnetic interference and is regulated to provide the cleanest signal path. Problems in the reference voltage or signal return path can cause unusual problems and multiple fault codes from all the sensors sharing the Vref and ZVR circuits. "Shorted high or low" and "voltage high or low" are typical out-of-range fault code descriptions produced by several sensors that share common shorted or grounded Vref and ZVR pathways. This happens because the voltage supplied to the sensors has changed. Less than +5 volts or the absence of a ZVR distorts the ECU's ability to properly sense correct signal voltages. If the ZVR is connected to chassis ground, voltage fluctuations and electromagnetic interference can sometimes distort electrical signals and measurement of voltage drops across the sensor circuits. A single defective sensor may have an internal short circuit to ground and supply the ZVR with +5 volts, which can interfere with the operation of all sensors sharing a common Vref or ZVR. Disconnecting a defective sensor can sometimes cause the multiple fault codes to disappear. The use of an LED diode installed in series with the ZVR circuit at each sensor can detect a malfunctioning circuit or sensor device if the polarity-sensitive LED lights in both directions when connected to the defective sensor. Normally it should light when connected in only one direction.

Just because a control module does not log a fault code does not mean that no problems exist in the electronic control system. Because the normal signal range (within 85%) used to diagnose most sensor circuits spans the entire operating range of the sensor, it is possible for the sensor to produce a signal that does not measure the actual operating condition and, therefore, is not identified with a fault code. A good strategy to identify problems is to monitor signal voltage using a scanner or software data list while comparing observed values with expected values reported in a shop manual.

Quick-testing to determine whether a fault code is generated by defective wiring, pin connectors, or sensor can be performed using jumper wires. While monitoring sensor signal voltage using an electronic service tool, the signal voltage values should change when either disconnecting the sensor or jumping sensor signal wires to ZVR or +5 Vref. If no change is observed when momentarily grounding the signal wire or supplying the signal wire with +5 Vref, the wiring or ECU pin connections in the circuit are suspect. Some manufacturers recommend using a calibrated resistor in series with the jumper wire when performing these tests to prevent damage to sensitive control modules.

Three-Wire Sensor Circuit Monitoring

Three-wire circuits, whether digital or analog, passive or active, use a reference voltage, signal, and ZVR wire, also referred to as ground return by some manufacturers. Voltage out-of-range faults (FMI 3 and 4) are detected when the signal voltage from a sensor typically falls outside of the 0.5–4.5 volts out-of-range fault threshold (**TABLE 24-3**). Most three-wire sensors typically measure signal voltage between the positive voltage on the signal wire and the ZVR wire across a pull-down resistor (**FIGURE 24-66**). However, some active three-wire sensors with digital outputs, such as Hall-effect sensors and several manufacturers of pressure sensors, supply a high-frequency digital signal

---

TABLE 24-2 Out-of-Range Voltage Fault Code Descriptions Using a Pull-Up Resistor (i.e., two-wire NTC thermistor)

Condition	Observation	Code Description
Sensor disconnected	Signal voltage higher than 4.5 volts	FMI 3: Out-of-range high, shorted high
Signal wire shorted to positive voltage (12V battery or +5 volts reference)	Signal voltage higher than 4.5 volts	FMI 3: Out-of-range high, shorted high
Sensor open	Signal voltage higher than 4.5 volts	FMI 3: Out-of-range high, shorted high
Sensor signal wire shorted to ground	Signal voltage lower than 0.5 volts	FMI 4: Out-of-range low, shorted low
Sensor internally shorted to ground or ZVR	Signal voltage lower than 0.5 volts	FMI 4: Out-of-range low, shorted low

TABLE 24-3 Out-of-Range Voltage Fault Code Descriptions Using a Pull-Down Resistor (i.e., three-wire potentiometer)

Condition	Observation	Code Description
Sensor disconnected	Signal voltage lower than 0.5 volts	FMI 4: Out-of-range low, shorted low
Signal wire shorted to positive voltage (12V battery or +5 Vref)	Signal voltage higher than 4.5 volts	FMI 3: Out-of-range high, shorted high
Sensor open	Signal voltage lower than 0.5 volts	FMI 4: Out-of-range low, shorted low
Sensor signal wire shorted to ground	Signal voltage lower than 0.5 volts	FMI 4: Out-of-range low, shorted low
Sensor internally shorted to ground or ZVR	Signal voltage lower than 0.5 volts	FMI 4: Out-of-range low, shorted low

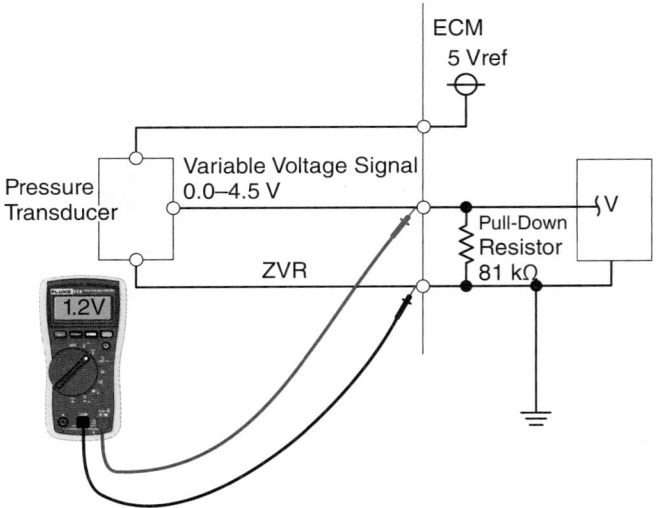

FIGURE 24-66 A low-bias sensor using a pull-down resistor. The sensor voltage is measured across the pull-down resistor.

voltage of +5 Vref at the signal wire. A resistor must be placed between the Vref and the signal voltage to measure a wave form. These sensors do not have a voltage that varies proportionally to speed or pressure (**FIGURE 24-67**).

To measure signal voltage of three-wire sensors involves using a pull-up or pull-down resistor located in the ECU. In the case of a circuit using a pull-down resistor, a voltage-measuring microcontroller connected in parallel across the pull-down resistor measures voltage drop across the resistor between the positive signal wire and the negative ZVR. Because there is only one pull-down resistor, all the voltage supplied by the signal wire is dropped across the pull-down resistor. This means that a defective active-type sensor has a fault code of FMI 4 for low voltage or shorted low if either of the +5 Vref and ZVR circuits are open (**FIGURE 24-68**). Because no current is supplied to the active sensor with either an open Vref or ZVR, internal sensor circuits cannot operate and supply a varying positive polarity signal voltage. Voltage in this case is 0, which is below the 0.5 volt fault threshold for low voltage.

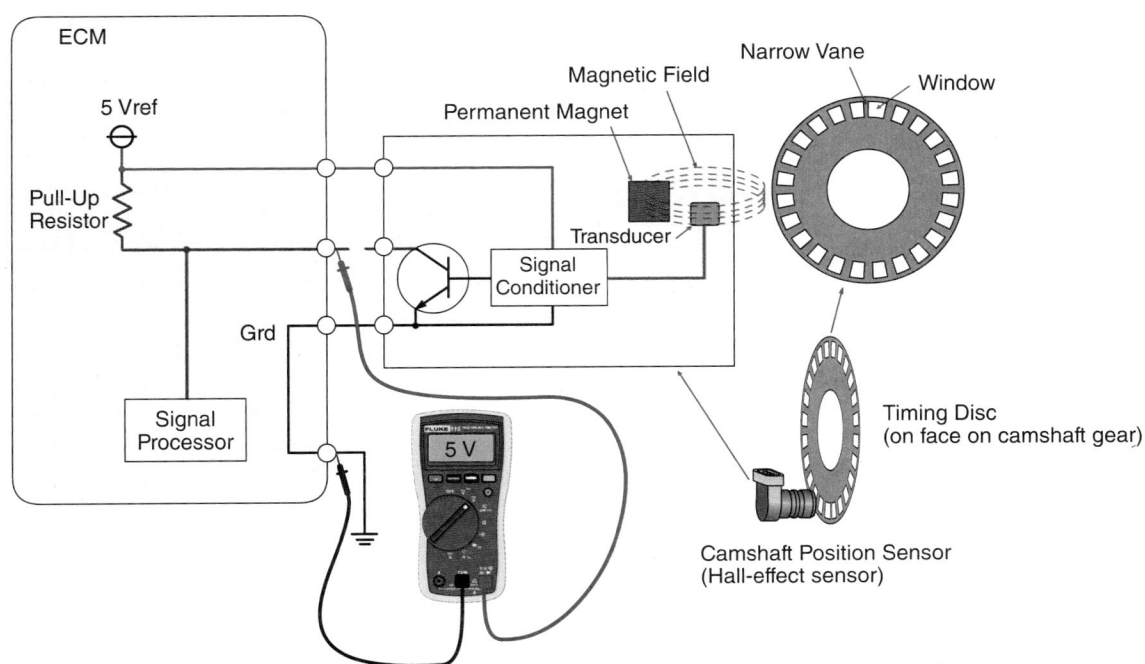

FIGURE 24-67 Use of a resistor between the Vref and signal to measure a digital waveform from a Hall-effect sensor with a digital output. Disconnecting the sensor produces an out-of-range +5 volts signal, which makes it a high-bias three-wire active sensor. Grounding the signal wire produces a 0 volt signal.

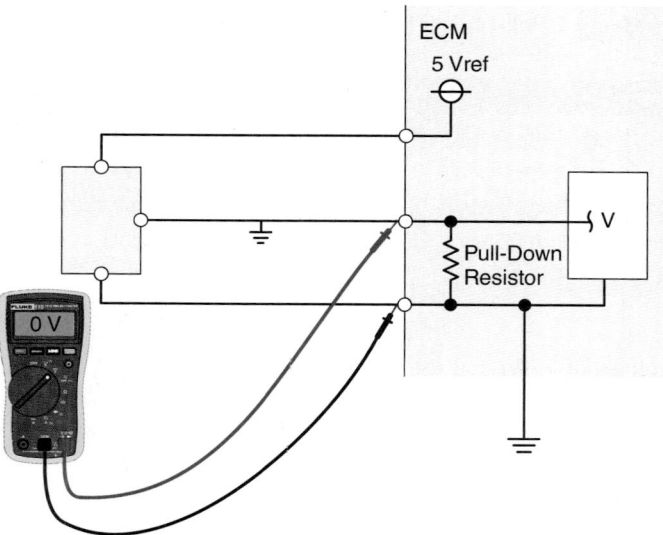

FIGURE 24-68 A signal wire of a three-wire active sensor shorted to ground produces a fault code of FMI 4: shorted low, voltage low.

A short-to-ground signal wire produces an identical shorted low, voltage low FMI fault code.

If the same three-wire sensor is connected to an ECU containing a pull-up resistor connected between a +5 Vref and signal, a disconnected sensor produces a voltage high, shorted high FMI fault code for the signal. In this instance, the active sensor does not work, and the microcontroller sees all the +5Vref drop across the microcontroller and internal ground. The open circuit produces a fault code of FMI 3: voltage high, shorted high, as illustrated in Figure 24-67.

High- and Low-Bias Sensors

Whenever a sensor is disconnected or open, the out-of-range voltage code is either high or low. If the arrangement of the pull-up or pull-down resistor causes signal voltage to go high when disconnected, it is considered a high-bias resistor. That is, it has a bias or tendency to produce a fault code of out-of-range high, voltage high, or FMI 3. If the tendency for a sensor circuit is to produce a voltage low code when disconnected, it is considered a low-bias sensor. Generally, high-bias sensors use a pull-up resistor and low-bias sensors monitor signal voltage with a pull-down resistor.

Circuits using pull-up and pull-down resistors have the added advantage of limiting excessive current flow to a sensor to protect the wiring, sensor, or control module if a short to ground or battery positive takes place. Excessive current flow is reduced by the resistor when a fault condition exists. By limiting excessive current flow during shorted conditions in sensor circuits, Vref and ZVR circuits are protected as well.

More comprehensive circuit monitoring also takes place between the Vref and ZVR in some but not all control systems. Open, shorted to ground, or shorted to voltage source or resistive circuit pathways result in fault codes for these circuits. Because ZVR is common to the sensors, problems with the + reference voltage to a specific sensor circuit may only be detected.

After performing a repair to an electronic control system, the repair should be validated before returning a vehicle to service to confirm the fault code does not reappear. In HD-OBD systems, repair validation requires operating the circuit or device under the enabling conditions for a major system monitor to run and obtain a system readiness code. Make sure the conditions to operate the device or run the monitor are met during the testing procedure. These procedures are outlined in the service manual. For a simple sensor replacement, the comprehensive component monitor, which continuously evaluates circuits, runs the instant the key is switched on. If no fault is detected, the code disappears and the malfunction indicator lamp (MIL) generally extinguishes. Double-check that no codes are pending or waiting to illuminate a MIL. Occasionally, diagnostic codes can be set during routine service procedures or by problems outside the electronic control system. Always clear codes and confirm that they reset prior to circuit troubleshooting.

► TECHNICIAN TIP

Minimum tools required for fault isolation pinpoint testing include a digital volt-ohmmeter (DVOM) and some test leads or jumper wires. Proper break-out harness or pin connectors are also needed to access the various connectors and components to be tested. Using improper tools can result in damage to pins and connectors and faulty meter reading, causing misleading diagnosis and produce even more diagnostic codes.

► TECHNICIAN TIP

If an intermittent fault is suspected, a physical check of the suspect circuit can be performed by flexing connectors and harnesses at likely failure points while monitoring the circuit with a multimeter, service software or an oscilloscope. Graphing meters with glitch-testing capabilities can also identify and record the circuit fault in microseconds. If the problem is related to temperature, vibration, or moisture, the circuit or control module can be heated, lightly tapped, or even sprayed with water to simulate the failure conditions. Some testing software feature pull test capabilities, which can provide an audible alert when brief interruption in circuit voltages takes place when pulling or bending wiring harnesses.

Pinpoint Testing of Sensors

LO 24-10 Outline procedures for pinpoint testing of sensors.

The on-board diagnostic system capabilities are limited and can only narrow a fault to a circuit or system. After that, the technician must identify what the nature of the problem is that produced the diagnostic fault code. Servicing of sensor faults involves performing pinpoint electrical tests and making other observations to identify precisely where and what caused the fault. This stage of diagnostic testing is called off-board diagnostics or pinpoint testing.

Testing of Pressure Sensors

Diagnostic tests of pressure sensors are similar to other strategies for evaluating three-wire sensors. On-board diagnostic systems identify problems in the circuits. Scan tools can then measure real-time data to observe abnormal but in-range functional problems and retrieve fault codes associated with the circuits (**TABLE 24-4**).

TABLE 24-4 Fault Code Descriptions for a Two- or Three-Wire Sensor

Condition	Observation	Code Description
In-range voltage but signal not valid	No rationality or plausibility when data compared with normal system behavior or other sensor inputs	In-range fault

Pinpoint tests using break-out harnesses are performed on live circuits too. Resistance tests are used to identify shorted or open wires in harnesses to these sensors. However, because these are active sensors with sensitive electronic circuits, it is not possible to perform resistance tests with an ohmmeter on the sensors themselves or while the vehicle battery is connected. The wiring harness should be checked to verify +5 Vref and ZVR are supplied to the sensor using a voltmeter.

Fault Code State Change

One of the most effective ways of differentiating between a defective sensor, a wiring harness, or even a defective ECU is through **fault code state change**. Fault code state change is the process of creating the opposite fault code than the reported one to differentiate problems in sensors, harnesses, and ECUs. Using the fault code state change method for two- and three-wire sensors involves disconnecting a sensor harness from the sensor, and then using a jumper wire to short out the sensor harness after it is disconnected.

When a sensor circuit fault is identified the first step for the fault code state change is to:

1. Disconnect the sensor while monitoring the fault or sensor signal using diagnostic software or a scanner. If the fault code changed, the problem is likely in the sensor.
2. After the sensor is disconnected and no change of state is observed when monitoring the sensor data, use a jumper wire to short the +5 Vref to the signal wire. The code should switch a three-wire sensor with a voltage low code to voltage high. A two-wire sensor where +5 Vref is shorted to ZVR should switch from voltage high to low. If the change of state does not take place, the problem is in the wiring harness or ECU (**FIGURES 24-69, 24-70**).
3. Similar to the previous step, check the ZVR return path. Use a jumper wire to connect the disconnected sensor signal wire to chassis ground. A voltage high code should change to voltage low for a two- or three-wire sensor if the ZVR wire is open.
4. If the codes have not changed, disconnect the ECU harness and use a jumper wire to short the signal or ZVR and +5 Vref together at the appropriate ECU pins for the sensor. On a three-wire sensor, the code should switch from low to high. Jump the signal pin on the ECU to chassis ground to get a voltage high code to switch to voltage low. If the codes do not switch, the ECU is likely defective (**FIGURE 24-71**).

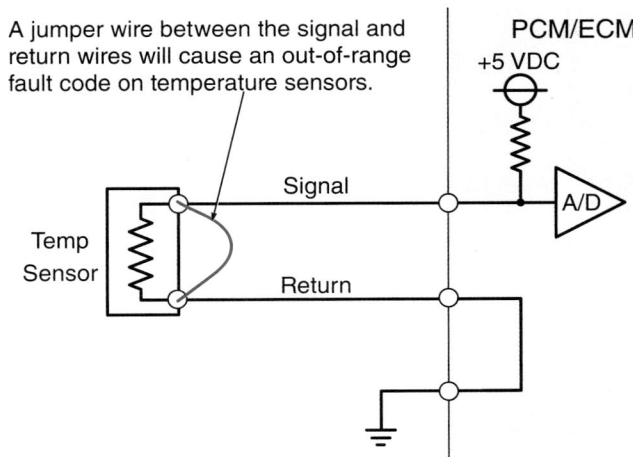

FIGURE 24-69 A voltage low code should switch to a voltage high when a two-wire sensor is disconnected. Shorting the disconnected wiring harness +5 Vref to the signal return or ZVR should switch the code from high to low voltage if the sensor is defective.

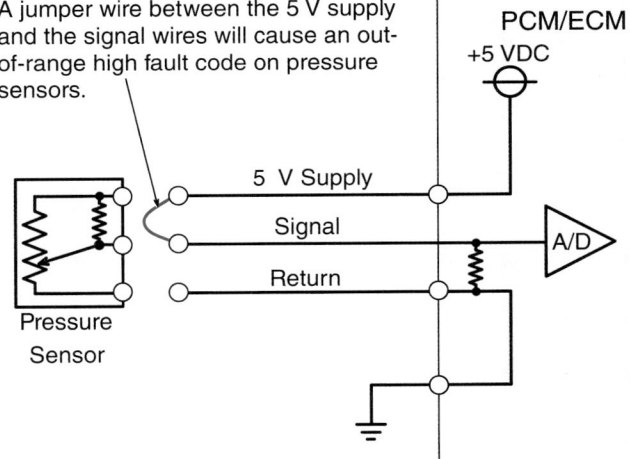

FIGURE 24-70 On a pressure sensor, a voltage high code should switch to voltage low when the sensor is disconnected if the sensor is defective. If not, short the +5 Vref and signal wire together. If the code does not change, the harness is likely shorted.

Pinpoint Testing of Thermistors

The range of resistance values of a thermistor varies by manufacturer and what temperature range the sensor measures. The change in resistance is not linear or directly proportional to temperature, either (**TABLE 24-5**). At the low and high ends of temperature range, small changes in temperature produce large changes in resistance, while changes in midrange temperature values produce smaller changes to sensor resistance. Several

FIGURE 24-71 Shorting the pins for sensor signal to +5 Vref and ZVR should produce a fault code state change if the ECU is working correctly.

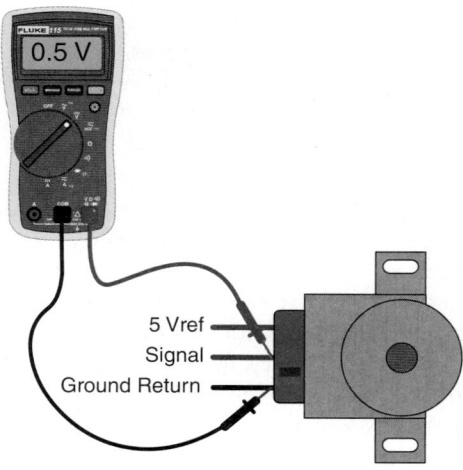

FIGURE 24-72 Signal voltage when pinpoint testing is always measured between the ground return and signal wire for all sensors.

TABLE 24-5 The Inverse and Non-linear Relationship Between Temperature and Resistance of a Thermistor

Temperature		Resistance
°Celsius	°Fahrenheit	Ohms
100	210	185
70	160	450
38	100	1600
20	70	3400
−4	40	7500
−7	20	13,500
−18	0	250,000
−40	−40	100,700

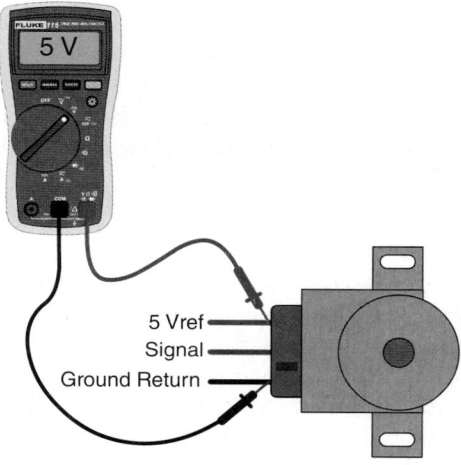

FIGURE 24-73 Confirming the availability of +5 Vref is an important step in pinpoint diagnostics to isolate a fault. Five volts can be measured from either chassis ground or sensor ground return. To confirm both signals are accurate, measure ground return and +5 Vref.

temperature and resistance values are typically supplied by the manufacturer service literature to properly evaluate a thermistor when testing using an ohmmeter.

Pinpoint Testing of Variable Reluctance Sensors

Variable reluctance sensors are two-wire passive sensors. The coil of wire surrounding a magnet should be tested for continuity and its resistance measured. Resistance is high because there are hundreds of wire-winding turns and the wire diameter is very small. The output of the sensor can be measured with an alternating-current voltmeter. As the reluctor speed increases, the voltage produced by the sensor rises proportionally, and so does the frequency of the voltage.

A broken magnet causes a low voltage reading. Likewise, an improper air gap between the sensor and reluctor causes sensor output failure. Iron filings at the magnet of the sensor also causes an inadequate change in sensor reluctance, generating insufficient voltage. Simply removing, cleaning, reinstalling, and adjusting the sensor air gap can sometimes correct erratic sensor signals.

Variable reluctance sensor operation can often be evaluated from a scan tool, service software or waveform graphing meter. For example, if an engine speed sensor is defective, engine speed data cannot be observed from a scanner. Graphing meters can compare known good sensor waveforms with observed waveforms to detect sensor faults.

Pinpoint Testing of Hall-Effect Sensors

Diagnostic testing of Hall-effect sensors follow similar diagnostic strategies for any other three-wire active sensor (**FIGURE 24-72**). Out-of-range faults on the sensor can be pinpoint tested with a voltmeter by first verifying +5 Vref and ZVR are available to the sensor (**FIGURE 24-73**). After disconnecting the sensor and harness plug, a quick check to differentiate between a defective sensor and defective wiring harness is to short the +5 Vref to the signal return circuit. While monitoring sensor voltage using software or a scanner connected to the diagnostic data link connector, the signal voltage shows five volts or an "on" state. If there is no change in the voltage, the wiring harness or connector plugs are likely defective. Shorts of any of the circuit wires to ground, battery voltage, or to one another are checked using either an ohmmeter when the vehicle battery is disconnected or measuring voltages in the sensor harness when the circuit is live.

Another important check of Hall-effect sensors is made using a graphing meter. Sometimes the circuit board within the sensor can fail and produce a waveform unrecognizable to the ECU, such as when the edges of a normally square waveform are not sharp and well-defined. This often happens during hot soak period, and the vehicle does not start until the engine cools. A graphing meter allows examination of the waveform for comparison between known good waveforms.

To verify the correct wave form of a Hall-effect sensor, it is necessary to install a resistor between the signal and +5 Vref and then graphing meter or oscilloscope leads across the resistor. The sensor needs to be operated by turning a wheel or running an engine to observe the wave form. This unique situation is necessary since the digital signal is pulled high between the +5 Vref and signal wire.

Pinpoint Testing of Mass Airflow Sensors

MAF sensors produce waveforms or data that can be observed by using a graphing meter. Sensor operation can also be monitored using a scanner, OEM software, or a multimeter with a break-out harness. A digital waveform may be observed on some digital MAF sensors when a resistor is placed between the signal and +5 Vref while the sensor is flowing. Diagnostics of MAF sensors follow those of any three-wire active sensor. It is also important to remember turbulence and airflow velocity variations can give false signals. For example, dirty heater wires or hot film or film wires can cause incorrect readings. Screens placed within the sensor to reduce turbulence can catch debris. These parts require cleaning or replacement to restore proper operation. If the heater wire is intermittently breaking open, tapping the sensor to disconnect the wire reveals the glitch if the sensor output is observed on a graphing meter or scanner.

Wrap-Up

Ready for Review

▶ Devices that convert one form of energy into another are called transducers. Sensors are a type of transducer because they convert physical conditions or states into electrical data. Pressure, temperature, angle, speed, and mass are just a few of the physical variables about which sensors supply electrical data to processors.

▶ A sensor is considered active or passive depending on whether it uses power supplied by the ECU to operate.

▶ Reference voltage refers to a precisely regulated voltage supplied by the ECU to sensors. It is significant to microcontroller operation because the value of the unknown resistance can be calculated by measuring voltage drop across the resistor with a known input voltage.

▶ Other classifications of sensors include resistive sensors, voltage generators, switch sensors, variable capacitance pressure sensors, and piezo-pressure and piezoresistive sensors.

▶ Switches are the simplest sensors of all because they have no resistance in the closed position and infinite resistance in the open position. Switches are categorized as sensors whenever they provide information to an electronic control system.

▶ The simplest digital signal is a single pole single throw (SPST) switch. It is found in either an open or closed state.

▶ When a switch is connected between the ECU and a battery positive, it is known as a pull-up circuit. A pull-down circuit is constructed when current to the switch is connected between the ECU and a negative ground current potential.

▶ Resistive sensors belong to the class of sensors that condition or change the value of a voltage signal supplied to the sensor. Many types of resistive sensors exist.

▶ A thermistor is a temperature-sensitive variable resistor commonly used to measure coolant, oil, fuel, or air temperature. The most common type of thermistor is a negative temperature coefficient (NTC) thermistor.

▶ Rheostats are two-wire variable resistance sensors. They are not commonly used as input devices to an ECU but instead are used for sending units, such as fuel level, oil pressure, and some temperature gauges.

▶ Three-wire sensors, regardless of how they appear or what function they perform, have a common wiring configuration. One wire provides reference voltage to the sensor. The second wire provides a negative ground signal to the ECU. The third wire is a signal return from the sensor. The advantage of using three-wire sensors is that they provide comprehensive diagnostic information about the sensor and its circuit operation.

▶ Potentiometers are similar to rheostats in that they vary signal voltage depending on the position of a sliding contact or wiper moving across a resistive material. However, they are three-wire sensors with the signal wire connected to the internal wiper. Potentiometers supply analog data to processing circuits.

▶ Pressure measurements, such as intake manifold boost, barometric pressure, and oil and fuel pressure, use two types of sensor technology. One is a variable capacitance sensor and the other uses strain gauge resistive sensors. These are both active sensors that produce analog output signals.

- Strain gauge measurements record small changes in the resistance of tiny wires caused by stretching or contraction of the wires.
- Piezoresistive sensors rely on the ability of certain mineral crystals to produce voltage or change resistance when compressed. Rather than using a strain gauge resistor wire construction, these sensors use a piezoresistive crystal arranged with a Wheatstone bridge to measure the change in resistance of the piezo crystal. The advantage of these sensors is their ability to measure very high pressures.
- A variable capacitance sensor is an active pressure sensor used to measure both dynamic and static pressure.
- Voltage generators are passive and produce an analog signal of varying voltage or AC frequency.
- Variable reluctance sensors are used to measure rotational speed. Wheel speed, vehicle speed, engine speed, and camshaft and crankshaft position sensors are common applications of these sensors.
- The ability of a material to conduct or resist magnetic lines of force is known as reluctance. Variable reluctance sensors use changing sensor reluctance to induce current flow by changing magnetic field strengths inside the sensor.
- Like variable reluctance sensors, Hall-effect sensors are commonly used to measure rotational speed of a shaft. Though they are more complex and expensive to manufacture than variable reluctance sensors, they produce a digital signal square waveform and have strong signal strength at low shaft rotational speeds.
- Oxygen sensors are used to adjust EGR flow on diesels and are an input to engine and aftertreatment system operation.
- NOx sensors are constructed and operate similarly to wide-range planar oxygen sensors, except that different concentrations of alloys are used in the sensor walls.
- Constructed like a wide-range planar NOx or oxygen sensor, an ammonia sensor uses an aluminum oxide substrate, rather than a ZrO_2 element to detect and generate a voltage for ammonia in a range from 0 to 100 ppm.
- The mass airflow (MAF) sensor measures the weight of air entering the engine intake. Its unique design also reports data about air density, and to some extent, the vapor content.
- MAF sensors are common on engines operating at stoichiometric air-fuel ratios. However, on diesel engines operating with an excess air ratio, the MAF is used as part of the HD-OBD component monitor for the EGR. A variety of electrical signals originate from MAF sensors, but all work using a hot-wire operating principle.
- A thermistor's resistance value varies by manufacturer and the substance being measured.
- Variable reluctance sensors are two-wire passive sensors. The output of the sensor can be measured using an alternating-current voltmeter. As the reluctor speed increases, the AC frequency and voltage produced by the sensor rises proportionately.

- Hall-effect sensors can be tested and diagnosed in a similar way to any three-wire active sensor.
- MAF sensors produce waveforms that can be observed by using a graphing meter. Sensor operation can also be monitored using a scanner or a multimeter. Diagnostics of MAF sensor follow those of any three-wire active sensor.

Key Terms

active sensor A sensor that uses a current supplied by the ECU to operate. An internal microcontroller conditions the sensor's electrical signal.

ammonia sensor A sensor used by selective catalyst reduction (SCR) systems that provides data to the ECU used to measure ammonia slip.

fault code state change A diagnostic technique where the opposite fault code is introduced than the reported one to differentiate problems in sensors, harnesses, and ECUs.

hall-effect sensor A sensor commonly used to measure the rotational speed of a shaft; it has the advantage of producing a digital signal square waveform and has strong signal strength at low shaft rotational speeds.

idle validation switch (IVS) A throttle input circuit used for safety reasons to verify throttle position.

Nernst cells A technology used by exhaust gas sensors that measures the unknown gas concentration by comparing it to a known gas concentration.

NOx sensor A sensor that detects oxygen ions originating from nitric oxide (NOx) from among the other oxygen molecules present in the exhaust gas.

passive sensor A sensor that does not use a current supplied by the ECU to operate.

piezoresistive sensor A sensor that uses a piezoresistive crystal arranged with a Wheatstone bridge to measure the change in resistance of the piezo crystal; these sensors are adapted to measuring vibration and dynamic or continuous pressure changes.

pull-down switch A switch connected between the ECU and a negative ground current potential.

pull-up switch A switch connected between the ECU and a battery positive.

ratiometric This sensor has an output signal that changes in proportion to the supply voltage.

reductant quality (RDQ) sensor A sensor that measures the quality of diesel exhaust fluid (DEF).

reference voltage (Vref) A precisely regulated voltage supplied by the ECU to sensors; the value is typically 5 V DC, but some manufacturers use 8 or 12 volts.

rheostat A variable resistor constructed of a fixed input terminal and a variable output terminal, which vary current flow by passing current through a long, resistive, tightly coiled wire.

sensor count A unit for sensors digital output that is proportional to an analog signal output.

thermistor A temperature-sensitive variable resistor commonly used to measure coolant, oil, fuel, and air temperatures.

variable capacitance pressure sensor A type of active sensor that measures both dynamic and static pressure using a fixed and movable capacitor plate.

variable reluctance (VR) sensor A sensor used to measure rotational speed, including wheel speed, vehicle speed, engine speed, and camshaft and crankshaft position.

virtual sensor A sensor that does not physically exist but data from the sensor is made to appear real using software. A virtual sensor uses predictive algorithms to report data, meaning it calculates an estimated value for a physical variable that usually cannot be directly measured.

wide-range planar sensor A type of sensor technology that uses a current pump to calculate relative concentrations of oxygen, nitric oxide, and ammonia in exhaust gases.

Review Questions

1. Which type of input sensor is used by the engine control system and uses power supplied by the vehicle's ECU?
   a. Active
   b. Passive
   c. Inactive
   d. Delta

2. Which of the following is the most common voltage used for Vref?
   a. +5 volts
   b. +8 volts
   c. 500 milliamps
   d. +12 volts

3. A smart switch has a 10-ohm resistor connected across the pins of a single pole single throw switch. The switch pole is connected to +12 volts and the throw is connected to the ECU. Which of the following measurements will the ECU make if the smart switch is closed?
   a. 0 volts
   b. +12 volts
   c. +2 volts
   d. 10 ohms

4. What is the purpose of a voltage dividing circuit inside an ECU?
   a. It measures circuit amperage.
   b. It measures the voltage drop across a resistor with an unknown value.
   c. It prevents ground loop interference.
   d. It supplies multiple sources for Vref to sensors.

5. Which of these devices measures small changes in the resistance of tiny wires caused by stretching or contraction?
   a. Strain gauge
   b. Wire gauge
   c. Potentiometer
   d. Thermometer

6. What is the sensor signal voltage range of a typical three-wire active sensor?
   a. −0.5 to +4.5 volts
   b. 0 to +5 volts
   c. +0.5 to +4.5 volts
   d. 0 to 4.8 volts

7. What type of switch is connected between the ECU and a negative ground current potential?
   a. pull-down
   b. pull-up
   c. digital
   d. analog

8. What is the name for the sensor that increases its resistance as its temperature decreases?
   a. Negative temperature coefficient thermistor
   b. Positive temperature coefficient thermistor
   c. A thermocouple
   d. Piezoresistor

9. In a variable capacitance pressure sensor, which of the following produces the change in the signal voltage?
   a. The distance between two metal plates
   b. The resistance of strain gauge wires
   c. the type of sensor dielectric material
   d. A reference chamber with atmospheric pressure or vacuum

10. Which of the following fault conditions is reported for the signal circuit if an active three-wire pressure sensor is disconnected?
    a. Signal shorted high or voltage high
    b. Vref shorted to ZVR
    c. Signal voltage shorted low or voltage low
    d. Out of range

ASE Technician A/Technician B Style Questions

1. Technicians A and B are discussing the symptoms of a defective throttle position sensor in a late-model truck. Technician A says that if a resistive track in a throttle position sensor has worn out and is open, the engine only idles. Technician B says that if only one track is worn out, the engine accelerates, but there may be a fault code. Who is correct?
   a. Technician A
   b. Technician B
   c. Both Technician A and Technician B
   d. Neither Technician A nor Technician B

2. Two technicians are discussing engine control input sensors. Technician A says that switches are the simplest sensors of all, because they have no resistance in the closed position and infinite resistance in the open position. Technician B says that a zero-volt switch signal represents a closed switch, while 12 volts represents an open switch. Who is correct?
   a. Technician A
   b. Technician B

c. Both Technician A and Technician B
d. Neither Technician A nor Technician B

3. Technician A says that a pressure sensor with a vacuum chamber measures pressure at sea level as close to 14.5 psi (1 atmosphere). Technician B says that a pressure sensor with no vacuum reference chamber measures atmospheric pressure as close to 14.5 psi (1 atmosphere). Who is correct?
a. Technician A
b. Technician B
c. Both Technician A and Technician B
d. Neither Technician A nor Technician B

4. Technician A says that a pressure differential sensor senses a pressure drop across a venturi as gas velocity increases. Technician B says that a pressure differential sensor combined with a temperature sensor can measure gas mass. Who is correct?
a. Technician A
b. Technician B
c. Both Technician A and Technician B
d. Neither Technician A nor Technician B

5. Technician A says that a variable reluctance sensor used to measure wheel speed can be tested by measuring its resistance when the wheel is spinning. Technician B says a variable reluctance sensor can be tested by ranging a meter to measure less than 12 volts DC and measuring sensor voltage when the wheel is spinning. Who is correct?
a. Technician A
b. Technician B
c. Both Technician A and Technician B
d. Neither Technician A nor Technician B

6. Technician A says that switches are categorized as sensors whenever they provide information to an electronic control system. Technician B says that switch data may indicate a physical value, such as open or closed, up or down, high or low, or on or off. Who is correct?
a. Technician A
b. Technician B
c. Both Technician A and Technician B
d. Neither Technician A nor Technician B

7. Technician A says that the concentration of an unknown gas can be determined using voltage signals generated by two galvanic-type electrochemical cells and applying Kirchhoff's Law to determine the voltage from the cell with the unknown gas concentration. Technician B says that a Nernst cell measures the concentration of an unknown gas compared to a known gas concentration. Who is correct?
a. Technician A
b. Technician B
c. Both Technician A and Technician B
d. Neither Technician A nor Technician B

8. Technician A says that a fault code for a coolant temperature sensor indicates the sensor is defective and requires replacement. Technician B says that fault codes are not that specific and only narrow the fault down to a circuit. More pinpoint testing is likely needed. Who is correct?
a. Technician A
b. Technician B
c. Both Technician A and Technician B
d. Neither Technician A nor Technician B

9. Technician A and B are discussing a fault code for an oil pressure sensor with a steady signal voltage of +3.2 volts. Technician A says that it is a logical or plausibility error-type fault. Technician B says it is an out-of-range fault. Who is correct?
a. Technician A
b. Technician B
c. Both Technician A and Technician B
d. Neither Technician A nor Technician B

10. Technicians A and B are discussing the results of testing a thermistor with an FMI code of 4. The signal voltage from an NTC thermistor for the lubricating oil is +5 volts after the Vref and ZVR wire are shorted together. Technician A says that the sensor is defective. Technician B says the wiring likely has a problem. Who is correct?
a. Technician A
b. Technician B
c. Both Technician A and Technician B
d. Neither Technician A nor Technician B

CHAPTER 25

Understanding and Servicing Electronic Control Systems

Learning Objectives

- **LO 25-1** Identify and explain the purpose, operating principles, and organization of electronic control systems used in electrical systems on commercial vehicles.
- **LO 25-2** Identify and describe areas of electronic control.
- **LO 25-3** Identify and describe principles, types, and subtypes of electronic control loops.
- **LO 25-4** Identify and describe multiple-input multiple-output (MIMO) control systems and their disadvantages.
- **LO 25-5** Identify and describe principles of model predictive control.

- **LO 25-6** Describe the construction and operation of microcontrollers.
- **LO 25-7** Identify and describe the functions of microcontrollers.
- **LO 25-8** Differentiate between the construction, organization, and operation of microcontrollers and microprocessors.
- **LO 25-9** Describe the procedures and equipment used for field replacement and programming of electronic control units (ECUs).

You Are the Technician

In the heavy-truck dealership where you are a technician, you are designated to a skill group for diesel engine repair with specialized skills related to servicing exhaust aftertreatment systems. Daily you not only diagnose and service complaints for the dealer OEM, but also vehicles referred to you by other shops. Those problems are often related to incorrect service practices for replacement of particulate filters, sensors, and diagnosing diesel exhaust fluid (DEF)-related fault codes. Those trucks arrive at your shop because of the priority given to aftertreatment-related faults that can quickly result in loss of engine power and even shut down. Trucks are also critical to businesses serving customers and generating revenue, and it's enormously disruptive when there is a high frequency of fault codes associated with certain models and production dates that cause considerable aggravation to customers. One manufacturer in particular has a high frequency of aftertreatment system-related complaints from its latest vehicles. Several fault codes are associated with DEF quality, and exhaust gas sensor faults are derating the engine to operate at only idle speed. The sensors and most of the exhaust system parts have been replaced and there are no defects found when diagnostic pinpoint tests outlined in fault code diagnostic trees are completed. While a number of shops often deal with such difficult problems by reflashing engine control modules (ECMs) with unauthorized third-party calibration files that shut off fault monitoring in the aftertreatment system or modify software switches to ignore some faults, one vehicle has the latest generation of microcontroller software with boot and flash loaders having anti-tampering security features that are uncrackable. This means the root cause of the problem must be properly identified and corrected. As you consider what approaches to use to diagnose the problem vehicle, consider the following questions:

1. How are the aftertreatment faults likely identified and set on this vehicle?
2. What are some options the manufacturer is likely to offer as a solution to this problem?
3. Identify some common diagnostic and repair strategies built into original equipment manufacturers (OEM) service and diagnostic software that can be used to prevent the faults codes from re-occurring.

Introduction

An earlier chapter explained how today's commercial vehicles can be described as computers on wheels. Technicians are just as likely to use a computer as they use a wrench to service vehicles. Not a single vehicle system operates without complete, or at least an extensive degree of electronic control. In fact, industry observers attribute 80% of new features in the latest vehicles are made possible using advanced electronic control systems. This has not always been the case. Until recent years, mechanical devices, such as levers, springs, linkage, gears, cables, or diaphragms, controlled the operation of engines, braking, instrumentation, or transmissions (**FIGURE 25-1**). Electrical systems using microcontroller-based controls now replace mechanical components with operational capabilities far exceeding any mechanical system and can complete many more tasks with greater precision, efficiency, and reliability (**FIGURE 25-2**). The dominance and sophistication of electronic control makes skill development related to servicing control system technology one of the most important priorities for successful technicians. In fact, a new area of technology called **mechatronics** deals with the latest category of components where microcontrollers are embedded into mechanical systems, creating unique operational capabilities and functions. Components from steering gears, DEF dosing units, turbochargers, and exhaust gas recirculation (EGR) actuators are just a few of the many examples of mechatronic technology on today's commercial vehicles (**FIGURE 25-3**).

Technicians do not repair or need detailed knowledge of electronic components in electronic control systems, but they need to understand basic functionality because they interact with them daily through electronic service tools and servicing problems with mechatronic components or systems operated by microcontrollers. Software reprogramming of electronic control modules is also an important service issue within a vehicle's lifecycle because updating software calibrations for major control modules is a powerfully effective repair strategy to solve operating problems and repair faults. In fact, in many instances, service reprogramming of ECUs is increasingly important since it is the only repair method to correct control system related complaints

Because so many vehicle systems are now operated by programmable microcontrollers embedded in mechanical components, or mechatronic devices, understanding microcontrollers operation and service is now practically essential for technicians (**FIGURE 25-4**). Background information about electronic control systems using microcontrollers is foundational for understanding and identifying control system-related complaints, developing proper service practices, choosing correct diagnostic strategies, effectively using service tools, and making sound repair recommendations. This chapter provides a brief overview of the construction and operation of electronic control systems by outlining general concepts and principles to help technicians better understand the technology that informs service practice. Because technicians can expect to use service literature dealing with control systems and take advanced courses provided by manufacturers, many of the technical terms and concepts introduced in this chapter are background information for technical explanations likely encountered in training courses and service literature.

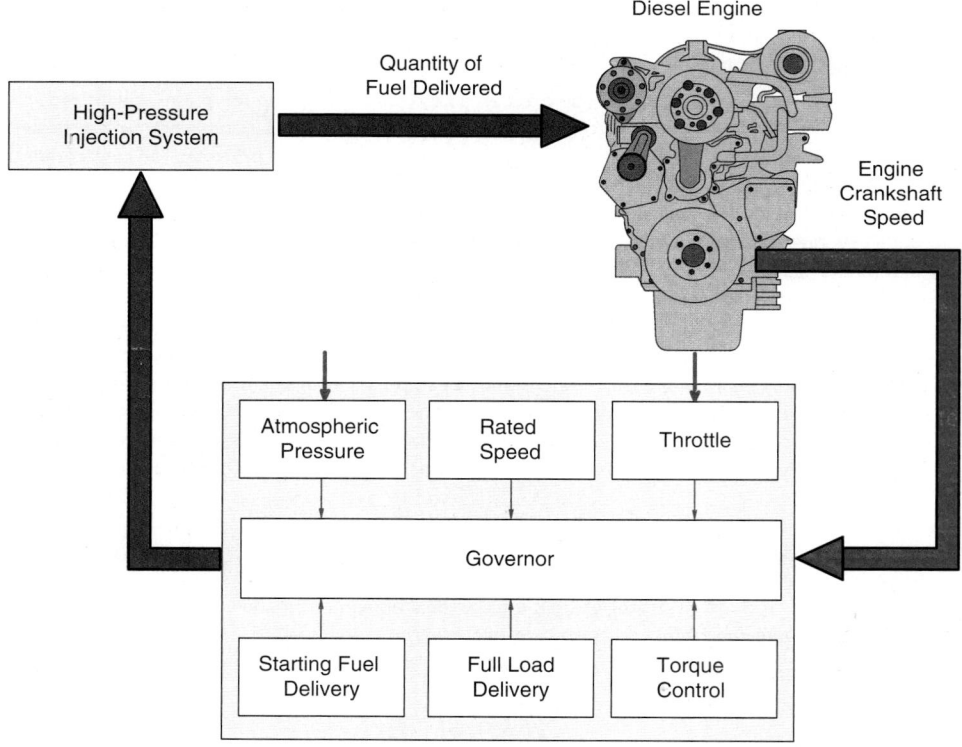

FIGURE 25-1 Mechanical control systems have been replaced by electronic control.

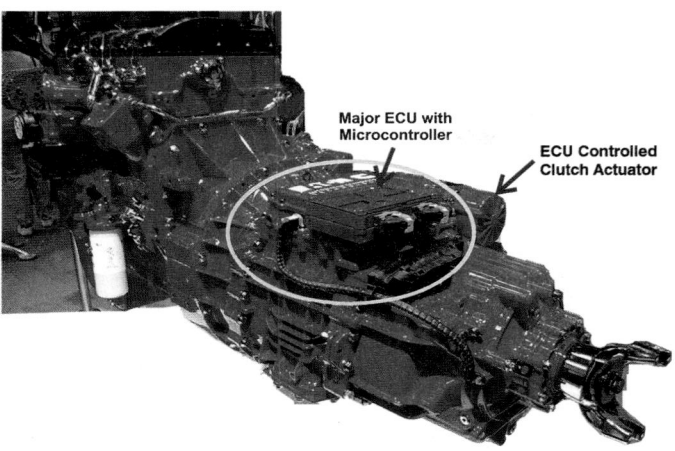

FIGURE 25-2 ECUs containing programmable microcontrollers now operate major components and systems.

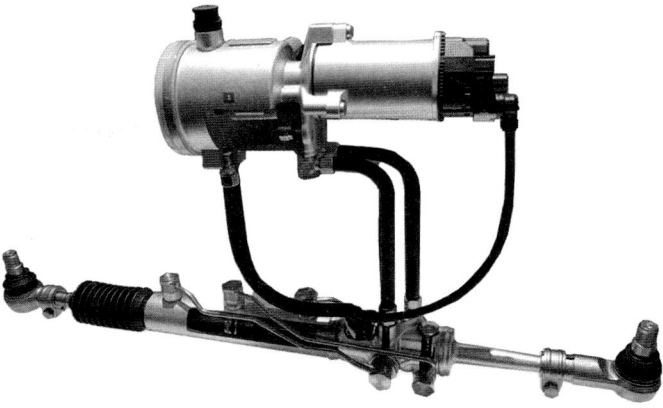

FIGURE 25-4 This electronically controlled steering rack for a rear axle steering system is an example of an embedded system. Embedded systems use advanced microcontrollers to operate a device or electronically regulate a systems operation.

FIGURE 25-3 This electronically controlled coolant pump combining mechanical and electrical components with embedded electronic control is an example of a mechatronic device. New capabilities and features are made possible using mechatronic technology.

Courtesy of MAHLE GmbH

Electronic Control Systems

LO 25-1 Identify and explain the purpose, operating principles, and organization of electronic control systems used in electrical systems on commercial vehicles.

The function of any **electronic control system** is to automatically regulate the operation of a component or system output to maintain it within a desired operating range. Another name for the targeted or desired operating range is **set-point** (**FIGURE 25-5**). This means that if the control system senses a device or system operation moving away from the desired set-point, the controller, which is like the system's brains, changes its output signals to restore or correct the set-point value. Set-points vary for many components and systems, but

electronic microcontrollers change the properties of electrical signal outputs, correcting errors or maintaining a set-point based on data from input signals. For example, the set-point for an alternator typically maintains the charging system output voltage at 14.1 volts by using a voltage regulator. However, as vehicle electrical loads change, so do current demands on the system and the charging current. Because the voltage regulator sense changes to charging system output voltage caused by varying current demands and changing engine speed, it can measure the difference or error between the set-point and the actual system voltage. This discrepancy or error between those two values enables the voltage regulator to increase or decrease the amount of electrical current supplied to the alternator's rotor and correct deviations from the set-point voltage (**FIGURE 25-6**). Regardless of the system or component that is electronically operated, the output signals from an electronic control system are varied to correct deviations of the system or device operation from its desired set-point. In the example of the voltage regulator, output charging system voltage is an input signal used to determine whether a control system needs to change the rotor's magnetic field strength to maintain alternator charging set-point voltage.

Organization of Electronic Control Systems

Unlike a mechanical system, the operation of electronic control systems can look mysterious because they are built with a variety of sensors, wires, electrical actuators, and electronic control modules, which are all operated by invisible electrical signals. However, to understand how electronic control systems operate, it is helpful to review and observe that the functioning of any electronic control system can be broken down into three major divisions (**FIGURE 25-7**):

1. Sensing
2. Processing
3. Output or actuation (**FIGURE 25-8**)

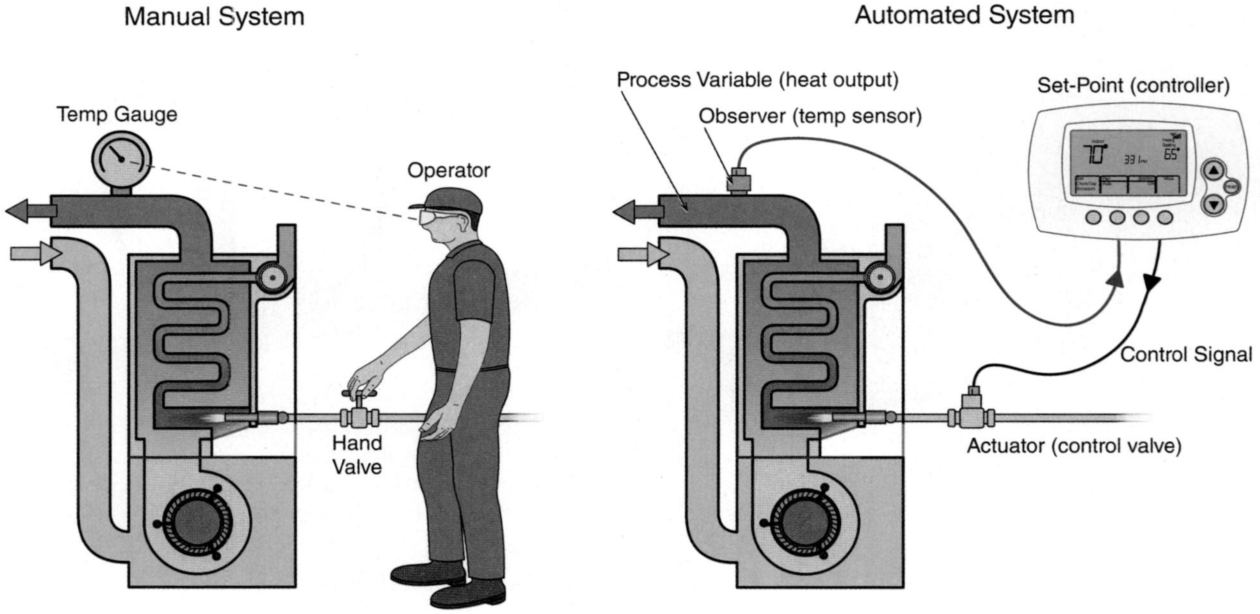

Manual System

Automated System

FIGURE 25-5 Comparing a manual and electronic control system. The thermostat establishes the set-point temperature for the house. The temperature is automatically regulated by switching the furnace on and off.

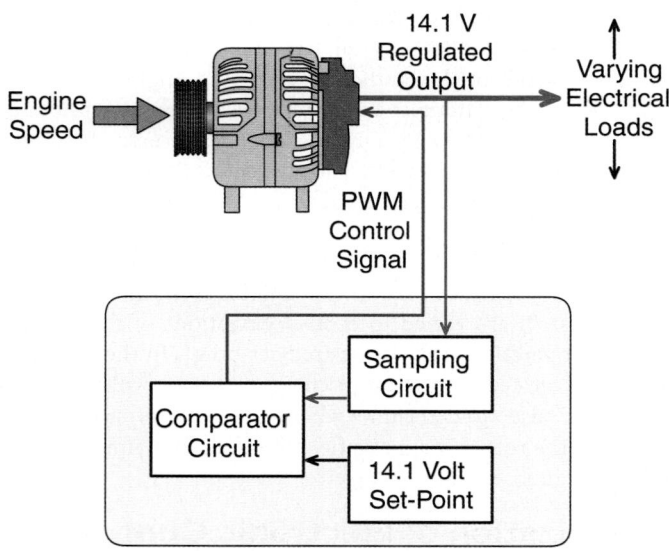

FIGURE 25-6 The charging system uses set-point regulation of the output voltage. The comparator circuit varies the signal to the rotor to correct for deviations from set-point.

Sensing Functions

In electronic control systems, sensors are input devices that convert some physical property or form of energy into an electrical signal. A term sometimes used interchangeably with sensor is transducer. Transducers are devices converting one form of energy into an electrical signal, but sensors are devices with a wider number of applications than only energy conversion. Sensors function to collect data about a system operating conditions or the state of a device by measuring some value, such

as temperature, position, speed, pressure, flow, level, angle, and magnetic field strength. Sensor inputs also include driver or passenger demands that are sensed through devices, such as switches, potentiometers, position sensors, touch panels, or even voice commands. Various types of electrical signals from sensors provide input data to an electronic control unit. As outlined in the previous chapters on sensors and electronic signal processing, the types of input signals supplied to the processing stage of control include:

- Varying analog alternating current (AC) or direct current (DC) voltage
- Varying frequency
- Digital signal (open/closed, on/off 1 or 0)
- Serial data (digital—binary or hexadecimal)
- Pulse-width–modulated signal
- Radio waves

Processing Functions

Processing refers to the second major element of the control system that collects sensor data, analyzes it, and determines what the control system outputs should be based on simple electrical logic, a set of logical instructions, or more advanced software programs. The processing function of electronic control systems is located in an electronic control unit or module. The simplest definition of an Electronic Control Unit, or ECU, is it is an electronic device that produces electronic signals that controls or regulates the operation of an electrically operated device or system. In a commercial vehicle, an ECU can consist of anything from a few electronic components, such as transistors, diodes, capacitors and resistors, soldered together, often onto a circuit board, to larger, more sophisticated devices with

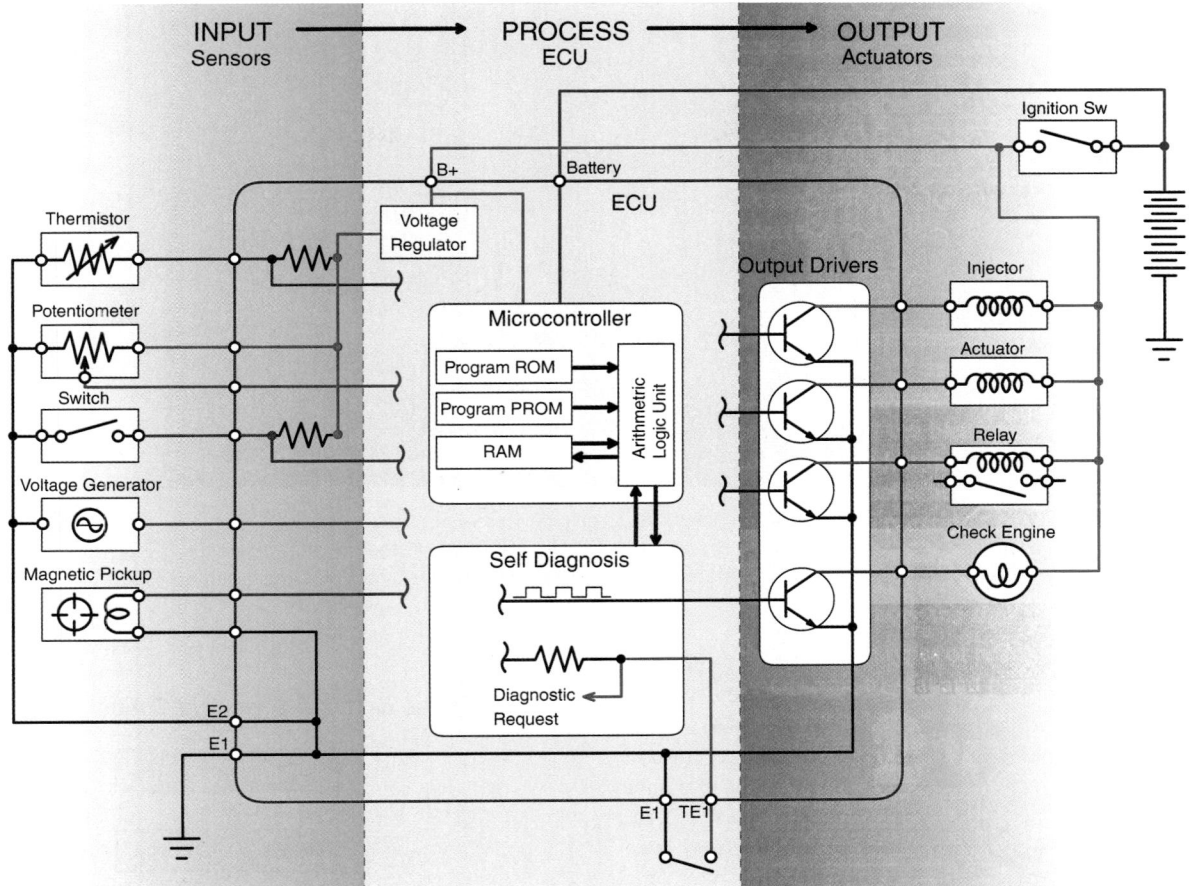

FIGURE 25-7 Three stages of signal processing. Sensors form input signals, software-controlled microprocessors are used to manipulate data, and electrically operated output devices carry out instructions of the processor.

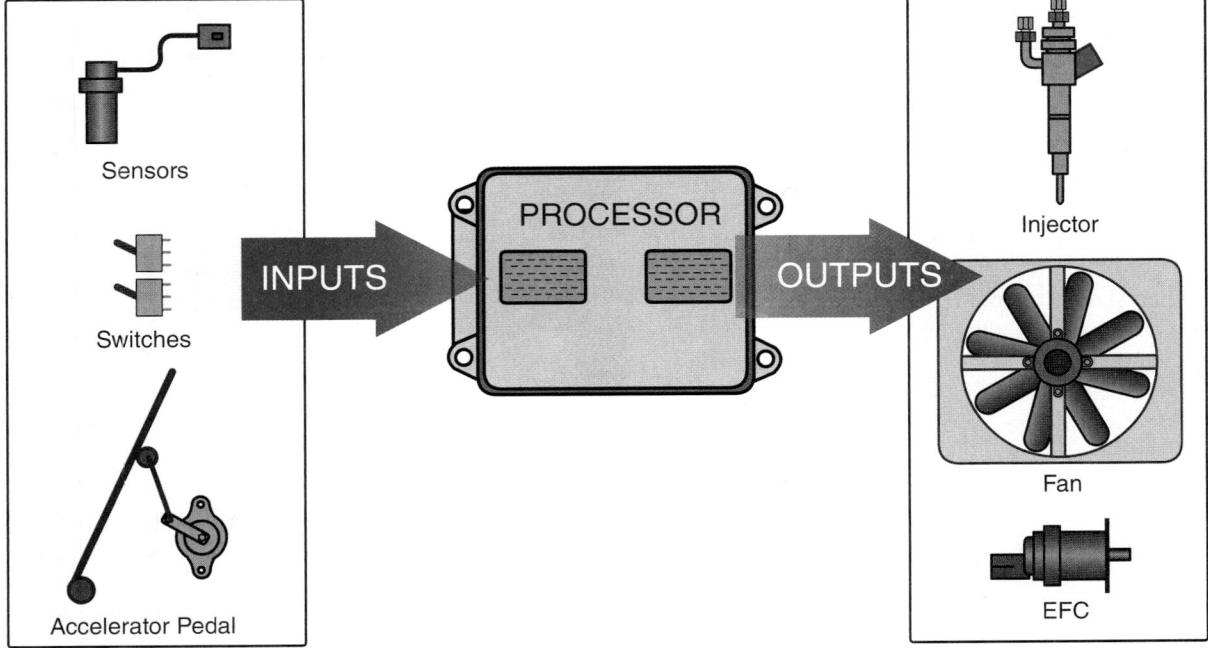

FIGURE 25-8 All electronic control systems process electrical signals in three distinct stages: data collection from sensor inputs; data processing inside an electronic control module; and production of output signals for electrically operated devices.

FIGURE 25-9 This major ECU contains electronic devices, such as capacitors and transistors, plus small integrated circuits (ICs) and large-scale integrated circuits with limited memory. Microcontrollers have more memory and programmable capabilities, and greater processing power than ICs.

multiple or folded circuit boards containing integrated circuits, or microcontrollers running software (**FIGURE 25-9**). More complex ECUs with sophisticated tasks control the operation of major components, such as engines and transmissions that have many sensors and output devices, and an extensive set of programmed instructions stored in software code. They may even control the entire electrical system. Simpler ECUs may only control some lights, the dash gauges, or the speed and intermittent delay time of a windshield wiper motor.

Processing Algorithms   At the center of almost every contemporary electronic control unit's operation is a microcontroller. This advanced electronic component is made from integrated circuits and, for now, can be simply compared to a calculator or, in most instances, an advanced programmable calculator that has memory storage capabilities. A microcontroller is comparable to a calculator because it solves mathematical problems using algorithms. An algorithm, as defined previously in this textbook, is a mathematical formula used to solve a problem or answer a question (**FIGURE 25-10**). Some simple questions could be: How much fuel should be injected? When should the malfunction indicator lamp (MIL) switch on? When should the next transmission upshift or downshift take place? Or, what speed is the vehicle traveling (**FIGURE 25-11**)? To illustrate how an algorithm answers the question about how fast the vehicle is traveling, remember that electrical pulses are generated by the speed sensors located at the wheel ends or on the transmission output shaft. These input signals can be counted by the microcontroller and the length of time between the generation of each electrical pulse. Using an internal clock measuring the time between pulses or the time that a fixed number of pulses are transmitted, the microcontroller can calculate vehicle speed using the mathematical formula, which is a type of algorithm: Speed = Distance/Time or # of tooth pulses/time.

Cruise Control—Executive Control Chart

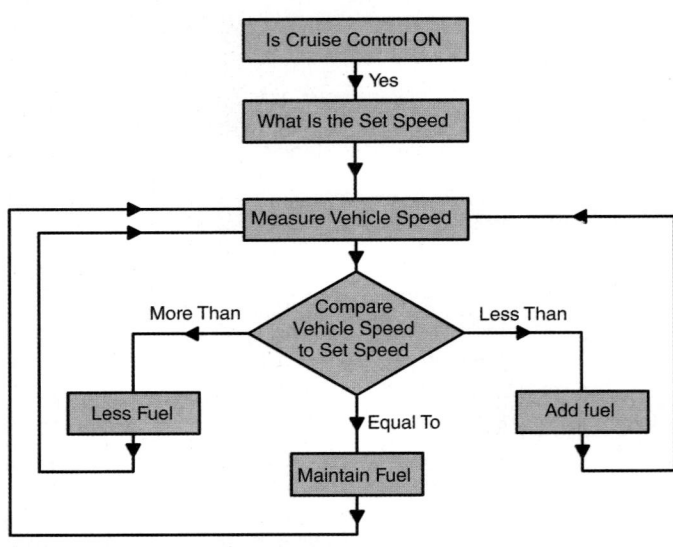

FIGURE 25-10 An algorithm provides clear steps for how to solve a problem. A flowchart for an algorithm answers the question: How does the cruise control operate?

Processors can also use logic or a stored set of conditions to do the job of analyzing the input data to calculate a specific output signal. Something as simple as an open switch or circuit for the transmission neutral-gear signal will prevent a microcontroller from energizing a starter relay needed to crank the starting motor. In the example of the microcontroller paired with the speed sensor, the microcontrollers output could be signals used by the instrument cluster speedometer or a digital signal from the antilock brake system (ABS) critical to other processing functions requiring vehicle speed data.

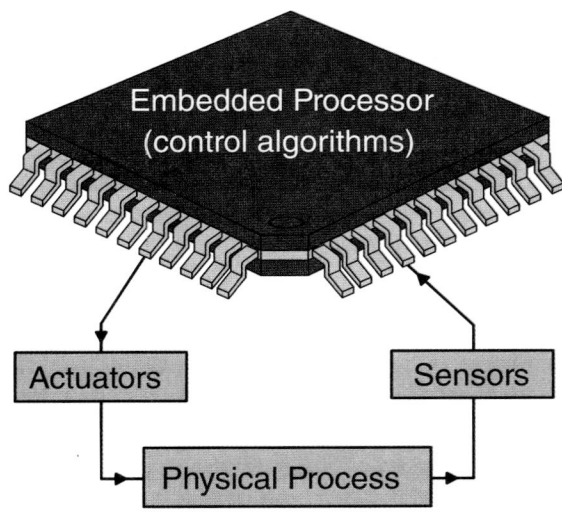

FIGURE 25-11 Algorithms inside the microcontroller contain mathematical algorithms regulating the operation of a controlled system.

Output Functions

The third functional element of a control system is creating an output signal inside the ECU that can be used to control the operation of an electrically operated component or system. These outputs may be signals used to operate anything from a single light-emitting diode (LED) light, digital display of numeric or alphabetic information, or electric current to operate solenoids, relays, injectors, actuators, motors, digital display, or other electromechanical devices. Like input signals, output signals can be analog or digital. Signal types can vary in terms of voltage, amperage, and frequency. Digital signals, such as serial data used to communicate with other ECUs over onboard networks, is another category of output signal. Electrical signals from the ECU drivers are monitored by a diagnostic system, which evaluates voltage drops and current flow to output devices to determine whether out-of-range-type faults are present in output devices and circuits.

Output Drivers Output drivers are commonly switching-type transistors that turn current on and off to output devices. Output drivers can be categorized as high, low or, push-pull type, depending on the current polarity available at the ECU pin (**FIGURE 25-12**). High-side drivers switch or drive current using positive polarity. This means that a load connected to a constantly supplied negative ground is switched on and off by supplying a matching positive polarity current. Low-side drivers switch or drive a load on and off if it is connected to a constantly supplied positive polarity current. The decision to use a driver that is either high- or low-side depends on a variety of factors, such as whether the load is high- or low-amperage, voltage-sensitive, has inductive or resistive properties, or has other special electrical characteristics and requirements. Push-pull drivers switch or drive sharply defined square-shaped waveforms, such as serial data or piezoelectric injectors, by switching current using both

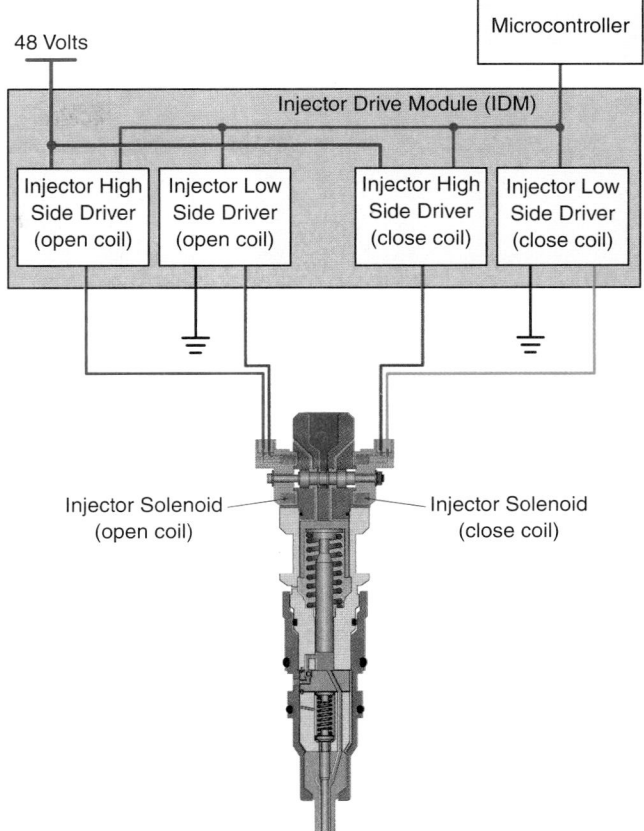

FIGURE 25-12 For this HEUI injector a low-side output driver swtiches a negative polarity current source to an injector coil while a high-side driver switches positive polarity current.

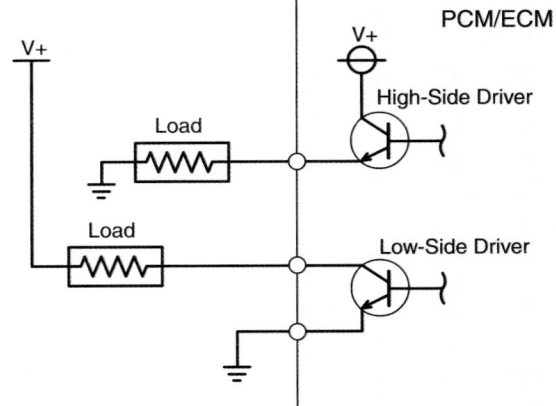

FIGURE 25-13 Push-pull drivers switch both positive- and negative-polarity current to produce sharp-edge-shapedwave forms.

negative and positive polarity (**FIGURE 25-13**). Another term commonly used to describe a set of four transistors switching the polarity of a voltage applied to a push-pull load is a **H-bridge**. These circuits are often used to operate injector solenoids or

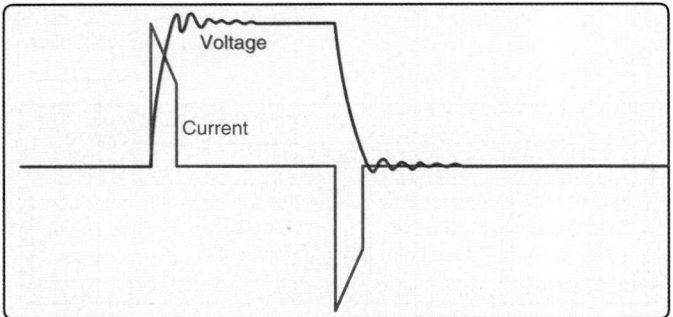

FIGURE 25-14 A push-pull driver circuit switches current polarity to a piezoelectric injector to produce a rapid end to an injection event.

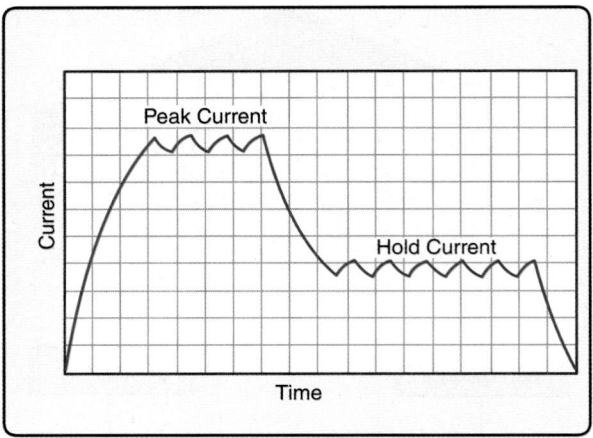

FIGURE 25-15 The waveform of an inductive-type injector coil uses a peak-and-hold-shaped waveform to reduce heat buildup.

enable DC motors to reverse direction. In training materials or service literature, manufacturers often describe what type of signal is supplied by an output driver to a device. Understanding what type of signal an output driver is expected to have is helpful when choosing test instruments and analyzing electrical signals with graphing meters, using software, programs to observe signal waveforms, or on scanners, or using simple voltmeters to perform quick checks for output signal voltage **FIGURE 25-14**.

Output Driver Transistors Very low voltage output signals are produced by the microcontroller inside the ECU and often need amplification to operate circuits with high current requirements. Output devices with high current demands, such as solenoids, relays, electric motors, power inverters, digital displays, heater circuits in gas sensors, and lights, are supplied current or the appropriate electrical signals by output drivers. Output drivers are typically transistors that can amplify the much smaller amounts of current at a micro-amp level for signals produced by a microcontroller. Using a driver circuit to amplify output signals reduces potentially damaging high current flow through a microcontroller and enables further conditioning of the output circuit signals to match the circuits characteristics. For example, if the output signal is through a wire coil, the load has inductive resistance. In this application, a peak and hold or sawtooth waveform from the driver is preferred (**FIGURE 25-15**). The peak voltage quickly builds a magnetic field by initially pushing high current flow through a device, but dropping the voltage shortly afterwards. This strategy prevents excessive current consumption through a device, potentially causing overheating and shortened service life. Electrical characteristics of inductive loads are different from a low voltage-resistive load, such as simply switching an LED indicator light on and off. Drivers for resistive load circuits do not use a peak-and-hold current rate shape instead, they use sharp on-off edges for square-shaped current waveforms.

▶ **TECHNICIAN TIP**

In older ECUs using a single bipolar-type transistor as an output driver, an output signal that is shorted to ground or another power source can quickly overheat the transistor, permanently damaging the ECU. When testing output components connected to older ECU, do not use jumper wires to supply grounds or positive battery voltage to devices that are connected to an ECU. Always disconnect the device from an ECU before performing pinpoint electrical tests.

In circuits requiring very high output current, a single bipolar-type transistor may not be used since it requires a high amount of current supplied to the base to switch current flow through the emitter collector circuit. A small integrated circuit or microcontroller may not be capable of supplying this current. Instead, an output driver may consist of two paired transistors, such as a negative-positive-negative (NPN) or positive-negative-positive (PNP) pair, or two field effect transistors (FETs) connected together, in what is called a Darlington pair configuration (**FIGURE 25-16**). Using this arrangement of transistors, a low voltage signal from a microcontroller applied to the base or gate of one transistor is used to switch current flow through another transistor. The output current from the first transistor is supplied to the base or gate of a second transistor. This arrangement multiplies the low-voltage signal from the microcontroller. Darlington pair transistor configurations can have very high DC gains. **Transistor gain** refers to the ratio of current flow between collector (output) and the transistor base current used to switch current flow through the emitter collector circuit. In Darlington pairs, transistors can achieve a gain ratio of several hundred to several thousand times the amount of micro-amperage applied to the a transistor base.

In addition to using single transistors or Darlington transistor pairs, FETs, referred to as metal oxide semiconductor field effect transistors (MOSFETs), are more commonly used as output drivers (**FIGURE 25-17**). (The construction and operation of MOSFETs is described more completely in the Semiconductors chapter.) In contemporary ECUs, MOSFETs are exclusively used as output drivers (**FIGURE 25-18**). Unlike a bipolar transistor requiring a current supply to the transistor base to switch the transistor open or closed, a MOSFET gate, the equivalent to the base of the bipolar transistor, is only voltage and not amperage or current sensitive. This means it needs almost no amperage applied to the gate to allow or block current flow through the source–drain channel. Also, unlike bipolar-type semiconductors with a resistive junction area separating positive (P) and negative (N) material, MOSFETs are comparatively far less resistive and drop little voltage through current channels. Because of this feature, MOSFETs operate much cooler and waste less current through resistive heating. Because switching a MOSFET channel to open or close requires virtually no current, only voltage, an almost limitless number of MOSFET gates can be connected in parallel to switch or drive output devices with no significant increase in current consumption through a microcontroller

signaling circuit. MOSFETs are also high-impedance devices, which means it requires high voltage externally applied to the ECU output pin to damage the MOSFET source–drain channel. However, the gates of MOSFETs can be easily damaged by electrostatic discharge of current.

N-channel enhancement-type MOSFET, are commonly used since the channel conducting current flow is normally blocked until a positive bias voltage is applied to the gate (**FIGURES 25-19, 25-20**). When the gate is biased by a positive-polarity voltage signal, current flow through the channel from the source to drain is opened. The quantity of current allowed to pass through the channel varies proportionally to the voltage applied to the gate, with increasing voltage needed to move the gate from only minimal resistance then to almost no resistance.

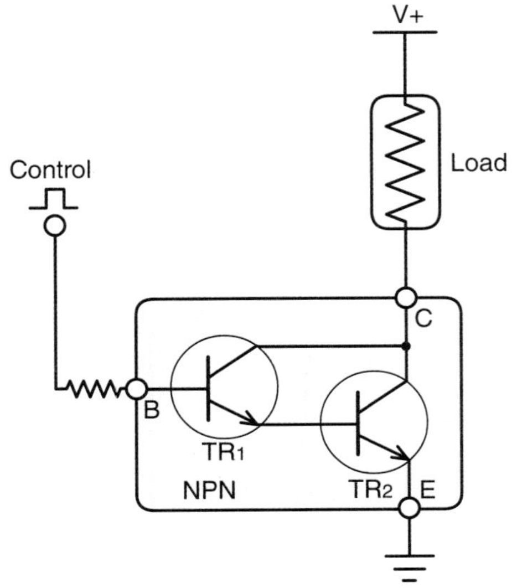

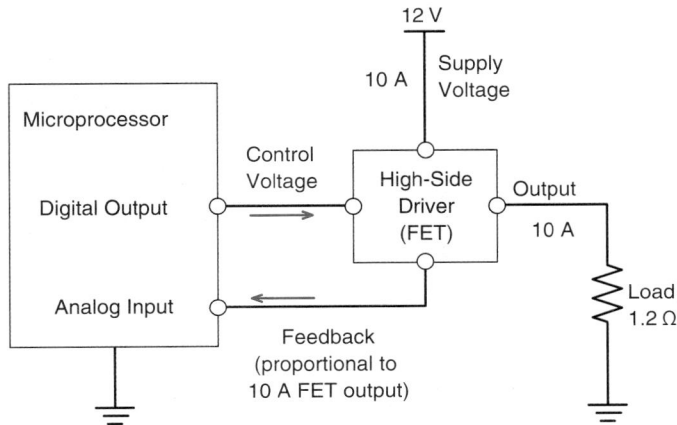

FIGURE 25-16 A Darlington pair of transistors multiplies the output signal of one transistor by another. Bipolar transistors are shown here but this can also be a pair of FETs.

FIGURE 25-17 Field effect transistors used as output drivers can measure amperage through a circuit and provide feedback to a microcontroller.

FIGURE 25-18 The FICM for 6.6 L DMAX diesel CRS2 injectors. The module controls injector events and steps up battery voltage to a level high enough to energize injectors.

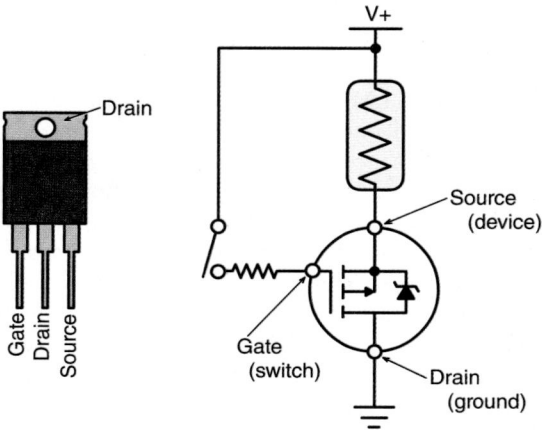

FIGURE 25-19 This "P" channel MOSFET opens the circuit to the load when the switch is closed. A Zener diode protects the circuit from excessive voltage.

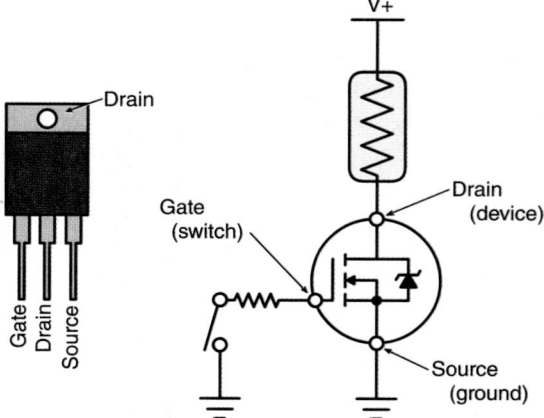

FIGURE 25-20 This "N" channel MOSFET closes the circuit to the load when the switch is closed. A Zener diode protects the circuit from excessive voltage.

▶ **TECHNICIAN TIP**

While the source-drain channels of MOSFETS can handle high current flow and are not sensitive to electrostatic discharge (ESD), the same is not true for the gates. Voltage-sensitive gates in FETs are easily destroyed by ESD. Microcontrollers and other integrated circuits using MOSFET circuits have voltage-sensitive gates. Whenever one works with ESD-sensitive components, always use protocols to prevent ESD, such as wearing grounding straps, discharging any ESD through metal vehicle parts by grabbing bare metal before handling sensitive instrument clusters, and keeping parts in electrically conductive mylar bags until they are ready for installation.

Areas of Electronic Control

LO 25-2 Identify and describe areas of electronic control.

Microcontrollers are found almost everywhere on commercial vehicles. They range from simple controllers inside a speedometer, auxiliary heater, or window motor, to mechatronic components and ECUs. Major system ECU's circuit boards can use a single controller or several sophisticated microcontrollers supported by a dozen or more smaller controllers. Major system controllers, such as those for the electrical system, transmission, or engine, are called **domain controllers** because they regulate the operation of multiple system-related components. Because microcontrollers are the most essential component in control systems and ECUs, or the brains of the control system, they need to be examined more closely. Increasingly ECUs and their microcontrollers are requiring more service work associated with malfunctioning systems, poor system performance, failure to generate fault codes, or false failures. Not only is it important to identify control system-related issues and differentiate them from component-level malfunctions, but control systems are requiring more frequent calibration updates. The next section primarily focuses on the construction and operation of microcontrollers found in ECUs for medium-to-large control systems having multiple inputs and outputs.

ECU Domains

Major ECUs are used in commercial vehicles to perform tasks dedicated to specific areas of control. These major areas of control are sometimes referred to as domains, which may contain multiple ECU units. In commercial vehicles, ECUs are used in at least these five major areas:

1. Engine and transmission or powertrain control
2. Body and electrical system control
3. Aftertreatment Control
4. Chassis Control, which operate vehicle stability controls associated with braking, traction, steering, suspension systems and air system accessories. More advanced systems integrating a variety of other driver-assistance control systems include collision avoidance or roll-over protection systems (**FIGURE 25-21**).
5. Infotainment—Onboard entertainment and navigation systems use inputs from satellites, cell towers, information storage systems, passengers, and operators to provide advanced visual and audio data outputs.

Manufacturers are attempting to reduce the number of ECUs by integrating smaller segmented control areas into larger domains using a single, more sophisticated ECU with faster processing capabilities. Engine ECU and aftertreatment ECUs are examples where the aftertreatment module functions are now integrated into the engine ECU in the latest vehicles. However, the five large control areas are frequently broken down into more limited areas of subcontrol using smaller, simpler, and less expensive types of ECUs. For example, a modern diesel engine has an electronic control unit that may be complemented by a module controlling only the injectors, or glow-plugs, EGR system, or the turbocharger. The control areas and modules are not isolated from one another because the modules exchange information with one another using several methods of communication. At the smallest level, all microcontrollers have the capability to transmit and receive information between the pins of a serial data communication port. Serial data can

FIGURE 25-21 Some areas and domains where ECU's control the operation of major chassis systems of on-highway and vocational vehicles.

be exchanged between a microcontroller and another system device, such as a liquid-crystal display (LCD) (**FIGURE 25-22**). In vehicles with multiple ECU's, these communication pathways are called networks, and the wires or fiberoptic cables that carry the communication signals are called data buses. Two of the most common methods for network communication are the local area interconnect (LIN), the simplest network arrangement that is described more completely in the chapter on Onboard Networks (**FIGURE 25-23**), and the controller area network (CAN). CAN, the most important network required by legislation, connects major vehicle control modules together

using the Society of Automotive Engineers (SAE) J-1939 standard as a template for the network's design and operation. European built vehicles use, the International Organization for Standardization (ISO) 11783 standard for network rules, governing such things as how each of the network components are constructed, how data is exchanged, and how fault codes are described and reported (**FIGURE 25-24**).

Several other SAE and ISO standards apply to vehicle electronics for passenger and vehicle safety. They are intended to prevent catastrophic failures, such as a vehicle of engine runaway condition if an ECU fails, or if software code becomes

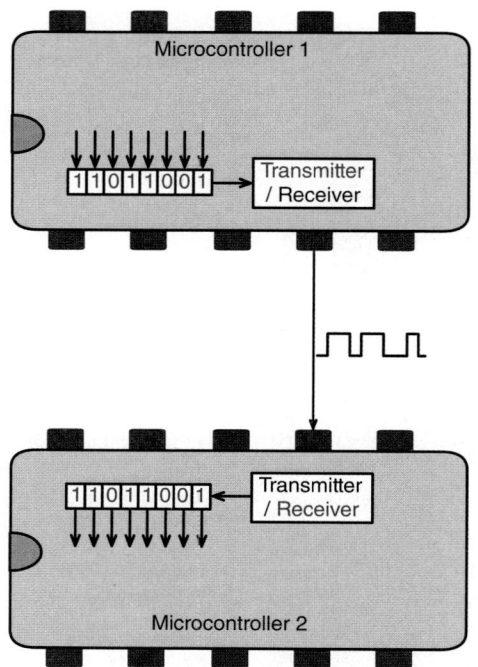

FIGURE 25-22 Microcontrollers can exchange information between themselves or with other devices through a standardized serial communication port located on at least two pins of the controller package Tx (transmit) and Rx (Receive).

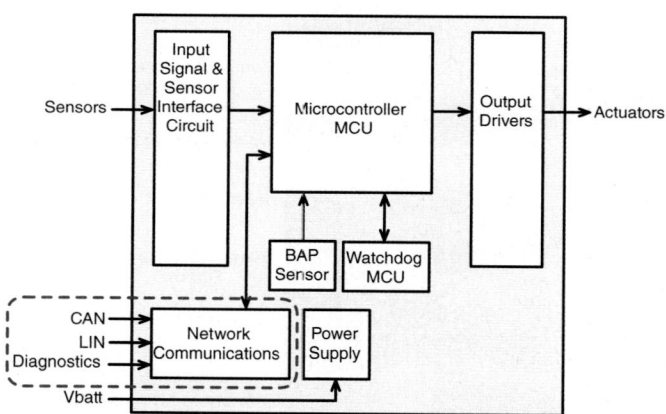

FIGURE 25-23 Microcontrollers and ECUs communicate with one another and other devices over network communication pathways called data buses.

corrupted, plus protect the costly ECUs from over-voltage conditions, reverse polarity electromagnetic interference, high temperatures, moisture, mechanical shock, short circuits, etc.

Principles of Electronic Control Loops

LO 25-3 Identify and describe principles, types, and subtypes of electronic control loops.

As outlined earlier in the chapter, the purpose of any electronic control system is to automatically regulate the operation of a component or system output to maintain it within a desired

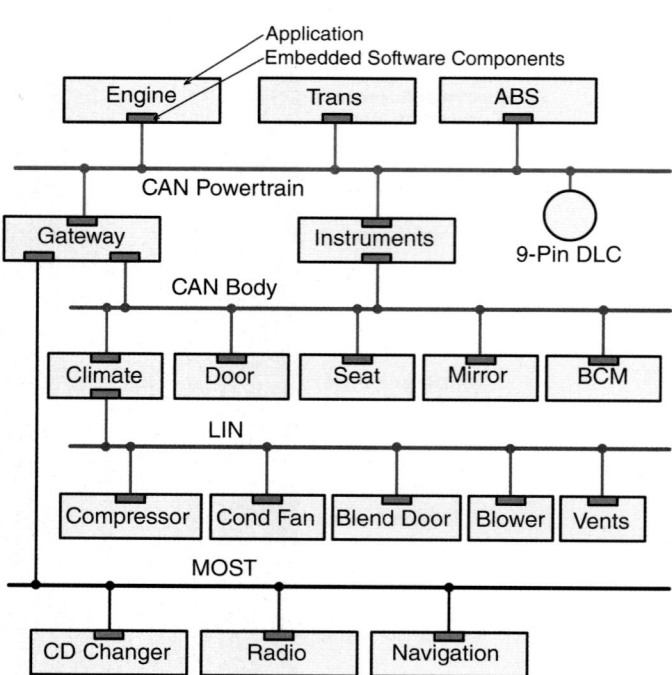

FIGURE 25-24 The controlled area network (CAN) data bus is the communication pathway for safety-related and major system ECUs.

operating range (**FIGURE 25-25**). One of the most effective ways it can control a process is to monitor its actual output and compare it with a desired output. For example, if a cruise control system is expected to maintain road speed a driver sets at 50 mph (80 kph), feedback from a vehicle speed sensor is essential to monitor and maintain the vehicle speed in its desired range. An arrangement in which a feedback signal is used to adjust a process generating an output signal is called a closed-loop control system. Closed-loop control systems monitor and compare a control system's actual output with the desired output to make corrections or adjustments to the control unit's output signals (**FIGURE 25-26**).

This example of a control loop regulation in the speed control system seems simple enough and it functions well every day for most users. But consider how well the system might respond if a vehicle is traveling over hilly terrain with many bumps or over a gravel road and the trip is accompanied by headwinds and cross winds. Frequent corrections to the output signals controlling engine speed are required. How quickly the system responds to the outside influences affecting speed could change the speed control system's operational smoothness and accuracy. If there was electromechanical linkage moving a throttle lever, changes to its mechanical resistance, return spring tension, and how well it responds to electrical signals will influence the quality of the corrections made by speed control to achieve the desired speed. If the control loop system is not well-designed, speed control could be inaccurate and the vehicle speed could surge, travel too slow or fast compared to set speed, or change speed too abruptly. This example of the types of disturbances affecting closed-loop control is intended to help technicians begin to think about other factors that are involved in the operation of a closed-loop control

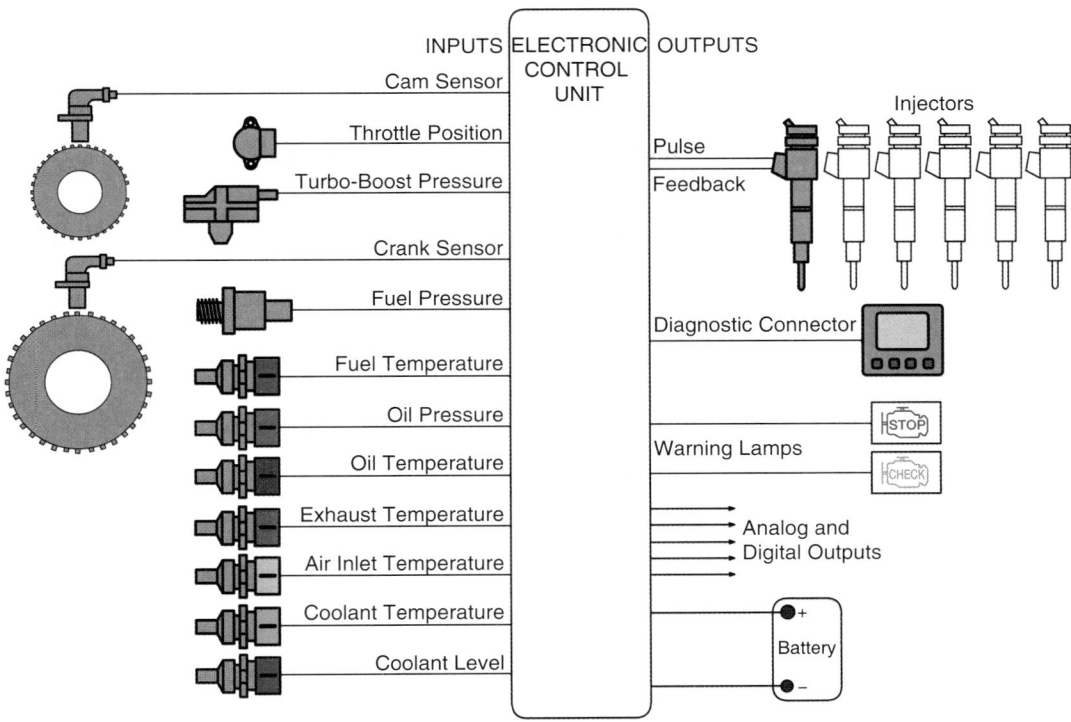

FIGURE 25-25 While the high-pressure injection system meters the fuel supplied to the combustion chamber, the governor controls the quantity of fuel injected based on a variety of inputs and control logic stored in software instructions.

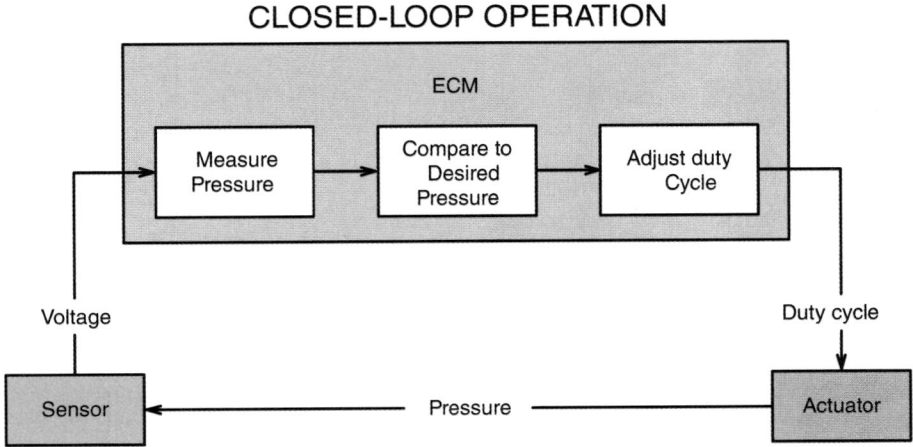

FIGURE 25-26 Closed-loop control uses sensor data supplied to the ECU to regulate the actuator or system output.

system (**FIGURE 25-27**). There are a set of problems that closed-loop control of vehicle speed can have that extend to other looping controls used by engines, transmissions, ABS/automatic traction control (ATC), and other vehicle systems operating with electronic controls. This next section about electronic control examines the types and operation of electronic control loop systems, problems encountered in control loops, and the latest methods to regulate system operation of much more complex control systems with multiple-input multiple-output (MIMO).

Open- and Closed-Loop Control System Error

Before looking more closely at closed-loop control system, which traditionally has dominated electronic control systems, it's valuable to understand an open-loop system first. Manufacturers use the term open loop in service and training literature to describe a control system where no monitoring of the system output takes place to change input signals or influence a control

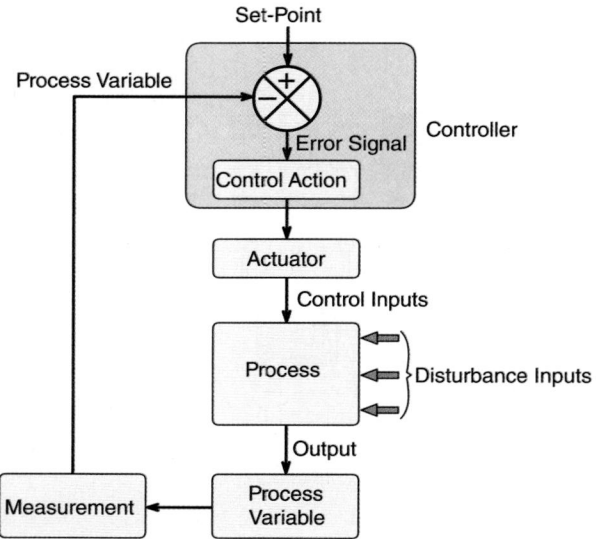

FIGURE 25-27 Components of a closed-loop control system. Closed-loop control helps correct for system disturbances that move an output from its set-point.

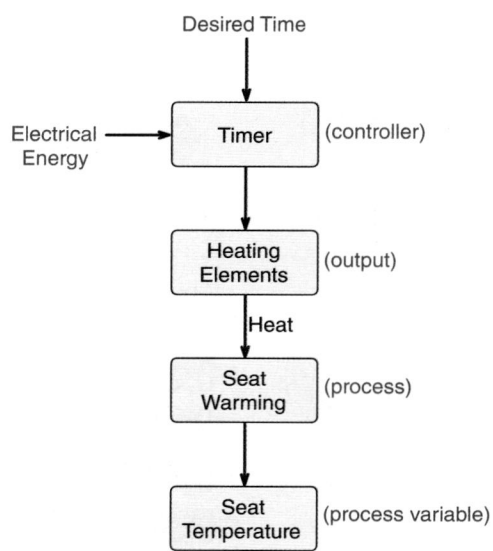

FIGURE 25-28 An open-loop system is a type of non-feedback control in which the output has no influence or effect on the input signal.

systems action. Measurements of system process variable (PV) or outputs are not performed and not "fed back" to correct output signals, nor are they compared to a desired output condition. Because the control loop does not close, with its output remaining unconnected to an input, open-loop systems are referred to as non-feedback-type systems. An example of open-loop control is the use of a timer to control a windshield electric defrost grid or heated seat (**FIGURE 25-28**). The timer controls the flow of electric current for heating, but the defrost grid or seat is not shut off when the driver is comfortable or the windshield is clear. The timer supplies current to ensure the heating elements reach a set-point of "hot" and typically remain hot for a specified time, regardless of what was the desirable temperature or visibility.

If the seats were especially cold and there was extra-thick frost on the windshield, a large difference is expected between the system results before the timer shuts off and what the driver desired. This difference between the actual result and desired outcome is called **system error**. To correct the error, the driver manually cycles the timer on again if the seat is not warm enough when the timer expired. The seat may be too hot before the timer shuts off the heating elements, which is also a control system error. This manual or open-loop control contributes to further error if the heating cycle is again not long enough, or too long. In contrast to open-loop control, **closed-loop systems** are designed to correct error to produce and maintain the desired output condition or variable. It does this by comparing its actual measured condition, called the process variable, with a set-point or desired condition. A closed-loop system corrects for error between set-points and PVs by generating an **error signal** (**FIGURE 25-29**). In the case of the heated seat and window, the error could be the difference between too hot versus just right or a clear windshield versus foggy but not frosted. An error signal, however, is the difference between the process variable and a set-point value for the input. Carefully note the error signal,

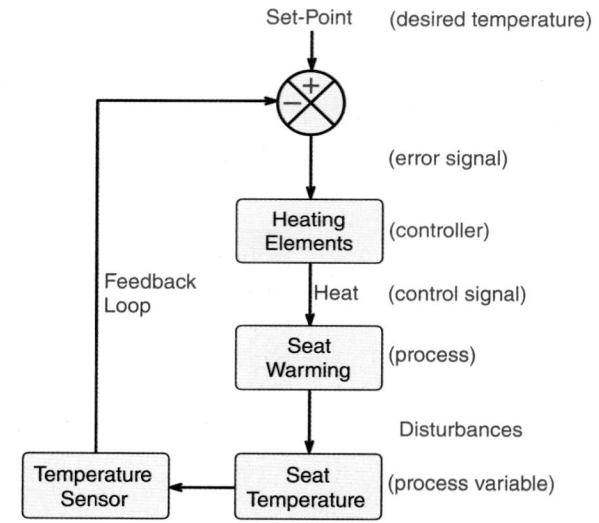

FIGURE 25-29 Error signal data is used to recalculate the controller input signal as the value of measured error is either added or subtracted from the value of the set-point.

which is used to produce a correction factor that is applied to the input signal is based on the measurement of output error. A comparator circuit generates data for the error signal and either adds to or subtracts some value from the original set-point data, which is fed into the controller. By modifying the controller input signal data from its original set-point value, the correct PV is achieved. If the error requires reducing the value of the set-point (e.g., shortening the seat and window heating time), it is a negative feedback signal. If heating time is added to the original set-point value (lengthening the heating time), then the error signal is considered a positive feedback signal (**FIGURE 25-30**).

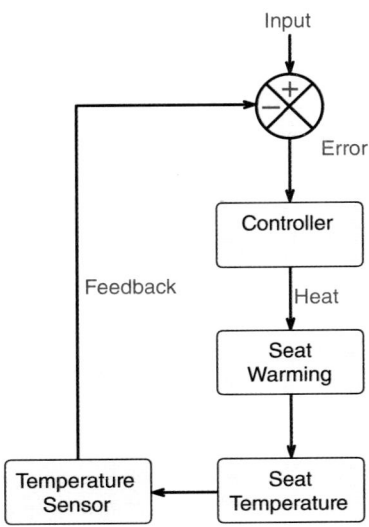

FIGURE 25-30 Error signals are either subtracted from or added to the set-point.

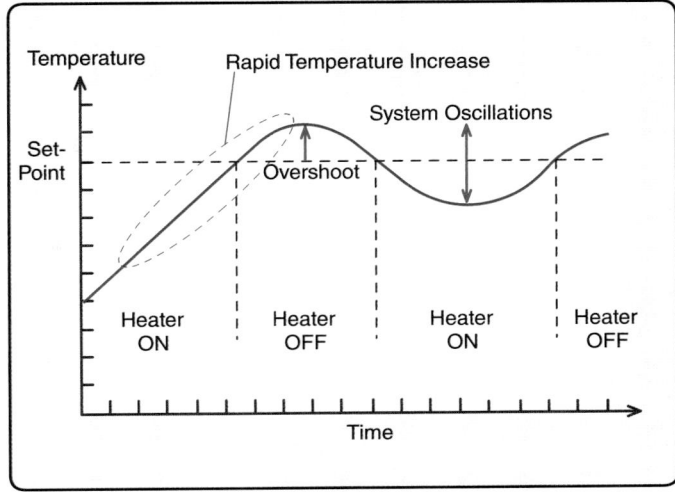

FIGURE 25-31 If the slope of temperature change is too fast near the set-point, the system is unstable and oscillates. The actuator controlling the process moves too rapidly near the set-point.

Closed-Loop Feedback and System Disturbances

To convert the open-loop heating of the driver's seat and windshield to closed-loop, the output or process variable needs to be measured and fed-back to a controller in order to adjust heating time. If it was practical, a temperature sensor could be added to each of the systems to provide data about the seat or windshield temperature. When feedback about an output state is supplied by a sensor, the system is better able to correct system for error caused by system disturbances. **Disturbances** are uncontrolled outside factors influencing a process that interferes with a control system task. In this case, disturbances that could influence the process of seat heating are the driver hopping in and out of the cab to make deliveries, preventing the seat from properly warming up. High humidity in the cab or very cold winds are process disturbances that could also slow the process of defrosting the windshield.

Compared to open-loop systems, closed-loop systems can reduce a control system's sensitivity to external disturbances, which gives them an advantage over open-loop systems. The disadvantage is closed-loop systems are more complex after adding sensors for feedback and a mechanism to mathematically and electronically store and then correct a set-point value using an error signal.

▶ TECHNICIAN TIP

When observing unusual system behaviors, remember that control systems that normally operate using closed control loops may operate for some time in open loop or be forced into open loop. For example, the absence of correct data or inaccurate data, such as when exhaust gas sensors are too cold to generate a reliable signal, causes any closed-loop to operate using preset open-loop set-points. Engines may sound and perform differently when cold or restarting when warm compared to a fully warmed-up condition. Some transmissions may likewise shift differently until the fluid is fully warmed-up. The loop closes when the system controller judges the gas sensors to supply reliable data.

Problems Encountered by Closed-Loop Feedback Controls

While the use of closed-loop control appears to be an ideal arrangement for any control system, there are several factors that can influence the quality of system performance. The most obvious factors are:

- How sensitive is a system to measuring and correcting error?
- How quickly and accurately can a system make corrections to process variables?
- How forcefully can a correction to a process variable be made to reduce or eliminate error? (The rate of change made when correcting error.)
- How responsive is an output actuator to output signals from the controller (e.g., Are there problems caused by binding, worn, or deteriorated actuators)?

In the field, design characteristics of closed-loop feedback controls can either improve or worsen the quality of system control response. For example, if the change to the system output signals is too large in comparison to the feedback signal error, the response of an output actuator becomes exaggerated and the system can become unstable (**FIGURE 25-31**). Consider another control system loop to help understand this condition—the engine idle speed control. If an electrical load is switched on and loads the alternator or the AC compressor clutch is released, the amount of fuel injected in a diesel engine must change to maintain a consistent idle speed. Diesel engine speed is particularly sensitive to very small changes in fueling; even the smallest adjustment can dramatically change no-load engine speed. A closed-loop system used to maintain a precisely set idle speed can become unstable and the engine speed begins to oscillate or rhythmically change its speed as it tries to correct for error caused by the system disturbances. Cutting back the fuel slows the engine speed after the speed signal is fed back as negative error signal. If the engine speed decreases below its idle speed set-point due to decreased fueling, positive error signals increase fueling, which is followed again by a negative feedback signal. The control system term describing the size of this difference between the change that takes place between the input error signal and output signal is called **gain**.

Controller Gain

Controller gain is a change that takes place between the input error signal and output signal. When the difference between the input and output signals grows larger, or is amplified, gain is said to increase. Using a controller with a large amount of gain is helpful when a big discrepancy exists between a desired and the actual output because high controller gain control rapidly closes the gap. However, there is a point when excessive gain makes the controller unstable if the gain is overcorrecting a small error. When controller gain is excessive, it is considered too sensitive to changes in its input commands or signals. A high-gain system can start to oscillate as it overshoots its set-point as the controller tries to over-correct small error signals (**FIGURE 25-32**). Not only will the controlled system have an undesirable output, but the condition can potentially lead to a mechanical failure in some systems due to excessive actuator force and process variable output oscillations. The opposite condition can take place if there is inadequate controller gain. A feedback loop that has low gain or is insensitive responds too slowly or not at all to error caused by disturbances if the error is too small.

Proportional Feedback Control

To correct the problem caused by a control system with either too much or too little gain, the most commonly used control algorithm varies the controller gain according to the amount of error or distance between actual output and the set-point. This means that if there is discrepancy between a set-point and value of the measured process variable, the algorithm evaluates the size or magnitude of the error and adjusts the gain upwards or downwards, depending on the discrepancy between set-point and the process variable. If there is a large discrepancy, gain increases allowing the controller to close in faster on the set-point. When the error diminishes as the PV approaches the set-point, the algorithm reduces the controller gain, slowing the speed at which the error is reduced. In other words, the force and speed the controller uses to respond to the error is proportional to the size of the error. The control strategy of adjusting gain up or down in proportion to the size of error lends this type of controller the name **proportional feedback control**. The operation of proportional control when used by the cruise/vehicle speed control system is very noticeable when there is a large difference between actual vehicle speed and cruise control set speed. In that situation, a cruise control system aggressively accelerates the vehicle until it gets closer to its set-point (**FIGURE 25-33**). A more comfortable driving experience is achieved by gradual tapering of the rate of acceleration, or reducing controller gain, while it is approaching its set-point. This behavior of the cruise control system is common and an easily observed application of a proportional feedback control algorithm (**FIGURE 25-34**).

Proportional-Integral (PI) Feedback Control

Proportional feedback control can work well in many feedback loops. However, under some circumstances, system disturbances can be very high and long-lasting. Returning to the example of the cruise control system, strong headwinds and steep hills can translate into a long delay reaching set-points because the error signal becomes smaller when the PV or vehicle speed approaches the cruise control set-point speed. Because the amount of controller gain is sharply reduced near the cruise control set-point, strong resistance by system disturbances could cause the cruise control to operate below set-point for a long time, or even prevent the controller from reaching the set-point, since a larger error is needed to generate the controller response or force necessary for corrective action. Traveling downhill with a

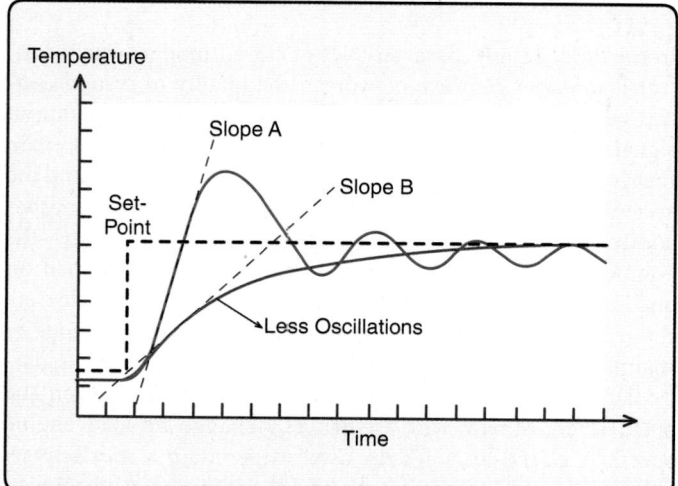

FIGURE 25-32 Slope A gain is high and causes system oscillation. Slope B is flatter and gain is reduced as the process variable nears set-point.

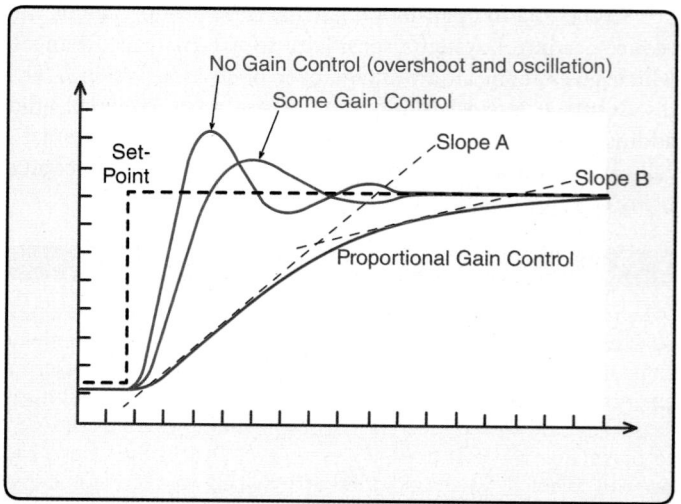

FIGURE 25-33 Note the two different slopes of the line with no oscillation. Proportional control reduces the controller gain as the error between set-point and process variable is reduced.

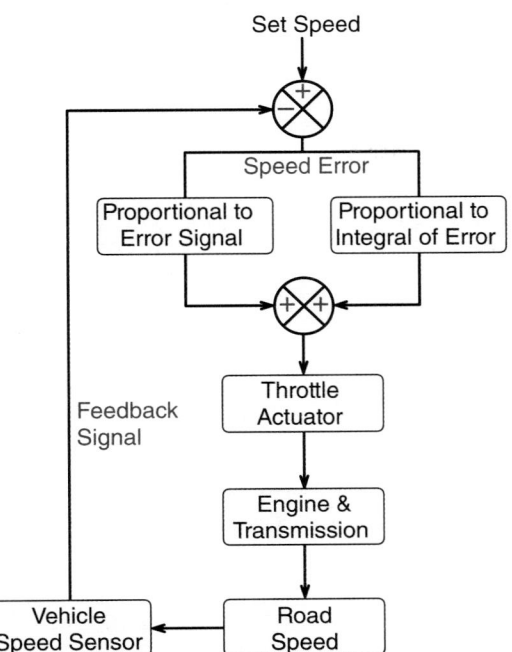

FIGURE 25-34 A block diagram of a cruise control system with proportional gain. The integral is the area between the PV line and set-point (SP).

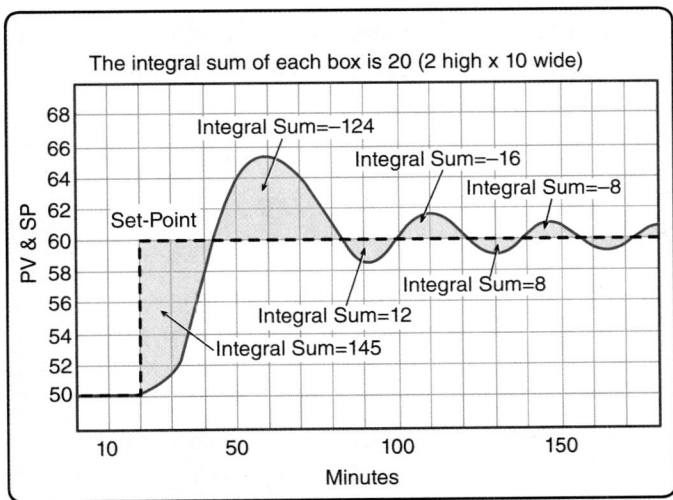

FIGURE 25-35 Integral control algorithms measure how long a PV error exists. The area between the PV and set-point is measured using an integral function. Controller input signals are corrected based on the size of the integral; controller gain changes according to the integral area.

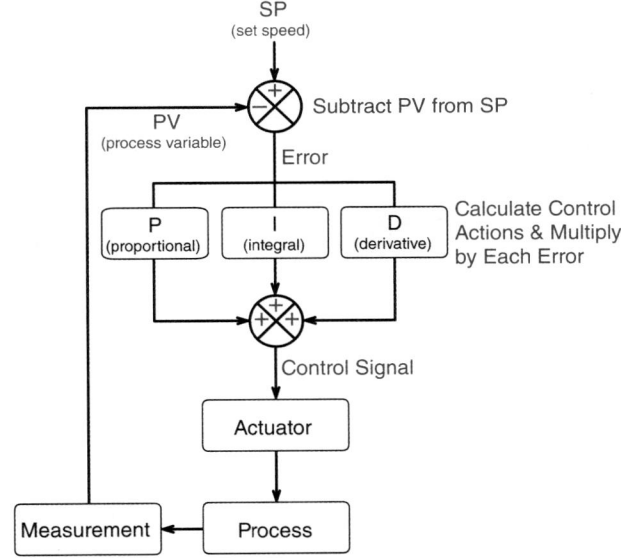

FIGURE 25-36 Error signal is calculated by subtracting PV from set-point. The P, I, and D correction factors are added together and multiplied with the error signal to produce a control signal.

tailwind has the opposite effect and potentially causes the proportional controller to overshoot the set-point and maintain a small over-speed error. To correct these types of small errors above or below the set-point that can remain for a long time, another algorithm is added to proportional control. The algorithm, called **integral feedback control**, analyzes the time that error deviations are present above or below the set-point (**FIGURE 25-35**). Greater correction force or correction rate change is added to the controller error signal relative to the time that error is present. The error analysis is performed by calculating the area between the two plotted lines of the set-point and PV or actual controller output. You may recall from high school math that to find this area beneath a curve, an integral of the functions (a mathematical equation) for the two lines is calculated, which lends the name integral feedback control. Integral feedback combined with proportional feedback control is called proportional-integral (P-I) control.

Proportional-Integral Derivative (PID) Control

Derivative feedback control is another type of closed-loop control mechanism used to correct for PV error. What is different about derivative control from the other controller strategies is it corrects for potential future error and not current error. In a sense, the derivative algorithm used by the controller is predictive or future orientated. It is, however, based on current error signals and designed to reduce the rate of change of current error to zero. Derivative control algorithms correct for future error by continuously calculating the trajectory of error for the process variable. If the slope of the trajectory for the system process variable error is too steep, it remembers where the error signal has been in the past and applies a correction factor to an anticipated future error signal. The pattern for future direction or steepness of a plotted line for the PV is calculated using a math function called a derivative. The derivative algorithm applies a correction factor to the error signal to dampen the predicted rate of change, based on previous performance, and reduces set-point error. Derivative correction factors are combined with proportional-integral algorithms to collectively achieve **proportional-integral derivative (PID) control** (**FIGURE 25-36**).

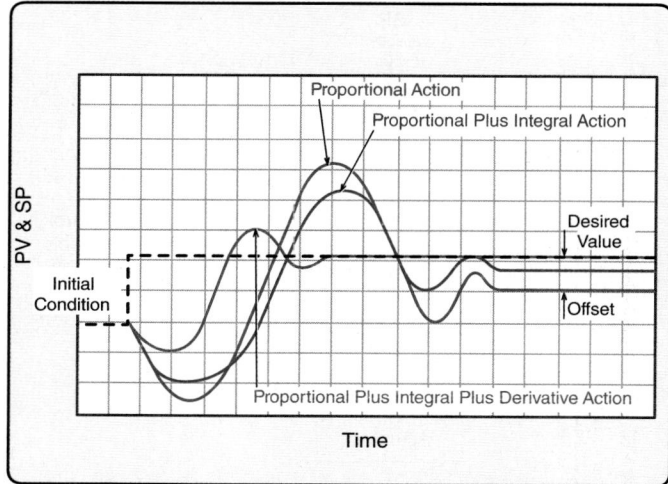

FIGURE 25-37 Combining all three P, I, and D algorithms together (PID) achieves the smoothest and most stable control system.

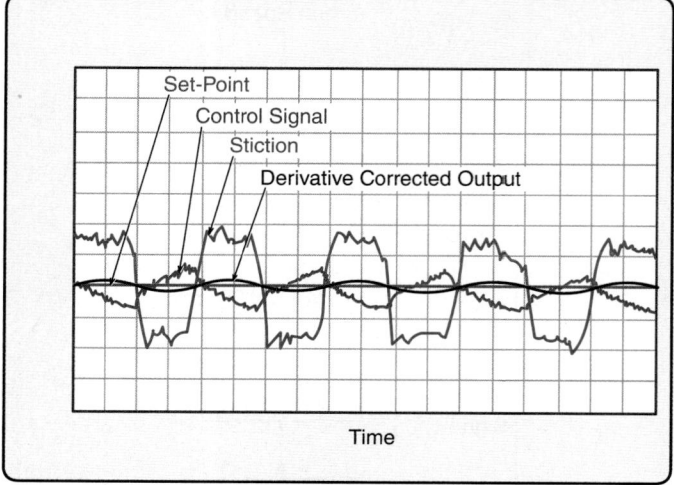

FIGURE 25-38 Cyclic changes to a process variable caused by an unanticipated disturbance, such as stiction, can be removed using derivative control algorithms combined with proportional and integral controls.

When all three PID algorithms are used by a controller, they minimize the error signal to produce the fastest responding, smoothest, most stable, reliable, and precise process variable (**FIGURE 25-37**). To achieve the best outcomes, **PID tuning** is a process performed by calibration engineers on instrumented systems where the algorithms are adjusted under experimental conditions. Average PID values are developed to accommodate a wide variability in stock component response to control signals. Engine performance enthusiasts undertake PID tuning to achieve optimal process variables when modified high performance parts replace stock components. Factory control algorithms for performance injectors and turbochargers simply do not enable the best control of performance components using electrical signals generated by stock PID algorithms. However, PID controllers are complex to calibrate and used for only the most sensitive systems. Proportional control is not commonly used by itself. Proportional and integral control are most often combined. Combining proportional and derivative control is complex to develop from a calibration standpoint, expensive to implement electronically, and uncommonly used except in sensitive applications.

Situations where **stiction** can occur, a term for static friction caused by binding, sticking actuators, can be minimized by adding derivative control algorithms to feedback signals. Controller force will build-up and then suddenly overcome a sticking or binding actuator when only PI controls are used. A predictable sawtooth output signal pattern is produced, which can be tuned out using a PID controller. Even if there is no stiction present, the PID control can be triggered if the condition arises (**FIGURE 25-38**).

▶ TECHNICIAN TIP

Poor system performance and slow response complaints due to unanticipated disturbances, such as fluid leakage, soot build-up in intake manifolds, misadjusted slacks, increased mechanical and electrical resistance, component deterioration and wear, can often be corrected with an updated reflash of an ECU with a newer calibration file containing P, I, P-I, or PID algorithms. Even in relatively new vehicles, it is often not

failed components causing complaints or generating fault codes but unanticipated changes in situations such as an injector's responses to electrical signals, frictional coefficients of components like transmission clutch pack discs, bands, lock-up torque converter friction discs, and fluid friction modifiers. In many situations, the control algorithms simply were not designed to adequately correct error resulting from in-use deterioration or unanticipated interactions with other worn, deteriorated components. Always check for calibration software updates or reflash a control system module when investigating complaints potentially related to a control system operation.

Multiple-Input Multiple-Output (MIMO) Control Systems

LO 25-4 Identify and describe multiple-input multiple-output (MIMO) control systems and their disadvantages.

To review, a closed-loop control to function, several essential elements are needed:

- An output device (an electrical actuator) or signal
- Sensors to supply data about the system process variable or how the actuator is actually functioning
- Set-points, which are desired values for system operation
- ECU with control logic (PIDs) and addressable memory storage

Previous sections have examined the operation of the above control loop elements and control loop operation by looking at a single-input single-output (SISO) device like the cruise control. This simple example has only one output controlled by one control signal. A vehicle speed sensor supplies a feedback for an error signal to a controller, which commands engine speed using a controller-generated output signal. The output could be completely electronic or a linear actuator connected to the throttle lever on a mechanically governed engine. The set-point for the system is established by the driver toggling a set-speed

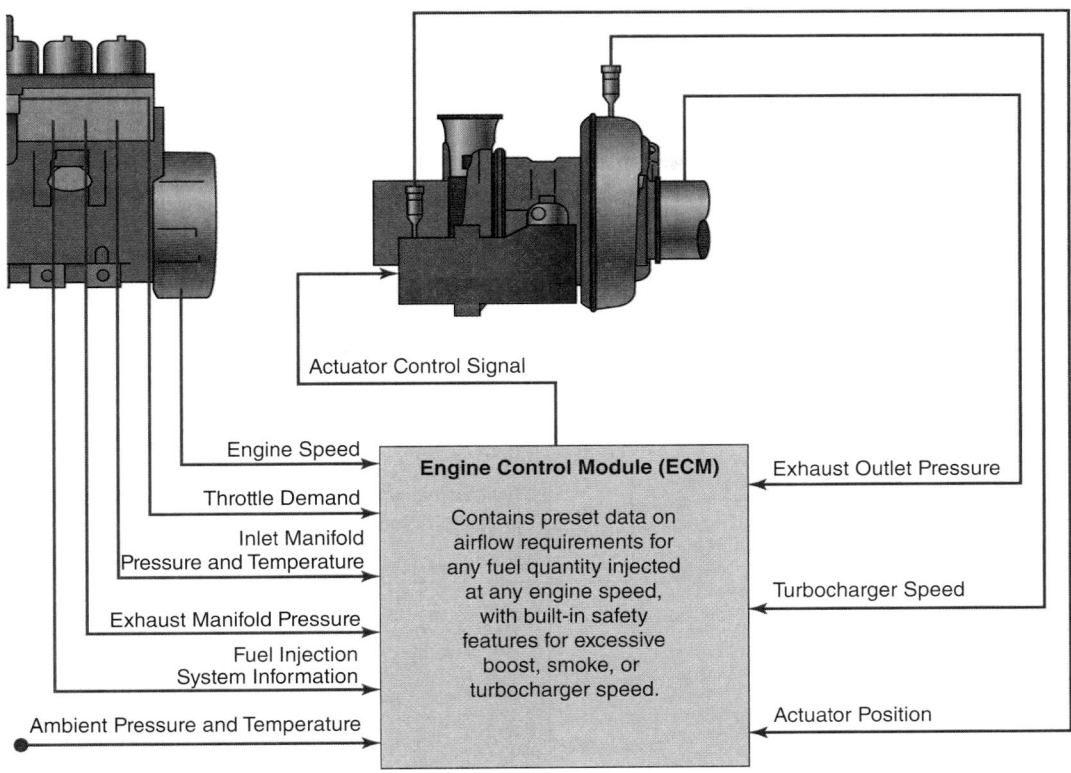

FIGURE 25-39 A multiple-input and multiple-output (MIMO) system has more than one input to control several output variables, such as turbocharger and EGR valve position, injection timing, and fuel rates.

switch that stores the desired road speed in memory. MIMO control systems, however, are more complex. Consider the example of a diesel engine injection system. Determining the optimal set-point in the combustion cycle for when the start of injection (SOI) should begin and how much fuel to inject–injection quantity (IQ) depends on many more input variables to achieve good performance, low emissions, combined with low fuel consumption (**FIGURE 25-39**).

These variables include, but are not limited to, collecting sensor data about how much air is available for combustion (turbocharger boost pressure) and what is the current engine speed, engine temperature, driver demand (throttle position), etc. The optimal set-point for injection timing and quantity may also need to consider other factors, such as limiting noise, improving engine reliability, and reducing vibration. How the engine responds to changes in the SOI and IQ are not linear; incremental changes to either variable can have much larger or smaller effects, depending on operating conditions. Feedback signals for these control systems are not as clear either. Crankshaft sensors can measure speed and how fast the engine accelerates when fueling, but the engine and injector may not always have the capability to supply feedback signals for identifying the precise crankshaft position when combustion begins after the start of injection.

Calibration Files and Look-Up Tables

To determine the set-point for MIMO systems, optimal set-point values are calculated using a wide range of possible combinations for various operating conditions and arranged in

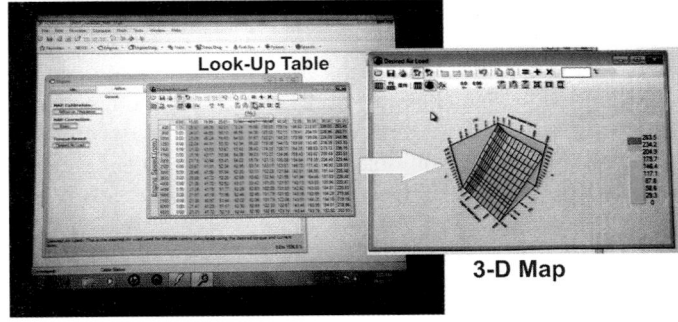

FIGURE 25-40 Calibration files for MIMO systems use look-up tables that are visualized with three-dimensional maps.

what are called **look-up tables** (**FIGURE 25-40**). Look-up tables are mathematical shortcuts used by an ECU controller to provide answers to complex questions or solutions to mathematical problems solved elsewhere. A look-up table in this situation contains a set-point: What should be the SOI at 20 psi of boost pressure and 45% throttle position demand? This set-point value is determined during preproduction calibration testing by running an engine on an experimental test bench while manipulating different input values. The optimal set-point is determined by measuring process variables, such as horsepower, torque, fuel consumption, and emissions, plus any other relevant criteria. The process of looking for a set-point in look-up table data is faster and requires less ECU processing capabilities than performing complex and intensive calculations using

Speed Density Calculation

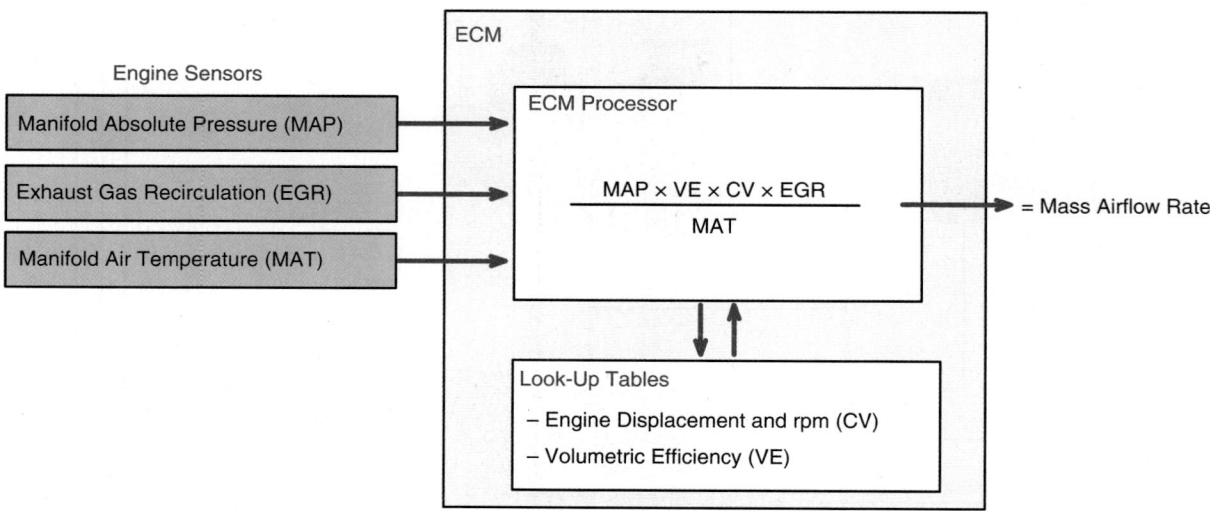

FIGURE 25-41 An example of a multiple-input control system and algorithm used to calculate desired mass airflow rate.

advanced algorithms that may not account for all possible input variables (**FIGURE 25-41**). This process of using a look-up table is very fast and can be compared to the high-school exercise of looking up data in the back of a math textbook. A business or math class may have a student look up a decimal equivalent for a trigonometric angle or how much the cost of a mortgage is reduced for a given interest rate. The efficiency is gained because the calculation is already completed and the look-up table value is simply plugged into a formula. The use of look-up data tables for a control system is also a method to improve the efficiency while reducing the cost of ECU modules. If processing output signals for dozens of devices every millisecond was done without the use of look-up tables, the processing power required for control modules would make them even more costly. Microcontrollers with much more sophisticated capabilities would be required. The ECU would need very fast clock speeds and enormous memory capacity to keep up with calculations that are not only used by the engine, ABS, instrumentation displays, touch screens, etc., but also for diagnostic systems and communication interfaces. The cost and complexity of an ECU is kept to a minimum with the use of look-up tables stored in programmable memory chips.

Text-only data stored in look-up tables is developed during a process called **calibration**. The calibration process determines what group of set-point values are optimal for a system to achieve the desired outputs. During the calibration process, an analysis asks about what tasks the control system is performing and how those tasks are carried out. Traditionally, generating calibration data was done manually by performing experiments where components are operated in labs, on a test bench, or with dynamometers before fine-tuning the look-up table set-points in the field. Major components such as transmissions, engines, and vehicles with ABS/ATC are instrumented with sensors to log how a system performs when individual variables, among dozens, are manipulated one at a time. When an optimal set of outcomes are identified after each variable is manipulated, the set-points for

the systems are included in a look-up table. Data logs from test instruments helped generate set-points for determining what kind of signals are needed to produce a specific actuator movement, control valve operation, shift schedules, clutch pressures, and slippage of a torque converter for transmissions, what frequency of ABS modulator valve operation will best stop a vehicle on different slippery surfaces, etc.

It's important to understand that as control systems needed to become more sophisticated with new demands placed on their performance, calibration efforts became more labor- and time-intensive. Part of the explanation is that the effects of calibration variables are interdependent, which make it almost impossible to develop calibrations for major control systems, such as engines, stability control, and transmissions, by simply optimizing one variable at a time in a look-up table because of the enormous complexity of interactions between those systems. The optimal setting for one variable may require trade-offs to improve the outcomes of another. Optimal set-points also compete with needs for driver comfort, system reliability, durability, safety, noise, vibration, and harshness encountered under various environmental conditions, such as temperature, altitude, and operating speed.

To illustrate the difficulty of developing a calibration process for a diesel engine using just two sensors to control three outputs of engine speed, SOI, and injection pressure, experimental manipulations of control system variables would need 10,000 possible permutations of operating conditions to generate the appropriate look-up table. With 15 control outputs and 22 actuators, the number of permutations for set-point measurements explodes exponentially to more than a trillion data points to generate a complete look-up table (**FIGURE 25-42, TABLE 25-1**).

One shortcut to generate large sets of look-up table set-points is to use three dimensional maps. Data for look-up tables are visualized by using calibration maps. Fewer experimental manipulations of control system variables or parameters are needed for producing data tables because coordinates on a map

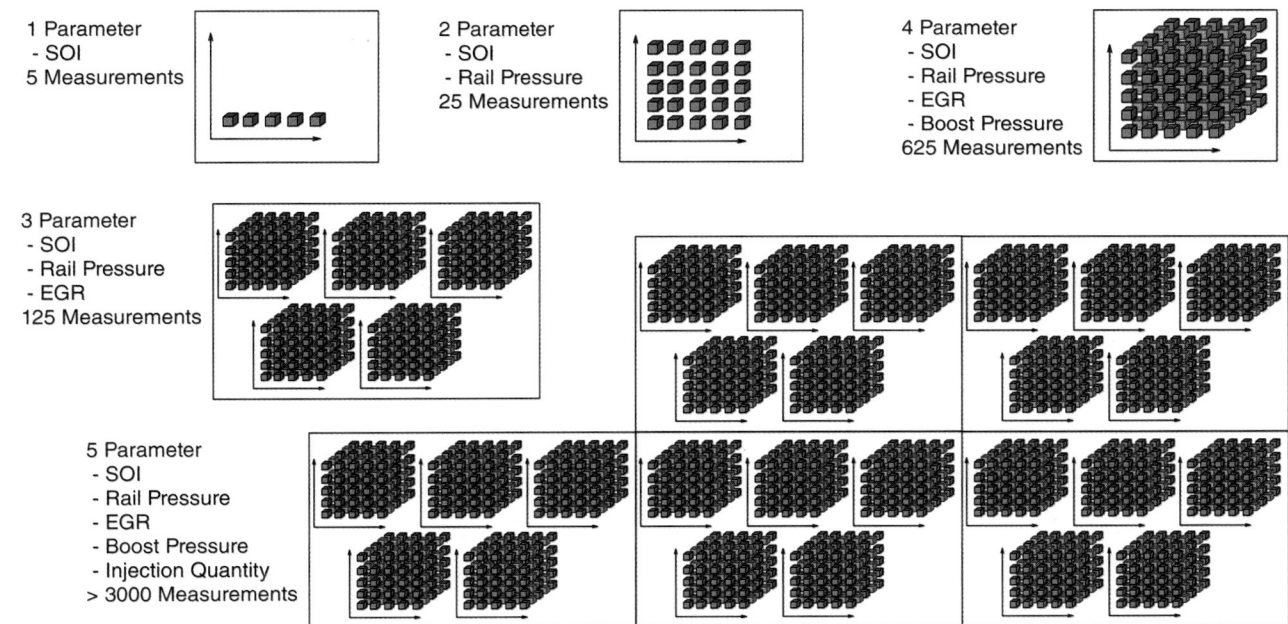

FIGURE 25-42 Each time the number of sensors, actuators, and controlled output devices increases, the number of set-points in a look-up table increases exponentially to the point where they become impractical to develop.

TABLE 25-1 Parameters

Year	Number of Sensors	Number of Actuators	Control Variables	Control Outputs	Look-Up Table Data Test Points
1998	2	8	Speed, Load, Injection Timing & Pressure	3	10,000
2002	4	10	Speed, Load, Injection Timing & Pressure, EGR	3	100,000
2004	8	15	Speed, Load, Injection Timing & Pressure, EGR, Turbocharging Control	5	1,000,000
2007	10	19	Speed, Load, Multiple Injection Timing, Injection Pressure, EGR, Turbocharging Control, Particulate Filter Regeneration	11	1,000,000,000
2010	12	22	Speed, Load, Multiple Injection Timing, Injection Pressure, EGR, Turbocharging Control, Aftertreatment Controls	15	>1,000,000,000,000
2015++	18 plus virtual sensors	NA	ADAS, 3–8 different injection events to shape injection rate, injection pressure & timing, EGR, air mass flow, PM regeneration, SCR dosing, fault tolerant systems	NA	NA

(Source: Some data extracted from Detroit Diesel Corporation Presentation 11th Annual DEER Conference, August 2005.)

are used to interpolate a greater number of set-points. (Interpolation simply means estimating data at a point between two other data points.)

Principles of Model Predictive Control

LO 25-5 Identify and describe principles of model predictive control.

MIMO system look-up tables are impractical to develop once a system moves beyond having a few controlled outputs and sensors. The difficulties encountered by the complexity of developing PID control system calibrations and accompanying look-up

tables in recent years have caused an enormous shift in methods for developing calibration files and operating strategies used by major control systems. In addition to the impracticality of needing to test and calculate values for potentially billions of set-points in MIMO systems, other industry demands are making the use of PID-type controls in major ECU domains obsolete. Legislative demands to make vehicles cleaner, more fuel efficient, and safer means adding more hardware, components, and controls for each control system domain. Control systems for the exhaust aftertreatment, diesel air pathways with EGR, chassis ABS/ATC, automated and automatic transmission, plus vehicle stability, and collision avoidance systems have multiplied the number of sensors and control variables. The result of the enormous new complexity and system interactions is control calibration optimization that cannot be developed primarily on test benches and dynamometers by manipulating a single variable. Such tasks would be, among other problems, too time-consuming. Other pressures to make control system operation and calibration even more difficult include added durability requirements for emission systems. Control systems need to be able to compensate for age and deterioration of components, which means a fixed set-point look-up table would require frequent updates. Manufacturers have also been forced to adopt new methods to operate control systems due to:

- Competitive industry pressures to increase performance, efficiency, and safety, while adding more comfort and convenience features that can supply more even more vehicle information to enhance telematic capabilities.
- Added hardware, which increases control system complexity, production costs, and exponentially more calibration time and engineering resources.
- Adding hardware and systems that require more sensors to form feedback loops and sensor redundancy for onboard diagnostics.
- Sensor design, costs, and reliability demands that have sharply increased, which means fewer sensors are preferred, and virtual sensors that can estimate a process variable are better.
- Needing computational efficiency from ECUs to reduce costs. Increased system inputs and outputs work against greater economy in ECU processing speeds, memory, and capacity to execute more instructions.
- Aftertreatment dynamics differ significantly from other engine systems. (Very complex control is required for nonlinear relationships between emission production and engine operation.)
- Tightened heavy-duty onboard diagnostics (HD-OBD) emission detection thresholds, which means control systems need to be more sensitive to faults; detecting them faster at lower thresholds without causing false alarms or nuisance codes.

Manufacturers have moved away from PID control to a new control system strategy called **model predictive control (MPC)**. MPC is a control system method that relies on a data generated from a mathematical model of expected system behavior to generate control system signals. Rather than using experiments to provide set-point for hundreds of potential control loops, only a very limited set of variables from just a few sensors, called **state observers**, are used to predict and generate the optimal set of control signals. State observers do not provide feedback to form control loops but provide reference points in the model of operation to predict what an optimal set of output signals should be used. (**FIGURE 25-43**).

While industry pressures forcing the innovations in control system design are of little concern to technicians, they help explain recent changes in the number of "smart" (networked) mechatronic components on vehicles. The change also means system behavior and service practices are different too.

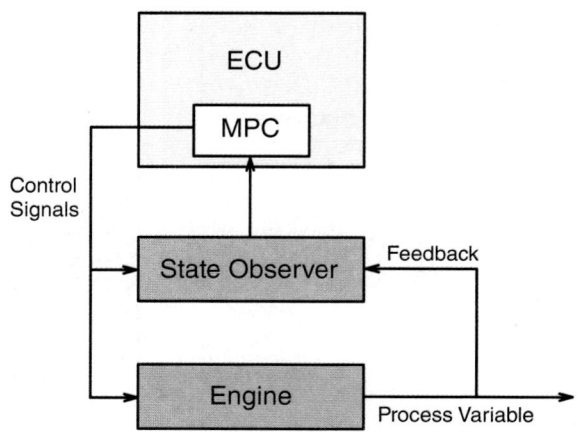

FIGURE 25-43 State observers supply feedback from the engine or other system process variable used to decide or predict what the next best control step should be. A mathematical model of how the system should behave, rather than set-points in a fixed look-up table, is the reference point for generating output signals.

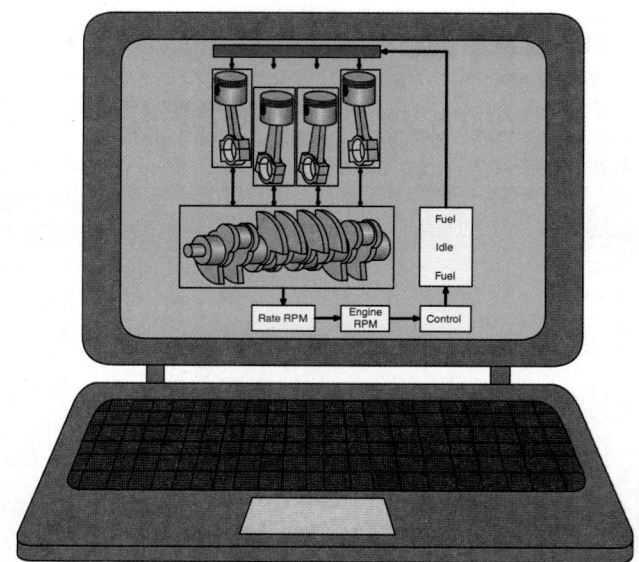

FIGURE 25-44 An example of a virtual engine model. Software simulates engine operation with data that represent objects that are animated by algorithms according to physical laws.

This alternate approach to control system design and operation has created new categories of diagnostic codes and code descriptions. New diagnostic strategies, service techniques, and repair recommendations are necessary to correct problems in MPC systems when they are encountered.

MPC Operation

MPC calibration methods essentially develop a mathematical model of a component or system operation describing the complete system with all its properties and behaviors. Like a video game, this model is virtual, meaning the component or system does not physically exist, but software makes it appear real (**FIGURE 25-44**). The idea of a virtual model can be compared to a computer animation or video game displayed on a screen. If it is an engine, the movement and operation of components, such as pistons in cylinders, flywheel rotation, and combustion events, valve action, are predicted and represented by data detailing each object's size, shape, construction material, and mass. Mathematical formulas based on what are called first-order physical laws animate the virtual objects corresponding to actual components and predict operating behaviors. All potential input variables, disturbances, deterioration, and operating conditions are anticipated and modeled with physical laws associated with motion, electricity, magnetism, hydraulics, and chemistry. Using the stored model as the set-point template, the control system ECU is capable of more simply and efficiently generating all possible outputs signals for all time using the model to estimate output signal values in real-time. The control pathway, that is, the steps the controller follows and the output signal values it generates, is predetermined by the model outline for system behavior. The absence of a PID-type closed-loop feedback control gives MPC open-loop-like control characteristics, except that the control steps are much better adapted to accurately predict the behavior of the controlled device or system.

MPC provides computational efficiency for ECUs by using a model where all the intensive calculations are done upfront during model development. This is not unlike the computational efficiencies derived using look-up tables, but a virtual model provides a much richer data set that is dynamic, meaning it simulates actual working characteristics. The model simplifies problem solving for the ECU by creating mathematical shortcuts and solutions built into the model, enabling it to generate the best set of output signals faster and more frequently. Using virtual objects joined together within the mathematical model that represent actual components and their operating behaviors is one effective way to reduce an ECU's need for complexity and processing power. Using data from just two or three sensors functioning as state observers to drive the model predictions for selecting the best set of output signals further reduces processing demands on the ECU. State observer inputs, rather than dozens of other sensor inputs, to a well-designed model can more accurately predict a pattern or likely set of output signals for all system actuators. If the comparison of MPC to a video game is extended, just as game software creates virtual models of characters as objects controlled by algorithms based on physical laws of motion and constrained by rules around normal human movement, a modeled control system animates the electrical and mechanical components. And just as output actions on screen are initiated by moving a joystick or pressing a few buttons on a controller, MPC state observers cause output actions derived from the model to drive the system hardware or components.

Role of State Observers in MPC

The job of state observers is key to understanding what drives the predictive abilities to generate a complete set of control signals. State observers are sensor inputs used to predict the operational state of a system whether it is the engine, braking, ADAS,

transmission, or other major control system. For engines, a state predictor determines among other operating conditions, whether the vehicle is operating at a steady speed and load along an interstate highway or in urban driving conditions with stop-and-go, varying load operation. Each of these circumstances requires different demands for the amount of EGR used, injection timing, fuel quantity, injection rate shape, boost pressure, particulate filter soot loading, and SCR dosing. Transmissions, collision avoidance, stability control systems, and the ABS/ATC require different control strategies based on unique operating conditions predicted by state observers. For example, a steering angle sensor can predict the forward direction of vehicle movement and whether it might collide with an object or roll over. How quickly a wheel locks-up can predict the type of road surface a vehicle is operating over and how best to cycle the modulator valves to apply, hold, and release the brakes. Even a rain sensor can predict when to switch wipers on and off, the sweep interval, or the optimal speed for wipers to clean a windshield (**FIGURE 25-45**).

To give one a sense of the creative spark that led to development of state observers, it's useful to know that MPC originated from old industrial control methods used by factory managers. For example, a baker or other decision maker in a large bakery may look at the calendar on December 1 and decide to switch from making apple pies to baking Christmas cake. His decision is based on only a single piece of data—the date. The calendar date is like a state observer and is the single most important piece of predictive data about how resources and labor should be used. Note a state observer and not dozens of other variables, such as whether there are orders on hand from grocery stores for Christmas cake determines the start date. The limited data derived from a calendar more efficiently and accurately predicts the best production decision and all subsequent control decisions made at the bakery. The baker can confidently predict the orders will arrive shortly and product will be available because it is near Christmas. Think also about a decision for choosing a route to drive home after work in a busy, traffic-congested city. Two pieces of data are critical to the route choice that can be best predicted by answering the questions: Which day of the

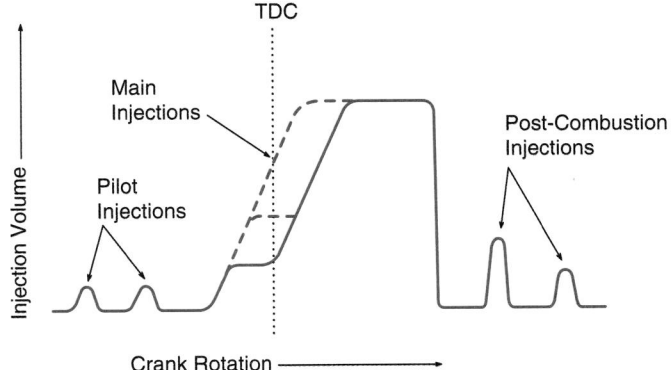

FIGURE 25-45 Two pilot injections enable the use of retarded injection timing while maintaining adequate combustion time. The first reduces soot formation by maintaining high cylinder temperatures.

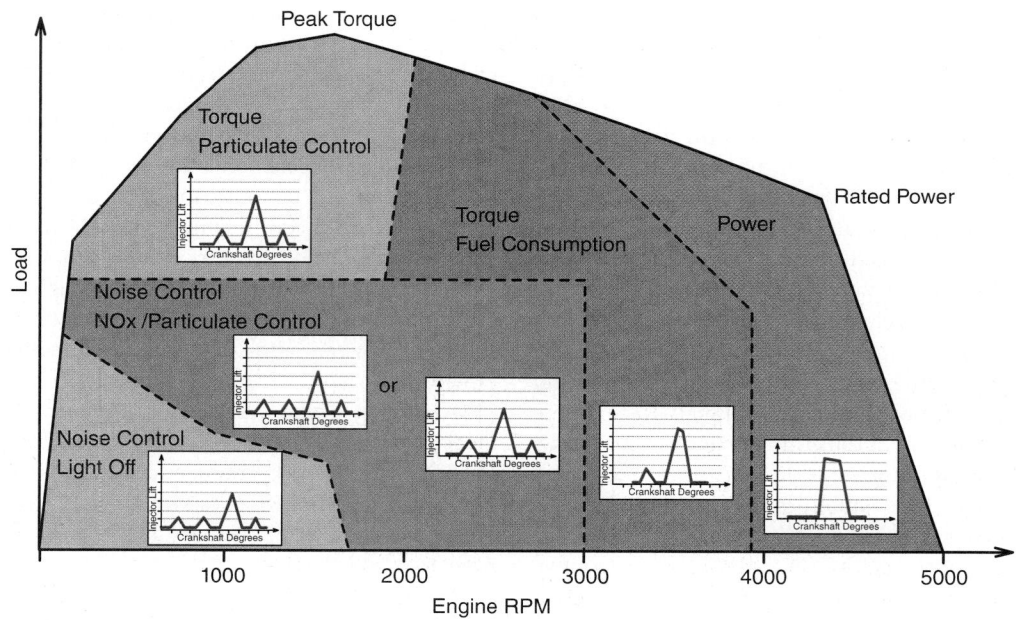

FIGURE 25-46 State observers are used to help predict what is the optimal injection rate shape—how many pilot, main, or post main injection events.

week and what time of day is the drive taking place? Is it Saturday or Wednesday? Or, is the drive home taking place after finishing a night or day shift?

Transmission state observers that predict shift schedules are engine torque output and driver torque demand. Diesel engines using MPC typically now use only exhaust gas sensors, intake manifold pressure, and throttle position to predict and then generate the optimal set of all output signals for fuel, airflow, EGR, and aftertreatment system operation. These signals are generated by the virtual model predictions for how it should operate under an identical situation. Other sensors are still needed to detect faults and provide diagnostic information but are not essential to system operation. Feedback from sensors is also used to optimize the model performance and, in most cases, update the model to help correct for system wear and deterioration (**FIGURE 25-46**).

▶ TECHNICIAN TIP

The complexity of aftertreatment system operation has demanded the use of MPC. MPC is also used to diagnose aftertreatment system faults that technicians must be made aware of to understand fault diagnostic and specialized service procedures. For example, models of soot loading in a DPF are compared with actual data from the particulate filter's pressure differential sensor. If the data from the model and sensor do not match, a fault is set. To correct the fault, the filter and sensor must be checked. If no physical faults are found, the model is likely incorrect and requires updating through an adaptation procedure. SCR dosing and catalyst deterioration is also modeled. NOx sensor codes and ammonia slip codes may sometimes only be remedied by updating the model stored in the ECU. Again, this often only involves reteaching the ECU or causing the model to readapt or relearn how the SCR breaks down DEF fluid (**FIGURE 25-47**).

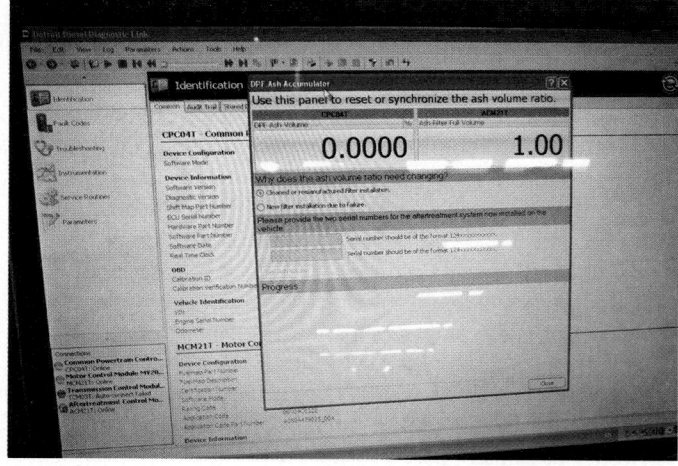

FIGURE 25-47 When replacing a DPF, the model for filter restriction must be readapted to account for the new filter restrictions.

▶ TECHNICIAN TIP

Reports from investigations into the discrepancies between standardized emission test results used for certifying vehicle and engine compliance and the results of emissions measured on the road suggest model predictive controls may account for the dual-mode operation. It is possible for MPC state observers to identify whether a vehicle is operating on an emission test cycle due to predictable stop-start and load schedules used by test protocols. Engine controls, aftertreatment systems, and onboard diagnostic tests must operate to ensure compliance with emission standards under emission test conditions. Outside of emission test cycle operating states, it's possible for MPC to generate a different set of output signals using a model for on-highway, off-road, high altitude, or other non-test conditions for any engine. If controls operate to allow excessive emissions, the control system is considered to use an auxiliary emission control device (AECD), sometimes known as an emission defeat device. Any commercial vehicle, but more commonly only fire trucks and other emergency vehicles, is allowed to run AECDs with EPA permission.

Mapped and Mapless MPC

An enormous amount of academic and industry research has developed a wide variety of methods to implement MPC system. Each has specific advantages when applied to a particular control system. But for technicians, it is useful to know commercial vehicles use two basic versions of MPC: **Mapped MPC** and **Mapless MPC**. While both types generally do not use a fixed set of look-up tables for operational control, a mapped MPC system is like a hybrid version of PID control and MPC. It combines PID with MPC by generating look-up tables on the fly or while the system is in operation. The set-points in the look-up tables are virtual and are generated by an algorithm that is selected and modified according to the operating state of the system. For example, the set of look-up tables used for high-altitude engine operation are different than one generated at sea level. Urban driving conditions maps are generated by examining the frequency of stopping and starting plus the amount of time spent at idle. These maps are different than ones used to operate at steady state on-highway. A variation of the mapped system selects from a stored set of calibration maps with set-points optimized for a unique operating condition. Map selection is predicted according to operating state which is predicted by the state observer.

Mapless MPC is the latest, most advanced control system. There are no look-up tables generated or used by the model. Instead, a highly accurate, well-refined predictive model is used, along with a mechanism to correct model discrepancy or errors, that updates the model in real-time (**FIGURE 25-48**). The update mechanism is frequently called an optimizer function or adaptive learning function. Mathematical functions generate lines

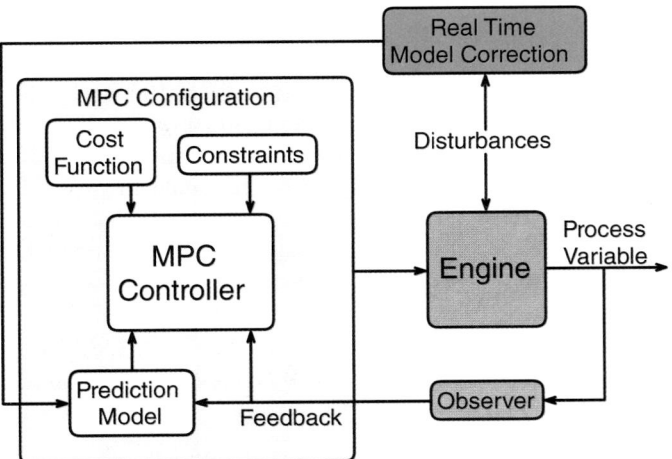

FIGURE 25-48 Mapless MPC systems do not use look-up tables but instead use a very refined, highly developed model to predict set-points. Another mechanism is used to update the model or correct model error set-points in real-time.

and coordinates for maps used by the model for identifying set-points for anything from system faults to the pulse width or voltage to operate an actuator.

Machine Learning and Model Optimization

While models need to adapt to components built with slight differences due to manufacturing tolerances and changes caused by wear and deterioration over time, it's also valuable if models can learn from previous control decisions. To help a control system produce better, more reliable, repeatable decisions and results, models may also include an updating feature called the model optimizer. Another name for this is machine learning. It works by feeding back measured PVs, such as emissions output, fuel consumption, and performance variables. Predictive algorithms used by MPC in engine ECUs can generate several possible control system paths or a set of output signals to achieve desired outcomes in terms of performance, fuel economy, and emissions. If a particularly set of control steps recently produced a better, more desirable set of outcomes, such as lower emissions, increased power, or reduced emissions, the optimizer performs a cost-benefit analysis—deciding which trade-offs, based on priority for each, are acceptable to improve the model. The pathway that offers the optimal outcome is chosen a few milliseconds to several seconds before the output signal is generated (**FIGURE 25-49**). Optimization or machine learning is particularly useful in ADAS and automated driving systems to help improve system performance. Learning how to recognize patterns and optimize results is a vital feature of more advanced MPC systems since MPC is future-oriented and not simply designed to correct error. This future-orientated, predictive characteristic also lends MPC the name over-the-horizon predictive control. The question being continuously asked and answered by the software is: What should be the next best control step signal based on the current operating state? MPC can even look around the corner to anticipate roadblocks. MPC includes work-around strategies for worn-out parts and malfunctioning components that could interfere with proper system operation. If there are defective parts or components, it can automatically reroute and use another set of control steps.

Mapless MPC systems can also use virtual sensors to estimate what the output signal should be for any given system state. For example, virtual sensors estimating NOx production calculate NOx output using estimates of cylinder pressures and temperatures. Exhaust NOx concentrations derived from a virtual sensor is used to dose the aftertreatment systems with diesel exhaust fluid.

MPC Virtual Objects

As mentioned, MPC uses virtual objects and virtual sensors to operate. Assembled together, the various objects, which represent hardware components in a system, create a model. Like a character, person, or instrument, such as a car in a video game, objects are programmed with data sets and algorithms that cause the object to operate according to physical, electrical, hydraulic, electronic, and chemical laws. Objects are constructed using simulation software without a need to create a physical

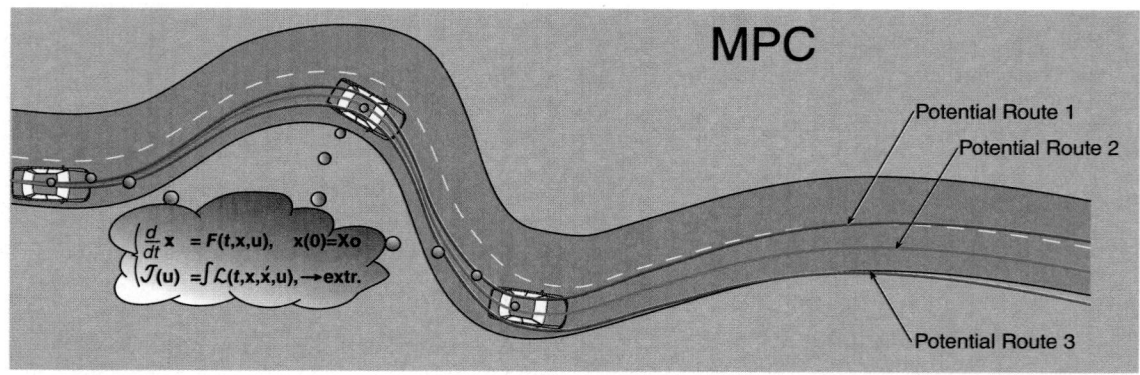

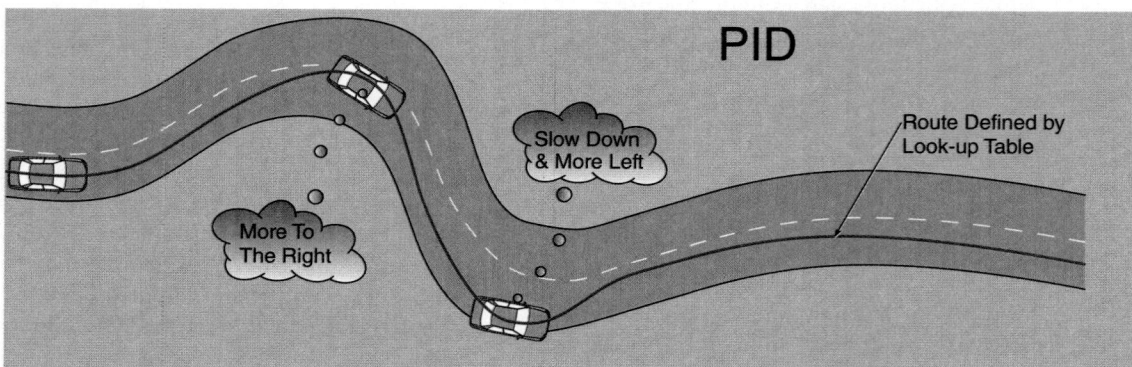

FIGURE 25-49 Much more processing time and complex steps are required for PID controls compared to MPC. MPC generates control pathway options in advance, rather than continuously checking for and correcting error.

replica for preliminary testing. Only at the final stages of model calibration development is the ECU model tested on hardware and fine-tuned in the field through a process called "Hardware in the Loop." Virtual objects include components, such as EGR valves, variable geometry turbochargers, aftertreatment systems, injectors, and transmissions with its internal components. Objects are programmed with knowledge of system interactions with other objects, which not only enables the model to work smoothly, but enables relatively easy updating of an entire model with new objects. Instead of requiring a long complex calibration process generating new experimental sets of control set-points required by PID controls using real hardware, virtual objects are like building blocks in a Lego set that allow sensors and hardware to be easily replaced or updated in a model. In other words, virtual objects can be plugged in and out of the major model without the disruptive and glitchy effects caused by updating traditional calibrations with new parts.

Accurate representations of components with virtual objects not only enable the model to operate a system more efficiently, but also much faster than PID controls. Because the ECU does not consume as much time and resources performing all the complex calculations necessary for a PID system to identify and correct deviations from set-points, MPC actuators can be operated more quickly and frequently to achieve better process variables. Often, significant error is needed in a proportional control system to cause a correction to take place. And unless an integral-type correction is combined with proportional control, error correction can take much more time (**FIGURE 25-50**).

Adaptation Adjustments

The precise requirements for operating precision explain why even small mechanical differences, due to the manufacturing tolerances, can greatly influence the performance of the latest-generation engines and transmissions. Calibration codes for injectors, control modules for exhaust gas sensors, and serial number changes for particulate filters are just a few examples of where MPC adjusts its knowledge of virtual objects and adapts the model for optimal operation. This also helps explain why ECUs are coded with a vehicle serial number and cannot be interchanged between vehicles. Virtual models stored in the ECUs are vehicle-specific and are interdependent with other ECU data to integrate their operation to maintain safe vehicle control. For example, the vehicle weight and size are stored in ECUs for stability control. They may also send high-priority CAN messages to de-rate an engine or disengage an engine retarder. If the engine ECU or engine was changed, and the engine no longer had a retarder, serious consequences could result.

Actuator Adaptation Adjustments and Model Predictive Control

MPC requires very precise representations of an object's response to signals. For example, the limits of a valve opening and closing must be precisely known to correctly position it during operation. Sticking actuator valves and linkage, and valves not fully closing or opening, can not only be damaged

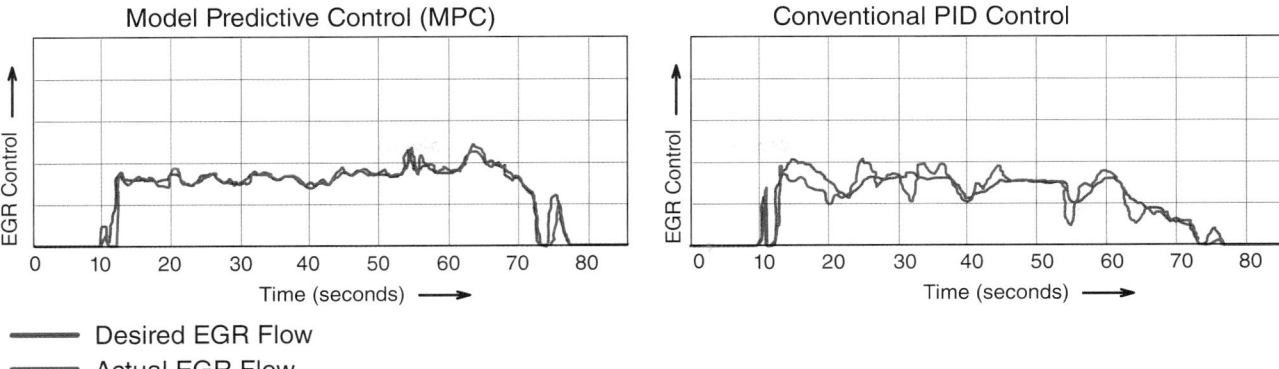

Model Predictive Control (MPC)   Conventional PID Control

━━━━ Desired EGR Flow
━━━━ Actual EGR Flow

FIGURE 25-50 Comparing desired versus measured EGR flow in an MPC- and PID-controlled system. MPC actuators move more quickly, frequently, and accurately.

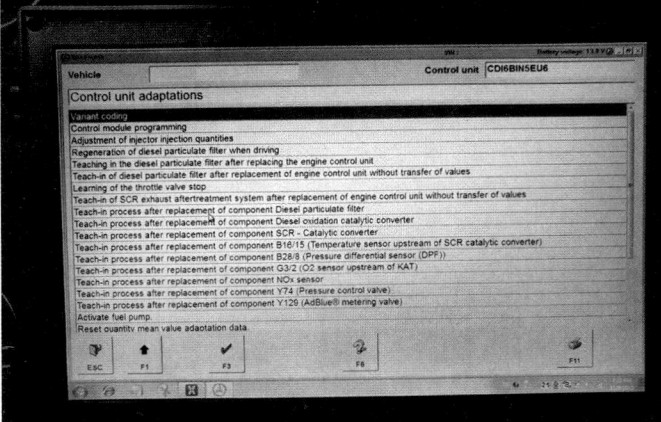

FIGURE 25-51 A screen shot of the service menu for various adaption strategies available to a common rail ECU.

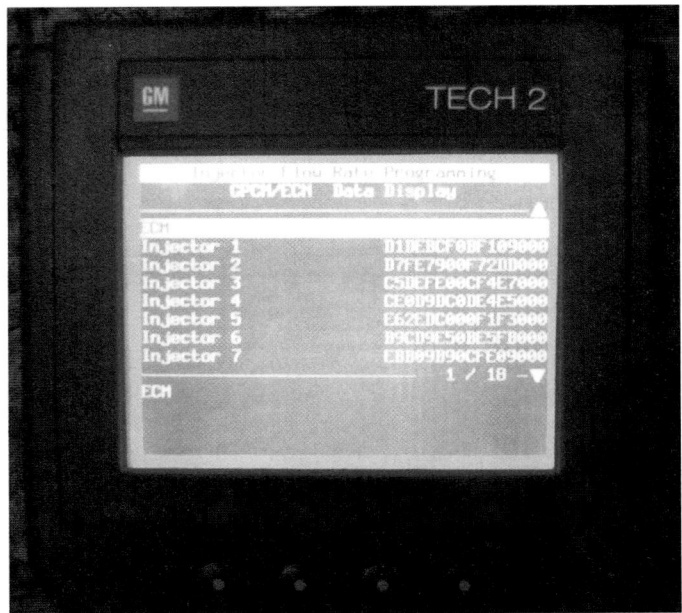

FIGURE 25-52 Installing or transferring injector calibration codes updates the model of injector behavior with operating characteristics unique to each injector.

by overdriving them with electrical signals, but they can disrupt proper system operation and cause enormous distortions in vehicle performance. Wear and deterioration are expected to happen, but the model is designed to adapt to these changes but needs to learn where what the problems are, and how worn something is, in order to adjust control paths with a deterioration factor. This explains why adaption routines in service and diagnostic software are used by manufacturers to ensure the models knowledge of a virtual object is complete and can accurately generate control signals. In other words, adaptation procedures that update information about model objects representing components must be made to "learn" the components' real-world characteristics (**FIGURE 25-51**).

Component adaptation or model optimization takes place in three fundamental ways:

1. Fast adaptation when the key is cycle on or off; turbocharger, EGR, and throttle actuators are common examples.
2. Service adaptation when parts are replaced and information, such as calibration codes, are updated. Fuel injectors, actuators, gas sensor modules, and parts with an embedded microcontroller are examples (**FIGURE 25-52**).

3. Slow adaptation when the model relearns a component's characteristics through a model with an optimizing feedback loop. This process is performed while the vehicle is in service and takes place continuously over many driving cycles. Air filter air flow, injector calibration code updating, and transmission shift schedules are typical examples of slow adaptation strategies.

Fault codes for aftertreatment system components can often be repaired by performing an adaptation procedure to force the model to update its knowledge about system operation. When any parts are replaced, the model must learn the new part's characteristics and introduce it to the other objects in the system. To perform a service adaptation procedure, follow the steps in **SKILL DRILL 25-1**.

SKILL DRILL 25-1 Performing a Service Adaptation Procedure

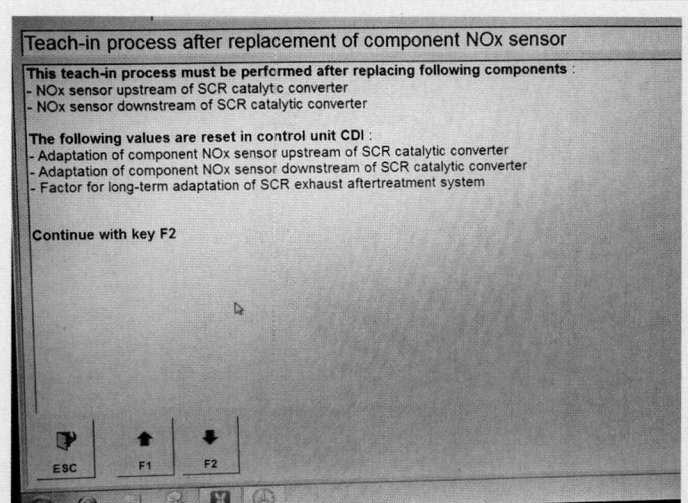

1. Check service literature or documentation arriving with the part. Determine if the manufacturer requires a component adaptation to be performed after a part has been replaced.

2. Search relevant service information literature to determine what specific procedures are required to perform a component adaptation after the part is replaced or to correct a fault code.

3. Determine whether information, such as vehicle serial numbers or calibration numbers from the old part, must be transferred to the new part and if software is required.

4. Identify and locate equipment and software necessary to perform the service adaptation.

5. Navigate to appropriate service menus for performing service adaptations. These are usually associated with a major domain ECU controlling the component.

6. Identify any alternatives to service adaptation using prescribed software and equipment if it is not available. Specifically check for methods to place a system in an adaptive learning mode, such as using a sequence of throttle pedal sweeps, switching instrument cluster switches on and off, opening and closing doors, or moving the transmission range selector.

7. After component replacement and adaption, operate the vehicle to verify the complaint is corrected by matching the road test conditions to conditions when the component operates. Check that there are no fault codes before releasing the vehicle to the customer.

► TECHNICIAN TIP

When replacing any control system parts or components with embedded microcontrollers with a new one, the MPC controller must first be made to "learn" and store the new part's characteristics. Components must also be made to recognize one another. If this is not done, parts can fail to operate, generate fault codes, or cause drivability complaints that can seem to be unrelated to the repair.

► TECHNICIAN TIP

Unusual noises from mechanical linkage and stepper motor-controlled devices are routinely heard when a key is switched on and off. Engines using MPC relearn new limits for control valve movement and the electrical signals required to correctly position a device during these actuator sweeps. Relearning or adaption is necessary to correct for wear and component deterioration to ensure the model takes these factors into account when it generates output signals. This fast adaptation process updates the knowledge the model uses for critical virtual objects, such as throttle plates, EGR valves, and turbocharger actuators. After performing the adaptation or relearn process, new values are stored for virtual object's behavior and can accommodate even minor faults.

Model-Based Diagnostics

One of the greatest advantages of MPC is in the area of fault diagnostics. Model-based deviation between a theoretical model of expected behavior and measured feedback about actual operation are used to determine fault conditions. What that simply means is that diagnostics have moved to comparing whether the system behavior matches the expected model behavior. The advantage of the approach is that it's cheaper to implement because complex algorithms to predict failures are not required.

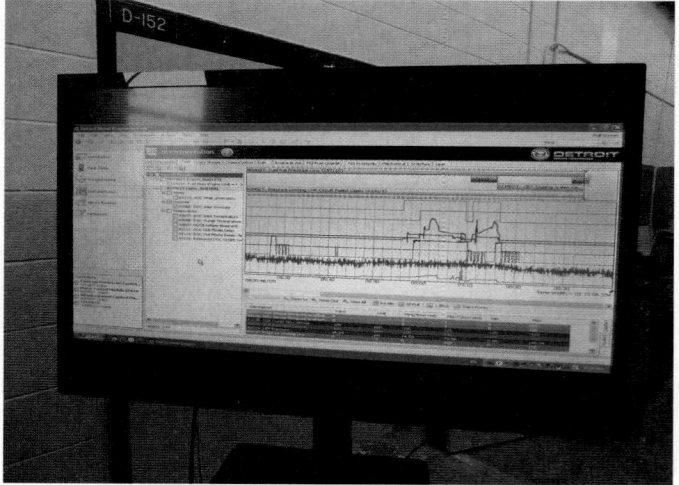

FIGURE 25-53 Waveforms from sensors and output actuators are carefully compared with models of failures for identical parts. This enables MPC to predict imminent failures.

The incidence of false failures and nuisance fault codes is sharply reduced used MPC to identify faults. Faults can also be predicted, and an imminent failure identified. A single piece of data, such as a momentary, but atypical, waveform from a sensor or output actuator that matches a model for a predictable failure, enables identification of an imminent failure (**FIGURE 25-53**).

Fault-Tolerant Systems

MPC can not only more accurately identify faults and predict imminent faults, but also has the ability to adjust system operation to compensate for a fault and keep a system within a normal operating range. When a control system has the ability to adjust its operation to accommodate a fault, it is considered to be a **fault tolerant system**. To understand a fault-tolerant system, consider the problem caused by a sticking EGR valve, or one that does not open completely. This type of fault could potentially increase NOx emissions. The control system could respond in several ways. First, it could identify the fault and illuminate a MIL. If the fault was serious enough, the engine power could be de-rated, taking the vehicle out of useful service. Another response is to accommodate the fault and minimize its influence on system operation. A fault-tolerant system can accommodate some less serious faults and enable the engine emissions to stay within legislated limits by choosing a different control pathway. It could, for example, compensate for a defective EGR valve by delivering more DEF to the aftertreatment system. Boost pressure, injection timing, pressure, or injection rate could also be altered to produce less engine-out NOx. Accommodating faults requires engine subsystems to have a high **degree of freedom**. Having a high degree of operational freedom means the model is able to select from a wide range of variables to change its forward control paths to compensate for faults or optimize performance of a system (**FIGURE 25-54**).

▶ **TECHNICIAN TIP**

Fault codes with descriptions, such as "Adaptation Limit Surpassed" or "Adaptation Control Position Exceeded Learning Limit," are examples of faults in MPC control systems where adaptive learning takes place and indicate the control system is likely fault-tolerant. Adaption or learning limits are programmed limits to the degrees of freedom to which a model can adjust for wear and deterioration. When a fault is reported

it usually means that the controller has reached the end of its ability to compensate for a system fault. However, with MPC, the problem may or may not be in the component with the fault but caused by another problem with the system. Carefully follow diagnostic troubleshooting procedures when pinpointing the root cause of these codes to avoid unnecessary parts replacement and wasted diagnostic time.

▶ **TECHNICIAN TIP**

MPC can compensate for component wear and deterioration by generating a new set of look-up tables or generating a new map. This keeps the MIL off and potentially minimizes the likelihood of a related repair. However, when fault accommodation takes place, the vehicle loses performance and increases fuel consumption. Sometimes, no MIL is generated to identify the problem and the complaint is only symptom-based. It's important to study engine data during a road test to diagnose MPC fault-tolerant systems, "**fault healing**" strategies, which may reduce power output and increase fuel consumption. Compare data values with other vehicles in known good condition to identify the discrepancy and diagnose which component or system may be changing the MPC virtual look-up tables.

Construction and Operation of Microcontrollers

LO 25-6 Describe the construction and operation of microcontrollers.

The operation of control systems is centered in an ECU. An ECU, in turn, is constructed around microcontrollers. Before more closely examining ECUs, it's helpful to understand more about the construction and operation of microcontrollers, which are basic building blocks for any control system (**FIGURE 25-55**).

As the name suggests, microcontrollers are a general category of integrated circuits designed and constructed to control the operation of electrical components and systems. Like other

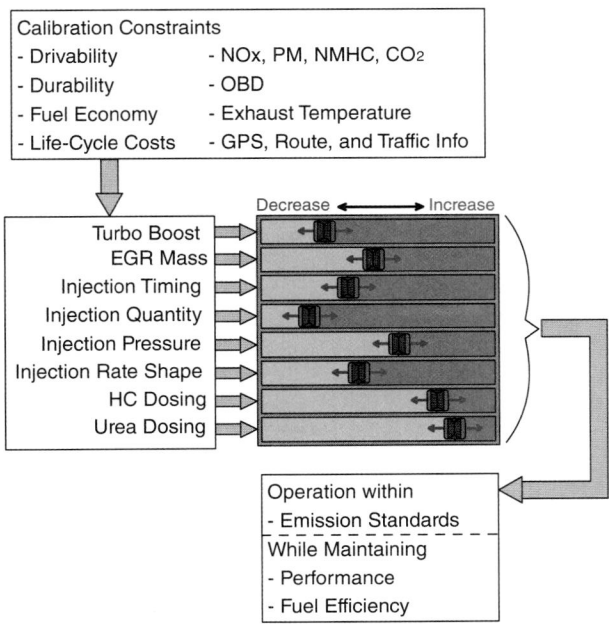

FIGURE 25-54 A fault-tolerant system can change a wide number of variables to work around a fault. The variable positions for control signals represented by knobs on sliding controls help visualize how dozens of alternate control pathways are selected to potentially minimize the effects of a fault.

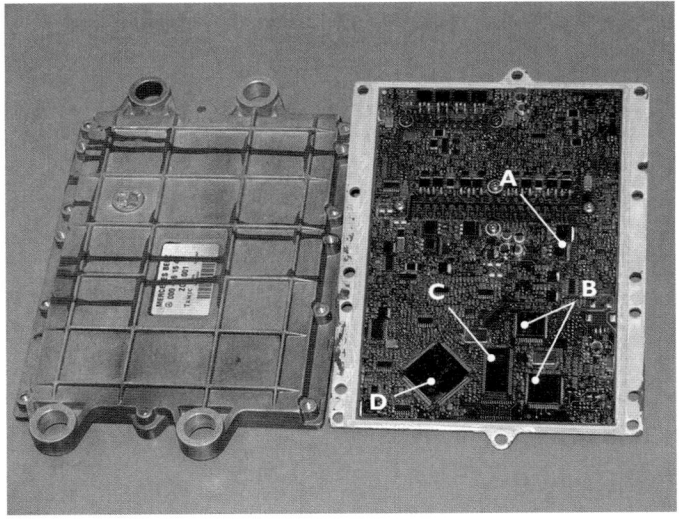

FIGURE 25-55 Microcontrollers are the most important elements of an ECU.

integrated circuits, they miniaturize many discrete electronic devices, such as transistors, diodes, resistors, capacitors, and inductors, by integrating them into multiple layers on a silicon chip. Because the number of circuits integrated into silicon chip is scalable, there can be anywhere from a few dozen to millions of discrete devices packed into a single chip wafer. This means microcontrollers can vary enormously in terms of their size, operating speed, sophistication, capabilities, and functions. For example, the type of microcontroller used in a tire pressure sensor, which senses and wirelessly transmits tire temperature and pressure data, is different from a microcontroller used in an engine, transmission, chassis, or cab electrical system controller having potentially hundreds of input and output signals plus several communication channels. Microcontrollers in major control domains are also constructed differently from microcontrollers regulating sound output from a vehicle entertainment system or driving the display of an instrument cluster for the driver information center.

Types of Microcontroller Memory

Microcontrollers store program information and calibration data in memory either on the silicon chip or by using additional memory located near a microcontroller. Memory can be divided into two basic categories, depending on whether the memory requires battery current to retain storage information. Volatile memory requires a constant supply of current to remain intact while non-volatile memory (NVM) does not. When the ignition key is switched off and the ECU loses power, volatile memory disappears. This explains why NVM is used to store program code in addition to important data, such as

fault codes, that need to remain available after an ignition key cycle. One might reasonably wonder whether all memory in a microcontroller or ECU should be the non-volatile type. Until recently, the use of memory for reading, writing, and storing information was constrained by the number of times memory registers could be erased and rewritten before wearing out. NVM capable of being erased and rewritten or flashed could only tolerate flashing from between 1000 to 10,000 times. Volatile memory types can be flashed upwards of more than a million times but have technical issues with how quickly they can be read or rewritten to.

Volatile memory and NVM can be further categorized into the type of information they can best store and the method used to erase and write to memory registers. Further categories of ECU memory include:

- Read-only memory (ROM)
- Random-access memory (RAM)
- Programmable read-only memory (PROM)
- Electrically erasable, programmable, read-only memory (EEPROM)
- Flash memory or non-volatile RAM (NVRAM), which is a ROM/RAM hybrid that can be written to, but which does not require power to maintain its contents

Read-Only Memory (ROM)

Traditional ROM is a category of NVM used for permanent storage of program data (**FIGURE 25-56**). It is called read-only because it is not designed to be regularly erased and rewritten to. ROM memory storage generally includes all program-related data.

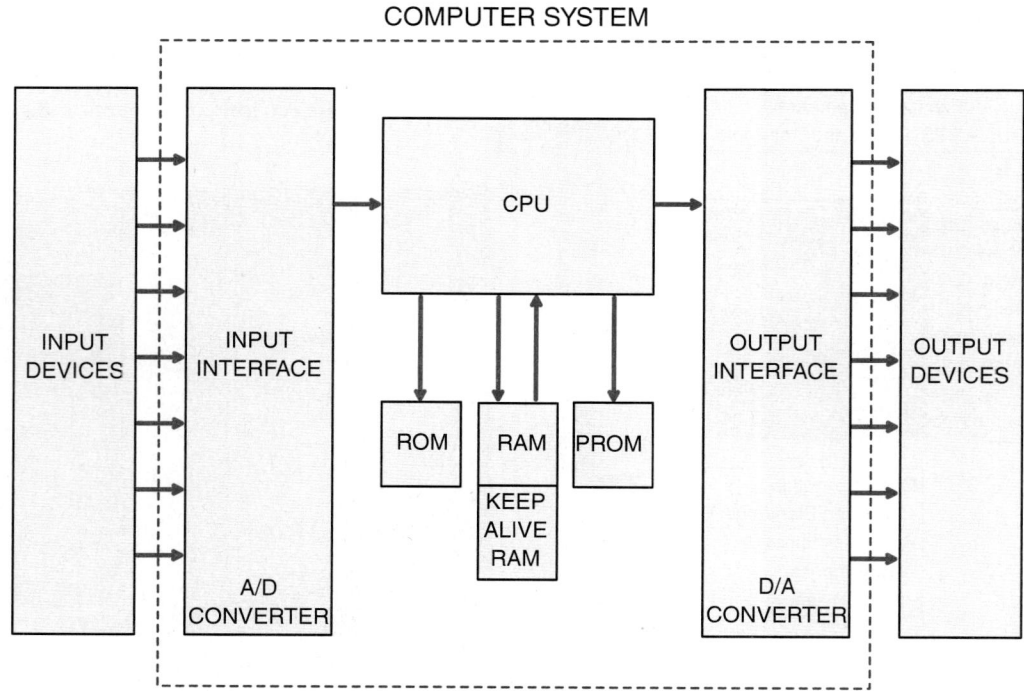

FIGURE 25-56 Non-volatile memory (NVM) means the information is not lost when power to the ECM is disconnected or the ignition is switched off. Keep-alive memory (KAM) refers to memory that is retained only due to a constant supply of current to the ECM when the ignition is switched off.

The CPU reads the program instructions with control system logic stored in the ROM, but it does not write to or change the instructions contained in ROM during its normal operation. ROM program code and control logic is typically built into the ECU during the manufacturing process for smaller, task-specific chips, such as those performing analog-to-digital signal conversion, voltage regulators, or as a tire pressure sensor. Program data in larger sophisticated chips is uploaded into the ECU by a system programmer or manufacturer using specialized tools and software designed for that purpose.

Random-Access Memory (RAM)

Random-access memory (RAM) is a temporary storage place for information that needs to be quickly accessed. RAM memory is both quickly readable and writable. Input data from sensors is commonly stored in RAM awaiting processing by the ECU since it cannot process all sensor data simultaneously. When used for temporary storage for data awaiting processing, RAM is called a buffer memory. Most RAM memory is designed to be lost when power is interrupted, such as turning the ignition key off. That characteristic explains why RAM is often used only as temporary storage of memory. However, NVRAM retains its information even when the power is removed. Volatile RAM data can also be stored in the ECM after the key is shut off by providing a continuous battery supply to an ECU, in addition to power supplied by the ignition circuit. If battery power is used to keep the RAM intact when the key is off, it is also known as keep-alive memory (KAM) (**FIGURE 25-57**).

EEPROM and Flash Memory

Electrically erasable programmable read-only memory (EEPROM) was developed to allow manufacturers to change the program instructions operating the ECU electronically instead of physically fixing it into the ECU during its construction. Rather than retain memory placeholder values of 1 and 0 using electrons, digital EEPROM information is stored as a magnetic field.

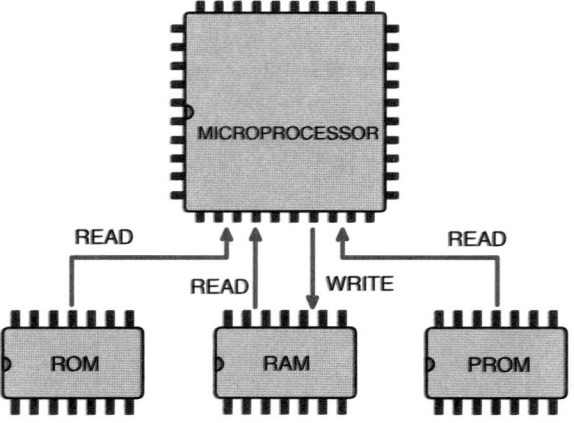

FIGURE 25-57 Data memory is required to store calibration data for operating the microcontroller. This memory stores software code or control logic, giving the ECU and the system or component it controls its unique operational characteristics.

In recent years, flash memory, which is non-volatile EEPROM, is used. This memory chip is almost identical to the type used by a universal serial bus (USB) memory stick. It has enormous shock resistance and durability and is able to withstand intense pressure, extremes of temperature, and immersion in water, which are conditions found in commercial vehicles. It also offers the convenience of easily reprogramming or recalibrating the ECU, which has already been mentioned as the process known as flashing or flash programming. ECUs can access separate memory chips containing EEPROM mounted next to microcontrollers to increase the memory capacity of the control unit.

Most of the time, flash programming of ECUs in the field involves only the installation in the ECU of calibration data, such as models for MPC, look-up tables for PID controls, references to diagnostic fault codes, and countless pieces of vehicle- or component-specific information, such as injector calibration codes.

> ▶ **TECHNICIAN TIP**
>
> When reprogramming an ECU, multiple bar graphs of uploads to an ECU may show up on the software menu screens. While this might be alarming to initially see, it is normal since multiple bar graphs indicate multiple memory locations in the ECU are being erased and rewritten, which is called a memory reflash.

Microcontroller Functions

LO 25-7 Identify and describe the functions of microcontrollers.

Microcontrollers that store and carry out instructions are commonly needed to perform a list of tasks, such as:

- answer problems posed by mathematical algorithms and logic conditions,
- communicate with other electronic devices,
- process input and output electrical signals supplied to chip package pins,
- store programmed instructions, plus retrieve and store new data, and
- time or set the pace and track the execution of program instructions.

Virtually all microcontrollers today are constructed using P-type and N-type metal–oxide–semiconductor material to form gates and channels. Constructing microcontroller silicon chips using complementary metal–oxide–semiconductor (CMOS) technology enables the devices to have low power consumption, plus form reliable memory storage areas, logic gates, and other digital circuits. Because the construction and functions performed by microcontrollers look identical to a personal computer, it's convenient to consider vehicle ECUs as "computers." However, at an operational level and for service considerations, it is important to understand the differences. An important question to answer, then, is what are the differences between a microcontroller and microprocessor? Both devices have many things in common, but key differences include the following:

1. Microcontrollers are generally designed to perform a specific task. Unlike microprocessors used in desktops and

laptop computers running multiple types of software, such as Windows, plus a diverse variety of applications, such as word processing or playing media, microcontrollers are commonly dedicated to one task or function and run one specific program to control the features, actions, or operation of a device. Some common microcontroller tasks are voltage regulation, converting analog sensor data to digital data, or producing electrical signals to operate an electric motor. Built-in task specificity and comparatively limited programmability enables production of very inexpensive microcontrollers, often costing less than a dollar, compared to a microprocessor costing hundreds of dollars.

2. Microcontrollers are complete computers on a chip typically having a CPU, internal programmable memory, a clock, communication channels, external interface pins, and internal capabilities assembled in a package to process input and output signals (**FIGURE 25-58**). In contrast, microprocessors have one or more CPUs that are more sophisticated and are used to support an operating system, such as Windows, while also executing large, complex software application programs. A microprocessor is not a complete computer on a chip like a microcontroller though. A microprocessor requires external memory and data buses to store the operating system and software programs, and requires peripherals, such as keyboards, video displays, or printers, to process inputs and outputs.

3. Microcontrollers contain a single or multiple CPUs, but its design is simpler, yet capable of performing both arithmetic and logic operations. Mathematical operations may be simple addition, multiplication, and division or more complex operations. More complex mathematical problem solving can also be programmed into a microcontroller by breaking down functions into simpler steps solved using basic math. Logic functions enable the CPU to answer questions like whether one numerical value is equal to, greater than, or less than the other. Processors with more sophisticated logic functions using complex conditional statements and math operations use a specialized arithmetic logic unit (ALU). Regardless of the processor sophistication, math and logic functions involve the use of what are called logic gates: AND, OR, XOR, and NOT. Operation of logic gates is covered in the chapter on Electronic Signal Processing (**FIGURE 25-59**).

4. Microcontrollers and ECUs, when combined with vehicle or mechanical devices, are called **embedded** devices and are capable of stand-alone control. As mentioned, microprocessors require additional support systems. Countless numbers of consumer products, including televisions, microwaves, clock radios, refrigerators, etc. use microcontrollers that are embedded devices because the product's operation depends on the integration of electronic, mechanical, and electrical control. This means that when a microcontroller is operating to regulate electrical or mechanical components from the inside, it's termed "embedded" into a device. Similarly, an ECU is tasked with a dedicated function regulating and operating parts within a larger mechanical or electrical system. A vehicle ECU is considered an embedded device because it is integral to a vehicle's electrical and or mechanical control system. So much integration of electronic and mechanical systems is taking place in today's commercial vehicles that a new term has been created; mechatronics. Mechatronics was defined earlier in the chapter and combines the term mechanical and electronics. Mechatronics refers to the integration of mechanical components, electronic devices, and microcontrollers into a single component or system. A considerable portion of a vehicle's value and service work is now tied to the mechatronics technology in items as simple as seating and cab controls to as complex as automated driving systems, stability and engine control systems integrating electronics with hydraulic, pneumatic, and other mechanical systems.

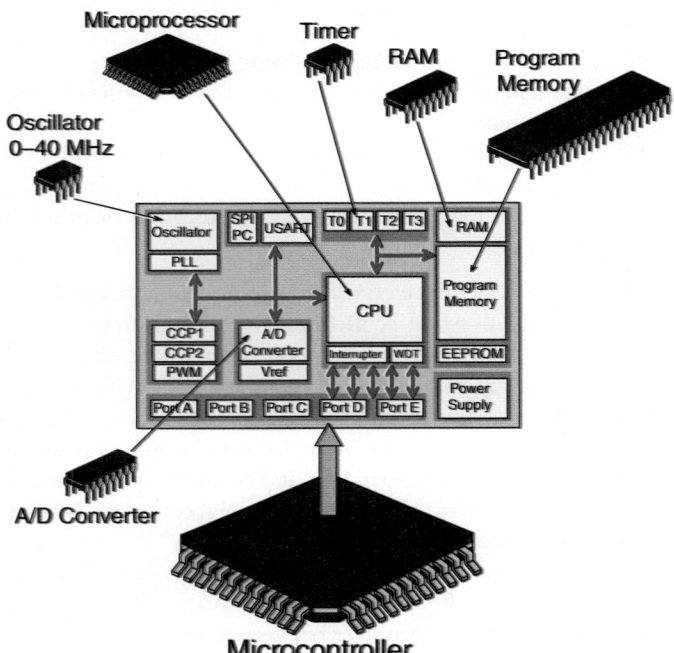

FIGURE 25-58 A microcontroller is a complete computer on a chip. A microprocessor requires external devices and external memory storage to operate.

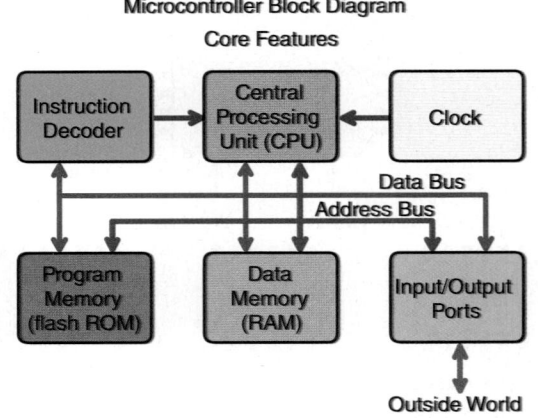

FIGURE 25-59 Elements of a typical microcontroller.

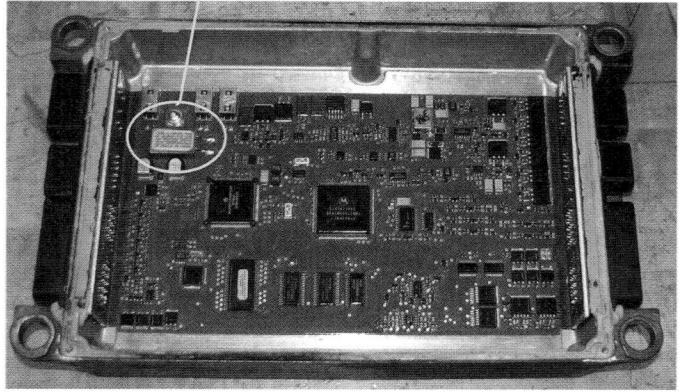

FIGURE 25-60 A lithium battery is soldered to the circuit board of this DDEC-IV ECM to keep volatile memory alive when the battery is disconnected.

FIGURE 25-61 A Gortex fabric filter is below the black button of this ECU. The fabric filters air passing in and out of the ECU because a barometric pressure sensor located inside must be vented to the atmosphere.

5. Microcontrollers usually have low-power requirements since many devices they control are battery-operated. Because microcontrollers can store memory that must be maintained when the ignition is switched off, they can continuously consume power, but the demand must be kept low to prevent excessive drain from the battery (**FIGURE 25-60**). When connected to a vehicle network and placed in **sleep mode**, ECU power consumption is at its lowest level, but some amount of current measured in milliwatts may still be consumed. Traditionally, microcontrollers have operated at 5 volts; however, to further reduce key-off power consumption and prevent damage to much smaller integrated circuit transistors, 3.3 volts is becoming more commonplace.

6. Microcontrollers used in ECUs of commercial vehicles have ruggedized construction. While the choice of components and construction of an ECU is to be as inexpensive as possible, it must operate in a harsh environment and replacement costs are not cheap. Overvoltage reverse polarity and short circuit protection is built into most circuits to improve reliability. Temperature ranges under which they must flawlessly operate are extreme, ranging from less than −40°F (−40°C) to 180°F (80°C) in the engine compartment. Vibration can loosen contacts and chemical action from moisture or air can lead to internal corrosion. This explains why a Gortex fabric, a material that can block moisture penetration, is often used to cover a ventilation hole into an ECU (**FIGURE 25-61**). Components are all surface mounted to a circuit board and may be glued with resin, using no wire leads that can vibrate and break due to fatigue failure. A protective chemical coating or polymer film barrier, called a **conformity coating**, is often sprayed onto the circuit board and components to insulate them from chemical contaminants and moisture and also to dampen some vibration (**FIGURE 25-62**).

▶ TECHNICIAN TIP

Some advanced ECUs use lithium batteries soldered to the circuit board to maintain power to program memory when the key is switched off or the battery is disconnected. When the real-time clock (RTC) option is enabled, for time and date-stamps, trip information and fault codes, the lithium battery current is used whenever the battery is removed. Because the life cycle of the circuit board battery is just a few years, program memory can be lost and the ECU is disabled after the battery is drained. Another common name for this disabled condition is called a "bricked" ECU because it generally cannot be reprogrammed in the field and must be replaced. To prevent this disabling condition, often requiring an ECU replacement, the RTC logging feature of trip information would need to be disabled. If the RTC is enabled, a fault is set before the battery is completely drained. When it is set, have the ECU repaired before the battery is completely depleted. Some aftermarket ECU repair facilities can replace the battery and prevent the need for an ECU repair.

▶ TECHNICIAN TIP

ECUs with internal batteries have a limited shelf life. This means that an ECU cannot be left stored on a parts shelf indefinitely or the battery drains and the program information is lost. Electronic stability control systems are one common type of ECU that can quickly drain the internal battery and make the ECU useless. Allowing a vehicle battery to drain with the key-on or leaving a vehicle battery dead are two other conditions known to "brick" an ECU.

▶ TECHNICIAN TIP

Water contamination, and even oil or fuel contamination, of an ECU can take place. Liquids sloshing inside a control module can cause unusual complaints pointing to an electronic problem, such as stalling, setting of fault codes, or warning lights suddenly appearing when the vehicle brakes or decelerates. To check for contamination, remove the ECU and shake it to listen for liquids. Because of the potential for hazardous or safety-related failures, a contaminated ECU should always be replaced. Remember to never directly

FIGURE 25-62 The glossy shellac coating covering components on this ECU board is an example of a protective conformity coating.

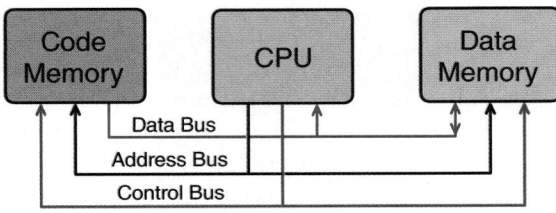

FIGURE 25-63 The architecture of the microcontroller that allows it to simultaneously access internal program or control logic, and application memory makes the microcontroller start and operate faster than a microprocessor, which only has one path to external memory.

power wash an ECU with high-pressure water, and quickly repair engine coolant and fuel and oil leaks, particularly if liquids are dripping onto an ECU.

Microcontroller Versus Microprocessor Architecture

LO 25-8 Differentiate between the construction, organization, and operation of microcontrollers and microprocessors.

One of the most significant distinctions between microcontrollers and processors is the use of two fundamentally different types of architecture or organization of digital data processing structures used by each device to access program and calibration memory. Memory is needed by both microcontrollers and microprocessors to store program instructions, which is control system logic and calibration- or application-specific data. It is important to understand that these two types of data work together but are distinctly different and have very different purposes. The CPU of a microcontroller stores the two types of data in memory into two distinctly separate register locations. However, the microcontroller is designed to access the two different sets of memory in the separate registers at the same time using two separate internal pathways, called data buses (**FIGURE 25-63**). One data bus or communication pathway connects the CPU to program memory that contains step-by-step control logic and instructions for how it is to complete the tasks it is to perform. A second separate data

bus connects to the memory register location where application or calibration data is stored. Calibration data containing information unique for an application is also simply called data memory and serves a different function than program memory. But data and program memory are required to work together in a microcontroller. Accessing both sets of memory registers at the same time using two different data buses provides the microcontroller with a processing speed advantage. In contrast, microprocessors generally use only one memory data bus connected to a large single external storage area for memory. The data bus to connect the CPU to memory in a microprocessor is a single pathway used to retrieve and store both operating system data and application program memory stored in the same location—usually a hard drive. Knowing names for the types of architecture using dual versus single storage location and pathway for data bus interconnections between the CPU and memory are not important, but it's noteworthy and important to understand because of the enormous influence on how fast microcontrollers can complete the jobs they are tasked with in comparison to microprocessors. For example, the arrangement explains why quickly after switching on the ignition, ECU-containing microcontrollers are operating and do not require a long boot-up period. The unique architecture or structure of a microcontroller also changes the service techniques and methods for replacement, reprogramming, or recalibrating microcontrollers, compared to the method most people are familiar with who use personal computers.

Firmware and Calibration Data

Different terminology is used by the electronic industry for the two separate memory registers and types of memory used by microcontrollers. Program data or control logic is called firmware and calibration data or application memory is called data memory. **Firmware** is the microcontroller's operating system stored in program memory. Firmware contains machine-level instructions that perform all control, arithmetic, logic, and data manipulation operations. Compared to a microprocessor, firmware is like the Windows operating system. Firmware is also more closely associated with operating the controller's physical electronic circuits or hardware. With the exception of the simplest microcontrollers, almost all microcontrollers contain some firmware.

In contrast to firmware, application or data memory contains task or application specific information such as component features, model objects, PID look-up tables, fault codes, operating parameters, and customized data. The information is unique to a control system, vehicle model, horsepower rating, tire size, vehicle weight, size, gear ratios, etc. Application or calibration data is used by the firmware or to perform system control operations.

Firmware and calibration data must not be lost when the ignition key is switched off or the battery is disconnected. This explains why the content of both memories is stored in NVM devices, such as ROM, EPROM, or flash memory. Firmware and calibration data were once commonly burned into ROM during the manufacturing process. If that is the situation, the memory is permanently installed and cannot be changed after manufacture. ROM circuits or chips must be physically replaced or, in the case of erasable flash memory, reprogrammed through firmware or calibration software updates, if possible. Updating or changing microcontroller firmware memory may rarely, if ever, be done because it infrequently changes. Replacing and reflashing a microcontroller with new application-specific information, or calibration information, is more common. Updating memory storage of either firmware or calibration information can be done independently of one another or at the same time. Note that during a reprogramming event, changes and updates of memory commonly require complete erasing of all contents in each memory address before new memory can be installed (**FIGURE 25-64**).

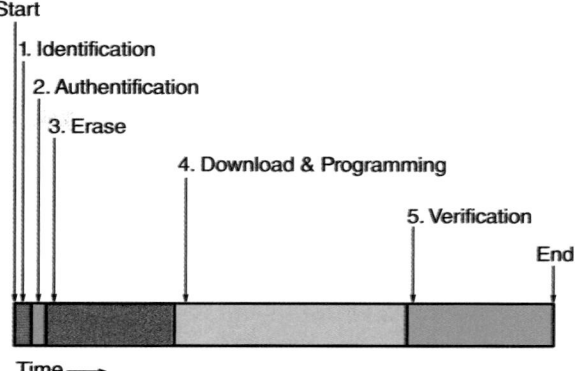

FIGURE 25-64 General sequence of reprogramming a microcontroller.

is called a data flash or **D-flash** event. The latest software tools can selectively identify and update portions of each of these separate memory storage areas to replace digital data stored in each.

Microcontroller Memory Data Buses and Addresses

The size or width of the data bus, reported in bits, is often used by OEMs to indicate how powerful a control module is. Data bus size inside a microcontroller is like counting the lanes of a highway in that the higher the bit count (a bit is a 1 or 0), the more lanes of highway are available to handle traffic. The significance of the data bus size lies in measuring how much information can be moved in and out of the CPU at any one time. That means the size of the data bus determines the maximum number of memory addresses that can be used when executing an instruction. Microcontroller data buses are commonly 2, 4, 8, 16, or 32 bits in size, with the larger data buses having a bigger data pipeline or more lanes of a highway to transmit information. A wider data bus is best accompanied by matching the bus size with the same number of memory registers of either 2, 4, 8, 16, or 32 bytes (note that each byte equals 8 bits of data), and a CPU is capable of handling a corresponding amount of data contained in one instruction set of either 2, 4, 8, 16, or 32 bits in length. Larger data bus width, memory registers, and CPU-processing capabilities measured in bit sizes are capable of processing more information and using more memory contained in any instruction set during execution of a programs control logic.

Microcontroller Memory Addresses

At a minimum, microcontrollers store a limited set of instructions in firmware program memory that enables it to interpret inputs signals and controls output signals. Unlike personal computers running Windows or OS Apple software, a microcontroller uses much fewer types of instructions and only those specific to the functions the controller is designed to handle. For example, if the controller is switched on and operates an LED that lights up when a button is pushed, instructions include steps, such as measuring a switch input pin voltage, converting it to digital hexadecimal value, and using logic steps to determine whether the switch voltage is above or below a specific value before determining whether a transistor should be biased to supply current to the light. A sequence of instructions or control logic creates a program. The program data is stored in memory registers organized into row and columns. The column height and row width of the memory registers are designated by hexadecimal coordinates of numbers and letters (**FIGURE 25-65**). A simple coordinate for 4-byte memory locations is 0X0000 with the first number designating the column location and the second letter designating the coordinate for row. (Memory registers with higher bit counts, such as 8, 16, and 32, have longer rows and wider columns for greater memory storage capacity.) The sequence beginning the execution of program instructions takes place after the controller powers on or boots up. Unlike a personal computer, ECUs are required to quickly operate after the ignition is switched. To do this, a specialized set of instructions, called a boot loader, stored in its own unique memory location, decides whether the program will begin executing lines of instruction in program code. If it does, program code

instructions are automatically read from the first program register with an address 0X0000. When the instruction is completed, a program counter, which tracks the execution of instructions, automatically requires the next instruction to be read, or the first instruction requires the CPU to read some other instructions from another address location. After the instruction is executed, the program counter automatically increments the next read-memory register for program code by a value of 1 to keep the program executing until the addresses are all read. This means the second instructions at address 0X0001 are fetched, read, and executed after the first.

Contents of Program and Calibration Memory

In sophisticated ECUs operating the engine, transmission, or ABS, the idea that the CPU processes input data according to programmed instructions is straightforward. However, for service considerations, such as when ECU software is updated, it is very important to understand each what type of information is stored in each memory register. Read-from memory locations generally consist of two parts: Program and calibration memory. In other words, two different sets of memory registers are read and used by the ECU to operate: program and data. The contents of each of the memory storage areas can be of different sizes and composed of different types of memory technology (**FIGURE 25-66**). While program and data memory are typically stored in two separate and distinct areas of memory (Harvard architecture), both memories can be simultaneously accessed by the microcontroller. Program memory can be understood to describe *WHAT* should be done, while the data memory explains *HOW* to do it. For example, the "what" part of the instruction could be "measure and calculate the voltage signal" at a specific microcontroller pin. The "how" part would be "using a special mathematical coefficient of XX.X" stored in calibration memory. The next program instruction "what" could be to "give the voltage signal a name," the calibration memory executed for the "how" part could be "using the name in calibration address location 2F X 0304." The label used by the program instruction retrieved from the data memory

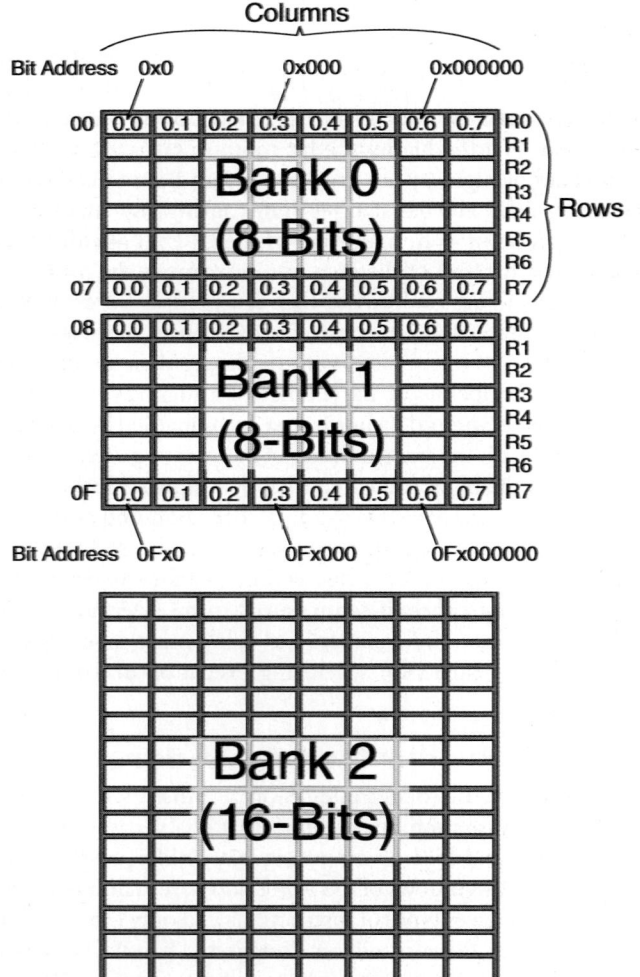

FIGURE 25-65 Microcontroller memory is stored in pages that are addressed according to row and columns. Addresses are read using a hexadecimal numbering system.

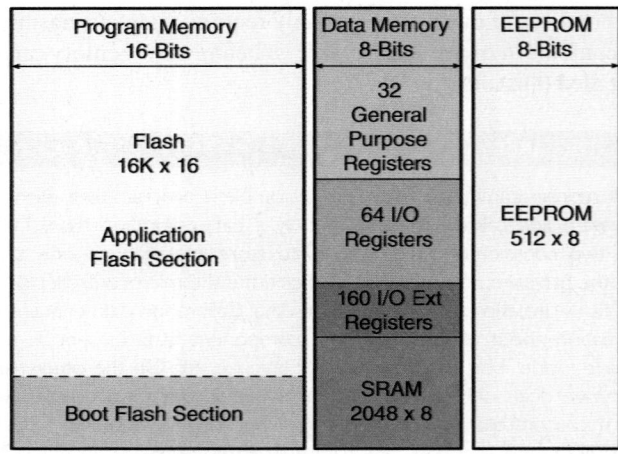

FIGURE 25-66 Calibration data and program or firmware are stored in two separate locations which can be of different size and secured separately.

register could be battery voltage or whatever was specified by the information stored in the data address.

Calibration or data memory can be made up of information stored while the ECU is operating but, more importantly, it contains specific information provided by a manufacturer in the form of models with objects, or look-up tables, or calibration files. Look-up tables are simply mathematical shortcuts used to quickly solve problems, such as: What voltage should be supplied to an actuator or other output device at a specific engine speed and load? How much time should elapse between an ABS brake "hold" and "release" event for a particular vehicle speed?

Modifying Program Versus Data Files

ECU module manufacturers supply ECUs to vehicle manufacturers. To be economically efficient, ECU manufacturers build units using generic microcontroller hardware that can be used for a wide variety of purposes or meet the requirements of several vehicle applications. The function of input and output pins is programmable and the internal firmware programs can have software code installed to perform a wide variety of tasks. This explains why an identical-looking module is used for controlling the cab electrical system and may also be used as a transmission control unit, or as a controller for the ABS or exhaust aftertreatment system. Generic multipurpose ECUs that are built blank, having no instructions stored in memory, require the installation of both program/firmware and data/calibration files (P-flash and D-Flash). Firmware files are developed by the ECU builder and stored in an ECU for a specific purpose, such as engine, transmission, or body control, that can be used by multiple vehicle manufacturers. But data in calibration files containing vehicle-unique information are developed for a specific chassis or component and then uploaded into the ECU (D-flash). ECU makers use separate security features using a program in the microcontroller called the **boot loader** to lock down proprietary firmware files and data files so they cannot be changed except by authorized persons using proprietary equipment. A boot loader is a small but secure set of instructions stored in a separate area of memory that decides if there is a set of valid program and data files stored in the microcontroller (**FIGURE 25-67**). If there is a valid application, the microcontroller continues to execute commands and operate. If there isn't, it looks for files transmitted over the vehicle data link connector (DLC) and install them using another program, called a flash loader. Vehicle manufacturers install data files during the vehicle build or during a service replacement procedure or service update (P-flash) using the boot loader. To have the boot loader begin to erase a either program or data memory registers and store new files, it needs to be unlocked before a set of memory reprogramming instructions is transmitted

To change the firmware or application memory, the boot loader may only require a simple password in order to protect the files from unauthorized changes. Often, firmware has additional levels of security before the ECU is handed the over to the vehicle OEM to install its calibration files. The most recent boot loaders for major domain ECUs are unlocked using multi-factor authentication involving the use of credentials from OEM dealer employees and encryption keys as complex as 2048-bit

that are unique for each vehicle identification number (VIN) ECU. Encrypting access to a controller is also done through network gateways. Manufacturers are using secure gateways now to prevent the possibility of what is called a "CAN hack." CAN hacking involves a remote user accessing the CAN communications and take control of a vehicle.

ECU Tampering

When ECUs are tampered with by third parties, called tuners, a new piece of firmware or calibration file is created from the original files to add new features or unlock hidden functionalities. Most often, engine tuners alter calibration files to increase engine power output, shut-off fault code logging, or change transmission shift points. It is generally the less-complex calibration files stored in data memory that are altered and not the more complex and heavily secured firmware program files. Third parties producing unauthorized software extract calibration files, and occasionally firmware, producing a memory dump. The files are transferred from a microcontroller to a personal computer using one of two different communication interface devices used to program microcontrollers with the following communication protocols:

- JTAG (Joint Test Action Group)
- BDM (Background debug mode)

Both these interfaces use a short cable attached to the circuit board. The cable and communication adapter supply a voltage signal applied to a specific microcontroller pin on the circuit board to connect and access a communication port to either download or upload files when the ECU is removed from the vehicle. Calibration and firmware data are then analyzed using JTAG or BDM programmers or other specialized windows software to identify data for alteration, such as software switches that shut off fault codes or emission monitors, look-up tables

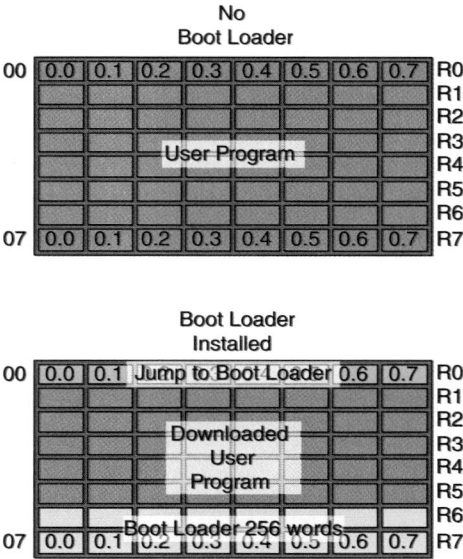

FIGURE 25-67 A boot loader is a security feature to prevent unauthorized installation of calibration or program files. The boot loader is the first instruction read by a microcontroller when it is powered up.

for boost pressure, fuel rates, etc. After modifying the calibration or data memory, it must be uploaded using the BDM or JTAG communication interfaces, along with the boot and flash loader program instructions. To validate whether the changes to memory are authorized, a common security technique is to use a check-sum digit in the memory files. A check-sum digit or string of digits is like a secret password that must match the boot loader's calculation for the correct check-sum before the files are stored in memory registers.

▶ TECHNICIAN TIP

To understand what calibration and program files do, programmers give descriptions of what logic steps do, identify data types, explain conversion rules for converting data into physical units, etc. Description labels are also given to virtual objects, characteristic curves, and specific maps. Descriptive information is stored in an industry-standard file called an ASAP2 description file, abbreviated to A2L. The file format is in hexadecimal code that people with specialized skills, such as tuners and engineers, can read using specialized programming software and by some OEM software applications.

Field Replacement and Programming of Electronic Control Units (ECUs)

LO 25-9 Describe the procedures and equipment used for field replacement and programming of electronic control units (ECUs).

ECUs now dominate the electrical system control. And while these devices have tremendous reliability, using features to enable them to withstand mechanical shock, corrosion, wide temperature swings, short circuited inputs and outputs, plus over-voltage protection, they may still fail and require replacement. Replacing a major ECU module in the latest vehicles typically involves reprogramming it with new data. Reprogramming ECUs is also necessary to repair electrical system problems or correct unintended faults that not only annoy users, but could lead to control system failures, malfunctions, and safety issues that could damage a vehicle or harm occupants or another road user. Long development cycles between creating firmware and calibration data and deployment in vehicles may also require updating ECU programming to correct bugs or compensate for unanticipated performance of deteriorated components. Understanding the differences between the types of programs and data that these control units may contain provides background for the service methods used.

▶ TECHNICIAN TIP

When flashing an ECU, battery voltage is critical. Switching the ignition switch off during reprogramming or low battery voltage can potentially corrupt the erase of old memory files or the upload of new files, as well as corrupt the flash and boot loader programs. If the files are corrupted, the ECU is said to be "bricked," meaning it is useless and may not be reprogrammable (**FIGURE 25-68**).

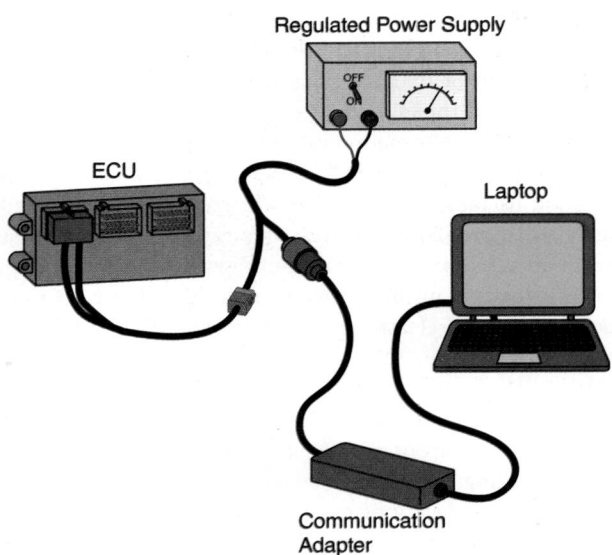

FIGURE 25-68 On-bench and vehicle reprogramming should be performed with a regulated power supply to prevent low battery voltage from "bricking" the ECU.

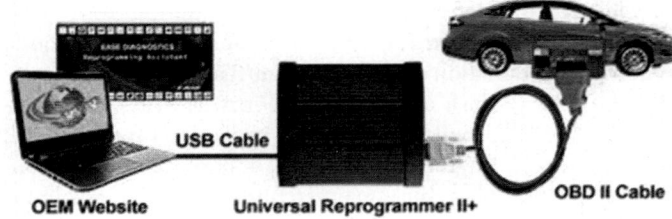

FIGURE 25-69 Onboard programming is performed through the vehicle data link connector. The files are downloaded from the manufacturer and uploaded by a pass-thru programmer.

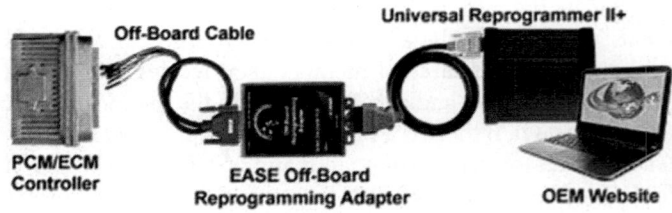

FIGURE 25-70 Offboard programming is performed on an individual ECU using a special adapter cable to connect with only the ECU terminals.

Bench Versus On-Vehicle Programming

As mentioned, reprogramming ECU modules when either new calibration data, firmware, or both are installed is called **flashing**. Two methods are commonly used to flash ECUs.

1. Using a pass-thru programmer or purpose-built communication adapter connected to the onboard network through the vehicle DLC (**FIGURE 25-69**).
2. Offboard programming or bench programming of the control module alone (**FIGURE 25-70**).

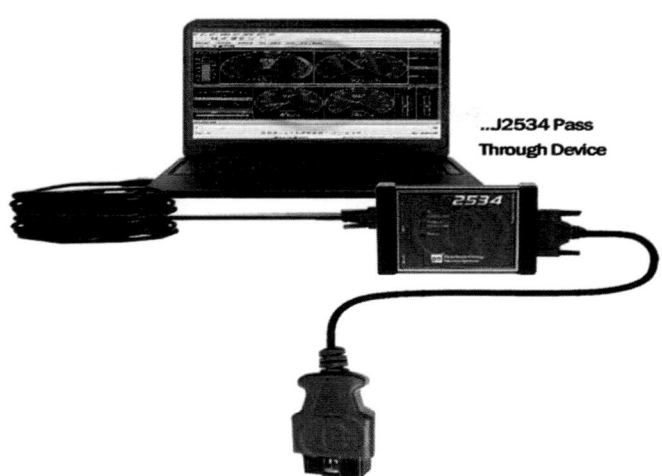

...J2534 Pass
Through Device

FIGURE 25-71 A pass-thru programmer is a communication device capable of uploading calibration and firmware files, reading diagnostic codes, and performing other service-related procedures for any of the vehicle's ECUs.

Offboard programming is performed by a technician or parts supplier by connecting a purpose-made wiring harness to a control module and connecting the other end of the harness to a device called a **pass-thru programmer**. When connected to a Windows-based computer, the programmer retrieves the correct calibration or appropriate firmware file from an OEM server and transmits it to the microcontroller memory addresses. A paid subscription service is usually required to unlock the boot loader and to provide access to OEM-supplied calibration files for engine and other chassis ECUs. Because the files most often are secured to prevent unauthorized tampering, the tool uses security protocols defined by the SAE J-2534 standard. The EPA has mandated all heavy- and light-duty vehicles to adopt this standard to reflash any ECU that can potentially influence emissions. For convenience, OEMs use this protocol for non-emission-related ECUs. J-2534's purpose is to create an Application Programming Interface (API) by defining features of a vehicle communication device, enabling repair facilities to reflash ECUs without the need for a dealer-only or OEM-specific tool (**FIGURE 25-71**).

Onboard servicing programming procedures are similar to offboard in that a pass-thru programmer or, in the case of engine control modules, a vehicle communication adapter can be used if it conforms to the same standards as pass-thru protocols. One or more ECUs can be programmed through the vehicle DLC. The pass-thru programmer typically silences the onboard communication of all other modules to prevent corruption of program and calibration files caused by communication interference.

▶ **TECHNICIAN TIP**

Aftermarket software is widely available to access and modify data files and perform D-flash updates of ECUs. One example of a PC program used to modify embedded controllers is WinOLS. This software is one of many used by the microcontroller programming industry and is capable of reading ECU data files to search for, view, identify the function of look-up tables, and label data maps. The software contains features that also enables it to modify the check-sum digits, firmware, or calibration file contents of ECUs. The Windows-based software derives its name from the file extension used for the data, ".OLS," which is a file format for look-up tables, maps, and hexadecimal ECU data.

Calibration Coding Numbers

It is important to note again that many major control modules on today's vehicles are electronically tied to a VIN using an OEM calibration coding system. This means that an identical control module cannot be transferred to another vehicle even if there are no differences. Other modules will not communicate with the orphan module, and its functions will not be enabled unless it stores a VIN that matches the vehicle and a VIN used by other modules. A network gateway module may perform this task, or it is done by individual modules. The purpose of the coding system is to prevent calibration errors that could mismatch of features in a module affecting vehicle and occupant safety. It also prevents trade in the use of unauthorized, tampered, or illicit parts from other vehicles. From a dealer perspective, a module must be replaced with a new part and reprogrammed with an OEM service tool that calculates a correct key to unlock the boot loader to enable reprogramming of the ECU. Third parties are always working on software that will enable an old defective ECU with good calibration files to be cloned into a used ECU in proper working order. Another alternative method is to remove the calibration software number from a good, used ECU to allow it to be programmed for reuse.

Types of Service Programming

Depending on the type of ECU, such as whether it is a major or minor unit, and the data it contains, there are four general update or replacement methods. Manufacturers have variations on each of these methods:

- Service programming update to repair or reconfigure an ECU
- ECU replacement without any additional service programming operation
- ECU replacement with manual reprogramming
- ECU replacement with user parameter transfer (cloning)

1. Service programming update is performed to repair or update, but not to replace a module. Long timelines between the development of firmware and calibration files and final production may require module updates. The module may also have some memory corrupted. Often, after performing symptom-based diagnostic checks to investigate poor system performance, and finding no fault, the ECU can be reflashed to return the system to normal operation. Newer calibration files incorporate fixes to operating bugs or correction factors to older worn mechanical parts that were not included in the original files.
2. ECU replacement without any additional service programming operation is performed on the most basic ECUs. These

ECUs are not configurable and are exchanged with replacement pre-programmed modules over the counter. Using only minimal vehicle information, such as the VIN, a control unit code, part number, or major component identification number for the transmission or even the climate control system, is required to select the correct module.

3. ECU replacement with manual reprogramming is performed on control units that have firmware installed but no calibration data. Information cannot be transferred into the new module from the defective module. Instead, the technician manually enters information into the module or computer interface, such as the VIN, component serial number, odometer reading, axle ratios, tire size, injector calibration codes, or major component serial number. An installation wizard selects the appropriate calibration data from a server using this data and then installs the correct calibration files into the module. Some engine ECUs, injector drive modules, ABS/ATC modules, or instrument cluster modules are examples where manual data entry is required before the module calibration files can be uploaded.

4. ECU replacement with user parameter transfer is performed when data is transferred from a current ECU or stored file template. A fleet of anywhere from a few vehicles to hundreds of vehicles can have an ECU recalibrated with newer flash files using a template with customized customer or factory programmable parameters. The operation of the electrical system, electrical accessories, and features, such as the vehicle speed limit, tire size, rear axle ratio, idle shut-down time, and other features either switched off or on, can be effectively cloned into a blank ECU.

To transfer the programming from an old ECU to a new one, follow the steps in SKILL DRILL 25-2.

SKILL DRILL 25-2 Transferring Calibration Files to a New ECU (On Vehicle)

1. Connect to the vehicle DLC with a J-2534-compliant communication adapter capable of reflashing an ECU on the vehicle.
2. Transfer information from the old control unit to the computer hard drive by navigating the service programming menu for "Read or load from ECU."
3. Select a menu option "Customer Parameters Settings" to read and download calibration data from the old ECU.
4. Select a file folder or memory card to store the download template.
5. End the read and download session.
6. Install and connect the new control unit.
7. Reconnect the J-2534-compliant communication adapter to the new control unit.
8. Navigate to the parameters page and select "Parameters setting: write in the ECU." A display screen should prompt you to select a programming file on the computer.
9. Select OK to upload the calibration or firmware file to transfer it to the new ECU.
10. After the programming is completed, switch off the ignition key and restart the vehicle.
11. Confirm the correct operation of the control unit by operating the system associated with the module.
12. Attach a mandatory service programming label to a vehicle if the engine- or emission-related control module was updated.

Wrap-Up

Ready for Review

▶ The purpose of electronic control systems is to automatically regulate the operation of a component or system output to maintain it within a desired operating range.

▶ If the control system senses a device or system operation moving away from the desired set-point, the controller, which is like the system's brains, changes its output signals to restore or correct the set-point value.

▶ Set-points vary for many components and systems, but electronic microcontrollers change the properties of electrical signal outputs, correcting errors or maintaining a set-point based on data from input signals.

▶ Mechatronics is a new category of components where microcontrollers are embedded into mechanical systems, creating new operational capabilities and functions. Many components on commercial vehicles now use mechatronic controls.

▶ Steering gears, DEF dosing units, turbochargers, and exhaust gas recirculation (EGR) actuators are just a few of the many examples of mechatronic technology on today's commercial vehicles.

▶ Reprogramming of electronic control modules is also an important service issue because updating software calibrations for major control modules is a powerfully effective repair strategy to solve operating problems and repair faults. Service reprogramming of electronic control units (ECUs) is increasingly important since it is the only repair method to correct control system-related complaints.

▶ Because so many vehicle systems are now operated using embedded components, or mechatronic devices, understanding microcontroller's operation and service is now essential for technicians.

▶ At the center of almost every contemporary electronic control unit's operation is a microcontroller. A microcontroller is an integrated circuit operating like an advanced programmable calculator with memory storage capabilities.

▶ Output drivers are commonly switching-type transistors that turn voltage on and off to output devices. Output drivers can be categorized as high, low, or push-pull type, depending on the current polarity available at the ECU pin.

▶ Transistor gain refers to the ratio of current flow between the collector (output) and the transistor base current used to switch current flow through the emitter collector circuit.

▶ In Darlington pairs, transistors can achieve a gain ratio of several hundred to several thousand times the micro-amperage applied to the transistor base by a microcontroller.

▶ Major ECUs used in commercial vehicles are dedicated to specific areas of control. These major areas of control are sometimes referred to as domains.

▶ An arrangement in which a feedback signal is used to adjust a process generating an output signal is called a closed-loop control system. Closed-loop control systems monitor and compare a control system's actual output with the desired output to make corrections or adjustments to the control units output signals.

▶ Open-loop control systems do not close because they do not monitor system outputs and output signals have no influence on control system action.

▶ Closed-loop systems are designed to correct a process variable's error to produce and maintain the desired output condition or variable. It does this by comparing its actual measured condition, called the process variable (PV), with a set-point or desired condition.

▶ A closed-loop system corrects for error between set-points and PVs by generating an error signal.

▶ An error signal is the difference between the PV and a set-point value for the input. The error signal is used to produce a correction factor that is applied to the input signal.

▶ When feedback about an output state is supplied by a sensor, the closed-loop system is better able to correct the system for error caused by system disturbances. Disturbances are uncontrolled outside factors influencing the control system task.

▶ Closed-loop systems use specialized algorithms to optimize the system performance and correct set-point error.

▶ The most common control algorithms correcting error and optimizing closed-loop operation are: proportional, integral, proportional-integral (P-I), and proportional-integral derivative (PID).

▶ Multiple-input and multiple-output (MIMO) control systems are more complex than single input and single output systems.

▶ To determine the set-point for MIMO systems, optimal set-point values are experimentally derived using a wide range of possible combinations for various operating conditions and arranged in what are called look-up tables.

▶ Look-up tables are mathematical shortcuts used by an ECU controller to provide answers to complex questions or solutions to mathematical problems solved elsewhere.

▶ The process of looking for a set-point in look-up table data is faster and requires less ECU processing capabilities than performing complex and intensive calculations using advanced algorithms that may not account for all possible input variables.

▶ As MIMO systems increase in the number of controlled outputs and sensors, they become impractical to use because too many data set-points are needed to develop a proper look-up table that developed during a calibration process.

▶ The labor-intensive, time-consuming work developing MIMO calibrations have caused manufacturers of control systems to move from PID control to model predictive control (MPC).

▶ MPC uses a mathematical model of how the system should behave, rather than set-points in a fixed look-up table, as the reference point for generating output signals.

▶ MPC provides computational efficiency for ECUs by using a virtual model of a system where all the intensive calculations are done upfront during calibration development. Computational efficiencies are using a virtual model of system operation that provides a much richer data set that is dynamic, meaning it simulates a system's actual working characteristics.

▶ All potential input variables, disturbances, deterioration, and operating conditions are anticipated and modeled in MPC systems using physical laws associated with motion, electricity, magnetism, hydraulics, and chemistry.

▶ State observers are selected sensor inputs used by MPC to predict and generate the next best set of control signals.

▶ Mapless MPC is the latest, most-advanced control system. There are no look-up tables generated or used by the model. Instead, a highly accurate, well-refined predictive model is used, along with a mechanism to correct model discrepancy or errors, that updates the model in real-time.

▶ Learning how to recognize patterns and optimize results is a vital feature of more advanced MPC systems since MPC is future-oriented and not simply designed to correct error. This future-orientated, predictive characteristic also lends MPC the name over-the-horizon predictive control.

▶ MPC can not only more accurately identify faults and predict imminent faults, but also has the ability to adjust system operation to compensate for a fault and keep a system within a normal operating range.

▶ Model-based deviation between a theoretical model of expected behavior and measured feedback about actual operation are used to determine fault conditions.

▶ When an MPC control system can adjust its operation to accommodate a fault, it is considered to be fault tolerant.

▶ Microcontrollers are a general category of integrated circuits designed and constructed to control the operation of electrical components and systems.

▶ Microcontrollers are generally designed to perform a specific task. It is a complete computer on a chip. A microprocessor requires external devices and external memory storage to operate.

▶ One of the most significant distinctions between microcontrollers and microprocessors is the use of two fundamentally different types of architecture used by each device to access program and calibration memory. One register is for just the programmed instructions to operate the microcontroller called the firmware, the other is calibration data.

▶ The microcontroller is designed to access the two different sets of memory in the separate registers at the same time using two separate internal pathways called data buses.

▶ Reprogramming the ECU may be either a complete programming event of replacing the firmware and calibration data, or only replacing calibration data.

▶ A boot loader inside a microcontroller is used to lock down proprietary firmware files and data files so they cannot be changed except by authorized persons using proprietary equipment.

▶ To have the boot loader begin to erase either program or data memory registers and store new files, it needs to be unlocked before a set of memory reprogramming instructions is transmitted.

▶ Reprogramming microcontrollers involves using a pass-thru programmer or purpose-built communication adapter connected to the onboard network through the vehicle DLC.

▶ There are four general update or replacement methods for ECUs.
  • Service programming update to repair or reconfigure an ECU
  • ECU replacement without any additional service programming operation
  • ECU replacement with manual reprogramming
  • ECU replacement with user parameter transfer (cloning)

Key Terms

boot loader A small but secure set of instructions stored in a separate area of microcontroller memory that decides if there is a set of valid program and data files stored in the microcontroller. The boot loader determines whether the ECU begins to operate or not.

calibration A process of refining data used by a control system to optimize system performance.

closed-loop systems A control strategy to correct for system error by using feedback from the system output to adjust a process generating the output.

conformity coating A protective chemical coating or polymer film barrier sprayed onto the circuit board and components to insulate them from chemical contaminants and moisture and also to dampen some vibration.

degree of freedom The extent an engine control system is capable of accommodating faults by adjusting control variables. A high degree of operational freedom means the model is able to select from a wide range of forward control paths to compensate for faults.

derivative feedback control An error correction method that calculates the trajectory of current error to correct future error.

D-flash (data flash) A category of reprogramming or memory update of only the data or calibration information in an ECU or microcontroller.

disturbances Uncontrolled outside factors influencing a process that interferes with a control system task.

domain controllers ECUs used in major control systems, such as the engine or electrical system, that regulate the operation of multiple components or other subsystem ECUs.

electronic control system An arrangement of electronic and electrical devices designed to automatically regulate the operation of a component or system output and maintain it within a desired operating range.

error signal A term describing the modified input signal to a controller with a correction factor based on the output error. Error signal is calculated by adding or subtracting from the controller's set-point input signal.

fault healing The specific strategy used by an MPC system to compensate for a fault in a fault tolerant system.

fault-tolerant systems A feature of a control system enabling it to accommodate a fault without significantly affecting its operation.

firmware Program files stored in the microcontroller that contains machine code instructions to operate the circuits of a microcontroller.

flashing The process of installing new or reprogramming calibration or firmware data in an ECU's flash memory storage area.

H-bridge A control circuit taking its name from the shape of four transistors arranged to switch the polarity current applied to a load. It is often used to change the direction of DC electric motors or rapidly open and close injector solenoids.

integral feedback control An error-correction algorithm that analyzes the time that error deviations are present above or below the set-point, and increases controller gain if error is not quickly corrected.

look-up tables Groups of set-point values arranged in a table used by control system as a reference point to adjust system output signals. Look-up tables are also used by the ECU as mathematical shortcuts to provide answers to complex problems.

mapless MPC An advanced type of model predictive control system that does not use look-up tables and has a model-optimizing mechanism to correct model errors in real time.

mapped MPC A type of model predictive control system that generates the optimal set of control signals using virtually generated set-points or predicts which set of look-up tables to use as set-points.

model predictive control (MPC) A category of control system method that relies on a data model of expected system behavior to generate control system signals.

P-flash (program flash) A category of reprogramming or memory update of only the program information in an ECU or microcontroller.

pass-thru programmers A vehicle communication device compliant with the SAE standard J-2534 to flash or reprogram ECUs.

PID tuning A process performed on instrumented systems during calibration where the control algorithms are adjusted under experimental conditions to achieve optimal system outputs.

proportional feedback control An error-correction algorithm that adjusts controller gain up or down in proportion to the size of error.

proportional-integral derivative (PID) controls Error-correction algorithms comprised of proportional-, integral-, and derivative-type calculations.

set-point A term for the targeted or desired operating range of a controlled system.

sleep mode A state of a microcontroller or ECU when power consumption is lowest.

state observers A limited number of sensors that are used by MPC systems to predict operating state or conditions.

stiction A term for static friction caused by binding actuators.

system error A term describing the difference between a system output or process variable and its desired or set-point value.

Review Questions

1. Mechatronics best refers to:
   a. mechanical components operated with electrical signals.
   b. mechanical components with embedded microcontrollers.
   c. mechanical components operated by PID-type controllers.
   d. mechanical components capable of motion that are electronically controlled.
2. Which of the following statements best describes a control system set-point?
   a. The output signal from a controller
   b. The error-corrected input signal to a controller
   c. The desired value for a system output
   d. The measured value of a system output
3. Which element of a control system uses logic to perform its job?
   a. Sensors or input circuits
   b. Processing
   c. Output
   d. Output drivers
4. Which type of control loop uses sensor data to adjust a control system output?
   a. Closed-loop
   b. Open loops
   c. Derivative feedback
   d. Proportional feedback

5. How is an error signal produced?
   a. When the system output value deviates from the set-point
   b. When the desired output is different from the actual measured output
   c. By adding or subtracting a correction factor from the set-point value
   d. When a system disturbance affects the system output
6. Consider a bus traveling along a highway and the driver is using the cruise control to regulate vehicle speed. How does a strong headwind affect the control system?
   a. It acts as a system disturbance.
   b. It changes the vehicle speed set-point.
   c. The headwind generates an error signal.
   d. The headwind forces the cruise control into open-loop operation.
7. Consider the cruise control system when there is a large error between set-point speed and actual vehicle speed. What is the controller's best response to the error?
   a. The controller measures how long an error is present before responding.
   b. The controller should measure the trajectory of the error signal to calculate a correction factor for future error.
   c. The controller should quickly respond and reduce the amount of error as quickly as possible.
   d. The controller should rapidly reduce the amount of error but slow down the rate of error reduction as the vehicle reaches its set-point.
8. Which control system is most likely to use look-up tables and three-dimensional maps?
   a. Single-input, single-output systems
   b. Model Predictive Control
   c. Closed-loop control
   d. Multiple-input and multiple-output control systems
9. Which control system uses virtual objects as reference points to generate output signals?
   a. Proportional control systems
   b. Proportional integral control systems
   c. Proportional integral derivative control systems
   d. Model Predictive Control systems
10. What is likely to happen during a reflash of an ECU if the battery voltage drops too low?
    a. The reprogramming event ends and requires restarting.
    b. All memory reverts to its original state it had before the reflash.
    c. The file for reflashing the ECU needs to be downloaded from a web site once more.
    d. The ECU does not function and cannot be recovered.

ASE Technician A/Technician B Style Questions

1. Technician A says that multiple-input multiple-output systems, like the current diesel exhaust aftertreatment systems, are too complex to use PID controls and now require closed-loop-type controls that provide sensor feedback

to the controller. Technician B says that Model Predictive Control systems are used by exhaust aftertreatment systems to correct dosing error using proportional-integral feedback loops. Who is correct?

a. Technician A
b. Technician B
c. Both Technician A and Technician
d. Neither Technician A nor Technician B

2. Technician A says that ECUs in commercial vehicles wake-up fast when the ignition is switched on because they operate using microprocessors. Technician B says that the fast wake-up of ECUs is explained by their use of microcontrollers, which generally do not have an operating system to load during boot-up. Who is correct?

a. Technician A
b. Technician B
c. Both Technician A and Technician B
d. Neither Technician A nor Technician B

3. Technicians A and B are researching the procedure to replace an ECU that was operational but developed a large crack after a collision. Technician A says that files in the ECU can be downloaded and transferred to the unit. Technician B says that a pass-thru programmer is likely needed to upload program and data files to flash memory. Who is correct?

a. Technician A
b. Technician B
c. Both Technician A and Technician B
d. Neither Technician A nor Technician B

4. Technicians A and B were performing an inspection of a new bus and noting the large number of sensors on the engine and exhaust systems. Technician A said that only a few of the sensors were essential for the control system to operate the engine. Technician B said that all the sensors were necessary to operate control-system feedback loops for the engine to properly run. Who is correct?

a. Technician A
b. Technician B
c. Both Technician A and Technician B
d. Neither Technician A nor Technician B

5. Technician A said that any fault in a contemporary control system with multiple inputs and outputs will shut down the control system and set fault codes. Technician B said that most faults in major control are often ignored without any disruption to the system operation. Who is correct?

a. Technician A
b. Technician B
c. Both Technician A and Technician B
d. Neither Technician A nor Technician B

6. While investigating a customer complaint about surging and irregular vehicle speed only when the cruise control was set, Technician A said it was likely caused by a system disturbance. Technician B said the problem was likely with an incorrectly programmed or calibrated controller. Who is correct?

a. Technician A
b. Technician B
c. Both Technician A and Technician B
d. Neither Technician A nor Technician B

7. Technician A says that MPC is the best control system to predict what type of injection rate shape is most suited to a particular operating condition. Technician B says that MPC uses state observers to help predict which set of output signals is best suited for an operating condition. Who is correct?

a. Technician A
b. Technician B
c. Both Technician A and Technician B
d. Neither Technician A nor Technician B

8. While checking the electrical signals to the injectors of an engine that would not start, Technician A said the graphing meter could show a signal that has a saw-tooth shape and has two different voltage steps for energizing current. Technician B said that the injectors use an H-bridge driver that switches the polarity of current energizing the injectors to rapidly open and close the injector nozzle. Who is correct?

a. Technician A
b. Technician B
c. Both Technician A and Technician B
d. Neither Technician A nor Technician B

9. Technician A says that microcontrollers can communicate with other microcontrollers using serial data. Technician B says that only ECUs can communicate with one another. Who is correct?

a. Technician A
b. Technician B
c. Both Technician A and Technician B
d. Neither Technician A nor Technician B

10. While checking data from an engine ECU, Technician A found letter and number combinations with $ symbols and said the data was corrupted. Technician B said that the letter and number combinations with a dollar sign at the beginning was an example of binary code. Who is correct?

a. Technician A
b. Technician B
c. Both Technician A and Technician B
d. Neither Technician A nor Technician B

CHAPTER 26

Onboard Vehicle Networks and Electronic Service Tools

Learning Objectives

After reading this chapter, you will be able to:

- **LO 26-1** Identify and describe classifications of onboard vehicle networks.
- **LO 26-2** Identify and explain the purpose, and advantages, of vehicle networks and multiplex technology.
- **LO 26-3** Identify and explain the purpose, function, construction, and operating principles of vehicle networks.
- **LO 26-4** Identify and explain the construction and operation of controller area networks (CANs).
- **LO 26-5** Identify and describe the Unified Diagnostic Service network protocol.
- **LO 26-6** Identify and explain common data bus problems.
- **LO 26-7** Identify major components and outline the function of Smartplex network components.
- **LO 26-8** Describe Navistar's Diamond logic electrical system.
- **LO 26-9** Identify and explain the operation of wireless network technology.
- **LO 26-10** Identify and explain the purpose of programmable logic controller (PLC) network technology.
- **LO 26-11** Explain the operating principles of electronic service tools.

You Are the Technician

After arriving at a customer's yard for a service call, you are asked to diagnose a problem with a brand-new Class 8 highway tractor. The vehicle will start and run, but the engine will not accelerate above idle speed. After the engine is started, a red warning light immediately flashes for 30 seconds before the engine shuts down. You perform typical visual inspections of the vehicle, inspecting the exhaust systems and wiring harnesses and checking for fuel, coolant, air, and oil leaks. According to the dash gauge and visual verification, the selective catalytic reduction (SCR) tank is three-quarters full. Nothing seems amiss, but you realize that certain emission-related faults and engine protection system-related faults will produce these symptoms. Without being able to easily return to the shop with the vehicle to access diagnostic software and service information, finding the fault that is specifically causing the severe engine power de-rate conditions and shutdown is challenging. Before calling for a tow truck to bring the tractor to the shop, consider the following questions:

1. What are two procedures that can be used to retrieve fault codes other than using original equipment manufacturers (OEM) or other types of diagnostic software?
2. Explain why the red engine warning lamp—the stop engine lamp—is flashing before the engine shuts down.
3. Are SAE J-1939 fault codes retrievable from this vehicle without OEM software? Explain your answer.

Introduction

Commercial vehicles have been transformed by the explosive growth of electronic control units (ECUs) used to operate almost every chassis and powertrain system. Whether it is one or more ECUs controlling the operation of an engine, transmission, antilock brake system (ABS), instrument cluster, or ECUs coordinating the electrical system operation, there are tremendous advantages and an almost endless number of functions and features made possible when ECUs are connected to communicate and share information. Today's commercial vehicles use one or more communication pathways connecting ECUs to form what are called onboard networks (**FIGURE 26-1**).

In concept, a vehicle network is somewhat like a social network, in which people are connected through websites or organizations that allow them to exchange information and collaborate to accomplish tasks or reach goals otherwise unachievable when disconnected. The idea of the "whole being greater than the sum of its parts" applies to vehicle networks too. Extensive use of microcontrollers operating or assisting driver control of vehicle systems is leveraged with network communication to provide a huge number of benefits not possible when unconnected or operating as stand-alone modules. In fact, the introduction and evolution of onboard networks is one of the most important developments of heavy-duty (HD) chassis systems after application of electronic controls because of the features, new capabilities, and efficiencies it enables.

The name for the main network transmitting the most important messages exchanged by ECUs is called the controller area network (CAN). This standardized onboard communication tool enables ECUs to transmit their messages over what is called a network data bus, consisting of a pair of twisted wires connected in parallel to ECUs belonging to the CAN (**FIGURE 26-2**). A CAN data bus is also appropriately called the network backbone. Like a telephone line or conference call shared by multiple users, each ECU takes turns sending and listening to information transmitted over the CAN data bus. If more than one module tried to talk at the same time, like a conference call or in classroom, the messages would be garbled. Allowing multiple signals and users to share the data bus is

FIGURE 26-1 Today's electrical systems are much more advanced than those of even a few years ago. **A.** Telematics module. **B.** Engine control. **C.** ABS and dynamic vehicle control. **D.** Transmission. **E.** Body electrical control module. **F.** Cab electrical control. **G.** Air and suspension system control. **H.** Infotainment system. **I.** GPS navigation. **J.** Collision avoidance systems.

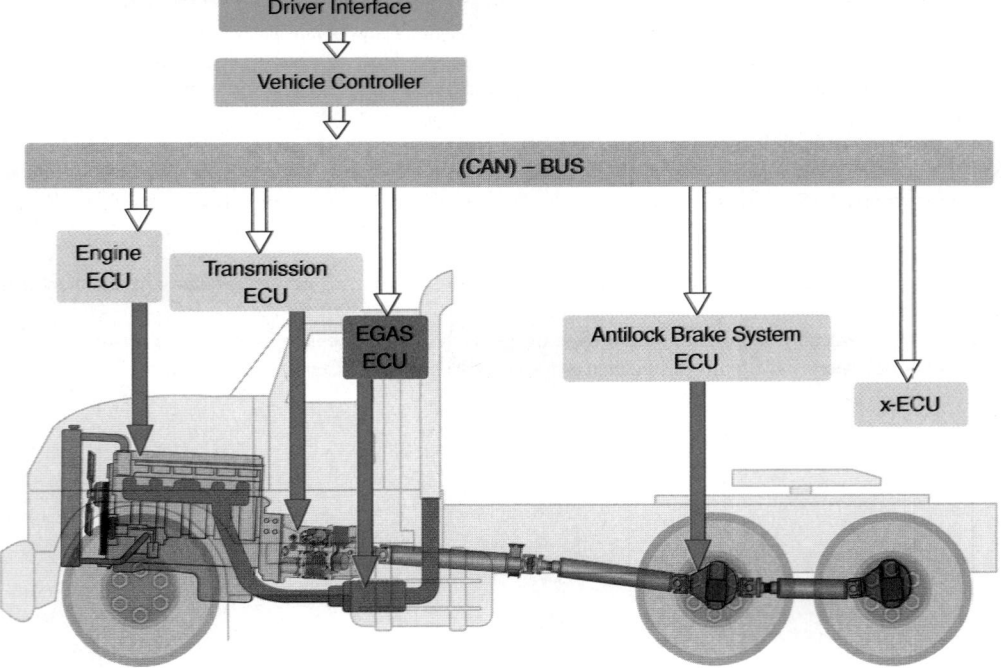

FIGURE 26-2 ECUs communicate with each other using a CAN data bus.

made possible by a process called **multiplexing**—a method that enables transmission of different electrical signals over the same communication channel.

Other networks and data pathways are used on commercial vehicles, but the CAN has legislated operating standards critical for enabling electronic service to easily communicate with ECUs having functions related to the emission system.

The original intent of electronic communication between modules was not to access emission-related information or add features to increase passenger comfort or safety, but to reduce and simplify the electrical system wiring. Because of their length and distance between the driver and engine, transit buses at one time used an enormous amount of electrical wiring, bundled in

harnesses, which took considerable time to design and install (**FIGURE 26-3**). Not surprisingly, buses were the first commercial vehicles to use network communication, which reduced the number of wires and wiring weight by as much as 500 lb (**FIGURE 26-4**). An estimated two-thirds reduction in manufacturing cost and assembly time was achieved by eliminating most of the wiring between the driver's area and the rear of the bus. Lighting signals, signage, plus onboard communications between the driver and engine and transmission was conducted using two wires connecting an electronic module at the front of the bus to a module at the rear.

Later, onboard networks gained more prominence with the introduction of electronically controlled engines. Servicing and

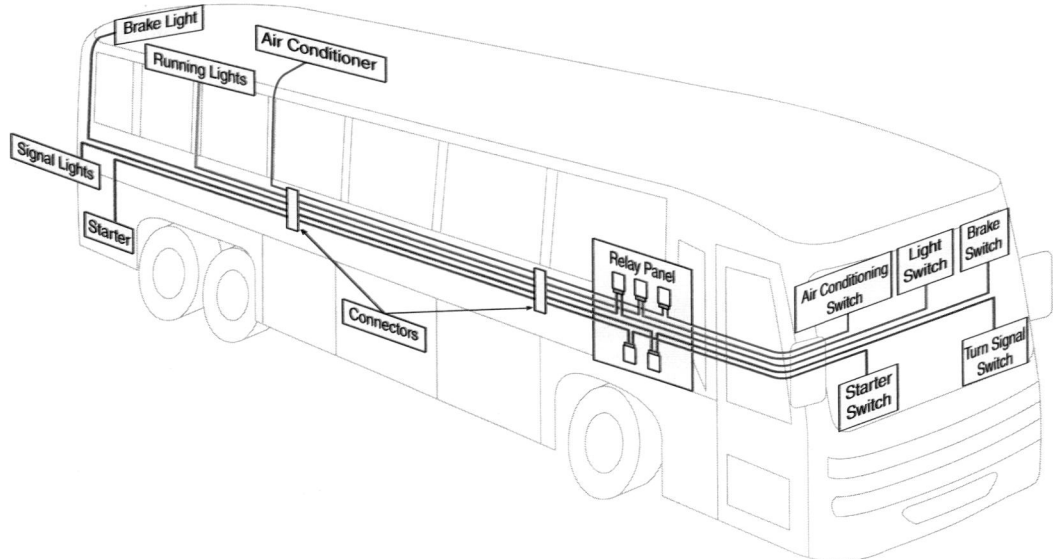

FIGURE 26-3 A point-to-point wiring system with relay logic controls are used on older electrical systems.

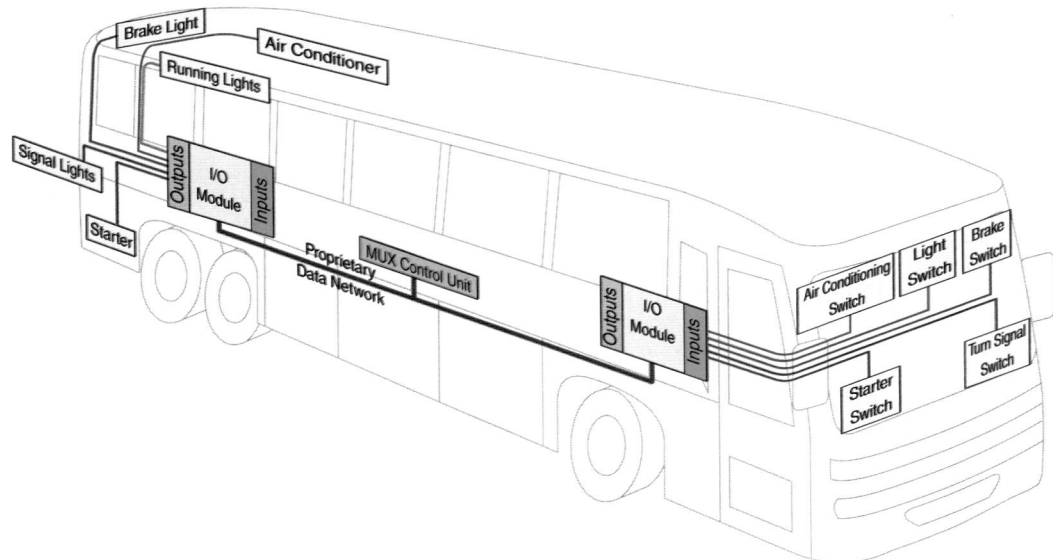

FIGURE 26-4 Using two electronic control modules communicating over a pair of wires dramatically reduced the amount of wiring between the front and rear of a bus.

diagnosing engine problems required communication with a diagnostic data link connector (DLC) in the cab (TABLE 26-1). Bi-directional, or two-way, communication between an electronic service tool and the engine prompted the development of legislated standards used to enable network communication between these two electronic devices (see Figure 26-4). Today, commercial trucks and buses, forestry, mining, construction, military, power generators, fire and rescue vehicles, and industrial machines use a legislated standard for their CANs defined by the **SAE J-1939** or **ISO-11898**. But there are other networks commonly onboard current on-highway trucks and buses that are examined in this chapter.

Technicians interact with onboard networks every time they connect an electronic service tool to the DLC to check for fault codes, scroll though service menu screens containing vehicle data, update maintenance information, or download trip information. Replacing electrical control modules, changing customer programmable parameters, performing ECU calibration updates to correct system bugs or glitches, adding vehicle accessories, or just using diagnostic blink codes to troubleshoot a problem are just a few of the many tasks of the onboard network, shaping the work of technicians. Given the integration of networks into vehicle control systems and technician duties, this chapter provides the background information about onboard networks—how they are built, operate, and are serviced. This chapter also examines the construction and operation of electronic service tools used to interact with vehicle networks, to help technicians develop the skills needed to service networked vehicles.

Early Network Concept

LO 26-1 Identify and describe classifications of onboard vehicle networks.

Low-voltage digital network communication between electrical control modules was originally intended to solve the problem encountered using bulky wiring harnesses on transit buses. Before networks were used, bus and other commercial vehicle chassis connected electrical components together using a **point-to-point wiring** of the electrical system (FIGURE 26-5). That meant switching on a single light required a circuit connecting the battery to a fuse, a switch, plus wires connecting the switch to the light, a connection to chassis ground, and an operator input to decide to switch the light on. Regardless of where the light and the switch were located, wire connected each terminal of the light or lighting circuit.

TABLE 26-1 Progression of the Use of Commercial Vehicle Electronics

Generation	Development
First Generation— Simple electronics	The addition of simple electronics to improve the efficiency of vehicle operation. Examples: electronic voltage regulators, electronic instrument gauges, two-speed axle shift module, and LED lights.
Second Generation— Control modules	Incorporating electronics into control modules used to operate engines, transmissions, climate control, and antilock braking system.
Third Generation— Onboard integration of control modules into controller area networks (CANs)	Development of control module networks used to provide greater safety, efficiencies, and capabilities than any control module can perform on its own. Information and processing capabilities are shared between modules. An ABS module will sense wheel speed lock-up and deactivate the engine brake. A traction control module will reduce engine power output when wheel slip is detected.
Dedicated Short-Distance Radio Communication (DSRC) For V2V and V2I communication	A wireless network communication system for intelligent transportation system (ITS) enabling secure, interference-free high-speed vehicle-to-vehicle (V2V) and vehicle-to-infrastructure (V2I) communication. A basic safety message is exchanged between vehicles indicating location, speed, direction of travel, and brake system status. Communication with the CAN takes place using transponders known as onboard units (OBUs) or roadside units (RSUs). V2V enabled truck platooning, beginning in 2019, and improvement to automated driving systems.

FIGURE 26-5 A highway coach's electrical distribution panel using a point-to-point method to connect the electrical system.

Solution to Point-to-Point Wiring Failure

Understandably, point-to-point wiring technique results in very large, heavy wiring harnesses throughout the vehicle. Each connection in the circuit and length of wire also produces electrical resistance and a source of potential failure. Corrosion, loose connections, and chafed wiring were common electrical system failures, and the technique created a notoriously unreliable system that was difficult and time-consuming to not only troubleshoot but also repair.

Point-to-point wiring construction created unique problems for urban transit and highway coach buses in which the driver is at the front of the vehicle, and engines and transmissions are located at the rear. Many miles of electrical wire were needed to operate the electrical systems. Adding electrical relays to control other simple 12/24-volt circuits built further complexity into the electrical system, which accounted for as much one-half of engineering time and 15% of vehicle assembly cost, according to one transit bus manufacturer.

To eliminate the problems created by point-to-point wiring and relay logic systems, bus chassis were the first commercial vehicles to use onboard networks. Bulky wiring harnesses were replaced with electronic, microcontroller-operated lighting modules strategically positioned near the light circuits or other electrical devices (**FIGURE 26-6**). A signal input processor module near the driver acquired signals and input data from switches, throttles, gear selectors, and other devices. The output signals produced by the module near the front of the bus sent low-voltage, Morse-code-like binary digit signals over two wires to another electronic control unit (ECU) at the rear of the bus. This communication method, using binary digits of "1s" and "0s," sent one after another, is called **serial data**. The module at the rear interpreted the messages supplied by serial data and produced output signals to energize the lighting systems, operate engine and transmission controls, and other electrical devices.

Serial Data

The radically new approach to electrical system design of the early networked buses has evolved into architecture of the modern distributed control, electrical system (**FIGURE 26-7**). Onboard vehicle networks are formed by connecting vehicle electronic control modules to one another to communicate and exchange information.

Module-to-module communication is commonly done over a pair of wires called a data bus. Microcontrollers, as well as ECUs, can communicate over data bus using serial data. Serial data described earlier in Chapter 24 is composed of binary code. Binary code is used by microcontrollers to process alphabetical and numerical data by converting numbers or letters into a defined set of 1s and 0s. When microcontrollers send and receive binary-coded messages made up from long strings of 1s and 0s, sent one after another in series, it is called serial data. In a sense, serial communication

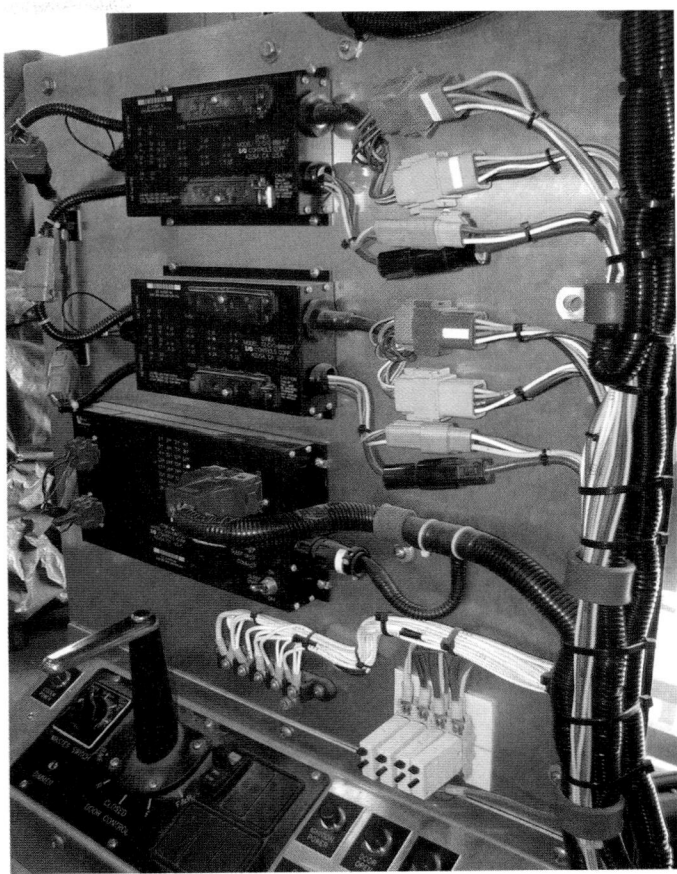

FIGURE 26-6 A multiplex electrical control system for a transit bus consolidates thousands of wires and relays into a few input-output control modules.

is like electronic Morse code. Unlike Morse code, which uses dots and dashes, 0s and 1s are transmitted in a series, one after another, using voltage pulses to represent the two digits (**FIGURE 26-8**). Data strings are very long, but the rapid speed microcontrollers send, receive, and then process these messages compensates for the cumbersome use of binary-coded data.

Network Electrical System Control Advantages

LO 26-2 Identify and explain the purpose, and advantages, vehicle networks and multiplex technology.

Increased complexity of vehicles and market demands for improved reliability have driven the use of networked control of an electrical system. Manufacturers can also lower the cost of vehicle design and production by eliminating much of the vehicle wiring. In fact, both Navistar, with its Diamond Logic Electrical System, and Freightliner, with its Smartplex system, claim a 40% reduction in the amount of wiring. Since the original use of networked control of the electrical system, all manufacturers of trucks and buses have discovered more competitive

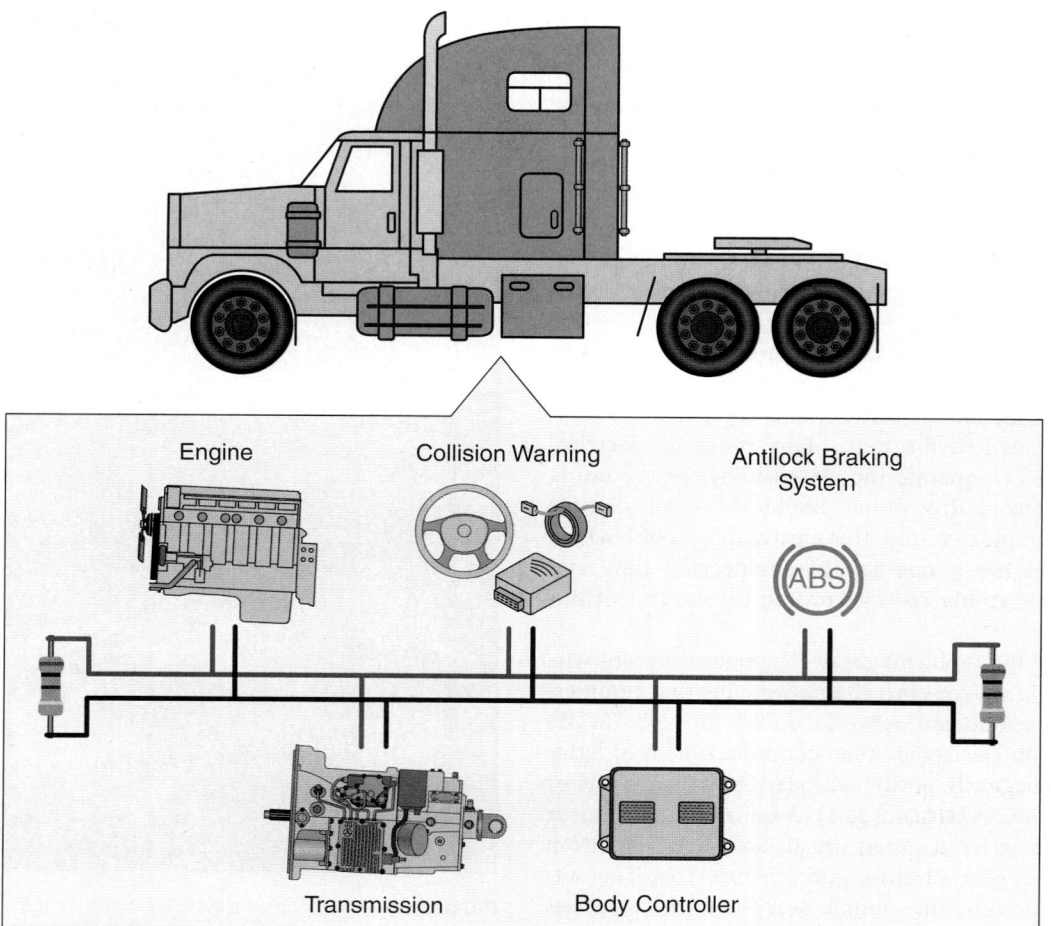

FIGURE 26-7 Onboard networks connect multiple ECUs together to communicate with one another, which distributes the control of the electrical system.

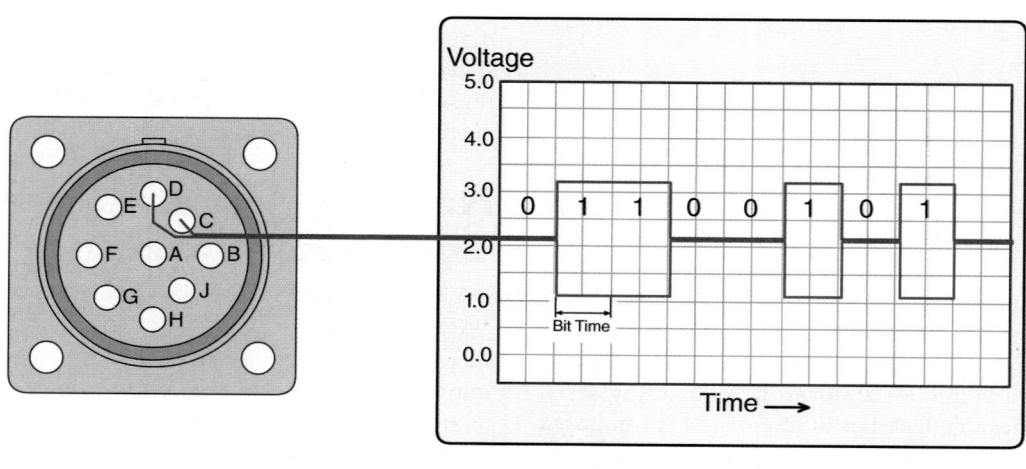

Binary Code=01100101

FIGURE 26-8 Serial data consists of binary code represented by voltage pulses appearing one after another, in series, from the data link connector.

reasons for adopting networked electrical system control. These advantages include:

- Software-driven control logic of the electrical system and features
- Enabling the mandatory use of onboard diagnostics
- Ease of connecting electronically controlled accessories and devices
- Reduction in number of sensors

Software Control of Electrical System

When using networks, electrical system control logic and complexity is absorbed by software instead of a huge array of hardwired components and circuit boards. The electrical system occupies less space, is lighter in weight, and is easier to design, install, troubleshoot, and repair. New automatic functions and features are added to enhance operator comfort, convenience, and safety. Industry observers claim that as much as 80% of new features in today's vehicles are driven by software innovation. The newest vehicle communication networks permit enhanced features and control of every electrical subsystem, from vehicle lighting, steering, braking, and body controls (e.g., wipers, door locks, windows) to advanced driver assistance systems (ADAS), such as collision avoidance systems. By adding only software and a twisted pair of wires to connect modules, they can communicate and share processed information. Network communication also enables more precise and sophisticated electrical control of ABS, electrical system controller (ESC), instrument gauges, air- and hydraulic-operated accessories, climate control, inter-axle differentials, and engine and transmission operation. Examples include:

- Power door lock activation above 5 mph (8 kph) for occupant protection in the event of a crash.
- Placing the transmission in reverse or engaging the power take-off (PTO) automatically mutes the radio volume to prevent driver distraction and allows the driver to hear warnings while backing-up. The radio is muted because communication takes place between the transmission and an infotainment control module.
- Intermittent wiper speeds default to the slowest sweep frequency when the parking brake is set, regardless of wiper switch position. This feature, enabled by communication between the body electrical control and ABS module, reduces wiper blade replacement and wear on the wiper mechanism.
- To prevent a vehicle roll-away situation, the horn honks if the driver's door is opened and the park brake is not set.
- A wheel slip event detected by the ABS module sends a message to the engine ECM to disable engine brakes or reduce engine power, while the ABS module applies the brakes to the slipping wheel, enabling torque transfer to non-slipping wheels.

Countless examples of interoperability between electrical system inputs and outputs provide enhanced safety for passengers and operators and prevent vehicle damage.

Tremendous gains in operating efficiency, reduced vehicle design complexity, and construction costs are enabled by networking modules that distribute electrical system control over multiple ECMs.

Onboard Diagnostics (OBD) and Network Communication

Legislation setting ever-lower limits on exhaust emissions required a greater level of precision of diesel engine operation. Those lower limits are only attainable through the extensive use of electronically controlled engine components, such as injectors, turbochargers, exhaust gas recirculation (EGR) valves, and advanced exhaust aftertreatment systems. The problem with diagnosing and repairing electronic systems, in comparison to mechanical ones, is the relatively invisible and silent operation of electricity. Broken mechanical systems are often diagnosed visually or with mechanical tools, such as pressure gauges and dial indicators. However, a defective engine sensor or broken wire in a harness is not so easily detected, and it can be a time-consuming operation to diagnose based on only symptoms and using a multimeter to sequentially test every circuit. Self-monitoring or self-diagnostic capabilities are, therefore, built into electronic control systems to help technicians perform faster diagnostic checks and repairs. ECUs can easily evaluate the voltage and current levels of circuits to which they are connected and determine whether the data makes sense and is in the correct operational range. These self-diagnostic capabilities are referred to as **onboard diagnostics (OBD)** systems (**FIGURE 26-9**).

All electronically controlled engines and power train components have built-in self-diagnostic capabilities. To communicate this data to an electronic service tool from even a single module requires the use of duplex or **bidirectional communications**, meaning two-way multiplex communication can take place between service tools and ECUs. As modules for transmissions, antilock braking, and other electronic controls were

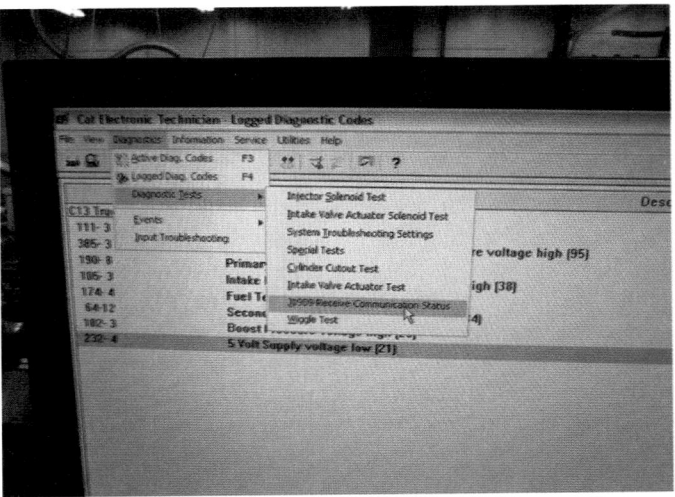

FIGURE 26-9 OBD relies on network communication with service tools to report fault codes and emission-related information.

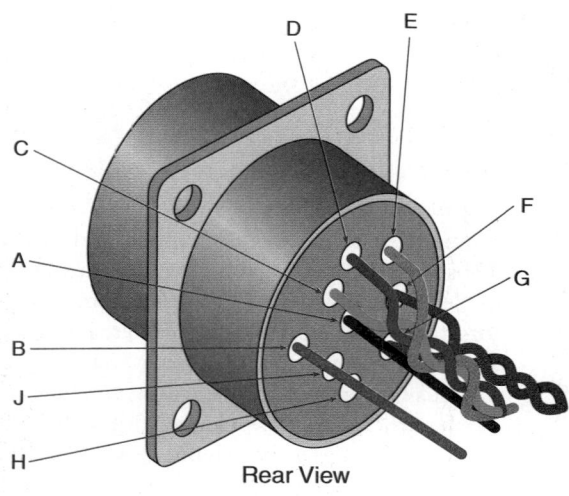

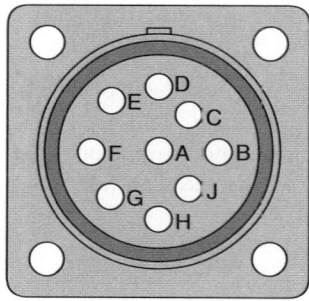

Front View

A Battery Ground
B 12V DC
C J1939 Data Link (+)
D J1939 Data Link (−)
E J1939 Shield
F J1587 Data Link (+)
G J1587 Data Link (−)
H Plug
J Plug

FIGURE 26-10 The 9-pin DLC enables service tool communication with the vehicle network.

added, network communication allowed these modules to communicate fault codes and data to a single diagnostic DLC (**FIGURE 26-10**).

OBD Legislation and Network Standards

Because a variety of modules can impact the vehicle's emissions, network communication enables easy identification of specific faults using electronic service tools connected to the DLC. For example, incorrect or missing vehicle speed data supplied by the ABS control module can interfere with speed-dependent injection timing and quantity, leading to excessive emission production. A transmission may not shift correctly, causing the engine speed to remain higher than it should, which, in turn, produces more emissions. When a malfunction is detected, diagnostic information is stored in the control module associated with the system containing the fault. The ECU identifies the fault to assist pinpoint testing to isolate the root cause and repair of the malfunction. The legislative standard used by the Environmental Protection Agency (EPA) in North America and the EURO I–VI standards for heavy-duty vehicles in Europe are based on protocols developed by the Society of Automotive Engineers (SAE—world body). In North America, the standard is referred to as heavy-duty onboard diagnostics (HD-OBD). A World Harmonized OBD (WH-OBD) standard exists for both North American and European commercial vehicles. This same legislation regulates the operation of mandatory onboard networks to access emission-related information stored in various modules. Currently, these network standards are a part of the SAE J-1939 and ISO-11898. The HD-OBD and WH-OBD standards outline network-related requirements, all intended to help quickly repair emission-related failures by reducing the

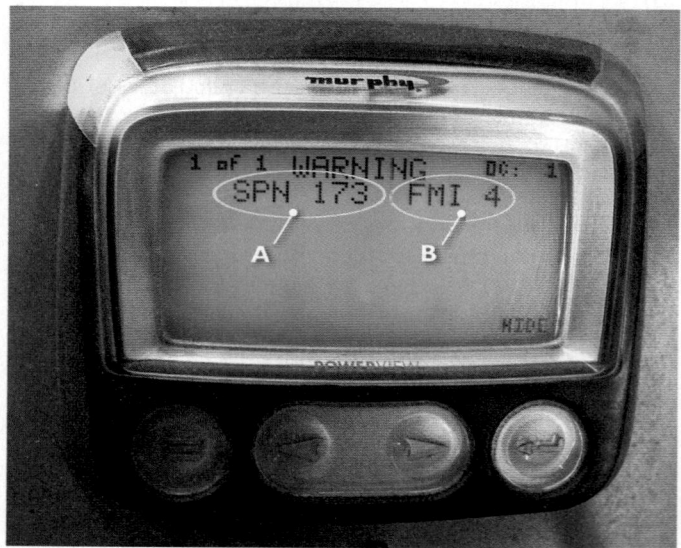

FIGURE 26-11 This dash-mounted Murphy gauge displays fault codes and other vehicle information stored in electronic control modules. It uses only two wires connected to the network to retrieve and transmit information.

cost and difficulties for independent repair facilities to access fault codes, retrieve emission-related data, and recalibrate or program control modules. Consequently, standards are established for the CAN communication—among other requirements for its construction and operation, mandatory data reporting, fault code structure, the configuration of the DLC, and software code used by the network and electronic service tools (**FIGURE 26-11**).

Network Connecting of Electronically Controlled Accessories

Network control of the vehicle electrical systems makes it easier to add accessories at the factory or aftermarket without any complex programming or vehicle modification using onboard networks. Connecting many electrical devices and ECUs to the vehicle can take place automatically at specific connection points designated by the manufacturer, or by using electrical system control module programming software. Larger ECUs controlling major domains now require coding to lock them to a specific vehicle identification number (VIN) to prevent unintended interactions with the vehicle or network that could cause the vehicle to operate unsafely (**FIGURE 26-12**). An example is an ABS module with vehicle dynamic control functions, such as roll-over protection and stability control. Coding of the module contains unique and critical chassis information, such as weight, yaw limits, and acceleration sensor parameters. When a new or replacement network-compatible ECU is introduced to

a network, it has or receives a unique identifier or name so other modules can recognize its messages and send it messages containing the identifier address. After its presence is introduced to the network through what is called a digital hand shake, connections made in the network provide access to information it needs to perform its job.

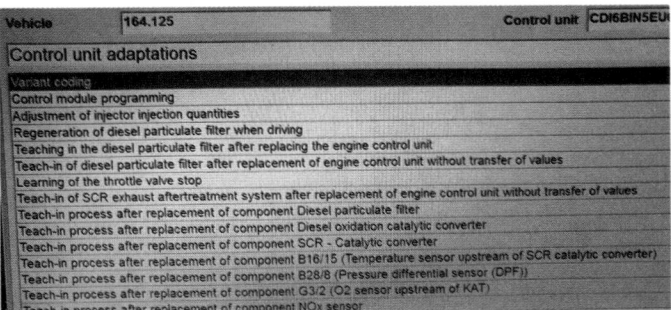

FIGURE 26-12 Variant coding of a module contains unique chassis information, such as weight, VIN, yaw, and acceleration sensor parameters. Once the control unit "learns" its variant coding, it is permanently and irrevocably locked down.

The ease of vehicle customization provided by network communication has resulted in a long list of special features used to enhance vehicle productivity, safety, and comfort. A few

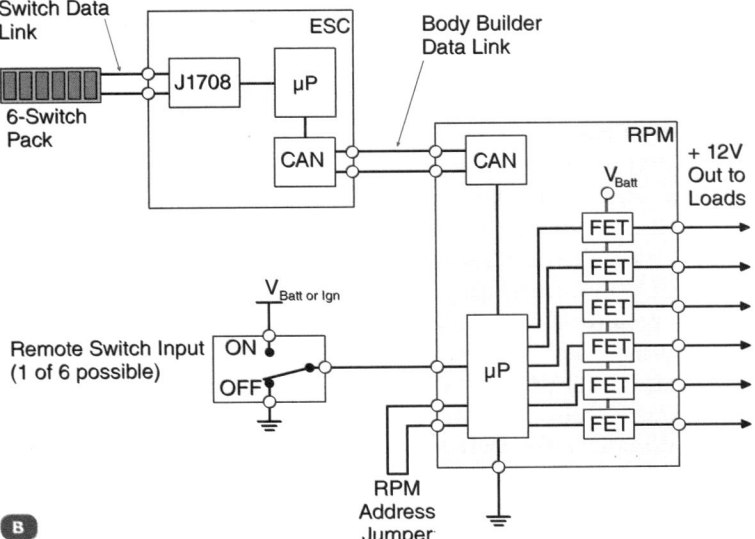

FIGURE 26-13 A. The remote power module controls the electrical outputs for an aftermarket-mounted body. **B.** Diagram for remote power module.

examples of hundreds of new safety and convenience features made possible by network communication include:

- Headlights that are automatically switched on with wiper activation to meet road safety regulations
- Interior bus lighting that automatically dims at night to minimize interior windshield glare
- A dome or work light that shuts off after 10 minutes with door open and key off to protect against battery run-down
- Air solenoids controlling air-operated accessories shutoff under certain faults for truck and driver protection
- Interlocked controls for equipment and operator protection. Transfer case gears, for example, are programmed to prevent changing unless the vehicle is parked. Bus passenger doors cannot be opened unless the vehicle is stopped.
- Air suspensions, which cannot be dumped above 10 mph (16 kph), or power divider locks that limit vehicle speed to protect the vehicle against costly damage.
- Virtual fusing of electrical circuits. Special field effect transistors (FETs) in output modules can be programmed to open at specific current thresholds. Additional rules, such as the time allowed before current reset takes place, is also programmable. Wiring and current-sensitive devices are thus protected from damage from excessive current flow.

▶ TECHNICIAN TIP

It is no longer an acceptable practice to simply splice an accessory into any available power or ground circuit on a commercial vehicle. All accessory circuits monitor current to the accessory, and electrical system fault codes will shut down electrical circuits if the wiring resistance or current consumption is different from specification. In some cases, wiring damaged by a splice requires the replacement of the entire electrical harness. Use OEM service literature to locate termination points to correctly connect any electrical accessories. Consult equipment dealers to reprogram the electrical system, customize new switch functions, and add circuits for current supplied to new electrically operated accessories.

Reducing Sensor Numbers Using Networks

Sensor data can be shared across many devices connected into a network. This network feature eliminates duplication of sensors needed by a module. A simple example is the use of a vehicle speed sensor. This data is required by many vehicle systems and devices. The instrument gauge cluster, transmission, engine, and ABS all require vehicle speed data, as does the entertainment system, which might lower or raise the radio volume, depending on road speed (**FIGURE 26-14**).

Using one electronic module to sense and process speed sensor data, then distribute the information over the network, reduces the construction cost and associated wiring required to connect a sensor to each device needing road speed data. Note, too, that the information-processing and control capabilities are distributed over many modules, which enhances the processing power of the total network. Instead of numerous modules

FIGURE 26-14 The instrument cluster is a network device that can retrieve and display chassis and sensor information to the driver.

performing the same task—such as calculating vehicle speed data—only one module does it, which frees the processors in other ECUs to perform different work.

Network Construction

LO 26-3 Identify and explain the purpose, function, construction, and operating principles of vehicle networks.

All networks have in common the concepts of interconnected modules and the use of serial data to enable digital communication between each module. But there are many other elements that make up a network and not all networks are constructed, organized, connected, or operated the same way. Some of the ways networks are different from one another includes how they are connected; how messages are addressed and shared; the time length of each bit transmission; or how the data is transmitted, such as its operating speed, physical characteristics, and even on which vehicle application it can be used. This collection of standards or rules that govern the construction and operation of a network is called the network protocol. As previously mentioned, the SAE J-1939 or ISO-11898 protocols outline network design and operation for current HD commercial vehicles. Breaking protocols down further, technicians can expect to encounter descriptions of the network protocol differences by visualizing the network in layers like the layers of a cake. Layers are an abstract concept that groups various sets of rule design and operating features used by a protocol. Each layer is composed of a subset of standards within an ISO or SAE protocol governing one aspect of the network operation. Layers are further arranged into what is called a stack made up of multiple layers. One layer describes network message construction, another layer defines fault codes, and another how those messages are communicated. To help visualize the network, layers arranged into stacks are described from the bottom up beginning with the physical characteristics defined as the lowest layer of the stack. The J-1939 SAE standard for networks, which corresponds to an ISO-11898 standard, has five layers. Technicians do not need to know anything about network layers or stacks, but the information each contains has practical applications. Network layers and stacks are also terms technician can expect to encounter in advanced courses and service literature. This next section describes some important features of the networks used on commercial vehicles.

Network Typology

Typology describes how modules communication pathways are connected to one another (**FIGURE 26-15**). Most often, the typology refers to the physical shape of the way a network is connected. A star network interconnection is shaped just like that—with star-shaped interconnections (**FIGURE 26-16**). Ring and bus networks are other common layouts of connection configurations for the channels exchanging data. The word **data bus** when used in network typology describes a network connection that looks just like a bus route. It has stops, called network nodes, where modules are connected. Traffic or serial data is two-way and passes along parallel paths over the bus route. Bus typology is used by the SAE J-1939 network and by all commercial vehicles today. An older network, J-1708, which is just the physical layer standard for networks prior to about 2001, also uses bus typology.

Physical Layers

The physical layer of a network stack outlines its construction details. It's also the lowest or most basic layer. The physical layer standard for the J-1939 network defines, among other things:

- Length of the data bus, also called the network backbone—40 meters

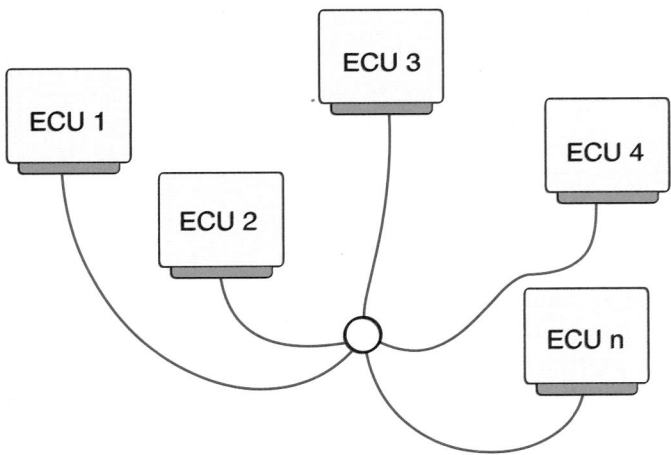

FIGURE 26-15 The typology of a star network is shaped like a star.

- Length of stubs, that is, harnesses connected to the network backbone—3 meters
- Network termination—two 120-ohm resisters
- Maximum number of nodes or modules—30

Data bus or backbone twists per inch of wire, shielding, shielding termination, connector dimensions, wire color, etc. are included in the J-1939 standard's physical layer.

The J-1939 standard is mandatory on HD vehicles and for off-highway equipment (**FIGURE 26-17**). Prior to J-1939's introduction on HD vehicles in 2001, J-1708, a physical layer protocol, and J-1587, a fault code protocol, were used on HD vehicles. Both 1708 and 1587 protocols communicated using serial data available at two pins on a standard American Trucking Association (ATA) 6-pin DLC. Until recently, HD trucks and buses used both protocols with network serial communication available at pins in the 9-pin DLC. The adoption of the most recent version of the J-1939 protocol, operating more than a thousand times faster and supporting much larger messages, has made the network obsolete on current vehicles.

Local Interconnect Network (LIN)

While the J-1939 network uses twisted wire pairs, other networks, such as the simpler **local interconnect network (LIN)**, examined later, use a single wire to control devices like glow plug controllers, voltage regulators, power mirrors, windows, and door locks (**FIGURE 26-18**). Other networks connect wirelessly, or even communicate using fiber optics. Physical layer standards exist for each type of network.

Centralized or Distributed Network Control

Networks may also be classified by whether network operation is (a) dependent on one master module directing the operation of several other slave modules, or (b) if control of the vehicle's electrical system is shared among the vehicle's ECUs. Most late-model vehicles and equipment have, in fact, multiple onboard networks using a combination of network types. Master-slave networks are referred to as centralized network control. LINs are the most common example of a centralized network. This

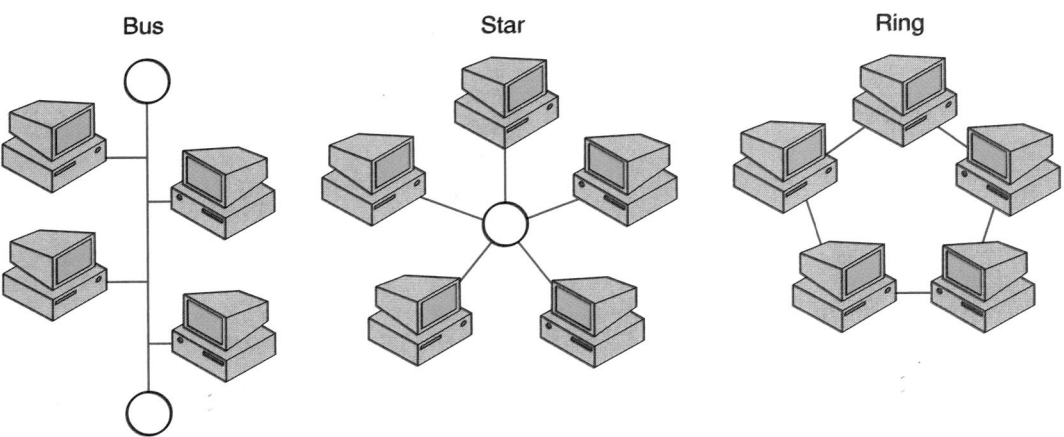

FIGURE 26-16 Network typology refers to the shape taken by the module interconnections.

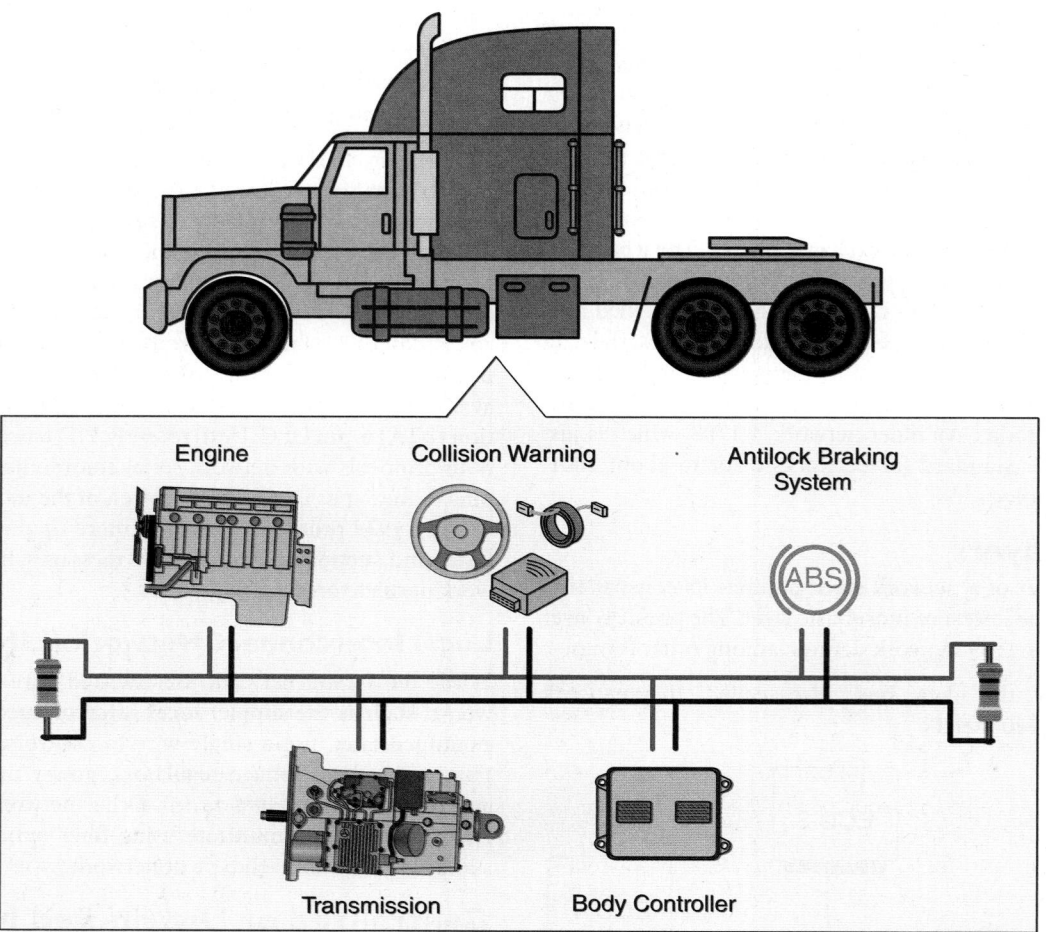

FIGURE 26-17 A J-1939 network uses distributed control of the vehicle's electrical system.

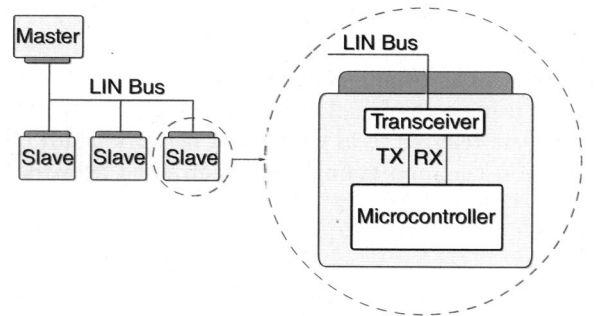

FIGURE 26-18 A local interconnect network (LIN) uses a centralized control.

network is popular for applications where low-cost and simplicity are all that is required. A LIN uses two microcontrollers—a master and slave. The master microcontroller or module sends **serial data** to various other less-sophisticated control modules, or mechatronic devices which contain only simple, inexpensive microcontrollers to carry out instructions. Data speeds on LINs are low, operating at up to 20 kilobits/second. The master module typically first receives an input from the driver or a major system ECU. It then makes requests for information

or sends commands to be executed by a slave module. Because the master controls the LIN network operation, a slave module responds only to requests by the master or central control module. A single wire is all that is used to connect all the slave modules to a master module, enabling every module to receive and transmit serial data. To prevent confusion between messages among slave modules, the master microcontroller uses the slave module's identity or address in serial communication to exchange messages. An example of a command from the engine ECU to a slave glow plug controller instructs the glow-plug controller slave to energize glow plugs for a specific electrical time duration of 5 seconds. The slave module carries out the command using it's unique programming to energize the plugs in a specific sequence and pulse width signal to prevent excessive current consumption. Next, the master controller, in this case, the engine ECU, asks the slave, glow-plug controller if the task was completed. The master expects an answer, or perhaps an answer or a network communication error is logged. It may also ask the glow-plug controller if there are any burnt-out or open glow plugs. The slave must report and acknowledge each of the communications to the master controller (**FIGURE 26-19**).

In contrast to a LIN, distributed CANs do not control the network operation with a single master ECU. Instead, CAN

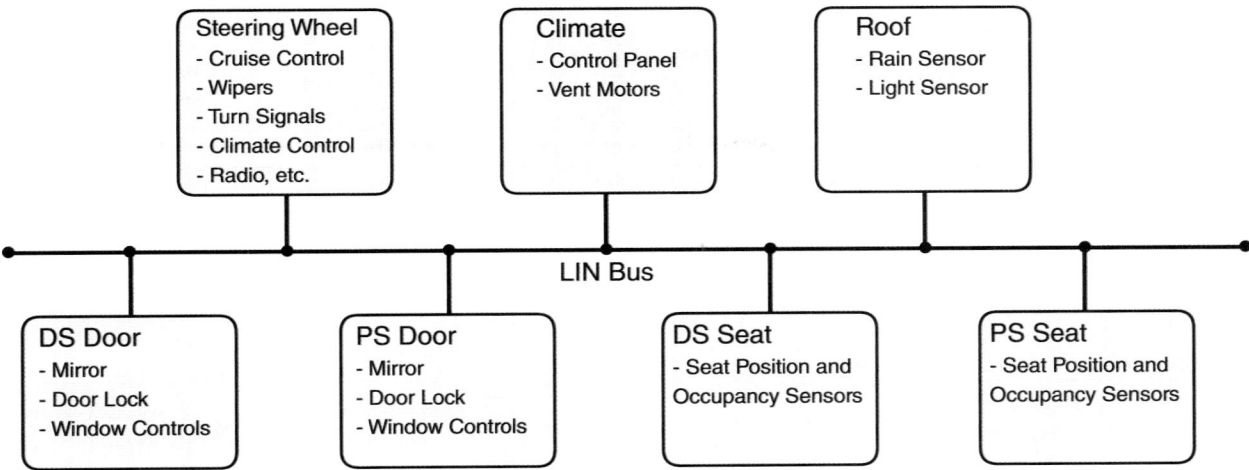

FIGURE 26-19 LINs use a single wire to communicate information between a master and several slave microcontrollers.

vehicle operation and the electrical system control use several to a couple of dozen ECUs, all sending and receiving information to produce output signals to electrical devices. Modules often depend on data from other network ECUs to provide input information to perform their tasks. For example, a wheel lock-up event during braking sends a message to the engine ECU to disable the engine brake and reduce engine torque, and to the turbocharger to open turbocharger vanes. Note that adding J-1939 CAN capabilities to a module adds significant cost and complexity to a module, which explains why LINs using microcontrollers costing less than a dollar are often used to carry out simpler tasks.

Network Domains and Gateway Modules

Networks are also formed based on organizational priorities. Modules are grouped by area or function, are called **domains**, and include areas of major control such as the engine, transmission, ABS, climate control, instrumentation, entertainment devices, or body electrical control. Within each domain are often, but not necessarily, smaller sub-control modules. An example described earlier is an engine ECU with a sub-control glow plug module. An engine ECU could also communicate and control an EGR, turbocharger, or alternator control module, but only the engine ECU would connect to the CAN and transmit information from these modules.

Network Congestion and Data Priority

With the amount of data that is sent over the network, the number of signals can congest the data bus with message traffic. Not all information has high priority or immediate importance. For example, information that affects vehicle or occupant safety, such as the ABS braking system, engine, or transmission, has priority over non-critical network traffic, such as a request for air conditioning. To prevent network traffic congestion and ensure critical messages are responded to instantly, lower-priority messages are shifted to operating on other vehicle networks. Mission-critical, safety-related messages transmitted over high-speed networks do not typically share the same network as one involving data exchange for the less critical climate control, lighting control modules, or the onboard navigation system. Still, some information needs to be exchanged between the various networks to allow optimal vehicle functionality. To enable communication between different onboard networks, and sometimes individual control modules, a **gateway module** is used. The job of this module, as the name suggests, is to redirect and translate communication between various onboard networks operating with different protocols or transmission speeds before they are allowed onto the main CAN. Inter-network communication is made possible with the gateway module. Without the gateway module, access to various networks through the CAN data link connector using electronic service tools would not be possible. For example, vehicles using J-1708 network connected to slower speed devices connect to the central gateway. This allows a service tool operating on the J-1939 network at the 9-pin DLC to request J-1708 data and translate J-1587 fault codes (**FIGURE 26-20**). Before the use of a gateway network, a separate connection to the DLC was needed to communicate with electronic service tools. Technicians connecting to vehicles with gateway modules will discover the gateway modules are used to map the network for a service tool. The network map is then used to access information in a specific module, such as one for the suspension system, climate control, and ABS (**FIGURE 26-21**).

Multiple Network Capabilities

Today, multiple networks exist on most vehicles. Rarely does contemporary equipment utilize only a single CAN for powertrain- and emission-related functions. While network congestion is the most important reason to move to multiple networks, cost is another. Modules used on CANs have far more sophisticated microcontrollers, software, and related electronics to operate on these networks with the complexity of communication protocols required by CAN. Manufacturers can produce cheaper modules, called nodes, or devices for centrally controlled networks than distributed CANs. Furthermore, manufacturers

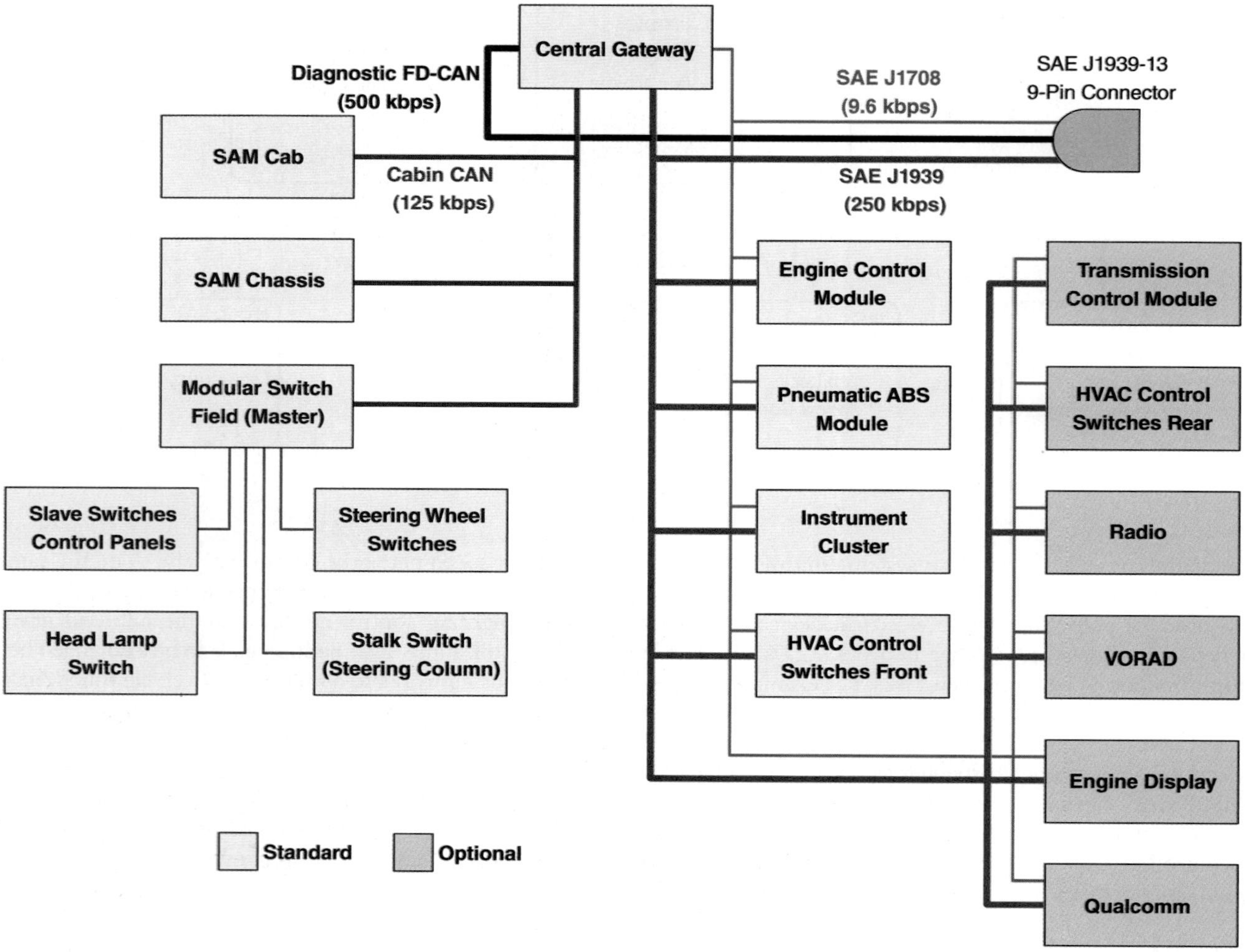

Diagnostic FD-CAN **(500 kbps)**

Central Gateway

SAE J1708 **(9.6 kbps)**

SAE J1939-13 **9-Pin Connector**

SAM Cab

Cabin CAN **(125 kbps)**

SAE J1939 **(250 kbps)**

SAM Chassis

Modular Switch **Field (Master)**

Engine Control **Module**

Transmission **Control Module**

Pneumatic ABS **Module**

HVAC Control **Switches Rear**

Slave Switches **Control Panels**

Steering Wheel **Switches**

Instrument **Cluster**

Radio

Head Lamp **Switch**

Stalk Switch **(Steering Column)**

HVAC Control **Switches Front**

VORAD

Engine Display

Standard   **Optional**

Qualcomm

FIGURE 26-20 A gateway module enables communication between different onboard networks and between different protocols. A recent version does not connect J-1708 or J1922 to the DLC.

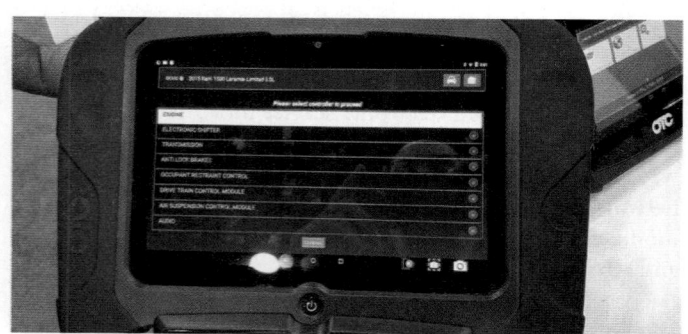

FIGURE 26-21 A gateway module maps the network to identify modules accessible through the CAN.

often use their own in-house or proprietary networks for controlling unique OEM electrical devices on the network.

For control of electrical accessories, OEMs design their operation using ladder logic, a software-based control system that replicates relay-based electrical system operation. Where wiring diagrams once illustrated battery current flow through electrical connections and devices and showed relays switched

open or closed, ladder logic shows rules for software logic to control devices. For example, to operate a starting motor, the electrical system control software would need to confirm that a specific set of conditions is met by verifying a set of true/false statements, such as these: The ignition switch is in the start position = true/false; the transmission is in neutral = true/false; Battery voltage is above 10.6 volts = true/false; the clutch is depressed = true/false. Using ladder logic, customized operational features, such as International Truck's PTO, can be programmed with up to 42 rules of engagement, disengagement, and re-engagement, along with operator warnings and alarms. Controlled differential locks release above road speeds of 25 mph (40 kph) to prevent power divider damage. Features can be added or deleted, switches can be relocated, and programmable parameters can be changed. The vehicle's new file is stored in centralized vehicle configuration data storage.

Freightliner heavy-duty vehicles use multiple onboard networks having inter-network communication capabilities (**FIGURE 26-22**). In Freightliner's signals detect and acquisition module (SAM), output signals to electrical system devices in the cab and those on the chassis are controlled separately by

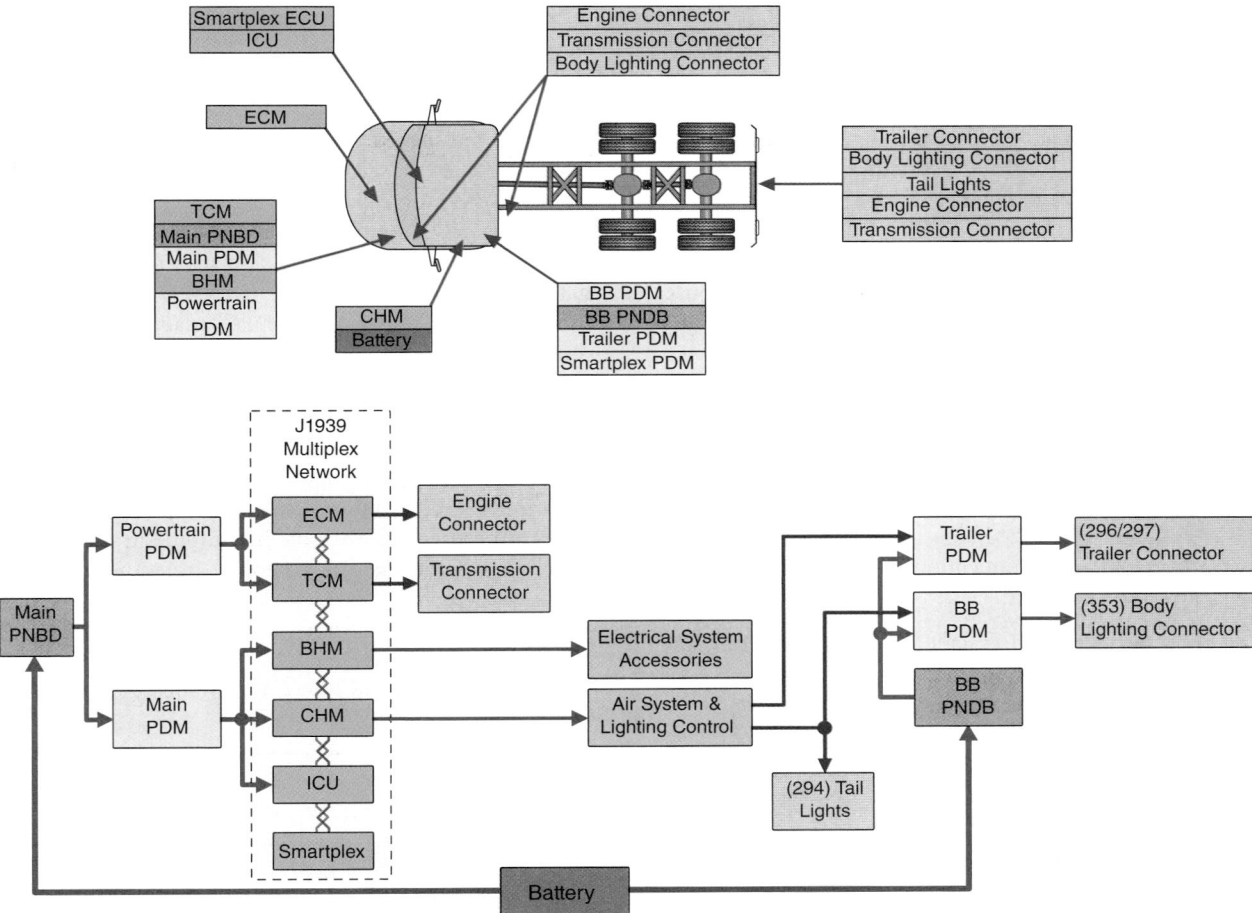

FIGURE 26-22 Freightliners M2 networked truck chassis using a chassis control module and a bulkhead control module.

two modules to prevent congestion from excessive amounts of data using only one network: One SAM module controls chassis electrical system devices, such as lighting or air system, while another operates devices inside the cab. On the latest vehicles, these networks communicate using **Universal Diagnostic Service (UDS)**, a globally used universal network protocol. UDS networks send data at different speeds than the J-1939 backbone network used by the engine and other power train systems. To enable internetwork communication, a gateway module translates information for each network compatible with its own transmission speed and message format. In the latest models of trucks, such as the Cascadia, Freightliner has moved to using a single SAM (sSAM) module located inside the cab.

Controlled Area Networks (CANs)

LO 26-4 Identify and explain the construction and operation of controller area networks (CANs).

The term, **controlled area networks (CANs)**, earlier described briefly, is a distributed network control system used by J-1939 and ISO11898. This means no single central control module is used. Instead, each module or node on the network has

processing capabilities that can initiate electrical control for faster response and synchronize their operation with other network modules. Therefore, each module on the network has memorized the SAE and ISO protocols of how and what it can do. Because the network has no central control, the connected components will still operate if parts of it are severed. It can even operate with limited capabilities with one of the data bus wires broken or shorted.

CANs are the most widely used type of network for integrating power train operation of all the latest vehicles. Since 2002, heavy-duty on-highway vehicles have used J-1939 CAN in North America. These networks integrate LANs through gateway modules, which are vehicles using multiple types of networks on a single chassis, such as UDS or other specialized proprietary networks connecting manufacturer-specific equipment. Because there is no central control module coordinating communication or controlling network devices, each CAN module has built-in processor capabilities to process input and output data while simultaneously receiving and transmitting data to the network. A built-in clock and transceiver in each CAN module helps synchronize multiplex communication between modules, so each takes an appropriate turn using the data bus to send and receive messages.

Other processing functions built into every CAN module allow it to interpret other network communication data and control the messages it sends to the data bus. This degree of sophistication makes CAN nodes more expensive to build. Engine, transmission, and ABS modules are the largest and most common types of CAN modules. Other onboard networks are built to reduce costs and increase CAN speed.

J-1939 Versus J-1708/1587

Two different types of CANs used by on-highway trucks, buses, and highway equipment are the SAE network standards J-1939 and J-1587/1708. The J-1587/1708 CAN is identified by the six-pin DLC. It is an older network that transmits data at the relatively slow speed of 9600 bits per second (bps). This speed was satisfactory when only one to three ECUs were used on a vehicle. J-1708 refers to the standards for the physical layer, or just specifications for data bus construction. J-1957, which accompanies J-1708, has standardized fault codes and uses an SAE set of rules to govern the communication over the J-1708 physical network. The J-1708 data bus:

- Contains two twisted wires using 18 American Wire Gauge (AWG) color-coded orange and green
- Links all electronic modules on the vehicle
- Communicates at 9600 bps
- Transmits at a maximum distance of 131' (40 m)
- Connects up to 20 modules or nodes

Beginning in 2001, the J-1939 using CAN 1.0 replaced the J-1708 standard for data bus. The J-1939:

- Uses two twisted wires of 18 AWG color-coded yellow and green
- Connects only modules that are compatible with the J-1939 standard
- Requires terminating resistors
- CAN 1.0 communicates at between 125,000 bps and 256,000 bps
- CAN 2.0 or flexible data rate CAN (CAN-FD) communicates at 500 kbps to 1000 kbps
- Transmits at a maximum distance of 131' (40 m)
- Connects up to 30 modules or nodes
- Stub connections to the twisted wire backbone are limited to 3' (0.9 m) in length

J-1939 defines not only the construction of the data bus, but all features and characteristics of the network. Contrasted to J-1957/1708, J-1939 is like high-speed Internet access compared to dial-up in terms of the amount of data carried per second. J-1587 and J-1939 use serial data communication protocols, which have similar characteristics but differ in relation to rules about such things as message structure, data transmission speed, connectivity hardware configuration, and diagnostic fault codes.

CAN 2.0, CAN-FD

Beginning with some models, such as Volvo in 2015 with WH-OBD, the latest commercial vehicles began using a faster CAN J-1939 protocol. CAN 2.0, also called flexible data rate of CAN-FD, doubles the maximum speed for data rate transmission from a maximum of 250 kbps on CAN 1.0 to over 500 kbps. The maximum size of the bits in data packet transmission has increased to over eight times more than CAN 1.0 (**FIGURE 26-23**). Faster CAN communication with shorter bit transmission time is necessary to accommodate network traffic on commercial trucks typically using 20 ECUs. To designate the new CAN-FD, the cab DLC is colored green. It is sometimes called a Type II connector or CAN 500 connector. In contrast, the older CAN 1.0 DLC is black and has one larger pin that does not fit into the newer CAN-FD plug (**FIGURE 26-24**). This means the older 9-pin DLC adapter cables do not fit into a CAN-FD DLC, but the newer CAN FD cables are backward-compatible with the older CAN 1.0 DLC.

The newer CAN-FD connector is green to make technicians aware that older communication adapters connected to scanners or network bridges to a personal computer (PC) are not compatible. The faster data rate and packet size of messages often cannot be used with older equipment, resulting in communication errors or disconnecting from the network after a few seconds.

Other changes that have accompanied the CAN-FD is the use of multiple CAN channels. Some manufacturers, such as Freightliner, Volvo, and PACAAR, are using three J-1939 CAN

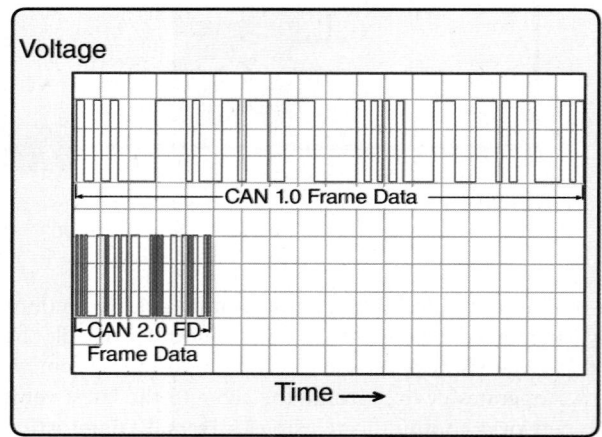

FIGURE 26-23 CAN-FD can transmit much more data in a shorter time than CAN 1.0.

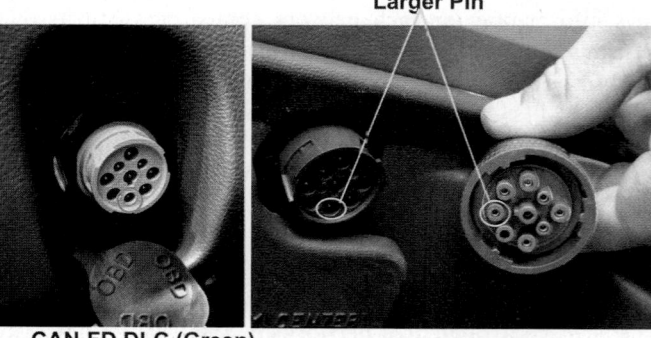

FIGURE 26-24 The latest CAN-FD protocols, or CAN 2.0, use a green-colored DLC that is backward-compatible with CAN 1.0.

networks beginning in 2017: CAN 1, CAN 2, and CAN 3. The powertrain or diagnostic CAN-FD is called the CAN 3 channel while other slower CAN 1.0 networks are moved to CAN 1 and 2 channels (**FIGURE 26-25**). This arrangement eliminates the older J-1708 data bus. CAN-FD and diagnostic CAN are now connected directly to the DLC. A gateway module connects all three CANs. UDS (Universal Diagnostic System) is also used on these vehicles. UDS is a diagnostic and service protocol that can operate on its own over a separate data bus or over a CAN with J-1939. UDS messages are inserted between CAN messages.

Differential Voltage and Serial Communication

Serial communication is like electronic Morse code. Instead of dots and dashes, 0s and 1s are transmitted in a series, one after another, using voltage pulses. Because there is only one pair of wires making up the data bus, serial data is transmitted one bit at a time, one bit after another, or in series (**FIGURE 26-26**).

The J-1939 data bus uses two wires: one wire called CAN-HI, and the other CAN-LO. By manipulating the polarity

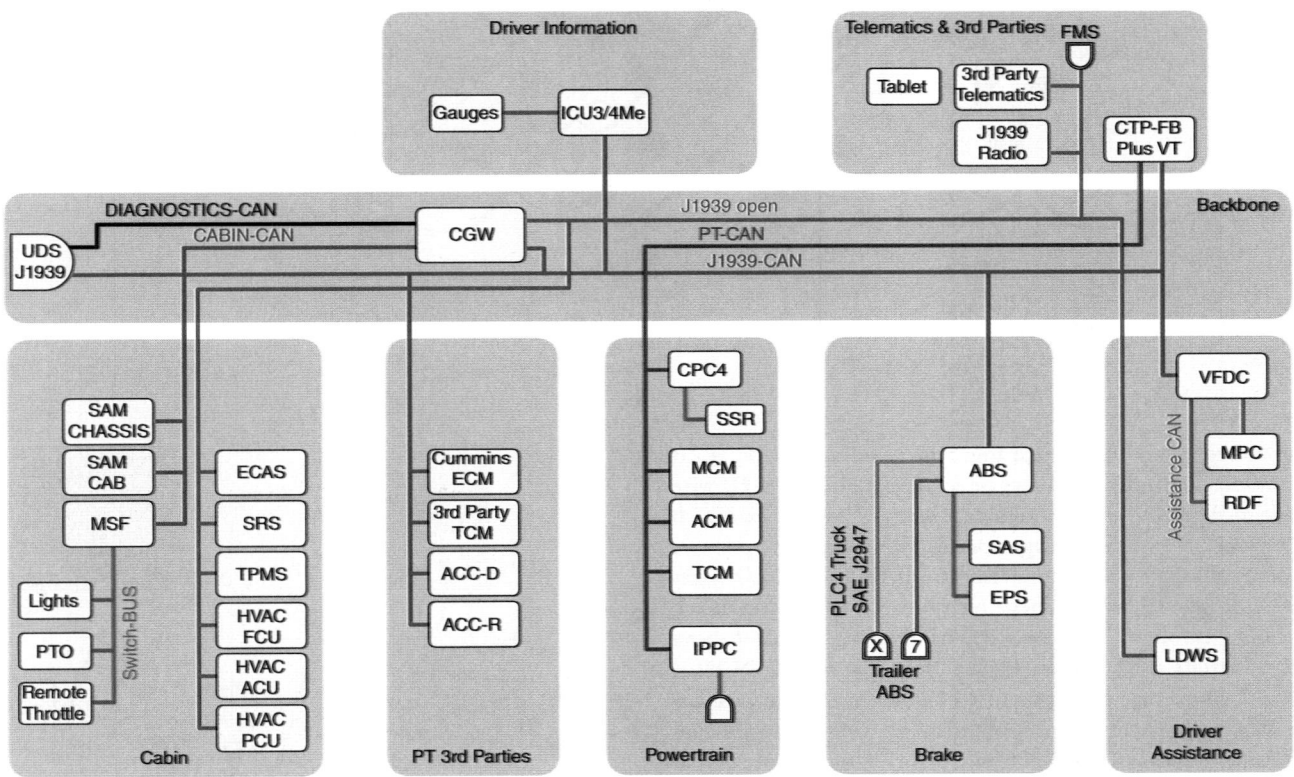

FIGURE 26-25 Three J-1939 channels are used on the latest HD tractors. UDS now operates over the CAN.

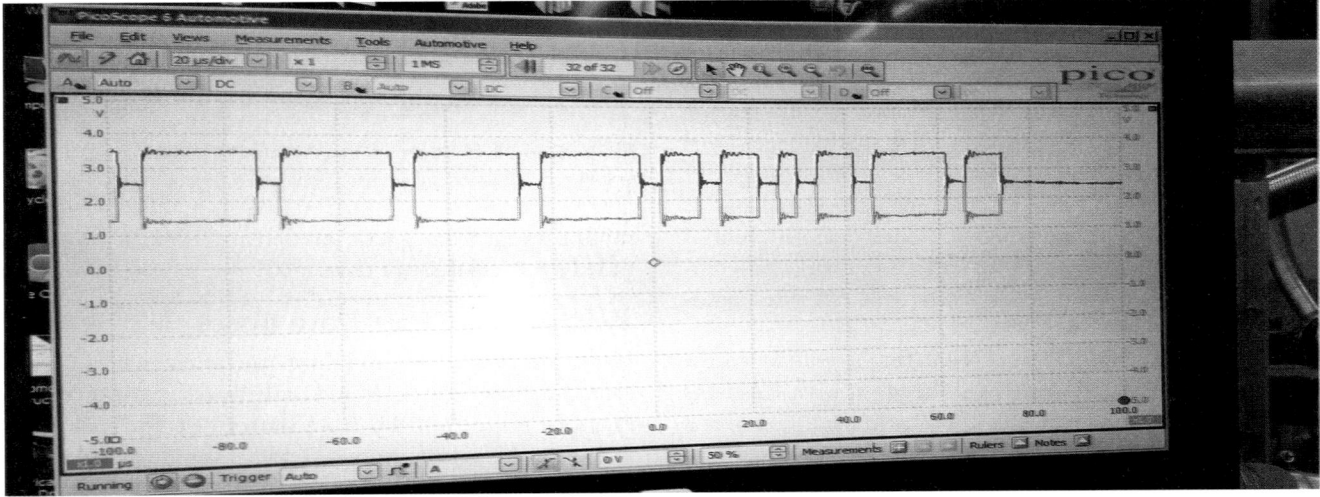

FIGURE 26-26 A serial data waveform from a J-1939 network.

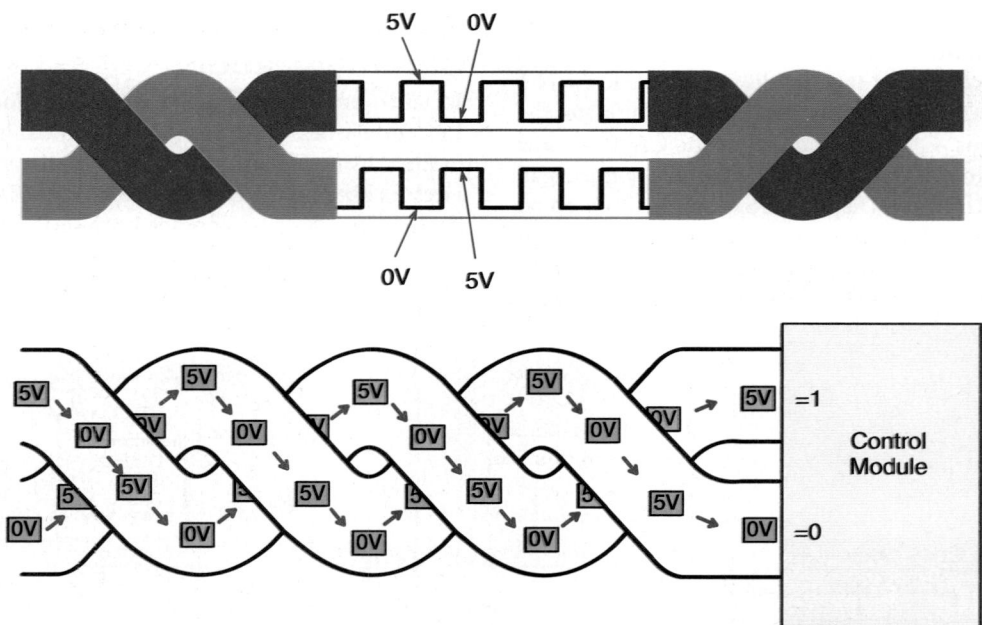

FIGURE 26-27 Differential voltage, or differential mode transmission, of serial data ensures that a clear, crisp electrical signal is transmitted over the data bus.

of the voltage in both wires, a logic bit of either "0" or "1" is transmitted. To produce a binary bit value of 1, the CAN-HI wire is made more positive than a resting voltage of both lines, which is +2.5 volts when referencing ground. This means the positive lead of a voltmeter placed on either the CAN HI and LO wires will both display +2.5 volts if negative voltmeter lead is connected to chassis ground. Pulling the CAN-HI wire HI makes it more positive than its resting voltage. This means when a CAN-HI is pulled HI, its voltage moves from +2.5 volts to +3.5 volts. Likewise, the CAN-LO wire is made more negative, it is pulled negatively from +2.5 down to 0 volts. Each wire has a mirror opposite charge of the other, with a 3.5 volt differential when communicating a "1" logic bit. To transmit a logic bit of "0", no differential voltage is present. The CAN HI and LO remain at +2.5 volts.

When the voltage on the paired data bus wires is pulled more negatively or positively to create a polarity that is mirror opposite of one another, it produces a sharp, crisp differential voltage of 3.5 volts that is easily understood by the control modules (**FIGURE 26-27**). When the differential voltage signal reaches its destination, network modules detect the voltage difference between the two wires to determine if the signal logic is a 1 or 0. This signal processing method is known as **differential mode transmission**. Note that J-1587/1708 networks differential voltage is also measured between the two CAN wires, but is slightly higher than J-1939 signals.

On the J-1939 CAN, the CAN-HI (high) wire is yellow and carries positive voltage (CAN+). The green wire, CAN-LO (low) (CAN−), is negative. Signals could be transmitted over a single wire if one of the wires were broken or grounded out, but using the voltage-differential mode of transmission provides a better signal quality capable of very high rates of data transmission. Using differential voltage and twisting the wires

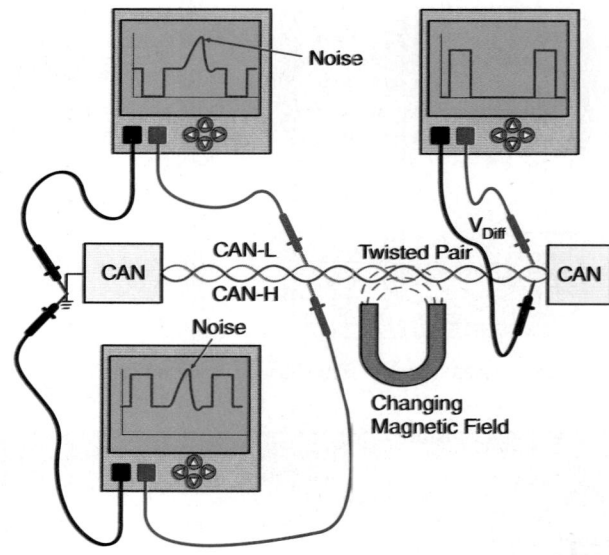

FIGURE 26-28 EMI sources that can affect the data bus. Differential voltage transmission minimizes signal interference.

minimizes electromagnetic interference (EMI) in the wires, also called electrical noise or cross talk.

Twisted Wire Pair Data Buses

Wires are twisted to minimize electromagnetic interference caused by magnetic fields and radio waves (**FIGURE 26-28**). For example, magnetic fields from starters, electric motors, injectors, or radio signals from CB radios can penetrate the wires and induce voltage. Distortions to differential voltage signals can garble or change network messages. A cancellation effect on any induced voltage is achieved using differential mode transmission, because the two wires carry equal and opposite voltage polarity. For example, if a slightly higher positive or negative voltage is induced in the wires, both will move in the same direction. The +3.5 CAN-HI could become +3.9, but the negative CAN-LO would also become +0.4 volts. In this instance, the voltage differential of 3.5 volts remains the same. Twisting the wires also helps the voltage differential in both wires stay the same when interference, affecting both wires the same way, is produced by magnetic induction.

EMI introduced into the wires tends to affect both wires equally when wires are twisted five turns per inch or two turns per centimeter. The low-voltage signal of the CAN-FD data bus is even more susceptible to EMI due to the average transmission speed of 256 kbps to 800 kbps. Wires are not only twisted together to resist induction of current, but, on earlier vehicles, they were also covered in a metal foil to absorb EMI signals. A third wire attached to the foil drained away induced current flow in the foil to chassis ground. This is like the use of the braided shielding wire used on TV cable. With the TV cable, the inner wire carries the signal and the outer braided wire shields the inner cable from interference that would produce a static-filled, distorted picture.

▶ **TECHNICIAN TIP**

Only one connection to ground should be made on the J-1939 drain wire. If more than one connection is made to ground, the outer shielding can become a circuit pathway. This, in turn, intensifies EMI interference if electrical current moves through the shielding conductor from one drain ground to the other.

Terminating Resisters

To further minimize signal distortion, at each end of the J-1939 CANbus, there is a 120-ohm resistor that extinguishes or dampens out voltage signals to prevent their reflection through the data bus (**FIGURE 26-29**). Similar to a light bulb, which converts current to heat and light, the resistors absorb the signal's energy to quickly extinguish it once it has passed though the data bus. Quickly extinguishing the signals prevents interference with new signals, which, in turn, increases data transmission speed over the data bus.

Network signals are distorted and slowed if terminating resistors are missing or defective. An ohmmeter is used to measure the resistance of the J-1939 data bus to determine whether network problems are caused by the data bus. Two 120-ohm terminating resistors connected in parallel across the CAN+ and CAN– wires provide 60 ohms of total bus resistance. Note, the resistance of the CAN-HI and CAN-LO wires can only be measured after the battery is disconnected. Disconnecting either of the terminating resistors causes the bus resistance to rise to 120 ohms. If the resistance of the data link is 120 ohms, then there is either an open bus circuit somewhere, or a terminating resistor is missing. Pinched, cut, or shorted data bus wires will extinguish any network communication. The outer foil should have continuity with chassis ground and none to either of the twisted wire pair. Repairs to the bus need to be performed according to prescribed manufacturer procedures. Field experience has demonstrated that if only one J-1939 terminating resistor is missing, the network or vehicle does not typically have any operational problems, but communication is slowed, which is commonly observed when using electronic service tools that require long response times. However, if both terminating resistors are missing, no communication is possible (**FIGURE 26-30**). Older CAN 1.0 networks used terminating

FIGURE 26-29 A terminating resistor for a J-1939 network.

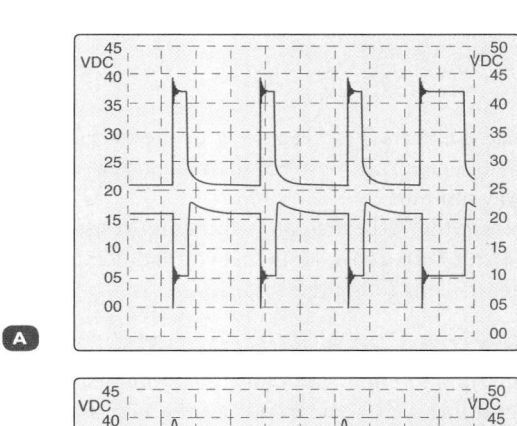

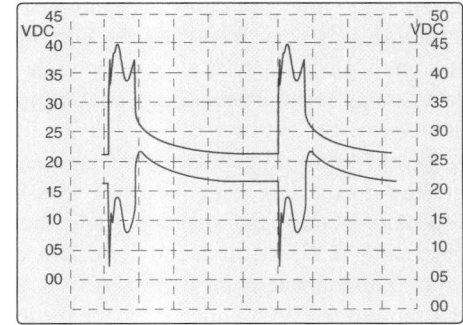

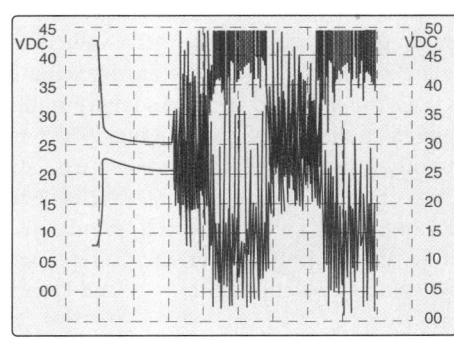

FIGURE 26-30 Waveforms when resistors are missing from a J-1939 data bus. **A.** Two resistors. **B.** One missing resistor. **C.** No resistors (all resistors missing).

SKILL DRILL 26-1 Measuring Resistance of Terminating Resistors

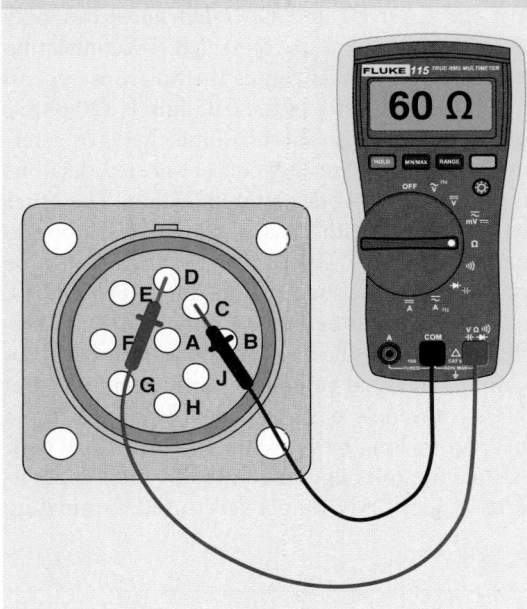

1. With the ignition off, disconnect the batteries.
2. Connect the leads of a digital multimeter (DMM) to pins C and D of the 9-pin diagnostic connector.
3. Set the multimeter to read in ohms.
4. Measure and record the resistance. Normal resistance should be 60 ohms; 120 ohms indicates one missing resistor; 45 ohms indicates an extra resistor. With both resistors removed, there should be a high resistance of more than 10,000 ohms from current flow through modules, but not infinite resistance, which indicates open circuited modules.

resisters located externally at each end of the data bus. In the latest CAN-FD networks, the terminating resisters are located in the gateway module.

To measure the resistance of terminating resistors, follow the steps in **SKILL DRILL 26-1**. Note that you should perform this test only after disconnecting the batteries.

Multiplexing Data Bus Signals

It may be puzzling to understand how the same two wires connected to multiple ECUs can send and receive information, apparently simultaneously, especially considering the enormous volume of data passing over the networks. If communication took place simultaneously, the positive and negative voltage pulses representing 0s and 1s would collide, canceling one another or generally garbling any message, a lot like a noisy classroom when everyone is speaking at once and no one is understood.

However, using an electrical signal communication strategy called multiplexing overcomes the problem. **Multiplexing (MUX)** simply refers to a concept where transmission of more than one electrical signal or message takes place over a single wire or pair of wires. In modern vehicles, thousands of messages are exchanged every second between a dozen or more ECUs over the onboard networks where multiplex communication enables sharing of the data bus. MUX requires the modules and other network devices to take turns, sharing time on the data bus communication pathway (**FIGURE 26-31**). Only one module can talk, and all other modules must listen until it is their turn to talk. This should remind you of a well-ordered classroom where there is cooperation around communication rules; no one interrupts anyone else until they are finished speaking. Data transfer back and forth along the data bus does not take place simultaneously, but each device transmits and receives data by cooperating to time-share a common signal

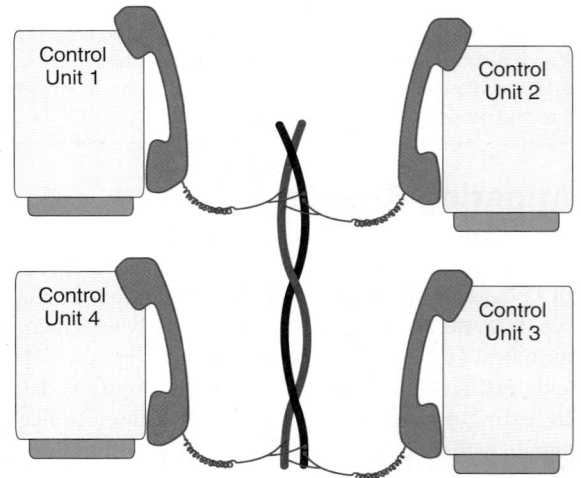

FIGURE 26-31 Time division multiplexing (TDM) is like a phone call where modules share a phone extension.

path (**FIGURE 26-32**). The speed at which the data exchange takes place makes communication appear to occur simultaneously, although it does not.

Two common multiplex strategies are used by the CAN and other onboard networks. One is time division multiplexing (TDM), the other uses ethernet principles.

Time Division Multiplexing

In case of **time division multiplexing (TDM)**, the use of the data bus is allotted to one module for a fixed time slot. If there are 20 modules, each module is given a time slot of 1/20th of a second and each module takes a turn in a timed sequence to use the data bus. This means that after one second, each module has

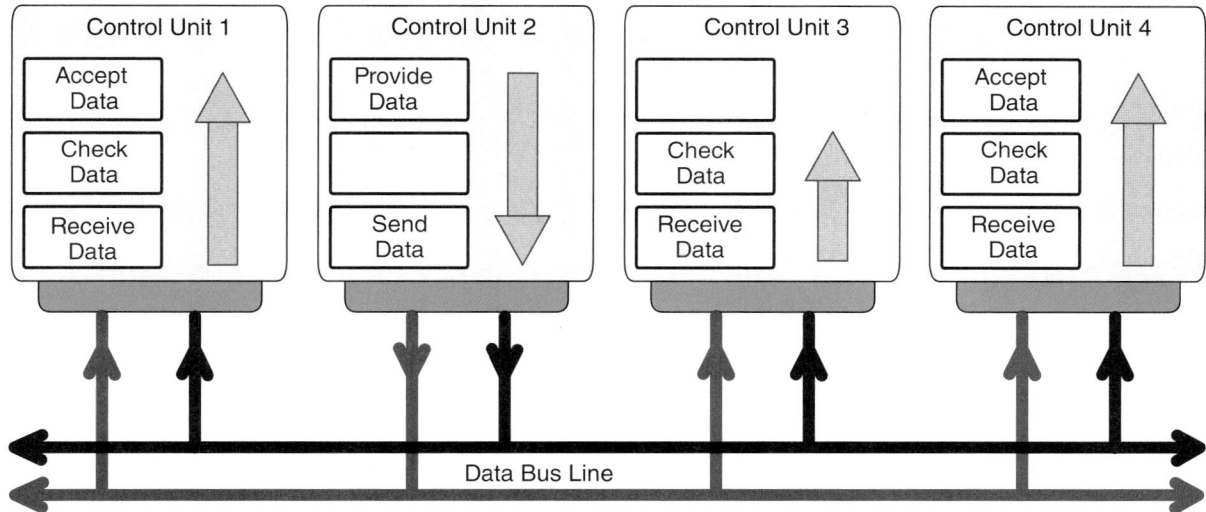

FIGURE 26-32 The rule of TDM allows only one module to send information, while the remaining modules receive.

broadcast any messages it had to every other module and every module has listened to all the information shared over the data bus. TDM is acceptable for slow transmission speeds because there is a big gap between each of the time slots allotted to a module and all the allotted time is unlikely to be used. Time could be better used if other modules could use the idle time on the network data bus. If TDM were used in all onboard networks works, the time available to each module is the number of modules divided by the time available each second or whatever time frame is acceptable.

Ethernet Principles of MUX

A better method of multiplexing signals on the data bus is to use ethernet principles of time sharing. Like the TDM method, networks using ethernet principles allow each module to take a turn transmitting data and afterwards listening to all other communication over the data bus. However, rather than waiting for a designated time period to elapse before it broadcasts information, a module can begin to transmit data once its transceiver detects no other module is transmitting over the network. This method uses network time more efficiently and increases the possibility of greater data transfer volume.

Priority Bits and Data Bus Arbitration

To prevent collisions or signal interference using ethernet-type communication, message importance is prioritized. For example, if two modules begin transmitting data at exactly the same time, priority is assigned to the more important or critical network broadcast messages. Priority bits indicating the relative importance of a message are found in the first frame of a longer multi-frame CAN message. Safety-related information obviously has the highest priority, and lower priority is given to information for things like a command to roll a window up or down. Deciding which module is allowed to transmit information and which one must stop is a process called **bit arbitration**.

As soon as the data bus is free (i.e., the telephone line is not busy), any node or module using ethernet, like MUX, can begin

transmitting information. If two or more modules start transmitting at once, the message is formatted to start with several priority bits used to decide which message has the most urgency to access to the data bus. For example, a wheel lock-up event or a traction control module message indicating excessive wheel slip will have priority to transmit to the data bus and send a message to the engine ECM to reduce engine torque. Modules with lower priority messages automatically switch from transmitting to receiving, and repeat their broadcast as soon as the data bus is free again.

CAN messages are divided into frames, with each frame containing specific information. The first data bits of the start frame contain priority bits with highest ranking priority bits designated to begin with 1 and lower priority messages designated to begin with numbers, such as 2, 3, or 4 (**FIGURE 26-33**).

Network Messages

Using CAN networks is like shouting a message in a well-ordered room crowded with people. Everyone can hear the broadcast message, but not everyone will respond or is permitted to speak at once because of message rules. Using the CAN protocols, however, is not as potentially confusing as a room full of shouting people. Instead of people, modules are communicating with one another operating under a strictly defined set of rules to control communication. Messages sent and received over the network are constructed in frames with a maximum data frame message length now of 64 bits in CAN-FD. This maximum message length is, by digital data standards, short, taking about 0.2 milliseconds to transmit a message with 32 bits of data. A short message ensures the wait time for each message is as brief as possible. To keep the data length time short, data carried on the CANbus has several distinct message formats:

- Priority bits—Tells which message should be transmitted first in the event of a collision when two modules begin to transmit simultaneously. Its message format is: "My ABS wheel lock-up event is more important than a message to roll-up the window."

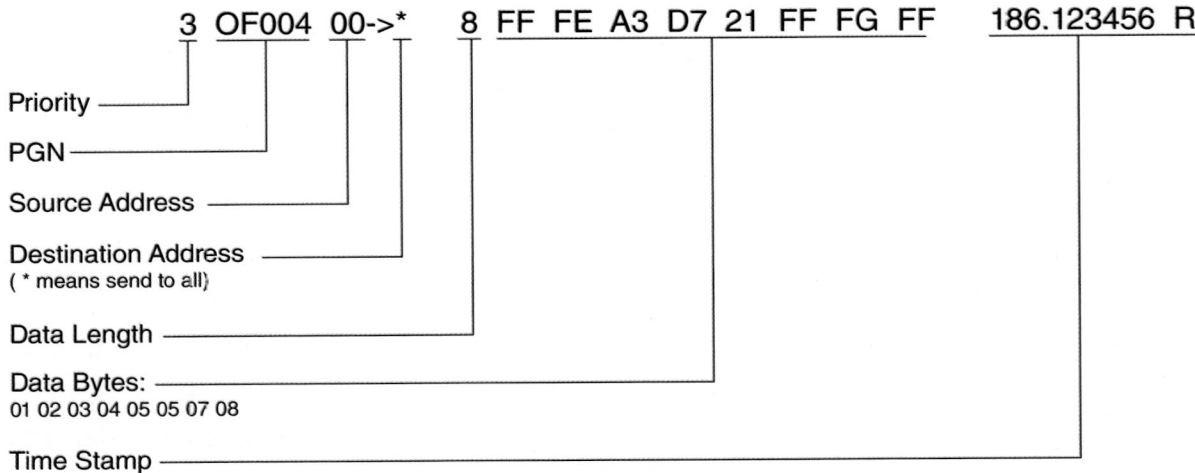

FIGURE 26-33 Construction of a CAN message. Note the position of priority bits.

- Parameter Group Number—It identifies itself and contains information from a major domain ECU. Its message format could be something like this: "Hello, everyone, here's some information from control module Y with a box full of data labeled X, I hope it's useful!"
- Data frame—It contains the actual message. It holds the contents in the box labeled data X.
- Remote frame—Is a request for information and it may contain the address of a specific module it wants the information sent from. Its message format is something like this: "Hello, everyone, (or ABS module), can somebody (ABS module) please send the information labeled Y?"
- Error frame—Its message format is something like this: (Everyone out loud but one at a time in sequence) "Can you repeat that?" This message is sent by modules that do not understand a message, if the information is garbled or is not sent according to rules.
- Overload frame—Its message format is something like this: "I'm a very busy transmission control module sending something more important, could you please wait for a moment?"

Using these message formats that determine which module is transmitting or receiving data, eliminates problems with message transmission while communicating huge quantities of information. A check sum digit is used to calculate whether the data in the message is accurate and uncorrupted. A simple check-sum security check uses a mathematical formula that adds up the numbers in the message and checks whether all the other modules agree that sum corresponds with the sum they calculated. Start and end frames help the other modules know when they can begin or end broadcast messages (**FIGURE 26-34**).

All modules can acknowledge the receipt of information when requested by a module by transmitting the message "there were no corrupted messages." This is like ending a telephone call with the message, "Did you hear what I said? Everyone says OK and good-bye."

No centralized special software controls the network communication. Operating instructions are embedded in the memory chips used by any CAN module connected to the network.

Manufacturers supplying devices connected to the network must ensure the devices are constructed to design specifications that make them network compatible. This enables the use of the plug-and-play feature of the network.

SAFETY TIP

On J-1939 CAN networks, any module connected to the network must be certified as compatible. Non-compatible modules may work, but they can cause unusual, and even catastrophic, problems. For example, security systems or remote starters connected to the network can suddenly and unexpectedly cause a vehicle to stop operation. "Footprint errors" shutting down the network are produced when incompatible devices are connected to the network too. The latest networks simply do not recognize or allow modules to communicate over the network unless they are properly programmed with the correct module identifying information and correct hand shake messages.

▶ TECHNICIAN TIP

The use of electronic service tools, such as scanners, PCs, and other devices, to communicate with modules connected to the vehicle network is critical to the diagnosis and repair of emission-related faults. Fault codes, communication language, and other features of the onboard network are standardized by EPA legislation to make it easier for technicians to repair a wide variety of vehicles with a minimum amount of electronic service tools. The right to repair aspects of the EPA legislation enabled aftermarket tool manufacturers—not just the OEMs—to supply service tools to communicate with the network.

Unified Diagnostic Service (UDS)

LO 26-5 Identify and describe the Unified Diagnostic Service network protocol.

A problem encountered by manufacturers of components and global truck and bus platforms is having a worldwide standard for communicating, diagnosing, and reprogramming embedded devices. Embedded devices described in earlier

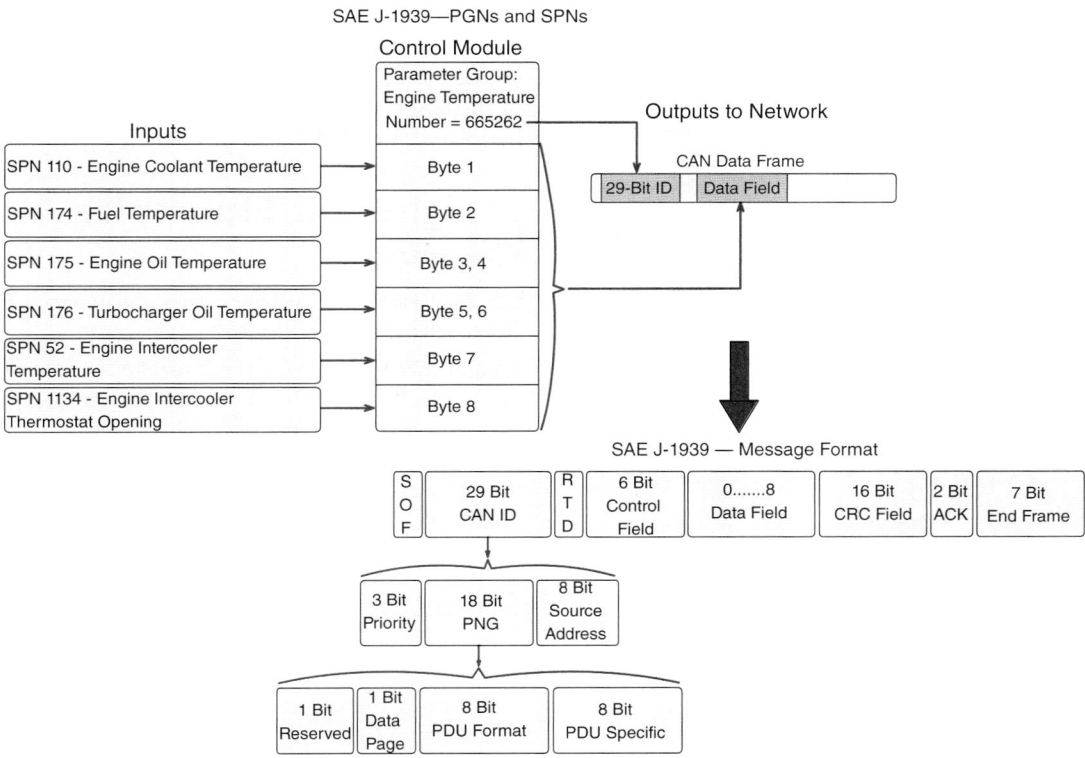

FIGURE 26-34 Construction of a J-1939 network CAN 1.0 message. Message information also includes whether the data is a fault code or simply system information.

chapters are components using microcontrollers to operate often these embedded devices are mechatronic components having mechanical, hydraulic, or pneumatic action directed by microcontrollers. Because network communication is often regulated according to emission legislation, it has regional differences that global producers, parts rebuilders, and service tool manufacturers find cumbersome to work with. To overcome this problem, Unified Diagnostic Service (UDS) ISO 14229 was developed as a global standard for, among other purposes, establishing network communications, identifying and retrieving fault codes (called blame codes in UDS), analyzing problems with microcontrollers and refreshing them with new firmware and calibration data, reprogramming ECUs reading network data, and creating a universal standard programming interface for electronic service tools. UDS is currently used by truck and bus makers and often called a "private network." It is considered private because a layer called "Security Access Service," which is a security feature, can be added to prevent access to network communication data, microcontroller calibration data and firmware programming except by the OEM. This feature is expected to be very important with the growth of autonomous vehicles because it prevents CAN hacking—a situation where a remote hacker with a wireless device establishes itself as a network node and takes control of a vehicle through its network.

UDS protocols allow it to communicate over CAN networks, between CAN messages, without needing a separate data bus. It can also operate on its own network data bus.

Common Data Bus Problems

LO 26-6 Identify and explain common data bus problems.

Problems on networks commonly originate from the following causes:

- Shorted or defective CAN modules
- Shorts to ground, power or CAN+ HI and CAN− LO wires
- Missing terminating resistors
- Additional terminating resistors

When network problems are present, the symptoms can vary widely from vehicle to vehicle, depending on the fault and manufacturer (**FIGURE 26-35**). The vehicle may not start at all or may accelerate slowly (if it accelerates at all), the transmission may not shift properly, lights may be out, etc. (**FIGURE 26-36**). Disconnecting modules one by one can help identify a module that is shorting out the CANbus. But the best initial diagnostic routine to identify a network problem is to perform resistance and voltage checks of the CANbus at the DLC. The HD-OBD system monitors the CANbus voltage and reports network faults if the voltage measurements are not correct or if there is a problem with the data. These faults are reported as network codes. The failure of a service tool to communicate with the DLC requires a check of the voltage between the CAN Hi and CAN Lo pins, which should be a minimum of one volt for J-1939 and slightly more for the J1708 data bus. After disconnecting the batteries to remove all vehicle power, resistance checks of the terminating resistors can be performed. Too many or too few resistors give an incorrect resistance reading, as do shorted modules. The proper resistance should be close to 60 ohms.

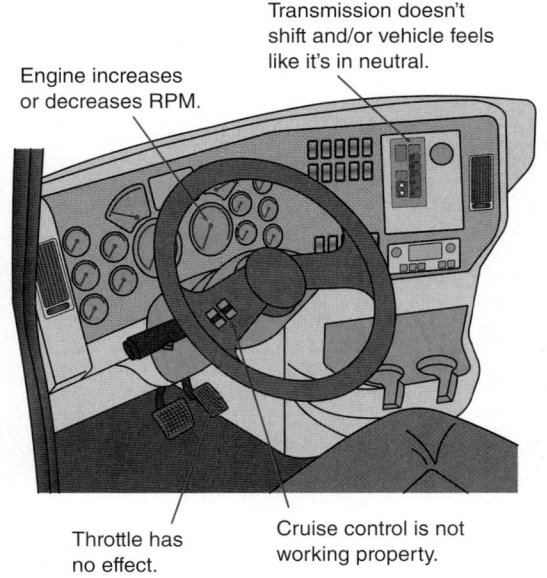

Engine increases or decreases RPM.

Transmission doesn't shift and/or vehicle feels like it's in neutral.

Throttle has no effect.

Cruise control is not working property.

FIGURE 26-35 Symptoms of a CANbus network problem.

To perform a DLC voltage check, follow the steps in **SKILL DRILL 26-2**. This test checks whether enough voltage is available on the DLC CAN lines to transmit data. And to check for shorts in the CAN, follow the guidelines in **SKILL DRILL 26-3**. Again, perform this test only after disconnecting the batteries.

Freightliner Smartplex Network Overview

LO 26-7 Identify major components and outline the function of Smartplex network components.

Freightliner uses several versions of advanced network control of the electrical system that demonstrate the combined effectiveness of several network typologies and protocols. It markets several versions of its onboard vehicle networks under the name SmartPlex. The following is a general overview of Freightliner's Smartplex electrical control systems used on its M2 and heavy-duty tractors.

Smartplex Elements

All electrical system components, such as motors, relays, switches, accessories, and lights are connected to two ECUs essential to the network operation. These two control modules monitor and regulate all electrical system operation in the

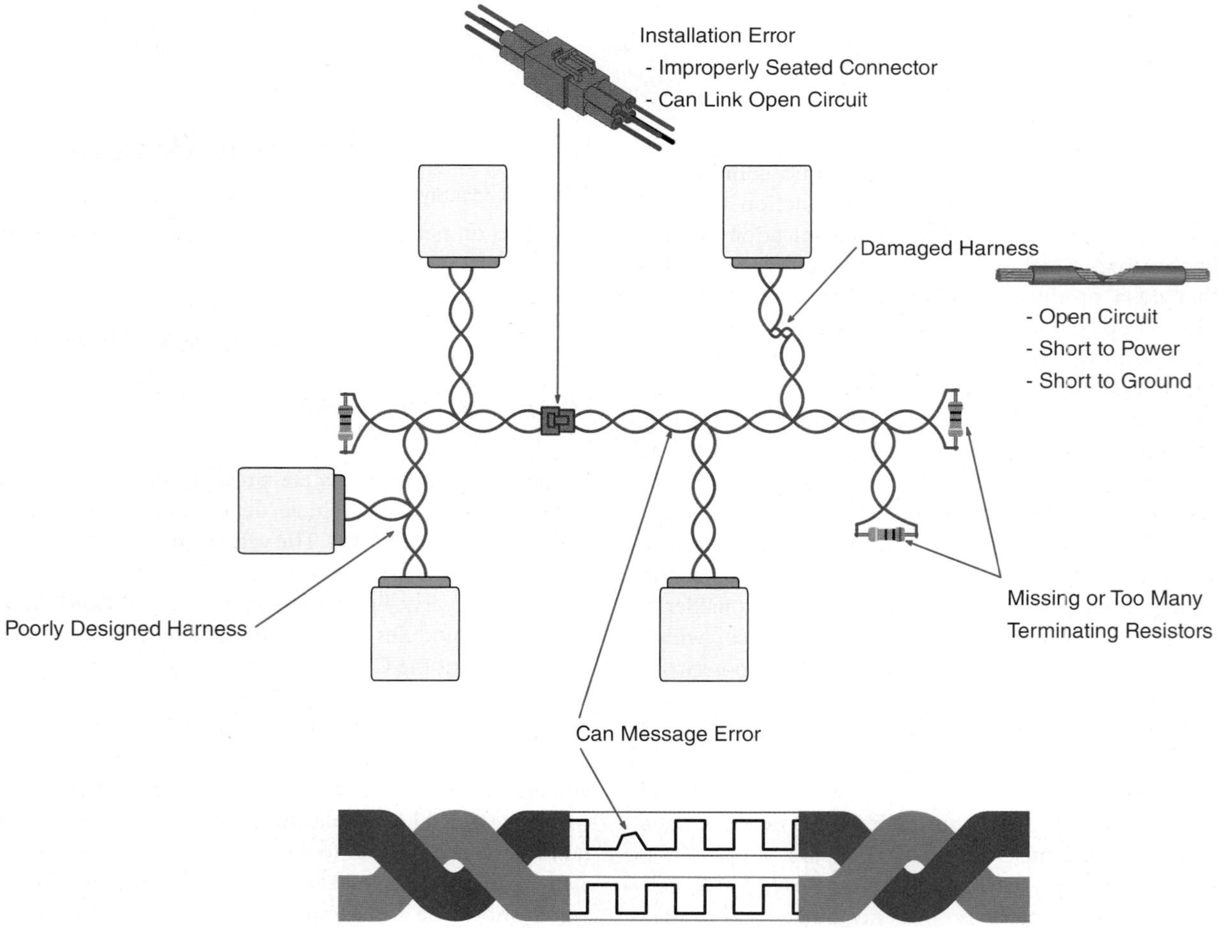

Installation Error
- Improperly Seated Connector
- Can Link Open Circuit

Damaged Harness

- Open Circuit
- Short to Power
- Short to Ground

Poorly Designed Harness

Missing or Too Many Terminating Resistors

Can Message Error

FIGURE 26-36 CANbus defects.

SKILL DRILL 26-2 Performing a DLC Voltage Check

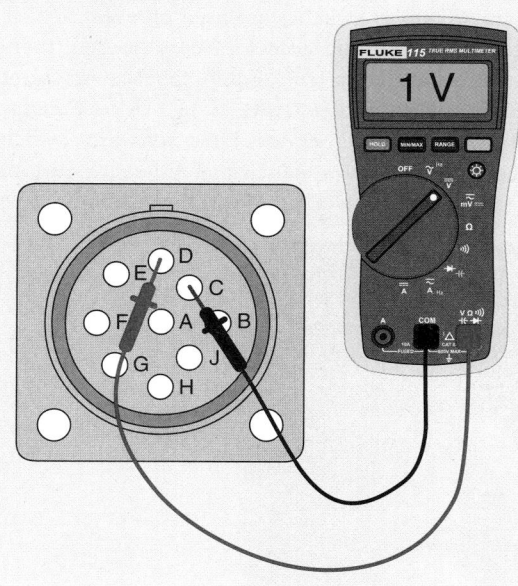

1. Set the digital multimeter (DMM) to read in volts.
2. With the ignition on, connect the leads of a DMM to pins C and D (yellow and green wires) of the 9-pin diagnostic connector.
3. Measure and record the voltage. The voltage should be more than 1 volt but close to +2.5 volts. When working correctly, the meter averages the CAN wire voltage, so it may appear unstable. If there is no voltage, there is no network communication taking place.

SKILL DRILL 26-3 Checking for Shorts in the CAN

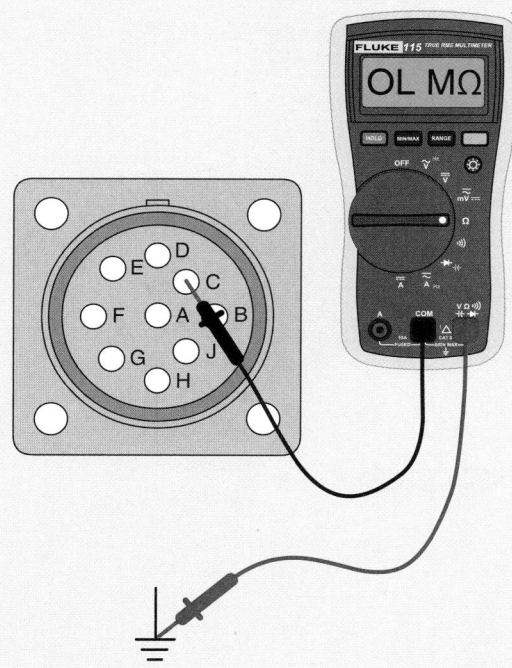

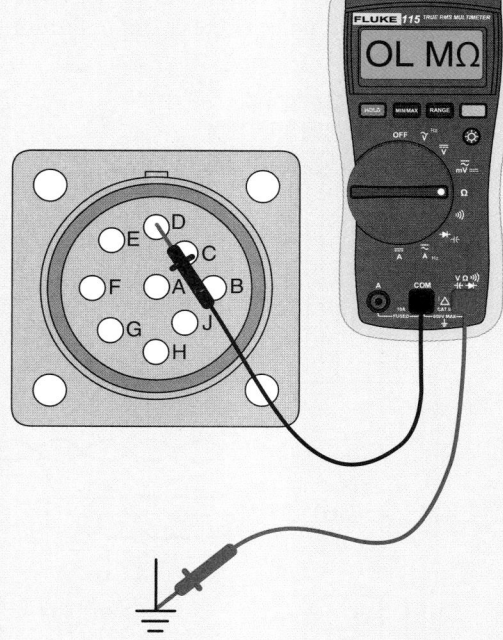

1. With the ignition off, disconnect the batteries.
2. Connect one lead of a DMM to pin C of the 9-pin diagnostic connector.
3. Connect the multimeter lead to chassis ground.
4. Set the DMM to read in ohms.
5. Measure and record the resistance.

6. Connect one lead of a DMM to pin D of the 9-pin diagnostic connector.
7. Connect the other DMM lead to chassis ground.
8. Measure and record the resistance. The resistance between chassis ground and either pins C or D should be infinite or out-of-limit.

cab and chassis. In the M2 class of trucks, a bulkhead module (BHM) is the master control module for the SmartPlex electrical system. As the master controller, it contains all programmed system parameters, controls current flow, and provides circuit protection for the electrical system. The BHM communicates with other modules over a J-1939 CAN and coordinates the activity of another module called the chassis control module (CHM) and an optional switch expansion module. On older tractors, Freightliner uses two electrical system control modules called **signal detection and actuation module (SAM)**. One is for the cab and the other is dedicated to chassis system electrical control (**FIGURE 26-37**).

Driver inputs to the electrical system are through smart switches. These are low-current switches that supply input signals to the SAM or BHM. Smart switches are available in two- and three-position configurations, momentary contact, and with a latching feature. A two-position switch supplies an on or off signal to the SAM-BHM and a three-position switch allows for an up/down/off signal to the SAM-BHM.

Each smart switch has an internal printed circuit board that contains:

- Three precision resistors that are used to indicate the switch position and identify the switch to the BHM using a unique voltage signal produced by the resistive value of the switch.
- An LED for backlighting the switch when the switch is activated, closed, or on, or when the headlights are turned on or activated. A solid light status indicates the circuit or feature

is activated. If a fault is present, the LED blinks warnings regarding the functioning of the switch circuit operation.

A set of standard smart switches are used on every vehicle but if additional equipment and accessories are needed, more switch packs can be installed by a Truck Equipment Manufacturer (TEM) for specific applications (**FIGURE 26-38**). Using Freightliner's proprietary web-based Service Link software, switch functions and other electrical system capabilities are custom programmed. An optional networked switch expansion module

FIGURE 26-37 Location of the chassis SAM and PDM on the cab firewall.

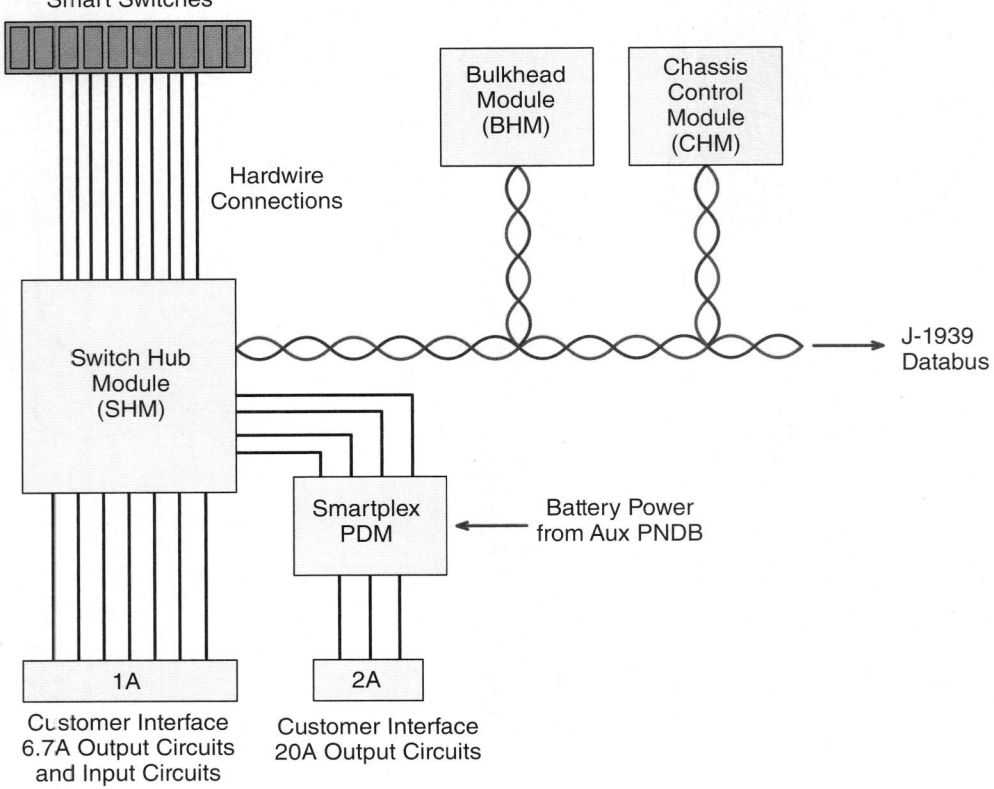

FIGURE 26-38 Programmable switch packs enable customization of switch functions.

provides an interface to the network for the switches. In its tractors, Freightliner uses a standard equipment switch interface module called the **modular switch field (Master) (MSFM)**.

The instrument cluster and its integrated gauges is also a network device. Gauges are driven by J-1939 network data and the drivers information center can pull-up chassis information (**FIGURE 26-39**).

Power distribution modules (PDMs) incorporating inputs and power outputs with 20 amps or more of current-carrying capacity are useful programmable output devices for body builders. Modules containing **field effect** transistors (FETs), which operate like a combined solid-state relay and a circuit breaker, also have virtual fusing for circuit protection. When current is applied to the gate, an FET can switch current flow like a regular switching transistor. However, a fourth leg or terminal on an FET allows monitoring of current levels through the FET. This means that, if the programmed maximum current is exceeded, the control logic software monitoring current flow will switch off the FET.

FIGURE 26-39 The instrument cluster is a network input and output device.

Power Distribution Module

What is commonly known as a power distribution box, containing fuses, circuit breakers, and relays, Freightliner calls it a main Power Distribution Module (PDM). This device distributes battery power to the various control modules on the vehicle. The PDM contains fuses to protect the wiring circuits connected to the electrical system control modules. Four connectors supply current to the SAMs or BHM and CHM modules for their output devices If any fuses or breakers in the PDM are open, all circuits are affected since current from each of the fuses and breakers is distributed through the BHM and CHM modules. This arrangement explains why several unrelated electrical system complaints take place simultaneously if a fuse or breaker is blown or tripped.

Power Net Distribution Box (PNDB)

The power net distribution box (PNDB) is used on Freightliner tractors in addition to the PDM. Current for the PDM is switched through the PNDB and major circuits powered directly by the battery are connected and protected against overload by the PNDB. A control module integrated into the PNDB ensures power is maintained to keep-alive circuits when the vehicle is shut down. For example, the DEF purge system, which drains DEF fluid from the SCR delivery system to prevent lines from freezing, is one example of an important keep-alive circuit.

Air Management Unit

Like other truck builders, Freightliner uses an electronically controlled air management unit. Air control modules like this control air pressure to air operated devices through electrically controlled solenoid valves. The air management unit essentially provides general-purpose ECU control of air-operated body equipment accessories. Not only do these modules minimize the number of air lines, but they also eliminate the need for air lines to connect to switches located in the dash (**FIGURE 26-40**).

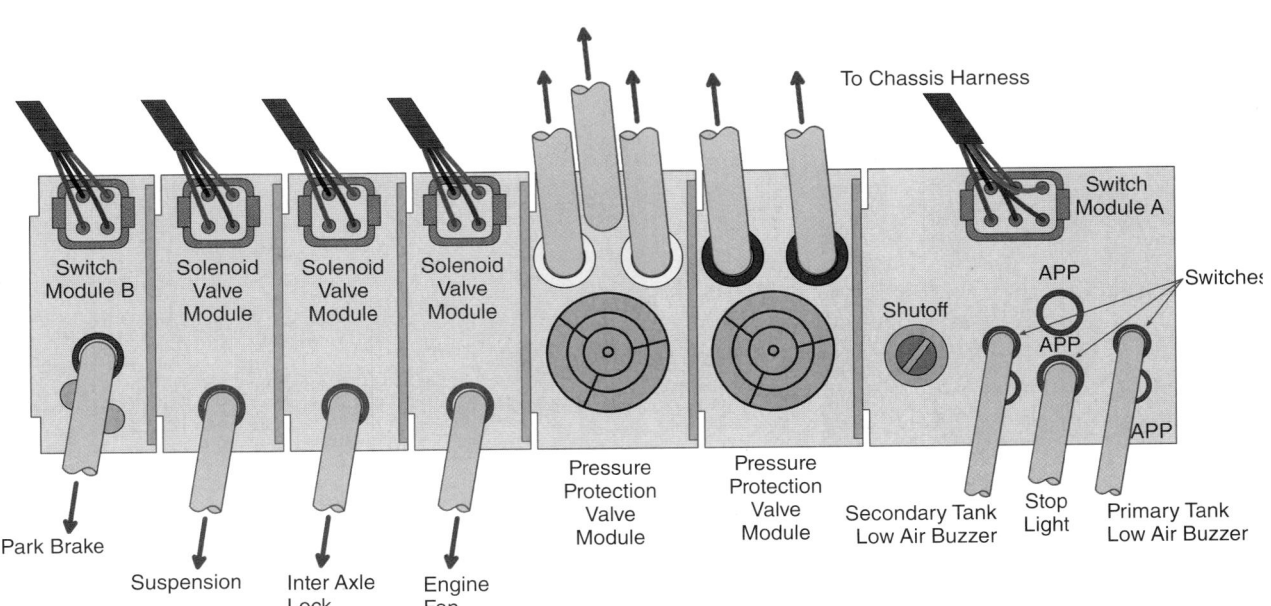

FIGURE 26-40 The air management unit controls air accessories and is a network device.

Navistar's Diamond Logic Electrical System

LO 26-8 Describe Navistar's Diamond logic electrical system.

Navistar's Diamond Logic electrical system uses a single main electrical system controller (ESC) (**FIGURE 26-41**). The ESC is a master control module for one or more modules either inside or outside the cab, called a Remote Power Module (RPM) (**FIGURE 26-42**). The RPM provides connection points for body builders and other electrical system accessories. Communication between the ESC and the RPM takes place over a J-1939 CAN. These remote power modules are supplied network data and can switch multiple outputs up to 30 amps through virtual fuses, each switched using programmable switches in the dash. Expansion switch packs can also be used to add electrically operated accessories (**FIGURE 26-43**). Outputs operating devices, such as lights, hydraulic and air controls, and relays, can be programmed to fit the unique application of the vehicle (**FIGURE 26-44**). RPMs can be daisy chained together to provide access points for multiple electrical accessories.

FIGURE 26-43 Laser-labeled and factory-programmed switches are used in the top row of this Navistar dash. An unprogrammed expansion switch pack is in the bottom row.

FIGURE 26-41 The ESC for this Navistar vocational chassis is located behind the driver's seat.

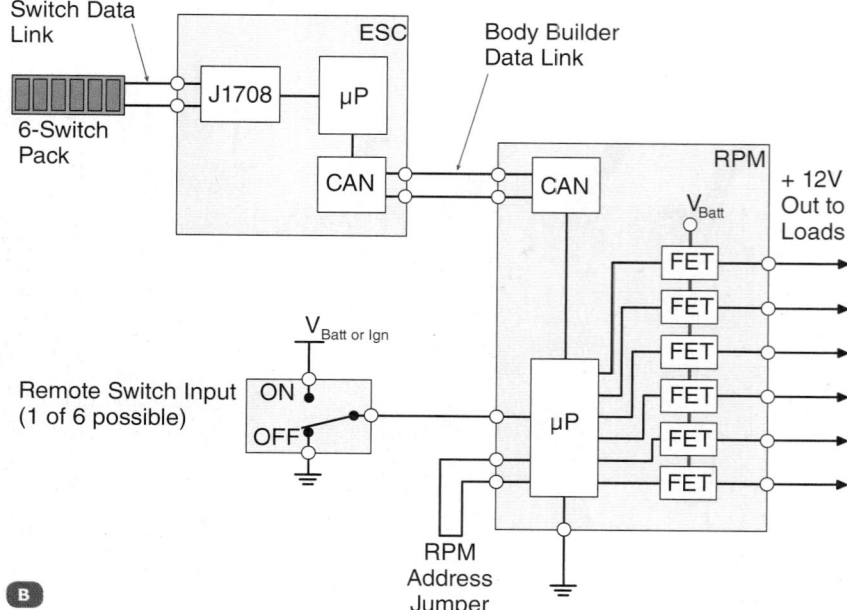

FIGURE 26-42 A. The remote power module controls the electrical outputs for electrical accessories. **B.** Diagram for a remote power module.

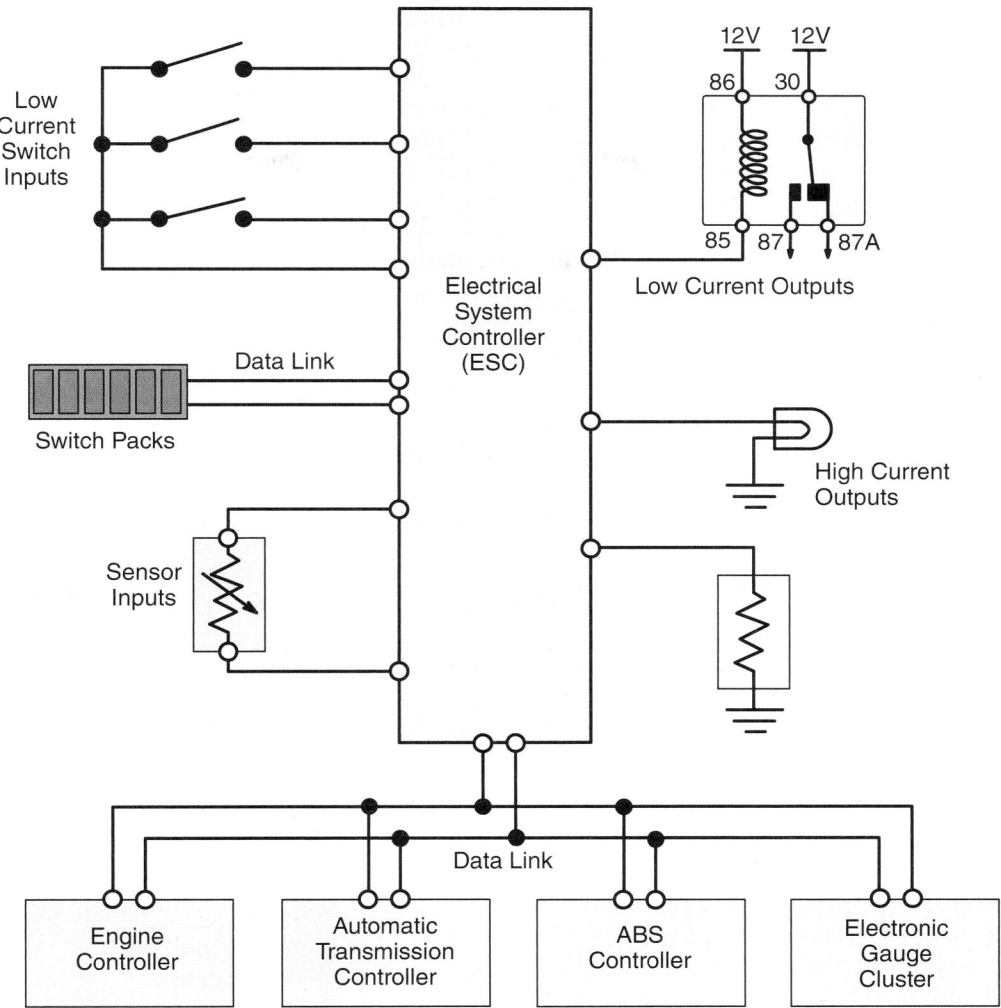

FIGURE 26-44 Navistar's electrical system controllers (ESCs).

Wireless Network Communication

LO 26-9 Identify and explain the operation of wireless network technology.

Cell phone, Internet, and Bluetooth technology are three additional methods of network communication using wireless network interface. A Bluetooth-equipped phone, when recognized and connected by a dedicated network node, will turn down the volume of a radio, and can transmit the call to the entertainment system for hands-free communication. Similarly, many aftermarket consumer devices, such as navigation systems, entertainment devices, security alarms, media players, and pagers, can be connected to the vehicle network with a touch of a button, or even with voice commands. Bluetooth communication technology is used to connect these devices to the networks and supply information for them to operate properly or to enhance functionality. Cell phone technology is also used in system interface. **FIGURE 26-45** shows a telematics technology that continuously

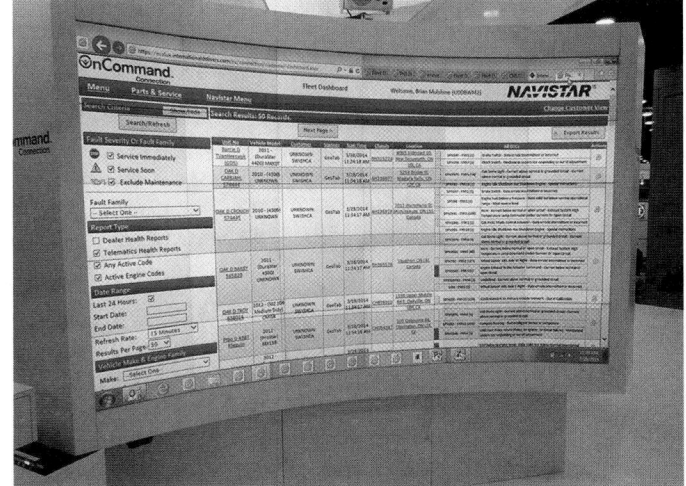

FIGURE 26-45 Navistar's telematics solution for remote fleet monitoring.

transmits network information to a central dispatch where the data is monitored. A CAN-compatible wireless cell phone module or node transmits CAN data, as well as receive and transmit internet signals over the cell phone radio signals (**FIGURE 26-46**).

The vehicle network modules provide features, such as:

- Remote vehicle diagnostics
- Remote door unlocking
- Locating lost or stolen vehicles
- Remote ignition lock-out if the vehicle is stolen
- Remote monitoring of trip reports, including distances, activity, logbook details, speed, fuel consumption, and start and end positions/times
- Navigation around traffic jams
- Real-time positions, speed, status, and activities of a vehicle
- CANbus data acquisition, wired trailer recognition, wireless trailer temperature monitoring, etc.

Bluetooth Technology

Bluetooth is a short-range wireless technology that can automatically connect a device to a network. Cell phones are a common application for Bluetooth technology, used to connect a phone with the audio system using the onboard network. Many vehicles today are equipped or retrofitted with a wireless communication module connected to the data bus of the onboard vehicle network to communicate with Bluetooth and other radio devices, such as key fobs and cell networks. Instead of using wires to communicate with the network, Bluetooth-enabled devices, such as cell phones, use radio frequencies. Communication from the cell phone to network is also multiplexed over a wide number of shifting radio frequencies. Frequency shifting happens much like changing the radio station several times every second, with both the network and the cell phone simultaneously exchanging data on different frequencies. To start a connection, the Bluetooth device sends a signal on a predefined radio frequency, telling the wireless module or node it wants to communicate. The module, in turn, sends back a mathematical formula to the Bluetooth device telling it which frequencies to use and when. Communication can then begin between the wireless **network node** and the Bluetooth device. The communication formula determining which radio frequencies to use and when to use them is constantly updated during the interaction.

Electronic service tools are a type of network communication node. When an electronic service tool connects to the network, it is called a network bridge. The security and dependability of Bluetooth radio signals makes it ideal for bridging onboard networks to android, Apple OS, or PC applications. Most OEM engine manufacturers now have apps enabling technicians and operators to access basic service and diagnostic information from the network (**FIGURES 26-47** and **26-48**).

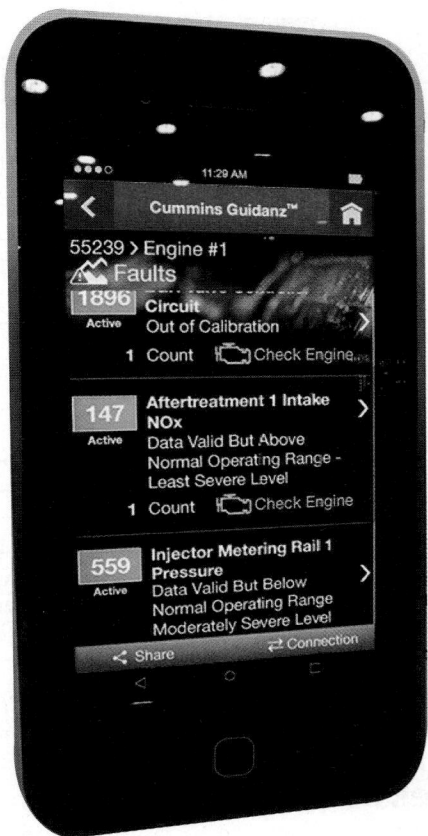

FIGURE 26-47 A Cummins engine app for retrieving fault codes and engine data.

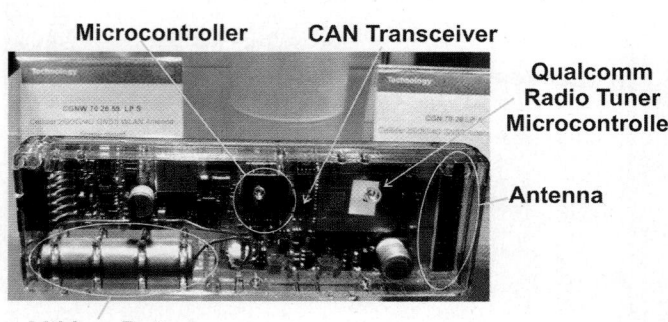

FIGURE 26-46 A wireless communication module connects to the CAN network and will communicate over cell phone or wireless Internet bandwidth.

FIGURE 26-48 This Bluetooth adapter is a wireless network bridge for the Cummins app and any other J-1939 network.

Power Line Carrier (PLC) Communication SAE J2497

LO 26-10 Identify and explain the purpose of programmable logic controller (PLC) network technology.

PLC4TRUCKS is another commonly used multiplex system used to provide a J-1939 connection between the tractor and trailer, primarily to power the in-dash ABS trailer lamp mandated in 2001. PLC is an acronym for power line carrier technology, which enables multiplex communication over constantly powered wires on the J-560 trailer plug. Many more functions can potentially be incorporated into this PLC communication bridge between the tractor and trailer, but few are currently implemented. Network communication, when enabled, takes place over the brown and green (tail light and right turn signal) wires of the J-560 trailer plug. Two modules, called bridges, which are located in the tractor and trailer, are used to enable communication. The system can operate in conventional mode when either a pre-2001 tractor or trailer is connected to one another. When both units are equipped with network bridges, communication can take place between the units in "smart mode." Establishing smart mode is performed automatically—no operator action is required.

PLC Smart Mode Operation

When the ignition key is turned on, the tractor bridge computer starts with J-560 outputs in conventional mode. This means the circuits to the trailer are powered as they would be during traditional operation. The blue, or auxiliary, circuit powers the trailer bridge computer. Subsequently, the trailer bridge computer also starts in conventional mode, but cycles a 5-ohm resistor in and out of the blue circuit at a rate of 20 Hz, producing a 20-Hz, 2.5-amp current pulse on the constant power blue circuit. The 20-Hz pulse causes the tractor bridge to listen for J-1939 communication on the green and brown circuit's tail lamp/right turn signal circuit, and respond to the trailer bridge module.

If the trailer bridge computer receives these messages, it sends an acknowledgment. Both bridges then switch to smart mode. If either bridge fails to receive these messages within a set period of time, the trailer bridge ceases pulsing, and the blue circuit and both bridges return to conventional mode. In smart mode, six of the seven J-560 circuit functions change. Four are used fulltime to power all the lighting circuits, and two are used for J-1939 communication. Both tractor and trailer bridges are responsible for operating the right turn and tail lamp circuits with power from the remaining four circuits, while the green and brown tail and right turn circuits are used for J-1939 communication between the trailer ABS and tractor network. The existing ground circuit remains unchanged.

Electronic Service Tool

LO 26-11 Explain the operating principles of electronic service tools.

Communicating with the onboard network with off-board electronic service tools requires establishing the tool as a network node. This applies to whether the tool is a PC, cell phone, or hand-held code reader connected directly to the DLC. Next, the node needs to establish a connection to the network to enable communication between the tool and other ECUs on the network. This step requires what is called an API, which is an acronym for Application Programming Interface. APIs are software applications that allow two applications to talk to each other. Each time you use an app on a cell phone to retrieve weather information or send a text message, an API is used. A network API connects to the onboard network and sends a request for data to the ECUs. The API then retrieves the requested data, interprets it, and processes the information to make it readable. APIs are used from simple code readers to more elaborate Windows-based PCs (**FIGURES 26-49** and **26-50**).

RP-1210 API

In North America, the most commonly recognized API conforms to a "Recommended Engineering and Maintenance Practice" by the Technology & Maintenance Council (TMC) of the American Trucking Association (ATA) RP-1210. It is a recommended practice that is supported by most commercial trucking companies, OEMs, and suppliers. TMC's open source Recommended Practice RP-1210 API is used by electronic service tools, particularly Windows-based software used on PCs and laptops to establish a network bridge. That means a device using the RP-1210 API bridges the communication pathways between the CAN and electronic service tool. RP-1210 has three

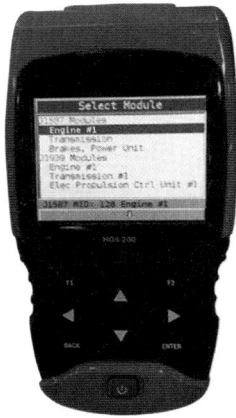

FIGURE 26-49 Service menu of a hand-held scanner for HD commercial vehicles.

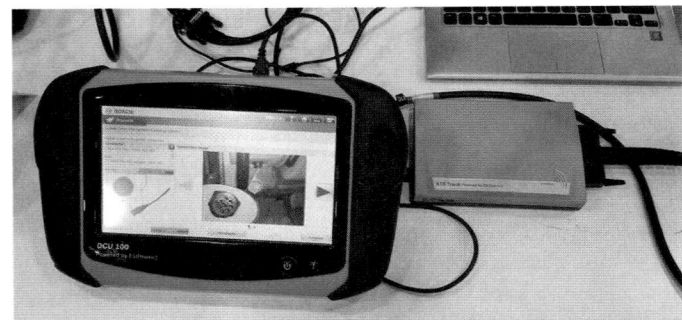

FIGURE 26-50 A more advanced HD vehicle scanner with touch screen and a pass thru programmer to the left of the scanner.

FIGURE 26-51 Serial communication adapters are network bridges using an RP-1210 API to access network communications.

versions: A, B, and C. The latest version RP1210c is compatible with and supports the latest CAN-FD network protocols. Data link or serial communication adapters can communicate primarily with J-1939, J-1708, and other ISO network protocols using RP-1210 drivers (**FIGURE 26-51**). Requests for information, reading of CAN data, and diagnostic routines can be initiated by devices using a network bridge. Binary data from the CAN network is read by the RP-1210 compliant device and converted into hexadecimal format.

CAN DBC Files

A problem any scanner or software has after it receives the hexadecimal network traffic data is interpreting the data. CAN message identifiers and the data they contain need to be translated from a hexadecimal value into a readable format. A file called a data base container (DBC) contains reference information that is used to convert the message identifier and the data accompanying it into a readable format. An example of a hexadecimal coded message is:

0x0CF00400FF FF FF 68 13 FF FF FF

A DBC file can identify the parameter group number, data labels, and data message content to convert this above hexadecimal code into engine speed of 621 rpm.

Standard SAE fault codes and emission-related information can be applied across many vehicles to convert most network data. However, for proprietary CAN messages, such as OEM-specific fault codes that manufacturers are not required to disclose publicly, only the OEM typically have the DBC conversion rules. Tool companies are sometimes allowed to purchase the information but, more often, the OEM software is needed to service and diagnose.

Wrap-Up

Ready for Review

▸ Onboard vehicle networks are formed by connecting vehicle electronic control modules to one another to communicate and exchange information.

▸ Communication takes place between all the modules and devices connected to the network using an electrical signal-processing strategy called multiplexing (MUX).

▸ Onboard networks can be categorized by typology, their physical layer, their network protocol, or by whether they have centralized or distributed control.

▸ Networks are formed based on organizational priorities, with modules grouped by area or function, such as those involved in engine, transmission, ABS, climate control, instrumentation, entertainment devices, or body electrical control.

▸ The type of multiplexing used in onboard networks works by dividing the time available to each network module or device to transmit and listen to information. Only one module is allowed to talk, and all other modules must listen until it is their turn to talk.

▸ Advantages of multiplexing include simplified software control of the electrical system, to enable onboard diagnostics, ease of connecting electronically controlled accessories and features, and reduction in number of sensors.

▸ Controlled area networks are the most widely used type of network for integrating power train operation of all the latest vehicles.

▸ Two different types of CANs used by on-highway trucks, buses, and highway equipment are the SAE network standards of J-1939 and J-1587/1708.

▸ In serial communication, one wire, called CAN-HI, has a more positive voltage than the other, which is CAN-LO. Each wire has a mirror opposite charge of the other when communication takes place.

▸ Wires are twisted to minimize electromagnetic interference caused by magnetic fields and radio waves. To further minimize signal distortion, at each end of the J-1939 CANbus there is a 120-ohm resistor that extinguishes multiplex voltage signals to prevent their reflection through the data bus.

▸ J-1939 CAN 1.0 transmitted data at 125 to 250 kbps, but is now replaced by CAN-FD or CAN 2.0 with more than 500 kbps data rate using much larger messages.

▸ Network signals are distorted and slowed if terminating resistors are missing or defective.

▸ Data carried on the CANbus has several distinct message formats: data frame, remote frame, error frame, and overload frame. Messages sent and received over the network are constructed in frames with a maximum transmission rate of over 500 kbits/sec.

▸ Messages are prioritized to prevent data collision between positive and negative signals canceling one another.

▸ Cell phone and Bluetooth technology are two levels of network communication using wireless network interface.

▸ Disconnecting modules one by one can help identify a module that is shorting out the CANbus, but the best diagnostic routine to identify a network problem is to perform resistance and voltage checks of the CANbus at the DLC.

▶ RP-1210 is a recommended practice for an application programming interface (API) to bridge an electronic service tool with an onboard network.

Key Terms

bit arbitration The process of deciding which messages have priority to transmit over the network to prevent data collision between positive and negative signals canceling one another.

bidirectional communication Two-way multiplex communication. A communication channel between an electronic service tool and vehicle network where commands are sent and data received by the service tool.

Bluetooth A short-range wireless technology that can automatically connect a device into a network.

controlled area network (CAN) A distributed network control system in which several control modules exert varying degrees of control over common chassis electrical components.

data bus The typology forming the communication pathway of electronic control modules in a network.

differential mode transmission A digital signal transmission technology in which network modules detect the voltage difference between two wires to determine if a signal is a 1 or a 0.

field effect transistor (FET) A unipolar transistor that uses an electric field to control the conductivity of a semiconductor material.

gateway module A module that translates communication protocols to enable inter-network communication between different networks operating on-board a vehicle.

Multiplexing (MUX) Transmission of more than one electrical signal or message that takes place over a single wire or pair of wires.

network node A point on a network.

onboard diagnostics (OBD) Self-diagnostic capabilities of electronic control modules that allow them to evaluate voltage and current levels of circuits to which they are connected and determine if data is in the correct operational range.

serial communication Communication using zeroes and ones to transmit data in a series, one bit after another in sequence.

serial data Pieces of data sent by the master module.

time division multiplexing (TDM) A type of multiplexing used in onboard networks and that works by dividing the time communication available to each network module or device.

typology Refers to the arrangement of communication pathways between electrical control units.

Review Questions

1. What terminals of the 9-pin diagnostic connector are connected to a digital multimeter (DMM) to check the resistance of the terminating resistors used for the CANbus?
   a. A and B
   b. 14 and 16
   c. C and D
   d. 3 and 4

2. Which communication strategy enables network ECUs to share information without causing message transmissions to collide and interfere?
   a. Networking
   b. Multiplexing
   c. Communication
   d. Linking

3. The rules or standards used to communicate over the networks are called:
   a. network protocol.
   b. typology.
   c. physical protocol.
   d. CAN (controller area network).

4. Electronic control modules can easily evaluate the voltage and current levels of circuits to which they are connected and determine whether the data makes sense and is in the correct operational range. These self-diagnostic capabilities are referred to as?
   a. CAN (controller area network)
   b. OBD (onboard diagnostics)
   c. Network protocol
   d. Typology

5. What format of digital communication is sent and received by control system modules to transmit information over the CAN?
   a. Scan tool
   b. Multiplexing
   c. Serial data
   d. Parallel data

6. When a twisted pair of wires is connected in parallel to all modules in the network, the typology forming the communication pathway is called a:
   a. bus.
   b. network.
   c. system.
   d. circuit.

7. What communication method requires the modules and other devices to take turns, sharing the data bus communication pathway?
   a. Data sharing
   b. Time division multiplexing
   c. Network
   d. Circuit

8. Which of the following connectors do technicians use to access the onboard network on the latest model trucks?
   a. 6-pin diagnostic connector
   b. 16-pin DLC (data link connector)
   c. 9-pin black-colored diagnostic connector
   d. 9-pin green-colored diagnostic connector

9. All electronically controlled engines and power train components have built-in self-diagnostic capabilities. To communicate this data to an electronic service tool from even a single module requires the use of:
   a. bidirectional communications.
   b. factory scan tool.
   c. direct communication.
   d. personal computer.

10. What format is network traffic converted into by communication adapters?
    a. Decimal
    b. Hexadecimal
    c. Binary
    d. Windows-based

ASE Technician A/Technician B Style Questions

1. Two technicians are discussing checking the voltage at the 9-pin diagnostic connector or datalink connector (DLC). Technician A says that voltage is checked with the ignition on at terminals C and D. Technician B says that the voltage at terminals C and D should be 12.6 volts. Who is correct?
    a. Technician A
    b. Technician B
    c. Both Technician A and Technician B
    d. Neither Technician A nor Technician B

2. Technician A says that a CAN is required on all commercial vehicles to reduce the amount of wiring. Technician B says that the CAN is required by emission legislation. Who is correct?
    a. Technician A
    b. Technician B
    c. Both Technician A and Technician B
    d. Neither Technician A nor Technician B

3. Technician A and B are discussing a method to determine whether an ABS module on a late-model bus is defective.

Technician A says that exchanging the suspect module with a new module sitting on the parts department shelf would be the best idea. Technician B says that it's a better idea to exchange it with a working one from another bus. Who is correct?
    a. Technician A
    b. Technician B
    c. Both Technician A and Technician B
    d. Neither Technician A nor Technician B

4. Two technicians are discussing truck serial data communication. Technician A says that trucks using the J1939 SAE standard establish a connection between the tractor and trailer, to power the in-dash ABS trailer lamp using power line carrier (PLC) technology. Technician B says that the PLC system can illuminate a tractor ABS light only when connected to a 2001 or later tractor or trailer. Who is correct?
    a. Technician A
    b. Technician B
    c. Both Technician A and Technician B
    d. Neither Technician A nor Technician B

5. Technician A says the black-colored 9-pin plug on the hand-held scanner cannot connect to the green-colored 9-pin DLC connector in the cab. Technician B says that the scanner probably will not work anyway, even if the cable did connect to the DLC. Who is correct?
    a. Technician A
    b. Technician B
    c. Both Technician A and Technician B
    d. Neither Technician A nor Technician B

6. Two technicians are discussing truck serial data communication and networks. Technician A says that the engine ECM is the master control module on most truck and bus onboard networks and that all communication from the vehicle's ECUs is coordinated by the ECM. Technician B says that a network control module coordinates the activity of ECUs on a CAN. Who is correct?
   a. Technician A
   b. Technician B
   c. Both Technician A and Technician B
   d. Neither Technician A nor Technician B

7. Technician A says a J-1939 CAN data bus uses a green and yellow wire twisted together plus a shielding foil wrapped on the outside of the wires. Technician B says that CAN networks never use shielding foil to minimize EMI interference with CAN signals. Who is correct?
   a. Technician A
   b. Technician B
   c. Both Technician A and Technician B
   d. Neither Technician A nor Technician B

8. Technician A says serial data on CANs is made up of binary digits of 0s and 1s. Technician B says that fault codes messages are transmitted in hexadecimal code over the network. Who is correct?
   a. Technician A
   b. Technician B
   c. Both Technician A and Technician B
   d. Neither Technician A nor Technician B

9. Two technicians are describing the use of electronic service tools. Technician A says that fault codes, communication language, and other features of the onboard network are standardized by EPA legislation. Technician B says that only the truck manufacturer's specific scan tool or software can read the legislated fault codes. Who is correct?
   a. Technician A
   b. Technician B
   c. Both Technician A and Technician B
   d. Neither Technician A nor Technician B

10. Technician A says that WiFi and telematic data is transmitted by a radio node on the CAN. Technician B says that a cell phone and router need to be connected to the network to transmit network data. Who is correct?
   a. Technician A
   b. Technician B
   c. Both Technician A and Technician B
   d. Neither Technician A nor Technician B

CAUTION

HEAT TREATED
ALLOY. DO NOT
WELD TO RAIL
OR DRILL
FLANGES.
CRACKS MAY
RESULT

SECTION 3
Suspension, Steering, and Brakes

CHAPTER 27   Commercial Vehicle Tires

CHAPTER 28   Wheel Rims and Hubs

CHAPTER 29   Front Axles and Vehicle Alignment Factors

CHAPTER 30   Truck Frames

CHAPTER 31   Suspension Systems

CHAPTER 32   Steering Systems and Integral Steering Gears

CHAPTER 33   Braking Fundamentals and Air Brake Foundations

CHAPTER 34   Air Brake Circuits and Valves

CHAPTER 35   Servicing Air Brake Air Systems

CHAPTER 36   Servicing Air Brake Foundation and Parking Brake Systems

CHAPTER 37   Antilock Braking, Vehicle Stability, and Collision Avoidance Systems

CHAPTER 38   Fundamentals of Hydraulic and Air-Over-Hydraulic Braking Systems

CHAPTER 39   Fifth Wheels and Hitching Devices

Courtesy of Bridgestone Corporation

CHAPTER 27

Commercial Vehicle Tires

Learning Objectives

After reading this chapter, you will be able to:

- **LO 27-1** Explain the purpose and function of commercial vehicle tires.
- **LO 27-2** Identify and explain the hazards associated with tire service and maintenance.
- **LO 27-3** Identify and describe the different classifications of commercial vehicle tires.
- **LO 27-4** Identify and explain tire identification and sizing terminology.
- **LO 27-5** Identify and describe tire construction features and their purpose in radial tubeless tires.

- **LO 27-6** Identify and explain tire inflation factors.
- **LO 27-7** Explain the purpose and operation of TPMS.
- **LO 27-8** Identify and outline common service procedures associated with tire service and maintenance.
- **LO 27-9** Outline procedures to inspect the wheel assembly for air loss.

You Are the Technician

While working at a truck lease operation you notice there is an increase in tire-related maintenance costs. There is an above-average replacement of tires for conditions, such as cupping on one side of the tire, the tread depth varying around the tires, and irregular tire wear. As you investigate possible causes, you examine the tire inspection preventive maintenance (PM) program. Tires are regularly checked for the correct inflation pressure at least once a month and the tires are rotated per manufacturer's recommendations. However, there are a variety of complaints that are even more frequently made that could be tire-related. Drivers are complaining of a steering wheel shimmy from side to side, tramping noise, and general vibration at highway speeds. As you consider the mounting costs of both tire replacement and labor spent diagnosing vibration complaints, you are considering adding more inspection items to the PM inspection related to tires. Include answers to the following in your recomendations.

1. What inspection procedures would you consider adding to a general PM inspection for the tires? Justify your recommendation.
2. The wheels of the lease vehicles are regularly removed to inspect brake shoe wear, brake pads, calipers, hardware, and so on. How might this inspection program contribute to accelerated complaints related to tire vibration?
3. How might installation procedures of wheel rims affect the balance of wheel and tire assemblies?

Introduction

Tires are a major component of what the trucking industry calls the wheel end. Together with hubs and rims, tires have the job of safely supporting the vehicle weight over a wide range of speed, load, and road conditions. The importance of tires alone to operating costs and maintenance practices is highlighted by studies showing tires are the second highest fleet operating costs after fuel. As **TABLE 27-1** shows, tires are also the most common reason for breakdowns on the road, and they rank second in terms of mechanical defects related to accidents. It is easy to understand the importance of competently maintaining and servicing tires from an economic perspective.

Preventing tire failures and minimizing tire wear can save considerable expense from downtime and roadside repair. The percentage of avoidable mishaps involving tires is detailed further in Bendix's reasons for recommending tire pressure monitoring systems (TPMS). Bendix data indicates that:

- Only 44% of all truck tires are within 5 psi of their target inflation.
- 90% of all tire failures are a result of tire underinflation.

The tire wheel rim and hub make-up the vehicle wheel end.

- 20% underinflation reduces tire carcass life by 30%.
- 20% underinflation reduces tread life by 25%.
- 20% underinflation reduces fuel mileage by 2%.

In addition, proper maintenance of tires is critical for safety. Statistical data demonstrates that, at the worst, one in 1000 serious accidents results in a death. If an accident involves a tire or wheel separation, that rate increases to one in 10 accidents resulting in a fatality. Liability for proper tire and wheel maintenance in many jurisdictions is the responsibility of maintenance technicians. Canadian provinces fine truck fleets up to $50,000 for each wheel separation occurrence.

Because of the wide variety of tasks vehicles are expected to perform, there are enormous variations in tire technology that technicians need to properly understand in order to promote lower operating costs, increase vehicle reliability, safety, and extend tire service life.

Fundamentals of Commercial Vehicle Tires

LO 27-1 Explain the purpose and function of commercial vehicle tires.

Understanding tires used on heavy-duty commercial vehicles begins with understanding the differences between heavy-duty tires and those used on light-duty vehicles. A good starting point for technicians is to understand the functions of tires.

Commercial Tire Principles

Two major differences exist between larger commercial vehicle tires and light-duty tires. Commercial vehicle tires contain larger air volume and produce a larger **contact patch** with the road. The larger air volume contained in heavy-vehicle tires means

TABLE 27-1 Ranking of Reasons for Roadside Service Calls

Reason for Service Call	Percentage of All Service Calls
Tires	51.3%
Jump or pull start	7.6%
Air line or hose	4.7%
Alternator	4.1%
Wiring	3.9%
Fuel filter	3.7%
Fuel	3.5%
Brakes	2.4%
All other issues	Less than 1%

Source: www.Truckinfo.net/trucking/stats.htm

that a tire can support more weight with the same (or even less) tire pressure compared to other types of tires. Also, the larger road contact patch of a truck tire, of perhaps 80 square inches (203 cm²), means less power is transmitted through each unit of contact area. Commercial truck tire construction is different than, for example, a motorcycle tire, which concentrates more weight per unit of contact patch area and transmits more torque through each unit of area in contact with the road. **FIGURE 27-1** shows the power per unit of contact pressure for different applications of tires.

A larger air volume and bigger contact patch with the road are the two major differences explaining why truck tires typically last much longer than tires on cars and motorcycles—even while carrying more weight and transmitting more power either through engine or brake torque.

Tire Functions

Tires have four basic functions, listed here and illustrated in **FIGURE 27-2**:

- Supporting the vehicle load
- Transmitting braking and traction forces to the road surface
- Absorbing road shocks
- Providing directional control of the vehicle.

As depicted in **FIGURE 27-3**, trapped air volume within the tire acts as a cushion to support the vehicle load and absorbs road shock. **FIGURE 27-4** shows that the larger air volume contained in tires used by commercial vehicles supports more weight with less tire pressure compared to other types of tires.

A wide variety of tires are made to provide unique operational features for specific vehicle applications. For example, tires for on-highway trucks carrying heavy loads are different, depending on whether they are used on a steering axle, drive axle,

or even trailer axles, where tires are pulled rather than steered and transmit no drive torque. The type of road surface, loading factors, fuel economy requirements, driving speed, ride characteristics, and even weight legislation are also factors influencing tire selection and design. However, the most significant factor

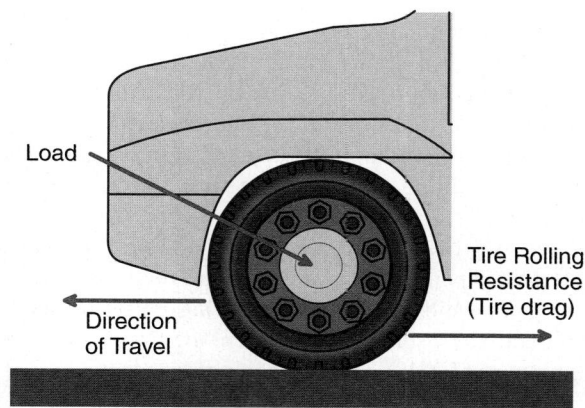

FIGURE 27-2 Tires support the vehicle load, transmit braking and traction forces to the road surface, absorb road shock, and provide directional control of the vehicle.

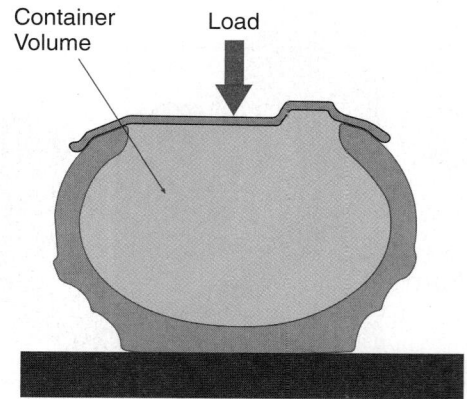

FIGURE 27-3 Trapped air volume supports the load and absorbs road shock.

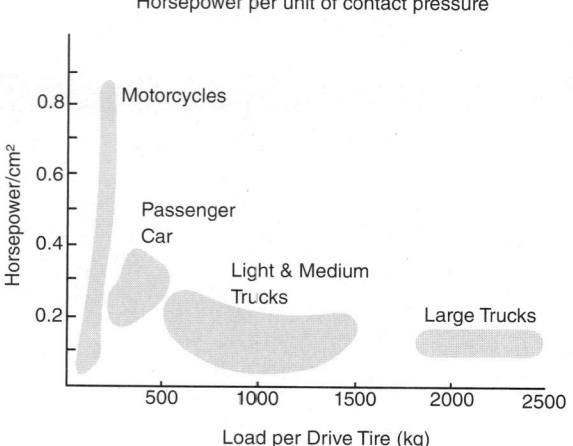

FIGURE 27-1 Horsepower per centimeter versus load per drive tire. The larger contact patch area of a truck tire means less power is transmitted through each unit of contact area.

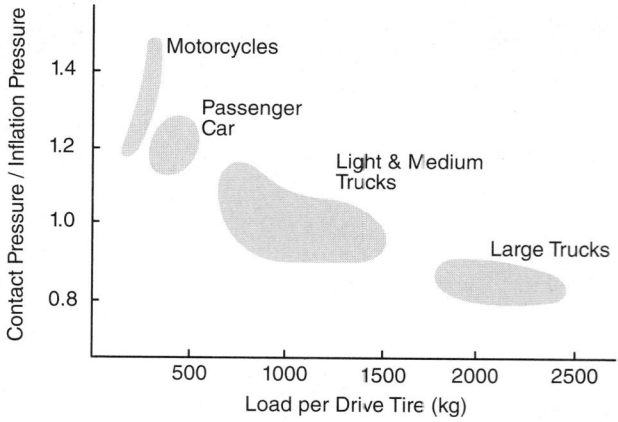

FIGURE 27-4 Load on driving tires compared to the ratio of contact pressure to inflation pressure.

influencing tire design is the axle where the tire is mounted. As shown in **FIGURE 27-5**, the three basic positions are:

- Steering
- Drive
- Trailer

Tires at each position experience different rolling resistances. As illustrated in **FIGURE 27-6**, a tire under load is not perfectly round. In fact, it is quite flat at the bottom where the tire tread is in contact with the road surface. As a result, the tire is said to have **rolling resistance**, which means it resists rolling naturally. The greatest rolling resistance is encountered by tires carrying the greater proportion of vehicle weight. This means more wear is expected on tires as vehicle weight increases.

Tire Service Safety

LO 27-2 Identify and explain the hazards associated with tire service and maintenance.

OSHA has a safety standard for tube- and tubeless-type tires, as well as for installing multipiece tire rims. Employers are obligated by law to properly train all employees working with tires

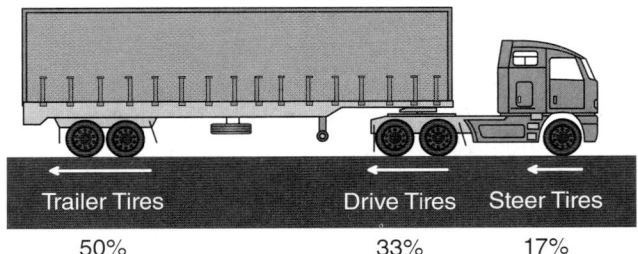

FIGURE 27-5 Rolling resistances by tire position.

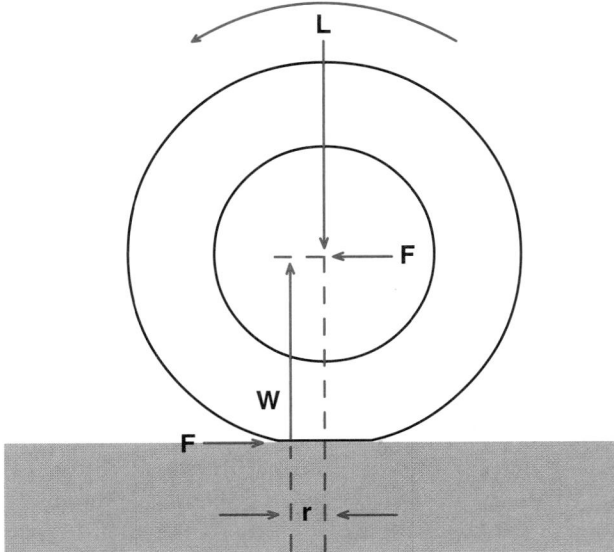

FIGURE 27-6 Tire rolling resistance.

in safe tire inflation procedures before they begin working with tires. This includes making sure both workers and equipment reliably adhere to safety standards.

Inflated tires contain an enormous amount of stored energy. The sidewall of a typical commercial vehicle tire inflated to 100 psi (689 kPa) has over 34 tons (31 metric tons) of force acting on it. Tires are designed to safely contain this potential force. When tires are damaged, operated even for brief times when flat, or underinflated, however, they can pose a serious safety threat.

Force from exploding tires is typically released at an angle of up to 45 degrees from the rupture. That produces a destructive blast of compressed air accompanied with a shower of high-speed particles and parts. **FIGURE 27-7** shows the direction of the explosion paths for a tire depending on how it is positioned. An unrestrained wheel with a tire failure can fly as much as 66' (20 m) through the air, striking any bystander with lethal force. Failures of multi-piece or split rim tires have caused numerous technician fatalities.

The potential for lethal or serious injuries when working with tires cannot be overstated. Tire work should only be carried out by technicians trained in tire safety and service procedures prior to working with tires. Common hazards associated with tire work include hazards related to deflating, inflating, lifting, and moving tires.

Compressed air and debris can be released when deflating tires. Air escaping from tires while being deflated is under high pressure and releases a jet of air that can inflict serious injury by propelling dirt and debris at high speed.

While inflating tires, there is a risk of exploding tire debris and parts. Compressed air in inflated tires can explode with tremendous force. Explosion or separation of multi-piece wheel rims can occur when misassembled, damaged, or deteriorated rim and wheel assemblies fail to restrain the force of the compressed air. To avoid accidents when inflating tires, always use a safety cage and a remote clip-on style air hose with an accurate pressure regulator. Securing a commercial tire during inflation can be done with a horizontal restraint or a vertical safety cage while maintaining the safe operating perimeter (**FIGURE 27-8**). As shown in all three illustrations, no one should enter the area of potential trajectory when tires are being inflated.

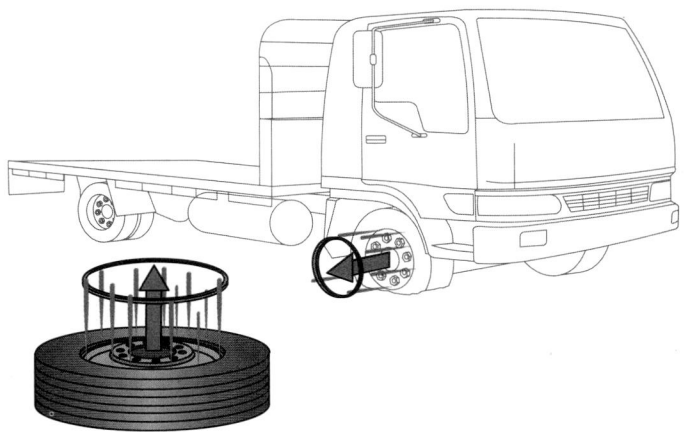

FIGURE 27-7 Explosion paths.

FIGURE 27-8 Tire cage used to safely inflate tires.

Unfortunately, the use of tire cages has declined in recent years due to the elimination of multi-piece or split rims, and the use of radial tires. Radial tires, however, are not indestructible, and defects can lead to tires disintegrating with explosive force. Safety cages should still be used, even for these tires. Always inflate tires with a clip-on chuck having an inline tire pressure gauge that enables technicians to remotely monitor tire pressure. Also, initially inflate tires to only 20 psi (138 kPa) to check for leaks and bead sealing.

Weight of the tire and rim assembly also poses a safety risk to the technician. Commercial vehicle tires and rim assemblies are very heavy and require proper lifting techniques. Finally, improper or inadequate inspection procedures and installation procedures causing wheels to separate from a vehicle are additional hazards resulting from the absence of comprehensive technician training associated with tires and wheel rims.

Tire Arrangements

Wheel and tire combinations used on heavy-duty vehicles must comply with government regulations. The reason for the regulations is that, when wheels and tires are used in an incorrect arrangement, a vehicle can become unstable in certain road conditions. Regulations state that radial tires and bias-ply tires should never be used on the same axle because of the tires' different handling characteristics.

Ideally, the tires on the same axle should be of the same brand and tread pattern. This is important because the handling characteristics between tire brands vary due to different construction techniques and materials each manufacturer uses. Having different tread patterns between tires even with the same dimensions on the same axle causing instability under certain road conditions. **FIGURE 27-9** shows correct and incorrect combinations.

Classifications of Commercial Vehicle Tires

LO 27-3 Identify and describe the different classifications of commercial vehicle tires.

Commercial vehicle tires come in two basic types—tube or tubeless. Tube tires cost much less and are much easier to repair, but in North America, no tube-type tires have been produced for years. However, many container-type trailers and vehicles in developing countries commonly use inner tubes in tires. The following discussion is necessary to address the prevalence of tube-type tires still used.

Comparing Tubeless and Tube-Type Tires

Commercial vehicle tires are either tube or tubeless, with tubeless tires by far the most common and practical to use. What differentiates the two types of tires is how the air is sealed inside the tire. If the air is sealed inside using an inner tube separate from the tire casing, the tire is a **tube-type tire**. If the air is not sealed in an inner tube, the tire is a **tubeless tire**.

Tube and tubeless tires use similar construction with one major exception. On a tubeless tire, a liner of rubber is applied to the inside of the tire to create an air-tight seal with the casing. This, and some other construction differences, enables tube tires to weigh comparatively less. Different wheel rim configurations are also used with each type of tire. As illustrated in **FIGURE 27-10**, tubeless tires use a single-piece, **drop-center wheel rim**, also called a semi-drop center, which is a type of wheel rim that has a deep channel in the rim center with a diameter smaller than the rim diameter. The dropped rim center is used to ease tire installation by allowing one side of the tire bead to be placed into this dropped center channel so that the tire can slide over the rim enough to allow the opposite side of the tire to slip over the rim edge. (Wheel rims are covered in greater detail in the chapter Wheel Rims and Hubs.) Tube-type tires use a multi-piece, flat-wheel rim assembly, such as the one depicted in **FIGURE 27-11**. Stiff sidewalls of bias ply tires make it difficult to pull a tire over a drop center rim and require a flat-base rim with one or two side-split rings to lock the tire onto the rim. Tube-type tires also require a **tire flap**. This piece of rubber wraps around the rim to protect the inner tube from chafing, pinching, and cracking caused by friction between the valve stem slot in the rim and the edges of the tire bead.

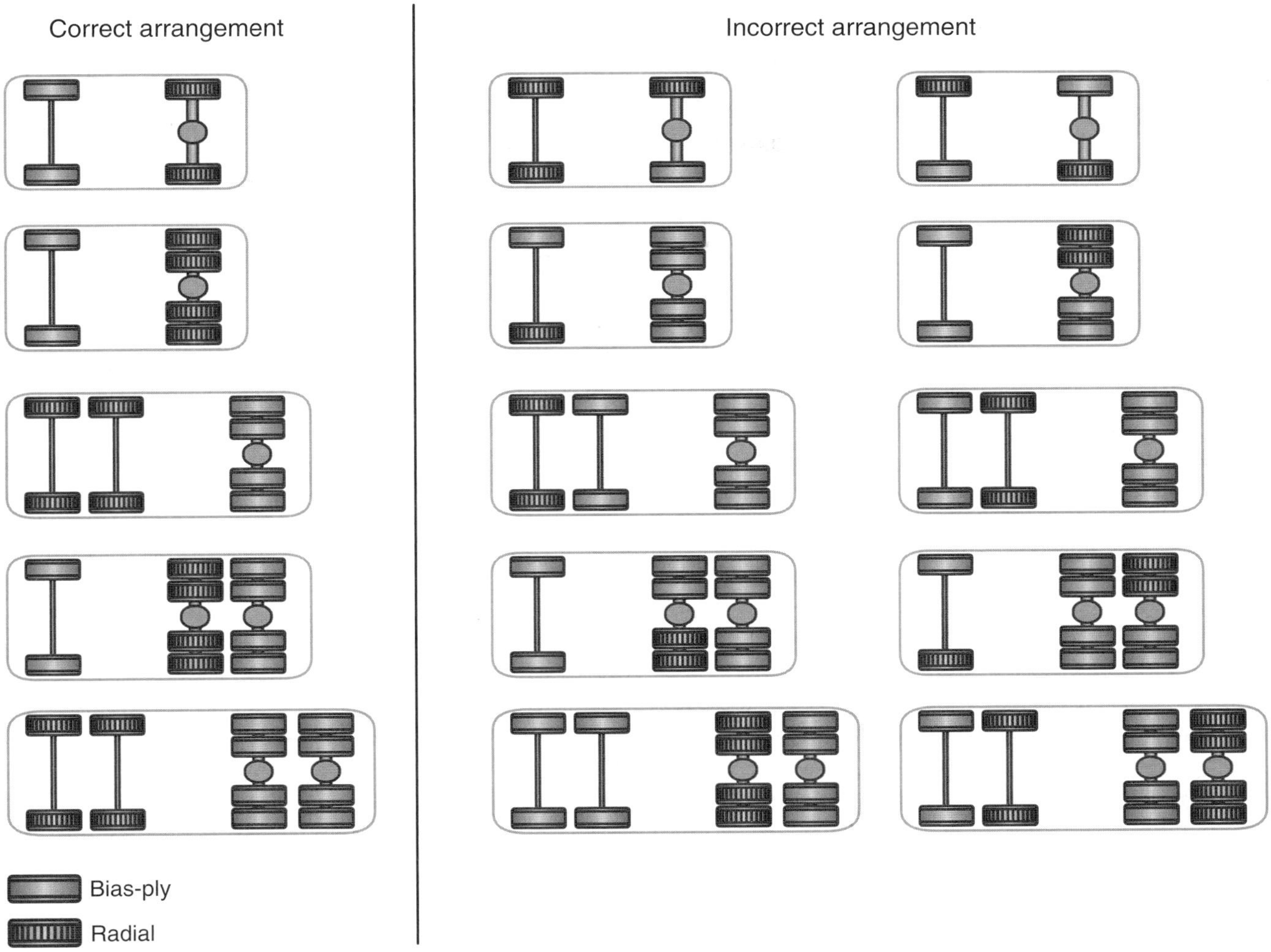

Correct arrangement   Incorrect arrangement

Bias-ply

Radial

FIGURE 27-9 Correct and incorrect tire arrangements.

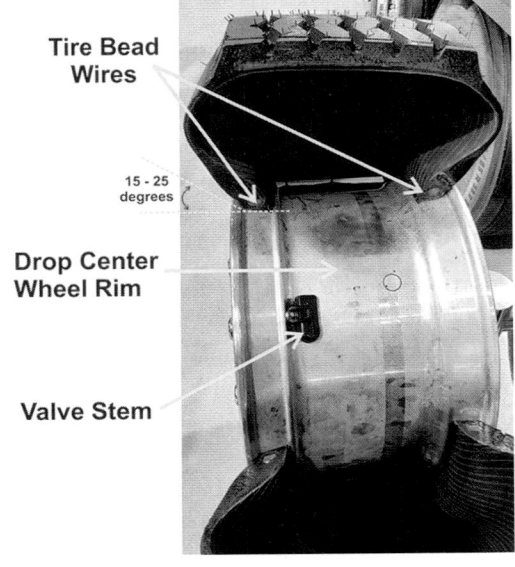

FIGURE 27-10 Tubeless tires seal air inside the tire using a tire bead to rim seal. The configuration is much simpler compared to tube tires.

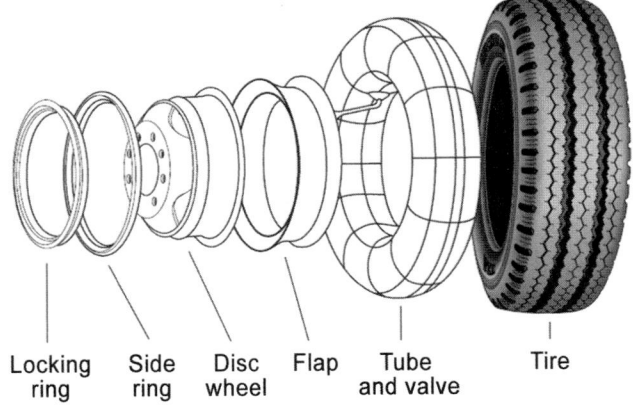

Locking ring | Side ring | Disc wheel | Flap | Tube and valve | Tire

FIGURE 27-11 Tube-type tires use multi-piece rims and need a flap to prevent chafing of the tube against the wheel.

The **tire bead** is the inner circumference of the tire sidewall and is the part of the tire that centers the tire contact onto the rim.

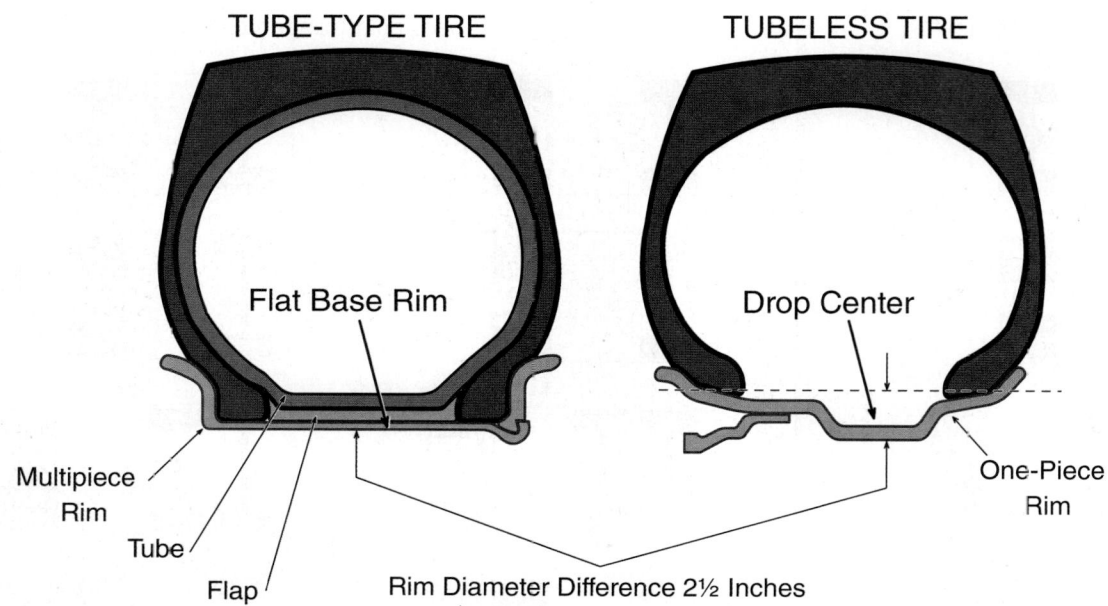

FIGURE 27-12 Tube-type tires compared to tubeless tires.

FIGURE 27-12 provides a side-by-side comparison of tube-type and tubeless tires. Note the multi-piece rim and requirement for a flap in a tube-type tire and the flat rim base. Additionally, tire sidewall height and width are smaller in the tubeless tire.

When compared using equivalent sizes, both types of tires can support the same loads at the same inflation pressure. Tubeless tires are the most commonly used because they have several advantages. These include:

- A lighter tire and wheel rim assembly.
- Fewer flats caused by tire punctures.
- Greater tire bead durability is achieved through reduced heat transfer from hot brake drums using tubeless tires and rims.
- Reduced internal tire friction results in lower tire temperatures, thus improving tire life.
- Better lateral stability due to a reduced sidewall height compared to identically sized tube-type tires.
- The use of an uncomplicated single-piece wheel rim in comparison to multi-piece rims used for tube-type tires.

This last advantage plays a key role in tire safety. Fewer parts and reduced hazards due to mismatched rim components are benefits with tubeless tires. Tube-type tires use multiple-piece split rims to enable the installation of the tire over the wheel rim. Two- and three-piece styles are most common. Split rim components are not interchangeable and must be carefully matched together (**match mounting**). Mismatching components can cause the locking split-ring to separate from the wheel with explosive lethal force. **FIGURE 27-13** shows two- and three-piece rim configurations.

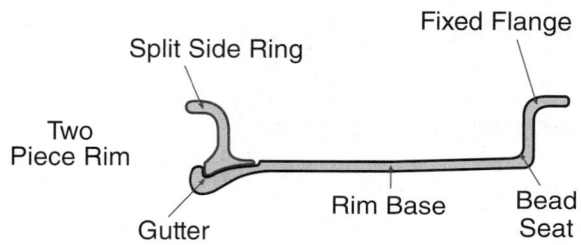

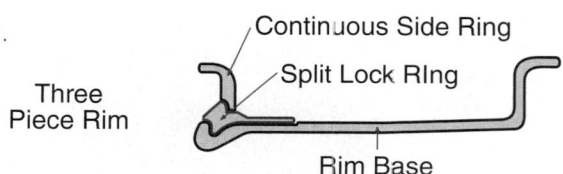

FIGURE 27-13 Two- and three-piece split rim configurations for tube-type tires.

Tire Identification and Sizing

LO 27-4 Identify and explain tire identification and sizing terminology.

Several dimensions are important in tire sizing. The **overall diameter** is the diameter of an inflated tire at the outermost surface of the tread. The **nominal diameter** is a size code figure for reference purposes only, as indicated in the tire and rim size designation. **Section width** is the distance between the outside of the sidewalls on an inflated tire without any load on it, and **section height** is simply the height of the sidewalls.

Standard Aspect Tires

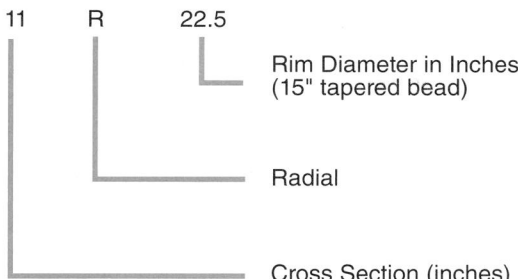

11   R   22.5

Rim Diameter in Inches
(15" tapered bead)

Radial

Cross Section (inches)

Low Profile Tires

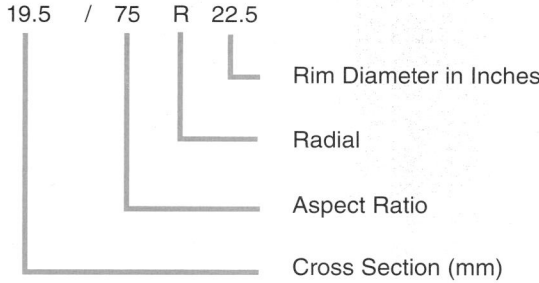

19.5   /   75   R   22.5

Rim Diameter in Inches

Radial

Aspect Ratio

Cross Section (mm)

FIGURE 27-14 The system for designating tire size.

Static radius is the distance from the tire center to ground level. Measurements are checked on fitted tires inflated to the specified tire pressure. **Rolling circumference** is the distance covered by one revolution of the tire.

Most truck tire sizes are indicated by the section width and diameter, either in inches or millimeters, followed by R for radial, followed by the rim or wheel diameter in inches. As illustrated in **FIGURE 27-14**, the placement of each number and digit corresponds to specific information about the tire. For example, a designation of 11R 22.5 indicates that this tire is 11" (26.5 cm) across, from the widest point of its outer sidewall to the widest point of its inner sidewall, when mounted and measured on a specified width wheel. This is sometimes called the cross section of the tire or, as mentioned above, this measurement is referred to as the tire's section width. The R designates a radial tire while the 22.5 refers to the rim diameter on which the tire is mounted. In this case, that is 22.5" (57.2 cm).

Tire sizes and other important data are molded into the sidewalls of tires, as shown on the tire in **FIGURE 27-15**. **FIGURE 27-16** illustrates the standard tire identification markings on a new tire and provides a legend for what each marking signifies.

TABLE 27-2 shows the marking system mandated by the U.S. Department of Transportation (DOT) for new tires, and **TABLE 27-3** shows the same for retreaded tires.

The most important markings of those illustrated in Figure 27-16 are 295/75 R 22.5 tubeless. These letters and numbers indicate the following:

- 295 = tire width in mm
- 75 = cross-sectional ratio H:W in percent
- R = radial design
- 22.5 = nominal rim diameter of a 15-degree tapered rim (code)
- Tubeless = tubeless tire type
- Other legal and standardized markings used on the tire sidewall:
  - 156 = 8819 lb (4000 kg) tire load capacity S (single tire configuration)
  - 150 = 7386 lb (3350 kg) tire load capacity D (dual tire configuration)

Hand Holes

Drop Center

FIGURE 27-15 The tire diameter, width, and aspect ratio are molded into this tire's sidewall.

- L = acceptable speed of 75 mph (120 km/h)
- M = acceptable speed of 81 mph (130 km/h)

Note that the tire load capacity may be given as two numbers: 150/156. The smaller number is for dual tires, which may be unexpected, but dual tires carry less load since they cannot release heat as quickly as a single tire. Closely spaced dual tires do not allow the sidewalls to radiate as much heat as a single tire on a wheel end can.

Tire Aspect Ratio

Determining a tire profile begins by determining the aspect ratio for the tire. The **aspect ratio** refers to a comparison between the height of the sidewall (section height) to the section width expressed as a percentage. Aspect ratio is calculated by dividing the section height by the section width. The lower a tire's aspect ratio, the wider the tire becomes in relation to the height of the sidewall. For example, a tire with a section width of 11" (265 mm) and an aspect ratio of 80% has a sidewall height of 8.8" (212 mm). The same tire with an aspect ratio of 75% has a sidewall height of 8.25" (209 mm).

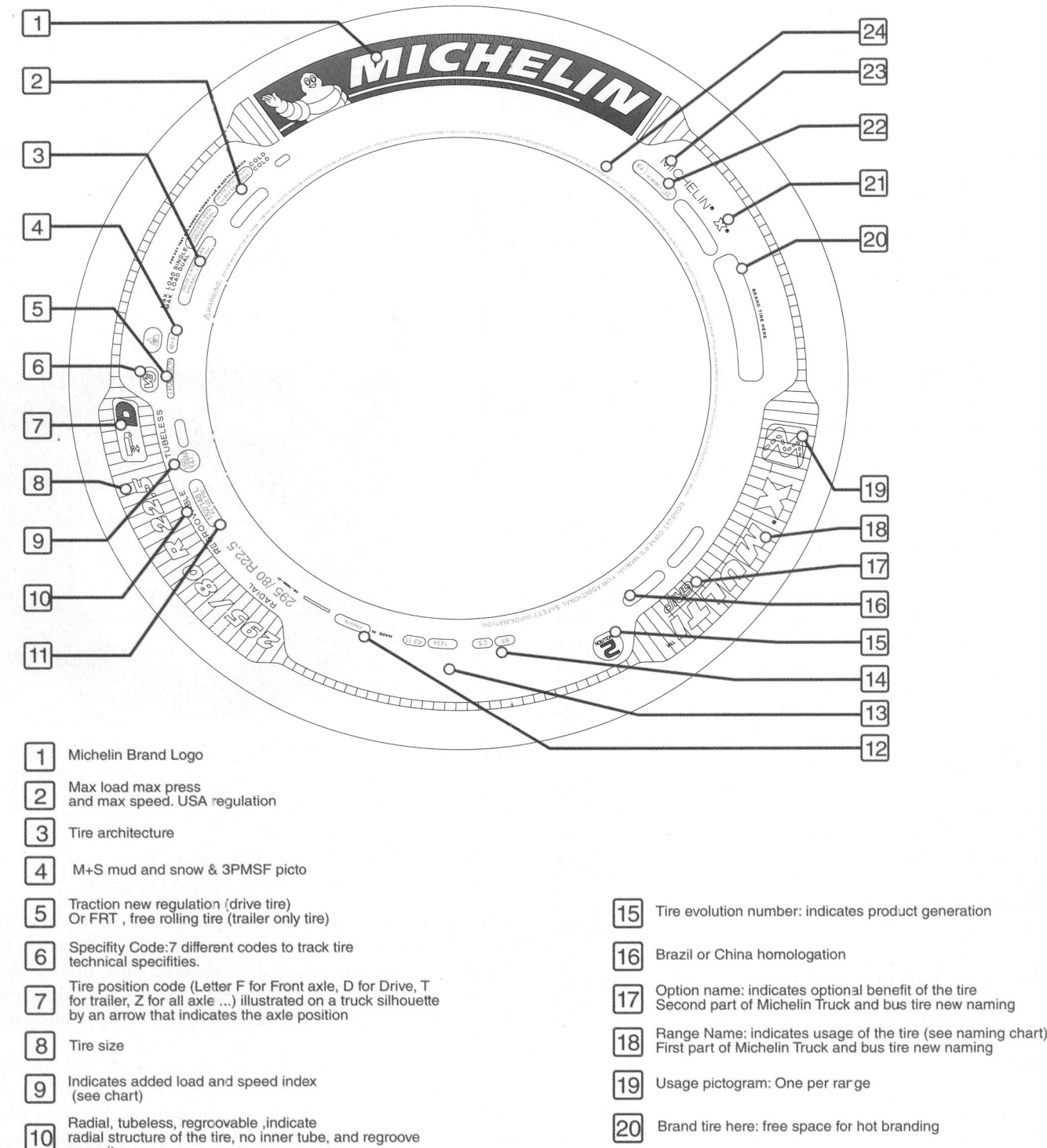

1   Michelin Brand Logo

2   Max load max press
    and max speed. USA regulation

3   Tire architecture

4   M+S mud and snow & 3PMSF picto

5   Traction new regulation (drive tire)
    Or FRT , free rolling tire (trailer only tire)

6   Specifity Code:7 different codes to track tire
    technical specifities.

7   Tire position code (Letter F for Front axle, D for Drive, T
    for trailer, Z for all axle ...) illustrated on a truck silhouette
    by an arrow that indicates the axle position

8   Tire size

9   Indicates added load and speed index
    (see chart)

10 Radial, tubeless, regroovable ,indicate
    radial structure of the tire, no inner tube, and regroove
    capacity

11 Load and speed index (see chart)

12 Made in ..... : indicates where was the tire Manufactured

13 Place for logistic information: vignette, barcode
    and matricule number ex:PRZ6596G

14 DOT: departement of transport the last 4 numbers indicate
    tire manufacturing   date 43: week 11: year 2011

15 Tire evolution number: indicates product generation

16 Brazil or China homologation

17 Option name: indicates optional benefit of the tire
    Second part of Michelin Truck and bus tire new naming

18 Range Name: indicates usage of the tire (see naming chart)
    First part of Michelin Truck and bus tire new naming

19 Usage pictogram: One per range

20 Brand tire here: free space for hot branding

21 X®: symbole of MICHELIN radial tire. it's a registred brand

22 E2....: CEE homogation number

23 Michelin registred brand

24 Warning: gives user information

FIGURE 27-16 Explanation of standard tire identification markings.

TABLE 27-2 New Truck Tire Markings Required by the Department of Transportation (DOT)

DOT	XX	XX	XXX	>0100
Meets DOT standards	Manufacturer 2-digit identification mark	Tire size 2-digit (mold/chamber) identification mark	Tire type Code (optional)	Date of manufacture (week/year) identification mark

TABLE 27-3 Retread Truck Tire Markings Required by the Department of Transportation (DOT) and the States

Department of Transportation Requirements for Truck Tire Retread Markings				
R	XX	XX	XXX	0100
Indicates retread	Manufacturer 2-digit identification mark	Tire size 2-digit (mold/chamber) identification mark	Tire type Code (optional)	Date of manufacture (week/year) identification mark

Additional State Requirements for Truck Tire Retread Markings					
R	XX	XX	XXX	0100	RS F2
Indicates retread	Manufacturer 2-digit identification mark	Tire size 2-digit (mold/chamber) identification mark	Tire type Code (optional)	Date of manufacture (week/year) identification mark	RS indicates retread was produced under Industry Retread Standards. F2 indicates the tire is acceptable for steer axle use and has been retreaded

Low Profile Tires

Low profile (LP) tires refer to a type of tire that has a shorter sidewall height than conventional tires. Also called low aspect ratio tires, these tires have shorter, stiffer sidewalls, resulting in less heating and tread squirm (that is, the flexibility in the tire tread between the surface of the tread and the tire carcass). These features enable the tires to have lower rolling resistance, which improves fuel economy. LP tires also have a better contact patch with the road surface. Since the sidewall is shorter, LP tires offer more responsive steering and tire stability due to greater lateral stability of tire sidewalls. That is, the sidewalls do not flex as much compared to conventional tires.

The ratio of tire section height to section width for low aspect ratio tires is generally 70% to 45% of the tire tread width. This means the tire is much wider than the height of the sidewall. LP construction offers the following advantages:

- Reduced tread wear and less irregular wear on steer and trail axles. Shorter sidewalls are stiffer, resulting in less tread squirm and heating plus a better contact patch with the road surface.
- Improved steering and tire stability due to greater lateral stability of tire sidewalls.
- Lighter weight.
- Smaller tire diameters, which enable trailer cube volumes to increase—potentially generating more revenue for loads.

LP tires cost more and have greater potential for sidewall damage through contact with curbs and rim damage if the tire cannot cushion the rim against contacts with road objects or deep pot holes at high speeds.

Wide-Base or Super Single Tires

Wide-base tires, or **flotation tires**, are large tires with a low aspect ratio. **FIGURE 27-17** shows a wide-base tire. The most common application for this profile of tire is on vehicles with high front-axle loads that exceed the loading capacity of standard tires. Dump trucks and refuse haulers that have front-axle capacities ranging from 18,000 to 20,000 lb (8165 to 9072 kg) typically use these tires.

The most common sizes of wide-base single tires used in North America are 385/65R22.5, 425/65R22.5, 435/50R22.5, 445/50R22.5, and 445/65R22.5. In many regions, depending on load regulations, wide-base LP tires are used to replace two single tires on a drive axle.

Super single tires are wide-base LP tires. Super singles are used to replace two conventional single tires on an axle to save weight and reduce wheel end parts. About 1000 lb (454 kg) of weight are saved using these tires on a tandem-axle bulk-hauler application. Tire wear remains about the same as conventional dual tires, but lower rolling resistance translates into some marginal fuel savings.

When compared with standard dual tires, super single or wide-base single tires shift the bearing load centerline outward

FIGURE 27-17 Wide-base tires replace dual tires to reduce wheel end weight and reduce rolling resistance.

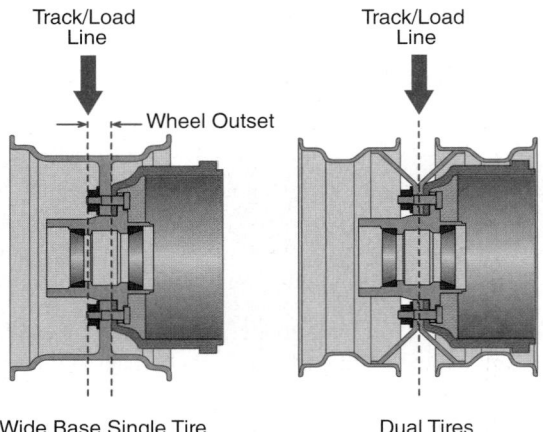

FIGURE 27-18 Wide-base tires shift the bearing load centerline compared to dual tires.

to the axle end (**FIGURE 27-18**). This produces increased bearing and potentially more axle housing wear. Widening the tire track with these tires increases hub and axle spindle loading, resulting in increased loading of the outer wheel bearings. Bearing life can potentially be reduced, and wheel ends require more frequent inspection.

Construction of Commercial Vehicle Tires

LO 27-5 Identify and describe tire construction features and their purpose in radial tubeless tires.

Construction techniques and materials used by each tire manufacturer are chosen to provide operating features specific to a tire's function. For example, tire tread design influences noise, braking, torque transmission, rolling resistance, and cornering. Tire tread design even influences traction on wet surfaces and

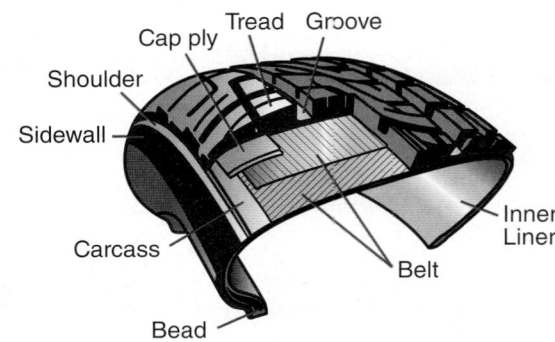

FIGURE 27-19 The tire itself is generally composed of the tread, sidewalls, inner liner, and bead.

in mud or snow. So, depending on where and how the tire is used, each application needs careful analysis and selection to deliver the best performance.

Basic elements of a heavy-duty commercial vehicle tire include the tire casings, the belt, beads, sidewalls, inner liner, and tread. **FIGURE 27-19** illustrates these principle construction elements of a tire and more.

Tire Casings

The **tire casing** forms the foundational body of the tire and consists of several layers of fabric cord, called plies, encased with a rubber compound. Common cord materials are polyester, nylon, or rayon cords, which add more strength to the tire than simply using a rubber mold to form the case. The tread, belt system (radial or bias-ply), and sidewalls are added to the tire casing.

As a foundation, the casing must withstand all the mechanical damage from impact, twisting, and rolling forces during driving. Tubeless casings are superior in strength to a separate inner tube once commonly used to hold air. Tubeless casings easily provide the mechanical strength needed for road service, and they seal air inside the tire without the need for a tube. Lightweight casings are preferred because they reduce internal heat build-up, which leads to deterioration of rubber. The quality of tire casing construction is a factor determining how often tires can be retreaded.

Casing Belt System

The belt system is attached to the tire casing. The role of the belt system is to provide stability to the tread area of the tire. Belt design, in turn, contributes to the wear, handling, and traction characteristics of the tire. Belts also work together with the tire sidewall to influence traction and cornering capabilities.

There are three basic types of tire construction: bias-ply, radial-ply, and bias-belted. The construction of the different types is illustrated in **FIGURE 27-20**. A **bias-ply tire** is constructed in a latticed, crisscrossing structure, with alternate plies crossing over each other and laid with the cord angles in opposite directions. In bias-ply tires, the tread and tire sidewalls share the same casing and plies. **Radial-ply tires** have two or more layers of casing plies and cord loops running radially from bead

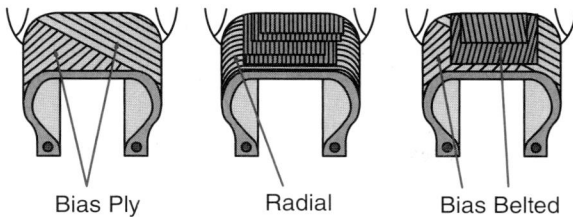

FIGURE 27-20 Bias-ply, radial-ply, and bias-belted construction.

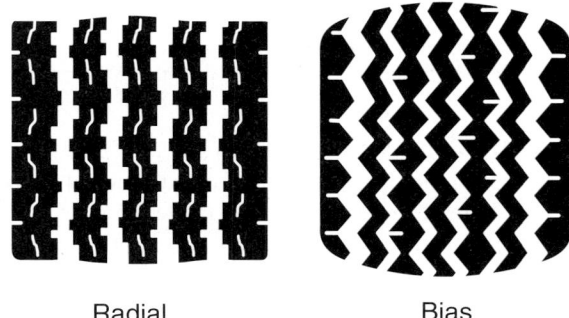

FIGURE 27-21 Contact patch for a radial and bias tire.

to bead. As such, radial tires separate the mechanical action of the tread and sidewalls, which results in a better contact patch formed between the tire and road, as shown in **FIGURE 27-21**. Consequently, radial tires have better fuel economy. Additionally, rolling resistance is reduced, producing longer tread life and reduced fuel consumption.

Today, most commercial on-highway vehicles use what are known as **radial-belted tires**. That is, tires where the belts are placed at 90 degrees to the tire centerline and wrapped from side to side around the tire beads. Braided steel is the most common belt material used today. Steel belts provide the best strength and stability to the tread area without adding excess weight to the tire.

Bias-Ply Tires

Bias-ply tires are an early tire construction technique that is still used today, but rarely, and mostly by tube-type tires. Bias-ply belt design places tread belts at an angle or diagonally to the tire centerline. Bias-ply belt construction provides the advantage of a stiffer tread and sidewall area for improved wear and puncture resistance for off-road and even military applications. Stiffer sidewalls provide better driver handling and feedback from the road surfaces and less frequent damage to sidewalls from road hazards, snags, or even rusting of steel belts used in radial construction.

Bias-ply is an inexpensively manufactured tire design used today in some applications for trucks, trailers, and farm equipment. Although inexpensive, the design has a significant disadvantage. Because the tread and tire sidewalls share the same casing and plies, sidewall flexing under load is transferred to the tread. This transfer deforms the tread formation under load.

Contact patch friction, tire wear, and rolling resistance all increase as well. In addition, the belt cords have what is known as high hysteresis energy loss. Hysteresis, or unpredictable tread movement in this instance, is the loss of energy through heat caused by flexing and friction. This results in the cords having high rolling resistances and heat-up when the cords are flexed. When excessive heat is generated by the tire, tread life and fuel economy are reduced. The high sidewall stiffness also requires bias-ply tires to use multipiece rims, since the tire cannot be easily stretched over a rim edge like a drop center rim used by tubeless tires. Instead, the tire is forced over a flat rim and a second rim flange is installed with one or two split rings to hold the rim flange in place, which secures the tire onto the rim. As mentioned, this is a complex rim system with a high potential to cause severe injury and death to anyone caught in the trajectory of a split-rim ring, if it spontaneously disengages from the rim.

Radial Tires

Radial tires have a belt system that arranges plies at right angles to the tread centerline. Belts may or may not be layered diagonally below the tread. Radial plies separate the mechanical action of the tread and sidewalls, which results in a better contact patch formed between the tire and road, which, in turn, reduces rolling resistance and improves fuel economy. Reduced rolling resistance results from constructing tires this way because it enables the smaller, shorter-casing cords to deflect more easily under load, thereby generating less heat while providing better high-speed traction. Tread stiffness is added in the belt area, increasing tread life while improving handling characteristics. Radial tires are a more complex design than bias tires. Consequently, radial tires have higher material and manufacturing costs.

In summary, radial tire belt construction provides:

- Reduced tread wear
- Improved potential for retreading, which is discussed in the section Retreading Tires
- Less rolling resistance for improved fuel economy
- A superior road contact patch for better traction characteristics

Bias-Belted Tires

In the bias-ply belted tire, as shown in Figure 27-21, the manufacturer attaches circumference belts over the bias and below the tread, much like the radial tire does. The major difference in the bias-ply tire comes from a rigid belt, usually of synthetic fabric, that is added. Bias-ply belted tires are reputed to have longer tread life than plain bias-ply tires for the same reasons that belted radial-ply tires do—less flexing and movement of the tread.

Tire Beads

Tire bead bundles sit on the wheel rim and help form an airtight seal between the tire and rim. Individual tire beads are formed from steel wire wound together to form a cable, as illustrated in **FIGURE 27-22**. Belt plies are looped around the bead bundles holding them in place. The rim for a radial tire has a bead

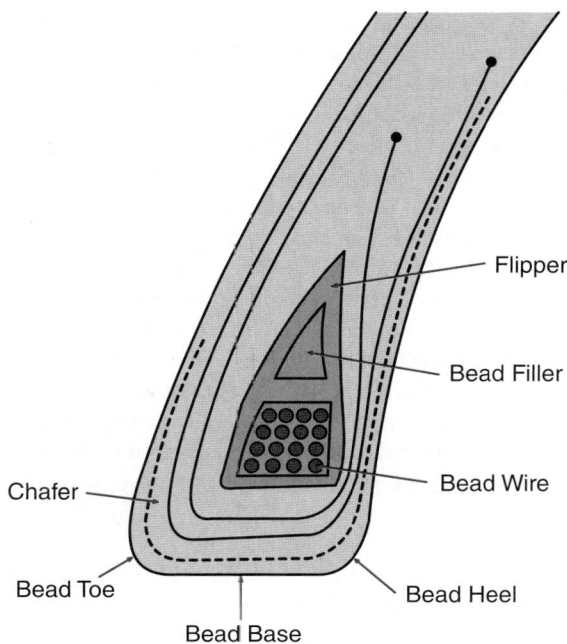

FIGURE 27-22 Features of a tire bead.

channel where the bead sits. On the outside edge of the channel is a vertical flange with a 15-degreee angle that keeps the bead from sliding off the rim.

A specialized rubber compound called bead filler is incorporated into the bead and extends into the sidewall area. The rubber compound used in the bead area is usually harder than other rubber materials making up the tire. Bead filler is harder so that it can withstand the potential damage from mounting and dismounting tires from the rim, as well as sustain deflection when the tire is heavily loaded. Beads require lubrication during installation to prevent damage from tools used to stretch the bead over the rim. Beads can also be damaged from heat transferred from the brake drums resulting in unpredictable tire blow-outs.

Sidewalls

Sidewalls use a specialized rubber compound applied to the casing. This is used to add flexibility and weathering resistance. Steel and/or nylon inserts can be added to provide quicker steering response.

Inner Liner

The primary function of the inner liner is to seal air inside a tire and keep moisture out. A specially compounded rubber material is used. The inner liner layer has no cord reinforcement and serves a function like an inner tube. Abrasives, and even some aftermarket tire-balancing materials, rolling around inside a tire can quickly erode the liner and lead to leakage. If a damaged inner liner allows water to leak into the tire, the wheel rim can rust. The inner liner does not do a perfect job sealing the tire, however. All tires leak a small quantity of air through the inner liner. Roughly 1% to 3% of inflation pressure is typically lost per month. That translates to about 1 psi (6.9 kPa)

in a large commercial vehicle tire. Weekly checks of inflation with a properly calibrated, direct-reading pressure gauge are recommended.

Tire Tread

Tread is a cap of molded rubber compound attached to the top of the belt system. Tread is typically made from an abrasion resistant, high-grip rubber compound, formulated to combine the best traction, tire longevity, and low rolling resistance for superior fuel economy. Tread on commercial vehicle tires is replaceable for drive and trailer tires, but should not be used for steer tires. The tire casing can be recycled to reduce operating costs and limit the environmental impact of disposing of worn tires.

Two basic tire tread designs are the block and rib style. Block-style tread is used for the drive tires to grip the road better for improved torque transmission. Ribbed tires do not transmit torque and must roll with little resistance when the direction of the tire is changed. Other tread designs are the rib-lug and lug. **TABLE 27-4** compares those four basic tread designs, as well as the rib-block tread design.

Most tread patterns are designed for specific applications. Traction tires are used on drive axles, and steer tires are used on front axles. Trailering tires do not require steering or transmitting drive torque. **TABLE 27-5** compares the features and benefits of drive, steer, and trailering tire treads. Application factors that affect tread selection can include:

- Long Haul—Travel on state/interprovincial highways and normal highways at maximum speeds, with runs over 250 miles (402 km)/trip.
- Regional Service—Travel on state/interprovincial highways at normal and lower speeds, with runs under 250 miles (402 km). Vehicle may make many sharp turns and maneuvers in tight turning radiuses.
- Urban—Most travel between and around city areas. High maneuverability required.
- On-Off-Road—Travel on some highway and secondary roads with travel on gravel, muddy, snow packed, and dirt roads.

Tire Construction and Fuel Economy

As a tire rotates, it flexes. Friction between tire plies and belts causes energy to convert to heat. Loss of energy through hysteresis accounts for approximately 90% of energy losses through

TABLE 27-4 Comparison of Common Tread Design

Type	Rib	Block	Rib-Block	Rib-Lug	Lug
Pattern					
Profile	Grooves cut around the circumference of a tire	Tread is chunked into individual blocks that are arranged in a pattern	Pattern combines block-type tread in the center with a shoulder rib	Combination of rib and lug patterns	Grooves cut in a lateral direction across tread
Features	• Improved driving stability • Lower rolling resistance • Lowest tread noise • Best water drainage performance for less skidding and hydroplaning	• Good drive and braking forces • Best traction on normal paved road	• Low rolling resistance • Smooth comfortable ride • Relatively low noise production • Good traction on snow or muddy terrain	• Rib-type pattern increases steering stability and prevents skidding • Lug-type pattern transfers traction drive and braking forces effectively	• Excellent drive and braking forces • Strongest traction force • Better resistance to tread cuts
Applications	• Best for driving on smooth cemented roads and highways • Ideal for steering or trailer tires	• Good traction performance when driving on asphalt and cement roads	• Good performance when driving on normal cemented roads • Improves fuel economy and has low tread wear	• Suitable for driving on normal cemented, asphalt roads and gravel roads at a middle/low speed	• Suitable for driving on all normal surfaces and best for muddy, off-road surfaces

TABLE 27-5 Comparison of Drive, Steer, and Trailering Tire Treads

Drive Tire Tread	Steer Tire Tread	Trailering Tire Tread
• Long tread wear • Long high-speed runs • Fuel economy • Wet traction • Noise reduction • Resistance to irregular wear • Dry traction • Snow traction • Wet traction	• Responsive steering • High-speed runs • Long tread wear • Resistance to cutting/chipping • Resistance to road hazard penetration	• Resistance to irregular wear • Fuel economy • Long highway speed runs • Noise reduction • Resistance to rib tearing • Resistance to curbing

rolling resistance. The remaining 10% energy loss takes place in the tread as the tire tread is deformed by road surface irregularities. (In other words, smoother roads have less rolling resistance.) Harder tread materials do not flex as easily and take more energy to deform to accommodate road irregularities. Softer tread material rubber compounds provide better fuel economy but lower wear resistance than harder compounds. Low profile (LP) tires also have less rolling resistance. When deflected sideways, more energy is transmitted to the road with a stiffer sidewall than with one that flexes. Radial tires have lower rolling resistance than diagonal bias-ply tires.

The arrangement of tire plies in radial tires at 90 degrees to the tire centerline means plies flex easier with less friction. Hysteresis energy losses are reduced, improving fuel economy in radial-ply construction. LP tires improve fuel economy even more. LPs that have a low aspect ratio may have a harsher ride but are more responsive because they transmit steering inputs quicker and produce less flexion of the sidewalls.

Hysteresis is also related to the hardness of the tire compound. Soft tire tread has less friction loss since it easily changes shape. Hard compound has higher friction loss but has longer service life. Softer tires have better traction due to adhesion or

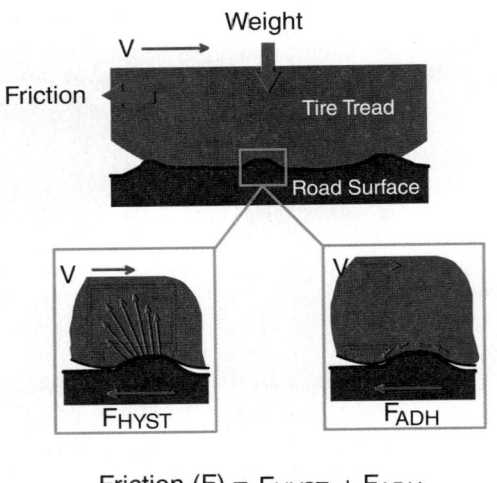

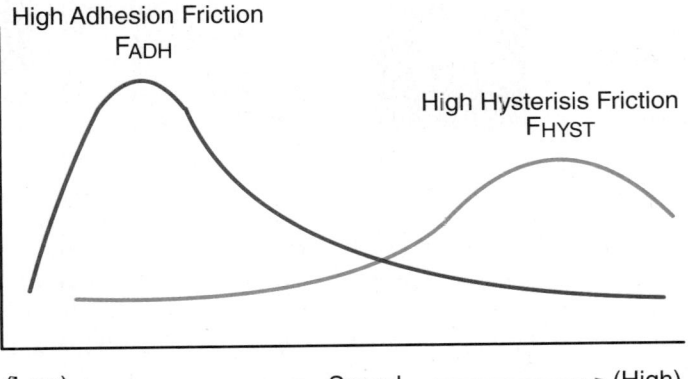

Friction (F) = F$_{HYST}$ + F$_{ADH}$

FIGURE 27-23 Types of friction at increasing levels of road speed.

stickiness at low speeds. **FIGURE 27-23** illustrates the shift from adhesion friction to hysteresis friction as speeds increase. Optimal tread compound (hard or soft) is designed to match operating conditions, such as speed and the type of road surface the vehicle regularly encounters.

Friction plays a vital role in the traction motion of the tires and vehicle. At low speed, the friction is regarded as having a "high-adhesion" rate. But as the speed increases, the frictional qualities tend to decrease. The type of road surface is a crucial factor with fictional adherence.

Fuel economy also relates to tread type and tire wear. Rib-type tread encounters less rolling resistance than block-type tread. That is because there is less movement, or squirming, of the rib-type tread in the contact patch area. Worn tires also have less rolling resistance than new tires. The tread pattern stiffens as it wears down, leading to less flexing and deformation in the tread area.

The use of fuel-efficient tires on all axle positions can make a significant impact on fuel consumption. A 10% reduction in rolling resistance results in approximately 3% reduced fuel consumption. This means consumption drops approximately 0.2 gallons/62 miles (0.9 liters/100 km) on a vehicle that consumes eight gallons/62 miles (30 liters/100 km).

Changing tires can produce incorrect speedometer readings and influence fuel economy because tire revolutions per mile (rpm) may no longer be correct. Even tires with the same labeling, when supplied by different manufacturers or using different types of tread, have different rolling circumferences. Data supplied to several vehicles' electronic control units (ECUs) also depend on accurate tire sizes—the ABS, traction control, engine, transmission, instrument cluster, and so on. Changing tire sizes more than 3% generally requires changing axle ratios to ensure the engine torque curves are properly matched with vehicle speed, too. After changing tires or ECUs, tire size or rpm may need to be reset. To properly determine tire rpm, tire suppliers should provide accurate information. Dual-inline package (DIP) switches on a speedometer are often used

FIGURE 27-24 Retreading tires involves applying new tread to the casing.

to change tire rpm stored in the speedometer memory. Newer vehicles only require software to modify the calculation performed by the engine or ABS module to convert pulses per mile (or kilometer) of the speed sensor to correctly report vehicle speed on the speedometer.

Retreading Tires

Retreading tires, illustrated in **FIGURE 27-24**, involves recycling the tire casing to extend its service life and is sometimes known as a "cap," "recap," or a "remold." Retreaded tires cost significantly less than the cost of a new tire (typically 40% of the cost of new) and are, therefore, widely used in commercial fleet operations. According to the Tire Retread and Repair Information Bureau, retreaded truck tires represent a savings of over $3 billion US dollars annually in North America. Retreads are also environmentally friendly. Consider that it requires approximately 22 gallons (83 liters) of oil to manufacture one new truck tire. Most of this oil is used to produce the casing which is reused in the retreading process. By contrast, a retread only takes seven gallons (26.5 liters) of oil to produce. Retreading wide-base tires saves even more production costs. Some tires can be retreaded as often as ten times.

There are two main processes used for retreading commercial vehicle tires:

- Hot curing, also known as mold cure
- Cold curing, also known as precure

Both retread processes start with the inspection of the tire to determine its serviceability. Damage to sidewalls or the belt system disqualifies the tire as a candidate for retread. Once a tire is deemed serviceable, its old tread is removed. The casing is then buffed to clean it and prepare its surface to receive the new tread.

When **hot curing**, the casing is covered with uncured rubber and then placed in a mold where it is heated. The heating process binds the tread to the casing and cures the tread. A more commonly used process is called **cold curing**, which uses a molded, precured tread strip or tread ring that is glued to the casing.

The tire is then placed in a rubber envelope or container with a vacuum applied to the entire tire to prevent it from burning during the next step. Next, the enveloped tire is placed in a heated chamber to bind the tread to the casing. **TABLE 27-6** compares the processes of hot- and cold-curing retread. **FIGURE 27-25** compares the two processes used to retread tires.

TABLE 27-6 Comparison of Hot and Cold Curing Retread Processes

Hot-Curing Retread	Cold-Curing Retread
One-piece tread rubber is bonded directly to the casing	Precured, preformed tread rubber is glued to the tire casing by a thin piece of cushion gum
One-piece rubber is applied evenly around the tire casing No splices improves tire circumference uniformity	Precured rubber ends are glued together by a process called stitching Can be performed easier in the field
Less heat is applied to the sidewall during the curing process	High heat to the sidewall during the curing process

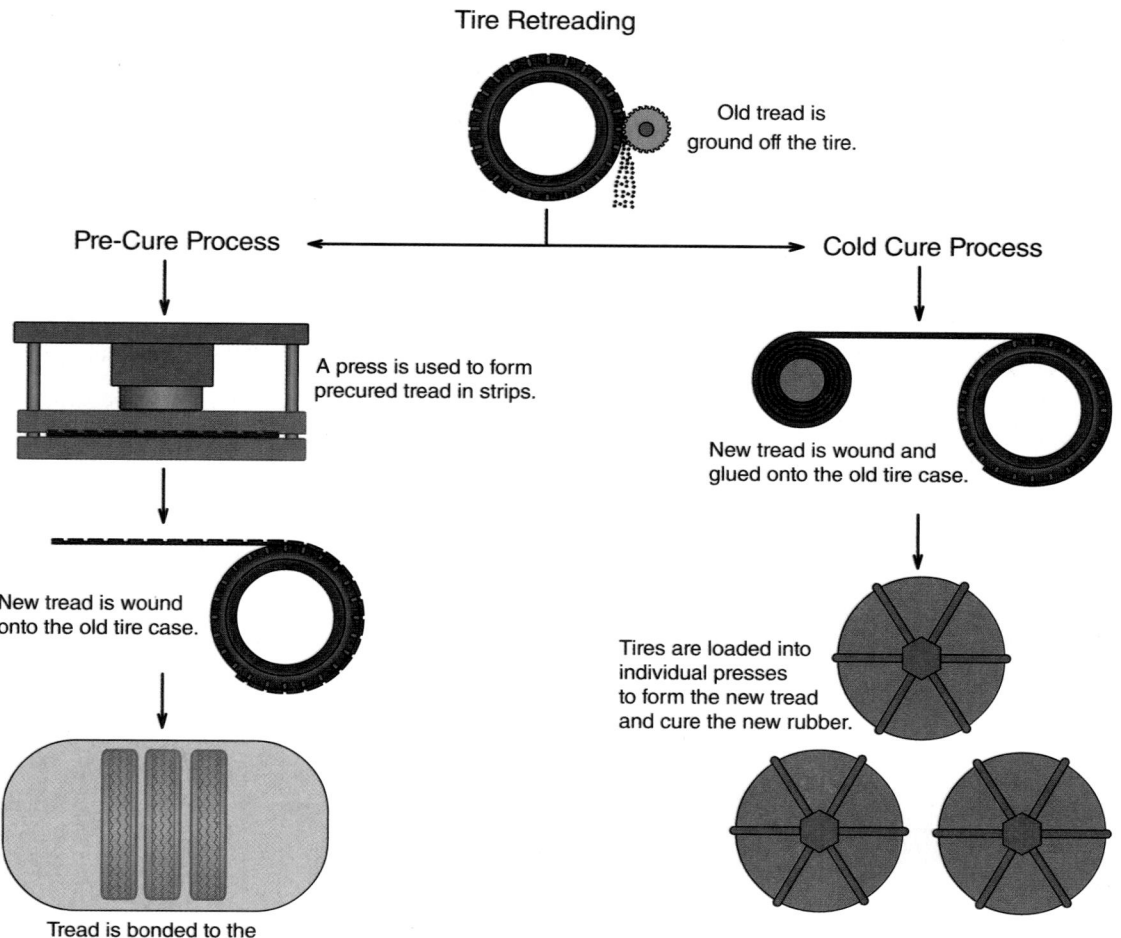

FIGURE 27-25 Comparing two different processes used to cure tires.

Tire Tread Separation

Tire tread separation describes the separation of the tread from the tire casing. Tire retreads or recaps are often mistakenly blamed for "road alligators," like those shown in **FIGURE 27-26**, which can litter the highway. These separated tire treads originate most often from medium- and heavy-duty commercial tires. Several studies, including a National Highway Traffic Safety Administration (NHTSA) study, have determined that tire debris on highways is not caused by retreads. Analysis of tire fragments and casings collected demonstrated that tire debris from retread tires and original equipment manufacturers (OEM) tires is similar to the proportion of retread and OEM tires in service. This means both new tires, without retread caps, and retread tires separate at identical rates. Still, retreads have a bad reputation.

Tread separations are caused by several factors, as listed in **TABLE 27-7**. Tread separations caused by heat generated by underinflation start at the edges of the steel belts next to the sidewalls, where heat and stress fatigue affect the tire the most. A bump forms in the tread area where the tread is separating, causing the defective tire to become unbalanced. This bump is a visual indicator that the tread is going to separate. Expansion of this bubble increases until tire failure occurs. Another type of failure, known as a zipper rupture, is illustrated in **FIGURE 27-27**. Zipper ruptures are caused by impact with road debris at high speeds.

FIGURE 27-26 Separated tire treads known as road alligators.

TABLE 27-7 Tread Failure by Cause of Separation

Cause of Tread Separation	Percentage of Failures
Road hazard	36% to 38%
Operational problems	32%
Manufacturing defects	16%
Excessive heat	30%

> ▶ TECHNICIAN TIP

Drive tires experience the most fatigue due to longer service life and higher heat loads from heavier tread and higher drive torque. High drive torque contributes to more casing fatigue, compared with moderate fatigue on steer positioned tires and lowest fatigue for trailer tires. To prevent tire tread separation, these tires are the most critical to frequently check for correct inflation pressure.

Tread Depth

Minimum tread groove depths are specified by Federal Motor Vehicle Safety Standard 119. FMVSS 119 requires manufacturers to include six evenly spaced tread depth indicators, more commonly called wear bars, around the circumference of a highway tire. Illustrated in **FIGURE 27-28**, wear bars are designed to have the same thickness of the tire tread when only 1/16"

FIGURE 27-27 Zipper rupture tire failure.

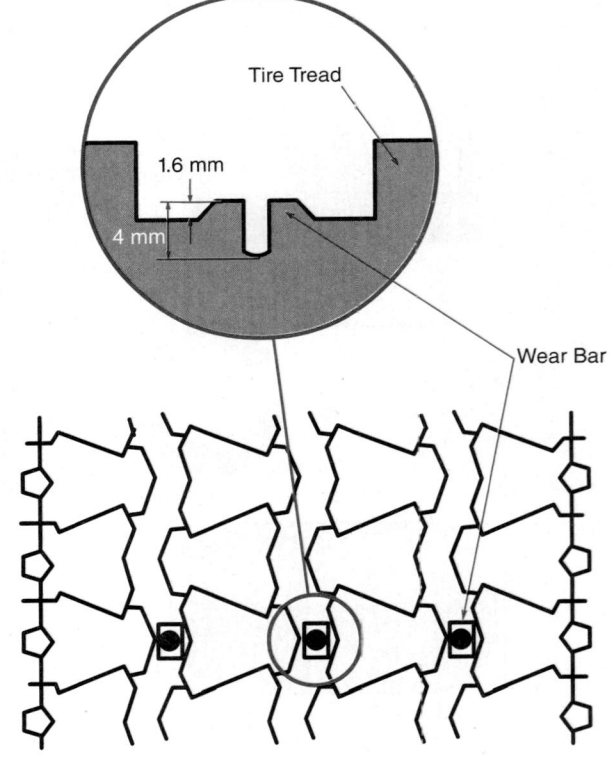

FIGURE 27-28 Tire wear bars or tread depth indicators inside the tire.

(1.59 mm) of tread groove depth is remaining. Vehicle operators are required to maintain at least 1/8" (3.18 mm) of tread groove depth on the front tires of any bus, truck, or truck tractor and 1/16" (1.59 mm) remaining tread depth on any other wheel positions. **FIGURE 27-29** shows a tread measuring device.

Tire Regrooving

Regrooving is a process that uses a heated cutting tool to carve new tread or add stripes to a tire. Regroovable tires are manufactured to extend the tire tread life and have adequately thick tread compound between the bottom of the original tread grooves and the top of the uppermost breaker or belt depth. The depth of this area, called **undertread**, permits regrooving. It must allow a minimum of 3/32" (2.38 mm) of rubber material to cover and protect the cord after regrooving. If a tire is regroovable, a label on the sidewall (as discussed in the Tire Identification and Sizing section) designates it as such. Tire regrooving is infrequently performed today, but when it is, regrooving is performed on tires used by intercity coach service, rather than in truck fleets.

Tire Inflation Factors

LO 27-6 Identify and explain tire inflation factors.

Maintaining the correct tire pressure for a commercial vehicle is an important factor determining the load its tires can safely carry. Maintenance of correct tire pressure means the tire supports vehicle weight without a problem. Fuel economy, vehicle dynamics, tire durability, and tread life are affected by inflation pressure.

Too little tire pressure, the most common condition, also eventually causes catastrophic tire failure. This happens as the individual layers of fabric and steel encased in rubber are forced to stretch beyond the elastic limits of the fabric and steel reinforcing cords. Excessive bending and flexing of tire layers during underinflation causes this condition. In addition, excessive heat produced by friction between layers within the tire builds and causes the bonds between the various materials to weaken. The combination of mechanical stress and heat build-up eventually leads to premature deterioration and failure. **FIGURE 27-30** charts the effects of tire inflation pressure on tire life.

Even if a tire does not fail immediately, once weakened, it remains damaged, even after being properly inflated. In fact, some manufacturers recommend that a tire be replaced, not re-inflated, if allowed to run with less than 20% of its inflation pressure for any length of time. As mentioned in the Inner Liner section, all tires leak a small quantity of air through the inner liner—typically close to 1% to 3% of inflation pressure per month—and should, therefore, be checked weekly.

Determining Inflation Pressure

Vehicle weight is the primary determinant of **tire inflation pressure**. Heavier loads require higher inflation pressure to properly support the load. All tire manufacturers supply load/inflation tables that can be used to determine the proper inflation pressure at various vehicle weight loads. Faster vehicle speeds also increase forces that can damage tires, which means less weight can be safely supported at higher vehicle speeds.

FIGURE 27-29 Measuring tread depth. Note the location of a wear bar.

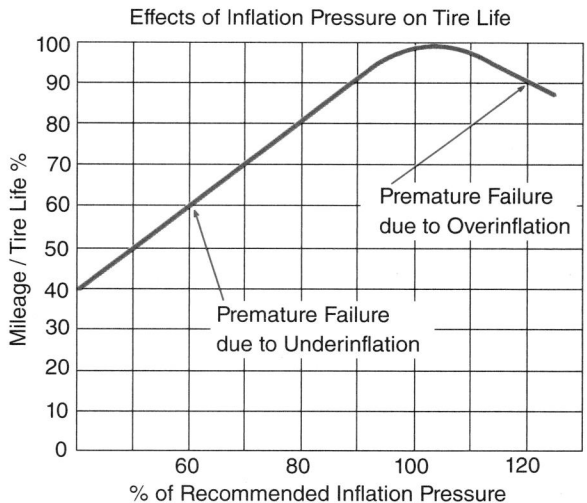

FIGURE 27-30 Tire life versus recommended inflation pressure.

TABLE 27-8 Load Ratings for Commercial Vehicle Tires								
Load Index	148	149	150	151	152	153	154	155	156
Load capacity (lb/tire)	6945	7165	7385	7606	7826	8047	8267	8543	8818
Load capacity (kg/tire)	3150	3250	3350	3450	3550	3650	3750	3875	4000

TABLE 27-9 Speed Ratings for Commercial Vehicle Tires

Speed index	F	G	J	K	L	M	N
Speed in mph	50	56	62	68	75	81	87
Speed in kph	80	90	100	110	120	130	140

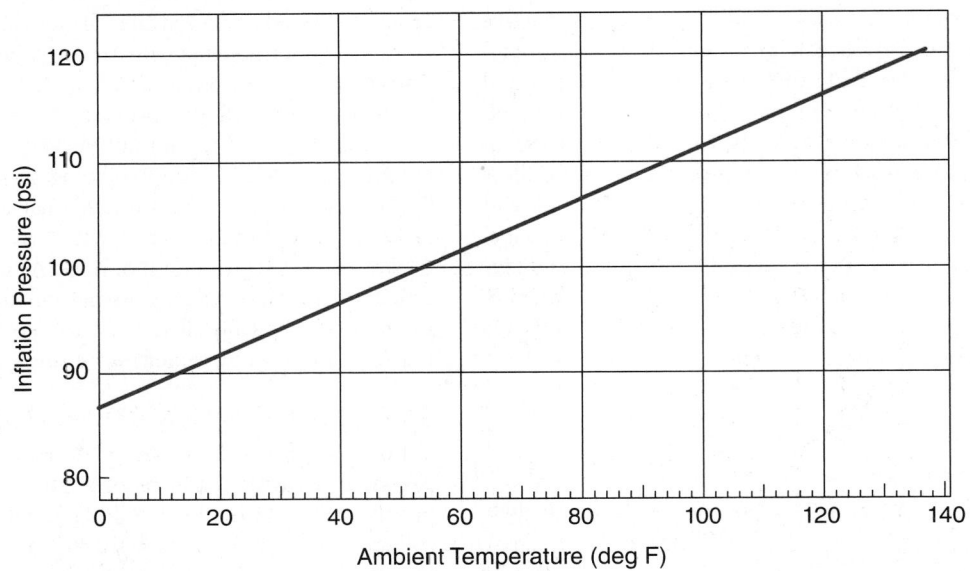

FIGURE 27-31 As tire temperature increases, so does inflation pressure.

TABLE 27-8 shows the load ratings for commercial vehicles and **TABLE 27-9** shows the speed ratings. Load index and speed ratings are part of a mandatory group of markings, such as tire sizes and serial numbers, required by the US DOT for tires.

Temperature and atmospheric pressure can affect tire pressure, too. For example, a tire initial inflation pressure of 100 psi (689.5 kPa) at 60° F (16° C) ambient temperature increases approximately 2 psi (13.8 kPa) for every 10° F (−5.6° C) increase in temperature. In the summer, a tire commonly runs at pressure 15 to 20 psi higher than its cold inflation pressure. Inflation pressures are always measured when cold, so air pressure should not be bled from a tire when warm because commercial vehicle radial tires are designed to accept this pressure change. **FIGURE 27-31** shows the effect of ambient temperature on inflation pressure.

On dual-wheel assemblies, maintaining identical tire inflation pressure is critical for normal tire wear. Even as little as a 5 psi (34.5 kPa) pressure difference produces a 5/16" (7.94 mm) difference in rolling diameter. Over one mile, the rolling diameter distance is equivalent to causing a tire to scuff (that is, a tire mark caused by applying enough power to a wheel to make it spin) 13' (3.96 m). And over 100,000 miles (160 km), that amounts to 246 miles (396 km) of scuffing!

Correct tire inflation levels are critical for safety, operation, and fuel economy. An underinflated tire cannot maintain its shape and becomes flatter than intended while in contact with the road (**FIGURE 27-32**). If a vehicle's tires

7 " (17.8 cm) long @ 100 psi
= optimum fuel economy

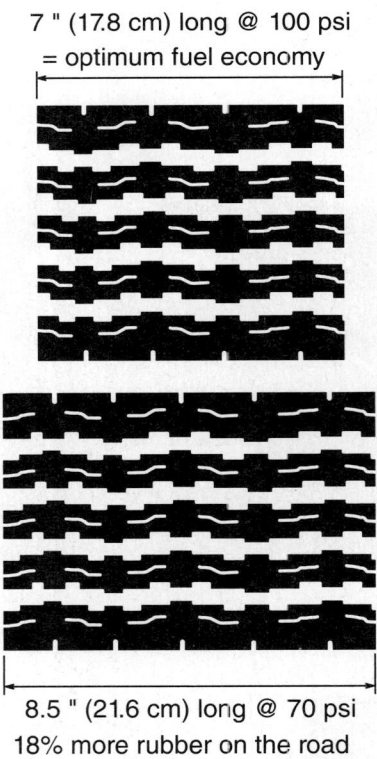

8.5 " (21.6 cm) long @ 70 psi
18% more rubber on the road
= decrease in fuel economy

FIGURE 27-32 Lower tire pressure increases the contact patch area, which in turn increases rolling resistance and tire wear.

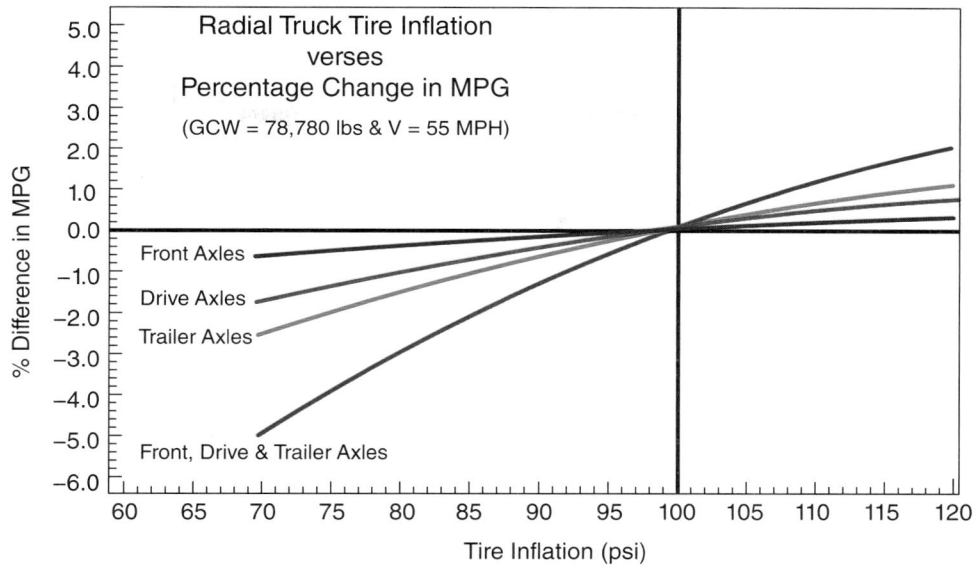

FIGURE 27-33 Proper tire inflation affects fuel economy. Underinflation increases tire rolling resistance.

nominally inflated to 100 psi (689.5 kPa) are underinflated by 20 psi (1379 kPa), the tires may fail. A significant loss of steering precision and cornering stability also accompanies underinflation. Additionally, the tire's tread life may be reduced by as much as 25%. Lower inflation pressure allows the tire to deflect or bend more as it rolls. Energy used to distort the tire shape is converted to heat. Rolling resistance increases when inflation pressure is low and causes a reduction in fuel economy of up to 5%. For these reasons, it is imperative to keep air pressure at an appropriate level to suppress unnecessary distortion and minimize energy loss. **FIGURE 27-33** shows the impact of tire inflation on fuel economy.

An overinflated tire is stiff and unyielding, and it has a poor contact patch with the road. If a vehicle's tires are overinflated by 20 psi (137.9 kPa), the tires can be damaged more easily when running over potholes or road debris. Additionally, higher inflated tires cannot isolate road irregularities well, causing a harsher ride. To a point, however, higher inflation pressures usually provide an improvement in steering response and cornering stability. Tire pressure must be checked with a quality air gauge because inflation pressure cannot be accurately estimated through visual inspection or hitting it with a solid heavy object. **FIGURE 27-34** compares the different effects of underinflation, overinflation, and proper inflation.

Automatic Tire Inflation Systems

Given the importance of correct tire inflation to fuel economy, tire life, and safety, automatic tire inflation systems are used to adjust tire inflation pressures using the air stored in a trailer or tractor reservoir. Most commonly, automatic inflation systems are installed on trailers, particularly in applications, such as liquid air, chemical tankers, or fuel haulers, where a tread separation could have catastrophic consequences.

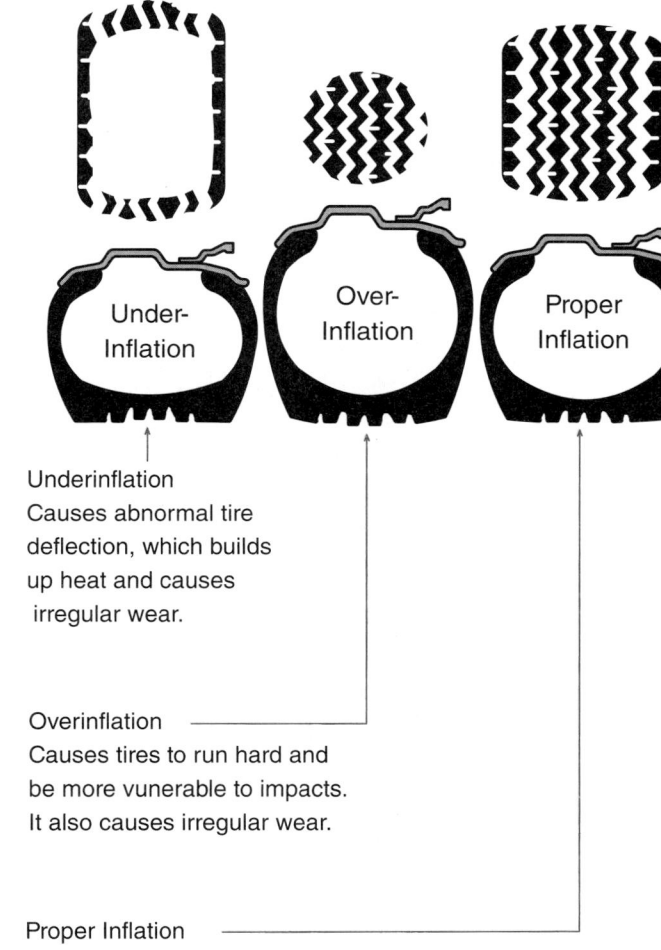

Underinflation
Causes abnormal tire deflection, which builds up heat and causes irregular wear.

Overinflation
Causes tires to run hard and be more vunerable to impacts. It also causes irregular wear.

Proper Inflation
The correct profile for full contact with the road promotes traction, braking capability and safety.

FIGURE 27-34 Effects of various levels of tire inflation.

The latest automatic inflation systems alert the driver through a warning light if the system is used on a trailer. Tires on the trailer are filled by the reservoir air supply to maintain inflation pressure constantly at the correct level while the vehicle is moving. If tire air pressure falls below a preset level, air is automatically supplied through a pressure control box and then into the axle through air lines. The air is then distributed to each tire on an axle end through a rotary air valve mounted inside the wheel hub that redirects air from an air line routed through the axle housing to each tire (**FIGURE 27-35**). Drive axles in tractors make it more difficult to pass air lines through axle housings. On drive axles where the axle shaft interferes with air line routing, the air is supplied by a rigid air hose over the outside of the tire to the rotary air valve, which is also called a stator.

If a tire suddenly loses pressure, due to a puncture or other major cause, one-way check valves at each tire prevent all tires from losing pressure. Only the leaking tire draws air from the air control system. A pressure control valve supplying air from the trailer reservoir cuts off air to the system if air pressure falls below 80–100 psi so the operation of air brake components supplied by the reservoir are not limited. An electrically controlled pressure protection valve notes the sudden loss in air pressure and can switch on a warning light at the front of the trailer, if equipped.

Meritor combines an automatic inflation system with a thermal warning alert for overheated hubs, which also switches on the warning light (**FIGURE 27-36**). If a wheel end loses oil and heat builds up in the axle spindle, a heat-sensing plug melts,

allowing air to leak from the wheel end. Because the plug is also supplied with air, identification of the hot spindle and hub is made by listening for an air leak from the hub with a melted thermal plug that previously sealed air.

Tire Pressure Monitoring Systems

LO 27-7 Explain the purpose and operation of TPMS.

Maintaining proper tire pressure is essential for the safety and performance of a vehicle. Tire inflation pressure is the air pressure in the tire that provides it with load-carrying capacity that affects overall vehicle performance. It also plays a significant role in decreasing fuel consumption, reducing carbon dioxide (CO_2) emissions and extending tire life. All tires lose inflation over time around the tire beads and through the inner liner. Making the problem worse are modern vehicles' contemporary operating practices that have extended chassis lubrication service intervals, which can allow tires to become dangerously underinflated unless regularly, or more frequently, checked by technicians or the vehicle's driver.

In addition to increased fuel consumption and tire wear, long periods of driving with low tire pressure can cause additional stress on the tire sidewalls. This results in increased operating temperatures that can lead to premature tire failure. Tires operating with low pressure can also affect the handling and performance of the vehicle. In a worst-case scenario, underinflation can lead to a tire blowout or tread separation.

The automated **tire pressure monitoring system (TPMS)** provides a means of reliable and continuous monitoring of the tire pressure and is designed to increase tire life, decrease fuel consumption, and improve vehicle performance. A TPMS monitors the tires for low air pressure, and often tire temperature, to alert the driver when one or more tires are lower than (or in some cases, pressure and temperatures are higher than) the designated thresholds. This alert can be an illuminated warning lamp or a chime. A vehicle can be equipped from the factory with a TPMS or it can be added as an accessory to all vehicles using conventional and run-flat tires (**FIGURE 27-37**). With some TPMS, drivers can monitor the tire pressures and temperatures from the driver's seat to ensure that the tires are properly inflated under all operating conditions. The TPMS is designed to ignore normal pressure variations caused by changes in ambient temperature.

There are two basic configurations used to monitor the vehicle's tire pressures: direct and indirect. A **direct TPMS** measures the tire pressure via a sensor that is installed inside each wheel, which helps protect the TPMS from damage (**FIGURE 27-38**). Each wheel sensor is equipped with an antenna that wirelessly relays the information it senses to receivers located within the vehicle, as illustrated in **FIGURE 27-39**. The receivers send the signal to the control unit. The sensor can respond to a drop-in pressure of as little as 2 psi (14 kPa). The control unit sends an

Air Supply Through Axle

Rotary Type Air Distribution Valve

Tire Air Supply Hoses

FIGURE 27-35 A cross sectional view of a wheel end with an automatic tire inflation system.

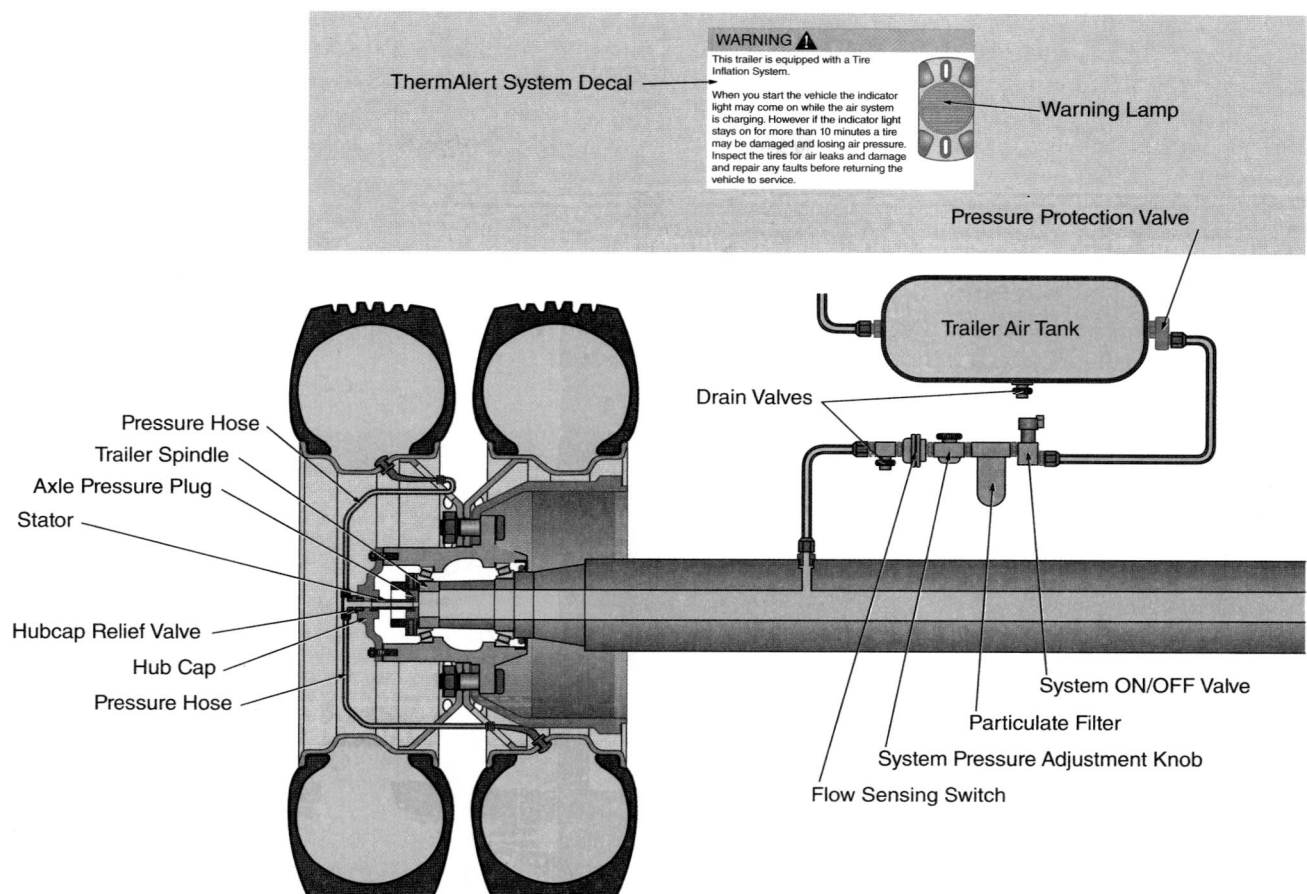

FIGURE 27-36 Note the components for an automatic tire inflation system combined with temperature-sensitive heat plugs. Plugs detect an overheated spindle and melt, releasing air, which switches on a warning light. A rapidly leaking tire also switches on the warning light.

appropriate signal to the driver's information circuit or, in some vehicles, the onboard computer, which in turn illuminates a display in the vehicle's multifunction screen to warn the driver of low tire pressure in a certain wheel. An audible and visual warning alerts the driver, allowing time for the vehicle to stop or be driven to a service station.

The sensors are powered by an internal battery that is designed to last between 5 and 10 years. The use of a **centrifugal switch** in the sensor allows the sensor to go to sleep when the vehicle stops, which extends battery life. When the battery goes dead, it needs to be replaced, which usually means that the entire sensor must be replaced, because the battery is typically sealed inside the sensor. Sensors that are activated by tire rotation can be expected to last as long as 6 to 10 years, whereas sensors that are constantly on, such as those installed in valve stem caps, last less than 5 years.

A direct TPMS can be of two types: one-way communication or two-way communication. In one-way communication, the TPMS sensor can only transmit to the receiver; it cannot receive any information. In this type of system, the sensors usually use a centrifugal switch to turn them on and off to conserve the battery energy. In a two-way communication TPMS,

the sensor can receive signals, as well as transmit signals. This allows the control unit to send signals to wake up or cause the sensor to sleep, thus extending the sensor's battery life.

An **indirect TPMS** indirectly monitors tire air pressure by monitoring wheel speed. If only a single wheel is installed on an axle end, the wheel speed antilock brake systems (ABSs) can measure the difference in the rotational speed of the four wheels. A wheel that is rotating faster than the others indicates that the tire has lower pressure than the other tires. This is because, if a tire loses pressure, its rolling radius is reduced, which increases the speed of rotation. Since it is rolling faster than the other tires, the wheel-speed sensor sends a slightly faster wheel-speed signal for that wheel to the ABS control unit. The control unit monitors the changes in wheel speed, and, when a low tire pressure failure is detected, it sends a signal to the low tire pressure light and/or chime on the dashboard.

SmarTire® TPMS

Bendix CVS SmarTire® TPMS is a popular system available as original equipment or as a retrofit kit (**FIGURE 27-40**). It uses tire sensors mounted on each wheel rim to measure pressure and temperature every 12 seconds. Collecting temperature and pressure data enables the system to correct for natural changes in tire pressure accompanying temperature change. Tire data is wirelessly transmitted every three to five minutes, unless there is more than a three psi pressure drop within the interval. If a rapid depressurization is detected, data is immediately transmitted to a driver display with an audible warning sound to alert the driver. In addition to the tire sensors, the system uses what is called a gateway receiver. This device picks up low-frequency radio signals transmitted by the tire sensors and compares it with user-stored settings for pressure. Radio signals used by the gateway receiver are not Bluetooth but are transmitted by pressure sensitive radio frequency identification (RFID) tags. If a tire is underinflated or running over temperature, the gateway sends an alert through both the vehicle data network and to what Bendix calls the SmartWave display unit. A correction factor for temperature is calculated by the gateway module and applied to the pressure reading to determine if the data is in an acceptable range.

Because the SmarTire TPMS can be used on trailers, as well as straight trucks, several three different driver warning or display units are used. The first is a SmartWave display unit in the dash (**FIGURE 27-41**). The display unit is connected directly to the gateway receiver, which picks up radio signals using an external antenna. A navigable menu allows the driver to identify the tire, its pressure and temperature, and identify faults (**FIGURE 27-42**).

A smaller two-lamp in-dash display fits into the opening the size of a large toggle switch and is also connected to the gateway receiver. Driver alerts from this display unit must be read using an electronic service tool. The third display is for use on trailers and is integrated with the ABS warning light (**FIGURE 27-43**).

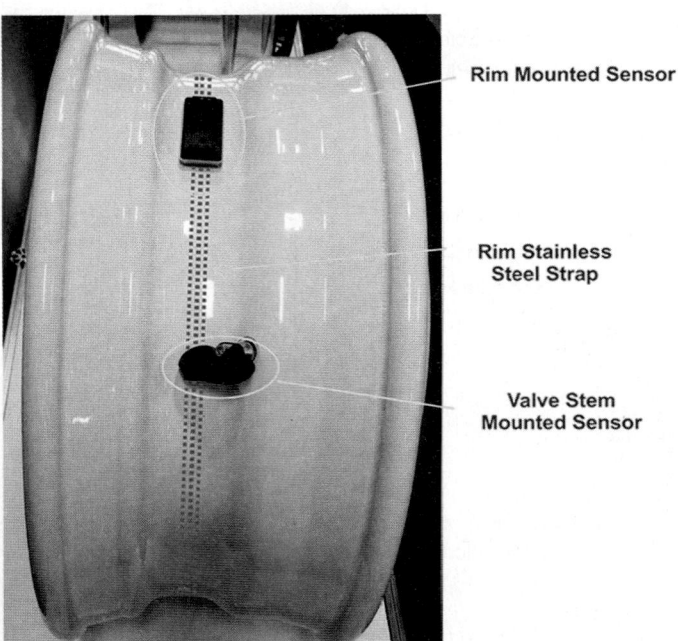

FIGURE 27-38 Tire pressure sensors are either mounted on the rim with a stainless-steel strap (gear-type hose clamp) or a sensor integral to the valve stem.

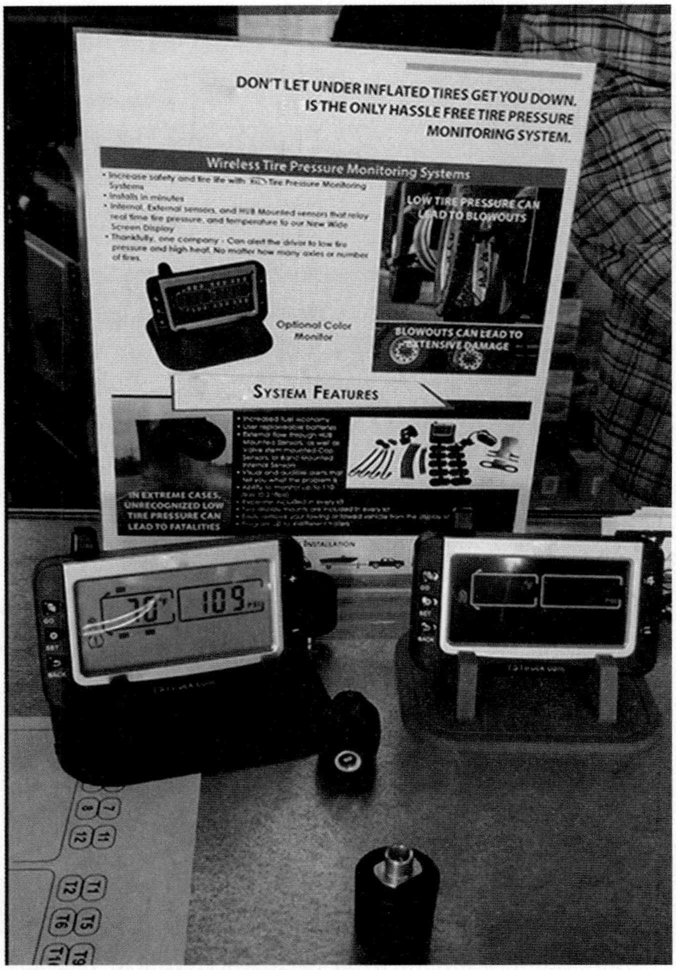

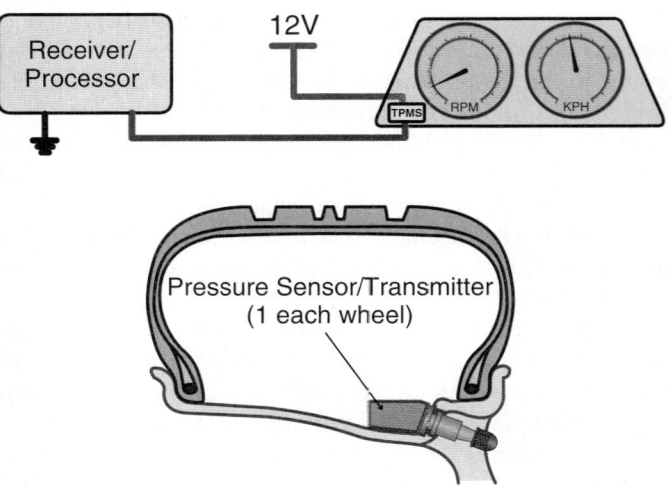

FIGURE 27-39 The tire pressure monitoring system (TPMS).

FIGURE 27-37 One of many aftermarket types of TPMS.

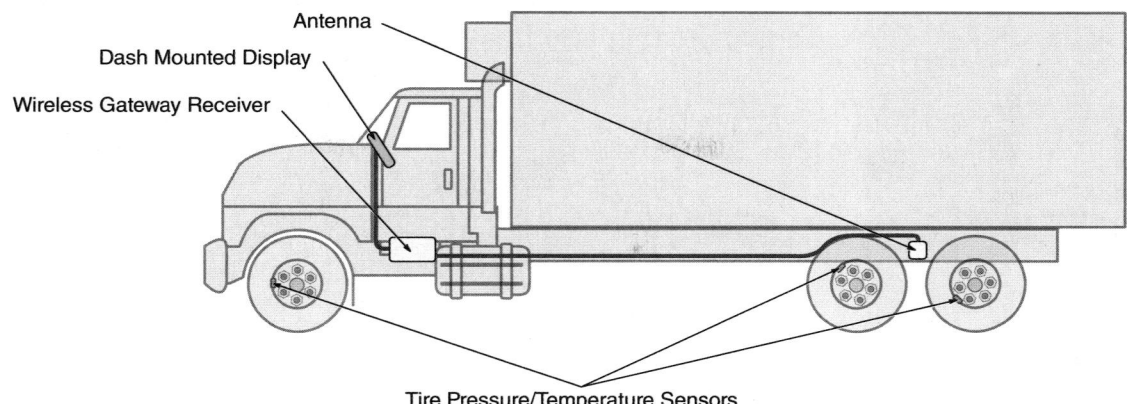

FIGURE 27-40 Bendix's TPMS has three major components: wheel-speed sensors, a gateway module receiving radio signals, and a driver display with audible alerts for fault.

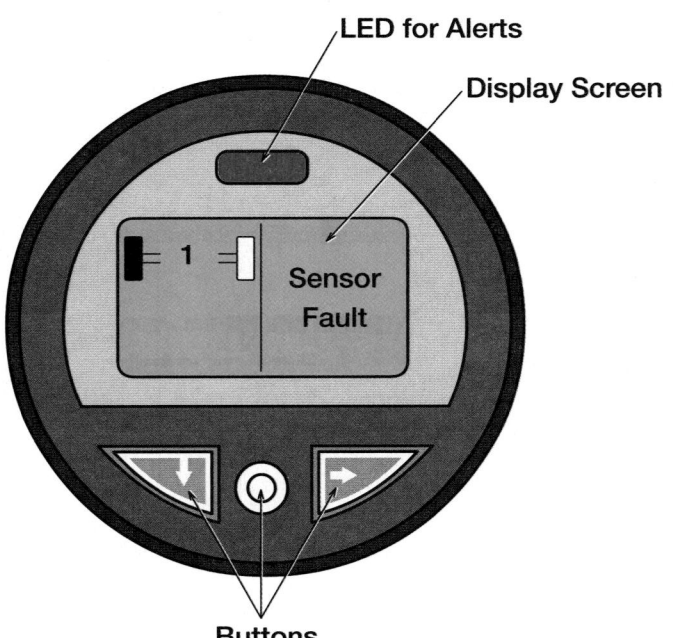

FIGURE 27-41 The dash display unit of the SmarTire TPMS fits into an opening the size of a regular instrument gauge and has a navigable menu.

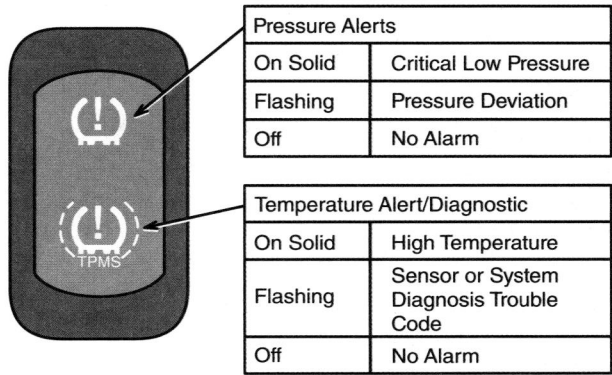

FIGURE 27-42 Warning lights for Bendix SmartTire TPMS can be displayed in dash mounted toggle switch.

Pressure Alerts	
On Solid	Critical Low Pressure
Flashing	Pressure Deviation
Off	No Alarm

Temperature Alert/Diagnostic	
On Solid	High Temperature
Flashing	Sensor or System Diagnosis Trouble Code
Off	No Alarm

A handheld electronic service tool to display fault codes, identify sensors, and perform maintenance procedures is available. Windows-based software can be downloaded for comprehensive diagnostics and setup of the system. To reset the TPMS to have it learn a new sensor, test a sensor, or relearn a new procedure, follow the steps in **SKILL DRILL 27-1**.

To enable correct identification of each sensor on wheel ends with dual wheels, it's critical that tire sensors are located at 180 degrees apart. This means that during sensor installation, the sensor is installed next to the tire valve stem (**FIGURE 27-44**).

Trailer Lamp

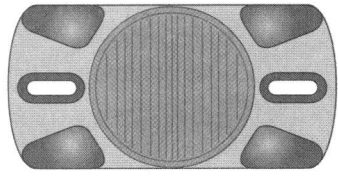

System Alerts	
On Solid	Critical Low Pressure
Flashing Rapidly	Pressure Deviation
Flashing (Twice then long delay)	Sensor or System Diagnosis Trouble Code
Off	No Alarm

FIGURE 27-43 SmarTire warning displays can blink out flash codes to alert the driver to tire pressure and temperature faults.

SKILL DRILL 27-1 TPMS Sensor Testing and Learning

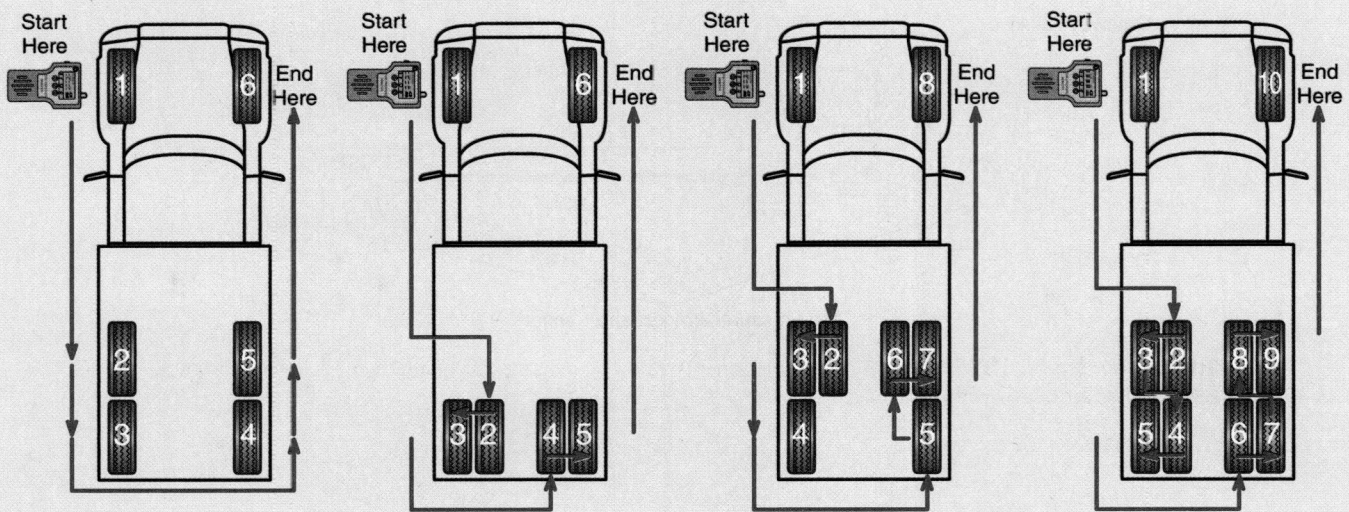

After a tire is installed or relocated on the same vehicle or another vehicle, the tire sensor's position on each axle requires identification. Using a handheld electronic service tool, called the SmartWave tool, each sensor's unique identification number and position can be learned and stored on a tire map. During the procedure, the radio transmitter in the tool activates the closest sensor and requests sensor data. The following is a general outline for three common maintenance procedures.

A. Sensor Testing and Learn Procedure

This procedure can be used to test each sensor's operation by selecting individual sensors or to store new sensor data.

1. After switching on the SmartWave service tool, place the tool's antenna against the tire sidewall close to the wheel rim at the valve stem location.
2. Press and release the "Initiate" button on the tool. A signal is sent to the nearby sensor to activate it. Wait for the sensor data transmission, which takes 3–5 seconds.
3. The tool should receive an eight-digit sensor identification, along with the tire pressure within two psi of actual tire pressure, and the tire's temperature. If received, the sensor is operating correctly.
4. Repeat the previous steps above on any remaining sensors to validate sensor operation.

B. Walk-Around Learn Procedure

Whenever tires are rotated or replaced, the TPMS must re-learn the position of each sensor in each tire. The Walk-Around Learn procedure is used to activate each sensor and store new location data in the gateway module through a cable upload. To do this, the technician must walk around the vehicle in a U-shaped pattern, starting at the left (driver's) front-most tire location.

1. Select the "Walk-Around Learn" icon from the tool menu.
2. Select the number of tires on the vehicle when prompted.
3. Activate each of the vehicle's wheel sensors in the correct order by moving in the correct direction and pressing the "Learn" button. In learn mode, only the sensor ID is displayed. If there are

dual tires, begin with the inboard tire location and move to the outboard tire using the same steps outlined in procedure A.
4. Once the tool has learned the tire sensor ID for the given position, it prompts the user to move to the next tire position. Repeat until all the tires have been learned.
5. After the last tire has been learned, press the down arrow. The tool is now ready to transmit this information to the vehicle's tire pressure-sensor receiver.
6. Using the supplied cable, connect the tool to the diagnostic port of the tire pressure-sensor receiver.
7. Press the check mark to begin downloading the new tire sensor IDs into the receiver.

C. Gateway Module Sensor Identification

This procedure is used to store sensor identification numbers and locations inside the module without the download from the SmartWave handheld service tool. Windows-based software is used to initiate the sensor learn procedure. Using the gateway module method to identify the sensors is slower, but it is not necessary to remove tires to record sensor IDs and enter them manually.

1. Connect a Windows-based computer to the gateway module diagnostic connector using a J-1939 compliant communication adapter.
2. Enter the set-up configuration using the Bendix software. Enter the number of axles and dual wheels into a tire map of the vehicle.
3. Select the tire that requires a new sensor identification number to be associated with and select the "Learn" command for the module to detect the sensor's ID.
4. Using a SmartWave handheld tool or other RFID initiator tool, trigger the appropriate sensor to send a transmission to the module using a "Learn" command from the handheld tool placed near the tire sensor.
5. Up to 30 seconds may be required for the gateway module to learn the new sensor identification. Wait until the tire symbol displayed by the software turns from red to green.
6. The sensor programming is completed when all tire positions are highlighted in green after storing correct sensor identification numbers.

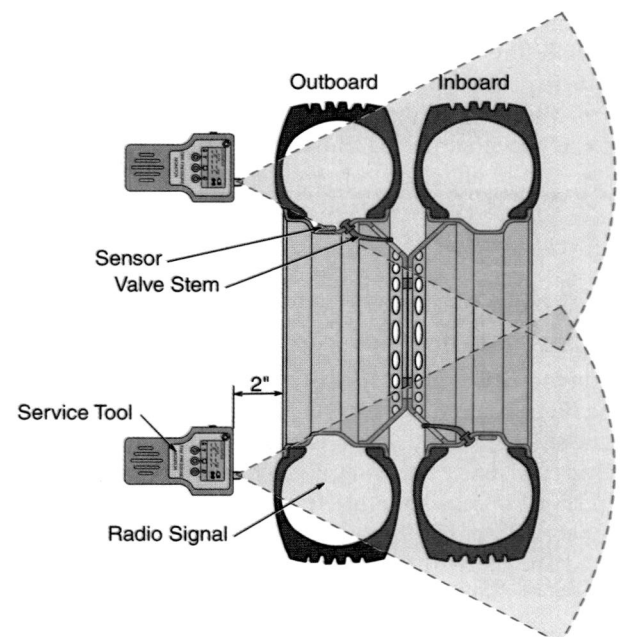

FIGURE 27-44 Tire pressure sensors must be located 180 degrees opposite one another to enable electronic service tools to learn whether the sensor is located inside the inboard or outboard tire after a tire is installed.

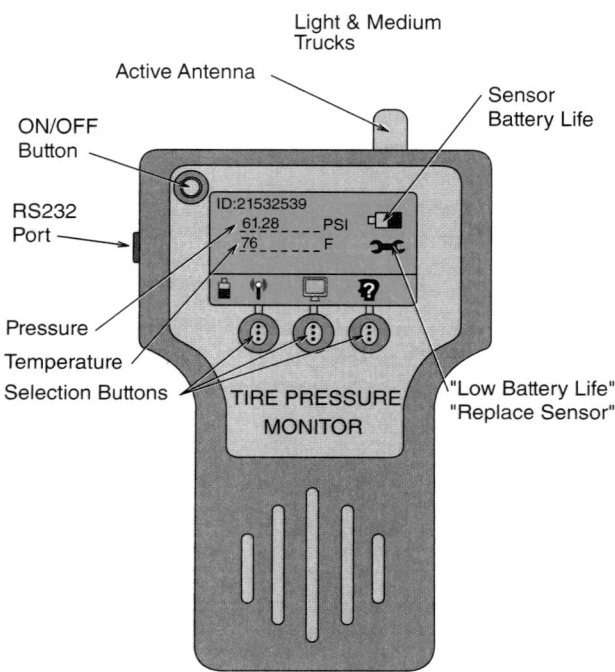

FIGURE 27-45 The SmartWave electronic service tool uses an antenna that communicates with the gateway module and identifies each tire sensor serial number and position—whether it's inboard or outboard on each wheel end.

When the wheel is installed, the normal correct position for the tire valve stem for each tire is accessible in opposite hand holes of wheel rims. The result is the sensors are automatically positioned 180 degrees apart. After the tires and wheels are installed, the service tool is placed against the sidewall of the tire and a radio signal requests the identification number for the sensor.

If the sensor has been installed next to the valve stem, the proximity of the sensor to the tool's antenna enables correct identification and location of the sensor as either inboard or outboard. An alternative procedure is to record tire sensor numbers during installation, or remove the tire to read the sensor number, and then manually enter the sensor number using the software or the handheld tool (**FIGURE 27-45**).

Tire fault codes are automatically set and displayed. Robust and weatherproof in design, the wireless gateway can be conveniently mounted to the vehicle's chassis and can be connected to the vehicle's J1939 communications network to provide messaging for display and control functions.

Maintenance and Service of Commercial Tires

LO 27-8 Identify and outline common service procedures associated with tire service and maintenance.

Tires are one of the most maintenance-intensive parts of a vehicle. They require regular visual inspections, pressure inspections, and rotations. Visual inspections of the tires and wheels

should be made whenever a vehicle comes into a workshop for any work. It is common to check for any unusual wear patterns and for any embedded objects or other signs of damage. If the vehicle is not equipped with a TPMS, then the operator should be encouraged to check the pressure at least monthly. Another task is rotating the tires. Most manufacturers recommend that the tires be rotated at each oil change to even out the wear and extend the life of the tires. Research the vehicle and service material for more information.

Tire Service Tools

To service wheels and tires in an efficient manner, you must have the appropriate tools and equipment. The basic equipment list should consist of:

- **Tire pressure gauge:** Used to check the air pressure in tires
- **Tire inflation tool:** Connected to a preset air regulator to limit maximum tire pressure. It must have a clip-on air chuck with a hose long enough to remotely monitor inflation
- **Tread depth gauge:** Used to measure a tire's tread depth
- **Valve stem tool:** Used to remove and install tubeless valve stem in rims
- **Valve core tool:** Used to remove and install Schrader valve cores in valve stems
- **Tire-changing machine capable of handling the range of tires that the workshop stocks:** If the shop handles run-flat tires, then the tire-changing machine must be designed to handle the more robust bead and sidewalls.

- **Tire dunk tank:** Used to locate leaks in tires and rims
- **Tire spreader:** Used to spread the sidewalls of a tire for easier access during tire patching
- **Air tire buffer:** Used to lightly buff the inside surface of the tire as preparation for tire patching
- **Patch stitching tool:** Used to apply pressure to the patch when positioning it
- **Tire inflation cage:** Used to contain the tire and rim during tire inflation and prevent injury or death in the event of a tire explosion
- **Wheel balancing machine:** capable of handling the range of tires that the shop services
- **Variety of wheel weight styles:** To cover the various styles of wheels
- **Tire rim hammers:** To unseat beads
- **Tire irons:** A set of pry bars used to remove and install tubeless tires
- **Wheel weight hammer:** Used to remove and install wheel weights onto rims
- **TPMS reset tool:** Used to reset the TPMS (not required on all TPMS-equipped vehicles)

Common Tire Service Issues

Common tire and wheel issues include:

- **Air loss:** The most common issue with tires is air loss. Tires normally lose a small amount of air over time and require periodic refilling. Punctures occur that cause leaks of various sizes. Valve stems and tire beads can also allow air to leak from the tire.
- **An out-of-balance tire or wheel:** The wheel and tires should be balanced, with the weight equally distributed throughout. When a tire rotates, any points of unequal weight cause the tire to be out of balance, placing stress on the shocks, bearings, and wheel assembly. A static imbalance causes the wheel to hop, creating a tramping noise as the heavy spot contacts the road surface. A dynamic balance in the front tires causes the wheel to shake from side to side. Rear tire dynamic imbalance can be felt by a vibration in the driver's seat. Additionally, the vehicle vibrates at speeds of about 50 to 60 mph (80 to 97 kph) and above, it has a rough ride, and the steering wheel may vibrate. A wheel balancer is used to identify and correct wheel imbalances.
- **Excessive loaded radial run-out on the tire, wheel, and hub assembly:** With radial run-out, the tire is out of round and the tread moves up and down. It is caused by incorrect manufacture or by damage to the tire, such as a broken belt. Correction involves replacing the tire.
- **Excessive lateral run-out on the tire, wheel and hub assembly:** Run-out occurs when a part of the wheel assembly becomes bent or was manufactured improperly. The result is a wobble. When lateral run-out occurs, the only method for fixing it is to replace the bent or improperly manufactured component.

- **Heavy pulling of a vehicle to either the left or the right while the customer is driving:** This is an indication of these possible problems:
  - Mismatched front tire sizes or pressures
  - Tire with broken or misaligned belts
  - Out-of-alignment wheels
  - Worn suspension or steering components
  - A dragging front brake assembly

Adjusting Tire Pressure and Using Pressure Gauges

Even brand new high-quality tires lose air over time. It's estimated that a minimum of one to three psi is lost per month on new heavy-truck tires, which means tire pressure needs to be checked and adjusted periodically. It is good practice to measure tire pressure at least monthly to identify a leaking tire. When equipped with a TPMS, each individual tire is automatically checked and alerts the driver of a problem if a tire's pressure is outside of the specified limits. These vehicles may have specific tire inflation pressures and a TPMS learn/reset procedure required by the manufacturer if the pressure sensor is changed, inflation pressure changes, or the tire is rotated out of its learned position.

Tires are inflated through a valve stem located in each tire rim or inner tube. A Schrader valve is a one-way check valve located at the outside end of the valve stem with a pin that must be pressed inward to either inflate the tire or release air from it. The valve is threaded into the valve stem and can be removed with a purpose-made tool to rapidly deflate a tire or to replace the valve if it leaks or the pin becomes bent. Gauges or inflation tools used to check tire pressure or fill tires with air have an end called an air chuck that has a purpose-made pin that pushes directly on the Schrader valve to open the valve. Topping up the air pressure is performed outside a safety cage only if the rim is securely attached to the hub. If a tire has been operated at less than 80% of its recommended operating pressure, the Schrader valve core should be removed to completely deflate the tire.

Before the tire is reinflated, it must be demounted and inspected internally, as well as externally, for damage, such as broken belts, bulged sidewalls, or shifted belts and plies. There are two main types of **tire pressure gauges**: gauges that are combined with a tire inflation air chuck and gauges-only tools (**FIGURE 27-46**). To access the valve stems of both the inner and outer dual wheel with Schrader valve pointing in opposite directions, tire gauges and inflation gauges are double-sided. Double-sided air chucks on the gauge or inflation tool enables the air chuck to seals around the Schrader valve to be pushed onto the inner tires valve stem or pulled onto the outer tires to check pressure or inflate. A clip-on air chuck and a hose of sufficient length must be used when inflating tires in safety cages. This enables the technician to remotely monitor tire pressure while remaining outside any trajectory path of an exploding tire. Actual tire inflation should be controlled from 10 feet away using an extension hose and a clip-on chuck.

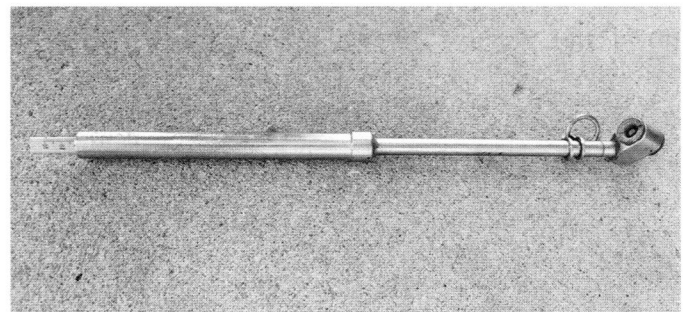

FIGURE 27-46 Tire pressure and inflation gauges.

MANUFACTURED BY		KILOGRAMS / POUNDS		SUITABLE TIRE - RIM CHOICE				THIS VEHICLE CONFORMS TO ALL
				TIRE SIZE	RIM SIZE	KPA COLD	PSI	APPLICABLE FEDERAL MOTOR VEHICLE
PETERBILT MOTORS CO.	GVWR	22680.0	50000	295/75R22.5G	22.5X8.25	760	110	SAFETY STANDARDS IN EFFECT ON THE
DIVISION OF PACCAR INC.	FR. GAWR	5443.2	12000	295/75R22.5F	22.5X8.25	620	90	DATE OF MANUFACTURE
	2ND. GAWR	8618.4	19000	295/75R22.5F	22.5X8.25	620	90	
DATE MFG. 02/2017	3RD. GAWR	8618.4	19000					VIN 1XP-BDK9X-7-J D451542
	4TH. GAWR			LABEL 22-01467				TYPE VEH. TRUCK TRACTOR

FIGURE 27-47 A mandatory tire inflation chart is posted on the driver's door pillar listing cold and hot tire inflation pressures according to tire size and load-carrying capacity.

Each tire pressure gauge measures pressure in kilopascals (kPa), pounds per square inch (psi), or bars. One bar is equivalent to 100 kPa or 14.5 psi. One psi is equivalent to approximately 7 kPa.

The tire pressure varies between tire sizes and load-carrying weight. Recommended tire pressures are required to be posted on a decal around the driver's door, usually on the door pillar (**FIGURE 27-47**). The maximum tire pressure is located on the tire sidewall. Never inflate the tire above the maximum pressure listed on the sidewall.

▶ TECHNICIAN TIP

If tire pressures are checked after the vehicle has been driven and the tires are warm or hot, do not release this excess pressure. If you bleed the tire pressure down to the manufacturer's recommendation, it is underinflated when the tire is cold or at normal operating temperature. This could cause premature wear on the tires and potential tire damage. Most tire manufacturers recommend checking tire pressures before the vehicle has been driven more than one mile (1.6 km). Tire inflation pressure decals list cold and hot pressures to provide guidelines to determine thresholds for over and under inflation.

▶ TECHNICIAN TIP

Tire pressure should be checked when tires are cold (around 70° F [21° C]). On average, the pressure in a tire increases or decreases by about 12.5 kPa for each 2° when the tire is above or below its normal operating temperature.

Inspecting Tire Wear Patterns

Normal tire tread should take place consistently and evenly across the tread over the expected tread life. Common irregular tire wear patterns indicate problems with steering angles or worn suspension and steering components. Several common problems include feathering of ribs or blocks, wear on only one side of the tire, cupping, center wear, and edge wear on both sides of the tire.

Feathering is observed on steering tires where a tire rib has a slightly rounded edge on one side and a sharp edge on the opposite. This condition may be easier to identify if the technician runs the palm of his or her hand across the tire in both directions, feeling for the sharper raised edges in only one direction of hand movement across the tread. Feathering is most commonly a result of the tires set with excessive toe-in or toe-out. If the tire's sharp edge is toward the outside edges of the treads, then the tire is excessively toed out. If there are sharp edges toward the inside of the treads, then the tire is excessively toed in.

Wear on only one side of the tire tread—either a steering, drive, or trailering tire—indicates that the wheels are not properly aligned. In this case, the tire is dragged sideways down the road due to misalignment between the vehicle direction of travel and the tire's orientation. More information about tire wear due to misalignment is covered in the chapter on front steering axles and vehicle alignment factors.

Cupping is the appearance of dips around the edge of the tread, on one or both outer sides of the tire. This wear can occur if the tire is too lightly loaded due to an incorrect position of the fifth wheel, or even high road crowns. A leaking or worn-out shock absorber also allows a cupping wear to take place because even a slightly out-of-balance tire bounces rhythmically up and down if the axle is lightly loaded. Tire center wear is when the ribs in the middle of the tire wear faster than those on each side. It results from driving on overinflated tires. To evaluate for abnormal tire wear patterns, follow the steps in **SKILL DRILL 27-2**.

Tire wear, particularly in radial-ply tubeless tires, is due to a range of reasons, which are commonly caused by tire imbalance, incorrect inflation, uneven loading of axles or tires, and misalignment problems. **TABLE 27-10** shows a range of conditions and the wear signs for each condition.

Dismounting a Tire

Dismounting a truck tire can be performed manually with bead unseating tools and a set of tire irons on tubeless tires. Center post-type tire machines are becoming more common and can supply over 1000 ft-lb of torque to rotate a large truck rim while compressing a tire sidewall to break the bead loose from the rim. The machine rotates the rim while the bead of a deflated tire is forced off or over the rim flange during removal and installation. Several other types of tire machines are available, which means technicians must become familiar with several machine operations, which vary between manufacturers (**FIGURE 27-48**). To dismount a tire using a drop center-type rim, follow the steps in **SKILL DRILL 27-3**.

SKILL DRILL 27-2 Evaluating Abnormal Tire Wear Patterns

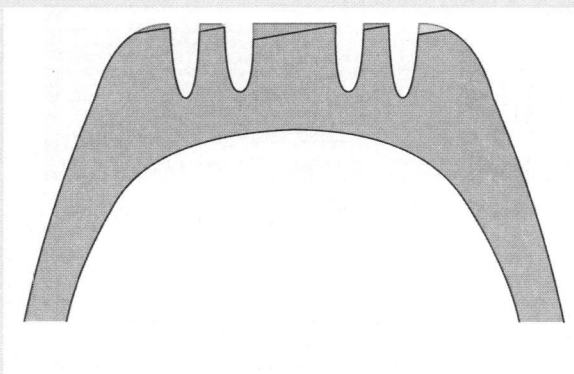

1. Inspect the tires for embedded objects in treads and remove them. If any object penetrates the tread, mark the hole with a tire crayon.
2. Visually examine all tires for evidence of unusual wear.
3. Measure and record the air pressure in the tires.
4. Measure and record the tread depth in several spots across the width tread. Most tires have wear indicator bars incorporated into the tread pattern. Inspect the wear indicator bars. Front tires

should have at least 4/32" (3.18 mm), while drive or trailer tires must have a minimum of 2/32" (1.59 mm). The wear indicator bars are normally set at this depth. If the tread is worn down to that level, the tires are unserviceable and must be replaced.

5. Examine the tread wear patterns. Common causes of uneven wear can include faulty shock absorbers, incorrect front alignment angles, out-of-balance tires, and incorrectly loaded axles. Uneven tread and bald spots can indicate over- or underinflated tires and poor alignment. Certain erratic wear patterns, called river wear, can show on trailer tires and are caused by unusual thrust forces that can be related to trailer axle alignment.
6. Inspect the sidewalls of the tires for signs of weather cracking, separation, and gouges from sharp objects.
7. Carefully examine the tread area for separation. This is usually identified as bubbles under the tread area or large cracks at the intersecting point between the tread and sidewall.
8. Spin the wheel and see if it is running true. Use a block of wood or another fixed object, such as a long hammer handle placed alongside the tire when it is spun, to quickly visually inspect for lateral run-out. A stationary block of wood placed on the floor near the raised wheel can be used to visually inspect for radial run-out of the tire. Alternatively, a dial indicator may be used for precise measurements of observations and recording.

TABLE 27-10 Ride and Wear Problems and Incorrect Tire Pressures

	Cause	Set/Condition	Result
	Toe	Excessive toe-in Excessive toe-out	Excessive outside shoulder wear with feather edges pointing inside Excessive inside shoulder wear with feather edges pointing outside
	Camber	Excessively positive Excessively negative	Excessive outside shoulder wear Excessive inside shoulder wear Pulling to the side

TABLE 27-10 Ride and Wear Problems and Incorrect Tire Pressures (Continued)

	Cause	Set/Condition	Result
	King-pin offset	Edge wear	Excessive tire wear
	Over inflation	Incorrect tire pressure	Excessive tire wear
	Under inflation	Incorrect tire pressure	Excessive tire wear, which can lead to operational instability
Heel (worn) / Toe	Tandem rear axle parallelism	Tires not parallel to one another	Toe-in/toe-out type wear (different side to side)
	Uneven axle loading	Excessive load weight that is offset over the tires	Tractor pulling to the side with excess and uneven load

SAFETY TIP

OSHA requires the use of a restraining device for inflating tires on multi-piece rims. Safety cages safely restrain tires and rims in the event of an explosive release of air, which propels the rim and tire apart with very high force. Underlining the potential amount of energy contained in a tire and wheel assembly, OSHA requires the restraining device or barrier, which includes cages, to have the capacity to withstand the maximum force of 150% of the maximum tire specification pressure. With the safety cage, OSHA also requires employers to provide an air line for tire inflation consisting of a clip-on chuck, an in-line control valve with a pressure gauge, or a preset air regulator to limit maximum inflation pressure. The line must be long enough to allow the technician to stand outside the trajectory of any explosion, which is at least 10 feet away. When using cages, technicians should keep the following tips in mind:

- Do not alter your tire inflation cage in any way.
- Cages must be freestanding and at least three feet from other objects; permanently mounting an inflation cage to the floor or near a wall prevents equal dissipation of energy released in all directions if a tire explosion takes place.

SKILL DRILL 27-3 Manually Dismounting a Tubeless Tire (Drop Center Rim)

1. Remove the Schrader valve core from the tire valve stem and remove the deflated tire and wheel assembly from the vehicle.
2. Lay the tire and wheel assembly on the floor, preferably over a mudflap, and unseat both beads directly opposite the TPMS sensor, if equipped. A variety of different **bead breaker** tools are used to unseat the tire bead from the rim. The tools are used to pry, drive, or pull a wedge between the tire bead and edge of the rim and then push down on the tire sidewall.
3. If the tire has a TPMS sensor, note its location. Normally the pressure sensor is located near the valve stem. A rim-mounted decal may also indicate the sensor's location. Do not attempt to begin unseating the bead using tire irons near the sensor or valve stem.
4. Ensure that the mounting side of the wheel is facing upward. This is the side where wheel nuts clamp the wheel onto the hub of the wheel. With the mounting side up, this typically positions the drop center section of the wheel rim to be as

high as possible. It's necessary to have this deep channel up as high as possible or it is difficult to lift the second tire bead up over the rim, allowing the tire to be removed from the rim. Using another position permanently gouges or damages the tire bead.

5. Apply bead lubricant to the bead area, which is a nonpetroleum-based grease or soap-like substance, to lubricate the tools to prevent damage to the bead caused by friction with the tools.
6. Insert one or two long tire irons beneath the tire bead near the TPMS sensor and pry the top tire bead over the wheel rim flange. Progressively pry and lift the top bead over the rim by working away from the sensor location until the top bead is free. Use caution to prevent contact between the sensor and the tire irons.
7. Repeat the same process for the bottom tire bead. Begin near the sensor to lift the tire bead over the rim flange until the tire is removed from the wheel. Use the tire lever to pry the tire bead over the rim while pushing down on the sidewall on the opposite side of the tire.

Using a Center Post Tire Machine

1. After removing the deflated tire and wheel assembly from the vehicle, unseat the beads directly opposite the sensor and valve stem with a swing arm of the machine. Do not break the bead at or near the sensor and valve stem.
2. Lubricate the tire bead and position the tire-wheel assembly on the machine.
3. Lift the bead over the rim flange with the bead-lifting bar and then turn the tire to dismount the top bead.
4. Repeat the bead-removal procedure for the second bead until the entire tire is removed from the wheel rim. Be careful not to make contact with the TPMS sensor.

FIGURE 27-48 A salesperson demonstrating the operation of center post automatic tire machine. The salesperson is observing the bead-rolling tool push the tire bead up over the rim flange.

To fit a tire to a wheel rim (tubeless), follow the guidelines in **SKILL DRILL 27-4**.

> ### ▶ TECHNICIAN TIP
>
> Always remove any balance weights from both sides of the rim before mounting it on the tire changer. If they are not removed, the bead remover could drag the weights around the rim, causing damage to the rim face. This is particularly important with alloy rims. The damage done by the balance weights is not repairable and usually requires the rim to be replaced, costing the shop a lot of money.

Replacing a Schrader Valve

Tire valve stems have a one-way check valve to allow air to enter a tire through an air chuck or release air when using a pressure gauge. Schrader, also called valve cores, contain elastomer-type washers or O-rings that deteriorate and require replacement when new tires are installed. To replace the Schrader valve, the entire tire valve stem should also be replaced when a tire is changed.

To change the valve stem, the wheel must be removed from the vehicle. The tire is then deflated, and the top bead broken. The old valve stem is cut out or the nuts holding it in the rim are removed. A new valve is pulled or tightened into place with new sealing washers to seal the hole in the wheel rim. The tire is reassembled and inflated to the recommended pressure inside a safety cage. To leak check the new valve, soapy water is sprayed around the valve stem and core to detect air leaks after the tire is inflated.

In some instances, only the Schrader valve or valve stem core requires replacement. A purpose-made tool is used to unscrew the core and used to tighten the new core. To replace a screw-in valve stem, follow the guidelines in **SKILL DRILL 27-5**.

Tire Balance

When a tire rotates, its mass should ideally be evenly distributed around the centerline of rotation. However, because of a less-than-perfect tire design and manufacturing process, some spots are heavier and others are lighter. Uneven weight distribution around the rotating center becomes exaggerated with increased speed and distance from the tire's center of rotation. Just a few ounces or grams of weight becomes exponentially much heavier as the tire speed and wheel diameter increases. The effect is wheel vibration that causes either a lateral and side-to-side shake in the wheel, or an up-and-down vibration producing an effect called tire tramp—a thumping sound made when a heavy spot of the tire contacts the road with

SKILL DRILL 27-4 Fitting a Tire to a Wheel Rim (Tubeless)

1. Inspect the bead seats on the wheel rim to ensure that the bead seats properly. Place the rim on the floor with the wider side at the bottom, ensuring that the seats are clean and free from dirt.
2. Lubricate the first bead of the tire and the upper bead seat of the rim and push the first bead into the wheel rim, using the narrower drop center radius, as far down as possible. The remaining section of the bead must be pushed into position using a tire iron.
3. Fit part of the second bead to the rim and use vice grips to hold it in place. Be sure not to damage the rim with the vice grips.
4. Fit the rest of the tire onto the rim and apply the recommended lubricant to the beads as required.
5. With the valve core still removed, place the wheel and tire assembly into a cage and inflate the tire to seat the beads. Then install the valve core and complete inflation according to manufacturer's recommendations.

SKILL DRILL 27-5 Replacing a Screw-In Type Schrader Valve

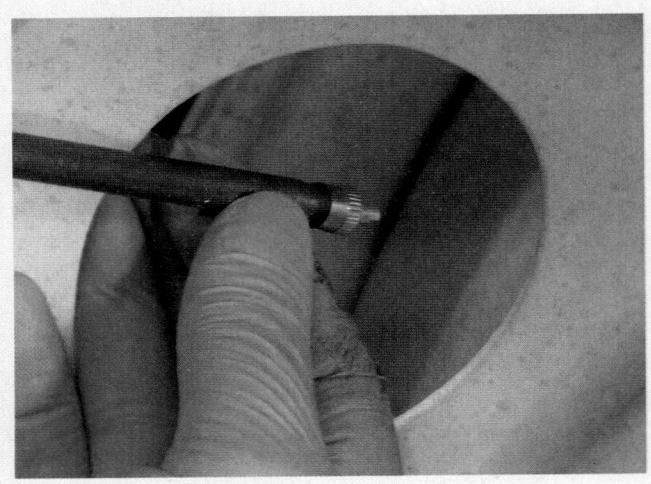

1. If the valve stem is a screw-in valve stem, remove the wheel from the vehicle, deflate the tire, break the top bead using the tire machine, and mount the wheel on the tire machine.
2. Unscrew the nut that holds the valve stem to the rim. Remove the valve stem from the inside of the rim.
3. Discard the old sealing washers and replace them with new ones. Place the valve stem with one new sealing washer through the hole on the inside of the rim.
4. Place a new sealing washer over the valve stem and thread the nut on by hand. Tighten the nut to the specified torque.

greater force than the rest of the tire. Two types of imbalance conditions can be present separately or together. One is static imbalance and the other is dynamic imbalance (**FIGURE 27-49**).

A tire that is dynamically imbalanced occurs when a spot on either the inside or the outside of the tire's centerline is heavy. This induces a side-to-side force imbalance in the tire as it rotates, which can cause a vibration, as well as the steering wheel to shimmy. **Dynamic imbalance** is usually a result of manufacturing variations, but it can be caused by a damaged tire or wheel. Accumulations of mud inside the wheel rim can suddenly produce a dynamic imbalance condition. Obviously, dynamic imbalance reduces ride quality and tends to increase wear on the tires

and on steering and suspension system components. Dynamic balancing of the tires is performed when new tires are installed on the vehicle, as well as any time that tire imbalance is suspected.

Dynamic balancing is performed on a tire balancer that can spin the tire and then identify the location and weight of any dynamic imbalance. A weight equal to the weight causing the imbalance is placed directly opposite the heavy spot on the tire or rim. The effect of adding a weight is to counter-balance dynamic imbalance in the tire by creating a force that is equal to, but opposing, the force causing the first imbalance condition.

Static imbalance takes place when a heavy spot on the tire is in the vertical centerline of the tire. The imbalanced force throws the tire up and down, but not side to side. To correct a static imbalance condition, a weight equal to the imbalance weight is divided equally in two and placed on opposite sides of the rim directly opposite the heavy spot of the tire. Like the correction for the dynamic imbalance condition, an equal-but-opposite force is generated to oppose the static imbalance.

Various designs of wheel weights are used, depending on the type of wheel rim. If the weights attached to the wheel are not the correct type, they fly off when the vehicle is driven. It is good practice to use new wheel weights when balancing a wheel. To balance a tire, follow the steps in **SKILL DRILL 27-6**.

To perform on-vehicle wheel balancing, follow the steps in **SKILL DRILL 27-7**.

Tire Repairs

Driving a short distance on a tire while it is severely underinflated causes the tire to overheat, as well as weaken the sidewall belts, creating a dangerous, non-repairable condition. The damage is not visible from the outside, so every tire needing repairs must be removed

FIGURE 27-49 Comparing the cause and effects of static and dynamic tire imbalance.

Static Imbalance   Dynamic Imbalance

Heavy Spots   Shimmy
Centered   Offset
Tramp   Tramp
Center Lines

SKILL DRILL 27-6 Balancing a Tire

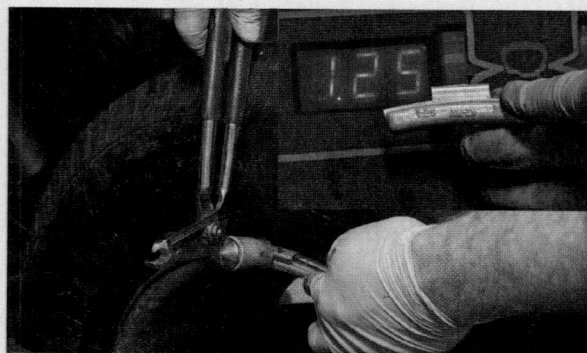

1. Check and adjust the tire pressure before balancing the tire.
2. Mount the wheel and tire on the balancer, putting the inside part of the wheel toward the balancer, in most cases. Secure the wheel by screwing the hub nut assembly on the balancer shaft.
3. Calibrate the balancer to the wheel by measuring the width of the rim with a rim caliper, using the gauge on the balancer to determine the location of the flange on the wheel (offset), and the diameter of the wheel as listed on the tire.

4. Input this data into the balancer's computer, if fitted, according to the manufacturer's instruction manual. If no computer is fitted, set the balancer adjustments manually according to the instruction manual.
5. If equipped, lower the safety hood over the wheel.
6. Spin the wheel. Read the balancer's analysis, which is normally displayed visually on the machine. It tells you whether the wheel is out of balance and, if so, how much weight to use and where to put it to balance the wheel. If the wheel is out of balance, you should remove the old weights and recheck the balance of the wheel before adding new weights.
7. Install new weights recommended by the machine's display, usually by hammering them onto the edge of the rim where indicated, although some are held in place by tape on the back side of the weight.
8. Now re-spin the wheel to check for accuracy of the balancing job and to confirm that balance has been achieved. A reading of zero on both sides of the wheel means the wheel is ready to reinstall on the vehicle. Repeat the process for the rest of the wheels and tires.
9. Reinstall and tighten the wheel-mounting hardware using the recommended procedure and correct specification.

from the wheel for inspection and to assess its serviceability. The tire needs to be inspected externally first, then internally for any signs of serious damage, such as chaffing of the sidewalls or cords sticking through the inner liner. If the inspection shows no signs of non-repairable failure, then the tire can be repaired in accordance with the procedures recommended by the tire associations.

- Repairs from any nail or similar object should be limited to the actual tread area. Among the criteria to perform a proper repair are:
- Repairs are limited to the tread area only.
- Puncture injury cannot be greater than 6 mm in diameter. Larger punctures damage the belts and the tire carcass must be scrapped.
- Repairs must be performed by removing the tire from the rim/wheel assembly to perform a complete inspection to assess all damage that may be present.

- Repairs cannot overlap. This means that if there are two or more repairs required to fix the tire, then each repair patch must not overlap.
- A rubber stem, or plug, must be applied to fill the puncture injury, and a patch must be applied to seal the inner liner. A common repair unit is a one-piece unit with a stem and patch portion. A plug by itself is an unacceptable repair.

To patch a tire, it needs to be removed from the wheel. You also need a buffer to clean the inside of the tire, glue for attaching the patch, and a tire plug patch. The tire plug patch is a superior product to the old-fashioned tire plug, and, in many places, it is the only legal way to repair a hole in a tire. It is more expensive but is a much safer alternative for repairing a tire because it patches the inside of the tire, in addition to filling the hole in the tire. To patch a tire, follow the steps in **SKILL DRILL 27-8**.

SKILL DRILL 27-7 Performing On-Vehicle Wheel Balancing

1. Raise the vehicle and position the balancer against the wheel so that the center of the balancer drive drum is on the tire's shoulder.
2. Position the electronic sensor as close as possible to the king pin on the inside of the axle.
3. Commence the actual wheel balancing by following the manufacturer's instructions and activating the balancer.
4. Once the wheel is rotating at the desired speed, disconnect the balancer drive drum from the wheel as per the method recommended by the balancer manufacturer.
5. Push the balancer flash button and move the machine away from the wheel. When the button is pushed, the stroboscopic flashes are stopped, and balance values are automatically shown on the balancer's display.
6. Attach the appropriate weight vertically above the center of the wheel as per the balancer instructions.
7. Repeat steps five through seven to ensure that the wheel is properly balanced.
8. Disconnect and remove the balancing equipment.

SKILL DRILL 27-8 Patching a Tire

1. After marking the location of the air leak on the tread of the tire, and the position of the tire and weights on the rim, remove the tire from the rim assembly so that an internal patch can be used seal the puncture.
2. Mount the tire in a tire spreader so that the puncture hole can be accessed from both the inside and the outside of the tire.
3. Use drill bit to open and clean the hole where the puncture is located.
4. Use a tire buffer to smooth the area inside the tire around the puncture cleaning an area slightly larger than the size of the tire patch.

SKILL DRILL 27-8 Patching a Tire (Continued)

5. After completing the buffing process, clean out all the accumulated debris. A vacuum works well for this.

6. Liberally apply the liquid cleaning solution to a clean rag and scrub the area just buffed. Some patching systems use a liquid cleaner that is applied to the tire and scraped off with a scraper. Repeat this step once or twice, as needed.

7. Apply vulcanizing cement evenly to the inner buffed surface of the tire and work it into the hole. Doing so prevents water from entering the hole and moving its way into the tire's tread. As with most contact-type cements, it needs to time until the cement is relatively dry and is only tacky to touch.

8. After selecting the appropriate tire patch, remove the plastic protective cover that is on the sticky side of the tire patch.

9. Take the pointed part of the patch and push it through the inner side of the tire's hole that was previously drilled, pushing it through to the outside of the tire.

10. Using a pair of pliers, grip the stem of the patch and pull it out so that the disc portion of the patch contacts the cemented area. Pull this narrow part of the patch away from the tire's tread. The sticky side of the patch has now been tightly pressed onto the buffed surface.

11. Use a stitching tool and roll the inner side of the tire patch tight onto the inner surface of the tire. Start at the center of the patch and work outward. This removes any air bubbles from between the sticky side of the patch and the buffed surface. The patch is now installed properly onto the tire. It is a good practice to cover the buffed area and newly applied patch with a rubber patch sealant. Doing so ensures a long-term, airtight repair. Trim the plug material even using a diagonal side cutter.

12. After the rubber patch sealant has dried, the tire can be reassembled onto the rim in its original position and inflated to the recommended pressure.

SKILL DRILL 27-9 Inspecting the Wheel Assembly for Air Loss Using the Spray-Bottle Method

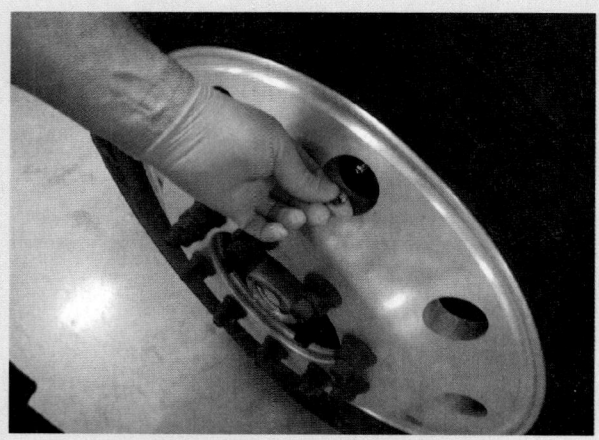

1. Remove the tire from the vehicle and inflate it to its proper pressure.
2. Using a spray bottle of soapy water, spray the valve stem and core, tire tread, and tire bead area.
3. Inspect the tire, valve stem, and wheel assembly for bubbles, which indicates a leak.
4. Mark any leaks in the tire with a tire crayon.

Inspecting the Wheel Assembly for Air Loss

LO 27-9 Outline procedures to inspect the wheel assembly for air loss.

A frequent tire-related complaint is caused by tires with slow leaks. To efficiently check the suspect tire, it must be removed from the vehicle and inflated to no more than 20 psi.

A preliminary check for leaks is performed with a spray bottle of soapy water. Spray the soapy water around the tread, valve stem and core. In addition, spray around the bead area.

If there is any air leakage, soapy air bubbles indicate where the problem is. Mark the tire with a wax crayon where the air bubbles are coming from so that the repairs can be carried out. To inspect the wheel assembly for air loss using the spray-bottle method, follow the steps in **SKILL DRILL 27-9**.

Measuring Wheel, Tire, and Hub Flange Run-out

Run-out is the side-to-side (lateral) or up-and-down (radial) variation in rotating wheel dimensions. In many cases, run-out issues cannot be observed when the vehicle is stationary on the ground. Instead, run-out problems can be felt as a vibration while the vehicle is being driven, usually more noticeable as speed is increased. If the vibration is primarily observed in the steering wheel as side-to-side wheel shimmy, the run-out is most likely in one or both front wheel assemblies.

Vibration felt primarily in the back of the driver's seat or throughout the entire vehicle suggests that the problem is with one or both rear drive wheels. To measure tire run-out, follow the steps in **SKILL DRILL 27-10**.

To measure wheel run-out, follow the steps in **SKILL DRILL 27-11**.

SKILL DRILL 27-10 Measuring Radial Tire Run-Out

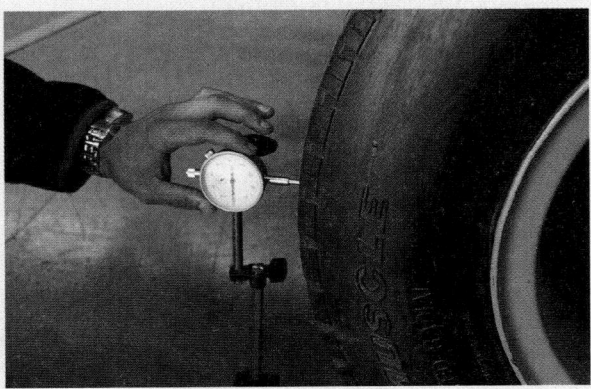

1. Research the procedure and specifications for measuring tire run-out in the service information. Raise the vehicle on a hoist or place a jack under the vehicle at a suitable lifting point and raise the vehicle. If using a jack, be sure to place safety stands under the frame of the vehicle and slowly lower the vehicle onto the stand.
2. Select the run-out gauge or dial indicator, attachment, and bracket that fits the purpose of measuring run-out.
3. Mount the dial indicator on a firm surface to stabilize it.
4. Adjust the dial indicator so the plunger is 90 degrees to the tread of the tire.
5. Press the dial indicator gently against the tire and rotate the tire one full turn. Keep pressing until the plunger settles about halfway into the indicator.
6. Verify that the plunger is still 90 degrees to the tire and lock the indicator assembly into position.
7. Carefully rotate the tire a couple of times while observing the dial readings. If the pointer hovers around a single graduation on the dial, the tire has minimal run-out or surface distortion and the test is complete. If the pointer moves significantly in and out, record the variations.
8. Find the point of maximum movement to the in and move the dial so that zero is over this point.
9. Continue to rotate the tire. Find the point of maximum movement out and record the reading. This measure indicates the run-out value. Confirm this value by rotating the tire several more times to verify the zero point and high point. The result is the radial run-out measurement for the tire.
10. Compare these values with the manufacturer's specifications. If the deviation is greater than the specifications, the wheel and/or hub run-out must be measured.

SKILL DRILL 27-11 Measuring Lateral Wheel Run-Out

1. Select a run-out gauge or dial indicator and bracket. Mount the dial indicator on a firm surface beside the wheel to anchor it. Adjust the dial indicator so the plunger is 90 degrees to the wheel rim.
2. Press the dial indicator gently against the wheel and rotate the wheel one full turn. Keep pressing until the plunger settles about halfway into the indicator. Verify that the plunger is still 90 degrees to the wheel and lock the indicator assembly into position.
3. Carefully rotate the wheel several times while observing the dial readings. Record the maximum and minimum gauge measurements and subtract the maximum from minimum measurements. The result is the lateral run-out measurement for the wheel.
4. Compare these values with the manufacturer's specifications. If the deviation is greater than the specifications, the hub flange run-out must be measured to determine if the wheel or the hub is the problem.

Wrap-Up

Ready for Review

- Tires are responsible for supporting the vehicle load, transmitting braking and traction forces to the road surface, absorbing road shock, and providing directional control of the vehicle.
- A wide variety of tires are made to provide unique operational features for specific vehicle applications.
- Inflated tires contain an enormous amount of stored energy, and serious safety precautions must be taken when working with them.
- Compressed air and debris can be released when deflating tires. While inflating tires, there is a risk of exploding tire debris and parts.
- When wheels and tires are used in an incorrect arrangement, a vehicle can become unstable in certain road conditions.
- Maintaining proper tire pressure is essential for the safety and performance of a vehicle, as well as decreasing fuel consumption, reducing CO_2 emissions, and extending tire life.
- The automated tire pressure monitoring system (TPMS) continuously monitors tire pressure to increase fuel economy and safety.
- Commercial vehicle tires are either tube or tubeless to seal air inside the tire.
- Tire sizes and other important data are molded into the sidewalls of tires. Different marking systems are used for new and retreaded tires.
- The lower a tire's aspect ratio, the wider the tire becomes in relation to the height of the sidewall.
- Low-profile tires offer more responsive steering, better fuel economy, and tire stability due to greater lateral stability of tire sidewalls.
- The role of the belt system is to provide stability to the tread area of the tire.
- Three basic types of tire construction are bias-ply, radial-ply, and bias-belted.
- Bias-ply belt construction provides a stiffer tread and sidewall area.
- Radial tires produce less rolling resistance while providing better high-speed traction. They also have increased tread life and improved handling characteristics.
- The primary function of the inner liner is to seal air inside a tire and keep moisture out. Tread is typically made from an abrasion-resistant, high-grip rubber compound, formulated to combine the best traction, tire longevity, and low rolling resistance for superior fuel economy.
- The profile of tread used on a tire depends on the type of axle to which the tire is attached. Tread is designed for either steering, drive tires, or trailering tires.

- Retreaded tires cost significantly less than the cost of a new tire (typically 40% of the cost of new); they are widely used in commercial fleet operations.
- Tires can be retreaded using a hot-curing or cold-curing method.
- Retreaded tires do not fail at higher rates than OEM tires; the failure rates are comparable.
- The depth of tire tread grooves is mandated by Federal Motor Vehicle Safety Standard 119.
- Manufacturers include wear bars around the circumference of the tire to enable technicians to determine how much tread groove depth remains.
- Regroovable tires are manufactured to extend the tire tread life and have adequately thick tread compound between the bottom of the original tread grooves and the top of the uppermost breaker or belt depth.
- Maintaining the correct tire pressure for a commercial vehicle is an important factor determining the load its tires can safely carry.
- Too much or too little tire pressure can cause catastrophic failure, and the combination of mechanical stress and heat build-up eventually lead to premature deterioration and failure.
- Loss of energy through hysteresis accounts for approximately 90% of energy losses through rolling resistance. The remaining 10% energy loss takes place in the tread as the tire tread is deformed by road surface irregularities.

Key Terms

aspect ratio The ratio of sidewall height to section width of a tire.

bead breaker A tool used to break the tire bead seal from the rim.

bias-ply tire A type of tire ply construction where plies are arranged in a latticed, crisscrossing structure, with alternate plies crossing over each other and laid with the cord angles in opposite directions.

cold curing A retreading process that uses a molded, pre-cured tread strip or tread ring, which is glued to the casing.

contact patch The area of the tire that is in actual contact with the road.

direct TPMS A type of automated tire pressure monitoring system that measures tire pressure, and possibly temperature, via a sensor installed inside each wheel.

drop-center wheel rim A type of wheel rim design used by tubeless tires to ease installation of a tire over a rim. The center section of the wheel between the two bead seats has a smaller radius area.

dynamic imbalance A condition of a rotating assembly, such as a tire, wheel, or flywheel, where its weight is not symmetrically balanced around the center line of rotation and is offset from the vertical axis center.

flotation tire Large tires used on the front axle with a low aspect ratio. Also called *wide-base tire*.

hot curing A retreading process in which the casing is covered with uncured rubber and then placed in a mold and heated. Also called *mold curing*.

indirect TPMS A type of automated tire pressure monitoring system that uses the anti-lock braking system of a vehicle to measure the difference in the rotational speed of the four wheels to determine tire pressure.

low profile (LP) tire A type of tire that has a shorter sidewall height than conventional tires.

nominal diameter A size-code figure, for reference purposes only, as indicated in the tire and rim size designation.

overall diameter The diameter of an inflated tire at the outermost surface of the tread.

radial-belted tire A tire construction with belts placed at 90 degrees to the tire centerline, wrapped from side to side around the tire beads.

radial-ply tire A tire with two or more layers of casing plies and cord loops running radially from bead to bead.

regrooving A process that uses a heated cutting tool to carve new tread or add stripes to a tire.

retreading The process of applying new tread to an existing tire casing to extend the service life of the tire.

rolling circumference The distance covered by one revolution of the tire.

rolling resistance The tendency of a tire to resist rolling along naturally when under load.

section height The height of the sidewalls.

section width The distance between the outside of the sidewalls on an inflated tire without any load on it.

static imbalance A condition of a rotating assembly, such as a tire, wheel, or flywheel, where the weight is not symmetrically balanced around the center line of rotation and the offset is at the vertical axis center.

static radius The distance from the tire center to ground level.

super single tire Wide-base, low-profile tire used to replace two conventional single tires on an axle to save weight and reduce wheel end parts.

tire bead A rubber section of the tire that contacts the wheel rim. The rubber bead contains steel wire wound together to form a cable; when bundled together, they sit at the wheel rim to form an airtight seal between the tire and the rim.

tire casing The foundational body of the tire, consisting of several layers of fabric cord, called plies, encased with a rubber compound; a network of cords that give the tire shape and strength; also known as casing cords.

tire flap A piece of rubber that wraps around the rim to protect the inner tube from chafing, pinching, and cracking caused by friction between the valve stem slot in the rim and the edges of the tire bead.

tire inflation pressure The level of air in the tire that provides it with load-carrying capacity and that affects overall vehicle performance.

tire pressure gauge A gauge used to measure the air pressure within a tire.

tire pressure monitoring system (TPMS) A system within wheel sensors that monitors tire inflation pressure and temperature.

tire tread separation The separation of the tread from the tire casing.

tread A cap of molded rubber compound attached to the top of a tire's belt system.

tubeless tire A tire in which the air is sealed by only the wheel and tire.

tube-type tire A tire in which an inner tube containing the air is separate from the casing.

undertread The depth of the area between the bottom of the original tread grooves and the top of the uppermost belt.

wide-base tire Large tire with a low aspect ratio. Also called *flotation tire*.

Review Questions

1. Which of the following statements about heavy-duty commercial vehicle tires is correct?
   a. Fewer than half of all truck tires are inflated within 5 psi of their target pressure
   b. 75% of all tire failures are a result of tire under-inflation
   c. 20% under-inflation reduces tire casing life by 80%
   d. 10% under-inflation reduces tread life by 25%
2. The most common type of tire construction used by today's on-highway class 8, heavy-duty commercial vehicles are:
   a. tube-type.
   b. bias-ply construction.
   c. radial-ply construction.
   d. retreaded tires.
3. When servicing tires, which of the following are the best combination of safety precautions to use?
   a. Use a safety cage during inflation and a remotely connected air chuck.
   b. Wear safety glasses, steel-toed boots, and a bump cap.
   c. Use tire bead lubricant and OEM-approved pry bars.
   d. Chain tires to rims when inflating and stay out of potential tire trajectory path if it explodes.
4. What is the approximate tread width of an 11R 22.5 tire?
   a. 22" (59 cm)
   b. 11" (28 cm)
   c. 45" (114 cm)
   d. 0.78" × 11" (1.98 cm × 27.9 cm)

5. Consider a tire with a sidewall marking of 445/50R 22.5. What is the sidewall dimension of the tire?
   a. 11" (28 cm)
   b. 222 mm (8.74")
   c. 445 mm (17.5")
   d. 8.8" (22.4 cm)

6. Consider a tire with a sidewall marking of 445/65R 22.5. What classification of tire is this?
   a. Low-profile radial
   b. Bias-ply
   c. High hysteresis
   d. A drive-axle tire only

7. Which of the following is an advantage of a diagonal bias-ply tire?
   a. It resists punctures and road damage better than other tires
   b. Lower rolling resistance
   c. Longer tread life
   d. Better road contact patch for superior traction

8. What is the most likely cause of excessive wear of one tire of a dual-wheel tire pair on the same axle end?
   a. Uneven vehicle loading
   b. Unbalanced tires
   c. Uneven tire sizes
   d. Lateral tire run-out

9. What is the most common cause of tire tread separation?
   a. Using retreaded tires
   b. Improperly cured tire retread-caps
   c. Underinflation
   d. Excessive torque

10. What is the correct service recommendation for a tire that is found to have only 60 psi of air, yet is required to have an inflation pressure of 100 psi cold, which is indicated by the driver's side door decal?
    a. Scrap the tire.
    b. Inflate the tire on the vehicle to 100 psi and check for leaks.
    c. Deflate and dismount the tire, inspect, and re-inflate in a safety cage if no defects are found.
    d. Inflate to 20 psi and check for leaks, then inflate to 100 psi.

ASE Technician A/Technician B Style Questions

1. Technician A says that commercial truck tires support less weight per square inch (cm) of contact patch and transmit less drive torque per square inch (cm) than a motorcycle tire. Technician B says truck tires last longer and carry more weight while transmitting more torque than a typical car tire. Who is correct?
   a. Technician A
   b. Technician B
   c. Both Technician A and Technician B
   d. Neither Technician A nor Technician B

2. Technician A says "road alligators" are road debris that could be eliminated if re-tread tires were banned from use. Technician B says "road alligators" are not just produced by the caps of a retread tire separating from the case, but are caused by underinflation of any tire. Who is correct?
   a. Technician A
   b. Technician B
   c. Both Technician A and Technician B
   d. Neither Technician A nor Technician B

3. Consider one wheel of a dual-wheel combination that has been removed from a trailer to repair a flat tire. Technician A says the tire should be first inflated in a safety cage with a clip-on, remote inline air chuck. Technician B says the tire should be first dismounted and inspected for damage before re-inflating. Who is correct?
   a. Technician A
   b. Technician B
   c. Both Technician A and Technician B
   d. Neither Technician A nor Technician B

4. Technician A says that tires are marked with a mandatory load index of 150 and a J speed rating can carry more weight than a tire with a load index of 156 and M speed rating. Technician B agreed that tires carry mandatory load index markings, but a tire with an L speed rating and load index of 156 can travel faster with more weight than a J speed rating and load index of 150. Who is correct?
   a. Technician A
   b. Technician B
   c. Both Technician A and Technician B
   d. Neither Technician A nor Technician B

5. Technician A says that a TPMS can save the owner fuel over a period of time. Technician B says that a TPMS helps prevent blowouts. Who is correct?
   a. Technician A
   b. Technician B
   c. Both Technician A and Technician B
   d. Neither Technician A nor Technician B

6. Technician A says that a Bendix TPMS uses pressure-sensing RFID tags located inside tires to transmit radio signals to a gateway receiver using Bluetooth radio signals. Technician B says Bendix's TPMS sensors can be "wakened" to transmit radio signals when performing diagnostic tests using a handheld radio transmitter-receiver. Who is correct?
   a. Technician A
   b. Technician B
   c. Both Technician A and Technician B
   d. Neither Technician A nor Technician B

7. Technician A says that the tires worn down to the level of a wear bar should be replaced. Technician B says tire tread depth should be measured to determine when it should be replaced. Who is correct?
   a. Technician A
   b. Technician B
   c. Both Technician A and Technician B
   d. Neither Technician A nor Technician B

8. Technician A says that it does not matter if you mix brands of tires on a steering axle if the tires are the same size. Technician B says that the driver should check the tire pressures at least every three months. Who is correct?
   a. Technician A
   b. Technician B
   c. Both Technician A and Technician B
   d. Neither Technician A nor Technician B

9. Technician A says that excessive tire wear on the inside and outside edges of a tire is due to a problem with steering angle alignment. Technician B says that excessive tire wear is most likely caused by over inflation of the tire. Who is correct?
   a. Technician A
   b. Technician B
   c. Both Technician A and Technician B
   d. Neither Technician A nor Technician B

10. Technician A says that dynamic wheel imbalance can result in steering wheel shimmy. Technician B says that static wheel unbalance could cause wheel tramp to occur. Who is correct?
    a. Technician A
    b. Technician B
    c. Both Technician A and Technician B
    d. Neither Technician A nor Technician B

CHAPTER 28
Wheel Rims and Hubs

Learning Objectives

- **LO 28-1** Identify and explain the fundamentals of wheels and rims.
- **LO 28-2** Identify the types, features, and applications of commercial vehicle wheels.
- **LO 28-3** Explain how wheels can be classified by their dimensions and load carrying capacity.
- **LO 28-4** Identify and describe the types of wheel centering systems and explain features of hub and stub piloted wheels.
- **LO 28-5** Identify and explain the wheel retention methods used by hub piloted wheels.
- **LO 28-6** Identify and explain wheel nut torque versus clamping force.

- **LO 28-7** Identify and explain service techniques for inspecting wheels and hubs.
- **LO 28-8** Identify the types of hubs and differentiate between concepts of bearing preload and end play.
- **LO 28-9** Identify and describe the construction of standard hubs and service methods for adjusting wheel bearing end play.
- **LO 28-10** Identify and describe the construction of preset hubs and service methods for adjusting wheel bearing end play.
- **LO 28-11** Describe and explain construction features of cast spoke hubs and rim retention system.
- **LO 28-12** Describe and explain the purpose of hub seals and lubricant.

You Are the Technician

A reputable truck fleet operation recently had a wheel separation on one of its trucks that caused extensive damage to other vehicles on the road. Although a wheel separation is uncommon, it can be disastrous, if not fatal, if a separated wheel hits another vehicle, building, or person. The incident has left you concerned about the safety practices and procedures you follow in your shop whenever wheels hubs are reinstalled.

Like other technicians that service truck-bus wheels and hubs in the shop, you have received wheel end installation service training as required by the Occupational Safety and Health Administration (OSHA) regulations. But you are considering how best to perform preventative maintenance inspections on all wheels and hubs to make sure the assemblies are safe and in good working order. You are also contemplating revising the service standards you will use when replacing wheels and hubs. As you prepare plans for the steps to take, consider how you would answer the following questions:

1. What specific points of inspections would you carry out for the three major types of wheels and hub assemblies serviced by your shop in the future?
2. In addition to correctly tightening the wheel fasteners, what other factors would you consider to ensure you obtain proper clamping force on wheels and rims?
3. How would you ensure that the wheel bearing end play is within the acceptable range for each vehicle?

Introduction

Wheel rims, tires, and hubs are names given to major components making up the axle **wheel end**. **FIGURE 28-1** is an image that identifies the major components of the wheel end that function to support the vehicle weight rolling and steering over irregular surfaces under a wide range of loads and operating conditions. A number of factors determine the design and construction of the wheel end; the most basic is constructing a wheel end capable of properly supporting the vehicle weight while rolling, steering, or supplying traction in steering, trailer, or drive axle positions.

Regardless of where it is positioned, problems in wheel ends can potentially result in complaints, such as premature or uneven tire and brake wear, brake pull, seal leaks, wandering steering, wheel separations, and even vehicle fires. In the case of vehicle fires, the situation is often caused by overheated tires. Enormous amounts of heat are transferred from hubs and dragging brakes or when a wheel bearing fails. Heat passes from the brake drum and hub into the rim, and then melts, or even ignites, a tire.

Wheel ends are one of the most crucial vehicle systems to competently maintain and service from both a safety and economic perspective. Wheel-end failures and wheel separations can also have catastrophic consequences, not only to the vehicle and its occupants, but to other users of the roadway. In fact, the importance of proper service and maintenance of wheel ends is underlined by the OSHA Regulation 29 CFR 1910.177, which requires mandatory training for all technicians servicing tires and wheels. In many jurisdictions, wheel separations can incur fines up to $50,000 per incident, with potential for imprisonment in the case of serious negligence.

With the wide variety of tasks commercial vehicles perform, there is a corresponding difference in the design technology used to construct wheel ends. And, because of the importance of wheel ends to each vocational task performed by commercial vehicles, it is important for technicians to properly understand wheel-end construction, service, and maintenance techniques, along with the causes of wheel-end failures.

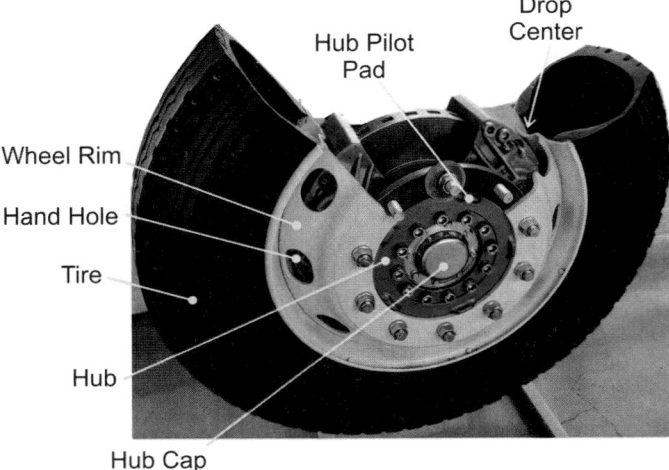

FIGURE 28-1 Major components of wheel ends include the tire, wheel rim, and hub assembly.

Fundamentals of Wheels and Rims

LO 28-1 Identify and explain the fundamentals of wheels and rims.

The general purpose of a wheel assembly is first to smoothly roll over irregular surfaces to enable vehicle mobility. Rolling wheels have some resistance but reduce sliding friction and increase a vehicles weight carrying capacity. Wheels also can turn to steer a vehicle and transfer the rolling vehicle weight from the hubs to the tires while simultaneously transmitting driving torque to the road through wheel traction. Combined stress from the force of driving torque transmitted through drive axles and the weight of a vehicle means the same wheel used in a non-driving position, such as a trailer, can support more weight than a drive axle.

Factors that determine the design, construction, and selection of wheels include:

- Load rating or gross vehicle weight
- Position of the wheel, such as whether it is attached to a steering, driving, or trailer axle
- Application: off road, on highway, construction, mining, refuse hauling, etc.
- Dual- or single-wheel system
- Hub mounting system used to center and attach the wheel to the hub
- Tire type: tube, tubeless, or bias ply
- Tire size and inflation pressure
- Type of braking system: drum or air disc brake (ADB)
- Vehicle steering or handling characteristics
- Appearance and ease of maintenance
- Regional regulations and standards

Wheel Types

LO 28-2 Identify the types, features, and applications of commercial vehicle wheels.

Medium- and heavy-duty (HD) buses and trucks use only two basic types of wheels:

1. Open center or demountable rim: An **open center rim**, also called a **demountable rim**, only consists of the metal rim band (**FIGURE 28-2**). Because these wheels do not have

FIGURE 28-2 A demountable or open center rim.

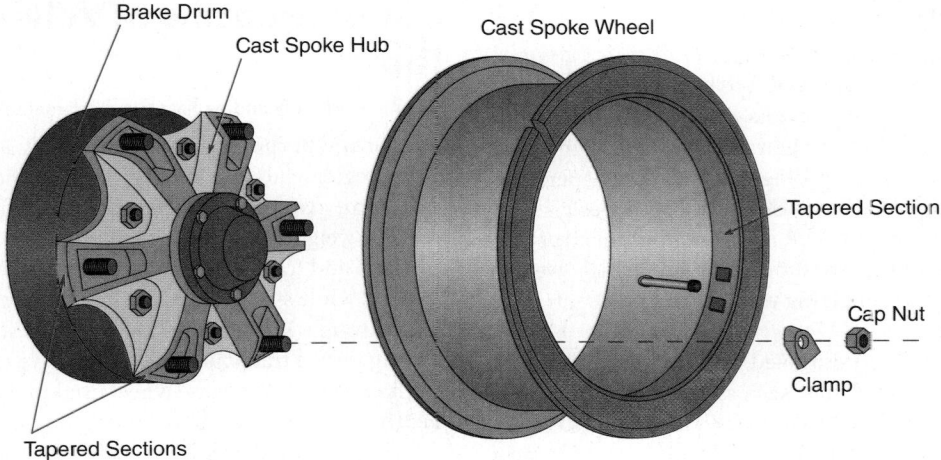

FIGURE 28-3 Single demountable rim on a cast spoke hub.

a center disc, they are called open center rims. Open center rims are only used with **cast spoke** hubs, which integrate three, five, or six cast iron spokes with the bearing hub. Together the rim, wedged and clamped over a cast spoke hub, form the wheel (**FIGURE 28-3**). The wheel spokes support either one or two tire rims. Depending on the type of tire used by the vehicle, the rim may be a single or multi-piece configuration made of one, two, or three pieces. Tires with tubes and bias ply tires use multi-piece rims with a flat rim base and one or two split rings to secure one side of the tire onto the rim (**FIGURE 28-4**). The opposite side the tire is positioned by the rim flange. Tubeless radial tires use single piece, drop center rim. The drop center rim enables easier installation of a radial tubeless tire over the rim.

Different terms are used when identifying this rim. It's technically important to first note that the terms *wheel* and *rim* are often used interchangeably. There is, however, a difference because the **wheel rim** refers only to the flat horizontal section of a wheel having an outer circular lip of metal on which the inside edge of the tire is mounted. The purpose of the rim is to seal and hold the tire onto the wheel. Occasionally the name "Dayton" is attached to open center wheels, but the term refers to an early manufacturer of cast spoke hubs and is not a wheel type.

2. Disc Wheels—This wheel design has both a rim and a disc in the wheel center. The disc is attached around its circumference to the rim (**FIGURE 28-5**). The disc center construction lends the **disc wheel** its name. Disc wheels are a one-piece design made from steel or aluminum. Occasionally, the term "Budd" wheel is applied to these wheels, particularly when they are made from aluminum, but that name refers only to an early manufacturer of disc wheels and is not a wheel design. The disc attaches to the hub using wheel studs and nuts.

Disc-type wheels have closed centers and contain holes for studs used to clamp the wheel to the hub with nuts. Only eight or ten

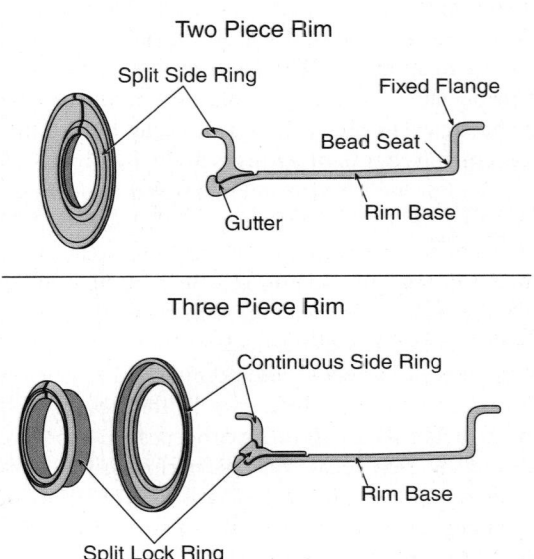

FIGURE 28-4 Multi-piece open center rims use either one or two split rings. Three-piece rims use a flange ring with a split ring.

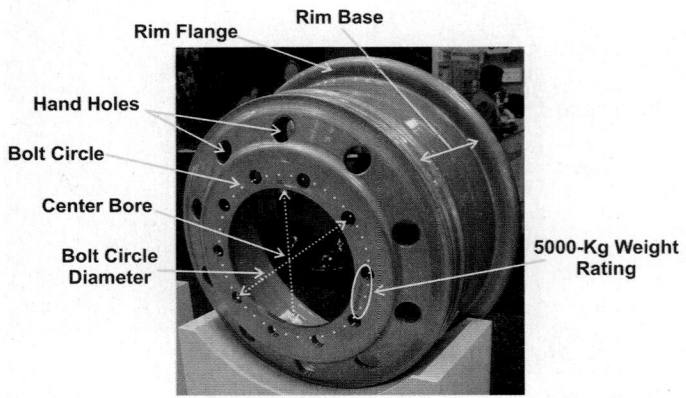

FIGURE 28-5 Elements of a disc wheel.

stud holes are found in commercial vehicle wheel discs. In the center of the disc is a large single hole called the center bore. The center bore allows the wheel to pass over a hub to help center the wheel and is used to transfer vehicle weight to the hub on hub piloted disc wheels. Additional hand holes in disc wheel provide access to the tire valve stem on single and dual wheels. Removal of material to create hand holes helps lighten the weight of a wheel, but there is a trade-off between the number and size of hand holes and the wheels' weight carrying capacity.

For decades, the strength of cast spoke hubs with open center rims dominated the commercial wheel industry. Disc wheels have almost completely displaced open center rims and open center rims with potentially dangerous split rings. Many open center rims are still in service, particularly in the heavy hauling, off-road construction industry. In developing countries, bias ply tires with tubes use open center rims that are preferred because of their ability to withstand abuse, taking cuts and remaining inflated and in service after an inner tube replacement. It is important to note that split, or multipiece, open center rims must be properly serviced to prevent explosive separation of rings and rims, causing severe physical injury and death.

Wheel Dimensions

LO 28-3 Explain how wheels can be classified by their dimensions and load carrying capacity.

Wheels can be further classified by their dimensions and load carrying capacity. A wheel's load capacity or weight the wheel can support is measured in kilograms (k) or pounds (lb). This critical capacity is usually stamped on the wheel and is strongly influenced by wheel dimensions. A variety of wheel dimensions also have an influence on how well the vehicle can maneuver, transmit torque, and travel over irregular surfaces while carrying a payload. In Europe and North America, standardizing regulations for tires, rims, and valve parts are established by Tire and Rim Associations (TRAs) in their respective countries. The European TRA regulations are used by EURO and Asian manufacturers.

Wheel Dimension Terminology

Important standardized dimensions include:

1. **Wheel Diameter**—A wheel is sized according to its diameter measured across the center of the wheel from each bead seat on the rim flange (**FIGURE 28-6**). The **rim diameter** measurement does not include the thickness of the edge rim flange. The most common diameter for HD commercial vehicles is 22.5". For historical reasons, the diameter is stated only in inches in North America and Europe. Highway tractors with aggressive down-speeding (high torque rise engines with rear axle ratios geared to run fast at low engine rpm) may use 24.5" diameter wheels to further reduce engine rpm. Low floor and gooseneck trailers used to float construction equipment, or vehicles with high cubic volume capacity, such as car haulers, may use specialized 17.5" and 19.5" diameter wheels.

2. **Rim width**—Refers to the distance across the rim flanges at the bead seat. The **bead seat** is the edge of the rim that creates a seal between the tire bead and the wheel. The **rim flange** is the exterior lip that holds the tire in place. The width of the rim is also commonly stated in inches for historical reasons. A typical rim width for a 22.5" diameter wheel is between 7.5" to 14".

3. **Bolt Circle**—The center of every bolt hole is arranged around the circumference of a dimension called the bolt circle. A bolt circle is identified by its diameter or the distance across the center of the rim to an opposite bolt hole in the bolt circumference. Typically, the diameter is expressed in millimeters. In North America, two common bolt circle diameters for a hub piloted 22.5" wheel is 275 mm (10.83") and 285.75 mm (11.25"). Commercial vehicle wheels on European vehicles are built to a different dimensional standard, with the most commonly used bolt circle diameter for 10 bolts being 335 mm (13.2") on HD vehicles (**FIGURE 28-7**). Bolt circle specifications are usually published with the number of bolts in the circle, which is either eight or 10 bolts. Wheels using eight bolts

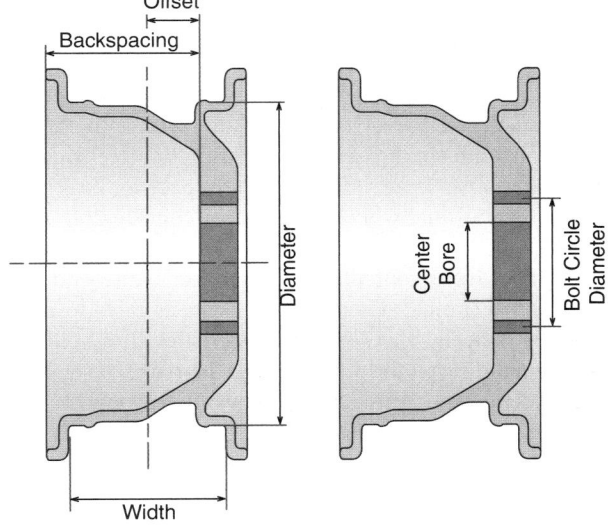

FIGURE 28-6 Wheel dimensions for diameter bolt circle and center bore.

FIGURE 28-7 The standard wheel dimensions for the center bore and bolt circle are different between a European and North American wheel.

have the 275 mm (10.83") bolt circle while 10-bolt wheels use the wider 285.75 mm (11.25") circle diameter. Stated as 8 x 275 mm, the specification is a bolt circle with 8 bolts having a diameter of 10.83" or 275 mm. Bolt circle is also less commonly referred to as the bolt pitch. Rarely used stud piloted wheels use only 10 bolts to retain the wheels on 22.5" and 24.5" diameter wheels. These wheels also only use a 285.75 mm (11.25") bolt circle diameter.

4. **Center bore**—The center bore of a wheel is the size of the hole in wheel disc that centers the wheel over the mounting hub. In North America, the standard opening for a center bore for 22.5" and 24.5" diameter wheels is 8.722" or 221 mm. This center bore diameter is identical for hub and stud piloted wheels. The standard center bore in Europe for the same size wheel is 281 mm or 11.06". If the wheel is centered using the axle hub and center bore, it is referred to as a hub piloted wheel. Machined pads on a hub identify a wheel end using a hub piloted wheel.

Because stud and hub piloted wheels share the same **bolt circle pattern** and center-bore diameter, it is possible to interchange the wheels. Stud piloted wheels use a different size stud and bolt hole shape compared to hub piloted wheels. No pilot pads are used on stud piloted hubs.

Wheel Offset

On disc-type wheels, the disc may be positioned directly in the vertical centerline of the wheel or offset either towards the brake assembly or towards the outside or street side of the wheel. Using offset is necessary to create space for brake drums or rotors. When dual wheels are used, a considerable amount of offset is necessary to mount the discs against one another to keep the tires from contacting one another while under load. In fact, non-technical descriptions of wheels refer to them as "deep-dish" wheels. Handling characteristics of a vehicle can change, depending on the direction and degree of offset, because the vehicle weight is projected downwards through a vertical centerline of the wheel. How and where the wheels centerline can intersect with the kingpin-inclination (KPI) angle influences steering and tire wear characteristics. This same line of projected weight can influence bearing loads. Offset can place the wheel weight nearer to the outboard end of the axle stub and outer wheel bearing or closer to the inner wheel bearing (**FIGURE 28-8**).

Defined, **wheel offset** is the horizontal distance from the wheel disc surface where it attaches to a hub, to the true vertical centerline of the wheel. Offset can be positive, negative, or zero (**FIGURE 28-9**). **Negative offset** places the disc closer to the brake side of the wheel, while **zero offset** places the wheel centerline and disc along the same vertical centerline. Front steer axle wheels use **positive offset** and place the disc nearer the street side or outboard of the wheel. Positive offset in this case creates space for the brakes while placing the vehicle load closer to the inner wheel bearing. The overall width of the front axle and wheels together is shorter when wheels with positive offset are used. If negative offset was used, the wheels would extend beyond the fenders and the vehicle weight would project farther

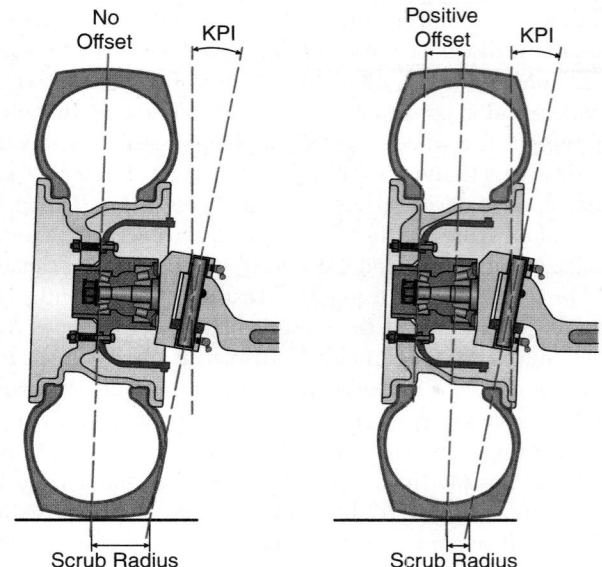

FIGURE 28-8 The direction and amount of wheel disc offset influences the scrub radius and where the wheel bearing load is.

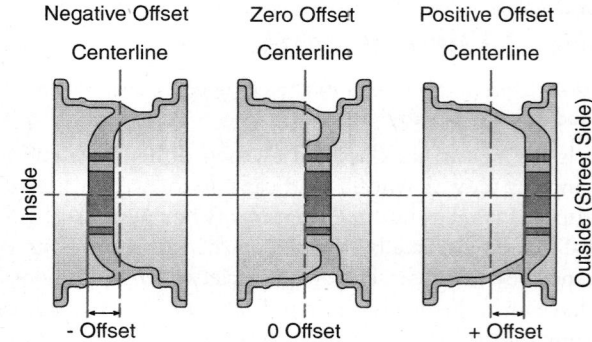

FIGURE 28-9 The position of the wheel disc establishes hub offset.

out from the KPI. Dual wheels take two identical wheels with positive offset and turn the outboard disc wheel 180-degree around to install a negative offset wheel against a positive offset wheel. This arrangement of two identical wheels having one negative and the other with positive offset is the only way to position two discs next to one another. Drum and disc brakes require space inside the wheels, so additional offset is required, particularly with ADB assemblies where the rotor is attached to the hub (**FIGURE 28-10**).

Minimum Dual Spacing

A term related to wheel offset is **minimum dual spacing** or dual spacing, which refers to the minimum allowable distance between the wheel centerlines in a dual-wheel arrangement (**FIGURE 28-11**). This lateral distance from wheel centerline to centerline is determined by adding offset distance of disc wheels. On cast spoke hubs, the width of a spacer band establishes dual spacing. Spacing is a critical dimension because tires should not contact one another when loaded.

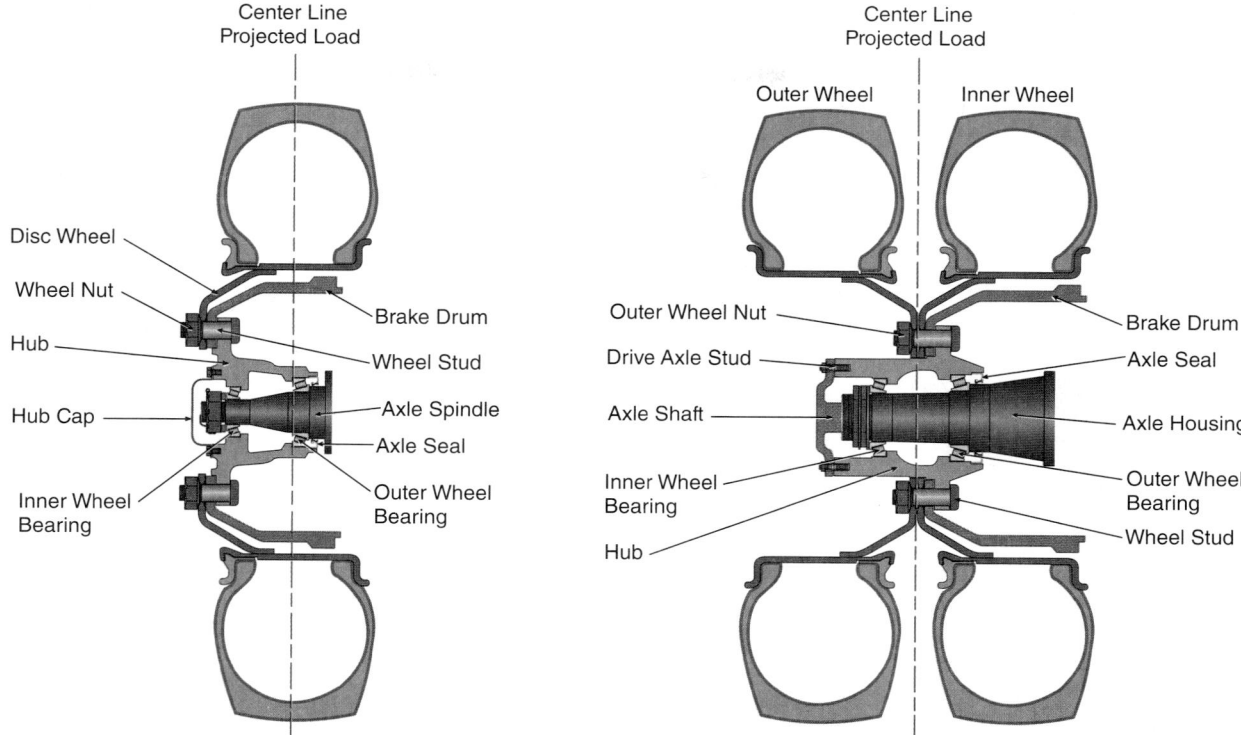

FIGURE 28-10 Positive offset is used on the front wheels to create space for brakes and place the vehicle load closer to the larger inner wheel bearing. Dual wheels use a positive and negative offset to space dual tires.

Hub and Stud Piloted Disc Wheels

LO 28-4 Identify and describe the types of wheel centering systems and explain features of hub and stub piloted wheels.

Two types of disc wheels are used on commercial vehicles; hub piloted and **stud piloted disc wheels**. The terms Uni-Mount or Metric are sometimes used to described hub piloted disc wheels, but they are not accurate technical terms. The two wheels are differentiated by the method used to center the wheel over the hub. If a wheel is stud piloted, the wheel studs, combined with cone-shaped nuts, center the wheel on the hub. Vehicle weight is carried by the studs and the stud-nut combination clamps the wheel to the hub. In the case of a **hub piloted disc wheel**, the wheel slides over precision-machined **pilot pads** on the hub used to make the wheels axis of rotation concentric with the rotational axis of the hub (**FIGURE 28-12**). Without aligning the hub and wheels rotational centers, the result is wheel imbalance, causing vibration from the up and down or elliptical-shaped rotation of the wheel. Radial runout of a wheel is checked to verify that no misalignment is present between the wheel and hub.

Bolt holes in a hub piloted wheel are straight because of the design of the wheel retention hardware. Regardless of whether it is a single or dual wheel, hub piloted wheels use either eight or 10 splined studs driven into the hub and a single, two-piece nut for each stud or bolt hole (**FIGURE 28-13**). The combination

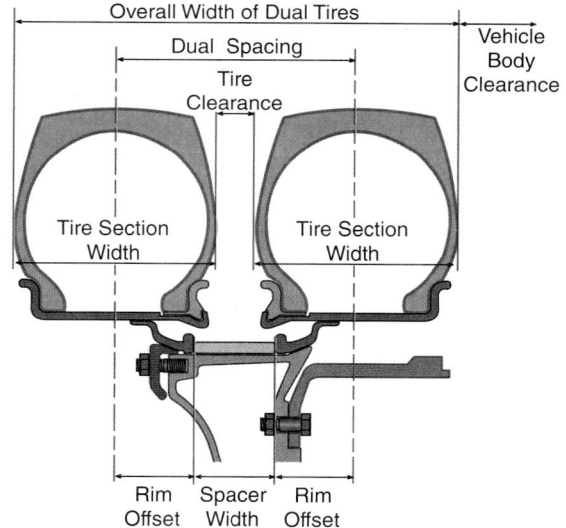

FIGURE 28-11 Minimum dual spacing is the smallest allowable distance between two-wheel centerlines. Spacing is needed to prevent dual tires from contacting one another under load.

of single two-piece nut and stud creates a bolted connection, clamping together the wheel and the hub. Note the hub piloted bolted joint does not transfer wheel weight to the hub—the weight is transferred primarily through the pilot pads. This means the bolted joint only clamps the wheel to the hub and is not stressed by vehicle weight.

Hub Pilot Pads

Wheel Stud

Hub Assembly

FIGURE 28-12 A hub piloted wheel is centered over the hub using pilot pads. Wheel loads are transferred to the hub through the pads.

Pilot pads can wear out on a hub piloted wheel. The result is radial runout. Always check for radial runout when wheel vibration occurs. The use of a selective set of feeler blades to act as temporary shims between pilot pads and the wheel center bore can help re-center a wheel when diagnosing vibration due to radial runout of hub piloted wheels.

Stud Piloted Wheel Mounting

If studs are used to center the wheel, it is called a **stud piloted** wheel. On a single disc wheel, a stud with splines is driven into the hub and a second inner nut with internal and external threads is tightened over the stud after the wheel is installed (**FIGURE 28-14**). The inner nut has a tapered cone-shaped face to center the wheel hole over the stud when it is tightened. Wheel bolt holes are not straight. To center the wheel with the

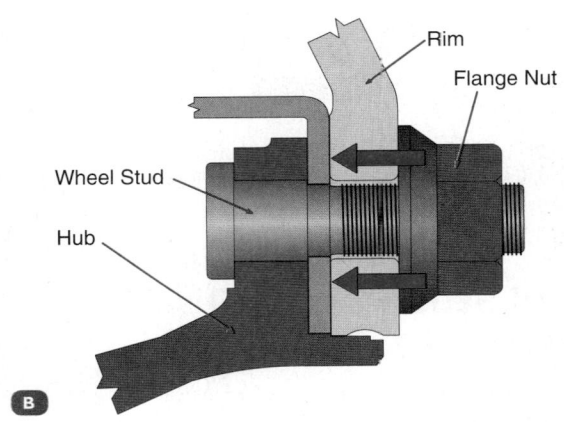

FIGURE 28-13 A. Hub piloted disc wheel. **B.** Components of a hub piloted disc wheel.

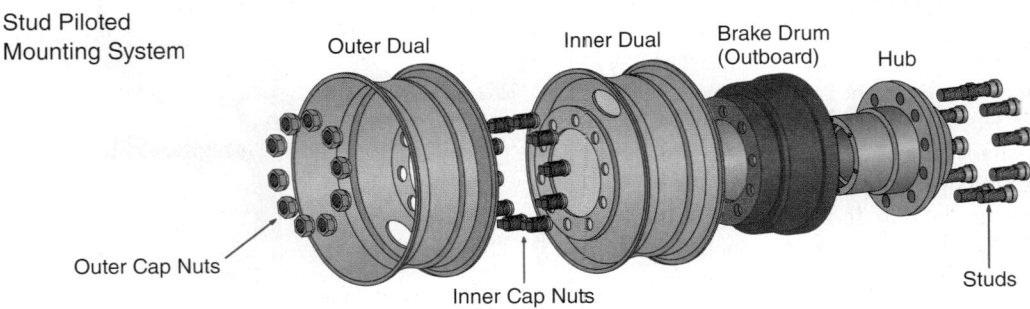

FIGURE 28-14 Features of a stud piloted wheel centering and retention system.

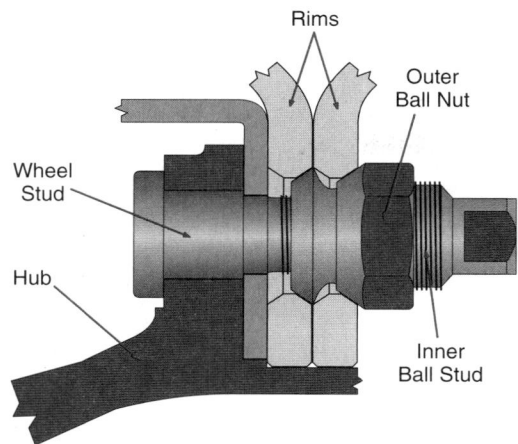

FIGURE 28-15 Stud piloted mounting systems use tapered holes for ball-type studs and nuts. Cap nuts with square heads are used to retain the inner wheel on dual wheel axle ends.

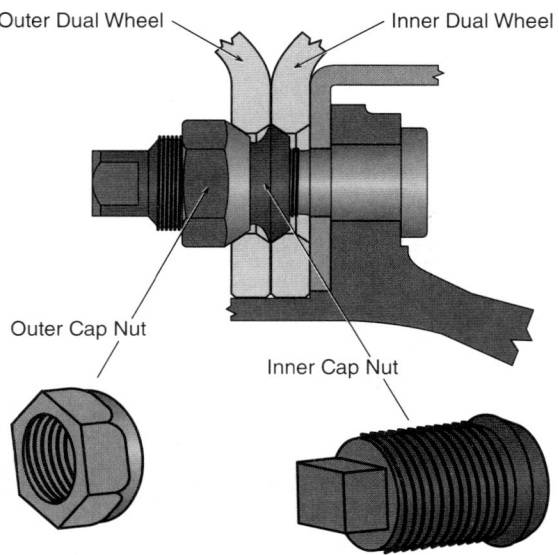

FIGURE 28-16 The inner nut has internal and external threads to tighten it onto the wheel stud fastened to the hub. When dual wheels are used, the outer ball nut is threaded onto the inner nut.

cone-shaped nut, the wheel hole facing the nut also needs be cone-shaped to fit the nut (**FIGURE 28-15**). Because the studs center the wheel, they also support and transfer vehicle weight to the hub which explains why 22.5" to 24.5" wheels use 10 and not eight bolt holes. Stud piloted wheel studs have additional stress because they not only support vehicle weight but create a bolted joint to retain the wheel.

Dual stud piloted wheels require an additional outer ball nut, which means there are three fasteners for each bolt hole. Inner and outer ball nuts are required to hold a dual-wheel assembly together for a total of 20 per dual, plus the stud in the hub (**FIGURE 28-16**). Stud piloted wheels use left- and right-hand threaded nuts to prevent wheel nuts on the left side of the vehicle from loosening. Different types of ball nuts and studs are used on steel and aluminum wheels, along with different angles of taper seats. Aluminum

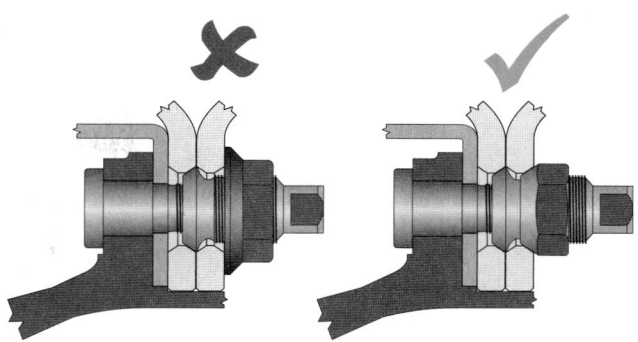

FIGURE 28-17 Hardware for stud piloted and hub piloted systems are different and should not be interchanged.

wheels require longer studs due to the greater thickness of aluminum wheel discs. And, as illustrated in **FIGURE 28-17**, the hardware used to retain hub piloted and stud piloted wheels is different and should never be interchanged. Stud piloted wheels use a ball seat stud to retain and support the inner wheel, while a ball seat nut is used on the outer wheel. If a hub piloted wheel is installed using cone-shaped nuts, the nuts quickly loosen and cause wheel separation.

Stud piloted wheels were very common more than two decades ago but are now rarely used. Hub piloted wheels have displaced stud piloted wheels, having advantages, such as requiring fewer wheel nuts and studs, a better safety record, less expensive to produce, lighter, and simpler to maintain and service.

▶ **TECHNICIAN TIP**

Stud piloted wheels use left-hand threaded studs, and inner and outer nuts on the left side of the vehicle. The use of left-handed threads prevents the nuts from loosening due to the phenomenon of clocking and, in fact, can help tighten the nuts. Whenever brake work is performed, and the hubs are removed, it is critical the correct hub with left-hand stud threads is installed on the left side of a vehicle. If the left- and right-hand hubs are interchanged, the wheel will separate—often within the first day of service.

Hub Piloted Wheel Retention

LO 28-5 Identify and explain the wheel retention methods used by hub piloted wheels.

Wheels are fastened to the hubs by threaded studs and wheel nuts. **Wheel studs** are attached at one end to the hub and use a nut to provide the clamping force necessary to hold the wheel against the hub (**FIGURE 28-18**). To prevent wheel separation and ensure reliable and durable service life, several features are designed into the construction of hub piloted fasteners. First, wheel studs and nuts are made from heat-treated, high-grade alloy forged steel. Heat treating anneals just on the outside, threaded portion of the stud making it a little softer than the rest of the stud. Softening the thread minimizes the likelihood of stripping the threads. Another feature is the threads between the studs and the nuts are fine, close-fitting, and accurately sized, which provide stronger clamping force because they

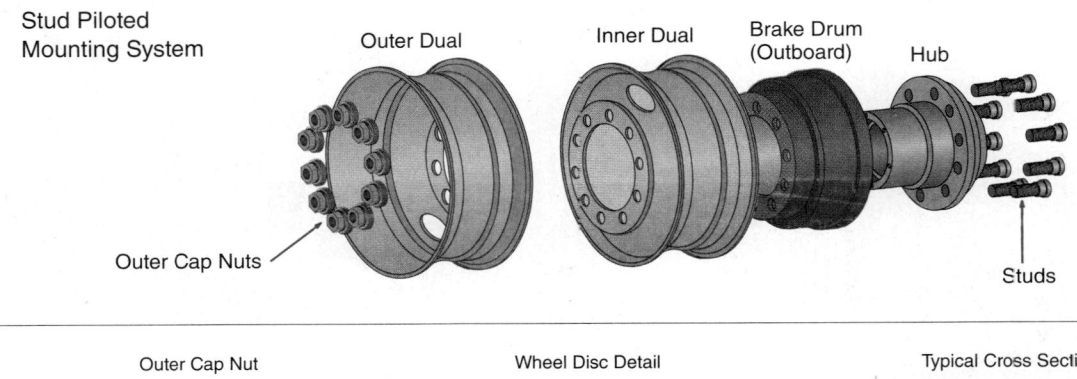

FIGURE 28-18 Features of hub piloted wheels and hub retention systems.

can be tightened with more torque. Inadequate clamping force caused by loose nuts or damaged studs allows the wheel to separate from the hub and failure can take place through several mechanisms.

Clocking

The first condition that leads to nut loosening is a condition called **clocking**. This takes place where a small amount of movement between the wheel discs and hub is allowed by a gap between the studs and wheel. Relative back and forth movement between the hub and wheel produces incremental rotation of the outside edge of wheel nuts, which can potentially loosen them (**FIGURE 28-19**). Accelerating and decelerating the wheel during driving and braking torque is the primary cause of nut loosening due to clocking. One helpful way to visually identify this condition when it takes place is using wheel nut indicators (**FIGURE 28-20**). After properly installing and tightening the wheel nuts, position indicators are installed. When inspected daily, the arrow pointers should remain orientated in the same direction as when they were installed.

Two solutions to prevent clocking-related loosening are related to the nut design. Hub piloted wheels universally use a two-piece flange nut that is crimped together. A wide flange below the hex-shaped head distributes nut clamping force over a wider area than the nut, but the flange can also rotate independently of the head (**FIGURE 28-21**). This means that when the wheel moves relative to the stud during clocking, and attempts to turn the nut, only the flange rotates, but not the nut. A drop of oil placed between the flange and head is important to prevent clocking and increase the clamping force applied through the flange when the nut is tightened.

A second method to reduce clocking-related loosening of wheel nuts is to use a sleeved nut. The nut sleeve extends

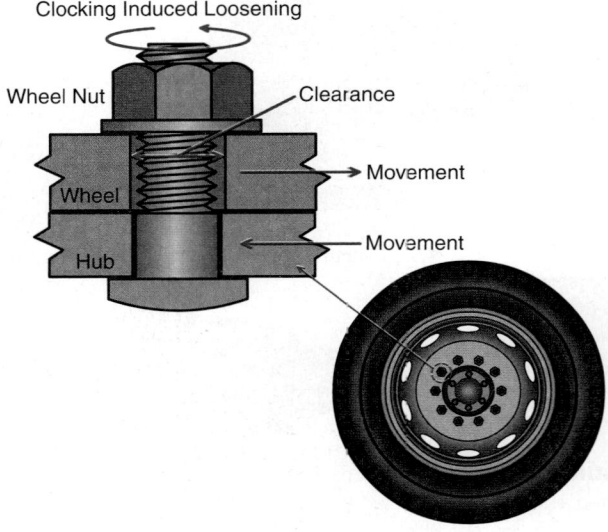

FIGURE 28-19 A gap between the wheel stud and wheel allows incremental back and forth movement when the hub is turning in the opposite direction of the wheel, such as when accelerating and braking. The movement can loosen wheel nuts.

into the wheels bolt hole to eliminate any space around the bolt hole. The idea is eliminating the space in the bolt hole prevents wheel-hub movement, which produces clocking-related loosening of nuts (**FIGURE 28-22**).

Loss of clamping force can also take place if too much paint or foreign material is trapped between the wheels and hub or between two dual wheels. When wheels rotate, the normal flexing of disc wheels between disc and the hub squeezes out dirt and paint, leaving a small clearance (**FIGURE 28-23**). When clearance is increased, clamping force is reduced, which can result in loose wheel nuts. This explains why it is important to clean rust and

FIGURE 28-20 Wheel nut position indicators can help visually identify nut clocking or loosening.

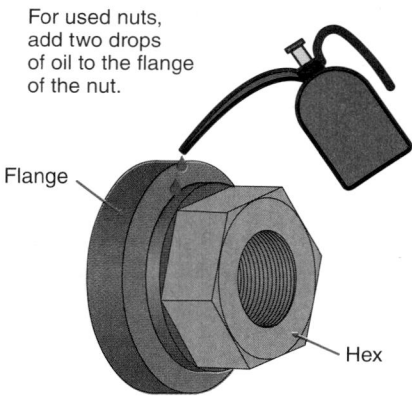

FIGURE 28-21 Hub piloted wheels use two-piece flange nuts to prevent nut loosening from clocking.

dirt from mating surfaces of wheels and hubs when assembling them. Paint having a thickness of more than 0.003" can cause a loss of clamping force. The use of grease should be avoided for the same reason.

▶ **TECHNICIAN TIP**

Wheel paint helps minimize wheel corrosion and enhances their appearance. However, re-conditioned wheels are often repainted with too much paint. Thick paint between multiple wheel surfaces, such as the hub and between discs, can be squeezed out creating an unwanted clearance. This clearance produces loose wheel nuts. The maximum amount of paint on the disc-hub surface should be no more than 0.003"

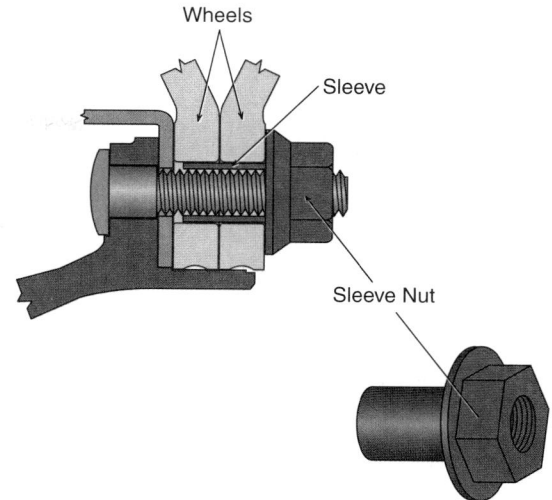

FIGURE 28-22 A sleeve nut minimizes clocking by eliminating space between the wheel hole and stud.

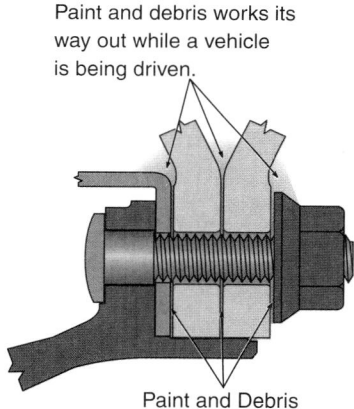

FIGURE 28-23 Areas where dirt, grease, and paint can squeeze out between wheels and hubs, causing wheel nuts to loosen.

(0.076 mm), which is about the thickness of a page from a magazine. To tell if the paint is too thick, which can lead to nut loosening, check whether number stampings on the wheel are legible or not. If not, the paint is too thick and must be removed before assembling wheels.

Disc Wheel Separator Plates

One exception to the placement of any material between the wheels and hub that could potentially loosen wheel nuts is the use of a purpose made gasket to prevent wheel corrosion. When steel and aluminum wheels are assembled together, galvanic corrosion can quickly take place, destroying the aluminum wheel. To prevent this, a mylar- or nylon-like separator plate is installed between the wheels to minimize corrosion. This gasket is approximately 0.040" (1.016 mm) thick and is positioned between the hub and wheel, outboard brake drum and wheel, or combined with a second gasket between two dual wheels. It should not be installed between hub and brake drum. Because the gasket is made from dense mylar, it will not squeeze out from between tightly clamped discs or hubs.

> ▶ **TECHNICIAN TIP**
>
> Corrosion of aluminum wheels in a dual-wheel arrangement is accelerated whenever they are installed with steel wheels. The aluminum wheel is installed on the outside for appearances and the relatively inexpensive steel is installed on inside. Galvanic corrosion can cause the wheel nuts to loosen and allow the wheels to separate. To minimize the likelihood of this situation, always install a mylar gasket between the aluminum and steel wheels.

Wheel Nut Torque Versus Clamping Force

LO 28-6 Identify and explain wheel nut torque versus clamping force.

Wheel studs and nuts form a bolted joint to clamp the wheel to the hub. Stud tension produces clamping force between a wheel and hub. Because clamping force is what keeps the wheel attached to the hub, it is critical that studs are properly tensioned using a wheel nut. Tightening the nut stretches the stud to tension it, giving it a preload force, which allows it to behave like an elastic band. As mentioned, it is critical that the correct torque be used on wheel nuts to achieve the correct tension or preload force on the stud, thus maintaining its elasticity (**FIGURE 28-24**).

Under-tightening wheel nuts allows wheels to run loose, eventually pounding and deforming wheel bolt holes and studs. Cracks can also form in the bolt hole areas. If nuts are not adequately tightened, studs break from fatigue failure caused by continuous bending and stretching cycle from a low preload tension to a high preload tension and back again. Like bending a piece of metal repeatedly, studs will break from fatigue when frequently cycled from low to high tension and back again. In contrast to a loosely tensioned stud, a correctly tensioned stud does not bend or stretch as easily as a loose one. This means a loose stud can break due to fatigue failure more quickly than even a slightly over tightened fastener.

Note that severely overtightening wheel fasteners also causes problems. Overtightening wheel nuts can stretch studs beyond their yield strength. When overstretched and deformed, the stud is no longer in an elastic state and easily breaks.

One common way overtightening can happen is not only to fail to use a torque wrench and follow correct procedures, or to use lubricant on stud threads when it should not be used. On some wheel studs, such as stud piloted wheels, torque specifications are given for tightening dry threads. Using lubricant on these fasteners is believed to assist loosening of studs and nuts. Applying lubricant to the threads of a stud or nut when the torque specifications and procedure requires dry threads enables more of the twisting force, tightening the nut to stretch the stud further than it should (**FIGURE 28-25**). Force normally needed to overcome dry thread friction is instead redirected into turning the wheel nuts and the stud and can break due to

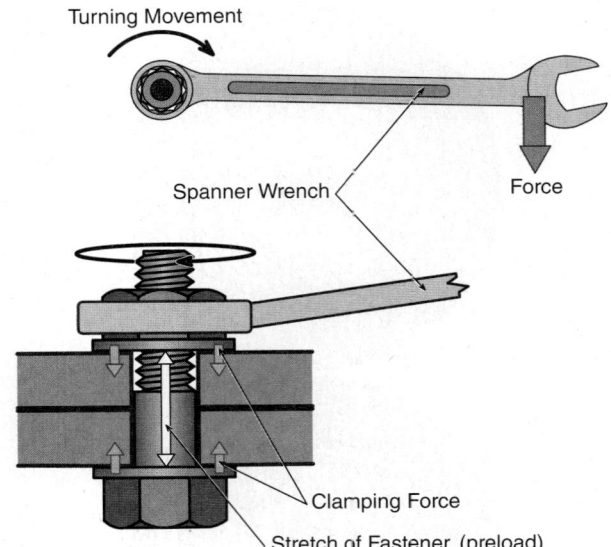

FIGURE 28-24 Tightening a bolted joint stretches the stud. Stud tension is also called preload and protects the joint from damaging cyclic loading resulting in fatigue failure.

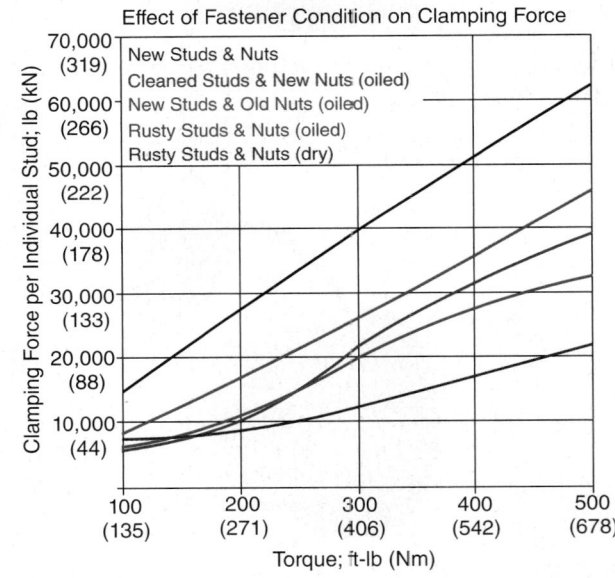

FIGURE 28-25 The effects of mounting hardware condition on wheel clamping force. A properly cleaned and lubricated fastener will clamp the wheel tighter and prevent separation.

excessive tensioning and stretching beyond its tensile strength. Similarly, torque specification requiring thread lubricant takes into account the fact that more twisting force converts to stretching and preloading of the fastener. The absence of thread lubricant, or attempting to tighten studs with threads that are rusty and have excessive friction—even with lubricant, leads to inadequate stud tension. When lubricant is specified, 30W oil is recommended.

As illustrated in **FIGURE 28-26**, the best way for a technician to produce the clamping force necessary to keep the wheels

FIGURE 28-26 A wireless Bluetooth transceiver-equipped torque wrench. Clamping force is produced by tightening a fastener.

on the vehicle is through correct preparation of fasteners and the use of a torque wrench. Torque is the measure of twisting force applied to wheel fasteners and is a function of the length of a wrench and the force applied to it. Preload on the bolt—the amount of stretch—is proportional to the torque applied to the nut through the wrench.

All wheel nuts must be tightened to the correct torque and in the proper sequence, while following other important cleaning and installation techniques to minimize the likelihood of a wheel separation event.

Wheel Fastener Tightening Sequence

To prevent a wheel from warping during installation and create more consistent clamping force on all studs, a star pattern tightening sequence is best followed when nuts are initially snugged, partially tightened, and then finally tightened (**FIGURE 28-27**). By lightly tightening or snugging-up the first wheel nut, then tightening the nut opposite it at 50 to 100 ft-lb (68 to 136 Nm) of torque, clamping force on the wheel is evenly distributed. The wheel nuts should be tightened in stages of 100 to 150 ft-lb (135.6 to 203.3 Nm) increments on wheels requiring 400 to 600 ft-lb (542.3 to 813.5 Nm) of nut torque. A typical M 22 × 1.5 wheel nut used on hub piloted wheels is tightened to between 510 to 600 ft-lb (691.5 to 813.5 Nm). If all the bolts are completely tightened beginning on one side and follow a circular pattern, the wheel will bend and remain tilted at an angle.

FIGURE 28-27 The star pattern sequence of tightening wheel nuts to ensure consistent clamping force and avoid wheel damage.

Bending happens when the nuts opposite the first nuts are finally tightened, and a gap between the hub and wheel of the nuts tightened last allows the wheel to bend, causing clamping force to be inconsistent.

After hub piloted wheel nuts are tightened to specification, the wheel and fasteners tend to settle, resulting in less clamping force. Wheel nuts should be retightened after the first 50 to 100 miles (80 to 160 km) of operation to verify torque setting. Wheels should be periodically retightened at 150,000 mile (190,000 km) intervals. See **SKILL DRILL 28-1**.

▶ TECHNICIAN TIP

Focusing primarily on correctly tightening bolted joints using a torque wrench can lead to wheel separation. Other service practices must be included before correct tightening of wheel studs can be effective. An

SKILL DRILL 28-1 Preparing to Install a Wheel

1. Chock the vehicle wheels and support the axle on safety stands.
2. Visually inspect the wheels for cracks, severe corrosion, missing or broken fasteners, leaks, or incorrect fitting wheels.
3. Both tires of a dual-wheel assembly should be completely deflated before loosening nuts for removal from the hub. Remove the valve stem core to deflate the tire.
4. Run a piece of wire through the valve stem to be sure there are no obstructions and that tire deflation is complete.
5. Loosen wheel nuts with a few turns using a "star" or "crisscross" pattern. When all the nuts are loose, remove the nuts.
6. Remove the wheel from hub, using caution to prevent damage to the wheel studs.

SKILL DRILL 28-1 Preparing to Install a Wheel (Continued)

7. Reinspect the wheel for cracks around the bolt holes or the center bore of the wheel. Check for elongated bolt holes and damaged bolt holes.
8. Remove debris and foreign material from all mating surfaces with a wire brush.
9. Clean or verify the mating face of the hub, rotor, and/or drum are properly cleaned and not damaged or cracked.
10. Inspect all wheel and fastener components for damage or signs of excessive wear.
11. Lubricate flange nuts with two drops of oil between the flange and hex nut.
12. If installing a dual wheel, offset the outer wheel so that the handhold openings allow access to the tire valve stems.
13. Snug the lug nuts in a star pattern to seat the wheel on the hub. This step requires no more than 50 to 100 ft-lb (68 to 136 Nm) of force to seat the wheels.
14. Torque the lug nuts to specification using a calibrated torque control tool. Tighten the wheel nuts to specifications in three or more steps.

acronym developed by the Tire Industry Association to help remember the correct procedures is R-I-S-T. RIST stands for:

R = Remove debris from mating surfaces and clean.
I = Inspect components for damage or excessive wear.
S = Snug the fasteners in a star pattern.
T = Torque to specification.

SAFETY TIP

Installing wheel hardware requires special attention be given to correctly tightening wheel nuts using torque wrenches. Stud and hub piloted wheel nuts are not interchangeable. The tapered face of the wheel nut must face the tapered seat of stud piloted wheels. Re-torque of hub piloted wheel nuts is essential after 50 miles (80 km) of operation since the wheels and mounting hardware settles and loosens after initial installation.

Wheel Service

LO 28-7 Identify and explain service techniques for inspecting wheels and hubs.

Service and maintenance procedures for wheels generally involves removal, inspection, and installation of wheels and rims. Identifying wheel imbalance conditions caused by damaged wheels or incorrect installation procedures requires measuring wheel runout. Potential for serious injury servicing multi-piece wheels requires careful attention to ring inspection and installation procedures. Before inspecting the wheels for runout conditions, the hubs should be checked to determine whether the bearings are loose. Loose wheel bearings or even loose king pins may be confused with wheel, rim, or tire defects. Wheel and hub assemblies are heavy and should not be removed without mechanical assistance from devices like a wheel dolly shown in **FIGURE 28-28**.

FIGURE 28-28 A wheel dolly is used to remove and reinstall wheel and hub assemblies.

Hub Quick Inspection

When wheels are installed or while identifying vibration-related complaints, it's important to inspect wheels and rims for lateral and radial runout conditions. Before checking for runout, it is important to first check for problems in the hub, such as loose wheel bearings. Steps to use to perform a quick inspection of the hub include:

1. Lift and support the axle. Chock other wheels and release the park brakes.
2. Rotate the wheel to determine that is turns freely and smoothly.
3. Listen and feel for any indication of rough operation or vibration while turning the wheel. Place your finger tips on the hub while turning to help identify roughness felt in the wheel bearings.
4. Inspect for excessively loose wheel bearings by identifying movement in the hub. This is done by tilting the wheel using a

pry bar to lift the bottom of the tire while placing your hand on the top of the tire (**FIGURE 28-29**). If any movement is detected or a chucking sound is heard, the bearings and king pins should be further inspected. Excess movement in the hub requires removing a vehicle from service until repairs are made.

Lateral Runout Inspection

Lateral runout is a side-to-side movement or wobble of a wheel from its vertical rotational axis. A quick check of lateral and radial runout is performed with the wheel raised from the ground and the axle properly supported. Using the edge of an axle stand or long hammer handle placed stationary but close to the wheel rim, the wheel is spun. Ideally, 1/8" (3.175 mm) or less lateral runout should exist, and total indicated runout should not exceed 1/4" (6.355 mm). Because the commercial vehicle wheels and tires do not rotate as fast due to their large diameter, it is surprising that in service, lateral runout of as much as 1/2" (12.7 mm) on many wheels does not produce driver complaints (**TABLE 28-1**). The cause of runout should be identified, especially during installation, since lateral runout can originate from improper mounting or contact between the hub and wheel. Dirt, metal burs, bent wheel discs, and a bent hub wheel mounting flange can cause lateral runout. The wheel should be removed, cleaned, and inspected and the hub runout measured with a dial indicator. If no significant runout is detected in the hub and the wheel still

has runout after cleaning and reinstallation with the proper procedures, the wheel is likely bent.

Radial Runout Inspection

Radial runout is an up and down movement of a wheel from its horizontal axis. Operationally it is observed as "wheel hop" and produces tire flat spots. The procedures for inspecting for radial runout are identical to lateral runout except the inspection tool or dial indicator is placed on the tread surface or inside edge of the rim.

When rims are installed on cast spoke hubs, the lateral runout needs to be checked and adjusted first. Rim clamps should be first installed and tightened in a star pattern to wedge the rim against the tapered spokes. **FIGURE 28-30A** shows the correct sequence for a three-spoke wheel, **FIGURE 28-30B** shows the sequence for a five-spoke wheel, and **FIGURE 28-30C** shows the sequence for a six-spoke wheel.

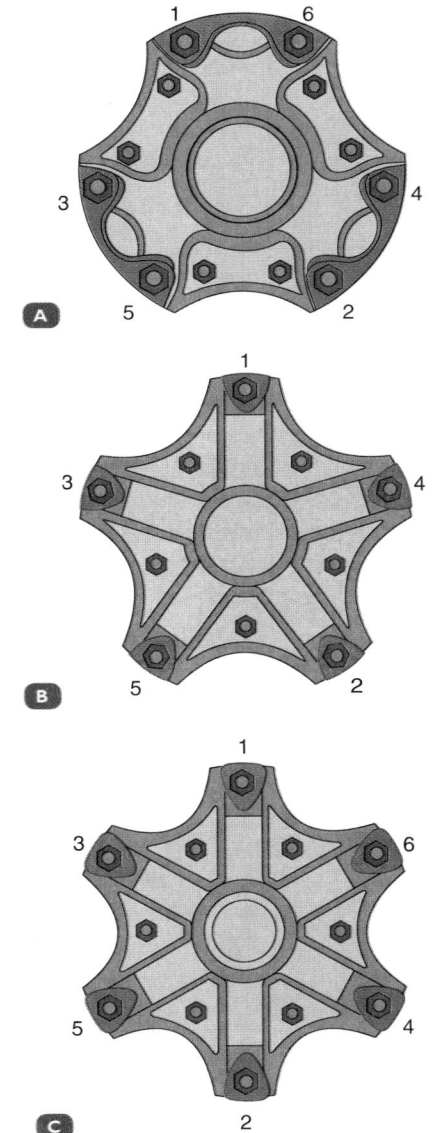

FIGURE 28-29 A quick check of the hub and bearings requires tilting the wheel back and forth at a 45-degree angle. Any movement requires further investigation for the root cause.

FIGURE 28-30 Proper torque sequence for a cast spoke hub with: **A.** three spokes; **B.** five spokes; and **C.** six spokes.

TABLE 28-1 Lateral and Radial Runout Specifications

Lateral and Radial Runout Limits	On Highway	Off-Road	Wide Base Single
Steer	0.080" (2.032 mm)	0.110" (2.794 mm)	0.125" (3.175 mm)
Drive - Trailer	0.125" (3.175 mm)	0.125" (3.175 mm)	0.125" (3.175 mm)

If the rim has not had clamps tightened with consistent and even force, the rim may become radially distorted or elongated (egg-shaped). Radial runout should be checked to determine if this condition exists and requires rim replacement. Measuring the radial runout is performed by using a dial indicator gauge or some object next to the tire tread and rotating the tire to observe whether there are high and low spots.

Multi-Piece Rim Inspection

Rims using tubes use a flat base rim rather than a drop center-type rim. Only one side of the multi-piece rim has a flange to locate the tire on the rim and split rings are used to hold the tire on after it is placed over the rim. The rims may use one or two retention rings. These rings vary according to manufacturer, tire size, and rim design and must be correctly matched to the rim. Rings may appear to fit but they, in fact, do not fit properly on the rim base. Matching must be done using wall charts with part numbers that match stamping numbers on the rim base and parts. Failure to properly match tire and rim sizes or rim parts is extremely dangerous. An incorrectly matched, damaged, or incorrectly installed ring can slip. The result is an explosive release of tire air pressure, which throws the ring and tire more than twenty feet in the air. If the tire or parts hit anyone, the result is severe injury or death. Before even thinking about working on any multi-piece tire and rim assembly, be sure you are trained according to legislated standards and completely familiar with all safety guidelines.

FIGURE 28-31 illustrates areas of the rim base that should be cleaned and inspected before assembling. Metal surfaces on the rim and rings should be cleaned to remove rust or corrosion buildup that prevents parts from properly fitting together. Any cracks or severely corroded metal parts, bent rim flanges and side rings, or gouges in the rim caused by tools are conditions requiring the parts to be destroyed and discarded.

Disc Wheel Inspection

Before installing a wheel, it should be checked to verify the mounting system matches the wheel type. Stud and hub piloted wheels and fasteners are not interchangeable. Disc wheels and open center rims are inspected for radial and lateral runout. Before installing a disc wheel, it should be inspected for cracks between: hand holds, hand holds to bolt holes, and between bolt holes. Cracks may cause air leakage (**FIGURE 28-32**). Circumferential cracks in the rim, at the valve stem, or along welds allow a tire to lose pressure.

Bolt holes should be carefully inspected as well. Elongated bolt holes indicate a wheel that has operated with loose fasteners. Damage around bolt holes may indicate the installation of incorrect wheel fasteners.

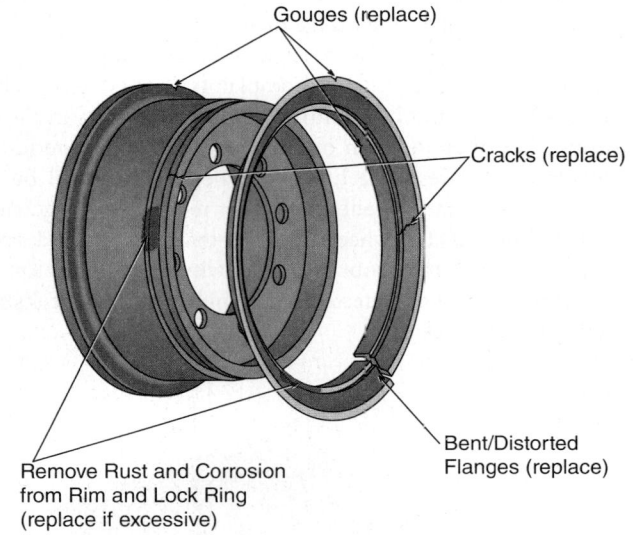

FIGURE 28-31 Conditions to check for when examining multi-piece rims.

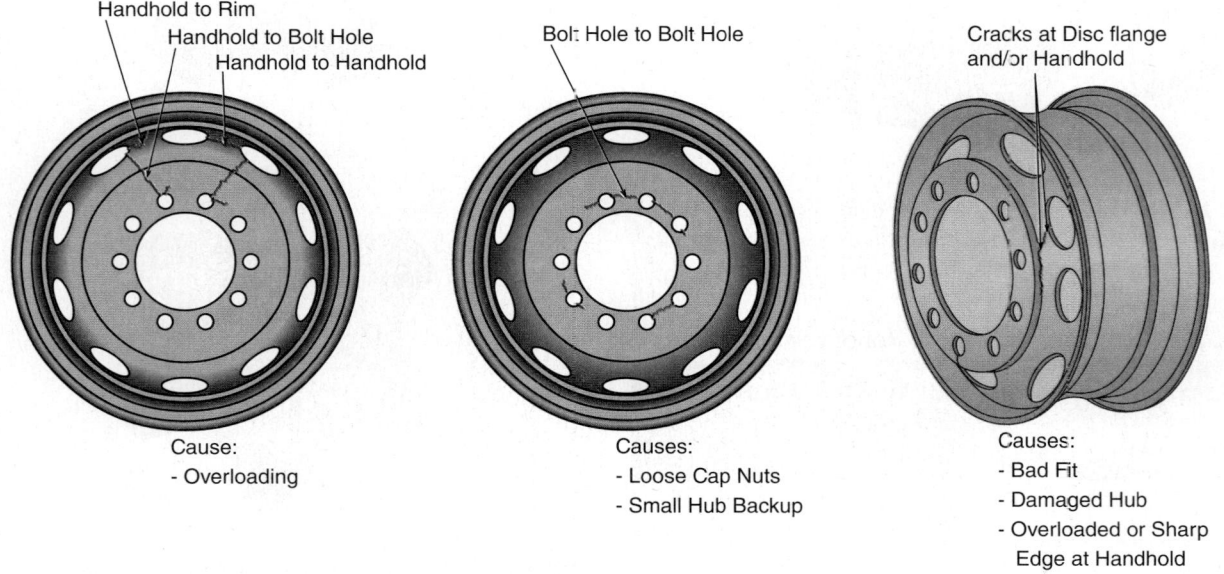

FIGURE 28-32 Causes of cracks in areas where disc wheels should be inspected.

Hub System Fundamentals

LO 28-8 Identify the types of hubs and differentiate between concepts of bearing preload and end play.

Hubs or bearing hubs are another major wheel end component. These precision components transfer vehicle weight to the axle while reducing friction between the stationary axle and a rotating wheel using a set of wheel bearings. Hubs also provide an attachment point for brake drums, antilock brake system (ABS) reluctor rings, and drive axles to transfer torque to the wheels. In **cast spoke wheels**, the hub makes up part of the wheel and is a mounting point for the rim. Subcomponents of a hub are precision-manufactured bearings, seals, lubricant, and an oil cap. Differences between hubs depend on which axle they are positioned, steer, drive, or trailer. Common materials are iron or weight-saving aluminum, which dissipates heat generated by wheel bearing friction.

Hubs use a pair of tapered roller bearings designed to transfer radial and axial loads evenly from all directions while rolling (**FIGURE 28-33**). The use of two tapered-shape wheel bearings having an adjustable preload force creates a very rigid bearing configuration that remains dimensionally stable under heavy load. **Preload force** is the pressure present between the bearing cup and cone of a tapered wheel bearing. Tightening a bearing adjusting nut increases the force applied to the bearing cone and increases preload pressure. Loosening the nut reduces preload force or creates a clearance between the cup and cone. Friction and heat buildup in the hub are minimized using optimized roller shapes in tapered roller bearings, which have the highest capacity of any bearing to absorb combined radial and axial loads.

Unlike hubs in light-duty vehicles, the bearings in all heavy-duty hubs are arranged to support and transfer weight entirely to the axle housing and not to a drive shaft. This bearing configuration is called a full-floating bearing. Full-floating axles are used exclusively on heavy-duty commercial vehicles because of the superior weight-bearing capabilities this hub configuration has. **FIGURE 28-34** shows a wheel hub with a full-floating bearing configuration in which the weight of the vehicle is supported by the bearings.

Hub Classification

In addition to a hub's position and construction material, four types of hubs are used on commercial vehicles:

1. Cast spoke hubs
2. Conventional or standard hubs with manually adjusted bearings
3. Preset hubs using a precision spacer and close-tolerance bearings, which eliminates the need to manually adjust bearings
4. Hub assemblies with limited-maintenance spindle locking nut

A significant amount of design effort has gone into development of hub bearing systems that can maintain correct bearing preload over the service life of a vehicle. Given the weight carried by bearings and the long distances travelled, these are not small achievements. So before examining the varieties of hub systems, it is important to understand how critical wheel bearing preload and adjustment is to the durability of hubs and vehicle safety.

Wheel Bearing Preload

Several studies conducted in Canada and the United States examining the causes of wheel separation have estimated the loss of hub lubricant causes between 50% and 80% of wheel separation events. Problems related to wheel fasteners and wheel separations contribute the remaining 20% to 50% of separation events. The reason for the loss of lubricant might not appear to be directly related to bearings, but it is very important to understand that precise adjustment of wheel bearing preload is necessary to maximize bearing life and prevent wheel seal leaks (**FIGURE 28-35**). Even a slightly loose bearing allows the hub seal to operate in an elliptical plane on the axle spindle, prematurely wearing the seal. Also, if a bearing is loose, or excessively tight, the wheel bearing cannot receive proper lubrication, which allows it to overheat and fail. Even before the bearing fails, heat

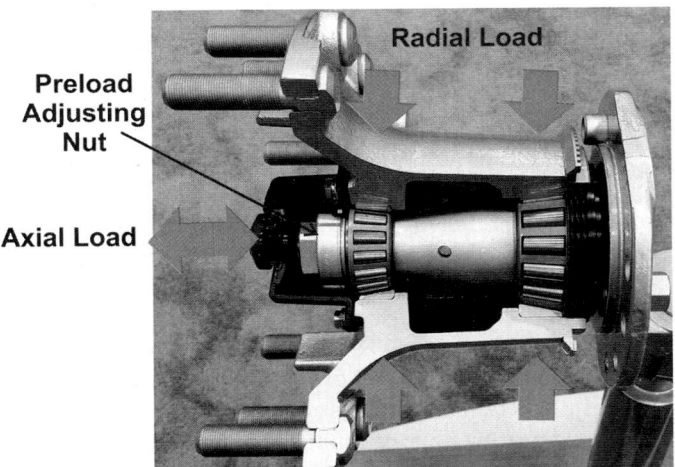

FIGURE 28-33 A tapered roller bearing is the strongest bearing design to support combined radial and axial loads while remaining dimensionally stable under heavy load.

FIGURE 28-34 A. Bearing cup. **B.** Cone. **C.** ABS tone ring. **D.** Oil seal. **E.** Retaining nut. **F.** Hub.

FIGURE 28-35 Oil flung from a leaking wheel seal distributes itself over the inside tire.

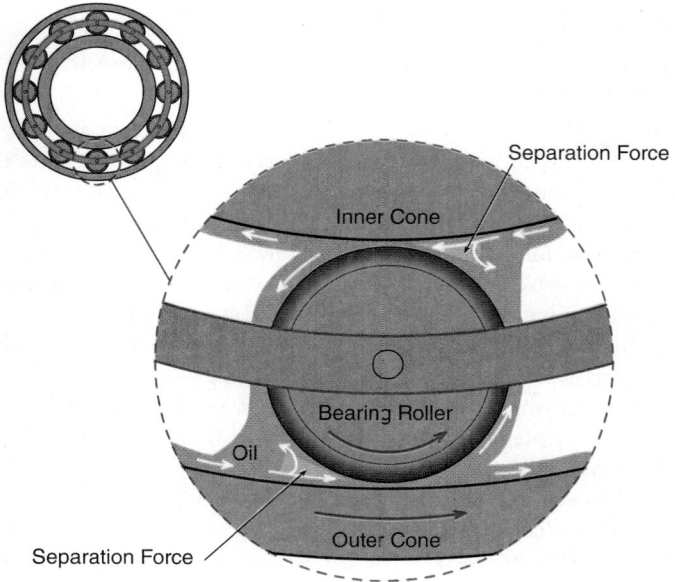

FIGURE 28-36 Correct bearing preload is needed to create a proper oil film. Bearing rollers must turn while under load, enabling them to pick up lubricant.

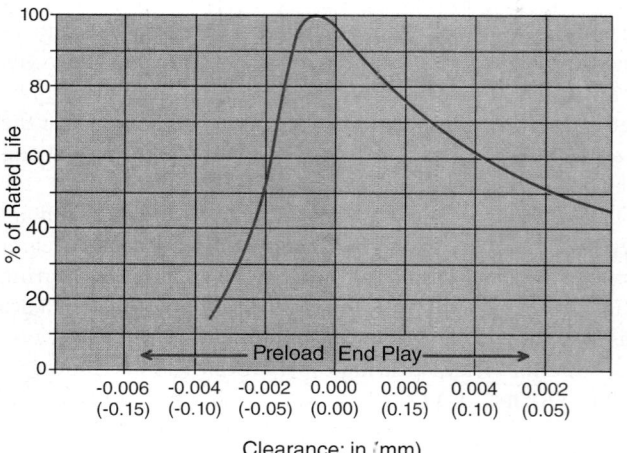

FIGURE 28-37 A slight negative preload extends bearing life by strengthening the hydrodynamic wedge.

thins hub lubricants and can damage many types of seal material. To avoid harming the hub seal, lubricant, and wheel bearing, precise adjustment of wheel bearing preload is necessary to maximize bearing life and prevent wheel seal leaks.

Preload is a bearing load factor established when wheel bearings are adjusted, usually by turning a threaded nut ahead of a set of tapered roller bearings. **Bearing preload** is not a clearance; it's the load applied to a bearing before any vehicle weight or rolling loads are applied. Turning the adjusting nut to apply pressure to the contact line between a roller and race applies an axial load to the bearing. Without adequate preload, the bearings do not roll properly—some force needs to be applied to the bearing to give its rollers traction to rotate around a bearing race or cup. When the bearing rotates, a hydrodynamic oil wedge is created between the bearing rollers and race that separates the two metal parts (**FIGURE 28-36**).

A condition of zero preload is present when hub bearings have only reached an adjustment point where there is no end play. Tightening an adjusting nut further increases the load applied to the bearing. Preload can be measured in terms of the weight or pressure applied to the bearing, or the distance the bearing moves after the nut is turned past zero preload. **FIGURE 28-37** shows how bearing life is extended by a slightly negative preload that strengthens the effect of the hydrodynamic wedge.

Preload and Hydrodynamic Wedge Lubrication

It is important to note that proper lubrication of a bearing and the lowest friction takes place when there is less than zero preload. This condition is present when the bearing has pressure applied by the adjusting nut and no end play exists. Some bearing specialists refer to this as negative preload. However, because negative preload cannot be measured in the field, some end play must be adjusted into the preload force applied by the bearing's adjusting nut. A proper hydrodynamic wedge between the roller and race is a function of the pressure contact between the roller and race with moderate contact pressure exerting

the greatest force separating moving metal parts. This may seem counterintuitive, but with little to no preload, the force of the hydrodynamic oil wedge is low because the rollers do not turn. Sliding friction also increases between the rollers and race, which produces heat. Understanding the requirement for bearing rollers to rotate to receive proper lubrication film helps explain why even a hub filled with oil or grease allows loose bearings to quickly fail. It is equally important to remember that excessive preload destroys a bearing since a lubricating wedge cannot form between the rollers and bearing race.

Wheel bearing preload cannot be accurately measured by a technician, but bearing end play can. End play is adjusted manually by technicians, but preload cannot be accurately measured. If negative preload is established, because the adjusting nut is tightened too much, the bearing could fail since oil could not separate the rollers and race. For this reason, bearing end play is adjusted to between 0.001" and 0.005" (0.025 and 0.127 mm) is measurable with a dial indicator. With that amount of end play, both the bearings and the seals have longer service life (**FIGURE 28-38**).

Correctly set bearing end play reduces:

- tire wear because the wheels do not toe out.
- the likelihood of seal leaks.
- the possibility of catastrophic bearing failure and unscheduled maintenance.
- brake vibration because the brake drum and shoes are parallel.

Standard Hubs

LO 28-9 Identify and describe the construction of standard hubs and service methods for adjusting wheel bearing end play.

Standard hubs are precision-machined aluminum or cast iron castings used in drive, steer, and trailer configurations (**FIGURE 28-39**). Two bearing cups are press-fitted into the housing with two tapered roller bearing cones. A seal is installed on the inboard side of the hub, which is used to retain oil or grease in the hub. To adjust the wheel bearings and ensure the

adjustment does not loosen or "back-off," the hub uses a pair of adjusting nuts that are accompanied by a lock washer or large flat washer. When used, the flat washer provides a flat, smooth, bearing-like surface to contact the outer wheel bearing and distributes the pressure of the adjusting nuts evenly to the bearing. Should the bearing turn during service, it will not contact and turn the adjusting nut, which could lead to loosening of the wheel bearings. Replacement bearings are installed and manually adjusted using an industry standard procedure defined by **TMC RP 618**, which is discussed further in the Manually Adjusting Wheel Bearings section.

On a standard hub, brake drums can be mounted either inboard or outboard. Outboard drums are installed over the hub and pilot on the same studs as the wheel. This means the hub does not require removal in order to replace the brake drum. Only the wheel is removed, leaving bearings and wheel seals undisturbed. Inboard drums are bolted to the inside surface of the hub, requiring hub removal during brake drum replacement.

FIGURE 28-39 A. Standard hub. **B.** Preset hub with a precision sleeve.

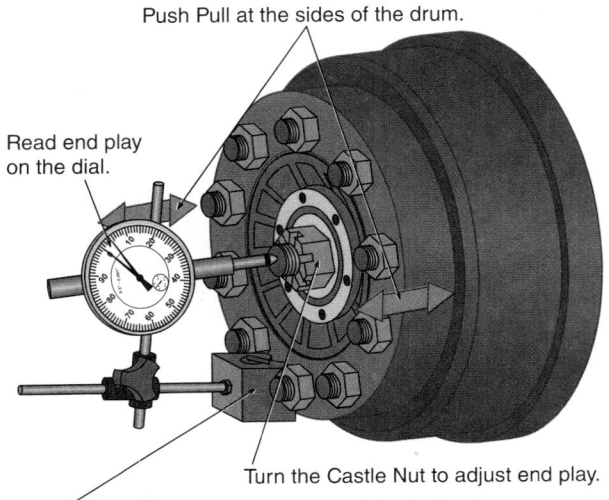

Push Pull at the sides of the drum.

Read end play on the dial.

Turn the Castle Nut to adjust end play.

Mount Dial Indicator to bottom of the brake drum.

FIGURE 28-38 Bearing endplay measured with a dial indicator. The hub is pushed in and out while the dial indicator's needle measures movement at the end of the spindle.

SKILL DRILL 28-2 Manually Adjusting Wheel Bearings Using the TMC 618 Procedure

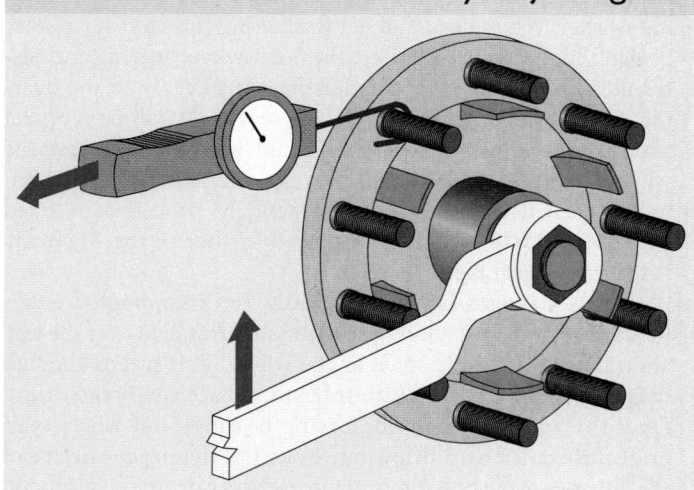

1. Lubricate the bearings with clean lubricant of the same type used in the axle sump or hub assembly.
2. Install the wheel hub and bearing onto spindle and torque the inner adjusting nut to 200 ft-lb (271 Nm) while rotating the hub assembly.
3. Back off the inner adjusting nut one full turn.
4. Re-torque the inner adjusting nut to 50 ft-lb (68 Nm) while rotating the wheel hub assembly.
5. Back off the inner adjustment nuts as per **TABLE 24-3**.
6. Install the locking washer.
7. Install and torque the outer jam nut as per **TABLE 24-3**.
8. Verify hub end play with a dial indicator.

TABLE 28-2 Final Back-Off for Adjustment Nuts by Axle Type and Threads per Inch

Axle Type	Threads per Inch	Final Back-Off	Jam Nut Torque
Steer (front non-drive)	12	1/6 turn* (with cotter pin)	No jam nut used. Use cotter pin.
	18	1/4 turn* (with cotter pin)	
	14	1/2 turn (with less than 2 5/8" [6.67 cm] nut)	200–300 ft-lb (272–408 Nm)
	18	1/2 turn (with less than 2 5/8" [6.67 cm] nut)	
Drive	12	1/4 turn	With dowel-type washer 300–400 ft-lb (408–544 Nm)
	16	1/4 turn	Tang washer 200–275 ft-lb (272–374 Nm)
Trailer**	12	1/4 turn	Over 2 5/8"
	16	1/4 turn	300–400 ft-lb (408–544 Nm)

* Install cotter pin to lock the nut.

** For positive adjustment wheel bearings (a Rockwell product), use 250–300 ft-lb (339–407 mm) on adjusting nut and jam nut, as listed in the Rockwell field maintenance manual No. 14.

Manually Adjusting Wheel Bearings

TMC bearing RP 618 is an industry-established procedure for obtaining a wheel end play of between 0.001" and 0.005" (0.025 mm and 0.127 mm). Tightening the bearing retaining nut controls end play by loading or, more accurately, preloading the bearing before the vehicle load is applied. Optimum bearing and seal life are obtained using 0.001" to 0.005" (0.025 mm to 0.127 mm) preload. To manually adjust wheel bearings, follow the steps in **SKILL DRILL 28-2**, in conjunction with **TABLE 28-2**.

Bearing adjusting nuts on some axle ends may use a cotter pin with a locking tab to prevent backing off of the lock nut, as illustrated in **FIGURE 28-40**. When installing the cotter pin, never tighten the adjusting nut to align it with the cotter pin slot in the spindle. This can add excessive preload to the wheel bearings and cause a premature bearing failure. Back-off the adjusting nut instead to align the cotter pin hole.

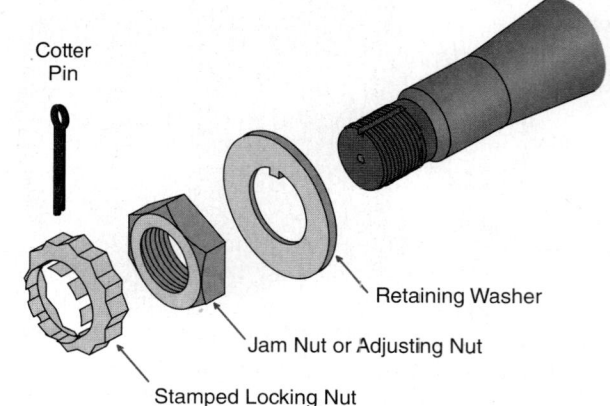

FIGURE 28-40 A conventional spindle nut on a steer axle is locked into place with a locking nut and cotter pin.

SKILL DRILL 28-3 Measuring Wheel End Play

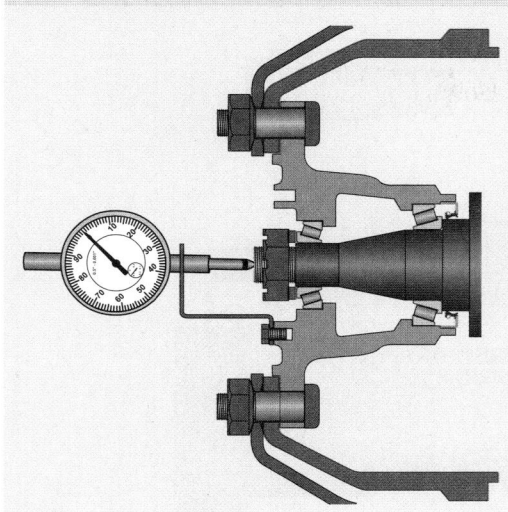

1. Attach a dial indicator with its magnetic base to the wheel hub.
2. Adjust the dial indicator so that its plunger or pointer is against the end of the spindle, with its direction approximately parallel to the axis of the spindle.
3. Grasp the wheel assembly at the 3 o'clock and 9 o'clock positions. Push the wheel assembly in and out and rock it at 45-degree angle while oscillating it to move the bearings.
4. Note how far the pointer plunger is pushed in and how far it extends. Subtracting the difference between the maximum and minimum values is total bearing end play.

Measuring Wheel End Play

Wheel end play is the free movement of the wheel hub assembly along the axle spindle axis. A large variety of wheel end retaining nuts are used to precisely adjust the wheel bearing end play and lock the adjustment in place. For example, the Stemco Pro-Torq nut is a popular wheel retaining nut system that enables precise location and locking of the retaining nut for achieving correct end play. To measure wheel end play, follow the guidelines in **SKILL DRILL 28-3**.

▶ TECHNICIAN TIP

Often one of the first indicators of loose wheel bearing adjustment is ABS wheel speed sensor codes. Loose bearing allows the hub to contact the speed sensor and increase the air gap until the signal becomes erratic. Pushing the speed sensor back into the spring-loaded retainer only temporarily corrects the problem. The wheel bearing adjustment should always be checked whenever a wheel speed sensor code is set.

Preset Hubs

LO 28-10 Identify and describe the construction of preset hubs and service methods for adjusting wheel bearing end play.

Standard hubs were used for decades but, beginning in the late 1990s, a new method was introduced to establish correct wheel bearing end play. By using bearing cups, cones, and bearing bores machined seat-to-seat to precise tolerances in a climate-controlled factory, a metal sleeve placed between the bearing cones could precisely establish end play. These new hubs, called preset or unitized hubs, are illustrated in **FIGURE 28-41**. **Preset hubs** are manufactured as a single piece unit and replaced as a unit. If they are disassembled and parts replaced, they must be serviced as a standard hub and bearing adjusted to obtain the correct end play. Parts should never be interchanged with these hubs. **TABLE 28-3** compares the features of standard hubs and preset hubs.

FIGURE 28-41 Preset hub unit.

TABLE 28-3 Comparison of Standard and Preset Hub Features

Standard Hubs	Preset Hubs
Individual components are assembled by a technician	Hub assembly is completely assembled from factory
Least-accurate wheel bearing adjustment	Bearing end play is factory pre-set for improved accuracy
Wheel end play adjustment depends on technician skill	Adjustment made at factory and no end play errors
Labor-intensive operation	Faster installation and no further maintenance required

Using a precision-machined bearing sleeve placed between the inner bearing races establishes a predetermined distance between the bearing cones. Spacer sleeves are precisely machined for a precise width between the bearings, as shown in

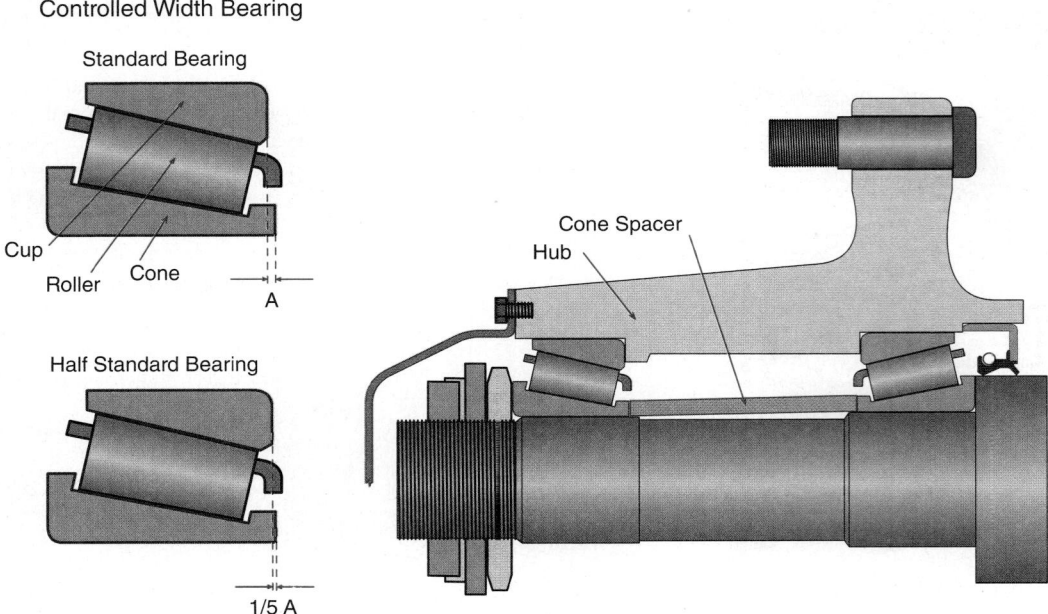

FIGURE 28-42 Precision preset hubs have precisely machined ledges for bearing cup and cone installation. The distances between the ledges and the bearing spacer maintain precise bearing preload.

FIGURE 28-42. Because the spacer is not a collapsible sleeve, its width does not change during normal operation.

When bearings or other hub components require service, a completely new hub is installed on to the spindle and the bearing retaining nut is typically torqued only once to 250 to 300 ft-lb (339 to 407 Nm). Wheel bearing end play is automatically set when the nut is tightened. Lubricant is added, and a hubcap is installed. The precision of bearing preload exceeds the accuracy obtainable for standard hubs using a manual bearing adjustment method. Preset hubs offer simplified installation procedures, improved wheel seal and bearing life, plus lower maintenance requirements. Note that preset bearings are not interchangeable with standard hub bearings; preset hubs use half-stand bearings. Half-stand bearings are precision bearings manufactured to a tighter tolerance than standard bearings. The prefix HS in the bearing number designates half-stand bearings.

Limited Maintenance Locking Nut

Another strategy to achieve and maintain reliable wheel bearing preload is the use of low or no maintenance locking nuts. There is no designated term for this type of hardware used in the evolution of new methods to establish and maintain wheel bearing locking systems, but several systems are commonly used. As an alternative to the TMC 618 method to adjust wheel bearings, low or no maintenance adjusting nut systems help technicians quickly and accurately establish correct wheel bearing end play. The intent of designs is to adjust end play in just a couple of simple steps that do not require the use of a dial indicator to validate correct end play. When maintenance is required, the adjusting mechanism provides a method to incrementally tighten the bearing preload to correct for bearing wear. In addition to the conventional double-nut locking configurations are Stemco's

FIGURE 28-43 Comparing the ProTORQ and Zip TORQ bearing lock nuts.

PRO-TORQ™ and Zip TORQ locking device (**FIGURE 28-43**). The Pro-Torque™ nut is a six- or eight-sided nut that is torqued into place; a mechanical locking spring is then installed into the body of the nut, locking it into position on the spindle (**FIGURE 28-44**). The Zip TORQ is a similar device that replaces the locking spring with a locking mechanism to prevent the nut from backing off. ConMet offers a preset spindle nut that is tightened to 300 ft-lb (407 Nm). A locking snap ring is placed in the nut to prevent the adjustment from loosening.

Correct end play is 0.001" to 0.005" (0.025 to 0.127 mm). Note: End play when using a ProTorq Nut is 0.001" to 0.003" or (0.025 to 0.076 mm).

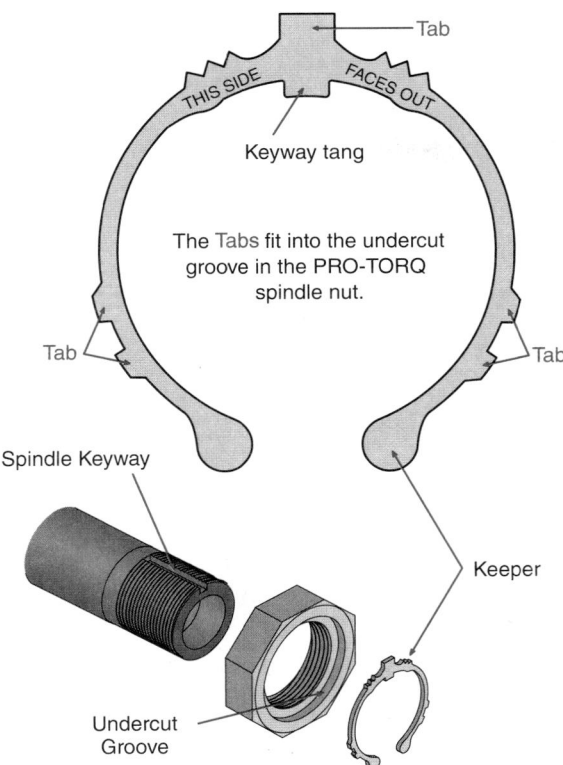

FIGURE 28-44 Stemco® PRO-TORQ® nut system.

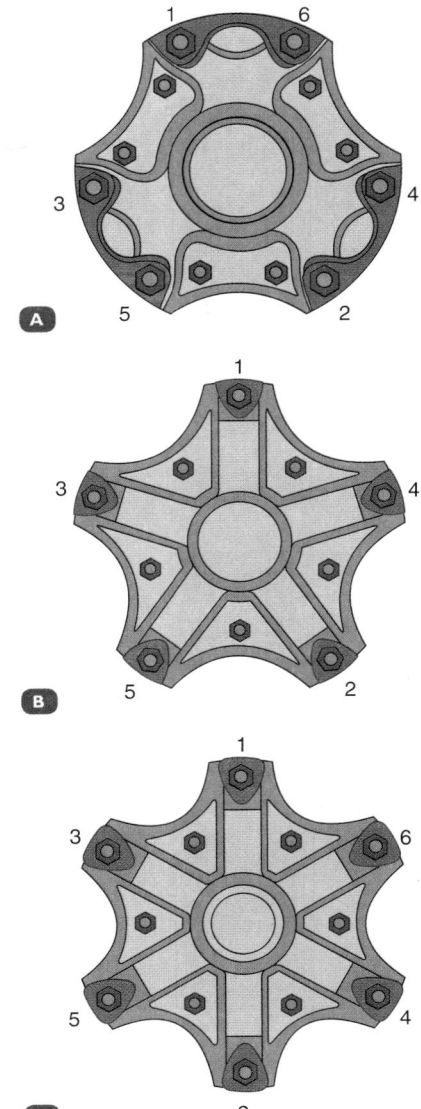

FIGURE 28-45 Proper torque sequence for a cast spoke hub with: **A.** three spokes; **B.** five spokes; and **C.** six spokes.

Cast Spoke Hubs

LO 28-11 Describe and explain construction features of cast spoke hubs and rim retention system.

Cast iron spoke hubs are also part of the wheel for open center rims. These hubs are preferred in off-road or heavy-duty construction vehicle applications, such as dump trucks, heavy equipment hauling, or logging because they have the highest load-carrying capacity. This hub design is one of the oldest and most rugged types of modern wheel and hub configurations. The design has traditionally the fewest incidences of "wheel-off" failures due to the use of clamps to hold the rims in place.

The spokes on a cast spoke hub support the tire rim. This means that more spokes provide increased capacity of the wheel to support weight. Small-diameter wheels used on equipment trailers may have only three spokes. Larger-diameter wheels hauling heavier loads use five spokes (**FIGURE 28-45**). The heaviest loads are supported with wheels using six spokes.

The cast spoke wheel, such as the one shown in **FIGURE 28-46**, incorporates a hub containing wheel bearings. Brake drums are bolted to the cast spoke. Open center rims are installed over the beveled spokes to prevent the inboard side of the rim from sliding off the rim. Friction between the rim and the increasingly larger-diameter spoke holds the rim tightly. The rim is locked in position using wedge-shaped clamps attached to the wheel with studs and nuts. Wheel clamps force the rim onto a taper-shaped hub to secure the wheel and prevent it from rotating under drive or braking torque forces. If the rim and hub

do rotate separately, raised wheel stops on the rim limits the rim rotation to prevent shearing the tire valve stem.

When dual tires are used on a cast spoke wheel, a rim spacer, such as the one shown in **FIGURE 28-47**, is used between the rims to transfer the clamping force of wheel clamps to the inner rim. The spacer also spaces the dual wheels, preventing the tires from contacting one another during vehicle operation.

Spacers are available in different widths and must be properly matched to the tire rim width and spoke width. If a spacer collapses due to excessive clamping force, the rims may move under brake or drive torque. The moving rims will then contact the stops on the rim. Under this condition, a clunking noise originates from the wheel when braking or accelerating. Collapsed or worn spacers can also lead to loose wheels and sheared tire valve stems.

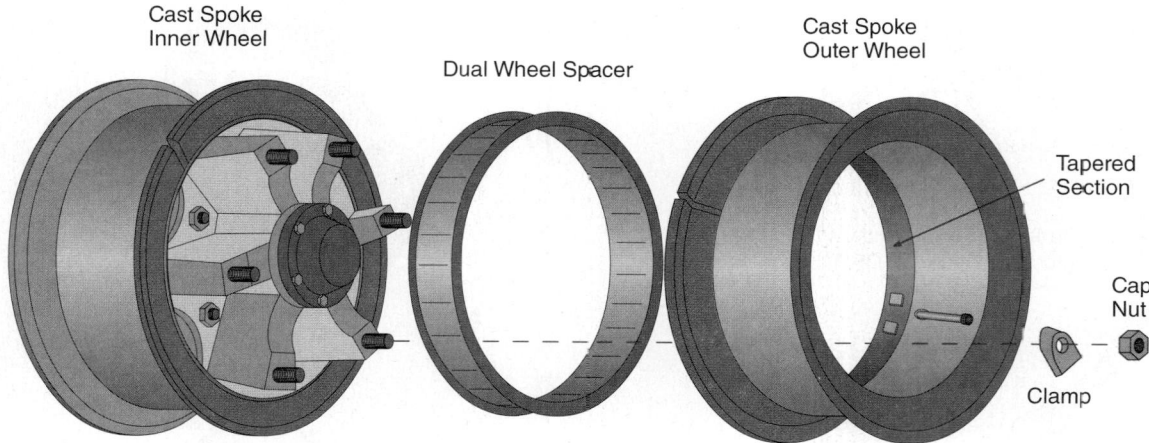

FIGURE 28-46 Dual demountable rim on a cast spoke hub.

FIGURE 28-47 Corrugated spacers used with cast spoke hubs.

The wheel clamps retaining demountable rims on spoke-type wheels are under very high spring-like tension. When a wheel clamp is loosened, the spring forces retaining the wheel rim over the tapered spokes are rapidly released and cause the clamp to fly off the wheel stud with considerable force. To prevent physical injury from flying wheel clamps, do not completely remove the nuts initially. Instead, first release tension on the rim by backing off the retaining nuts on all the clamps. The nuts should stay on the wheel studs with no less than two or three threads. Then, when the tension is released, hit the clamps with a hammer to loosen before removing the retaining nuts completely.

Hub Seals and Lubricant

LO 28-12 Describe and explain the purpose of hub seals and lubricant.

Two principle operations of maintaining wheels and hubs are replacing hub seals and regularly inspecting the lubricant level in the hub. Hub seals are an integral part of hubs used to keep

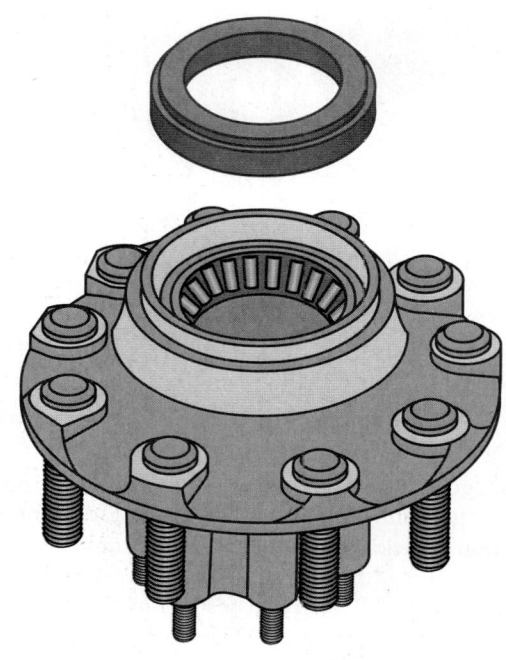

FIGURE 28-48 Dynamic oil seals are pressed into the hub to seal lubricant inside and prevent dirt and water from entering.

oil or grease from leaking out between the wheel spindle and the rotating hub. Wheel seals also function to keep out dirt, water, and other contaminants. However, if water does enter a hub cavity and is noticed by the presence of milky-colored lubricant. This dangerous condition requires hub disassembly and inspection of wheel bearings.

Hub seals are dynamic-type seals. Dynamic seals are used in places where there is relative motion between the mating surfaces being sealed. **FIGURE 28-48** illustrates a dynamic seal.

Hub seals are typically made from metal and specialized Teflon or rubber-like materials. A replaceable metal wear ring is commonly used to restore a spindle surface damaged by seal wear, cuts, or burrs to prevent seal failure. Functionally, wheel seals must do the following:

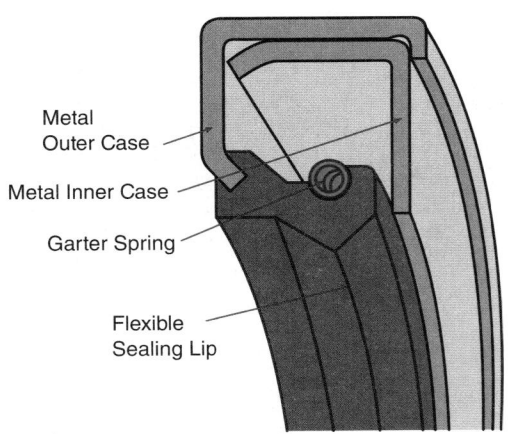

FIGURE 28-49 The hub seal is pressed into a step or ledge in the hub bore. A garter spring helps maintain a positive pressure seal between the seal lip and axle spindle.

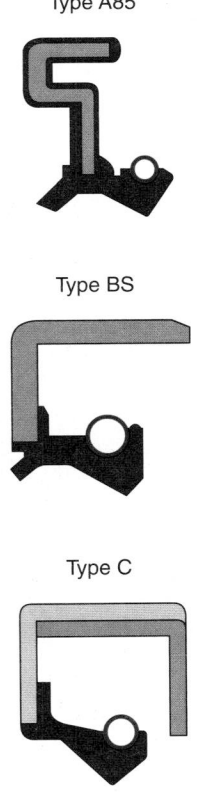

Type A85

Type BS

Type C

FIGURE 28-50 Various single- and double-seal lip configurations are used to seal out dirt and liquids while keeping lubricants from leaking out of the hub cavity.

- Withstand high temperatures produced during braking
- Be compatible with various hub lubricants that can degrade rubber materials
- Endure harsh operating conditions, such as extreme temperature changes and abrasion from metal particles and road grit for extended travel distances.

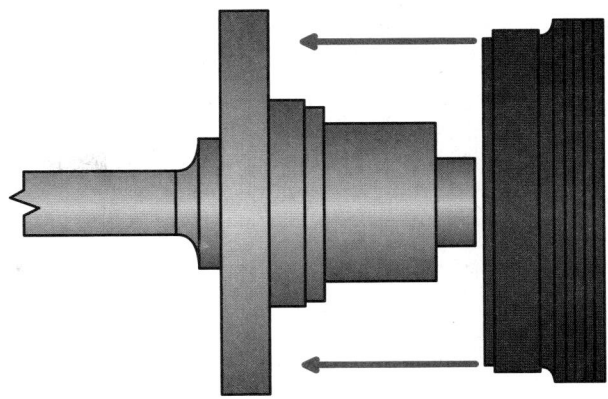

FIGURE 28-51 Seal driver.

Types of Hub Seals

A variety of seal types are available. They are classified depending on how sealing is performed, the type of installation tools used, materials the seal is made from, and whether the seal is pressed into the hub or onto the spindle shaft.

Most seals are lip-type seals, which use a flexible piece of material to seal the rotating shaft. A garter spring is installed behind the seal lip to hold the seal firmly against the shaft, as shown in **FIGURE 28-49**. Any gas pressure inside the hub is used to force the seal tighter against the spindle. A small amount of hub lubricant leaks through the lip area and forms an oil film between the lip and shaft. This feature helps prevent leaks when gas pressures are high, such as when the oil or grease in the hub assembly becomes hot and expands. Various lip-type seals are illustrated in **FIGURE 28-50**.

When pressure is low, and leaks are unlikely, the lower tension on the lip reduces seal and shaft wear. A slight oil film on the spindle reduces seal and shaft wear, plus provides additional sealing capabilities. A good quality seal, installed properly, does not allow any oil to pass the seal lip. Because dirt and contaminants must be kept out at the same time oil is sealed in the hub, most seals use a double lip design. One lip performs each function. Seal drivers, like the one in **FIGURE 28-51**, are often used to install wheel seals. Alternatively, hub seals are hand-pressed into the hub.

Seal Failures

Wheel-end seal leaks are one of the biggest maintenance concerns among heavy-duty commercial vehicle operators. Wheel seal leaks can quickly cause a wheel end to come off. Regularly inspecting wheel seals is critical preventive maintenance. When inspecting seals, a slight amount of oil weepage around the seal bore is usually acceptable, but drops or significant wetting are not permitted. The most common failure mode for most bearings is a lack of or improper lubrication caused by leaking wheel seals. As noted several times already, wheel bearing adjustment is critical to extending seal service life. Another leading cause of premature wheel seal failure is installation error. Damage to the seal during installation includes:

- Not lubricating the seal properly during installation
- Failing to drive the seal squarely into the hub
- Failing to correctly adjust wheel bearing end play
- Using a seal incompatible with hub lubricant
- Dirty or contaminated lubricant

Lack of lubricant on the seal lip quickly overheats the seal and destroys the sealing lip, so it is important to lubricate sealing surfaces during assembly.

Dozens of seals are available and are selected according to quality and expected longevity. But installation techniques are highly variable and include:

- Installing the seal using seal drivers
- Seals pressed by hand into a seal bore
- Seals installed first on the spindle and inserted into the seal bore when the wheel bearing adjustment nut is tightened

After seal installation, the oiler cap for steer and trailer axles have a removable plug to fill the hub with oil. The wheel should be rotated while filling the hub cavity with the correct type and grade of oil. After several minutes of filling, it is important to recheck the oil level to verify the level is stable. If a drive axle seal is replaced, the hub cavity must be filled with oil from the differential housing. To do this, raise the side of the axle opposite to end that had the seal replaced. This enables oil to flow into the hub cavity. Recheck the differential oil level afterwards (**FIGURE 28-52**).

Wheel Hub Lubricants

Gear oil and grease are used to lubricate wheel bearings. Good quality grease resists corrosion and water entry into the hub. Grease also helps absorb bearing shock loads and resists melting when hot.

Semi-liquid synthetic grease is commonly used in pre-set hubs. This grease is a semi-solid lubricant that is thick enough to stay in the bearings and provide lubrication, but thin enough to flow between parts. Lubricants used for wheel bearings generally contain the extreme-pressure (EP) additive lithium or lithium soap. Lithium is a metallic element that provides additional lubrication and corrosion protection. Lubricant levels are inspected through the sight glass of oiler caps. Oil level is indicated on lines used in the face of the oil cap (**FIGURE 28-53**).

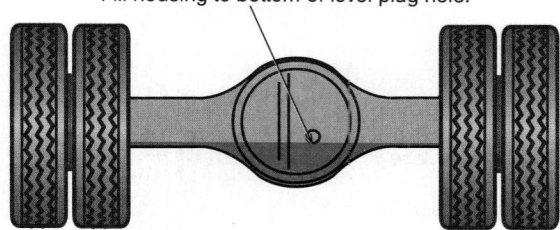

Fill housing to bottom of level plug hole.

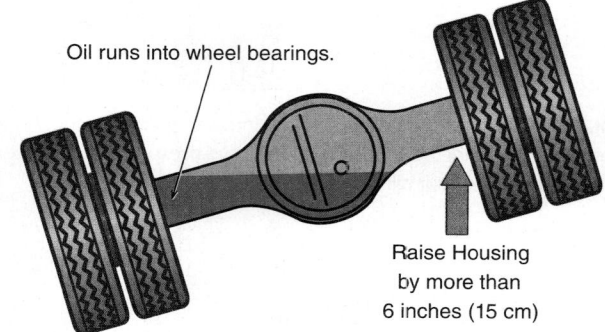

Oil runs into wheel bearings.

Raise Housing by more than 6 inches (15 cm)

FIGURE 28-52 To fill the drive axle hub with oil, raise the axle housing on the side opposite the end requiring oil. This enables oil to flow from the differential housing into the hub.

FIGURE 28-53 Lines on the site glass face of the oiler cap indicate oil level.

Wrap-Up

Ready for Review

- The role of the hub is to transfer the vehicle weight from the wheels to the axle ends and enable the wheel to rotate on the axle end.
- Wheel offset is important because it is typically used to bring the tire centerline into close alignment with the larger inner wheel bearing, and it reduces load on the stub axle. The offset can be either zero, positive, or negative.
- Wheels are fastened to the hubs by wheel studs and wheel nuts. Wheel studs and wheel nuts are highly stressed by loads from the weight of the vehicle and the forces generated by its motion.

- Undertightening wheel nuts allows wheels to run loose, eventually pounding and deforming wheel bolt holes.
- Overtightening wheel nuts can stretch studs and cause them to fail. Applying excessive lubricant to the threads of a stud or nut can cause excessive tightening.
- The best way for a technician to produce the clamping force necessary to keep the wheels on the vehicle is through correct preparation of fasteners and the use of a torque wrench.
- Cast iron spoke wheels are preferred in off-road or heavy-duty construction vehicle applications, such as dump trucks, heavy equipment hauling, or logging. These wheels have the highest load-carrying capacity.
- On a cast spoke wheel, friction between the taper-shaped rim, wheel clamps, and the increasingly larger-diameter spoke hold everything together.
- When dual tires are used on a cast spoke hubs, a rim spacer is used between the rims to transfer the clamping force of wheel clamps to the inner rim.
- When rims are installed on spoke hubs, the lateral runout needs to be checked and adjusted.
- Disc wheels are simple, single-piece, stamped steel or aluminum rims onto which the tire is mounted. They can be hub piloted or stud piloted.
- Stud piloted disc wheels are the oldest type of disc wheel and no longer used on new equipment. They can use up to twice as many nuts as a hub-piloted system.
- Because stud piloted wheels transfer weight through the studs, there is a greater likelihood of breaking wheel studs and losing a wheel if the proper service procedures and hardware are not used.
- Hub piloted disc wheels use pilot pads instead of studs and nuts to center the wheel. Hub-piloted wheel nuts and studs only clamp the disc to the hub and do not support vehicle weight.
- Wheel hubs contain bearings used to reduce the friction between the stationary axle and rotating wheel.
- Bearing preload is necessary to cause the taper bearing rollers to rotate and create a hydrodynamic wedge.
- Technicians cannot adjust bearing preload, but they can adjust and measure bearing end play, which closely predicts bearing preload force.
- Precise adjustment of wheel bearing end play is necessary to maximize bearing life and prevent wheel seal leaks.
- Standard hubs are precision-machined aluminum or cast iron castings and are used in drive, steer, and trailer configurations. Wheel bearings on standard hubs must be manually adjusted.
- Preset hubs have correct bearing end play engineered into their design and manufacture. The bearing cup and bearing bores, along with a collapsible metal sleeve, are machined seat-to-seat with close and precise tolerances in a climate-controlled factory.
- Preset hubs offer simplified installation procedures, improved wheel seal and bearing life, plus lower maintenance requirements.

- Wheel seals are an integral part of hubs used to keep oil or grease from leaking out between the wheel spindle and the rotating hub. Wheel seals also function to keep out dirt, water, and other contaminants.
- Wheel seals are classified depending on how sealing is performed, the type of installation tools used, materials the seal is made from, and whether the seal is pressed into the hub or onto the spindle shaft.
- Leaking wheel seals can quickly cause the wheel to separate from the vehicle. Regularly inspecting wheel seals is critical preventive maintenance.
- Gear oil and grease are used to lubricate wheel bearings. Semi-liquid synthetic grease is commonly used in preset hubs. This grease is a semisolid lubricant that is thick enough to stay in the bearings and provide lubrication but thin enough to flow between parts.

Key Terms

bead seat The edge of the rim that creates a seal between the tire bead and the wheel.

bearing preload The load applied to a bearing before any vehicle weight or rolling loads are applied.

bolt circle pattern The number and spacing of the wheel nuts or wheel studs on the wheel hub on the wheel rim.

cast spoke wheel A type of heavy-duty commercial wheel that uses three, five, or six cast iron spokes integrated with a bearing hub.

demountable rim A type of wheel rim that can be removed from the cast iron spoke hub attached to the axle. Also called an *open center rim*.

disc wheel A closed center steel or aluminum wheel that supports a tire and attaches to the hub using wheel studs and nuts.

hub piloted disc wheel A type of disc wheel that uses a series of machined pads on the hub to help center the wheel.

negative offset When the hub mounting surface is towards the inboard or brake side or of the wheel's centerline.

open center rim A type of wheel rim that can be removed from the cast iron spoke hub attached to the axle. Also called a *demountable rim*.

pilot pad The lugs attached to the bearing hub to center the wheel assembly correctly during assembly.

positive offset When the plane of the hub mounting surface is shifted from the centerline toward the outside or outboard side of the wheel.

preset hub A wheel hub that uses a precision spacer and close-tolerance bearings to eliminate the need for manual adjustment.

rim diameter The distance across the center of the rim, from bead seat to bead seat. Also known as *wheel diameter*.

rim flange The exterior lip that holds the tire in place.

rim width The distance across the rim flanges at the bead seat.

standard hub   A wheel hub that uses manually adjusted wheel bearing end play.

stud piloted disc wheel   A type of disc wheel that retains the disc using studs attached to the hub and a tapered, or ball-type, wheel nut to center the disc onto the hub.

TMC RP 618   A procedure established by The Maintenance Council for obtaining acceptable wheel bearing end play of 0.001" and 0.005" (0.025 mm and 0.127 mm).

wheel end   The assembly at the end of the axle.

wheel end play   The free movement of the wheel hub assembly along the axle spindle axis.

wheel offset   The distance from the hub mounting surface to the centerline of the wheel.

wheel rim   The outer circular lip of the metal on which the inside edge of the tire is mounted.

wheel studs   The threaded fasteners that attach the wheel to the vehicle.

zero offset   When the plane of the hub mounting surface is even with the centerline of the wheel.

Review Questions

1. On which type of wheel are open center demountable rims used?
   a. Stud piloted
   b. Disc wheels
   c. Hub centered wheels
   d. Cast spoke
2. Which type of wheel will use the largest diameter bolt circle?
   a. 10-hole stud piloted
   b. 10-hole hub piloted
   c. 10-hole European wheels
   d. 10-hole North American disc wheels
3. Two-piece flange nuts are used primarily to
   a. Prevent nut loosening due to clocking
   b. Distribute nut torque evenly around the bolt hole
   c. Center a stud piloted wheel around its bolt holes
   d. Center a hub piloted wheel around its bolt holes
4. How many wheel nuts are used on two sets of dual wheels using stud piloted centering system?
   a. 16
   b. 20
   c. 30
   d. 40
5. How much wheel bearing end play can be measured on a wheel end having a slight negative bearing preload?
   a. 0.001" to 0.005"
   b. 0.005" to 0.008"
   c. Zero
   d. −0.001" to −0.003"
6. What is acceptable wheel bearing end play after adjusting using the TMC RP 618 procedures?
   a. 0.001" to 0.003"
   b. 0.001" to 0.005"
   c. 0.001" to 0.008"
   d. 0.005" to 0.008"

7. Which of the following reasons best explains the requirement for some wheel bearing preload?
   a. To prevent the wheels from developing excessive toe-out
   b. To create a hydrodynamic wedge to separate bearing rollers and races
   c. To increase sliding friction and decrease rolling friction
   d. Preload is measurable and enables verification of correct bearing adjustment
8. Which of the following parts is unique to a preset hub?
   a. A long-life hub seal
   b. A metal sleeve between the tapered roller bearings
   c. A specialized adjusting nut
   d. A ProTORQ adjusting nut
9. What is the purpose of a corrugated rim spacer?
   a. Prevents tire valve shearing
   b. Establishes wheel offset
   c. Prevents wheel separation
   d. Establishes dual tire separation
10. Which of the following is the most common reason for wheel separation?
    a. Hub seal leaks
    b. Loose wheel fasteners
    c. Broken wheel studs
    d. The use of hub piloted wheels

ASE Technician A/Technician B Style Questions

1. Technician A says that cast spoke wheels are preferred by off-road operators and users of construction trucks. Technician B says disc wheels are a better choice because they are a stronger wheel design. Who is correct?
   a. Technician A
   b. Technician B
   c. Both Technician A and B
   d. Neither Technician A nor Technician B
2. Technician A says that stud piloted wheels use more fasteners to clamp the wheel and, therefore, have no lateral runout. Technician B says hub piloted wheels have more frequent wheel separations because they use fewer nuts to retain a wheel. Who is correct?
   a. Technician A
   b. Technician B
   c. Both Technician A and B
   d. Neither Technician A nor Technician B
3. Technician A says that less radial and lateral wheel runout is acceptable on steer axle wheels. Technician B says that the same wheel on a trailer can support more weight than it can on a drive axle. Who is correct?
   a. Technician A
   b. Technician B
   c. Both Technician A and B
   d. Neither Technician A nor Technician B
4. Technician A says that wedges are used to hold a rim on a cast spoke hub wheel. Technician B says that wedges are under tension and can injure a technician when the retaining nuts are removed. Who is correct?

a. Technician A
b. Technician B
c. Both Technician A and B
d. Neither Technician A nor Technician B

5. While checking a hub for loose wheel bearings, Technician A says that lateral movement of the wheel indicates loose bearings. Technician B says that the kingpins should be checked too to see if they are causing wheel movement Who is correct?
a. Technician A
b. Technician B
c. Both Technician A and B
d. Neither Technician A nor Technician B

6. Technician A says that bearings with some preload operate cooler than bearings with more than 0.005" end play. Technician B says that additional end play helps the bearing roller receive more lubricant to run cooler. Who is correct?
a. Technician A
b. Technician B
c. Both Technician A and B
d. Neither Technician A nor Technician B

7. Technician A says that a bias ply tire with a tube uses a wheel with a flat rim base and has split rings holding one side of the tire onto the rim. Technician B says that multi-piece rims are very dangerous to service. Who is correct?
a. Technician A
b. Technician B
c. Both Technician A and B
d. Neither Technician A nor Technician B

8. Technician A says that replacing a bearing in a preset hub requires a wheel bearing adjustment like a standard hub. Technician B says using a half stand bearing allows the preset hub to be reused and no special adjustment procedure is needed. Who is correct?
a. Technician A
b. Technician B
c. Both Technician A and B
d. Neither Technician A nor Technician B

9. Technician A says that after initial installation, only hub piloted wheels require retightening after 50 miles (80 km) when a wheel separator gasket is used. Technician B says that only stud piloted wheel fasteners need retightening after 50 miles (80 km) of operation. Who is correct?
a. Technician A
b. Technician B
c. Both Technician A and B
d. Neither Technician A nor Technician B

10. Technician A says that wheel bearing preload is correctly adjusted at between 0.001" and 0.005" (0.025 and 0.127 mm). Technician B says that correctly adjusted wheel bearing end play of a ProTORQ adjusting nut is between 0.001" and 0.003" (0.025 and 0.076 mm). Who is correct?
a. Technician A
b. Technician B
c. Both Technician A and B
d. Neither Technician A nor Technician B

CHAPTER 29

Front Axles and Vehicle Alignment Factors

Learning Objectives

After reading this chapter, you will be able to:

- **LO 29-1** Identify and describe the classification, construction, and functions of non-drive axles.
- **LO 29-2** Identify and describe the purpose, classification, and operation of lift, tag, and pusher axles.
- **LO 29-3** Identify, describe, and explain factors affecting wheel and vehicle alignment.
- **LO 29-4** Identify and describe the purpose, function, and adjustment of the wheel alignment factor called toe.

- **LO 29-5** Identify and describe the purpose and function of the front axle construction factors called king pin and steering axis inclination angles.
- **LO 29-6** Identify and describe the purpose of steering geometry and differentiate it from vehicle alignment factors.
- **LO 29-7** Identify, describe, and outline procedures used to measure and adjust wheel alignment.
- **LO 29-8** Identify, describe, and outline procedures involved in inspecting and adjusting vehicle alignment.

You Are the Technician

A driver with a tandem axle straight truck complains that the steering of the truck tends to pull toward the curb side of the road. After performing a visual inspection, you notice most of the tires have uneven tread wear. A vehicle alignment indicates a 5 degree difference from recommended specification of the included angle on the right-side steer axle.

1. List some likely causes of the vehicle pulling to one side of the road.
2. List the alignment angles that could cause the vehicle to pull to the right and indicate how those angles would be different.
3. What service recommendation would you make based on deviation from specifications of the included angle?

Introduction

Axles are straight shafts to which the wheels and hubs are attached. As such, front axles are part of the vehicle's steering system, as shown in **FIGURE 29-1**. Axles perform several functions related to:

- Driving (combined driving and steer axle)
- Braking
- Steering and alignment

Another major function of axles is to transfer the vehicle weight from the wheel ends to the suspension system. However, a critical function of axles and, in particular, the front axle, is to maintain the correct position of the wheels relative to each other and the vehicle body.

Types and Functions of Non-Drive Axles

LO 29-1 Identify and describe the classification, construction, and functions of non-drive axles.

There are two main categories of axles used on commercial vehicles. Live (drive) axles are axles that are powered and can move the vehicle, like those shown in **FIGURE 29-2**. Live axles include the differential gearing and components used to transmit torque to the wheel ends. These are covered in detail in the

chapter Heavy-Duty Drive Axles. The discussion of axles in this chapter focuses on non-driving steering axles.

In contrast to live axles, **non-drive (dead) axles** do not have the capability to drive the vehicle. That is, non-drive axles do not transmit power. A typical non-drive (dead) axle is depicted in the illustration of the steering system in Figure 29-1.

FIGURE 29-2 Two steering axles with one functioning as a steering and drive axle are combined into the front axles. This configuration for a concrete pump truck supports greater loads and offers better off-road traction and maneuverability.

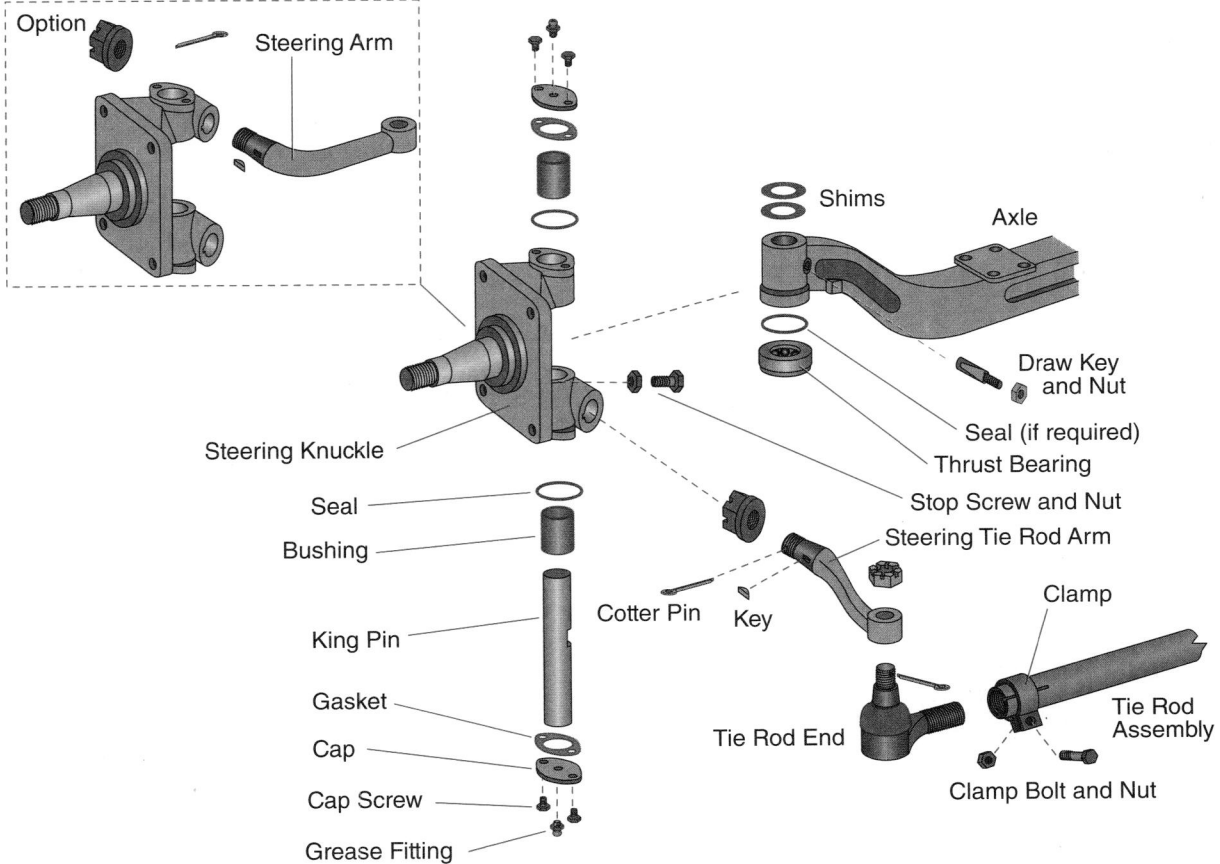

FIGURE 29-1 Typical medium- and heavy-duty steering system.

Non-drive (dead) axles perform two main functions critical to the operation of the vehicle. First, dead axles provide a connection point for wheel ends. Second, dead axles align the vehicle wheels so that the vehicle steers in a straight line and turns correctly. Non-drive axles also perform the important function of transmitting brake-reaction torque forces from the tire-wheel assembly to the rest of the vehicle through the suspension system. In addition, vehicle weight is distributed through the entire vehicle through both its driving and non-driving axles. Axles are used to support the weight of a fully loaded vehicle, so they must be properly designed to carry the load and resist distortion from brake "wind-up" or the opposite effect of torque reaction as well. Finally, connection points for the suspension system are located on the axle.

There are several common types of dead axles, including:

- Steering axles (front axles)
- Lift, tag, and pusher axles (rear axles)
- Trailer axles (rear axles)

Steering axles are primarily located in the front of heavy-duty vehicles. On heavily loaded vehicles distributing weight over multiple dead axles, the vehicles can be equipped with non-drive steering axles. Lift, tag, and pusher axles are rear dead axles that can have self-steering features allowing the wheel ends to articulate and follow the direction of the vehicle. More often, trailer axles use self-steering lift axles to support additional trailer weight while minimizing the side scrub of tires and excessive side thrust loading of hubs when turning.

Steering Axles

Steering axles are used for the front axle of medium- and heavy-duty commercial vehicles. The most common configuration is the **solid I-beam**, also called a forged I-beam design named for its rigid I-shaped profile, as shown in **FIGURE 29-3**. Nominal axle weight capacities for steering axles typically range from 6000 lb (2722 kg) to 26,500 lb (12,020 kg). Very heavy commercial vehicles, such as concrete mixers and mobile cranes, often use two steering axles (see Figure 29-2).

In addition to the extreme loads, steering axles must absorb significant and frequent brake torque (**FIGURE 29-4**). The axles must be able to endure frequent load cycles without fatiguing and breaking. For those reasons, steering axles are typically made from hot forged steel alloys that resists cracking and produces a high strength-to-weight ratio. In the event of an impact, forged steel axles bend and do not fracture.

Newer technologies have produced fabricated steer axles that substantially reduce axle weight. A rigid, but hollow box-shaped cross section of the axle helps resist horizontal, vertical, and torsional twisting forces. That resistance, in turn, helps

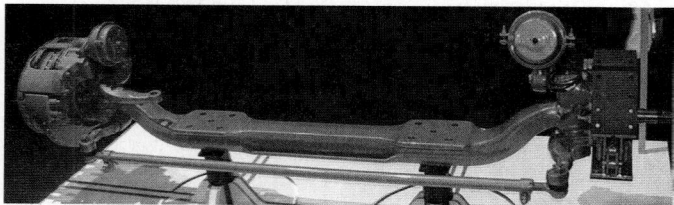

FIGURE 29-3 Solid I-beam steering axle with a drop-center design.

manage the increased brake torque loads that have resulted from the shortened stopping distances mandated by changes made in 2010 to the Federal Motor Vehicle Safety Standard (FMVSS) 121.

Steering Knuckles and King Pins

Each end of the I-beam uses an articulating attachment point that connects the front wheels to the axle. This device is commonly called a steering knuckle, and it enables the rotation of the wheel end around the end of the axle. It is the turning, or articulation, of the steering knuckle that gives directional control of the vehicle to the steering system.

Each steering knuckle is connected to the I-beam through the **king pin** and rotates around the king pin, as illustrated in **FIGURE 29-5**. The steering knuckle also contains connection points for steering arms and the tie-rod, which is a tube that ties or connects the left and right steering arms together at each wheel end. Tying the steering arms together with a tie-rod

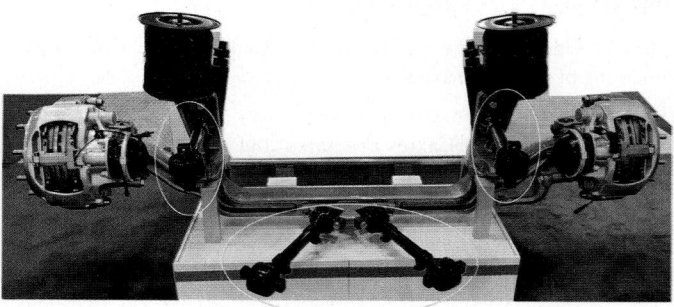

FIGURE 29-4 This drop center I-beam front axle with an air suspension system uses four stabilizer bars or torque control arms to resist axle wind-up caused by brake torque.

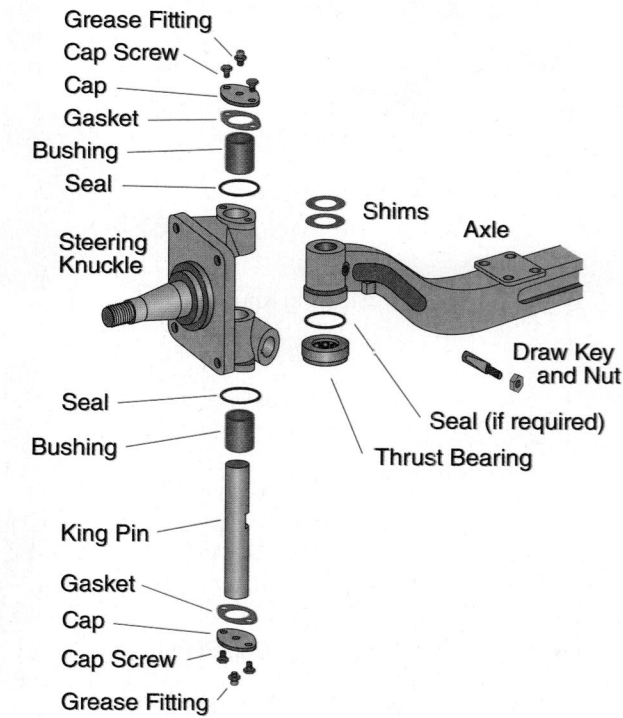

FIGURE 29-5 Steering knuckle assembly.

synchronizes the movement of the steering knuckles, as shown in **FIGURE 29-6**. Two common methods are used to remove the tie rod end from the steering arm. One technique is to strike the steering arm with a heavy hammer or air-operated hammer. This loosens the tapered joint. The other method is to use a tool called a fork or pickle fork. This tool is simply a wedge placed on both sides of the tie rod stud. Striking the fork with a hammer separates the tie-rod from the steering arm (**FIGURE 29-7**).

A single bearing located between the steering knuckle and axle transfers the weight supported by the wheel end to the axle. Without it, excessive friction between the axle and knuckle quickly wears the two components and dramatically increases steering effort. Selective shims, located on the upper part of the axle I-beam between the knuckle and axle, as illustrated in Figure 29-6, take up any excessive clearance between the two parts. Improperly shimmed steering knuckles or knuckles missing shims have excessive vertical movement and create a clunking sound over each bump in a road.

King Pin Profiles and Materials

Steering knuckles using king pins have the advantage of being able to support much heavier weights compared to a ball-joint suspension and permits knuckle rotation. The most common profile of a king pin is a straight king pin. Bushings in the upper and lower part of the knuckle form a replaceable wear surface for the king pin. One or two tapered draw keys are used to lock the straight king pin to the axle. **FIGURE 29-8** shows various

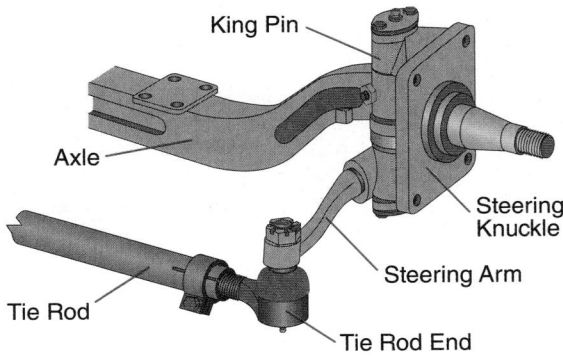

FIGURE 29-6 Tie-rods are ball-and-swivel joints that distribute steering force to each wheel end.

FIGURE 29-7 A tool with a wedge-shaped separator placed between the tie rod end and the steering arm can separate the two components.

FIGURE 29-8 Service kit for a straight king pin with a single lock. **A.** Hub seals. **B.** Straight king pin. **C.** King pin bushing. **D.** Tie rod end. **E.** Steering knuckle bearing. **F.** King pin draw keys. **G.** Steering knuckle shims. **H.** King pin gaskets.

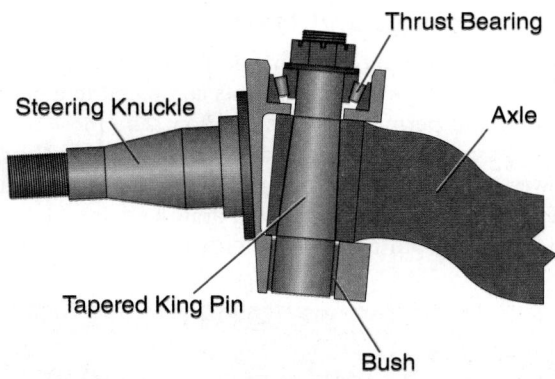

FIGURE 29-9 Tapered king pin used in a steering knuckle.

replaceable service parts for a straight king pin with a single lock. Brass bushings are used in this service kit.

Another shape of king pin is the tapered king pin. Tapered king pins have an adjusting nut that is used to adjust clearances between the pin and knuckle bushings, as illustrated in **FIGURE 29-9**. Unlike straight king pins, tapered pins do not use a tapered draw key to lock the pin in place, but generally can rotate in the axle spindle. Tapered king pins are used on some applications, such as on some heavy-duty Volvo front axles. The advantage of the tapered king pin is it has a threaded end or uses an adjusting nut that can be turned to compensate for king pin and bushing wear and to minimize excessive operating clearances.

King pin bushings are made using several materials. Most commonly, they are constructed from bimetal (brass and steel), nylon and steel, or similar composite materials. The steel outer shell provides strength for the bushing while the brass and nylon on the inside bushing surface provide a compatible wear surface for smooth steering rotation.

Steel-backed bronze (bimetal) bushings **FIGURE 29-10A** provide longer service life in severe service and can tolerate more dirt contamination. Bimetal construction makes these bushings ideal for aggregate haulers and refuse-handling vehicles. Pin-to-bushing clearances are obtained either by honing and or reaming the bushing. The king pin is never machined to fit the bushings or axle spindle.

Nylon bushings have the advantage of producing low steering effort and ease of installation because they often do not need to be reamed to fit the king pin. Instead, they use a tight, hand press fit operating clearance. But these bushings typically wear out faster than bronze bushings and are only used in light-duty, on-highway applications.

Composite bushings are currently the most commonly used by axle manufacturers. Using a steel backing, the inside diameter has a layer of plastic, such as low-friction acetyl resin polymer, applied to the steel back. Dimpling and grooving the coating enables improved grease distribution and retention compared to bronze bushings.

Reamers, such as the one shown in **FIGURE 29-10B**, may be needed to fit the king pin into the bushing, but not always. After the upper and lower bushings are installed in the steering knuckle, the king pin is hand-fitted into the knuckle. A snug fit is required between the pin and bushings. If the pin cannot be installed

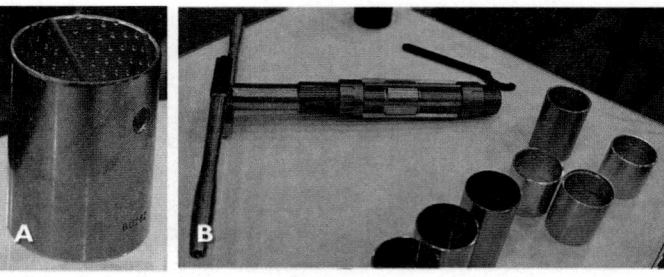

FIGURE 29-10 A. Bushing. **B.** Hand reamer.

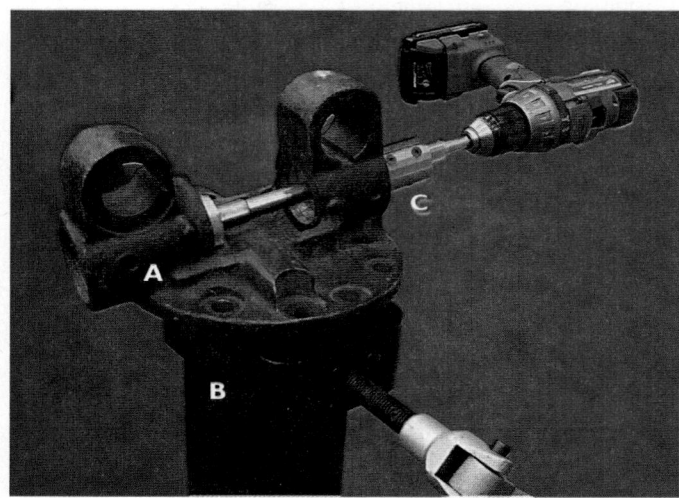

FIGURE 29-11 A cordless drill is used to drive a king pin bushing reamer, removing material from the bushing. **A.** Steering knuckle. **B.** Holding fixture. **C.** Bushing reamer.

into the bushings by hand, or the pin is too tight, the bushings require reaming (as shown in **FIGURE 29-11**), not the king pin. The reamer is used to remove a small amount of material from inside the bushing to establish the correct bushing to king pin fit.

Steering Stops

Steering stops are used to limit the turning angle of the steering knuckle. Adjustment of knuckle travel against the steering stops depends on the clearance of the tires and steer-axle components with the frame rails and suspension components. Power-steering gears have poppet relief plungers, which are adjusted to relieve power assist at the end of steering travel. This reduces pump wear and excessive stress on steering linkage components. Automatic pressure relief plungers in the steering gear set after a steering stop are correctly adjusted. Stops are adjusted to cut power assist with an additional clearance remaining of 1/8" to 3/16" (3.2 mm to 4.8 mm) between the axle spindle stop and the axle. It's important that the steer stops, shown in **FIGURE 29-12**, are correctly adjusted first before the steering gear poppets are set to protect the power steering system. Incorrect adjustments to the stops and steering gear could cause the steering linkage to bind or allow tires to contact the frame or steering linkage. Incorrect adjustment could also cause the steering angle to be unnecessarily limited in its travel or, worse, cause excessive pressure to be applied to the steering linkage, potentially causing damage.

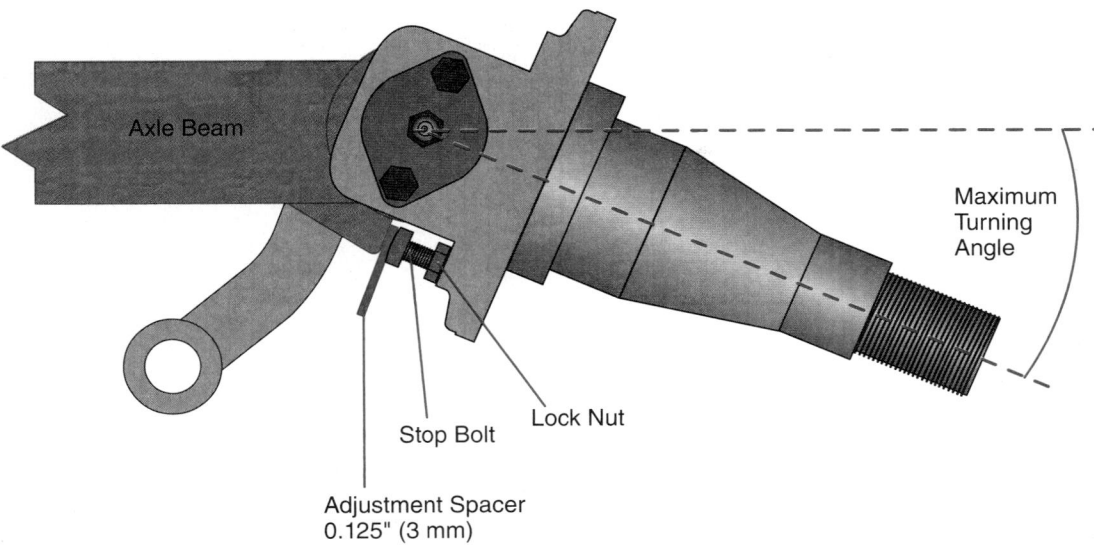

Axle Beam

Maximum
Turning
Angle

Lock Nut

Stop Bolt

Adjustment Spacer
0.125" (3 mm)

FIGURE 29-12 A thin spacer plate placed between the stop and axle spindle is used to correctly adjust automatic steering gear poppets.

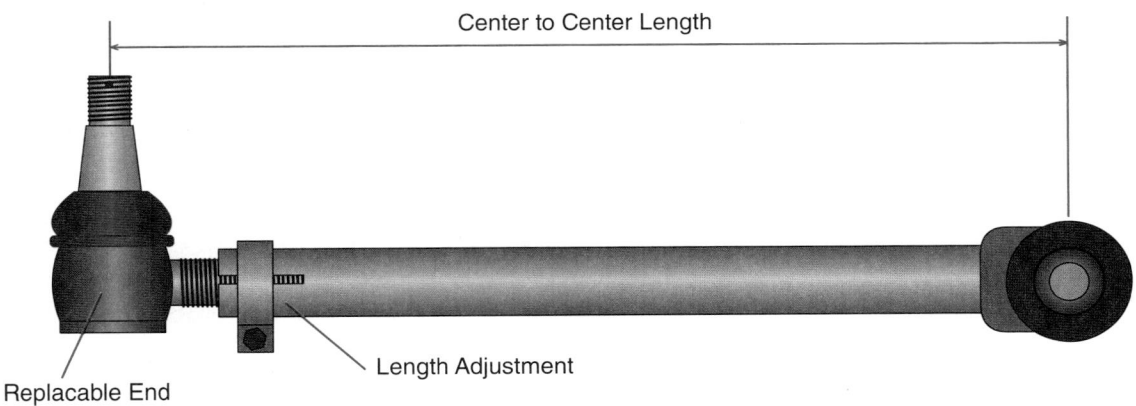

Center to Center Length

Length Adjustment

Replacable End

FIGURE 29-13 Measuring a drag link for correct replacement.

Pitman Arm

The **pitman arm**, sometimes called the **drop arm**, transfers the steering box output shaft motion to the steering linkage by converting rotational movement into linear motion. The pitman arm is typically splined to the steering gear output shaft, called the sector shaft, at one end and connected through a ball stud joint to the drag link. For additional safety, a snap ring, large nut, or set screws are often used to secure the pitman arm to the steering shaft to prevent the arm from disconnecting. A slightly tapered spline on some steering gear sector shaft requires the arm to be pressed on and off the shaft, which also helps ensure the arm does not accidently disconnect, resulting in a loss of vehicle control.

Drag Link

The **drag link**, illustrated in **FIGURE 29-13**, is connected to the steering arm at one end and the pitman arm at the other to transfer steering gear force to the steering arm. Drag link length can vary, depending on the distance between the steering gear and the front axle. For a typical drag link, the center-to-center length is critical to maintain the same number of turns from the vehicle straight-ahead position to the steering stop. Some drag links are also adjustable in order to center the straight-ahead position of the wheels with the steering box center of travel. This means the adjustable link has a threaded adjusting sleeve, which is used to center the steering wheel, with the straight-ahead position of the front axle wheels.

When installing an adjustable drag link, the front tires must be squared with the chassis frame. This can often be done using a measuring tape or a large framing square. In addition, the steering wheel spokes must be correctly orientated in a straight-ahead position, and the steering box must be centered so that the equal number of turns on the steering input shaft moves the box to the right or left. The drag link, illustrated in **FIGURE 29-14**, is adjusted to the correct length to connect to the pitman arm and steering arm without moving the tires or steering gear.

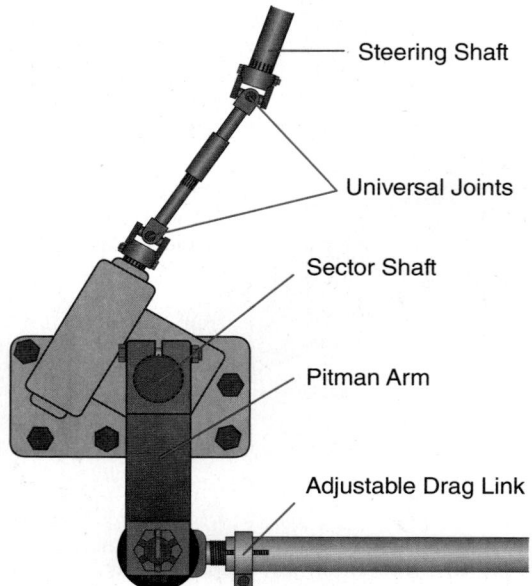

FIGURE 29-14 Connection of the draglink and pitman arm to the sector shaft and steering box.

Lift, Tag, and Pusher Axles

LO 29-2 Identify and describe the purpose, classification, and operation of lift, tag, and pusher axles.

Lift, tag, and pusher axles are used to supplement the load-carrying capacity of a vehicle when required. As such, they are rear non-drive axles. What determines if an axle is a lift, tag, or pusher axle is the axle's position in relation to the drive axle and whether it always remains in contact with the road surface. **Tag axles** are mounted behind the drive axle, and **pusher axles** are mounted in front of the drive axle. Tag and pusher axles are also often **lift axles** that can be mechanically raised and lowered to meet the regulated requirements for maximum weight loads per axle when needed. When the vehicle is empty, turning, or lightly loaded, these dead axles are raised to save tire wear and fuel. Likewise, when the vehicle is full or heavily loaded, the axles can be lowered to distribute the weight over a tire contact patch that has a larger surface area.

Tag and pusher axles commonly use a pair of airbags to lower the axle onto the roadway. Air pressure regulated by the driver and supplied to the suspension air springs, shown in **FIGURE 29-15A**, determines what percentage of the load the axle shares with the vehicle's other axles. As the air pressure increases, the axle lowers. Conversely, the axle is lifted by a separate set of airbags, shown in **FIGURE 29-15B**, after the suspension air springs are deflated.

Features are added to axles to better suit a particular application. For example, drop centers are used to accommodate a driveshaft tunnel for a lift axle. **FIGURE 29-16** shows a self-steering axle that uses a large caster angle to give the axle the self-steering capability to follow the front steer axle. Self-steer axles can be used on trailers and as pusher axles on straight trucks.

FIGURE 29-15 A. Lift axle air springs. **B.** Self-steering lift axle.

FIGURE 29-16 A self-steering trailer axle.

Fundamentals of Vehicle Alignment

LO 29-3 Identify, describe, and explain factors affecting wheel and vehicle alignment.

Wheel alignment, sometimes called **tracking**, refers to the positioning of the tires relative to the vehicle. The purpose of aligning and adjusting wheel position is to give heavy-duty commercial vehicles predictable, straight-line directional stability, and the ability to correctly turn, while minimizing tire wear and improving vehicle handling characteristics. Changes in vehicle loading and uneven loading alter wheel alignment, so those variables need to be taken into account by various alignment factors. Without correct wheel alignment vehicles:

- Consume more fuel due to additional rolling resistance
- Wear tires faster since misalignment produces uneven pressure and drag forces on tires
- Experience directional instability, as alignment strongly influences steering control
- Experience premature suspension and steering-component wear due to excessive forces applied to the components from wheel drag
- Cause increased driver fatigue due to the need to continuously correct vehicle direction, a condition known as counter-steer (illustrated in **FIGURE 29-17**), and cause increased effort required to steering the vehicle

The positioning of the wheels and tires in relation to the vehicle results in a set of angles that, taken together, determine the vehicle's total alignment. Therefore, before one can check a vehicle's total alignment, one needs to know what the wheel alignment angles are and how they and their geometric relationships affect vehicle operation and steering.

Alignment Angles

Tire alignment angles change as a result of vehicle loads. Front-axle components, therefore, contain many built-in features that enable them to optimize tire alignment for improved directional stability and vehicle handling when loaded.

Alignment angles fall into one of two categories: primary or secondary. Primary alignment angles refer to the positioning of the wheels relative to one another and to the vehicle. Manufacturers generally provide a mechanism to adjust some of those angles, but not all are always adjustable. Often, but not always, the following primary angles are adjustable:

- Camber
- Caster
- Toe

Secondary angles refer to the non-adjustable steering geometry of the vehicle produced by the design and operation of its steering and suspension components. Secondary angles include:

- King pin or steering axis inclination
- Included angle
- **Ackermann angle** or tire **toe-out on turns**
- Track width
- Thrust angle
- Frame angle

Camber

Camber is the side-to-side vertical tilt of the wheel. It is viewed from the front of the vehicle and is measured in degrees. Camber causes a tire to roll like a cone either inward or outward from the vehicle centerline. **Positive camber** exists when the tires are closer together at the bottom and farther apart at the top, as illustrated in **FIGURE 29-18A**. **Negative camber** exists when the tires are closer together at the top, as illustrated in **FIGURE 29-18B**.

A vehicle with camber pull pulls in the direction of the greatest positive camber. To picture why the vehicle pulls in this direction, think of a paper cone lying on its side. When the cone is rolled, it turns in the direction of the narrower end of the cone. Tires do the same thing in regard to their camber, which can place more weight on the outside or inside edge of the tire. Camber is affected by ride height on wheels with independent suspensions and can be observed by looking at the inward or outward vertical tilt of the wheel on vehicles that are loaded. The tires tilt further inward at the top, making the camber more negative when the suspension height is lowered (**FIGURE 29-19**).

All heavy-duty commercial vehicles use positive camber because a loaded vehicle bends the axle slightly at its center. That bend causes the wheels to tilt inward at the top, as shown in **FIGURE 29-20A**. Without some positive camber, a loaded vehicle places more force on the inside of the tire tread, prematurely wearing out the tire. With positive camber, a loaded vehicle allows the tire to run flatter against the road after the axle bends. When bending, the axle then places more vehicle weight on the larger inner wheel bearing. Less steering effort is required when loaded, since the load is closer to the vehicle center and wear

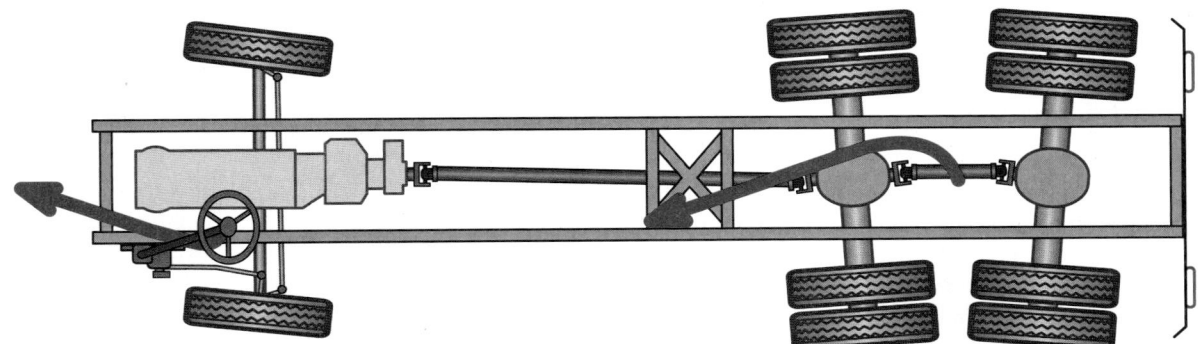

FIGURE 29-17 Misalignments require counter-steer to keep the vehicle straight.

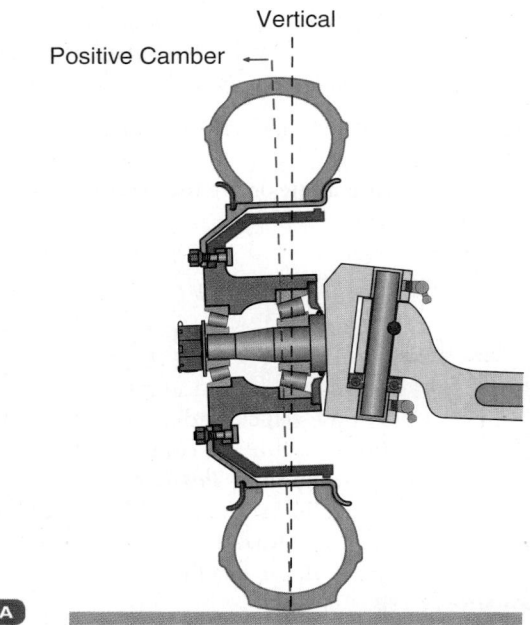
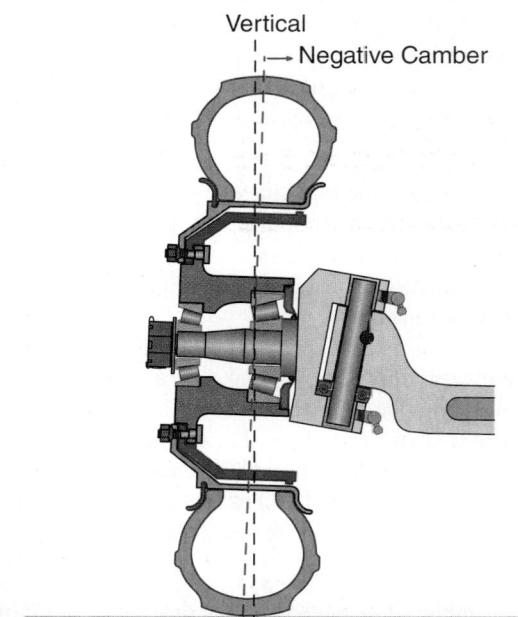

FIGURE 29-18 A. Positive camber. **B.** Negative camber.

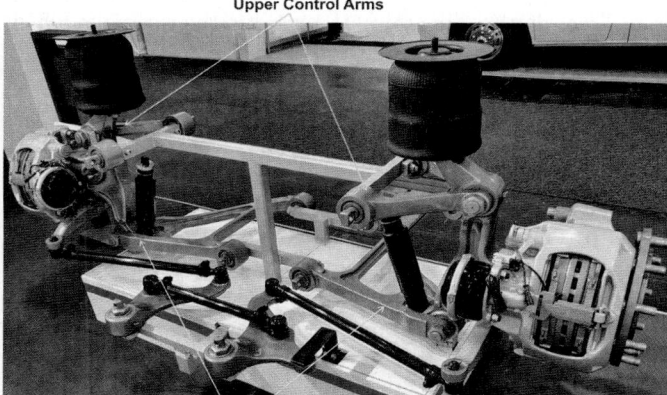

FIGURE 29-19 The lower and upper control arms of this independent suspension used on a transit bus are moved in and out relative to one another to adjust camber.

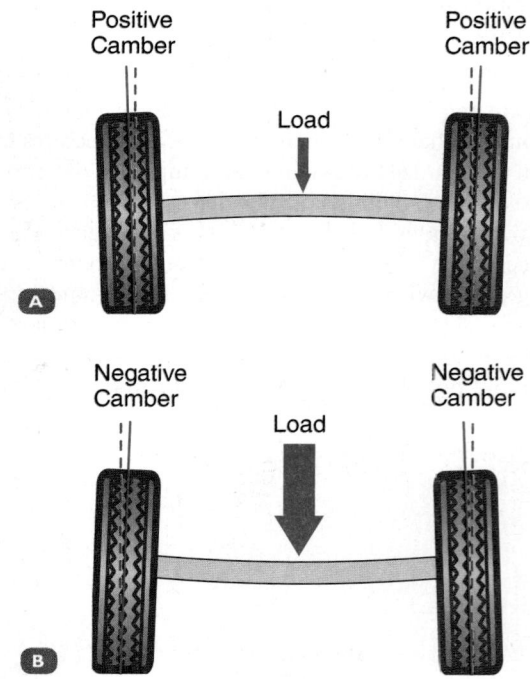

FIGURE 29-20 A. Heavy loads have a neutralizing effect on positive camber. **B.** Under heavy loads, negative camber results in more weight being placed on the inner end of the axle spindle where a larger wheel bearing is used.

of the wheel bearing and spindle is also minimized. Axles with no camber, such as trailer axles, use identically sized inner and outer tapered roller bearings in the axle hubs.

Camber and Vehicle Handling Characteristics

Even though negative camber is not used on heavy vehicles, a positive or neutral camber can turn negative when the vehicle is loaded, as illustrated in **FIGURE 29-20B**. One other benefit of negative camber is improved cornering capabilities. Camber actually causes the tires to have slightly different rolling radiuses, depending on whether the inside or outside shoulder of the tire has the greatest weight loaded against it. (Recall the

analogy of the paper cone.) For example, high positive camber means that more weight is applied to the outside edge of the tire, thus reducing its rolling diameter slightly compared to the inside edge. In this case, the tires tend to roll out and away from the vehicle centerline. Negative camber causes tires to roll inward toward the centerline. Because camber is a tire-wearing angle, optimal camber angles are needed to produce the least tire wear while improving steering and directional stability.

Also, because roads are crowned to improve water drainage, the traffic lane is lower on the curb side than in the center. That curve allows rainwater to run off the road. Slightly reducing the degree of positive camber on the right-side wheel compensates for the crown in the road, as shown in **FIGURE 29-21**. Without that adjustment, driving on a crowned road causes weight on a heavy vehicle to transfer to the right in left-hand drive vehicles, which, in turn, causes the vehicle to pull, or drift, toward the curb.

With less positive camber on the right side, relatively more positive camber is used on the left wheel to correct the effects of road crown. A difference of 0.25-degree more positive angle on the left wheel compared to the right wheel is typically used. The small difference between the right and left side camber angle does not influence rolling direction on a flat road surface. However, excessive positive or negative camber produces uneven tire wear on either side of the tire, depending on whether the camber is excessively positive or negative. **TABLE 29-1** shows the relationship between camber setting and tire life. Notice from the table how additional positive camber on the left wheel compensates for road crown. Improved straight-line directional stability is achieved with slightly more positive camber on the left than right wheel. Tire life is extended using correct camber and toe-in angles. (Toe-in angles are discussed in the Toe section later in the chapter.)

Camber angle is often adjusted into an axle when it is forged. A slight inward or outward twist of the axle end spindle establishes camber and is not adjustable after manufacturing. Some repair facilities attempt to bend the axle in the field to change camber angle, but experience indicates that the metal eventually returns to the shape it had prior to the bending operation.

Caster

Caster is viewed from the side of a vehicle and is the forward or rearward tilt of the steering axis from true vertical, as illustrated in **FIGURE 29-22**. When using king pins, caster angle is formed between a true vertical line and an imaginary vertical line passing through the king pin. Stated another way, caster angle is seen as a line connecting the upper and lower steering knuckle pivot points. **FIGURE 29-23** illustrates the difference between caster and camber.

When the upper pivot point of the steering knuckle is more rearward compared to the lower pivot point, caster is positive. If the upper pivot point is forward of the lower pivot point, caster is negative. Typically, no difference in caster angle is adjusted between the left and right side; however, no more than maximum side-to-side variation of ±0.5 degrees is recommended on most vehicles. Unlike camber, caster is not a tire-wearing angle under most operating conditions.

Caster and Vehicle Stability

Today's vehicles all use positive caster for straight-line directional control stability and steering-return ability. Using a positive amount of caster at both wheels provides directional

TABLE 29-1 Relationship of Camber Setting to Tire Life

Camber Setting (in degrees)		
Left	Right	Tire Life %
−3/4	−1	90%
−1/4	−1/2	89%
+1/4	0	100% (Optimal)
+3/4	+1/2	78%
+2	+1-3/4	73%

Source: *The Maintenance Council*

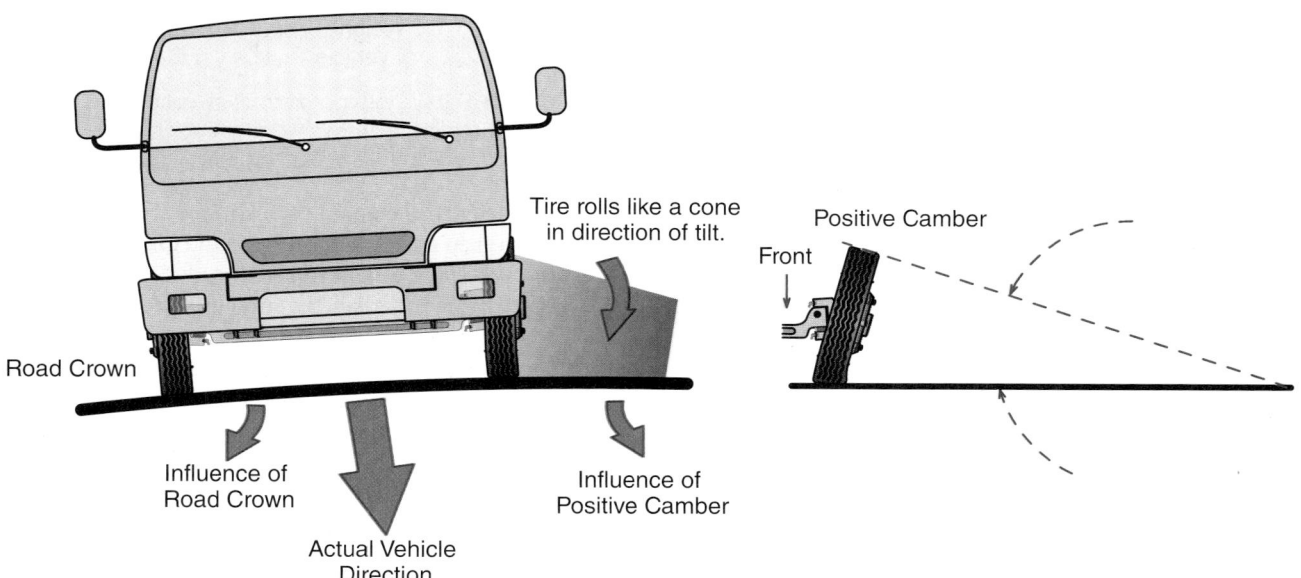

FIGURE 29-21 Less positive camber or more negative camber at the right wheel helps mitigate the effects of road crown.

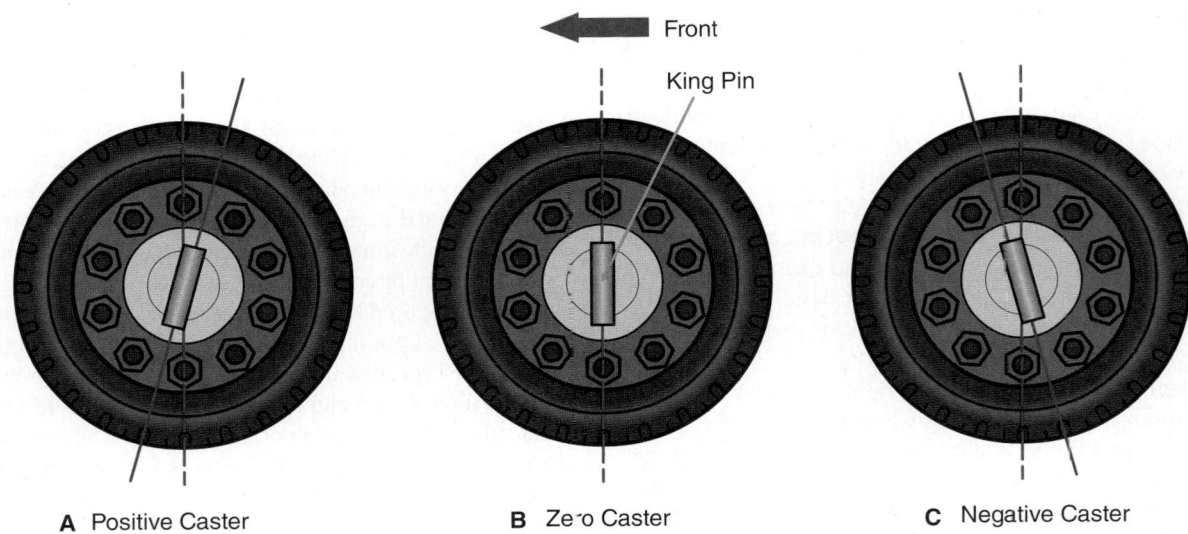

A Positive Caster   B Zero Caster   C Negative Caster

FIGURE 29-22 A. Positive caster. **B.** Zero caster. **C.** Negative caster.

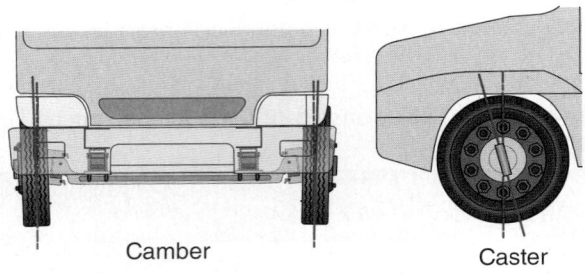

Camber   Caster

FIGURE 29-23 Comparing camber and caster steering angles.

stability and forces the wheels to return to a straight forward point if the steering knuckle is turned to the left or right. This happens for a couple of reasons. First, straight-line directional stability is enhanced because positive caster projects the weight of the vehicle ahead of the point where tires contact the road. In other words, with positive caster, the tires resist wandering because the contact patch of the tire follows the projected weight of the vehicle, as illustrated in **FIGURE 29-24**.

Positive caster also produces a weight shift on the tires when moved away from a straight-line direction. That shift forces the wheel to return to straight-ahead position. When turning left, a positive caster angle causes the left side of the vehicle to lift and the right side to lower. That occurs because positive caster causes the rotation of the left steering knuckle spindle to swing downward and lift the left side on left turns but swing upward and lower the left steering knuckle when turning right. As the left steering knuckle lifts the vehicle it tilts the top of left tire outward. The opposite happens on the right side. When turning left, the right tire tilts inward at the top because the spindle end of the steering knuckle swings upward and tilts inward at the top at the same time. These actions on the left and right side cause a weight shift to the outside edge of the left tire and to the inside edge of right the tires. The weight shift to tire edges combined with forward directional movement produces force on the tires to return the wheels to the direction of straight-line travel.

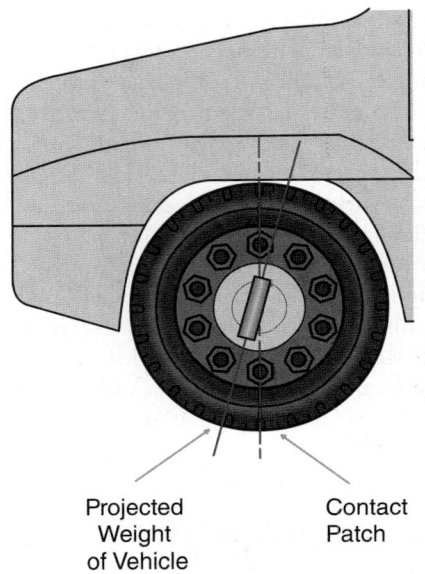

Projected Weight of Vehicle   Contact Patch

FIGURE 29-24 Positive caster projects the weight of the vehicle ahead of the point of contact between the tire and the road.

Weight transfer to the edges of both tires stops when the tires return to an even and level position found only in a straight-line direction. While the weight transfer produced by a large degree of positive caster increases the amount of effort required for cornering, it has the advantage of providing even more steering wheel return force in heavily loaded vehicles to automatically center the steer tires to a straight-line direction after either a left or right turn is completed. A common caster angle for a HD tractor is 3.5 degree positive on both left and right sides.

Like camber, a slightly different caster angle between the right and left wheels may sometimes be used to help compensate for road crown. The right side is adjusted with slightly more positive caster to produce a difference of no more than 0.5 degree difference between left and right.

The basic method for measuring caster angle on alignment equipment is to measure the angle of tilt when a wheel is turned. As caster angle increases, the degree the wheel tilts or leans vertically in or out at the top, compared to the bottom of the wheel, changes proportionally. As caster angle increases, the outside wheel tilts inward—even more so when the wheel is straight and parallel to vehicle centerline. This means when turning right, the left wheel tilts inward at the top and the bottom turns outward. The opposite effect is seen when turning left. The caster angle is measured using turning plates and is basically the difference between a wheel's vertical tilt when the wheels are straightened and when they are turned at 20, 30, or 45 degrees.

Caster Shimmy

While a little caster is good, excessive caster is dangerous. Excess positive caster is responsible for a condition called **caster shimmy** that can be dangerous to vehicle control and directional stability. The effect of excess positive caster and caster shimmy is observed on furniture casters and shopping cart wheels. If you have ever tried to maneuver a cart experiencing caster shimmy, you have likely noticed the rapid side-to-side movement of the wheel, as illustrated in **FIGURE 29-25**. As the vehicle moves faster, the tires cannot quickly "find" the projected track they should follow and begin to swing from left to right in an attempt to find a straight-ahead direction. In a heavy vehicle, this shimmy is felt in the steering wheel.

As positive camber increases, the vehicle weight is projected farther ahead of the tire's contact patch. With increasing positive caster, there is a greater likelihood for caster shimmy and increased shimmy intensity. This also happens because caster angle affects the radius of camber roll. Coincidently, a high degree of positive caster also produce proportional increases in the intensity and frequency of shimmy, particularly after hitting a bump.

FIGURE 29-25 Excessive caster causes wheel shimmy.

Another common cause of caster shimmy is an increase in vehicle load over the rear axle. When this happens, the rear frame and suspension are lowered, and the steering knuckle tilts backward, adding more positive caster. Shock absorbers, like those shown in **FIGURE 29-26**, are occasionally used on the tie-rod to minimize caster shimmy on axles with a high degree of positive caster, such as self-steering axles.

Adjusting Caster

Caster angle is primarily built into the shape of the steering axle spindle where the king pin passes through the steering axle or king pin bore. Major changes to caster require twisting the axle. Because metal tends to return to its original forged position (the shape it had when originally manufactured), any changes in the field typically revert to original axle shape. Another reason for not bending axles to adjust caster is that bending the axle leads to metallurgical damage to the axle. That can ultimately result in sudden catastrophic failure. For that reason, manufacturers explicitly forbid any bending of axles in the field to adjust caster. However, small changes in caster can be made by using tapered shims placed between the suspension springs and the axle. Placement of these selectively sized shims can rotate the axle slightly around its horizontal centerline.

Frame Angle

LO 29-4 Identify and describe the purpose, function and adjustment of the wheel alignment factor called toe.

Even though it is a secondary angle, **frame angle** can be considered with caster, since the frame angle can influence caster angle. Frame angle refers to the vehicle's frame relative to horizontal measurement to the ground. A **positive frame angle** is the condition where the frame's rear is higher than the front, as illustrated in **FIGURE 29-27A**. **Negative frame angle** is present when the frame's rear is lower than the front, as illustrated in **FIGURE 29-27B**. It is important to note that manufacturer alignment specifications are often recommended for loaded conditions because that is the normal operating condition for the vehicle. This explains why a vehicle should be loaded when measuring alignment angles if it is recommended by the manufacturer of the alignment equipment. Frame angle generally remains unchanged on vehicles with air suspension, as automatic

FIGURE 29-26 Shock absorbers minimize caster angle-related shimmy.

leveling valves adjust ride height for any given load. Under some conditions, however, any suspension system's normal ride height may change, which, in turn, affects adjustments to the steering geometry or the readings when the vehicle is unloaded.

Toe

LO 29-4 Identify and describe the purpose, function, and adjustment of the wheel alignment factor called toe.

By itself, the term **toe** is a measurement, in degrees, of how much the front wheels are turned in or out from a straight-ahead position. Toe is referenced from a position directly above the tires and facing forward. When the wheels are closer together at the front and farther apart at the rear, a **toe-in** condition exists (**FIGURE 29-28A**.) When the wheels are closer together in the rear than in the front, a **toe-out** condition exists.

Some toe angle is necessary on almost all commercial vehicles because clearances in steering linkage and wheel bearings allow the tires to turn outward from a straight-line position when moving. Due to a positive scrub radius found on front steer axles of almost all commercial on-highway vehicles, the tires are forced to turn outward when the vehicle moves forward. This would cause the tires to be dragged sideways down the road and rapidly wear out the tires if the toe adjustment does not correct for this situation. Adjusting the tires to toe-in slightly compensates for toe-out movement of tires due to positive scrub radius and allows the tires to rotate in parallel (**FIGURE 29-28B**). Rolling down the road, tires naturally toe-out to a zero toe position due to positive scrub radius.

Toe and Tire Wear

When traveling forward, toe should be zero degrees to prevent tire wear. Excessive toe-out wears the inside edge of both tires as the tire is dragged slightly sideways when traveling. Too much toe-in wears the outside edge of tires for the same reason. The difference between toe wear and camber wear is that toe wear creates a "feathering" of the tread because it is dragged sideways while uneven pressure on tire edges caused by camber wear does not feather tire edges. Toe problems affect both tires, while camber wear affects one tire, unless both tires have incorrect camber. **TABLE 29-2** shows the life expectancy of tires based on toe dimensions.

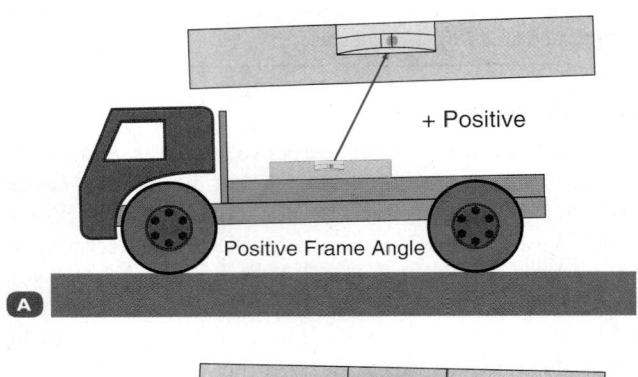

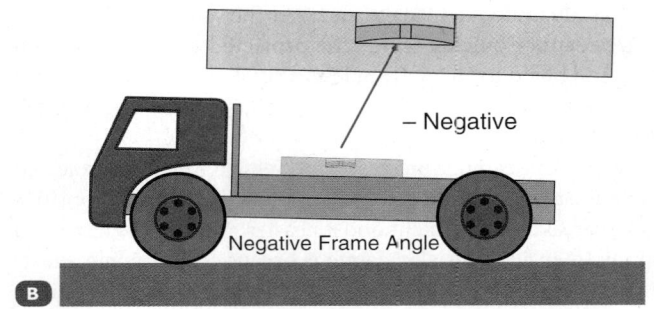

FIGURE 29-27 A. Positive frame angle. **B.** Negative frame angle.

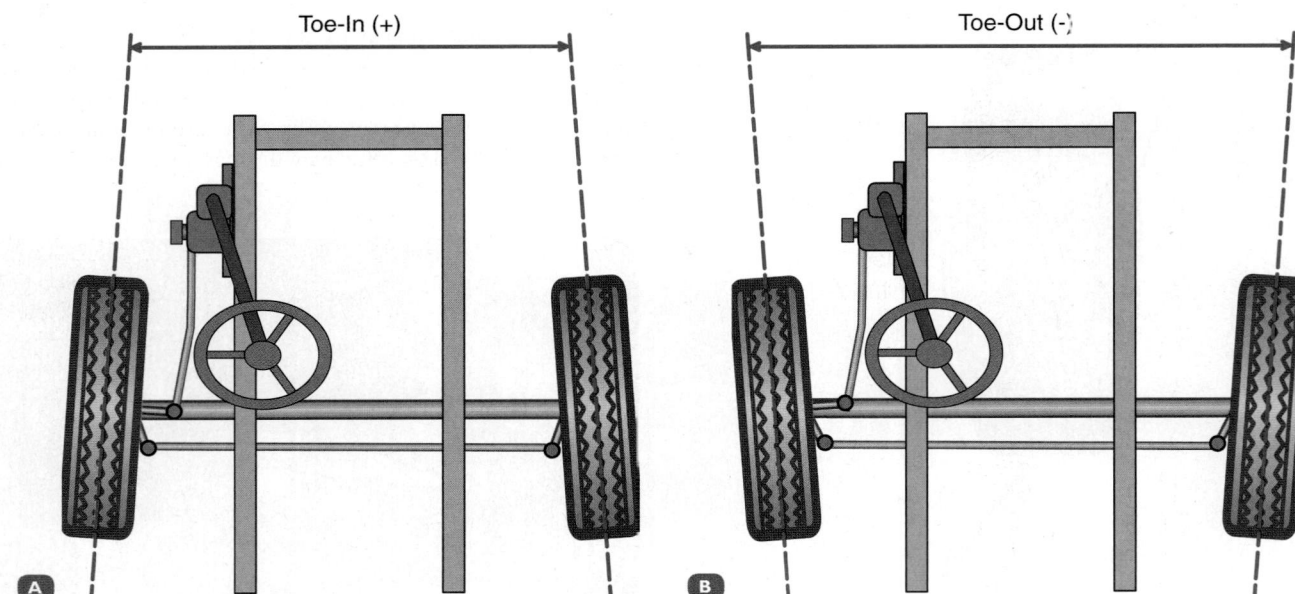

FIGURE 29-28 A. Toe-In. **B.** Toe-Out.

As with some other angles, toe can be adjusted by changing the length of the tie-rod. The length is, in turn, changed by shortening or lengthening the tie-rod ends threaded into the tie-rod. **Tie-rod ends** are ball-and-socket joints attached to the steering knuckle steering arms. The tie-rod ends are connected together by threading into a cross tube. Each side uses a left- or right-hand thread to enable adjustment of tire toe by turning the cross tube that connects the tie-rod ends. As shown in **FIGURE 29-29**, tie-rod ends are manufactured in several designs that prevent contact with the steering linkage.

King Pin and Steering Axis Inclination Angles

LO 29-5 Identify and describe the purpose and function of the front axle construction factors called king pin and steering axis inclination angles.

Steering axis inclination and king pin inclination are industry terms used interchangeably since they refer to the same steering angle. Both terms refer to the axis around which the wheel assembly swivels as it turns to the right or left. On vehicles

equipped with king pins, this angle is naturally referred to as the **king pin-inclination angle (KPI)**. KPI is the angle formed between true vertical and the angle of the king pin. This angle is formed into the axle during manufacture when the king pin bores are reamed. As such, the KPI is not adjustable. As with steering axis inclination, KPI is formed by drawing a line through the center of the upper and lower king pin pivot points of the suspension assembly, as shown in **FIGURE 29-30**. As one would expect, then, the **steering axis inclination angle (SAI)** or KPI, while described similarly to caster angle, is viewed from the front of the vehicle and not the side, like caster angle (**FIGURE 29-31**).

KPI has the most influence on directional stability since it works with caster to lift or lower the steering knuckle during turns, enhancing the self-centering action of the steering system. Combined with positive caster, the KPI angle helps return

TABLE 29-2 Life Expectancy of Tires Based on Toe Dimensions

Toe-In	Tire Life Expectancy
0.03125" (0.794 mm)	100%
0.125" (3.175 mm)	82%
0.25" (6.35 mm)	76%

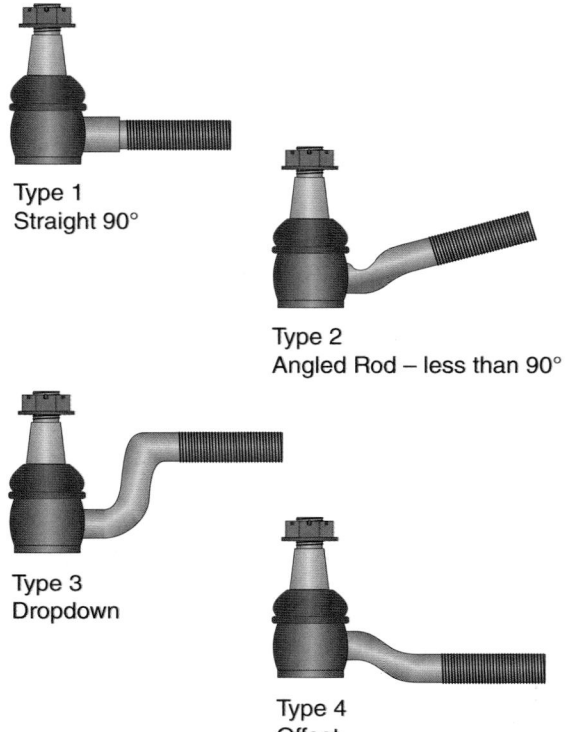

Type 1
Straight 90°

Type 2
Angled Rod – less than 90°

Type 3
Dropdown

Type 4
Offset

FIGURE 29-29 Types of tie-rod ends.

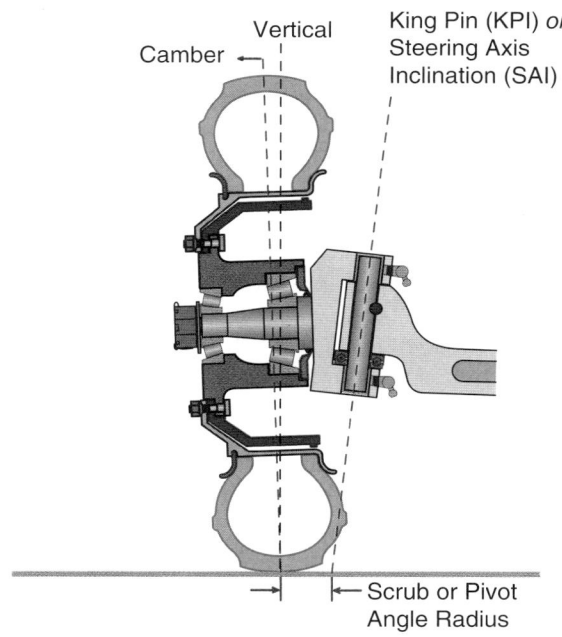

FIGURE 29-30 The axis around which the wheel assembly swivels as it turns to the right or left is called the king pin-inclination angle. It is formed by drawing a line through the centerline of the king pin.

Bubble Leveler **Optical Head With Target and Laser Site** **Turn Plate**

FIGURE 29-31 A turntable is used to measure the direction of wheel rotation in degrees. When the wheel is turned to a specific angle, the caster angle and SAI are measured.

the steering to a straight-line direction after turning the wheels. This happens because the KPI, along with a positive caster angle, lifts the wheel up in an arc-like direction during turns. Weight transfer to the left and right tire edges during turns then causes the steering knuckle to want to return to a straight-line direction. KPI angles are larger than camber angles and allow caster angles to be smaller. That relationship between KPI and caster results in reduced steering effort. KPI also causes the wheels to rise and fall in an arc on bumps rather than in a straight-line, which would be the case if no KPI were present. This means KPI helps prevent directional instability.

Included Angle

The angle formed between the KPI and the camber line is called the **included angle**. As depicted in **FIGURE 29-32**, the included angle is found by adding the KPI angle and the camber angle together. If the camber angle is specified as negative, then it is subtracted from the KPI angle. The included angle is not adjustable and is provided as a reference specification. When measured, the included angle can help determine if any parts are bent, such as an axle, steering knuckle spindle or control arm.

Scrub Radius

In addition to its influence with caster, the KPI angle also determines the scrub radius of a tire. The **scrub radius** is the difference between the intersection of a point on the tire contact patch between true vertical and the KPI angle. Scrub radius forms the pivot point for the tire contact with the road. A **positive scrub radius** is formed when the KPI angle is projected inside the tire's vertical centerline, as shown in Figure 29-32. This means the KPI is closer to the vehicle centerline than the tire's centerline. A **negative scrub radius** is produced when the

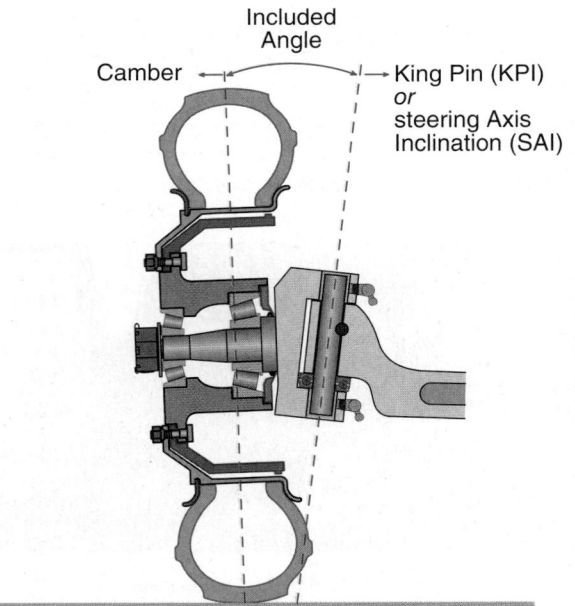

FIGURE 29-32 The included angle is the combination of the KPI and the caster angle. Although not adjustable, it can be useful in identifying bent components.

Camber — Included Angle — King Pin (KPI) *or* steering Axis Inclination (SAI)

KPI projects outside the tire's vertical centerline. Whether the **scrub angle** is negative or positive it affects the transmission of "road feel" back to the driver through the steering wheel. Positive scrub radius transmits better steering road feel back to the driver and helps self-center the tires. For this reason, almost all heavy-duty commercial vehicles use a positive scrub so that, when rolling forward, the positive scrub radius causes the tire to turn outward away from the vehicle centerline. As mentioned earlier, positive scrub radius tends to turn tires outward and causes all the clearances in the front axle, such as in wheel bearings and tie-rod ends, to be taken up, since the tires to toe-out. In addition, turning right or left increases turning resistance applied to the steering linkage, which is transmitted to the steering wheel. Because moving the steering from a straight-line position also produces increased steering resistance due to positive scrub radius, turning resistance is sensed by the driver as feedback from the road. Negative scrub radius produces what some drivers refer to as "numb" steering or little steering feedback.

Zero scrub radius is possible without an inclined king pin, but it requires a deeply dished wheel that places the king pin in the vertical centerline of the wheel. It is more practical to incline the king pin, use a less dished wheel, and maintain the self-centering effect of positive scrub radius.

Basic Steering Geometry

LO 29-6 Identify and describe the purpose of steering geometry and differentiate it from vehicle alignment factors.

The relationships between the steering system, the wheel positions, and the suspension system form what is called the steering geometry. **Steering geometry** is a geometric arrangement of linkage in the steering of a vehicle designed to solve the problem of keeping the wheels properly oriented through various dynamic driving positions of the steering and suspension systems. As the wheels move up and down relative to the chassis, the steering linkage must also swings vertically through an arc. Without compensation by some steering geometry, the wheel would turn in and out as the vehicle goes over bumps. With steering geometry, the suspension components and steering linkage travel together in a similar arc. That symmetrical motion allows the wheel to track straight ahead, or in a consistent direction if it is in a turn. Note there is a difference between steering geometry and vehicle alignment factors. Whereas steering geometry deals with the dynamics of linkage and steering system components, vehicle alignment factors have more in common with the position of axle components.

Ackermann Principle and the Ackermann Angle

The **turning radius** of a vehicle depends on the pivot point of the vehicle, the angle the wheels turn, plus the distance between the steering wheels and pivot point. For example, since a vehicle's pivot point is at the center of the rear axle, long wheel base vehicles have wide turning radiuses while shorter wheel base length vehicles have tighter turning circles. Efficient turning with the least tire wear and a change in vehicle direction proportional to the steering angle requires the outside wheel to turn at a smaller angle than the inner wheel. The Ackermann angle, illustrated in **FIGURE 29-33**, is also called tire toe-out on turns. It refers to the **Ackermann principle**, which states that the inner wheel should have a greater turning angle than the outside wheel since it has a smaller turning radius.

This is accomplished by changing the angle and length of the Ackermann or steering arms. The ideal angle for the steering arms is produced by drawing a line between the pivot point at the center of the rear axle and through the angled steering arm when the vehicle is steered straight ahead. In tandem-axle vehicles, the pivot center is between the two axles. Theoretically, changing the wheel base requires a different steering arm. Generally, however, manufacturers use only one steering arm, regardless of vehicle wheel base. **FIGURE 29-34** shows the Ackermann angle. Ackermann angle producing toe-out on turns is a non-adjustable angle. If it is not correct according to the manufacturer's specifications, then the steering linkage is likely bent, typically the steering arm. This also causes the tires to scrub when turning corners.

> ▶ **TECHNICIAN TIP**
>
> The Ackermann angle is not considered a tire-wearing angle under most conditions. The wrong arm, however, accelerates tire wear for vehicles doing extensive turning, such as those operating in a city or on secondary highways with high road crowns, requiring the driver to turn the wheels slightly to correct drifting to the curb.

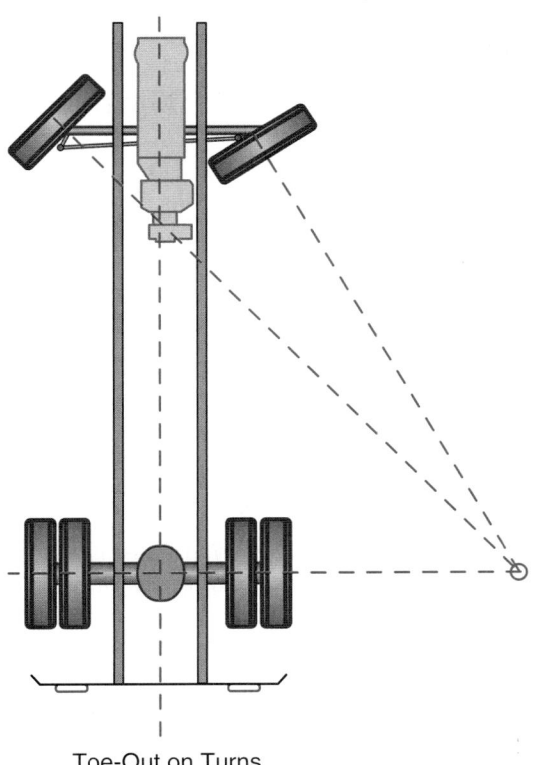

Toe-Out on Turns

FIGURE 29-33 For toe-out on turns to be correct, each wheel must be able to trace its own true arc when turning a corner.

Axle Setback

Axle setback, also referred to simply as **setback** or **skew** setback, is the difference in distance between any axle end and the perpendicular centerline. For example, on left-hand drive roads, some trailer axles may have 0.125" (3.175 mm) set back toward on the right or curb side. When the distance from the end of the right axle is measured from the trailer king pin, the right-side axle is pulled slightly forward than the left if the measured distances are all made equal. This kind of setback pulls the right side of the axle slightly forward to compensate for high road crown, as illustrated in **FIGURE 29-35**. Axle setback can also be due to mismatched rims.

Trailer Axles and Axle Tracking

Trailer axles, like most steering axles, are categorized as dead axles. This means they do not transfer torque to wheel ends. Axle tracking, which refers to the ability of all vehicle and trailer tires to follow the same path, depends on axle parallelism and

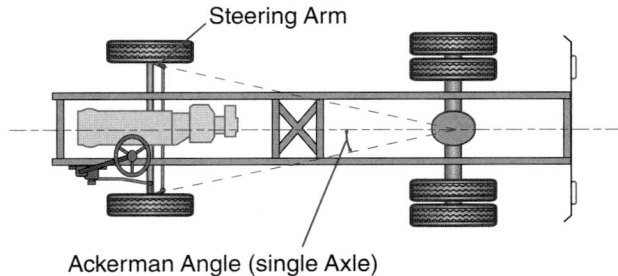

Ackerman Angle (single Axle)

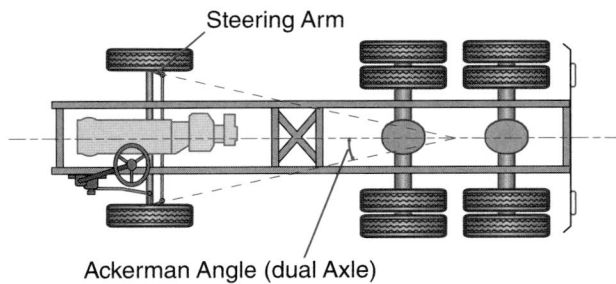

Ackerman Angle (dual Axle)

FIGURE 29-34 Ackermann angle.

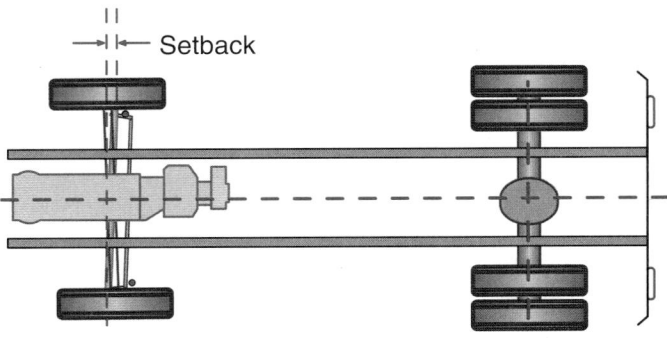

Setback

FIGURE 29-35 Axle setback to the right helps vehicles compensate for road crown.

sharing a common centerline. Proper vehicle tracking requires all axles to be parallel with one another and to have similar amounts of offset from either the vehicle centerline or a centerline running between all axles. Tandem axles need to be parallel to within ±0.125" (3.175 mm) difference measured through the axle center line from both the left and right side of the vehicle when measured at the axle end.

Axles should be perpendicular to chassis centerline within 0.125" (3.175 mm) when measured between axle center and chassis centerline. Alternatively, there should be no more than 0.25" (6.35 mm) difference between the axle end when measured from left side of frame to right-axle end and vice versa. The nominal toe setting is 0" ± 1/32" (0 ± 0.794 mm). This variation is smaller than a steer axle since there is no steering linkage.

▶ **TECHNICIAN TIP**

In extreme conditions of axle offset creating a thrust angle, the tracks the rear tires make are both offset to one side of the tracks made by the front tire. This condition is known as crabbing and can cause diagonal tire pattern wear on the rear tires, as well as vehicle instability, in some driving conditions. A vehicle that is crabbing appears to be driving slightly sideways down the road.

Types of Wheel Alignment

LO 29-7 Identify, describe, and outline procedures used to measure and adjust wheel alignment.

Performing a wheel alignment requires the use of a precision alignment machine. In the past, simpler devices (such as using a measuring tape or a piece of string to set wheel toe) were used to align the vehicle's wheels. Today's vehicles and tires are sensitive to the position of the wheels, so simply using a tape measure to set toe and adjust steering linkage is unacceptable.

Vehicle alignment equipment ranges in type from simple and inexpensive trammel bars and tire line scribing tools to sophisticated and expensive electronic systems using a variety of optical sensors, like that shown in **FIGURE 29-36**. Electronic alignment can identify either the vehicle centerline or vehicle frame as an alignment reference point.

Alignment is a regular part of the maintenance regimen for all heavy-duty vehicles. In addition, anytime a part that has an adjustment for alignment angles is removed or replaced for any reason, an alignment should be performed. For example, if the front axle has elongated adjustment slots for the spring saddles, and is being replaced, an alignment needs to be performed once the new axle is installed to ensure the correct wheel alignment angles are restored. If you are unsure if replacing a particular part requires an alignment once the new part is installed, refer to the manufacturer's service information.

The three basic types of wheel alignment are: (1) geometric centerline (thrust angle) alignment; (2) frame centerline alignment; and (3) loaded versus unloaded alignment.

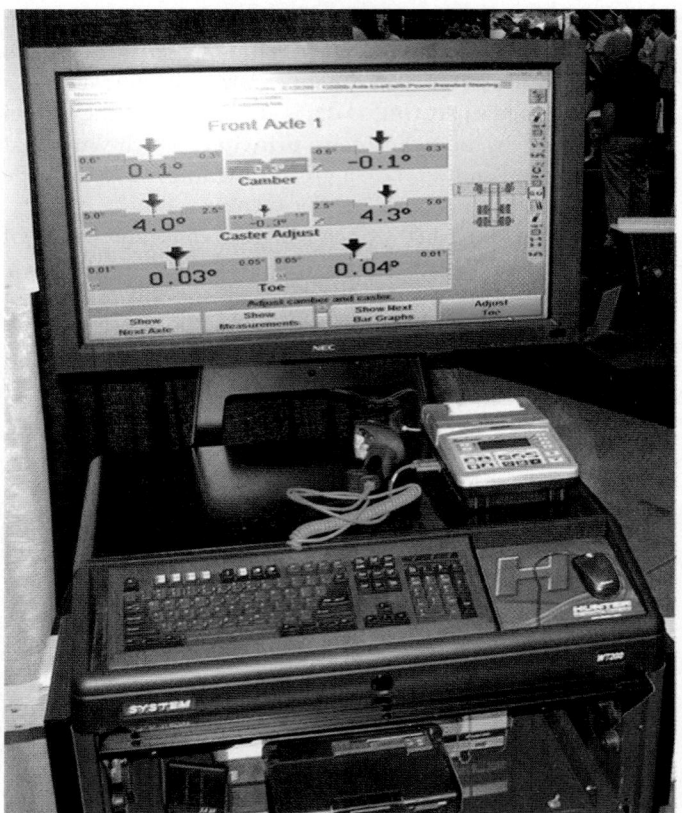

FIGURE 29-36 This Hunter alignment system uses optical sensors to measure vehicle alignment factors. Laser light beams project light onto camera-like photo sensors to measure alignment angles.

Geometric Centerline Alignment— Thrust Angle

Geometric centerline alignment is a method where a vehicle's centerline is established by placing a line from the midpoint of the front axle and the midpoint of the rear-most axle. The geometric centerline is commonly used as a reference for total wheel alignment. This method does not use frame rails or frame cross member as reference points. Instead, the alignment system establishes the geometric centerline reference point for adjustments. Ignoring the frame as a reference point eliminates error due to a bent or damaged frame.

Geometric centerline total alignment allows wheels and axles to be adjusted relative to one another to obtain the correct **thrust angle**—the angle formed between the geometric centerline and the thrust line of an axle, is illustrated in **FIGURE 29-37**. The term **thrust line** refers to the direction in which the rear wheels are pointing. It represents the direction the axle "points" compared to the centerline of the vehicle. Vehicles with solid, adjustable rear axles can use this method.

Frame Centerline Alignment

Unlike geometric centerline alignment, the **frame centerline alignment** method uses the vehicle frame and not its axles as the reference point for making alignment adjustments. In the

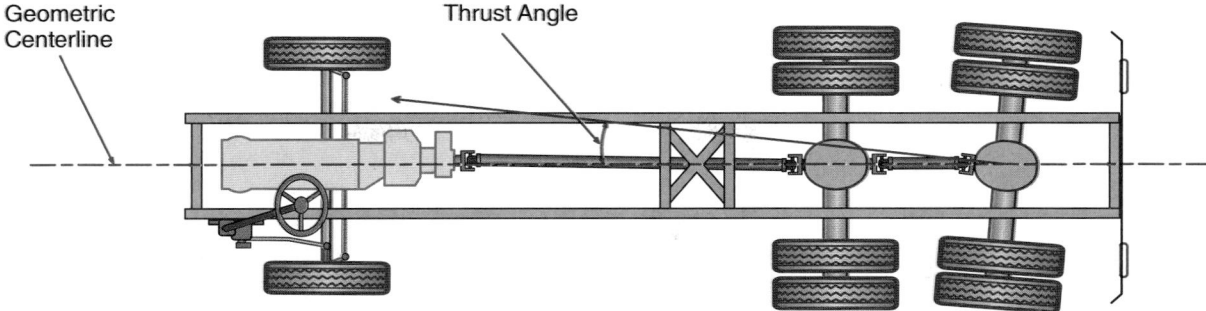

FIGURE 29-37 The thrust angle is formed between the geometric centerline and the thrust line and indicates the direction the axle will travel.

FIGURE 29-38 This alignment system uses laser light beams that hit target sensors in each optical head to determine geometric centerline, for measuring caster, camber, and toe.

field, frame centerline alignments (or checking for frame centerline alignment) can be made without using sophisticated alignment equipment. Technicians do, however, need to make very careful measurements and observations to complete the necessary calculations and interpret their results before making changes to axle alignment.

An economical electronic version uses two self-centering frame gauges hung at a right angle to the frame, one in the front and one in the rear. The gauges contains reflective targets used to identify the frame centerline. Cameras or lasers measure the angle the axles are positioned relative to the centerline of the frame. This system does not compensate for wheel run-out, which must be manually performed on each wheel using a bubble level, but the method allows for faster checks of alignment (**FIGURE 29-38**).

Loaded Versus Unloaded Alignment

Alignment specifications may or may not be set for unloaded vehicles. As a vehicle's load changes, however, its wheel alignment changes. That is particularly true for the front axles and other vehicle alignment factors. As the load increases, the axles begins to bend slightly. The bending causes the camber, king pin inclination, and caster to change. Because axles and spring weight ratings vary by vehicle application, different alignment settings may be required to obtain the best loaded alignments.

Performing Vehicle Alignments: In-Service Wheel Alignment

LO 29-8 Identify, describe, and outline procedures involved in inspecting and adjusting vehicle alignment.

Wheel alignment for modern on-highway commercial vehicles involves more than just aligning the wheels on the steer axle. Total alignment of all vehicle wheels is necessary since, without it, tire scrub increases rolling resistance, which in turn increases fuel consumption. Vehicles that do not correctly track can also increase the amount of cross-sectional area exposed to wind, which increases fuel consumption and affects vehicle handling. Premature or abnormal tire wear indicates the need for alignment, but alignment should be checked whenever new steer tires are installed. Steer axles, drive axles, trailer axles, and dolly axle alignment is required to complete a vehicle total alignment. In the total alignment procedure, every axle and wheel angle on the vehicle is measured and the axles are adjusted to be parallel so that all the wheels roll in the same direction and rolling resistance is minimized.

Tire life and fuel economy are improved by maintaining correct specifications for the following vehicle alignment parameters:

- Toe
- Rear tandem parallelism

- Camber
- Rear tandem **axle perpendicularity** (axles square with the frame)

TABLE 29-3 shows The Maintenance Council's (TMC) recommended practices for drive–axle alignment.

Over its working life, every heavy vehicle needs to be inspected for alignment to ensure optimal performance, safety, and fuel efficiency. Outside of routine maintenance and inspections, drivers and technicians may notice one or more handling issues related to alignment, as outlined in **TABLE 29-4**.

TABLE 29-3 Recommended Practices for Drive–Axle Alignment

Type of Axle	Recommendation for Drive–Axle Alignment
Steer Axles	Toe-in with a range 0–0.125" (0–3.175 mm)
Drive Axles	Tandem axles to be parallel within 0.125" (3.175 mm) measured at axle end. Axles should be perpendicular to chassis centerline within 0.125" (3.175 mm) when measured from axle end to chassis centerline, or within 0.25" (6.35 mm) when measured from left frame rail to the right axle end.
Trailer Axles	Tandem axles to be parallel within 0.125" (3.175 mm) difference between the axle's centers measured on the left and the right side of the vehicle and measured at the axle end. Axles should be perpendicular to chassis centerline within 0.125" (3.175 mm) when measured between axle end and chassis centerline. Alternatively, there should be no more than 0.25" (6.35 mm) difference between the axle end when measured from left side of frame to right axle end and vice versa. Nominal toe setting: 0" ± 1/32" (0 ± 0.794 mm). This figure is lower than a steer axle since there is no steering linkage.

Source: *The Maintenance Council*

TABLE 29-4 Handling Issues and Possible Causes

Complaint	Possible Cause	Complaint	Possible Cause
Wander or shimmy,	• Worn tie-rod ends • Worn drag link ends • Worn king pins or king pin bushings • Loose or shifted suspension • Weak shock absorbers • Weak or broken front springs • Incorrect front-end alignment—Caster is incorrect • Loose steering gear • Incorrectly installed or adjusted steering gear • Incorrectly installed pitman or drop arm • Loose or worn steering column slip yoke and joints • Loose wheel bearings • Improperly lubricated fifth wheel • Low or unequal tire pressure • Unequal sized tires • Linkage binding • Steering gear binding • Front axle shifted on the springs • Looseness in steering linkage • King pins binding in steering knuckles • Rear axle shifted on the springs • Rear axle housing bent • Vehicle frame diamond-shaped • Loose U-bolts • Loose spring shackle pins and bushings • Uneven vehicle loading • Uneven tire wear	Thumps and knocks from front suspension	• Loose or worn king pins and bushings • Broken steering knuckle thrust bearing • Missing or worn steering knuckle shims • Loose front suspension attaching bolts • Loose shock absorber mountings • Worn spring bushings • Worn or seized steering column slip yoke
		Irregular or excessive tire wear	• Incorrect front wheel or total vehicle alignment • Worn king pins or king pin bushings • Loose front suspension attaching bolts • Weak shock absorbers • Weak front springs • Bent drop arm or pitman arm • Loose or worn steering slip shaft and joints • Worn tie-rod ends • Improper position of fifth wheel • Incorrect camber or toe adjustment • Under or over inflation • Incorrectly distributed vehicle load
		Vehicle pulls to one side	• Unequal tire size • Unequal tire inflation • Unequally loaded vehicle • Incorrect or unequal caster, camber, or toe-in • Defective wheel bearing • Weak or broken spring • Brakes dragging on one side • Bent steering arm or steering knuckle • Misaligned vehicle frame • Worn suspension spring bushings • Worn suspension arm bushings • Misaligned suspension torque arms • Shifted rear axle

Faced with one or more handling issues, a technician might be tempted to jump straight to performing a vehicle alignment. Before doing so, however, the technician should perform a series of inspections, measurements, and checks to determine the scope and type of alignment work that needs to be done. To perform a prealignment inspection, follow the steps in **SKILL DRILL 29-1**.

Measuring Toe-In and Toe-Out

As discussed earlier in the chapter, steering geometry must be within the manufacturer's specifications for the vehicle to operate correctly. For that reason, it is important that a vehicle's toe-in and toe-out are regularly measured. Follow the steps in **SKILL DRILL 29-2** to measure toe-in and toe-out using a toe tester or trammel bar.

SKILL DRILL 29-1 Performing a Prealignment Inspection

1. Locate and follow the procedure in the service manual.
2. Remove any heavy items from the vehicle. Do not remove any item or equipment that is supplied with the vehicle and normally kept in the vehicle.
3. Check all tires for proper tire size and adjust tire pressure to specifications.
4. Check the vehicle's ride height. It is impossible to carry out a successful wheel alignment when the vehicle's ride height is incorrect.
5. Check the free-play of the steering wheel. Excess free-play must be corrected before undertaking the wheel alignment.
6. Inspect all suspension and steering components according to service information, including the wheel bearings. Repair or replace all damaged or worn suspension components prior to aligning the vehicle.
7. Position the vehicle, making sure the front tires are centered and positioned correctly on the turntables.
8. Attach the wheel end sensors of the alignment equipment to the wheels.
9. Perform manufacturers set-up procedures, such as leveling the sensors, correcting for wheel run-out, or wheel roll compensation.
10. Compare manufacturer specifications with actual measurements.

SKILL DRILL 29-2 Measuring Toe-Out Using a Trammel Bar

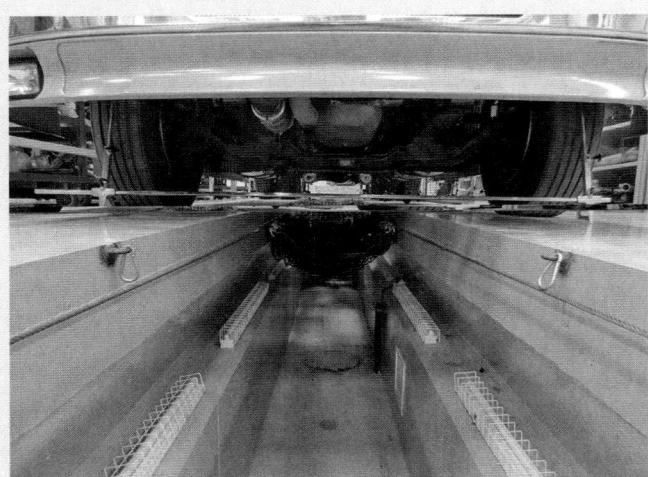

1. Locate and follow the procedure in the service manual.
2. Perform system pre-checks, as per SKILL DRILL 29-1.
3. Park the vehicle on a level surface in a straight-ahead position over a pit, if possible.
4. Mark the tire at the approximate center of the tread flange at a position that is in line with the center of the wheel.
5. Repeat step 3 on the other front tire.
6. Set up the trammel bar per the manufacturer's specifications placing the measuring pins on the marks that you have made on the front tires.
7. Tighten the slider on the trammel bar.
8. Remove the trammel bar and move the vehicle forward so the wheels rotate through 180 degrees, and place the trammel bar behind the tires over the marks made on the tires.
9. Measure the difference between the front and rear points on the tires in this position. An increase in the rear measured dimension is the toe-in amount. Take the measurement and compare it with the manufacturer's specifications.
10. Adjust the toe-in dimension to manufacturers specification, loosening and adjusting the tie rod by turning it.
11. Repeat the measuring process to ensure that the corrective action is within specifications.
12. List the test results and/or recommendations on the job sheet or work order.
13. Clean the work area.

Checking KPI and Included Angle

As mentioned previously, the KPI is the angle formed by an imaginary line running through the upper and lower steering pivots relative to a true vertical center line through the tire. KPI cannot be adjusted, though a technician will, on occasion, be asked to check the KPI to ensure it is within the manufacturer's specifications after an accident or axle repair. Generally, KPI should not vary more than half a degree, plus or minus. If KPI is incorrect, check for a bent spindle or steering knuckle. If incorrect, KPI produces a complaint that the steering wheel is not returning to center after cornering. To check KPI and included angle, follow the steps in **SKILL DRILL 29-3**.

Axle Tracking and Parallelism

Tracking refers to the tire path followed by all the tires on a vehicle. Ideally, all tires should move in the same path. Tires that do not take the same path often have different or incorrect axle offsets, or the vehicle axles are not parallel.

In the straight-ahead position, the rear wheels of a vehicle should follow the front wheels in a parallel manner. This is referred to as **axle parallelism**. If either the rear or front axle of a vehicle is not at right angles to the chassis centerline, the front tires are affected and have misalignment wear since the steering tires are correcting for an improper thrust angle. Failure of the wheels to correctly track is usually due to the following causes:

- Broken or shifted main leaf spring
- Loose or broken spring center or U-bolts
- Incorrectly installed springs—back to front reversed
- Bent or twisted frame
- Locating rods, track bars, or torque rods are improperly adjusted, or have worn bushings
- Worn suspension bushings for springs and torque rods

To inspect axles for correct tracking and parallelism, follow the steps in **SKILL DRILL 29-4**.

SKILL DRILL 29-3 Checking KPI and Included Angle

1. Locate and follow the procedure in the service manual.
2. Position the vehicle on the alignment equipment turning plates.

3. Attach the wheel sensors on the vehicle to the locations specified by the alignment equipment manufacturer and compensate for tire and wheel rim run-out.
4. Follow the alignment machine instructions for measuring the KPI and compare them with the vehicle manufacturer's specifications. Typically, the KPI reading requires turning the wheels to a specified angle from straight-ahead center while on the turning plates.
5. KPI is a non-adjustable angle; no changes can be made. The angle helps the technician to verify that steering components are not bent.
6. Calculate the included angle, if the alignment machine does not, by adding or subtracting the positive or negative camber reading of each wheel to the KPI of each wheel and compare with specifications.
7. List the test results and/or recommendations on the job sheet or work order.

SKILL DRILL 29-4 Inspecting Tandem Axles for Parallelism and Tracking

1. Park the vehicle on a flat surface. Clamp a long straight edge across the frame in front of the front axle of the tandem at exactly 90 degrees to the vehicle center line.
2. Drop a plumb bob line from the straight edge in line with the front axle hub. Using a trammel bar measure the distance from the line to the hub, and tighten the trammel.
3. Repeat the procedure on the other side of the vehicle. Compare the measurements; they should be equal to within 0.125" (3.175 mm). Adjust as necessary.
4. Using the trammel, check the distance between the two hubs of the tandem on the left side. Compare with the right side. Measurements should be within 0.125" (3.175 mm). Adjust as necessary.
5. Variation of more than 0.125" (3.175 mm) must be corrected. Note that, typically, only one side of the axles is adjustable.

Front Axle Inspection

King pins, tie-rod ends, and drag links are checked for looseness or wear prior to alignment or if non-repeatable alignment measurements are observed. When properly greased, no movement between the king pin and steering knuckle or between the tie-rod joint and steering knuckle should be observable (**FIGURE 29-39**). To perform an inspection of the king pins, follow the steps in **SKILL DRILL 29-5**. To lubricate the king pins, follow the steps in **SKILL DRILL 29-6**.

FIGURE 29-39 Rather than use sledge hammers, this hydraulic press can be used to remove seized king pins from the steering knuckle and axle spindle.

▶ TECHNICIAN TIP

When greasing king pins, apply grease to the fittings on both the lower and upper part of the steering knuckle. A small amount of grease should flow between the knuckle and axle to purge water and dirt from the joint. The wheel end must be raised from the ground to allow grease to evenly flow around the bushing and out between the knuckle and axle joint. If this procedure is not followed, the steering knuckle sealing cap gasket will blow due to high pressure beneath the cap, which prevents any further lubrication of the steering knuckle. If blown, the sealing cap and sealing O-ring or gasket needs replacement before additional attempts to lubricate the joint are made.

SKILL DRILL 29-5 Inspecting the King Pins for Wear

1. After supporting the front axle weight on safety stands, measure the axial (up and down) and radial (side-to-side) movement of the steering knuckle to evaluate king pin wear. Any visible axial (vertical) movement generally indicates wear in the lower thrust bearing between the steering knuckle and axle. Vertical movement measured between the knuckle and axle of more than 0.040" requires

re-shimming, bearing replacement, and possibly bushing and pin replacement. A small amount of radial movement is permissible. More than 0.015" radial (side-to-side) movement between the knuckle and axle requires king pin bushing and pin replacement. New bushings have approximately 0.002"–0.005" radial clearance.

2. Have a helper apply the service brakes to differentiate wheel bearing movement from king pin bushing wear.

3. Use a dial indicator to make precise measurements. Place the dial indicator at the top and bottom of the wheel or tire to make two separate measurements.

4. Grasp the top of the tire and move the tire in and out to measure lateral movement of the king pin. Perform the same check on the bottom of the tire to measure lateral movement of the lower end of the king pin.

5. Measure vertical movement of the steering knuckle to check for a damaged or worn spindle bearing or worn axle-steering knuckle. Pry the tire up and down with a pry bar. No movement of the knuckle assembly should be felt and no "clunking" sound should be heard. Place a dial indicator against the lower or upper end of the steering knuckle to measure vertical movement.

6. Check OEM specifications for maximum limits of movement in the steering knuckle assembly. Note that loose wheel bearings can give a false indication of worn bushings. Therefore, it is necessary to have someone apply the brakes while checking king pin movement. When the brakes are applied, only movement in the steering knuckle is detected.

Inspecting and Servicing Tie-Rods and Tie-Rod Ends

Tie-rod ends and tubes should be checked for bending, cracks, looseness, and weakness at every lubrication service. To inspect and service tie-rods and tie-rod ends, follow the steps in **SKILL DRILL 29-7**.

To perform a geometric centerline alignment, follow the steps in **SKILL DRILL 29-8**.

SKILL DRILL 29-6 Lubricating King Pins

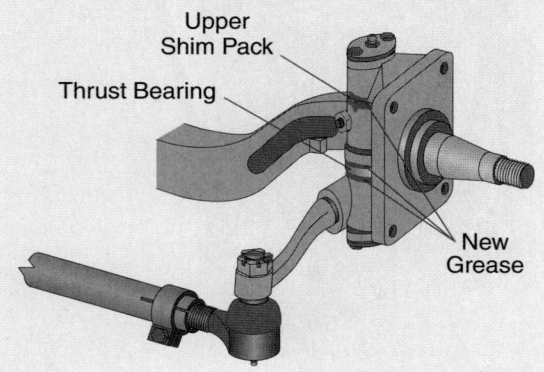

Upper Shim Pack
Thrust Bearing
New Grease

1. Relieve weight on the front axle by lifting the wheels from the ground and supporting the axle with safety stands.
2. Perform an inspection of the king pin and steering knuckle assembly by measuring vertical and radial movement.
3. Using a grease gun, begin lubricating the king pins by purging water and grease from the pin with a couple of pumps of grease.
4. Stop greasing when only clean grease begins to flow from the joint connection between the lower and upper end of the steering knuckle. Do not over lubricate the assembly. Excess grease attracts abrasive dirt, which can wear out the joint.

SKILL DRILL 29-7 Inspecting and Servicing Tie-Rods and Tie-Rod Ends

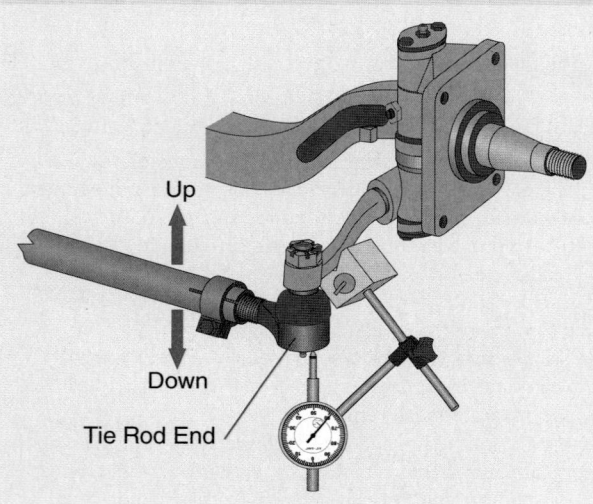

Up
Down
Tie Rod End

1. If removed or disabled, ball studs should have a minimum of 5 in-lb (0.565 Nm) of resistance when turning. Shaking the steering wheel slightly back and forth while the wheels are on the ground while measuring lateral movement when the steering wheel is rocked back and forth should not indicate any visible free play.
2. If play is detected, use a dial indicator to measure any vertical or lateral movement. Lateral movement exceeding 0.030" (0.762 mm) is unacceptable.
3. Tie-rod ends, like other articulating steering system joints, are ball-and-socket type. A castellated nut enables the use of a cotter pin to lock the nut for added safety. Secure the thread engagement in the tube with a clamp.
4. Check that the tie-rod end is threaded adequately and equally on both sides into tie-rod so that no gap can be observed between the end of the tie-rod and the open slot of the tube.
5. Replace any joint with a cracked rubber boot. When lubricating the joint, grease should purge the boot of dirt through a bleed hole.

SKILL DRILL 29-8 Performing a Geometric Centerline Alignment

1. Mount and locate the sensors on the front steer and rear axle to measure the thrust angle, if present.
2. Adjust the rear axle as it is the first to point the thrust line down the vehicle centerline. The rear axle now becomes a reference point for aligning the other axles.
3. Align the front steer axle using the rear axle as a reference.
4. To adjust parallelism, loosen front axle U-bolts and shift the axle over the slightly oversized alignment holes in the spring seats.
5. Align the second drive axle after the steer axle is adjusted.
6. Adjust additional axles using the rear axle as a reference point.

Wrap-Up

Ready for Review

▶ Axles transfer the vehicle weight from the wheel ends to the suspension system and assist maintaining the correct position of the wheels to one another.

▶ There are two main categories of axles—live (drive) and dead (non-drive). Live axles are powered and can move the vehicle; non-drive axles provide a connection point for wheel ends and align the vehicle wheels properly.

▶ Heavy-duty vehicles commonly use I-beam front axles. Each end of the I-beam is outfitted with a steering knuckle that enables articulation of the wheel end.

▶ Steering knuckles on medium- and heavy-duty vehicles use king pins since they can support heavy loads.

▶ Lift, tag, and pusher axles are used to supplement the load-carrying capacity of a vehicle when required. They are rear non-drive axles.

▶ Tag and pusher axles commonly use a pair of airbags to lower the axle and control axle loading.

▶ Wheels need to be aligned to give heavy-duty commercial vehicles predictable, straight-line directional stability and the ability to correctly turn while minimizing tire wear and improving vehicle handling characteristics.

▶ Tire alignment angles can change as a result of vehicle loads. Primary alignment angles are camber, caster, and toe.

▶ All heavy-duty commercial vehicles use positive camber because a loaded vehicle bends the axle slightly. When normally loaded, bending the axle reduces the camber angle, often to a negative camber angle.

▶ Today's vehicles all use positive caster for straight-line directional control stability and steering-return ability. Positive caster produces a weight shift on the left- and right-side steer tires when moved from a straight-line direction.

▶ Excess positive caster causes caster shimmy that can be dangerous to vehicle control and directional stability.

▶ Clearances combined with a positive tire scrub radius in steering linkage and wheel bearings allow the tires to turn outward from a straight-line position when moving.

▶ When traveling forward, toe should be zero degrees to prevent tire wear. Excessive toe-out wears the inside edge of both tires. Too much toe-in wears the outside edge of tires.

▶ Caster angle has the most influence on directional stability because it works with KPI to lift or lower the steering knuckle during turns, enhancing self-centering action of the steering system.

▶ Almost all heavy-duty commercial vehicles use a positive scrub, which causes the tire to turn outward when rolling forward from the vehicle centerline.

▶ The relationships between the steering system, the wheel positions, and the suspension system form what is called the steering geometry. Whereas steering geometry deals with the dynamics of linkage, vehicle alignment factors have more in common with the position of axle components.

▶ The turning radius of a vehicle depends on the pivot point of the vehicle, the angle the wheels turn, plus the distance between the steering and drive axles. According to the Ackermann principle, the inner wheel should have a greater, sharper turning angle than the outside wheel since it has a smaller turning radius.

▶ Alignment is a regular part of the maintenance regimen for all heavy-duty vehicles. Performing a total wheel and vehicle alignment requires the use of an alignment machine.

▶ The three basic types of wheel alignment are: (1) geometric centerline (thrust angle) alignment; (2) frame centerline alignment under either loaded or unloaded conditions.

Key Terms

Ackermann angle The angle the steering arms make with the vehicle center line. The angle should project towards the center of the rear axle. Also called *toe-out on turns*.

Ackermann principle The geometric alignment of a vehicle's steering arms that enables the wheels to toe out on turns with the inside wheels of a turn rotating in a smaller turning radius than the wheels on the outside.

axle The shaft of the suspension system to which the hubs and wheels are attached; used to transmit driving torque to the wheels.

axle parallelism When the rear wheels of a vehicle follow the front wheels in a parallel manner.

axle perpendicularity When the axles are square with the vehicle frame.

axle setback The difference in distance between any axle end and the perpendicular centerline. Also called *setback* or *skew*.

camber The side-to-side vertical tilt of the wheel. It is viewed from the front of the vehicle and measured in degrees. See also *negative camber* and *positive camber*.

caster The angle formed through the wheel pivot points when viewed from the side in comparison to a vertical line through the wheel.

caster shimmy The rapid, side-to-side movement of the steering wheel resulting from excess positive caster.

drag link A connecting linkage that transfers movement of the pitman arm to the upper steering arm.

drop arm An arm that transfers the steering box output shaft motion to the steering linkage by converting rotational movement into liner motion. Also called the *pitman arm*.

frame angle The horizontal angle the vehicle's frame has compared with a level horizontal measurement. See also *positive frame angle* and *negative frame angle*.

frame centerline alignment An alignment method that uses the vehicle frame and not its axles as the reference point for making alignment adjustments.

geometric centerline alignment An alignment method that establishes a vehicle's centerline by placing a line from the midpoint of the front axle and the midpoint of the rear-most axle.

included angle The angle of camber added or subtracted to the king pin inclination angle.

King pin The main pivot in the steering mechanism of a vehicle.

King pin inclination angle (KPI) The angle formed between true vertical and the angle of the king pin. Also called *steering axis inclination angle*.

lift axle A non-drive (dead) axle that can be mechanically raised and lowered to meet requirements regulated for maximum axle weight loads.

negative camber When the top of the tire is closer to the center of the vehicle than the bottom of the tire.

negative frame angle The condition where the frame's rear is lower than the front.

negative scrub radius A condition in which the projected KPI intersects with the road surface outboard from the tire's vertical centerline.

non-drive (dead) axle An axle that does not supply power to the wheels.

pitman arm A pitman arm connects the steering sector shaft to the steering linkage. It converts the sector shaft movement to a sweeping arc to produce linear steering linkage movement. Also called a *drop arm*.

positive camber When the tires are closer together at the bottom and farther apart at the top when viewed from the front of a vehicle.

positive frame angle The condition where the frame's rear is higher than the front.

positive scrub radius A condition in which the projected KPI point of contact intersects with the road surface inboard of the tire's vertical centerline.

pusher axle A non-drive rear mounted axle, ahead of the drive axle.

scrub angle The distance between two imaginary points on the road surface—the point of centerline contact between the road surface and the tire, and the point where the king pin inclination angle projects its contact with the road surface. The difference between the two points is either positive or negative, depending on whether the KPI line is inside or outside of the tire centerline. See also *positive scrub radius* and *negative scrub radius*.

setback The distance one wheel end is set back from the axles perpendicular angle with the frame.

skew The difference in distance between any axle end and the perpendicular centerline. Also called *axle setback* or *setback*.

solid I-beam A type of solid steering axle named for its forged I-beam design.

steering axis inclination angle (SAI) The angle formed by an imaginary line running through the upper and lower steering pivots relative to vertical as viewed from the front. The angle is measured between true vertical and the angle of the king pin. Also called *king pin inclination angle (KPI)*.

steering axle An axle that has articulating steering knuckles that allows the vehicle to turn.

steering geometry A geometric arrangement of linkage in the steering of a vehicle designed to solve the problem of keeping the wheels properly oriented through various positions of the steering and suspension system travel.

steering stops Adjustable bolts used to limit the turning angle of the steering knuckle.

tag axle A rear non-drive axle mounted behind the drive axle.

thrust angle The relationship between the centerline of the vehicle and the angle of the rear axle.

thrust line The direction in which the rear axle wheels are pointing.

tie-rod end Articulating ball-and-socket joints attached to each end of the tie-rod.

toe A measurement of how much the front wheels are turned in or out from a straight-ahead position. The angle is referenced from a position directly above the tires and facing forward.

toe-in A condition that exists when, as seen from above, the wheels are closer together at the front and farther apart at the rear.

toe-out A condition that exists when, as seen from above, the wheels are closer together in the rear and farther apart at the front.

toe-out on turns A geometric steering concept that the inner wheel should have a greater turning angle than the outside wheel. Also called *Ackermann angle*.

tracking The directional pathway taken by the axles and wheel.

trailer axle A non-drive axle used by trailers that generally has no steering linkage unless it is a self-steering axle.

turning radius The diameter of a circle the vehicle can turn in when the steering wheel is turned to the limit.

wheel alignment The positioning of the tires relative to the vehicle. Also called *tracking*.

Review Questions

1. What is the most common configuration of the front steering axle used on medium- and heavy-duty vehicles?
   a. Solid I-beam
   b. Solid H-beam
   c. Solid rectangular beam
   d. A hollow round tube.

2. Which of the following types of king pin bushings are currently the most commonly used by axle manufacturers?
  a. Nylon
  b. Composite
  c. Bronze
  d. Brass

3. The pitman arm is typically splined to the steering gear output shaft at one end and connected through a ball stud to the:
  a. center link.
  b. steering link.
  c. drag link.
  d. tie rod.

4. Which of the following statements best describes a lifting tag axle?
  a. A dead axle located behind the rear drive axles that is always in contact with the road
  b. A dead axle located in front of the rear drive axles that is raised when turning corners
  c. A live axle located in front of the rear drive axles that is always in contact with the road
  d. A dead axle located behind the rear drive axles that is always raised when turning corners

5. Which of the following angles produces a steering wheel shimmy if it is not correctly adjusted?
  a. Caster
  b. Camber
  c. Thrust angle
  d. Toe angle

6. Which reason best explains why an alignment specification would place a slightly more positive camber angle on the left wheel?
  a. To increase the positive scrub radius
  b. To compensate for the effect of a high road crown
  c. To provide improved directional stability on flat road surfaces
  d. To minimize tire wear

7. Concerning caster, what is the maximum side to-side variation that is recommended for most vehicles?
  a. Plus or minus 0.1 degree
  b. Plus or minus 0.2 degree
  c. Plus or minus 0.3 degree
  d. Plus or minus 0.5 degree

8. Which of the following alignment angles, when misaligned, produces feathered tire wear on the outside edge of the front steering tires?
  a. Camber
  b. Caster
  c. Toe-in
  d. Toe-out

9. Which steering geometry angle causes the tires to toe-out on turns?
  a. Toe
  b. Ackerman
  c. SAI
  d. Included

10. Consider a vehicle with 1/8" (0.125") (3.175 mm) of toe-in. What happens to the distance of the two front tires between the front and rear of the tires when the vehicle travels over the road?
  a. The distance becomes nearly the same between the front and rear.
  b. The front of the tires remain closer than the back.
  c. The back of the tires remain closer than the front.
  d. The tires tilt outward at the top and do not change the distance between the front and rear.

ASE Technician A/Technician B Style Questions

1. Technician A says a key function of axles is to maintain the position of the wheels relative to each other and the vehicle body. Technician B says there are two main categories of axles, which are drive and non-drive. Who is correct?
  a. Technician A
  b. Technician B
  c. Both Technician A and Technician B
  d. Neither Technician A nor Technician B

2. Technician A says the steering knuckle enables the articulation of the wheel end. Technician B says the steering knuckle is connected to the I-beam through the master pin. Who is correct?
  a. Technician A
  b. Technician B
  c. Both Technician A and Technician B
  d. Neither Technician A nor Technician B

3. Technician A says a snug fit is required between the king pin and bushings. Technician B says if the pin cannot be installed into the bushings by hand, or the pin is too tight, the king pin should be machined slightly smaller. Who is correct?
  a. Technician A
  b. Technician B
  c. Both Technician A and Technician B
  d. Neither Technician A nor Technician B

4. Technician A says steering stops are used to limit the turning angle of the steering knuckle. Technician B says stops are adjusted to cut power assist with zero clearance remaining between the spindle stop and the axle. Who is correct?
  a. Technician A
  b. Technician B
  c. Both Technician A and Technician B
  d. Neither Technician A nor Technician B

5. Technician A says when installing an adjustable drag link, the front tires must be squared with the chassis frame. Technician B says the steering wheel spokes must be correctly oriented in a straight-ahead position, and the steering box must be centered. Who is correct?
  a. Technician A
  b. Technician B
  c. Both Technician A and Technician B
  d. Neither Technician A nor Technician B

6. Technician A says wheel alignment refers to the positioning of the tires relative to the vehicle. Technician B says rolling resistance and correct wheel alignment is not an issue with regard to fuel consumption. Who is correct?
   a. Technician A
   b. Technician B
   c. Both Technician A and Technician B
   d. Neither Technician A nor Technician B

7. Technician A says caster can be adjusted by heating and slightly bending the axle. Technician B says caster can be adjusted by using tapered shims placed between the suspension springs and the axle. Who is correct?
   a. Technician A
   b. Technician B
   c. Both Technician A and Technician B
   d. Neither Technician A nor Technician B

8. Technician A says when traveling forward, toe should be zero degrees to prevent tire wear. Technician B says too much toe-in wears the inside edges of tires. Who is correct?
   a. Technician A
   b. Technician B
   c. Both Technician A and Technician B
   d. Neither Technician A nor Technician B

9. Technician A says the Ackerman angle refers to a steering principle that states the inner wheel should have a greater turning angle than the outside wheel because it has a smaller turning radius. Technician B says the Ackermann angle producing toe-out on turns is an adjustable angle. Who is correct?
   a. Technician A
   b. Technician B
   c. Both Technician A and Technician B
   d. Neither Technician A nor Technician B

10. Technician A says the geometric centerline (thrust angle) alignment method has the advantage of eliminating alignment error due to a bent or damaged frame. Technician B says vehicles with solid, adjustable rear axles cannot use this method. Who is correct?
    a. Technician A
    b. Technician B
    c. Both Technician A and Technician B
    d. Neither Technician A nor Technician B

CHAPTER 30

Truck Frames

Learning Objectives

- **LO 30-1** Explain the fundamentals of truck frame design and strength.
- **LO 30-2** Describe truck frame construction.
- **LO 30-3** Explain attachment procedures for truck frames.
- **LO 30-4** Describe frame inspection and maintenance procedure, including out-of-service criteria.
- **LO 30-5** Explain frame alignment inspection and repair procedures.
- **LO 30-6** Describe procedures for welding on frames.

You Are the Technician

A vehicle is brought to your repair facility for inspection before it is bought by a customer as a used vehicle. As you inspect the vehicle, you notice that there has been some body repair in the front right corner of the vehicle. The body repair included a new bumper and looks like it was professionally done. You road test the vehicle and notice a slight pull to the right. As you inspect the front suspension components to find out why it is pulling, you notice that the front leaf spring shackles do not seem to be at the same angle from one side to the other.

1. What can you conclude from your observations?
2. What do you think has happened to this vehicle?
3. What next steps would you take to confirm your suspicions?
4. What is the likely repair that is required on this vehicle?
5. What abnormal wear problems could occur if the vehicle is not repaired?

Introduction

A vehicle frame is the backbone of the vehicle. It provides the structure to which all other vehicle components can be attached, as illustrated in **FIGURE 30-1**. The suspension, drivetrain, and vehicle body are all supported by the frame. Engineering a vehicle frame seems very simple if all that is required of the frame is to be strong enough to carry the loads. However, a vehicle frame must be capable of much more than just carrying the load of the components attached to it.

Every heavy-duty vehicle frame must be able to handle all the forces thrown at it as the vehicle is being driven. Road shocks and bumps can more than quadruple the forces acting on the frame, so the frame must be strong enough to withstand all those forces and more. While negotiating uneven road conditions, the frame must be flexible enough to allow some twisting as the suspension articulates over the bumps. After twisting, the frame must always return to its original shape without permanent deformation. Flexibility is critical—a frame that is too rigid risks failing due to fracture. The frame must also allow for this repeated flexing without succumbing to failure due to fatigue.

Fundamentals of Frame Design

LO 30-1 Explain the fundamentals of truck frame design and strength.

Several frame designs can be used in the heavy-truck market. Depending on the intended vehicle use, frames can be constructed from C-channel, box rails, or I-beams, all of which are illustrated in **FIGURE 30-2**. **C-channel** is a C-shaped steel frame rail. **Full-box rails** are box-shaped frame rails, and **I-beams** are I-shaped frame rails. The strongest type of rail is the I-beam, but it is usually found only in very heavy off-road equipment and in some heavy hauler flatbed trailers. Some specialized heavy-duty vehicles use tubular steel frame designs, which are even stronger than I-beams, but tubular rails are not normally found in on-highway trucks. The most common frame design for heavy-duty trucks is the **ladder-type frame** constructed of two parallel C-channel steel rails held together by a series of cross members. The frame construction resembles a ladder, with the cross members being the rungs, as shown in **FIGURE 30-3**.

All frames, regardless of their design, must be strong enough to withstand multiple forces millions of times over. In addition, the frame must be able to support not only the load that the vehicle is designed to carry, but also support all the vehicle components connected to the frame itself. The engine, transmission, axles, suspension, cab, and the body are all attached to and, therefore, supported by the frame. At the same time the frame is supporting all of these vehicle components, it is also subjected to tremendous stresses during a normal operating day.

Forces Acting on the Frame

Road forces from uneven terrain, combined with cornering, braking, and acceleration forces, all cause twisting and bending stresses that the frame must be able to withstand without permanent deformation. Vehicle design engineers carefully calculate all the forces—including tension and compression—that are imposed on any particular frame. The engineers' goal is to ensure that the frame is strong enough to handle the intended vehicle loading and vocation.

Tension and Compression

Forces are exerted on multiple areas of a truck frame, but the flanges of the frame rails are particularly susceptible to heavy forces. Flanges are the flat areas at the top and bottom of the frame rail and are subjected to the greatest levels of tension and compression, depending on how the frame is loaded. **Tension** is a force trying to stretch, or pull, the rail apart, and **compression** is a force trying to crush, or squeeze, the rail together. As illustrated in **FIGURE 30-4**, the forces acting on a frame alternate from compression to tension, depending on where the load is placed and where the suspension supports the frame. In most vehicles, the majority of the lower-frame flange experiences tension, while most of the upper flange experiences compression forces.

During vehicle operation, the top and bottom flanges of the frame are under either tension or compression stress, depending on exactly where the load is placed and where the frame is supported by the suspension. The load pushing down on the frame creates compression on the top flange of the frame rail and tension on the bottom flange. The frame supports (the suspension system) push up against the frame in the opposite direction, causing compression on the bottom flange of the rail and tension forces on the top flange.

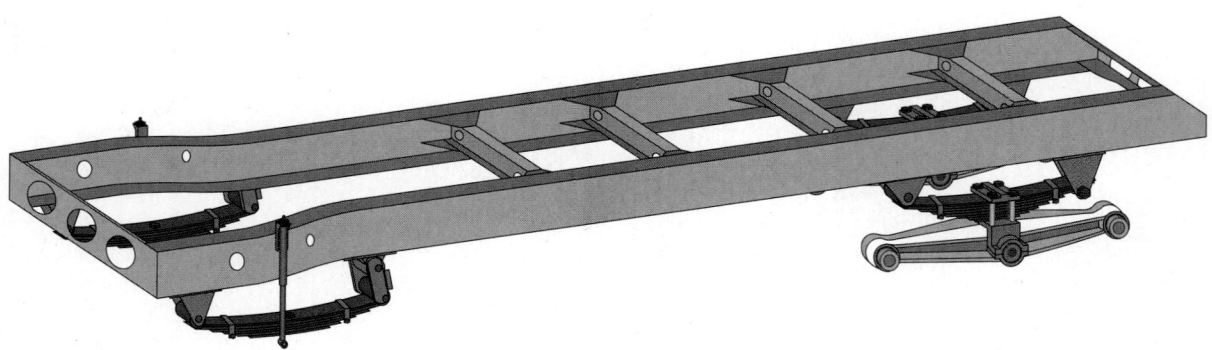

FIGURE 30-1 The frame is the backbone of the vehicle.

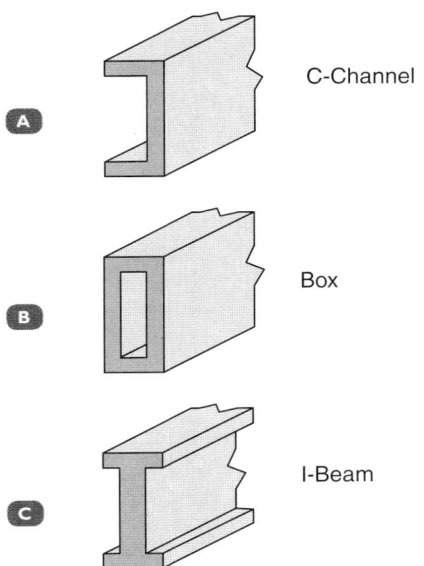

FIGURE 30-2 Frame rail design can be: **A.** C-Channel. **B.** Box.
C. I-beam. The C-channel rail design is the most popular of these.

FIGURE 30-3 Ladder-type frame/chassis.

Notice in Figure 30-4 that the forces at the top flange and the bottom flange are opposite each other. As a result, the forces cancel each other at the center of the **frame rail web**, which is the upright section of the frame rail. Specifically, the forces cancel out in the middle of the frame rail web in an area called the **neutral axis** or **neutral fiber**. No matter how much force is placed on the frame rails, the forces are the lowest at the neutral axis. For this reason, all of the mounting holes for **cross members** (cross members are metal braces that join the two frame rails together) and the other vehicle components are located as close as possible to the center of the web of the rail, where the forces acting on the rail are lowest.

A **stress riser**, also called a **stress concentration**, is anything that reduces or changes the integrity or strength of the material. Stress risers can lead to a crack in the rail, which is a serious safety risk. For this reason, any time a frame must be raised by a jack or a hoist, the frame should be protected from damage by using wooden blocks, nylon straps, or similar cushioning devices. Extreme care should be used *anytime* work is performed around the frame that could result in a scratch or gouge, which could cause a stress riser.

Similarly, no extra holes should be drilled in a vehicle frame unless necessary. If holes are needed in the frame, they should be drilled as close as possible to the neutral axis of the web, and as far away from the highest stress areas of the frame as possible. Holes should *never* be drilled in the rail flanges.

> ▶ **TECHNICIAN TIP**
>
> Given the role of the frame and the extreme forces it must withstand, there are no holes in the flanges. Furthermore, no drilling or cutting should ever be performed on the flanges because doing so drastically reduces the ability of the rail to resist these forces. Even a gouge or serious scratch in the flange, for example, caused by careless jacking or handling of heavy components around the frame rails, can significantly weaken the rail and result in a stress riser.

Other Frame Stresses

As mentioned previously, the stresses that act upon a frame are varied. Components that are mounted to the outside of the frame rails exert forces that try to twist the frame rail outwards.

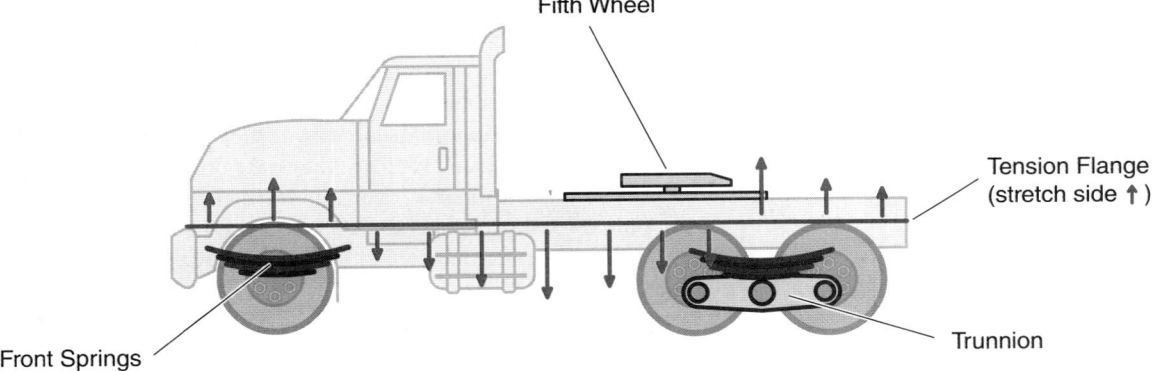

FIGURE 30-4 Tension and compression forces along the frame.

Components installed between the frame rail try to twist the frame inwards. Loads placed on the frame exert a downward force that wants to cause the frame to sag. That downward force is opposed by an upward force exerted by the suspension, which in turn tries to bow the frame upward. As the vehicle is driven, these forces are amplified many times by the bumps in the road. That means a vehicle frame must have significant extra capacity to withstand the inevitable flexing and twisting forces without sustaining permanent damage. These forces are directly affected by anything that is attached to the frame rail.

Calculating Frame Strength

Three basic variables used in frame design determine the strength of a given frame—resist bending moment (RBM), section modulus, and yield strength. Although frame design is not a necessary skill for technicians, an understanding of these three terms helps when diagnosing frame damage, deciding on frame modifications, and determining repair strategies.

Resist Bending Moment (RBM)

The first of the terms used in frame design is resist bending moment or RBM. A moment is the torque or twisting/bending force applied to any component around a pivot point. The use of moment may seem strange, but it is based on an older meaning of the word. Long ago, the word moment was often used to mean "of great significance or importance," such as in "this was a discovery of great moment." (Today, this meaning comes through in the word momentous, as in "Graduation is a *momentous* occasion.")

The use of the word *moment* to describe a force, then, refers to the importance of the force in terms of where it is acting on the component. In the context of a vehicle frame, the **resist bending moment (RBM)** is the ability of the frame to support the force trying to bend it at the point where this bending force is greatest. The RBM of a frame is the actual measure of the strength of the frame. RBM is calculated by multiplying two other variables in frame design—section modulus and yield strength.

Section Modulus

Section modulus is an engineering term used to describe the strength of the shape of a certain component. As such, section modulus has absolutely no relationship to the material the component is made of. For example, the section modulus calculation is identical for a C-channel made of plastic and for a C-channel of the exact same size made from **high-carbon steel**—steel alloyed with carbon at levels of 0.9% to 2.5%. Therefore, section modulus is a measure of the strength of the *design*, not the material.

The section modulus calculation produces a constant for a shape, so the units used for the calculation do not matter. Section modulus can be stated as inches, centimeters, and so on. Two types of section modulus calculations are possible. The first is the elastic section modulus and the second is the plastic section modulus. Elastic section modulus is used for frame design, so that calculation is used here.

For C-channel frames, the section modulus (SM) is calculated as follows:

$$SM = \frac{BH^2}{6} - \frac{bh^3}{6H}$$

Where B is the overall width of the channel at the flange; H is the overall height of the channel from flange to flange; b is the width of the inside of the flange from the inside of the web to the flange edge; and h is the height of the inside of the web between the inside of the two flanges.

If you play around with the SM equation for C-channel, you can quickly see that the height of the web has a much larger effect on the outcome than the width of the flanges. To demonstrate this, let's run the equation using the following figures for the C-channel:

$$B = 2$$
$$H = 6$$
$$b = 1.5$$
$$h = 5$$

The calculation using those figures is as follows:

$$SM = \frac{2 \times 6^2}{6} - \frac{1.5 \times 5^3}{6 \times 6}$$
$$= \frac{72}{6} - \frac{187.5}{36}$$
$$= 12 - 5.2$$
$$= 6.8$$

If we switch the figures to make the flange wider than the web is high, the outcome is much different.

$$B = 6$$
$$H = 2$$
$$b = 5$$
$$h = 1.5$$

The calculation for the wider flange is as follows:

$$SM = \frac{6 \times 2^2}{6} - \frac{5 \times 1.5^3}{6 \times 2}$$
$$= \frac{24}{6} - \frac{16.875}{12}$$
$$= 4 - 1.4$$
$$= 2.6$$

The difference in the results shows that the height of the component is much more important than the width, which makes sense. Imagine a typical 2" × 6" (38 × 140 mm) wooden beam used in construction. If that beam is placed on its narrow edge between two supports (such as with floor joists), it holds a much larger load than if we place the board on its wider flat side between the two supports. The same is true in the context of a vehicle frame using C-channel rails. Making the web taller allows the frame to carry a bigger load than making the flange wider.

Yield Strength

The second variable required to calculate RBM is the yield strength of the material used to construct the frame.

Yield strength is the amount of force required to permanently deform the material. Until a material reaches its yield strength, the material can deform, but returns to its original shape when the load is removed. Once the yield strength is exceeded, the deformation is permanent.

Yield strength is determined by placing a piece of the material with a specific cross-sectional area—typically one square inch—in a machine that gradually exerts increasing force on the material in an attempt to pull the material apart. When the material reaches its yield strength, the material shape permanently deforms and is incapable of rebounding to its original shape. That point is also known as the elastic limit of the material.

Yield strength varies depending on the material being tested. Medium-carbon, high-tensile steel yields and deforms at approximately 50,000 psi (345 MPa). **Medium-carbon steels** are alloys with carbon at levels of 0.25% to 0.6%. **Tensile strength** is the amount of force required before a material breaks. **Heat-treated alloy steel** yields at 110,000 psi (758 MPa) or higher. Most heavy-truck frames today use heat-treated alloy steel frames with 110,000 or 120,000 psi (758–827 MPa) yield strength. Heat-treated alloy steel allows the frame material to be thinner and lighter, and the frame to retain the necessary RBM or structural strength.

Actual Frame Strength

To determine the actual strength of a particular frame, the RBM must be calculated and then compared to the total force acting on the frame. The RBM should be higher than the total force. In fact, RBMs must be high enough to support three times the maximum load of the frame.

To calculate the RBM, multiply the yield strength of the material by its section modulus.

$$RBM = SM \times YS$$

For example, imagine a truck has a frame with rails made of a heat-treated alloy steel rated at 110,000 psi (758 MPa) yield strength. The section modulus of that steel is 14.8, which is a typical section modulus of a 10 5/8" (270 mm) C-channel frame. The resulting RBM is:

$$RBM = 14.8 \times 110,000 \ (758)$$
$$= 1,628,000 \ \text{in-lb} \ (183,939 \ \text{Nm})$$

Before specifying this frame for an application, the maximum force acting on the frame must be found and then compared to the RBM of the frame. The force the frame must be capable of supporting is determined in two steps. The first step is finding the maximum load on the frame. The second step is multiplying the maximum load by the distance in inches from the load point to the frame support point. That distance is the length of the lever arm or "moment" arm trying to twist the frame rail.

The amount of load placed on the frame is relatively easy to determine, but the point at which that force is concentrated on the frame is not as easy to identify. That point is called the **maximum bending moment** and is simply the maximum bending stress put on a vehicle frame. As illustrated in

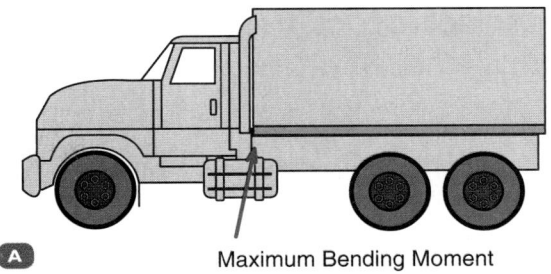

A Maximum Bending Moment

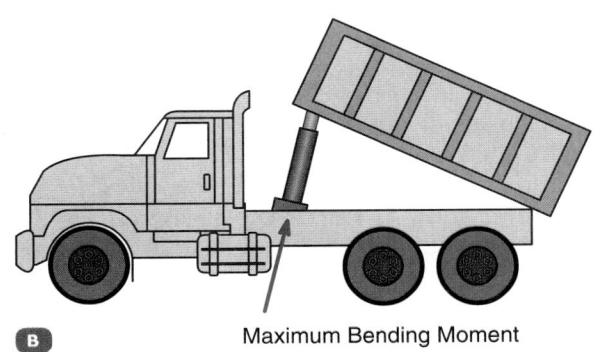

B Maximum Bending Moment

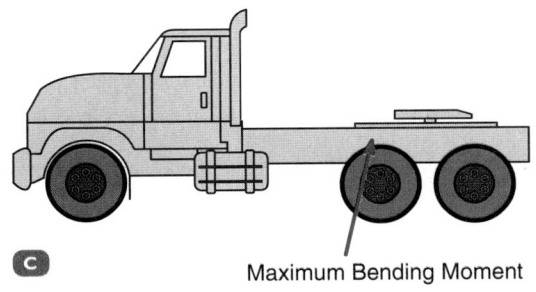

C Maximum Bending Moment

FIGURE 30-5 Maximum bending moment on a: **A.** Straight truck. **B.** Dump truck. **C.** Tractor.

FIGURE 30-5, the maximum bending moment is different for every style of vehicle. The maximum bending moment for any vehicle depends on its design and where the load is placed on the vehicle, so straight trucks, dump trucks, and tractors have very different maximum bending moment locations.

The maximum bending moment of the vehicle is the point where the load is acting on the frame at the maximum distance from the support points. The maximum bending moment is calculated by multiplying the load by the distance in inches from the support point. For example, a 34,000 lb (15,455 kg) load at a distance of 18" (460 mm) from the support point equals 612,000 in-lb total (69,147 Nm), or 306,000 in-lb (34,573 Nm) of bending force per frame rail.

Frame strength is critical for heavy-duty trucks. The frame must be designed with sufficient strength to support the load placed on it and have a significant margin of safety to ensure long service life.

Construction of Frames

LO 30-2 Describe truck frame construction.

The design and construction of truck frames is critical in ensuring the safe and efficient operation of the truck over its service life. The design of the components, their configuration, and the material from which they are made, are all important considerations in frame construction.

Frame Material

Medium-duty truck frame rails are generally constructed using medium-carbon steels with yield strengths of up to 50,000 psi (345 MPa). To carry heavier vehicle loads, the steel plate used to manufacture these frames must be thicker. Using a thicker plate increases the frame's section modulus, which in turn increases the RBM of the frame.

Increasing the RBM of a frame by using a thicker plate has some disadvantages, however. A key disadvantage of using a thicker plate to increase the SM of the frame rail is higher weight. For example, a frame rail made of medium-carbon, high-tensile steel with 50,000 psi (345 MPa) yield strength and an SM of 24 has an RBM of 1,200,000 in-lb (135,581 Nm). That means the frame weighs approximately 2.45 pounds per inch (0.44 kg per cm). Continuing to run the figures, the total weight of a frame 180" (457 cm) long is 882 lb (401 kg) for both frame rails.

By contrast, a frame formed from high-performance alloy steel with 85,000 psi (586 MPa) yield strength cuts the frame weight by 30% to 40%, and it is still able to carry the same load. That is because the frame steel is thinner and weighs less per inch.

A frame made of heat-treated chrome-molybdenum-alloy steel causes the SM to drop even more, further reducing frame weight. Consider a heat-treated alloy-steel frame with a yield strength of 110,000 psi (758 MPa) and an SM of just 11. Again, this frame's height and flange width is the same, but the steel plate is thinner. The RBM of that type of frame rail is 1,210,000 in-lb (136,712 Nm). Because the SM of the heat-treated, chrome-molybdenum frame is smaller, the frame weighs only 1.125 pounds per inch (0.22 kg per cm), for a total weight of 405 lb (184 kg). This heat-treated frame weighs less than half the weight of the medium-carbon-steel frame in the first example, yet the RBM strength is higher. The reduced frame weight also allows the vehicle to carry larger payloads.

Aluminum-alloy frames have yield strengths of 60,000 psi (414 MPa) and, with sufficient section modulus, can carry the loads required by today's heavy trucks. **Aluminum alloy** is aluminum mixed with other metals to increase its strength. The weight savings are even greater when compared to the chrome-molybdenum, alloy-steel frames. The cost of aluminum, however, can be a deterrent.

The best compromise between weight and cost for manufacturers today is the heat-treated, alloy-steel frame. Most, if not all, medium- and heavy-duty trucks currently in production are equipped with this type of frame. Lighter-duty trucks may still be equipped with medium-carbon and or heat-treated medium-carbon steel frames.

Welding on medium-carbon steel frames to alter frame length and to attach aftermarket components, such as lift gates, is a common practice in the truck industry today. Whenever modifications are made to the vehicle, care must be taken to protect the RBM of the frame. Most manufacturers prohibit welding on heat-treated frame rails and consider additional welds as voiding the vehicle's warranty. The heat from the weld can destroy the heat treatment and, thereby, reduce frame strength. Despite the risks, frame modifications are common in the industry, and many aftermarket shops perform this work on a regular basis.

Although manufacturers prohibit welding on heat-treated frame rails, they nonetheless offer instructions on frame lengthening and modifications that require welding. Clearly, there is some controversy as to the correct method of completing this kind of work—or if the work should be performed at all. Some industry experts insist it is necessary to reinforce a welded frame at and beyond the weld in both directions to bring the frame RBM back to specification. Other experts maintain that a reinforcement drastically increases SM and leads to a stress riser and frame cracking. Frame welding is discussed in more detail in the Maintenance and Service of Truck Frames section of this chapter.

Rails, Cross Members, and Fasteners

As mentioned at the beginning of the chapter, C-channel frames, like that illustrated in **FIGURE 30-6**, are the most common configuration for heavy vehicles. The C-channels of the ladder frame may be formed of medium- or high-carbon steel, but today they are typically made of heat-treated alloy steel with exceptionally high yield strength. The C shape of the channel rails provides an extremely strong beam to support the vehicle components. The flat top and bottom areas of the C shape are known as the upper and lower flanges and the upright side of the C is known as the **web**.

Some C-channel ladder-type frame designs are known as drop front or drop forward. As shown in **FIGURE 30-7**, the web height of the C-channel drops off near the front of the rails and/or the rails curve lower at the front. Both drop-front and drop-forward designs allow a lower mounting position for the engine and drivetrain, which in turn lowers the vehicle's center of gravity.

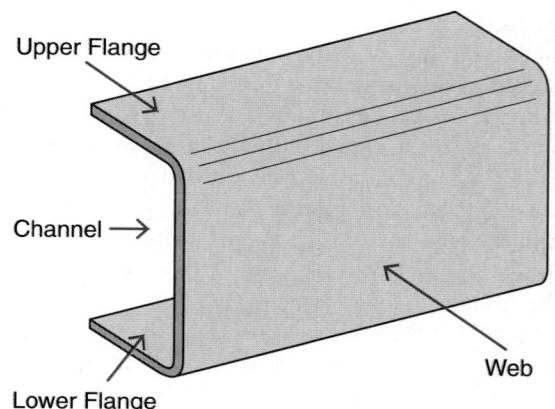

FIGURE 30-6 C-channel frame rail.

In a variation of the C-channel, ladder-type frame, the front sections of the rails bow outward symmetrically. That means the sections bow the same amount on each rail. This configuration was shown in Figure 30-1. In yet another variation of the C-channel, ladder-type frame, the front sections of the rails bow out asymmetrically. That is, only one rail is bowed outward. Asymmetrical configurations accommodate the engine package and front suspension.

The frame rails of the C-channel, ladder-type frame are the main load-bearing components of the frame. The connecting cross members tie the rails together, both to maintain their alignment and to stop them from twisting under the heavy loads the rails must carry. Frame cross members also help to control torsional stresses on the frame rails by flexing and transmitting some of the twisting stress from one rail to the other.

Frame cross members can be box, hat (**FIGURE 30-8**), or C-channel shaped. They may also be straight or shaped to accommodate vehicle systems, such as the driveline. Often the front cross member that supports the engine is lowered. This is called a drop-center cross member, and it allows the engine and driveline mounting to be lower. As with asymmetrical ladder frames, the ability to lower the mounting of the driveline lowers the vehicle's center of gravity. The cross members also provide mounting locations and protection for vehicle wiring and other components, such as air valves and piping.

Fasteners

Cross members are bolted, riveted, or attached to the rails with Huck® brand fasteners (**FIGURE 30-9**). Despite appearances, **Huck® fasteners** are not nuts and bolts. Rather, the fasteners are

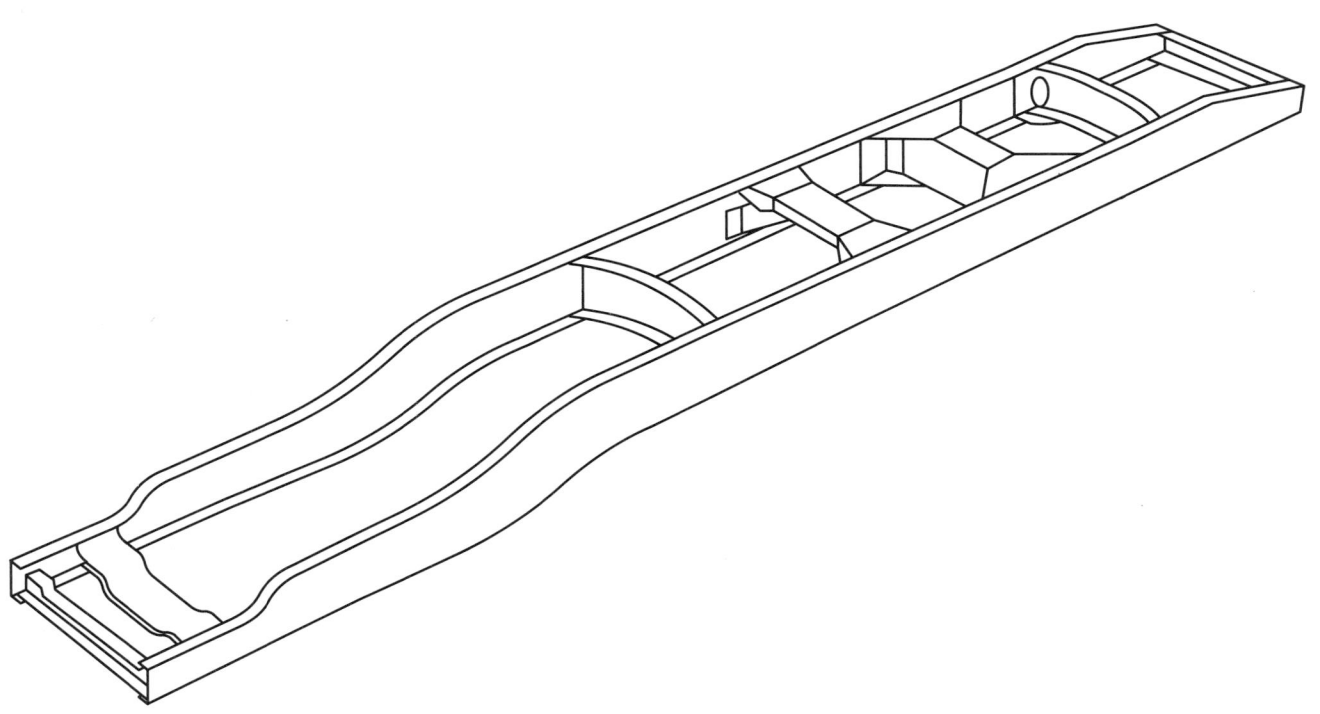

FIGURE 30-7 A drop-front frame.

FIGURE 30-8 Hat-style cross member.

FIGURE 30-9 Huck® brand fastener.

more like a riveted connection in that the Huck® bolt has ridges instead of threads. In addition, the Huck® nut is **swaged** onto the bolt, meaning that the metal of the nut is deformed by the installation tool to precisely fit the Huck bolt. Therefore, the collar cannot be tightened after the fastener is installed. As a result, these fasteners are one of the most secure attaching systems available and should last for the life of the vehicle.

Huck® fasteners were originally designed for use by NASA in the space program. Their versatility has caused them to be adopted for use in many industries, including the truck market. Huck® bolt fasteners cannot be re-torqued by traditional methods. Nonetheless, the bolts need to be inspected for looseness and for rust streaking from the frame components that are held together. Streaks can indicate movement between the components in contact. If rust streaking is found, further investigation is necessary to find out if the fasteners are loose.

Reinforced Frame Rails

In exceptionally heavy applications, manufacturers may reinforce frame rails to increase RBM by installing extra C-channel rails that fit inside the original C-channel. Two or three C-channels can be bolted together to increase the SM and, therefore, the RBM of the frame rails. The use of multiple channels bolted together allows the frame to be more flexible than using single extra-thick channel to increase frame RBM. Another profile of reinforcement is the **L-plate**, or inverted L-plates, which are L-shaped beams that can be bolted to the outside of the C-channel to increase the rails' RBM. **FIGURE 30-10** shows several applications of different reinforcement profiles.

Reinforced frames are typically only found in off-road and heavy-hauler applications because of the weight penalty they carry. Frames with three and four channels bolted together can weigh as much as 4 or 5 pounds (1.8 to 2.3 kg) per inch of rail.

Frame Reinforcement

If necessary, frame rails can also be locally reinforced when installing vehicle accessories. Local reinforcements include C-channel, L-channel plates, or fishplates. A **fishplate** is a flat, steel-plate reinforcement bolted usually inside, and sometimes outside, the frame rail.

Great care must be taken when installing reinforcements so as not to create stress risers. The secret to successful reinforcement is tapering. That is, the edges of the reinforcing plate should be angled to spread out the stress concentration. When reinforcing a frame, the plate used should be long enough to pass the area required to be reinforced by at least half the height of the frame web. From there, it should taper away from those points at a rate of 25 to 60 degrees, with the longest side at the tension flange of the rail. All reinforcements and bolts should be tapered and staggered. Tapering spreads out the change in section modulus and reduces the stress riser (**FIGURE 30-11**).

The reinforcement plate should be bolted in place using as many existing holes as possible. Only grade 8 flange-head bolts and hardened-steel washers should be used. (Soft washers lose their torque, and using no washers damages the frame rail.) Bolt holes should be 1/32" (0.03125 cm) wider than the bolts. Leaving space around the bolt allows the bolt to act as a torsion member, adding to frame flexibility; a body-bound bolt increases localized stress.

In no case shall the holes be closer to the flanges than the factory frame holes. Never should the holes be closer than 1.5" (2.7 cm) from the flange. Remember that going from flexible to stiff in any component leads to concentrated stress. The more the reinforcement can be tapered, the better in terms of reducing the stress risers. Always stagger and taper the reinforcement plate and the attaching bolts, if possible.

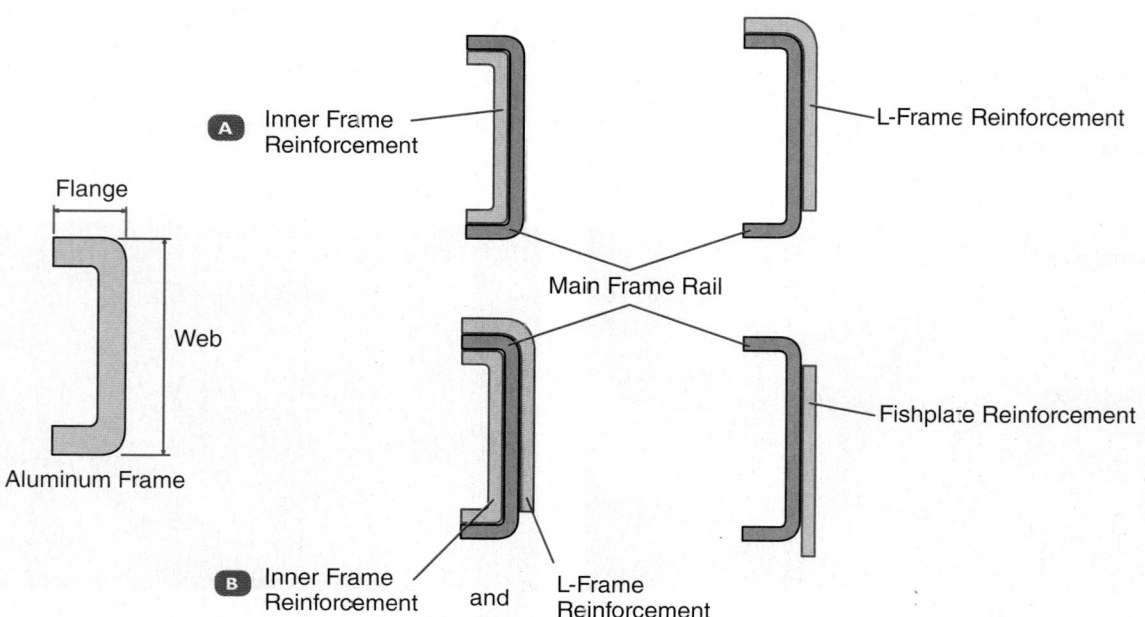

FIGURE 30-10 Reinforced frame rails using: **A.** C-channel, L-plate. **B.** L-plate with C-channel, Fishplate.

If holes are drilled, they should be staggered, so that they are not in a vertical line, if possible. Never drill more holes in a vertical line than the largest number of holes drilled at the factory. Holes should be separated from each other by at least 2.5 times the diameter of the hole. The holes should be drilled as close to the neutral fiber (the center of the web) as possible. The hole should be no closer to the edge of the reinforcing plate than twice the bolt's diameter.

Frame-Supported Attachments

LO 30-3 Explain attachment procedures for truck frames.

There are four general ways in which a vehicle body can be attached to the chassis frame: U-bolt clamps, outrigger-type mounts, fishplates, and spring-loaded resilient mounts. The choice of body mount is determined by the type of truck body being installed.

When the body is relatively flexible, such as with van bodies, it can be mounted to the frame in one of three ways: with U-bolts, outriggers, or fishplates. The least recommended, yet most common, of these is the U-bolt mounting system (**FIGURE 30-12**).

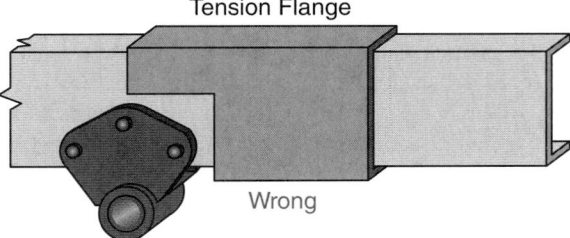

Tension Flange

Wrong

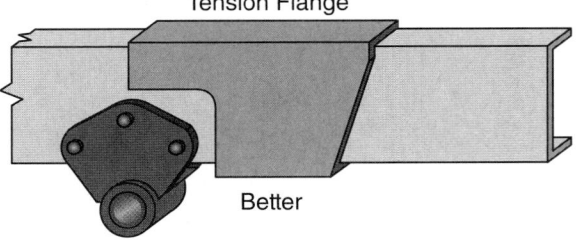

Tension Flange

Better

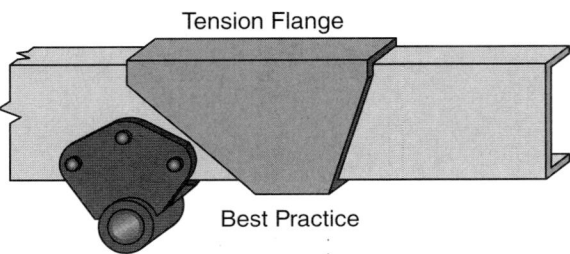

Tension Flange

Best Practice

FIGURE 30-11 Always taper and stagger reinforcements and attaching bolts as much as possible.

U-bolt Mounts

U-bolts are the least secure mounting system, but their ease of installation makes them popular with builders of truck bodies. When a body is placed on the frame, a semi-flexible material is used between the body and the frame. Polyurethane can be used, but most often the material is a strip (or strips) of hardwood, such as oak. There are three primary benefits to adding semi-flexible material. First, it protects the frame flange from damage. It also adds to the flexibility of the vehicle. Finally, it helps to spread the load along the length of the frame without causing any localized stress points on the frame due to any unevenness in the body construction.

The U-bolts go over a sub-frame attached to the vehicle body and down both sides of the frame rail. They are then clamped at the bottom flange of the rail. The wood or polyurethane is clamped between the body subframe and the actual chassis frame. U-bolt mounting systems use friction between the frame, the spacer, and the sub-frame of the body to locate the body longitudinally. As a result, the body can sometimes move relative to the frame (**FIGURE 30-13**).

When a U-bolt mounting is used, it is also recommended that solid spacers be inserted inside the frame C-channel to stop the frame flanges from collapsing when they are clamped by the U-bolt. Steel spacers are recommended over wood because, over time, wooden blocks may contract and fall out. Again, in practice this is rarely done, and most bodies attached with

FIGURE 30-12 U-bolt mountings.

FIGURE 30-13 This U-bolt strap has moved due to impact.

U-bolts have no spacers installed at all. Quite often, the lower frame flange is bent at the U-bolt clamp point, as shown in **FIGURE 30-14**.

Bent flanges greatly reduce the frame strength. Flanges can bend more in vehicle service, leading to a loose U-bolt and a body that can move along the frame. U-bolt body-mounting systems are almost universal because they are easy to install and require no drilling of the frame, but these systems are the poorest of the three available choices. It is not unusual to see a U-bolt-attached body that has shifted in operation because of the short cuts taken at installation. Frame flanges that are collapsed (and therefore weakened) because a spacer was not used when installing U-bolt clamps can lead to the frame cracking at the weakened section.

U-bolt body mounting can be successful, however, if done correctly. Even though this is rarely the case, U-bolt mounting systems have been known to last for the life of vehicles with no visible problems.

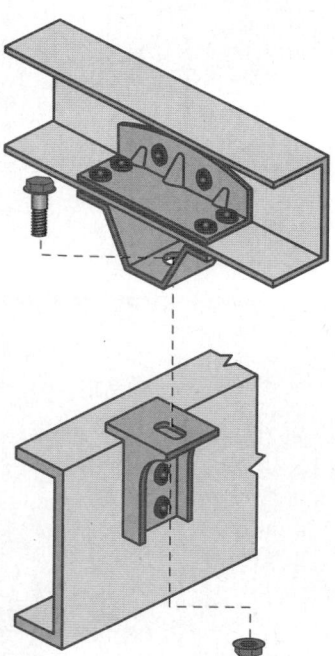

FIGURE 30-14 A bent frame rail flange.

Outrigger Mounts

Outrigger mounting is the recommended method of attaching flexible bodies to a ladder-type frame. Outrigger mounting is the most secure body mounting because the body is positively prevented from moving longitudinally. In addition, outrigger mounts cause no damage to the frame itself.

Outrigger brackets are welded to the vehicle body and then bolted to the frame web. Alternately, the outriggers may bolt to another bracket that, in turn, is bolted to the frame web **FIGURE 30-15**. Again, a wooden or polyurethane strip is usually used between the body sub-frame and the upper flange of the chassis frame rail. The strip spreads the load along the frame and absorbs any high or low spots in the body sub-frame. Obviously, this system requires substantially more work to install than the U-joint system. Mounting holes must be drilled in both the frame web and the body sub-frame, adding several hours of labor to the job.

To prevent longitudinal movement, it is recommended that four outrigger-type mounts be installed at the four corners of the body. Outrigger mounts firmly attach to the frame web and prevent fore and aft movement. In practice, however, outrigger mounts are rarely used.

Fishplate Mounts

Fishplating is the second recommended choice for flexible body mounting. This mounting system, as illustrated in (**FIGURE 30-16**), uses fishplates that are bolted to the body sub-frame and the vehicle frame web. Fishplates are flat plates used to re-inforce the frame rail. Fishplate mounts also use a wooden or polyurethane strip between the body sub-frame and the upper flange of the vehicle frame to insulate the frame and absorb any manufacturing deviations in the body sub-frame.

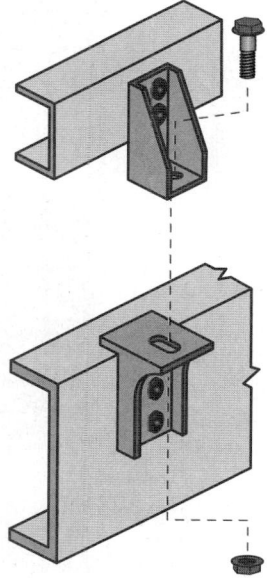
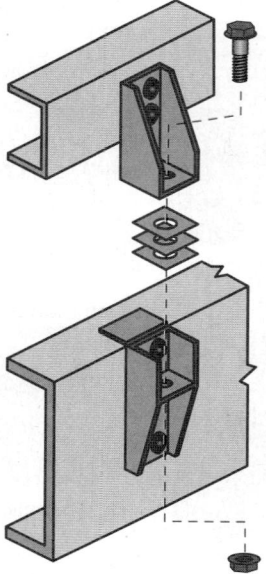

FIGURE 30-15 Outrigger mounting system.

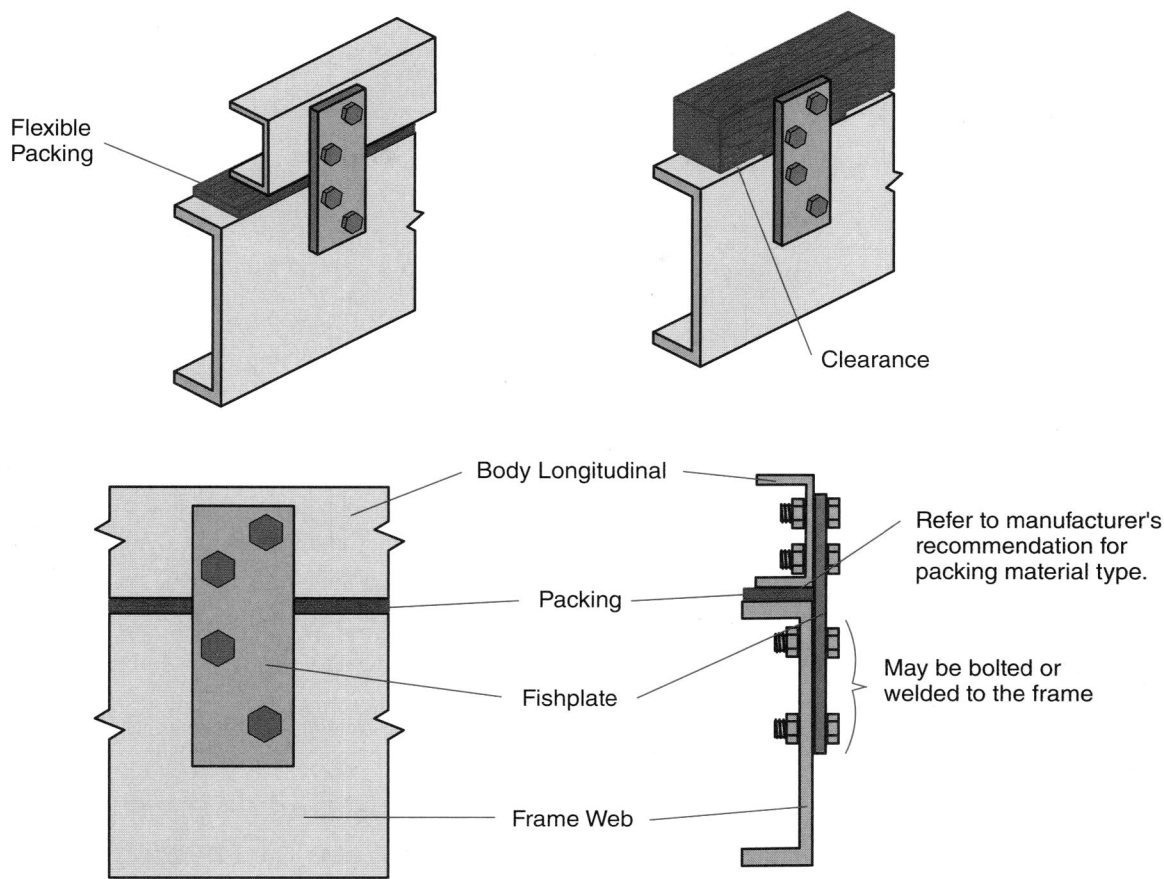

FIGURE 30-16 Fishplate mounting system.

Fishplate systems are very secure. Like the outrigger systems, however, fishplates require holes to be drilled in the frame web and the body sub-frame. That drilling adds to the labor hours required to install the body. The extra time involved for these mounting systems is the major disadvantage that causes them to be rarely used in body installations.

Resilient Mounting Systems

When mounting a body that has reduced or very little flexibility, it is necessary to provide some movement or flexibility at the mounting points so that the body does not prevent the vehicle frame from flexing normally. Typically, installing these rigid bodies requires resilient mounting systems—these are outrigger-type mounts with a flexible medium that allows the body to move slightly up, down, or side to side.

Resilient mounts can be spring-loaded or made with rubber or polyurethane elements that accommodate movement. Resilient mounts are perfect for rigid bodies, such as tankers or garbage packers. These bodies are extremely stiff and require that the mounts provide the flexibility. Tanker bodies can be mounted in a three- or four-point system that uses flexible rubber or polyurethane components. These components allow the vehicle frame to flex as necessary. Semi-rigid bodies can also use resilient outrigger mounts. **FIGURE 30-17** shows a garbage packer using spring-loaded resilient mounts. This allows some movement of the body as the frame flexes.

FIGURE 30-17 A garbage packer with spring-loaded outrigger mounts.

Sometimes a semi-rigid or rigid vehicle body is mounted on a frame that experiences more than normal bending and flexing because of the vehicle vocation. In those situations, another type of resilient mount, called a vertical mount, can be used to allow greater-than-normal vertical movement of the body, while maintaining the body's longitudinal position. These mounts have friction material between the vertical elements that restrict the up-and-down motion. The mounting bolts are in slotted holes that allow greater-than-normal vertical movement. That movement is stopped when the bolt meets the end of the slotted hole in the vertical bracket.

Stresses Caused by Frame Attachments

Almost all the components installed on a vehicle are attached to the frame and add to the weight the frame must support. These attachments; hydraulics, dump boxes, winches, and so on, as shown in **FIGURE 30-18**, add varying levels of side-bending forces that the frame must also withstand. Components attached to the frame tend to concentrate stresses at the attachment point.

Consider the frame of a truck as it operates on a highway. The heaviest load is resting on the truck frame at the maximum bending moment for the particular design of vehicle. The suspension supports the frame by pushing upwards against the downward motion. The frame rails flex and twist between these two points, and the length of the frame rail between the points has a direct influence on the amount of flexing that takes place.

If large components are bolted to the frame rail halfway between these two points, however, the frame rail loses some flexibility. The mass of the component's mounting bracket restricts natural flexing movement of the frame rail at the point where it is attached. That means the frame has less distance over which it can absorb the forces by flexing. In fact, it flexes normally up to the point the attaching bracket begins, and then its flexibility decreases. This additional force causes stress risers at the beginning and end of the mounting bracket. Fatigue failures of most metal components typically occur at a stress riser.

Other components, such as pinion and axle shafts, experience this type of failure as well. Fatigue failure of those components usually occurs where the section (shape and size) of the component changes. For example, typical breakage points are found where a spline is machined into the shaft or where a shaft reduces from a raised section that supports a bearing.

FIGURE 30-18 Attachments, such as hydraulics, dump boxes, and winches add varying levels of side-bending forces to the frame.

These breakage points occur because stress is always concentrated where the shaft widens or narrows and the shaft's ability to flex is changed.

Shaft manufacturers attempt to reduce the stress concentration by the actual design of the shaft itself. They gradually increase or decrease the shaft size by using a radius transition from the thinner to thicker part. That gradual change tends to spread out the effects of the stress concentration through the area of the radius. The same thinking is used when dealing with a frame rail. That is, forces should be spread over the rail to reduce the effects of stress risers or concentrators.

As a technician, it is important for you to understand the stresses a frame is subject to and avoid causing or increasing stress risers. Remember that the upper and lower flange alternate between compression and tension, depending on the positioning of the load maximum bending moment and the suspension supports. The tension flange is always under more stress than the compression flange. The center of the frame web (the neutral fiber) deals with the least amount of stress because the compression and tension forces cancel each other out. Therefore, any attachments should be made as close to the center of the web as possible, and care must be taken to reinforce the rails, if necessary, to minimize or nullify any stress riser that may be created by large attachments.

Inspection, Service, and Maintenance of Truck Frames

LO 30-4 Describe frame inspection and maintenance procedure, including out-of-service criteria.

Frame maintenance starts with a visual inspection of all the frame components as described in **SKILL DRILL 30-1**. All frame components (side rails, cross members, and brackets) should be checked for breaks, cracks, excessive corrosion, distortion, elongated holes, fastener looseness, and damage before needed repairs can be determined. If any of these defects are found, they must be repaired according to manufacturer's recommendations.

Out-of-Service Criteria for Truck Frames

Before engaging in any service activities, it is critical to understand the out-of-service criteria for truck frames. The Commercial Vehicle Safety Alliance (CVSA) is a North American organization that sets out-of-service criteria for commercial vehicles, in concert with all vehicle stakeholders and enforcement agencies. The criteria apply to drivers' licensing qualifications, hours of work, and medical condition, as well as the physical condition of the vehicle. The following are the CVSA out-of-service criteria specifically for vehicle frames.

The vehicle shall be rendered out-of-service if any of the following defects are present on the vehicle at the time of inspection:

■ Any cracked, sagged, loose, or broken side rail that allows the vehicle body to contact moving components or otherwise suggests imminent frame collapse

SKILL DRILL 30-1 Conducting Exterior Inspections of Frame

1. Check the vehicle frame and the frame members for bending or other types of deformities, and for any cracks and excessive rust or scale.
2. Check frame members for cracks, breaks, looseness, or sagging. In addition, inspect them for any loose or missing fasteners, including fasteners attaching functional components, such as the engine, transmission, steering gear, suspension, body parts, and fifth-wheel components.
3. Check for any condition that causes the body or frame to be in contact with a tire or any part of the wheel assemblies, and for missing or unengaged locking pins in adjustable axle assemblies.

- Any broken, cracked, or loose frame member that adversely affects the support of any suspension, steering, driveline, or body component
- Any crack 1.5" (38 mm) in length or larger in the frame web that projects towards the bottom flange of the rail
- Any crack in the frame web that extends around the radius and into the lower flange
- Any crack 1" (25 mm) or larger in the bottom flange of the side rail
- Any condition that causes the vehicle body or frame to be in contact with any part of the vehicle tires or wheel assemblies, including excessive loading

The CVSA states that a vehicle shall not be put back into service until the defects are repaired.

Types of Frame Damage

Cracked frames are usually caused by fatigue failures, caused by stress risers and/or chronic overloading. Localized crack repair by welding is covered in the Crack Repair section at the end of this chapter. There are five other general types of frame damage that can occur when dealing with ladder-type frames: sag, bow, diamond, twist, and sidesway.

Sag

Frame **sag** is a downward bend of the frame rails caused by one of two factors (**FIGURE 30-19A**). The primary cause of sag is static overload, which occurs when the load on the vehicle is more than the frame can handle. The other cause of sag is shock load to the frame, caused by the vehicle dropping into a depression in the terrain; the load consequently bends the frame. Sag can also be caused by a weakening of the frame RBM; for example, by drilling too many holes in the web, by holes being too close to the flanges, or by welding the frame rails and negating the properties of their heat treatment. A definitive sign of frame sag is wrinkles in the compression flange of the rail at the point of sag.

Types of Chassis Frame Damage

Sag
The frame
is bent
down in
the middle.

Diamond
One frame rail
has moved ahead
of the other rail.

Twist
The front of the
framerolls to one
side while the
rear of the frame
rolls the other way.

Sidesway
The frame
is bent to
one side.

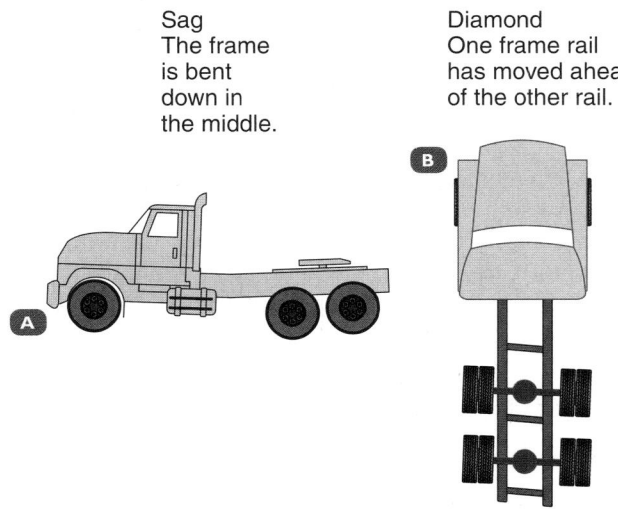
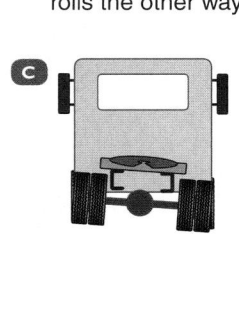
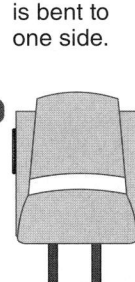

FIGURE 30-19 A. Sag. **B.** Diamond. **C.** Twist. **D.** Sidesway.

Bow

Bow is the opposite of sag. It is the upward bending of the frame rails and can be caused by uneven loading of the frame. This can occur in dump truck applications when the box is raised. The rear contact point of the box can cause the frame to bend at that point and bow upwards at the suspension. A definitive indication of frame bow is wrinkling of the lower frame flange at the point that bowing occurs.

Diamond

Diamond is a condition when one frame rail is further forward than the other (**FIGURE 30-19B**). Diamond usually occurs because of impact from a collision or from a poorly reinforced plough mounting on a snow removal vehicle. Diamond can also be caused by trying to free a stuck vehicle carrying a heavy load by chaining the vehicle, but to only one frame rail.

Twist

Frame **twist** occurs when one frame rail is lower than the other and can be caused by collision damage (**FIGURE 30-19C**). Sometimes, what seems to be frame twist, is not. For example, a broken spring gives the indication of a twisted frame, but the frame usually returns to its correct alignment when the broken spring is repaired. A truly twisted frame is one of the most difficult to repair because the rails must be simultaneously pushed and/or pulled in more than one direction to straighten them.

Sidesway

Sidesway is when the vehicle frame is bowed outward when viewed from the top (**FIGURE 30-19D**). As with other types of frame damage, sidesway is usually caused by accident damage sustained during a side-impact collision. Shock loading while using a snowplow can also cause sidesway.

Corrosion Damage

Corrosion, like that shown in **FIGURE 30-20**, is a constant threat to the integrity of the frame metal. Normal surface rusting of a frame does not greatly affect its strength. Always inspect the frame for rust damage while conducting vehicle service, as excessive corrosion compromises the frame's strength.

Rust is less of a problem for today's heavy vehicles than it was in the past. Today's heat-treated high-tensile-strength frames

FIGURE 30-20 Excessive corrosion.

are typically powder-coated or painted using an electrophoretic process. Both of those processes lead to a much more resilient paint coating. As such, they are much less likely to sustain rust damage than older frames. Still, improper or careless work practices around the frame can damage the paint surface and cause eventual rusting. Always use due care to avoid scratching, or otherwise damaging, the frame coating and exposing the base metal when working on a vehicle.

A particularly troublesome type of corrosion is **galvanic corrosion**, which is the corrosion of material caused by the electrolytic effect that can occur when two dissimilar metals are in contact. This electrolytic effect can result in a heavy corrosion problem with certain chassis frames that use elements constructed from different metals.

Galvanic corrosion occurs when there are dissimilar metals in contact when an electrolyte is introduced between them. During galvanic corrosion, one metal becomes the anode and the other becomes the cathode. The metals form a galvanic cell similar to a battery. An electrical current created by the oxidation of the anode flows through the electrolyte from the anode to the cathode. The electrolyte can be anything that conducts electricity, such as plain water or water mixed with road salt—either of which can be a powerful electrolyte.

The most common occurrence of a galvanic cell in a truck frame is aluminum in contact with steel. When water or salt water is present between the two, the aluminum becomes the anode and the steel is the cathode. The anode (the aluminum) oxidizes, resulting in a current flow, but at the expense of the aluminum component.

To prevent this, anytime aluminum is used in the vehicle construction, for example, as a frame cross member, there must be an insulator between the two metals to prevent a galvanic cell from occurring. Typically, the metals are separated by a polymer, such as Mylar. Alternatively, the two metals are coated with a corrosion-resistant insulating sealer, like Tectyl-400C™, before they are assembled. The attaching bolts and washers are also coated with the sealer at all points where they are in contact with the aluminum.

Any time work is performed on vehicle components with dissimilar metals, it is essential that these separators and sealers are replaced and reapplied on reassembly, as required. Otherwise, corrosion results. Galvanic cells can be created whenever any two dissimilar metals are in contact. On trucks, the most common combination is aluminum and steel, but be aware that other combinations of metal can lead also to galvanic cells. For that reason, all dissimilar metals should be insulated from each other. Needless to say, technicians working with aluminum frames must be extremely diligent to avoid creating galvanic cells and their resultant corrosion; aluminum frames are most often associated with flatbed trailers.

Frame Alignment

LO 30-5 Explain frame alignment inspection and repair procedures.

To determine if a frame has had damage due to impact or collision, it is necessary to check frame alignment. A frame that is out of alignment causes numerous problems. When the frame is misaligned, the axles are no longer perpendicular to the direction of vehicle travel, meaning that tire scrub occurs. This leads to poor fuel economy, rapid tire wear, and excess wear and tear on the entire vehicle driveline. Driver fatigue increases, as the operator has to fight the steering wheel to keep the vehicle in a straight line.

Several commercial vehicle alignment systems are available to check frame alignment, but it can also be checked using a simple method requiring only a plumb-bob and a chalk-line. This method involves projecting reference points on the vehicle frame to the floor and then comparing centerlines and distances. To manually check frame alignment, follow the steps in **SKILL DRILL 30-2**. The procedure described is typical, but may

vary for a particular vehicle. Prepare to do the manual check with the following preliminary steps:

- Check the vehicle's tire pressure and adjust each tire as required.
- Confirm that the wheel height is the same from side to side and front to back.
- Visually inspect for any obvious frame or suspension damage and repair as necessary.
- Ensure that the vehicle is on a smooth, level surface and that the front wheels are in the straight-ahead position.
- Roll the vehicle back and forth by hand to neutralize the suspension.

SKILL DRILL 30-2 Checking Frame Alignment Manually

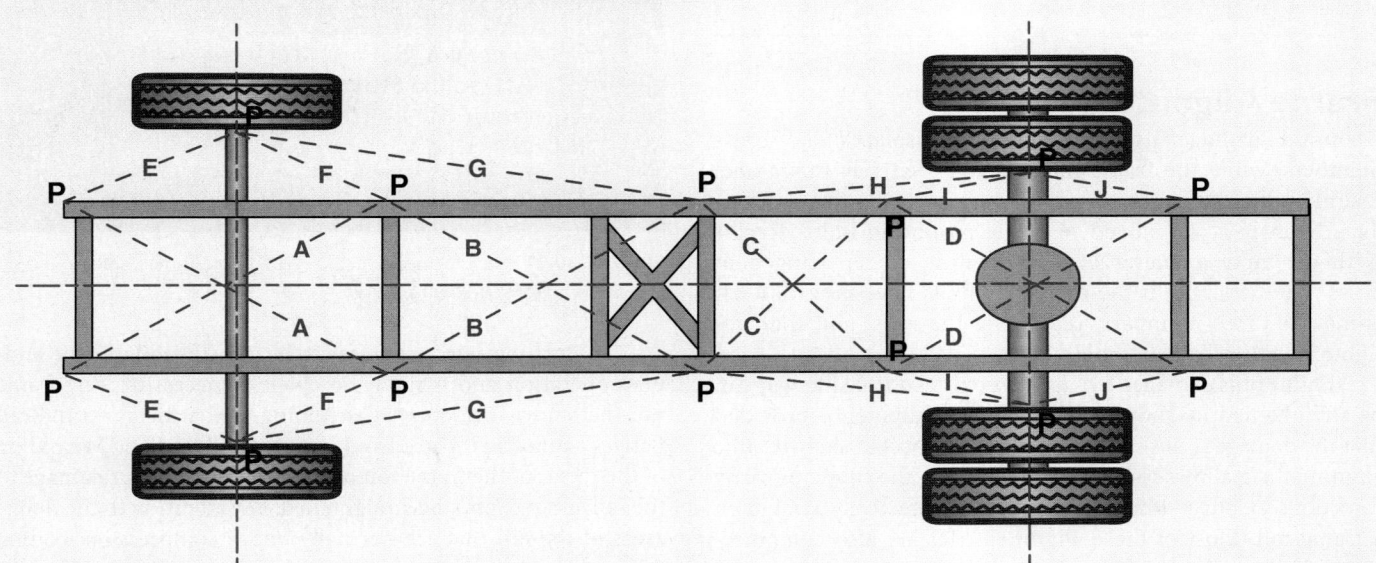

1. Select the reference points on the frame that are to be projected to the floor. (The reference points vary from vehicle to vehicle, but the points used must be the same points on each side of the frame.) Project as many reference points as possible—using more points increases accuracy.
2. If the frame being checked has rails that bow outward at the front, then use the front spring mounts as reference points to find the vehicle centerline. Reference points include, but are not limited to:
   - Front suspension
   - Front and rear spring mounting bracket bolts
   - Mounting bolts on the frame cross members (use the same position bolt on each side rail)
   - Rear suspension spring mounting bracket bolts, front and rear.

   Several other reference points can be used if they are at the same point on each of the frame rails: using more reference points makes the alignment check more accurate. A straight edge can be clamped square to the frame rails, if enough reference points cannot be found.

3. Hold a plumb-bob string in place at each of the reference points on the frame. Ensure that you are at the same side of each bolt head or rivet and that the reference point is the same on each side. If the string of the plumb bob is at the apex of the bolt hex on one side and on a flat on the other side, the points are not the same. Hanging the plumb bob from the washer on the bolt, rather than the bolt head, is more accurate. Also, ensure that the reference point is the same distance from the frame rail on each side, and then project its location to the floor with the plumb bob.
4. Stick a piece of tape to the floor directly beneath the plumb-bob and mark the spot on the tape or the floor. Be very precise and consistent with the marks or the test is useless. Continue marking until all the reference points are projected to the floor.
5. Carefully move the vehicle away from the marked spots on the floor. Measure the distance between the front plumb-bob marks from the right- and left-side rails. Carefully mark the exact center between these two points. That is the centerline of the frame and the front.

SKILL DRILL 30-2 Checking Frame Alignment Manually (Continued)

6. Measure the distance between the rear right and left plumb-bob marks and mark the exact center between these two points. That is the centerline of the frame at the rear.
7. Using a chalk line, carefully pull the line between the two marked centers and snap the line on the ground. This is now the truck frame centerline.
8. Pull the chalk line diagonally between the plumb-bob marks (i.e., between the last mark at the left rear and the second last mark at the right rear). Snap a line.

9. Pull the chalk line between the last mark at the right rear and the second last mark at the left rear. Snap a line.
10. Continue marking chalk lines until all the plumb-bob marks are diagonally connected to form a series of Xs along the length of the frame centerline, as shown in the diagram. If the frame is in alignment, the exact center of the Xs should be at the frame centerline plus or minus 1/8" (2.75 mm).
11. Measure the length of the pairs of intersecting diagonals. The intersecting lines should be equal to within 1/8" (2.75 mm). If they are not, frame diamonding is present.

▶ TECHNICIAN TIP

Out-of-alignment frame sections can easily be determined by the Xs that do not coincide with the frame centerline or intersecting diagonals of differing lengths.

Frame Alignment Repair

Diamond damage usually bends or displaces the cross members, while the frame rails remain relatively unscathed. Examine the frame cross members very carefully to see if they have been bent or moved on their mounting bolts. Repair is then simply a matter of straightening or replacing bent cross members and, if the mounting bolts have moved, loosening the cross members, realigning the rails, and then re-tightening the cross members.

Frame rails damaged by sag, bow, twist, and/or sidesway can be straightened by shops with specialty equipment—provided that the damage is not severe. This type of specialized hydraulic alignment rig allows forces to be applied to the frame in many directions at once, which is required to effectively straighten a frame rail. Most of these alignment rigs are also computer-assisted. The operator follows detailed setup instructions laid out by the computer, which greatly increases the success rate of the repair.

Manufacturers recommend that frame straightening be done cold, but some shops attempt to straighten frame rails by applying heat. This practice is not sanctioned by manufacturers and usually results in a loss of frame strength in heat-treated frame rails. In fact, most manufacturers prohibit heating or welding of any frames, unless specifically authorized by their engineering department, as shown by the warning label in **FIGURE 30-21**.

▶ TECHNICIAN TIP

Manufacturers have specific recommendations for frame service; most call for damaged rails to be replaced. Heating or welding of heat-treated frames is prohibited by manufacturers without express permission. Further, any liability arising from work performed on their vehicle frames without written authorization of the manufacturer is solely the responsibility of the company and person who performs the work. Careful consideration must be taken before embarking on any frame work that falls outside of manufacturer recommendations.

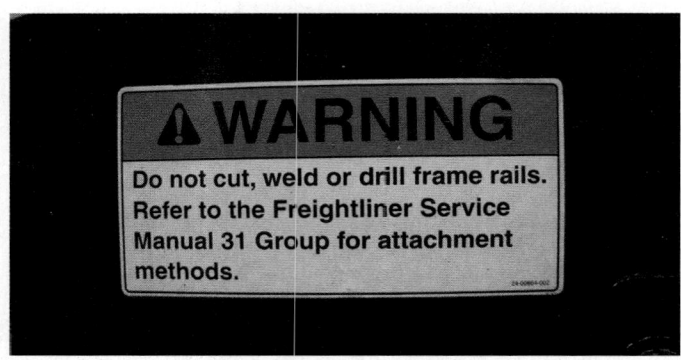

FIGURE 30-21 Manufacturers forbid welding on frames unless approved by their own engineers.

Trying to straighten a frame by heating the rails is a hit-and-miss operation and is rarely completely successful. Any frame rail that shows evidence of wrinkling of the metal on the rail flanges cannot be repaired and requires replacement. Wrinkling of the metal of the frame rail indicates severe impact damage to the rail and it cannot be straightened. Pay attention to the flange areas of the rail that are normally under compression loading to check for wrinkling. Some shops attempt blacksmith-style repairs on wrinkled frame rails to correct the buckling of the web or the flange by using heat and sledge hammers, but this kind of repair is not recommended by any manufacturer.

Whenever a frame has been straightened, it is essential that any damaged bolts or rivets be replaced with grade 8 attaching hardware using flange bolts and hardened steel washers. All frame fasteners should be re-torqued to specification after straightening. If a frame is assembled with rivets (lighter-duty frames) that have loosened, the rivets need to be removed and replaced with bolts. Always follow the manufacturer's recommendation for bolt grade when replacing rivets with bolts. These installations may call for grade-5 bolts. Be aware that substituting grade 8 for grade 5 may reduce the frame flexibility at that point.

SAFETY TIP

Read and understand these welding precautions before attempting any welding procedure on the frame or vehicle:

■ Avoid welding near the fuel tank, fuel lines, or brake lines.
■ Any components near the welding area that may be damaged by excessive heat must be removed or adequately protected.

- Always disconnect the battery or battery's positive and negative terminal posts.
- Check manufacturer's recommendation to protect the vehicle electronics, including disconnecting computer module grounds.
- Keep the ground connection of the arc welding machine as close to the work area as possible.
- Before welding the frame, remove the paint and or powder coating from the weld area.
- After welding, apply an anti-corrosion finishing compound to the weld and surrounding area.

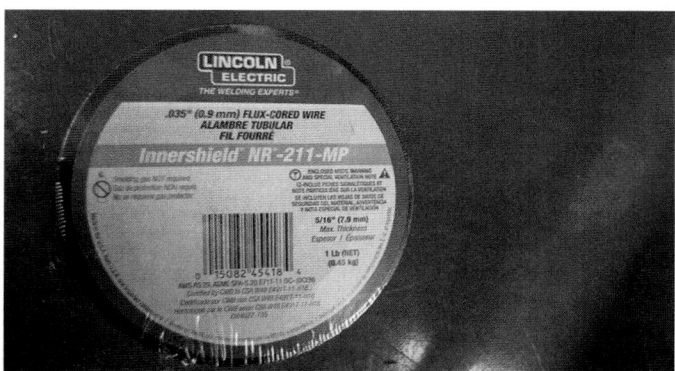

FIGURE 30-22 Flux-cored filler wire used in frame repair.

Welding Frames

LO 30-6 Describe procedures for welding on frames.

Most manufacturers do not recommend welding of any kind on frames, especially on heat-treated frames, and failure to follow their recommendations results in voided warranties, where the frame is concerned. When attaching optional equipment to a frame, they should be bolted using existing bolt holes and not welded. Any welding likely weakens the frame strength. However, with that said, there are shops that consistently splice and weld frames to extend their length and customize a vehicle, and others that use welding techniques to repair cracked or damaged frames to save costs. The following is not a recommendation for these procedures but merely an outline of how they are done.

Splicing Frames

Most manufacturers prefer that a vehicle be specified with the correct length frame so that lengthening and splicing is not necessary. Nonetheless, this practice has long been the norm for truck-body builders and modifiers. Most, if not all, medium and heavy truck frames in production are heat-treated. Cutting and welding on heat treated frames is not generally recommended by manufacturers. Only highly competent welders, such as those certified by the American Welding Society, who understand the welding process and the properties of the metal being welded, and with experience and proper training in pre-heating, heat treating, and tempering, have the necessary skills to cut and weld heat-treated steel, while maintaining the steel strength. The welded frame must be carefully preheated before welding, then heat-treated, quenched, and tempered after welding at very precise temperatures.

Welders also must know the correct filler metal for the frame material and how much heat to apply. Using the wrong filler wire results in a weld that is weaker than the frame metal and, as such, susceptible to breakage. Typical filler wire is shown in **FIGURE 30-22**. Too much heat at the weld site can harden the metal at the edge of the weld to a point where it becomes brittle and cracks. Incorrect preheating and cooling removes the heat-treating benefit of the steel and the frame steel strength is reduced at that point. For example, a heat-treated frame with 110,000 psi (760 MPa) yield strength can be reduced to 36,000 psi (250 MPa) by improper welding and finishing techniques.

In most cases, frames are welded to extend their length, and typically the design of the box or body being installed on the lengthened frame does not concentrate stress near the weld areas. That makes bringing the frame back to original strength not as critical. Manufacturers issue guidelines on frame lengthening or splicing to limit the risk of a frame failure because of welding. Following those guidelines helps to minimize frame weakness at weld joints by spreading out the joint and, therefore, ensuring that stresses are not concentrated at welds.

Frames are regularly cut and welded with straight cuts using a butt splice with few problems because the frame RBM is much greater than the load it carries. If a frame is subjected to large loads near the weld area, however, it can break at the splice. Most experts recommend that the frame rail web section should be cut at a 45- to 60-degree angle so that bending forces are spread out over a much larger area of the welded section.

According to a major truck manufacturer, when splicing a frame, the rails should be cut on an angle following the template in **FIGURE 30-23** to avoid a concentrated stress riser in the rejoined frame. The dimensions here are for a 10.06" (25.55 cm) frame. The diagram shows the left rail. The cuts on the right rail have opposite dimensions.

The flange section of the cut should be angled at 30 degrees from front to back. Some welders run the angles on the right and left rails in opposite directions to further spread out the load across the welded frame. Opposite-side staggering is recommended by certain manufacturers. Most manufacturers also insist that if a frame is lengthened, the splice must be reinforced to attempt to bring the frame back to its original strength. In practice, however, frame splicing is quite often done without reinforcements.

The theory behind not using reinforcements is that reinforcements stiffen the frame and create a stress concentrator (riser) at the point where the reinforcement begins. Fatigue failure of the frame (cracking) is a common occurrence at a stress riser. If lengthening a frame, careful calculation is required to make sure that the vehicle's maximum bending moment is not anywhere near the welded area.

Extending a frame to carry a long body tends to spread the load over a longer surface of the frame. That is typically the reason for most frame extensions, but if heavy loads are concentrated near the weld, it is likely to fail. Most experts agree that a frame welded without reinforcements fails at the tension-flange side of the weld, if the frame is heavily loaded at the weld point. For that reason, reinforcement of the weld is recommended.

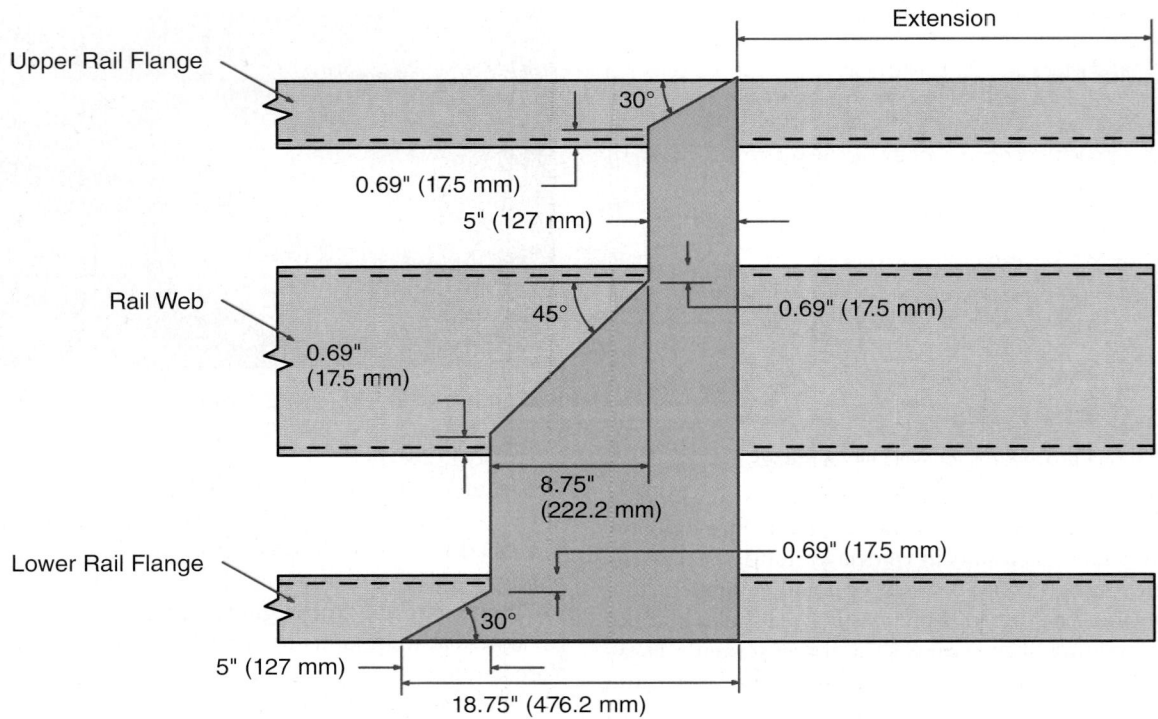

NOTE: If the extension is less than 6", a straight-cut butt splice can be used.

FIGURE 30-23 Template for splicing a frame.

Reinforcement should be bolted—not welded—and carried out in the manner depicted in the earlier section on reinforcement using fishplate. (Recall that using fishplate allows the frame flanges to flex more than using C-channel.) Frame reinforcements should extend past the weld point at least twice the web height, and should taper away from that point at 45 degrees. Reinforcements should be made with a metal equal in thickness (never use a thicker plate as reinforcement) and yield strength to the original frame metal. Staggering the bolts and tapering the reinforcement as much as possible avoids stress concentrators and is recommended, or failure is very likely. Some manufacturers even recommend reinforcements that extend the length of the whole rail.

Regardless, reinforcements should never stop at or before a cross member or other section stiffener, as doing so leaves a SM gap, causing a stress riser. As illustrated in **FIGURE 30-24**, the reinforcement should go past the cross member; sometimes this requires shortening the cross member to accommodate the reinforcing plate. Recall that Figure 30-10 showed proper reinforcements.

Crack Repair

Most manufacturers' preferred procedure for any heat-treated frame that has cracked due to fatigue failure, like that illustrated in **FIGURE 30-25**, is replacement of the frame rails, although most do offer instructions on repairing a cracked or otherwise damaged frame rail by welding. Fatigue cracks are usually caused by chronic overload or a **section change** in the frame rail, which causes a weak point. Be sure to investigate the cause before releasing the repaired vehicle, or it will likely be back. Repairing frame cracks by welding is a common practice in the industry for medium-carbon-steel frames and even for heat-treated alloy steels used in most heavy-truck frames.

When repairing cracked frame rails, one of the following welding processes should be used:

- Shielded metal arc welding (SMAW)
- Gas metal arc welding (GMAW), also known as metal inert gas (MIG) welding
- Gas tungsten arc welding (GTAW), also known as tungsten inert gas (TIG)

For high-strength, low-alloy steel with tensile strengths of up to 80,000 psi (5515 MPa), weld the crack with the appropriate low-hydrogen filler wire or electrode according to the information in **TABLE 30-1**. Correct amperage and voltage recommendations are shown in **TABLE 30-2**.

The frame metal surrounding the crack should be preheated to a temperature of 500°F to 600°F (260°C to 315°C). The Tempilstick™ shown in **FIGURE 30-26** is a tool that melts at a specific range of temperature, and so helps to achieve the correct temperature. Preheating helps to prevent the metal surrounding the weld from becoming brittle.

Remember to follow the welding precautions previously mentioned.

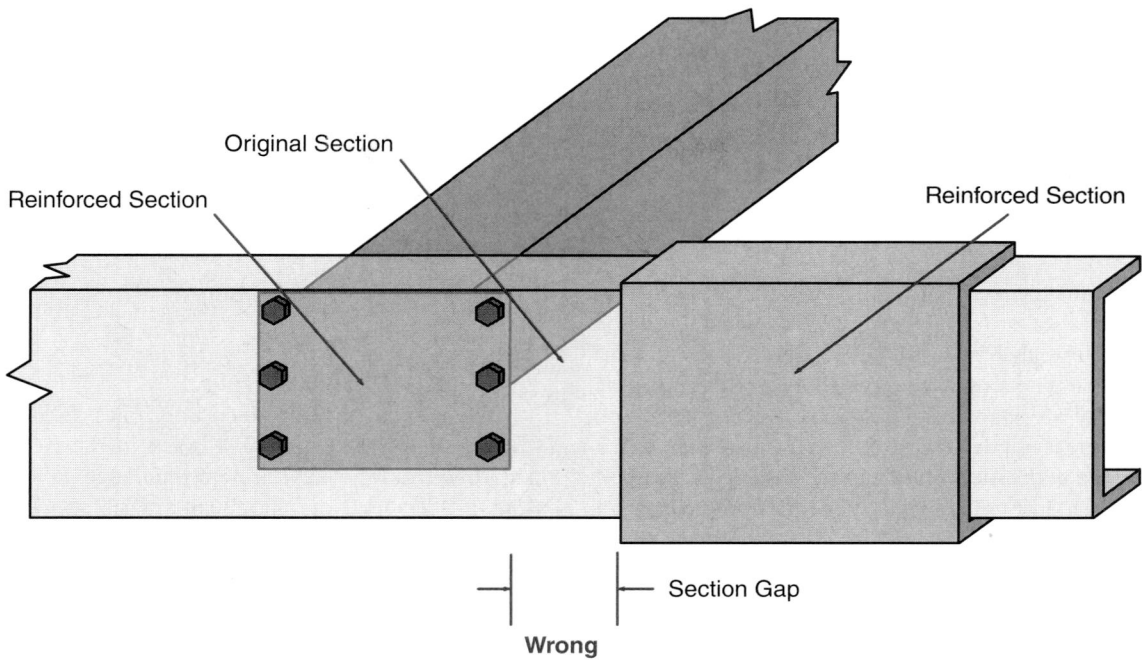

FIGURE 30-24 Reinforcements should extend past a cross member and be staggered.

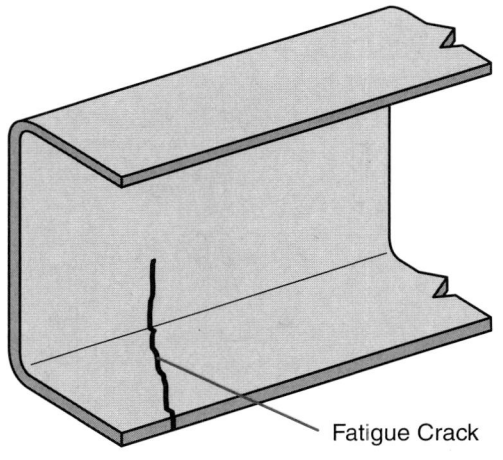

FIGURE 30-25 A fatigue crack.

TABLE 30-1 Recommended Electrodes and Wires

Material Strength (psi)	Recommended Electrode and Wire	
	SMAW	GMAW
50,000	E7018	E70S-3
60,000	–	E70S-1B
70,000	E8018	E80S-D2

FIGURE 30-26 A Tempilstick™.

TABLE 30-2 Amperage and Voltage Recommendations for Welding

SMAW Method (High-Strength, Low-Alloy [HSLA] Frames)				
Position	Electrode size in inches	Welding Current		Speed (In/Min)
		Amperes	Volts	
Flat	0.125	–	–	–
Horizontal and Vertical	0.125	110/140	20/14	24
GMAW Method (HSLA Frames)				
Position	Electrode size in inches	Welding Current		Speed (In/Min)
		Amperes	Volts	
Flat	0.035	–	–	350/400
Horizontal and Vertical	0.035	190/220	20/30	350/400

The first step in crack repair is to clean the area in and around the crack by removing all traces of rust, paint, grease, and oil. The goal is to ensure that the crack does not continue to spread after repair. Next, determine the type of crack to be repaired. Three types of frame cracks are:

- A web crack between two bolt holes or openings
- A flange crack
- A web crack that extends to or through the flange area

It is important to note that a cracked frame indicates an overload, a stress riser, or frame damage. The vehicle should be examined carefully to determine the cause of any crack failure to avoid the problem repeating itself; repairing a crack in a frame that is chronically overloaded can turn into a repetitive failure, if the original issue is not dealt with. After a frame failure, check to see if it cracked at the location of a newly installed accessory, or if the vehicle had just undergone a change in vocation, which may have caused overload. Also, check if there has been a serious repair, such as suspension, and investigate to see if these situations might have contributed to the failure. Remember that even a deep gouge in a frame rail can cause a stress riser, leading to a crack forming at the gouge or scratch.

▶ **TECHNICIAN TIP**

There is controversy over frame weld reinforcement. Unless the weld is performed perfectly and with the right filler material, a loss of strength is very likely to take place on a heat-treated frame. If you undertake to reinforce a frame, be sure to stagger reinforcements and install them properly so they do not cause a stress riser. Paying careful attention to the placement and installation of reinforcements lessens the chance of failure of the weld in most cases.

To repair a crack between bolt holes, follow the steps in **SKILL DRILL 30-3**. To repair a crack in the web or flange or extending from the web through the flange, follow the steps in **SKILL DRILL 30-4**. Note that the Skill Drill 30-4 includes all the steps as Skill Drill 30-3, with an added procedure for drilling a relief hole in the frame rail or web to stop the progression of the crack.

SKILL DRILL 30-3 Repairing a Crack in a Frame Between Bolt Holes

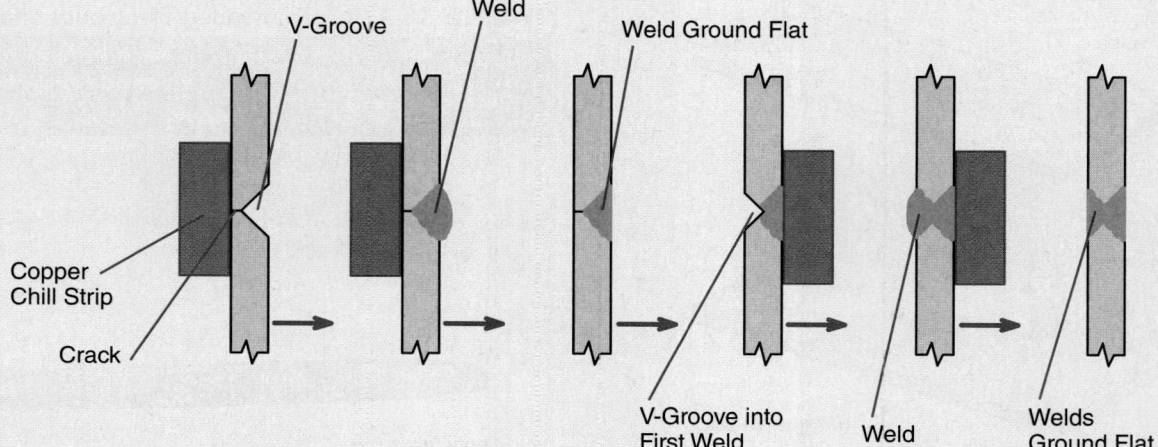

1. Clean the entire area around the crack of all rust, paint, oil, or grease.
2. Grind a 'v' groove into the frame rail to a depth 1/8" (3.175 mm) less than the rail metal thickness. Clamp a chill strip made of aluminum or copper to the backside of the rail from the groove.
3. Grind the finished weld flush with the frame rail. Leaving a weld "cap" protruding on either side of the rail produces a stress riser because of the frame thickness. As a result, its section modulus is increased at that point, so the weld cap must be ground flat. Grind the weld in the direction of the frame rail length to minimize stress risers at the weld.
4. Repeat step 1 through step 3 for the other side of the crack. Start by grinding the "v" groove deep enough to reach the first weld material.
5. Weld the groove with the appropriate filler wire and again grind the weld flush. When welding heat-treated frames with tensile strengths of 110,000 to 120,000 psi (758 to 827 MPa), use a low-hydrogen electrode with higher-than-average crack resistance, such as AWS-E-11018.
6. After welding to repair a frame, reinforce the rail with fishplate or channel to reestablish the frame strength. (Follow the guidelines outlined in the Frame Reinforcement section found earlier in the chapter.) Remember that staggering and tapering the frame reinforcement plates is essential. Otherwise, they create a stress riser and lead to failure, due to increased stiffness at the reinforcement.

SKILL DRILL 30-4 Repairing a Crack in the Web or Flange

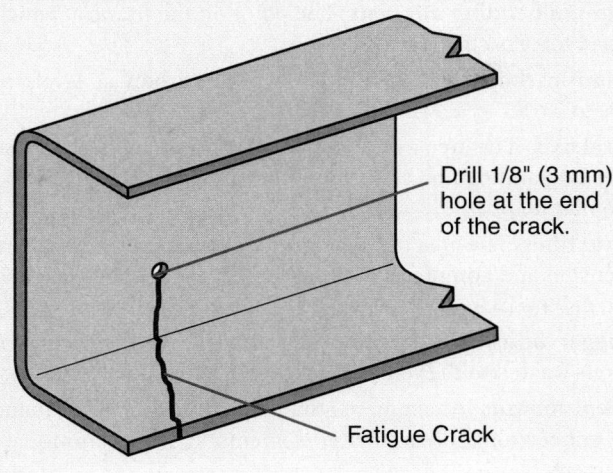

Drill 1/8" (3 mm) hole at the end of the crack.

Fatigue Crack

1. Follow the steps in Skill Drill 30-3 for repairing a crack in a frame between bolt holes.
2. After cleaning and grinding the first groove in the crack, determine the exact end of the crack and drill a small 1/8" (3.175 mm) hole. This stops the crack from proceeding past the weld point. Then continue the above-outlined repair procedure.
3. Crack repairs that extend to the frame flange should be reinforced with staggered C-channel or L-plate that reinforces the flange area, as well as the web of the frame rail.

Wrap-Up

Ready for Review

▶ Most medium- to heavy-duty vehicles use a ladder-type frame consisting of two long rails connected by a series of cross members that keep the rails in alignment.
▶ The frame supports all the vehicle's components. The body, vehicle driveline, and all the suspension equipment are attached to the frame.
▶ Frames must be strong enough to carry these components, plus the load that the vehicle is expected to carry. Frames must also be flexible enough to bend and twist in reaction to various forces, without deforming, as the vehicle moves along the road.
▶ The most common type of frame rail is C-channel, but I-beam (usually for heavier applications) and box channel can also be used.
▶ Frame rails can be reinforced with a L-plate, fishplate, or even another C-channel fitted inside the rail, when required.
▶ When the frame is loaded, one flange is subject to compression-loading, trying to compress the flange together, and the other flange is subject to tension-loading, trying to pull the flange apart.
▶ All frame attachments should be made as close as possible to the neutral fiber.
▶ Frame strength is calculated using three engineering terms: section modulus, yield strength, and resist bending moment (RBM). RBM is actual strength of the frame and is calculated from the frame's section modulus and its yield strength.
▶ Frames can be made from mild steel that has yield strength of 50,000 psi (345 MPa) (usually light-duty vehicles); heat-treated steel that has a yield strength

of 110,000+ psi (758 MPa) (used for most heavy-duty vehicles); or aluminum alloy, which has a yield strength of 60,000 psi (414 MPa).
▶ Aluminum-alloy frames are lighter than steel and are usually I-beam shaped for increased strength.
▶ Frame cross members hold the rails in alignment and can be box channel, C-channel, I-beam, or hat-shaped. Cross members are often curved to allow passage of wiring, piping, and other vehicle components.
▶ Frame body attachments can be U-bolts, fishplates, or resilient mounts.
▶ U-bolts are the least recommended, but most common, method of frame body attachment. When U-bolts are used, the body can move longitudinally, unless outrigger mounts are also used to hold it in place.
▶ Resilient mounts are spring-loaded or have an elastic component, and are used when the body is not flexible. This allows the frame to flex independently of the vehicle body.
▶ The Commercial Vehicle Safety Alliance, a North American organization, establishes service criteria for commercial vehicles, including for vehicle frames. Any vehicle whose frame does not meet the criteria must be removed from service until repaired.
▶ Frame damage includes sag, bow, twist, diamond, and sideway. In addition, damage can be in the form of corrosion from road salt, or from galvanic cells created by dissimilar metals in contact.
▶ Manufacturers insist that frame straightening be done cold, but it is common practice in the field to use heat, even though heat can severely reduce the yield strength of a frame rail.

▶ Frame realignment is normally performed with the use of sophisticated computer-alignment machines. It can also be performed manually by taking precise measurements of the frame and projecting them onto a flat floor.

▶ Manufacturers forbid welding on heat-treated frames because the yield strength can be reduced from 110,000 to 36,000 psi (758 to 248 MPa) by excessive heat.

▶ Frame splicing is a common practice to increase frame rail length to install longer bodies or extra equipment. Frame splicing is not endorsed by manufacturers.

▶ Galvanic corrosion can occur when two dissimilar metals are in contact and an electrolyte is introduced between them. This creates a situation where one metal becomes the anode and the other becomes the cathode of the resulting galvanic cell. This situation can quickly lead to serious corrosion of the metals involved.

Key Terms

aluminum alloy Aluminum mixed with other metals to increase its strength.

bow A type of frame damage characterized by the upward bending of the frame rails that can be caused by uneven loading of the frame. The opposite of sag.

C-channel C-shaped steel beam that is the most common frame rail in heavy trucks.

compression A force that pushes down on the top flange of a frame rail between two support points, which tends to squeeze the flange of the frame rail together.

cross members Cross beams that join the two frame rails together to form a ladder-type frame.

diamond A type of frame damage characterized by one frame rail moving forward or backward in relation to the other.

fishplate Flat plate used to re-enforce the frame rail, or a plate bolted to the frame rail web to attach components to the frame.

frame rail web The upright section of the frame rail. Also called *web*.

full-box rail A box-shaped frame rail.

galvanic corrosion Corrosion of the material caused by the electrolytic effect that can occur when two dissimilar metals are in contact.

heat-treated alloy steel Highly engineered steel with a yield strength of at least 110,000 psi (758 MPa).

high-carbon steel Steel alloyed with carbon at levels of 0.9% to 2.5%.

Huck® fastener A riveted connection with ridges instead of threads and with the nut swaged onto the bolt, preventing the collar from being tightened after the fastener is installed.

I-beam I-shaped beam used for frame rails on heavier vehicles; can be aluminum or steel.

L-plate L-shaped beams that can be bolted to the outside of the C-channel to increase the rails' RBM.

ladder-type frame A frame consisting of two rails joined together by a series of cross members.

maximum bending moment The point on the frame at which the load force is concentrated.

medium-carbon steel Steel alloyed with carbon at levels of 0.25% to 0.6%.

neutral axis The area in the middle of a frame rail web where the tension and compression forces cancel each other out. Also called *neutral fiber*.

neutral fiber The area in the middle of a frame rail web where the tension and compression forces cancel each other out. Also called *neutral axis*.

outrigger brackets A frame-body attachment consisting of brackets welded to the vehicle and then bolted to the frame web.

resilient mounts Attachments that are spring-loaded or made with rubber or polyurethane elements that accommodate movement.

resist bending moment (RBM) The frame strength calculated using the section modulus of the frame rail and its yield strength.

sag A type of frame damage characterized by the downward bending of the frame rail between two support points. The opposite of *bow*.

section change A point where a component becomes thicker or thinner or rigid, forming a weak point where breakage can begin.

section modulus An engineering calculation used to determine the strength of a frame rail based only on its shape, height, width, and thickness.

sidesway A type of frame damage characterized by a sideways bending or deformation of the frame.

stress concentration Anything that reduces or changes the integrity or strength of the material. Also called *stress riser*.

stress riser Anything that reduces or changes the integrity or strength of the material. Also called *stress concentration*.

swaged When two metal components are fitted together by deforming the metal of one to fit the other precisely.

tensile strength The amount of force required before a material deforms or breaks.

tension A force that tries to pull apart the bottom flange of a frame rail supported between two points.

twist A type of frame damage that occurs when one rail bends up and the other rail bends down.

U-bolt A frame-body attachment that goes over a sub-frame attached to the vehicle body and down both sides of the frame rail before being clamped at the bottom flange of the rail.

web The upright portion of the frame rail. Also called *frame rail web*.

yield strength An engineering term used to describe the amount of force required to permanently deform a material. Yield strength occurs at the material's elastic limit—the maximum force a material can withstand and still return to its original configuration.

Review Questions

1. A frame's load-carrying ability can be determined by multiplying which of the following?
   a. The section modulus by the material yield strength
   b. The section modulus by the RBM
   c. The yield strength by the RBM
   d. None of the choices are correct

2. Which of the following is a desirable characteristic of a frame?
   a. It should be rigid to prevent fatigue failure.
   b. It should be able to flex and twist.
   c. It should have holes drilled in the flanges for easy attachment of accessories.
   d. It should have just enough strength to support the vehicle body and accessories.

3. Resist bending moment, or RBM, on truck frames refers to which of the following?
   a. The actual strength of the frame
   b. The maximum load a vehicle can carry
   c. The minimum load the vehicle is designed to carry
   d. The thickness of the frame

4. Which of the following most correctly describes section modulus when discussing truck frames?
   a. An engineering formula based on the material shape and thickness
   b. An engineering formula based on the material length and thickness
   c. An engineering formula based on the material type and thickness
   d. An engineering formula based on the material type and shape

5. Most truck frames are constructed from which of the following?
   a. Box channel
   b. Tubular channel
   c. C-channel
   d. K-channel

6. Before welding a crack on a steel frame, what must be done?
   a. Drill out the ends of the crack with a 1/8" drill bit to stop its progression
   b. Seal the crack with epoxy
   c. Spread the crack with a chisel
   d. Monitor the crack through several days of vehicle operation to make sure it has finished cracking

7. To give a gradual increase in section modulus, frame reinforcement plates should be:
   a. cut on a 45-degree angle.
   b. cut square.
   c. circular.
   d. rectangular.

8. When drilling holes into a frame, where is the best place to drill?
   a. As close as possible to the top flange
   b. As close as possible to the bottom flange
   c. In the flanges
   d. As close as possible to the neutral fiber

9. When drilling holes in a frame, it is best to do which of the following?
   a. Stagger the holes, so no holes are in a vertical line
   b. Put only four holes in any vertical line
   c. Make sure the holes are as close together as possible
   d. Never stagger the holes, as it weakens more than one section of the frame

10. What precaution must you take when bolting a steel accessory to an aluminum frame?
   a. Use Tectyl-400C™ or a similar compound to protect against electrolytic corrosion
   b. No precautions are required
   c. Use copper washers to protect against electrolytic corrosion
   d. Use high-strength aluminum bolts

ASE Technician A/Technician B Style Questions

1. Technician A says that actual frame rail strength can be calculated by multiplying the section modulus by the yield strength. Technician B says that to determine actual rail strength, the RBM is multiplied by the section modulus. Who is correct?
   a. Technician A
   b. Technician B
   c. Both Technician A and Technician B
   d. Neither Technician A nor Technician B

2. Technician A says that most frame fatigue cracks are caused by overloading of the frame. Technician B says that cracks often occur at a section change, where the frame becomes less flexible. Who is correct?
   a. Technician A
   b. Technician B
   c. Both Technician A and Technician B
   d. Neither Technician A nor Technician B

3. Technician A says that welding heat-treated frames changes the frame strength and is not sanctioned by the manufacturer. Technician B says that damaged heat-treated frame rails should be replaced, not repaired. Who is correct?
   a. Technician A
   b. Technician B
   c. Both Technician A and Technician B
   d. Neither Technician A nor Technician B

4. Technician A says that the frame rail top flange is under compression when a load is placed on it. Technician B says that the frame rails bottom flange is under tension where the suspension mounts to the frame. Who is correct?
   a. Technician A
   b. Technician B
   c. Both Technician A and Technician B
   d. Neither Technician A nor Technician B

5. Technician A says that the neutral fiber refers to the center of the frame web. Technician B says the neutral fiber is where most of a frame rail stress is concentrated. Who is correct?
   a. Technician A
   b. Technician B

c. Both Technician A and Technician B
d. Neither Technician A nor Technician B

6. Technician A says I-channel frames are the most common configuration for heavy vehicles. Technician B says connecting cross-members tie the rails together both to maintain their alignment and to stop them from twisting under the heavy loads the rails must carry. Who is correct?
   a. Technician A
   b. Technician B
   c. Both Technician A and Technician B
   d. Neither Technician A nor Technician B

7. Technician A says Huck® fasteners are a type of nuts and bolts. Technician B says Huck® fasteners are one of the most secure attaching systems available and should last for the life of the vehicle. Who is correct?
   a. Technician A
   b. Technician B
   c. Both Technician A and Technician B
   d. Neither Technician A nor Technician B

8. Technician A says U-bolts are the most secure mounting system for attaching a truck body to a frame. Technician B says U-bolts and their ease of installation makes them popular with builders of truck bodies. Who is correct?
   a. Technician A
   b. Technician B
   c. Both Technician A and Technician B
   d. Neither Technician A nor Technician B

9. Technician A says outrigger mounting is the recommended method of attaching flexible bodies to ladder-type frames. Technician B says outrigger brackets are welded to the vehicle body and to the frame web. Who is correct?
   a. Technician A
   b. Technician B
   c. Both Technician A and Technician B
   d. Neither Technician A nor Technician B

10. Technician A says fishplates are flat plates used to reinforce the frame rail. Technician B says a fishplate mount does not require holes to be drilled in the frame web and the body sub-frame. Who is correct?
    a. Technician A
    b. Technician B
    c. Both Technician A and Technician B
    d. Neither Technician A nor Technician B

CHAPTER 31

Suspension Systems

Learning Objectives

After reading this chapter, you will be able to:

- **LO 31-1** Explain the fundamentals of heavy-duty vehicle suspensions.
- **LO 31-2** Describe heavy-duty vehicle suspension system components.

- **LO 31-3** Describe leaf-spring suspension systems.
- **LO 31-4** Describe equalizing beam suspension systems.
- **LO 31-5** Describe air springs and air spring suspension systems.
- **LO 31-6** Explain electronically controlled air spring suspensions.
- **LO 31-7** Describe suspension system inspection and explain service procedures.

You Are the Technician

A highway tractor is brought to your shop. The driver complains that one of the rear airbags has torn. He tells you that this is the second airbag he has had to replace since the last time the vehicle was in for a major service. You confirm the complaint—it is definitely a torn airbag. When you inspect the vehicle, everything else looks fine. The shock absorbers are new, and the torque and track rods are in good shape. Explain why you might use each of the following procedures to diagnose the problem.

1. Why might you check the airbags for the proper application?
2. Why might you check that nothing is rubbing against the air spring?
3. Why might you check the shocks for proper application?
4. Why might you check all the rear suspension components for looseness?
5. Would it make sense to talk to the airbag supplier to see if there is a problem with these particular airbags? Why or why not?

Introduction

History has romanticized the horse-drawn chariots of ancient Rome with images of the hero speeding to victory in his chariot drawn by four thoroughbred horses, as shown in **FIGURE 31-1**. The reality, however, is a much different story. Roman chariots had rudimentary suspension systems, and as their speed increased, every bump from the uneven road surface was transmitted to the vehicle and its driver. In fact, the chariot races were attended not so much to see the victor, but rather to view the spectacle of drivers being thrown from their speeding vehicles (sometimes to their death) as they lost control of the bumping, rattling chariot.

Since those times, various inventors have tried to tackle the problem of a suspension system. The earliest form of suspension was a box-shaped carriage supported on a wheeled cart by means of chains attached at each corner. This hanging box arrangement swings back and forth freely as bumps are encountered, meaning that the occupants had better not be prone to motion sickness. Next was the stagecoach, which mounted the "coach" on heavy leather straps, called through braces, that helped to insulate the passengers from road shocks. The steel leaf spring appeared in the 17th century and the leather supporting straps were then fixed to springs, instead of directly to the undercarriage, which further insulated the passengers and cargo from the road. Since those days, much advancement has been made in suspension systems, allowing vehicles to travel at greater speeds, while still protecting the vehicle, the load, and the passengers.

Fundamentals of Suspension Systems

LO 31-1 Explain the fundamentals of heavy-duty vehicle suspensions.

Suspension systems must tolerate a huge number of forces when a vehicle is being driven down the road. Think about all a vehicle's weight being supported by the suspension system, and then subjecting the parts in that system to the normal cornering,

FIGURE 31-1 Most chariots had rudimentary suspension systems, so they were very unstable.
Image © Dorling Kindersley/Getty Images.

accelerating, and braking forces. On top of that, add in the abnormal forces encountered when traversing unusual hazards, such as potholes or speed bumps. **Elasticity** is a required characteristic of a suspension system. An object displays elasticity if, after applying a sufficient force to the object to deform its shape, it then returns to its original shape when the force is removed. Elasticity is the property of a material, in this instance a spring, which causes it to be restored to its original shape after distortion. A material is said to be more elastic if it restores itself more precisely to its original configuration. The **elastic limit** of a material is the amount of force required to permanently deform the material. Vehicle suspension systems generally use the elastic properties of special metals, or air springs, to provide the springing medium that a suspension system requires.

Springs are located between the frame/chassis and the axle assemblies and are shaped to suit specific applications. For instance, leaf springs are formed into an arc and are designed specifically to absorb the applied force (pressure of the load) by flattening out when under load and then returning to their original shape when a load is removed.

Functions of a Suspension System

A vehicle's suspension must perform several important functions. The first is the spring must be capable of supporting weight of the vehicle and cargo. A suspension must connect the axles securely to the vehicle frame. The vehicle's suspension must control the axle torque reaction when accelerating and decelerating, and maintain the vehicle's lateral (side to side) stability. A suspension system must also ensure that the vehicle's tires always maintain contact with the road, or the vehicle loses traction and becomes unstable. Additionally, the suspension must be able to perform all of those functions satisfactorily, whether the vehicle is empty or fully loaded.

Support the Sprung Weight

The suspension system must support the sprung weight of the vehicle and cargo while stopped or moving. The **sprung weight** is the weight of the vehicle components supported by the springs. The sprung weight includes basically everything on the vehicle, except the axles and wheel ends. The suspension must support the sprung weight, regardless of the forces acting on it, all the while insulating the vehicle body, driver, passengers, and cargo from excessive road shocks. The suspension must absorb the shocks and vibrations from uneven road surfaces to ensure driver comfort and to protect the vehicle load from damage. Excessive vibration and shocks transmitted to the vehicle frame and body leads to fatigue failures of these components.

Connect the Axles to the Frame

Another basic function of the suspension system is to securely connect the axles to the frame of the vehicle. The suspension must maintain the axle spacing and alignment as the axles articulate over uneven road surfaces and bumps. Maintaining the alignment and spacing of the axles adds to vehicle stability. Axles that do not retain their alignment while articulating cause the vehicle to have very poor handling capabilities and excessive tire wear, and are very hard for a driver to control.

Control Axle Torque

The suspension must control axle torque or wind-up caused by acceleration and braking forces. As the vehicle accelerates, the rear axles tend to wind up with the front of the axle rising with the torque load. Under braking effort, the axles tend to wind-down, with the front of the axle lowering. These winding torque forces must be transferred to the vehicle frame by the suspension to avoid fatigue failures of components and excessive changes in driveline angularity.

Maintain Lateral Stability

The suspension system must maintain a vehicle's **lateral stability**, which is the vehicle's ability to be stable from side to side. As a vehicle enters a turn, centrifugal force pushes the vehicle toward the outer circumference of the turn. The springs must be strong enough that this force does not cause the vehicle to topple over.

Springs determine if the suspension is stiff or soft and, therefore, how the vehicle responds. Stiffer suspensions improve lateral stability at the expense of ride comfort. Softer suspensions offer a more comfortable ride but, in some instances, such as higher road speed cornering, a soft suspension can increase the possibility of rollover.

Ensure Contact with the Road

The suspension must ensure the vehicle's tires stay in contact with the road surface. The **contact patch** between the vehicle tires and the road is relatively small—approximately 1 square foot (125 cm²) or less for most truck tires, as shown in **FIGURE 31-2**.

These contact patches provide the traction (frictional contact) through which all the acceleration, braking, and cornering forces are transferred to the road surface. If the tires lose this frictional contact with the road, the vehicle loses control. Therefore, maintaining contact is essential. As the wheels move upward and downward over bumps, they tend to continue moving due to inertia. This rhythmic up and down motion caused by road shock is called **oscillation**. If a suspension system is not able to absorb

these forces and stop the oscillation quickly, the wheels start to hop uncontrollably. **Wheel hop** caused by excessive suspension oscillation can lead to loss of control and extreme tire wear.

Basic Suspension Terms

Knowing a few common terms associated with suspension systems provides a background for the discussion of suspension systems that follows.

Sprung Weight and Unsprung Weight

As mentioned earlier in the chapter, sprung weight is any portion of the vehicle that is supported by the suspension springs. This usually includes the chassis frame and the vehicle body. Sprung weight greatly affects the vehicle-handling characteristics, especially during hard acceleration, braking, and cornering. **Unsprung weight** is the portion of the vehicle that is not supported by the suspension system springs. Unsprung weight includes the drive and steer axles, wheels, tires, brakes, and parts of the suspension system itself. **FIGURE 31-3** illustrates the difference between sprung weight and unsprung weight.

> ▶ **TECHNICIAN TIP**
>
> An ideal vehicle suspension is soft enough for a comfortable ride and load protection, and firm enough for vehicle stability. Air suspension systems come close to the perfect balance of soft and firm suspension, but they are expensive and don't always respond quickly enough to the inertial shifting of the load on turns, leading to some instability. Leaf-spring suspension systems are most economical, and when firm enough, add stability to avoid rollover. In normal driving situations, however, they are stiff and give a rough ride. So, the end result is often a compromise based on cost, stability, and comfort.

The heavier the unsprung mass, the harder the vehicle is to control. Consider which is easier to control: a beach ball versus a bowling ball. When large and heavy wheel assemblies encounter a bump or pothole, they experience a larger reaction force. In some cases, that reaction force is large enough to make the tire lose contact with the road surface. If the tires are not in contact with the road, they have lost all traction and cannot control the vehicle's direction of travel, which creates a potentially dangerous situation.

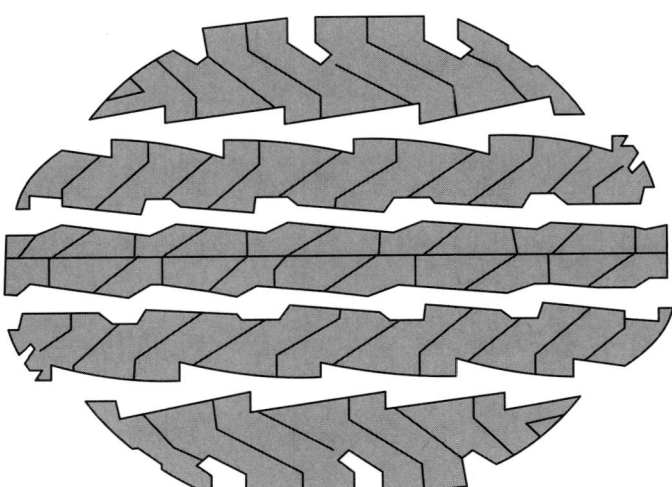

FIGURE 31-2 The road contact patch for a tire is relatively small.

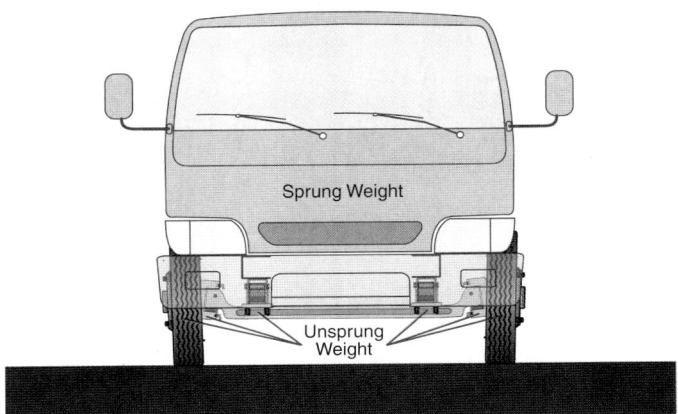

FIGURE 31-3 Unsprung weight versus sprung weight.

Lower unsprung weights allow the tires to follow the road contour more easily without bouncing. Heavier unsprung weights can lead to severe road shocks being sent through the suspension system. Manufacturers try to keep unsprung weight to a minimum by specifying lighter-weight aluminum wheels and lighter axle components, but the axles and the brakes must also be strong enough to support and stop the vehicle and its load. Unsprung weight is always a tradeoff between comfort and practicality.

Overslung and Underslung

Overslung suspension systems have the spring attached in position above the axles. **Underslung** have the springs attached to the underside of the axles.

Jounce

Jounce is the upward motion of the wheel, axle, and suspension system when the vehicle encounters a bump in the road. Most suspension systems have jounce bumpers or blocks that prevent the suspension from being compressed so much that the axles contact the frame of the vehicle. When a jounce occurs, the spring absorbs the energy as it flexes and straightens out. That energy is then given back as the spring rebounds, or returns, to its normal shape.

Rebound

Rebound is the downward movement of the wheels and axles as the spring recovers from compression caused by road bumps or hitting a pothole or depression in the road. As such, rebound is the spring's reaction to a jounce. Together, jounce and rebound cause the suspension system to oscillate until the energy absorbed by the spring has been dissipated, as illustrated in **FIGURE 31-4**. It is the same as what happens when a person jumps on a trampoline. The person continues to bounce up and down until the energy of the jump is gone.

One of the major functions of a suspension system is to minimize suspension oscillation. That is achieved either through **self-dampening** friction or with the use of a **shock absorber**, which, in this instance, is a hydraulic piston and cylinder arrangement designed for that exact purpose. Both methods absorb the springs' oscillation by converting the energy from jounce and rebound to heat. The heat conversion occurs in one of two ways. **Interleaf friction**, caused by the individual leaves in a multi-leaf spring pack rubbing together, can dissipate unwanted oscillation; this is called self-dampening. (Multi-leaf spring packs are discussed in greater detail in the section on Springs.)

Kinetic energy generated by the shock absorber action is converted into another form of energy (typically heat) by the compression and displacement of hydraulic fluid in shock absorbers. Some suspensions use a combination of both heat conversion methods.

If a suspension fails to absorb the energy promptly, the spring oscillations may cause the wheels to hop off the ground due to the uncontrolled bouncing. This makes it very hard to control the vehicle.

Spring Rate and Load Range

Spring rate refers to the movement of the spring when it is loaded. A high spring rate corresponds to a stiffer suspension with higher lateral stability, and a low spring rate to a more comfortable ride. The amount of deflection is linear in constant-rate springs. So, if a load of 440 lb (200 kg) causes the spring to deflect 1" (2.54 cm), then a load of 880 lb (400 kg) deflects the spring 2" (5.08 cm). **FIGURE 31-5** illustrates this deflection.

A spring with a high spring rate deflects less when loaded than a spring with a low spring rate. The load range of a spring refers to the load the spring can carry. Adding leaves to a spring pack, or thickening the leaves or the coils, increases the load range and the spring rate. A spring with a low spring rate leads to a softer ride, but also decreases the vehicle's load-carrying capacity and lateral stability.

As mentioned in the section, Maintain Lateral Stability, when a vehicle starts to turn, centrifugal forces push the load toward the outside of the turning circle. That puts more load on the outside spring. In vehicles with a low spring rate (softer ride), the vehicle sags on the outside (lateral instability),

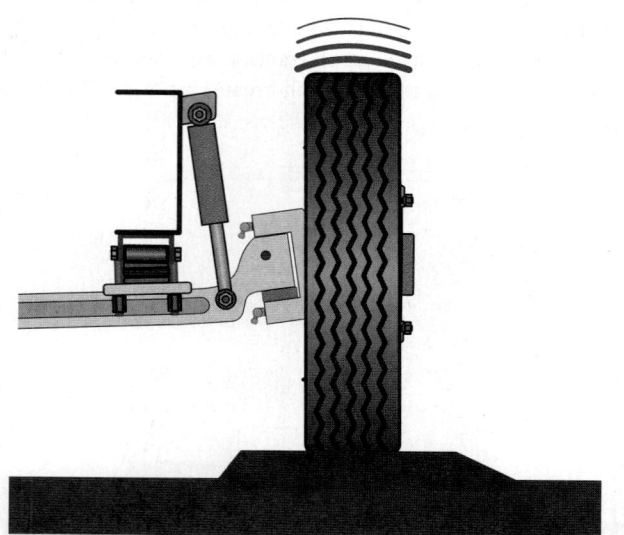

FIGURE 31-4 A suspension system must absorb and stop spring oscillation to maintain vehicle control.

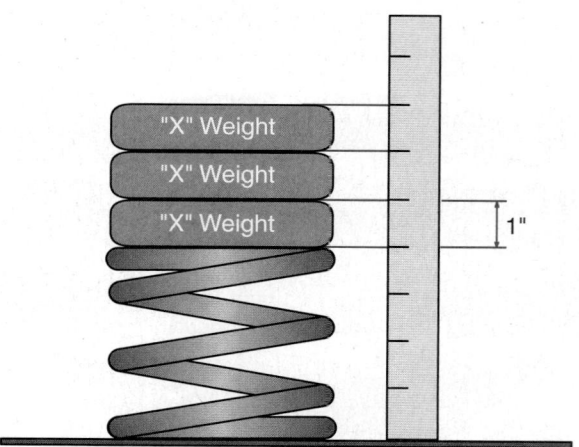

FIGURE 31-5 Spring rate equals "X" weight versus deflection.

increasing the possibility of a rollover. By contrast, a high spring rate suspension adds greatly to load capacity and lateral stability in turns, but makes for a stiffer, bumpier ride. Suspensions are designed as a compromise to allow the best ride possible, and with the necessary load capacity and stability for the vehicle's expected vocation.

Parallelogram

Parallelogram is a term used quite often in suspension systems. A parallelogram is a four-sided figure in which each of the two opposite sides is parallel with each other. In suspensions, parallelograms are used to keep the wheels and axles at the proper angle or pitch during jounce and rebound.

Most light-duty, and some heavy-duty vehicles, use parallelogram front suspension systems that keep the front wheels at the correct camber angle as the vehicle encounters bumps in the road. The most common type of front suspension used for this purpose is the double wishbone system. In the double wishbone system, two A-frame control arms attach to the frame at two points each, and the apex of the A-frames attach to the top and bottom of the spindle. As the wheel goes over a bump, the wheel moves up. In response, the upper and lower control arms (the A-frames) both pivot the same amount, moving closer to the frame but essentially maintaining the camber angle of the wheel. (There are slight changes to the steer angle due to tie rod position, king pin inclination, and so forth.)

In heavy trucks, the term parallelogram is more associated with the rear suspension and uses a combination of torque rods and track rods or **trailing arms** so that, as the rear wheels encounter a bump, the suspension parallelogram keeps the rear axle housing at a fixed pitch angle. **FIGURE 31-6** shows a suspension parallelogram.

All rear-wheel-drive vehicle suspensions tend to squat during the forces of acceleration, as the pinion gear physically tries to climb up the crown or ring gear in the drive axle. The parallelogram suspension design limits the axle wind-up and the corresponding frame movement during the forces of acceleration. Limiting wind-up ensures that the drive pinion U-joint angles remain within the design specifications. This, in turn, reduces the chance of driveline vibrations caused by the suspension.

The situation changes during braking. The vehicle momentum tends to cause the rear of the vehicle to rise and the axle to wind in the opposite direction. The force on the axle builds

to a point where the springs are loaded until they eventually rebound. That rebound causes the tires to lose traction with the road, leading to a condition known as wheel hop. Wheel hop is especially problematic on leaf-spring suspensions, which are explained in greater detail in the Leaf Springs Systems section of this chapter. Wheel hop can reduce vehicle directional stability and braking effort.

Careful design and positioning of the torque and track rods can greatly reduce wheel hop. Anti-squat and anti-wheel hop ideals are usually at odds with optimum vehicle ride characteristics. Parallelogram rear suspension systems attempt to carefully balance spring rate, anti-squat, and anti-wheel hop characteristics to optimize vehicle handling and control, while providing a good ride and load protection.

Components of a Suspension System

LO 31-2 Describe heavy-duty vehicle suspension system components.

There are several primary components of a suspension system. Components include springs, torque rods, axle stops (or jounce blocks), and shock absorbers.

Springs

The spring is the suspension's main flexible component. Basic types are leaf springs, coil springs, rubber springs, air springs, and torsion bars. A **leaf spring** consists of a semi-elliptically curved spring steel plate clamped to an axle at its middle and attached to the vehicle sprung weight components at both ends so that it supports the body of the vehicle. When more than one steel plate or leaf is stacked together and used for a spring, it is called a **multi-leaf spring** or a **spring pack**. **Coil springs** are metal rods or bars that are twisted into a coil, coil springs can be specifically designed for a particular application. **Rubber springs** are high-density rubber blocks that act as the elastic component of a suspension and come in many different shapes and sizes to suit the application. **Air springs** are tough rubber bags filled with air and come in many designs for different applications. Air springs are sometimes used in concert with leaf springs for certain applications. **Torsion bars** are strong spring steel bars attached to the suspension and usually anchored on the vehicle frame. Torsion bars twist in response to the movement of the wheels and axles to absorb their vertical movement.

Light-duty commercial vehicles usually use heavy coil springs or torsion bars at the front and leaf springs at the rear. Heavy-duty commercial vehicles predominately use leaf springs, rubber springs, or air suspension. Some Original Equipment Manufacturers (OEM) use the torsion bar suspension in preference to the leaf-spring configuration. We discuss each type of spring in more detail later in this chapter.

Torque Rods

Torque rods are used on most suspension systems to keep the axles in alignment with each other and with the frame. They also transfer axle acceleration and braking forces to the frame.

FIGURE 31-6 A suspension parallelogram.

FIGURE 31-7 Adjustable torque rod.

FIGURE 31-8 Rubber jounce block or axle stop.

Torque rods can be mounted longitudinally to control alignment, or transversely to control centrifugal forces during turns. When mounted transversely, torque rods are called **track rods**. Some systems have torque rods mounted diagonally to control both.

Torque rods are usually adjustable. **FIGURE 31-7** shows an adjustable two-piece threaded torque rod. Torque rods can also be adjusted by placing shims at the mounting locations or by turning eccentric washers at the mounting pins.

Torque rods are mounted between the frame and the axles with rubber bushings. The rubber allows some movement while absorbing shock. The resilience of the rubber brings the axles back to alignment very quickly. This movement also allows tandem, or tridem, axles to follow a more natural route during turns. As a tandem-axle vehicle enters a turn, the cornering forces tend to push the front axle of the tandem to the outside of the turn. At the same time, the cornering forces push the rear axle toward the inside of the turn. The rubber bushings in a suspension system can allow up to 3" (7.5 cm) of lateral movement, so each axle follows a more natural turn. Once the vehicle returns to straight-ahead driving, the rubber bushings return the axles to alignment.

Axle Stops or Jounce Blocks

All suspensions limit axle movement with a rubber or solid stop mounted between the frame and the axle, as shown in **FIGURE 31-8**, or between the frame and the springs. This stop is called an **axle stop**. (Axle stops are also known as **jounce blocks**.) If the suspension is allowed to articulate with no limit, the axles bang into the frame when severe bumps are encountered. **Articulation** is the movement of the suspension due to road bumps and terrain. The axle articulation must be stopped before contact with the frame or it could lead to failure of the frame itself. Air-spring suspensions sometimes have the stops inside the air springs and are not visible from the outside.

Shock Absorbers

Some multi-leaf suspension systems rely on self-dampening caused by strong interleaf friction to dissipate the spring oscillation energy. Although these springs are quite effective at dampening oscillations, the interleaf friction leads to a very stiff and bumpy ride, particularly when a vehicle is partly or lightly loaded. In the past, heavy-duty trucks relied on this self-dampening

FIGURE 31-9 Hydraulic shock absorber.

more frequently, but today, more manufacturers are using leaf springs, with little or no interleaf friction, to provide a softer ride. Leaf springs and multi-leaf spring packs are discussed in greater detail in the section on Leaf-Spring Systems.

Hydraulic Shock Absorbers

Leaf springs with little or no interleaf friction must use hydraulic shock absorbers such as those shown in **FIGURE 31-9**.

Hydraulic shock absorbers absorb the spring oscillation that is not controlled by self-dampening to stop the wheels from bouncing off the ground. Air-spring suspensions offer absolutely no self-dampening effect and must use shock absorbers or other dampers to stop spring oscillation. Otherwise, the wheels bounce uncontrollably.

Most hydraulic shock absorbers are designed with an inner and outer tube. The outer tube is also known as the reserve tube or reservoir, and it holds a supply of hydraulic fluid. The inner tube has a piston and a base valve installed. The inner tube is full of fluid above and beneath the piston.

Shocks are dual acting. That means they absorb energy by converting it to heat on both the compression and the rebound stroke. The piston is designed with a series of orifices that allow fluid to pass through the piston at a specific rate. All shock absorbers today are velocity sensitive. In other words, the piston orifices are controlled by flexible discs. The faster the shock compresses or extends, the more the piston restricts fluid flow. That restriction makes the shock stiffer when the compression or extension of the shock is faster.

▶ TECHNICIAN TIP

The double-acting shock absorber dampens spring oscillation by forcing fluid through small orifices in the piston valve. The energy is transformed into heat from the resulting fluid friction, and then the heat dissipates into the atmosphere. A quick way to tell if shocks are working is to feel them to see if they are warm after the vehicle has been driven for a while over rough roads. A shock absorber on the same axle that feels noticeably colder than the other is probably defective.

SAFETY TIP

Hard-working shocks can reach 350° F (177° C) and can cause burns. To be safe, use an infrared temperature reader when measuring the temperature of shocks—not your hands.

The piston is connected to the push rod, which in turn is connected to the upper mounting eye of the shock absorber. The upper mounting eye has a rubber bushing that is bolted to the vehicle frame. The lower mounting eye of the shock is welded to the base of the outer tube. The lower mounting eye also has a rubber bushing, and it is bolted to the vehicle axle. The base valve at the bottom of the inner tube has a specifically sized orifice that allows fluid to flow into and out of the reserve tube, as necessary, to keep the area beneath the piston full of fluid.

When a jounce (bump) is encountered by the wheel, the axle moves upward. That motion causes the shock to compress. During this compression, the hydraulic fluid is forced through the piston orifices from the area beneath the piston to the area above. Because the diameter of the piston rod takes up space, not all the fluid can be forced through the piston orifices. Some of the fluid flows through the base valve into the reserve tube or reservoir, as illustrated in **FIGURE 31-10**.

The turbulent flow resulting from the fluid being forced through the orifices absorbs the energy of the jounce and transforms it into heat in the fluid. This heat is dissipated through the walls of the shock absorber out to the atmosphere.

On rebound, the opposite happens. The shock extends, and the piston is pulled upward, forcing the fluid above the piston to flow through the orifices to the area beneath the piston.

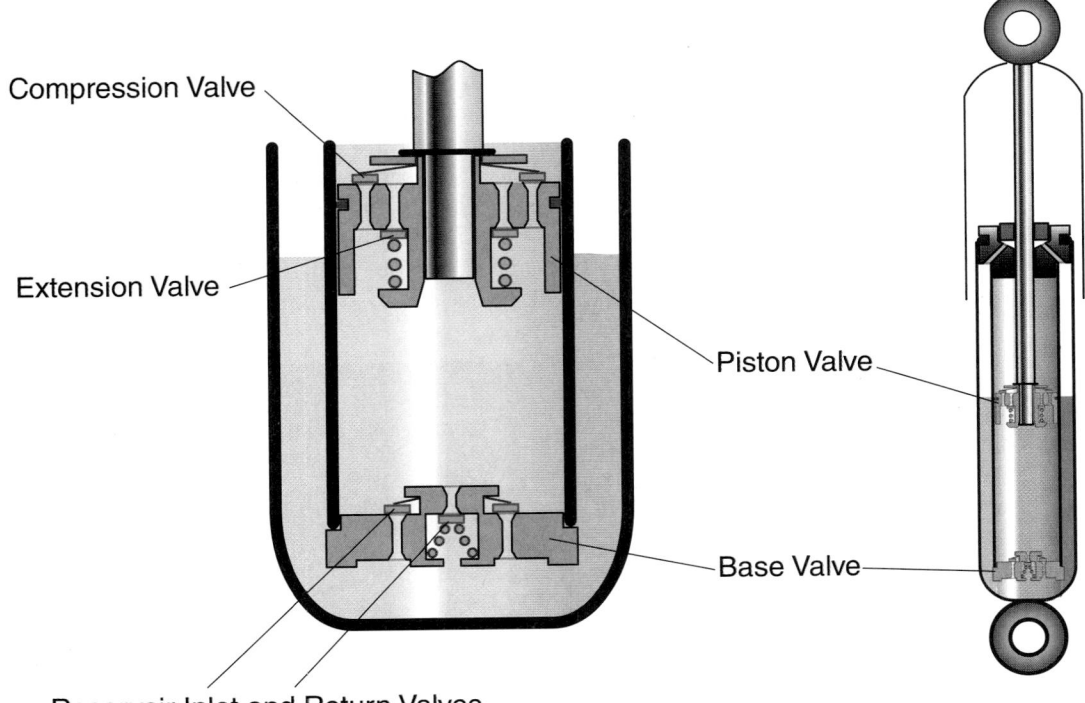

FIGURE 31-10 Shock absorber valves.

That reverse flow again absorbs the energy of the spring rebound, turning it into heat. The piston rod is taking up space in the area above the piston, so, as the piston rises, the fluid above the piston is insufficient to fill the area below the piston. Fluid is then drawn through the base valve to compensate.

Due to hysteresis, the rebound force of the unsprung weight is less than the jounce force. **Hysteresis** occurs when something is deflected, but does not rebound with the same force, usually due to the internal friction inherent in the material as it deflects. Many parts of the vehicle suspension system display hysteresis—the tires, rubber mounting bushings, and even the springs themselves.

Although it is dual acting, the piston valve of the shock absorber is usually biased. That means it is harder to draw the fluid back through the valve on rebound than it is to push the fluid through the valve when a jounce is encountered. Biasing the valve this way allows the shock absorber to compress more easily and not transmit a bump through the shock absorber to the frame. The suspension can then do the job of absorbing the impact of a bump in the road.

Bias is also necessary on the extension stroke. On the extension stroke, the shock is trying to control the movement of the vehicle sprung weight. The shock absorber then absorbs a greater amount of energy on the rebound, creating more heat as the fluid is pulled through the piston orifices. By absorbing a greater amount of energy, the shock absorbers slow the spring oscillations much more quickly, allowing for better vehicle control.

Gas Shock Absorbers

As a fluid-filled shock absorber works, the fluid can become aerated due to the turbulence and the suction at the base valve. Aerated fluid can severely diminish the effectiveness of a vehicle's shock absorbers. Gas shocks are designed to reduce or eliminate this aeration. Manufacturers charge the shock absorber with 100–150 psi (690–1043 kPa) of nitrogen gas. This pressure collapses the air bubbles and prevents the fluid and air from mixing, leading to more consistent shock absorber operation. Gas shock absorbers can be found on most light commercial and medium-duty vehicles and are increasingly popular on heavy trucks.

Electronic Shock Absorbers

Electronically controlled shock absorbers have been available in the automotive market since the 1980s. Today, they are available in the heavy-truck market and can be found on some trucks with air suspension systems.

The electronic shock absorber system uses sensors that monitor vehicle acceleration, brake pressure, speed, and the pressure in the air spring bellows. The system then uses solenoids that control the orifice sizing in the shock absorber valves. As a result, electronic shock absorber systems can control the rate of shock dampening in milliseconds.

Electronic shock absorbers greatly increase vehicle stability by reducing vehicle diving and squat caused by braking and acceleration. The system also enhances lateral stability by selectively increasing the stiffness of the shocks on the outside of the vehicle during turns. Electronic shock absorber control is optimized when integrated with electronically controlled air-spring suspension systems. (Air suspension systems are discussed in greater detail in the Air-Spring Suspension Systems section later in this chapter.)

The following are popular types of suspension systems commonly used in the trucking industry:

- Steel leaf-spring systems with single or multiple leaves
- Composite leaf springs (mostly found on semi-trailers)
- Equalizing beam suspension systems: solid, rubber, and leaf spring
- Solid rubber-cushion suspension systems, such as the Hendrickson HAULMAAX® suspension
- Air-spring suspension systems
- Combination air- and leaf-spring systems
- Electronically controlled air-spring systems

The following sections of this chapter go into each suspension type in greater detail, and the final section discusses Suspension System Inspection and Maintenance.

Leaf-Spring Systems

LO 31-3 Describe leaf-spring suspension systems.

The first steel leaf spring was introduced in the seventeenth century to support the body of horse-drawn coaches. Today, springs are manufactured from low-alloy, medium-to-high carbon steel that has very high yield strength, allowing the steel to return to its original shape after it has been deflected without deformation. Leaf-spring leaves are **shot-peened**, a process that bombards the metal with small beads at high speeds, in manufacturing to reduce surface stress and lessen the possibility of a stress riser that could lead to a cracked or broken spring.

Multi-Leaf Spring Packs

A multi-leaf spring pack is a stack of spring steel leaves held together with a center bolt, as shown in **FIGURE 31-11**. The spring pack may also have several spring alignment clips to keep the leaves parallel to each other. The top leaf, or plate, of the spring usually has an eye formed at one or both ends for attachment purposes. Each subsequent leaf in the stack is shorter than the one above, so the spring pack has a half-diamond shape.

FIGURE 31-11 A multi-leaf spring.

The number of leaves in a stack directly affects the spring's capacity or load rate. Multi-leaf springs that are tightly clamped together have a self-dampening characteristic. As the spring is deflected under load and jounce conditions, the leaves straighten out, causing each leaf to move against the next leaf in the pack. Interleaf friction results. The friction between the leaves absorbs the energy from spring oscillations and transforms it into heat.

This self-dampening can be very effective, so much so, in fact, that in certain applications, no other shock absorbers are needed to control spring oscillations caused by jounce and rebound. If a vehicle relies on interleaf friction for the dampening of the spring oscillations, the leaves must be kept tightly clamped together, and there should never be any lubricant placed between the individual leaves, if they are to be effective.

Using interleaf friction as a sole method of shock absorption, however, causes a rougher ride. The friction tends to stop the spring's motion when a bump is encountered. Because of this, most manufacturers today use leaf-spring arrangements that lessen the self-dampening effect.

The taper leaf, shown in **FIGURE 31-12**, and parabolic leaf springs produce less interleaf friction, leading to a softer ride. These types of springs use fewer leaves, usually two or three, to lessen interleaf friction, and some springs are even assembled with nylon slipper pads between the leaves to further reduce interleaf friction. While the ride is better when the self-dampening effect is reduced, it is necessary for these springs to use carefully selected hydraulic shock absorbers to counter spring oscillation during jounce and rebound.

Composite Leaf Springs

Composite leaf springs are made from fiberglass, carbon fiber, and epoxy formed into one large semi-elliptical leaf with steel re-enforced contact points. **FIGURE 31-13** shows a composite leaf spring.

Composite springs offer a large weight savings over traditional leaf springs made of steel. Composites weigh up to 75% less than a comparable steel leaf spring! They also last longer because they are not subject to fatigue damage, as steel springs are. Pricing for composite leaf springs is similar to their steel counterparts. However, even with the obvious benefits of composite springs, they have only made small inroads into the heavy-truck market and are not often seen on heavy-duty commercial vehicles. Composite springs can be used on any axle instead of steel leaf springs. They are most commonly found on tandem trailer systems that need to take advantage of the weight savings that composite springs afford.

Constant-Rate Leaf-Spring Assemblies

Constant-rate springs are single or multi-leaf spring packs that have one or more leaves rolled into an eye at each end. As illustrated in **FIGURE 31-14**, the spring packs are attached to the vehicle frame through a fixed pin at one end and a shackle at the other. The fixed pin maintains axle alignment, while the shackle allows the spring length to change as it is loaded. Constant-rate springs have a fixed rate of deflection. That is, as load is placed upon the spring, the spring's deflection is consistent. If a load of 200 lb (91 kg) causes the spring to deflect 1" (2.5 cm), then a load of 400 lb (182 kg) causes the spring to deflect 2" (5 cm).

FIGURE 31-12 A taper leaf.

FIGURE 31-13 Composite leaf springs.

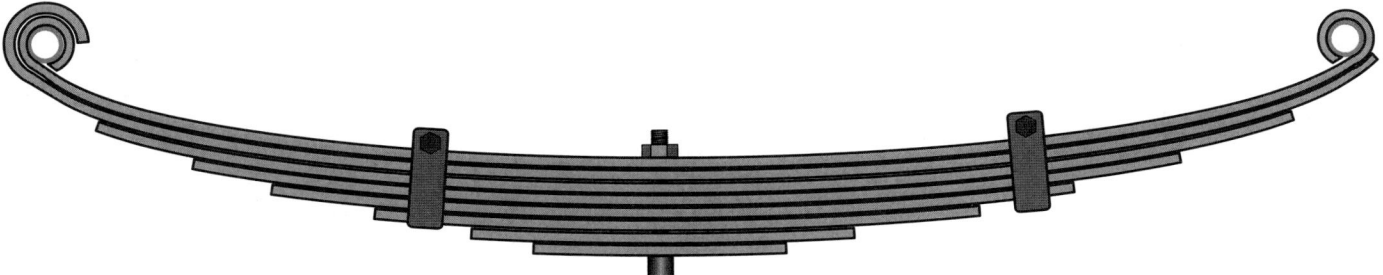

FIGURE 31-14 Constant-rate leaf spring with eyes formed on both ends.

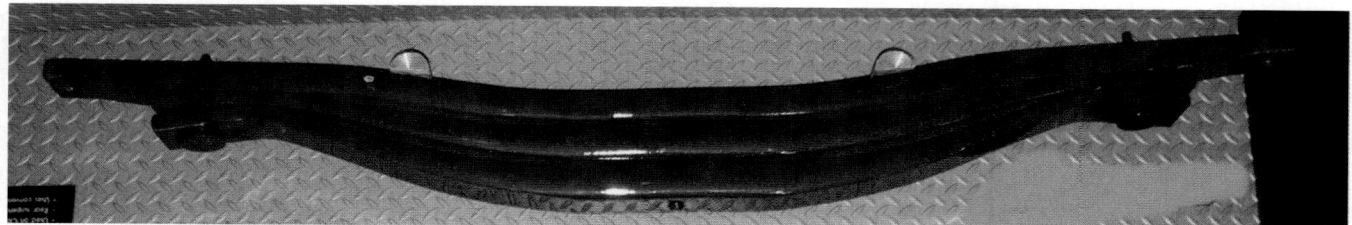

FIGURE 31-15 Parabolic leaf spring.

Doubling the load on the spring doubles the spring's deflection. This is in accordance with Hooke's law of elasticity, which states that the compression or extension of a spring is directly proportional to the load it is subjected to. For constant-rate springs to support a fully loaded vehicle, they must have a high load rate or spring capacity. Unfortunately, this means that when the vehicle is lightly loaded or empty, constant-rate springs are extremely stiff and provide little shock absorption, leading to a very rough ride. For that reason, constant-rate springs are not as common as variable-rate springs today. Variable-rate springs are discussed in more detail in the Variable-Rate or Progressive-Rate Leaf Springs section of this chapter.

Taper Leaf and Parabolic Leaf Springs

Taper leaf springs, like the ones in Figure 31-12, consist of a leaf-spring pack in which the leaves have a varying thickness. Specifically, they are thinner at the outer ends of the leaf and get progressively thicker toward the center of the leaf.

The individual leaves are separated by low-friction spacers. That separation reduces interleaf friction and gives this spring type a softer ride. At the same time, because the leaves are full length, they can still carry the load of an equivalent semi-elliptical multi-leaf spring. Taper leaf springs are not variable-rate, yet the lack of interleaf friction gives the spring a softer ride throughout its operating range.

Parabolic leaf springs can be mono-leaf or multi-leaf, such as the one in **FIGURE 31-15**. Parabolic leaf springs are very similar to taper leaf with one key difference, the spring taper is parabolic, meaning that the taper is engineered to precisely control the spring rate.

The width of the spring leaves can also be parabolic. That is, the width can change, leading to even more precise engineering of spring rate. Parabolic multi-leaf springs can be separated by low-friction blocks to reduce interleaf friction and lead to much improved ride characteristics during all operating conditions. While reducing weight (as compared to multi-leaf spring packs), they can still carry the same loads as a much heavier multi-leaf spring pack, when required, because of the equal length spring leaves.

Variable-Rate or Progressive-Rate Leaf Springs

There are a couple of different types of variable-rate springs. The most common type uses a semi-elliptical spring pack that is not shackled to the vehicle frame. One leaf, called a torque leaf, is pinned to the front spring bracket to maintain axle alignment.

FIGURE 31-16 Multi-leaf spring with cam brackets.

(Torque rods may be used to maintain alignment instead of a torque leaf.) The vehicle weight rests on the remainder of the spring pack's leaves through what are known as cam or hanger brackets.

The cam (hanger) brackets are semi-elliptical supports that allow the spring's contact points to easily slide along the bracket. These brackets are usually, but not always, replaceable. When the vehicle is unloaded, the ends of the spring pack rest in these hangers. As the load increases, the springs flatten out and lengthen. As that happens, the spring's contact points slide along the brackets closer to the center of the spring pack, as shown in **FIGURE 31-16**.

As the leaf springs flatten out, the cam (hanger) brackets cause the weight to be supported closer to the thicker part of the spring pack (the center). Spring rate increases and deflection decreases, ensuring that the spring capacity, or load rate, increases as the vehicle weight increases.

Other variable-rate springs have leaves that are separated from the main pack so that, under light loads, only one or two leaves support the load. Increasing the load, however, causes more leaves to compress, leading to increased spring rate and higher spring capacity. These types of springs allow a lower spring rate when lightly loaded, adding to driver comfort, while still being able to support a fully loaded vehicle when required. Both of these types of springs also offer improved vehicle handling characteristics when compared to traditional leaf springs.

Auxiliary Springs

Auxiliary springs are mounted on top of a carefully selected variable-rate spring. Auxiliary springs use cam brackets as contact points, making them variable-rate. As vehicle load increases, the springs can carry more weight.

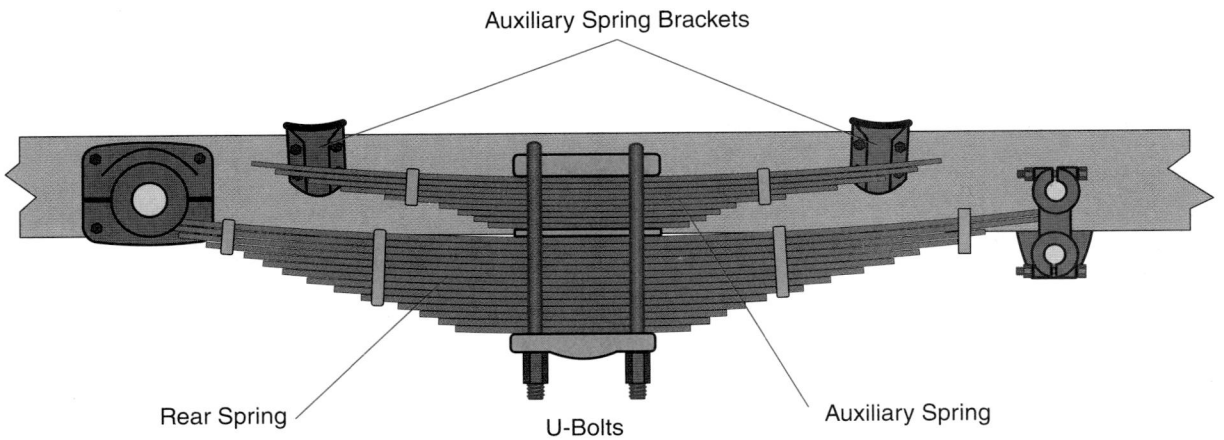

Auxiliary Spring Brackets

Rear Spring   U-Bolts   Auxiliary Spring

FIGURE 31-17 Typical auxiliary spring layout.

The auxiliary spring is not in contact with its cam brackets when the vehicle is lightly loaded. As the load increases, however, contact results, as depicted in **FIGURE 31-17**. A suspension system using auxiliary springs allows a lower (softer) spring rate for driver comfort and vehicle control when unloaded, yet is still able to carry as much load as a much stiffer spring pack when required.

Leaf Spring Mounting Systems

Combination leaf-spring and air systems, such as Kenworth's AG130 and Hendrickson's AIRTEK® system, are making inroads into the market, as are fully independent air-spring front suspensions, such as Hendrickson's IFS™. These systems are examined later in the chapter, after first concentrating on typical leaf-spring front suspension systems.

Front Steering-Axle Leaf-Spring Suspensions

The front suspension systems on heavy-duty trucks in North America are almost exclusively solid I-beam type with leaf springs. The solid I-beam of the front axle is usually connected to the vehicle frame through two leaf springs, as shown in **FIGURE 31-18**. The leaf springs normally have at least two or more leaves for safety reasons. (If one leaf breaks, the other still supports the vehicle.) The leaves may have an insulating material between each leaf to stop wear and reduce interleaf friction to obtain the smoothest ride.

Some newer front suspensions are even equipped with **mono-leaf springs** (leaf springs with only one leaf) to eliminate interleaf friction altogether. Multi-leaf springs are held together with a center bolt and the top two leaves at the front and the top leaf at the back are rolled to accept a bushing and a steel spring pin or a rubber mounting bushing. A typical front leaf-spring suspension system is illustrated in **FIGURE 31-19**.

The front end of the spring is supported in the front spring bracket, which is bolted to the vehicle frame using either the steel spring pin or the rubber bushing and bolt. Systems that use the steel spring pin attachment need to be lubricated on a regular basis. Systems that use the rubber bushing and bolt method are maintenance-free.

FIGURE 31-18 Solid I-beam leaf-spring suspension.

The spring usually has two or more alignment clips installed to hold the leaves parallel. The spring center bolt locates the spring in the lower **shock bracket**, which is the bracket that the shock absorber bolts to. Sometimes the shock bracket is above the spring, under the upper plate. The shock bracket locates on the spring spacer that is positioned above the **caster adjusting shim**. The caster adjusting shim is used to roll the axle forward or rearward, as needed, to set the caster angle during initial alignment of the vehicle. On top of the spring is the upper plate, which locates on the spring center bolt and usually incorporates an axle stop. **FIGURE 31-20** shows an axle stop preventing the axle from banging against the frame during extreme spring motion.

Two large U-bolts and nuts with hardened-steel washers clamp the upper plate, spring, shock bracket, spacer, and caster shim to the I-beam axle, positively locating the axle to the spring. The axle is at exactly 90 degrees longitudinally to the frame. The rear of the spring is attached to the frame in one of two ways. The first way uses a spring pin that is inserted through the rolled eye of the spring leaf. As with the front of the spring, a rubber bushing and bolt may be used instead of a

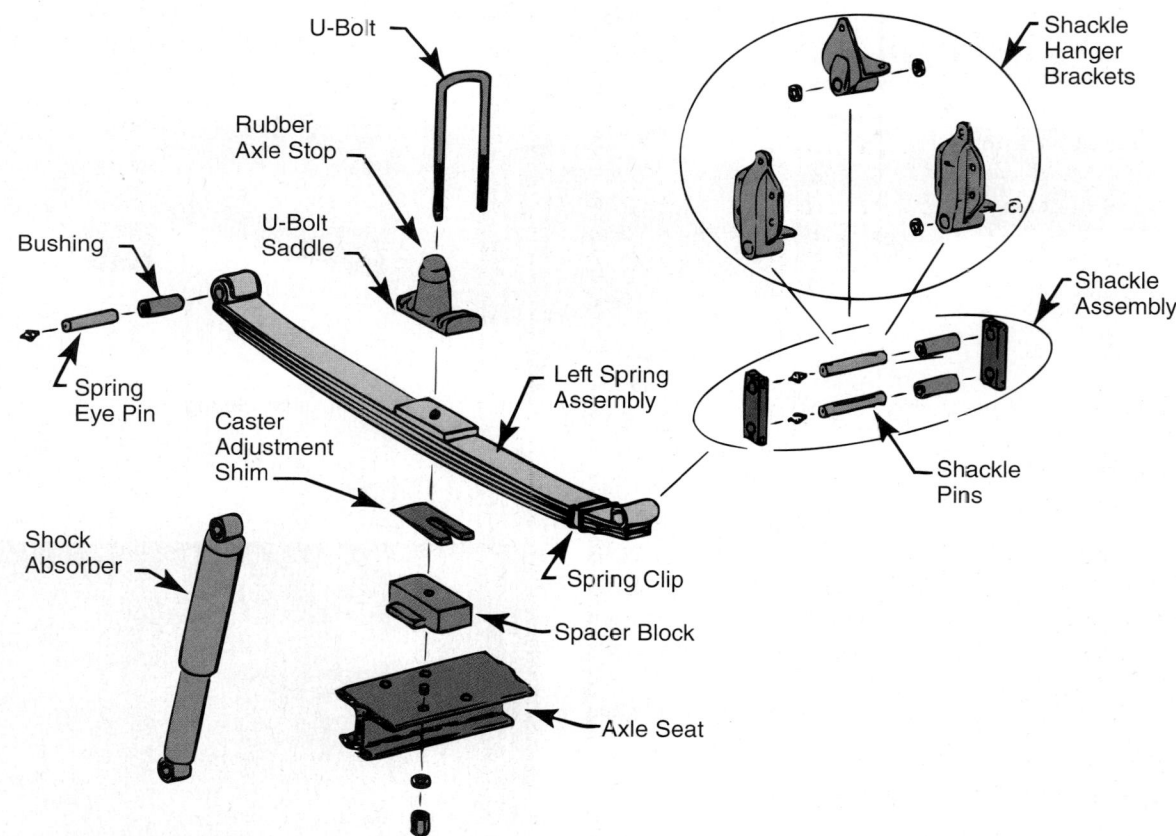

FIGURE 31-19 Front leaf-spring suspension.

FIGURE 31-20 Typical front suspension: **A.** Jounce block/upper plate. **B.** The shock mount. **C.** The caster shim.

spring pin, depending on the manufacturer. This pin or bushing is attached to a **swing shackle**, which, in turn, is attached to the rear spring bracket that is bolted to the frame. The swing shackle allows for the lengthening and shortening of the spring as it cycles through jounce and rebound.

The second way to attach the rear of the spring is to position the top leaf of the spring straight, instead of rolling it into an eye. The top two straight leaves are supported in a rubber insulator block that allows the spring length to change. This second method offers the advantage of being variable rate because the rear contact point of the spring leaves changes as the vehicle is loaded.

Drive Axle Leaf-Spring Suspensions

When leaf springs are used as the suspension system on drive axles, typically variable rate springs are used. Using variable rate springs allows the suspension to handle a heavily loaded vehicle when necessary, but also it allows a softer rate and desirable drive characteristics when the vehicle is lightly loaded or empty. Drive-axle leaf-spring suspensions can be designed for single-drive axles and tandem-drive axles.

Single-Drive Axle Leaf-Spring Suspensions

A typical single-drive axle leaf-spring suspension has a leaf spring attached to the drive axle housing in much the same way as the leaf spring in a front I-beam suspension. That is, the spring is clamped on with large U-bolts. The spring mount has a top and a bottom plate and a spring seat. The spring seat may also have an incorporated torque rod mounting bracket. There may also be an angled shim used to set the axle angle for drive-line angle adjustment (sometimes the lower spring seat is beveled so it alone controls the drive axle angle).

The front and rear of the spring is supported in cam (hanger) brackets bolted to the frame. As the spring is loaded and straightens out, the cam (hanger) brackets allow the spring contact point to slide as the spring lengthens. The contact point between the spring and the bracket is, therefore, closer to the center of the spring pack. This arrangement gives the spring a variable rate—a lower spring rate for a softer ride when the vehicle is lightly loaded, and a higher spring rate for a stiffer ride and increased lateral support when the vehicle is fully loaded.

The cam (hanger) brackets may or may not have replaceable wear pads where the springs contact the brackets. Axle alignment is usually controlled by torque rods, which are bolted to the spring seat and the bottom of the front spring hanger bracket. There are three methods of controlling axle alignment using torque rods, adjustable threaded torque rods, eccentric mounting washers, and shims. The threaded torque rod method has a fixed torque rod on one side and an adjustable torque rod on the other. Axle alignment is controlled by lengthening or shortening the threaded torque rod.

When an eccentric washer is used with torque rods, axle alignment is controlled by loosening the mounting bolt and rotating the eccentric washer, which pushes the axle forward or backward. The third method of axle alignment control is using shims between the torque rod and its mounting pad; adding shims pushes the axle back and removing shims brings the axle forward. Besides maintaining axle alignment, the torque rods also transmit acceleration and braking forces to the frame to maintain axle rotational position. The torque rods are mounted through rubber bushings, which help to absorb the shock of these forces. Some drive axle leaf-spring suspensions do not use torque rods for axle alignment. Instead of torque rods, each of the leaf springs has one leaf that has a formed eye that is, in turn, bolted to the spring mounting bracket. This is called a torque leaf. Torque leaves transfer braking and acceleration forces to

the frame and help to maintain axle alignment. **FIGURE 31-21** shows a torque leaf and a cam (hanger) bracket for a leaf-spring suspension. The axle may also be equipped with transverse torque rods to control centrifugal cornering forces on the axle.

Tandem-Drive Leaf-Spring Suspensions

When a tandem-drive axle uses a standard leaf-spring suspension system, the spring is attached to the axle in the same way as for a single-drive axle with one exception, the rear of the front spring and the front of the rear spring are supported in what is known as an **equalizer**. As illustrated in **FIGURE 31-22**, the center of the equalizer itself is supported in an **equalizer bracket**

FIGURE 31-21 A. Spring cam/hanger bracket. **B.** A torque leaf.

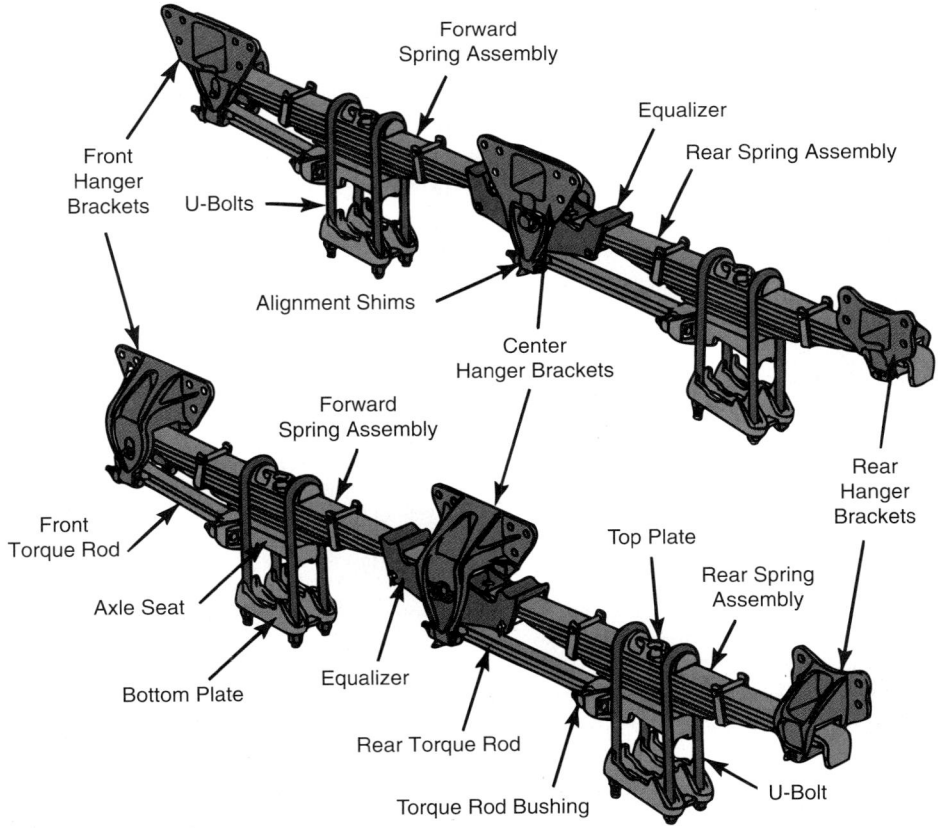

FIGURE 31-22 Typical equalizer suspension. Alignment of the axles is controlled by torque rods.

(also known as the center hanger bracket). The equalizer is mounted on a pin so that the equalizer can pivot backward and forward.

The equalizer bracket is bolted to the vehicle frame and has internal stops that limit the equalizer's pivoting movement. The equalizer ensures that both tandem axles are equally loaded. As the front axle encounters a bump and moves upward toward the frame, the rear of the front spring pushes the equalizer upward at the front and the equalizer's pivoting action forces the front of the rear spring downward. That action spreads the load of the vehicle equally between the front and the rear springs and axles and helps to keep all four wheels in solid contact with the road.

Equalizing suspensions are commonly referred to as a load-sharing type suspension. The pivoting action also reduces the severity of the bump at the equalizer bracket by reducing some of the upward motion. The tandem axles are held in alignment by torque rods. As with a single axle, the torque rods can have three possible adjustment methods: they can be threaded on one side, use shims, or be mounted using eccentric washers.

Equalizing Beam Suspensions

LO 31-4 Describe equalizing beam suspension systems.

Equalizing beam, also known as (**walking beam**), suspension is a very common tandem suspension system. In this type of suspension, two large equalizing beams placed between the two axles equalize the load between the four wheels. There are four basic types of **equalizing beam suspensions**:

1. Solid mount, with no spring at all
2. Leaf-spring type
3. Rubber-spring type, as shown in **FIGURE 31-23**
4. Air-spring type

Each of these types of suspensions, except for the air-spring type, is discussed in more detail in its own subsection. Air-type equalizing beam suspensions are covered in the Air-Spring Suspension Systems section. Equalizing beam suspensions are used on tandem-drive axles and use the lever principle to reduce the impact of road surface irregularities.

Typical equalizing beam suspensions have the equalizing beams mounted under the axles of the tandem. The beams, one on each side, connect the two axles together. Beam end connection points usually feature rubber bushings. The elasticity of the rubber allows for some movement under strain but quickly returns to the original shape to maintain alignment of the axles. The low mounting position lowers the center of gravity of the vehicle, adding to lateral stability.

The centers of the beams are fitted with bronze and steel or rubber bushings and are mounted to the large spring saddles held in place by saddle caps. The center bushing allows the beam to pivot at the saddle. The large saddle holding the beam is, in turn, attached to the vehicle frame either directly, as is the case of a solid-mount system, or through a leaf-spring, rubber-spring, or air-spring system.

The two equalizing beams are joined at the center bushings by a cross tube. The rubber bushings used at the attachment points of these suspension systems allow lateral movement as the vehicle turns a corner. As the vehicle enters a turn, the axles can move as much as 3" (7.62 cm) from side to side. This is because, while tandem axles go through a turn, the pivot point is not at either axle, but at an imaginary point between the two axles, so the forces tend to push the front axle to the outside of the curve and push the rear axle toward the inside. The elasticity of the rubber bushings in the torque rods and beams bring the axles back to alignment quickly when the vehicle returns to straight-ahead driving. This transition is illustrated in **FIGURE 31-24**.

The lever principle employed by equalizing beam suspension systems reduces the road shocks to the frame by 50%. When the front axle encounters a bump in the terrain, it moves up by the size of the bump. As illustrated in **FIGURE 31-25**, when a vehicle hits a bump 6" (15.24 cm) high, the axle moves up the equalizing beam. Because the equalizing beam pivots at the rear mounting bushing in this scenario, the beam acts as a lever. The center of the beam, therefore, only moves up 3" (7.62 cm). The impact to the saddle that is attached to the vehicle frame is only half of the impact to the axle. This reduces the shock to the vehicle and the cargo.

FIGURE 31-23 Rubber-spring equalizing beam suspension.

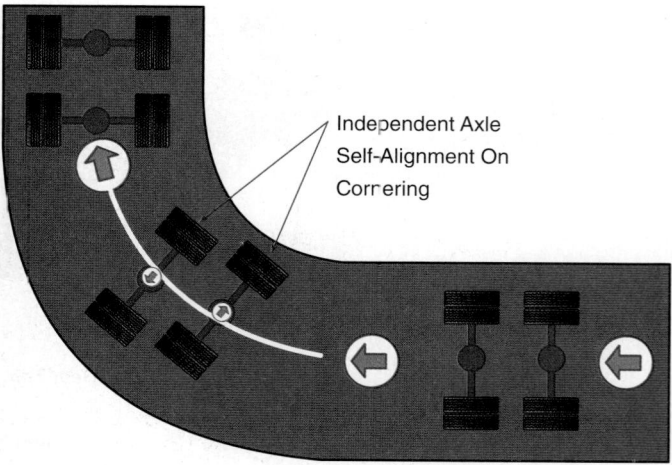

Independent Axle Self-Alignment On Cornering

FIGURE 31-24 Rubber bushings help bring the axle back to alignment.

Equalizing beam suspensions typically offer a large range of suspension articulation. The wheels can move as much as 17" (43.18 cm) on some systems, when required, so they can be used in very rough off-road conditions while still equalizing the load on each wheel and maintaining tire contact. Several manufacturers produce equalizing beam (also known as walking beam) suspensions, all of similar construction.

Solid-Mount Equalizing Beam Suspensions

Solid-mount equalizing beam suspensions have the beam saddle bolted directly to the vehicle frame. As a result, they have very limited capabilities for absorbing shock energy, other than the lever principle mentioned previously. That means they have a rough ride compared to other systems. Solid-mount systems do offer a large degree of lateral stability, high load-carrying capacity, and excellent durability from the suspension system. The suspension usually has two or more torque rods to transfer the acceleration and braking forces to the frame.

Solid-mounted systems can be found in vehicles that have a high center of gravity. They are also common in vehicles

typically operated at lower speeds in off-road environments requiring a large degree of suspension movement. Similarly, solid-mounted systems are found in applications where very heavy load capacity is required, such as concrete mixers, cranes, and boom trucks.

Leaf-Spring Equalizing Beam Suspensions

In equalizing, or walking, beam suspensions that utilize leaf springs, each beam's saddle is clamped to the center of a multileaf spring pack that usually has a rolled eye at the front. The front of the spring is mounted to the front spring hanger by a pin. The pin can be rubber or solid mounted, as shown in **FIGURE 31-26**. The rear of the leaf spring rides on a cam (hanger) bracket in the rear spring hanger, which allows the contact point to change as the spring is loaded so the spring has a variable rate. This suspension system can be a constant-rated system, identified by the main leaves being shorter and only supported by the rear spring hanger. The vari-rate version has extended main leaves that are initially supported on the auxiliary spring hangers. Hendrickson uses these extensively and identifies the variations by using RT to designate the constant-rated system and RTE for the vari-rated system.

The suspension has two or more torque rods to transfer acceleration and braking forces to the frame. A leaf-spring equalizing beam suspension gives slightly better ride characteristics than a solid mount.

Rubber-Spring Equalizing Beam Suspensions

Rubber equalizing beam suspensions, like the one illustrated in **FIGURE 31-27A**, are similar to the leaf-spring style; however, they use a variety of rubber cushion elements to absorb road shock.

The rubber components are mounted between the saddle and the frame hangers and are usually variable rate. As the load

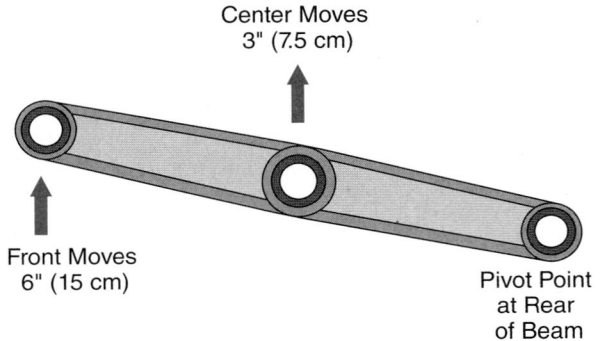

FIGURE 31-25 Lever principle employed by equalizing beams.

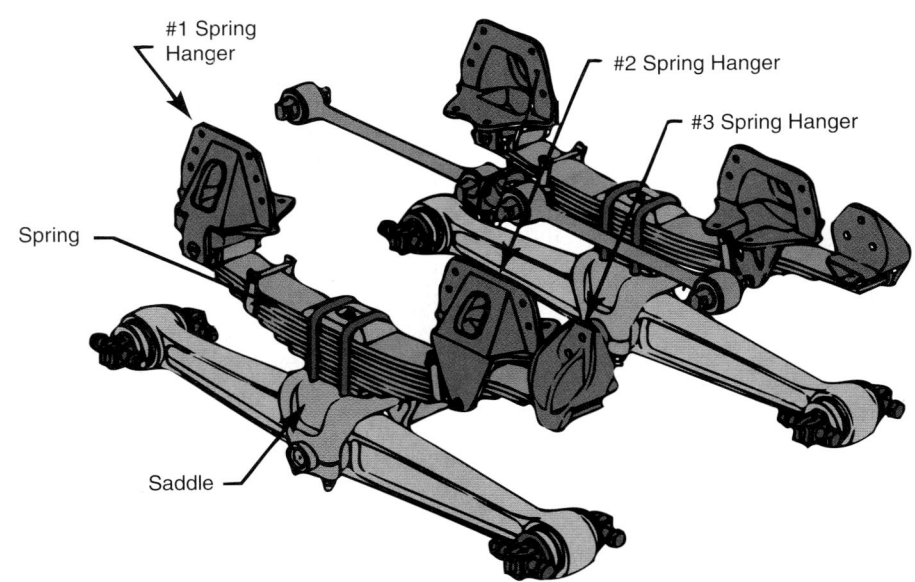

FIGURE 31-26 Leaf-spring equalizing beam suspension.

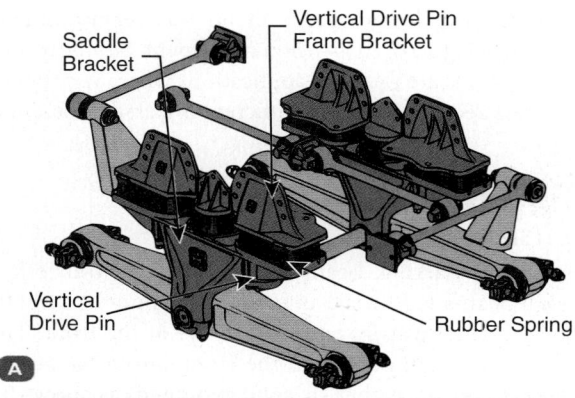

FIGURE 31-27 A. Rubber-spring equalizing beam suspension. **B.** Angular rubber bolster springs.

FIGURE 31-28 Chalmers can attachment system showing: **A.** Restrictor can. **B.** Rubber spring. **C.** Equalizer beam.

increases, more and more of the rubber element is compressed. That makes for good light-load characteristics and excellent heavy-load lateral stability.

Rubber equalizer beam suspensions usually have four vertical drive pins attached to frame hangers. The drive pins pass through the rubber springs and engage drive pin bushings in the saddle. The drive pins keep the beam saddles in alignment as the rubber spring compresses and rebounds. The drive pins have rebound stop nuts and nylon bumpers. The nuts and bumpers limit the upward motion of the drive pins when the suspension encounters greater than normal rebound conditions and excessive lateral forces that tend to pull the pins out of the saddles. The drive pins are very important for maintaining the spring and axle positioning, and they transfer some accelerating, braking, and cornering (lateral) forces to the frame. The newer style of rubber-spring systems uses angular mounted "bolster" springs to transfer drive and braking forces through the suspension. Notice the metal plates encased in the cutaway rubber bolster spring shown in **FIGURE 31-27B**. This design has eliminated the vertical drive pins associated with older rubber-spring systems.

Chalmers Rubber-Spring Equalizing Beam Suspensions

Chalmers Suspension International manufactures an equalizing beam suspension that is unique in its design. The Chalmers system uses equalizing beams that are not solidly attached to the axles. Instead, they ride in brackets, called saddles, that are welded to the axles.

Chalmers suspension also uses cylindrical rubber springs that are variable rate. As the springs compress, their spring rate increases. The rubber-spring elements are enveloped by spun metal restrictor "cans," such as those shown in **FIGURE 31-28**. The cans restrict the springs' outward motion as the springs are compressed. As such, the cans modify the spring rate as they approach maximum compression. The can attachment system is much simpler than a typical equalizer beam suspension and so is easier to service and maintain.

The rubber springs in a Chalmers suspension are free-floating. They are not attached to the frame or the equalizing beams. Instead, they are compressed between a beam spring plate, which is held to the beam by two bolts, and the restrictor can, which rides free against the frame bracket. The two axles of the tandem are held in longitudinal and lateral alignment by eight torque rods mounted to cylindrical spigots.

Four torque rods are mounted below the axles. Those four torque rods transfer brake and acceleration forces to the vehicle frame through the large saddle brackets, called triangular A-frames, which are, in turn, bolted to the frame. This set of four torque rods is also responsible for axle alignment to the vehicle frame. Two of the rods are adjustable to accomplish this.

The four other torque rods are mounted diagonally at the top of the axles. The ends of each pair of rods are attached to a tower welded to each axle close to its center. The other ends of this set of rods are attached to the vehicle frame near the rails, forming a V shape with the rods for each axle, as shown in **FIGURE 31-29**. These upper torque rods control axle lateral alignment. All eight torque rods are mounted by rubber bushings and held in place by spigot caps, which compress the bushings when torqued to specification.

The rubber bushings allow exceptional articulation of the axles while still maintaining vehicle alignment. The elasticity of the bushings returns the axles to their relaxed position very quickly. As such, the Chalmers suspension system boasts one of the highest levels of wheel articulation in the market. The **variable spring rate** of the rubber springs adds excellent lateral stability. As the vehicle load shifts to one side, the spring rate on that side gets stiffer and stiffer. The more load that is applied, the more the restrictor can comes into play by intensifying the spring rate even more to stop the load shift.

FIGURE 31-29 Torque rods in a Chalmers suspension system. **A.** Frame attachments (2). **B.** Rubber bushings (2). **C.** Spigot washers (2). **D.** Axle attachment.

FIGURE 31-30 Wear pads on a Chalmers suspension system.

As shown in **FIGURE 31-30**, the Chalmers equalizing beams are not physically attached to the axles. They are held in place by the saddle brackets on the axles. The only fasteners used on the beams are the bolts that hold the beam spring plates that locate the rubber springs. Because the equalizing beams are not fixed to the axles, they allow for excellent articulation and less maintenance than competing systems. When the beams wear past specifications, wear pads can be welded into place to repair them.

The Chalmers suspension is extremely light when compared to standard leaf- or air-spring equalizer beam suspensions. The Chalmers system is also exceptionally easy to service—the entire system can be repaired and/or replaced using normal shop tools, without using any expensive specialized equipment. The rubber springs are easily changed by taking the load off the springs and removing the two bolts attaching the beam spring plate to the beam. When unloaded, the plate, spring, and restrictor can slide out and be removed together. The 16 rubber bushings attaching the torque rods are also easy to replace. The tension on the rubber bushing is caused by the spigot caps. Once the caps are removed, the torque rod can be easily slid off the spigots, and the bushings can be removed by simply prying them out with a screwdriver or similar tool. Furthermore, the system requires absolutely no lubrication, making it a zero-maintenance system.

Periodic inspection of the system is required, however. The restrictor cans are subject to corrosion, depending on the

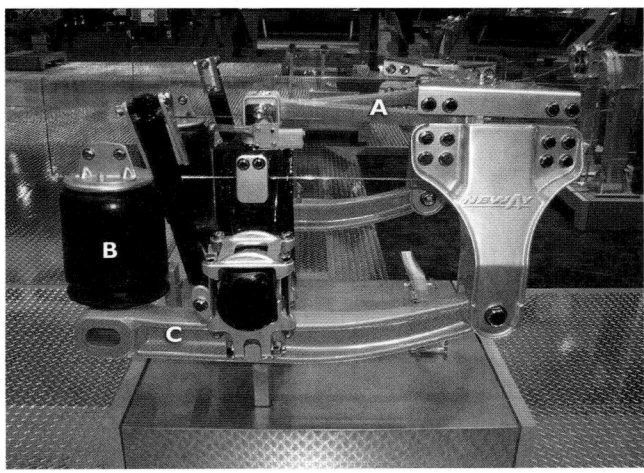

FIGURE 31-31 Typical air-spring suspension, including: **A.** Upper torque rods. **B.** Air spring (bellows). **C.** Trailing arm.

operating environment, and must be replaced when necessary. The rubber torque rod bushings should be checked for play while the suspension is neutralized (no torque or side loading). They should be checked for play by hand only—do not use a pry bar. If any play exists, the bushing should be replaced. Chalmers claims the rubber springs it uses are indestructible and only require replacement if they are damaged by solvent or other chemical attack. Never use oil-based lubricants on this system. The only other components of the Chalmers system are the equalizing beams, which should be periodically checked for wear at the saddle contact area and for cracks. Excessive wear can be repaired by welding wear pads onto the beams; cracks, however, warrant replacement of the beams.

Air-Spring Suspension Systems

LO 31-5 Describe air springs and air spring suspension systems.

Air-spring suspensions, such as the one shown in **FIGURE 31-31**, are becoming the most popular suspension systems for on-highway vehicle operation. Indeed, even for vocational use, these systems are being utilized more and more.

The reason air-spring suspension systems are so popular is because they provide better shock isolation than any of the other suspension systems mentioned previously. Two main advantages of air-spring suspension are that the load is better protected and driver comfort is optimized. Air-spring systems help prevent losses due to excessive load agitation or shock damage. The softer-ride air springs also go a long way to keeping drivers content. Fleet operators recognize that competent professional drivers are rare and the investment in air-spring suspensions is money well spent.

Air-spring systems offer superior spring equalization when compared to other systems. The air **bellows**, also known as simply the **airbags**, are the actual spring element in these suspension systems. All the airbags are connected by air lines. As the pressure increases in one bag because of a jounce, the pressure also increases in the other bags providing perfect equalization.

To absorb road shocks, the multi-ply rubber bellows are filled with air compressed by the vehicle's air system. The air-spring pressure is adjustable within design limits so that the vehicle ride height remains constant, whether loaded or unloaded.

When a leaf-spring suspension is loaded, the operating angles of the driveline's universal joints can become more severe. Severe angles can lead to vibrations and eventual failure of these and other driveline components. This does not occur with air-spring suspensions, unless the ride height is intentionally changed. As a result, the driveline components usually require service less frequently.

The adjustable air pressure also means that the spring rate for air springs is infinitely adjustable, within design limits. One of the drawbacks of air-spring suspensions is that, with their lower (softer) spring rate, they offer lower lateral stability in turns. As the vehicle weight shifts to the outside during cornering, the outside spring flattens. The vehicle is then more susceptible to rollover. Note that vehicle speed when cornering plays a significant factor with this phenomenon, as it does with any suspension configuration. Manufacturers combat this drawback by using transverse torque rods, **stabilizer bars**, and carefully selected **reversible sleeve pistons** (also known as **rolling lobe pistons**) in the airbags, which change the spring-rate profile of the air spring. Another issue with air-spring systems is that they lack the self-dampening characteristics found on leaf-spring systems. Air-spring systems must use shock absorbers or other dampening systems to dissipate spring oscillations.

Air-Spring Construction

Although the concept of an air spring was first thought of at the turn of the century, the first viable air spring was patented by Firestone in 1938. Today's air springs are manufactured from a highly durable multi-ply rubber similar in construction to the sidewall of an automotive tire. The walls of the airbags consist of at least four layers of corded plies and a smooth air-proof inner liner.

Bellows come in two basic configurations—reversible sleeve (rolling lobe) and **convoluted air spring**. The reversible sleeve air bellows, shown in **FIGURE 31-32**, has only a top bead plate. At the bottom is a sleeve-type piston that pushes up into the bellows as it is compressed. The convoluted type has a bottom bead plate and a top bead plate. The convoluted type also has one or more girdle hoops that wrap around the bellows, effectively breaking the length of the bellows into two or more sections. One girdle hoop is used for a double convoluted style and two for a triple convoluted style. **FIGURE 31-33** shows triple convoluted air spring

The convoluted style of air spring is not as commonly used as the reversible sleeve type, which is the most popular type of air spring in on-highway use. The reversible sleeve-type air spring has a piston at the bottom that is forced up into the bellows as a jounce is encountered. The spring rate of the reversible sleeve-type air spring can be somewhat controlled by manipulating the shape of the sleeve or piston. Outward flaring the bottom of the piston, as illustrated in **FIGURE 31-34**, results in a spring rate that

FIGURE 31-32 Reversible sleeve (rolling lobe bellows). **A.** Combo stud. **B.** Attachment stud. **C.** Top bead plate. **D.** Reversible sleeve.

FIGURE 31-33 Convoluted bellows. **A.** Air connection. **B.** Top bead plate. **C.** Girdle hoop. **D.** Bottom bead plate.

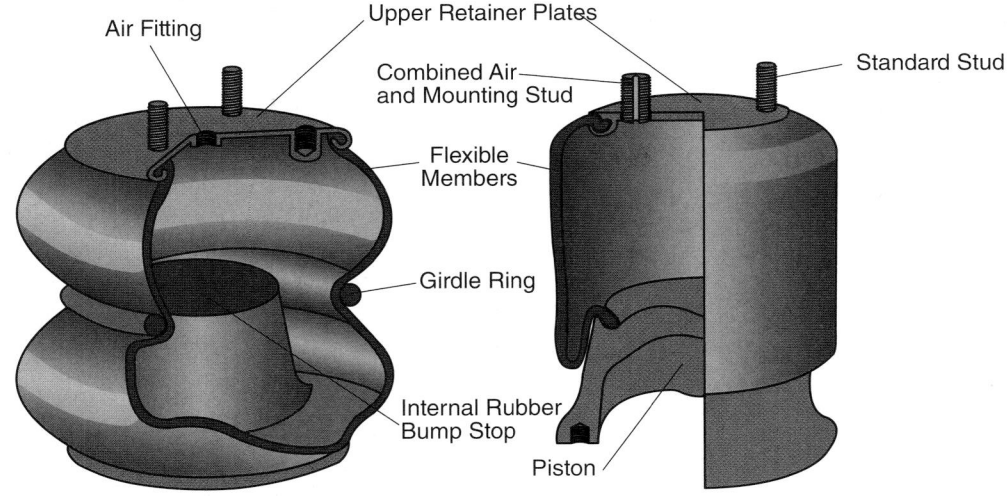

FIGURE 31-34 Cut away of a convoluted air spring with internal stop bumper and a reversible sleeve type, the shape of the reversible sleeve piston determines the spring rate of the air spring as it compresses.

gets stiffer as the spring is compressed, adding to lateral stability during turns. The multi-ply material of the air spring is held in place by bead plates at the top and bottom (in the convoluted type) or by a bead plate at the top and a clamp plate that attaches the bottom of the bellows to the piston (in the reversing lobe type).

The top bead plates have attachment studs or threaded blind holes and an air fitting to supply compressed air to the bellows. The air fitting is sometimes fashioned into one of the attachment studs. In that case, it is called a **combo stud**. The bottom bead plate on the convoluted-type also has blind attachment holes; the reversing sleeve-type has the lower attachment holes in the bottom of the piston. The reversing sleeve piston can be aluminum, plastic, steel, carbon fiber, or hardened rubber. Air-spring suspension systems generally use rubber jounce blocks that restrict the maximum upward motion of the axles. These jounce blocks can be incorporated inside the air spring or may be separately mounted.

Until recently, air springs were strictly used for the rear axles of either a power unit (tractor) or for trailer suspensions. Today, air springs, or at least combination air and leaf springs, are becoming common on front axles, as well. When air springs alone are used on drive axles, they are typically mounted at the rear of large, box-frame-designed **trailing arms**, which are held in place by rubber bushings installed in mounting brackets. Trailing arms refer to large and very strong beams. The front of the beam attaches to the vehicle frame and the beam trails behind. The axle is attached to the beam approximately halfway along its length, and the end of the beam has a spring medium, usually air, between the beam and the frame. The trailing arms keep the axle aligned during suspension articulation. The trailing arm mounting brackets are bolted to the frame. Axle alignment is controlled by threaded torque rods that are adjustable. If the rods themselves are not adjustable, they are mounted to the vehicle

FIGURE 31-35 Combination leaf/air-spring suspension system. **A.** "Z" leaf spring. **B.** Air spring.

using shims or eccentric bushings to allow for adjustment to control axle alignment.

Air-spring oscillations are not dampened by the springs themselves. This is one reason why they offer such a soft ride. Rather, they must use heavy-duty, dual-acting shock absorbers at each air spring to dissipate the spring's energy. Air-spring suspensions typically have transverse torque rods and/or stabilizer bars to control sidesway and add lateral stability during turns and excessive suspension articulation.

Combination Leaf/Air-Spring

Combination leaf/air-spring suspension systems are becoming the norm in drive-axle air-suspension systems. In these systems, the air spring is mounted on a specially modified Z-shaped leaf spring that takes the place of the trailing arm. The leaf spring may be a single leaf or a two- or three-leaf pack and the air spring is mounted at the rear of the leaf, as shown in **FIGURE 31-35**. Combination-spring suspension systems incorporate the best of both worlds. The suspension can gain the excellent lateral stability of a high-spring-rate leaf-spring system, while still offering the excellent shock isolation offered by air springs.

As the vehicle encounters lateral forces, the leaf-spring component resists the side loading by acting as a torsional member and twisting as the load shifts to the side. This action, along with carefully selected rolling lobe pistons, enhances rollover protection and allows suspension engineers considerable latitude when designing suspensions for a particular installation.

For a long time, air-spring suspensions were not considered for steer-axle applications, because the uncontrolled oscillations of a typical air-spring system could lead to very poor vehicle control or worn shocks. In addition, excessive loads cause poor handling due to the front axle bouncing uncontrollably.

The introduction of combination leaf/air-spring systems have now opened the front-axle market to air-spring manufacturers. Several manufacturers now offer many leaf/air-spring designs that combine the softer ride characteristics of air springs with the characteristic stability of traditional leaf springs.

As with traditional front leaf suspensions, combination systems use a traditional leaf spring clamped to the front axle. The leaf spring has a rolled eye at the front, which is connected to the front spring hanger with a rubber bushing. The rear of the spring also has an eye connected to a traditional swinging shackle. The front spring connection maintains axle alignment, while the rear shackle allows for changes in the leaf length due to oscillation. The air-spring bellows are mounted between the spring top plate and the frame. As the leaf-spring oscillates, it also compresses the bellows, as shown in **FIGURE 31-36**. The air spring maintains ride height under all conditions and provides a low (soft) spring rate, while the leaf spring has a higher (stiffer) spring rate. The two spring types together give the suspension all the desirable characteristics of both systems. The leaf springs also add lateral stability by operating as torsional devices as the vehicle experiences side forces due to turns or excessive articulation.

Air-Spring Equalizing Beam Suspensions

Air-spring equalizing beam suspensions are also relatively new. They utilize air springs as the shock absorbing element used with a traditional walking beam suspension. Utilizing air springs offers a better ride on vocational vehicles, during all operating conditions, over vehicles that traditionally use rubber- or leaf-spring equalizing beam suspensions.

In this type of suspension system, the saddle that normally attaches to the leaf spring is replaced with a longer design saddle that attaches to the front frame hanger with an eccentrically mounted rubber bushing. (The bushing is eccentric to allow for axle alignment.) Two air springs are mounted between the saddle and two of the frame hangers, one directly above the axle and the second further back.

The air springs provide the same excellent ride conditions offered by other air-spring suspension systems, whether the vehicle is loaded or unloaded. In addition, the suspension has longitudinal and transverse torque rods that transfer braking, acceleration, and lateral forces to the frame. Air-spring oscillation is controlled by heavy-duty, dual-acting, hydraulic shock absorbers. Hendrickson currently offers a retrofit kit to change its equalizer beam suspensions with leaf springs to an air-spring equalizer beam system.

Air-Spring Control

Because air-spring suspensions utilize compressed air inside a bellows as the spring medium, an air-control system is needed to make the system operate. The control system must keep the air springs inflated at the proper level, regardless of vehicle load. Proper inflation is critical for maintaining correct vehicle ride height during all operating conditions.

The air-control system consists of at least a pressure protection valve (a valve that protects the air brake system from pressure loss if there is a major leak in the air spring system), **height-control valve** (a valve that maintains ride height), and the connecting lines (**FIGURE 31-37**). The control system may have other options, such as a **dump valve** (a valve that allows rapid release of air-spring pressure, usually part of the height-control valve) and a pressure regulator valve (sometimes

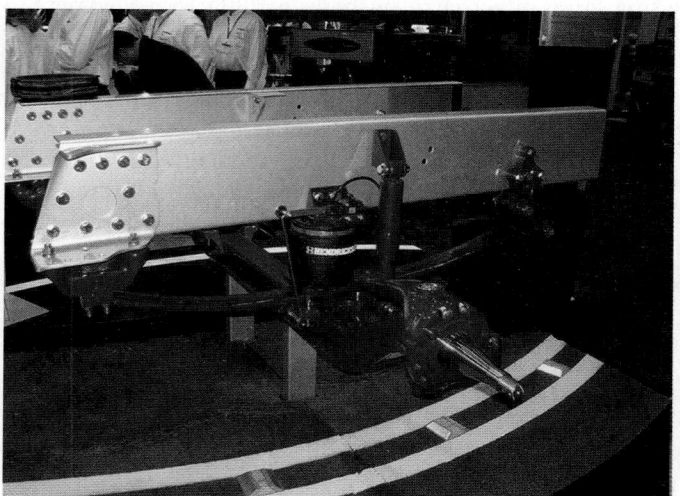

FIGURE 31-36 Combination leaf/air front suspension.

FIGURE 31-37 The height-control valve is attached to the frame and connected to the suspension by a link.

incorporated into the pressure protection valve). The vehicle air system supplies the compressed air to operate the system.

To allow the vehicle to build pressure on start-up, compressed air flow to the air-spring system is blocked by the pressure protection valve, like the one shown in **FIGURE 31-38**, until the air system builds to a minimum pressure of usually 65 psi (448 kPa). Once this threshold pressure is reached, the valve opens and allows compressed air to flow to the height-control valve. The pressure protection valve protects the vehicle's air system from a major pressure loss in the air-suspension system. The valve does not allow air to flow to the suspension until the threshold pressure is reached, and shuts if pressure drops below that level.

The height-control valve, illustrated in **FIGURE 31-39**, is the central command for the air system. The valve is mounted solidly to the vehicle frame and controls air flow to and from the air springs. At one end of the valve, a lever is attached; the other end is fixed through a link to the rear axle or the suspension components.

At the correct ride height, the height-control valve lever is usually horizontal to the ground. As the suspension is loaded, the frame lowers. That drop causes the lever to be pushed up and the height-control valve to meter air into the air

FIGURE 31-38 Pressure protection valve.

springs to re-establish the correct ride height. The springs are inflated until the lever is once again horizontal. As the vehicle is unloaded, the opposite occurs. The frame is lifted by the air spring when the load is decreased, forcing the height-control valve lever downward. That action causes the valve to exhaust air from the springs again until the lever returns to its starting, horizontal position.

The lever and the valve have a certain amount of free travel (0.25–0.375" or 6–9 mm) before the valve takes corrective action by inflating or deflating the springs. There is also a delay feature inside the valve. The delay is usually controlled by the movement of a viscous fluid that slows the opening and closing of the actual valve to keep the suspension from trying to adjust pressure in reaction to every single bump in the road.

Air-spring pressure may be limited to 100 psi (690 kPa) by using pressure-regulating valves in combination with the pressure protection valve. When necessary under extreme loads, other systems can be inflated up to full air-system operating pressures. It is important to note that when an air spring encounters a jounce, the spring collapses on itself, increasing the pressure in the spring. Because all the springs are connected by the air lines, the pressure increases simultaneously in all the bellows, making for excellent load equalization between the wheels. Note that the maximum pressure an air spring is designed to contain is 200 psi (1379 kPa)—whether by inflation or by compression caused by road shocks. If the air-spring inflation pressure is higher than 100 psi (690 kPa), it could indicate that the maximum pressure may be reached more easily, leading to spring failure.

Electronically Controlled Air-Suspension Systems

LO 31-6 Explain electronically controlled air spring suspensions.

Electronic control of air-spring suspension systems, such as the one in **FIGURE 31-40**, has been available for over 17 years. These systems use three or more height sensors to determine (a) vehicle ride height and (b) differences between front and rear and

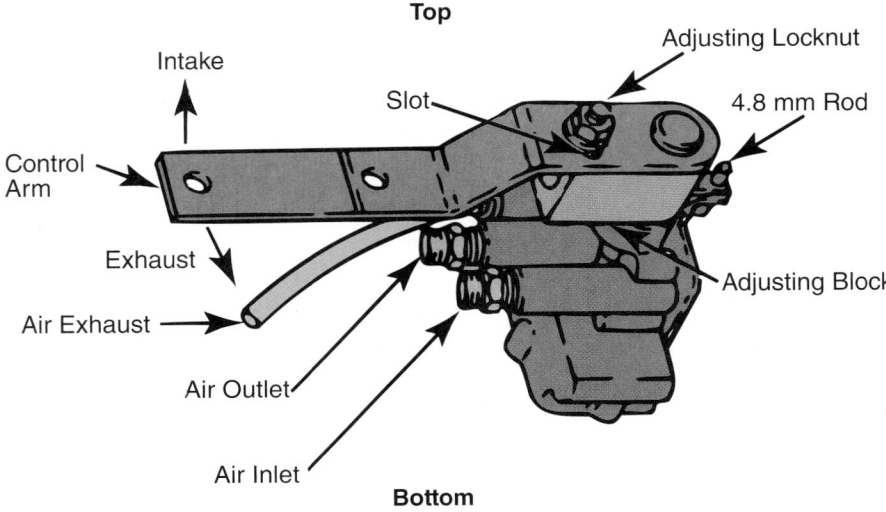

FIGURE 31-39 Height-control valve.

side-to-side ride levels. When a deviation is detected, the system electronic control unit (ECU) corrects the discrepancy by activating solenoids that control air pressure to the right or left rear air springs or to the front air springs. Those adjustments allow the system to maintain optimal ride height whether the vehicle is loaded, unloaded, or unevenly loaded from side to side.

The system ECU uses pressure sensors to monitor the vehicle load. The sensors measure the pressure in the air springs. That data is then converted to a perceived axle load. If the vehicle is equipped with a tag or a pusher axle, that axle can be automatically lowered or raised, when necessary, to match the load.

The latest models of these systems integrate with the ABS and traction control systems. Under operating conditions in which there is danger of losing drive traction, the pressure in the air springs on the pusher or tag axle can be reduced by the system to give more traction to the drive axles. The makers of these systems claim that the system can lead to fuel economy savings because the system uses air more sparingly than conventional systems; therefore, the air compressor does not have to be as active.

Electronically controlled air-spring systems usually have other selectable features, such as automatic leveling while loading or unloading, and a selectable vehicle ride height. Depending on how the vehicle is set up, these features can be selectable at the dashboard or remotely.

▶ TECNICIAN TIP

Dock walk is a dangerous phenomenon that can occur with air-spring suspension-equipped trailers or straight trucks. As the vehicle is being unloaded, typically involving a forklift, the suspension articulates from the weight of the forklift. Since the wheels cannot turn when the brakes are applied, this articulation tends to cause the vehicle to move away from the loading dock very slightly with each down and up motion of the suspension. Eventually, this can lead to a dangerous gap between the dock and the vehicle. Many systems have been designed to combat this problem. The most common system is simply a dump valve that allows the driver to release the air from the springs while the vehicle is being unloaded, this bottoms out the suspension, eliminating "dock walk." Dumping the air, however, sometimes leaves the trailer too low for the dock. Manufacturers now have systems that still dump the air, but as the driver initiates the dump, levers move into place that hold the suspension at the optimum dock height. When the suspension is aired up again, the levers return to their original position, so they don't interfere with suspension operation. Other methods of preventing dock-walk are anchor systems that physically restrict the trailer from moving away from the dock and compensating dock ramps that extend further if the trailer creeps away.

Kenworth Air Spring Systems

Kenworth is using a new in-house-designed type of air suspension system that utilizes twin air springs at each wheel. This system has a large stabilizer bar that transfers load from one side to the other during turns and as the suspension articulates over rough terrain. This type of stabilizer is more akin to the stabilizer found on light-duty vehicles using coil spring suspensions. The Kenworth system also uses two large diagonally mounted top-mounted torque rods to maintain axle alignment. The angle of the upper torque rods helps to prevent squatting at the rear under acceleration. The system is modular in that a single axle suspension carries spring saddles that accept a second axle. **FIGURE 31-41** shows the Kenworth design.

Independent Front Suspension

An Irish company, Timoney Technology, has teamed up with Chalmers suspensions to market a fully independent heavy-truck front suspension system that is currently quite successful

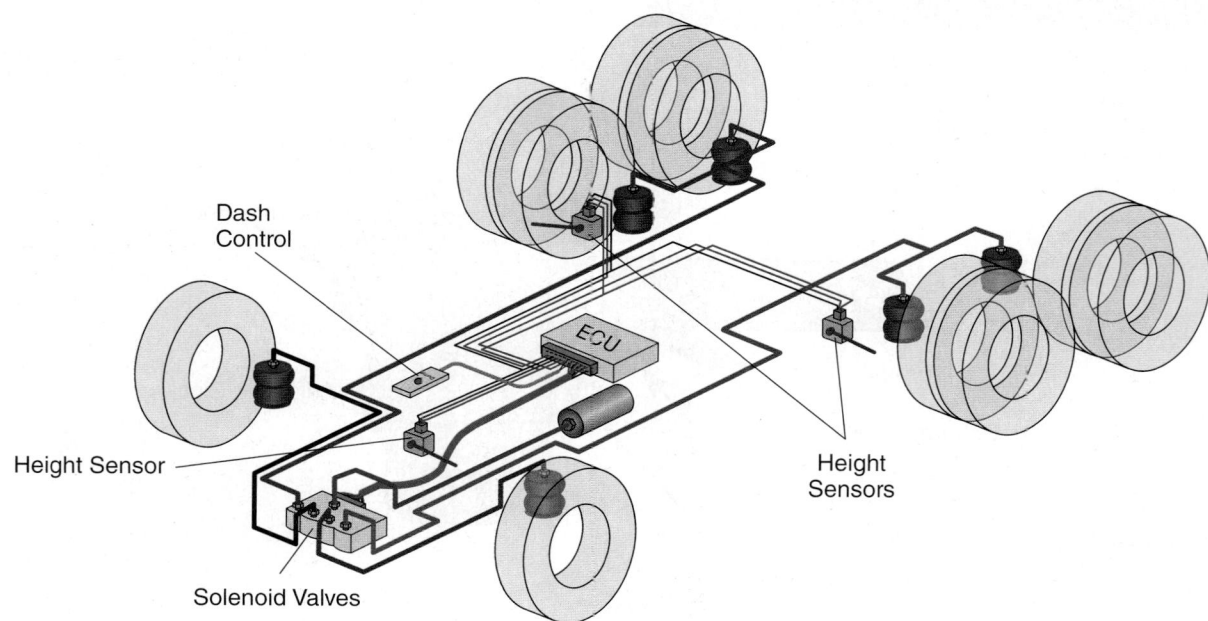

FIGURE 31-40 Electronically controlled leveling system.

FIGURE 31-41 Kenworth's in-house combination air/leaf spring suspension design for tractor drive axles. Note the large stabilizer bar attached to the axle and supported in the front brackets.

FIGURE 31-42 Fully independent front suspension systems for heavy-duty vehicles like the one shown here from ZF are offered by several manufacturers.

in specialized world markets. The system utilizes coil springs and double wishbone construction, making it very similar to many automobile front suspension systems. Timoney has extensive experience in building and marketing these suspension systems for municipal fire trucks, airport service and emergency vehicles, and heavy military applications. Many North American end users are looking at these suspensions for certain applications, mostly large fire trucks. The ride quality and handling characteristics of these suspensions are immediately apparent and noticeably better than their solid I-beam counterparts. Whether they make a large impact in the marketplace with this axle remains to be seen. The Hendrickson IFS is a fully independent suspension system for buses, and ZF also manufactures an independent front suspension. These two systems are again double wishbone and coil spring design. Currently, Meritor markets a fully independent suspension drive axle for military equipment only, where its superior ride and handling capabilities in off-road and rough terrain make it an excellent choice for these applications. Hendrickson also markets independent front suspension for the military and for the heavy motorhome markets. **FIGURE 31-42** shows the ZF independent front suspension system.

Suspension System Inspection and Maintenance

LO 31-7 Describe suspension system inspection and explain service procedures.

Most of today's truck suspension systems use rubber mounting bushings, which require very little maintenance. However, all suspension systems should be thoroughly inspected for signs of damage and wear. Some systems, for example, those using bronze and steel pin bushings, require periodic lubrication of bushing and hangers. This section provides a brief overview of suspension inspection procedures and recommended suspension service. In no way should it be considered a complete listing of inspection and service procedures. Always check the individual manufacturer's service manual for a comprehensive list of service procedures for the vehicle being inspected.

The most common problem in suspension systems is play or looseness of the parts. Although many of the parts are designed with special connections that allow for movement (for example, to accommodate movement of the wheels), excessive play is actually a bad thing. Excessive play magnifies the feel of road imperfections and makes the steering less responsive to steering wheel input. Excessive play is potentially very damaging. It causes wear on the connecting parts and tires. Naturally, any amount of play in a fixed part is problematic and is frequently a result of part failure. Remember, unwanted looseness in the suspension system can be extremely dangerous and should be corrected as soon as possible. In some cases, the vehicle should not be driven until the vehicle has been repaired. Repair of excessive play typically means replacement of the worn or loose part(s).

Out-of-Service Criteria for Suspension Systems

The Commercial Vehicle Safety Alliance (CVSA) is a North American organization that sets out-of-service criteria for commercial vehicles in concert with all vehicle stakeholders and enforcement agencies. The criteria apply to drivers' licensing qualifications, hours of work, and medical conditions, as well as the physical condition of the vehicle.

According to the CVSA, the vehicle shall be rendered out of service if any of the following defects are present on the vehicle's suspension system at the time of inspection, and the vehicle shall not be put back into service until the defects are repaired.

- Any U-bolts or other spring-to-axle clamping bolts missing, cracked, or broken
- Any axle positioning components, axle housing, axle, or spring hanger is missing, cracked, loose, or broken, allowing the axle position to shift
- Any leaf spring with 25% or more of the leaves cracked or broken
- Any leaf spring with a main leaf broken; a main leaf extends to the load-bearing components attached to the frame (hangers or equalizers) or to the spring eye
- Any leaf spring with a separated or missing leaf or portion thereof

- Any spring with a broken torque or radius rod leaf
- Any broken coil spring
- Any missing rubber spring
- Any spring leaf displaced in such a manner that it could come in contact with the frame, rim, brake drum, or the tire
- Any deflated air spring or springs
- Any broken or cracked torsion bar on torsion bar suspensions
- Any fiber composite spring with intersecting cracks (a crack 90 degrees to the spring length)
- Any crack in a fiber-composite spring that extends more than ¾ of the spring length, viewed from the side or the top, as illustrated in **FIGURE 31-43**
- Any torque or radius rod associated with axle alignment or their mounting brackets that is missing, broken, cracked, or loose, and any missing bushing in torque rods, sway bars, or track rods
- Any adjustable (sliding) axle sub-frame with more than 25% of the attaching pins missing or not engaged

There may be other out-of-service criteria enforced in certain jurisdictions. The above list of out-of-service criteria is not meant to be a standard for vehicle maintenance targets, and should in no way be construed as a measure of vehicle suitability for safe operation.

SAFETY TIP

In addition to the aforementioned out-of-service criteria, it is incumbent upon authorized inspection personnel to declare any vehicle out-of-service if the loading or operation of said vehicle is, in their opinion, likely to lead to an accident or breakdown.

Inspecting the Suspension System

Before beginning any inspection, familiarize yourself with basic safety and procedural practices, such as the following:

- Manufacturers recommend that any fasteners that are removed during suspension servicing be replaced with fasteners of the same grade and sizing. Used fasteners should be discarded. **No suspension fasteners should be reused for any reason**.
- Before performing any service on suspension systems, the technician should have a good understanding of the system. Disconnecting suspension components when the system is under load can lead to severe injury or death from sudden release of spring tension or collapse of the vehicle support. **Only authorized, knowledgeable technicians should perform suspension service**.
- Never use a cutting torch or heat when removing suspension fasteners or components. Use of heat alters the strength of the components and could lead to eventual failure, causing loss of vehicle control. Seized components can be removed by obtaining the correct tool for the job at hand.

Inspecting Leaf-Spring Systems

Before a new vehicle is put into service for the first time, a leaf-spring suspension system should be inspected. To inspect leaf-spring suspensions, follow the steps in **SKILL DRILL 31-1**.

Conducting an In-Service Inspection of a Suspension System

In-service inspection should be carried out on a regular basis but, at a minimum, once a year. Technicians should be on the lookout for deep scratches and/or gouges that can form stress

A: Side to side crack extending more than 3/4 of the spring length.

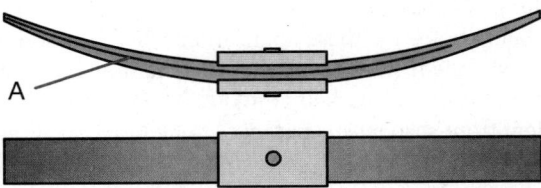

B: Top to bottom crack extending more than 3/4 of the spring length.

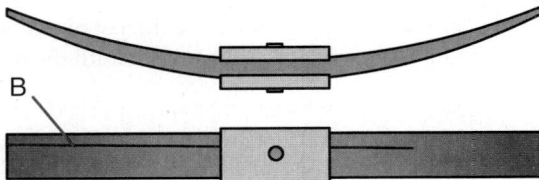

C: Intersecting cracks of any length

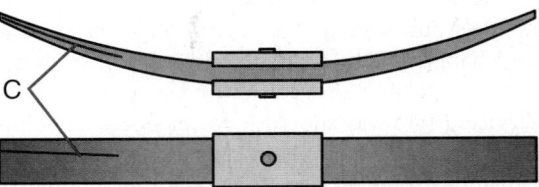

FIGURE 31-43 Out-of-service criteria for composite leaf springs.

SKILL DRILL 31-1 Inspecting a Leaf-Spring System

1. Inspect the entire system for broken or missing components, such as fasteners, bushings, spring clamps, or clips.
2. Inspect for proper spring alignment in the hangers and for suspension interference with the vehicle frame, attachments, or brake components.
3. Check and re-torque frame hangers, springs, and shock absorber mounting hardware. Most late-model frames use "Huck" brand fasteners at the frame hangers. Inspect Huck bolt fasteners for looseness. (Recall from the Heavy-Duty Truck Frames chapter that Huck bolt fasteners cannot be re-torqued by traditional methods.)
4. Check for rust streaking from the frame hanger. Streaks can indicate movement between the hanger and frame. If rust streaking is found, investigate further to find the loose fasteners.

risers and lead to spring leaf breakage. (Spring leaf breakage on a mono-leaf [single-leaf] spring leads to loss of vehicle control.) Technicians should also look carefully for excessive abrasive wear on the individual leaves and spring packs. Follow the steps in **SKILL DRILL 31-2** to conduct an in-service inspection.

Unloading a Suspension for Measuring Play

Play in the suspension system can be damaging to other components or can be a major safety hazard on the road. Testing for play requires the proper technique for the results to be accurate. For play to be measured, the joint must be unloaded. This means

SKILL DRILL 31-2 Performing an In-Service Inspection of a Suspension System

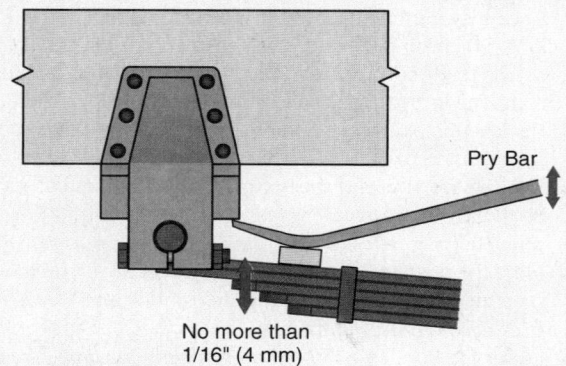

Pry Bar

No more than
1/16" (4 mm)

1. Check the leaf springs for missing or cracked leaves.
2. Check for deep gouges or scratches in the leaves, particularly in mono-leaf (single-leaf) springs.
3. Inspect parabolic leaf springs for missing inter-leaf spacers and/ or anti-friction pads.
4. Check the spring leaves for abrasive wear. Replace any spring that shows excessive abrasive wear. Replace the individual leaves or the entire spring pack per manufacturer's recommendations.
5. Check the spring mounting fasteners, top plates, axle pads, and axle spacers for cracks and/or looseness.
6. Re-torque mounting U-bolts and hardware to specification following the pattern shown. (Most suspension manufacturers recommend that leaf-spring mounting U-bolts and hardware torque be re-checked every 20,000 miles (32,000 km).) Springs should be under load while U-bolts are torqued. Failure to tighten in the correct order can lead to failure of the U-bolt.

7. Check spring hangers for spring alignment and signs of side rubbing in the hangers; this could indicate worn mounting bushings.
8. Use a pry bar (as shown) to check steel pin and bronze spring mounting bushings for wear and movement. Excessive movement (greater than 1/16" or 4 mm) usually requires bushing replacement, but always check the manufacturer's specification.
9. Determine if bronze and steel pin bushings require lubrication. They should be lubricated as part of the vehicle's regular oil change and lube schedule. Check for looseness before lubricating the bushing.
10. Check rubber-spring mounting bushings for any free movement. Bushings are made of rubber encased by inner and outer steel sleeves. Therefore, the spring moves slightly when a pry bar is used. Any bushing that allows the spring to move freely, however, should be replaced.
11. Check that the inner and outer metal sleeves of the bushing are not in contact with each other. If they are, replace the bushing.
12. Check the rubber of the bushings for end shredding, which results from excessive movement.
13. To replace shredded bushings. Remove the spring. Press the bushing out using a press then press a new bushing into place. Special tools are available to remove and insert bushings while the spring is still attached to the axle.
14. Check the rear spring shackle on front suspensions for any sideways movement, or looseness of the spring or shackle at the mounting points on the frame and at the spring. There should be no perceptible movement.

SKILL DRILL 31-2 Performing an In-Service Inspection of a Suspension System (Continued)

15. Check unusual tire wear on the vehicle. River wear and/or cupping can indicate suspension problems (wandering and wheel hop). If the tire balance is correct, carefully examine the suspension system to determine the cause.

16. Check spring hanger slipper pads for excessive wear. Wear at the slipper pads is normal. Replace only when wear is excessive.

17. Check the insides of the spring hanger legs. Abrasive wear indicates the spring is not aligned properly or is loose in its mounting bushing. The spring should not contact the inside of the hanger legs in normal operation.

18. Visually inspect shock absorbers for oil leaks, damaged rubber bushings, and broken mounts.

---

the joint cannot be under compression or tension forces. In the case of suspension ball joints, the joint cannot be supporting the weight of the vehicle or the force from the vehicle spring when measuring the play. Some suspension inspections need to be conducted with an unloaded suspension system. Check the service manual if you are unsure.

Removing and Replacing Front Spring Components

To remove and replace front spring components, follow the steps in **SKILL DRILL 31-3**.

Inspecting Rear Spring Suspension Components

To inspect rear spring suspension components, follow the steps in **SKILL DRILL 31-4**.

Inspecting Equalizer Beam Suspension Systems

Equalizer beams in suspension systems are subjected to extreme compression load on the top of the beam and equally extreme tension loads on the bottom of the beam. Failure of the beam

SKILL DRILL 31-3 Removing and Replacing Front Spring Components

1. Locate and follow the appropriate procedure in the service manual.

2. Complete the appropriate job sheet or work order with all pertinent information.

3. Chock the rear wheels, set the parking brake, and remove the ignition key.

4. Jack up the front of the vehicle and support the frame (not the axle) with axle stands. The frame should be high enough to lift the front wheels 1" to 2" (25 to 50 mm) from the floor.

5. Support the front axle with a floor jack.

6. Disconnect the shock absorber from lower mount. Check the condition of the shock by stroking the shock both directions. In most cases, you want to install new shock absorbers during a spring or spring-pin replacement.

7. Remove U-bolts from spring assembly. *Note:* If U-bolts are extremely rusted, they will be very difficult to remove. Since they must be replaced, it may be faster, and, in the long run, cheaper for the customer, to cut the U-bolt with a cutting torch, but be sure not to heat any of the suspension components that are not being replaced.

8. Remove the pinch bolts and drive the pins out of the rear shackle assembly.

9. Remove the front spring eye pins. Remember, these pins may be threaded-type, requiring you to screw them out of the spring bushing. Refer to manufacturer's service manual.

10. Note the position of the caster shim and record it on the job sheet or work order. (Thick edge to front or rear?) *Note:* The thick edge is usually to the rear.

11. Lower the front axle and remove the spring assembly from the vehicle.

12. Record the following information on the job sheet or work order:
- Vehicle make
- Vehicle year and model
- Front axle capacity (axle weight ratings may be found on the VIN label, usually located inside the driver's door frame)
- Spring width
- Number of leaves
- Pad thickness
- Length (long end and short end)

Note: Refer to the manufacturer's parts book and/or spring manufacturer's catalog to make sure you obtain the correct parts.

13. Replace spring assembly with correct part for the application.
- Clean the axle seat and locating dowel hole.
- Remove and install bushings with a suitable bushing driver. *Note:* Some spring bushings must be welded in place. Refer to the service manual for detailed instructions.

SKILL DRILL 31-3 Removing and Replacing Front Spring Components (Continued)

- Install new pins and secure with pinch bolts. Now is a good time to lubricate the pins. Since there is no weight on them, grease can easily flow around the entire surface of the pin.
14. Position the caster shim and spacers in their original position.
15. Raise the front axle and install the top plate and U-bolts.
16. Remove the jack stands and lower the vehicle to the floor.

17. Torque the pinch bolts, U-bolts, and shock bolt to specifications. Record the recommended torques on the job sheet or work order.
- U-bolts (diameter and torque)
- Pinch bolts (diameter and torque)
- Shock mounts (diameter and torque)
18. List the test results and recommendations on the job sheet or work order, clean the work area, and return tools and materials to their proper storage.

SKILL DRILL 31-4 Inspecting Rear Spring Suspension Components

1. Locate and follow the appropriate procedure in the service manual.
2. Complete the accompanying job sheet or work order with all pertinent information.
3. Chock the front wheels, release the parking brakes (must have at least 100 psi in air-brake reservoirs), and remove the ignition key.
4. Inspect U-bolts for corrosion, missing nuts or washers, and the correct location in the spring saddle. Torque the nuts to the manufacturer's specifications. Important: U-bolts should be torqued with the weight of the vehicle resting on the springs.
5. Record your findings about the U-bolts on the job sheet or work order. Include the following information:
- U-bolt condition (OK, broken, or damaged)
- Does U-bolt fit top plate correctly?
- U-bolt diameter and thread pitch
- Torque specifications
6. Visually inspect the rear spring assemblies. Look for broken leaves, cracks, nicks, corrosion, and missing spring clips. Sagging (worn out) springs may cause the vehicle to lean to the right or left.
7. Record your findings about the rear spring assembly on the job sheet or work order. Include the following information:
- Spring assemblies (OK, cracked, broken, damaged, or sagging)
- Spring clips (OK, missing, or damaged)

8. Visually inspect shock absorbers. Look for oil leaks, damaged rubber bushings, and broken mounts. If the vehicle has just been driven (50 miles [80 km] or more), the shock absorber should be warm to the touch. A cold shock absorber is not working properly.
9. Record your findings about the shock absorbers on the job sheet or work order. Include the following information:
- Shock absorbers (OK or leaking)
- Rubber mounts (OK, damaged, or missing)
10. Inspect the torque arms or torque leaves and bushings. Remember, torque arms have bushings on both ends. Worn bushings can be detected by prying on the torque arm or leaf; there should be very little looseness.
11. Record your findings on the job sheet or work order. Include the following information:
- Torque arms (OK, missing, or damaged)
- Torque leaves (OK, broken, or center bolt sheared)
- Bushings (OK, worn out, or missing or loose bolts)
12. Inspect the spring mounts. Jack up the rear of the vehicle and support the frame with axle stands. Visually inspect the front and rear hanger spring cam surfaces. Use a pry bar to check the equalizer bushing; it should have very little looseness. Check equalizer slipper pads for excessive wear. Check the frame hanger mounting bolts.
13. Record your findings on the job sheet or work order. Include the following information:
- Front hanger (OK, broken, damaged, or loose or missing bolts)
- Center hanger (OK, broken, damaged, or loose or missing bolts)
- Equalizing arm (OK, broken, damaged, bushing worn out, or slipper pads worn)
- Rear hanger (OK, broken, damaged, or loose or missing bolts)
14. Make replacements on required components as approved. Record findings on job sheet or work order.
- Replace damaged U-bolts with new grade 8 U-bolts, hardened washers, and deep nuts. Use anti-seize compound to coat the threads.
- Spring assemblies and shock absorbers should always be replaced in pairs.
15. List the test results and/or recommendations on the job sheet or work order, clean the work area, and return tools and materials to their proper storage.

can lead to loss of vehicle control and catastrophic accidents and damage. Therefore, careful inspection of the beams themselves is a crucial part of suspension maintenance procedures.

There have been numerous failures of equalizer beams from deep gouges or scratches caused by road or accident damage. Scratches and gouges can cause stress risers, which concentrate the tension forces at the scratch or gouge on the lower beam surface, leading to cracking or complete breakage. Beams that exhibit heavy gouging or scratches should be replaced.

SAFETY TIP

Never try to repair a cracked, gouged, or deeply scratched equalizer beam by welding the crack or building up the scratch or gouge. The heat can detrimentally affect the beam strength leading to catastrophic failure. Replace beams that are damaged.

Longitudinal and transverse torque rods should be inspected for damage from impacts. Bent or badly damaged rods should be replaced. Check the rod end mounting bushings for looseness—no excessive movement is allowed. Torque rod bushings can be either a straddle mount or tapered stud mount. Longitudinal torque rod bushings can be checked for movement by hand using a pry bar, or may be checked with the

suspension loaded by rocking the vehicle back and forth under power. Transverse torque rods should be checked with a pry bar. Any significant movement indicates replacement is necessary. The bushings, whether taper stud or straddle mount style, are replaced by pushing them out with a press after the torque rod is removed from the vehicle. Then a new bushing is pressed into place and the rod is re-installed. Axle alignment on equalizing beam suspensions is typically set by shimming the beam ends so alignment is not necessary after torque rod bushing replacement.

Inspecting Rear Beam Suspension Components

Beam suspensions may be one of two types: spring or rubber load cushions. The equalizing (walking) beams are inspected the same way with both systems. After you identify which system you are inspecting, follow the correct procedure in the service manual. To inspect rear beam suspension components, follow the steps in SKILL DRILL 31-5.

Inspecting Frame Hangers

Most new rubber-spring suspension systems utilize diagonally mounted rubber "bolster" springs, which allow the acceleration and braking forces to be controlled by the spring and the torque rods. Older rubber-spring equalizing beam suspensions use

SKILL DRILL 31-5 Inspecting Rear Beam Suspension Components

1. Locate and follow the appropriate procedure in the service manual.
2. Complete the accompanying job sheet or work order with all pertinent information.
3. Remove all grease and dirt from suspension area using a high-pressure washer.
4. Park vehicle on a level surface, chock the front wheels, and remove the ignition key.
5. Identify whether suspension is spring-type (a) or rubber cushion-type (b), then follow the corresponding instructions below.
   a. If the suspension is a spring-type, inspect the spring hanger, forward spring hanger pin, cam brackets, and spring eye bushings for excessive wear or damaged parts.
   b. If the suspension is a rubber cushion-type, visually inspect the rubber pads or cushions for cuts or damage.

   Note: The load cushions are made of butyl and natural rubber and are not resistant to petroleum products. If the cushions become saturated with these products, they split and disintegrate.

6. On rubber-spring suspensions with frame-mounted drive pins, check all the frame hangers for cracks, paying particular attention to the drive pin hangers. Cracks usually appear between bolt holes or from a bolt hole to the edge of the hanger bracket.
7. Check carefully for signs of rust emanating from the rubber-spring mounting area or from the drive pins and bushings. Rust streaks can indicate cracks or movement between components.
8. Using a jack, raise the frame slightly. If the drive pin or hanger bracket is cracked through, it separates, and it can be easily detected during this check.

   Note: Issues with any of the items checked in steps 5–8 require hanger replacement.

9. Inspect equalizer beam for cracks, gouges, or other damage.
10. With the vehicle loaded, check the equalizing beam rubber end bushings. The bushings are under compression on the top side. The bottom of the rubber is relaxed, so the ends of the rubber show a gap in the mounting bracket. This is normal.
11. Check the bushings for wear by placing a small jack under the beam end. Place a soft material between the beam and the jack to protect the beam from scratches. Try to raise the beam. If the inner sleeve of the bushing moves, the bushing must be replaced. Remember that the bushing is rubber-mounted. Compression of the rubber is expected, but the inner sleeve should not move. Check rubber center bushings by placing a jack under the saddle cap of the beam. If the saddle raises 1/8" (3.1 mm) before the beam is raised, the bushing is worn and must be replaced.
12. Check torque on all attaching hardware according to the manufacturer's recommendations.
13. List the test results and recommendations on the job sheet or work order, clean the work area, and return tools and materials to their proper storage.

vertical drive pins in the rubber-spring frame hangers that pass down through the rubber springs to the spring saddles. They are secured in the saddles by drive pin bushings. This arrangement allows the saddles to move up and down, but the drive pins and bushings maintain alignment of the saddles. All acceleration, braking, and cornering forces are transferred through the drive pins and bushings to the frame and, therefore, they require meticulous inspection.

Replacing Rubber Center Bushings

Steel and bronze equalizing beam end and center bushings are used in older applications of equalizing beam suspensions. These bushings add longevity to vehicle suspensions that are subjected to heavy loads and extremely tight turning situations. These conditions can wear out rubber bushings quickly. Steel and bronze bushings must be lubricated on a regular basis during the normal vehicle oil and lube schedules. These bushings are checked

in the same way as rubber beam bushings, but note that there is no rubber in these bushings, so all movement is wear.

Rubber center bushings allow lateral movement of up to 3" (7.5 cm) on turns. Excessive lateral movement allows the inside of the vehicle rear tires to contact the frame. Any contact between the inside of the tire sidewalls and the frame or suspension is another indication that the rubber center bushings must be replaced. To replace rubber center bushings, follow the procedure found in the vehicle service manual.

Inspecting and Maintaining Air-Spring Systems

Air-spring systems usually require very little maintenance other than visual inspection, although ride height may need to be checked and adjusted from time to time. Before a new vehicle is put into service for the first time, air-spring suspension systems should be inspected following the steps in **SKILL DRILL 31-6**.

SKILL DRILL 31-6 Inspecting and Maintaining Air-Spring Systems

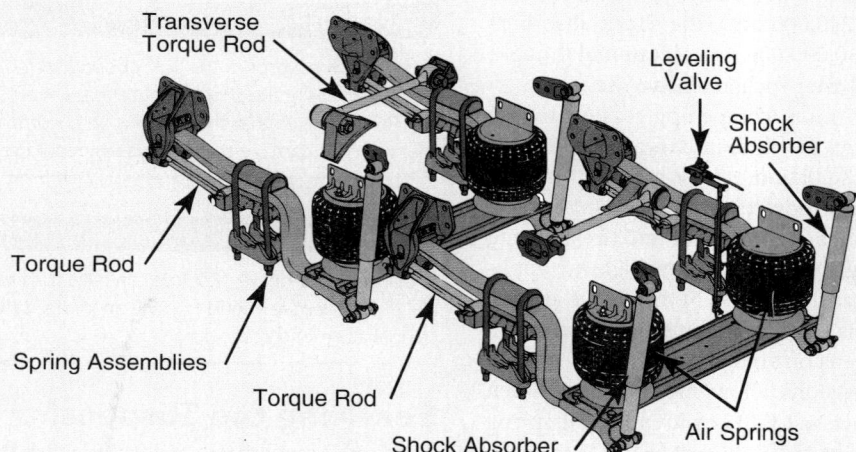

1. Inspect the entire system for broken or missing components, such as fasteners and bushings.
2. Check the air-system hoses and valves for proper routing, mounting, and connections.
3. Air-spring system stroke from jounce to rebound can be much longer than other suspensions, so inspect very carefully for suspension interference with the vehicle frame or attachments and brake components. Pay particular attention to the air springs themselves for abrasion. Air springs fail rapidly if they are chaffing.
4. Check and re-torque frame hangers, air-spring, and shock absorber mounting hardware. Inspect Huck fasteners for looseness. Check for rust streaking from the frame hanger. Streaks can indicate movement between the hanger and frame. If rust streaking is found, further investigation is necessary to find the loose fastener.
5. Check and re-torque all suspension attaching bolts, pivot bolts, and torque rod bushing bolts.
6. Check air beam-to-axle mounting components for torque and alignment.
7. Inspect all welded connections on axles, including torque-rod brackets and frame-hanger brackets on trailer suspensions.

8. Inflate the suspension to at least 75 psi (517 kPa) and check for any air leaks in lines, connections, valves, and the air springs themselves using a bubble mixture, if necessary.
9. Inspect the cross tube or channel connections for fastener torque. Check for any unusual signs of looseness, rust streaking, or metal shavings.
10. Check the height-control valve for secure air connections and proper mounting. Check the height-control linkage for damage for impact or abuse (for example, bent or broken linkage and interference with surrounding components).
11. Check the support beam (Z-spring or trailing arm) for dents, heavy scratches, or gouges, and/or signs of interference with other components.
12. Check the mounting bushings and brackets for any sign of side wear or abrasion from metal-to-metal contact.
13. Check the fasteners on all torque-rod bushings for proper torque. Check the bushings for rubber shredding, metal-to-metal contact, or excessive movement. No free movement is allowed.
14. Replace the bushings if any of the preceding conditions exist.
15. Check all suspension components for impact damage, dents, bending, or heavy scratches or gouging. All damaged components should be replaced.

Before disconnecting ANY air components on an air-spring suspension system (i.e., air lines, valves, air springs), it is essential that the air-spring system be completely deflated, or serious injury could result from explosive release of pressure and or collapse of the suspension.

Inspecting and Maintaining Shock Absorbers

Not all truck suspensions use shock absorbers, but shocks are becoming commonplace in most new trucks. Shock absorbers are essential for air-spring suspensions, which do not have any self-dampening capabilities. Unfortunately, shocks are quite often overlooked by service personnel as a maintenance item.

The Maintenance Council (TMC) has established recommended practice RP 643, which suggests that fleets include shock absorber replacement as part of a regular maintenance schedule. The reason is that, during operation, a shock absorber loses some of its fluid due to normal misting. Oil leaks around the top seal are, by design, to help lubricate the shock push rod. Over time, the shock's dampening capability is reduced.

When is the right time to change a shock? On a vehicle that has traveled 150,000 miles (240,000 km), the shock absorbers have stroked approximately 30,000,000 times! Rational thought dictates that they be replaced after such extensive use.

However, there are even more compelling reasons to pay attention to shock replacement. Shock absorbers are responsible for stopping excess spring oscillation, wheel hop, and irregular tire wear. Shocks are also responsible for increasing vehicle stability. Unusual tire wear, such as river-wear and tire-cupping wear, is becoming increasingly prevalent in on-highway applications. This type of wear can be caused by tires that are out of balance, but frequently this wear is attributed to worn shock absorbers on air-spring suspension systems.

Newer air-spring suspensions allow movement between jounce and rebound of as much as 13" (33 cm). Older leaf-spring suspensions allowed movement of 3" (7.6 cm) or less. When the shocks get weak, their ability to control oscillation and stop wheel hop is diminished, which leads to the unusual tire wear.

This type of wear can more than halve the life of a tire's tread. Unfortunately, this type of wear shows up rather slowly, and once it is discovered, even changing the shocks does not extend the tire's life. That is because the wear pattern is self-propagating. That is, the tire continues to wear the same way once the wear pattern has been established. The discovery of this type of wear has led to the recommendation that shocks be changed at the same time as the tires. The relatively low cost of a set of shock absorbers is a small price to pay to protect the large investment in a set of new tires, especially if this wear cannot be traced to tires being out of balance. When changing shocks, as with any parts, it is essential that the correct replacement shocks are installed. Shock absorbers used with air-spring suspensions are responsible for restricting the maximum oscillation of the air spring. If a shock is installed that is slightly longer than the original, it can lead to torn airbags caused by over-extension, so it is even more critical that they are correct for the particular installation.

Nonetheless, in-service shock absorbers should be checked following the steps in **SKILL DRILL 31-7** every 25,000 miles (40,000 km) or at least once a year.

Some shock absorbers are the rebound stops for air-spring suspensions. Before removing the shock, ensure that the air spring is contained by the vehicle weight, or that the suspension is completely deflated, or serious injury and/or damage to the air spring could result.

Shocks that are heavily worked can have fluid temperatures up to 350° F (177° C). Exercise caution or use an infrared thermometer to check the temperature of the shock.

Servicing the Suspension System

Although most heavy-suspension work these days is performed by specialty shops with specialized equipment and tooling, there are a couple of procedures that the technician should be

SKILL DRILL 31-7 Inspecting and Maintaining Shock Absorbers

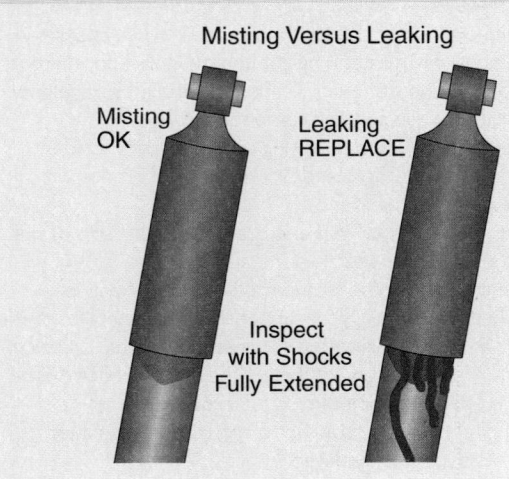

Misting Versus Leaking

Misting OK

Leaking REPLACE

Inspect with Shocks Fully Extended

1. Check the shock mounting fasteners for correct torque. Check mounting brackets for cracked welds and metal-to-metal contact caused by worn bushings. Replace the shock if the bushing allows free movement.

2. Check the shocks for dents or bends caused by road impact. Damage to the shock casing can cause internal or external chaffing, or it may stop the shock from working altogether. Replace shocks displaying this kind of damage.

3. Check shocks for leaking fluid. Misting of oil on the inside of the dust cover and the push rod is normal and necessary for seal and rod lubrication. Any dripping fluid, however, indicates a failed shock that should be replaced. Suspect shocks can be checked using the heat method after a 15-minute road test. If the shock is working correctly, the action of the shock causes the fluid to heat up. A weak or defective shock stays relatively cool. If a shock on the same axle is cooler than its mate, the pair should be replaced.

familiar with, namely, air-spring ride height adjustment and the principles of rear axle and rear tandem-axle alignment.

Adjusting the Ride Height

The height-control valve, or leveling valve, is the brains of the air-spring control system; inflating and deflating the air springs, as necessary, to maintain vehicle ride height. The valve has an internal delay mechanism so that correction to height does not take place during normal spring oscillation.

The ride height of a vehicle can only be measured if it has matching tires, which are properly inflated, and no additional weight in the vehicle. Once these issues are taken care of, the ride height can be measured as specified by the service information.

If the measured ride height is greater or less than specified, the vehicle is not in correct alignment and may be causing or contributing to the customer's concern. The use of a measuring tape from a fixed point on the frame or body of the vehicle to the component in question can help determine the cause of improper ride height. If the ride height issue is related to the airbag, then replacement of the airbag(s) may be necessary.

Follow all safety procedures outlined in the service manual. The inspection and adjustment should be performed on an unloaded vehicle. To inspect and test an air-suspension system and replace the leveling valve, follow the steps in **SKILL DRILL 31-8**. If the ride height needs to be adjusted, follow the steps in **SKILL DRILL 31-9**.

SKILL DRILL 31-8 Inspecting and Testing an Air-Suspension System and Replacing the Leveling Valve

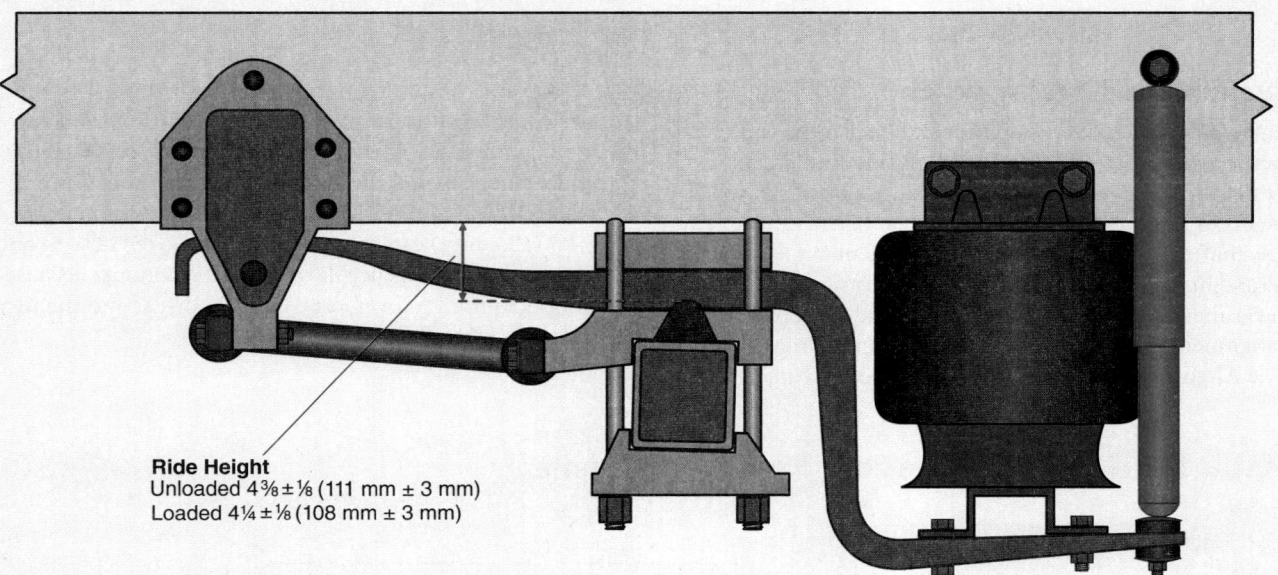

Ride Height
Unloaded 4⅜ ± ⅛ (111 mm ± 3 mm)
Loaded 4¼ ± ⅛ (108 mm ± 3 mm)

Note: The following procedure is typical; however, it is general in nature only. It is essential that you check the service manual for your vehicle for the correct procedure.

1. Locate and follow the appropriate procedure in the service manual.
2. Complete the accompanying job sheet or work order with all pertinent information.
3. Move vehicle to level floor area.
4. Free and center all suspension joints by slowly moving the vehicle back and forth several times without using the brakes. When coming to a complete stop, make sure the brakes are released.
5. With air-system pressure at 100 psi (690 kPa), remove ignition key and chock the front wheels.
6. Inspect lines, fittings, and valves for looseness and damage.
7. Test lines, fittings, and valves for air leaks using soapy water.
8. Purge the air pressure from the suspension system, mark the air lines for proper locations, and then remove the air lines from the leveling valve.
9. Remove the leveling valve link from the valve by removing the nut and washer. Procedures differ, so use the correct manufacturer's service manual for instructions.
10. Remove locknuts, washers, and bolts that connect the leveling valve to the frame.
11. Remove brass air fittings from the leveling valve.
12. Install brass air fittings into the new leveling valve.
13. Assemble bolts, washers, and locknuts that connect the valve to the frame.
14. Connect air lines to the leveling valve. (Making sure the air lines are in the correct locations.)
15. Assemble leveling valve threaded extension rod to leveling valve and assemble lock washer and nut.
16. Air up the system and release the parking brakes.
17. Check the ride height as recommended in the service manual to specification, as shown in the diagram. This system checks ride height between the bottom of the frame and the lower edge of the Z spring (main support member).
18. If the specification is correct, no further action is required. If it is not correct, proceed with Skill Drill 31-9.

SKILL DRILL 31-9 Adjusting the Ride Height

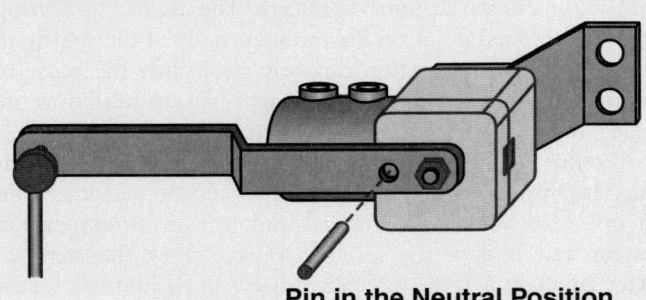

Pin in the Neutral Position

Note: The procedure here is for one type of height-control valve only. Other adjustment procedures are slightly different.

1. Loosen the height-control linkage and disconnect it at the valve or the axle, as required.
2. Manually raise or lower the valve lever until the ride height is correct.

3. When the ride height is correct, pin the valve in the center position.
4. Center the horizontal control lever on the height-control valve in the neutral position and pin it into place with a 1/8" (3 mm) pin or drill bit.
5. Adjust the valve linkage so it can be connected with the valve in the center position and then tighten.
6. Re-connect the valve linkage.
7. Remove the pin or drill bit and ensure that the ride height has remained within specification.
8. Road test the vehicle for 5 or 10 minutes and recheck the ride height using the above procedure. If the ride height is not within specification, repeat the procedure.

CAUTION: Remember to remove the pin when the job is complete! Failure to remove the pin results in a broken valve and permanent damage to the height-control valve.

Adjusting and Aligning Axles

When a vehicle requires an alignment, either front end or rear, the best course of action is to use one of the commercially available electronic alignment machines that use laser-sighted electronic heads mounted at the front and rear of the vehicle. These ensure that each of the axles is perpendicular to the vehicle frame and in exact alignment. It is possible, however, to perform rear axle alignment in the shop with minimal equipment. (Front axle alignment is covered in the Introduction to Front Axles and Vehicle Alignment Factors chapter and is not discussed here.)

Always consult the manufacturer's manual for the suspension being worked on. A general procedure for checking rear axle alignment is given in **SKILL DRILL 31-10**. A general procedure for adjusting the rear axles alignment is given in **SKILL DRILL 31-11**. It is important to note that an axle out of alignment by ½" (12.6 mm) can decrease tire life by over 24%. In addition, that small of a difference decreases fuel economy because of the energy required to overcome the side thrust and the increased rolling resistance.

SKILL DRILL 31-10 Checking Rear Axle Alignment

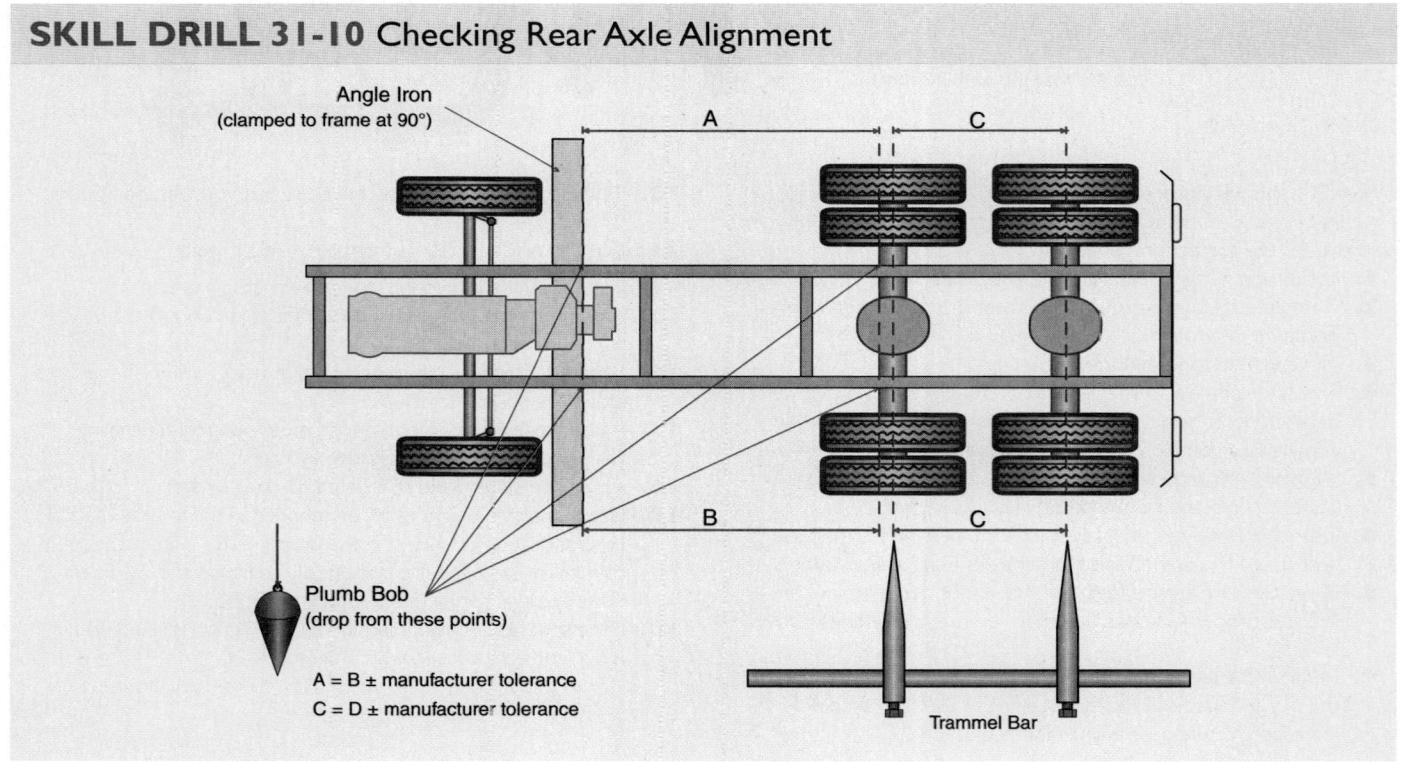

Angle Iron
(clamped to frame at 90°)

Plumb Bob
(drop from these points)

A = B ± manufacturer tolerance
C = D ± manufacturer tolerance

Trammel Bar

SKILL DRILL 31-10 Checking Rear Axle Alignment (Continued)

1. Park the vehicle on a level floor. Do not apply the parking brakes. Roll the vehicle backward and forward by hand to relieve stress on the suspension. Chock the front wheels to keep minimal load on the rear axle(s). Check and adjust tire pressures to the recommended level.
2. Lift the rear wheels with a jack and check for run-out, and correct as necessary. Ensure the front wheels are in the straight-ahead position.
3. Using a framing square, clamp a long straight edge to the vehicle frame in front of the rear axles. Ensure that the straight edge is exactly 90 degrees to the frame rails.
4. Suspend a plumb bob from the outer edge of the frame at the straight edge on both sides of the vehicle. Measure the

distance from plumb bob to the front rear axle on both sides (measurements A and B on the diagram). The distances should be equal to within 1/16" (1.5 mm). Compare the readings with the manufacturer's specification for the vehicle.
5. If the axle is a tandem, then measure the distance between the center of the front rear axle wheel and the rear wheel on the rear axle (measurements C and D in the diagram).
6. Use an adjustable trammel bar to take these measurements. This dimension should be equal to within 1/16" (1.5 mm). This specification is typical. Check the manufacturer's specification for the axle. If the front rear or rear axle needs to be adjusted, then proceed to Skill Drill 31-11.

SKILL DRILL 31-11 Adjusting Rear Axle Alignment

1. Determine the alignment adjustment point. This may be threaded torque rods on one side (A), shimmed torque rods on one side (B), or eccentric mounting bolts on one side on torque rods or trailing arm-suspension systems (C).
2. Once the correct method is determined, adjust the front rear axle alignment to the frame.
3. Adjust the rear axle to the front rear axle.

Wrap-Up

Ready for Review

▶ Suspension systems are designed to protect the passengers, the vehicle, and the load from road shocks.
▶ A suspension must deal with all the forces that act on it and minimize the impact to vehicle operation, including acceleration, braking and cornering force, and road shocks.

▶ A suspension must ensure that the vehicle tires remain in contact with the road.
▶ The suspension must support the vehicle body, the drivetrain, the load, any added accessories, and the passengers. This is known as the vehicle sprung weight.

▶ The unsprung weight of the vehicle refers to all the components not supported by the suspension: the wheels and tires, axles, and brakes. The mass of the unsprung weight can greatly affect vehicle stability, so manufacturers try to keep it as low as possible, while still providing adequate braking and support.

▶ Jounce and rebound are the terms used to describe the suspension system's reaction to road bumps. An upward motion of the tire and wheel caused by a bump in the road is a jounce, while the opposite motion, as the tire moves back down or into a depression in the road, is known as a rebound.

▶ Oscillation is the uncontrolled jouncing and rebounding of a suspension. It must be dissipated by using friction between the leaves of a leaf spring or by shock absorbers to maintain adequate vehicle control.

▶ Suspension systems use torque rods and track rods to maintain axle alignments and to transfer braking acceleration and cornering forces to the vehicle frame in heavy-duty rear suspensions. A parallelogram design strives to keep the rear drive axle at a constant angle as these forces impact the vehicle.

▶ In heavy-duty suspension systems, trailing arms refer to large and very strong beams. The front of the beam attaches to the vehicle frame and the beam trails behind. The axle is attached to the beam approximately halfway along its length, and the end of the beam has a spring medium, usually air, between the beam and the frame. The trailing arms keep the axle aligned during suspension articulation.

▶ Axle stops are used to prevent the axles from contacting the frame during severe jounce incidents. These rubber or nylon bumpers should not normally contact the frame. If they do, the vehicle is very much overloaded, or the suspension requires service.

▶ In the past, some heavy vehicles relied on strong interleaf friction to dampen suspension system oscillation. Today, shock absorbers are the primary method used to dampen system oscillations. Electronic shock absorbers are built with electronically changeable orifices that can react to dampen oscillations more effectively in certain conditions.

▶ Spring rate refers to the distance a spring is deflected when placed under load: high spring rate refers to a spring that requires a larger load to deflect, and low spring rate means the spring deflects easier. High spring rates provide more stability, especially in turns; however, the ride is noticeably rougher. Soft or lower spring rates provide more comfort, but at the expense of stability. Springs that take advantage of both softer ride and vehicle stability are known as variable-rate springs.

▶ Leaf springs come in many forms: single or mono-leaf, multi-leaf or spring packs, taper leaf, and parabolic. Leaf springs can have a variable rate or constant rate, depending on design and installation.

▶ Auxiliary springs are used to help support the vehicle only when fully loaded. They are typically mounted above a variable-rate leaf spring, but do not have any effect until the vehicle is close to its load limit. They are themselves usually variable rate.

▶ Equalizers are pivoting brackets, attached to the vehicle frame, that support the rear of the front leaf spring of the tandem and the front of the rear leaf spring of the tandem. As the front spring encounters a bump, the rear of the front spring pushes up the equalizer and it pivots, pushing the front of the rear spring down and equalizing the loads they each are carrying.

▶ Equalizing beam, or walking beam, tandem suspensions reduce the effect of road bumps on the frame. As the front axle moves up over a bump, the front of the equalizer beam moves up with it, but the other end of the beam is attached to the rear axles, and it pivots on the rear axle connection. The beam then acts as a lever, and the center of the beam, where it attaches to the vehicle frame, only moves up 50% of the distance the front axle moves, reducing the impact to the frame, the vehicle body, and the load.

▶ Rubber springs are a very common spring medium used in very heavy-duty applications. These springs are manufactured to be variable rate.

▶ A Chalmers suspension system is a rubber-spring suspension system that boasts the highest amount of articulation of any current suspension systems, and is extremely easy to service.

▶ Air springs, also known as air bellows or airbags, have instant and complete equalization in tandem applications, provide the softest ride, and yet can carry very heavy loads, when required. Air springs maintain a constant vehicle ride height (loaded or unloaded), and protect the load better than any other system, while providing much greater driver comfort. One drawback of air-spring systems is a slight loss of lateral stability, so many manufacturers are combining leaf springs with air springs to achieve improved stability and ride.

▶ Electronic suspension systems provide even better control of ride height and load distribution. These systems combine with ABS and traction-control systems to optimize vehicle control. They can change ride height from side to side, if necessary, to account for uneven loading, and can even increase pressure in the air springs on the outside of the curve during cornering to improve stability.

▶ Independent front suspension systems were once solely within the sphere of light-duty vehicles, but more and more manufacturers are producing these systems for the heavy-duty market. The increased control and comfort of these systems make them attractive, but their price and complexity are drawbacks from the standpoint of fleet operators.

▶ Suspension systems should be inspected on a regular basis for any component that is cracked, broken, or missing. Suspension maintenance usually involves lubrication of joints and re-torqueing of components, but technicians should always check the appropriate OEM manual for precise instructions.

▶ It is essential to maintain proper axle alignment. Misalignment of ½" (12.6 mm) can decrease tire life and severely reduce fuel economy. Alignment is normally performed using computerized alignment machines, but can be accomplished relatively easily in the repair shop.

▶ The CVSA issues a list of out-of-service criteria for essential vehicle systems. For suspension, the list basically covers any broken, cracked, or missing component in the suspension or its attaching components. If the vehicle has any of these criteria, it is taken out of service until repaired.

Key Terms

airbag The spring component of an air-spring suspension; a tough rubber bag filled with air. Also called *air spring* and *bellows*.

air spring The spring component of an air-spring suspension; a tough rubber bag filled with air. Also called *bellows* or *airbag*.

auxiliary spring A second leaf spring in a leaf-spring suspension that does not take any of the weight until the vehicle is close to fully loaded.

axle stop A rubber (usually) bumper that stops the axle from contacting the vehicle frame during severe suspension articulation. Also called *jounce block*.

bellows The spring component of an air-spring suspension; a tough rubber bag filled with air. Also called *air spring* and *airbag*.

caster adjusting shim An angular shim used at the front leaf-spring mount to roll the I-beam axle forward or back to set the caster angle.

coil spring A helical metal spring.

combo stud A mounting stud attached to an air spring that also receives the fitting to fill the spring with air.

contact patch The area of the tire that is in actual contact with the road.

convoluted air spring An air spring with a top and bottom mounting plate and one, two, or three girdle hoops. The girdle hoops add lateral stability to the spring.

dump valve A driver-operated air valve to release the air from an air suspension system while at the loading dock.

elastic limit The amount of force required to permanently deform a material.

equalizer The support for a tandem-drive axle, using a standard leaf-spring suspension system; it supports the rear of the front spring and the front of the rear spring.

equalizing beam A beam with each end attached to the axles of a tandem-axle arrangement and its center attached to the frame directly or through a spring system. The beam reduces the impact of road bumps to the frame by 50% and equalizes the load carried by each of the axles. Also called a *walking beam*.

equalizer bracket A bracket connecting the rear of the front leaf spring to the front of the rear leaf spring on a tandem-axle suspension; used to equalize the loading of each axle during suspension articulation.

equalizing beam suspensions Used on tandem-suspension systems; two large equalizing beams between the two axles equalize the load between the four wheels.

height-control valve An air valve that maintains air-spring suspension ride height.

hysteresis This occurs when something is deflected, but does not rebound with the same force, usually due to the internal friction inherent in the material as it deflects.

interleaf friction Friction caused by the leaves in a multi-leaf spring pack rubbing together during suspension articulation; can be effective in stopping unwanted oscillation.

jounce The upward motion of the wheels and axles in reaction to road bumps or terrain.

jounce block A rubber (usually) bumper that stops the axle from contacting the vehicle frame during severe suspension articulation. Also called *axle stop*.

lateral stability The vehicle's ability to be stable from side to side.

leaf spring A spring formed by elliptical steel leaves; can be single leaf or multi-leaf.

mono-leaf spring A leaf spring with a single leaf; usually found in front spring applications only.

multi-leaf spring A leaf spring with more than one steel plate or leaf stacked together and used for a spring. Also called a *spring pack*.

oscillation The rhythmic up and down motion of the suspension caused by road shock. It must be stopped by dampening or vehicle stability could be lost.

overslung A suspension where the leaf spring sits on top of the axle.

parallelogram A design element in suspension systems to keep the wheels or the axles in alignment throughout suspension articulation.

rebound The downward motion of the wheel and axle after a road bump or shock has occurred.

reversible sleeve piston A type of air spring with a piston that pushes into the air-spring bag or bellows as the suspension articulates. Also known as a *rolling lobe piston*.

rolling lobe piston A type of air spring with a piston that pushes into the air-spring bag or bellows as the suspension articulates. Also known as a *reversible sleeve piston*.

rubber spring A suspension system utilizing rubber as the spring medium; commonly found on heavier vehicles.

self-dampening The interleaf friction in a leaf-spring pack that helps to stop spring oscillation.

shock absorber A (usually) hydraulic piston and cylinder arrangement designed to minimize spring oscillation.

shock bracket A bracket, usually part of the spring mount, that the shock absorber bolts to.

shot-peened A metal surface treatment to prevent stress fractures. Steel shot is blasted at a metals surface to close any microscopic pores.

spring pack A leaf spring with more than one steel plate or leaves stacked together and used for a spring. Also called a *multi-leaf spring*.

spring rate The amount of force required to deflect the spring; a low spring rate means a softer spring and, therefore, ride; a higher spring rate adds more lateral stability, but gives a harsher ride.

sprung weight The portion of the vehicle supported by the springs; includes the frame, the body, the load, and any accessories.

stabilizer bars Transversely mounted bars that control axle alignment and add lateral stability while the vehicle is turning by transferring some of the load from the side of the vehicle on the outside of a turn to the side on the inside of the turn.

swing shackle A spring mounting system consisting of two upright flat bars side-by-side. The top of the bars is pinned to the frame spring bracket and the bottom of the bars are pinned to the rear leaf-spring eye. Shackles allow the leaf-spring length to change as the suspension oscillates.

torque rod A rod that transfers acceleration, braking, and lateral forces from the axle to the frame and maintains axle alignment. Torque rods can usually be adjusted by one method or another to realign the axles, when required.

torsion bar Bars in a vehicle's suspension system that twist in response to the movement of the wheels and absorb their vertical movement.

track rod Typically, transversely mounted torque rods that counteract lateral forces acting on the vehicle.

trailing arms Refers to large strong beams attached to the vehicle frame and to the axle, they support the spring medium.

underslung A suspension system where the leaf spring is mounted under the axle.

unsprung weight The vehicle weight not supported by the suspension system; includes the axles, the tires, wheels, and the brakes.

variable spring rate A spring or suspension system where more force is required to deflect the spring as load is added; allows a soft rate when unloaded and a much stiffer suspension when loaded.

walking beam A beam with each end attached to the axles of a tandem-axle arrangement and its center attached to the frame directly or through a spring system. The beam reduces the impact of road bumps to the frame by 50% and equalizes the load carried by each of the axles. Also called an *equalizing beam*.

wheel hop A situation where the wheels literally hop off the ground and lose their contact with the road, usually caused by excessive suspension wind-up due to extreme braking, but can also occur on acceleration.

Review Questions

1. The purpose of a shock absorber is to:
   a. absorb road shock.
   b. support vehicle weight.
   c. control spring oscillations.
   d. increase spring capacity.
2. Which of the following is the most common type of front suspension on class 8 trucks?
   a. Twin I-beam
   b. Independent
   c. Semi-independent
   d. I-beam
3. Cam/hanger-type spring brackets are used with which type of springs?
   a. Constant-rate springs
   b. Air springs
   c. Variable-rate or progressive-rate springs
   d. Composite springs
4. Equalizers reduce the upward motion of road shocks to the vehicle frame by doing which of the following?
   a. Using the lever principle
   b. Absorbing the shock
   c. Using shock absorbers
   d. Transferring the motion to the drive axle
5. Why is interleaf friction important on older leaf-spring installations?
   a. Interleaf friction adds to lateral stability.
   b. Interleaf friction dampens spring oscillations.
   c. Interleaf friction increases road feel.
   d. Interleaf friction is not desired and springs leaves should be lubricated to avoid it.
6. Which of the following conditions would not require you to remove a vehicle from service?
   a. Deflated airbag
   b. Broken spring leaf
   c. Broken torque rod
   d. A 6" (15 cm) crack in a fiber-composite spring.
7. Hysteresis occurs when:
   a. the leaves in a multi-leaf spring pack rub together during suspension articulation.
   b. something is deflected, but does not rebound with the same force.
   c. the upward motion of the wheels and axles reacts to road bumps or terrain.
   d. spring oscillations are uncontrollable.
8. The function of the torque rod is to:
   a. maintain axle alignment and transfer lateral forces to the frame.
   b. transfer acceleration and lateral forces to the frame.
   c. maintain axle alignment and transfer acceleration, braking, and lateral forces to the frame.
   d. transfer lateral and braking forces to the frame.

9. Which air valve is known as the central command for the air-suspension system?
   a. Master control valve
   b. Weight control valve
   c. Pressure control valve
   d. Height control valve

10. An axle that is out of alignment by _____ can decrease tire life by over 24%.
    a. 1/4" (6.3 mm)
    b. 1/2" (12.6 mm)
    c. 5/8" (15.9 mm)
    d. 3/4" (18.9 mm)

ASE Technician A/Technician B Style Questions

1. Technician A says that all multi-leaf spring packs are variable rate. Technician B says that auxiliary springs are usually variable rate. Who is correct?
   a. Technician A
   b. Technician B
   c. Both Technician A and Technician B
   d. Neither Technician A nor Technician B

2. Technician A says that higher spring rate aids in lateral stability. Technician B says that higher spring rates lead to a much softer ride. Who is correct?
   a. Technician A
   b. Technician B
   c. Both Technician A and Technician B
   d. Neither Technician A nor Technician B

3. Technician A says that variable-rate multi-leaf springs change rate because the contact point between the springs and the cams changes as load is added. Technician B says that some mono-leaf springs can be variable rate. Who is correct?
   a. Technician A
   b. Technician B
   c. Both Technician A and Technician B
   d. Neither Technician A nor Technician B

4. Technician A says that all torque rods are adjustable to control axle alignment. Technician B says that usually torque rods are only adjustable on one side. Who is correct?
   a. Technician A
   b. Technician B
   c. Both Technician A and Technician B
   d. Neither Technician A nor Technician B

5. Technician A says suspension systems must tolerate a huge number of forces when a vehicle is being driven down the road. Technician B says vehicle suspension systems generally use the elastic properties of special metals or air springs to provide the springing medium that a suspension system requires. Who is correct?
   a. Technician A
   b. Technician B
   c. Both Technician A and Technician B
   d. Neither Technician A nor Technician B

6. Technician A says the suspension system must ensure the vehicle's tires stay in contact with the road surface. Technician B says wheel hop caused by excessive suspension oscillation can lead to loss of control and extreme tire wear. Who is correct?
   a. Technician A
   b. Technician B
   c. Both Technician A and Technician B
   d. Neither Technician A nor Technician B

7. Technician A says a basic function of the suspension system is to securely connect the axles to the frame of the vehicle. Technician B says the suspension system must maintain the axle spacing and alignment as the axles articulate over uneven road surfaces and bumps. Who is correct?
   a. Technician A
   b. Technician B
   c. Both Technician A and Technician B
   d. Neither Technician A nor Technician B

8. Technician A says a shock absorber is effective in minimizing suspension oscillation. Technician B says interleaf friction in leaf springs is not effective in minimizing suspension oscillation. Who is correct?
   a. Technician A
   b. Technician B
   c. Both Technician A and Technician B
   d. Neither Technician A nor Technician B

9. Technician A says torque rods are used to keep the axles in alignment with each other and with the frame. Technician B says torque rods are usually not adjustable. Who is correct?
   a. Technician A
   b. Technician B
   c. Both Technician A and Technician B
   d. Neither Technician A nor Technician B

10. Technician A says most hydraulic shock absorbers are designed with an inner and an outer tube. Technician B says the outer tube is also known as the primary tube, and it does not hold a supply of hydraulic fluid. Who is correct?
    a. Technician A
    b. Technician B
    c. Both Technician A and Technician B
    d. Neither Technician A nor Technician B

CHAPTER 32

Steering Systems and Integral Steering Gears

Learning Objectives

After reading this chapter, you will be able to:

- **LO 32-1** Identify the purpose and major components of the steering systems.
- **LO 32-2** Describe the classifications of steering systems.
- **LO 32-3** Identify and describe the major components of the steering system.
- **LO 32-4** Identify and describe the types of steering gears and outline their basic operation.
- **LO 32-5** Explain the operation of integral power steering gears systems.

- **LO 32-6** Outline the advantages, disadvantages, and operation of rack and pinion type steering systems.
- **LO 32-7** Identify and describe the purpose and function of mechanical steering linkage in steering systems.
- **LO 32-8** Identify and explain the purpose and operation of steering system hydraulic components.
- **LO 32-9** Identify and explain the recommended service and maintenance procedures associated with steering systems.
- **LO 32-10** Identify and explain the recommended service and maintenance procedures associated with the hydraulic system.

You Are the Technician

A driver with an on-highway tractor arrives to the shop and complains the steering wheel moves forcefully to the right and left every time the vehicle hits a bump or crosses a pothole. You immediately recognize the driver's complaint as a condition called bump steer. That is, the vehicle's steering moves erratically after hitting a bump. After performing a visual inspection of the steering linkage with the wheels on the ground, you notice a new power steering hose has been installed. The driver explains the problems began after a leaking power steering hose was replaced. After listening to the driver and performing the inspection, consider the following:

1. What is likely the cause of the bump steer?
2. How will you correct the condition?
3. What other steering system inspections and service procedures would you recommend to the driver?

Introduction

While the concept of controlling vehicle direction by turning a steering wheel is familiar to every vehicle operator, steering is a "life and limb" system having significant consequences for road safety. The responsibility of technicians to choose safe work practices is needed to protect not only the operator and vehicle, but other road users. To properly assume these responsibilities, technicians need to be very knowledgeable about the purpose, construction, and operation of steering system components of various types of steering systems. Equipped with this knowledge, technicians can properly choose the correct service practices and tools when performing inspection, maintenance, or repairs on steering systems.

Fundamentals of Steering Systems

LO 32-1 Identify the purpose and major components of the steering systems.

The **steering system** includes the steering wheel, column, steering gear, its power assist mechanism, and steering linkage connecting the steering gear to the steer axle wheels. These are the major steering components used to maintain directional control of a vehicle. Mechanically speaking, the purpose of the **steering gear** is to convert and multiply the rotational force from the steering wheel to operate the steering linkage. The gear should also function to help maintain directional stability of the vehicle, especially when it encounters bumps and irregular road surfaces while transmitting some **road feel** and minimizing road shock and vibration to the driver. Road feel is force transmitted from the tires back through the steering system to the driver.

> **SAFETY TIP**
>
> Because of the sheer size and weight of a commercial vehicle, any fault in its steering system that results in a loss of steering control has catastrophic consequences, not only for the vehicle operator, but also for other road users. It is the responsibility of the technician to choose service practices that do not endanger the safety of the vehicle, its occupants, and other road users.

Heavy-duty steering systems include a combination of the following components:

- Steering wheels, columns, miter boxes, and intermediate shafts with optional tilt and telescopic options (miter boxes are used in high-angle steering columns to connect to the steering gear in specialized applications, such as low-entry vehicles)
- Single or dual power steering gears; the term steering gear is also used interchangeably with steering box
- Pitman arms, drag links, tie-rods, and other steering linkage (drag links are a connecting linkage that transfers movement of the pitman arm, also called a drop-arm, to the upper steering arm)
- Power steering pumps and lines

FIGURE 32-1 Convenience switches on the steering wheel require the use of a clock spring to maintain an electrical connection between the wheel and steering column wiring harness.

- **Steering-angle sensors** for the vehicle stability control systems
- Steering wheel clock springs, which are used when a vehicle is equipped with steering wheel mounted switches or driver's side airbag (the **clock spring** supplies a movable electrical connection between the steering wheel controls for the cruise, radio, cell phone, airbag, and electrical system) (**FIGURE 32-1**)

Even though all heavy-duty steering systems contain the same basic components, various classifications of steering systems use different combinations of those components.

Steering System Classifications

LO 32-2 Describe the classifications of steering systems.

Steering systems are typically classified by the arrangement of the steering linkage and type of steering gear or power-assist mechanism. Steering linkage arrangements vary with the vehicle weight and application, and whether the steering axle is solid or, in rare instances, the vehicle has independent suspension systems at the steer tires. Some vehicles, such as concrete mixers and crane carriers, have two steering axles, which significantly changes the system arrangement. A **conventional steering system**, with a solid I-beam front axle and a single steering gear, is illustrated in **FIGURE 32-2**.

Today's trucks and buses exclusively use power steering gears rather than manual gears, which have no power assist. The benefit of power steering gears is that hydraulic force, produced by a power steering pump, help multiply driver input force, and thereby reduce overall steering effort. The three major power steering gear systems are the integral piston system, the external power-assist system, and the rack-and-pinion system. Of these, the majority of systems use an integral piston-type power steering gear—which means the power-assist piston and gear assembly are incorporated into a single unit.

The integral piston classification of steering systems uses a hydraulic servo piston, also called power piston, as part of

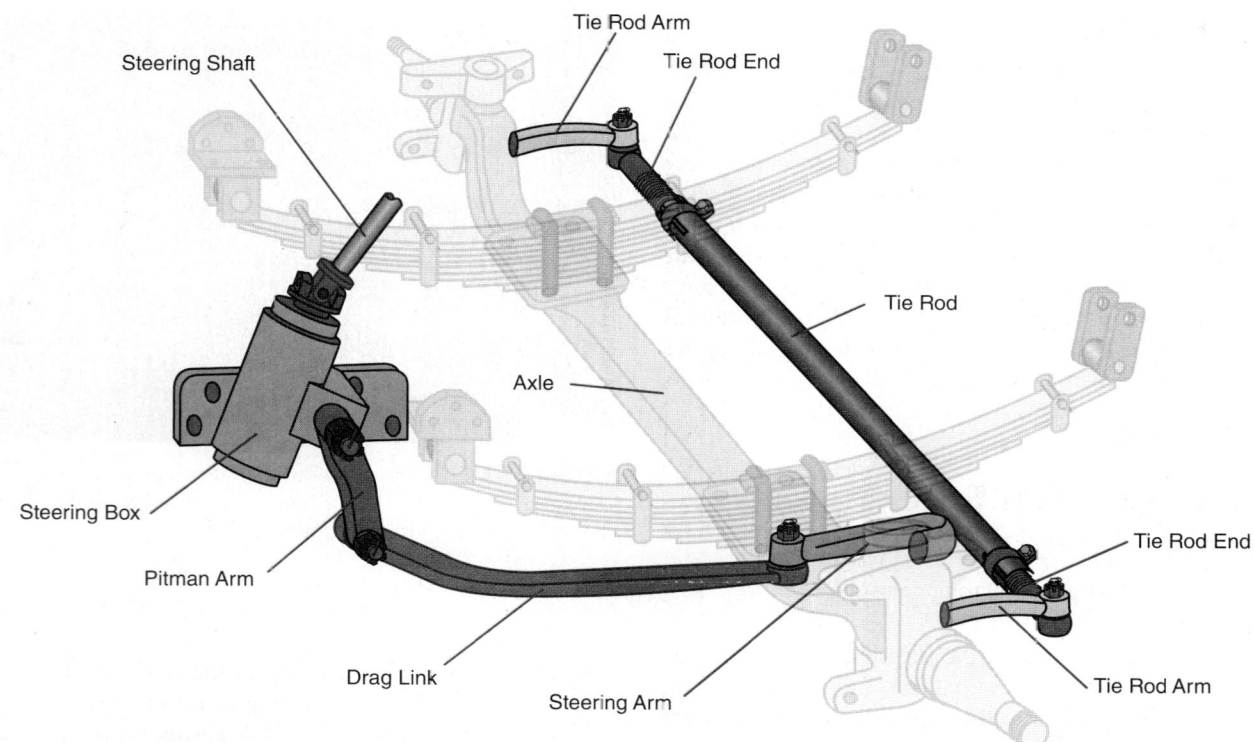

FIGURE 32-2 A conventional steering system.

FIGURE 32-3 A conventional integral steering system with an integrated power piston within the steering gear.

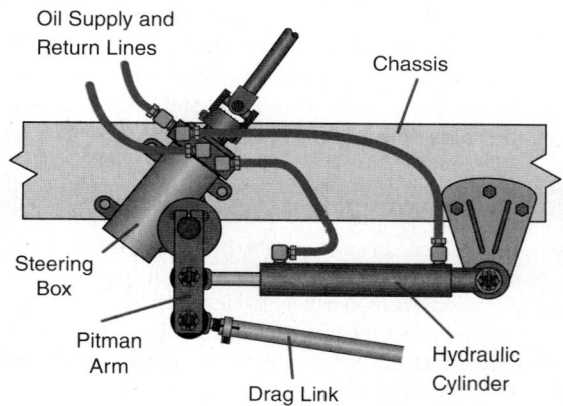

FIGURE 32-4 Diagram of a steering system using a hydraulic-assist cylinder to provide steering assist.

the steering gear. This system, as shown in **FIGURE 32-3**, uses a solid, straight steering axle and a simplified steering linkage arrangement. The hydraulic servo piston multiplies the driver input force using hydraulic pressure supplied by the power steering pump.

The external power-assist steering system uses a conventional worm-gear steering box as its base. It then adds an air or hydraulic-assist cylinder attached to the steering linkage, as illustrated in **FIGURE 32-4**. That cylinder provides the power assistance to the steering gear. Either a manual or power steering gear can be used with this type of steering system. A control valve integrated into the drag link directs fluid or pressurized air flow into the assist cylinder. Hydraulic lines connecting the assist piston to the steering gear control valve causes the piston to operate in tandem with the steering gear to supplement the steering gear force.

Rack-and-pinion steering integrates a power steering-assist mechanism into the steering linkage. A rack-and-pinion steering system has the advantage of providing more precise directional control. Achieving a sharper turning radius is also an advantage of rack-and-pinion steering. This system has been intermittently offered by Freightliner on the Century Class, Coronado, Columbia, Classic, and Classic XL. The primary reason front axle rack and pinion steering is not used on truck and bus cabs mounted on a heavy steel frame is related to the distance between the control rack and steering linkage. Unlike automobiles, which often mount the rack on the body, truck racks require mounting on the front axle. Excessive movement between the cab and axle quickly wears out the long section of linkage connecting the steering wheel to the rack. Relative movement between the rack and cab also interferes with the steering inputs because cab roll turns the steering linkage. Bosch and ZF currently market rack-and-pinion steering systems in Europe and North America. An electronically controlled steering rack is becoming popular in Europe for steering rear pusher and tag axles (**FIGURE 32-5**).

Components of Basic Steering Systems

LO 32-3 Identify and describe the major components of the steering system.

A basic steering system has three main assemblies: the steering wheel and steering column; the steering gear box; and steering linkage. Due to the vehicle weight and the high steering effort required to turn the steer axle tires, heavy-duty vehicles must add a power-assist system (usually hydraulic) to that basic steering system to reduce steering effort (**FIGURE 32-6**). Manual steering capabilities are built into every steering system in the event of a loss of power steering assist. If a hydraulic line breaks

or the engine stalls, a vehicle can be steered, with higher effort, to the side of the road without the hydraulic assist.

Movement of the steering system starts with the driver applying effort to the steering wheel (by turning it). The steering column transmits that effort from the steering wheel through the steering column down to the steering gear. The steering gear converts the rotary motion of the steering wheel to the linear sweeping motion of the pitman arm, which is needed to pivot the wheels. The steering gear also uses principles of gear reduction to give the driver mechanical advantage to overcome the high steering effort of tire resistance to turning, making it easier to steer the vehicle (**FIGURE 32-7**). The linear sweep of the pitman arm, connected to the steering gear output shaft, is then transmitted to the wheels by the drag link. Steering force is transmitted through the drag link to the **steering knuckle** by the upper steering arm. Steering arms on each of the steering knuckles are moved in unison by the tie-rod.

Steering Wheels

Trucks and buses have significantly larger steering wheels than automobiles or light-duty vehicles. Larger steering wheels provide greater mechanical advantage because more torque is required to turn steering axle wheels due to heavier vehicle weight. The larger-diameter wheel is critical in the event of a power steering-assist failure. If the power-assist fails, only manual steering is available to control the vehicle. Steering wheel diameters of 19" to 26" (48 cm to 66 cm) are common.

Size is not the only differentiating factor between the steering wheels on heavy- and light-duty vehicles. The angle of inclination is also different. In contrast to automobiles, in heavy-duty vehicles, the wheel is placed at approximately a 30-degree angle or more to the driver, as shown in **FIGURE 32-8**, which makes it easier to turn if power assist is ever lost. Typically, the steering wheel is splined to the steel shaft of the steering column. That attachment, however, is made without a

FIGURE 32-5 ZF's rack-and-pinion steering system.

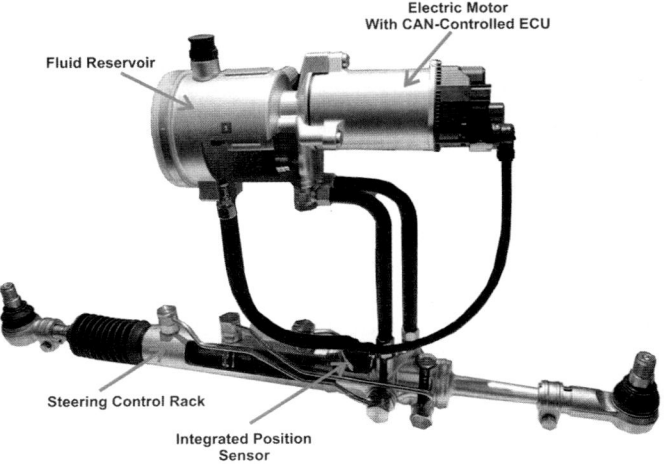

FIGURE 32-6 This stand-alone servo hydraulic rack-and-pinion steering for rear axles is operated by controller area network (CAN) signals from the driver's steering wheel.

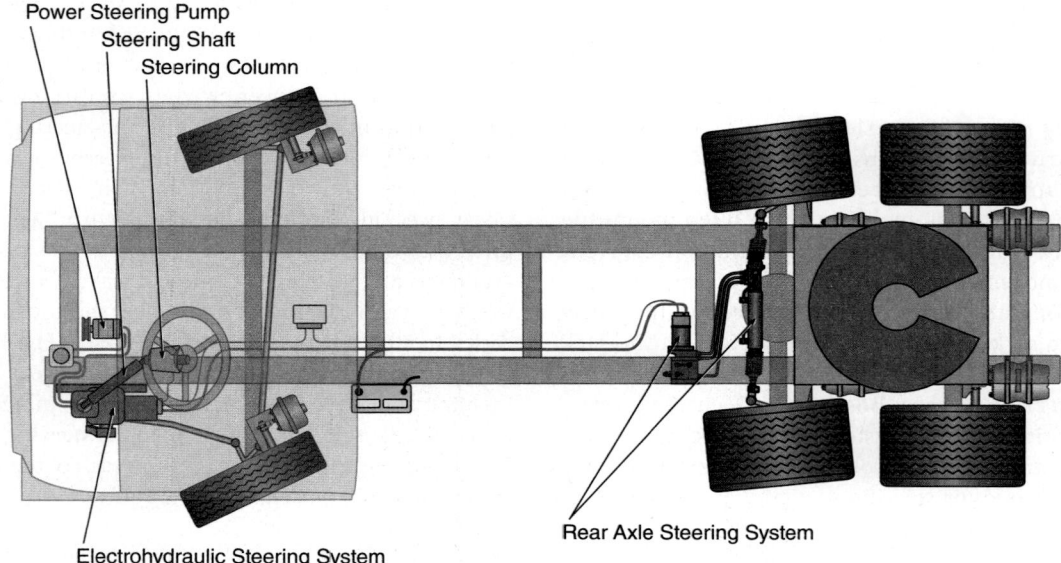

FIGURE 32-7 Connecting the vehicle front steering to a rear steering rack supplies new driver assist functions platooning of vehicles, and is part of the progression to full autonomous steering. When integrated with the stability control system, the second steering gear can automatically correct or compensate for a lateral force disturbance, such as side winds. Lane keeping and a traffic jam assist function where the rear axles can turn in the opposite direction of the front axle steer tire at low speeds is made possible through the additional steering control.

FIGURE 32-8 A larger steering wheel is used by heavy-duty (HD) commercial vehicle. This steering wheel has a supplemental restraint system (SRS) air bag.

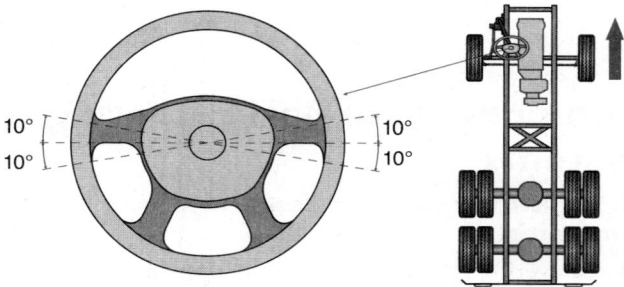

FIGURE 32-9 Steering wheel spokes should be symmetrically aligned to the vehicle straight-ahead position.

master spline. The steering wheel can, therefore, be removed, so that technicians can relocate spokes to a straight-ahead position, as illustrated in **FIGURE 32-9**, if adjustments to steering linkage, such as a tie-rod or adjustable drag link, are made. Always use a purpose-specific steering wheel puller to remove the steering wheel. Never use a hammer, heat the wheel, or pry the wheel off the spline.

Steering Columns and Shafts

Effort applied to the steering wheel is transferred down the **steering column**, which is made of two or more **steering shafts**, to the steering gear. Steering shafts make up the steering column, which is typically a combination of two or more steering shafts.

Steering columns in today's heavy-duty vehicles have unique and sometimes more advanced functions than previous generations of vehicles. First, heavy-duty steering columns must be capable of changing length to adapt to the flexion between the cab and frame-mounted steering gear. A sliding splined section of the column is incorporated into a pair of steering shafts, as illustrated in **FIGURE 32-10**. The sliding mechanism is commonly equipped with a grease fitting for lubrication. To enable an electrical connection between the rotating steering wheel and the stationary electrical wiring, a clock spring mechanism is used to connect steering wheel switches (**FIGURE 32-11**).

Additionally, the movement of the steering column must be capable of changing the angle between the steering wheel and gear. Since movement between the cab and steering gear takes place continuously as the vehicle absorbs road shock and

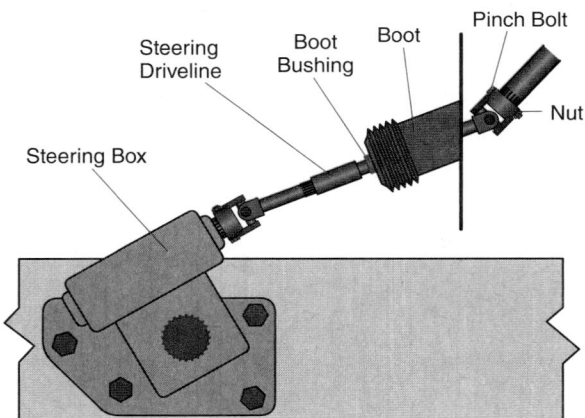

FIGURE 32-10 Steering column with flexible joint.

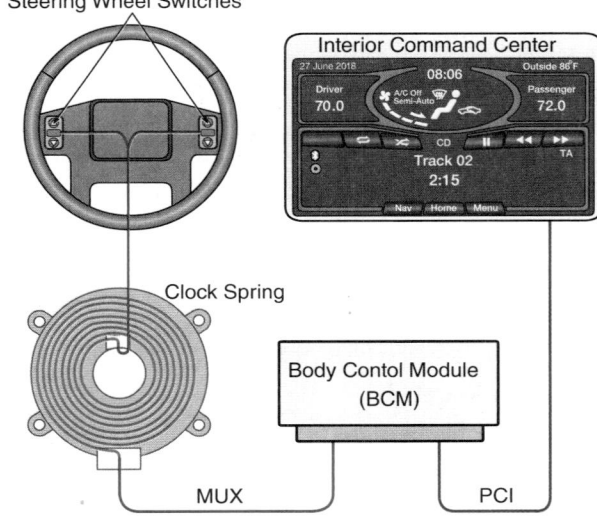

FIGURE 32-11 A clock spring is a long coil of wire that winds and unwinds whenever the steering wheel is turned. Switch signals are multiplexed through a pair of wires to communicate with the radio or other vehicle ECMs.

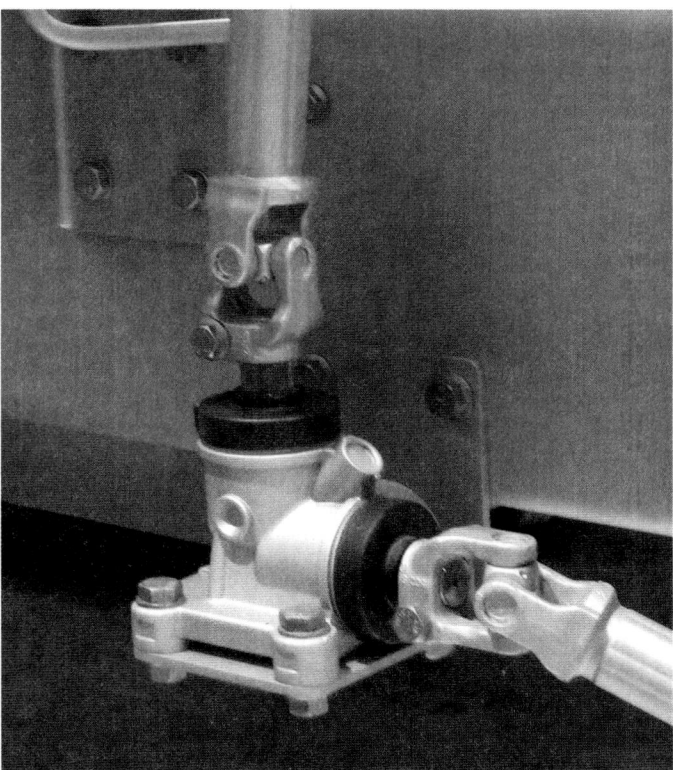

FIGURE 32-12 Miter box.

vibration, changes take place between the angles of the steering gear input shaft and the steering wheel. One or more **universal joints** (also called **U-joints**) are placed in the column to allow movement between the frame-mounted steering gear and steering column. Enabling flexion of the steering column prevents cab movement from being transmitted into the steering input shaft. When two universal joints are installed in the column, they must be phased. This means the crosses and bearing caps of the joints must exactly align with one another. If they are not aligned, the steering shafts movement can bind, which prevents the vehicle from being properly steered.

Multi-shaft steering columns using shafts connected on sliding splines, called slip yokes, enable the column to change in length. This feature is not only important to enable movement between the cab and frame-mounted gear, but it is a safety feature as well. A single, straight, steering shaft could be driven into the driver during a collision. With sliding splines, however, the shafts simply slide inside one another, shortening the shaft and preventing injury to the driver.

The location of the steering gear relative to the column sometimes requires the use of a miter box to connect the two components. **Miter boxes** are gear arrangements used to sharply change steering column angles. They are available in various angles and so enable the use of specialized cab configurations. Miter boxes are often used on cab-over-engine chassis where the steering gear is below the steering wheel, as shown in **FIGURE 32-12**.

► **TECHNICIAN TIP**

Ensuring steering column universal joints are properly aligned is a first step during column inspection. Out-of-phase steering column U-joints can cause a cyclical-like tightness, binding, or torque variations at the steering wheel. Proper phasing means the U-joint crosses and bearing caps must be precisely parallel to one another after the steering shafts are assembled into the column. During disassembly, separated shafts must be match-marked. During reinstallation, match-marking shafts enables correct alignment of column parts to turn smoothly together.

► **TECHNICIAN TIP**

When tapered studs are used to attach the articulating joints, such as tie-rod ends to steering linkage, a wedge fork can be used to separate the drag link from a steering arm (or pitman arm) or tie-rod ends from the steering knuckle. Common workshop practice is to shock the tie-rod end loose by striking with a large hammer. For safety reasons, castellated nuts crossed with cotter pins are used to lock the ball stud and nut together.

Steering Gears

LO 32-4 Identify and describe the types of steering gears and outline their basic operation.

Steering gears fall into one of two basic categories: manual or power (assisted). Manual steering gears were occasionally used in a few applications, primarily because of their simplicity, reliability, and low maintenance. Manual steering gears provide no assistance to the driver's turning effort and rely on a high mechanical gear ratio to reduce steering effort. This means more turns of the steering wheel are required to change the direction of the steer tires. Power steering does provide assistance to the driver's effort and fewer turns of the steering wheel are required to move the steer tires. Given the weight and size of heavy-duty commercial vehicles, manual steering gears are seldom, if ever, used in heavy commercial vehicles.

Power steering gears can steer the vehicle without power assistance. Power-assisted steering systems use one of three types of gearing technology. The first is a manual recirculating-ball steering gear. Even though this gearing type is manual, the principles of its design and construction are used by all steering gears, whether manual or power. The second type of gearing technology used in power-assisted steering systems is a power recirculating-ball gear, and the third type is the rack-and-pinion steering gear.

Autonomous Drive Steering Gears

The autonomous or semi-autonomous, self-steering vehicles were first developed in the early 2000s for agricultural vehicles using global positioning system (GPS)-based steering systems. These systems can now work together with software integrating a vehicle's cameras, radar, GPS, and other sensing systems to provide various levels of automation or assistance to the driver. Steering systems are now incorporated into collision avoidance to avoid hitting oncoming vehicles, keep the vehicle on the road if the driver is unable to, prevent vehicle roll-overs, and stabilize vehicle. Agricultural autonomous steering systems are typically hydraulically controlled, but systems introduced for commercial vehicles are electrically assisted. This means an electric motor is used to substitute driver input to the steering gear when automatic functions are desired or required (**FIGURE 32-13**).

FIGURE 32-13 An electric motor replaces driver input to the steering gear for autonomous and semi-autonomous drive trucks.

component. Replace the component with original equipment only. Do not straighten any bent steering system component.

Federal Motor Vehicle Safety Standards (FMVSS) require that all vehicles are capable of being steered manually if the loss of power assistance occurs, such as during an engine or hydraulic failure. For this reason, power steering gears contain a manual steering system that is useful to examine before studying power steering systems. In this section, we first cover the basics of steering ratios and then move into a more detailed discussion of the three types of steering gears and gear boxes.

Steering Ratio

In manual- and power-assisted steering systems alike, steering gears play a major role in converting the rotational movement of the steering wheel into a linear motion at the pitman arm. The force to turn the wheels of a heavily loaded vehicle requires the gear to supply a significant amount of mechanical advantage to allow the driver to safely maneuver the vehicle.

On heavy-duty vehicles, the **steering ratio** refers to the mechanical advantage produced by the gear. An example of a 20:1 steering ratio means a steering wheel turned 360 degrees turns the wheels 18 degrees (360 degrees rotation of the steering wheel/divided by the ratio constant of 20 = 18 degrees of wheel turn at a 20:1 ratio) ($20 \times 18 = 360$). Typical commercial vehicle ratios are between 16:1 and 23:1.

Although it does not transmit desirable feedback about the road conditions, a high steering ratio reduces road shock to the steering wheel and steering effort. A low ratio allows the steering to be more responsive to driver input and turn more quickly with less steering wheel movement.

In addition to being high or low, steering gears can either use a constant or a variable ratio. **Variable-ratio steering gears** use sector shafts with long and short lengths of teeth, as illustrated in **FIGURE 32-14B**. **Constant-ratio steering gears**, illustrated in **FIGURE 32-14A**, use sector shafts with teeth of equal length. Variable-ratio steering produces small amounts of

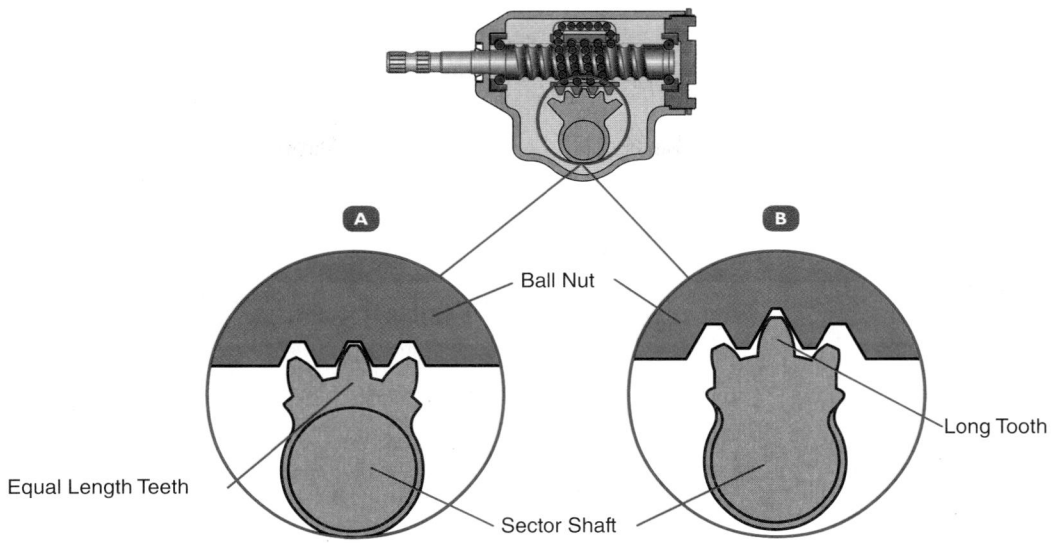

FIGURE 32-14 A. Constant-ratio steering gear. **B.** Variable-ratio steering gear.

movement near the steering center and larger movement of the sector shaft near the ends of the worm gear or power piston travel. The longer teeth reduce the ratio near the steering center, while the shorter teeth increase the steering ratio.

Variable-ratio steering gears move relatively little when the vehicle is traveling in a near-straight direction. For this reason, drivers prefer variable-ratio steering—little steering movement is required most of the time. Because variable-ratio gears move only slightly, they minimize a condition called oversteer—an overreaction to driver input when the steering wheel is first turned. Having a high steering ratio near the center of travel reduces the tendency of a vehicle to wander when traveling straight ahead. As the vehicle wheels are turned farther from center, the steering ratio increases.

▶ TECHNICIAN TIP

Variable-ratio steering gears found on most vehicles have a wider center tooth on the sector shaft and narrower teeth toward the ends. During service, it is important that all steering components are aligned and adjusted for steering in a straight-ahead direction. Pitman arms require matching of alignment marks on the steering sector shaft, as shown in Figure 32-27.

Steering ratios are magnified in power-assisted systems. Power-assisted steering provides a force multiplication of typically over 2000 lb (907 kg) of force at the sector shaft of the steering gear! When running, the power steering pump supplying hydraulic assist forces a constant low-pressure oil flow through the steering gear, providing an immediate response to driver input, absorbing road shock transmitted through the steering system, and eliminating steering wheel kick.

▶ TECHNICIAN TIP

Typical unresponsive motion in late-model steering gears is between 1/2" to 1 1/2" (1.3 cm to 3.8 cm). Checking unresponsive steering motion is measured at the rim of the steering wheel. Loose and worn

steering column components increases free play, which increases unresponsive motion. Before evaluating unresponsive free play, which is movement of the steering wheel required to produce tire movement, the steering column, gear mounting bolt torque, and linkage should be inspected. An unresponsive free play check is performed with the engine idling, on a smooth floor, and checked on both right and left wheel cuts.

Manual Recirculating-Ball Steering Gears

The principles behind manual recirculating-ball steering gears are the same principles used by all steering gears—manual and power assisted. **Recirculating-ball steering gear** systems consist of a steering box with a worm gear inside a metal block, called a ball-nut rack, with a threaded hole in it.

The **worm gear** is a helical (spiral), grooved shaft that is attached to the steering column and meshes with the **ball-nut rack**. The worm gear and ball-nut operate like a nut and bolt. In this case, the helix-shaped groove on the worm moves the ball-nut one tooth for each revolution of the worm. The helix-shaped groove provides smooth and quiet steering operation for the driver. It converts the rotary motion of the steering wheel to the linear motion needed to turn the wheels.

The worm gear is surrounded by a metal block, or ball-nut, containing ball bearings. The metal block has gear teeth cut into one outside edge. Those teeth mesh with another set of teeth cut into the sector shaft gear, as illustrated in **FIGURE 32-15**. Moving the input shaft of the steering gear is like threading a bolt into a nut—only in this case the worm gear is the bolt and the metal block is the nut. Although the nut-and-bolt analogy works for envisioning the shapes and orientation of the worm gear and the metal block, it is not entirely accurate.

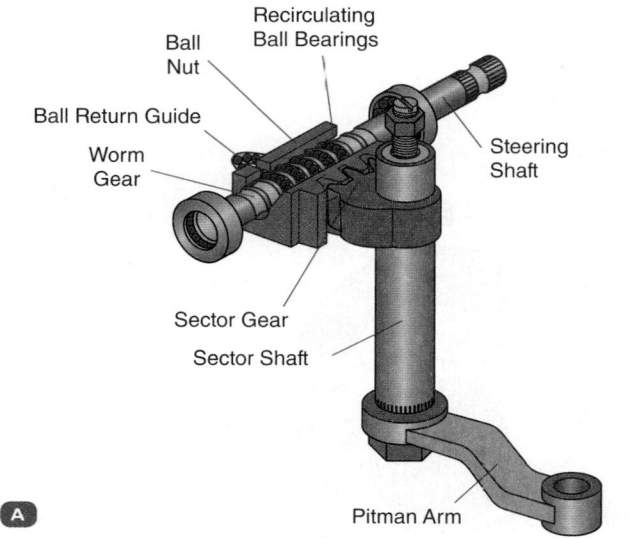

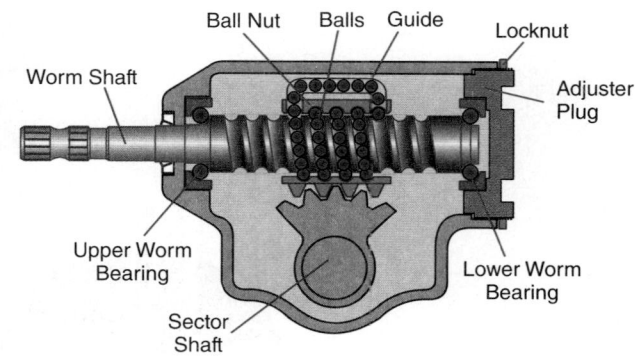

FIGURE 32-16 A cross section of a basic worm-type steering gear.

FIGURE 32-15 A. Recirculating-ball steering gear. B. Recirculating-ball steering gear with worm gear showing.

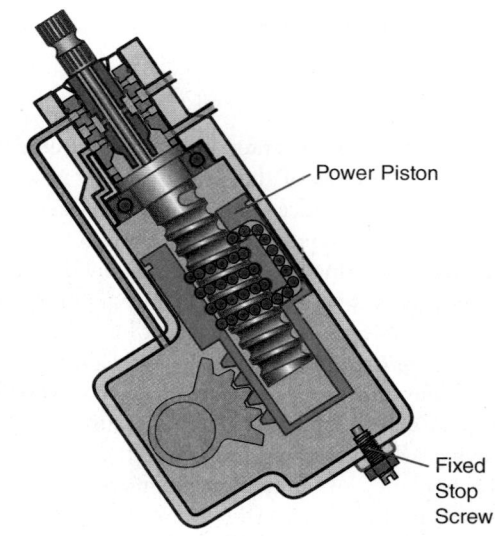

FIGURE 32-17 Stop screw in a power piston.

Unlike a nut-and-bolt arrangement, turning the steering wheel spins the worm gear in the box. As the worm gear spins, teeth on the metal block, which are engaged with the sector shaft, sweep back and forth. That back-and-forth movement causes the sector shaft to rotate. Another difference is found in the "threads" of the worm gear and ball-nut. Ball bearings are placed between the threads of the worm gear and ball-nut. As the steering wheel is turned, ball bearings recirculate around the worm gear inside the ball-nut. That is, the balls leave the rack at one end and pass through a channel or guide back into the rack at the opposite end, hence recirculating-ball steering. A cross-section of a basic worm steering gear is illustrated in **FIGURE 32-16**.

Using recirculating ball bearings has two primary advantages. First, recirculating ball bearings reduce friction between the worm gear and block. Lower friction reduces the steering effort, especially when a high-level steering effort is required (e.g., at low speeds in tight turns). Gear oil filling the steering gear also helps reduce friction. The second purpose served by recirculating-ball bearings is to allow almost zero clearance between the worm gear and block. If the two parts were simply threaded, some clearance would be required, producing excessive free play in the steering system.

Power Recirculating-Ball Steering Gears

LO 32-5 Explain the operation of integral power steering gears systems.

Power steering in a recirculating-ball system operates similarly to a manual system. A key exception is the level of output force. In a power steering system, pressurized hydraulic fluid multiplies the output force of the worm gear located inside a power piston by applying pressure to a power piston moving back and forth inside the steering gear. As shown in **FIGURE 32-17**,

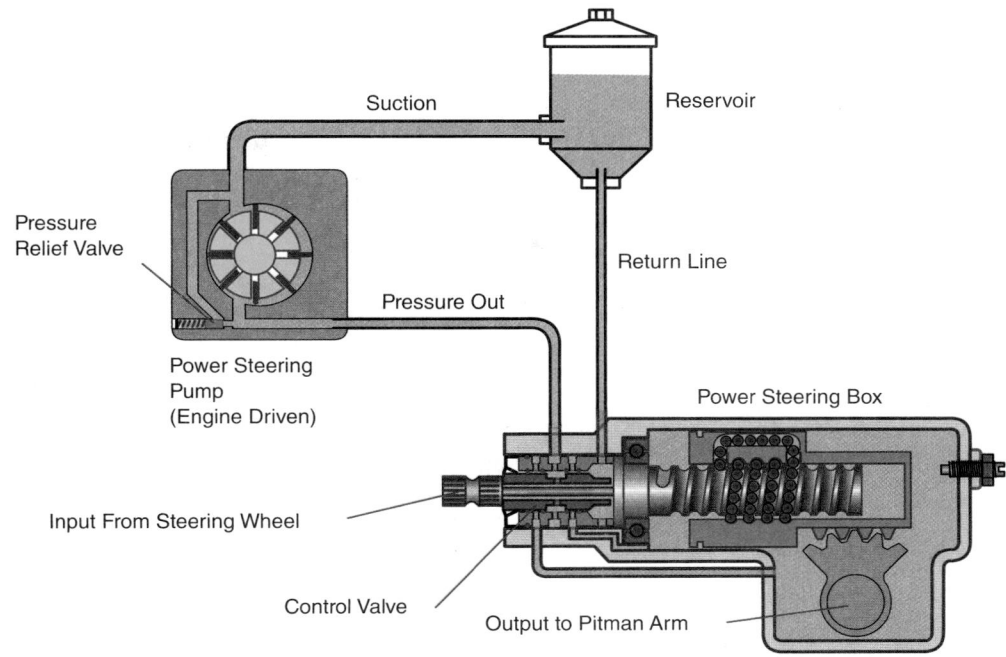

FIGURE 32-18 Hydraulic assist to the steering gear.

FIGURE 32-19 Power steering rotary valve and torsion bar.

the power piston has teeth machined into one side, just like the ball-nut, and those teeth engage the sector shaft teeth. The same recirculating-ball mechanism, using a worm gear and ball-nut, is located in a power steering gear; the major difference is the power piston has replaced the ball-nut.

Assist is provided by supplying higher-pressure fluid to one side of the piston. Which side of the piston receives the fluid depends on the direction the gear is expected to move. Power steering systems only engage to assist the steering effort of the driver when the driver is turning the steering wheel. This means when no turning force is being applied by the driver, such as when driving in a straight line, the hydraulic system only recirculates fluid and no assist is provided.

A schematic of hydraulic assist to the steering gear is shown in **FIGURE 32-18**.

Two critical components of the hydraulic control mechanism of all power steering gears are the **rotary valve** (also called a **spool valve**) and the torsion bar. Together, the rotary valve and torsion bar, shown in **FIGURE 32-19**, are responsible for controlling the flow of hydraulic pressure inside the steering gear.

Rotary Valve

The rotary valve, also called the spool valve, senses the change in force applied to the steering wheel at the beginning of a turn. Essentially, this valve directs pressurized fluid to either side of the power piston when turning is initiated. A steering rotary valve is illustrated in **FIGURE 32-20**.

The complete valve assembly, a cross section of which is illustrated in **FIGURE 32-21**, consists primarily of a rotary-shaped valve centered inside a valve body. The inner and outer section of the valve can move in relation to one another. The inner part of the valve is attached to the steering input shaft, while the outer part of the valve is connected to a component called the torsion bar. The torsion bar can slightly twist and transmit steering shaft input torque to the worm gear. Ports on the rotary valve body direct fluid from the power steering pump to either end of the power piston. When the steering wheel is not being turned, low-pressure hydraulic fluid is applied equally to both sides of the power piston inside the steering gear housing.

If the steered wheels receive a road shock, the shock forces are transmitted through the sector shaft to the piston and into to the **worm shaft**, and then into the rotary valve.

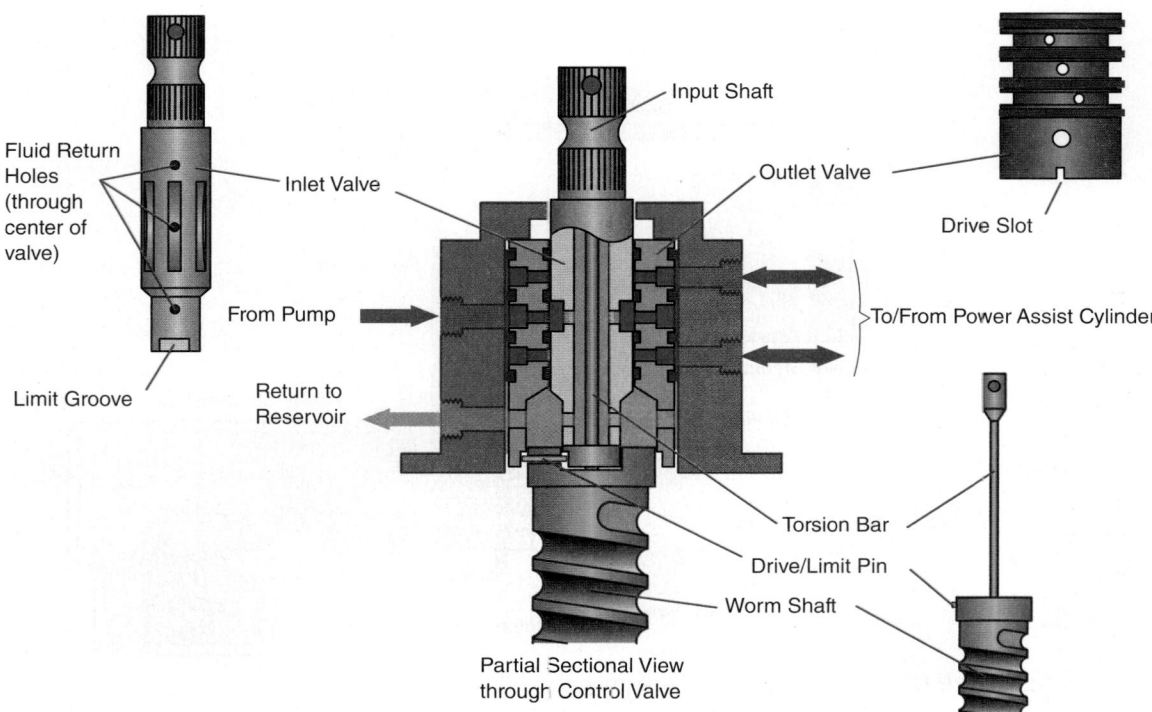

Fluid Return Holes (through center of valve)

Inlet Valve

Input Shaft

Outlet Valve

Drive Slot

From Pump

To/From Power Assist Cylinder

Return to Reservoir

Limit Groove

Torsion Bar

Drive/Limit Pin

Worm Shaft

Partial Sectional View through Control Valve

FIGURE 32-20 Steering rotary valve.

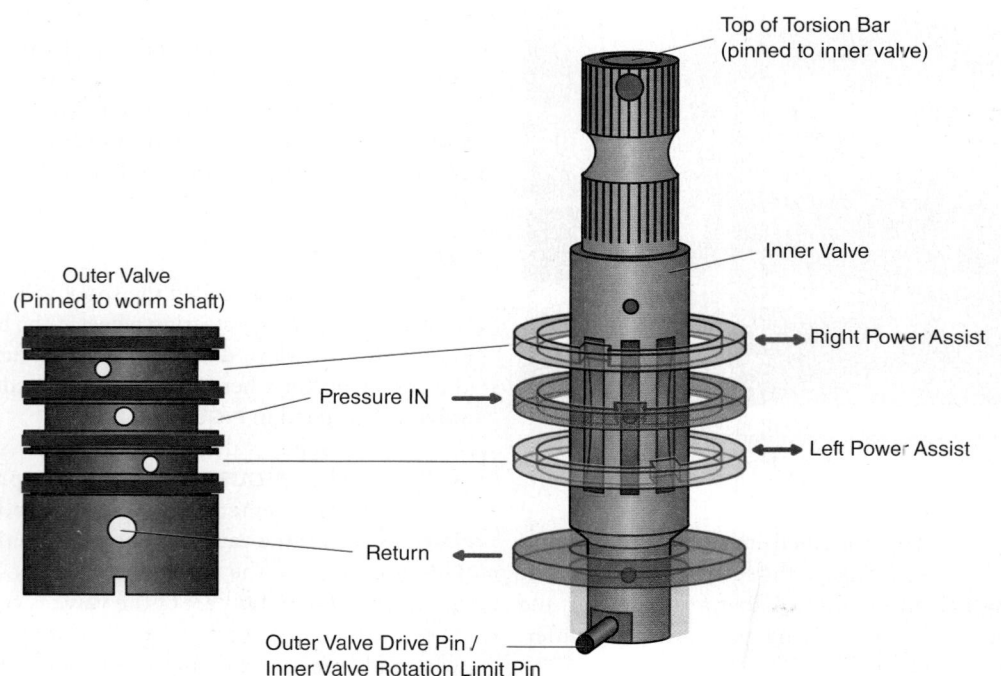

Top of Torsion Bar (pinned to inner valve)

Inner Valve

Outer Valve (Pinned to worm shaft)

Right Power Assist

Pressure IN

Left Power Assist

Return

Outer Valve Drive Pin / Inner Valve Rotation Limit Pin

FIGURE 32-21 Cross-section of rotary valve and ports.

Since the steering input shaft is not being turned, the torsion bar twists and changes the alignment between the ports on the rotary control valve, as shown in **FIGURE 32-22**. The rotary-control valve is designed to respond to the valve deflection by sending high-pressure fluid to the end of the power piston to counteract and resist the road shock forces. Hydraulic shock absorption by the gear prevents bump steer and steering wheel kick, which is a normal feature of manual steering gears. The hydraulic circuits in a steering gear are illustrated in **FIGURE 32-23**.

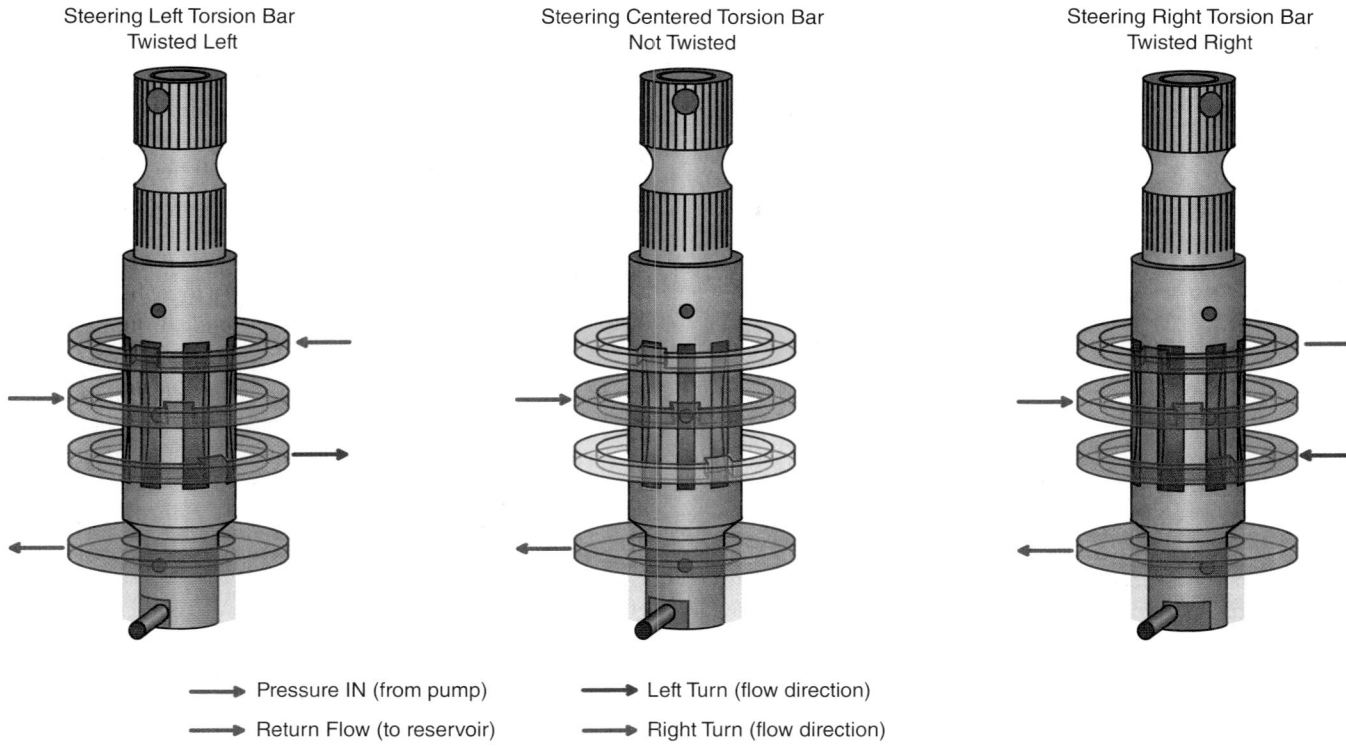

Steering Left Torsion Bar
Twisted Left

Steering Centered Torsion Bar
Not Twisted

Steering Right Torsion Bar
Twisted Right

→ Pressure IN (from pump) → Left Turn (flow direction)

→ Return Flow (to reservoir) → Right Turn (flow direction)

Power assist flow and pressure are always proportional to the amount of twist in the torsion bar.

FIGURE 32-22 Various alignments on rotary valves.

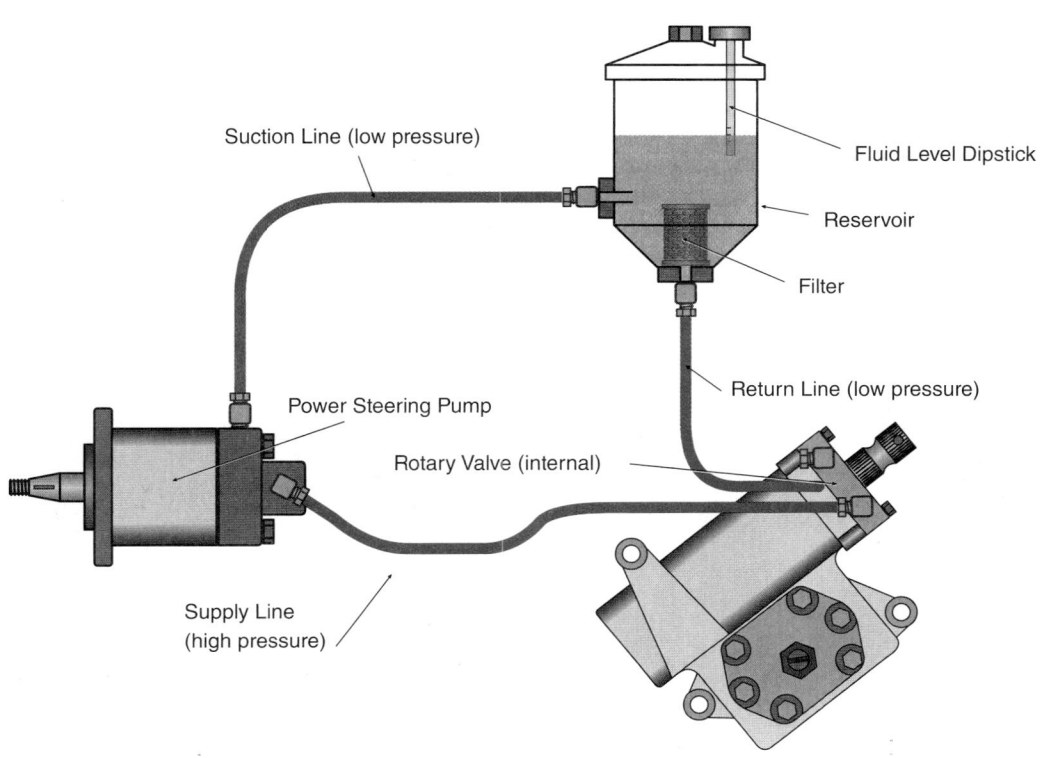

Suction Line (low pressure)

Fluid Level Dipstick

Reservoir

Filter

Return Line (low pressure)

Power Steering Pump

Rotary Valve (internal)

Supply Line
(high pressure)

FIGURE 32-23 Hydraulic circuits for a power steering system using an integral steering gear.

Torsion Rod

The job of the torsion rod is to move one of the two parts of the rotary (spool) valve, which directs hydraulic fluid to either side of the power piston. The **torsion rod** is a thin, spring-like metal rod that connects to the outside section of the rotary valve. The bottom of the rod is attached to the rotating worm gear. The torsion rod turns the worm gear when the input shaft turning force is transmitted to the torsion bar through the rotary control valve. Recall that the worm gear moves the power piston back and forth, and that motion turns the wheels. With or without hydraulic pressure, any difference between the torque applied to the input shaft and the force required to turn the steer tires twists the torsion rod.

The more torque the driver uses to turn the steering wheels, the more the rod twists. One or two degrees of steering wheel operation does not twist the rod very much to provide assist. This absence of hydraulic assist during small deflection of the torsion rod is what provides some feedback about steering effort, which is sensed by the driver as "road feel." Road surface irregularities, and even the resistance of the road surface to tire direction change, can be felt by the driver to greater or lesser degrees, depending on how much movement is required in the control valve before power assistance takes place. After three or more degrees of rotation or twisting of the torsion bar, control-valve deflection takes place and the valve begins to produce hydraulic assist. How much steering feedback, or road feel, a driver receives is built into the torsion rod and rotary control-valve design. The torsion bar, shown in **FIGURE 32-24**, is pinned inside of a steering gear input shaft. The input shaft is attached to the inside half of a two-piece rotary valve.

Both the torsion bar and the input shaft can move a limited amount independently of one another—depending on the twisting force applied to the input shaft. Increasing turning torque applied to the input shaft, combined with resistance from the worm gear, produces a proportional deflection in the valve-port alignment inside the rotary valve. This means the greatest input effort fully opens the appropriate hydraulic ports supplying hydraulic pressure to one side of the power piston. Depending on the direction of the twist, pressurized fluid passes through the valve to the top or bottom end of the steering gear power piston. If the torsion rod is broken, power assist is not possible. However, even if the torsion rod is broken, the design of the rotary-control valve allows the continuous transmission of torque from the input shaft to the worm.

Rack-and-Pinion Steering

LO 32-6 Outline the advantages, disadvantages, and operation of rack and pinion type steering systems.

Rack-and-pinion steering systems have been used in automobiles for decades and, in recent years, adapted for a few heavy trucks. The compact design of the system has a number of advantages. On heavy trucks, the system is 45 lb (20 kg) lighter than conventional integral steering. Rack-and-pinion steering has fewer parts and pivot points than conventional integral steering systems. Because the system has fewer parts, it also has fewer joints, which provides more precise steering response and greater reliability. The ZF rack-and-pinion steering gear, shown in **FIGURE 32-25**, is used by an independent suspension system in a cab-over-engine heavy-duty truck.

Rack-and-pinion steering systems do not include a pitman arm or a drag link. So, because the rack is parallel with the front axle, the problem of bump steer is minimized. **Bump steer** can occur when a wheel hits a bump and the axle lifts or drops through an arc on the side where the steering gear is located. The up-or-down axle movement changes the distance between the upper steering arm and the end of the pitman arm. This change in length between these two points can cause the drag link to push or pull on the steering arm, which, in turn, causes the vehicle to dart to one side of the road as the steering linkage is pushed or pulled. Steering pull can also sometimes occur when an axle twists due to braking torque. Without the drag link or pitman arm, which rack-and-pinion steering eliminates, steering pull is minimized.

Freightliner's rack-and-pinion steering system consists of a horizontal tube containing a geared rack. A pinion gear intersects the rack at a 90-degree angle. The pinion gear is connected directly to the steering wheel through a plunging column that slides up and down with the suspension. Tie-rods protrude from each end of the tube and connect with the steering arms on the steering knuckle. A power-assist piston is integrated into the rack.

FIGURE 32-24 Rotary valve and torsion bar.

FIGURE 32-25 ZF rack-and-pinion steering gear.

Turning the steering wheel causes the pinion gear to move the rack either to the left or right. A rotary-control valve, such as the ones found in the integral steering gears, supplies pressurized oil to two ports, one on either side of the rack piston. Without the hydraulic assist, the rack is moved left or right by only the torque transmitted from the steering wheel and into the pinion gear and rack. A torsion bar in the rack's rotary control valve varies the hydraulic pressure applied to the power piston proportionally to driver-input torque.

Steering Linkage

LO 32-7 Identify and describe the purpose and function of mechanical steering linkage in steering systems.

The final basic components of any steering system are the **steering linkage**. The parts that make up the steering linkage are the pitman (drop) arm, drag link, tie-rod ends, and the upper and lower steering arms. These components were introduced in the Front Steering Axles and Vehicle Alignment Factors chapter. We extend that introductory discussion in this section.

Pitman Arm

Recall that the pitman arm, also called the drop arm, is attached to the output shaft, which is more correctly referred to as the sector shaft of the steering gear. The steering linkage is illustrated in **FIGURE 32-26**. The function of the pitman arm is to convert and transfer the rotational movement of the sector gear to linear motion that moves the steering linkage. The arm is splined to the sector shaft and tightened with either a pinch bolt, set screws, or a specialized nut with a lock tab. **FIGURE 32-27** shows a pinch bolt locking the pitman arm to the sector shaft on this gear. Note the index lines on the sector shaft, which must be lined up with the pitman arm. If not properly aligned, the steering gear is not able to rotate the steering wheel evenly between left and right turns.

It is critical that the connection of the pitman arm to the steering box sector shaft is secure. The splined shafts are often tapered to create a tighter connection. Set screws can be used to lock the arm to the sector shaft to add further security to the connection. The connection is so tight that it requires a

specialized puller to remove the pitman arm from the sector shaft. An illustration for a pitman arm puller is shown in **FIGURE 32-28**.

An aligning mark is often used on the sector shaft and pitman arm to correctly center the wheels with the steering gear. The length of the arm affects the leverage of the steering gear on the linkage. Heavier vehicles use longer arms. On dual-box systems, the arms are different length and the right-side arm, used on the slave steering gear, must always be longer than the left. If the wrong arm is installed, the slave gear creates a wheel shake on left turns because the turning radius of each wheel is different. Correct pitman arm alignment/timing and drag link length is critical to prevent a similar condition.

Drag Link

Recall from the Introduction to Front Axles and Vehicle Alignment Factors chapter that the drag link is a steering linkage rod connecting the pitman arm at one end to the upper steering arm at the other. In addition to the basic bridging function, the drag link performs a leveling function. The sweeping arc the drag

FIGURE 32-27 A pitman arm being locked to sector shaft by a pinch bolt.

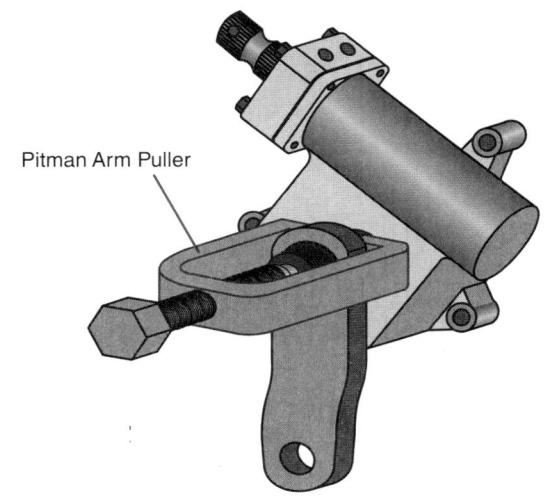

Pitman Arm Puller

FIGURE 32-28 A pitman arm puller for a Sheppard model steering box.

FIGURE 32-26 A steering linkage.

link moves through is enabled by the articulating ball joints at each end of the drag link. As the vehicle's suspension height adjusts as the chassis is loaded or the vehicle encounters bumps on the road, the drag link moves up and down and maintains the link between the pitman and steering arm.

While many drag links are fixed in length, others are adjustable. Adjustable drag links use a threaded center coupler or threaded rod end that enables changing the links length. On a single steering box, an adjustable link is turned to enable a technician to center the steering wheel so its position corresponds to the high point or center of the steering box travel. On dual-box systems, adjustable links enable changes to equalize the turning radius of each wheel to left or right.

Tie-Rod Ends

Tie-rod ends, such as the one shown in **FIGURE 32-29**, are ball-and-socket joints attached to both the left and right steering knuckle's lower steering arms. The ends are connected together

by threading them into a cross tube called the **tie-rod**. Each side uses a left- or right-hand thread to enable adjustment of tire toe by turning the cross tube, which connects the tie-rod ends. Since the steering gear pushes or pulls on the upper steering arm only on one side, the movement is transferred to the opposite side through the tie-rod. Synchronizing the movement of both steering knuckles using the tie-rod means the articulating joints of the tie-rods move quite a bit. The weight of a vehicle combined with constant movement of the tie-rod ends means these parts wear the fastest of any piece of steering linkage. Frequent lubrication and maintenance inspections of these two critical joints are important to maintaining precise vehicle steering control.

A hydraulic steering dampener, illustrated in **FIGURE 32-30**, is sometimes connected to the tie-rod. The dampener, which operates like a shock absorber, minimizes steering wheel shimmy caused by high positive camber. Under conditions when the rear of the vehicle is heavily loaded, the frame angle may change, and the front wheels' kingpin-inclination angle (KPI) tends to tilt back, which increases positive camber. Caster shimmy becomes even more exaggerated as vehicle speed increases. The dampener prevents exaggerated caster shimmy and loss of steering control.

Pitman arms, tie-rods, and drag links are often designed with sharply curved shafts to prevent interference between steering or suspension components when wheels are cut sharply. Dropped tie-rod ends, illustrated in **FIGURE 32-31**, and tie-rod centers decrease link-to-attachment point angles. The dropped design also solves the steering geometry problem of enabling sharp turning radiuses without linkage interference by increasing the clearance between the steering arm and the tie-rod.

FIGURE 32-29 Tie-rod ends.

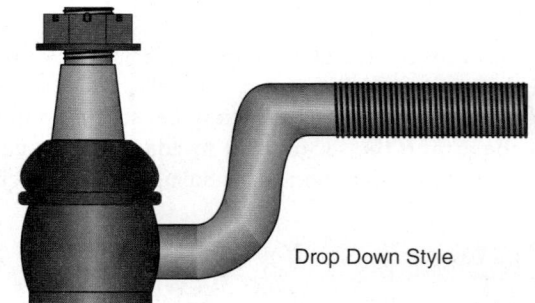

Drop Down Style

FIGURE 32-31 Drop-style tie-rod end.

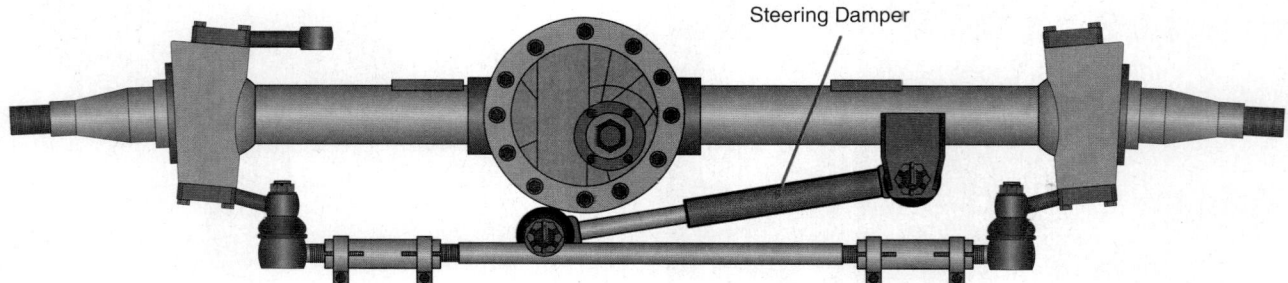

Steering Damper

FIGURE 32-30 Hydraulic steering dampener.

Steering Arms

Steering arms, also called tie-rod arms, are heavy stamped-steel arms that extend from the steering knuckle. The tie-rods connect to the lower steering arms to synchronize steering knuckle rotation. Two steering arms are used on the left-side steering knuckle: an upper arm and a lower arm. A single steering arm, also called the Ackermann arm, is used on the right when single steering boxes are used. Both lower arms are attached to the knuckle using tapered shafts and a keyway to prevent movement in the steering knuckle. A castellated nut and cotter pin are used to tighten and secure the shaft.

The lower steering arms are forged at an angle that, ideally, is unique to the wheel base of the chassis, as illustrated in **FIGURE 32-32**. By drawing an imaginary line through the shaft, the line should intersect at the vehicle's pivot point at the center of the rear axle's turning radius. Forming the shaft at this angle produces a slightly different turning radius for each wheel, with the outside one toeing out on turns and the inner wheel turning more sharply, with a smaller turning radius, than the outside wheel of the turn. The name given to this important angle and feature of the steering arm enabling toe-out on turns is called the Ackerman angle. Tandem-axle steering arm angles should intersect with the centerline between the two axles. While the ideal steering arm angle corresponds to an angle that intersects with the center of the rear differential, in practice, manufacturers use a steering arm common to a wide range of wheel-base lengths.

Kingpins

On vehicles with an I-beam front axle, the kingpin passes through the steering knuckle's upper arm, through the opening of the I-beam, and then through the knuckle yoke's lower arm, as illustrated in **FIGURE 32-33**. A retaining bolt keeps the kingpin in place and locks the pin in the I-beam axle. A thrust bearing is also used between the I-beam and lower arm of the knuckle so that the end of the I-beam rests on the bearing.

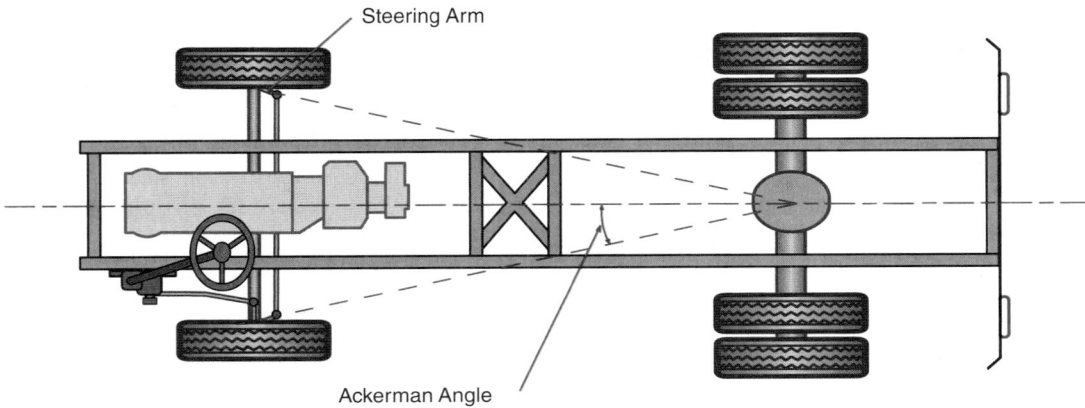

FIGURE 32-32 Ackermann arm angles are shaped to match the wheel base of the chassis.

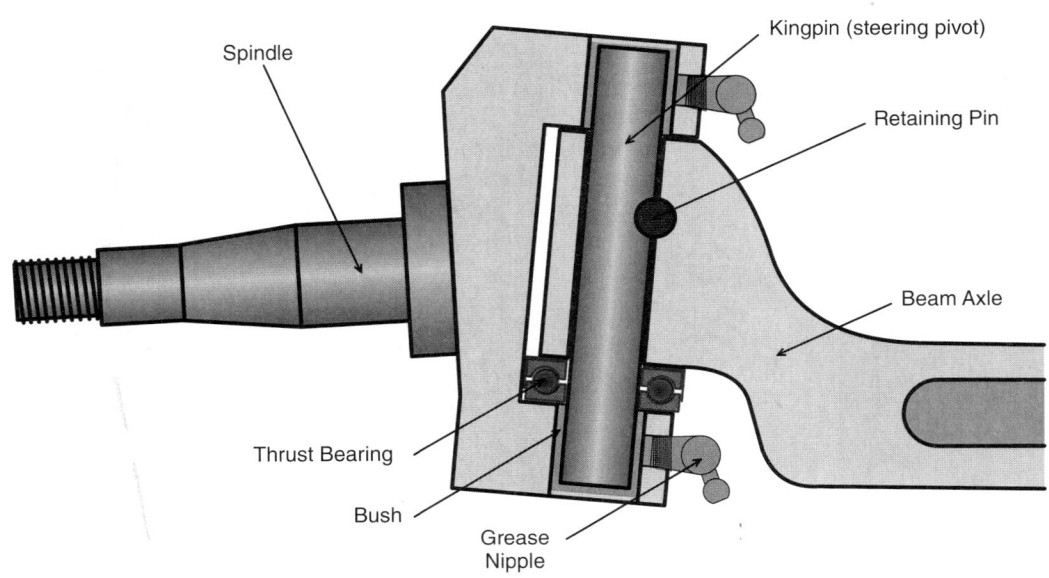

FIGURE 32-33 Kingpin assembly.

Steering Knuckle

Steering knuckles with kingpins have the advantage of being able to support much heavier weights compared to the ball-joints used by light-duty suspension systems. To enable the least amount of friction between the knuckle and axle, a single bearing is located between the steering knuckle and axle, which transfers the weight supported by the wheel end to the axle. Without it, excessive friction between the axle and knuckle quickly wears the two components and dramatically increases steering effort. The knuckle also uses adjustable **steering stops**, which limit the maximum rotation of the knuckle when turned. This prevents the steer tires from contacting the frame, steering linkage, or suspension components.

Hydraulic Components of Power Steering Systems

LO 32-8 Identify and explain the purpose and operation of steering system hydraulic components.

Power steering reduces the amount of physical effort required by the driver to steer the vehicle. A good power steering system not only reduces the effort required to steer the vehicle, but also provides good steering feedback (road feel) to the driver.

The latest steering systems with driver-assisted features use electric pumps to supply steering assist when the engine is off. However, the most common type of power steering has an **engine-driven hydraulic pump** that delivers hydraulic fluid to the **power unit** at the steering gear through connecting hoses

and pipes. The power unit is the hydraulic-assist portion of the steering gear. When the driver rotates the steering wheel, hydraulic pressure supplied by the pump increases due to the restriction in the fluid passageway in the rotary control valve. Return hoses, high-pressure hydraulic lines, the fluid reservoir, and a variety of valves in the pump and steering gear make up the remaining components of the hydraulic system.

Hydraulically Assisted Power Steering

Hydraulically assisted power steering uses hydraulic fluid under pressure to assist the driver in steering the wheels. This design, illustrated in **FIGURE 32-34**, is especially helpful at slower vehicle speeds when the effort required to turn the steering wheel is much higher. Two lines connect the pump to the steering gear control valve: a pressure and fluid return. A remotely mounted reservoir receives fluid returning from the pump before filtering it and supplying the pump inlet. The fluid reservoir can be mounted on the pump, or it can be remotely mounted. With the engine running, fluid flows continuously from the **power steering pump** to the steering gear control valve and back to the power steering pump. With the steering wheel in the neutral position, minimal pump pressure circulates fluid to and from the steering gear and requires little engine power to operate.

Power Steering Fluid and Hoses

The hydraulic fluid in a power steering system transmits the pressure from the power steering pump to the working chambers in the power steering gear or rack. The fluid must withstand high temperatures and pressures and, at the same time,

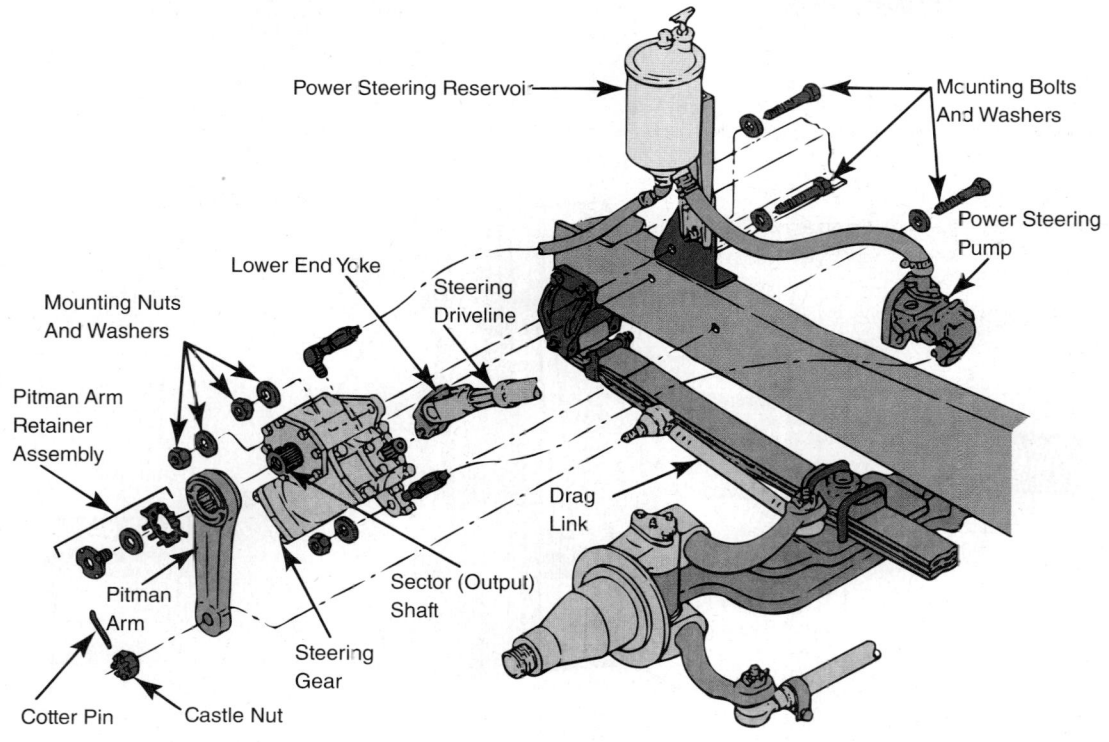

FIGURE 32-34 View of major power steering components.

lubricate the pump and steering gear, while preserving the system seals and pressure hoses. The fluid must also flow freely at very cold temperatures. Manufacturers have specified either engine oil or automatic-transmission power steering gear fluid, like that shown in **FIGURE 32-35**, for their power steering systems. Most engine-driven pumps use engine oil to avoid the risk of contaminating engine oil with automatic-transmission fluid.

Regardless of the type of oil, it becomes contaminated with rubber and metallic particles from internal wear in the system. Because of this, a replaceable filter is installed in the fluid reservoir.

Power steering hoses carry power steering fluid from the pump to the steering gear. This hose is usually made of flexible, steel-braided hose material. The return hose from the steering

FIGURE 32-35 Power steering fluid.

gear back to the pump reservoir carries fluid under much lower pressure and is not usually reinforced. These hoses must also allow movement between the engine and chassis, so they cannot be too stiff.

Over time, power steering hoses become weak or damaged. If they leak, they cause a loss of vehicle control. For this reason, hoses should be inspected for seepage or wear during each service. Also, some power steering hoses use an O-ring to seal the end of each hose to the pump and steering gear. These seals can wear or leak, requiring replacement of the O-ring.

As illustrated in **FIGURE 32-36**, when the steering gear is in the neutral or non-steering position, equal low pressure is being applied to both ends of the steering gear piston. The oil is circulating at back pressure only and provides a hydraulic cushion for the steering gear. Circulating oil is cooled in the reservoir or through a small heat exchanger, which is usually a tube in the low-pressure return line wrapped with cooling fins to help cool the oil.

▶ TECHNICIAN TIP

A power steering reservoir is often equipped with a filter needing periodic replacement. Restricted filters lead to over-heating of power steering oil, pump cavitation, or air leaks on the suction side of the system.

With the engine running and the steering in the neutral position, fluid flow is directed into the valve assembly through drilled holes in the outer sleeve, like those shown in **FIGURE 32-37**. As soon as the steering is turned to the left or right, the slight relative movement occurs between the inner and the outer parts of the valve due to the action of the torsion rod. In the neutral position, the inner part of the valve connected to the steering input shaft lets fluid pass equally to both sides of the piston through internal passages and return to the fluid reservoir. Equal but low pressure is applied to both sides of the power piston.

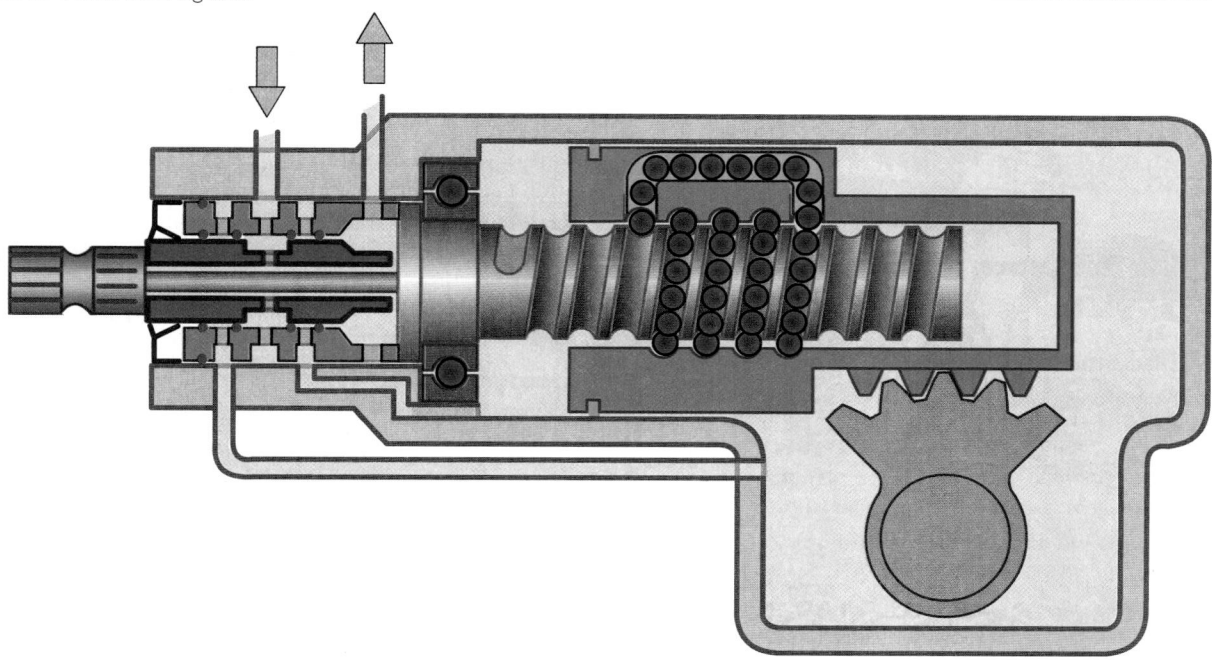

FIGURE 32-36 With the steering gear in the neutral or non-steering position, equal low pressure is being applied to both ends of the steering gear piston.

When the steering wheel is turned, fluid is restricted from returning to the to the reservoir. This happens due to the action between the twisting torsion rod and the outer half of the rotary control valve. Fluid is then directed to the side that matches the turning action. At the same time, fluid on the opposite side is directed to the return circuit—back to the reservoir. Slight rotation of the valve gives a small amount of assistance, which becomes progressively greater as the torsion bar flexes when more assistance is needed.

Power Steering Pumps

To provide the hydraulic force necessary to assist steering effort, an engine-driven hydraulic pump is used. Gear-driven pumps are more popular due to the reliability of a direct connection versus a belt-driven system. Gear pumps can be mounted at either end of the engine, as well. These pumps can be either the vane, gear, or roller.

Engine speed can vary, so unregulated pump output volume can be too low or excessively high. To compensate for this, the pump is designed to produce more volume than needed at idle and is regulated by a **flow-control valve**. A pressure-relief valve is also incorporated into the pump to prevent excessively high pressures, such as when the steering is turned to the end of the steering stops. In addition to the pressure relief valve in the power steering pump, steering gears are equipped with relief valves that relieve pump pressure when the wheels near the steering stops at a full wheel cut. Without pressure relief, the steering system components are severely stressed and power steering oil overheats.

Power steering reservoirs should always be located above the level of the power steering pump. Lines should always be located at a level below the reservoir. Typically, 10w-30, 15w-40, or automatic-transmission fluids are used as oils. Since chemical additives in various oils may not be compatible with steering gear, hose, or reservoir materials, it is not a recommended practice to mix oils.

Power Steering Coolers

Pressurizing the power steering oil produces heat that can damage the oil. Overheated oil oxidizes and forms sludge, as well as hardens hoses and other rubber-based parts. Heated oil loses its viscosity and leaks between small clearances, causing a loss in power-assist. On heavy vehicles, an oil cooler is used to prevent overheating.

▶ TECHNICIAN TIP

Engine-driven power steering pumps use two seals on the drive shaft. One deflects engine oil from being pulled into the gear by pump suction, and the other prevents oil from leaving the gear. If the engine-side seal is damaged or cut from by abrasive metal filings or dirt, the pump pulls engine oil from the engine and overfills the power steering reservoir. Engine oil laden with black soot contaminates the reservoir.

Types of Hydraulic Pumps

To provide the hydraulic force necessary to assist steering effort, an engine-driven hydraulic pump and reservoir are used. Gear-driven pumps are more popular due to the reliability of a direct connection compared to that of a belt-driven system. Gear pumps can be mounted at either end of the engine too. Pumps are one of the following types:

- vane-type, illustrated in **FIGURE 32-38**
- roller-type, illustrated in **FIGURE 32-39**
- gear-type, as illustrated in **FIGURE 32-40**

In vane- and roller-types, the vanes or rollers rotate inside an eccentric cam, pulling oil in one side and forcing it out the other side as the volume between the rollers or vanes changes. As the vanes or rollers spin, hydraulic fluid is pulled from the return line at low pressure and forced into the outlet at high pressure.

Depending on engine speed, pump output volume can be too low or excessively high. Therefore, the pump uses a flow-control valve designed to compensate for normally low-volume output at idle and decrease output volume at high pump speeds. Regulating pump volume is a flow-control needle that throttles the flow of fluid at the pump's outlet. The needle valve's position

FIGURE 32-37 Drilled passageways through the outer sleeve of the rotary valve.

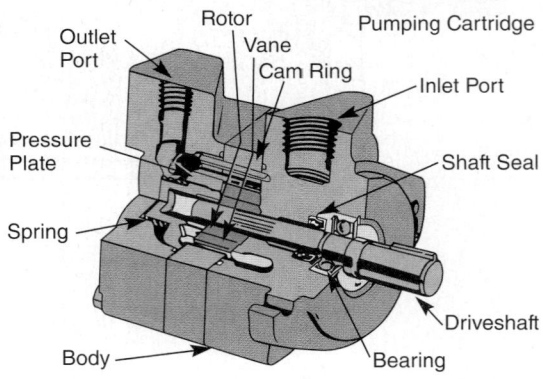

FIGURE 32-38 Exploded view of a rotary-vane power steering pump.

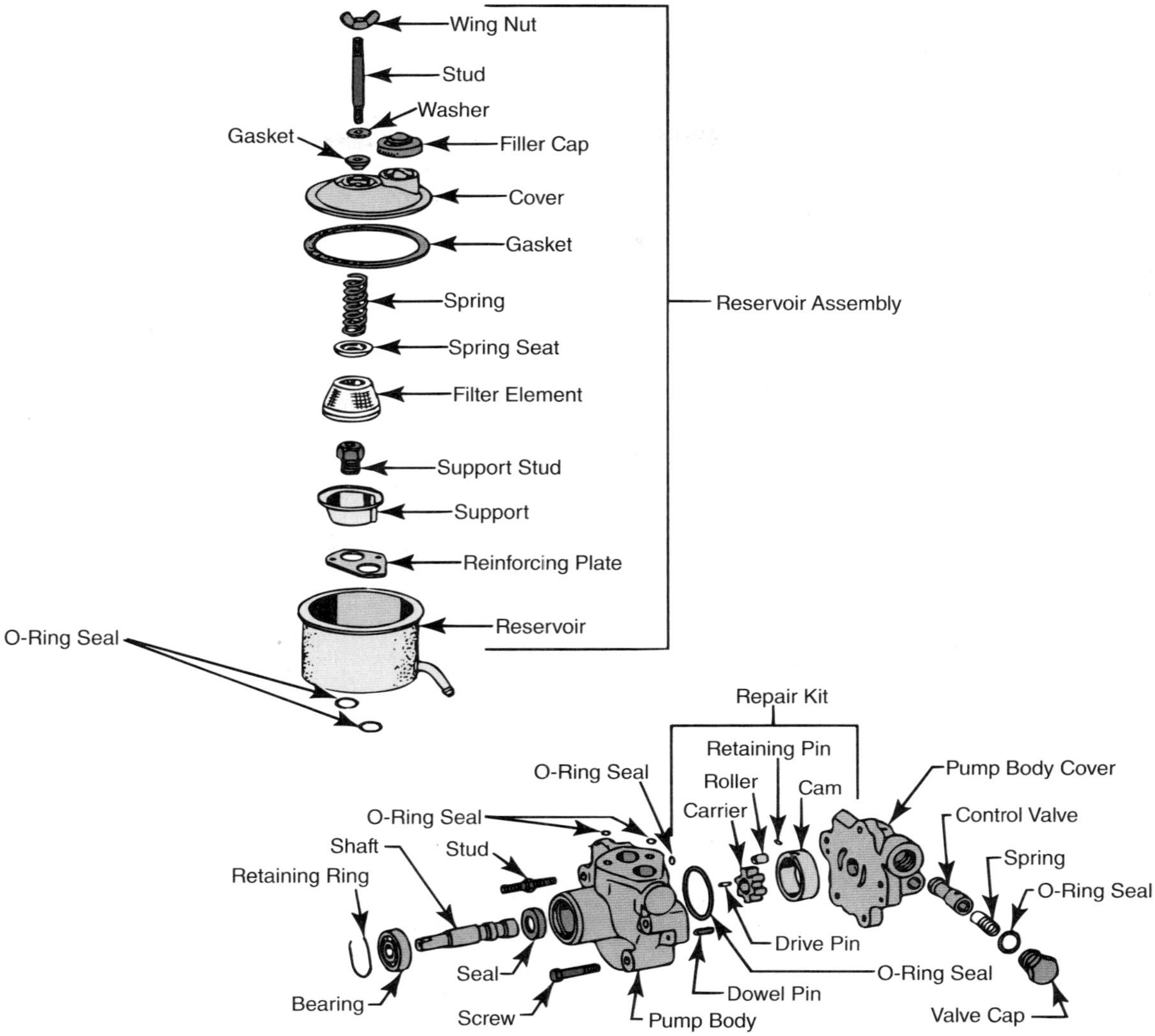

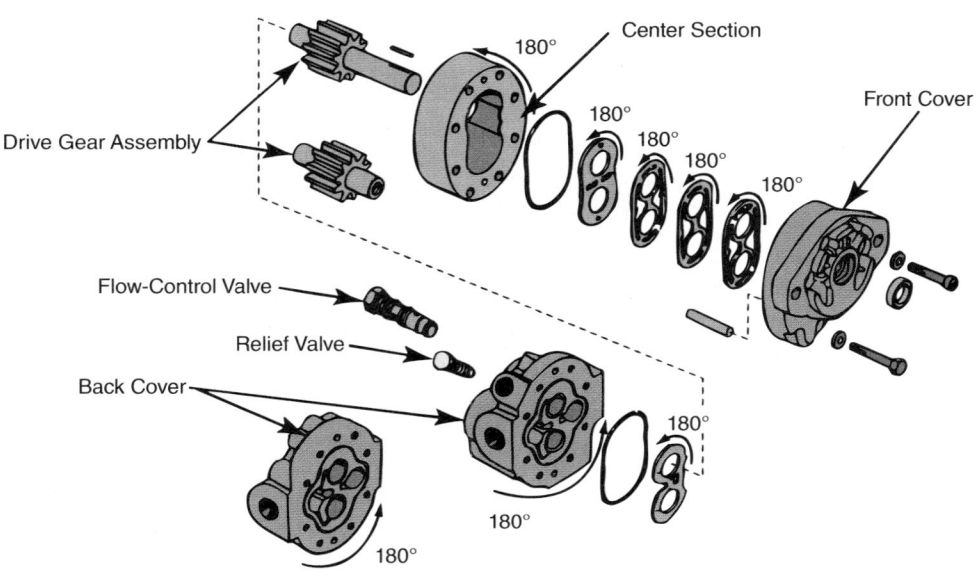

Wing Nut
Stud
Washer
Gasket
Filler Cap
Cover
Gasket
Spring
Spring Seat
Filter Element
Support Stud
Support
Reinforcing Plate
Reservoir
O-Ring Seal
Reservoir Assembly

Repair Kit
Retaining Pin
Roller
Cam
O-Ring Seal
Pump Body Cover
O-Ring Seal
Carrier
Control Valve
Shaft
Stud
Spring
Retaining Ring
O-Ring Seal
Seal
Drive Pin
O-Ring Seal
Bearing
Screw
Dowel Pin
Pump Body
Valve Cap

FIGURE 32-39 Exploded view of a roller power steering pump.

Center Section
180°
Front Cover
180°
180°
180°
180°
Drive Gear Assembly
Flow-Control Valve
Relief Valve
Back Cover
180°
180°
180°

FIGURE 32-40 Exploded view of a gear power steering pump.

is balanced between pump outlet pressure and the position of the high-pressure regulating valve. The valve position at idle is illustrated in Figure 32-40.

When both outlet flow and output pressure are low, the flow-control valve is moved to the right by the regulating valve. This allows more fluid to flow through the valve to the steering gear. **FIGURE 32-41** shows high-output pressure forcing the

pressure-regulating valve to move left and redirect fluid back to the low-pressure pump-return circuit. At the same time, the flow-control valve blocks fluid flow out of the pump.

If pump outlet pressures exceed the control valve's ability to regulate pressure, an internal relief valve opens and dumps pump pressure directly back into the reservoir, as illustrated in **FIGURE 32-42**.

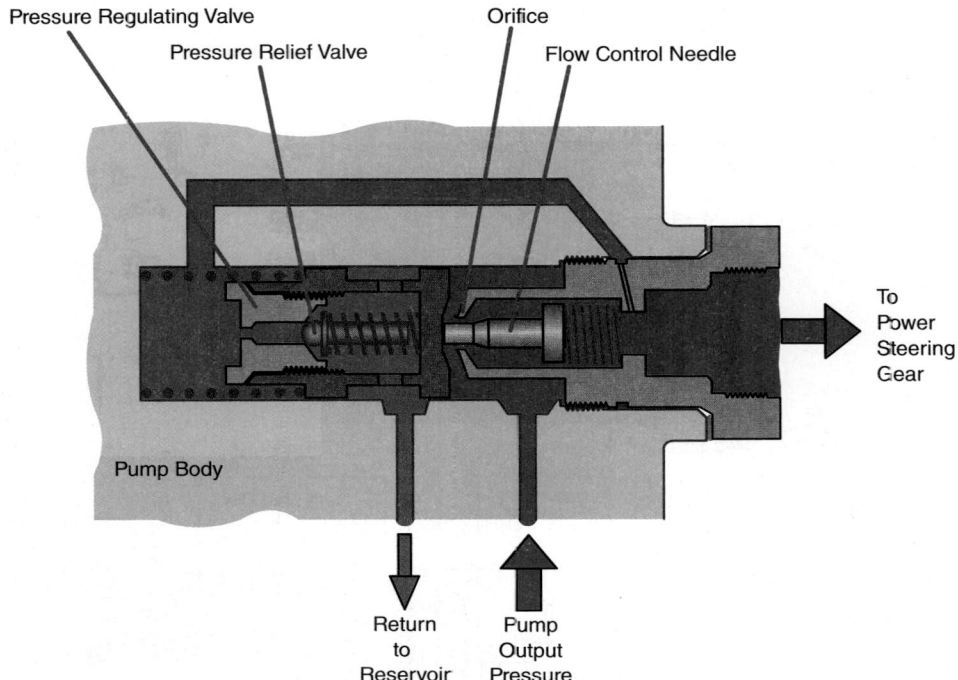

FIGURE 32-41 The flow-control valve's movement regulates hydraulic pressure and volume to the steering gear by moving a spring-loaded needle valve located in the outlet fitting of the pump.

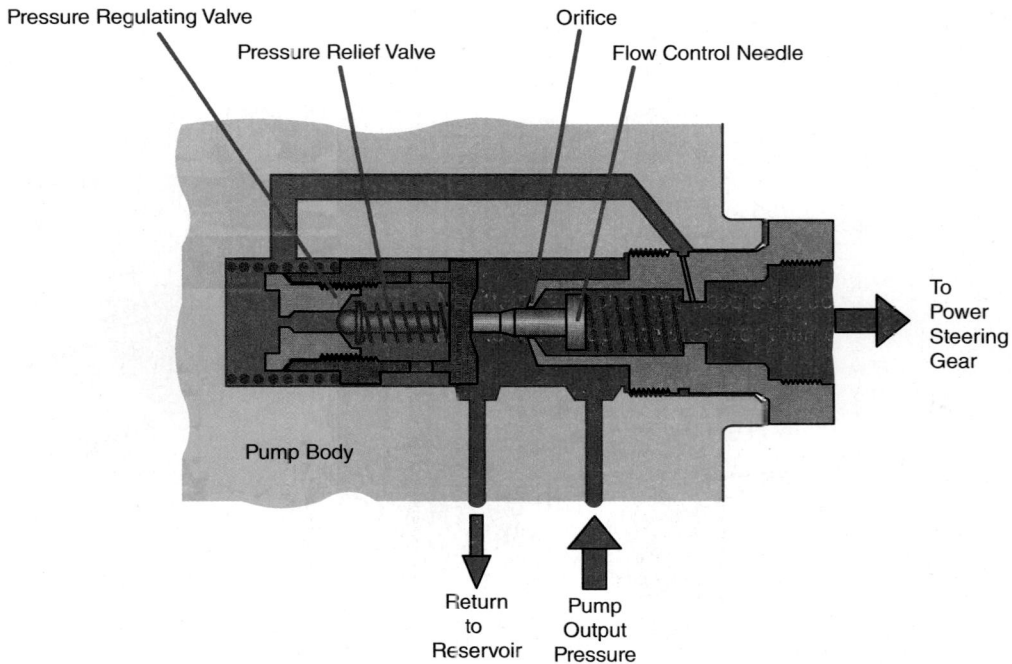

FIGURE 32-42 Flow-control valve with the steering wheel at full lock.

Electronically Controlled Variable Displacement Pump

The introduction of a steering system electronic control unit (ECU) also makes it possible to use an electronically controlled variable displacement power steering pump. These pumps rotate an eccentric cam ring surrounding the pump rotors to vary the output pressure and volume. An electronically controlled spool valve uses hydraulic pressure to pivot the cam ring (**FIGURE 32-43**). The benefits are reduced parasitic power loss to the steering system by the engine and lower power steering fluid temperature to conserve energy.

Semi-Automated Steering Gears

The steering system, like almost every other chassis system, is transforming and adding new functions with the application of electronic controls. New driver-assistance functions are possible by the addition of a servo-electric motor at the steering gear input shaft to combine steering inputs from the driver and motor (**FIGURE 32-44**). Bosch is an example of one manufacturer that has designed and built a line of HD commercial steering gears that use a conventional hydraulic-assisted recirculating-ball steering gear or rack, but add an electric motor to supplement driver input. Two steering sensors integrated into the steering column sense turning angle and driver steering torque input (**FIGURE 32-45**). Information from these sensors is supplied to a CAN connected steering ECU that combines steering data with vehicle speed, load, the stability control system YAW sensor data, lane departure sensing system information, etc. After the data is processed, the electric motor assists the steering wheel movement by adding or subtracting a steering shaft input

torque to optimize steering functions. Additional functions and features include:

- Speed-sensitive steering where high assistance is provided at low road speeds and progressively less assistance with increasing road speed to transmit more road feel.
- Programmable steering stops to prevent overloading the steering gear when the wheel is locked at the end of each turn.
- Side wind disturbance correction.
- Lane departure assistance to return the vehicle to its lane if it leaves.
- CAN communication can replace hydraulic lines to a second steering box on another front or rear steer axle having either a tag or pusher axle.
- Semiautonomous steering functions, such as during platooning several vehicles.
- Reduced driver fatigue caused by frequent steering correction and high steering effort.

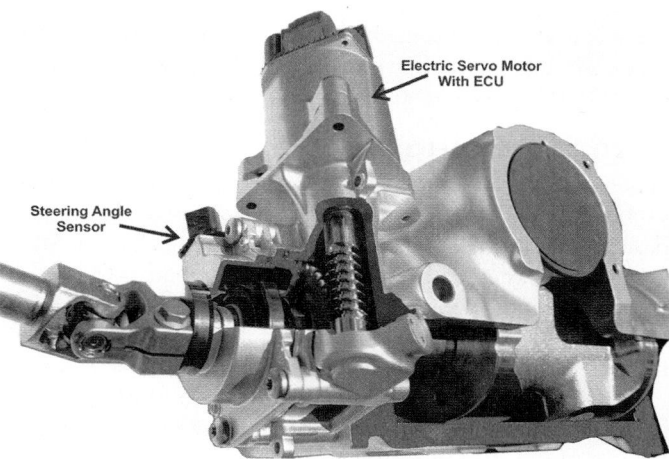

FIGURE 32-44 Bosch's recirculating-ball steering gear with a CAN-controlled servo electric motor to combine driver input with electric assist.

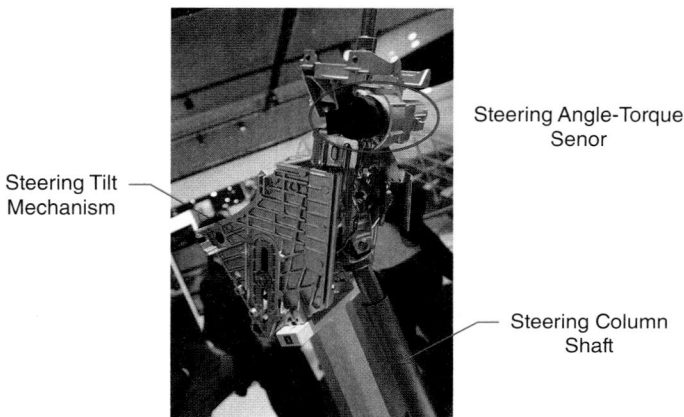

FIGURE 32-45 A sensor combining steering angle and input torque sensing functions is used by semi-automated steering gears.

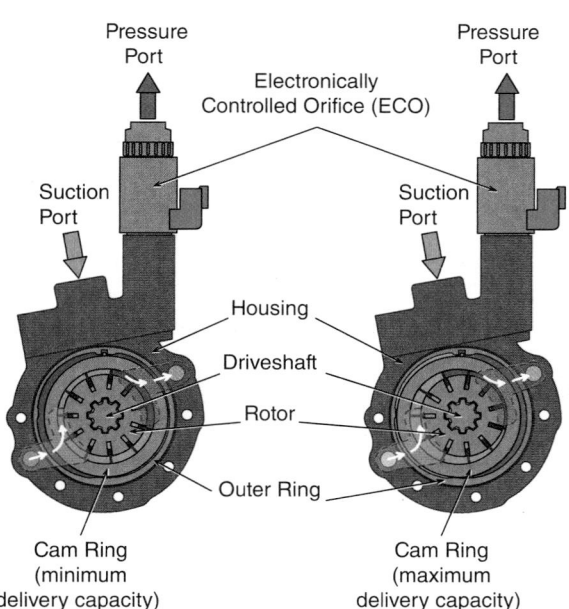

FIGURE 32-43 Rotating the eccentric cam ring surrounding the rotor vanes electronically varies pump displacement.

Maintenance and Service of the Steering System

LO 32-9 Identify and explain the recommended service and maintenance procedures associated with steering systems.

The steering system is critical to a vehicle's safe operation. Always follow manufacturer procedures when working on a steering system. To maintain a vehicle in safe operating condition, it is essential to regularly inspect the steering components. This can be performed both by visually inspecting the components and joints for damage, looseness, or leakage and by operating the steering system.

To prevent dirt or other foreign matter from entering the hydraulic system, clean around dipstick filler caps before checking power steering oil level. Investigate and correct any external leak, no matter how minor, in the steering system. Comply with manufacturer's specifications and instructions for servicing the steering system. If inspection or testing of the steering system, particularly the steering gear, reveals evidence of abnormal wear or damage, or if you encounter any unusual circumstances or are unsure about choosing the correct service procedure, STOP! Then consult the vehicle manufacturer's service manual and other OEM service literature.

Steering Complaints

When a driver presents a complaint about a steering-related problem, as with any diagnosis, it is important to collect some basic information. It is important to determine what the steering is doing, when and where the problem occurs, and how the vehicle responds. A visual inspection of fluid levels, hoses, linkage, and signs of leaks is always performed first before proceeding with more-specific diagnostic procedures.

Preliminary system checks, including tire inflation pressure, tire condition, power steering level, and a visual inspection of the suspension system, should precede any major diagnostic test. For on-highway tractors, the fifth wheel should be checked to make sure it has been greased because binding between the trailer and tractor causes hard steering. Chassis parts to be checked for excessive wear or damage include:

- Kingpins
- Spring leafs, shackles, and pins
- Suspension height
- Suspension U-bolts
- Drag link(s)
- Tie-rod ends
- Steering stops
- Steering gear mounting
- Steering column slip joints and universal joints

Steering complaints fall into the following descriptive categories:

- Hard steering
- Binding
- Bump steer
- Shimmy
- Excessive turning radius
- Oversteer or understeer
- Pulling or wandering
- Noise

TABLE 32-1 provides descriptions of each of these common complaints and their possible causes.

Steer-Axle Steering-Stop Adjustment

All medium- and heavy-duty steering systems use steering stops to limit the range of motion of the wheels. Steering stops are adjusted to achieve a maximum wheel cut while maintaining a minimum of 1" (2.5 cm) clearance between the tires and any part of the chassis. To prevent damage to the high-pressure pump, gear, and steering linkage, the stops are used to adjust internal pressure-relief valves in the steering gear. Power steering gears are equipped with internal-pressure relief valves, which relieve or unload hydraulic pressure as the steering linkage approaches the stops.

Automatic stops, which are now built into most steering gears, are set the first time the steering wheel is turned completely from stop to stop. To check this, the vehicle, when parked, should have the steering wheel turned to the maximum wheel-cut on either the left or the right. If correctly adjusted, the chassis frame rail on the side the wheels are turned to should not flex at the end of wheel travel. If it does, the automatic plungers must be reset. If the turning radius is reduced on either side, check the gap between the axle stop and the axle. When adjusted correctly, the stops should have a small 1/8" to 3/8" (3.2 mm to 9.5 mm) gap between the stop and the contact point on the front axle just before turning effort increases. This happens because the relief

TABLE 32-1 Common Steering-Related Problems

Concern	Possible Cause	Remedy
Hard Steering	• The driver describes the steering with phrases, such as "won't turn unless moving" • The vehicle steers, but with difficulty • Measured at the steering wheel center nut, effort requiring more than 100 in-lb (11.3 N m) at the steering wheel rim is considered excessive	• Faulty supply pump • Tight or seized kingpins • High oil operating temperature • Front-end load too great • Low oil level in reservoir • Air in system • Caster angle adjusted incorrectly
Binding	• Any cyclical-like tightness, locking-up, or torque variations at the steering wheel	• Steering column U-joints not phased • U-joint working angles greater than 25 degrees • Seized or tight kingpins • Seized or tight steering linkage joints
Bump Steer	• The steering wheel kicks whenever the vehicle goes over a bump in the road and oscillates back and forth	• Air in steering system • Incorrect drag link, misadjusted drag link, or mismatched drag link and upper steering arm
Shimmy	• The steering wheel rhythmically shakes back and forth at low and or high speeds	• Incorrect caster angle—too much positive caster • Incorrectly loaded vehicle • Air in system • Excessive toe-in • Incorrect steering gear adjustments Wheels out of balance
Excessive Turning Radius	• The vehicle wheel cut is at a sharper angle than normal	• Steering stop relief plungers not adjusted • Steering stops not correctly adjusted
Oversteer	• The vehicle turns more than the driver wants compared to steering input • The vehicle suddenly and rapidly changes direction or darts when turned	• Oil pressure too high • Air trapped in steering gear • Looseness; worn steering linkage • Front-end alignment not adjusted correctly • Overloading • Axles not parallel • Mismatched or incorrect tire and wheel rims
Understeer	• The vehicle does not respond enough to normal steering input • Steering seems sluggish	• Oil flow too low • Air trapped in steering gear • Looseness; worn steering linkage • Vehicle alignment angles not adjusted correctly • Overloading • Axles not parallel • Mismatched or incorrect tire and wheel rims • Loose or worn pitman arm splines • Loose steering gear
Pulling or Wandering	• The vehicle requires constant wheel correction to keep the vehicle traveling in a straight-line direction • The vehicle pulls consistently in a single direction (e.g., to the right) • The steering can also appear to be loose, meaning there is a loss of motion in the steering system	• Vehicle angles alignment not adjusted correctly • Improper loading or tire pressure • Loose, broken, or damaged suspension (i.e., broken leaf spring center bolt) • Loose or worn steering linkage • Loose or worn pitman arm splines • Loose steering gear mounting • Loose wheel bearings • Wrong tires for application
Noise	• Clunks, buzzing, hissing, and other sounds	• Restricted oil filter • Low hydraulic fluid level • Air in system

valve only begins to unload the hydraulic pressure as the stop approaches the contact on the axle.

Automatic stops, such as those pictured in **FIGURE 32-46** electronic control unit, may need resetting in cases when, for example, larger tires have been installed or a gear is replaced. Automatically adjusted pressure-relief valves in the pump can only be adjusted once. If the valves have been automatically set before, the plungers need to be tapped out with a small drift punch to enable them to properly reset. Plugs are often located in most gears that allow this procedures to be performed without disassembling the steering gear.

Centering the Steering Gear

Sector shaft contact needs to be centered with the teeth of the power-assist piston so that the gear turns the maximum range in each direction. Centering the gear contact is even more

FIGURE 32-46 Automatic steering stops (circled) adjust the first time the wheels are cut and the relief valves contact the end of the steering box.

important on variable-ratio steering gears because the teeth have different lengths and are responsible for transferring the correct road feel. Incorrect centering can lead to steering wander, excessive looseness, and even binding of the steering gear. Even if the steering gear sector shaft and assist piston are centered, incorrect positioning of the tie-rod ends and incorrect length of the drag link can cause the steering to operate off-center. To verify on-center operation, follow the procedure in **SKILL DRILL 32-1**.

Worm Gear Preload Adjustment

Clearances between the worm gear and the supporting bearings are minimal. Tight clearances prevent unnecessary movement and looseness in the steering gear. Loose ball bearings cause steering to wander, requiring constant wheel correction by the driver. Worm gear preload is set at the factory and may need readjustment if worm-gear parts are replaced or disassembled. Bearing preload is measured with an inch-pound (newton meter) torque wrench when the sector shaft is removed from the gear. Selective shims or a jam nut is used to set the preload to manufacturer specifications. When the bearing preload is adjusted, a needle and beam-type torque wrench is used to check that the steering input shaft has approximately 6 to 15 in-lb (67 to 169 N cm) of resistance.

> ▶ **TECHNICIAN TIP**
>
> Worm-gear preload adjustment is critical to eliminate any looseness in the gear, while allowing just enough pressure against the bearing without binding, and still allowing oil between parts.

SKILL DRILL 32-1 Centering the Steering Linkage

1. Square the tires with the frame so the tires are tracking in a dead straight-ahead position. This can be done by measuring the distance of the front and rear of the tire to adjust for the same distance from the frame rail.
2. Disconnect the drag link at both ends.
3. Disconnect the steering gear input shaft.
4. Check the timing mark on the pitman arm and sector shaft to verify that they line up.
5. Turn the input shaft with a 12-point socket, and count the number of turns. Precisely find and mark the halfway point between the travel limits of the input shaft.
6. Measure the distance between the hole of the pitman arm and the steering arm used by the drag link. It must be exactly the same length as the drag link. If not, the correct drag link or an adjustable drag link must be installed and adjusted.
7. Reconnect the steering input shaft, ensuring that the steering wheel spokes are aligned for a straight-ahead position.
8. If the steering wheel is not centered, remove the steering wheel and reinstall it with the spoke properly aligned to a straight-ahead position.

Over-Center Adjustment

Teeth on the sector shaft and power steering gear are tapered, and proper clearance between them requires adjustment. After worm-bearing preload is completed and the sector shaft is installed and centered, the over-center adjustment can be performed. As with the worm-gear preload, over-center adjustment is done with a torque wrench. A left-hand-thread adjusting screw on the cover at the rear of the sector shaft moves the sector shaft towards or away from the assist piston. To adjust preload to the manufacturer's specifications, rock the sector shaft through the center point using a 12-point socket to turn the input shaft. Once preload is adjusted on the sector shaft, the amount of resistance measured with an inch-pound (newton meter) torque wretch at the input shaft can be compared with manufacturer's specifications, as shown in **FIGURE 32-47**. Total torque applied to the input shaft through the center point of the steering gear is called **total mesh adjustment**. When the torque is correct, the steering-gear preload is in the proper range.

Maintenance and Service of the Hydraulic System

LO 32-10 Identify and explain the recommended service and maintenance procedures associated with the hydraulic system.

Oil pressure and volume requirements are established during the design of the steering system. When diagnosing steering problems, oil pressure and flow must meet certain specifications. Pressure levels determine how much force the steering system can apply to linkage, and flow, or volume, determines the speed at which the work is done. Pressure and flow specifications vary from vehicle to vehicle, but generally systems operate at a flow rate of 2.5 to 6 gallons per minute (gpm) (9.5 to 22.7 liters per minute [lpm]) and approximately 1500 psi (10,342 kPa).

System pressure and operating temperature must be considered during the diagnosis of the steering system. High system pressure creates heat, which thins out the oil and reduces the efficiency of the steering pump and gear. Thin oil leaks past the power piston and vanes or rollers of the power steering pump, increasing steering effort, while at the same time reducing steering speed.

Power Steering System Analyzer (PSSA)

Determining whether a steering problem is present in a gear or pump, requires the use of a **Power Steering System Analyzer (PSSA)** gauge, like that illustrated in **FIGURE 32-48**, during diagnostics. The PSSA tool is a combination flow meter, shut-off valve, and pressure gauge. It enables a technician to measure hydraulic-flow pressure in the steering system and to apply a load to the pump using the system's hydraulic lines. In other words, the PSSA provides pressure (psi or kilopascals) and flow data (gpm or lpm) when it is installed in series with the high-pressure line at the steering gear. A shutoff valve simulates a load on the system. The PSSA typically consists of a pressure gauge rated at 3000 psi (20,684 kPa) and a flow meter with a capacity of 10 gpm (37.8 lpm).

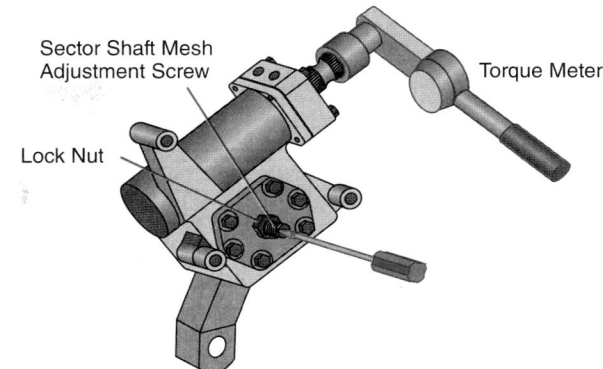

FIGURE 32-47 Over-center adjustment.

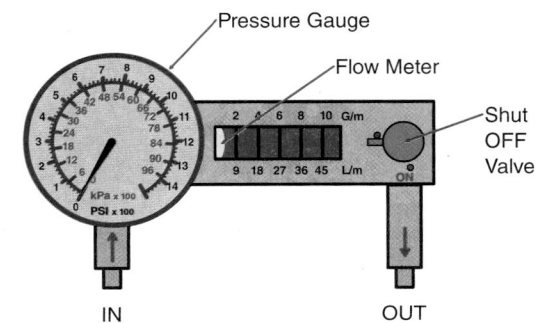

FIGURE 32-48 A power steering system analyzer.

SAFETY TIP

It is important to take the following precautions when performing hydraulic tests with a PSSA:

- Familiarize yourself with all moving parts that could cause personal injury.
- During test procedures, do not allow the fluid reservoir to run low on oil.
- Before beginning tests, check all components, hoses, and fittings for tightness and leaks.
- Wear appropriate safety glasses.

A shutoff valve placed downstream from the pressure gauge allows the power steering pump to be isolated from the steering gear. That separation facilitates checking the pump relief pressure. A simple thermometer placed in the reservoir, as illustrated in **FIGURE 32-49**, shows system temperature.

Since the analyzer is connected in series, only one hose connection is opened—either at the pump output or at the pressure input—to the power steering gear housing.

To use a PSSA, follow the steps in **SKILL DRILL 32-2**. When thinking about hydraulic diagnostic work, it is helpful to remember the following:

To use a PSSA to measure pump maximum-relief pressure, follow the steps in **SKILL DRILL 32-3**.

To use a PSSA to test flow volume, follow the steps in **SKILL DRILL 32-4**.

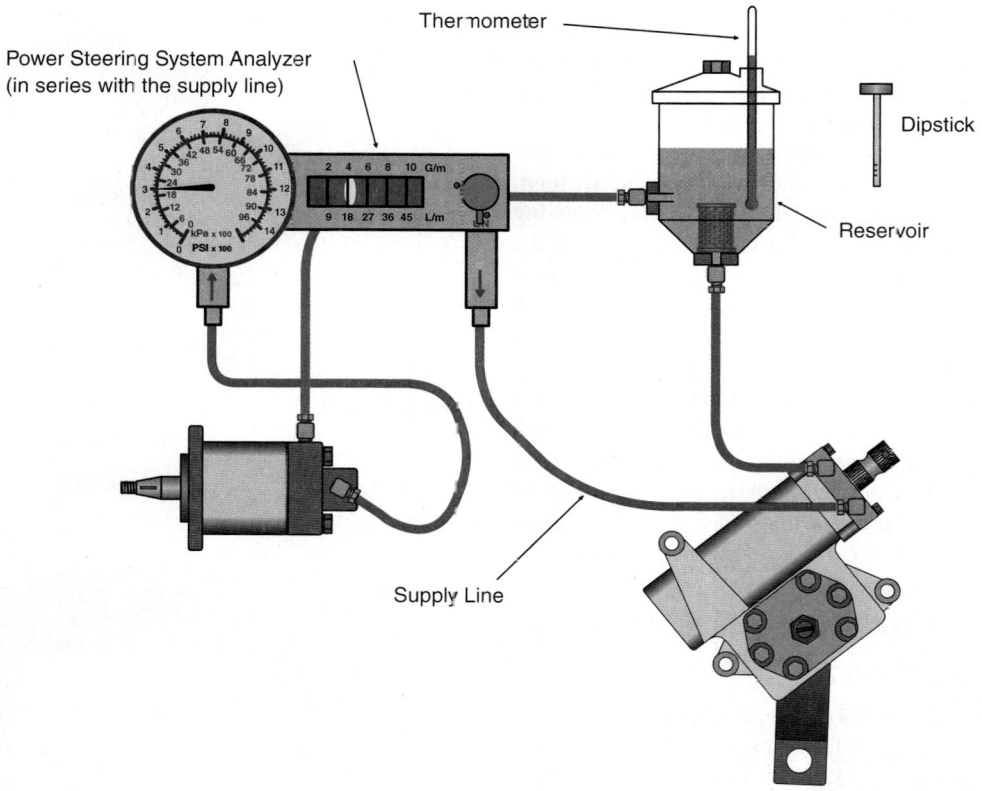

FIGURE 32-49 A thermometer in the reservoir.

SKILL DRILL 32-2 Using a Power Steering System Analyzer

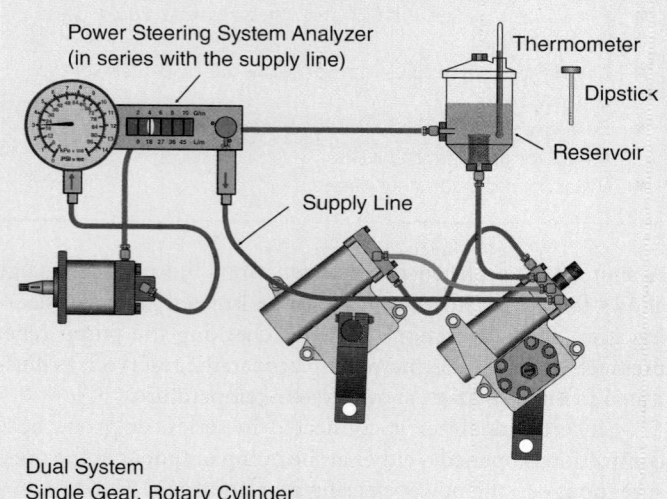

Dual System
Single Gear, Rotary Cylinder

1. Connect the PSSA gauge in series with the output pressure line of the power steering pump.
2. Start and idle the engine and check the system reservoir oil level. Also, observe whether the oil is flowing in the correct direction through the gauge using the arrow on the flow meter.
3. Place a thermometer in the reservoir. A digital-type thermometer with a wired probe is ideal.
4. While the engine is at idle speed, warm the system oil. This is performed by slowly closing the shutoff valve until a pressure reading of approximately 1000 psi (690 MPa) is reached. Hold this pressure until system temperature reaches 180°F (82°C). Fluid should never reach 250°F (121°C). If it does, testing must be suspended until the fluid cools.
5. Completely re-open the shutoff valve when the temperature is 180°F (82°C).
6. Measure and record system pressure when the valve is opened, also referred to as back pressure. Normal system back pressure is between 0 and 100 psi (0 and 690 kPa) with the engine idling and no steering input. Dual-steering gear systems should have slightly higher back pressure.
   - Pressure: The amount of force the steering gear can apply to linkage.
   - Flow: Speed of steering, which is related to how far the piston can be displaced by oil.

A defective pressure relief valve or missing relief valve may not relieve pump pressure when the shutoff valve is closed. This potentially can result in damage to the pump and rupture hoses. Observe the pressure gauge closely while closing the shutoff valve. If the pressure rises too rapidly or reaches 2500 psi (17,237 kPa), immediately open the valve.

Before beginning testing or starting the engine, always verify the shutoff valve is open.

Testing for Internal Leakage

To determine whether the steering gear has internal defects, such as worn power-assist piston seals or a worn gear cylinder, an internal leak test should be performed. This test is performed almost identically to the steering pressure-relief valve test procedures. One exception is during testing; one must prevent the steering relief valves inside the steering gear from unloading as the gear is turned from stop to stop. To test a system for internal leakage, follow the steps in **SKILL DRILL 32-5**.

On dual-gear systems, the steering gears must be isolated if pump leakage occurs at a rate exceeding two gallons (7.6 liters) per minute. To identify which steering gear is bypassing the oil, block the lines to the slave cylinder after testing both gears together. If the slave cylinder is defective, installing plugs in the lines to the slave cylinder should reduce leakage to less than one gallon (3.8 liters) per minute.

It is critical to install a spacer between the steering stops when performing the internal gear leakage test. Without the spacers, the high system pressure cannot be reached when turning the wheels, and a false failure results as the steering arm unloads after contacting the steering stops.

SKILL DRILL 32-3 Measuring Pump Maximum-Relief Pressure

1. With the engine at idle, slowly turn the PSSA shutoff valve until it is closed.
2. Measure and record the maximum pressure. This reading corresponds to the pressure at which the relief valve opens. Be sure to open the shutoff valve as quickly (within 15 seconds) as possible to avoid overheating the oil or damaging lines or the steering pump.
3. Compare observations with manufacturer's specifications. Pump output volume is measured under four conditions:
   • At idle and with normal back pressure
   • At idle under a 1500 psi (10,342 kPa) load applied with the shutoff valve
   • Flow at full-governed rpm with back pressure only
   • Flow at full-governed rpm under a 1500 psi (10,342 kPa) load applied with the shutoff valve

SKILL DRILL 32-4 Testing Flow Volume

1. Connect the PSSA gauge in series with the output pressure line of the power steering pump.

2. Start and idle the engine and check system reservoir oil level. Also, observe whether the oil is flowing in the correct direction through the gauge using the arrow on the flow meter.
3. While the engine is at idle speed, warm the system oil. This is performed by slowly closing the shutoff valve until a pressure reading of approximately 1000 psi (6900 kPa) is reached. Hold this pressure until the system temperature reaches 180°F (121°C). Fluid should never reach 250°F (121°C). If it does, testing must be suspended until the fluid cools.
4. Completely re-open the shutoff valve when the temperature is 180°F (121°C).
5. Read the flow gauge, which measures output volume of the pump. Flow is measured in gallons or liters per minute.
6. Raise the engine speed to 1500 rpm and record the volume observed on the flow gauge.
7. Compare observations with manufacturer's specifications.

SKILL DRILL 32-5 Testing for Internal Leakage

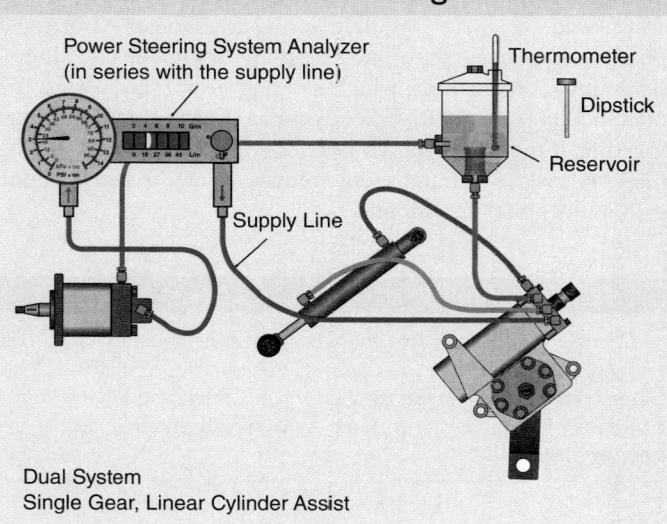

Power Steering System Analyzer
(in series with the supply line)

Thermometer

Dipstick

Reservoir

Supply Line

Dual System
Single Gear, Linear Cylinder Assist

1. Place a 1" (2.5 cm) thick steel spacer or other suitable spacer between the steering stop and axle contact point to prevent contact with the stops and relieve steering pressure.
2. With the engine at idle, turn the steering wheel with approximately 20 lb (9.1 kg) of input effort against the spacer between the stops.
3. Observe and record pressure and flow volume for each left and right turn. Pressures should be very near the pressures achieved during the steering relief-valve pressure checks.
4. If flow volumes exceed one gallon (3.8 liters) per minute at the steering stops, the gear is bypassing oil internally and should be replaced.

Checking Oil Aeration

Air mixed with the oil (aerated oil) in the steering system is inspected visually. Oil should appear clear without any signs of foaming. Entrained gas bubbles cause the fluid to compress and take on elastic qualities. Steering effort increases and bump steer becomes exaggerated as the air compresses and releases. A common cause of air leakage into the system is loose hose connections on the suction side. A power steering reservoir contains a filter needing periodic replacement. Restricted filters lead to over-heating of power steering oil, pump cavitation, and air leaks on the suction side of the system.

Bleeding Air from the Steering System

Whenever a steering gear is serviced, any air in the system must be purged to restore proper operation. Turning the wheels from stop to stop while the vehicle is parked and its engine is running does not remove air. The wheels should be lifted from the floor. Only then can the wheels can be turned to help purge air. Low-pressure fluid flow through the gear gradually purges most air from the gear.

Another way to purge air from the system is by moving the wheels by hand while the engine is idling. That should only be done, however, after the steering stops are set. While the engine is idling, air-bleed screws located on top of steering gears can be loosened to also purge air.

Dual-steering boxes are more difficult to bleed. After steering stops are set, a recommended method to purge air is to disconnect the drag link at each gear and force the pitman arm from stop to stop several times while the engine is idling. Pushing fluid through the steering gear this way, when it is not pressurized by the gear during a turn, effectively removes air where circulating fluid carries air to the reservoir for purging.

▶ TECHNICIAN TIP

Moving the wheels by hand from steering stop to stop while the engine is running and the wheels are raised from the shop floor is more effective at purging air than if the steering wheel is turned while the wheels are on the ground. That is because, when the wheels are on the ground, high fluid pressure required to operate the steering gear when turning causes air to compress and break up inside the box. Smaller dispersed bubbles are much more difficult to purge.

Removing and Replacing the Supplemental Restraint System

In North America, heavy-duty trucks are not yet required to have supplemental restraint systems (SRS), also known as airbags. Some manufacturers, such as Volvo, do install them in their heavy-duty vehicles. These systems are sure to become increasingly popular in heavy trucks in the future.

An airbag in an SRS is inflated by an explosive charge and deploys in as little as 0.03 seconds. If the bag deploys unexpectedly, its explosive force can cause serious injury. For this reason, it is essential that the technician disable the airbag system before working around a steering column equipped with SRS.

The steering wheel-mounted SRS has a clock spring mounted in the column under the steering wheel to connect the airbag, the horn button, and any steering wheel-mounted controls. The steering-angle sensor used for the vehicle-stability system may also be part of, or attached to, the clock spring. The clock spring winds and unwinds to allow the steering wheel to turn. Over time, the wires in the clock spring can break, and the spring requires replacement. SKILL DRILL 32-6 discusses how to remove safely and replace the SRS, the steering wheel, and the clock spring.

SKILL DRILL 32-6 Removing and Replacing Steering Wheel and Center/Time the SRS Coil

1. Find and remove the SRS fuse. Verify by turning the key on and observing that the SRS light remains lit for at least 30 seconds and does not go out. Make sure the wheels are straight ahead. Turn the key off.

2. Remove the negative battery cable and allow a minimum of five minutes to pass to let the SRS system's capacitors discharge. Do not use a memory minder or auxiliary power source!

3. Locate the SRS connector at the bottom of the steering column and disconnect. Remove upper and lower trim panels.

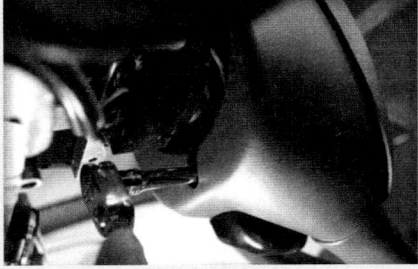

4. Locate the bolts or spring clip on the back of the steering wheel that hold the airbag to the steering wheel, and remove or release them.

5. Lift the airbag from the steering wheel, and disconnect the airbag connector to the steering wheel harness.

6. Set the airbag on a bench, face up, in a safe place.

7. Remove the fasteners that hold the steering wheel on.

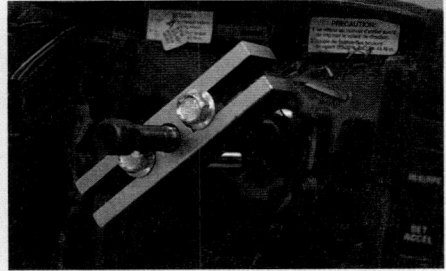

8. Remove the steering wheel with the manufacturer's recommended puller (this information can be found in the service information).

9. Remove the clock spring screws or snap ring and lift the clock spring from the steering column shaft. Attach a thin wire to the clock-spring connector (airbag connector was disconnected earlier) at the base of the steering column and pull the clock spring and connector up through the steering column.

SKILL DRILL 32-6 Removing and Replacing Steering Wheel and Center/Time the SRS Coil (Continued)

10. Gently pull the clock-spring harness down through steering column.

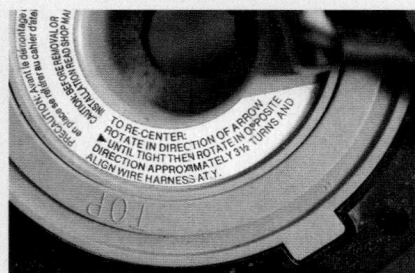

11. If the anti rotation key is still installed, skip to Step 13. If the anti rotation key is not installed, center the clock spring following the manufacturer's procedure. In this case, we gently rotate the inner rotor counterclockwise until it stops.

12. Rotate the inner rotor clockwise the required number of turns—in this case four full turns. Verify that all the marks are aligned in their specified positions.

13. Reinstall the clock-spring assembly in the proper orientation and secure it with the screws or snap ring. Reinstall components in the reverse order of removal, ensuring that torque specifications are followed. Also remove the anti rotation key at the appropriate step.

Wrap-Up

Ready for Review

▶ Steering systems are life-and-limb systems, meaning failure of the technician to inspect and maintain the system, or to choose the correct service procedures and tools, can result in catastrophic personal injury and death.

▶ Steering systems multiply the rotational force applied to the steering wheel, provide directional control of the vehicle, reduce road shock to the steering wheel, and provide steering feedback to the driver, called road feel.

▶ Miter boxes are used in high-angle steering columns to connect the steering gear to the steering column.

▶ Pitman arms, drag links, and tie-rods are steering linkage common to all conventional truck-steering systems.

▶ All heavy-duty commercial vehicles use integral power steering gears, which means the power steering assist and gear mechanism are incorporated into a single steering box.

▶ Hydraulic steering pumps provide the main force to multiply driver input torque to the steering system.

▶ All integral power steering gears use a recirculating-ball steering gear.

▶ Recirculating-ball steering gears mechanically multiply input force and use a worm gear with a ball-nut.

▶ Rack-and-pinion steering is rarely used on heavy-duty commercial vehicles.

▶ A mechanism that enables the steering gear to steer the vehicle in the event of a loss of power assist is designed into every steering gear.

- ▶ Heavy-duty commercial vehicles use larger-diameter steering wheels, which are positioned at a 30-degree or greater angle to the driver to make them easier to turn.
- ▶ Most heavy-duty commercial vehicles use multi-piece steering columns composed of two or more splined steering shafts with universal joints, which enable changes in column angle caused by movement between the cab and frame-mounted steering gear.
- ▶ Sliding splines in the steering column are called slip joints; they allow the column length to change due to movement between the cab and the frame-mounted steering gear. Sliding slip yokes also enable the steering column to shorten, and thus protect the driver during collisions.
- ▶ Correct phasing or alignment of steering-column universal joints is necessary to prevent steering-column binding.
- ▶ A clock-spring and steering-angle sensor are electrical devices located beneath the steering wheel in many late-model vehicles.
- ▶ The rotary electronic control unit control valve directs pressurized hydraulic oil to either side of a power piston to multiply driver steering effort.
- ▶ The torsion bar connects at one end to the outer half of the rotary-control valve and the lower end to the bottom of the worm gear.
- ▶ The steering input shaft is connected to the inner section of the rotary-control valve.
- ▶ Twisting of the torsion bar causes deflection between the two sections of the rotary-control valve and changes the direction of pressurized hydraulic oil to either side of the power piston.
- ▶ The direction of input force twisting the torsion bar changes the alignment between two sections of the control valve which, in turn, redirects pressurized oil in the steering gear.
- ▶ Road feel describes the feedback a driver receives through the steering system about the resistance the tires encounter in steering direction.
- ▶ The power steering pump uses flow control and pressure-relief valves.
- ▶ The steering gear has internal pressure-relief valves, which unload pump pressure when the steering linkage has contacted the steering stops.
- ▶ Steering stops are used to limit steer tire movement, which could bring the tires in contact with the suspension, frame, or steering linkage.
- ▶ Pitman arms connect to the steering gear output shaft called the sector shaft.
- ▶ Drag links connect the pitman arm to the upper steering arm and transmit steering force to the steering knuckle through the upper steering arm.
- ▶ Two lower steering arms have a unique angular shape called an Ackermann angle. The angle causes the steer tires to toe out on turns where the inner tire follows a tighter turning radius than the outer tire.
- ▶ Alignment marks on the pitman arm are used to properly center the steering linkage.
- ▶ Centering of the steering wheel can be done by changing the length of an adjustable drag link or turning the tie-rod.
- ▶ A Power Steering System Analyzer is used to diagnose hydraulic-related problems in the power steering system by measuring pump flow and pressure under different operating conditions.
- ▶ Worm-gear preload adjusts bearing clearances in the steering input shaft bearing.
- ▶ The over-center adjustment adjusts the clearances between the tapered sector shaft gear teeth and the teeth on the power piston.
- ▶ When measured with an inch-pound (newton meter) torque wrench, worm-gear preload plus the over-center adjustment establishes the total mesh adjustment.

Key Terms

ball-nut rack A metal block with a threaded hole that is part of the recirculating-ball steering system.

bump steer The undesired condition produced after hitting a bump which pushes or pulls steering linkage. The steering wheel may also be violently forced from the driver's grip during severe bump steer.

clock spring A special rotary electrical connector located between the steering wheel and the steering column that maintains a constant electrical connection with the wiring system while the vehicle's steering wheel is being turned.

constant-ratio steering gears Steering gears that use sector shafts with teeth of equal lengths.

conventional steering system A steering system with a solid axle and a single steering gear.

engine-driven hydraulic pump A power steering pump driven by a belt or gear driven by the engine.

flow-control valve A valve used in power steering pumps to regulate the volume of fluid flow out of the power steering pump.

miter boxes A gear arrangement that allows sharp angle changes in the steering column.

power steering pump A hydraulic pump that provides hydraulic pressure to the steering gear, which reduces the force required by the driver to turn the steering wheel.

Power Steering System Analyzer (PSSA) A combination flow meter, shut-off valve, and pressure gauge used to diagnose hydraulic problems in power steering systems.

power unit The hydraulic assist portion of the power steering gear.

rack-and-pinion steering system A type of steering gear arrangement that uses two gears. A smaller round pinion gear located at the end of the steering shaft connects to a linear gear, called the rack. The pinion gear moves the rack from side-to-side as the pinion rotates. The side-to-side motion of the rack controls the direction of the steer tires.

recirculating-ball steering gear   A steering gear that uses a worm gear inside a metal ball-nut having a threaded hole for the worm. Gear teeth are cut into one outside edge of the ball-nut, which engages the sector shaft.

road feel   The force transmitted from the tires back through the steering system to the driver.

rotary valve   A valve connected to the input shaft of the steering gear that controls the direction of pressurized fluid through the steering gear. Along with the torsion bar, changes in torque applied to the steering wheel. Also called a *spool valve*.

spool valve   A valve connected to the input shaft of the steering gear that controls the direction of pressurized fluid through the steering gear. Along with the torsion bar, changes in torque applied to the steering wheel. Also called a *rotary valve*.

steering-angle sensor   A sensor that measures the rotational angle of the steering wheel.

steering arm   An arm that extends from the steering knuckle. The tie-rods connect to these arms in order to steer the wheels.

steering gear   A device that converts the rotary motion of the steering wheel to the linear motion needed to steer the vehicle.

steering knuckle   A device that connects the front wheel to the axle; it pivots on the top and bottom, thus allowing the front wheels to turn.

steering linkage   Steel rods that connect the steering box to the steering arms on the steering knuckle.

steering ratio   The mechanical advantage produced by the steering gear, which converts large turns of the steering wheel into smaller turns of the tire to ease steering for the driver.

steering shafts   The shaft that connects the steering wheel to the steering gear assembly of a vehicle.

steering stops   Bolts used to limit the turning angle of the steering knuckle.

tie-rod   A shaft that transfers motion between the steering arms at the front wheels.

tie-rod end   Articulating ball-and-socket joints attached to each end of the tie-rod.

torsion rod   A thin, spring-like metal rod that connects to one end of the rotary valve to the worm gear.

total mesh adjustment   A setting of the appropriate depth for the sector shaft tapered teeth with power piston teeth to prevent tooth binding and excess steering free play.

variable-ratio steering gears   Steering gears that use sector shafts with long and short lengths of teeth.

worm gear   A gear with a helical, threaded shaft used in a steering gear and meshes with a ball nut that transfers motion from the steering wheel to the steering linkage. Also called the *worm shaft*.

Review Questions

1. On an integral power steering gear, which of the following indicates excessive clearances between the sector shaft teeth and the power piston?
   a. Lost range of motion within steering gear
   b. Steering wheel shimmy
   c. Excessive steering effort
   d. Noise from the power steering pump when hot
2. A driver complains the steering wheel moves violently whenever the vehicle encounters a bump in the road. Which of the following is the most likely problem?
   a. An out-of-phase steering column
   b. Air in the steering gear
   c. Incorrect vehicle-alignment angles
   d. A misadjusted tie-rod
3. A shock absorber-like device is attached to the tie-rod. Which of the following is most likely the purpose of the device?
   a. Helps center the steering wheel
   b. Minimizes road shock and vibration to the driver
   c. Minimizes caster shimmy
   d. Prevents bump steer
4. Which of the following is the most likely problem if a steering tire contacts a drag link on sharp right turns?
   a. A misaligned steering column
   b. A steering wheel off-center
   c. A drag link that is adjusted to the wrong length
   d. An incorrectly adjusted steering stop
5. What is the most likely cause for a power steering reservoir to overflow with oil?
   a. A defective power steering pump shaft seal
   b. Air in the steering gear
   c. Fluid that has become too hot
   d. Mixing engine oil and automatic-transmission oil in the reservoir
6. Steering-gear seal leakage on power steering gears due to dirt abrasion (wear caused by dirt rubbing against the seals) is minimized by
   a. using the correct viscosity of power steering fluid.
   b. greasing the steering-sector shaft and input-shaft seals with chassis grease during service.
   c. using a power steering fluid oil cooler.
   d. changing the power steering filter regularly.
7. When the steering gear is in a straight-ahead position and the engine is running, how much pressure is applied to each end of the internal power piston of a recirculating-ball steering gear?
   a. Full pump pressure is applied to both ends of the piston to keep it cantered.

b. High pressure is applied to the lower end, but moderate pressure is applied to the opposite.

c. The rotary valve prevents flow so no pressure is applied to either end of the piston.

d. Only the low pressure of recirculating pump flow is applied equally to both ends of the piston.

8. Which of the following are the points of attachment for each end of the torsion bar?

a. The power piston and the input shaft

b. The lower end of the worm gear and the rotary valve

c. The outside half of the rotary valve and the recirculating-ball cage

d. The center section of the rotary valve and the input shaft

9. Consider a vehicle traveling in a straight-line direction along the road. One wheel drops into a pothole and forces the wheel 5 degrees to the right. What happens to fluid pressure inside the integral steering gear?

a. Fluid pressure is applied to only one side of the piston to resist steering gear movement because the torsion bar twists and redirects flow through the rotary valve.

b. Fluid on both sides of the power piston is trapped by the rotary valve to resist piston-gear movement.

c. The driver must turn the input shaft to enable the rotary valve to provide fluid pressure before any gear movement is resisted.

d. No change in pressure because road feel must be transmitted back to the steering wheel.

10. How wide a gap should be present between the steering stop and front axle when the pressure-relief valve in the steering gear begins to relieve pump pressure?

a. 1" (25 mm)

b. 1/2" (13 mm)

c. 1/4" (6.35 mm)

d. 1/8" (3 mm)

ASE Technician A/Technician B Style Questions

1. Technician A says if the steering column input shaft is not aligned correctly, it has tight spots or binds when turned. Technician B says if the power steering fluid level is low, there is a noise when turning the steering wheel. Who is correct?

a. Technician A

b. Technician B

c. Both Technician A and Technician B

d. Neither Technician A nor Technician B

2. Technician A says if the kingpins are not lubricated, the vehicle is hard to steer. Technician B says clunking noises when turning the steering wheel are acceptable. Who is correct?

a. Technician A

b. Technician B

c. Both Technician A and Technician B

d. Neither Technician A nor Technician B

3. Technician A says if the steering effort is high whenever the steering wheel is turned, one of the power steering pressure-relief valves in the steering gear is defective. Technician B says if the steering gear has excessive internal leakage, the vehicle is hard to steer. Who is correct?

a. Technician A

b. Technician B

c. Both Technician A and Technician B

d. Neither Technician A nor Technician B

4. While discussing possible causes of wandering steering, Technician A says it could be caused by a loose over-center adjustment. Technician B says a more likely cause is air in the power steering fluid. Who is correct?

a. Technician A

b. Technician B

c. Both Technician A and Technician B

d. Neither Technician A nor Technician B

5. Technician A says that the reason the steering wheel is hard to turn in one direction only is likely a misadjusted steering-relief valve. Technician B says that a more likely cause of the complaint is a broken torsion bar. Who is correct?

a. Technician A

b. Technician B

c. Both Technician A and Technician B

d. Neither Technician A nor Technician B

6. Technician A says rack-and-pinion steering systems do not include tie rods. Technician B says rack-and-pinion steering systems do not include a pitman arm or a drag link. Who is correct?

a. Technician A

b. Technician B

c. Both Technician A and Technician B

d. Neither Technician A nor Technician B

7. While checking the fluid levels during a service, the power steering reservoir contained soot-thickened engine oil and the reservoir was almost overflowing. Technician A says the reservoir was likely incorrectly filled with waste engine oil. Technician B says that a more likely cause is a defective power steering pump-shaft seal. Who is correct?

a. Technician A

b. Technician B

c. Both Technician A and Technician B

d. Neither Technician A nor Technician B

8. Technician A says that a lack of lubricant on the fifth wheel can potentially cause a loss of ability to properly steer a vehicle. Technician B says that a lack of grease on the table of a fifth wheel only makes it difficult to back-up a trailer. Who is correct?

a. Technician A

b. Technician B

c. Both Technician A and Technician B

d. Neither Technician A nor Technician B

9. Technician A says that the frame rail where the steering gear is mounted should twist whenever the wheels are turned and the steering stops make contact with the front axle. Technician B says that if the frame rail twists when the wheels are turned, and the steering stops contact the front axle, the steering gear-relief valves are incorrectly adjusted. Who is correct?
   a. Technician A
   b. Technician B
   c. Both Technician A and Technician B
   d. Neither Technician A nor Technician B

10. Technician A says that tie-rod ends must only use a left-hand thread on the right-side end and a right-hand thread on the left. Technician B says tie-rod ends use the same thread on each end to enable the tie rod to turn when centering the steering wheel or adjusting the toe. Who is correct?
    a. Technician A
    b. Technician B
    c. Both Technician A and Technician B
    d. Neither Technician A nor Technician B

CHAPTER 33

Braking Fundamentals and Air Brake Foundations

Learning Objectives

- **LO 33-1** Identify and describe physical concepts and the effects of vehicle speed and weight on braking performance.
- **LO 33-2** Identify types of braking systems.
- **LO 33-3** Identify, describe, and compare air brake foundation systems.
- **LO 33-4** Identify and describe the construction and operation of S-cam brake components.
- **LO 33-5** Identify and explain the causes of brake fade.
- **LO 33-6** Identify and explain the concepts of brake torque and brake balance.
- **LO 33-7** Identify and describe the purpose and construction of brake drums.
- **LO 33-8** Identify and describe the types, purpose, construction, and adjustment of brake chambers and actuators.
- **LO 33-9** Classify and describe the types, purpose, construction, and operation of slack adjusters.
- **LO 33-10** Identify and describe the construction and operation of air disc brakes.
- **LO 33-11** Identify and describe the design and operation of wedge brakes.

You Are the Technician

A late-model tractor-trailer combination vehicle is brought to your repair facility, and the driver complains that the tractor rear brakes are grabbing when he applies the brakes. He can hear the antilock brake system (ABS) modulators chuffing air while the vehicle is slowing down—even though he is not applying heavy pressure to the brake pedal. You accompany the driver on a road test and confirm the driver's concern—the rear tractor brakes seem as if they are about to lock up when the brakes are applied. The driver informs you that the rear tractor brakes have recently been replaced. To make a correct service recommendation, consider the following in your response.

1. What inspections would you make of the brake system?
2. How would you confirm that all the vehicle brakes are, in fact, working correctly?
3. How would you determine if the rear tractor brakes are working harder than the rest of the vehicle brakes?

Introduction

The enormous amount of energy contained in a heavily loaded truck or bus moving at highway speeds requires an equally powerful and reliable braking system to slow and bring the vehicle to a controlled stop. After the vehicle has stopped, the braking system of heavy trucks—not the drive train—is used to keep the vehicle parked. Even under emergency conditions, such as the loss of air or brake fluid, failure of components, or even the breakaway of a trailer, commercial vehicle braking systems are expected to slow and stop the vehicle safely without catastrophic consequences posed by a runaway vehicle laden with freight or passengers.

To accomplish this, brakes convert the vehicle's kinetic energy into heat energy using friction, as shown in **FIGURE 33-1**. Heat in brake components is dissipated to the atmosphere through brake design factors, as depicted in **FIGURE 33-2**. Unless the build-up of heat in brake parts is minimized, heat accumulations lead to a loss of braking efficiency and damage to brake components. Legislation for truck and bus brake systems specifies brake performance standards. The most recent changes in rules for brake system performance require shorter stopping distances, as shown in **FIGURE 33-3**, with a higher level of vehicle stability while braking.

Innovations in technology have placed even more demands on braking systems. Improved vehicle aerodynamics, low-profile tires with reduced rolling resistance, plus drive trains with substantially lower friction, means the mechanism that once helped slow a vehicle are absent and this work is now almost entirely placed on the brake system. Demanding even more effective braking systems are legislative standards establishing ever-increasing levels of vehicle safety with the use of antilock brake control, automatic adjusting mechanisms, and shorter stopping distances. An example is a collision avoidance system that automatically applies the brakes when an obstacle is detected or a collision is imminent. European laws have made this feature standard equipment on trucks for several years and the

same regulation is contemplated for North American heavy commercial vehicles.

The example of integration between a vehicle's brakes and a collision avoidance system highlights the evolution of braking systems to do more than just stop a vehicle. Braking systems are also integral to vehicle stability control, rollover protection, and traction control systems. To incorporate these sophisticated features, the braking system now has a large element of electronic control capable of operating the braking system with virtually no driver input. Later chapters cover the technology of more advanced brakes, but this chapter is intended to lay the foundations for basic principles used by braking systems to provide the necessary background to effectively maintain, service, and diagnose commercial vehicle brake systems.

How Brakes Work

LO 33-1 Identify and describe physical concepts and the effects of vehicle speed and weight on braking performance.

Just as an engine uses heat to produce power, the braking system takes vehicle power stored as **kinetic energy** (the energy of a body in motion) and converts it back into heat through friction. Using brake drums or discs attached to the wheels, friction is produced by forcefully applying heat-resistant braking material against these rotating components. Friction's by-product—heat is then dissipated into the air. Because a vehicle must be capable of stopping faster than it can accelerate, a tremendous amount of braking force is needed. With the heavier weight and the speed commercial vehicles travel, the power generated by the brakes must be several times that of the engine. **FIGURE 33-4** shows that many times more power is required to slow and stop a vehicle than is required to accelerate a vehicle. Just as horsepower is used to measure the energy used to bring a vehicle up to speed, the retarding force required of the braking system can be estimated using horsepower to get an idea of the energy required by the braking system.

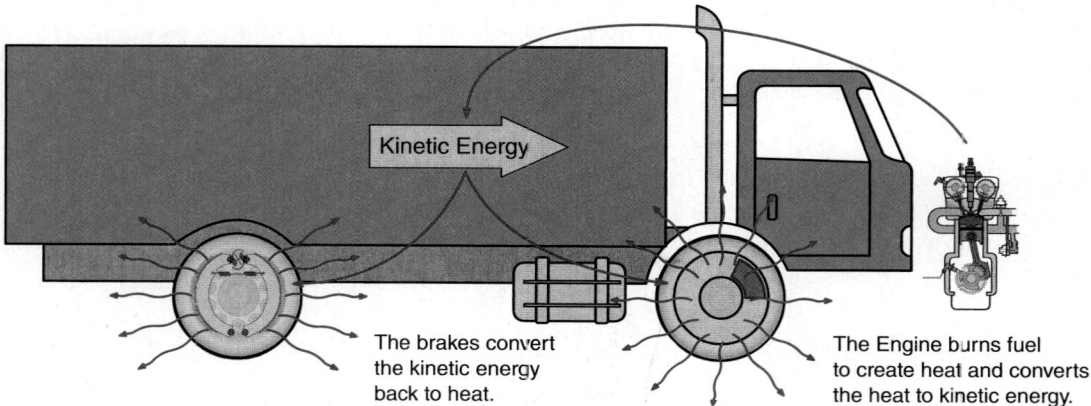

FIGURE 33-1 While the engine converts combustion heat to mechanical force, brakes convert a vehicle's moving energy into heat energy.

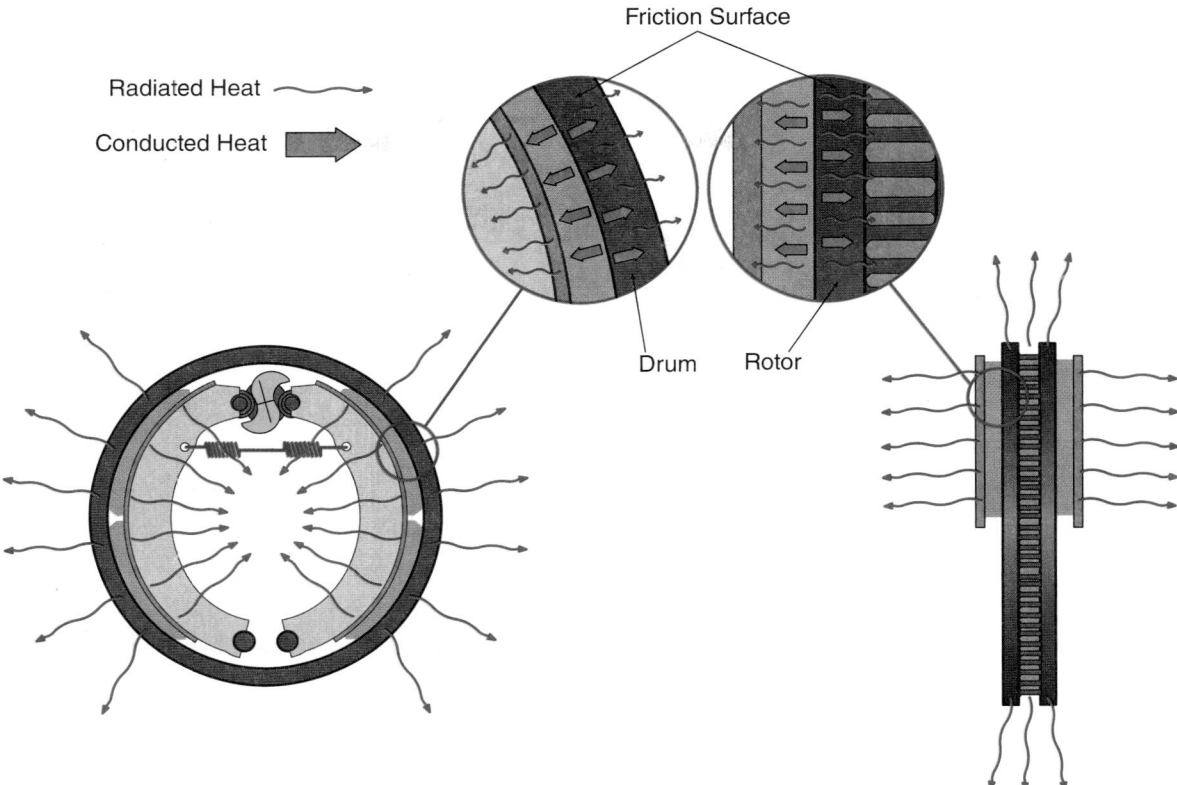

FIGURE 33-2 Unless the build-up of heat in brake parts is minimized, heat accumulations lead to a loss of braking efficiency and damage to brake components.

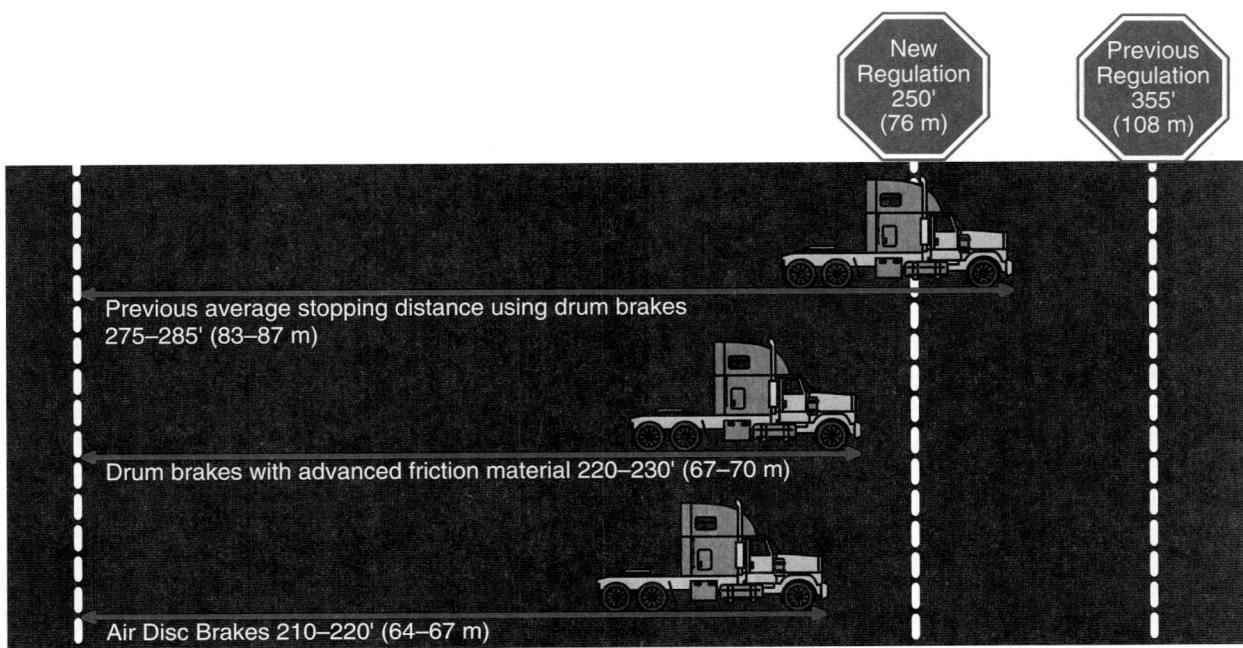

FIGURE 33-3 Legislation for truck and bus brake systems specifies brake performance standards.

FIGURE 33-4 Many times more power is required to slow and stop a vehicle than is required to accelerate a vehicle. Braking power can also be measured in horsepower used to decelerate a vehicle, rather than accelerate a vehicle.

To better understand this concept, consider a truck with a 350 hp engine used to accelerate a loaded vehicle to 60 mph (97 kph) in 60 seconds. To slow and stop the vehicle in an emergency condition takes approximately 6 seconds—a tenth of the time used to accelerate the unit. The vehicle is also decelerated at 10 times the rate of acceleration. Calculated together, the brakes require 10 times the power of the engine. Or, in this example, the brakes exert 3,5000 hp of retarding force!

Influence of Vehicle Weight and Speed

The forces involved in decelerating a vehicle are considerable. Looking more closely at the factors influencing brake system capabilities, it is important to note increasing amounts of energy are required as a vehicle's weight and speed increase. Using the engineering formula used to calculate the energy of motion, kinetic energy, it can be demonstrated that, as the weight of the vehicle is doubled, the kinetic energy converted into heat energy is also doubled. **FIGURE 33-5** shows the influence of vehicle speed and weight on required braking force. Doubling vehicle weight or speed needs twice the braking power for the same deceleration rate. When weight and speed are both doubled, braking force must increase by a factor of eight. If the brakes cannot adequately absorb and dissipate the additional heat produced by increasing vehicle weight, braking performance and safety suffers. This explains why heavy-duty brakes are specified not by the type of vehicle, but by the weight carried by an axle and its location on the vehicle.

Increasing vehicle speed has a greater effect than vehicle weight on the braking system power. Calculations of kinetic energy show braking power requirements increase by a factor

of four as speed doubles. This means four times as much power is required to decelerate from a speed of 40 mph (64 kph) compared to 20 mph (32 kph). A stop from 60 mph (97 kph), which is three times the speed of 20 mph (32 kph), needs nine times the energy. It is understandable, then, why increased vehicle weight and speed need greater braking system pressure, larger friction surfaces, and greater capacity to absorb, as well as dissipate, heat. **FIGURE 33-6** shows the influence of higher vehicle speeds on stopping distances. **FIGURE 33-7** compares different brake foundation technologies and their influence on stopping capabilities.

Brake Torque and Inertia Shift

Appling brakes has two effects on a vehicle. One is the transfer of torque from the slowing wheel end to the axle through the brake mechanism. Axles twist, and the suspension system is used to control axle movement. Components used to attach the brake mechanism need to be capable of repeated torque transfer from the brake to the axle.

Deceleration during braking also produces a shift in vehicle weight from the rear to the front of a vehicle. The effect, called **inertia shift**, moves weight from the rear axles and transfers it forward. This effect is observed when, during hard braking, the rear suspension lifts, and the rear wheels tend to lock up easily. The front of the vehicle dives, as weight transfers from the rear to front axles. Shifting weight changes axle loads as weight transfers forward. Weight transfer that lightens rear axles and makes forward axles heavier, in turn, change how much traction is available to a tire. Wheel lockup can take place, as the rear tires lose traction during inertia shift.

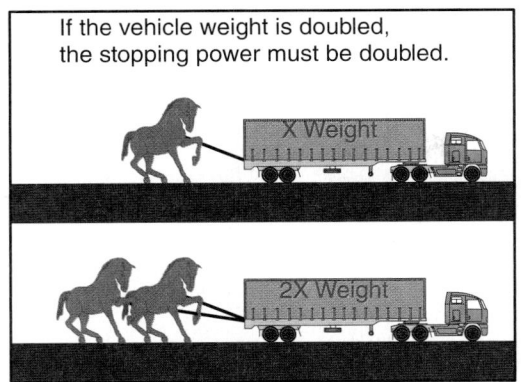

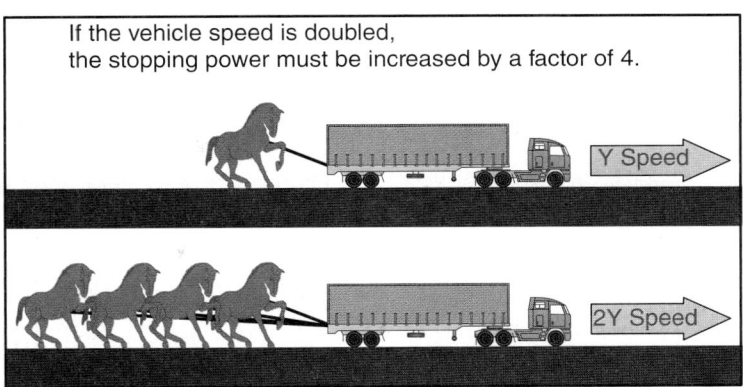

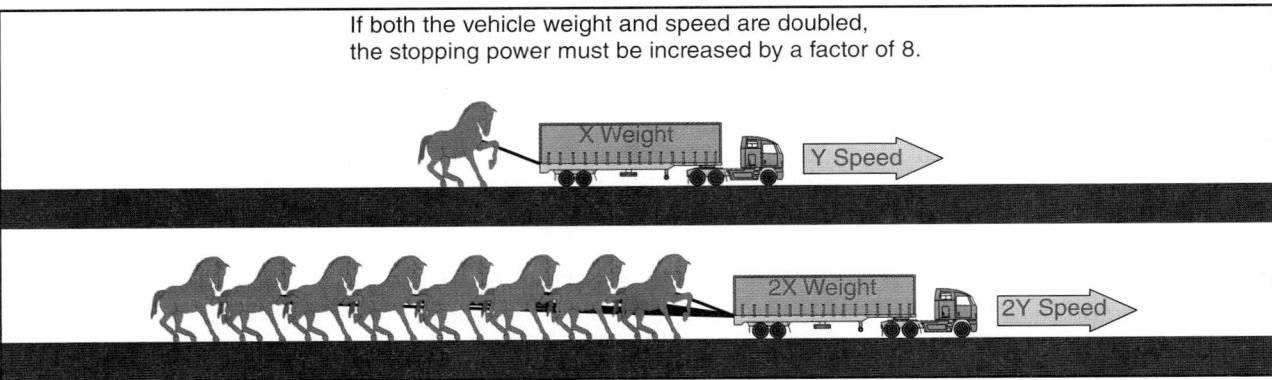

FIGURE 33-5 Note the influence of vehicle speed and weight on required braking force. When weight and speed are both doubled, braking force must increase by a factor of eight times.

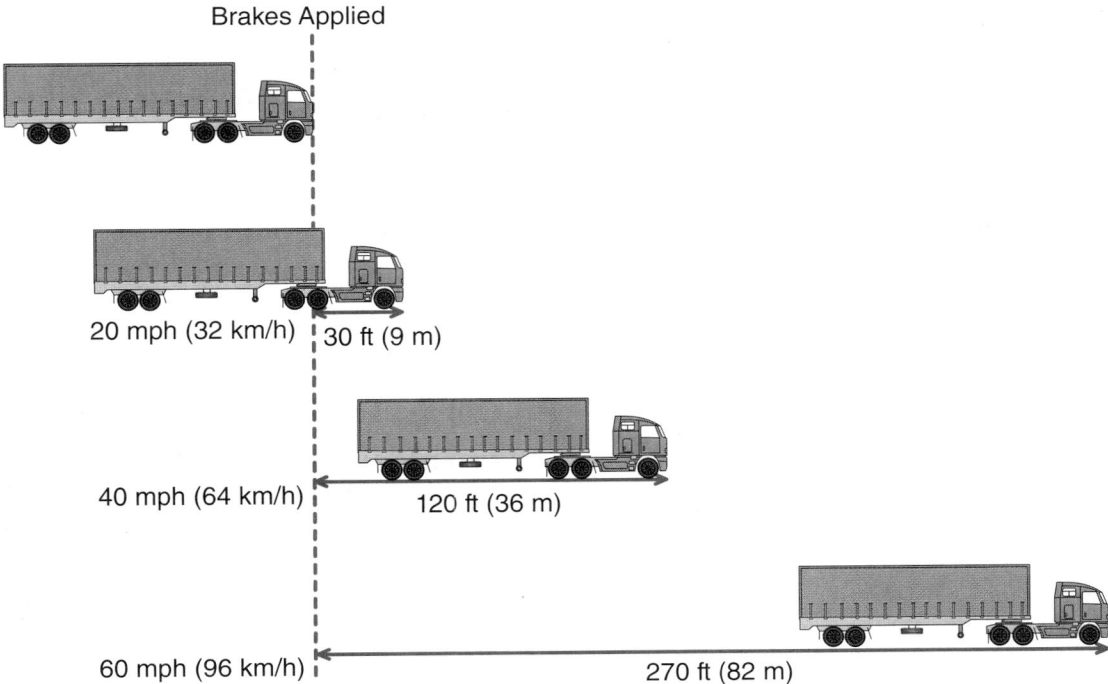

FIGURE 33-6 Higher vehicle speeds and weights require increasing stopping distances.

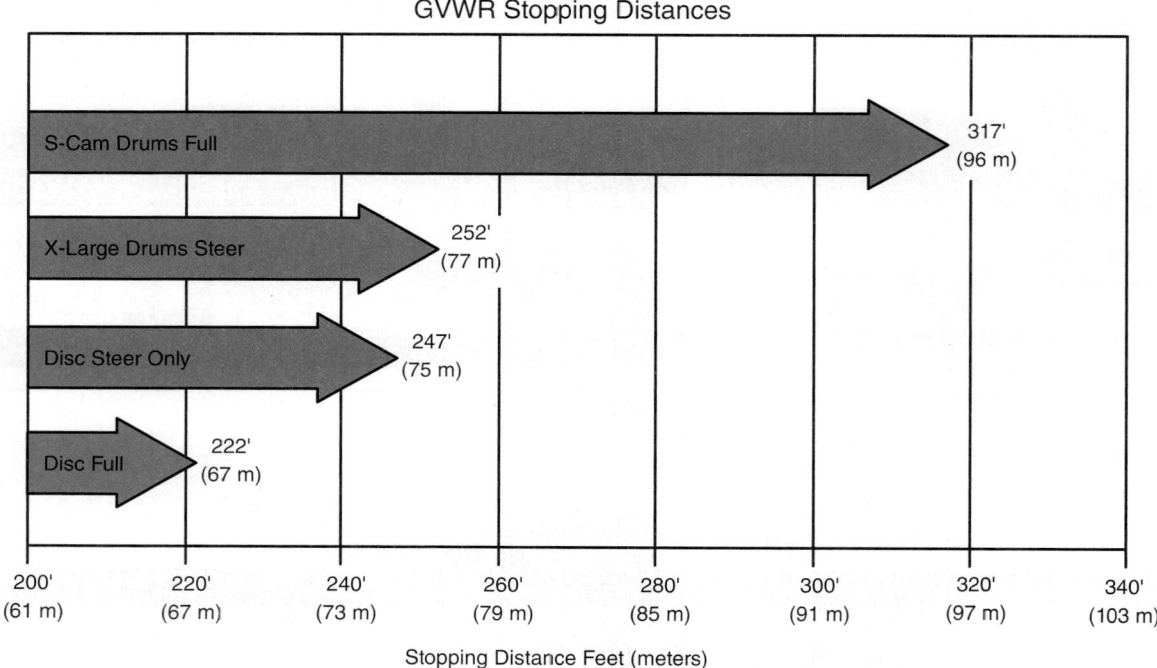

FIGURE 33-7 Comparisons between different brake foundation technologies and their influence on stopping capabilities.

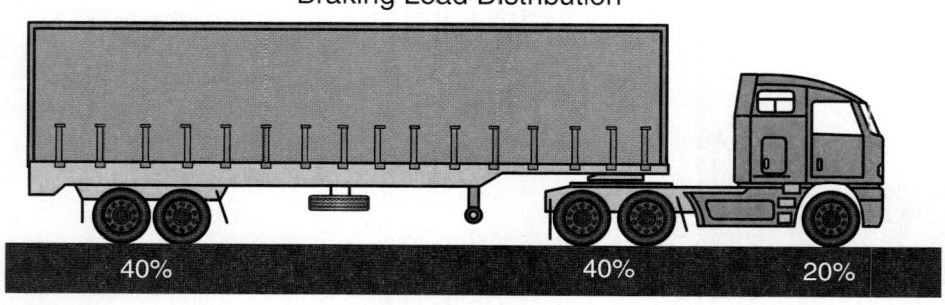

FIGURE 33-8 Shifting load weight during braking can lead to vehicle instability so the amount of braking must be correctly distributed over each axle.

The consequence of wheel lock-up is that the tires begin to skid, and the driver loses the ability to steer the vehicle. The mandatory use of antilock braking systems and other components incorporated into the braking system minimizes the likelihood of a wheel lockup event. Other design factors—including brake size, brake type, valve opening pressures, use of specialized valves, and so on—are brake system elements that take into account the effects of inertia shift on braking and must be maintained by a technician. **FIGURE 33-8** shows how vehicle weight is distributed over each axle. Too much braking performed by the front axle can cause jack-knifing. Too much braking done by the rear axles can cause the trailer or rear axles to swing out. **FIGURE 33-9** shows the brake torque reaction to braking force. Axles twist in the opposite direction to the force applied to the rotating drum or rotor used to slow and stop the vehicle.

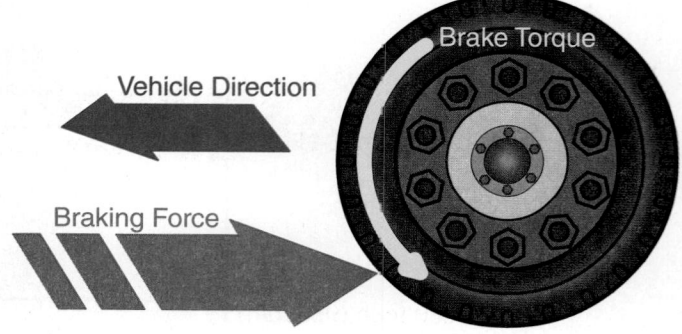

FIGURE 33-9 Brake torque is the reaction force to braking force. Axles twist in the opposite direction to the force applied to the rotating drum or rotor used to slow and stop the vehicle.

Types of Braking Systems

LO 33-2 Identify types of braking systems.

Because brakes require a much greater force than can be applied by the driver to slow a vehicle, brakes must multiply the input force of the driver's leg. Force multiplication is performed several ways in a braking system, but two primary methods for forcing friction material against drums and discs are using hydraulic fluid or using air pressure. Another term for brake application force is actuation pressure. A few midrange trucks produced in Europe and Asia use both air and hydraulic pressure to multiply brake force applied to the brake pedal by the driver. However, air pressure is more often used to supply force multiplication in vehicles above Class 4 (above 14,000 lb or 6351 kg gross vehicle weight [GVW]).

FIGURE 33-10 depicts the force multiplication needed by the braking system to multiply the brake pedal input force enough to effectively apply the brakes. **FIGURE 33-11** shows how hydraulic multiplication of driver input force can multiply brake pedal force and supply pressure to multiple wheel cylinders or brake caliper pistons. However, extra brake chambers

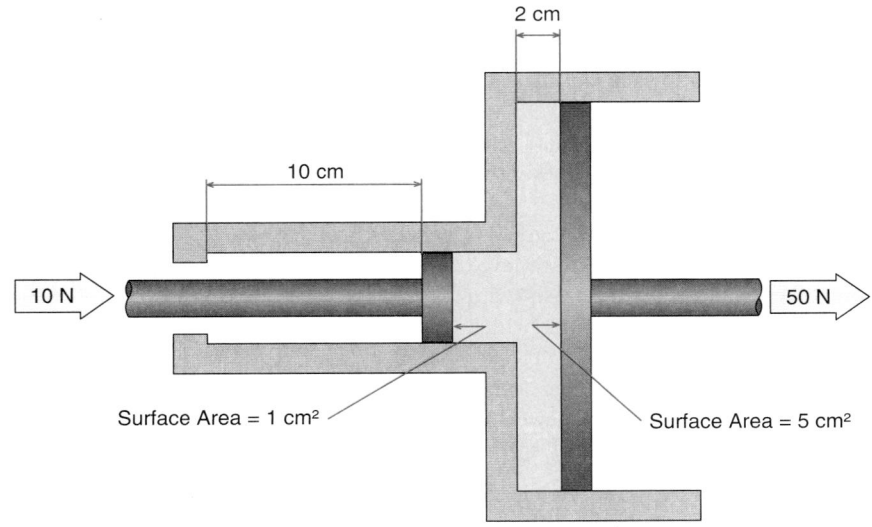

FIGURE 33-10 Force multiplication is needed by the braking system to multiply the brake pedal input force enough to effectively apply the brakes.

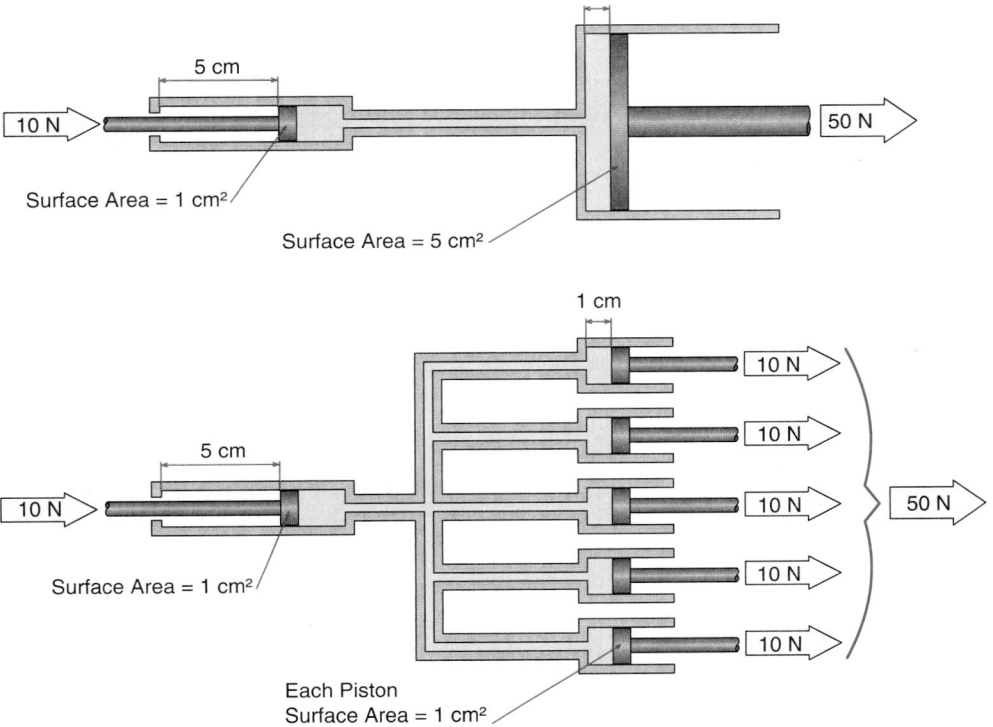

FIGURE 33-11 Hydraulic multiplication of driver input force can multiply brake pedal force and supply pressure to multiple wheel cylinders or brake caliper pistons.

used by multiple axles on heavy trucks and buses have higher flow requirements, making air pressure a better medium to multiply force.

Comparing Air and Hydraulic Braking Systems

Air and hydraulic braking systems each have operating characteristics that make one or the other ideal for certain applications. In heavy-duty combination vehicles, air is the best choice because of the large volume of liquid that is needed, instead of air, to actuate all the brake chambers at each axle end.

Air systems also have the following advantages:

- The supply of air is limitless, which allows for minor leaks without the loss of braking.
- Connecting the tractor and trailer braking systems is easier using air lines rather than hydraulic hoses, as shown in **FIGURE 33-12**.
- Air brake systems are not sensitive to altitude changes. Air can be compressed at high altitudes, as well as sea level, so no loss of pressure takes place. This contrasts with hydraulic brake systems using vacuum boosters, which lose efficiency at high altitudes.
- Simpler foundation brakes—shoes, drums, and other components at the wheel ends—are simpler and fewer.
- Air can be compressed and stores energy like a coil spring, as shown in **FIGURE 33-13**.

Air systems are not without disadvantages, however, which include the following:

- The air must be pressurized, filtered, and stored in large, multiple reservoirs. This means more components are required, increasing the system complexity and cost when using air.
- The speed of air pressure transmission is much slower than a hydraulic system, which produces a longer delay between brake pedal application and brake shoe/pad actuation.
- Control of air pressure through brake circuits requires more valves and components, which adds complexity and cost to the air brake system.
- Some driver dissatisfaction with the delay occurs when an air system is empty and needs to build up pressure after the engine is started.
- Little to no feedback comes from the brake pedal about braking effort.
- Larger brake system components and diameter lines are required because air systems operate at lower pressures than hydraulic systems.
- Air brake system complexity requires that technicians have more knowledge and skill when servicing. For similar reasons, driver training and certification to operate a vehicle with air brakes is mandatory in most jurisdictions.

Air brakes system performance and safety standards are legislated by the **Federal Motor Vehicle Safety Standard 121 (FMVSS 121)**. To ensure safe braking performance under normal and emergency conditions, compliance with the standard is required by all air brake systems at the time of manufacture.

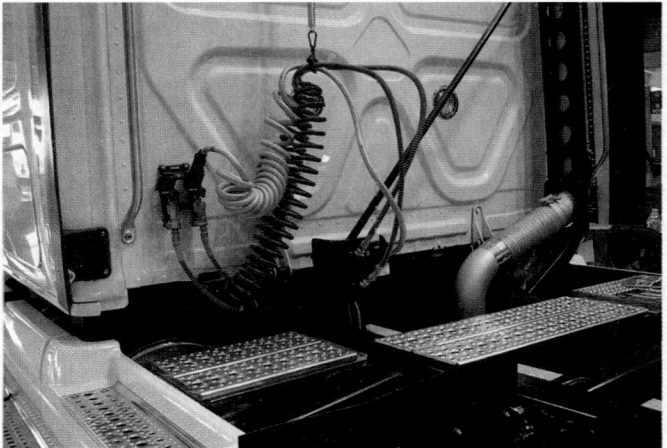

FIGURE 33-12 Connecting the tractor and trailer braking systems is easier using air lines, rather than hydraulic hoses. This tractor supplies air to the trailer through the red Emergency/Trailer supply hose and the blue service brake hose.

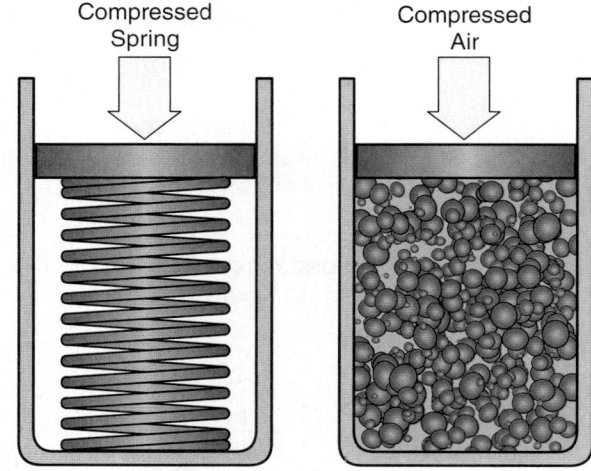

FIGURE 33-13 Air can be compressed and stores energy like a coil spring.

Hydraulic systems have the following advantages:

- Higher line pressures, enabling the use of smaller components.
- Faster force transmission through smaller lines. Hydraulic fluid is not compressible like air, and almost no delay takes place between brake pedal application and friction material actuation.
- Improved feedback during braking application. As the pedal is pushed further, resistance increases more than in an air system. The disadvantage is that hydraulic systems transmit annoying pressure pulsations, caused by warped rotors and out-of-round brake drums, back into the brake pedal.
- Lower initial cost due to fewer and smaller components.

Hydraulic brake performance and safety standards are governed by FMVSS standards 105, 106, 116, and 135.

Hydraulic brake systems, as shown in **FIGURE 33-14**, are used on single-drive axle vehicles under 14,000 lb (6364 kg)

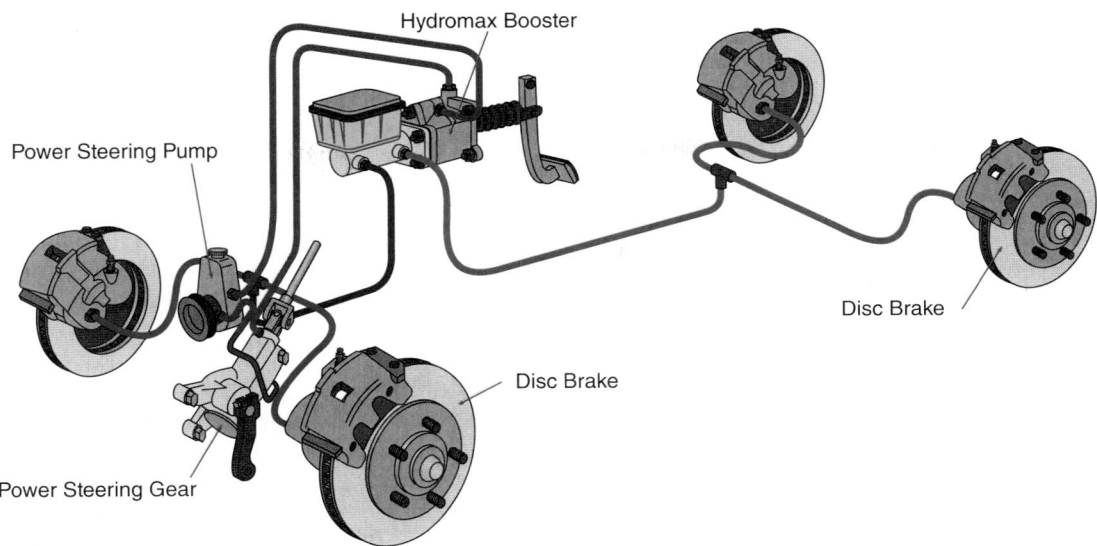

FIGURE 33-14 Hydraulic brakes are used on single-axle vehicles under 14,000 lb (6364 kg) GVW. An electric or hydraulic brake booster is used on diesel-powered vehicles since no engine vacuum is available to help multiply driver input force applied to the brake pedal.

GVW. An electric or mechanical brake booster is used on diesel-powered vehicles, as no engine vacuum is available to help multiply driver input force through the brake pedal. Note the dual-hydraulic brake circuits. There is one circuit each for the front and rear axle.

Brake System Subsystems

Regardless of the type of braking system, all braking systems have the following subsystems.

- *Brake foundations*—**Brake foundations** are the braking components found at the wheel ends. Foundation brakes use either a drum or brake shoe combination or discs and pads. (Discs are also called rotors.) Vehicles also use combinations of drum and disc for foundations.
- *Dual-brake circuits*—Whether the actuation system is hydraulic or air operated, two separate brake circuits control the front and rear axle braking systems. Separate circuits are used to prevent a total loss of braking if a failure occurs. Only half of the brakes is affected by a failure, and the vehicle can still be brought to a safe controlled stop. In air brake systems, the primary circuit controls the rear brakes, and the secondary circuit controls the front axle brakes. Trailers receive air pressure supplied by the secondary circuit in early-model trucks. Late-model vehicles supply air to the trailer from the reservoir with the highest pressure.
- *Parking brakes*—With the exception of trucks using a driveline park brake, all vehicles use the foundation brakes for keeping a vehicle stationary when parked.

Air Brake Foundation Systems

LO 33-3 Identify, describe, and compare air brake foundation systems.

Three basic types of brake foundation configurations found in medium- and heavy-duty commercial vehicles are:

- Cam brakes
- Air disc systems
- Wedge brakes

(This chapter examines the brake foundation system. Air brake circuits and valves are covered in a separate chapter.)

In air brake foundation systems, air pressure proportional to brake pedal travel is supplied by the primary and secondary air systems. Foundation brake components are located at the wheel ends and provide the braking action needed to slow and stop a vehicle. The wedge brakes in **FIGURE 33-15** use shoes and rollers for the brake foundation. **Wedge brakes** use leverage to multiply braking force. A wedge pushed between two ramps, as shown in **FIGURE 33-16**, multiplies brake force proportional to the angle of the brake wedge. Rollers used between the ramps and wedge reduce friction force.

FIGURE 33-15 Foundation brake components are located at the wheel ends and provide the braking action needed to slow and stop a vehicle. The wedge brakes in this illustration use shoes and rollers for the brake foundation.

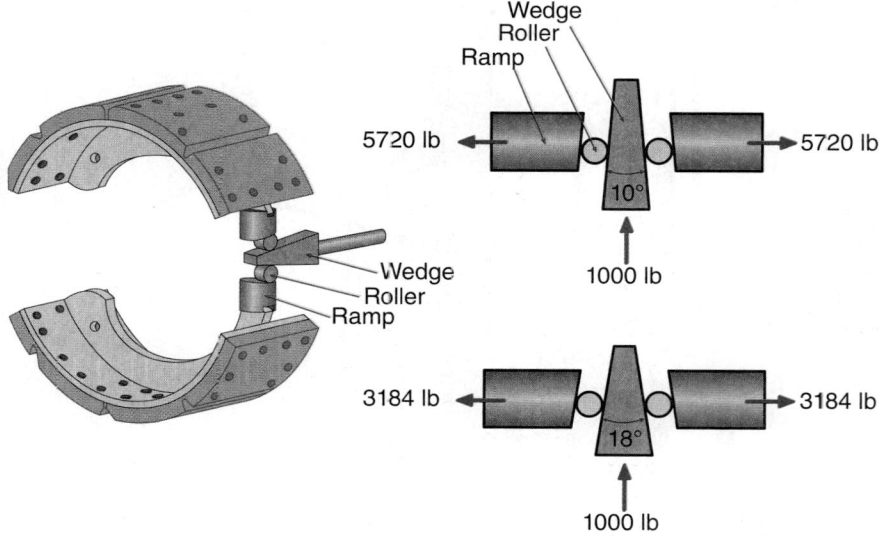

FIGURE 33-16 Wedge brakes refer to the leverage principle used to multiply braking force. A wedge pushed between two ramps multiplies brake force proportional to the angle of the brake wedge. Rollers used between the ramps and wedge reduce friction force.

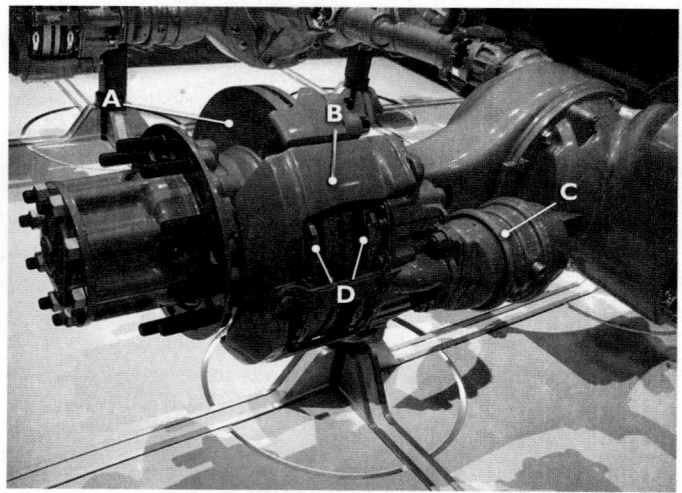

FIGURE 33-17 Disc brakes squeeze brake pads against a rotor attached to the wheel to produce braking action. Higher application force by brake pads against the rotors make disc brake systems more efficient than other types of foundation brakes. **A.** Brake rotor. **B.** Brake caliper. **C.** Actuator chamber. **D.** Brake pads.

Disc brakes squeeze brake pads against a rotor attached to the wheel to produce braking action. Higher application force by brake pads against the rotors makes disc brake systems more efficient than other types of foundation brakes. Shorter stopping distances are easier to achieve using disc brake systems. **FIGURE 33-17** shows a typical heavy-duty truck disc brake.

Cam brakes are the most common foundation brake found on heavy trucks today. These brake systems use an "S"-shaped cam that twists between two rollers to expand a set of brake shoes to apply the brakes. Because they are the most common foundation brake system, our discussion focuses primarily on the S-cam foundation brake, followed by a shorter examination of disc and wedge brakes.

Cam Brake System Operation

LO 33-4 Identify and describe the construction and operation of S-cam brake components.

Cam brakes consist of an air brake chamber, automatic slack adjuster, S-camshaft, brake hardware, shoes and linings, spider, and brake drum. The name cam brake is given because of an "S"-shaped camshaft, or **S-cam**, used to force brake shoes onto the brake drum. When torque is applied to the camshaft through the S-shaped cam ramps, rollers on the brake shoes ride up the cam, causing the shoes to contact the brake drum. Shoe-to-drum friction slows and stops the vehicle. **FIGURE 33-18** shows the components of a typical S-cam brake foundation system.

Cam brakes are commonly used with 15" and 16.5" diameter drums and in varying widths from 4" to 7". **TABLE 33-1** shows stopping distance requirements prior to 2011. Revisions to the year 2011 FMVSS 121 standard introduced a 30% reduction in stopping distance from the previous year. More powerful brake configurations are now necessary to meet the revised stopping distance standards. The common 16.5" × 7" rear axle brake may be replaced by an optional 16.5" × 8" or 16.5" × 8.62" brake. Traditional front axle brakes using 15" × 4" drums and brake shoes may move up to 16.5" × 5" brakes.

These stopping distance requirements must also be met with a stability requirement. During certification, the vehicle must stay within a 12' (365 m) lane with no part of the vehicle leaving the lane during braking. It should be noted that the superior stopping power and fade resistance of air disc brakes (ADB) will likely displace the cam brake in most applications.

Cam brake shoes use either a single- or double-anchor pin. Today's anchor pin holes are open ended to enable quick changing of brake shoes. Older shoes used closed shoe anchors, which were prone to seizing and labor-intensive to remove during brake replacement. Figure 33-18 shows an S-cam brake foundation brake using double-anchor pins. The S-cam shown in **FIGURE 33-19**

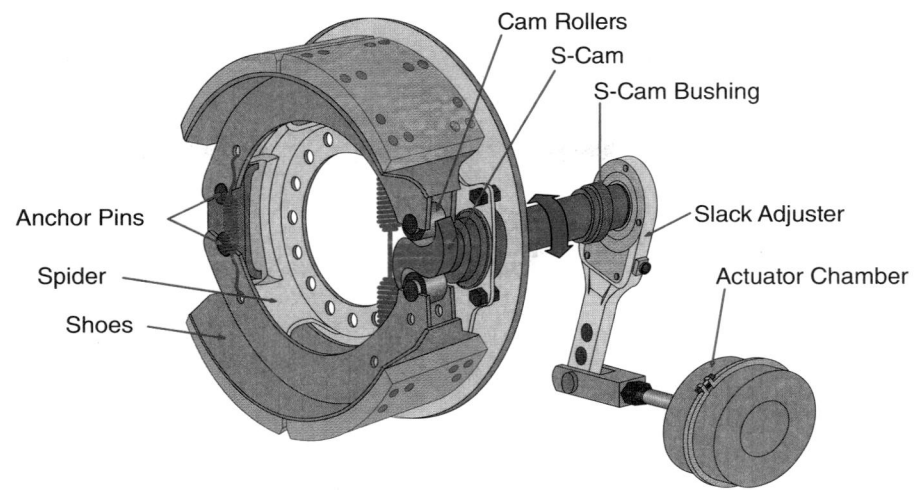

FIGURE 33-18 Components of a typical S-cam brake foundation system.

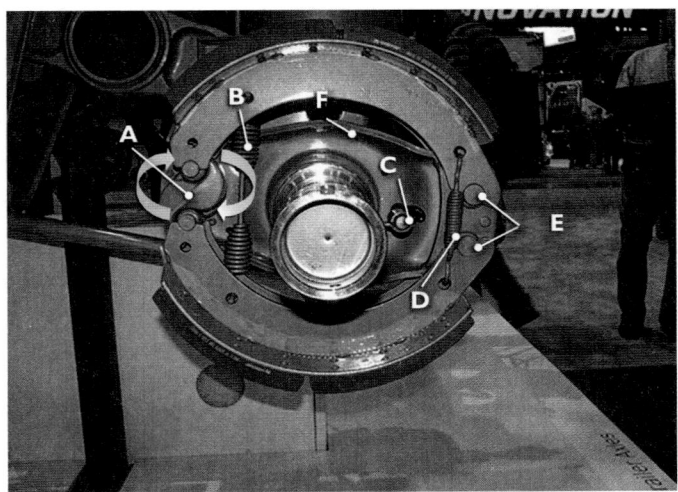

FIGURE 33-19 An S-cam brake foundation using double-anchor pins. The S-cam rotates in a clockwise direction, which makes this cam a right-hand cam. **A.** S-cam. **B.** Shoe return spring. **C.** ABS speed sensor. **D.** Shoe return spring. **E.** Anchor pins. **F.** Spider.

FIGURE 33-20 An S-cam brake foundation using a single-anchor pin (circled). The S-cam rotates in a counterclockwise direction, which makes this cam a left-hand cam. (Note: The actuator chamber is in front of and below the axle.)

TABLE 33-1 Stopping Distance Requirements (60 mph [97 kph] to 0 mph [0 kph]) Prior to 2011

Service Brakes	Stopping Distance (feet [m])
Loaded & Unloaded Buses	280 [85]
Loaded Trucks	310 [94 m]
Empty Trucks & Tractors	335 [102 m]
Loaded Tractors	355 [108]
Emergency & Failed Systems (except bobtails)	**Stopping Distance (feet [m])**
All except Bobtails (no trailer)	613 [187 m]
Bobtail Tractors	720 [219 m]
Automobiles (for reference) Empty or Loaded	215 [66 m]

rotates in a counterclockwise direction, which makes this cam a left-hand cam. **FIGURE 33-20** shows a single-anchor S-cam brake. Note, the actuator chamber is in front of and below the axle.

Self-Energization

Cam brakes use a primary-secondary shoe design with fixed anchor points for each shoe opposite the camshaft end of the shoe. Both shoes are identically shaped and use two different lengths and shapes of brake lining on each shoe. What is different between the primary and secondary shoe is the direction of drum rotation acting on each shoe during brake application.

On the primary shoe, the shorter section of brake lining contacts the drum first, as it is rotated on its anchor pin against the rotating drum. Because the forward edge of the shorter lining is contacting the drum first, the direction of drum rotation causes an action, called **self-energization**, to take place. Self-energizing causes shoe-drum friction to rotate the brake shoe into the drum with more force. The effect is the brake applies "harder" or "bite" into the drum with greater force, thus increasing friction. Opposite the primary shoe is the secondary shoe. When it is forced against the drum, the direction of brake drum rotation forces the lining away from the drum, and less friction is produced. Self-energization can cause uneven brake shoe wear. The secondary shoe can either be on the top or the bottom position of the wheel end, left or right, depending on the location of the camshaft. **FIGURE 33-21** shows the effect of self-energization.

Left- and Right-Hand Camshafts

Camshafts are classified two ways. One is by the direction they rotate to force the brake shoes against the drum. Depending on which direction the camshaft rotates to force the primary shoe against the drum, the cam is referred to as a left- or right-hand camshaft. Left-hand cams rotate counterclockwise, while right-hand cams turn clockwise. To make it easier to remember, simply consider which hand you would turn the hands of a clock at 12-oclock?, clockwise or counterclockwise? **Left-hand camshafts** and **right-hand camshafts** are found on either side of the vehicle, and it is critical when performing a brake job to ensure the correct camshaft is used when replacing or reassembling brakes on a wheel end.

Another way camshafts are classified is how they are positioned relative to drum rotation. A **cam-same** camshaft rotates in the same direction as the drum to energize the brakes. The primary brake shoe rollers are pushed out and down. A **cam-opposite** camshaft rotates opposite the drum's rotation to energize the brakes. The opposite rotation pushes the shoe roller up and out. Cam-opposite positioning produces more brake torque, but causes the brake shoe to contact the drum at the cam end, rather than closer to the center. The result is uneven brake shoe wear. **FIGURE 33-22** shows the two cam positions.

The major reason for different camshaft rotations is the position of the brake chambers. Some suspension systems simply do not allow enough room above or below the wheel end or in front or behind for the chamber. Positioning the chamber where the best clearances are obtained requires an appropriate type of camshaft. The location of the actuator chamber relative to the axle determines the camshaft direction of rotation. Left-hand cams turn counterclockwise (**FIGURE 33-23A**); right-hand camshafts rotate clockwise (**FIGURE 33-23B**).

S-Cam Brackets

To support the camshaft between the brake chamber and the brake spider at the wheel end, a support bracket is used to enclose the camshaft. At least two support bushings are located at each end of the bracket. Grease seals at each end of the tube are designed to allow grease to exit at the slack adjuster end of the bracket, but prevent grease from getting into the brakes.

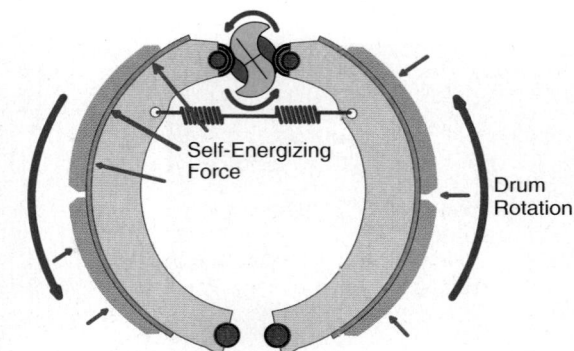

FIGURE 33-21 Self-energizing causes shoe-drum friction to rotate the brake shoe into the drum with more force. The effect is that the brake applies "harder" or "bite" into the drum with greater force, thus increasing friction.

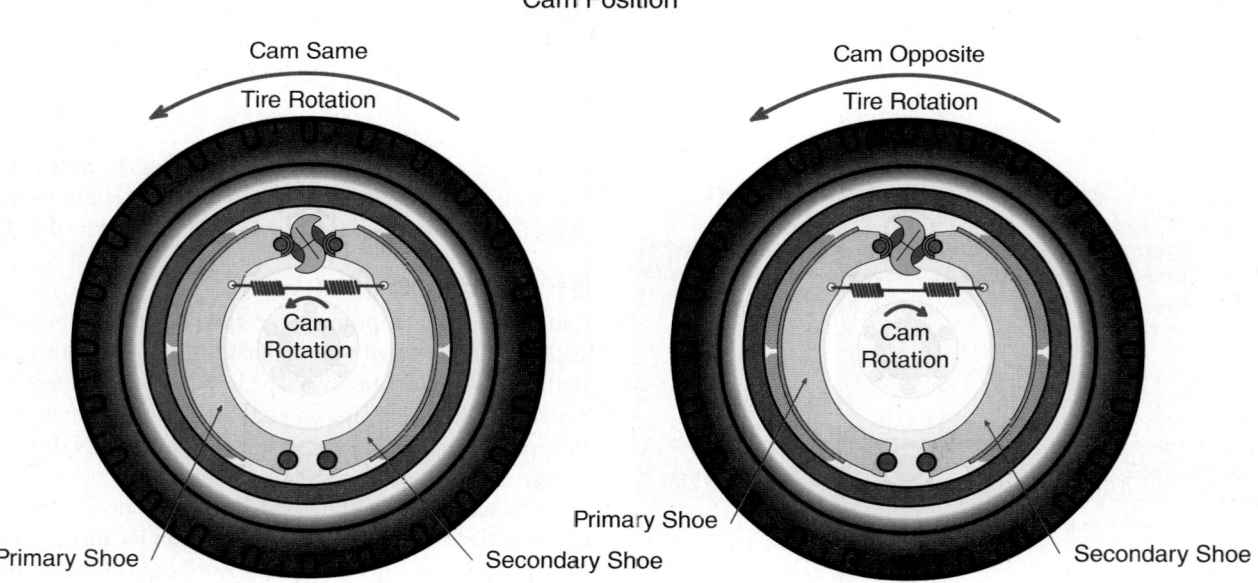

FIGURE 33-22 Cam positioning can change the amount of brake torque by changing the contact point between the shoe and brake drum. The cam-opposite position pushes the brake rollers out with more application force to produce greater brake torque. The downside of cam-opposite S-cam positioning is uneven brake shoe wear.

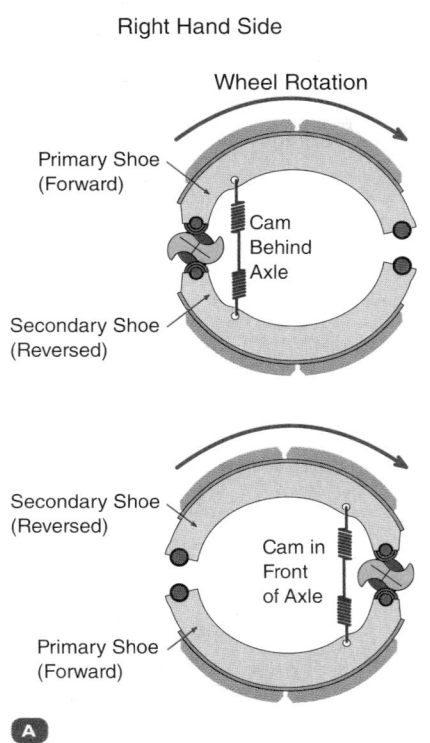

Right Hand Side

Wheel Rotation

Primary Shoe
(Forward)

Cam
Behind
Axle

Secondary Shoe
(Reversed)

Secondary Shoe
(Reversed)

Cam in
Front
of Axle

Primary Shoe
(Forward)

A

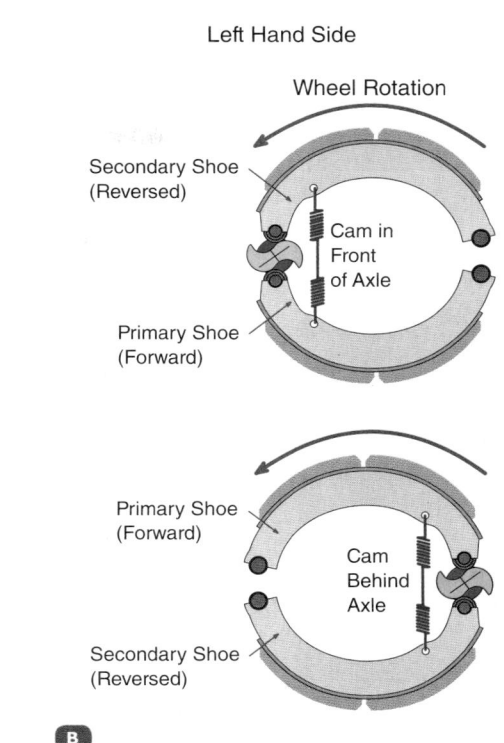

Left Hand Side

Wheel Rotation

Secondary Shoe
(Reversed)

Cam in
Front
of Axle

Primary Shoe
(Forward)

Primary Shoe
(Forward)

Cam
Behind
Axle

Secondary Shoe
(Reversed)

B

FIGURE 33-23 A. Right-hand and **B.** Left-hand S-camshaft classification is determined by the direction the cam rotates to apply the brakes. The location of the actuator chamber relative to the axle determines the camshaft direction of rotation. Left-hand camshafts turn counterclockwise. Right-hand camshafts rotate clockwise.

Grease nipples are installed in the brackets to lubricate the bushings. When the bushings or camshafts wear out, movement of the S-cam has some linear linear, rather than only a rotational, motion, which introduces more brake chamber stroke travel. Even when camshaft and bushing wear is within acceptable limits, "wheel-up" brake adjustment is a good practice to avoid adjustment error due to even slightly worn bushings. Making wheel-up adjustments involves tightening the slack adjusters with the wheels off the ground until a slight amount of brake shoe drag is obtained.

S-cams are shimmed with washers to prevent any excessive end play along the cam bracket. After installation, selective shims are placed between the slack adjuster and clip holding the slack adjuster onto the end of the S-cam. The S-cam bracket, shown in **FIGURE 33-24**, supports the S-cam and has an attachment point for the actuator chamber. Note the grease fitting in the bracket used to grease support bushing located at each end of the bracket. **FIGURE 33-25** shows the S-cam nylon bushings at each end used to support the S-cam. Bushings require lubrication and do wear, which requires the actuator chamber to extend the pushrod farther to compensate for cam deflection. Selective shims installed at the end of the S-cam are used to minimize any cam end play; **FIGURE 33-26** illustrates the shim positioning.

Brake Shoes

Cam brakes use brake shoes that are made in different sizes to match an axle weight rating. The shoes have two ends—a cam and anchor pin end—and have either one or two pieces of lining attached. One or two pieces of friction material are attached

FIGURE 33-24 The S-cam bracket (circled) supports the S-cam and has an attachment point for the actuator chamber. Note the grease fitting in the bracket used to grease support bushing located at each end of the bracket.

to the brake shoe table and are called either **brake block** or **brake lining**. Brake lining and block differ in that a block is 3/4" thick and lining is 1/2" thick. Two pieces of block are required to reline a shoe, but only one piece of lining.

Block and lining are riveted, bolted, or glued to the brake shoe table. While glued friction material, called bonded lining, can withstand high temperatures, riveted lining is considered superior in heavy-duty applications because it is mechanically held to the shoe. The web is the support perpendicular to the bottom of the brake shoe table. A single or double web is used to support the brake table, depending on the width of the shoe. **FIGURE 33-27** shows the subcomponents of an air brake

FIGURE 33-25 S-cam brackets contain nylon bushings at each end used to support the S-cam. Bushings require lubrication and do wear, which requires the brake chamber to extend its pushrod farther to compensate for cam deflection.

FIGURE 33-26 Selective shims are installed at the end of the S-cam to minimize any S-cam end play.

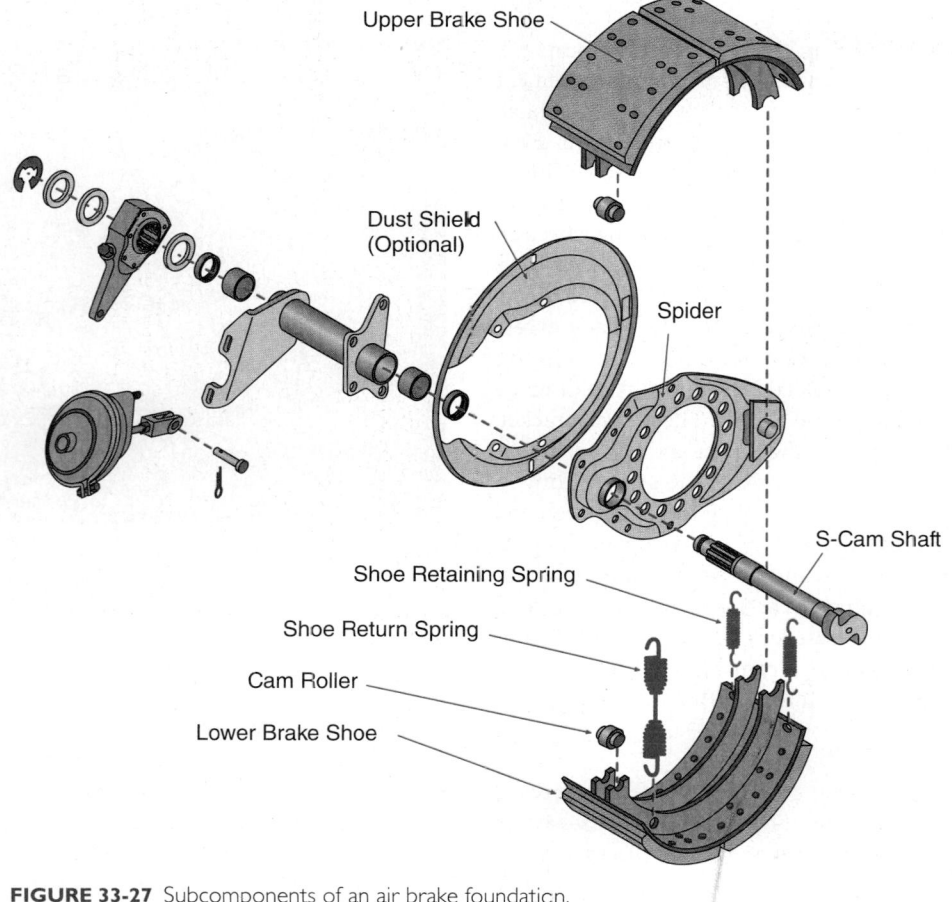

FIGURE 33-27 Subcomponents of an air brake foundation.

foundation. Brake block refers to 3/4" thick brake shoe friction material, which is either bolted or riveted to brake shoes. Brake block, like lining, is composed of a variety of materials to match a service application. For example, in frequent braking applications, such as a transit bus, lining materials may make the friction element more fade-resistant and wear-resistant but may generate more noise and brake drum wear. **FIGURE 33-28** shows various types of brake block and brake lining.

When inspecting new or rebuilt brake shoes for wear, follow the steps in **SKILL DRILL 33-1**. To remove the brake shoes, follow the steps in **SKILL DRILL 33-2**.

Coefficient of Friction (CoF)

Brake friction material is classified several ways, such as by its composition, whether it is riveted or bonded, and so on. One of

FIGURE 33-28 Brake block refers to 3/4" thick brake shoe friction material that is either bolted or riveted to brake shoes. Brake block, like lining, is composed of a variety of materials to match a service application.

SKILL DRILL 33-1 Inspecting Brake Shoes

1. Determine if the shoe tables are warped or bent. Check for any small gaps between the lining and the shoe table.
2. Check for elongated rivet holes, which can cause movement between the shoe table and the lining.
3. Check for corrosion of the shoe table. Inspect for uneven fit between the lining and the shoe table. Look for visible rust at the edges.
4. Check for web-end wear, uneven, or mushroom ends. Check both the anchor pin end and the roller end for wear and elongation. Use gauges to verify the proper distance between the web ends.
5. Check for loose or broken welds. Look for cracks in the welds between the shoe table and the web.
6. Check for chips or cracks in the corrosion-resistant paint. Make sure the paint is even and that there is solid coverage.

SKILL DRILL 33-2 Removing Brake Shoes

1. After backing off the brakes using the slack adjuster, the S-cam is rotated to its start position. This enables the cam roller to be easily unclipped and removed from the shoes. Lifting the upper brake shoe slightly using a pry bar provides additional clearance to remove the cam rollers.
2. The larger, single brake shoe return spring is disconnected from pins on the brake shoes after the cam rollers are removed.
3. Rotating the lower shoe downward allows the two smaller return springs to be disconnected. The shoes are freely removed from the brake spider.

the most important characteristics, though, is its **coefficient of friction (CoF)**. CoF refers to the amount of force required to move an object while in contact with another. Stated another way, CoF describes how slippery the surface is between two objects. If an object weighs 100 lb (45 kg), and a force of 40 lb (18 kg) is required to keep it moving while it remains in contact with another body, the CoF between the two bodies is said to be 40% or 0.4. If only 35 lb (16 kg) force is required, the CoF is 35% or 0.35.

Changes to the CoF take place when the condition of the surfaces between the objects varies. For example, the introduction of oil, grease, or heat between two dry, flat metal surfaces changes the CoF between them, as they become more or less slippery. CoF, as depicted in **FIGURE 33-29**, is defined as a ratio between the force required to move an object compared to its weight. In the illustration, a 45 lb (25 kg) force applied to the 100 lb (45 kg) load generates a 0.45 or 45% CoF.

Brake Block Material

Brake friction material is made from a wide variety of materials to provide a varying CoF to match an application and provide other desirable performance characteristics. The perfect friction material would have the correct coefficient maintained constantly for its service life under all operating conditions of pressure, speed, temperature, and humidity. Perfect lining would not score or wear the brake drum, would operate quietly and wear slowly, and would not fade or emit a noxious odor. Friction material is made from heat-resistant adhesive resin blended with materials, such as glass fiber, Kevlar, mineral wool, aramid fibers, ceramic fibers, carbon fibers, slag, bronze, steel, and elastomer-like compounds. Asbestos is not used in any friction material today.

Two broad categories for friction material are **non-asbestos organic (NAO) lining** and **semi-metallic linings**. Because the CoF of metallic particles in lining increases when hot, heat-resistant, semi-metallic blends are used for higher temperatures and load service ratings. The downside for semi-metallic linings is that they wear brake drums faster, have a poor CoF when cold, and can be noisy. Vocational trucks that stop and start frequently, such as buses and garbage trucks, use the severe-service semi-metallic materials. Brake block for these

vehicles contain a high percentage of steel wool fibers, for high-temperature fade-resistance, along with some graphite to extend service life while reducing noise.

It's not uncommon to have these vehicles undergo as many as four brake jobs a year, each job separated by as little as 50,000 miles (31,250 km). NOA linings are more commonly used in line-haul tractors where far less braking takes place, so that brake replacement service interval may be as long as 500,000 miles (312,500 km).

Selection of brake block material is made by taking in the axle weight and service condition—severe, heavy, and moderate. The **AL factor**, depicted in **FIGURE 33-30**, is another consideration. AL refers to the size or surface area of a brake chamber multiplied by the length of the slack adjuster in inches. Larger chambers and longer slack adjusters exert more pressure against the brake lining. It is critical to maintain the OEM-specified length of slack adjusters and other components. Changing the length, as shown in **FIGURE 33-31**, alters the torque applied to the brakes, as well as the stroke length required to apply the brakes.

Edge Codes

All brake block friction material is identified by a stencil on its edge and called an **edge code**. The friction class is indicated by two letters. The first letter represents a cold CoF and the second the hot CoF. **FIGURE 33-32** shows a typical brake shoe edge code. The "GG" refers to the CoF produced by the brake block to drum contact. **TABLE 33-2** lists the edge codes for various CoFs.

The friction code has no relationship to the quality of the brake block. The manufacturer name or identification code is also stenciled into the edge of the block. When reading edge codes, note the first part is the manufacturer's identification, and the next alphabetic code indicates the composition or material the block is made from. The third two-letter code is the friction class. The first letter represents a "normal" coefficient, and the second letter represents the "hot" CoF. Each letter

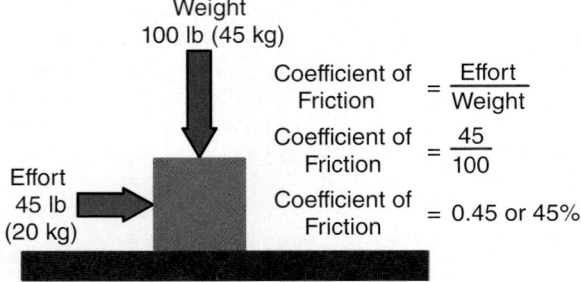

Weight
100 lb (45 kg)

$$\text{Coefficient of Friction} = \frac{\text{Effort}}{\text{Weight}}$$

$$\text{Coefficient of Friction} = \frac{45}{100}$$

$$\text{Coefficient of Friction} = 0.45 \text{ or } 45\%$$

Effort
45 lb
(20 kg)

FIGURE 33-29 Coefficient of friction is a ratio between the force required to move an object compared to its weight. In the illustration, a 45 lb (25 kg) force applied to the 100 lb (45kg) load generates a 0.45 or 45% coefficient of friction.

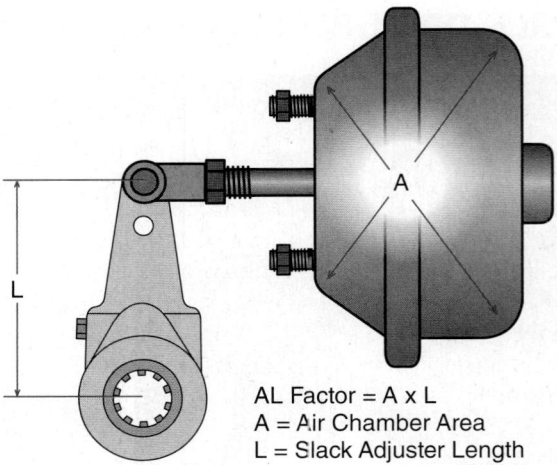

AL Factor = A x L
A = Air Chamber Area
L = Slack Adjuster Length

FIGURE 33-30 The AL factor refers to the size or surface area of a brake chamber multiplied by the length of the slack adjuster. Larger chambers and longer slack adjusters exert more pressure against the brake lining.

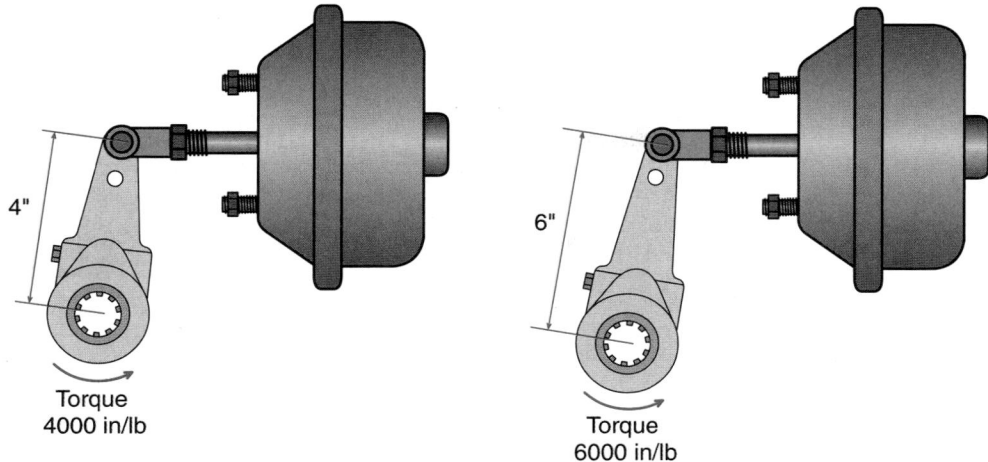

Torque
4000 in/lb

Torque
6000 in/lb

FIGURE 33-31 It is critical to maintain the OEM-specified length of slack adjusters and other components. Changing the length of slack alters the torque applied to the brakes, as well as the stroke length required to apply the brakes.

FIGURE 33-32 Brake shoe edge codes (circled), such as the "GG" in reference to the coefficient of friction produced by the brake block to drum contact.

TABLE 33-2 Coefficient of Friction Edge Codes

Coefficient of Friction	Edge Code
Over 0.25, but not over 0.35	E
Over 0.35, but not over 0.45	F
Over 0.45, but not over 0.55	G
Over 0.55	H

indicates an average CoF. Manufacturers calculate these averages from laboratory test data, where a one-square-inch sample of the lining is applied under pressure against a moving drum. As the drum heats up, normal range data to calculate cold CoF is collected between 200°F (93°C) to 400°F (204°C). The hot CoF coefficient is averaged using data from 300°F (149°C) to 650°F (343°C). Brake temperatures can climb as high as 1000°F (538°C).

Occasionally, two different pieces of block are used on one shoe to give it different characteristics. Combination lining, as it is called, also has a direction of rotation arrow stamped on the shoe to ensure correct installation.

Brake Fade

LO 33-5 Identify and explain the causes of brake fade.

Brake fade is a problem that can be described as the inability of the brakes to maintain their effectiveness. An operator describes fade as the need to push the pedal harder to get the same braking effectiveness. Good quality brake linings fade slightly upon each brake application, but immediately return to their initial state after cooling. However, the CoF of the lining may change during its service life. When the lining's CoF decreases, the vehicle develops what is known as a "hard pedal." Brake fade occurs for several reasons. During brake fade, the brakes' stopping power is reduced, as shown in **FIGURE 33-33**, due to problems, such as overheated brake drums and shoes, contaminated lining, or changes to the friction material, such as glazing of linings. Common types of brake fade are heat, water, mechanical, and chemical fade, as well as glazing of lining.

> ▶ **TECHNICIAN TIP**

Brakes can emit noises for a large variety of reasons. Much of the noises have one common source, though—vibration. High-frequency vibration between metal brake parts or vibrating brake drums produces a loud, unpleasant noise. Loose and worn parts, hard brake lining, and the absence of lubrication between some metal parts are the source of most vibration-related noise. To minimize noise, technicians should use lubricants between moving parts of brake shoes and brake hardware. Anchor pins and cam rollers are two places where the absence of lubricant is most likely to emit noise. Lubricants dampen high-frequency vibration between the parts by absorbing vibration and resist transmitting mechanical vibration between parts. Never-Seez, a graphite-based lubricant, salt-resistant grease, or high-temperature silicone grease is recommended at points of friction and movement in the brake to prevent noise. Strong, low-frequency vibration in the driving axle brakes and affecting the entire vehicle may occur at low speeds just before the vehicle stops. This type of vibration is caused by masses outside the foundation brakes being brought onto the same vibration frequency.

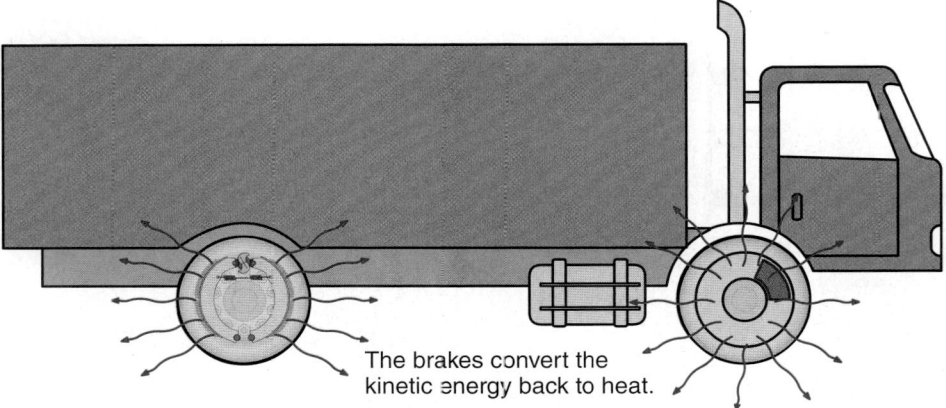

The brakes convert the
kinetic energy back to heat.

FIGURE 33-33 Brake fade takes place when the brake's stopping power is reduced due to problems, such as overheating brake drums and shoes, contaminated lining, or changes to the friction material, such as glazing of linings.

Heat Fade

Heat fade is the loss or reduction in the CoF as the brake temperature increases. The lining may become "slipperier," and heating of the brake drum causes its expansion and increases its internal diameter. To get an idea of the conditions producing heat-related fade, consider this: a single full-stop brake application from 60 mph (97 kph) raises drum temperatures to approximately 600°F (316°C)—the general limit for safe brake operation. If an axle is heavily loaded or braking is not properly distributed to all the wheels, some drums reach 800°F to 1000°F (427°C to 538°C). When heated, the internal diameter of the drum increases approximately 0.01" (2.5 mm) per 100°F rise above 50°F. This means at 600°F (316°C), the brake drums are 0.055" (1.4 mm) larger than at 50°F (10°C). Depending on the length of the slack adjuster, brake chamber pushrod stroke increases about 0.40" (10 mm), or close to half an inch (13 mm). The angle formed between the slack adjuster and chamber push rod is reduced, causing a loss in the leverage or the mechanical advantage of the normally 90-degree angle between the slack adjuster to brake pushrod. The smaller slack adjuster to pushrod angle means the driver must push harder against the brake pedal to compensate for the lost leverage, which progressively deteriorates with increased brake drum temperature.

Gradual and predictable fade is engineered into lining and is a desirable characteristic. Controlled fade prevents the lining from overheating and destroying itself by maintaining its CoF. When the operator senses fade, it is a warning that the brakes have overheated and should be cooled to allow them to recover. Operating overheated brakes results in damaged linings and drums and decreased overall performance. Disc brakes are not immune to fade, but they are less affected by heat and water than drums.

Heat fade can also take place in hydraulic brake systems due to the boiling temperature of brake fluid. Because brake fluid is hygroscopic—that is, it attracts water—moisture contained in brake fluid can turn to steam when heat transfers from the caliper piston into the fluid. Bubbles in the master cylinder can indicate the brake fluid is boiling out moisture. Alternatively, fluid that absorbs considerable heat can, in turn,

boil. Specifications for brake fluids, such as DOT 3, DOT 4, and DOT 5, differ primarily in boiling point. The highest DOT specification, DOT 5, uses silicone-based fluid and has the highest boiling point. Silicone-based fluids are hydrophobic, which means they do not attract water and do not damage paint. The latest specification, DOT 5.1, is polyethylene glycol, which is hygroscopic. **TABLE 33-3** shows boiling point specifications for different brake fluids.

Anti-fade is an opposite condition of heat fade, where the CoF increases as the brakes get hotter. If the increase in friction is too large, braking effectiveness becomes unpredictable, which can potentially cause vehicle instability problems, especially if the lining is installed on steering axles. **FIGURE 33-34** shows how disc brakes are more resistant to heat fade than drum brakes. In the illustration, stopping distances become longer with each successive brake application. Heat deteriorates drum brake performance at a greater rate than disc brakes.

Disc brakes are resistant to brake fade for a few reasons. Better cooling through ventilation of the disc or rotor dissipates heat faster. Fins or nubs connecting one side of the disc to the other, as shown in **FIGURE 33-35**, increase surface area, which releases more heat faster.

Water Fade

Brake fade is not always due to overheating. **Water fade** occurs when water gets between the friction surfaces and the drum and acts act as a lubricant, reducing braking efficiency. Water can also be absorbed by the lining and braking efficiency does not

TABLE 33-3 Dry and Wet Boiling Points of Brake Fluid

Dry Boiling Point	Wet Boiling Point (Contains 3.7% Moisture)	
DOT 3	401°F (205°C)	284°F (140°C)
DOT 4	446°F (230°C)	311°F (155°C)
DOT 5	500°F (260°C)	356°F (180°C)
DOT 5.1	500°F (260°C)	356°F (180°C)

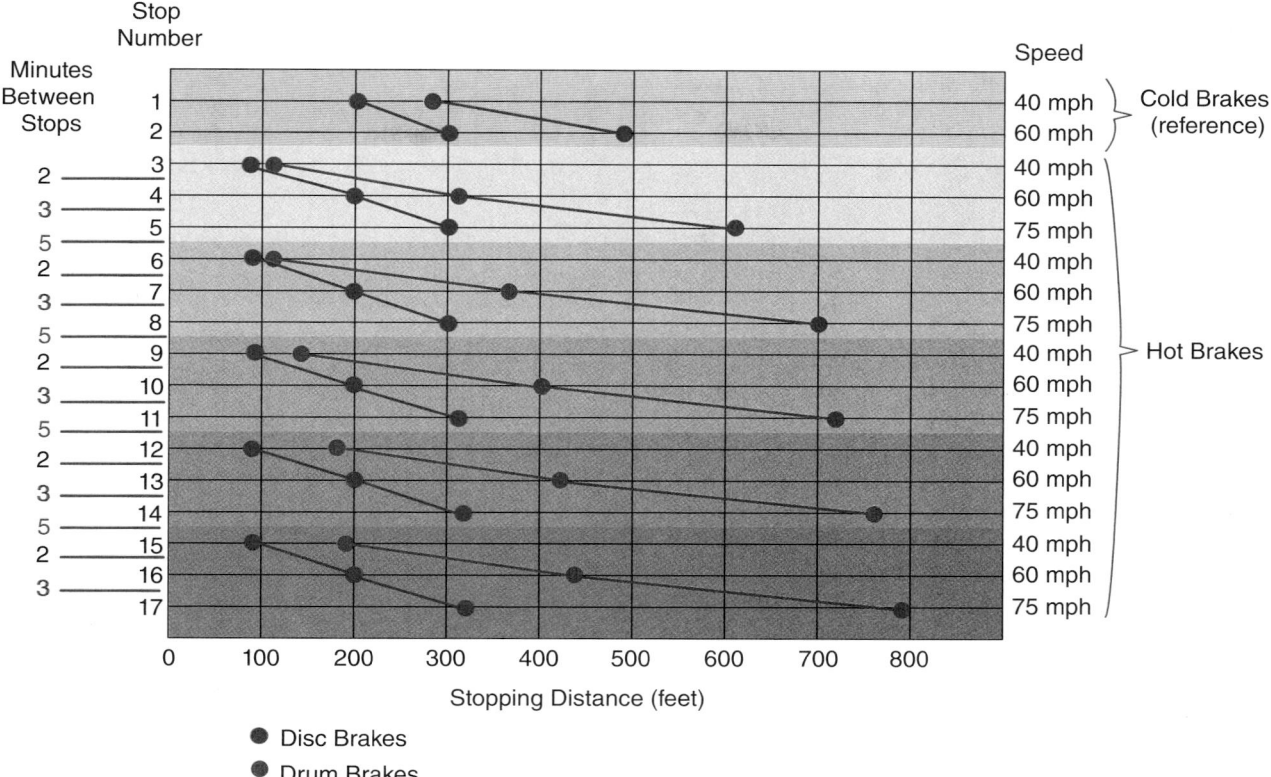

FIGURE 33-34 Disc brakes are more resistant to heat fade than drum brakes. In the illustration, stopping distances become longer with each successive brake application. Heat deteriorates drum brake performance at a greater rate than disc brakes.

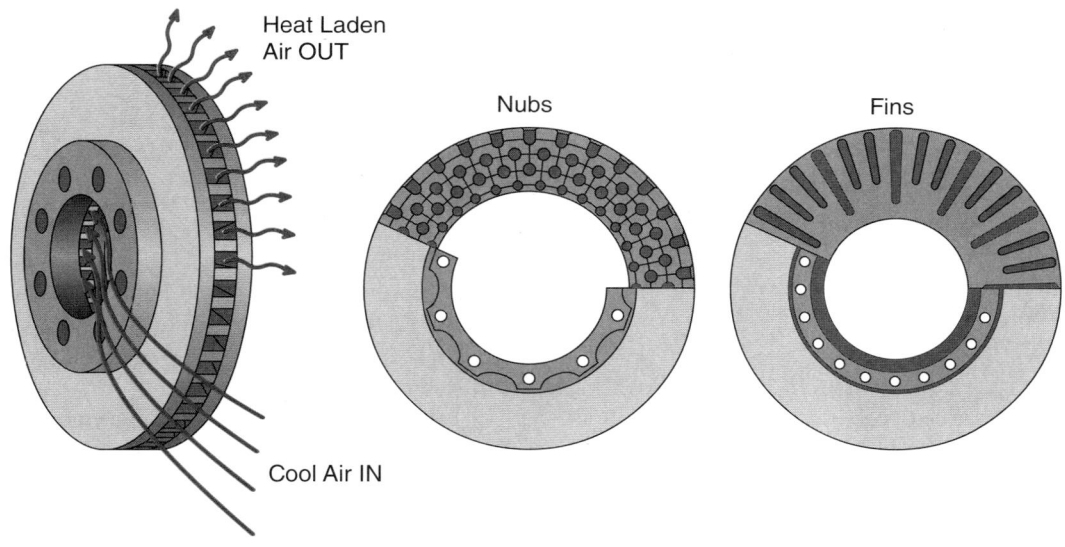

FIGURE 33-35 Disc brakes are resistant to brake fade for a few reasons. Better cooling through ventilation of the disc or rotor dissipates heat faster. Fins or nubs connecting one side of the disc to the other increases surface area, which also speeds up heat dissipation.

return to normal until the water has vaporized. Related to water fade is an erratic high friction reaction during the first two or three stops. This takes place because some linings are sensitive to humidity. Brake dust also tends to attract moisture, allowing iron oxide (rust) to form on the drum after a vehicle is parked overnight.

Mechanical Fade

Mechanical fade occurs when drums expand due to heat. The problem is made worse as the brake chamber pushrod travel lengthens to compensate for the larger internal drum diameter.

Chemical Fade

Chemical fade takes place when steam or gases from vaporized lining materials form between hot lining and the drum, reducing the CoF.

Glazing of Brake Lining

Glazing is characterized by a hard, glassy burnt appearance to the lining surface. This hard, glassy surface is a condition causing brake fade and a "hard" brake pedal. Glazed linings are produced by slow brake applications or a brake that is lightly dragging along a drum. When this happens, the lining temperature becomes hot enough to melt resins binding the friction material, but the pressure is not adequate to wear away friction material and expose new lining surfaces.

Increasing the work per square inch of lining forces the brake to operate with higher pressure per unit of area, which wears away and renews the lining surface. This explains why some glazing can be removed through several hard brake applications. More often, sanding the lining surface, or replacing the lining, is the only remedy to correct fade or "hard pedal" conditions. The undelaying cause of high brake temperatures combined with low application force also needs correction. Defective quick release or relay valves are a common cause for glazed lining. Linings with a high CoF glaze easier than low CoF linings because less force is required to produce the same braking effect.

Brake Torque and Balance

LO 33-6 Identify and explain the concepts of brake torque and brake balance.

Brake torque refers to the force applied to the foundation brakes during braking. It is calculated by the vehicle manufacturer using several variables, including:

- Designed axle weight
- Diameter and width of the brake drum/shoes/disc
- Brake lining CoF or brake pad characteristics
- Foundation brake system design, i.e., S-cam, air disc, wedge
- Length of slack adjuster
- S-cam dimensions

Too much or too little torque or uneven torque across wheel ends and axles affects vehicle stability during braking. Brake torque needs to be balanced to have each axle or wheel end contributing consistent and even braking force for each axle, which varies with axle loading or supported weight and inertia shift of weight. For example, when considering S-cam brakes, the torque is calculated relative to drum capacity, drum area, and lining area; in the case of air disc brakes, torque is relative to rotor and brake pad characteristics. More torque is needed for axles carrying heavier loads, such as the rear drive axles. This means larger capacity brakes using more torque are used. On the front axles, which carry less weight, smaller drums and narrower brake shoes are used because less braking is done by the front axles.

Understanding the need to balance brake torque over all axles should help technicians understand why it is critical to replace friction material, slack adjusters, and any other part affecting torque with original parts. It is recommended that friction material on all axles be replaced at the same time. In fact, modifying the brake system in any way by using incorrect parts, or parts not intended for the vehicle or application, changes the manufacturer's certified design factors. A repair facility can potentially become liable for any adverse consequences related to the modification.

> ▶ **TECHNICIAN TIP**
>
> When diagnosing brake complaints, such as pulling to one side, hard pedal, poor braking, and "grabby-brakes," even application of brake torque should be included in the checks. In the field, brake torque is practically measured with an infrared thermometer. After performing several hard stops, the temperatures of each brake drum or rotor can be measured. The temperatures should be consistent across all axles. Cooler or hotter brakes indicate brake torque is not consistent, and the cause should be investigated.

Brake Drums

LO 33-7 Identify and describe the purpose and construction of brake drums.

Next to brake shoes, brake drums are the other critical friction-producing component in the braking system. As considerable heat is generated during braking, drums must:

- Resist distortion and brake fade
- Resist wear, scoring, and heat damage
- Absorb heat and transfer it to the outer surface

Two types of brake drums are:

- **cast drums** made from cast iron
- **centrifuge drums** made with a cast-iron core surrounded by a steel band

Strength and lighter weight are the advantage of a more expensive centrifuge drum. A typical drive wheel brake drum made of cast-iron weighs 110 lb (50 kg), and a typical steel-shelled version weighs 94 lb (43 kg). For the steer axle, a typical cast-iron brake drum weighs 77 lb (35 kg), while a steel-shelled brake drum weighs 67 lb (30.5 kg).

Brake drums are dynamically balanced at the factory. At the factory, the drum is either machined to balance or uses welded weights to balance. Both methods provide identical performance characteristics. **FIGURE 33-36** shows the terminology used for brake drums. **FIGURE 33-37** shows the two types of brake drums—inboard or outboard—mounted on disc-type wheels. Inboard-mounted drums are attached to the hub on the inner hub surface and held in place with studs and nuts. The hub must be removed to replace the drum when inboard drums are used. When outboard drums are used, it is only necessary to remove the wheels to replace the drum; the hub seal and bearings are left undisturbed. **FIGURE 33-38** shows an example of an outboard-mounted brake drum that is installed over studs in the wheel hub and clamped against the hub by the wheels. A maximum brake drum internal diameter is cast into the brake drum.

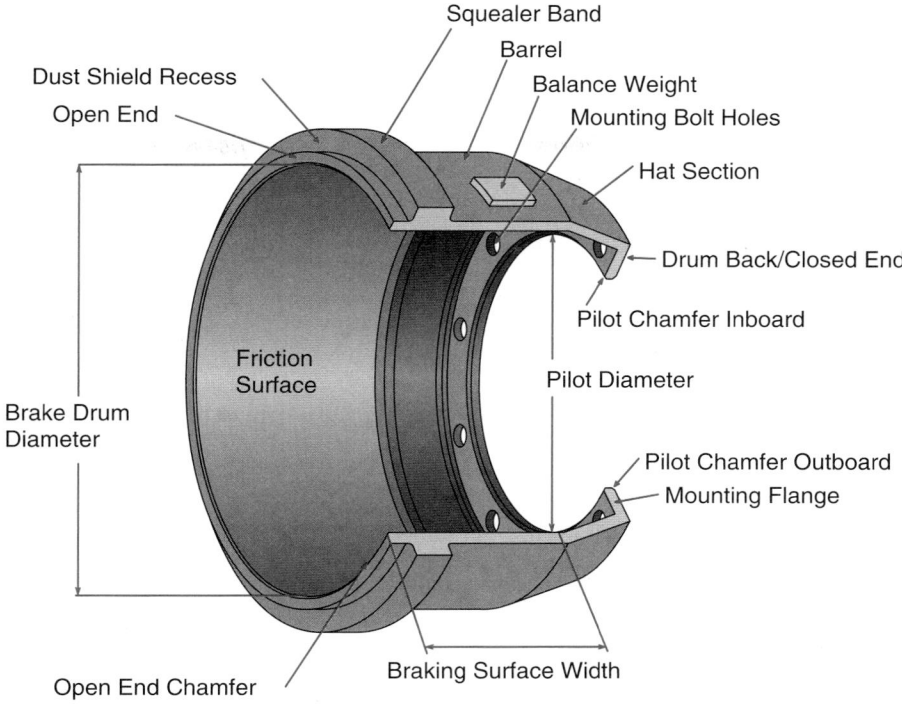

FIGURE 33-36 Brake drum terminology.

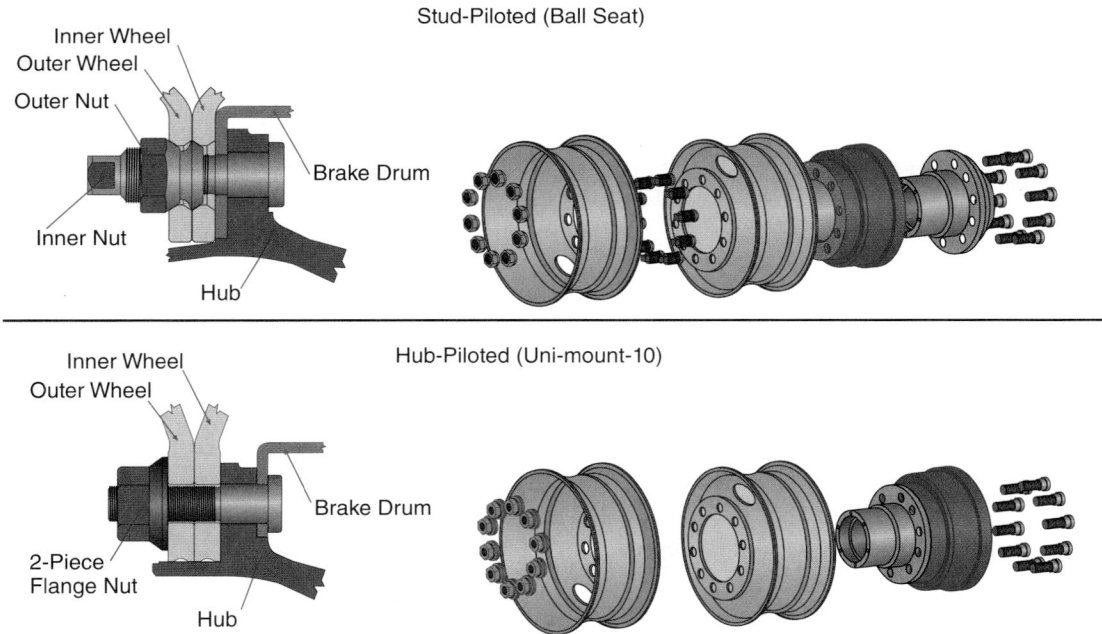

FIGURE 33-37 Brake drums can be mounted inboard or outboard on disc-type wheels. The hub must be removed to replace the drum when inboard drums are used. Outboard drums can be replaced by simply removing the wheels. The hub bearings and seal are not disturbed during brake service.

Brake Drum Mounting

The type of wheel-end a drum is mounted to changes the features of a drum. On disc wheel hubs, drums can be mounted inboard or outboard of the wheel hub. Outboard-mounted drums are simpler to remove and replace since the hub does not require removal. Drums are attached to the wheel using either a hub-piloted or stud-piloted method. For the stud-piloted drum,

a ball seat is machined into the drum to accommodate a ball-type nut used to center the drum.

Cast-spoke drums are bolted to the hub. The hub is removed, and the drum nuts and bolts are loosened to replace the drum. Correct hub and drum combinations are required to prevent loose wheels, broken bolts, and damage to drums.

When brake drum types, weights, and brands are interchanged, braking can be adversely affected because the heat-dissipation properties of the drum change. To maintain optimal brake performance, always change drums in pairs on axles, and do not mix brake drums.

Brake Chambers and Actuators

LO 33-8 Identify and describe the types, purpose, construction, and adjustment of brake chambers and actuators.

Applying the brakes supplies air pressure to actuator chambers proportional to brake pedal travel. Brake chambers then take the air pressure and convert it to mechanical force used to apply the brakes. A rubber diaphragm inside the chamber seals the pressure and acts against a push-plate, which in turn moves a pushrod that, finally, acts on the foundation brakes.

Actuators are like brake chambers, except they have additional components, such as **power springs** used to apply park brakes or internal pushrod lock mechanisms. **Spring brake** actuators, as shown in **FIGURES 33-39** and **33-40**, are used on rear drive axles to apply park brakes, which are also referred to as "maxi-brakes." These actuators have dual chambers. On vehicles less than 52,000 lb (23,636 kg) GVW, spring brakes are required on only one drive axle. On vehicles with over 52,000 lb (23,636 kg) GVW, spring brakes are used on both rear drive axles, enabling the brakes to meet the FMVSS 121 standard. Each parking brake must be capable of producing brake force equal to 14% of the gross axle weight rating, and together they must be able to hold the vehicle stationary on a 20% grade, loaded or empty.

Brake chambers are available in a variety of diameter sizes to supply a wide range of output forces and stroke length. The effective diaphragm diameter identifies the size of brake chamber, which is proportional to its application force. For example, a "type 30" brake chamber has a diaphragm diameter of 8" (20.3 cm), which gives it 30 square inches (193 square cm) of effective piston area. This means the chamber's output force is 300 lb (136.4 kg) if 10 psi (69 kPa) of air pressure is supplied. If more or less air is supplied, application force changes. Brake chambers range in size from a 9 series with a 9 square inch (54 square cm) diaphragm surface to a 36 series with a 36 square inch (232.25 square cm) surface area.

Long Stroke Chambers

A standard brake chamber has a 2.5" stroke travel. Some 3" stroke chambers are manufactured and are called **long stroke chambers**. Traditional short stroke chambers with 2.5" (63.5 mm) travel should travel no more than half that distance with the brake properly adjusted and at 90 degrees to the chamber pushrod. Travel greater than 1.25"

FIGURE 33-38 An example of an outboard-mounted brake drum that is installed over studs in the wheel hub and clamped against the hub by the wheels. A maximum brake drum internal diameter is cast into the brake drum.

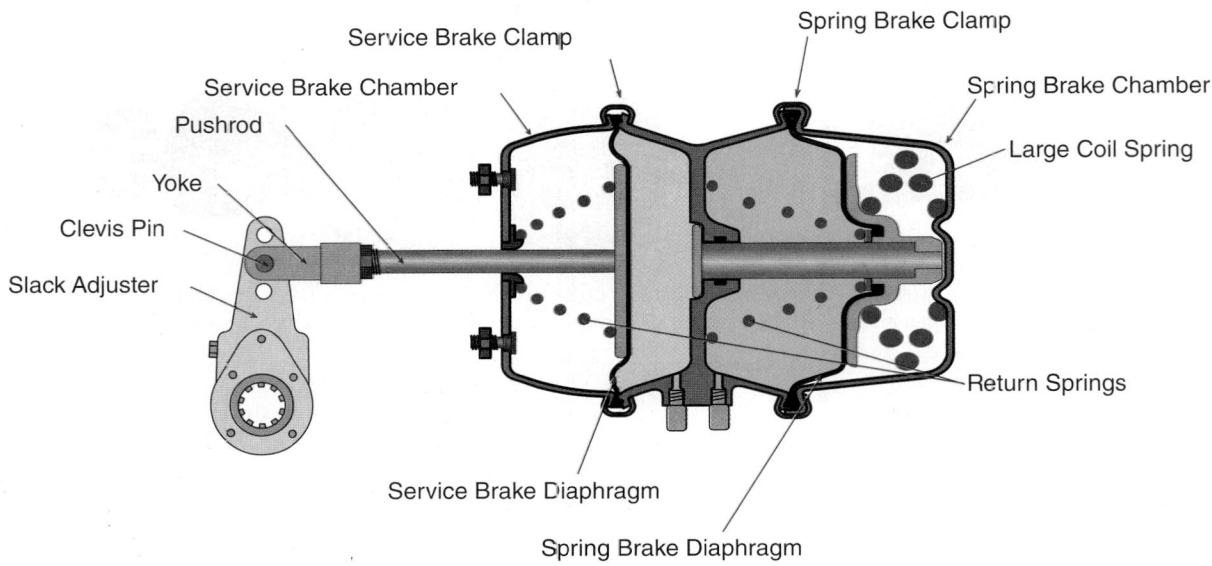

FIGURE 33-39 Applying the brakes supplies air pressure to actuator chambers proportional to brake pedal travel.

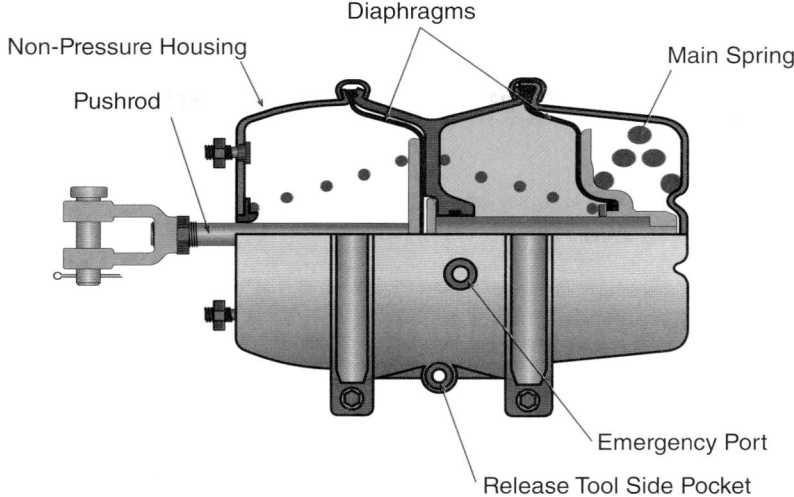

FIGURE 33-40 Components of a combination or dual spring brake and service brake actuators.

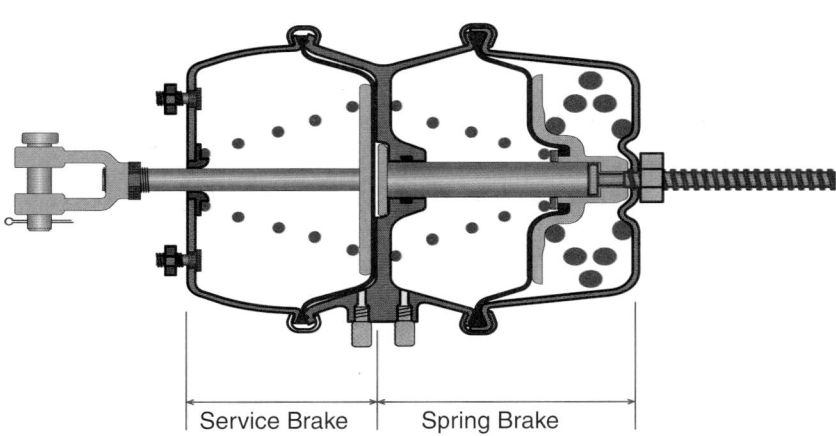

FIGURE 33-41 Spring brake and service chambers work in opposite ways—the service chamber requires air pressure to *apply the brakes*, while the park or emergency spring brake needs air pressure *to release the brakes*.

(31.75 mm) causes the chamber's effectiveness to drop and increases the potential for "bottoming out," meaning that the pushrod travel prevents full application of brake torque.

Long stroke chambers are built to help minimize the hazard of an inadequate brake stroke for a misadjusted slack adjuster or worn brakes that require a longer stroke. Operational differences between these chambers do not allow for mixed use on a vehicle. Long stroke chambers have special identifying features, such as square-shaped air inlet ports and yokes that are welded to the pushrod.

Dual-Brake Chambers

When a brake chamber uses only a single chamber, it is called a service chamber. Dual-brake chambers contain a spring brake actuator and have two separate air and mechanical actuators in a single housing. In addition to their normal parking functions, spring brakes can function as a service brake under emergency conditions. The rear section of the dual-brake chamber contains a powerful spring that is compressed using air pressure or released by removing air pressure. A pushrod extending from the rear chamber into the front service chamber is designed to push against the forward service chamber push plate and apply the brakes when no air is compressing the spring. This means the spring brake and service chambers work the opposite way—the service chamber requires air pressure to **apply** the brakes, while the park or emergency spring brake needs air pressure to **release** the brakes, as shown in **FIGURE 33-41**. When the park brakes are applied, air is exhausted from the rear chamber, allowing the power spring to force the actuator pushrod forward and apply the brakes. Approximately 75 psi (517 kPa) of air pressure is needed to release the spring brake, which loads the spring with at least 2250 lb (1023 kg) of compression force in a type 30 chamber.

A correctly adjusted brake has only 1/2" (1.27 cm) of slack, leaving 2" (5.08 cm) of reserve chamber stroke. When slack reaches 1" (2.54 cm), the brakes must be adjusted. This is referred to as a driver's most important inch of life. Consider that during brake heat fade, the drum expands and can add close to another 1/2" (12.7 mm) of clearance. Lining worn, the thickness of three sheets of paper adds another 1/4" (6.35 mm) of clearance, and it is not hard to imagine how easily a brake chamber could bottom out. Most jurisdictions have legislation requiring drivers of air-braked vehicles to check manual and automatic slack adjusters daily during the pre-trip inspection. It's also required by law for drivers to check brakes before driving down steep grades that are posted with regulatory signs.

FIGURE 33-42 shows a single-service brake chamber that contains a single diaphragm used to seal air in the actuator. Supplying air pressure to the actuator causes the diaphragm to push against the chamber piston rod assembly, which moves the slack adjuster. Brake chambers are available in a variety of diameter sizes to supply a wide range of output forces and stroke length. The effective diaphragm diameter identifies the size of the brake chamber, which is proportional to its application force, as shown in the chart in **FIGURE 33-43**. For example, a "type 30" brake chamber has a diaphragm diameter of 8" (20 cm), which gives it 30 square inches (193 square cm) of effective piston area.

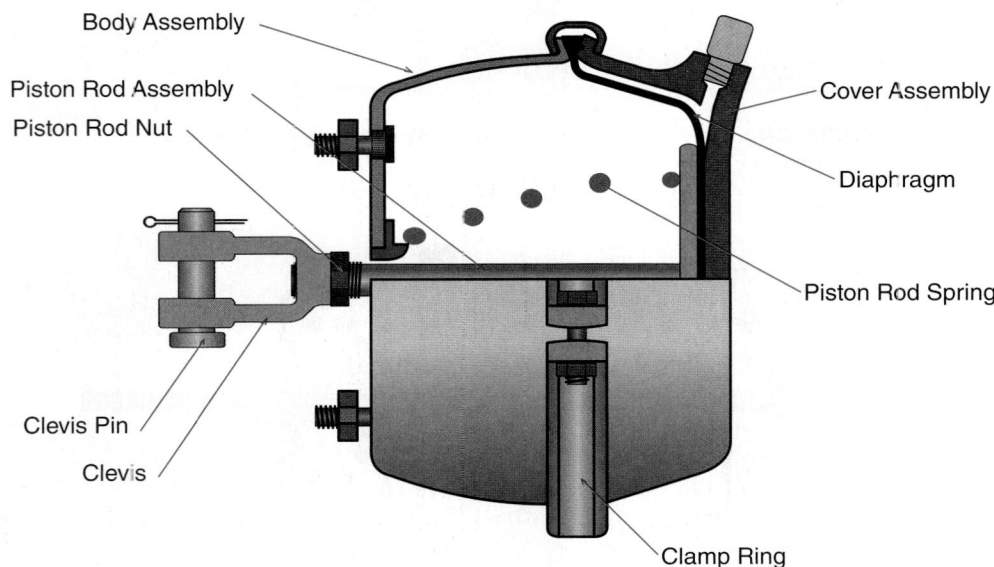

FIGURE 33-42 A single-service brake chamber contains a single diaphragm used to seal air in the actuator. Supplying air pressure to the actuator causes the diaphragm to push against the chamber piston rod assembly, which moves the slack adjuster.

Braking Forces
Effect of Brake Chamber and Roto Chamber Sizes

Clamp Ring Type Brake Chamber		9	12	16	20	24	30	36	
Roto Chamber		9	12	16	20	24	30	36	50
Effective Area of Diaphragm (sq inches)	6	9	12	16	20	24	30	36	50
Pounds Force Developed with 60 P.S.I.	360	540	720	960	1200	1440	1800	2160	3000

FIGURE 33-43 Brake chambers are available in a variety of diameter sizes to supply a wide range of output forces and stroke length. The effective diaphragm diameter identifies the size of the brake chamber, which is proportional to its application force. For example, a "type 30" brake chamber has a diaphragm diameter of 8", which gives it 30 square inches of effective piston area.

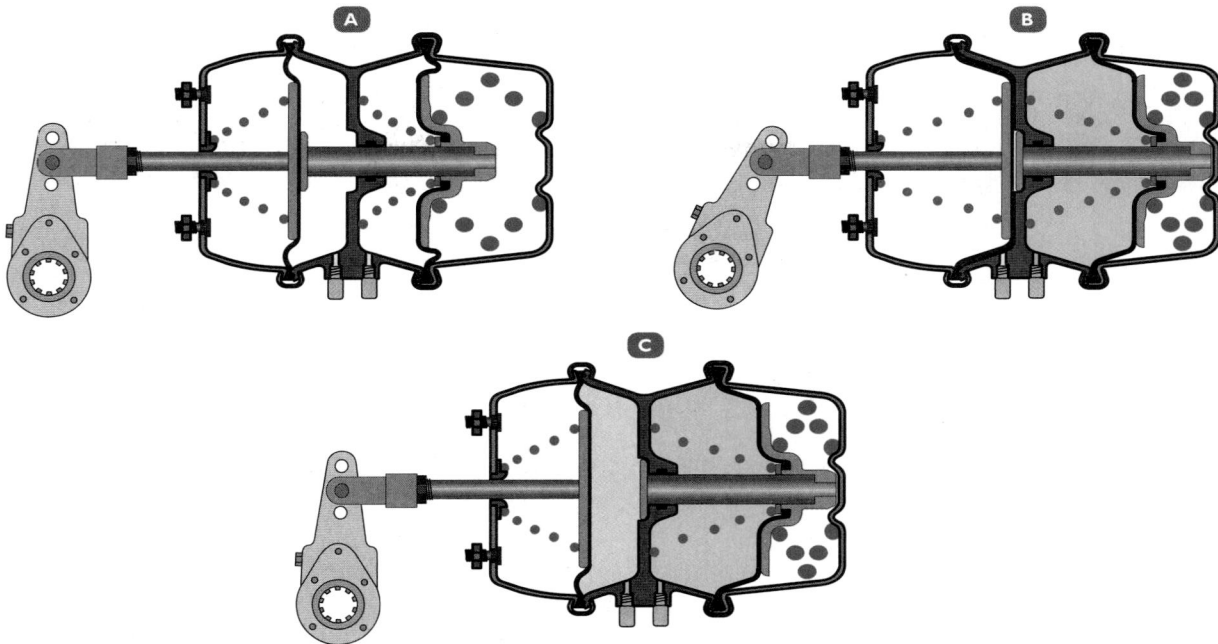

FIGURE 33-44 Sequential operation of the emergency spring brake chamber and service chamber. **A.** The spring brake is applied because no air is supplied to the chamber. In **B** and **C**, the emergency spring brake is released using air pressure. The service chamber is released in **B** and applied in **C**.

FIGURE 33-44 shows the sequential operation of the emergency spring brake chamber and service chamber. In **FIGURE 33-44A**, the spring brake is applied since no air is supplied to the chamber. In **FIGURE 33-44B** and **33-44C**, the emergency spring brake is released using air pressure. The service chamber is released in B and applied in C. The power spring is in the rear brake chamber and is used to apply the park/emergency brake. The power spring (blue) is shown caged in **FIGURE 33-45**. Supplying air to the actuator below the diaphragm compresses the spring to release the brake.

To inspect, test, and replace a spring brake actuator, follow the procedure in **SKILL DRILL 33-3**.

Release (Caging) Bolts

In the event of a loss of vehicle air pressure and the ability of the air system to build pressure, the power spring applies the brakes. If the vehicle needs to be moved for towing, the power spring can be released by inserting a **release bolt** into the spring and tightening the bolt. Tightening the bolt compresses the spring and releases the park brake. If the diaphragm for the service chamber is replaced, the release bolt can be used to compress the power spring to safely remove the rear spring brake chamber.

A release or caging bolt, as shown in **FIGURE 33-46**, is generally attached to every dual-chamber brake actuator. A power spring in the rear chamber requires compressing to move a disabled vehicle without an air supply. Inserting and turning the release bolt into a keyed receptacle in the power spring,

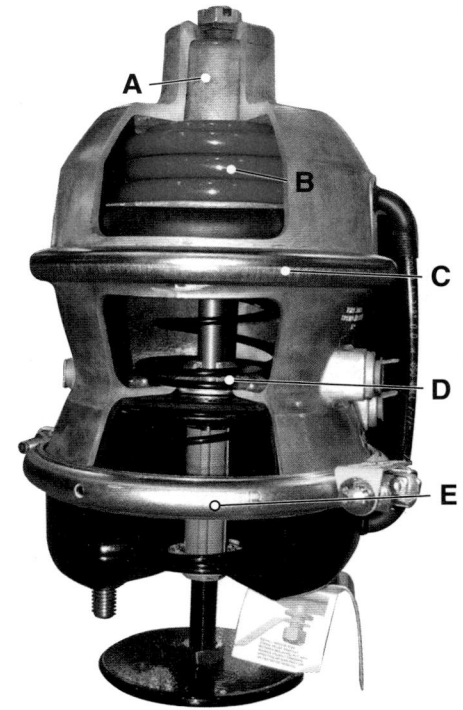

FIGURE 33-45 The power spring is in the rear brake chamber and is used to apply the park/emergency brake. Supplying air to the actuator below the diaphragm compresses the spring to release the brake. **A.** Cage bolt. **B.** Caged power spring. **C.** Single-piece spring brake chamber clamp. **D.** Chamber separation seal. **E.** Service chamber clamp.

SKILL DRILL 33-3 Inspecting, Testing, and Replacing a Spring Brake Actuator

1. Locate and follow the appropriate procedure in the service manual.
2. Complete the accompanying job sheet or work order with all pertinent information.
3. Move vehicle into the shop, apply the parking brakes, and block the vehicle wheels.
4. Inspect brake chamber operation and check for air leakage
5. Start the engine and charge the air system to the compressor governor valve cut-out point.
6. Stop the engine and release the parking brakes.
7. Have an assistant apply and hold the brake pedal.
8. Apply a soap solution around the air brake chamber clamp and breather holes.
9. Verify that no bubbles appear.
10. If the bubbles appear, overhaul or replace the rear air brake chamber.
11. Remove the rear brake chamber.
12. Raise the vehicle and support with safety stands.
13. Cage the power spring on the parking (spring) brake chamber.
    a. Remove plug from the release tool keyhole in the center of the spring brake chamber.
    b. Remove the release tool assembly from the side pocket of the adapter. *Caution:* Do not attempt to cage the power spring when the rear air brake chamber shows structural damage. Caging the power spring or disassembly of the spring brake chamber may result in the forceful release of the power spring and the chamber contents, which may cause severe personal injury. Remove the entire rear air brake chamber, if it has structural damage, and replace with a new unit.
14. With the parking brakes released, insert the release stud through the keyhole in the rear air brake chamber. Bottom out stud and turn the release stud 90° (1/4" turn) clockwise.

15. Pull on the release stud to ensure the release stud crosspin is properly seated in the pressure plate. Assemble the release stud washer and nut on the release stud finger tight.
16. Measure the release stud length beyond the release stud nut. Check service manual for correct length. *Caution:* Do not over torque the stud nut.
17. Fully release the air brake automatic slack adjuster and remove air brake chamber clevis pins.
18. Drain air from air reservoirs and disconnect air lines from the brake chamber.
19. Remove mounting nuts and washer from the rear air brake chamber and remove chamber.
20. Disassemble brake chamber to replace service brake diaphragm and install new spring brake chamber.
21. Mark the adapter and service hosing in relation to the clamp ring assembly.
22. Pull out the pushrod and clamp it using locking-type pliers.
23. Remove nuts and bolts on clamp ring assembly and remove clamp ring.
24. Remove diaphragm and spring brake chamber.
25. Clean and inspect parts for rust and cracks. *Caution:* Never disassemble the spring brake assembly; always replace with a new assembly.
26. Install new service brake diaphragm and new spring brake assembly.
27. Install clamp ring assembly and torque nuts and bolts.
28. Remove locking-type pliers.
29. Install brake chamber to the chamber/camshaft support bracket.
30. Install mounting washer and nuts to the rear air brake chamber and torque (108 Nm).
31. Install air brake chamber clevis pins and connect air lines.
32. Adjust slack adjuster to adjust the brakes.
33. Start the engine and charge the system to the air compressor governor valve cut-out point and release the parking brakes; stop engine.
34. Uncage the spring brake and unscrew the release stud nut and washer from the release stud.
35. Turn the release stud one-quarter turn counterclockwise, remove it from the keyhole, and install in the storage pocket. Install dust plug into the keyhole.
36. Remove safety stands and lower vehicle.
37. Check for proper brake operation and leaks.
38. Set parking brakes and remove wheel blocks.
39. List the test results and/or recommendations on the job sheet or work order and clean work area and return tools and materials to proper storage.

and then tightening the bolt, compresses the power spring. **FIGURE 33-47** shows a power spring from the emergency/park brake actuator. The power spring is more commonly called a "maxi spring," forming part of the "maxi-brake."

Roto-Chambers

Roto-chambers, shown in **FIGURE 33-48**, are actuators with a unique diaphragm construction that delivers consistent output force, regardless of the pushrod position. To achieve this, the

FIGURE 33-46 A. A release or caging bolt is generally attached to every dual-chamber brake actuator. **B.** Inserting and turning the release bolt into a keyed receptacle in the power spring, and then tightening the bolt, compresses the power spring.

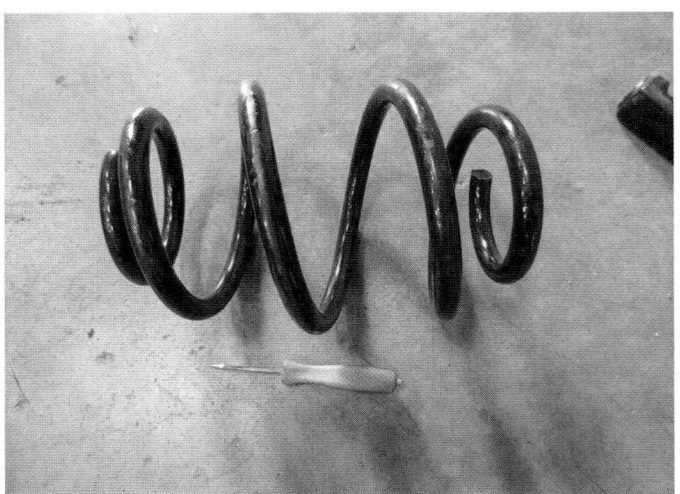

FIGURE 33-47 A power spring from the emergency/park brake actuator. The power spring is more commonly called a "maxi spring," forming part of the "maxi-brake."

spring in the rear chamber is under high compression force, disassembling that chamber and suddenly releasing the spring has been proven many times to be lethal or to result in serious physical injuries. To protect people and equipment from damage caused by a flying power spring, the clamp and chamber have safety features to minimize the likelihood of releasing the spring. THE REAR CLAMP MUST NEVER BE REMOVED! It is recommended that the release or caging bolt be installed to compress the spring anytime a chamber is removed.

SAFETY TIP

A spring brake or combination service/spring brake must be disarmed before disposal—and not simply disposed with other garbage. Forceful release of the power spring may occur without warning after disposal. Specialized cages enable the power spring to be cut with a torch prior to disposal, which removes the likelihood of the potentially lethal spring causing property damage or severely injuring someone.

▶ TECHNICIAN TIP

Broken power springs often puncture the diaphragm in the spring brake chamber, as well as prevent adequate parking brake force. Several techniques are used to inspect chamber power springs. One is to remove the end plug from the release-bolt access hole at the rear of the spring brake chamber. Using a trouble light, examine the spring to determine if it is broken. A broken spring does not allow the release-bolt key hole, located at the rear of the spring, to line up with the access hole. Brake chamber stroke can also be checked while applying and releasing the parking brake. If the anticipated range of motion is not observed, the spring may be broken. If a rattle is heard after tapping the chamber with a hammer or shaking the chamber after it is removed, the spring is probably broken.

chamber has a much larger diaphragm that "unrolls" during operation. It is clamped on both the outer chamber body and the inner push plate. The rolling-type diaphragm used in roto-chambers also provides a longer service life in comparison to traditional brake chambers. Roto-chambers are frequently found on transit buses where very high braking frequency is the norm, and safety is especially critical.

SAFETY TIP

Brake chambers can be disassembled by removing a clamp holding two dish-shaped halves of the chamber. Worn, leaking diaphragms are easily changed by disassembling the chamber. Because the power

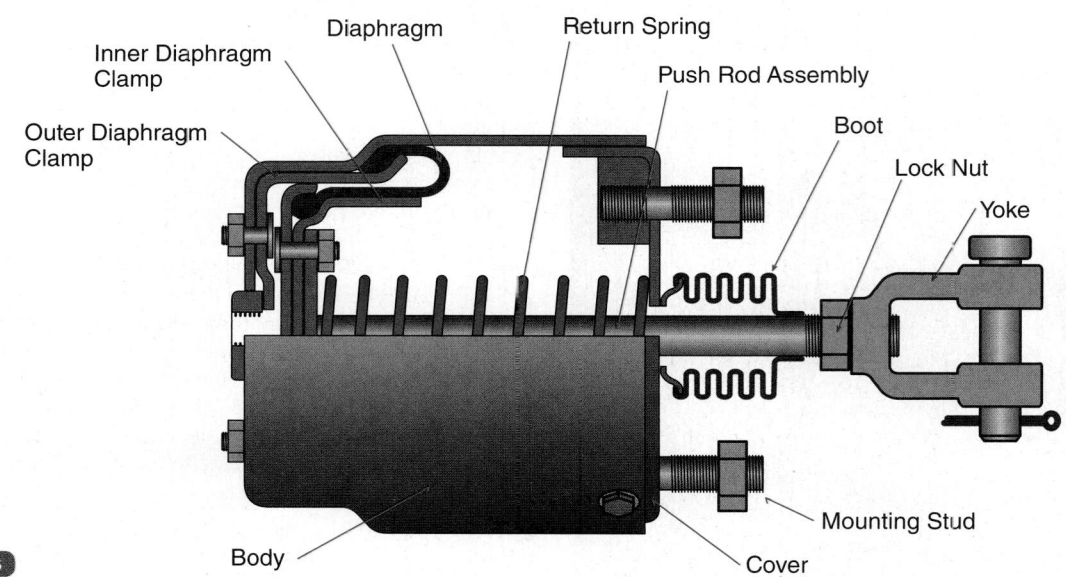

FIGURE 33-48 A. Roto-chambers are brake chamber actuators with a much larger diaphragm that "unrolls" during operation. **B.** The construction of a roto-chamber provides consistent output pressure, regardless of brake pushrod position.

Slack Adjusters

LO 33-9 Classify and describe the types, purpose, construction, and operation of slack adjusters.

The **slack adjuster** is a mechanical lever between the brake chamber and the foundation brake assembly. The slack adjuster's primary function is to multiply the force from the brake chamber to the camshaft of the foundation brakes. A second critical function is to remove excessive chamber pushrod travel to maintain minimal clearance between the brake shoe and drum on a cam brake system. As brakes wear, the clearance between drums and shoes increases, which means the distance travelled by the brake chamber pushrod increases. Increased pushrod travel changes the angle between the pushrod and the slack adjuster, which diminishes the torque applied to the foundation brakes. Most brake chambers have a maximum stroke of 2.5" (6.35 cm), so worn brakes that have not had an adjustment

could bottom out the chamber pushrod, resulting in a further loss of braking force.

In an air disc system, the slack adjuster also adjusts the clearance between the brake pads and rotor disc. Two basic types of slack adjusters are used—automatic or manual. **Manual slack adjusters**, the first type used, are now obsolete, but can occasionally be found on older equipment. The second type is an automatic slack adjuster (ASA). ASAs have been mandatory on air brake vehicles since 1994. Both types remove excess free play due to brake drum-lining wear.

The stroke indicators attached to the chamber bracket in **FIGURE 33-49** are used to visually inspect maximum pushrod travel. When the brakes are applied, the pushrod clevis pin should not travel any farther than the most distant stroke indicator. Note that the most efficient braking action is obtained when the slack adjuster arm is approximately 90 degrees to the brake chamber pushrod.

Manual Slack Adjusters

As the name suggests, slack adjusters correct excess pushrod travel caused by increased drum-to-lining clearance produced by brake wear. Most standard slacks are 5" (12.7 cm) in length, while 6" (15.25 cm) are popular on specialty applications. One, two, or three holes with bushings can be in the arm to match specific length requirements for an application. Various arm configurations and spline types to fit camshafts are made. Bendix uses a number to designate a torque rating. For example, a type 20 represents a 20,000 in-lb (2260 Nm) of torque, and a type 30 represents 30,000 in-lb (3390 Nm). A grease fitting is used to lubricate the adjusting mechanism and splines. Manual slacks have an adjusting screw that is locked in place by a sliding collar. To adjust, the collar is pushed inward, and the screw is turned with a 9/16" wrench. A worm gear turns the slacks internal spline to reposition the camshaft.

FIGURE 33-49 Slack adjusters are used to maintain correct drum-to-shoe clearance and correct pushrod travel. The stroke indicators attached to the chamber bracket are used to visually inspect maximum pushrod travel. When the brakes are applied, the pushrod clevis pin should not travel any farther than the most distant stroke indicator.

Automatic Slack Adjusters (ASA)

When installed, **automatic slack adjusters (ASAs)** compensate for wear in brake shoe linings caused by normal braking operation. ASAs are used because shoe-to-lining clearance increases, and the brake chamber pushrod return stroke exceeds safe travel limits. To prevent this, the slack adjuster automatically adjusts brake stroke to maintain the correct shoe-to-drum clearance and reset the stroke to the correct length with each brake application. If the air brake chamber pushrod stroke is within limits during operation, no adjustment occurs. Two types of ASAs are used.

1. *Stroke-sensing*—**Stroke-sensing ASAs** adjust slack based on the measured rotation between a brake application and release. Stroke-sensing slack adjusters were some of the earliest used, but have several problems, making them nearly obsolete in new vehicles. Stroke-sensing slacks adjust based on the total amount of slack travel. Many factors can change the total slack travel distance. Brake lining compression, deflection of the S-cam bracket, heat expansion of the drum, and distortion of the brake component can all increase travel distance. The increased travel distance can cause the slacks to over-adjust, leading to no running clearance for the brake shoes.

2. *Clearance-sensing*—**Clearance-sensing ASAs** reduce pushrod travel based on torque input to the ASA. Drum-to-shoe clearance is sensed between the mechanical position of the slack when it first moves and the point when the torque increases as the shoes contact the drums. Manufacturers use a variety of adjusting mechanisms to rotate the slack's spline gear and reduce chamber stroke travel. Correction to pushrod travel happens either during brake application and stops, adjusting as resistance to S-cam rotation increases, or as the slack is released. Most manufacturers offer clearance-sensing ASAs because they can more accurately maintain a nominal shoe-to-drum clearance, which is approximately one-third of total chamber stroke. This happens because slack adjustment is made before braking, when the brake drums are coolest and bending of the brake system components under high torque is minimal. Over-adjustment does not easily take place with this adjuster. **FIGURE 33-50** shows four of the most popular ASAs.

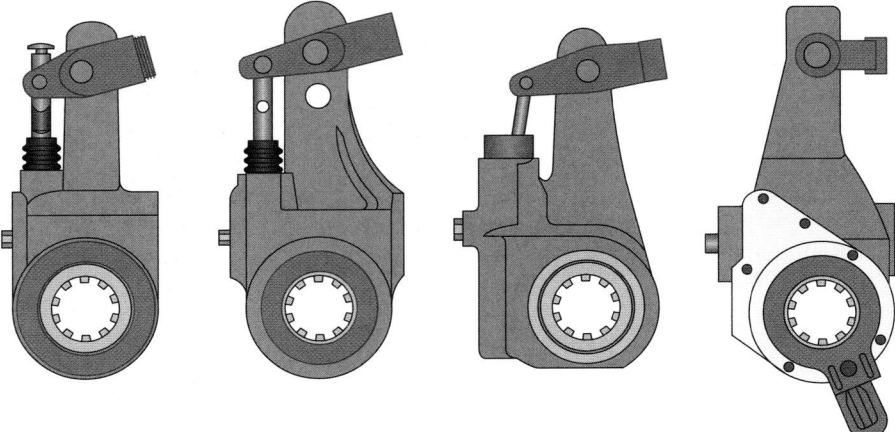

FIGURE 33-50 Four of the most common types of automatic slack adjusters (ASAs). To maintain correct drum-to-brake shoe clearance, ASAs are either stroke-sensing or clearance-sensing.

When the automatic slack adjusters need replacing, start by parking the bus, truck, or trailer on a level surface, and chock its wheels. Then follow the steps in **SKILL DRILL 33-4**.

FIGURE 33-51 shows an internal view of a Bendix clearance-sensing slack. When pushrod travel becomes excessive and enough pressure is placed against the slack, the adjustment arm moves and causes a mechanism to rotate the S-cam splines inside the slack. **FIGURE 33-52** shows an example of a stroke-sensing ASA. When pushrod travel becomes excessive, the actuator rod lifts and rotates the slacks adjusting mechanism. While this slack can adjust for wear in brake foundation parts, it can also over-adjust when brake drums expand after becoming hot. These conditions cause the brakes to drag when the drum cools and contracts.

A correctly adjusted brake has only 1/2" (1.27 cm) of slack, leaving 2" (5.08 cm) of reserve chamber stroke.

SKILL DRILL 33-4 Replacing Automatic Slack Adjusters

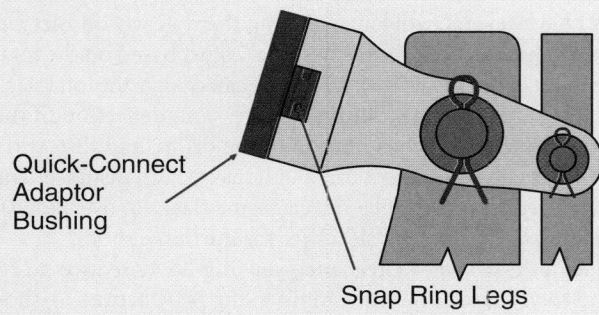

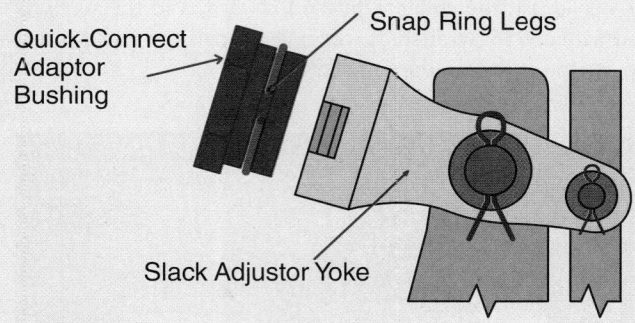

1. Release the spring brakes. If the brakes are left applied, the spring brake needs to be caged before removing the slack adjuster.

2. Disconnect the slack adjuster attaching hardware. Most slack adjusters are locked onto the S-camshaft using a removable snap-ring. Disconnect the clevis yoke clevis pins and the yoke from the chamber pushrod. If the slack used a quick-connect type clevis, it should ideally be replaced with a standard threaded type, since quick-connect clevises loosen over time, contributing to longer brake stroke travel or over stroking.

3. Remove the slack adjuster from the S-cam. Slack adjusters that have been on a long time or left unlubricated may be seized and require a purpose-made puller to remove. Otherwise, the slack may require the use of a large hammer or cutting torch to coax the slack from the splines on the S-cam.

4. Inspect other brake foundation components. Remove the backing plate, if equipped, to check the condition of the brake foundation assembly. There should be adequate brake lining. The S-cam should not have excessive play due to worn bushings. The brake chamber should also be inspected for cracks, leaks, proper centering, and bent pushrods.

SKILL DRILL 33-4 Replacing Automatic Slack Adjusters (Continued)

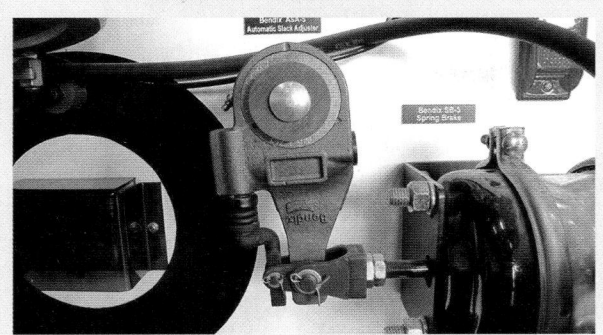

5. Choose the correct parts. Models, types, and brands of slack adjusters should never be mixed on the same axle since it can lead to variations in brake stoke travel and brake torque imbalance. Replace both slack adjusters on an axle if the matching identical slack cannot be found. Some slack adjusters are made specifically for right or left side of vehicle applications. The shape of these slack adjusters is designed to provide clearance for axle parts.

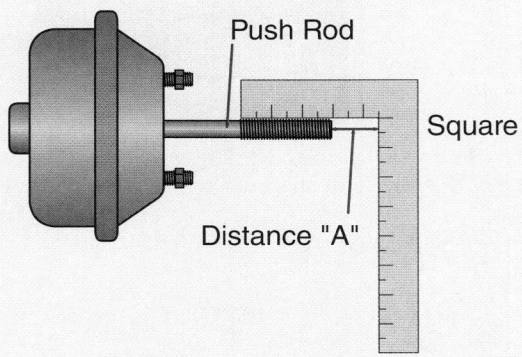

Slack Adjuster Arm Length	"A" Std Quick Connector or Easy-ON Adaptor	"A" Extended Easy-ON Adaptor
5"	1 15/16"–3 1/32"	2 7/16"–3 17/32"
5 1/2"	1 15/16"–3 3/16"	2 7/16"–3 11/16"
6"	1 3/16"–3 1/16"	2 11/16"–3 11/16"

6. Before mounting the slack adjuster on the camshaft, confirm that the brake chamber pushrod length allows a 90-degree angle between the slack adjuster and chamber, or whether pushrod shortening or replacement is required. To perform this check, follow one of the following two methods:

Method 1:
- Place carpenter's square so that one edge is parallel to the actuator pushrod and the other edge of the square passes through the centerline of the camshaft.
- The hole of the clevis and the vertical leg of the square must pass through the centerline of the S-cam. If not, the brake chamber pushrod needs cutting or replacement, depending on whether it's too long or short.

Method 2:
- Measure the distance from the end of the pushrod without the yoke to the edge of the square that passes though the camshaft centerline. Determine the distance needed to attach the yoke. That distance depends on the slack adjuster arm length—between 5" (12.7 cm) and 6" (15.2 cm)—and requires comparison between the slack length and the manufacturer's service information for the type of clevis yoke used.

7. Install the slack after cleaning and lubricating the S-cam with anti-seize compound. Install the large flat washers and shim the slack adjusters to enable approximately 0.05" (1.27 mm) movement of the slack along the S-cam.

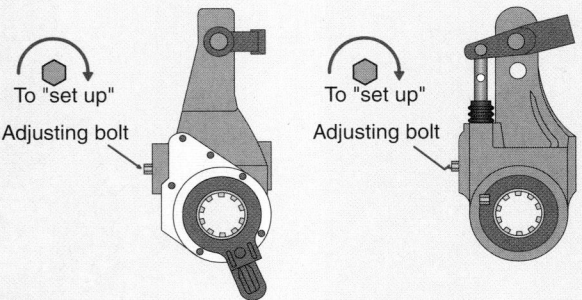

8. Replace the clevis yoke on the pushrod and manually adjust the slack until its clevis and link holes align with those in the clevis. Adjust the brake.

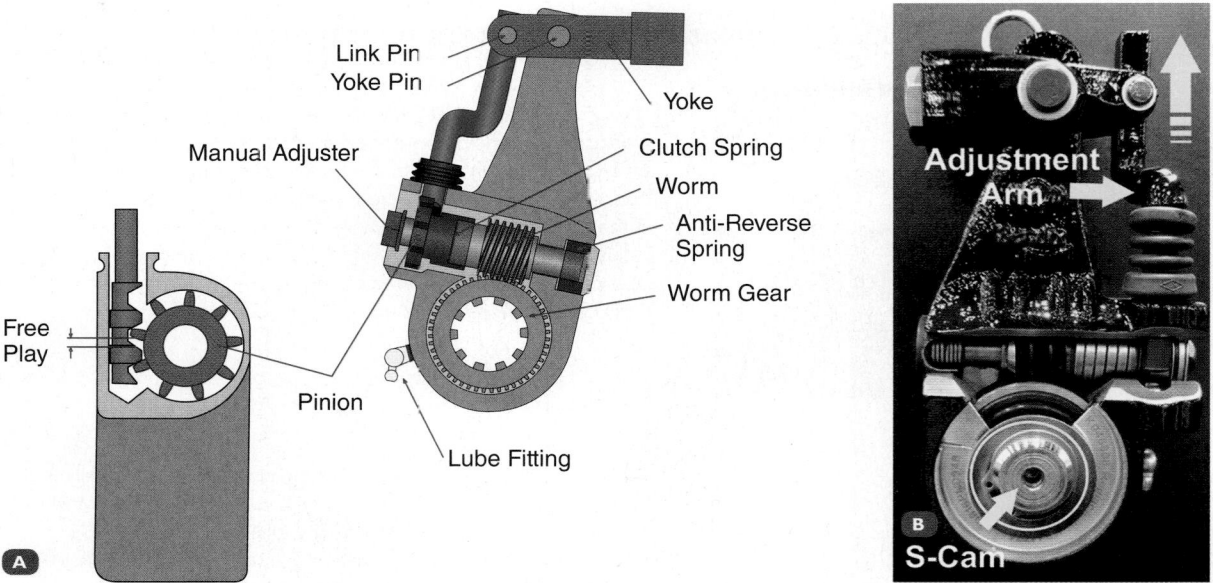

FIGURE 33-51 A. An internal view of a Bendix clearance-sensing slack. When pushrod travel becomes excessive and enough pressure is placed against the slack, the adjustment arm moves **B.** and causes a mechanism to rotate the S-cam splines inside the slack.

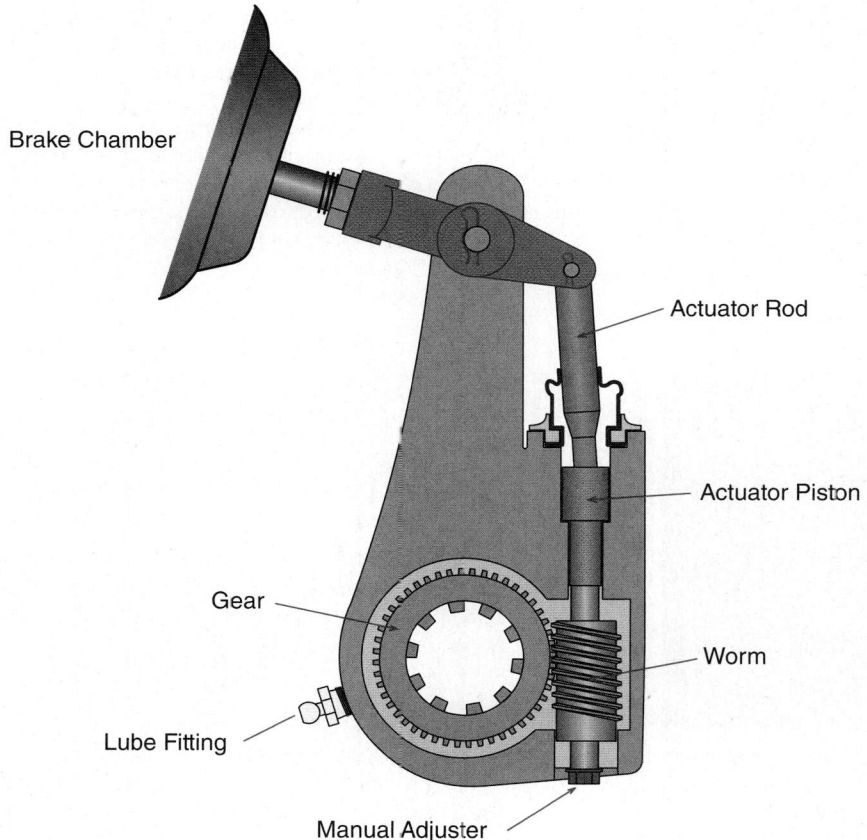

FIGURE 33-52 An example of a stroke-sensing ASA. When pushrod travel becomes excessive, the actuator rod lifts and rotates the slacks adjusting mechanism. While this slack can adjust for wear in brake foundation parts, it can also over-adjust when brake drums expand after becoming hot. These conditions cause the brakes to drag when the drum cools and contracts.

When slack reaches 1" (2.54 cm), the brakes must be adjusted. **FIGURE 33-53** shows the correct way to measure stroke. **FIGURE 33-54** shows a manual slack adjuster. To adjust, a locking ring is pushed down, and the adjusting screw is turned to obtain the correct stroke or brake shoe-to-drum clearance.

ASA Maintenance

ASAs may or may not have a grease fitting, as manufacturers move to low- and no-lube sealed slack adjusters. Stroke travel should be regularly inspected by drivers and technicians. Once initially adjusted, ASA slacks should never need readjusting.

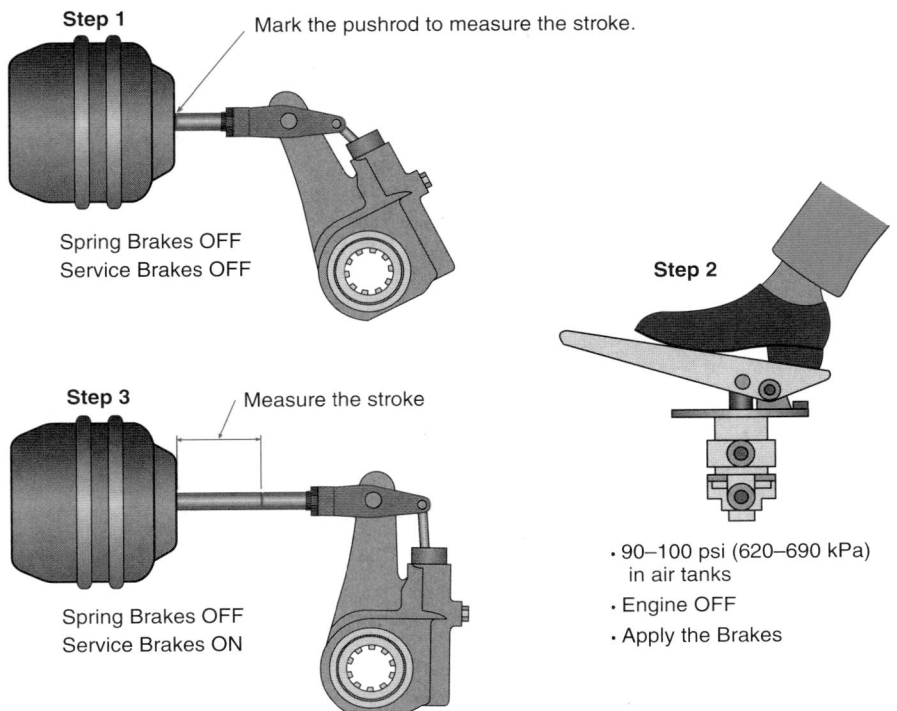

FIGURE 33-53 A correctly adjusted brake has only 1/2" (1.27 cm) of slack, leaving 2" (5.08 cm) of reserve chamber stroke. When slack reaches 1" (2.54 cm), the brakes must be adjusted.

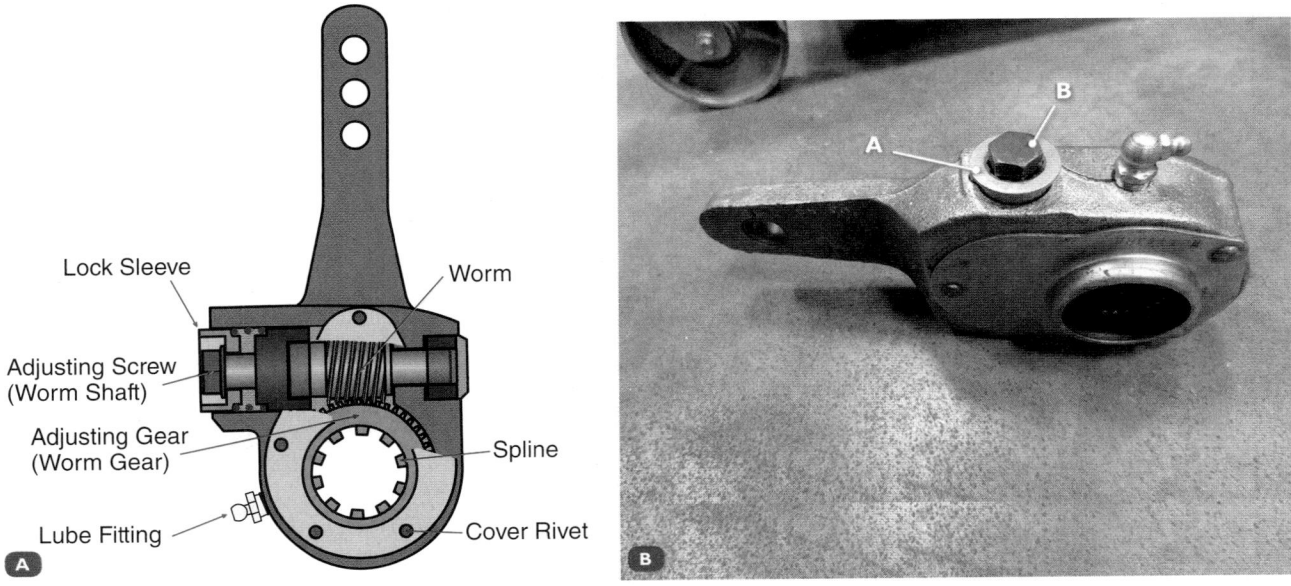

FIGURE 33-54 A. Manual slack adjusters are no longer used but may be found on older equipment. **B.** To adjust, a (A) locking ring is pushed down and the (B) adjusting screw is turned to obtain the correct stroke or brake shoe-to-drum clearance.

If manual adjustment is required during the service life of the slack, or if stroke travel differs between two slacks on the same axle, both slacks should be replaced.

Air Disc Brakes (ADB)

LO 33-10 Identify and describe the construction and operation of air disc brakes.

Disc brakes have been commonly used on hydraulic brake systems for decades and until recently were used only on a few air-braked vehicles. However, beginning in 2011, new legislation reducing stopping distances of heavy trucks by one-third, which means larger, more powerful brakes are needed to meet the new safety standards. **TABLE 33-4** shows the new standards. Higher vehicle speeds are common now, with many regions having 70 mph (113 kph) speed limits, which puts even more demand on braking systems.

The need for improved braking capacity means changes to traditional S-cam systems are underway. Air disc brakes (ADBs) are becoming more prevalent because of the following advantages:

- *Better side-to-side consistency in braking torque.* Disc brakes minimize the effects of different CoFs between left and right brakes.
- *Lower potential for heat- and mechanical-related brake fade.* Unlike drum brakes, as heat builds up in an air disc brake rotor, the rotor expands toward the pads, not away. Contact between the friction surfaces remains consistent even as the discs warm up. In fact, field tests prove ADB stopping perfomance far exceed drum brakes at high speed and loads normally causing heat and mechanical fade.
- *Better cooling with air disc brakes.* ADBs use vented rotors, which dissipate heat faster than drum brakes.
- *Consistent actuation force.* ADBs have fewer moving parts transferring brake force, which results in more consistent brake application and release.
- *Shorter service time.* Changing brake pads and rotors is done in much less time than changing drums and shoes.

Disc brakes, shown in **FIGURE 33-55**, use rotors instead of drums. Greater force can be applied to the rotor without causing mechanical damage. Higher clamping forces, in turn shortens stopping distances. Brake fade is minimal in air disc systems because rotors are squeezed by brake pads, rather than using shoes pushed outwards into the drums. More surface area is available in ventilated rotors for cooling to minimize heat fade. In some earlier ADB systems, greater mechanical advantage was provided by a disc pad actuator when combined with an ADB-specific slack adjuster. The actuator rotated a screw-type mechanism that squeezed the brake pads against the rotor. In addition to a screw-type application mechanism, a brake wedge could be used to multiply force applied to the brake pads. Early ADB systems had many problems related to maintenance and operation due to corrosion of slider pins, inconsistent operation of adjusting mechanisms, undersized rotors, and poor part availability because the system was not common. Unless regularly lubricated, parts would seize, leading to very costly repairs.

Bendix ADB series ADB22X™, SN7™, SN6™, and SK7™ are examples of a design change widely used for a new generation of ADB. Refer to **FIGURE 33-56** for a contemporary **floating caliper** ADB design (the caliper floats on two pins), which consists of two major parts: the caliper and the carrier.

Disc Brake Actuation—Brakes Applied

(See Figure 33-56B) The Bendix ADB system has an air chamber used as an actuator. It is screwed into or bolted to the carrier housing containing an eccentric lever and pressure piston. The brake multiplies force from the actuator and has a fulcrum point that is supported by an eccentrically shaped roller bearing to minimize friction and variations to input brake force. When the actuator is supplied with air pressure, braking force is transmitted through two pressure pistons to the inboard brake pad by a bridge, distributing the force, through threaded spindles in the caliper piston.

The result is both brake pads are squeezed into the rotor and the opposite pad is pressed in as the brake caliper slides along guide pins as it reacts to the pressure applied to the inboard pad. Braking force is a function of air pressure, the size of the actuator piston, and the multiplication ratio of the brake lever.

Two pistons are used rather than one to eliminate taper wear of brake pads that occurs when only one piston is used.

Disc Brakes Released

When the brake actuation has finished, the brake caliper returns to its initial position. A return spring located inside the power piston moves the brake lever to its non-brake position.

No pressure is exerted against the brake pad when released, and a small air gap exists between the pad and rotor.

TABLE 33-4 Heavy Truck Stopping Rules

Phase	Axle Configuration	GVWR (lb)	New Requirement (feet)	Compliance Date
Phase 1	Standard 6×4	Below 59,600	250	August 2011
Phase 2	6×4 Severe Service	59,600–70,000	250	August 2013
	6×4 Severe Service	Above 70,000	310	August 2013
	All 4×2 Heavy Tractors	All	250	August 2013

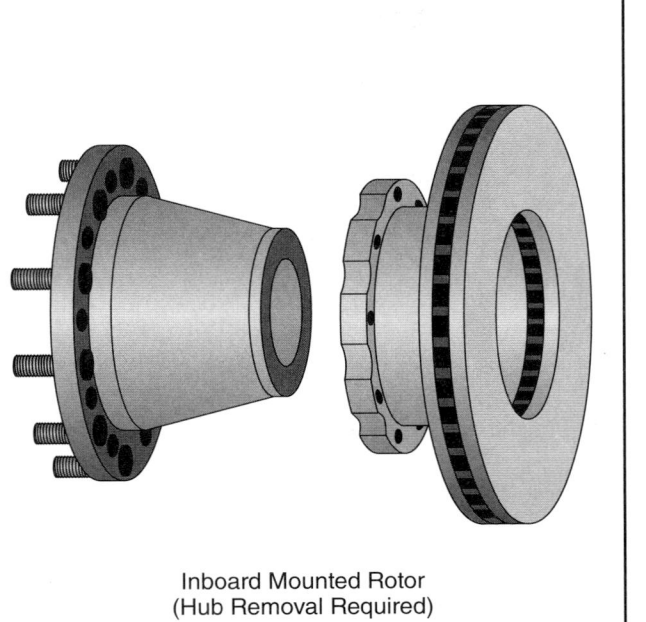

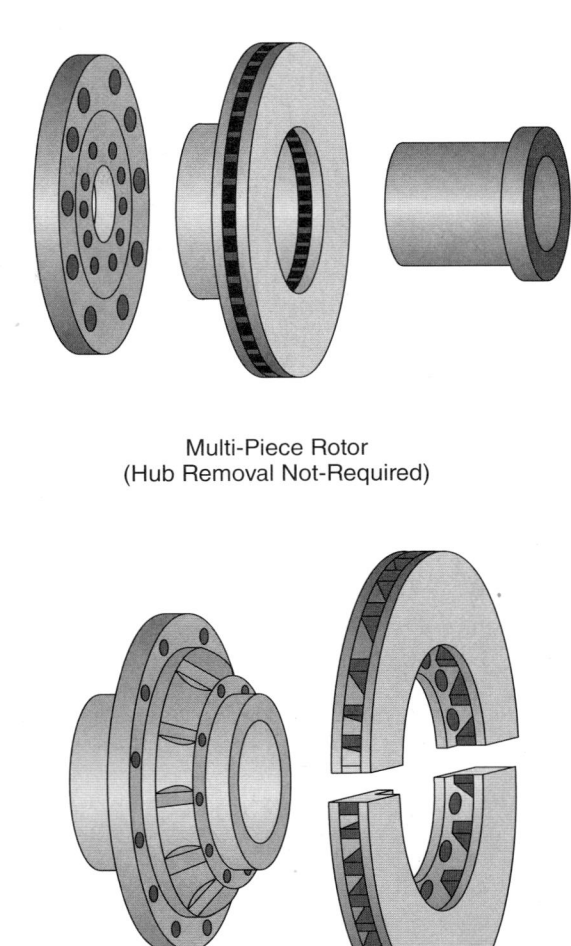

Multi-Piece Rotor
(Hub Removal Not-Required)

Inboard Mounted Rotor
(Hub Removal Required)

FIGURE 33-55 Disc brakes use rotors instead of drums. Greater force can be applied to the rotor, which shortens stopping distances. Brake fade is minimal in air disc systems because rotors are squeezed, rather than pushed outward like drums. More surface area for cooling also helps minimize heat-related brake fade.

The full-floating caliper design allows the caliper to slide along the caliper pins and release pressure against the outboard pad.

Auto-Adjustment of Disc Brakes

To compensate for wear from the caliper's initial position, which uses a small air gap between the brake pad and rotor, an internal automatic clearance-sensing adjusting mechanism is used. Clearance between the pads and rotor is maintained to ensure that the position of the brake lever is the same at the beginning of each brake application. The adjustment mechanism consists of threaded spindles, also called tappets, which are used to set the air gap between the pads and rotor. These spindles can be turned manually to establish the caliper's non-braked position. Spindle movement is synchronized by a chain connecting the two threaded tappets. A ratcheting helix mechanism inside the tappet causes the actuating beam to rotate the tappets whenever clearance increases between the pads and rotor. Rotation

of the tappets is a function of piston movement. The tappets could overtighten as the caliper components are squeezed and piston travel increases. However, any preload pressure on the tappets from over-adjustment does not permit tappet rotation. This takes place only when zero force is applied against the tappets when the brake is released.

Meritor's ADB system, shown in **FIGURE 33-57**, is used on late-model vehicles to shorten stopping distances. **FIGURE 33-58** shows a Bendix ADB system used on the front axle of a late-model truck.

FIGURE 33-59 shows the Bendix® ADB Models ADB22X™, SN7™, SN6™, and SK7™. Two tappets spread braking force evenly across the surface of the inner brake pad. The sliding caliper design distributes braking forces equally between the inboard and outboard brake pad. As pads grip the rotor, the vehicle decelerates. Wear sensors supply a continuous voltage signal that measures pad and rotor thickness.

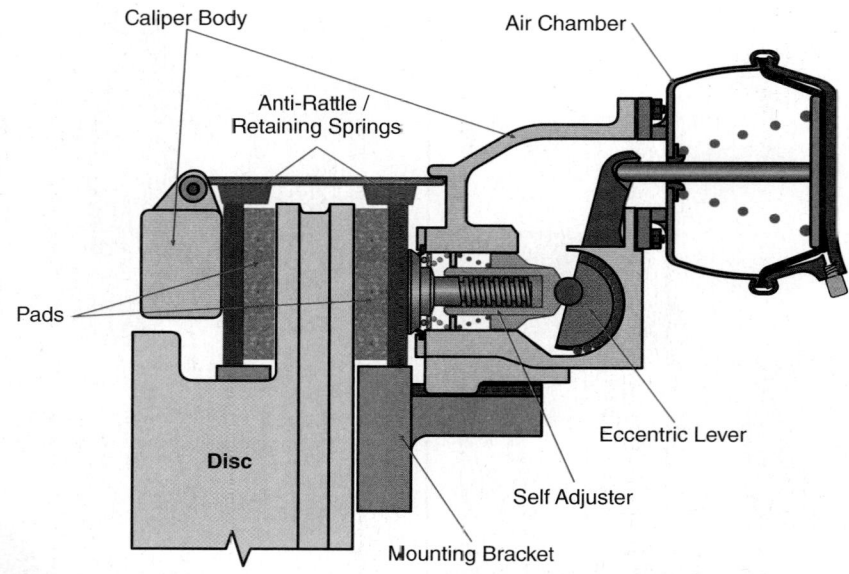

FIGURE 33-56 A. Schematic of a floating caliper system. **B.** Bendix ADB design.

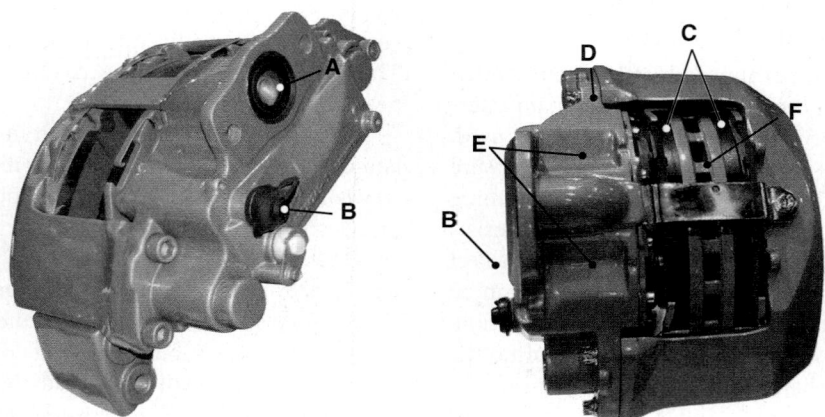

FIGURE 33-57 Meritor's air disc brake system is used on late-model vehicles to shorten stopping distances. **A.** Chamber attachment point. **B.** Adjusting release screw. **C.** Brake pads. **D.** Caliper. **E.** Dual air pistons. **F.** Ventilated rotor.

FIGURE 33-58 A Bendix air disc brake system used on the front axle of a late-model truck.

FIGURE 33-59 Bendix uses wear sensors in some of its ADBs, which supply a continuous voltage signal that measures pad and rotor thickness. Pad and rotor wear sensor lead pins are circled.

Simplex Wedge   Duplex Wedge

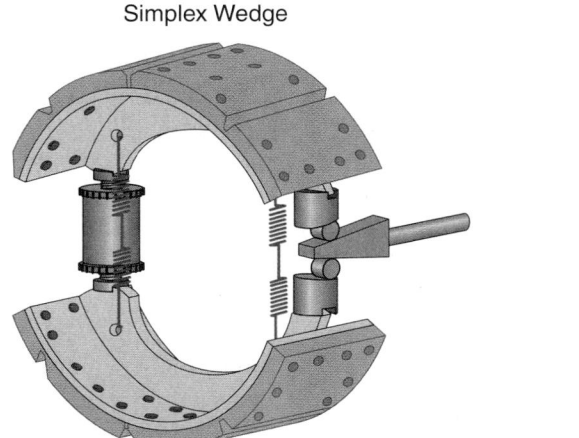
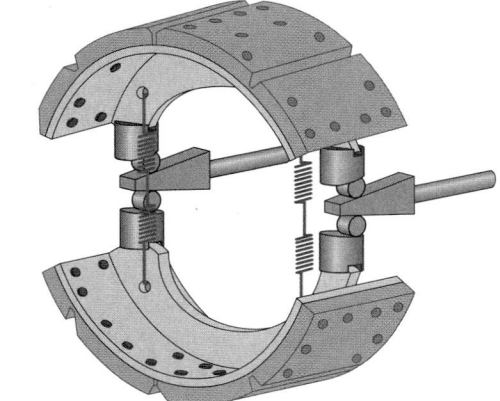

FIGURE 33-60 Two types of wedge brake systems used for shoe and drum brake systems.

Wedge Brakes

LO 33-11 Identify and describe the design and operation of wedge brakes.

Before the most recent shorter stopping requirements were introduced, S-cam brakes comprised 95% of all heavy-duty North American air brake systems. A smaller niche drum brake system is the wedge brake. These systems use a ramp-and-roller design inside a wheel cylinder to multiply force supplied by an air chamber. Two wedge brake systems were built but have not been available for more than a decade. One, called the simplex system, used a single actuator, and duplex systems used dual actuators. With greater complexity, cost, and unpredictable release, wedge brakes have not had much popularity. The wedge brake's adjusting mechanism is incorporated into the housing of the brake itself. **FIGURE 33-60** shows the simplex and duplex style of wedge brakes.

Wrap-Up

Ready for Review

▶ A moving vehicle has a tremendous amount of kinetic energy.

▶ To stop a vehicle, the kinetic energy must be converted into heat energy through the braking system.

▶ Weight and speed have different effects on braking requirements; doubling the weight requires double the braking force but doubling the weight and the speed requires eight times the braking force.

▶ To operate, brakes must turn kinetic energy into heat, but they must also be capable of dissipating the heat quickly, or they quickly lose their effectiveness.

▶ As a vehicle brakes, its weight shifts from back to front. Brakes must be designed to be able to handle this inertia shift.

▶ All brake systems use some force to multiply the braking effort applied to the brake pedal by the driver. This force can be compressed air, hydraulic pressure, or a combination of the two.

▶ Compressed air is the primary method of choice to multiply brake force for highway trucks.

▶ Air brake systems are very versatile and can be easily connected to trailers, plus there is no worry of leaks or spills, as in hydraulic systems.

▶ Air brake systems can handle small system leaks without adverse effects.

▶ All brake systems are dual-brake systems, meaning that if one system fails the other can still stop the vehicle.

▶ Because of their simplicity, cam brakes are the most popular air brake foundation brake system in on-highway trucks.

▶ Air brake systems are subject to federal regulation under the Federal Motor Vehicle Safety Standard (FMVSS) 121.

▶ S-cam used in cam brakes can be left- or right-handed.

▶ Brake friction material is edge-coded to ensure the material used is matched to the vehicle.

▶ Brake chamber size and slack adjuster lever length combine to deliver a twisting force to the brake camshafts.

▶ Brake chambers are air-operated diaphragm chambers used to apply pressure to the brakes.

▶ Actuators have dual chambers with one containing a power spring to operate the emergency or parking brake system.

▶ Spring brake chambers must be disarmed before they are discarded by cutting the power spring with an acetylene torch.

▶ Slack adjusters are used to keep the brake chamber stroke adjusted; all modern vehicles are equipped with automatic slack adjusters.

Key Terms

AL factor The size or surface area of a brake chamber multiplied by the length of the slack adjuster in inches.

anti-fade An opposite condition of heat fade where the coefficient of friction increases as the brakes get hotter.

automatic slack adjusters (ASAs) Automatically adjust brake stroke to maintain the correct shoe-to-drum clearance.

brake block Brake friction material that is 0.75" (19 mm) thick.

brake fade The inability of the brake to maintain its effectiveness. Brake fade causes a need for increased pedal application force to maintain the same braking effectiveness.

brake foundations The braking components found at the wheel ends.

brake lining Brake friction material that is 1/2" (13 mm) thick.

brake torque The force applied to the foundation brakes during braking.

cam brakes An "S"-shaped shaft head that twists between two rollers to expand a set of brake shoes.

cam-opposite A cam brake where the cam rotates opposite the drum's rotation to energize the brakes.

cam-same An arrangement where the cam rotates the same direction the drum's rotation to energize the brakes.

cast drums Brake drums made from cast iron.

centrifuge drums Brake drums made with a cast-iron core surrounded by a steel band.

chemical fade A type of brake fade that takes place when steam or gases from vaporized lining materials form between hot lining and the drum, reducing the coefficient of friction.

clearance-sensing ASA A type of automatic slack adjuster that reduces pushrod travel based on torque input to the ASA.

coefficient of friction (CoF) The amount of friction between two objects in contact; calculated by dividing the force required to move the object by the weight of the object.

edge code A code representing the CoF of a brake lining and its composition.

Federal Motor Vehicle Safety Standard 121 (FMVSS 121) Performance and safety standards legislation for air brakes.

floating caliper A disc brake caliper that is both supported and slides along on two pins.

glazing A cause of brake fade characterized by a hard, glassy, burnt appearance to the lining surface, diminishing its CoF.

heat fade The loss or reduction in the CoF as the brake temperature increases.

inertia shift Weight that moves from the rear of the vehicle to the front during braking.

kinetic energy The energy of a body in motion.

left-hand camshafts S-cams that rotate in a counterclockwise direction to apply the brakes.

long stroke chambers Brake chambers manufactured with a 3" (76 mm) maximum stroke travel.

manual slack adjusters A manually adjusted lever between the brake chamber and the S-cam; to maintain brake shoe to drum clearance.

mechanical fade Loss of brake effectiveness that occurs when drums expand due to heat.

non-asbestos organic (NAO) lining Brake friction material commonly used in line-haul tractors where far less braking takes place.

power springs Springs in brake actuators used to apply park brakes or internal pushrod lock mechanisms.

release bolt A bolt that compresses the power spring of spring brakes and releases the park brake.

right-hand camshafts Camshafts that rotate in a clockwise direction to apply the brakes.

roto-chambers Actuators with a unique diaphragm and piston construction that delivers consistent output force, regardless of the pushrod position.

S-cam A camshaft used to force brake shoes against the brake drum.

self-energization A braking effect that causes the shoe-drum friction to rotate the brake shoe into the drum with more force.

semi-metallic lining Brake friction material comprising heat-resistant semi-metallic blends that are used for higher temperatures and severe service ratings.

slack adjuster A mechanical lever between the brake chamber and the foundation brake assembly.

spring brake Brakes commonly used on rear drive axles that contain power springs that are used to apply park brakes. They are also referred to as "maxi-brakes."

stroke-sensing ASA A slack adjuster that adjusts shoe to drum clearance based on the slack adjuster stroke length.

water fade A type of brake fade that occurs when water gets between the friction surfaces and the drum that acts as a lubricant and reduces braking efficiency.

wedge brakes Brakes that use a wedge pushed between two rollers as a lever to apply the brakes.

Review Questions

1. Which of the following best describes how brakes transform energy?
   a. Brakes convert rotational tire movement into friction.
   b. Brakes convert kinetic energy produced by the engine into heat.
   c. Brakes convert tire rotational energy into heat.
   d. Brakes convert vehicle kinetic energy into heat.

2. Which of the following describes the relationship between braking force and vehicle speed?
   a. Braking force is directly proportional to vehicle speed.
   b. Doubling vehicle speed requires two times more braking force.
   c. Doubling vehicle speed requires four times more braking force.
   d. Doubling vehicle speed requires eight times more braking force.

3. How much more additional braking force is required by a vehicle weighing 40,000 lb (18,144 kg) braking from 50 mph (80 kph), compared to the force required to brake when it weighs 80,000 lb (36,287 kg)?
   a. The same amount of brake force is required
   b. Two times more braking force required
   c. Four times more braking force is required
   d. Half the braking force is required

4. How does inertia affect the operation of brakes on a tandem-axle trailer?
   a. More braking torque is required by the rear axle because inertia transfers weight to the rear axle.
   b. Wheels can lockup easier on forward axles because load and traction on the forward axle tires increases, compared to the rear axle.
   c. More braking is done by forward axle, compared to the rear axle.
   d. Less brake torque is needed by forward axles, compared to rearward axles.

5. Which of the following statements is correct?
   a. A left-hand S-cam camshaft turns clockwise to apply brakes.
   b. A left-hand S-cam camshaft turns counterclockwise to apply brakes.
   c. A right-hand S-cam shaft turns counterclockwise to apply brakes.
   d. A right-hand S-cam shaft turns clockwise to release brakes.

6. Consider a bus with air brakes operating at 5280 ft (1609 m) altitude. What effect does the lower atmospheric pressure have on the brake system operation?
   a. Maximum air tank pressure is lower
   b. Brake application force is lowered
   c. There is no change on air system pressure or application force
   d. The transmission speed of air through brake lines is reduced

7. What is the effect on the brake application force if an automatic slack adjuster with a longer arm is installed?
   a. Application force increases, and brake chamber stroke length remains the same
   b. Application force decreases, but brake stroke length increases
   c. Application force increases, but brake stroke length decreases
   d. Application force increases, and brake stroke length increases

8. Which of the following explains why excess heat in brake foundations causes brake fade?
   a. Increased drum-to-brake lining clearances increases brake chamber stroke length.
   b. Brake block and lining coefficient of friction increases as friction material becomes stickier.
   c. Heated air in brake chambers becomes thinner and more compressible.
   d. A fade factor caused by heat is designed into brake friction materials.

9. Which of the following describes braking from a brake chamber containing a power spring?
a. A spring released and air-applied parking brake
b. A spring applied and air-released parking brake
c. A spring released and air-applied service brake
d. A spring applied and air-released service brake

10. Which of the following is a reason that stroke-sensing automatic slack adjusters are almost obsolete?
a. They are prone to over adjustment.
b. They may not adjust at all.
c. They leave too much clearance between the drum and the shoes.
d. They have a high failure rate.

ASE Technician A/Technician B Style Questions

1. Technician A says that heavy trucks and buses require more power to stop than they do to accelerate. Technician B says that a doubling vehicle speed and weight requires eight times more braking force to decelerate over the same distance. Who is correct?
a. Technician A
b. Technician B
c. Both Technician A and Technician B
d. Neither Technician A nor Technician B

2. Technician A says that the latest legislative requirements for truck brake systems demand shorter stopping distances. Technician B says that, to achieve shorter stopping distances, all drum brakes are legally required to be replaced by disc brakes. Who is correct?
a. Technician A
b. Technician B
c. Both Technician A and Technician B
d. Neither Technician A nor Technician B

3. While trying to determine whether the braking force is balanced between two axles of a tractor using an infra-red thermometer, Technician A says that a hotter brake drum indicates a wheel end with increased brake torque. Technician B says that a wheel end with a cooler drum has more brake application force. Who is correct?
a. Technician A
b. Technician B
c. Both Technician A and Technician B
d. Neither Technician A nor Technician B

4. While recommending repairs to a truck with oil-contaminated brake lining caused by a leaking wheel seal, Technician A says the lining should be replaced, not just cleaned, on the contaminated wheel end. Technician B says that the brake lining should be replaced on both sides of the same axle with the contaminated lining. Who is correct?
a. Technician A
b. Technician B
c. Both Technician A and Technician B
d. Neither Technician A nor Technician B

5. While examining a set of brake linings that were glazed, Technician A said that the cause could be the use of a replacement

slack adjuster with an arm that was too long. Technician B says the cause was likely a slack adjuster that was over tightening and allowing the brakes to drag. Who is correct?
a. Technician A
b. Technician B
c. Both Technician A and Technician B
d. Neither Technician A nor Technician B

6. Technicians A and B were estimating the cost of parts and labor to provide a quote for a brake job on a tandem-axle dump truck. Technician A says that if the truck uses outboard drums, wheel seals and brake drum hardware, such as nuts, bolts, and washers, do not need to be replaced. Technician B says that if the truck uses inboard drums, the cost for replacing hub seals and drum hardware needs to be included in the quote. Who is correct?
a. Technician A
b. Technician B
c. Both Technician A and Technician B
d. Neither Technician A nor Technician B

7. Technician A says that air brake systems are better than hydraulic in tractor trailer applications because it is easier to connect and disconnect tractors from trailers. Technician B says that air brake systems respond more slowly to driver input from the brake pedal, compared to hydraulic brakes. Who is correct?
a. Technician A
b. Technician B
c. Both Technician A and Technician B
d. Neither Technician A nor Technician B

8. Technician A says that slack adjusters do not have more than a 90-degree angle when correctly adjusted to 1/2" (13 mm) stroke length. Technician B says a slack adjuster with a stroke indicator should not allow the clevis pin to travel further than the first of two pins of stroke indicator, which is closest to the brake chamber. Who is correct?
a. Technician A
b. Technician B
c. Both Technician A and Technician B
d. Neither Technician A nor Technician B

9. Technician A says that air disc brakes don't create as much brake fade as drum brakes because brake pads squeeze a rotor. Technician B says that disc brakes experience as much or more heat fade due to increased friction and shorter stopping distance standards. Who is correct?
a. Technician A
b. Technician B
c. Both Technician A and Technician B
d. Neither Technician A nor Technician B

10. Technician A says that right-hand S-cams are used on the right side of a vehicle and left-hand cams on the left side. Technician B says right- and left-hand S-cams can be used on either side of a vehicle. Who is correct?
a. Technician A
b. Technician B
c. Both Technician A and Technician B
d. Neither Technician A nor Technician B

CHAPTER 34

Air Brake Circuits and Valves

Learning Objectives

- **LO 34-1** Outline the advantages and disadvantages of air brake systems on commercial vehicles.
- **LO 34-2** Identify and list air brake subsystems and control circuits.
- **LO 34-3** Identify and describe the purpose, construction, and operation of components used by the air supply system.
- **LO 34-4** Identify and describe the purpose, construction, and operation of components used by the air delivery and control systems.

- **LO 34-5** Describe pneumatic brake balance.
- **LO 34-6** Identify and describe the purpose, construction, and operation of components used by the park/emergency braking circuits.
- **LO 34-7** Identify and describe the purpose, construction, and operation of components used in trailer air circuits.

You Are the Technician

You have recently begun working at a mixed fleet operation with a wide variety of medium and heavy trucks modified for specialized purposes in the mining and oil exploration industry. Some trucks were originally built as on-highway tractors but now have frame extensions to accommodate installation of 20' (6.1 m) boxes, plus a fifth wheel for towing short trailers. Other chassis have had specialized installations of hydraulic booms, large air compressors, power generators, and drilling equipment. Some straight trucks have had additional axles installed, some self-steering, and others enhanced with a combination of tag and pusher axles equipped with air brakes. While most of these trucks operate in off-road conditions on rough gravel roads, a few are licensed to operate on public roads.

There have been a few complaints from operators that the braking systems are not effective and that the vehicles become unstable and difficult to steer when braking. Some vehicles take too long to stop and require very high brake application pressures to slow the vehicles. The tire costs for the fleet are excessively high because many vehicles have tires regularly damaged with flat spots, likely due to the brakes locking up.

1. Briefly outline the steps you might take to begin to verify the operator complaints and begin to analyze potential causes of the vehicle control problems reported by the drivers.
2. List and identify problems with the braking system. What do you think could be wrong with the trucks' air brake circuits that would account for the operator complaints?
3. List the items you believe should be inspected, tested, and included in a proper preventative maintenance programs for air brakes.
4. Identify some of the diagnostic tests you might use to validate the correct operation of the air brake system components and operation in the fleet of trucks. Give reasons for using the tests.

Introduction

Compressed air brake systems have been used since the 1870s when George Westinghouse first built air brake systems for heavy locomotives. Not long afterwards, air brakes were used in on-road vehicles. Since then, air brake systems have undergone numerous refinements to make them a highly reliable, effective braking system preferred for heavy-duty commercial vehicles because of their superior stopping power and safety.

The concept of compressed air brake systems is relatively simple. Air is drawn into an air compressor where it is pressurized, sent to a storage tank, and held at approximately 125 psi (862 kPa). When needed for braking, compressed air is piped through lines and valves to the wheel end brakes. Air-operated cylinders, or brake chambers, at the wheels convert the energy-stored compressed air into mechanical force used to apply the brakes. As illustrated in **FIGURE 34-1**, compressed air can store energy much like a coil spring. Air brake systems multiply and transfer brake pedal force using the properties of air pressure. Because large vehicles also require an emergency brake system, compressed air is used to release heavy mechanical spring pressure supplying very high mechanical force that can apply emergency/park brakes.

The basic principles of air brake systems are straightforward. In practice, however, safe, effective, efficient, and reliable air brake system operation relies on three major subsystems and a variety of components unique to each of those systems. This chapter specifically covers:

- Air supply system, which consists primarily of the air compressor and reservoirs
- Air delivery system, which is composed of valves and air lines arranged into specific circuits
- Emergency and park brake system, which is designed to maintain vehicle control when air is lost and to hold the vehicle when parked

The trailer air brake system is a fourth subsystem of the air brake system and works in parallel with the tractor air brake systems when a trailer is towed.

Advantages of Air Systems

LO 34-1 Outline the advantages and disadvantages of air brake systems on commercial vehicles.

In heavy-duty combination vehicles, air is used to transmit pressure and multiply the force of a driver's foot on the brake pedal during brake application. **FIGURE 34-2** illustrates how brake systems multiply force, depending on the pressure and the surface area. For example, a 4:1 pressure differential multiplies 12 lb (5.4 kg) of air pressure per square inch into 48 lb (21.8 kg) of braking force. Air is an ideal medium for transmitting and multiplying force, compared to hydraulic fluid, in large vehicles due primarily to the heavier vehicle weights and the greater number of wheel ends. Much more force needs to be applied at more wheel ends than in single-axle, light-duty vehicles equipped with hydraulic brakes.

Air pressure can be stored in an uncomplicated reservoir when a vehicle is not braking. Therefore, the greater stopping power requirements of heavy commercial vehicles are easily stored in reservoirs onboard after being supplied and by an engine-driven air compressor. In comparison, braking a loaded heavy-duty vehicle using hydraulic fluid would be much less efficient. It would require moving large quantities of liquids through lines and require a complex force and volume multiplication system to convert the driver's input to braking force at each wheel. When it comes to heavy-duty commercial vehicles, air brake systems have several other advantages:

- The supply of air is limitless, which allows for minor leaks without the loss of braking. If small leaks do occur, the air can be replenished without a loss of braking.

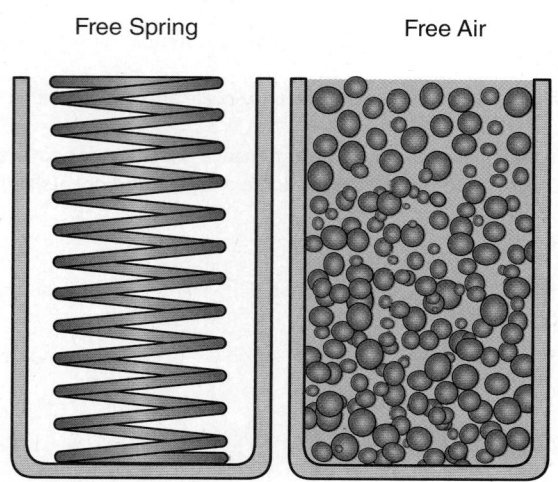
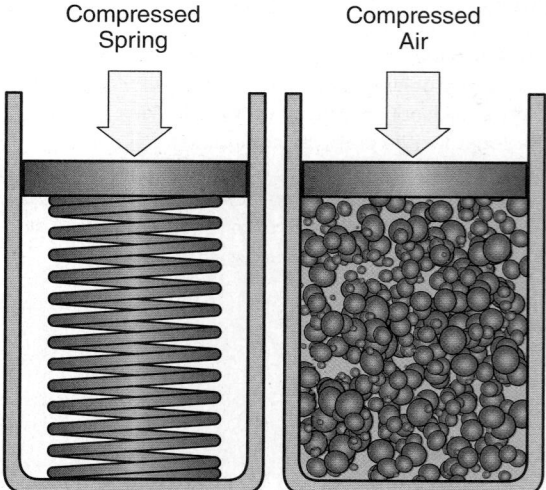

Free Spring   Free Air   Compressed Spring   Compressed Air

FIGURE 34-1 Compressed air can store energy much like a coil spring. Air brake systems multiply and transfer brake pedal force using the properties of air pressure.

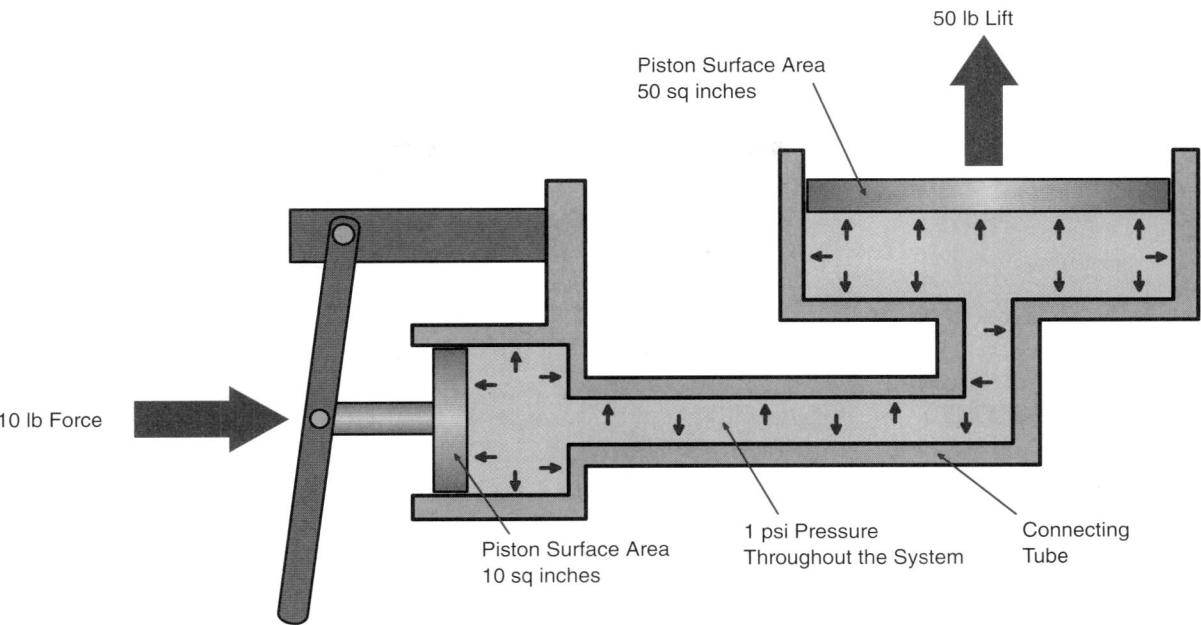

FIGURE 34-2 Braking force is a result of the air pressure multiplied by the surface area.

- Air brake systems enable easier and faster coupling and uncoupling of trailers from the tractor unit. Air lines can be disconnected, and only air is lost. Hydraulic systems require bleeding of air each time they are opened to connect to another vehicle.
- Air systems use simpler foundation brakes, as shoes, drums, and other components at the wheel ends are simpler and fewer.
- Air brakes can maintain brake pressure at high altitudes since an air compressor multiplies atmospheric air pressure. Vacuum boosters used with hydraulic brakes lose effectiveness with increased altitude.

Disadvantages of Air Systems

Despite all the advantages to air brake systems, air brakes do have some disadvantages:

- The air must be pressurized, filtered, and stored in large, multiple reservoirs. **Brake lag** creates a delay between driver application and brake actuation because the speed of air pressure transmission is much slower. An even longer lag exists with air brakes between brake pedal application and actual braking. Hydraulic force has little or no delay compared to air.
- Control of air pressure through air brake circuits requires more valves and components, which adds complexity and cost to the air brake system.
- Some drivers express dissatisfaction with the delay when an air system is empty and needs to build up pressure after the engine is started.
- There is little to no feedback from the brake pedal about braking effort.
- Air systems operate at lower pressures than hydraulic systems, so larger brake system components and diameter

lines are needed. Noise accompanies the movement and exhausting of air, as well.
- The complexity of air brake systems means more knowledge and skill are required of technicians who service the systems. For similar reasons, driver training and certification to operate a vehicle with air brakes is mandatory in most jurisdictions.
- Air can become contaminated with moisture and cause brake valves and other components to freeze up in cold-weather operation.

The performance and safety standards of air brake systems are legislated. For instance, in the United States, the Federal Motor Vehicle Safety Standard 121 (FMVSS 121) sets the standards. Other countries also have standards to which all vehicles must comply. To ensure safe braking performance under normal and emergency conditions, compliance with the set standards is required by all air brake systems at the time of manufacture.

Air Brake Subsystems and Control Circuits

LO 34-2 Identify and list air brake subsystems and control circuits.

Four distinct air brake circuits are used in trucks, buses, and trailers:

- Air supply system
- Air delivery and control system
- Park-emergency/supply brake system
- Trailer air brake system and its subsystems

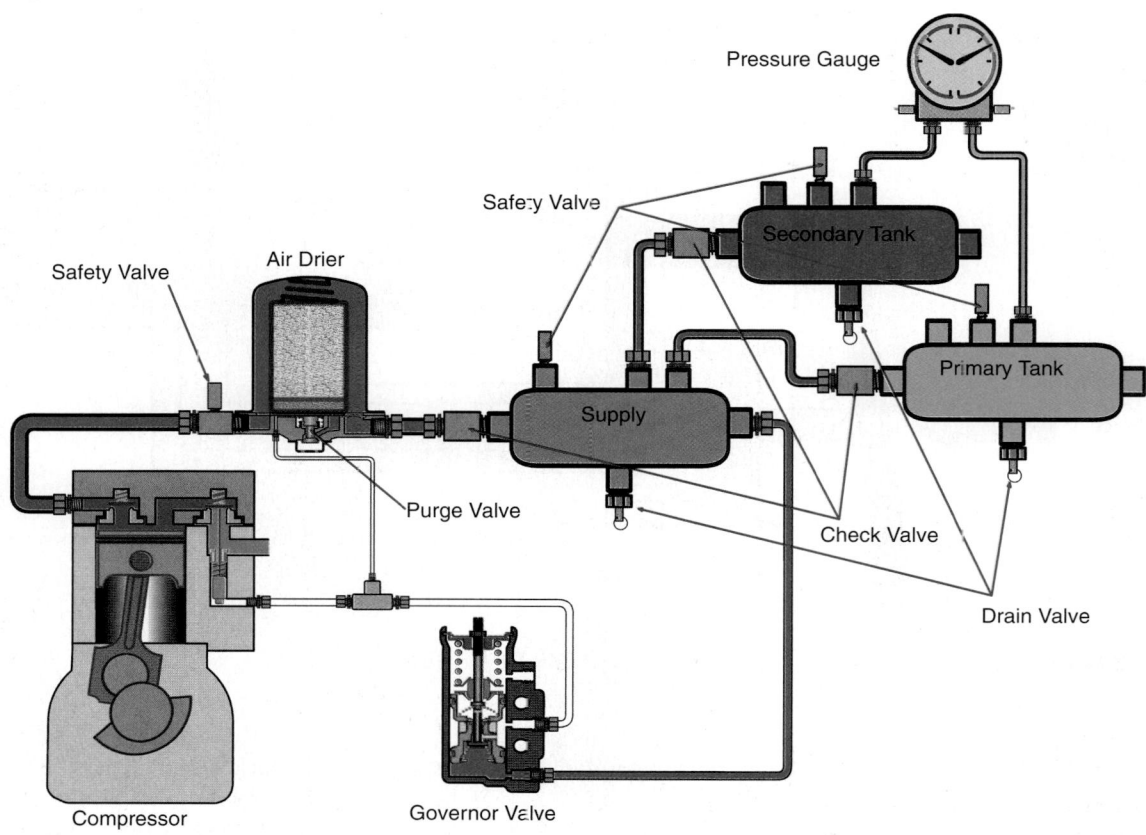

FIGURE 34-3 Components of the air supply, or charging system, of a typical circuit air brake system used in commercial vehicles.

Each of these circuits is discussed in greater detail in the remaining sections of this chapter.

Air brake circuits are also divided into two separate systems—**primary circuit** and **secondary circuit**. A **dual-circuit system** configuration improves air brake system safety by duplicating braking system operation using two separate circuits, with either circuit capable of stopping the vehicle if one circuit should fail. **FIGURE 34-3** illustrates the components of the air supply or charging system of a typical circuit air brake system used in commercial vehicles. The supply reservoir receives air and distributes it equally to the primary and secondary air reservoirs. Generally, as depicted in **FIGURE 34-4**, the primary air brake circuit supplies air to the rear axle and trailer brakes. The secondary system supplies the front brakes. To prevent an air leak or component failure in one system from causing a total loss of braking, the two systems can function independently of one another to bring the vehicle to a safe controlled stop.

How the primary and secondary circuits are divided generally depends on the type and manufacturer of the vehicle. There are several exceptions to the generalizations outlined next, but it can be helpful to first visualize the arrangement in a straight truck (a truck that does not tow a trailer). In a straight truck, the primary circuit provides air pressure to the rear brakes and the secondary circuit to the front axles. The opposite is the case with a tractor towing a trailer. The secondary circuit supplies pressure to the tractors rear brakes and the trailer air brakes. Navistar is one of several OEM exceptions. It uses the primary air circuit to supply pressurized air to the rear brakes and trailer, while secondary air supplies the front brakes.

Primary brake circuits are commonly color-coded as green air lines. Secondary circuits generally are designated orange. **TABLE 34-1** lists the typical colors associated with air brake circuits. Most air supply lines are fabricated from materials, such as **Synflex**, which is a brand name for tubing made from nylon and which is shown in the system in **FIGURE 34-5**.

For both trucks and tractors, the **emergency brake circuit**, also called the **park brake circuit**, holds the truck/trailer or tractor stationary when parked. It's called the emergency circuit because it also provides a back-up emergency braking system in the event of a loss of air pressure in the secondary braking system of a tractor or the primary system of a truck. **FIGURE 34-6** shows a dual-chamber actuator. The power spring in the dual-chamber actuator supplies the force used by the emergency/park brake circuit to hold the truck/trailer or tractor if air pressure is lost.

Antilock braking, traction, stability control, and adaptive cruise-braking systems are also integrated into the air brake system. These elements of a contemporary brake system ares covered in the Antilock Braking, Vehicle Stability, and Collision Avoidance Systems chapter.

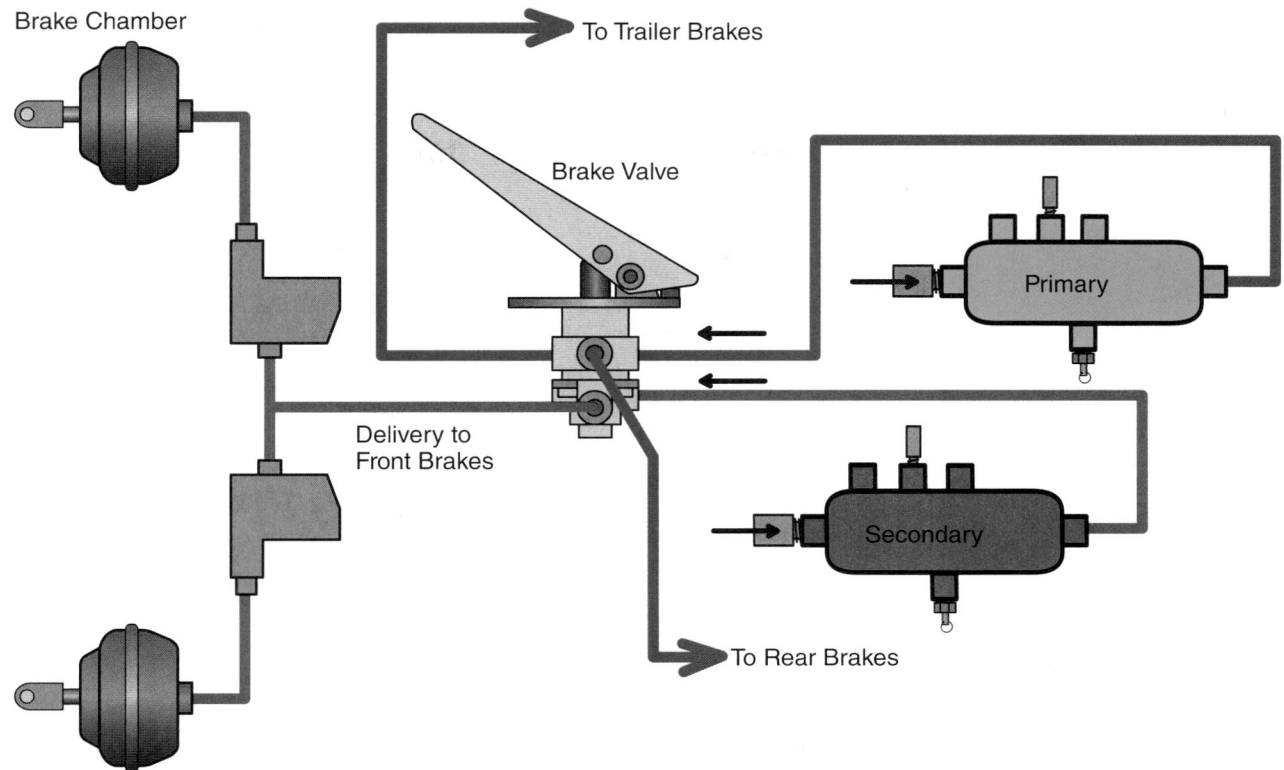

FIGURE 34-4 Primary and secondary circuits in a dual-circuit air brake system.

TABLE 34-1 Typical Air Line Color Codes Used to Designate Air Brake Circuits

Air Line Color	Brake Circuit
Black	Supply charging
Green	Primary
Orange	Secondary
Red	Park-emergency and trailer reservoir supply tank
Blue	Trailer control/service brake
Yellow	Park-emergency brake control

Components of the Air Supply System

LO 34-3 Identify and describe the purpose, construction, and operation of components used by the air supply system.

The air supply compresses, conditions, and stores the air for the vehicle's braking circuits and other air-operated accessories. The air supply system includes the following components:

- An engine-driven air compressor
- An air compressor governor controlling minimum and maximum reservoir air pressure
- Air reservoirs or tanks for both the primary and secondary systems

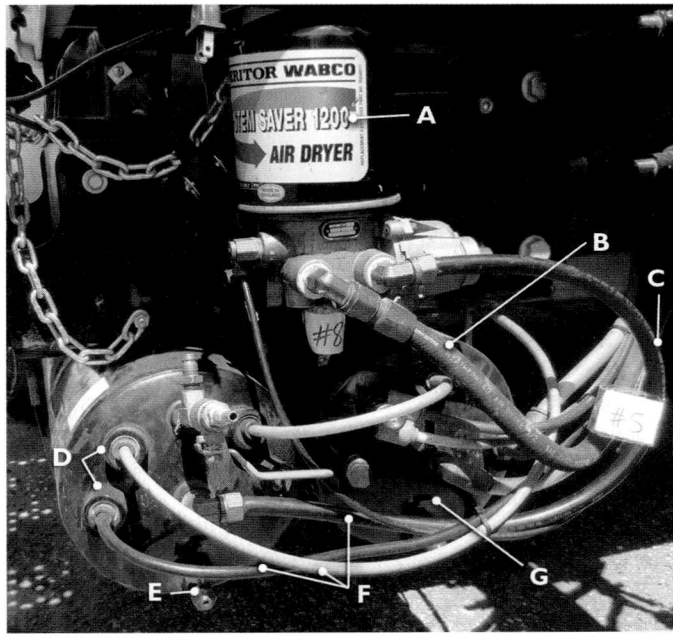

FIGURE 34-5 FMVSS121 standard requires a drain valve on all air tanks. Synflex tubing is a type of flexible nylon tubing commonly used for air lines. **A.** Replaceable dessicant filter. **B.** Braided steel air line from compressor. **C.** Air dryer line out. **D.** Quick connect air fittings (2). **E.** Drain valve. **F.** Nylon Synflex tubing. **G.** Secondary tank.

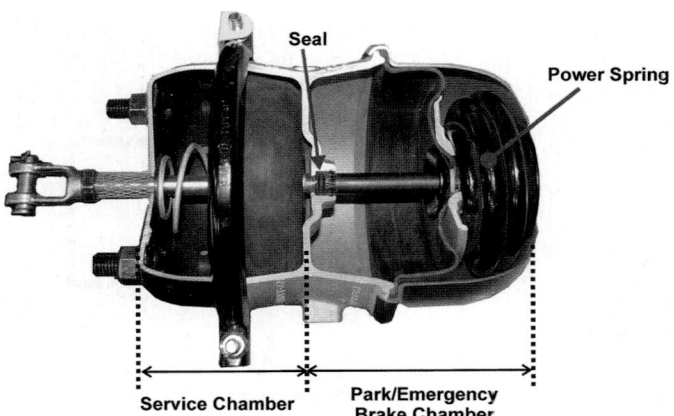

FIGURE 34-6 The power spring supplies the force used by the emergency/park brake circuit. **A.** Seal. **B.** Power spring.

- Pressure protection and check valves
- An air dryer to remove moisture and small oil droplets to prevent air supply contamination

Other vehicle systems may also use the supply of compressed air. For example, the air suspension, transmission controls, or interaxle differential lock might use compressed air. Air reservoirs for the trailer braking system receive air from the secondary air circuit supplied through the dedicated trailer air supply. The red-colored air line connecting the tractor to the trailer fills the trailer reservoir after a manually operated valve in the tractor is activated by the driver.

Air Compressors

Air compressors are the source of power for the air brake system. Compressors are engine driven. They use either a belt or drive gear and can rotate in either direction. Most compressors are integrated with the engine's cooling and lubrication system. The most common configuration for an air compressor is a two-cylinder reciprocating-piston design. Small air systems may use a single cylinder, and larger systems can use four-cylinder compressors in either a "V" or inline design. Output is measured in cubic feet of air pumped per minute (CFM) (or liter per minute [lpm]).

To meet FMVSS 121 standards, a compressor must be capable of building up system air pressure from 85 psi to 125 psi (586 kPa to 862 kPa) in a minimum of 25 seconds at governed engine speed. Correct compressor capacity is determined by the volume of the vehicle's air reservoirs and air-operated accessories. The limiting factor to a compressor's size is its expected duty cycle. Since compressors are designed to operate a maximum of 25% duty cycle—that is, 25% "on time"—the compressor output volume rated in cubic ft/minute (CFM) must be high enough to meet and exceed air system requirements without exceeding the 25% threshold. **FIGURE 34-7** shows the relationship between vehicle type and air usage. If heat produced during excessive compressor loading period is not given adequate time to dissipate, the

compressor prematurely wears out. Single-cylinder, like the one shown in **FIGURE 34-8A**, and multiple-cylinder compressors, such as the one shown in **FIGURE 34-8B**, are used to increase capacity.

The compressor typically consists of three major sections: a cylinder head, crankshaft, and the crankcase. Cast iron is used to construct the compressor. An oil line from the engine lubricates the crankshaft bearings and cylinder walls. Piston rings help form a gas-tight seal to compress air and scrape oil from the cylinder walls, directing it back into the crankcase. Engine coolant circulates through the compressor to remove heat build-up. In most applications, a flange on the compressor crankcase provides a mounting surface to bolt the compressor onto the engine. Most compressors are coupled to the engine using a drive gear because a gear-driven coupling has the highest durability and reliability. Some single-cylinder compressors may require timing to the engine to minimize vibration caused by the inertia of the reciprocating piston. Though not as reliable or efficient, belt-driven compressors may be used in older vehicles or medium-duty vehicles with smaller air supply systems.

Compressor Operation—Loading and Unloading

The compressor is an essential component for the air brake system and operates by loading and unloading as the air passes through it. Air is pulled into the compressor cylinders through the air intake valves during the piston downstroke. During the upstroke, air is pushed out of the cylinders through the spring loaded, one-way air discharge valves.

As illustrated in **FIGURE 34-9A**, on upstrokes, increasing cylinder air pressure closes the spring-loaded air intake valves while the discharge valves normally closed by spring tension are opened. **FIGURE 34-9B** illustrates the downstroke. During downstroke, the intake valves are opened by a pressure differential between the cylinders and air pressure at the intake port. Atmospheric air pressure pushes its way into the cylinders through an open intake valve during the intake stroke due to the pressure differential between the intake port and cylinder. Pressurized air from an engine's turbocharged intake manifold air pressure also pushes its way into the cylinders. Spring tension closes the discharge valves at the end of the intake stroke to prevent air from leaking back from the reservoirs through the air compressor.

Compressor Discharge Line

High air temperatures from the compressor discharge port are initially lowered by heat radiating from annealed copper tubing connecting the compressor with an air dryer or air reservoir. Annealed, or softened copper, easily transfers heat to the atmosphere and does not harden with time and vibration, so it should not crack. In vehicles having five or less axles equipped with air brakes, a 1/2" (12.7 mm) inside diameter (ID) annealed copper discharge tube of between 6" (1.8 m) and

Air Usage	Compressor Duty Cycle	Example of Vehicle Type
Low Air Use 5 axles or less	Less than 15% (% of engine running time that the compressor builds up air pressure)	- Line haul single trailer without air suspension - Air-over-hydraulic brakes 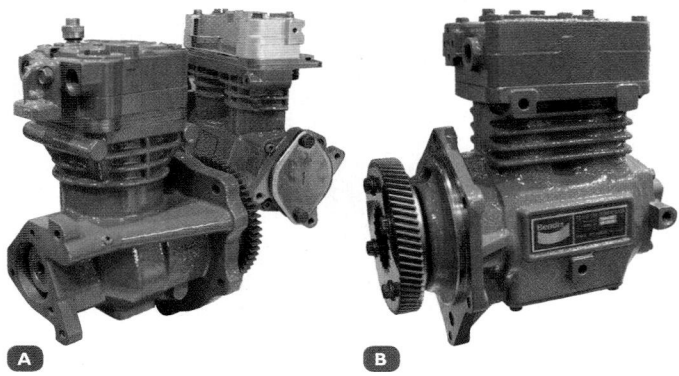
Low Air Use 5 axles or less	Up to 25 %	- Line haul single trailer with air suspension - School bus
High Air Use 8 axles or less	Up to 25%	- Double/triple trailer. / Open highway Coach/RV / Yard/terminal jockey - Off highway / construction. - Concrete mixer / Dump truck / Fire truck, etc.
High Air Use 12 axles or less	Up to 25%	- City transit bus - Refuse truck - Bulk unloaders - Low boys, etc.

FIGURE 34-7 An air compressor's capacity must be selected to limit the cycle time (on/off time). Undersized compressors build air pressure too slowly and wear out prematurely.

FIGURE 34-8 A. Single-cylinder compressor. **B.** Two-cylinder compressor.

9" (2.7 m) length is used. Larger systems use 5/8" (15.9 mm) or 3/4" (19.1 mm) diameter tube up to 15' (4.6 m) long. The copper tube should slope downward from the compressor to prevent a build-up of moisture that could freeze in the line. A stainless-steel flex line is often used after the solid-copper line ends. The flex line absorbs engine vibration and flexing between the engine and frame-mounted air dryer caused by torque reaction or chassis twisting.

Because an air compressor's cylinder walls are oil-lubricated, some oil always carries over into the discharge tube. The result is hot discharge lines that can carbonize oil inside on the walls of the line and lead to discharge-line restriction.

Air Compressor Governor

The air compressor is coupled to the engine and turns continuously, but a **governor** controls air system pressure by stopping and starting the build-up of air pressure inside the compressor. When the compressor builds-up pressure, the process is called loading. The state when the compressor is driven, but is not building air pressure, is called unloaded. The governor also controls purging of the air dryer. Current FMVSS 121 air brake standards require vehicle air pressure to fall no lower than 85 psi (586 kPa) and reach 125–130 psi (862–896 kPa) when the compressor unloads or cuts out. Cut-in pressures are generally 20 to 25 psi (138 to 173 kPa) below cut-out pressure.

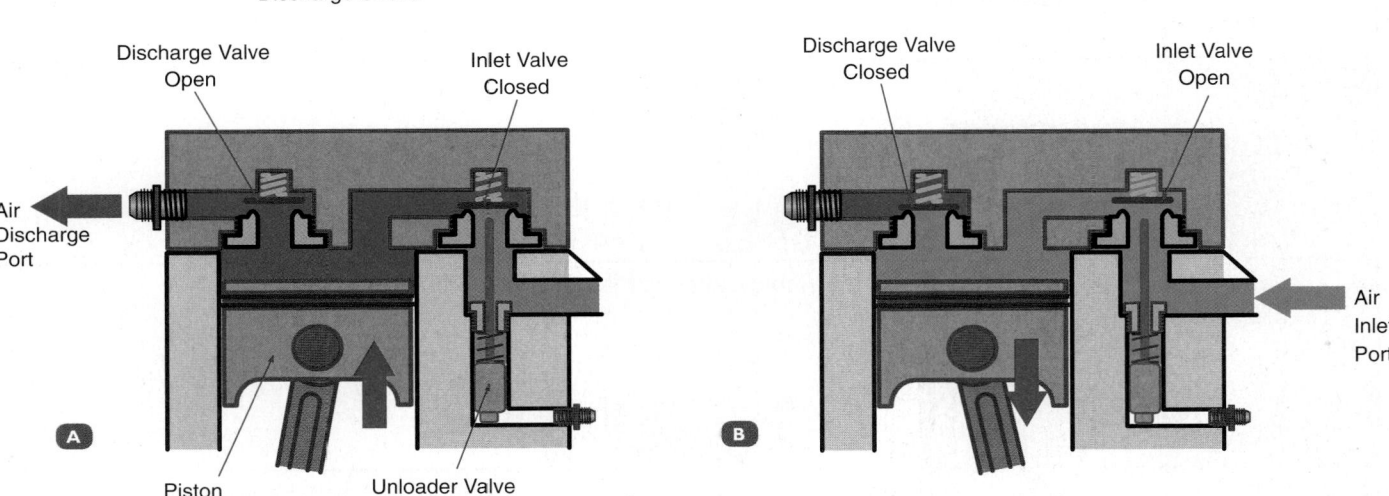

Discharge Stroke

Discharge Valve Open

Inlet Valve Closed

Air Discharge Port

A

Piston

Unloader Valve

Intake Stroke

Discharge Valve Closed

Inlet Valve Open

Air Inlet Port

B

FIGURE 34-9 One-way check valves are used to regulate air entering and leaving the air compressor. **A.** Check-valve position during the upstroke. **B.** Check-valve position during the downstroke.

That means a vehicle with a cut-out pressure of 125 psi (862 kPa) can be expected to have a cut-in pressure of 100 to 105 psi (689 to 724 kPa). Governors control the cut-in and cut-out pressures of the compressor by opening or closing the unloader valves, using air pressure supplied by the air reservoirs. Unloader valves are air-operated valves usually located in the intake port of the compressor. Air pressure is supplied to the compressor unloader valves and air dryer purge valves through the governor unloader port. The unloader port supplies air at system pressure to switch the compressors operation from loading to unloaded. In the unloaded state, air pressure supplied by the governor holds the compressors intake air check valves open, preventing them from closing during an upward stroke of the compressor pistons. Opening unloader valves allows air to cycle in and out of the compressor cylinders, preventing air from compressing and leaving through the discharge port's one-way check valve.

As illustrated in **FIGURE 34-10**, the governor has three ports:

- **Reservoir**—Inlet port for the air system pressure connected to the supply-service or primary air reservoir to sense system pressure.
- **Unloader**—An air outlet port supplying air at system pressure (85 to 130 psi range [586 to 896 kPa]) only when cut-out pressure is reached. Air system pressure in the line or at this port is exhausted and switches to atmospheric pressure when governor cut-in pressure is reached.
- **Exhaust**—An outlet port that vents air from the unloader port when the air system transitions to cut-in pressure.

Governor Loading and Unloading Operation

Loading and unloading the compressor is determined by whether atmospheric or reservoir air pressure is supplied

FIGURE 34-10 Governor valve with **A.** Reservoir port. **B.** Mounting bolts. **C.** Unloader port. **D.** Exhaust port. **E.** Top cover.

to the unloader valves. The supply of either source of air is controlled by the position of the governor piston. As the air system pressure builds when the compressor is loaded, reservoir pressure is supplied to one side of the governor piston, which is opposed by spring pressure (**FIGURE 34-11**). The piston operates more like a spool valve with a cavity surrounding

COMPRESSOR LOADED

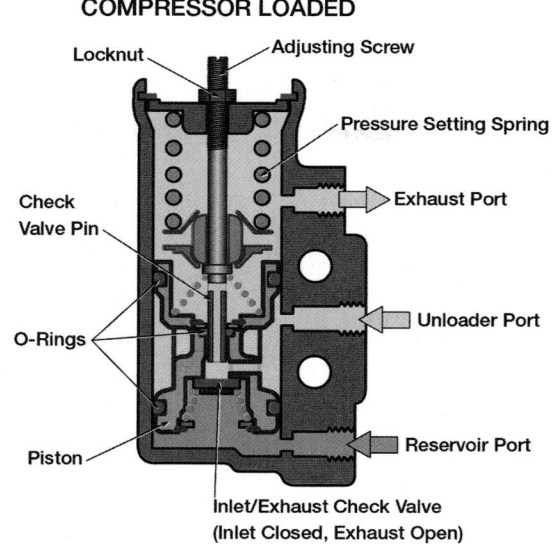

Locknut — Adjusting Screw — Pressure Setting Spring — Exhaust Port — Unloader Port — Reservoir Port

Check Valve Pin — O-Rings — Piston

Inlet/Exhaust Check Valve
(Inlet Closed, Exhaust Open)

COMPRESSOR UNLOADED

Locknut — Adjusting Screw — Pressure Setting Spring — Exhaust Port — Unloader Port — Reservoir Port

Check Valve Pin — O-Rings — Piston

Inlet/Exhaust Check Valve
(Inlet Open, Exhaust Closed)

FIGURE 34-11 Movement of the governor piston by reservoir pressure against the pressure spring tension controls the cut-in and cut out pressure.

the center of the valve. Either pressurized air from the reservoir or atmospheric air pressure can enter the cavity surrounding the governor piston. As the governor piston spring is compressed by increasing air pressure on one side of the piston, supplied through the reservoir port, the governor piston moves upwards against pressure spring tension. Built into the end of the piston is a small one-way check valve with two seats—an inlet and exhaust, which has two functions. This explains why a single check valve is called an inlet and exhaust check valve. The valve is located at the end of a pin that extends through the governor piston. Movement of the pin simultaneously opens or closes the check valve on the inlet or exhaust seat so that either atmospheric or reservoir air pressure can enter the cavity surrounding the governor piston. During loading, the check valve allows only atmospheric pressure to surround the piston cavity. It seats on the inlet seat to close the passage from the reservoir air pressure. At the same time, it opens the air passage around the exhaust seat and internally connects the unloader port to atmospheric pressure supplied to the governor through the governor's exhaust port. However, when cut-out pressure is reached, the upward movement of the governor piston allows the check valve pin controlling the opening and closing of both valve seats to contact the governor pressure adjusting screw pin. Contact with the adjusting screw closes the exhaust seat passage to the atmospheric pressure at the governor's exhaust port while simultaneously opening the inlet check valve seat to reservoir pressure. At that point, reservoir pressure replaces atmospheric pressure surrounding the governor piston at the unloader port. Pressurized air from the compressor's unloader port then mechanically forces open the compressor's intake unloader valves. This effectively ends compressor loading or build-up with air.

To load the compressor, reservoir pressure acting on the governor piston diminishes as air is used by the chassis and the state of balance between system air pressure and governor spring pressure force changes. Governor piston movement allows the governor pin to simultaneously open the exhaust check valve seat while closing the inlet check valve seat at cut in pressure. Pressurized air in the unloader port area can be heard venting to the atmosphere. Closing the exhaust passage while simultaneously opening the inlet passage enables reservoir pressure to flow around the governor piston from the inlet valve and to the unloader port. **FIGURE 34-12** illustrates the governor circuit.

A governor can be installed on the air compressor or remotely. An unloader line connects the governor to the compressor's unloader port.

▶ **TECHNICIAN TIP**

Governors are generally non-serviceable. Any abnormal change to system cut-in and cut-out pressures require governor replacement and not an adjustment. An adjustable governor has an adjustment screw with a lock nut. Cut-in and cut-out pressures are adjusted at the same time by turning the screw clockwise to decrease pressures and counterclockwise to increase pressure.

Compressor Unloader Valves

Air intake and discharge valves are in the cylinder head. Compressor discharge or exhaust valves are one-way check valves ensuring air pushed out of the cylinder only goes to the air discharge line. The valve is opened by high compressor cylinder pressure and closed by a negative pressure differential between the discharge line and cylinder pressure. The intake valves can also function as one-way check valves, except they can be mechanically held open, allowing air to pump in and out of the cylinder through the valves. Air pressure acting on small pistons beneath the compressors intake valves hold the intake valves open when the compressor is unloaded by the governor. When system air pressure is needed, the air beneath the pistons is vented to atmosphere, allowing the compressor intake valves to function as one-way check valves. These pistons, controlling intake valve operation, are called **unloader valves (FIGURE 34-13)**. **Unloading** refers to the state when an air compressor is not pumping air—or is unloaded. As illustrated

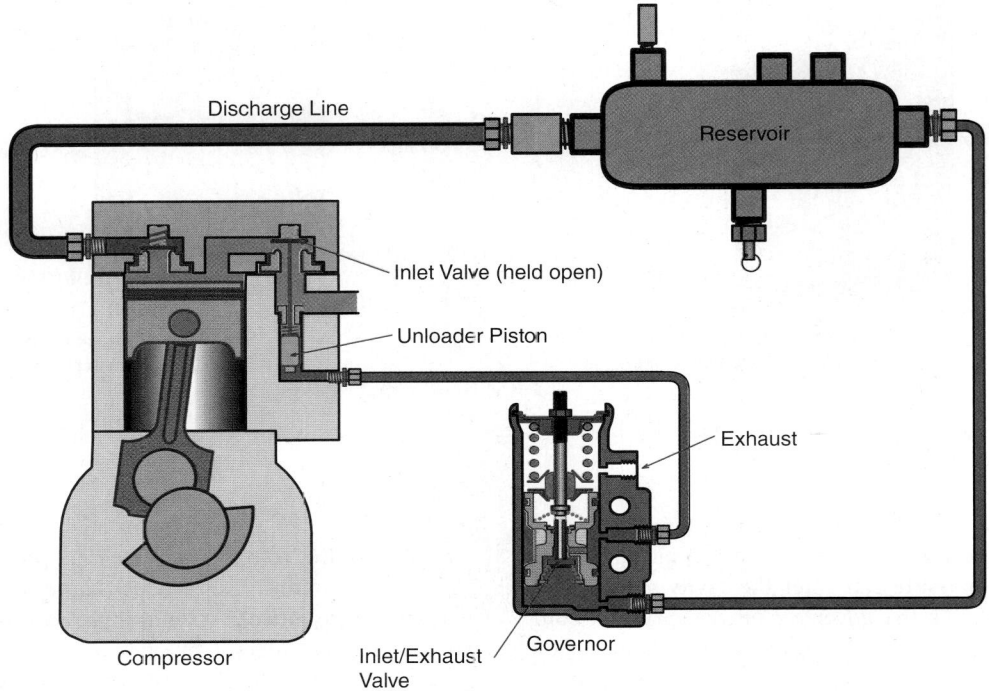

FIGURE 34-12 A Bendix D2 governor circuit. Pressurizing the unloader port causes the unloader valves to hold open the inlet check valves. Opened inlet valves do not allow system air pressure to build.

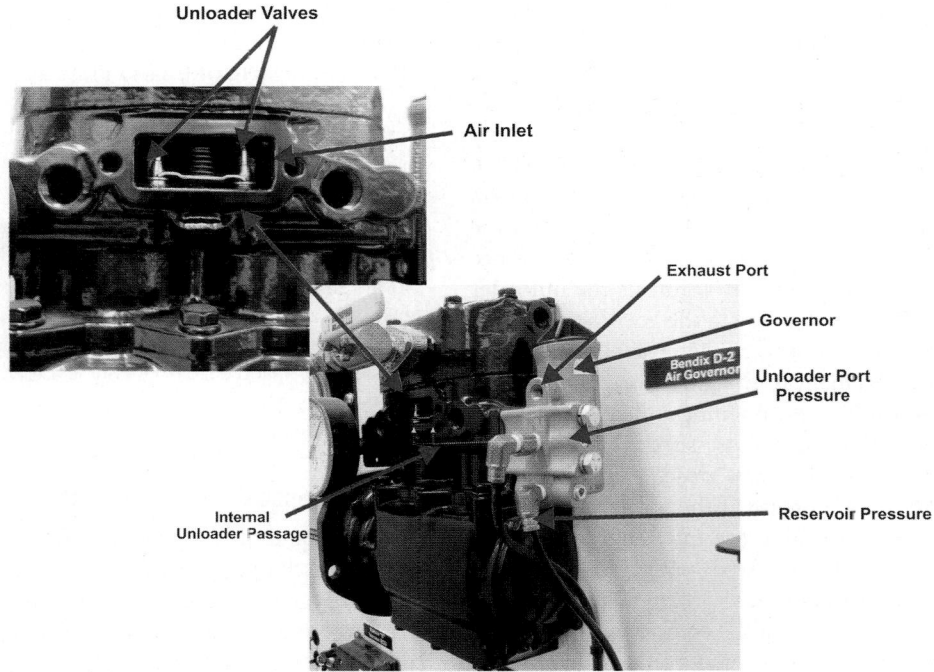

FIGURE 34-13 Pressurized air is supplied to the compressor unloader valves by the governor. Pressurized air acting on the unloader valves forces and holds open the compressor's air inlet check valves.

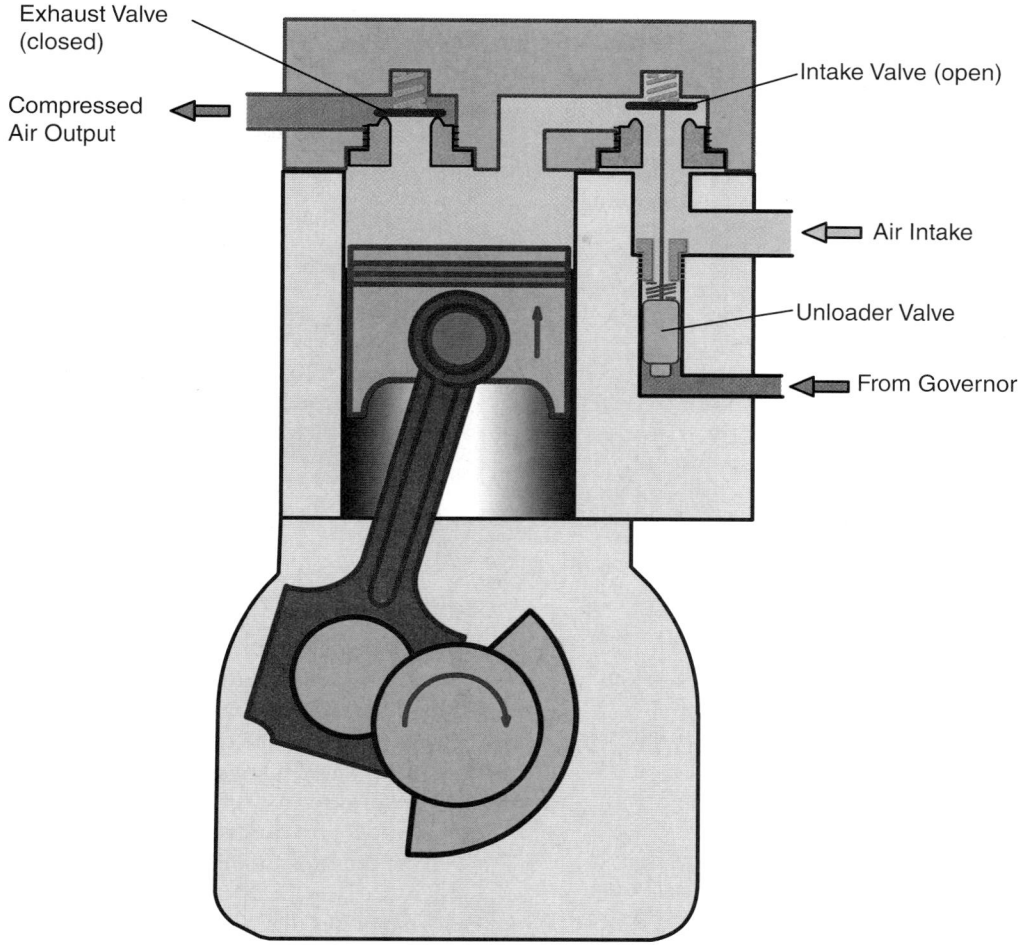

FIGURE 34-14 Supplying air pressure to the unloader valve forces the air inlet check valve open and prevents the compressor from loading or building air pressure.

in **FIGURE 34-14**, when the compressor is **loading**—that is, building up system air pressure—unloader valves have no air pressure applied to them and are retracted.

Unloader valves in some air compressors, such as Meritor's, use a sliding plate or leaf valves to load and unload the compressor (**FIGURE 34-15**). When unloaded, a sliding leaf opens an internal passageway during the upstroke, which allows air in the cylinder to pass back into the opposite cylinder on a down stroke. Air drawn into the cylinders simply pushes back between the two cylinders when unloaded and pressure cannot build in the cylinders. When system cut-in pressure is reached, air is exhausted from the unloader port of the governor and the sliding leaf closes the passageway that had allowed air to bypass the inlet check valves. This means air must pass through the compressor discharge valve or one-way check valves to leave the cylinders.

▶ TECHNICIAN TIP

Slow build-up time from an air compressor may not be due to a worn compressor or a defective governor. Leaking or stuck unloader valves are often to blame. If valves have carbonized oil around their seats, or if the O-ring seals around the valves are deteriorated and allow air to

leak past the valve, the result is poor compressor efficiency since intake air is pushed out the partially open intake check valves when loading. If shop air pressure is applied to the governor unloader port on the air compressor, it *should not be heard* leaking around the unloader valves. A defective discharge valve should not leak air either. And, if air is applied to the compressor discharge port, there should be no audible air leaks through the air intake port of the compressor. A leaking discharge valve can allow reservoir pressure to leak back through the compressor and drain the reservoir.

Inlet Regulating Valve

Air supplied to the compressor is filtered through the engine air filter or the air compressor's own air filter. To build up air pressure faster and prevent slow build-up of system pressure at high altitudes, the compressor can receive its air from the engine's turbocharged boosted intake manifold. An **inlet pressure regulating valve** located in the compressor intake port limits air pressure to approximately 10 psi (69 kPa) if supplied with turbocharged air. The 10 psi (69 kPa) limit reduces the compression temperatures of the compressed air, which can potentially damage the compressor and lead to excessively high air discharge temperatures.

Discharge Check
Valves

Air Discharge
Port

Piston

Crankshaft

Air Inlet Ports

BLOCK SIDE OF COMPRESSOR VALVE BODY
Compressor Loaded

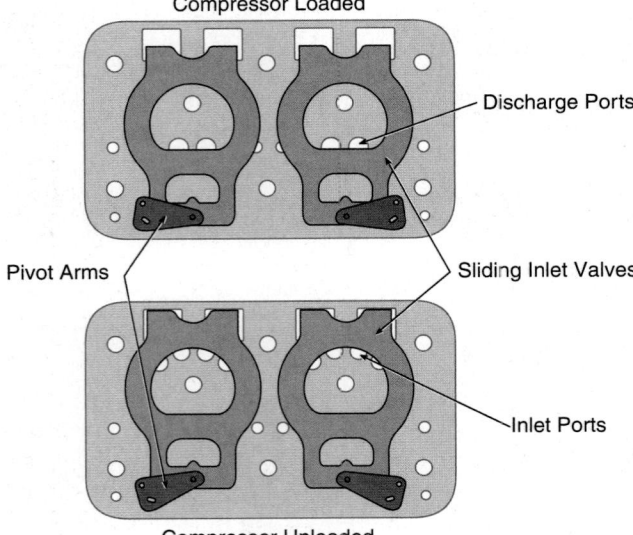

Discharge Ports

Pivot Arms

Sliding Inlet Valves

Inlet Ports

Compressor Unloaded

FIGURE 34-15 A sliding plate covers and uncovers the discharge and intake ports of this Meritor compressor.

FIGURE 34-16 The turbo cut-off valve is typically integrated with the air dryer inlet.

Turbocharger Cut-Off Valve

On turbocharged engines, which are supplied air from the pressurized intake manifold, boost air pressure can also pass through the compressor inlet and leak out the exhaust port of the air dryer when the compressor and air dryer are unloaded. To prevent a loss of engine intake boost pressure through the compressor when it is unloaded, pressurized air from the governor unloader port closes a valve in the compressor discharge line when the compressor unloads. **Turbocharger cut-off valves** are located in either the air compressor or internal to the air dryer. On compressors that have an air inlet connected to atmospheric pressure, the cut-off valve eliminates the "puffing" noise of air passing in and out of the compressor cylinder when unloaded. **FIGURE 34-16** shows a turbocharger cut-off valve.

To inspect and test the air compressor unloader circuit for leakage, follow the steps in **SKILL DRILL 34-1**.

SKILL DRILL 34-1 Inspecting and Testing the Air Compressor Unloader Circuit for Leakage; Replacing Unloader Valves as Needed

1. To diagnose the cause for too frequent cycling of the compressor and air dryer purge within the system cut-in and cut-out pressures, use the following procedures as a general guideline.
2. Properly chock the vehicle's wheels and charge the system to normal governor cut-out pressure (120 psi [830 kPa]).
3. Inspect the governor, gasket, unloader lines, and reservoir lines to the governor for kinks and damage. Verify that the primary reservoir line to the governor is connected to the top of the reservoir.
4. Drain both the primary and secondary air reservoirs and leave the drain valves open.
5. Connect a fitting with a shut-off valve to the governor's unloader port to supply the unloader port with pressurized shop air.
6. Connect an air pressure gauge to another fitting on the unloader port or connect the gauge to a "T" type fitting supplying the unloader port with shop air.
7. Pressurize the unloader port with air and, with the engine off, listen and feel for air leakage from the air dryer purge valve

exhaust port and the air intake of the air compressor. Verify no leaks are detected.
8. Observe the air pressure gauge readings after closing the shut-off valve trapping air in the unloader port.
9. Note any drop in air pressure after 30 seconds. No drop in air pressure should be observed.
10. If air is leaking from the air dryer purge valve, recommend purge valve replacement and/or air dryer replacement or overhaul.
11. If no air is leaking from the air dryer purge valve, but air pressure drops in the unloader port, disconnect and remove the governor.
12. Connect "T" type air fitting with a shut-off valve to the air compressor's governor unloader port. Connect the other end of the fitting to a supply of shop air pressure to supply pressurized air to the unloader port.
13. With the air supply shut-off valve closed, air pressure should be retained in the compressor unloader port. Disconnecting

SKILL DRILL 34-1 Inspecting and Testing the Air Compressor Unloader Circuit for Leakage; Replacing Unloader Valves as Needed (Continued)

the shop air supply line and opening the shut-off valve allows air pressure to drop to atmospheric pressure in the unloader port.

14. Connect an air pressure gauge to a second unloader port on the compressor to measure air pressure supplied to the governor unloader port.

15. Run the engine to operate the compressor.

16. Open and close the shop air shut-off valve to load and unload the compressor. Listen and observe dash pressure gauges for the compressor response. Verify the compressor unloads when

air is supplied to the governor and loads when air pressure drops to atmospheric pressure in the unloader port.

17. Shut the engine off and supply shop air to the governor unloader port.

18. Close the shut-off valve to trap air in the unloader port and observe the air pressure gauge readings.

19. Verify that the unloader port retains air pressure, noting any pressure drop after 30 seconds.

20. If the unloader port does not hold air pressure, the unloader valves or unloader valve "O-ring" are leaking and require replacement.

Air Reservoirs

Air reservoirs or air tanks on a vehicle store compressed air, allow it to cool, and provide a place for water and oil droplets to condense out of the air. FMVSS 121 standards require that the combined volume of all service reservoirs and supply reservoirs must be at least 12 times the combined volume of all service brake chambers at full stroke. This means the size of reservoirs is determined by the number of axles on the truck/tractor and trailer.

Reservoirs are designated as **service reservoir** (or **supply reservoir**), **primary reservoir**, and **secondary reservoir**, according to the circuits they supply. Each reservoir must be equipped with a manual drain valve to remove condensed water and oil unless a third tank, the supply tank, is used. The supply tank, also called the **wet tank**, is the first reservoir receiving air from the compressor. Its function is to condense and collect any remaining water and oil left in the compressed air, which lends it the name—wet tank.

The tank has at least two valves. One is an air pressure **safety relief valve**, which releases air if the tank pressure climbs above 150 psi (1034 kPa). The second valve is a one-way check valve between the service tank and the primary or secondary tank. Only one-way flow of air pressure, from the primary to secondary tanks, is permitted using the check valve. This valve

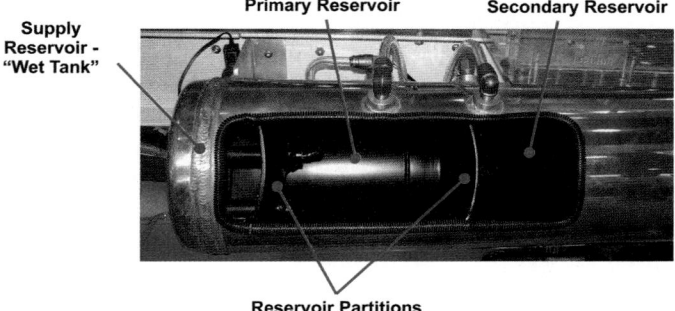

FIGURE 34-17 A combined wet, primary, and secondary reservoir with internal check valves.

prevents air from leaking back from either the primary or secondary tank if there is a failure causing the wet tank to lose air. Air can leave the wet tank, but it cannot flow back into the wet tank from the primary or secondary reservoir (**FIGURE 34-17**). Some reservoirs have an integral wet tank combined with a primary and secondary reservoir. An internal baffle separating the two tanks contain an integral one-way check valve, which is not serviceable.

FIGURE 34-18 shows a reservoir safety valve.

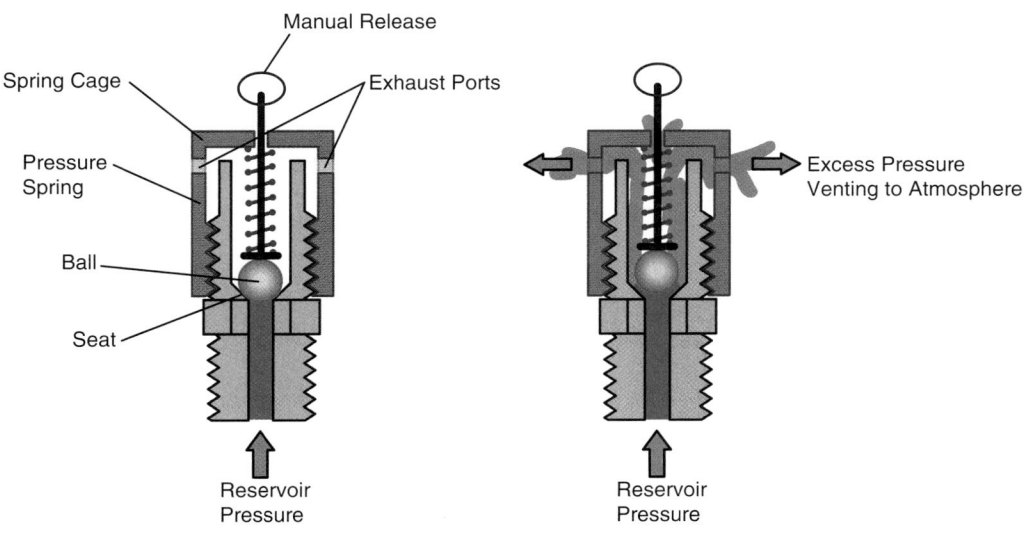

FIGURE 34-18 An air reservoir pressure relief safety valve.

Reservoir Air Control Valves

In addition to the safety relief valve, several other important one way check valves are used to protect the air supply system. For example, the wet tank often has a **one-way check valve** located at its inlet to prevent a loss of air from the wet tank through a failed air dryer or compressor supply circuit. Operation of the one-way check valve after the service tank can be checked by opening the drain valve on the wet tank and draining the air pressure. By observing the air pressure gauges in the cab, both the primary and secondary tank pressures should remain at cut-out pressure.

Quick-connect air fittings, such as the ones shown in **FIGURE 34-19**, are now commonly used to connect air lines to reservoirs and valves. These fitting are a "push-to-seal" type connecter. Simply inserting the line into the fitting and pushing automatically seals the line. Disconnecting the fitting involves pushing the line into the fitting slightly while pushing a sliding collar around the fitting. When the collar is pushed in, the line can be pulled to release the line.

Pressure Protection Valves

Pressure protection valves, such as the one illustrated in **FIGURE 34-20**, are normally closed, pressure-sensitive air control valves. When air is shared between two reservoirs or an auxiliary air circuit, such as the air suspension or even the air horn circuit, the valve flows air only above the closing setting of the valve. A typical valve setting is 70 to 85 psi (483 to 586 kPa). This means that, until reservoir pressure is above the valve setting, no air flows to the circuit or air accessory.

Pressure protection valves can be used in many different applications but are typically used to protect or isolate one reservoir from another. If an air accessory is rapidly losing air, or the driver is using the horn for too long, such as in a fire truck application, the remaining air reservoir pressure is protected from loss of pressure since the accessory air supply is cut off. They do this by closing automatically at a preset pressure. The valve is also commonly used to delay the filling of auxiliary reservoirs until a preset pressure is achieved in the primary or secondary air reservoirs. Reservoir pressure can then build faster to release the park brakes. Air-operated accessories that are not part of the air brake system must use a pressure protection valve to prevent a loss of air from affecting the braking system.

Drain Valves

Each reservoir must be equipped with a drain valve, such as the one shown in **FIGURE 34-21**, to remove water and oil that may contaminate supply system air. The tanks should be drained regularly between 30 and 90 days. **Automatic drain valves**

FIGURE 34-19 Quick connect fittings (circled).

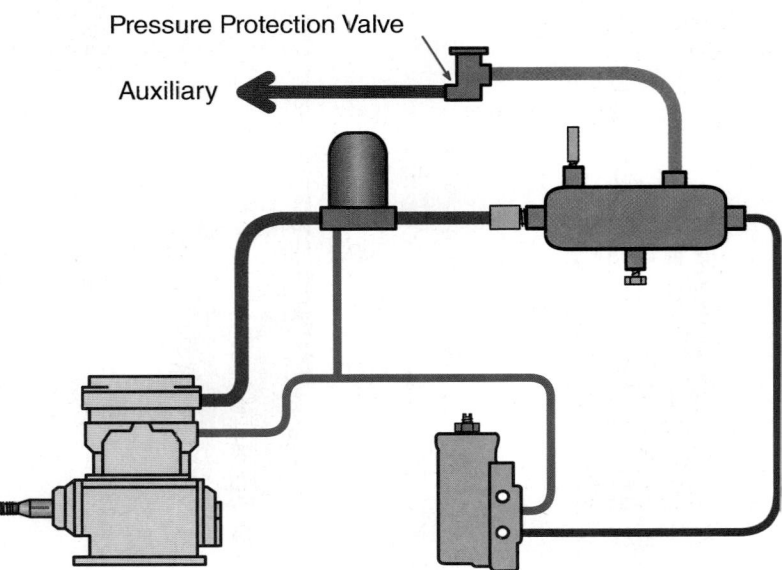

FIGURE 34-20 Pressure protection valves are normally closed pressure sensitive air control valves. These valves are typically used to protect or isolate one reservoir from another if an air leak occurs.

are also used to drain sludge-like residues as they accumulate. As illustrated in **FIGURE 34-22**, a typical automatic drain valve purges sludge every time the tank pressure rises and falls. An inlet valve connected to the sump of an automatic drain valve opens when reservoir pressure is low. This allows any contaminants to drain into the valve. Sludge drains into the valve until governor cut-out pressure is reached. When reservoir pressure drops 2 psi (14 kPa), an exhaust valve in the drain valve opens

FIGURE 34-21 Reservoir drain valve.

due to a slight pressure differential between the upper and lower surfaces of the valve's diaphragm. The pressure drop in the reservoir causes the sludge accumulated in the valve sump to drain. The length of time the exhaust valve remains open, and the amount of sludge purged from the reservoir, depends on the air pressure in the sump when the drains intake valve closes, and how frequently the air pressure in the reservoir changes.

Air Dryers

Air dryers are like an in-line filtration system used to remove air contaminants passed by the air compressor. Water and oil droplets discharged from the compressor can form sludge that fouls valves, blocks lines, and generally interferes with the operation of the air delivery system. Furthermore, in winter temperatures, moisture freezes and blocks proper airflow through lines and valves.

To prolong the service life of the air brake system and reduce maintenance costs, systems generally include an air dryer. The air dryer provides clean, dry air to the components of the brake system. Daily draining of the reservoirs using manually operated drain valves can usually be eliminated when using air dryers.

Air dryers use a replaceable desiccant cartridge to trap oil and water discharged from the compressor by a process known as **adsorption**. The dryer **desiccant** is made up of tiny silica beads that are a tough granular material capable of adsorbing water and oil into their surface. Adsorption means that the water

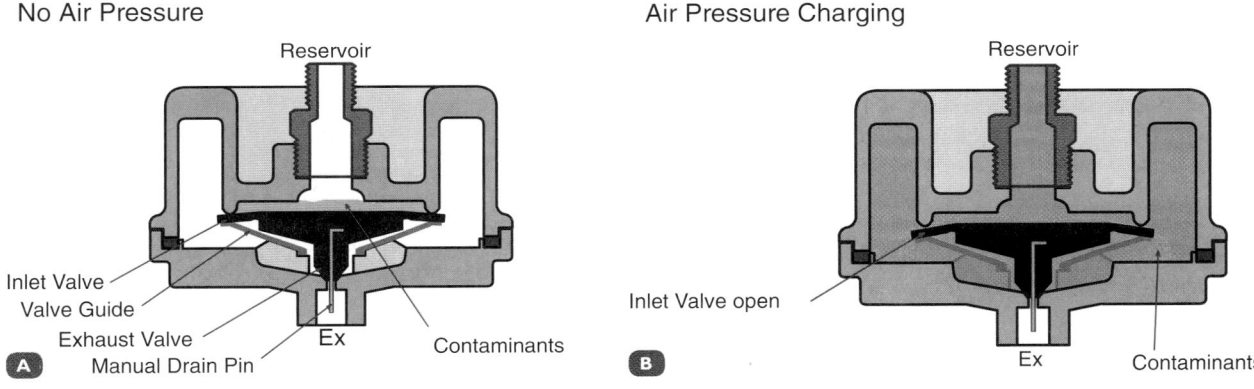

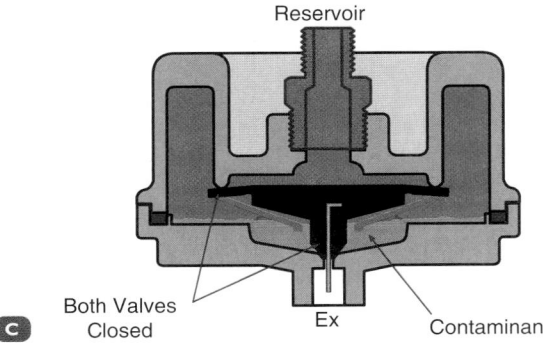

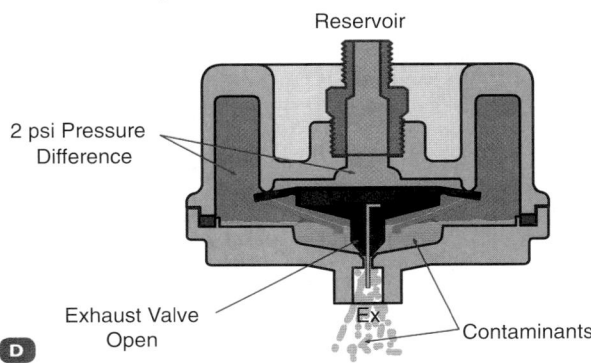

FIGURE 34-22 Automatic drain valve operation. **A.** No air pressure in reservoir. **B.** When reservoir pressure builds, contaminants increase. **C.** At cut-out pressure, inlet and exhaust valves are closed. **D.** A 2 psi (14 kPa) pressure decrease drains the valve.

and oil basically sticks to the surface of the beads. **FIGURE 34-23** shows the millions of beads that make up a desiccant cartridge and give the air dryer enormous adsorption capabilities.

Most oil droplets are first removed by the metal oil separator as the air passes into the air dryer. As shown in **FIGURE 34-24**, metal fibers trap oil even more effectively than desiccant. After entering the dryer, air passes through the desiccant before moving into the service reservoir. Water and any remaining oil stick to the desiccant beads as air passes through the desiccant.

Air Dryer Charge and Purge Cycle

Air enters the dryer during the charge cycle when the compressor is loading. In its base, the dryer contains a **purge valve**. An air signal line connects the governor's unloader port to the dryer's purge valve. During this charging period, the purge valve is closed. When the compressor unloads, the dryer purge valve opens and causes the air volume trapped in the dryer to blast out the bottom of the dryer. The air carries oil and water out with it. The burst of air from the dryer lasts just a few seconds but indicates the finish of a **purge cycle**. Air may take as long as 30 seconds to completely drain from the desiccant.

The turbo cut-off valve, which is often integrated into the dryer inlet port, closes when the compressor unloads. This action prevents any further entry of air into the dryer from the compressor and prevents a loss of boost pressure from the engine intake manifold into the dryer through the open compressor intake valves unload. A check valve at the air dryer's outlet air line prevents any reservoir air from leaking back into the dryer after it is purged. The air dryer charge cycle is illustrated in **FIGURE 34-25** and the purge cycle in **FIGURE 34-26**.

FIGURE 34-23 **A.** Desiccant in an air dryer. **B.** Purge valve.

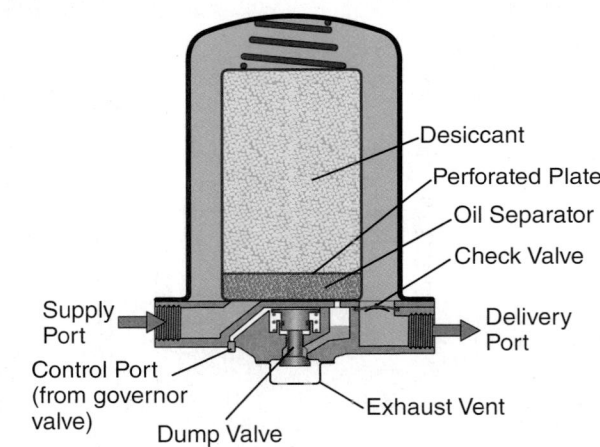

FIGURE 34-25 Air dryer charging cycle.

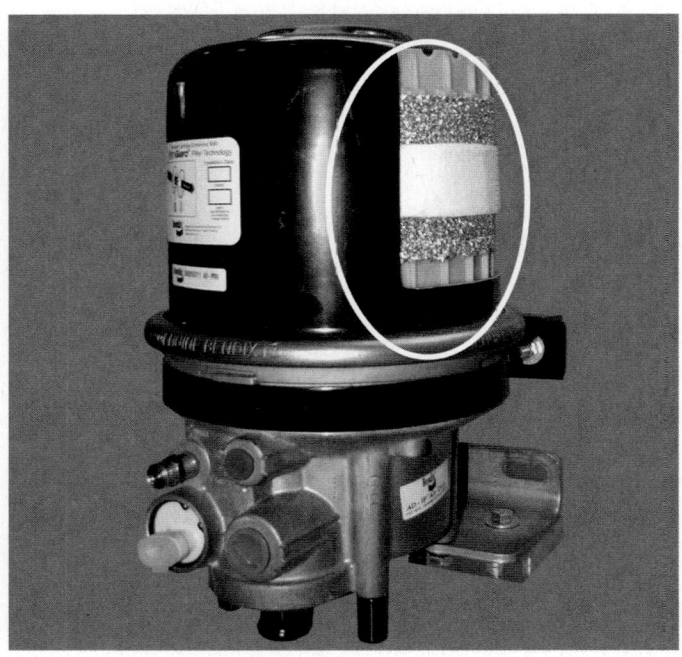

FIGURE 34-24 Air dryer with oil separator (indicated).

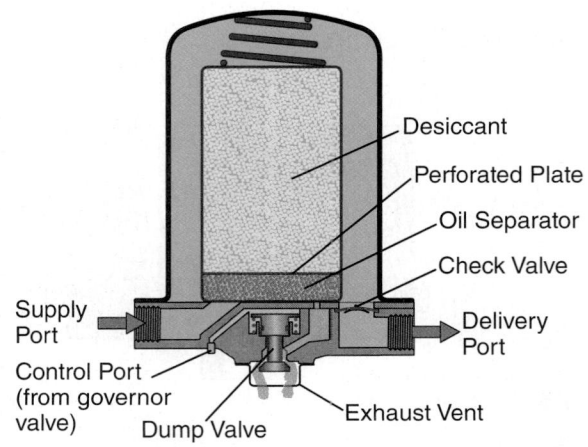

FIGURE 34-26 Air dryer purging cycle.

Since moisture passes by the purge valve before exhausting out of the dryer, the purge valve can potentially freeze open in cold weather. If this happens, an open purge valve does not allow the air system pressure to build. Air simply passes directly out of the purge valve. To prevent this freezing, a thermostatically controlled electric heating element is embedded in the air dryer housing. Heating elements and other parts should be replaced during rebuild procedures. Overhaul kits containing purge valves, electric heaters, thermostats, and other components are available for overhaul.

▶ TECHNICIAN TIP

Most air dryers today use easy-to-replace, spin-on replaceable desiccant cartridges. It is important to replace cartridges at recommended service intervals and whenever an air compressor has failed. A slow air build-up may also be due to air flow restriction caused by contamination inside the dryer desiccant. For safety reasons, always completely drain air from the vehicle's air brake system, since cartridges can suddenly "blow-off" the dryer housing when removed for service. Also, slowly disconnect the air lines and "wiggle" fittings before the last few threads are loosened to release any trapped air.

SAFETY TIP

One-way check valves between the service tank, air dryer, and even the air compressor, allow air pressure to remain in the dryer connecting lines, even after draining all air reservoirs. Use caution when disconnecting these lines to minimize the hazard of whipping lines and blasts of air pressure. Lines should be slowly loosened and allowed to drain before completely disconnecting. Also, make sure the purge valve is in the unloaded position before removing the cartridge.

Advanced Air Dryer Technologies

Along with every other vehicle system, air dryers have evolved technologically to improve fuel economy, reduce emissions, add new features, or simplify air system design and operation.

One air dryer design by Bendix integrates the spin-on desiccant cartridge, turbocharger cut-off valve, governor, and four pressure-protection valves into a single component. The **Air Dryer Integrated System (AD-IS)** dryer by Bendix, shown in **FIGURE 34-27**, works with the air supply system to also isolate air brake reservoir circuits against complete pressure failures.

Since every reservoir is supplied through the dryer, pressure protection valves set to 70 psi (483 kPa) automatically close to isolate a reservoir if pressure falls below that level. Even if all brake circuits fail, the dryer maintains at least 100 psi (689 kPa) in one reservoir. That minimum level of pressure allows the vehicle to have some limited braking ability while being moved in an emergency. Without this reservoir protection feature, a loss of air pressure in a single tank could potentially provide only a few limited brake applications before the emergency/park brakes applied. **FIGURE 34-28** illustrates this process in the AD-IS air dryer.

FIGURE 34-27 Bendix AD-IS air dryer.

The **Dryer Integrated Module (DRM)** is another version of the AD-IS dryer. As **FIGURE 34-29** illustrates, the DRM features an additional small supplemental reservoir to provide additional purge volume to the dryer desiccant cartridge. Because the desiccant cartridge itself typically does not have adequate purge volume, dried air in the supplemental reservoir is used to supply additional air to purge more moisture and contaminants from the dryer.

The Bendix **Electronic Air Control (EAC)**, shown in **FIGURE 34-30**, is an air supply system consisting of an electronically controlled air compressor clutch, air dryer, unloader valve, and multiple air circuit protection controls. The EAC is designed to help manufacturers meet the 2016 Greenhouse Gas Emission Standards by optimizing when the air compressor engages and disengages. The compressor clutch operates much like an on/off fan clutch except that the system collects data from a variety of vehicle sensors to calculate the optimum timing for compressor loading and unloading events. The system is also connected to the vehicle's controller area network (CAN) backbone, which provides input to software embedded into a control module.

The software contains algorithms (mathematical formulas used to solve problems) that ensure the compressor completely disengages from the engine when no air is required. This means that fuel is not wasted even due to the slight frictional losses from reciprocating pistons while unloaded.

One example of a strategy to reduce energy consumption is to have the compressor load during vehicle-engine deceleration. In the EAC, the mechanical governor is replaced with electronic control of an unloader valve, so compressor cycling is precisely controlled. Consequently, the frequency of overall compressor cycling drops. That reduction extends compressor life and generates up to 3% in fuel savings. Programmability of the system enables customized air pressure control and distributions based on customer priorities and information collected over the vehicle CAN.

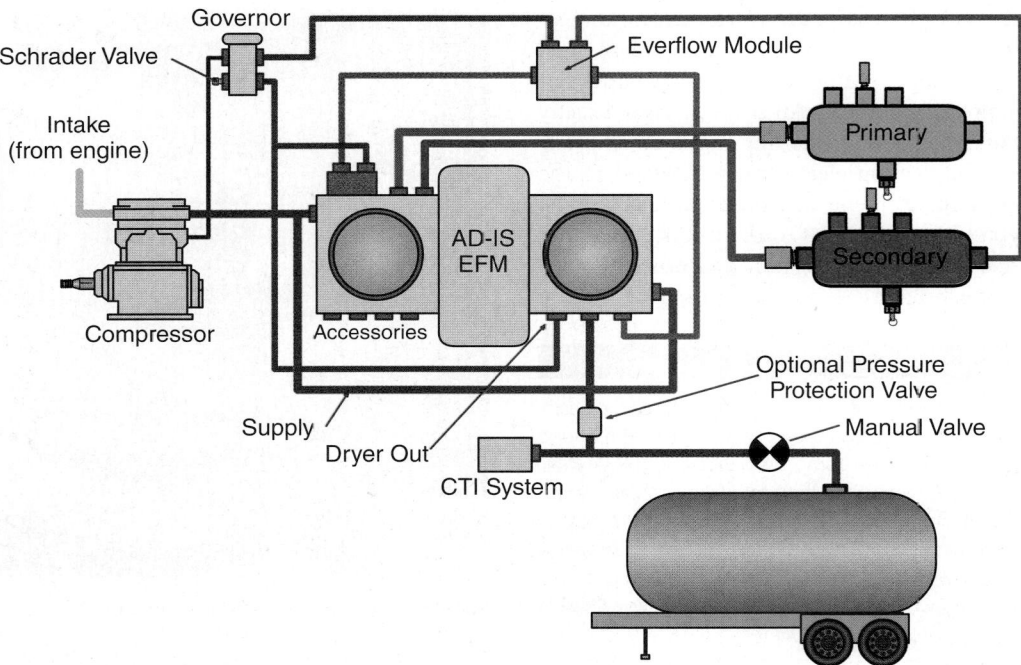

FIGURE 34-28 Schematic view of the Bendix AD-IS air dryer.

Air Dryer (during charging cycle)

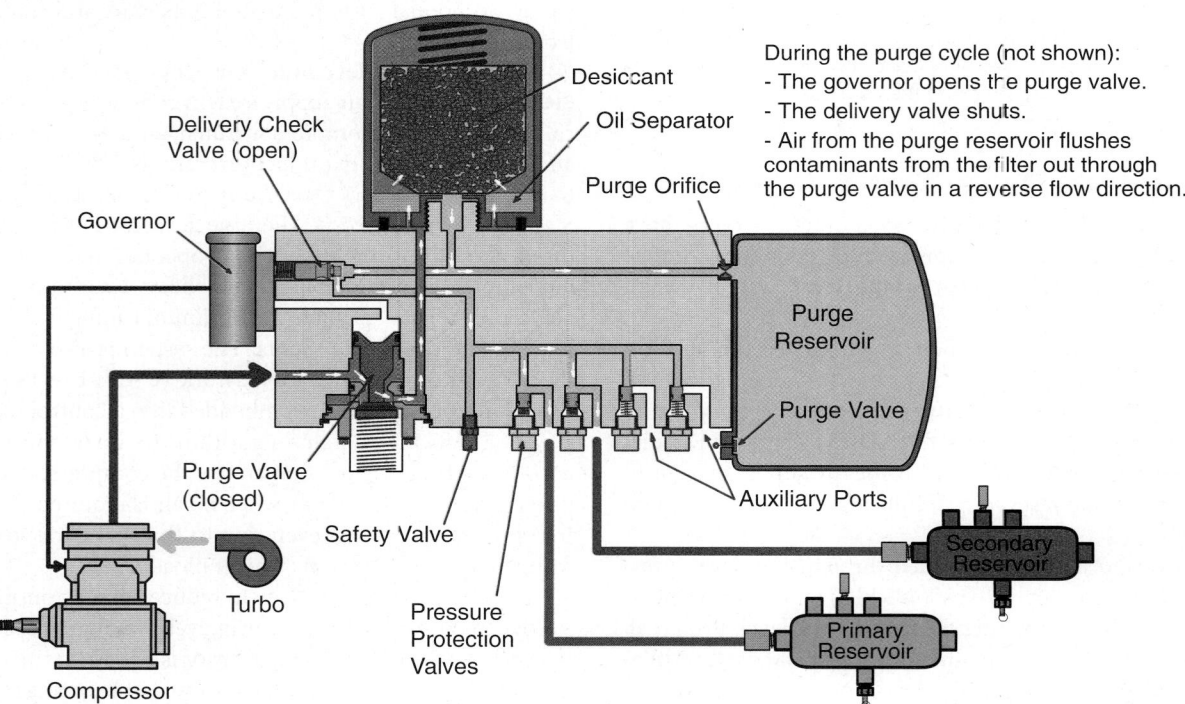

During the purge cycle (not shown):
- The governor opens the purge valve.
- The delivery valve shuts.
- Air from the purge reservoir flushes contaminants from the filter out through the purge valve in a reverse flow direction.

FIGURE 34-29 Schematic of operation of an AD-IS air dryer with a Dryer Integrated Module (DRM) during charge and purge cycles. Note the role of the integrated air reservoir used to purge the compact desiccant cartridge.

Another Bendix system called the Bendix **Pneumatic Booster System (PBS) Injection Booster**, shown in **FIGURE 34-31**, uses an air-injection booster with the EAC dryer and compressor to reduce emissions and improve fuel economy. The Bendix PBS works by injecting a blast of air into the intake manifold during the turbo lag period. The extra air supplements turbocharger boost pressure, which enhances combustion efficiency, thereby reducing both emissions and fuel consumption. When the EAC dryer, air compressor with on/off clutch, and the PBS air-injection booster system are used together, Bendix claims that a vehicle achieves up to an 8% reduction in fuel consumption.

▶ **TECHNICIAN TIP**

A leaking air dryer purge valve allows air to leak from the unloader port of the governor, causing frequent compressor cycling and air dryer purging. Likewise, a leaking air signal line from the air reservoir to the governor, a leaking governor gasket, or leaking unloader valves in the air compressor causes frequent purging of the dryer. Defective O-rings sealing unloader valves in the compressor's cylinder head can also leak air from the unloader port, resulting in unnecessary compressor cycling. Be sure to perform complete and comprehensive diagnostic checks recommending any parts replacement when these complaints are presented.

FIGURE 34-30 The control unit and air dryer of a Bendix Electronic Air Control (EAC) air supply system.

FIGURE 34-31 The Bendix Electronic Air System (EAS) also uses an air-injection booster with the EAC dryer and an on/off compressor to reduce emissions and improve fuel economy.

Diagnosing Problems in the Air Supply System

Troubleshooting problems in the air supply system begins with the dash gauges. Separate pressure gauges located in the driver's view in the instrument panel are required to indicate primary and secondary tank pressures. As **FIGURE 34-32** shows, the gauges are typically color-coded and labeled to distinguish pressure in the two circuits. An application air pressure gauge is sometimes located in the dash to measure air pressure applied to the service brake chambers. Pressure sensors in the reservoirs also allow monitoring of system pressure using service software.

Another important item to monitor is the low-pressure switch, such as the one in **FIGURE 34-33**. Both the primary and

FIGURE 34-32 Two dash gauges are required by FMVSS 121 standards to indicate pressure in the primary and secondary air reservoirs.

FIGURE 34-33 The low-pressure warning switch is used to operate a buzzer and warning light when air pressure is too low—typically less than 65 psi (448 kPa).

secondary tanks use a low-pressure switch to operate a low air pressure warning system. If either tank pressure falls below 65 psi (586 kPa), the low-pressure switch illuminates a warning light in the driver's view and causes an audible alarm to sound.

Not all potential problems can be identified from the dashboard. For example, because oil is carried over from the air compressor and intake air has moisture, it is normal to have accumulations of oil in the reservoir tanks. To determine if the amount of oil is excessive, two oil drain tests can be performed.

The first test involves the use of a piece of paper held over the air inlet port. When the compressor is loaded, some oil droplets spit out onto the paper. More than four or five droplets during a loading cycle of the compressor indicate an abnormal oil discharge. The likely cause is worn-out cylinders and worn or broken piston rings.

A second test involves draining and measuring the quantity of oil accumulated in an air reservoir, then comparing the quantity of oil accumulated in the reservoir at a later service interval. After collecting the oil drained from the wet tank reservoir in a bottle, the amount of oil is compared against a calibrated oil level marked on the bottle. Depending on hours in service, there is a specific corresponding quantity of oil that is considered normal. Excessive accumulations are likely caused by a defective air compressor.

To inspect air supply system performance, follow the steps in **SKILL DRILL 34-2**.

Components of Air Delivery and Control Systems

LO 34-4 Identify and describe the purpose, construction, and operation of components used by the air delivery and control systems.

In addition to having an effective air supply system, the air brakes must also have a reliable air delivery system. The delivery system transmits controlled air pressure from the reservoirs to the brake chambers. A typical system is illustrated in **FIGURE 34-34** and consists of:

- A foot-operated brake valve and often an additional hand-operated trailer service brake control valve
- Relay valves that increase the speed and volume of air supplied to brake chambers
- Anti-compounding system design to prevent both the service brakes and the parking brakes being applied at the same time
- Proportioning valves to adjust braking force when a tractor is not pulling a trailer
- Quick-release valves to assist in releasing the brakes quickly
- Push-pull hand-operated valves for parking using the spring brakes and trailer air supply

---

SKILL DRILL 34-2 Inspecting Air Supply System Performance

1. Drain all the air reservoirs using the manual drain valve located on each air reservoir—wet, primary, and secondary tanks. Then close the reservoir drain valves.
2. Verify the low-pressure warning buzzer and light are operating. Do this by switching the ignition key to the "on" position with the engine off (KOEO).

3. Measure the air pressure build-time. Start the engine and bring the engine to high idle, which is its maximum no-load rpm. Record the following observations while building air pressure to cut-out pressure when the compressor unloads:
   - The air pressure when the warning light and buzzer shut-off.
   - The time it takes the air pressure to build between 85 psi (586 kPa) and 100 psi (689 kPa).
   - The compressor unloading or cut-out pressure.
   - Air pressure should reach no less than approximately 60 psi (414 kPa) before the buzzer and light are activated.
   - The 85 to 100 psi (586 to 689 kPa) build time should be less than 25 seconds at governed engine rpm. If the build-up time exceeds 45 seconds, the system must be taken out of service.
4. Validate the compressor unloading cut-out pressure by recording the system pressure on both the primary and secondary reservoir dash gauges. The compressor should cut-out at between 120 and 135 psi (827 and 931 kPa).
5. Validate the compressor cut-in pressure. Do this by pumping the service brakes to deplete the primary and secondary supply reservoirs. Listen for the compressor to begin loading and or observe the dash gauges to record cut-in pressure. The difference between cut-in and cut-out pressure should be 25 psi (172 kPa) or less. Compare your observations to the manufacturer's specifications.

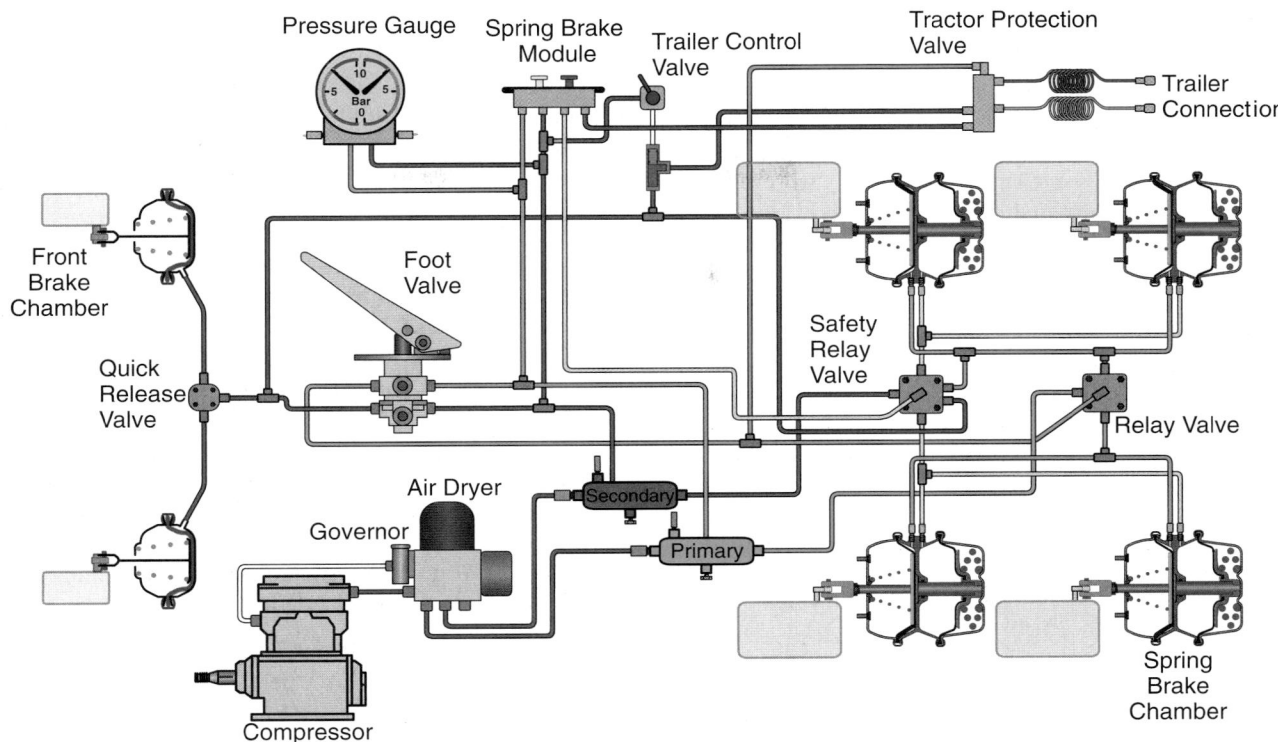

FIGURE 34-34 A simplified schematic of a typical air brake circuit for a tandem-axle tractor.

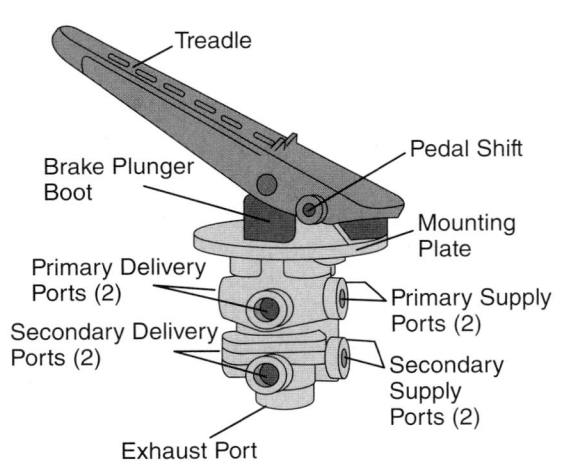

FIGURE 34-35 Treadle and brake application valve.

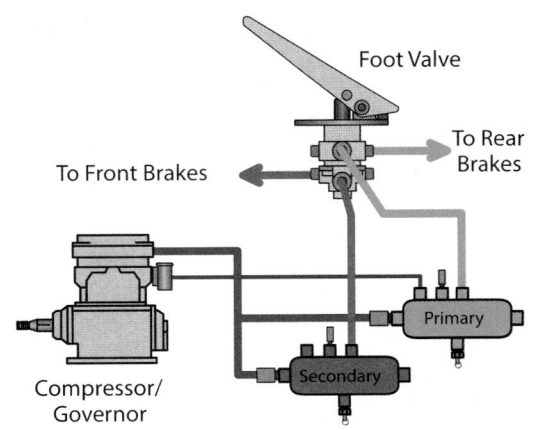

FIGURE 34-36 The foot valve includes a treadle, or pedals, operated by the driver to control braking. Primary and secondary supply and delivery lines connect to the valve.

Foot Valves

The **foot (treadle) valve**, like that illustrated in **FIGURE 34-35**, is the center of the delivery system. It distributes air to the brake chambers and controls the air pressure supplied for braking. When the operator depresses the brake pedal, the foot valve delivers air pressure proportional to pedal travel. That means the further down the operator pushes the foot valve, the more air pressure is delivered to the brake chambers. Since all air brake vehicles use dual circuits, there are two foot valves integrated into a single housing—one each for the primary and secondary circuits.

Two sets of ports corresponding to the primary and secondary circuits are incorporated into the foot valve. The first set includes a supply port from each of the primary and secondary air reservoirs. The second set includes two delivery ports for the primary and secondary air circuits. **FIGURE 34-36** shows how a foot valve is connected to the supply and delivery systems.

Foot Valve Construction

The top part of the foot valve always contains the primary circuit control valve. The bottom part always contains the secondary control circuit. This division is done for safety reasons. The primary circuit should activate sooner than the secondary to time the brake application events from the rear of the vehicle and then sequentially on forward axles. Also, if the primary circuit fails, pressure needs to be mechanically transferred to the secondary circuit's control plunger, rather than through air pressure. Brake pedal "feel" is supplied by either a rubber or metal spring outside the valve, next to the primary piston. Spring tension increases the harder the pedal is pushed.

Foot valves can be either floor-mounted or suspended to the firewall or bulkhead of the cab. **FIGURE 34-37** shows a foot valve suspended from the firewall. The foot valve is spring-loaded. Therefore, the operator generally feels only the spring pressure—not the pressure of the brake application as in a hydraulic brake system. Depending on the application—transit

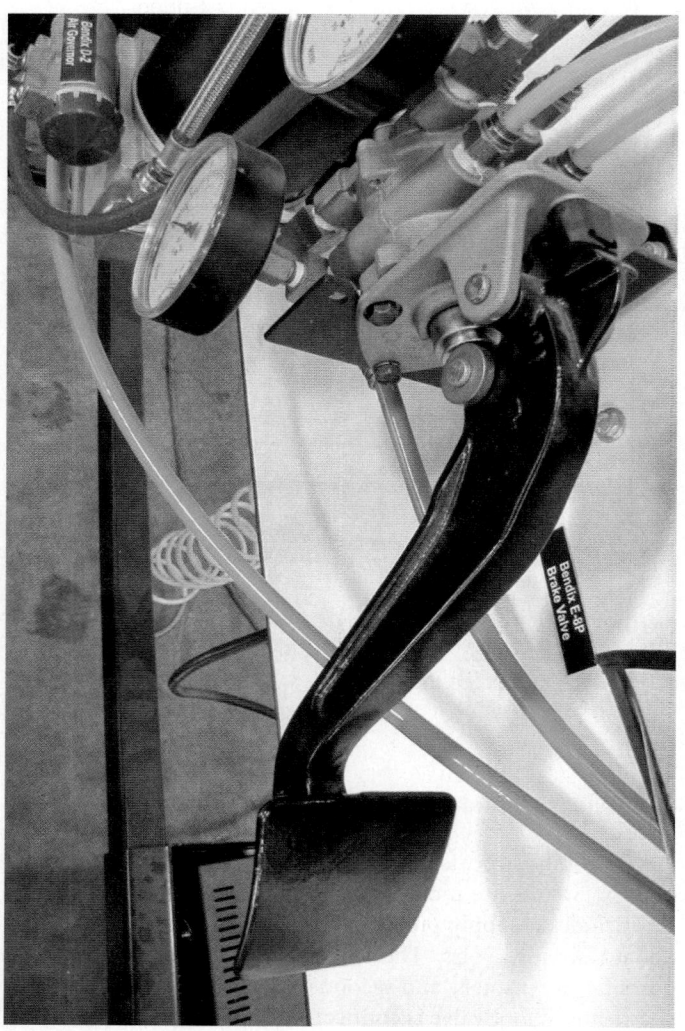

FIGURE 34-37 Foot valve designed to be mounted to the firewall.

bus or on-highway truck—the valves are designed to be sensitive to pedal travel. Valves for transit applications use more pedal travel to supply the same pressure than truck valves do. More pedal travel in a bus allows the operator to apply the brakes even more gradually for smoother and less-sensitive brake application. Smooth braking protects passengers from abrupt stops.

Foot valves are self-balancing or **pressure-balanced** devices. This concept, which applies to many brake valves, is important to understand. Pressure-balancing refers to the way regulation of air delivery pressure takes place. In practice, pressure-balanced foot valves continuously supply and regulate the brake application air pressure at a constant pressure to maintain consistent brake application force. Even if a small leak occurs in the signal air circuit leaving the valve during a brake application, the foot valve maintains application pressure, even as the amount of air volume leaving the valve increases because of the leak.

It's also worthwhile to note that maximum brake application pressure can be no higher than the system reservoir pressure. When the foot valve is released, the brake application is released.

A foot valve can also incorporate electrical switches for the automatic transmission retarder system. Retarders are used to slow forward motion of the vehicle above 5 mph (8 kph). Most retarders redirect the flow of hydraulic fluid through the torque converter. Retarders also increase drive-line resistance using a small internal brake in the output section of the transmission. Since retarders are typically electrically activated, specialized foot valves can properly sequence the operation of several internal electrical switches to control retarder operation, with each stage increasing drive-line resistance.

Foot Valve Operation

Operating the foot valve involves applying the brakes, either through the primary or secondary circuit. In normal primary circuit operation, when the foot valve is depressed, a plunger in the top of the valve pushes on a spring with graduating tension that provides "brake feel" to the driver. The graduated spring, in turn, pushes against the primary circuit piston, which closes an exhaust valve. At the same time the exhaust valve closes, the primary circuit air inlet valve is opened and routes primary air supply to flow out the primary circuit delivery port. This process is illustrated in **FIGURE 34-38**. Pushing on the brake treadle valve compresses the graduating spring and transmits pedal force to the primary piston. An air bleed passageway from the delivery side of the primary valve supplies air pressure to push against the secondary piston.

A normal secondary circuit operation involves opening its air inlet valve when the secondary piston is moved. Doing so enables air to pass through a calibrated air bleed passage and pressurize the piston cavity above the secondary piston. As air pressure moves the secondary piston, which, like the primary circuit, closes an exhaust valve, the secondary air inlet valve is simultaneously opened. Secondary air flows out of the secondary delivery port. Because only a small volume of air is required

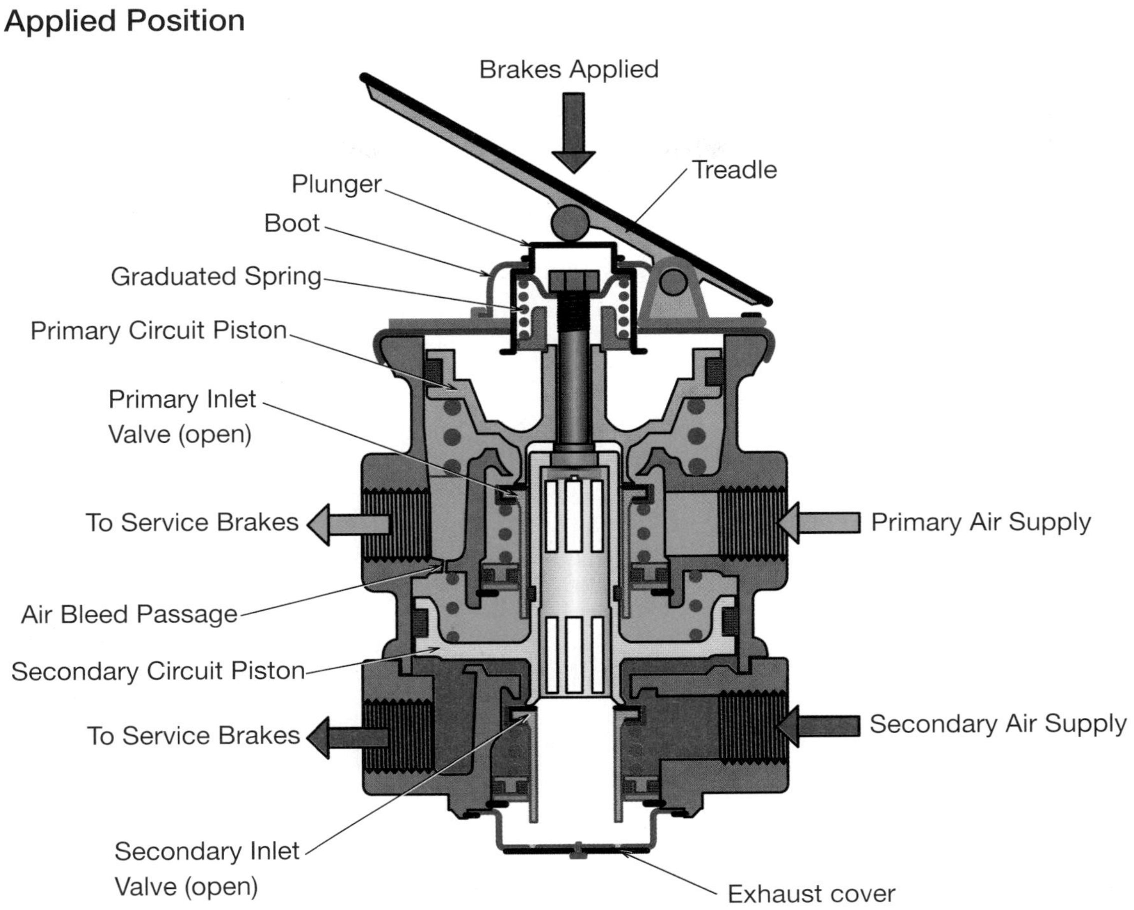

Applied Position

FIGURE 34-38 Applying the foot valve in normal operation.

to move the secondary piston, movement of the secondary piston takes place almost simultaneously with the primary circuit portion.

When the delivery pressure for the primary circuit acting below the piston is balanced equally with the mechanical force acting on the brake pedal, the delivery air pressure returns the primary piston to a position that closes the air inlet valve. This action stops the flow of air into the primary circuit and delivery pressure stabilizes. As illustrated in **FIGURE 34-39**, the exhaust valve remains closed and no air is released through the exhaust port. The piston moves again to open the inlet air valve if the pressure differential between the delivery pressure and foot valve pressure changes. This means that if air pressure drops at the delivery port, unbalanced spring tension above the piston pushes against the piston to open the air inlet valve and supplies more air to the delivery port to pressure compensate the delivery port—signal line pressure. If the foot valve is fully depressed, both the primary and secondary inlet valves remain open and full reservoir pressure is delivered to the brake chambers.

Air leaves the foot valve through a narrow-diameter supply line, called the signal line. Signal line pressure is proportional to the force the driver uses to push against the foot valve. Next the air travels to a relay valve that supplies air to brake chambers at the wheel ends. The relay valve is also **pressure-compensating** to ensure air pressure from the relay valves delivery ports is proportional only to the air signal line pressure, which is proportional to pedal travel.

When the brake pedal is released, as illustrated in **FIGURE 34-40**, the mechanical forces acting on both the primary and secondary pistons is removed. That is, releasing the brake pedal produces a pressure imbalance on both the primary and secondary circuit inlet and exhaust valves. Both primary and secondary circuit pistons are forced upwards by both air and spring pressure. This action opens the exhaust valves, allowing all delivery line pressure to vent through the exhaust valve.

Troubleshooting Problems with the Foot Valve

Two common problems occur with the foot valve. The first is a loss of air pressure in the primary or secondary circuit. The second relates to an overly sensitive switch at the delivery port that activates the stop lights.

Balanced Position

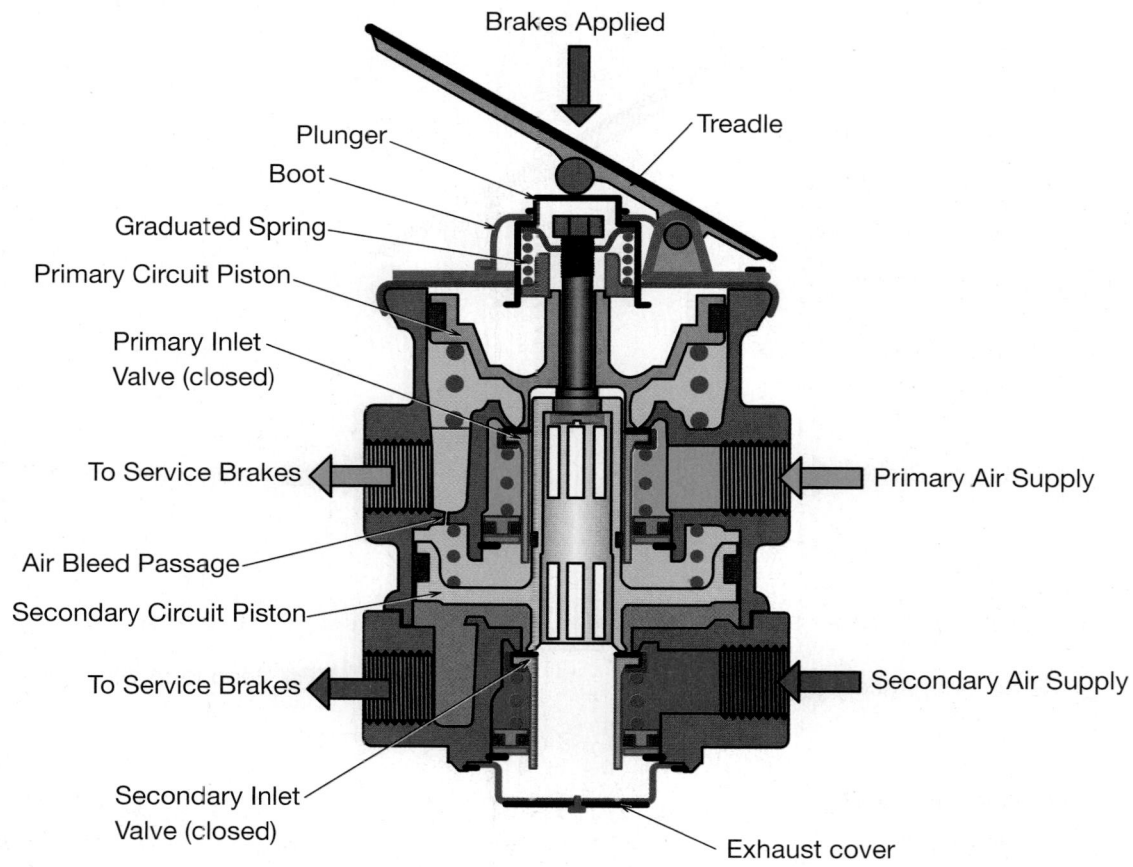

FIGURE 34-39 The foot valve in the balanced position.

In the case of loss of air pressure, the foot valve can still operate. That is true whether air pressure is lost in the primary or secondary circuit. If air is lost in the secondary circuit, the primary circuit still functions, but without the air-relay effect against the secondary piston. If air is lost in the primary circuit, the pedal can mechanically push the primary piston directly into the secondary piston to operate the secondary circuit. This means when primary air pressure is lost, mechanical, rather than air pressure, moves the secondary piston downwards.

Sometimes a pressure-sensitive electrical switch located at the delivery port activates the stop lights. The switch closes at less than 0.5 psi (3.4 kPa) pressure. This switch is also often located on the tractor protection valve. When a double check valve is used to supply pressure from either primary or secondary circuits, the stop light switch can be used to detect air pressure from either brake circuit. As shown in **FIGURE 34-41**, the switch is mounted at the outlet of a double check valve. Pressure from either circuit flows to the outlet port of the valve and switches the stop lights on and off.

To inspect and test the brake treadle (foot valve), fittings, and mounts, and adjust or replace as needed, follow the steps in **SKILL DRILL 34-3**.

To inspect and test the tractor protection valve and replace as needed, follow the steps in **SKILL DRILL 34-4**.

Relay Valves

Like an electrical relay that uses a small amount of current to switch a larger amount, air relays use the small volume of air from the foot valve delivery port to signal or switch a larger volume of air supplied by the reservoir tanks. A circuit with an air relay is illustrated in **FIGURE 34-42**. Relay valves use a small amount of air volume to control larger volumes of air flow.

Relay valves are critical devices used to speed up the flow and increase the volume of air supplied to brake chambers during brake applications and release. Since the air lines from the foot valve to brake chambers are long, the time it takes to apply and release brakes increases. FMVSS 121 standards require less than 0.040 seconds delay between the application

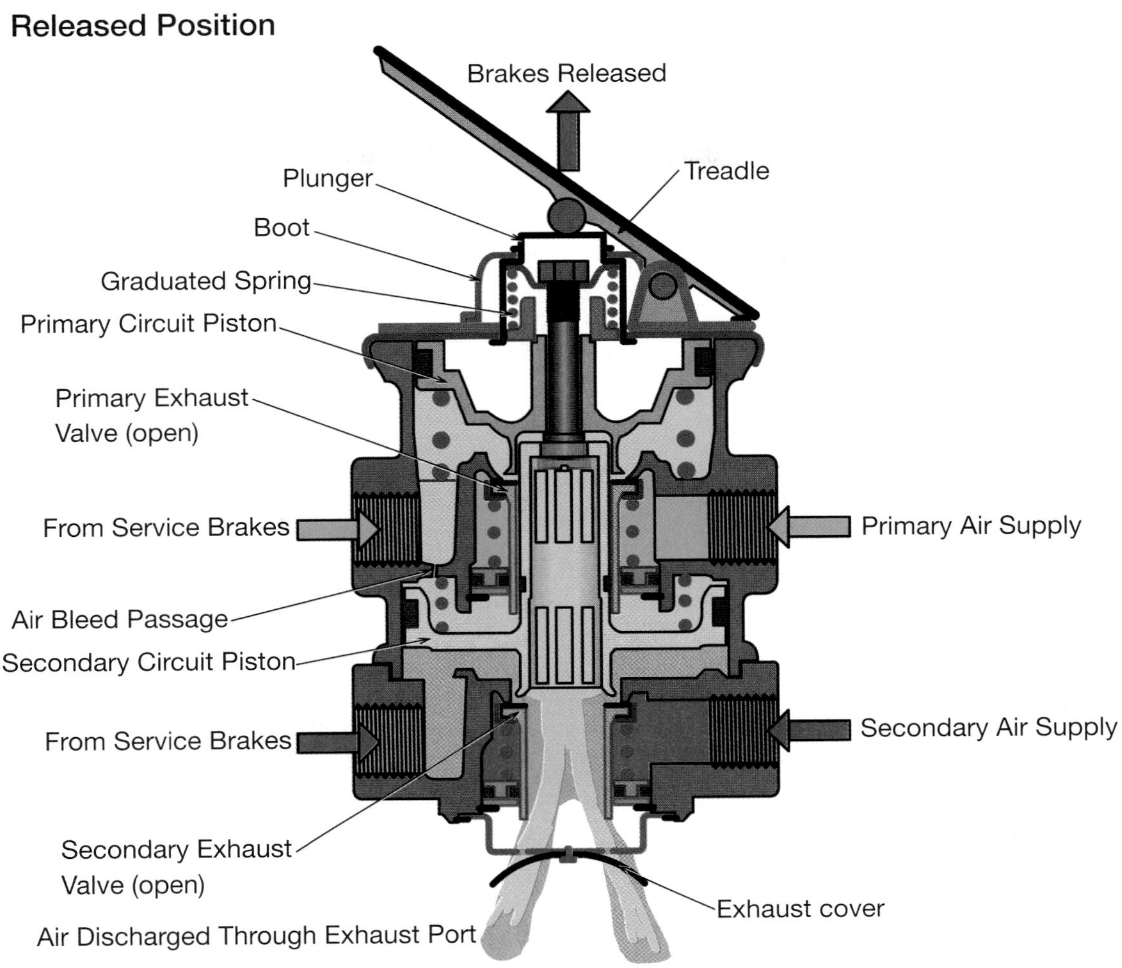

Released Position

Brakes Released

Plunger

Boot

Treadle

Graduated Spring

Primary Circuit Piston

Primary Exhaust
Valve (open)

From Service Brakes

Primary Air Supply

Air Bleed Passage

Secondary Circuit Piston

From Service Brakes

Secondary Air Supply

Secondary Exhaust
Valve (open)

Exhaust cover

Air Discharged Through Exhaust Port

FIGURE 34-40 Releasing the brake pedal.

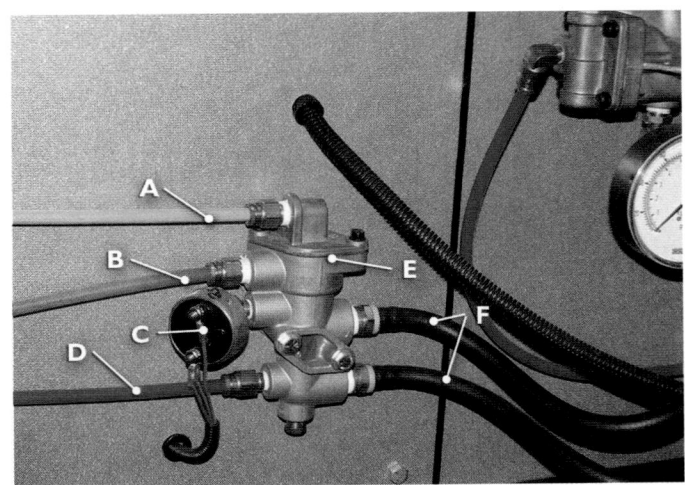

FIGURE 34-41 A pressure-sensitive electrical switch for the stop lights is located at the delivery port of this tractor protection valve. The switch closes at less than 0.5 psi (3.4 kPa) pressure. **A.** Primary circuit. **B.** From-cab trailer valve. **C.** Stop light switch. **D.** Secondary circuit. **E.** Tractor protection valve. **F.** To-trailer air lines.

of the foot valve and movement at the brake chambers. When brakes are released, the time required for draining air from the chambers and lines through the exhaust port of the foot valve take even longer than a brake application. To speed up brake application and release, relay valves are used for the rear brakes, and a quick-release valve is used for the front brakes. A single relay valve, like the one shown in **FIGURE 34-43**, usually supplies tandem rear axles.

The relay valve supplies the same air pressure to the brake chambers provided by the signal line from the foot valve delivery port. It can speed up application for several reasons. First, signal lines from the foot valve use narrow diameter lines to connect the foot valve to the relay valve. Because the line has a low volume, it can pressurize quickly. By quickly pressurizing the signal line, the relay valve can transmit a pressure signal to the relay valve in less time. Likewise, an exhaust valve built into the relay valve can also drain air from the brake chambers, rather than having it return and drain out the exhaust port of the foot valve.

SKILL DRILL 34-3 Inspecting and Testing the Brake Treadle (Foot) Valve, Fittings, and Mounts; Adjusting or Replacing as Needed

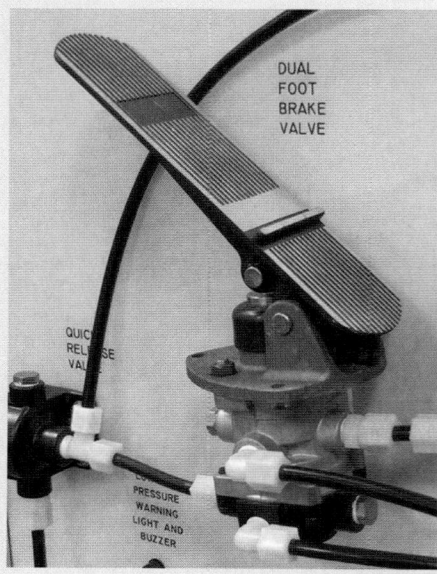

1. Clean dirt, gravel, and other foreign material from the base of the brake pedal. Verify any floormats or loose articles in the cab do not interfere with the valve operation.
2. Inspect the pedal clevis pin, roller, and pedal to verify the pedal moves freely and is not seized or binding.
3. Connect air pressure test gauges to the primary and secondary delivery ports or signal lines from the foot valve.
4. Build air primary and secondary reservoir pressure to 120 psi (830 kPa).
5. Depress the pedal to several graduated positions with increasing pedal force while observing the pressure on the test gauges. Confirm that delivery pressure varies equally from primary and secondary ports and proportionately with the movement of the brake pedal.

6. Fully depress the brake pedal and confirm reservoir pressure and delivery pressure are the same.
7. Release the brake pedal and confirm pressure immediately drops to 0 psi.
8. Spray the exhaust port and body of the valve with a soapy solution, to check for leakage. Make and hold a pressure application of 80 psi (550 kPa) and check the valve's exhaust port, body, and fittings for leaks. Leakage from the exhaust valve is limited to a 1" bubble every three seconds.
9. If the brake valve does not function as described above, or if leakage is excessive, replace as follows:
    a. Drain all the air reservoirs.
    b. Tag the brake valve air supply and delivery lines for assembly reference.
    c. Disconnect the air lines from the brake valve and seal them with tape to keep out contaminants.
    d. Note the locations and positions of the double check valves and elbows, then remove them from the brake valve. Clean dirt and old sealant from the threads.
    e. Remove mounting hardware from the valve body and remove the valve from the mounting bracket.
    f. Select a replacement valve using tags on the valve and confirm selection using OEM part numbers.
    g. Apply a small quantity of pipe sealant to the male threads of each fitting, the double check valves and the elbows.
    h. Install the double check valves and elbows in the ports of the brake valves. Attach the brake valve and mounting bracket to the cab wall or floor where the valve is mounted.
    i. Using a light oil, lubricate the brake pedal roller and roller pin.
    j. Install brake pedal; move the pedal as needed to align the hole in the brake pedal and the mounting bracket.
    k. Connect the air lines as previously marked. Tighten the nuts finger-tight. Using a wrench, further tighten the nuts.
10. Start engine, charge up the air system, inspect for air leaks, and verify the brake system is correctly operating during a road test.

SKILL DRILL 34-4 Inspecting and Testing the Tractor Protection Valve; Replacing as Needed

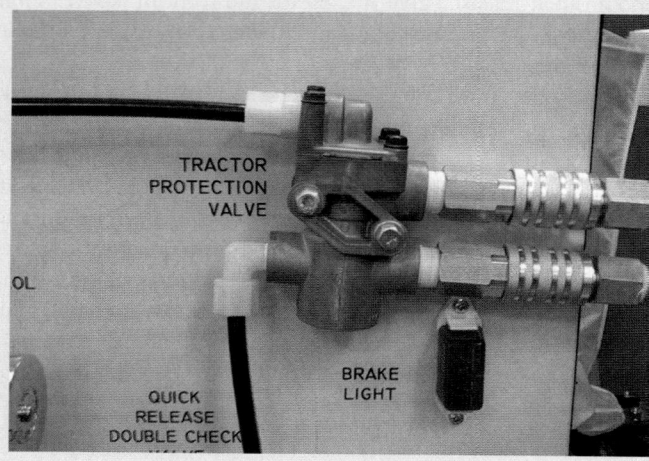

1. To validate the correct operation of the tractor protection valve, which protects the tractor from a loss of air pressure if the trailer loses air pressure or disconnects from the tractor, use the following guidelines.
2. With the tractor and trailer connected, properly chock the tractor and trailer wheels and ensure system pressure is within its normal operating pressure range (between 105 and 135 psi [724 and 931 kPa]).
3. All park and service brakes must be released, and all pull-push dash valves pushed in.
4. Disconnect the red trailer supply line from the tractor to the trailer at the trailer gladhand coupling.
5. Confirm that when the gladhand couplings are disconnected, the trailer air supply from the tractor closes automatically. In most cases the trailer air supply stops almost immediately. In older systems, air continues to leak for a short time and then stop.

SKILL DRILL 34-4 Inspecting and Testing the Tractor Protection Valve; Replacing as Needed (Continued)

6. Listen to confirm and/or observe the automatic application of the trailer spring brakes. The spring brake valve on the trailer should apply the spring brakes automatically as soon as the trailer air supply line is disconnected. If the brakes do not apply, the trailer spring brake valve is defective or air circuits to the valve are not correctly connected.

7. After the trailer air supply line from the tractor is disconnected, confirm there is no air leaking from the supply/emergency gladhand coupler on the trailer back from the trailer. Air leaking from the trailer gladhand coupler indicates that the trailer spring brake control valve is defective.

8. Observe the tractor's dash pressure gauges and record the pressure at which the air stops escaping from the trailer supply line.

9. Confirm that in no instance should air continue to leak from the trailer supply-emergency line from the tractor when either the primary or secondary pressure gauge falls below 45 psi (310 kPa). Failure of the tractor protection valve to close and isolate the tractor air system when pressure drops to below 45 psi (310 kPa) means the valve is defective or the air circuits to the valve are not correctly connected.

10. Disconnect the blue service/control line to the trailer.

11. Apply the service brakes and hold the pedal fully down. With the trailer air supply push-pull valve out, no air should be delivered out of the blue service/control brake hose to the trailer.

12. Push in the trailer air supply valve after the red trailer supply hose is reconnected to the trailer.

13. Reapply the service brakes with the blue service/control hose disconnected. Air should release from the trailer service hose proportional to brake application pressure when the tractor's service brakes are applied.

14. To replace the valve, drain all air reservoirs, disconnect, and remove the trailer hose assemblies from the valve. Disconnect and remove the brake light switches from the tractor protection (TP) valve.

15. Disconnect the tractor service and supply lines. Label the air lines and tape the line ends closed to prevent contaminants entering the lines.

16. Remove the fasteners attaching the valve to the vehicle. Remove the valve.

17. Install new valve on the vehicle and attach it with mounting bolts and tighten.

18. Connect lines and switches to valve as marked and tighten. Ensure all male fittings have Teflon sealant applied to the threads to prevent leakage.

19. Close the drain cocks to the air reservoirs.

20. Start engine and build system air pressure to 120 psi (830 kPa).

21. Retest new valve by using the previous steps.

22. Set parking brakes and remove wheel chocks.

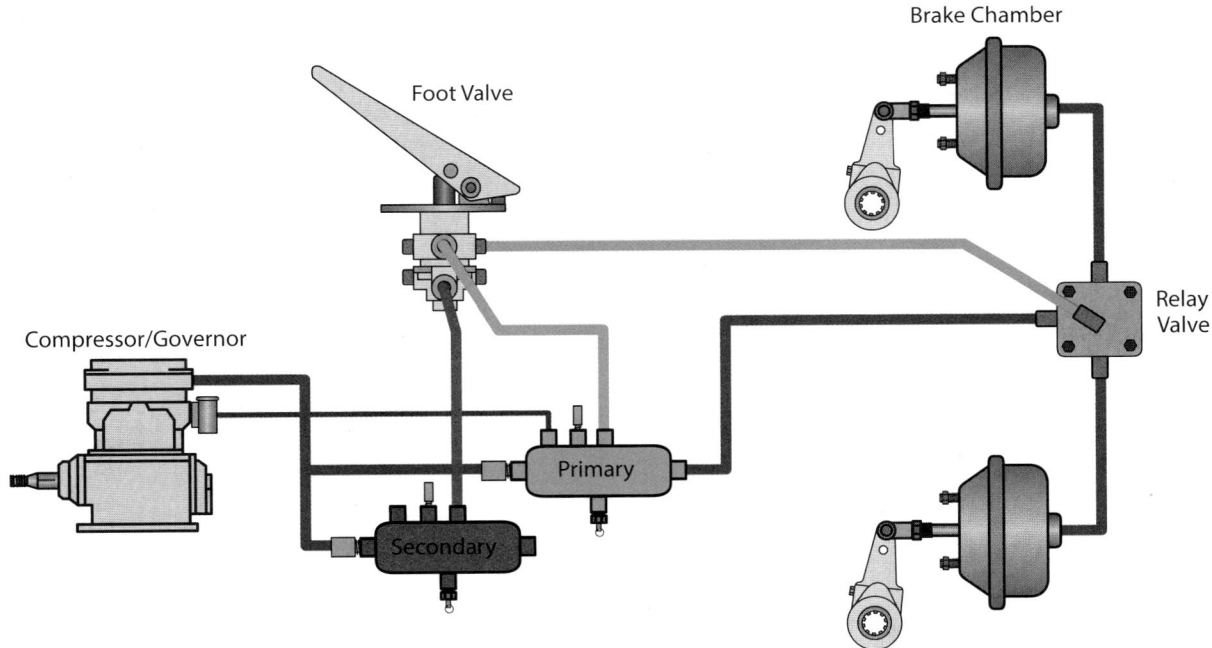

FIGURE 34-42 An air circuit with a relay valve.

A second reason for the speedier delivery is that the relay valve is supplied by a large, high-volume air supply line connected to the air reservoir. The line is typically 5/8" (15.9 mm) or 3/4" (19.1 mm) in comparison to the 1/4" (6.4 mm) signal line from the delivery port on the foot valve. Because four brake chambers commonly require actuation from a single relay valve, the relay valve can supply more air faster than through a distant foot valve filling chambers with a 1/4" (6.4 mm) diameter air line.

Relay Valve Operation–Applying Brakes

Air pressure from the foot valve (signal air) is supplied to a service-control port on the relay valve. Reservoir air pressure arrives at the supply port of the relay valve. Signal air enters a cavity above the relay piston, which pushes the piston down against the spring pressure proportionally to the signal air pressure. This means the relay valve piston moves a distance corresponding to the force applied to the foot valve by the driver. An exhaust valve inside the relay valve seats simultaneously with the piston's downward movement, sealing off an exhaust passageway. At the same time, an air inlet port in the valve opens, so reservoir air supply flows past the open air inlet valve and into the brake chambers.

FIGURE 34-43 Air line connections to a relay valve.

Pressure Compensating Balance

When pressure at the relay valve's outlet or delivery port equals the pressure supplied by the now-open air inlet valve, air pressure beneath the relay piston equals the signal air pressure above the piston. This action causes the piston to lift slightly, which in turn closes the spring-loaded air inlet valve. That action is much like the inlet valve in the foot valve.

If no more air enters the cavity above the piston, the inlet valve remains seated and the exhaust valve remains closed, too. Air pressure to the brake chambers is held constant when inlet pressure and delivery pressure are equal. If there is a small leak at the chamber, the delivery port pressure drops and unbalances the pressure acting on the piston. The inlet valve opens again until the state of balance returns. The **pressure-compensating balance valve** feature of air brake valves ensures a consistent delivery of air pressure is maintained, in spite of leaks in the delivery system lines or air chambers.

Relay Valve Operation—Releasing Brakes

When signal pressure from the foot valve drops due to reduced application pressure, air pressure in the cavity above the relay piston is lowered more than pressure below the piston. This condition lifts and unseats the exhaust valve, as is illustrated in **FIGURE 34-44**. Opening the exhaust passage vents air pressure in the brake chambers, which is expelled out the exhaust valve port, releasing the brakes.

Pneumatic Brake Balance

LO 34-5 Describe pneumatic brake balance.

Pneumatic balance, or the supply of the same air pressure to all wheels when braking, is a critical aspect of brake balance. Timing brake applications in the correct sequence on each axle,

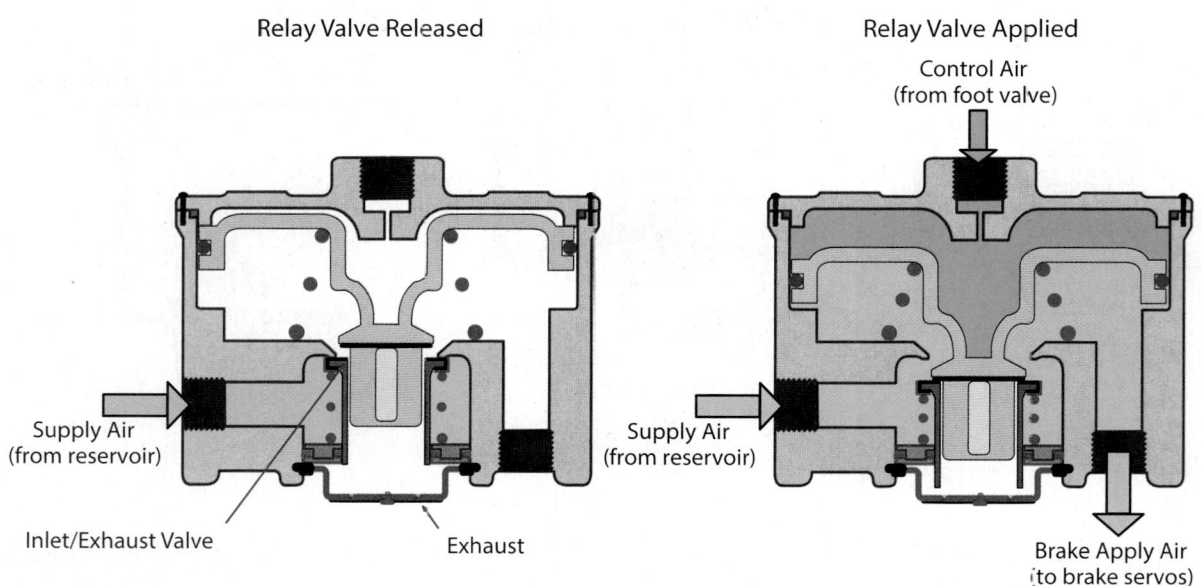

FIGURE 34-44 Application and release of the relay valve.

and having equal brake pressure at all wheel ends, are necessary for safe vehicle operation. Without pneumatic balance, some brakes work harder than others and brakes on an axle can lock up, leading to vehicle instability during braking, brake fade, and brake fires. Unequal application pressure leads to uneven brake wear and some brakes overheating.

Without pneumatic balance, a vehicle tends to either jack-knife or have the trailer swing out during hard braking events. Jackknifing occurs when the tractor's drive axle brakes have higher braking force than the trailer axles. If imbalance is present when road conditions are slippery or during a hard-braking event, the tractor drive axles lock up while the trailer axles are still rolling. Locked tractor axle brakes cause the tractor to lose directional stability, as the tractor is sliding on the tires. A heavily loaded unbraked trailer then pushes the tractor around the king pin.

During **trailer swing-out** the opposite occurs. Trailer swing-out occurs when the trailer brakes have higher levels of braking force than the tractor brakes. When trailer brakes are locked and directional stability is lost, the tractor drags the trailer, causing it to swing out and into another lane.

Relay Valve Crack Pressures

To design an air braking system with good brake timing, where brake application occurs in the correct axle sequence, relay valves are available with different crack pressures. **Crack pressure** refers to the signal pressure required by the relay valve to begin supplying air to the brake chambers.

By changing the relay piston spring tension within the valve, which the signal line air pressure must exceed before air is delivered to the brake chambers, timing of the brake application for tractor and trailer axles is varied. Ideally, the relay valve farthest away from the tractor has the lowest crack pressure because air takes longer to travel that far. In fact, a crack pressure as low as 0.25 to 0.5 psi (1.72 to 3.45 kPa) is used on some trailer valves to ensure they begin braking first, and quickly, in spite of the distance air signal pressure travels.

As expected, tractor relay valves have a slightly higher crack pressure because signal air pressure reaches those valves later. Consider that 95% of brake applications are made at less than 25 psi (172 kPa), with 10 to 20 psi (69 to 138 kPa) being most common. At those levels, a difference of crack pressure as little as 4 psi (28 kPa) between tractor and trailer is enough to cause significant pneumatic imbalance, leading to uneven brake torque.

Technicians interpreting driver complaints, making service recommendations and selecting replacement parts need to understand the importance of pneumatic brake balance. Pneumatic balance is produced when air pressure is equal at all wheel ends. This means pneumatic imbalance results if relay valve crack pressures are significantly different. For example, a tractor may use a relay valve that has a 10 psi (69 kPa) crack pressure and a trailer being towed uses a 1 psi (7 kPa) crack pressure relay valve. Since frequent brake applications are made at less than 10 psi (69 kPa), generally only the trailer brakes apply during controlled brake applications.

Testing done by University of Michigan Transportation Research Institute recommends that **snub braking** should be the braking technique used when downhill braking. This method requires that the truck brakes should be applied hard to slow the truck down to about 5 mph (2 kph), then hard braking should continue to be repeatedly applied and released until the bottom of the hill is reached. The goal is to avoid lightly and continuously applying the brakes. The amount of heat energy produced by the brakes is the same whether the brakes are applied hard for a short time or lightly for a long time. All of the brakes are not, however, equally applied in the light and continuous application situation.

If brake application pressure is between 20 and 30 psi (138 and 207 kPa), all the relay valves open, and all the brakes—not just the trailer brakes—work and dissipate heat. As more brakes are used by the braking system, each operates cooler. Remember that contaminants and alcohol in the air system can also cause higher than normal crack pressures.

Pneumatic Brake Imbalance

A brake imbalance condition can be uncovered by inspecting the brake linings. If a **pneumatic imbalance** exists, the brake linings on some axles wear faster than others. If the variation exists only between brake ends on each axle, a brake torque imbalance is likely present. Brake torque can be determined by measuring the brake drum temperatures with an infrared thermometer after a couple of hard brake applications. Drums should be close to the same temperatures if brake torque is similar.

Crack Pressure

Nominal crack pressure (NCP) refers to the input air pressure required to produce delivery air pressure. Relay valves commonly have crack pressures varying from 2.5 psi to 10.5 psi (17.2 to 72.4 kPa), which are intended for specific applications, depending on which axle the valve controls the braking pressure for. Brakes farthest away from the foot valve require the lowest pressure because signal air pressure takes the longest time to reach those valves. To produce nearly a simultaneous application of brakes, crack pressure increases as the valve is placed closer to the foot valve. Special attention must be paid when replacing valves because different crack pressures can lead to brake imbalance.

SAFETY TIP

Installing a "will fit" relay valve with an incorrect crack pressure can lead to a severe imbalance in brake application timing, which contributes to abnormal wear and even potentially unsafe vehicle braking. Always select the correct replacement valve originally specified by a manufacturer.

Anti-Compounding Relay Valves

Applying service and spring brakes at the same time combines spring brake and service brake force. Together, spring and service brake force applied to the slack adjuster is excessive and can lead to premature failure of the slack adjusters, or overtightening of automatic slack adjusters. To prevent foundation brake damage, an **anti-compounding valve** is used to prevent simultaneous application of the two forces. Essentially the use of this valve in the air supply to the spring brake chambers causes the spring brakes to release when the service brakes arev applied. The valve also causes the spring brakes to reapply when the service brakes are released. Anti-compounding valves are generally incorporated into the spring brake relay valve, as shown in **FIGURE 34-45**.

An anti-compounding valve. like that illustrated in **FIGURE 34-46**, is a type of **double check valve**. As such, it has two supply ports and one delivery port. The double check valve

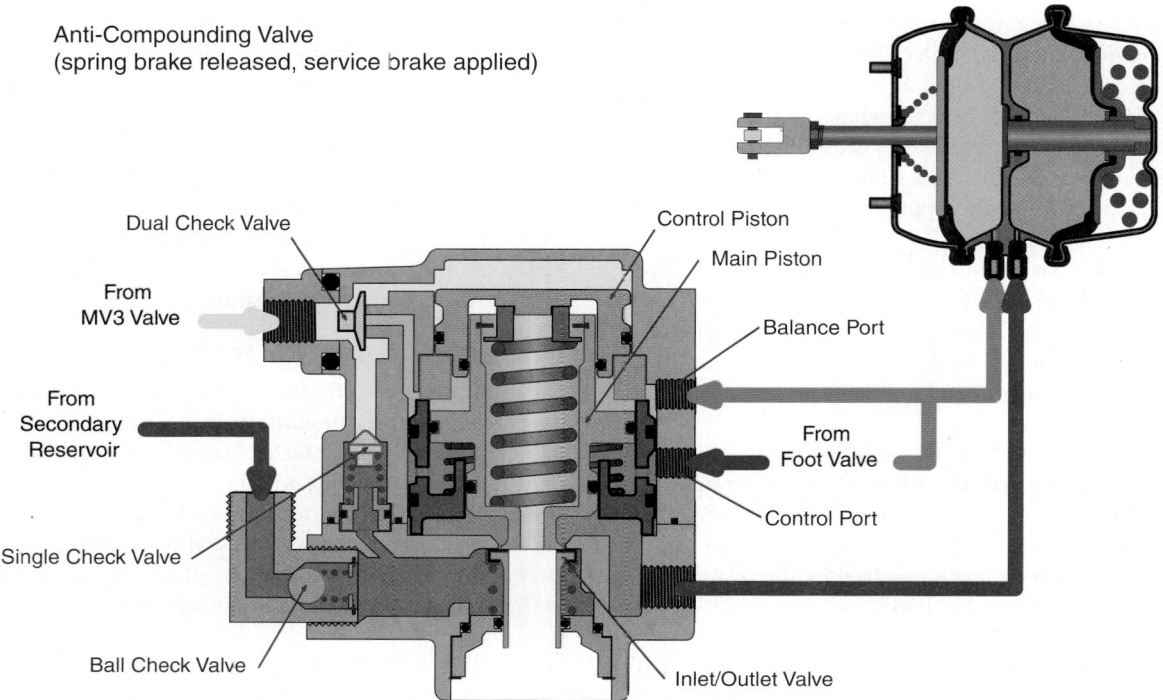

Anti-Compounding Valve
(spring brake released, service brake applied)

FIGURE 34-45 Anti-compounding feature prevents the service and spring brakes from applying pressure together, which would produce excessive force against the slack adjuster.

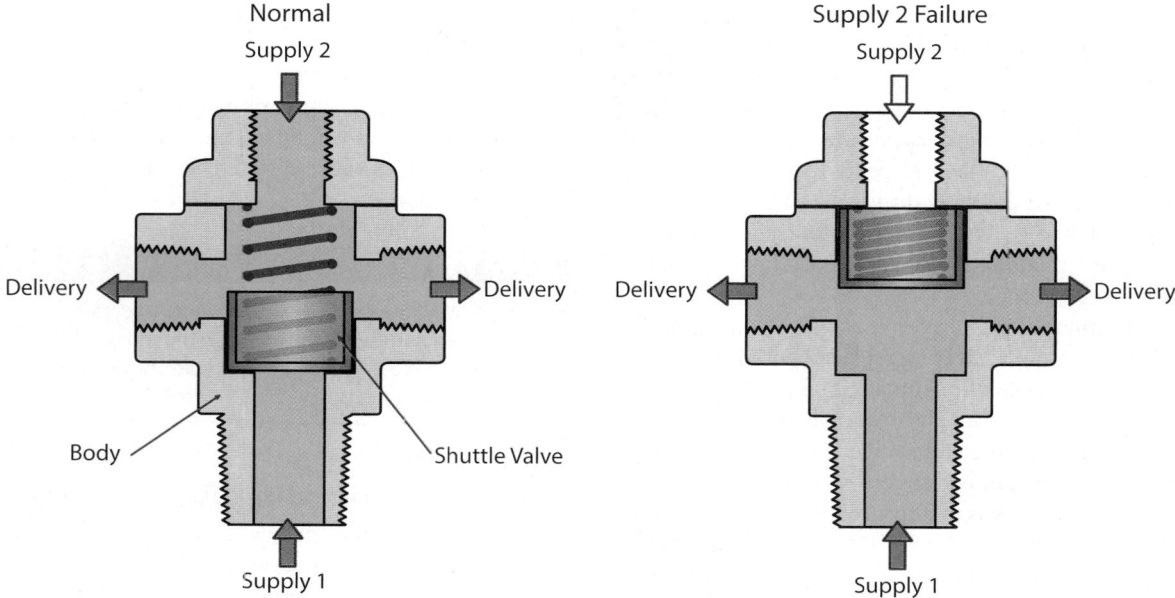

FIGURE 34-46 A relay valve with a double check valve used to prevent brake failure. The double check valve normally blocks secondary pressure, unless the primary circuit fails.

only allows air to flow from either supply port to the delivery port. Air cannot change direction and flow from the delivery port to either of the supply ports. Neither can air flow from one supply port to another supply port.

One supply port of the anti-compounding valve is connected to the parking brake valve in the dash. The other supply port of the anti-compounding valve is connected to the rear axle service brake pressure signal. Pressure from either supply source activates the spring brake relay valve and fills the spring brake chambers—thus releasing the spring brake. So, if the service brakes are applied at the same time as the spring brakes, the service brake signal applies the service brakes and releases the spring brakes. Anti-compounding double check valves can be used separately, or incorporated into a relay valve, or even into quick-release valves.

For additional safety, a single-axle bus or truck can also be equipped with a double check valve to apply brakes in the event of either a primary or secondary circuit failure. The input to the double check-equipped relay valve is connected to both the primary and secondary signal circuits supplied by the foot valve. In normal operation, the primary circuit supplies the double check valve with air pressure first and prevents secondary circuit air from signaling the valve. In this normal circumstance, the valve blocks the secondary circuit signal. If the primary circuit fails and no air is supplied to the valve, the secondary circuit signal operates the relay valve, enabling the vehicle to brake normally.

▶ TECHNICIAN TIP

Just because a service brake relay valve is leaking air out of its exhaust port, it does not mean the valve is at fault. Sometimes a spring brake is leaking air past a seal between the rear spring brake and service chamber when the spring brake is released. If this happens, air used to release the spring brake travels past the seal, then into the service brake hose and out the exhaust port of the relay valve. Before replacing a valve that has air leaking from its exhaust, disconnect or pinch the delivery lines from that service brake chambers when the park brakes are released to determine if air is being fed back from a leaking brake chamber seal. Trailer spring brake valves can also encounter this condition.

To inspect and test a service brake relay valve and replace as needed, follow the steps in **SKILL DRILL 34-5**.

SKILL DRILL 34-5 Inspecting and Testing a Service Brake Relay Valve; Replacing as Needed

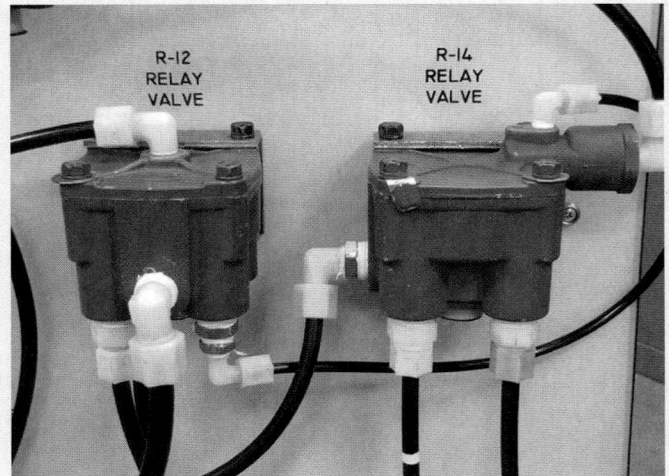

1. Apply the parking brakes and chock the vehicle wheels.
2. Charge the air reservoir pressures to governor cut-out pressure (120 psi [830 kPa]) and release parking brakes.
3. Make several service brake applications and check for prompt, simultaneous application and release of the brakes, while inspecting the operation of the relay valve. Verify air from the service chambers is exhausting from the exhaust port of the relay valve.
4. With the service brakes released, apply a soapy water solution to the exhaust port of the relay valve and check for excessive leakage.
5. While holding a full-service brake application, apply a soapy water solution to the exhaust port and check for air leaks.
6. Using a duplex air gauge or two air pressure gauges, "T" in an air gauge fitting to the relay signal port, also called the service port.

Connect a second air pressure gauge to the delivery port of the relay valve by installing a "T" fitting.
7. Gradually make a service brake application and apply the service brake to make a full brake application while observing and recording the following observations:
   a. The relay valve crack pressure—the pressure at the signal port required to produce air pressure at the delivery ports.
   b. Relay signal pressure compared to delivery pressure. Both should be proportional for a non-proportional type of relay valve.
   c. Verify that at full signal pressure the relay valve applies full reservoir.
   If the relay valve fails the above tests, recommend replacement. To replace the relay valve, use the following guidelines:
8. Disconnect and tag all air hoses from the relay valve. Seal the hose ends with tape. Label the connection ports of the tagged hoses for correct reassembly. *Caution:* Open the air reservoir drain valve to drain air from the system before disconnecting any lines or fittings.
9. Remove the valve mounting bolts and remove the valve.
10. Replace the old valve with a new valve recommended by the manufacturer.
11. Attach the new relay valve to the vehicle using the bolts, washers, and nuts; torque to specifications.
12. Transfer any fittings to the new valve and seal all male ends of fittings with pipe sealant, such as liquid Teflon. Connect the air hose fittings to the valve ports and tighten according to manufacturer specifications.
13. Close the air reservoir drain valves and charge the air reservoirs to governor cut-out pressure.
14. Re-test relay valve operation using previous steps to verify correct relay valve operation.

Brake Proportioning Relay Valves

When a tractor is traveling without a trailer (**bobtailing**), the absence of weight over the rear axles can easily cause the wheels to lock up, even under slight brake applications. To prevent that from happening, a relay valve for tractors is designed to reduce normal service brake applications when no trailer is towed.

When the vehicle is operating in a bobtailing condition, a special **bobtailing proportioning relay (BPR) valve** is used to assist in controlling the braking performance. The valve, which is known in some locations as a "bobtailing valve," is a combination of two valves in a single housing. A typical BPR valve is shown in **FIGURE 34-47**. The lower half of the valve contains a conventional service brake relay valve. The upper half has an additional port connected to the cab-mounted, push-pull trailer air supply valve. It also contains a **proportioning valve**. When the trailer valve port is pressurized with air, the proportioning valve functions to change service brake application pressure. When the tractor is bobtailing, the absence of trailer-supplied air pressure to the brakes reduces the tractor's rear service brake application pressure relative to signal pressure from the foot valve. The opposite condition is enabled when the trailer-supplied air and relay operation reverts to normal with application pressure becoming proportional to signal pressure. The relationship between the service brake chamber pressure and the brake valve delivery pressure is charted in **FIGURE 34-48**.

Limiting apply pressure to the rear service brakes helps to avoid the brakes locking the rear wheels, resulting in skidding and loss of control when there is no trailer loading the rear service brakes. When the tractor is pulling a trailer, weight over the tractor's rear axles allows the relay valve to resume normal operation.

Front Axle Limiter Valves

Like the rear axle service brake relay valve using a proportioning valve, a **limiter (ratio) valve**, such as the one illustrated in **FIGURE 34-49**, is used on the steer axle of a tractor air brake system. A front-axle ratio-control valve (limiter valve) works

FIGURE 34-47 BPR relay valve.

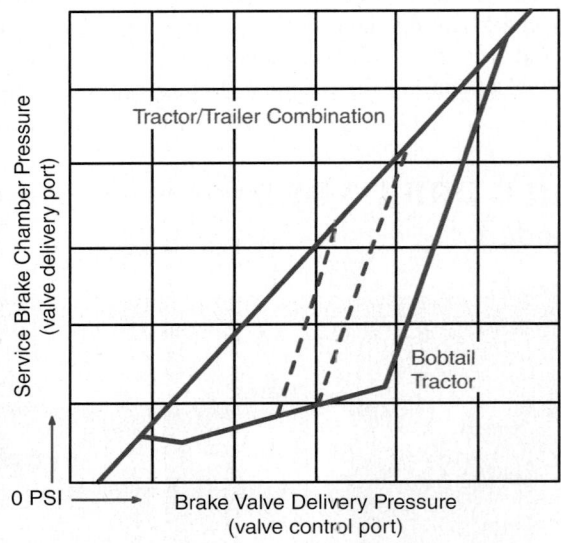

FIGURE 34-48 Changes to brake application pressure supplied by a proportioning relay valve with and without a trailer connected.

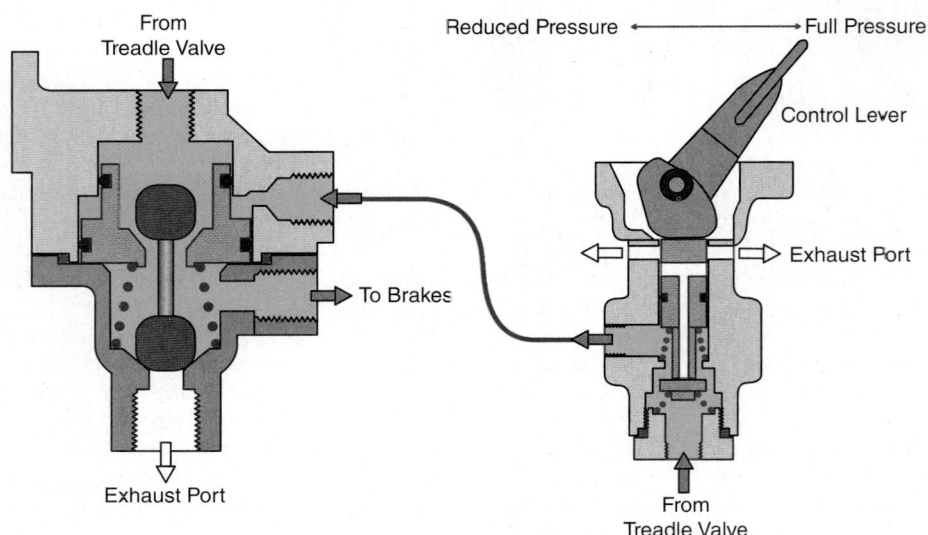

FIGURE 34-49 Manual front wheel limiter valve.

opposite the BPR valve. Instead of reducing air pressure to the front axle during bobtail operation, the limiter valve automatically increases brake application air pressure to improve braking lost with the reduction of rear brake torque. Full brake pressure is available to the steer axle service brakes, while reduced pressure is available when towing a trailer. Limiting front brake pressure only takes place when a trailer is towed by a tractor.

Another feature built into a limiter valve improves timing of the front-axle brake application. The **limiter** or **ratio control valve** holds off front-axle pressure until 4 or 5 psi (28 or 34 kPa) of pressure reaches the valve. By doing this, the front brake application pressure is delayed so that the rear brakes apply at the same time as the front brakes. Otherwise, the rear brake application would be delayed because of the time it takes for the air to reach the rear brakes and apply them.

Quick-Release Valves (QR valve)

Quick-release (QR) valves are designed to speed up the exhaust of air from brake chambers and some other air valves. Without a quick-release valve or a quick-release function built into the relay valves, air would need to flow back to the foot valve or park brake valve to vent from the brake chambers. As **FIGURE 34-50** shows, common QR valves have three ports—a supply port at the top and two delivery ports at the side.

The operation of the QR valve is simple. When air pressure is supplied to the valve inlet, a spring-loaded diaphragm is pushed

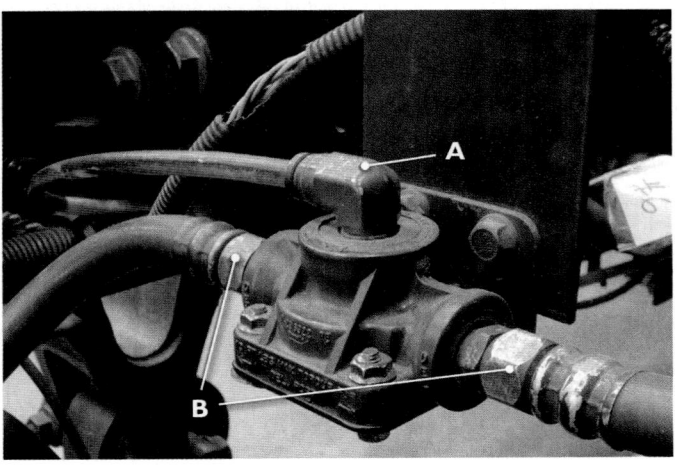

FIGURE 34-50 Quick-release valve. **A.** Air supply. **B.** Air delivery.

downward to seal the exhaust port, as illustrated in **FIGURE 34-51A**. Air flows out of both delivery ports to the brake chamber. When supply pressure is removed, as illustrated in **FIGURE 34-51B**, spring and air pressure below the diaphragm lift the QR valve diaphragm and open the exhaust passageway. Air from both the supply line and brake chambers vent from the exhaust passage.

To inspect and test the QR valve and replace as needed, follow the steps in **SKILL DRILL 34-6**.

Park/Emergency Brake Circuit

LO 34-6 Identify and describe the purpose, construction, and operation of components used by the park/emergency braking circuits.

The **park/emergency braking system** has two major functions. The first is to control spring brake operation for parking the vehicle. Spring brakes use coiled steel power springs located in the rear axle brake chambers to mechanically apply the brakes.

Air pressure of at least 30 to 45 psi (207 to 310 kPa) is needed to begin releasing the spring brakes by compressing the springs using air pressure acting on a diaphragm in the spring brake chamber. In straight trucks that do not tow trailers, the circuit shown in **FIGURE 34-52** also has the capability to enable several "controlled brake applications" using the spring brakes, instead of the normal service system air brake chambers, if there is air loss to the rear brakes or primary reservoir.

Push-Pull Control Valves

Push-pull park/emergency and **trailer supply control valves** are mounted in the vehicle dash of a tractor unit, as shown in **FIGURE 34-53**. Supply and delivery port connections are on the valves. Both color- and shape-coded valves are normally closed to prevent air flowing through the valves unless they are depressed or pushed in. When traveling over the road, the park/emergency valve button is pushed in to release the truck spring brakes, and it is pulled out for parking. Pulling the valve button out exhausts air from the air signal port connected to the spring brake relay valve. The trailer supply valve is depressed to supply air to the trailer to release its spring brakes.

The valves are pressure-sensitive. That is, the valves automatically return to the exhaust, or "button out," position, when reservoir supply pressure for the spring brakes is below the required minimum to hold off or release the spring brakes. When reservoir pressure is reduced, the valve buttons pop out

Quick Release Valve: Applied

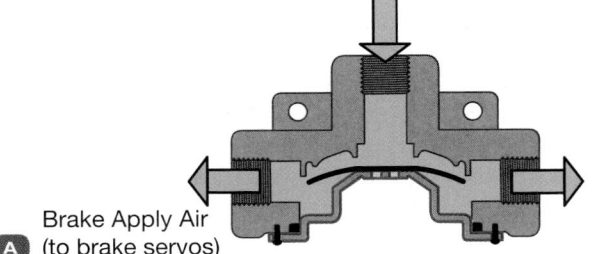

Quick Release Valve: Releasing

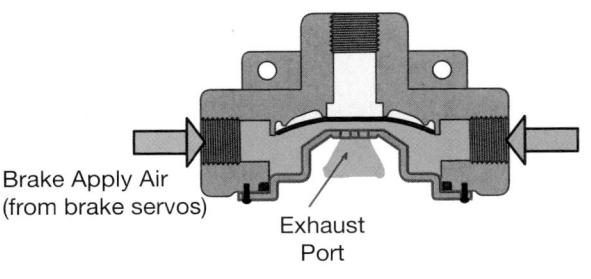

FIGURE 34-51 A quick-release valve during **A.** Application and **B.** Release.

SKILL DRILL 34-6 Inspecting and Testing the Quick-Release Valve; Replacing as Needed

1. Locate the QR valve for the axle in the brake system.
2. To test the valve for leakage and correct operation, have an assistant apply the service brakes to inspect the valve exhaust port for leaks with the brakes applied.

3. No leaks from the exhaust port should be heard or felt from the valve with the brakes applied.
4. Release the brakes. Check that air from the brake chambers exhausts from the valve when it is properly working.
5. To further test the valve for air leaks, spray the valve and exhaust port with a soapy water solution.
6. Apply and hold the brakes; a leakage of up to 1" bubble in three seconds is permitted from the exhaust port. No leakage is permitted anywhere on the valve body, or between valve body and cover plate over the exhaust port.
7. To replace the valve, tag and disconnect the three air lines from the QR valve.
8. Remove the mounting bolts and the valve.
9. Match the old valve with a correct replacement valve using the OEM-specified valve.
10. Install the QR valve with the exhaust port facing down. Securely tighten the mounting bolts.
11. Connect the airlines to the QR valve in the locations previously marked.
12. Repeat the operating and leakage tests using previous steps to validate correct operation.

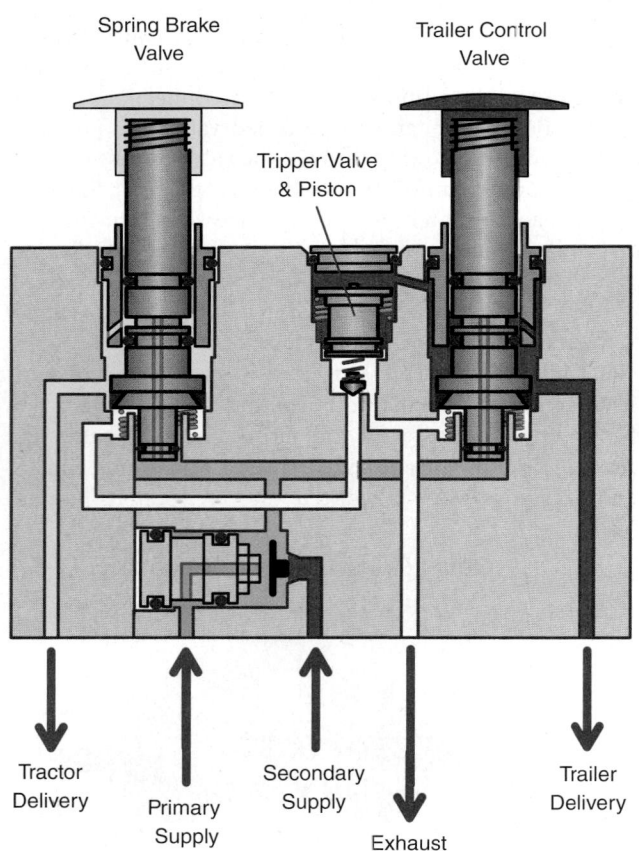

FIGURE 34-52 A single-axle straight truck or bus uses a single park brake valve.

FIGURE 34-53 Push-pull park/emergency and trailer-supply control valves.

and the spring brakes are applied. This feature ensures that the vehicle can come to a controlled stop if there is a loss of air pressure in the park brake reservoir. The park/emergency and trailer supply valve are interconnected in such a way that, if the tractor suffers enough air loss to cause the park/emergency valve to pop out, the trailer supply valve pops out also, applying the trailer spring brakes. If the air loss is in the trailer, however, the trailer supply valve only pops out, applying only the trailer spring brakes. Contrary to what is commonly portrayed in the movies, an air-braked vehicle does not completely lose brakes if there is a rapid loss of air pressure. Holding either valve in when reservoir pressure is adequate supplies air to the spring brake relay valve and begins to release the brakes. An integral **double check valve**

SKILL DRILL 34-7 Inspecting and Testing the Parking Brake Push-Pull Valve (PP1); Replacing as Needed

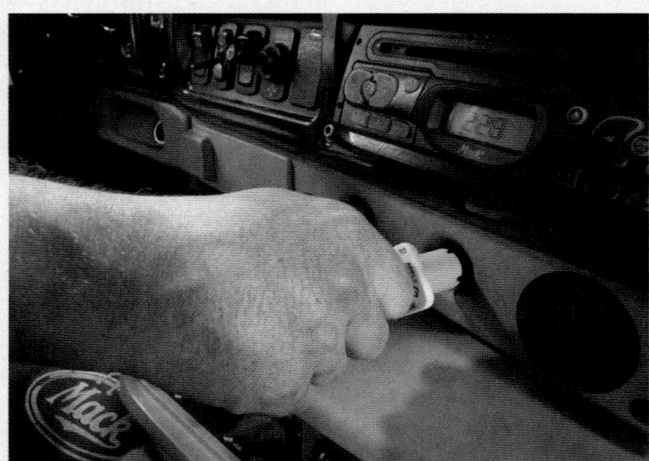

1. Move vehicle into the shop, apply the parking brakes, and chock the vehicle wheels.
2. Charge air system pressure to governor cut-out pressure (120 psi [830 kPa]).
3. Remove any dash panels to access the hand control push-pull (PP1) parking brake valve.
4. Test the valve for air leaks. With air pressure at 120 psi (830 kPa) and valve button pulled out, coat the exhaust port and the plunger stem with a soapy solution. Air leakage at any point should not exceed one bubble every five seconds.
5. Repeat the above procedure with the valve pushed in to release the brakes.
6. Open the primary air reservoir drain valve to completely drain the primary air reservoir while observing the operation of the PP1 valve. Repeat the procedure while draining the secondary reservoir after the primary reservoir has drained.

7. Observe the air reservoir pressure displayed by each of the dash gauges. Verify the PP1 valve pops out to apply the spring brakes only when both supply reservoir pressures drop to no less than between 20 to 30 psi (140 to 210 kPa).
8. Charge the air reservoir pressures to governor cut-out pressure (120 psi [830 kPa]) and release parking brakes.
9. Push in the PP1 button and have an assistant verify that the spring brakes correctly release.
10. If spring brakes do not release, "T" in an air pressure gauge to the spring brake relay valve's service or signal port to measure pressure from the PP1 valve.
11. With the PP1 valve button pushed in to release the spring brakes, confirm whether the air pressure supplied to the relay valve is equal to reservoir pressure.
12. If valve does not work as described, or does not pass the air leak test, replace the valve. Caution: Drain air reservoirs before disconnecting air lines.
13. Disconnect and tag all air hoses connected to the PP1 valve. Seal the hose ends with tape. Label the connection ports of the tagged hoses for correct reassembly.
14. Transfer the square yellow button to the new valve by turning the button counterclockwise to remove it from the valve stem.
15. Verify the new valve is the correct valve for the application according to OEM specifications.
16. Install new valve assembly in the instrument panel and install mounting screws.
17. Use Teflon sealant on any male fittings before connecting the air lines and fitting to the correct valve ports. Tighten the fittings according to OEM specifications.
18. Retest new valve by using the previous steps to validate correct operation.

is used to supply air from either the primary or secondary circuit reservoirs to release spring brakes. Automatic pressure settings vary, depending on application. Generally, however, the valve pops out when pressure is as low as 20 to 30 psi (138 to 207 kPa).

To inspect and test the parking brake push-pull valve and replace as needed, follow the steps in **SKILL DRILL 34-7**.

Inversion Valve

An **inversion valve** is a common name given to the valve used to control spring brake operation in the park/emergency circuit of straight trucks—the **spring brake relay valve**. **FIGURE 34-54** shows an inversion valve. The valve enables several controlled brake applications using the spring brakes if service air pressure is lost to the rear brakes supplied by the secondary air reservoir. Primary circuit air pressure is used instead to supply air pressure to release the spring brakes. A service brake application releases air, holding off the spring brakes, to enable the springs to apply the brakes. Inversion valves are required because the front axle or primary circuit brakes alone cannot supply adequate braking force to stop the vehicle quickly enough to meet the FMVSS 121 requirements for

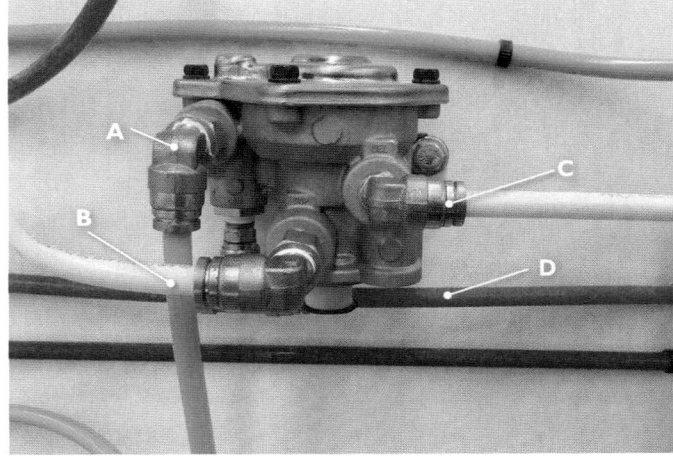

FIGURE 34-54 The inversion valve, more correctly called the spring brake valve, detects the primary circuit air loss and uses the spring brakes to apply as many as five to eight brake applications. **A.** Primary applied. **B.** Secondary applied. **C.** To spring brake relay valve. **D.** From park/emergency dash valve.

emergency stopping. Inversion valves are not required on tractors because trailer brakes that are supplied air from both the primary and secondary reservoirs can help the tractor meet the required FMVSS 121 emergency stopping requirements and slow the tractor.

The label "inversion valve" is given to a normally open valve that requires air pressure to close. Inversion valves operate the opposite way most other air valves work—which are normally closed and require air to open. Because the spring brake valve reverses, or "inverts," the service-park brake operation when service air pressure is lost, the name "inversion valve" is commonly given to the valve, though not technically correct.

The spring brake/inversion valve detects the secondary circuit air loss and uses the spring brakes to apply five to eight brake applications, depending on the primary reservoir size.

The spring brakes, not the service brakes, are used to slow the vehicle. Pressure proportional to front brake pressure applies the spring brakes whenever the brake pedal is pushed. The inversion valve supplies primary circuit air pressure to release the spring brakes when the brake pedal is not applied. The inversion valve then allows the springs to apply the brakes by releasing air from the spring brake chambers as a brake pedal application is made. Air from the primary reservoir supplying the front axle is used to operate the inversion valve. Spring brake valves on straight trucks also limit maximum spring brake release pressure to 90 to 95 psi (621 to 655 kPa), rather than allowing the full system air pressure to release the spring brake.

To inspect and test the spring brake inversion relay valve and replace as needed, follow the steps in **SKILL DRILL 34-8.**

SKILL DRILL 34-8 Inspecting and Testing the Spring Brake Inversion Relay Valve (IR-2); Replacing as Needed

1. Move vehicle into the shop, apply the parking brakes, and chock the vehicle wheels.
2. Charge air system pressure to governor cut-out pressure (120 psi [830 kPa]).
3. Release the spring brakes by pushing in the dash-mounted park brake button. Verify the spring brakes completely release.

4. To inspect the relay function of the spring brake relay valve (IR-2), apply the spring brakes by pulling out the dash-mounted park brake button. Confirm the combined inversion spring brake relay valve exhausts all air in the spring brake chambers from the exhaust port of the valve. Confirm the spring brakes apply.
5. To validate the anti-compounding feature of the valve, the spring brakes should release when a service brake application is made. To do this, connect a pressure gauge to the delivery port of the IR-2 valve and make a gradual service brake application with the spring brakes applied.
6. Confirm that the IR-2 valve supplies air pressure to the delivery port to release the spring brakes when the service brake is applied.
7. To validate the correct operation of the inversion valve function of the IR-2, connect an air pressure gauge to the signal port for the IR-2 valve's secondary air control circuit. Allow the air pressure gauge to remain connected to the delivery port or install a second air pressure gauge to the delivery port of the valve supplying air to the spring brake actuators.
8. Release the spring brakes by pushing in the button for the park brake valve. Drain the primary air reservoir by opening the reservoir drain valve. The inversion valve can now respond to a loss of air pressure in the primary circuit by using secondary circuit air pressure to exhaust air from the spring brakes.
9. Make a gradual service brake application with the spring brakes released (dash valve button in). Verify the brake application exhausts air from the spring brakes by confirming air in the spring brake chambers leaves the exhaust port of the valve.
10. Confirm that the spring brake delivery port has air pressure after the signal or control port for the secondary circuit brakes rises above 10 psi (69 kPa).
11. Check the valve ports, fittings, covers, and seals with soapy water to check for leaks when the spring brakes and service brakes are applied.
12. If the valve does not function correctly to operate as a combined relay and inversion valve with an anti-compounding feature, replace the valve. Replace a leaking valve or remove and reseal any leaking fittings.
13. Follow the same procedures as Skill Drill 34-5 to replace the IR-2 spring brake valve.

Trailer Air Circuits

LO 34-7 Identify and describe the purpose, construction, and operation of components used in trailer air circuits.

The trailer park and service brakes are controlled by the tractor. Components in the brake circuit include:

- Gladhands
- Trailer air hoses
- Trailer reservoir tanks
- Pressure protection valves
- Relay valves
- Push-pull trailer air supply valve
- Trailer brake control valve (TV)

Air is supplied to the trailer circuit by the tractor's secondary air reservoir. As shown in **FIGURE 34-55**, two color-coded flexible hoses connect the tractor and trailer air system. Red is for the supply/emergency circuit and blue is for the service brakes. The blue line supplies an air signal for the service brakes and the red line supplies air for the trailer air reservoir, as well as the supply/emergency brake circuit. A service and spring brake reservoir is used on the trailer. It's helpful to remember that the red emergency trailer supply hose is always located on the outside of the tractor and trailer. The idea is that, in the case of a trailer jackknife, the line breaks or disconnects first. If that happens, the air supply to the trailer spring brakes is lost and the trailer is automatically brought to a stop.

Supply air to the trailer is controlled through a red octagonal-shaped tractor-mounted push-pull valve. Sending air to the trailer from the cab-mounted push-pull automatically begins to release the trailer spring brakes and begins filling the trailer reservoir, if empty. Depending on the type of trailer spring valve used, priority can be given to releasing the spring brakes before the brake reservoirs are filled or vice versa—the spring brakes cannot be released until the trailer air supply reservoir is filled first. The tractor and trailer have separate valves to release and apply their respective spring brakes. Each valve can release the spring brakes independently of one another but pulling out the square yellow **tractor park/emergency control valve** pops out both valves and applies both the trailer and the tractor spring

brakes. Either valve can be pushed in separately to release the spring brakes, but both require pushing in to move a tractor connected to a trailer.

Trailer service brakes can be additionally activated by air pressure supplied by the blue trailer hose. An air pressure signal identical to the one supplied to the tractors rear axle service brakes is transmitted to the trailer. Over the road, a hand-operated trailer brake control valve can also be used to apply just the trailer service brakes, independent of any other brake application. **FIGURE 34-56**. Sometimes called the "broker brake" because it saves wear on tractor brakes by applying only trailer brakes, this valve is mandatory in some jurisdictions, like Canada, but not always in others.

FMVSS 121 specifies that all trailers have a means of activating the trailer brakes under trailer breakaway conditions. The loss of a trailer could potentially cause a major loss in air pressure for the tractor. To satisfy both requirements to protect the tractor and trailer, a TP valve isolates the tractor during a breakaway condition, while enabling the loss of trailer air pressure to activate the spring brakes for emergency stopping. Both trailer air hoses are connected to the TP valve. The blue service line is closer to the tractor center, while the red emergency/supply hose is always the outside line between the two units.

Gladhands

Gladhands are the air couplers attached to the trailer hoses connecting the tractor and trailer air systems. Pictured in **FIGURE 34-57**, they are called "gladhands" because they resemble a pair of hands during a handshake when coupled. Gladhands use a flexible rubber-like seal, shown in **FIGURE 34-58**, to prevent air leaks between coupler halves when the couplers are connected.

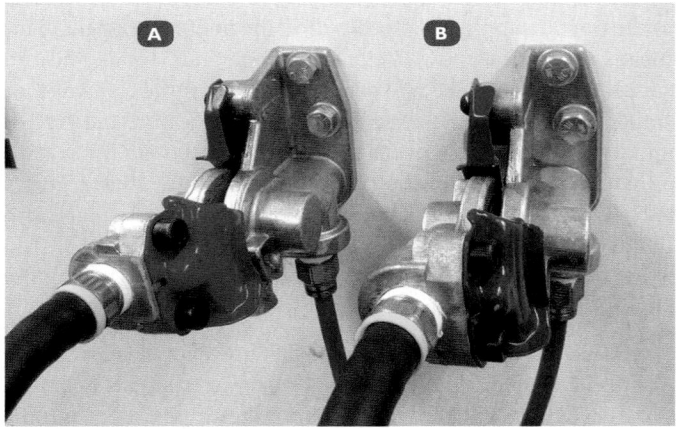

FIGURE 34-55 Color-coded hoses are used to differentiate brake systems. **A.** Park/emergency line. **B.** Service line.

FIGURE 34-56 The trailer brake control valve is a hand-operated pressure regulating valve that enables separate control of trailer service brakes.

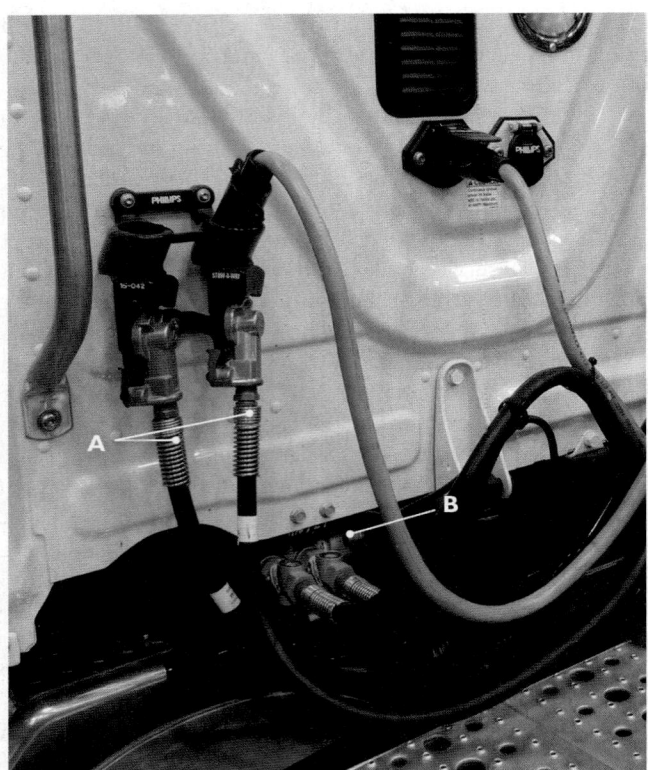

FIGURE 34-57 Gladhand holders on the rear of a tractor. Red, or emergency-trailer supply, is always on the inside, the service line is on the outside. **A.** Trailer gladhands (2). **B.** Tractor protection valve.

Trailer System Valves

Tractors that pull semi-trailers and/or straight trucks that pull full trailers require several valves to supply and control the air service brake and the spring brake systems on the trailer. Regardless of which towing vehicle is being discussed, these valves include a valve to actuate the trailer service brakes, a valve to supply air to the trailer reservoirs, and a valve that protects the towing vehicle air system.

Trailer Brake Control (TC) Valve

The trailer brake control (TC) valve is mounted on the steering column or in the dash near the driver. Only the trailer service brakes are applied whenever this hand-operated valve is moved by the driver. **Trailer brake control valves** typically use a cam-and-spring mechanism to control a graduated delivery of air pressure to the trailer. Returning the handle up to a rest position releases service brakes, while moving the valve handle down increases trailer-only service brake application. Some drivers use the valve to apply only trailer brakes to reduce tractor brake wear. However, the TC valve should never be used for parking.

Trailer Air Supply Valve

The red octagonal-shaped **trailer supply valve** is used to control the TP system and route air from the secondary brake reservoir to the trailer brake reservoir. Like other push-pull control valves, the trailer air supply valve is a pressure sensitive, on-off

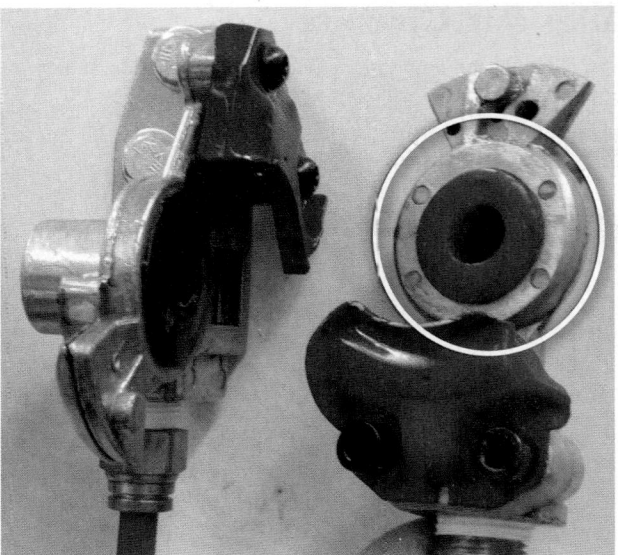

FIGURE 34-58 Gladhands contain seals that can leak air. Seals (circled) should be regularly inspected and replaced, if found worn or defective.

control valve that automatically pops out when reservoir supply pressure falls too low.

When the valve button is out, the trailer spring brakes are applied. FMVSS 121 requires the trailer air supply to be interlocked with the tractor park brakes. This means the tractor spring brakes cannot be applied without the trailer spring brakes also applying. This feature prevents the trailer from unexpectedly rolling away during disconnection. A two-button module combination incorporating a trailer and tractor spring brake release is most often used. This module contains the tractor park/emergency valve with the trailer supply valve. The combination valve reduces the number of air lines and fittings required.

Tractor Protection Valves

The primary function of **tractor protection (TP) valves** is to prevent a rapid loss of air from the tractor during a trailer breakaway condition, or when either the tractor or trailer develops a severe air leak. When 45 psi (310 kPa) or more of air is available at the tractor supply port to the valve, the inlet valve opens. This means the valve is now in the normal or "run" mode and can supply a trailer service brake application from the foot valve or trailer control valve. The valve is used every time the tractor and trailer are disconnected, shutting off the trailer service and supply lines when the park/emergency and trailer supply valves are pulled out. A schematic of the TP valve is illustrated in **FIGURE 34-59**.

The valve incorporates several air control functions into a single valve. These include:

■ A service line shut-off feature that prevents a trailer service brake application when tractor air pressure falls below 45 psi (310 kPa) in the tractor. Until the air pressure from the trailer air supply valve increases above 45 psi (310 kPa), the valve remains closed to service signal pressure.

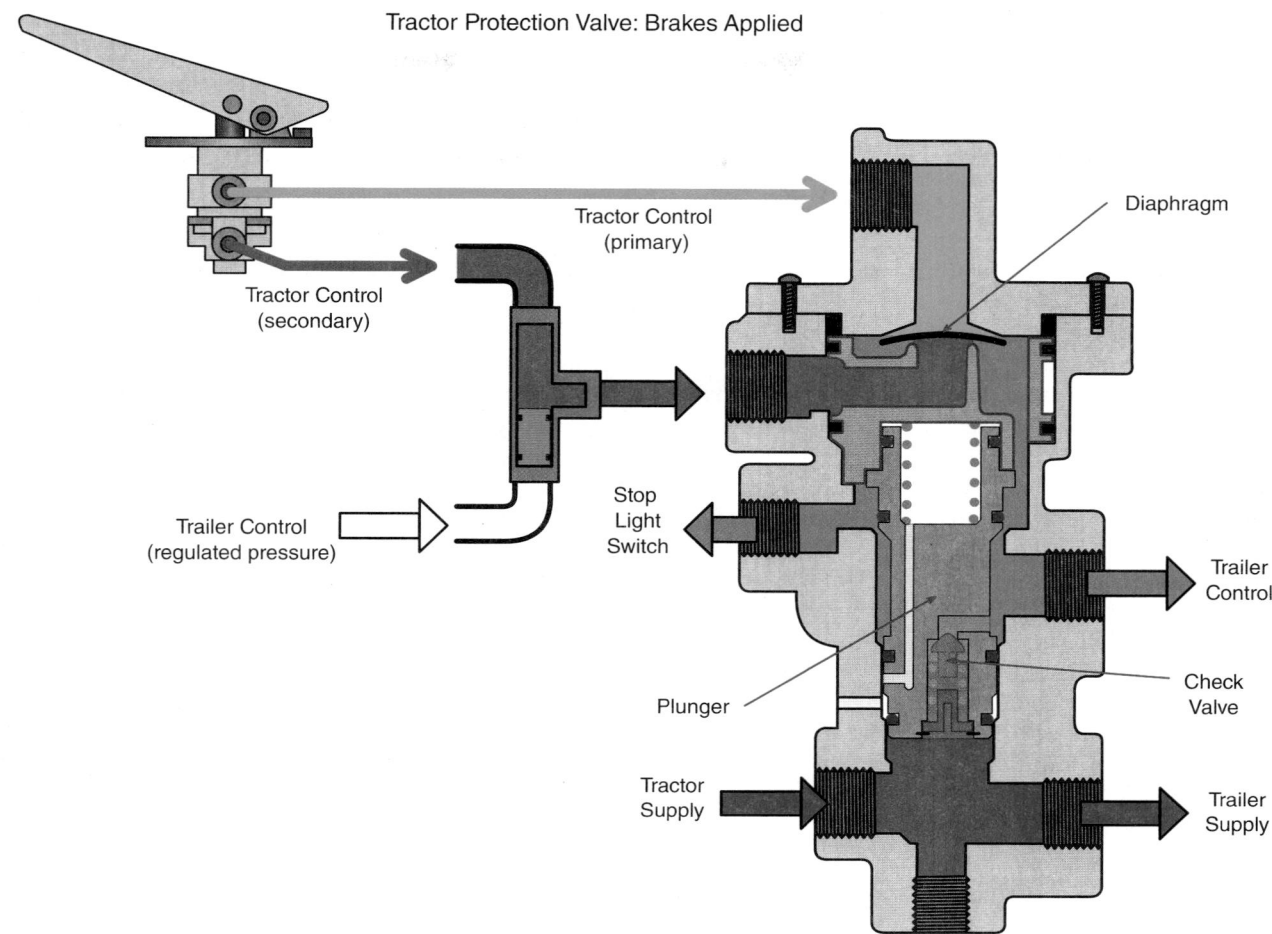

FIGURE 34-59 Air flow through a tractor protection valve with the trailer brakes released and the service brakes applied.

- A quick-release valve for the trailer service line. This prevents air from becoming trapped in the service hose when the trailer is parked and speeds up trailer service brake release.
- Double check valves to prevent compounding of trailer service and park brakes.
- Double check valves to divert the highest service air pressure from either the tractor's front or rear brake circuits or the trailer valve.
- A stop light port for a stop light switch.

Two checks can be made of the valve operation. One is to build up tractor air pressure from 0 psi (0 kPa) while the gladhands are disconnected. While pushing the trailer supply valve in, no air should pass through the red tractor hose until approximately 45 psi (310k Pa) of tractor air pressure is reached. After building up air pressure in the tractor, with the trailer supply valve pushed in, the supply/emergency gladhand should release air from the tractor until pressure falls to approximately 45 psi (310 kPa). With the tractor service brake applied, air should be released from the blue service hose and shut-off at the same time as air is cut off for the supply/emergency hose.

With just the blue service hose disconnected and the trailer charged with air, the hand-operated trailer control valve can be activated to check for air pressure delivery out the service hose.

Trailer Spring Brake Valves

Trailer spring brake valves are relay valves designed for use in trailer air brake systems to control the supply/emergency brake circuit. What is different about these valves, as compared to tractor spring brake valves, is that they are generally designed to be mounted on a trailer reservoir to regulate the filling of the reservoir(s), in addition to the other valve functions. Trailer spring brake valves typically use internal pressure protection and check valves to isolate a reservoir failure, which is intended to prevent automatic application of the trailer spring brakes if the spring brake reservoir suddenly loses air pressure. In that situation, the service brake reservoir or trailer air supply from the tractor can hold off the trailer spring brakes.

Priority of Trailer Spring Brake

An internal valve in the trailer spring brake valve may control whether the air reservoir for the service or spring brake is filled first. The valve can determine whether releasing the spring brakes is done only with the trailer supply air from the trailer supply/emergency line first or using only reservoir pressure to release the spring brakes. A choice is offered since a trailers brakes may be still applied or drag when the tractor is moved without the driver realizing the trailer supply tank was not filled with adequate air pressure to release the brakes. Allowing the trailer spring brakes to release using only the air supplied by the red trailer supply/emergency line can result in the temporary absence of trailer service brakes until the reservoir is filled. So, the choice of the spring brake valve is made between prioritizing safety and potential damage to tires and equipment. When trailer spring brakes are released by only the tractor's supply of air through the trailer supply/emergency line, the arrangement is referred to as having **spring brake priority**. If the trailer air reservoir must be filled before the trailer spring brakes are released, the spring brake valve is said to have **service brake priority**. An anti-compound feature preventing application of service and park brake application together is part of these valves.

The situation with the choice of trailer spring brake valve features arose when FMVSS 121 regulations in North America changed in the 1990s allowing for more simplified trailer system circuit plumbing by requiring only one reservoir, not two, to supply air for the service and supply/emergency brake system on some trailers. **FIGURE 34-60** illustrates that circuit. Depending on when the trailer was manufactured, manufacturers and customers could decide whether to supply air pressure to both the trailer service brakes and the spring brake from a single reservoir, or give priority to the spring brake release before the reservoir filled with adequate air pressure to operate the service brakes, too.

As already discussed, when equipped for spring brake priority, enabling air supplied from the tractor to release the spring brakes first before filling the reservoir to supply the service brakes. The advantage of spring brake priority systems is that they enable the trailer to be towed without waiting for the trailer air reservoirs to first fill. The disadvantage is that a trailer could be traveling without adequate air pressure to operate the service brakes. If there is a major loss of air to the trailer service brakes in a spring brake priority system, the spring brakes may remain released while no service brakes are available on the trailer. The only way to apply brakes on the trailer is to close the trailer supply valve, which causes the trailer's spring brakes to apply automatically.

Trailers with service brake priority fill the trailer air reservoir before supplying the spring brake chambers. This arrangement ensures enough air is available to operate the service brakes before the spring brakes can be released and the trailer is towed. The driver, however, may be inconvenienced a little longer, before being able to pull away with a trailer, while the reservoir is filling.

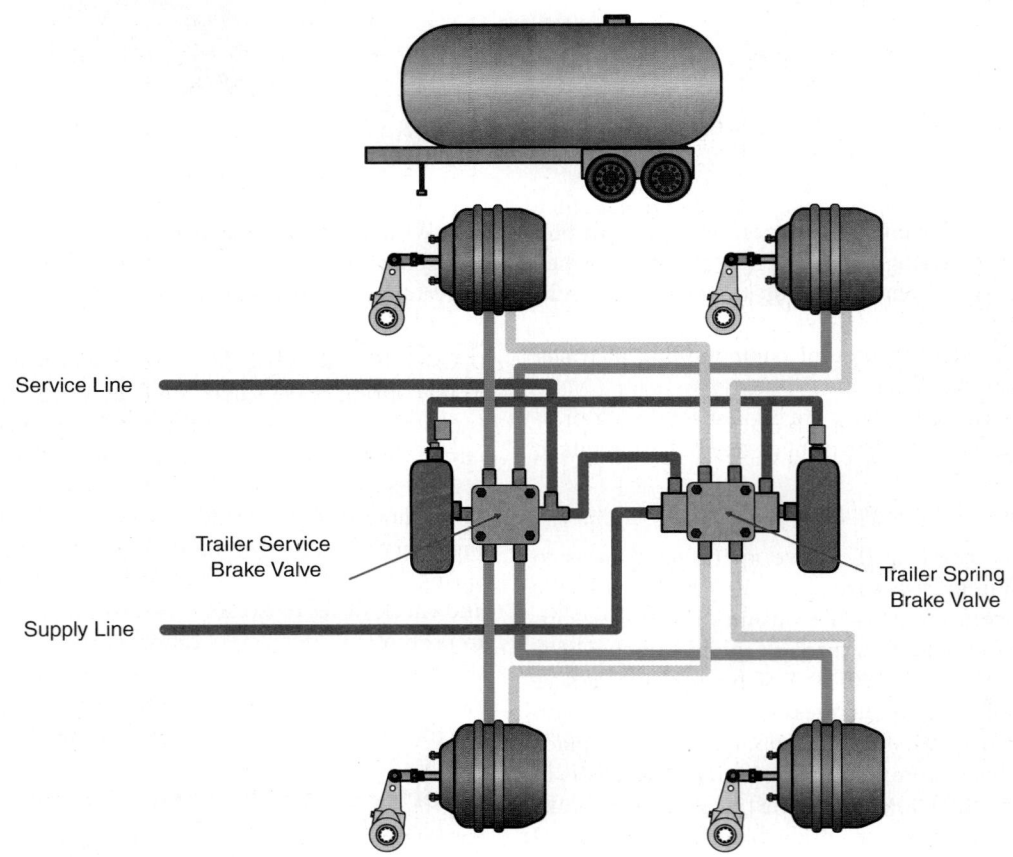

Service Line

Trailer Service
Brake Valve

Supply Line

Trailer Spring
Brake Valve

FIGURE 34-60 A typical air circuit for a trailer.

A popular trailer spring brake valve performs the following functions:

- Provide a fast application of the spring brakes when parking.
- Isolate trailer brake reservoirs from air pressure loss in the event of a loss of trailer supply line air pressure.

- Prevent automatic application of spring brakes if pressure is lost only from the trailer reservoirs. Spring brakes are released with only trailer supply air pressure from the tractor.
- Allow anti-compounding of service and spring forces when the trailer supply line is at atmospheric pressure.
- Limit spring brake "hold-off" pressure to 90 to 95 psi (621 to 655 kPa).

Wrap-Up

Ready for Review

▶ Air pressure is an ideal medium used to multiply and transmit driver braking effort.

▶ Commercial vehicles use dual-circuit, primary, and secondary split brake systems for safety reasons. Failure in one circuit allows the remaining functioning circuit to bring a vehicle to a safe and controlled stop.

▶ The major air brake circuit subsystems include air supply, air delivery, the park/emergency brake system, and trailer air brake system.

▶ The air supply system consists of an engine-driven air compressor, a governor controlling minimum and maximum air pressure, an air dryer to remove moisture and small oil droplets, air reservoirs or tanks (primary and secondary system), pressure protection, and check valves.

▶ Air compressors are reciprocating pumps that are most often gear driven for reliability.

▶ One-way check and pressure protection valves protect all the reservoirs from completely draining if a major air leak occurs. Pressure relief valves protect the reservoirs from rupturing if the compressor does not cut out at the predetermined pressure.

▶ When the compressor is building air pressure, it is loading. When the compressor stops pressurizing air, it is unloading. A governor controls the cut-in and cut-out systems' pressures to determine when the compressor loads and unloads.

▶ Unloader valves, which are small air-operated pistons, hold the compressor inlet check valves open to unload the compressor.

▶ Three air reservoirs are commonly used: a service-supply reservoir (often called a wet tank), a primary reservoir, and a secondary reservoir.

▶ The primary system circuit supplies air for the rear brakes, while the secondary system supplies air for the front brakes. Both systems can supply air to the trailer brakes and the park/emergency circuit.

▶ Air dryers condition system air by removing oil and water contamination. Desiccant material traps contaminants, which are purged from the dryer when the air compressor unloads.

▶ To meet Greenhouse Gas Emission Standards phased in in 2016, air compressors are frequently equipped with

electronically controlled governors and on-off clutches. This change reduces parasitic load on the engine when the compressors are moving when unloaded. The compressors also build air pressure during more optimal conditions to improve fuel economy, such as when the engine decelerates.

▶ Relay valves also contain quick-release valves whose function is to speed up transmission of air brake application.

▶ Foot valves, relay valves, and some other valves have a pressure-compensating feature that enables brake application pressure to remain consistent, even when slight leaks are present in the brake lines and chambers.

▶ Tractors towing trailers use specialized relay valves called proportional relay valves that reduce brake application pressure to the rear brakes and increase front-axle brake application pressure when no trailer is towed.

▶ An anti-compounding feature prevents the application of the service and spring brakes together. A double check valve enables the service brakes to release the parking circuit spring brakes when the park brakes are applied.

▶ Pneumatic brake balance refers to the air system capability to supply the correct pressure to each brake at the correct time. Air brake systems use pneumatic balance, which causes the rear-most brakes to require the least signal pressure and to apply first. Progressively more signal pressure is applied the closer the brake is to the front of the vehicle. Correct pneumatic brake balance helps prevent tractor jackknifing and trailer swing-out.

▶ Dash-mounted push-pull valves control the park brake operation for the truck-tractor and trailer spring brakes. The valves automatically apply the park brakes when brake pressure falls to 30–45 psi (207–310 kPa).

▶ A red octagonal push-pull valve in the cab supplies air to the trailer reservoir and controls the park brake operation.

▶ Trailer air systems can be designed for spring brake priority or service brake priority valving. Spring brake priority enables the trailer air supply to release the trailer spring brakes without first filling the reservoirs. Service priority valving ensures the service brake reservoir is filled first, before the spring brakes are released.

Key Terms

adsorption A process in which material collects on the surface and the air dryer adsorbs moisture from the air and then discharges it in the purge cycle.

Air Dryer Integrated System (AD-IS) An air supply system component that contains an air dryer and several pressure protection valves to regulate charging of the air reservoirs.

anti-compounding valve An air control system design feature that prevents simultaneous application of the service and spring brakes.

automatic drain valve A drain valve located on the bottom of the air system reservoirs that automatically drains any accumulations of water or oil whenever the air reservoir cycles.

bobtailing A tractor traveling without a trailer.

bobtailing proportioning relay (BPR) valve A specialized relay valve used to reduce delivery pressure to the rear brakes of a tractor when no trailer is towed.

brake lag The time delay between driver brake pedal application and brake actuation due to the slower speed of air pressure transmission through air lines and valves.

crack pressure The air signal pressure required to begin delivery of air pressure from a relay valve.

desiccant Silica beads used in the air dryer to trap and hold moisture and oil until the dryer is purged.

double check valves A brake valve with two air inlets and one air outlet. Only the higher inlet pressure leaves the single valve outlet.

dryer integrated module (DRM) An AD-IS-type dryer with the addition of an air reservoir used to assist purging of the spin-on dryer desiccant cartridge.

dual-circuit system A split between the primary and secondary air brake circuits on commercial vehicles done for safety purposes. A failure in one circuit does not affect the operation of the second air or hydraulic brake circuit.

Electronic Air Control (EAC) A controller area network (CAN)-operated air supply system that regulates the air compressor load and unload cycle, plus additional optional air supply system components.

emergency brake circuit The air circuit responsible for the application and release of power springs in the brake chambers. Also referred to as the spring brake circuit or *park brake circuit*.

foot valve The foot-operated valve that controls the application and release of brakes. The foot valve is the center of the brake delivery system and is also called the *treadle valve*.

gladhands The air couplers attached to the trailer hoses connecting the tractor and trailer air systems.

governor An air control valve that regulates the air compressor cut-in and cut-out pressure. The governor also controls the purging of the air dryer.

inlet pressure regulating valve Regulates the maximum air intake pressure supplied to the air compressor from a turbocharged engine's intake manifold.

inversion valve A normally open valve that requires air pressure to close. Another name often given to a *spring brake relay valve*.

limiter valve An air pressure proportioning valve used to increase brake application pressure to the front brakes when a trailer is not towed by a tractor. Also known as a *ratio valve*.

loading The state of the air compressor when it is building system air pressure. The unloader valves are not active.

Nominal Crack Pressure (NCP) The minimum air signal pressure required to begin delivery of air pressure from a relay valve.

one-way check valve A valve with the purpose to protect the air reservoirs and other air system storage units from completely draining if a leak occurs downstream of one reservoir.

park brake circuit The air circuit responsible for the application and release of power springs in the brake chambers. Also referred to as the spring brake circuit or *emergency brake circuit*.

park/emergency braking system The air circuit responsible for the application of the spring brakes for parking. It also has the capability to enable several controlled brake applications if a major air leak occurs in either the primary or secondary air brake circuits.

Pneumatic Booster System (PBS) Injection Booster An option for the Bendix EAC system, which injects a blast of compressed air into the engine intake manifold to reduce turbocharger lag.

pneumatic balance The correct timing of brake application air pressure to each vehicle axle at the correct pressure.

pneumatic imbalance The incorrect timing of brake application air pressure to vehicle axles or brake application at the wrong pressure. Pneumatic imbalance leads to tractor jackknifing or trailer swing-out.

pressure-balanced A feature of air control system valves that ensures air application pressure is consistently maintained to the brake chambers, even when small leaks drain air from delivery components, such as lines and chambers.

pressure-compensating balance valve A term identical to the pressure-balanced valves feature of air brake valves that ensures a consistent delivery of air pressure is maintained despite leaks in the delivery system lines or air chambers.

pressure-compensating relay valve A relay valve having a pressure-balanced inlet and exhaust valve to ensure consistent air delivery pressure to the brakes.

pressure protection valve A normally closed valve that opens after a preset pressure is reached. Pressure protection valves are used to limit maximum charging pressure of air system reservoirs or circuits draining out of the reservoir.

primary circuit Refers to the split brake circuit system used on commercial vehicles. The primary circuit generally operates the rear brakes, while the *secondary circuit* operates the front brakes.

primary reservoir One of two air reservoirs responsible for holding pressurized air for the dual-circuit air brake system.

proportioning valve Valves used mostly on older vehicles equipped with rear drum brakes to reduce rear wheel hydraulic brake pressure under hard braking or light loads. Located in line with the rear brakes.

purge cycle The time between the closing and opening of the dryer purge valve, or the loading and unloading of the air compressor. Oil and moisture trapped in the dryer desiccant are purged when the air compressor unloads.

push-pull park/emergency control valve Hand-operated dash valve used to control the operation of the spring brakes for a straight truck, tractor, and/or trailer.

quick-release (QR) valve An air valve that is used to speed up the release of air pressure from air lines. The valve exhaust closes when supplied air and then opens when air pressure drops.

ratio valve An air pressure proportioning valve used to increase brake application pressure to the front brakes when a trailer is not towed by a tractor. Also known as a *limiter valve*.

relay valve Critical air control valve s used to speed up the flow of air during brake application and release. It uses a small signal pressure to control a larger volume of reservoir pressure.

safety relief valve A pressure relief valve located in the service-supply or wet tank; used to prevent tank rupture from over-pressurization. The valve typically opens at pressures above 150 psi (1,034 kPa).

secondary circuit Refers to the split brake circuit system used on commercial vehicles. The *primary circuit* generally operates the rear brakes, while the secondary circuit operates the front brakes.

secondary reservoir One of two air reservoirs responsible for holding pressurized air for the dual-circuit air brake system.

service brake priority A trailer spring brake relay valve that does not allow the park-spring brakes to release until the trailer air reservoir is filled.

service reservoir The first air reservoir to receive air from the air compressor or dryer. Water and oil condense in this tank, which supplies the primary and secondary air reservoirs. Also called the *supply reservoir*.

snub braking A braking technique that should be used when downhill braking. It requires the truck brakes to be applied hard to slow the truck down to about 5 mph (2 kph), then continued repeatedly until the bottom of the hill is reached.

spring brake priority A trailer spring brake relay valve that allows the park-spring brakes to release with only air supplied by the trailer supply valve.

spring brake relay valve A specialized relay valve that is used to supply air to hold off the spring brakes or release air and apply the spring brakes. Also called an *inversion valve*.

supply reservoir The first air reservoir to receive air from the air compressor or dryer. Water and oil condense in this tank, which supplies the primary and secondary air reservoirs. Also called the *service reservoir*.

Synflex A reinforced nylon material used to make flexible air lines.

tractor protection (TP) valves A valve that controls the supply of air to the trailer from the tractor. The valve automatically isolates the tractor air reservoirs from being completely drained if a trailer breaks away from a tractor.

trailer brake control (TC) valve A hand-operated, cab-mounted control valve used to manually apply the trailer service brakes.

trailer supply valve A push-pull valve in the cab used to supply air pressure to the trailer air brake reservoirs.

trailer swing-out A condition caused by incorrect pneumatic balance between a tractor and trailer. Typically, trailer brakes are applied at too high a pressure, locking the trailer brakes. The trailer tires slide and cause the trailer to swing out into an adjacent lane.

treadle valve The center of the brake delivery system. Also called the *foot valve*.

turbocharger cut-off valves An air-operated valve that closes the air inlet to the air dryer to prevent engine intake boost pressure from leaking out the dryer's purge port.

unloader valves Air-operated piston-like valves used to physically hold open the air compressor's air intake check valves.

unloading The state of the air compressor when it is not building air pressure. Unloader valves hold the check valves open.

wet tank Another name for the service or supply air reservoir. It is called a wet tank since moisture and vaporized oil condense in this tank.

Review Questions

1. Which of the following statements best describes a dual-circuit air brake system used on a tractor-trailer combination vehicle?
   a. The front axle brakes operate independently using a separate air circuit from the rear axle and trailer brakes.
   b. The loss of air pressure in one brake circuit enables the brakes to be applied on a wheel on the same axle but on the opposite side.
   c. Brake circuits are color coded.
   d. Air-braked vehicles have a separate service and a park-emergency circuit.

2. Which of the following events can take place as the compressor transitions from loaded to unloaded operation?
   a. The compressor stops building air pressure, the air dryer purges, and the turbocharger cut-off valve closes.
   b. The compressor starts building air pressure, the air dryer purge valve closes, and the turbocharger cut-off valve opens.

c. Air is exhausted from the compressor unloader valves, the air dryer purge valve, and turbocharger cut-off valve.

d. Air is supplied to the compressor unloader valves and exhausted from the air dryer purge valve and turbocharger cut-off valve.

3. The pressure relief valve on the service air reservoir releases air pressure every 10 seconds. Which of the following is the most likely explanation?

a. A defective air governor

b. Leaking compressor unloader valves

c. Leaking air intake check valves

d. A defective reservoir one-way check valve

4. When draining the air reservoirs on a vehicle equipped with an air dryer, an excessive amount of water is discovered in the reservoirs. What is the most likely cause?

a. A missing air intake filter

b. A coolant leak from the compressor head gasket

c. Excessive compressor discharge temperatures

d. A defective air dryer purge valve

5. It takes 30 seconds to build up primary and secondary system air pressure from 85 to 125 psi (586 to 862 kPa) at maximum engine rpm. What is the most correct service recommendation?

a. Replace the compressor

b. Adjust the compressor governor and retest

c. Service the air dryer and retest

d. Replace the primary tank one-way check valve and retest

6. Which of the following vehicles is most likely to use an air compressor with an electronically controlled, on-off drive coupling?

a. A 2015 and earlier highway tractor

b. A 2010 and later city transit bus

c. A 2015 or earlier medium-duty straight truck

d. A 2016 and later highway tractor

7. When a tractor is bobtailing, the rear axle brakes lock-up under the slightest brake application. What is the most likely cause?

a. The proportioning relay valve for the rear brakes is defective.

b. The limiter-ratio valve for the secondary brake circuit is defective.

c. The tractor protection valve is defective.

d. An anti-compounding valve is defective.

8. In a properly functioning dual-circuit air brake system, which of the following is used to move the foot valves secondary circuit piston downward to apply the brakes?

a. Spring tension

b. Air pressure

c. Contact with the primary piston

d. Mechanical linkage connected to the secondary piston

9. Consider a service brake chamber with a cut and leaking supply hose. What will happen to the air delivery pressure from a relay valve supplying the brake chamber if it has a pressure compensating feature?

a. Air delivery is cut-off to the leaking chamber.

b. Air delivery pressure from the relay valve drops to that line only.

c. Air pressure remains proportional to signal line pressure to all relay valve delivery ports.

d. The relay valve inverts spring brake operation.

10. Which of the following situations is possible if a trailer is equipped with a spring brake valve with a service priority feature?

a. The trailer reservoir does not require filling before the spring brakes can be released.

b. The trailer can be moved after the trailer air supply button is pushed but the trailer will have no service brakes.

c. The spring brakes are released almost immediately after air is supplied to the red supply/emergency trailer line.

d. The trailer cannot be moved until the trailer reservoir is filled to supply air to release the spring brakes.

ASE Technician A/Technician Style Questions

1. Technicians A and B were discussing the advantages and disadvantages of air-braked vehicles. While considering a truck with turbocharged diesel engine and an air compressor air intake connected to the engine's pressurized intake manifold, Technician A says that the truck will lose air pressure at higher altitudes. Technician B says that pressure is not affected, but it will take more time to build up air pressure when the engine is under load. Who is correct?

a. Technician A only

b. Technician B only

c. Both Technician A and Technician B

d. Neither Technician A nor Technician B

2. A bus has service brakes that release slowly. Technician A says that a relay valve is defective and not exhausting air from the brake chamber. Technician B says an air leak in a brake chamber is the cause. Who is correct?

a. Technician A only

b. Technician B only

c. Both Technician A and Technician B

d. Neither Technician A nor Technician B

3. Technician A says the service and spring brakes are both applied when the brake pedal is pushed while the spring brakes are applied. Technician B says the service brakes application will release the spring brakes. Who is correct?

a. Technician A only

b. Technician B only

c. Both Technician A and Technician B

d. Neither Technician A nor Technician B

4. While discussing the loss of secondary reservoir pressure supplying the rear brakes of a tandem-axle truck, Technician A says that the spring brakes are automatically applied. Technician B says that applying the service brakes will release air from the rear spring brake chambers to apply the rear brakes. Who is correct?

a. Technician A only
b. Technician B only
c. Both Technician A and Technician B
d. Neither Technician A nor Technician B

5. Technician A says that spring brake relay valves limit spring brake release pressure to 90 to 95 psi (621 to 655 kPa). Technician B says that full reservoir pressure is supplied to the chambers to release spring brakes. Who is correct?
a. Technician A only
b. Technician B only
c. Both Technician A and Technician B
d. Neither Technician A nor Technician B

6. Technician A says that a compressor with 130 psi (896 kPa) cut-out pressure can be expected to have a cut in pressure of 85 to 100 psi (586 to 689 kPa). Technician B says that the cut in pressure should typically be not less than 20 to 25 psi (138 to 172 kPa) below cut out pressure. Who is correct?
a. Technician A only
b. Technician B only
c. Both Technician A and Technician B
d. Neither Technician A nor Technician B

7. Technician A says that leaking O rings around the compressor's unloader valves will cause the air dryer to frequently purge when there is little or no drop in reservoir air pressure. Technician B says that a leaking governor gasket will cause the air dryer to purge too frequently. Who is correct?
a. Technician A only
b. Technician B only
c. Both Technician A and Technician B
d. Neither Technician A nor Technician B

8. Technician A says that even a small leak in the primary air circuits signal air line from a foot valve will result in a loss of application pressure to the rear brakes of a vehicle. Technician B says that a small leak in the signal line to the service brake relay valve will not result in any change in brake application pressure. Who is correct?
a. Technician A only
b. Technician B only
c. Both Technician A and Technician B
d. Neither Technician A nor Technician B

9. Technician A says that pneumatic brake balance is achieved when all brakes are supplied the same air pressure when braking. Technician B says that pneumatic brake balance requires the selection of relay valves with crack pressures having 4 or more psi (28 kPa or more) difference between the tractor and trailer. Who is correct?
a. Technician A only
b. Technician B only
c. Both Technician A and Technician B
d. Neither Technician A nor Technician B

10. Technician A says that a trailer can jackknife when the trailer's braking force is significantly higher than the tractor's. Technician B says the trailer will swing-out into the adjacent lane when the tractor's braking force is significantly higher than the trailer's. Who is correct?
a. Technician A only
b. Technician B only
c. Both Technician A and Technician B
d. Neither Technician A nor Technician B

CHAPTER 35

Servicing Air Brake Air Systems

Learning Objectives

- **LO 35-1** Identify and explain safety hazards, precautions, and procedures to be observed when servicing air brakes.
- **LO 35-2** Identify and describe common categories of brake system complaints.
- **LO 35-3** Identify common air brake system component failures, associated symptoms, and corrective actions.
- **LO 35-4** Identify and describe preliminary inspection and diagnostic procedures used to identify air brake system faults.

- **LO 35-5** Describe the testing procedure for the automatic emergency brake system.
- **LO 35-6** Identify and describe procedures used to perform inspections for correct brake balance.
- **LO 35-7** Identify and describe common failures and inspection procedures for components in the air supply system.

You Are the Technician

You have recently begun receiving used trucks and buses at your service location and are performing a complete inspection of the equipment for resale. You note, however, that some vehicles have had specialized chassis equipment removed. Others do not have the required "Vehicle Completed" decal located on the driver's side B pillar indicating that the vehicle conforms to all applicable Federal Motor Vehicle Safety Standards (FMVSS). The decal indicates that certification procedures, required by law, have been completed and are designed to ensure the purchaser that their completed or modified vehicle is safe, reliable, and durable.

You remember that some vehicles can leave the factory classified as "incomplete" vehicles because they undergo additional stages of manufacturing to install bodies, specialized accessories, hydraulic, lighting, and other components needed to make them comply with federal standards for completed vehicles. Nonetheless, you want to make sure all vehicles sold at your service location conform to all FMVSS air brake safety standards.

1. Identify the air circuits and components you will focus on to ensure the air brake air circuits are in FMVSS compliance.
2. Identify several diagnostic tests you could use to validate the correct operation of the air circuits in a brake system and that the air system complies with FMVSS 121 standards. Provide reasons for using each of the tests.
3. Describe several complaints drivers would likely report if there were deficiencies in the operation of the air brake circuits. Explain the likely causes for each complaint.

Introduction

Because brake systems are critical to the safe and effective operation of every heavy-duty vehicle, brake system failures can have catastrophic results. This means inspecting, maintaining, and servicing air brake systems are the most critical safety-related operations technicians perform.

Brake system inspection, maintenance, and service includes three major subsystems. First, service must be performed on the system's air supply, air circuits, and air valves, which is outlined in this chapter. Second, technicians must routinely service the brake foundations. Components of the foundation brakes include the slack adjusters, camshafts, brake chambers, shoes, drums, retaining hardware, brake rotors (or discs), and brake pads. Brake foundation service is covered more extensively in the next chapter. Finally, technicians need to ensure that the brakes on every vehicle they service are balanced. **Brake balance** is the ability of the braking system to apply the correct amount of braking torque to each wheel end at the correct time. Ideally, air should supply all the vehicles brake chambers at the same time and pressure. Proper brake balance involves coordination between the brake foundation and air system operation.

This chapter outlines common brake system complaints and describes methods to test air supply and circuit operation that can identify air circuit and supply system malfunctions. It also provides an overview of comprehensive testing and service procedures of air brake circuits commonly undertaken by the commercial vehicle technician.

Safety During Brake System Service

LO 35-1 Identify and explain safety hazards, precautions, and procedures to be observed when servicing air brakes.

Before undertaking any brake inspection, maintenance, or repair, it is essential that the technician have a complete understanding of safe shop practices for these activities. Brake repairs, inspection, and maintenance are some of the most critical life-and-limb, safety-related operations technicians perform. Not only is there a risk to public safety when a vehicle's braking system fails to operate as designed, but brake service work itself has unique safety risks to technicians. Brake dust hazards, sudden release of pressurized air, and unintended vehicle movement are just a few potential hazards facing technicians. A disciplined approach to understanding and following the best work practices and procedures during service work ensures safe vehicle operation and minimizes the likelihood of personal injuries.

When working on or around a brake system and its related components, the following precautions should be observed:

- Wear safety glasses and use a respirator or face mask avoid inhaling brake dust.
- Brake chamber pushrods and slack adjusters may apply when system pressure drops. Keep hands away from chamber and related parts.

- Because a burst of air pressure may whip lines around as air escapes, never connect or disconnect a hose or line containing air pressure. Similarly, do not remove a component or pipe plug unless all system air pressure has been depleted.
- Spring brakes contain a powerful spring that can easily maim or kill someone if released from a brake chamber. Use only the recommended procedures, proper service tools and observe all precautions when performing any service work with these components.
- Do not attempt to disassemble a component until all recommended service procedures are read and understood.
- Always validate all repairs with a thorough road test.

Brake Dust Hazards

The latest types of brake lining are no longer manufactured with any asbestos fibers. Instead, these linings contain a variety of ingredients, such as glass fibers, mineral wool, aramid fibers, ceramic fibers, brass, and carbon fibers. Dust produced by these materials is not specifically regulated by the Occupational Safety and Health Administration (OSHA) and are considered nuisance dusts.

Nonetheless, evidence indicates that certain diseases can develop in individuals who experience long-term exposure to some non-asbestos fibers. Manufacturers recommend that technicians use caution to avoid creating and inhaling dust. Never use compressed air or dry brushing to clean brake parts or assemblies. Doing so sends dust particles airborne. Working in the open air away from other operations is good practice. Never use compressed air or dry sweeping to clean the work area, either.

As a further precaution, the National Institute of Occupational Safety and Health (NIOSH) recommends technicians wear an **N-95 disposable face mask**, such as the one shown in **FIGURE 35-1**. **N-95 masks** filter 95% of all airborne particles. Technicians should wear the respirator from removal of the wheels through final reassembly.

Filtering is not reserved for personal protective equipment (PPE), however. OSHA recommends using filter cylinders to enclose the entire brake end. These cylinders have vacuums with high-efficiency particulate assistance (HEPA) filters and arm sleeves through which the technician can slide his arms while performing inspection and repairs. The arm sleeves enable the technician to work on the wheel end without coming into direct contact with parts and dust.

If individual HEPA filter cylinders are not available, then use an industrial vacuum cleaner with a HEPA filter system to clean dust from the brake drums, shoes, backing plates, and other brake parts. Then, remove any remaining dust with a rag soaked in water or by power washing the wheel end. Even hosing down the wheel ends with a water hose can reduce breathing hazards posed by fine brake dust.

After having worked on brakes, vacuum work clothes and wash them separately from other clothing. Wash your hands before eating, drinking, or smoking. Dust residue on your hands can be ingested and lead to digestive system problems.

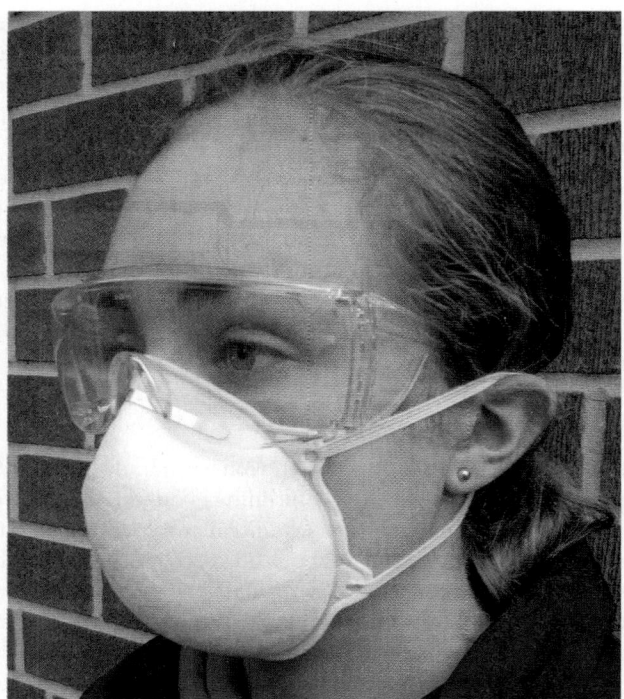

FIGURE 35-1 An N-95 air mask filters 95% of airborne dust particles 3 microns in size and larger.

Vehicle Preparation

When undertaking any brake service activity, it is important to prepare the vehicle correctly. Vehicles should be parked on a level surface and wheels blocked with purpose-made wheel chocks to prevent the vehicle from moving. Locking-type safety stands to support the vehicle must have the appropriate weight capacity for the vehicle. **FIGURE 35-2A** shows the appropriate placement of axle support stands, and **FIGURE 35-2B** shows correct placement of wheel chocks. Never work under a vehicle supported only by jacks—even for a moment. Jacks can easily slip and fall over without warning. Serious personal injury, death, and damage to a vehicle can result.

Preventing serious injury or death caused by the release of stored energy from hazards such as compressed air, power springs, batteries, or running engines is required by health and safety legislation. In the United States, OSHA legislation states that before a technician "performs any servicing or maintenance on a machine or piece of equipment where the unexpected energizing, start-up or release of stored energy could occur and cause injury, the machine or equipment shall be isolated from the energy source and rendered inoperative" (OSHA's Control of Hazardous Energy Sources final rule in 1989).

When this standard is applied to servicing and maintaining air brake systems, hazardous energy refers to, among other possibilities, mechanical movement of the vehicle or components and potential energy due to pressure stored in air reservoirs or power springs. Properly trained, conscientious technicians also regularly disconnect battery cables, relieve air pressure, chock

FIGURE 35-2 **A.** Correct placement of axle support stands. **B.** Correct placement of wheel chocks.

wheels, remove the ignition key, and undertake a number of similar stored energy-control preventative measures anticipating hazards in order to protect themselves, other workers, and equipment.

It is also important when preparing a vehicle to not overlook technology that can interfere with test procedures. For example, on vehicles with automatic traction control (ATC), the ATC can transfer power from a spinning wheel supported on a safety stand to one on the ground. The result is sudden unexpected vehicle movement. So, before performing any dynamic testing where wheels are turning to check components like ABS wheel speed sensors, or testing on a brake dynamometer, the ATC function must be disabled. This means the ATC indicator lamp should be on after removing a fuse or disconnecting a wiring harness to the ATC module. Similarly, collision-avoiding radar, such as Bendix Wingman, should have the power removed to the radar element. This prevents the sudden unintended application of brakes while on a dynamometer.

Diagnosing Brake System Malfunctions

LO 35-2 Identify and describe common categories of brake system complaints.

Many parts of the brake system can be at fault when a complaint is made about braking system performance. It is important to follow a logical sequence in dealing with the complaint to identify the source of the problem. The following are brake system-related complaints that a technician is likely to be asked to diagnose and correct on a regular basis.

Common Brake System Complaints

Brake system inspection is recommended when any complaints about soft brakes, braking noise, pulling, or general air system malfunction are made. Such complaints commonly indicate a defect is likely present in the braking system.

Soft Brakes

Soft brake complaints (also called hard braking) are made when the brakes are applied and the vehicle is not slowing or stopping effectively. Typical causes of soft braking can originate in the foundation brake system, the brake linings and drums, or in the air system itself.

The following defects in the foundation brakes can result in soft braking:

- Brake misadjustment that caused by malfunctioning or incorrectly adjusted brakes, defective adjustment mechanism, incorrect brake parts, or incorrect assembly.
- Worn foundation components, such as brake clevis pins and yokes, camshaft bushings, and S-cams.
- Broken park brake springs producing glazed or hardened brake linings.
- Incorrect chamber size and type.
- Incorrect slack adjuster length.

Soft braking can also result from certain brake lining and drum conditions, including:

- Glazed lining
- Polished drum surface
- Incorrect use of friction material
- Oil- or grease-contaminated linings
- Excessively worn brake lining, cracked or loose brake block

Air system malfunctions can also lead to soft braking. For example, air leaks or restrictions in the application or supply systems can decrease the air pressure available for braking. Contaminated, malfunctioning, or worn air valves can lead to the decrease in air pressure, which results in soft braking.

Braking Noise

All air brake systems make noise—and much more noise than hydraulic brakes. The forces and amount of mechanical movement involved in braking a heavy-duty commercial vehicle are much greater than those found in an automobile. Air brake noise results from the build-up, application, and release of air pressure combined with the movement of mechanical components.

Brake noises from loading air compressors, purging air dryers, and air exhaust from valves are all normal sounds. However, continual air leakage and frequent compressor unloading, and grinding noises from the brakes require corrective action. With training and field experience, a technician can differentiate normal brake noise from unusual or abnormal sounds created when the brakes are applied or normal air system operation.

When diagnosing brake noises, technicians should pay careful attention to the type of noise. For example, observe whether the noise is grinding, squealing, or hissing. Brake squeal is most commonly produced by some type of vibration. Correctly tightened and properly lubricated components normally do not cause brake squeal. However, some brake linings used in severe-service, high-temperature, frequent-stopping applications, such as a transit bus, can be expected to often generate noise.

Technicians should also carefully observe noise volume and whether it is a low or high frequency. Also, technicians should try to locate where in the system the noise is occurring, as well as when the noise takes place. For example, are the brakes warm or cold when the noise occurs? Is the compressor loading or unloading? Is the noise occurring at high or low vehicle speed, or at the beginning or end of the brake application? Finally, the technician needs to determine the braking condition that produces the noise. For example, is the noise heard when applying light, moderate, or heavy brake pressure? And does the noise change as the brakes are being applied? All these observations and inquiries help the technician start to understand the essence of the noise complaint.

The sources of squealing and grinding noises are very different. Squealing noise is typically caused by vibrating parts. Lubricant, such as dielectric grease or antiseize compound, on shoe rollers, anchor pins, and contact points between the shoes and brake spider minimizes noise created at these metal-to-metal contact points. Other typical causes of brake squeal during brake applications include the following:

- Glazed lining and or drums. **Glazing** is a mirror-like finish produced through high temperature, low pressure contact between lining and brake drums.
- Loose lining, brake block, or shoes.
- Loose anchor pins, bushings, camshafts, and support brackets.
- Missing or defective brake shoe return springs, which allow shoes to drag.
- Brake drum design and weight.
- Incorrect lining for the application.
- Poor lining-to-drum contact.
- Improper alignment of foundation parts.
- Imbalanced brakes causing one axle or wheel to perform a disproportionate amount of the braking.

- Dragging brakes or failure of brakes to release.
- Brake shoes rubbing against a rotating drum.

Typical causes of a grinding noise when the brakes are applied include:

- Foreign material embedded in friction material.
- Dislocated brake parts, such as a return spring, roller, or table pin.
- Metal-to-metal contact between brake shoe and brake drum.
- A broken brake shoe or other foundation part failure.

Pulling

Brake pull, also called **brake steer**, is an unintended left or right direction change by a vehicle during a brake application. Not all brake steer is caused by a problem in the braking system. For example, lose or worn steering linkages, wheel bearings, or king pins can be incorrectly attributed to brake pull, since the problem is exaggerated or has a more pronounced effect during braking. Likewise, if the suspension shifts during over the road operation, the vehicle will pull when braking. Broken leaf springs, sheared center bolts, loose U-bolts, broken or loose torque arms, and incorrect axle alignment are a few other common causes of suspension-related brake-pull.

Other potential causes of brake pull include the following:

- Oil- or grease-contaminated lining
- Improperly adjusted brakes or incorrect drum/shoe clearances
- Incorrect brake balance or brake torque
- Mismatched, defective, or worn foundation components, such as brake lining, mixed slack adjuster length, type and brands, and defective air chambers.
- Damaged, kinked, pinched, or undersized brake hoses and or lines
- Defective or incorrect replacement of air system components

Typical causes of pulling brakes:

- Mismatched brake lining or drums on either side of the vehicle
- Glazed lining and drums
- Misadjusted, defective, incorrect type, brand, or mixed use of slack adjusters
- Spring brakes not fully releasing due to a broken spring, air leak, or insufficient release pressure
- Slow release or slow application on one side of an axle (worn foundation brake components, such as camshaft and bushings, binding shoe, a defective quick release or relay valve, pinched or kinked brake line, or seized anchor pin on a closed shoe hole)

Braking Odors

Complaints about smell generally indicate rapid brake wear. Smells are typically related to overheated brake lining. As the brake lining overheats, the resins binding the friction material in the brakes begin to vaporize. This condition can also cause gas-related brake fade because the trapped gasses prevent proper contact between lining and drums-rotors. Similarly, excessive grease from over-lubrication of camshafts or leaking wheel seals can contaminate the friction material with oil or grease. Having grease on the friction material when the linings overheat can produce complaints related to smell.

Linings can wear faster than normal when the driver aggressively brakes or frequently brakes at high-speed. Using an incorrect lining for particular application, dragging brakes, or brake torque imbalance can all contribute to accelerated lining wear as well.

Troubleshooting Air Braking Problems

LO 35-3 Identify common air brake system component failures, associated symptoms, and corrective actions.

Troubleshooting problems in a vehicle's braking system must be undertaken methodically. **TABLE 35-1** is a starting point for identifying common complaints in the air braking system. The information may assist in the diagnosis of air brake systems by identifying common faults and causes, along with possible remedies. Always consult manufacturers' specific information for the vehicle you are working on.

Conducting Preliminary Inspections on Brake Systems

LO 35-4 Identify and describe preliminary inspection and diagnostic procedures used to identify air brake system faults.

Before establishing a diagnosis and recommending repairs, it is important to conduct a series of preliminary tests to inspect the performance of the air brake system. By conducting the preliminary inspections, tests, and measurements described in this next section, a clearer understanding of potential causes for braking complaints will emerge and enable the technician to make appropriate adjustments and effective repair recommendations. After preliminary inspections are performed, more advanced pin point testing can identify specific system faults.

Preliminary Testing Procedures

Conducting preliminary tests help eliminate potential problem areas and help the technician arrive at an accurate diagnosis of the problem. Preliminary tests include inspecting air brake system performance, identifying air leakage, measuring oil consumption, and **brake stroke length**, which is the distance the service brake pushrod travels. During preliminary tests, parking brake function, emergency brake function, and antilock braking performance should also be inspected.

Testing Air Brake System Performance

A starting point for brake inspection during a preventative maintenance inspection is the FMVSS 121 Dual Air Brake System Test. This inspection should be performed on a flat level surface after chocking the vehicle's wheels to prevent it from moving.

TABLE 35-1 Complaints and Possible Causes in Air Brake Systems

Component	Complaint	Possible Causes—Remedy

Compressor	Builds pressure above cut-out pressure	• Verify dash gauge accuracy.
		• Inspect governor operation.
		  • Verify the governor pressurizes the unloader port when cut-out pressure is reached.
		• Inspect unloader/plungers for leaks.
		  • Replace unloader valves, cylinder head, or governor.

	Will not load or build air pressure	• Verify dash gauge accuracy. • Inspect compressor drive coupling (on-off electric operation and mechanical type). • Inspect unloader valve operation. • Inspect exhaust and intake valve operation. • Inspect compressor cylinders for scoring, excessive wear, broken rings, or damaged pistons. • Verify the governor depressurizes the unloader port when cut-in pressure is reached. • Replace unloader valves, cylinder head, air compressor, or governor.
	Slow pressure build-up	• Verify dash gauge accuracy. • Inspect compressor drive coupling (on-off electric operation and mechanical type). • Inspect discharge line for restriction. • Inspect unloader valve operation. • Verify unloader valves and unloader port are not leaking. • Inspect compressor inlet and exhaust valves. • Inspect condition of compressor cylinder walls and rings.
	Pumps excessive oil in reservoirs	• Inspect oil return for restriction, kink, or loop. • Inspect for gasket obstructing drain. • Inspect for undersize return line. • Inspect intake vacuum of the compressor. • Measure engine crankcase pressure for excessive pressure (poor engine ventilation). • Inspect compressor cylinder walls for excessive wear, scoring, or ring wear. • Replace compressor.
Excessive Wet Tank Contamination	Excess oil accumulation	• See Complaint—Pumps excessive oil.
	Excess water accumulation	• Service air dryer desiccant or replace cartridge. • Drain daily. • Install automatic drain on wet tank.
Low-Pressure Buzzer or Warning Light Not Working at Pressures below 65 psi (448 kPa)	Won't operate	• Inspect circuit ground and wiring to low-pressure switch. • Inspect a test sensor operation for three-wire pressure sensor. • Replace switch or buzzer/light. • Inspect dash gauge for accuracy. • Replace switch or buzzer/light.
Safety Relief Valve	Frequently releases pressure	• Verify correct system cut-out pressure is reached or exceeded. • Inspect governor and unloader circuit operation.
	Releases pressure at less than 140 psi (965 kPa)	• Test and replace.
	Leaks	• Replace.
	Does not relieve excess pressure	• Inspect and test periodically: • Remove and test above 150 psi (1035 kPa) with shop air. • Replace if non functional.
Manual Reservoir Drain Valve	Leaks	• Replace.
	Won't drain	• Repair or replace.
Automatic Reservoir Drain Valve	Won't drain in cold weather	• Replace with heated unit.

TABLE 35 -1 Complaints and Possible Causes in Air Brake Systems (continued)

Component	Complaint	Possible Causes—Remedy
	Leaks or malfunctions	• Repair or replace. • Periodic testing: • With system pressure stabilized (compressor unloaded), no leak evident at discharge port; make several foot-brake applications to reduce wet tank pressure. Moisture should automatically drain from discharge port.
Governor	Irregular cut-in and out pressures	• Verify dash gauge accuracy. • Inspect and measure unloader line diameter and compare with manufacturer's specifications. • Inspect unloader circuit for leakage. • Inspect unloader valve operation. • Check operation of other air-actuated accessory. • Inspect governor reservoir line for kinks, restrictions, and verify connection is to top of reservoir. • Repair, adjust, or replace governor.

Single Check Valve	Defective if it allows air to leak back from primary or secondary reservoir to a wet tank	• Periodic test:
		• Drain air pressure from the wet tank and verify primary and secondary pressure are maintained by the one-way check valves.
		  • Bleed the primary supply reservoir and observe gauges. Only the primary reservoir pressure should drop.
		  • Repeat the same procedure with the secondary air reservoir after recharging pressure in all reservoirs.
		  • One-way check valve should maintain air pressure in the secondary reservoir.
		• Replace the check valve if test results show unintended draining of air from the reservoirs.

Primary and Secondary Reservoir	Excess oil/water	• Drain as required. • Check automatic drain valve on wet tank for proper operation. • Replace desiccant cartridge in the air dryer. • Inspect air compressor for pumping oil.
Air Gauge	Incorrect reading	• Verify correct air pressure with master gauge. • Replace gauge if deviation greater than 2%.
Foot (Treadle) Valve	Leaks at the exhaust port when the trailer hand valve is applied	• Inspect and test double-check valve; repair or replace.
	Leaks at exhaust with all brakes released	• Inspect anti-compound double-check valve for unintended reverse flow. • Repair or replace double-check valve. • Inspect foot valve for inlet valve leak. • Repair or replace if inlet valve leaking.
	Leaks at exhaust with foot brake applied	• Foot valve defective. • Repair or replace.
Quick-Release Valve	Leaks air out exhaust port when service brakes are applied	• Replace service brake quick-release valve.
	Leaks air from exhaust port when spring brakes are released	• Replace quick-release valve or spring brake relay valve with integral quick-release valve.
Service Brake Chamber	Leaks when brakes are applied	• Replace diaphragm or chamber actuator.
	Sluggish application or release	• Inspect brake foundation for broken springs and seized anchor pins • Inspect for air-line restriction/leak. • Inspect service chamber broken return spring. • Inspect relay and foot valve operation.

TABLE 35-1 Complaints and Possible Causes in Air Brake Systems (continued)

Component	Complaint	Possible Causes—Remedy
		• Inspect pushrod to slack adjuster angle.
		• Angle should approach 90 degrees on application.
		• Check for improper chamber or obstruction.
Slack Adjuster	Over-tightens or does not adjust for correct clearance	• Replace the slack adjuster. • Inspect S-cam mechanism for loose or worn parts. • Inspect the brake chamber pushrod length and chamber angle using an OEM template.
	Adjusting screw will not turn	• Replace slack adjuster.
	Cracked housing	• Inspect spring brake anti-compound system for compound braking. • Inspect and verify air chamber is the correct size. • Replace with correct size if larger or smaller than original size.
	Worn clevis pin and bushing	• Replace bushing and clevis pin.

Relay Valve	Leaks at exhaust port without brakes applied	• Check pushrod seal in spring brake for back-flow of spring release pressure through service port to open exhaust on valve.
		  • Replace.
		• Check inlet valve in relay valve for leak.
		• If reservoir inlet section of valve shows evidence of contamination, check supply lines for rusty fittings or carbon deposits.
		  • Repair or replace.

	Leaks at exhaust port with service brakes applied	• Exhaust valve not seating properly. • Repair or replace.
Spring Parking Brake (only service chamber side of spring brake)	Parking brake drags or won't release	• Check for: improper adjustment, restrictions, or broken line. • Diaphragm failure. • System pressure too low. • Broken return spring (service spring side). • Quick release of relay valve malfunction. • Broken power spring. • Replace entire unit or piggy-back power spring section.

	Sluggish park application	• Check for:
		  • Failed spring brake diaphragm.
		  • Broken power spring.

	Leaks when pressurized for park and brake release	• Check for:
		  • Ruptured spring-side diaphragm.
		  • Push rod seal leakage.

	Service chamber malfunction	• See service brake chamber.
Park Control Valve (yellow push-pull valve)	Leaks at exhaust port	• Replace.
	Parking brake won't release	• Check for full system pressure delivery through valve.
	Parking brakes won't apply	• Replace valve if it does not exhaust pressure from spring brake relay valve.
Trailer Supply Valve (red octagonal push-pull valve)	Leaks at exhaust port	• Replace push-pull valve.

TABLE 35 -1 Complaints and Possible Causes in Air Brake Systems (continued)

Component	Complaint	Possible Causes—Remedy
	Driver may "over-ride" automatic trailer brakes when tractor air is below 20 psi (140 kPa)	• Replace tractor-protection (TP) valve.
	Won't apply trailer immediately when "pulled"	• Replace if it won't exhaust. • Repair or replace after verifying the TP valve and tractor-only park valve is functional.
Tractor Protection Valve	A slow leak from the trailer supply hose does not shut off trailer air supply at between 40 psi and 20 psi (275 kPa and 140 kPa)	• Inspect trailer supply push-pull valve, to verify it "pops" out at between 20 psi and 40 psi (275 kPa and 140 kPa). • Repair or replace TP valve
	Leaks at exhaust port	• Repair or replace.
Hand Control Valve-Trailer Service Brakes	Leaks at exhaust port when in applied or release position	• Repair or replace.
Stop Light Switch	Leaks	• Replace.
	Fails to signal, wiring and air pressure OK, bulbs check OK	• Replace.
Inversion Relay Valve	Function test: Inversion relay valve with the loss of rear service supply; spring brakes should provide a rear brake application along with front service brakes when applying the service brakes	• Periodically test by bleeding rear service tank and observing front brake and rear spring brake application when depressing foot pedal.
	Leaks	• Repair or replace.
Air Dryer	Air leaking constantly from purge valve	• Purge valve seal damaged. Replace purge seal. • Purge valve frozen. Inspect electric heating element. • Replace the purge valve or air dryer.
	Heater inoperative	• Blown fuse. • Check fuse and replace with 8-correct amperage fuse. Broken wires or poor connections. • Repair or replace wiring to heater.
	Slow wet tank build-up	• Filter and/or desiccant plugged. • Service dryer.

The vehicle's parking spring-brakes are applied, the transmission is in neutral, and supply reservoirs completely drained of air. To conduct a test of air brake system performance, follow the guidelines in Skill Drill 35-2.

Testing for Air Leakage

Technicians need to test for air leakage to determine if the amount of leakage is within acceptable levels. To conduct an air leakage test, follow the steps in **SKILL DRILL 35-1**. The results indicate if the vehicle has an acceptable or unacceptable level of air leakage.

The acceptable level of air leakage in two minutes from either the primary or secondary supply reservoir depends on the vehicle. For a single-axle vehicle with the brakes applied, the limit is no more than 4 psi (28 kPa). For a tractor/trailer combination vehicle, a leak of no more than 6 psi (41 kPa) is allowed, and for a tractor with two trailers, no more than 8 psi (55 kPa). If leaks are detected, they should be repaired, and the vehicle retested to confirm the correct repair has been made. Soapy water can be used to pinpoint leaks.

Air leaks can take place at many points in the vehicle air system. Air leaks from anywhere on the vehicle should be

SKILL DRILL 35-1 Testing for Service Brake Air Leakage

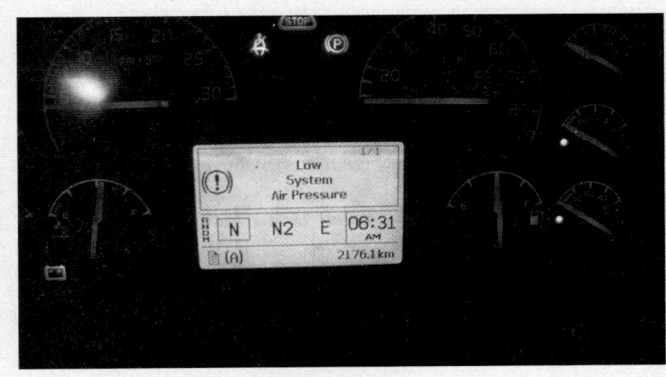

1. Build the system pressure to cut-out pressure.
2. Allow the system pressure to stabilize for one minute.
3. Observe and record the pressure drop on the primary and secondary gauges after two minutes without the service brakes applied.
4. Air leakage should not exceed 2 psi (14 kPa) per minute with single vehicles and 4 psi (28 kPa) for combination vehicles.
5. Fully apply the service brakes and allow the pressure to stabilize. Hold the brake pressure for two minutes.
6. Observe and record the changes in air pressure on both gauges over two minutes after the service brakes are applied.
7. With brakes applied, leakage should be no more than 4 psi (28 kPa) for single vehicles, or 6 psi (41 kPa) for combination vehicles.

identified and repaired, including at the supply reservoirs, vehicle accessories, transmission controls, power divider shift cylinders, parking brake chambers, supply lines, fittings, dash gauges, all brake valves, governor, and compressor discharge valves. As shown in **FIGURE 35-3A**, spring brake chambers use a seal to prevent air leakage from the power spring chamber into the service chamber. A leaking seal causes air to continually leak from the quick release valve or the exhaust port of a relay valve associated with the service brake when the brakes are released. (**FIGURE 35-3B**).

In addition, air accessories, such as the air suspension, power take-off controls, and even the air seats, should be investigated when inspecting for loss of air pressure. Connections to air reservoirs for vehicle accessories are one of many possible sources of air leakage. On the schematic for a coach shown in **FIGURE 35-4**, the number of air reservoirs located throughout the chassis means an extensive inspection for air leaks is required.

Air shift controls for transmissions can leak, also. Worn leaking "O"-rings for range control cylinders can leak inside a transmission and can be hard to pinpoint. Blocking the air supply line to the transmission to determine whether the pressure loss stops leaking can help identify a transmission as a source of leak.

Not all air leaks can be detected using soapy water or easily listening for hissing noises. Leaks behind cab instrument panels and dash, body cavities, and inside transmissions and power dividers due to defective O-rings

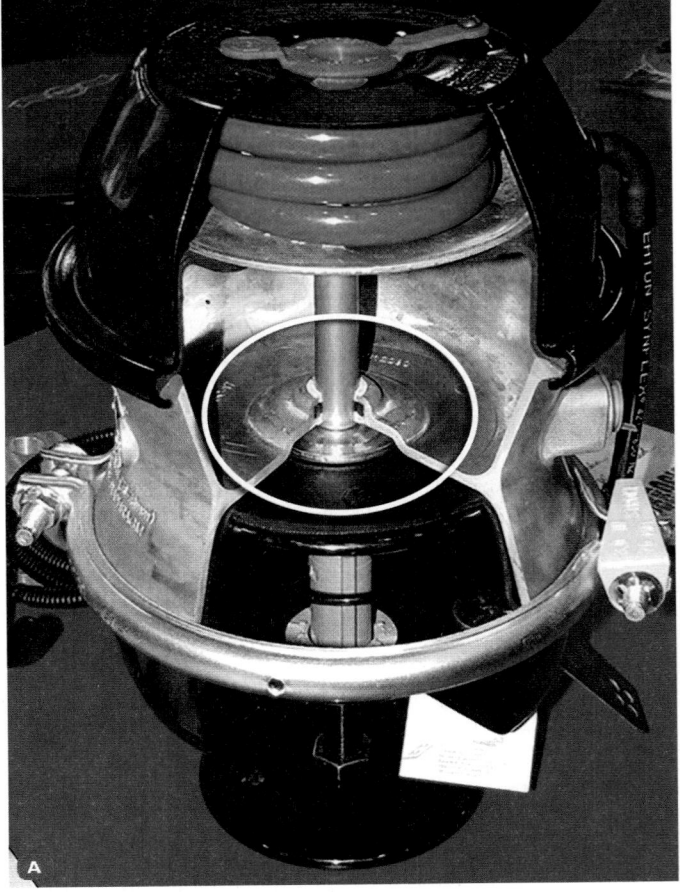

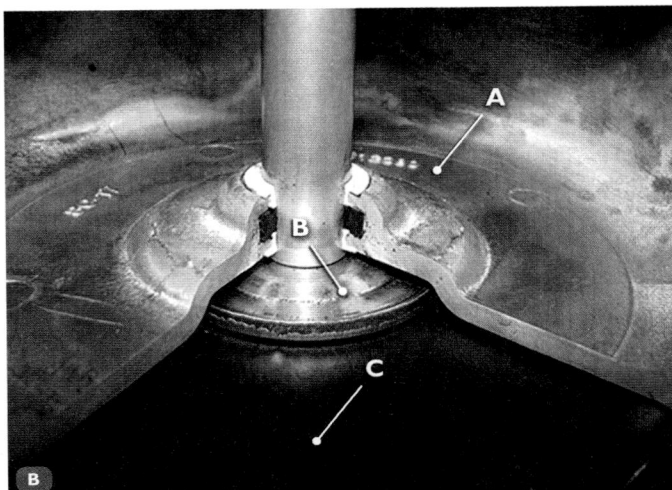

FIGURE 35-3 A. Spring brake chambers with air seal (circled). **B.** Close up of seal with (A) spring brake chamber, (B) seal, and (C) service brake air diaphragm.

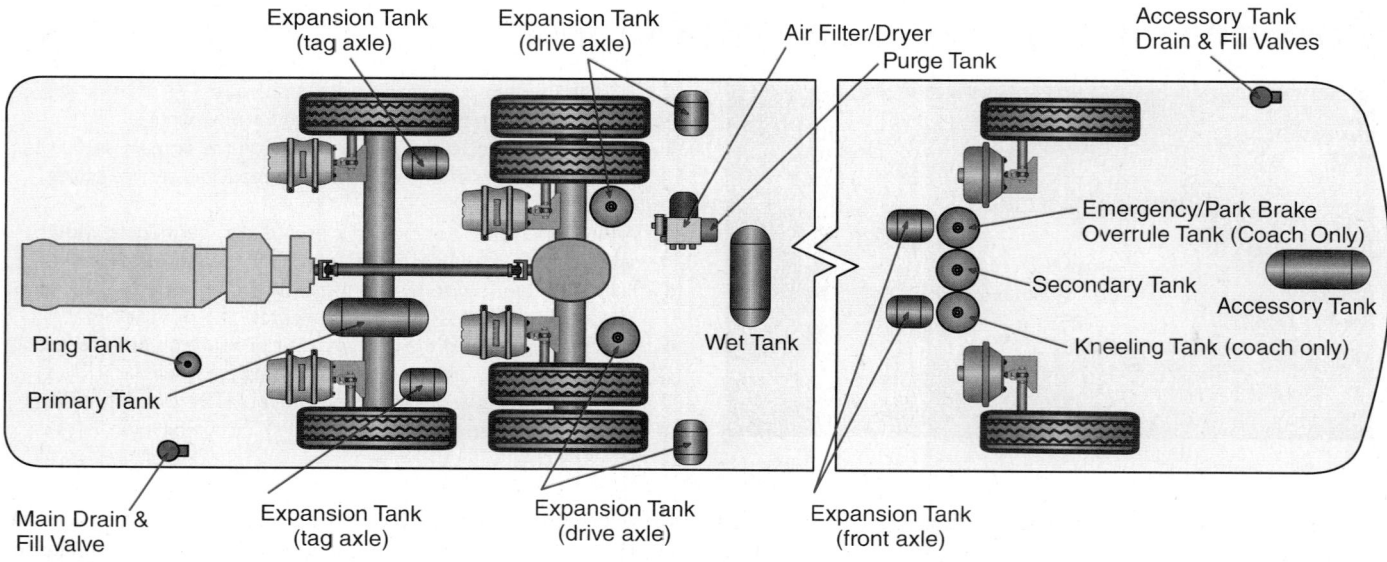

FIGURE 35-4 The number of air reservoirs on a coach presents many possible sources for air leaks.

on shift mechanisms are often difficult to identify. Moving the vehicle to quiet location outside a shop can help a technician detect the sound of smaller leaks. Also helpful for locating some slow leaks causing air to leak-down over several hours are ultrasonic noise detectors. These are more commonly used to locate engine vacuum and air conditioning refrigerant leaks. A technique more often used is to isolate air circuits by disconnecting or pinching air lines. Suspected air circuits can be temporarily pinched using purpose-made tools that do not damage flexible nylon airlines. When the leakage stops, the correct circuit supply line can be traced to precisely pinpoint the air leak.

▶ TECHNICIAN TIP

Air leakage from lines and air reservoirs is the number one cause for compressors to pump excessive amounts of air. The result is that a compressor runs too hot and passes oil vapor into the system. To conduct a thorough air system leakage check, the brake pedal should be applied for two minutes while observing the air pressure gauges. An application pressure of approximately 90 psi (621 kPa) should be used. After releasing the pedal, the gauges should be watched for two additional minutes. When the brakes are released, air leakage should not exceed 2 psi (14 kPa) per minute with single vehicles and 4 psi (28 kPa) for combination vehicles. With brakes applied, leakage should be no more than 4 psi (28 kPa) for single vehicles, or 6 psi (41 kPa) for combination vehicles.

Testing for Oil Consumption

Some oil is normally pumped from the air compressor. The air dryer is responsible for removing oil passed into the air supply by the compressor. Some oil can end up in the air reservoir if the oil volume is excessive, as shown in **FIGURE 35-5**. Oil can mix with water and gum-up air valves. Oil carbonizes in the hot air discharge line and restricts air flow from the compressor. At one time, a cardboard card placed over the compressor's air outlet

FIGURE 35-5 Annual amount of oil that can end up in the air reservoir.

was used to diagnose excessive oil discharge. Too many droplets of oil on the card originating from the air compressor cylinders was the justification to replace the compressor. This test is now obsolete, but when the paper card technique was used, an excessively worn compressor would leave more than two or three drops of oil inside a target area on a paper card, which was placed over an open air compressor inlet.

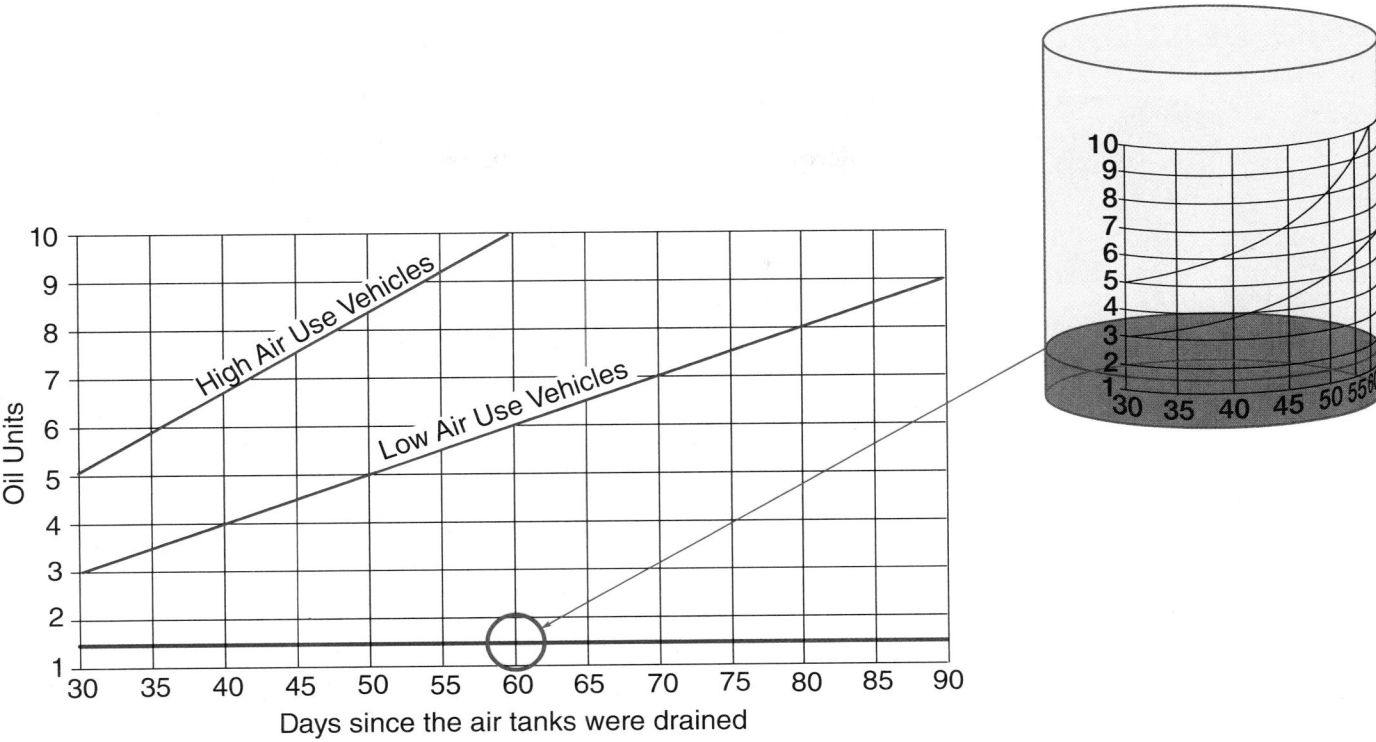

FIGURE 35-6 An oil accumulation chart is printed on the face of a BASIC. Using the amount of oil collected in a BASIC and the time elapsed from the last oil reservoir drain interval, determines the amount of oil passed by an air compressor. The chart is used to evaluate whether oil use is within an acceptable range.

Today, a more reliable and less subjective test recommended by Bendix involves the use of the Bendix Air System Inspection Cup (BASIC). After checking an engine for external oil leaks and the air system for air leaks, the oil in the air system reservoirs is drained into the BASIC as the air tanks are drained. The chart on the side of the cup allows the technician to determine if the level of oil in the reservoir is acceptable.

If more than one unit of oil or a cloudy oil water emulsion is drained, the vehicle's air dryer desiccant should be replaced, and an air leakage test of the entire air system performed. If less than one unit of oil or oil emulsion is drained, the technician uses the chart on the cup to determine if the amount of oil passed by the compressor is within an acceptable range. To make that determination, the technician must know the number of days since the reservoir was last drained. **FIGURE 35-6** shows the chart. Note in the figure that the technician has drained a low level of oil from the reservoir and that it has been 60 days since the air tank was last drained. Because the decision point is under the diagonal line for the acceptable level, the oil level in the air reservoir is acceptable.

Testing the Automatic Emergency Brake System

LO 35-5 Describe the testing procedure for the automatic emergency brake system.

Inspecting the operation of the automatic emergency brake system has two benefits. It helps determine whether the spring brakes will apply during a loss of system pressure. The inspection also helps identify whether several controlled applications of the brake pedal can be used to help slow a vehicle encountering a sudden severe drop in air pressure. Without the split- or dual-circuit feature of the braking system, the controlled or modulated stop feature using only one air reservoir would not be possible, since loss in air pressure in would affect the entire the entire system air pressure.

A variety of valves and circuits are evaluated during this test. Single and double check valves, tractor protection, park control, tractor control, relay, antilock modulators, trailer spring brake, inversion valves, and spring brake relay valves are needed for the proper operation of this circuit. To test the functioning of the automatic emergency brake system, follow the steps in **SKILL DRILL 35-2** for performing a **dual-circuit integrity test**.

Testing the Antilock Brake System (ABS)

Operation of ABS modulator valves can be checked during the initial cycle of the ignition switch. After applying and holding the brakes when the ignition switch is off, the ignition is switched on. During this time, the ABS control module briefly energizes the modulator valve solenoids to test the electrical circuit operation. With the service brake applied, air pressure exhausts from the modulator, making a short, "chuffing" sound. (This test is called the **chuff test**.) Identification of a defective modulator valve can easily be pinpointed by the absence of a "chuff" sound or an unusual noise made by the valve.

Since the modulators are energized in a specific sequence, the location of the valve can be identified using a service manual

SKILL DRILL 35-2 Performing a Dual-Circuit Integrity Test

1. Charge both supply reservoirs to full pressure. With the engine stopped, drain the front axle reservoir (primary or secondary depending on the manufacturer) to 0 psi. Verify the following:
   • The rear axle reservoir does not lose any pressure.
   • On a tractor and trailer combination, the trailer air reservoir remains charged.
   • Tractor and trailer brakes should not apply automatically.
2. With air pressure in the front axle reservoir at 0 psi, fully depress the brake pedal to make a brake application and then release the pedal. During this time, verify the following:
   • Rear axle brakes should apply and release.
   • Trailer brakes should also apply and release on combination vehicles.
   • The brake lights should light up and go out.
3. Slowly drain the rear axle reservoir pressure using the reservoir drain. Verify the following events take place:
   • The front brake reservoir does not lose any pressure
   • The park brake push-pull control valve should pop out to apply spring brakes at between 35 psi and 45 psi (241 kPa and 310 kPa).

   • Tractor protection valve on a combination vehicle should also pop-out to close the trailer supply at between 20 psi and 45 psi (138 kPa and 310 kPa) and the trailer air supply hose (red) should be exhausted, usually through the tractor protection valve exhaust port.
   • Trailer park brakes should apply only after tractor protection valve closes.
   • When the test is performed with a full front axle brake reservoir, the front axle reservoir should not lose pressure.
4. After closing both reservoir drain valves, build up system air pressure. Stop the engine and drain rear axle reservoir to 0 psi. With no air pressure in the rear axle reservoir, apply and release the service brake pedal to make a brake application. Verify the following events take place:
   • Front axle brakes should apply and release.
   • On combination vehicles, the trailer park brakes should also apply and release.
   • The inverting relay spring brake control valve on straight trucks should cause the rear axle brakes to apply and release in unison with the front brake application and release.
5. On tractors and other towing vehicles, an additional test of the tractor protection valve includes disconnecting the red trailer supply/emergency airline and draining air from the tractor reservoir.
6. Record the pressure at which the octagonal-shaped, dash mounted, push-pull trailer supply valve pops out during a service brake application. Perform this test after the supply reservoirs are both charged to cut-out pressure. Disconnecting the red tractor-trailer supply/emergency circuit gladhand while the service brakes are applied must eventually cause the trailer supply valve in the cab to pop-out at between 20 psi and 45 psi (138 kPa and 310 kPa).

or by simply listening and pinpointing the valve without a correct "chuff." Note that the chuff test does not work unless the vehicle is stationary. **FIGURE 35-7** shows a modulator. Moving the vehicle prevents performance of the test.

Conducting Advanced Brake Balance Testing

LO 35-6 Identify and describe procedures used to perform inspections for correct brake balance.

After completing preliminary tests, more comprehensive test procedures can be performed to evaluate brake balance. Correct brake balance is achieved when all brakes apply and release at exactly the same time, with each brake applying the correct braking force or torque required, according to axle load. Brake balance has two main elements—torque and pneumatic balance. Torque balance is related to the braking force applied by the brake friction materials at each axle end. Ideally, each brake end equally applies its designed braking force to the wheel for any given load, when properly balanced. Wheel ends, such as the front axle with smaller drum, shoe, and brake chambers actuators, exert less brake torque than the drive axle wheel ends

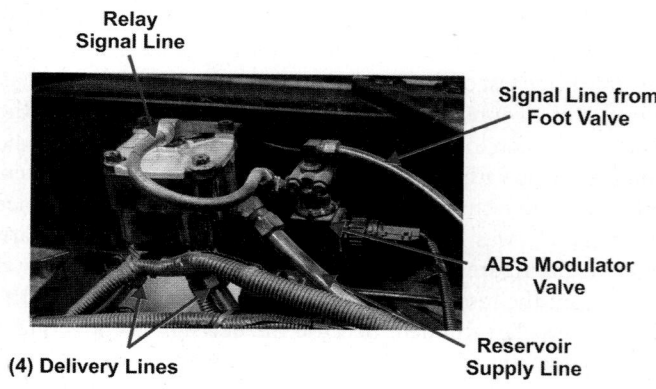

FIGURE 35-7 Modulator.

with larger brakes, but the drive axles can be expected to support more weight, requiring greater braking force.

Pneumatic balance is related to the supply and timing of the air pressure at each brake chamber. The same pressure should be supplied at the same time to all wheels when correct pneumatic balance is achieved. Brake balance is important to vehicle safety, particularly on combination vehicles.

For example, a tractor and trailer with unbalanced brakes that applies the tractor's brakes faster and more aggressively than its trailer can cause jackknifing. Uneven lining wear takes place with the most rapid wear on wheel ends supporting the most load and doing the greatest amount of work. Testing brake balance, which involves measuring brake torque, air pressure, and timing of air signals, is more complex diagnostic procedures, but ones that are sometimes necessary to identify unusual brake system faults.

Testing Pneumatic Brake Balance

The purpose of measuring air brake pressure between different axles is to verify correct pneumatic brake balance of the brake system. Pneumatic imbalance causes some wheel ends or axles to work harder to brake than others, and imbalance is present when brake applications at the wheel ends are not synchronized. Significant pneumatic brake imbalances can lead to vehicle instability during braking, brake fade, and even brake fires.

If a tractor's drive axles have a higher level of braking force than the trailer axles, the tractor drive axles can brake too aggressively and may lock up and cause a loss of directional stability. Since steering can take place only when tires are rolling, locked tires behave more like snow skis or a water board, preventing effective steering control. Even if the tractor's tires

have not locked, but the brakes are applying more braking torque than the trailer's, the unrestrained rolling trailer tires and trailer weight enable the trailer to push the tractor and rotate it around the king pin. This condition is called jackknifing and is shown in **FIGURE 35-8A**. A similar condition takes place when the trailer, rather than the tractor's, brakes lock-up. In this situation, the trailer loses directional stability as the tractor drags the trailer, causing the trailer to swing out into another lane, as shown in **FIGURE 35-8B**.

Two main contributors to correct brake balance are proper torque balance and pneumatic balance. Proper brake **torque balance**, which refers to the actual application force or retarding power at the wheel end, is produced using properly matched and maintained air and foundation system components, correctly adjusted brakes, plus properly loaded vehicles. The lack of uniform friction-material to friction-surface contact means some wheel braking torque is greater than others. In other words, if a truck, bus, or trailer unit has a torque imbalance, some of the brakes will not work well at all, resulting in longer stopping distances. Other brakes may work harder and lock up easier than others, leaving destructive flat spots on tires. Unequal-length slack adjusters, oil-contaminated linings, or mismatched linings can contribute to brake torque imbalances between wheel ends.

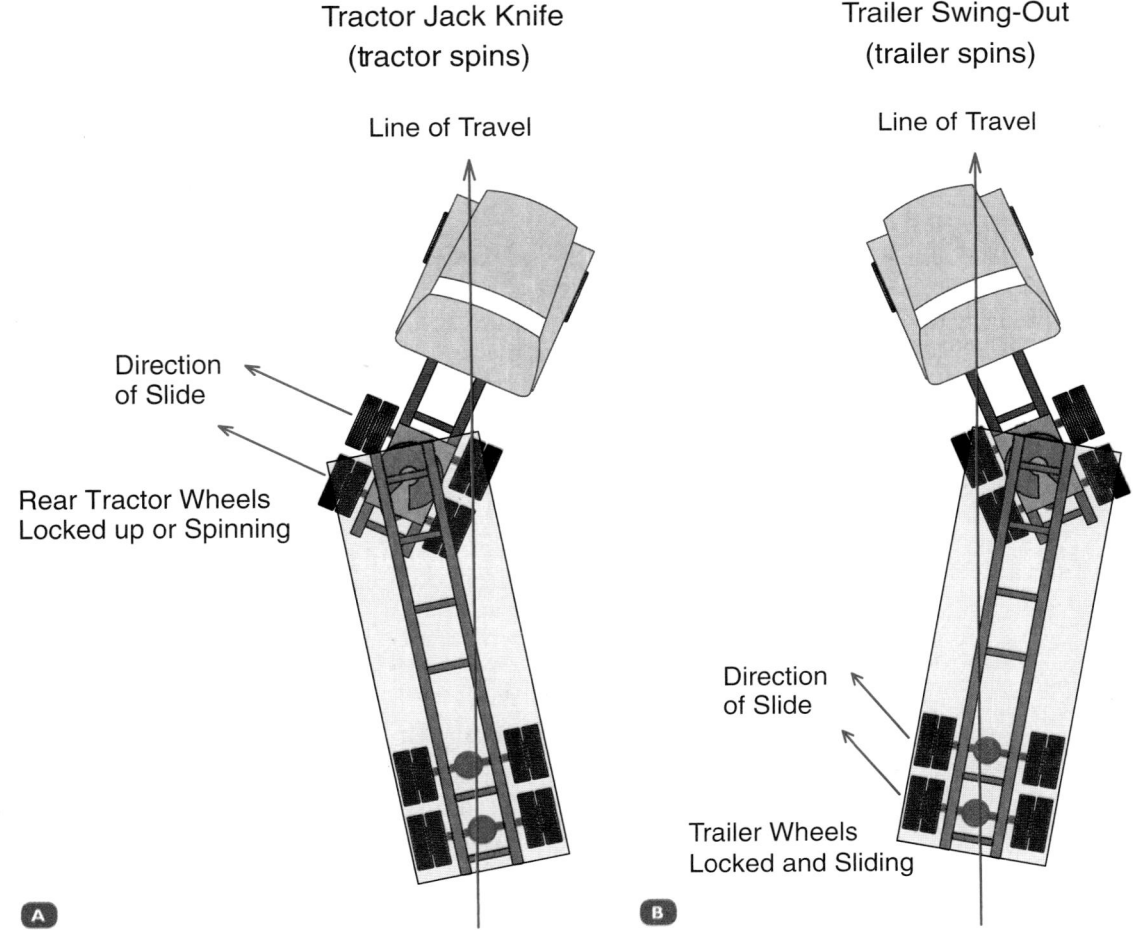

Tractor Jack Knife
(tractor spins)

Line of Travel

Direction
of Slide

Rear Tractor Wheels
Locked up or Spinning

Trailer Swing-Out
(trailer spins)

Line of Travel

Direction
of Slide

Trailer Wheels
Locked and Sliding

A

B

FIGURE 35-8 A. Tractor jackknife. **B.** Trailer swing-out.

Unlike torque balance, **pneumatic balance** is created by having equal air pressure at all wheel ends supplied at the same time. The distance air signals and air pressure must travel over the length of a combination vehicle can delay the application of brakes farthest away from the foot valve. A vehicle with a pneumatic imbalance allows some brakes to work harder by applying sooner than others, and lock up easier than others. Of course, the opposite situation can be present, when pneumatic imbalance allows brakes to apply too late or with inadequate application pressure. Incorrect pneumatic balance problems typically affect only one axle or a set of axles, such as the tractor tandem drive axles or the trailer axles, or the front axle and single rear axle.

While ABS can prevent over-braked wheels from locking-up, ABS is not a substitute for balanced braking. High application pressure braking of an ABS-equipped tractor connected to a non-ABS-equipped trailer, or a trailer with a non-functioning defective ABS, can lock its brakes, causing it to rapidly swing out of its lane.

Common causes of torque imbalance include:

- Oil- or grease-contaminated friction material
- Polished drums or rotors
- Glazed friction material
- Mixing friction capabilities of brake linings or pads at one or more wheels
- Oversized drums and thin rotors
- Improper brake adjustment
- Mismatched brake chambers and automatic slack adjusters
- Improperly installed automatic slacks or unequal length arms on slack adjusters
- Defective or inoperative ABS wheel speed sensors
- Restricted air lines or incorrectly operating air circuit valves

A brake torque imbalance can be discovered by inspecting the brake linings. If a torque imbalance exists, the linings at some of the wheel ends wear faster than others. Another effective technique is to make several hard-braking applications and measure brake drum or rotor temperature. Variations of more than 20° F (11° C) from side to side on the same axle, or 100° F (56° C) from steer to drive axles that a, indicate a torque imbalance.

FIGURE 35-9 A metal tag on a relay valve designating crack pressure. Tractors and trailers use relay valves with different crack or opening pressures.

Identifying Brake Timing Imbalance

A **brake timing imbalance** occurs when some brakes receive air faster than others. FMVSS standards require that a 60 psi (414 kPa) application air pressure at each brake chamber should not be delayed more than 0.45 seconds for trucks and buses and 0.50 seconds in the case of trailers when timed from the initial application of the service brake treadle valve.

Brakes must also release quickly. With 95 psi (655 kPa) of air pressure in each brake chamber, application pressure must fall to 5 psi (34 kPa), taking no longer than 0.55 seconds for trucks and buses when measured from the initial release of the treadle valve. On trailers, the same pressure reduction is required within 1.00 second. Slightly longer times are allowed in multiple-trailer combinations.

The distance air signals and reservoir air volume must travel in long combination vehicles can interfere with the ability of brakes to apply at the same time with the same pressure. Air signal time can lag and air pressure in long lengths of lines drops as distance increases or as the air changes direction. To speed-up brake applications and help correctly time or synchronize brake applications, tractors and trailers use relay valves with different crack or opening pressures. These crack pressure differences are depicted in **FIGURE 35-9**. Crack pressure is the signal air pressure required to enable the relay valve to begin supplying air to brake chamber actuators. It takes time to transmit air pressure over a longer distance to the trailer. Therefore, having a lower crack pressure on the trailer than on the tractor helps the brakes to apply at the same time across the vehicle. Front-axle crack pressures should be the highest. Otherwise, the front axle uses a limiting valve, which reduces air pressure by approximately 50% when application pressures are below 40 psi (276 kPa), or when towing a trailer.

▶ TECHNICIAN TIP

Air pressure loss in piping takes place due to friction between the air and the pipe walls. Like electrical circuits carrying amperage, air circuit pipe diameter must increase to prevent a loss of air pressure and volume supplied to valves and air chambers. The use of fittings and bends in pipe, plus the change of air direction through valves, also has significant effect on air pressure and volume. Depending on the air velocity and diameter of pipe, a 90-degree fitting in an air line causes as much as a 15% drop in air volume and pressure due to a drop in air velocity. A T fitting can be close to twice the loss of a sharp 90-degree elbow. The loss of air velocity through valves and fittings does not add up, but has a compounded effect on system performance. Avoid the use of sharp bends in air lines and the use of fittings, which contribute to loss in air pressure and volume.

Testing Air Brake Pressure Balance

Pneumatic or air pressure imbalance occurs when the tractor's or trailer's air system either delivers incorrect air pressures to brake chambers on a combination vehicle or delivers the pressure at the wrong time or out of the correct sequence with other axles. The most common causes of pneumatic imbalance are incorrect or malfunctioning relay valves. Quick-release valves can also malfunction in ways that interfere with air pressure balance. Pinched or kinked air lines, air leaks, leaking gladhand seals, air system contamination, and a variety of other valve-related problems can contribute to pneumatic imbalance.

Pneumatic imbalance is measured with a duplex gauge, such as the one shown in **FIGURE 35-10**. The **duplex gauge** is essentially two air gauges in a single housing. Two color-coded hoses approximately 35' long are connected to corresponding and similarly color-coded gauge indicators. This configuration allows the pressure in both lines to be observed simultaneously by a technician. Input and output air pressure at separate points in the brake system can be measured with duplex gauge. Air restrictions, pressure imbalances, or inadequate air pressure are also commonly measured when diagnosing air system complaints using a duplex gauge. Comparing pressure between two points enables a relative comparison of air pressure and the time it takes for air pressure to arrive at components.

The duplex gauge can measure the pressure balance from the front steer to rear drive axle. After installing the duplex gauge to the service side of a front and rear air brake chamber, the service brakes are applied in 10 psi (69 kPa) increments up to 80 psi or 90 psi (552 kPa or 621 kPa). The pressure difference between the front and rear brakes should not exceed 2 psi (14 kPa). Since industry studies have observed 80% of all braking applications are 20 psi (138 kPa) or less, the 2 psi (14 kPa) recommendation identifies consistent braking application force, especially important at low application pressures.

Another useful tool is the gladhand test unit. It can measure air pressure supplied to the trailer, as well as the time it takes to build and release air pressure in the service line. **FIGURE 35-11** shows a gladhand test unit.

Unbalanced trailer brake pressures are typically caused by the following:

- Malfunctioning relay valves
- Malfunctioning brake application/foot valve
- Kinked or restricted lines

Consider a couple of scenarios that a technician is likely to face about testing air brake pressure balance. In one scenario, a driver visits the shop complaining that the trailer of his combination vehicle seems to be pushing the tractor. The customer describes a delay in the brake application in the trailer or a brake application with lower pressure than the tractor results in an alarming bump by the trailer into the tractor. The bump takes place because the trailer pushes the tractor power unit. If the imbalance is large enough, the bump can potentially push the tractor off the road on slippery wet or icy roads when braking through a curve. Imbalance results in a jackknife condition, or the combination unit is run off the road. In the situation described by the driver, the tractor brakes are likely applying sooner and at a higher pressure than trailer brakes. To validate the problem, connect one end of the duplex gauge to points 1 or 2 as shown on **FIGURE 35-12** to check application timing and pressure. If the trailer application pressure is suspected to be higher, then connect the other duplex gauge line to measure points 2 and 3. If the pressures are the same, measure between 3 and 4. If pressures are the same on the trailer, the problem is in the tractor system, which is sending a higher-than-normal signal pressure.

Still using Figure 35-12 as a guide, consider a different complaint. This time, the trailer brakes are slow to release. Connect the duplex gauge to points 2 and 3. Make a brake application while closely observing the slack adjuster arm. If the gauges return to zero quickly together, but the slack adjuster only moves after air is exhausted, there is likely a binding mechanical condition in the brake foundation. Weak brake shoe return springs, chamber defects, and dry cam bushings are several possible causes.

Inspecting and Servicing Air Brake Valves

Variations in pneumatic balance and brake timing are magnified on slippery road conditions. Not only is jackknifing and trailer "swing out" more likely to happen, but a trailer

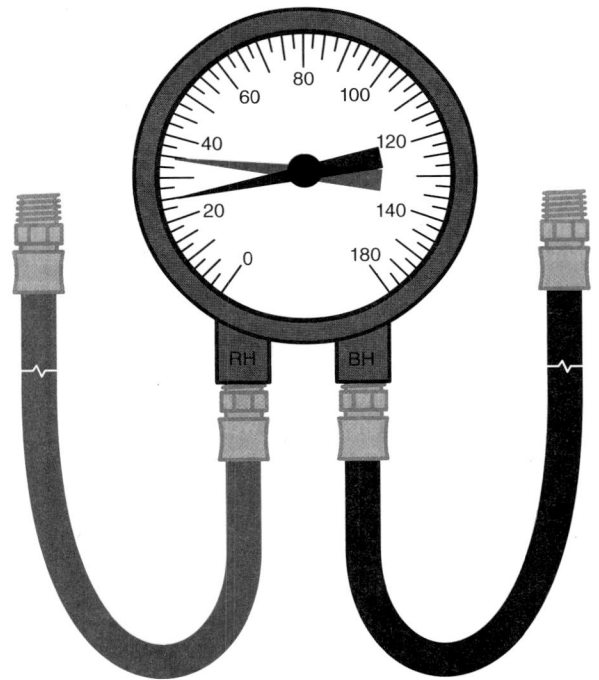

FIGURE 35-10 A duplex gauge.

Gladhand Test Unit

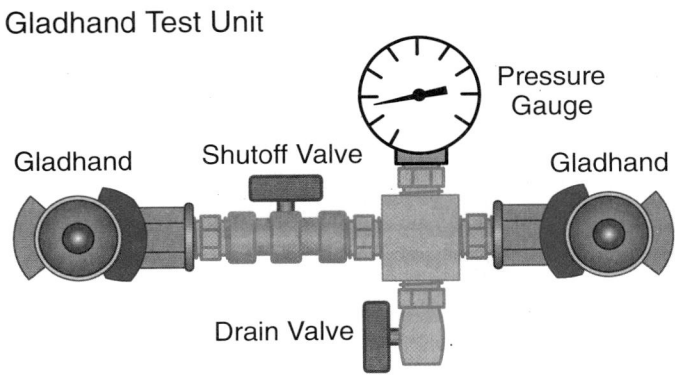

FIGURE 35-11 Gladhand test unit.

Tractor Test Points

Trailer Test Points

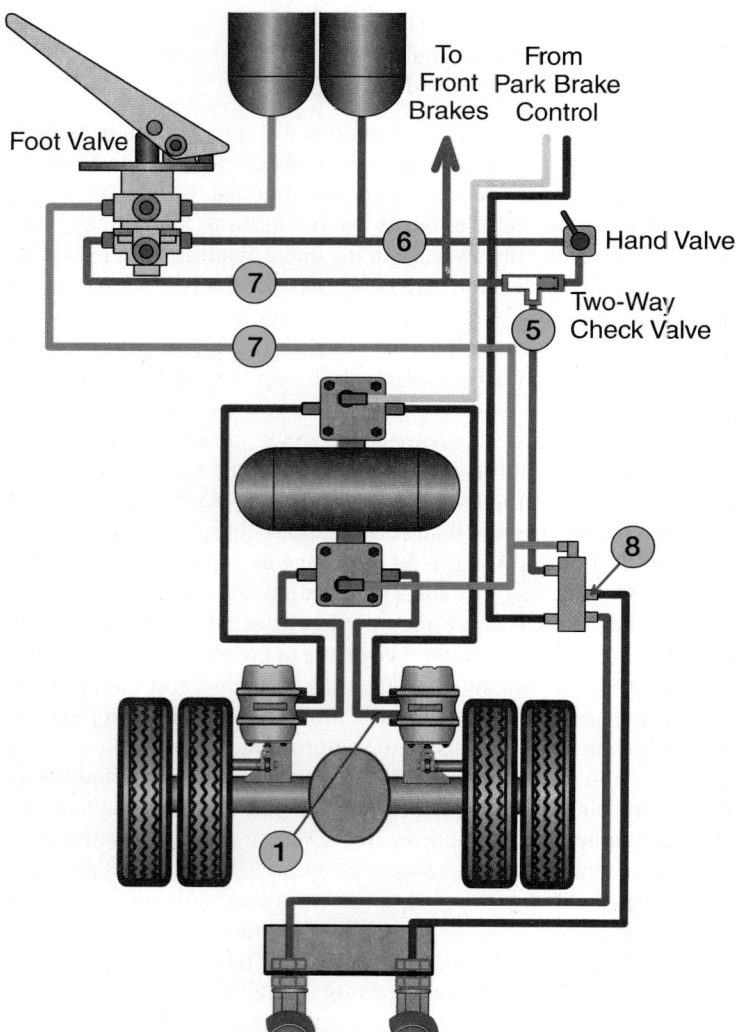

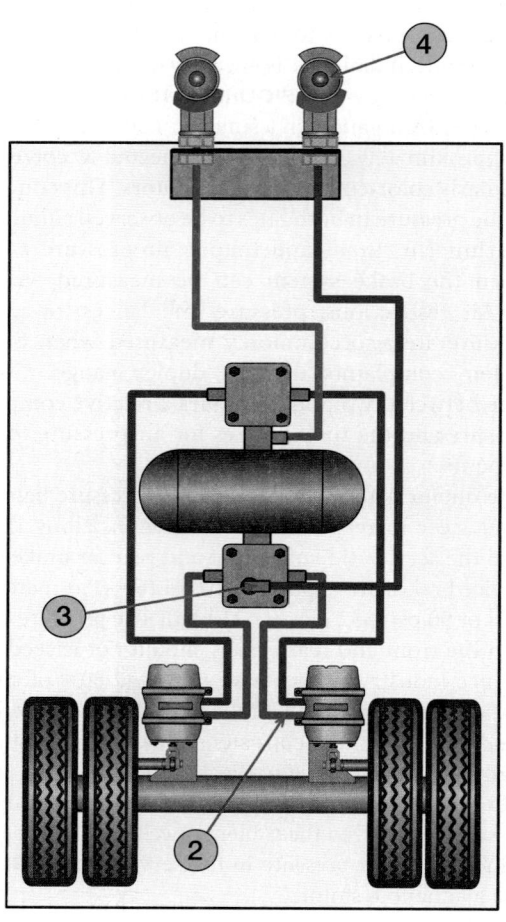

FIGURE 35-12 Pneumatic balance duplex gauge check points.

can push a tractor off the road on a curve or into the ditch if brake balance is poor. Synchronization of braking applications requires careful selection of replacement brake valves and lines—assuming a tractor and or trailer was correctly built by the manufacturer.

For instance, relay valves are especially important for pneumatic balance and timing. Relay valves not only influence brake timing but also are used to speed-up both application and release of air brake pressure. By varying the air pressure signal supplying the relay valves control port, making it proportional to brake pedal movement, the delivery air pressure to brake chamber actuators can be graduated to vary brake torque to each axle. The pressure required to initiate delivery of air pressure from the relay valve is an important design feature of relay valves and the air system. Relay valve crack pressure refers to

the minimum air pressure required to trigger the relay valve to begin air delivery.

Technicians must be especially attentive to a relay valve's crack pressure to provide correct pneumatic brake balance to an air system. Not all relay valves or any relay valve are the same, even though they may appear identical. There are dozens of valves to choose from with different crack pressures. Tractors use higher crack pressures than trailers to make sure the more distant brake valves of the trailer open at the same time as the tractor. This is necessary since control air signals take longer to travel to the more distant trailer valves. Lengthening signal transmission time is the dimeter of large lines requiring greater air fill volume. Trailer signal lines are typically 1/2" (13 mm) in diameter, compared to tractor control lines at 3/8" (9.5 mm), to compensate for the effect of pressure drop in air signals encountered in narrow lines travelling long distances. A trailer with a high crack pressure relay valve has a significantly slower or later brake application than the tractor and tends to push the tractor when braking. Since 1991, FMVSS 121 regulations require all brake valves to contain labeling or tags stating crack pressures. Technicians must ensure the crack pressure of valves removed from equipment is the pressure specified for the trailer, and ensure a replacement valve has identical specifications.

Higher crack pressures also increase the differential between control signal air pressure and delivery air pressure. A tractor valve may have a crack pressure as high as 15 psi (103 kPa), while trailers typically use valves between 1 psi and 4 psi (7 kPa and 28 kPa). When replacing brake valves, both new and rebuilt valves must have a metal tag with a detailed part number identifying valve characteristics. Once the valve is confirmed as defective, it is critical to replace one with exactly the same performance specifications.

▶ TECHNICIAN TIP

Electronic control of air brakes can eliminate brake balance problems because the system can transmit an electrical signal to the relay valves, which can immediately respond to driver demand to apply a brake and do it more quickly. Superior brake balance, plus many other features and advantages, are offered by electronic brakes, but current FMVSS 121 regulations require a full pneumatic back-up system to any electronic control. Duplicating the electronic controls of electronic braking systems with a pneumatic brake system puts electronic braking at a significant cost disadvantage. This explains why electronic braking is currently not commonly used in on-highway vehicles and will likely be used only when vehicle has an automated or autonomous driving system use only electronic signals to apply the brakes.

The Skill Drills 35-1 and 35-2 described how to inspect, test, and, if necessary, replace a variety of air brake system valves.

Servicing the Air Supply System Components

LO 35-7 Identify and describe common failures and inspection procedures for components in the air supply system.

A primary function in servicing any brake system is being able to service the components of the air supply system. A technician needs to be familiar with the unique servicing issues of the air compressor, governor, air reservoirs, pressure gauges, air dryers, and evaporator and injection systems.

Air Compressor

The air compressor often drives the engine fuel pump. Sometimes the air compressor even drives the power steering pump bolted to the rear section of the compressor. The compressor crankshaft is designed to accept a drive-coupling placed between the compressor and fuel pump. A defective fuel pump or power steering pump drive seal can leak into the compressor's crankcase. Lubricating oil inside the compressor can also be pulled into the power steering pump or fuel pump. So, when searching to pinpoint the cause of these unusual conditions, do not overlook this area where fluids can leak back and forth between what seems like completely unconnected systems. Lubricating oil for the compressor's crankshaft and pistons is supplied to the compressor by a line from the engine cylinder block oil gallery connected to the air compressor. A crankcase sump in the compressor returns oil to the oil pan through a drain hose, or drains oil into the front geartrain through the compressor crankcase.

Compressors are typically driven by the front- or rear-engine geartrain, which is a more reliable coupling than a belt-driven drive. Unlike belt-driven drives, no maintenance is required on a direct-drive gear coupling. The latest compressors use a controller area network (CAN)-controlled clutch to reduce parasitic power drawn by the compressor when it is operating and to optimize the operating cycle time of an air compressor for improved efficiency.

Engine coolant is commonly supplied to the compressor through two flexible hoses that are connected to engine water jackets. A compressor with a damage head gasket can over-pressurize the engine cooling system, giving the engine symptoms of a leaking head gasket or cavitated cylinder liner or cylinder wall. This condition is best detected by measuring cooling system pressure with the engine running and the air reservoir drains opened. A reduction in engine cooling system pressure indicates the compression leak into the cooling system is originating from the compressor. Alternatively, the coolant lines to the compressor can be crimped with purpose-made tools. Temporarily cutting coolant flow from the compressor to the engine reduces cooling system pressure in the engine resulting from a compression leak from the compressor.

Other common compressor problems include compressor noise and a broken compressor crankcase. Less obvious, but still common are compressor problems include pumping oil and slow air build-up time due to worn or scored cylinders, defective unloader valves, and leaking unloader and discharge valves.

Pumping Oil

A compressor is said to flood when its crankcase overfills with oil. This situation is often caused by a blocked or restricted oil drain. When the compressor's crankcase is flooded with oil, oil is forced past the piston rings. The compressor then produces oil discharge. Another cause for a flooded compressor is a restricted air intake. When restricted, the negative intake air pressure causes the compressor to pull air up from the crankcase and past the piston rings.

A worn-out engine produces excessive piston ring blowby, causing high compressor crankcase pressure. Blowby contains oil droplets that pushes past the compressor's piston rings only when the compressor is unloaded. When loading, air pressure in the cylinders prevents oil from moving past the rings. Conversely, a worn-out air compressor can increase engine crankcase pressure.

An optional intake check valve is available on some models, which can hold 4 or 5 pounds of air pressure in the compressor cylinders when unloaded. The additional air pressure in the compressor cylinders surges back and forth through the unloaded or open intake valves from one cylinder to the other, reducing any parasitic power draw from the engine. Oil is also prevented from passing around the piston rings and into the cylinders.

A compressor that is pumping oil does not pump it out the air intake while it is loading. That's because its air intake valves are closed during the compression stroke. Instead, oil is passed out the compressor discharge line. Note that a defective compressor piston with a hole in it, or one with worn cylinders or broken rings, can also allow pressurized intake manifold air into the engine crankcase. Air in the engine crankcase can dramatically increase engine crankcase pressure and cause the intake manifold to lose boost pressure. Many engines have been unnecessarily rebuilt due to a defective air compressor after an assumption has been made that high engine crankcase blowby is only caused by a worn-out engine. Closing the intake passage from the intake manifold to the compressor inlet is critical when performing blowby testing of engines, or identifying the cause of excessive engine oil leaks.

> ▶ **TECHNICIAN TIP**
>
> A defective air compressor can mimic specific engine failures, resulting in unnecessary engine repairs. Head gasket leaks in an air compressor overpressurizes the engine cooling system. Unless properly investigated, the leak is often assumed to be in the engine. Likewise, a worn-out compressor with broken rings and scored cylinders pressurizes the engine crankcase, which can appear to be caused by a worn-out engine, instead. Any time high engine crankcase pressure or cooling system pressure complaints are reported, good practice is to isolate the air compressor to eliminate it as a source of the complaints.

All air compressors pass a small amount of oil. Discharged oil may collect in the discharge line, where it is baked by high-temperature air. Baked oil gradually turns to carbon and restricts the discharge line. This explains why manufacturers recommend replacing the discharge line whenever a compressor is replaced. The compressor discharge line fitting temperature operates normally between 200° F and 360° F (93° C and 182° C) when charging. The copper line at the compressor end is annealed to prevent cracking due to vibration and thermal cycling. The line also enables compressed air to cool before entering the dryer. Note that the line should slope downwards to prevent the condensation of water, which can potentially freeze and block the line, as shown in **FIGURE 35-13**.

> ▶ **TECHNICIAN TIP**
>
> Thoroughly clean and de-burr any air line, including the discharge line, before connecting it to the air system. Small metal particles can easily pass through the system and damage brake valves. When disturbing the discharge line, care should be taken to prevent any carbon from entering the air system by disconnecting the line at the air dryer first. After running the new compressor, the discharge line fitting temperature operates normally between 200° F and 360° F (93° C and 182° C) when charging.

Excessive Air Build-Up Time

A compressor must build-up air pressure from 85psi (587 kPa) to 100psi (690 kPa) in less than 25 seconds at high idle speed. Excessive compressor buildup time is typically caused by one of the following:

- Worn or scored cylinder walls or broken piston rings
- Restriction on the air inlet side of the air compressor
- Excessive air leaks
- Loose or slipping drive belts
- Malfunctioning unloader valves
- Defective discharge valves or restricted discharge lines

In addition, restricted air intake filters and hoses are a common factor in slow buildup time. Kinked or restricted discharge lines increase air pressure buildup time. The discharge line must maintain a constant slope down from the compressor to the air dryer inlet fitting to avoid low points where ice may form and

FIGURE 35-13 Compressor discharge line (indicated) should slope downward to prevent condensation.

block the flow. If carbon buildup in the discharge line is more than 1/16", the line should be replaced.

An excessively restricted air discharge line caused by such conditions as ice or carbon plugging causes compressor discharge pressure to increase to the point where the connecting rod may break and blow a hole in the side of the compressor.

Unloader valves can have O-ring seals leak or carbon and gum-up from oil residue, preventing the intake valves from properly operating when loading. When the intake valves are partially held open, the compressor cannot efficiently operate. Unloader valve kits are available to service worn, leaking, and defective unloader valves without requiring a complete compressor replacement. Likewise, defective discharge check valves can draw air back into the cylinder during an intake stroke.

► TECHNICIAN TIP

Turbocharger boost pressure can be lost through a compressor connected to the engine intake system if it has damaged cylinders. Boost pressure passes through the compressor and increase engine crankcase pressure, causing the engine to appear worn out. Unnecessary engine overhauls are frequently performed due to misdiagnosed compressor problems. To isolate a high engine crankcase pressure fault or loss of boost pressure to the air compressor, disconnect the air intake pipe to the compressor. Crankcase pressure drops and boost pressure increases if the compressor is defective.

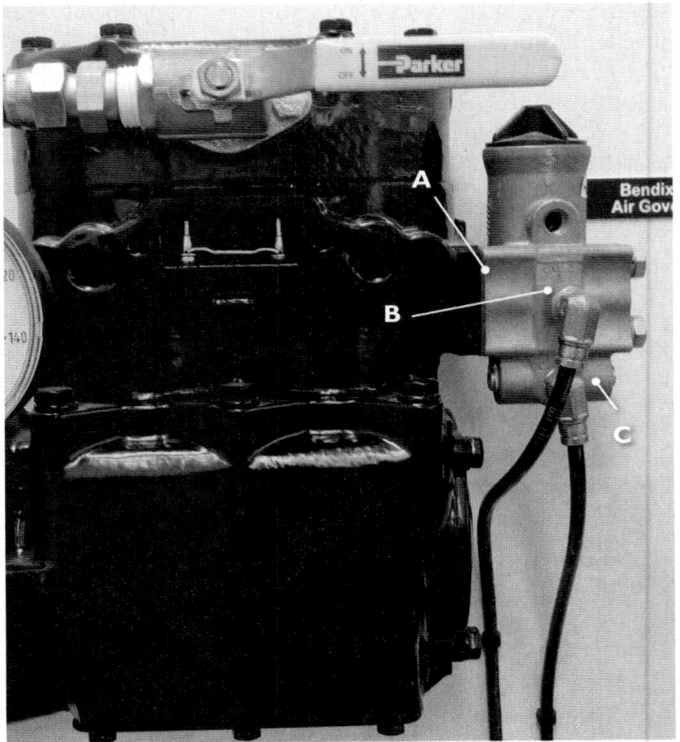

FIGURE 35-14 The governor gasket is located between the compressor and governor body. A leaking gasket, unloader valve, or unloader line causes the compressor to cycle frequently. **A.** Governor gasket. **B.** Unloader port. **C.** Reservoir port.

Governor

The pressure at which the governor loads is called the **governor cut-in pressure**, and the pressure at which it unloads is called the **governor cut-out pressure**. Both should be verified against vehicle OEM specification, but governors should begin loading at no less than 100 psi to 105 psi (689 kPa to 724 kPa) and unload at 120 psi to 135 psi (827 kPa to 931 kPa). If the governor is malfunctioning, it should be replaced, not adjusted. (Note: The newest greenhouse gas [GHG] engines, introduced in 2015, use CAN-controlled compressor on-off clutches and fully electronic governors that do not follow conventional cut-in and cut-out pressures as part of operational strategies to reduce fuel consumption.)

The reservoir line to the governor should always be connected to the top of the primary air reservoir. If the air dryer and compressor are frequently loading and unloading, check the governor gasket for leakage. Unloader valves can also leak air between the governor unloader ports and the unloader valves, which causes frequent cycling of the dryer and compressor. **FIGURE 35-14** shows the governor gasket and the unloader and reservoir ports.

Leaking air dryer purge valves and governor air lines can have the same effect as a leaking governor gasket—it allows the unloader line pressure to fall faster than reservoir pressure. To check for leaking compressor unloader valves, charge the unloader port with an air hose or through a Schrader valve connected to the governor unloader port. Shut off the air supply and observe whether there is a reduction in air pressure through the unloader circuit of the governor. A pressure gauge connected to the air hose is helpful when performing this inspection. A steady pressure reading indicates no air leakage is taking place through the unloader circuit. A loss of pressure indicates possible leaking unloader valves, a defective governor, leaking unloader lines, or a leaking air dryer unloader valve.

It is possible to fill the air reservoir without a running engine. The remote mounted governor in **FIGURE 35-15** is equipped with a Schrader valve connected to the reservoir port.

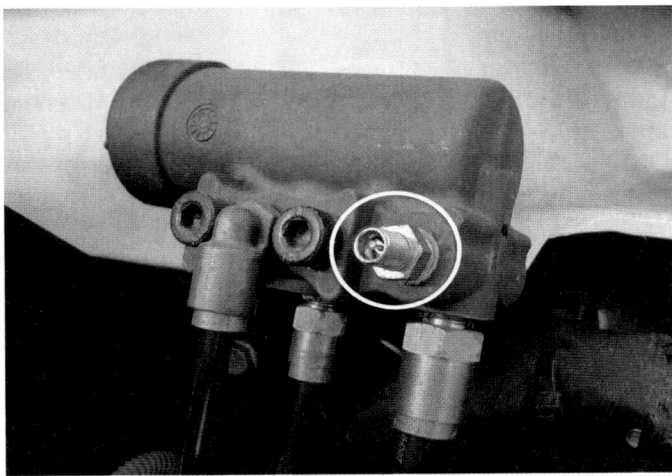

FIGURE 35-15 Remote mounted governor with a Schrader valve (circled).

A shop air line can easily be clipped onto the valve and the reservoirs charged to enable the brakes to be released without a running engine or to minimize build-up time in a shop.

Air Reservoirs

Both primary and secondary air tanks, plus any accessory and wet air tanks, should be drained during a pre-trip inspection. Good practice requires draining air tanks at the end of each day and leaving them open all night. In tanks equipped with automatic drain valves, reservoirs should be purged at every 12,000 miles (19,200 km) or once every year. If automatic drain valves are installed, their operation should be checked before the weather turns cold. The reservoir's pressure relief valve should be removed yearly, and its operation should be verified and compared against OEM specifications—typically opening to release excess reservoir pressure at 150 psi (1034 kPa).

Oil and water contamination in the air reservoirs is detrimental to the entire air system. Valves and lines sludge-up and fail to properly operate. Excessive water in the air reservoirs is typically caused by one of the following:

- Improper reservoir draining intervals
- Malfunctioning air dryer (i.e., the desiccant is not removing contaminants)
- Excessive air compressor duty-cycle (over 25 percent)
- An air dryer purge valve frozen closed
- High inlet air temperatures to the air dryer, which prevents water condensation
- A leaking air compressor head gasket or cracked cylinder head

To minimize these causes, some vehicles use an automatic air reservoir drain valve, such as the common DV-2 model of drain valve. An automatic air reservoir drain valve ejects moisture and contaminant accumulations from air reservoirs. It operates automatically, removing contaminants every time the reservoir cycles between a pressure buildup and pressure reduction. When charging, the inlet valve opens and the exhaust valve closes due to the increasing air pressure inside the valve. Contaminants accumulate in the sump of the valve as long as the pressure continues to increase.

When pressure stops increasing, both the inlet and exhaust valves are closed. As air is depleted from the reservoir, a minimum of a 2 psi (14 kPa) difference in air pressure above the inlet valve and the valve sump causes the exhaust valve to open, as pressure in the sump cavity is higher than the pressure above the inlet valve. Contaminants are ejected from the valve sump until the pressure loss in the sump drops enough to close the exhaust valve again. The amount of contaminants ejected varies with the reservoir pressure drop taking place each time air is drained from the system.

Dash Pressure Gauges

The dash gauge accuracy can be verified with a calibrated test gauge installed in the appropriate air reservoir. A gauge requires replacement if there is a difference of +2% or 2 psi to 3 psi

(14 kPa to 20 kPa), compared with measurements made with an accurate master gauge. Pressure sensors in air reservoirs are used to provide data to the vehicle control modules to operate electrically controlled air circuits and electronic air compressor clutches and governors.

Air Dryers

The dryer's purpose is to remove moisture, dirt, oil, and other contaminants that could damage the air system components before the air enters the system reservoir. A buildup of water or ice in the reservoirs could reduce reservoir capacity, leading to frequent compressor cycling. Water can interfere with proper brake system operation and can freeze in valves and lines.

Desiccant cartridges contained by dryers should be regularly replaced. Typical air dryer cartridge replacement schedule is every 3 years/300K miles (480K km) for low-air-use vehicles and every year/100K miles (160K km) for high-air-use vehicles.

When inspecting the air dryer, note that it should purge when the compressor unloads. Purging is identified by the sudden rapid exhaust of air draining from the dryer. The exhaust contains contaminants and moisture. Unloader line pressure is applied to the purge valve, forcing the valve open and keeping the valve open while the compressor is unloaded. Leaking O-rings in the purge valve drain pressure from the unloader circuit, causing both the dryer and air compressor to frequently load and unload. In cold weather, water and contaminants in the exhaust enable a purge valve to often freeze in the open position if the electric heater or thermostat circuit is inoperative. Service calls to temporarily allow the vehicle to build-up air pressure involve bypassing the dryer with a fitting to join the dryer inlet and outlet lines. If the dryer does not purge, possible causes include:

- Malfunction of the air purge valve in dryer
- Governor malfunction
- Improper governor control line connection to the reservoir

Frequent dryer purging accompanied by compressor unloading could be caused by any of the following:

- A compressor unloader mechanism malfunction (typically leaking unloader valve seals)
- An air dryer purge valve or inlet check valve malfunction
- Excessive air system leakage

FIGURE 35-16 shows an air dryer with a desiccant cartridge, purge valve, inlet port, and heating element.

Alcohol Evaporator and Injector Systems

A cold weather air system accessory is the alcohol injection system. The system sends methanol into the air system to prevent moisture from freezing in the system. An evaporator is placed in series between the air dryer and primary reservoir containing the alcohol. The alcohol is atomized by the air passing from the compressor.

Alcohol evaporator systems send approximately 1 to 2 ounces (30 to 60 ml) of alcohol per hour into the air brake system whenever the compressor is loaded. Air brake antifreeze is made only from methanol, not ethanol, combined with some lubricant, which should not corrode metal valves and is compatible with other air system materials but needs daily replenishing. If the system is using too little alcohol, it means the system is not receiving enough freeze protection. Excessive alcohol use wastes alcohol. City pick-up and delivery vehicles cycle the air compressors more frequently due to stop-and-go driving, and so use more alcohol. On-highway vehicles use less methanol because the brakes are not used as often, so the compressor does not operate as frequently.

Air Lines and Hoses

It is helpful to remember when diagnosing a problem with a specific brake circuit that nylon airline tubing is color coded to designate which air circuit it belongs. **TABLE 35-2** provides a guide to the color coding. Nylon line, or Synflex, is flexible, chemically resistant to deterioration, durable, and weather resistant. **FIGURE 35-17** shows nylon tubing entering a truck cab and connecting to a bulkhead suspended foot valve. When replacing an air line, use nylon tubing only where it has been used previously. Nylon air lines must never be routed in areas where temperature could exceed 200° F (93° C).

TABLE 35-2 Nylon Airline Color Designation Chart

Air Brake Circuit Color	Air Circuit
Red	Secondary
Green	Primary and delivery
Yellow	Parking brake
Blue	Suspension
Black	Accessory
Brown	Trailer brake

FIGURE 35-16 A commonly used Bendix AD-9 dryer. Its **A.** desiccant cartridge, **B.** purge valve, **C.** inlet port, and **D.** electric heating element can be replaced during rebuild procedures.

FIGURE 35-17 Nylon tubing entering a truck cab and connecting to a bulkhead suspended foot valve.

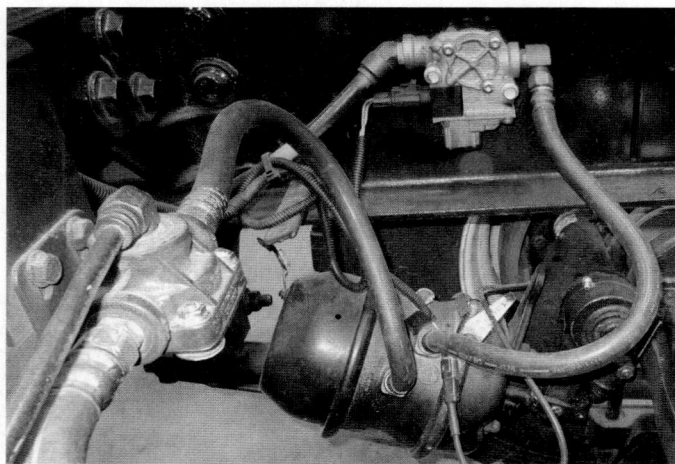

FIGURE 35-18 Rubber flex hoses with fabric-reinforced walls are used in highly flexible air connections.

FIGURE 35-19 Springs are used to prevent kinking and relieve strain on some hoses that have sharp bends.

Complaints, such as slow brake application or slow brake release, can indicate an air line is kinked, restricted, or clogged. To check for this condition, the suspected tube or hose should be disconnected at both ends and blown through to clear any blockage. Tubing and hoses can be inspected for partial restriction caused by dents or kinks. If Teflon-braided or stainless-steel hoses used in the engine compartment are replaced, they should be serviced with only the same type of hose material.

Flexible hoses like those in **FIGURE 35-18** are typically used where there is constant flexing, such as for brake chamber hoses. When visually inspected, any hose that is chafed, worn, or kinked should be replaced.

All air lines should be checked for damage from cuts, swelling, kinks, and deterioration due to time and exposure to harsh operating environments. Inspect for pinched lines and the correct use of retaining clips, brackets, and ties to support hoses. Hose spring guards, such as the one in **FIGURE 35-19**, are used where air lines are highly flexed and should be in good condition and not distorted.

Wrap-Up

Ready for Review

- Brake service is one of the most critical tasks that a technician must perform because the life of the driver and all other road users is jeopardized if mistakes are made.
- Brakes must be balanced—both torque, or mechanical, balance and pneumatic balance are required for proper braking to occur.
- Safety is paramount when working on braking systems. Dust, whipping air lines, uncontrolled vehicle movement, and the spring brake power spring are just a few of the potential hazards for the technician.
- Common brake complaints include soft brake pedal, noisy brakes, pulling brakes, and odors from the brake system.
- FMVSS 121 legislation specifies standards for brake systems, including air buildup time, air leakage rate, and brake adjustment settings.
- All air compressors pump some oil into the air brake system, but excessive oil pumping must be corrected.
- Several procedures are used to test the functioning of air brake systems, such as buildup time, leakage rate, dual-circuit integrity check, park brake application test, and emergency brake application test.

- Brake torque balance is maintained by the proper maintenance of the foundation brake system and brake actuators.
- Brake pneumatic balance is checked by using a duplex gauge that measures air pressure at two points at once.
- FMVSS 121 stipulates brake apply and release timing. Tractor brakes must apply within 0.45 seconds and trailer brakes within 0.5 seconds. Tractor brakes must release within 0.55 seconds and trailer brakes within 1 second.
- Relay valve crack pressure may vary from front to rear so that all the brakes apply at once.
- When any relay valve is replaced in the system, it is essential that the new valve has the same crack pressure as the old one.
- Compressor discharge lines can become restricted with carbon build up and should be replaced with the compressor.
- Air tanks should be drained daily unless equipped with automatic drain valves.
- Air hoses are color coded, so technicians will know what system they are connected to.
- Trailer jacknifing and swing out are caused by pneumatic brake imbalances between the tractor and trailer.
- Defective air compressors having worn-out cylinders and leaking head gaskets can appear to be faults in the engine. Air compressors should be isolated from the engine to identify faults in the air compressor.

- Leaking governor unloader circuits or reservoir line pressure to the governor cause the air compressor to frequently load and unload.
- The desiccant material in an air dryer should be replaced at regular service intervals or whenever the reservoirs are accumulating excessive water and oil.

Key Terms

chuff test A test performed on the antilock braking systems that results in air pressure being exhausted from the modulator and making a short chuffing sound.

dual-circuit integrity test A test performed to verify the functioning of the automatic emergency brake system.

duplex gauge Two air gauges in a single housing.

governor cut-in pressure The pressure at which the governor loads or starts the compressor operation.

governor cut-out pressure The pressure at which the governor unloads or ends the compressor operation.

N-95 mask A face mask that filters out 95% of all airborne particles.

pneumatic balance The correct timing of brake application air pressure to each vehicle axle at the correct pressure.

Review Questions

1. If a relay valve is to be replaced, which of the following is an important check?
   a. That the crack pressure of the replacement valve is the same as the OEM manufacturer specifications
   b. That the new relay valve doesn't have any extra outlet ports
   c. That the relay valve is made from aluminum or plastic materials
   d. That there is a port for the reservoir and service lines

2. Which of the following are stored energy sources that need to be isolated and removed from a vehicle when servicing air brakes?
   a. The engine, transmission, and air reservoirs
   b. Air pressure, battery current, and power springs
   c. Hydraulic actuators, air actuators, and the ignition switch
   d. Spring brakes

3. When inspecting the air brake compressor build-up time, the maximum amount of time allowed for air pressure to rise from 85 psi (586 kPa) to 100 psi (690 kPa) is _____ seconds.
   a. 15
   b. 25
   c. 45
   d. 60

4. What is the maximum amount of air leakage allowed in two minutes from a tractor and one trailer combination vehicle with brakes applied?
   a. 1 psi (7 kPa)
   b. 2 psi (14 kPa)
   c. 4 psi (28 kPa)
   d. 6 psi (41 kPa)

5. After opening the manual drain valve to deplete the air in the fully charged primary reservoir, the fully charged secondary reservoir began to drain when the primary reservoir pressure reached 60 psi (414 kPa). Which of the following answers best explains the observation?
   a. There is no fault, the secondary reservoir should drain through the primary reservoir.
   b. There is a defective pressure protection valve in the secondary air circuit.
   c. There is a defective one-way check valve between the reservoirs.
   d. There is a defective automatic drain valve in the secondary reservoir.

6. At what air pressure should a low-pressure warning device activate?
   a. 65 psi (448 kPa)
   b. 75 psi (517 kPa)
   c. 85 psi (586 kPa)
   d. 95 psi (655 kPa)

7. Which of the following best describes the procedure for performing an ABS modulator chuff test?
   a. Air system charged, apply service brake with ignition key off, then turn the ignition on.
   b. Air system charged, turn ignition on, and then apply the service brakes.
   c. Air system charged, road test the vehicle, and try to lock up the brakes.
   d. Air system charged, run vehicle on dyno, and use the dyno to lock the brakes.

8. Crack pressure on relay valves is different so the timing of brake applications can be simultaneous. Which of the following would be the most acceptable crack pressures for a tractor and a trailer relay valves?
   a. 10 psi (69 kPa) for the tractor and 10 psi (69 kPa) for the trailer
   b. 4 psi (28 kPa) for the tractor and 10 psi (69 kPa) for the trailer
   c. 10 psi (69 kPa) for the tractor and 0.5 psi (3.4 kPa) for the trailer
   d. 10 psi (69 kPa) for the tractor and 15 psi (103 kPa) for the trailer

9. Which of the following is a likely cause for a restriction in the air discharge line from an air compressor?
   a. A compressor pumping excess oil
   b. A restricted air filter
   c. Leaking unloader valve O-rings
   d. A restricted intake air hose

10. What is the most likely complaint caused by leaking air dryer purge valve O-rings?
   a. There is no air pressure build-up in the reservoirs.
   b. The air dryer and air compressor frequently cycle between load and unload, but reservoir pressure drops very little.
   c. Excessive accumulations of water and oil in the air reservoirs
   d. The air dryer does not purge.

ASE Technician A/Technician B Style Questions

1. Technician A says that brake balance can be upset by replacing brakes on one wheel end only. Technician B says that brake balance can be upset by replacing an air line with one of a larger size. Who is correct?
   a. Technician A
   b. Technician B
   c. Both Technician A and Technician B
   d. Neither Technician A nor Technician B

2. Technician A says that brake dust no longer contains asbestos, so it is not necessary to be concerned with inhaling brake dust as much as it was in the past. Technician B says that brake dust should be vacuumed off the wheel end with a HEPA filter-equipped vacuum cleaner. Who is correct?
   a. Technician A
   b. Technician B
   c. Both Technician A and Technician B
   d. Neither Technician A nor Technician B

3. Technician A says that brake squeal generated when brakes are lightly applied is likely caused by loose parts or lack of lubricant between parts, like the brake rollers. Technician B says that brake squeal is likely caused by shoe friction material designed for severe service in transit buses or refuse pick-up trucks. Who is correct?
   a. Technician A
   b. Technician B
   c. Both Technician A and Technician B
   d. Neither Technician A nor Technician B

4. Technician A says that when testing for brake leakage, a single-axle vehicle with brakes applied should leak no more than 4 psi (28 kPa) in two minutes. Technician B says that the acceptable leakage for a tractor and one trailer combination is no more than 6 psi (41 kPa) in two minutes. Who is correct?
   a. Technician A
   b. Technician B
   c. Both Technician A and Technician B
   d. Neither Technician A nor Technician B

5. Technician A says that a leaking air line fitting at the air dryer purge valve will cause the compressor to frequently load, even though reservoir pressure has not dropped below cut-in pressure. Technician B says that leaking O-rings around the compressor unloader valves will cause the compressor to frequently load without the reservoir pressure falling below cut-in pressure. Who is correct?
   a. Technician A
   b. Technician B
   c. Both Technician A and Technician B
   d. Neither Technician A nor Technician B

6. Technician A says that an air line rupture in a line connected to the secondary reservoir brake circuit will completely drain both the primary and secondary reservoir. Technician B says that the primary reservoir is pressure-protected and will not fall below 65 psi (448 kPa) if the secondary air reservoir has a large air leak. Who is correct?
   a. Technician A
   b. Technician B
   c. Both Technician A and Technician B
   d. Neither Technician A nor Technician B

7. Technician A says that the likely cause of a trailer to jackknife is the crack pressure of the trailer relay valve is much higher than the tractor's is. Technician B says a jackknife condition is caused by a combined failure of the trailer ABS and relay valve crack pressure that are higher on the tractor than the trailer. Who is correct?
   a. Technician A
   b. Technician B
   c. Both Technician A and Technician B
   d. Neither Technician A nor Technician B

8. To validate whether a compressor should be replaced due to high oil consumption caused by worn cylinders, Technician A suggested a paper test. This involved placing a piece of paper over the compressor's air intake port and counting the number of oil droplets accumulated after one minute. Technician B suggested that measuring the amount of oil accumulated in the reservoirs is a better method. Who is correct?
   a. Technician A
   b. Technician B
   c. Both Technician A and Technician B
   d. Neither Technician A nor Technician B

9. Technician A suspects that a crack in an air compressor cylinder head could be causing the engine's cooling system to over pressurize. He suggests that leaving the air reservoir's drain valve open while measuring cooling system pressure should result in a lower cooling system pressure if the compressor is the fault. Technician B suggests that crimping the coolant lines to the air compressor will eliminate pressurization of the engine cooling system. Who is correct?
   a. Technician A
   b. Technician B
   c. Both Technician A and Technician B
   d. Neither Technician A nor Technician B

10. While performing a test of brake pressure between the front and rear axles of a transit bus, using a duplex gauge, the rear axle air brake pressure was found to have 5 psi (34 kPa) difference at low-to-moderate application pressures (at up to 50 psi [345 kPa] brake application pressure). A 15 psi (103 kPa) difference was measured with a full brake application. Technician A said that the results were normal and recommended returning the bus to service. Technician B said the results were abnormal and insisted the bus should be taken out of service. Who is correct?
    a. Technician A
    b. Technician B
    c. Both Technician A and Technician B
    d. Neither Technician A nor Technician B

CHAPTER 36

Servicing Air Brake Foundation and Parking Brake Systems

Learning Objectives

After reading this chapter, you will be able to:

- **LO 36-1** Outline common procedures used to safely prepare a vehicle to perform service work on its foundation brakes.
- **LO 36-2** Outline common inspection areas and procedures used to perform a preliminary inspection of brake foundation components.
- **LO 36-3** Identify and describe the procedures used to inspect and perform an adjustment of brake stroke travel.
- **LO 36-4** Outline the procedures used to perform functional tests, inspection, and service on spring-type parking brakes.
- **LO 36-5** Identify and describe inspection and service procedures used to replace brake drums.
- **LO 36-6** Identify and describe inspection and service procedures used to replace S-cam-actuated brake shoes.

- **LO 36-7** Identify and describe inspection and service procedures used to replace S-type camshafts.
- **LO 36-8** Identify and describe the types of slack adjusters, inspection, and service procedures used to replace and adjust automatic slack adjusters.
- **LO 36-9** Outline inspection and service procedures for air disc brakes.
- **LO 36-10** Identify and explain the purpose and procedures used to inspect, measure, and adjust disc brake pad to rotor running clearance inspection.
- **LO 36-11** Outline the procedures used to replace disc brake pads, inspect automatic adjusters, and perform an initial brake adjustment.

You Are the Technician

Recently, several trucks in a fleet you service were taken out of service during road-side safety blitzes by law enforcement agencies. The safety defects were related to misadjusted brakes with all the trucks having automatic slack adjusters (ASAs) on the drum brakes that were over-stroking. Given that daily inspections of brake stroke are required by safety legislation, follow-up with a review of service records, drivers, and technicians found that the slack adjusters were regularly and frequently lubricated and inspected. However, the drivers of the vehicles reported they frequently adjusted the slack adjusters before trips. In fact, the vehicles with out-of-service brakes had drivers daily readjusting the brakes to achieve ½" to ¾" (12.7 mm to 19 mm) brake chamber pushrod travel measured using the free stroke method. Before reporting what you determined to be the root cause of the out-of-service condition of the brakes, consider the following questions:

1. Name and outline, in point form, the steps to follow for the only acceptable method that is used to accurately measure brake stroke travel.
2. What effect would daily readjustment have on the brake stroke adjustment mechanism of the ASAs used by the trucks?
3. Outline the procedure for performing functional tests of ASAs to determine whether the slack adjuster's adjusting mechanism is faulty.

Introduction

Brake friction components, such as brake block, lining, drums, pads and rotors at wheel ends, are designed to wear, and, consequently, are expected to require regular and more frequent maintenance than any other area of the brake system. The service life of the foundation brakes depends on many factors, such as the characteristics of brake block or lining, type and quality of drums and brake hardware, type of vehicle operation (transit, on-highway line haul, vocational, pick-up and delivery, etc.), and more (see **FIGURE 36-1**). Aggressive driving accompanied by hard braking also accelerates brake wear, as does carrying of heavy loads, which increases the work required by the brake foundation system. If operating conditions require frequent braking, or transporting heavier loads, brake lining replacement intervals are, therefore, shorter. Unbalanced braking also requires more frequent replacement of brake block, lining, drums, pads and rotors on axles doing the most work.

Brake actuators, such as camshafts, camshaft bushing, slack adjusters, spring brakes, and calipers, which are other important elements of the brake foundation system, require frequent inspection, maintenance, and service by technicians to ensure safe, reliable brake system operation. These brake foundation components operate with significant mechanical action as they function to adjust, apply, and release the brakes, and encounter wear, generally in proportion to friction materials contact with drums and rotors (**FIGURE 36-2**).

This chapter examines common brake foundation diagnostic, service, and maintenance procedures. Content in this chapter builds on brake inspection and diagnostic procedures for air system service outlined in the previous chapter.

Vehicle Preparation and Safety During Brake System Service

LO 36-1 Outline common procedures used to safely prepare a vehicle to perform service work on its foundation brakes.

Before beginning any service procedure, it is critical that the vehicle be properly prepared and that its servicing needs are correctly estimated to determine the equipment, labor time, information service systems and other service resources required to complete repairs. Important safety procedures and practices used during brake system service, discussed in the Air Brake Air System Service chapter, should be reviewed.

Particularly relevant to servicing foundation brake systems is the importance of parking a vehicle on a level surface and chocking the wheels with purpose-built chocks to prevent any vehicle movement. Spring brakes should be caged on all axles to place the park brakes in a released position when serviced. This is important to prevent the brakes from being incorrectly adjusted when foundation work is completed, and to ensure parts are positioned correctly during installation. The air should be drained from all air reservoirs after caging the spring brakes and the engine cranking system locked-out to prevent it from turning over and starting. Axles should be raised and supported on safety stands at a height that allows the tires to only clear the ground and not higher. Locking-type safety stands being used should be in proper working condition, and the appropriate stand weight capacity must be used to support the axles. Verify the cargo-loading compartments are empty before supporting the vehicle with stands that can collapse if inadvertently loaded with excessive, but unexpected, weight or uneven weight distribution. An overloaded stand may not collapse immediately and may take hours to slowly bend before suddenly collapsing. Slack adjusters should be backed off until the S-cam rollers and S-cams return to the start position of the S-cam rotation. And, when servicing other systems, follow all the procedures outlined in the vehicle service manual for removing wheels, drums, and rotors.

Preliminary Brake Inspection

LO 36-2 Outline common inspection areas and procedures used to perform a preliminary inspection of brake foundation components.

Determining the service requirements of the foundation brakes involves making a series of preliminary visual inspections. During regular service inspections, an inspection sheet containing a checklist of inspection items should be used. An inspection involves examining the foundation braking system for damage or defects caused by debris, component failure, or wear and deterioration. To identify brake components that are damaged, missing, or malfunctioning, a technician should be familiar with the normal appearance and operation of the foundation brake components and indications of imminent failures. Areas of

FIGURE 36-1 Brake block, which makes up the friction element of brake shoes, has edge codes to best match its characteristics with an application.

FIGURE 36-2 ASA slack adjusters, cam bushings, rollers, and other frequently wearing parts of the brake foundation.

the foundation braking system for inspection should include a variety of items in the following categories:

- Verifying brake-lining/block to drum contact and release
- Inspecting brake-lining/block conditions
- Inspecting for brake-lining/block contamination (i.e., wheel seal leaks, grease from the S-cam lubrication, and embedded gravel)
- Measuring brake-lining/block thickness
- Inspecting for broken or cracked brake drums and rotors
- Inspecting air brake chambers for
  - audible air leaks
  - cracks, severe corrosion, and non-manufactured holes
  - mismatched or incorrectly sized air brake chambers
  - mismatched slack adjuster brands, types, and length
  - broken power springs in spring brake chambers
- Inspecting brake hoses and tubes for damage, wear, securement, and whether air lines are connected or repaired with incorrect fittings

A good inspection sheet identifies several items associated with brake shoes, such as minimum thickness, the condition of lining face, and whether the shoes have mechanical damage, such as broken welds. Brake block and lining should be examined for excessive wear, cracks, glazing, and contamination from oil or grease. No movement between the brake lining and the shoe is permissible. Inspect the brake shoes for the presence of a **cam-over condition**, which can take place when the linings and brake drums are worn enough to allow the S-cam to rotate past the rollers when the brakes are applied. If this condition takes place, the S-cam rollers crest, or pass over, the highest point of S-cam and prevent the cam from reversing direction. A cam-over condition on a wheel end locks up the brakes in an applied position, requiring disassembly and replacement of the brake components in the wheel end. Roller and anchor pin contact points should be inspected for excessive wear. S-cam wear should also be checked and measured, if it is approaching wear limits. Camshaft tubes and slack adjusters should be properly lubricated.

When inspecting the foundation brakes, verify that components used or intended for replacement are correct for the application. Brake chambers should have the proper length of pushrods and match one another on the same axle for correct size. The inspection plug in the rear section of the spring brakes should be removed to inspect for a broken power spring, which is generally indicated by a misaligned receptacle in the guide plate for the caging bolt or the failure of the receptacle to center closely below to the inspection hole **FIGURE 36-3**. Air leaks from the chamber need to be checked when the park brake spring is released by air pressure.

The brake drum or rotor should be cleaned and inspected for the following conditions:

- Braking surfaces should be free of scoring, excessive heat checking, and cracks.
- The drum diameter or rotor thickness should be within the maximum limits cast or stamped on the drum or on the rotor. It is recommended that at least 0.40" (10 mm) below maximum diameter or thickness should remain as a wear allowance before reusing.

- Brake drum mounting holes and pilot surface must be round and concentric.
- The mounting surface must be clean and flat.

When diagnosing brake noises, technicians should pay careful attention to the type of noise. For example, observe whether the noise is a grinding, squealing, or hissing. Brake squeal is most commonly produced by some type of vibration. Correctly tightened and properly lubricated components normally do not cause brake squeal. However, some brake linings used in high-temperature, frequent-stopping applications, such as a transit bus, can be expected to often generate noise and strong odors from resin binding friction material together.

▶ **TECHNICIAN TIP**

Brake block and brake lining is made from materials to match operating conditions. Friction material with greater wear-resistance may often be harder and more prone to noise. A trade-off for quieter brakes is softer friction material accompanied by shorter friction material life. Softer friction material, however, can prolong brake drum service life.

Inspecting and Adjusting Air Brakes

LO 36-3 Identify and describe the procedures used to inspect and perform an adjustment of brake stroke travel.

The brake adjustment is the starting point for a brake system inspection and a critical service procedure. Regular brake inspections by qualified inspectors are mandated by law, and legislation applying to North America and around the world requires slack adjusters be checked daily, during the pre-trip inspection, and before driving down steep grades that are posted with regulatory signs. Since 1996, all commercial trucks and trailers with air

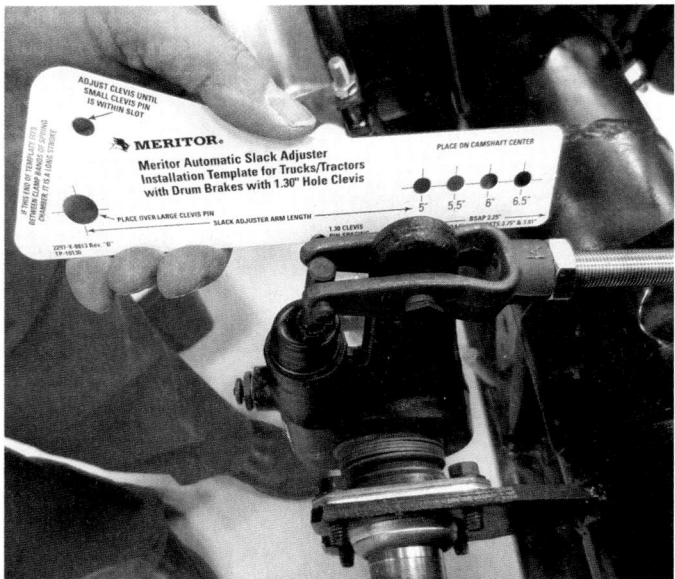

FIGURE 36-3 This template is aligned with the pushrod clevis pins and the centerline of the S-cam to determine whether the pushrod yoke requires adjustment.

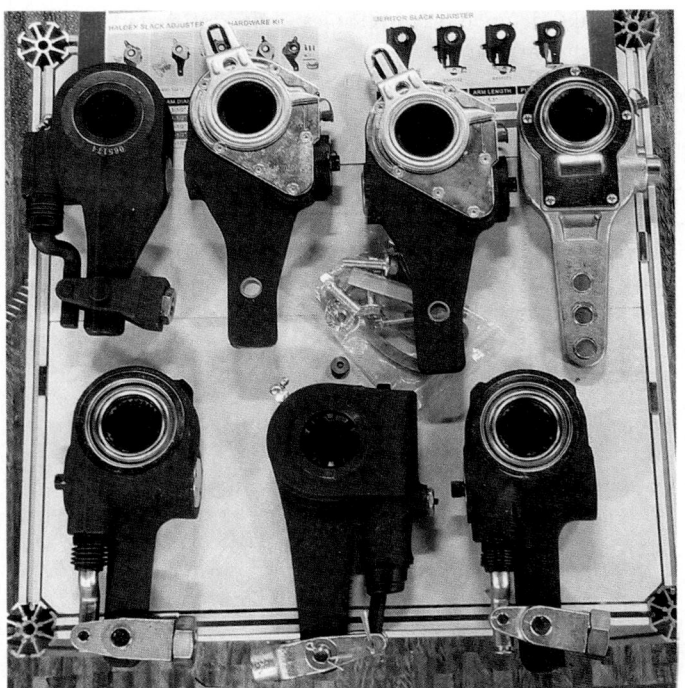

FIGURE 36-4 ASAs use different adjusting mechanisms and have different initial adjustment procedures that technicians must be familiar with.

brakes are manufactured with automatic slack adjusters (ASAs). ASAs maintain brake drum-to-shoe clearance more reliably than manual slack adjusters. After correct installation, ASAs should not need any further manual adjustment. (**FIGURE 36-4**). Chapter

36 New figure ASA If an ASA is found to allow a brake stroke beyond the maximum allowable limit, the slack is likely defective and requires replacement. Even if the slack is temporarily adjusted, a defective slack adjuster brake stroke quickly returns to a misadjusted position, most often lengthening or over-stroking, rather than shortening, the brake stroke, and travels quickly past its maximum limit. There are some exceptions, but a quick visual check of the brake adjustment can generally be done by estimating the angle between the slack adjuster and brake chamber pushrod. **FIGURE 36-5** illustrates the relationship between stroke length and brake force. As the brake lining wears, pushrod travel lengthens to the point where maximum torque through a 90-degree angle disappears, and the brake chamber actuators maximum brake stroke reaches its travel limit. Brake force rapidly diminishes when stroke travel reaches its maximum limit.

The Most Important Inch

To understand just how critical a correct brake adjustment is, consider the following. A correctly adjusted brake has only ½" (1.27 cm) of pushrod stroke travel, leaving 2" (5.08 cm) of reserve chamber stroke for a Type 30 brake chamber. When the slack allows 1" (2.54 cm) of brake stroke, it is mandatory that the brake be adjusted. This is referred to as a driver's most important inch of life (**TABLE 36-1**).

Brake torque is already reduced if a slack is adjusted to 1" of stroke travel. This happens because slack adjuster arm moves only ¼" and not ½" as the arm angle passes beyond 90-degrees. A loss of application force takes place due to the smaller arm angle and component stretching. Consider also that a cast iron drum also expands when heated, so heat fade can add close to

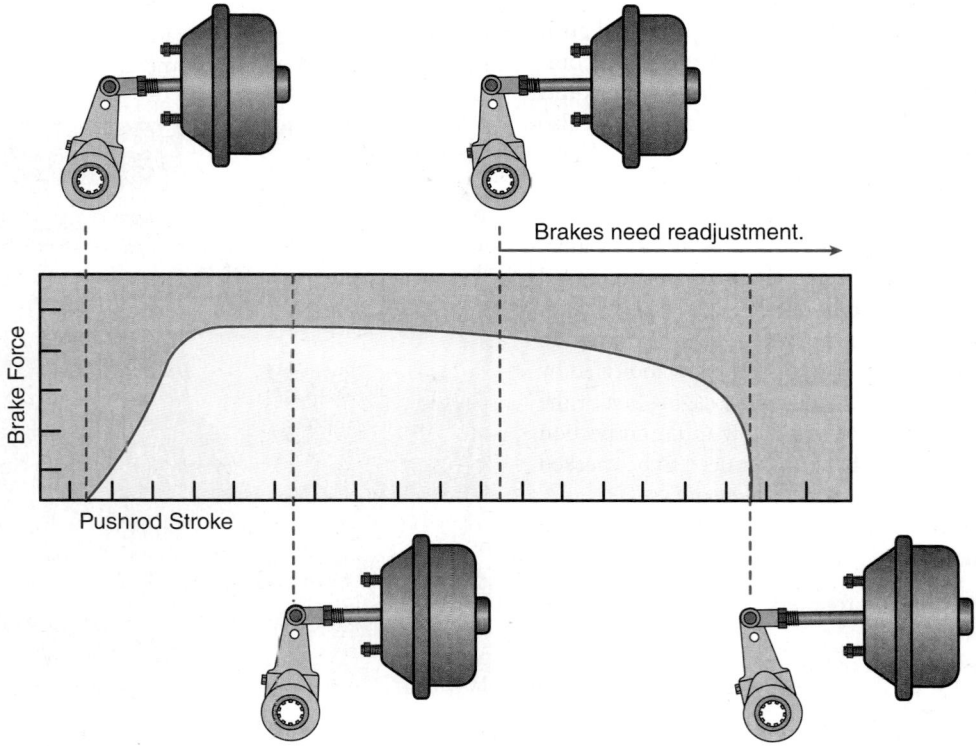

FIGURE 36-5 Air brakes are initially adjusted to obtain the shortest pushrod travel distance without the brake shoes dragging against the drum.

TABLE 36-1 Drum Brake ASA Stroke Measurement and Adjustment Criteria

ASA Brake Stroke Adjustment/Measuring Condition	Brake Stroke Travel
Initial installation by technician	½" to ¾"
Typical observed in-service brake stroke measurement	⅝" ¾" to ¾" 90-degree angle (±10 degrees) between pushrod and slack adjuster arm
Maximum allowable brake stroke before mandatory adjustment	1"
Out-of-Service Criteria for Type 30 brake chamber	2"

a ½" of clearance to the diminishing brake chamber force. This leaves only ¼" reserve stroke before the chamber pushrod potentially bottoms out. If not corrected by an ASA, lining worn the thickness of 3 sheets of paper adds another 1" to 4" (25.4 mm to 101.6 mm) of pushrod travel.

Measuring Brake Stroke

Verifying that brake chamber pushrod travel or **brake stroke length** is correct is a daily requirement for a trip inspection. Stroke travel indicates whether the brakes are properly adjusted to obtain optimal drum-shoe clearance. When brakes are properly adjusted, the angle formed between the brake chamber pushrod and the arm of the slack adjuster is approximately 90 degrees (±10 degrees) with an 80–100 psi brake application pressure.

Brake chamber stroke length is commonly measured in one of three ways:

- Free stroke measurement
- Using stroke indicators
- Applied stroke measurement

Free Stroke Measurement Method

Free stroke measurement method measures the pushrod stroke length using a lever to move the slack adjuster. A technician inspects a brake's free stroke using a purpose-made lever, or a long combination wrench to move the slack adjuster arm until the brake shoes contact the drum. A chalk mark is first made on the brake chamber pushrod at the chamber face with the park brakes released and the wheels chocked. The chamber pushrod is then pulled by hand to its travel limit. A short pry bar or wrench can be used to assist pulling on the pushrod, using the slack adjuster as a fulcrum point. Purpose-made tools are also used to pull the brake chamber pushrod from a retracted position to the point where the shoes contact the brake drum. The pushrod of a properly adjusted brake typically should never move more than ¾" (19 mm) using this method. Note this check can only be used as a quick inspection method to check for severely out-of-adjustment brakes. Free stroke measurement is not a recommended practice to check for proper brake stroke adjustment.

FIGURE 36-6 A red zip tie (circled) is used to assist measuring brake stroke travel. **A.** Service brake chamber. **B.** Stroke indicator.

Proper brake chamber stroke measurement should be conducted by methods that apply the brakes with normal application pressure. Various types of visual stroke indicators are used to assist measuring brake stroke travel. The simple red plastic tie seen in **FIGURE 36-6** is attached to the brake chamber pushrod at the chamber face. When the brake is applied, the stroke travel can be measured with a tape or steel ruler between the chamber face and the plastic tie.

Applied Stroke Measurement Method

When the **applied stroke measurement** method is used, the pushrod stroke length with a minimum 90 psi (621 kPa) service brake application is the most acceptable procedure recommended for measuring brake stroke length and validating correct brake adjustment. The method is commonly used by roadside inspectors and is recommended by commercial fleet maintenance supervisors to perform brake adjustments for manual and automatic slack adjusters. Because the applied stroke method uses a service brake application to measure pushrod stroke travel, it requires two persons—one to apply the brakes and one to measure stroke travel.

To check brake stroke length using applied stroke measurement, follow the steps in **SKILL DRILL 36-1** using the data in **TABLE 36-2**, which shows the maximum permissible applied brake stroke travel before requiring the brake becomes ineffective. Note that these dimensions are out-of-service limits. A typical 30-series chamber is initially adjusted to have ½" to ¾" (12.7 mm to 19 mm) applied brake stroke travel using an ASA. Once this initial drum-to-shoe clearance adjustment is established on drum brakes, an ASA

SKILL DRILL 36-1 Measuring Brake Stroke Length Using Applied Stroke Measurement Technique

1. Using the dash gauge as a guide, adjust the air system pressure to between 80 to 100 psi.
2. Measure and record the distance between the face of the service brake chamber and the center of the slack adjuster clevis pin.
3. Have an assistant make a full-service brake application. While holding the applied brake pressure, measure and record the distance from the brake chamber face to the center of the pushrod clevis pin.
4. Subtract the measured brake release stroke distance from the applied stroke and record. Compare your findings to the information on Table 36-2. Repeat at all wheel locations.
5. On trailers, use the hand or trailer valve to apply the service brakes to measure pushrod angle.

TABLE 36-2 Actuator Stroke Table

Standard Stroke Actuator	
Brake Actuator Size	Maximum Operating Stroke
30	2" (5 cm)
24	1.75" (4.45 cm)
20	1.75" (4.45 cm)
16	1.75" (4.45 cm)
12	1.375" (3.5 cm)
Long Stroke Actuator	
30LS	2.5" (6.35 cm)
24L	2" (5 cm)
24LS	2.5" (6.35 cm)
20L	2" (5 cm)
16L	2" (5 cm)

Source: Bendix.

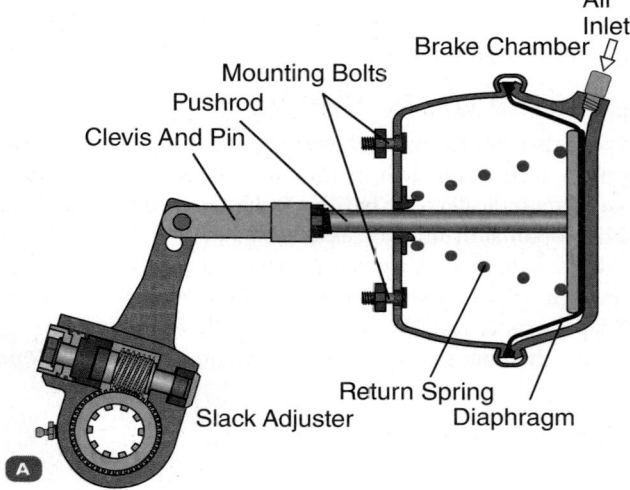

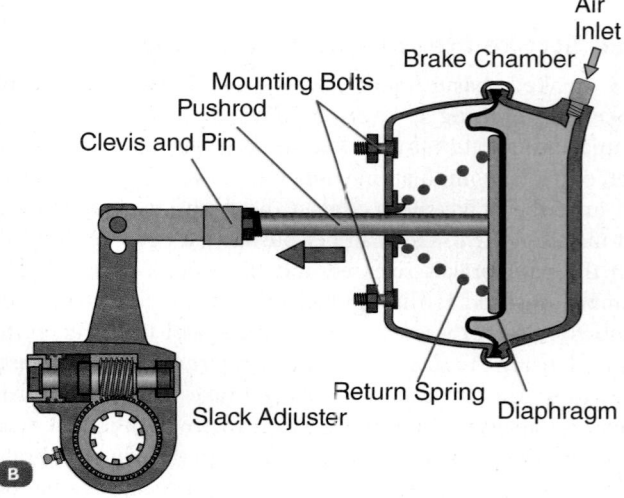

FIGURE 36-7 The position of the slack adjuster with the brakes released and applied. **A.** Brake released. **B.** Brake applied.

either maintains this initial adjustment or adjusts the brake stroke to the correct stroke length designed into it by the manufacturer. This in-service stroke length is commonly ⅝" to ¾" (15.9 mm to 19 mm) of brake stroke travel (see Table 36-1). In addition to the stroke-sensing mechanism an ASA uses, this final brake stroke position depends on a variety of factors that vary the force through an ASA, such as chamber diameter, application air pressure, and slack arm length. As the brake lining wears, and the stroke length increases, either a stroke- or clearance-sensing mechanism adjusts an ASA to maintain the adjustment established for its applied stroke travel.

During daily inspections, when the park-spring brakes are applied, spring brake pressure applies the brakes forcefully enough to measure either the stroke distance or the angle between the brake chamber pushrod and the slack adjuster arm. As shown in **FIGURE 36-7**, when the brakes are

FIGURE 36-8 The ASA adjustment locking pin must first be retracted before the adjusting screw is turned.

FIGURE 36-9 Correct ASA adjustment and brake stroke travel depends correctly adjusting the length of the chamber pushrod and yoke to obtain a precise position of ASA clevis pins. Pushrod and yoke length must be correctly adjusted before initial ASA adjustment.

FIGURE 36-10 Visual stroke indicator.

applied, an approximately 90-degree angle is formed between the slack adjuster and the brake chamber pushrod. The angle may vary slightly on some vehicles to prevent interference with other components.

If the angle is more than 90 degrees, the slack adjuster likely requires adjustment and must be checked. If the adjustment is incorrect and the slack adjuster is an automatic type, further investigation is required to determine the reason for the misadjustment and the reason it does not have a 90-degree installed angle. Either condition could be caused by a variety of problems, ranging from a defective slack adjuster "backing-off" or problems in the brake application mechanism, such as a deposit on the "S-cam," binding, worn or loose components, to an incorrect initial adjustment of an ASA or improperly installed brake chamber using a pushrod cut too long or too short (**FIGURE 36-8**). Measure and record the distance from the brake chamber face to the center of the clevis pin with the brakes fully released. Repeat at all wheel locations. Use an OEM template to match the slack adjuster clevis pin holes on the template to determine whether the length of the pushrod or yoke requires adjustment (**FIGURE 36-9**). When the large and small clevis pin of an ASA align with the holes of a template placed over the S-cam centerline, the pushrod yoke and pushrod length are correctly set. If not, the pushrod yoke attached to the slack may require adjustment, or the pushrod itself may need shortening or lengthening.

Brake Adjustment Indicators

Newer air brake chamber pushrods have a bright marking on the pushrod at the face of the brake chamber. If the pushrod travel becomes excessive, the mark is used as a visual indicator that a brake adjustment must be done immediately. **FIGURE 36-10** shows another visual stroke indicator used to inspect the applied stroke length. The maximum pushrod travel measured at the clevis pin should be no more than the distance between the two yellow tabs.

▶ **TECHNICIAN TIP**

Using the parking brake control valve and the trailer supply valve to release spring brakes during an adjustment can produce an incorrect brake adjustment. Some parking brake control valves and trailer supply valves supply air to spring brake chambers with as little as 20 psi (138 kPa) air reservoir pressure, which actually leaves the spring brakes partially applied. This explains why it is necessary to verify that air pressure is at least 90–100 psi (620–670 kPa), and that all parking brakes are released before checking or making a brake adjustment.

▶ **TECHNICIAN TIP**

With the brakes applied, a 90-degree angle between the center of the slack adjuster arm and the brake chamber pushrod when the brakes are applied may not always be a satisfactory indication that the brake adjustment is correct. The 90-degree angle depends more on the length of the chamber pushrod than the actual brake adjustment. To prevent interference between the slack adjuster and suspension or axle parts, some chamber to slack adjuster angles vary plus or minus 10 degrees, as shown in **FIGURE 36-11**.

When measuring applied stroke, a reference mark is made on the pushrod at the brake chamber's face when the brakes are released. When the service brake is applied with approximately

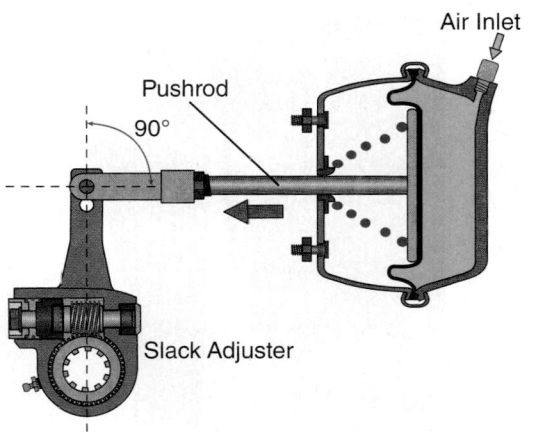

FIGURE 36-11 Some configurations of pushrod and slack adjuster use larger angles to prevent interference with the axles and attachments.

80–90 psi (552–621 kPa) air pressure, the pushrod travel is measured. Application pressure is adjusted by pumping the brakes to deplete the air reservoir until desired pressure is reached on the dash gauge. If the slack has 1" (2.54 cm) or more travel, legislated safety standards require that it must be adjusted. Slightly more travel before adjustment is required is allowed by the applied stroke measurement (normally no more than ¾" or 19 mm) due to component stretch during a brake application.

As shown in **FIGURE 36-12**, applied brake stroke travel is longer than the free stroke limit. With air pressure applying the brakes, greater force is used against the braking mechanism, which produces a slightly longer stroke.

Testing Parking Brake Function

LO 36-4 Outline the procedures used to perform functional tests, inspection, and service on spring-type parking brakes.

During inspection and service, verifying the park-spring brakes are quickly applied and released validates the correct operation of park control, tractor protection, and the spring brake relay valve with an anti-compounding feature. The operation of brake lines, hoses, spring brake chambers, and supply reservoirs are also indirectly evaluated.

On straight trucks, with air system at full pressure and the engine idling between 600 and 900 RPM, the push-pull park control valve is applied and released during this inspection. Brakes must apply and release promptly when the valve is pushed in and out. For tractor and trailer combinations, the red, octagonal, tractor-protection control valve in the cab is used to supply air to the trailer reservoir, as well as apply and release the trailer spring brakes. Again, the brakes must respond quickly to the valve being pushed in and out.

This test requires two technicians. One needs to check brake operation when the wheels are chocked, while the other operates the dash valves. Alternatively, the speed of park brake

Free Stroke = B − A

Applied Stroke = C − A

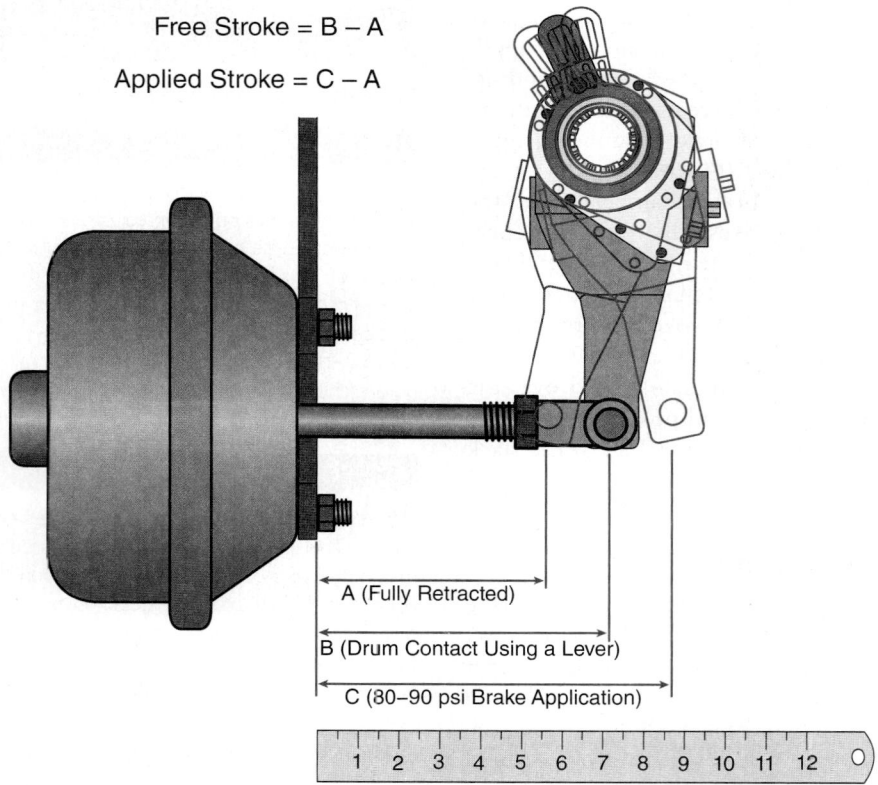

A (Fully Retracted)

B (Drum Contact Using a Lever)

C (80–90 psi Brake Application)

FIGURE 36-12 Applied stroke is longer than free stroke.

release and application can be performed by allowing the vehicle to slowly roll while in gear to no more than 3 mph. The park brake can then be applied and released to evaluate system operation.

Spring Brake Servicing

Removing the spring brake chamber or actuator requires caging the power spring. This is a simple procedure, but technicians must use extreme caution when performing this task, as the caged power spring is under extreme pressure and can explosively release with incredibly lethal force. **FIGURE 36-13** shows the correct procedure for "caging" a spring brake chamber to release the parking brake. The power spring in the rear chamber is compressed by a pressure plate when tightening the caging bolt. *Note*: only use hand tools. Do not use impact wrenches or air ratchets, and do not over tighten the bolt. Over-tightening the bolt damages the pressure plate, which could potentially cause the spring to explosively release. If the pressure plate is damaged, it can result in an improper stroke travel adjustment or the misaligned or damaged pressure plate in the park brake chamber, which can cause a brake to drag. A good practice is to remove the access plug from the rear of the chamber to verify the pressure plate is properly seated in the chamber.

When installing parking brake chambers, the correct chamber position and pushrod length are critical to achieve effective brake application. When replacing a complete spring brake actuator, the pushrod on the new chamber must be cut to length. To determine the correct chamber pushrod length, two measurements are required: brake stroke length and the point where the centerline of the slack adjuster intersects with the chamber pushrod when the brake is applied. A small carpenter's square can be used to measure the intersection point when the slack adjuster is at 90 degrees to the pushrod. The maximum brake stroke length x is subtracted from the pushrod length to find the cutting point. **FIGURE 36-14** shows the correct procedure for measuring and cutting the pushrod.

When threading the clevis pin yoke onto the brake chamber, care must be taken to ensure an adequate amount of thread holds the pushrod onto the yoke. If, however, the clevis pin yoke is threaded too far, the pushrod can potentially interfere with the slack adjuster travel. The pushrod should be threaded into the clevis at least ½" (13 mm) but should not protrude into the clevis yoke by any more than ⅛" (3.18 mm), as shown in **FIGURE 36-15**.

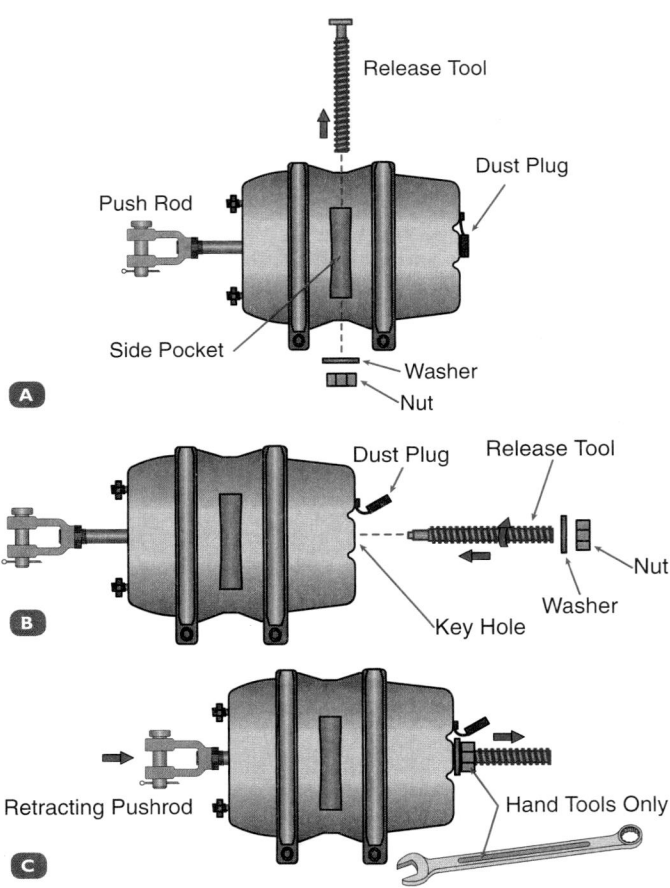

FIGURE 36-13 **A.** Insert the release tool. **B.** Release the stud by turning a quarter-turn clockwise. **C.** Retract the pushrod.

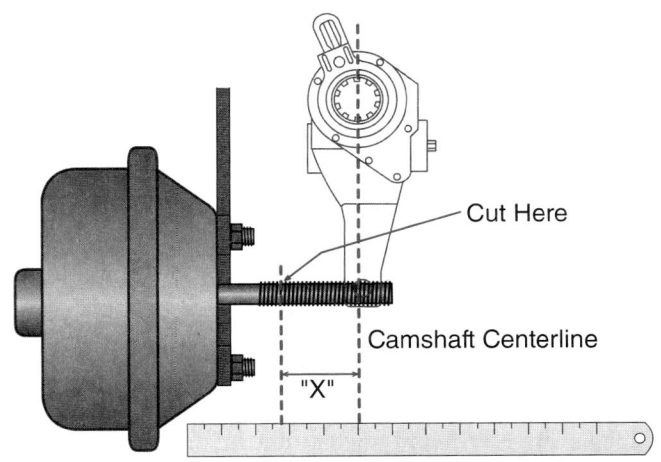

Slack Adjuster Length	"X" Dimension
5"–5½"(127–139 mm)	2¼" (57.15 mm)
6"–7" (152.4–177.8 mm)	2½" (63.5 mm)

FIGURE 36-14 Correct procedure for measuring and cutting the pushrod.

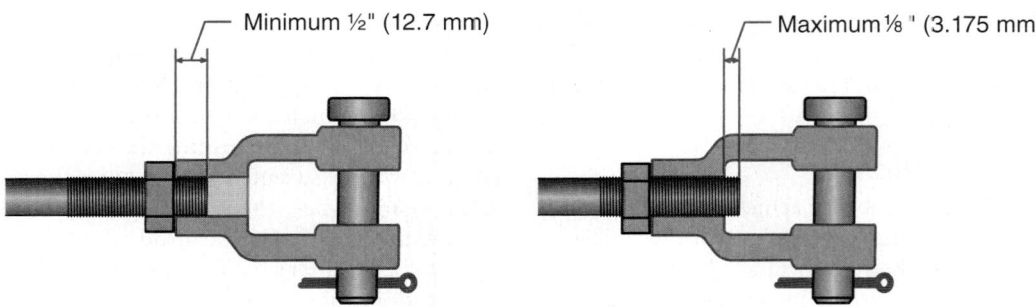

FIGURE 36-15 Pushrod should be threaded into the clevis yoke by at least ½". Pushrod should not protrude into the clevis yoke by more than ⅛".

FIGURE 36-16 Brake drum.

Brake Drum Service

LO 36-5 Identify and describe inspection and service procedures used to replace brake drums.

Correctly servicing brake drums (**FIGURE 36-16**) is another critical procedure to effectively service air brake foundations. The service limit for maximum wear on brake drums is cast into most brake drums. Drum wear is measured using an inside bore gauge or drum micrometer. When placed inside a drum, either of the gauges measure maximum diameter. The maximum worn diameter requiring drum replacement should be less than 16.120" for most 16.0" × 7" (42 cm × 17.8 cm) drums. Drums generally should not require reboring or machining to an oversized inside diameter. But, if any boring is required, such as under some circumstances to ensure correct brake balance, machining should leave the drum 0.040" (10 mm) under the maximum inside diameter. This guideline should be applied regardless of the reason for the boring, such as to remove scoring, heat checks, or light cracking. A minimum thickness must be maintained for additional wear.

As an example, when checking brake drum diameter for wear, the discard diameter is 0.120" over the original diameter

for a 16.0" drum. However, when reboring brake drums, the finished diameter should not exceed the original diameter by more than 0.080". This leaves 0.040" or 10.2 mm of material to wear in-service before it reaches the discard diameter. Removing more than this amount of material increases the likelihood of brake fade and a cam-over condition can result. (Cam-over takes place when the drum is too large, and the S-cam rotates too far and traps the rollers against the concave side of the S-cam. The camshaft cannot rotate back to release the brakes and the brakes are locked on.) For a new 16.5" drum, therefore, the maximum inside diameter is 16.580" (42.1 cm). That is, 16.5" + 0.080" = 16.580". If 0.40" (10.2 mm) remains for a wear allowance, the replacement diameter is 16.620" (42.2 cm) because the drum cannot be machined and maintain an adequate thickness for in-service wear. Brake drum run out does not cause a brake pedal pulsation like out of round drums produce on hydraulic brakes because air in lines cushions pulsations from the brake shoes; however, a drum should not exceed a total of 0.025" (0.635 mm), because contact between friction material and the drum deteriorates with increasing runout.

> ► **TECHNICIAN TIP**

Sometimes brake defects are found on only one axle end. Leaking wheel seals contaminating brake lining, a defective slack adjuster, a cracked drum, or a damaged shoe on only one wheel might seem more efficiently and economically repaired by replacing only the affected parts. However, braking performance is affected because brake torque changes whenever brake parts are different at each axle end. When performing brake repairs, consistent brake balance or applied brake torque at both ends of a common axle MUST be maintained. This means that if the brake shoes are replaced at one end, the shoes on the opposite end should also be replaced. If a brake drum is machined or replaced, the other drum should also be machined to the same dimension, or both replaced, to maintain consistent braking performance.

A condition called Martensite spotting takes place when the drum braking surface is rapidly heated. When it is formed, the drum surface material changes composition to produce a dark, very hard crystalline structure scattered over the drum's wear surface. The hardness of Martensite makes it very

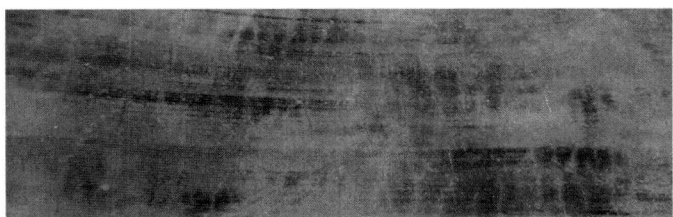

FIGURE 36-17 Martensite spotting can prevent drums from being machined.

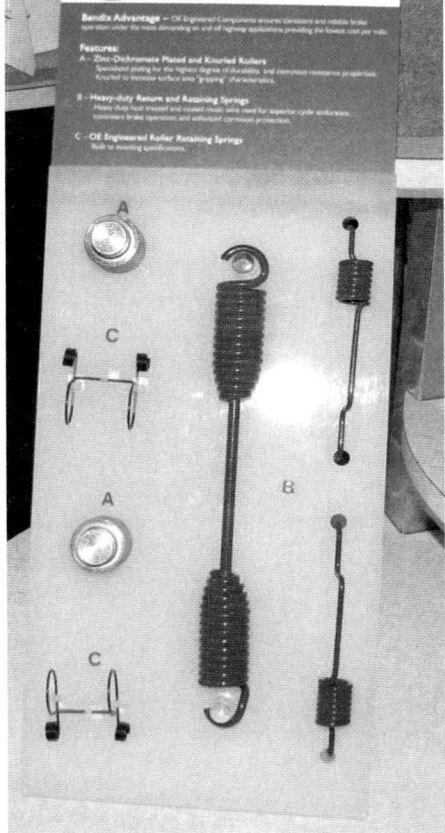

FIGURE 36-18 Foundation brakes typically are replaced with a service kit containing new or remanufactured shoes and hardware.

difficult to machine and may prevent consistent, even drum wear. **FIGURE 36-17** shows an example of Martensite spotting that may require drum replacement

The use of extended brake life brake parts using heavier drums and thicker linings lengthens the service intervals between brake replacements. Inexpensive standard drums for normal service weigh approximately 60–100 lb (27–45.5 kg). Heavy-duty drums weigh approximately 120 lb (54 kg) each, and drums for severe service can reach 135 lb (61kg) each!

When foundation brakes need to be replaced, a service kit, such as the one shown in **FIGURE 36-18**, is commonly used. The kit typically includes new or remanufactured shoes and hardware.

FIGURE 36-19 This brake drum is not correctly installed on the hub pilot pads. When the wheel is tightened, the drum face can crack, and the wheel become loose. The circled area shows incorrect brake drum fit.

When replacing drums, it is critical that the type of drum is matched correctly with its hub. Correct matching is critical for the proper centering of wheel rims and to prevent "wheel-off" accidents, loose or broken mounting studs, and dragging brakes.

Hub-piloted brake drums rest tightly on and are centered by pilot pads located on the outside of the wheel hub and have larger stud holes in the brake drum. The tight fit between the drum and the wheel hub pilot pads ensures a more precise fit for centering the drum over the brake shoes. Because the position of the drum can interfere with the wheel position on its hub pilot pads, it is very important to verify the drums seat properly on the drum pilot pad before installing wheels. **FIGURE 36-19** shows an incorrectly installed brake drum. Failure to install an outboard-mounted drum properly on the drum pilot pads can cause the brake drum holes to crack on the drum face, as shown in **FIGURE 36-20**.

Ball-seat-type bolt holes are used by drums with stud-piloted wheels and have a tighter fit on studs. New drum designs enable the use of the same drum for ball-seat and hub-piloted wheels. However, new drum designs cannot always be used with some older stud-piloted hubs. Carefully following manufacturer directions concerning replacement parts is essential. In **FIGURE 36-21**, note the presence of two distinctly different hub pilot pads. One is for the wheel and the other for the brake drum.

Corrosion forming between wheel hubs and the chamfer of the brake drum pilot pad is a concern when installing the more commonly used hub-piloted brake drums. The location of this type of corrosion generally results from improper installation, which can prevent the drum from correctly centering squarely onto the hub and against the hub flange. After the wheel nuts are tightened, the brake drum can crack, as shown in **FIGURE 36-22**. Cracking can lead to brake drum failure as in **FIGURE 36-23**.

FIGURE 36-20 Cracked brake drum holes on the drum face.

FIGURE 36-21 A wheel hub with two sets of pilot pads. **A.** Wheel pilot pads. **B.** Drum pilot pads.

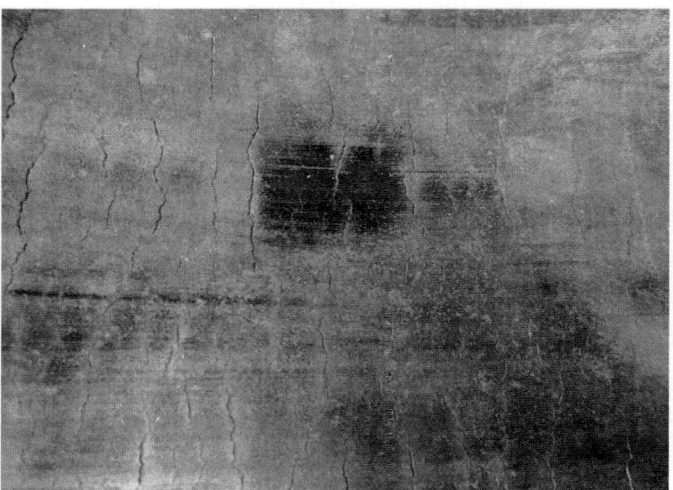

FIGURE 36-22 Light heat cracking is a normal wear condition. The cracks do not deeply penetrate the drum braking surfaces.

FIGURE 36-23 A broken brake drum casting.

Improper drum installation also causes irregular braking because the centerline of the drum and hub are not aligned. To prevent this, good service practice is to completely remove hub and pilot pad corrosion prior to installing the brake drum. Corrosion is best removed by chipping it and then cleaning the hub with a wire brush. Corrosion is especially a problem with aluminum hubs, which require more careful cleaning to prevent damage to the aluminum.

Brake drums need to be discarded if they have any of the following conditions:

- Scoring
- Severe heat checking
- Cracking through the hat section
- Cracking through the side wall.

TABLE 36-3 Drum Service Guidelines

Condition	Cause	Remedy
Deep, uniform drum wear	Brake drag Brake imbalance on worn wheel ends Dirt and contaminants embedded in the brake lining Incorrect braking and or driving technique—not snubbing brakes or downshifting on hills Braking with hand valve on trailer brakes only	Replace the drum Install dust shields backing plates
Eccentric drum wear (i.e., drum worn on one side only)	Brake drum dropped, bent, or machined out-of-round Drum not centered on drum wheel hub pilots	Replace the drum
Worn brake drum bolt holes	Insufficient torque applied to wheel nuts, which also causes hub and drum pilots to wear	Replace the drum
Uniform heat checking (fine cracks)	Heavy braking	Replace the drum
Uniform hot spotting (black spots) on the drum's surface (Martensite spots)	Brake lining to drum contact surfaces burnished too slowly during break-in Dragging brakes Extremely hard linings Lining swell from poor-quality linings, causing brake drag	Replace the drum
Polished or glazed drums (mirror-like shine)	Low-pressure braking Incorrect brake block material for application—too soft	Replace the drum
Scoring (Grooving) Deep grooves in the drum's surface that exceed the drum's maximum diameter Drum can appear to be in good condition	Dirt or contaminants in the brake system Linings worn to the rivets or not OEM-approved	Replace the drum Scoring in the drum's braking surface that is deeper than 0.10" (2.54 mm) and wider than 0.030" (0.76 mm) requires both drum and lining replacement
"Blue" Drum Inside of the brake drum has "blue" color from excessive heat Components can be deformed or damaged	Caused by extremely high temperatures due to brake imbalance Poor driver techniques Too-soft brake lining Brake drag	Replace the drum
Cracked drum	A drum can crack when the parking brake is set while the brakes are extremely hot; the cooling drum contracts on the brake shoes with enough force to crack the drum	Replace the drum
Oil- or grease-contaminated lining and drums	Oil and grease spots have penetrated the drum's surface The brake drum probably is discolored	Replace the drum

TABLE 36-4 Drum Inspection Replacement Guide

Nominal Diameter	Discard Drum At
16.5"	16.620"
16"	16.120"
15"	15.120"

Brake drum service guidelines are given in **TABLE 36-3**, and **TABLE 36-4** contains a drum replacement guide.

Brake Shoe Service

LO 36-6 Identify and describe inspection and service procedures used to replace S-cam-actuated brake shoes.

As illustrated in **FIGURE 36-24**, replacement or relining of brake shoes is required when lining thickness at the center of the shoe has reached $\frac{5}{16}$" (7.94 mm) ($\frac{1}{4}$" [6.35 mm] for extended service lining). A wear line on some shoes placed at $\frac{1}{4}$" (6.35 mm) thickness is measured at the center of the shoe and can be used as a visual guide. Alternatively, brake shoe wear can be determined by inserting a go/no-go gauge into the backing plate hole (**FIGURE 36-25**). Lastly, **FIGURE 36-26** shows an optional wear indicator switch sensor in a brake shoe. When the brake shoe wears to less than 50%, the sensor grounds out against the brake drum, which triggers a warning indicator. Rivets or bolts attaching the brake block or lining to the shoe table should never be permitted to contact the drum.

Inspecting and Removing Brake Shoes

When inspecting new or rebuilt brake shoes for wear, follow the guidelines in **SKILL DRILL 36-2**. To remove the brake shoes,

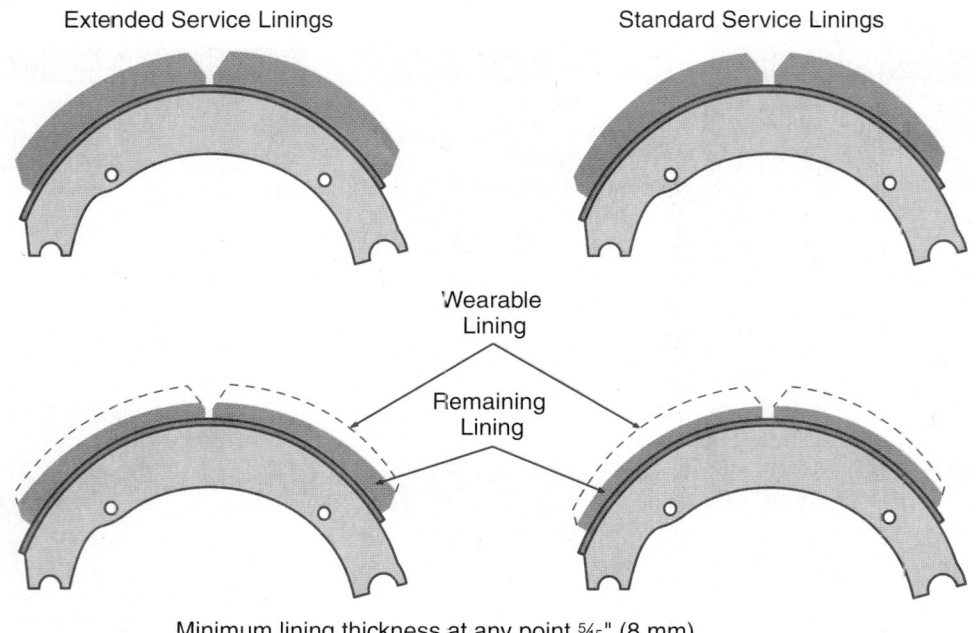

Extended Service Linings

Standard Service Linings

Wearable Lining

Remaining Lining

Minimum lining thickness at any point ⁵⁄₁₅" (8 mm)

FIGURE 36-24 Standard lining thickness is tapered at each end of the shoe. Extended service line is uniform in thickness.

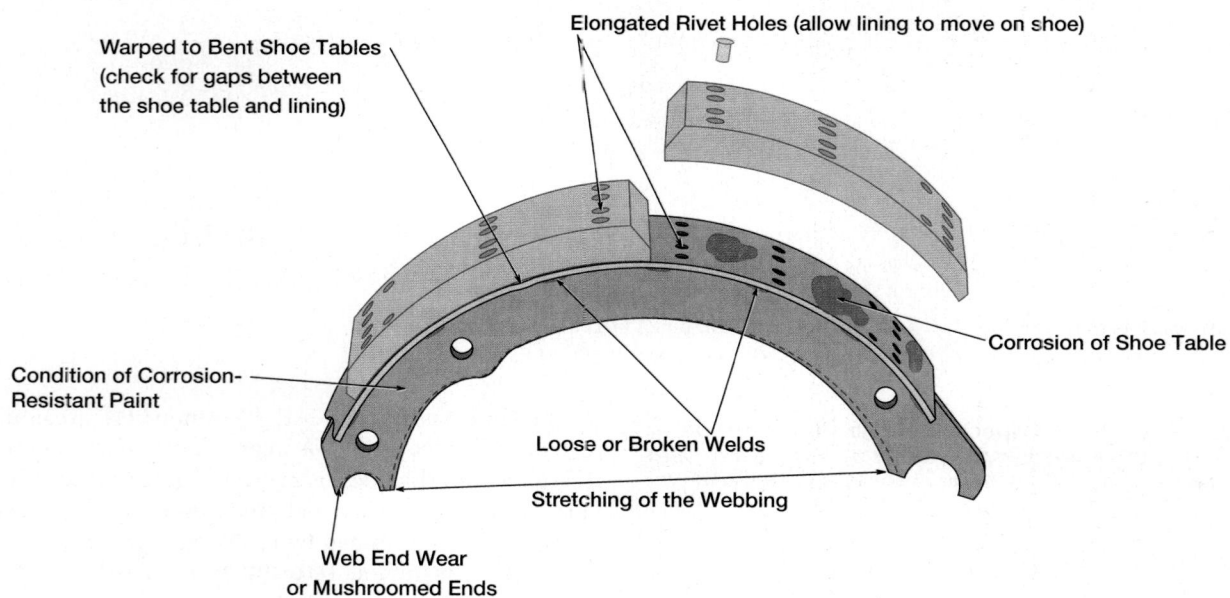

Warped to Bent Shoe Tables (check for gaps between the shoe table and lining)

Elongated Rivet Holes (allow lining to move on shoe)

Corrosion of Shoe Table

Condition of Corrosion-Resistant Paint

Loose or Broken Welds

Stretching of the Webbing

Web End Wear or Mushroomed Ends

FIGURE 36-25 Points to inspect on a brake shoe for serviceability.

follow the steps in **SKILL DRILL 36-3**. Alternatively, brake shoes can be quickly removed by pushing out the anchor pins using a punch and hammer (**FIGURE 36-27**). These brakes use a single center return spring and have a closed hole in the shoe for an anchor pin. Enclosed anchor pin holes are called "P"-type shoes. Semicircular anchor pin holes are called quick release brakes or a "QR" brake, which refers to the faster shoe replacement enabled by open anchor pin holes.

Disassembling Brakes

Two methods are used to disassemble brakes. The most common method requires only a pry bar as a lever to remove

FIGURE 36-26 An optional wear indicator switch sensor (circled) on a brake shoe.

shoe rollers. To disassemble brakes using a pry bar, follow the steps in **SKILL DRILL 36-4**.

An alternate method for disassembling brakes involves a tool resembling a heavy-duty screwdriver with a V-shaped notch cut into the bottom of the blade. The notched screwdriver is used to disconnect both brake-retain springs from the anchor pin end of brake shoes (**FIGURE 36-28**). With this method, the brake shoe springs are stretched and removed from retaining holes. The tool helps technicians avoid the pinching hazard associated with removing cam rollers while the return springs are connected. The springs can cause the shoes to snap back into position while removing the rollers and pinch fingers if a technician is not cautious. After this, the upper and lower brake shoes are pulled off the anchor pins and freed from the spider.

Installing Brake Shoes

If brake shoes are defective or need to be replaced, follow the guidelines in **SKILL DRILL 36-5**. New or "green" brakes require a

SKILL DRILL 36-2 Inspecting Brake Shoes

1. Determine if the shoe tables are warped or bent. Check for any small gaps between the lining and the shoe table.
2. Inspect the shoe foundation for elongated rivet holes, which can cause movement between the shoe table and the lining.
3. Inspect the shoe foundation for corrosion of the shoe table. Inspect for uneven fit between the lining and the shoe table. Look for visible rust at the edges.
4. Inspect the shoe foundation for web-end wear, or uneven or mushroom ends. Check both the anchor pin end and the roller end for wear and elongation. Use gauges to verify the proper distance between the web ends.
5. Inspect the shoe foundation for loose or broken welds. Look for cracks in the welds between the shoe table and the web.
6. Inspect the shoe foundation for chips or cracks in the corrosion-resistant paint. Make sure the paint is even and that there is solid coverage.

SKILL DRILL 36-3 Removing Brake Shoes

1. After backing off the brakes using the slack adjuster, the S-cam is rotated to its start position. This enables the cam rollers to be easily unclipped and removed from the shoes. Lifting the upper brake shoe slightly using a pry bar provides additional clearance to remove the cam rollers.
2. The larger, single brake shoe return spring is easily pulled and disconnected from an anchor pin on the brake shoes after the cam rollers are removed.
3. Rotating the lower shoe downwards allows the two smaller return springs on the opposite end of the shoes to be disconnected. The shoes are freely removed from the brake spider.

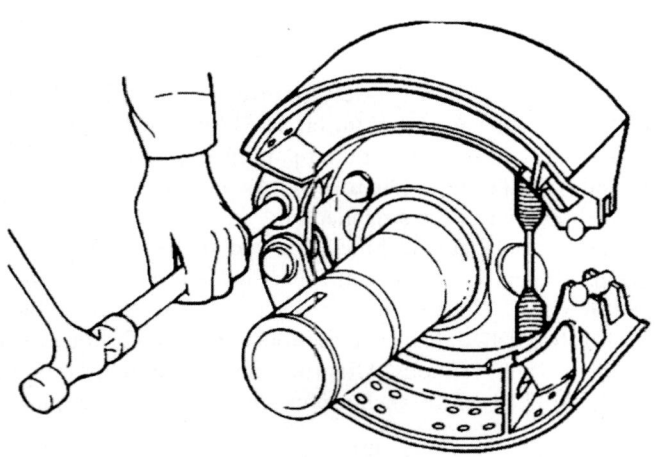

FIGURE 36-27 Pressing out anchor pins to remove brake shoes.

break-in procedure called burnishing. This involves driving the vehicle at moderate speeds and repeatedly snubbing the brakes hard using 20 psi or greater application pressure. The brake adjustment should be rechecked after burnishing the drums and shoes.

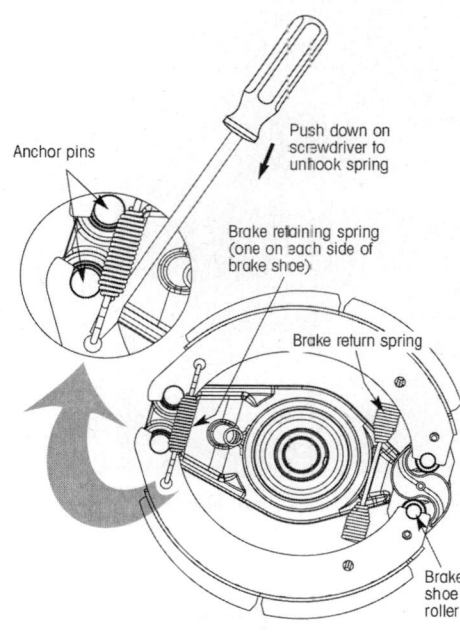

FIGURE 36-28 The use of a notched screw driver to remove brake shoe return springs.

SKILL DRILL 36-4 Disassembling Brakes with a Pry Bar

1. Insert the pry bar between one of the shoes and the axle shaft, or camshaft. Lift the shoe and remove the roller. Repeat the procedure for the opposite shoe. Generally, when performing a brake shoe replacement, cam rollers, return springs, and other brake hardware is included in a kit accompanying shoes. Any used brake hardware is discarded.
2. The larger upper return spring is easily removed from its pins since there is no spring tension after the rollers are removed.
3. Shoes are rotated backwards or lifted off the anchor pin to remove two smaller return springs at the anchor pin end of the shoes.
4. Anchor pins are pushed out of the brake spider. Lubricate the new pins with never-seize to minimize friction and absorb vibrations, which lead to brake squeal and other noise.

SKILL DRILL 36-5 Installing Brake Shoes

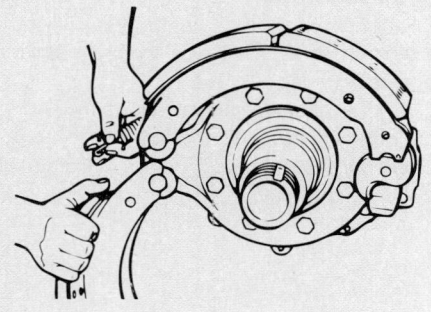

1. Install the anchor pin into the spider, centering the pin in the spider. Use never-seize lubricant when installing the anchor pin.

SKILL DRILL 36-5 Installing Brake Shoes (Continued)

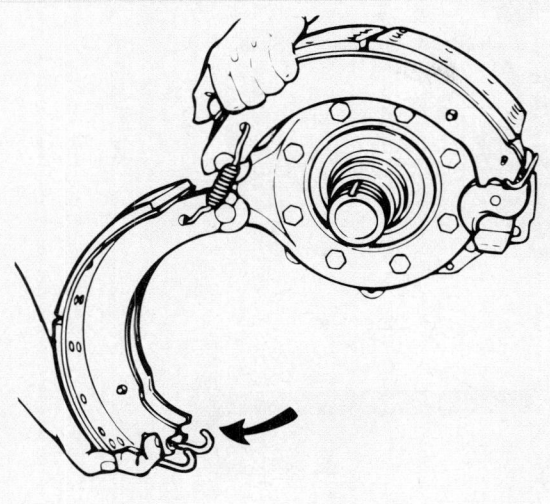

2. Install two new brake shoe retaining springs in the anchor pin end of the shoes.

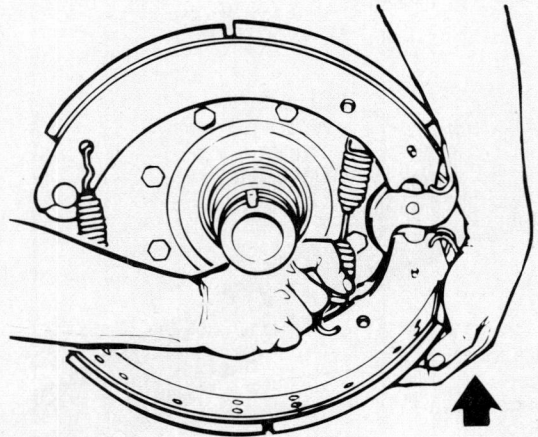

3. Place the top shoe onto the anchor pin in the brake spider. The opposite end of the shoe rests against the S-cam. Swing the lower shoe, with return springs attached, onto the anchor pin for that shoe and then continue swinging the end of the shoe toward the S-cam. Return spring tension should hold the shoes in this position.

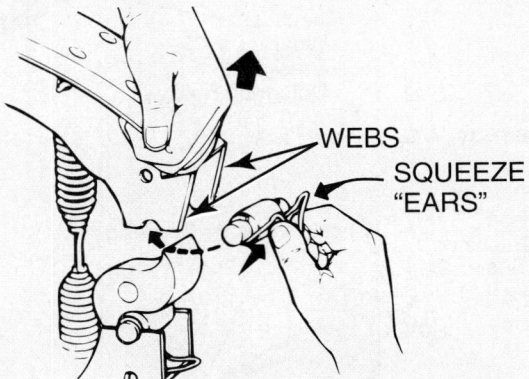

4. Connect the hook of the larger brake shoe return spring onto the return spring pin at the cam end of the upper shoe. While holding the shoes against the S-cam, connect the other end of the hook to the return spring pin of the other shoe.

5. Using a pry bar inserted between the cam end of one of the brake shoes and the spider, pry the shoe from the cam until the brake shoe roller and pin can be installed between the S-cam and the slots in the end of the brake shoe. Duplicate the procedure on the other shoe. Only the roller ends connecting with the shoes require never-seize lubricant.

6. Turn the slack-adjuster adjusting screw until the brake chamber pushrod yoke clevis pin aligns with the correct hole in the slacks arm. The clevis pin should be lubricated with never-seize compound and a new cotter pin installed. Adjust the S-cam until the cam rollers are in lowest position on the S-cam.

7. The brake drums and wheels can now be installed and torqued to manufacturer's specifications.

8. While slowly spinning the wheel, the slack adjuster can be adjusted until a slight amount of drag is sensed as the shoe and drum clearance becomes smaller. When the service brakes are applied, both slack adjusters should move in unison, stopping at identical angles with the same pushrod stroke travel. The brakes should apply and release simultaneously.

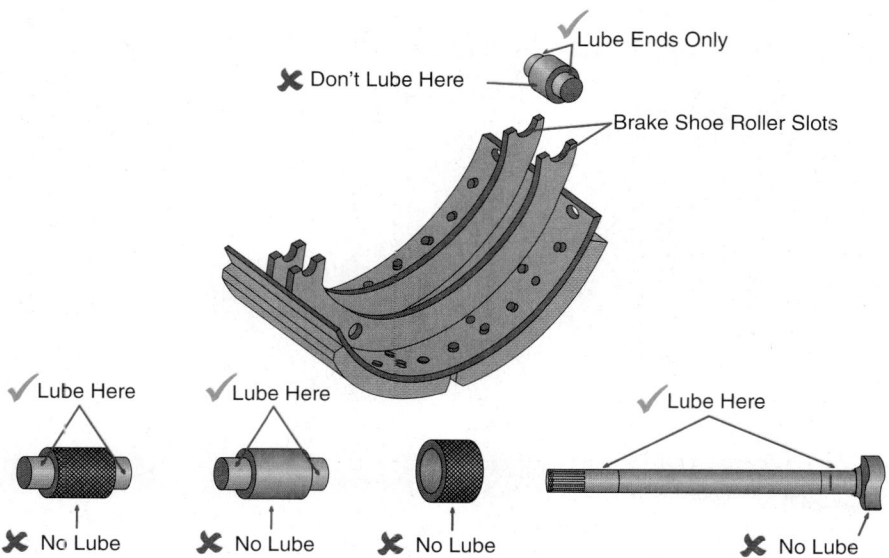

FIGURE 36-29 Not all parts in a brake shoe installation should be lubricated. In fact, some should specifically *NOT* be lubricated.

When installing brake shoes, anti seize lubricant is applied to each of the brake shoe ends to minimize friction and noise production from the cam rollers and anchor pins connection points. It is important to lubricate only certain of the component parts during assembly. Lubricant can attract and retain abrasive grit and dirt, so it should not be used on friction surfaces directly exposed to high amounts of contaminants. **FIGURE 36-29** is a guide of which parts to lubricate when installing brake shoes.

Camshafts

LO 36-7 Identify and describe inspection and service procedures used to replace S-type camshafts.

The S-cam bushings and camshaft bushing surfaces must be inspected regularly for signs of axial and radial wear at the points indicated in **FIGURE 36-30**. If any of the points are observed to be worn, the cam must be discarded. Camshafts and bushings are inspected for axial (in and out along the camshaft axis) and radial play (up, down, and sideways). The specifications shown are general and should be checked against specific manufacturers' recommendations. Likewise, the support bracket should be checked regularly for broken welds, cracks, and straightness, as shown in **FIGURE 36-31**.

Radial free play, which is up and down or sideways movement of the camshaft, should typically be no more than 0.030" (0.76 mm) movement. Allowable radial play varies between manufacturers, but rarely is more than 0.030". Camshaft end play typically is a minimum of 0.005" and a maximum of 0.030". Check camshaft play using a dial indicator with a flexible mount, as shown in **FIGURE 36-32**. If bushings are excessively worn, both the camshaft and bushings should be replaced. Camshaft bushing surfaces should be free of wear and corrosion. Any visible wear or roughness that can be felt requires replacement. The cam head should have no cracks, and its roller surfaces should be free of flat spots, brinelling, or ridges.

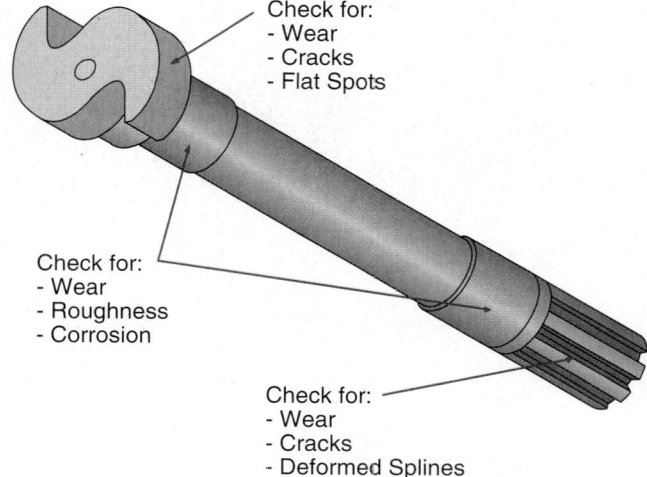

FIGURE 36-30 Wear points on a camshaft.

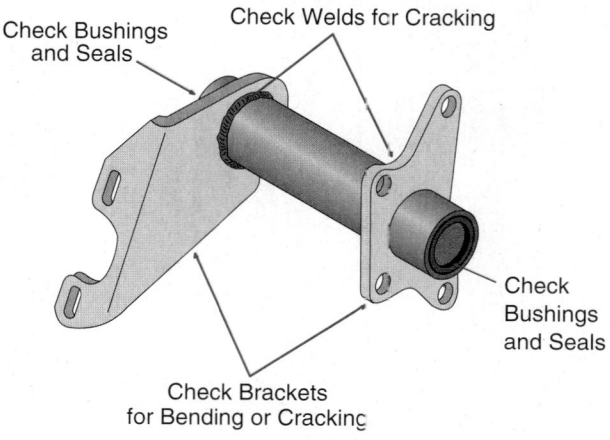

FIGURE 36-31 Wear points on the camshaft support bracket.

Removing the Camshaft

To remove the camshaft, follow the steps in **SKILL DRILL 36-6**.

Installing a Camshaft

Camshafts are classified as left- or right-hand rotation, according to the direction they rotate when the brakes are applied. Left-hand camshafts rotate counterclockwise (CCW), and right-hand camshafts rotate clockwise (CW). Camshaft rotation is illustrated in **FIGURE 36-33**. Failure to identify the correct direction of rotation and the appropriate installation location is a common cause of a major waste of labor time by novice technicians when performing camshaft replacement.

When replacing a camshaft and its bushings, two camshaft grease seals are replaced, one at each end of the cam tube. The direction of the seal lip placement is critical. To minimize grease entering the wheel end, which can contaminate the brake shoes, the seal lip at the cam end should point inboard towards the tube center. **FIGURE 36-34** shows the orientation of the lip seals.

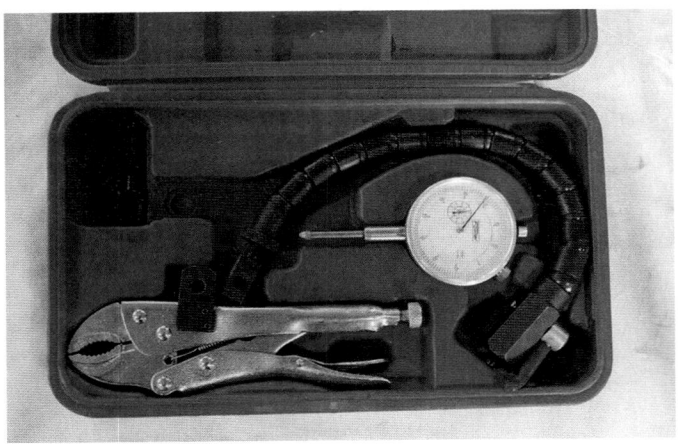

FIGURE 36-32 Check camshaft for radial play using a dial indicator..

The seal lip at the splined end should point away from the slack to enable venting and purging of old grease and contaminants into the center of the support tube during service. It is critical to ensure that the grease holes of the bushing line-up with two grease fittings at each end of the tube. When assembling the camshaft, coat camshaft journals with a light film of chassis lube. Grease the support bracket tube until grease is forced out into the gap between the slack adjuster and support bracket tube. Grease should not appear at the cam end of the shaft where the brake shoes are. If it does, the seals have not been properly installed.

Camshaft end play is adjusted using shims. A thick D-shaped camshaft flat washer, such as the one shown in **FIGURE 36-35**, is placed over the splined end first. This washer deflects grease away from the shoes and, like a thrust bearing, protects the grease seal from damage from the rotating cam lobe. Another large washer is installed between the slack adjuster and the camshaft seal. A shim pack to adjust the camshaft end play is placed between the slack adjuster and tube or split between this area and the slack adjusters snap-ring retention clip. It is vital to verify no lateral angle exists between the slack adjuster and chamber pushrod due to the placement of the shims. End play of the cam shaft should be adjusted to between 0.005" (0.127 mm) and 0.030" (1 mm) by using the appropriate number of spacer washers. After the slack adjuster is installed, a new snap ring is seated into the groove at the splined end of the camshaft.

Inspecting the Spider Plate

The brake spider plate that is attached to the axle end should be inspected for cracks or broken surfaces on the spider at the cam, anchor pin, and mounting bolt holes. Lining wear tapered from side to side across a shoe table indicates a bent spider, which can take place at the anchor pin end. The steel spider can be easily bent if it is heated and hammered to remove seized anchor pins. A purpose-made C-shaped press operated with

SKILL DRILL 36-6 Removing the Camshaft

1. Disconnect the slack adjuster from the brake chamber yoke. Removing the clevis pin or pins frees the slack arm from the yoke.
2. Remove the snap ring and washer at the splined end of the camshaft before pulling the slack adjuster from the cam shaft. If the slack adjuster has worn into the camshaft splines or is seized to the camshaft by corrosion, a puller may be required. Purpose-made pullers are available to remove slack adjusters.
3. Remove the spacer shims used to adjust axial end play. Also, remove the thick washer between the cam support bracket and shims.
4. Slide the camshaft out of the support bracket tube from the axle end. Remove the backing plates, if equipped.

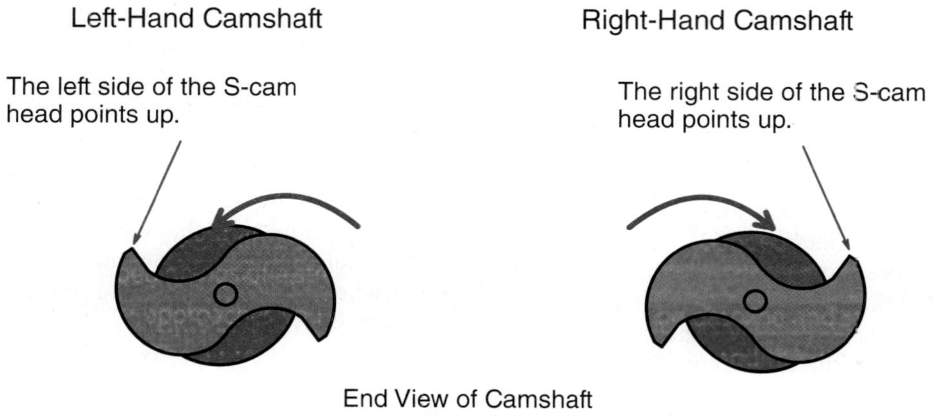

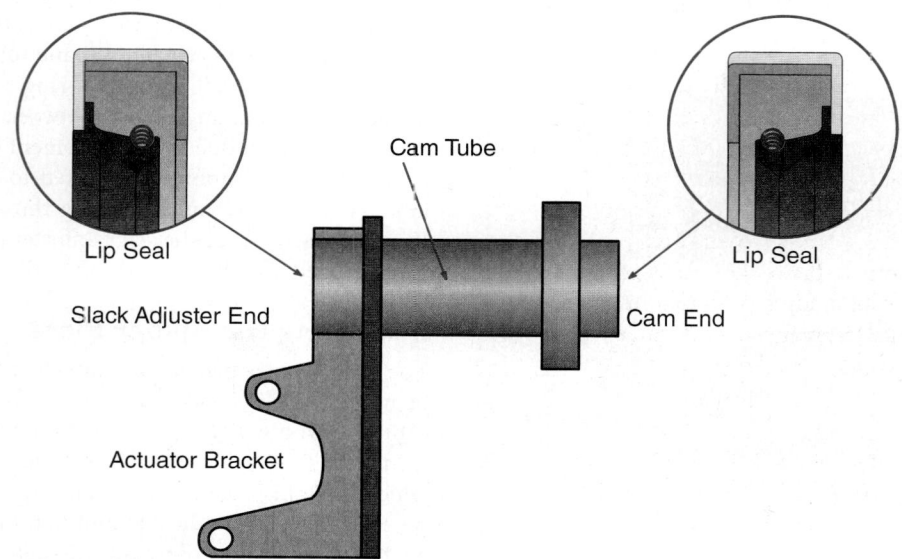

Left-Hand Camshaft

The left side of the S-cam head points up.

Right-Hand Camshaft

The right side of the S-cam head points up.

End View of Camshaft

FIGURE 36-33 Camshafts are classified by the direction of rotation required to apply the brakes.

Cam Tube

Lip Seal

Slack Adjuster End

Lip Seal

Cam End

Actuator Bracket

FIGURE 36-34 Lip-type grease seals are installed at each end of the camshaft bracket. To prevent grease from contaminating brake shoes and drums, outer wheel end grease seals are installed with lips facing the inboard—toward the slack adjuster.

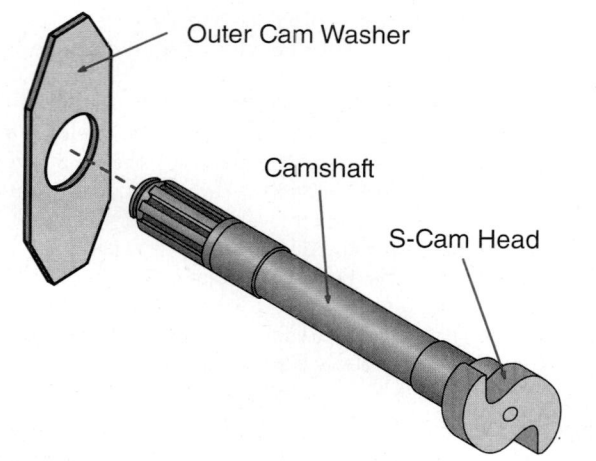

Outer Cam Washer

Camshaft

S-Cam Head

FIGURE 36-35 A large washer is located just behind the S-cam lobe.

an air impact gun can be used to push out seized anchor pins. Radial clearance around the anchor pins in excess of 0.010" (0.25 mm) indicates excessive wear, requiring brake spider replacement.

Slack Adjuster Inspection and Maintenance

LO 36-8 Identify and describe the types of slack adjusters, inspection, and service procedures used to replace and adjust automatic slack adjusters.

Correct brake stroke adjustment and maintenance, a fundamental function of slack adjusters, is critical to effective vehicle braking and road safety. Since 1994, all air brake systems used on highways have required ASAs.

Two types of ASA's uses are classified according to whether they adjust the brake stroke by sensing the clearance between the brake drum and shoe or sensing the stroke length. Clearance-sensing ASAs are more popular since there are fewer problems associated with brake over-adjustment. Regardless of the type, when inspecting slack adjusters, they should be observed to fully apply the brakes without binding or interference with other part and should return to the full released position. Inspect for looseness between the brake chamber pushrod yoke, adapter bushings, and the yoke clevis pins. Both clevis pins, if used, should be free to rotate and be lubricated with anti seize compound. When an adjuster link is used, seals and dust boots should be present and not damaged. The slack should appear to have grease squeezed out of the splined collar from regularly scheduled lubrication intervals using the correct grade of grease.

To determine whether the slack adjuster is properly adjusting the brake, measure the distance from the brake chamber face to the largest clevis pin with the brakes released, and again after a full brake application. The difference between the two measurements is the chamber stroke or applied stroke measurement. Manufacturers emphasize that a slack adjuster that is over-stroking—which means the stroke length is too long, should never be readjusted because it can indicate a defect in the adjustment mechanism. Readjusting a defective slack does not restore the proper drum to brake shoe clearance, but quickly "backs-off." Instead, the slack adjuster should be replaced—in pairs on an axle—or a functional test performed of the slack adjuster operation.

Adjusting Automatic Slack Adjusters

ASAs maintain shoe-to-drum clearance established during an initial adjustment. Depending on the type and construction of the slack, a correctly installed ASA moves to obtain the optimal stroke length it was designed for. Not all slack adjusters can be relied on to correct for errors made during initial adjustment at installation. Following OEM setup procedures or establishing the correct brake stroke adjustment during installation is essential to proper brake system operation. As already mentioned, two types of ASAs are used, which have an internal adjusting mechanism to monitor and maintain the proper clearance between the brake linings and drum. **FIGURE 36-36A** shows an ASA with external bracket actuation, and **FIGURE 36-36B** shows one with link-rod activation. Because slack adjusters use different adjusting mechanisms and designs, brands of slack adjusters should never be intermixed on the same axle. Ideally, a vehicle uses the same type or brand of slack adjuster and ones of identical age on a vehicle. That means when one slack is replaced due to wear or improper operation, all should be replaced.

Pushrod stroke with ASAs is typically slightly longer than older manual slack adjusters. Using a common type 30 air chamber and an ASA, pushrod travel of more than ¾" (1.9 cm) during a free stroke measurement, or more than 2" (5.08 cm) using applied stroke method, requires ASA replacement if the initial adjustment was correctly performed. Long stroke (LS)

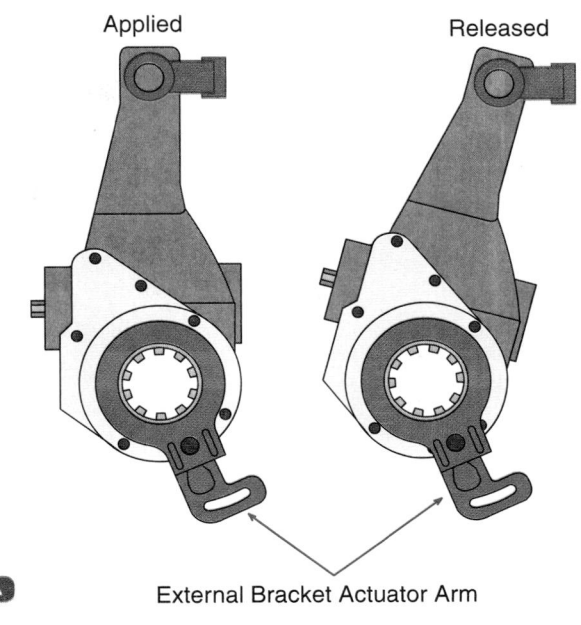

External Bracket Activation

Applied   Released

A   External Bracket Actuator Arm

Link Rod Activation

Link Rod

B   Applied   Released

FIGURE 36-36 A. External bracket actuation. **B.** Link rod activation.

chambers have square-shaped inlet ports or a tag on a clamp bolt but use the same stroke limits.

ASAs are best initially adjusted using the applied stroke method of brake adjustment. If an adjustment needs backing off, the turning force required to back off a slack is much more than a manual slack and can prematurely wear or damage the adjustment mechanism, if performed repeatedly.

If the slack adjuster uses a square-shaped adjusting bolt, a spring-loaded mechanical pawl or lock that meshes with internal teeth may need to be removed first, before the ASA can be adjusted. One type of pawl, which prevents reversal of the

FIGURE 36-37 To adjust some types of ASAs, a locking pawl must be first disengaged. This pawl uses a hexagonal cap.

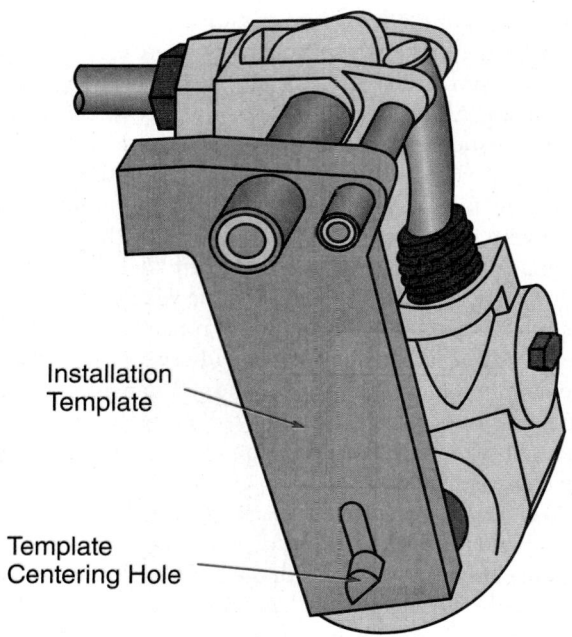

FIGURE 36-38 A Gunite brand template for aligning the slack adjuster link and yoke.

adjustment, is disengaged by removing a ¾" (1.9 cm) hexagonal-shaped cap located on the side of the adjuster. Other adjusters using these hex caps use a round-shaped "button," which can be pried out approximately ⅟₃₂" (0.8 mm) with a flat-bladed screwdriver, as illustrated in **FIGURE 36-37**.

An ASA should be manually adjusted only after a brake shoe or drum is replaced or removed. Frequent manual adjustment reduces the durability of the internal adjusting mechanism. ASAs should be lubricated whenever chassis lubrication services are performed, so at 25,000 miles (40,000 km) or three months, whichever occurs first. The latest automatic adjusters are using an updated mechanism to minimize potential damage to the adjuster mechanism when it is backed off for brake service.

Stroke-Sensing Slacks

Stroke-sensing slack adjusters sense and adjust pushrod stroke distance. Excessive stroke travel activates the adjusting mechanism to maintain drum-to-lining clearance. The problem with stroke-sensing slack adjusters is over-adjustment and shortening of the stroke length can take place when brake parts are worn. As parts deflect farther due to wear and deterioration, the longer sensed stroke is over-corrected by the adjuster, even though drum-to-lining clearance is correct. If camshaft bushing wear is present, which lengthens stroke, or air chamber bracket deflection takes place, over-adjustment reduces drum-to-shoe clearances to the point where the brake drags and overheats.

▶ TECHNICIAN TIP

When installing the pushrod yoke, some manufacturers provide a template, as shown in **FIGURE 36-38**, for use in aligning the slack adjuster adjusting link and yoke to obtain the correct mounting angle between the adjuster and pushrod. The template helps a technician adjust the pushrod yoke to the correct position or alerts the technicians to an incorrect length of chamber pushrod. Other manufacturers use a special

procedure to properly position and adjust the ASA's external adjusting lever or bracket. Consult manufacturer's service literature for the specific steps to adjust the external arm.

Clearance Sensing

Most ASAs currently manufactured adjust lining-to-drum clearances until the force applied to the brakes, through the slack adjuster is high. The ability to adjust stroke travel during the initial part of each brake application and stop adjusting as resistance to brake cam rotation builds is a clearance-sensing adjustment principle. The advantage of clearance-sensing slack adjuster mechanisms is pushrod stroke length, and problems caused by brake wear and flexing of brake parts are less of influence. Adjustment of clearance-sensing slacks begins to take place before the rapid rise in brake force torque (**FIGURE 36-39**). Adjusting mechanisms in clearance-sensing slacks rotate an internal adjusting mechanism when the brake is released.

Functional Testing of ASAs

To differentiate whether an over-stroked automatic slack is simply misadjusted or defective, manufacturers publish a service procedure to test or measure the functionally of their particular slack adjuster. Consult the manufacturer's product service bulletins for specific procedures for the ASA model being evaluated. To illustrate, a common functional test procedure involves backing off the slack adjuster to allow it to over-stroke. Typically, turning the adjusting screw counterclockwise ¾-turn is enough. When backing off the adjustment, a ratcheting sound should be heard, accompanied by high turning resistance. Remember, a locking pawl may need to be removed before the adjusting screw can be moved. Next, the adjusting screw and slack

FIGURE 36-39 The clutch of this clearance-sensing slack-adjusting mechanism opens and turns the adjuster mechanism under rapid heavy brake application force. Bendix has an improved mechanism for establishing brake shoe-to-drum clearance and reduced likelihood of damage when backed off.

adjuster body are marked with chalk or scribed with a mark. Marking both parts is done to enable a technician to observe the direction of rotation for the adjusting screw as the brakes are repeatedly applied and released in the next step. For a properly functioning slack, the adjusting screw turns clockwise when the brakes are repeatedly applied and released to reestablish the correct stroke length. The screw should typically not turn when the brakes are released. The screw also rotates more as the brakes are applied and the stroke length is longest. Shortening of the stroke length causes the screw to turn less with each brake application until the correct brake stroke length is obtained. At that point, rotational movement of the screw stops.

Another functional test of the slack adjuster involves the use of a torque wrench to measure the amount of resistance in the adjustment screw when either backing off or tightening the adjustment screw. Too little turning resistance, when compared to specifications, means the slack adjustment mechanism is damaged or excessively worn, which requires replacement of the slack.

Replacing Automatic Slack Adjusters

When the ASAs need replacing, start by parking the bus, truck, or trailer on a level surface, and chock its wheels. Then follow the steps in **SKILL DRILL 36-7**. Specialized tools, such as those in **FIGURE 36-40**, can be used to remove slack adjusters seized to the camshaft or seized clevis pins.

SKILL DRILL 36-7 Replacing Automatic Slack Adjusters

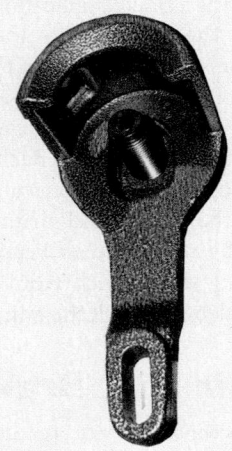

1. Properly chock the vehicle wheels and release the spring brakes. If the brakes are left applied, the spring brake needs to be caged before removing the slack adjuster.
2. Disconnect the slack adjuster attaching hardware. Most slack adjusters are locked onto the S-camshaft using a removable snap-ring. Disconnect the clevis yoke clevis pins and the yoke from the chamber pushrod. If the slack used a quick-connect type clevis, it should ideally be replaced with a standard threaded-type, since quick connect clevises loosen over time and can contribute to longer brake stroke travel or over-stroking.
3. Remove the slack adjuster from the S-cam. Slack adjusters that have been on a long time or left unlubricated may be seized and require a purpose-made puller to remove. Otherwise, the slack

may require the use of a large hammer or cutting torch to coax the slack from the splines on the S-cam.
4. Inspect other brake foundation components. Remove the backing plate, if equipped, to check the condition of the brake foundation assembly. There should be adequate brake lining. The S-cam should not have excessive play due to worn bushings. The brake chamber should also be inspected for cracks, leaks, proper centering, and bent pushrods.
5. Choose the correct parts. Models, types, and brands of slack adjusters should never be mixed on the same axle since it can lead to variations in brake stoke travel and brake torque imbalance.
6. Replace both slack adjusters on an axle if the matching identical slack cannot be found. Note that some slack adjusters have offset arms that are made specifically for the right or left side of vehicle applications to provide clearance for axle parts.
7. Before mounting the slack adjuster on the camshaft, confirm that the brake chamber pushrod length allows a 90-degree angle between the slack adjuster and chamber, or whether pushrod shortening or replacement is required. To perform this check, follow one of the following three methods.

Method 1:
- Place a carpenter's square so that one edge is parallel to the actuator pushrod and the other edge of the square passes through the centerline of the camshaft.
- The hole of the clevis and the vertical leg of square must pass through the centerline of the S-cam. If not, the brake chamber pushrod needs cutting or replacement, depending on whether it's too long or short.

SKILL DRILL 36-7 Replacing Automatic Slack Adjusters (Continued)

Method 2:

• Measure the distance from the end of the pushrod, without the yoke, to the edge of the square that passes though the camshaft centerline. Determine the distance needed to attach the yoke. That distance depends on the slack adjuster arm length—between 5" (12.7 cm) and 6" (15.2 cm)—and requires comparison between the slack length and the manufacturer's service information for the type of clevis yoke used.

Method 3:

Most manufacturers provide a plastic template with two clevis pin holes that are used to help ensure the correct installation angle is maintained between the slack adjuster and pushrod. One larger hole is for the slack arm and the other smaller hole is for the linkage for the slack adjuster mechanism. A centering hole may be used on the template to identify the center of the camshaft. Follow the template instructions to verify the camshaft center and clevis holes in the template provide a correct angle between the slack and pushrod. If not, the brake chamber pushrod yoke may require adjustment, or the brake chamber push rod requires cutting or replacement.

8. Ensure the slack adjuster is centered on the S-cam directly in front of the brake chamber pushrod. Slide the slack adjuster onto the camshaft to check this. If it is not centered, shimming with flat washers and shims is required during the next step.

9. Install the slack after cleaning and lubricating the S-cam with anti seize compound. Install the large inner flat washers between the slack and S-cam bracket first, then install the slack and shim the slack adjuster with outer washers to enable approximately 0.05" (1.27 mm) axial movement of the slack along the S-cam.

10. Manually adjust the slack until the clevis and link holes align with the pushrod yoke. Verify alignment using any accompanying plastic template required to align with the holes in the slack and yoke clevis.

11. Adjust the brake by tightening the slack adjuster until the shoes contact the brake drum. Back off the adjuster to achieve the correct brake pushrod stroke.

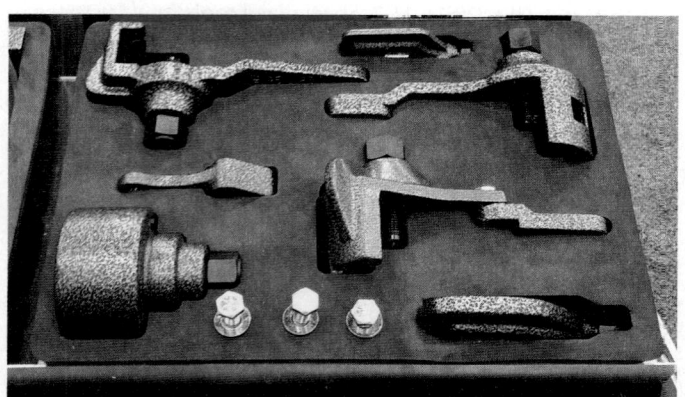

FIGURE 36-40 Pullers that can be operated with hand or air tools can remove seized slack adjusters and clevis pins.

> ▶ TECHNICIAN TIP

An ASA that does not maintain stroke adjustment is either faulty or the foundation brake has a problem. Technicians need to determine why a defective adjuster is over-stroking—meaning it has excessive stroke—and make the appropriate repairs, or perform a functional test. Simply readjusting a self-adjusting brake adjuster, or replacing it, does not ensure that the problem is corrected. The problem may exist in the foundation brake system.

Manual Slack Adjuster Adjustment

Manual slack adjusters are still occasionally found on old trailers and some off-road equipment. These slack adjusters must be frequently manually adjusted to maintain acceptable brake stroke length. The adjustment screw uses a spring-loaded locking sleeve around the screw to lock the adjustment and prevent the slack from unwinding the adjustment to an over-stroke position. The lock sleeve is pressed in and held down before the ⁹⁄₁₆" (14.3 mm) adjusting screw can be turned. How the slack is

orientated determines the correct direction to turn the adjusting screw—CW or CCW. Using a ⁹⁄₁₆" (14.3 mm) wrench, the locking sleeve around the adjusting screw is pressed inwards while the adjusting screw is turned. The slack rotates the camshaft when turning the adjusting screw. Rotating the adjuster in the correct direction to shorten brake stroke rotates the S-cam in the same direction as a brake application.

While turning the adjuster in the correct direction, rotating the adjuster screw stops after the brake shoes have contacted the drum. By looking through an inspection hole on the back of a dust shield, a technician can visually verify that the linings have contacted the drum. Backing off the adjusting screw about ⅓ to ½ of a turn should establish correct running clearance between the lining and drum. The brake stroke travel should then be measured to verify pushrod stroke is acceptable. Removing the wrench from the adjusting screw enables the locking sleeve to lock the adjusting screw in place.

Servicing Air Disc Brakes

LO 36-9 Outline inspection and service procedures for air disc brakes.

Servicing air disc brakes involves inspecting or replacing brake pads and rotors, measuring pad and rotor thicknesses and pad to rotor running clearance. Measuring brake pad wear is necessary for determining remaining service life of the friction materials and whether they require replacement. Measuring running clearances is important to determine whether the brake is correctly adjusted or requiring further service.

Brake Pad Inspection

On most air disc brakes, brake pads can be visually inspected without removing the wheels. Newer-model air disc brakes, such as those shown in **FIGURE 36-41**, allow the technician to check brake pad thickness visually. When the wheels are removed for a thorough inspection, the thickness of the friction material can also be measured or estimated. The pad friction material is typically allowed to wear to less than the thickness of the pads steel backing plate (**FIGURE 36-42**). If it is less, the pads must be replaced. Minimum thickness, however, depends on the type of pad being used and manufacturer specifications, and the manufacturer's service information must be used to determine the correct minimum thickness specification to allow a pad to remain in service. New service tools, such as the type in **FIGURE 36-43**, can measure the rotor and pad wear with the wheel on or off. A pair of sliding calipers on the tool can be slipped over the rotor to measure its thickness while another end of the tool can be inserted into the caliper to measure the combined thickness of the two brake pads using two reference points on the caliper. The advantage of the service tool is it reports a percentage for the remaining friction material service life.

When inspecting pads, it's useful to note that minor damage at the edges is permitted, but pads must be replaced if significant damage is present on the surface of the pad. All brake pads on an axle must be replaced at the same time to prevent any side-to-side variations in brake torque causing brake pull.

Alternate Measurement Methods for Brake Pad Wear

Disc brake pads can usually be visually inspected with little effort; however, certain manufacturers have other indicators to assess wear. Notches cut in to the sliding caliper and the caliper bracket and or the extension of bushings on the caliper pins can be used to indicate when pad replacement is required

(**FIGURE 36-44**). Electronic wear indicators, such as the ones shown in **FIGURE 36-45**, are commonly used to measure brake pad wear. **Electronic pad wear indicators** measure brake pad and rotor wear electronically and send signals to the antilock braking system (ABS) module which communicates with the driver's information center to alert the driver when excessive wear occurs. These indicators come in one of two types. One is simply an on-off switch that signals the driver when a pad has worn to a predetermined wear point. The second type uses a potentiometer to measure progressive wear; with this type, the driver receives ongoing information on brake wear. Unlike mechanical wear indicators, electronic wear indicators using potentiometers can account for both pad and rotor wear.

For on-off indicators, a sensor is placed in a groove of the brake pad at the factory or by the technician when replacement pads are installed. When the pad wears away through use, a minimum wear point is reached when the sensor contacts the rotor. Normally closed and normally open indicators are used, which either open or close the circuit for a warning light or buzzer. Sensor contact with the rotor opens or closes the circuit, depending on the type of switch. Sensors should be replaced when the new pads are installed.

FIGURE 36-41 Brake pad thickness is easily checked by visually inspecting the pads in the calipers.

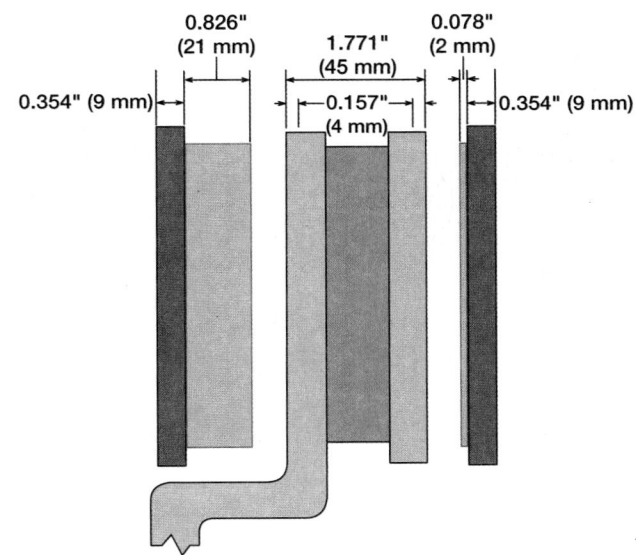

FIGURE 36-42 Measurable dimensions of the brake pad and rotor during inspection. No less than 2 mm of brake pad is allowed for this wheel end.

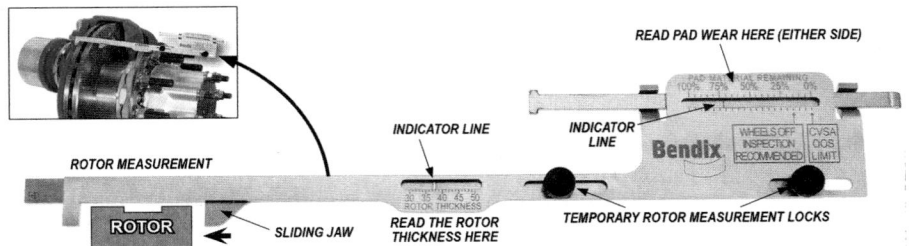

FIGURE 36-43 The brake rotor and pad measurement tool can measure the thickness of brake rotors and pads with the wheel on. The thickness and percentage of remaining service life is determined by a scale on the tool.

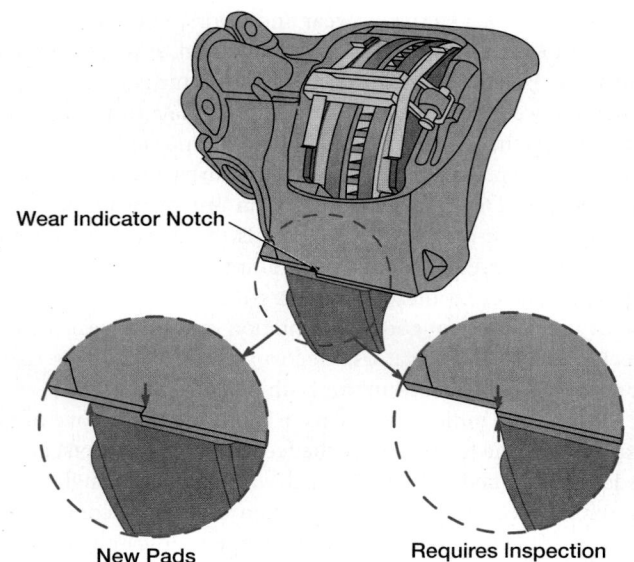

Wear Indicator Notch

New Pads   Requires Inspection

FIGURE 36-44 Brake pad and rotor wear can be observed using wear indicator notches on some calipers.

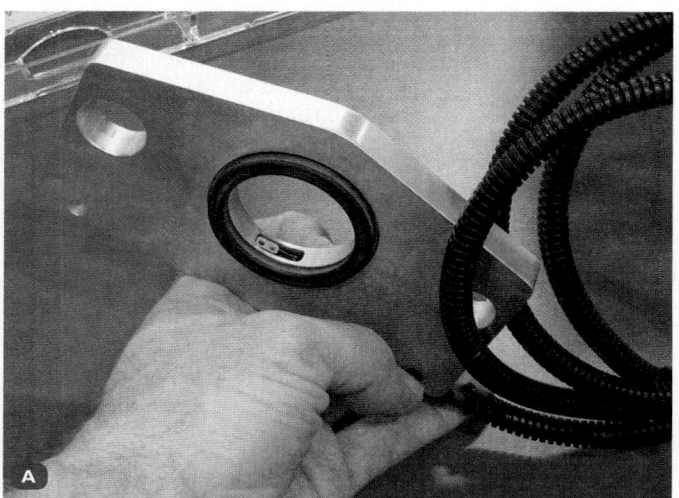

A

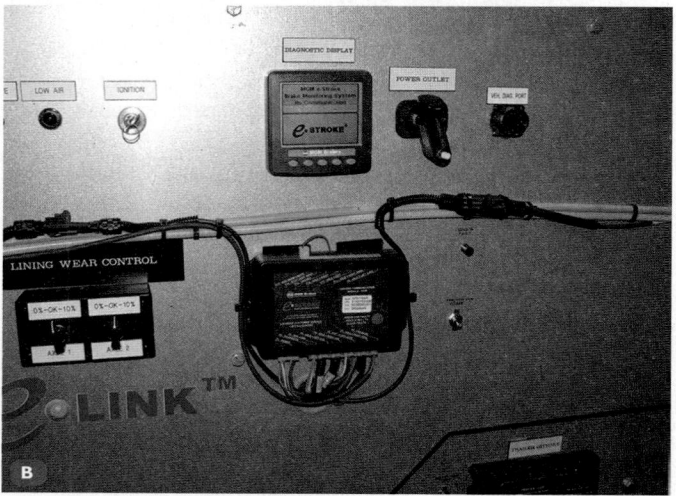

B

FIGURE 36-45 Electronic wear indicator systems manufactured by MGM Brakes. **A.** Sensor. **B.** Control system.

FIGURE 36-46 A potentiometer-type wear indicator and a wiring harness connector.

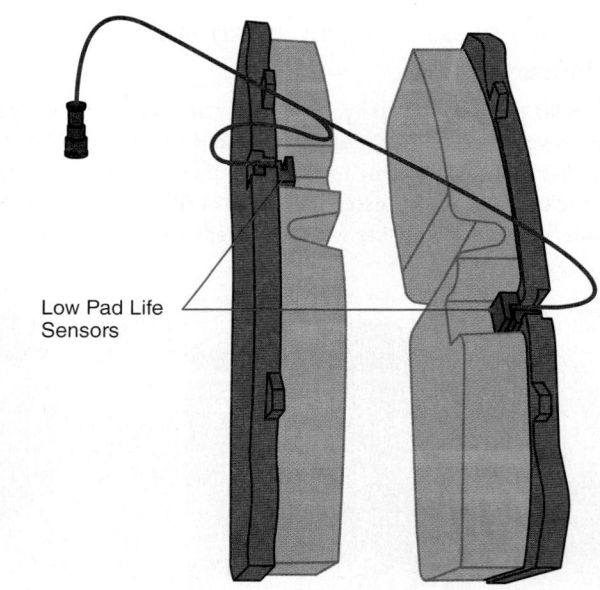

Low Pad Life Sensors

FIGURE 36-47 A switch embedded into a brake pad alerts the driver when the pad is reaching minimum thickness.

A potentiometer-type sensor measures the progressive movement of the brake pad towards the rotor. A hand-held diagnostic tool can check individual wheel circuits or six separate circuits. A check of the potentiometer can also be performed using the tool. As shown in **FIGURE 36-46**, a potentiometer-type wear indicator for air disc brakes measures brake pad thickness and progressive brake pad wear. An electronic service tool can read brake wear information from a system control module or monitor the function of an individual wheel sensor.

A simple type of electronic brake wear indicator uses a switch embedded into a brake pad, as illustrated in **FIGURE 36-47**. The driver is alerted when pad wear is approaching minimum thickness. When the switch at the brake pad contacts the brake rotor, the circuit is grounded and provides a warning signal for the driver.

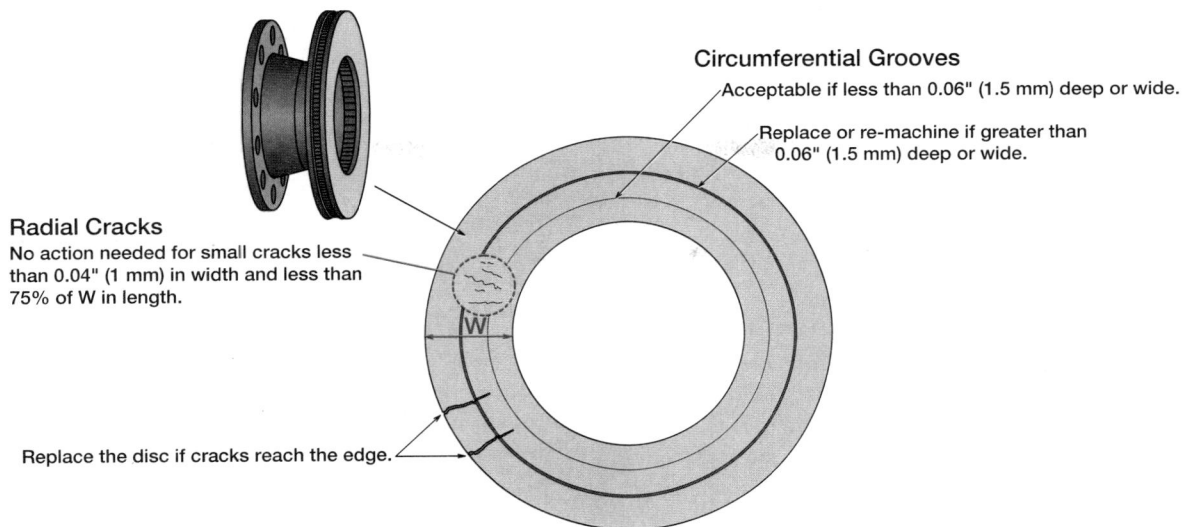

Radial Cracks
No action needed for small cracks less than 0.04" (1 mm) in width and less than 75% of W in length.

Circumferential Grooves
Acceptable if less than 0.06" (1.5 mm) deep or wide.

Replace or re-machine if greater than 0.06" (1.5 mm) deep or wide.

Replace the disc if cracks reach the edge.

These values are a guide only; always check manufacturer wear limit specifications.

FIGURE 36-48 Inspection points and criteria for evaluating the serviceability of a rotor.

Rotor Surface Inspection

Rotors are inspected whenever pads are replaced. Cracked and overheated rotors should be replaced. Some cracking and scoring are permissible, depending on the rotor area affected and the depth and length of cracks and scoring (**FIGURE 36-48**). Heat checking and small cracks are caused by the constant thermal cycling of rotors from hot to cold. These can wear away and reappear. However, small cracks may grow into larger unacceptable cracks or when very high brake temperatures are encountered by the rotor. Large wear grooves in a rotor may reduce the rotors available friction area for new pads, so turning rotors (grinding and cutting material from the surface of the rotor) can be useful, but normally is not necessary. If turning is performed, a brake lathe, such as shown in **FIGURE 36-49**, can cut rotors while on the wheel end. Machining rotors on the vehicle is a best practice because it minimizes lateral runout due to hub and bearing irregularities caused when a rotor is transferred from an off-vehicle machine to the axle end. A minimum rotor thickness is stamped into the rotor. A measuring tool called a rotor micrometer is specifically built to measure rotor thickness and is used to evaluate the rotor for minimum thickness serviceability (**FIGURE 36-50**). A rotor must have a minimum thickness, usually cast or stamped into the rotor, before it can be returned to service or after machining. Another number can also be stamped into the rotor to identify its discard thickness. Without adequate thickness, the rotor cannot absorb and dissipate heat, resulting in rotor warpage, potential brake fade, and heat damage to the caliper.

Rotor Replacement

Rotors are inspected and replaced for the following defects:

- Excessive wear (measured with a rotor micrometer)
- Overheating (blue discoloration or burnt)
- Deep heat checking (light heat checking is acceptable)
- Deep cracks (small shallow cracks are acceptable)

FIGURE 36-49 A brake lathe.

- Deep wear grooves
- Visual damage
- Contamination from wheel seal leaks or excessive rusting

Unless the wheel or the brake pads are removed, only the inner side of the rotor can be visually inspected with the wheel on. Rotor thickness should be measured across any deep groove. If the thickness across the groove is less than the minimum discard dimension stamped on the rotor casting, the rotor requires replacement. If a rotor requires replacement, the caliper assembly and brake chamber must be first removed. Bolts attaching the caliper carrier to the spindle are the most convenient point to remove the caliper assembly

(**FIGURE 36-51**). Rotors are attached to the hub either using bolts or are stud-mounted (**FIGURE 36-52**). For stud-mounted rotors, a brass or synthetic hammer is used to remove or press out the hub-to-rotor studs to prevent damage to the reusable studs. Bolt-mounted rotors simply require removal of bolts attaching the rotor to the hub. The brake is reassembled in reverse order.

Inspecting Caliper Sliders for Movement

Some side-to-side movement of the brake caliper should be present on all disc brakes to establish some running clearance between brake pads and the rotor after the brakes are released. The lateral sliding movement of a caliper is necessary to allow it to recenter the pads over the rotor as components wear. Without some side-to-side movement in the caliper, the pads drag against the rotor and overheat, causing

THICKNESS MEASUREMENT

1.626" (41.3 MM) MINIMUM THICKNESS

Applies to solid or vented rotor.

MICROMETER

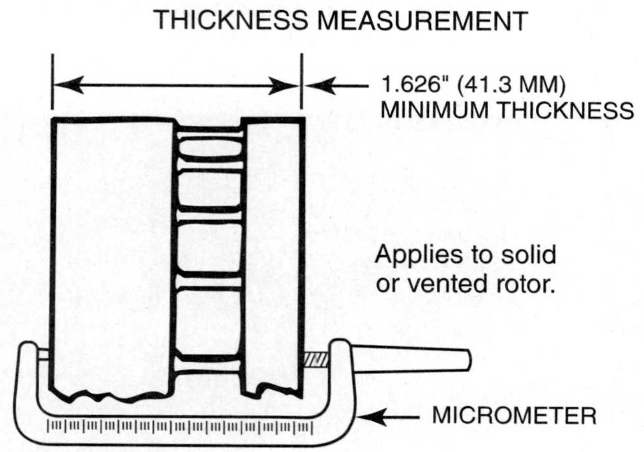

FIGURE 36-50 A rotor micrometer is used to measure the thickness of a rotor to determine whether it can be returned to service or must be scrapped.

premature wear and, potentially, heat damage. Lateral sliding movement of the caliper takes place over a sturdy set of lubricated pins called guide pins or caliper slider pins. The pins pass through a caliper carrier, which is bolted to the spider plate attached to the steering knuckle spindle, or the steering knuckle itself. The arrangement of attaching the caliper to the caliper carrier enables the caliper to float or slide sideways over the rotor to recenter the caliper after brake applications. If caliper movement is not present, the caliper sliders or guide pins are likely seized, lacking lubrication, and need servicing (**FIGURE 36-53**). Excessive wear of only one brake pad at a wheel end usually indicates a caliper that is binding on the slider pin. If only one pin is binding, the pads have end-to-end taper wear, with one end of both pads worn more than the other. Inspect dust seals and O-rings to make sure they are present and not leaking. Inspection mirrors can be used to check these parts when the wheel is not removed.

With the wheels chocked and the parking brakes released, check the caliper movement by grasping the caliper and pushing it back and forth. Some sideways movement of the caliper along the slider pins should be observed. Movement can also be measured with a dial indicator and the observed side-to-side movement or lateral travel compared to specifications (**FIGURE 36-54**). If adequate caliper movement is not detected, the caliper pins or bolts must be removed, cleaned, and lubricated. Rubber seals and O-rings used to keep water out of the pin sliding surfaces and causing corrosion should be inspected or replaced. Inspect the guide-pin bushings and replace all bushings and pins if wear, pitting, bending, or excessive corrosion is observed. Silicone dielectric grease having high-temperature resistance, consistent temperature viscosity, and resistance to chemical change can be used to lubricate pins after they are cleaned. Alternatively, high-temperature marine grease, capable of resisting contamination from road salt, can be used for lubricant.

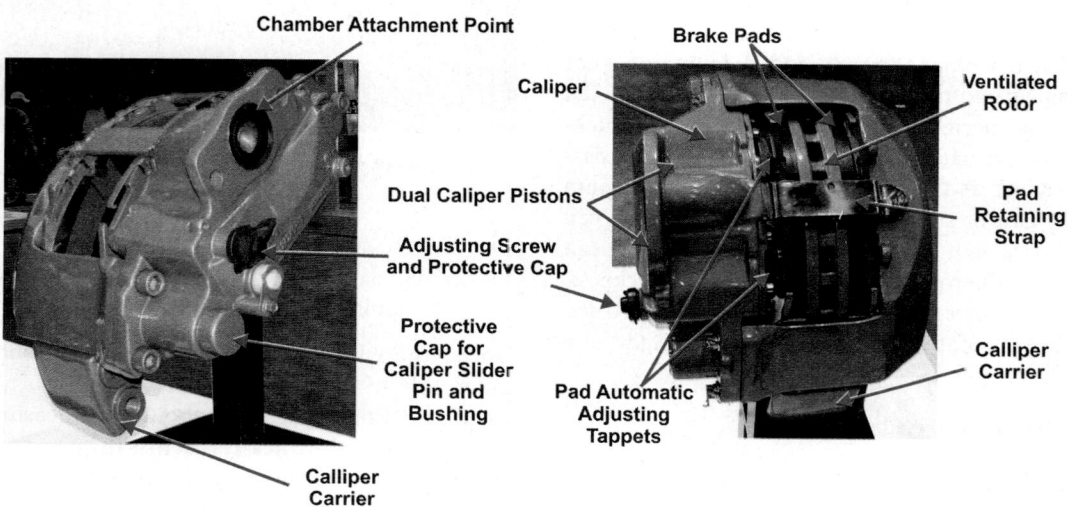

FIGURE 36-51 Components of a Bendix caliper assembly.

A: Stud-Mounted Rotor

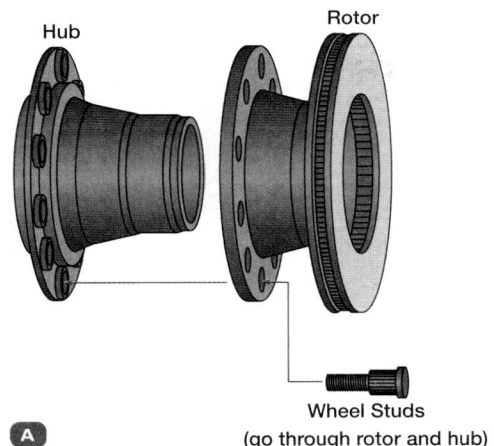

A

Wheel Studs
(go through rotor and hub)

B: Bolt-Mounted Rotor

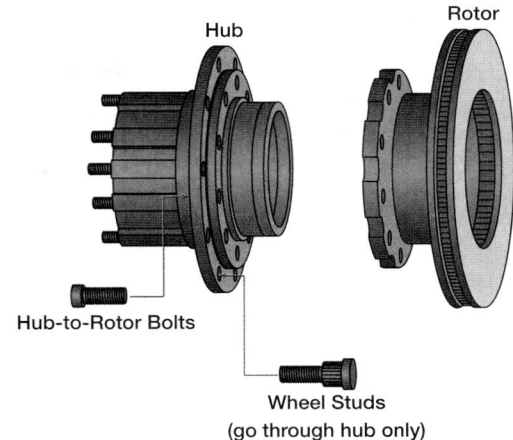

Hub-to-Rotor Bolts

Wheel Studs
(go through hub only)

A: Stud-Mounted Rotor

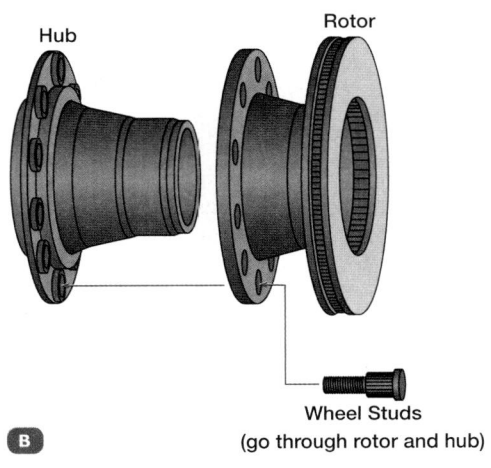

B

Wheel Studs
(go through rotor and hub)

B: Bolt-Mounted Rotor

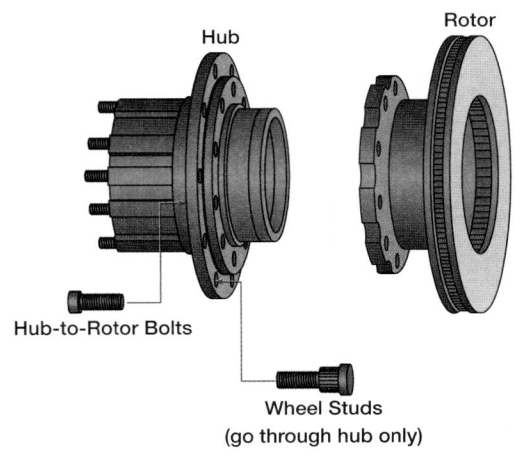

Hub-to-Rotor Bolts

Wheel Studs
(go through hub only)

FIGURE 36-52 A. Stud-mounted rotors are typically used on drive axle hubs. **B.** Bolt-mounted rotors.

Inspecting and Measuring Brake Pad-Rotor Running Clearance

LO 36-10 Identify and explain the purpose and procedures used to inspect, measure, and adjust disc brake pad to rotor running clearance inspection.

Disc brake calipers use automatic adjusting mechanisms that sense and maintain the correct clearance between pads and rotors. This running clearance between the brake pads and rotor is a crucial operating clearance for effective braking. When the brakes are released, a slight clearance should be established to minimize brake drag caused by friction between the brake pads and rotor. If the clearance is excessive, extra brake chamber stroke length is required to take up the clearance, which can lead to inadequate braking or brake failure. Without adequate running clearance, friction prematurely wears the pads and rotor and may even result in brake overheating. One method to check pad running clearance is to insert two feeler or thickness blades between the pad and

tappets or plate behind the pad (**FIGURE 36-55**). This is done after only the inboard pad has been pushed away from the rotor and the tappets or backing plate behind the pad. A space between the thickness of a nickel and a dime should be measured between each pad and the tappet. Manufacturer's specifications differ between brake models, but a typical nominal clearance is 0.030" (0.75 mm). Acceptable movement during a check of the caliper sliders means no further inspection of pad running clearance is required because the absence of adequate running clearance does not allow side-to-side caliper movement. If the running clearance is not correct, the brake must be adjusted, and the clearance rechecked, after the brakes have been moderately applied with a 30-psi (2-bar) application 10–20 times. This number of applications is required by the adjustment mechanism to establish the correct pad running clearance. If the running clearance is not correct, there is likely a problem in the adjusting mechanism and the caliper needs to be replaced or inspected. Caliper repair is possible using specialized repair kits and tools that are available.

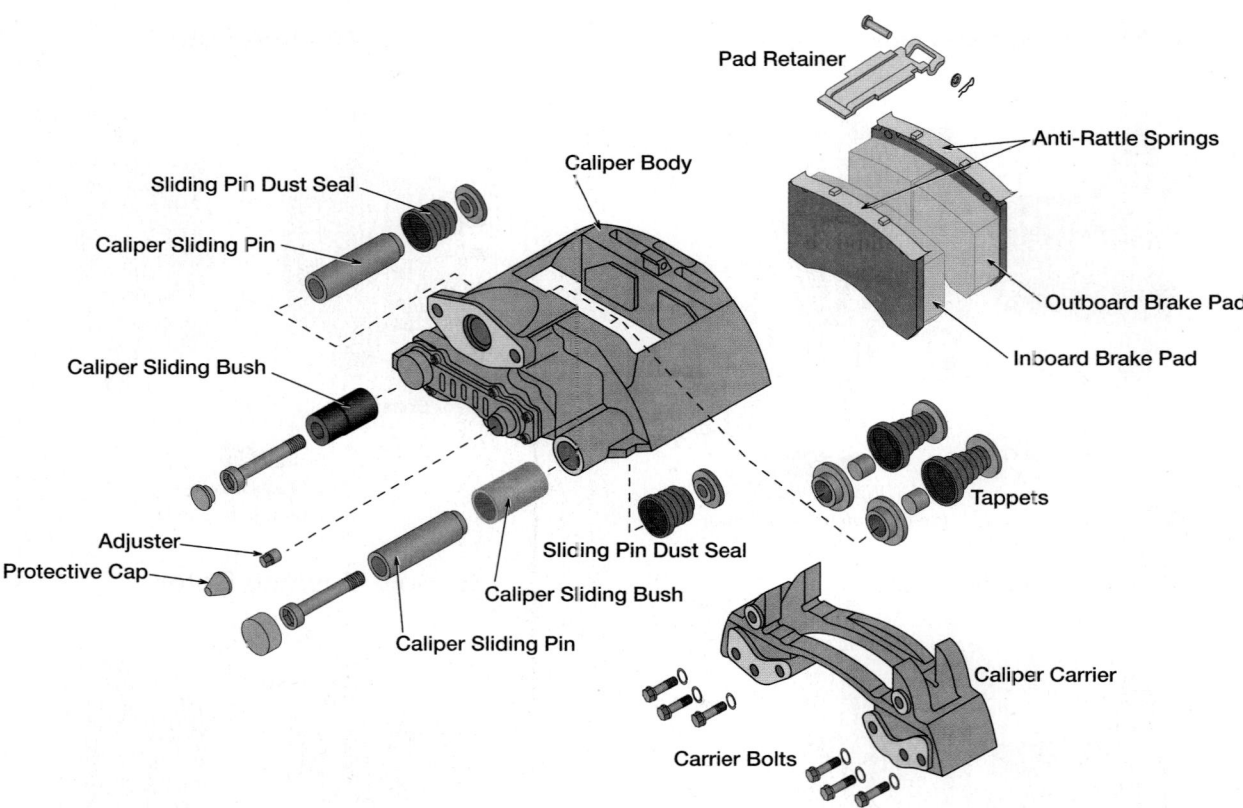

FIGURE 36-53 Slider pins and bushings enable the caliper to re-center over the rotor before and after a brake application. Free movement is essential to maintain pad running clearances.

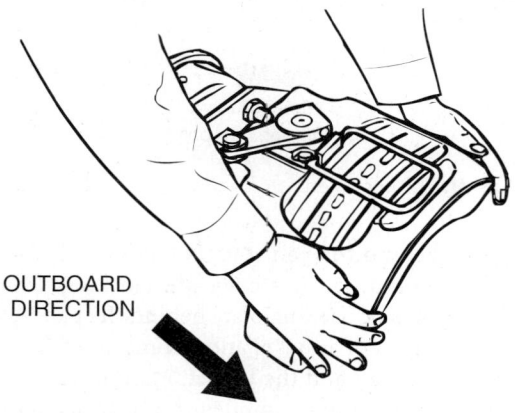

FIGURE 36-54 Grasping the caliper and pushing it back and forth sideways over the sliding pins checks the condition of the caliper slide pins.

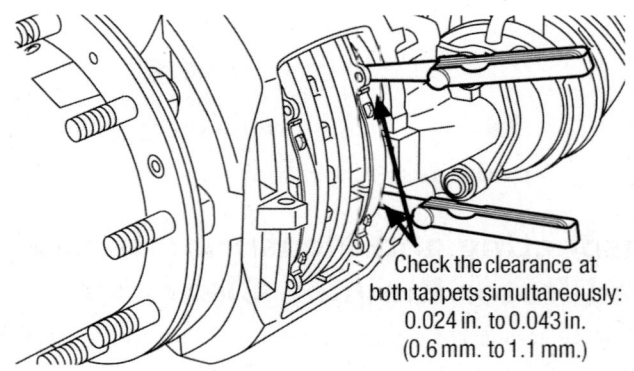

FIGURE 36-55 Feeler blades inserted behind the inboard brake pad are used to measure the running clearance between the rotor and caliper.

Performing a Pad to Rotor Running Clearance Adjustment

Pad to rotor running clearance on air disc brakes is related to the brake adjustment. Before checking the running clearance, measure the amount of brake chamber stroke on calipers that have externally accessible brake chambers and pushrods. New caliper designs do not have externally accessible linkage but, when possible, this measurement can be done with an assistant applying and releasing the brakes. The distance from the bottom of the air chamber to the center of the slack adjuster clevis pin when the brakes are both applied and released is measured. Subtracting the smaller from larger number provides the brake chamber stroke length. The measured stroke length is compared to specifications. If the pushrod stroke travel is too much or too little, pad to rotor running clearances is not correct, either. To establish the correct running clearance, the brake is adjusted with a 6-mm Allan key on Meritor calipers to either increase or decrease clearances. On Bendix calipers, a 10-mm, 6-point boxed end wrench is used over a shear screw to adjust the brake

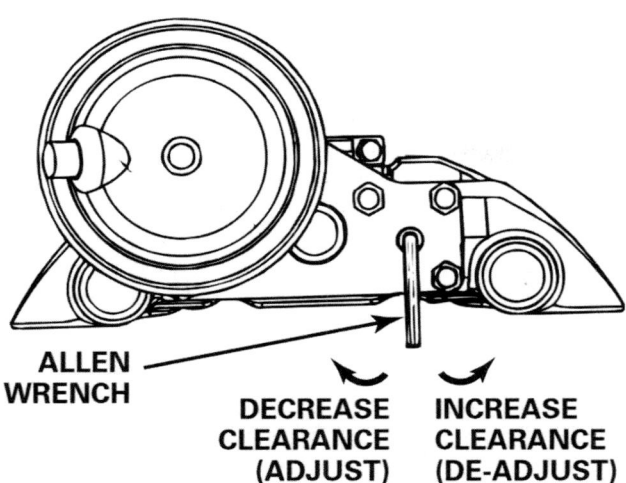

FIGURE 36-56 An Allan key is used to move the adjusting mechanism on a Meritor caliper, which is located behind a plug on the caliper. Turning the Allan key clockwise or counter clockwise changes the pad-to-shoe running clearance.

FIGURE 36-57 Location of the shear screw for adjusting Bendix disc brakes.

(**FIGURE 36-56** and **FIGURE 36-57**). Verify the park brakes are released and the wheels are chocked before attempting to adjust the running clearance. After the brake is adjusted, it should be applied 10–20 times at a moderate application pressure to check whether the automatic adjusting mechanism is working correctly. If running clearances are not correct after the brake applications, the caliper likely needs replacement.

Disc Brake Pad Replacement

LO 36-11 Outline the procedures used to replace disc brake pads, inspect automatic adjusters, and perform an initial brake adjustment.

One of the advantages of most air disc brakes is the ease with which the pads can be replaced. The caliper generally does not need to be removed, but only inspected to verify the sliding pins allow the caliper to freely move. To replace brake pads, the brake adjusters are backed off after the park brakes are released. The retaining bar over the pads is removed and the pads lifted out of place prior to installation of new pads (**FIGURE 36-58**). The rotor's thickness can be measured, and the rotor inspected on both sides for cracks and excessive heat checking. If necessary, the rotor should be replaced or machined. Dust boots and seals for automatic adjuster tappets and slider pins should be inspected to see whether they are missing, leaking, or cracked. Wear sensors can be inspected to determine whether they are worn or damaged before they are transferred to the new pads. Pads should be installed verifying the friction material and not the backing plate contacts the rotor. Verify the anti-rattle clip on the top of the pad maintains some slight tension; it is used to clamp the pad in place and prevent noise caused by pad movement. After reinstalling the retaining bar, the brake pad-rotor running clearances can be adjusted according to the manufacturer's recommended procedure. Note, if the retaining strap is missing, the pads can "climb" out of the caliper and contact the

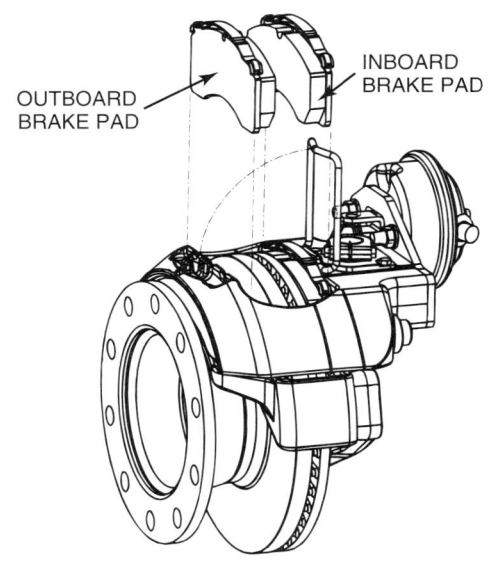

FIGURE 36-58 Pads are removed with the caliper in place. After removing the retaining strap and backing off the brakes, the pads are lifted out of place.

wheel, resulting in severe damage and loss of braking. Recheck the running clearance of the pads after making 10–20 applications of the brakes at approximately 30 psi. The running clearance inspection verifies the automatic running clearance adjusting mechanism is working correctly.

Disc Brake Adjuster Inspection

Before performing a brake adjustment, it important to verify the correct operation of the automatic brake adjusters. On both Meritor and Bendix brakes, this test method allows a technician to visually observe the movement of the automatic brake adjuster screw. This test is like the functional test of the ASA used by drum brakes. To inspect the automatic adjuster mechanism in each caliper, first tighten the adjusting screw clockwise until

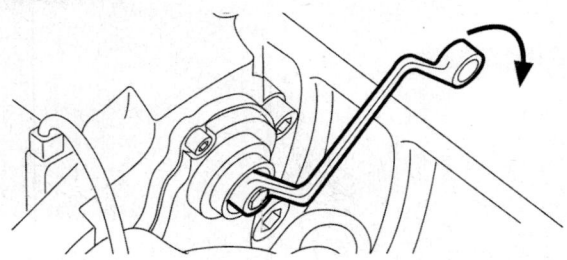

FIGURE 36-59 The automatic adjuster is checked by observing clockwise movement of a box end wrench. When backed off, the brake adjuster should automatically turn clockwise with each brake application.

the pads contact the rotor. Next, turn the adjuster three clicks counterclockwise to back off using a box wrench, hex key, or socket. This corresponds to about ¾ of a turn on the adjusting screw. Leave the wrench or socket on adjuster and positioned so that it can turn clockwise without contacting another part (**FIGURE 36-59**). Check that the automatic adjuster reduces the increased running clearance by applying the brakes with a moderate brake application of approximately 30 psi (2 bar) 5 to 10 times. Each time the brake is applied and released, the wrench should turn clockwise if the adjuster is properly functioning. A failed adjuster is indicated if a wrench does not turn, turns only on the first brake application, or turns forward and backward with every brake application. In these last instances, the adjuster has failed and the caliper requires replacement or overhaul.

If this procedure is not followed, the brake adjustment needs to be rechecked after the initial adjustment. After the initial brake adjustment has been established, the brakes should be applied 10–20 times at moderate application pressure and the running clearances between the pads and rotors rechecked to verify they are the same as the initial adjustment. Correct clearance indicates the automatic adjuster is not backing off the brake.

Disc Brake Adjustment

As outlined in the previous paragraphs, an initial adjustment of the brakes is needed when pads are replaced. A ratcheting-type adjuster beneath an adjuster cap moves the automatic clearance-sensing adjusting mechanism. When properly adjusted, the clearance-sensing automatic adjusting mechanism built into each caliper should maintain the correct pad to rotor running clearance. Only after the park brakes are released and the wheels chocked can the running clearances of the pads be adjusted to manufacturers' specifications, as shown in **FIGURE 36-60**. Automatic adjustment of excessive running clearances can take place after the initial adjustment. To adjust the brakes, a typical procedure involves tightening the automatic adjuster mechanism clockwise to remove running clearance. The ratcheting adjuster is then backed off about three clicks or ¾ of a turn. Next, the brakes are operated 10–20 times and the running clearances are rechecked. The rotor or wheel should turn freely after this step. If the clearance is not correct, the brake is readjusted and rechecked again. As previously discussed, if the running clearance is not established correctly after cycling the brakes,

the adjustment mechanism is likely defective and the caliper requires removal, replacement, or overhaul.

It is helpful to note that when the brake is backed off, the limit of the adjuster screw counterclockwise rotation can be sensed by a technician by very high resistance when attempting to turn the adjuster screw. Even more resistance is felt if the parking brakes are applied because the force on the adjuster mechanism prevents movement of the adjuster. To prevent accidental damage to the adjuster screw caused by attempting to adjust the running clearance or backing off the brake with the park brake applied, Bendix uses a shear adapter over its 8-mm and 10-mm hex head adjusting screws. The shear adapter is like a splined removable cap placed over the adjusting screw that strips the internal splines in the cap if too much torque is applied to the cap. The shear adapter can be removed with a pair of needle-nose pliers and replaced, if it is stripped.

▶ **TECHNICIAN TIP**

A shear adapter cap is used over the adjusting screw of Bendix disc brakes adjusting screw. The adjusting screw does not move if the park brakes are applied or the adjuster is seized. If too much force is applied to the adapter, splines inside the adapter strip. Shear adapters are replaceable and can be removed with a pair of needle-nose pliers. To prevent stripping, always verify the park brake is released or caged and the wheels are chocked before backing off or adjusting a disc brake. Always reinstall the protective dust cover with some lithium-based grease to prevent water entering the adjuster mechanism.

FIGURE 36-60 The location of the brake adjuster on air disc brakes is below a dust cap. After replacing brake pads, the brakes require initial adjustment, which is automatically maintained by an internal adjustment mechanism.

Wrap-Up

Ready for Review

▶ When installing a new brake actuator, the technician must cut the pushrod precisely to size so that the brake functions correctly.

▶ Brake torque balance is maintained by the proper maintenance and replacement practices of the foundation brake system and brake actuators.

▶ Brake drum wear limits are 0.120" (3.05 mm) over nominal diameter on a 16" drum.

▶ Some newer air brake systems have wear indicators and/or stroke sensors to warn the driver if the brakes are worn or need adjustment.

▶ Manufacturers recommend that brake stroke be measured with the brakes applied and released.

▶ The distance between the face of the brake chamber and the largest clevis in the slack adjuster is measured with the brakes applied and released. The difference between the two measurements is the applied brake stroke travel.

▶ All vehicles manufactured today are equipped with automatic slack adjusters (ASAs). It is essential that all adjusters on an axle are of the same type and model, so both brakes adjust to the same brake stroke length.

▶ Applied brake stroke measurement using an 80–90 psi brake application is the recommended procedure to measure the length of brake stroke.

▶ ASAs use either clearance-sensing or stroke-sensing mechanisms to adjust brake stroke.

▶ In use, a typical applied stroke measurement observed for an ASA is ⅝" to ¾".

▶ A slack adjuster must be adjusted whenever brake stroke exceeds 1".

▶ Most ASAs are adjusted by technicians to obtain ½" to ¾" brake stroke when initially installed. The slack adjuster adjusts to its designed brake stroke after the initial adjustment.

▶ When brake drums are installed, it is critical that they fit properly over their pilot pads on the hub.

▶ Brake S-cam camshafts should be checked for radial and axial play.

▶ If an ASA is not maintaining brake adjustment, technicians should diagnose the slack adjuster and the foundation brake system to determine the cause.

▶ A functional test of the ASA can be performed to determine whether an ASA is defective, if it is found misadjusted.

▶ Disc brake calipers should move freely from side to side by hand on their slider pins when the pads are removed. Any resistance to caliper side-to-side movement requires an inspection of caliper running clearances and slider pins.

▶ The absence of side-to-side movement of the caliper requires the caliper sliding pins to be inspected and lubricated.

▶ Measuring rotor-to-pad running clearance determines whether a disc brake is correctly adjusted.

▶ Shear adapters used on Bendix brakes strip if the brake adjuster is forced to turn with the park brakes applied or if the adjuster is seized.

▶ A failure of a caliper to maintain correct running clearance indicates its internal automatic clearance- or stroke-sensing adjustment mechanism is not working correctly.

▶ A functional test of the caliper adjusting mechanism should move the adjustment screw clockwise when the brakes are applied and there is excess running clearance between the pads and rotors.

Key Terms

applied stroke measurement   The pushrod stroke length with a 90 psi (621 kPa) service brake application.

brake stroke length   The distance traveled by the brake chamber pushrod.

cam-over conditions   When the linings and or brake components are worn enough to allow the cam to rotate past the rollers.

electronic pad wear indicators   Devices that measure brake pad wear electronically and send signals to the driver information display.

free stroke measurement   The brake pushrod stroke length using a lever to move the slack adjuster.

Review Questions

1. When the brakes are fully applied, the angle between the slack adjuster and the brake chamber pushrod should be _____ degrees.
   a. 45
   b. 60
   c. 75
   d. 90

2. Which of the following is the correct combination of values used for an automatic slack adjuster for a drum brake using a type 30 brake chamber?
   a. 2" maximum brake stroke with a 1" initial brake stroke adjustment
   b. ⅝" to ¾" observed in-service brake stroke with a 1-inch maximum allowable
   c. ½" to ¾" in-service observed brake stroke with a ⅝" to ¾" initial adjustment
   d. 1" out of service brake stroke with a ¾" in-service maximum brake stroke

3. Under which of the following conditions does an automatic-type clearance-sensing slack adjuster make an adjustment to brake stroke travel?
   a. During brake application, but not during brake release
   b. During brake application and release
   c. When stroke travel exceeds a design factor
   d. Only when the pushrod stroke travel exceeds the initial brake stroke adjustment

4. What is the stroke limit on a standard size 30 brake actuator before it is out of service?
   a. 1.375" (3.5 cm)
   b. 1.5" (2.54 cm)
   c. 1.75" (4.45 cm)
   d. 2" (5 cm)

5. Which of the following is the most acceptable method to measure brake chamber stroke?
   a. By hand with a lever
   b. Free stroke method
   c. Applied stroke method
   d. Using stroke indicators

6. Which of the following conditions is necessary for a cam-over condition?
   a. An oversized brake drum and a slack adjuster that is over-stroking
   b. Worn brake shoes and a slack adjuster that is over-stroking
   c. Worn brake shoes and drum
   d. A defective slack adjuster and worn cam bushings

7. Which of the following is the most correct service recommendation for a 16.5" drum worn to 16.575"?
   a. Discard the drum
   b. Return the drum to service if no major cracks or scoring are observed
   c. Machine the drum to remove any light cracking or scoring
   d. Inspect the drum for an out-of-round condition that could cause a brake pulsation

8. What is the correct service recommendation for repairing oil-contaminated brake shoes on the left side of one axle of a tandem-drive tractor?
   a. Replace the oil-contaminated brake shoes
   b. Clean the oil-contaminated brake shoes with solvent and reinstall
   c. Replace the brake shoes on both sides of the axle with oil-contaminated lining
   d. Replace all the brake shoes on both drive axles

9. What is the correct service recommendation for a recently replaced automatic slack adjuster that has been found to have 1" of brake stroke travel?
   a. Replace the slack adjuster
   b. Replace the slack adjuster on both ends of the axle
   c. Perform a functional test of the slack adjuster to determine if it is defective
   d. Manually readjust the slack adjuster and recommend the driver return to have the adjuster rechecked after a week of operation

10. Which of the following is the most likely cause of a caliper that has no lateral or side-to-side movement when pushed by hand force?
    a. Seized caliper slider pins
    b. A failed automatic adjusting mechanism and seized caliper slider pins
    c. A misadjusted brake
    d. A defective automatic adjuster

ASE Technician A/Technician B Style Questions

1. Technician A says that spring brakes should be caged in preparation for a brake service replacing brake drums and shoes. Technician B says that if the brake chamber is not replaced, it is wasted labor time to cage the brake. Who is correct?
   a. Technician A
   b. Technician B
   c. Both Technician A and Technician B
   d. Neither Technician A nor Technician B

2. Technician A says that a cam-over condition can be caused by a failed automatic slack adjuster. Technician B says that a cam-over condition can cause a seized brake condition where the brakes won't release. Who is correct?
   a. Technician A
   b. Technician B
   c. Both Technician A and Technician B
   d. Neither Technician A nor Technician B

3. Technician A says that a left-hand S-cam turns counter-clockwise to apply a brake. Technician B says that a left-hand camshaft turns clockwise when applying the brake. Who is correct?
   a. Technician A
   b. Technician B
   c. Both Technician A and Technician B
   d. Neither Technician A nor Technician B

4. Technician A says that a plastic installation template is often used when replacing many automatic slack adjusters to adjust the initial brake stroke travel. Technician B says that the template is used to adjust the position of the pushrod yoke. Who is correct?
   a. Technician A
   b. Technician B
   c. Both Technician A and Technician B
   d. Neither Technician A nor Technician B

5. Technician A says that a used 16" brake drum measured to be 16.020" in diameter can be returned to service. Technician B says that there is not enough material remaining in the drum to allow for wear if new brake shoes are installed. Who is correct?
   a. Technician A
   b. Technician B
   c. Both Technician A and Technician B
   d. Neither Technician A nor Technician B

6. While discussing possible causes for stripped splines on a shear adapter for a brake adjuster, Technician A says that the shear adapter was likely damaged because an adjustment was attempted when the parking brake was applied. Technician B says that the automatic adjusting mechanism could likely have seized. Who is correct?
   a. Technician A
   b. Technician B
   c. Both Technician A and Technician B
   d. Neither Technician A nor Technician B

7. Technician A says that the only acceptable method to determine whether brake pads require replacement is to visually inspect the pads with the wheel removed. Technician B says that the wheel does not need to be removed to determine whether brake pads and rotors require replacement. Who is correct?
   a. Technician A
   b. Technician B
   c. Both Technician A and Technician B
   d. Neither Technician A nor Technician B

8. Technician A says that the largest of two numbers stamped on a rotor refers to the minimum thickness of a rotor that it's allowed to be machined to. Technician B says the smallest of the two numbers refers to the smallest thickness the rotor can be machined to. Who is correct?
   a. Technician A
   b. Technician B
   c. Both Technician A and Technician B
   d. Neither Technician A nor Technician B

9. While discussing a method to check the operation of an automatic brake adjuster for disc-type brakes, Technician A said that the adjusting screw should be turned clockwise to back off the brake and then observe whether the screw turns counterclockwise when the brakes are repeatedly applied. Technician B says that the adjusting screw should not turn after the brake adjustment is backed off because no brake wear takes place. Who is correct?
   a. Technician A
   b. Technician B
   c. Both Technician A and Technician B
   d. Neither Technician A nor Technician B

10. Technician A says that hub-piloted brake drums fit tightly around the studs on the inboard side of a hub. Technician B said that hub-piloted drums fit loosely around the studs on the outboard side of a hub. Who is correct?
   a. Technician A
   b. Technician B
   c. Both Technician A and Technician B
   d. Neither Technician A nor Technician B

CHAPTER 37

Antilock Braking, Vehicle Stability, and Collision Avoidance Systems

Learning Objectives

After reading this chapter, you will be able to:

- **LO 37-1** Describe the fundamentals of an antilock braking system (ABS).
- **LO 37-2** List the system requirements for ABS.
- **LO 37-3** Describe the components of a basic ABS and their functions.
- **LO 37-4** Define ABS configurations.
- **LO 37-5** Identify and describe the purpose and operation of vehicle dynamic control systems.

- **LO 37-6** Identify and describe the construction and operation of rollover protection systems.
- **LO 37-7** Identify and describe the construction and operation of directional stability control systems.
- **LO 37-8** Identify and describe the construction and operation of collision avoidance systems (CAS).
- **LO 37-9** Recommend maintenance and service procedures for antilock braking, vehicle stability, and CAS.

You Are the Technician

A relatively new, late-model tractor has been brought to your original equipment manufacturer (OEM) service facility after it was involved in a rear-end collision with a school bus. The highly experienced driver of the tractor has had more than 25 years of accident-free driving. He claims he was braking the tractor when the brakes suddenly released, resulting in the unfortunate collision. The tractor brakes had already been inspected by two other repair facilities and no fault was found. Your inspection report is the final step of investigation. If, like the other technicians, you find no fault with the brakes, the driver could be fired, and the company would become engaged in costly litigation.

Given the sophistication and degree of electronic control of the braking system, you balance the probability of a failure in the braking system's reliability against the integrity and skill of the driver. A few scenarios come to mind in which a new vehicle could have some previously undetected assembly errors, such as incorrectly connected air lines and wiring harnesses. You conduct a road test and apply the brakes dozens of times until they lock up. However during your test, you discovered that the brakes did, in fact, briefly release on one occasion after they were applied.

To isolate the fault, consider the following:

1. Identify how electronic controls of the braking system operate to apply and release the brakes and under which condition.
2. Outline what steps or procedures should be taken to verify the correct operation and connections of the vehicle's braking system circuits used by the ABS, ATC, RSC, and CAS.
3. List the components or inspection points you believe would help isolate the possible causes of the brake system failure.

Introduction

The ability of tires to steer and brake are severely diminished when sliding or skidding along a road surface. Without rolling tires gripping the road or having adhesive traction, a coasting vehicle is only pushed in the direction of inertia forces. The same is true during braking. Tires that are turning at a slow speed stop a vehicle faster than tires locked-up by brake application force. These principles of vehicle control have been well understood, but it wasn't until the development of reliable technology in the 1990s that electronic control of braking systems could prevent powerful air brakes from locking up the tires under slippery conditions or during panic stops. **Antilock braking systems (ABSs)**, also called **Electric Brakes Systems (EBSs)** in Europe, monitor wheel speed to help the brake system maintain traction between the tire and the road. The use of ABS greatly enhances vehicle stability and safety on slippery road surfaces or during panic stop situations.

Antilock brakes are one of the earliest chassis systems adapted with electronic controls. The same control valves, electronic control units (ECU) and sensors found in original ABSs are used today along with a few additional devices to provide more enhanced vehicle control features. **Electronic stability control (ESC)** systems that optimize braking and steering functions in emergency situations and build on ABS architecture are now required in new truck tractors, school buses, and intercity buses in North America since June 2018. Collison Avoidance Systems, also called Advanced Emergency Braking Systems, have been mandatory on heavy-duty commercial vehicles in Europe since 2013. The same legislation is contemplated for North American commercial vehicles for 2022 implementation. What this means for technicians is understanding the ABS operation, diagnostic techniques, and service practices are essential skills. To help develop these skills, this chapter examines fundamentals of ABSs and the progressive development of vehicle dynamic control and collision avoidance systems (CAS) centered in the ABS architecture.

The Evolving ABS

As the ABS evolved, more capabilities have been added to the basic ABS. With the addition of just a few other components, software algorithms, and more powerful ECUs, the ABS can provide automatic traction control, improve vehicle stability, prevent rollovers, and even help avoid collisions. Analyzing **vehicle dynamics**, which is the study of vehicle movement in response to road conditions and driver inputs, has enabled development of even more sophisticated control of vehicle stability using the ABS. Microcontrollers today can not only assist driver braking, but, under specific circumstances, respond to potentially dangerous conditions by providing dynamic control strategies far more rapidly and superior to any a human driver can undertake.

The progressive development of vehicle dynamic control and CAS have built on the ABS architecture. Dozens of marketing names are given to the systems by each of their manufacturers and generic terms are used in this chapter. But their development is examined in sequence. **Automatic Traction Control (ATC)** is the first stability control system added to ABSs to reduce the potential for tractor-trailer jackknifing. Among other causes, jackknifing can happen when one drive wheel excessively spins during acceleration around curves. If the loss of traction beneath the tractor's drive wheels at low vehicle speeds is sensed by the ABS, the ATC momentarily and automatically applies the brake on the spinning wheel to transfer drive torque to the wheel with traction. If both drive wheels have poor traction, the ATC automatically reduces engine power until the tires can again grip the road surface.

Rollover Stability Control (RSC) monitors wheel speed and adds two sensors. One sensor measures the steering wheel's steering angle and the other measures the lateral or sideway acceleration of the tractor (**FIGURE 37-1**). If the ECU matches the current vehicle dynamic conditions with critical thresholds stored in program logic for a rollover event, it can selectively apply control options, such as reducing engine power, activating the engine brake, and automatically applying individual drive

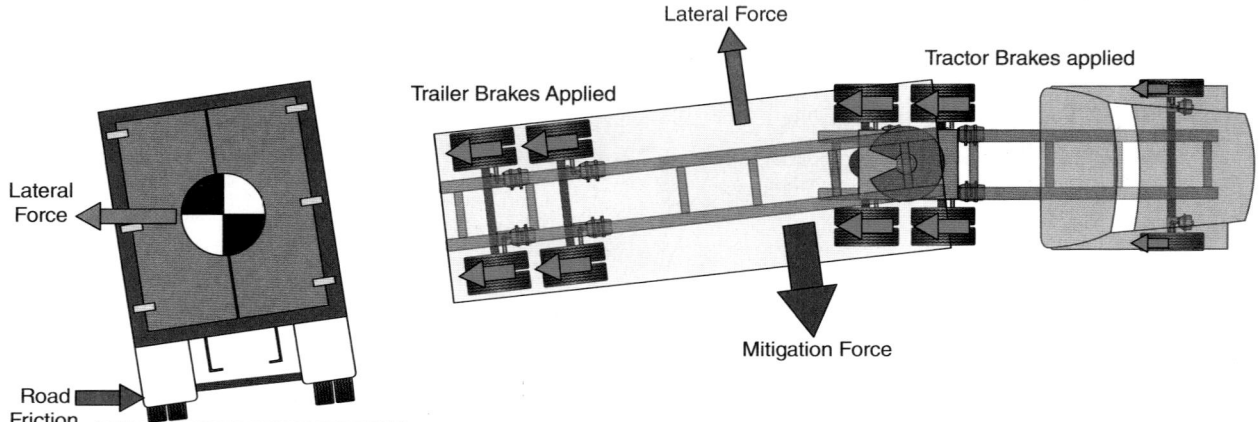

FIGURE 37-1 By applying the trailer brakes and engine brakes, the vehicle speed is reduced to prevent a rollover.

axle and trailer brakes (**FIGURE 37-2**). When the critical conditions have passed, normal vehicle operation resumes, but the events are recorded in a data log.

Directional Stability Control (DSC) systems do not need to detect a rollover condition before activating. Straight trucks and buses, as well as tractor-trailer combinations, change out the lateral force sensor used for rollover protection for a yaw sensor. The yaw or rotational force sensor is used to detect the potential for a vehicle to turn around its center point (**FIGURE 37-3**). DSC minimizes the likelihood of a vehicle drifting sideways on slippery road surfaces or losing control when rapidly changing lanes. Selective application of control options for the engine brake or tractor or trailer brakes at each wheel end can bring the vehicle dynamics back into control.

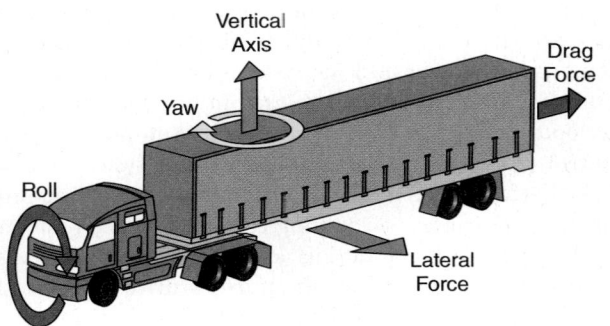

FIGURE 37-2 ESC can apply individual brakes at wheel ends to create a force reversing the tendency of an unstable vehicle to rotate around its center point.

The latest application of the ABS to vehicle dynamic control adds short and long-distance radar signals to ABS inputs. **Collison avoidance systems (CAS)**, or collision mitigation systems as they are sometimes called, detect objects in front of and around a truck or bus to alert a driver of impending collisions. If the driver does not respond quickly, the system reduces engine power and applies the brakes to avoid a collision, or at least reduce the collision's damage. Automatically applying the brakes in circumstances like this lends the system another name—**Emergency Braking System (FIGURE 37-4)**. Use of this system today does not need to wait for a rare condition, such as an imminent collision. The same components and algorithms used by the CAS are used today by the **adaptive cruise control (ACC)** system. When the vehicle is in cruise control, the vehicle speed is adjusted to prevent rear end collisions with vehicles ahead of the truck or bus.

Fundamentals of Antilock Braking Systems

LO 37-1 Describe the fundamentals of an antilock braking system (ABS).

A vehicle's **antilock braking system (ABS)** is an electronic control system that works with the service brake system to monitor and automatically limit wheel lockup events during vehicle braking. **Wheel lockup** occurs when the drive or steer tires have stopped rotating when braking. Rolling tires with adhesive traction to the road surfaces can be steered better. They also

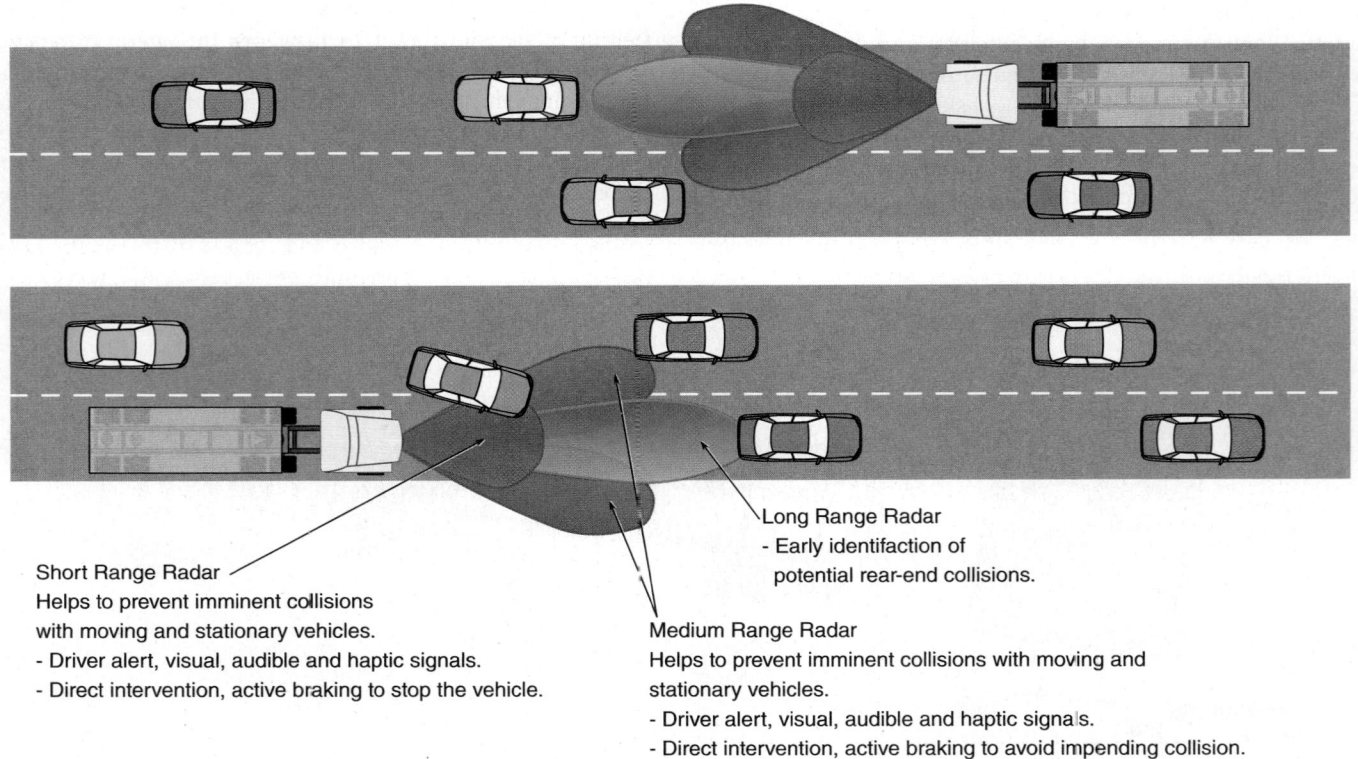

Short Range Radar
Helps to prevent imminent collisions with moving and stationary vehicles.
- Driver alert, visual, audible and haptic signals.
- Direct intervention, active braking to stop the vehicle.

Medium Range Radar
Helps to prevent imminent collisions with moving and stationary vehicles.
- Driver alert, visual, audible and haptic signals.
- Direct intervention, active braking to avoid impending collision.

Long Range Radar
- Early identifaction of potential rear-end collisions.

FIGURE 37-3 Emergency braking systems use short- and long-distance radar to detect objects and apply the vehicle brakes to avoid collisions.

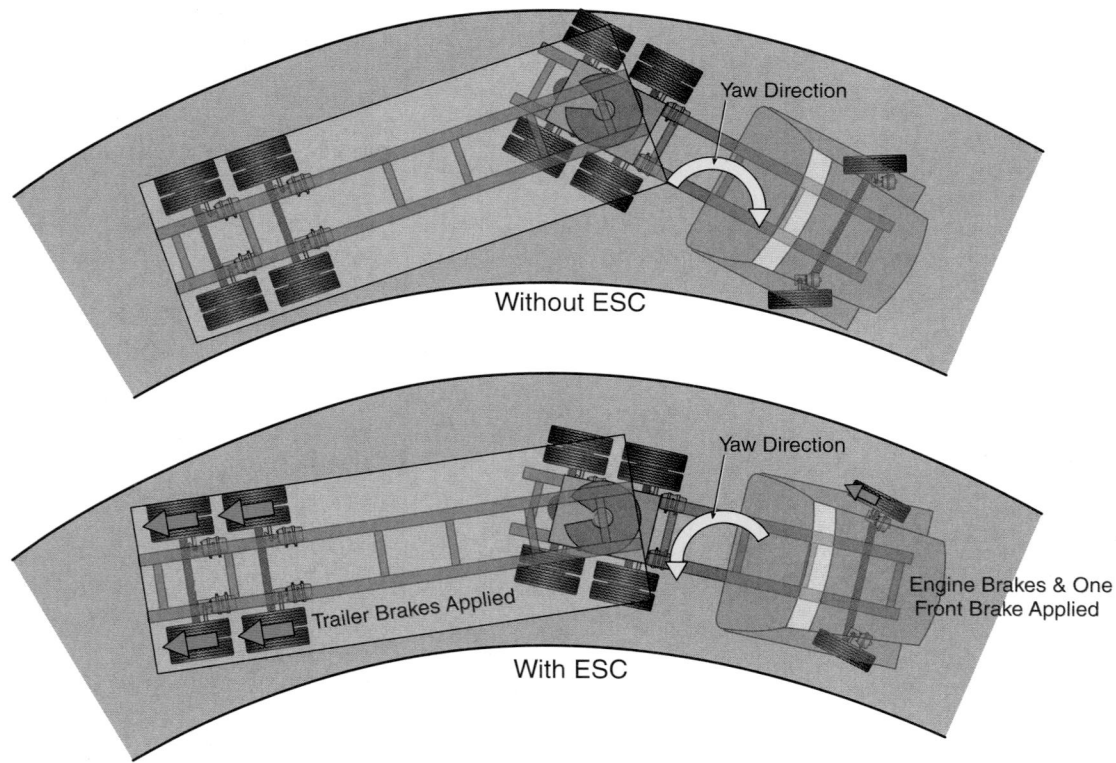

FIGURE 37-4 Yaw rotation is a movement in the center of a truck or bus around its vertical axis. Excessive yaw force changes the direction the vehicle is pointing, moving it either to the left or right of its intended direction of travel.

transfer more braking force than locked-up, skidding tires. For those reasons, ABS dramatically enhances vehicle control and safety. In other words, a truck, bus, or trailer behaves more like a sled when wheels lockup; ABS minimizes the loss of control that takes place when tires stop rotating.

Today's ABSs incorporate multiple features that improve the operation of the vehicle from both a functional and a safety perspective. Since the first failed attempt to introduce ABS in 1975, until the first mandatory use in 1997, regulations and requirements for vehicle dynamic control have driven development for increased sophistication of the technology.

ABS Features and Benefits

ABSs provide multiple benefits to the vehicle and the driver. In addition to preventing wheel lockup in regular driving conditions, ABSs decrease longer stopping distances on slippery surfaces, such as wet, muddy, or snow-covered roads. ABSs also enhance steering control during hard braking, as illustrated in **FIGURE 37-5**. Another benefit of the ABS is extended tire life. Using ABS prevents the formation of flat spots and uneven tread wear caused by intense, localized friction on locked, skidding tires. The likelihood of a tractor **jackknife** or **trailer swing-out** situation is minimized using ABS as well. **TABLE 37-1** shows the key features of an ABS and the benefits they provide.

The ABS works simply by electronically measuring individual wheel speeds to provide feedback to brake valves electrically controlling air application pressure to the brake chambers.

Braking force applied to a wheel end is automatically reduced whenever a wheel's speed approaches lockup (or 0 rpm under hard braking conditions). The deceleration rate of the wheels is greater during an aggressive or hard brake application, or if the vehicle is on a slippery surface. Controlled braking takes place because the control logic inside the ECU can distinguish between normal and abnormal deceleration using an algorithm to calculate whether decelerating wheels are likely to lockup. Once slowed, wheels can begin to rotate faster after brake application pressure is electronically reduced. The system cycles brake applications automatically to reapply braking force until wheel lockup speed is approached again. This cycle of releasing and applying the brakes, illustrated in **FIGURE 37-6**, takes place rapidly until the brake pedal is released.

▶ TECHNICIAN TIP

During slippery road conditions, drivers should be aware that pumping the brake pedal to simulate ABS operation is not as effective as a hard and steady brake application. Even with sophisticated control algorithms and hardware found on today's vehicles, air application pressure to the brake chambers can never be more than what the operator is using to apply the brake pedal. This means that to enhance the effectiveness of the ABS operation, maximum steady air pressure to the service chambers should be made available to electronically controlled brake valves by using a full application pressure. The ECU can then electronically modulate or vary brake pressure, which responds to wheel lockup and skid faster than the driver possibly can.

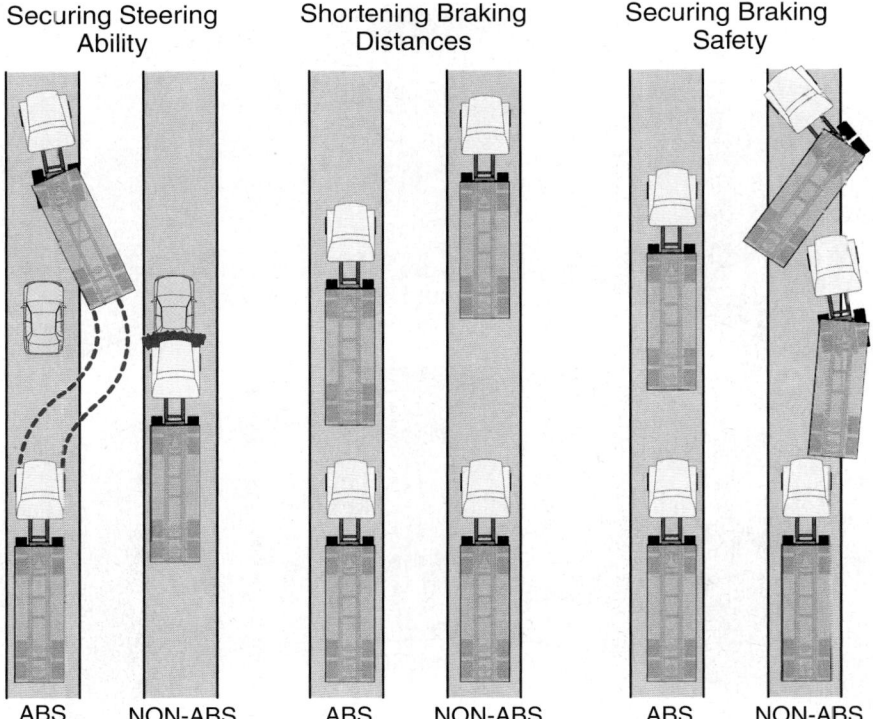

FIGURE 37-5 Antilock braking systems not only shorten stopping distances, but enhance vehicle steering control during emergency braking.

TABLE 37-1 ABS Features and Benefits

Feature	Benefit
Electronic control of brake force to wheel ends	• Prevents wheel lockup and skidding during braking • Improves steering control and vehicle stability during panic braking and slippery conditions • Minimizes the likelihood of tractor jackknifing and trailer swing-out • Prevents tire flat spotting
Traction control	• A feature that uses the ABS components to minimize wheel spin during acceleration on slippery surfaces • Minimizes the likelihood of "fishtailing" or spin-out to improve steering control and directional stability • Reduces the likelihood of shock load damage to driveline components after a wheel spin
Electronic control brake system operation	• Faster response than driver to wheel lockup and spin; ABSs can "pump" the brakes on individual wheels (or pairs of wheels), independently, and with greater speed and accuracy, than a driver • Default to normal braking when fault detected in electronic control system • Adaptive fault accommodation shuts off the ABS only to wheel ends with ABS faults • Self-diagnostic capabilities and communication to interface with off-board diagnostic tools

Antilock Braking System Requirements

LO 37-2 List the system requirements for ABS.

The first truck air brake ABS was introduced in 1975, but mandatory ABS capabilities were only legislated in phases beginning in the late 1990s and early 2000s. FMVSS 121 has introduced shorter stopping requirements for heavy trucks beginning in 2015—stopping distances have been reduced from 355' (108 m) to as little as 250' (76 m) in 2015. New standards include stricter

vehicle stability requirements. Systems must prevent trailer swing-out and jackknifing, and tractors and trailers currently need to remain within a 12-foot-wide (3.7-meter-wide) lane under hard braking conditions.

In addition to the stopping distance and stability regulations implemented in 2015, FMVSS 121 ABS performance requirements include:

■ The ABS on tractors and full trailers must control the braking pressure to at least one front axle and one rear axle. The system must further control braking on one of

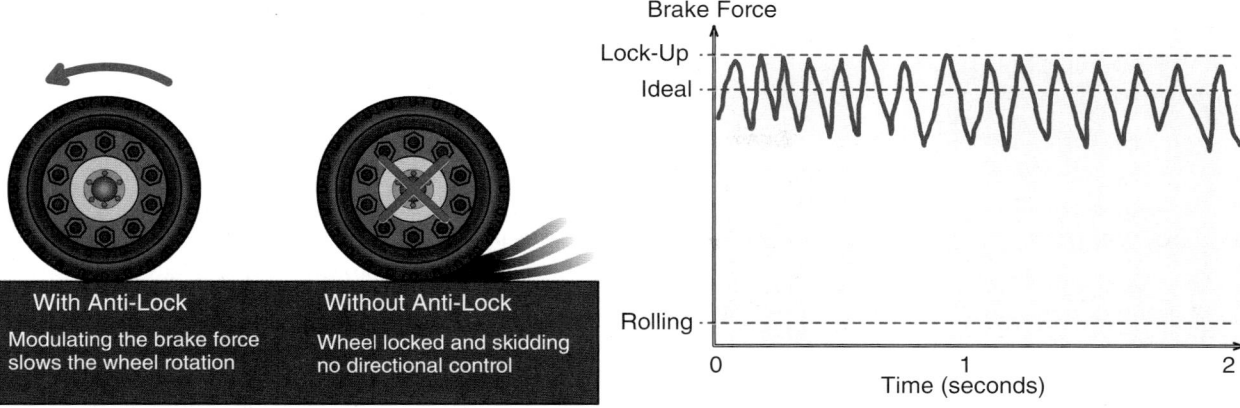

FIGURE 37-6 The ABS works by rapidly applying and releasing the brakes to create a maximum braking force just below a threshold where the wheels lockup.

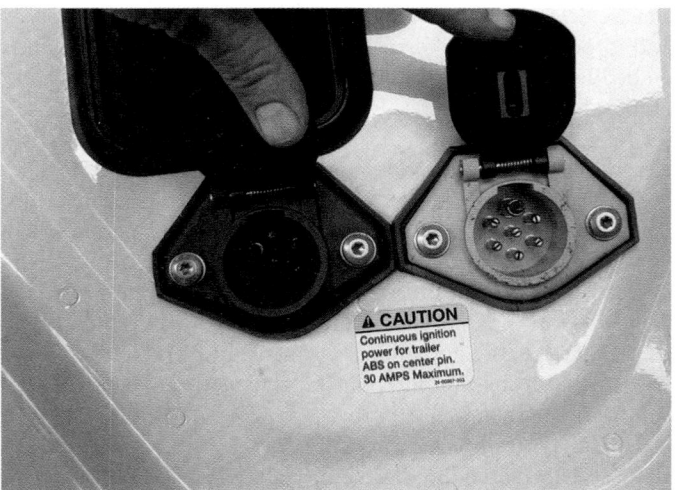

FIGURE 37-7 Trailers equipped with ABS modules can receive power through the brake light circuit, pin #4 of the J-560 trailer connector, or the center pin #7.

FIGURE 37-8 In-cab ABS warning lights alert the driver to a fault in the ABS in either the trailer (tractors only) or truck ABS.

the rear axles using two modulator valves. These are ABS air control valves used to electronically regulate the air pressure supplied to service brake chambers. By opening and closing the supply of air to the brakes, the modulator valves enable independent control of brake pressure at each end of the axle. Other performance requirements of FMVSS 121 can require an ABS on additional axles.

- ABS on semi-trailers and converter dollies must control at least one axle of the trailer.
- ABS electronic control modules on trailers must be capable of being powered by the trailer's stop lamp circuit. A second brake light power-up source is required to ensure trailers equipped with ABS still function when connected to an older, non-ABS tractor. In addition to using brake light power, tractors built after March 1, 1997 provide a constant 12-volt current to the trailer through a #7 pin of the J-560 trailer connector, which is a trailer cord receptacle located at the rear of the tractor. As shown in **FIGURE 37-7**, the yellow-green trailer plug connector is used to connect

trailers with ABS since it supplies a constant power source to the ABS module. The black connector color is designated for use by non-ABS trailers and can use the #7 pin to supply accessories, such as an electrically operated lift axle. A larger ground pin on ABS tractors and trailers accommodates higher electrical loads on trailers using ABS.

- ABS-equipped vehicles must have a dedicated amber-colored ABS malfunction indicator lamp. The lamp should illuminate only during an ABS malfunction. On tractors, the ABS malfunction lamp must be in front of and in clear view of the driver, such as shown in **FIGURE 37-8**. On trailers, an external yellow indicator is located on the left side of the trailer, near the rear side marker lamp, as shown in **FIGURE 37-9**. For dollies, the lamp needs to be located on the left side and visible at a distance 10' (3 m) from the lamp. On older vehicles, when the ignition key is first switched on, the bulb illuminates for a few seconds to validate the bulb is operating properly. Depending on the system, the light can remain on until the vehicle moves fast enough to provide wheel speed data to the control module. At that point the light goes out, unless a fault is detected. Since February 2009, the light should come on for a couple of seconds and then go out if no faults are present. Until then, the wheel speed sensor input signal was required for the light to extinguish. Likewise, on models manufactured

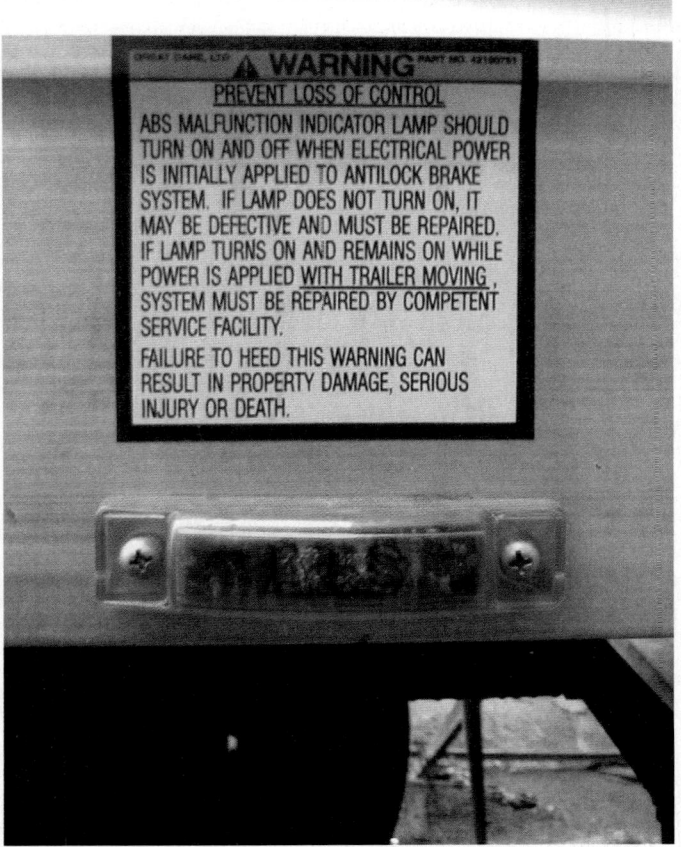

FIGURE 37-9 The ABS warning light on a trailer is located near the rear lower left or corner of the trailer wall. A failure in the trailer ABS illuminates the light.

after March 2009, an external ABS light for the trailer or dolly is not mandatory, because the tractor has a trailer ABS light on the dash that switches on if there is an issue with the trailer ABS.

- Air-braked tractors and trucks that tow other air-braked vehicles and that were built after March 1, 2001, must communicate with an in-cab ABS malfunction indicator lamp, which alerts the driver to any malfunction in a towed vehicle's ABS.

ABS is used by both air and hydraulic braking systems and has been required by law on air-braked tractors since 1997, all other air-braked trucks and buses since 1998, and in hydraulic systems on vehicles over 10,000 lb (4536 kg) gross vehicle weight (GVW) since 1999.

Antilock Braking System Components

LO 37-3 Describe the components of a basic ABS and their functions.

Electronic control of brake application force enables an ABS to adjust brake application pressure faster and more accurately

than a driver. Depending on the sophistication of the ABS and vehicle configuration, a basic ABS improves vehicle braking using the following common components:

- ECU
- Wheel speed sensors with exciter rings—used to measure wheel speed
- Modulator valves, which electronically change application air pressure supplied to the brake chambers
- ABS trailer cords
- ABS malfunction indicator lamp

The next section describes a basic ABS before examining, in more detail, the operation of more advanced ABS configurations in the Enhancements to Antilock Braking Systems section.

Electronic Control Units (ECU)

The vehicle's ECU collects information from the sensor inputs and processes the information using specialized algorithms embedded in software stored in the ECU. Algorithms are mathematical formulas used to solve a problem. In the case of ABS, the formula solves the problem of when and for how long to apply electrical signals to the modulator valves to prevent wheel lockup.

Based on sensor inputs and instructions programmed into software, the ECU produces output signals to operate brake valves and warning lights and communicate with the vehicle network. Self-diagnostic capabilities built into the ECU can supply technicians with ABS performance data as well as generate ABS fault codes and other diagnostic information. ECUs are constructed to be mounted on the chassis frame or inside the environmentally protected cab.

ECUs typically operate using supply voltages of between 12 and 24 volts, depending on the model of the ECU. An ignition on/off current supply and a separate continuous battery current input are commonly connected through a three- to five-amp fuse and a 30-amp fuse, respectively. Often the ECUs use two ground inputs. One is for the ECU electronics, and the second is for a safety-related interlock of the ABS warning light circuit and ECU. Normally, the ECU grounds out the ABS warning light whenever a fault is detected. However, with the double ground ECU input, the ABS wiring harness is purposely designed to automatically short the ABS warning lamp circuit to ground if the ECU connector is disconnected from the ECU.

ECU Configuration

ECU configurations vary depending on system configurations for the number of sensors and modulator valves required for a particular chassis. Other features, such as traction control, engine torque limiting capability, diagnostic outputs, and other switch inputs, add more complexity and pins to the ECU. In addition to varying by their processing speeds and memory size, ECUs can also vary according to whether they have the following features:

- An output for a cab- or dash-mounted tractor or trailer ABS warning lamp (the trailer warning light is required for all tow vehicles manufactured after March 1, 2001)

- An output for a dash-mounted automatic traction control (ATC) status/indicator lamp
- Integration with a service brake relay valve
- An optional blink code activation switch
- An optional ABS and ATC off-road switch
- Integration with a traction control valve
- J1939 serial communication to the vehicle network
- An engine brake or transmission retarder inhibit relay connection
- A stop lamp switch input (stop lamp switch status may be read from the J-1939 network data)
- An odometer function that records accumulated distance
- Automatic or manual calibration of ECU software
- Optional Hill Start Feature with an interface between the transmission and braking system to help prevent the vehicle from rolling backwards from a stop position on steep inclines
- Integrated barometric pressure, temperature, accelerometers, and yaw sensors for stability control systems
- Integration with brake load demand and application pressure sensors at the foot valve or in brake lines
- Integration with radar units for CAS

More sophisticated ECUs detect a system configuration immediately after the ignition is switched on. For example, the number of wheel speed sensors and modulator valves are immediately identified and the sound of electrical solenoids cycling modulator valves open and closed can be easily heard.

ABS configuration of Meritor Wabco systems can be determined using blink codes. **Blink codes**, also called **flash codes**, are a fault-reporting strategy in which a fault indicator light blinks on and off to report a fault code number. Short pauses between light flashes separate numbers; long pauses separate fault codes. After the ABS diagnostic switch in the dash is pressed and released for three seconds, the module enters the clear fault mode. When pressed again for at least three seconds, then released, the system displays eight quick flashes followed by a system configuration code, if the code clearing process was successful. An ECU does not perform the blink code test when vehicle speed is detected. Bendix uses light-emitting diode (LED) lights on some of their controllers to indicate faults and report system status.

ECU and Onboard Network Communication

Many vehicle features use wheel speed data, so the ABS module averages speed data and broadcasts it over the J-1939 network. Speedometers, entertainment systems, CAS, and safety interlock systems used by door locks, power dividers, and outriggers, need not duplicate vehicle speed sensors if they can simply use ABS data. ATC uses engine torque limiting, which is a strategy in which the ABS ECU communicates with the engine ECU to reduce power when the wheels slip. (Torque limiting is covered in the Torque Limiting section.) A hardwired connection to an electrical relay also enables the ABS ECU to disable the engine brake or driveline retarder, which can also cause the wheels to lockup.

Since March 1, 2001, all tractors must have an in-cab, trailer ABS malfunction indicator lamp. To transmit the status of the trailer ABS over the J-560 tractor/trailer electrical connector, ABS commonly use power line carrier technology. **Power line carrier (PLC) technology** is a data transmission technology enabling data exchange between the tractor and trailer ABS. PLC is needed to alert the driver, using an in-dash warning light, about any potential malfunction of the trailer ABS.

> ▶ TECHNICIAN TIP

Engine-based braking systems, such as exhaust brakes and compression release brakes, can promote wheel lockup conditions when activated. Driveline retarders used by automatic transmissions lockup wheels on slippery surfaces as well. The ABS module has capabilities to inhibit, or shut-off, engine brakes and driveline retarders either through onboard network communication, such as over the J-1939 data bus, or directly through the use of electrical relays, which can electrically disable these devices.

The data is not like serial digital communication over a standard controlled area network (CAN). Instead, PLC signals change (modulate) both the frequency and amplitude of a distinctly different voltage signal than is normally carried over the J-560 trailer plug #7 blue constant power wire between the trailer and tractor. When #7 pin current flow is paused, the PLC modules exchange bursts of data via high frequency voltage "chirps" in milliseconds of time. For the PLC to function, tractors and trailers must both be equipped with PLC. The amplitude and frequency-modulated voltage signal varies between 100 KHz and 400 KHz and is transmitted both ways between the trailer and tractor ABS control modules. **FIGURE 37-10** shows the differences between a power line with PLC and one without PLC.

In addition to ABS software, specialized communication adapters can be used to check for correct PLC communication between the trailer and tractor and perform system diagnostics. One example is Bendix's Trailer Remote Diagnostic Unit (TRDU). This unit not only provides blink codes to diagnose ABS problems but can clear codes and provide system configuration settings and odometer readings. If it does not establish communication due to a problem with PLC communication or a problem with the ABS ECU, the LED lights on the TRDU illuminate in a clockwise pattern until the ABS ECU communication is established (**FIGURE 37-11**).

Engine Retarders and ABS Control

One other critical ability of an ABS not covered by legislation is to control the operation of the driveline retarder and engine brake, which is also called a retarder. When operating on slippery, low friction coefficient surfaces, activating the engine brake or driveline retarder causes several of the drive wheels to lockup. To prevent this from happening, the ABS needs to have some method to communicate with the engine ECM when it senses a lockup event. Even activating the modulator control valves at the locked wheels will not release the brakes if the driveline rotation is resisted by the engine or transmission. The use of rapid network communication over J-1939 networks allows the exchange of high-priority messages from

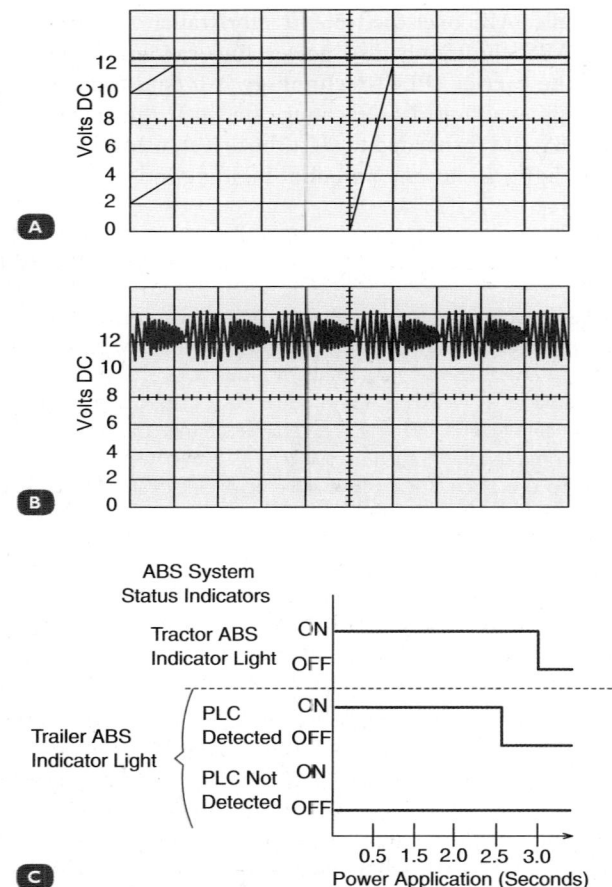

FIGURE 37-10 Power line carrier (PLC) technology that changes (modulates) both the frequency and amplitude of the #7 blue power wire between the trailer and tractor. PLC technology is used to meet the 2001 requirement to provide a tractor-located trailer ABS malfunction lamp. **A.** Power line without PLC signal. **B.** Power line with PLC signal. **C.** ABS status indicators.

the ABS ECU to disable the engine brake or driveline retarder. Older vehicles with slower J-1708 network communication, or none at all, uses an external relay to switch off power to the engine brake. If equipped with a relay-controlled engine brake, the ABS ECU supplies a ground signal to the relay, causing it to switch off power to dash switches in the cab. Without 12-volt power supplied to the engine brake on/off switch, the brake is disabled.

More advanced vehicle dynamic control requires the ABS ECU to activate the engine brakes to decelerate a vehicle if it senses an impending rollover or the wheels are spinning.

ECU Programming Major system ECUs today have the vehicle identification number (VIN) and other unique identifying information to validate the correct configuration of ECU is used on a vehicle. Given the complexity of today's ECUs, mismatched ECUs with incorrect programming variables not only prevent proper system operation but can adversely affect vehicle dynamics. In other words, the wrong ECU is a safety hazard to vehicle occupants and other road users. A defective ECU is identified by following correct diagnostic procedures outlined in the OEM service information. Often the process

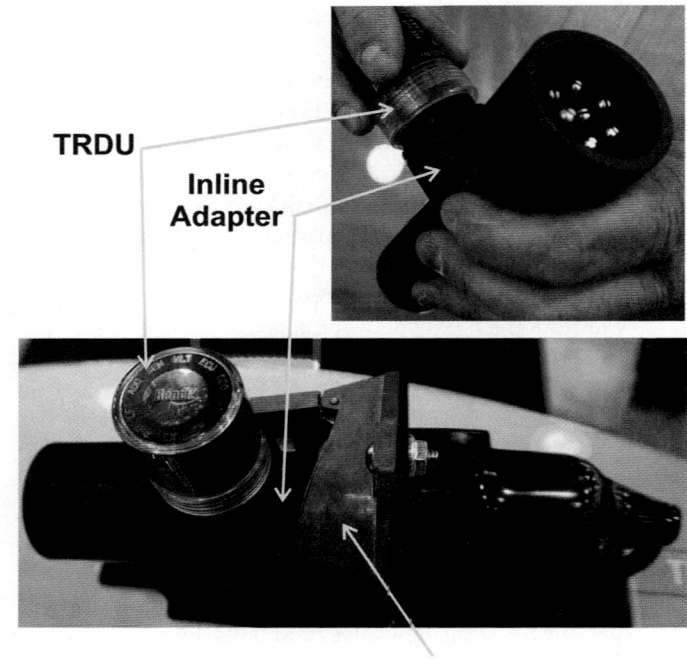

FIGURE 37-11 The TRDU adapter attaches to an inline connecter between the trailer cord and plug to read trailer fault codes.

eliminates faults in every other system component, harness, and power supply before isolating the cause as an ECU. Strong indications of a defective ECU are ABS, TCS, and other lights that remain on and do not blink after the ignition is switched on, or communication errors. Replacing an ECU from stock cannot be done any longer because the programming is performed by the ECU manufacturer or parts supplier. Since replacement ECU could result in a long down-time, waiting for an ECU to be built and shipped, some programming capabilities are given to dealers who can download secure files from servers. Multiple checks are performed to ensure the correct calibration is uploaded to a replacement ECU. Another alternative offered for aftermarket replacement programming is the use of partially programmed ECUs. These ECUs can be quickly configured for use on a wide variety of vehicles using electronic service tools, such as Meritor's proprietary TOOLBOX service software.

▶ TECHNICIAN TIP

Testing whether an ECU may be defective by replacing it with one from another vehicle or stock parts is often not possible. Today's vehicles' ECUs may store the VIN automatically when they are switched on or after several initial key cycles. The stored VIN is cross-checked to verify the ABS ECU VIN matches the VIN supplied by the other vehicle controllers. If not, the ECU generates an ECU Internal VIN Mismatch diagnostic trouble code (DTC) and does not operate. The intent of this procedure is to prevent mismatching of controllers from different vehicle configurations that could result in unexpected, but dangerous, system interactions. A controller with the wrong program can result in unsafe or unstable vehicle operation. When ordering a replacement controller, the VIN and other relevant data must be forwarded to the supplier to obtain the correct configuration.

Tire Rolling Circumference Adaptation   Because wheel speed data is critical to the ABS and so many other vehicle systems, the ECU requires a precise rolling circumference ratio for steer axle and drive axle tires to perform correctly. Tire size adaptation uses data from the vehicle speed sensor on the output shaft of the transmission to recalculate tire rolling diameter to verify it is within the correct range. This is performed whenever the vehicle enabling conditions are met, such as speed is greater than approximately 12 mph. No acceleration or deceleration is taking place and there are no active faults present. The adaptation process recalibrates tire size every trip when the enabling conditions are met. If the rotations per mile are not within maximum and minimum anticipated values, a fault code is set.

Wheel Speed Sensors

Wheel speed sensors are variable reluctance-type sensors used to produce wheel speed data. Variable reluctance sensors use changes in a sensor's magnetic field strength to generate an alternating current (AC) signal. The frequency of the AC pulses is converted by the ECU into wheel speed data. As illustrated in **FIGURE 37-12**, two main parts make up the wheel speed sensing system. One is a reluctor wheel, also called the tone or exciter ring. The other part is the variable reluctance sensor itself.

As illustrated in **FIGURE 37-13**, the **reluctor wheel**, also called an **exciter ring**, is simply a ring of raised iron teeth or a gear-like ring that moves past the sensor when the wheel rotates. The reluctor wheel (exciter ring) is pressed onto the inner wheel hub or cast into a brake drum. The ring must be pried off the hub to transfer it to another hub or brake rotor. Some of the latest exciter rings are held in place with a snap ring to make it easy to transfer it to another rotor or hub. The **variable reluctance (VR) sensor** consists of a permanent magnet wrapped with hundreds of coils of very fine wire. The sensor is placed in close proximity to the exciter ring, where metal shutters or iron teeth on the exciter ring intensify the magnetic field strength in the sensor.

Magnetic fields can pass through iron much easier than through air. The magnetic lines of force increase in density when passing through the raised iron tooth. That increase in density results in intensification. Then, as the raised tooth moves past the sensor, the field weakens and contracts. Movement of the magnetic field like this, both weakening and intensifying the field, causes magnetic lines of force to cut across the wire conductors, which induce AC flow in the coil surrounding the magnet.

When an exciter ring tooth and gap move past the sensor tip, an AC voltage "cycle" is generated. AC frequency depends on the wheel speed and the number of teeth in the exciter. Both are analyzed by the ECU using an algorithm to detect when wheel lockup is about to happen. Note that it is the AC cycle frequency—not the voltage—that is analyzed by the ECU. Voltage levels for generated AC depends on the sensor air gap between the tip of the sensor and the surface of the exciter ring. Sensor voltage increases as the sensor gap decreases and vice versa. For example, a sensor air gap of 0 to 0.015" (0 to 0.381 mm) produces approximately five volts with a minimum specification of 0.4 volts at 100 Hz frequency, corresponding to seven mph (11.3 kph) with a 100-tooth ring. To test a wheel speed sensor, follow the steps in **SKILL DRILL 37-1**.

Exctor Ring   Wheel Speed Sensor

FIGURE 37-12 Wheel speed sensors are typically located on the axle hub and are either a straight or elbow-shaped design. Sensors use a variable reluctance-type design to generate an AC voltage. **A.** Wheel speed sensor. **B.** Wheel end reluctor or exciter ring.

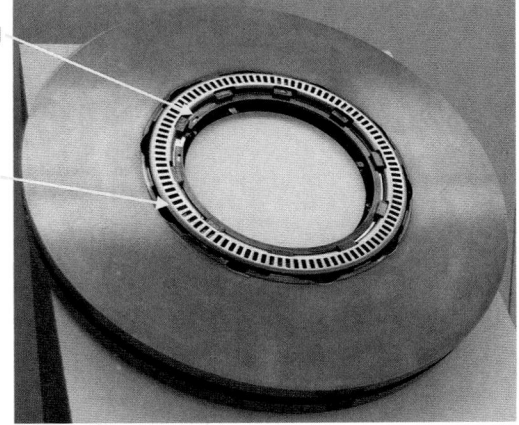

Snap Ring

Exciter Ring

FIGURE 37-13 The wheel speed sensor generates wheel rotational velocity data by counting the number of teeth passing by the sensor per unit of time. One wheel rotation is typically 100 teeth. **A.** Removable exciter ring. **B.** Snap ring.

Wheel speed calculations using an exciter ring with 100 teeth are typically based on a default tire size of 510 revolutions per mile. This number is an average approximation of actual rolling circumference of tires with a radius of 22.5" to 24.5" (57.2 to 11.4 cm). A precise number commonly varies between 460 and 650 rpm, depending on tire size, pressure tread wear, and vehicle load. The ABS sensitivity to detecting wheel lockup is reduced when tire rolling circumference is excessive on all wheels or tire rpm is low. **FIGURE 37-14** shows the relationship between tire size and revolutions.

SKILL DRILL 37-1 Testing Wheel Speed Sensor Codes

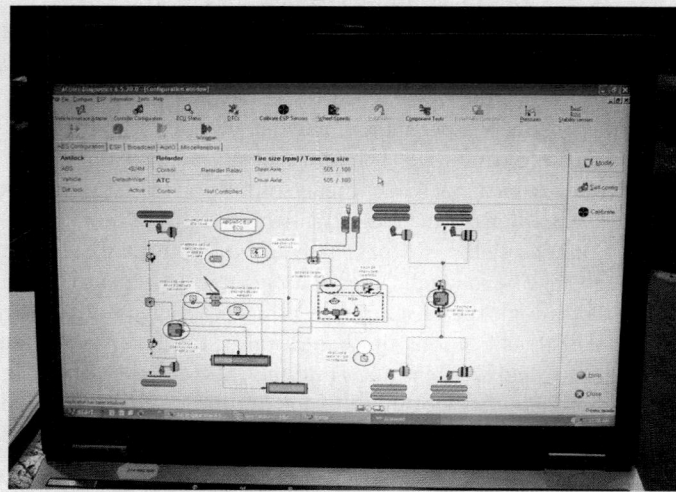

When a wheel speed sensor code is identified using an electronic service tool or blink codes, the following are general steps to follow to pinpoint and correct the fault condition.

1. Visually inspect the sensor. Confirm that the condition of sensor head is acceptable, correct installation of exciter ring, condition and number of exciter teeth, proper bearing wheel bearing end-play, sensor lead routing, and clipping.
2. Inspect sensor connectors for damaged, corroded, or bent pins. Verify harness routing and the ECU connectors are snuggly connected.

3. Inspect the condition and retention of the sensor in the clamping sleeve. Clean the sensor of iron filings while visually inspecting the sensor. Filings sticking to the internal magnet can affect sensor signals.
4. Inspect for excessive air gap. Remove and inspect the sensor head for damage. Reinstall a sensor that appears acceptable by pushing the sensor into the sensor block against the exciter ring to contact the exciter ring.
5. Measure sensor voltage output. Rotate wheel at one-half revolution per second. Use a multimeter ranged to AC volts to verify a minimum of 0.25 volts AC (VAC) sensor output per second. Replace any sensor with no signal voltage and recheck.
6. Inspect the sensor for open or shorted condition. Using an ohmmeter, measure and compare sensor resistance against specifications. Common resistance values are between 1500–2500 ohms across sensor leads. Confirm there is no continuity between sensor leads and the sensor case.
7. Check mechanical function of brake. Inspect brake chamber pushrod travel, correct chamber operation, and check for kinked or restricted airlines.
8. Confirm the tire size is correct and the tire is at the correct inflation pressure.
9. Inspect the condition of ECU pins and harness. Measure the sensor lead resistance at the ECU harness pins. Use an ohmmeter to verify the harness circuit to the sensor is not shorted, open, or grounded.
10. Confirm the system is configured correctly with the ECU identifying the correct number of sensors.

Wheel Rotational Speed @ 62 mph (100 kph)

FIGURE 37-14 Tire size changes the number of sensor pulses per mile from wheel speed sensors. It is recommended that tires vary no more than 0.75˝ (19.05 mm) diameter on 100 tooth reluctor rings.

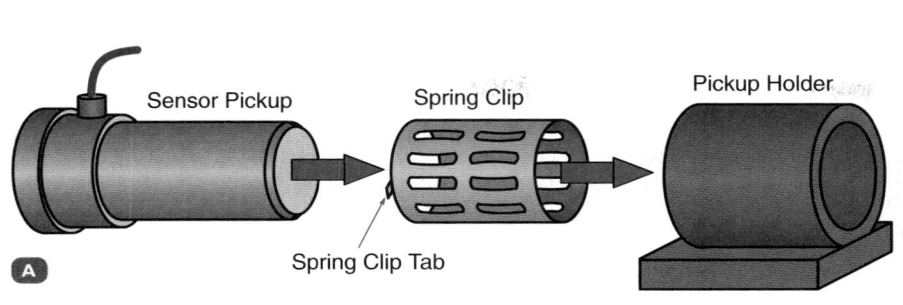

FIGURE 37-15 A. Wheel sensor assembly. **B.** Wheel sensor.

Wheel Speed Sensor Position

When referencing a speed sensor or modulator valve position, the driver's seat is the vehicle's reference point. Sensors themselves are typically installed in mounting blocks welded to the axle housing. A spring-like stainless steel clip clamps the sensor with a friction fit inside the mounting block. **FIGURE 37-15A** illustrates the friction fit of a wheel sensor and **FIGURE 37-15B** shows a wheel sensor in place. An air gap is established by pushing the sensor against the exciter ring. **FIGURE 37-16** illustrates the air gap. As the rotating exciter contacts the sensor, the sensor is pushed back slightly. Normal wheel bearing end play further "bumps" the sensor away from the exciter, establishing an operating sensor air gap. Loss of correct sensor air gap is a common ABS-related complaint. Sensors should be checked to see whether they are firmly in place and whether a loose wheel bearing may be interfering with the air gap.

When the ABS configuration equips the wheels of only one tandem axle with wheel speed sensors, the sensors are usually located on the axle whose wheels are most likely to lockup first during braking. This means that on a tandem axle with a four-spring suspension, the sensors are generally on the lead or forward axle. On a tandem axle with air suspension, the sensors are generally located on the trailing axle.

> ▶ **TECHNICIAN TIP**
>
> An ABS module generates fault codes if the rpm is too low or high. To prevent tire size fault codes from being generated, the actual rolling circumference of front axle steer axle tires is compared to the drive axle tires and must also be within a 0.85:1.15 ratio.

> ▶ **TECHNICIAN TIP**
>
> A common root cause of wheel speed fault codes is loose wheel bearings. A loose bearing allows the wheel hub to push the sensor away from the exciter ring causing excessive sensor air gap, which weakens the wheel speed signal. Always check wheel bearing end play when speed sensor faults are set.
>
> After servicing wheel ends and hubs, it is important to adjust the wheel bearings to achieve correct end play. The sensors should be pushed firmly into place after working on a wheel end to prevent sensor fault codes from suddenly appearing.

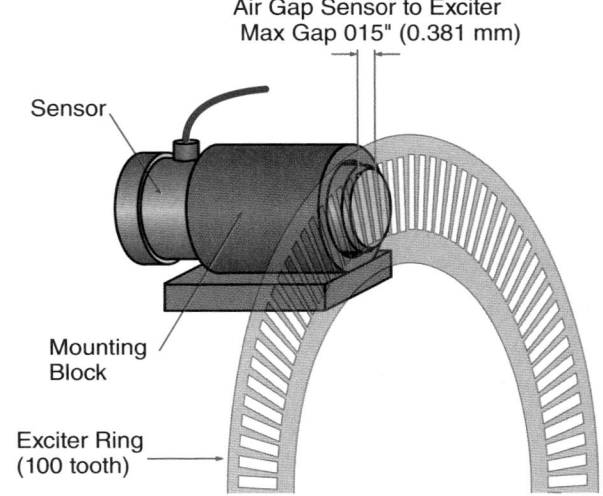

FIGURE 37-16 Acceptable wheel sensor air gap.

Modulator Valves

ABS modulator valves are high capacity, on/off air valves that contain a pair of electric solenoids used to control air brake application pressure. As these two "inlet-air" and "exhaust-air" solenoids are energized and de-energized by electrical signals from the ABS ECU, the controller simulates "pumping the brakes". That is, the controller signals to apply and release braking pressure on both axles, wheel ends on each axle, or at individual wheel ends connected to the modulator valves. **FIGURE 37-17** graphs the braking action as pressure is applied to the various braking components on the vehicle.

During normal braking applications, the modulator valves are not active. When activated on air brake systems, modulators adjust braking force by taking the air pressure supplied by the foot valve and doing three things with it. Modulators use air pressure to:

- hold the supplied brake pressure in the service chambers,
- release or dump brake pressure supplied to the service chambers, and
- reapply brake pressure to service chambers after it has been dumped.

ABS modulator valves are physically closer to the brake chambers than the driver's foot valve. Consequently, braking response is substantially faster with ABS brakes. Plus, the electronic control makes braking decisions faster and more precise because ABS ECU's can adjust braking air pressure to each wheel or set of wheels on an axle to achieve optimal braking effectiveness **FIGURE 37-18**.

Modulators can be used to control the braking function at individual service chambers, on a pair of chambers on a single axle, or on two chambers on the same side of a tandem axle. When controlling braking at individual wheel ends, the modulator is the last control valve through which air passes before entering the brake chamber. **FIGURE 37-19** shows a single channel modulator valve used to control a single brake chamber. When controlling air supply to two chambers, the modulator is often connected in series after a quick release valve. This arrangement provides a faster release of exhaust during normal service brake applications. **FIGURE 37-20** shows the location and configuration of front axle modulator valves, with and without a quick release valve.

Modulator Valve Construction

Individual modulators are typically constructed from diecast aluminum body and contain two solenoids: one normally open and one normally closed solenoid. Three electrical pins connect to the solenoids and they share a common ground connection. The valves can be integrated into a conventional relay valve too. Like other relay air valves, they have a variety of control, inlet, reservoir, and supply ports depending on how the system is configured. The modulator valve itself contains an air inlet

and exhaust valve whose position is controlled by a solenoid. **FIGURE 37-21** shows a trailer ABS module along with the modulator valve and sensors from a training board.

Operation Modulator Valves During Non-Antilock Braking

During normal service braking, both modulator inlet and exhaust valve solenoids are de-energized. The normally open inlet solenoid controlling the inlet diaphragm position enables air to pass through the valve and out the delivery port past the

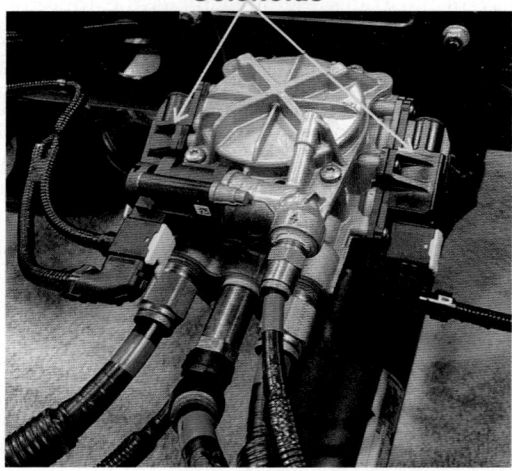

FIGURE 37-18 This rear drive axle relay valve integrates ABS control solenoids into the valve for fast brake response.

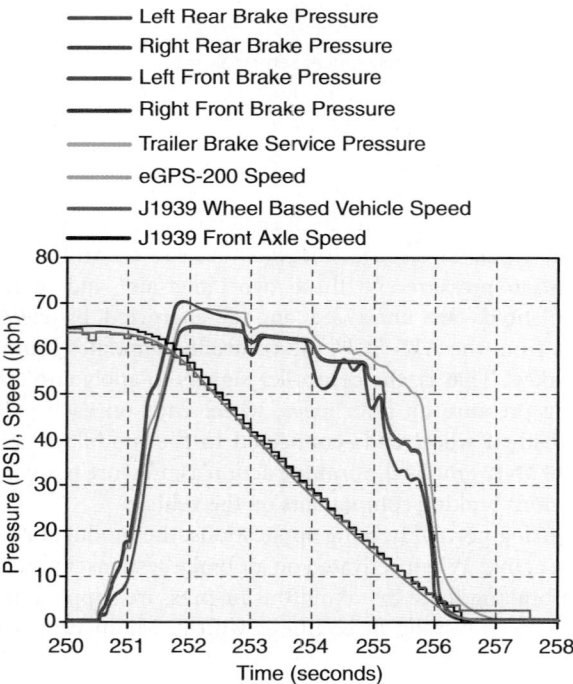

—— Left Rear Brake Pressure
—— Right Rear Brake Pressure
—— Left Front Brake Pressure
—— Right Front Brake Pressure
—— Trailer Brake Service Pressure
—— eGPS-200 Speed
—— J1939 Wheel Based Vehicle Speed
—— J1939 Front Axle Speed

FIGURE 37-17 The vehicle has decelerated from over 43 mph to 0 mph (70 kph to 0 kph) in less than five seconds. Note the small, incrementally stepped decrease in front axle and vehicle speed made due to the changing brake modulator valve pressure in the trailer, rear, and front axle brake chambers.

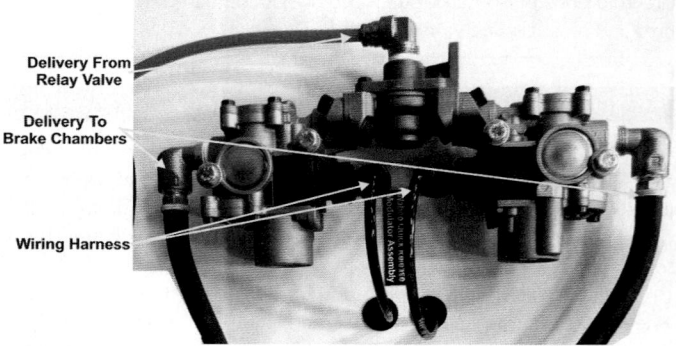

FIGURE 37-19 A left and right single-channel modulator valve joined and supplied air through a quick release valve.

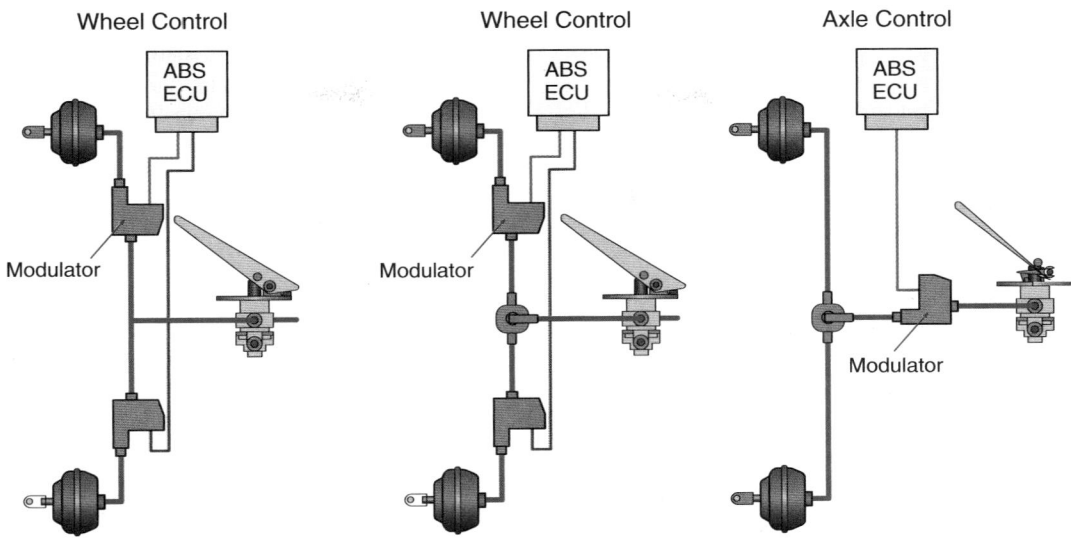

FIGURE 37-20 A location and configuration of front axle modulator valves with and without a quick release valve.

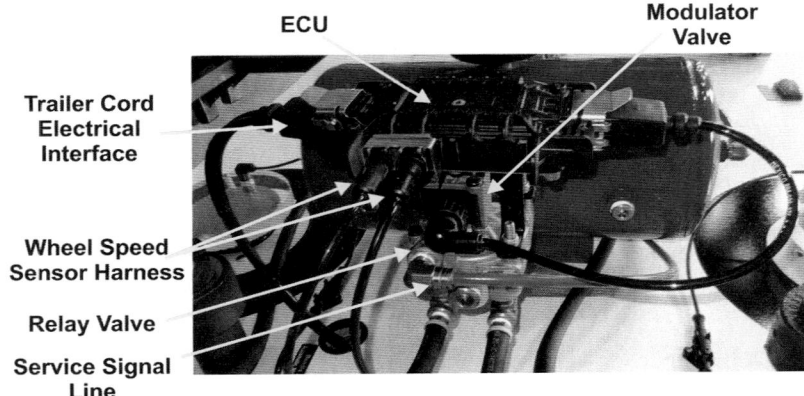

FIGURE 37-21 A trailer ABS module with a modulated control signal air supply inlet valve mounted on a service relay valve.

normally closed exhaust valve. In a modulated relay valve, the combined modulator-relay valve behaves like a regular relay valve. However, the control signal air pressure is modulated by an inlet and exhaust solenoid valve that either exhausts the signal air pressure or admits it into the valve (**FIGURE 37-22**).

Operation of Modulator Valves During Antilock Braking

There are three distinct aspects of the antilock braking process:

- Exhaust
- Hold
- Reapply

Pressure changes during these phases are shown in the chart in **FIGURE 37-23**.

Before the first phase begins, the system is inactive, as shown in **FIGURE 37-24A**. The first phase is antilock *exhaust* and is illustrated in **FIGURE 37-24B**. When wheel lockup is detected or imminent, the ECU energizes both the inlet air supply and exhaust solenoids in the modulator. Energizing the supply

FIGURE 37-22 An ABS modulator valve mounted on top of the service brake relay valve. The valve modulates inlet air pressure at the signal or control port of the relay valve.

solenoid prevents inlet air flow into the normally open valve and opens the normally closed exhaust port to atmosphere. The modulator remains in the antilock exhaust mode until the ECU senses an increase in wheel speed. At that point, the ECU can de-energize the exhaust solenoid and either open or close the air inlet solenoid. De-energizing the inlet solenoid rebuilds brake chamber air pressure, which reapplies the brakes if wheel speed becomes excessive. To chuff test the modulator valve, follow the steps in **SKILL DRILL 37-2**.

The ECU can change the modulator control status by putting the solenoids into a *hold* air pressure position, as illustrated in **FIGURE 37-24C**, the ECU does this when it senses the correct wheel speed has been achieved using the brake application pressure used at that moment. In hold mode of operation, the modulator air supply inlet solenoid remains energized, which blocks air flow into the valve. At the same time, the exhaust solenoid is de-energized. That prevents air in the brake chamber from exhausting out the service chamber(s). De-energizing the exhaust solenoid closes the exhaust outlet port. No air can be released from the chambers or supplied though the closed inlet valve. The modulator can change to an exhaust or reapply mode from the antilock hold mode.

In the antilock *reapply* mode, if the ECU senses that wheel speed has increased to the point when re-application of braking pressure is necessary, it de-energizes the supply and exhaust solenoids. With both solenoids de-energized, the modulator re-supplies air pressure to the chambers as it does in a normal braking condition. In this state, the exhaust valve is closed, and the air inlet valve is open. Reapply mode is illustrated in **FIGURE 37-24D**.

Steer Axle Control During some ABS events, such as when the steering tires are on surfaces with different frictional coefficients (one tire is on a more slippery surface), the steering wheel can pull left or right and potentially cause directional instability. Because each front wheel has a wheel speed sensor and modulator valve, the air application pressure is blended at both wheel ends to balance out and minimize pull on the steering wheel this means that the application pressure is progressively increased on the wheel with the greatest traction rather than suddenly with full force. The feature attempts to optimize both stopping distance and directional control. Bendix refers to their use of this patented brake application control as **Modified Individual Regulation (MIR)**.

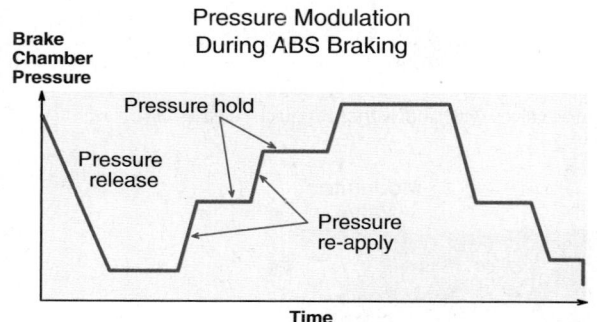

FIGURE 37-23 Operation of the modulator valves to control brake application pressure.

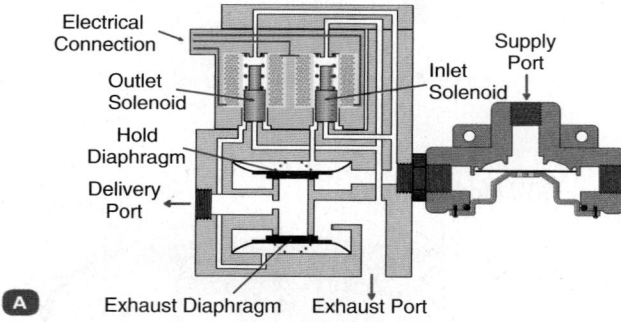

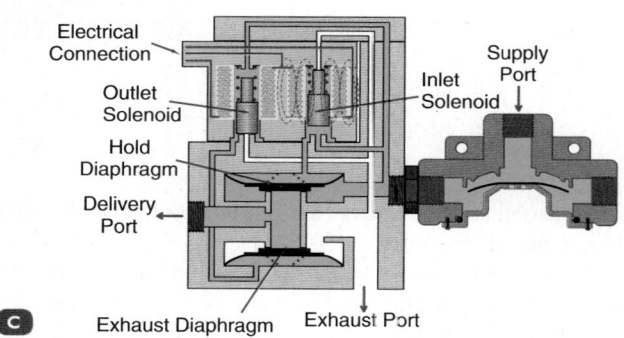

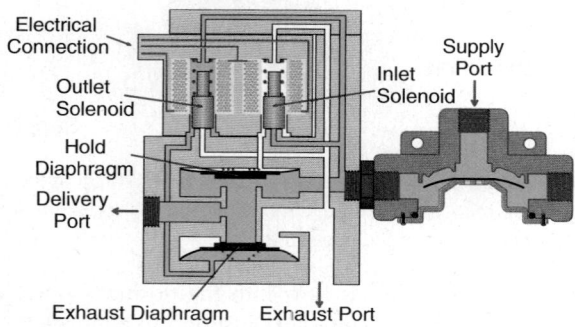

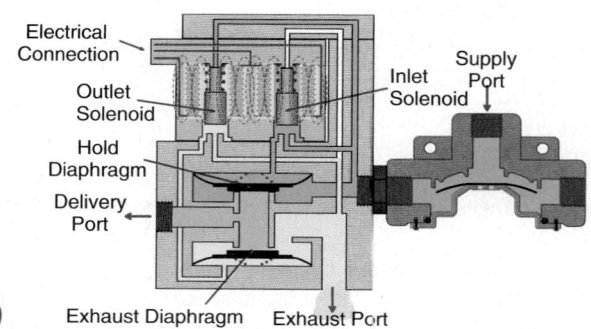

FIGURE 37-24 Modulator function. **A.** Before braking. **B.** During apply mode. **C.** During hold mode. **D.** During exhaust mode.

SKILL DRILL 37-2 Performing the Modulator Valve Chuff Test

The Chuff Test is an electrical and pneumatic modulator valve test that can help technicians validate correct modulator valve operation, wiring, and installation. To perform a Chuff test, use the following as a general outline:

1. Confirm service brake air pressure is at least 105 psi.
2. Chock the wheels and release the park brakes.

3. Press the service brake pedal to obtain a full brake application and hold the pedal down.
4. Switch the ignition to the on position but do not start the engine.
5. Listen for a correctly operating modulator valve by observing whether each valve emits a sharp, loud exhaust of air as the ECU cycles each modulator valve on and off.
6. Listen for one distinct chuff noise and two thumping noises from each valve as the air inlet solenoid operates typically twice and the exhaust solenoid once.
7. To identify any defective valve location, note the sequence of valve activations. Note the sequence to also verify the valve is connected correctly. Typically, the valves test:
   - Steer axle right and left
   - Drive axle right and left
   - Second Drive axle right and left
   - Repeat—the sequence is performed twice during a key-on event.
8. Note that no chuff test is performed by the ECU if any wheel speed data is detected.

ABS Trailer Cords

The trailer cords used in antilock braking systems are subject to Society of Automotive Engineers (SAE) standards. Specifically, the **SAE J-560 standard** applies to the dimensional and functionality requirements for seven-pin tractor/trailer electrical connectors. It is more commonly known as the standard for the trailer electrical cord, plugs, and sockets, as well as for transfers of ABS signals between the tractor and trailer. **TABLE 37-2** shows J-560 standards for plugs, connectors, and cords.

Prior to the introduction of ABS, the #7 (blue) wire conductor was intended for auxiliary power purposes. Lift axles and other trailer accessories could be supplied current through this wire and switched on and off by a dash toggle switch. After the introduction of ABS, legislation required the #7 blue auxiliary power circuit be dedicated to supply continuous current to the trailer ABS. The minimum wire gauge size increased to

12 American Wire Gauge (AWG). Since many auxiliary electrical devices, in addition to the current demands of the ABS, increased the total trailer power consumption, the minimum diameter of the ground white wire conductor was also increased to 8 AWG. A green-colored trailer cord identifies a cord meeting SAE standards for ABS trailer cords with larger diameter conductors and ground pins. The function of each pin is illustrated in **FIGURE 37-25**.

FIGURE 37-25 Power is constantly supplied through the #7 pin after the key is switched on. Each pin communicates different information. **A.** Pin 1: Ground Circuit. **B.** Pin 2: Clearance, Sidemarker, ID. **C.** Pin 3: Left-Hand Turn Signal. **D.** Pin 4: Stop Lamp Circuit. **E.** Pin 5: Right Turn Signal and Hazard Signal. **F.** Pin 6: Tail Lamp, Marker Lamp, License Plate Lamp. **G.** Pin 7: Continuous Power or Auxiliary Circuit (Activated in "Key On" Position).

TABLE 37-2 J-560 Standards for Trailer Plugs, Connectors, and Cords

J-560 Pin Number	Color	Purpose	Wire Gauge
1	White	Ground	8 AWG
2	Black	Clearance, marker, and ID	12 AWG
3	Yellow	Left turn	12 AWG
4	Red	Stop	10 AWG
5	Green	Right turn	12 AWG
6	Brown	Tail	12 AWG
7	Blue	Auxiliary and ABS	10 AWG

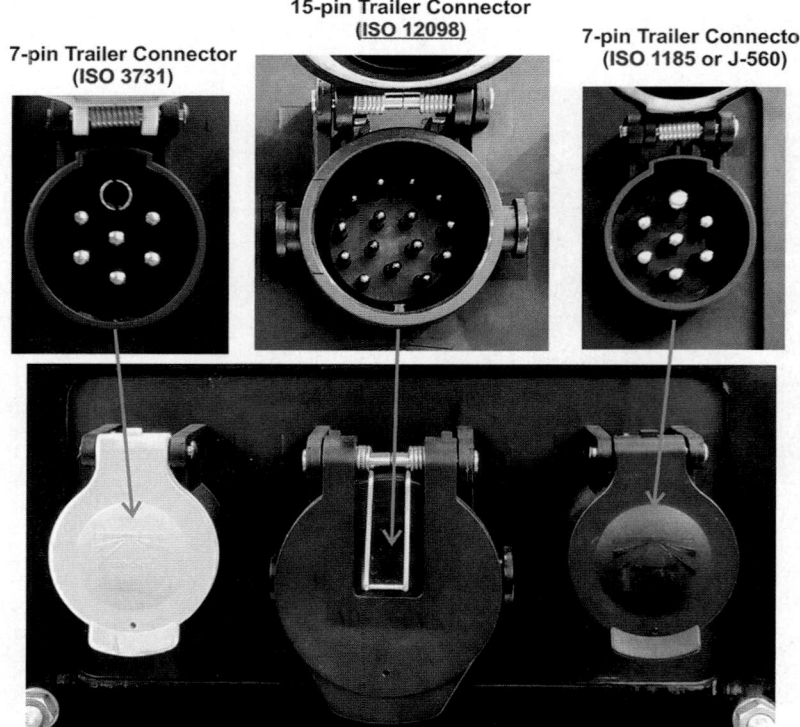

FIGURE 37-26 Three to five different trailer plugs are found on European trailers, depending on whether they are 12- or 24-volt system, single or double trailers.

▶ **TECHNICIAN TIP**

Modulator valve and other ABS fault codes may not be related to a problem in an ABS component at all. Problems in the wheel end and brake foundation show up as ABS faults. Examples include a slack adjuster that has backed off; grease or oil on brake linings; kinked, restricted air lines; or a defective brake chamber that prevents correct ABS operation. An automatic slack adjuster that has backed-off does not allow a wheel speed change when the valve is activated. In this case, the electronic control system assumes the valve is mechanically defective when the root cause is a defective or misadjusted slack adjuster. Eliminate possible mechanical causes in the wheel end first when performing diagnostic checks.

▶ **TECHNICIAN TIP**

When the ignition switch is first cycled to the on position, the ECU learns or rediscovers the ABS configuration and performs a self-test of the solenoids. All the solenoids to the modulator valves are cycled in a particular sequence wherever they are on the chassis. By making a full brake application when the ignition is initially switched on, the sound of air supplied to the modulator valves is amplified by the exhaust of air from each valve. The "chuffing" sound made by the modulator valves is a useful functional test of the ABS to validate the modulator valves are functioning correctly both electrically and pneumatically. Otherwise, without the brakes applied, only electrical continuity of solenoid coils is done by the ECU.

An **ISO 11446 connector** is commonly used in Europe as a 13-pin trailer cord connector but only occasionally in North America. The addition of two more pins to form the later 15-pin

European version is built according to ISO 12098, replacing the ISO 11446 cable. Freightliner is one example of a manufacturer providing the 13-pin plug alongside the J-560 plug in North America (**FIGURE 37-26**). The ISO 11446 uses a multi-pin tractor-trailer electrical connector with conductors and pins that can also transfer ABS ECU communication signals. This is particularly important for coordinated response between a tractor and one, or even two, trailers to a loss of directional stability or rollover conditions. Brakes in each of those trailers can receive signals from a tractor ECU, as well as transmit message requests for torque reduction (**TABLE 37-3**). This connector carries power, ABS fault lamp status, and serial communications to and from trailer ABSs.

Another common plug on European trailers conforms to ISO 7638-1 or 2 for 24- or 12-volt vehicles. Pin 5 on the plug carries ABS fault lamp information. If the voltage on pin 5 is less than five volts, the dash-mounted fault indicator lamp for trailer ABS illuminates (**FIGURE 37-27**).

Indicator Lights and Switches

The final components in an ABS are the indicator lights and the off-road switch. The ABS indicator lamp (amber-colored) indicates the status of the ABS. The light can illuminate to indicate normal operation or to signal a system fault. After the ignition is switched on, the ABS indicator light typically remains lit for several seconds, and then goes out if the system is functioning correctly. In addition, ABS lights are diagnostic output devices, as was discussed in the ECU Configuration section.

TABLE 37-3 ISO Pin Numbers for ISO 12098 Trailer Plugs

Pin #	15-Pin ISO 12098 Electrical Signals	Color
1	Left Turn	Yellow
2	Rear fog lamps	Blue
3	Negative Ground (-) Pins 1 - 8	White
4	Right Turn	Green
5	Right-side tail lamps, clearance-marker lamps, license plate lamp	Brown
6	Stop lamps	Red
7	Left-side tail lamps, clearance-marker lamps, license plate	Black
8	Back-up lamps, control current to block surge brakes when reversing	Pink
9	+12V Constant Power	Orange
10	+12V Ignition Power	Grey
11	Ground (-) for pin 10	Black/White
12	Reserved for future allocation	Light Grey
13	Ground (-) for pin 9	Red/White
14	CAN HI ISO 12098 (Europe only)	Green/White
15	CAN LO ISO 12098 (Europe only)	Brown/White

Source: ISO standard per OEM product bulletin for trailer cords.

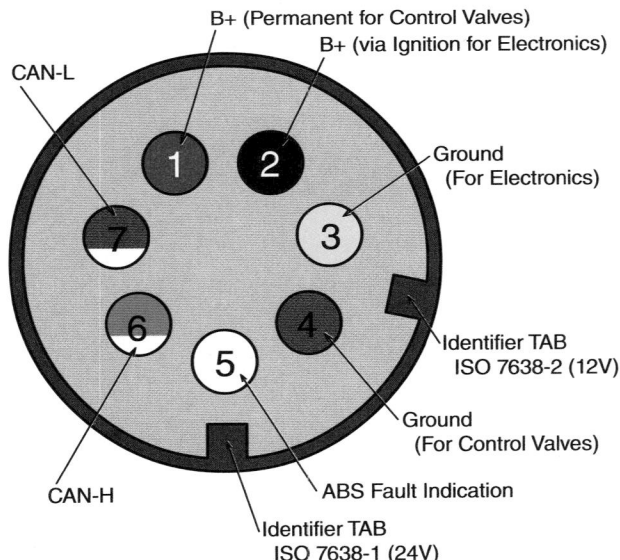

FIGURE 37-27 Pin #5 carries ABS fault information. If less than five volts is measured at the pin, the tractors trailer ABS light illuminates.

The ABS warning light for the trailer/dolly is not required for an in-cab light on vehicles built before March 2001. An external trailer/dolly indicator lamp is used and mandatory on vehicles built from 1998 to 2009. On vehicles built after March 2009, the external ABS light is not required.

On some vehicles, an off-road ABS switch is used to improve ABS function on poor traction surfaces, such as loose gravel, sand, snow, and dirt. The switch allows more wheel lockup, due to loose gravel and mud, which actually reduces stopping distances in off-road conditions. Switching to off-road mode takes into account the braking effect added by the accumulation of loose road material or snow that piles-up in front of the tire when braking. In the latest systems, model predictive control of ABS eliminates the need for an off-road switch because it is also able to predict what type of road surface the vehicle is operating over by observing the rate of wheel deceleration.

ABS Configurations

LO 37-4 Define ABS configurations.

ABS configuration is defined by the location and number of wheel sensors and modulator valves used. The most common configurations for tractors are:

- Four sensors/four modulators (4S/4M) **FIGURE 37-28**
- Six sensors/four modulators (6S/4M) **FIGURE 37-29**
- Six sensors/six modulators (6S/6M) **FIGURE 37-30**

Common configurations for trailers are 2S/1M, 2S/2M, 4S/2M, and 4S/3M.

Some tractors use a 4S/6M ABS. In that system, rear drive axle wheel speed sensors are located on the front drive axle only. During hard braking, front tires are less likely to lockup first since vehicle weight is transferred by inertia to the front drive axle, from the rear drive. With the additional axle weight caused by inertia weight shift, the front drive axle grips the road better, and effectively controls the vehicle longer than the rear drive, which quickly lockup as weight is removed. If sensors were located on the rear drive axle, the ABS would prematurely go into antilock brake mode. In that case, braking would be less efficient because both sets of drive tires would experience brake pressure modulation.

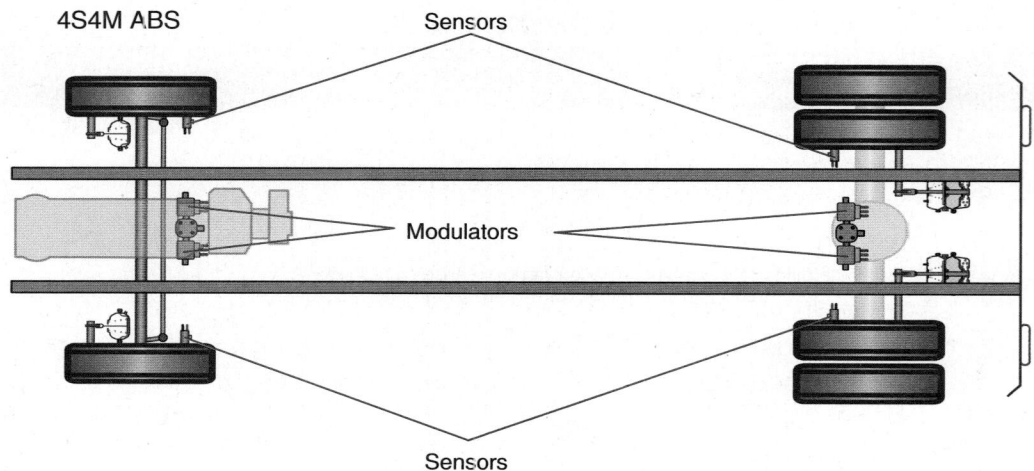

FIGURE 37-28 4S/4M ABS configuration.

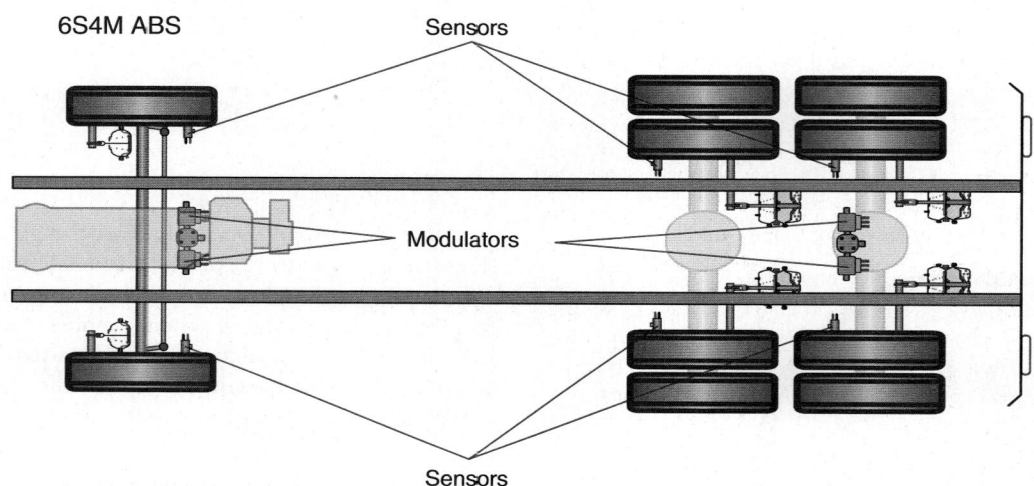

FIGURE 37-29 6S/4M ABS configuration.

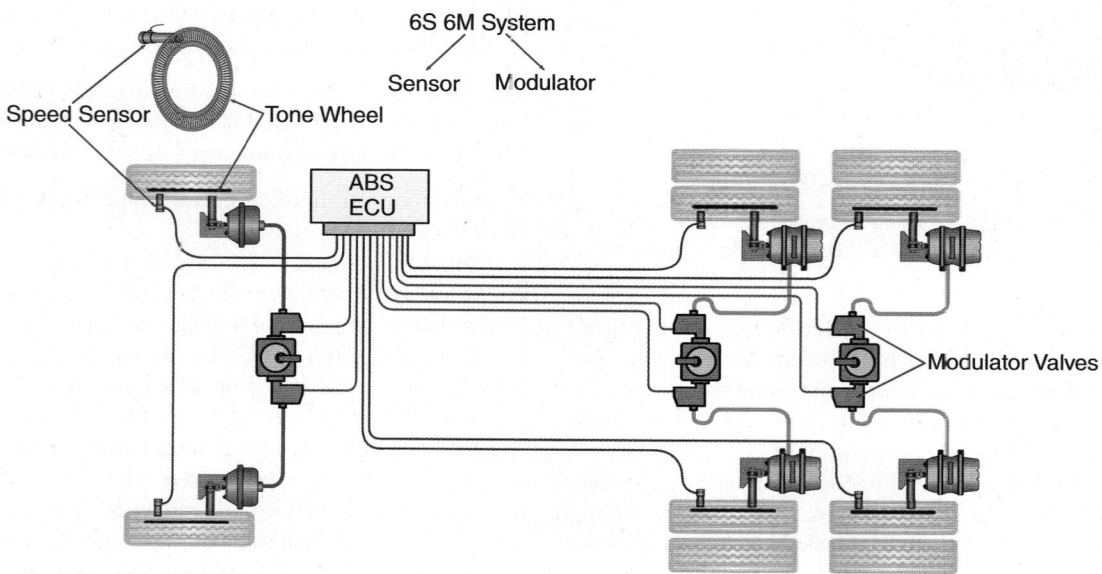

FIGURE 37-30 6S/6M ABS configuration.

Vehicle Dynamic Control Systems

LO 37-5 Identify and describe the purpose and operation of vehicle dynamic control systems.

ABSs became the basic building block for further development of dynamic control systems. When a few more sensors, control valves, and advanced algorithms are integrated into the ABS ECU, the hardware can provide additional safety and vehicle control features. One of the primary adaptations of ABS improves vehicle traction, as well as braking capabilities. **Automatic slip regulation (ASR)**, or ATC, improves traction and vehicle stability by minimizing wheel spin. Adding the traction control feature to ABSs requires only the addition of a single solenoid-controlled air valve and some software to an enhanced functioning ECU. With the addition of a couple other sensors, ABS can also be leveraged to provide rollover protection, electronic stability control, and CAS.

Traction Control

Traction control is an enhancement to the ABS used to improve vehicle stability when accelerating. The only significant change in system hardware requirements for traction control is the addition of an electrically controlled air valve, which supplies air at reservoir pressure to the control port on an ABS modulator-relay valve. This is necessary because the driver's foot is on the accelerator pedal instead of the brake pedal and the driver likely cannot detect wheel spin. Because the brakes are applied without a driver input, the normally closed traction control air valve is electrically opened and closed by ECU commands to apply or release the brakes (**FIGURE 37-31**).

TCSs also include an enable/disable switch that allows the operator to engage or disengage the TCS, as necessary. The switch may be used to either engage or disengage the TCS while the vehicle is in motion, such as in an off-road condition where more wheel slip is expected. Although the traction control disengages while the vehicle is in motion, it does not re-engage (even with the switch in the engaged position) until the vehicle comes to a complete stop.

Traction Control System Operation

The ABS constantly measures and compares individual wheel speeds to prevent wheel lockup. That activity is also useful in controlling **wheel slip** or **wheel spin**, produced when excess torque from the drivetrain causes the tire to break free from the road surface. With traction control, a tire that has lost traction and is spinning too fast is instantly identified by comparison with the other wheel speeds on the vehicle, both front and rear. If wheels spin, unacceptable torque steering by the drive axles can take place.

Traction control systems commonly use two strategies to control wheel spin: torque limiting and differential braking. Both strategies use messages exchanged between the ABS ECU and engine ECM. The ABS ECU commands the engine ECM to reduce torque by exchanging information over the J-1939 network.

Vehicles with traction control have an indicator lamp on the dash. When the vehicle ignition is first turned to ON, the ATC lamp comes on for a few seconds to verify the bulb works. If the lamp goes out after a few seconds, the ATC system is ready; if the lamp stays on, it indicates a malfunction in the system. If wheel spin occurs at any speed above 25 mph (40 kph), the ECU instantly blinks the traction control dash lamp to advise the driver that a wheel spin is occurring. If the torque limiting feature is enabled, the ECU signals the engine control module to reduce engine torque to a level suitable for the available traction. The ECU generally does not signal the ATC control valve to apply the brakes even slightly when wheel speed is above 25 mph (40 kph).

Torque Limiting

Torque limiting is basically a reduction in engine power. During a wheel slip condition, uneven wheel speeds prevent proper forward motion and can cause the vehicle to lose directional stability, as illustrated in **FIGURE 37-32**. The resulting understeer or oversteer risks pushing a vehicle outside its lane. Limiting engine torque until traction is restored is an effective method to maintain directional stability.

Torque limiting enables drive axle tires to regain traction and maintain vehicle stability by minimizing sideways drift or fishtailing, also known as **power jackknifing**. **Fishtailing** is a condition in which the drive axles of a vehicle push the rear of a vehicle to the left or right, often when turning corners. Directional steering control is lost when one wheel excessively spins. An oversteer condition is present when the unequal drive torque from the drive axles rotates the vehicle around its vertical center point. During oversteer, the

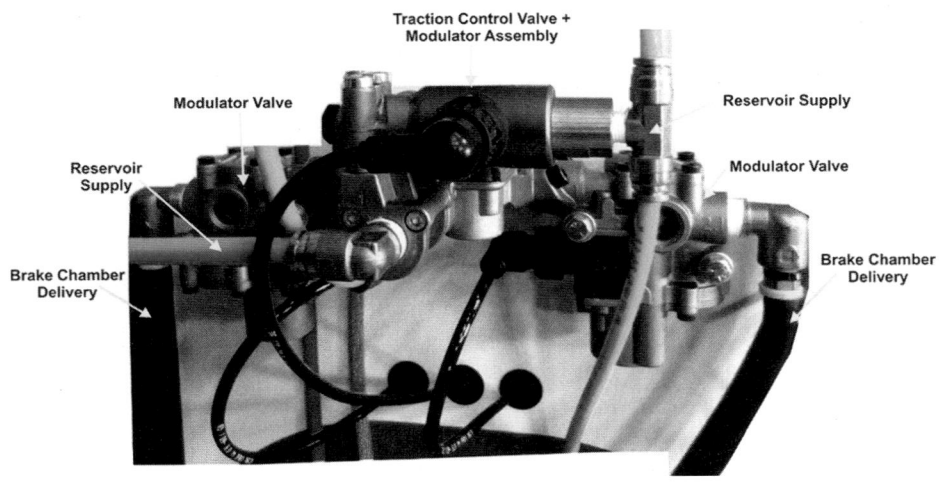

FIGURE 37-31 A traction control valve provides an air signal to the drive axle relay valve.

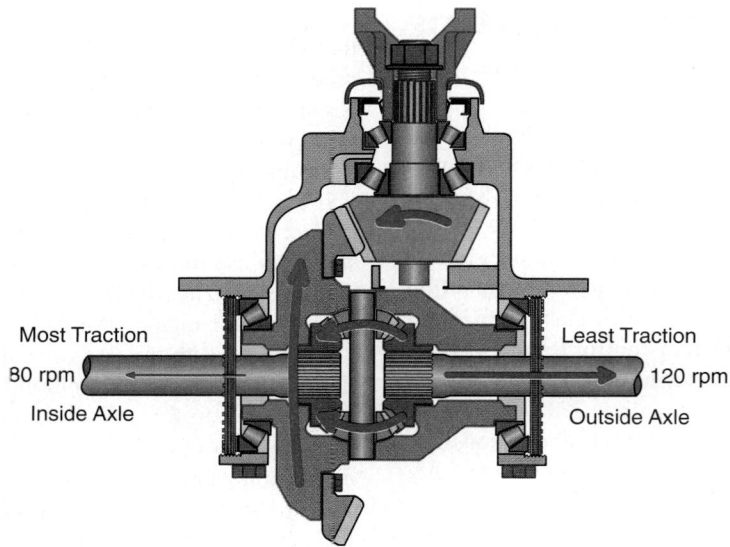

FIGURE 37-32 Uneven wheel speeds at the inside and outside of the axle prevent proper forward motion from taking place.

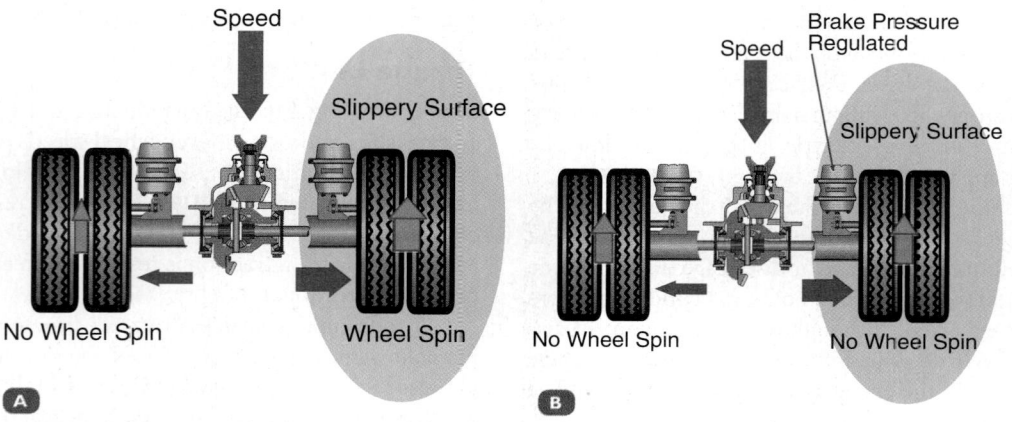

FIGURE 37-33 Distribution of torque during differential braking. **A.** Without traction control. **B.** With traction control.

steering inputs are exaggerated; slight turns of the steering wheel when cornering during oversteer situations produce even more dramatic changes in vehicle direction during a turn.

When the ABS first identifies a wheel slip condition, the ECU signals the engine to reduce the power output. With reduced engine power, the tires again begin to grip the road surface. When both drive wheels are spinning because traction is low or absent, the ATC automatically reduces engine power through J-1939 network communication to re-establish tire-to-road traction. If the wheels continue to slip, the ATC automatically applies and releases the brakes.

Differential Braking

Differential braking is a second strategy used by TCSs only at low speeds when one wheel is spinning on a slippery surface. During differential braking, the brakes are only applied on a slipping wheel to transfer torque to a stationary or slowly turning wheel with traction. ABS modulator valves are independently activated to apply a single brake to the slipping wheel. Applying one brake on the axle with the slipping wheel causes drive torque to transfer to a non-slipping wheel through the differential or inter-axle differential. **FIGURE 37-33** shows how differential braking redistributes torque.

When a differential braking feature is configured into the system, the ABS ECU energizes a solenoid in the ATC valve that supplies air to the relay valve delivering air to each of the rear axle modulator valves, or the ATC valve supplies air directly to each modulator valve. **FIGURE 37-34** illustrates a system with the ATC valve supply air to a relay valve. Because the ATC valve and modulator valves are controlled by the common ECU, the solenoid valves in the appropriate modulator are opened and closed to block air application pressure to a wheel that has traction, but gently applies and releases the brake on the spinning wheel only. The gentle brake application transfers torque from the slipping

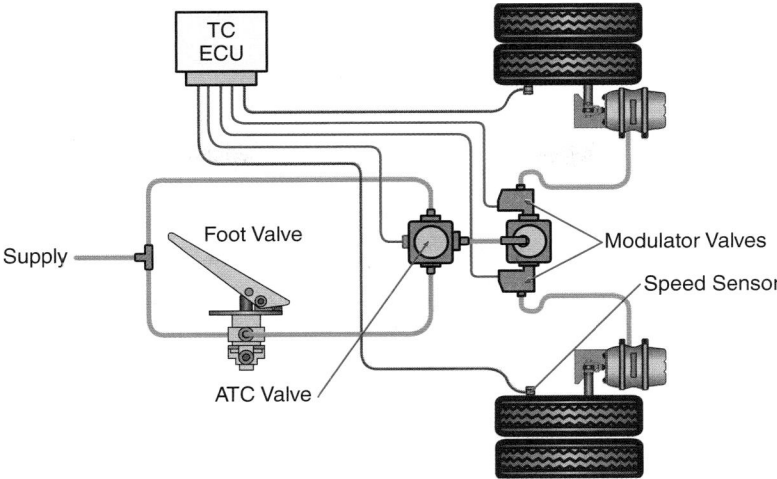

FIGURE 37-34 The ATC valve is connected to the signal port of a service brake relay valve. Air pressure is constantly supplied to the valve. When required, a normally closed solenoid in the ATC valve opens and applies air pressure to the signal port to apply the brakes in response to an electrical signal.

FIGURE 37-35 ATC valves located on the service brake relay valves. **A.** Modulator valve. **B.** Service brake relay valve. **C.** Traction control valve. **D.** Wiring harness. **E.** Air supply from service reservoir.

FIGURE 37-36 The ECU, conventional relay valve, and ATC valve are integrated into a single unit. **A.** ABS/Traction control module. **B.** ATC valve. **C.** Service brake relay valve.

wheels through the axle differential to drive the stationary or more slowly spinning wheel.

Sometimes ATC valves are located on the service brake relay valves as shown in **FIGURE 37-35**. In this position, they apply air pressure to the relay valves control signal port in response to an electrical signal from the ABS/ATC control module. **FIGURE 37-36** shows an ECU, a conventional relay valve, and an ATC valve integrated into a single unit.

Advanced ATC Control

In off-road conditions, an off-road ATC strategy allows more wheel slip in loose sand, mud, snow, and gravel. Generally, allowing more off-road wheel slip minimizes the nuisance of engine de-rating.

Advanced ATC systems adapt the amount of wheel slip for a particular operating condition by anticipating the driver's intention. More wheel slip is permitted when the accelerator pedal is above a preset threshold than when the vehicle is lightly throttled. Faster acceleration and traction are enabled with this strategy. When driving through a curve, yaw sensors in the ECU decreases the amount of allowable wheel slip to maintain vehicle stability.

The ATC can cause overheating of a brake if it is applied for too long. A situation where this takes place could be a transit bus climbing a long, steep, icy hill for several minutes. To prevent this, the ATC deactivates differential braking after three minutes. A two-minute cool-down period is necessary before differential braking resumes.

Rollover Stability Control (RSC)

LO 37-6 Identify and describe the construction and operation of rollover protection systems.

Another stability and safety enhancement system is the use of the ABS to minimize the likelihood of vehicle rollovers. **Roll stability control (RSC)** is a vehicle control system that measures lateral acceleration of a vehicle and compares it to thresholds for when a rollover situation can take place. More data is collected by the RSC, such as steering wheel angle, lateral acceleration, average vehicle speed, and travel direction, to predict the likelihood of a vehicle to rollover. This means the system adds only two new sensors, a lateral acceleration and steering angle sensor, plus more advanced ECU capabilities to operate the RSC system. If a rollover is imminent, the ECU corrects the vehicle dynamics through a combination of braking, use of an engine retarder, and reduction of engine torque, which send messages to de-rate engine power output. When the RSC applies individual brakes automatically on wheels to slow down sideways slide, or lateral vehicle acceleration, it does this even before the driver is aware of a potential rollover.

Lateral Acceleration Sensor

The system uses data from the wheel speed sensors and from a lateral acceleration sensor, or "G" sensor to detect potential rollover conditions. Its operating concept is not much different from the effect that a sudden sharp cornering has on a coffee cup sitting on a friction surface inside a vehicle. Inertia reaction to the lateral acceleration force are strong enough to push sideways against the cup and even empty it. Likewise, the lateral acceleration sensor measures inertia forces reacting to lateral acceleration by measuring the response of a heavy mass, called a seismic weight (**FIGURE 37-37**). The weight compresses a spring-like device when the direction of sensor movement changes. The degree of spring compression is electrically measured and is proportional to the force of lateral acceleration. Merging sensor data with other onboard information and comparing it with the known thresholds that cause rollovers,

determines whether a rollover event is impending. This unique sensor is not serviceable separately because it is located inside the control module. Because it measures the response of a mass to a change of direction, the correct orientation of the ECU is critical. An adjustment procedure is available to properly calibrate its position if it is moved or replaced.

Tripped Versus Untripped Rollovers

The RSC can only minimize the likelihood of a tripped rollover, *not* stop it. Tripped rollover events are different from **untripped rollovers** that occur when outside disturbances increase the likelihood of a rollover. High and uneven trailer loads, suspension defects causing the vehicle to lean, heavy gusty winds, and rapid movement of the steering wheel back and forth at high speeds are just a few of many conditions that can cause untripped rollovers. If road traction is good but a truck strikes a curb and then rolls down an embankment, the untripped rollover condition is not preventable by the RSC system. If the impact energy from a vehicle collision is high enough and directed above the vehicle's center of gravity, the vehicle can also roll.

RSC Trailer Braking Strategies

Simpler RSC systems activate only the rear brakes of a tractor or truck through the ATC valve. To provide a trailer with stability control, a second electrically controlled air valve is connected between the tractor foot valve and the tractor protection valve to operate the trailer brakes. If a rollover condition is anticipated, the valve opens and supplies air from the secondary air reservoir to activate the trailer brakes, slowing the vehicle and minimizing the likelihood of a rollover. The drag force created by the trailer brake application cancels out some of the lateral acceleration force.

More sophisticated trailer rollover protection systems use advanced algorithms, which include estimates of the trailer's mass derived from air pressure in the air suspension system. A pressure sensing load valve installed in the suspension air bag helps the ECU modify modulator valve action and the timing of brake application force to the rear brakes.

When a high lateral acceleration situation is detected, the system may briefly and gently apply the trailer brakes to test the rollover potential. If rollover is pending, the system simultaneously applies full braking pressure on the outer side of the trailer that is rolling over and lowers application pressure to the brakes on the inner side of the trailer. It applies unequal braking pressure because the wheels on the inside of the curve are lightly loaded. Applying high application pressure to the inside wheels is counterproductive because centrifugal force of the turn lifts the inside wheels upward away from the ground, thus transferring the weight to the outside tires. Unequal brake application force also has the effect of creating a stabilizing twisting force on the trailer, tractor, truck, or bus as it slows down one side of the vehicle more than the other. This reaction opposes the force rolling the vehicle over (**FIGURE 37-38**).

Modulation of brake application pressure by the ABS may also help slow the trailer much faster if the tires are lightly loaded as they lift. If the trailer is stable, the system recognizes that, and no speed change takes place. Note that

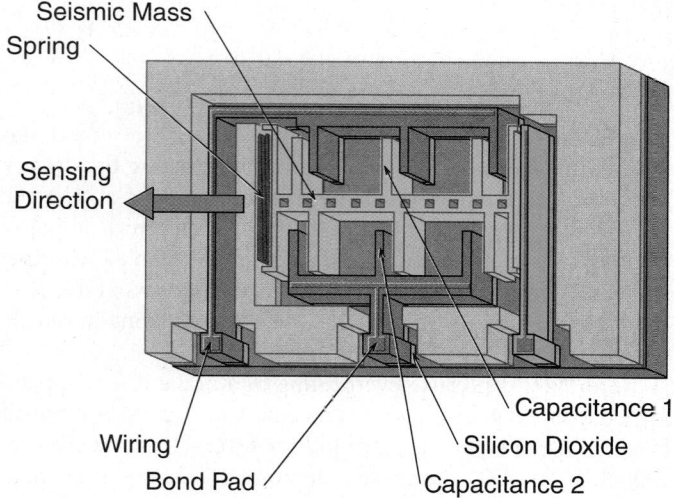

FIGURE 37-37 A lateral acceleration sensor measures the inertial response of a heavy mass to a change in sideways movement.

Seismic Mass
Spring
Sensing Direction
Wiring
Bond Pad
Capacitance 1
Silicon Dioxide
Capacitance 2

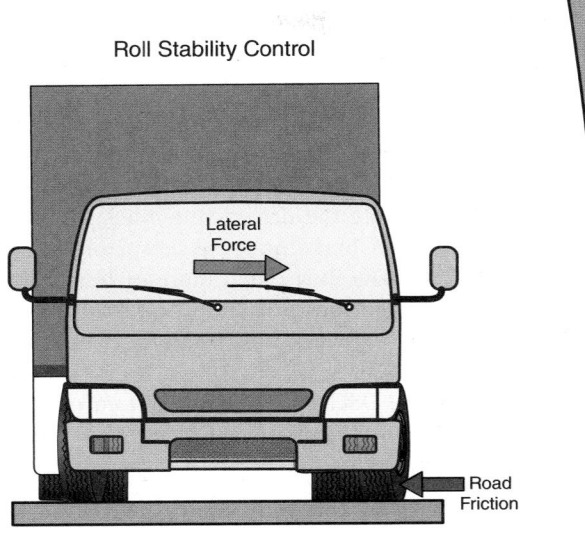

Roll Stability Control

Lateral
Force

Road
Friction

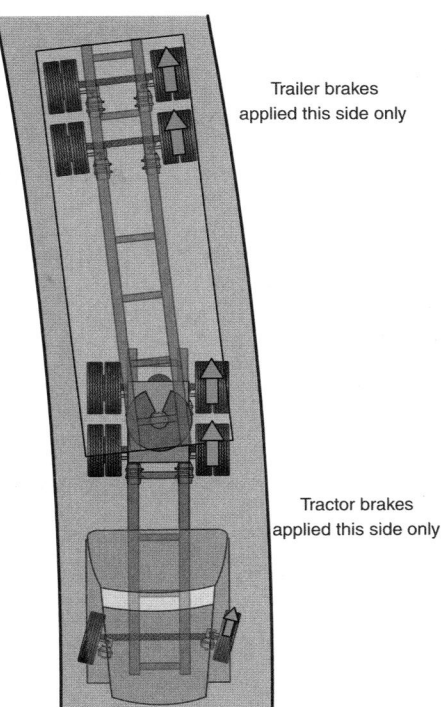

Trailer brakes
applied this side only

Tractor brakes
applied this side only

FIGURE 37-38 Braking on the side of a vehicle that is rolling over can counteract the lateral force of acceleration.

the driver's braking inputs have priority. If the driver applies the brakes at a greater force than the rollover protection system, the system switches off. Some trailer rollover stability systems can operate independently of the tractor's braking system, if the tractor is operating with or without its own stability-enhancing system.

When disconnecting or removing the steering column of a vehicle with RSC, it is important to remember that the calibration of the steering wheel angle sensor is a critical input to the RSC algorithm. Brakes can often spontaneously apply when the steering wheel is moved if the sensor adjustment or calibration is disturbed. The directional stability control system may not function properly either, which can result in a loss of vehicle control. After any service work is done to the steering system, always recalibrate and adjust the steering wheel angle sensor according to OEM procedures.

Steering Angle Sensor Calibration

A steering angle sensor is used to interpret the direction of travel using a steering wheel angle. A straight-ahead direction is 0 degree. But to correctly measure steering angle and orientate it to a straight-ahead position, the steering angle sensor must learn or requires calibration about where the steering center and right and left stops are. If the angle is incorrectly estimated, the RSC interprets the data incorrectly and spontaneously applies the brakes. Not only that, but the rollover stability feature is lost. It's important that a recalibration or relearn procedure is performed whenever:

- The steering angle sensor is replaced or removed during service.
- After completing any work on the steering column that could disturb the alignment of the sensor to the column
- After any adjustment or replacement work is completed on the steering linkage
- After a wheel alignment or wheel track
- After an accident that may have bent the steering linkage or damaged the steering angle sensor

OEM software from Bendix, such as AСom or Meritor's TOOL-BOX, are needed for recalibrating any of the vehicle dynamic control sensors (**FIGURE 37-39**).

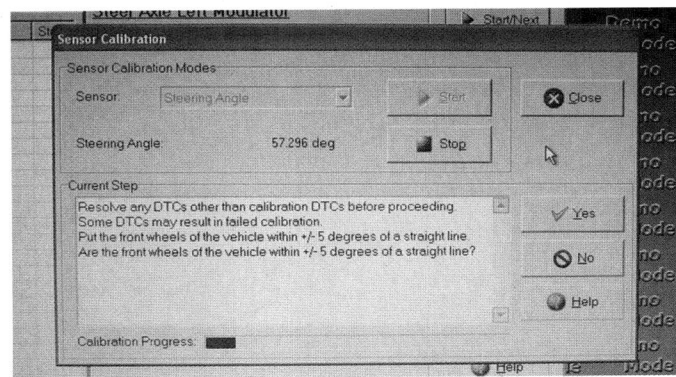

FIGURE 37-39 Sophisticated stability control systems use a steering angle sensor as an additional input. It must be calibrated any time the steering systems is serviced.

Directional Stability Control (DSC)

LO 37-7 Identify and describe the construction and operation of directional stability control systems.

Rollover stability systems work best when tires have good road traction, but when traction is poor on slippery surfaces, the risk to stability is yaw control. **Directional stability control (DSC) systems** assist the driver in maintaining a vehicle's intended driving path by controlling yaw. **Yaw** simply refers to the rotation of a vehicle around its vertical axis. It is the difference between the vehicle's steered (intended) direction and the actual direction of travel. The difference between these two directions is called the **directional slip angle**. The purpose of DSC is to increase vehicle stability during maneuvers, such as cornering and lane changes, where the slip angle is potentially highest. Commercial vehicles, having high center of gravity and heavy loads, are at risk of exaggerated yaw movement. This is particularly important travelling through curves.

Yaw Control

Ideally, there is never a difference between intended and actual direction of travel. If, however, a vehicle is moving through a curve and its tires lose traction, the tires slide sideways and the vehicle tends to spin. Good **yaw control** gives the driver the ability to steer a vehicle through a curve. Without good yaw control, in slippery conditions on a curve, or while turning at high speed, a vehicle may not respond to steering input. In fact, the vehicle may drift out of a lane, or plow out on the curve due to understeer. Or, if a trailer pushes a tractor through a curve, the tractor may rotate too much, and the vehicle jackknifes due to oversteer. **FIGURE 37-40** shows how DSC affects a vehicle traveling through a curve.

In terms of components, the lateral acceleration sensor in a rollover stability system is upgraded to a yaw sensor in a directional stability control system. As shown in **FIGURE 37-41**, directional stability control includes a steering wheel angle sensor, brake application pressure sensor, and an air supply valve to the front axle modulator valves, which operate like an ATC air valve. The use of additional sensors enables the ECU to calculate the driver's intended pathway to help steer the vehicle. A brake pressure sensor provides data for the ECU to calculate how much more or less brake application force is required to precisely control the vehicle in emergency situations. **TABLE 37-4** lists and describes the additional sensors in a DSC.

The DSC strategies select from options, such as decrease engine torque, differential braking, activate engine braking, or operate individual brakes. DSC modules are installed close to the vehicle's center of gravity and contain an internal yaw sensor. The sensor more sensitively measures lateral acceleration around the yaw axis, which is a vertical centerline through a vehicles center of gravity. Unlike the RSC lateral acceleration sensor, a yaw can detect movement in several axes of vehicle rotation using gyroscope-like sensor design. Two vibrating tuning forks change their vibration frequency relative to one another as they are turned or moved out from a vertical axis. The differences between the fork vibration frequency is translated into a signal

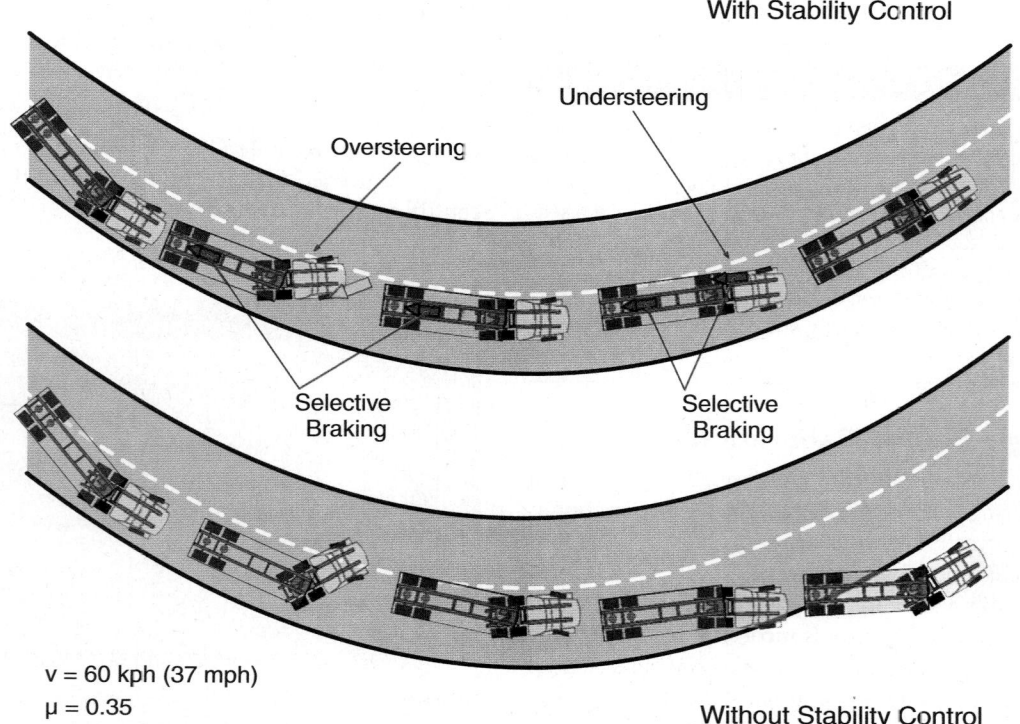

With Stability Control

Oversteering   Understeering

Selective Braking   Selective Braking

v = 60 kph (37 mph)
μ = 0.35

Without Stability Control

FIGURE 37-40 The ECU selectively applies individual brakes to maintain directional stability on a curve.

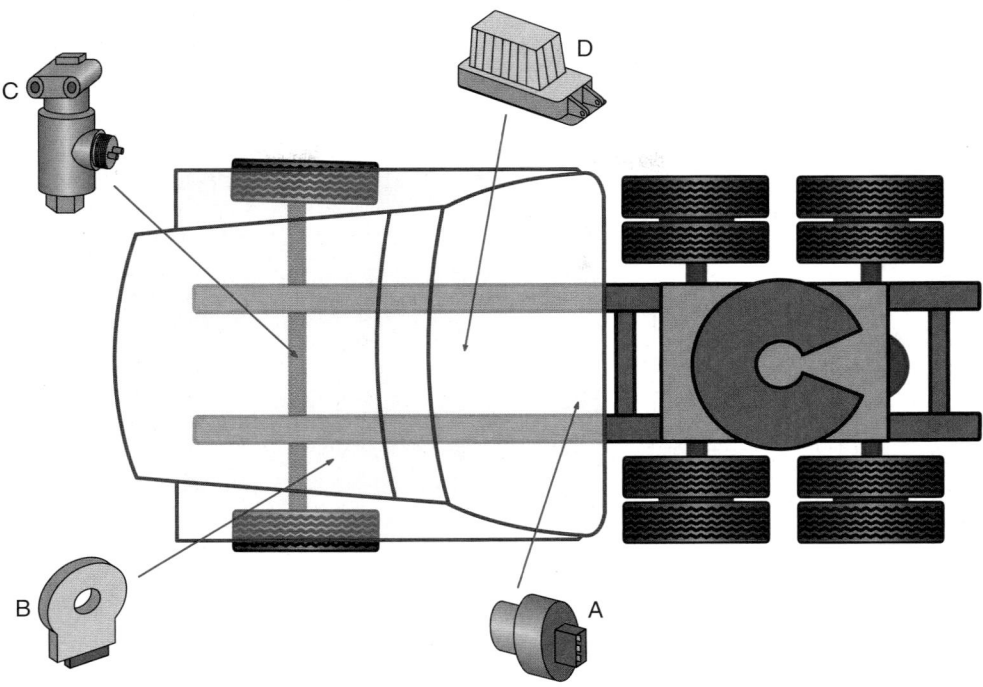

FIGURE 37-41 Components of a typical directional stability control system. **A.** Brake demand pressure sensor. **B.** Steering angle sensor. **C.** Front axle solenoid valve. **D.** ESC module.

TABLE 37-4 Additional Sensors in a Directional Stability Control System

Sensor	Purpose	Function	Application
Wheel speed sensor	Monitors the wheel rotation at individual wheels	Allows the system to determine vehicle speed and monitor wheel lockup to optimize braking	ABS, ATC, RSC, vehicle stability control
Lateral acceleration sensor (yaw sensor)	Senses the side or lateral forces acting on the vehicle		Vehicle stability control
Brake demand pressure sensor (BPS)	Senses air brake application pressure	Used to calculate lateral acceleration force	Stability control systems
Load Sensing Pressure Sensor	Senses air pressure in air springs	Supplies data to modify brake application force and timing according to vehicle load	RSC DSC vehicle stability control
Steering angle sensor (SAS)	Measures steering wheel angle	Used to calculate yaw angle	RSC, DSC stability control systems
Yaw sensor (inside the electronic stability control [ESC] module)	Processes ABS, ATC, and stability control data	Processes sensor inputs and produces output signals to modulator valves and warning lights	ABS, ATC, RSC, DSC stability control systems

proportional to the degree of yaw, roll, and pitch movement (**FIGURE 37-42**). This sensor technology explains why module installation and orientation in the chassis is critical and requires correct leveling during installation. Modules can face either the front or rear of the vehicle and contain information about the vehicle dimensions and other parameters. Modules should never be moved to a different location on the vehicle. If they are, the module must be recalibrated to learn its new position (**FIGURE 37-43**).

Collision Avoidance Systems

LO 37-8 Identify and describe the construction and operation of collision avoidance systems (CAS).

According to the National Highway Transportation Safety Administration (NHTSA), rear-end collisions account for over 20% of all heavy truck crashes. In approximately 60% of these accidents, the truck is striking another vehicle. Two common causes for these accidents are driving too fast for the conditions or following too closely.

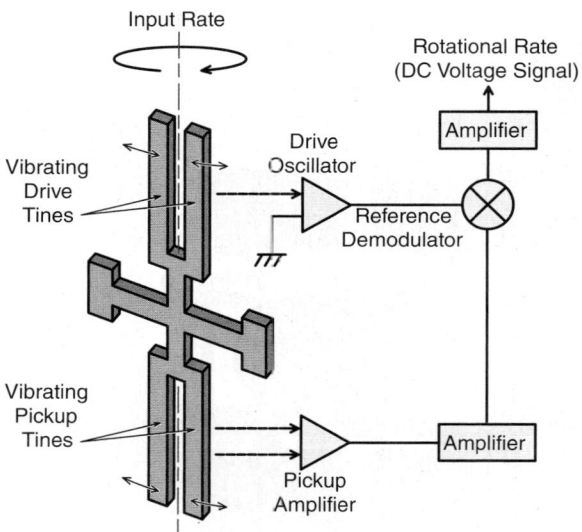

FIGURE 37-42 A functional block diagram for the operation of a Yaw sensor.

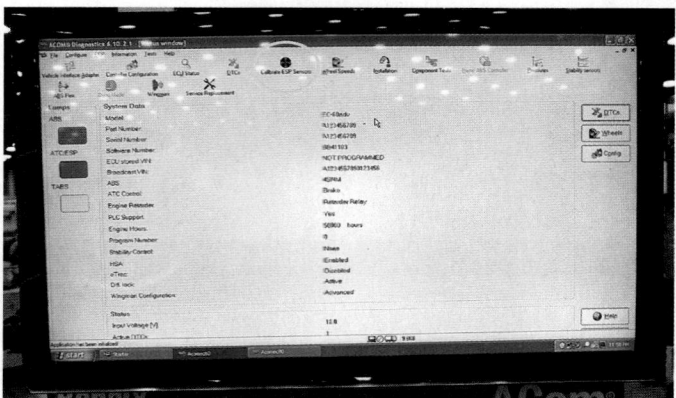

FIGURE 37-43 This version of ACom is used to recalibrate ECU position steering angle, yaw, lateral acceleration, brake demand and load pressure sensors.

FIGURE 37-44 Collision avoidance sensors. **A.** Side-mounted radar. **B.** Front-mounted radar.

Collision avoidance systems are vehicle stability control systems that detect objects beside and in front of a vehicle that have the potential to collide with the vehicle. CASs minimize the likelihood of collisions two ways. The first is by alerting the driver when a preset following distance is shortened. A second feature in some systems is to apply the vehicle's brakes to slow the truck down safely and reestablish a safe following distance. Drivers are alerted to unsafe following distances using audible alarms and by activating the engine brake.

A key component of CAS is radar that can detect fixed and moving objects from 500' (152 m) to a kilometer (0.6 miles) away. An ECU collects radar data to determine if another object or vehicle is within the detection range. The ECU calculates the distance to the lead vehicle and the difference in speeds of the two vehicles. The radar can measure the direction and distance from the target vehicle and combines that information with data about the road curvature estimated

from the tractor's measured yaw rate. The system uses an algorithm to calculate the time to collision and implements a collision avoidance strategy if an object is identified as being in the same lane as the truck. **FIGURE 37-44** shows collision avoidance radar. These sensors can monitor the area in front of a vehicle, as well as the side in the driver's blind spot. The additional blind spot located sensor can help prevent collision during lane changes.

Radar Adjustments

An unobscured view of the road and precise vertical and lateral alignment of the radar sensor on a vehicle is critical to proper operation. Radar alignment must be within the range of –0.5 degree to –2.0 degrees downward to reflect a return signal and laterally aligned to have a field of view exactly center of the vehicle. Lateral adjustment corresponds to a range of +0.8 degree from center. Misalignment in older sensors causes false warnings, prevents the systems from properly functioning, and generates a DTC if the signal doesn't reflect back to the sensor correctly. Newer sensors have some self-correcting signal capabilities. There cannot be any interference with the radio signals from any other vehicle components, such as the front bumper, animal bumpers, winter fronts, or decorations. A common problem is the front bumper of the vehicle pushes against snowbanks or parked machinery, which not only momentarily deflects the bumper, but puts the sensor out of alignment. Vertical and lateral adjustment screws are located beneath the plastic cover over the sensor. These can be adjusted with the use of proprietary diagnostic service software or with an alignment tool (**FIGURE 37-45**). To align the sensor, follow the steps in **SKILL DRILL 37-3**.

Adaptive Cruise Control (ACC)

Adaptive cruise control (ACC) is an advanced driver assistance feature providing a specialized cruise mode that enables the vehicle to recognize potential collisions with vehicles or objects it is following and reduces the vehicle speed. When the lead vehicle speeds up or changes lane, the set cruise speed resumes and the vehicle automatically speeds up. Essentially, it is a non-emergency application of the CAS. Using the CAS, a driver can set the ACC in one of two ways. The first option is to select the maximum vehicle speed with no objects in front of the vehicle. The second option regulates the cruise control speed according to vehicles in front of the truck or bus. If a vehicle is

SKILL DRILL 37-3 Aligning a Front Radar Sensor

Use the following procedure as a general guideline when inspecting or adjusting the vertical and lateral alignment of a front radar sensor for a CAS of adaptive cruise control.

1. To verify vertical radar alignment, first park the vehicle on a level floor and verify the suspension system is at the correct ride height.

2. Remove the protective front cover from the radar sensor.
3. Position the laser leveling tool over the sensor using the magnetic tripod. The radar alignment tool measures vertical alignment with a leveling bubble and lateral alignment with a laser light (see the second image).
4. After attaching the tripod to the mounting base where it straddles the sensor, check the vertical alignment bubble. Verify the leveling bubble just touches the leveling line closest to the vehicle. This should provide a one-half to two-degree angle downward.
5. Loosen the vertical alignment lock bolts and adjust the vertical alignment, if necessary. Retighten the locking bolts.
6. To verify lateral alignment: Using a tape measure or ruler, measure out from two symmetrical points on the frame that are equal distances from the radar. The receiver for tow hooks provides ideal points.
7. Switch on the lateral laser level light and aim it at the ruler or tape measure placed against the frame.
8. Observe and record the distance from the frame where the laser light reflects onto the ruler or tape measure.
9. Swivel the laser 180 degrees and aim it at the ruler or tape measure on the opposite side of the radar. Repeat step 7 and record the measurement.
10. Compare the two measurement. They must be within 1/8" (3.2 mm) of one another to have acceptable lateral alignment.
11. Reinstall the front protective cover and clear any system fault codes.

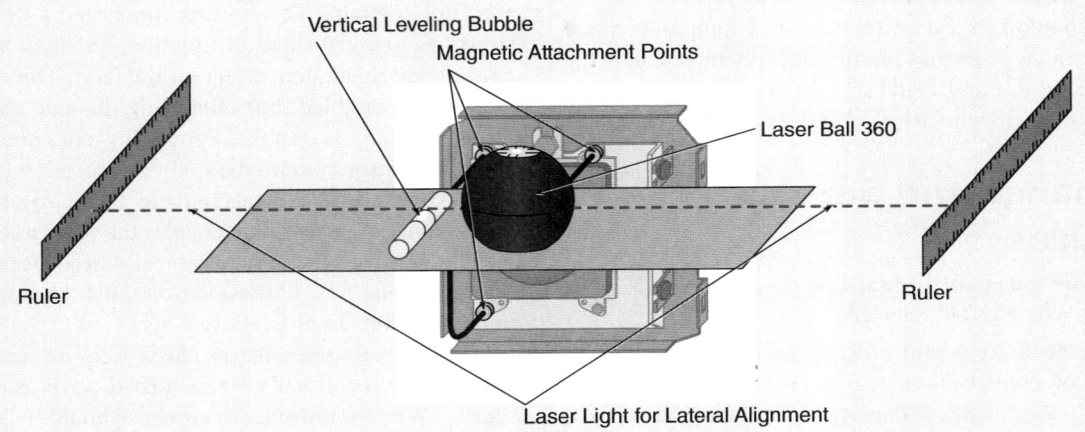

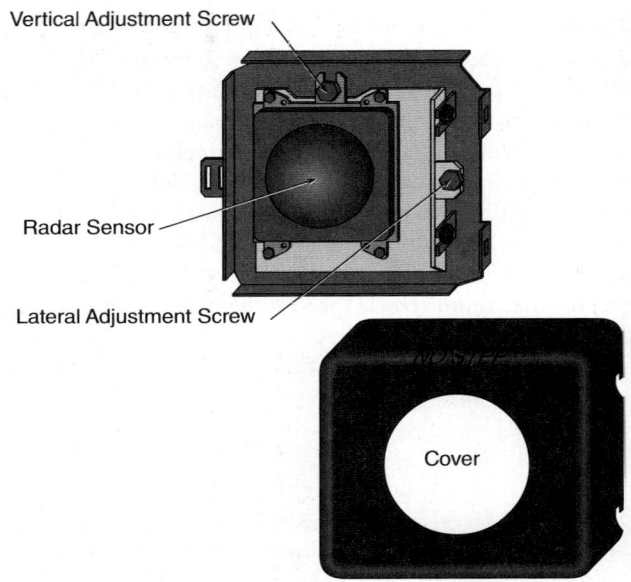

FIGURE 37-45 The lateral and vertical adjustment of the radar sensor is made using two adjustment screws.

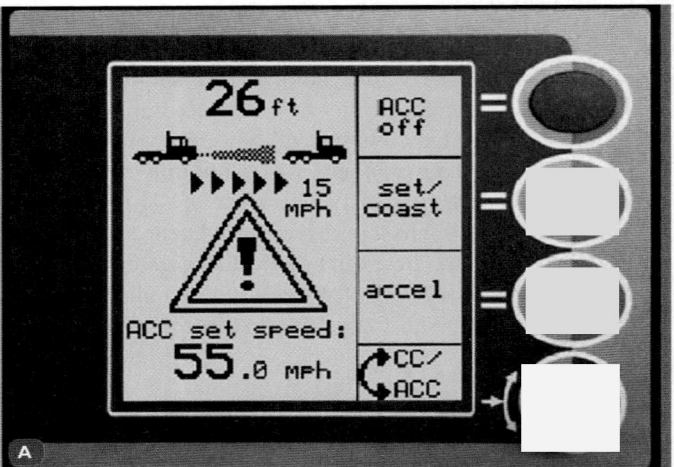

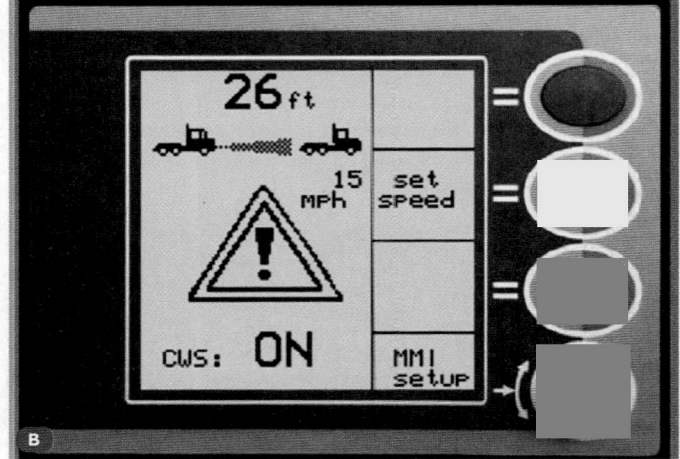

FIGURE 37-46 A screen from an ACC CAS. **A.** Under normal conditions. **B.** Alerting the driver to the activation of the CAS.

detected, the cruise control adjusts vehicle speed to maintain a safe traveling distance. The vehicle can de-rate the engine whenever the gap between two vehicles becomes too close, or it can activate the engine brake for a faster reduction in vehicle speed.

The driver operates the ACC system in a manner like conventional cruise control (CCC). Rather than selecting a constant speed for the truck to automatically maintain, with ACC, the driver is selecting a maximum speed, which the truck maintains when there is no lead vehicle in the lane in front of the truck. A display screen, such as the one shown in **FIGURE 37-46A**, keeps the driver informed about the system's status. The display indicates when the system is active and its maximum set speed. If a lead vehicle is detected, the system tells the driver of the other vehicle's presence, its speed, and the gap between the two vehicles. If the truck is closing on the lead vehicle, as shown on the screen in **FIGURE 37-46B**, the system reduces the vehicle speed to match that of the lead vehicle and maintains the following distance. To do so, the system first decreases engine torque. It can also apply a transmission retarder or engine brake, downshift the transmission (if it is automatic), and apply the service brakes. If the vehicle is closing rapidly, the system can alert the driver through audible and visual signals. When there is a fault, the display also informs the driver, and the system shuts down.

Maintenance and Service Procedures

LO 37-9 Recommend maintenance and service procedures for antilock braking, vehicle stability, and CAS.

Basic and enhanced ABSs and other stability control systems generally have no regular maintenance. OEM software displays system configuration data, active and inactive system faults, service procedures, and activates system outputs to validate operation. Calibration of various stability control system sensors is also performed by the software. **FIGURE 37-47** shows the screen from OEM software.

When a system fault is detected, ABS and ATC functions are fault tolerant. This means the systems develop adaptive strategies to allow them to function, but they may be fully or partially disabled, depending on the fault. The entire system is not usually disabled, but often only the axle with a sensor or modulator fault is disabled; remaining axles are still operating. In a four-sensor system, ABS on the affected wheel is disabled, but ABS on all other wheels remains active. In a six-sensor tractor system, one sensor fault enables the ABS to remain active by using input from the remaining rear wheel speed sensor on the same side. The ATC is, however, disabled. **TABLE 37-5** shows the impact of faults in different sensors.

Sensor adjustments on ABSs require special attention anytime the wheel ends are disturbed, such as during a brake service. When removed, sensor clips should be lubricated with dielectric-type grease. This is grease that is non-electrically conductive, not chassis grease. In some instances, sensors require special attention:

- Steering Angle Sensors (SAS)—Whenever front-end alignment or steering system work is performed, SAS need recalibration.
- Yaw Rate Sensor—Whenever the electronic control module is removed or disturbed in any way, it must be reinstalled in the same precise location and in the same orientation. A recalibration process with OEM software is used.
- Stability Control Modules—These contain an internal yaw sensor and should never be moved to a different location on the vehicle.

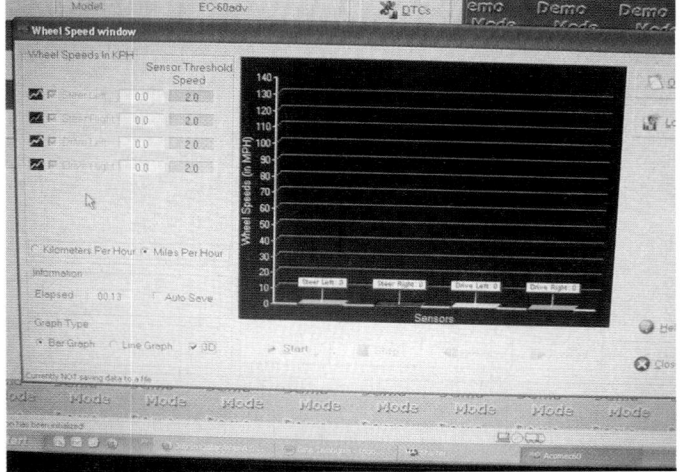

FIGURE 37-47 When servicing ABS, ATC, and ESC systems, diagnostic software is used to measure system data, such as wheel speed, as well as test output devices.

- Front Sensor of CAS—Shown in **FIGURE 37-48**, this sensor is in the front bumper and can easily be misaligned when the bumper contacts other objects. The sensor requires directional calibration to ensure it is aimed at the correct point in front of the vehicle on the roadway.
- Sensor air gap—Loss of correct sensor air gap is a common ABS-related complaint. Sensors should be checked to see whether they are firmly in place and whether loose wheel bearings may be interfering with the air gap.

Another common check to perform is on the warning lamps. Ensure the ABS malfunction lights are operating every time the vehicle is started. When the ignition is switched on, the ABS lamp should illuminate momentarily. The tractor ABS lamp can also be used to display tractor blink code diagnostics. The ATC and RSC/ESC functions may use the same dash indicator lamp, so understanding how the ABS and ATC/RSC/ESC lamps work is important. Generally, if the vehicle is equipped with ATC—but not RSC/ESC—the ABS and ATC lamps illuminate for approximately three seconds when the ignition is turned to the ON position and then both go out together. When equipped with ATC and RSC/ESC, both lamps illuminate when the ignition is switched on but the ATC/RSC/ESC lamp stays on a moment longer after the ABS lamp goes out.

Finally, the ABS/ATC control modules require a precise rolling circumference ratio between steer axle and drive axle tires for ABS and ATC to perform properly. Therefore, if tire size changes, new tire data should be entered into the system using OEM software. A default tire ratio value of 1.00 is programmed into the unit. If the automatic tire size alignment calculates a different value, the original value is overwritten in the memory to adapt the ABS and ATC function with different tire sizes on the vehicle.

TABLE 37-5 Fault Location and Impact on Antilock Braking System

| Failed Device | System Still Operating (Yes/No) | | | | | |
| | ABS Front | | ABS Rear | | Traction | Standard Braking |
	Left	Right	Left	Right		
RF Sensor	Yes	Yes	Yes	Yes	No	Yes
RM Sensor	Yes	Yes	Yes	Yes	No	Yes
LF Sensor	Yes	Yes	Yes	Yes	No	Yes
LM Sensor	Yes	Yes	Yes	Yes	No	Yes
RR Sensor	Yes	Yes	Yes	No	No	Yes
LR Sensor	Yes	Yes	No	Yes	No	Yes
RF Modulator	Yes	No	Yes	Yes	Yes	Yes
LF Modulator	No	Yes	Yes	Yes	Yes	Yes
RR Modulator	Yes	Yes	Yes	No	No	Yes
LR Modulator	Yes	Yes	No	Yes	No	Yes
Controller	No	No	No	No	No	Yes
Traction Solenoid	Yes	Yes	Yes	Yes	No	Yes
Engine Control Module[1]	Yes	Yes	Yes	Yes	No	Yes
Voltage[2]	No	No	No	No	No	Yes

[1] ABS is available in six-sensor system if mid sensor is functional.
[2] When ECM voltage or wiring "corrects" itself, system is restored.

FIGURE 37-48 The front sensor of the collision avoidance system.

▶ **TECHNICIAN TIP**

During dynamometer testing of a vehicle, the ATC must be disabled. This deactivates the ATC brake torque transfer and engine de-rate strategies used by the ECM. A test mode is used to avoid torque reduction or torque increase and brake activation when the vehicle is on a dynamometer.

Using Blink Codes

In the absence of more sophisticated electronic service tools or software, technicians can communicate with the ECU using blink codes. Codes are obtained by either cycling the ignition switch on and off, or pressing the ATC disable switch or a blink code switch. The controller has several modes that the technician can select to access fault or calibration information. Codes flash the ABS or ATC warning lights a specific number of times that corresponds to a numerical digit. A brief pause separates two-digit codes. All codes are then separated by two seconds of lamp OFF.

Diagnostic Modes

To enter the various diagnostic modes, use the following chart:

Mode	Mode Description	Description	Ignition Cycles (1 second ON/1 second OFF)
1	Simple or Wheel Speed Mode	Shortened list of up to three active codes display at one time	ON, off, ON
2	Active Faults	Displays up to nine fault codes	ON, off, ON, off, ON
3	Stored Faults/ Clear Mode	Displays all stored faults switching ignition power off and on twice during the 10 seconds of lamp energization clears codes	ON, off, ON, off, ON, off ON
4	Configuration Mode	Displays a blink code corresponding to a configuration code number listed in service literature	ON, off, ON, off, ON, off, ON, off, ON

Wrap-Up

Ready for Review

▶ Vehicle control, steering, and braking are better maintained when tires are rolling rather than locked. Antilock braking systems (ABS) monitor and automatically limit wheel lockup events during vehicle braking.

▶ Tractor jackknife or trailer swing-out condition is minimized using ABS. Jackknifing can take place when the tractor brakes lockup and the trailer pushes the tractor around the king pin. Trailer swing-out happens when the trailer brakes lock and the trailer drifts into another lane.

▶ Automatic traction control (ATC), automatic slip regulation (ASR), and electronic stability control (ESC) are names given to the same refinement to the ABS, which prevents drive wheels from slipping, losing traction, or breaking free from road contact due to excessive drive torque.

▶ Wheel speed sensors measure tire speed and are used by the ABS electronic control unit (ECU) to calculate an impending wheel lockup event.

▶ Modulator valves are electrically controlled air valves that either exhaust, hold, or build-up air pressure in the brake chambers. The ABS ECU regulates the operation of the modulator valves to limit wheel speed lockup by maintaining the optimal amount of air pressure in the service brake chambers to slow the vehicle while minimizing wheel speed lockup.

▶ The ABS malfunction light illuminates whenever a fault occurs in the ABS. Fault codes can be extracted from the ABS ECU through the ABS malfunction light, which blinks out a sequence of short and long light flashes.

▶ A tractor requires a separate in-dash malfunction indicator lamp for the trailer ABS. The trailer has a yellow ABS malfunction light located on the left, lower, rear quarter of the trailer, which illuminates whenever there is a fault in the trailer ABS.

▶ Power line carrier (PLC) for trucks is a communication technology that transmits data from the trailer ABS ECU to the tractor. The data is carried over the #7 blue wire.

▶ Power for the trailer ABS ECU is supplied by the dedicated current flow on #7 blue wire of the J-560 trailer plug. The stop lamp circuit #4 on the J-560 plug can also supply power to the trailer ABS when the brakes are applied. Trailer ABS cords are color-coded green and have different-sized conductors than non-ABS trailer cords.

▶ Wheel speed data processed by the ABS ECU is used by many other vehicle modules when it is shared over the J-1939 onboard network.

▶ Traction control systems (TCS) use ABS components plus the addition of an electrically signaled air valve, which supplies air to the modulator valve.

▶ Wheel slip caused by excessive driver torque is reduced by the TCS in two ways. The first is to reduce engine power output. The second is to apply the brakes on the wheel end that has lost traction. Braking the slipping wheel transfers torque to other wheels through the differentials.

▶ Yaw refers to the difference between the vehicle's steered direction of travel and the actual direction it is moving. A yaw sensor is used by a directional stability control system to detect whether the vehicle may slide laterally from its lane.

▶ Stability control systems help prevent vehicle rollovers. By adding a steering wheel angle sensor and a lateral acceleration rate sensor to the TCS, brakes can be selectively applied automatically to affected wheels and the engine de-rated to prevent a rollover.

▶ Directional control systems share similar hardware to stability control systems. The stability control system uses a lateral acceleration sensor, but the directional stability system uses a yaw sensor to measure the difference between the vehicle's intended steered pathway and its actual direction.

▶ Collision avoidance systems use radar technology to detect obstacles the vehicle could potentially collide with. The collision detection system can be integrated into the cruise control system to slow a vehicle down, or even brake, if a collision is impending.

Key Terms

adaptive cruise control (ACC) A specialized cruise mode that enables the vehicle to recognize potential collisions with vehicles or objects it is following and reduce the vehicle speed.

antilock braking system (ABS) An electronic control system that works with the service brake system to monitor and automatically limit wheel lockup events during vehicle braking.

automatic slip regulation (ASR) A traction control system that minimizes wheel spin.

automatic traction control (ATC) A traction control system that minimizes wheel slip or spin due to excessive drive torque. Also called *electronic stability regulation (ESR)*.

blink code A method of providing fault code data for a specific system that involves counting the number of flashes from a warning lamp and observing longer pauses between the light blinks. Also called *flash code*.

collision avoidance system (CAS) A vehicle stability control system that detects objects beside and in front of a vehicle that have the potential to collide with the vehicle.

differential braking Applying the brakes on an individual slipping wheel to transfer torque to a stationary or slowly turning wheel with traction.

Directional slip angle The difference between the vehicle's steered (intended) direction and the actual direction of travel. The difference between these two directions is called the directional slip angle.

directional stability control (DSC) systems A stability control system that assists the driver in maintaining a vehicle's intended driving path by controlling yaw.

electronic stability control (ESC) A general term for vehicle control systems that optimize braking and steering in emergency situations and minimizes the likelihood of a rollover, loss of vehicle direction, and wheel slip.

fishtailing A condition when the drive axles of a vehicle laterally push the rear of a vehicles and steering control is lost. Also called *power jackknifing*.

flash code A strategy used by ECUs to report fault codes by flashing or blinking fault lamps, using long and short pauses between the light flashes to represent numerical fault codes. Also called *blink code*.

ISO 11446 connector A type of connector commonly used in Europe that uses dedicated pins to transmit ABS information between the tractor and trailer.

jackknife A condition when the drive axles of a vehicle push the rear of a vehicle around its center point and steering control is lost. Generally caused by aggressive over braking or lockup of the trailer wheels, which folds the orientation of the combination vehicle into a shape of a pocket-knife. Also called *fishtailing*.

Modified Individual Regulation (MIR) A method to prevent brake pull of the steering caused by unequal ABS acting on the front steer axle.

power line carrier (PLC) technology A data transmission technology enabling data exchange between the tractor and trailer ABS.

reluctor wheel The toothed wheel mounted on the wheel hub, which is used by the wheel speed sensor to generate wheel speed data. Also called the *exciter ring*.

roll stability control (RSC) A vehicle control system that measures lateral acceleration of a vehicle to minimize the likelihood of a vehicle rollover.

SAE J-560 standard The SAE standards for the configuration of trailer electrical cables and plugs.

torque limiting A reduction in engine power out; used as strategy to reduce wheel slip or loss of directional control.

traction control An enhancement to the ABS that is used to improve vehicle stability when accelerating.

trailer swing-out   A situation when the trailer leaves it's lane due to aggressive or over braking of the tractor.

untripped rollovers   A vehicle rollover condition produced when an unavoidable outside disturbance causes the rollover.

variable reluctance (VR) sensor   A sensor used to measure rotational speed, including wheel speed, vehicle speed, engine speed, and camshaft and crankshaft position.

wheel lockup   A condition where the drive or steer tires have stopped rotating when braking.

wheel slip   A condition in which excess torque from the drive-train causes the tire to break free from the road surface. Also called *wheel spin*.

wheel spin   A condition in which excess torque from the drive-train causes the tire to break free from the road surface. Also called *wheel slip*.

yaw   The rotation of a vehicle around its vertical axis; the difference between the vehicle's intended direction and the actual direction of travel.

yaw control   Minimizing the slip or difference between the desired or steered direction of a vehicle and actual direction a vehicle is moving.

Review Questions

1. Which vehicle dynamic control system adds a steering angle and lateral acceleration sensor to ABS architecture?
   a. Automatic traction control
   b. Rollover stability control
   c. Collison avoidance system
   d. Directional stability control

2. Consider a tractor and semitrailer combination vehicle. If the tractor were equipped with an ABS but the trailer was not, which of the following situations would most likely occur under a hard braking condition?
   a. Jackknife
   b. Oversteer
   c. Understeer
   d. Trailer swing-out

3. What type of electrical signal is supplied to the ABS ECU by wheel speed sensors?
   a. Digital
   b. Serial data J-1939
   c. Low voltage direct current (DC)
   d. Low voltage alternating current (AC)

4. ABS modulator valves contain:
   a. an electrically controlled inlet and exhaust valve.
   b. only an electrically controlled air inlet valve.
   c. only an electrically controlled exhaust valve.
   d. a normally closed inlet and exhaust valve.

5. Traction control systems minimize wheel slip by:
   a. reducing engine power when the wheels spin.
   b. selectively applying brakes to slipping or spinning wheels.
   c. modulating brake pressure to wheels with traction.
   d. selectively braking slipping wheels and reducing engine power.

6. A lateral acceleration sensor, or "G" sensor, is a system input sensor used only by the:
   a. ABS.
   b. automatic traction control (ATC) system.
   c. roll stability control (RSC) system.
   d. directional stability control (DSC) system.

7. A yaw sensor is an input used by the directional stability control system to:
   a. detect whether the vehicle's center of gravity has become too high.
   b. measure the steering wheel angle.
   c. measure the difference between "steered" and actual vehicle direction.
   d. measure the rotation of a tractor around the trailer king pin.

8. Which of the following is the air gap setting for a typical truck wheel speed sensor?
   a. 0.005"
   b. 0.010"
   c. 0.015"
   d. There is no air gap setting.

9. Which of the following test instruments is used to measure the output signal of a wheel speed sensor?
   a. An ohmmeter
   b. A DC voltmeter
   c. An AC voltmeter
   d. An oscilloscope

10. Automatic traction control differential braking will normally not occur when which of the following conditions exist?
    a. Road speeds above 25 mph (40 kph)
    b. Road speeds below 5 mph (8 kph)
    c. Only when there is a defective front wheel speed sensor
    d. When only one wheel is spinning

ASE Technician A/Technician B Style Questions

1. Technician A says that the ABS only exhausts air pressure from a brake chamber when the wheel is about to lockup or has locked-up. Technician B says that the modulator valve can exhaust, hold, and rebuild air pressure in a service chamber when the wheels are approaching lockup or have locked-up. Who is correct?
   a. Technician A
   b. Technician B
   c. Both Technician A and Technician B
   d. Neither Technician A nor Technician B

2. Technician A says that a modulator code fault could be caused by a defective solenoid inside the valve. Technician B says a modulator fault code can be caused by a misadjusted slack adjuster. Who is correct?
   a. Technician A
   b. Technician B
   c. Both Technician A and Technician B
   d. Neither Technician A nor Technician B

3. Technician A says that an ABS trailer electrical cord is color-coded green. Technician B says that trailer electrical cords are different only as to the wire size of the conductors. Who is correct?
   a. Technician A
   b. Technician B
   c. Both Technician A and Technician B
   d. Neither Technician A nor Technician B

4. Technician A says that a rollover protection system can only use a yaw sensor. Technician B says that only a directional stability control system uses a lateral acceleration sensor. Who is correct?
   a. Technician A
   b. Technician B
   c. Both Technician A and Technician B
   d. Neither Technician A nor Technician B

5. Technician A says that wheel speed sensors are usually Hall-effect sensors. Technician B says that wheel speed sensors create a digital signal. Who is correct?
   a. Technician A
   b. Technician B
   c. Both Technician A and Technician B
   d. Neither Technician A nor Technician B

6. Technician A says that ABSs are regulated under FMVSS 121. Technician B says that every axle of a tractor-trailer system must have ABS. Who is correct?
   a. Technician A
   b. Technician B
   c. Both Technician A and Technician B
   d. Neither Technician A nor Technician B

7. Technician A says that ABSs must have a red warning lamp on the dash that lights up when an ABS malfunction occurs. Technician B says the ABS warning lamp must come on for a few seconds when the key is switched on and then go out if the system is functioning correctly. Who is correct?
   a. Technician A
   b. Technician B
   c. Both Technician A and Technician B
   d. Neither Technician A nor Technician B

8. Technician A says that, since March 2001, vehicles that tow ABS-equipped trailers must show a trailer ABS malfunction on a dash indicator light. Technician B says that trailer ABSs communicate with the tractor by using power line carrier technology. Who is correct?
   a. Technician A
   b. Technician B
   c. Both Technician A and Technician B
   d. Neither Technician A nor Technician B

9. Technician A says that tractor ABS modulator valve solenoids are cycled when the ignition is first turned on. Technician B says that applying the brake pedal and then switching the ignition on allows the operator to check that the solenoids are exhausting air as they should. Who is correct?
   a. Technician A
   b. Technician B
   c. Both Technician A and Technician B
   d. Neither Technician A nor Technician B

10. Technician A says that blink codes must always be used to check for ABS malfunctions. Technician B says that ABS wheel sensor air gap is set by loosening a lock nut and then adjusting the gap. Who is correct?
    a. Technician A
    b. Technician B
    c. Both Technician A and Technician B
    d. Neither Technician A nor Technician B

CHAPTER 38

Fundamentals of Hydraulic and Air-Over-Hydraulic Braking Systems

Learning Objectives

After reading this chapter, you will be able to:

- **LO 38-1** Identify and explain the features and advantages of hydraulic power brake systems.
- **LO 38-2** Categorize and describe the types of hydraulic brake system configurations.
- **LO 38-3** Describe and explain the purpose, advantages, and construction of brake-by-wire hydraulic brake systems.
- **LO 38-4** Describe the construction and operation of conventional hydraulic brake systems.
- **LO 38-5** Identify and describe the properties of hydraulic brake fluid.
- **LO 38-6** Identify, and describe the components of hydrualic foundation braking systems.
- **LO 38-7** Describe and explain the construction and operation of wheel cylinders.
- **LO 38-8** Identify and explain the advantages and features of disc brake systems.
- **LO 38-9** Identify and describe the types, construction, and operation of hydraulic brake power assist systems.
- **LO 38-10** Identify and describe the construction, and operation of a hydraulic brake antilock braking system (HABS).
- **LO 38-11** Identify and describe the components, construction, and operation of a full power hydraulic brake system.
- **LO 38-12** Describe the purpose, construction, and operation of parking brake and emergency braking systems.
- **LO 38-13** Outline the steps and procedures for a hydraulic brake system inspection.

You Are the Technician

As a technician in an urban truck repair facility, many of the service center's work involves the repair of single-axle straight trucks operating as pick-up and delivery vehicles in urban cores. Because the trucks have short life cycles in this severe service and are in Class 4–6 range, the busy independent business owner-operator will choose less complex hydraulic brakes. Frequent stopping and starting and hard braking are common to this type of vocational operation, resulting in more frequent brake service. And, one of the most frequent braking complaints to diagnose and service is a low-brake pedal. A package delivery truck has arrived with a low brake pedal complaint and a brake warning light is on. As you consider preparing an estimate for brake work after diagnosing the brake system problems, outline the following:

1. List the most likely causes for the low-brake pedal.
2. What conditions are likely to illuminate the brake warning light?
3. What steps are required to bleed the antilock brake system (ABS) brake modulator valves?

Introduction

The basic concept of hydraulic brakes uses the force the driver's leg applies to the brake pedal and distributes it to the brakes at each wheel end through a hydraulic component known as a master cylinder. When the master cylinder has pedal force applied to it, an internal hydraulic piston moves and pressurizes brake fluid inside the cylinder (**FIGURE 38-1**). Pressure is distributed through hydraulic brake lines connected to braking components at each wheel. Brake fluid pressure acts on hydraulically operated slave cylinders or **caliper pistons** at each wheel, which either squeezes brake pads against a turning rotor or pushes brake shoes against a rotating brake drum.

In contemporary brake systems, driver effort to apply the brakes is assisted by a vacuum, air, or hydraulic servo mechanism that multiples the driver's input force at the brake pedal. These servo systems are called power assist systems that form hydraulic power brakes (HPBs). HPBs not only reduce the pedal effort needed to apply the brakes, but also reduce stopping distances.

Hydraulic brakes, like other vehicle systems, have undergone major technological changes. Stopping distance requirements first introduced in the 1980s were progressively shortened to today where a maximum stopping distance is limited to of 230" (70 m) from 62 mph (100 kph). However, the latest heavily loaded hydraulically braked vehicle can now commonly stop in less than 4 seconds over 177" (54 m) from a 60 mph (99 kph) speed. Mandatory use of antilock brakes was added in 1999. Adding collision avoidance and stability control systems have incorporated the vehicle controller area network (CAN) into braking, and now an Advanced Driver Assistance System (ADAS) uses an electric actuator to regulate brake fluid pressure from the master cylinder based on an integrated pedal stroke sensor and input signals from CAN communication. With new ADAS features added to hydraulic braking systems, not only do technicians need to be competent in traditional service and maintenance practices, but also require new skills related to understanding the operation, servicing, and diagnostic techniques

for braking systems having advanced electronic controls. Transfer of these skills and knowledge is necessary to service hydraulic clutch controls and hydraulic and electric trailer brakes, which share operating principles with the conventional braking system (**FIGURE 38-2**). To help technicians develop the necessary skills to work with all these systems, this chapter examines the conventional hydraulic brake systems operation and service. More advanced information about the latest brake-by-wire hydraulic braking systems provides the information to develop service practices related to advanced driver assistance features of hydraulic brakes.

Features and Advantages of Hydraulic Power Brakes

LO 38-1 Identify and explain the features and advantages of hydraulic power brake systems.

Hydraulically operated brakes are a common braking system used on medium-duty trucks, school buses, and motor homes with gross vehicle weights up to Class 7—33,000 lb. Unlike vehicles equipped with air brakes, a separate driver's licensing system is not needed to qualify drivers to operate vehicles with hydraulic brakes, which makes hydraulic brakes popular for rental trucks, urban delivery vehicles, and motor homes.

A more significant advantage for hydraulic brakes over air brakes is the use of highly pressurized brake fluid to apply drum or disc foundation brakes (**FIGURE 38-3**). Because hydraulic brakes are applied using higher pressures of between 700 psi (4826 kPa) to over 2300 psi (15,858 kPa), hydraulic components are more powerful and compact, and the overall system weighs much less than an air brake system. The complexity and cost of air supply systems, valving, and brake lines is comparatively less for a hydraulic braking system. Brake lag, the time delay between applying the brakes and when actual braking force occurs, is shorter too. Lag is mostly caused by delay in the transmission of braking application force through fluid or air.

Delay is insignificant for faster moving and more powerful pressure waves of hydraulic fluids. Compared to the almost instantaneous transmission of hydraulic pressure, air brakes require

FIGURE 38-1 A master cylinder is at the center of a hydraulic brake system. It is mounted on the firewall in front of the driver.

FIGURE 38-2 A clutch and brake bulkhead module for a tilt cab medium-duty truck.

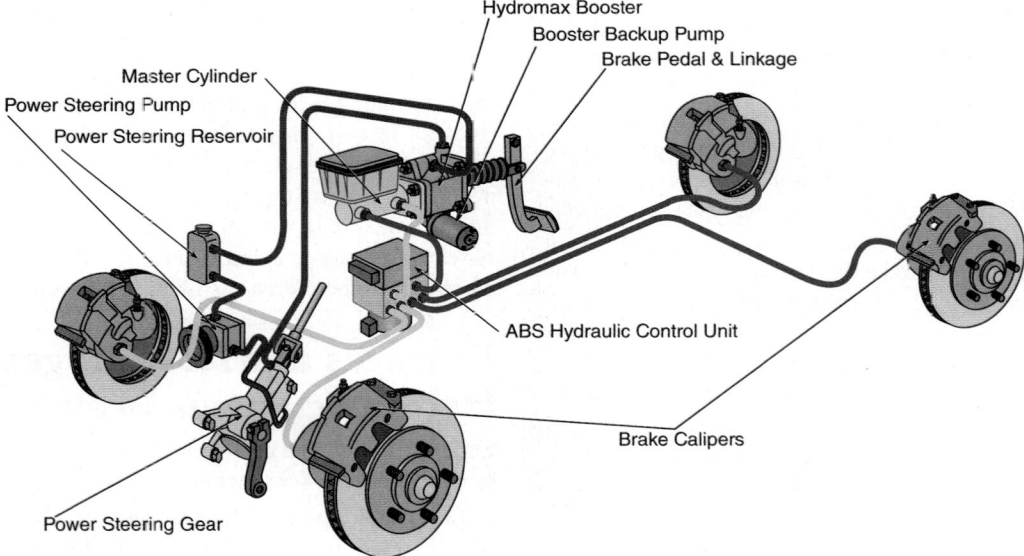

FIGURE 38-3 A typical hydraulic brake system configuration on a medium-duty truck or bus with disc brakes.

more time to build up and deliver adequate air volume to multiple brake chambers before brakes are fully applied. This means brake pedal response is faster, and stopping distances are potentially shorter, using hydraulic brakes. The solid column of fluid connecting the brake components at the wheel transmits better brake "feel" or braking action feedback to the driver. Transfer of force through hydraulic fluid also translates into less mechanical movement and accompanying wear and deterioration in a hydraulic system compared to air-operated systems. And because the driver supplies the force to push hydraulic fluid through the system when brakes are applied, the complexity of adding a compressor, air reservoirs, and conditioning the air to remove moisture and contaminants is eliminated, along with a greater number of additional maintenance requirements required by air brakes compared to hydraulic brakes.

In addition to the benefits provided by hydraulic brake systems, the latest hydraulic brake system incorporates advanced electronic control features and advanced driver assistance systems, such as:

- Collision avoidance and stability control assistance
- Antilock braking system (ABS)
- Drag torque control (DTC) (disabling of the engine retarder by the ABS)
- Electronic brake dorce distribution (EBD) (provides opt-mal brake balance to each wheel end or axle)
- Four-wheel automatic traction control (ATC)
- Hill holding capability
- Electrically operated power parking brakes
- Electronic control of for ADAS systems

Hydraulic Braking System Configurations

LO 38-2 Categorize and describe the types of hydraulic brake system configurations.

Hydraulic braking systems use hydraulic pressure or fluid power to transmit braking force, supplied by the driver, to

FIGURE 38-4 Disc brakes, consisting of a rotor caliper and brake pads, are the most common brake foundation used on commercial vehicles since 2005.

wheel end braking components. As vehicle weights increase, more force is required to apply the brakes to produce safe controlled stops. Development of braking systems that supplement the driver's braking efforts and skills helps categorize the various configurations of hydraulic brake systems. In addition to the effort and/or technology used by driver assistance systems, hydraulic brake systems are classified according to the type of foundation braking system used at the wheel ends. Brake foundations use either drums and shoes or disc brakes using a brake rotor with calipers and brake pads (**FIGURE 38-4**). **Servo mechanisms**, which are simply electrical, mechanical, or hydraulic force multipliers, are used to supplement the driver's braking effort. Servos use a smaller or weaker driver pedal force and multiply force through a servo mechanism to increase brake application pressure. Another name for a servo mechanism used by hydraulic brake systems is a **brake booster**. On

Dual Diaphragm
Vacuum Booster

Brake Fluid
Reservoir

Fluid Level
Sensor

Master Cylinder

Brake Pedal
Push Rod

FIGURE 38-5 A dual chamber vacuum booster and master cylinder for a Class 5 truck chassis using a gasoline engine.

hydraulic brake systems, the challenge of servo brake booster is to multiply braking effort proportional to the driver's pedal effort or brake pedal application force. Servo brake booster types include vacuum- and air-powered boosters, hydraulic pump boosters driven by either an electric motor or combined with pressurized hydraulic fluid from the power steering pump. Power assistance systems include:

- Vacuum assisted (Bendix Hydro-Vac)
- Hydraulically assisted with electric pump backup (Delco Hy-Power, Bosch-Bendix Hydro-Max)
- Hydraulically assisted with a gas accumulator backup (Bosch/Bendix Hydro-Boost Meritor WABCO HPB)
- Combined hydraulic and vacuum assistance (Delco Dual Power)
- Air-over-hydraulic assistance (indirect and direct acting)
- Full brake power systems (Wabco: Navistar, Freightliner)

Safety regulations for braking systems mandating minimum stopping distances and antilock braking mean contemporary brake systems only use disc brakes and electrohydraulic assisted brakes, which provide power assistance even when the engine is not operating.

Vacuum Boosters

The **vacuum-boosted** hydraulic braking system reduces the amount of pedal pressure or driver effort needed for braking. Pedal effort is supplemented by force applied by one or more large diaphragms enclosed in a round metal cannister (**FIGURE 38-5**). The diaphragm multiplies the driver's pedal application force acquired through a vacuum servo arrangement. A pressure differential of atmospheric pressure on one side of the diaphragm and the low pressure supplied by a vacuum pump or engine vacuum available below the throttle plate of gasoline engine is used to generate servo force. While vacuum-boosted brakes are still commonly used on automobiles, they have not been used by most medium-duty commercial vehicles since the 1980s. The lack of power assistance supplied by an engine or engine-driven

vacuum pump when the engine was shut off limited a vacuum-boosted system's safety, effectiveness and reliability. Compared to a hydraulic-assisted braking system, vacuum-boosted assistance is mechanically more complex, not as powerful, and unable to meet stopping distance requirements. When the vehicle engine is a diesel without the availability of intake manifold vacuum, a vacuum pump is required, along with a dash-mounted vacuum gauge and warning system indicating the availability of vacuum and a driver alert for low vacuum.

Hydraulically Assisted Braking Systems

Hydraulically assisted braking reduces driver pedal effort using pressurized hydraulic fluid to supplement the driver's pedal effort. Either gas accumulators storing hydraulic pressure built-up by electric motors or engine-driven hydraulic pumps are used to provide servo power assistance (**FIGURE 38-6**). Various marketing names are used by system suppliers; however, one of the most common uses hydraulic pressure supplied by the vehicle's power steering pump and a hydraulic accumulator to provide the servo power assistance when the engine is off or stalled. Contemporary vehicles with a hydraulic brakes back-up the power steering pumps assistance with a separate electrohydraulic pump integrated into the master cylinder. In either system, when the driver presses the brake pedal, a valve controlling the release of hydraulic pressure supplies pressurized fluid to multiply the driver's pedal application force. Pressurized hydraulic fluid combines with the driver's pedal force to push brake fluid to the hydraulic wheel end components to reduce the driver's brake application effort.

Air-over-Hydraulic Braking Systems

Air-over-hydraulic braking systems are another servo-assisted braking systems that are no longer used. Long vehicle service life, combined with the widespread use of the systems made primarily by original equipment manufacturers (OEMs), such

Brake Pedal Pushrod

Power Steering Pump Booster

Nitrogen Gas Accumulators

Master Cylinder

FIGURE 38-6 This combination hydraulic power assist and master cylinder circulates power steering fluid through the booster. Brake fluid reservoir attachment points are circled.

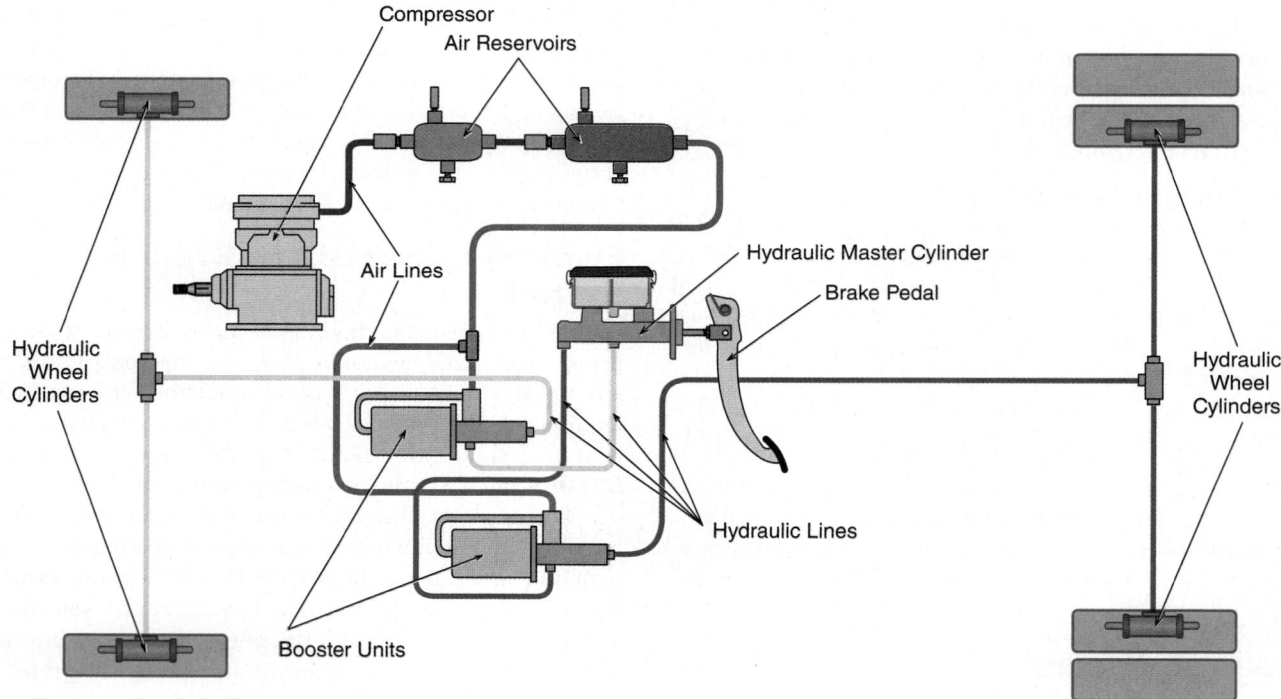

Compressor

Air Reservoirs

Hydraulic Master Cylinder

Brake Pedal

Air Lines

Hydraulic Wheel Cylinders

Hydraulic Wheel Cylinders

Hydraulic Lines

Booster Units

FIGURE 38-7 A direct acting air-over-hydraulic system uses brake fluid pressure to signal an air control valve. Air pressure then applies force to the master cylinder piston to provide power assistance to reduce brake pedal effort.

as Hino and Mitsubishi, means many of these vehicles are still in service. These systems used pressurized air supplied by an engine-driven air compressor to reduce driver pedal effort. Air-over-hydraulic systems were available in two different configurations based on the type of control circuit used to apply the brakes. Either hydraulic pressure supplied by a pedal-operated cylinder is used to signal an air-operated servo piston applying application force to the master cylinder or a foot-operated air valve supplied actuation pressure to a master cylinder (**FIGURES 38-7** and **38-8**).

Both air-over-hydraulic systems need the same air brake supply system components as full air brake systems, which are covered in the chapter on Air Brake Foundation Systems and Air Brake Circuits—a compressor, air dryer reservoir tanks, and lines.

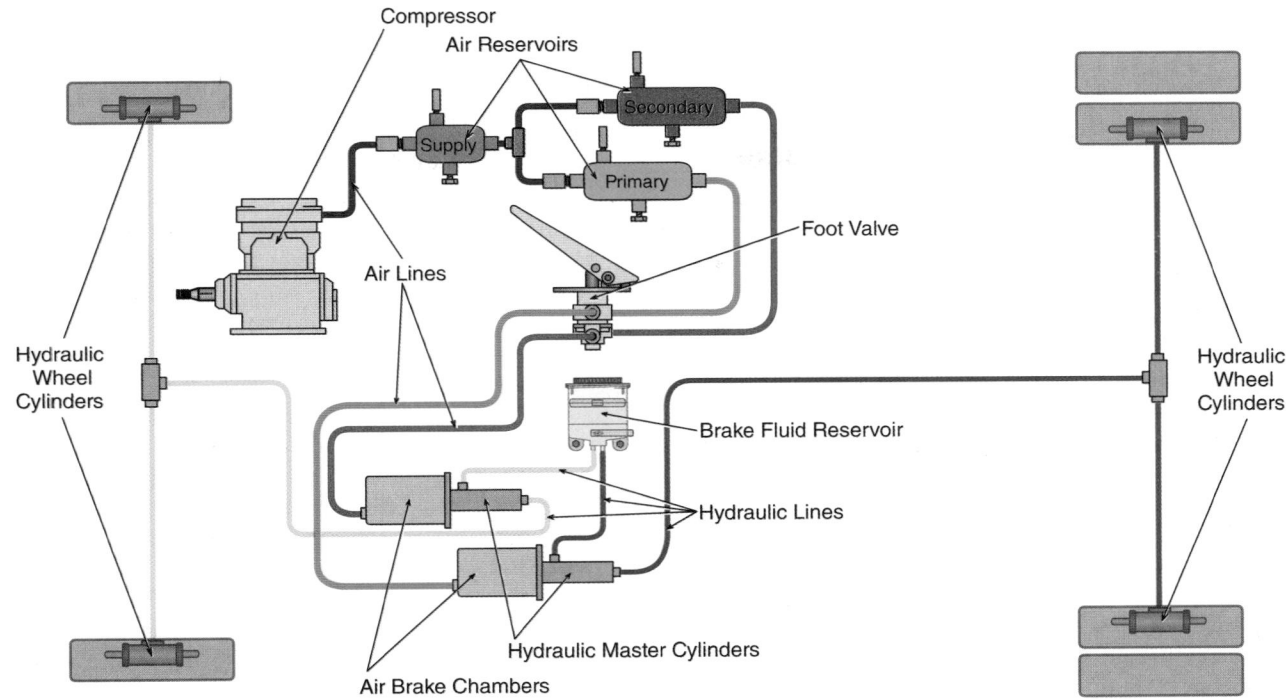

FIGURE 38-8 An indirect acting type booster is the second type of air-over-hydraulic system control uses an air-operated foot valve to control air pressure operating a master cylinder.

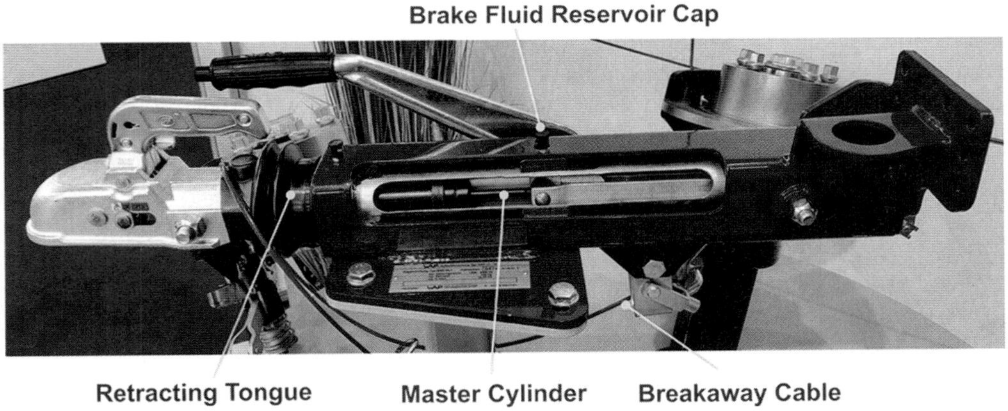

Brake Fluid Reservoir Cap

Retracting Tongue   Master Cylinder   Breakaway Cable

FIGURE 38-9 Surge brakes use the inertia force of a decelerating trailer to compress a pushrod of a master cylinder supplying brake pressure to trailer brakes.

Surge Braking Systems

When a hydraulically braked vehicle is towing a trailer heavy enough to require its own braking system, the trailers must be equipped with a braking system. Surge brakes are one type of trailer hydraulic braking system that operate using the deceleration force of the trailer generated when the tow vehicle brakes. Attached to the tongue of a trailer with surge brakes is a master cylinder with linkage that compresses the master cylinder pushrod against the drawbar, forcing brake fluid through the brake lines to the wheel cylinders (**FIGURE 38-9**). When equipped with a trailer breakaway safety device, the master cylinder on the trailer has a cable attached to the tow unit. If the cable is pulled during a trailer separation, a safety mechanism trips, causing the master cylinder to apply the trailer brakes. When backing a trailer up a grade or incline, the brakes can apply and prevent reverse movement. To eliminate this natural action, a braking override feature in manually activated to prevent the brakes from applying.

Trailers also use a hydraulic braking system operated remotely by an electronic brake controller located in the cab of the tow vehicle. A hydraulic pump on the trailer is used to force brake fluid to the brakes at the correct pressure to match the tow vehicle's deceleration rate. The controller uses a pendulum-type sensor that detects a change in vehicle inertia. Voltage proportional to the inertia created during deceleration signals the hydraulic pump.

Electric Trailer Brakes

Trailers also use electric brakes that do not use hydraulic brake circuits but share similar components to hydraulic drum brakes. Instead of activating brakes using a master cylinder, electric trailers are energized by an electronic brake controller typically located in the tow vehicle cab. The controller senses the rate of deceleration and advanced controllers have other input signals from vehicle CAN communications. After processing the signals, the controller sends direct current (DC) to electromagnets in each wheel end proportional to the deceleration rate or braking force of the tow vehicle. When energized to no more than 12 volts, the electromagnet drags along the inner vertical surface of the drum face. Because the electromagnet is attached to a lever that pries against the primary brake shoe, the brakes are applied with force proportional to the magnetic field strength. A stronger magnetic force creates more drag between the drum and magnet, pulling the actuating lever with increased force. The secondary shoe is applied by movement of the primary shoe (**FIGURE 38-10**).

Electric brake controllers require calibration to increase or decrease what is called the controller gain. Increasing gain raises controller output voltage while decreasing gain does the opposite. A controller's gain should be adjusted to achieve the highest braking force without locking up the wheels when braking.

Full Brake Power Systems

The Hydraulic Power Brake system by Wabco, called Full Power Brake system by Navistar, is used by Class 4–7

vehicles, including Freightliner models. This system does not use hydraulic pressure supplied by the power steering pump for servo brake force assistance. Instead, it uses two electric motors to store pressurized brake fluid inside nitrogen gas-charged accumulators (**FIGURE 38-11**). The system uses a conventional master cylinder and another unique electronically controlled major hydraulic component called the hydraulic compact unit (HCU) that supplies pressurized brake fluid to the brake calipers. Pressurized fluid is delivered according to brake fluid pressure signals supplied by the master cylinder and advanced control algorithms. Essentially, the master cylinder provides only pilot signals to open and close hydraulic relay valves inside the HCU. The HCU is mounted on the chassis and can integrate signals from the master cylinder and other chassis system control modules to provide ABS, stability, and traction control features, plus electronic brake force distribution. Electronic brake force distribution adjusts brake pressure to each caliper, or according to axle loading, to achieve balanced brake application force on each wheel end. The use of either eight or an optional 10 control valves in the HCU determines if the control unit can maintain proper brake balance at each wheel end or two wheel ends and an axle plus enable ATC control. Another optional features appearing with the Full Power Braking System is the Spring Applied/Hydraulic Release, or SAHR power parking brake system built by Bosch. Drag torque control and hill holding capabilities can also be integrated into the HCU operation. Because brake application pressure signals are transmitted by CAN communications, the advanced electronic control module in this system potentially has the capability to "brake by wire," which means it could initiate driverless brake applications by integrating signals from the collision avoidance systems, much like it already does for ATC. Autonomous and semi-autonomous braking capabilities are a small developmental step for this system.

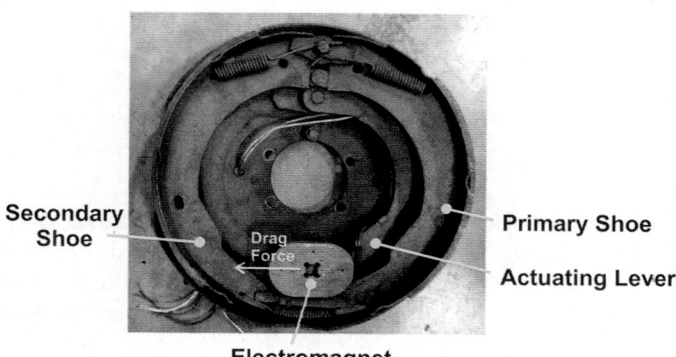

FIGURE 38-10 When energized by a brake controller, the electromagnet drags along the brake drum face and pulls an actuating lever that applies the brakes.

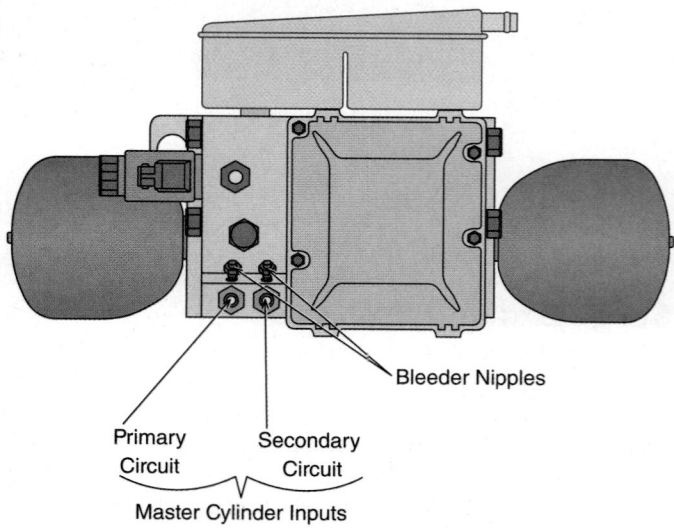

FIGURE 38-11 The Hydraulic Compact Unit (HCU) from Wabco.

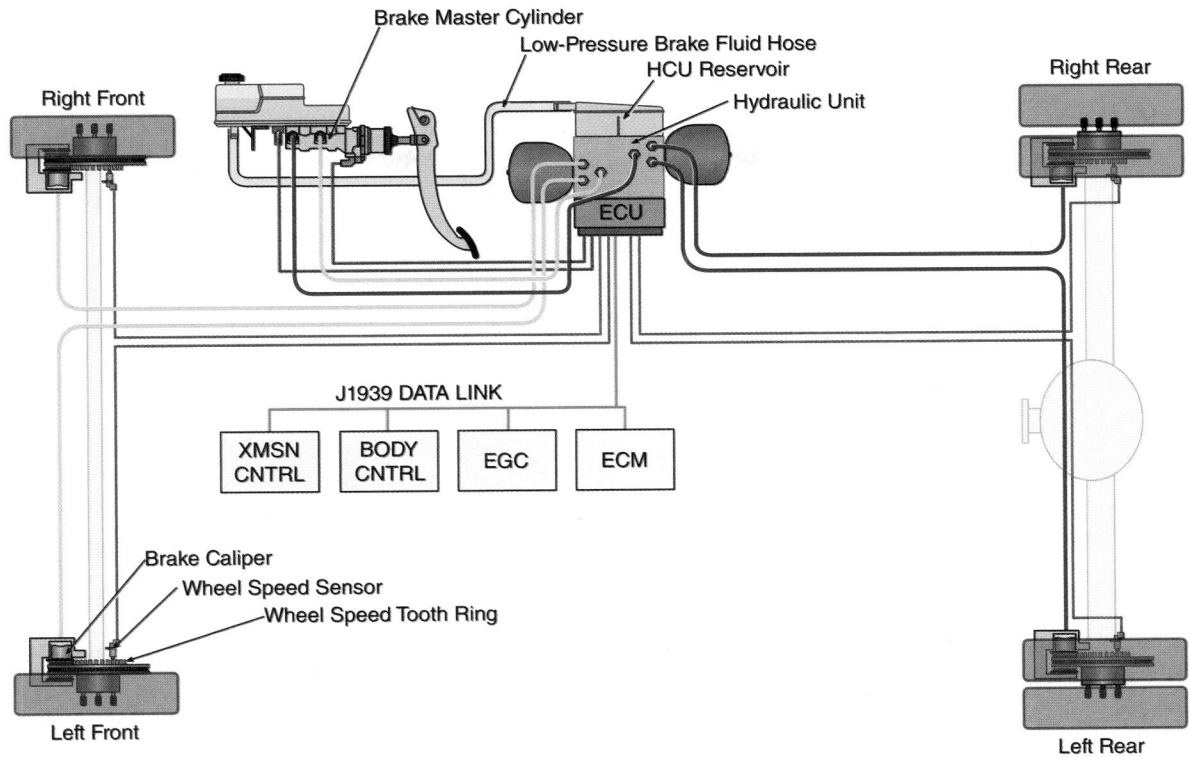

FIGURE 38-12 CAN data input from other control system modules to the Full Power hydraulic brake system control unit can add new features and enhance braking effectiveness.

Brake-by-Wire Braking Systems

LO 38-3 Describe and explain the purpose, advantages, and construction of brake-by-wire hydraulic brake systems.

Brake-by-wire technologies enable faster hydraulic brake response by eliminating delays in brake application force introduced by mechanical components. Using electrical signals supplied to valves and components located closer to the wheel ends, rather than hydraulic pressure from a distant master cylinder, provides faster and more precise brake system response. Using CAN communication from other control modules, input variables from the engine and transmission can enhance brake balance and add new features, such as disengagement of an engine retarder if wheel slip is detected or provide hill assist braking to prevent vehicle rollback on inclines (**FIGURE 38-12**). In North America, brake-by-wire technology cannot eliminate completely the hydraulic system operated by the driver since legislation requires a backup or redundant braking system in the safety-critical brake systems in the event of a failure in the electronic system. However, with the introduction of ADAS systems featuring autonomous intelligent cruise control as part of the evolution or development of fully autonomous vehicles, brake-by-wire systems are expected to appear side by side with conventional mechanical, driver-actuated, braking systems. Electric vehicles using regenerative braking also simulate brake "feel" or feedback to the driver through the pedal using electronic actuators that can "push back" against the driver's effort,

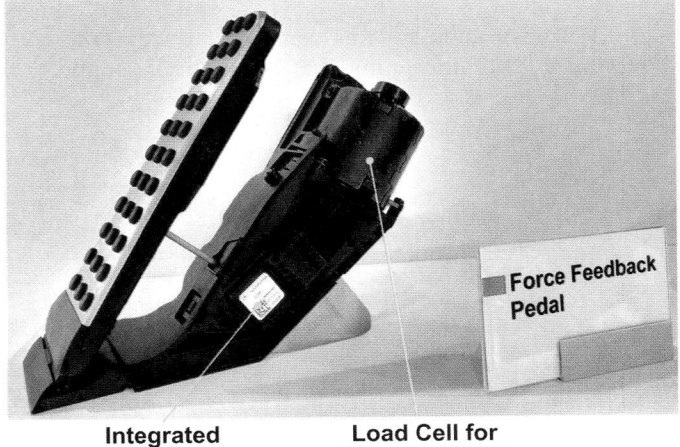

FIGURE 38-13 Vehicles with regenerative braking use a brake pedal with an integrated stroke sensor and provide haptic feedback or force to simulate brake feel.

modeling regenerative braking with the feel of hydraulic braking (**FIGURE 38-13**).

Brake-by-wire is a mature technology when applied to electronic power parking brakes (**FIGURE 38-14**). These brakes can eliminate cables and levers controlling the parking brake mechanism located inside a drum in the driveline or wheel end. The SAHR brake is one example, but many medium-duty vehicles also integrate electric parking brake control into calipers. Either an electric actuator mechanically applies the brakes using a motorized mechanism built into the brake caliper or the park brake is applied using a short cable or drum brake mechanism (**FIGURE 38-15**). These systems can integrate with idle stop systems to hold the vehicle automatically when the engine shuts off or if a hill-hold assist function is enabled. They can then automatically release the parking brake when the vehicle is commanded to move again. Electronically controlled park brakes can even integrate with collision avoidance systems to apply the brakes to prevent or minimize the severity of a collision by automatically applying the park brakes when commanded by the collision avoidance system through CAN communication.

Brake-by-Wire System Construction

Three fundamental configurations used to construct brake-by-wire systems include, but are not limited to:

- Electric-only systems using brake caliper clamping rotors with high-speed electric motors used to apply and release brake pads (**FIGURE 38-16**). While no brake fluid is necessary, a redundant hydraulic circuit can be maintained in the caliper to apply the brakes under driver control when the electric system has failed. Because the caliper controls the braking event and supplies electronic control feedback to a control unit, these systems require several additional feedback control devices, including brake temperature, clamping force, and actuator position sensors in each caliper.
- Electrohydraulic systems using an electronically controlled hydraulic pump that builds brake application

pressure using power from electric motors. The system stores pressurized brake fluid used for brake application in gas-charged accumulators. Brake applications are controlled by signaling fast-responding hydraulic control valves.

- Electromechanical system using a conventional braking system with an electronically controlled but powerful brake actuator applying brake force though a master cylinder. These systems are currently used in off-road vehicles and in electric and hybrid electric vehicles.

Sensor and data inputs for brake-by-wire systems include:

- Wheel speed sensor
- Electric vehicle battery state of charge
- Yaw and steering angle
- Brake pedal stroke sensor
- Master cylinder pressure
- Brake caliper hydraulic pressure or clamping force sensors
- Brake caliper motor position and speed sensors
- Vehicle speed and throttle position

Electromechanical Braking

In current hybrid electric vehicles using brake-by-wire systems, a braking event begins with the vehicle operator pressing the brake pedal. A pedal stroke sensor measures the pedal travel distance and speed and compares it to models of braking situations, such as a panic stop or normal braking. A hydraulic actuator converts pedal movement into proportional braking pressure applied to the master cylinder piston. Advanced control algorithms can integrate data from vehicle sensors to provide antilock braking, vehicle stability, and traction control.

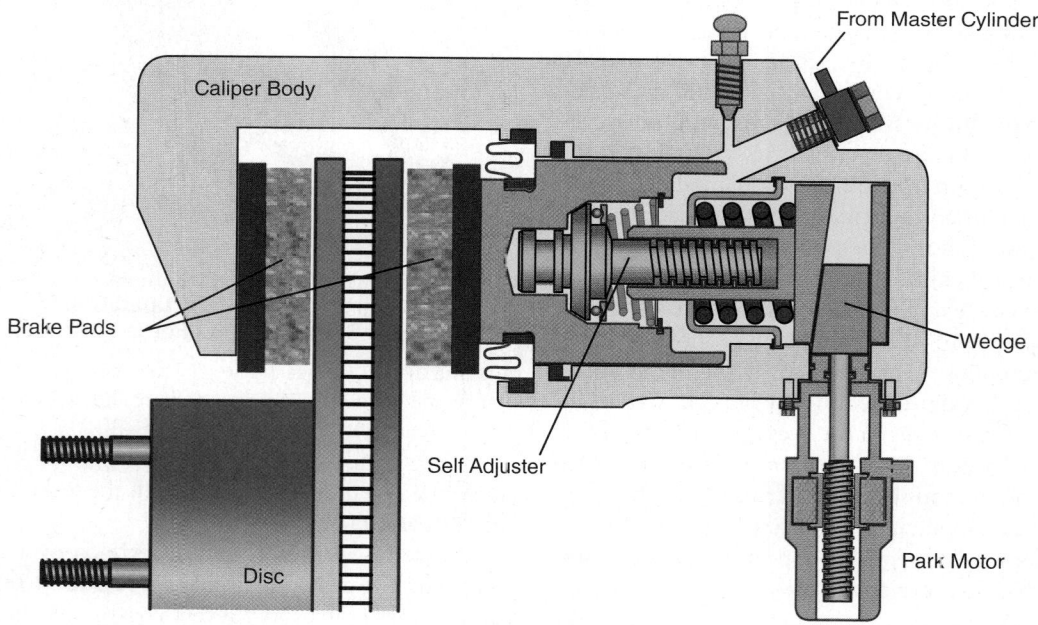

FIGURE 38-14 Basic electrically operated hand brake.

FIGURE 38-15 This fixed piston-type caliper uses either an electric actuator or hydraulic fluid to apply and release the parking brake cable.

FIGURE 38-16 This brake-by-wire caliper uses high-speed actuators to apply the brakes faster than hydraulic fluids using only electrical signals.

Conventional Hydraulic Braking Systems

LO 38-4 Describe the construction and operation of conventional hydraulic brake systems.

All hydraulic braking systems on medium-duty commercial vehicles include the following major components:

- A brake pedal or lever
- A master cylinder assembly containing a piston assembly (made up of either one or two pistons, a series of seals, O-rings, and a fluid reservoir)
- Brake fluid
- Hydraulic brake lines
- A brake warning system
- Brake foundations of either disc or drum and shoe brakes. Disc brake assemblies at each of the wheels consist of a brake caliper that clamps or pinches a pair of brake pads onto a **rotor** (which is also known as a brake disc) or **wheel cylinders** that push **brake shoes** into **brake drums**

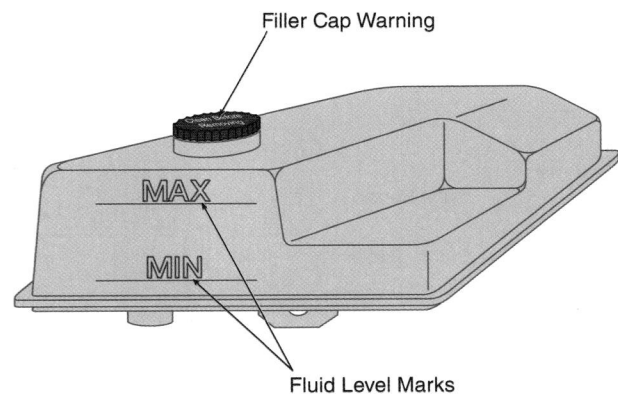

FIGURE 38-17 A master cylinder reservoir must have a minimum and maximum level marking. The fill cap should also be labeled to direct cleaning around the cap before removing it to fill.

that is attached to wheels. In both types, the movement of the brake pads or shoes is designed to bring the vehicle to a controlled stop.

Federal Motor Vehicle Safety Standard (FMVSS) 105 standard for hydraulic brakes requires a warning system for a drop in the level of **brake fluid** in any master cylinder reservoir compartment to below either an OEM set level or one-fourth of the fluid capacity of that reservoir. Separate reservoir compartments are also required for each service brake circuit supplied by the master cylinder, which means two in most vehicles. Loss of fluid from one compartment should not result in a complete loss of brake fluid from another compartment (**FIGURE 38-17**).

Master Cylinder Operation

When the operator presses the brake pedal that is attached to a pushrod connected to the master cylinder, the linear pushrod movement exerts pressure against a rear-most piston in the master cylinder (**FIGURE 38-18**). This piston, called the **primary piston**, is one of two pistons used in a master cylinder. A **secondary piston** is located ahead of the primary piston. Brake fluid trapped between the primary and secondary piston creates a solid hydraulic link that causes forward movement of the secondary piston whenever the primary piston is pushed through the brake pedal travel. Forward movement of both primary and secondary pistons pushes brake fluid out to brake lines connected to external ports in the master cylinder (**FIGURE 38-19**). The master cylinder pistons have seals at each end, called cups, which resemble O-rings with lip-type sealing. Two cups are located on each end of the two pistons and it is important to note the lips of these cups are angled to control fluid movement. Brake fluid pressure acting against the lips causes the lips to press harder against the bore of the master cylinder when pressure acting on the cup. However, the cup lip shape causes it to flatten when pistons are retracted as the brakes release.

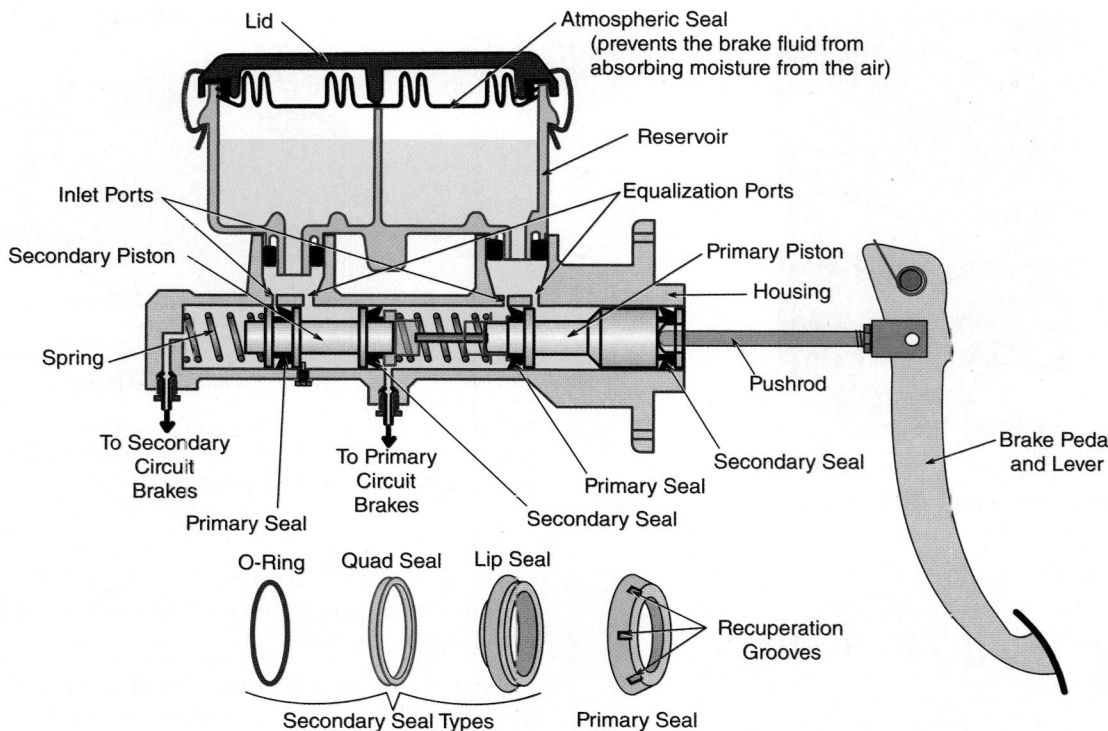

FIGURE 38-18 Components inside a dual-circuit, tandem master cylinder.

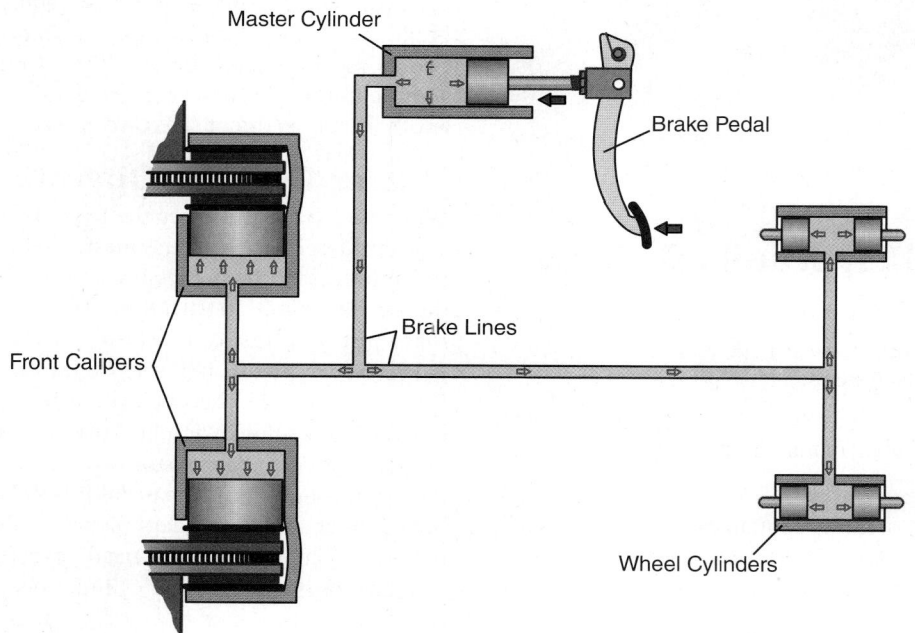

FIGURE 38-19 Example of a basic hydraulic braking system.

Brake fluid for the brake application is supplied to the cavities surrounding the master cylinder pistons by the brake fluid reservoir. When the brakes are released, gravity feeds brake fluid through a passageway ahead of the piston from the brake reservoir located above the master cylinder. This passageway is called the inlet port. A second set of ports called the equalization port allows brake fluid behind the pistons to return to the reservoir. Without the equalization ports, the pistons could not return to their resting position and open the inlet ports.

Master Cylinder: Brake Application

Pushing the primary piston forward pressurizes brake fluid between both cups of the primary piston. Forward movement of the primary piston causes the rear-most cup to glide past and seal the inlet port, trapping brake fluid between two primary piston cup seals. Fluid is pressurized in the primary brake line proportional to the force acting on the brake pedal and delivered out to the rear-most brake line of the master cylinder.

To prevent a negative pressure forming behind the primary and secondary piston cups, which would interfere with forward piston movement, an equalization port behind the piston cups allows brake fluid to back fill behind both pistons.

Fluid trapped between the primary and secondary piston forms the solid hydraulic link between the primary and secondary pistons, causing secondary piston movement that begins almost immediately after the primary piston begins forward movement. Fluid trapped by the secondary piston is forced out the front-most brake line of secondary brake circuit duplicating the actions of the primary piston.

Master Cylinder: Brake Release

Releasing the brake pedal causes a sharp reduction in brake pressure within the master cylinder. A combination of brake shoe return spring tension or caliper O-ring tension, and slight lateral runout of the rotor, pushes the primary and secondary pistons back into a resting position against internal piston stops. Brake fluid is returned to the reservoir through equalization ports first and then finally residual line pressure is returned to the reservoir through the inlet ports. The edges of the forward traveling sealing cups fold back, which helps reduce resistance to rearward piston movement. Recuperation grooves on the piston cups further help the folding of cup lips and rapid piston return travel.

Brake Fluid Leakage

A gradual drop in the brake fluid reservoir level takes place as brake pads wear. As the caliper pistons move outward to compensate for pad wear while maintaining close pad to rotor clearances, the equivalent volume of displaced fluid does not return to the reservoir. This explains why a low brake fluid reservoir is an indication of the amount of brake pad wear. However, a leak in the primary or secondary brake circuits causes disruption to the operation of the master cylinder. To prevent a catastrophic loss of brakes if a leak in a brake line or caliper takes place, two brake

circuits—the primary and secondary circuit, are always used. If one circuit fails, a backup circuit can still brake the vehicle and bring it to a controlled stop. A split circuit system ensures that a leak or failure in one circuit allows the other circuit to stop a vehicle—although braking effectiveness is lost. Trucks typically use a **front/rear split** dual-circuit brake system where the primary piston of the master cylinder section pressurizes the front caliper pistons and the secondary piston to pressurize the rear caliper pistons (**FIGURE 38-20**). This front-rear split configuration also provides better brake balance for the weight transfer to the front brakes when braking.

If a leak takes place in the primary circuit, the solid hydraulic column of brake fluid is lost. To operate the secondary circuit, the primary piston continues to move forward but mechanically contacts and pushes the secondary piston to pressurize fluid. Longer brake pedal travel takes place when the primary circuit fails. The divided brake fluid reservoir generally prevents all fluid loss to the leak.

If the secondary brake circuit leaks, the primary circuit still operates and pushes against the secondary piston. However, the brake pedal travel is limited by primary circuit pressure. The symptom of secondary brake circuit fluid leakage is a spongy brake feel and loss of brake effectiveness (**FIGURE 38-21**).

Pressure Differential Switch

Safety regulations require that a loss of brake fluid or leak in a brake circuit is accompanied by a warning to alert the driver. A warning light is mandatory and may include an audible alert if the system has an electronic brake monitoring system. A pressure differential switch is used to detect brake fluid leak from a between the primary and secondary circuit through a line, caliper, or wheel cylinder. The switch contains a valve with a notched piston centered in a cylinder. Brake fluid from each circuit acts on either end of the piston centered between two springs (**FIGURE 38-22**). When brake pressure remains the same in both circuits, the piston remains centered in the cylinder. However, a leak causing a pressure drop in one circuit during the brake application forces the piston off-center, pushing a switch pin onto a ramp. When the piston ramp pushes the pin, it closes the switch and grounds out an electrical circuit to the brake

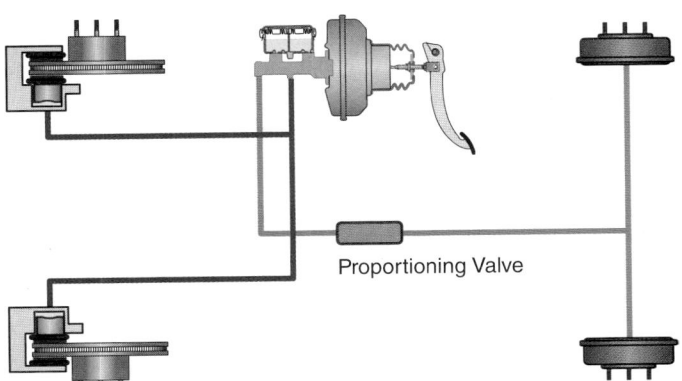

FIGURE 38-20 Front to rear split brake circuits. A proportioning valve is not used in all disc brake systems.

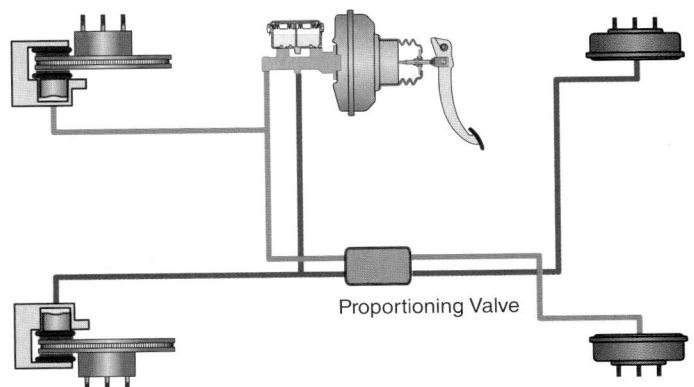

FIGURE 38-21 A diagonal split system separates brake circuits into left-front and right-rear or right-front left-rear circuits to achieve controlled stops.

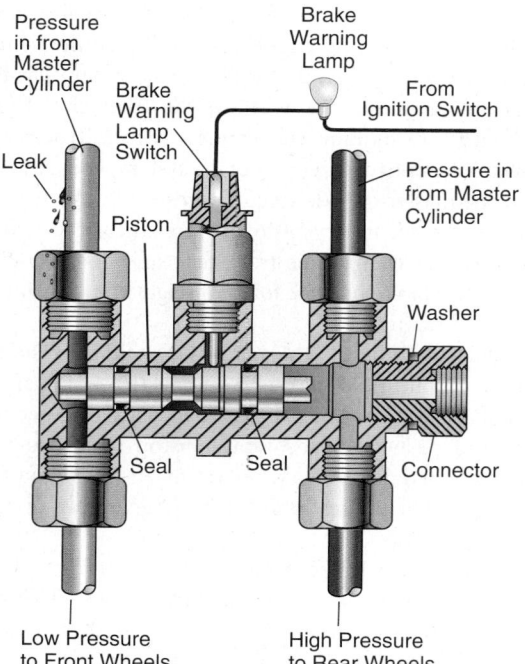

FIGURE 38-22 The pressure differential switch piston is centered between two springs. Piston movement caused by a brake pressure differential causes the electrical circuit to ground.

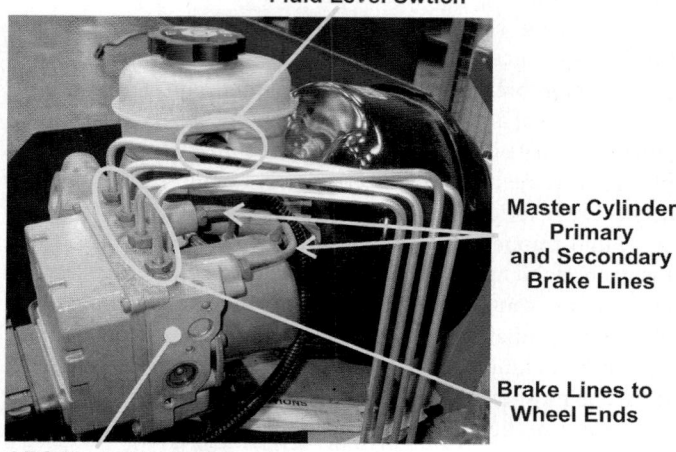

FIGURE 38-23 The location of a low brake fluid level switch.

warning light or module. The light remains illuminated until the switch is recentered. This can only happen after any system leak is repaired and normal brake application pressure between the primary and secondary circuits equalize. The light may illuminate during brake bleeding operations but should equalize and extinguish the light when the brakes are applied.

Low Fluid Warning

If the level of brake fluid in the master cylinder reservoir is low, it can indicate a brake fluid leak or potentially excessive brake pad wear. Low fluid level can allow air to enter the brake system, which causes the loss of brake application pressure. Because air is compressible, brake fluid takes on a spongy, elastic-like properties. To prevent this, a brake fluid level switch is used to alert the driver through a warning light that the brake fluid level is critically low. The switch is commonly a float with a magnetic reed valve. If the float level is low, the magnet closes a metal switch contact and grounds out the circuit (**FIGURE 38-23**).

Hydraulic Brake Fluid

LO 38-5 Identify and describe the properties of hydraulic brake fluid.

Brake fluids are used by hydraulic braking and clutch systems. FMVSS standards do not specify the composition of brake fluid or how it should be packaged but only outline performance specifications. Some important properties include its ability to resist freezing and boiling. Since fluid can absorb heat from caliper pistons, vapor bubbles formed when fluid boils result in a sudden loss of brake application force and spongy brakes. Cold

fluid should remain viscous enough to move easily. Fluid should also prevent corrosion of internal metal components so additives like borate are included in fluid formulations.

To prevent corrosion due to water entering the brake system, brake fluid is formulated to absorb moisture, rather than allowing it to stay in free droplet form and sink into low spots in the system. This ability to absorb water means brake fluid is **hydroscopic**. If the fluid has absorbed water, the water can boil out of the fluid and, unfortunately, form vapor bubbles. A specification for brake fluid limiting this boiling point is called the wet boiling temperature.

Most brake fluids are made from glycol esters, which combine alcohol and an antifreeze-like fluid base (**TABLE 38-1**). The ester-glycol-based combination is a powerful solvent, which makes brake fluids particularly hazardous to paint, behaving like paint stripper. Categories of brake fluid are classified by the US Department of Transportation (DOT) according to their performance specifications outlined by FMVSS 116 standards for brake fluid. Only DOT 3 through 5.1 are used in truck brake systems. Because of the ability to absorb heat from caliper pistons, DOT 3 minimum should be used in commercial vehicle brake systems, but DOT 4, 5, or 5.1 are better choices due to high brake temperatures these vehicles encounter. A silicone-base fluid was preferred until the recent introduction of DOT 5.1 fluid, a glycol based fluid lime DOT 4. The DOT 5.0 silicone fluid previously had the highest resistance to boiling and a more stable viscosity index over a wider temperature range. Silicone does not damage paint but is **hydrophilic**, meaning it does not absorb moisture.

▶ TECHNICIAN TIP

Brake fluid, except for silicone-based DOT 5, will peel and strip paint. Always use caution when pouring brake fluid to avoid contaminating and damaging painted surfaces. Brake fluid's hydroscopic properties make it easily absorb water so opened bottles and cans must be tightly resealed. Contaminated brake fluid turns from a clear or light amber color to darker red and brown when it has absorbed water. Contaminated fluid must be discarded.

TABLE 38-1 Brake Fluid Properties

Department of Transportation Specification	Dry Boiling Point	Wet Boiling Point	Composition
DOT 2	374° F (190° C)	284° F (140° C)	Alcohol/Castor Oil (Obsolete)
DOT 3	401° F (205° C)	311° F (155° C)	Glycol Ester
DOT 4	446° F (230° C)	311° F (155° C)	Glycol Ester with Borate
DOT 5	500° F (260° C)	356° F (180° C)	Silicone
DOT 5.1	500° F (260° C)	356° F (180° C)	Glycol Ester with Borate

Source: Data from FMVSS 116 appearing in 49 CFR Standards for Brake Fluids.

▶ TECHNICIAN TIP

Because brake fluid is designed to absorb water introduced by condensation, it is recommended that fluid should be changed every two years. One manufacturer has determined that as little as 3% percent contamination can lower the boiling point by 50%. When contaminated by water condensation, the fluid loses the ability to prevent corrosion of metal parts and rust can form. Not only is rust an abrasive that damages seals and cups, rusty fluid also damages other hydraulic seals, leading to leakage. To identify rusty fluid, it is important to remember rust turns black in brake fluid and blackened fluid indicates brake fluid service and system inspection is required.

▶ TECHNICIAN TIP

Minimum brake fluid standard for commercial vehicles is DOT 3 fluid. Higher performing DOT 4+, DOT 5, and DOT 5.1 with greater resistance to boiling are preferred because of the heavier loads, greater brake torque, and multiple caliper pistons capable of transferring more heat into brake fluid. DOT 5 fluid made from silicone cannot be mixed with other brake fluids.

Brake Lines and Hoses

In a hydraulic system, rigid steel **brake lines** and flexible hoses conduct brake fluid to wheel end components. Zinc-plated malleable steel lines run along the chassis from the master cylinder and along axles housing, but flexible lines connect to the brake foundation to allow for suspension travel and side-to-side movement when turning wheels. Flexible lines are made in several grades from materials, such as vinyl, Kevlar, Teflon, and braided stainless-steel (**FIGURE 38-24**). An outer weather guard layer of protective vinyl material is used on most hoses. Brake hoses all have fittings attached at each end that are either threaded or banjo-style ends to seal against the brake caliper with a non-reusable copper sealing washer. Regardless of their construction, new and aftermarket brake lines, fittings, and flex hoses must meet safety standards outlined in FMVSS 106 and Society of Automotive Engineers (SAE) J1401 standards for brake hoses and fittings.

Important elements of these safety standards include:

1. Flex hose markings: Also called torque stripes. These markings are used to prevent installation errors caused by twisted hoses. Every aftermarket-produced flex line must have at least two clearly identifiable stripes of at least ¹⁄₁₆" in width, placed on opposite sides of the brake hose along its length. OEM hoses do not require the stripes, but the presence of stripes highlights the importance of installing smooth curves on flexible brake hoses.

2. Burst pressures: Aftermarket and OEM hoses must be designed to withstand a water pressure of 4000 psi (27,579 kPa) for two minutes without rupturing. Hoses that are ⅛" (3 mm) or smaller are tested at 7000 psi (48,263 kPa).

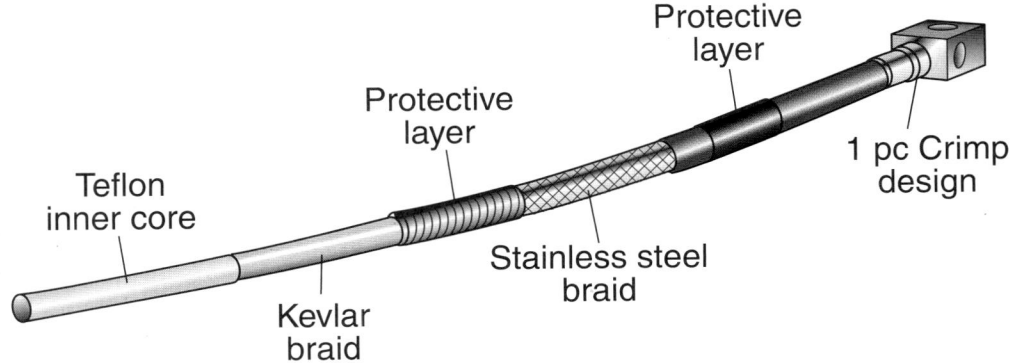

FIGURE 38-24 A typical flex line construction uses a Teflon inner seal layer protected by Kevlar and reinforced with braided steel mesh to resist swelling during brake applications.

3. Whip testing: The importance of hose durability is evidence by hoses designed to withstand cracking or damage after 35 hours of continuous bending on a flexing machine.
4. Tensile strength: Flexible hydraulic brake hose must withstand a rapid pull force of a minimum of 325 lb (147 kg) without separation the line and fittings separating. A second slower pull test requires the same performance at 370 lb (168 kg) without separation.
5. Cold weather, resistance to chemical deterioration, and fitting corrosion are other tests brake hoses are required to pass.

There is no recommended service interval for brake lines and hoses. Instead, visual inspection is required to identify problems. Most failures of flex hoses take place at fitting ends, which require bubble crimping—a mechanically secure machine attachment method using a bubble-shaped die to bond a hose to a fitting. Pinching hoses with locking pliers is another potential way to internally damage a hose not designed for this stress. Tears in the inner liner can also create one-way check valves that cause brakes to drag due to slow release time through restricted internal diameters of a hose.

Flex hoses should be inspected to identify:

■ Cracks: Even small shallow cracks in the outer weather guard allow water into the inner hose, which causes deterioration.
■ Blisters or bubbles: Any hose that has a blister or bubble when the brakes are pressed must be replaced.
■ Leaks: Brake hoses should never leak or even weep brake fluid. A leak is lost braking force and an entry point for air and moisture. Air in the fluid is dangerous because air is compressible. This increases the amount of pedal travel that's necessary to apply the brakes, and may increase it to the point where a spongy pedal hits the floor before the brakes effectively apply.

Pre-flared and cut-to-length lines with fittings can save time by eliminating the flaring process, but sometimes they can be difficult to source due to flare, fitting, and length considerations.

> **▶ TECHNICIAN TIP**
>
> Any air or gas bubbles in hydraulic brake systems is dangerous. Gas in liquid brake fluid takes away the fluid's non-compressible property and prevents the transmission of hydraulic braking force throughout the system. Because gas bubbles are compressible, air gives brake fluid an elastic property that translates into a "spongy" or spring-like feel to brake application pressure. Air can enter through loose bleeder screws, worn or damaged calipers piston seals, brake cylinder cups, and O-rings. Brakes are especially vulnerable to the entry of air when the system is opened during parts replacement of as a caliper, wheel cylinder, or brake hose. Water also turns to vapor when heated and becomes trapped in the hydraulic system—especially behind valves and accumulators in the ABS modulator assembly. When servicing brakes, follow OEM recommended procedures for bleeding brakes. Always bleed modulator valves and hydraulic parking brakes in the correct sequence. Follow recommended service intervals for flushing and replacing brake fluid from brake systems.

Steel Brake Lines

At one time, lead was used to plate brake lines to prevent corrosion, but zinc has replaced lead on flexible steel lines. Steel lines have threaded nuts at each end to connect with flex hoses, master cylinders, wheel cylinders, or other fittings. An inverted 45-degree double flare end shape is formed in the line end and seated with a nut. This double flare shape is used to seal a brake line and nut where it connects to a master cylinder, flexible brake hose, or other fitting. The unique geometric shape of the double inverted flare is necessary to form a seal for up to several thousand psi (kPa) of brake fluid pressure (**FIGURE 38-25**). An interference fit of three to five degrees difference between the male and female line sealing surfaces further helps create a deformable seal. At the master cylinder, several loops of coiled steel brake line are used to enable the line to absorb flexion between the chassis and cab, as well as from vibrations, which can lead to premature line cracking. When lines have two different lengths of nut, the longer, more stress resistant nut connects to fixed components, such as the master or wheel cylinder.

Steel lines can corrode from the outside when pitted by road gravel and other debris. Corrosion takes place internally if brake fluid has absorbed water. If brake lines are corroded, they require replacement before a failure occurs. Brake lines can either be fabricated from rolls of steel tubing using new fittings or using precut lines with flared ends. Bending new lines requires the use of line-bending tools to prevent crimping and restricting the line.

Flaring Procedures

A flaring tool is used to form SAE 45-degree flares for custom-made lines. A bubble-shaped ISO flare used on European products and some North American cars uses a different procedure (**FIGURE 38-26**). After the correct diameter line is cut to length with a tube cutter, the end of the line is deburred with a deburring tool often incorporated into the tube cutter. The

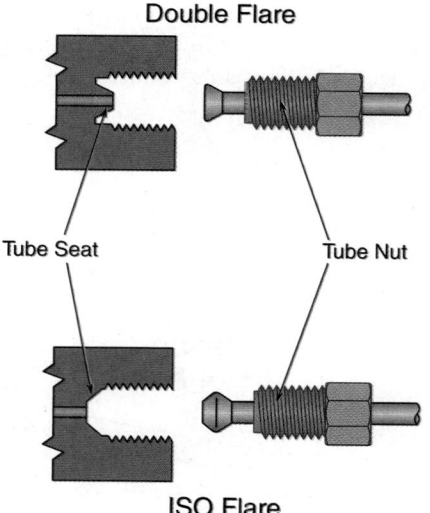

Double Flare

Tube Seat   Tube Nut

ISO Flare

FIGURE 38-25 SAE and ISO standards use two differently shaped flares to seal steel brake lines.

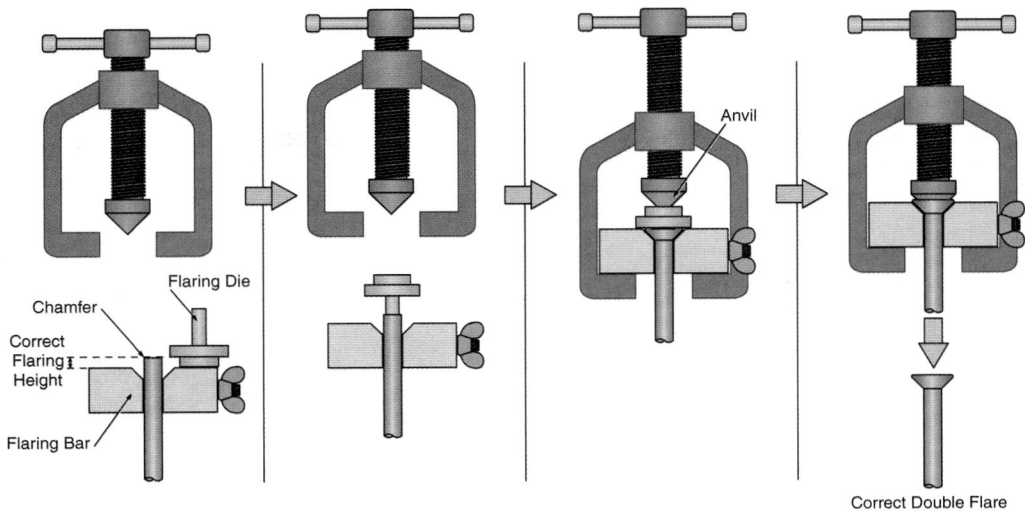

FIGURE 38-26 Steps used to create a 45-degree SAE flare in a steel brake line.

correct size line nut is installed on the line with the threaded end toward the flare. Next the end of the line is clamped in a flaring bar using the correct diameter opening for the line. While the leg of the bar used with a flaring tool is clamped tightly in a vice, the line end is filed smooth and square with a metal file. To make the first of two flares or folds in the line, a metal die is pressed over top of the line that protrudes slightly above the flaring bar surface. The protrusion height of the line is determined by a stepped ridge on the die. Next, the die is removed and a cone in the flaring tool forcing screw is pressed into the line.

Foundation Components of Hydraulic Braking Systems

LO 38-6 Identify, and describe the components of hydrualic foundation braking systems.

As mentioned, two types of brake foundation systems used are drum brakes and disc brakes. Stopping distance requirements introduced in the 1980s have almost eliminated the use of drum brakes on medium-duty commercial vehicles. Disc brakes using rotors and pads have displaced drum brakes due to their ability to apply greater clamping force to rotors, particularly when hot when brake fade naturally takes place with drum brakes. Expanding rotors are literally pinched tighter by the calipers and brake pads, minimizing brake fade caused by heat. This section explains the purpose, operation, and construction of different components of each type of foundation braking system.

Drum Brakes

Drum brakes are the earliest modern commercial vehicle brake design. The brake drum is attached to a rotating wheel that revolves around a set of brake shoes moved outward against the drum when brakes are applied. Brake drum widths commonly range from 4" to 6" (10 cm to 15 cm) and 12" to 15.5" (30.5 cm to 39 cm) brake drum diameters (**FIGURE 38-27**). A drum brake has two brake shoes with a riveted friction lining attached to a

FIGURE 38-27 A two-wheel cylinder hydraulic brake using double-acting wheel cylinders.

metal shoe table. Higher brake temperatures of heavily loaded vehicles demand the mechanical bond of rivets rather than bonded lining, which only glues friction material to the shoes. Brake shoes are pushed out against the brake drum by one or two hydraulic wheel cylinders. Since friction is proportional to the force applied by the shoes, higher hydraulic pressure in wheel cylinders translates into increased friction and stopping power. One advantage of drum and shoe foundations is the potential to use self-energizing brake friction force on brake shoes and servo brake friction action. Both these forces cause the shoes to increase the brake torque and frictional coefficients between the shoe and drum. Less hydraulic brake application pressure is necessary using self-energization and servo brake action to stop the vehicle, which was an advantage when power assist systems were not available or worked poorly compared to today's systems.

When self-energizing takes place, the leading edge of the primary brake shoe—the first part of the lining to contact the drum, grips the drum and attempts to rotate with the drum.

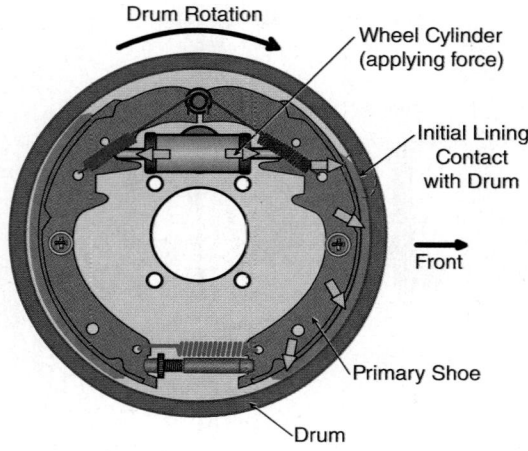

FIGURE 38-28 The primary shoe lining grips the drum with its leading edge causing pressure and rotational force that pushes the shoe harder into the drum.

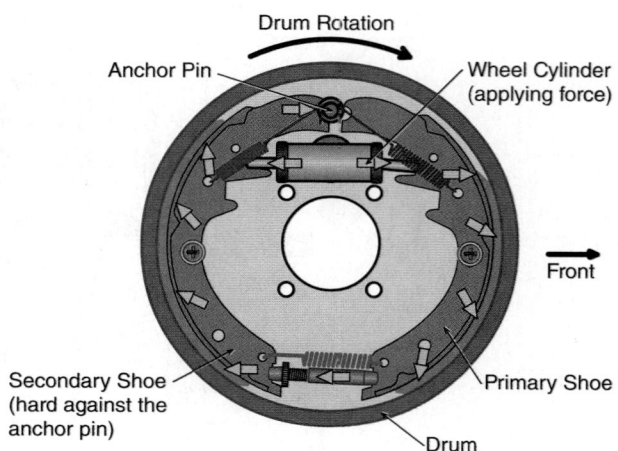

Drag forces from the drum rotate both brake shoes in the direction of drum rotation. In the forward direction the secondary shoe comes to a stop against the anchor pin. In reverse the primary shoe stops against the anchor pin.

FIGURE 38-29 Servo action takes place in the secondary shoe as the primary shoe rotation pushes the heel of the secondary shoe into the brake drum.

This action slightly tips the shoe into the drum and rotational pressure on the leading edge of the brake lining causes a mechanical action to press the shoe harder into the drum face. Self-energizing action operates like a wedge with increasing drum rotational force driving the shoe harder into the drum (**FIGURE 38-28**).

Servo brake action takes place in the secondary shoe where the self-energizing action of the primary shoe causes rotational force acting on it to transfer into the heel of the secondary shoe. Rotational force from primary shoes self-energizing action is transmitted through a movable brake adjuster or linkage into the secondary shoe causing it to push harder against the drum rotation. The leading edge of the secondary shoe, now opposite the wheel cylinder, has much more force applied to it through the primary shoe, which, in turn, produces self-energization action in the secondary shoe. When the secondary shoe lining contacts the drum, primary shoe rotational force continues to transfer into the secondary shoe and the rotational force from the brake drum multiplies brake shoe pressure application force, increasing brake torque. Both self-energizing and servo action literally can jam the shoes into the brake drum, increasing brake application force, which multiplies brake torque (**FIGURE 38-29**). Close lining-to-drum clearance is necessary to prevent excessive self-energization and servo forces overwhelming the brake anchoring devices and destroying the brake assembly.

> ▶ **TECHNICIAN TIP**
>
> Maintaining close brake drum to shoe contact is critical not only to prevent a low brake pedal complaint, but to prevent excessive self-energizing and servo brake shoe action, which can tear apart the brake shoes and brake components in the wheel end. A large shoe-to-drum clearance can cause the leading edge and heel of the brake shoes to become so great, the force of drum rotation pushes the shoes hard enough to break shoe anchors and shear bolts holding down wheel cylinders. "Grabby" brakes or brakes that quickly lock up under light application is a symptom accompanying excessive drum-to-shoe clearance in brakes using servo brake action.

Drum Brake Fade

Brake fade caused by heat, which increases the brake drum diameter, is a major disadvantage of drum-shoe foundations. Heat from the shoes and drums must dissipate through the drum, which takes more time than a rotor having two surface areas and internal air vents. Heat fade can result in chemical fade too as gases from hot shoes trapped between the lining and drum decrease drum-lining friction coefficients. Heat can even cause brake lining to liquefy and produce a slippery glaze on the friction material, which results in mechanical fade. (Remember that brake fade is the increase of braking effort required by the driver to produce the same brake torque.) Dragging brakes or inadequate pressure of the brake lining against the drum resulting in prolonged and increased brake temperatures are common causes of glazed brake lining. Brake fade is experienced as the increased effort required to prevent the gradual loss of brake stopping power during prolonged or strenuous use. Very high temperatures are produced at the brake drum, and that causes deterioration in the frictional value of the lining or pad material.

Brake Shoe Configurations

The design of common brake shoe systems on medium- to heavy-duty vehicles can be in the form of one of these basic designs:

- Leading and trailing brake shoe configuration
- Two-leading-shoe configuration

Single-Leading- and Trailing-Shoe Configuration

The single-leading-shoe (SLS) drum brake, which is also known as a **leading/trailing shoe drum brake arrangement,** is a basic type of drum brake design. The term primary shoe, which is the first shoe to contact the drum and is located on the forward side of the brake, also corresponds to the leading shoe. The secondary shoe corresponds to the trailing shoe. This shoe arrangement is typically found on the rear wheels of drum brake vehicles. An advantage of an SLS brake is that it is equally effective whether the vehicle is traveling forward or in reverse. An SLS brake is less powerful than a **twin-leading-shoe drum brake**, because it uses only a single, double-acting wheel cylinder and has self-energizing action in only one shoe. A rigid anchor point opposite the wheel cylinder prevents transmission of rotational force from one shoe to another, preventing servo action. However, this arrangement is acceptable in vehicles where high brake torque is not critical on the rear brakes, such as when lightly loaded vehicles with excessive braking force could cause the rear wheels to lock.

The term "leading/trailing" is used because there is one shoe that is "leading," that is, self-energizing in the direction of the drum's rotation in the forward direction. When this happens, the leading shoe is dragged into the friction surface of the drum because the lining contacts the drum on its leading edge. Self-energization wedges the shoe into the drum and brake torque increases with greater hydraulic brake pressure and drum rotational force. The other shoe is "trailing," that is, the lining contacts the drum on its trailing edge, which prevents self-energization. Drum rotation pushes the shoe away from the drum's friction surface and the lining does not grip the drum as effectively as the leading shoe.

When the vehicle is moving in reverse, the role of the leading and trailing shoes is switched. What is the **leading shoe** when the vehicle is traveling forward becomes the **trailing shoe,** and vice versa. The leading shoe can be identified by observing the hydraulic wheel cylinder's mounted position and the drum brake's direction of rotation, where the hydraulic wheel cylinder forces the brake shoe outwards to contact the drum and self-energize (**FIGURE 38-30**).

Two-Leading Brake Shoes

The two-leading brake shoe can also be referred to as having two "primary" shoes, both operating using principles of self-energization that help wedge the shoe lining into the brake drum when the drum is rotating in the forward direction. This brake shoe configuration is identified using two, single-acting wheel cylinders (**FIGURE 38-31**).

Each brake shoe in this arrangement is forced outward, to contact the drum at a point on the leading edge of the lining. Self-energization takes place in both shoes. There is no brake **servo action**, but self-energization action in both shoes provides a powerful and consistent brake torque. The self-energizing effect develops in the two-leading-shoe arrangement because the leading shoes are effectively dragged into the brake drum's friction surface to achieve maximum braking torque.

Drum Brake Adjusters

Brake shoe adjusters have access points in the shoe backing plates to allow technicians to initially adjust the brake lining to brake drum clearance. Maintaining a small clearance minimizes brake pedal travel because less fluid is needed to expand the shoes to contact drums. Excessive clearance is the main cause for a low brake pedal—one that requires a long stroke before the brakes begin to contact the drums. Brake pull causing the vehicle to steer left or right when braking is commonly produced when the adjusters are not correctly positioned to achieve equal shoe to drum clearances. Another hole in the backing plate is usually present to allow inspection of this critical clearance. Generally, adjusters are initially rotated until the shoes make firm contact with the drum and them backed off an equal number of turns or degrees of rotation on each wheel end to obtain the correct clearance, usually between 0.010" and 0.020" (0.024 cm to 0.051 cm), the thickness of a piece of paper and credit card. Another method involves tightening the adjuster to lock the wheel and then backing off the adjuster until the raised wheel turns with a slight amount of drag.

Three types of brake shoe adjusting mechanisms commonly used are:

- Star wheel-type adjuster with a left- and right-hand threaded mechanism
- Wedge-type adjuster

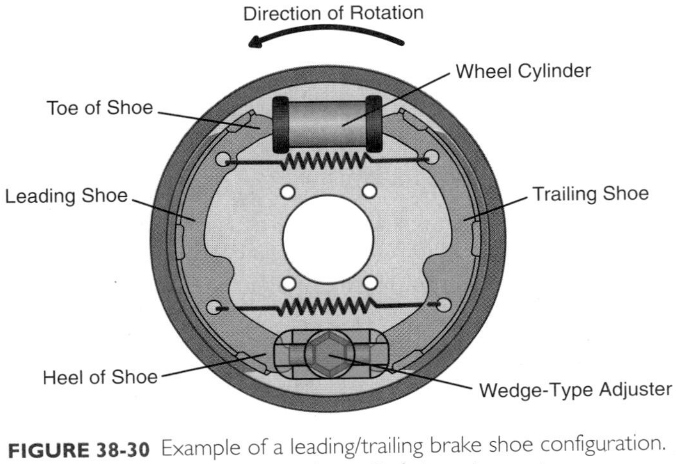

FIGURE 38-30 Example of a leading/trailing brake shoe configuration. The leading shoe self energizes, the trailing shoe does not.

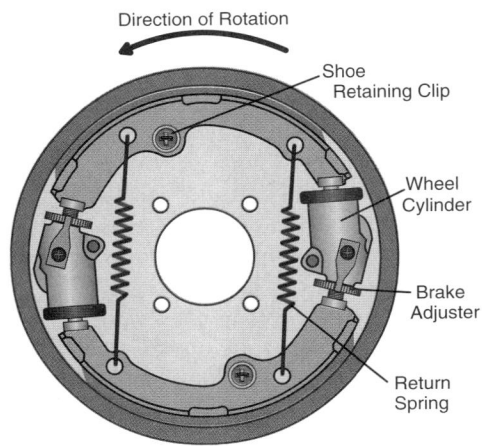

FIGURE 38-31 Example of a two-leading brake shoe configuration.

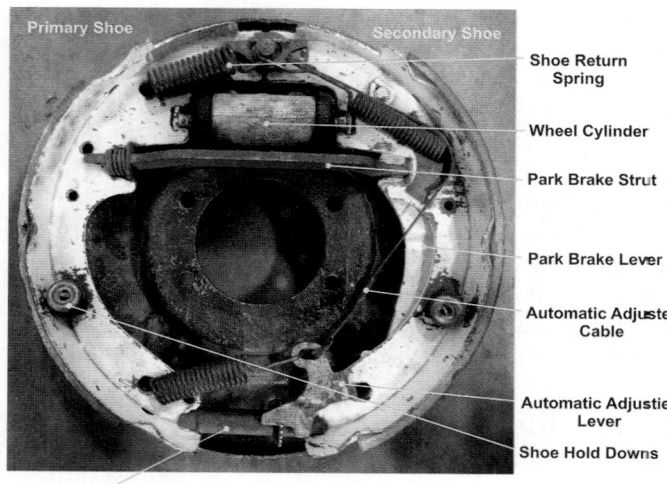

FIGURE 38-32 A servo brake arrangement. The cable of the automatic adjuster mechanism tightens and pulls the automatic adjustment lever if drum-to-shoe clearance is excessive.

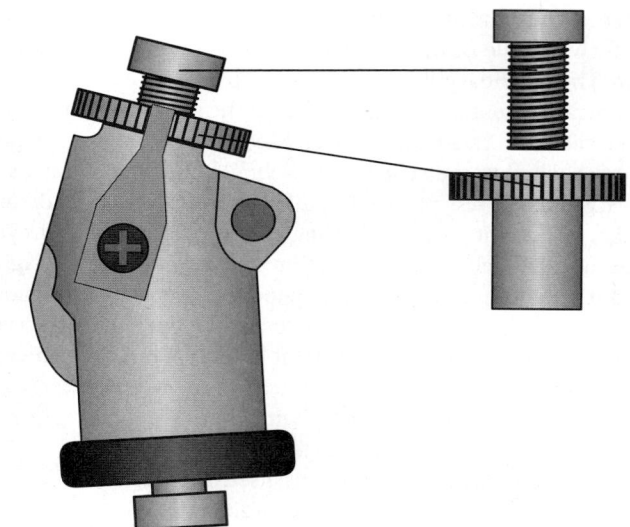

FIGURE 38-33 Example of a star-type adjuster.

- Cam-type adjusters, which are used as an eccentric cam behind the shoe table that is turned to move the shoes in or away from the drum to obtain the correct drum-shoe clearance.

All three types of adjusters are used by large- and medium-size brake drums. Automatic adjusters use the rotation of shoes to pull linkage, which rotates a star wheel adjuster. Shoes with greater drum to shoe clearance rotate more inside the drum than tight shoes. Depending on how far the shoes rotated when braking—often when traveling in the reverse direction, the adjuster cable or lever is pulled further if clearances are excessive. Connecting an adjuster cable to an adjustment lever increments the star wheel rotation to lengthen the adjuster and reduce shoe-drum clearance (**FIGURE 38-32**).

Star Wheel-Type Adjuster

It is important to maintain a specified drum-to-lining clearance at all times. In later-model vehicles, this function is carried out automatically. But, after a brake service, the adjusters require initial adjustment maintained by automatic-type adjusters.

An excessively large clearance between drums and linings results in a low brake pedal and a delay in the brakes applying. However, if clearances are too small, the brakes drag and overheat. Also, if the brake adjustment is not equal on both sides and in front and back, then vehicle stability is an issue under heavy braking. Small incremental steps in the star adjusting screw is useful to obtain precise brake balance.

The star adjusting screw consists of a threaded bolt and two nuts (**FIGURE 38-33**). They are marked either "L" (for left hand, counterclockwise [CCW] rotation) or "R" (for right hand, clockwise [CW] rotation). Because each end of the adjuster is in contact with a brake shoe, the clearance decreases or increases as the screws are turned. Access to the adjusting star wheels is through holes in the brake **backing plate**; the holes are located

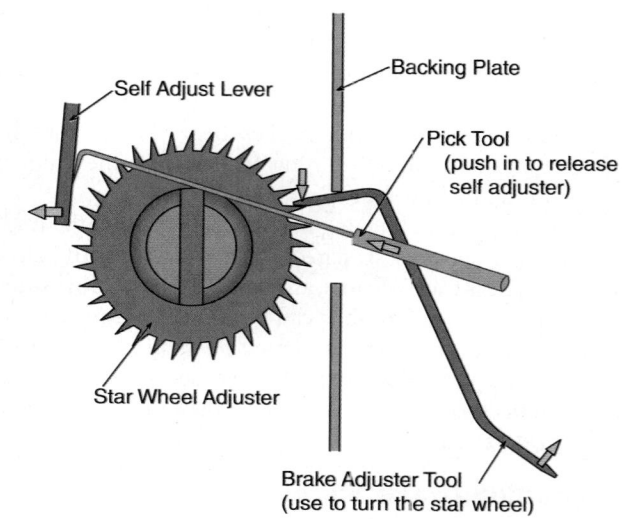

FIGURE 38-34 To back-off a brake with an external star wheel adjuster, the external adjusting lever needs to be pushed away before the start wheel is rotated.

on the bottom and top of the wheel on both the front and the rear brakes of drum brake systems.

Automatic star wheel adjusters can use either internal or external adjusting mechanisms. Internal adjusters are built into a mechanism located inside a wheel cylinder. The ratcheting adjusting mechanism has a helical-shaped groove tracked with a pin that will rotate the star wheel whenever the piston travel becomes excessive. When external linkage is used to adjust the star wheel, a release tool is first needed to push the adjusting lever away from the star wheel before the adjuster can be turned to retract brake shoes from the drum. This step is performed before removing a brake drum with a ridge worn into it from contact with the shoes. When adjusting the shoe-to-drum clearance after drum installation, the star wheel freely ratchets over the external adjusting lever but does not back-off and increase shoe to drum clearance (**FIGURE 38-34**).

Wedge-Type Adjuster

The wedge-type adjuster consists of a taper-shaped wedge that can be screwed in or out from the back of the backing plate between the tappet rollers that adjust the brake lining to brake drum clearance (**FIGURE 38-35**). Moving the wedge inboard reduces lining-to-drum clearances. The wedge-type adjuster mechanism tends to easily seize, and its use was displaced by the star wheel adjuster.

Brake Springs

Brake springs are used to pull the brake shoes back to a resting position away from the brake drums when the brakes are released. Strong spring tension is necessary to force brake fluid from the wheel cylinder back to the master cylinder. Springs are color-coded to indicate their strength. Black is the strongest spring tension, followed by red. Green has a moderate tension, followed by yellow and white, which has the least tension. Spring color is important to enable the brake shoes to follow a correct sequence of mechanical action when applying and releasing the brakes. Automatic adjusting mechanism often depends on the spring color to operate correctly.

Brake Drums

Brake drums for hydraulic brakes are often heavier and thicker than drums for air brakes due to higher hydraulic force application pressure. Steel bands often wrap cast iron drums to prevent expansion and distortion during high-temperature brake applications. Because the drums have premium features and materials, the cost to replace these components is often more than the cost to machine drums with irregular, heat-checked, bell-mouthed or scored brake surfaces. Before machining the drums, to restore a smooth flat drum contact surface, the drum diameter should be measured to determine whether it is within maximum diameter limits that are stamped on the drum. Once machined, an allowance of a minimum of 0.030"

(0.08 cm) of material is needed for wear before the drum reaches maximum diameter.

Wheel Cylinders

LO 38-7 Describe and explain the construction and operation of wheel cylinders.

A wheel cylinder is a hydraulic actuation component in a drum brake system that forces brake shoes against the brake drum. One or two are in each wheel end, usually at the top, and if a second one is used, it is at the bottom of the shoes. Adding the second cylinder increases the force applied to the shoes and increases brake torque (**FIGURE 38-36**). Small rods or grooved flanges protrude from the wheel cylinder pistons to transit hydraulic force to the shoes. If the cylinder has only one piston, it is single acting (**FIGURE 38-37**). Two pistons give the cylinder double-acting capabilities. The construction inside is simple with one or two short steel pistons sealed from behind on the fluid side with cup-type radial lip seals. Each piston requires a seal, so a double-acting cylinder with two pistons has two seals and a single cup seal is used in a single-acting cylinder. An expander spring between the cups and pistons maintains a slight pressure on the

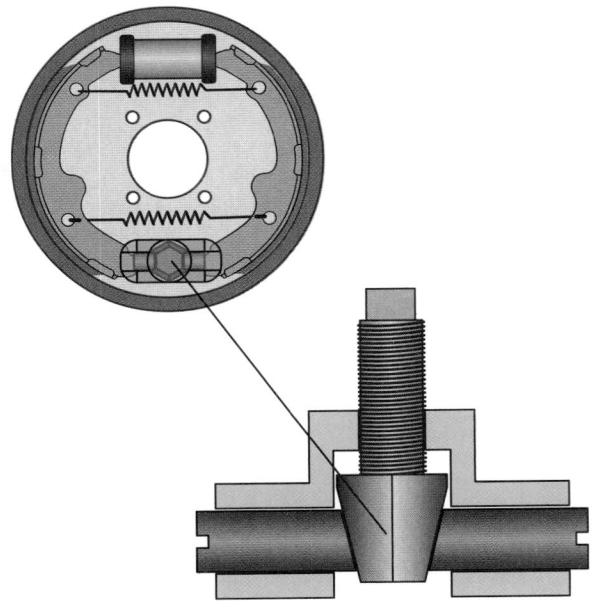

FIGURE 38-35 Example of a wedge-type adjuster.

FIGURE 38-36 Dual-wheel cylinder with star-wheel automatic adjusters.

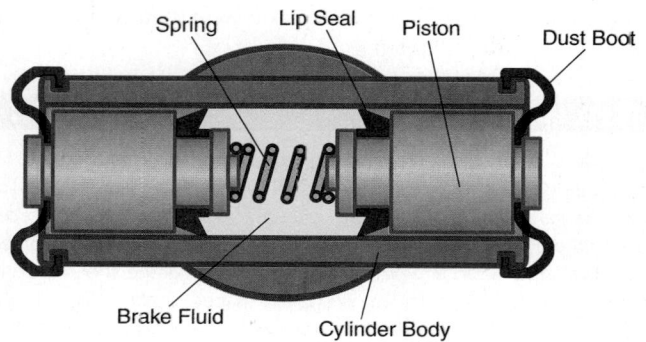

FIGURE 38-37 Dual-action/double cylinder with a piston at each end.

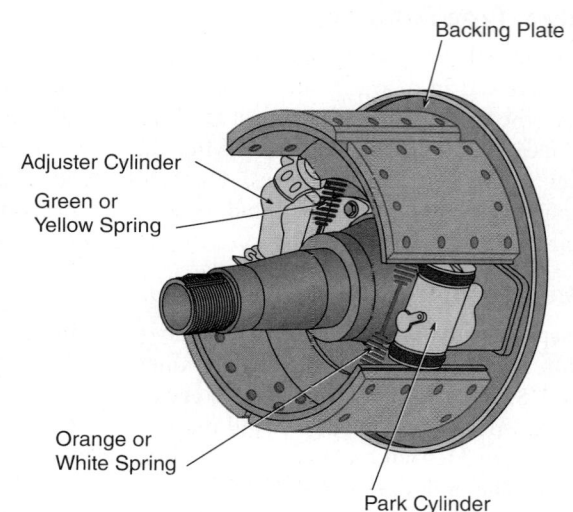

FIGURE 38-38 A Lucas Girling hydraulic brake system uses a wheel cylinder with separate park and adjusting functions.

cup seal lips to prevent the cylinders from leaking when no brake fluid pressure is available to flatten the cup seal lips against the walls of the wheel cylinder. A flexible rubber or silicone boot allows for linear piston movement while preventing dust and moisture from contaminating fluid in the cylinder.

Wheel cylinders are usually made of cast iron. Extreme pressures and temperatures generated during braking can contribute to shortened cylinder and seal life, resulting in leakage from the cup seals. If two-wheel cylinders are used, a hydraulic jumper line connects the top and bottom wheel cylinders. A bleeder screw is located at the highest point of the cylinder to allow air to be bled from the wheel end.

Lucas Girling and Bendix A2L Hydraulic Drum Brakes

One popular hydraulic drum brake system configuration used on many medium-duty vehicles in North America and Europe is produced by Lucas Girling and Bendix (**FIGURE 38-38**). This hydraulic brake foundation system is unique for its use of a

power spring-type park brake released by hydraulic pressure (**FIGURES 38-39** and **38-40**). An engine-driven hydraulic pump and reservoir filled with automatic transmission fluid releases the park brake's spring. A heavy power spring applies the park brakes through a park brake wheel cylinder with a wedge-type actuator. During brake applications, the park brake spring in the park brake pedestal is released and the cylinder is supplied brake fluid pressure from a conventional master cylinder with a hydraulic boost mechanism (**FIGURE 38-41**). A second hydraulic cylinder containing automatic "twin-stop" adjusters applies the brakes (**FIGURE 38-42**). These adjusters, located in the wheel cylinder at the end of the pistons, are stroke sensing, which means they rotate an adjusting screw automatically

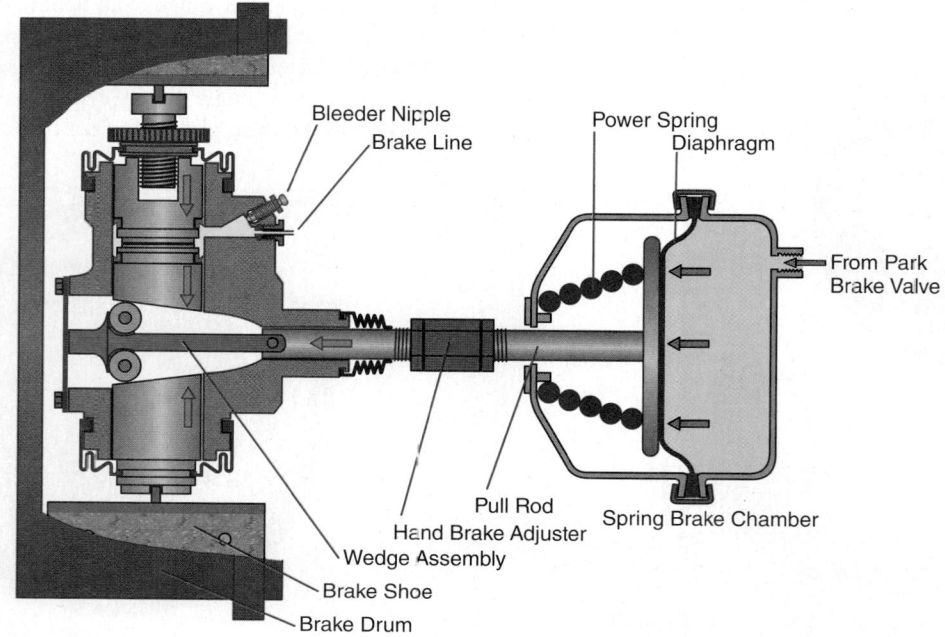

FIGURE 38-39 A spring-applied, hydraulically released park brake cylinder and park brake pedestal action. Brakes are not applied.

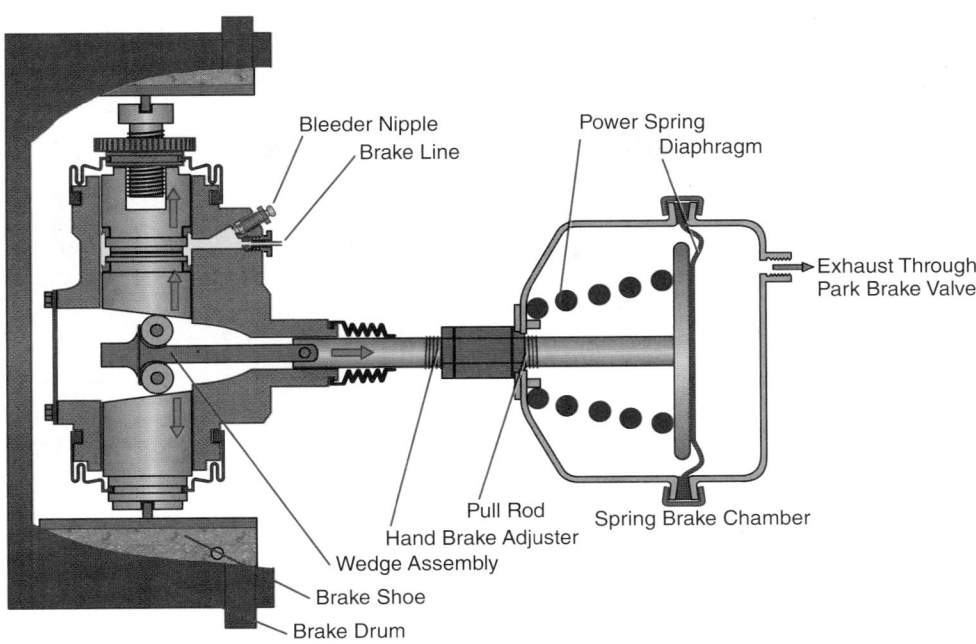

FIGURE 38-40 Park brake in the applied position—hydraulically un-compressed compressed park brake spring in the park brake pedestal.

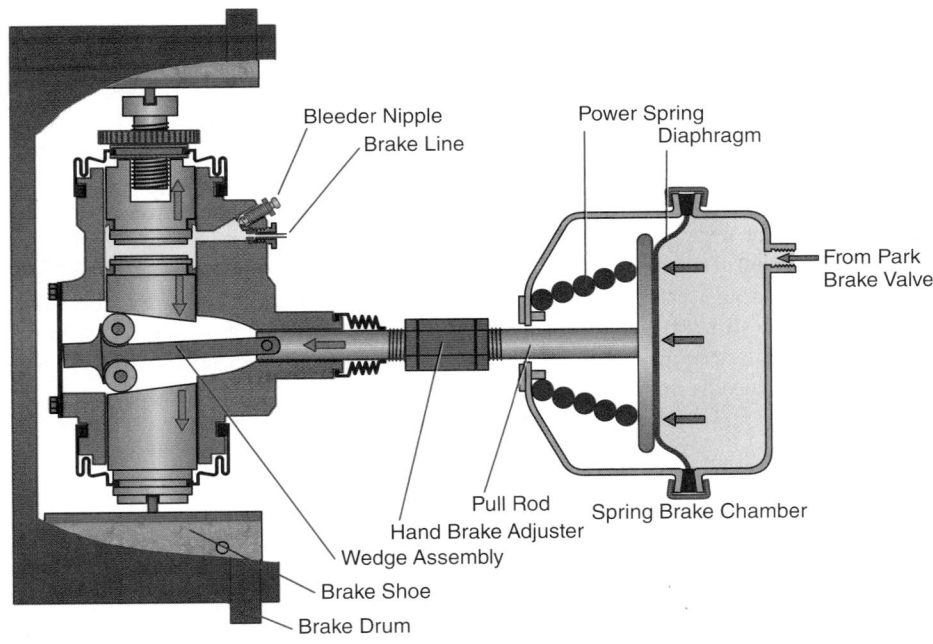

FIGURE 38-41 Park brake in the released position. Park brake spring is compressed by hydraulic fluid. Service brake is applied.

whenever the excessive drum-to-brake clearance is present. The adjusters positioned at the end of the wheel cylinder pistons have a helical groove cut along the length of the adjuster body. A small screw with a grooved end, called a pawl, follows the helical grooves and causes the adjuster to turn whenever it moves in and out during braking events. Once the piston stroke becomes excessive due to brake wear, the adjuster body turns far enough to enable the screw to lift and turn the adjuster to switch to another set of parallel grooves. A threaded screw between the adjuster and cylinder piston lengthens the adjuster mechanism when the shoe clearance is excessive, thus maintaining a constant drum-to-shoe clearance.

The brakes also use two brake shoes with a color-coded yellow and white return spring. A hydraulic jumper line connects the park and adjusting hydraulic cylinders together, which both operate to apply the brakes.

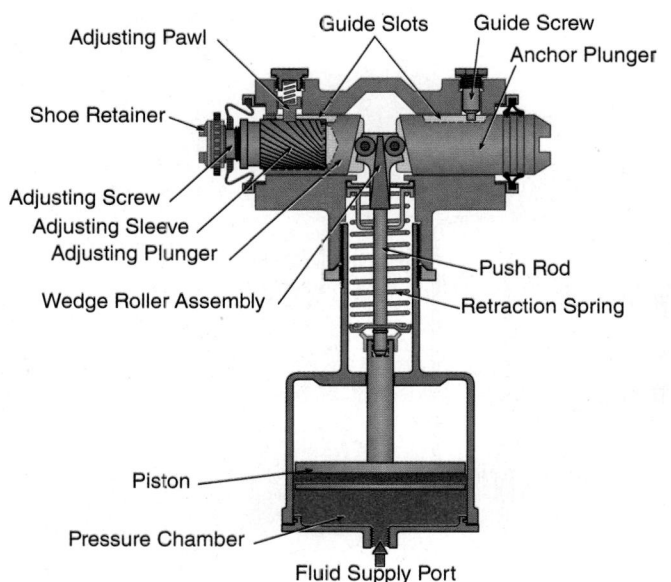

FIGURE 38-42 A Lucas Girling "twin-stop" automatic brake adjuster.

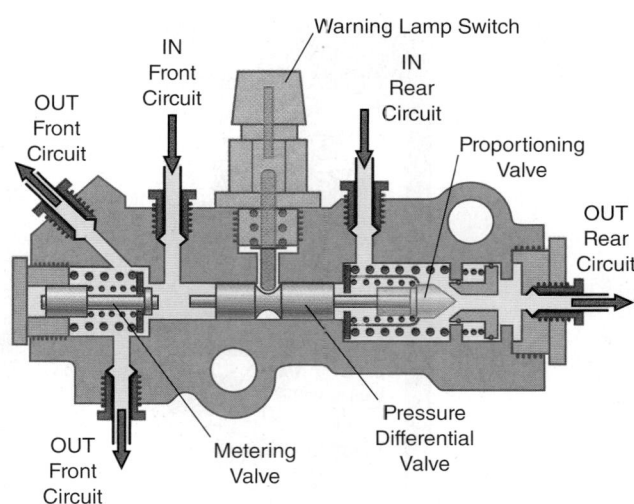

FIGURE 38-43 A combination valve included a metering, proportioning, and pressure differential switch.

Brake Metering and Proportioning Valves

To enhance vehicle stability during braking, two different hydraulic brake valves were once commonly used on various drum brake systems to control brake pressure to the front and rear brakes. A brake pressure **metering valve** was used to help delay the onset of brake application force to the front brakes until after the rear brakes were applied. By applying the rear brakes first, vehicle stability was enhanced because the front end of the vehicle tended not to dive or sink as far with inertia shifting of vehicle weight to the front. It also meant the rear of the vehicle would not be as likely swing out since drag exerted by the application force of rear brakes improved straight-line directional stability. The metering valve operated by requiring brake fluid pressure from the master cylinder to exceed a minimum threshold before fluid was allowed to pass through to the front brakes.

Rear-brake proportioning valves are another type of valve that was once used to enhance vehicle stability at the rear brakes. Unlike the metering valve, it worked by limiting maximum brake fluid pressure to the rear brakes. This was necessary because high brake pressure could result in excessive rear brake torque and lock-up the rear brakes. Metering and proportioning valves plus a pressure differential switch were often incorporated into a single unit called a **combination valve** (**FIGURE 38-43**). Later, variable pressure proportioning valves were used on light trucks and vans, which connected the proportioning valve to linkage attached to the frame. Changes in ride height caused by increasing or decreasing loads would vary the proportioning valve's limiting pressure up or down to increase brake torque when loaded and reduce it under unloaded conditions. Both metering and proportioning valves are inspected with hydraulic pressure gauges installed in the brake lines. Brake line pressure is compared against specifications to determine whether a valve was correctly operating. To inspect metering valve operation, follow the steps in **SKILL DRILL 38-1**.

SKILL DRILL 38-1 Testing the Metering or the Proportioning Valves

1. Research the testing procedure and specifications in the appropriate service information.
2. Disconnect the inlet line and outlet line from the metering valve or proportioning valve. Use a flare nut wrench to loosen the brake lines.
3. Connect the valve pressure tester to the inlet port and outlet port of the metering valve or the proportioning valve. Reconnect the inlet line to the valve, with the pressure gauge teed into it.
4. Operate the brake pedal and observe both pressure gauge readings; compare the findings to specifications.

Advantages of Disc Brakes

LO 38-8 Identify and explain the advantages and features of disc brake systems.

The introduction of reduced stopping distance requirements for vehicles over 10,000 lb gross vehicle weight (GVW) in the 1980s meant the end of drum brakes, which are not as effective as disc brakes. For the lighter range of medium-duty vehicles, drum brakes continued in use on rear axles until the mid-1990s when stopping distance and braking stability requirements became even stricter and ABS was mandated. By then, disc brakes, which are not as prone to brake fade, displaced drum brakes from medium-duty commercial vehicles. Disc brakes have an advantage over drums because squeezing hot shoes and rotors doesn't reduce brake torque as much as it does for drum brakes. Heat generated during braking expands a rotor's thickness, which helps pinch shoes tighter against pads. In drum brakes, heat expands the drum, increasing the clearances between brake linings and drums. Recovery time from heat effects is faster for disc brakes because the rotor's surface area is much larger and can radiate more heat and faster than a drum, which traps heat and must pass through thick drum walls before air can remove brake-generated heat. Rotors on commercial vehicles are typically internally ventilated, which further improves resistance to heat fade. Disc brakes also recover more quickly from immersion in water. This is an important feature because wet brakes are less effective than dry brakes. Maintenance requirements for disc brakes are fewer plus, the lighter, relatively less complex disc brake systems have a built-in automatic rotor-to-pad adjustment feature that maintains close contact between brake pads and rotors each time the brake is operated.

No special valving is used by disc brakes like drum brakes required in very old cars and trucks. The brake balance between axles is now established by the OEM selection of the diameter and number of caliper pistons, rotor diameter, and master cylinder bore diameter. Because there is no self-energizing and servo action in disc brakes, braking is proportional to driver pedal effort. This feature translates into better feedback to the driver about brake action. The latest electronically controlled brake systems can even balance brake torque between each wheel end by analyzing wheel speed data from ABS sensors to adjust hydraulic braking pressure.

Major components of the hydraulic disc brake foundation system include (**FIGURE 38-44**):

- Calipers
- Rotors
- Brake pads
- Lines and hoses
- Optional parking brake mechanisms

Disc Brake Wheel-End Components

At the wheel end are several major components associated with the disc brake system. In addition to the wheel hub assembly, rotor, and caliper are a torque plate and optional dust shield. The torque plate is bolted to either the steering knuckle or flange on the rear axle housing. Torque plates, sometimes called anchor plates, serve as a solid attachment point for the calipers

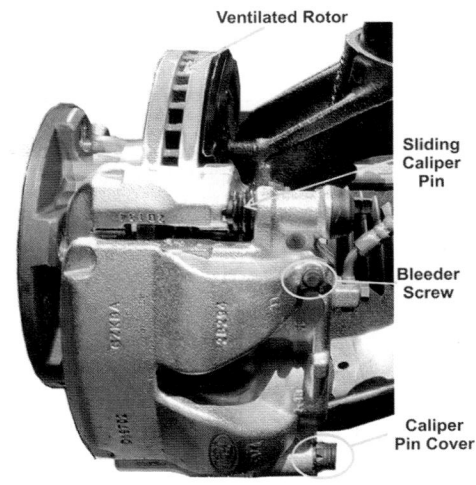

FIGURE 38-44 Heavy-duty vehicle disc brake system.

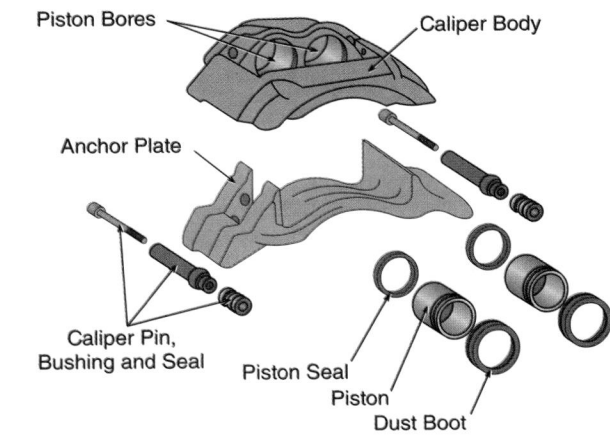

FIGURE 38-45 A floating caliper design using sliding pins.

to transfer brake torque from the calipers to the axles and chassis. These heavy parts are made from malleable steel that bends rather than cracks when shock loaded. The ABS wheel speed sensor is also placed in the torque plate. An optional dust shield minimizes the entry of abrasive road debris into the wheel-end brake components to reduce unnecessary wear. Commercial vehicles use two main types of calipers and are classified according to the method used to attach them to the torque plate:

- Floating calipers, also called reaction beam
- Fixed calipers

Floating Calipers

Floating calipers, which move freely in a lateral direction back and forth across the rotor, are identified by several distinctive features. First, there are two slots or at least two pins used to position the caliper over the rotor. The pins, which pass from the anchor plate into the caliper, allow the caliper to smoothly move back and forth across the rotor along the lubricated pins. This sliding action takes place whenever the brakes are applied lends the sliding name to this caliper design (**FIGURE 38-45**).

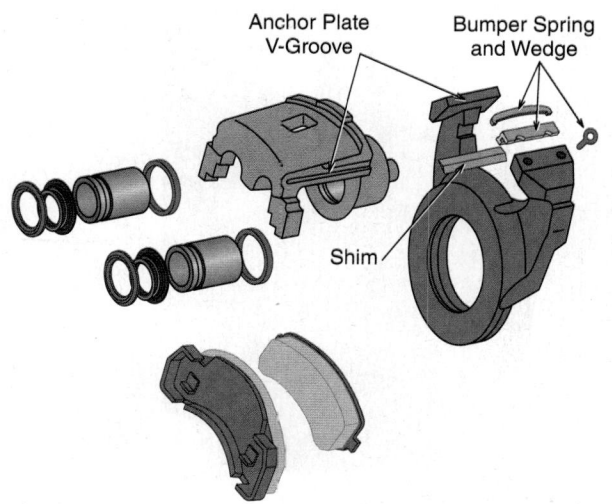

FIGURE 38-46 A floating caliper design using wedges and a spring to retain the caliper on the anchor plate while allowing it to slide along grooves.

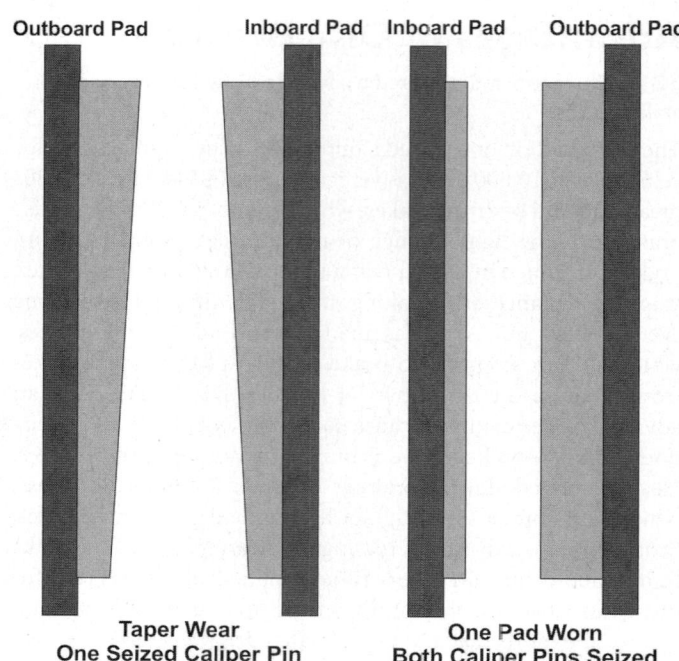

FIGURE 38-47 Uneven brake pad wear caused by sticking or binding in a single caliper slider pin.

Meritor also calls this caliper design a **reaction beam**. The caliper uses sliding guide pins, which pass through a carrier, or saddle, bolted directly to the torque plate.

If pins are not used, lubricated grooves or slots in the anchor plate are cut to match with edges on each end of caliper. A wedge may be inserted between the two parts to retain the caliper on the anchor plate. This arrangement provides a sliding action to center the caliper over the rotor, lightly holding the caliper in position while allowing it enough freedom of movement to slide back and forth. Additionally, to prevent the caliper from bouncing and making noise in the grooves, a bumper spring, retaining wedge, and selective shim can be used to maintain a snug fit with minimal pressure between the anchor plate and caliper (**FIGURE 38-46**).

Floating calipers use pistons that are located on only one side—the inboard side. During braking, the entire caliper moves inboard when the pistons move outboard to apply the brakes, squeezing two brake pads located on each side of the rotor. Floating calipers work well, but their size and construction limits having no more than two pistons. Given the limited piston surface area, the maximum brake torque floating calipers are capable of producing is adequate for most applications, but it is less than the fixed caliper examined next. The sliding pins may also require maintenance between brake pad replacement if they begin to stick and not slide. Corrosion and dirt accumulations can cause pins to corrode and wear, particularly if the seals retaining grease around the caliper sliding pins allow water and other contaminants into the caliper bushings. Road salt is particularly harsh and can chemically harden some lubricants or cause sticking between pins and bushings along which the pins slide. When the sliding pins stick and bind, the caliper cannot fully retract away from the brake pads and brake drag friction continues after braking. This sticking–binding sliding pin condition is identified by excessive premature wear on the inboard brake pad. Taper wear of brake pads is caused by just a single pin sticking (**FIGURE 38-47**). It also produces excessive heat, capable of warping the rotor and causing increased fuel consumption.

To inspect a caliper for sticking slider pins, the brake pads are examined to determine whether the wear on each is the same and symmetrical. A caliper should also be gripped and moved laterally back and forth to verify movement takes place.

Reaction-Beam Calipers

Meritor builds floating calipers it calls reaction-beam calipers. The reaction-beam hydraulic disc brake caliper slides over sealed and lubricated guide pins and sleeves attached to another component Meritor calls the carrier a saddle plate. The carrier, in turn, is bolted directly to the torque plate or anchor. The torque plate is bolted onto the axle or may be a part of the axle. When the Meritor caliper is removed, the caliper and carrier are unbolted and removed together as an assembly (**FIGURE 38-48**).

Fixed Calipers

Fixed calipers, as the name suggests, don't slide back and forth across the rotor. Instead, they are bolted to the torque plate and do not move. This design eliminates problems associated with wear and sticking of slider pins and bushings. When brake pad changes are required, only the pad retention bolts are removed, and the new linings can be dropped into the caliper. Because the caliper housing is not removed, the brake hose is untouched during brake service.

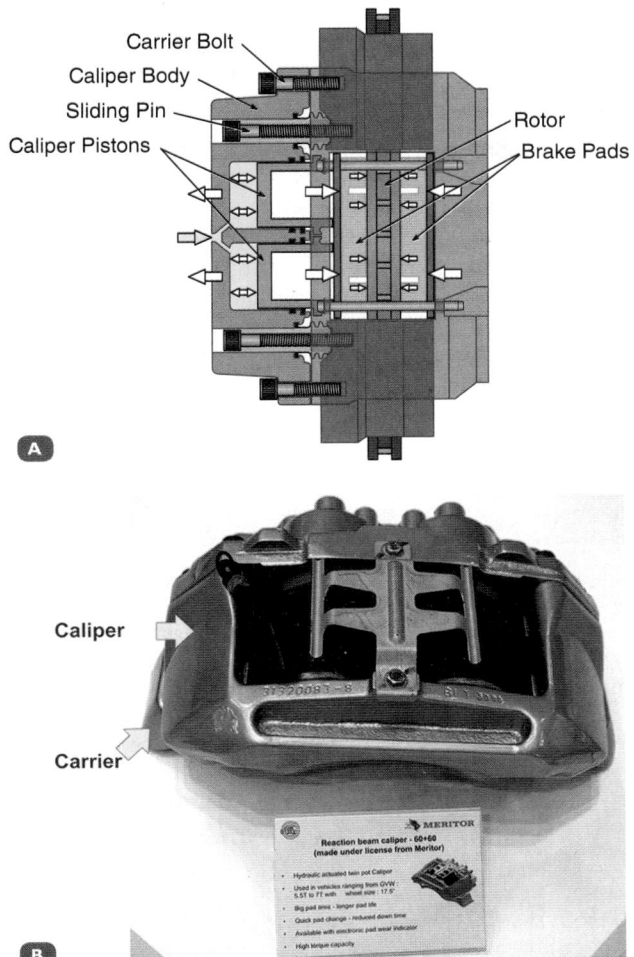

FIGURE 38-48 A. Meritor's reaction-beam caliper is a type of floating caliper. Note the arrows showing the direction of force and movement in a floating caliper. **B.** A reaction beam caliper designed by Meritor requires both the caliper and carrier removal at the same time

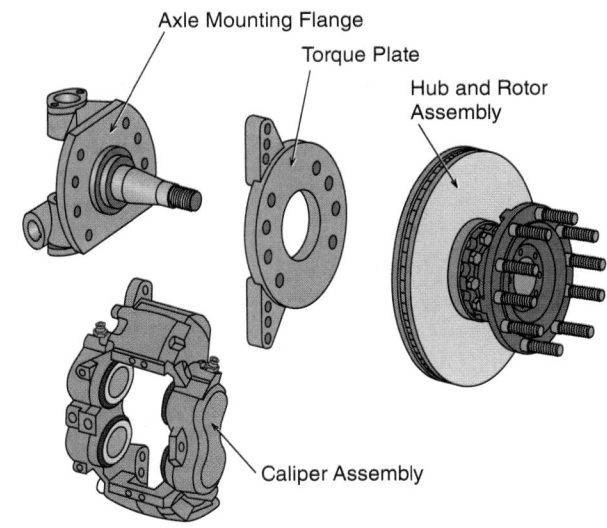

FIGURE 38-49 A fixed caliper is bolted directly to the torque plate. Only the pistons, but not the caliper, move to center the brake pads over the rotor.

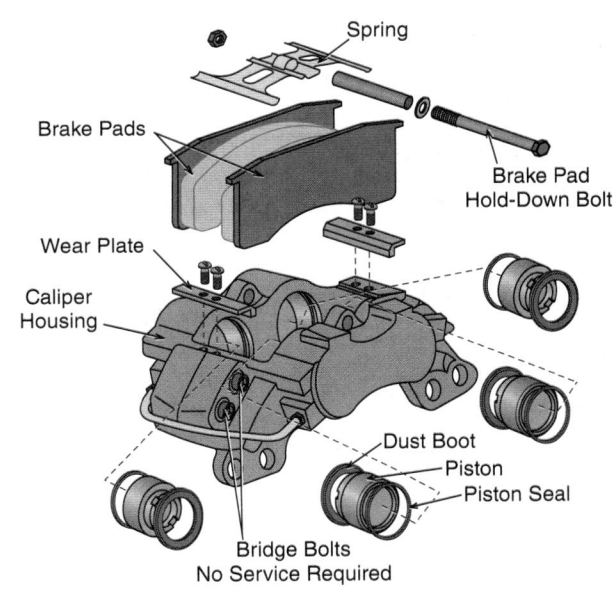

FIGURE 38-50 Parting halves of the fixed rotor are assembled with non-serviceable bridge bolts.

To enable brake pads to center over the rotor, the caliper pistons are arranged on both sides of the caliper to clamp brake pads against the rotor when the brakes are applied. The use of four or more pistons in the caliper doubles the surface area that pressurized hydraulic fluid acts against. The larger surface area providing greater clamping force explains why fixed calipers are considered high performance calipers useful on commercial vehicles operating with heavy loads. These calipers are also a popular aftermarket upgrade on light trucks with large tire sizes to compensate for the reduce braking effectiveness caused by oversized tires (**FIGURE 38-49**).

Using pistons on both sides of the calipers requires a crossover brake line to connect the inboard and outboard halves of the calipers to supply brake fluid to the outboard pistons. Both bleeders must be opened during brake bleeding service to remove air, but it is critical that all hydraulic components upstream of these calipers, such as the hydraulic parking brake, must be bled as well. This operation can only be performed using OEM software, such as Bendix ACOM or WABCC Toolbox, to command brake valves and actuators to move and purge air following specific sequence of prompts in software menus (**FIGURE 38-50**).

During a brake application, the hydraulic pressure behind the pistons of floating or fixed calipers is evenly applied to the all pistons to clamp the brake pads against the rotor. When the brakes are released, the pistons retract and allow the rotor to turn freely. If any brake wear has taken place, the pistons do not retract to a previous position but incrementally move closer to the rotor to maintain the same pad to rotor clearance.

Caliper Pistons

Brake calipers are constructed from cast iron or plated cast iron to provide an attractive finish. Piston bores in the casting have a sealing ring in each bore to prevent fluid leakage past the piston. Pistons placed in the bore are made from aluminum, chrome-plated steel, and high-temperature-resistant plastic-like materials called **phenolic**. A dust boot over the piston prevents abrasive dirt and contaminants from entering the area between the piston and the piston bore (**FIGURE 38-51**). Calipers are rebuildable and service kits are available to replace the piston and seals during an overhaul. Caliper cores must be carefully inspected and the caliper bore lightly honed to remove any pitting or light scratches. Calipers with heavily pitted, rusted, or deeply scratched piston bores caused by abrasive wear and particles must be discarded.

No adjusting mechanism is used to maintain brake pad-to-rotor clearance. Instead, the calipers' pistons use a square-cut O-ring around the piston circumference that not only seals brake fluid in housing but also is involved in retracting the piston when the brakes are released (**FIGURE 38-52**). During

braking, the piston seal located in a groove within the caliper housing clings to the piston and is stretched as the square seal grips the piston. Piston movement causes the seal to twist as the piston moves toward the brake pads. When the brakes are released, the elastic stretching action behaves like a return spring to help retract the piston back into the bore. The result is the close pad-to-rotor clearance is maintained. Eventually pad and rotor wear could increase rotor-to-pad clearance. To enable the piston to reposition the pads closer to the rotor, the O-ring must slip over the piston body. This happens whenever the piston moves farther than the sealing ring can stretch or the caliper can vibrate over road bumps to help reposition the piston. Often a slightly low brake pedal returns to its normal position if a vehicle is lightly braked while driving it over rough gravel or bumpy road surfaces.

▶ TECHNICIAN TIP

Low brake pedal, where braking action takes place only after a long pedal stroke, is a common complaint with hydraulic brakes. It has several causes, but one overlooked problem is a caliper piston that does not correctly adjust or is pushed back too far by lateral rotor runout or rotor thickness variations after every brake application. Operating a vehicle with a low brake pedal over rough gravel roads allows vibration to help reposition a sticky caliper piston O-ring over the piston and restore normal brake pedal travel. Lateral rotor runout and rotor thickness variations causing a low brake pedal must be checked at each wheel end using a precision dial indicator.

Brake Rotors

Brake rotors, called discs due to their circular shape, work with the pads and caliper to create friction during braking. Sliding and adhesive friction between the pads and rotor that is bolted to the wheel hub converts rotating movement into heat energy. Rotors are commonly made from several grades of alloyed cast iron. Cast iron has stable, heat-resistant properties and long-wearing capabilities, making it ideal material for making rotors. Iron's coefficient of friction and ability to withstand temperatures up to 2100° F (1149° C) are easily handled by brake temperatures that can just exceed 1000° F (538° C) under prolonged hard braking. Better quality, longer wearing rotors have more carbon content, less silicon, and are alloyed with more corrosion-resistant metals to resist rusting from humidity and road salt. Other materials, such as steel, laminated steel, and ceramic alloyed rotors, are only used in high end performance racing and not on commercial vehicles.

To dissipate heat, commercial vehicle rotors are ventilated with air passageways between each face of the rotor that circulate air using centrifugal force (**FIGURE 38-53**). Air drawn into the rotor center flows out from its faster-turning outside diameter to help cool the rotor. Another important factor to resisting heat is the rotor thickness. The mass of the rotor determines how much heat a rotor can absorb before overheating and potentially cracking or warping. Thinner worn rotors are more likely to end up heat damaged and can contribute to brake fade. Minimum rotor thickness specification is stamped into the rotor, often along with a minimum thickness, after machining operations

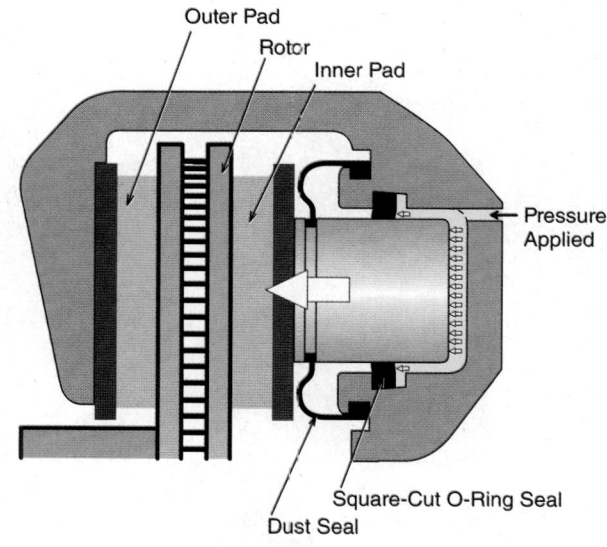

FIGURE 38-51 A cross-sectional view of a caliper piston and seals.

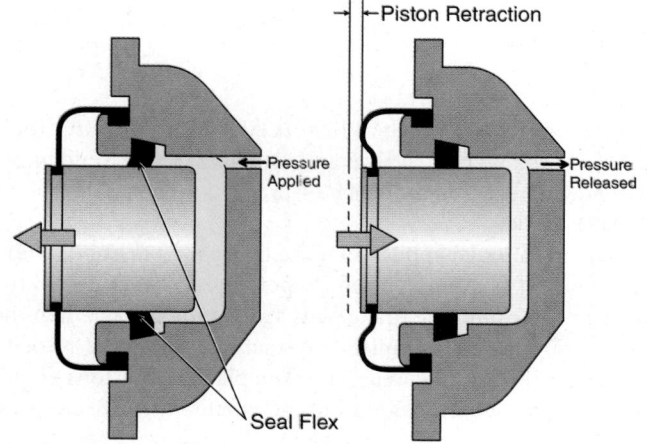

FIGURE 38-52 A square-cut O-ring is used to help slightly retract the piston from the rotor when the brakes are released.

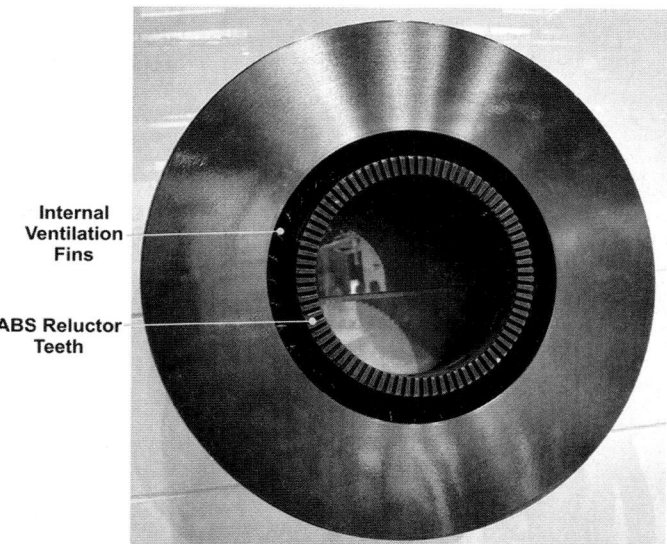

FIGURE 38-53 This flat rotor contains an ABS relocator ring and internal ventilation passages to centrifugally cool the rotor.

FIGURE 38-55 The raised center of the rotor is called the hat.

FIGURE 38-54 The hat section of this commercial vehicle brake rotor combines a drum surface for the park brake shoes.

to straighten warped rotors, rotors with irregular thickness or clean surface imperfections.

Rotors are made either flat or with a raised center hat section (**FIGURE 38-54**). The hat section is built to allow the rotor to fit over a wheel hub (**FIGURE 38-55**). Special care must be taken when assembling the rotor that the hat section or the area of a flat rotor that fits on a wheel hub is properly prepared. The surfaces on the rotor and hub must be clean, free of corrosion, and flat. Using an air-powered tool to buff the areas with fiber pads is a good practice to prevent the rotor from warping due to trapped contamination beneath the center section after the rotor is tightened to specifications using a torque wrench.

Rotor Service

Rotors are inspected using several methods. Visually, rotors are examined for excessive pitting corrosion, cracking, and deep

heat checks (**FIGURE 38-56**). Any damage that cannot be easily removed by machining and leaving adequate thickness of rotor for further wear should be discarded. To do this, the thickness of a rotor between it's thinnest points where corrosion or pitting is present is measured with a brake micrometer or Vernier (**FIGURE 38-57**). Thickness should be measured over at least three points and compared with specifications (**FIGURE 38-58**). A rotor's nominal thickness is its narrowest allowable dimension after machining, which provides for further wear before it reaches a minimum thickness—the thickness when it should be discarded. The minimum thickness and often the nominal thickness or minimum machine thickness are stamped into the rotor. Lateral runout is measured using a dial indicator and obtained while turning the rotor (**FIGURE 38-59**).

OEM maximum lateral runout specifications generally range from as little as 0.0012" to 0.015" (0.003 mm to 0.381 mm) total indicated runout (maximum lateral – minimum lateral dimension) measured ¼" in from the outer diameter of the brake rotor. No runout is ideal. However, runout and thickness variations causes brake pulsation and low brake pedal, it should be removed by machining.

Brake Pads

Brake pad friction materials must brake effectively when either cold or hot, deliver long rotor and pad service life, and operate noiselessly. Brake dust created by the pads should not accumulate around brake and wheel parts and should not be a health hazard. Often there is a trade-off between good braking performance and service life of pads and rotors. Pads with high frictional coefficients can have excellent braking performance but quickly wear out rotors.

Ceramic and semi-metallic pad materials are more commonly used in today's commercial vehicles because of excellent braking properties needed for heavy vehicles. The pads are riveted or bonded to steel backing plates. Softer organic pads used on automobiles made of natural materials, such as Kevlar, glass,

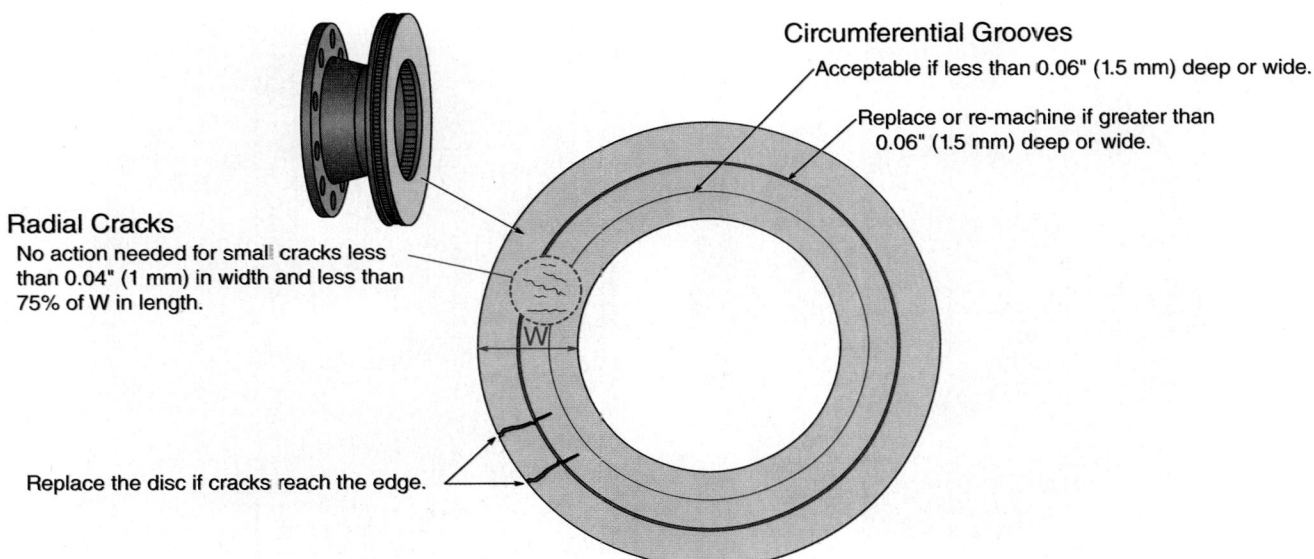

Circumferential Grooves
Acceptable if less than 0.06" (1.5 mm) deep or wide.

Replace or re-machine if greater than 0.06" (1.5 mm) deep or wide.

Radial Cracks
No action needed for small cracks less than 0.04" (1 mm) in width and less than 75% of W in length.

Replace the disc if cracks reach the edge.

These values are a guide only; always check manufacturer wear limit specifications.

FIGURE 38-56 Visual inspection criteria for commercial vehicle rotors.

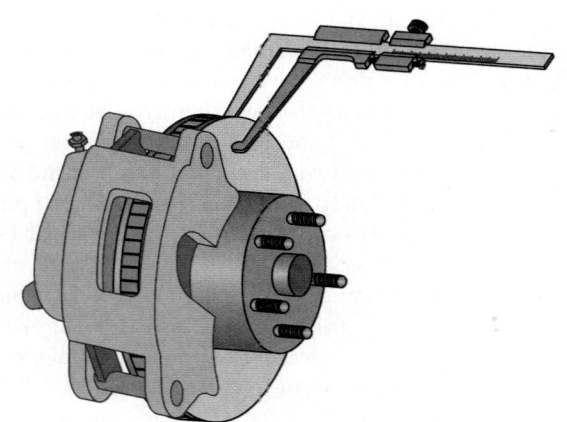

FIGURE 38-57 Measuring rotor thickness with a Vernier.

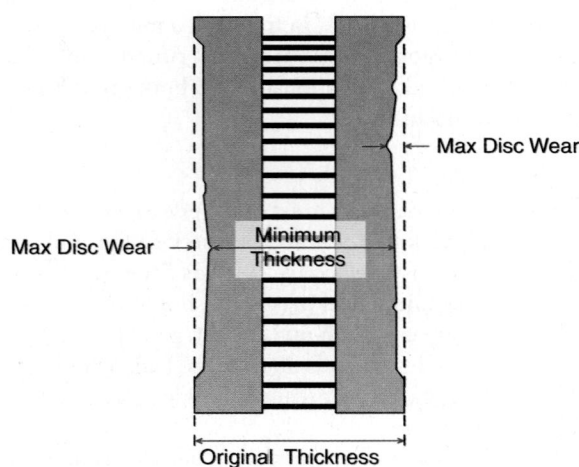

Max Disc Wear

Max Disc Wear

Minimum Thickness

Original Thickness

FIGURE 38-58 Rotor thickness should be measured at the thinnest point of a rotor where corrosion or pitting is present.

rubber, and resins, wear too quickly. Semi-metallic brake pads are composed of between 30% and 65% of various metals. The metal gives the pad excellent heat resistance, particularly when they are hot, by creating more adhesive or sticky friction. Metals may include steel wool or wire, iron, brass, graphite, and copper combined with a bonding material. The disadvantage of metal friction material is it aggressively wears rotors and can produce brake squeal and other noises.

Ceramic composite pads are longer lasting and quieter, but more expensive, than semi-metallic pads (**FIGURE 38-60**). Ceramic pads friction material resembles clay-like pottery material. They are typically made from clay and porcelain mixed with copper flakes and wire. Copper fibers in ceramic composites produce a brake pad that reduces the type of friction between the pads and rotors, which causes the rapid rotor wear and high frequency squeal of steel-based composites. As ceramic pads wear, less visible dust is produced, and it does not stick to wheels. Ceramic pads are longer lasting than steel-based composites because ceramic materials are also more resistant to heat-related wear.

Brake Pad Features

Chamfer pad edges and slots cut vertically, diagonally, or horizontally in the pads are designed to minimize noises. Insulator shims behind the pads can further dampen noise but are also critical insulators to prevent heat transfer into the caliper pistons and lower brake fluid temperatures. Anti-rattle springs are often placed over pads to firmly hold them in position in the caliper to prevent rattling noises. Tabs on the edges of the brake pads are used to locate the brake pads on the caliper and often require bending with a hammer and punch after installation (**FIGURE 38-61**). Bending the tabs is necessary to tighten pads in position to ensure the pads do not move during operation with the brakes released, which could produce rattling noises as well.

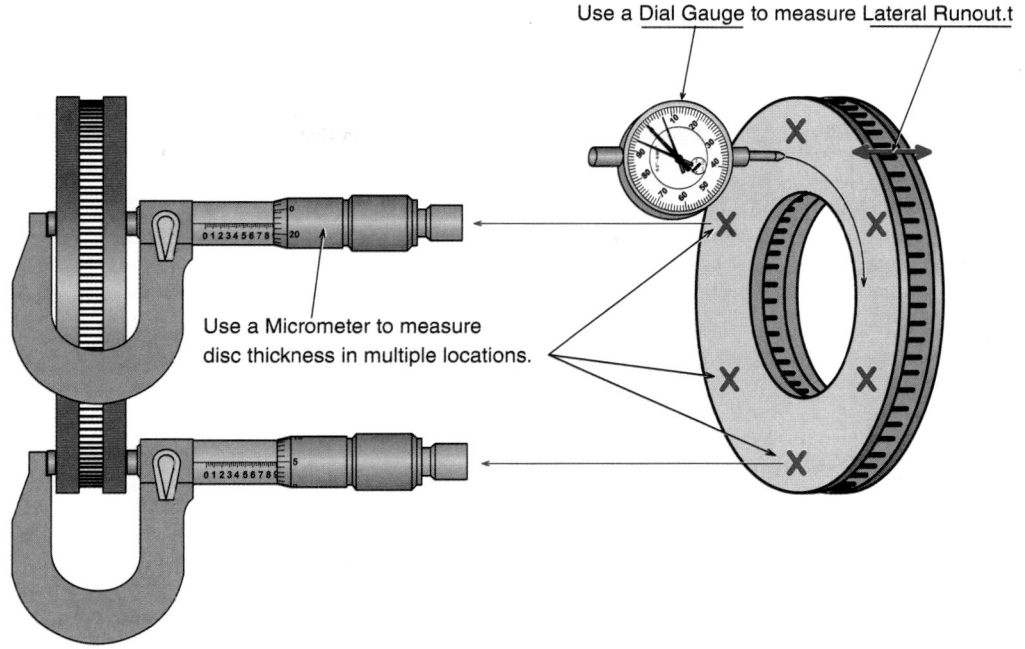

FIGURE 38-59 Measurement operations for a brake rotor involve measuring lateral runout and thickness.

FIGURE 38-60 A bonded ceramic pad is glued to the steel backing plate.

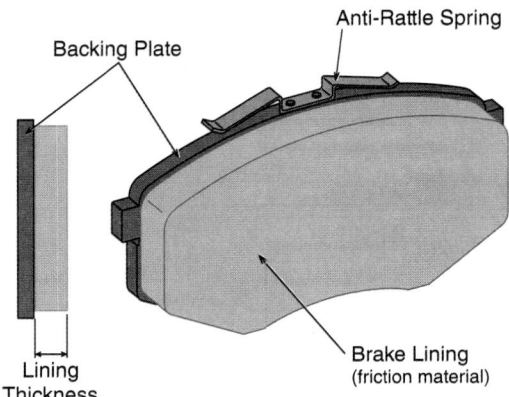

FIGURE 38-61 A brake pad for disc brakes has a much smaller surface area but higher loading. An anti-rattle spring minimizes brake noise.

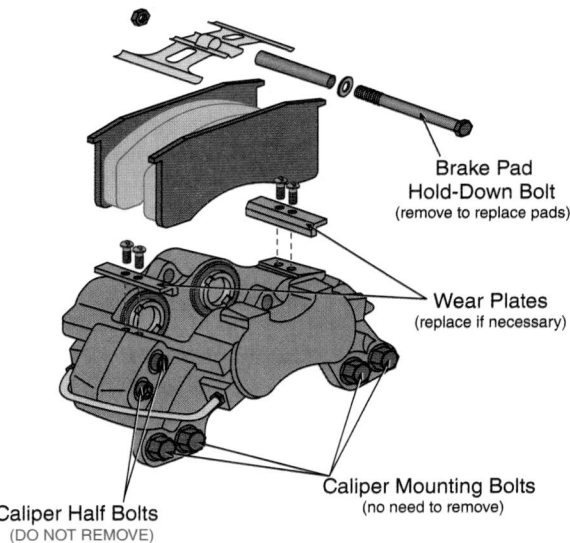

FIGURE 38-62 Fixed-type brake calipers do not require removal to replace the pads. After pushing back the caliper pistons, only a single bolt requires removal to replace pads.

Note that when replacing brake pads, floating calipers generally require removal to remove and replace the pads. Rotors that are in relatively good condition do not need machining between pad replacement unless the rotor finish is likely to prematurely wear a brake pad. Rusty, pitted, and distorted rotors require machining or replacement. When removing the caliper, never allow the flex brake line to support the weight of the caliper. Always use an elastic cable to suspend the caliper from the chassis and do not twist the line during reinstallation. Fixed calipers do not require removal to replace the pads. Only a single bolt requires removal to change brake pads (**FIGURE 38-62**).

When brake pad friction material is worn to a thickness of no less than ⅛" (3.2 mm), above the steel backing plate, the pads must be replaced. Alternatively, measure pad and backing plate thickness with a Vernier. Compare specifications with measured dimensions to make a service recommendation. When replacing pads, they should be replaced in axle sets to maintain brake balance on an axle.

SAFETY TIP

Brake pads can create a lot of toxic brake dust that should not be inhaled. Always wear personal protective equipment when working on brakes, such as HEPA breathing masks. Wash down wheel ends and brake parts with water before working on brakes. Never use compressed air to clean brakes because it produces enormous clouds of hazardous brake dust that others in a work area may inhale.

▶ TECHNICIAN TIP

How long a brake rotor lasts also depends, in part, on how the brakes are used. Aggressive braking, which is hard and frequent pedal application force, accelerates brake wear and wears out brake pad rotors faster than a moderate, but longer, brake application force. Other factors to explain premature brake wear include:

- Road and traffic conditions: Urban driving versus on-highway
- Topographic and climate conditions: Hilly versus flat, wet and salty roads versus dry, clean roads
- The degree of dirt and contamination: Off-road or coarse gravel without backing plates versus clean on-road with backing plates
- Quality of the brake rotors' casting material
- Brake pad friction material: Semi-metallic versus ceramic
- Condition of sliding pins and bushings, and use of lubricant: Free caliper pins versus sticking and binding calipers
- Piston seal and bore condition: Scored and contaminated versus clean and freely moving piston

Hydraulic Brake Power Assist Systems

LO 38-9 Identify and describe the types, construction, and operation of hydraulic brake power assist systems.

As mentioned at the beginning of the chapter, medium- to heavy-duty vehicles require a large amount of brake torque to stop. It's beyond most driver's leg strength to comfortably supply the hydraulic pressure needed to create that stopping power. Air brake systems can naturally assist driver effort to apply the brakes because the system multiplies driver pedal force. However, when hydraulic brake systems are used in commercial vehicles, the brake system requires some kind of power assist—be it vacuum, hydraulic, or air—to achieve the needed braking force. All vehicles with hydraulic brakes require these devices and a backup system to allow the driver to brake the vehicle if they fail. This next section examines more closely four types of power assist systems—commonly called brake boosters, used with hydraulic brakes.

Vacuum Brake Booster

A vacuum power assist system uses a vacuum booster, as shown in **FIGURE 38-63**, to assist the driver by increasing the braking force applied to the brake pedal. Vacuum boosters, alternatively called vacuum servos, use principles of pressure differential to multiply braking force applied to the pushrod of the brake master cylinder.

The vacuum used to power a vacuum booster is generated by either an engine-driven vacuum pump or derived from the intake manifold pressure of a throttled spark ignition engine. Vacuum is transferred to the booster along semi-rigid rubber, metal, or plastic lines and is stored in the reservoir of the booster. Vacuum storage pressure is maintained using a one-way check

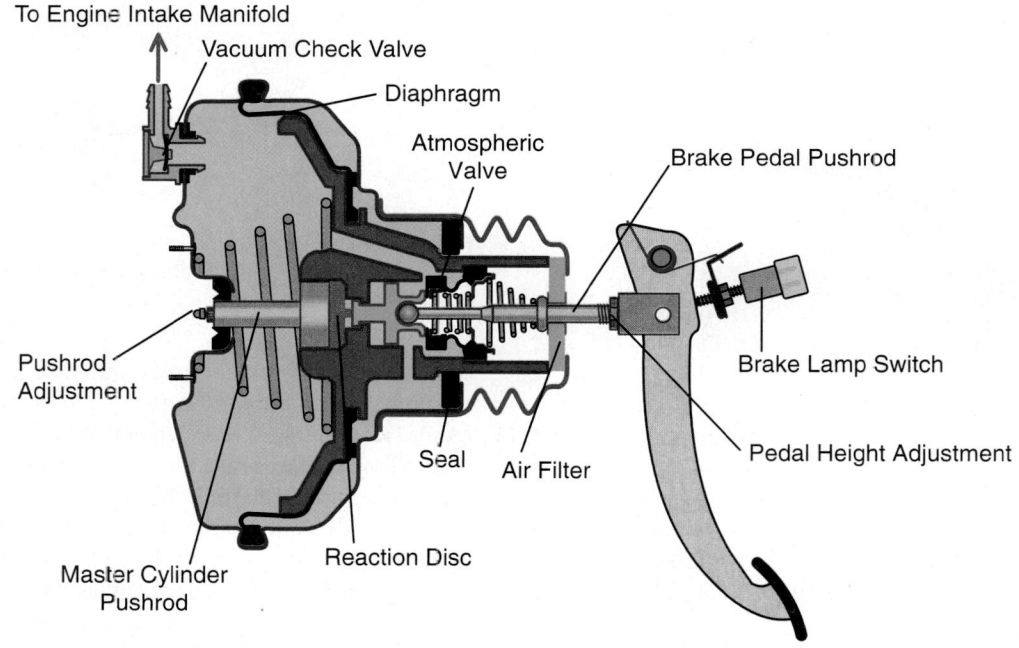

FIGURE 38-63 Cutaway of a typical vacuum brake booster.

valve at the reservoir. The vacuum power booster uses a large diaphragm, or sometimes two diaphragms in tandem, to supply a very large surface area for the supplied vacuum to operate against it. Although these systems are called vacuum boost systems, it is actually atmospheric pressure that does the work of amplifying the braking force.

The most common booster, shown in Figure 38-63, is positioned between the brake pedal and master cylinder. When the engine is running, vacuum is supplied through an inlet check valve to both sides of the large diaphragm in the vacuum booster, creating equal low pressure on both sides. When the brake pedal is depressed, a pushrod opens the atmospheric control valve, allowing atmospheric air pressure to enter only the pedal side of the diaphragm. The atmospheric air pressure pushes the diaphragm and the master cylinder pushrod toward the master cylinder, increasing the pressure on the master cylinder pistons the level of assistance this power-boost gives depends on the pressure applied to the brake pedal. The vacuum-assist booster has three stages of operation depending on the driver's input:

1. In stage 1, the driver's foot is off the pedal, and the atmospheric valve is closed. Vacuum enters both sides of the diaphragm. Vacuum pressure on both sides is equal so there is no power assist, and the system is primed to assist when necessary.
2. In stage 2, the driver pushes on the pedal. The atmospheric regulating valve in the center of the booster that's acted on by the pedal push rod opens proportionally to pedal travel. Atmospheric pressure gradually enters the rear side of the diaphragm and the pressure differential on either side of the booster diaphragm begins to push toward the master cylinder, creating a power assist.
3. In stage 3, the driver holds the pedal at a certain point. This allows the atmospheric valve to close to a position that maintains a pressure differential between the two sides, so the assist pressure holds at a steady level. The reaction disc is a mechanically sensitive part of the atmospheric valve that determines how much pedal effort is required to open and close the atmospheric valve.
4. Lifting the brake pedal allows the vacuum to re-enter the atmospheric side of the booster reservoir and replenish vacuum lost during the braking event.

In heavier vehicles, the master cylinder is used to provide a proportional brake pressure signal to a second master cylinder. Due to its size and additional need for vacuum reservoirs, the

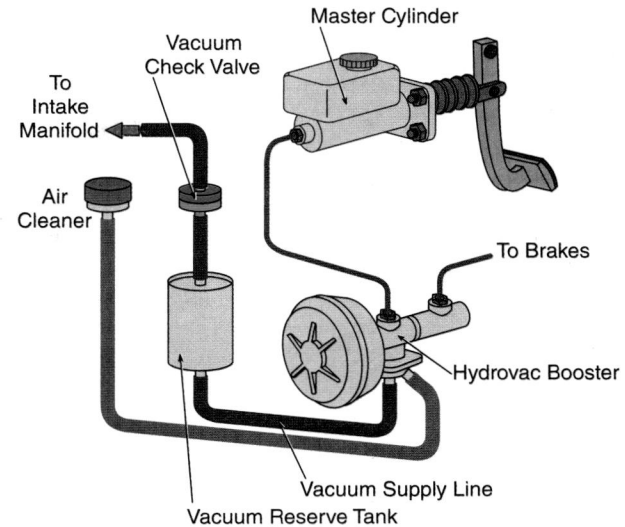

Master Cylinder
Vacuum Check Valve
To Intake Manifold
Air Cleaner
To Brakes
Hydrovac Booster
Vacuum Supply Line
Vacuum Reserve Tank

FIGURE 38-64 A larger, more powerful, hydraulic brake system requires additional vacuum reservoir capacity.

relay-like second master cylinder is located somewhere else on the chassis, beneath the cab (**FIGURE 38-64**). The large amount of air moving in and out of the vacuum reservoirs is filtered to prevent contamination when vehicles are operated in dusty off-road conditions.

Vacuum Brakes Servo Integrity Test

If the engine stops running, the booster's inlet check valve holds the vacuum in the booster. Boosters are designed with enough reserve capacity to allow two to three full-brake applications before the entire vacuum reservoir supply is lost. To check the booster system for operating integrity, follow the steps in **SKILL DRILL 38-2**.

Hydraulic Assist Systems

Many North American Class 4 to Class 6 vehicles use a hydraulic brake system equipped with hydraulic assistance. The Hydromax or Hydroboost power assist brake boosters are marketing names used by Bosch and Bendix. Hydraulic assist systems use pressurized hydraulic fluid rather than vacuum to provide brake power assist (**FIGURE 38-65**). The system has a hydraulic servo mechanism connected in series with a dual-circuit master cylinder. A typical hydraulic assist

SKILL DRILL 38-2 Checking Booster System for Operating Integrity

1. Press the brake pedal and fully apply the brake with the engine running.
2. Shut off the engine and compare the pedal movement with another full-brake application. The pedal movement should remain the same in both cases. Also, immediately after the vehicle is shut off, listen carefully for any hissing sound near where the brake pedal pushrod enters the booster. A hissing sound indicates

that the atmospheric valve is leaking and that the booster should be replaced.
3. Pump the brakes repeatedly with the engine off to deplete the vacuum reservoir. With the brakes still applied, start the engine. The brake pedal should fall as vacuum enters the booster. If the pedal remains hard, there is a problem with the vacuum supply or the booster.

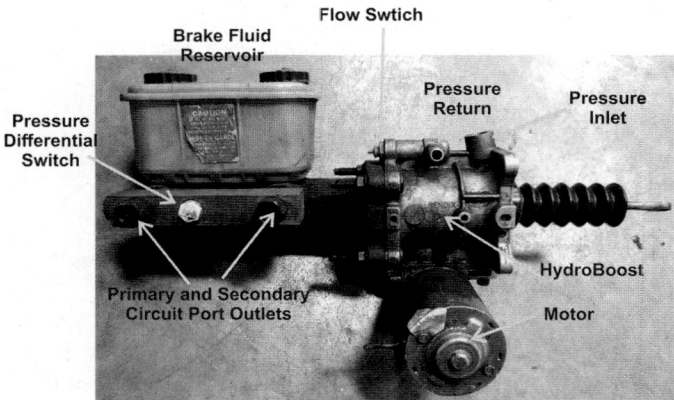

FIGURE 38-65 Hydraulic booster chamber connected in series with a dual-circuit master cylinder.

system is shown in **FIGURE 38-66**. The booster unit is bolted to the firewall, and the master cylinder is bolted to the front of booster.

The hydraulic pressure used for power assist is usually supplied by the vehicle's power steering pump. Some installations, however, use a dedicated hydraulic pump to supply pressure because the demands on the pump from the simultaneous use of the power steering and brake systems can be quite substantial. The booster unit used with hydraulic systems is equipped with an electrical backup motor should hydraulic pressure be lost for any reason. Effort is increased with the motor only operation, but not as much as when both the hydraulic pressure and hydroelectric pressure assist are lost. If the engine stalls and the electric motor fails to operate, braking can still take place, but without assistance and requires considerable effort to fully apply the brake (**FIGURE 38-67**).

On lighter medium-duty vehicles, a hydraulic accumulator is used to supply a reserve of hydraulic pressure in the event of a failure in the engine-driven hydraulic pump. The accumulator uses a heavy spring to store fluid under pressure. This addition provides the system with power assist for a couple of brake applications before it is depleted (**FIGURE 38-68**).

Following are five operating modes for an electrohydraulic assist system. Details of the electrohydraulic assist system are illustrated in **FIGURE 38-69**.

Hydraulic Assist System Operating Modes

1. In the first mode with the engine running and no brake application, hydraulic pressure is delivered to the inlet of the booster and travels through the unit unrestricted. The hydraulic pressure then returns to the pump reservoir (**FIGURE 38-70**). As the fluid exits the booster unit, the fluid opens a flow control switch that interrupts the electrical circuit to the backup electrical motor. No electrical or hydraulic brake assist occurs during this mode.
2. During the second mode (braking mode), the driver pushes the brake pedal. That action closes the booster's throttle valve, which restricts the fluid trying to exit the booster and causes pressure inside the booster to rise. The rising pressure pushes on the booster's power piston, amplifying

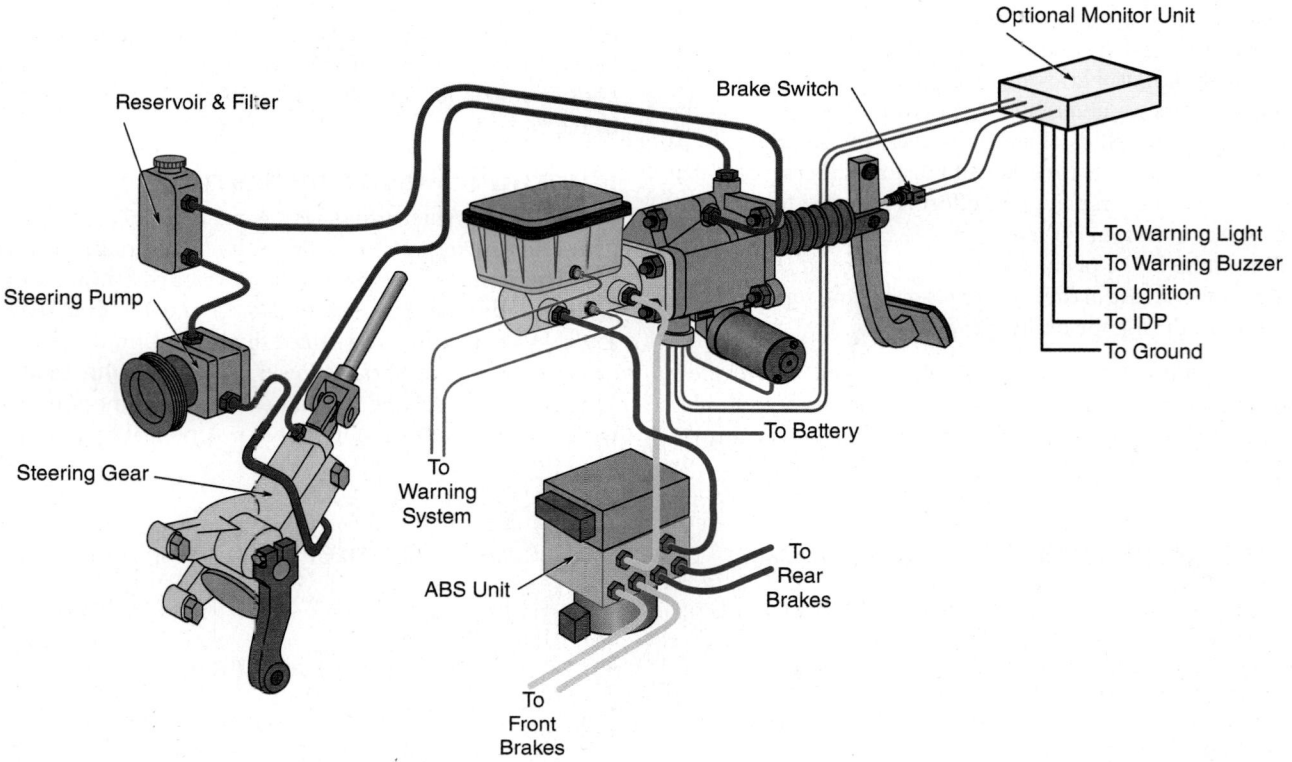

FIGURE 38-66 A typical Hydroboost system with ABS.

the brake pressure delivered to the master cylinder piston. Consequently, brake application pressure increases. Closing of the throttle valve takes place simultaneously with pressure applied to the reaction piston. Pressure applied to the reaction piston regulates how far the throttle valve closes. As pressure rises and pushes the power piston toward the master cylinder, the pressure simultaneously pushes back against the reaction piston and toward the driver's brake pedal. This gives the driver feedback or "feel" for the forcefulness of the brake application.

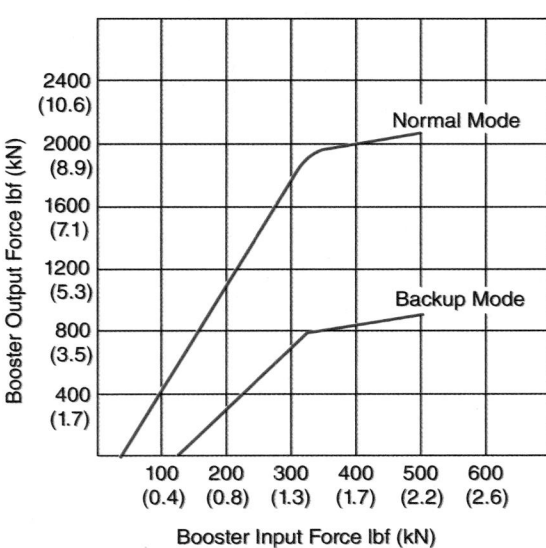

FIGURE 38-67 Hydraulic assist input force supplied by the electric motor is less than half the hydraulic pump-supplied assistance.

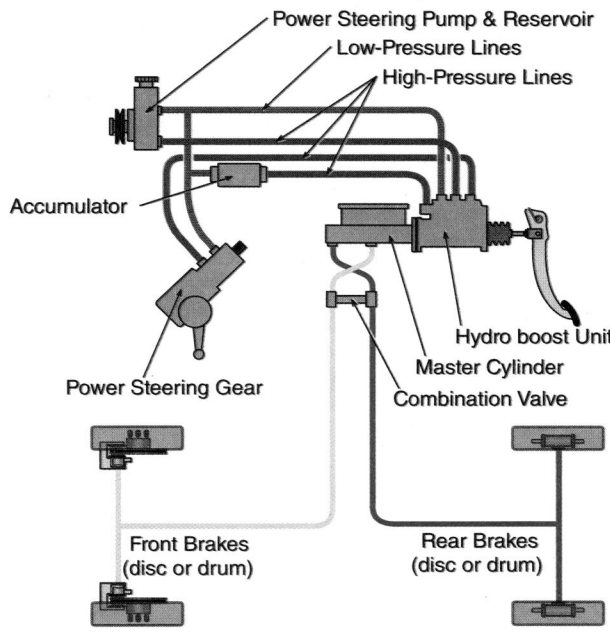

FIGURE 38-68 Layout of the hydraulic circuits for a Hydroboost hydraulic brake assist unit.

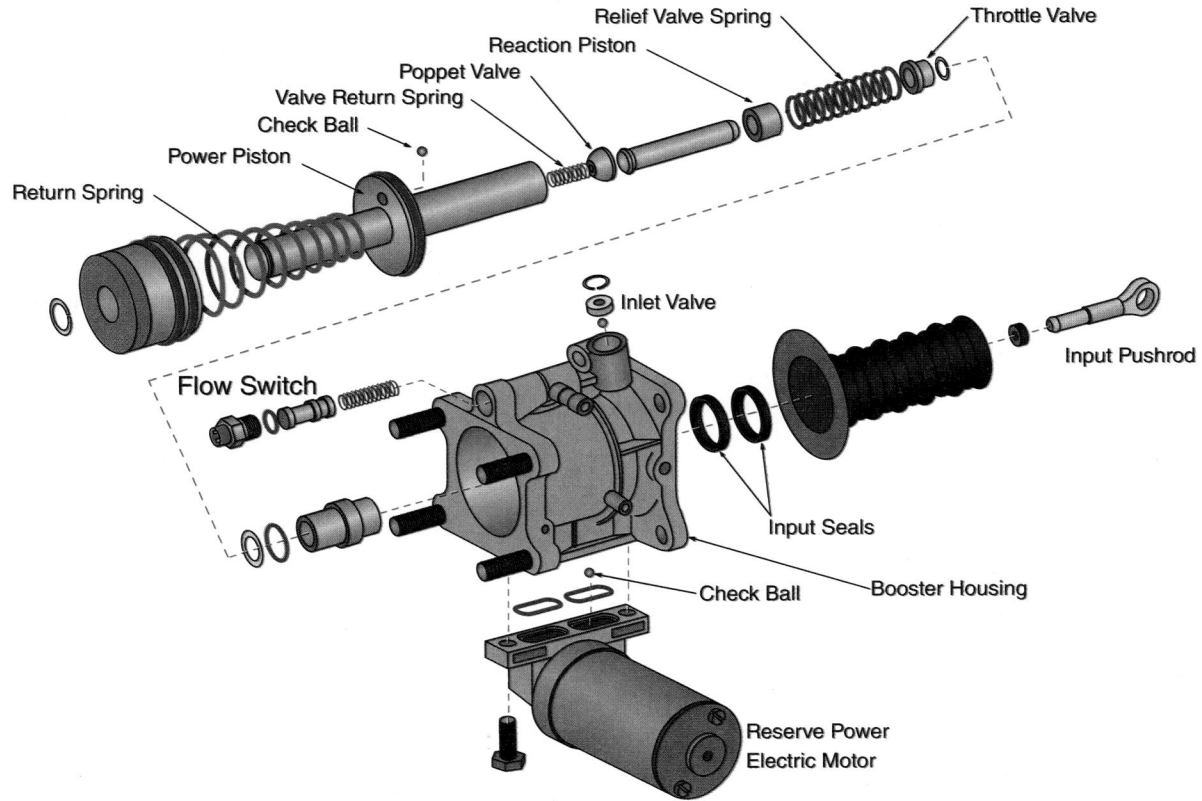

FIGURE 38-69 Subcomponents of a Hydroboost hydraulic brake assist unit.

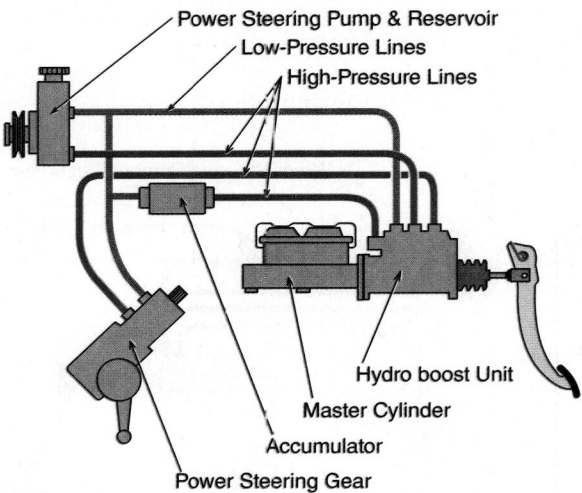

FIGURE 38-70 Fluid flow through various circuits of a hydraulic assisted brake booster.

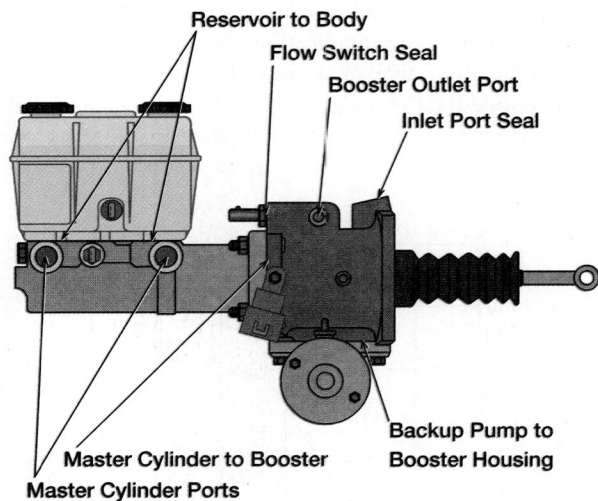

FIGURE 38-71 Inspection points for leaks on a hydraulic brake booster.

3. The third mode of operation is when the driver holds the brake pedal down at any point. Doing so holds the throttle valve at a precise open/closed position, which establishes a steady assist pressure.

4. The fourth mode of operation is the assist from the electrical backup motor. If there is an interruption in the hydraulic pressure exiting the booster during either an engine failure or hydraulic system failure, the flow control switch in the booster unit closes. The circuit to the backup electrical motor is therefore complete. If the driver pushes the brake pedal during this condition, the brake light switch signals a relay to send electric current to the backup motor. The electric motor drives a small hydraulic pump to supply pressure to the booster. In these circumstances, the brake assist works the same as in mode 2 and mode 3 but the assistance pressure is less than half. If the driver pushes the brake pedal in this vehicle without the key on or without the engine running, the backup motor works in the same way. The backup motor provides emergency brake booster operation as long as the battery can supply the motor.

5. With no hydraulic or electric assist, the pedal pushrod compresses the linkage inside the hydraulic boost unit to directly act on the master cylinder pistons. Braking can take place but is severely limited due to the reduced force the driver applies to the pedal compared to the assisted modes.

Hydraulic assist systems should be routinely checked for brake assist level—both with the engine running and shut off (to check the backup motor)—and for leakage at the connecting hoses, switches, and joints. Also check for leakage at the connection to the master cylinder reservoir bolted to the master cylinder. Leakage between the master cylinder and booster should be examined carefully. If it is brake fluid, the rear seal of the master cylinder is leaking, and the unit requires replacement. If it is hydraulic fluid, the booster requires rebuilding or replacement (**FIGURE 38-71**).

Inspecting a Hydraulic Assist Booster System

1. With the engine off and the key in the "on" position, apply the service brakes.

2. Listen for the backup electric pump to operate. The indicator lamp on the instrument cluster should illuminate when the electric pump backup is operating and an audible warning may accompany the light warning.

3. Start the engine. The backup motor and any backup pump indicators, if equipped, should switch-off after the engine starts. This indicates that the brake power assist is working correctly.

Air–Hydraulic Booster

As mentioned at the beginning of the chapter, classifying brake systems air-over-hydraulic, or, in some cases, hydraulic-over-air system, are divided into two general categories. One system uses an air-operated foot valve to provide proportional brake pressure to an air cylinder acting on the master cylinder. The second system uses hydraulic pressure to control an air-operated relay valve, which operates a pneumatic cylinder supplying proportional pressure to the hydraulic master cylinder. Split hydraulic brake systems require two separate air cylinders acting on a master cylinder. When the air actuator is used to supply proportional brake application pressure and acts directly on the master cylinder, it is called a **direct-acting** system. This configuration is seen in **FIGURE 38-72**.

A slight variation of the direct-acting cylinder is an indirect-acting system, which uses an air to air to hydraulic sequence to apply proportional braking pressure to the master cylinder. The use of an air-operated foot valve controlling an air relay to supply air pressure proportional to driver effort is used to vary brake pressure output from the master cylinder. This system is seen in **FIGURE 38-73**. The use of an air-operated foot valve and

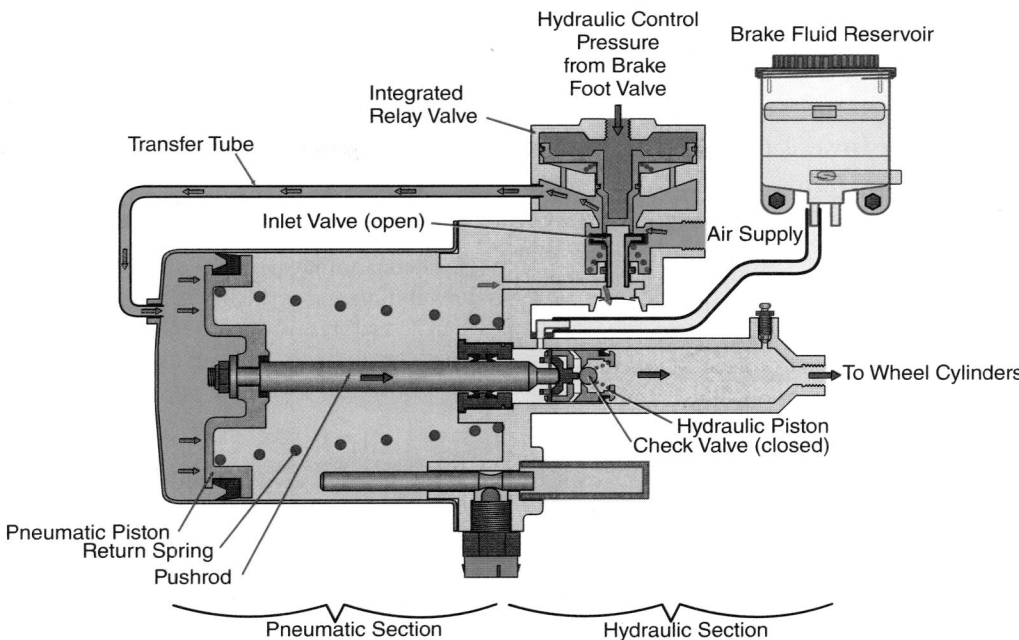

FIGURE 38-72 A directing acting air booster assembly when the brakes are applied.

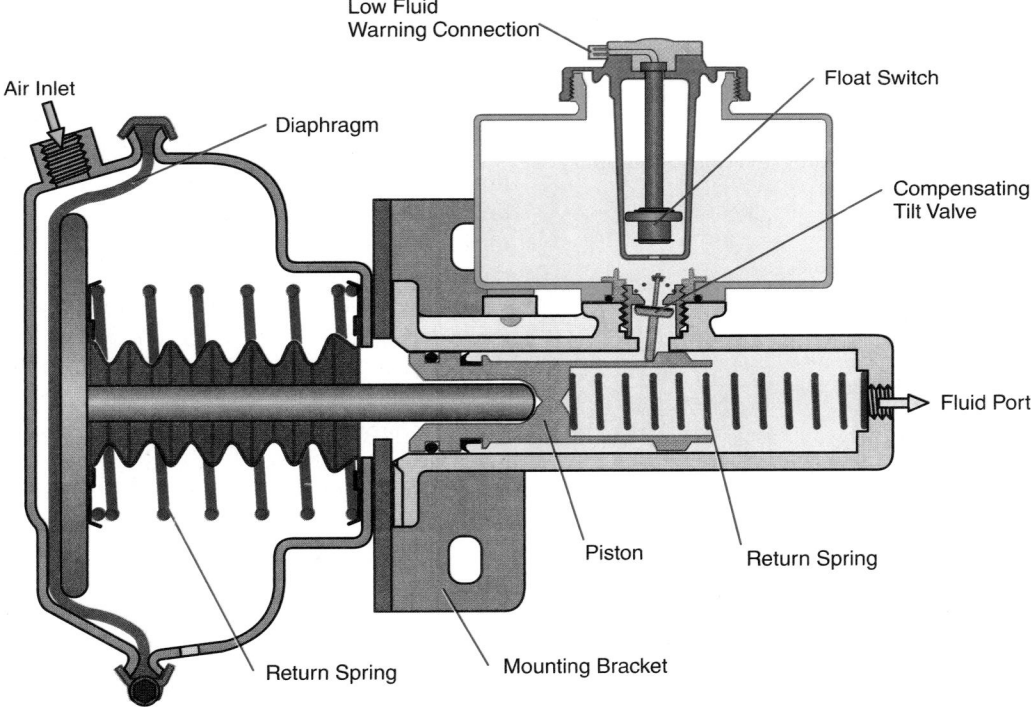

FIGURE 38-73 An indirect acting-type booster in the applied mode.

air relay valve eliminates the need for another hydraulic circuit and master cylinder.

Air Powered Booster Inspection

Air components of air-hydraulic brake booster system should be inspected the same way any part is inspected in a full air brake system. When performing a quick inspection of hydraulic components, there is no practical way to verify the power units converting air pressure to hydraulic pressure are correctly functioning other than to operate the brakes and confirm they have adequate brake fluid in the reservoirs. No brake warning indicator lamps should be illuminated when the system is operating correctly.

Hydraulic Brake Antilock Braking System (HABS)

LO 38-10 Identify and describe the construction, and operation of a hydraulic brake antilock braking system (HABS).

If equipped with hydraulic brakes, hydraulic antilock braking systems (HABS) are required by commercial vehicles over 10,000 lb GVW since 1999. Regardless of the type of power assist system used, the HABS system operates with the conventional primary and secondary hydraulic brake circuits to prevent wheel lockup. This means that if the HABS system fails, traditional non-ABS braking can take place. Directional stability and shortened stopping distances on slippery surfaces are provided by any ABS to improve vehicle safety. The operating principles of an ABS are relatively simple. Wheel speed sensors supply tire rotation speed data to an ABS electronic control module. The data is analyzed for potential wheel lockup, identified when wheel speed drops to zero while other tires are rotating. A modulator or brake pressure control valve cyclically releases and applies brake pressure to the locked wheel to enable the tire to rotate again, but maintains maximum braking capabilities to match road surface conditions that may be slippery due to ice, snow, mud, or loose sand (**FIGURE 38-74**). Maintaining a minimum tire rotation speed is necessary because a locked-up tire-wheel cannot maintain road traction and prevents proper steering control provided by tires with adhesive friction. Without tire traction, only sliding friction provides braking force on slippery surfaces. Compared to the adhesive friction of a rolling tire, sliding friction on slippery surfaces increases stopping distances.

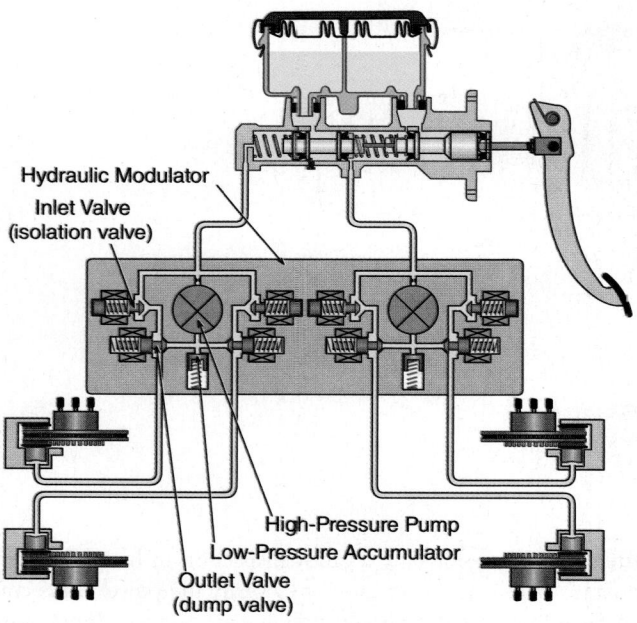

Hydraulic Modulator
Inlet Valve
(isolation valve)

High-Pressure Pump
Low-Pressure Accumulator
Outlet Valve
(dump valve)

FIGURE 38-74 A modulator valve contains two separate valves—an isolator valve that opens and closes the supply of pressurized brake fluid to the wheel end, and a dump valve to exhaust brake fluid pressure to release the brake.

HABSs are transparent to the driver, which means a driver does not need to do anything to activate the HABS. However, a driver must maintain steady pedal pressure when the HABS is activated and not release the brake or, simultaneously, tap the throttle while the ABS is actively braking. ABS logic is confounded on a few earlier systems when both the brakes and throttle are operated at the same time in vehicles with full electronic engine and braking control.

Understanding HABS operation is foundational to understanding and servicing more complex, advanced, driver-assistance features included in the vehicle stability control, traction control, and collision avoidance systems because they all use ABS components and operating strategies.

Hydraulic ABS Configurations

HABS requirements were introduced in stages, so several different technologies are used to meet each requirement. Since 2005, FMVSS 105 requires shorter stopping distances and the performance requirement to remain within a 12-foot-wide (3.7 m) lane when braking in a curve at 30 mph (48 kph) has demanded the use of four-channel, four-sensor, four-wheel disc brakes using HABS at each wheel. A four-channel system means there are four modulator valves controlling brake pressure to four wheel ends and four wheel speed sensors providing the HABS module feedback about rotational speed at each of those wheels (**FIGURE 38-75**). Each modulator valve assembly contains two valves—an isolator or inlet valve and a dump valve. The first valve, the isolator or inlet valve is a normally open valve that allows fluid to enter the caliper. Energizing the valve closes it, which blocks pressurized flow of brake fluid. This means the isolator valve either holds brake fluid pressure or increases it during an ABS event by opening the valve to admit higher brake pressure. The second valve, the dump valve, is normally closed. When energized, it exhausts or dumps pressurized brake fluid from the caliper to release the brake during an ABS wheel lock-up event.

Prior to the 2005 standard, the first HABS requirement in 1999 allowed commercial vehicles to meet stopping distance rules and provide stability control using a speed sensor on all four wheels, and a separate modulator valve for each of the front wheels, but only one modulator valve to control braking in the rear wheels. This is considered a three-channel, four-sensor system with the number of modulator valves designating a channel of control. However, the lightest vehicles between Class 3 and 5 built prior to 2001 allowed the ABS to only control the brakes on the rear drive axle using a single sensor in the driveline. Wheels on other axles of the vehicle were not controlled by the ABS. This is a single-channel, single-sensor system.

Hydraulic Braking Control Components

As already mentioned, in addition to the master cylinder, a HABS uses modulator valves and an electrohydraulic pump to pressurize brake fluid (**FIGURE 38-76**). Each modulator valve or circuit to a wheel end uses a pair of valves—an isolator and dump valve (**FIGURE 38-77**). Unlike the air brake ABS, the hydraulic system does not have an almost endless supply of pressurized brake fluid

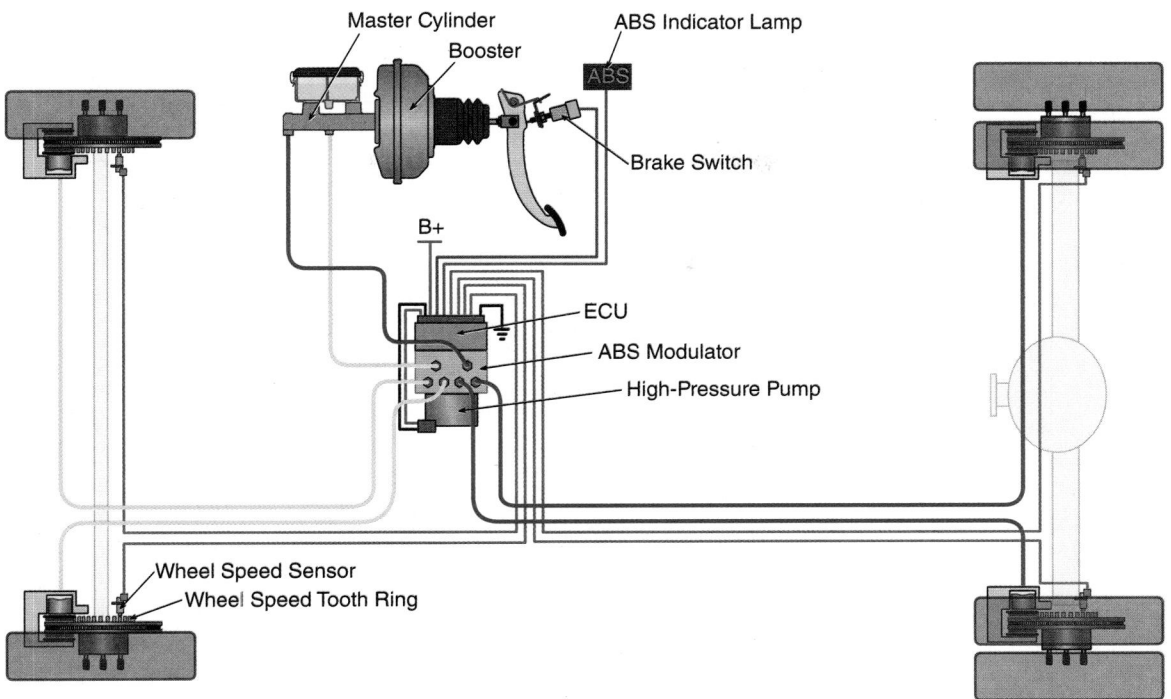

FIGURE 38-75 The configuration of a contemporary four-channel, four-sensor HABS.

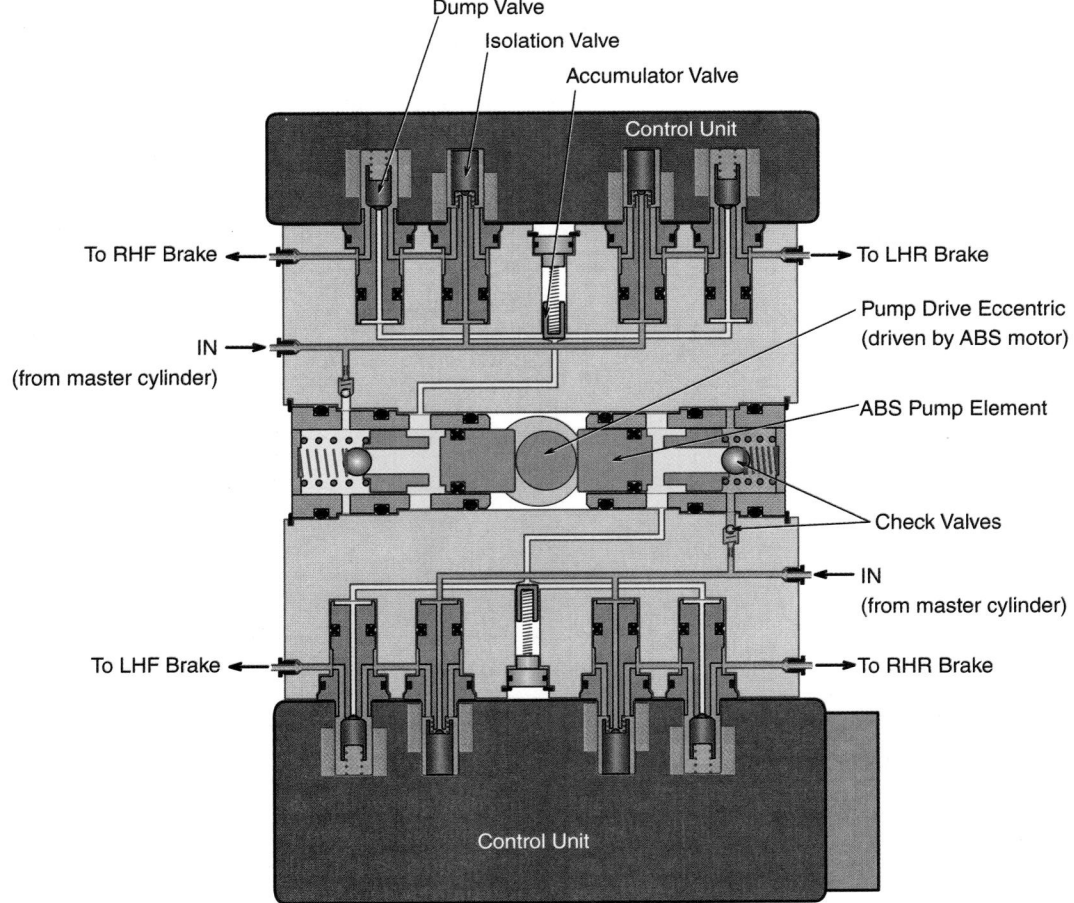

FIGURE 38-76 A modulator valve assembly for a common split circuit brake system contains the electrohydraulic pump, check valves, two low pressure accumulators, and four pairs of modulator valves.

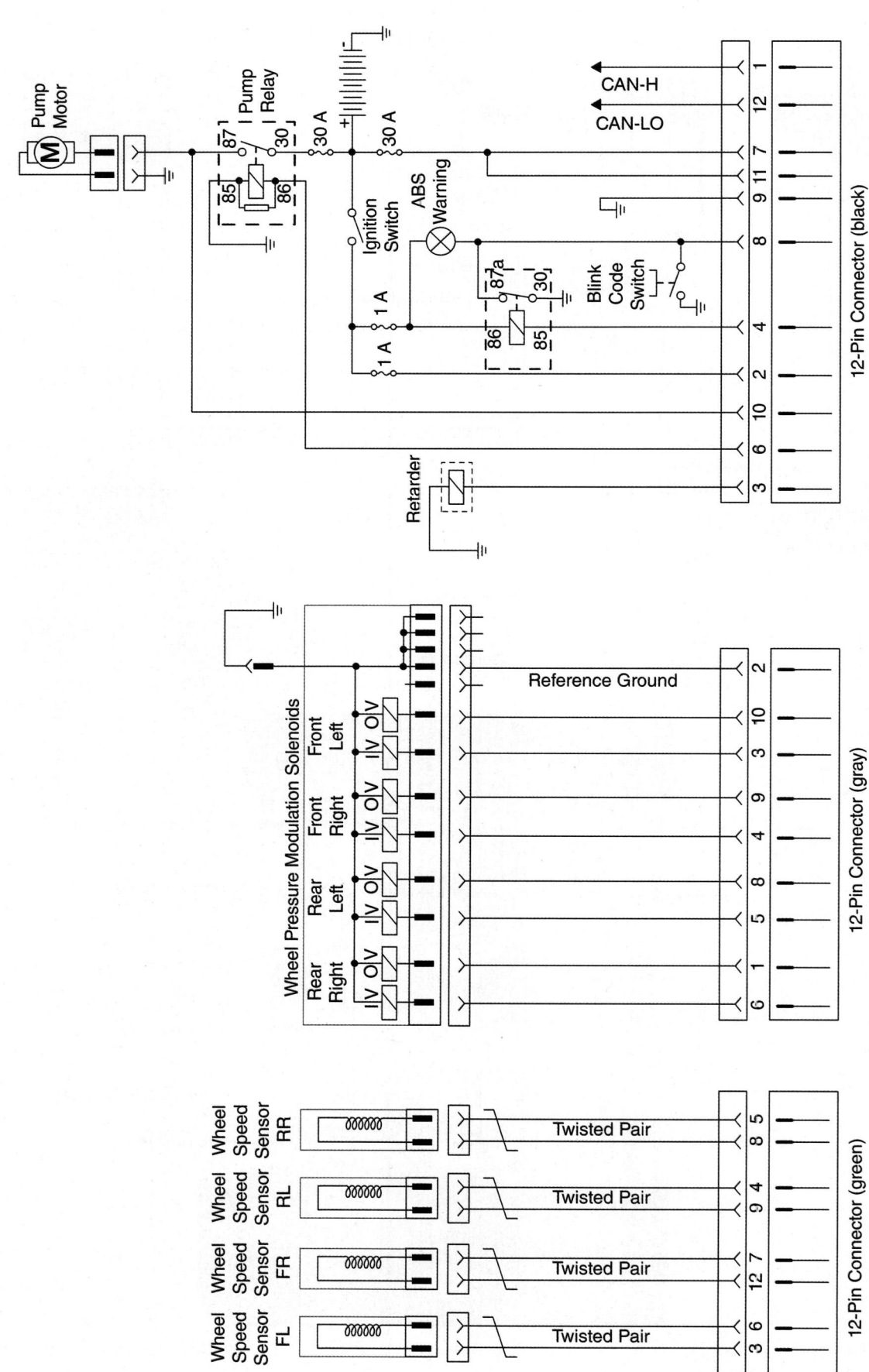

FIGURE 38-77 A HABS modulator assembly contains four pairs of modulator valves with each modulator consisting of an isolation or inlet valve and a dump or outlet valve.

to exhaust and reapply the brakes when multiple apply-release cycles are required by an ABS event. A hydraulic pressure resupply system is essential (**FIGURE 38-78**). Without resupplying the brake application pressure, the master cylinder piston would continue to displace brake fluid, the brake pedal would sink to the floor, and finally bottom out during a prolonged ABS event. In this situation, there would quickly be no brake pressure and the brakes would need to be released and reapplied by the driver. To prevent this, HABS use an electrohydraulic, high-pressure pump to supply the extra brake fluid pressure to reapply the brakes after a modulator valve releases pressure for the first time. When this happens, brake application pressure using brake fluid is not supplied by the master cylinder but instead by the high-pressure pump circuit. During an HABS event, the master cylinder pushrod does not move any further than the original brake application. To do this, the pump circuit collects brake fluid released from the dump valves when the wheel has locked up. Next, the pump re-pressurizes this fluid and supplies it back to the inlet or isolation valves supplied by an accumulator. Pressurized fluid is pumped into and stored in an accumulator whenever a pressure-sensitive switch detects low fluid pressure in the accumulator. The antilock pressure switch is responsible for switching the high-pressure pump on and off to maintain accumulator pressure in an acceptable range. During each key-cycle when the vehicle is moving above 12 mph (20 kph), the high-pressure pump operates for approximately one-half second to validate operation of the motor and pressure switch.

A set of one-way check valves in the primary and secondary circuits are closed by pressurized brake fluid from the high-pressure pump outlet circuit. Closing these check valves prevents the brake pedal from sinking during HABS events and ensures almost no pressurized fluid from the pump returns to the master cylinder. The pulsing brake pedal felt by the driver during a HABS event is the hydraulic action of these check valves sealing against the electrohydraulic action of the pump combined with the operation of the isolation and dump valves. The high-pressure electric motor-driven pump on a HABS modulator valve is seen in **FIGURE 38-79**.

HABS System Operation

The sequence of hydraulic brake control described in the previous section is outlined here. Dampening of hydraulic brake pressure pulsations is achieved by using spring-loaded hydraulic accumulators. In some systems, the fluid from the dump valve can return directly to the master cylinder reservoir or to the pump inlet, but the pump draws brake fluid from the brake reservoir.

1. **Normal Brake Mode**—Brakes released. During normal brake operation without an ABS event, the normally open isolation valve allows fluid to flow from the master cylinder through the valve and to the calipers. The normally closed dump or outlet valve blocks brake fluid from flowing back to the accumulator, brake reservoir, or pump. During normal braking, the inlet valve remains open and the outlet valve remains closed (**FIGURE 38-80**).

FIGURE 38-79 A HABS modulator assembly showing an electrohydraulic motor, control module and brake lines for a split circuit brake system .

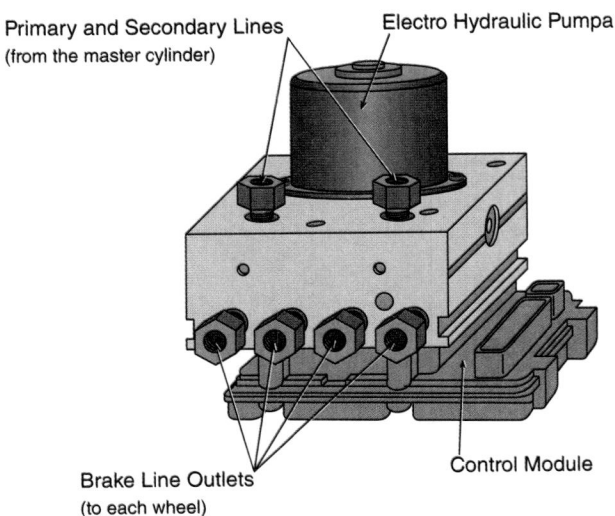

FIGURE 38-78 A four-channel HABS modulator assembly has input from two master cylinder circuits and separate outputs to each wheel.

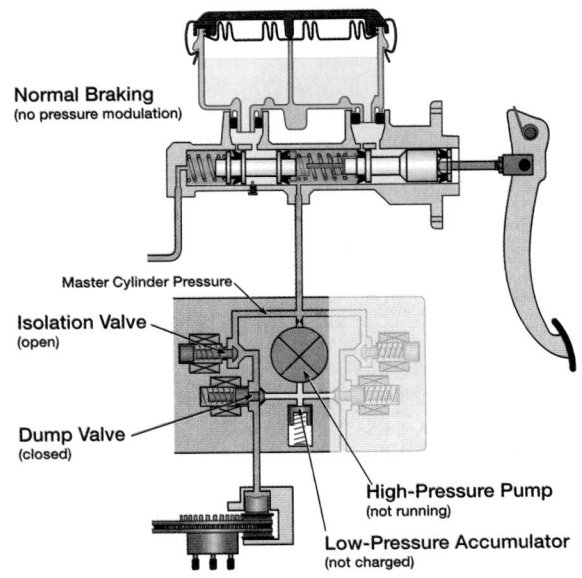

FIGURE 38-80 In normal mode, both control valves are deenergized. The isolation valve is open, the dump valve is closed. The high-pressure pump is off.

2. **Isolation Mode**—Brakes applied and an imminent lock-up is sensed. Both the isolation and dump valves are closed. Brake fluid is held in the caliper and none can return to the accumulator, reservoir, or pump. During a panic stop mode or on slippery surfaces, as the wheel nears lock-up, the inlet and dump valves remain closed (**FIGURE 38-81**).

3. **Dump Mode**—Brakes are released after the wheel has locked up. Pressure drops to the wheel end and the brake is released because the dump valve is opened. The isolation valve remains closed, but the dump valve is energized to open, allowing fluid from the caliper to return to the high-pressure pump inlet to charge an accumulator or, in some models, return to the master cylinder. If the accumulator pressure is low, the high-pressure motor is energized (**FIGURE 38-82**).

4. **Reapply Mode**—To quickly restore braking pressure, pump pressure, not master cylinder pressure, is supplied to the brake caliper by de-energizing and reopening the isolation valve, as needed. The dump valve is also de-energized and closed. Brake fluid pressure builds up in the brake caliper to apply the brakes. Reapplying the brake slows the wheel rotation (**FIGURE 38-83**).

Bleeding HABS Assemblies

The HABS modulator assembly must be mounted below the master cylinder and above the wheel cylinders to prevent air from becoming trapped in the assembly. WABCO recommends that the orientation of the assembly's motor end is tilted up from the horizontal plane between 5 and 30 degrees. Despite this recommendation, vapor bubbles from boiled fluid, leaks through caliper seals, and accumulation of other gases from chemical decomposition still become trapped in the HABS modulator assembly. The result is a low and spongy brake pedal that

gradually develops over time. Pedal firmness or sponginess varies according to the amount of trapped gases. During scheduled brake service or when brake fluid is replaced, it is important that the modulator assembly is bled as well to restore a normal brake pedal feel (**FIGURE 38-84**). This is done by energizing the isolation and dump solenoids during a bleeding process

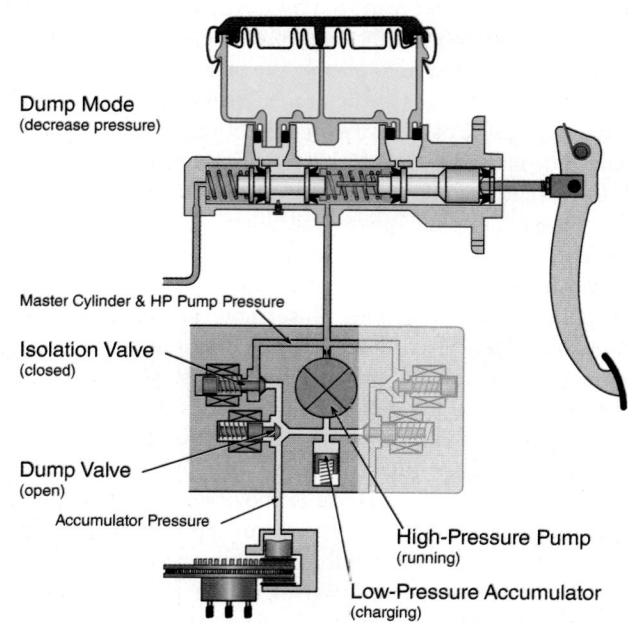

FIGURE 38-82 In release or dump mode, both valves are energized to close the isolation valve but open the dump valve. The high-pressure pump may be activated to maintain pressure in the accumulator supplying pressurized brake fluid.

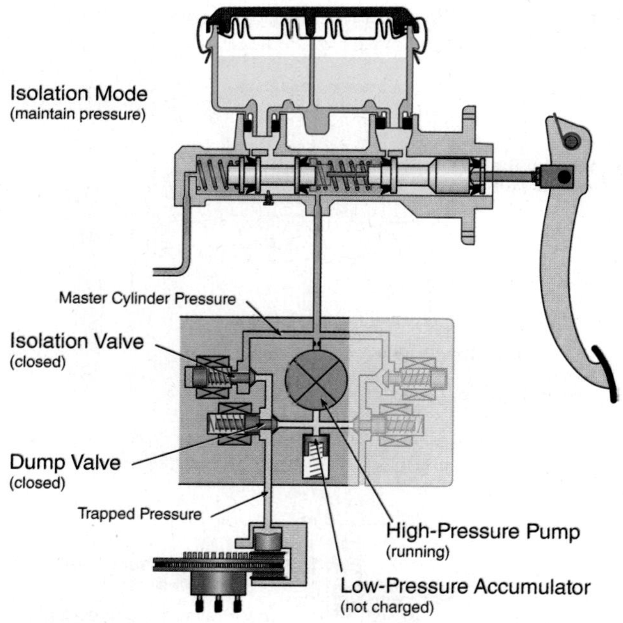

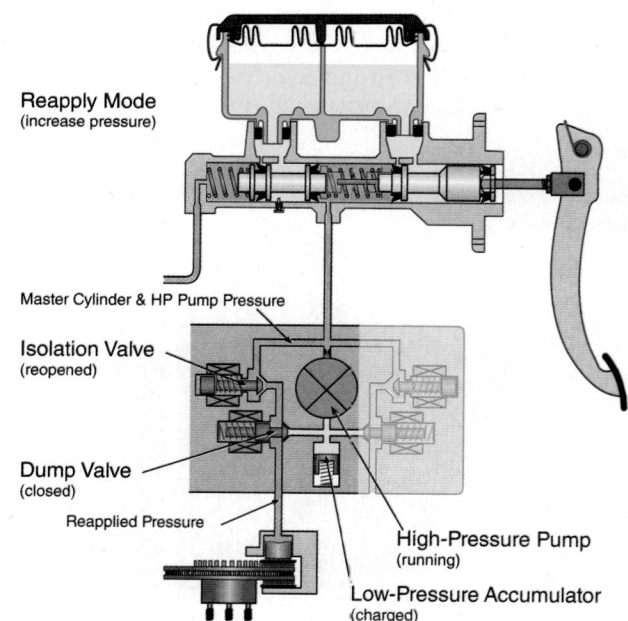

FIGURE 38-81 In isolation mode, both the dump valve and isolation valves are closed. Only the isolation valve is energized to close. The pump remains off unless the accumulator pressure switch detects low accumulator pressure.

FIGURE 38-83 In reapply mode, the high-pressure pump charges the accumulator with brake fluid supplied earlier by the open dump valve. Both the isolation and dump valves are de-energized, leaving the isolation valve open and the dump valve closed.

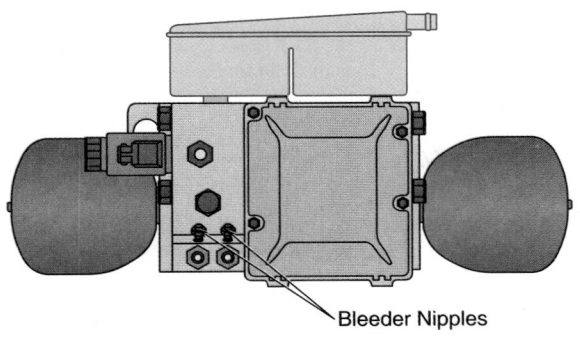

FIGURE 38-84 Points on the WABCO HPB HCU to bleed the master cylinder.

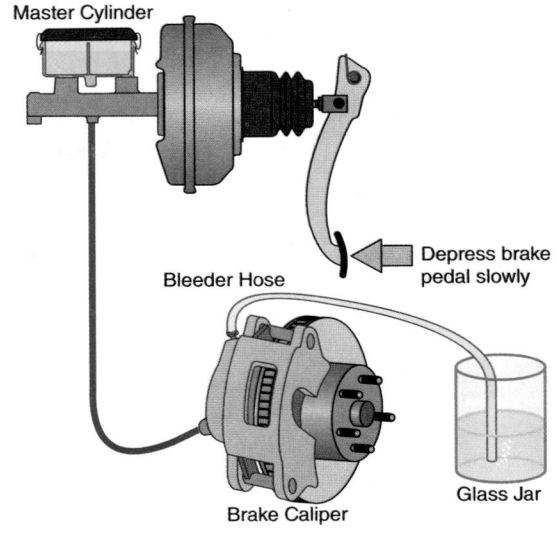

FIGURE 38-85 Air is removed from the brake system from bleeder screws at the calipers. A hose placed over the bleeder with an end in brake fluid prevents air from re-entering the system.

to purge trapped vapor from behind the valves in the assembly. Free downloads of OEM service and diagnostic software, such as WABCO's Toolbox or Bendix's ACOM, are available with a menu item to provide guided directions for bleeding HABS. Generally, the bleeders' screws at the caliper are opened one at a time at a wheel identified by software service prompts (**FIGURE 38-85**). Once the brake pedal is pushed and the brake light switch closes, the electrohydraulic pump is energized to help purge trapped air from the bleeder screws at the calipers.

Full Power Hydraulic Brake System

LO 38-11 Identify and describe the components, construction, and operation of a full power hydraulic brake system.

The refinement and development of more sophisticated feature-rich hydraulic brake systems has produced WABCO's

Hydraulic Power Brake (HPB) system. Introduced to meet the 2005 revised FMVSS 105 brake standards for class 4 to 7 trucks and buses, the latest version of the full power hydraulic brake system adds improved pedal feel, shorter stopping distances, ABS, traction control, and electronic brakeforce distribution, and the system can easily be integrated into stability control and collision avoidance system operation (**FIGURE 38-86**). Navistar refers to this system as

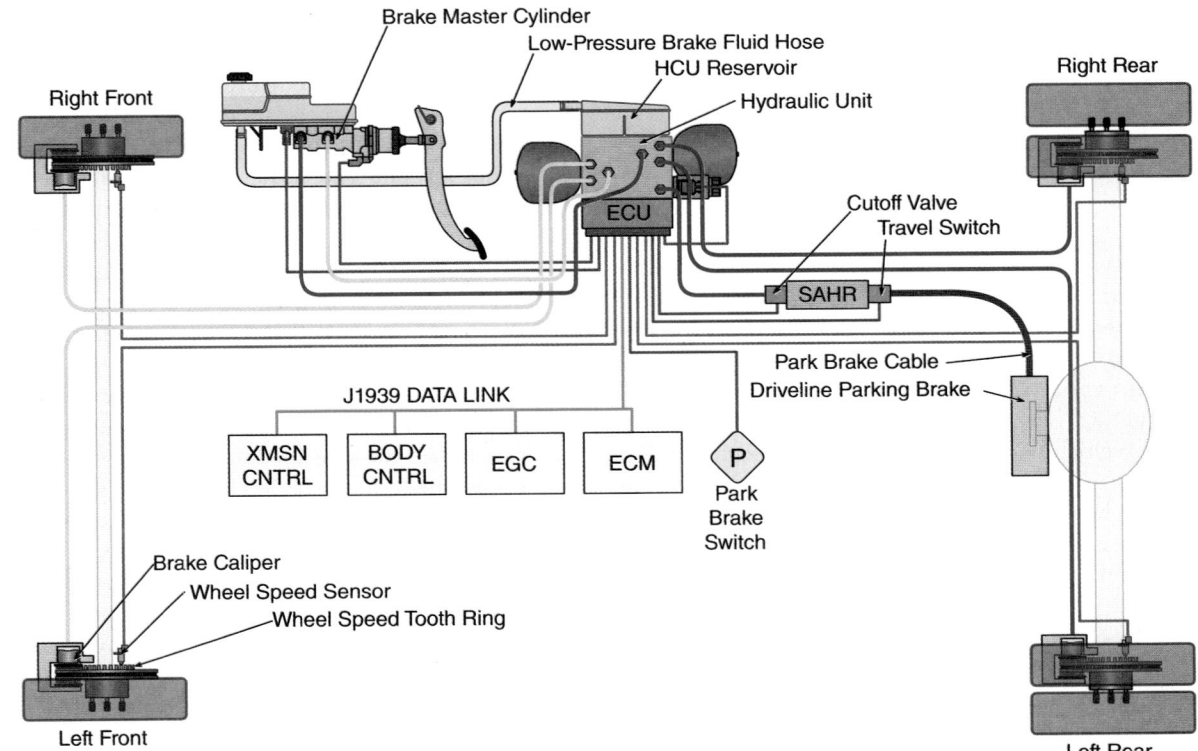

FIGURE 38-86 Component layout of a Navistar full power braking control system.

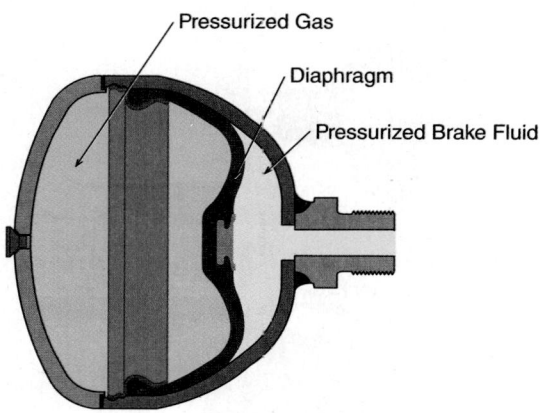

FIGURE 38-87 A cross-sectional view of a gas accumulator used to pressurize brake fluid.

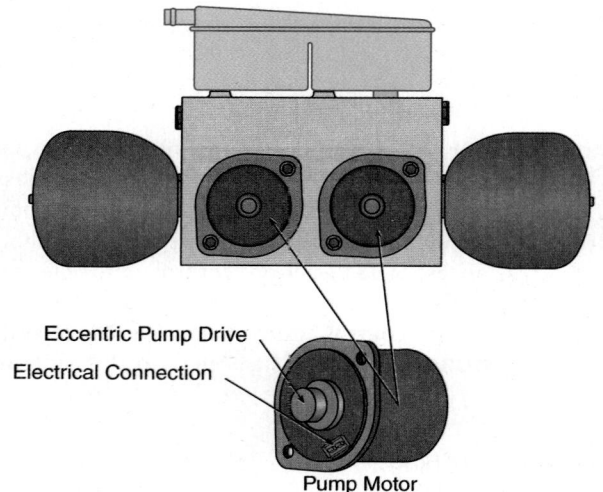

FIGURE 38-88 Electric motors are used to pump and pressurize brake fluid in the accumulators. Braking pressure is supplied by stored and pressurized fluid.

full power hydraulic brakes because it is not assisted by an external hydraulic power steering pump. Instead, all (full) hydraulic pressure required to apply the brakes is stored by high-pressure hydraulic pumps in hydraulic accumulators, which maintains available brake pressure between 1770 and 2320 psi (11,721 and 15,996 kPa) (**FIGURE 38-87**). Switching on the vehicle's ignition energizes two electrohydraulic pumps used to charge two nitrogen gas accumulators with pressurized brake fluid (**FIGURE 38-88**). Improved brake response time is a result of storing hydraulic braking energy in the accumulators and closely coupling them with mechanical and electronically controlled brake valves. As mentioned earlier in the chapter, this brake system is particularly unique because it uses CAN communication to improve control of braking events and add significant new features using CAN data. Early units did not use CAN communication and non-CAN-controlled units are available.

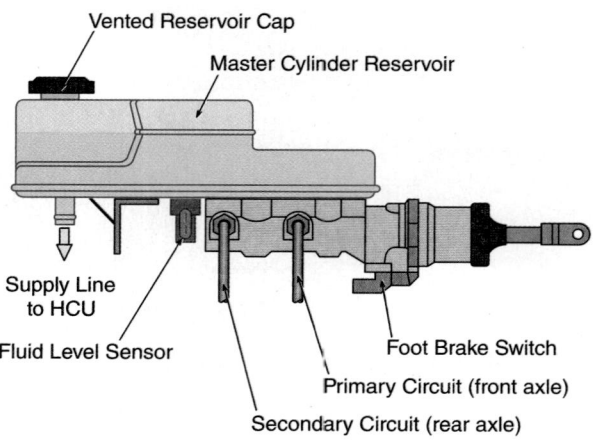

FIGURE 38-89 A master cylinder only supplies hydraulic pilot signals to the HCU. The HCU and master cylinder reservoir are connected through a low-pressure fill line.

HPB System Components

The HPB system uses a split-circuit master cylinder with primary and secondary brake circuit lines supplying only pilot hydraulic signals to provide braking demand signals (**FIGURE 38-89**). An electronically controlled HCU at the center of the system receives pressure signals from the master cylinder, but its brake circuits are not directly connected to the brake calipers. Master cylinder circuits are dead-headed or blocked at two hydraulic relay valves in the HCU (**FIGURE 38-90**). Like an electrical relay that uses a small amount of current to switch a larger amount, hydraulic relays valves operate like hydraulic pressure amplifiers. Master cylinder pressure is stepped up to higher pressure and volume proportional to the master cylinder supplying brake demand or pilot signals using the mechanically operated hydraulic relay valves (**FIGURE 38-91**).

Even though there are only two brake circuits, a primary and secondary, the HCU electronically controls pressure to each of the four calipers to achieve balanced braking for shorter stopping distances and reduce uneven brake pad wear. Two control valves in each brake circuit to the calipers—an inlet (isolator) and (outlet) dump valve can vary brake torque by changing brake pressure supplied to each caliper by cycling the valves open and or closed three times per second (**FIGURE 38-92**). However, the control valves use an operating strategy almost identical to the one described in the previous section on ABS. This feature, called Electronic Brakeforce Distribution, can also compensate for axle loading imbalances by monitoring ABS sensor data to measure deceleration rates at each wheel. Wheel speed data analysis allows individual tailoring of brake application pressure. For ATC events, two additional ATC pressure control valves can open and close to supply highly pressurized brake fluid from the accumulators to the isolation and dump valves at each brake. Eight electrohydraulic control valves are used in HCU without ATC and ten valves are needed by the HCU to provide ATC features. When required, hydraulic brake pressure is supplied and released to the correct brake caliper to achieve the desired operational effect.

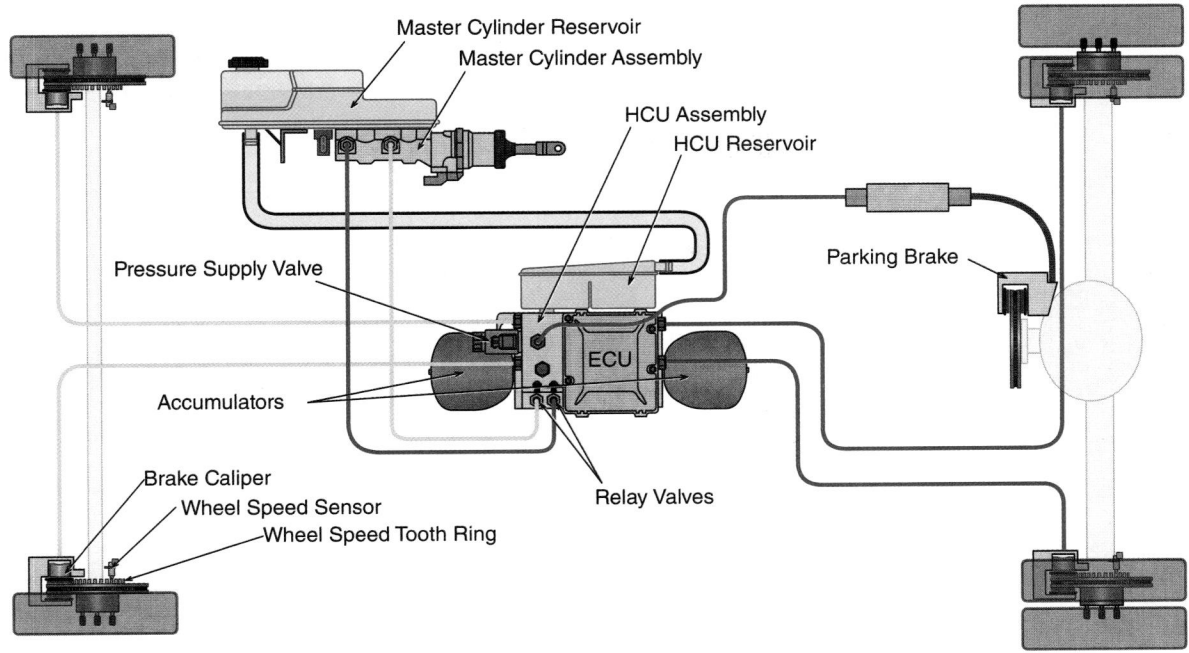

FIGURE 38-90 The mechanically operated hydraulic relay valves are located in the HCU unit and amplify pilot pressure signals from the master cylinder.

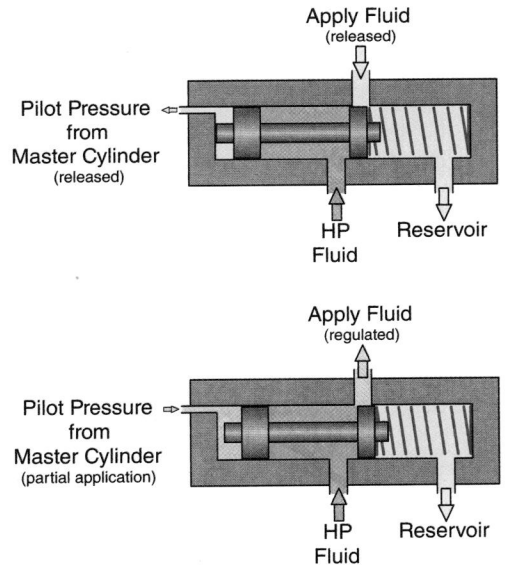

FIGURE 38-91 The principle of a hydraulic relay valve. Small volumes and pressure of hydraulic fluid are mechanically multiplied in a hydraulic relay. Moving a piston or spool valve proportionally opens a larger pressurized fluid port.

A brake fluid reservoir on the HCU is connected to the master cylinder reservoir through a low-pressure fill line. When the pedal is applied or released, brake fluid moves back and forth to the reservoir from the brake calipers. Several fail-safe modes are used by the HCU in the event of power failure because no backup braking circuits are directly connected from the master cylinder to calipers. If a major fault does occur, the unit automatically applies a parking brake to stop the vehicle. The SAHR parking brake also automatically applies when power to the system is lost. Internal pressure sensors in the HCU sense available accumulator brake fluid pressure to provide operational and diagnostic strategies.

Normal Braking Mode—No Brakes Applied

Without the brakes applied, all the modulator valves in the HCU are resting in a non-energized state. Only pressurized brake fluid is present between the accumulator outlets and the relay valves. The position of pistons in the relay valve blocks pressurized brake fluid in the accumulators from entering the lines connected to the calipers. This allows unpressurized brake fluid to flow back from the brake calipers past the modulator valves and into two return ports of the HCU reservoir.

Normal Braking Mode—Brakes Applied

When the brakes are applied after the brake pedal is pressed, two primary and secondary pilot signals from the master cylinder are transmitted to the two HCU relay valves. Fluid pressure in the signal lines only applies pressure to the mechanical relay valves. Pistons in the relay valve are moved by the pilot signals and open a larger passageway connecting the pressurized brake fluid from the accumulators to the normally open ABS inlet (isolation) valve for each wheel end. The outlet valve (dump) is normally closed. Again, the relay valves are built to apply brake pressure to the wheel end calipers proportional to the pressure and displacement volume of pilot signals developed by the master cylinder.

When the brake pedal is released, the relay valves pistons close to block the passage of pressurized brake fluid from the accumulators to the calipers. Pressurized brake fluid in the calipers can return to the HCU reservoir through the open ABS inlet valve and through a port on the hydraulic relay valve.

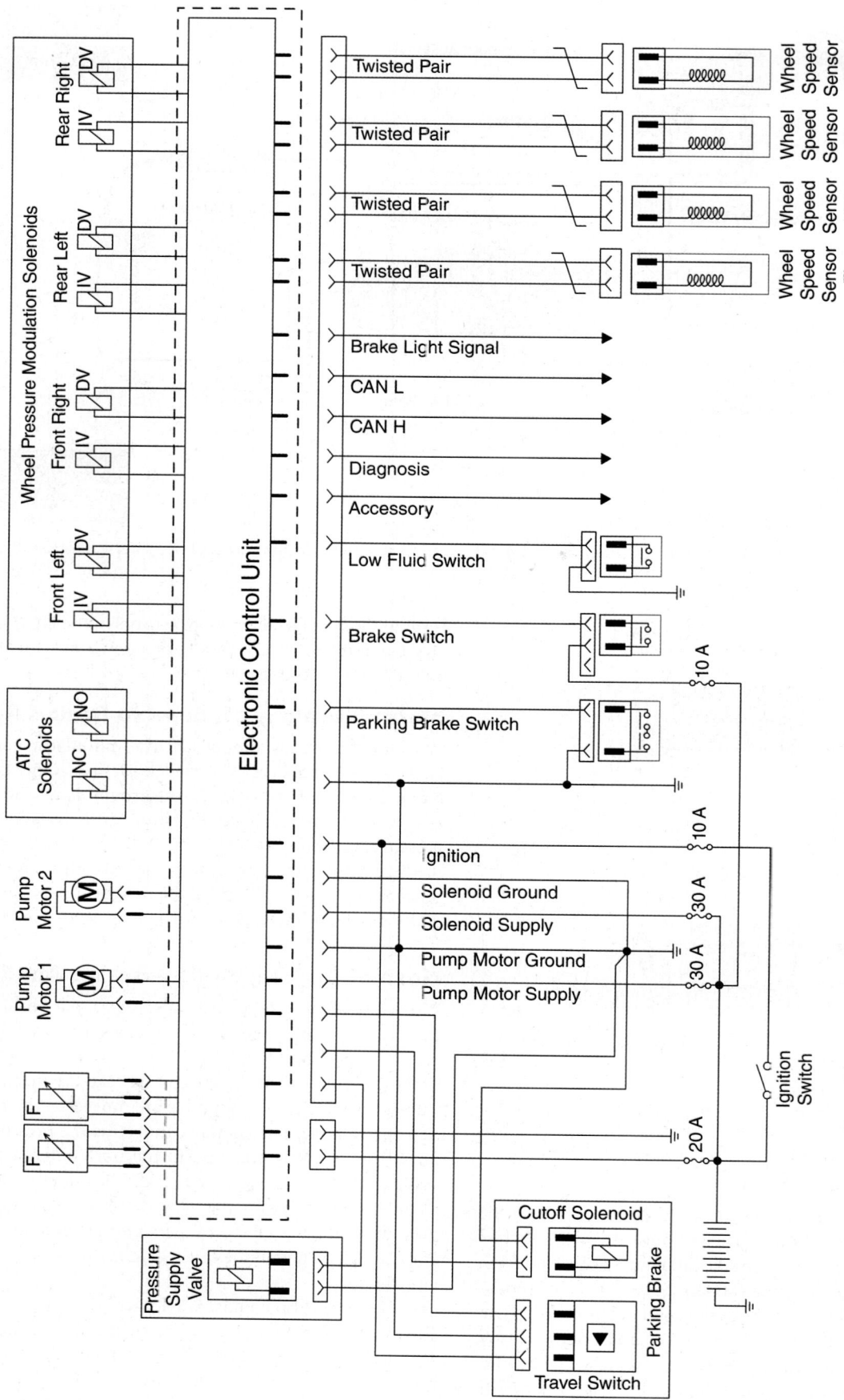

FIGURE 38-92 The schematic view of the modulator valves in the HCU. Note: An additional pair of valves in the ATC modulator supplies a second pressure source to the ABS modulator valves.

ABS Braking Mode—Brakes Applied

When an ABS event occurs, braking begins normally but the electronic control unit (ECU) has identified a wheel speed is near lock up. If the brake pedal switch is closed, ABS operation takes place energizing and de-energizing the solenoid-controlled inlet and outlet valves that control brake fluid flow to each wheel end. Modulator valve cores for the inlet (isolation) and outlet (dump) valves are part of the HCU assembly and operated by electromagnetic fields in coils in the ECU bolted to the HCU. The ECU adjusts the brake torque by electronically cycling through hold, decrease pressure, and increase pressure three times per second. Operation of these valves is the same as described in the ABS braking section. This strategy prevents the wheels from locking, while maximizing brake application pressure to stop the vehicle.

ATC Mode—No Brakes Applied

If equipped and programmed for ATC, the HCU has an ATC modulator valve consisting of another inlet valve and outlet valve. When energized, the normally closed ATC inlet valve supplies a second hydraulic brake pressure input to the hydraulic relay valve for the primary and secondary circuits. The ATC modulator is in the HCU and operates with the rear ABS inlet and outlet valves to restore traction using differential braking. If the brake pedal is up and the brake switch is open, the ECU analyzes wheel speed data to identify whether a left or right rear wheel is slipping due to lost traction or excessive engine torque. A traction control switch in the dash should also be in the "enable" position and wheel speed must be below 31 mph (50 kph). When these conditions are met, differential braking is used to transfer torque from the slipping wheel to the wheel with more traction. To provide differential braking, the ATC inlet valve is energized and opened, and its outlet valve is closed. This allows pressurized brake fluid to flow from the accumulator to the relay valve for the rear brakes. Normally, all four calipers would receive brake pressure, but the other ABS inlet valves are energized to block the flow of brake pressure to all wheels except the slipping wheel. If the left wheel is slipping, the ABS inlet valve on the left wheel is energized to open, but the remaining inlet valves are closed. Both inlet and outlet valves for the left wheel are cycled open and closed by the ECU to gently apply the brake to the slipping left wheel. Applying a moderate braking force to the left wheel and causes torque to transfer through the rear axle differential to the right-side tire with more traction.

When the ATC dash switch in the DISABLE or MUD and SNOW position, normal traction control features are disabled or in reduced sensitivity mode. This off-road mode allows a greater amount of wheel slip in poor traction conditions.

Spring Applied Air Released Park Brake

The Spring Applied/Hydraulic Release, or SAHR, powered parking brake system is an option available with the HPB system. This device is controlled by the optional pressure supply valve (**FIGURE 38-93**). Bendix produces an SAHR canister containing a strong brake spring used to tension a parking brake cable, which applies the parking brake. The HPB assembly has

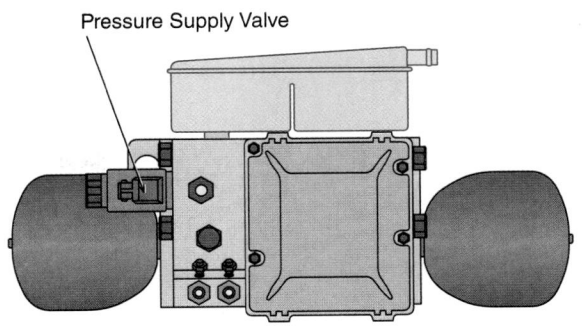

FIGURE 38-93 The optional pressure supply valve controls the release and application of the park brake cylinder.

a control valve that routes pressurized brake fluid to the SAHR canister to release the internal spring and relax the parking brake cable. A "drive-away" function is built into the system that automatically releases the parking brake when the vehicle is driven. This SAHR parking brake canister is typically located inside the driver's side frame rail, forward of the rear axles. Vehicles not equipped with hydraulic parking brakes have mechanical or air (Spring Applied/Air Released, SAAR) parking brakes.

HPB Inspection

Quick testing of the full-power electrohydraulic pumps and gas-filled accumulators, such as the WABCO HPB, is performed by verifying the correct system responses to brake pumping the brake pedal. With the ignition and engine off and then switching the ignition on but having the engine off, the brake pedal is pumped quickly multiple times to deplete the accumulators of brake fluid pressure. Listening to confirm the flow of fluid from the accumulators as the brakes are applied and released is a first step. Fluid flow should be easily heard. While pumping the brakes, also verify that as pressure drops in the nitrogen-filled accumulators. This is observed as both electric brake fluid pumps are energized when pressure-sensitive switches detect the pressure drop. The pumps do not need to begin operating at the same time, but both must operate. Pressure sensors in the HCU allow self-priming to take place for up to three minutes. If there is insufficient brake pressure boost assistance sensed by the internal pressure sensors, the HCU shuts off. Further diagnostic checks for the system must be performed using OEM software or Meritor-WABCO's diagnostic and service software called Toolbox.

HPB Bleeding Procedures

Because the master cylinder circuit to HCU circuit or the HCU-to-caliper circuit are separate, the master cylinder cannot be bled through the calipers. Instead, both primary and secondary circuits of the master cylinder are purged of air by opening two bleeder screws above the HCU relay valve. Isolation of the master cylinder also means a spongy or spring-like brake pedal caused by air in the HCU to caliper circuit cannot be felt. After the master cylinder is bled, the HCU to caliper circuits are bled from the brake calipers beginning from the longest circuit to the shortest. If the vehicle has an SAHR parking brake, it must be bled after the master cylinder but before the caliper circuits.

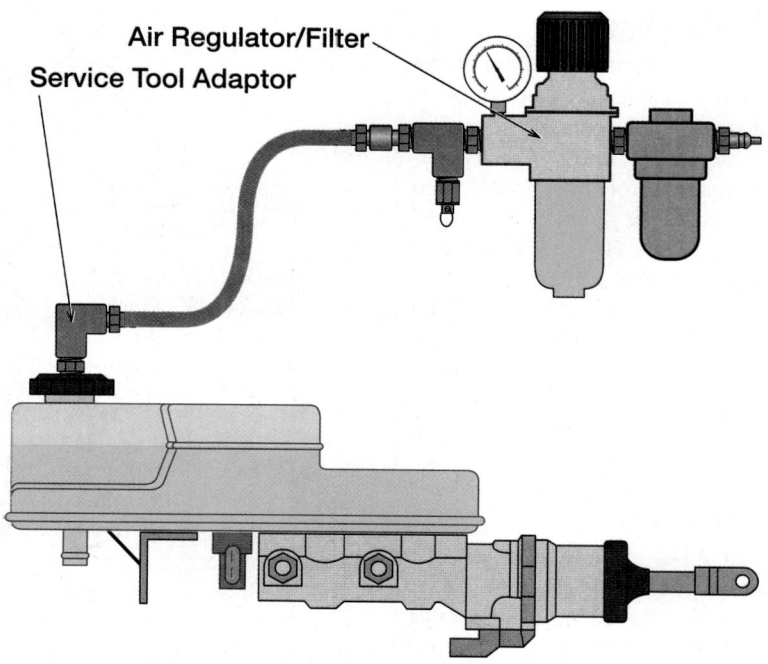

Air Regulator/Filter
Service Tool Adaptor

FIGURE 38-94 To pressure bleed with air over fluid, a regulated supply of positively pressurized air or nitrogen is applied to the master cylinder reservoir using a purpose-made adapter that covers and seals the reservoir.

Before bleeding the master, the batteries must be disconnected or the fuses removed from the electrohydraulic motors to prevent the HCU from operating. Next, a hose is placed over the primary circuit of the master cylinder bleeder screws at the HCU and the other end into a bottle of brake fluid. To push brake fluid and air from the system, the brake pedal is not pushed. Instead, pressure bleeding is recommended (**FIGURE 38-94**). This involves using either:

1. Fluid-over-fluid pressure at the master cylinder filler cap. Brake fluid pressure stored in a pressure bleeder ball—a device pressurizing brake fluid, is pushed through the master cylinder under a slight positive pressure.
2. Dry nitrogen or pressurized air over fluid. This technique applies gas pressure to the filler cap of the master cylinder to push fluid through.

Once approximately 8.5 ounces (251 ml) of fluid have drained from the bleeder screws, and no bubbles are released from the bleeder hose in the bottle, the process is completed.

To bleed the HCU to caliper circuit, the HPB system must be re-pressurized by reconnecting the batteries or reinstalling the fuses to run the pumps. Once pumped up, a procedure called "Deplete Accumulators" is performed using service software. While following service menu prompts, the internal ATC inlet valve is automatically opened to apply pressure to all the brake calipers. Caliper circuits are bled beginning with the longest circuit and ending with the shortest circuit. If the vehicle is not equipped with ATC, the procedure is performed with the brake pedal fully applied throughout the bleeding process. This action causes the hydraulic relay valves to continuously supply brake fluid pressure to the calipers. Pressure sensors in the HCU allow self-priming of the accumulators

to take place for up to three minutes. If there is insufficient brake pressure sense by the internal pressure sensors, the HCU shuts off.

▶ **TECHNICIAN TIP**

Many of the HCUs ECUs have a limited shelf life and storage life due to programming that is maintained by keep-alive current. Batteries soldered to the circuit board supply current when the control unit is not connected to vehicle battery power. If the programming is lost due to the lack of keep-alive current, the ECU becomes "bricked." To prevent this from happening, use a trickle charger to maintain battery voltage when a vehicle is in storage. Do not leave a vehicle in storage without a battery connected or the charge in the circuit board battery will deplete.

HCU Memory Log

Electronic memory built into the HCU tracks all events in the brake system. Because the electric motors have a limited number of service cycles, a maintenance interval is set for the motors and accumulators. The status of the components is checked using service software. Whenever the motors are replaced, a cycle counter logging of the operating cycles of the motors must be reset (**FIGURE 38-95**).

Parking Brake and Emergency Braking Systems

LO 38-12 Describe the purpose, construction, and operation of parking brake and emergency braking systems.

All commercial vehicles are required to have a park brake system that can also act as an emergency brake if there is a failure of the service brakes. FMVSS requires that a park brake must

HPB Counters		_□X
Operating Time (hours)	219	
Pump Motor		
Pump Motor Hours	1.8	Clear Pump Hours
Brake Event Counters		
Decel < 0.2g	188	
Decel 0.2g - 0.5g	227	Clear Counters
Decel > 0.5g	50	
Miscellaneous Counters		
ABS Events	46	Clear ABS Cycles
Ignition Cycles	87	Clear Ignition Cycles
	Close	

FIGURE 38-95 A screen image from Toolbox tracking activity of the HPB motors.

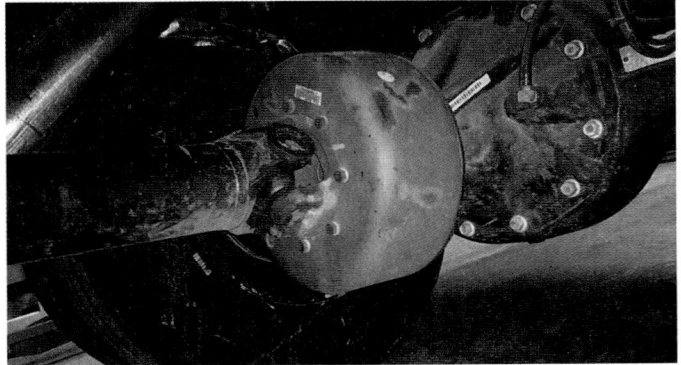

FIGURE 38-96 Drive shaft hand brake system.

FIGURE 38-97 Basic manually operated hand brake.

hold a vehicle stationary on as much as a 30% grade in the forward and reverse direction for a test limit of five minutes. Lighter vehicles are only required to remain stationary on a 20% grade.

The park brake system must be separate from the service brakes, so devices like aftermarket brake line locks that hold hydraulic pressure cannot be used. In many hydraulic braking systems, this park or emergency brake is the mechanically operated hand brake. A park brake drum with brake shoes is installed on the driveline (**FIGURE 38-96**). A cable-operated lever in the cab is pulled to apply the brake shoes, which have both self-energizing and servo brake action to increase holding power (**FIGURE 38-97**). The brake lever must be capable of locking in the applied position using a latch, ratchet, or an over-center locking mechanism. Cables can also operate parking brake levers

on calipers (**FIGURE 38-98**). Initial hand brake adjustment using this arrangement is achieved by lengthening or shortening the threaded yoke on a cable.

Spring Applied Hydraulic Release Brake

The Bendix A2L brakes and Lucas Girling hydraulic brakes use a spring applied and hydraulic release brake pedestals at each of the rear axle wheel ends (**FIGURE 38-99**). Pressure to compress the power spring is supplied by an engine-driven hydraulic pump using pressurized automatic transmission fluid.

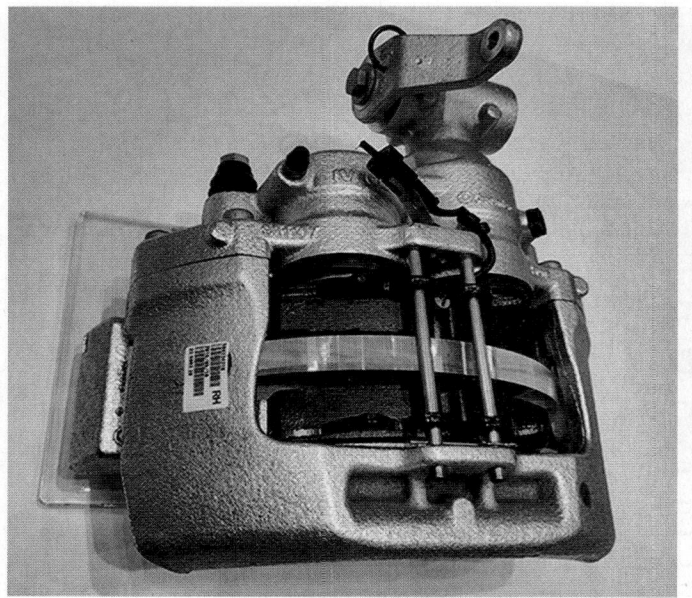

FIGURE 38-98 A cable-operated park brake of a caliper used on an Iveco truck.

This park brake configuration uses a wedge-shaped-type pushrod with rollers extending into a dedicated park brake wheel cylinder. In a park brake-type wheel cylinder, the cylinder pistons are ramp-shaped to enable brake pushrod movement to apply or release the brakes by rolling over the piston ramps. Ramped piston and pushrod movement are seen in **FIGURES 38-100** and **38-101**. This design enables application of the park brakes after hydraulic pressure is released that compresses the power spring in the spring brake pedestals. The park brake also applies force to expand the wheel cylinders and, thus,

FIGURE 38-99 A typical spring brake pedestal with an adjusting nut in the center contains an internal power spring. It is mounted on the rear axle of a medium-duty truck. A pushrod extends from the chamber to the dedicated park brake wheel cylinder.

apply the service brakes when transmission fluid is vented from the park brake pedestals.

Hydraulic Brake System Inspection

LO 38-13 Outline the steps and procedures for a hydraulic brake system inspection.

Most brake system complaints are outlined in **TABLE 38-2**. When making service recommendations, a brake system inspection should be performed first. A typical brake inspection procedure includes four main areas or steps.

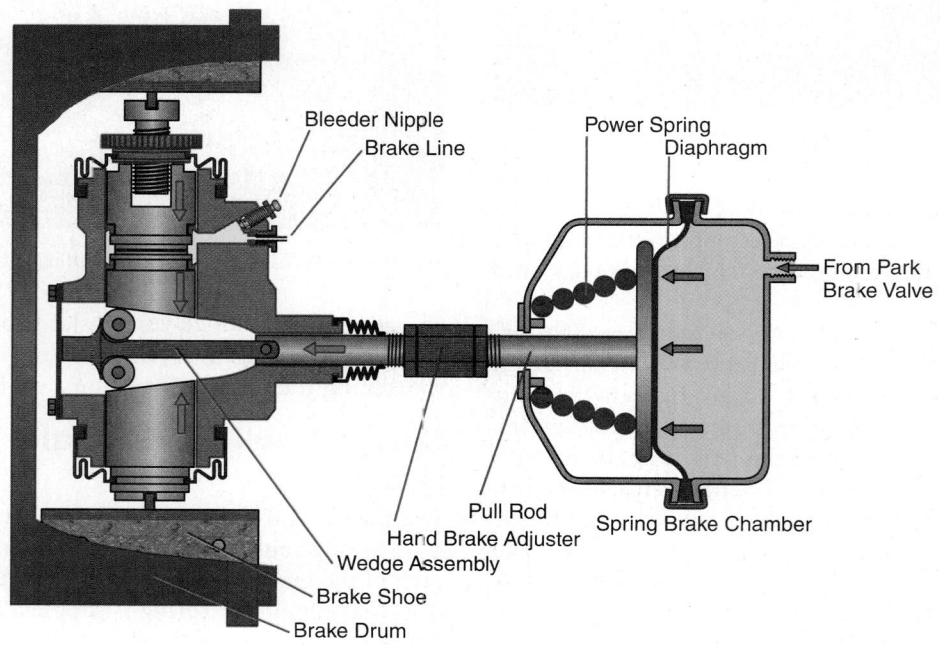

FIGURE 38-100 Park brake in off position.

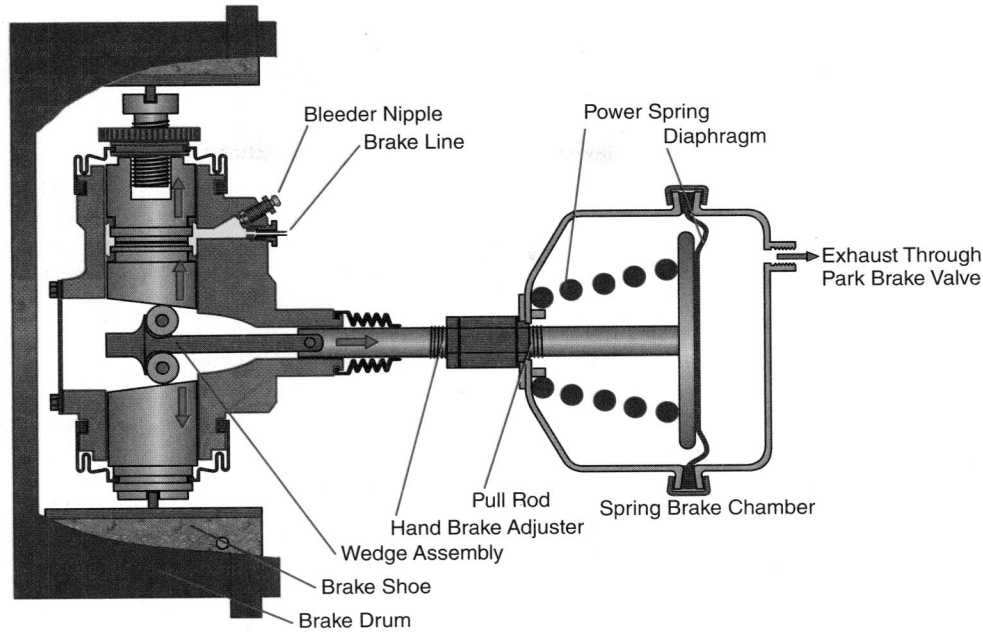

FIGURE 38-101 Park brake in the applied position.

TABLE 38-2 Common Brake System Complaints and Remedies

Complaint	Possible Causes	Remedy
Low Brake Pedal	Air in brake fluid Brake shoes out of adjustment Excessive lateral runout of calipers Seized caliper pistons Sticking or seized caliper sliders Worn out brake pads or shoes Oversized worn drums Low brake fluid level Defective wheel bearing Brake fluid leak	Bleed brakes, modulator valve, and SAHR park brake Inspect and or replace rotors and drums Remove, inspect, clean, and lubricate slider pins and bushing Inspect for brake fluid leaks Top up master cylinder Inspect and replace wheel bearings, as necessary Inspect for leaks and repair, as necessary
Spongy Brake Pedal	Air in brake fluid or brake valves Bulging flex line Defective master cylinder seals Worn or misadjusted brakes Sticking or seized slider pins	Bleed brakes, modulator valve, and SAHR park brake Inspect and replace brake lines, as necessary Inspect master cylinder and booster for leaks Service slider pins by removing, cleaning and lubricating
Little or No Power Assistance	Brake booster is inoperative or defective Low power steering fluid level Low power steering pump pressure Glazed brake friction materials Pads worn below minimum thickness Brake caliper piston seized Contaminated brake friction materials	Perform brake booster diagnostics Install new pads Inspect power steering level and top-up, as necessary Inspect power steering system for leaks Perform power steering pump pressure and flow analysis Inspect or replace the brake pads or shoes Install new pads and shoes in axle sets. Inspect or replace brake calipers
Pedal Pulsation	Excessive lateral runout of brake rotor High spots or low spots on the rotor Excessive rotor thickness variations Transfer of brake friction material to rotor Cracked rotor	Measure rotor runout with a dial indicator—Replace if necessary Measure rotor thickness in several places with a Vernier or micrometer—Replace if necessary Machine rotor or replace, as necessary Inspect and replace rotor, as necessary

TABLE 38-2 Common Brake System Complaints and Remedies (continued)

Complaint	Possible Causes	Remedy
Brakes Grab and Lock	Contaminated friction material lining	Install new pads in axle sets
	Mismatched brake friction material	Install new pads in axle sets
	Rough rotor surfaces on one rotor	Resurface or replace rotor in axle sets
	Seized caliper pistons	Disassemble caliper and repair or replace, as necessary
	Loose caliper	Inspect caliper hold down and repair, as necessary
	Excessive rotor thickness variation or runout	Resurface or replace rotor
	ABS system defective	Check ABS for codes
	Drum brakes out of adjustment	Inspect and adjust brakes, as necessary
Uneven Brake Pad Wear	Misaligned caliper	Inspect and reposition brake caliper
	Sticking slider pins and bushings	Inspect, clean, and lubricate slider pins with dielectric grease
	One or more pistons sticking	Inspect piston movement and repair or replace calipers, as necessary
Brakes Squeal	Loose brake components	Inspect brake pads, calipers, and shoes for looseness
	Lack of lubricant between metal-to-metal parts contact	Lubricate all shoe-to-backing plate contact points
		Lubricate caliper sliding pins and anchor points
	Missing pad shims	Install shims behind pads
	Missing anti-rattle spring	Install missing anti-rattle springs and clips
	Glazed friction material	Inspect pads and linings for glaze, replace, as necessary
	Gravel embedded in friction material	Inspect and clean friction material, as necessary
Brake Pull Left or Right	Uneven tire pressure or tire size	Equalize to recommended pressures, install correct size tires with good tread
	Restricted flex hose or line	Examine the hoses and lines, and replace, as necessary
	Front end out of alignment	Perform total vehicle alignment
	Loose or worn front end components	Inspect front end suspension and steering components, repair or replace, as necessary
	Defective wheel bearing	
	Mismatched brake parts	Inspect brake parts for correct application and match
	Leak in one brake circuit	Inspect system for leaks and repair, as necessary

1. Inspect wheel-end, chassis, and under-hood components.
   - Inspecting the wheel-end brake involves visually evaluating the thickness of brake friction material
   - Condition of drums and rotors and brake hardware, such as springs and hold-downs
   - Brake adjustment
   - Checking for brake and hydraulic fluid leaks
   - Inspecting brake hoses and lines
   - Inspect the brake power assist system for proper assist, leakage, missing or damaged components, fluid levels, brake assist backup system operation, and electrical connections
   - Brake fluid level in the master cylinder
   - Brake fluid color and condition of brake fluid for contamination
   - Condition of seals, such as the filler cap of master cylinder for swelling
   - Operation of power steering system
2. Inspect the function of brake indicator and warning lamps.
   - Engine off key off, cycle the ignition switch to run.
   - Verify all warning and indicator lamps illuminate. All lamps should remain on except the ABS warning light, which should only remain on for two to three seconds and then switch off. The ABS light will illuminate again if active codes are present.
   - Start the engine and, with the ignition switch in the run position, release the park brakes.

   - Verify the park brake indicator lamp switches off.
   - Observe other brake indicator lamps, such as the vacuum, ATC or brake booster warning lamps. Confirm all brake indicator lamps switch off.
   - Reapply the park brake and confirm the park brake lamp switches on.
3. Validate the brake pedal reserve height is correct.
   - With the engine running, firmly apply the brake pedal using about 50 lb (23 kg) of application force and hold the pressure for approximately 10 seconds.
   - Confirm no brake indicator lights illuminate and observe the height of the brake pedal above the floor is normal. The pedal should not continuously sink or require a long travel stroke to apply the brakes. Compare observations with OEM specifications
4. Inspect the brake power assist unit and verify its operation.
   - Follow the steps outlined in each section of brake assist boosters for vacuum, hydraulic, and HPB system functional checks outlined in the chapter.
   - Inspect the booster unit for fluid or vacuum leaks.
5. Inspect the parking brake.
   - Apply the parking brake and slowly attempt to move the vehicle in both the low forward and reverse gear without touching the throttle. The vehicle should not roll in either gear.
   - Inspect the parking brake actuator for air or hydraulic fluid leaks.

Wrap-Up

Ready for Review

▶ Medium- to heavy-duty vehicle hydraulic braking systems need power assist to operate satisfactorily; the power assist can be supplied by vacuum, hydraulic pressure, or air pressure.

▶ Hydraulic braking with vacuum assist is typical for lighter-duty vehicles. Hydraulic assist systems and air-over-hydraulic systems are used on medium- and heavy-duty vehicles.

▶ In all hydraulic braking systems, a pushrod exerts force on the piston(s) in the master cylinder, causing an increase in fluid pressure that results in force being applied to the brake pads and shoes.

▶ Vacuum-assisted braking systems use a pressure differential between vacuum and atmospheric pressure to amplify pedal force to reduce braking effort.

▶ Hydroboost systems use hydraulic pressure supplied by the power steering pump or a dedicated pump to intensify braking effort.

▶ Air-over-hydraulic brake systems use a conventional hydraulic brake system. Compressed air pressure provides the assistance force to multiply brake pedal effort.

▶ Hydraulic brake system components selected depending on whether the system uses drum or disc brakes. Drum brakes use brake shoes and disc brakes use pads and rotors.

▶ Today, drum brakes are generally not used on new vehicles but commonly found on an older vehicle's rear wheels.

▶ The drum brake has two brake shoes, with a friction material attached using rivets or glue. Rivets provide a stronger bond for attaching brake friction lining. Shoes expand against a brake drum's inside surface to slow the wheel.

▶ Disc brakes slow rotation of the wheels by the friction generated through squeezing brake pads against a brake rotor using a hydraulic caliper.

▶ Disc brakes offer better stopping performance than drum brakes and provide a much higher braking force.

▶ Disc brake performance does not deteriorate like drum brake performance deteriorates as the components heat up.

▶ Hydraulic brake systems can use a variety of valves to control system operation. These include proportioning valves, metering valves, pressure differential valves, and/or combination valves.

▶ Air-over-hydraulic systems also include systems for air supply, a foot brake valve, air booster units, and fail-safe systems.

▶ Air brake boosters can be indirect or direct. Indirect are found on heavier trucks, and direct are generally found on lighter trucks. Boosters have three positions: released, applied, and balanced.

▶ As a fail-safe, hydraulic and air-over-hydraulic braking systems are required by regulation to use a dual circuit system design so that one system can stop the vehicle if the other fails.

▶ All vehicles are required to have a park brake system that can also act as an emergency brake should there be a failure of the service brakes.

▶ Most hydraulic brake systems today are equipped with four-channel ABS, meaning that each of the four wheel brakes is controlled individually.

▶ Vehicles with ABS can also use the ABS to operate an electronic stability system to enhance vehicle safety.

▶ ABS components can also be used to provide traction control on lighter vehicles.

▶ **Full power hydraulic brakes** do not use an external hydraulic power steering pump. Instead, all (full) hydraulic pressure required to apply the brakes is stored by high-pressure hydraulic pumps in hydraulic accumulators.

▶ **Full power hydraulic brakes** store brake pressure between 1770 and 2320 psi (11,721 and 15,996 kPa) that is directed to each brake through mechanically operated hydraulic relay valves.

▶ Switching on the vehicle's ignition energizes two electrohydraulic pumps used by **full power fydraulic brake** system to charge two nitrogen gas accumulators with pressurized brake fluid improved brake response time in **full power hydraulic brake** systems is a result of storing hydraulic braking energy in the accumulators and closely coupling them with mechanical and electronically controlled brakes

▶ A typical brake inspection procedure includes four main areas or steps.

Key Terms

air-over-hydraulic braking system   A braking system that uses compressed air to provide power assistance to the hydraulic components in the braking system.

backing plate   A metal plate covering the inboard side of brake foundation components in the wheel end.

brake drum   A short, wide, hollow cylinder that is capped on one end and bolted to a vehicle's wheel; it has an inner friction surface that the brake shoe is forced against.

brake fluid   Hydraulic fluid that transfers forces under pressure through the hydraulic lines to the wheel braking units.

brake lines   Made of seamless, double-walled steel, and able to transmit more than 1000 psi (6895 kPa) of hydraulic pressure through the hydraulic brake system.

brake shoes   A combined steel table and brake lining friction material that apply force to the brake drum during braking.

caliper piston   A hydraulic device that uses pressure from the master cylinder to apply the brake pads against the rotor.

combination valve   A valve that combines either all or some of the following into one housing—the proportioning valve, the metering valve, and the pressure differential valve.

front/rear split   A brake system in which the front brakes operate on one hydraulic circuit and the rear brakes from the other.

hydrophilic   A material property indicating it resists absorbing water

hydroscopic   A material property indicating it absorbs water.

leading shoes   An arrangement for brake shoes where they are self energize in the forward direction of brake drum rotation.

leading/trailing shoe drum brake arrangement   A type of brake shoe arrangement where one shoe is positioned to self energize and the opposite shoe does not.

metering valve   A valve that delays brake application pressure to the front disk brakes until a certain level of pressure builds in the system.

phenolic   A lightweight synthetic plastic made of high-temperature-resistant material.

primary piston   A brake piston in the master cylinder moved directly by the pushrod or the power booster; it generates hydraulic pressure to move the secondary piston.

rotor   The main rotating component of a disc brake system that is attached to the wheel hub.

secondary piston   A piston that is moved by hydraulic pressure generated by the primary piston in the master cylinder.

servo action   A drum brake design where one brake shoe, when self energized, applies an increased energizing force to the other brake shoe, in proportion to the initial energizing force; further enhances the self-energizing feature of some drum brakes.

trailing shoes   Brake shoes installed so that they are applied in the opposite direction to the forward rotation of the brake drum; not self-energizing and less efficient at developing braking force.

twin-leading-shoe drum brake   Brake shoe arrangement in which both brake shoes are self-energizing in the forward direction.

vacuum booster   A vacuum-operated power assist system for hydraulic brakes.

wheel cylinders   A hydraulic cylinder with one or two pistons, seals, dust boots, and a bleeder screw that pushes the brake shoes into contact with the brake drum to slow or stop the vehicle.

Review Questions

1. Which of the following is the purpose of a metering valve in a hydraulic brake system?
   a. Delays application of the rear brakes
   b. Delays application of the front brakes
   c. Delays the return of brake fluid
   d. Delays the activation of the warning lamp

2. Which of the following is normally used to move the secondary piston in a master cylinder when the brakes are applied?
   a. Brake fluid pressure
   b. Contact with the primary piston
   c. Accumulator pressure
   d. Direct action of the master cylinder pushrod

3. What effect does air in the hydraulic brake circuit have on the brake pedal?
   a. A hard and high brake pedal
   b. A low and hard brake pedal
   c. A low and spongy brake pedal
   d. It is difficult to detect when air is in the primary circuit

4. During normal operation, a hydraulically boosted master cylinder is typically assisted by which of the following?
   a. The vehicle's power steering pump
   b. The engine's oil pump
   c. An electric motor
   d. A hydraulic accumulator

5. Which one of the following conditions activates the brake warning light in the instrument panel?
   a. A low brake pedal
   b. A twisted brake hose at a front caliper
   c. A park brake switch stuck closed
   d. A defective ABS wheel speed sensor

6. What effect does the loss of vacuum have on the brake pedal feel with a vacuum-assisted brake booster?
   a. A hard and high brake pedal
   b. A low and hard brake pedal
   c. A low and spongy brake pedal
   d. A long brake pedal stroke

7. Which of the following color of paint on a brake spring indicates the strongest spring tension?
   a. White
   b. Black
   c. Yellow
   d. Green

8. Which hydraulic caliper design provides the highest brake application force?
   a. Reaction beam
   b. Floating caliper
   c. Fixed caliper
   d. Sliding caliper

9. Which of the following service tools is essential to bleeding the ABS modulator valves?
   a. A purpose made pressure bleeder
   b. A bleeder hose and jar of brake fluid
   c. A nitrogen or air pressure regulator
   d. OEM software

10. During normal brake applications, which of the following pressurizes brake fluid in a full power hydraulic brake system?
    a. Electro hydraulic pumps
    b. A hydraulic relay valve
    c. A power assisted master cylinder
    d. A master cylinder

ASE Technician A/Technician B Style Questions

1. Technician A says that excessive drum-to-lining clearance causes a low brake pedal. Technician B says that there would be a delay in the brakes applying if there were an excessively large drum-to-lining clearance. Who is correct?
   a. Technician A
   b. Technician B
   c. Both Technician A and Technician B
   d. Neither Technician A nor Technician B

2. Technician A says that if the drum-to-lining clearance is too tight, the result would be dragging brakes. Technician B says if the drum-to-lining clearance is too tight, the result would be overheated brakes. Who is correct?
   a. Technician A
   b. Technician B
   c. Both Technician A and Technician B
   d. Neither Technician A nor Technician B

3. Technicians A and B were discussing service recommendations for brake service on a truck that had 90% service life remaining in rear brake linings. A wheel cylinder failed and contaminated the brake linings on one wheel. Technician A says that the brake linings on both rear brakes must be replaced. Technician B says that only the contaminated lining needs replacement because the lining is almost like new. Who is correct?
   a. Technician A
   b. Technician B
   c. Both Technician A and Technician B
   d. Neither Technician A nor Technician B

4. Technician A says that black, darkened brake fluid indicates the brake fluid is contaminated with rust. Technician B says that black brake fluid indicates the brake's fluid was overheated and burned. Who is correct?
   a. Technician A
   b. Technician B
   c. Both Technician A and Technician B
   d. Neither Technician A nor Technician B

5. Technicians A and B were examining brake pads on a school bus that had heavily worn inboard pads but lightly worn outboard pads. Technician A says that abnormal wear was likely caused by frequent and aggressive brake applications. Technician B says the caliper sliding pins are likely sticking and need service when the pads are replaced. Who is correct?
   a. Technician A
   b. Technician B
   c. Both Technician A and Technician B
   d. Neither Technician A nor Technician B

6. Technician A says that a defective ABS accumulator pressure switch would prevent the operation of the electrohydraulic motor in an ABS modulator valve. Technician B says that a defective motor would be detected whenever the vehicle first operates above 12 mph (20 kph) motor. Who is correct?
   a. Technician A
   b. Technician B
   c. Both Technician A and Technician B
   d. Neither Technician A nor Technician B

7. Technician A says that most types of brake fluid are designed to absorb water. Technician B says that most types of brake fluid are designed to prevent water absorption. Who is correct?
   a. Technician A
   b. Technician B
   c. Both Technician A and Technician B
   d. Neither Technician A nor Technician B

8. Technician A says the only method available to bleed the master cylinder on a full power hydraulic brake system requires OEM software. Technician B says that the master cylinder can be bled manually. Who is correct?
   a. Technician A
   b. Technician B
   c. Both Technician A and Technician B
   d. Neither Technician A nor Technician B

9. Technician A says that the reserve height of a brake pedal disappears, and the brake pedal should slowly sink to the floor, when an ABS system detects a wheel lock-up event. Technician B says that the brake pedal should not sink at all when the ABS system is activated during a wheel lock-up. Who is correct?
   a. Technician A
   b. Technician B
   c. Both Technician A and Technician B
   d. Neither Technician A nor Technician B

10. Technician A says that a popular park brake system on school buses uses an electrically controlled, hydraulically applied, spring-released, cable-operated parking brake. Technician B says that the most common cable-operated park brake mechanism used on hydraulic brake systems is spring applied, and released using pressurized brake fluid. Who is correct?
    a. Technician A
    b. Technician B
    c. Both Technician A and Technician B
    d. Neither Technician A nor Technician B

CHAPTER 39

Fifth Wheels and Hitching Devices

Learning Objectives

- **LO 39-1** Identify common configurations for combination vehicles.
- **LO 39-2** Identify key factors used to determine axle spacing and maximum weight ratings for medium- and heavy-duty commercial vehicles.
- **LO 39-3** Identify and describe various types of hitching mechanisms used by combination vehicles.
- **LO 39-4** Identify and describe the types, features, and applications of fifth wheels and upper couplers.
- **LO 39-5** Explain the purpose of fifth wheel weight and capacity ratings.

- **LO 39-6** Identify and describe the construction and operation of fifth wheels and upper couplers.
- **LO 39-7** Identify and explain the factors considered and methods used to mount and reposition fifth wheels.
- **LO 39-8** Identify and explain common complaints and failures of fifth wheel locking mechanisms.
- **LO 39-9** Identify and describe the inspection methods and service procedures used to maintain fifth wheels and upper couplers.
- **LO 39-10** Identify and describe the purpose and operation of trailer landing gear.

You Are the Technician

After reading some inspection report histories of several tractors and trailers in a fleet operation, you discover a consistent pattern of problems contributing to unusually high maintenance costs. Some of the problems include:

- Abnormal tire wear patterns on the front axle tires, leading to frequent replacement.
- Excessive tire wear on only the drive axle set of tires, resulting in frequent tire replacement.
- Steering and vehicle handling complaints, leading to unnecessary replacement of steering and suspension parts, such as steering gears, which were later found to have no fault.
- Damage to the front corners of several trailers and crush damage to tractor's vertical muffler.
- Damage to trailer landing gear and tractor mud-flap brackets torn off several tractors.

The company has also received several fines for overloaded axles at highway inspection weigh scales.

One of the possible causes that could account for the pattern of complaints and repairs is an incorrectly positioned fifth wheel, leading to unequal distribution of load weight over the tractors' axles. As you begin to perform an inspection of the vehicles with the highest number of complaints, consider the following:

1. How would each of the above complaints relate to an incorrectly positioned fifth wheel?
2. Which complaints would be specific to a fifth wheel moved too far forward, rearward, or both?
3. Outline what items should be inspected to verify that the fifth wheel can be properly adjusted to properly distribute loads over the tractors axles.

Introduction

To prevent damage caused by overloaded vehicles to the pavement and structure of roadways and bridges, the maximum vehicle weight supported by tires and axles is limited by legislation. Two principles guiding the technical details of the legislation are that tires should apply no more than 600 psi (272 kg/cm²) to its road contact patch. Second, the weight of a vehicle supported by a single axle should almost never exceed 20,000 lb (9072 kg).

A limited number of vehicle factors and operating conditions change the general rule for maximum axle weight. However, the best solution to enable transportation of heavier loads is to add more axles to the vehicle configuration. Adding more axles minimizes damage to road surfaces caused by concentrating too much weight onto a small surface area beneath the tire or a narrow section of a bridge structure. Similarly, adding additional tires to an axle end or much wider tires, such as super singles, redistributes the vehicle weight over a larger road surface area.

Adding more axles to a rigid chassis is not without challenges, however. For vehicles loaded with tens of thousands of pounds of cargo, steering and maneuvering could become almost impossible. To solve this dilemma, trailers are used that allow the vehicle to articulate, or bend when turning. Connecting trucks with trailers form **combination vehicles**, such as the tanker shown in **FIGURE 39-1A**. When a truck pulls a trailer, it is called a tractor. In a combination vehicle, the trailer is the towed unit, hence the term tractor-trailer is often used to describe a combination vehicle. Fifth wheels and a variety of coupling devices are needed to connect or hitch trailers to tractors while allowing articulation between the tractor and towed units. A fifth wheel is a plate-type coupler with locking jaws that both

grips a trailer and supports the weight of a semi-trailer which enables articulation or bending movement between the tractor and trailer. In **FIGURE 39-1B**, the front of the trailer is supported by the tractor and articulates on the fifth wheel.

Fifth wheels and coupling devices are used to connect vehicles together into a combination vehicle. Combination vehicles allow the tractor, sometimes called the power unit, to be used to pull a variety of loads (dry goods, liquid bulk, or aggregates, for example) which makes the vehicle more versatile, reduces dead time (when the vehicle is waiting between loads), and increases profitability for the owner. Vehicles can be connected by using various types of hitches, couplers, and fifth wheels. This next section discusses the different types of combination vehicles and how they are connected.

Common Configurations for Combination Vehicles

LO 39-1 Identify common configurations for combination vehicles.

To understand when and where various coupling devices and fifth wheels are used, it is important to learn common configurations for combination vehicles. Combination vehicles can be divided into categories according to their towing arrangement. Tractors, trailers (semi and full), and converter dollies.

Tractors

The term "tractor-engine," which was given to a motorized vehicle pulling wagons, has been replaced by the term tractor. A **tractor** is a commercial motor vehicle chassis designed to exclusively tow trailers. Having usually just a cab and no capability to carry cargo, tractors use high torque output engines and a fifth wheel, which is used to support the front end of a trailer.

Pulling trailers today is not fundamentally different than the wagons of a bygone era. Tractors are commonly constructed using high torque rise engines and transmissions with deep gear reduction ratios to produce substantial traction power at low speeds for hauling heavy loads through one or two drive axles. Depending on where and how the tractor is used, the cab may have a sleeper unit for the driver or driving team. A day cab, or conventional tractor, such as the one shown in **FIGURE 39-2**, does not have a sleeper unit and is used for short-distance hauling. Aerodynamic fairings reduce energy losses due to wind resistance and increase fuel economy.

A common tractor configuration places the engine ahead of the cab. This **cab forward (CF)** design provides the driver favorable ride characteristics and easier access to the cab. **Cab-over-engine (COE)** tractors have the engine located beneath the cab. This design is less commonly used in North America, but is used almost exclusively in Europe because COE tractors are shorter and more maneuverable. **FIGURE 39-3** shows a cab over engine tractor.

Legislation limiting vehicle length means longer trailers can be used with COE tractors. Placing the cab over the steer axles means the tractor is more easily turned in tight spaces. A disadvantage, however, is that suspension bounce and jounce are more powerfully transmitted to the cab. The wheel base length

FIGURE 39-1 A. Combining vehicles requires specialized hitching equipment. **B.** A semi-trailer connects to the tractor using a fifth wheel.

and location of the fifth wheel on a tractor are critical since the weight of the trailer must be distributed over all the axles, so that no axle exceeds the maximum legal weight. Legal weight limits are covered in the Vehicle Weight Ratings and Capacity section.

A **terminal tractor**, also known as a **shunt truck** or yard tractor, is built to move semi-trailers around a warehouse yard or intermodal facility. As shown in **FIGURE 39-4**, terminal tractors use unique suspensions and fifth wheels designed to get under a semi-trailer and lift a trailer without the need to raise the trailer landing gear. A hydraulic lifting mechanism integrated into the fifth wheel is designed to lift the trailer 15" (38.1 cm) with as much as 70,000 lb (31,818 kg) of force. To improve visibility, a single-person cab is offset to the left of the engine.

Trailers

Trailers are the cargo-carrying portion of a combination vehicle. The most familiar combination configuration in North America is a tractor with a semi-trailer. **Semi-trailers** use one, two, or even three axles, depending on their length and load-carrying capacity. Because the trailer's load is actually carried by the tractor, it is referred to as a *semi-trailer*. Different from a semi-trailer, a **full trailer** has axles at the front and rear of the trailer to support the entire weight of the trailer. **FIGURE 39-5** shows a full trailer. This allows the trailer to be pulled by a vehicle with an appropriate hitching system.

The position of the axles can often be moved forward and backward along the trailer to achieve proper and even weight distribution over the axles. This is particularly useful if the load is an irregular size or weight.

The front of the semi-trailer is supported and towed by a fifth wheel, which may or may not always be attached directly to a tractor. Some trailer configurations are also constructed with fifth wheels that can support a second trailer. When not connected to the tractor, the trailer's landing gear supports the front of the trailer. The **landing gear** is a set of retractable legs attached to the trailer, which support a semi-trailer when it is not resting on a fifth wheel. Landing gear is illustrated in **FIGURE 39-6**.

Converter Dollies

Full trailers are most often semi-trailers that are converted to full trailers using a **converter dolly**, which is a fifth wheel supported by one or two axles. The converter dolly may also use self-steering axles having a high degree of positive caster to maintain straight-line directional stability. Whenever a converter dolly is used to connect two trailers, the lead trailer is equipped at the rear with a pintle hook-type hitch, like the one in **FIGURE 39-7**. Pintle hooks are covered in the Pintle Hooks and Couplers section.

FIGURE 39-2 Conventional cab-forward tractors locate the engine in front of the cab.

FIGURE 39-3 Cab-over-engine tractors are shorter and more maneuverable, but transmit more road shock to the driver.

FIGURE 39-4 A shunt truck or yard tractor has a hydraulically lifted fifth wheel and is used to move trailers around a yard without needing to raise the trailer's landing gear.

FIGURE 39-5 A full trailer is located behind the semitrailer in this picture. A converter dolly beneath the front of the last trailer converts a semi-trailer into a full trailer.

FIGURE 39-6 Landing gear is a set of retractable legs attached to the trailer.

FIGURE 39-7 This tractor has a fifth wheel and a single point hitch for a rear coupler or pintle hook, which enables it to connect and pull a trailer through an A-train hitching configuration.

Trailer-Train Combinations

Combination vehicles may also have multiple trailers, referred to as **A-, B-, or C-trains**. The various train types are differentiated by the hitching mechanism connecting them to the trailers. The geometric shape of the connection is what distinguishes the different classifications of trailer combinations. On A- and C-type trailer trains, a **draw bar**, which is a rigid steel tow bar with a round-shaped eyelet at one end, is used to connect the converter dolly of the second trailer to a lead trailer, which is usually a semi-trailer in North America. This means both A and C trailers are full trailers connected to a lead trailer. A single draw bar is used to connect an A-train converter dolly to the lead trailer, while two draw bars connect the dolly of a C-type train to the lead trailer. Visually, the shape of the single point connection of an A train resembles the letter A, while the two connection points of a C-train resembles the letter C.

A-Type Trailer Combinations

An **A-train** is a three-unit combination of a tractor plus two trailers. The second trailer is a full trailer unit connected by a draw bar to a single hitch point to the lead, or the first, trailer. The shape of the articulation point—the "A" shape of the draw bar on the converter dolly—lends the name to the tractor trailer combination. When connected to a trailer, A-type converter dollies form A-trains. A-trains have a significant disadvantage due to the use of a single draw bar connection point. A single connection point creates a greater potential for the rear trailer to become unstable and drift from the lead trailer track. For this reason, A-trains are not allowed to operate in many jurisdictions. **FIGURE 39-8** shows the connection point of an A-train.

One exception to the uncommon use of an A-type trailer hitching configuration is by haulers transporting grain and

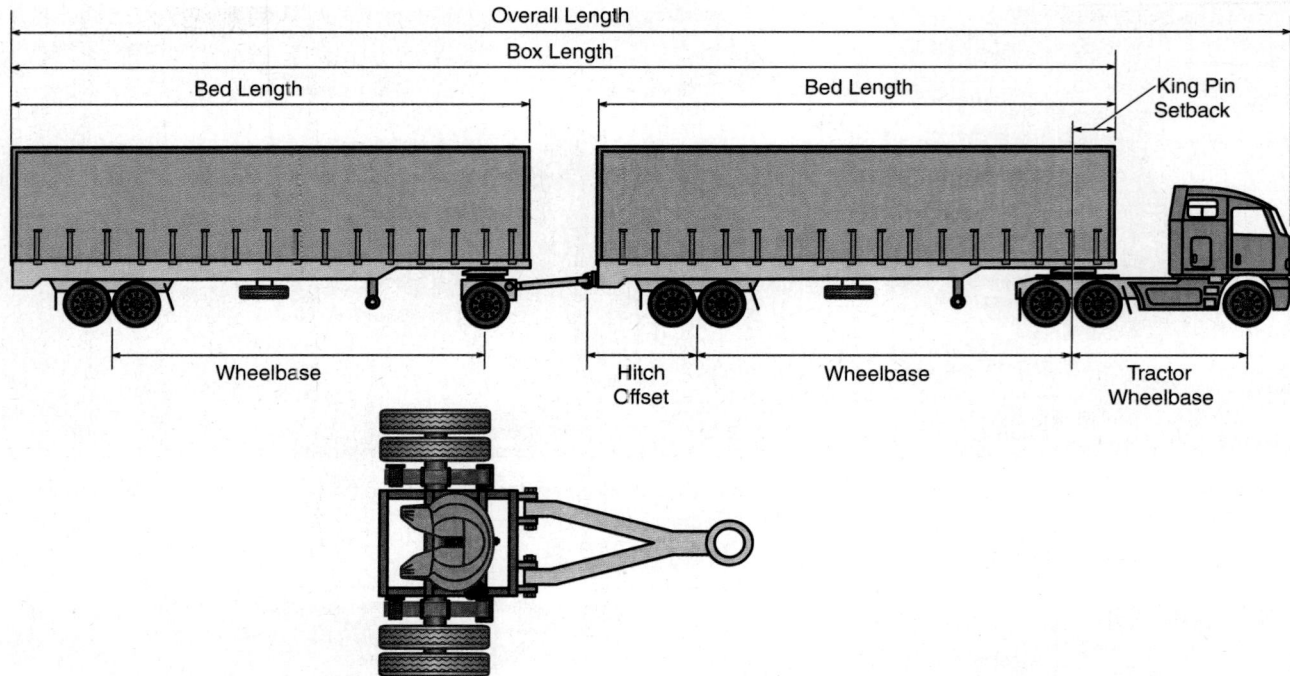

FIGURE 39-8 An A-train consists of a tractor pulling a semi-trailer and a second, full trailer, behind the semi-trailer using a single draw bar. A converter dolly converts a semitrailer to a full trailer.

Pup Trailer

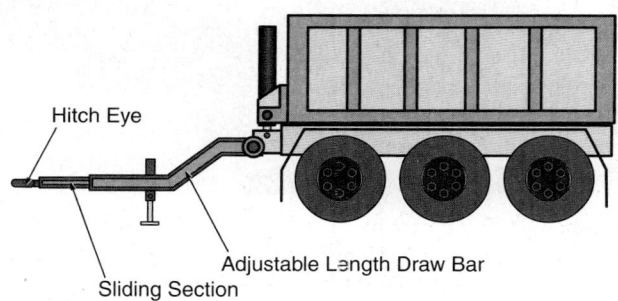

FIGURE 39-9 The draw bar of a pup trailer has a single connection point. The bar is usually integrated with the trailer frame.

aggregate material. A pup trailer, also called stiff pulled trailer, pony trailer, end dumps, or by some other local name, is towed behind a semi-trailer or dump truck using an adjustable length draw bar. The pup trailer is shorter than a full trailer but supports a load on its own axles like a full trailer. Its draw bar is typically made from box channel steel integrated with the trailer frame (**FIGURE 39-9**). Air lines and electrical cables pass through the draw bar to protect it from material dumped from the lead vehicle. The sliding draw bar is a key feature that can be shortened to make the trailer more maneuverable, but lengthened when required to meet standards for bridge formula. The most important reason for the use of the longer draw bar is it allows the pup trailer to be easily jackknifed at 90 degrees

when it is backed-up to enable the tow vehicle to dump a load of product. When the lead vehicle is empty, the pump trailer is dumped. The draw bar has a built-in angle that keeps the draw bar close to the ground to minimize interference with the tailgate of the tow vehicle when it opens. Most draw bars connect using a pintle hook and eye hitch, but for off-road applications, a swivel-type rubber coupler enables the bar to articulate when the trailer twists over uneven ground surfaces.

B-Type Trailer Combinations

A B-train is the second trailer of a three-unit combination of a tractor and two trailers. B combinations are simply another semi-trailer connected to a fifth wheel attached to the rear section of the first trailer. The B-train does not use a converter dolly. Instead, a section of the rear frame of the lead trailer is built to extend out to support the second trailer with a fifth wheel. The extension with the fifth wheel can retract beneath the lead trailer whenever it is not used. Given its function, the extension frame or tail section of the lead trailer with the fifth wheel is often referred to as the "bridge."

B and C combinations are frequently used in North America. Since B-trains use a fifth wheel, they can support and distribute higher trailer weights than a C-train. One study found that using B-trains achieves a 78% increase in payload using only 25% more fuel. The B-train configuration is the most stable of the three combination vehicle types because a fifth-wheel connection between trailers is the best at resisting the rollover of the second trailer. **FIGURE 39-10** shows the connection point of a B-train.

C-Type Trailer Combinations

C-type trailer trains use converter dollies having two separate draw bars attached to each side of the converter dolly. The lead trailer uses two pintle hooks, one on each side of the trailer, to serve as a hinge-like attachment point for the draw bars. The C-dolly's two horizontal parallel connection points give a C-train greater stability than an A-train. Compared to a B-train, however, the C-train is not quite as stable since the hinge joint permits greater vertical articulation. However, the two parallel draw bars of the C-dolly ensure that the C-train does not move from a horizontal plane when towed. A C-train is similar to the A-train except that the C-train has two draw bars attached to two points on the lead trailer (**FIGURE 39-11**).

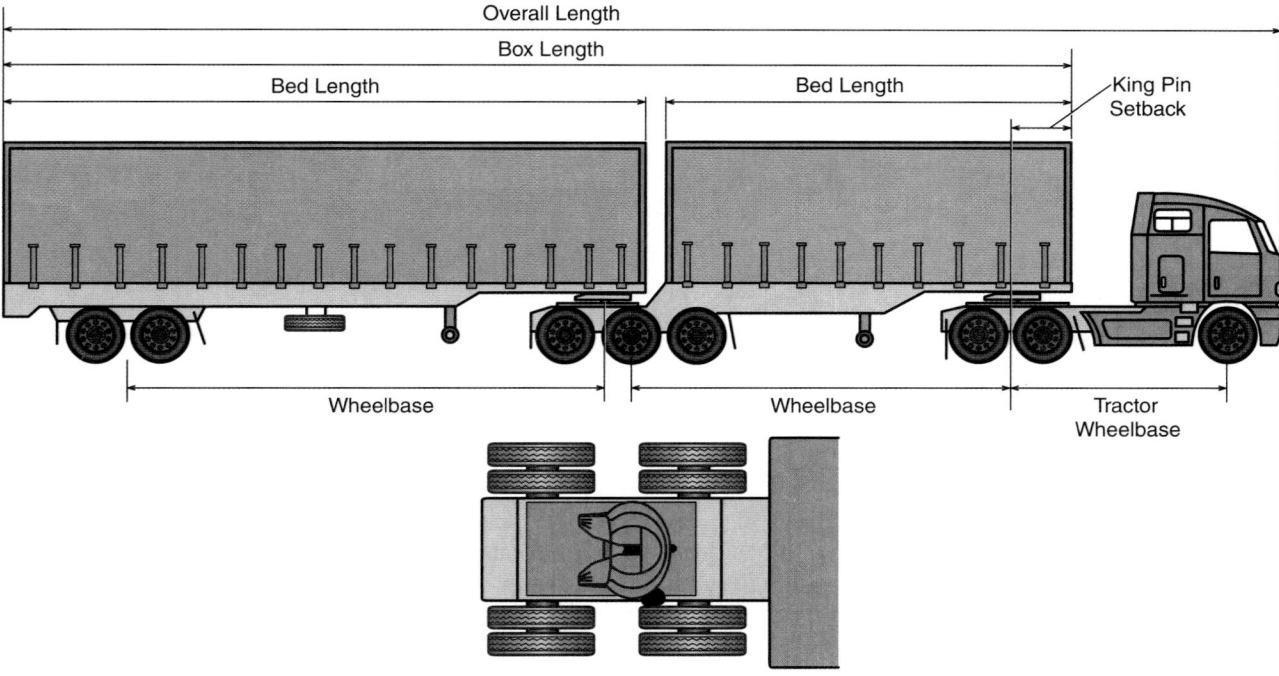

FIGURE 39-10 A B-train consists of a tractor pulling a semi-trailer and a second, full trailer, behind the semi-trailer.

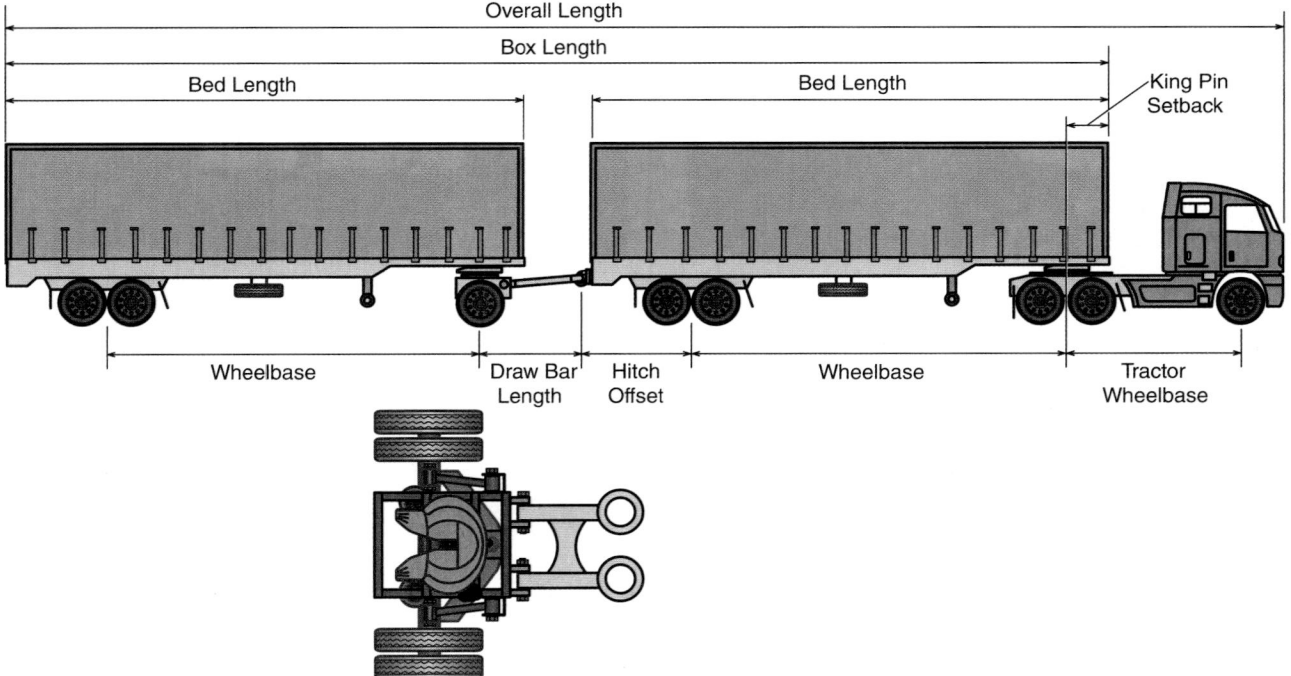

FIGURE 39-11 A C-train uses two draw bars to connect the rear trailer to the lead trailer.

A major safety hazard is created whenever grease or oil are used to lubricate a pintle hook coupler. NEVER grease or lubricate the draw bar eye or pintle hook of a coupler. Grease, oil, or other types of lubricant easily attract and retain dirt and sand, which forms a rapidly abrasive material that shortens the coupler service life. Dust- and sand-covered grease also makes it very difficult to perform a visual inspection of the coupler for cracks and excessive wear.

Vehicle Weight Ratings and Capacity

LO 39-2 Identify key factors used to determine axle spacing and maximum weight ratings for medium- and heavy-duty commercial vehicles.

In the early 20th century, vehicle weight limits were legislated to protect dirt and gravel roads from damage caused by the heavy wheel weights of commercial vehicles. As truck traffic and load weights increased continually, truck weight limits began to focus primarily on gross weight limits to protect bridges from damaging truck weights. **Gross weight limits** are the maximum legal weight of a loaded vehicle that can travel on roads and bridges.

By the mid-1970s, a law was passed to limit the weight-to-length ratio of heavy trucks to protect roads and bridges from the damage caused by the concentrated weight of shorter trucks. The law created the **Federal Bridge Gross Weight Formula** (also known as **Bridge Formula B** and the **Federal Bridge Formula**). Those formulas established the maximum weights for a commercial motor vehicle (CMV) based on the number of axles the vehicle had and the spacing between those axles.

The formula is part of US/Canadian weight and length regulations regarding interstate/interprovincial commercial traffic. Axle spacing is as important as axle weight in bridge design. Consider a vehicle with two axles carrying significant weight. If not spaced far enough apart, those two axles act like a single axle in terms of loading road surfaces. The longer the **axle spread**—a distance measured from axle center to axle center—the better weight distribution is achieved to prevent road and bridge damage.

The bridge formula, therefore, allows motor vehicles to be loaded to maximum weight only if each group of axles and their spacing also satisfy the requirements of the formula. In North America, the weight limit is typically 20,000 lb (9072 kg) for a single-axle vehicle with a total weight on one or more axles that are not more than 40" (101.6 cm) apart. For **tandem axles** (a two-axle tractor or trailer configuration), the total weight limit is typically 34,000 lb (15,422 kg) for a vehicle with its full weight on two or more consecutive axles that are between 40" and 96" (101.6 cm and 243.8 cm) apart.

Vehicle Weight Ratings

Numerous configurations of trucks, tractor-trailers, and even buses can be classified by length, weight, number of axles, and number of wheels. In North America, one of the most common ways trucks are categorized is by **gross vehicle weight (GVW)**. GVW refers to the maximum design weight of a vehicle including a full tank of fuel, fully loaded to its capacity, and with all passengers. **TABLE 39-1** shows the classifications of vehicles by GVW. The heaviest classification using this method is GVW Class 8 vehicles. Class 8 includes vehicles weighing more than 34,001 lb (14,969 kg), which are usually considered heavy trucks.

Gross Vehicle Weight Rating

A similar classification system based on weight is **Gross Vehicle Weight Rating (GVWR)**. GVWR is the design rating specified by a manufacturer as the recommended maximum weight of a vehicle when fully loaded. Trucks or tractors (power units) are classified primarily into a class between 4 and 8 based on their GVWR.

General legislation in North America limits the GVW of a vehicle, or a combination of vehicles, according to the number of axles and the distance between the axles. Those limits are listed in **TABLE 39-2**.

Many exceptions and variations are made to the general rule. As an example of how axle spacing affects maximum load, consider that vehicles with multiple axles whose centers are less than 4' (1.2 m) apart are classified as a single axle unit. The situation is even more complex for triaxle combinations. When a vehicle has a single drive axle with center-to-center distances closer than 10' (3.0 m) (or a steering axle closer than 9' [2.7 m]) to a triaxle unit, the single axle is considered part of that triaxle. The presence of the additional axle does not increase the allowable legal load capacity of that triaxle unit.

TABLE 39-1 Classification of Chassis by Gross Vehicle Weight (GVW)

Class	Gross Vehicle Weight
1	6000 lb (2721.6 kg) or less
2	6001–10,000 lb (2722–4535.9 kg)
3	10,001–14,000 lb (4536.4–6350.3 kg)
4	14,001–16,000 lb (6350.7–7257.5 kg)
5	16,001–19,500 lb (7257.9–8845.1 kg)
6	19,501–26,000 lb (8845.5–11,793.4 kg)
7	26,001–34,000 lb (11,793.9 kg–14,968.5 kg)
8	34,001 lb (14,969 kg) or more

TABLE 39-2 General Law Gross Weight Limits

Number of Axles	Weight Limit
2	34,000 lb (15,422.1 kg)
3	54,000 lb (24,494 kg)
4	69,000 lb (31,297.9 kg)
5	80,000 lb (36,287.4 kg)
6	100,000 lb (45,359.2 kg)

Gross Combined Vehicle Weight

The gross combined weight rating (GCWR) is a specific maximum weight limit determined by the vehicle manufacturer. Unlike other weight ratings, the GCWR takes into account two individual (yet attached) vehicles—the tow vehicle, or tractor, and the trailer.

Types of Fifth Wheels and Coupling Devices

LO 39-3 Identify and describe various types of hitching mechanisms used by combination vehicles.

A variety of vehicle factors and operating conditions can change the general rules for determining maximum axle weight. The accepted approach for transporting heavier and larger loads is to add more axles to the vehicle configuration in order to minimize damage to road surfaces. Adding more axles is best accomplished by arranging combination vehicles and trailers in a way than allows them to articulate, or bend, when turning. Fifth wheels and a variety of coupling devices connect or hitch trailers to tractors and allow articulation between tractor and towed units. Depending on the size and type of trailer or the product transported, a number of hitching devices have been developed to tow full trailers and specialized equipment. These devices

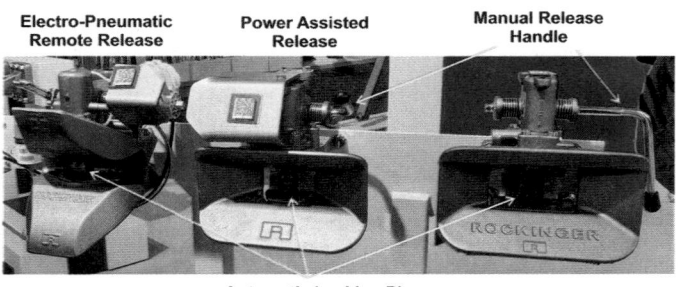

FIGURE 39-12 Automatic couplers used on European vehicles drop a locking pin into the draw bar eyelet after it engages the hitch.

include pintle hooks and couplers, ball hitches, etc. Fifth wheels and upper couplers are used to connect and tow semi-trailers. We first discuss coupling systems used with full trailers.

Pintle Hooks and Couplers

Pintle hooks are trailer hitching devices that use a fixed towing horn, which connects with a draw bar attached to the towed vehicle. Pintle hooks are coupled by raising the draw bar eyelet over the pintle horn and locking it closed with a pivoting latch. Automatic-type couplers are popular in Europe. These devices automatically drop a pin into the draw bar eyelet after it engages the hitch. **FIGURE 39-12** shows how the manual or automatic release mechanism disconnects the pintle hook. **Couplers** are hitching devices that look like pintle hooks except the towing horn pivots and is not fixed. Since the wider-opening coupler connects easier to a draw bar eyelet than a pintle hook, couplers are especially useful in applications with frequent trailer coupling and uncoupling. **FIGURE 39-13** shows a pintle hook and a coupler. Pintle hooks and couplers are selected by towing and vertical weight.

To minimize shock loads when initially moving a trailer or during braking, a **snubber**, or load dampener, can be used. As shown in **FIGURE 39-14A**, rubber cushions or heavy springs are integrated into the device to permit some movement along the centerline and some side-to-side strain relief. An air-cushioned pintle hook, such as the one pictured in **FIGURE 39-14B**, is a rigid pintle hook equipped with an air chamber connected to a plunger, which removes the slack between the pintle horn and draw bar.

Draw bars are used to connect tow vehicles to a tractor or lead towing unit. Draw bars are illustrated in **FIGURE 39-15**. Bars are typically fabricated box-like structures or solid malleable steel material, which bends, but does not crack or break, under heavy strain. The bar has an eyelet or a lunette, as shown in **FIGURE 39-16**, welded or bolted to the bar, which can connect to a pintle, coupler, or pin on the tow vehicle.

Ball Hitches

Ball hitches are used on light- and medium-duty vehicles having a 12,000 lb (5455 kg) towing weight capacity. The ball requires

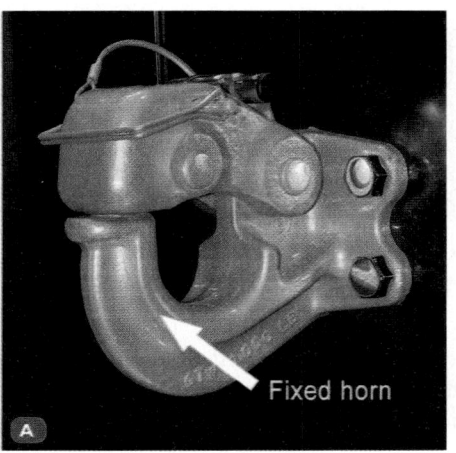 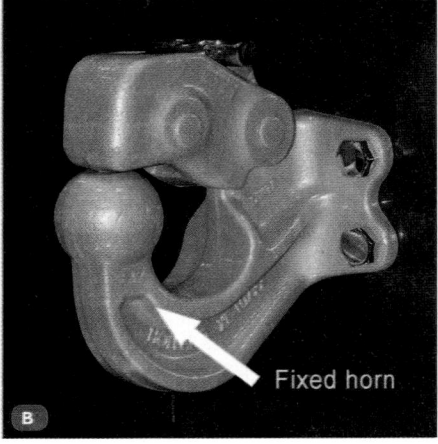 

FIGURE 39-13 A. Pintle hook with a fixed horn. **B.** Pintle hook with a ball hitch. **C.** Coupler.

Snubber spring

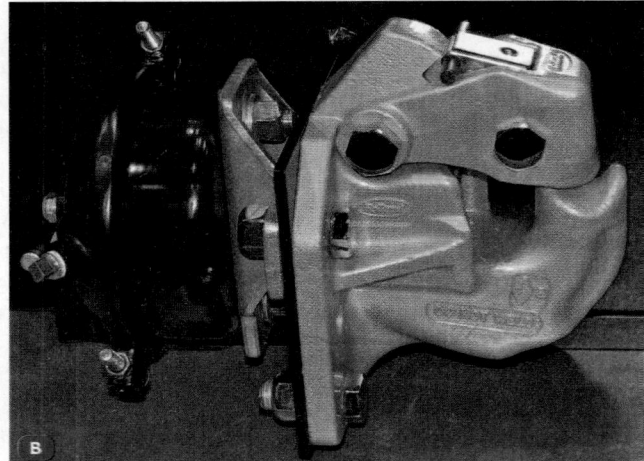

FIGURE 39-14 A. Snubber. **B.** Air-cushioned pintle hook.

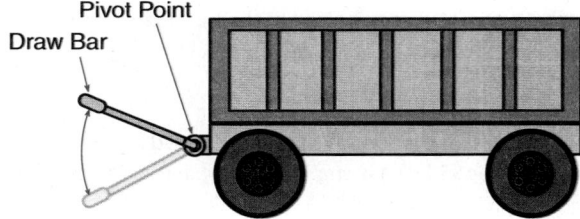

Pivot Point

Draw Bar

FIGURE 39-15 Draw bar.

a tongue-type tow bar, which loops over a ball. Ball hitches have the advantage of providing a positive no-slack fit because the draw bar has a spring-loaded tensioner at the connection point with the ball. Ball hitches, pintle hooks, and couplers typically use rigid couplers.

Ball hitches are classified by the weight supported by the ball or **tongue weight (TW)** and the **gross trailer weight (GTW)**, which is the weight of the trailer and cargo. Different sizes of balls are used depending on the category of hitch. A 2⁵⁄₁₆" (5.9 cm) diameter ball coupler is the largest size for a Class 4 hitch. Class 4 hitches are classified as a hitch with weight carrying rating of up to 10,000 lb (4545 kg) gross trailer weight and 1000–1200 lb (455–545 kg) tongue weight. Gooseneck trailers, such as those hauling large motor homes,

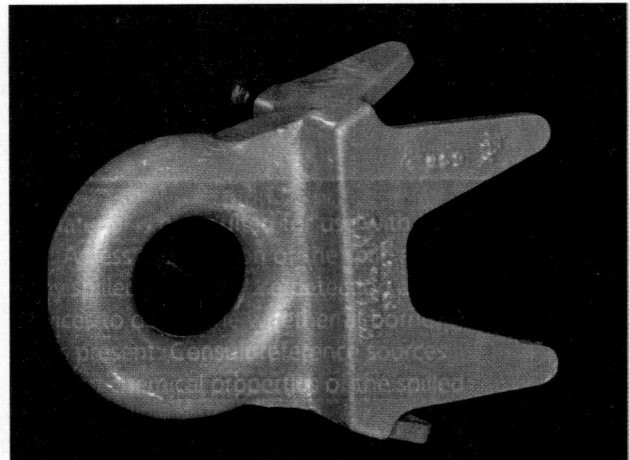

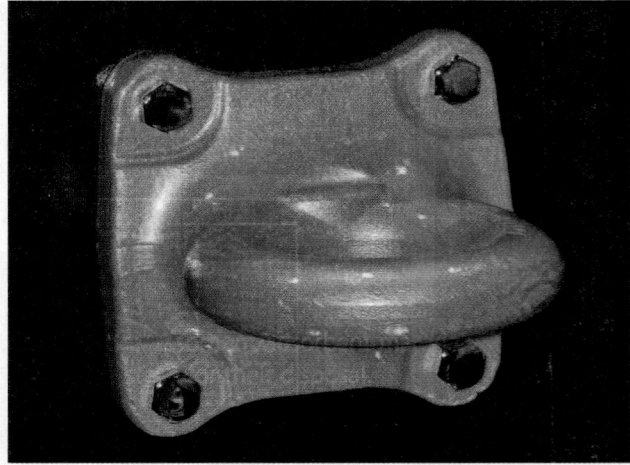

FIGURE 39-16 Draw bar eyelets, also called lunettes, are made in a variety of configurations for attachment to a towing draw bar.

can use ball hitches mounted to the bed of a pickup truck. The ball is fastened to a frame section or receiver plate of the tow vehicle, which is called a receiver (see **FIGURE 39-17**). However, for vertical loads exceeding 10,000 lb (4545 kg), fifth wheel couplers are a more practical hitching system, even in light-duty configurations. The fifth wheel shown in **FIGURE 39-18** is attached to the bed of a pickup and pulls gooseneck trailers. The various types of fifth wheels are described in the following sections.

Safety chains must supplement the ball hitch, pintle, or coupler connection in the event the trailer connection breaks away. When fabricating safety chains, the length of safety chains should be no longer than needed to provide a small amount of slack for cornering. As illustrated in **FIGURE 39-19**, chains are crossed beneath the tow bar to prevent it from dropping to the ground if the coupling system disconnects. Chains must be attached to the tractor and tow vehicle frame and not attached to the pintle hook or other device.

Tongue Weight

Tongue weight, or TW, is the load the draw bar places on the pintle hook, coupler, or ball hitch. As a general rule, the vertical load on the trailer tongue should be estimated to be at least 10% of the gross trailer weight. When loaded properly, the weight of the load assists in stabilizing the draw bar for improved directional control when cornering, and reduces the wear-out effect of surging caused by speed changes. Excessive vertical load results in accelerated wear on the tongue and

tow bar. As illustrated in **FIGURE 39-20**, the capacity of the hitching device must match or exceed the maximum anticipated load.

FIGURE 39-17 A 2" receiver tube is in the hitch plate to accept various ball-type couplers.

FIGURE 39-18 This fifth wheel is attached to the bed of a pickup and pulls gooseneck trailers.

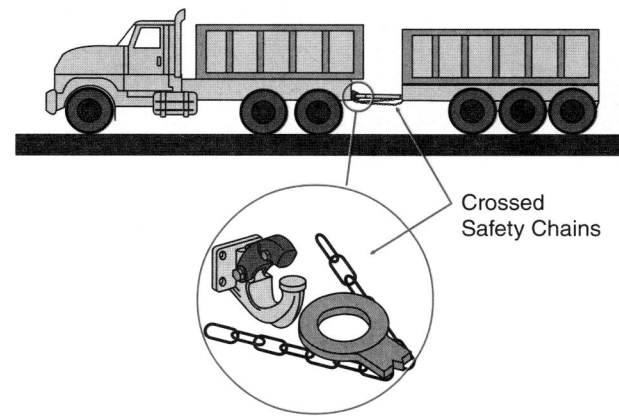

FIGURE 39-19 Chains should be of a length that can be crossed below the tow bar and short enough to prevent the tow bar from contacting the ground if disconnected.

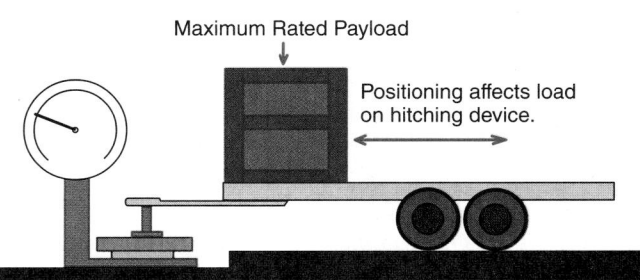

FIGURE 39-20 The capacity of the hitching device must match or exceed the maximum anticipated load. The position of a load affects the weight applied to a hitching device.

Fifth Wheels are Plate-Type Coupling Devices

LO 39-4 Identify and describe the types, features, and applications of fifth wheels and upper couplers.

Fifth wheels are plate-type coupling devices designed to support the weight of a semi-trailer and lock the trailer to the tractor or tow unit. **FIGURE 39-21A** pictures a fifth-wheel coupler. On tractors, the fifth wheel is mounted on the rear frame of a tractor above the drive axles and can use several different types of locking jaws to fasten the trailer king pin to the plate. As shown in **FIGURE 39-21B**, to properly distribute trailer weight over all the tractors axles, the center of the fifth wheel is located ahead of the center point between the two rear drive axles. This position enables that both the steer and drive axles distribute trailer weight.

The fifth wheel articulates against the upper coupler plate, attached to the trailer, and rotates around the upper coupler king pin. Both the trailer plate and king pin together are referred to as the **upper coupler**. This device distributes the trailer load through the fifth wheel onto the tractor suspension while enabling articulation between the tractor and trailer when changing direction or steering. (More information on upper couplers can be found in the Upper Couplers section.)

To allow free and easy rotation of the trailer upper coupler and reduce wear on the fifth wheel top plate, lubrication is required. Grease grooves built into the fifth wheels top plate typically retain and help distribute grease. Not all fifth wheels use grease, however. For example, "no lube" fifth wheels use a special Teflon-like, antifriction plate or insert on the top plate, such as the one pictured in **FIGURE 39-22**. Antifriction plates are common on aluminum fifth wheels because the low-friction Teflon-like pads form a replaceable wear surface to extend the service life of the softer aluminum fifth wheel.

Fifth wheels must maintain a secure connection when the trailer rolls slightly about its horizontal axis, such as when cornering. Fifth wheels must also resist the forces of braking and acceleration. To ensure this strong connection, fifth wheels should have approximately three to six degrees of rotation around a horizontal axis, as illustrated in **FIGURE 39-23**. This clearance is achieved through the flexion of rubber bushings surrounding the steel

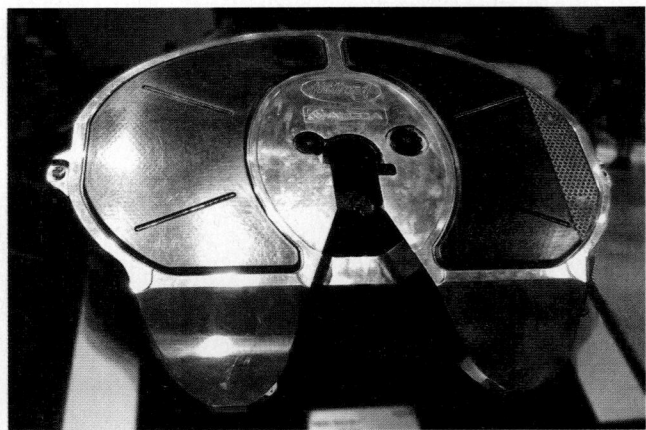

FIGURE 39-22 Fifth wheel with an antifriction plate in the place of grease grooves.

FIGURE 39-21 A. Fifth wheels are plate-type couplers. The fifth whee is mounted securely to the rear frame of the tractor. **B.** Fifth wheel center is mounted ahead of the center point between the two drive axles.

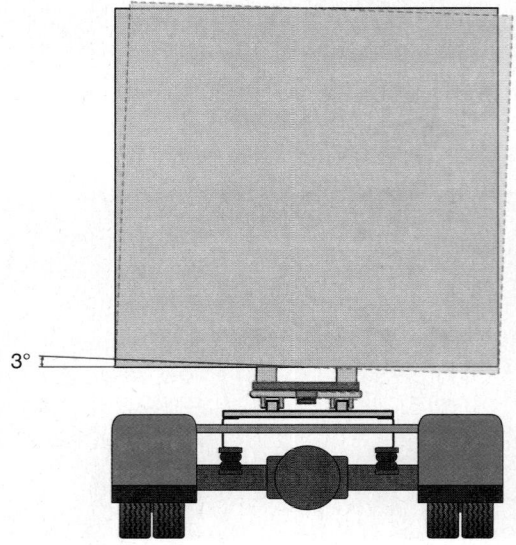

FIGURE 39-23 The fifth wheel should be able to flex three to six degrees around a horizontal axis.

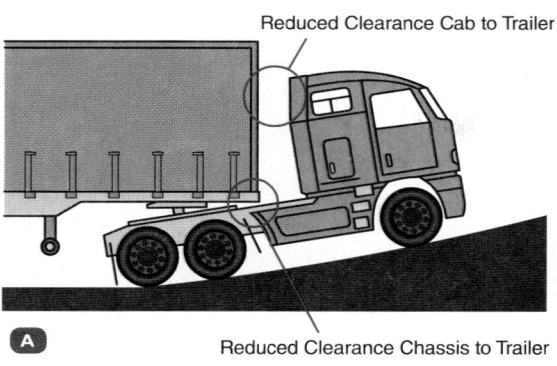

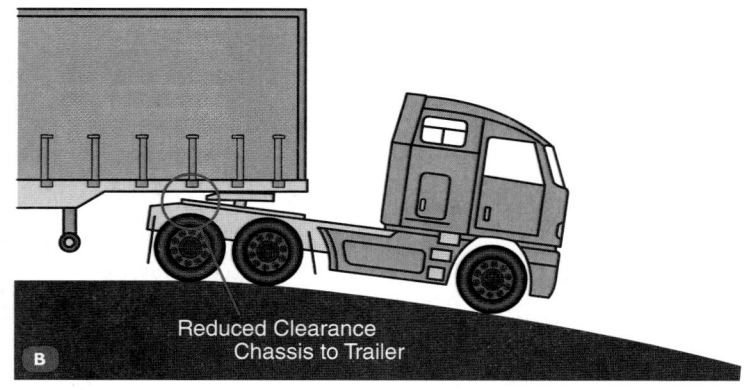

FIGURE 39-24 Clearance angles on fifth wheels should prevent **A.** tipping and **B.** tilting.

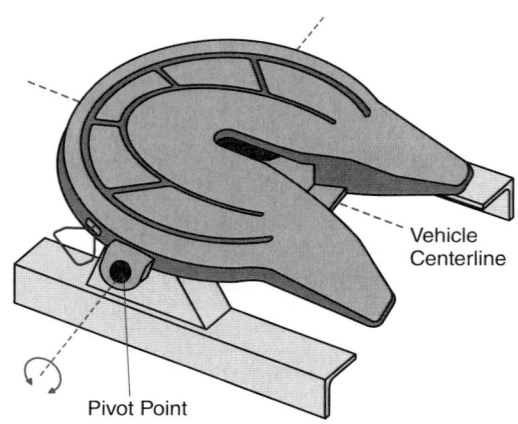

FIGURE 39-25 The semi-oscillating plate can rotate longitudinally along the vehicle's centerline to adjust to inclines and bumps in the road surface.

pins that secure the fifth wheel to the tractor. To enable the trailer to pivot when moving up (**FIGURE 39-24A**) or down relative to the tractor (**FIGURE 39-24B**), such as when moving over sharp inclines, fifth wheels also pivot or tilt along a longitudinal axis.

Semi-Oscillating Type

Fifth wheels that pivot slightly in both a horizontal and longitudinal axis are called **semi-oscillating fifth wheels** and are the most common type of fifth wheel used in on-highway applications. Semi-oscillating plates can move several degrees vertically and horizontally along the vehicle's centerline. By moving vertically and horizontally, the vehicle is able to adjust to inclines and bumps in the road surface. **FIGURE 39-25** shows a semi-oscillating plate and the pivot point around which it rotates.

Fully (Double) Oscillating Fifth Wheel

Fully oscillating fifth wheels are a type of fifth wheel designed to provide more front-to-rear and side-to-side movement between the tractor and semi-trailer than semi-oscillating plates. The additional capacity to articulate along these planes prevents the trailer body from twisting. The result of enhanced oscillating capacity means fully oscillating fifth wheels are ideally suited for vehicles operating in off-road conditions, such as mining or logging. Liquid tankers also use fully oscillating fifth wheels to minimize cracking of the tank barrel caused by twisting of the barrel over uneven road surfaces. **FIGURE 39-26A** shows the basic design of a fully oscillating fifth wheel, and **FIGURE 39-26B** shows one in a tanker application.

Rigid-Type or "No-Tilt"

Having a fifth wheel with the capacity to oscillate is not always desirable. For this reason, a **rigid fifth wheel** is built that does not oscillate about either axis of the vehicle. This means it does not articulate from side-to-side or front-to-back. Instead, it is fixed in location. **FIGURE 39-27** shows a rigid fifth wheel.

In applications that require a rigid fifth wheel, the articulation is provided by an articulating upper coupler on the trailer. That design combination prevents excessive trailer rotation around a horizontal axis, which could increase the likelihood of a roll-over.

Frameless dump trailers are an example where the upper coupler articulates. A simple flip-type mechanism beneath the top plate can convert the no-tilt or rigid wheel to a standard semi-oscillating fifth wheel. **FIGURE 39-28** shows a rigid fifth wheel in use on a dump trailer.

Note that a rigid fifth wheel that does not oscillate is different from a rigid mounted fifth wheel. The latter type is unmovable on the tractor frame and is rigidly bolted in place, preventing both longitudinal and horizontal movement over the vehicle drive axles.

Two-Height Fifth Wheels

Two-height fifth wheels are a specialty stationary fifth wheel that can be either air or hydraulically operated. Two-height fifth wheels are made for low frame height tractors that haul trailers

FIGURE 39-27 A rigid-type fifth wheel.

FIGURE 39-26 A. A fully oscillating fifth wheel, with pivot points (circled). **B.** Tankers often use fully oscillating fifth wheels to eliminate twisting between the tractor and trailer.

FIGURE 39-28 A rigid fifth wheel in use on a frameless dump trailer.

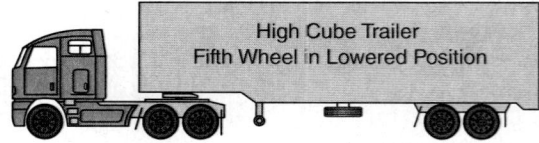

FIGURE 39-29 The height of these specialty fifth wheels is adjustable. Shunt tractors use these fifth wheels to eliminate the need to raise and lower landing gear while moving trailers.

of different heights. For example, as illustrated in **FIGURE 39-29**, the same tractor could haul 117" (297.2 cm) high cubic capacity trailers or pull standard 110" (279.4 cm) height van trailers. A high cubic capacity trailer carries light loads, such as wood or potato chips. In the lowered position, the two-height fifth wheel pulls the higher cubic capacity trailer. When in the raised position, the two-height fifth wheel enables the same tractor to move standard van trailers.

Fifth Wheel Ratings and Capacity

LO 39-5 Explain the purpose of fifth wheel weight and capacity ratings.

Fifth wheels have maximum operating limits and capacities. These limits are expressed in terms of vertical load and draw bar capacity **Vertical load** acts downward on the fifth wheel through the trailer upper coupler. There is no vertical load applied through the king pin. **Draw bar capacity** or **"D" capacity** is the maximum horizontal pulling force that can be safely applied to the fifth wheel.

Fifth wheels are rated anywhere from 50,000 to 70,000 lb (22,727 to 31,818 kg) vertical load capacity, and from 80,000 to 200,000 lb (36,367 to 90,909 kg) draw bar capacity.

Manufacturers typically rate their product in terms of operating service conditions, as illustrated in **FIGURE 39-30**. For example, a moderate or standard-duty coupler is suitable for

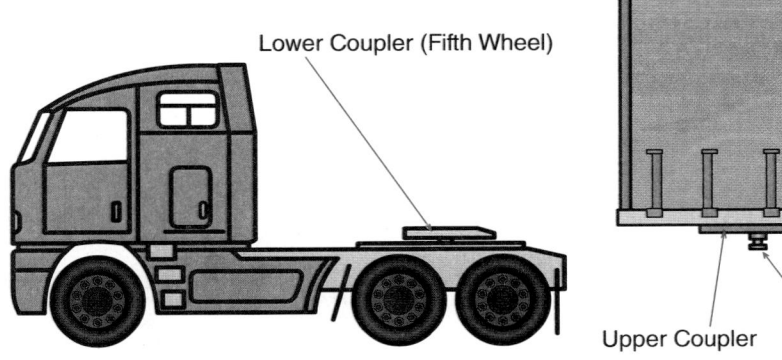

Severe Duty — Use where axles on towed vehicle = 5

Standard Duty — Use where axles on towed vehicle = 2

Moderate Duty — Use where axles on towed vehicle = 3

FIGURE 39-30 Fifth wheel capacity and ratings is based on anticipated road conditions and the number of axles pulled by the fifth wheel.

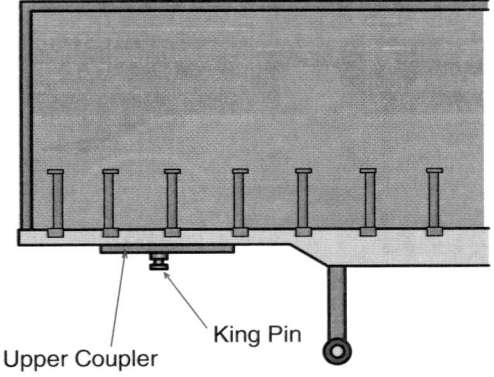

Lower Coupler (Fifth Wheel)

King Pin

Upper Coupler

FIGURE 39-31 Upper coupler, lower coupler, and king pin of a fifth wheel.

most on-highway applications, while severe-duty service equipment is required for applications using multiple additional axles on trailers and abnormal stresses, such as operating off-road or where frequent hook/unhook cycles are encountered. A heavy load pulled over paved roads is less severe than a lighter load pulled in off-highway conditions where continual pounding of coupling jaws and bushings is anticipated.

Upper Couplers

The upper coupler is often referred to as the upper half of the fifth wheel. It is the steel plate, load-bearing surface on the underside of the front of a semi-trailer. The upper coupler rests on the fifth wheel of a tractor or converter dolly. The upper coupler is either bolted or welded to the trailer body. **FIGURE 39-31** illustrates how the upper and lower couplers connect to hitch the tractor to the semi-trailer.

The king pin is attached to the upper coupler, as shown in **FIGURE 39-32**. King pins come in a variety of shapes, depending on the method of attaching the pin to the upper coupler. Three basic styles are common: mushroom, bolted, or cruciform. Mushroom-shaped king pins are welded in place above the coupler **FIGURE 39-33**. Cruciform king pins are larger, heavier, cross-shaped pins that are welded in place in a separate enclosure in the trailer subfloor.

King pins are either 2" or 3.5" (5.1 or 8.9 cm) in diameter. The larger 3.5" (8.9 cm) pins are only used in specialized off-road applications. Pins are either bolted into the upper coupler using a backing plate, or welded in place. A flange on the bottom of the pin prevents the pin from pulling out of the fifth

FIGURE 39-32 An upper coupler of a flat deck trailer. Note the bolts retaining the upper coupler to the trailer frame and the bolts enabling easy replacement of the king pin.

FIGURE 39-33 A king pin in the upper coupler plate of a trailer.

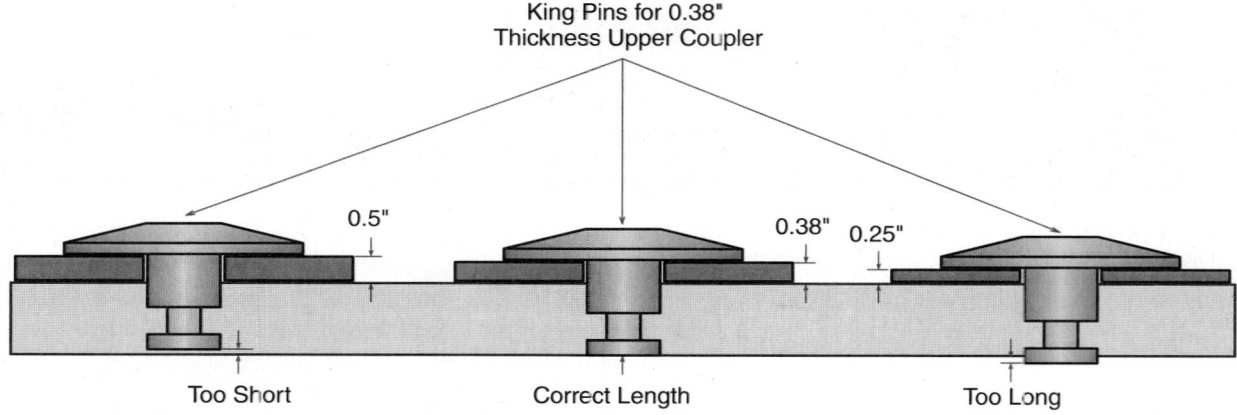

FIGURE 39-34 King pin length must be appropriate for the thickness of the upper coupler plate.

wheel locking jaws. As illustrated in **FIGURE 39-34**, the length of a king pin must be properly selected to match the thickness of the upper coupler plate. The pins are forged from specialized steel alloys and hardened on the exterior, not only to give the pin wear resistance but to minimize the likelihood of breaking if shock-loaded. Welding or heating repairs of any type affect the strength and wear resistance of the king pin.

Construction of Fifth Wheels

LO 39-6 Identify and describe the construction and operation of fifth wheels and upper couplers.

Fifth wheels consist of several major sections:

- Top plate
- Locking mechanism
- Mounting plate

The major components of a fifth wheel are illustrated in **FIGURE 39-35**. The fifth wheel is also referred to as the lower coupler since it works together with the trailer's upper coupler containing the king pin.

Top Plates

Fifth wheel top plates, such as the one in **FIGURE 39-36**, are made from either stamped or cast steel. Forged aluminum wheels are also available for specialized applications. Stamped steel plates use reinforcing bars beneath the plate to increase its strength without the weight penalty of a cast iron plate.

The weight of the trailer is supported on the outer circumference surfaces of the top plate. The center section of the fifth wheel where the locking jaw mechanism is located is recessed to prevent it from carrying any vertical load applied by the trailer. A weakened or "bowed" upper coupler plate can contact the center of the top plate. That contact concentrates the trailer load onto the center of the fifth wheel and can interfere with its operation. As illustrated in **FIGURE 39-37**, center-loading can cause the fifth wheel to flex like a beam, which leads to fatigue failure and top plate cracking. Shiny areas caused by coupler-to-plate contact near the center of the plate can indicate center loading is taking place.

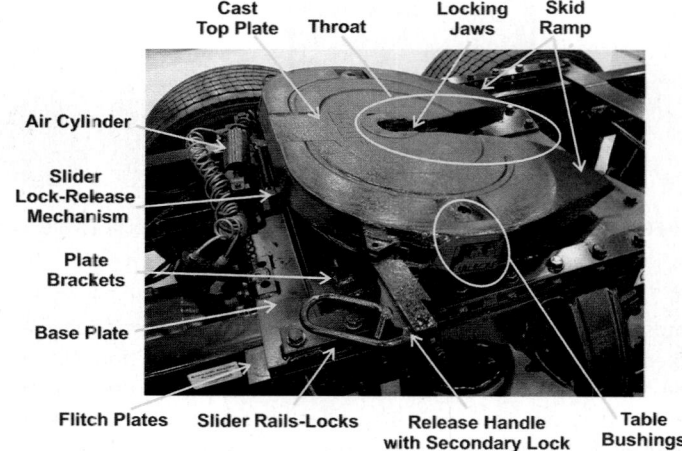

FIGURE 39-35 Fifth wheel layout.

FIGURE 39-36 This cut-away of a fifth wheel is cast steel and has grooves in the top plate to retain grease.

Every fifth wheel assembly uses a locking mechanism to securely hold the trailer king pin to the fifth wheel. Locking mechanisms include coupling jaws, A- and B-type locks, and no-slack coupling.

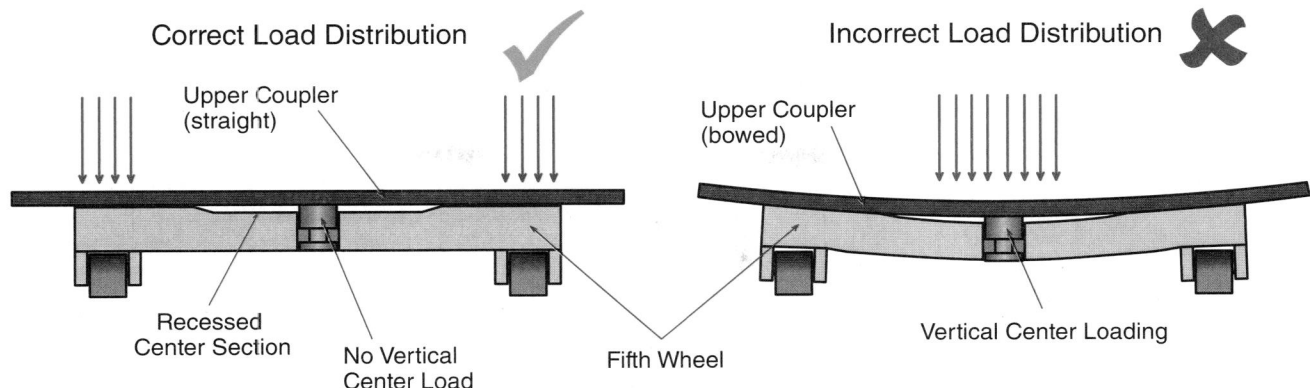

FIGURE 39-37 Proper and improper loading of the fifth wheel.

Locking Mechanisms and Coupling Jaws

One method of locking the fifth wheel into place is by using coupling jaws. Backing the tractor beneath the trailer pushes the king pin into the fifth wheel throat. That action automatically locks the jaws around the pin. Jaws must prevent separation of the trailer from the fifth wheel assembly unless a positive-type manual release is activated.

A fifth wheel release lever is located on the fifth wheel, as shown in **FIGURE 39-38**, and may have a remotely released air cylinder that can be activated by the driver inside the cab. Air release mechanisms are interlocked with the parking brake to prevent accidental unlocking of the jaws unless the vehicle is stopped and parked. Manual-release mechanisms often use a **secondary safety latch** to minimize the likelihood of an unintended jaw release. This means a second mechanism is needed to release the lever or fifth wheel jaws, not just one. The release mechanism has the option of a left- or right-hand operation, which refers to the side of the vehicle where the release latch is located. Jaws accommodate an industry standard 2" (5.1 cm) king pin, which has a minimum tow rating of 80,000 lb (36,364 kg).

A-Type Lock Jaw Mechanism

SAF Holland, manufacturer of a popular fifth wheel, uses two types of locking mechanisms. The **A-type lock** as shown in **FIGURE 39-39**, has a single swinging lock jaw and plunger for simple operation. When the king pin enters the fifth wheel, pressure applied to a yoke causes the lock jaw to swing closed around the king pin. A manually adjustable plunger wedges the swing jaw closed around the king pin after it snuggly encompasses the king pin. Approximately 300 lb (136 kg) of force is required to close the lock. On some plates, a replaceable wear ring in the throat area is used to extend the life of a plate, which is worn by repeated hammering of the king pin into the plate throat.

B-Type Lock

Another common, but heavier, lock mechanism used by SAF Holland is the **B-type lock**. As shown in **FIGURE 39-40**, this mechanism uses two swinging jaws and a yoke to lock the jaws securely around the king pin. When the king pin enters the plate's throat, the open jaws pivot closed around the king pin.

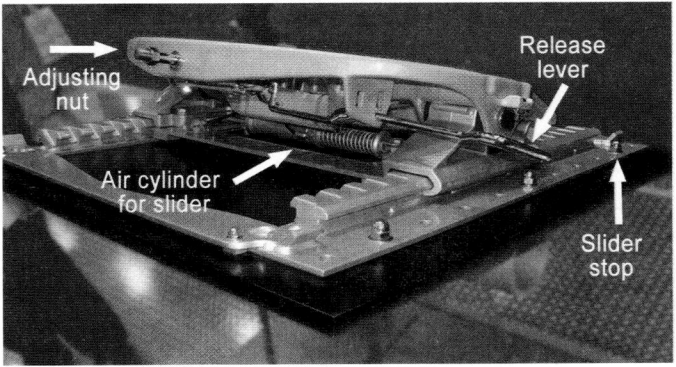

FIGURE 39-38 The jaw release lever can be located on either the right or left of a fifth wheel. A two-stage release of the lever is often required to prevent accidental release.

A spring-loaded yoke slides between the jaws and a part of the top plate casting beneath the plate to lock the jaws closed to prevent any jaw opening by rearward king pin force. Manually retracting the yoke allows the jaws to release when the king pin is moved rearward against the closed jaws. The resting closed position of the yoke is adjustable, which determines the clearance between the king pin and the jaws. Using the wedge shape of the sliding yoke behind the jaws, adjustment of the clearance between the yoke wedge and the jaws determines how snug or loose the jaws wrap around the king pin. **FIGURE 39-41** shows the underside of a Holland fifth wheel using a B-type lock.

No-Slack Coupling

ConMet, Fontaine, and Jost are all manufacturers that offer fifth wheels with a locking-bar locking mechanism called a **no-slack coupler**. As shown on the fifth wheel pictured in **FIGURE 39-42**, the mechanism uses a hardened steel bar, which slides behind the king pin to lock it into place. An automatically adjusting serrated wedge device tightens the locking bar against the king pin, almost eliminating any clearance around the king pin, which otherwise accelerates wear between the king pin and locking bar.

A no-slack lock mechanism uses serrated edges between the locking bar and wedge. To release the locking mechanism, the wedge is simply pivoted away from the lock's serrations and

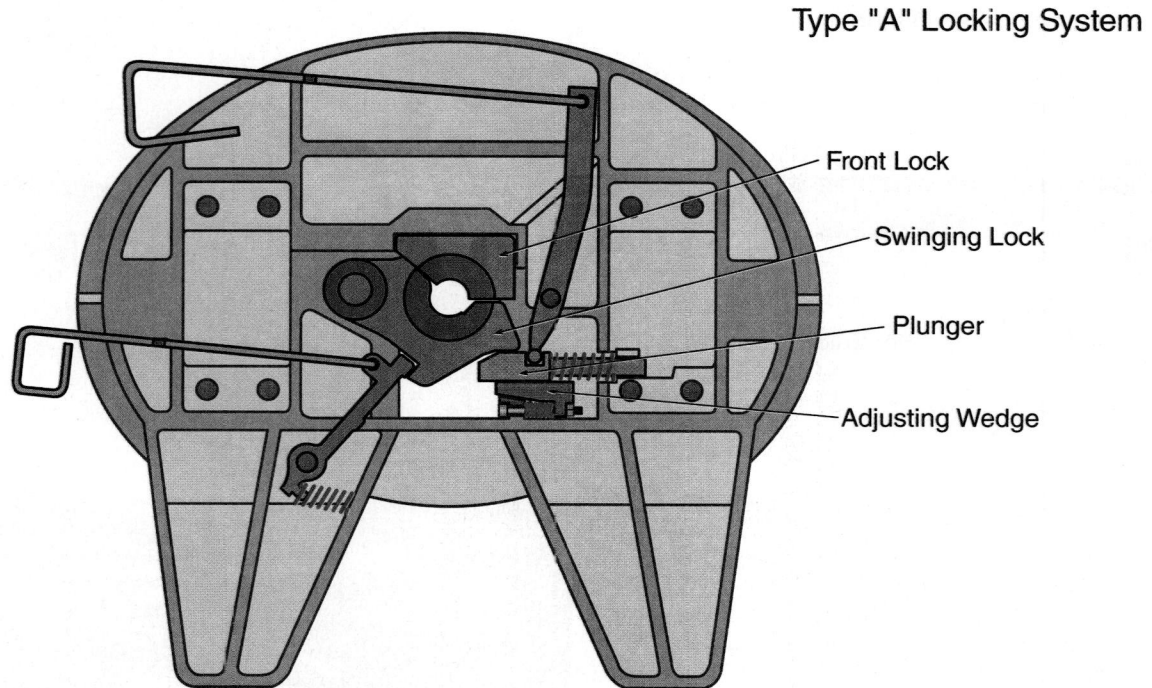

Type "A" Locking System

- Front Lock
- Swinging Lock
- Plunger
- Adjusting Wedge

FIGURE 39-39 An A-type lock mechanism.

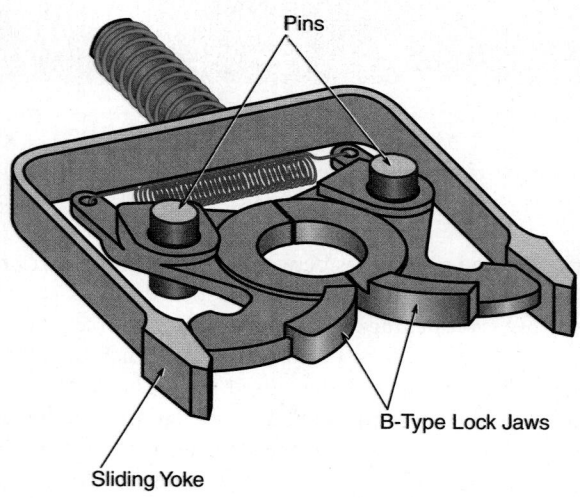

Pins

Sliding Yoke

B-Type Lock Jaws

FIGURE 39-40 A fifth wheel with a B-type lock. Note the two large pins in the plate, which are pivot points for the lock jaws.

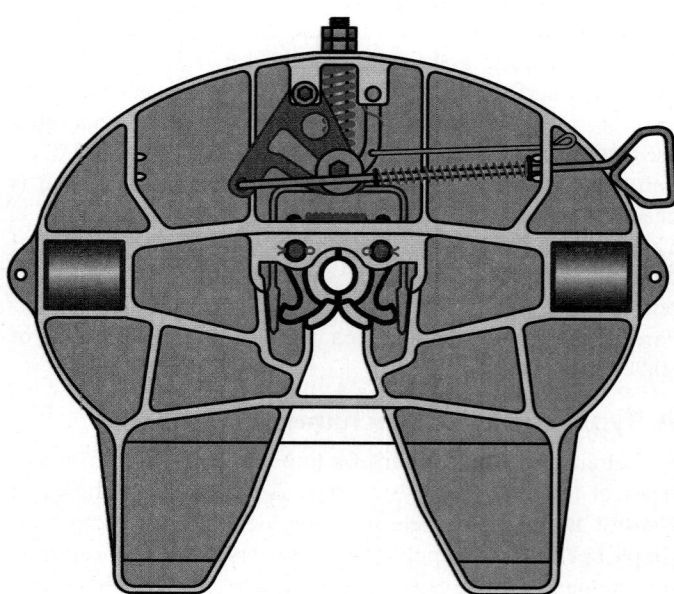

FIGURE 39-41 The underside of a Holland fifth wheel using a B-type lock mechanism.

retracted into an unlocked position. Without the wedge clamping the lock in position, the king pin is easily moved rearward.

This mechanism provides the snuggest automatic fit of locking mechanisms around the king pin since the spring-loaded wedge's pressure pushes the coupling into the king pin until almost no clearance is available. A wedge stop rod is adjusted at the factory and should be maintained to leave a 0.25" (6.35 mm) gap between the wedge and the stop rod. If the locking bar becomes stuck and prevents the fifth wheel from unlocking, the stop rod can be hit with a hammer to push the wedge open. **FIGURE 39-43A** shows a wedge-type coupling in the locked position, and **FIGURE 39-43B** shows it in the unlocked position.

Mounting Fifth Wheels

LO 39-7 Identify and explain the factors considered and methods used to mount and reposition fifth wheels.

Fifth wheels are attached to a baseplate typically through brackets containing a steel pin and heavy rubber bushing, as illustrated in **FIGURE 39-44**. **Flitch plates** attach the mounting base plate to the vehicle frame, as shown in **FIGURE 39-45**. Flitch plates are typically pieces of angle iron bolted to the tractor

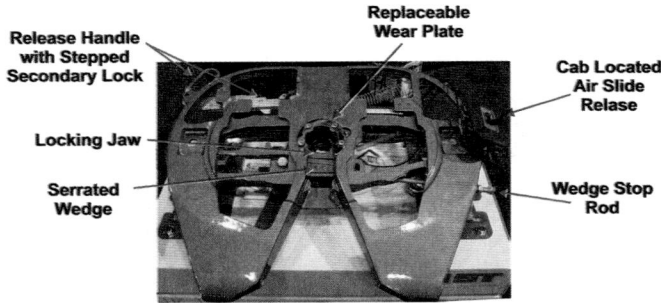

FIGURE 39-42 A no-slack wedge-type lock mechanism. Serrated edges on the wedge lock the jaw in position around the king pin.

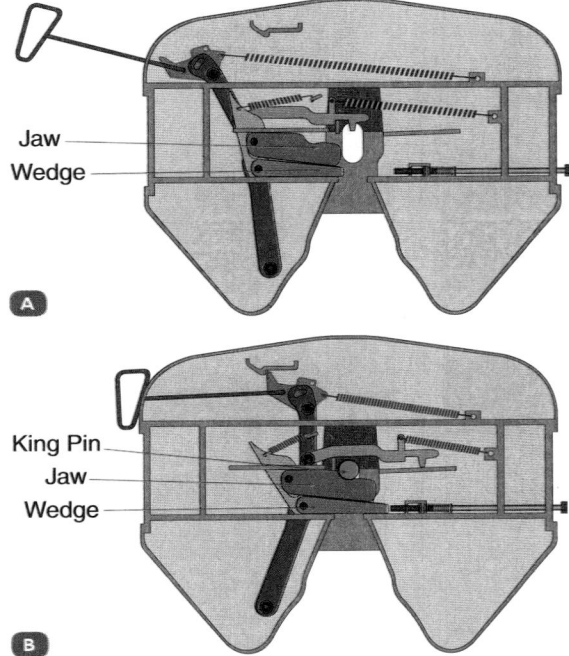

FIGURE 39-43 Operation of wedge-type automatically adjusting coupling. **A.** Locked position. **B.** Unlocked position.

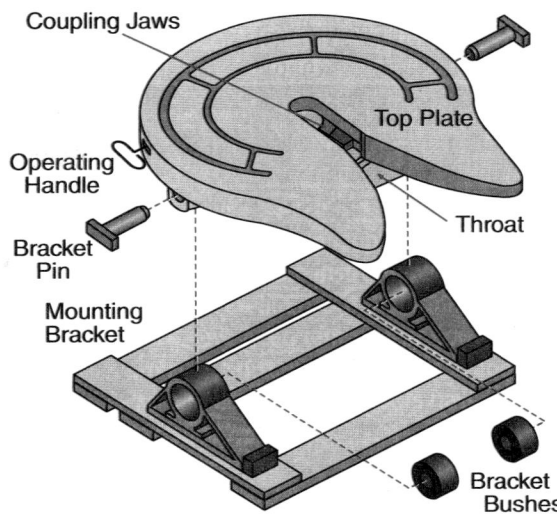

FIGURE 39-44 Fifth wheel mounting system.

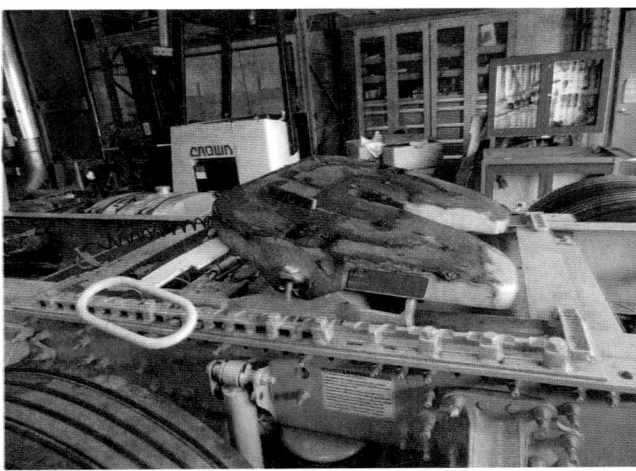

FIGURE 39-45 Flitch plates are pieces of angle iron that attaches the fifth wheel base plate to the frame.

frame, and then the base plate is welded or bolted to the angle iron. Plates must be secured to the frame of the vehicle with properly designed brackets, mounting plates, or additional pieces of angle iron and properly tightened with bolts of adequate size and grade. Society of Automotive Engineers (SAE) Grade 8 bolts or ISO 10.9 is the minimum tensile strength of bolt used. The installation should not cause cracking, warping, or deforming of the vehicle frame. If the fifth wheel is a sliding type, the installation must include top plate stops or a mechanism to prevent the fifth wheel from shifting or sliding off the baseplate frame to which it is attached.

The height of the bracket is critical to obtain correct coupling height. Generally, the fifth wheel plate, when level, should be at 47" (119.4 cm) when measured from the ground with a correctly adjusted suspension system height. Ramps on the tractor frame may be used to guide the trailer onto the fifth wheel and should

allow the trailer to contact the wheel without interference from the ramps. If the coupling height is too low when connecting to the tractor, the trailer king pin may not lock properly or may prevent the trailer from properly articulating. Excessive coupling height damages the trailer as it is lifted onto the tractor chassis during coupling. Coupler height is measured with the fifth wheel level and parallel with the ground. Overall trailer height should not exceed 13'6" (4.1 m), including the fifth wheel coupler height.

Fifth Wheel Sliders

The fifth wheel can be moved forward or backward to accommodate different trailer lengths having different king pin set-back distances. King pin set-back refers to the distance between the front trailer wall and the king pin centerline. The setback dimension varies the **swing clearance** of the trailer, which refers to the clearance between the trailer and tractor during turns. Moving the fifth wheel is necessary when using some trailers to prevent the trailer from contacting the cab or cab fairings, or the trailers landing gear striking the rear mud flap hangers. The location of the fifth wheel can also be moved to enable even distribution of weight over the tractor's drive axles and front steer axle. To reposition the fifth wheel, a **slider mechanism** enables the top plate to move forward and backward along a base frame. Sliders are a set of rails with a ratchet-like mechanism that enables the fifth wheel to move back and forth just ahead of the centerline between a pair of tandem axles. Sliders enable the proper distribution of trailer weight over all tractor axles. The sliding mechanism is locked in position by plungers, which intersect with the lock mechanism of the base frame. A manual or air slider release mechanism is used to unlock the slider and allow the fifth wheel to move back and forth over the drive axles. **FIGURE 39-46** shows a manual slide release in the locked and unlocked positions. Tandem-drive tractors typically are equipped with sliding mechanisms. Single-axle tractors with a shorter wheel base generally use a fixed or rigid mounted fifth wheel that does not move.

Fifth Wheel Location

Proper fifth wheel positioning by the slider and during initial installation is critical. An incorrectly positioned fifth wheel unequally loads axles. If it is positioned too far ahead, the front axles are overloaded, and steering becomes harder to turn. Uneven tire wear takes place on the rear drive and steering axles because the tires are unequally loaded with weight. Additionally, with the trailer too far ahead, interference between the tractor and trailer landing gear can take place. The front corners of the trailer can make contact with the tractor cab and damage both units, since positioning the wheel closer to the cab reduces trailer swing clearance. As illustrated in **FIGURE 39-47**, the position of the fifth wheel,

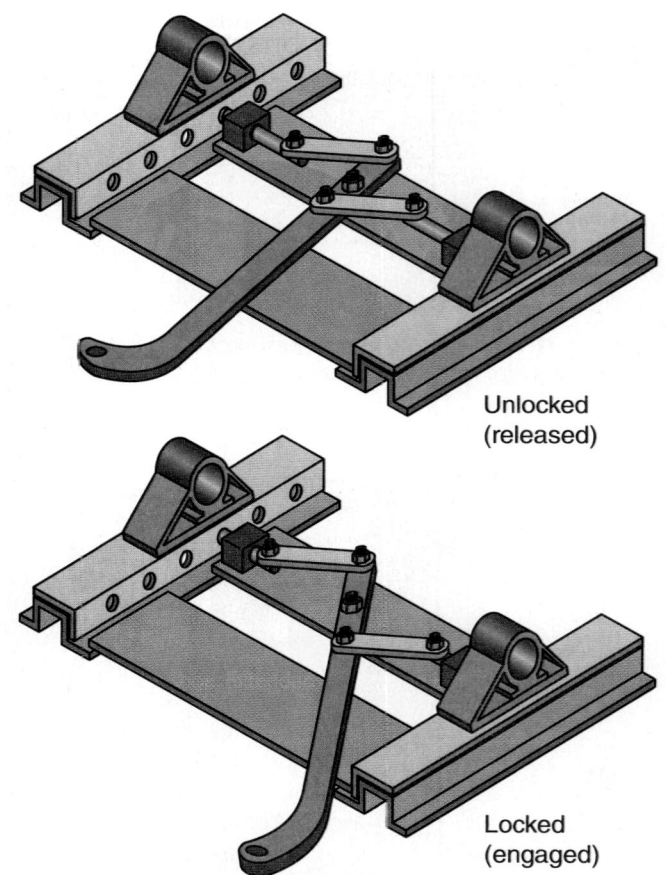

Unlocked
(released)

Locked
(engaged)

FIGURE 39-46 Manual slide release.

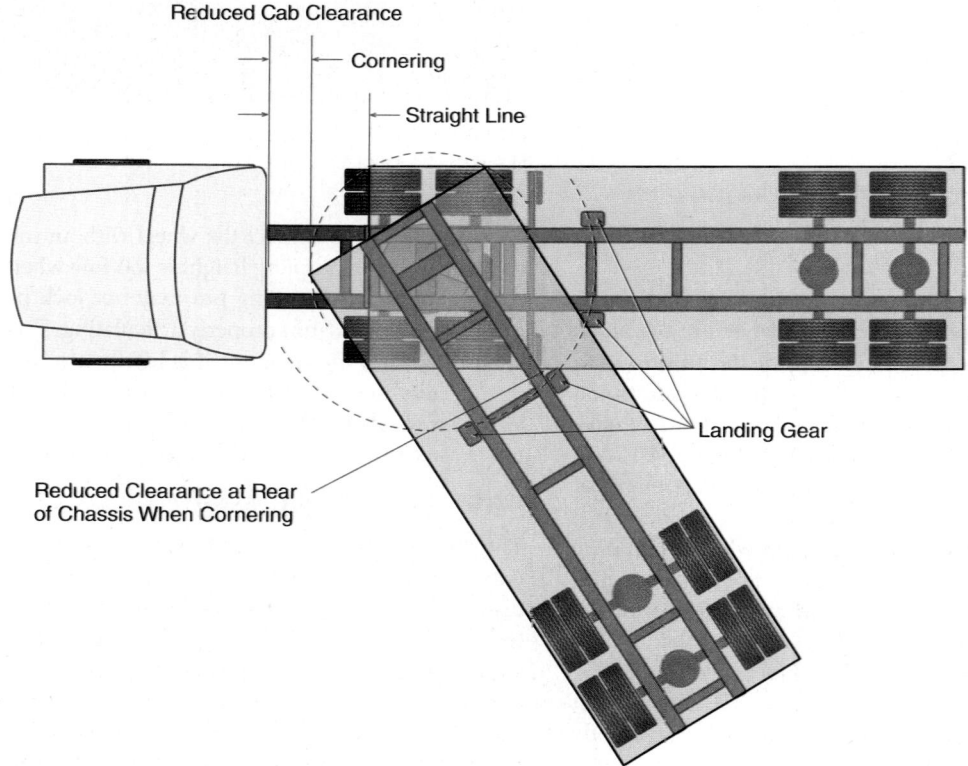

Reduced Cab Clearance

Cornering

Straight Line

Landing Gear

Reduced Clearance at Rear
of Chassis When Cornering

FIGURE 39-47 The position of the fifth wheel affects the swing clearance of the trailer in relation to the tractor.

whether rigidly mounted or on sliders, must allow adequate swing radius clearance between the trailer and the tractor, as well as between the tractor with the landing gear legs when turning. The swing radius is determined by the distance between the king pin and the front of the trailer

Positioning the fifth wheel too far rearward creates another set of problems. Excessive clearance between the tractor and trailer creates power-robbing wind drag between the tractor and trailer. Drivers may prefer to move a fifth wheel farther rearward than it should be because it actually lightens the load on the front axle and reduces steering effort. If the fifth wheel slide length is too short, however, the fifth wheel may not shift far enough forward to load the front axle with heavier trailer weight. The rear axles may be overloaded and poor tire contact takes place on the front axle as it becomes "unloaded." Surprisingly, poorly loaded front tires do not develop a good contact patch with the road surface, which can result in unusual uneven front tire wear patterns.

When installing a fifth wheel, the device should be placed in the rearmost position of the slider mechanism. At this point, the fifth wheel center should be located no further back than 1" (2.5 cm) ahead of the centerline, between the tandem rear axles, to achieve proper weight distribution. Stops are welded to the slider mechanism to prevent the fifth wheel from moving to any position farther back along the tractor frame. The technician must take into account the swing radius of the trailers towed by the tractor when making final calculations for identifying the stop positions before they are welded in place.

Troubleshooting Fifth Wheel Locking Complaints

LO 39-8 Identify and explain common complaints and failures of fifth wheel locking mechanisms.

Two primary complaints regarding fifth wheels relate to locking. Either the trailer fails to lock into the fifth wheel or fails to unlock from it. Sometimes problems relate to a complete failure to lock or unlock and sometimes the trailer simply has difficulty locking or unlocking from the fifth wheel. **TABLE 39-3** includes causes and remedies for locking problems, and **TABLE 39-4** includes causes and remedies for unlocking problems.

Maintenance and Service of Fifth Wheels and Upper Couplers

LO 39-9 Identify and describe the inspection methods and service procedures used to maintain fifth wheels and upper couplers.

Periodic visual inspection of the fifth wheel and the security of the coupling is required by law. Incorrect coupling can allow the trailer to disconnect with catastrophic consequences. It is an inadequate test of the fifth wheel coupling to only perform a "tug" test—pulling the trailer with the tractor and quickly braking to check if the trailer is properly coupled. A trailer can rest on the fifth wheel without properly locking to the fifth wheel. It is critical to visually examine the lock jaws to verify they have closed around the king pin after the trailer is connected.

TABLE 39-3 Causes and Remedies for Locking Problems Related to Fifth Wheels

Potential Cause	Remedy
Fifth wheel lock is closed	Pull both primary and secondary release handles. Open locks with a pry bar.
	Check operation of the air release cylinder. It must open and close correctly.
Lock release lever bent and binding	Inspect lever and straighten or replace, as necessary.
	Check for correct handle operation according to manufacturer's service literature.[1]
Bent king pin	Check king pin with king pin gauge or "go–no go gauge."
Trailer too high and not allowing the king pin to enter lock properly	Lower trailer landing gear.[2]
Rusted, grimy, sticking lock mechanism	Clean mechanism with a solvent. Lubricate with light engine oil or diesel fuel. Open and close the lock mechanism several times to free up operation.
Misadjusted jaw locks	Adjust lock mechanism per manufacturer instructions.
Worn-out fifth wheel lock mechanism	Remove, disassemble, and rebuild per manufacturer's instructions.
	Replace top plate and bracket bushings.
Distorted upper coupler plate	Check for warping or distortion of coupler with 48" (122 cm) straight edge.
Fifth wheel too far forward	Reposition fifth wheel.
No-lube plate too thick for king pin	Measure king pin length and determine whether a lube plate can be used with the trailer king pin. Remove lube plate if king pin length is inadequate.

[1] Normal operation for some release handles is to return "in" after unlocking the fifth wheel.
[2] The fifth wheel should lift the front of the trailer only slightly when connecting to the tractor.

TABLE 39-4 Causes and Remedies for Unlocking Problems Related to Fifth Wheels

Potential Cause	Remedy
Fifth wheel lock is closed	Pull both primary and secondary release handles. Open locks with a pry bar.
	Check operation of the air release cylinder. It must open and close correctly.
Bent king pin	Check king pin with king pin gauge or "go–no go gauge."
Rusted, grimy, sticking lock mechanism	Clean mechanism with a solvent. Lubricate with light engine oil or diesel fuel. Open and close the lock mechanism several times to free up operation.
Jaw locks adjusted too tightly	Adjust lock mechanism per manufacturer instructions.
Worn-out fifth wheel lock mechanism	Remove, disassemble, and rebuild per manufacturer's instructions.
	Replace top plate and bracket bushings.
Distorted upper coupler plate	Check for warping or distortion of coupler with 48" (122 cm) straight edge.
Lock release lever bent and binding	Inspect lever and straighten or replace as necessary.[1]
Lock release handle needs to be held in unlock position to disconnect	Check for correct handle operation according to manufacturer's service literature.[1]
Tractor putting pressure on locks when releasing	Back up tractor into the trailer again with the trailer brakes applied. Reattempt to disconnect from fifth wheel after moving the primary and secondary release lever to unlock.

[1] Normal operation for some release handles is to return "in" after unlocking the fifth wheel.

When coupling, the fifth wheel must at least slightly lift the front of the trailer. If the trailer is not lifted, coupling problems can result. For example, to make it easier to couple a trailer, tractors with air suspension are often coupled after the suspension air is "dumped" by using a manually operated dump valve. The problem with this practice is the fifth wheel may not properly lock around the king pin because the trailer is too high. The fifth wheel lock jaws may also be damaged by the lower flange on the king pin. Always inflate the tractor suspension air bags.

Fifth wheel and upper coupler inspection is recommended every three months, or 30,000 miles (18,750 km). Inspection of the fifth wheel includes:

- Checking the tightness of mounting hardware and replacing any missing or damaged bolts. All bolts holding fifth wheels and coupling devices must be a minimum of Grade 8 tensile strength.
- Checking for broken or distorted components and repair or replace, as needed.
- Inspecting the fifth wheel for bent, worn, or broken parts.
- Checking the adjustment of the fifth wheel locks and adjusting them using the recommended service tools and procedures. If the locks cannot be properly adjusted due to wear, the fifth wheel must be rebuilt or replaced.

Lubricating the Fifth Wheel

Checking the fifth wheel may also involve applying grease to the fifth wheel plate. Light oil is used to lubricate the locking mechanisms and sliders. Pin bushings have grease fittings, which use chassis grease. The actual load-bearing surface between the fifth wheel top plate and support brackets is steel on steel. Because contact between the top plate and mounting brackets is steel to steel, it requires lubrication. However, most

fifth wheels are held in place with rubber bushing around a urethane-sleeved pivot tube. A pin passes through the top plate and the bushing sleeve to connect the plate with the mounting bracket. This sleeve compresses as load is applied either up or down, so about 0.5" (1.3 cm) of movement of the pin in the bushing is normal on most models. Top plate bushings can be checked using a pry bar. When lifted upwards, normal travel should not exceed a 0.5" (1.3 cm) with moderate pressure applied to the bushing. To lubricate a fifth wheel, follow the steps in **SKILL DRILL 39-1**.

Upper Coupler Checks

The upper coupler and the king pin need to be checked for shape, size, and wear. The upper coupler also needs to be checked for flatness. This upper coupler plate check can be performed with a 48" (122 cm) straight edge or flat bar. The flatness needs to be checked in all directions. Any bumps, valleys, or warping causes uneven loading of the fifth wheel, which could result in damage to the top plate and poor lock life. Rippled or bent plates also absorb grease, reducing the amount of lubrication available to the coupling. **FIGURE 39-48** shows the allowable curvature for a fifth wheel upper coupler.

In addition to checking the upper coupler, the king pin also needs to be checked for straightness, length, and wear. A critical tool for checking a king pin is the king pin gauge shown in **FIGURE 39-49**.

Checking King Pin Straightness, Length, and Wear

To inspect the straightness of a king pin, use a framing square or king pin gauge check to see if the king pin is bent, as shown in **FIGURE 39-50**. If a trailer has rolled or nearly tipped, the pin

SKILL DRILL 39-1 Lubricating a Fifth Wheel

1. Grease the top plate contact surfaces using water-resistant lithium-based grease. Note that the grease fitting is on the side or under the front of the top plate. Grease the bracket supports through the fittings.

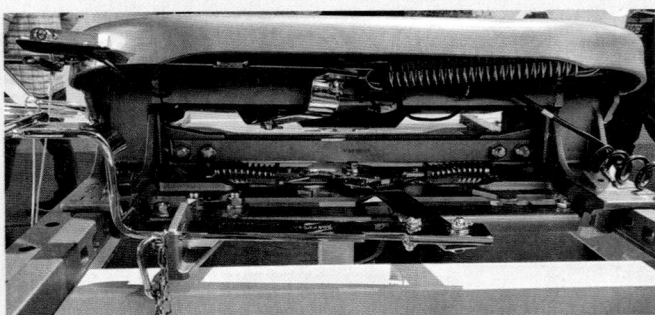

3. Lubricate the sliding fifth wheel lock track and linkage pivots with a light oil.

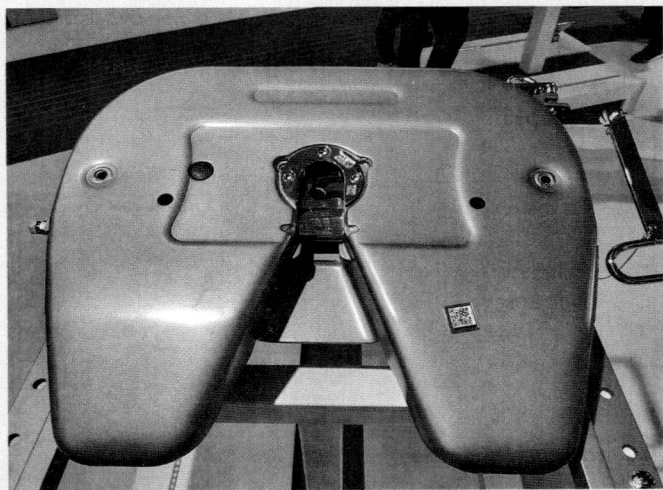

2. Fill the reservoirs with grease fittings, if applicable.

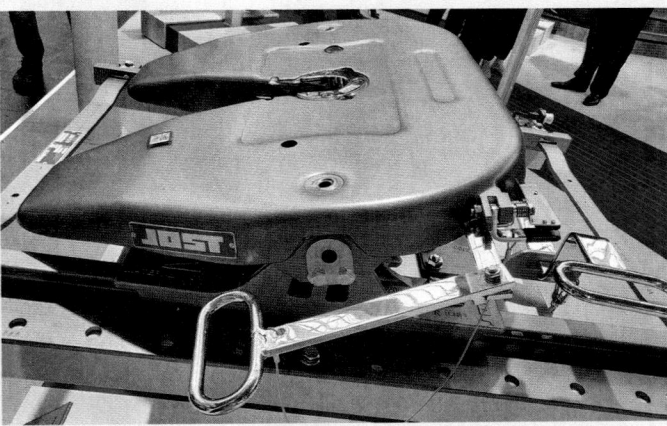

4. On sliding fifth wheels, spray a light oil on the rack and slide path.

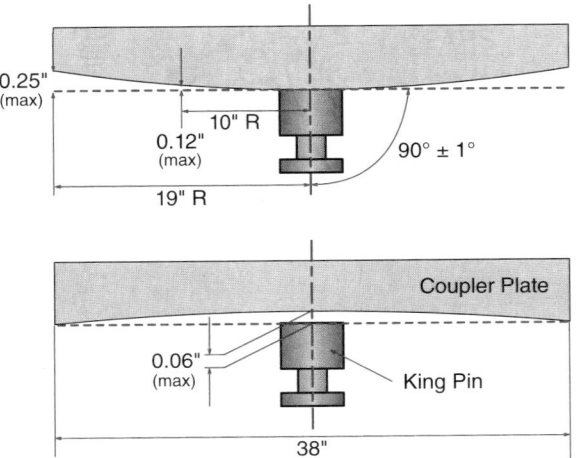

FIGURE 39-48 Typical installation position for king pins and tolerances allowed for upper coupler plate flatness.

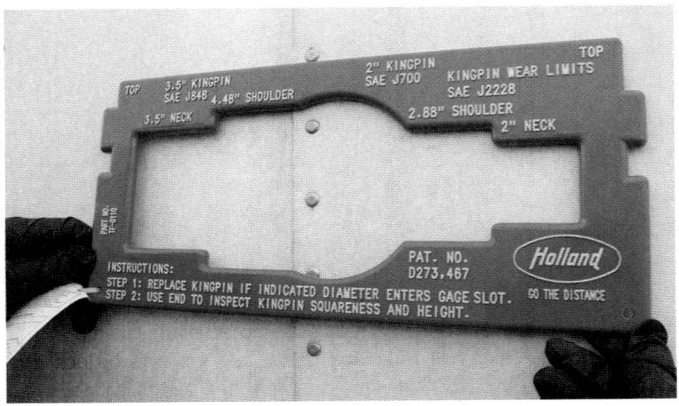

FIGURE 39-49 The king pin "go–no go" gauge is a common instrument for checking the king pin.

FIGURE 39-50 Use a king pin gauge to check for straightness.

can bend. A bent king pin increases locking jaw wear and could also prevent the fifth wheel from properly locking. It is recommended that the king pin should be replaced if it exceeds one degree from square in any direction. After king pin replacement, the pin length should be double checked since pins must match with the coupler plate thickness. Incorrect king pin length prevents proper coupling if it is too short, and trailer instability if it is too long. A king pin gauge can also be used to check the king pin's length. **FIGURE 39-51** shows the dimensions of a SAE standard king pin.

King pins are made to an industry standard of 2" (5.1 cm) diameter. If the king pin slides into the 2" (5.1 cm) neck diameter slot of the go–no go gauge, it is worn out and requires replacement. Excessive wear of ⅛" (3.175 mm) requires pin replacement since a loose pin becomes noisy due to chucking and damages locking jaws from excessive play. If a fifth wheel

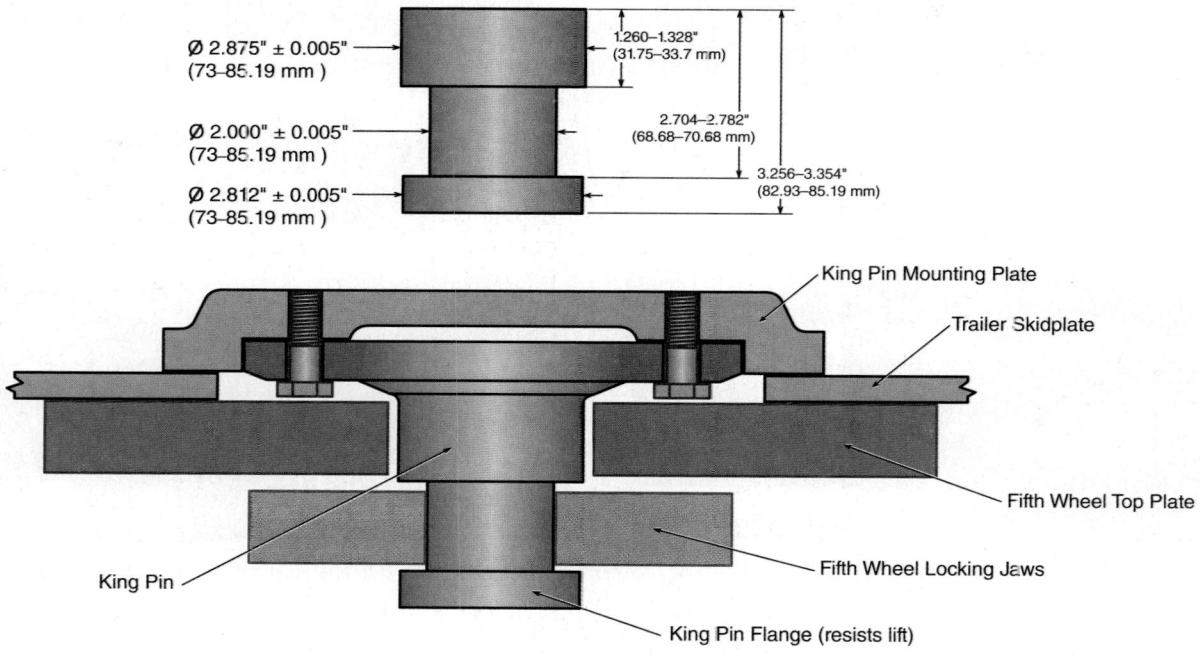

FIGURE 39-51 Dimensions of a king pin built to SAE standards.

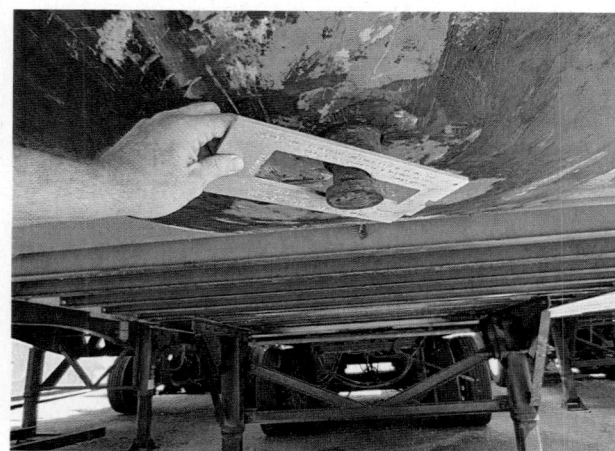

FIGURE 39-52 Use a king pin gauge to check for wear.

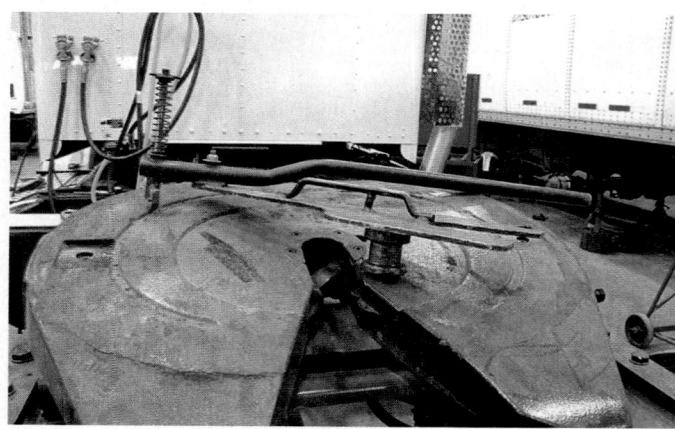

FIGURE 39-53 A king pin service tool can be used to check drag in the locking jaws.

is adjusted to fit a worn pin, it may not release from a trailer when a pin that is dimensionally correct is used. A micrometer or a go–no go gauge is used to check for wear, as shown in **FIGURE 39-52**.

In addition to checking the king pin itself, the locking jaws around the king pin must be checked. A king pin service tool, such as the one shown in **FIGURE 39-53**, is used to measure the amount of drag in locking jaws, to check for excessive free play, and to test the unlock–lock mechanism. **FIGURE 39-54** illustrates how to use the tool for this check. Engaging the hook and pushing the handle causes the locking jaws to open and close. Excessive effort required to release jaws or failure of the jaws to completely close indicates an adjustment or rebuild is required. To inspect a king pin, follow the steps in **SKILL DRILL 39-2**.

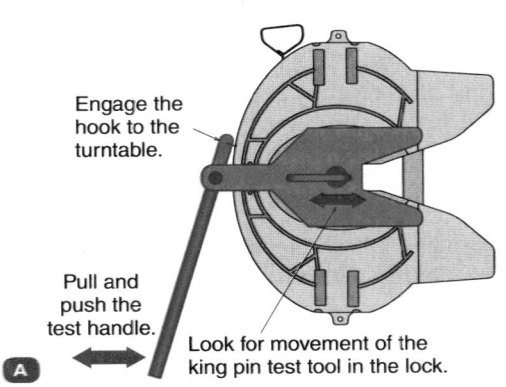

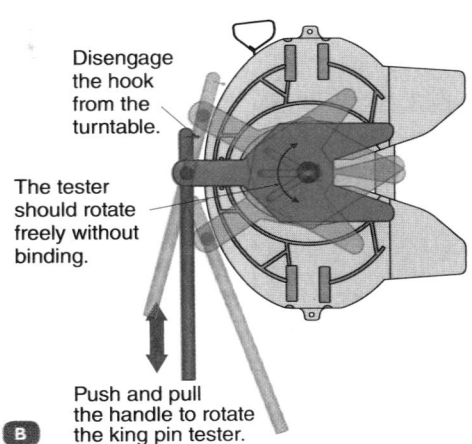

FIGURE 39-54 A. Engaged hook. **B.** Disengaged hook.

SKILL DRILL 39-2 King Pin Inspection Procedures

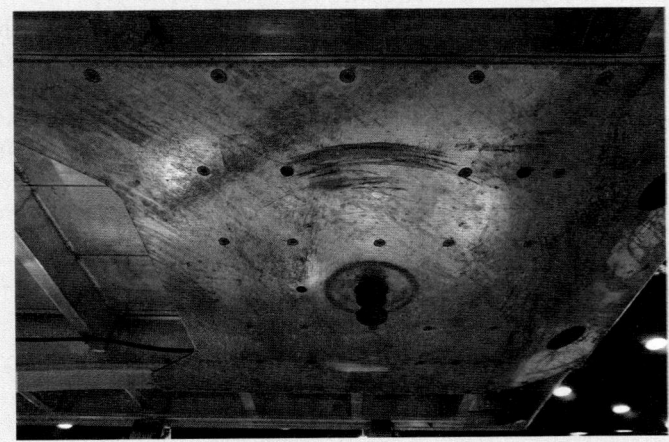

1. Check the upper coupler plate for flatness. Using a 48" straight edge, place the gauge edge against the upper coupler plate to check for flatness in all directions. Note any warpage or indentations of the plate that could cause excessive or uneven loading of areas of the fifth wheel. Give particular attention to irregularities and deformities that could damage the locking jaws or reduce lock service life. Compare with specifications from the trailer manufacturer and replace the coupler plate if it exceeds specifications.

2. Inspect the king pin for squareness. Using a carpenter's square or a purpose-made king pin gauge, check to see if the king pin is at 90 degrees to the upper coupler plate. A bent king pin can result from a tractor or trailer roll-over or excessive coupling speed. Note that a bent king pin can interfere with proper coupling and uncoupling, as well as rapidly wear the lock mechanism. Replace any king pin that is more than one degree from square with the upper coupler in any direction.

3. Inspect the king pin length. The king pin must be the correct length to properly couple with the fifth wheel. Using a king pin gauge or carpenters square, measure the length of the king pin and compare with SAE specifications. If a plastic aftermarket lube plate is used on the fifth wheel top plate, pay particular attention to whether the pin can compensate for the plate thickness. King pins that are not the correct length can interfere with coupling and rapidly wear the locking mechanism.

4. Inspect the king pin for wear. Using a king pin gauge, micrometer, or precision Vernier caliper, measure the king pin diameter. Replace any king pin that is worn ⅛" (3.175 mm) or more in any direction. Note, an excessively worn king pin enters the gauge slots of a king pin gauge.

5. Inspect the king pin attachment to the upper coupler. Inspect the king pin to verify it is securely attached to the upper coupler. A loose king pin can be mistaken for a misadjusted fifth wheel because a loose attachment creates noise when accelerating and braking. Reinstall or replace any king pin that is not securely attached to the upper coupler.

6. Visually inspect the king pin for damage. Visually examine the king pin to identify any nicks, gouges, cracks, indications of heating from welding, or other deformities that may lead to sudden failure. If any damage is observed, replace the king pin.

Fifth Wheel Service Adjustments

Fifth wheels need to be adjusted from time to time. When a king pin is excessively worn or the jaws are loose and require adjustment, drivers complain about a banging noise from the fifth wheel each time the tractor is accelerated and decelerated. Jaws that are too tight do not easily release a king pin or jaws remain locked. The adjustment procedures are different depending on the type of locking mechanism the fifth wheel uses—A, B, or no-slack locks.

A-Type Lock Adjustment

The lock adjustment screw is found in the throat of the upper plate. After the lock is closed with a lock testing tool or a 2" (5.1 cm) "dummy" pin, the adjustment screw should be turned clockwise until tight. Backing out the screw 1.5 turns adjusts the fifth wheel jaws. The adjustment should be verified by locking and unlocking the jaws several times with a lock tester, as illustrated in **FIGURE 39-55**. When an A-type lock is correctly

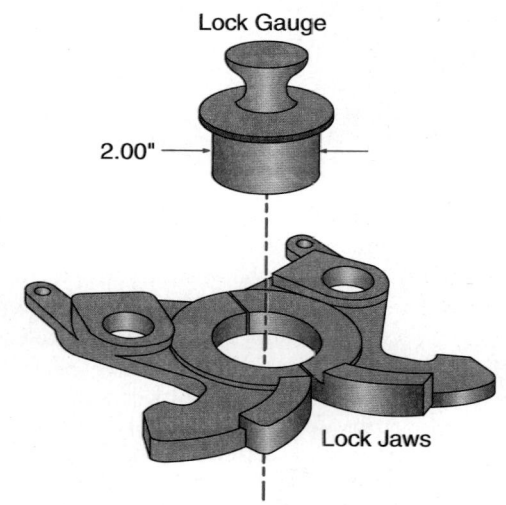

FIGURE 39-55 Lock gauge for testing locking jaw diameter.

adjusted, the jaws must fully enclose the king pin and the locking plunger should be visible when inspected from the rear of the fifth wheel.

B-Type Lock Adjustment

After closing the locks around a 2" (5.1 cm) "dummy" pin, the pin should fit snugly in the jaws and should rotate with some hand force. If the pin is loose, turn the adjusting nut at the top of the plate counterclockwise until there is adequate drag on the pin. A slight gap between the flat washers and rubber bushings below the adjusting nut should be present after the adjustment is completed. The adjustment should be verified by locking and unlocking the jaws several times with a lock tester. When properly adjusted, the jaws should have no more than a 0.5" (1.3 cm) gap between each jaw after closing around the king pin, as illustrated in **FIGURES 39-56** and **39-57**.

No-Slack Locks

To adjust a Fontaine model no-slack lock, after closing the fifth wheel with a standard 2" (5.1 cm) king pin tool, push on the wedge stop rod until it contacts the wedge. When correctly adjusted, it should move in 0.25" (6.4 mm) with hand pressure, then spring back out. If the 0.25" (6.4 mm) clearance is not available, adjust by turning the bolt until the free travel is 0.25" (6.4 mm). The adjustment should be verified by locking and unlocking the jaws several times with a lock tester. If the automatic adjusting feature of the Fontaine is not working, it is likely the jaw and wedge serrations have worn beyond tolerances. **FIGURE 39-58** is a schematic of a Fontaine-style no-slack lock.

As with the automatic feature of a Fontaine no-slack fifth wheel, an adjustment screw is used to set the locking bar travel on a Jost no-slack locking mechanism. The adjustment is first checked by using a lock testing tool. Rocking the tool back and forth in the locks determine whether it is correctly adjusted. If there is too much fore and aft free play, the lock is too loose and the adjustment screw located on the outside edge of the fifth

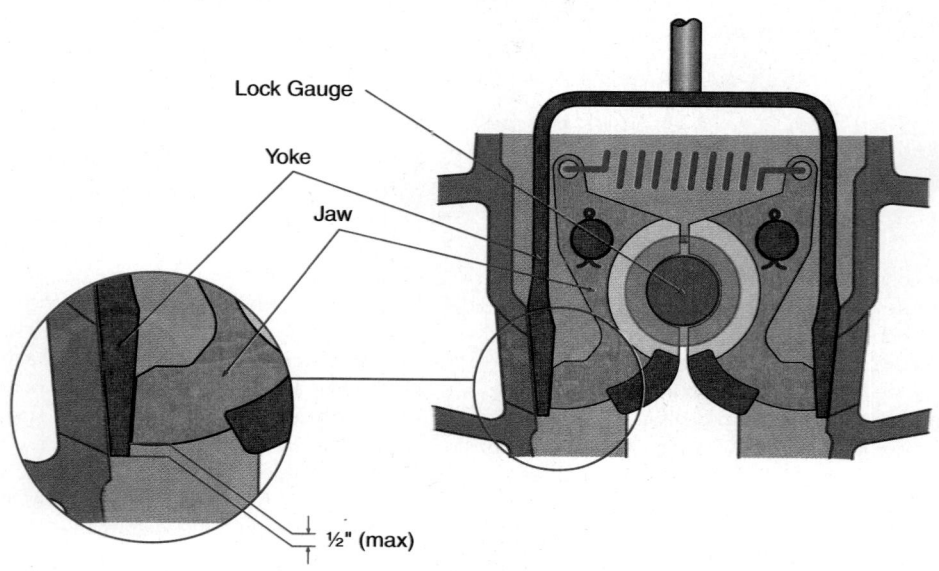

FIGURE 39-56 The locking mechanism of a B-type lock.

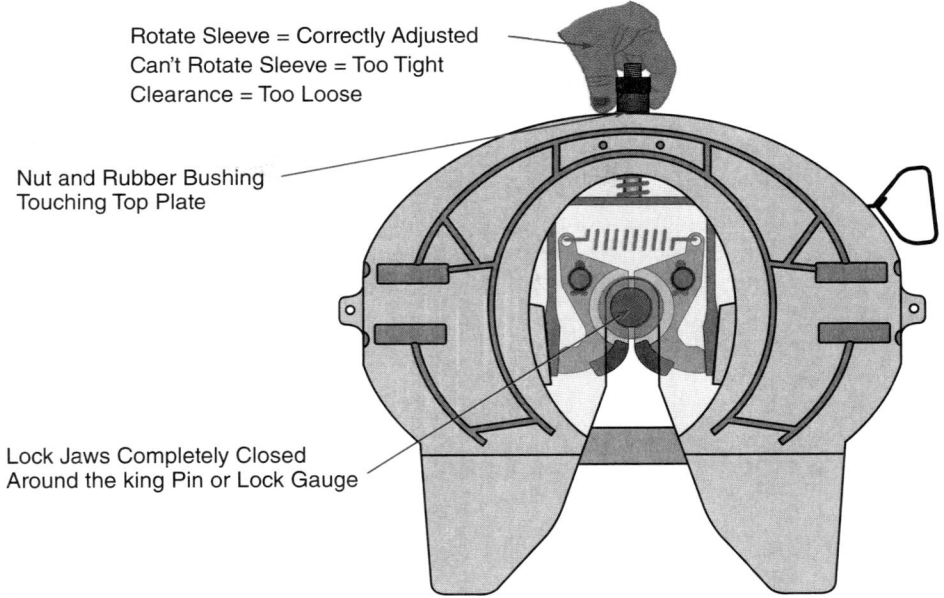

Rotate Sleeve = Correctly Adjusted
Can't Rotate Sleeve = Too Tight
Clearance = Too Loose

Nut and Rubber Bushing
Touching Top Plate

Lock Jaws Completely Closed
Around the king Pin or Lock Gauge

FIGURE 39-57 When properly adjusted, a B-type lock allows the adjusting nut and a new uncompressed bushing to touch the top plate when the jaws are locked.

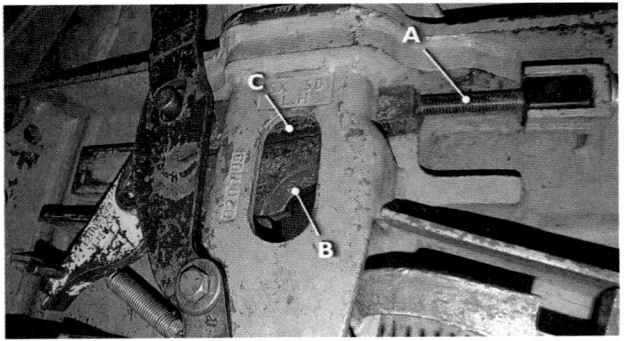

FIGURE 39-58 A no-slack fifth wheel using a wedge as a locking bar to prevent the jaws from opening. **A.** Wedge stop. **B.** Jaw. **C.** Wedge.

wheel top plate is turned counterclockwise one turn. If excessive drag is felt on the pin while turning the tool in the locks, the adjustment is too tight. In that case, the adjusting screw is tuned clockwise one turn. The adjustment should be verified by locking and unlocking the jaws several times with a lock tester. Con-Met no-slack fifth wheel locks are adjusted in a similar fashion.

Sliding Fifth Wheel Mounting

The sliding fifth wheel mounting (if equipped) should be checked for excessive play or movement. Any extra movement here leads to rapid wear caused by the trailer pushing and pulling against the slider as the vehicle is in motion. Follow the steps in **SKILL DRILL 39-3** to inspect the slider mechanism.

SKILL DRILL 39-3 Inspecting the Slider Mechanism on a Fifth Wheel

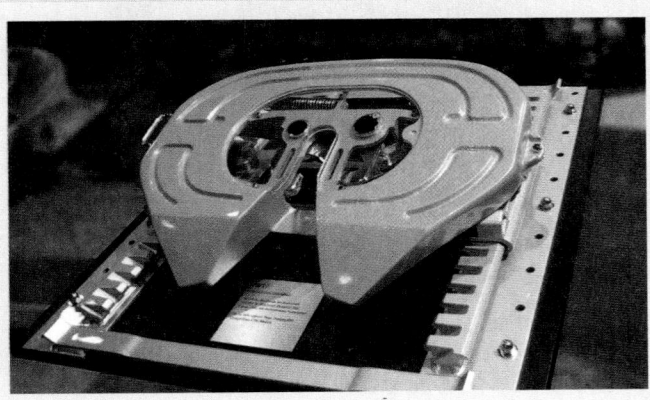

1. With trailer attached, check for excessive motion at the slider bracket plungers by moving the trailer back and forth.

2. If excessive movement is present, disconnect the trailer and conduct the following inspections.
  • Inspect all the slider mounting brackets for cracks or missing or damaged parts.
  • Inspect the locking plungers for full engagement.
  • Check the locking mechanism for proper operation—both releasing and engaging.

3. Adjust the plungers or replace the parts, as required. In some cases, the locking plungers can be adjusted; in others, replacement is the only solution.

Landing Gear

LO 39-10 Identify and describe the purpose and operation of trailer landing gear.

An integral part of the coupling system is the use of trailer landing gear. Landing gear on a trailer are the retractable legs that are extended to support the weight of the trailer before the fifth wheel is uncoupled from the tractor. Landing gear remains extended until the trailer couples to the fifth wheel. Afterwards, the legs are retracted by operating a crank handle. A two-speed gear mechanism connected to the crank handle is used to lower and raise the landing gear. High gear is for rapid movement of the gear when no load is resting on the legs. Low speed has a higher gear reduction ratio for partially lifting the trailer's vertical load from the fifth wheel when uncoupling. **FIGURE 39-59** shows the two-speed gearing mechanism.

Several grease fittings are typically installed on the landing gear to lubricate the long internal lifting screw and the gear reduction mechanism. As shown in **FIGURE 39-60**, a bar connects the left- and right-side landing gear legs to synchronize movement of the left and right landing gear legs. Occasionally, the landing gear binds when lifting or lowering. A common problem with landing gear is that trailers fall on legs that have not been extended far enough when uncoupling. The shock load typically bends the long screws in the landing gear leg and damages teeth in the gear reduction mechanism. Disconnecting the connecting bar between the legs help differentiate whether the problem is in one or both landing gears since one may move freely, but the other not. Legs can be rebuilt with service kits or replaced when mechanisms are damaged or worn out. **FIGURE 39-61** shows a landing gear with several types of replaceable foot. Feet are built to support trailer weight on sand, concrete, asphalt, or uneven surfaces.

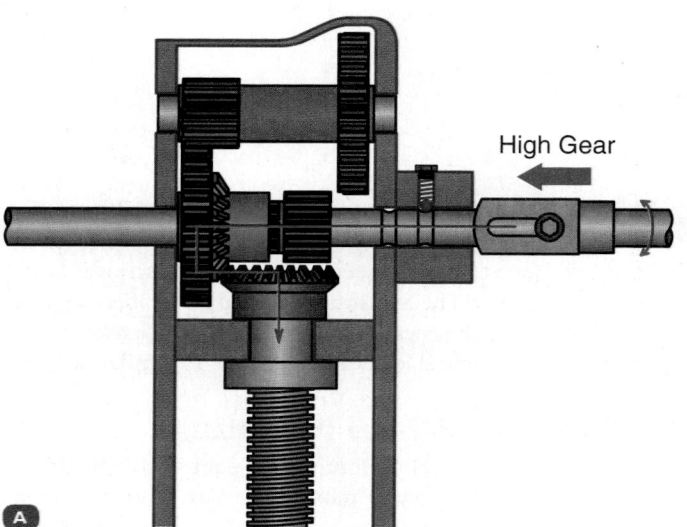
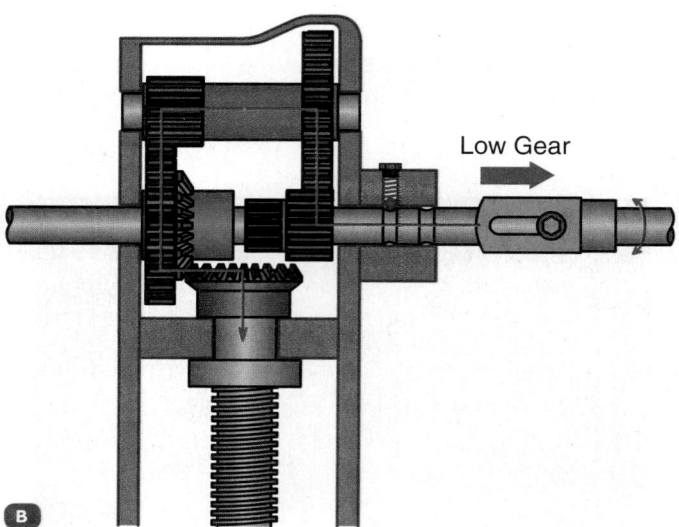

FIGURE 39-59 Landing gear mechanism in **A.** high gear and **B.** low gear.

FIGURE 39-60 A cross shaft between the landing gears synchronizes the movement of the landing gear mechanism.

FIGURE 39-61 The leg of this landing gear uses a replaceable-type foot. The height adjustment screw, as well as the leg mounting system, is damaged when a trailer is dropped on the landing gear.

Wrap-Up

Ready for Review

- Connecting trucks and tractors with trailers form what are known as combination vehicles. Combining vehicles is necessary for commercial vehicles to meet legislated requirements limiting axle weight by adding more axles to distribute vehicle weight. Fifth wheels and various other hitching devices are needed to form combination units.

- Fifth wheels are used to connect semi-trailers to tractors and support the weight of the trailer while allowing articulation between tractor and trailer. The trailer has a steel plate that rests on the fifth wheel, which is called an upper coupler. Welded or bolted to the upper coupler is an industry standard 2" (5.1 cm) king pin, which is locked into the fifth wheel when the trailer is towed.

- Full trailers are formed by using a converter dolly to support the front of a semi-trailer with one or two axles. The converter dolly uses a fifth wheel to support the trailer weight.

- Converter dollies enable a second trailer to attach to a lead trailer. Converter dollies are configured into A and C types according to the geometric shape of the connection points. A-trains have a single connection point to the lead trailer, while C-trains use two.

- B-trains are a type of combination vehicle composed of two trailers plus one tractor. A second semi-trailer attaches to the lead trailer through a fifth wheel mounted to a stub frame of the lead trailer.

- B-trains substantially increase the cargo-carrying capacity of a combination vehicle with only a small increase in fuel consumption.

- Pintle hooks are trailer-hitching devices that use a fixed towing horn, which connects with a draw bar attached to the towed vehicle. Couplers are hitching devices that look similar to pintle hooks except the towing horn pivots and is not fixed.

- Pintle hooks and couplers may use shock-dampening devices, such as rubber insulators called snubbers or air chambers, to take away any free-play in the trailer connection.

- Draw bars are used to connect tow vehicles to a tractor or lead towing unit. The bar has an eyelet or a lunette welded or bolted to the bar, which can connect to a pintle, coupler, or pin on the tow vehicle.

- Ball hitches are used on light and medium-duty vehicles having a 12,000 lb (5443 kg) towing weight capacity. The ball requires a tongue-type tow bar, which loops over a ball. Ball hitches have the advantage of providing a positive no-slack fit. Safety chains are used with ball

hitches to protect against complete loss of the trailer in the event of a break-away.

- It is important to lubricate the top plate of a fifth wheel or use a low friction, "no-lube" plate on top of the fifth wheel. Without the lubrication, articulation between the fifth wheel and trailer encounter high resistance. Steering the vehicle is difficult and the trailer can push the tractor out of its lane when cornering. Lubrication is necessary to reduce wear on the fifth wheel top plate and trailer upper coupler.

- Fifth wheel top plates are made from cast iron, stamped steel, or aluminum. The type of jaw mechanism that locks and holds the trailer king pin in the fifth wheel varies between manufacturers. Most locking jaw mechanisms require periodic inspection and adjustment to compensate for jaw wear. No-slack lock mechanisms are automatically adjusting.

- Fifth wheels must be properly positioned on the frame when installed to prevent interference between the trailer and tractor, as well as to obtain proper distribution of trailer weight among the tractor axles. A fifth wheel should not move any farther rearward on a chassis than 1" (2.5 cm) ahead of the center between the rear tandem axles.

- The height of a fifth wheel should not allow the trailer to exceed 13' 6" (4.1 m). The height should also enable the trailer to couple properly with the tractor.

- Semi-oscillating fifth wheels are the most common type used on-highway for pulling dry cube trailers. The semi-oscillating wheel articulates several degrees side-to-side and back-to-front. Full oscillating fifth wheels articulate much more and are typically used for bulk liquid tankers to prevent tanker barrels from twisting and cracking. Rigid-type fifth wheels do not articulate and allow only the flexible upper coupler to move and are used on dump trailers.

- Upper couplers attach to the trailer and hold the king pin. King pins are available in 2" (5.1 cm) and 3.5" (8.9 cm) for specialized applications. Upper couplers are checked for flatness during inspection.

- King pins are inspected for straightness, length, and wear—typically with a go–no go gauge.

- Trailer landing gear is composed of two legs, which must support the weight of the trailer when uncoupling. The landing gear has a two-speed gear reduction mechanism to quickly raise the legs (fast speed up) and reduce the load on the fifth wheel when uncoupling (slow speed–high gear reduction) to lift the trailer slightly from the fifth wheel. Legs can be replaced or rebuilt when damaged. The gear mechanism requires periodic lubrication with chassis grease.

Key Terms

A-, B-, or C-train A three-unit combination of tractor plus two trailers.

A-type lock A single swinging lock jaw and plunger for simple operation.

axle spread The distance between the centerline of two axles.

B-type lock A fifth wheel locking mechanism that uses two swinging jaws and a yoke to lock the jaws securely around the king pin.

ball hitch A single-point connection configuration for a hitch that uses a tongue-shaped draw bar, which loops over a ball connected to the tow vehicle.

Bridge Formula B See *Federal Bridge Gross Weight Formula*.

cab forward (CF) A tractor with the engine located ahead of the cab.

cab-over-engine (COE) A tractor with the engine located beneath the cab.

combination vehicles Two or more combined or coupled vehicle units.

converter dolly A single or set of dual axles that supports a fifth wheel. Converter dollies convert semi-trailers into full trailers.

coupler Trailer hitching device, similar to pintle hooks, but in which the towing horn pivots and is not fixed.

"D" capacity The maximum horizontal pulling force that can be safely applied to the fifth wheel. Also called *draw bar capacity*.

draw bar capacity The maximum horizontal pulling force that can be safely applied to the fifth wheel. Also called *"D" capacity*.

draw bars Bars used to connect tow vehicles to a tractor or lead towing unit.

Federal Bridge Formula See *Federal Bridge Gross Weight Formula*.

Federal Bridge Gross Weight Formula Laws that limit the weight-to-length ratio of heavy trucks with the goal of protecting roads and bridges from the damage caused by the concentrated weight of shorter trucks. Also known as *Bridge Formula B* or *Federal Bridge Formula*.

flitch plates Angle iron that is attached to the fifth wheel on one side and is bolted to the frame on another side.

full trailer A trailer that is supported at both ends with an axle and does not rest on a fifth wheel.

fully oscillating fifth wheel A type of fifth wheel designed to provide front-to-rear and side-to-side movement between the tractor and semi-trailer.

gross trailer weight (GTW) The maximum carrying capacity of a trailer calculated by measuring the trailer weight and load.

gross vehicle weight (GVW) The maximum design weight of a vehicle including a full tank of fuel, fully loaded to its capacity, and with all passengers.

Gross Vehicle Weight Rating (GVWR) The design rating specified by a manufacturer as the recommended maximum weight of a vehicle when fully loaded to capacity, including all passengers and a full tank of fuel.

gross weight limit The maximum legal weight of a vehicle that can travel on roads and bridges.

landing gear Retractable legs attached to the trailer, which support a semi-trailer when it is not resting on a fifth wheel.

no-slack coupler A type of fifth wheel lock mechanism that uses serrated edges between the locking bar and wedge to ensure no play in the coupling.

rigid fifth wheel A type of fifth wheel that does not oscillate about either axis of the vehicle. It does not articulate from side-to-side or front-to-back. It is fixed in location.

secondary safety latch An additional mechanism used as an added step to unlatch or release a fifth wheel locking jaw.

semi-oscillating fifth wheel Fifth wheels that pivot slightly in both horizontal and vertical directions; the standard type of fifth wheel used in on-highway applications.

semi-trailer A trailer that has some of its load carried by the tractor through a hitching device.

shunt truck A tractor designed to move semi-trailers around a warehouse yard or intermodal facility. Also known as a *terminal tractor*.

slider mechanism A plate the fifth wheel is attached to that has a ratchet-like set of plungers that enable the fifth wheel to be repositioned forward or backward along the tractor frame.

snubber A shock-absorbing insulator used to absorb shock loads transmitted by the trailer when the tow vehicle is accelerating or decelerating.

swing clearance The clearance remaining between a trailer and tractor when the combination vehicle is cornering.

tandem axle A two-axle tractor or trailer configuration.

terminal tractor A tractor designed to move semi-trailers around a warehouse yard or intermodal facility. Also known as a *shunt truck*.

tongue weight (TW) The weight supported by the ball (tongue) in a ball hitch.

trailer The cargo-carrying portion of a combination vehicle.

two-height fifth wheel A specialty stationary fifth wheel that can be either air or hydraulically raised or lowered.

upper coupler A steel plate and a king pin fastened to the underside of the forward portion of a semi-trailer frame and designed to tow and support the weight of the trailer.

vertical load The weight supported by a hitching device, which is applied downwards by the weight of the trailer.

Review Question

1. Which of the following is the maximum weight load a single axle on a Class 8 combination vehicle is permitted to carry?
   a. 80,000 lb (36,287 kg)
   b. 42,000 lb (19,051 kg)
   c. 20,000 lb (9072 kg)
   d. 10,000 lb (4536 kg)

2. Which of the following is used to connect a single semi-trailer to a tractor?
   a. A fifth wheel
   b. A converter dolly
   c. A pintle hook
   d. A draw bar

3. What classification of combination vehicle is used by a converter dolly connecting to a lead trailer with a single draw bar?
   a. A semi-oscillating
   b. A B-train
   c. An A-train
   d. A C-train

4. What minimum grade of fasteners is required to fasten all fifth wheels and hitching devices to the frame?
   a. SAE Grade 14
   b. SAE Grade 8
   c. SAE Grade 5
   d. Corrosion-resistant plated fasteners

5. The height of the fifth wheel from the ground should:
   a. not allow the trailer height to exceed 13'6" (4.1 m).
   b. be between 3'6" and 60" (1.1 and 1.5 m).
   c. be capable of being varied by adjusting air or hydraulic pressure.
   d. provide adequate swing clearance between the tractor and the trailer.

6. Side-to-side articulation of a semi-oscillating fifth wheel is provided by:
   a. compression in the rubber bushing beneath the top plate.
   b. a cradle mechanism supporting the top plate of the fifth wheel.
   c. pivoting of the top plate around steel pins in the plate brackets.
   d. flexing of the upper coupler plate.

7. Which of the following complaints are reported when a fifth wheel locking jaws are too loose and require adjustment?
   a. The fifth wheel does not release.
   b. The fifth wheel does not correctly lock.
   c. The driver complains about a banging noise during acceleration and deceleration.
   d. The rubber bushing on the adjustment bolt is more than ½" (12.7 mm) away from the top plate.

8. Which of the following is the correct position for the rear-most travel of a fifth wheel?
   a. The centerline of the fifth wheel should align with the centerline between the tandem drive axles.
   b. The fifth wheel centerline should allow approximately two meters of swing clearance between the trailer and cab.
   c. The fifth wheel centerline should travel no farther back than one foot ahead of the center between the drive axles.
   d. The fifth wheel centerline should travel no farther back than one inch ahead of the center between the drive axles.

9. Which of the following is the correct diameter of a new on-highway SAE king pin where it engages the lock jaws?
   a. 2" ± 0.005" (50 mm ± 0.127 mm)
   b. 2.85" ± 0.005" (71.12 mm ± 0.127 mm)
   c. 3.5" + 0.005" (88.9 mm ± 0.127 mm)
   d. 2.25" + 0.005" (57.15 mm ± 0.127 mm)

10. Which of the following is the most likely consequence of dropping a trailer onto its landing gear?
   a. A bent leg
   b. Broken leg mounting bolts
   c. A bent internal screw
   d. Only one leg will extend

ASE Technician A/Technician B Style Questions

1. Technicians A and B were discussing the position of a fifth wheel on a conventional cab forward tractor compared to a cab-over-engine tractor. Technician A says that the position of the fifth wheel has to move farther forward on a cab forward tractor to distribute trailer weight evenly over the axles. Technician B says that a cab forward tractor needs to move the fifth wheel farther back than a cab-over-engine tractor. Who is correct?
   a. Technician A
   b. Technician B
   c. Both Technician A and Technician B
   d. Neither Technician A nor Technician B

2. Technician A says that a fully oscillating fifth wheel is the best fifth wheel to use for a frameless dump trailer with an articulating upper coupler. Technician B says that a rigid-type fifth wheel is safer. Who is correct?
   a. Technician A
   b. Technician B
   c. Both Technician A and Technician B
   d. Neither Technician A nor Technician B

3. Technician A says that a semi-oscillating fifth wheel is the most commonly used fifth wheel on tractors towing semi-trailers. Technician B says that a fully oscillating fifth wheel helps prevent liquid tanker barrels from cracking. Who is correct?
   a. Technician A
   b. Technician B
   c. Both Technician A and Technician B
   d. Neither Technician A nor Technician B

4. A fifth wheel king pin is checked with a go–no go gauge. The 2" (5.1 cm) pin easily slipped into both the wider and narrower slots of the gauge. Technician A recommends replacing the king pin. Technician B says all fifth wheel lock jaws are designed to safely accommodate and adjust to variations dimensions of king pins. Who is correct?
   a. Technician A
   b. Technician B
   c. Both Technician A and Technician B
   d. Neither Technician A nor Technician B

5. Technician A says the A-train configuration uses a fifth-wheel mounted onto a converter dolly to support the front of the rear most trailer. Technician B says the B-train configuration is the least stable of the three combination vehicle types. Who is correct?
   a. Technician A
   b. Technician B
   c. Both Technician A and Technician B
   d. Neither Technician A nor Technician B

6. Technician A says that, in North America, a common method to classify trucks is by gross vehicle weight (GVW). Technician B says that GVW refers to the maximum design weight of a vehicle including a full tank of fuel, fully loaded to its capacity, and with all passengers. Who is correct?
   a. Technician A
   b. Technician B
   c. Both Technician A and Technician B
   d. Neither Technician A nor Technician B

7. Technician A says pintle hooks are coupled by raising the draw bar eye over the pintle horn and locking it closed with a pivoting latch. Technician B says a snubber or load dampener was used in the past to minimize shock loads but are no longer being used. Who is correct?
   a. Technician A
   b. Technician B
   c. Both Technician A and Technician B
   d. Neither Technician A nor Technician B

8. Technician A says that ball hitches are used on light- and medium-duty vehicles having a 16,000 lb (6350 kg) or less towing weight capacity. Technician B says that ball hitches have the advantage of providing a positive no-slack fit because the draw bar has a spring-loaded tensioner at the connection point with the ball. Who is correct?
   a. Technician A
   b. Technician B
   c. Both Technician A and Technician B
   d. Neither Technician A nor Technician B

9. Technician A says that tongue weight (TW) is the load the draw bar places on the pintle hook, coupler, or ball hitch. Technician B says that, as a general rule, when estimating the vertical load of the trailer tongue it should be at least 30% of the gross trailer weight. Who is correct?
   a. Technician A
   b. Technician B
   c. Both Technician A and Technician B
   d. Neither Technician A nor Technician B

10. Technician A says that a complete king pin replacement is necessary when the king pin is excessively worn. Technician B says that a worn king pin can be acceptably repaired by spray welding and machining the king pin to the correct dimension while it is still attached to the trailer. Who is correct?
    a. Technician A
    b. Technician B
    c. Both Technician A and Technician B
    d. Neither Technician A nor Technician B

SECTION 4
Drivetrains

CHAPTER 40   Heavy-Duty Clutches

CHAPTER 41   Servicing Heavy-Duty Clutches

CHAPTER 42   Basic Gearing Concepts

CHAPTER 43   Standard Transmissions

CHAPTER 44   Servicing Standard Transmissions

CHAPTER 45   Automated Manual Transmissions

CHAPTER 46   Torque Converters

CHAPTER 47   Planetary Gear Concepts

CHAPTER 48   Hydraulically Controlled Automatic Transmissions

CHAPTER 49   Electronically Controlled Automatic Transmissions

CHAPTER 50   Maintaining Automatic Transmissions

CHAPTER 51   Heavy-Duty Drive Shaft Systems

CHAPTER 52   **Heavy-Duty Drive Axles**

CHAPTER 53   **Servicing and Maintaining Drive Axles**

CHAPTER 54   **Electric Drive Vehicles and AC Traction Motors**

CHAPTER 55   **Autonomous Driving and Advanced Driver Assistance Systems for Commercial Vehicles**

CHAPTER 56   **Hybrid Drive Systems and Series-Type Hybrid Drives**

CHAPTER 57   **Allison EV Drive and Series-Parallel Hybrid Systems**

CHAPTER 40

Heavy-Duty Clutches

Learning Objectives

After reading this chapter, you will be able to:

- **LO 40-1** Explain the fundamentals and function of a clutch assembly.
- **LO 40-2** Describe the various types and design of clutches.

- **LO 40-3** Describe the various components of clutch assemblies.
- **LO 40-4** Explain the purpose and function of clutch brakes.
- **LO 40-5** Describe and explain the function of various clutch actuation systems.

You Are the Technician

A customer brings his two-year-old Freightliner truck to your shop and complains that he hears grinding from the transmission when he shifts into either first range or reverse. He says that the grinding does not happen as he is driving down the road shifting to any other gear; just first and reverse. He tells you that the problem started and has been getting worse and worse since his brother-in-law has been driving some shifts in the truck for him. You check out his complaint and find that, sure enough, there is grinding from the transmission when trying to select either first or reverse from neutral.

1. What component do you think may be to blame for this situation?
2. How would you verify your suspicion?
3. What advice could you give the driver to avoid a repeat concern?
4. What repair should be done?

Introduction

The clutch is an indispensable part of all power systems. It is the link between the power plant (the engine) and the rest of the vehicle driveline. All of the torque and power the engine produces must travel through the clutch. The correctly functioning clutch must provide many miles of faithful service without failure. It is the duty of every technician to fully understand the functioning, maintenance, and, when necessary, the replacement of this vital component. This chapter will help the technician to understand the purpose, function, and construction of the modern clutches commonly found in the medium- to heavy-duty truck industry.

Fundamentals of Heavy-Duty Clutches

LO 40-1 Explain the fundamentals and function of a clutch assembly.

The origin of the simple friction clutch dates back to the middle of the 19th century, circa 1835 to 1845. At that time, clutches were used for the same purposes we use them today—to connect and disconnect a power device from a mechanical system. In those days, however, clutches were typically connecting and disconnecting machinery from a steam engine. There were a multitude of designs—expanding shoe and drum types, a flat friction disc clamped against a flywheel similar to today's clutches, and the cone-type clutch.

The cone-type clutch, illustrated in **FIGURE 40-1**, was one of the more popular designs in its day. The cone-type clutch consisted of a female member (the cup) attached to the power source, which was usually a steam engine. A male member (the cone) was attached to the gearing of the machine that needed to be driven. The cup and cone had a running clearance in the disengaged position. When the clutch lever was moved into the engaged position by the operator, the cone slid along the driven shaft splines until it engaged the cup and was held in that position by the spring. The friction material on the cone would grab onto, or "clutch," the driving cup, and thereby transferred power to the machinery. To disengage the clutch, the release lever

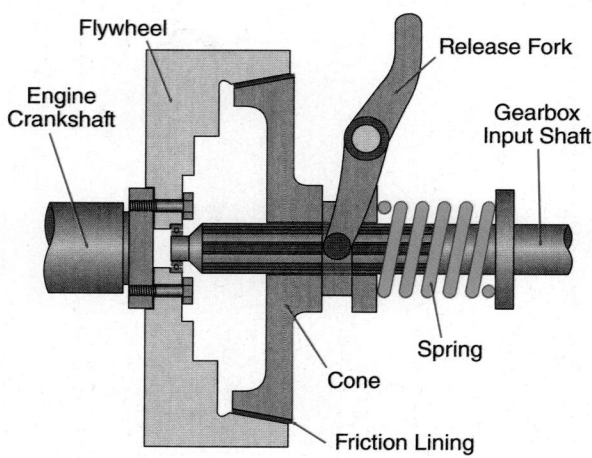

FIGURE 40-1 Early cone-type friction clutch.

moved back in the opposite direction, compressing the spring, and was locked in that position; this reestablished the running clearance, freeing the driven shaft once again and interrupting the flow of power to the machinery.

The cone-type clutch was an extremely important technological development. Prior to the invention of the clutch, machinery was typically directly connected to the engine. The machinery was started by closing a valve, which allowed the steam pressure to build up and provide the necessary power to drive the machine. Heavy loads hindered the start of the machinery. The innovation of the clutch allowed the engine to be started and build up momentum in its flywheel before the load was applied. The clutch also allowed the machinery to be stopped without shutting down the engine.

Modern Clutches

The dictionary definition of clutch is to "grab or hold tightly," and this is exactly what we need a clutch to do—to grab onto a component from a running engine and transfer its motion to the driveline of the vehicle. Most people understand this to be the essential function of a clutch, but if the only purpose of a clutch were to connect two components, the vehicle could be built more simply with just a solid connection from the engine to the driveline. The clutch could be eliminated altogether.

The real purpose of the clutch is to enable the engine to be disconnected from the driveline in order to stop the vehicle or to change gears and/or direction. In simplest terms, the main job of the clutch is to connect and disconnect the engine from the driveline. (The clutch does have other important functions. These functions are discussed later in this chapter.)

The clutch accomplishes its job by squeezing one or more driven members or discs that are splined to the transmission **input shaft** between the flywheel and one or more driving plates that are driven by the engine.

The motive power clutch uses at least two, and sometimes more, driving components; the flywheel is the engine-side driving component, and the pressure plate is the clutch-side driving component. The flywheel and the pressure plate are responsible for transferring engine power to the driven element of the clutch. Clutches can have more than one plate that transfers power to the driven members, but more on that later. The **flywheel** is a heavy, round, metal disc bolted to the end of the engine crankshaft. **FIGURE 40-2** shows a typical flywheel.

The flywheel has several purposes. First, it must be heavy enough to provide sufficient inertia to keep the engine turning between power impulses. Second, the flywheel's weight is also used to absorb and smooth out the torsional vibrations caused by the engine's power pulses. Third, the flywheel provides a mounting area for the clutch itself. Last, it also provides one of the friction surfaces used to transmit power to the front of the clutch-driven disc, more commonly known simply as the **clutch disc or friction disc**. The clutch disc is a plate or disc that has friction material on both sides and is splined to the transmission input shaft. The clutch disc, or discs, is/are the clutch assembly's only driven element(s).

The **pressure plate** is the friction surface of the clutch assembly and it is used to squeeze the clutch disc against the

FIGURE 40-2 The flywheel serves many important functions.

FIGURE 40-3 Modern dual-disc clutch assembly with an Eaton transmission.

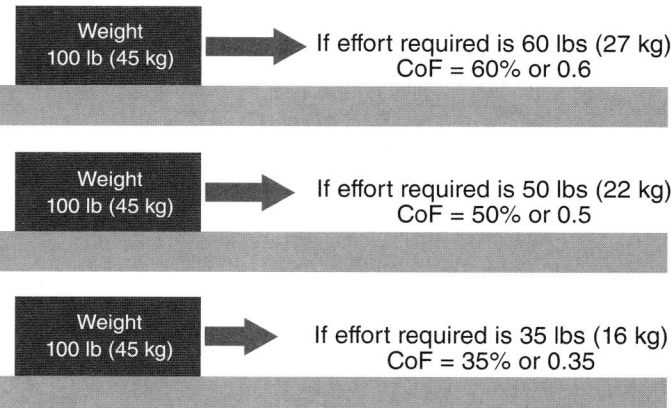

Coefficient of Friction (CoF) = Load/Effort

| Weight 100 lb (45 kg) | → If effort required is 60 lbs (27 kg) CoF = 60% or 0.6 |

| Weight 100 lb (45 kg) | → If effort required is 50 lbs (22 kg) CoF = 50% or 0.5 |

| Weight 100 lb (45 kg) | → If effort required is 35 lbs (16 kg) CoF = 35% or 0.35 |

FIGURE 40-4 The coefficient of friction depends on the pull, or force, required to move an object across a given surface.

flywheel. The pressure plate transfers the power from the rotating clutch assembly to the rear of the clutch disc. The **clutch cover** is the outside part of the clutch bolted to the flywheel and holds all of the clutch components except the clutch disc. It is mistakenly, but commonly, called the pressure plate. The pressure plate is actually one of the components contained inside the clutch cover. The clutch cover also contains all the other parts of the clutch, including the pressure springs and release springs. Because the clutch cover is bolted to the engine flywheel, the cover, pressure plate, and all the components attached to or part of the cover always rotate with the engine. Together, these components work to squeeze the friction disc(s); as mentioned earlier, some clutches have more than one disc, between the two (or more) driving elements of the assembled clutch. As noted previously, the friction disc or discs is/are the only driven element(s) in the assembled clutch. When the friction discs are squeezed between the driving elements, power is transferred to the disc(s) and, because the friction disc(s) are splined to the transmission input shaft, this action connects the engine and the transmission so that torque can be sent to the transmission and on to the driveline. **FIGURE 40-3** shows a newer electronically actuated clutch design that has eliminated the need for a clutch pedal.

The Role of Friction

The clutch performs its duty by using **friction**, which is the relative resistance to motion between any two bodies in contact with one another. In simple terms, the more friction that there is between two bodies, the harder it is to move the bodies in contact. The **coefficient of friction (CoF)** is a measure of the friction that exists between two bodies in contact. As illustrated in **FIGURE 40-4**, the CoF is calculated by dividing the force required to move an object across a given surface by the weight of the object being moved.

Engineers carefully select friction material used in the clutch disc so that the CoF between the disc(s) and the driving elements give the desired result. The clutch should engage smoothly. This requires that the clutch allows some slippage as it is first engaged so the driveline is not shocked. The clutch must also not slip when fully engaged and transmitting increasing torque to the driveline. Several factors affect the CoF, such as the surface conditions of the objects. For example, rough surfaces have different CoF than smooth surfaces, as do wet and dry surfaces. Two blocks of smooth steel in contact are easier to move than two rough-surfaced bricks of the same weight. If lubricating oil is placed between the two steel blocks, they move even more easily. The CoF is tailored to the specific clutch application to allow the desired operating performance.

Basic Clutch Functions

As mentioned previously, clutches do more than just connect and disconnect the engine to the driveline. A clutch must allow a certain amount of slippage at engagement while the load is being taken up and the vehicle starts to move. Slippage occurs as the driver is allowing the clutch to engage by slowly, but steadily, releasing the clutch pedal in a controlled manner. The ability to control the clutch slip is a desirable skill in any driver. The CoF of the particular clutch affects this ability somewhat—a higher CoF clutch engages more abruptly than one with a lower CoF.

This initial slippage is known as **kinetic friction** and prevents driveline shock. Kinetic friction, however, has a serious drawback, and that is heat. Think about when you rub your hands together quickly, they get warm, right? The same thing happens when a clutch disc is slipping, but too much heat can quickly cause a clutch to burn out and fail. This kinetic or sliding friction allows a smooth engagement and adds to operator comfort by giving the driver a feel for the clutch, but too much slippage destroys the clutch very quickly, so there must be a balance between comfort and slip control. The only time a clutch really wears is during slip, when a clutch is fully engaged and not slipping, no wear occurs on the friction surface, but while slipping, wear can happen very quickly. A clutch must offer a long service life and perform hundreds of thousands of engagements and disengagements, so it is critical that the CoF is correct for the application, and that the driver is skilled at the clutch's operation.

Besides engaging and disengaging the engine and the driveline, one of the most important functions of a clutch used in today's applications is to absorb damaging driveline torsional vibrations. Torsional vibrations are powerful vibrations caused by the engine firing impulses. **FIGURE 40-5** is a depiction of torsional vibrations.

Every time a cylinder fires, the force from the firing twists and accelerates the crankshaft. Torsional vibrations have increased as engine torque has increased and engine cruising rpm has diminished. Torsional vibrations must be managed or the entire driveline sustains fatigue damage. Think about bending a coat hanger back and forth many times, the hanger eventually breaks due to fatigue failure; the same is true for a vehicle driveline. Some manufacturers believe that managing torsional vibrations is the single most important job of the clutch, and even more important than its connect and disconnect functions.

Clutch Capacity

Clutch capacity is the amount of torque a clutch can transmit before it starts to slip. Clutch capacity must be matched to the particular application or slippage and clutch failure may result.

In highway truck applications, there are many different horsepower and torque ratings available. Each engine and torque rating requires a clutch that is capable of handling the torque produced. Always compare the torque capacity of the clutch with the torque rating of a particular powertrain. Be especially careful if the engine has been rerated to a higher torque capacity. Quite often the stock clutch may not handle the increased torque output. Generally speaking, clutch capacity is affected by three factors: CoF of the materials used in the clutch's manufacture, surface area of the clutch disc's friction material that is in contact with the flywheel and pressure plate, and clamp load provided by the application springs. All automotive clutches are manufactured with cast iron flywheels and pressure plates, so the CoF of the clutch disc facings and the clamp load are the important elements here. The larger the surface area of the components in contact with each other, the more torque can be transmitted. That is the reason that many clutches are manufactured with dual discs. Dual discs like those shown in **FIGURE 40-6** double the surface contact area and, therefore, double the ability of the clutch to transmit torque without slipping.

Clamp force (clamp load) is the amount of force pushing the clutch against the pressure plate and flywheel. The harder the clutch is squeezed between the pressure plate and the flywheel, the greater the torque the clutch can handle. The clamp load, or force, however, must consider the force required to release the clutch. The more the clamp force, the greater the release force required to cage the clamping springs. This problem can be compensated for by using larger levers in the clutch release system to gain mechanical advantage, but as levers get longer, the movement they provide gets shorter. Some manufacturers

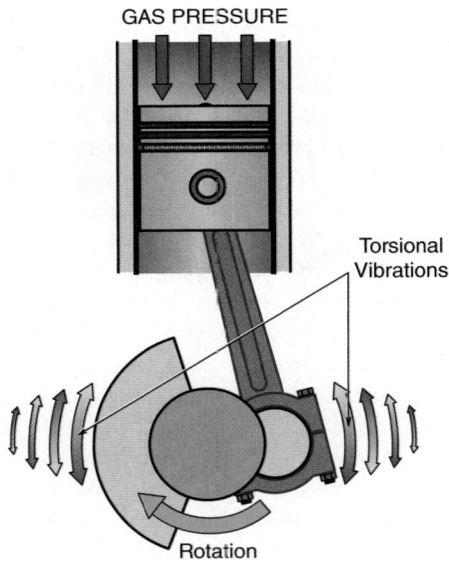

FIGURE 40-5 Torsional vibrations can cause wear and damage in a driveline and must be absorbed.

FIGURE 40-6 Two friction discs double the clutch's torque carrying capability, or clutch capacity, without increasing the diameter of the clutch.

use hydraulically actuated clutch release systems to compensate when the force required to release the clutch is high.

Types and Design of Clutches

LO 40-2 Describe the various types and design of clutches.

Two basic types of clutches are used in the medium- and heavy-duty commercial vehicle industry. They are the push-type and the pull-type. The push and pull refer to the direction the release fingers or levers have to be moved in order to disengage the clutch. In a **push-type clutch**, the release fingers or levers are pushed toward the engine flywheel to release the clutch; in the **pull-type clutch**, the levers are pulled away from the flywheel to disengage.

The single-disc push-type clutch illustrated in **FIGURE 40-7** is used primarily in light-duty applications, but it can be found in trucks up to class 4, 5, and 6. Increasingly, though, a large version of the push-type clutch is being used with automated transmissions in class 7 and 8 vehicles. The Volvo I-Shift, the Mack mDrive™, the ZF AS Tronic, and the new Eaton Endurant™ transmissions all use a single-disc, push-type clutch. The single disc used with these clutches is approximately 17" (430 mm)

in diameter. Push-type clutches are also available with dual friction discs for more severe-duty applications. **FIGURE 40-8** shows the single disc push-type clutch from a Volvo I-Shift. Using dual discs allows the clutch capacity to be increased without changing the overall diameter of the clutch or the clutch clamp load.

Pull-type clutches, such as the one shown in Figures 40-9 and 40-10, are used almost exclusively in class 6, 7, and 8 trucks that use unsynchronized transmissions. Using a pull-type clutch allows the use of a clutch brake to slow and stop the transmission gearing when first or reverse gear is being selected. We will explain clutch brakes in greater detail in the Clutch Brakes section. **FIGURE 40-9** shows a drawing of an angle spring pull-type clutch, while **FIGURE 40-10** shows a cutaway view of a diaphragm spring pull-type clutch.

Pull-type clutches are also available in dual-friction disc designs for increased clutch torque capacity. A dual-disc clutch must use an **intermediate plate** (sometimes known as a separator plate) between the two discs. An intermediate plate is a cast iron plate that is connected to the flywheel or the clutch cover. An intermediate plate provides a means to transfer torque from the engine to the back of the front clutch disc and the front of the rear clutch disc. Multiple-disc clutches (clutches with more than two friction discs) are available for certain applications where extremely high torque transfer capacity is needed. A multiple-disc clutch requires a separator plate between each pair of clutch friction discs. As yet, however, multiple-disc clutches are not prevalent in the on-highway truck market.

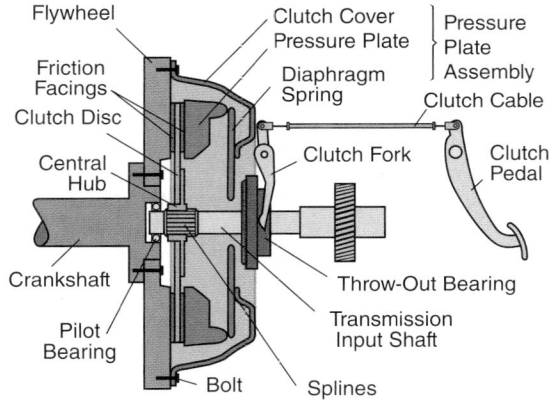

FIGURE 40-7 A standard push-type vehicle clutch.

FIGURE 40-8 The Volvo I-Shift uses a 17" (430 mm) single-disc push-type clutch.

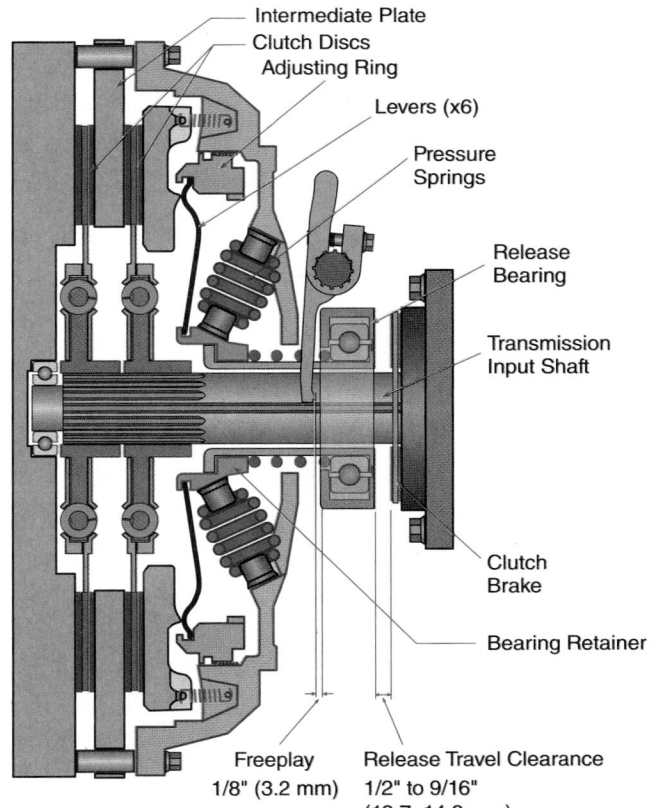

FIGURE 40-9 Angle spring pull-type clutch.

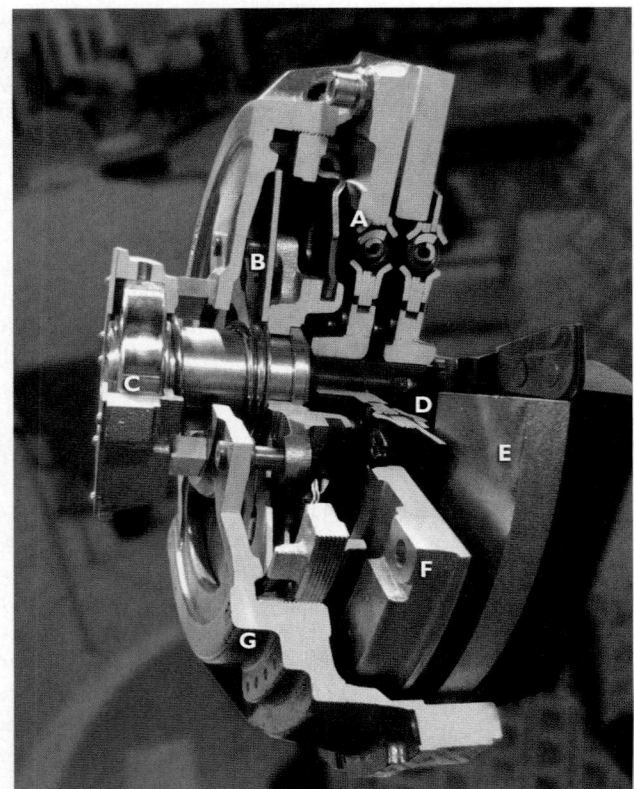

FIGURE 40-10 Dual-disc pull-type clutch. **A.** Torsional dampening springs. **B.** Diaphragm spring (supplies clamp load). **C.** Integral (attached) release bearing. **D.** Friction discs. **E.** Intermediate plate. **F.** Pressure plate. **G.** Clutch cover.

FIGURE 40-11 The clutch cover contains most of the parts of the clutch.

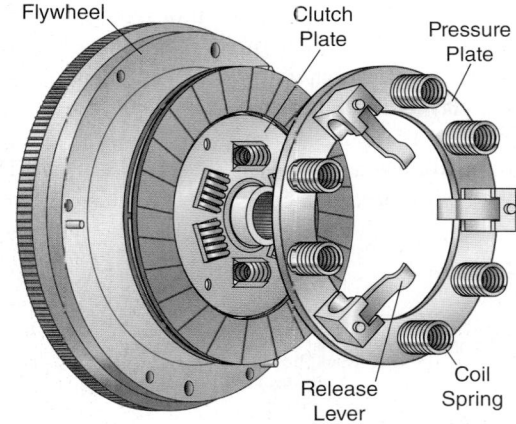

FIGURE 40-12 The coil spring pressure plate uses coil springs to create the disc clamping pressure and uses release levers to cage the coil's springs and free the clutch disc.

Clutch types are also described by the type of cover the clutch has. The clutch cover is the component that houses the functioning parts of the clutch: the actuating levers, the springs, and the pressure plate. **FIGURE 40-11** shows a typical stamped steel clutch cover.

The clutch cover is commonly referred to simply as the pressure plate; however, the pressure plate is just one of the components in the clutch cover. There are three broad design categories for clutch covers:

- The coil spring style, available in push- or pull-type
- The diaphragm spring style, available in push- or pull-type
- The angle spring style, a pull-type clutch patented by the DANA Corporation; however, now mostly associated with Eaton.

These style designations refer to the method used to clamp the friction disc(s) between the flywheel and the pressure plate(s). There are self-adjusting versions of each design category as well.

Coil Spring-Style Push-Type Clutch

The **coil spring-style clutch** uses coil springs mounted perpendicular (90 degrees) to the pressure plate. These coil springs act directly against the back of the plate to supply clamping force. Angle spring clutches also use coil springs, but their design is quite different, so they are put into a separate category to

distinguish them from perpendicular coil spring clutches. In a push-type coil spring clutch, such as the one illustrated in **FIGURE 40-12**, a series of levers are attached to a pivot point, which is attached to the clutch cover. The outer edges of the levers are attached to the pressure plate.

When disengagement is required, the release bearing is pushed against the inner surface of these levers. The **release bearing** is a ball bearing mounted on a hollow housing that is pushed against the release levers to disengage the clutch that supports the bearing. The release bearing housing is installed on the input shaft sleeve of the transmission and can be slid back and forth along the sleeve. In a push-type clutch, the release bearing is normally stationary until the bearing contacts the release levers to disengage the clutch. When the driver pushes on the clutch pedal, the clutch release system (mechanical, cable, or hydraulic) pushes the release bearing against the release levers of the clutch. Because the levers are attached to the clutch cover, pushing the inner part of the lever toward the flywheel causes the outer edge of the levers to move toward the transmission. The levers are connected to the pressure plate at their outer edge, so this action causes the pressure plate to move toward the transmission as well. As the plate is pulled away from the flywheel, the coil springs are caged (or collapsed); this action frees the clutch disc and allows it to rotate independently of the flywheel and pressure plate.

The same method is used in a pull-type coil spring clutch, except the pivot point and contact point of the levers are merely reversed. The pivot point of the levers is now at their outer edge and the attachment point to the pressure plate is further inboard. In both push- and pull-type clutches, as the friction discs wear, the pressure plate moves closer to the flywheel to compensate. The movement of the pressure plate toward the flywheel as disc wear occurs causes the coil springs to extend in order to keep contact with the pressure plate, this lengthening reduces the clamp load exerted by the springs and, therefore, clutch capacity is also reduced slightly.

Hooke's law states that the force delivered by a spring to an object is directly related to its compression or extension (see **FIGURE 40-13**). That means that the more the spring is compressed, the more force it delivers to the pressure plate. As the friction disc wears, the coil springs extend. That extension of the springs reduces the force against the pressure plate. Therefore, the more that the clutch disc wears, the less clamping force and clutch capacity it has. To compensate for wear, coil spring clutches are built with very strong springs. The strong springs can make coil spring clutches more difficult for the driver to disengage.

In any clutch, the clutch cover is the component that is bolted to the flywheel, so the driving torque must be transferred from the cover to the pressure plate. Coil spring-style clutches transfer this torque to the pressure plate in one of two ways, depending on whether the cover is formed from stamped steel or is cast. The stamped steel version normally has pockets or notches formed in the stamped steel cover and drive lugs cast into the pressure plate, as shown in **FIGURE 40-14**. This allows positive torque transfer, while allowing the pressure plate to move forward and backward as it engages and disengages. A clutch with a cast iron or aluminum cover may use a similar arrangement to transfer torque to the pressure plate, or it may have cut outs in the cover that engage notches in the pressure plate. Because of their loss of capacity as they wear and the difficulty in operating, coil spring clutches have mostly given way to diaphragm or angle spring clutches as the first choice of vehicle manufacturers.

Diaphragm Spring Clutch

The **diaphragm spring clutch** uses a single diaphragm spring (also known as a Belleville spring) to provide the clamping force. **FIGURE 40-15** shows a diaphragm spring resting on a pressure plate, the clutch cover has been removed for clarity; note the circular mark left on the spring from the pivot ring in the clutch cover and the drive strap attachment points.

A diaphragm spring clutch may have a stamped steel, cast iron, or aluminum cover. The cover is bolted to the engine flywheel and, therefore, turns with it. Normally, in both the push-type and pull-type diaphragm style, driving torque is transmitted to the pressure plate through a series of drive straps attached to both the cover and the pressure plate.

FIGURE 40-14 The driving force must be transferred from the clutch cover to the pressure plate. **A.** Formed notches in the stamped steel cover engage the cast iron pressure plate to transfer driving torque. **B.** Lugs on the pressure plate.

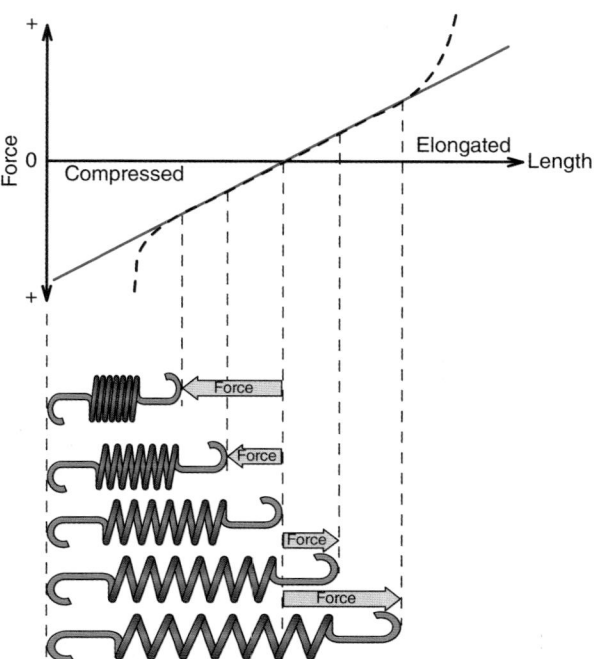

FIGURE 40-13 The force delivered by a spring is directly proportional to the length of its compression.

FIGURE 40-15 The finger-like segments of the diaphragm spring act as the release levers for the clutch.

These straps are made from laminated spring steel and have two functions. The first is to linearly transfer the driving torque to the pressure plate, as mentioned above. The second function of the straps is to act as return springs and move the pressure plate away from the clutch disc when it is disengaged. **FIGURE 40-16** shows a Volvo I-Shift, electronically controlled, single-disc, diaphragm spring, push-type clutch. Note the size of the full-face organic disc compared to the quarter on the clutch disc center hub. The full face is nearly 17" (43 cm) in diameter.

In their normal, relaxed position, the drive straps are straight. As the clutch is engaged, the pressure plate moves toward the flywheel and the straps bend slightly. When the clutch is disengaged, the straps straighten out and pull the pressure plate back. As shown in **FIGURE 40-17**, these straps must be strong enough to withstand maximum engine torque with a safety margin. If the drive straps are overloaded, they can permanently deform or bend. This prevents the strap from pulling the pressure plate back when the clutch is released, so the clutch cannot fully disengage. Bent drive straps can lead to gear clash while shifting and clutch overheating because the friction disc may stay in contact with the flywheel and pressure plate while disengaged.

A diaphragm spring clutch creates clamp load with the use of a single diaphragm spring pushing on the pressure plate. The spring on this clutch is a single cone-shaped spring, like the one shown in Figure 40-15. Its outer edge rests against the pressure plate, and the inner part of the spring is cut into segments called fingers. These fingers act as the release levers. A pivot ring is installed inside the clutch cover between the outside edge of the spring and the fingers.

To disengage the push-type diaphragm clutch, the release bearing is pushed against the release fingers. The pivot ring acts as a fulcrum, and the outer edge of the spring is pulled away from the pressure plate. The plate drive straps return to their normal straight shape, pulling the pressure plate away from the clutch disc, as illustrated in **FIGURE 40-18A**.

When the driver releases the clutch pedal the diaphragm spring forces the pressure plate against the clutch disc squeezing it between the plate and the flywheel and the clutch is engaged as seen in **FIGURE 40-18B**. Rather than lose pressure as disc wear occurs, which happens in the coil spring type, the diaphragm spring clutch is designed to increase loading on the pressure plate as disc wear occurs, until it is 50% worn. At that point, the pressure gradually decreases again for the second 50% of wear, until the pressure returns to the original loading. This varying clamp load is accomplished through the changing contact point of the outer edge of the diaphragm spring with a specially designed lobe on the pressure plate and the pivot ring contact, which changes the effective lever length of the spring as the disc wears.

The pull-type version of the diaphragm spring-style clutch, shown in **FIGURE 40-19**, arranges the diaphragm spring differently. The pivot point changes to the outer edge, and it engages the pressure plate further in toward the center. This has the effect of reversing release direction. In the pull-type diaphragm

FIGURE 40-16 Volvo I-Shift clutch. **A.** Torsional dampening springs. **B.** Stamped steel clutch cover. **C.** Diaphragm spring. **D.** Clutch disc. **E.** Drive straps.

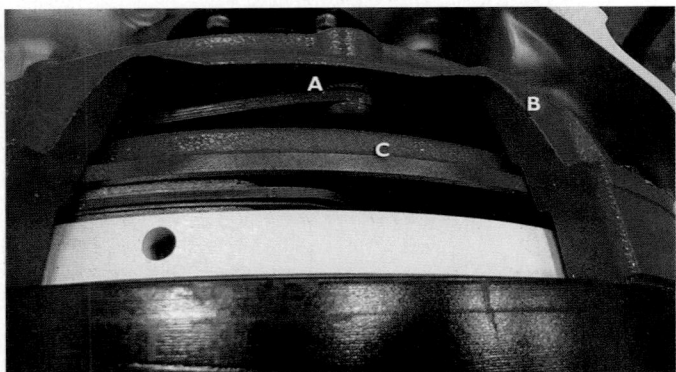

FIGURE 40-17 Normal flexing of the drive strap for an engaged clutch; the drive strap can be permanently distorted if the clutch is overloaded or shock loaded. **A.** Drive strap. **B.** Clutch cover. **C.** Pressure plate.

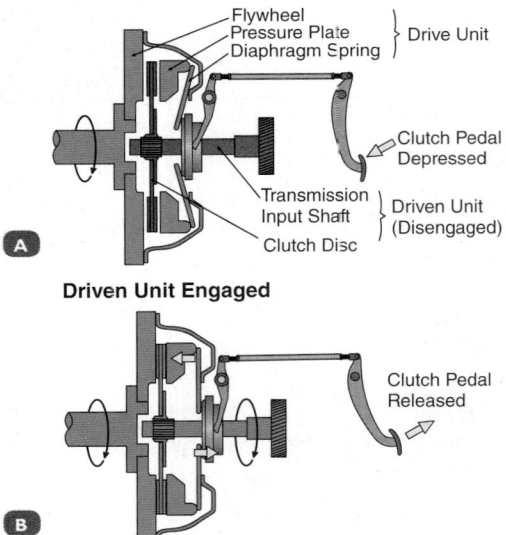

FIGURE 40-18 A. Depressing the clutch pedal releases the clamp load. **B.** Releasing the clutch pedal reapplies the clamping force and reconnects the engine and transmission, firmly clamping them together to continue rotating as a unit.

FIGURE 40-19 Rockwell pull-type diaphragm spring clutch. **A.** Release bearing. **B.** Threaded adjusting ring. **C.** Diaphragm spring. **D.** Adjusting ring lock strap. **E.** Drive strap.

FIGURE 40-20 Eaton Easy Pedal Advantage angle spring clutch. **A.** Angled pressure springs. **B.** Disengagement assist (Easy Pedal) springs. **C.** Clutch cover. **D.** Integral release bearing. **E.** Quick-adjust mechanism for internal clutch adjustment. **F.** Pressure plate return springs (1 of 4).

spring-style clutch, the drive torque may be transferred to the pressure plate through either drive straps or pockets in the cover and lugs on the pressure plate. If the clutch does not have drive straps, several small coil springs attached between the cover and the pressure plate pull the plate away from the friction disc when the clutch is disengaged.

Angle Spring Clutch

The **angle spring clutch** was patented by the DANA corporation in the 1960s. Since then, many changes in ownership and mergers have occurred, and now the clutch is manufactured by the Eaton Corporation. The original patent has expired and, therefore, there are many companies marketing angle spring clutches today, but their designs are all relatively similar or the same as the original.

The angle spring clutch uses three pairs of angled springs pushing against the pressure plate through levers to supply the clamp load. The angle spring pull-style clutch is by far the most popular in heavy-duty on-highway trucks that use non-synchronized transmissions. Its design allows for a near constant clamp load throughout the life of the clutch discs as long as the adjustment is correct. The angle spring clutch in most applications uses dual-discs for increased clutch capacity.

Six angle-mounted coil springs push axially against the bearing retainer. In turn, the bearing retainer pushes against the inner edge of six equally spaced levers. The fulcrum of the levers is at their outer edge on the adjusting ring. The length of the levers multiplies the pressure of the springs and increases the force against the pressure plate to create the clamp load. Driving torque is transferred to the pressure plate by lugs and pockets.

The use of the levers in the clutch design allows increased clamp load with a decreased pedal effort to disengage the clutch. Eaton claims that clutch actuation effort has been reduced by 50% over the years through innovation in the clutch design. The Eaton angle spring clutch, shown in **FIGURE 40-20**, also uses three assist springs that function to reduce pedal effort

after clutch release. The three assist springs are arranged so that, as the clutch releases, the springs help to hold the clutch in the release position. In fact, once the clutch is released, only 30% of the pedal effort required for disengagement is needed to hold the clutch pedal down. For that reason, this type of clutch is known as the "Easy Pedal Advantage®" clutch.

To understand the operation of the Angle spring clutch, refer to Figure 40-9 while reading the following passage. To disengage the clutch, the integral (attached) release bearing is pulled by the release fork, which pulls the inner edge of the release levers toward the transmission. The release levers are pivoted off the adjusting ring at their outer edge and this action takes the pressure off the pressure plate, allowing the small return springs to pull the pressure plate away from the clutch discs. The discs are now free to turn inside the clutch assembly. To engage the clutch, the driver releases the clutch pedal and the three sets of angle springs push the bearing retainer and the inner edge of the levers toward the flywheel. The levers pivot off the adjusting ring and contact the pressure plate, forcing it forward toward the flywheel clamping the clutch disc(s) between the flywheel, the pressure plate, and the intermediate plate (in dual-disc clutches).

Self-Adjusting Clutches

Self-adjusting clutches have an automatic adjusting system that relies on pressure plate movement to cause an adjustment. There are two major North American suppliers of self-adjusting clutches commonly found on today's medium-duty and heavy-duty vehicles. They are Eaton's Solo clutch, now known as the Advantage® Self-Adjust, shown in **FIGURE 40-21**, and Meritor's AutoJust clutch, which is no longer in production. In Europe, ZF Sachs AG markets the Twin XTend™ self-adjusting clutch, which operates very similarly to the Eaton Solo.

The Eaton Solo clutch incorporates a fixed and a movable cam ring that takes the place of the internal threaded adjusting

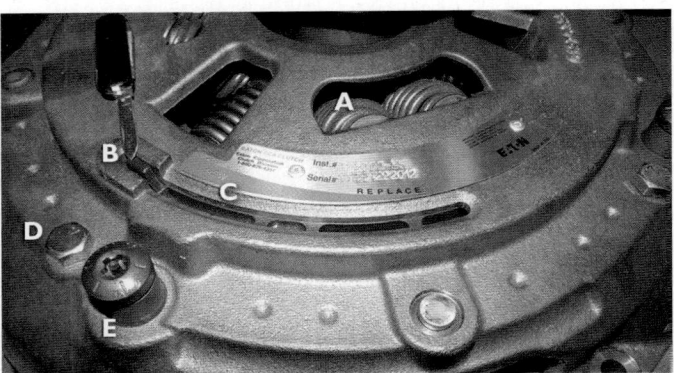

FIGURE 40-21 Eaton self-adjusting clutch. **A.** Angle springs. **B.** Self-adjust indicator tab. **C.** New to replace scale. **D.** Shipping bolts (one of four). **E.** Wear sensors.

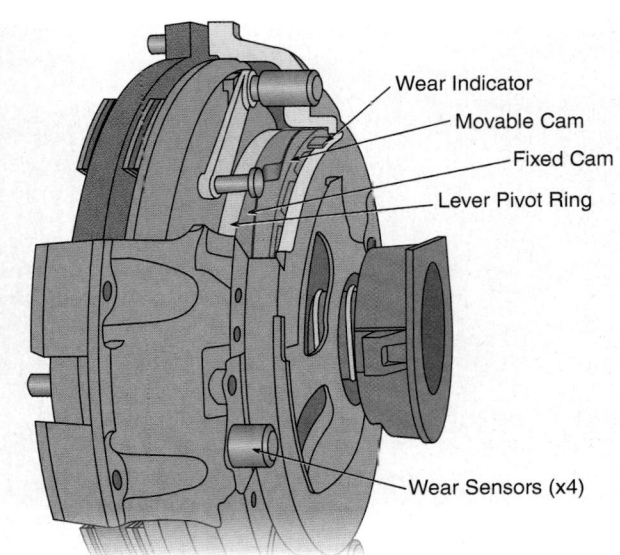

FIGURE 40-22 The ramped cam rings in the solo self-adjust clutch take the place of the threaded adjusting ring.

ring. The rear cam ring adjusts automatically as wear is sensed. The Eaton Solo operates similarly to the angle spring clutch with the exception of the self-adjust feature. The Arvin Meritor AutoJust clutch uses a diaphragm spring, and its operation is identical to the operation of the previously described pull-type diaphragm spring clutches, again with the exception of the self-adjust feature. The ZF Sachs AG self-adjusting clutch, called Twin XTend, was marketed through Meritor until the companies parted ways fairly recently. ZF now supplies the Twin XTend directly to the North American market. The self-adjust feature of these clutches is discussed in more detail in the Heavy-Duty Clutch Servicing chapter. **FIGURE 40-22** shows the cam rings in the solo clutch.

Components of Clutches

LO 40-3 Describe the various components of clutch assemblies.

Clutches include several other components critical to their function, including friction discs, flywheels, intermediate plates, pilot and release bearings, and clutch brakes. Additionally, regardless of type, every clutch has an actuation system that is mechanically, hydraulically, or automatically controlled.

Clutch Friction Discs

Clutch friction discs are the only driven member of the clutch assembly. The friction discs must transfer all the engine torque to the driveline without slipping. Today's clutch discs must also absorb damaging engine torsional vibrations, cushion shock loads, and prevent gear rattle at idle. The clutch disc must do all this for many years of vehicle operation. For these reasons, the clutch discs can be thought of as the heart of the clutch. They are essential to successful clutch operation. Different types of clutch discs contribute varying benefits to the clutch system.

The friction facings on the clutch discs come in two distinct categories—organic and ceramic—both of which are available in rigid and or dampened disc styles. The dampened disc style provides torsional vibration control.

Organic Facings

Organic facings are made of various natural materials, such as cotton fibers, rubber material, aluminum, glass fibers, copper or

FIGURE 40-23 Organic friction discs.

brass fibers, and carbon material. These materials are blended together and formed into solid discs, such as the ones shown in **FIGURE 40-23**, which are then bonded or riveted to the outermost edge of the friction disc. Organic friction discs are made from a variety of carefully selected materials to give them the correct coefficient of friction.

Organic facings are usually attached to what are commonly called cushion segments, which are properly named marcel springs. The cushion segments or marcels are waved to create a slight space between the front and rear friction facing, as shown in **FIGURE 40-24**. On clutch engagement, these segments compress, allowing a gradual increase in clamp load and, therefore, friction. That gradual increase gives the vehicle a smoother start. As their name suggests, cushion segments cushion the engagement of the clutch and assist in release of the discs on clutch

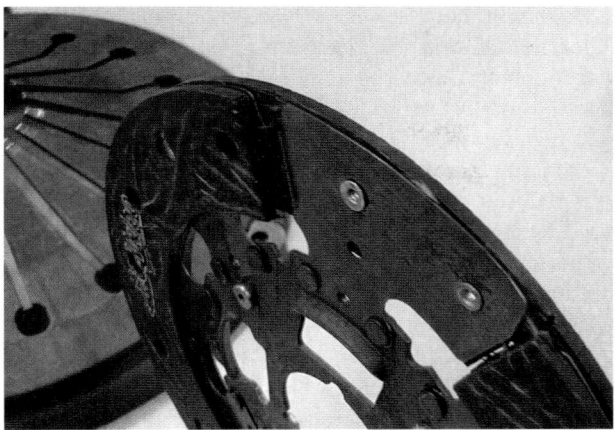

FIGURE 40-24 Cushion segments (marcel springs).

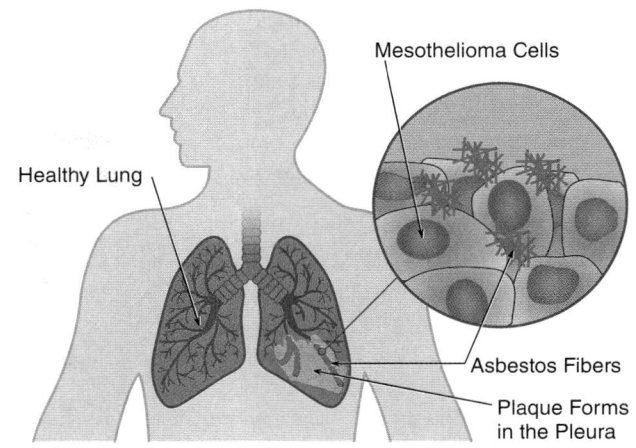

FIGURE 40-25 Mesothelioma is almost always fatal.

disengagement. Cushion segments are not normally used in heavy applications.

Organic facings are full-face linings. That means that the outer area of the disc is completely covered by the facing material. Organic facings normally have grooves cut into the facing from the central hub to the outside edge to allow for heat dissipation and removal of debris by centrifugal force. Although a clutch facing (clutch lining) is very thin when new—less than 1/8" (3–4 mm)—quite a large amount of dust and debris is present in the clutch housing when the clutch has worn out.

Dangers of Organic Facings

Asbestos used to be the material of choice in the production of friction materials because of its high heat resistance; however, in the late 1970s, asbestos was banned from use in friction materials in North America because of its carcinogenic qualities—a carcinogen can cause cancer. The ban has actually been lifted, but manufacturers in North America still voluntarily abstain from using asbestos in automotive friction materials. It is important to note that friction materials manufactured overseas and installed on imported new vehicles may still contain various amounts of asbestos. Therefore, use of some imported clutches or brake linings may expose a technician to asbestos. Exposure to asbestos fibers is known to cause asbestosis, which affects the lungs and is a precursor to lung cancer. Asbestos exposure is also a known cause of mesothelioma, a rare and almost always fatal condition affecting the outer lining of the lungs, the pleura, or the lining of the chest cavity (**FIGURE 40-25**). Asbestos can also affect the peritoneum, which is the lining of the stomach cavity.

Much debate surrounds the long-term effects of exposure to the newer organic friction material that contain no asbestos, but may contain other fine fibers, such as glass. Some critics argue that new materials are even worse than asbestos. The long-term effect of exposure to ceramic friction material dust is also not fully understood.

The safest bet for technicians is to protect themselves when servicing any vehicle by always wearing a National Institute of Occupational Safety and Health (NIOSH)-approved respirator and coveralls that protect street clothes from being contaminated by dust. Technicians should also vacuum any dust using a

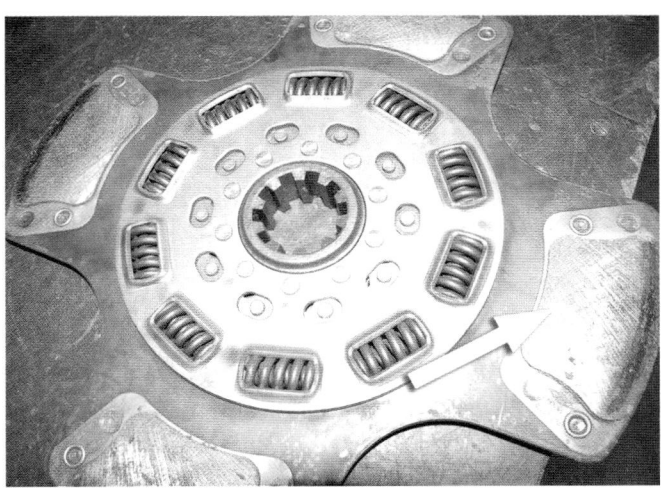

FIGURE 40-26 Ceramic facing.

vacuum with a HEPA filter, or wash dust off with a low-pressure water and contaminant containment system before working on clutches or brakes. After service, friction dust should be disposed of as a hazardous waste.

Ceramic Clutch Facings

In most medium-to-heavy applications, organic clutch discs have been replaced by discs with ceramic facings, such as the one shown in **FIGURE 40-26**. **Ceramic friction facings** are made mostly of man-made materials specifically designed to produce desirable characteristics. Specifically, ceramic facings have a much higher CoF and do not normally have a full-face lining.

Ceramic facings are made by mixing various man-made materials together, forming the material into the shape required, and then baking it. The material is then attached to a steel backing plate before being riveted to the disc. Ceramic facings have a much higher CoF and, therefore, do not require full-face linings to give satisfactory clutch torque capability. Consequently, ceramic discs have several pads or buttons around the disc surface with spaces in between. The spaces allow for excellent cooling and better debris removal.

Ceramic facings are very rarely full-face linings. Some extreme-duty applications, such as racing, may call for full-face linings. Ceramic facings are not attached to cushion segments in the way that some organic facings are. The lack of attachment to cushion segments or marcels, combined with their higher CoF, results in a much more abrupt clutch engagement when ceramic facings are used.

Rigid and Dampened Disc Styles

Both ceramic and organic discs are available in rigid and or dampened disc styles. **FIGURE 40-27** shows a dampened disc and a rigid disc. Dampened discs have a set of torsional dampening springs around their center hub. The springs are designed to absorb engine torsional vibrations. By contrast, rigid discs do not absorb these vibrations. Rigid discs are used in some severe-duty applications where dampened discs would not survive, and so are not usually found in on-highway vehicles.

Vibration Control

Every time an engine cylinder fires, it causes the crankshaft to twist, resulting in engine torsional vibrations. The twisting causes first an acceleration, then a deceleration of the engine crankshaft on each power stroke. The more torque the engine produces, the more severe the twisting force. Torsional vibrations can be responsible for severe driveline damage, including wearing of the input shaft spline, transmission input gear set, and drive axle gearing, as well as leakage of the transmission gasket and pinion seal.

These vibrations are exacerbated by engines that produce high torque at lower rpm. Manufacturers are trying to maximize fuel economy by downspeeding drivelines from a norm of 1425 rpm to as low as 1125 rpm. This means that a vehicle can be operated at highway speeds, but the engine is running at 1125 rpm. Fuel economy increases by 1% for every 100 rpm the operating rpm is reduced. But this fuel saving comes at a cost; driveline experts say that downspeeding from 1425 rpm to 1125 increases driveline torque by 36%. Even lower rpm are expected in the near future further increasing driveline torque. The primary defense against these damaging torsionals is the dampened clutch disc.

A dampened disc is constructed of several components attached together. The central hub is splined to the transmission input shaft, but it is not driven directly by the friction discs. Another disc, called the driven plate, sits around the central hub. The driven plate has a large slot that rotates around the central hub. This driven plate has slots for the torsional springs. The springs are usually coaxial, which simply means a spring inside a spring, so that the dampening force can be precisely selected for the application. The friction material is attached to this driven plate. **FIGURE 40-28** depicts a torsional dampening clutch disc.

Sandwiched on both sides of the drive plate are two or more spring cage plates that hold the torsional springs in place. These plates are rigidly attached to the central hub and contact the springs in the driven plate. The power flow for this arrangement then flows from the flywheel and pressure plate to the friction material attached to the driven plate. The flow continues through the coaxial torsion springs to the spring cage or cover plates and onto the central hub and the input shaft.

This means that the drive goes through the springs before it reaches the input shaft. The springs compress to absorb the acceleration of the crankshaft due to the firing pulses, effectively dampening the oscillations before they reach the driveline. Notice in **FIGURE 40-29** that the cutout in the clutch disc for

FIGURE 40-27 A. Rigid disc. **B.** Dampened disc.

1: Torque is transferred from flywheel/pressure plate to friction facing on the clutch plate.

2: Torque is transferred from the clutch plate and cover to the damper springs.

3: Damper springs compress to absorb torsional vibrations.

4: The damper springs transfer the torque to the splines hub.

Engine Coast

Compressed (during firing pulse)

Splined Hub

Damper Springs

Clutch Cover Plate (riveted to clutch plate)

Clutch Plate

Friction Facing

FIGURE 40-28 Manufacturers claim that over 90% of a clutch's duty cycle is absorbing torsional vibrations.

the splined hub is quite a bit larger than the hub. This allows the torsional springs to be compressed as they transfer drive to the hub, thereby absorbing torsional vibrations. There are stop pins that limit how far the driven plate can move around the central hub to protect the torsional springs.

The disc in **FIGURE 40-29** is only one design used for dampening. Many manufacturers use different designs, such as the one shown in **FIGURE 40-30**, but the effect is the same in that the friction material can only drive the input shaft through torsional springs, thereby dampening the vibrations. Regardless of the style used, **dampening discs** all allow the driven disc to rotate against springs before the drive reaches the driven hub, absorbing and dampening damaging torsional vibration before it reaches the transmission and the rest of the driveline.

In some applications, more dampening is required, particularly in today's engines that can achieve extremely high torque at relatively low rpm. When an engine produces high torque at low rpm, the amount of torque produced for each firing pulse must be larger. This causes greater twisting of the crankshaft and, therefore, more torsional vibration. When peak torque is reached at lower rpm, the likelihood of the driveline being in a resonant condition is also much greater. All drivelines have a **resonant frequency**, which is the point at which the driveline enters into a resonant condition, where all the components start to oscillate in unison.

The best example of **resonance** is an opera singer hitting high C and shattering a crystal glass. The frequency of the singer's voice matches the resonant frequency of the crystal and the crystal's molecules vibrate wildly until the glass shatters. For vehicles, resonance is the frequency at which the driveline's vibrations are the most damaging. Driveline resonance occurs when the frequency of the engine's firing pulses matches the resonant frequency of that particular driveline. The matching frequencies greatly amplify the damaging twisting forces delivered by the crankshaft and can very quickly cause extreme driveline damage, such as spline wear, shaft breakage due to fatigue, and vibration-induced oil leaks. Many factors influence the resonant point of a driveline; configuration; whether 6 × 4 or 6 × 2 drive, driveshaft and u-joint sizing, axle ratios, wheel base, and more affect the resonant frequency of a particular driveline.

Clutch manufacturers have engineered what are commonly known as **soft-dampened clutches** to combat this situation. Soft-dampened clutches have much longer travel when dampening, which allows them to better combat resonance in a driveline. Soft-dampened clutches can be recognized by the larger windows in the spring cage plates that surround their stop pins. **FIGURE 40-31** shows a dampened clutch with a normal travel damper and a soft dampened clutch disc with a long travel damper. Compare the images. Notice the difference in the available travel of the dampening discs before they contact the stop

FIGURE 40-29 The large cutout in the clutch disc allows it to rotate around the splined hub in the center.

FIGURE 40-31 A. Normal travel damper. **B.** Long travel damper. Stop pins are circled on each.

FIGURE 40-30 A dampening disc.

pins. These clutches have the tendency to lower the rpm of the resonance point for the driveline and put it out of the normal rpm operating range of the vehicle.

Some manufacturers also use **friction dampening**. Friction dampening involves controlling torsional vibration by placing friction material between the spring cage plates of the clutch disc and the friction driven plate. In order to start dampening movement, this friction must be overcome, and that process helps to further dampen the oscillations. Some manufacturers of lighter-duty vehicles use a dual-mass flywheel, such as the one shown in **FIGURE 40-32**, to further reduce these torsional vibrations. A **dual-mass flywheel** has one section of the flywheel that is bolted to the engine crankshaft. This section drives a series of coaxial springs that, in turn, transmit that drive force to a second section to which the clutch assembly is bolted. Dual-mass flywheels, such as the one in Figure 40-32, are not currently being used on heavy-duty applications. When a vehicle is equipped with a dual-mass flywheel, it may use a rigid clutch disc or a dampened disc to enhance the vibration absorption.

Another problem associated with high-torque, electronically controlled engines is that of transmission gear rattle at idle caused by torsional accelerations of the crankshaft. The damper springs used to absorb loaded torsional vibrations are too strong to absorb these unloaded accelerations. Consequently, the transmission gears rattle at idle. The latest clutch discs have an added set of very light dampening springs that are in series with the normal torsion-dampening springs in the clutch disc. These light dampening springs must be compressed for the normal dampening springs to react. In no or very light load situations, such as idle, these springs absorb the torsional vibrations associated with gear rattle. Eaton, ZF Sachs AG, and Meritor call this **"pre-dampening."** **FIGURE 40-33** shows pre-dampening springs on a clutch disc.

The lengths manufacturers go to reduce these vibrations shows that they are a very serious concern. It is important for the technician to remember, when replacing any of these components, to replace them with new parts that meet or exceed the manufacturer's specifications.

Flywheels

As defined earlier in this chapter, a flywheel is a heavy round metal disc attached to the end of the crankshaft. The flywheel has several purposes. First, it normally has the ring gear attached to it so that the engine can be started. Second, it provides an inertial mass that keeps the engine rotating between firing impulses. Third, the flywheel's resistance to acceleration and deceleration helps to smooth out torsional vibrations, and last, the flywheel provides a mounting place for the clutch assembly.

Flywheels also have the surface against which the clutch friction disc is clamped. Flywheels are quite heavy, the weight is tailored to the application and, because of this, the flywheel carries considerable inertia as it rotates. That is, once they are rotating at a certain speed they tend to keep rotating, and this allows the engine to run smoothly in between firing cycles. The flywheel's inertia also helps in torsional dampening because of their mass. The accelerations of the crankshaft caused by torsional vibrations are somewhat subdued by the energy required to try to accelerate and decelerate the heavy flywheel.

Flywheels come in two basic designs. **Flat-type flywheels**, such as the one shown in **FIGURE 40-34**, have all of the clutch components inside the clutch cover and the cover bolts to the flywheel. This is the most common type of flywheel in use today. The second type is the 14" (35.6 cm) pot-type flywheel shown in **FIGURE 40-35**. In the **pot-type flywheel**, the clutch friction discs and the intermediate plate are installed into the "pot" shape of the flywheel and the clutch cover containing the pressure plate bolts to the back of the flywheel. If the flywheel has a raised bolt circle where the clutch cover mounts, it is extremely important

FIGURE 40-32 Dual-mass flywheel.

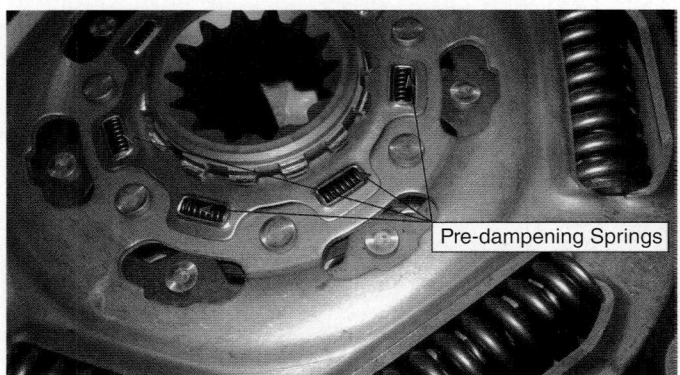

FIGURE 40-33 Pre-dampening springs absorb idle torsional vibration to prevent gear rattle.

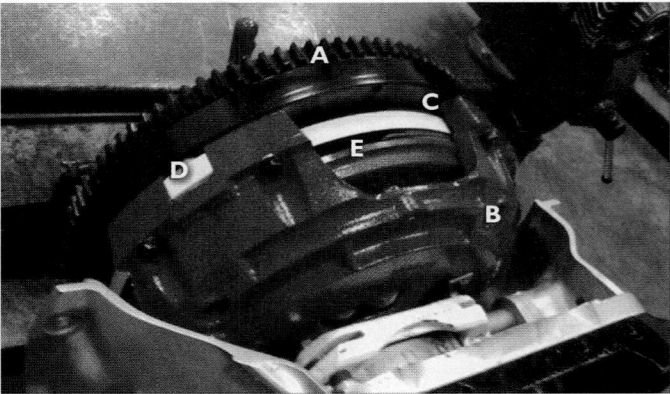

FIGURE 40-34 Flat-type flywheel. **A.** Flywheel. **B.** Clutch cover. **C.** Intermediate plate. **D.** Intermediate plate drive lugs. **E.** Friction discs.

that, when the flywheel face is resurfaced, the raised bolt circle is machined by the same amount in order to maintain the correct clamp load. If the bolt circle is not ground down by the same amount, the flywheel friction surface is further away from the clutch pressure plate. That distance causes the springs to extend, reducing clamp load.

Intermediate Plates

The intermediate plate is the plate that contacts the back of the forward clutch friction disc and the front of the rear friction disc on dual-disc clutches. This cast iron plate is necessary for all dual-disc designs and creates a "friction sandwich" of flywheel, front friction disc, intermediate plate, rear friction disc, and the pressure plate. Torque is transferred to the intermediate plate either directly from the clutch cover through lugs that engage slots in the cover or through drive straps. In older pot-type flywheel designs, the intermediate plate is driven by **drive pins** installed in the flywheel itself. Intermediate plate drive lugs and drive pins are indicated on the flywheels shown in Figures 40-34 and 40-35.

Pilot Bearings and Release Bearings

Pilot bearings are so called because they carry the pilot end of the input shaft. This often-overlooked bearing is extremely important. It allows the input shaft to be supported straddle style. That is, the front of the shaft is supported in the pilot bearing and the rear of the shaft is supported in the transmission input bearing mounted in the transmission case. This holds the shaft solidly when the clutch discs are disengaged and ensures the shaft remains centered.

The pilot bearing may be as simple as a brass bushing or needle bearing mounted in a pocket formed in the rear of the crankshaft, as is common on light-duty vehicles. Larger vehicles more commonly use a ball bearing mounted in the center of the flywheel, as shown in **FIGURE 40-36**. Regardless of the type, this bearing should always be replaced when replacing the clutch, even if it seems to be fine. The added cost to replace it during a clutch servicing is incidental compared to the costs that would be incurred to replace the bearing separately at a later date, should it fail.

As its name implies, the release bearing is used to release clamp force on the clutch friction discs. In lighter-duty applications, the release bearing may also be called the throw-out bearing. But in heavy applications, release bearing is a more common term. This bearing allows a stationary clutch fork to apply pressure to a rotating clutch's release levers or fingers. The pressure allows the clutch to cage the pressure plate spring(s) and interrupt power flow to the transmission. In a push-type clutch, the release bearing is part of a housing with a hollow center. The hollow part of this housing rides on a sleeve that is part of the transmission input bearing cover. The input shaft passes through this sleeve, and the release bearing housing is on the outside of the sleeve.

The release bearing itself is a ball bearing that is specially designed so that it can withstand both axial and radial loading. The push-type clutch release bearing, shown in **FIGURE 40-37**, is typical, in that it is a sealed unit. That means that it cannot be lubricated periodically, but there may be a grease fitting to lubricate the release bearing housing where it slides on the input shaft sleeve. The **release fork** (or **yoke**), also shown in Figure 40-37, is the lever that is actuated by the clutch linkage and moves the release bearing. On push-type clutches, the release fork engages a groove in the release bearing housing.

The release lever is mounted on a cross shaft or on a pivot in the clutch bell housing so that when the driver pushes the clutch pedal down, the release bearing and its housing move

FIGURE 40-36 Pilot bearing.

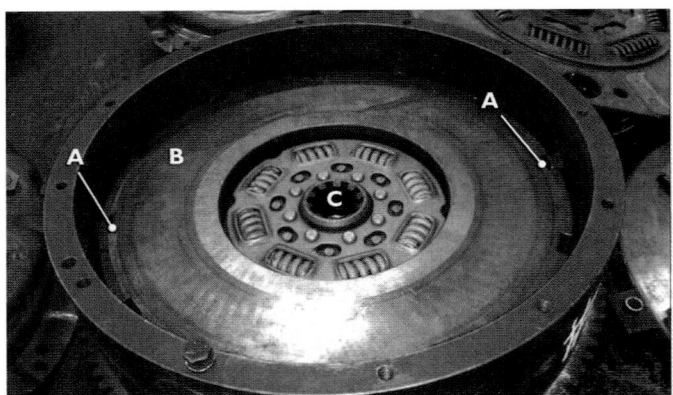

FIGURE 40-35 Pot-type flywheel. **A.** Intermediate plate drive pins. **B.** Intermediate plate. **C.** Front driven disc.

FIGURE 40-37 Push-type clutch release bearing with housing lubrication hose and fork with cross-shaft.

toward the clutch release levers or fingers. The release bearing in a push-type clutch typically does not actually rotate until in comes in contact with the release fingers or levers of the pressure plate. This is important to remember when diagnosing clutch noise complaints. Once the bearing is pushed against the fingers or levers with sufficient force, the pressure plate spring(s) is (are) caged, and the clutch is disengaged. Even though the push-type clutch release bearing is more expensive than a pilot bearing, the release bearing should always be replaced when a clutch is replaced. That is because, like the flywheel pilot bearing, replacing the release bearing during a clutch replacement is less expensive than doing it separately because of failure later.

SAFETY TIP

The release bearing in a push-type clutch is designed only for periodic rotation when disengaging the clutch. If the driver rides the pedal or the clutch adjustment is incorrect, the bearing is constantly rotating. That constant rotation causes it to overheat and causes the permanent lubricating grease to liquefy and run out of the bearing, leading to premature bearing failure.

In a pull-type clutch, the release bearing performs the same function as in a push-type clutch—to release the clutch—but the pull-type's design is quite different. The pull-type clutch release bearing is integral to the clutch. That means it is permanently attached to the clutch cover and, in most cases, is not serviced separately (**FIGURE 40-38**). The release bearing, again, is a ball bearing designed to handle axial and radial thrust loads. The transmission input bearing cover used with a pull-type clutch does not have a sleeve, as it does in the push-type clutch. Instead, the release bearing is encompassed in a hollow housing. The outer race of the bearing is attached to the housing itself, and the inner race is attached to a sleeve. Inside the sleeve, there are two bronze bushings that allow the sleeve to ride on the transmission input shaft. This sleeve, in turn, attaches to what is commonly referred to as a retainer. It is the retainer that actually engages the release levers. Pull-type clutch release bearings usually require periodic lubrication. It is important to not overlook this service procedure.

The release fork in a pull-type clutch with mechanical clutch linkage is "U" shaped and is attached to a cross shaft that is mounted inside the clutch bell housing. As shown in **FIGURE 40-39**, the "U" shape of the fork fits closely over the outside of the release bearing housing from the top, holding it stationary.

As noted earlier in this section, the inner race of the release bearing is attached to the sleeve and the retainer inside the clutch. The retainer is fixed to the release levers, so all three turn with the clutch. Consequently, the inner race of the release bearing is rotating any time the engine is running.

To disengage the clutch, the driver actuates the clutch pedal. Actuating the pedal causes the cross shaft and the "U" shaped fork to rotate the ends of the "U" contact wear pads located on the front of the release bearing housing and pull the bearing to the rear. This action pulls the retainer and the release levers to the rear, which cages the pressure plate spring(s), disengaging the clutch. Most pull-type clutch release bearings need to be lubricated as part of regular maintenance procedures and are equipped with a grease fitting to allow this. There are, however, some permanently lubed designs as well. In some installations, a hose is attached to the release bearing and connected to a grease Zerk, or grease nipple, on the outside of the bell housing so that the bearing can be lubricated more easily. Figure 40-39 shows a release bearing with an attached grease hose. In later-model

FIGURE 40-39 The release fork fits over the non-rotating release bearing housing in a pull-type clutch. **A.** Release bearing. **B.** Release fork. **C.** Cross shaft. **D.** Clutch housing. **E.** Clutch brake. **F.** Transmission front bearing cover.

FIGURE 40-38 Pull-type clutch release bearing. **A.** Lubrication tube. **B.** Release bearing.

trucks equipped with pull-type clutch and hydraulic linkage, a different style of release fork is used. This release fork is referred to as a catapult fork or lever because of it shape.

A catapult release fork and a typical older-style release fork are shown in **FIGURE 40-40**. The catapult fork is mounted on a pivot at the bottom of a specially formed clutch bell housing that has an opening where the hydraulic clutch actuation cylinder bolts to and engages the release lever. It is important to note, however, that when a hydraulic clutch actuator is used, the driver does not experience loss of free pedal in the cab to indicate clutch wear **FIGURE 40-41**. This is because the hydraulic actuator always keeps the release fork in light contact with the release bearing, even as the clutch discs wear. Because of this, the clutch can be out of adjustment with no visible indication.

FIGURE 40-40 A. A catapult clutch release fork. **B.** A traditional clutch fork.

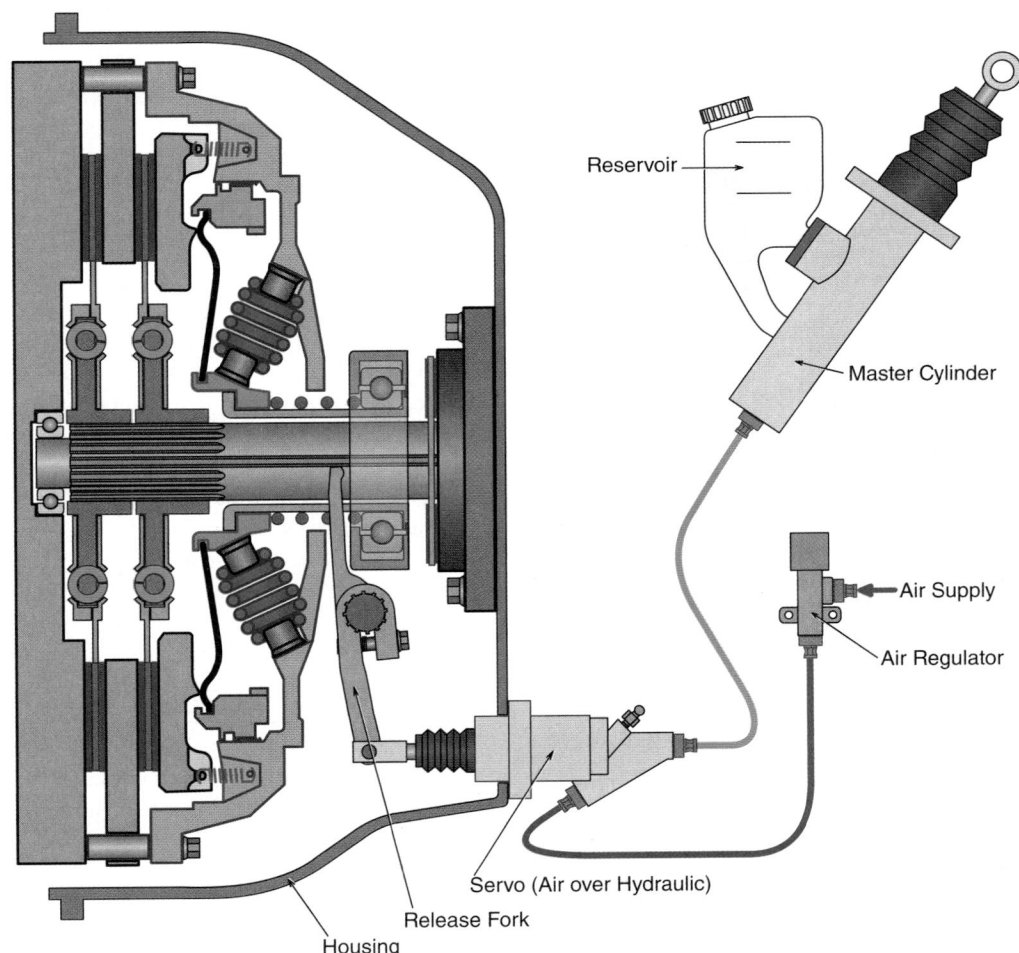

FIGURE 40-41 Many manufacturers are going to hydraulic clutch actuation systems, like this one from Eaton.

These installations must be monitored carefully on a regular basis to ensure that clutch adjustment is correct, or should use self-adjusting clutches, such as the Solo clutch.

Housings

The clutch and all its components are contained inside the flywheel housing and the clutch housing. These are the two mating housings between the engine and the transmission. The flywheel housing is the circular housing that is bolted to the engine and surrounds the flywheel. The flywheel housing is usually constructed from either cast iron or cast aluminum and typically has an opening to accept the starter motor, which bolts to the housing. The flywheel housing may or may not contain an inspection opening and an installation point for an engine barring tool (a small gear bolted to the housing that can be used to manually turn the engine flywheel). There may also be mounting holes in the housing for sensors and lock/positioning pins to be installed. The clutch housing (also sometimes known as a clutch bell housing) is also constructed of cast iron or cast aluminum and is bolted to the front of the transmission. In most transmissions, it is replaceable without transmission disassembly. In some of the newer automated transmissions, however, it forms part of the transmission housing and replacement requires transmission over-haul. The clutch housing usually has a removable inspection cover that allows access to inspect the clutch and to lube the release bearing. The clutch housing also contains the support system for the clutch release fork, where required. In most applications, this is a cross-shaft that is supported in bores in the housing. **FIGURE 40-42** shows a typical clutch housing.

FIGURE 40-42 A typical clutch housing bolted to a transmission.

TABLE 40-1 SAE Flywheel Housing Bore Size Chart		
SAE NUMBER	**BORE DIAMETER**	
	Inches	Millimeters (mm)
00	31.0	787.4
0	25.5	647.7
1/2	23.0	584.2
1	20.0	511.2
2	17.625	447.7
3	16.125	409.6

Flywheel housing and clutch housing mate together precisely to maintain alignment of the crankshaft centerline and the transmission input shaft centerline. The clutch housing has a raised pilot that fits into a precise bore on the flywheel housing to ensure this alignment. Misalignment of the crankshaft and transmission input shaft can lead to seal failures and shaft and/ or bearing damage in the transmission. The flywheel and clutch housings are sized according to SAE specifications, as shown in **TABLE 40-1**.

Clutch Brakes

LO 40-4 Explain the purpose and function of clutch brakes.

Pull-type clutches can be found in many sizes of trucks from class 5 all the way to class 8, but they are usually found on most class 7 and 8 trucks (with the exception of those that are equipped with certain automated manual transmissions). Most class 7 or 8 trucks that have manual transmissions are equipped with twin, or even triple, countershaft non-synchronized gear boxes. Unlike most light-duty transmissions that have synchronizers to prevent gear clash (or grinding) while shifting, these types of transmissions require the driver to match shaft and gear speeds manually during a shift, or gear clashing occurs. The input shaft, the countershafts, and all the main-shaft gearing are rotating when these vehicles are idling in neutral with the clutch engaged. When the driver wants to select first gear or reverse, he first depresses the clutch pedal to disengage the engine. The inertia of the rotating components tends to keep them rotating, however, so if the driver tries to engage a gear, the difference in speed between the rotating gear and the stationary main shaft causes tremendous clashing. The rotating components have no load on them and little resistance to rotation, so they may continue to rotate for over a minute before a clash-free shift can be made.

Pull-type clutches facilitate the use of a clutch brake that can alleviate this problem. A **clutch brake** is a small frictional brake usually mounted on the transmission input shaft and designed to slow down or stop the transmission rotation when the driver wishes to engage first or reverse from a neutral position. The clutch brake is mounted on the input shaft between the release bearing and the transmission input bearing housing.

The input shaft has two splines that run its entire length, and the clutch brake has two matching teeth that fit into the splines. The rear of the release bearing housing has a smooth surface, as does the front of the transmission input bearing cover. The clutch brake has friction material on the front and back sides that contact these smooth surfaces. **FIGURE 40-43** shows a typical clutch brake and the bearing cover frictional surface.

As the driver disengages the clutch, the release bearing moves backward toward the transmission. If the driver pushes the clutch pedal all the way to the floor, the clutch brake is squeezed between the release bearing housing and the transmission input bearing cover so that the input shaft rotation is stopped. This allows the driver to select first or reverse gear without gear clash. Stopping the input shaft with the brake saves

FIGURE 40-43 The clutch brake is squeezed between the back of the release bearing and the front of the transmission bearing cover to slow the input shaft and the transmission gearing.

FIGURE 40-45 Torque-limiting clutch brake.

FIGURE 40-44 Three two-piece clutch brakes and one torque-limiting clutch brake (bottom right).

the time needed to wait for the shafts and gears to stop spinning on their own.

A clutch brake may pose a problem for the inexperienced driver, however. The clutch brake is actuated within the last 1" (2.5 cm) of clutch pedal travel. If the driver pushes the clutch pedal to the floor when making upshifts as the vehicle is moving, the clutch brake is destroyed very quickly. When engaged while the vehicle is moving and in gear, the clutch brake is attempting to stop the input shaft. When in gear, the input shaft is connected through the transmission gearing to the rear axle of the vehicle. The result is that, for the second before the driver actually shifts to neutral to make the shift, the clutch brake is trying to stop the entire vehicle. If the driver hits the clutch brake on upshifts and downshifts, the brake usually fails within days.

There are three general types of clutch brakes: conventional, torque-limiting, and limited torque. There are also aftermarket replacement brakes that are in two pieces so they can be installed without removing the transmission. **FIGURE 40-44** shows a variety of clutch brakes.

Conventional Clutch Brake

The conventional clutch brake is a solid piece of metal with friction material on either side. To install a conventional clutch brake, the transmission must be removed. In order to avoid the associated labor costs, aftermarket versions of this brake are made in a two-piece design that allows them to be replaced without removing the transmission. When installing a two-piece clutch brake, the original clutch brake is carefully cut off of the input shaft using a die grinder or an oxyacetylene torch. The two pieces are then put into place and connected together.

SAFETY TIP

Extreme caution must be taken to not damage the input shaft if using an oxyacetylene torch inside the clutch bell housing. An accumulation of grease, oil, and clutch dust can also result in a fire. Therefore, always clean the area first and be prepared with a fire extinguisher to douse any flames, should fire erupt. It is much safer to use a die grinder or other cutting tool for this purpose, but again exercise extreme caution to not damage the input shaft.

Torque-Limiting Clutch Brake

The torque-limiting clutch brake, like that shown in **FIGURE 40-45**, is the brake of choice of most manufacturers. The reason it is preferred is that it is designed to slip should the torque applied exceed its setting—typically 25 ft-lb (34 Nm). The brake consists of an outer housing. Attached to the housing are the friction material and a separate inner hub that is splined to the input shaft. Two Belleville (diaphragm spring)-type spring washers are placed inside the housing on either side of the inner hub to exert pressure against the hub. The brake is designed so that when approximately 25 ft-lb (34 Nm) of torque is twisting against the inner hub, the hub slips inside the housing protecting the clutch brake. This design allows a modicum of tolerance for an inexperienced driver who hits the clutch brake while upshifting. A key advantage of the torque-limiting clutch brake, therefore, is that it allows some latitude for driver error and lasts longer than the conventional clutch brake if the driver actuates the brake while the vehicle is moving. If the driver hits the clutch brake repeatedly while shifting, however, even this design fails. Driver training on the proper use of clutch brakes is essential.

Limiting Torque Clutch Brake

The limiting torque design of clutch brake is, for all intents and purposes, obsolete today; it was used for the same purposes as the brakes listed above and was also designed to assist in upshifts. **FIGURE 40-46** is an illustration of this type of clutch brake, which was also called an upshift brake.

Limiting torque clutch brakes allowed a highly experienced double-clutching driver to quickly reduce engine speed in neutral during an upshift. At that point in the shift, the transmission main shaft is slowing faster than the engine and main shaft gearing because of heavy loading or steep grades. The limiting torque clutch allowed a fractional increase in shifting speed when used by a highly skilled driver.

Eaton Corporation is using this faster upshifting strategy in some of its newer UltraShift transmission models. UltraShift transmissions use a computer-controlled clutch system that also controls either an electrical inertia brake mounted on the side of the transmission or a low-capacity inertia brake (LCIB) mounted where a traditional clutch brake would be to manipulate engine and shaft speeds during upshifts. An electric **inertia brake** (**FIGURE 40-47**) is a type of transmission shaft brake geared to one countershaft, which controls gearing rotational speed while shifting. The LCIB (**FIGURE 40-48**) is actuated by the electric clutch actuator moving the release bearing in much

the same way as a traditional clutch brake. Regardless of the brake type used, the result is a slight increase in shifting speed. Computer control allows perfect speed matching of gears and shafts and provides clash-free shifts—even with the most inexperienced driver.

Clutch Actuation Systems

LO 40-5 Describe and explain the function of various clutch actuation systems.

Different clutches use different actuation systems. Most clutches in heavy-duty vehicles are actuated by mechanical linkage systems, but hydraulic, air-assisted hydraulic, automatic, centrifugal, electrical, and wet clutch actuation systems are also in use.

Mechanical Linkage

Most medium- to heavy-duty truck clutches are actuated by mechanical linkage systems. The actuation system starts with the clutch pedal. The pedal is usually a first or second-class lever that helps the driver to overcome the tremendous clamp loads associated with modern clutches. Clamp loads can be more than 4000 lb (1814 kg). Without leverage, a driver would not be able

FIGURE 40-47 Electrically operated inertia brake.

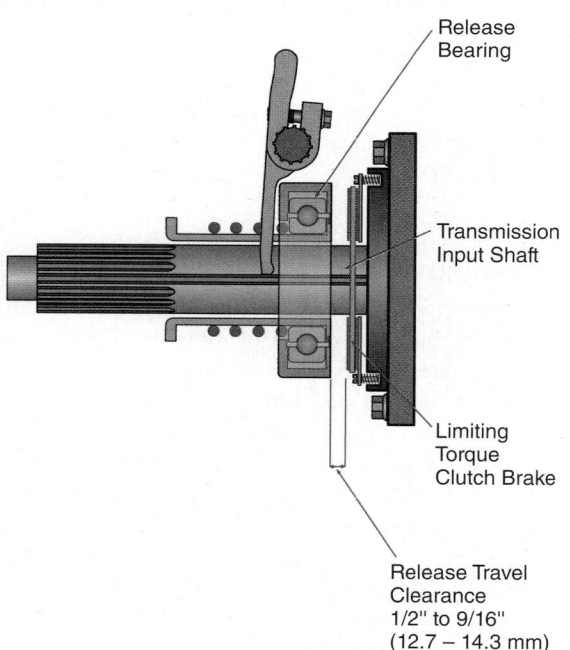

FIGURE 40-46 The design for a limiting torque (upshift) clutch brake.

Release Bearing

Transmission Input Shaft

Limiting Torque Clutch Brake

Release Travel Clearance 1/2" to 9/16" (12.7 – 14.3 mm)

FIGURE 40-48 Low-capacity inertia brake (LCIB) used on Eaton's latest UltraShift transmissions.

to release the clutch. As illustrated in **FIGURE 40-49**, the clutch pedal attaches to a series of rods, bellcranks, and levers supported by the vehicle body and frame. Those components are, in turn, attached to the cross-shaft at the clutch bell housing. The release fork is rotated by the cross-shaft to pull the release bearing.

The levers in the clutch linkage and inside the clutch assembly compound the force of the driver's foot on the pedal. That leverage allows a force of around 50 to 60 lb (22 to 27 kg) to cage the 3200 lb or 4000 lb (1451 kg or 1814 kg) clamping force. But, as we know when we use levers to compound force, we give up something in return. In this case, we sacrifice distance.

The driver may push the pedal through 10" or 11" (25 or 28 cm) of travel, but the release bearing only moves 0.5" (1.3 cm) or so. The pressure plate inside the clutch cover usually only moves 0.15" to 0.20" (0.381 to 0.508 cm) and allows approximately 0.05" (0.127 cm) clearance on each side of each clutch disc in order for it to spin freely. With such a small amount of clearance for the discs, it is clear that any warping or damage to the discs could cause the discs to stay partially pressed against the flywheel or pressure plate when disengaged—which could cause clashing shifts. In some cases, the rods, levers, and

bellcranks of a mechanical linkage system can be replaced by a cable, as illustrated in **FIGURE 40-50**. Cable linkage allows more flexibility in component location and the connection of components, but cable linkage systems are not as popular as mechanical linkage in heavy-duty vehicles.

Hydraulic Actuation Systems

Hydraulically actuated clutches, such as the one as illustrated in **FIGURE 40-51**, consist of a clutch master cylinder and push rod that is connected to the clutch pedal. A clutch **slave cylinder** is mounted at the transmission to actuate the cross-shaft and a hydraulic circuit connects the two. At least a portion of this circuit has a flex hose so that movement of the driveline does not affect the solid hydraulic line. When the driver pushes the pedal, two simultaneous actions occur: the hydraulic circuit is pressurized and the slave cylinder push rod pushes the cross-shaft lever. Mechanical advantage is gained in two ways. First, it is gained by the effective lever length of the pedal. Second, mechanical advantage is increased by using a larger piston in the slave cylinder than in the master cylinder. Many manufacturers are now using hydraulic actuation systems with the catapult release lever shown earlier.

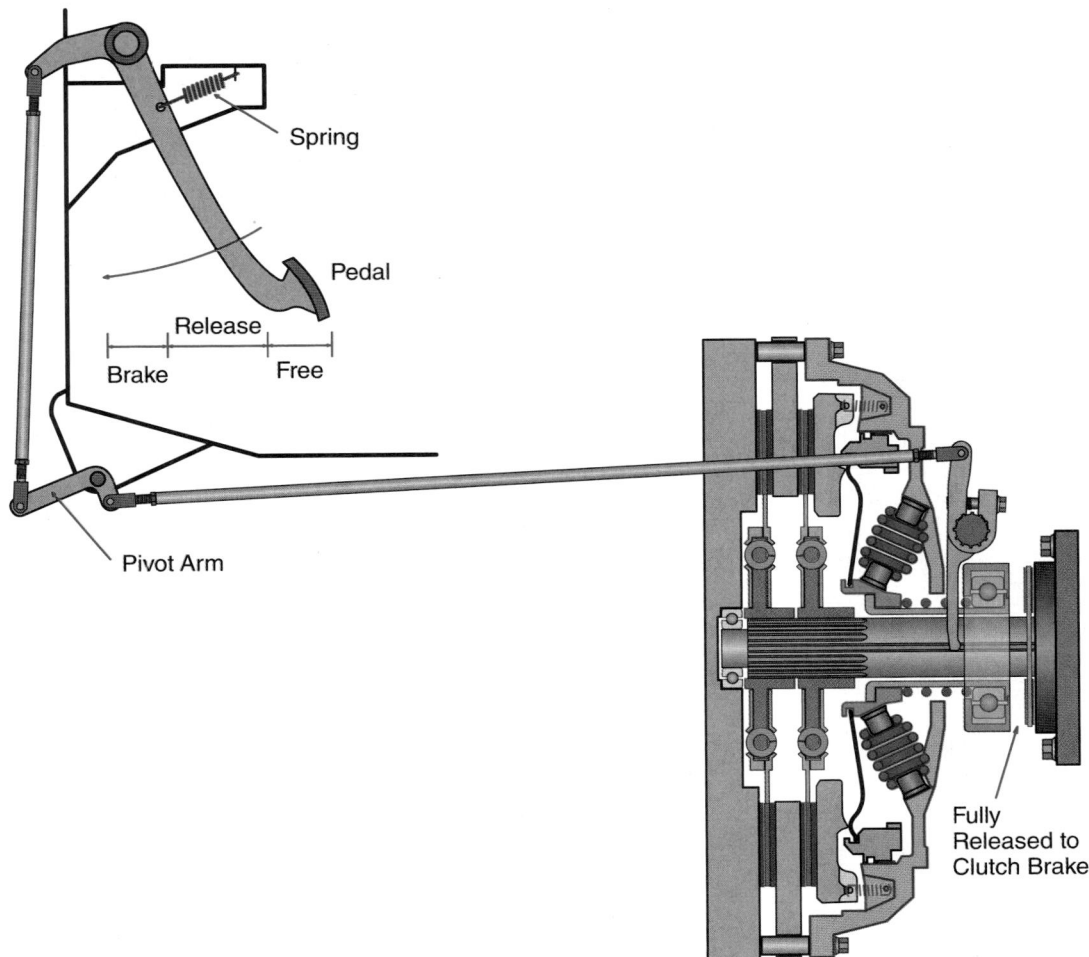

FIGURE 40-49 Mechanical linkage is the most popular actuation system for on-highway trucks, although hydraulic actuation systems are becoming more and more popular.

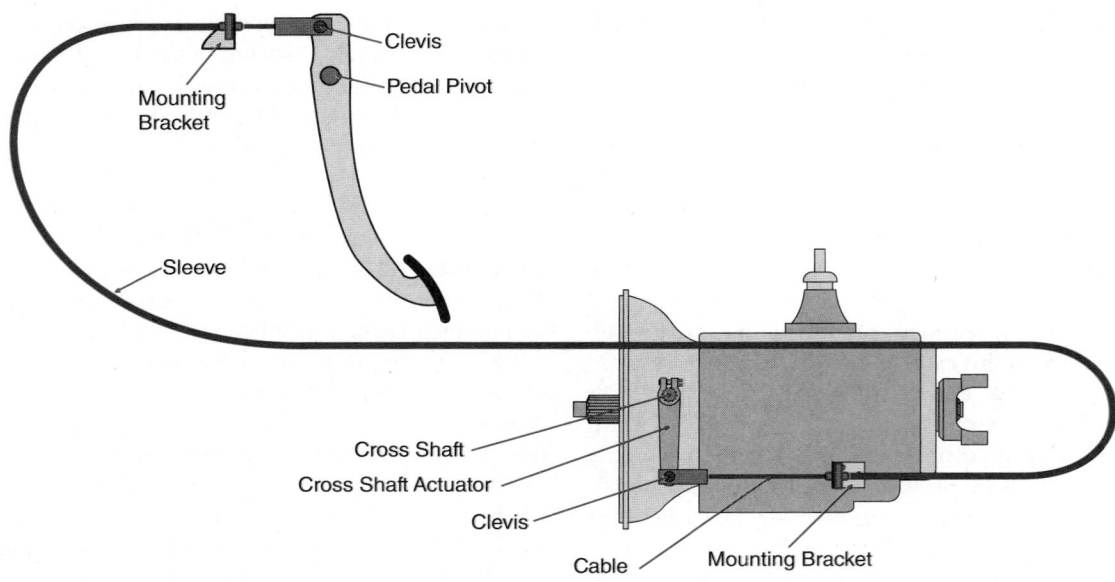

FIGURE 40-50 Cable linkage clutch actuation system.

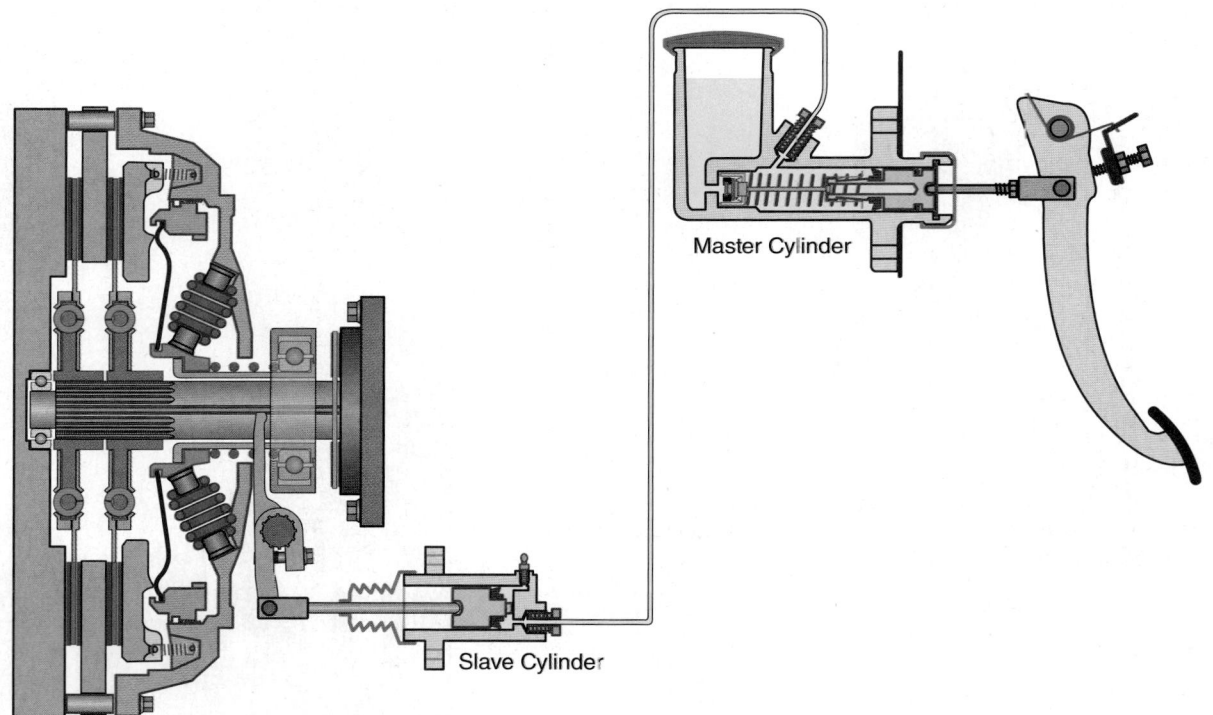

FIGURE 40-51 Hydraulic clutch actuation systems are becoming more popular today.

Air-Assisted Hydraulic Actuation Systems

Air-assisted hydraulic actuation systems are generally similar to hydraulic systems with one important difference—instead of the master cylinder pressure acting directly on the slave cylinder and the cross-shaft lever, the master cylinder controls a reaction plunger and a pilot valve, which allows air pressure to act on a servo piston to move the cross-shaft lever.

As the driver pushes on the pedal and pressure in the circuit increases, the reaction plunger moves first to seal off the air exhaust port. Further movement of the pedal moves the pilot valve and allows air to act on the servo piston. As pressure builds in the servo piston chamber, it pushes back against the reaction plunger, which then seats the pilot valve. Consequently, air pressure is held. In this way, the driver can control how much pressure is exerted on the clutch and gains a feel for the clutch pedal. When the driver eases up on the pedal, the reaction piston and the pilot valve move to seal off the air inlet and open the exhaust port, allowing the clutch to engage.

Automatically Actuated Clutches

Vehicles equipped with automated manual transmissions—that is, transmissions that shift themselves with little or no input from the driver—usually require automatically operated clutches. Three-pedal auto-shift systems from Eaton were equipped with a clutch pedal, and the driver was required to use the clutch only when starting off in first or reverse. Newer systems are fully automated, but even though there is no clutch pedal, there is still a clutch. The following are the clutches used with these fully automated transmissions.

Two-Pedal Centrifugal Clutch Actuation System

The Eaton two-pedal UltraShift transmission system was the first system on the market that did not use a traditional clutch pedal. Instead, it used a self-engaging clutch called the DM AutoClutch, also known as the data mechanical clutch (pictured in **FIGURE 40-52**). The clutch has no release bearing and is equipped with four heavy spring-loaded weights that serve to engage the clutch.

When the engine is rotating below approximately 850 rpm, the springs keep the weights inboard and the clutch remains disengaged. As the engine speed passes 850 rpm, the weights overcome the spring force and move outward with the increasing centrifugal force. The rollers on the weights ride against the ramps on the pressure plate, forcing it to move toward the flywheel clamping the clutch discs. The clamp force increases with engine rpm until approximately 1200 rpm, at which point the peak clamp force of around 4000 lb (1814 kg) is achieved. As the engine is decelerated, the springs force the weights inboard, starting at approximately 1100 rpm and continuing until the rpm passes 850, at which time the rollers move off the ramps on the pressure plate and laminated drive straps pull the pressure plate back toward the transmission, releasing the clutch discs.

It is important to note that this clutch is in a disengaged position at rest. When installing the clutch, a jack bolt must be used to clamp the pressure plate and hold the friction discs

in place after they have been centered by the clutch disc alignment tool. When these clutches were first introduced, they were used on the heavy-duty, twin-countershaft, UltraShift models. Medium-duty, single-countershaft, UltraShift transmissions used an electric clutch actuator. This AutoClutch had a couple of problems when it was introduced. First, the clutch uses two ceramic-faced clutch discs with a high CoF and, subsequently, it had a very abrupt engagement. Second, if a driver tried to be conscientious and avoid the abrupt engagement by feathering the throttle, the clutch experienced significant wear and overheating. Because of these concerns, this clutch is no longer offered in new builds and has been replaced by the electronic clutch actuator.

Electrically Actuated Clutches

Eaton Corporation now uses an electronic clutch actuator (ECA), as shown in **FIGURE 40-53** on all medium- and heavy-duty UltraShift transmission models. The ECA uses an electric

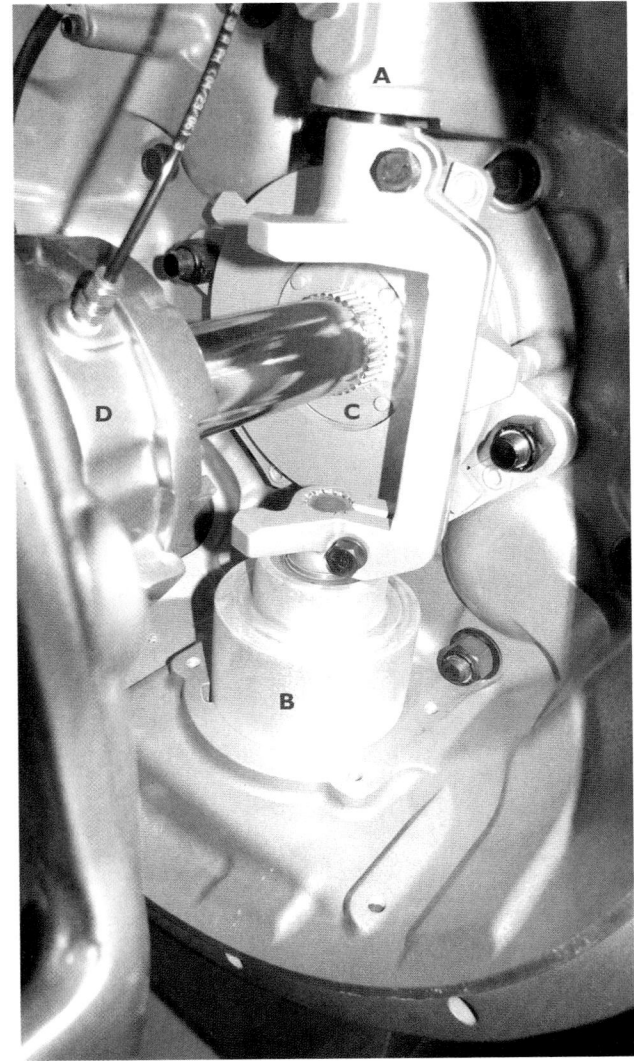

FIGURE 40-53 An electronic clutch actuator (ECA). **A.** Cross shaft. **B.** ECA. **C.** Heavy-duty inertia brake (clutch brake). **D.** Release bearing.

FIGURE 40-52 A disassembled DM AutoClutch. **A.** Weights. **B.** Rollers and springs. **C.** Pressure plate. **D.** Ramps.

motor driving three interconnected planetary gear sets to release the clutch and to actuate the new heavy-duty inertia brake on the input shaft. The three interconnected planetary gears allow the motor to achieve a gear reduction of approximately 30:1.

This computer-controlled actuator is used to move the release bearing to a released position and to engage the clutch. The ECA is a 41-volt stepper motor equipped with on board electronics that make it a mechatronic device, that is, the motor can give feedback to the transmission ECU about its functioning and position. **FIGURE 40-54** shows a partially disassembled ECA.

The computer-controlled actuator also applies an input shaft-mounted inertia brake (similar to a clutch brake) when needed. This allows the computer to control engine speed precisely by manipulating the inertia brake on upshifts while in neutral, leading to incrementally faster upshifts. Eaton claims that by using this procedure, its UltraShift transmission can shift through 18 speeds on a 15% grade while pulling 160,000 lb (72,574 kg)—a feat that very few professional drivers could accomplish. Many manufacturers are experimenting with automatic clutches. The latest versions of these auto-clutches feature different designs—air-actuated, electrically actuated, or computer-controlled hydraulic actuation.

Wet Clutches

Eaton's transmission model FO-8406-ASW uses a computer-actuated wet clutch. Wet clutches have been used in the past by Mack and many European manufacturers. Those wet clutches were typically multi-disc clutches actuated by a clutch fork in the same way as today's dry clutches. In older wet clutches, however, an air-actuated reservoir introduces cooling fluid to cool and lubricate the clutch during engagement and disengagement. As shown in **FIGURE 40-55**, the Eaton wet clutch is a much more sophisticated device. It consists of a hydraulically actuated wet clutch pack more similar to the type used in automatic transmissions.

FIGURE 40-54 The ECA is a mechatronic device capable of reporting its function and position to the transmission controller.

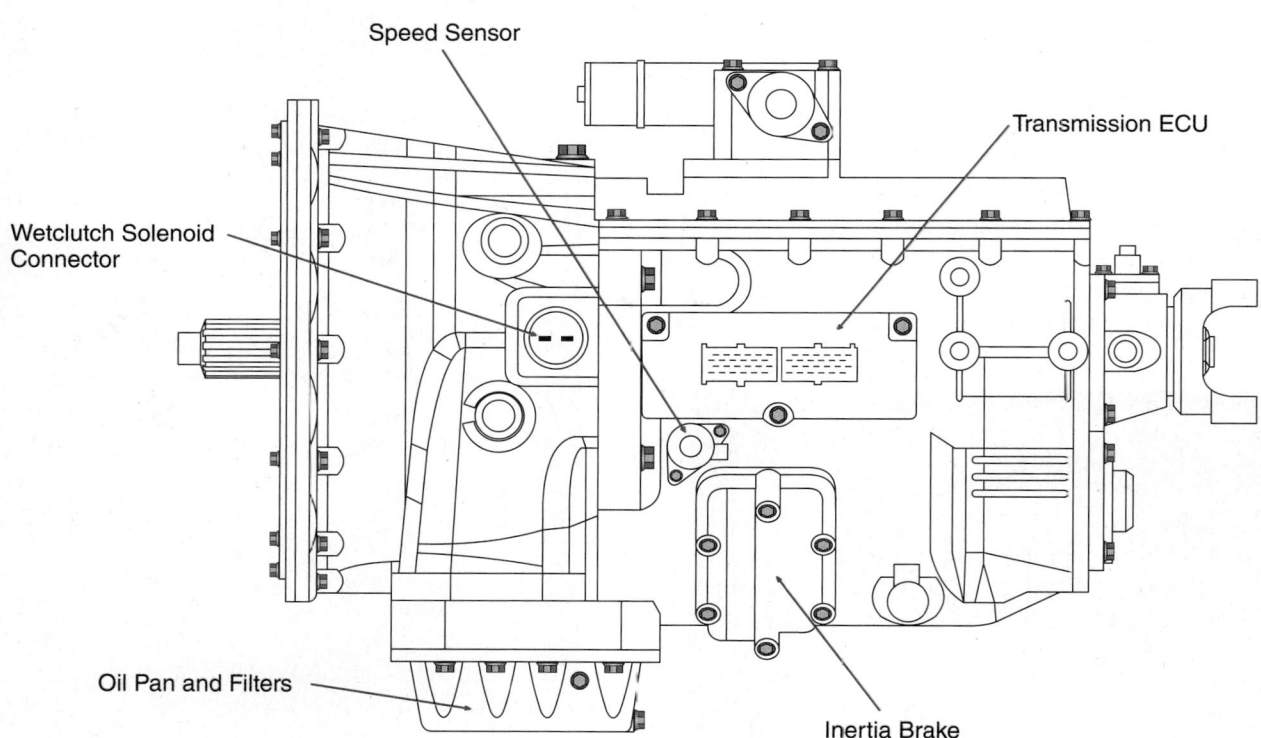

FIGURE 40-55 The Eaton FO-8406-ASW models use a hydraulically actuated multi-disc wet clutch similar to an automatic transmission clutch pack.

The FO-8406-ASW has a hydraulic pump to supply actuating pressure and engagement and disengagement are controlled by the transmission computer. This type of wet clutch allows more control of torque transfer at vehicle take-off. These types of electronically controlled auto-clutches can even be programmed with what is known as "urge to move," which makes their operation in a vehicle equipped with a manual transmission almost indistinguishable from vehicles equipped with traditional automatic transmissions.

Wrap-Up

Ready for Review

▶ A friction clutch has two basic functions. The first function is to transmit torque from the engine to the driveline and the second is to allow the engine and the driveline to be disconnected, when required.

▶ Clutches operate by utilizing friction, which is the resistance of motion between two bodies in contact to transmit torque.

▶ Clutches must absorb and dissipate increasingly powerful torsional vibrations that tend to twist driveline components every time an engine cylinder fires.

▶ Clutch capacity, or the amount of torque a clutch can handle without slipping, is affected by the coefficient of friction (CoF) of the material used, the surface area in contact, and the clamp load.

▶ Clutches can be push-type or pull-type. This refers to the direction a clutch release bearing moves while the clutch is being disengaged.

▶ Coil springs can be used to supply clamping load for the clutch. As the clutch discs wear, they lose their clamping force.

▶ Diaphragm spring clutches are a better choice in most push-type clutch applications, as their clamp load is not diminished as the disc wears.

▶ The easy-pedal angle-spring pull-type clutch from Eaton is arguably the most popular clutch used in North American heavy-duty applications; its design prevents a reduction in clamp load, as long the clutch is correctly adjusted.

▶ Pull-type clutches allow the use of clutch brakes. Clutch brakes are splined to the input shaft of a non-synchronized transmission.

▶ For years, clutch friction facings were made with asbestos, which is a known carcinogen. Today, clutches manufactured in North America contain no asbestos. The long-term effects of exposure to clutch dust from modern facing materials is unknown. Technicians should always wear NIOSH-approved respirators when working in any dust-laden environment.

▶ Some clutches today are self-adjusting and require little or no maintenance. The Eaton Solo (Advantage® Self-Adjust) is one example.

▶ Two general types of friction materials are used today: organic and ceramic. Ceramic facings have higher CoF than organic, but provide a more abrupt engagement.

▶ Today's manufacturers of clutches have developed clutch systems that are very good at smoothing out driveline vibrations caused by engine torsionals, both under load and at idle.

▶ Engine flywheels have several important functions. They offer a friction surface for the clutch, provide inertia, and smooth out power pulsations from the engine.

▶ Flywheels come in two predominate designs: a flat-style flywheel and a pot-style flywheel.

▶ Dual-disc clutches use an intermediate plate that provides a friction surface for the rear of the front friction disc and the front of the rear disc.

▶ Pilot bearings support the front end of the transmission input shaft and should be replaced whenever the clutch is replaced.

▶ The release fork (release yoke) is the lever that actually moves the release bearing to disengage the clutch.

▶ The release bearings in push-type clutches slide on a sleeve that surrounds the input shaft and only rotate when the clutch is being disengaged. The release bearings in a pull-type clutch are integral, and the inner bearing race rotates whenever the engine is rotating.

▶ Most on-highway trucks contain clutches that can be actuated by mechanical linkage. Clutches can also be actuated by cable or hydraulics.

▶ Automated transmissions still use clutches, but in some cases they are automatically actuated by centrifugal force, air, electric, or hydraulic actuators. Automatically operated clutches have no clutch pedal.

Key Terms

angle spring clutch A clutch manufactured by Eaton/Spicer Corporation that uses three pairs of angled springs pushing against levers to supply the clamp load.

ceramic friction facings Friction facings made mostly of man-made materials specifically designed to produce desirable characteristics.

clamp force The force squeezing the clutch disc between the pressure plate and the flywheel. Also called *clamp load*.

clamp load The force squeezing the clutch disc/s between the pressure plate and the flywheel. Also called *clamping force*.

clutch brake A small frictional brake usually mounted on the transmission input shaft; designed to slow down or stop the inertia of the transmission gearing so shifts into first or reverse can be made without clashing.

clutch capacity The amount of torque the clutch can safely handle without slipping.

clutch cover The outside part of the clutch that is bolted to the flywheel and that holds all the clutch components, except the clutch disc. Mistakenly, but commonly, called the pressure plate.

clutch disc or friction disc A plate or disc that has friction material on both sides and is splined to the transmission input shaft.

coefficient of friction (CoF) The amount of force required to move an object while in contact with another.

coil spring-style clutch A clutch that uses coils springs mounted perpendicular to the pressure plate to provide the clamp load.

dampening disc A disc with a ring of torsional dampening springs around its hub designed to absorb engine torsional vibrations.

diaphragm spring clutch A clutch that uses a single diaphragm spring, also known as a Belleville spring, to provide the clamping force.

drive pin Pin used in a pot-type flywheel to drive the intermediate plate.

dual-mass flywheel A flywheel with two sections separated by torsional springs; one section attaches to the engine crankshaft and the clutch cover is bolted to the other section.

flat-type flywheel A flywheel that is predominately flat, with all its components inside the cover; the clutch cover bolts to it.

friction The relative resistance to motion between any two bodies in contact with one another.

friction dampening Controlling torsional vibration by using friction material in between the various plates in a clutch friction disc.

flywheel A heavy round metal disc attached to the end of the crankshaft to smooth out vibrations from the crankshaft assembly and provide one of the friction surfaces for a clutch disc used on manual transmission/transaxle applications.

Hooke's law A law of physics that states that force delivered by a spring to an object is directly related to its compression or extension; the greater the spring is compressed, the more force the spring delivers.

inertia brake A type of transmission shaft brake geared to one countershaft, which controls gearing rotational speed while shifting.

input shaft The component to which the clutch discs are splined.

intermediate plate A cast iron plate that is connected to the flywheel or the clutch cover, also known as a separator plate.

kinetic friction The friction between two surfaces that are sliding against each other.

organic facings Friction facings made of various natural materials, such as cotton fibers, rubber, aluminum, glass, copper or brass fibers, and carbon material.

pilot bearing A bearing that supports the front of the transmission input shaft; mounted in the flywheel or the rear of the crankshaft.

pot-type flywheel A flywheel shaped like a deep pot inside which all the components of the clutch are housed, except for the clutch cover.

pre-dampening A series of small torsional dampening springs designed to prevent gear rattle at idle.

pull-type clutch A clutch with an integral release bearing, which is pulled toward the transmission to disengage the clutch.

push-type clutch A clutch in which the release bearing is pushed toward the engine to release the clutch.

release bearing A hollow bearing through which the input shaft passes, which allows for the push or pull against rotating clutch release levers to release the clutch.

release fork (yoke) The actuator that moves the release bearing.

resonance The frequency at which the driveline's vibrations are the most damaging.

resonant frequency The frequency at which the driveline enters a resonant condition, where all the components start to oscillate in unison.

self-adjusting clutches Clutches with an automatically adjusting system that relies on pressure plate movement to cause an adjustment.

slave cylinder The hydraulic cylinder used to release the clutch in hydraulically actuated clutch systems.

soft-dampened clutch A clutch with extra-long travel windows for its dampening springs; used to combat resonance in a driveline.

Review Questions

1. Which of the following clutch types has an integral or attached release bearing?
   a. Push-type clutch
   b. Diaphragm-type clutch
   c. Lever-type clutch
   d. Pull-type clutch
2. What are the components found inside a clutch that allow us to release it with less pedal effort and also amplify clutch application pressure when it is engaged?
   a. Pressure plates
   b. Torsional springs
   c. Levers
   d. Pivot rings
3. The primary function of the coaxial springs mounted in a clutch disc hub is to do which of the following?
   a. Increase clutch clamp load
   b. Make the disc stronger
   c. Absorb torsional vibrations
   d. Assist the driver in releasing the clutch
4. The function of most types of clutch brakes is to do which of the following?
   a. Slow down or stop the transmission gearing while shifting to first gear or reverse
   b. Allow for easier up-shifting

c. Absorb engine torque

d. Allow for easier downshifting

5. What is the primary reason pull-type clutches are used in heavy-duty applications?

   a. Pull-type clutches last longer.

   b. Pull-type clutches are less expensive to manufacture.

   c. Pull-type clutches require less pedal effort than push-type.

   d. Pull-type clutches allow the use of a clutch brake.

6. Which of the following do not affect the capacity of the clutch to handle engine power without slipping?

   a. The coefficient of friction of the clutch disc material

   b. The surface area of the friction discs

   c. The number of friction discs

   d. The type of clutch release mechanism

7. Why do some clutches use two discs?

   a. To increase clutch capacity

   b. To allow a smoother engagement

   c. To double clutch life

   d. To increase flywheel inertia

8. Which type of clutch release system may use a catapult fork?

   a. A mechanical-linkage system

   b. A hydraulic-release system

   c. A cable-release system

   d. An electrical system

9. Which of the following clutch types provide constant pressure plate load, regardless of clutch disc wear, as long as adjustment is correct?

   a. Coil spring-type clutch

   b. Angle spring clutch

   c. Coaxial spring clutch

   d. Marcel spring clutch

10. A new clutch disc has very small springs mounted in a circle around the clutch disc hub; these springs are commonly referred to as _____ springs.

    a. torsional dampening

    b. anti-breakage

    c. engagement cushioning

    d. pre-dampening

ASE Technician A/Technician B Style Questions

1. Technician A says that a pilot bearing should always be replaced when a clutch is replaced. Technician B says that soft-dampened clutches are better at absorbing torsional vibrations. Who is correct?

   a. Technician A

   b. Technician B

   c. Both Technician A and Technician B

   d. Neither Technician A nor Technician B

2. Technician A says that since North American clutch manufacturers no longer use asbestos, there is no need to be concerned by clutch dust. Technician B says that compressed air is the best way to clean the clutch housing when performing a clutch replacement. Who is correct?

   a. Technician A

   b. Technician B

   c. Both Technician A and Technician B

   d. Neither Technician A nor Technician B

3. Technician A says that coil spring clutches are the best because the heavy coil springs provide exceptional clamp load. Technician B says that diaphragm spring-style clutches are a better choice because they do not lose clamp load. Who is correct?

   a. Technician A

   b. Technician B

   c. Both Technician A and Technician B

   d. Neither Technician A nor Technician B

4. Technician A says that the release bearing in pull-type clutches only rotates when disengaging the clutch. Technician B says that the release bearing in pull-type clutches is replaced whenever the clutch is replaced. Who is correct?

   a. Technician A

   b. Technician B

   c. Both Technician A and Technician B

   d. Neither Technician A nor Technician B

5. Technician A says that using dual discs in a clutch doubles the clutch capacity. Technician B says that increasing clamp load can increase clutch capacity. Who is correct?

   a. Technician A

   b. Technician B

   c. Both Technician A and Technician B

   d. Neither Technician A nor Technician B

6. Technician A says that most heavy-duty truck clutches use organic linings. Technician B says that the most common clutch type used in heavy trucks is the angle spring clutch. Who is correct?

   a. Technician A

   b. Technician B

   c. Both Technician A and Technician B

   d. Neither Technician A nor Technician B

7. Technician A says that most clutch brakes are installed to help the driver up-shift. Technician B says that clutch brakes can be replaced without removing the transmission. Who is correct?

   a. Technician A

   b. Technician B

   c. Both Technician A and Technician B

   d. Neither Technician A nor Technician B

8. Technician A says that a diaphragm spring clutch is a better choice than a coil spring-style clutch because it doesn't lose clamp load as the disc wears. Technician B says that diaphragm spring clutches are only found in light-duty vehicles. Who is correct?

   a. Technician A

   b. Technician B

   c. Both Technician A and Technician B

   d. Neither Technician A nor Technician B

9. Technician A says that some clutches are self-adjusting. Technician B says that all clutches with hydraulic actuation systems do not require periodic adjustment. Who is correct?
   a. Technician A
   b. Technician B
   c. Both Technician A and Technician B
   d. Neither Technician A nor Technician B

10. Technician A says that some hydraulically actuated clutches use a catapult release lever. Technician B says that a catapult lever is bolted to the clutch housing. Who is correct?
   a. Technician A
   b. Technician B
   c. Both Technician A and Technician B
   d. Neither Technician A nor Technician B

CHAPTER 41

Servicing Heavy-Duty Clutches

Learning Objectives

After reading this chapter, you will be able to:

- **LO 41-1** Describe and explain clutch system preventative maintenance requirements.
- **LO 41-2** Describe and explain common clutch problems and their causes.
- **LO 41-3** Explain the procedure for removing the transmission and clutch assemblies.
- **LO 41-4** Explain the inspection and repair of clutch components.
- **LO 41-5** Describe the installation procedures for single- and dual-disc clutches.
- **LO 41-6** Explain the installation and resetting procedures for self-adjusting clutches.

You Are the Technician

A class 8 tractor is brought to your shop for a clutch adjustment. The driver says there is something wrong with the clutch, but he is not sure what it is. He says, "It just doesn't 'feel' right." He says the clutch brake does not seem to be working anymore, and he has to wait a long time before shifting into first or reverse to avoid gear clash. From your experience, the free play in the cab seems normal for this vehicle. Pedal and linkage movement seem fine. When you inspect the clutch, you see that release-bearing travel is approximately 0.75" (187 mm). Fork to release-bearing clearance is correct at 0.125" (3.2 mm), and the clutch brake is still like new.

1. What can you conclude from your investigation?
2. Do you think you can solve the driver's problem?
3. What procedure would you undertake to repair the situation?
4. Do you think this vehicle requires a clutch replacement?

Introduction

Clutch servicing is a job that almost all heavy-duty truck technicians must perform during their careers. Servicing a clutch falls into one of two basic categories. The first category is maintenance procedures, such as clutch adjustments, release-bearing lubrication and inspection, and lubrication of the clutch actuation components. The clutch actuation components include the **clutch linkage** (the connection between the driver's clutch pedal and the clutch cross-shaft), the **cross-shaft** itself (the cross-shaft supports the release fork), and the release fork. Typical clutch actuation components are shown in **FIGURE 41-1**.

The second category of service involves clutch replacement. Timely clutch adjustments and maintenance can go a long way to preventing premature clutch replacement. Technicians should be aware of signs that indicate a clutch is not being used properly due to driver error or driver abuse. Some signs to watch for include: excessive dust buildup from friction material, worn clutch brakes on pull-type clutches, and any sign of overheating or burning of clutch components. If any of these indicators are present, further investigation is required to determine whether the driver or the equipment is at fault.

Preventative Maintenance of Clutches

LO 41-1 Describe and explain clutch system preventative maintenance requirements.

Clutch inspection and maintenance should be performed according to the manufacturer's maintenance schedule. This schedule varies, depending on the vehicle **vocation** (or the specific function the vehicle is designed to perform), but is usually every 8000 to 10,000 miles (12,000 to 16,000 km) for standard mechanical clutches.

Clutch preventative maintenance involves three basic elements:

1. **Clutch inspection.** Inspection of the clutch and its actuating system can allow a technician to prevent costly downtime by preventing potential problems. The clutch itself should be visually inspected for excess wear if possible (on 14" [35.6 cm] pot-style flywheels, the clutch discs cannot be seen), and replaced as necessary. All linkages should be inspected for wear and repaired, as necessary.
2. **Lubrication.** During a vehicle service, all moving components of the clutch actuation system should be lubricated, as should the release bearing, clutch-release fork, and cross-shaft. Note that some systems have **sealed release bearings**. Sealed release bearings are those that do not require periodic lubrication, but still require inspection.
3. **Clutch adjustment.** Timely adjustment of the clutch is essential to its longevity. The clutch should be adjusted, as necessary, when the vehicle is in the shop for maintenance.

The following sections discuss the adjustment procedures for various types of medium- and heavy-duty clutches.

Clutch Adjustment

Many factors can affect the useful life of a clutch and its need for periodic adjustment. The life expectancy of the clutch and, therefore, how often adjustments are required, can vary widely, even on identical vehicles. Vehicle loading, driver skill, and highway or city operation are all important factors when it comes to clutch life, but one of the most important ways to ensure the clutch lasts as long as possible is correct and timely clutch adjustment.

Push-Type Clutch Inspection and Adjustment

A properly adjusted push-type clutch usually has a certain amount of **free play**, or clearance, between the clutch release levers, or the diaphragm-spring fingers, and the release bearing. (Note, however, that some newer hydraulically actuated push-type clutches run with no free play. This is because the actuation cylinder only retracts enough to unload the release levers or fingers.) **FIGURE 41-2** shows where the clearance is to be measured.

As the clutch friction disc(s) wear, the pressure plate must move toward the flywheel to compensate. Therefore, the outer edge of the release levers or diaphragm spring must move toward the flywheel also, to follow the pressure plate. This causes the inner edge of the release levers or the diaphragm-spring fingers to move toward the transmission and the release bearing. Eventually, their travel is stopped by the release bearing. Any further wear after this point of contact results in partially reducing clutch clamp load because the levers or the fingers cannot move any further back. This situation can lead to clutch slippage and early clutch failure. If the adjustment has too much free play, the clutch pedal may not have enough travel to fully release the

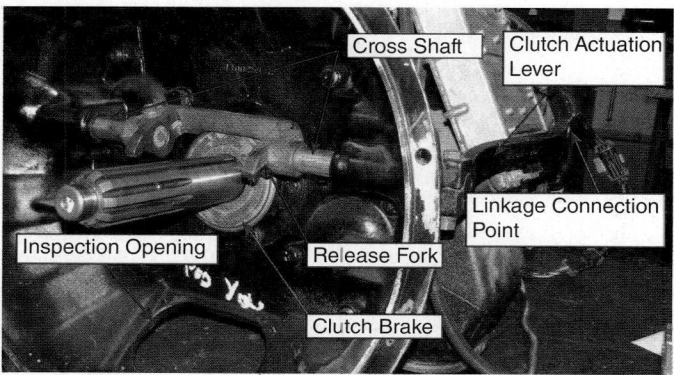

FIGURE 41-1 Typical clutch actuation components.

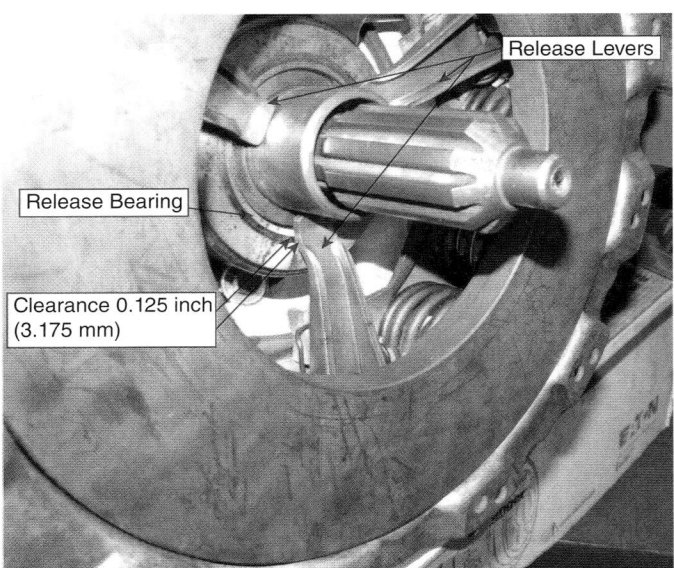

FIGURE 41-2 Typical push-type clutch adjustment requires 0.125" (3.175 mm) clearance between the levers and the release bearing.

pressure on the clutch disc, causing the gears to clash (grind) when shifting and resulting in heavy synchronizer wear. With this condition, the clutch starts to engage too close to the floor when releasing the pedal.

In a push-type clutch, clutch adjustment is accomplished by adjusting the cable or mechanical linkage in such a way as to gain approximately 0.125" (3.175 mm) clearance between the release bearing and the release levers or fingers. In some

hydraulically actuated systems, the slave-cylinder push rod is adjusted to gain the desired 0.125" (3.175 mm) clearance.

This adjustment typically leads to approximately 1-2" (2.5 to 5.1 cm) of free travel at the clutch pedal. Clutch adjustment should be performed as often as necessary. When an adjustment is performed, record the in-cab free pedal and inform the driver that when the pedal-free travel is reduced by half because of disc wear, another adjustment is required to reestablish normal clearance at the release bearing and the free pedal in the cab. As mentioned previously push-type clutches with hydraulic actuation systems may have an adjustable slave cylinder pushrod. However, some hydraulic systems may operate with no clearance at all. In that case, there is light contact between the bearing and the release levers and little or no free pedal in the cab. Some clutches are self-compensating for wear, while others require regular checking and adjusting. Always check manufacturer's specifications to be sure of the correct adjustment setting. It is important to check the clutch linkage mechanism for proper operation and correct the adjustment (free play) periodically. It is common to do so during every routine maintenance service.

To check and adjust a mechanical push-type clutch, follow the steps in **SKILL DRILL 41-1**.

Checking and Adjusting a Hydraulic Push-Type Clutch

It is important to check the clutch hydraulic system and components for proper operation and correct adjustment. It is common to do so during periodic routine maintenance service.

SKILL DRILL 41-1 Checking and Adjusting a Push-Type Clutch

1. Research the procedure and specifications for inspecting and adjusting the clutch linkage in the appropriate service information. You are looking specifically for the proper clutch-pedal height, the proper clutch-pedal free play, and the procedure for making adjustments.
2. Following the specified procedure, inspect the clutch linkage parts for damage, wear, or bent or missing components. Look for signs of binding, looseness, and excessive wear.

3. Start with the clutch-pedal assembly and inspect all components inside the cab. It is good practice to operate the clutch pedal while you are inspecting the components to observe any looseness or binding.
4. Check the clutch linkage components outside the cab for the same signs as the components inside the cab.
5. Measure the clutch-pedal height. Clutch-pedal height is normally measured from the floor pan to the top of the clutch-pedal pad with the clutch pedal released. Make sure there are no floor mats or other obstructions that affect the operation of the pedal. Compare your reading with the specifications and determine any necessary actions to correct any fault.
6. Measure the clutch-pedal free play. Pedal free play is normally measured from the top of the pedal at rest to where all play is taken up between the release bearing and the levers in the clutch assembly. This can be felt by hand or foot. Perform any adjustments as necessary, following the manufacturer's procedure.
7. Start the vehicle and depress the clutch. The clutch should engage at the proper height and have the proper free play. Make a gear selection to ensure the gears do not clash going into mesh. While in gear, slowly release the clutch and see how far the clutch pedal must travel before the clutch starts to engage in forward motion. Check the operation against the manufacturer's specifications and correct as necessary.

If the hydraulic clutch system is improperly maintained, clutch operation could be compromised in a similar manner as the operation of a mechanical-linkage clutch, resulting in pressure plate, friction disc, and transmission synchronizer failure. Also, improper or old fluid in the hydraulic system can cause master cylinder and slave cylinder damage.

To check and adjust a hydraulic clutch, follow the steps in **SKILL DRILL 41-2**.

▶ TECHNICIAN TIP

Make sure there are no floor mats or other obstructions that affect the operation of the clutch pedal.

▶ TECHNICIAN TIP

Note that the 0.125" (3.175 mm) clearance specification may vary by OEM. Some OEMs require their push-type clutches to be adjusted based on in-cab free pedal. Be sure to consult the manufacturer's documentation for the clutch you are working on.

Pull-Type Clutch Adjustment

A properly adjusted pull-type clutch has a certain clearance between the tips of the release fork and the wear pads on the release bearing. In a pull-type clutch, as the disc(s) wear, the pressure plate moves toward the flywheel to compensate, just as it did in a push-type clutch. However, because the release levers or diaphragm-spring pivot points are on their outer edge, and the point where they contact the pressure plate is further inboard, the contact point and inner edge of the levers or fingers and the integral release bearing all move toward the flywheel. The clutch release fork is in front of the release bearing. Eventually, therefore, it stops the release-bearing travel, if adjustment is not performed. Any further disc wear after the bearing contacts the fork causes decreased clamp load, which can lead to slippage and early clutch failure. Clutch adjustment reestablishes the correct free play of the release bearing and ensures the plate load is not affected by disc wear.

Pull-type clutch adjustment is significantly different than the push-type adjustment and must accomplish three things:

1. **Clutch-brake actuation**, or **squeeze** (if equipped). Clutch-brake actuation is affected by total pedal travel and is adjusted by adjusting the clutch linkage.
2. **Release-bearing travel.** This ensures that the release bearing moves far enough to completely disengage the clutch. This is usually the only adjustment necessary on a pull-type clutch.
3. **Clutch free travel**, or the play between the release fork and the release bearing. This establishes clutch-pedal free travel in the cab and ensures that the clamp load is not affected by disc wear.

Linkage Adjustment

It is a good idea to check the linkage adjustment, or clutch-brake squeeze, before a clutch adjustment, to ensure that the

---

SKILL DRILL 41-2 Checking and Adjusting a Hydraulic Push-Type Clutch

1. Research the procedure and specifications for inspecting and adjusting the hydraulic clutch components in the appropriate original equipment manufacturers (OEM) service information.
2. Inspect the clutch master cylinder for correct fluid level and check the quality of the fluid.
3. Inspect all line connections to the master cylinder. If a leak at the rear of the master cylinder is suspected, it may be necessary to remove the master cylinder from the firewall to inspect behind it for leaks (if no other visible external leaks are present).

4. Make sure no hydraulic lines are kinked or leaking at their connections. Any leak requires that the system be repaired and bled of any air.
5. Check all rubber hoses for dry rot, bulges, or leaks. Make sure all hydraulic components are secure in their mountings and that all support straps are secure.
6. Check the boot on the slave cylinder for seepage, which may indicate a leaking slave cylinder piston seal. Note: some newer hydraulic systems may have the slave cylinder inside the clutch housing.
7. Check clutch-pedal height. Clutch-pedal height is normally measured from the floor pan to the top of the clutch-pedal pad with the clutch pedal released. Compare your reading with the specifications and determine any necessary actions to correct any fault.
8. Measure clutch-pedal free play using a tape measure. Pedal free play is normally measured from the top of the pedal at rest to where all play is taken up between the pedal and the pressure plate. Compare your reading with the factory specifications and determine any necessary actions to correct.
9. Note that newer hydraulically actuated clutches run with no free pedal in the cab. Always check manufacturers' specifications for the vehicle you are working on before undertaking any servicing.

linkage has not been tampered with or previously used to adjust in-cab free pedal. If the linkage has been used to compensate for clutch wear, the clutch-brake squeeze is lower than normal, and/or the pedal may bottom out before squeeze occurs. Linkage adjustment should *rarely* be required during normal clutch service, so long as the linkage was properly set at the factory or during dealer prep. Pull-type clutch adjustment usually only requires resetting the release-bearing position using the clutch's internal adjusting ring or the external threaded sleeve (Lipe clutch).

The need for linkage adjustment is normally caused by wear in the linkage system. Once the worn components are replaced, adjustment is typically unnecessary. Linkage adjustment controls the total movement of the release fork and, therefore, when the fork pushes the release bearing against the clutch brake. This should occur in the last 1/2 to 1" (12.7 to 25.4 mm) of pedal travel. **FIGURE 41-3** depicts a check of clutch-brake squeeze.

To check the clutch-brake squeeze, insert a 0.010" (2.54 mm) feeler gauge or a business card between the clutch brake and the release bearing and have a colleague push the clutch pedal to the floor. While clamping the feeler gauge between the brake and the bearing, note the clutch-pedal position with a tape measure. Now have the colleague raise the pedal slowly and stop when the feeler gauge can be removed. Measure the height of the clutch pedal at this point. It should be 0.5" to 1" (12.7 to 25.4 mm) higher than the end of pedal travel noted previously. If that is not the case, the clutch linkage must be adjusted to gain proper brake squeeze. It is important that clutch-brake squeeze occurs close to the end of pedal travel so the driver does not hit the brake during

normal shifting, a brake that is set too high has a short lifespan. Lengthening the linkage lowers the squeeze point, and shortening the linkage raises the squeeze point.

Release-Bearing Travel

Once you establish that the linkage adjustment is correct and has not been tampered with, it is time to check the release-bearing travel. Release-bearing travel is the distance the release bearing moves as the clutch pedal is depressed to the floor. As the discs wear, the release bearing moves toward the flywheel with the pressure plate and the release levers. This increases release-bearing travel at the same time it reduces free play at the release fork. Release-bearing travel is typically 0.5" to 0.56" (1.25 to 1.4 cm) and is set by adjusting the clutch internally to move the release bearing back to where it started. Note: On some Eaton clutches, the release travel is listed at 0.490" to 0.56" (1.24 to 1.4 cm). **FIGURE 41-4** shows the view of the release bearing from the clutch inspection opening in the bell housing.

The most common form of internal adjustment involves turning a large **adjusting ring** inside the clutch cover. Clockwise movement of this adjusting ring moves the lever or diaphragm-spring pivot points closer to the pressure plate. That movement causes their inner edges and the integral release bearing to move toward the transmission. That resets the release-bearing travel to 0.5" to 0.56" (1.25 to 1.4 cm) and, if no linkage adjustment has been made, the release-fork free play is reestablished also.

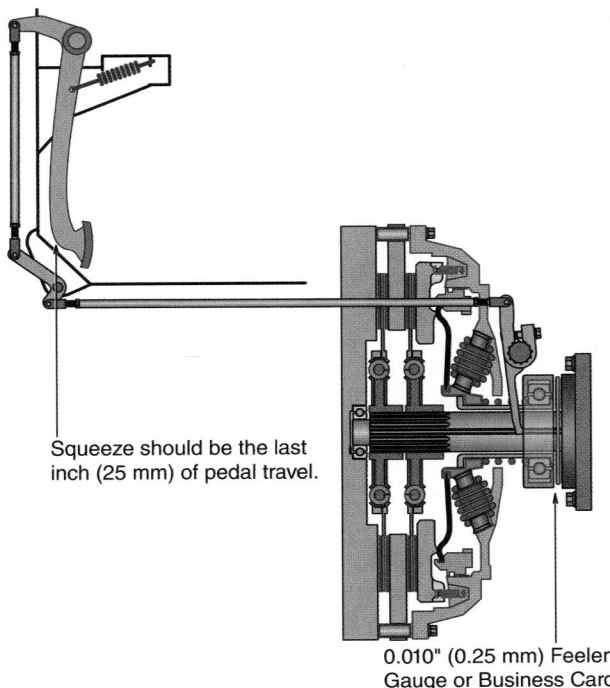

Squeeze should be the last inch (25 mm) of pedal travel.

0.010" (0.25 mm) Feeler Gauge or Business Card

FIGURE 41-3 Clutch-brake squeeze should occur within the last inch of pedal travel.

Release Fork

Clutch Free Travel

Clutch Brake

Release Bearing Travel

FIGURE 41-4 Release-bearing travel is the distance the release bearing moves before it contacts the clutch brake.

When adjusting a clutch using the internal adjusting ring, no matter which adjustment method is used, the clutch must be disengaged fully (clutch pedal to the floor) to turn the adjustment ring. Disengaging the clutch releases the clamp load and allows the adjusting ring to turn. Failure to disengage the clutch before trying to turn the adjustment ring can cause damage to the clutch components.

Angle-Spring Clutch Adjustment with Locking Tang

There are two adjustment systems for the angle-spring clutch. As shown in **FIGURE 41-5**, the first system uses a **locking tang** that is bolted to the clutch cover and rests between two of the square lugs that are formed on the adjusting ring. To adjust the clutch, the engine is first barred or turned over until the lock tang is at the clutch housing inspection cover opening. The lock tang is removed, and the clutch pedal is held to the floor. The technician then turns the large adjusting ring clockwise, when viewed from the rear (for a normal wear adjustment). The clutch normally has cast-in arrows showing the direction for normal wear adjustment. The adjusting ring can be turned using a pry bar or using a special prying tool that bolts to the lock tang bolt hole. To check the adjustment is correct, the clutch pedal must be released.

Angle-Spring Clutch Adjustment with Quick-Adjust Device

The second adjusting system is exclusive to Eaton/Spicer angle-spring clutches and uses a **quick-adjust** device, like that shown in **FIGURE 41-6**. This device consists of 5/8" (15.875 mm) bolt attached to a small pinion gear that meshes with internal teeth on the large adjusting ring (note that some quick-adjust mechanisms use a ¾" (19 mm) bolt. The 5/8" (15.875 mm) bolt has a spring-loaded locking sleeve that prevents it from moving by itself. The quick-adjust device is bolted to the clutch cover.

FIGURE 41-7 illustrates a properly adjusted pull-type clutch with 0.49" to 0.56" (12.4 to 14.2 mm) release-bearing travel.

To adjust the clutch with this system, the engine is again rotated until the quick-adjust is at the bottom and accessible through the clutch inspection cover. The clutch pedal is depressed to remove the clamp load and the technician uses a wrench or socket, first to depress the locking sleeve on the bolt, and then to turn the quick-adjust, which rotates the large adjusting ring in the clutch cover. The quick-adjust is rotated clockwise from the rear to adjust for worn clutch discs. One full turn of the quick-adjust equates to approximately a 0.125" to 0.2" (3.2 to 5 mm) difference in release-bearing travel. **SKILL DRILL 41-3** outlines the step-by-step procedure for adjusting an angle-spring pull-type clutch.

Remember that, in most cases, no linkage adjustment should be required. The internal adjustment is normally all that is needed to achieve proper adjustment of the clutch.

FIGURE 41-6 Quick-adjustment device. **A.** Adjusting ring. **B.** Quick-adjust device.

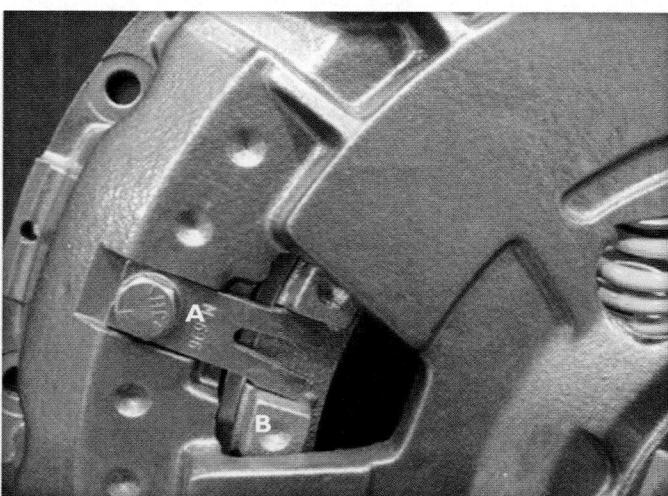

FIGURE 41-5 In this angle-spring clutch, the locking tang at point **A** is removed and the large adjusting ring at point **B** is turned clockwise to adjust for wear.

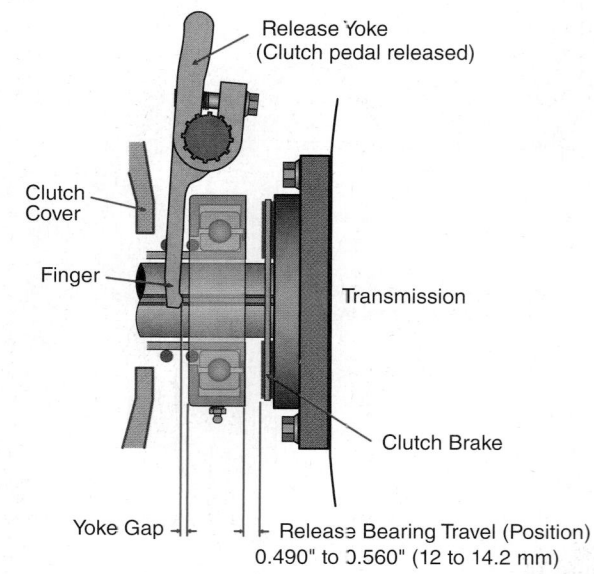

FIGURE 41-7 A properly adjusted pull-type clutch.

SKILL DRILL 41-3 Adjusting a Pull-Type Clutch

1. Remove the clutch bell-housing inspection cover. Bump the engine over until the clutch-adjusting mechanism is in line with the opening.
2. Insert a 0.010" (0.254 mm) feeler gauge between the clutch brake and the transmission front bearing cover. Have an assistant depress the clutch pedal as far as it goes while you clamp the feeler gauge.
3. Have your assistant measure and record the distance the clutch pedal is from the floor of the cab.
4. Tell the assistant to slowly let the pedal up until you can pull the feeler gauge from between the clutch brake and the bearing cover. Then tell him/her to stop and measure the pedal distance from the floor again.
5. The difference between the two measurements is the clutch-brake squeeze dimension. It should be between 0.5" and 1" (1.27 cm and 2.54 cm). If this dimension is correct, a linkage adjustment is not required. (A linkage adjustment is very rarely required on a pull-type clutch.)

6. Check the distance between the back of the release bearing and the clutch brake. This is the release-bearing travel dimension and should be approximately 0.5" (1.27 cm). As the clutch disc wears, that dimension increases.
7. To adjust the clutch for wear and reduce the release-bearing travel dimension, have an assistant hold the clutch pedal down to release the clutch clamp load. Use a wrench to push down on the quick-adjust bolt (see photo), if equipped, and turn the bolt clockwise 1/2 turn. Then let the pedal up and recheck the release-bearing travel dimension as in step 6.
8. Always ensure that the quick-adjust bolt returns to the out (locked) position after adjustment is complete. (Note: If the clutch does not have a quick-adjust bolt, remove the lock strap, and turn the large adjusting ring clockwise one notch at a time while your assistant holds the clutch pedal down. Then recheck the dimension with the pedal released.)
9. After correcting the release-bearing travel dimension to be 0.5" (1.27 cm), check that the clearance between the release-fork fingers and the contact patches on the release bearing is 1/8" (3.2 mm). (This dimension gets smaller as the clutch disc wears and gets larger as the release-bearing travel dimension is corrected for wear.) If this dimension is not correct and the release-bearing travel is set, then a linkage adjustment may be required. Be aware that increasing the fork-to-bearing clearance by adjusting the linkage decreases the clutch-brake squeeze dimension and vice versa.
10. Lubricate the release bearing until lubricant purges out the back of the bearing sleeve onto the input shaft. Reinstall the inspection cover.
11. Measure and record the pedal free travel in the cab. (Note: Some hydraulic actuation systems have little or no pedal free travel.) This measurement is the normal pedal free travel. Inform the driver to have the clutch readjusted when this dimension decreases by half.

Failure to depress the clutch pedal prior to trying to rotate the adjusting ring in a pull-type clutch causes damage to the quick-adjust mechanism. It must only be rotated with the clutch pedal fully depressed.

Lipe/Haldex Adjustment

The Lipe/Haldex brand of pull-type clutches uses a different system to adjust release-bearing travel. The release-bearing spider, or retainer, that holds the inner edge of the release levers, is attached to the release bearing by a threaded sleeve with an adjusting nut and a jamb nut. To reposition the bearing, the jamb nut is simply loosened, and the adjusting nut is turned. Those actions move the bearing back to its original location, thereby re-establishing release-bearing travel and release-fork free play. The jamb nut is then retightened. **FIGURE 41-8** illustrates a threaded release sleeve-type of clutch adjusted to achieve the same 0.5" to 0.5625" (1.27 to 1.43 mm) bearing free travel and 0.125" (0.32 mm) clearance at the release fork.

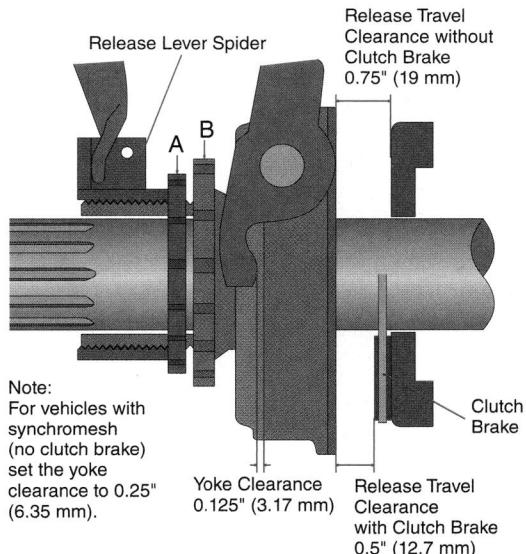

FIGURE 41-8 A properly adjusted threaded release sleeve-type of clutch.

Release-Fork Free Travel or Play

As mentioned in the Release-Bearing Travel section, the internal adjustment to reset release-bearing free travel normally results in the fork free play returning to its optimal setting of 0.125" (3.175 mm). This is because both are set by moving the bearing away from the fork with the adjusting ring inside the clutch. If fork clearance is not correctly re-established after the internal adjustment, total pedal travel may need to be adjusted by raising or lowering the clutch-pedal stops in the cab. The proper 0.125" (3.175 mm) free play at the fork usually equates to 2.0" to 2.5" (50.8 to 63.5 mm) of pedal free travel in the cab. Readjustment should be performed when in-cab pedal free play drops to half of the normal amount achieved after a correct adjustment.

> ► **TECHNICIAN TIP**
>
> Pedal free play is a result of proper adjustment and, therefore, may vary from vehicle to vehicle. Whatever pedal free play is established after a correct adjustment is made is the correct pedal free play for that vehicle. Drivers should be instructed to return for re-adjustment of the clutch when clutch wear causes a 50% drop in the in-cab free pedal.

Bleeding a Hydraulic-Clutch System

In the case of a hydraulic-clutch system failure, it may be necessary to bleed the air from the system. Bleeding is also needed whenever any hydraulic component is replaced, or the hydraulic fluid becomes unfit for use due to age or contamination. Not all systems are fitted with a bleeder screw due to how the system is constructed. It may be necessary to bleed the system from the line entering the slave cylinder.

Research the procedure and specifications for bleeding the hydraulic-clutch system you are working on. There are three types of bleeding: gravity bleeding, manual bleeding, and **pressure bleeding** (a pressure bleeder forces fluid under pressure through the hydraulic system). Determine the proper bleeding method to use by consulting the manufacturer's specifications. After bleeding the hydraulic-clutch system, fill the master cylinder to the correct level with the specified type of brake fluid.

Gravity Bleeding

Gravity bleeding uses gravity to push fluid and air from the master cylinder and lines out through the slave cylinder bleeder screw. In most vehicles, the clutch master cylinder is quite a bit higher than the slave cylinder. The weight of the fluid can, therefore, be used to supply the pressure to push fluid and air out of the system.

To bleed/flush a hydraulic clutch system using the gravity method, follow the steps in **SKILL DRILL 41-4**.

> ► **TECHNICIAN TIP**
>
> Be careful of the pressure that comes out of the slave cylinder, as it may splash or spray into your eyes. Also, brake fluid eats paint and some plastics, so, when handling brake fluid, quickly clean up any spilled fluid with generous amounts of water.

Manual Bleeding

The manual bleeding method uses the master cylinder to push fluid and air from the system. The procedure usually requires an assistant to hold the clutch pedal down while the other person opens the bleeder valve on the slave cylinder. Pumping of the pedal results in a single air bubble breaking up into smaller bubbles or foam, which requires more time to bleed the system properly.

To bleed/flush a hydraulic-clutch system using the manual method, follow the steps in **SKILL DRILL 41-5**.

Pressure or Vacuum Bleeding

The pressure or vacuum-bleeding method uses pressure or vacuum to push or pull fluid and air from the system. This method works well for systems that tend to trap air in the hydraulic system that cannot be bled manually. It does require special bleeding tools and equipment.

SKILL DRILL 41-4 Bleeding/Flushing a Hydraulic-Clutch System Using the Gravity Method

1. If the fluid needs to be flushed, use a suction gun or old antifreeze tester to suck the fluid out of the clutch master cylinder reservoir. Fill it with the specified fluid.
2. Open the bleeder screw on the slave cylinder.
3. Allow air and fluid to drain from the system into a container.
4. Keep the master cylinder filled.
5. Once all air and old fluid are removed, close the bleeder screw and operate the clutch pedal to check for normal operation.

SKILL DRILL 41-5 Bleeding/Flushing a Hydraulic-Clutch System Using the Manual Method

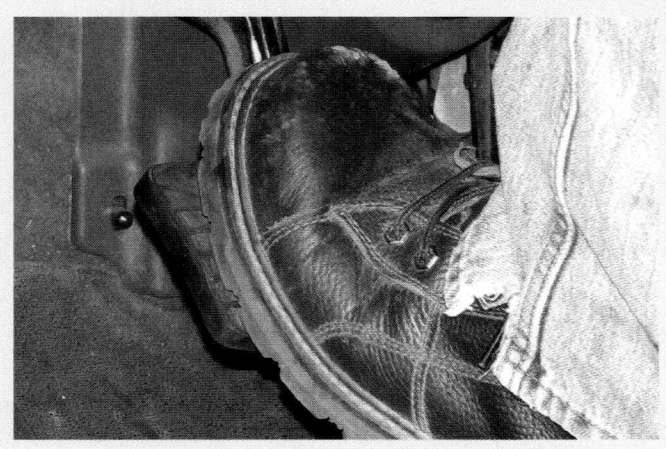

1. If the fluid needs to be flushed, use a suction gun or old antifreeze tester to suck the fluid out of the clutch master cylinder reservoir. Fill it with the specified fluid.
2. Have an assistant depress the clutch pedal slowly. Open the bleeder valve on the slave cylinder and let fluid run out into a container.
3. When all the fluid stops flowing, close the bleeder valve and slowly release the pedal.
4. Repeat this process until all air and old fluid are removed from the system.
5. After bleeding the clutch-hydraulic system, check for correct pedal feel, and fill the master cylinder to the correct level with the specified type of brake fluid.

SKILL DRILL 41-6 Bleeding/Flushing a Hydraulic-Clutch System Using the Pressure Method

1. Hook up the pressure or vacuum-bleeding tool to the vehicle with the correct adapters.
2. Apply pressure or vacuum to the system.
3. Open the bleeder screw and allow the fluid and air to be purged from the system. Capture the fluid in the bleeder or use a hose to direct it into a plastic container. Repeat this process as necessary.
4. After bleeding the hydraulic-clutch system, check for correct pedal feel, and fill the master cylinder to the correct level with the specified type of brake fluid.

To bleed a hydraulic-clutch system using the pressure method, follow the guidelines in **SKILL DRILL 41-6**.

Hydraulically Actuated Pull-Type Clutch Adjustment

In most cases, a vehicle fitted a hydraulically actuated pull-type clutch is equipped with a self-adjusting clutch. Because the newer hydraulic-clutch actuation system automatically keeps the release lever in light contact with the release bearing, there is no physical indication (like a loss of free pedal in a mechanical linkage) to the driver that an adjustment may be necessary. Using a self-adjusting clutch keeps the clutch adjusted correctly. However, if a hydraulically actuated system is retrofitted with a standard clutch, the clutch must be carefully monitored for required adjustment. This is easily done by checking the dimension between the clutch release bearing and the clutch brake and adjusting, as necessary, in the same manner as a mechanically actuated pull-type clutch. But it is up to maintenance personnel to check the need for adjustment, as the driver likely has no indication that adjustment is necessary until the clutch begins to slip.

Troubleshooting Clutch Problems

LO 41-2 Describe and explain common clutch problems and their causes.

The primary cause of clutch failure is excess heat. Excess heat causes the surface of the friction materials to liquefy, so they can no longer transfer torque. As a result, the disc starts slipping, which in turn causes more heat. At that point, complete failure occurs very rapidly. A severely burned clutch is shown in **FIGURE 41-9**. This amount of heat can cause the metal on the flywheel, the pressure plate, and the intermediate plate to get so hot that it begins to smear across the surface, as can be seen in **FIGURE 41-10**. For cast iron to flow, the temperature must reach at least 2100°F (1150°C). Excess heat can be caused by an inexperienced driver slipping the clutch too much on engagement or starting in the wrong gear. A clutch that is trying to carry a load that is higher than its capacity will slip, leading to excess heat, or a clutch that has not been adjusted regularly loses its clamp load and will start to slip, again causing excess heat and burning.

Clutch chatter is another common complaint for clutches. **Clutch chatter** is the intermittent grabbing and slipping of the clutch while it is being engaged. Clutch chatter can be caused by issues, such as a warped flywheel or pressure plate. One of the most common causes of chatter, however, is an oil-soaked clutch disc caused by leaking fluids. Shock loads can also cause severe damage to a clutch, and to the entire driveline, and must be avoided. Proper driver education is essential to a long and trouble-free clutch life, but the driver and the technician must work together to get the maximum life from the clutch. **TABLE 41-1** describes some common operator errors and the clutch problems they can cause.

TABLE 41-2 lists common clutch complaints, their causes, and remedies. This chart is in no way a comprehensive list of problems. Always check the manufacturer's manual when diagnosing a clutch system problem.

FIGURE 41-9 Once the ceramic friction material becomes burned, its coefficient of friction and, therefore, clutch capacity is greatly reduced.

FIGURE 41-10 For cast iron to smear like this, the temperature must reach at least 2 00°F (1150°C).

TABLE 41-1 Common Operator Errors and Clutch Problems

Operator Errors	Resulting Clutch Problems
Starting in too high a gear	This causes excess slippage in the clutch because the engine has insufficient torque to pick up the load in a higher gear. The clutch must slip to make up the difference. The correct gear is the one that allows the driver to pick up the load and start moving without increasing engine speed (or with minimal increase in speed).
Proper shifting techniques	If a driver shifts to a gear that is too far away in ratio from the vehicle speed, the clutch must slip to absorb the speed difference.
Overloading the clutch	All clutches have a maximum torque capacity. Exceeding the maximum load on a clutch causes the clutch to slip.
Riding the clutch	Pressure on the clutch pedal lowers pressure-plate clamp load and can lead to a slipping clutch and overheating.
Holding the vehicle on an incline by slipping the clutch	Purposely slipping the clutch has no value other than to overheat the clutch and cause premature wear. Operators should never engage in this practice.
Coasting in gear with the clutch disengaged	Operators should always have the clutch engaged, except when starting or shifting. Coasting in gear allows the speed difference between the engine and the clutch disc to vary uncontrollably. When the driver wishes to re-engage the clutch, the clutch must slip to make up the difference in speeds. Excessive disc speed can also occur by coasting down a loading ramp. For example, a vehicle with a 17:1 reverse gear ratio and a 4:1 final drive ratio has a total ratio of 68:1 so at 2000 rpm engine speed, the tire speed is 29.4 rpm. Heavy-duty truck tires rotate approximately 600 rpm, so in reverse, this vehicle can achieve a top speed of approximately 3 mph (5 kph). If the driver coasts the vehicle down the ramp at 15 mph (24 kph) in reverse with the vehicle in gear and the clutch released, the speed of the clutch disc increases to 10,000 rpm. That far exceeds the clutch's burst strength—causing the friction material to fly off the disc and leading to complete clutch failure.
Failure to request clutch adjustment or report erratic operation	The driver must be informed when the clutch is ready for a readjustment and must bring the vehicle in for service as soon as possible when it is required. The driver should also report any erratic behavior to the technician promptly, so it can be seen to.

TABLE 41-2 Common Clutch Complaints, Causes, and Corrections

Symptom	Cause	Correction
Clutch slips on engagement or during operation	Insufficient release-bearing clearance; no free play Riding the pedal Clutch worn out	Readjust clutch to gain correct clearance Instruct driver on proper techniques Replace worn-out clutch
Pedal hard to depress	Linkage binding Release-bearing wear pads grooved	Repair or replace linkage Replace release-bearing or clutch assembly
Clutch does not release completely	Insufficient release-bearing free travel Worn or damaged input shaft splines; discs hanging up Warped clutch disc or pressure plate Intermediate plate binding	Readjust clutch Replace input shaft Replace clutch as necessary Correct binding intermediate plate check drive pin on 14" (35.6 cm) clutch and drive slots on 15.5" (39.4 cm) clutch repair or replace, as necessary
Clutch chatters on engagement	Starting in too high a gear for the load Oil-soaked discs Warped or damaged pressure plate, flywheel, or clutch disc	Instruct the driver on proper operating techniques Repair source of oil contamination and clean or replace discs Replace warped or damaged components
Clutch noisy on disengagement	Worn or damaged release bearing Worn or damaged pilot bearing (noisy only when fully disengaged) Clutch adjustment incorrect on pull-type clutch	Replace release bearing Release pilot bearing If adjustment was made on pull-type clutch with linkage instead of internal adjustment, it can cause the retainer to contact clutch disc torsional damper—readjust correctly with the internal adjusting ring
Gear clash on shifting	Too much free play at pedal (push-type clutch) Not enough release-bearing travel (pull-type clutch) Discs warped or damaged Pilot-bearing binding	Adjust clutch linkage Adjust clutch internally Replace damaged components Replace pilot bearing

Clutch Repair and Replacement Procedures

LO 41-3 Explain the procedure for removing the transmission and clutch assemblies.

Every OEM has its own detailed instructions on clutch installation procedures. OEM-specific procedures should be followed to the letter. This section is merely a general outline of clutch replacement procedures that are common to most manufacturers.

Removing a Clutch

A clutch needs to be replaced when it is damaged, contaminated by leaking fluid, or when adjustment can no longer correct for a slipping clutch. The transmission must be removed to remove the clutch, meaning that the driver's **shift lever and tower** bolted to the top of the transmission must be removed. This requires replacement of the shift tower gasket. Care should also be taken to avoid fluid spills that could be caused by removing the tower and/or a slip yoke from the transmission output shaft. A **slip yoke** is a sliding drive-shaft yoke that sometimes seals the rear of the transmission on lighter-duty vehicles.

To safely and correctly remove and install a clutch requires **guide studs**, which are long threaded studs that support the clutch while the bolts are removed. Guide studs are supplied in some after-market clutch service kits, but can easily be made by cutting the head off an appropriate-size bolt and cutting a screw driver slot in it. In addition, you also need a **clutch-alignment tool**, or an old input shaft, to hold the friction discs in alignment for reassembly. An alignment tool is needed to line up the input shaft with the friction discs; otherwise, it is impossible to reinstall the transmission.

You also need **shipping blocks**, which are small wooden spacers that hold the release bearing of a pull-type clutch in the released position. These should be installed before the clutch-attaching bolts are removed to relieve the pressure on the pressure plate. If you are removing a SOLO or other self-adjusting clutch, four **shipping bolts** are required to cage the clutch-pressure plate for removal. NOTE: When reinstalling a Solo self-adjusting clutch, do not remove the alignment tool until the clutch is torqued to the flywheel correctly and the shipping bolts are removed. If the alignment tool is removed before the shipping bolts, the discs are not aligned. If you are replacing a **Data Mechanical (DM) centrifugal clutch**, used with an Ultra-Shift automated transmission, you need to make a **jack bolt** out of 3" of 3/8" Unified National Coarse (UNC) threaded rod. Place two nuts locked together on the threaded rod and install it into one of the four threaded jack-bolt holes adjacent to the installation bolt holes in the clutch cover. Tighten the jack bolt to 9 pounds foot. This forces the pressure plate forward and secures the clutch discs. Note, however, that on clutch removal, the front disc is free and can fall. Use the jack bolt to secure the disc again on reinstallation; after the clutch is bolted to the flywheel, install the jack bolt in the six o'clock position to maintain disc alignment before you remove the aligning tool. Do not forget to remove the jack bolt after the transmission is installed. Heavier clutches can weigh up to 182 lb (82.6 kg) and may require the use of a clutch jack. Make sure you have all the needed items before you begin the job.

To remove a typical transmission and clutch, follow the steps in **SKILL DRILL 41-7**.

SKILL DRILL 41-7 Removing a Manual Transmission and Clutch

1. Remove the transmission shift lever and shift tower. Cover the opening of the transmission with a suitable device to prevent ingress of contaminants.

2. Remove the driveshaft and mark the location of the drive and driven yokes so they can be realigned on reinstallation. If the transmission has a removable slip yoke connecting it to the driveshaft, it may be advisable to drain the transmission fluid or use a dummy slip yoke to avoid fluid spills. If separating a slip yoke, always mark the location of the two halves so they can be reassembled correctly.

SAFETY TIP

A sudden release of air pressure can cause serious injury due to blowing particles and or air lines whipping about, so drain the air tanks, as required, before continuing, if any air connections are to be removed. Even after the air tanks are drained, exercise caution, as some air may remain in the system.

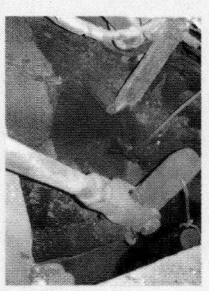

3. Disconnect the air supply and electrical connections from the transmission. If the clutch linkage has more than one possible mounting hole in the cross-shaft lever, mark the location and remove the linkage. If the clutch has a hydraulic-actuating system, remove the slave valve and support it by ties or wire.

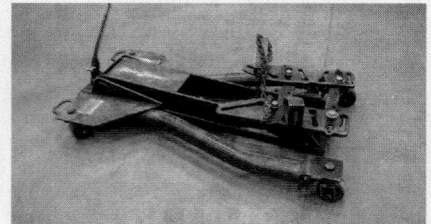

4. Support the transmission with a suitable jack. Note that the jack must have the correct attachments so that the transmission can be supported at its normal inclination. Use a safety chain to secure the transmission to the jack.

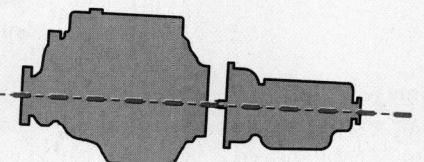

5. Remove the transmission frame supports. Remove the bolts securing the transmission to the flywheel housing. Pull the transmission straight back. Use extreme caution to ensure the transmission does not hang down from the input shaft, as damage to the transmission and/or clutch discs could result. Lower the jack and move the transmission out of the work area. Remove the clutch brake, if equipped. Inspect the clutch-release fork and cross-shaft for wear and smooth operation.

6. Before removing the clutch, inspect the clutch to determine what type it is. An Eaton Solo auto-adjust clutch, a SACH's Twin XTend, or a Meritor AutoJust clutch needs to have shipping bolts installed before removal. Failure to install the shipping bolts can lead to adjust-mechanism damage and or warping of the pressure plate.

SKILL DRILL 41-7 Removing a Manual Transmission and Clutch (Continued)

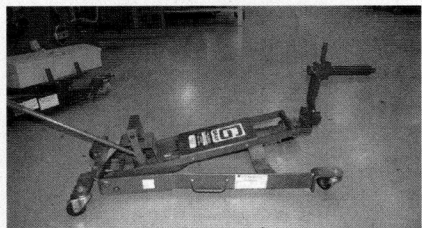

7. Install a clutch-alignment tool to hold the disc/discs centered. If an alignment tool is unavailable, use an old input shaft. If using a clutch jack, use the alignment tool that comes with the jack. Dual-disc 15.5" (39.4 cm) clutches can weigh more than 175 lb (79.4 kg), so it is advisable to use a clutch jack to take the weight of the clutch. Also, beware of pinch hazards as the clutch is being removed.

8. On Eaton Solo, SACH's Twin XTend, or Meritor AutoJust clutches, install the four shipping bolts in the holes provided. Consult OEM documentation for the locations and sizes, tighten bolts until they make contact, and then turn one more turn. On all other pull-type clutches, use a clutch yoke tool to pull the release bearing back and install two 5/8" (1.6 mm) or larger wooden shipping blocks to remove the spring pressure from the pressure plate. Failure to do so may cause pressure plate warping.

9. Remove the top two clutch-attaching bolts and replace them with guide studs. Note: Guide studs can be purchased, or you can cut the top off a long bolt of the correct size and thread for the particular clutch you are working on, and cut a slot in the end to accept a flat-tipped screwdriver.

10. Remove the rest of the attaching bolts following a crisscross pattern. If the clutch is not being replaced, mark the cover and the flywheel so the clutch can be reinstalled in the same location.

11. Pry the clutch back on the guide studs and remove with the clutch jack. On a 14" (35.6 cm) clutch with a pot-style flywheel, the front friction disc and the intermediate plate likely stays in the flywheel, but be careful that the components do not fall out when the pressure plate is removed. Use caution when you remove them from the flywheel.

12. Inspect the removed clutch carefully for signs of abuse, such as abnormal overheating, burst clutch facing, cracked friction-disc hubs, and excess wear on the release-bearing wear pads. All these signs can indicate clutch abuse. If any of those signs are present, make sure that the driver is notified so as not to repeat the failure.

13. If the flywheel is to be sent for resurfacing, remove it now. Use guide studs in the top two flywheel-attaching bolt positions and use caution to avoid pinching when removing.

14. Remove the pilot bearing using a puller.

SAFETY TIP

If removing a clutch without a clutch jack, get assistance and exercise extreme care. When removing a 15.5" (39.4 cm) clutch, the complete clutch, rear disc, intermediate plate, and front disc are removed all at once, and together they can weigh more than 175 lb (79.4 kg).

Component Inspection with Clutch Removed

LO 41-4 Explain the inspection and repair of clutch components.

Several components should be checked when the clutch is removed. Failure to do so could lead to poor clutch performance or even component failure. The transmission input shaft spline, as shown in **FIGURE 41-11**, should be inspected for wear. Any wear here can cause the friction discs to hang up and cause poor release. Replace the shaft if wear is excessive.

It is also important to inspect the **clutch bell housing**. The clutch bell housing is the housing that surrounds the clutch assembly and attaches to the flywheel housing. The **flywheel housing** surrounds the flywheel and bolts to the engine. It is necessary to inspect both housings for wear caused by excessive vibration. Unlike the flywheel housing wear, clutch bell housing wear cannot be measured. The technician must use his discretion when inspecting the clutch bell housing face and pilot for wear. The **clutch bell housing pilot** is the small protrusion that fits inside a mating recess in the flywheel housing, known as the **flywheel housing pilot**. Most wear occurs between the 3 and 8 o'clock positions, as illustrated in **FIGURE 41-12**. Identifying wear on the clutch bell housing is subject to the technician's discretion, as it cannot be effectively measured. If wear is significant,

the transmission hangs down slightly and causes damage to the clutch disc, the input shaft, and the input bearing. It can also lead to gear jump-out when the transmission is in direct gear. Replace the housing as necessary.

On non-synchronized transmissions, it is also important to check the input-shaft bearing cover for wear. From the clutch brake, measure the distance between the forward end of the input-shaft splines to the friction surface of the input-bearing cover. The distance should not exceed 8.71" (22.2 cm), as shown in **FIGURE 41-13**. The SAE-specified distance for dimension A is 8.657" (219.9 mm) nominal and should not exceed 8.71" (221.5 mm). If the distance is longer than the specification, a new bearing cover should be installed.

Cross Shaft Inspection and Repair

The release-bearing cross shaft and the fork should be inspected when the transmission is removed for any reason (**FIGURE 41-14**). The cross shaft is supported by bushings in the clutch bell housing, check the shaft and the bushing for wear; slight movement

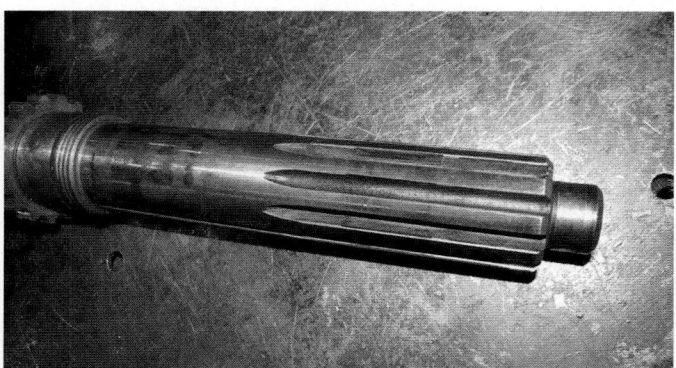
FIGURE 41-11 Inspect input shaft spline for wear.

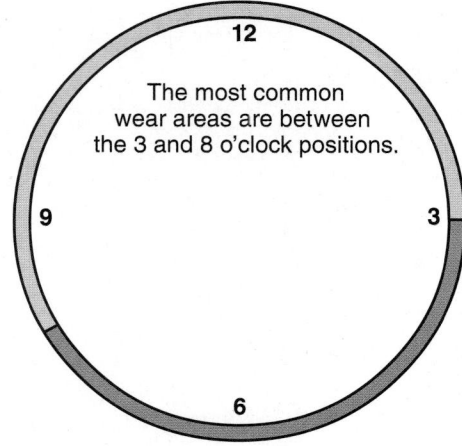
FIGURE 41-12 Common wear areas on a clutch bell housing.

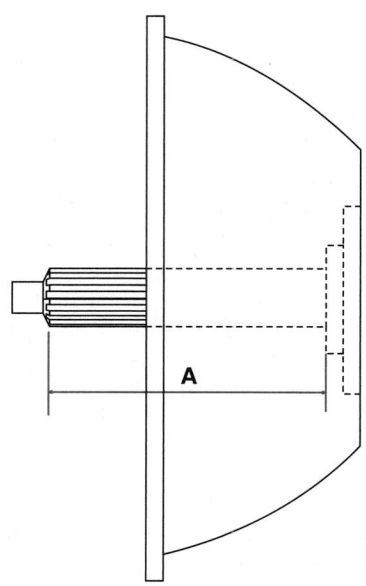
FIGURE 41-13 The SAE specification for dimension A is 8.657" (219.9 mm) nominal and should not exceed 8.71" (221.5 mm).

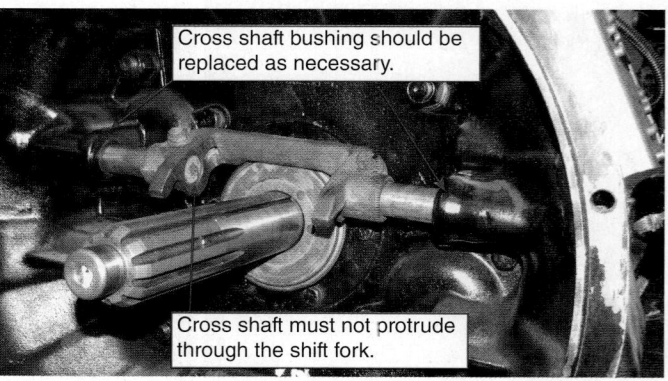
FIGURE 41-14 The fork, the cross shaft, and bushings should be inspected for wear anytime the transmission is removed.

between the cross shaft and bushing is normal, but excessive wear can cause side loading of the release-bearing and limit its lifespan. Worn bushings can also lead to poor clutch release and gear clash complaints. Replace bushings and the shaft when necessary. When replacing cross-shaft bushings, ensure that the grease opening aligns with the grease zerks on the bell housing. When reinstalling the clutch fork, be certain that the cross-shaft ends do not protrude into the area where the fork contacts the release bearing. This causes sideloading of the bearing and leads to failure. Always lubricate the cross shaft and check its full-range operation before re-installing the transmission.

Dial Indicator Checks

When replacing any type of clutch, the following dial indicator checks should be performed to ensure proper clutch operation and service life. While performing these tests, record the total indicated runout (TIR), which is the difference between the low and the high spots. Check for runout on the **flywheel friction surface**, where the clutch-friction disc runs. Check the pilot bearing bore in the flywheel for runout. The **pilot bearing bore** is the bore in the flywheel that receives the pilot bearing. Check runout on the flywheel housing pilot as well. The flywheel housing pilot is the small indentation in the flywheel housing that receives the clutch bell housing pilot. Also check the **flywheel housing face** where the transmission bolts to it for runout. Failure to perform these runout checks can result in transmission misalignment, leading to gear slip-out or erratic and unsatisfactory clutch operation. These checks ensure that the clutch discs do not hang up, and that the center line of the transmission is directly in line with the centerline of the engine. To perform dial indicator checks, follow the steps in **SKILL DRILL 41-8**.

SKILL DRILL 41-8 Performing Clutch Dial Indicator Checks

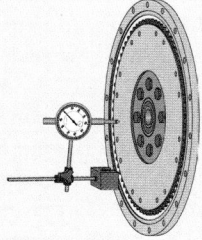

1. Begin by cleaning all the surfaces to be checked with a rag and a suitable solvent, if necessary. Attach a dial indicator to the flywheel housing face with the gauge pointer contacting the outer edge of the flywheel friction surface. Zero the gauge.

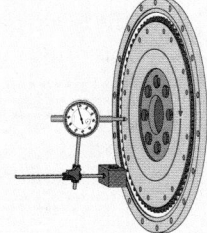

2. Rotate the flywheel one complete revolution—marking the high and low points. It is important that the crankshaft stays in either the most forward or the most rearward position during this test to avoid erroneous readings. Compare your results to the manufacturer's specifications for the typical maximum TIR. A typical maximum is 0.008" (0.2 mm).

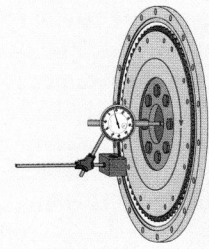

3. Again, with the gauge attached to the flywheel housing, move the pointer so that it contacts the inner surface of the pilot bearing bore. Rotate the flywheel one complete revolution marking the high and low points. TIR should not exceed 0.005" (0.127 mm).

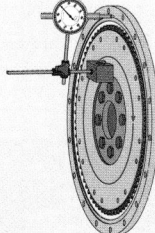

4. Attach the dial indicator to the flywheel face and position the pointer so that it contacts the flat face of the front of the flywheel housing. Be careful that the pointer is not actually in line with the bolt circle so as not to damage the gauge. Rotate the flywheel one complete revolution, marking the high and the low points. Remember to keep the crankshaft fully forward or rearward for this check. TIR should not exceed 0.008" (0.203 mm).

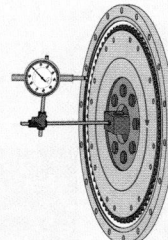

5. The last check is the flywheel housing pilot. With the gauge still attached to the flywheel face, move the pointer to contact the inner surface of the flywheel housing bore that accepts the transmission bell housing pilot, as shown. Rotate the flywheel one complete revolution, marking the high and low points. Again, TIR should not exceed 0.008" (0.203 mm).

Machining the Flywheel

During clutch service, the flywheel may need to be resurfaced if there is scoring or other damage. In some cases, flywheels may be machined several times during their service life. The cost of a new flywheel can be prohibitive, so this practice is unlikely to change. If the flywheel has a raised rim or section where the clutch mounting bolts attach, as is the case with a 14" (35.6 cm) pot-style flywheel, it is essential that the mounting area is machined by the same amount as the flywheel face, or clutch clamp load is changed. A pot-style flywheel is shown in **FIGURE 41-15**.

When the flywheel of a push-type clutch is properly resurfaced, there is virtually no impact to the clutch operation as the mounting position merely moves toward the engine with each successive machining. When angle-spring pull-type clutch flywheels are machined, however, it is not quite as simple. With each machining procedure the clutch and, therefore, the release bearing, moves closer to the engine. This means that the distance from the release bearing to the clutch brake gets longer.

Technicians must be careful of this, as adjusting the clutch according to specifications after flywheel machining moves the release bearing and the retainer further away from the clutch cover than normal, which can over-compress the pressure setting springs, causing an increase in pedal effort and possible clutch release issues. The only way to avoid this situation is to use a thicker clutch brake or shims between the clutch brake and the release bearing to make up for the thinner flywheel.

Although OEMs recommend simply replacing the flywheel if it needs excessive machining (more than 0.060" [1.524 mm]), the aftermarket supplies oversized clutch brakes and shims for this purpose. Clutch-brake thickness is normally 0.375" (9.525 mm), but clutch brakes are available up to 0.560" (14.224 mm), and shims in a variety of thicknesses are also available. If the flywheel is machined, it is important to realize that a truck flywheel could have been machined 3 or 4 times during its life, at 0.050" (1.27 mm)

approximately per time. That can add to 0.200" (5.08 mm) of extra room between the clutch brake and the bearing, leading to a clutch installation with too much spring compression during release, if shims are not used.

Therefore, if you, as a technician, come across a clutch installation with shims between the bearing and clutch brake and/or an oversize clutch brake, or if your flywheel requires machining, you may need to use shims in your clutch installation. Note: a flywheel that is machined excessively may cause contact between the flywheel mounting bolts and the front disc torsional damper. Always check the disc fit carefully by hand before installing the clutch.

Replacing Intermediate-Plate Drive Pins on a 14" (35.6 cm) Pot-Style Flywheel

Fourteen-inch (35.6 cm) clutch pot-style flywheels are unique in that the intermediate plate is driven by six drive pins installed in the flywheel. These drive pins should be replaced when the clutch is replaced.

To replace the drive pins, use an Allen wrench to remove the two set screws that secure each drive pin and knock the pins out using a suitable drift punch. After the flywheel is machined, install six new drive pins in the unused holes in the flywheel, ignoring the previously used holes. Use a drive-pin installation tool or a small carpenter's square to ensure the pin drive flanks are exactly perpendicular to the flywheel friction surface.

When all the pins are installed, place the flywheel flat on a work surface and place two 0.5" (12.7 mm) nuts opposite each other on the flywheel friction surface. This allows you to install and remove the intermediate plate easily without pinching your fingers. Next, test the fit of the intermediate plate on the drive pins, the plate must not hang up or stick on the pins. If the plate hangs or sticks, use a square to check that the pins are perpendicular to the flywheel friction surface.

Next, rotate the intermediate plate so that its drive slots are up against the pins. Using a feeler gauge, as shown in **FIGURE 41-16**, measure the clearance on the opposite side of each slot. The minimum clearance for the drive pin slots is 0.006" (0.1524 mm). Finally, lock all pins in place with two new set screws each.

FIGURE 41-15 If the bolt circle area is not machined by the same amount as the flywheel face, clamp load is changed.

FIGURE 41-16 Checking intermediate-plate drive pin clearance on a 14" (35.6 cm) clutch pot-style flywheel.

Never file the intermediate-plate drive slots or the drive pins to alleviate a sticking condition! Always check that the drive pins are square and, if so, find the other source of the problem. Filing the pins or the slots leads to unequal loading of the drive pins and could result in pin breakage and system failure.

Clutch Installation Procedures

LO 41-5 Describe the installation procedures for single- and dual-disc clutches.

Installing a new clutch is a relatively straightforward procedure, but remember that you require a clutch alignment tool to line up the clutch discs before the clutch is bolted to the flywheel. Otherwise, it is impossible to install the transmission as the discs do not line up to the input-shaft splines. If installing a Solo or other self-adjusting clutch, you must remove the shipping bolts after the clutch is bolted to the flywheel. Do not remove the clutch alignment tool until the clutch is torqued into place or the discs fall out of alignment.

Do not grease or oil the splines of the transmission input shaft. Any grease or oil is thrown outward by centrifugal force and ends up on the friction surfaces, leading to chatter on engagement and possible disc slippage. Most manufacturers insist that the spline be left dry, or you can wipe the shaft with an oily rag only.

Always test install the clutch discs onto the spline of the transmission input shaft before installing a new clutch to see if they fit correctly and that they do not bind. This is a simple step that can save a lot of aggravation. If you wait until you are installing the transmission to discover you have the wrong discs or that they bind on the input shaft, you have to start all over again.

Installing a Push-Type Clutch

With a push-type clutch, usually the clutch cover and the friction disc are installed at the same time. To begin, install a new pilot bearing, such as the one shown in **FIGURE 41-17**, with a high temperature Viton seal or better. Always replace the pilot bearing when replacing the clutch—even if the pilot bearing seems to be in good condition. The cost of replacing it is very small compared to the work required to replace it if it fails later. Also, check that the clutch friction disc fits into the flywheel recess and does not contact the attaching bolts.

The next step is to install two guide studs in the top two clutch attaching holes. Test fit the clutch friction disc into the flywheel recess using the clutch alignment tool to center the disc. Mount the clutch disc on the alignment tool and insert the tool into the pilot bearing. Press the disc against the flywheel and rotate it to make sure there is no contact between the disc and flywheel or the flywheel mounting bolts. Make sure the correct side of the disc is facing the flywheel. As shown in **FIGURE 41-18**, clutch friction discs are stamped with

either "flywheel side" or "pressure plate side" indications, so be sure to install the discs in the correct orientation.

Install a clutch alignment tool through the clutch cover and install the disc on the tool splines. With the alignment tool in place through the clutch cover and the clutch disc, install the disc and the clutch cover/pressure plate assembly over the previously installed guide pins. To support the cover assembly, be sure the pilot of the alignment tool enters the pilot bearing bore. Then install six attaching bolts in the open clutch attaching holes until they are finger tight (tightened by hand without using a tool). Remove the guide studs and replace them with the other two attaching bolts, again, finger tight.

Now, use an appropriate tool to tighten the bolts in a crisscross pattern, starting with one of the bottom bolts. Using a crisscross pattern to tighten the bolts allows the cover to be drawn in evenly without causing warping of the pressure plate. When all bolts are tight, torque them to the manufacturer's specification, again using a crisscross pattern, starting with one of the bottom bolts.

Once the plate is tightened, the alignment tool can be removed, as the clamped pressure plate holds the friction disc(s) in place. It may be necessary to tap the end of the tool with a

FIGURE 41-17 New pilot bearing.

FIGURE 41-18 Clutch friction discs are stamped to ensure they are correctly oriented.

rubber mallet to loosen it. Run the alignment tool into and out of mesh with the splines in the disc and the pilot bearing bore to ensure it does not hang up. That final check ensures that the transmission input shaft slides easily into place.

FIGURE 41-20 The intermediate-plate side of a clutch-friction disc.

▶ TECHNICIAN TIP

Some medium-duty push-type coil-spring clutches may have wooden shipping blocks installed between the release levers and the clutch cover, as shown in **FIGURE 41-19**. These blocks are loosened as the clutch cover is tightened to the flywheel. If they do not fall out by themselves, make sure you remove these blocks after installing the clutch cover and before the alignment tool is removed.

FIGURE 41-19 Remove wooden shipping blocks, if equipped, after installing the clutch and before removing the alignment tool.

FIGURE 41-21 Anti-rattle springs used on super-duty 14" (35.6 cm) clutches with pot-style flywheels.

the clutch is disengaged. If your clutch has these, install them now. Space them equally around the intermediate plate between the drive pins. The round edge of the anti-rattle springs' openings must point toward the flywheel, as shown in **FIGURE 41-21**.

▶ SAFETY TIP

The anti-rattle springs are placed between each pair of drive pins, with the semi-circular opening toward the engine flywheel. These springs are very sharp and must be pushed into place. Wear heavy gloves while installing them to avoid cuts.

Installing a 14" (35.6 cm) Dual-Disc Pull-Type Clutch

Different types of clutches have different installation processes. For a 14" (35.6 cm) dual-disc pull-type clutch, start by installing a new pilot bearing with a high temperature Viton seal or better. As with other clutch types, it is important to always replace the pilot bearing during clutch service on the 14" (35.6 cm) dual-disc pull-type clutch because the cost of replacing the bearing at this point is lower than the labor cost required to replace it later.

Next, install two guide studs in the top two clutch attaching bolt holes in the flywheel. Identify and test fit in the flywheel recess, the clutch-friction disc (single-disc clutch), or the forward clutch-friction disc (dual-disc clutches). Use a clutch alignment tool to center the disc and temporarily install the disc in the recess. As shown in **FIGURE 41-20**, the disc is marked "flywheel" side or "intermediate-plate" side. Make sure you install the disc in the correct orientation, and then rotate the disc. There should be absolutely no contact between the disc and the flywheel or bolts.

With this style of flywheel, you can leave the disc where it is supported by the alignment tool. Then install the intermediate plate over the drive pins. Certain heavy-duty 14" (35.6 cm) inter-mediate plates require three anti-rattle springs to be installed. **Anti-rattle springs** stop the intermediate plate from rattling when

Remove the alignment tool and install the rear friction disc with the side marked "intermediate plate" or "pressure plate" correctly oriented. Then reinstall the alignment tool through both discs. Be certain the tool pilot goes into the pilot bearing inner race. Slide the clutch cover over the alignment tool and the previously installed guide pins and install six attaching bolts in the open attaching holes and finger tighten them. Remove the guide studs, replace them with the other two attaching bolts, and, again, finger tighten them.

Tighten the bolts in a crisscross pattern starting with one of the bottom bolts to prevent warping of the pressure plate. When all the bolts are tight, as shown in **FIGURE 41-22**, torque them to OEM specifications in the same crisscross pattern. As the cover is drawn in, the two 5/8" (15.88 mm) shipping blocks beneath

FIGURE 41-22 Always torque the attaching bolts to manufacturer's specification.

FIGURE 41-23 Ensure any shipping blocks are removed after installation.

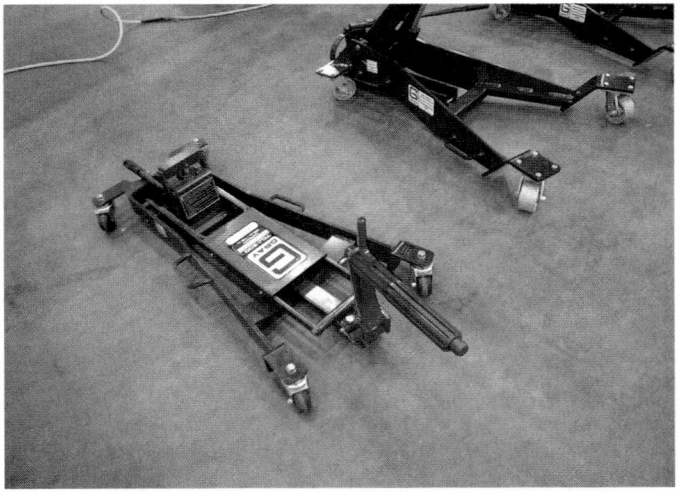

FIGURE 41-24 Dual-disc clutches can weigh upwards of 180 lb (81.6 kg). Use a clutch jack to support the clutch.

FIGURE 41-25 Intermediate plate drive slots in the clutch cover.

the release bearing, shown in **FIGURE 41-23**, should fall out. If they do not, be sure to remove them.

The alignment tool can now be removed, as the clamped pressure plate holds the friction discs in place. It may be necessary to tap the end of the tool with a rubber mallet to loosen it. Once again, run the alignment tool into and out of mesh with the splines in the discs and the pilot bearing race to ensure it is not hanging up.

Installing a 15.5" (39.4 cm) Dual-Disc Pull-Type Clutch

Although there are many similarities in installing a 14" (35.6 cm) and a 15.5" (39.4 cm) dual-disc pull-type clutch, it is important to recognize the difference in weight. A 15.5" (39.4 cm) clutch is extremely heavy and the use of a clutch jack is strongly recommended. Serious injury could result from trying to install this clutch alone without the use of a clutch jack like the one shown in **FIGURE 41-24**.

Installing a 15.5" (39.4 cm) clutch is almost the same procedure as a 14" (35.6 cm) clutch, but there are some differences. As with the 14" (35.6 cm) dual-disc pull-type clutch, start by

installing a new pilot bearing with a high temperature Viton seal or better. Then proceed to installing two guide studs in the top two clutch attaching holes. Once again, test fit the clutch-friction disc into the flywheel recess using the clutch alignment tool to center the disc, making sure the correct side of the disc is facing the flywheel and that there is absolutely no contact between the friction disc hub and the flywheel recess or the flywheel attaching bolts.

Because the larger clutch requires a jack, first install the correct alignment spline on the jack. Then install the release bearing and clutch cover over the alignment spline. Continue by installing the rear friction disc on the alignment spline. Make sure the side stamped "pressure plate" goes toward the clutch cover. Next, install the intermediate plate and check that it moves smoothly into and out of the clutch-cover drive slots, as shown in **FIGURE 41-25**. Always test fit the intermediate plate in the clutch-cover drive slots; failure to do so could lead to a clutch that does not release properly.

Install the front friction disc with the side marked "flywheel" toward the engine flywheel. Using the jack, raise the complete clutch into position and slide the clutch cover over the two guide studs, ensuring that the alignment tool pilot enters the pilot bearing bore in the flywheel. Note: rather than using a clutch jack, some technicians install the clutch assembly on the splines of the input shaft of the transmission and install the clutch and transmission together. This method is *not recommended* by OEMs.

Install six attaching bolts in the open attaching holes and finger tighten them. Remove the guide studs and replace them with the other two attaching bolts, again finger tightening them. Using an appropriate tool, continue tightening the bolts in a crisscross pattern, starting with one of the bottom bolts. Once all the bolts are tight, torque them to OEM specifications in the same crisscross pattern. Again, make sure that the wooden shipping blocks, like those shown in **FIGURE 41-26**, fall out. If they do not, use a release-bearing pulling tool to move the bearing until they do.

The alignment tool and jack can now be removed because the clamped pressure plate holds the friction discs in place. If needed, tap the end of the tool with a rubber mallet to loosen the alignment tool. Run the alignment tool into and out of mesh with the splines in the discs and the pilot bearing bore to ensure it is not hanging up.

Lightly tap the positive separator roll pins, shown in **FIGURE 41-27**, through the access holes in the clutch cover to ensure that the pins are flush against the flywheel. There is one pin in each intermediate-plate drive lug. This ensures that there is equal space on both sides of the intermediate plate when the clutch is disengaged. Pull-type clutches are the most popular clutch type used in heavy-duty trucks, as these vehicles normally have non-synchronized transmissions. Using a pull-type clutch allows the use of a clutch brake that is necessary with these transmissions.

Reinstalling the Transmission

Reinstalling the transmission can be accomplished by following the steps listed in Skill Drill 41-7 in reverse. It is recommended that you start by installing a new torque-limiting clutch brake on the input shaft, ensuring that the larger diameter side is toward the transmission bearing cover. Installing the transmission when a pull-type clutch is used requires that the release

fork be rotated enough so it passes over the release bearing as the transmission is mating up to the flywheel housing.

Place the transmission into gear prior to installing it. That way, you can turn the input shaft to line up the splines by turning the output yoke. Never let the transmission hang unsupported in the disc splines. Even slight warping of the disc hub can cause disengagement problems and damage the input shaft bearing. Never pull the transmission in with the attaching bolts. The transmission should fit snugly to the flywheel housing with little effort. If it does not slide in smoothly, stop! Investigate the cause and correct it before proceeding.

Do not raise the fork to the fully horizontal position as it may contact the clutch cover, damaging the fork or the cover. Some technicians use the release lever on the outside of the transmission as a tool to pull the transmission into the flywheel housing. This is an acceptable procedure for a normal clutch. However, if you are installing an Eaton Solo, SACH's Twin XTend, or a Meritor AutoJust clutch, you may cause the adjusting mechanism to

FIGURE 41-27 The positive separator pins must be flush against the flywheel after installation is complete. **A.** Separator pin. **B.** Access hole. **C.** Intermediate plate. **D.** Flywheel.

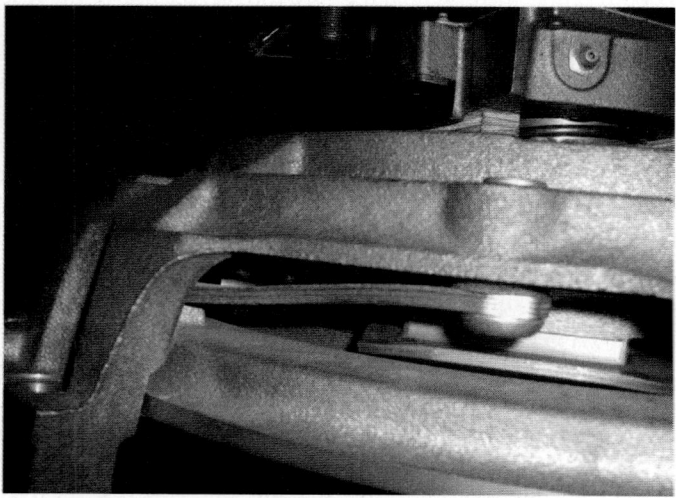

FIGURE 41-26 Shipping blocks must be removed after installation.

actuate, leading to an over-adjusted clutch that does not disengage. The clutch then needs to be reset.

Once the transmission is installed, follow the clutch-adjustment procedures outlined earlier in this chapter.

Self-Adjusting Clutch Repair and Replacement

LO 41-6 Explain the installation and resetting procedures for self-adjusting clutches.

The Eaton Solo clutch, SACH's Twin XTend, and Meritor AutoJust are types of self-adjusting clutches common in the trucking industry today. These clutches have an automatic adjusting system that relies on pressure plate movement to cause an adjustment. These clutches are packaged with shipping bolts, installed like those pictured in **FIGURE 41-28**. The bolts hold the pressure plate in a certain location and prevent any movement of the adjusting mechanisms.

These clutches are installed in the same manner as other dual-disc clutches with one exception. After the covers have been torqued to the flywheel, the shipping bolts must be removed for the clutch to operate. The shipping bolts are four yellow-colored or tagged bolts installed in the clutch cover. Do not remove the clutch alignment tool until these bolts are removed. While these bolts are holding the pressure plate caged or in the released position, the clutch discs can move out of alignment. These clutches are designed to require no manual adjustment other than initial setup procedures. These procedures are specific to each size of clutch and each manufacturer. Manufacturers publish these procedures in the installation instructions that accompany a new clutch and on their individual corporate websites.

When a self-adjusting clutch is removed, the shipping bolts must be installed before the cover attaching bolts are loosened. Otherwise, the clutch over-adjusts, and/or the pressure plate may be damaged. Keep the bolts from new installations for future use when you have to remove one of these clutches.

Operation of Self-Adjusting Clutches

The Eaton Solo, SACH's Twin XTend, and Meritor AutoJust self-adjusting clutches have replaced the large internal adjusting ring with a set of **movable cam rings**. These cam rings sense plate movement as disc wear occurs and compensate by sliding one cam over the other on clutch release to reposition the pressure plate, levers, and release bearing. The Solo self-adjusting clutch from Eaton has four wear sensors in the clutch cover. **FIGURE 41-29** shows the cam rings and the wear sensors in a Solo self-adjusting clutch.

The Solo's wear sensors are like large roll pins in the clutch cover; these wear sensors move toward the flywheel with the pressure plate as clutch-disc wear occurs, repositioning themselves as the clutch is re-engaged. When the wear sensors move, the cam rings adjust the next time the clutch is disengaged.

The maintenance on these clutches is usually limited to inspection for proper functioning (making sure they are adjusting) and lubricating the release bearing, cross-shafts, and fork wear pads.

A known issue with Solo self-adjusting clutches is that they can over adjust in certain circumstances—typically when the driver hits a loading dock hard or otherwise shock loads the driveline and pushes the clutch pedal at the same time. This can cause the Solo clutch to adjust too far, moving the bearing too close to the clutch brake. Complaints may be the clutch pedal is too high, the vehicle won't start (if the pedal is too high to actuate the clutch switch) or gear clashing. To check if the Solo has over-adjusted, check the distance between the release bearing and the clutch brake. If the dimension is less than 0.375" (9.5 mm), the clutch has over-adjusted and it must be reset. To reset an over-adjusted Solo clutch without removing the transmission, follow the steps in **SKILL DRILL 41-9**.

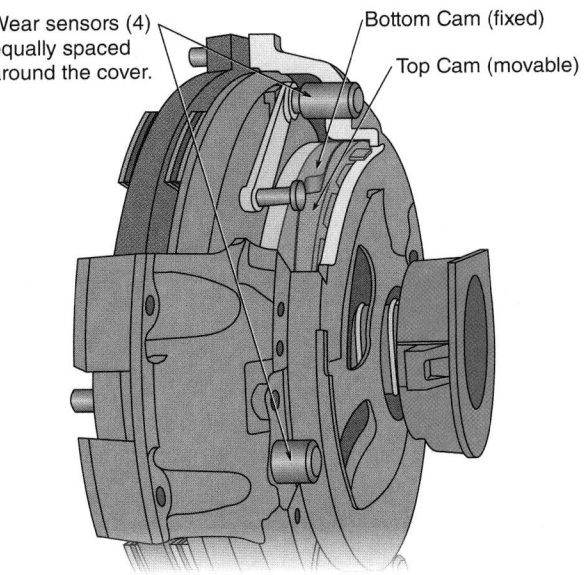

FIGURE 41-29 When wear occurs, the wear sensors reposition toward the flywheel as the clutch is engaged. The cam rings adjust the clutch the next time it is disengaged.

FIGURE 41-28 Shipping bolts (circled) on a Solo self-adjusting clutch.

SKILL DRILL 41-9 Resetting an Over-Adjusted Solo Clutch

1. With the vehicle on a hoist or over a pit, have an assistant depress the clutch pedal to the floor and hold it there.
2. Attempt to move the Solo wear tab to the "new" position. CAUTION: Use finger pressure only, do not try to force the tab, as it will break. If the tab moves to the new position, have the assistant release the clutch pedal. The tab should remain in the new position, if so move to step 8; if the tab does not move, continue with step 3.
3. You must get more movement from the release bearing for the tab to be repositioned. Start by supporting the transmission on a suitable jack.
4. Loosen all the transmission to flywheel housing attaching bolts by at least 0.5" (12.5 mm). Do not fully remove the bolts.
5. Carefully move the transmission back and place two 0.5" (12.5 mm) spacers between the flywheel housing and the transmission housing—one on the left side and one on the right. Note: You may have to adjust or disconnect the clutch linkage to accommodate the movement.
6. Snug up the two transmission attaching bolts on either side of each spacer. This gives you 0.5" (12.5 mm) of extra room to move the release bearing.
7. Reattach the linkage if removed and again have an assistant hold the clutch pedal down to the floor. Try to move the wear

tab on the Solo to the new position (if the tab does not move, it may be necessary to adjust the clutch linkage at this point to get the release bearing to move far enough to unload the adjusting cams). Once the tab is in the "new" position, have the assistant release the clutch pedal to hold the tab there.
8. The wear sensors must now be reset. Do not touch the clutch pedal until this process is finished, or the tab adjusts again.
9. Install the 4 shipping and resetting bolts that are shipped with each Solo (if you do not have a set of bolts, they are: 7/16 UNC 14 by 1¾" for the 15.5" Solo and 3/8 UNC 16 by 1¼" for the stamped-steel 14" Solo). The bolts are installed in the holes that are slightly inboard of and close to the four wear sensors on the clutch cover.
10. Tighten the resetting bolts incrementally using a crisscross pattern until all the bolts are snug. The wear sensors are pulled through the clutch cover as they reset.
11. When all four bolts are tightened, remove them again in a crisscross pattern. The wear sensors stay in the reset position.
12. Remove the spacers (if used) and retorque the transmission mounting bolts.
13. Adjust the clutch linkage until there is no play between the clutch fork and the release bearing.
14. Have an assistant push the clutch pedal to the floor and observe the wear indicator tab. It should move toward the replace position as the Solo clutch adjusts. Check the dimension between the back of the release bearing and the clutch brake. It should be between 0.490" and 0.590" (12.4 mm and 15 mm). If it is still more than 0.590" (15 mm), repeat step 14.
15. Adjust the linkage to have 0.125" (3.18 mm) clearance between the release fork and the release bearing.
16. Check that clutch-brake squeeze occurs in the last inch of pedal travel using the 0.010" (0.25 mm) feeler-gauge method. Place the feeler gauge between the release bearing and the clutch brake and have an assistant push the pedal to the floor and record the pedal position.
17. Slowly release the pedal until the feeler gauge can be pulled out. This should occur within the first inch of pedal movement returning from full stroke.

Wrap-Up

Ready for Review

▶ Proper and timely clutch maintenance can go a long way to extending clutch life. Clutches should be inspected and adjusted as per manufacturer's maintenance schedule.

▶ Adjusting push-type clutches involves adjusting the clutch-actuating mechanism to reestablish free pedal or release-fork clearance.

▶ Adjusting pull-type clutches usually does not require any linkage adjustment. The clutch is adjusted internally to re-establish release-bearing travel and release-fork clearance.

▶ Some newer hydraulic-clutch actuation systems run with no clutch-pedal free play. Always check the manufacturer's maintenance instructions.

▶ Release-bearing travel is the distance the release bearing moves while releasing the clutch on a pull-type clutch. This dimension gets smaller as the clutch discs wear.

▶ The most common cause of premature clutch failure is excessive heat. While a clutch is engaged and not slipping, heat is basically non-existent. But if the clutch slips or the driver allows the clutch to slip too much during engagement and disengagement, the clutch fails rapidly.

- When replacing a clutch, always follow manufacturer's procedures, which are usually available online or in written service manuals.
- When removing and installing the transmission, it is essential to keep it horizontal to the crankshaft centerline. If the transmission hangs unsupported, it can damage the input shaft splines, the clutch discs, and/or the transmission input bearing.
- Self-adjusting clutches have shipping bolts, usually yellow or tagged yellow, to cage the pressure plate. These bolts must be removed after the clutch is installed and before the disc alignment tool is removed.
- A DM clutch requires a jack-bolt to hold the discs in place when removing or installing.
- All clutch components should be inspected prior to the new clutch being installed. Pay attention to cross-shafts and bushing, input shaft splines, release forks, and pivots.
- Always replace the pilot bearing and the release bearing (push-type clutches). Their cost is far outweighed by the cost of having to again remove the transmission to replace them later.
- Dial-indicator checks should be performed on the flywheel friction surface, the pilot bearing bore, the flywheel housing face, and the flywheel housing pilot. Also, check the clutch bell housing on the transmission for excessive wear.
- Always check that the new clutch discs fit freely on the transmission input shaft splines and in the flywheel recess before the clutch is installed.
- Clutches are heavy. Use of guide studs can prevent you from dropping the clutch. These studs hold the clutch in place as you remove the rest of the bolts, and as you re-install the clutch. Guide studs can be made easily by cutting the heads off bolts, or they can be purchased from tool suppliers.
- Most manufacturers recommend using a clutch jack to remove and install heavy clutches. The use of a clutch jack can make the job a lot easier, but not all shops have them. Always ask for assistance if you require it.

Key Terms

adjusting ring A large threaded ring in the clutch cover of a pull-type clutch used to adjust the clutch internally.

anti-rattle springs Flat springs used to stop the intermediate plate from rattling on a 14" (35.6 cm) double-disc clutch with a pot-style flywheel.

clutch alignment tool A tool that holds the clutch discs in alignment as the clutch is installed and without which it is impossible to slide the transmission input shaft through the new clutch discs.

clutch bell housing The housing surrounding the clutch that bolts to the flywheel housing.

clutch bell housing pilot A small protrusion on the front of the clutch bell housing that fits into a mating recess in the flywheel housing.

clutch-brake actuation The point of clutch-pedal actuation on a pull-type clutch when the clutch brake is being actuated or squeezed. Also called *squeeze*.

clutch chatter The condition of the clutch alternately engaging and slipping quite rapidly when the driver engages the clutch.

clutch free travel The free play between the clutch fork and the release bearing.

clutch linkage The mechanical connection between the driver's clutch pedal and the clutch-cross shaft.

cross-shaft A rotating shaft that holds the clutch-release fork.

Data Mechanical (DM) centrifugal clutch A centrifugally actuated clutch, used with an Ultra-Shift automated transmission.

flywheel friction surface The flat friction surface of the flywheel face.

flywheel housing The round housing bolted to the rear of the engine to which the clutch bell housing is bolted.

flywheel housing face The part of the flywheel housing that mates to the clutch bell housing.

flywheel housing pilot A small recess in the flywheel housing that receives the clutch bell housing pilot.

free play Clearance between two components.

guide studs Long threaded studs that stop a component from falling while the attaching bolts are removed.

Jack bolt A bolt that forces the pressure plate forward and secures the clutch discs in a DM clutch.

locking tang A small flat piece of metal that stops the large internal adjusting ring from moving when the clutch is operating.

movable cam rings Rings used in self-adjusting clutches that take up the space of the threaded adjusting ring in the clutch cover.

pilot bearing bore The hole in the center of the flywheel that holds the pilot bearing.

pressure bleeder A device that bleeds a hydraulic system by pressurizing the fluid.

quick-adjust A small mechanism used to turn the large adjusting ring in the clutch cover when adjustment is required.

release-bearing travel The distance the release bearing moves while releasing the clutch in a pull-type clutch.

sealed release bearing A release bearing with no grease nipple or zerk.

shift lever and tower The shift lever and the tower that connects it to the transmission.

shipping blocks Wooden blocks that support the release bearing and cage the pressure plate on pull-type clutches.

shipping bolts Bolts used to cage the pressure plate of self-adjusting clutches, such as the Eaton Solo and the SACH's Twin Xtend.

slip yoke A splined tube that allows for driveshaft length changes.

squeeze The point of clutch-pedal actuation on a pull-type clutch when the clutch brake is being actuated or squeezed. Also called *clutch-brake actuation*.

total indicated runout (TIR) The difference between the high and low measurement of a flat surface, such as the flywheel friction surface.

vocation The type of service a vehicle is involved in.

Review Questions

1. Which of the following would be a driving condition most likely to cause a clutch to "burst," or throw the facings off the clutch disc?
   a. Coasting in gear with the clutch engaged
   b. Coasting in gear with the clutch disengaged
   c. Shock-loading the clutch
   d. Excessive torsional vibrations

2. Normally, a properly adjusted pull-type clutch should have how much clearance at the release fork?
   a. ¼" (6.36 mm) clearance between the release-fork fingers and the release bearing
   b. ½" (12.7 mm) clearance between the release-fork fingers and the release bearing
   c. ¾" (19.05 mm) clearance between the release-fork fingers and the release bearing
   d. ⅛" (3.18 mm) clearance between the release-fork fingers and the release bearing

3. Normally speaking, pull-type clutch release-bearing travel is adjusted internally and should be which of the following dimensions?
   a. ¾" to 1" (19.05 to 25.4 mm)
   b. ¼" to ¾" (6.36 to 19.05 mm)
   c. 1" to 1 ¼" (25.4 to 31.75 mm)
   d. ½" to ⁹⁄₁₆" (12.7 to 14.29 mm)

4. A clutch that has too much free play at the fork can cause which of the following?
   a. Wear on the clutch release fork
   b. Gear clash
   c. Clutch slippage
   d. Overheating

5. What must be done just before removing the alignment tool while installing a Solo self-adjusting clutch?
   a. The clutch mounting bolts should be hand tight.
   b. the clutch mounting bolts must be torqued.
   c. The release-bearing free travel dimension should be set.
   d. The shipping bolts must be removed.

6. Flywheel housing face total indicated runout cannot exceed which of the following?
   a. 0.005" (0.127 mm)
   b. 0.0005" (0.0127 mm)
   c. 0.001" (0.025 mm) per inch (25.4 mm) of housing diameter
   d. 0.008" (0.203 mm)

7. The total indicated runout for the pilot bearing bore should not exceed which of the following?
   a. 0.005" (0.127 mm)
   b. 0.008" (0.203 mm)
   c. 0.0005" (0.0127 mm)
   d. 0.0005" (0.0127 mm) per inch (25.4 mm) of flywheel diameter

8. A driver reports that the free pedal in his cab is only half as much as it used to be. What could be the problem?
   a. The clutch release bearing is seized.
   b. The torsional springs are damaged.
   c. The clutch is likely overheating.
   d. This is a normal condition caused by clutch disk wear.

9. Which of the following components transfers torque from the clutch cover to the pressure plate in most diaphragm spring-type clutches?
   a. Drive straps
   b. Cast lugs that protrude through the clutch cover
   c. The diaphragm spring
   d. The input shaft

10. An important purpose of the drive straps used in a clutch is to do which of the following?
    a. Provide higher clutch capacity
    b. Increase clutch slip on engagement
    c. Pull the pressure plate away from the clutch disk
    d. Absorb torsional vibrations

ASE Technician A/Technician B Style Questions

1. Technician A says that, when installing clutch discs, heavy grease should be used on the input shaft splines so the discs do not "hang up." Technician B says doing so can cause grease contamination of the discs and it is not recommended. Who is correct?
   a. Technician A
   b. Technician B
   c. Both Technician A and Technician B
   d. Neither Technician A nor Technician B

2. Technician A says that angle-spring pull-type clutches are adjusted by turning the large adjustment ring in the clutch cover. Technician B says that the adjustment changes the clutch-brake squeeze dimension. Who is correct?
   a. Technician A
   b. Technician B
   c. Both Technician A and Technician B
   d. Neither Technician A nor Technician B

3. Technician A says that clutch-brake squeeze should occur in the last inch (25.4 mm) of clutch-pedal travel near the floor. Technician B says that clutch-brake squeeze can be altered by a linkage adjustment. Who is correct?
   a. Technician A
   b. Technician B
   c. Both Technician A and Technician B
   d. Neither Technician A nor Technician B

4. Technician A says that a pull-type clutch with mechanical linkage should have 0.125" (3.2 mm) free play between the release fork and the release bearing. Technician B says that a pull-type clutch release-bearing travel dimension should be approximately 0.5" (1.27 cm). Who is correct?
   a. Technician A
   b. Technician B

    c. Both Technician A and Technician B
    d. Neither Technician A nor Technician B

5. Technician A says that if there is no free play at the fork on a pull-type clutch with mechanical linkage, premature clutch wear-out is possible. Technician B says that some hydraulically actuated clutches are designed to operate with no fork to release-bearing clearance. Who is correct?
    a. Technician A
    b. Technician B
    c. Both Technician A and Technician B
    d. Neither Technician A nor Technician B

6. Technician A says that a Solo self-adjusting clutch that has over-adjusted has less than 0.375" (9.5 mm), release-bearing travel. Technician B says that a Solo self-adjusting clutch must be removed to be reset if it has over-adjusted. Who is correct?
    a. Technician A
    b. Technician B
    c. Both Technician A and Technician B
    d. Neither Technician A nor Technician B

7. Technician A sees significant wear on the clutch bell housing face and recommends its replacement. Technician B states that wear in this location is normal and does not require replacement. Who is correct?
    a. Technician A
    b. Technician B
    c. Both Technician A and Technician B
    d. Neither Technician A nor Technician B

8. Technician A says that riding the clutch pedal can cause bent drive straps. Technician B says that bent or warped drive straps are caused by shock-loading the driveline. Who is correct?
    a. Technician A
    b. Technician B
    c. Both Technician A and Technician B
    d. Neither Technician A nor Technician B

9. Technician A says that coasting with the clutch disengaged is a bad driving practice. Technician B says that using the clutch brake to hold a vehicle on a hill is a safe practice. Who is correct?
    a. Technician A
    b. Technician B
    c. Both Technician A and Technician B
    d. Neither Technician A nor Technician B

10. Technician A says that Eaton Solo clutches can be adjusted manually, when required. Technician B says that Eaton Solo clutches are self-adjusting. Who is correct?
    a. Technician A
    b. Technician B
    c. Both Technician A and Technician B
    d. Neither Technician A nor Technician B

CHAPTER 42

Basic Gearing Concepts

Learning Objectives

After reading this chapter, you will be able to:

- **LO 42-1** Explain the fundamental design and functions and interaction of gears.
- **LO 42-2** Explain how to calculate simple and compound gear ratios and the relationship to speed and torque.
- **LO 42-3** Describe the various types of gears and explain their operating characteristics.

You Are the Technician

A truck is brought to your repair shop and the driver complains that he feels a significant vibration throughout the truck in first gear that seems to get worse as he drives faster. Once he shifts into second gear, the vibration goes away. You check the transmission fluid and although the level is correct, you notice the fluid has a silvery look. You recommend removing the transmission and its shift cover for a closer inspection of the components.

1. Would you recommend replacing the transmission bearings?
2. Would you inspect the gearing for wear?
3. What would you look for in the transmission to find the root of this problem?

Introduction

To properly diagnose and repair gear systems, technicians must have a fundamental knowledge of gearing concepts. Gears are essential to the operation of any vehicle. Gears are found in many areas on a vehicle, but primarily in the engine, transmission, and drive axle. The correct functioning of those gears makes the vehicle move. The basic function of a gear is to transfer torque and motion from a rotational input to a rotational output. Gears can be used to gain mechanical advantage to either increase output power or increase output speed or simply to transfer torque and motion unchanged. **Torque** is the twisting force generated by the engine's operation. **Mechanical advantage** is a mechanism that allows us to move greater distances or weight at the output of the mechanism with relatively lower speed or force at the input. There are many different types of gears, but all of them share common basic terms and principles. **FIGURE 42-1** shows a cutaway of a typical standard transmission exposing the gearing.

Historically, the first gears were simple wooden peg gears. As illustrated in **FIGURE 42-2**, one wheel of wood would have pegs installed perpendicular to its **axis** (the centerline that the wheel revolves around) and these pegs meshed with another wheel of wood on which the pegs were installed parallel to its axis. The intermeshed pegs of the driving wheel caused the driven wheel to turn. Motion could be transferred in this way.

As the pegs begin to mesh, however, the outer end of the driving peg contacts the driven peg first. As they continue through mesh, the driving peg slides along the driven peg until the centers of the two wheels align. After that point, the driving peg slides back out until it leaves mesh.

With the driving pegs sliding in and out of mesh, the distance from the center of the driving wheel's axis to the point of contact of the driven wheel's pegs is constantly changing. The constant change in distance from the axis causes the driven wheel to turn faster at the longer contact points and slower at the shorter contact points. As a result, the speed of the driven wheel is also constantly changing, speeding up as the peg starts to mesh and slowing down as they come in to full mesh, and then speeding up again as the peg leaves mesh.

Changing speeds has little effect on a simple system, such as a grain miller's grindstone being turned with a slow-moving water wheel. As speed increases, however, the constantly changing speed becomes a serious vibration. Imagine what that would mean for a vehicle; it would be totally unacceptable. The whole vehicle would be trying to speed up and slow down constantly. Imagine the vibration that would result!

Modern gears are specially formed to eliminate this anomaly, so the driven gear operates at a consistent speed. This chapter discusses basic gearing terminology and explains the construction and operation of gears in basic, universal terms. The chapter does not, however, discuss gear failure analysis. Gear failure is discussed in relevant chapters and sections on the vehicle systems that use gears.

Fundamentals of Gears

LO 42-1 Explain the fundamental design and functions and interaction of gears.

Because gears are such a foundational part of the mechanics of vehicle systems, it is important to understand how they are designed and made, how they interact, and how their ratios determine their functionality.

Gear Design

Gears can be made from a variety of metals. In medium- and heavy-duty vehicles, gears are typically made from steel or **cast ductile iron**. Ductile means that the iron is softer and relatively bendable, rather than hard and brittle. Gears can also be made of nylon or other plastics, depending on the application. In drivelines, gears are usually either cast iron or forged steel. Cast iron and steel gears undergo various methods of surface hardening. **Hardening** is a manufacturing process that makes the surface of a gear much harder than its core. Typically, the surface is hardened to a depth of not more than 0.050" (1.2 mm). The idea is to produce a gear with a surface hard enough to withstand the extreme pressures that come from the sliding, and then rolling, contact that gear teeth are subjected to. While the exterior surface of the gear must be extremely hard, the gear's core must be more ductile so that it can resist fracture and absorb shock loads.

Gear Nomenclature

All gears can be described with a core set of terminology. As you read this section, consult the labeled illustration of gears shown in **FIGURE 42-3**.

FIGURE 42-1 A six-speed Fuller single countershaft transmission.

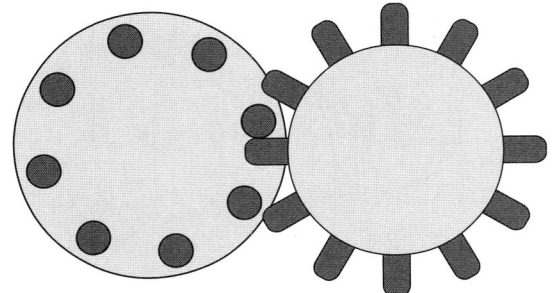

FIGURE 42-2 Wooden peg gears cause irregular speed of the driven gear.

The basic structure of the gear is its teeth, which, much as you might imagine, are the protrusions on the gear face. The apex of the tooth is called the **top land**. The tooth face is the area that actually contacts a mating gear. The tooth face may be parallel or at an angle to the gear's axis of rotation. The upper portion of the tooth contact area is called the **addendum** and the lower portion of the contact area is called the **dedendum**.

The root (also called **fillet radius**) of a gear is the bottom of the valley formed between two teeth. The precise design of the fillet radius provides a gradual change in section and determines the shape of the formed tooth. The filet radius minimizes stress risers (possible break points) to make the tooth stronger. The **root diameter** of a gear is the smallest circle of the gear measured at the fillet radius, or root, of the teeth.

Gear Face Contact During Mesh

As teeth on a gear engage, or mesh, with a mating gear, the contact starts at the addendum of the driven gear tooth and the dedendum of the driving gear tooth. The gears then slide into full mesh where the sliding motion stops and only rolling motion occurs between them. Then the gears slide out of mesh. At that point, contact ends between the dedendum of the driven gear tooth and the addendum of the driving tooth. The average contact point of a given tooth is its **pitch diameter** (also called the **pitch circle**). The pitch circle is the theoretical point where the sliding motion coming into mesh stops and only rolling motion exists. The pitch diameter is usually a point approximately half way up the tooth face from the fillet radius to the top land.

A gear's **pitch** is determined by the number of teeth per unit of diameter measured at the pitch circle of the gear. For example, a gear with 60 teeth and a pitch diameter of 10" (25.4 cm) is a six-pitch gear. This is important because only gears of the same pitch can mesh together properly. That means our example gear could only be in mesh with another six-pitch gear.

Involute Tooth Shape

Just as the peg gears mentioned previously, working gears have constantly changing points of contact. Modern gears are designed with a special tooth shape, called an **involute**, that compensates for the changing point of contact between the gears as they rotate through mesh. On an involute tooth, the dedendum (the lower part of the tooth) is thicker than the addendum (the upper part of the tooth). This special shape is how we eliminate the speed changes noted in the introduction. Let's follow two teeth in contact through mesh and see how this is done. **FIGURE 42-4** illustrates this process.

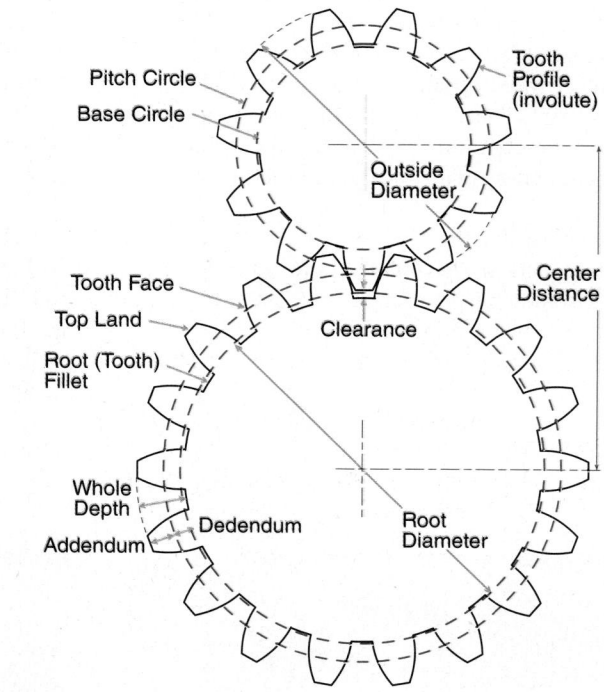

FIGURE 42-3 Anatomy of a gear.

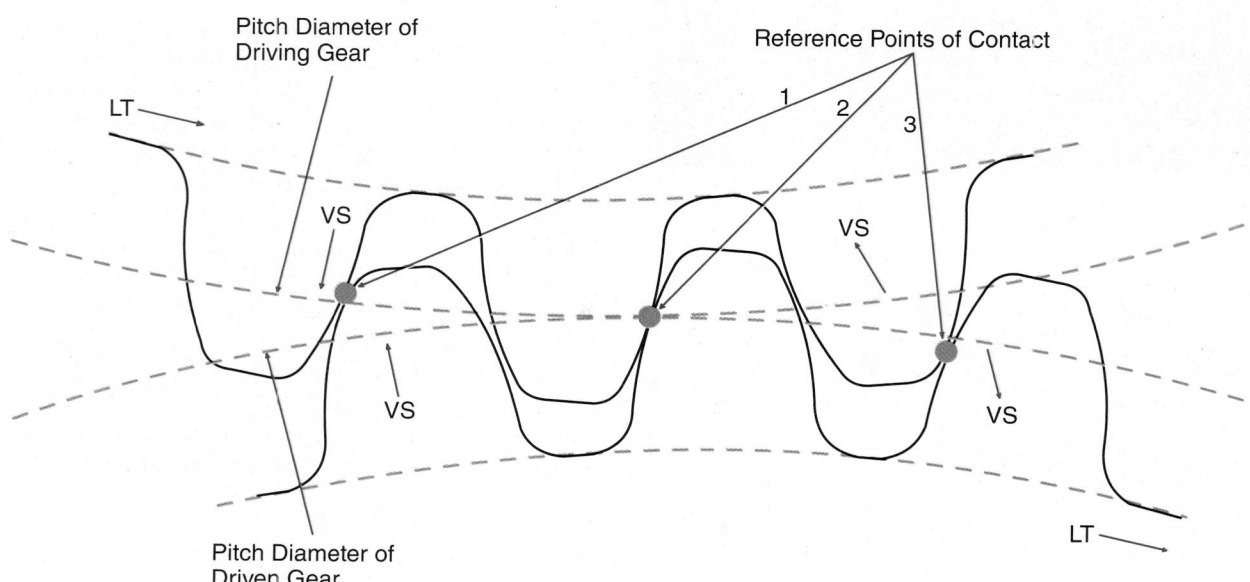

FIGURE 42-4 Involute tooth during mesh.

As the driving tooth comes into mesh with the driven tooth, the dedendum (thicker part) of the driving tooth contacts the addendum (thinner part) of the driven tooth. As the meshing continues, the driving tooth slides down the face of the driven tooth. That slide shortens the distance from the axis of the driving gear to the point of contact of the driving tooth—just as it did in the peg wheel example described in the introduction which should, theoretically, slow the driven gear's speed. As the driving tooth slides into mesh, however, the point of contact is moving toward the thicker part of the driven tooth. The thickening causes a minute acceleration of the driven gear, canceling out the deceleration caused by the changing point of contact.

This action continues until the point of contact reaches the pitch line where there is no more sliding contact, only rolling contact. As mesh continues, the reverse happens. The point of contact slightly lengthens, which should, theoretically, speed up the driven gear; however, the contact point of the driving tooth slides up to its addendum (thinner part) and the decrease in thickness causes a minute deceleration, cancelling out any acceleration caused by the increasing distance from the driving gear centerline.

What does all that mean? It means that, as the teeth go through mesh, the speed of the driven gear remains consistent, rather than speeding up and slowing down. It is important for the technician to understand that any change in the involute shape or axial positioning of the gears caused by wear may cause this speed oscillation of the driven gear. In high-speed equipment (such as a vehicle), this speed oscillation manifests as a vibration. Left unchecked, that vibration can cause catastrophic damage to the component—and any component connected to it—because of the constant torsional stress caused by the speed fluctuations.

Direction of Rotation

Gear rotation is described based on how the gear is moving when the flat face of the gear is viewed from the top. Rotation is normally referred to as **clockwise** when the viewed face on the gear moves to the right from the top. Rotation is **counterclockwise** when the viewed face on the gear moves to the left from the top. Clockwise rotation is usually referred to as forward rotation and counterclockwise rotation as reverse rotation.

When two external toothed gears, such as the ones shown in **FIGURE 42-5**, are in mesh with each other, the driven gear turns in the opposite direction to the drive gear. Not all gears are externally toothed, however. Some gears have internally facing teeth and are called ring gears or internal gears. When a gear with external teeth is in mesh with a ring or internal gear, the driven gear rotates in the same direction as the drive gear, as shown in **FIGURE 42-6**.

Gear Interaction

Gears can be mounted in many positions to accomplish the desired result. In medium- and heavy-duty vehicles, the most common mounting of gear sets is side-by-side on parallel axes. A notable exception to this is bevel gears, which are normally mounted at 90 degrees to each other. Gears must be mounted so that they have a certain amount of **backlash**, backlash is the clearance between the teeth of gears in mesh. As shown in **FIGURE 42-7**, backlash allows for a thin layer of lubricant between the tooth contact surfaces, and for expansion of the gears due to heat. Backlash must be closely controlled. Too little backlash does not allow lubricant in between teeth—leading to failure. Too much backlash can allow the gears to climb out of mesh and slip—again leading to failure. Backlash is controlled by tooth design or by moving the gears' axis closer together or further apart.

When thinking about gears, the simplest thing to compare them to is the lever. As shown in **FIGURE 42-8**, the **lever** is a simple machine that allows a larger object to be moved with less force or something to be moved a greater distance than the input distance. **Simple machines** are the simplest

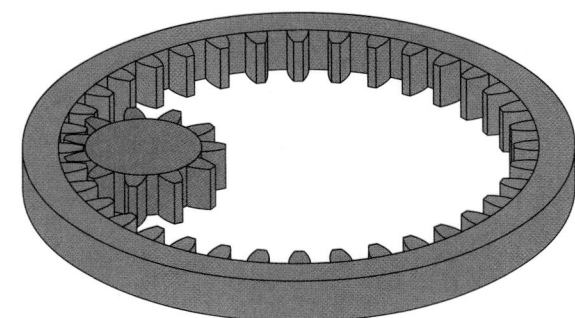

FIGURE 42-6 When an externally toothed gear is meshed with an internally toothed gear, both gears turn in the same direction.

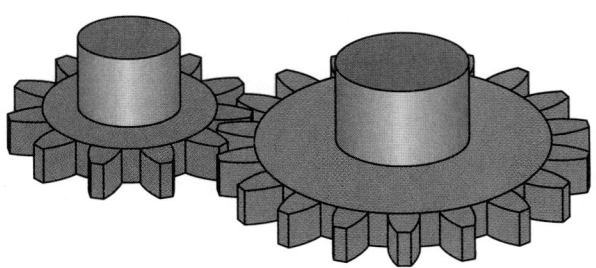

FIGURE 42-5 Two externally toothed gears in mesh rotate in opposite directions.

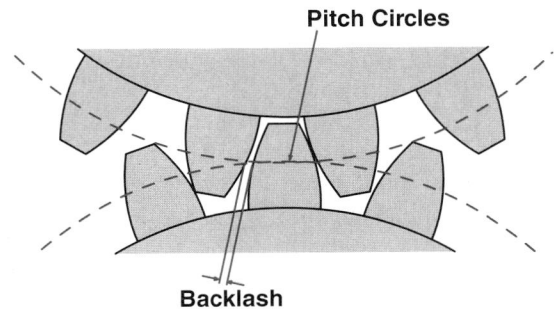

FIGURE 42-7 Backlash clearance in meshing gears.

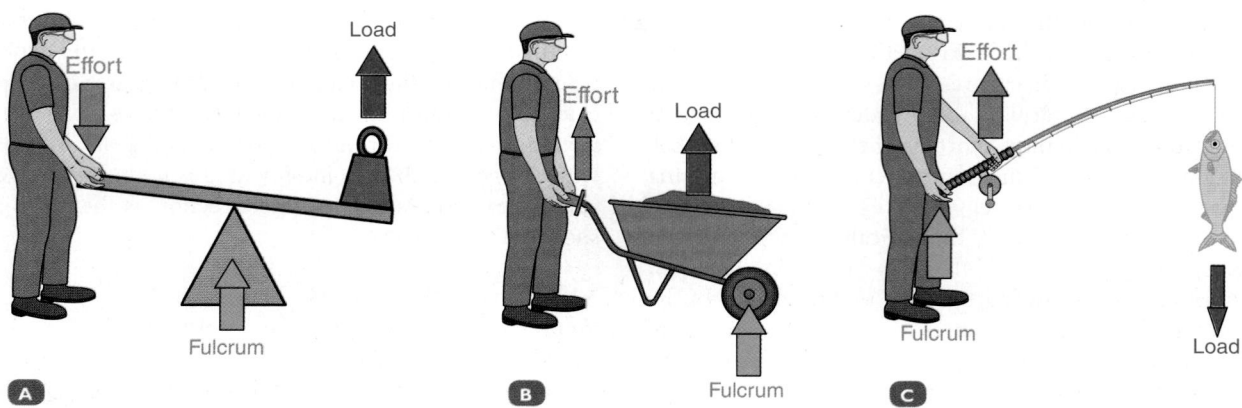

FIGURE 42-8 Levers are simple machines that we can use to gain mechanical advantage to move greater loads or increased distance. **A.** First-class lever. **B.** Second-class lever. **C.** Third-class lever.

mechanisms that allow us to gain mechanical advantage. A first-class lever **FIGURE 42-8A** has an effort arm (where the input force is applied), a load arm (where the weight to be moved is), and the fulcrum (or pivot) is in between the two. A see-saw or teeter totter is a good example of a first-class lever. A second-class lever **FIGURE 42-8B** places the load between the effort and the fulcrum. A wheelbarrow is a good example of a second-class lever. Both first- and second-class levers allow us to move something heavy with less input. A third-class lever **FIGURE 42-8C** places the effort between the fulcrum and the load. A fishing rod is a good example of a third-class lever. In this case, we increase the distance moved, not the weight. The tip of the rod moves much further than the distance we move our hands.

Gears are essentially first-class levers—the effort arm and the load arm are the distance from the tooth face to the center of the gear's axis of rotation. This is not easy to visualize because the gear is a circular lever. The fulcrum is the axis of rotation and the effort arm and the load arm are on opposite sides of the gear making them equal in length. Because of this, a single gear cannot offer mechanical advantage. Only when two or more circular levers or gears are used together can we gain mechanical advantage. Think of it as the load arm of one lever moving the effort arm of a second lever as shown in **FIGURE 42-9**. By changing the diameter of the gears and, therefore, the length of the effort and load arms, we can create the mechanical advantage we need.

Gears have evolved since the lever. As two gears in mesh rotate, the driving gear applies force or effort to each of the gear teeth in sequence. So, each tooth that comes in contact is a successive "lever" delivering force to the driven "lever." In practice, different lengths (gear diameter) of these "levers" provide different levels of output. That is, we can use the different lengths to gain mechanical advantage by increasing output torque, but decreasing output speed, when the driving gear is smaller than the driven gear, or by decreasing output torque while increasing output speeds when the driven gear is smaller than the drive gear. Gears of the same diameters can also be used to transfer speed and torque unchanged.

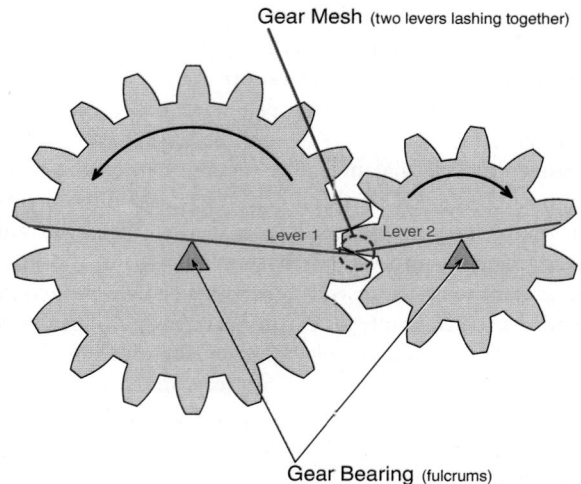

FIGURE 42-9 When two gears mesh it is like the output of one first-class lever inputting another first-class lever.

Gear Ratio Calculations

LO 42-2 Explain how to calculate simple and compound gear ratios and the relationship to speed and torque.

The sizing of the gears and the relationship between them is known as the **gear ratio**. One way to calculate the ratio between gears uses lever length (the distance from the center of the gears' axis to the tooth contact point). A much simpler method uses the number of gear teeth. Simple gear ratios are the relationship between one driving and one driven gear, while compound ratios involve more than one set of gears. Once the ratio is calculated, we can use it to calculate the torque and speed increase or decrease.

Simple Gear Ratios

Imagine a driving gear that has 15 teeth in mesh with a driven gear that has 30 teeth. Every time the driving gear rotates one complete turn, it moves the driven gear 15 teeth, or one-half of the driven gear's total teeth. Therefore, to move the driven gear one full turn, the driving gear must move 30 teeth—or two complete revolutions. The two gears in our example have a gear ratio of 2:1. Two turns of the driving gear equal one turn of the driven gear. This ratio is illustrated in **FIGURE 42-10**.

The formula to calculate this ratio is simple. Divide the number of teeth on the driven gear by the number of teeth on the drive gear:

$$30 / 15 = 2$$

The ratio is always compared to one revolution of the driven gear. Therefore, the two revolutions of the driving gear becomes a ratio of two to one and is expressed as 2:1.

What does this ratio accomplish? The ratio does two things. First, it is responsible for slowing down the speed of the driven gear. The speed of the driven gear is the speed of the driving gear divided by the ratio. In our example, that means the driven gear turns only half as fast as the driving gear.

Second, and more importantly, gear ratios are responsible for producing mechanical advantage. The mechanical advantage is the effort applied by the driving gear multiplied by the ratio. For example, a driving gear torque of 100 ft-lb (136 Nm) passing through a gear set with a 2:1 ratio becomes 200 ft-lb (271 Nm) at the driven gear. Any ratio with a first number greater than one is known as a **gear reduction** or **underdrive ratio**. The speed of the driven gear is reduced by the ratio, but available torque is increased by the same proportion.

But what happens if we reverse the two gears in our example and have the 30-tooth gear driving the 15-tooth gear? Every rotation of the 30-tooth driving gear turns the 15-tooth driven gear 30 teeth, or two complete revolutions. The formula for calculating the ratio remains the same. That is, the ratio is still calculated by dividing the number of teeth on the driven gear (in this case 15) by the number of teeth on the driving gear (in this case 30):

$$15 / 30 = 0.5$$

As with our earlier example, the ratio is always compared to one revolution of the driven gear. The 0.5 becomes 0.5 to 1 or

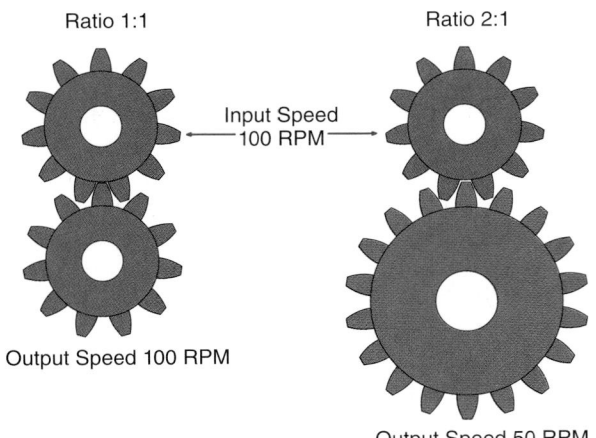

FIGURE 42-10 Gears with a 1:1 gear ratio, and with a 2:1 ratio.

0.5:1. What does this ratio accomplish? Again, the ratio does two things. First, it now speeds up the driven gear. That is, the speed of the driven gear is the speed of the driving gear divided by the ratio. That means the driven gear turns twice as fast as the driving gear, meaning we have gained mechanical advantage in terms of distance or speed.

By gaining speed, however, we give up the mechanical advantage of increased torque. The torque available at the driven gear is the torque available at the driving gear multiplied by the ratio. So, 100 ft-lb (136 Nm) of driving torque becomes 100 × 0.5 or 50 ft-lb (68 Nm) of torque at the driven gear. Any ratio in which the first number is less than 1 is known as an **overdrive ratio**. In gears with an overdrive ratio, the speed of the driven gear is increased by the ratio, but available torque is decreased by a corresponding amount.

Let's walk through the basic ratio, gear speed, and torque calculations for a simple gear arrangement. As we go through the calculations, we make the following assumptions:

- The drive gear has 20 teeth.
- The driven gear has 60 teeth.
- Input torque on the drive gear is 100 ft-lb (136 Nm).
- Input speed is 300 rpm.

Let's begin finding the gear ratio by dividing the number of teeth on the driven gear by the number of teeth on the drive gear:

$$60 / 20 = 3$$
$$3:1$$

That means the gear ratio is 3:1. Because 3 > 1, 3:1 is a reduction, or underdrive, ratio.

Next, let's calculate the torque available at the driven gear by multiplying the input torque by the gear ratio:

$$3 × 100 = 300 \text{ ft-lb (407 Nm) of torque available}$$
to the driven gear

Notice how the calculations prove the basic premise that reduction gears increase output torque. The gear ratio of 3:1 is a reduction ratio, and the torque output is higher than the torque input.

The next calculation we perform is to find the speed of the driven gear. To accomplish that, we need to divide the input speed by the ratio:

$$300 \text{ rpm} / 3 = 100 \text{ rpm}$$

As we expect, our underdrive gear ratio has caused a decrease in output speed.

Compound Ratios

In most applications, there are more than one set of gears involved in the transfer of speed and torque. When we have a ratio with more than one pair of gears involved, it is called a **compound ratio**. Let us examine briefly how compound ratios work. Consider the first gear power flow in a typical transmission. In this transmission, we assume the input gear has

27 teeth, and it drives a countershaft driven gear with 51 teeth. The countershaft first gear has 13 teeth, and it drives the main shaft first gear, which has 64 teeth. To summarize:

- Input drive gear has 27 teeth.
- Driven countershaft gear has 51 teeth.
- Countershaft first drive gear has 13 teeth.
- Driven main shaft gear has 64 teeth.

Following our formula, we divide the first driven gear by the first driving gear.

$$51 / 27 = 1.8888/1$$
$$1.89:1$$

Our gear ratio, therefore, is 1.89:1. This means that the input gear has to turn 1.89 times to turn the countershaft once.

Next, we calculate the ratio for the second set of gears. The second driven gear has 64 teeth and its driving gear has 13 teeth.

$$64 / 13 = 4.9230/1$$
$$4.92:1$$

So, the countershaft has to turn 4.92 times to turn the main shaft one complete turn.

If the input shaft must turn 1.89 times to turn the countershaft once, and the countershaft must turn 4.92 times to turn the main shaft once, to find the overall ratio we have to multiply how many times the input shaft must turn by how many times the countershaft must turn. Therefore,

$$1.89 \times 4.92 = 9.30$$

We see then that, to turn the main shaft one complete revolution, the input shaft must turn 9.30 times. That means the total, or compound, ratio of this gear train is 9.30:1.

There is an easier formula for compound gear sets. Rather than finding the ratios of each pair of gears and multiplying the two ratios together, we can multiply all the driven gears together and multiply all the drive gears together, and then divide the total of the driven by the total of the drive. Let's apply this formula to the four-gear compound ratio transmission setup above where the input gear has 27 teeth and it drives a countershaft driven gear with 51 teeth; the countershaft first gear has 13 teeth, and it drives the main shaft first gear, which has 64 teeth. Because this is a four-gear compound ratio the formula is as follows, the capital "D" represents driven gears and the small "d" represents drive gears.

$$\frac{D_1 \times D_2}{d_1 \times d_2}$$

To calculate the compound ratio then, we first multiply together the number of teeth on each of the driven gears:

$$51 \times 64 = 3264$$

Next, we multiply together the number of teeth on each of the driving gears:

$$27 \times 13 = 351$$

Finally, we divide the total of the driven gears by the total of the driving gears.

$$3264 / 351 = 9.299$$
$$9.3:1$$

Ratios are usually rounded after two decimals, so this result is the same as the first calculation—a compound ratio of 9.30 to 1, or 9.30:1. Because 9.3 is greater than one, this compound ratio is a reduction or underdrive. Therefore, the input shaft must turn 9.30 times for every one turn of the transmission main shaft. Available torque at the main shaft is input torque multiplied by the ratio. That means the available torque at the main shaft is 9.30 times greater than the input torque. The output speed on the main shaft, however, is the input speed divided by the ratio, or 9.30 times slower.

Compound ratios can often involve four, six, or even more gears in the transfer of power. Calculating ratios with that many gears is simply done by dividing the product of all the driven gears (all the driven gears multiplied together), D, by the product of all of the drive gears (all of the drive gears multiplied together), d. The formula for six gears looks like this:

$$\frac{D_1 \times D_2 \times D_3}{d_1 \times d_2 \times d_3}$$

The same formula can be used no matter how many gear sets are involved in a ratio. It simply becomes a larger calculation with the number of teeth on each driven gear multiplied together divided by the number of teeth on each of the drive gears multiplied together. **FIGURE 42-11** illustrates a typical transmission that uses compound ratios. For all ratios, except for direct, in this transmission, power comes in through the input gear, which drives the countershaft driven gear. The countershaft speed gear then drives the engaged main-shaft speed gear, so each of the ratios involve four gears.

In most vehicle systems, gears sets are used in combination to produce the desired gear ratio to move the vehicle. For example, any underdrive or overdrive ratio through a transmission has at least two ratios working together:

- The ratio of the input gear to the countershaft driven gear
- The ratio of the countershaft speed, or range gear, to its corresponding main shaft speed or range gear

Those two gears ratios combine to create a compound ratio.

Not all gears are overdrive or underdrive, however. When gears with exactly the same number of teeth are meshed, the resulting ratio is one to one (or 1:1). In this case, the gears transmit the exact speed of rotation, and torque remains unchanged.

Idler Gears

The gears used in most medium- and heavy-duty vehicle standard transmissions are almost exclusively externally toothed gears meshed together. When two externally toothed gears are in mesh, the driven gear turns in the reverse direction to the drive gear. That direction suits our purpose well for all gears except reverse.

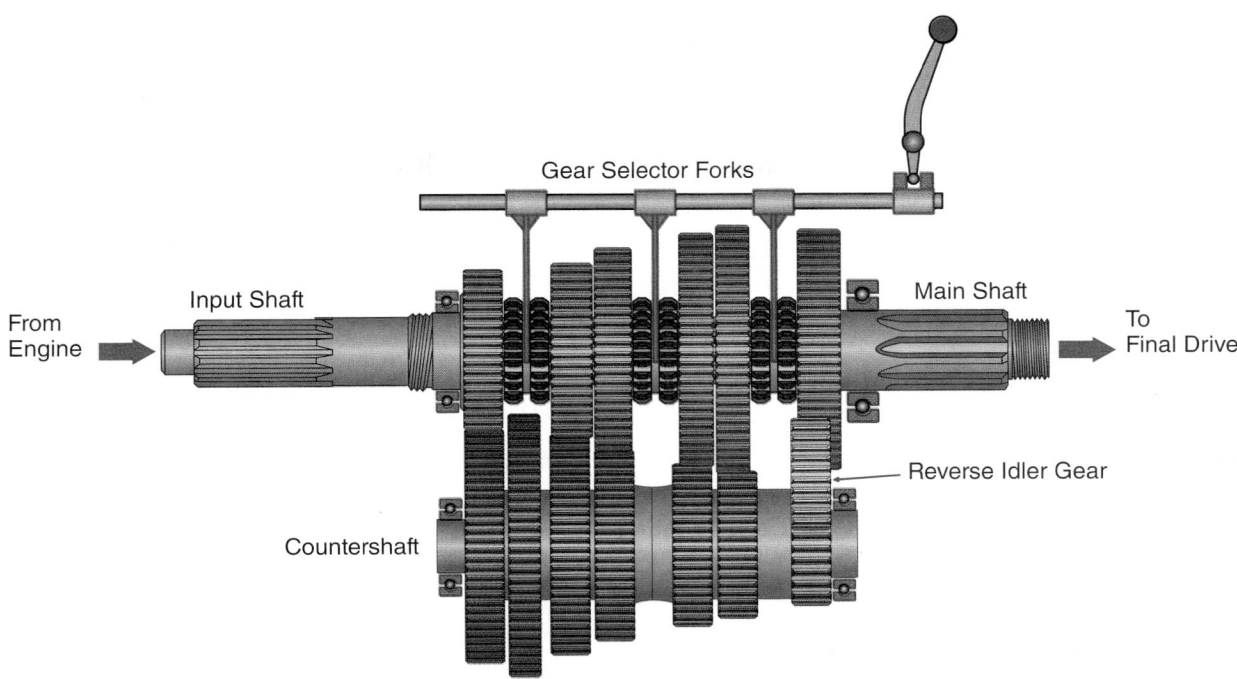

FIGURE 42-11 Compound gears.

By following the power flow, we can see how this works for us. The engine turns clockwise when viewed from the front. So too, does the transmission input shaft because it is connected to the engine through the clutch. The input shaft gear drives the countershaft driven gear counterclockwise. (That's why we call it a countershaft.) The countershaft first gear is part of the countershaft and so is also turning counterclockwise. Countershaft first gear is in mesh with the main shaft (output shaft) first gear. Therefore, the main shaft gear is driven in a clockwise direction, and the vehicle moves forward. These power flow directions of rotation are repeated for the rest of the transmission gear ranges.

In reverse, however, we must turn the output shaft counterclockwise to move backward. To do this, we use an idler gear. The purpose of idler gears is to act as a bridge between two gears and reverse the direction of rotation without changing the ratio. **Idler gears** are used in transmissions to drive a vehicle backward. As shown in **FIGURE 42-12**, an idler gear is placed in the power flow between the countershaft

reverse drive gear and the main shaft reverse gear. When the vehicle is in reverse, the input (countershaft) gear is turning counterclockwise. That causes the reverse idler gear to turn clockwise, which in turn makes the output (reverse main shaft) gear turn counterclockwise, as well. The vehicle, then, moves backward.

An idler is both a driven gear and a drive gear. An idler gear is driven by the countershaft reverse gear, and the idler gear drives the main shaft reverse gear. Because the idler gear functions in both of those capacities, it has no bearing on gear ratios.

To illustrate this point, let's use the same numbers we used for first gear ratio calculation in the Gear Ratio Calculation section. This time, however, we insert a 9-tooth idler gear into the first gear power flow and make it reverse.

Recall our assumptions:

- Input drive gear has 27 teeth.
- Driven countershaft gear has 51 teeth.
- Countershaft reverse drive gear has 13 teeth.
- Our newly introduced idler gear has 9 teeth.
- Reverse gear main shaft has 64 teeth.

First, we take the number of teeth on each of the driven gears and multiply them together:

$$51 \times 9 \times 64 = 29,376$$

Next, we take the number of teeth on each of the drive gears and multiply them together:

$$27 \times 9 \times 13 = 3159$$

Remember that the idler gear drives the main shaft reverse gear, so it is also a drive gear.

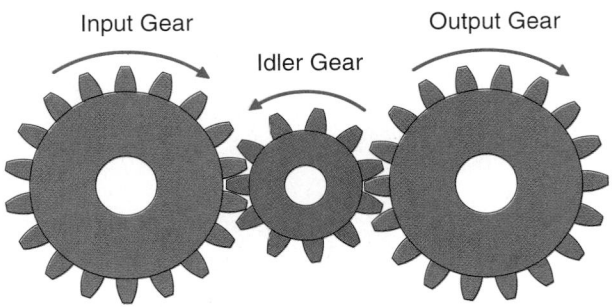

FIGURE 42-12 An idler gear.

Now we divide the product of all the driven teeth by the product of all the drive teeth. That is,

$$29{,}376 / 3159 = 9.299$$

$$9.3{:}1$$

That result, 9.3:1, is the exact same ratio that we had in the earlier calculation. Because an idler gear is both a drive and a driven gear, it cancels itself out in the calculation. Therefore, idler gears do not need to be included when calculating gear ratios.

Types of Gears

LO 42-3 Describe the various types of gears and explain their operating characteristics.

As you might expect, today's vehicles use many different types of gears in their various systems and engines. In this section, we discuss spur, helical, herringbone, bevel, worm, and rack-and-pinion gears.

Spur Gears

Spur gears are the simplest of modern gears used in vehicles today. As shown in **FIGURE 42-13**, a **spur gear** has teeth that are cut parallel to the gears axis of rotation. The advantages of spur gears are numerous. Spur gears are simpler and, therefore, less expensive to manufacture. Spur gears do not produce any axial thrust when they are in operation. **Axial thrust** is thrust that tries to move the gears apart along their axis. Spur gears in mesh merely produce **radial thrust**. That is, they tend to want to push away from each other radially, or perpendicular to their axis. Therefore, the shafts that support spur gears can be mounted on simple ball or roller bearings. This allows for simpler and less expensive manufacture of shafts, housings, and bearings.

Spur gears do, however, have some disadvantages. First, spur gears tend to be noisy in operation. As spur gear teeth come into mesh with each other, their meshing teeth tend to impact each other, causing a clicking sound. At higher speeds, the clicking becomes a high-pitched whine. For that reason, spur gears are seldom used in light-duty vehicle manufacture. Spur gear whine may be heard in some vehicles with standard transmissions while operating in reverse. Despite the whine, spur gears are commonly used for reverse gear in automobiles because the reverse gear train is usually operated for only short periods and at relatively slow speeds.

Another disadvantage of spur gears is that only one or two teeth are in mesh at any given time. That causes all the torque transfer to be carried by those one or two teeth. Consequently, the gear must be made larger or thicker so that one tooth can carry the load alone.

Helical Gears

Helical gears have teeth that are cut at an angle to their axis of rotation and because of the circular shape of the gear, the tooth is part of a helix or spiral in shape, hence the name. The design of a helical gear, such as the one shown in **FIGURE 42-14**, allows some advantages. First, when helical gears mesh, there is always more than one tooth in mesh at a time. As a result, helical gears do not make the characteristic whining noise that spur gears do. As the next set of teeth is coming into mesh, they do not click together. The effect is more of sliding motion as the teeth engage. Consequently, helical gears are much quieter in operation than spur gears.

Another advantage of helical gears is their strength. Because more than one or two teeth are in mesh at once, the individual teeth on a helical gear do not have to carry as much torque. Therefore, helical gears are stronger than equivalently sized spur gears. Furthermore, the design of helical gears allows gear width to be reduced with no loss of torque capacity. Transmission cases can be shorter and lighter in overall weight. Helical gears are manufactured with either a left-hand helix or a right-hand helix. To determine the hand, look at a helical gear from the top. A left-hand helix appears to move down to the left, and a right-hand helix appears to move down to the right.

FIGURE 42-13 Spur gears.

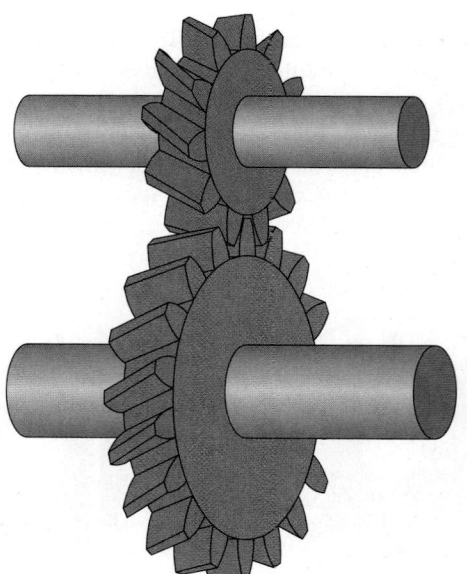

FIGURE 42-14 Helical gears.

When used together in side-by-side applications, a left-hand gear must mesh with a right-hand gear. When mounted at right angles to each other, however, two right-hand or two left-hand helices can mesh, as shown in **FIGURE 42-15**. This arrangement allows the power to turn a 90-degree corner.

The main disadvantage of helical gears is that they cause axial thrust. Axial thrust can be extreme under load and must be counteracted by tapered roller bearings and/or thrust bearings and washers. Another disadvantage of helical gears is their expense. Helical gearing is more expensive and more complicated to manufacture, leading to increased component cost.

Herringbone Gears

Herringbone gears, such as those shown in **FIGURE 42-16**, have opposite helices on each side of their face. That is, one-half of the tooth face is cut with a right-hand helix, and the other half of the tooth face is cut with a left-hand helix. Usually there is a groove cut at the apex of the "V" formed by the two helices to allow trapped lubricant to escape.

The advantages of herringbone gears are the same as helical gears with one key difference. The dual-cut helices on herringbone gears cause all axial thrust to be cancelled out.

These gears are obviously much more expensive to manufacture and, consequently, are not found in most vehicle applications. These gears can carry extreme loads and operate very quietly, with no axial thrust. Herringbone gears are used in specialized equipment, such as large turbines for generating electricity.

Bevel Gears

Bevel gears are gears cut on an angle and designed to allow the flow of power to turn a corner—usually 90 degrees. Therefore, bevel gears are primarily used in drive axles to send rotating force to the drive wheels. Bevel gear sets can be designed to allow for any degree of turning, up to 90 degrees. Bevel gears consist of a cone-shaped pinion gear (a **pinion gear** is a term used to describe a small driving gear) and a ring or "crown" gear. True bevel gearing is like spur-type gearing in that the teeth are straight cut. Bevel gears have the same inherent advantages and disadvantages of spur-type gearing—bevel gears are noisy and generally weaker, but cheaper to manufacture. **FIGURE 42-17** shows bevel gears.

Spiral bevel gearing attempts to minimize the disadvantages of bevel gears by using helically cut teeth. The spiral bevels' helical tooth configuration imparts the advantages of helical gearing to the bevel gear set, making them stronger and quieter, but they are more expensive to manufacture. **FIGURE 42-18** shows spiral bevel gears.

FIGURE 42-15 When mounted at right angles, two like-handed helical gears mesh.

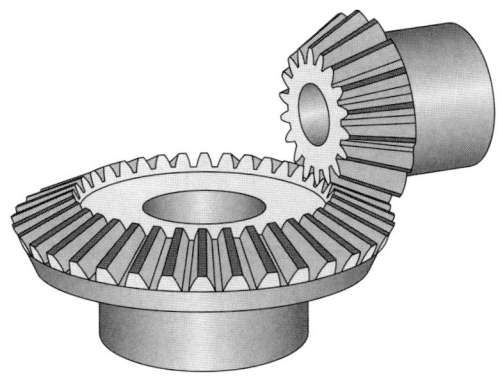

FIGURE 42-17 Bevel gears.

FIGURE 42-16 Herringbone gears.

FIGURE 42-18 Spiral bevel gears.

Durapoid, hypoid, generoid, and amboid gearing are all design improvements that make spiral bevel gearing stronger and more adaptable to use in drive-axle manufacture. These designs are discussed in more detail in the Heavy-Duty Truck Drive Axles chapter.

Worm Gears

Worm gears, such as the one illustrated in **FIGURE 42-19**, are another type of gear that allows the flow of power to turn a 90-degree corner. Worm gears consist of the worm shaft or screw, which meshes with the crown wheel. The outer edges of the crown wheel's teeth are scooped out at the center to allow for the shaft of the worm gear. That recess cut makes the wheel somewhat resemble a crown. Compared to bevel gearing systems, worm drive systems are capable of very large speed reductions with much smaller gears.

The ratio of worm gears is set by changing the number of tooth leads or starts on the worm. With a single-start worm, the driven crown wheel advances only one tooth with each revolution of the worm. So, a 20-tooth crown gear produces a ratio of 20:1. To achieve that reduction with bevel gears using a 12-tooth pinion, the crown gear needs 240 teeth. (Just imagine the size of such a gear!)

Most worm gears have a worm with three or four starts, which advance the crown gear three or four teeth per revolution, respectively. Worm gears are usually found in various types of machinery that require large reduction ratios.

One interesting feature of these gears is that, when a high ratio is used, the worm can drive the crown wheel easily, but extremely high resistance prevents the crown wheel from driving the worm. An example of this feature is the self-locking effect of the machine heads used for adjusting guitar strings.

In the past, worm gears were used in the drive axles of vehicles. At present, worm gears are not used in North American medium- or heavy-duty vehicles.

Rack-and-Pinion Gears

Rack-and-pinion gears consist of a flat rack with either spur or helically cut teeth on one side and a meshing circular pinion gear. **FIGURE 42-20** shows a rack-and-pinion gear. Rotation of the pinion causes the rack to move linearly or horizontally. Rack-and-pinion gears have, until recently, been predominately used in the steering mechanism of front-wheel-drive, light-duty vehicles; however, they are now becoming available in a variety of steering systems on medium- and heavy-duty vehicles as well.

Many combinations of gears are used in vehicle drivelines. As a result, a near infinite number of ratio combinations are possible to achieve the desired results. We can move a 120,000 lb (54,431 kg) load with an engine that produces only 1500 lb (680 kg) of torque. This is achieved by sacrificing speed for torque using reduction ratios. Alternatively, we can drive a vehicle at highway speeds with an engine that is only turning at 1400 rpm or less by sacrificing torque capability for increased speed using overdrive ratios.

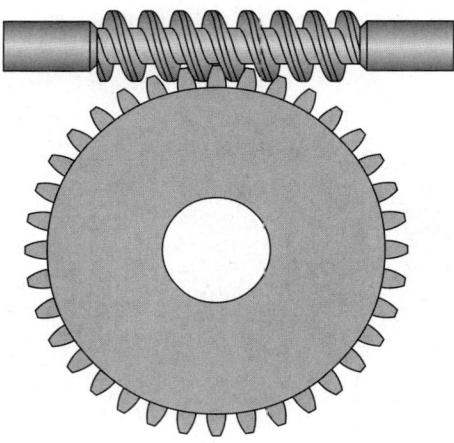

FIGURE 42-19 Worm gear.

FIGURE 42-20 Rack-and-pinion gear.

Wrap-Up

Ready for Review

▶ Gears are essential to the operation of any mechanized equipment—trucks and buses are no exception.
▶ Involute gear tooth design compensates for the natural tendency of two gears in mesh to turn at a constantly changing ratio of speed.

▶ Gear teeth spacing is known as gear pitch. Only gears of the same pitch can run in mesh with each other.
▶ Gears can have external or internal cut teeth. When externally toothed gears are in mesh, they rotate in opposite directions. A gear with internally cut teeth is known as a ring gear and, when in mesh with a gear with externally cut teeth, both gears turn in the same direction.

- Backlash is the clearance between the teeth of gears in mesh. Backlash is essential for lubrication and expansion, but must be tightly controlled to prevent gears slipping over each other's teeth.
- Gear design evolved from the lever—one of the six simple machines. Simple machines allow us to gain mechanical advantage to accomplish a task.
- Gear ratio is the comparison of the input to the output result of gears in mesh. The formula to calculate ratio is the number of teeth on the driven gear divided by the number of teeth on the drive gear. If input torque is known, output torque can be calculated by multiplying input torque by the ratio. Output speed can be calculated by dividing input speed by the gear ratio.
- Compound gear ratios are those that involve more than one set of gears. All ratios where the power flows through a transmission's countershaft are compound ratios. These can be calculated by multiplying all the driven gears together and dividing that figure by the product of all the drive gears.
- Idler gears are used to change direction of rotation. They have no influence on gear ratio, as they are both a driven gear and a drive gear.
- Spur gears are the simplest gears to manufacture. They have only radial thrust, but they are inherently noisy in operation.
- Helical gears are quieter and stronger than spur gears. Helical gears create both radial and axial thrust, and they are more complex to manufacture. Helical gears can be left-handed or right-handed.
- Herringbone gears have a left-hand helical cut on one side of the tooth surface and a right-hand helical cut on the other side of the tooth surface. These gears cancel out the axial thrust common to helical gears. The complexity of herringbone gears to manufacture makes them expensive and uncommon.
- Bevel gearing is used wherever a power flow must turn a corner, usually 90 degrees—at the drive axle, for example. Straight bevel gearing has the same problem as spur gears in that they are noisy in operation.
- Spiral bevel gearing is quieter and stronger in operation than bevel gearing. Many different types of spiral bevel gears have been developed over the years and are all improvements to basic spiral bevel design.
- Worm gears are capable of extremely large reductions in a very small package. Reductions of 40:1, or even 50:1, can be achieved in a relatively small space.
- Rack-and-pinion gears are quite popular as automotive steering systems and are starting to appear in some truck applications as well. This type of gearing gives excellent response when used in vehicle steering.

Key Terms

addendum The top, thinner part of an involute tooth contact area.

axial thrust Thrust that tries to move the gears apart along their axis.

axis The centerline that a gear or wheel revolves around.

backlash The clearance between teeth in mesh with each other.

bevel gear Gear cut on an angle allowing a power flow to turn a corner.

cast ductile iron Cast iron that is ductile (bendable), not brittle.

clockwise The clockwise direction of rotation of a gear as you look at it corresponding to the motion of the clock; also known as *forward*.

compound ratio Any gear ratio that involves more than one pair of gears.

counterclockwise The counterclockwise direction of rotation of a gear as you look at it corresponding to the motion of the clock; also known as *backward*.

dedendum The lower, thicker, part of an involute tooth contact area.

fillet radius The radius shape between the bottoms of two teeth. Also called *root*.

gear ratio The relationship between two gears in mesh as a comparison to input versus output.

gear reduction Any gear set that reduces output speed while at the same time increases output torque. Also known as *under-drive ratio*.

hardening A manufacturing process that makes the surface of a gear much harder than its core: typically, the surface is hardened to a depth of not more than 0.050" (1.2 mm).

helical gear A gear with teeth cut on an angle or spirally to its axis of rotation.

herringbone gear A gear cut with opposite helices on each side of the face.

idler gear Gear used in transmissions to drive a vehicle backward.

involute A gear design shape that compensates for the changing point of contact between gears as they rotate through mesh.

lever A simple machine that can allow a large object to be moved with less force.

mechanical advantage Occurs when we give up either speed or torque to increase either torque or speed through a machine.

overdrive ratio A ratio that provides a speed increase and output torque decrease.

pinion gear A small driving gear.

pitch The number of teeth per unit of pitch diameter on a gear.

pitch circle The theoretical point on the tooth face halfway between the root and the top land where only rolling motion exists. Also called the *pitch diameter*.

pitch diameter The theoretical point on the tooth face halfway between the root and the top land where only rolling motion exists. Also called the *pitch circle*.

rack-and-pinion gear A gear consisting of a flat rack with either spur or helically cut teeth on one side and a meshing circular pinion gear.

radial thrust Thrust that tries to push gears in mesh apart perpendicular to their axis.

root diameter The smallest circle of the gear measured at the fillet radius (root) of the teeth.

simple machine The simplest mechanism that allows us to gain mechanical advantage.

spur gear A gear with teeth cut parallel to its axis of rotation.

top land The apex of a tooth.

torque The twisting force applied to a shaft that may or may not result in motion.

underdrive ratio Any ratio that decreases output speed while increasing output torque. Also known as a *gear reduction.*

Review Questions

1. The input gear in a transmission has 24 teeth, the countershaft driven gear has 40 teeth. First gear countershaft has 12 teeth and main shaft first has 36 teeth. What is the first gear ratio?
   a. 1:5
   b. 0.55:1
   c. 1.8:1
   d. 5:1

2. If input torque is 1000 ft-lb (1356 Nm), how much torque is present at the output shaft when an input gear having 24 teeth is driving a countershaft driven gear with 48 teeth, and a countershaft second gear with 45 teeth is driving a main shaft gear with 60 teeth? Round up your answer to two decimals.
   a. 1750 ft-lb (2373 Nm)
   b. 2670 ft-lb (3620 Nm)
   c. 666 ft-lb (903 Nm)
   d. 571 ft-lb (774 Nm)

3. A gear having 48 teeth, which is rotating at a speed of 400 rpm, is driving another gear that has 78 teeth. Approximately how fast is the gear with 78 teeth rotating?
   a. 120 rpm
   b. 400 rpm
   c. 246 rpm
   d. 464 rpm

4. From which of the simple machines have gears basically evolved?
   a. The screw
   b. The inclined plane
   c. The wedge
   d. The lever

5. What does gear pitch refer to?
   a. The number of teeth per inch (2.54 mm) of pitch diameter
   b. The angle of the gear teeth
   c. The contact point of the gear teeth
   d. The shape of the gear teeth

6. What is the purpose of the involute shape of a gear tooth?
   a. Makes the gear contact smoother
   b. Adds strength to the gear tooth
   c. Makes the gear teeth last longer
   d. Makes the driven gear turn at a steady speed

7. Which of the following is NOT an advantage of helical gears?
   a. Quiet performance
   b. More than one tooth are in mesh at the same time
   c. Reduced axial thrust forces
   d. High strength

8. A gear with teeth machined straight and parallel to the shaft on which they are mounted are known as:
   a. spur gears.
   b. amboid gears.
   c. helical gears.
   d. spiral gears.

9. Which of the following is a disadvantage of spur gear sets?
   a. High thrust forces
   b. Torque losses
   c. Noise
   d. Expensive to manufacture

10. What could happen if a gear set has too much backlash?
    a. Overheating of the teeth
    b. Climbing out of mesh
    c. No lubrication of the teeth
    d. Bearing failure

ASE Technician A/Technician B Style Questions

1. Technician A says that the gear attached to the input shaft on a countershaft transmission is a drive gear and the gear it meshes with on the countershaft is a driven gear. Technician B says that all the countershaft speed gears are drive gears and all the main shaft speed gears are driven gears. Who is correct?
   a. Technician A
   b. Technician B
   c. Both Technician A and Technician B
   d. Neither Technician A nor Technician B

2. Technician A says a ratio that involves more than one set of gears is known as a compound ratio. Technician B says that the formula to calculate ratio is drive over driven. Who is correct?
   a. Technician A
   b. Technician B
   c. Both Technician A and Technician B
   d. Neither Technician A nor Technician B

3. Technician A says that all modern gearing uses an involute tooth shape. Technician B says the involute compensates for differing points of contact as a gear goes through mesh. Who is correct?
   a. Technician A
   b. Technician B
   c. Both Technician A and Technician B
   d. Neither Technician A nor Technician B

4. Technician A says that to calculate compound gear ratios you add all the driven gears together and divide by all the drive gears added together. Technician B says that idler gears are not used in gear ratio calculations. Who is correct?

a. Technician A
b. Technician B
c. Both Technician A and Technician B
d. Neither Technician A nor Technician B

5. Technician A says that externally toothed gears in mesh turn in opposite directions. Technician B says that idler gears are used to change the direction of rotation. Who is correct?
a. Technician A
b. Technician B
c. Both Technician A and Technician B
d. Neither Technician A nor Technician B

6. Technician A says that the meshing of peg gears causes an uneven speed in the driven gear. Technician B says that the distance between the contact point and the center of peg gears in mesh is constantly changing. Who is correct?
a. Technician A
b. Technician B
c. Both Technician A and Technician B
d. Neither Technician A nor Technician B

7. Technician A says that an underdrive ratio increases torque. Technician B says that an underdrive ratio creates a speed increase at the output. Who is correct?
a. Technician A
b. Technician B
c. Both Technician A and Technician B
d. Neither Technician A nor Technician B

8. Technician A says that an overdrive ratio increases torque available at the output shaft. Technician B says that an overdrive ratio is always less than 1:1. Who is correct?
a. Technician A
b. Technician B
c. Both Technician A and Technician B
d. Neither Technician A nor Technician B

9. Technician A says that bevel gears are used to make a power flow turn a corner. Technician B says that bevel gears are usually found in the drive axle. Who is correct?
a. Technician A
b. Technician B
c. Both Technician A and Technician B
d. Neither Technician A nor Technician B

10. Technician A says that rack-and-pinon gears are never found on heavy-duty trucks. Technician B says that herringbone gears are not normally used in heavy-duty trucks. Who is correct?
a. Technician A
b. Technician B
c. Both Technician A and Technician B
d. Neither Technician A nor Technician B

Learning Objectives

After reading this chapter, you will be able to:

- **LO 43-1** Describe the fundamentals and basic components of standard transmissions.
- **LO 43-2** Explain the various types of transmissions by range selection system, including sliding-gear, constant-mesh collar shift (also called sliding clutch or collar), and constant-mesh synchronized.
- **LO 43-3** Explain the operation of and power flows for single-countershaft transmissions.
- **LO 43-4** Explain the operation of and power flows for multiple-countershaft transmissions.

- **LO 43-5** Explain the purpose and function of auxiliary transmissions and describe their power flows.
- **LO 43-6** Describe air-shifting control systems for transmission auxiliary sections.
- **LO 43-7** Explain the function of FR series range-shift air-control systems.
- **LO 43-8** Explain the purpose and function of transfer cases and power take-off devices.

You Are the Technician

A driver brings his International Truck to your repair facility and complains that the transmission will not shift into high range. A road test confirms that this is the case. The transmission is one of the newer Fuller FR series 10-speed transmissions. You suspect the range synchronizer is to blame. Your boss tells you to go ahead and remove the auxiliary section for repair.

1. Is there anything you should do before removing the auxiliary section?
2. What things could cause the synchronizer to fail?
3. What advice should you give to the driver if it is a synchronizer failure?
4. If it is a synchronizer failure, what items would you expect wil require replacement?

Introduction

To diagnose and repair standard transmissions, a technician must have a firm grasp of basic transmission operating principles and power flows. Transmissions are not overly complex in their design, but they do have a certain mystique about them, as their operating components are hidden from view inside the transmission case.

Every day in North America, trucks are the method of choice to haul materials and products to various markets. In fact, everything that you have in your home or business at one point or another rode on a truck to get there. These truck loads can range from relatively light to extremely heavy—in some cases exceeding 120,000 lb (54,431 kg). Meanwhile, the largest on-highway truck engines produce only around 2100 ft-lb (2847 Nm) of torque. Without the torque multiplication provided by the transmission, moving these loads with 2100 ft-lb (2847 Nm) of available torque is impossible. The transmission, such as the one in **FIGURE 43-1**, is the component that allows us to move these heavy loads with apparent ease by using various gear ratios. This chapter attempts to open the "box" and allow the technician to view the internal components of the standard transmission, as well as learn how they function together.

Fundamentals of Transmissions

LO 43-1 Describe the fundamentals and basic components of standard transmissions.

The transmission allows us to move extremely heavy loads by using torque multiplication. However, a transmission must also allow us to move loads at speeds that are appropriate for the situation. For example, an off-road vehicle, like a bulldozer, may only need to move at a maximum of 20 mph (32 kph) to accomplish its function, whereas an on-highway truck must be capable of highway speeds of 65 mph (105 kph) or more.

Careful selection of the transmission can allow us to have the best of both worlds—low-speed pulling power and high-speed operation for highway use. Transmissions are tailored to the vehicle they are installed in to accomplish these goals. For example, an automobile equipped with a standard transmission may have only four or five forward speeds, or gear ranges. That range spread gives a car fairly good low- and high-speed operation. But step into a heavy-duty highway truck, and it likely has 13, or even 18, available forward speeds or gear ranges.

Why so many? The answer lies with the operating range of the engine. Most cars have a gasoline engine that has an operating range of 3000 to 4000 rpm. The diesel engine in the highway truck has an operating range of 1000 rpm or less. To operate the truck from a stop to highway speeds, the ratio difference between each gear, or range, to the next available gear, or the **ratio steps**, must be closer together than in the car. The truck engine can only accelerate 800 or 1000 rpm in each gear, so three or four times the number of steps are needed between low speed and high speed. **FIGURE 43-2** shows the gearing in a truck transmission.

Truck transmissions are specifically selected to match the vocation of the vehicle. Vocation is determined by many different factors. Does the vehicle spend most of its time at city speeds in stop-and-go traffic, or is it primarily an on-highway vehicle? Is the vehicle always heavily loaded or always lightly loaded? Factors like these and more are considered when specifying a vehicle's transmission.

Transmission Shafts

As illustrated in **FIGURE 43-3**, a basic transmission has at least four shafts running parallel to each other and installed in a housing known as the transmission case. They are the input shaft, the countershaft, the mainshaft or output shaft, and the reverse idler shaft. Engine torque is introduced to the transmission through the clutch disc or discs, which are splined to the input shaft.

The input gear is part of, or splined to, the input shaft. The **input shaft** is the input to the transmission driven by the clutch friction disc. The **countershaft** is the shaft inside the transmission that is driven by the input gear. The input gear is in constant mesh with the countershaft driven gear. That is, the gears are always in mesh and must turn together. The countershaft **range gears** are part of, or keyed to, the countershaft. Consequently, when the input gear turns the countershaft driven gear, all the countershaft gears turn with it.

FIGURE 43-1 The right transmission selection maximizes vehicle efficiency.

FIGURE 43-2 Trucks require transmissions with many more ranges than those required to operate automobiles.

Mainshaft

The **mainshaft** is the shaft that is driven by the countershaft and provides output for the transmission. For this reason, the mainshaft is also called the output shaft. The mainshaft usually supports the range or speed gears on bushings or bearings. The **speed gears** on the countershaft and the mainshaft create the transmission's ratios. Most modern transmissions have all the mainshaft gears in constant mesh with their mating countershaft gears and are, therefore, known as **constant mesh transmissions**. The speed gears are usually not splined to the shaft and, therefore, are free to turn. For rotational power to flow through the transmission, the mainshaft gears must be driven by the corresponding countershaft gears, and they then must transfer this power to the mainshaft. When a certain ratio is desired, that particular mainshaft speed gear is connected to the mainshaft.

There are several different systems used to connect the mainshaft gears to the mainshaft. Transmissions are generally described or typed by the gear connection or selection method they use. The three main types of transmission gear selection systems are the sliding-gear, sliding clutch or collar, and synchronized.

The first type is the sliding-gear transmission. In **sliding-gear transmissions**, a mainshaft gear that is splined to the mainshaft is slid into and out of mesh with a corresponding countershaft gear to create the ratio. Figure 43-3 shows a sliding-gear transmission. Sliding-gear transmissions require a great deal of skill to operate, as the driver is responsible for matching the speeds of the gears on the mainshaft with the speed of the gears on the countershaft while making a shift. Failure to match the speeds correctly results in loud clashing noises and transmission gear teeth damage, leading to their nickname as crash boxes. For this reason, these types of transmissions are all but obsolete these days.

The second-gear selection method is the **sliding clutch**—also known as the **sliding collar** or simply a **collar shift transmission**. In this type of transmission, the mainshaft speed gears are in constant mesh with the countershaft speed gears. The mainshaft gears are not splined to the mainshaft. The speed gears are connected to the mainshaft to create a ratio by sliding collars or clutches that are splined to the mainshaft. These collars or

clutches slide along the mainshaft to engage "dog" or clutching teeth on the gears to lock them to the shaft. The terms *sliding clutch* and *sliding collar* are used synonymously. However, to be correct, a sliding clutch has internal splines to connect it to the mainshaft and external clutching teeth to engage the internal clutching teeth of the mainshaft gear, whereas a sliding collar has only internal clutching teeth. The collar slides on an externally splined hub, which is in turn splined to the mainshaft, and held in place by snap rings. The internal clutching teeth of the collar engage external clutching teeth, known as dog teeth, on the mainshaft gear to lock the gear to the mainshaft. A sliding clutch and a sliding collar are shown in **FIGURE 43-4**. A sliding clutch or sliding collar transmission still requires driver skill to match the speeds of the gears and the clutches or collars while shifting, although they are much more forgiving than sliding-gear transmissions.

The third method of gear selection is the **synchronizer**. The **synchronized transmission** is again a constant mesh transmission, meaning that the mainshaft and countershaft speed gears are always in mesh. This transmission uses sliding clutches or collars for gear selection. The sliding clutches and collars are fitted over synchronizer hubs that are splined to the mainshaft. An important difference, however, is that synchronized constant-mesh transmissions have a method to match shaft and gear speeds before engagement to prevent gear clash. Some transmissions use a combination of one or more of these gear selection systems.

Reverse Idler Shaft

The final shaft essential for transmission operation is the **reverse idler shaft,** which supports the reverse idler gear. This gear is in mesh or slid into mesh (depending on the transmission) between the countershaft reverse gear and the mainshaft reverse gear to provide a means to move the vehicle backwards. Recall from the Basic Gearing Concepts chapter that the engine and the transmission input gear both turn clockwise when viewed from the front. The input gear turns the countershaft counterclockwise, and the countershaft gears then turn the mainshaft gears clockwise. The result is forward motion.

Sliding the idler gear in between the countershaft reverse gear and the mainshaft reverse gear means the countershaft

Input Shaft

Output Shaft

Countershaft

Reverse Idler Gear and Shaft

FIGURE 43-3 All transmissions have at least four shafts.

FIGURE 43-4 A. Sliding clutch. **B.** Sliding collar.

FIGURE 43-5 The shift pattern tells the driver which way to move the shift lever.

FIGURE 43-6 The shift finger sits in the shift gates, and each of these gates is attached to a shift rail. **A.** First and reverse gate. **B.** Spring-loaded reverse lock out. **C.** Second and third gate. **D.** Fourth and fifth gate. **E.** Shift finger.

reverse gear turns the idler clockwise. Then, the idler turns the mainshaft reverse gear counterclockwise to achieve reverse.

Shift Controls

Regardless of type, transmissions use many of the same basic types of controls. The transmission driver interface with a standard transmission is better known as the shift lever. The **shift lever** is a shift control the driver uses to change main box gear position. Typically, the shift lever has a knob with the shift pattern on it, as can be seen in **FIGURE 43-5**. The shift lever is the only part of the transmission shift mechanism that the driver sees daily.

There is much more to shifting the gears than just the lever, however. The shift lever may have the shift pattern displayed on the shift knob. If not there, the pattern is usually on a decal placed on the back of the driver's sun visor or in some other prominent position. The pattern tells the driver which way to move the lever to select a given range or gear.

The lever can be moved forward and back and side-to-side to engage the various ranges. The lever itself is mounted in a **shift tower**, a raised section with a pivot into which the shift lever fits. The shift tower has a spring-loaded pivot point just above the transmission shift bar housing. The shift tower may be part of, or bolted to, the shift bar housing of the transmission. The spring tends to return the shift lever to the neutral position when the transmission is not in gear.

Below the pivot point, the end of the shift lever forms the **shift finger**—a flat-sided piece that sits into the shift gates. It is important to note that because of the pivot point, moving the lever forward causes the shift finger to move back. Moving the lever to the right causes the finger to move left.

The **shift gates** are rectangular notches either formed into or attached to the shift rails. **FIGURE 43-6** shows shift gates and the flat end of the shift lever that forms the shift finger. The shift rails have the shift forks that select a particular range attached to them. **Shift forks** are forks that move the sliding clutches or collars in the transmission. Each rail and, therefore, each fork, is usually responsible for two ranges: one in the rearward position and one in the forward position. In a typical five-speed transmission, the rail on the right-hand side controls selection of first and reverse ranges, the center rail controls the selection of second and third ranges, and the left-hand side rail controls fourth- and fifth-range selection. With the transmission in neutral, the shift gates all line up with each other and the finger can be moved side to side in the gates.

To select first gear in the shift gates shown in Figure 43-5, the driver pulls the lever toward his side of the vehicle. That action moves the finger to the right-side gate. The driver then pulls the lever rearward, which moves the right shift rail to the

FIGURE 43-7 Shift forks attached to shift rails move the sliding clutches to engage the mainshaft gears.

front—engaging first range. Selecting reverse involves the same basic motion except that the driver pushes the lever forward, thereby moving the rail back. **FIGURE 43-7** shows shift forks attached to shift rails.

As the vehicle accelerates, the driver depresses the clutch, moves the lever back to neutral, and then selects the center gate and moves the lever forward to select second range, then rearward for third. The driver continues through the gears until fifth range (direct drive) is reached. Direct or fifth range is the range where the sliding clutch locks the input shaft to the mainshaft, giving us a 1:1 ratio. (A 1:1 ratio is normally called direct as the power flows directly from the input shaft through the sliding clutch to the output shaft.) This is the normal shift sequence for a typical five-speed transmission.

As the driver moves through the shifting sequence, the power flows through the transmission change. **Power flow** is the path that power takes from the beginning of an assembly to the end. In a transmission, power flow changes as different gears are selected by the driver. This is true for all transmissions.

Shift Rail Interlock

If the driver were to move more than one shift rail at once, the transmission would be in two ranges at once. In other words, the countershaft would be trying to drive the mainshaft at two different speeds. That would cause the transmission to lock up and experience catastrophic failure.

To prevent this from happening, the shift rails have an **interlock system** that prevents two rails from being moved from the neutral position at once. The interlock system also prevents the other two rails from moving if one rail is not in neutral. One of the simplest forms of interlock uses two balls and a pin and is illustrated in **FIGURE 43-8**.

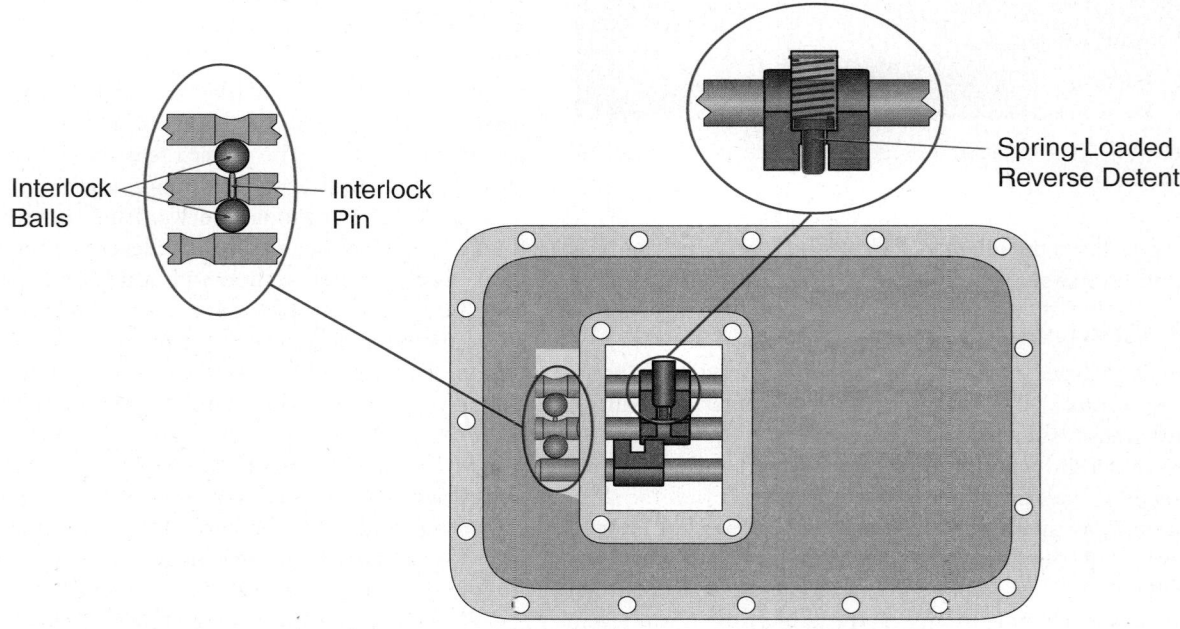

Interlock Balls

Interlock Pin

Spring-Loaded Reverse Detent

FIGURE 43-8 The shift rail interlock positively prevents two gears from being selected at the same time.

The shift rails are positioned parallel and close to one another. The two outside rails have a semicircular indent on their inside surfaces. Two steel balls are placed in the shift bar housing so that they fit into each indent. The center shift rail has a semicircular indent on both sides. In the neutral position, these indents line up with the indents on the outside shift rails. The center rail also has a small cross-drilled hole that extends from one indent to the other. Inside this hole is a sliding pin.

The steels balls are particularly sized so that, for one rail to move, it must force the ball over slightly. In operation, if the center rail is moved either forward or back, the two balls are moved out of its indents and are pushed further into the indents on the outside rails. The new position blocks any movement of the outside rails. If either outside rail is moved forward or back, as it is in Figure 43-8, its ball is forced further into the indent of the center rail, preventing the center rail from moving. This action also forces the pin in the center rail to move toward the other outside rail. The corresponding ball is forced into the outside rail indent by the sliding pin so it cannot move either.

In addition to those basic components, there may be other components in the shift bar housing as well. For example, mistakenly selecting reverse while driving forward could be very detrimental to the transmission.

Various methods are used to discourage this. These methods may be as simple as a spring-loaded system that requires an extra effort to select reverse, as was shown in Figure 43-5, or there may be a complex reverse interlock system that positively prevents reverse from being engaged when moving forward. Most shift bar housings also have spring-loaded **detent balls** that engage notches on the shift rails. **FIGURE 43-9** shows the detent balls and springs from a Fuller 18-speed transmission. By engaging the notches, the detent balls keep the shift rails in position when a shift is made to prevent vibration from moving the shift lever back to a neutral position.

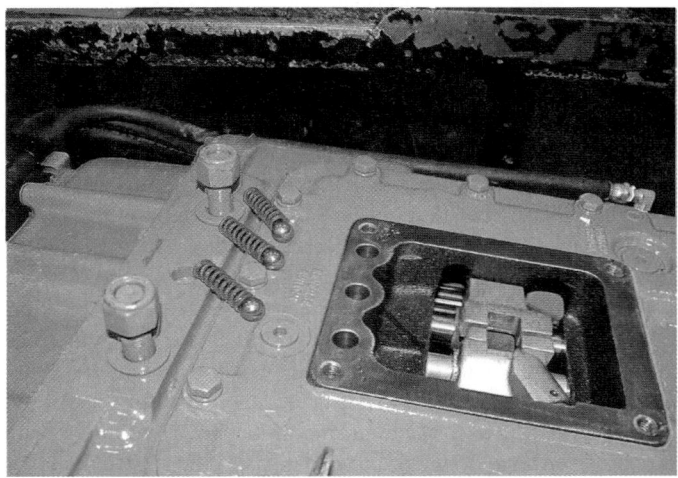

FIGURE 43-9 Spring-loaded detent balls help to hold the transmission in a selected gear.

Types of Sliding-Gear and Constant-Mesh Transmissions

LO 43-2 Explain the various types of transmissions by range selection system, including sliding-gear, constant-mesh collar shift (also called sliding clutch or collar), and constant-mesh synchronized.

As mentioned in the section on transmission fundamentals, transmissions are classified by the method of gear selection or engagement. Sliding-gear transmissions are generally obsolete and have been replaced by constant-mesh transmissions. However, technicians may still find sliding gears used for low and/or reverse range, (or gear), in some transmissions. In this section, we explain all three types of transmissions—the sliding-gear, the constant-mesh collar shift (also known as sliding collar or sliding clutch), and the constant-mesh synchronized transmission.

Sliding-Gear Transmissions

In the sliding-gear transmission, the mainshaft gears are splined to the mainshaft. In the neutral position, they are not in mesh with their matching countershaft gear. The mainshaft gear has a groove cut into one side and a shift fork installed in the groove. To select a range, the driver uses the shift lever to move the shift fork, sliding the gear along the mainshaft until its teeth mesh with the teeth of the corresponding countershaft gear. **FIGURE 43-10** shows a sliding-gear transmission.

The power flows from the clutch disc to the input gear, from the input gear to the countershaft driven gear, and then from the countershaft range gear to the mainshaft range gear. From there, power flows to the mainshaft, which doubles as the transmission output shaft, and then on to the driveshaft and the wheels. This transmission type works very well from a standing start when nothing inside the transmission is moving. Selecting a range when driving down the road, however, becomes a challenge, as all the gears and shafts are rotating at different speeds.

To shift ranges when this type of transmission is moving, the operator must use a **double-clutch** technique to synchronize gear and shaft speed. To double-clutch, the operator first disengages the clutch and moves the shift lever to the neutral position. Next, the driver re-engages the clutch and allows the engine speed to decrease to slow down the countershaft gears. That allows the speed of the countershaft gear to match the speed of the next higher range gear. The driver then disengages the clutch once more and moves the shifter into the next gear position. In this way, a clash-free shift can be made. The driver then engages the clutch again. Sliding-gear transmissions have a few disadvantages. For example, when downshifting, the countershaft gear is turning slower than the next lower mainshaft range gear. So, after re-engaging the clutch in the neutral position, the driver accelerates the engine to speed up the countershaft gears to match the speed of the desired mainshaft gear. Although that might sound simple, it actually involves considerable skill for the driver to get it right. These transmissions gained the nickname "crash boxes" because of the tendency of the gears to

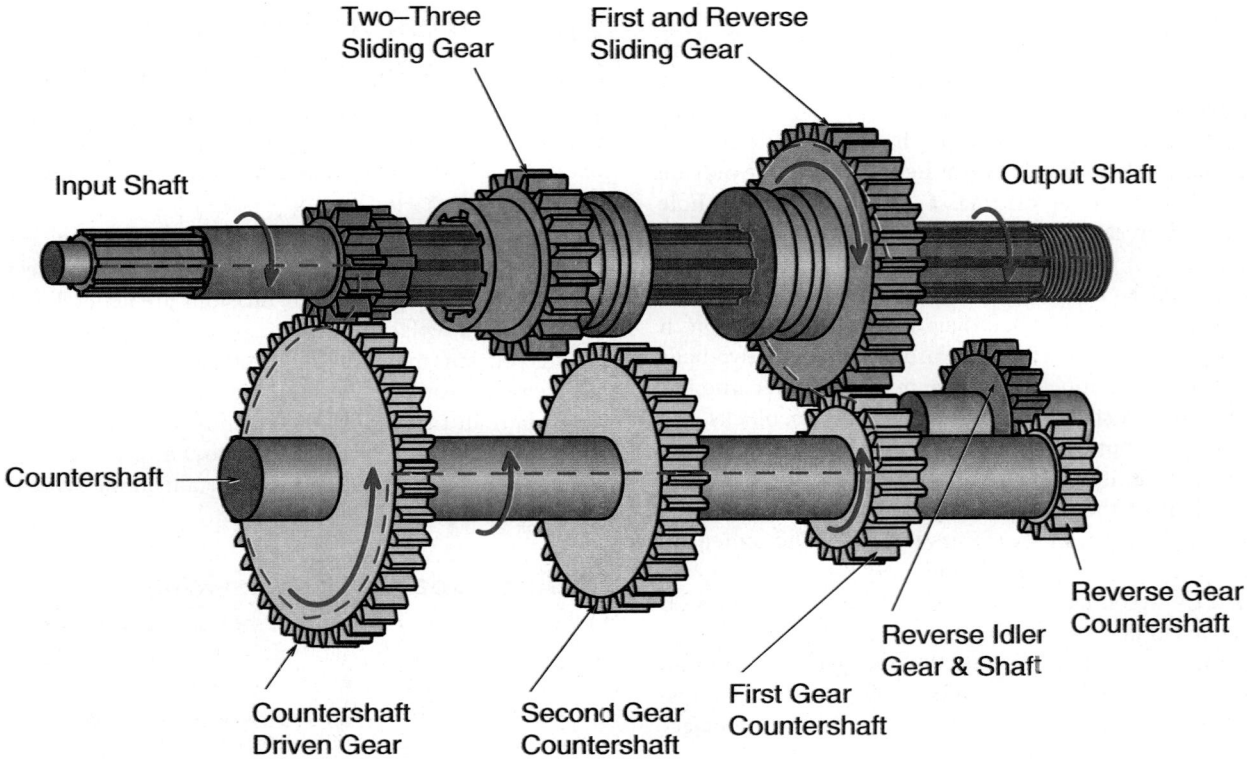

FIGURE 43-10 Sliding-gear transmissions are seldom seen today.

clash as shifts were being made. Even experienced drivers can run into trouble trying to match the gear speeds while shifting, leading to grinding noisy shifts.

Another problem with sliding-gear transmissions is that they can only use spur-cut gears and not quieter helical gears. (Helical gears cannot slide into mesh with each other while rotating.) As a result, sliding-gear transmissions tend to be noisy in operation and not as strong as they could be because of the spur gears.

Even though sliding-gear transmissions are no longer used in any North American vehicles, some constant-mesh transmissions do use a sliding-gear power flow for low range and reverse. As both these ranges are initiated from a stopped position with the clutch disengaged, nothing inside the transmission case is turning and gear clash is not a significant issue.

Constant-Mesh Collar Shift Transmissions

In a constant-mesh collar shift transmission, the mainshaft gears are constantly in mesh with their corresponding counter-shaft gears. All the mainshaft gears are turning at different speeds whenever the countershaft is turning. The differing speeds are based on the ratio between the range gears and their corresponding countershaft gears. Consequently, the mainshaft gears cannot be splined to the mainshaft. Otherwise, it would be trying to turn at several different speeds at once, which, of course, is impossible.

FIGURE 43-11 Sliding clutches (indicated) are splined to the mainshaft.

In a constant-mesh transmission, the mainshaft gears are free to turn on the mainshaft and are usually mounted on bearings or bushings. To select a range, sliding clutches or sliding collars are used. Sliding clutches have their inside surfaces splined to the mainshaft and have splines, or teeth, cut on their outside surface as well. These outer splines are also known as clutching teeth. The sliding clutches have a circumferentially cut groove in the center that is engaged by the shift fork. Sliding clutches are splined to the mainshaft in between two range gears and are used to lock one of the two gears to the shaft. As shown in **FIGURE 43-11**, there is a sliding clutch between each pair of mainshaft gears.

To make a gear selection, the sliding clutch is moved forward or backward, and its outside spline or clutching teeth are brought into mesh with matching internal splines, or clutching teeth, in the mainshaft gear. The mainshaft gear is then locked to the mainshaft, and the power flow comes from the countershaft gear to the selected mainshaft gear. The power flow then travels through the sliding clutch to the mainshaft and out to the driveshaft.

The terms *sliding clutch* and *sliding collar* are used interchangeably, and some manufacturers refer to the sliding clutches discussed above as sliding collars. Sliding collar, though, also refers to a ring that is splined on its inside surface. The sliding collar slides along a hub with a matching outer spline that is, itself, splined to the mainshaft. This means that the sliding collar and its hub always turn with the mainshaft. There is a sliding collar and hub between each pair of mainshaft gears. The outside of the sliding collar has a groove to accept the shift fork. To make a shift, the collar is moved by the shift fork and its internal splines slide over external teeth that are cut on the mainshaft gears. The external teeth are also called "dog teeth" because of their pointed shape. The movement of the shift fork and the internal splines of the collar locks the mainshaft gear to the mainshaft through the sliding collar's hub. The power flows from the countershaft gear to the mainshaft gear, through the shift collar to the collar's hub, then to the mainshaft, and out to the drivetrain. Sliding-gear constant-mesh transmissions and sliding-clutch/sliding collar constant-mesh transmissions are both unsynchronized. That is, to perform a proper clash-free shift, both types of transmission still need to be double-clutched to match gear speeds. This requires significant driver skill to match the speeds correctly and avoid gear clash while shifting.

The constant-mesh design of these transmissions allows for helical gears to be used. Helical gearing makes the transmission stronger because of the increased tooth contact. In addition, the wiping action of helical gears makes the transmission quieter in operation. Overall, transmission length can also be shortened because the helical gears do not need to be as wide as the spur-type gears to carry the same load. Transmission weight is reduced as a result. Helical gears, however, do increase friction in the drivetrain because of their wiping action while in mesh and they create significant axial thrust.

Constant-Mesh Synchronized Transmissions

A synchronized transmission is, again, a constant-mesh transmission. Synchronization eliminates the need for double-clutching techniques. The synchronizer is an assembly that matches shaft and gear speeds as a shift is being made for a clash-free engagement. The advent of synchronizers makes driving a vehicle with a standard transmission almost as easy as driving a vehicle with an automatic transmission. The shifting process for transmissions that use synchronizers is very similar to the sliding-collar shift system described in the Constant-Mesh Collar Shift Transmissions section. A key exception is the addition of the synchronizer components that match the speeds. There are four basic types of synchronizers: plain-type, block- or

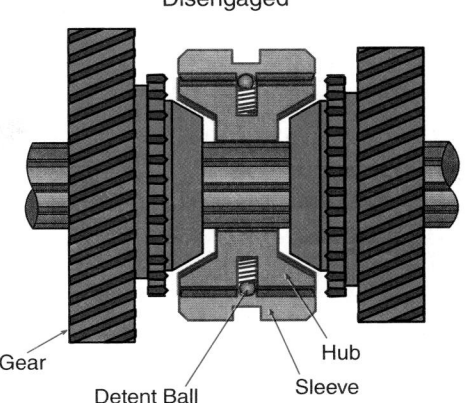

Disengaged

Gear   Detent Ball   Hub   Sleeve

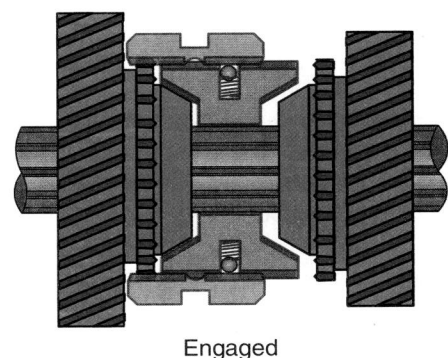

Engaged

FIGURE 43-12 Plain-type synchronizer.

insert-type, pin-type, and disc-and-plate-type. All the types rely on friction and some sort of shift delay system to synchronize the gear speeds.

Plain-Type Synchronizer

The plain-type synchronizer has a central hub that is splined to the mainshaft and a sliding collar that is splined to the hub. A plain-type synchronizer is illustrated in **FIGURE 43-12**. Several springs located in the hub force detent balls into a groove cut into the center of the collar's internal splines. These detent balls tend to stop the collar from moving past the center or neutral position.

The mainshaft gears have smooth, cone-shaped areas and a series of clutching teeth machined on their engagement side. Inside the plain-type synchronizer are two bronze cups that engage the cone-shaped machined area on the gear as the shift is initiated. The detent balls inside the sliding collar ensure that sufficient pressure is applied between the bronze cup and the smooth cone of the gear before the collar slides over the clutching teeth on the mainshaft gear. Ensuring the proper pressure beforehand allows the speeds to match before engagement, thereby reducing or eliminating gear clash.

Block- or Insert-Type Synchronizer

The block-type synchronizer, illustrated in **FIGURE 43-13**, is very similar to the plain-type, but the block-type has a more positive speed-matching system and a few more parts. The block-type

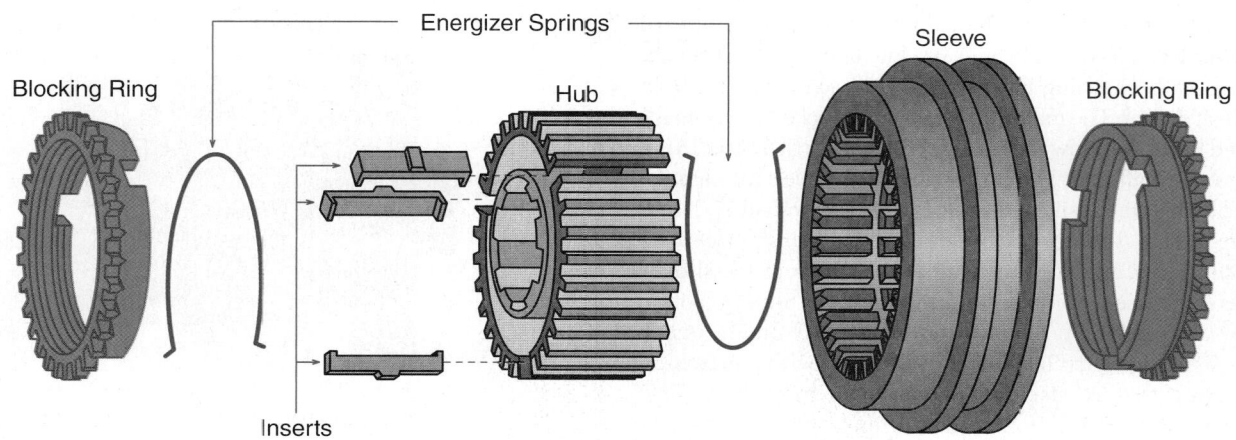

FIGURE 43-13 Block-type synchronizer.

synchronizer also has a central hub and a sliding collar like the plain type. Block-type synchronizers also have two bronze **blocking rings** (also known as blocker rings or baulk rings), parts that use friction to increase or decrease a gear's speed to match mainshaft speed so that the synchronizer sleeve can lock the gear to the shaft without clashing. Blocking rings have dog teeth on their outside circumference identical to the ones on the mainshaft gear. (Bronze, or a similarly soft metal, is usually used for blocking rings to prevent damage to the mainshaft gear as the lighter metal wears faster than the hardened mainshaft gear surface.) The block-type synchronizer also has three floating spring-loaded blocks, or inserts, set into grooves in the central hub. The blocks, or inserts, have a raised center that engages a groove in the internal splines of the sliding synchronizer collar. This arrangement keeps the collar in the neutral position until a shift is initiated.

The block-type synchronizer positively blocks gear engagement until the speeds match. As a shift is initiated, the shift fork moves the shift collar toward the intended gear. The groove in the moving collar drags the three blocks with it. The ends of the blocks engage three rectangular notches in the bronze blocker rings. These notches are specially sized so that the blocker ring can rotate slightly clockwise or counterclockwise in relation to the blocks or inserts. The pressure on the blocker rings forces them to contact the smooth cone-shaped surface of the mainshaft gear. The inside surface of the blocker rings is machined with sharp ridges that help cut through the film of lubricating oil on the gear's cone.

Pressure on the blocker ring causes friction between the two components. The friction causes the blocker ring to rotate slightly left or right, depending on whether the gear is turning faster or slower than the mainshaft and synchronizer. The size of the notches in the blocker rings allow this rotation to continue until the notch contacts the block. The rotation is equivalent to approximately one-half of the thickness of one dog tooth. When the block or insert contacts the edge of the notch, the dog teeth on the blocker ring no longer line up with the splines on the sliding collar. Therefore, the teeth block any further movement of the collar. Blocking action continues until the gear is speeded

FIGURE 43-14 A pin-type synchronizer.

up or slowed down sufficiently. Once the gear has accelerated or decelerated to match the mainshaft speed, its momentum carries the blocker ring in the opposite direction, allowing the dog teeth to align with the splines in the collar again. The collar then slides over the blocker ring dog teeth and the dog teeth of the mainshaft gear. The result is a positive clash-free shift.

Pin-Type Synchronizer

A pin-type synchronizer uses a sliding clutch or collar as its engagement device. The sliding clutch is splined to the mainshaft and has a groove or a disc that is engaged by the shift fork. The pin-type synchronizer is positioned between a pair of mainshaft gears and has two cone-shaped synchronizer friction rings. The surface of the friction rings can be made of bronze, aluminum, or a variety of synthetic materials. Grooves or notches are cut into the friction material to channel away lubricant and ensure contact with the gear.

The synchronizer friction rings have pins that are stepped. One section of each pin has a larger diameter and the other has a smaller diameter. A chamfer bridges the large and the small dimension. The pins fit into chamfered holes in the sliding clutch, and springs keep tension on the pins. A pin-type synchronizer is shown in **FIGURE 43-14**.

In the neutral position, the small dimension of each pin is held against the edge of the holes in the sliding clutch by spring tension. The mainshaft gear that the synchronizer controls may have a removable cup splined to its clutching teeth. The cup may either exactly match the synchronizer cone or simply have a surface machined to match the cone. When a shift is initiated, the sliding clutch is moved toward the intended mainshaft gear. The clutch pushes against the chamfered shoulder of the synchronizer ring pins, and that movement forces the ring to contact the mating cup on the gear.

The spring tension stops the sliding clutch from moving up onto the large diameter of the pin until sufficient pressure is applied to overcome the spring tension. Pressure causes enough friction to be generated at the mainshaft gear that the gear slows down or speeds up until it synchronizes with the sliding clutch. Further pressure causes the sliding clutch to force its way up onto the large-diameter shoulders of the synchronizer pins and engage the mainshaft gear with its clutching teeth.

There are several varieties of the pin-type synchronizer, with slight differences in their construction, but they all essentially operate in the manner just described.

Disc-and-Plate-Type Synchronizer

The disc-and-plate-type synchronizer has several components:

- The synchronizer gear—the input gear we want to engage
- The blocker—which is splined to and turns with the synchronizer gear
- The synchronizer drum—which is splined to and turns with the output gear
- The discs and plates

Several plates with external tangs, called separator plates, are placed into corresponding notches in the synchronizer drum and so turn with it. Disc-and-plate-type synchronizers are rarely seen today. An example of one is illustrated in **FIGURE 43-15**.

Between each set of plates are the synchronizer discs, which are internally splined to the blocker ring and, therefore, turn with it. The synchronizer drum has a circumferential groove that holds the shift fork. When a shift is initiated, the synchronizer drum is pushed toward the blocker and the input gear. In theory, this should move the blocker up the splines of the input gear.

The blocker, however, has a spring-loaded detent ball pushing into a groove on the splines of the input gear, so the blocker resists moving. That resistance causes the synchronizer discs to be squeezed between the separator plates. The resulting friction between the plates and discs causes the synchronizer gear to match speeds with the output gear. Further pressure overcomes the tension in the detent springs, and the blocker slides forward on the splines of the input gear. The splines in the synchronizer drum can now slide onto the input gear splines. Because the synchronizer drum splines are also still in mesh with the output gear, the gear is now engaged.

Most heavy-duty transmissions do not use synchronizers because synchronizers typically would not stand up to the heavy torque being transmitted by these transmissions and would wear out constantly. In many vehicles with heavy-duty transmissions, the driver must still **double-clutch** and have the skill required to match gear and shaft speeds.

Single-Countershaft Transmission Operation and Power Flows

LO 43-3 Explain the operation of and power flows for single-countershaft transmissions.

At the beginning of this chapter, we noted that a transmission must match the engine and vocational requirements of the vehicle into which it is installed. A transmission must also be economically feasible for that vehicle. As their name suggests, **single-countershaft transmissions** have only one countershaft and are the unit of choice for most light- and medium-duty vehicles manufactured in North America

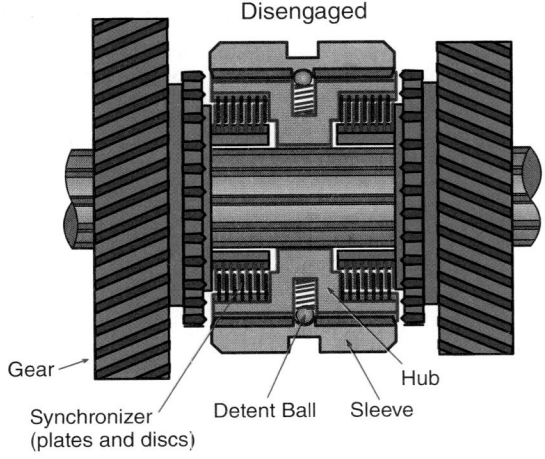

Disengaged

Gear

Synchronizer
(plates and discs)   Detent Ball   Sleeve   Hub

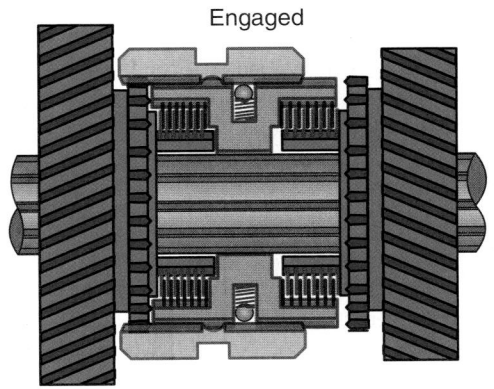

Engaged

FIGURE 43-15 Disc-and-plate-type synchronizer.

FIGURE 43-16 Eaton FS6406 six-speed single-countershaft transmission cutaway.

FIGURE 43-17 A bellcrank system on a Fuller six-speed transmission shift bar housing. **A.** Actual 5–6 shift rail and fork. **B.** Bellcrank. **C.** 5–6 shift gate rail.

because they are relatively inexpensive to manufacture and can usually handle the requirements of the vehicle. Single-countershaft transmissions are commonly available in four-, five-, and six-speed models, such as the one shown in **FIGURE 43-16**. Models with more forward ranges are also available.

Engines used in light- and medium-duty vehicles tend to have a wider operating rpm range than their heavier-duty counterparts. As a result, more ranges or ratio steps are not usually required. If the engine's rpm range is not enough on its own, a two-speed drive axle can be used to double the number of ranges. (A two-speed drive axle has a low and a high operating ratio. A two-speed drive axle can turn a five-speed transmission into a 10-speed—by first using the transmission gears in the **low**-axle ratio, and then shifting the axle to high and going through the transmission gears again. Two-speed drive axles are discussed in more detail in the Heavy-Duty Truck Drive Axles chapter.)

Overdrive Shifting

Several single countershaft transmissions are available with overdrive ratios. With overdrive ratios, the output shaft turns faster than the input shaft. To make that happen, a set of overdrive gears is typically installed on the mainshaft and the countershaft. Some manufacturers of light-duty, six-speed transmissions install the overdrive gear set after the reverse gear set. In truck applications, the overdrive gear set is usually installed in what is normally the fourth-gear position on the mainshaft.

The overdrive causes the high-range or top-speed gear position to no longer be in the direct position. The shift pattern becomes atypical. That is, instead of fifth range being with the shift lever in the rearward position (shift finger forward), we must move the lever forward (shift finger backward) to engage the overdrive gear set. A "U" type shift pattern is followed when shifting from third to fourth range or direct.

When the transmission is in third range, the shift finger is in the center gate with the shift lever rearward (shift finger forward). In fourth range, the shift finger is put into the

right-side gate and again the shift lever is rearward (shift finger is forward), to put the four–five sliding clutch into the direct position. Therefore, to make the shift from third to fourth, the operator must make an upside down "U" shape with the shift lever. Then, to shift into fifth (overdrive), the driver moves the shift lever forward, moving the shift finger rearward to engage the overdrive gear on the mainshaft.

The "U" pattern can be slightly confusing to a driver who is not used to it. Most manufacturers have now eliminated it by using a bellcrank system on the fourth–fifth gear shift rail. A **bellcrank** is a shaft or lever used in a mechanical linkage with a pivot in the center that reverses the normal direction of motion. The use of the bellcrank reverses the direction the shift lever must move to select the overdrive gear making the shift pattern "normal." The bellcrank standardizes the shift pattern for fourth and fifth on a five-speed overdrive transmission, or fifth and sixth on a six-speed overdrive transmission. The bellcrank in the Fuller six-speed transmission shift bar housing is pictured in **FIGURE 43-17**.

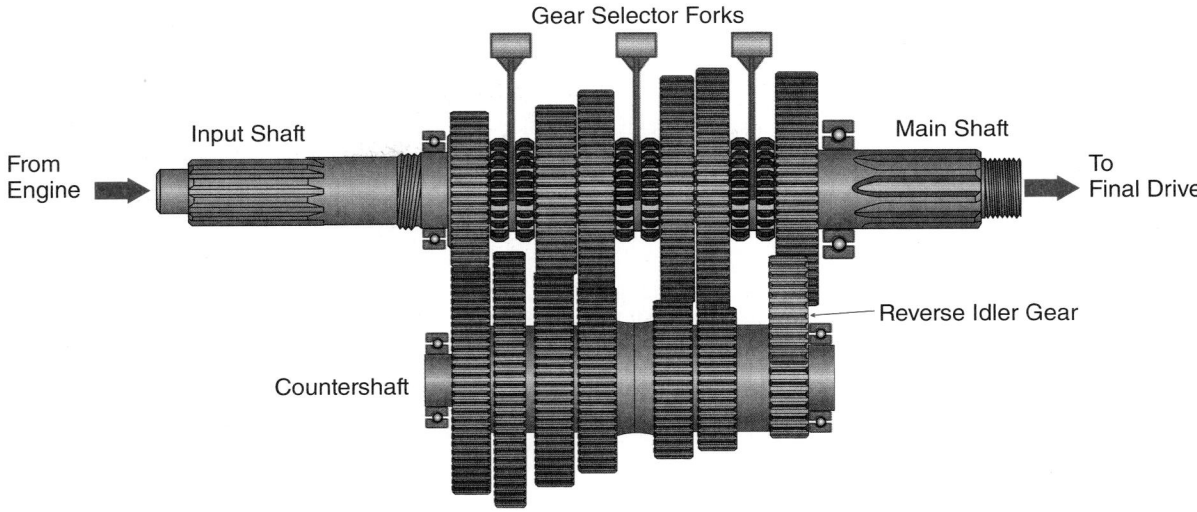

FIGURE 43-18 A five-speed, single-countershaft transmission in neutral.

In a shift cover with the bellcrank system, the four–five shift rail moves one end of the bellcrank, and the other end of the bellcrank moves the shift fork. When the shift lever is moved forward, the shift fork for the four–five sliding clutch actually moves forward instead of back. This simple system allows the shift pattern for an overdrive transmission to remain the same as for a non-overdrive model, making it easier on the operator.

Single-Countershaft Transmission Power Flows

Most of today's single-countershaft transmissions are constant-mesh and synchronized. (Several popular brands, however, still use a sliding gear for first range and reverse.) We now explain the power flows for a simplified version of a single-countershaft transmission.

The transmission depicted in **FIGURE 43-18** is a five-speed transmission that uses sliding clutches to engage all the mainshaft gears. In non-synchronized transmissions, the driver has to double-clutch when shifting gears to match the gear and shaft speeds, as there is no system installed to do so. To engage the gears, the driver slides a sliding clutch that is splined to the mainshaft into mesh with mainshaft gears, which are not splined to the mainshaft.

This type of transmission is quite popular in truck coach applications and is quite simple to understand. It is by no means, however, the only configuration used. Other transmission models used may be fully or partially synchronized, but the power flows are, for the most part, similar.

- *Neutral power flow.* In neutral, with the engine running and the clutch engaged, engine power is transmitted through the clutch to the transmission input shaft and the input gear. The input gear transmits the rotating power to the countershaft and the countershaft gears. The countershaft gears transmit the rotating power to the mainshaft gears and the

reverse idler gear. Because none of the mainshaft gears are engaged, the mainshaft stays stationary resulting in neutral.
- *Reverse power flow.* As illustrated in **FIGURE 43-19**, the reverse power flow starts from the neutral position. The driver pulls the shift lever to the far left and forward to the reverse gear position. (Certain transmissions may have special detents or the lever may need to be pushed downward as this action is completed; this helps to stop the inadvertent selection of reverse when shifting out of first gear.) This action moves the first and reverse sliding clutch on the mainshaft rearward and it engages the reverse mainshaft gear. The power flow is as follows: from the input shaft to the countershaft reverse gear to the idler gear to the reverse gear, and then first and reverse sliding clutch, and finally to the mainshaft. Use of the idler gear allows the direction of rotation of the mainshaft to change, leading to reverse.
- *First-gear power flow.* To select first gear, the driver depresses the clutch to disengage it and then he moves the shifter to the left and back to the first-gear position. This motion causes the first and reverse sliding clutch (splined to the mainshaft) to slide forward into engagement with first gear on the mainshaft. When the clutch is reengaged, the power flows from the input shaft to the countershaft first gear to the first and reverse sliding clutch first and then to the mainshaft. The first-gear power flow is illustrated in **FIGURE 43-20**.
- *Second-gear power flow.* To engage second gear, the driver moves the shift lever to neutral and then to the center shift gate and forward into the second-gear position. This action moves the first and reverse sliding clutch back to its neutral position and moves the two–three sliding clutch rearward to engage the second-gear clutching teeth. This locks second gear to the mainshaft so the power flows from the input shaft to the countershaft second gear to the mainshaft gear, through the two–three sliding clutch, and then to the mainshaft. The second-gear power flow is illustrated in **FIGURE 43-21**.

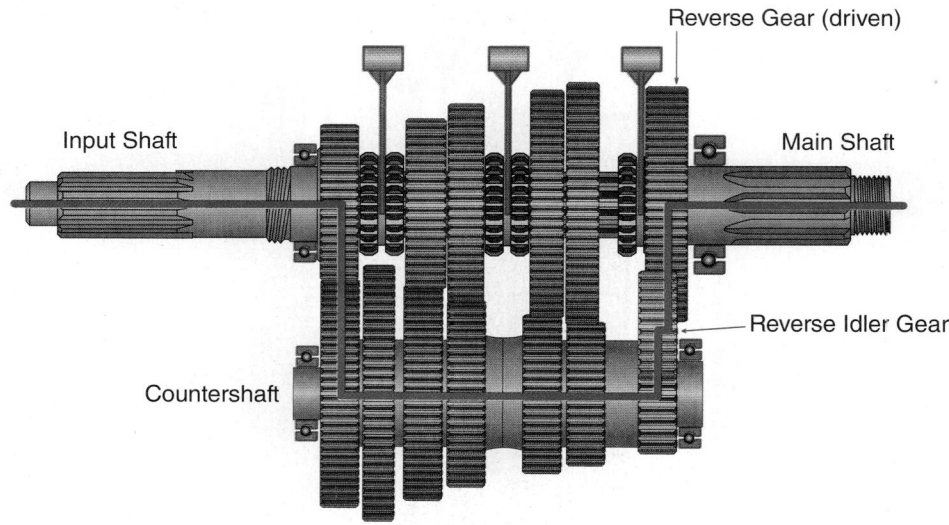

FIGURE 43-19 Reverse-gear power flow for a single, countershaft, five-speed transmission.

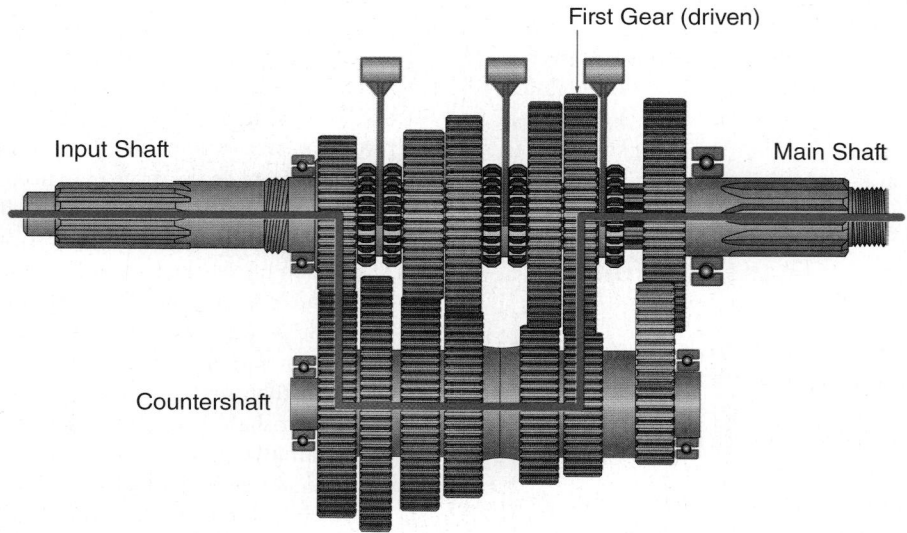

FIGURE 43-20 First-gear power flow for a single, countershaft, five-speed transmission.

- *Third-gear power flow.* To engage third, the driver pulls the shift lever rearward in the center shift gate. This action moves the two–three sliding clutch forward, which disengages it from the second-gear mainshaft and engages it into the third-gear mainshaft, locking third gear to the mainshaft. The power then flows from the input shaft to the third-gear countershaft to the third-gear mainshaft, through the two–three sliding clutch, and then to the mainshaft. The third-gear power flow is illustrated in **FIGURE 43-22**.

- *Fourth-gear power flow.* To engage fourth gear, the driver moves the shifter to the neutral position and then to the far-right shift gate and forward to the fourth-gear position. This action moves the two–three sliding clutch to the neutral position and slides the four–five sliding clutch rearward to engage the fourth-gear mainshaft and lock it to the mainshaft. The

power now flows from the input shaft to the countershaft fourth gear to the mainshaft fourth gear, through the four–five sliding clutch, and then on to the mainshaft. The fourth-gear power flow is illustrated in **FIGURE 43-23**.

- *Fifth-gear power flow.* To engage fifth gear, the driver pulls the shifter rearward in the far-right shift gate into the fifth-gear position. This action moves the four–five sliding clutch forward, causing it to disengage the mainshaft fourth gear and engage the clutching teeth in the back of the input shaft, effectively connecting the input shaft to the mainshaft. That is why we commonly refer to this gear range as direct. The power flow now flows directly from the input shaft through the four–five sliding clutch to the mainshaft. Power is still available through the countershaft to the mainshaft

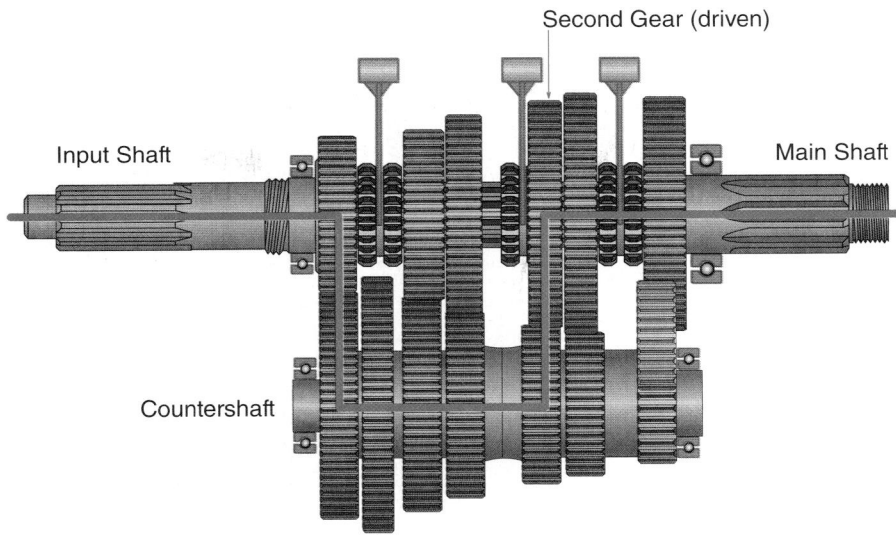

FIGURE 43-21 Second-gear power flow for a single, countershaft, five-speed transmission.

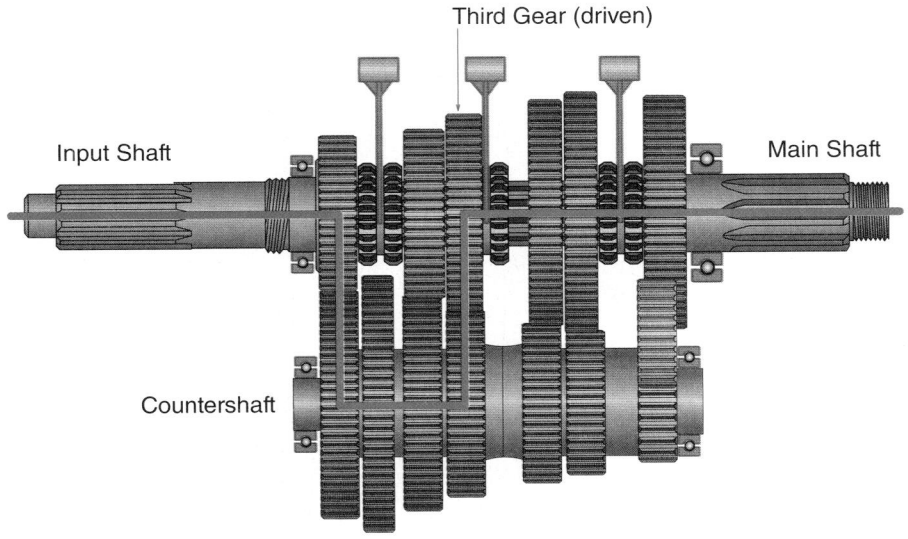

FIGURE 43-22 Third-gear power flow for a single, countershaft, five-speed transmission.

gears. No mainshaft gears are engaged, however, so the flow stops there. The fifth-gear power flow is illustrated in **FIGURE 43-24**.

Several manufacturers produce or have produced single-countershaft transmissions for the North American medium- and heavy-duty market, including Dana/Spicer, Rockwell/Meritor, Eaton Fuller, and ZF Friedrickshafen AG. Documentation for these transmissions is readily available on the Internet. Information on each manufacturer's products can be found at the following websites:

- Information on Spicer transmissions can be accessed through www.dana.com. Spicer now concentrates on the off-highway market.
- Information on Rockwell transmissions is available at www.meritor.com. Additionally, some information on ZF

transmissions used in North America can also be found at www.meritor.com.
- Information on Eaton/Fuller transmissions can be found at www.roadranger.com.
- ZF Friedrichshafen AG is a worldwide driveline manufacturing company. Until 2010, ZF marketed components for trucks in North America through Meritor. Information on those components can be accessed at www.ZF.com/us. ZF now markets directly to OEMs.

To access the correct documentation, you must have the model number of the transmission. The model number is located on the transmission's information plate. The model number indicates whether the transmission is an overdrive model or not, how many forward ranges it has, its torque capacity, and its ratio set.

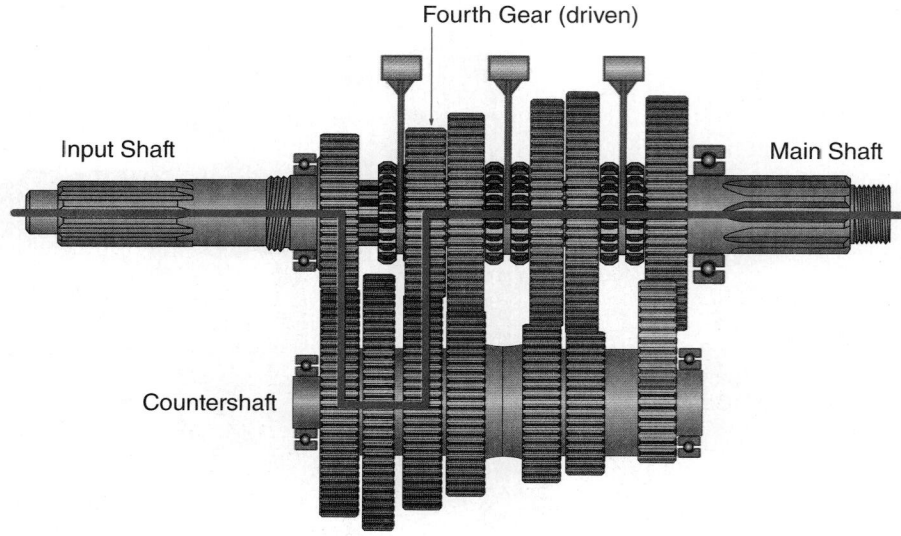

FIGURE 43-23 Fourth-gear power flow for a single, countershaft, five-speed transmission.

FIGURE 43-24 Fifth-gear, direct, power flow for a single, countershaft, five-speed transmission.

To understand the information contained in a transmission's model number, let's use the information plate shown in **FIGURE 43-25** as an example. The figure shows the plate for the popular Eaton Fuller medium-duty transmission; model number FS-5205-A. In this model number, each character or digit has significance:

■ "F" stands for Fuller.
■ "S" means the transmission is synchronized. If the transmission were an overdrive model, the S would be followed by an O.
■ The first "5" indicates the nominal input torque capacity. It is in hundred foot-pound units. That is, five multiplied by

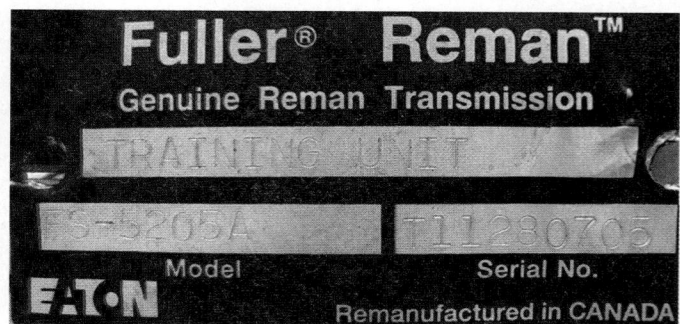

FIGURE 43-25 Information plate from a remanufactured Eaton Fuller transmission; model FS-5205A.

100 is the nominal input torque capacity in foot-pounds, so 500 ft-lb (678 Nm). If the digit were a "3," the transmission would have 300 ft-lb (407 Nm) of nominal input torque.

- The "2" is the design level.
- The "05" is the number of forward ranges.
- The A is the ratio set.
- The serial number is the manufacturing sequence number and is usually found beneath or beside the model number on the information tag. It may be helpful to have the serial number available when ordering parts for the unit.

Multiple Countershaft Transmissions

LO 43-4 Explain the operation of and power flows for multiple-countershaft transmissions.

As transport vehicle's loads have become heavier over the years, the work the transmission must perform has increased. With modern on-highway engines capable of producing more than 2250 ft-lb

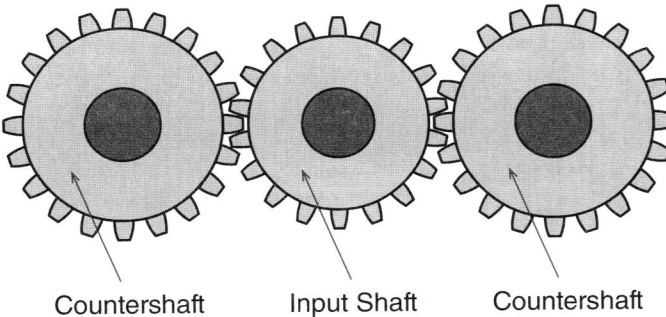

Countershaft   Input Shaft   Countershaft

FIGURE 43-26 Transmissions with two diametrically opposed countershafts split the torque load between the countershafts.

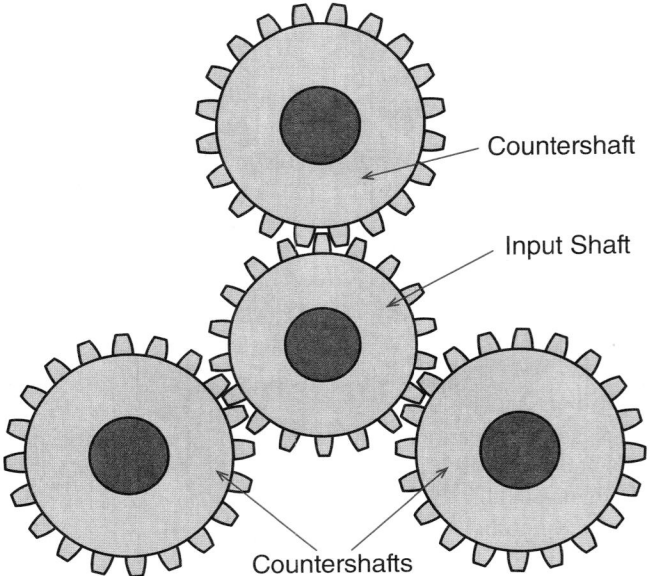

Countershaft

Input Shaft

Countershafts

FIGURE 43-27 The triple-countershaft transmission splits input torque between three countershafts.

(3051 Nm) of torque, the torque-handling capacity of transmissions has had to increase. The only conventional way to increase the torque capacity of a single-countershaft transmission was to increase the face width of the gears and increase shaft diameters inside the transmission, so they could handle the increased torque. Unfortunately, this would lead to longer and longer transmission cases to accommodate the larger gears. A more practical solution is to move to **multiple-countershaft transmissions,** transmissions that have more than one countershaft to distribute the torque between more teeth on the mainshaft and countershaft speed gears, increasing the torque carrying capacity of the transmission.

As shown in **FIGURES 43-26** and **43-27**, multiple-countershaft transmissions split the input torque between two or three countershafts spaced 180 or 120 degrees apart. This allows the input gear to have two or three sets of teeth involved in transferring torque to the countershafts at all times, so the load on each set of teeth is divided. Then, when the countershaft gears bring the torque back to the mainshaft, the torque is delivered to two or three sets of teeth on the mainshaft gear. The torque load is divided as more of the mainshaft gear teeth are used to transfer the load to the mainshaft. With more of the gear's teeth involved in torque transfer, the multiple-countershaft transmission gears' face-widths can be thinner than the gears used on a single-countershaft transmission capable of carrying the same load. This leads to a shorter overall transmission length and lighter weight. A twin-countershaft five-speed transmission capable of handling 1600 ft-lb (2169 Nm) of torque can be the same length and almost the same weight as a single-countershaft transmission that can handle only 900 or 1000 ft-lb (1220 or 1356 Nm) of torque. The only components that need to be strengthened to carry this load are the input shaft and the output shaft, as these shafts must carry the entire load. Strengthening those shafts can be accomplished simply by increasing their diameter.

The manufacturer who dominates the North American market for twin-countershaft transmissions is the Eaton Corporation. Its Fuller Roadranger transmissions have been installed in heavy-duty trucks for over 45 years. Rockwell, which later became Meritor, has also produced twin-countershaft transmissions in nine- and 13-speed models. Spicer also manufactured twin-countershaft models in the past, but does not produce on-highway models at this time. Mack (now Volvo/Mack) produces triple-countershaft transmission models for its own line of trucks.

Floating Mainshaft System

The extra countershaft, or shafts, in a multiple-countershaft transmission produces more benefits than just increased torque capacity. Because the mainshaft gears are supported between two diametrically opposed countershafts (or three equally spaced countershafts), the gears virtually float between those countershafts, as shown in **FIGURE 43-28**. Because the gears are floating, they do not need to be supported by the mainshaft and do not require any bushings or bearings to ride on. This makes the gears themselves and the mainshaft much simpler to manufacture.

In a single-countershaft transmission, when torque is being transferred between the countershaft gears and the mainshaft gears, the thrust forces try to push the gears apart, putting a heavy load on the mainshaft, its bearings, and the transmission case. The floating mainshaft system in a twin-countershaft model cancels these forces out. The mainshaft has no thrust forces acting on it, so it only must deal with the torque load.

When twin- or triple-countershaft transmissions are overhauled, it is essential to time the input gear and the countershaft gears to ensure that the mainshaft gears do float between the countershafts. Timing is a simple matter of lining up marked teeth on the countershaft driven gears with marked teeth on the input shaft drive gear for twins, or the fifth-speed gear for triples. If timing is done incorrectly, the gears will climb out of equilibrium, and the transmission will seize.

To time the gears on a twin-countershaft transmission, first find the marked tooth on each countershaft driven gear. The tooth is marked with a "0" and is directly above the countershaft keyway. Using a highly visible marking compound, select and mark the groove between any two teeth on the input shaft drive gear. Then, mark the groove exactly 180 degrees opposite, as shown in **FIGURE 43-29**. Upon installation, ensure that the marked countershaft teeth mesh with the marked input shaft gear teeth, and timing is correct. Timing triple-countershaft transmission is accomplished in a similar fashion.

Multiple-Countershaft Transmission Power Flows

In this section on multiple-countershaft transmission power flows, we will concentrate on the Eaton Fuller transmission, as

it dominates the industry. Most front sections, or main boxes, of twin-countershaft transmissions have five forward speeds or ranges. Depending on the transmission model, the gears may be listed as one, two, three, four, and five or as low, one, two, three, and four. Regardless of the nomenclature, the power flows are the same, so we will look at the main box power flow for a typical model, the RTLO-12713-A, as shown on the information plate pictured in **FIGURE 43-30**. This model's nomenclature follows:

- The "R" stands for Eaton Fuller Roadranger transmission.
- The "T" is for twin countershaft.
- The "L" is for low-inertia auxiliary section. (Auxiliary Sections are a supplementary transmission and are discussed in detail later in the chapter.)
- The "O" indicates main box overdrive.
- The number "12" is the nominal input torque multiplied by 100 and then adding 50. This transmission can handle 1250 ft-lb (1695 Nm).
- The number "7" is the design level. The number "6" would be **multi-mesh gearing** in the main box. In multi-mesh gearing, the mainshaft and countershaft gears have finer cut teeth—meaning more teeth are in mesh for increased strength. The number "7" shown in Figure 43-30 means the transmission has multi-mesh gears in the main box and helical gearing in the auxiliary section. If the number "9" were in this position, it would indicate that the transmission has an improved seal system.
- The number "13" indicates the number of forward speeds.
- The "A" is the ratio set, meaning the steps between shifts.

Main Box Power Flows

Recall that the Eaton Fuller transmission main boxes are all quite similar. They are twin-countershaft sliding-clutch transmissions with five forward speeds. Therefore, their power flows are identical except for main box overdrive transmissions and certain unique models, such as the Super Ten.

As mentioned previously, the names of the forward ranges vary, depending on the transmission model. For example, in 10-speed models, the ranges are 1, 2, 3, 4, and 5. In 13- and 18-speed models, however, the ranges are listed as

FIGURE 43-28 Mainshaft gears float between two countershafts.

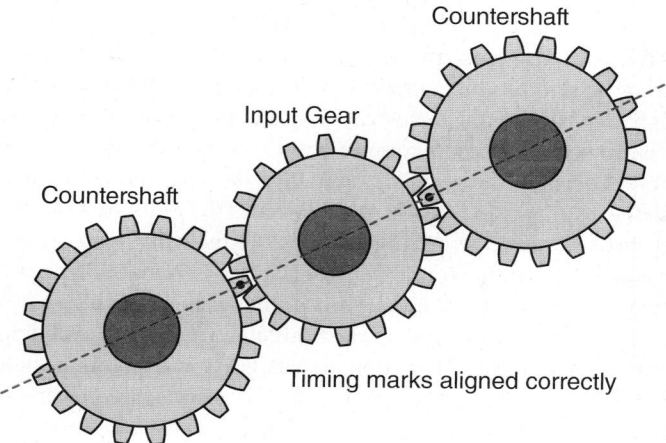

FIGURE 43-29 Properly timed drive gear set.

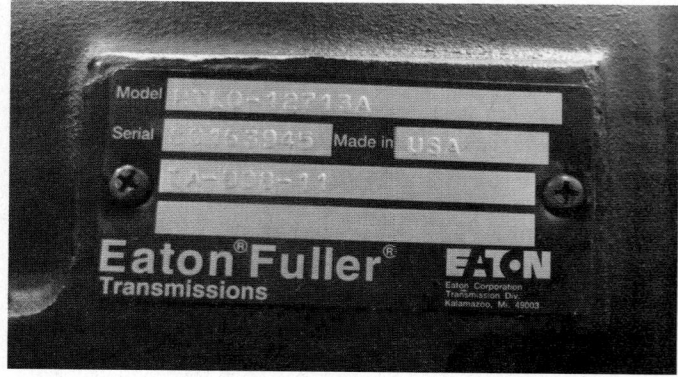

FIGURE 43-30 Information plate for an Eaton Fuller twin-countershaft transmission.

low, 1, 2, 3, and 4. Regardless of the names used, the flows are the same. Throughout this example, we use 1, 2, 3, 4, and 5 for simplicity.

The transmission uses three shift rails and forks, as shown in **FIGURE 43-31**, to control the position of three sliding clutches. The right rail controls the rear sliding clutch, which can engage either the first gear or reverse gear on the mainshaft. The center rail controls the next sliding clutch, which can engage either the second or third mainshaft gear. The left rail controls the front sliding clutch, which can engage the fourth mainshaft gear or engage the back of the input shaft to achieve direct or fifth range. Remember that the driver pulls the shifter left to select the right rail, etc.

The power flows are quite simple. The engine delivers torque to the transmission input shaft and the input gear transfers the torque to the twin countershafts. The countershafts are in constant mesh with their mating mainshaft gears. Therefore, the torque is transmitted from the countershaft to whichever mainshaft gear is locked to the mainshaft by its sliding clutch. The diagram in **FIGURE 43-32** depicts first range. The power flow for all ranges, except for direct, follows the same route and merely involves a different mainshaft gear.

Referencing Figure 43-32, the front section or main box mainshaft gears from back to front are reverse, first, second, third, and fourth. Fifth, or direct, range occurs when the four-five sliding clutch is engaged to the back of the input shaft and the power flows from the input shaft through the four-five sliding clutch directly to the mainshaft.

All main boxes generally share the same power flow. One exception is when a main box overdrive is installed. For a main box overdrive, the fourth mainshaft gear and its corresponding

countershaft gears are changed to create the overdrive ratio. The driver must then select direct before selecting the fourth-gear position (overdrive). In the past, the driver would simply alter the shift pattern by moving the shifter back to select direct and then forward to select the overdrive (in the normal fourth-gear position). Like the problem in single-countershaft transmissions, the awkward U-type shift pattern from third to fourth caused many unskilled drivers to continually select the wrong range first.

To eliminate driver error, all Eaton Fuller main box twin-countershaft overdrive transmissions now use a bellcrank, like the one shown in **FIGURE 43-33**, to move the four-five shift fork in the opposite direction so that the shift pattern is normal, which makes it easier for drivers. This is the same approach used in single countershaft transmissions.

FIGURE 43-31 The three shift rails and forks control the engagement of the three sliding clutches to lock the speed gears to the mainshaft.

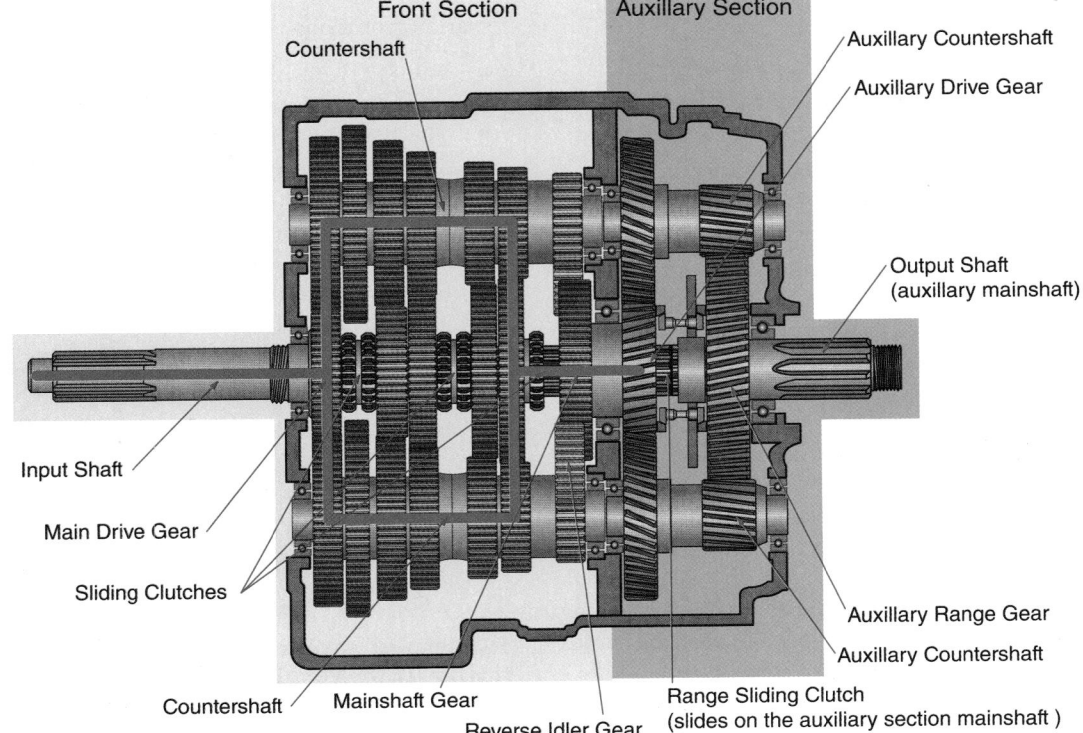

FIGURE 43-32 First gear, main box (front section), and power flow.

FIGURE 43-33 The bellcrank (circled) causes the actual shift fork to move in the opposite direction to the shift rail.

Auxiliary Sections

LO 43-5 Explain the purpose and function of auxiliary transmissions and describe their power flows.

Today's high-torque capacity engines have very short operating ranges. Maximum torque is normally achieved at approximately 1200 rpm, and rated speed may be as low as 1800 rpm. The efficient operating range is limited to 600 rpm, so these transmissions require many more speed ranges than their lighter-duty counterparts. All multiple countershaft transmissions are equipped with auxiliary sections that provide additional speed ranges. **Auxiliary sections** are bolted onto the main transmission and have two, three, or four ratios to multiply the ratios available to the driver through the primary transmission.

The auxiliary section is basically another transmission attached to the main transmission. As such, the auxiliary section has its own two, three, or four available ratios—meaning that the auxiliary section ratios multiply the available ratios from the main box by two, three, or four times.

In the past, auxiliary sections (then called auxiliary transmissions) were separate units attached to the main box by a short driveshaft. This arrangement required two shift levers in the cab

FIGURE 43-34 When assembled, this three-speed auxiliary section is bolted to the back of the Eaton twin-countershaft main box below it.

and considerable skill from the driver to coordinate the shifting of both transmissions at once when a **compound shift** (a shift maneuver involving both transmissions or sections) was required.

Auxiliary sections today are bolted directly to the main transmission and are controlled by air shift systems, making them much easier to operate. **FIGURE 43-34** shows an auxiliary section that is normally bolted to the back of an Eaton transmission. The main box or transmission of a twin-countershaft unit is typically a five-speed sliding collar/clutch type transmission and is almost identical in design to a single-countershaft five-speed, with the exception of the extra countershaft. The mainshaft gears are engaged by sliding clutches that lock the gears to the mainshaft.

Eaton makes several different transmission models tailored to various vocations:

- The 8LL with nine forward speeds, including a low-low range (for extreme pulling power).
- The 10-speed direct and overdrive models—probably the most popular model for delivery and linehaul applications.
- The 13-speed direct and overdrive transmissions—a versatile transmission usually used in line-haul applications.
- The 15-speed deep-reduction has five low-low ranges (deep-reduction) for off-road and 10 for on-highway (five in low range and five in high range).
- The 18-speed direct and overdrive transmission designed for high-speed, heavy line-haul operations.

The above are general model types; Eaton Fuller has many different versions of each type for specific vocations. Most of these transmissions use the same design of a five-speed main box and use different auxiliary sections with two, three, or four ranges to suit the application and provide the necessary range selections.

Two-Speed Auxiliary

The simplest auxiliary is the two-speed auxiliary, shown in **FIGURE 43-35**. The two-speed auxiliary is used in 10-speed transmission models—the five gear ranges in the front box are used twice each during acceleration, from start to highway speeds. The main box is shifted first through fifth with the auxiliary section in low range and then first through fifth main box is repeated with the auxiliary in high range.

The auxiliary section has its own mainshaft that is not connected to the mainshaft of the front section or main box. The auxiliary section also has twin countershafts. The auxiliary drive gear, which is splined to the output shaft of the main box, drives the countershafts of the auxiliary section. The low-range gears on the countershafts are in constant mesh with the large low-range gear on the auxiliary section mainshaft. Range selection is controlled by an air-actuated pin-type synchronizer with a sliding clutch, which is splined to the auxiliary section mainshaft.

With the synchronizer sliding clutch in the rearward position, the range gear is locked to the auxiliary section mainshaft. The power flows from the auxiliary drive gear through the countershafts to the range gear. In the forward position, the synchronizer sliding clutch locks the auxiliary section mainshaft to the auxiliary section drive gear. This provides high range or

FIGURE 43-35 Two-speed auxiliary used in 10-speed transmissions.

direct drive through the auxiliary. The countershafts and the range gears merely turn freely. **FIGURE 43-36** provides a basic illustration to anchor the discussion of auxiliary power flows.

Power Flow in a Two-Speed Auxiliary Section

The two-speed auxiliary has a low range and a high range. In low range, the power flows from the mainshaft of the main box to the auxiliary section drive gear splined to it. The auxiliary section drive gear transfers the power to the auxiliary section countershafts and, therefore, to the auxiliary section countershaft low-range gears. The auxiliary section countershaft's low-range gears are in constant mesh with the low-range gear on the auxiliary section mainshaft. The range synchronizer is in the rearward position, as illustrated in **FIGURE 43-37**. The range synchronizer's sliding clutch locks the range gear to the auxiliary section mainshaft. The power flows through the range synchronizer sliding clutch and onto the auxiliary section mainshaft.

In high range, the driver moves the range selector lever upward. The range synchronizer moves toward the front. This disengages the range gear from the auxiliary section mainshaft and allows the gear to turn freely around the mainshaft. With the synchronizer in this position, the synchronizer sliding clutch engages teeth in the back of the auxiliary drive gear. That engagement locks the gear to the auxiliary section mainshaft, as illustrated in **FIGURE 43-38**.

So, the power flows from the main box mainshaft to the auxiliary drive gear through the range synchronizer sliding clutch and directly onto the auxiliary section mainshaft. That power flow results in a direct range (straight through) in the auxiliary. The auxiliary countershaft and the range gear are still turning, as they are in constant mesh, but they are not connected to the auxiliary mainshaft.

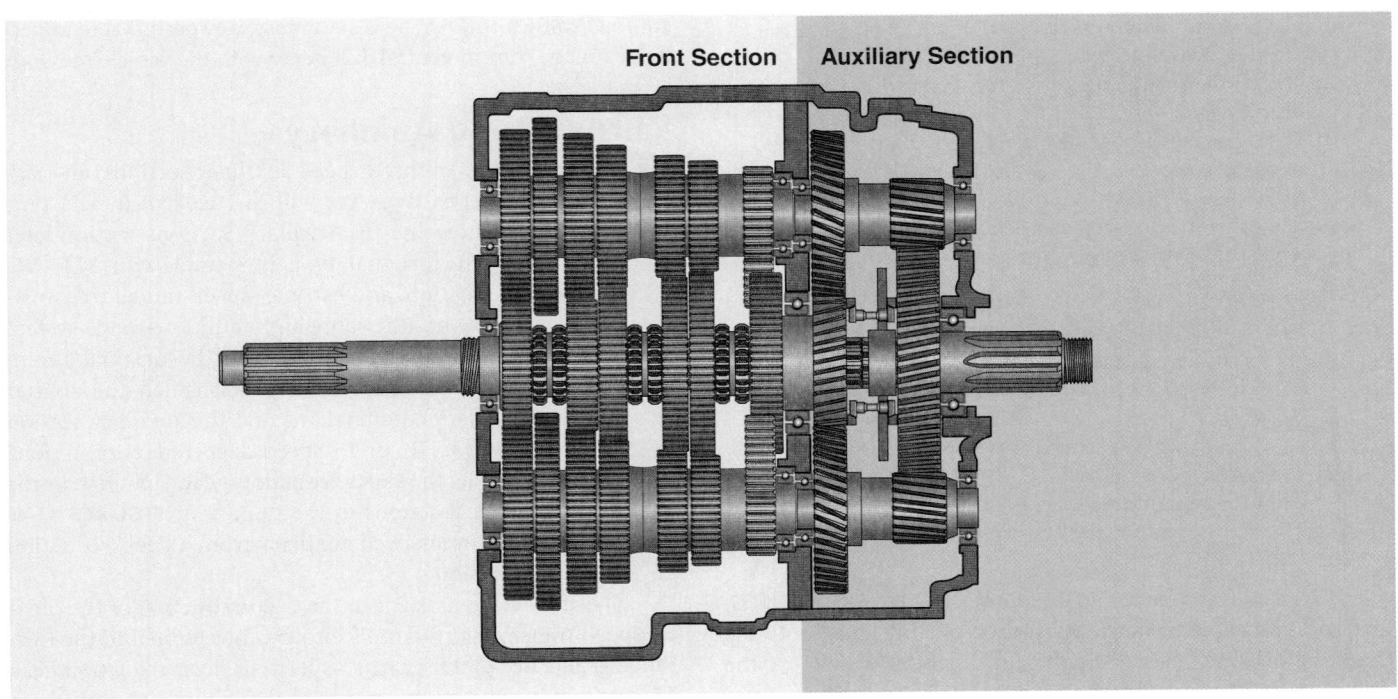

FIGURE 43-36 Auxiliary section power flows.

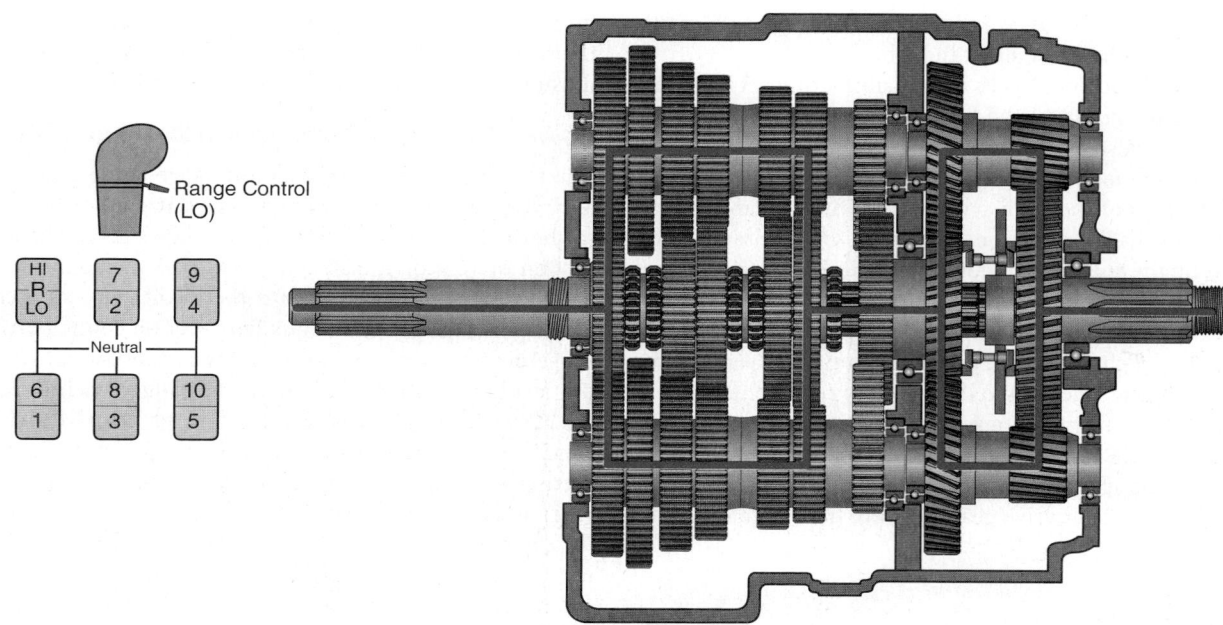

FIGURE 43-37 First-gear, low-range power flow, with first gear engaged in the main box and low range in the auxiliary.

It is essential to shift the auxiliary section properly to avoid serious damage to the range synchronizer. The driver must preselect the range shift while in gear. The range interlock does not allow the range to shift until the driver moves the shift lever to neutral. By preselecting the range shift, the shift is made immediately as the shift lever is moved to neutral, allowing the range synchronizer to do its job. If the driver incorrectly tries to change range after he shifts to neutral, the speed differences are too great and the range synchronizer suffers. The sequence is as follows:

1. Starting from a stop with the auxiliary in low range, the transmission main box is shifted through the desired gear ranges, using the double-clutch technique, until the main box top gear is reached.
2. Next, with the main box still in top gear, the driver moves the range control to the high-range position.
3. Then, double-clutching, the driver moves the shift lever through neutral to select the first-gear main box position again.
4. The range shift to high range is made automatically as the shift lever is moved to neutral.

The same sequence is used while decelerating:

1. With the auxiliary section in high range, the driver downshifts through the main box ranges, using the double-clutch technique, until he reaches the first-gear main box.
2. While still in first, the driver selects low range.
3. The driver double-clutches and shifts to the fifth-gear main box.
4. The auxiliary section shifts to low range automatically as the shift lever is moved to neutral.

The air shift system has an interlock, shown in **FIGURE 43-39**, that does not allow the auxiliary section to shift range until the transmission shift lever is in the neutral position. So, as the driver moves the lever through neutral, the range shift occurs automatically and very quickly. If the driver tries to change ranges after he moves the lever to neutral, the speed difference between the auxiliary mainshaft and the gears are too great and the range synchronizer is destroyed very quickly. Because it is unable to synchronize and shift, all the torque is trying to pass through the synchronizer blocker rings! When downshifting from high range, the gear shift lever is moved progressively down through the gears until the first-gear main box is reached. Next, the driver preselects the low-range position and then shifts the lever through neutral toward the fifth-gear main box position. As the lever moves through neutral, the range shift again occurs automatically. If the vehicle is stationary, it is permissible to perform a range shift in neutral, but never with the vehicle moving.

Three-Speed Auxiliary

There are two types of three-speed auxiliary sections: an original and a low-inertia type. We will discuss low-inertia type auxiliaries in the Low-Inertia Auxiliary Sections section later in this chapter. The original type was used with 8LL, 9L, 15-speed deep-reduction, and early 13-speed model transmissions. This auxiliary has the same high- and low-range system as the two-speed auxiliary. In addition, the original three-speed auxiliary has another set of gears, called the splitter gears, on the auxiliary countershafts and the auxiliary section mainshaft. In an 8LL, 9L, or 15-speed deep-reduction model, the gear is known as the deep-reduction gear, rather than the splitter gear, but it functions in the same way. **FIGURES 43-40** and **43-41** show a three-speed auxiliary from a deep-reduction 15-speed transmission.

The auxiliary mainshaft in the deep-reduction or the older 13-speed transmissions is split into two pieces behind the low-range gear. The splitter gear, 13-speed, or deep-reduction gear, 15-speed, is located on the rear part of the auxiliary mainshaft,

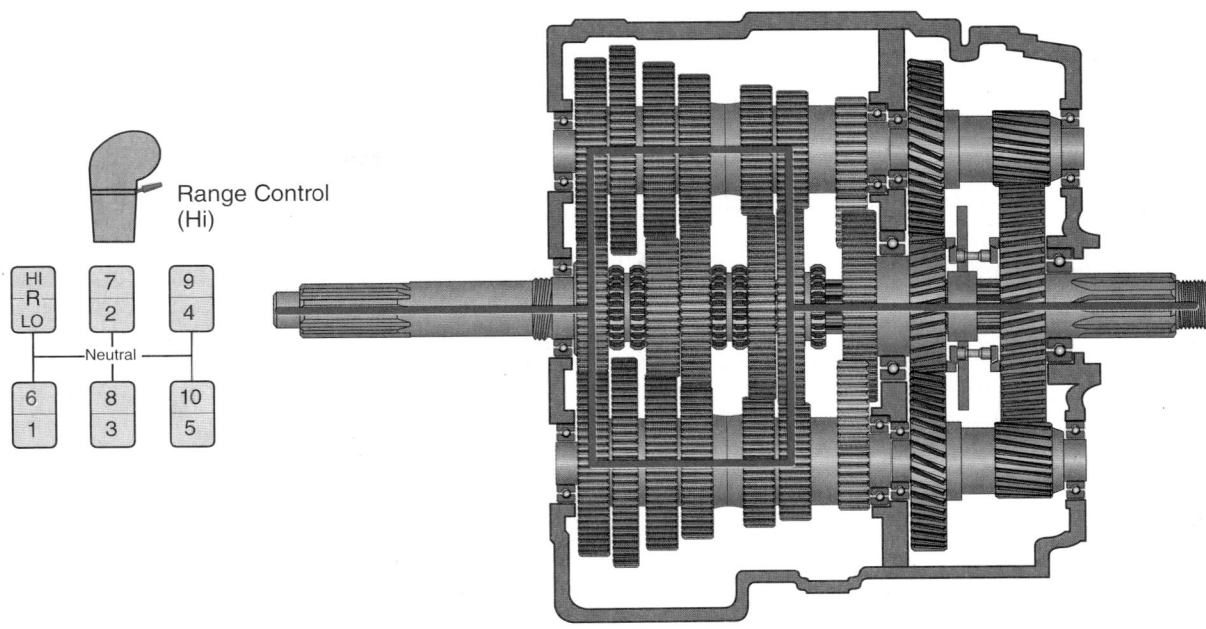

FIGURE 43-38 Sixth-gear power flow, first-gear main box, and high range (direct) in the auxiliary section.

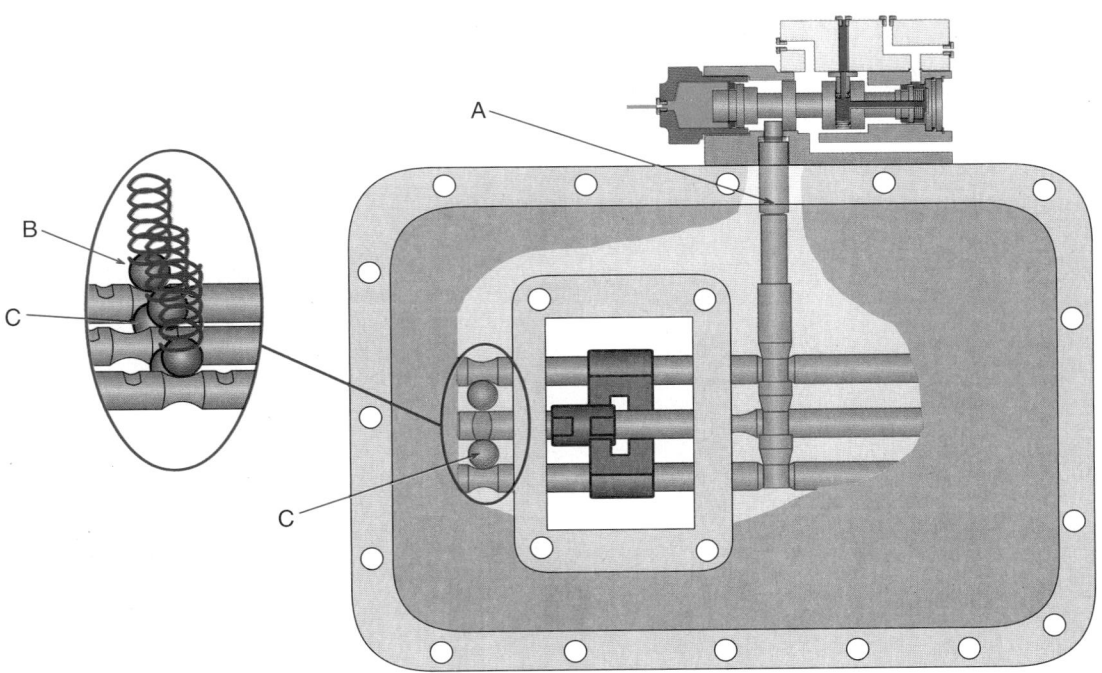

FIGURE 43-39 A. The range preselect lockout system that stops the slave air valve from moving while the transmission is in gear. **B.** Shift rail detent balls. **C.** Shift rail interlock.

and the low-range gear is located on the front part of the auxiliary mainshaft. The high- and low-range selection and operation are the same as in the two-speed, so we will concentrate on the splitter and deep-reduction gears.

In older 13-speed transmissions, the splitter gears may provide an overdrive or underdrive ratio that allows the driver to split a ratio while accelerating through the gears. The splitter function is only available in high-range on 13-speed models.

In the 8LL, 9L, and 15-speed deep-reduction, the gears in this position produce a lower ratio than low range and provide extra low-speed pulling power. In these models, the deep-reduction function is only available when the auxiliary section is in low range.

The shifting mechanism for the splitter or deep-reduction gears involves a sliding clutch actuated by an air-operated shift fork. When the fork is in the rearward position, the sliding clutch locks the splitter or deep-reduction gear to the rear part of the auxiliary section mainshaft. Power is forced to flow from the auxiliary drive gear to the auxiliary countershafts, to the splitter or deep-reduction gear, back to the rear section of the auxiliary mainshaft, and then out to the driveline. In this rearward position, the front part of the auxiliary section mainshaft is disengaged from the rest of the mainshaft and is free to turn.

In the forward position, the sliding clutch engages internal teeth on a coupler collar that is splined to the front part of the auxiliary mainshaft. That locks the front part of the mainshaft to the rear part of the mainshaft. As this occurs, the splitter, or

deep-reduction gear on the rear part of the mainshaft, is disengaged and is free to turn.

In the 8LL transmission, the shift progression is as outlined here. To begin, the main box is in low gear, the auxiliary section is in low range, and the deep-reduction gear is engaged. That starting position provides extremely low-speed and high-torque pulling power, if necessary. If this extremely low range is not required, the driver engages low-gear main box combined with low range in the auxiliary. This provides a normal pulling power low gear. During normal on-highway operation, the deep-reduction gear is not used, and usually the pulling power of the low gear in the main box is not required. In this case, the driver can start out in first-gear main box and low range in the auxiliary. The driver shifts through second, third, and fourth, and then operates the air control for high range while still in fourth. The driver then shifts through neutral back to the first-gear main box and goes through the gears again. Eight forward speeds are available, therefore, during normal operation.

The 9L model is identical except that low gear in the main box is used both in conjunction with the deep-reduction gear and by itself during low-range operation. Nine normal forward speeds are available with one deep-reduction gear position.

The deep-reduction transmission has 15 available speeds. The deep-reduction gear is engaged for off-road operation. With the auxiliary section in deep-reduction, the main box can be shifted through all five forward gears. Five low off-road ratios are produced. When highway operation is required, the deep-reduction gear is disengaged, and the transmission can be operated through all five forward gears, with the auxiliary in low range. The transmission can then be operated again

FIGURE 43-40 Three-speed deep-reduction auxiliary section.

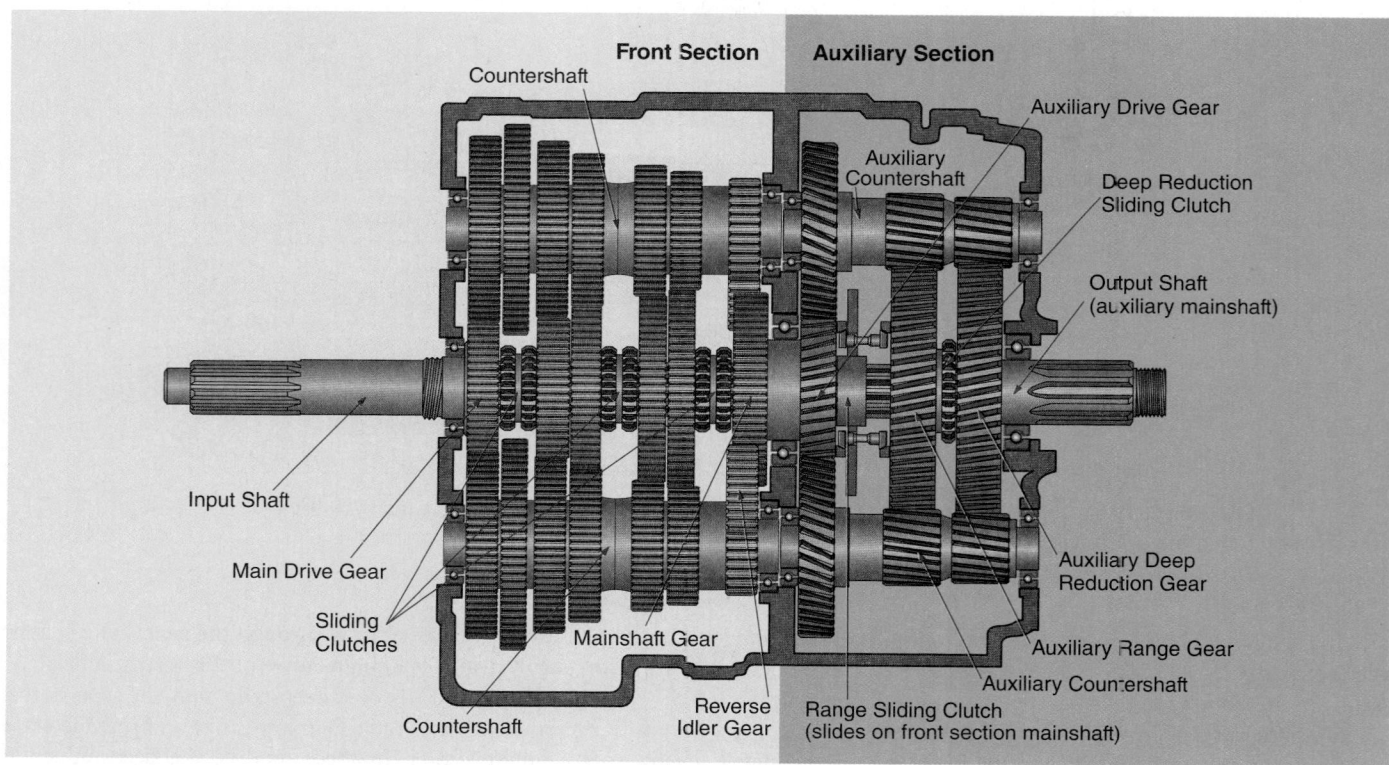

FIGURE 43-41 The deep-reduction gear set is at the back of the auxiliary section in a 15-speed deep-reduction transmission.

through all five forward gears, with the auxiliary in high range. Ten on-highway speed ranges are, therefore, available.

In all these transmissions, the shift control is interlocked to prevent shifting to deep-reduction mode unless the auxiliary section is in low range.

In 13-speed models, the splitter gears can only be used in high range. The driver starts out with the main box in low gear and the auxiliary section in low range. The driver then shifts through the main box gears to first, second, third, and fourth (direct). The driver then moves the range selector to high and shifts through neutral to the first-gear main box position again. (The low-shifter position is only used in low range.) This is now the sixth forward speed. The driver then moves the splitter button to high split while under load. To make the split shift happen, the driver very quickly releases and depresses the throttle. That quick action causes the air-shift mechanism to move the splitter sliding clutch rearward. When the splitter sliding clutch moves rearward, it detaches the front of the auxiliary transmission mainshaft from the rear and engages the splitter gear, which is then locked to the back half of the auxiliary mainshaft.

At this point, the power flows from the auxiliary drive gear to the auxiliary countershafts and back to the splitter gear. This is now seventh gear. The splitter creates a "half" gear step between six and eight. The driver then returns the splitter to low split and double-clutches while moving the shift lever to the

second-gear position. Eighth gear is achieved. The driver continues to move to high split for nine, etc., through the rest of the gears until the lever is in the fourth-gear position with high split, which is 13th gear. The driver reverses the sequence to downshift back to low gear.

Although these 13-speed transmissions were quite popular in the past, a technician is not likely to encounter a 13-speed transmission with the split auxiliary mainshaft today. Today's 13-speed transmissions are all low-inertia models that use a different type of auxiliary arrangement, which is covered a little later in this chapter. Because the deep-reduction 15-speed, the 8LL, and the 9L use the same split auxiliary mainshaft design, we continue our discussion by covering the power flow for the deep-reduction transmission.

Power Flowthrough a Deep-Reduction Three-Speed Auxiliary Section

Remember that, in a deep-reduction three-speed transmission like that shown in **FIGURE 43-42**, the auxiliary section mainshaft is in two pieces, which can be joined or disconnected, depending on whether the coupler is engaged by the splitter sliding clutch or not.

Deep Reduction Starting in low range with the deep-reduction gear engaged, the range synchronizer is rearward.

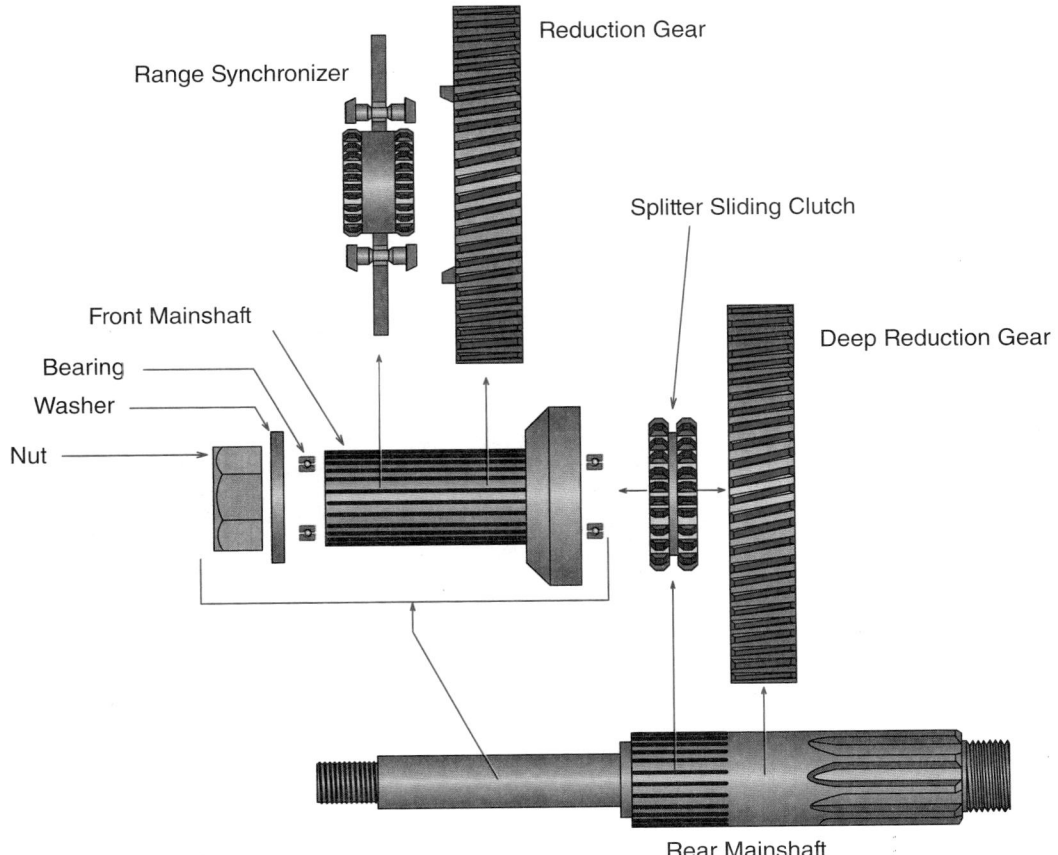

FIGURE 43-42 Two-piece deep-reduction auxiliary section mainshaft. The front part of the auxiliary mainshaft is supported by the rear part on bushings or bearings.

The synchronizer's clutching teeth engage the clutching teeth of the low-range gear, locking the gear to the front part of the split auxiliary mainshaft.

The deep-reduction sliding clutch is also in the rearward position. This motion does two things. First, the sliding clutch disengages from the shaft coupler, freeing the front half of the auxiliary section mainshaft from the rear. Second, the sliding clutch engages the deep-reduction gear clutching teeth, locking it to the rear part of the auxiliary section mainshaft, as illustrated in **FIGURE 43-43**.

The power flow is as follows. Power comes from the main box mainshaft to the auxiliary section drive gear, which is splined to it and in constant mesh with the auxiliary section countershafts. Power flows to the auxiliary countershafts and back to the deep-reduction gear set at the rear of the auxiliary section. Power then flows down to the engaged deep-reduction gear and through the deep-reduction sliding clutch to the rear part of the auxiliary section mainshaft. Power flow continues out to the driveline. Power also flows to the engaged range gear, but because the auxiliary mainshaft is uncoupled, the range gear is free to turn. This is the same auxiliary power flow for the LL position of an 8LL and the L position for a 9L.

Low Range   In low range, the deep-reduction gear is not selected, so the deep-reduction sliding clutch is in the forward position. This disengages the deep-reduction gear and engages the clutching teeth of the coupler. With the clutch teeth engaged, the two pieces of the auxiliary countershaft are locked together, as illustrated in **FIGURE 43-44**.

The range synchronizer is still in the rearward position, locking the range gear to the front part of the auxiliary mainshaft.

The power flows from the auxiliary drive gear, out to the auxiliary countershafts, down through the low-range countershaft gears, to the low-range gear on the auxiliary mainshaft. The power continues to flow through the range synchronizer sliding clutch, to the front part of the auxiliary mainshaft, then through the coupler to the rear part of the auxiliary countershaft, and out to the drive line.

High Range   In high range, the deep-reduction sliding clutch remains in the forward position. In that position, the clutch couples the two parts of the auxiliary mainshaft together, as illustrated in **FIGURE 43-45**. The range synchronizer moves forward. In the process, the range gear is disengaged, and the synchronizer's clutching teeth engage the teeth on the rear of the auxiliary drive gear. The power flows from the main box mainshaft to the auxiliary drive gear through the synchronizer sliding clutch to the front part of the auxiliary mainshaft. Power then flows through the coupler to the rear section of the auxiliary mainshaft and out to the drive line. The result is a direct, or one-to-one, power flow through the auxiliary section.

Low-Inertia Auxiliary Sections

The second type of three-speed auxiliary section is the low-inertia type pictured in **FIGURE 43-46**. **Low-inertia** designs allow the auxiliary to momentarily disengage from the main box during compound shifts, making it easier to move the shift lever. The low-inertia type is also available as a four-speed auxiliary for 18-speed transmissions, but the internal components are the same—only the ratios are different. Low-inertia auxiliary sections can have three or four usable ratios, but the gearing is similar. In the three-ratio unit, used

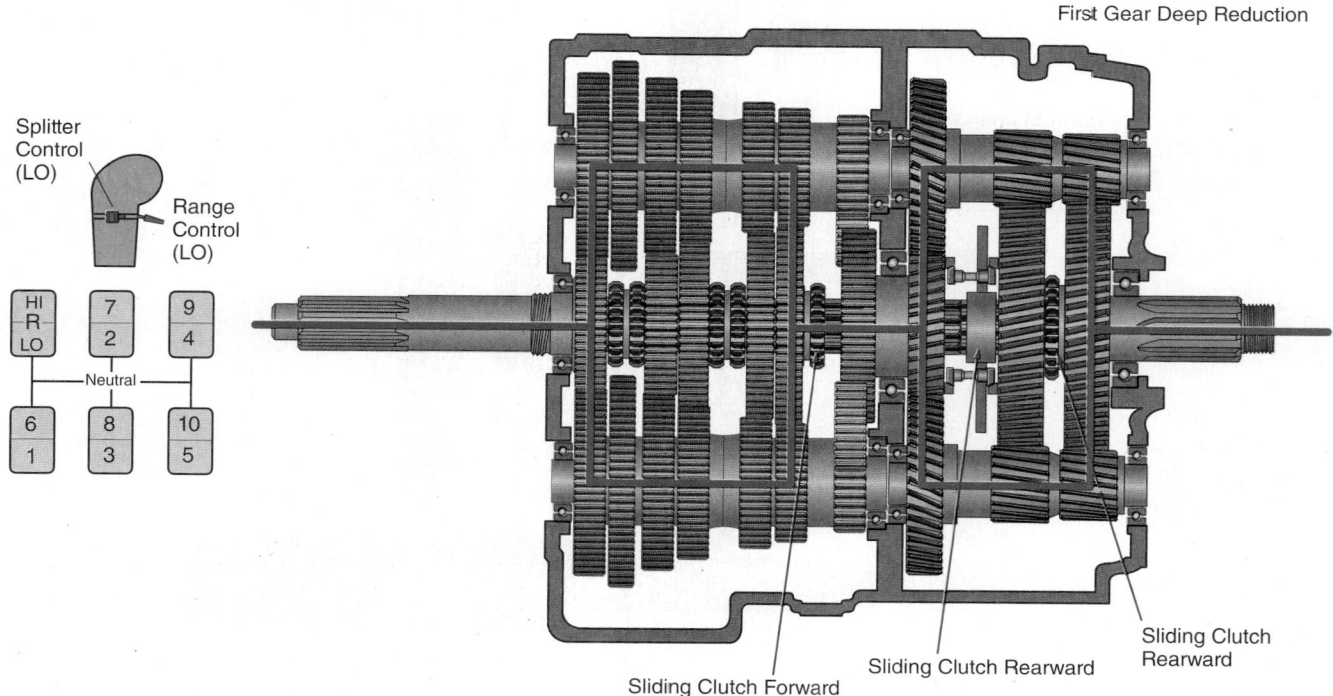

FIGURE 43-43 Power flow with the main box in first gear and auxiliary in deep-reduction.

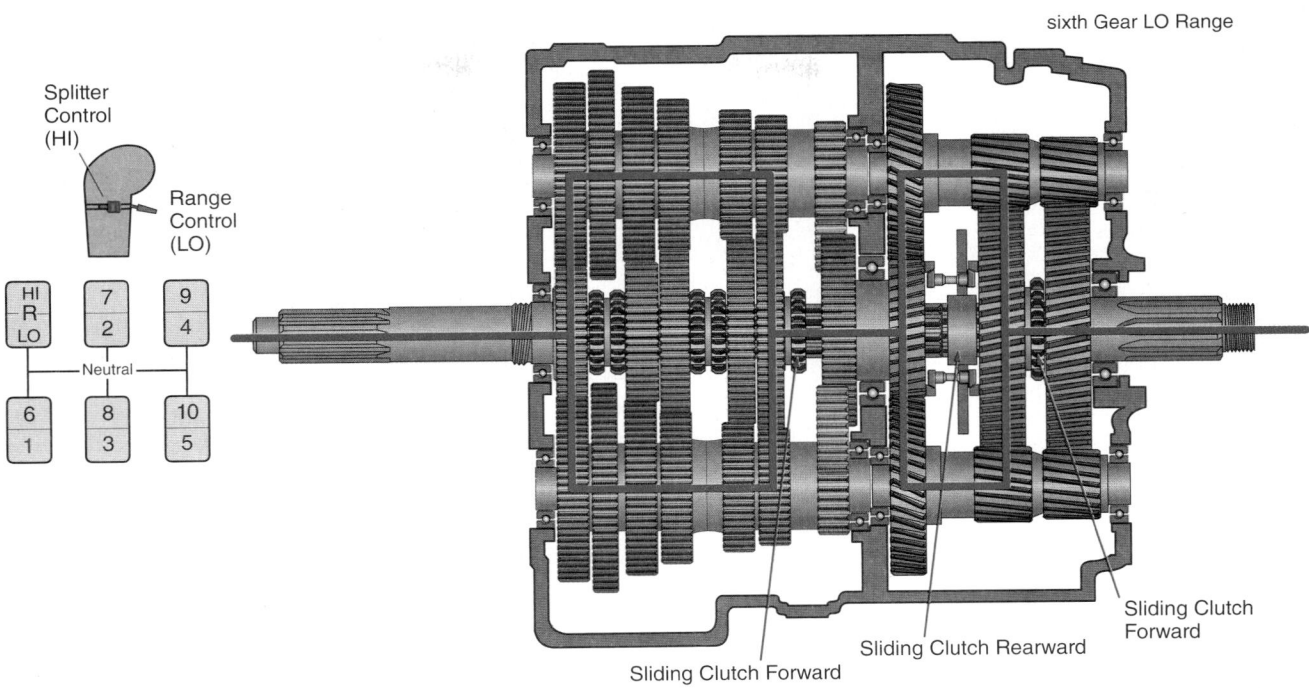

sixth Gear LO Range

Splitter Control (HI)

Range Control (LO)

HI	7	9
R	2	4
LO		

Neutral

6	8	10
1	3	5

Sliding Clutch Forward

Sliding Clutch Rearward

Sliding Clutch Forward

FIGURE 43-44 Power flow with the main box in first gear and the auxiliary section in low range.

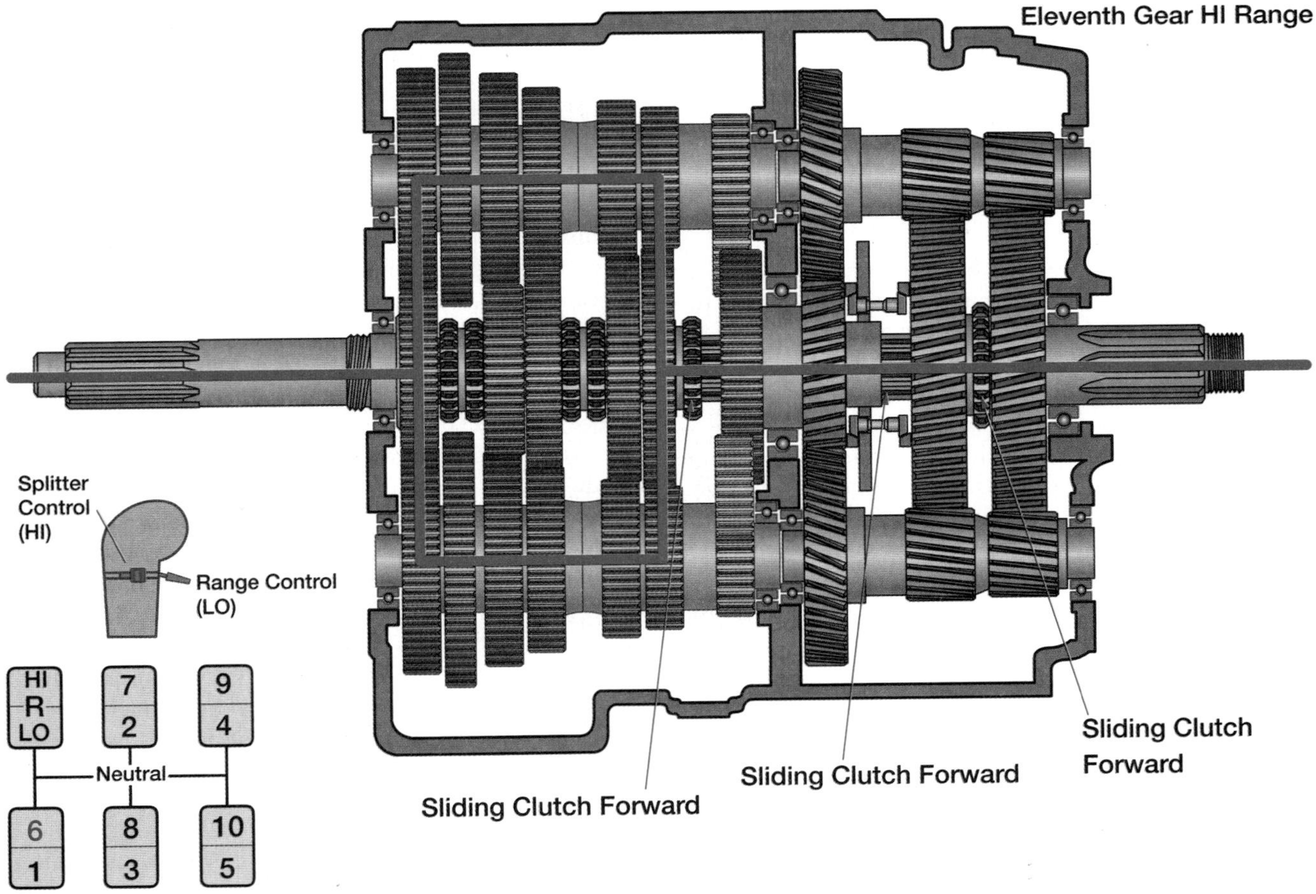

Eleventh Gear HI Range

Splitter Control (HI)

Range Control (LO)

HI	7	9
R	2	4
LO		

Neutral

6	8	10
1	3	5

Sliding Clutch Forward

Sliding Clutch Forward

Sliding Clutch Forward

FIGURE 43-45 Sixth-gear power flow in a deep-reduction main box is in the first gear position and the auxiliary is in the high range (direct).

FIGURE 43-46 Low-inertia auxiliary section.

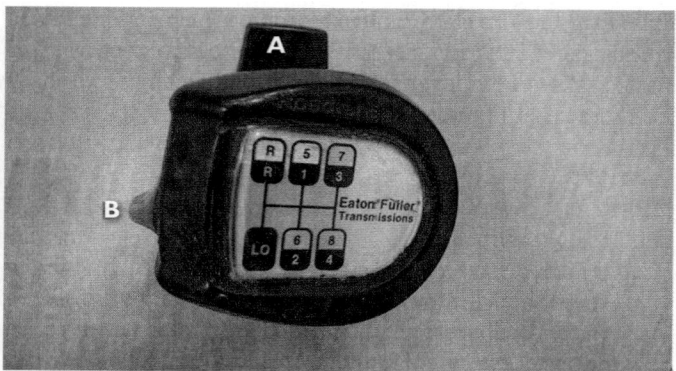

FIGURE 43-47 The driver shift knob incorporates the Roadranger valve, which controls the air shifts for the transmission. **A.** Range select lever. **B.** Splitter button.

with 13-speed transmissions, the splitter sliding clutch is only used in high range.

Low inertia refers to the fact that the auxiliary section gearing is not permanently connected to the main box gearing through the auxiliary drive gear. Because there is not as much weight or inertial mass, the driver can make compound shifts more quickly and smoothly. Remember that a compound shift occurs when two parts of the transmission are being shifted at once; for example, where both the driver's shift lever and the auxiliary section are shifting simultaneously. In these low-inertia auxiliary sections, the splitter sliding clutch is splined to the output shaft of the main box, and there are two different auxiliary drive gears: the front auxiliary drive gear and the rear auxiliary drive gear. The splitter air-shift mechanism determines which of these auxiliary drive gears input to the auxiliary section countershafts. In 13-speed models, the splitter is used only in high range, but in 18-speed models, it is used in both high and low range.

In the old style three-speed auxiliary section, the range gear was between the input gear and the splitter gear, and the auxiliary section mainshaft was in two pieces. In the low-inertia models, the range gear set is at the back of the auxiliary section, and the auxiliary mainshaft is one piece. The high- and low-range selection for these auxiliary sections is the same as for the previous three-speed auxiliary section. For low range, an air-operated synchronizer locks the range gear to the auxiliary section mainshaft in the rearward position. In the forward position, the synchronizer locks the auxiliary section mainshaft to the back side of the rear auxiliary drive gear. In the low split position, the splitter sliding clutch moves forward to lock the front auxiliary drive gear to the output shaft of the main box and transfer torque to the auxiliary countershafts. In the high split position, the splitter sliding clutch moves rearward and locks the rear auxiliary drive gear to the output shaft of the main box.

The presence of the splitter sliding clutch provides two different possible input ratios to the auxiliary section countershafts in high range. In high range and low split, the power flows from the front auxiliary drive gear to the auxiliary countershafts, down to the rear auxiliary drive gear, and out to the drive line. In high range and high split, the rear auxiliary drive gear is locked to the output shaft of the main box and the range synchronizer sliding clutch has locked the auxiliary section mainshaft to the rear side of the rear auxiliary drive gear, providing a direct power flow through the auxiliary section.

To operate an 18-speed transmission using all the forward gears, the driver first selects the main box low gear, with the auxiliary in low range and low split, and then accelerates. Next, the driver moves the splitter button to high split, while under load, and initiates the split shift by momentarily releasing and reapplying the accelerator.

The next shift is a lever shift. The driver first selects low split while under load and then depresses the clutch and moves the lever toward first gear position. During this process, the driver double-clutches to match the shaft and gear speeds. This is called a compound shift as both the main section and the auxiliary are being shifted at the same time. The driver continues up through the main box ranges, using low and high split in each until reaching fourth-gear main box, low range, and high split. At this point, the driver has gone through 10 forward speeds so far.

The next shift has three elements to it. While under load and still in fourth-gear main box, the driver moves the splitter to low split, switches to high range, and then double-clutches while moving the shift lever back to the first-gear main box position. As the shift lever moves through neutral, the range shift and the splitter shift occur. The driver continues through the remaining main box gears, using each in low, and then high, split until he reaches the fourth-gear main box again, in high range and high split. That gives the vehicle eight more forward ratios, for a total of 18 speeds. On deceleration, the driver simply reverses the process.

Depending on the load, it is not always necessary to utilize all the available ratios. Experienced drivers may skip ranges or splits, as required.

Thirteen-speed low-inertia models work in the same way, with the exception that the splitter is not available while the auxiliary section is in low range. The driver shift knob, pictured in **FIGURE 43-47**, incorporates the **Roadranger valve**, which controls the range and splitter shifts for the

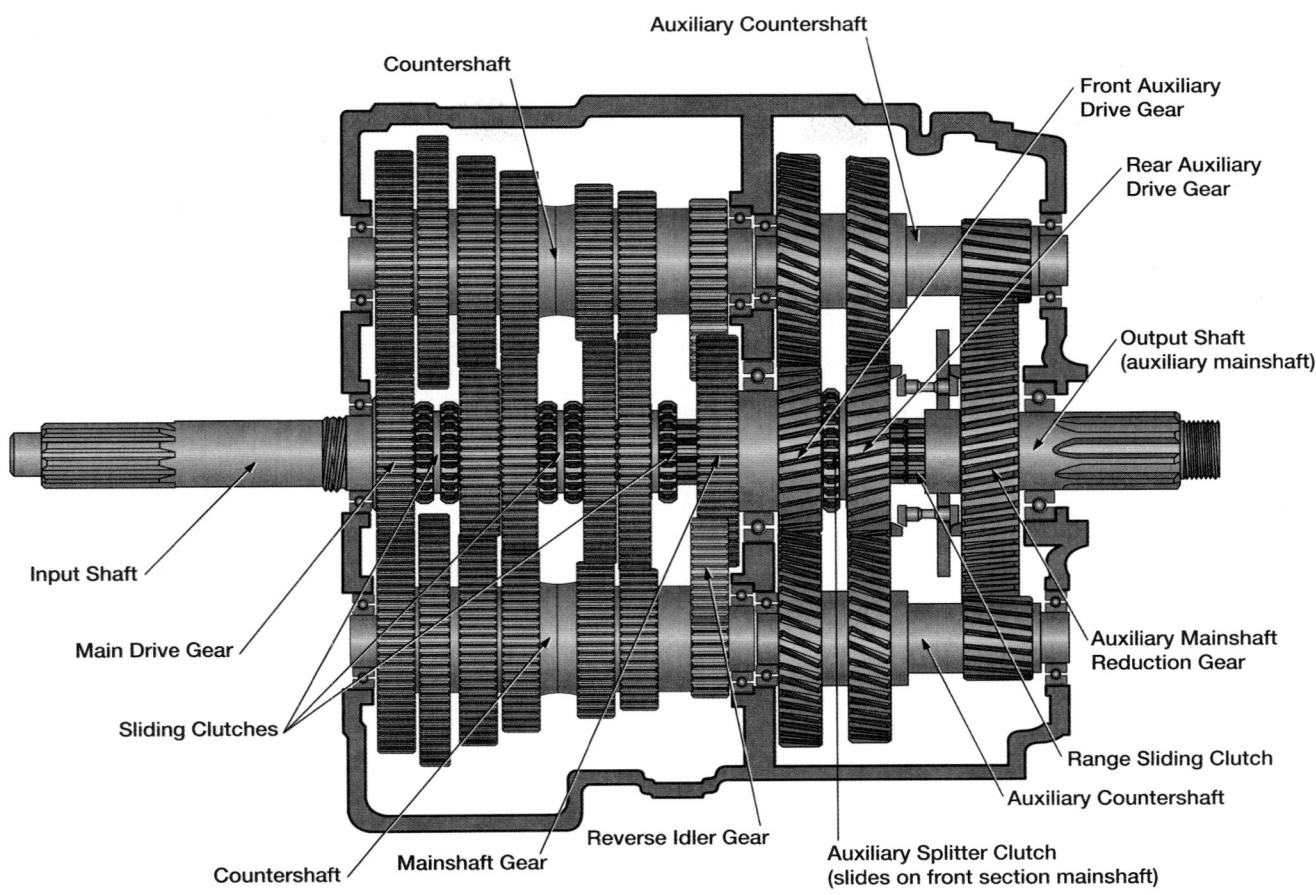

FIGURE 43-48 Cutaway of a transmission with a low inertia auxiliary section, modern 13 speed and 18 speed transmissions both use this design.

transmission. The Roadranger valve does not physically allow a splitter shift while in low range. The 13-speed low-inertia transmission provides five speeds in low range (from low to fourth) and then four lever positions and four splits in high range for eight more ratios, bringing the total number of ranges to 13.

Power Flows Through an 18-Speed Transmission with a Four-Speed Auxiliary

The 13-speed transmission's auxiliary section is identical to the 18-speed model, except for the gear ratios used. Before discussing the power flows, let's quickly review the positioning of all the components in this type of transmission as shown in **FIGURE 44-48**.

In the low-inertia auxiliary section, the mainshaft is one piece, and the range synchronizer sliding clutch is splined to the shaft. The low-inertia box has two selectable auxiliary drive gears: the front and the rear auxiliary drive gear. The front auxiliary drive gear rotates around the main box mainshaft. Even though it rotates around the mainshaft, the front auxiliary drive gear is not splined to it. The rear auxiliary drive gear, also known as the splitter gear, rotates around, but is not splined to, the auxiliary section mainshaft. The splitter sliding clutch sits between the two auxiliary drive gears and is splined to the

front box mainshaft. All the power exiting the main box must pass through the splitter sliding clutch to reach the auxiliary section. The position of the splitter sliding clutch determines which of the drive gears drives the auxiliary countershafts. The range synchronizer and its sliding clutch sit just behind the rear auxiliary drive gear and just in front of the range gear.

Now, let's examine all four power flows. Recall that 13-speed transmissions are mechanically prevented from using the splitter in low range by the Roadranger valve (the shift selector knob).

- *Low range low split.* In low range low split, the splitter sliding clutch, which is splined to the main box mainshaft, is forward, locking the front auxiliary drive gear to the main box mainshaft. The range synchronizer sliding clutch is rearward, locking the range gear to the auxiliary section mainshaft. The power flow is as follows. Rotational power flows from the main box mainshaft to the front auxiliary drive gear and out to the auxiliary countershafts. From the auxiliary countershafts, the power flows down to the engaged range gear, through the synchronizer sliding clutch to the auxiliary mainshaft, and out to the drive line. **FIGURE 43-49** shows the low-range low-split power flow.

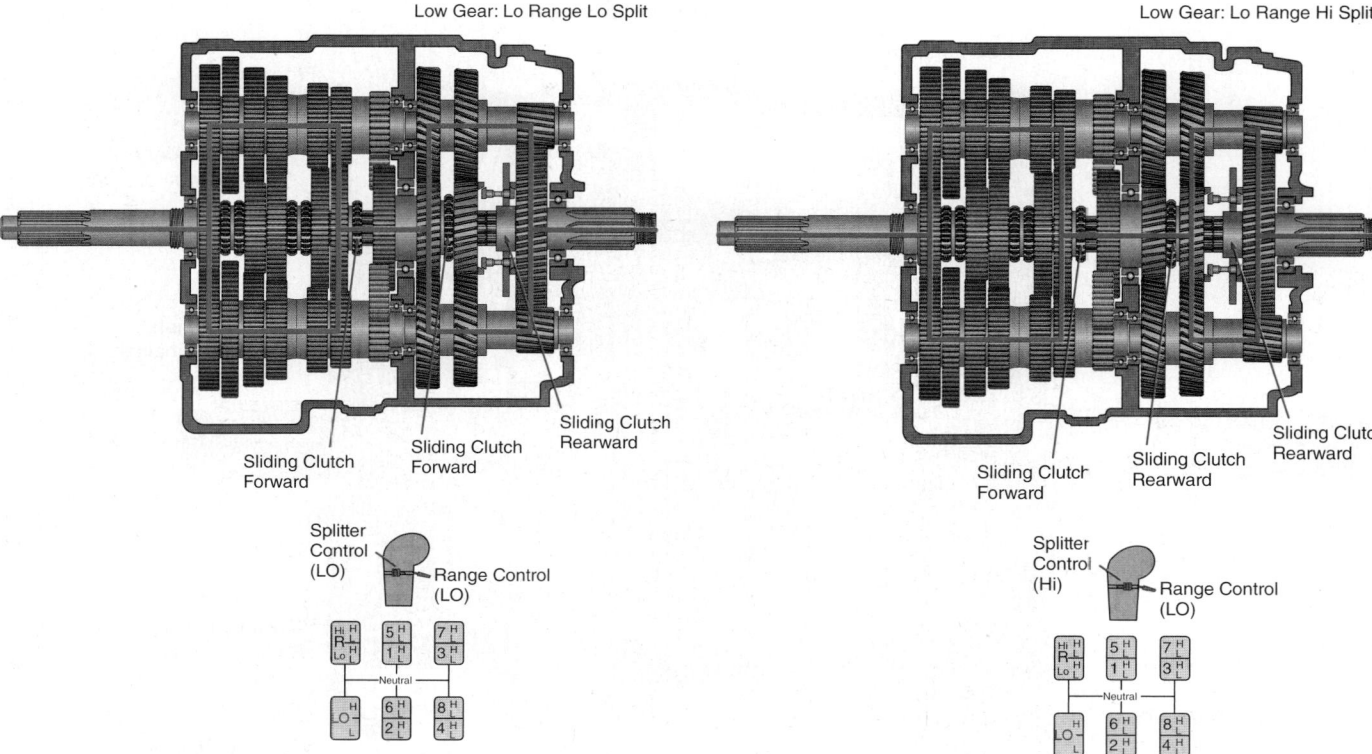

FIGURE 43-49 Low-range low-split power flow.

FIGURE 43-50 Low-range high-split power flow.

- *Low range high split.* In low range high split, the synchronizer sliding clutch remains rearward, thereby locking the range gear to the auxiliary section mainshaft. The splitter sliding clutch moves rearward and engages the rear auxiliary drive gear. That engagement locks the rear auxiliary drive gear to the main box mainshaft. The power flows from the main box mainshaft, through the splitter sliding clutch, to the rear auxiliary drive gear, and out to the auxiliary countershafts. The power then flows down to the range gear, through the synchronizer sliding clutch, to the auxiliary mainshaft, and out to the drive line. The driver splits between low and high split while moving up through the gears in low range. **FIGURE 43-50** shows the low-range high-split power flow.

- *Range shift.* The range shift is only made once during upshifting and once during downshifting. Upon reaching top gear in low range (fourth-gear main box and high split), the driver makes a compound shift by first moving the splitter button to low split while maintaining torque. The driver then preselects high range by pulling the Roadranger valve lever up. Next, the driver double-clutches while moving the shift lever back to the first-gear main box position. As the shift lever moves through the neutral position, the shifts occur automatically as the gears reach synchronous speed.

- *Power flow high range low split.* To move to high range, the range sliding clutch moves forward and engages the back of the rear auxiliary drive gear. That action locks the rear auxiliary drive gear to the auxiliary mainshaft

and allows the range gear to freewheel. In the low-split position, the splitter sliding clutch is forward. In that position, the splitter sliding clutch engages the front auxiliary drive gear and locks it to the mainshaft of the main box. The power flows from the main box mainshaft to the splitter sliding clutch, then to the front auxiliary drive gear, and out to the auxiliary section countershafts. Then, power continues to flow from the auxiliary section countershafts to the rear auxiliary drive gear, through the range sliding clutch to the auxiliary mainshaft, and out to the driveline. **FIGURE 43-51** shows a high-range low-split power flow.

- *Power flow high range high split.* Throughout high-range operation, the range sliding clutch stays forward, locking the back half of the rear auxiliary drive gear to the auxiliary mainshaft. To achieve high split, the splitter sliding clutch moves rearward and engages the front half of the rear auxiliary drive gear. This motion makes the rear auxiliary drive act as a bridge between the main box mainshaft and the auxiliary mainshaft, effectively connecting the two shafts together. The power flows from the main box mainshaft to the splitter sliding clutch, onward to the rear auxiliary drive gear. Power continues to flow through the range sliding clutch to the auxiliary mainshaft and out to the driveline. In high range high split, the auxiliary section is in direct drive. That means the output from the main box passes through the auxiliary unchanged. **FIGURE 43-52** shows a high-range high-split power flow.

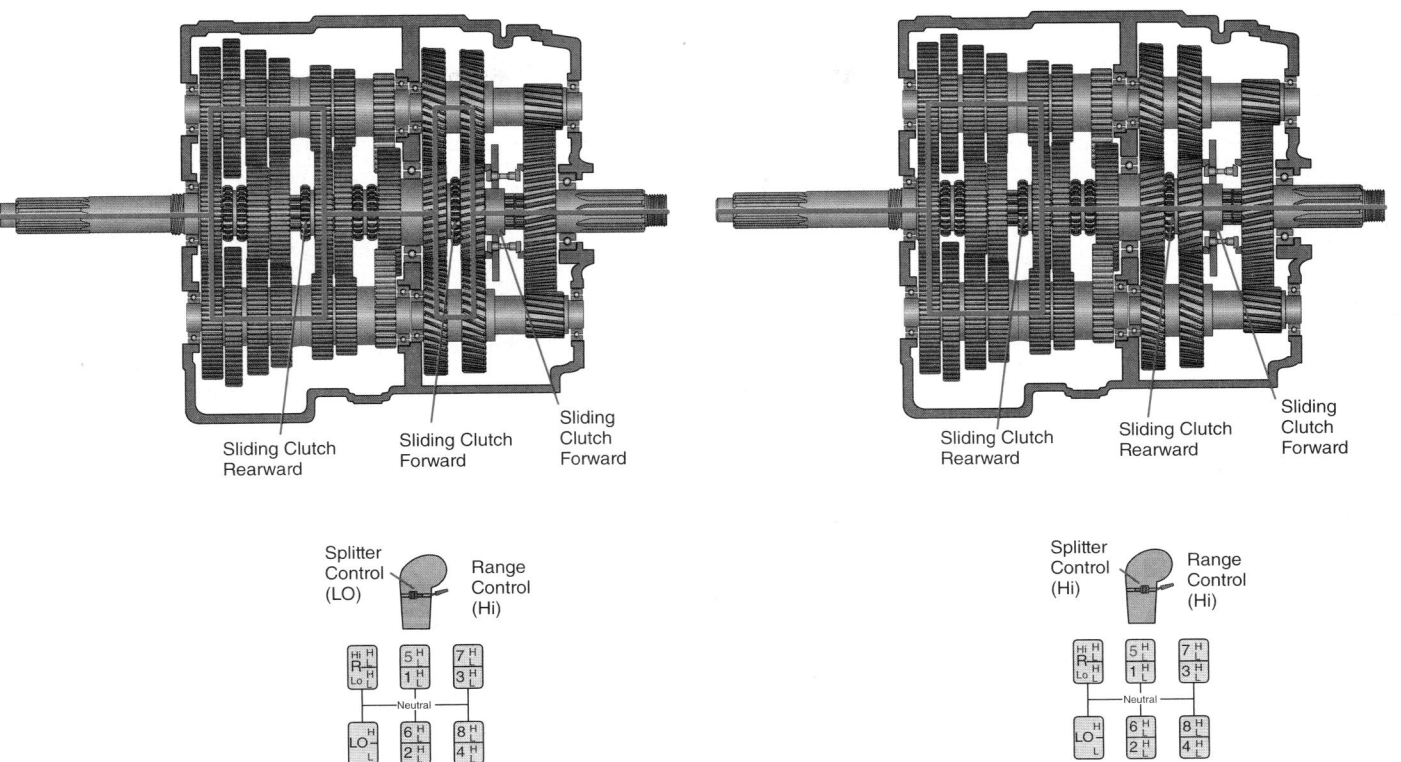

Fifth Gear: Hi Range Lo Split

Fifth Gear: Hi Range Hi Split

FIGURE 43-51 High range low split in a low-inertia auxiliary transmission.

FIGURE 43-52 High range high split (direct) in a low-inertia auxiliary transmission.

Auxiliary Section Air Control

LO 43-6 Describe air-shifting control systems for transmission auxiliary sections.

Pressurized air from the vehicle's air system is used to perform all auxiliary section shifting. The air control system starts with the master control on the shift lever. The master control is the driver's shift knob, called the Roadranger valve by Eaton. The air shifting system can be broken up into two distinct parts: range shift and splitter shifting. There are hundreds of Eaton Fuller transmission models for various applications and vocations. Some have slightly different air systems, but most of the air shift controls and shifting follow the descriptions in this section.

Range Shift Control

All Eaton Fuller twin-countershaft transmissions have a range-control switch consisting of a small lever. The lever is in the down position for low range and pulled up for high range. Air from the vehicle system is supplied to a combination **air filter/pressure regulator** that is mounted to the transmission, as illustrated in **FIGURE 43-53**. The pressure regulator/filter cleans the supply air and regulates it to between 58 and 63 psi (400 to 434 kPa).

Air from the pressure regulator is piped to the front of the **slave air valve**, a valve mounted on the side of the transmission that controls air flow to the range shift cylinder through a 1/4" (6.35 mm) air line. A spool valve-type piston is located inside the slave air valve. A center-drilled passage in that spool valve piston directs air to either the low- or high-range ports on the **range shift cylinder**. (The job of the range shift cylinder is to control the range shifts in the auxiliary.) The air supply to the slave air valve is also directed to the red 1/8" or 5/32" (3.175 or 3.969 mm) air line connected to the range shift control at port "S." With the range shift lever in the down (low-range) position, the air is allowed to pass through the range shift valve and out to the black 1/8" or 5/32" (3.175 or 3.969 mm) air line connected to the range shift control valve at port "P."

The air flows down the black line and acts on the backside of the spool valve piston inside the slave air valve. The same air pressure is now pushing against the front and the rear of the spool valve inside the slave air valve. The spool valve stays in the forward position because the surface area at the rear of the slave air valve is larger than the front, as illustrated in **FIGURE 43-54**. This directs the supply air through the spool of the slave air valve and through a 1/4" (6.35 mm) air line to the low-range (front) port of the range shift cylinder. The cylinder and its shift fork are moved rearward, which pushes the range synchronizer into low range by locking the range gear to the auxiliary output shaft.

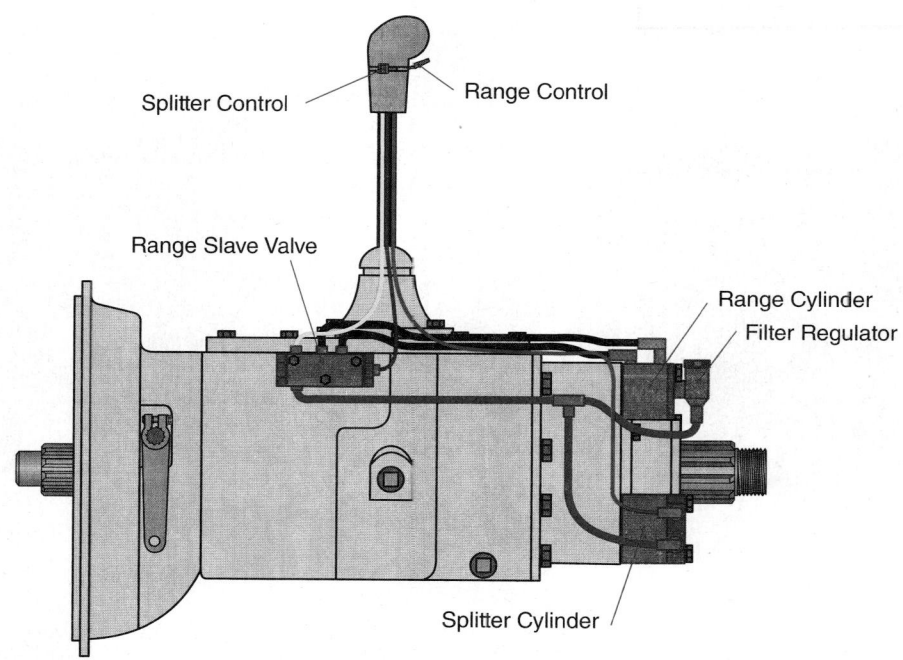

FIGURE 43-53 Air control systems are similar across most models of Eaton Fuller transmissions.

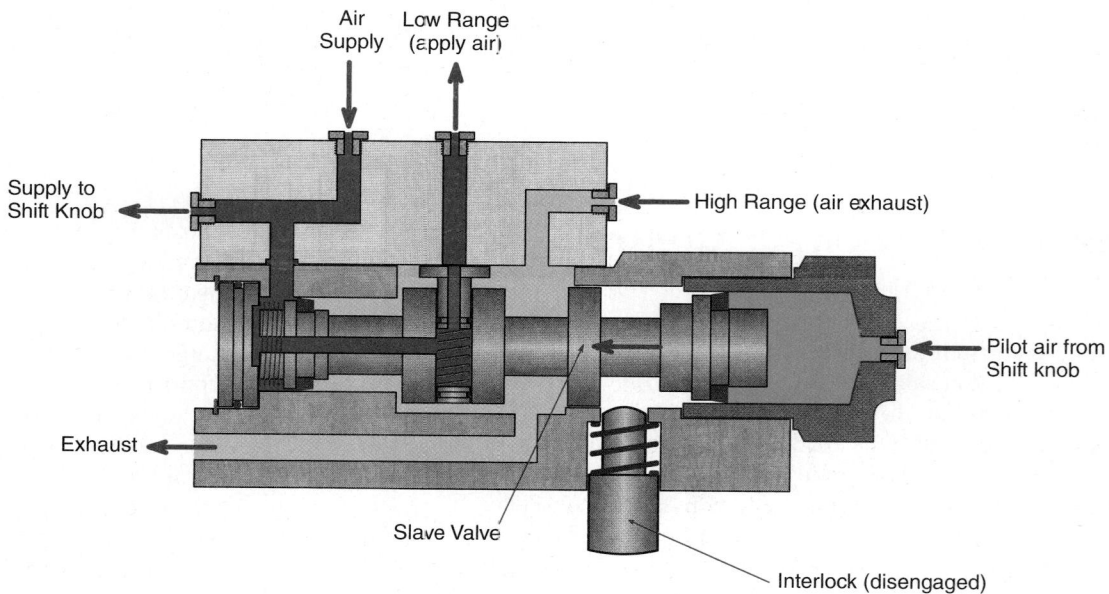

FIGURE 43-54 Slave air valve in low range.

When high range is selected, the range control valve seals off the supply of air to the black air line. The range control valve simultaneously exhausts the air in the black line at the master control from port "E," this exhausts the pressure that was acting on the back of the slave air valve spool valve. When this happens, the constant supply of air at the front of the slave air valve spool valve pushes the spool rearward, as illustrated in **FIGURE 43-55**. When the spool moves to the rearward position, it directs the flow of supply air through another 1/4" (6.35 mm)

air line to the high-range (rear) port of the range shift cylinder and exhausts the air in the low-range side of the cylinder at the slave air valve. This forces the range cylinder piston and fork forward. That forward motion moves the range synchronizer to high range by engaging the range sliding clutch in to the back side of the auxiliary drive gear.

All Eaton Fuller transmissions have an interlock system that prevents the slave air valve from moving unless the transmission is in neutral. The interlock system consists of a spring-loaded pin

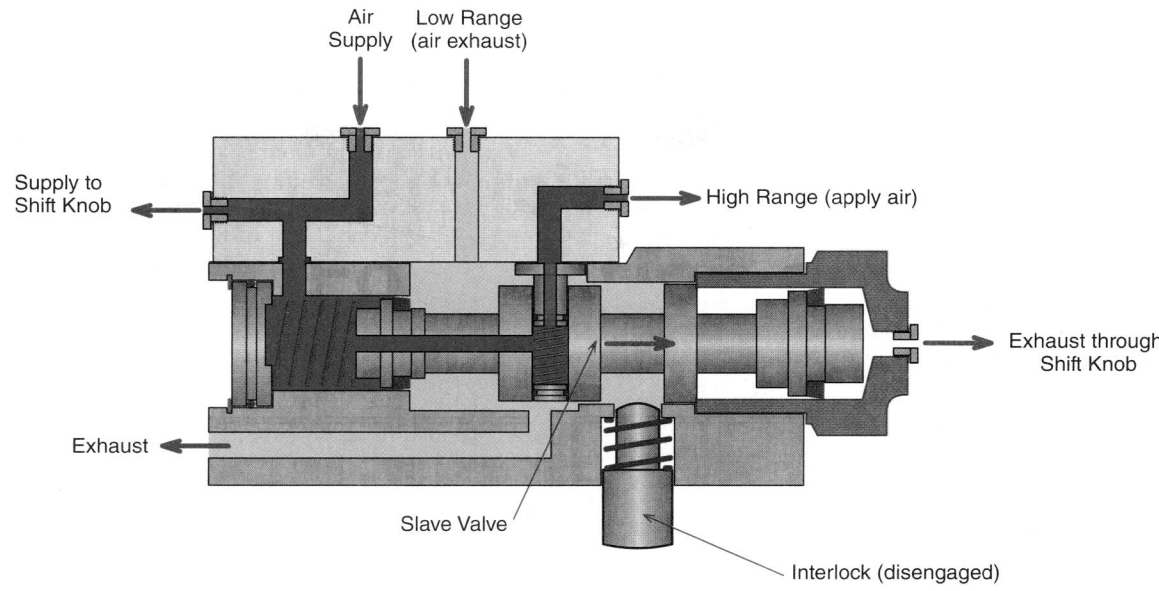

FIGURE 43-55 Slave air valve in high range.

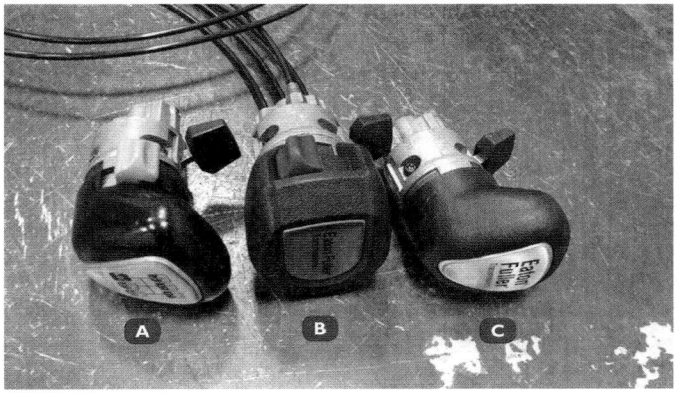

FIGURE 43-56 Color-coded Roadranger valve splitter buttons for: **A.** An 18-speed transmission (gray). **B.** A 13-speed transmission (red). **C.** A 10-speed transmission (no splitter button, only the range shift lever).

that is pushed out from the transmission and into the slave air valve spool valve. The pin physically stops the spool valve from moving while the transmission is in any gear other than neutral. It is essential that the range shift be preselected while the transmission is in gear. Then, as the shift lever moves through neutral, the range shift occurs automatically. The range lever can be moved from low to high and back again in neutral, if the vehicle is not moving, to check operation, but shifting the range in neutral while driving causes severe damage to the range synchronizer.

Splitter Shift Control

The splitter shift is controlled by a movable button on the master shift control. For low split, this button is moved rearward; for high split, the button is moved forward. Depending on the transmission model, this button may be blue, red, or grey. The 10-speed, 13-speed, and 18-speed shift knobs are shown in **FIGURE 43-56**.

The blue-colored button is used only for deep-reduction transmissions. An interlock system in the master shift control ensures the blue button on a deep-reduction transmission can only be used when the auxiliary section is in low range. The red button is used with a 13-speed transmission. Its master control interlock only allows the button to be used when the auxiliary section is in high range. The gray button is used with an 18-speed transmission and can be activated with the auxiliary section in both high and low range.

Splitter Air Control Operation

A constant supply of air from the air filter/regulator is delivered to the **splitter shift cylinder** cover and, through the cover, to both the front and the rear side of the splitter shift cylinder piston. (The job of the splitter shift cylinder is to control the splitter sliding clutch position.) The rear side of the piston has a larger surface area than the front, so this forces the piston and the splitter shift fork forward, resulting in low split. When high split is desired, the splitter button on the shift knob is pushed forward. That forward motion connects the air from the red 1/8" or 5/32" (3.175 or 3.969 mm) diameter air line at the range control lever to a third 1/8" or 5/32" (3.175 or 3.969 mm) air line connected to port "SP." The SP air line is usually blue. The other end of this air line is connected to the **splitter valve** attached to the splitter shift cylinder cover that controls the air flow to the front or rear of the splitter cylinder piston. A splitter valve is shown in **FIGURE 43-57**. The splitter valve allows air to flow to both sides of the splitter cylinder piston in low split and drains the air from the rear side of the cylinder piston in high split.

Note that, in 13-speed transmission models, the air to activate the splitter is delivered from a 1/8" or 5/32" (3.175 or 3.969 mm) air line, which is usually green in color. The green air line is connected to the high-range port of the slave air valve, which brings air to the "H/L" port of the Roadranger valve. This means that the air supply to activate the splitter valve is only available when the 13-speed transmission is in high range. In 15-speed deep-reduction transmissions, the green line to the Roadranger valve is connected to the low-range outlet port of the slave air valve, meaning that the air supply to control the splitter valve is only available when the 15-speed transmission is in low range.

This "pilot" air from the master control causes the splitter valve to move down in its bore, which both blocks the flow of constant supply air to the back side of the splitter piston and opens the backside of the splitter piston to exhaust at the splitter valve. The constant supply of air still operating on the

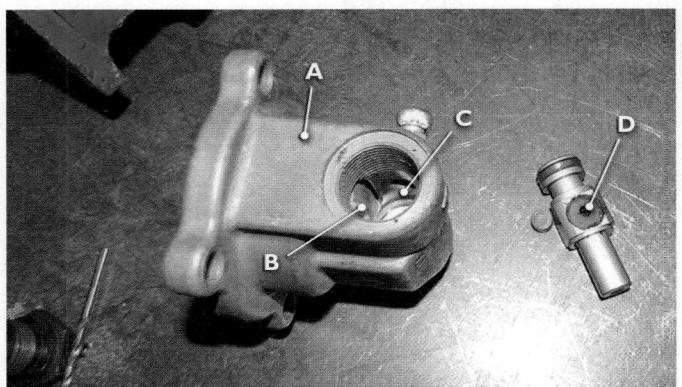

FIGURE 43-57 Splitter valve in a splitter cylinder cover. **A.** Splitter cylinder cover. **B.** Feed port to cylinder. **C.** Exhaust port. **D.** Splitter valve.

front side of the splitter piston forces the piston and the splitter shift fork rearward. The result is the high-split position on 18- or 13-speed transmissions, or the deep-reduction gear engagement on a 15-speed transmission.

The air system in the auxiliary section has four possible ratio selections. Each ratio has a unique configuration for the positions of the range and splitter cylinder and their sliding clutches. The following diagrams show the positioning of the range and splitter cylinder pistons and sliding clutches for 13- and 18-speed low-inertia auxiliary sections. For 15-speed deep-reduction, refer to the positioning in the 15-speed power flows depicted in Figures 43-33 through 43-35.

- *Air system low range low split.* The range sliding clutch is rearward and the splitter sliding clutch is forward, as illustrated in **FIGURE 43-58**.
- *Air system low range high split.* The range sliding clutch is rearward and the splitter sliding clutch is rearward, as illustrated in **FIGURE 43-59**. This ratio is only available on 18-speed transmissions.
- *Air system high range low split.* The range sliding clutch is forward and the splitter sliding clutch is forward, as illustrated in **FIGURE 43-60**.
- *Air system high range high split (direct).* The range sliding clutch is forward and the splitter sliding clutch is rearward, as illustrated in **FIGURE 43-61**.

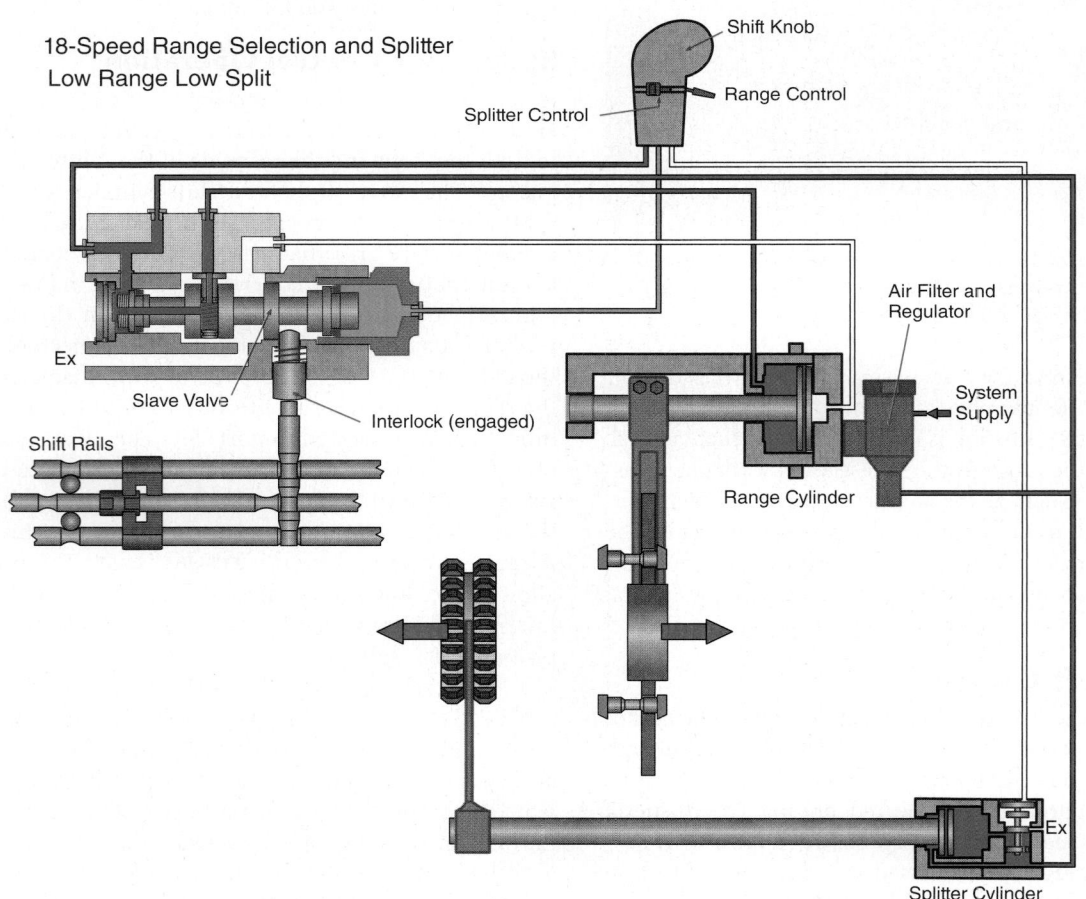

FIGURE 43-58 Air system low range low split.

18-Speed Range Selection and Splitter
Low Range High Split

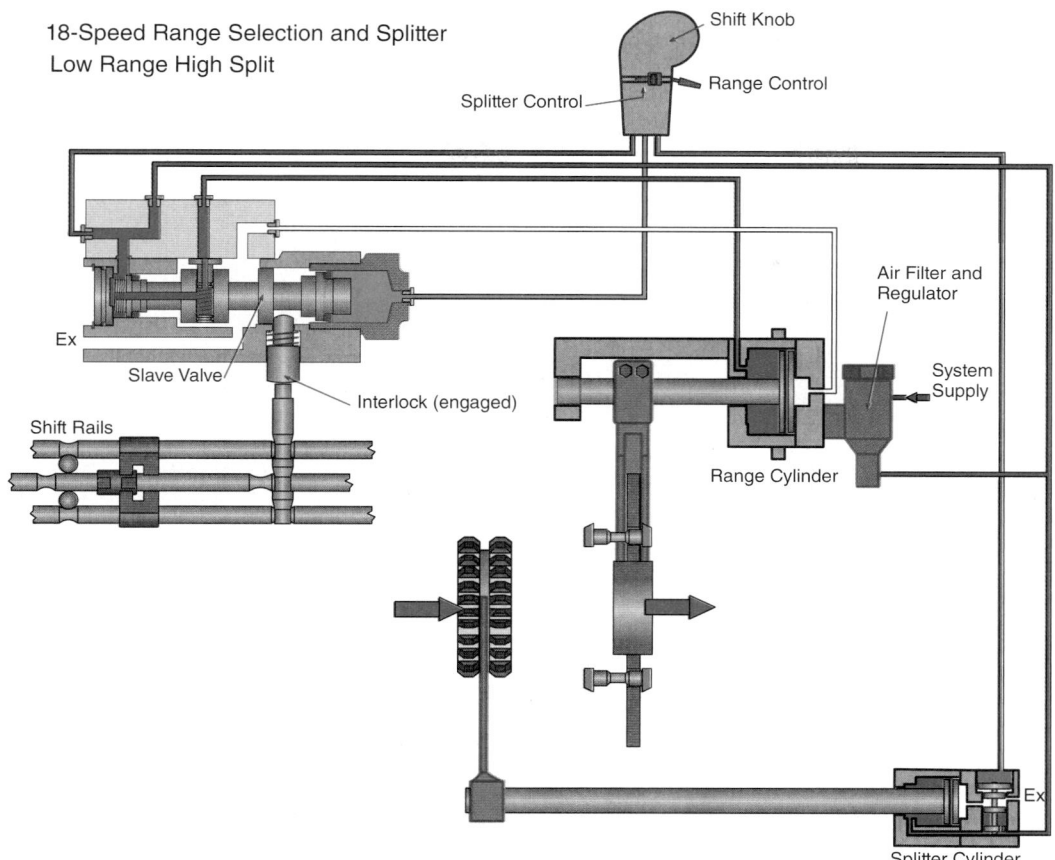

FIGURE 43-59 Air system low range high split.

18-Speed Range Selection and Splitter
High Range Low Split

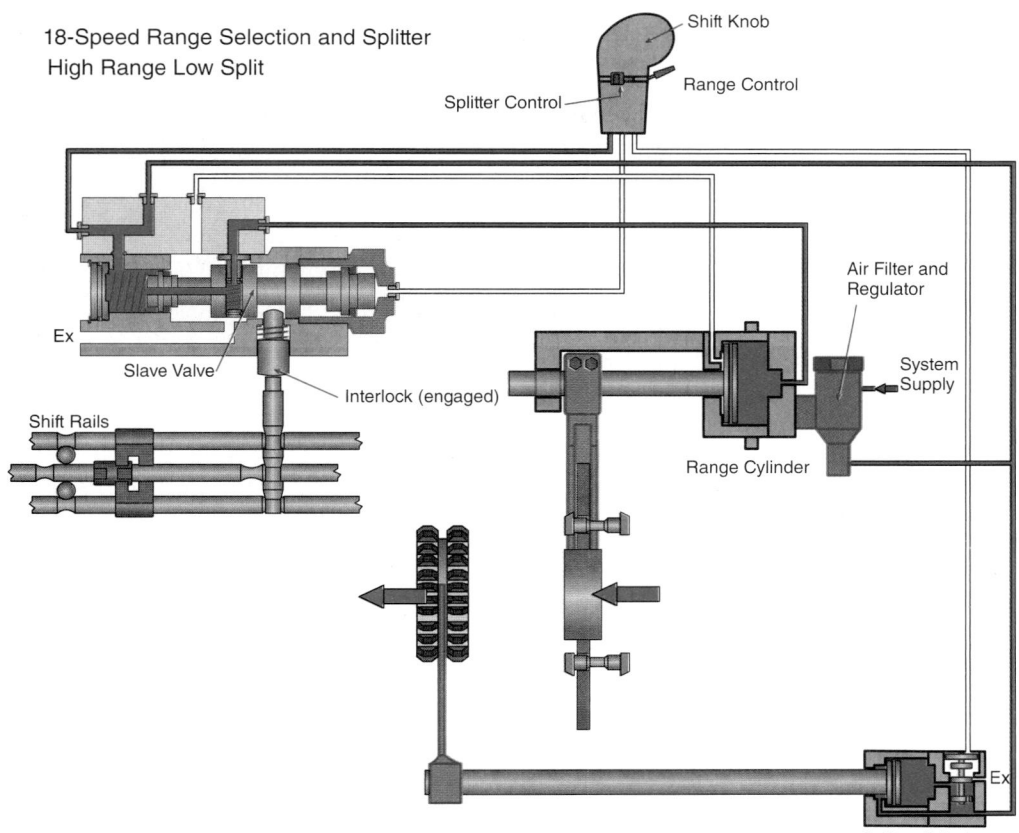

FIGURE 43-60 Air system high range low split.

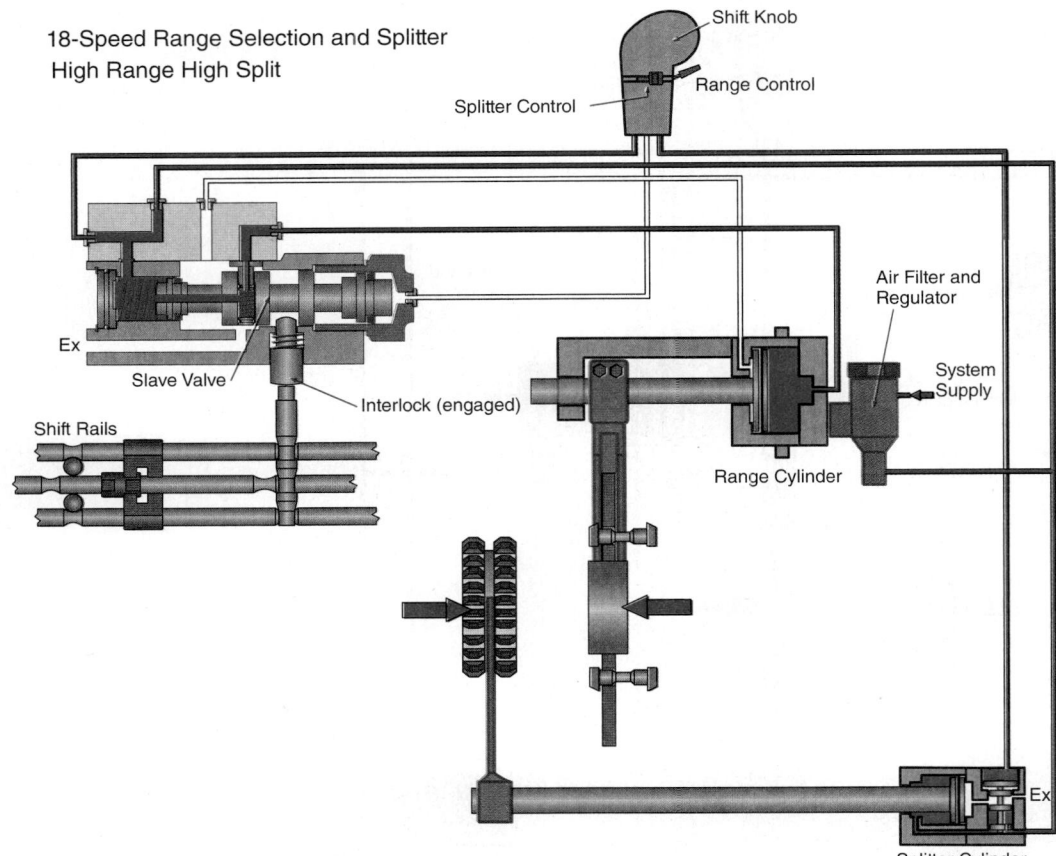

18-Speed Range Selection and Splitter
High Range High Split

Shift Knob

Range Control

Splitter Control

Ex

Slave Valve

Interlock (engaged)

Shift Rails

Air Filter and
Regulator

System
Supply

Range Cylinder

Ex

Splitter Cylinder

FIGURE 43-61 Air system high range high split.

FR Model Transmission Shift Controls

LO 43-7 Explain the function of FR series range-shift air-control systems.

The FR model transmissions from Eaton Fuller are 10-speed transmissions that have integrated all the air system components into a single module that is bolted to the top of the transmission shift cover. The **shift cover** is the cover on the transmission that holds the shift rails and forks. An air module from an FR-model transmission is pictured in **FIGURE 43-62**.

A schematic of the air module is illustrated in **FIGURE 43-63**. This air module holds the air filter, the pressure regulator, and the slave air valve. The high-range and low-range ports consist of holes drilled into the cover, which match up to ports in the air module. These ports are sealed by O-rings, as the module is bolted to the shift cover.

The air module also has an interlock system that does not allow range shifts to occur until the shift lever is moved to the neutral position. The shift cover in the FR series has only one shift rail, and the range cylinder is integrated with the cover, as can be seen in **FIGURE 43-64**, and the air module interlock finger rests against it. Whether the rail moves forward or back, the rail pushes on the interlock finger to prevent the range shift while in gear. As with the RT series of transmissions, the range shift must be preselected by the driver while the transmission is in gear. The range shift occurs automatically as the gear shift lever moves through neutral. Just as in the previously discussed

FIGURE 43-62 The air module on the shift bar housing of the FR-series Fuller transmission.

transmission models, failure to preselect the range shift can destroy the range synchronizer!

The single-module air system on the FR-series transmission has some differences to the normal range control that are described in the beginning of the section on Auxiliary Section Air Control. There are no external 1/4" (6.35 mm) lines carrying air to the range cylinder. Instead, there is only one supply line from the vehicle air system and two 1/8" (3.175 mm) lines going to and from the master shift control or Roadranger valve.

Reference Figure 43-63 as you read the following air system description. Inside the shift control module, we can see an air filter regulator system. Air is filtered and supplied to the shift control at a regulated pressure of 80 psi (552 kPa). The spool

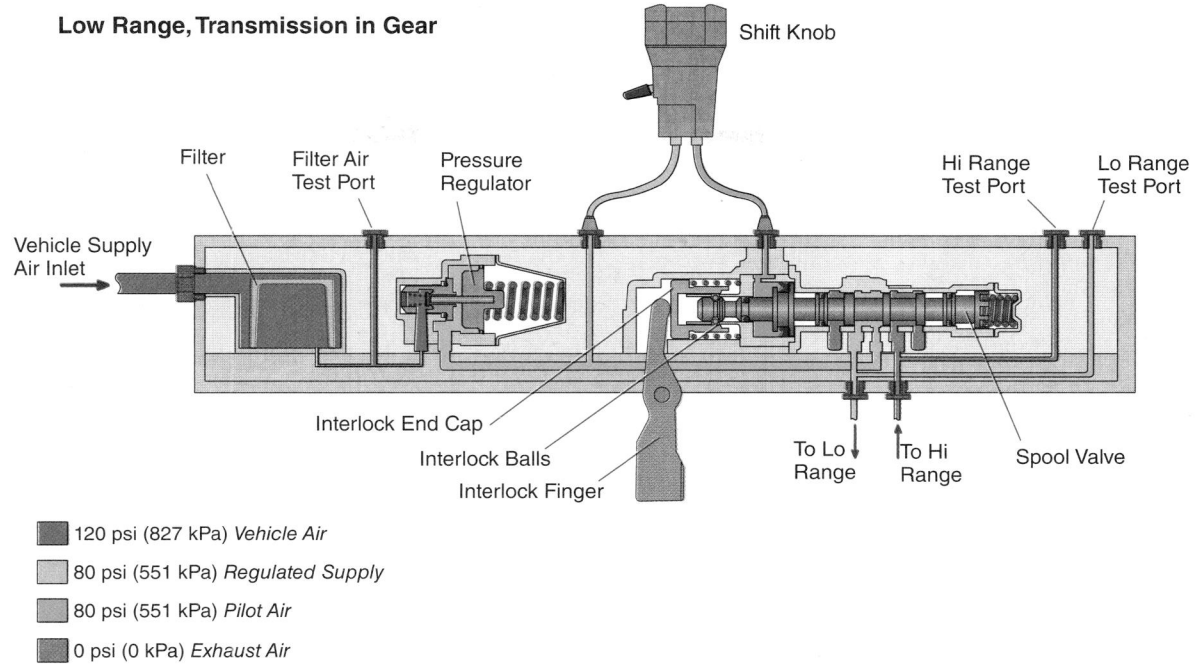

Low Range, Transmission in Gear

FIGURE 43-63 Schematic of air module in FR-model transmission.

120 psi (827 kPa) *Vehicle Air*

80 psi (551 kPa) *Regulated Supply*

80 psi (551 kPa) *Pilot Air*

0 psi (0 kPa) *Exhaust Air*

FIGURE 43-64 The range cylinder (circled) is in the shift bar housing on the Fuller FR-series transmissions.

valve inside the module has an end cap whose position is controlled by the interlock shift finger. When the transmission is in any gear, the interlock finger pushes the end cap to the right, and the interlock balls clamp the spool valve in position similarly to how a shop airline holds on to the coupler on an impact gun. As with other Fuller transmissions, the driver must preselect the range shift in gear before moving the shift lever through neutral.

As the transmission shifts to neutral, the interlock finger moves left at the top and releases the pressure on the end cap. That action frees the interlock balls, and the spool valve can move. In Figure 43-63, the transmission is in low range. Consequently, air flows from the supply to the Roadranger valve (in the shift knob). With the range shift lever in the down position, that air is directed to the pilot port and to the left side of the spool valve. The air forces the spool valve to the right against spring pressure. The spool in this position directs supply air to the low-range port and to the low side of the range cylinder piston. The range shift bar and synchronizer move rearward to

engage the low-range gear. Once the driver selects a gear, the interlock finger pushes the spool end cap to the right. That motion locks the spool in position.

To shift to high range, the driver moves the range lever up while in gear. That action stops the flow of pilot air to the spool valve. As the driver shifts through neutral, the interlock finger moves away from the end cap and spring pressure forces the spool valve to the left. The low-range air is exhausted and supply air is sent to the high-range port and the back of the range cylinder piston. That air forces the range shift bar and synchronizer forward and engages the high range.

SynchroSaver

If the driver manages to select a main box gear before the air system completes the shift to high range, it can cause the range synchronizer to be damaged. This is because if the range gear is not engaged, the power is trying to get to the range gear through the synchronizer's blocking rings friction material, where it quickly burns out. The FR-series transmission air module is equipped with a SynchroSaver feature designed to prevent that from occurring. If the driver achieves a main box gear shift before the high-range shift completes, the interlock finger pushes against the end cap of the spool and forces it to the right slightly. This movement aligns the spool valve outlet with both the low-range and the high-range ports. Air is then sent to both the front and the rear of the range cylinder at the same time. The rearward, or high-range, side of the piston has a larger surface area than the forward, or low-range, side. As the range cylinder moves to high range, the air pressure on the low-range side cushions the movement. The result is that the high range is engaged more smoothly with less burning of the synchronizer friction material.

Original models of the FR series had a movable pivot on the back of the auxiliary section that allowed removal of the auxiliary without first removing the shift cover. The pivot rotates the range synchronizer shaft so that it no longer engages the range shift cylinder piston shaft. Essentially, the pivot allowed the range shift bar to disengage from the range cylinder piston bar.

The pivot has two positions: locked and unlocked. Those positions are indicated by icons cast into the housing. A closed padlock symbol indicates the locked position, and an open padlock symbol indicates the unlocked position.

To remove the auxiliary, a technician must remove two bolts and rotate the pivot to the unlocked position. Then, the technician must reinstall one bolt to be sure it remains there. After the auxiliary section is reinstalled, the pivot is rotated back to the lock position. Current-production FR-series transmissions, as shown in **FIGURE 43-65**, do not have this pivot, so the shift bar housing must be removed to disengage the range synchronizer shaft prior to removing the auxiliary section.

SAFETY TIP

Technicians used to the RT- and RTLO-model transmissions may be accustomed to removing the auxiliary sections and replacing them with the transmission still installed. With the integrated system on the FR models, the transmission shift cover must be removed before the auxiliary section is removed. That is because the range shift piston shaft fits into a groove in the range synchronizer shaft. Damage and/or serious injury could occur from trying to force the auxiliary section out with the range shift piston still engaging the shift fork shaft.

Transfer Cases and Power Take Offs

LO 43-8 Explain the purpose and function of transfer cases and power take-off devices.

A **transfer case** is a gear box arrangement that is either attached to the back of the main transmission or connected to it by a short drive shaft. The transfer case allows the torque from the transmission to be split between the front and rear driving axles of a vehicle. The transfer case may also provide a lower gear ratio and power take-off options. A transfer case is pictured in **FIGURE 43-66**.

FIGURE 43-65 The shift bar cover must be removed to disengage the range shift shaft (circled) before removing the auxiliary section on newer FR-series transmissions.

Transfer cases are sometimes called a **dropbox**, as their design allows the front drive shaft to clear the bottom of the transmission to go to the front axle. The transfer case usually has at least four shafts:

- The input shaft
- The countershaft
- The front-axle drive shaft
- The rear-axle drive shaft

The four shafts are illustrated in **FIGURE 43-67**.

The transfer case may also contain reduction gearing to allow two speeds (low and high) through the case, when desired. A two-speed transfer case has two sets of gears that can drive the output shafts. These gear sets are selectable by the driver using a sliding clutch splined to the input shaft. The transfer case may or may not contain an inter-axle differential gear set to allow for speed changes between the front and rear drive axles. Speed differences between the front and rear drive axles can be induced by turning and/or unequal road conditions. If a vehicle is classified as all-wheel drive, it typically means that it is always in front- and rear-axle drive mode. Therefore, the vehicle must have an inter-axle differential. If the vehicle only uses the front drive axle in off-road or poor traction conditions, the vehicle is said to have part-time front-wheel drive. In that situation, an inter-axle differential is not always required. If an inter-axle differential is present, it normally has a lockout to prevent the differential from operating in poor traction conditions.

The front-axle engagement, two-speed shift control, and the inter-axle differential lockout are all controlled by the driver through a series of air or electric control valves on the dash. If the vehicle does not have an air system, electric motor controls only are used. It is important to note that part-time front-wheel drive systems should not be operated with the front-axle engaged under normal driving conditions. Part-time front-wheel drive should only be engaged in off-road and poor traction situations.

Transfer cases come in a variety of designs. Some come equipped with one or two power take-off shaft flanges that can be used to drive accessories on the vehicle. Transfer cases use splash lubrication systems in which the lower gears rotate in a bath of lubricant and splash a steady stream of lube onto the higher gears. Some systems use a lube pump that is filtered externally to supply pressurized oil to critical areas, such as the input shaft needle bearing and gears. This lubricant falls down through the transfer case and lubricates the other gears and shafts on the way down.

Power Take-Off Devices

Power take-off devices are quite popular in the trucking industry. These devices allow engine power to be rerouted to operate other equipment on the vehicle.

A **power take-off** (PTO) device, such as the one shown in **FIGURE 43-68**, is basically a device attached to the transmission that is gear-driven and can be used to run accessories. As such, a PTO is a gear box that is driven by the engine to power another mechanical or hydraulic component. Most PTOs are attached to the transmission through one of two provided SAE standard openings—the six-bolt or the eight-bolt opening. A PTO can be driven by the engine flywheel, or even by the front geartrain of the engine, but most are driven directly by the transmission's countershaft.

There are several different designs used in the manufacture of PTOs. One of the more common is the two-gear design. The two-gear design typically contains two shafts (the idler shaft and the output shaft) in the unit and three gears (the input gear, the drive gear, and the output gear). The PTO input gear is mounted on the idler shaft and is in constant mesh with the transmission countershaft gear. The output gear, also called the ratio gear, is attached to the output shaft. The drive gear is usually mounted on the input shaft, but not splined to it. A sliding clutch or collar splined to the input shaft is used to engage the drive gear, which is in constant mesh with the output gear. When the sliding clutch or collar engages the drive gear, power is transmitted to the output gear to drive the PTO output shaft. The PTO output shaft can be connected directly to a hydraulic pump or to a drive shaft to power a remote hydraulic or mechanical system. The sliding clutch can be moved mechanically or by an electric or air solenoid to engage the PTO. A typical PTO is shown in **FIGURE 43-69**.

The ratio gear may be fixed to the idler shaft or free to rotate on it. If the ratio gear is freely rotating, the sliding clutch locks it to the idler shaft to engage the PTO. (In some spur-tooth input-gear PTOs, the input gear is splined to the idler shaft and slid into mesh with the countershaft gear to engage the PTO. Those types are, however, less common.) The second shaft is the PTO output shaft, which has the PTO-driven gear keyed or splined to it. Most PTOs are designed to be used when the vehicle is stationary and in neutral.

The PTO generally is engaged by moving the sliding clutch to lock the input gear to the shaft. Some models use a different configuration and have a sliding gear on the output shaft for PTO engagement. The most common application of power take-offs is to drive hydraulic pumps directly. Power take-offs can also indirectly drive air compressors/vacuum pumps, pneumatic blowers, or other mechanical components, such as high-pressure water pumps through a driveshaft. The indirect type of PTO installation using a driveshaft must follow all the rules for driveshaft angles and limits mentioned in the Driveshaft Systems chapter.

FIGURE 43-66 Transfer case with: **A.** PTO shaft. **B.** Input from transmission. **C.** Rear drive axle. **D.** Front drive axle.

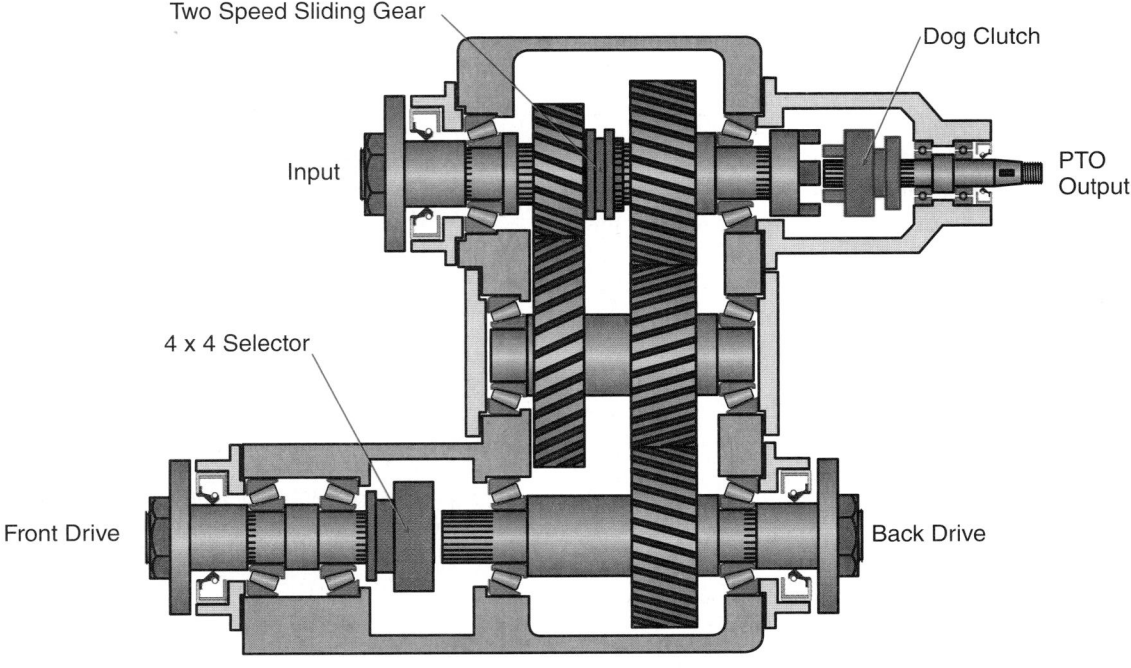

FIGURE 43-67 Schematic of a transfer case with a power take-off option.

FIGURE 43-68 A typical PTO driven by the transmission's countershaft.

FIGURE 43-69 A typical power take-off device. **A.** Constant-mesh gears. **B.** Sliding collar.

There are several other types of PTOs, such as front-mount belt-driven hydraulic pumps, and PTOs provided by transfer cases. One type of PTO common in off-road equipment is sandwiched between the engine and transmission. PTOs can be retrofitted to most vehicles, and they are usually quite easy to install, as long as there is sufficient clearance.

When installing a transmission-mounted PTO, care must be taken to provide the correct running clearance, or backlash, between the countershaft gear and the PTO drive gear. In most cases, this clearance runs between 0.006" and 0.018" (0.15 mm and 0.46 mm). A PTO mounted too tightly runs noisily and

ultimately fails. It can also damage the transmission in the process. Conversely, a PTO mounted too loosely (with too much backlash) runs the risk of skipping teeth under load. It, too, may cause catastrophic damage from pieces of metal broken off the gears running through the transmission and the PTO itself.

Deciding which type and size of PTO is correct for a given application is better left to the PTO manufacturer, who can give advice on PTO speed, horsepower capability, and suitability for a given vocation. Regardless of type, PTOs are a simple and effective way to use the powertrain of the vehicle to operate accessory devices, when necessary.

Wrap-Up

Ready for Review

- Different vehicles are designed for different vocations or purposes. On-highway, off-highway, delivery, heavy hauling, and other vocations have specific needs when it comes to torque multiplication requirements.
- Transmissions are designed with enough ratio steps or increases so that they can be operated under the necessary conditions for which the vehicle is designed.
- All transmissions have at least four shafts: an input shaft, a countershaft, a main or output shaft, and a reverse idler shaft.
- Transmissions are classified or typed by the method they use to select gear ratios.
- A sliding-gear transmission uses only spur gears and has all the speed gears splined to the mainshaft. The spur gears must be slid into mesh with their corresponding countershaft gears to select a ratio.
- Constant-mesh transmissions mainshaft speed gears are always in mesh with their corresponding countershaft gears. All the mainshaft gears turn freely on the mainshaft until they are locked to it by a sliding clutch, a sliding collar, or a synchronizer.
- Double-clutching is a technique to provide clash-free shifting. The driver disengages the clutch, shifts to neutral, and then re-engages the clutch again. The driver then tries to match the engine speed to the speed of the desired

mainshaft gear. The driver once again disengages the clutch, selects the gear, and re-engages the clutch. Double-clutching is used with sliding-gear transmissions and non-synchronized transmissions.
- Sliding clutches are internally splined to the transmission mainshaft. To select a ratio, the clutch's external clutching teeth engage internal clutching teeth on the mainshaft gears. This arrangement is a non-synchronized transmission.
- Sliding collars are splined to a hub that in turn is splined or keyed to the mainshaft. To select a ratio, the internal splines of the sliding collar slide over external clutching (dog) teeth on the mainshaft gear. This arrangement is a non-synchronized transmission.
- Synchronizers use friction to match shaft and gear speeds. Synchronizers simplify transmission operation by eliminating the need for double-clutching and the associated driver skill.
- Shift mechanisms include the shift lever, shift tower, shift cover, shift gates, shift rails, and shift forks. Two other components are also included in shift mechanisms. The shift rail interlock prevents two gears from being selected at once. The shift detents, usually spring-loaded balls, help the shift rail stay in gear.
- Overdrive transmissions sometimes present a problem for shift patterns. Most drivers are familiar with the standard H shift

pattern, but the overdrive ratio gears must be on the mainshaft, sometimes causing an awkward U-shape shift pattern. Manufacturers use methods, such as bellcranks, to reverse the movement of shift rails to maintain a standard shift pattern.

- ▶ All transmission power flows are compound flows. That is, more than one set of gears is involved in the ratio. Usually four gears are involved to create all ratios, except when in direct, or 1:1 ratio.
- ▶ In transmissions with auxiliary sections, up to eight gears are required to finalize the ratio being selected.
- ▶ Multiple countershaft transmissions split the input torque between two or three countershafts. They utilize many more teeth on the mainshaft gears to transmit torque to the mainshaft and allow the transmission to handle greater overall torque. The mainshaft, however, must be made stronger, as it must carry all of the torque by itself.
- ▶ Multiple countershaft transmissions allow the mainshaft to "float" or self-center, because all the mainshaft gears are directly supported by the two or three countershafts. The mainshaft in these transmissions carries no load until one of the mainshaft gears is locked to it by a sliding clutch. The sliding clutch centers the shaft when it engages.
- ▶ Auxiliary sections are used to multiply the number of available ratios from a transmission. Auxiliary sections typically have two, three, or four available ratios and so allow a transmission to which they are attached to have 10, 13, or even 18 forward ratios, respectively.
- ▶ Auxiliary section ratios are shifted by air cylinders. One air cylinder is used for range selection and one for splitter selection.
- ▶ It is essential that the driver preselects the range shift before shifting to the neutral position. Otherwise, the air-shift mechanism may not be able to complete the shift. Damage to the range synchronizer could result.
- ▶ The range shift from low to high range is used only once as the driver accelerates through the gears, and once on the way back down as he decelerates.
- ▶ The splitter shift provides a half-ratio step. It is used in both low and high range on 18-speed Fuller transmissions, but only in high range on 13-speed models.
- ▶ The Fuller FR-series transmissions are 10-speed fleet transmissions, and they use an integrated air module to control the range shift. The range cylinder in these models is part of the transmission shift cover.
- ▶ Transfer cases are used to split the output from the transmission and send the output to both the front and rear drive axles. Transfer cases can also have a high and low gear ratio, which can multiply the overall number of ratios available to the driver.
- ▶ Power take-off devices are used to power auxiliary devices on a vehicle, such as hydraulic pumps and conveyor systems. PTOs can be connected to the engine, the transmission, or the transfer case. The position of the PTO is usually dependent on when the auxiliary power is needed with the vehicle stationary, when the auxiliary power is needed with the vehicle moving, and how much power is required.

Key Terms

air filter/pressure regulator The Fuller air filter/pressure regulator cleans the pressurized air supply going to the transmission and regulates it to 58 to 63 psi (400 to 434 kPa).

auxiliary section A section bolted to the main transmission with two, three, or four ratios to multiply the ratios available to the driver.

bellcrank A shaft used in a mechanical linkage with a pivot in the center that reverses the normal direction of motion.

blocking ring A synchronizer part that uses friction to increase or decrease a gear's speed to match shaft speed, so that the synchronizer sleeve or collar can lock the gear to the shaft.

collar shift transmission A transmission that uses sliding clutches or sliding collars to select gear ratios.

compound shift A shift where two parts of the transmission are being shifted at once.

constant mesh transmission A transmission in which the main and countershaft gears are always in mesh.

countershaft The shaft inside a transmission driven by the input gear.

detent balls Spring-loaded steel balls that hold the shift rails in position.

dropbox A component that is bolted to the back of the transmission and connects the front and rear axles via the drive shaft; allows the output of a transmission to flow to both the rear and the front axles. Also called *transfer case*.

double-clutch A technique drivers use to synchronize gear and shaft speed.

input shaft The component to which the clutch discs are splined.

interlock system A system that prevents the transmission from engaging two mainshaft gears at once.

low-inertia A new design auxiliary section that momentarily disengages the auxiliary from the main box during compound shifts, making it easier to move the shift lever.

mainshaft The shaft that is driven by the countershaft and provides output for the transmission. Also called *output shaft*.

multi-mesh gearing Mainshaft and countershaft gears that have finer cut teeth—meaning more teeth are in mesh for increased strength.

multiple-countershaft transmission A transmission with more than one countershaft; used to distribute the torque between more teeth on the mainshaft and countershaft speed gears to increase torque capacity of the transmission.

power flow The path that power takes from the beginning of an assembly to the end. In a transmission, power flow changes as different gears are selected by the driver.

power take off (PTO) device A device attached to the transmission that is gear-driven and can be used to run accessories.

range gear Any speed gear; in Eaton transmissions, it refers to the low-range gear in the auxiliary section.

range shift cylinder The shift cylinder to control range shifts in the auxiliary.

ratio step The difference between one ratio and the next available.

reverse idler shaft   Shaft that supports the reverse idler gear.

Roadranger valve   The driver's shift knob that controls range and splitter shifting.

shift cover   The cover on the transmission that holds the shift rails and forks.

shift finger   A flat-sided piece that sits into the shift gates.

shift forks   The forks that move the sliding clutches or collars in the transmission.

shift gate   Rectangular notches either formed in or attached to the shift rails.

shift lever   The shift control the driver uses to change the main box gear position.

shift tower   A raised section with a pivot into which the shift lever fits.

single-countershaft transmissions   A transmission with only one countershaft.

slave air valve   The valve on the side of a Fuller transmission that controls air flow to the range shift cylinder.

sliding clutch   A device with splines on the inside and outside used as a gear-selection method for manual transmissions.

sliding collar   A device with splines on the inside only, used as a gear-selection method in manual transmissions.

sliding-gear transmission   A transmission with gears that are splined to a transmission mainshaft and are slid into and out of mesh with a corresponding countershaft gear.

speed gears   The gears on the countershaft and mainshaft that create the transmission ratios, also known as *range gears*.

splitter shift cylinder   The shift cylinder that controls the splitter sliding clutch.

splitter valve   A small valve in the splitter cylinder cover on a Fuller transmission that controls air flow to the front or rear of the splitter cylinder piston.

synchronized transmission   A transmission that uses sliding clutches or collars fitted over synchronizer hubs that are splined to the mainshaft to select gear ratios.

synchronizer   A device to match shaft and gear speeds for clash-free engagement.

transfer case   A component that is bolted to the back of the transmission or connected to it by a short drive shaft; allows the output of a transmission to flow to both the rear and the front axles. Also called *dropbox*.

Review Questions

1. What is the primary reason manufacturers use multiple-countershaft transmissions?
   a. Multiple-countershaft transmissions provide more ratios.
   b. Multiple-countershaft transmissions increase torque capacity.
   c. Multiple-countershaft transmissions are easier for the driver to operate.
   d. Multiple-countershaft transmissions are cheaper to produce.

2. Which of the following is NOT an advantage of multiple-countershaft transmissions?
   a. Multiple-countershaft transmissions shorten transmission length.
   b. Multiple-countershaft transmissions decrease transmission weight.
   c. Multiple-countershaft transmissions decrease the torque load on the transmission output shaft.
   d. Multiple-countershaft transmissions make the manufacturing process a little easier.

3. Which of the following BEST describes the role of the auxiliary section in a truck standard transmission?
   a. Reduction of torque output
   b. Multiplies the number of available gear ratios
   c. Reduces transmission length
   d. Enables faster road speeds in lower ranges

4. To rotate a countershaft transmission-driven gear in the same direction of rotation as the drive gear, which of the following is a requirement?
   a. The drive gear must be larger in diameter than the driven gear.
   b. There must be two gears, and both must have external teeth.
   c. There must be an idler gear between the drive and driven gears.
   d. Two gears must be in mesh, with one of them driving.

5. When a Fuller Roadranger low-inertia 13-speed transmission auxiliary section is in High range, Low split, in which position are the range and the splitter sliding clutches?
   a. Range sliding clutch forward, splitter sliding clutch rearward
   b. Range sliding clutch rearward, splitter sliding clutch forward
   c. Both sliding clutches forward
   d. Both sliding clutches rearward

6. When a constant-mesh transmission is in neutral, which of the following statements about the transmission's helical mainshaft gears is correct?
   a. They are splined to the main or output shaft.
   b. They are keyed to the main or output shaft.
   c. They are free to turn on the main or output shaft.
   d. They are keyed to the synchronizer hub.

7. When synchronizers are used in a transmission, the power flow is connected to the output shaft by the:
   a. countershaft.
   b. input shaft.
   c. synchronizer sliding collar or clutch and hub.
   d. synchronizer blocker ring.

8. What prevents transmission from being put in two gears at the same time?
   a. Shift rail detent balls and pins
   b. Shift rail interlock system
   c. Narrow shift gates
   d. A larger shift finger

9. When a sliding gear is used in a transmission, it is connected to the mainshaft by:
   a. splines in the sliding gear.
   b. a sliding clutch.
   c. a synchronizer.
   d. a shift fork.

10. When a Fuller Roadranger low-inertia 18-speed transmission auxiliary section is in Low range, High split, in which position are the range sliding clutch and the splitter sliding clutch?
  a. Range sliding clutch forward, splitter sliding clutch rearward
  b. Range sliding clutch rearward, splitter sliding clutch forward
  c. Both sliding clutches forward
  d. Both sliding clutches rearward

ASE Technician A/Technician B Style Questions

1. Technician A says that to make a range shift in a Road-Ranger transmission, you move the range selector valve lever first and then shift the transmission to the correct gear. Technician B says that you shift the transmission to neutral first and then move the range selector valve lever. Who is shifting the transmission correctly?
  a. Technician A
  b. Technician B
  c. Both Technician A and Technician B
  d. Neither Technician A nor Technician B

2. Technician A says that the splitter control button on a Fuller 13-speed transmission can be operated in both low and high ranges. Technician B says that the splitter control button on a Fuller 18-speed transmission can be operated in both high and low range. Who is correct?
  a. Technician A
  b. Technician B
  c. Both Technician A and Technician B
  d. Neither Technician A nor Technician B

3. Technician A says that the splitter piston in a Fuller 18-speed transmission moves forward for high split. Technician B says that the splitter piston in the 13-speed Fuller is rearward during low range. Who is correct?
  a. Technician A
  b. Technician B
  c. Both Technician A and Technician B
  d. Neither Technician A nor Technician B

4. Technician A says that the air shift system in a Fuller 13-speed RTLO-series transmission operates at 58–63 psi (393–434 kPa). Technician B says that the Fuller FR-series transmission's air system also operates at 58–63 psi (393–434 kPa). Who is correct?
  a. Technician A
  b. Technician B
  c. Both Technician A and Technician B
  d. Neither Technician A nor Technician B

5. Technician A says that the slave air valve in a Fuller 13-speed RTLO-series transmission is moved by air for both the low- and high-range positions. Technician B says that in the Fuller FR-series transmissions the spool valve in the shift control air module moves to the high-range position by spring pressure. Who is correct?
  a. Technician A
  b. Technician B
  c. Both Technician A and Technician B
  d. Neither Technician A nor Technician B

6. Technician A says that when the range sliding clutch is forward in a 13-speed auxiliary section, the transmission is in low range. Technician B says that when the splitter sliding clutch is rearward in a 13-speed transmission auxiliary section, the transmission is in high split. Who is correct?
  a. Technician A
  b. Technician B
  c. Both Technician A and Technician B
  d. Neither Technician A nor Technician B

7. Technician A says that the Fuller deep-reduction transmission has the deep-reduction gear at the rear of the auxiliary section. Technician B says that the auxiliary section mainshaft in a Fuller deep-reduction transmission is in two pieces. Who is correct?
  a. Technician A
  b. Technician B
  c. Both Technician A and Technician B
  d. Neither Technician A nor Technician B

8. Technician A says that in the low-split position, the splitter sliding clutch is forward in the 13-speed Fuller transmission. Technician B says that the range synchronizer is rearward when the 13-speed transmission is in low range. Who is correct?
  a. Technician A
  b. Technician B
  c. Both Technician A and Technician B
  d. Neither Technician A nor Technician B

9. Technician A says that, when a 13-speed fuller transmission auxiliary section is in low split, air is present at both sides of the splitter cylinder piston. Technician B says that, when the 13-speed Fuller transmission auxiliary section is in high split, air is present at the back of the splitter cylinder piston only. Who is correct?
  a. Technician A
  b. Technician B
  c. Both Technician A and Technician B
  d. Neither Technician A nor Technician B

10. Technician A says that air is present at both sides of the range cylinder piston in a Fuller 13-speed transmission auxiliary section when it is in low range. Technician B says that air is only present at the back of the range cylinder piston in a Fuller 13-speed transmission auxiliary section when it is in high range. Who is correct?
  a. Technician A
  b. Technician B
  c. Both Technician A and Technician B
  d. Neither Technician A nor Technician B

CHAPTER 44

Servicing Standard Transmissions

Learning Objectives

After reading this chapter, you will be able to:

- **LO 44-1** Explain the fundamentals of standard transmission lubrication.
- **LO 44-2** Describe standard transmission preventative maintenance procedures.
- **LO 44-3** Troubleshoot common standard transmission system problems.
- **LO 44-4** Diagnose and repair air shift system problems.
- **LO 44-5** Describe common transmission inspection procedures.
- **LO 44-6** Describe common repair procedures for standard transmissions.
- **LO 44-7** Explain and describe various transmission failures and their causes.

You Are the Technician

George's "Prostar" International tractor has 465,000 miles (748,345 km) and has come to your repair facility for a clutch replacement. The transmission is a Fuller Roadranger 13-speed model. After you remove the transmission and the clutch, you inspect all components looking for any abnormal wear or damage. You notice the input shaft splines are severely fretted where the clutch disks contact them. You recommend replacing the input shaft.

1. What could cause this kind of damage?
2. What could happen if the input shaft is not replaced?
3. Can you recommend anything to prevent reoccurrence of this problem?
4. What component would you be sure to check before reinstallation of the clutch?

Introduction

As a technician, you will need to put your practical understanding of heavy-duty truck systems to work each day. Although you may not be servicing transmissions every day, you will come close. This chapter covers the basic practices and procedures for maintaining and servicing standard transmissions used in heavy-duty vehicles. The focus is on establishing certain baseline guidelines for general transmission service and maintenance.

Even though the chapter title is Servicing Standard Transmissions, it is by no means intended to be a comprehensive guide or substitute for the original equipment manufacturer's service manuals. Any information contained in this chapter is to be superseded by original equipment manufacturer (OEM) information. It cannot be stressed enough how important it is to have access to the OEM manuals in order to properly service any transmission.

Fundamentals of Standard Transmission Lubrication

LO 44-1 Explain the fundamentals of standard transmission lubrication.

Before diving into a transmission maintenance or service procedure, it is critical that you understand the fundamentals of lubrication and how lubrication varies, depending on the vocation of the vehicle.

Today's medium- and heavy-duty transmissions are designed to give exceptional service and longevity. Manufacturers are warranting their products up to and including 750,000 miles (1,207,008 km), depending on vocation and load factors. These transmissions are expected to last the life of the vehicle—a life span of 2,000,000 to 3,000,000 miles (3,218,000–4,828,000 km) or more is not unheard of!

The only way these components can give this kind of service is with proper operation by the driver—and proper lubrication. Lubrication is the life blood of any mechanical component, and a transmission is no different. It is essential that the correct lubricant is used.

The most common lubricant recommended for medium/heavy-duty transmissions is SAE-50 weight engine oil—either petroleum-based or synthetic. Manufacturers today are almost exclusively using synthetic-based lubricants for extended vehicle operation. **Synthetic-based lubricants** are manufactured, rather than refined, and have a much longer service life. In fact, Eaton Fuller recommends its SAE-50 weight synthetic for use in all their models, and this is the lubricant their transmissions are filled with at the factory (**FIGURE 44-1**).

Transmissions that are filled at the factory with petroleum-based oils usually require an initial drain and fill after 5000 miles (8050 km) of operation. The early drain schedule is designed to remove small particles that are worn off the new gears as they wear-in. By contrast, units filled at the factory with synthetics can go up to 500,000 miles (805,000 km) before a fluid change is required. Transmissions with factory-filled synthetic are assembled with gearing that is manufactured to higher tolerances and the wear-in is not required.

Gear oils with **extreme pressure (EP) additives** should never be used in vocational transmissions, as they start to oxidize at elevated operating temperatures and cause transmission failure. Transmissions should not be consistently operated at sump temperatures of 250° F (121° C) or above, as this causes the loaded tooth contact temperature to rise to 350° F (177° C) or more. Temperatures at this level eventually destroy the heat treatment of the gears and lead to transmission failure. The following conditions may result in operating temperatures consistently over 250° F (121° C):

- Operating at high loads/slower speed/high torque for long periods
- High ambient temperature
- Restricted transmission air flow
- Exhaust system too close to the transmission
- High horsepower operation
- Engine retarder use

If operating temperatures are at or above 250° F (121° C), the use of an external transmission oil cooler is required. Oil coolers are recommended for any vehicle with an engine of 350 hp (261 kW) and above. Eaton Fuller requires that a cooler be used for any of the following configurations of vehicle:

- Engines of 400 hp (298 kW) and above and 90,000 lb (40,823 kg) gross combination weight (GCW) or greater
- Engines 400 hp (298 kW) and above and 1400 ft-lb (1898 Nm) or greater torque
- Engines 450 hp (298 kW) and above
- Engines with 1500 ft-lb (2033 Nm) torque ratings and above
- 18-speed Eaton Autoshift and Ultrashift transmissions require an Eaton-supplied oil-to-water cooler or equivalent.

Eaton Fuller FR-model transmissions can be fitted with an optional integral cooler, as shown in **FIGURE 44-2**.

Transmission Operating Angle

Transmission lubrication is dependent on the rotation of the countershaft(s) to cause splashing of the lubricant so it reaches the mainshaft gears and bearings (if applicable). It

FIGURE 44-1 Most, if not all, Eaton standard transmissions are now factory-filled with synthetic lubricant.

is important to note that when a transmission is operated at an angle (**FIGURE 44-3**), such as when operating in a pit, this so-called splash lubrication is affected.

Although several transmissions are equipped with a lube pump to augment the splash lubrication system, not all are. If the operating angle of the transmission is severe, 12 degrees or more, then the gearing at the high end of the transmission is

FIGURE 44-2 An integral oil cooler is an option with Eaton Fuller FR-series (fleet) transmissions.

FIGURE 44-3 When a vehicle operates at a steep angle, transmission lubrication can be affected.

starved for lubricant, as the oil is all toward the low end. Eaton recommends an oil pump for any transmission that consistently operates at 12 degrees or more. Be careful to take into account the transmission mounting angle relative to the vehicle frame, as well as the operating grade angle when determining the need for a pump, e.g., if the transmission is mounted at four degrees and the grade is equal to eight degrees, then the transmission is operating at 12 degrees and, therefore, requires an oil pump to ensure adequate lubrication.

Lubrication Service Interval Requirements

Most manufacturers have their own specific lubrication service interval requirements, based on the vehicle vocation. **Line-haul** vehicles spend most of their time in on-highway operation under medium to heavy loading. **Vocational** vehicles are subjected mostly to off-road operation and typically are heavily loaded. **Severe-duty service** vehicles are operated under extreme (maximum) loading most of the time or operate on heavy grades. **TABLE 44-1** lists Eaton Fuller's definitions of vehicle vocation, as well as servicing recommendations.

TABLE 44-2 lists Eaton Fuller's recommendations for lube change intervals based on the above vocations. Note that Eaton states that only synthetic SAE 50 fluid must be used in all automated transmissions and with engines of 1850 ft-lb (2508 Nm) or greater of torque. Oil cooler filters are to be changed at oil change intervals.

Proper lubrication is essential to transmission operation. Although Tables 44-1 and 44-2 are representative of a typical manufacturer's recommendation, they are by no means meant to replace OEM specifications. Always consult the OEM literature for the particular transmission being serviced to be sure the correct recommended procedures and schedules are followed.

It is important to have the transmission model and/or serial number to source the correct manual. Recall from the Standard Transmissions chapter, the model number is stamped on a data plate attached to the transmission. The model number provides a great deal of information about the transmission. **FIGURE 44-4** shows the breakdown of Eaton Fuller transmission's model numbers **nomenclature**; nomenclature refers to the meaning of the text and numbers in the model number.

TABLE 44-1 Vehicle Application Definitions		
Line-Haul (On-highway)	**Vocational (Off-highway)**	**Severe-Duty Service**
• High-mileage operation (over 60,000 miles [96,500 km] per year)	• Low-mileage operation (under 60,000 miles [96,500 km] per year)	• Consistent operation at or near maximum GCW or gross vehicle weight (GVW) ratings
• On-highway or good to excellent concrete or asphalt	• Off-highway or areas of unstable or loose, unimproved road surfaces	• Dirty or wet environments
• More than 30 miles (48 km) between starting and stopping	• Less than 30 miles (48 km) between starting and stopping	• Consistent operation on grades greater than 8%
• 4×2, 6×2, 6×4 tractor/trailer combinations and straight trucks	• Heavy-duty, off-road, or specialized application-type vehicles	
Check fluid levels and inspect for leaks at regular preventive maintenance intervals, not to exceed 12,000 miles (19,300 km)	Check fluid levels and inspect for leaks every 50 hours	Severe-duty service requires more frequent oil changes; most manufacturers recommend that change frequency be based on oil sampling

TABLE 44-2 Eaton Fuller's Recommendations for Lube Change Intervals

HEAVY-DUTY TRANSMISSIONS					
Product	Synthetic or Mineral	Lubricant	SAE	Change Interval for Line-Haul	Change Interval for Vocational
Automated and above 1850 ft-lb (2508 Nm)	Synthetic	PS-164 Rev 7 or equivalent	SAE 50	500,000 miles (805,000 km) or five years	180,000 miles (290,000 km) or three years (mobile applications) or five years (stationary applications)
Mechanical	Synthetic	PS-164 Rev 7 or equivalent	SAE 50	500,000 miles (805,000 km) or five years	180,000 miles (290,000 km) or three years (mobile applications) or five years (stationary applications)
Mechanical	Mineral	Heavy-duty engine oil	SAE 50 (HD engine oil), Mil 2104 H, Cat TO-4 (SAE 40 – SAE 50)	60,000 miles (96,600 km) or one year	60,000 miles (96,600 km) or one year (mobile applications) or 500 hours or one year (stationary applications)
MEDIUM-DUTY TRANSMISSIONS					
Product	Synthetic or Mineral	Lubricant	SAE	Change Interval for Line-Haul	Change Interval for Vocational
Automated (includes hybrid)	Synthetic	PS-164 Rev 7 or equivalent	SAE 50	500,000 miles (805,000 km) or 10 years	180,000 miles (290,000 km) or three years (mobile applications) or five years (stationary applications)
ASW clutch module	Synthetic	Dextron III Automatic transmission fluid (ATF)	N/A	150,000 miles (241,000 km) or three years	150,000 miles (241,000 km) or three years
Mechanical	Synthetic	PS-164 Rev 7 or equivalent	SAE 50	500,000 miles (805,000 km) or 10 years	180,000 miles (290,000 km) or three years (mobile applications) 2000 hours or five years (stationary applications)
Mechanical	Mineral	Heavy-duty engine oil	SAE 50 (HD engine oil), Mil 2104 H, Cat TO-4 (SAE 40 – SAE 50)	60,000 miles (96,600 km) or one year	500 hours or one year

▶ TECHNICIAN TIP

Transmission literature is widely available online, so there is no excuse for not having the correct and most up-to-date information for any particular transmission.

- For Eaton Fuller, visit http://www.roadranger.com/rr/CustomerSupport/Support/Literature Center/index.htm
- For Meritor products, visit https://www.meritor.com/literature-on-demand

Many more manufacturers have online applications that can be accessed for the required information.

Service Interval Using Fluid Analysis or Oil Sampling

Some fleets are choosing to use oil sampling to determine both the optimum transmission fluid/filter change frequency and early detection of malfunction or excessive wear. Fluid analysis is an excellent way to determine how much wear is occurring and whether the lubricant is maintaining the qualities that make it effective. Oil sampling can lead to extended lube change intervals, saving money and reducing the environmental impact. Sampling can also predict unit failure, allowing pre-emptive service, rather than an in-service breakdown. Note, however, that fleets must check with the manufacturer to determine whether their oil sampling program meets the warranty requirements for the OEM's specific products.

Oil sampling analyzes the oil for metal particles and other contaminants. Sampling also tests the quality of the oil by checking its viscosity, chemical make-up, and TBN/TAN or total base/acid number. TBN and TAN are usually more important in engine oil sampling, as the combustion by-products can affect these numbers significantly. In transmission samples, TBN and TAN are usually not as important, although the TAN number can increase as the oil degrades and oxidizes. Oxidized oil in transmissions is a sign of overheated operation. Oil viscosity is an important determinant of change frequency. Fluid contamination can reduce viscosity, while oxidation can increase the viscosity. Significant changes in viscosity require an oil change. In most cases of transmission wear, a high count of ferrous (iron), aluminum, bronze, chromium, and tin are found. High particle

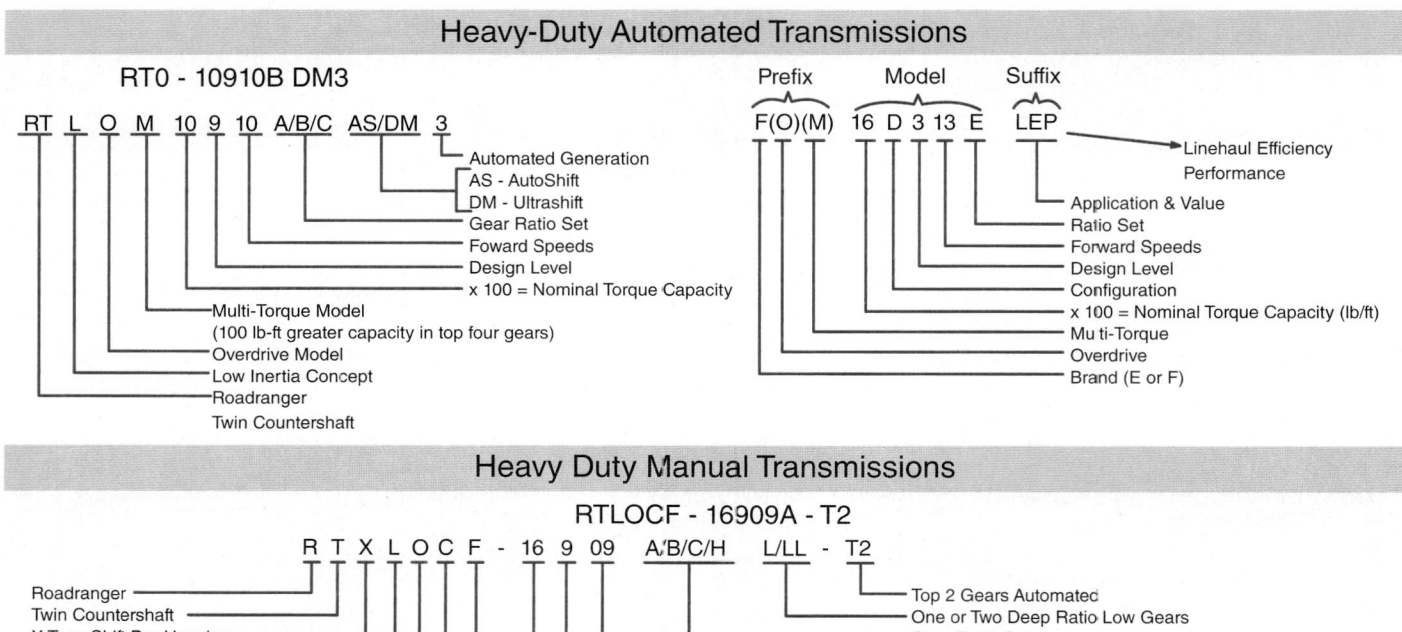

FIGURE 44-4 Manufacturers produce charts like these to explain the nomenclature of the transmission model number. Other manufacturers have similar nomenclature charts to identify their transmission models.

counts of these materials usually mean an overhaul is necessary. The fluid can contain liquid contaminants, as well, such as water, dirt, or anti-freeze from a leaking transmission cooler.

Eaton Fuller recommends that, if oil sampling is used to determine oil change interval on its transmissions that use synthetic oil, it should be performed every 50,000 to 60,000 miles or 80,000 to 100,000 km. The oil sample should be taken using a syringe designed to remove the sample from the center of the oil in the transmission with the fluid at operating temperature.

► TECHNICIAN TIP

Although some transmissions are equipped with oil pumps, almost all standard transmission lubrication is splash lubrication. This splash is caused by the rotation of the transmission's countershaft. As the countershaft turns, it churns through the oil in the bottom of the transmission case and throws this oil up onto the mainshaft and other components. The splash lubrication is assisted, in some cases, by oil rails and/or slingers inside the case that ensure oil reaches critical areas. When a vehicle breaks down and needs to be towed, be aware that, if the vehicle is towed on its drive wheels with the transmission in neutral and precautions are not taken, the mainshaft in the transmission is turning inside the case, but no other gears are rotating. Without the countershaft rotation, the mainshaft is starved for lubricant and failure is likely. When a vehicle with a standard transmission is towed on its drive wheels, it should have the driveshaft, or all axle shafts, removed to ensure that the transmission mainshaft does not turn. Alternately, the vehicle should be towed on its front (non-drive) wheels.

Preventative Maintenance of Transmissions

LO 44-2 Describe standard transmission preventative maintenance procedures.

Key to keeping any transmission in working order is following regular maintenance procedures. Preventive maintenance is the first step. As mentioned in the section on lubrication, proper lubricant is essential to transmission operation. A regularly scheduled maintenance program should be followed to ensure the lubricant is doing its job. The air tanks should be drained and checked for contamination on a daily basis. The transmission should also be visually inspected for oil leaks every day and repaired, as necessary. In addition to daily checks, the following preventative maintenance checks are recommended by Eaton at every service, or every 12,000 miles (19,000 km), whichever comes first. For off-road applications, the recommended service interval is every 50 hours of operation.

1. Air system and connections: Check the air system for leaks, worn air lines, loose connections, and bolts. Also, ensure the air system is not contaminated by water or oil. Check the air filter at the air filter regulator, if necessary. The sintered bronze air filter depicted in **FIGURE 44-5** easily shows contamination if it is present.

2. Clutch housing mounting: Check all mounting bolts of the clutch housing flange for looseness.

3. Clutch release bearing: Remove the hand-hole cover in the clutch bell housing and check radial and axial clearances in the release bearing.

4. Clutch pedal shaft and mechanism: Use a pry bar on the clutch release mechanism shafts to check for wear. If excessive movement is found, remove the clutch release mechanism and check bores and shafts on all bushings for wear. Check OEM documentation for correct clearances.

5. Lubricant: Check the lubricant level. A correct lubricant fill level is level with the bottom edge of the check hole, as illustrated in **FIGURE 44-6**. Always top up fluid levels with the correct lubricant. Never mix different type or brands. To check the fluid level of a manual transmission, follow the guidelines in **SKILL DRILL 44-1**. To change the transmission fluid, follow the guidelines in **SKILL DRILL 44-2**.

6. Oil filter: Inspect oil filter (if equipped) for damage or rust. Replace as necessary. Inspect oil filter adapter for damage or leakage. Replace as necessary. Replace the oil filter every 100,000 miles (161,000 km) and at every transmission fluid change. Most manufacturers recommend changing the filter at the same time as the transmission oil change intervals. Check the OEM manual.

7. Drain plugs: Check for leaks and tighten drain plugs securely.

8. Mounting and attaching bolts and gaskets: For applicable models, check all bolts, especially those on power take-off (PTO) covers and rear bearing covers, for looseness, which might cause oil leakage. Check PTO opening and rear bearing covers for oil leakage due to a faulty gasket.

9. Gear shift lever: Check for excessive looseness and free play in housing. If lever is loose in housing, proceed with check number 10.

10. Gear shift lever housing assembly: Remove the gear shift lever housing assembly from the transmission. Check that the tension spring and washer are secure and in good shape. Check the gear shift lever spade pin (pivot) and slot for wear. Check the bottom end of gear shift lever (shift finger) for wear and check slots of shift gates in shift bar housing for wear at contact points with shift lever.

11. Output shaft: Pry upward on the output shaft flange to check for radial clearance in the output shaft bearings; there should be none. Repair as necessary.

12. Rear bearing housing: Check the rear bearing housing and speedometer drive gear or speed sensor for oil leakage.

Troubleshooting Common Transmission System Problems

LO 44-3 Troubleshoot common standard transmission system problems.

The first step in any diagnostic activity is to diagnose the problem. Little good it does to start dismantling components without an idea of what could be causing the trouble! Diagnosing problems is a systematic activity that involves looking for and interpreting basic signs. As a technician, you will have to diagnose common transmission complaints, such as oil leaks, noise, vibration, hard shifting, gear slip, and problems with the air system.

Oil Leaks

Oil leaks are, of course, a cause for concern with any mechanical component because they lead to a decrease in lubricant. Still,

FIGURE 44-5 The sintered bronze air filter is easily accessible. Contamination here indicates problems with the truck air system.

Correct Lubricant Level

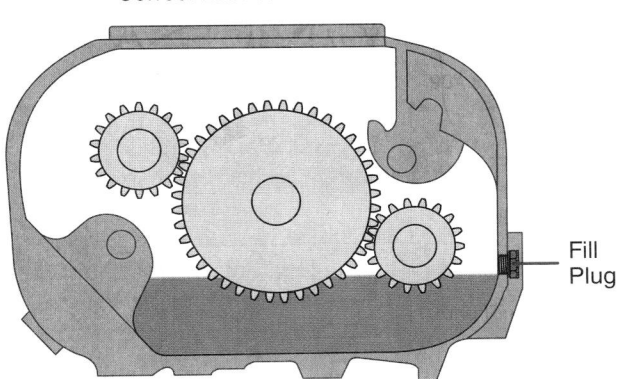

Fill Plug

Incorrect Lubricant Level

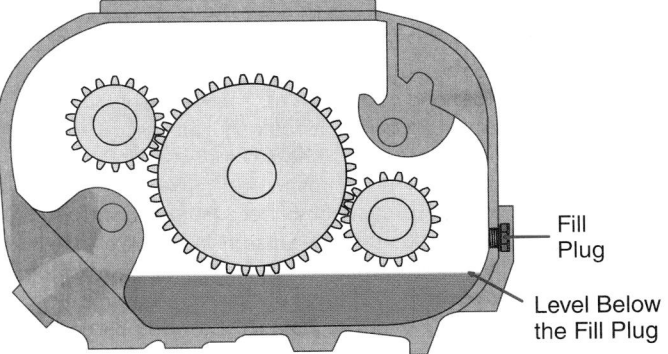

Fill Plug

Level Below the Fill Plug

FIGURE 44-6 Correct fluid level is even with the edge of the fill hole.

SKILL DRILL 44-1 Checking the Fluid Level of a Manual Transmission

1. Safely raise the vehicle on an approved lift, making sure it is secure. Check all lift specifications and operating mechanisms, including adapters, before the vehicle is elevated.

2. Perform a visual inspection of the transmission before checking the fluid level. The fluid level should be checked cold, between 60° F and 120° F (15.5° C and 48.8° C). Obtain a clean drain pan before removing the filler plug as fluid may spill out. If the fluid temperature is higher than recommended, then a fluid spill is likely.

3. Remove the filler plug using the proper wrench or ratchet to make sure the filler plug does not become damaged. Perform a visual inspection of the filler plug for thread damage and replace, if necessary. Inspect the threads in the transmission fill hole for damage also.

4. Some drain plugs are magnetic. If this is the case, examine the plug for signs of excessive metal and clean the plug before reinstallation.

5. If the transmission fluid begins to run out as the filler plug is removed, let the fluid flow into a suitable container until it stops. The cold fluid level should be even with the bottom of the filler plug hole. If the level is left over-full, aeration of the fluid could result, as well as build-up of pressure in the transmission, causing damage to the seals and/or gaskets.

6. If the fluid level is low, refill with the manufacturer's specified fluid, reinstall the filler plug, and wipe the area around the filler plug hole with a clean shop towel. Tighten the filler plug to the specified torque.

SKILL DRILL 44-2 Changing the Transmission Fluid

1. Raise the vehicle using an approved lift and make sure it is secure. Check all lift specifications and operating mechanisms, including adapters, before the vehicle is elevated. Obtain a clean drain pan to put the used fluid in.

2. Inspect the transmission for any leaks.

3. Remove the drain plug from the bottom of the transmission, being careful of the hot transmission fluid. Let fluid drain until it has stopped running out.

4. Replace the drain plug(s), tighten to the manufacturer's specification, and remove the fill plug(s).

5. Refill the transmission to the proper level using manufacturer-approved transmission fluid. Replace the fill plug and tighten to the manufacturer's specification. Use a shop towel to wipe away any spillage.

6. Road test the vehicle. If necessary, put the vehicle back on the lift and check for any leaks that may have resulted from the service. Always double check your work before returning the vehicle to the customer.

many unnecessary repairs are performed when there is only a slight weeping. An oil leak is different from an oil weep. An **oil weep** is a very minor oil seepage, usually caused by a wicking effect, and not usually a reason for repair. Oil weep can be recognized by a slight wetting of an area on the component. The area around the weep appears damp and oil has soaked into any dirt accumulated there—but there is no dripping of fluid.

An oil weep is usually not a cause for major concern. Eaton Fuller transmission rear seals, in fact, are designed to experience slight weeping, so when weeping is discovered on these transmission seals, no repair is needed. If an oil weep is discovered at a gasket, however, re-torque the attaching bolts and monitor the vehicle through its next few services. Depending on the state of the weep, it may not require a further repair. When dealing with and correcting a weep, always check and readjust the fluid level after the inspection and or repair.

By contrast, a leak is always associated with oil dripping and or an extremely wet area. Oil leaks must always be repaired. It may be difficult to see the actual path of the leak. Accumulated dirt and/or oil flow patterns may obstruct visibility.

Nonetheless, it is essential that the actual leak path is determined before deciding on a repair. Remove the excess dirt and clean the affected area with an approved degreaser. Refill the transmission lube to the proper level (even with the bottom of the fill hole). Road test the vehicle until it reaches normal operating temperatures and re-inspect the suspect area. Ensure that that area is not being contaminated by oil leaking elsewhere and splashing on the area. Once the source of the leak has been identified and repaired, repeat the process to verify the repair. Poor investigation into the actual source of a leak can cause considerable wasted effort, so take the time to properly diagnose any leak. Detailed steps for diagnosing oil leakage are provided in **SKILL DRILL 44-3.**

Transmission Noise Diagnoses

A certain amount of noise is expected from a heavy-duty transmission as it does its job. Excessive or unusual noises, however, are indications of a problem. It is quite common that noises that appear to be coming from the transmission may actually be originating elsewhere in the driveline. The transmission may simply be acting as an amplifier. Before undertaking transmission repairs, eliminate all possible sources of the noise before condemning the transmission.

Common noises in the Eaton Fuller twin-countershaft transmission include the gears rattling at idle, knocking sounds, whining, and growling. These noises can also occur in most other transmissions, as well.

SKILL DRILL 44-3 Inspecting for Leakage and Replacing Transmission Cover Plates, Gaskets, Seals, and Cap Bolts; Inspecting and Sealing Surfaces and Vents

1. Locate and follow the appropriate procedure in the service manual.
2. Complete the accompanying job sheet or work order with all pertinent information.
3. Move the vehicle into the shop, apply the parking brakes, and chock the vehicle's wheels. Observe lockout/tagout procedures.
4. If the vehicle has a manual transmission, place it in "neutral"; if it has an automatic transmission, place it in "park" or "neutral." Note: Some vehicles with automatic transmission do not have "park."
5. Clean the outside of the transmission to remove oil and dirt.
6. Operate the vehicle, if necessary.
7. Inspect the following areas for leaks:
   - PTO covers on the main case
   - Auxiliary case to main case
   - Main case and the clutch housing
   - Clutch housing to flywheel housing
   - Auxiliary countershaft covers
   - Slave valve to main case
   - Shift lever and tower assembly to the top cover
   - Top cover to main case
   - Fill and drain plugs

- Output shaft bearing retainer to auxiliary case
- Input bearing retainer to main case
- Speedometer bore or electronic speed pick-up in the output bearing retainer
- Output yoke and the oil seal in the output bearing retainer on the auxiliary case

(Note: Although the transmission must be installed to check for leaks, some of the areas where a leak might be detected cannot be "fixed" unless the transmission is removed.)

8. Remove the leaking component according to the service manual. (Note: If it is determined that there is a leaking oil seal, follow the procedures outlined in the service manual for replacing the seal.)
9. Use a scraper to remove all sealant/gasket material from both surfaces. Note: Do not get any dirt, sealant, or gasket material inside the transmission.
10. Clean the mounting surfaces with an approved solvent.
11. Fit the gasket in place over the studs or guide pins. The procedure may or may not require that sealant be applied to the surfaces. First check the service manual to be sure.
12. Some transmissions use sealant, instead of a gasket. If that is the case, apply applicable sealant with a sealant dispenser in a 0.125" (3.175 mm) bead. (Note: Make sure you put the sealant on the right surface; it may go on the case or cover.) Check the service manual. Make sure that you apply the sealant in the applicable pattern.
13. Install the component as described in the service manual. (Note: In most cases you need to apply a sealant to the attaching bolts before they are installed.)
14. Check condition of the breather vent:
    a. Check for damage.
    b. Remove the vent by unscrewing it from the top of the transmission.
    c. Remove all dirt and oil from the screen in the breather vent.
    d. Clean or replace, if necessary.
    e. Reinstall the vent using the correct thread sealant, as required.
15. List the test results and/or recommendations on the job sheet or work order, clean the work area, and return tools and materials to their proper storage.

Gear Rattle at Idle

A rough idling engine can cause gear rattle at idle because of the 0.006" to 0.015" (0.15 mm to 3.8 mm) clearance between the transmission mainshaft gears. The small torsional vibrations set up by rough running can cause the gears to strike each other, resulting in rattle.

This can be lessened or eliminated by smoothing out the engine operation. Another way to minimize gear rattle is by installing a clutch with pre-dampening vibration control. Pre-dampening clutch systems absorb minor torsional vibrations to prevent gear rattle at idle. To accomplish this, small torsional springs are added in the damper hub to react to idling torsional vibrations. **FIGURE 44-7** shows a clutch disc with pre-dampening vibration control. Finally, gear rattle can be reduced or eliminated by resetting the mainshaft clearances.

Knocking

Gears are sometimes damaged before or on installation. Gears can be damaged from some other cause as well, such as something that has impacted the gear teeth, for example. Damaged gears can have bumps or swells on the teeth as illustrated in **FIGURE 44-8**. These can cause a knocking or thudding sound as the gears go through mesh. Knocking is usually more pronounced when the vehicle is under load.

Bearings that have worn spots on the bearing races or damaged rollers or balls can cause a similar noise. A gear that is cracked or broken from shock loading can have the same type of knocking noise at low speeds. The noise changes to a howling sound as speed increases.

Whining

Spur-type gears have a natural tendency to whine. Eaton Fuller's introduction of multi-mesh gearing in design level six led to much quieter operation, as well as increased strength. Having more than one gear tooth in contact at a time helps reduce the tendency to whine. Regardless, as gear teeth wear and pitting occurs, whining usually begins. As the gear teeth continue to deteriorate, the whining becomes a louder howling.

Whining can also be caused by lack of backlash between gears. This is a common occurrence when a PTO is installed

with less than the recommended clearance. In addition, bearings that are improperly installed or "squeezed" (meaning they have insufficient clearance) can cause a whining noise.

Growling

A growling noise can be caused by bearings that are worn and badly damaged. Bearings can wear due to lube contamination, fatigue, or overloading. When bearing damage occurs, it typically affects all of the bearings throughout the transmission, so growling noise can be an indication that a complete overhaul is necessary. When bearings start to wear down, the resultant metal filings carried in the lube oil tend to wear the other transmission components, as well. The gear teeth faces, synchronizers, and shift forks can be worn down quickly by the abrasive particles. Growling can also be caused by timing issues, although an incorrectly timed twin or triple countershaft transmission usually does not turn at all. If a weld cracks or a key breaks on the countershaft, a gear may shift slightly. This results in a tooth-spacing error.

Vibration

In addition to noise, another problem that technicians must commonly diagnose is vibration. Although vibrations can occur in the transmission, it is very unlikely. Usually vibrations that occur elsewhere in the driveline are amplified in the transmission. Some sources of driveline vibration are driveshaft imbalance, U-joint angularity, unbalanced wheel or brake drums, defective engine mounts, and worn suspension.

The effects of driveline vibrations can readily show up in the transmission. Signs that there is vibration in the driveline include:

- Gear rattle at idle
- Fretted gear and shaft splines (worn where they contact each other)
- Fretted bearings or bores
- Repeated rear seal leakage

FIGURE 44-7 A clutch disc with pre-dampening vibration control may ease gear rattle at idle.

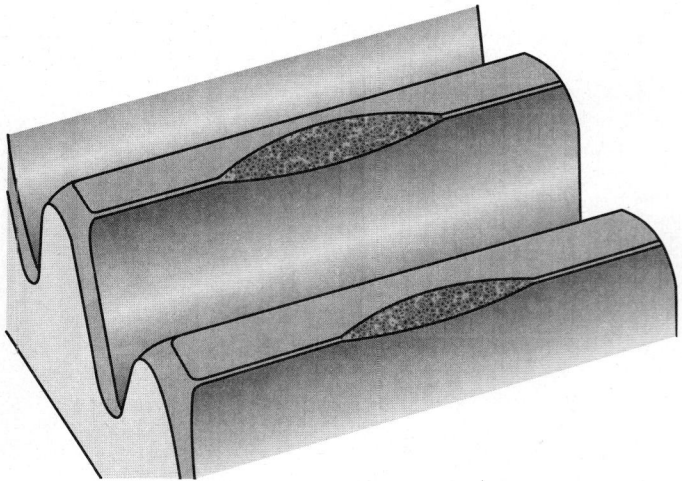

FIGURE 44-8 Bumps or swells on gear teeth due to abuse before assembly may cause a knocking sound.

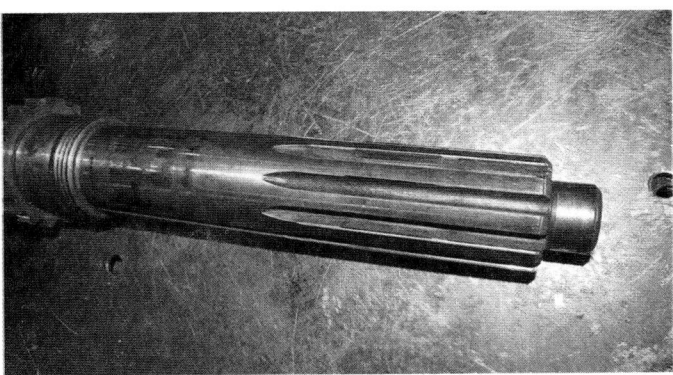

FIGURE 44-9 The spline wear on this input shaft is typically caused by driveline torsional vibrations.

- Broken or loose range synchronizer pins
- Repeated loosening of transmission bolts and mountings
- Input shaft spline wear where the clutch disks are mounted, as shown in **FIGURE 44-9**

Hard Shifting

Hard shifting can be caused by several factors, so it is important first to find out if the issue is inside or outside the transmission.

If the transmission has **remote shift linkage**, where the shift linkage is not directly on top of the shift cover, the remote shift linkage could be the culprit. To confirm that is the case, disconnect the remote shift linkage from the shift cover and try to move the shift rails inside the transmission. (*Note:* Do not allow the shift detent ball and spring to be forced up and out of the cover while moving the rails.) If the rails move freely, the problem is with the remote shift linkage. Follow the steps in **SKILL DRILL 44-4** to inspect, adjust, service, repair, or replace the remote shift linkage and control assembly brackets, bushings, pivots, and levers.

Hard shifting can also be due to internal causes, such as a sliding clutch that is binding. Sliding clutches tend to bind when the mainshaft spline has twisted, as shown in **FIGURE 44-10**. The mainshaft can twist in instances of heavy overloading or shock loading. A twisted mainshaft does not allow the sliding clutch at the twisted area to move freely. The twist occurs when the transmission is in a gear. As a result, the transmission typically remains in that gear or is very difficult to change out of that gear.

The movement of the sliding clutch can be affected by other deformities. The shift yoke for a particular gear can be bent and restrict the sliding clutch. The mainshaft key may be distorted and cause the sliding clutch to bind. Hard shifting can also be the result of the yoke bars or shift rails binding in the

SKILL DRILL 44-4 Inspecting, Adjusting, Servicing, Repairing, or Replacing Remote Shift Linkages and Control Assembly, Brackets, Bushings, Pivots, and Levers

1. Locate and follow the appropriate procedure in the service manual.
2. Complete the accompanying job sheet or work order with all pertinent information.
3. Disconnect linkages and remove the remote control assembly from the transmission according to manufacturer's recommended procedures.
4. Check shift linkage for straightness and rod pivot ends for wear. Replace if bent or worn.

5. Remove the set screw that fastens the outer shift lever to the shaft and remove the shaft.
6. Remove the two straps that fasten the boot to the housing and remove the boot.
7. Remove the lock wire and set screw from the inner shift lever and pull the shaft from the housing.
8. Inspect the shaft for wear and replace if excessively worn.
9. Remove and inspect the bushings in the housing; replace if worn or damaged.
10. Fill the housing between the two bushings with grease, as specified by the manufacturer.
11. Install the shaft through the housing.
12. Put the inner shift lever in position in the housing and tighten the set screw.
13. Install the boot over the shaft and on the housing and then install new straps.
14. Put the outer shift lever on the shaft, making sure that the outer shaft lever is aligned with the inner shaft lever. Tighten the set screw.
15. Install the remote shifter onto the transmission according to the manufacturer's recommended procedures.
16. Reconnect and adjust shift linkage according to the manufacturer's recommended procedures.
17. Torque fasteners to the manufacturer's specifications.
18. List the test results and/or recommendations on the job sheet or work order, clean the work area, and return tools and materials to their proper storage.

FIGURE 44-10 Hard shifting can be caused by a twisted mainshaft due to severe shock load.

FIGURE 44-11 Excessively worn clutching teeth caused by gear clashing on shifts.

shift housing because of a cracked housing or a sprung (bowed) shift rail. If it is hard to move the shift lever into the first and reverse shift gates only, the problem may be that the reverse detent plunger is over-torqued or binding due to burrs on the plunger. The reverse detent plunger purposely makes it harder to select this shift rail so that reverse is not selected inadvertently. Follow the steps in **SKILL DRILL 44-5** to inspect, adjust, and replace the transmission shift lever assembly, top cover, and shift bar housing.

Gear Slip Out

Gear slip out, or **jump out**, occurs when an engaged gear's sliding clutch moves out of engagement while the vehicle is pulling a load, causing the transmission to go into neutral. Gear slip out can occur in the main box and in the auxiliary section.

There are several reasons for gear slip in the main box. If the clutching teeth on the sliding clutch or the gear are badly worn from excessive gear clashing, slip out is very likely. **FIGURE 44-11** shows a clutch with badly worn clutching teeth.

SKILL DRILL 44-5 Inspecting, Adjusting, and Replacing Transmission Shift Lever Assembly, Top Cover, and Shift Bar Housing

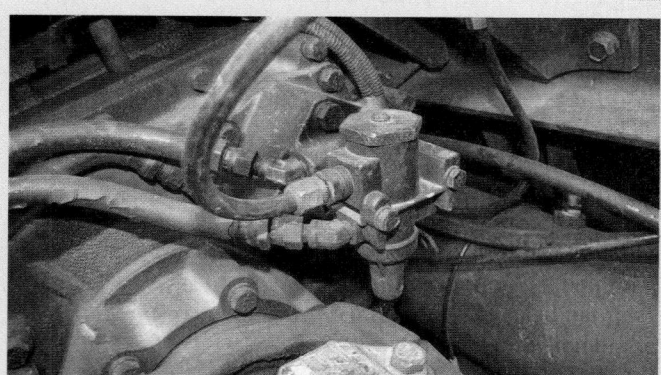

1. Locate and follow the appropriate procedure in the service manual.
2. Complete the accompanying job sheet or work order with all pertinent information.
3. Remove and inspect shift tower assembly:
   a. Place the transmission in "neutral" and deplete the air from the system.
   b. Disconnect the air lines that run to the shift knob at the slave valve.
   c. Remove the cap screws and washers that fasten the housing to the top cover.
   d. Remove the shift tower housing and lever assembly and gasket from the top cover housing.
   e. Refer to the service manual for disassembling and overhauling the shift lever tower assembly. (*Note:* Shift towers may be

made of cast iron or aluminum. Disassembly procedures differ, depending on the type of shift tower assembly.)
   f. Inspect components for cracks, tears, or other wear.
   g. Replace parts as required.
4. Remove and inspect the top cover and shift bar housing:
   a. Remove the three detent springs from the holes in the top cover. (*Note:* If a stronger heavy-duty detent spring is present, it is in the bore on the slave valve side of the transmission.)
   b. Remove a detent ball from each of the three holes using a magnetic probe.
   c. Remove the cap screws and washers from the top cover.
   d. Remove the top cover and shift bar housing from the transmission case.
   e. Refer to the service manual for disassembly, overhaul, reassembly, and reinstallation of the top cover and shift bar housing.
5. Reinstall shift tower assembly:
   a. Place the transmission in "neutral."
   b. Install the new gasket on the top cover housing.
   c. Place the shift tower housing onto the top cover housing. (*Note:* Make sure the bottom of the lower shift lever is installed between the forks and the sleeves in the top cover housing.)
   d. Install the mounting cap screws and torque to the manufacturer's specifications. (*Note:* Sealant may be required on the attaching bolt threads.)
6. List the test results and/or recommendations on the job sheet or work order; clean the work area, and return tools and materials to their proper storage.

The presence of excessively worn clutching teeth indicates that the driver is not shifting correctly.

Gear slip out can also occur because of worn shift forks or sliding clutch grooves that do not allow the sliding clutch to fully engage with mainshaft gears. Other causes of slip out include worn shift rail detents, weak or broken detent ball springs, or excessive whipping movement of long heavy shift levers, especially when operating over rough terrain.

Mechanical remote shift controls that are frame mounted can lead to slip out as the transmission moves under load. Eaton has modified the clutching teeth in later models so that the teeth have a back-taper shape, as shown in **FIGURE 44-12**. A **back-taper** is a profile of the teeth in which the outer edge is thicker than the inner edge. As the gear is loaded, the back-taper draws the sliding clutch into a deeper mesh, rather than trying to push it out of mesh.

In the auxiliary section, slip out usually occurs with the splitter gear and can be caused by worn clutching teeth. **FIGURE 44-13** shows a range synchronizer sliding clutch with badly worn clutching teeth caused by failure of the driver to preselect the range shift. Damage like this on a range sliding clutch can lead to range gear slip out/jump out or failure of range engagement in the auxiliary section. Other causes of gear slip out in the auxiliary section include defective air shift systems (low pressure) and incorrect shifting by the driver (namely, not preselecting the range shift or failure to break torque correctly during splitter shifts).

Diagnose and Repair Air Shift System Problems

LO 44-4 Diagnose and repair air shift system problems.

Different transmission models use different air shift system arrangements. FR-model transmissions have a range cylinder that is integral to the shift bar housing. When the shift bar housing is installed, the range piston shaft must engage the slot in the range shift bar, as shown in **FIGURE 44-14**.

The FR-model transmissions also use an air module bolted to the top of the housing, as shown in **FIGURE 44-15**. This module houses the slave air valve, the air filter regulator, and the range preselect interlock system. The small metal arm shown in Figure 44-15 is forced outward by the shift mechanism when the transmission is in any gear and locks the slave air valve piston in the module, preventing a range shift from occurring.

FIGURE 44-12 Back-taper (indicated) on the sliding clutch teeth helps to prevent gear slip out (jump out).

FIGURE 44-13 A range synchronizer sliding clutch with badly worn clutching teeth.

FIGURE 44-14 The range cylinder piston bar must engage the slot in the range synchronizer yoke bar. **A.** Range cylinder shaft. **B.** Range synchronizer shift bar.

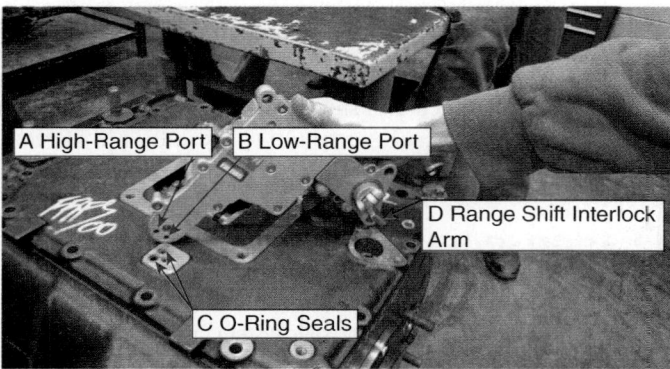

FIGURE 44-15 Single air module bolted to the shift bar housing on the FR-model transmissions. **A.** High-range port. **B.** Low-range port. **C.** O-ring seals. **D.** Range shift interlock arm.

When the transmission is shifted through neutral, the arm moves, freeing the slave air valve piston and the range shift occurs. Again, the driver must preselect the range shift while in gear. The shift happens automatically as the shift lever moves through the neutral position.

Most other transmission models use the standard type of range shift control. That is, the slave air valve is bolted to the side of the transmission and the range cylinder is mounted in the auxiliary section housing. Range shift failure can be caused by mechanical failure in the auxiliary section or by air shift problems. To locate the trouble spot, check for crossed air lines and air leaks with the engine off and the air system at operating pressure. Also check for leaks in the Roadranger valve. The Crossed Air Lines, Air Leaks, and Roadranger Valve sections that follow include general air troubleshooting procedures for 10-speed models with the slave valves mounted on the side of the transmission. Although these sections focus on the Eaton air system, other manufacturers' air system troubleshooting procedures are similar.

Air Filter/Pressure Regulator

A common cause of air shift system complaints is the air filter/pressure regulator being contaminated with oil or dirt. Since it is typically easy to access, this is always a good place to start when investigating air shift system problems. The filter in the air filter/regulator can be removed for cleaning by unscrewing the large end cap. Review Figure 44-3 for the location of the end cap. Drain or disconnect the air supply to the filter before servicing. The filter should be cleaned at every oil change and replaced, when necessary, as part of regular maintenance. If contamination is found, the source is likely elsewhere in the air system. After you clean the filter, investigate and repair the cause of the contamination.

A clogged filter can also affect regulator outlet pressure— low pressure can cause poor shifting. To check the pressure at the regulator, drain the air system or cut off the pressure to the air filter/regulator. Then, install a gauge at the outlet. As you build the vehicle pressure back to normal, check that the outlet pressure is between 58 and 63 psi (400 to 434 kPa). If the pressure is not in this range, drain the air system again, and remove and clean the

FIGURE 44-16 A steady leak at the Roadranger valve, like this one, while in the high-range position only, can indicate crossed air lines to the valve.

filter. Once again, rebuild system pressure and recheck. Never try to adjust the regulator pressure! If cleaning does not solve the problem, replace the assembly. With the air system at operating pressure, check the filter regulator for leaks. Any leakage at the breather port fails the regulator, and it should be replaced.

Crossed Air Lines

Crossed air line connections from the slave air valve to the Roadranger valve (driver shift knob), causes shift problems and can be easily detected. Move the range selection lever on the Roadranger valve up with the transmission in neutral. If the air lines are crossed, a constant leak of air is heard at the Roadranger valve while it is in high range. The leakage stops when the valve is returned to the low position.

If the air lines are crossed between the slave air valve and the range cylinder, the transmission is in high range when low range is selected, and vice versa.

Air Leaks

To check for air leaks, first turn the engine off, put the transmission in neutral, and ensure the air system is at operating pressure. Next, coat all air lines and fittings with a solution of soapy water. Covering all the lines and fittings allows you to check for leaks in both the high-range and low-range positions. If a leak is present, the soap starts to bubble or foam. If there is a steady leak from the exhaust port of the Roadranger valve, like the one shown in **FIGURE 44-16**, O-rings inside the valve or worn or defective parts of the valve are to blame. The solution is to overhaul or replace the valve, as necessary.

A steady leak from the breather of the slave air valve on the side of the transmission can be caused by defective piston O-rings in the valve. Again, the solution is to overhaul or replace the valve, as necessary. A leak from the transmission case breather in only low range can be caused by failure of the range yoke bar O-ring, causing pressure to leak into the transmission case.

Roadranger Valve

A thorough check of the Roadranger valve for air leaks involves checking it generally, and checking it during high-range and low-range operation.

To check the overall Roadranger valve operation, start at normal operating pressure in high range with the engine off and the transmission in neutral. Disconnect the 15/32" (12 mm) air line at the outlet, or P port, of the Roadranger valve. Then, move the lever to low range. A steady stream of air should flow from the P port of the valve, and it shuts off when moved back to high range. That indicates the Roadranger valve is functioning correctly. If the valve is not working correctly or leaks air in high range, repair or replace the valve. Reattach the air line.

To check the Roadranger valve for leakage at high-range operation, turn the engine off, put the transmission in neutral with the engine off, and ensure the air system is at operating pressure. Next, disconnect the high-range air line at the range cylinder. There should be no air present. Now, shift the Roadranger valve to high. You should hear a steady blast of air from the line. Shift the valve back to low, and the air should stop.

The next check tests the operation of the range preselect system. Recall from the Standard Transmissions chapter that the transmission has an interlock pin that prevents slave air valve piston movement while the transmission is in gear. The interlock pin is extended any time the transmission is in gear, and this physically prevents the valve piston from moving. This test ensures that this system is working correctly. Move the gear

shift lever to any gear position and then move the Roadranger valve to the high-range position. No air should be heard coming from the high-range air line, indicating that the slave air valve position is locked by the interlock pin. Then, move the lever to neutral. Air should be heard coming from the high-range line, indicating that the slave air valve has moved.

Checking the Roadranger valve for leakage at low-range operation involves running the same test as was done in high-range operation. Start again with the engine off, the transmission in neutral, and the air system at operating pressure. Select high range on the Roadranger valve, and then disconnect the low-range air line at the range cylinder. Next, select low range. You should hear a steady blast of air coming from the low-range line. Then, select high range, and the flow should stop. Next, place the transmission in any gear position and again select low range. No air should be heard escaping from the low-range line. When you move the lever to neutral, air should begin leaking again. Finally, select high range, and reconnect the air line.

If the air shift system does not operate as described in high and low range, the slave air valve, the range shift cylinder or components, or the range synchronizer is defective.

The final place to check for air leaks in the Roadranger system is in the range cylinder. As illustrated in **FIGURE 44-17**, the range cylinder consists of the yoke bar, the range piston, the

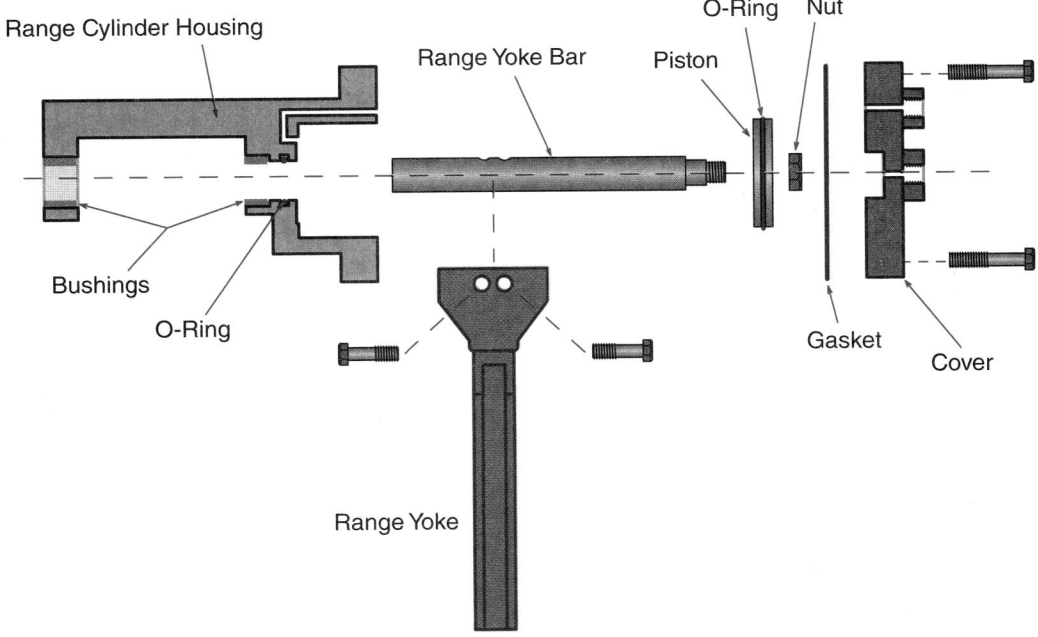

FIGURE 44-17 Range cylinder components.

housing, and the housing cover. The piston has an inner and an outer seal. If either of these seals is defective, range shifts to high or low are sluggish or may not occur at all. The yoke bar has an O-ring in the range cylinder housing to seal the low-range chamber of the housing from the case. If this seal fails, shifts to low range are sluggish or do not occur at all; in addition, the transmission case is pressurized when low range is selected. The cylinder housing cover is sealed by a gasket. If this gasket leaks, range shifts to high may be sluggish or may not occur at all. Plus, air is heard leaking from the cover when high range is selected.

Common Transmission Inspection Procedures

LO 44-5 Describe common transmission inspection procedures.

Transmission overhaul is not often performed in most shops. Still, it is important to have a basic understanding of what is involved in the process. The information required to successfully rebuild a transmission is very precise and unique to the model being worked on. For that reason, we will focus our discussion on general procedures for several transmission-related tasks commonly performed in repair shops.

> ▶ **TECHNICIAN TIP**

Information on overhauling or rebuilding particular transmissions is available from the manufacturers' websites. For information on the Eaton Roadranger, visit www.roadranger.com. For information on Meritor transmissions, visit www.meritor.com.

General Precautions and Procedures

As with any repair, it is critical that your work area be staged, orderly, and complete. Before beginning any maintenance or repair procedure on a transmission or auxiliary section, ensure that the following items are on hand and organized in your work area:

- The correct overhaul manual for the transmission model being serviced
- A clean dust-free area large enough to complete the repair
- All of the recommended tools found in the overhaul manual
- Replacement parts (i.e., gaskets, seals and/or bearings, snap rings, etc.) for parts that definitely or may be destroyed during disassembly

Before attempting any repair on any transmission, read and understand the following precautions and procedures:

- Bearings: Remove bearings with appropriate pullers. (*Note:* In certain models it may not be possible to use a puller to remove certain bearings, these may need to be driven from the shafts using a drift punch—THIS PROCEDURE DESTROYS THE BEARINGS and they MUST be replaced.) Carefully clean and inspect the bearings for damage and wear. Check races and balls or rollers for

pitting, heat discoloration, and other damage. If there is any doubt in the bearing's condition, replace it. If the bearing is to be reused, lubricate it and wrap it in protective material until ready to use. Before reinstallation, always check that the bearings fit in the bore and on its shaft. In Eaton Fuller transmissions, the bearings are a tight fit on the shaft and a light interference fit in the case bores.

- Assemblies: When disassembling various components, lay the pieces out on a clean surface in the order that they come apart and protect them from dirt and damage.
- Snap rings: Always remove snap rings with pliers designed for the job. Remember, even when they are removed correctly, snap rings are quite commonly distorted. Any distortion requires that the snap ring be replaced. Never reuse a sprung snap ring.
- Gears: Check all gear teeth for frosting or pitting. Frosting is a slight discoloration of the gear tooth face caused by tiny pits that occur naturally as the gears run together and find a common pitch line. Frosting and light pitting is usually not a cause for concern. As the gears continue to run together, frosting is usually replaced by a shiny smooth surface in a process known as healing. Moderate and heavy pitting, however, require gear replacement—especially if it is concentrated at the pitch line of the gear teeth. Check for cracks in the gears, and carefully inspect the clutching teeth for excessive wear from clashing. If clutching teeth are worn significantly, replace the gear. Do not mistake back-tapered clutching teeth for worn teeth. Back-taper teeth are wide on the outside edge and narrower on the inside edge. Clashing wear always progresses from the outside of the tooth to the inside.
- Splines: Check all shaft splines for wear, and replace as necessary.
- Cast iron parts: Check all cast iron components for cracks and or leaks. Replace as necessary.

Inspecting the Transmission Oil Cooler and Filter

Transmission oil not only lubricates a transmission's moving parts, but it may be used to cool the transmission. When oil passes over the moving parts in a transmission, it absorbs heat. In most cases, airflow over the transmission cools the oil. When that is not sufficient, oil is routed to a transmission cooler. The transmission cooler is a heat exchanger where the oil is cooled by engine coolant or airflow before returning to the transmission. Normally, a transmission cooler is needed if the transmission's continuous operating temperature is always more than 224° F (107° C), 275° F (135° C) at intermittent operation, or the engine has a lower rating of 392 hp (292 kW) or more. If airflow is restricted to the transmission due to the vehicle's configuration (aerodynamics), a transmission cooler may also be required. If a transmission cooler is used, it must be maintained in good working order. If the cooler is an airflow cooler, a fin comb may be required to assist in straightening the cooler's fins from time to time. To inspect the transmission oil filter and cooler, follow the steps in **SKILL DRILL 44-6.**

SKILL DRILL 44-6 Inspecting the Transmission Oil Filter and Cooler

1. Locate and follow the appropriate procedure in the service manual.
2. Complete the accompanying job sheet or work order with all pertinent information.
3. Move the vehicle into the shop, apply the parking brakes, and chock the vehicle's wheels. Observe lockout/tagout procedures.

4. If the vehicle has a manual transmission, place it in "neutral"; if it has an automatic transmission, place it in "park" or "neutral." (*Note:* Some vehicles with automatic transmissions do not have "park.")
5. Inspect and replace the transmission oil filter:
   a. Check transmission oil filter for leaks. If a leak is found, change the filter. (*Note:* If a filter is removed for any reason, a new one must be installed.)
   b. Place a drain pan under the filter if removal is necessary.
   c. Remove the oil filter using an oil filter removal tool and make sure the rubber seal from the old filter has not been left on the transmission filter housing.
   d. Wipe clean the mating surface on the transmission.
   e. Apply a thin coat of transmission oil to the new filter's rubber seal.
   f. Screw on the new filter. (*Note:* It may be necessary to drain the transmission main case prior to removing the filter.)
6. Inspect and replace transmission oil cooler:
   a. Check the cooler for signs of leaks. (*Note:* If there are leaks from the cooler, it may have to be replaced.)
   b. Check all lines and hoses for any signs of leaks.
   c. Check that the fins on the cooler's coils are straight, if equipped. Use a fin comb to straighten the fins, if necessary.
   d. Refer to the service manual for removal and replacement procedures if it is determined that a new cooler must be installed.
7. List the test results and/or recommendations on the job sheet or work order, clean the work area, and return tools and materials to their proper storage.

Inspecting the Air System

The need to troubleshoot the air shift system may become necessary if the transmission shifts too slowly or fails to shift into the desired range. Checking for leaks, proper airflow through the system, proper component operation, and the correct air system and air line connections are the primary methods for troubleshooting the system. When troubleshooting the air shift system, the engine should be turned off after building normal vehicle air pressure. Since procedures vary with the type of system (OEM differences), always consult the service manual before beginning any maintenance on the air shift system.

Air leaks can occur in any part of the air shift system. Leaks can occur at the range selector valve in the shift knob assembly, at the slave valve, range cylinder, air filter/regulator, in the air lines, or in the air line connections. The following procedure is general in nature. It is important to follow the procedure(s) outlined in the service manual for the type of transmission being serviced. Although the transmission must be installed to check for air leaks, most of the components where you might detect a leak cannot be repaired until the transmission is removed. To inspect, test, adjust, repair or replace air shift controls, lines, valves, regulators, filters, and cylinder assemblies, follow the steps in **SKILL DRILL 44-7**.

Inspecting the Power Take-Off

The final routine transmission inspection that is commonly undertaken in a shop is inspecting the power take-off (PTO). To inspect the PTO, follow the steps in **SKILL DRILL 44-8**.

Common Repair Procedures for Standard Transmissions

LO 44-6 Describe common repair procedures for standard transmissions.

The following section describes the procedures for the most common standard transmission repair procedures that are likely to be carried out in the shop. Some shops tackle more involved procedures, such as complete transmission overhaul, but in most cases, when there is catastrophic damage requiring complete overhaul, the shop merely remove the transmission and install a rebuilt unit. Installing a rebuilt unit reduces downtime, increases vehicle productivity, and is usually the cheaper option, in the long run.

Replacing the Input Shaft

Eaton Fuller twin-countershaft transmission input shafts are replaceable without dismantling the transmission. Input shafts

SKILL DRILL 44-7 Inspecting, Testing, Adjusting, Repairing, or Replacing Air Shift Controls, Lines, Valves, Regulators, Filters, and Cylinder Assemblies

1. Locate and follow the appropriate procedure in the service manual.
2. Complete the accompanying job sheet or work order with all pertinent information.
3. Move the vehicle into the shop, apply the parking brakes, and chock the vehicle's wheels. Observe lockout/tagout procedures.
4. Run the engine until normal vehicle air pressure is achieved.
5. Shut down the engine.
6. Check for air leaks in all fittings, lines, and connections:
   a. Place gear shift in "neutral."
   b. Coat air lines and fittings with soapy water.

   c. Move the range selector switch up or down.
   d. Identify air leaks at all fittings, lines, and connections.
7. Consult the service manual (air system schematics) and check that air lines are properly routed and connected.
8. Check the slave air valve to ensure that there is not a constant air leak out of the exhaust port. (*Note:* It is normal for there to be a quick release of exhaust when a range shift is made. Generally, some slave valves cannot be repaired and must be replaced if leaks are detected.) Consult the service manual for repair or replacement of the slave valve if a constant leak is detected.
9. Check the air filter/regulator for leaks:
   a. Place the gear shift in "neutral."
   b. Check that no air is leaking at the breather port.
   c. Replace the air filter/regulator if an air leak is detected. Refer to the service manual.
   d. If not replacing the air filter/regulator, check the filter element for contamination and replace, if necessary.
10. Check the range selector valve:
    a. Refer to the service manual for troubleshooting this valve.
    b. Repair or replace as required.
11. Check the range cylinder:
    a. Refer to the service manual for troubleshooting the range cylinder.
    b. Repair or replace as required.
12. List the test results and/or recommendations on the job sheet or work order, clean the work area, and return tools and materials to their proper storage.

SKILL DRILL 44-8 Inspecting the Power Take-off

1. Locate and follow the appropriate procedure in the service manual.
2. Complete the accompanying job sheet or work order with all pertinent information.
3. Move the vehicle into the shop, apply the parking brakes, and chock the vehicle's wheels. Observe lockout/tagout procedures.
4. If the vehicle has a manual transmission, place it in "neutral"; if it has an automatic transmission, place it in "park" or "neutral." (*Note:* Some vehicles with automatic transmission do not have "park.")
5. Check for proper engagement and disengagement of the PTO gearbox. It should shift smoothly without gear clashing.

6. Check that the PTO runs smoothly with no vibration or unusual noises.
7. Inspect linkage for looseness, broken brackets, missing clamps, security, and lubrication.
8. Inspect PTO seals and gaskets for leaks and the housing for cracks.
9. Inspect the driveline (if equipped) for loose U-joints and the correct driveline angle. (*Note:* Check the service manual for the procedure to check the driveline angle.)
10. Check for correct speed and output power.
11. Inspect shift system:
    a. Inspect hydraulic system (if equipped) fittings, cylinders, motors, and pump. Also check that there are no leaks.
    b. Inspect the air shift system (if equipped) for leaks and proper operation.
    c. Inspect the manual shift mechanism (if equipped); levers, cables, etc.
12. Inspect the electrical system wiring harness for cracks, security, and placement. Also check that connections are tight.
13. Inspect electrical components that control the PTO. (*Note:* Electrical components may include switches, gauges, overspeed protection system, etc.)
14. List the test results and/or recommendations on the job sheet or work order, clean the work area, and return tools and materials to their proper storage.

are commonly replaced due to excessive spline wear from the clutch disks caused by torsional vibrations or due to damage from the release bearing support bushings caused by lack of lubrication. To replace the input shaft, follow the steps in **SKILL DRILL 44-9.**

Replacing Rear Seals

Checking and replacing seals in the transmission is a general procedure that is commonly undertaken in the shop. To replace rear seals in a transmission, follow the steps in **SKILL DRILL 44-10.** The steps listed in Skill Drill 44-10 cover rear seal replacement with a speed sensor. The procedure is slightly different with a mechanical speedometer. Note that on transmissions with electronic speed sensors, the speedometer reluctor doubles as the sealing surface for the rear transmission seal. A reluctor is a toothed wheel used with a magnetic sensor, usually to measure shaft speed. If the reluctor has excessive wear from contact with the seal, it should also be replaced.

SKILL DRILL 44-9 Replacing the Input Shaft

1. Remove the transmission according to the procedure in the Servicing Heavy-Duty Clutches chapter. Remember not to let the transmission hang on the input shaft as it is removed. With the transmission suitably supported on a transmission jack or a workbench, remove the six nuts and four bolts that secure the clutch bell housing and remove the housing. Remove the six bolts securing the front bearing cover and remove the cover and gasket. Remove and discard the rubber lip seal if present. This seal is merely for shipping purposes and is not required further.

2. Using snap ring pliers, remove the front bearing snap ring from the input shaft. Use a soft iron maul to drive the input shaft to the rear as far as it goes (approximately 0.25" or 6.35 mm). A maul is a large 2" (5 cm) diameter bar approximately 8" (20 cm) long.

3. Grasp the input shaft and wiggle it. Try to move it forward as far as it goes. If it is difficult to move forward, tap the transmission housing front wall with the maul as it is pulled forward. This exposes the large snap ring on the outside of the input bearing; do not remove this snap ring.

4. Install the bearing puller #7070A kit (Owatonna tool company) or equivalent. This tool pulls on the large external snap ring on the bearing. Remove the input bearing.

5. Remove the bearing spacer from the input shaft. Remove the internal snap ring from the input drive gear using a small screwdriver. Remove the input shaft. The drive gear remains in place in the transmission case supported by the two countershafts.

6. Check and replace (as needed) the input shaft pocket bushing. This bushing supports the forward end of the mainshaft. Because the mainshaft "floats," the bushing rarely needs replacing. The input shaft has a spiral groove just in front of the bearing. The grooves are the oil return "threads." It is critical that they are clean and undamaged or the transmission may leak. Clean or replace as necessary.

SKILL DRILL 44-9 Replacing the Input Shaft (Continued)

7. To reinstall the input shaft, reverse the removal procedure. Insert the input shaft into the drive gear and reinstall the internal snap ring in the gear. Install the spacer on the input shaft against the snap ring.

8. Carefully examine the input bearing. Slide it over the input shaft and install it using bearing criver tool #5066 (Owatonna tool company) or equivalent. This driver has a large flange that contacts both bearing races and is recommended by Eaton Fuller. Drive the bearing until the bearing contacts the front case. (*Note:* It may be necessary to wiggle the input shaft forward in the case once or twice as in step 3 and drive the bearing again to fully seat the bearing and expose the snap ring groove.) Reinstall the input shaft snap ring to secure the bearing. Do not replace the rubber lip seal, if it was present—it is for shipping purposes only.

9. Reinstall the front bearing cover with a new gasket. Be careful to line up the oil drain return holes in the cover and in the gasket to the oil return hole in the transmission case. Apply Loctite 242 to the bolt threads and torque to 40 to 45 ft-lb (54 to 61 Nm). Reinstall the clutch bell housing and torque to specification. Reinstall the transmission as described in the Servicing Heavy-Duty Clutches chapter.

SKILL DRILL 44-10 Replacing Rear Seals

1. Disconnect the driveshaft at the output yoke of the transmission. Place the transmission in low gear low range. This helps prevent the yoke from turning. Remove the yoke nut using a 2.75" (70 mm) socket. Remove the yoke using a yoke puller tool.

2. Remove the vehicle speed sensor (VSS). Remove the speedometer reluctor (rotor) and the O-ring from the shaft. Carefully pry the seal out with a screwdriver or pry bar inserted into the seal groove. Do not pry against the seal housing.

3. Remove the oil slinger from the speedometer reluctor (rotor) using a suitable drift punch, if necessary. Check the sealing surface of the reluctor for grooving, burrs, or nicks. Do not try to repair the surface. If damaged, replace it.

SKILL DRILL 44-10 Replacing Rear Seals (Continued)

4. Install the seal into the housing using a suitable seal driver. The Eaton P/N 5564501 driver is for the 7-series transmission; the 9-series transmission uses a different driver. Check the OEM manual for the correct installer. Then, install the oil slinger onto the speedometer reluctor using the proper driver. The Eaton P/N 71223 driver is for the 7-series transmission; the 9-series uses a different driver. Check the OEM manual for the proper driver.

5. Install the O-ring and the speedometer reluctor. Install the speedometer sensor. If the sensor is the thread-in type, adjust it by turning the sensor in until it contacts a tooth on the reluctor. Then back it out one-half to one turn.

6. Install the output yoke and torque the nut to 450–500 ft-lb (9610–9677 Nm). If the nylon lock on the nut is damaged or worn significantly, replace the nut. Reinstall the driveshaft and top up the transmission with the correct fluid until the level is even with the fill hole.

Removing and Disassembling the Auxiliary Section

Even though a complete transmission overhaul is unlikely in most shops, you may find that you need to remove an auxiliary section for maintenance and light repair. It is critical to keep the components of the auxiliary section in order as you remove them so that you can reassemble them accurately and quickly. For example, when the auxiliary countershaft bearing covers are removed, keep the caps, shims, bearing race, and countershaft from each side separate so they can be reassembled correctly. Likewise, auxiliary section countershafts are identical, but they should be marked so they are reinstalled with the correct bearing and shim pack if the bearings are reused. Also note that the integral range cylinder in most Fuller 10-speed forward/reverse (FR) transmissions makes it necessary to remove the shift bar housing before removing the auxiliary section. (*Note:* If your FR transmission is equipped with a movable pivot for the range shift rail, it is not necessary to remove the shift bar housing. Simply remove the two bolts and rotate the pivot to the unlocked position and secure it there.) This unlock pivot device is shown in **FIGURE 44-18**.

To remove the auxiliary section from a Fuller 10-speed FR model, follow the steps in **SKILL DRILL 44-11**. To disassemble the auxiliary section, follow the steps in **SKILL DRILL 44-12**.

▶ TECHNICIAN TIP

If the auxiliary section is being completely replaced with a new one, do not remove the bearing covers in step 2 of Skill Drill 44-11, and step 3 is not necessary to remove the old unit. The countershafts, however, can catch on the main box case, so watch carefully as you move the auxiliary rearward to avoid this. The support straps need to be installed on the new unit, however, to install it properly.

Overhauling the Range Synchronizer

Once the auxiliary is removed and disassembled, the range synchronizer can also be disassembled, and the friction rings replaced, as needed. To disassemble the synchronizer, follow the guidelines in **SKILL DRILL 44-13**. Be sure to have a clean shop towel on hand to cover the synchronizer and prevent the tension springs from flying out into the shop.

Reassembling and Timing the Auxiliary Section

When reassembling and timing the auxiliary section, it is important to keep track of your progress at each step in the procedure. Have a means to mark the components that you remove so you are sure to reassemble them in the proper location. This is particularly

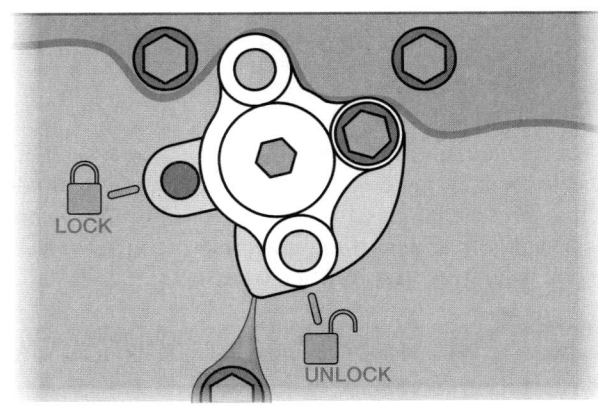

FIGURE 44-18 This unlock pivot device makes it unnecessary to remove the shift cover before removing the auxiliary section (only early-model FR transmissions were equipped with this).

SKILL DRILL 44-11 Removing the Auxiliary Section from a Fuller 10-Speed FR Model

1. Place the auxiliary section in low range. Drain the oil from the transmission. Support and then disconnect the driveshaft from the transmission output yoke. Move the driveshaft out of the way or remove it completely. Disconnect the speedometer cable or sensor. Drain the air tanks and remove the air lines going to the air module on the shift bar housing.

2. Remove the shift tower and the shift bar housing. Remove the auxiliary section countershaft bearing covers and shims. Do not mix the shims from side to side. Carefully mark the shim pack, bearing cover, bearing, and countershaft from one side so that they can be reinstalled in the correct side. Failure to do this means that the shim-setting procedure must be done on reassembly.

3. Attach countershaft support brackets (indicated) to each countershaft. Buy them or make them from 0.5" (13 mm) flat bar stock. These support the countershafts as the auxiliary section is removed. Supporting the countershafts properly prevents them from getting hung up in the main box case while removing the auxiliary. When you install the center bolt of the support brackets, tighten them fully and then back them off one-half to one turn so the countershafts can rotate as the auxiliary is removed.

4. Drive the two alignment dowels forward in the transmission case by 0.5" (13 mm) to break free any rust and ease removal. Do not drive them too far or they become loose. Remove the bolts attaching the auxiliary section to the main box. The bolts vary in length and must be replaced in their correct locations. Note the raised alignment shoulder.

5. Two or three threaded pusher holes in the auxiliary section flange area are covered with tape. Thread the longer removed bolts into these holes, and tighten evenly until the gasket seal is broken and the auxiliary is far enough back to install the auxiliary hanger bracket. Do not move the auxiliary back any further than necessary or it may drop. If practical, install the horizontal removal hanger bracket #5061 (Owatonna tool company) or equivalent to the top of the auxiliary section flange. This tool can also be constructed following Fuller instructions.

6. Connect a hoisting device to the tool and raise it until it supports the weight of the auxiliary. If supporting the auxiliary by a transmission jack, be sure the auxiliary section is firmly secured to the jack, so it does not fall. Carefully move the auxiliary section rearward to clear the main box and remove the auxiliary. Install the bottom flange of the auxiliary section to a brass-jawed vise for disassembly.

---

true when marking the teeth used to time the countershaft. Use a highly visible marking compound and be mindful that your marks may become obscured by the rear countershaft bearing and washer on some models. To reassemble and time the auxiliary section, follow the steps in **SKILL DRILL 44-14**.

▶ TECHNICIAN TIP

The main box and auxiliary sections on Eaton Fuller transmissions must be timed on assembly to ensure that the main or output shaft "floats" between the two countershafts. Failure to correctly time the transmission leads to transmission seizure. In fact, the transmission or the auxiliary usually does not even turn at all if incorrectly timed.

▶ TECHNICIAN TIP

Thirteen- and 18-speed model auxiliary sections have an additional gear set (the splitter gear set). Nonetheless, they follow a similar procedure for overhaul. Both the range and the splitter gear must be timed to the countershafts on reassembly. Consult the OEM manual for the particular model being serviced.

Reinstalling the Auxiliary Section

Once the auxiliary section is reassembled and timed, it can be reinstalled. To reinstall the auxiliary section, follow the steps in **SKILL DRILL 44-15**.

SKILL DRILL 44-12 Disassembling the Auxiliary Section

1. Remove the auxiliary section output yoke. Use a yoke puller, as needed. Place a clean shop towel into the Range gear mesh to stop the output shaft from turning. With yoke removed, remove the speedometer reluctor and the O-ring from the output shaft.

2. Use a maul and a soft bar to drive the auxiliary output shaft forward slightly (0.5" or 13 mm) to facilitate removal of the auxiliary countershafts. Remove the countershaft support straps one at a time while holding the countershafts. Remove each countershaft and its bearing race. Mark the countershafts so they can be reinstalled on the correct side.

3. Remove the range synchronizer, the yoke, and the range shift bar together from the front of the auxiliary and set aside. Drive the auxiliary output shaft forward with the maul and remove it. Do not misplace the large, steel bearing spacer. If not replacing the output shaft bearings, leave the front output shaft bearing in place, as shown.

4. If replacing the output shaft bearings, place the output shaft in a press with the range gear supported by blocks. Press the output shaft through the range gear and the bearing to remove it. (*Note:* The front and rear support bearings are different, so do not mix them up. The front support bearing inner diameter is slightly larger.) Remove the rear bearing cover from the auxiliary section housing.

5. Remove the rear output shaft support bearing and race. Some models have a one-piece outer and inner bearing race, as shown.

▶ **TECHNICIAN TIP**

Certain models have one chamfered hole in the rear bearing cover, so take note of its location. This chamfered hole is sealed by a nylon collar followed by a brass washer on the retaining bolt. When reassembling, a new tapered nylon collar must be used in the chamfered hole or the cover will leak.

SKILL DRILL 44-13 Overhauling the Range Synchronizer

1. Place the synchronizer on a bench with the large cone-shaped friction ring down. Cover the synchronizer with a shop towel. Carefully pull the smaller cup-shaped friction ring upwards until it separates from the synchronizer. Examine both friction rings for heat discoloration, loose pins, and glazed or worn areas. Replace as necessary.

2. Examine the splines and the clutching teeth of the synchronizer clutch and replace, if necessary.

3. To reassemble the synchronizer, slide the pins of the large friction ring into the three chamfered holes on the convex side of the synchronizer clutch. Place the synchronizer on the bench with the large friction ring down.

SKILL DRILL 44-13 Overhauling the Range Synchronizer (Continued)

4. Install the three tension-setting springs into the bores in the small friction ring. Place the small friction ring on top of the concave side of the synchronizer clutch with the springs resting against the pins of the large synchronizer ring.

5. Cover the synchronizer with a shop towel. With flat hands, twist the top friction ring counterclockwise very quickly while exerting downward force. This compresses the springs and causes the pins of the small friction ring to enter the other three holes in the synchronizer clutch. Essentially, just push down and twist. The shop towel prevents the springs from flying out if reassembly is unsuccessful.

SKILL DRILL 44-14 Reassembling and Timing the Auxiliary Section

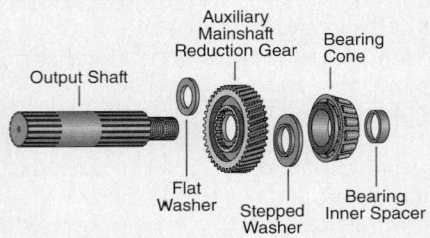

1. The auxiliary section countershafts have two of the low-range gear teeth marked with a 0. Carefully mark the inside groove between these two teeth on each countershaft with a highly visible marking compound. If there is any doubt as to the marked teeth's location, remove the bearings using a press, and then mark the teeth. Remember, it is the space between the teeth or the "groove" that is being marked.

2. Use the same marking compound to mark any tooth on the range gear and the tooth 180 degrees opposite. These teeth are timed to the two marked countershaft gear grooves on installation.

3. Assemble the output shaft as follows:
  a. With the shaft standing yoke-end up, install the flat range gear toothed washer.
  b. Next, install the range gear with the clutching teeth down.
  c. Install the stepped washer with the chamfered side up.
  d. Install the front-rear support bearing. Caution: The front and rear support bearings are different. The support bearings' inner diameters are different sizes. Do not mix them up. Heat the bearing to no more than 275° F (136° C) to install it or use an appropriate bearing driver. (Note: If the bearing is not being replaced it may still be necessary to fully reseat the bearing with a bearing driver, as it may have moved back slightly on disassembly of the auxiliary.)
  e. Install the inner bearing spacer on the shaft.

SKILL DRILL 44-14 Reassembling and Timing the Auxiliary Section (Continued)

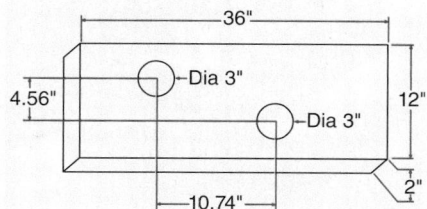

4. Fabricate a support for the countershafts from a 2" × 12" piece of wood with the dimensions shown. This support makes assembly much easier. Place the two countershafts into the support with the low-range gears up and the two marked tooth grooves to the center.

5. Slide the range synchronizer onto the assembled output shaft—low-range side up. Place it in between the two countershafts. Carefully time the assembly by meshing the two marked teeth on the range gear with the two marked grooves on the countershafts. The countershafts must be timed on installation to allow the floating mainshaft system.

6. Place the range shift fork in the synchronizer groove. Then, place the auxiliary section housing over the assembled gearing. Install the auxiliary countershaft bearing rear races and shims in their correct locations. Install the auxiliary countershaft support straps and snug the bolts. Do not over torque them. Make sure the bearing spacer is present on the output shaft behind the frontrear support bearing.

7. Install the one-piece rear support bearing raceways, then install the rear-rear support bearing either by heating to 275° F (136° C) or by using an appropriate driver. (*Note:* The two countershaft support holes are drilled into the work bench.)

8. Install a new seal in the rear bearing cover and install it with a new gasket, being careful to line up the oil return hole in the cover and the housing. (*Note:* If the rear bearing support came with a nylon collar and a brass washer on the bolt in the chamfered hole in the cover, be sure to replace them with new parts.)

9. Install the shaft O-ring and the speedometer reluctor.

10. Install the output yoke and torque to 450–500 ft-lb (610–677 Nm). To prevent the output shaft from turning, place the auxiliary section in low range and put a clean shop towel in the gear mesh. Hold the unit securely to avoid accidental damage while torque is being applied. It is essential that the output shaft is fully drawn into position before attempting to install the auxiliary or it may sag and misalignment may occur.

SKILL DRILL 44-15 Reinstalling the Auxiliary Section

1. Install the countershaft support straps on the auxiliary section countershafts. Snug the center bolts to center and hold the countershafts in position. Tighten the bolts securely, then back them off one-half to one turn. The output shaft and the countershafts must be able to turn for installation.

2. Drive the alignment dowel pins in the main box rearward. Ensure they are positioned correctly. The dowels have shoulders that should protrude approximately 0.5" (13 mm) to the rear from the main box. These shoulders are what center the auxiliary. Make sure also that the dowel pins are clean and free of rust.

3. Clean all rust and paint from the dowel pin holes in the auxiliary section housing. Lightly grease the dowel pins and the dowel pin holes in the auxiliary section.

4. Make sure the auxiliary section is in low range so that you can turn the countershafts using the output yoke.

5. Position a new gasket on the main box flange and dowel pins.

6. Use the hoisting tool to raise the auxiliary section level with the transmission main box or use a suitable transmission jack.

7. Position the auxiliary section level with the main case and slide the auxiliary section onto the dowel pins. Mesh the countershafts with the auxiliary drive gear as the housing is moved forward. Rotate the output yoke slightly to help the gears mesh. Slide the auxiliary forward until it is flush against the main box flange.

SAFETY TIP

The auxiliary should move into place with little effort. Do not force it, and never use the attaching bolts to draw the auxiliary section in. If resistance is encountered, the most likely cause is that the timing is incorrect. Retime the auxiliary and try again.

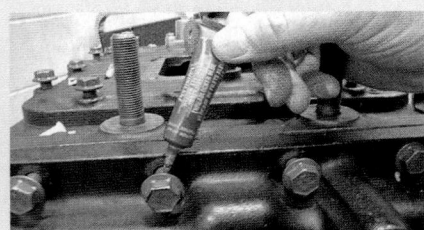

8. Apply thread sealant or equivalent to the all the retaining bolt threads. Install the bolts to secure and torque to 40–45 ft-lb (54–61 Nm).

9. Countershaft bearing endplay must be checked and reset with shims if any of the following components were replaced:

- countershafts
- countershaft bearings
- auxiliary housing

Countershaft bearing endplay must also be checked and reset with shims if the countershafts, bearings, or shims were not properly marked on disassembly and reassembled in the same location.

SKILL DRILL 44-15 Reinstalling the Auxiliary Section (Continued)

10. To shim the countershaft, use the following method:

   a. Clean all gasket material from the case and the countershaft bearing covers.

   b. Install each countershaft bearing cover using two bolts only 180 degrees apart with a shim. Torque the bolts to 7 in-lb (0.79 Nm) only. Do not over tighten! The cover can be easily broken!

   c. Alternately, use the shim setting tools available. These tools have a raised 0.100" (2.54 mm) section, so the shim does not need to be installed. The tools also double as countershaft support straps.

   d. Using feeler gauges, check the gap between the cover and the auxiliary housing gasket surface on both sides, as close to the bolts as possible, and average the two readings.

   e. Compare your reading to the shim-selection chart. Use **TABLE 44-3** to determine the correct shim by comparing the average feeler gauge reading to the chart.

   (*Note:* The oil pump shim is used when an auxiliary oil pump or PTO is mounted on the countershaft. The oil pump shims are smaller in outside diameter.)

   f. Select the proper shim and install it with a new Eaton Fuller gasket. Use thread sealant on the cover bolts and torque the bolts to specification, approximately 40–45 ft–lb (54–61 Nm).

   (*Note:* This procedure sets countershaft endplay at between 0.001" and 0.005" (2.54 and 12.6 mm) and relies on the compressed thickness of the cover gasket when calculating the shim thickness. Use of an aftermarket gasket instead of genuine Fuller parts may change the endplay and result in failure.)

11. If shimming is not required, remove the support straps and install the correct shim, new gasket, and countershaft bearing cover. Use thread sealant on the cover bolts and torque to 40–45 ft-lb (54–61 Nm).

12. Reinstall the shift bar housing with a new gasket, being careful to line up the range cylinder piston shaft with the range yoke bar slot. Use thread sealant on the cover bolts. Torque the bolts to specification; approximately 40–45 ft-lb (54–61 Nm).

13. Install the shift tower with a new gasket. Connect all removed air lines and the speedometer connections. Reinstall the driveshaft and refill the transmission with the correct lubricant until it is level with the fill hole.

TABLE 44-3 Shim Table

Feeler Gauge Average Gap (in inches)	Shim Thickness (in inches)	Standard Shim Part Number	Oil Pump Shim Part Number	Color Code
0.072–0.075	0.033–0.034	4302345	4302346	Gold
0.069–0.0715	0.036–0.037	21452	21472	Red
0.066–0.0685	0.039–0.040	21453	21473	Pink
0.063–0.0655	0.042–0.043	21454	21474	Brown
0.060–0.0625	0.045–0.046	21455	21475	Tan
0.057–0.0595	0.048–0.049	21456	21476	Orange
0.054–0.0565	0.051–0.052	21457	21477	Yellow
0.051–0.0535	0.054–0.055	21458	21478	Green

Analysis of Transmission Failure

LO 44-7 Explain and describe various transmission failures and their causes.

Failure analysis is a very important component of a technician's skill set. The ability to determine what specifically caused a failure to occur is essential to performing a complete repair. Correct diagnoses are also critical to preventing a repeat failure.

Drivetrain systems are frequently the subject of premature failures caused by overloading, driver error or abuse, or poor maintenance practices. Most manufacturers have guide books available to help determine the root cause of a failure. Remember that gears and shafts are made of ductile iron and are usually case or induction hardened, typically to a depth of no more than 0.050" (25.4 mm). The hardening allows the component's surface to resist wear, but the ductile core allows them to flex as they are loaded, so that they can absorb some shocks.

Several factors must be considered when determining the cause of failure: vehicle vocation, load, driver experience, road conditions, maintenance records, and an accurate report as to how and when the failure occurred. A more in-depth section on failure analysis is included at the end of the Servicing and Maintaining Drive Axles chapter.

Regular Wear or Maintenance Failures

Eaton Fuller twin-countershaft transmissions enjoy the largest market share in the heavy-duty commercial truck industry. These and, indeed, all twin- or triple-countershaft transmissions have certain unique wear characteristics when compared to single-countershaft transmissions. The surface of gear teeth may look smooth to the naked eye, yet all tooth surfaces are very irregular. They have numerous hills and valleys at the microscopic level. As teeth wear going through mesh with each other, these hills and valleys are worn away and the surface becomes increasingly smooth.

Spur-gear transmission wear patterns are slightly different than those with helical gears. Spur gear contact slides into mesh, then rolls against its mating tooth at full mesh (when tooth loading is highest). The spur gear then slides back out of mesh. By contrast, helical gears maintain continuous sliding- and wiping-type contact. The wiping contact of helical gears tends to make the surface smoother faster than with spur-type gears. Spur gear contact leads to extreme pressure between the teeth during their rolling contact. This type of load can break off, rather than wipe off, the microscopic surface irregularities. As a result, the tooth surface becomes dull, rather than shiny. As mentioned previously in the chapter, this condition is known as frosting. Frosting is quite a common occurrence with spur-gear contact; it is not usually a cause for concern. This frosting eventually heals. As the teeth continue to adjust to each other, the surface heals and becomes shiny once again.

Spur gear contact can also lead to minor pitting caused by the lubricant being forced down through microscopic peaks and valleys on the tooth surface. Small surface fractures of the tooth result, and eventually tiny pieces of metal are broken out. This condition is known as initial pitting. As the teeth adjust to each other, the initial pitting heals over and becomes shiny.

Twin- or triple-countershaft transmissions spread the torque load over several sets of teeth in contact, so the load on individual teeth is lower. The frosting and healing process can be slower than in single-countershaft transmissions—which means that wear can be observed much later in a transmission's lifespan. Also, sometimes the vocation of the transmission changes and it is subject to heavier loads. When that happens, the pitting process may restart, if the increased load causes the gear teeth to readjust to each other. Minor pitting again usually heals over time and is not a huge concern. Deep and concentrated pitting at the pitch line, however, indicates that these gears need to be replaced. When gear replacement is necessary, mainshaft gears and their matching countershaft gears must be replaced as a set.

In addition to friction, lubrication failures due to poor maintenance, incorrect lubrication, lack of lubrication, and/or contaminated lube always lead to eventual failure of tooth surfaces.

Abuse Failures

Transmission failure is not just the result of regular wear. It can be accelerated by abuses, such as sudden load increases, dumping the clutch, backing into a loading dock at speed, spinning out, and poor gear selection.

Shock load failures occur when a component is momentarily overloaded. When a load surpasses the base strength of the material, the material fails immediately. Driver abuse or inexperience is commonly a cause of shock load failures.

Dumping the clutch is common abuse that can be easily prevented. Dumping the clutch, instead of smoothly engaging it, puts enormous stress load on the entire driveline. The main failures that occur from this type of abuse are twisted mainshaft in the transmission (recall the image in Figure 44-9), driveshaft torsional failures, broken universal joints, and axle shaft torsional failures.

Backing into a loading dock at speed can cause shock failures, as can backing under a trailer too roughly. Likewise, shock failure can occur if the trailer is set too low, forcing the vehicle to attempt to lift the trailer as it hooks up.

Spinout, whether in a main differential or an inter-axle differential, is another source of driver abuse that can cause catastrophic damage to the transmission. When the driver allows the wheels to spin, the driveshaft and the differential side and spider gears are rotating at enormous speeds. If the wildly spinning wheels suddenly gain traction and stop, severe shock loads are transmitted to the transmission.

Poor gear selection by the driver can also lead to severe shock loads. If, as the driver tries to re-engage the clutch, the gear selection does not match the road speed, the driveline must absorb the shock. In that situation, failure is possible.

See the Servicing and Maintaining Drive Axles chapter for a more comprehensive look at gear and shaft failures and their causes.

Wrap-Up

Ready for Review

▶ Lubricant is the lifeblood of transmissions. It is essential that the quality and level be maintained for long transmission service.

▶ Most manufacturers now use synthetic-based lubricants, which allow a much longer service interval.

▶ Lubricants with extreme pressure (EP) additives are not normally recommended for heavy-duty transmission operation, as they can oxidize at common transmission operating temperatures.

▶ Many heavy-duty transmissions are fitted with internal or external oil coolers to deal with high operating temperatures resulting from high torque loads.

▶ Transmission model number nomenclature can give the technician valuable information about the transmission being serviced or repaired.

▶ Transmission preventative maintenance today typically involves a visual inspection of the transmission for leakage, checking the mounting components for integrity, and checking the shift mechanisms and the air shifting system for leaks and correct operation.

▶ The use of synthetic lubricant has resulted in lubrication and filter changes becoming less frequent.

▶ Noise from the transmission can come from a variety of causes. The type of noise—knocking, growling, whining, or rattling—can help the technician isolate the cause.

▶ Vibration can be caused by the transmission, but is more likely to be caused by other systems, such as torsional vibrations from the engine, driveline vibration from the driveshaft, or wheel-end vibrations due to imbalance.

▶ However, all these vibrations can cause transmission damage, and should be corrected as soon as possible.

▶ Gear slip out or jump out can occur if components, such as sliding clutches or shift forks, are worn. Wear on these components is frequently caused by driver error or abuse.

▶ Newer Eaton Fuller FR-model 10-speed fleet transmissions have a different air system than other transmissions. They use a one-piece air module to house all of the air control system components.

▶ FR models also have the range cylinder integral to the shift cover. It is essential that the shift cover is removed before the auxiliary section can be removed because the range shift bar interlocks with the range synchronizer shift rail.

▶ Diagnosing problems with the air shift system should always start with checking the air supply and air filter regulator for contamination and/or other problems.

▶ The Eaton Fuller transmission input shaft can be removed from the case without main box disassembly.

▶ When removing the auxiliary section, auxiliary countershaft support straps should always be used.

▶ The auxiliary section range gear and the main box input gear on Eaton Fuller Roadranger transmissions must be timed at installation to ensure that the gears are supported in equilibrium and allow the mainshaft system to float.

▶ After reinstalling the auxiliary section, the auxiliary countershaft end play must be set to specification.

▶ Frosting is a common phenomenon with twin-countershaft transmissions and is caused by microscopic imperfections on the tooth surfaces wearing off. The frosting generally heals over as the teeth continue to work together.

▶ Shock loads are extremely damaging to mechanical transmissions and are usually the fault of the driver. Dumping the clutch, engaging the wrong gear, and spinning the tires and then hitting solid pavement can all cause shock loads that can cause fatigue fracture, or even component breakage, to occur.

Key Terms

back-taper The tapered profile of the teeth on a sliding clutch such that the outer edge is thicker than the inner; the profile helps keep the clutch engaged under load.

extreme pressure (EP) additive   Additives usually found in hypoid gear lube and which should not be used in Fuller Roadranger transmissions and most heavy-duty transmissions because it tends to oxidize at relatively low temperatures.

gear slip out   The condition in which a transmission jumps out of gear and to neutral when under load, caused by worn components, such as sliding clutches and shift forks. Also called *jump out*.

jump out   The condition in which a transmission jumps out of gear and to neutral when under load, caused by worn components, such as sliding clutches and shift forks. Also called *gear slip out*.

line-haul   A truck that spends most of its time in on-highway operations transporting medium to heavy load.

nomenclature   The meaning of the letters and digits in truck transmission's model numbers.

oil weep   Very minor oil seepage usually caused by a wicking effect and not usually a reason for a repair.

remote shift linkage   A transmission shift linkage that is not mounted directly above the shift cover and that must be properly maintained and lubricated to prevent hard shifting.

severe-duty service   A vehicle that is operated under extreme (maximum) loading most of the time, or one that is operated on heavy grades.

synthetic-based lubricant   A lubricant that is manufactured, rather than refined, and so has much longer service life; it can be a blend of natural and synthetic materials.

vocational   A truck that is dedicated to a specific type of service job, or function.

Review Questions

1. What precaution must be taken when towing a vehicle with a standard transmission on its drive wheels?
   a. The axles or driveshaft must be removed.
   b. One axle should be removed.
   c. Leave the engine running.
   d. No precautions are necessary, as long as the distance towed is less than 50 miles or 80 km.
2. What must be removed before you can remove the auxiliary section on most Eaton Fuller FR-model transmissions?
   a. The input shaft
   b. The output yoke
   c. The shift bar cover
   d. The shift lever
3. When removing an auxiliary section in the vehicle, what is/are the recommended safeguards that you should install?
   a. Countershaft support straps
   b. Rear yoke support
   c. Guide studs
   d. Main box holding fixture
4. Which of the following could be the cause of hard lever shifting from first to second, if you have eliminated the shift linkage and shift bar housing as the problem on an Eaton Fuller twin-countershaft transmission?
   a. Burned synchronizer friction rings
   b. Broken detent springs
   c. Broken synchronizer pins
   d. Twisted mainshaft
5. While checking the Eaton Fuller Roadranger valve (shift knob) for correct operation of the high- and low-range shift, you find that air leaks constantly from the valve when in high-range only. What could be the problem?
   a. Leaking Roadranger valve
   b. Crossed air lines
   c. Defective slave air valve
   d. Defective range cylinder
6. Which of the following is responsible for lubrication of most standard transmissions?
   a. A gear pump
   b. An electric pump
   c. Submersion of all components in the fluid
   d. The splash caused by the countershaft's rotation
7. When assembling a 10-speed Fuller twin countershaft transmission auxiliary, you must time which of the following gears together?
   a. The range gear to the countershafts
   b. The input gear to the countershaft-driven gears
   c. The input gear to the range gear
   d. The range synchronizer to the range gear
8. Which of the following could cause a range synchronizer to have extreme wear on its clutching teeth?
   a. Air pressure too high.
   b. Shifting the range in neutral while the vehicle is stationary
   c. Skip shifting in the main box
   d. Failure to preselect the range shift
9. In the Fuller FR-series transmission, where is the range cylinder located?
   a. Inside the auxiliary section
   b. Bolted to the auxiliary section
   c. Bolted to the main box
   d. Inside the shift cover
10. Which of these parts should be removed before a damaged input shaft can be changed on a Fuller Roadranger twin-countershaft transmission?
    a. The shift bar housing
    b. The auxiliary section
    c. The mainshaft
    d. Clutch housing

ASE Technician A/Technician B Style Questions

1. Technician A says that normal non-synthetic lubricant can be used to top up a transmission that is equipped with synthetic oil. Technician B says that a transmission shipped from the factory with synthetic oil has a much longer service interval than one with mineral-based oil. Who is correct?
   a. Technician A
   b. Technician B
   c. Both Technician A and Technician B
   d. Neither Technician A nor Technician B

2. Technician A says that the correct lubricant level in a transmission should reach the bottom of the fill plug hole. Technician B says that as long as you can feel the fluid with the first digit of your finger the level is OK. Who is correct?
   a. Technician A
   b. Technician B
   c. Both Technician A and Technician B
   d. Neither Technician A nor Technician B

3. Technician A says that transmission rattling at idle can be caused by engine torsional vibrations. Technician B says that a clutch with pre-dampening can eliminate gear rattle at idle. Who is correct?
   a. Technician A
   b. Technician B
   c. Both Technician A and Technician B
   d. Neither Technician A nor Technician B

4. Technician A says that if an Eaton Fuller Roadranger transmission is an overdrive model, it has an O in the first four letters of its model number. Technician B says that an F in the third or fourth letter position of the model number means it is a five-speed model. Who is correct?
   a. Technician A
   b. Technician B
   c. Both Technician A and Technician B
   d. Neither Technician A nor Technician B

5. Technician A says that, for today's transmissions with synthetic lube, preventative maintenance is basically a visual inspection of all the transmission systems. Technician B says that transmissions equipped with straight mineral oil have oil-change intervals of 500,000 miles (805,000 kilometers). Who is correct?
   a. Technician A
   b. Technician B
   c. Both Technician A and Technician B
   d. Neither Technician A nor Technician B

6. Technician A says that when overhauling a Fuller 10-speed auxiliary section, the auxiliary drive gear must be timed to the auxiliary countershafts. Technician B says that auxiliary section countershaft support straps are necessary to reinstall the auxiliary section. Who is correct?
   a. Technician A
   b. Technician B
   c. Both Technician A and Technician B
   d. Neither Technician A nor Technician B

7. Technician A says that the air filter regulator is the first place to check if a Fuller 13-speed transmission air shift system is not working correctly. Technician B says that the air supply to the air filter regulator passes through a pressure protection valve. Who is correct?
   a. Technician A
   b. Technician B
   c. Both Technician A and Technician B
   d. Neither Technician A nor Technician B

8. Technician A says that you must line up the range cylinder shift bar in the shift cover with the range cylinder shift fork while installing the shift cover on a 13-speed Fuller transmission. Technician B says that the Fuller 13-speed transmission range shift cylinder is located at the back of the auxiliary section. Who is correct?
   a. Technician A
   b. Technician B
   c. Both Technician A and Technician B
   d. Neither Technician A nor Technician B

9. Technician A says that auxiliary countershaft end play must be checked and adjusted if the auxiliary countershaft bearings are replaced. Technician B says that the mainshaft end play should be checked before reinstalling the auxiliary section. Who is correct?
   a. Technician A
   b. Technician B
   c. Both Technician A and Technician B
   d. Neither Technician A nor Technician B

10. Technician A says that worn clutching teeth on the range synchronizer sliding clutch are normal and the clutch does not need to be replaced. Technician B says that worn range synchronizer clutching teeth are a sign of driver abuse. Who is correct?
    a. Technician A
    b. Technician B
    c. Both Technician A and Technician B
    d. Neither Technician A nor Technician B

CHAPTER 45

Automated Manual Transmissions

Learning Objectives

After reading this chapter, you should be able to:

- **LO 45-1** Explain the purpose and benefits of automated manual transmissions (AMTs).
- **LO 45-2** Explain the operations of AMTs.
- **LO 45-3** Explain the operation of dual-clutch transmissions.
- **LO 45-4** Explain the design and operation of three module transmissions.
- **LO 45-5** Describe the troubleshooting and service procedures for AMTs.

You Are the Technician

A driver brings his truck to your service facility. The vehicle is equipped with an Eaton 18-speed UltraShift automated transmission. The driver is new to this vehicle and complains that when he shuts the vehicle off, it sometimes will not start when he returns to the vehicle. He says that when he turns the key on and off a few times and releases the parking brake, it will then usually start. You examine the vehicle but cannot replicate the problem. What should be your next steps?

1. Should you observe the driver as he road tests the vehicle to see if he can replicate the problem?
2. Should you check the transmission for any active or inactive diagnostic trouble codes?
3. Why should you ask the driver to explain the shutdown procedure he uses for his vehicle?

Introduction

The automotive industry in general is under extreme pressure to reduce all harmful tailpipe emissions from vehicles. The trucking industry is not exempt from this pressure. Vehicles made in 2014 and later are the cleanest they have ever been. There are no further mandated reductions scheduled for traditional tailpipe emissions. The newest Environmental Protection Agency (EPA)-mandated reduction is now **carbon dioxide (CO$_2$)**, an odorless colorless gas.

Until recently, carbon dioxide was considered a harmless emission that simply occurred as one of the byproducts when a hydrocarbon fuel was burned completely, the other byproduct being H$_2$O (water). Today, however, carbon dioxide is considered a greenhouse gas that contributes to global warming and, therefore, the reduction of carbon dioxide emissions is of paramount importance to governments worldwide.

The only way a fossil fuel-burning vehicle can reduce its output of carbon dioxide is by increasing **thermal efficiency**. Increasing thermal efficiency means more of the fuel used is turned into power to drive the vehicle. Thermal efficiency is a hot topic in the trucking industry. Many new technologies and strategies are being used to achieve higher thermal efficiencies—from engine advancements to truck body shapes designed to reduce drag. Hybrid electric technology is also being used to reduce carbon dioxide emission. Using electricity to help power the vehicle reduces the amount of fossil fuel being burned. One of the strategies involving the driveline is the introduction of the electronically automated transmission, or what is commonly referred to as an **automated manual transmission (AMT)**. The shifting process for an AMT is controlled by the **transmission electronic control unit (ECU)**, also known as the **transmission control module (TCM)**. The ECU works in concert with the engine's control module to optimize shift points and strategies to maximize fuel efficiency. Even the most experienced driver would have trouble matching the precise shift control of a ECU. **FIGURE 45-1** shows an AMT manufactured by Eaton. This chapter introduces the student to the various types of AMTs and their operating systems.

FIGURE 45-1 Eaton Corporation's UltraShift transmission.

Benefits of Automated Transmissions

LO 45-1 Explain the purpose and benefits of automated manual transmissions (AMTs).

The electronically automated transmission comes in many varieties—some with a clutch pedal and some without. In the clutch-pedal types, the driver operates the clutch pedal for shifting from neutral to first or reverse only and the rest of the shifting is carried out by the transmission TCM or ECU. In models without a clutch pedal, a clutch is still used, but it is controlled by the ECU and the transmission's operation is entirely **shift by wire**. That is, shifting is controlled completely by the transmission electronic control. **FIGURE 45-2** shows the in-cab pedal configuration for a system with no clutch pedal.

The primary benefit of AMTs is improved fuel economy. It is estimated that AMTs improve a vehicle's fuel economy by 5% to 7% over conventional standard transmissions because of

FIGURE 45-2 Most AMTs have no clutch pedal.

their ability to use optimized shift strategies. Two other advantages of the AMT enhance safety: An AMT allows the driver to keep both hands on the steering wheel and AMTs are less tiring for the driver to operate because no shifting, clutching, or double clutching is necessary.

AMTs also reduce company expenditure on driver training. Learning to drive an 18-speed transmission can be a time-consuming and daunting task. AMTs drastically reduce the training time devoted to shifting gears. Furthermore, because the computer has control over shifting, the transmission is not subject to abuse commonly associated with unskilled drivers—and even occasionally with veteran drivers. The reduction in driver abuse means that AMTs experience longer transmission life, less down time for repairs, and higher vehicle resale value. Finally, the electronic control system also has a **self-diagnostic** capability, allowing easy troubleshooting of problems. In other words, the ECU is able to analyze its own functions.

The Role of Torque Break in Shifting

Most AMTs still use the conventional method of shifting. In other words, it is necessary to break torque—or unload the geartrain as a shift is being made. When the geartrain is under load or torque, it is nearly impossible to move the gearshift lever to disengage an engaged sliding clutch or collar. Before a shift can be made, the driver must unload the drivetrain or "break torque."

Breaking torque means the engine must be throttled back, and the throttle must be reapplied when the shift is complete. Changing the throttle position causes a delay in overall vehicle acceleration. The deceleration and acceleration required when changing the throttle position also causes a reduction in fuel economy. Several manufacturers now have AMTs on the market. Eaton, ZF, and Volvo all also offer **dual-clutch transmissions** capable of shifting without breaking torque, thereby improving fuel economy. Dual-clutch transmissions have two separate input shafts controlled by two separate clutches.

For years, experienced drivers have been shifting truck transmissions without using the clutch pedal except for starting from a stop. Although not recommended by any transmission manufacturer, this "**gear jamming**" technique is the basis for most AMTs. Essentially, what drivers were doing when making a shift was breaking torque by letting up on the accelerator in order to pull the gear stick to a neutral position. (Without breaking torque, the load on the gear shift components would make them impossible to move.) The driver would then carefully select the next gear as the engine rpm and the transmission mainshaft speeds synchronized. They would then complete the shift by jamming the transmission into the next gear.

To perform this technique properly required great skill and experience, and even the best drivers cause some damage to the shift collar or sliding clutch teeth. Matching the shaft speeds involved making a best guess and a less-experienced driver could destroy a transmission in very little time while "gear jamming."

Most automated transmissions use this gear jamming technique; they use computer controls to break torque and the computer then matches the shaft speeds with precision. The computer uses sensors to monitor the shaft speeds and then moves the shift forks with electric motors, air cylinders, or hydraulic cylinders. Gear jamming is done automatically, without gear clash, and with no damage to the transmission.

Types of Electronically Automated Manual Transmissions

The internal components and power flows of Fuller AMTs are practically identical to those used by standard transmissions. To review the internal functioning of standard transmissions, including gears and sliding clutches, consult the Standard Transmissions chapter. The Eaton Fuller Corporation still dominates the North American market for AMTs. Therefore, this chapter covers Eaton's range of AMTs in some depth. Several other manufacturers are now gaining an increasing share of the AMT market and many are discussed in this chapter.

Eaton Fuller's Automated Transmissions

Eaton entered the AMT market in 1993 with the **AutoSelect**. The transmission had limited electronics and used the older and slower J-1587 communications to enable the ECM to synchronize shaft speeds during driver-initiated shifting. J-1587 is the original Society of Automotive Engineers (SAE) communication protocol for commercial vehicles; J-1587 is quite slow in terms of data transmission at 9600 bits per second. Eaton next brought out a unique kind of transmission called the Super Ten and the Super Ten Top Two, pictured in **FIGURE 45-3**. The shift pattern of the Super Ten Top Two is illustrated in **FIGURE 45-4**.

The Super Ten transmission had automated control over the top two split gear ranges only, through a small electronic module that controlled the splitter cylinder. The control module for the top two gears is shown in **FIGURE 45-5**.

The control module provided some improvement to fuel economy and eased driver fatigue in long-haul operation. The driver did not have to constantly shift between ninth and tenth gears when approaching grades, for example. What made the Super Ten unique, however, was that its main box had just two

FIGURE 45-3 Eaton Fuller's Super Ten Top Two was introduced in 1994.

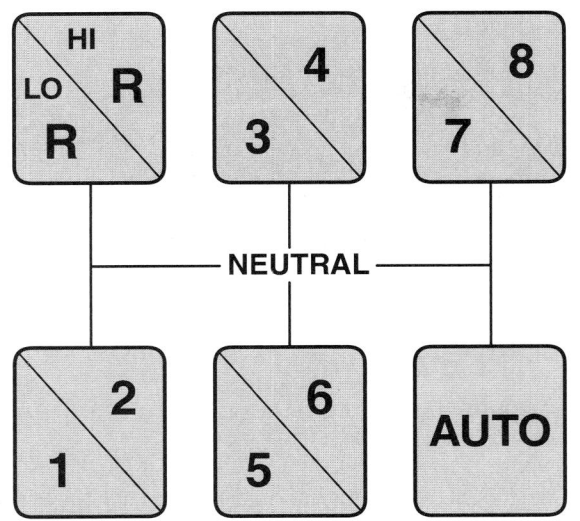

FIGURE 45-4 Super Ten Top Two shift pattern.

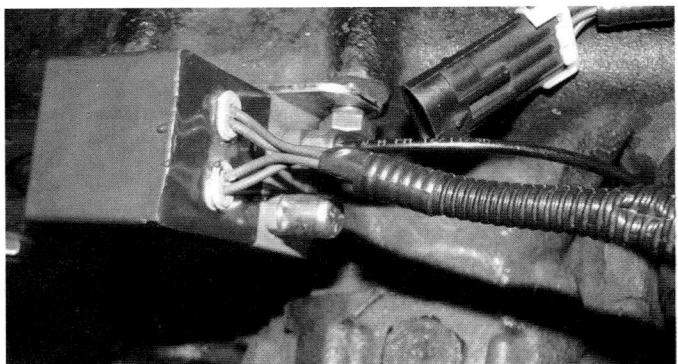

FIGURE 45-5 Top Two transmission's control module.

FIGURE 45-6 The Super Ten mainshaft has only two forward speed gears. **A.** Fourth gear. **B.** First gear. **C.** Reverse gear.

forward speed gears on the mainshaft—first- and fourth-speed gears only. That meant only three ratios were possible from the main box—low gear, fourth gear, and direct. The Super Ten mainshaft is shown in **FIGURE 45-6.**

The Super Ten transmission has a special shift mechanism that only moves two shift rails, even though the shift pattern remains traditional. Only the first/reverse and the fourth/direct

FIGURE 45-7 The shift rail of the Super Ten is arranged to reselect fourth gear mainshaft on the 5/6 to 7/8 shift. **A.** Fourth and fifth shift rail. **B.** First and reverse shift rail.

shift rail are moved in this transmission. The transmission also utilizes a four-speed auxiliary section. The shift pattern is a normal five-speed pattern, but the driver only must move through the pattern once to get to tenth gear. The driver can split each gear stick position with the splitter button.

To operate the transmission, the driver selects first gear, which engages the first gear mainshaft with the auxiliary section in low range low split. When an upshift is required, the driver moves the splitter to high split for second range. On the next upshift, the driver moves the splitter button back to low split and moves the stick to the third/fourth gear position. That stick shift engages the fourth gear in the main box, and the splitter moves back to low split again. The auxiliary is still in low range at this time. The driver then splits to high for fourth range. On the next upshift, the splitter button is again moved to low split and the gear stick is moved to the fifth/sixth gear position. Direct gear is selected in the main box. The splitter is back to low split for fifth range and then moved to high split for sixth range. On the next shift to seventh and eighth stick position, the driver splits back to low for seventh. Due to the special shift rail in the main box, however, the driver is actually reselecting the fourth gear position again in the main box. The shift rails for that gearing sequence are shown in **FIGURE 45-7.**

The ratio change occurs because, as the driver moves through neutral to the seventh–eighth shift gate, the shift rail contacts an air switch that causes an automatic range shift to high in the auxiliary section. That puts the driver in high range low split for seventh range. The auto range shift valve is shown in **FIGURE 45-8.**

As the driver continues to shift, he then splits to high split for eighth range. At that point, he can move to the auto position and let the Top Two technology take over shifting for ninth and tenth. Since the debut of the Super Ten, several Fuller Roadranger models have included the Top Two system, including 13- and 18-speed models.

The first fully automated standard transmission to hit the North American Market was the Eaton **AutoShift.** It was introduced in 1996/97 and featured the first generation of computer control. The AutoShift was a 10-speed model and had a standard dry double-disc clutch that was used only when starting

FIGURE 45-8 The auto range shift valve is actuated by the movement of the shift rail under the top cover. **A.** Actuating pin. **B.** Auto range shift valve. **C.** Mounting hole.

FIGURE 45-9 Eaton Fuller AutoShift 10-speed transmission.

from a standstill. Once the vehicle was moving, its transmission was capable of automatic shifting through the entire vehicle operating range—all the way to tenth gear and back down again, as necessary. **FIGURE 45-9** depicts an Eaton Fuller Auto-Shift 10-speed transmission. Note the orientation of the shift motors. Older generations had the rail select motor orientated on the right-hand side of the transmission. The present location on the left allows more room for complicated exhaust systems.

Since the debut of the AutoShift, Eaton Fuller has introduced several other models of automated transmissions ranging from six to 18 speeds and with or without clutch pedals. Eaton's latest automated transmission is the seven-speed Procision designed for the class 6 and 7 delivery truck market. This transmission is a dual wet-clutch transmission and is explained in greater detail in the Eaton Procision Automated Transmission section.

Meritor/ZF's Automated Transmissions

Meritor attempted to match Eaton's entry with a transmission model known as the **Engine Synchro Shift (ESS)** transmission. Although the driver still had to shift this transmission manually, the transmission's electronics allowed the engine speed to be manipulated during a shift. The shaft speed could be synchronized so that the clutch was only used for starting from a standstill.

Meritor then produced the **SureShift** line of transmissions, available in 9-, 10-, and 13-speeds. SureShift transmissions were electronics-over-air-actuated, three-pedal, fully automated transmissions. Meritor joined forces with ZF Friedrichshafen AG of Germany and produced ZF SureShift models of up to 16-speeds. Together, the two companies marketed the **Freedomline** of two-pedal automated transmissions available in both 12- and 16-speed models. All Freedomline transmissions used an air-operated clutch and shifting was controlled by the transmission computer. **FIGURE 45-10** shows a ZF/Meritor transmission from the Freedomline.

The partnership between ZF and Meritor dissolved in 2009. ZF now markets its transmissions directly to original equipment manufacturers (OEMs) in North America under their European names: the **AS-Tronic** series for light-, medium-, and heavy-duty applications; these are 12- and 16-speed two-pedal automated

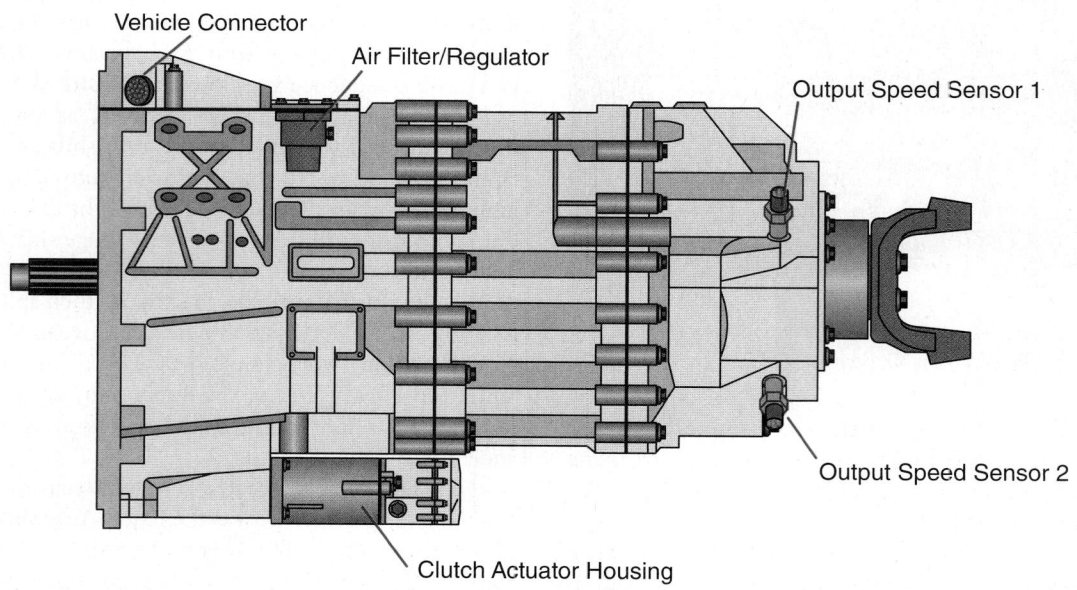

Vehicle Connector

Air Filter/Regulator

Output Speed Sensor 1

Output Speed Sensor 2

Clutch Actuator Housing

FIGURE 45-10 ZF/Meritor's Freedomline.

FIGURE 45-11 Traxon system with an optional hydraulic retarder called the ZF Intarder.

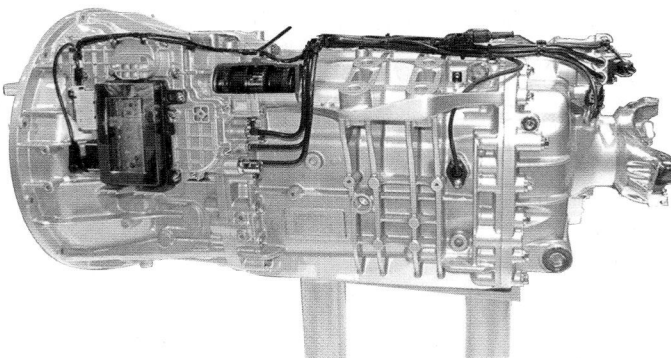

FIGURE 45-12 The Detroit Diesel DT-12 transmission.

FIGURE 45-13 Volvo I-Shift automated manual transmission.

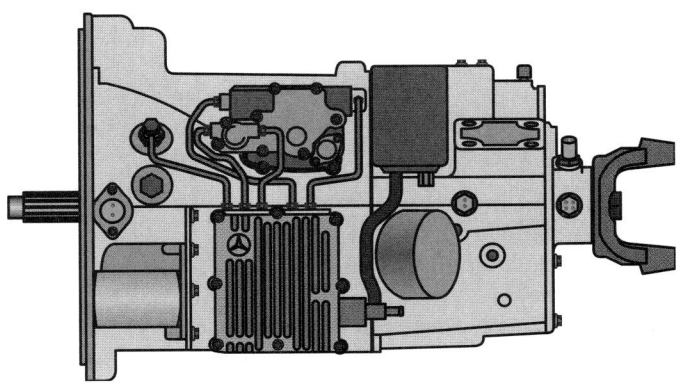

FIGURE 45-14 Daimler Trucks' AGS automated transmission.

transmissions. ZF also markets the torque converter-equipped **TC-Tronic** available with 12 speeds for extra-heavy-duty truck applications, although Europe is the primary market for these transmissions.

ZF now markets the latest version of the AS-Tronic, called the **Traxon** transmission, that has five optional input modules, a standard self-adjusting clutch, a dual-disc clutch, a torque converter module, an engine-driven power take-off (PTO) input module, and an electric traction motor that converts the system to a series hybrid. **FIGURE 45-11** shows a ZF Traxon transmission.

Detroit Diesel's DT-12

In 2013, Detroit Diesel released a transmission in the North American market called the **DT-12**, pictured in **FIGURE 45-12**. The DT-12 is a 12-speed automated transmission. It is the same transmission marketed by Mercedes in Europe in its Actros trucks. The design of the single countershaft transmission is very similar to that of the ZF transmission other than the missing second countershaft. The DT-12 system does not use a clutch pedal. Instead, the DT-12 relies on an air-actuated autoclutch. Shifting is accomplished by an electric solenoid over-air control system, which is also similar to the ZF control system.

Volvo Trucks' I-Shift

Volvo Trucks introduced the **I-Shift** automated transmission series in North America in 2004. As shown in **FIGURE 45-13**,

the I-Shift is a 12-speed, two-pedal design with electric-over-air actuation controlled by the TCU. The I-Shift is available in four models, including two with overdrive, and is capable of handling up to 2300 ft-lb (3118 Nm) of input torque.

Volvo's latest addition to its transmission line is the dual-clutch I-Shift. This 12-speed overdrive transmission has been available as an option in Volvo trucks in Europe since September 2014. It is similar to the Eaton Procision transmission with one key difference—the Volvo dual clutch uses two dry friction disc clutches instead of wet clutches.

Mercedes Benz's Automatic Gear Shift (AGS)

In 2004, Mercedes Benz, known in North America as Daimler Trucks, introduced the **Automatic Gear Shift (AGS)** two-pedal, six-speed automated transmission. The AGS was designed for medium-duty trucks with up to 60,000 lb (27,216 kg) gross vehicle weight (GVW). Shown in **FIGURE 45-14**, the AGS transmission uses an electronically controlled hydraulic clutch actuator for starting and stopping.

Operation of Automated Manual Transmissions

LO 45-2 Explain the operations of AMTs.

AMTs have unique operations and power flows compared to standard transmissions. And different makes and models of

AMTs operate differently from one another as well. This section covers the operation of the Eaton Fuller AutoShift, Ultra-Shift, Procision, and Endurant; the ZF AS-Tronic and Traxon; the Detroit Diesel DT-12; the Volvo I-Shift, dual clutch; and the Daimler AGS models.

Eaton Fuller AutoShift and UltraShift Operations

Eaton has two basic lines of AMTs available for the North American truck market. The three-pedal AutoShift line is now available in 10- and 18-speed models. The two-pedal **UltraShift** line is available in 5-, 6-, 9, 10-, 11-, 13-, 16-, and 18-speed models with either an electronically actuated clutch or a data mechanical (DM) clutch. DM clutches are operated centrifugally. The operating systems for the two lines are of such similar design that they are discussed together. The differences between each are highlighted.

The base transmission on each model is almost identical to a standard Eaton Fuller transmission. Additional components that make the transmission automated include:

- Transmission controller
- Shaft speed sensors
- Driver interface (electronic shifter)
- Start enable relay
- MEIIR (momentary engine ignition interrupt relay)
- Electric shift assembly, including the shift motors and the position sensors
- Electronically controlled range valve
- Electronically controlled splitter valve
- Inertia brakes
- Clutches used with electronically automated transmissions
- Shift strategies

Transmission Controller

The transmission control used with the first generation (Gen 1) of these transmissions consisted of a shift-control lever module, like that shown in **FIGURE 45-15A**, connected to a **system manager** ECU, comparable to that shown in **FIGURE 45-15B**. The system manager ECU was connected to the shift control ECU, like that shown in **FIGURE 45-15C**, on the transmission. Although the SAE recommended term for the transmission control is the TCM Eaton persists in calling it the transmission ECU so that term is used here.

In second generation (Gen 2) AutoShift transmissions, the system manager and the shift lever (or push-button pad) were combined. The number of electronic modules was reduced to two—one at the shift control and one at the transmission itself. Gen 1 transmissions communicated with the engine ECM over the J-1587 data link. Gen 2 models, launched in 1999, use the much faster **J-1939** data link for communication. The SAE J-1939 communication protocol features data transmission at a rate of at least 250,000 bits per second and up to 500,000 bits/second.

Shift initiation is handled by the shift control module at the driver interface. The shift control can be either push-button or lever-type. The controller communicates with the engine ECM to request a torque break to allow the shift. Shifts are initiated based on

FIGURE 45-15 First generation Eaton AMTs had three electronic modules: **A.** The shift control. **B.** The system manager. **C.** The transmission electronic control unit.

engine rpm and load factors. The transmission software basically monitors engine rpm and predicts an expected rpm decrease during the shift, identifying a target rpm at which to select the next gear.

If the engine rpm does not decrease quickly enough, the software can wait or initiate slowing the engine or the gearing with either the engine brake or an inertia brake, if one is installed. When the rpm falls to the target rpm of the shift, the shift controller tells the transmission controller to make the shift. The Eaton Ultrashift transmission uses sliding clutches with wider tooth spacing to make shifting easier and faster. Upon completion of the shift, the engine ECM resumes normal rpm control.

As more and more shifts are initiated, the transmission shift control learns the predictable rpm drop and responds accordingly. The driver can also request shifts to occur by pushing the push buttons on the shift controller or operating the transmission in the hold mode. The software then only shifts when requested by the driver.

The generation 3 (Gen 3) software, introduced in 2006, has only one module. As shown in **FIGURE 45-16**, it is mounted on the transmission. The driver interface is merely a series of switches that input to the controller, but the shift process is similar to previous generations.

The software has advanced with each generation. Gen 3 software is capable of **adaptive learning**, meaning that the software can learn and change strategy based on different factors. The software also has several pre-programmed operating modes for performance and fuel economy. The transmission control learns the terrain, the load, and the driving style of the driver and constantly adapts the shift strategies on the fly.

The ECU has self-diagnostic capabilities. It logs diagnostic trouble codes (DTCs) and produces a data **snapshot** of each incident. A data snapshot records all the relevant ECU data before and after a DTC is set to ease diagnoses. The controller is programmed to protect the transmission by prohibiting driver-initiated shifts that may damage the transmission, such as high-speed direction changes, high rpm shifts from neutral to range, or shifts that place the engine outside of its normal rpm operating range. The controller also has a fallback strategy that actuates when a problem is detected. Fallback strategies include shift inhibits, hold in gear, down shift to last held gear, and many others. Each fallback strategy permits failsafe, but limited, operation, if necessary.

Shaft Speed Sensors

For clash-free shifts to occur, the transmission control software must know the precise speed of the input shaft, the countershaft, the mainshaft gears, and the mainshaft itself.

The transmission has three speed sensors, like those shown in **FIGURE 45-17**, to accomplish this. The input speed sensor is at the front right corner of the transmission shift cover and targets the upper countershaft PTO gear. When the speed of the countershaft and the transmission ratios are known, the software can calculate the input shaft speed and the mainshaft gear speeds.

The mainshaft speed sensor is located at the left rear side of the transmission shift cover and targets the upper auxiliary countershaft driven gear. The mainshaft speed sensor monitors the speed of the auxiliary countershaft and sends that information to the transmission ECU. In turn, the transmission ECU can calculate the speed of the mainshaft and of the sliding clutches used to engage the mainshaft gears. The ECU uses all that information to tell the engine ECM to synchronize the speeds to perform a clash-proof shift.

The output speed sensor is positioned in the output shaft bearing support housing. The output speed sensor targets a tone wheel mounted on the shaft. The ECU uses this sensor to detect output shaft speed and confirm that shifts have been made.

Driver Interface

The driver shift control in Gen 1 and 2 software versions contained an electronic module responsible for shift scheduling while the transmission ECU handled the shifting. In Gen 3, these modules have been combined into a single module located on the transmission. The drivers shift control can be push-button or lever style. Single-module Gen 3 transmission ECUs require only a series of switches for driver input. The design of the switches varies depending on the OEM. **FIGURE 45-18** shows a transmission shift control from Freightliner.

Every shift control, regardless of the OEM, has several components to it. Each control has a display that alerts the driver to gear range and shifting status and also displays DTCs. The display can be integral to or remotely mounted from the shift control. The display indicates to the driver what gear the transmission is in.

FIGURE 45-16 The Eaton Gen 3 electronics are reduced to one small module mounted on the transmission.

FIGURE 45-17 The AutoShift and UltraShift transmissions have three speed sensors that input shaft speed information to the transmission ECU. **A.** Output shaft speed sensor. **B.** Mainshaft speed sensor. **C.** Input shaft speed sensor.

During a shift, the display indicates the target range as a solid number. As the transmission shifts to neutral, the target range starts flashing. Once the shift completes, the range number goes back to being solid. The control has up and down buttons for driver-initiated shifts and usually has five positions or push-button choices—R for reverse, N for neutral, D for drive, M for manual, and L for low range. Drive is the position used for fully automatic operation. Selecting M causes the transmission to remain in the current gear range. In manual, the driver can initiate shifts by using the up and down buttons. Selecting low when decelerating allows the transmission to downshift at the highest rpm for each range, giving maximum engine braking.

The driver can also use the up or down arrows in drive to select a different start-up gear than the one selected by the software. The control usually has a service light to alert the driver to transmission malfunctions. Some UltraShift transmission installations use an OEM-supplied shift control that may differ from the Eaton type. OEM shift controls are either resistive ladder-type controllers or J-1939 controllers. J-1939 controllers have communication capabilities and can interface directly with the transmission ECU. The transmission controller also uses multiplexing to communicate with all other vehicle modules through the controller area network (CAN) bus line.

Start Enable Relay

The **start enable relay** is an OEM-supplied relay usually mounted in the dash that is controlled by the transmission ECU. The start enable relay interrupts the circuit to the starter solenoid when it is not activated, preventing the vehicle from starting. When the driver turns on the key, the ECU through an initiation and self-check process. Next the ECU checks for neutral. When it has verified the transmission is in a neutral position, it turns on the start enable relay, allowing the vehicle's engine to be started. The ECU only turns on the start enable relay after the system initiation completes and it has verified that the transmission is not in any gear and that the transmission is, in fact, in neutral.

MEIIR Momentary Engine Ignition Interrupt Relay

The **momentary engine ignition interrupt relay (MEIIR)** is a relay supplied by the OEM and usually installed in the dash.

This relay is only supplied when the vehicle has an UltraShift transmission with a DM clutch. The relay is controlled by the transmission ECU and it interrupts the engine ignition (or fuel supply on diesel engines) in the event of a catastrophic failure of the DM clutch. In certain instances, a failure can occur that may cause the DM clutch to fail to disengage. The interruption of fueling or ignition by the MEIIR is designed to break torque to allow the transmission shift mechanism to pull to neutral. The relay is activated when the following occurs:

- When the driver has selected neutral
- When neutral is not achieved
- After 2.5 seconds have passed since the driver selected neutral
- When engine rpm is greater than 850 or when engine torque is more than 200 ft-lb (271 Nm)
- When the vehicle has an active J1939 fault

When these conditions are met, the ECU activates the relay, momentarily shutting off engine ignition/fueling to break torque to allow the shift control to pull to neutral. If neutral is not achieved, the system activates the relay again and again until the conditions no longer exist.

Electric Shift Assembly

The **electric shift assembly** consists of two shift motors: the shift finger and the shift finger position sensors. The shift motors perform the actual gear selection inside the AutoShift or UltraShift main box. There are two of these motors mounted on the top of the transmission shift cover. When shifting a normal standard transmission, the driver moves the shift lever in one of four different directions—left, right, backward, or forward. The twin shift control motors are responsible for moving the shift finger left to right along the shift shaft to select the correct shift rail and forward and back to select the desired gear. This mechanism is shown in **FIGURE 45-19**.

In a standard transmission, there is a shift finger at the bottom of the shift lever that engages one of the three shift rails when the lever is moved left to right. Each shift rail controls the position of one shift fork inside the transmission. Shift rail gates are shown in **FIGURE 45-20**. The shift fork engages with a sliding clutch that locks one gear to the transmission mainshaft, depending on whether the driver moves the lever forward or

FIGURE 45-18 Gen 3 shift control from Freightliner.

FIGURE 45-19 Shift finger and shift shaft in electric shift assembly.

FIGURE 45-20 Three shift rail gates. **A.** Left. **B.** Center. **C.** Right.

FIGURE 45-21 **A.** Shift rail nut. **B.** Recirculating ball tube.

back. The right rail moves the first and reverse shift fork. The center rail moves the second and third shift fork. The left rail moves the fourth and fifth gear shift fork.

In the Eaton AMT, the two shift motors accomplish the same thing. A shift finger is mounted on a shift shaft. One motor moves the shift finger left to right to select the correct rail. It is called the rail select motor. The other motor moves the shift finger forward and back to select the correct gear. It is called the gear select motor.

The motors are reversible DC motors, and both drive a worm shaft that controls the position of a recirculating ball nut. This type of nut is used because it provides very smooth and precise movement and longevity. A recirculating ball nut has a series of ball bearings running in the groove of the worm shaft. When in use, the bearings complete several circuits around the shaft. Their circuit is determined by the width of the ball nut. The bearings are returned to the beginning of the ball nut by a tube attached to the nut. The recirculating ball nuts move the shift finger from side to side and front to back to complete a shift. **FIGURE 45-21** shows a recirculating ball nut and the recirculating balls.

The electric shift assembly on earlier model AutoShift transmissions was oriented with the rail motor mounted laterally. The body of the motor protruded to the right side of the transmission case and the gear select motor protruded toward the front of the transmission. In contrast, Gen 3 AutoShift transmissions are oriented with the rail motor protruding toward the left side of the transmission case to allow more room for the installation of exhaust components on the right side.

Position Sensors

The precise positioning of the shift finger is essential to proper operation of an AMT. Therefore, two position sensors are used—the rail select position sensor and the gear select position sensor. Both sensors are shown in **FIGURE 45-22**. The rail select motor moves the shift finger left to right. The gear select motor moves the shift finger forward and back. In both cases, the travel distance is just over an inch (2.54 cm) in total, so exacting control is necessary.

The two position sensors are Hall Effect sensors that produce a digital signal and send it to the transmission ECU. Every time the transmission is powered down, the shift motors and

FIGURE 45-22 Position sensors provide extremely accurate shift finger position data to the transmission electronic control unit. **A.** Gear position sensor. **B.** Rail position sensor.

the position sensors work in concert to map the shift gate area. First, the sensors move across the gate to measure total distance from the left shift rail to the right shift rail. Next, the sensors push against the shift rail interlocks by trying to move the center and the right rail together, forward and back, and then by trying to move the center and the left-side shift rail together, forward and back. This recalibration procedure gives the transmission ECU a precise map of exactly where the gates and the rails are. Once the procedure is complete, the transmission is ready for the next power up and drive cycle. **FIGURE 45-23** illustrates the sequence of the recalibration process.

Electronically Controlled Range Valve

AutoShift and UltraShift models with 10 or more forward ranges have an auxiliary section and can be operated in high or low range, depending on the operating conditions. Shifting between high and low range is done pneumatically and was explained in the Standard Transmissions chapter. In the AutoShift and UltraShift models, the shifting is controlled by the transmission ECU.

The range cylinder cover is modified to accept an electrically operated air-control solenoid valve, as shown in **FIGURE 45-24**. The **air-control solenoid valve** has two electric solenoid valves that control the flow of air from the air filter/pressure regulator to the range cylinder piston. That is, the two electric solenoids direct air to the low- and high-range side of the cylinder piston

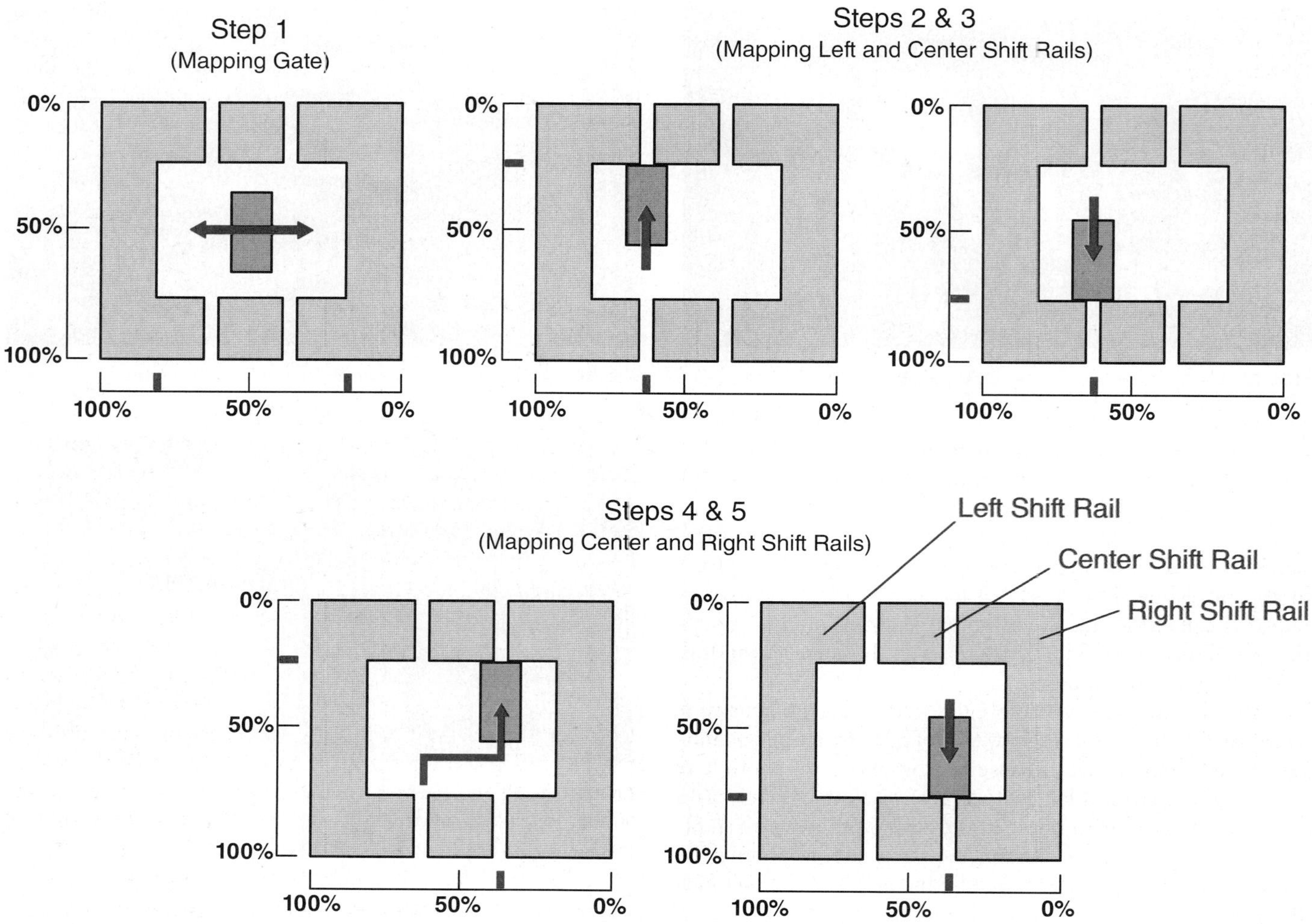

Step 1
(Mapping Gate)

0%

50%

100%

100%   50%   0%

Steps 2 & 3
(Mapping Left and Center Shift Rails)

0%

50%

100%

100%   50%   0%

0%

50%

100%

100%   50%   0%

Steps 4 & 5
(Mapping Center and Right Shift Rails)

0%

50%

100%

100%   50%   0%

Left Shift Rail
Center Shift Rail
Right Shift Rail

0%

50%

100%

100%   50%   0%

FIGURE 45-23 The recalibration procedure is performed on every system power down so the controller is ready to shift on the next drive cycle.

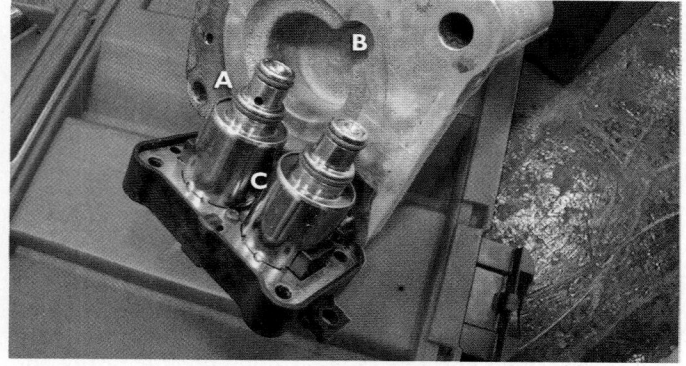

FIGURE 45-24 Electric solenoids in a range cylinder. **A.** Low-range port. **B.** High-range port. **C.** Solenoid pack.

as required by the control unit. The regulator holds the pressure between approximately 58 and 63 psi (400 and 434 kPa).

The operation of these valves is rather simple. To achieve low range, the transmission ECU energizes the low solenoid. Doing so allows air to flow to the front side of the range cylinder piston. The piston and its attached yoke move rearward to engage the low-range gear. The air behind the piston exhausts through the high-range solenoid.

When a shift to high range is required, the ECU de-energizes the low-range solenoid and energizes the high-range solenoid. Doing so exhausts air from the low side of the range cylinder piston through the low-range solenoid. Pressurized air is directed to the back of the piston, forcing it and the yoke forward. High range is then engaged.

Electronically Controlled Splitter Valve

On AutoShift and UltraShift models with more than ten forward speeds, there is a splitter cylinder that controls the position of the splitter sliding clutch. Recall that the splitter shift was discussed in the Standard Transmissions chapter. Review that chapter as needed to fully understand the operation of the splitter shift.

In AMTs, the splitter cylinder cover has been modified to hold the splitter shift solenoids. The splitter shift solenoids are electric solenoid over air control valves, are controlled by the transmission ECU, and are identical to the valves used for the range control. The ECU controls the solenoids to direct air supplied from the air filter/pressure regulator to send air to one or the other side of the splitter cylinder. Sending pressurized air to the front of the splitter cylinder piston engages the high split position and sending air to the rear of the splitter cylinder engages the low split position.

Inertia Brake

Medium-duty AutoShift and UltraShift transmissions and earlier heavy-duty UltraShift transmissions use an **inertia brake** to slow the rotational speed of the gears inside the transmission while shifting from neutral to reverse or a forward range. Slowing the gearing helps prevent gear clash. As shown in **FIGURE 45-25**, inertia brakes are typically mounted on the lower power take-off opening of the transmission.

The inertia brake can also be used to assist in gaining synchronicity of the transmission shafts and gears during upshift events. Quickly synchronizing shafts and gear speeds allows for slightly faster shift times. Fuller claims that an 18-speed UltraShift

FIGURE 45-25 The inertia brake mounts on the lower PTO opening of the transmission.

transmission can shift through all its gear ranges while pulling 160,000 lb (72,575 kg) on a 15% grade by using the inertia brake during upshifts. While climbing a hill under heavy load, the transmission mainshaft can slow faster than the engine and the mainshaft gears due to the loading. The inertia brake can reduce the mainshaft gear rpm more quickly, allowing faster shifts. Even the most skilled driver would be hard pressed to match such a feat.

The inertia brake is attached to the lower left side of the case. The brake's gear engages the lower main box countershaft. As illustrated in **FIGURE 45-26**, inside the brake are two rotating ramps separated by steel balls called the ball ramp. An electro-magnetic coil and a friction clutch pack are attached to the gear, so the gear rotates with the countershaft.

The electromagnetically operated ball ramp in the inertia brake assembly applies pressure to the friction plates to slow the transmission gearing. The transmission ECU actuates the inertia brake by energizing the electromagnetic coil. This slows one half of the ball ramp, which causes the balls to roll up the ramps. As the balls roll upward, the forward ramp is forced against the friction clutch pack. The gear slows and, because it is splined to the countershaft, both the countershaft and the transmission gearing are slowed. The ECU then, can speed up the synchronization process and, therefore, make the upshift more quickly.

Newer model UltraShift heavy-duty transmissions use an electronic clutch actuator (ECA). This allows the use of what is known as a low-capacity inertia brake. Instead of an inertia brake mounted on the countershaft, a large inertia brake is installed on the input shaft between the clutch release bearing and the transmission front bearing cover. Notice in **FIGURE 45-27** that the location is where a clutch brake used to be.

The low-capacity inertia brake serves the same purpose as a clutch brake. That is, the inertia brake stops the rotating gearing while the transmission is shifting into first or reverse gears.

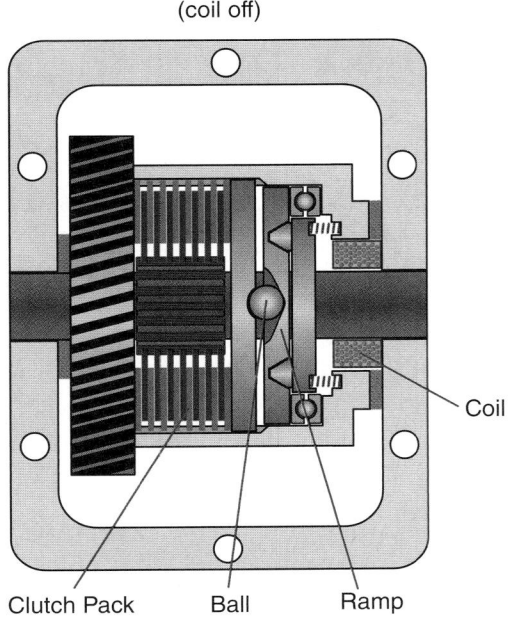
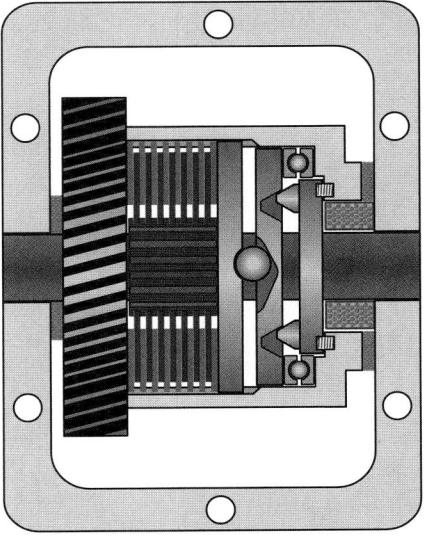

FIGURE 45-26 An inertia brake assembly.

FIGURE 45-27 Inertia brake in a new UltraShift transmission. **A.** Release fork. **B.** Inertia brake. **C.** Electronic clutch actuator. **D.** Release bearing.

FIGURE 45-28 Eaton SOLO self-adjusting clutch.

The low-capacity inertia brake can also be used during upshifts, when warranted by the operation of the vehicle. The ECA is not normally used while shifting, but in certain operating conditions it is utilized to increase the speed of upshifts.

Clutches Used with AutoShift and UltraShift AMTs

Four different clutches are used by Eaton Fuller in its AutoShift and UltraShift lines of electronically automated transmissions: SOLO, data mechanical, electronically actuated SOLO, and wet clutch.

The SOLO self-adjusting clutch is the only manually actuated clutch supplied with the AutoShift line of transmissions. SOLO clutches used with the AutoShift are three-pedal systems. They have a clutch pedal, which the driver must use when starting off shifting from neutral to reverse or forward only. The rest of the shifting is handled automatically by the transmission. **FIGURE 45-28** shows an Eaton SOLO self-adjusting clutch. The latest models of these clutches from Eaton are known as the Advantage Self-Adjust clutch and have several improvements over the original SOLO clutches.

The DM clutch is centrifugally applied by increasing engine rpm and is used with both medium- and heavy-duty models of the UltraShift line of transmissions. DM clutches use a two-pedal system with no clutch pedal. Four centrifugal weights apply the DM clutch as engine rpm increases; as the weights move out, they push against ramps built into the back of the pressure plate, which creates the clamp load. **FIGURE 45-29** shows the four weights in a DM clutch.

The DM clutch starts engagement at approximately 800 to 850 rpm. From there, it ramps up to full clamp load at approximately 1350 rpm. On disengagement, full clamp load remains until rpm has dropped to approximately 900 rpm. At that point, the clutch starts to release. By the time approximately 800 rpm is reached, the clutch is fully released.

▶ **TECHNICIAN TIP**

The DM clutch can be subject to abuse by an unskilled driver. If the driver tries to hold the vehicle on an incline by feathering the throttle to around 800 to 850 rpm, the clutch constantly slips and burns out in very little time. As always, proper driving training is essential with any new system.

FIGURE 45-29 A. Centrifugal weights and rollers in a DM clutch. **B.** Pressure plate. **C.** Ramps.

FIGURE 45-30 Eaton's electronically actuated clutch. **A.** Inertia brake. **B.** Clutch fork. **C.** Actuator.

The third type of clutch used on two-pedal models of Eaton Fuller AMT models is called an electronic clutch actuation device. An example is shown in **FIGURE 45-30**. An electronically actuated clutch contains an electronic module with an integrated electric stepper motor to operate a standard SOLO clutch. Because these transmissions are two-pedal models, there is no clutch pedal. Typically, the system only operates the clutch when starting from a standstill or when stopping. However, the transmission may occasionally activate the clutch during shifting to aid in synchronization. This is similar to the double-clutching technique discussed in the Heavy-Duty Clutches chapter.

Eaton Fuller Transmission Nomenclature

As a technician, it is important that you be able to decipher the nomenclature for the transmissions you will be working on. TABLES 45-1, 45-2, and 45-3 will help you decipher the nomenclature on Eaton Fuller 6-speed, 10-speed, and 13-speed transmissions.

As the company's line of transmissions has become more varied, new nomenclature is now used to reflect the variety of models available. TABLE 45-4 contains an example of Eaton Fuller's new nomenclature. The specific changes to Eaton Fuller's new nomenclature include the following:

- "E" or "F" has been added to the prefix to identify the brand as "Eaton" or "Fuller."
- "M" has been added to the prefix to identify this transmission is approved for use with multitorque engines.
- Configuration denotes the type of clutch the transmission uses. Configurations include:
  - D—Dry mechanical
  - E—Electronic clutch actuator
  - S—Wet shifting clutch
- The design level is now a combination of the gear box design and automation platform.
- The final suffix contains the application and value code. The application and value codes include:
  - L—Line-haul
  - H—Highway (and High in 2nd position)
  - P—Performance (and PTO in 2nd position)

- S—Severe duty
- ST—Standard
- V—Vocational (and Value in 2nd position)
- M—Multipurpose (and Mixer in 2nd position)
- C—Construction
- X—Extreme duty
- R—Recreational (motor home)
- G—Generator
- P—PTO
- U—Utility
- E—Efficient

Shifting Strategies

As with any new development in the automotive world, the switch to automated transmissions has been driven primarily by the need to meet increasingly stringent emission standards. AMTs help to achieve new standards by being more fuel efficient than their standard transmission predecessors.

Of course, to the fleet owner, fuel is the most expensive part of the daily operation. Improvements of 3% to 7% better fuel economy are very welcome. In fact, the significant savings help to offset the higher initial expense of an AMT.

Shifting strategies for every conceivable vocation for these transmissions have been developed to ensure that performance and fuel economy are optimized. The primary strategy is progressive shifting because it gives the best economy. For different vocations, however, more aggressive shift patterns are desired.

The transmission ECU can be programmed to allow a range of shift strategies, depending on the requirement. Most

TABLE 45-1 Nomenclature for Six-Speed FO-6406B-DM3

F	X-	X	4	06	X-	DM	3
Fuller	Overdrive, if present	Input torque × 100	Design level	Forward speeds	Gear ratio	Automated with DM clutch	Gen 3 electronics

TABLE 45-2 Nomenclature for 10-Speed RTO-16910A-DM3

R	T	O	IX	9	10	X	DM	3
Roadranger	Twin countershaft	Overdrive	Input torque × 100	Design level	Forward speeds	Gear ratio	Automated with DM clutch	Gen 3 electronics

TABLE 45-3 Nomenclature for 13-Speed RTLOM-16913A-DM3

RT	L	O	M	IX	9	13	X	DM	3
Roadranger twin	Low inertia	Overdrive	Multitorque 1750 ft-lb (2373 Nm) in top two gears only	Input torque × 100	Design level	Forward speeds	Ratio	Automated with DM clutch	Gen 3 electronics

TABLE 45-4 Nomenclature for UltraShift FOM-15D310B-LST

F	O	M	15	D	3	10	B	LST
Brand Eaton or Fuller	Overdrive	Multitorque	Input torque × 100	Clutch configuration	Design level	Forward speeds	Ratio	Application and value

transmission ECUs in use today are capable of sensing engine load, vehicle weight, and road grade or incline. The transmission ECUs monitor the fueling demand and other parameters over the J-1939 CAN bus line and adjust shifting strategies based on this information. The ability to change shifting as needed optimizes performance and fuel economy.

All AMTs have a manual shift mode that allows the driver complete control over shift points when required. Still, failsafe fallback modes exist to compensate for driver error, for example, if the engine is being lugged or running overspeed, the transmission controller initiates a shift to protect the engine.

AMTs are becoming increasingly popular. As their software becomes more sophisticated, it will become nearly impossible to find a driver capable of shifting with the skill and accuracy of an AMT while still reaching fuel economy targets. Today's AMTs have software that is fully interactive with the engine ECM and the other ECUs on the vehicle. This interaction allows features, such as, "Hill hold," which uses the vehicle ABS to ensure smooth starts without any roll back on slopes; "Urge to move," when the driver releases the foot brake the vehicle starts to move similar to an automatic car transmission; "Neutral coasting," allows the transmission to switch to neutral on downhill runs, slowing engine rpm to save fuel. Creep mode allows the vehicle to be maneuvered at extremely low speeds.

The latest systems are also using Model Predictive Control or MPC (MPC is fully discussed in the Understanding and Servicing Electronic Control Systems chapter). MPC allows the transmission controller to use predictive shifting based on model observations. Using MPC allows the transmission controller to adjust shift timing; skip shifting, when appropriate, based on learned load and terrain; vary clutch application pressures to facilitate smooth start off; use prediction for upshifting and downshifting to preserve driver safety and comfort; and to protect the cargo. The controller interacts with the cruise control system to predictively optimize shifting to enhance fuel economy. The model that the transmission controller uses constantly learns as the vehicle goes through its drive cycles and predicts the best possible shift strategies, making up for slight efficiency changes as the powertrain system wears or ages, such as clutch actuator, shift solenoid, or shift motor degradation.

Eaton Procision Dual-Clutch Automated Transmission

LO 45-3 Explain the operation of dual-clutch transmissions.

In September 2014, Eaton Fuller announced the addition of the new seven-speed **Procision**, a fully automated, dual-clutch transmission for the class 6 and 7 truck market. The transmission has been available in North America since early 2015.

Dual-clutch transmissions are not a new development. They have been used with great success in the automotive market since the early 1980s. There are two basic types of dual-clutch transmissions available. The first is a twin friction disc clutch design utilizing two separate friction clutches. The second type uses two hydraulically applied multi-plate wet clutches in a single rotating housing.

In both types, one of the clutches inputs a solid primary input shaft and the second clutch inputs a hollow secondary input shaft. The gearing is usually arranged so that odd-numbered gears are driven by the solid input shaft. Even-numbered gears are driven by the hollow secondary input shaft. This arrangement allows the transmission controller to engage the next gear before the shift occurs. To change to the next gear, the controller simply has to disengage one clutch and apply the other. The result is much smoother and faster shifting with no torque break losses. In normal automated transmissions, torque is broken to allow the shift and then reapplied—this wastes fuel. Eliminating torque break, therefore, leads to better fuel economy.

Volkswagen uses this type of transmission and calls it a direct shift gearbox (DSG). The advantage of these transmissions becomes apparent when you realize that a driver shifting a standard transmission must break torque by disengaging the clutch. That action uses approximately half a second, or 500 milliseconds, to complete the shift. An automated transmission improves that shift speed and the corresponding break in torque by 80% by shifting in approximately 100 milliseconds. The DSG dual-clutch transmission can shift in as little as 8 milliseconds with no torque break required.

The Eaton Procision transmission, shown in **FIGURE 45-31**, is capable of similar shifting speeds. The shifts occur under power (without torque break), and the transmission does not use a torque converter. For those reasons, Eaton claims on its website that the Procision transmission can achieve an 8% to 10% improvement in fuel economy over an automatic transmission when installed in a vehicle used for around-town deliveries.

Eaton Procision Operation

The Eaton Procision uses the second arrangement for a dual-clutch transmission. That is, the Procision has a dual-clutch module that contains the primary and secondary clutches. The dual clutch module is driven directly by a torsional damper bolted to the engine flywheel. **FIGURE 45-32** shows the dual-clutch module and the attached hydraulic pump drive gear.

The two clutches—one in front of the other in the rotating housing—drive two input shafts. The front clutch drives the hollow (secondary) input shaft, and the rear clutch drives the solid (primary) input shaft. The dual-clutch module rides

FIGURE 45-31 The Procision transmission from Eaton.

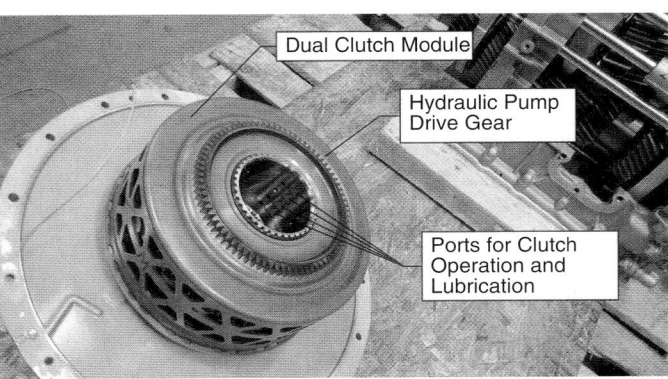

FIGURE 45-32 Each of the dual clutches drive one input shaft for the Procision.

FIGURE 45-33 The dual-clutch module rides on two roller bearings on the clutch support manifold.

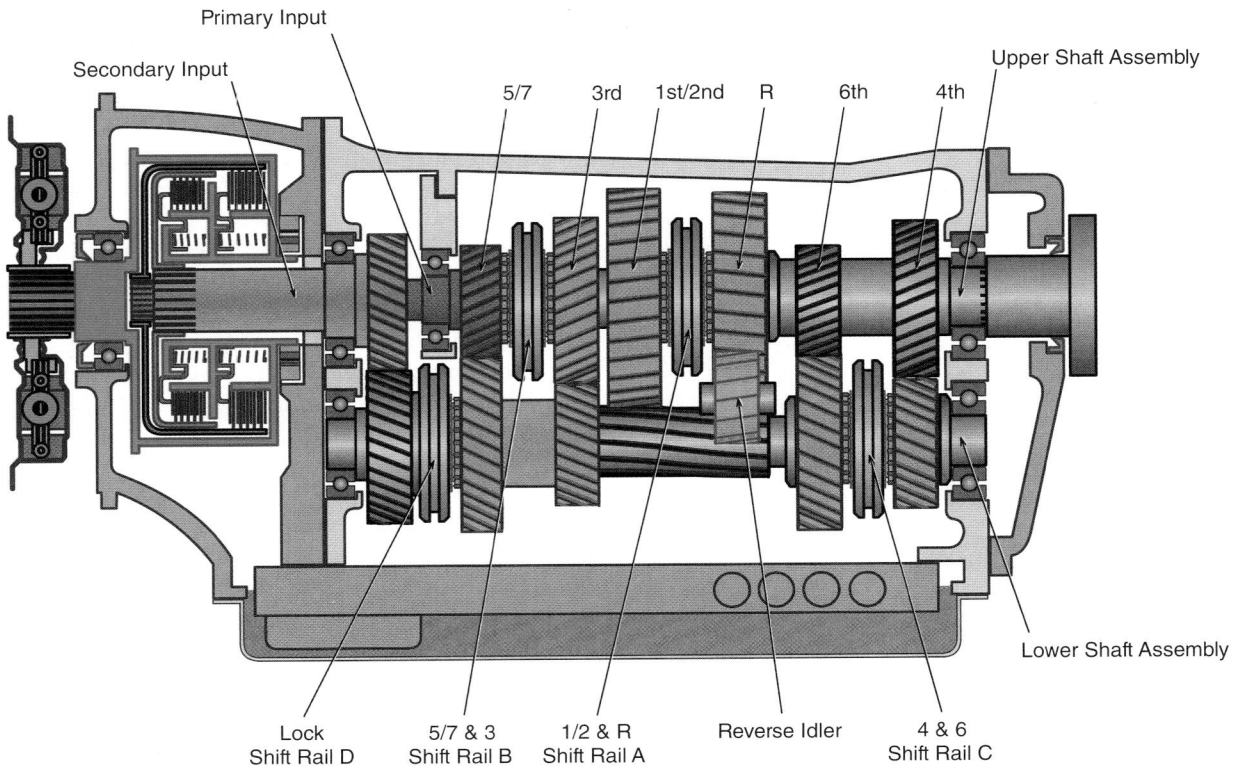

FIGURE 45-34 The dual-clutch transmission does not use traditional mainshafts and countershafts, rather it uses an upper shaft and a lower shaft.

on two straight roller bearings on the clutch support manifold, which also contains hydraulic passageways to cool, lubricate, and actuate the clutches. **FIGURE 45-33** shows the two input shafts and the hydraulic pump-driven gear and the dual-clutch support manifold.

Inside the transmission, then, are five shafts: the primary input shaft, the secondary input shaft, the main or output shaft (known as the upper shaft in this transmission), the lower shaft (because the transmission uses both the upper and lower shafts to select gears, the term countershaft is not used), and the reverse idler shaft. **FIGURE 45-34** depicts a cutaway view of the transmission—refer to this diagram to view the internal components.

The Procision transmission has four synchronizers, the lock synchronizer on the lower shaft, which locks the cluster gear to the lower shaft; the fifth/seventh and third synchronizer on the upper shaft; the first/second and reverse synchronizer, also on the upper shaft; and, finally, the sixth and fourth synchronizer on the lower shaft. The secondary input shaft inputs to the forward input gear, which is in constant mesh with the front lower shaft-driven gear. Because the front lower shaft-driven gear is fixed to the shaft, they always turn together. The primary input shaft's input gear is again in constant mesh with a cluster gear on the lower shaft. That cluster gear, however, is not fixed to the countershaft. To connect this gear to the lower shaft, the lock synchronizer, which is splined to the lower shaft, must be moved rearward to engage the clutching teeth on the cluster gear.

The next synchronizer shift mechanism is on the upper shaft. This synchronizer is moved rearward to engage third gear and forward for both fifth and seventh gears. Fifth gear in this transmission is direct. The next synchronizer is again on the upper shaft and moves rearward to engage reverse and forward for both first and second gears. The fourth and final synchronizer is on the lower shaft and moves rearward for fourth and forward for sixth gear.

The Procision has two oil pumps; a high-pressure gear pump and a high-flow gerotor pump. Both pumps are driven by the same shaft, which, in turn, is driven by a gear on the back of the rotating clutch module so that hydraulic pressure is available as soon as the engine is running. **FIGURE 45-35** shows the two pumps. The pumps are not individually serviceable and must be replaced as a unit.

Movement of the shift mechanisms and clutch operation is controlled hydraulically with pressure supplied by the high-pressure gear pump, while the transmission lubrication and cooling system is served by the high-flow gerotor pump.

FIGURE 45-35 Both the high-pressure gear and the low-pressure high-flow gerotor pump are driven by the same shaft.

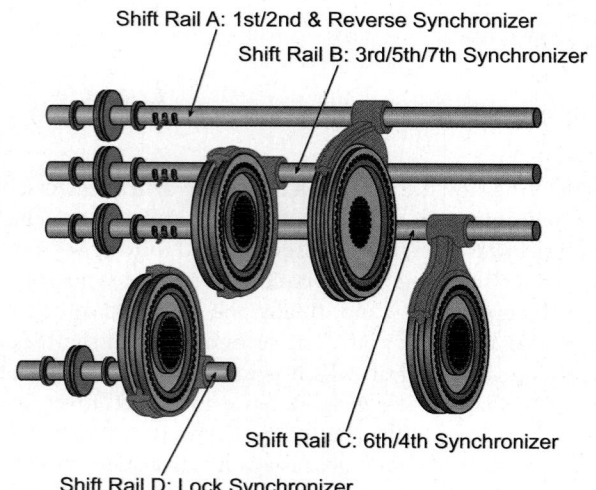

Shift Rail A: 1st/2nd & Reverse Synchronizer
Shift Rail B: 3rd/5th/7th Synchronizer
Shift Rail C: 6th/4th Synchronizer
Shift Rail D: Lock Synchronizer

FIGURE 45-36 The shift rails are operated by hydraulic pressure.

The transmission gearing is a departure from what technicians are used to seeing. Whereas, all the gears are fixed to the countershaft on most countershaft transmissions, the Procision lower shaft contains only two fixed gears. In the Procision, only the front lower shaft driven gear and the first and reverse lower shaft gears always turn with the lower shaft. The rear lower shaft driven gear is a cluster gear—two gears together—and is free to rotate on the lower shaft when it is unlocked. This two-gear block is locked to the countershaft only when the lock synchronizer is in the rearward position. Fourth gear and sixth gear are also not fixed to the lower shaft unless they are locked to it by the fourth–sixth synchronizer.

The mainshaft in this transmission is also an anomaly. In most transmissions, all the mainshaft gears are free to rotate around the mainshaft unless they are locked to it by a synchronizer or sliding clutch/collar, whereas, in the Procision transmission, the fourth and sixth mainshaft gears are fixed to the mainshaft and always turn with it, this is why the term upper shaft is used instead of mainshaft. Reverse, first, and third gear on the upper shaft are free to rotate around the shaft unless they are locked to it by the 3rd/5th/7th synchronizer or the 1st/2nd reverse synchronizer. This type of gearing arrangement, using both the upper and lower shafts to engage gears, is essential for dual-clutch transmissions to operate. The Procision has four shift rails, one for each of the four synchronizers. Shift rail A controls the 1st/2nd and reverse synchronizer, shift rail B controls the 3rd/5th/7th synchronizer, shift rail C controls the 6th/4th synchronizer, and shift rail D controls the lock synchronizer. The shift rail positions are operated by hydraulic pressure. **FIGURE 45-36** shows the shift rails.

Shift Control

Shifting and clutch operation is controlled by the **actuation control manifold (ACM)**, the valve body that holds all the control solenoids and valves. The Procision has 11 solenoids and 8 valves that are used to control the transmissions shifting, clutch actuation, and system cooling and lubrication. **FIGURE 45-37** shows the ACM.

Five solenoids are pulse-width-modulated solenoids that control pressures in the transmission. Two shift pressure solenoids, SPS1 and SPS2, control the pressure that moves the shift rails. The pressure control primary solenoid (PCPS) controls the primary clutch application pressure. The pressure control secondary solenoid (PCSS) controls the secondary clutch application pressure. The line pressure solenoid (LPS) controls the pressure in the high- and low-pressure hydraulic circuits. The shift rail positions are controlled by four valves and the position of the valves are controlled by four solenoids. The rail valve solenoids are on/off solenoids that are operated by the TCM to position the shift rails by moving the rail shift valves. Rail A valve solenoid (RAVS), rail B valve solenoid (RBVS), RCVS, and RDVS. The other solenoids and valves in the ACM are used to control cooling and lubrication circuits. **FIGURE 45-38** shows the schematic of the Procision hydraulic control circuits. Along with the solenoids and valves, the transmission also has a position sensor for each of the four shift rails. The transmission uses

FIGURE 45-37 The ACM contains all of the solenoids and valves that control the operation of the Procision.

four speed sensors. The secondary input speed sensor reads off the secondary input gear. The primary input speed sensor reads off the primary input gear. The engine speed sensor reads off a tone wheel attached to the rear of the dual oil pump shaft and the output speed sensor, which reads off the fourth gear on the upper shaft. All the speed sensors are Hall effect sensors for accuracy and longevity. The transmission uses a triple pressure sensor that measures line pressure and primary/secondary clutch actuation pressures. Lastly, the ACM has a temperature sensor to measure transmission sump temperature.

Procision Transmission Power Flows

Because the Procision transmission is unconventional compared to countershaft transmissions, it is worth reviewing its power flows. **TABLE 45-5** shows the position of the four shift rails and synchronizers for each gear, as well as the clutch applied.

- *Neutral:* On start up the transmission is in neutral, both of the wet clutches are released, and the transmission receives no input, as illustrated in **FIGURE 45-39**.
- *Reverse:* When reverse is selected, the first synchronizer on the lower shaft moves rearward to lock the second lower shaft driven gear (the cluster gear) to the lower shaft. The 1st/2nd and reverse synchronizer on the upper shaft also moves rearward to lock reverse gear to the upper shaft, as illustrated in **FIGURE 45-40**.

When the driver releases the brake pedal, the rear (primary) wet clutch starts to engage. The vehicle has an "urge to move" feel and hill-hold capability for a short period. As the driver steps on the throttle, the primary clutch fully applies, and reverse is fully engaged. The power flow is as follows: The primary clutch inputs the second input gear of the transmission. Then the power flows through to the second lower shaft driven gear, the cluster gear, which is locked to the lower shaft by the lock synchronizer. Next, the power is delivered to the reverse

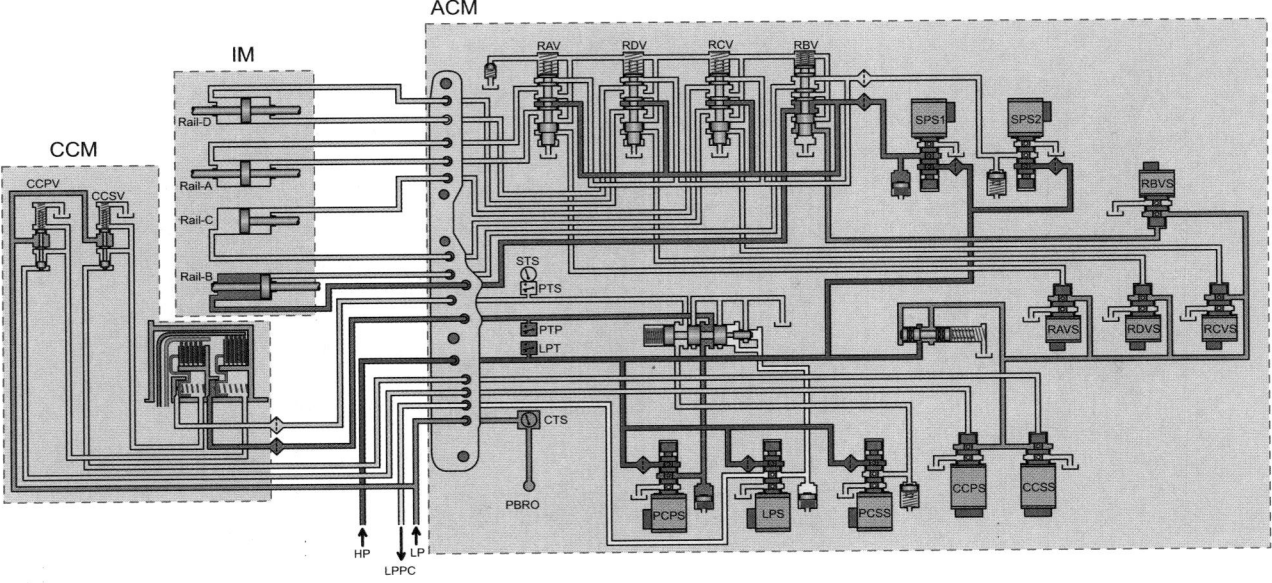

FIGURE 45-38 Procision hydraulic schematic.

TABLE 45-5 Position of Four Shift Rails and Synchronizers

Gear	Ratio	Applied Clutch	Rail A	Rail B	Rail C	Rail D
R	6.15	Primary	Rearward	Neutral	Neutral	Rearward
1	6.50	Primary	Forward	Neutral	Neutral	Rearward
2	4.17	Secondary	Forward	Neutral	Neutral	Rearward
3	2.53	Primary	Forward	Rearward	Neutral	Neutral
4	1.55	Secondary	Neutral	Rearward	Rearward	Neutral
5	1.00	Primary	Neutral	Forward	Rearward	Neutral
6	0.77	Secondary	Neutral	Forward	Forward	Neutral
7	0.64	Secondary	Neutral	Forward	Forward	Forward

No Clutches Applied

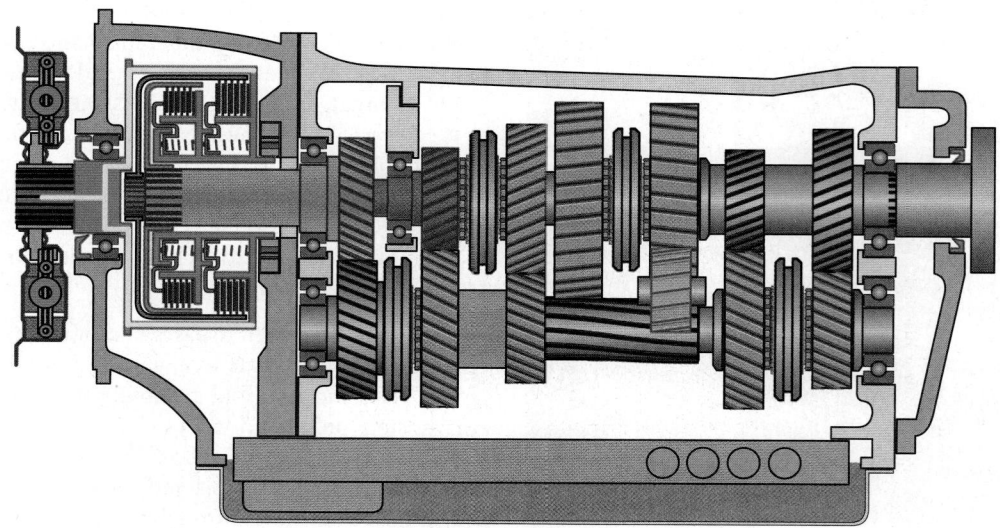

FIGURE 45-39 In Procision transmission, neither clutch is applied in neutral.

Primary Clutch Applied

Primary Input Shaft (driving)

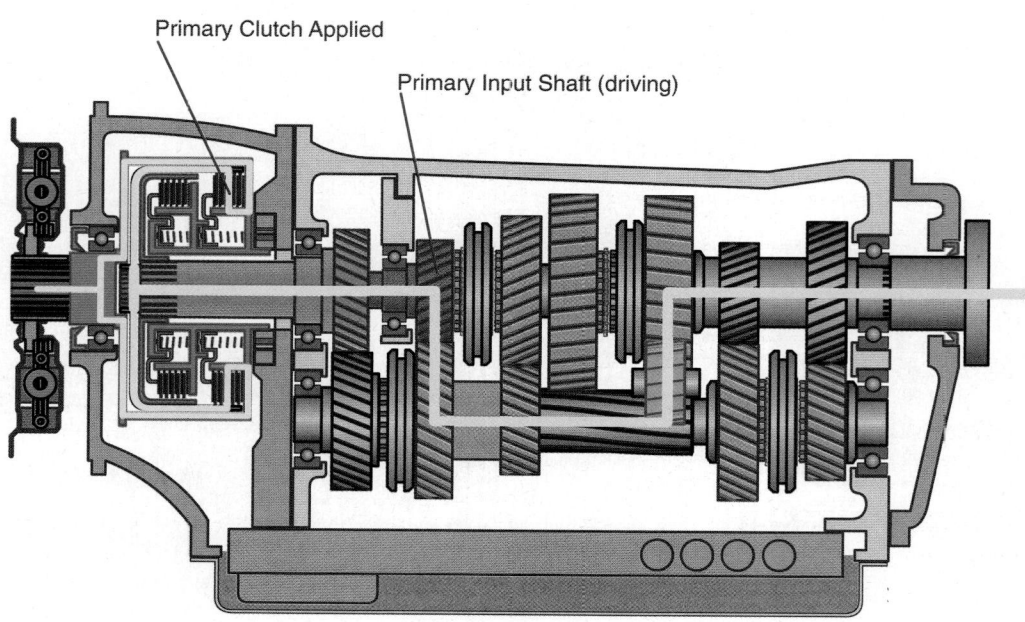

FIGURE 45-40 Reverse power flow in Procision transmission.

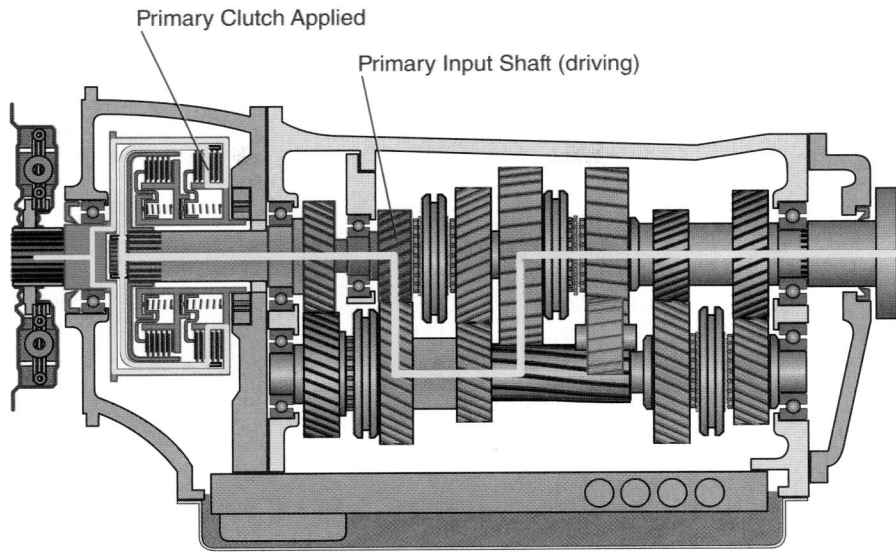

FIGURE 45-41 First gear power flow in Procision transmission.

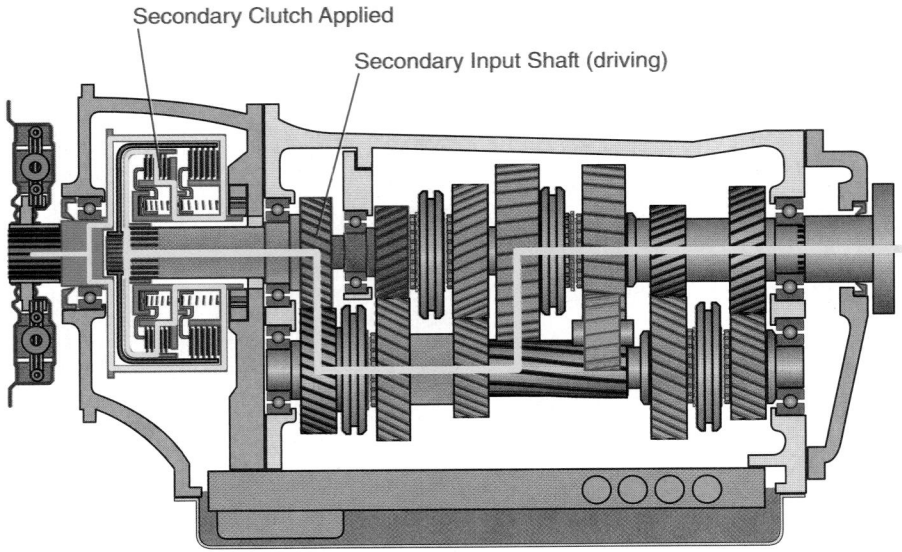

FIGURE 45-42 Second gear power flow in Procision transmission.

idler gear from the lower shaft first and reverse gear. Finally, power flows to the reverse upper shaft gear, which is locked to the upper shaft by the first/reverse synchronizer.

- *First gear*: When the driver selects first range, the lock synchronizer on the lower shaft moves rearward and locks the second lower shaft driven gear (the cluster gear) to the lower shaft. The first/reverse synchronizer on the upper shaft moves forward, locking first gear to the upper shaft, as illustrated in **FIGURE 45-41**. When the driver releases the brake, the primary clutch partially engages to provide urge to move and hill-hold capability for a short period. As the driver steps on the throttle, the primary clutch engages fully and the power flows from the primary clutch to the primary input gear and from there to the lower shaft through the second lower shaft driven gear, which is locked to the lower shaft by the lock synchronizer. Then

power flows from the lower shaft first/reverse gear to the first speed gear, which is locked to the upper shaft by the first/reverse synchronizer.

- *Second gear*: To achieve second gear, the transmission does not have to shift any gears or synchronizers; it merely switches the applied wet clutches. The primary wet clutch is disengaged, and the secondary wet clutch is engaged. The two synchronizers' positions used in first gear remain the same. The primary clutch is released, and the secondary clutch is applied with no torque interruption. This then sends the power from the secondary wet clutch, to the secondary input gear, and on to the front lower shaft driven gear. Power then flows from the lower shaft first and reverse gear to the still engaged first gear on the upper shaft. The difference in ratio between first and second is caused solely by the different input gear driving the lower shaft. See **FIGURE 45-42**.

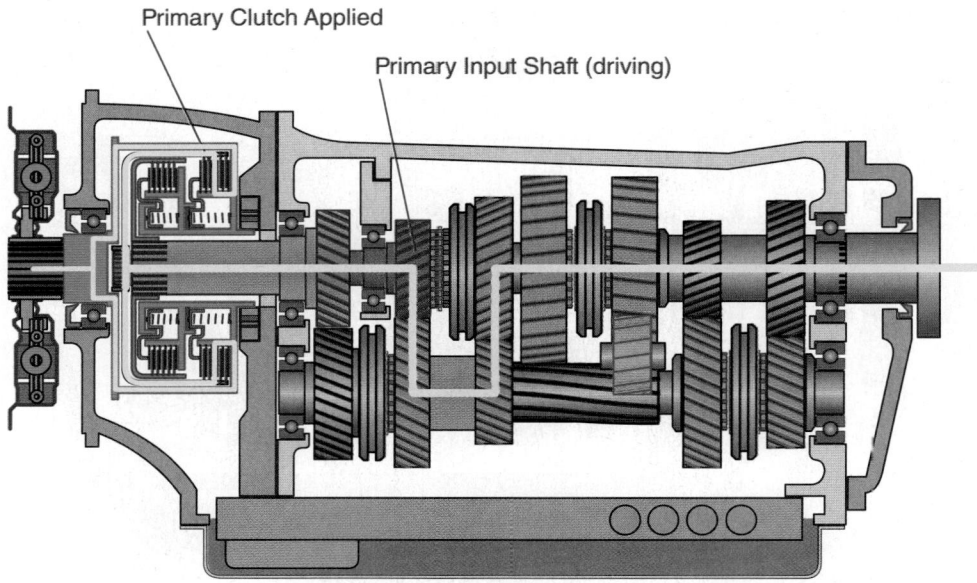

FIGURE 45-43 Third gear power flow in Procision transmission.

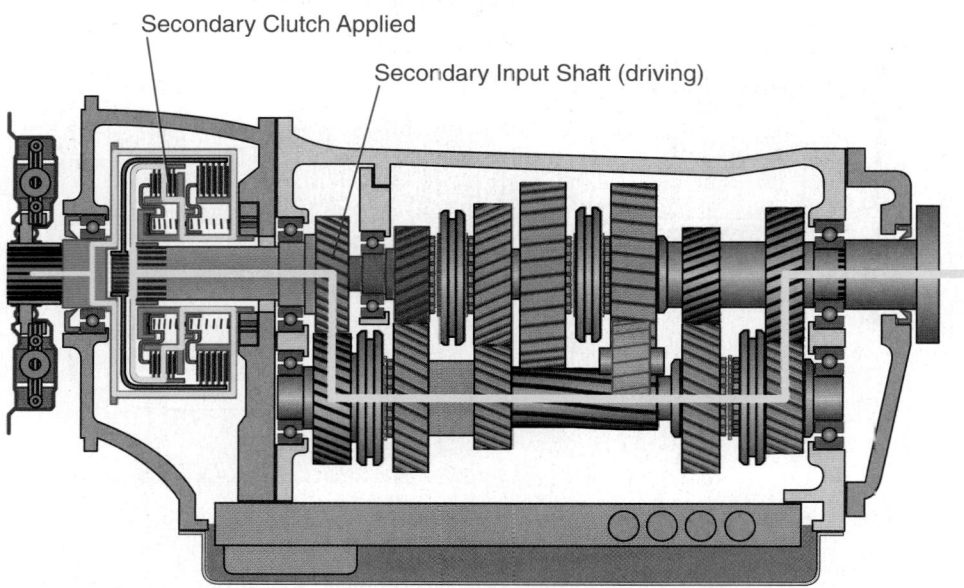

FIGURE 45-44 Fourth gear power flow in Procision transmission.

- *Third gear:* As the vehicle continues to accelerate, the transmission preselects third gear by moving the lock synchronizer to neutral and moving the 3rd/5th/7th synchronizer to the rear to engage the third gear on the upper shaft. When the shift to third is made, the transmission again merely switches input clutches from the secondary to the primary, as illustrated in **FIGURE 45-43**. The power flows from the primary input gear to the second lower shaft driven gear (the cluster gear). Because that gear and lower shaft third are one unit, power is sent up onto upper shaft third gear. The upper shaft third gear is locked to the upper shaft by the 3rd/5th/7th synchronizer. The lower

shaft is not involved in this power flow. The one-piece second lower shaft driven gear and the lower shaft third gear revolve around the lower shaft.

- *Fourth gear:* As the vehicle continues to accelerate, the transmission preselects fourth gear by moving the 1st/2nd and reverse synchronizer to the neutral position and moving the 4th/6th synchronizer to the rear to lock fourth gear lower shaft to the lower shaft. To make the shift, the transmission switches the input clutch from the primary to the secondary, as illustrated in **FIGURE 45-44**. The power flows from the secondary input gear to the lower shaft through the front lower shaft driven gear. Power then flows to the fourth lower

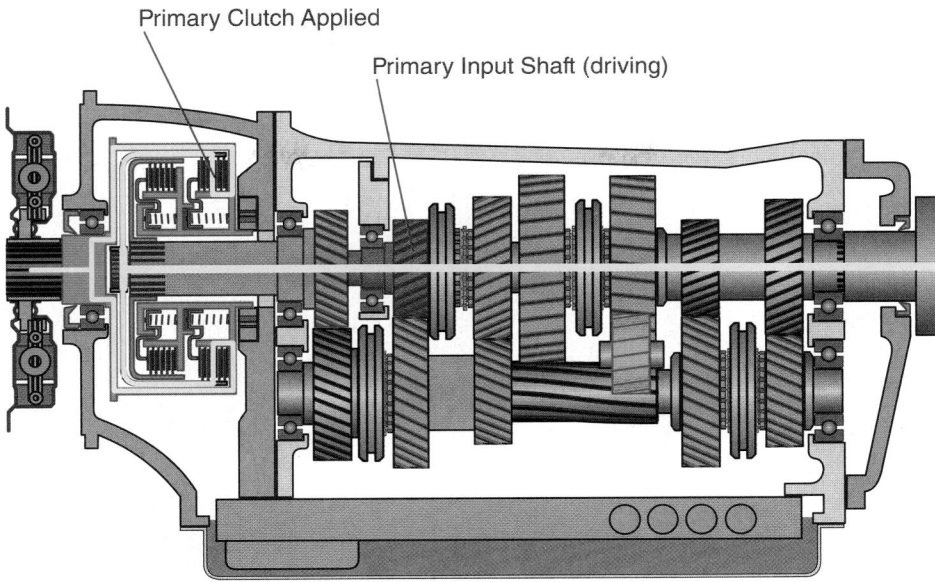

FIGURE 45-45 Fifth gear power flow in Procision transmission.

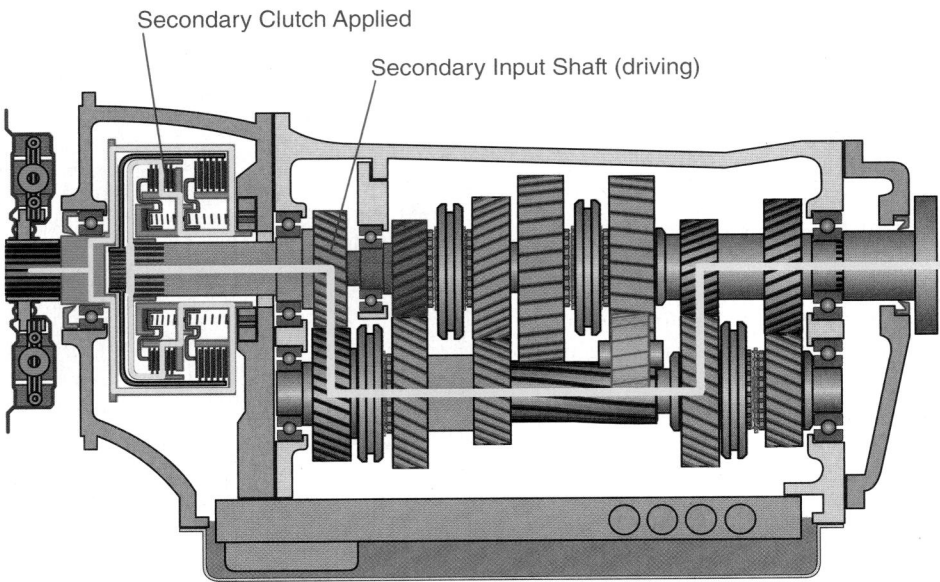

FIGURE 45-46 Sixth gear power flow in Procision transmission.

shaft gear, which is locked to the lower shaft by the 4th/6th synchronizer. Finally, power flows up to the upper shaft fourth gear, which is permanently fixed to the upper shaft.

- *Fifth gear:* As the vehicle continues to accelerate, the transmission preselects fifth gear by moving the 3rd/5th/7th synchronizer forward to lock the output shaft to the primary input gear. To make the shift, the transmission switches input clutches again—this time from the secondary to the primary clutch, as illustrated in **FIGURE 45-45**. The power is delivered to the primary input gear, which is locked to the upper shaft by the 3rd/5th/7th synchronizer. This power flow is direct. That is, it is a 1:1 ratio.
- *Sixth gear:* As the vehicle continues to accelerate, the transmission preselects sixth gear by moving the 4th/6th

synchronizer forward and locking the lower shaft sixth gear to the lower shaft. To make the shift, again the transmission switches the input clutch; this time, however, the transmission shifts from the primary to the secondary, as illustrated in **FIGURE 45-46**. The power flows to the secondary input gear and to the lower shaft through the front lower shaft driven gear. Power continues to the lower shaft sixth gear, which is locked to the lower shaft by the 4th/6th synchronizer. Finally, power travels up to the upper shaft sixth gear, which is permanently fixed to the upper shaft.

- *Seventh gear:* There is no preselect for the shift to seventh gear. This is the only shift in the Procision transmission that is not a full power shift. For this shift to occur, the

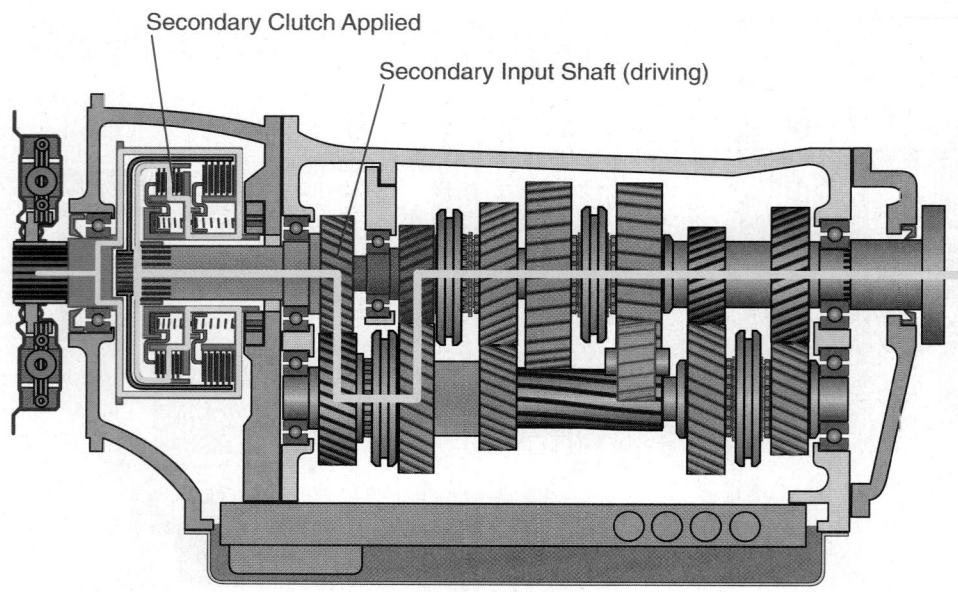

FIGURE 45-47 Seventh gear power flow in Procision transmission.

control system must break torque momentarily. The secondary clutch remains applied, and the transmission moves the 4th/6th synchronizer to the neutral position while moving the lock synchronizer rearward to lock the second lower shaft driven gear to the lower shaft. This process is illustrated in **FIGURE 45-47**. The power flows from the secondary input gear to the front lower shaft driven gear. Power continues to the second lower shaft driven gear, which is locked to the lower shaft by the lock synchronizer. Finally, power travels back up to the primary input gear, which is still locked to the output shaft by the 3rd/5th/7th synchronizer. The nomenclature for the Procision transmission model number EDCO-6F107A-M is explained in (**TABLE 45-6**).

Three Module Transmissions

LO 45-4 Explain the design and operation of three module transmissions.

Many manufacturers around the world produce transmissions that utilize a three-module design. These transmissions all have a split input section, a mainshaft section, and a planetary range section. The following section of this chapter discusses these transmissions in detail.

FIGURE 45-48 The new Eaton Endurant.

Eaton Endurant

In September 2017, Eaton introduced a brand-new automated transmission to its lineup called the Endurant, shown in **FIGURE 45-48**. Created through a joint venture with Cummins, this transmission was engineered from the ground up to be an

TABLE 45-6 Eaton Procision Nomenclature

Prefix			Model					Suffix
E	DC	O	-6F	I	07	A-		M
Eaton	Dual Clutch	Overdrive	Nominal Torque Capacity # × 100	Design Level	Forward Speeds	Gear Ratio Set		Transmission Parking Mechanism M = Non-park pawl vehicle GCW 35,000 lb

automated transmission unlike the AutoShift and UltraShift, which were basically standard transmissions adapted for computer control. Paccar is also marketing this transmission with their own branding. The Endurant was created specifically for the line-haul market and is capable of handling 1850 ft-lb (2580 Nm) of input torque and rated for as much as 510 hp. The transmission uses a 17" (430 mm) self-adjusting clutch, with a single organic-faced clutch disc similar to the one used by Volvo I-Shift.

The transmission has three sections. The first is a split input section that uses a synchronizer to select one of two input gear sets to drive the twin countershafts. The second is a mainshaft section with three gears (reverse, first, and second) that are free to rotate on the mainshaft; a sliding clutch is used between reverse and first gear so they can be locked to the mainshaft, and a second sliding clutch is used between second gear on the mainshaft and the rear input gear, which can either lock second gear to the mainshaft or lock the mainshaft to the rear split input gear. The third section is a planetary range section that is controlled by a third sliding clutch. This gearing arrangement gives the transmission 12 possible gear ratios; the gear ratios are discussed later in this section.

The position of the synchronizers and the sliding clutches are controlled by four shift rails, each of which are positioned by two pneumatic solenoids—one to move the rail forward and one to move the rail back—for a total of eight rail control solenoids. The control solenoids and rails are in the mechatronic control module, which is bolted to the top of the transmission. **FIGURE 45-49** shows the location of the mechatronic actuator.

The mechatronic module also houses the linear clutch actuator, which is controlled by four solenoids, two to apply the clutch, one for quick application and the other for slow application, and two to release the clutch—again one quick and one slow. The clutch solenoids can be actuated in concert or separately, depending on the requirements. The Endurant has an air-operated countershaft brake called an inertia brake to control shaft and gear speeds in the transmission to enable it to synchronize speeds for shifting. The countershaft brake is a multidisc clutch attached to the front end of the left countershaft inside the clutch housing of the transmission. The Endurant has specific software packages for whichever engine it is paired with that allow it to seamlessly integrate with the engine to optimize shifting. The integration allows the Endurant to have such features as hill-hold to prevent roll back on incline utilizing the vehicle ABS; creep mode, which allows the vehicle to be maneuvered at 1.5 kph (0.9 mph) for docking and other situations; and urge to move in which the vehicle starts to move when the driver releases the brake. It is also capable of skip shifting where warranted, neutral coast when safe, and look-ahead predictive shifting by anticipating terrain changes.

The Endurant comes equipped with a five-year, 750,000 mile (1,200,000 km), warranty for linehaul applications; a three-year, 350,000 mile (563,000 km) warranty for the clutch; and a 750,000 mile (1,200,000 km) lube interval. Although the Endurant is a new design using linear shift rails and clutch actuators, the basic gear arrangement to give it 12 speeds is not new. This gear arrangement of three section transmissions has been used for years by various manufacturers. ZF, Mercedes, Detroit, Volvo/Mack, and many others have used the three-section design with slight differences. The basic power flow of these transmissions is as follows: The front section is a split input section that allows the countershafts to be driven at two different speeds. The countershafts then drive two mainshaft gears, and the mainshaft can also be put into direct by locking it to the back of the rear split input gear. Therefore, in total, the first two sections can produce six different ratios. The third section is a planetary range section that can operate in two different ratios; low range in which the ring gear is held, the sun gear is input, and the carrier is output, giving an approximate 3.5:1 reduction, and high range in which the ring gear is locked to the carrier and power flows through the range section unchanged at 1:1 or direct. The planetary range section allows the six available ratios from the first two sections to be used twice—once in low range and once in direct, resulting in 12 available ratios. The following section on ZF transmissions goes into more detail on this type of transmission power flow. The Eaton Endurant has its own specific nomenclature. The Endurant model number EEO-17F112-C nomenclature is deciphered in **TABLE 45-7**.

Zahnradfabrik Friedrichshafen, ZF/Meritor

Eaton is not the only manufacturer of AMTs. Several other manufacturers have products on the North American market. Meritor marketed several AMTs in North America, as mentioned in the Introduction section of this chapter. Here, the transmissions Meritor marketed in partnership with ZF Friedrichshafen AG—the Freedomline and the AS-Tronic, are discussed.

ZF is a worldwide supplier of highly engineered and cutting-edge driveline and chassis components across all transportation sectors. The ZF company name is derived from its founding business Zahnradfabrik, which means "gear manufacture" in German, and the company's home town. Its headquarters are in the town of Friedrichshafen, Germany.

Mechatronic Control Unit

Transmission Control Unit

Linear Clutch Actuator

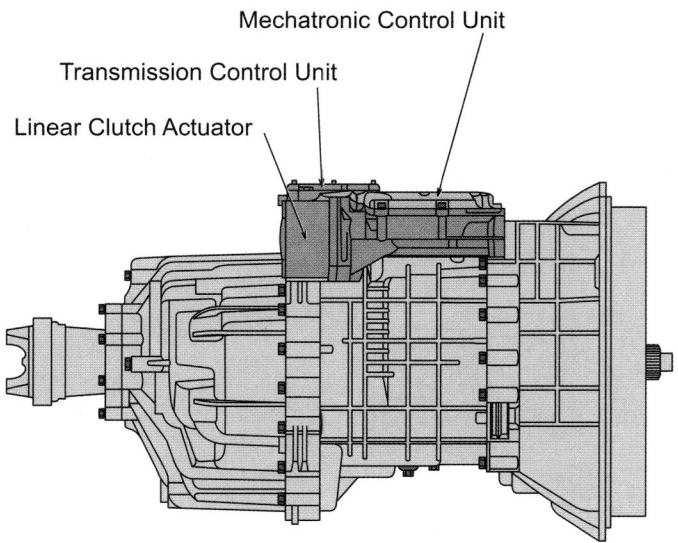

FIGURE 45-49 All the electronics and shift controls are internal to the transmission.

TABLE 45-7 Endurant Nomenclature

Prefix			Model				
E	E	O-	17	F	1	12	C
Eaton	Endurant	Overdrive	Torque Capacity # X-100+50	Units for Torque Ft-lb or Nm	Design Level	Forward Speeds	Gear Ratio (A/B/C/D)

ZF introduced its Freedomline of transmissions through Meritor, and Meritor was the exclusive North American supplier of the Freedomline series. In 2009, however, the partnership dissolved. ZF's truck transmission line is now known in the United States and in other parts of the world by two names, depending on vocation. ZF's AS-Tronic line is for light-, medium-, and heavy-duty applications. The TC-Tronic version with torque converter is used for heavy-truck applications and is primarily marketed in Europe.

The AS-Tronic is available in three basic formats: a 12-speed, a 12-speed with overdrive, and a 16-speed overdrive version. These are twin countershaft, heavy-duty transmissions with the latest models capable of accepting up to 2500 ft-lb (3400 Nm) of input torque. **FIGURE 45-50** shows the latest model of these transmissions from ZF called the Traxon.

They come equipped with a 17" (43.2 cm) organic-faced, single-disc, self-adjusting clutch that is operated pneumatically by the transmission electronic controller, otherwise known as the ZF Meritor Transmission Electronic Controller (ZMTEC). After the split with Meritor, the controller is now called ZTEC. The ZTEC transmission controller controls the flow of air to an air cylinder that actuates the clutch. The state of clutch adjustment is monitored every time the clutch is disengaged and engaged. An indicator on the dash tells the driver when clutch replacement is required. The clutch is equipped with a permanently lubricated release bearing, so no maintenance is required until clutch replacement.

As illustrated in **FIGURE 45-51**, the ZF transmission is modular in design with an input splitter section, a three-speed mainshaft section, and a planetary range section. As mentioned previously, it is very similar to the design of the Endurant discussed in the last section. Initial input to the countershaft from the input shaft is channeled through a splitter gear set at the front of the transmission. The front splitter gear is low split. In non-overdrive models, the rear splitter gear is high split. In

FIGURE 45-50 ZF's latest model transmission, the Traxon.

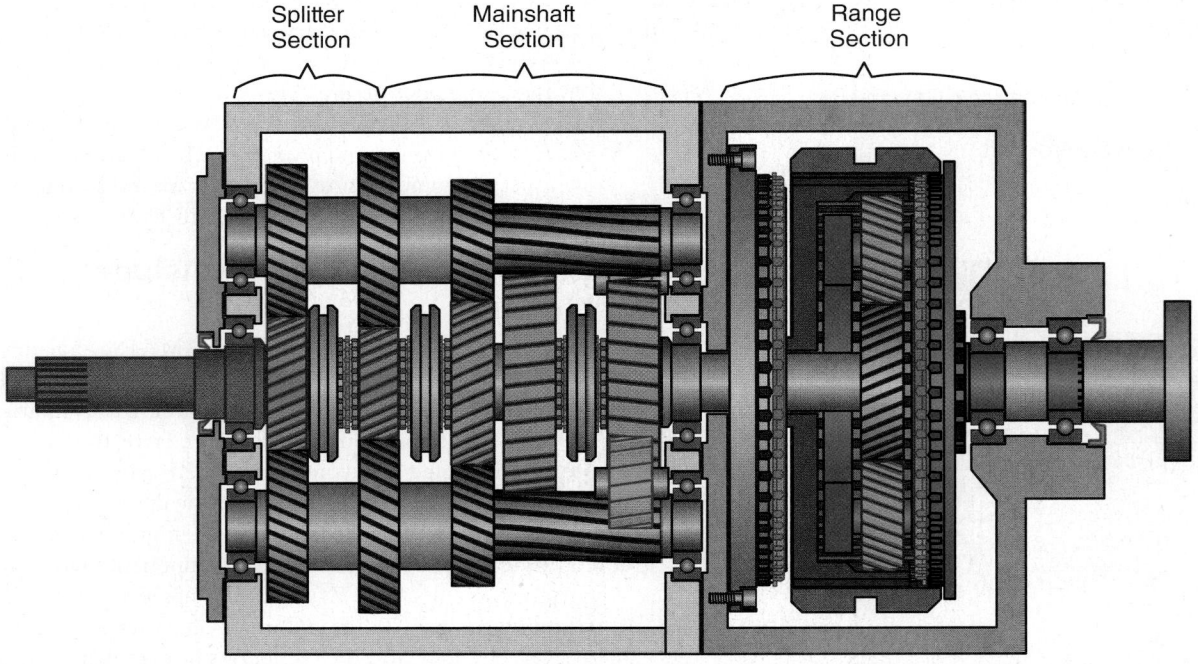

FIGURE 45-51 Several manufacturers market three-module design transmissions, such as the ZF shown here.

overdrive models, the front splitter is the high (overdrive) gear and the rear splitter gear is the low split. From the splitter gear set, the power is delivered to both countershafts.

In 12-speed models, the mainshaft has only two forward drive gears plus reverse. In 16-speed models, the mainshaft has three forward speed gears, plus reverse. From the mainshaft, the power is delivered to a planetary range gear set in the rear of the transmission. The rear planetary gear set provides low range by inputting the sun gear, holding the ring gear, and the carrier of the planetary gear set becomes output. In high range, the power passes the planetary gear set unchanged. **FIGURE 45-52** depicts an exploded view of the ZF transmission, the design uses each mainshaft gear four times—twice in low range and twice in high range.

The ZTEC controls shifting by using solenoids to control three air cylinders and a gate or fork selector that are integral with the transmission top cover. The air cylinders control gear selection and range and splitter shifts. The four solenoid-controlled air actuators, illustrated in **FIGURE 45-53**, position the shift rails when a ZF transmission shifts. Unlike the preceding Endurant transmission, the ZF design does not use linear actuators exclusively.

Power flows in the ZF AS-Tronic are relatively simple and are the same for every three-section design transmission. Each mainshaft gear is used four times. Take the 12-speed non-overdrive model as an example:

- In first range, power is delivered to the countershafts through the low-split gear set and delivered to the first gear mainshaft. Power than passes through the planetary gear set in low range.
- To move to second range, the splitter gear set is simply shifted to the high-split gear set.
- The third range returns input to the low-split gear set. The second gear mainshaft is selected and power passes once again through the planetary gear set in low range.
- For fourth range, the splitter gear is shifted to high split again.
- For fifth range, again the splitter gear set is shifted to low split. This time, however, the mainshaft is connected to the back of the rear splitter gear set and the countershaft speed gears are not used. Once more, the power flows through low range in the planetary range set.
- For sixth range, the splitter gear is shifted to high split. This puts the front section of the transmission into direct range. In other words, the input is connected to the front side of the rear splitter gear, and the mainshaft is connected to the rear of the gear. The power, however, is still flowing from the mainshaft through the low range of the planetary section.
- For seventh range, the planetary range section is put into high range, or direct. At that point, power passes through the range section unchanged. The front section of the transmission repeats the exact same sequence as above from first to sixth range, ending up with 12 forward ranges in total.

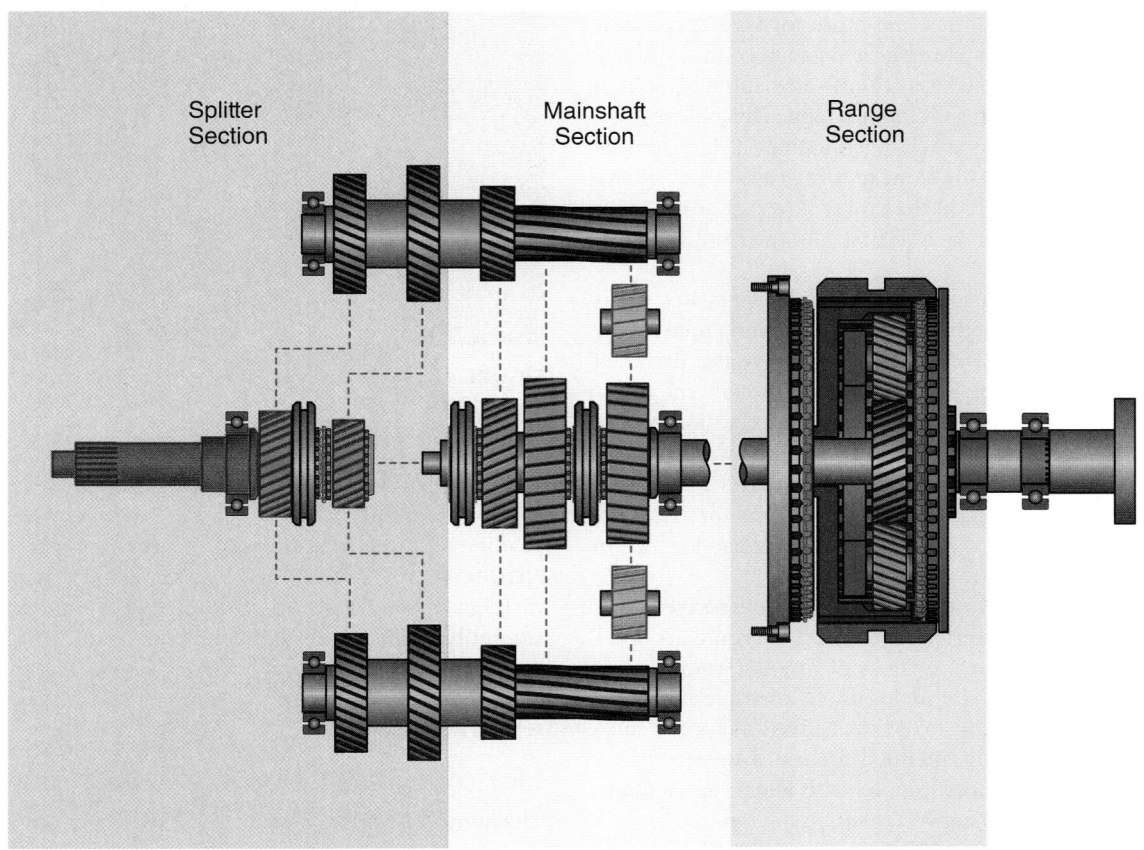

FIGURE 45-52 Exploded view of the ZF design.

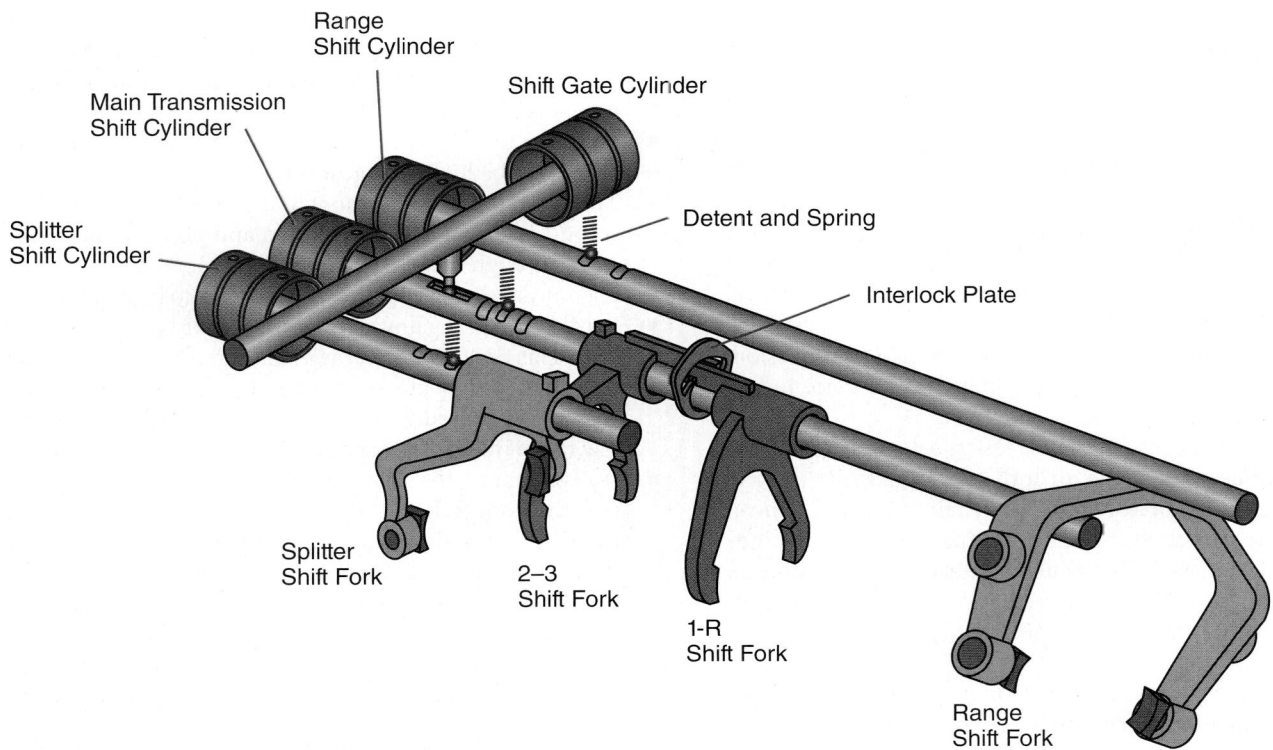

FIGURE 45-53 Four solenoid-controlled air actuators in a ZF transmission.

The only difference between the 12- and 16-speed models is that the 16-speed model has one more forward speed gear on the mainshaft and a matching gear on each of the countershafts. Each speed is still used four times—low and high split in low range and low and high split in high range. To achieve overdrive, the splitter gear ratios are changed so that the low-split set is the rear splitter gear and the front splitter gear is an overdrive gear set. The only difference in the power flow just described is that the rear splitter gear set is used first, and the front split gear set is used second.

These ZF transmissions use a two-pedal design, so there is no clutch pedal. Therefore, the transmission can operate totally automatically or can be switched to manual by the driver, if desired. As with all automated transmissions, though, the transmission has mechanisms to prevent abusive operation by the driver. The AS-Tronic and Traxon transmissions work to optimize shifting strategies for all road, load, and driver conditions. Latest versions of the control software utilize predictive shifting and global positioning system (GPS) look-ahead for terrain changes to improve shift strategies.

ZF also produces a heavy-duty 12-speed overdrive transmission with a torque converter called the TC-Tronic. Its operating principles are the same as those of the AS-Tronic except for the torque converter. The inclusion of a torque converter allows for extremely smooth take-offs, as well as torque multiplication, and is primarily intended for use with very heavy equipment. The converter is equipped with a lock-up clutch to eliminate any losses due to converter slip.

The latest offering from ZF is the Traxon with optional input modules. This system allows the customer to select

FIGURE 45-54 The dual-clutch module (left) and hybrid electric traction motor (right) for ZF Traxon transmissions.

from five different input modules, which allows much greater flexibility. Two of those modules, the dual-clutch module and the hybrid electric traction motor, are shown in **FIGURE 45-54**. As mentioned previously, the input can come through a single-disc self-adjusting clutch, a dual-clutch assembly (which can save fuel by power shifting), an engine-mounted PTO assembly, a torque converter module, or an electric traction motor that turns the transmission into a series hybrid system.

Meritor and ZF Nomenclature

The nomenclature for Meritor and ZF transmissions differs from the nomenclature of Eaton Fuller transmissions. **TABLES 45-8** and **45-9** list the nomenclature for two different transmissions.

TABLE 45-8 Nomenclature for Meritor RMX10-165-C2S002

R	M	X	10	165	C	2	S	002
Rockwell	M=manual S=ESS	X=overdrive no letter=Direct	# of forward speeds	Torque rating × 10	Ratio	Design level	Shift tower position	OEM specification

TABLE 45-9 Nomenclature for ZF O-16G10C-E18002

M	O	16	G	10	C	E	18	002
ZF Meritor	O=Overdrive no letter=direct	Torque rating X 100 + 50	Design platform	Forward speeds	Ratio	A=fully automated D=ESS/DDC E=ESS/ZF M=Manual S=SureShift	Highest torque in transmission × 100 + 50	OEM specification

Detroit Diesel's DT-12

Detroit Diesel introduced the DT-12 transmission to the North American market in 2012. The DT-12 shown in **FIGURE 45-55** is a 12-speed automated transmission. It is the same transmission marketed by Mercedes in Europe in its Actros trucks.

The design of the DT-12 single countershaft transmission is common to several transmissions produced in Europe. The DT-12 is a single countershaft design with three speed gears on the mainshaft. The input to the transmission goes through a two-speed splitter gear set, through one of the mainshaft speed gears, and then through a planetary hi–low range gear set at the rear of the transmission. The splitter gear set and the planetary range set both multiply the ratios available on the actual main-shaft by two, which results in a 12-speed transmission. The DT-12 system does not use a clutch pedal. Instead, the DT-12 relies on an air-actuated release bearing to control a large single- or dual-disc organic clutch. Shifting is accomplished by an electric over-air shift controller system.

The DT-12 is available in two sizes: A model, or "large transmission," capable of input torque up to 2050 ft-lb (2779 Nm), and the B, or "small transmission," capable of input torque up to 1650 ft-lb (2237 Nm). Both models are available as direct DT-12-DA or DT-12-DB, or overdrive models DT-12-OA or DT-12-OB.

The DT-12 was built in Germany by Mercedes for Detroit Diesel, but now this transmission is designed and built in North America. This allows the transmission to be better tailored to the North American market.

The DT-12 single countershaft, heavy-duty transmission comes equipped with a 17" (432 mm) organic-faced, single-disc, or a 14.7" (400 mm) dual-disc clutch that is operated by the transmission electronic controller. The transmission controller, called the TCM by Detroit, controls the flow of air to a self-contained air-actuated release bearing known as a concentric pneumatic clutch actuator (CPCA) that actuates the clutch, shown in **FIGURE 45-56**. The CPCA controls clutch adjustment. The clutch has two modes of operation: A slow actuation mode and a fast actuation mode. The TCM selects the mode based on the operating conditions. The transmission has a clutch learn routine that must be performed when the clutch, transmission, or TCM is replaced.

The state of clutch adjustment is monitored every time the clutch is disengaged and engaged. The DT-12 transmission uses a three-section or module design very similar to the Endurant and the ZF AS-Tronic. The DT-12 is illustrated in **FIGURE 45-57** and includes:

- a two-speed splitter gear input section.
- a two-speed mainshaft gear box module.
- a planetary range section for a low- and high-range output.

The transmission controller has an internal tilt sensor to aid the TCM in determining terrain and vehicle loading. This sensor aids in using the hill start feature where the vehicle

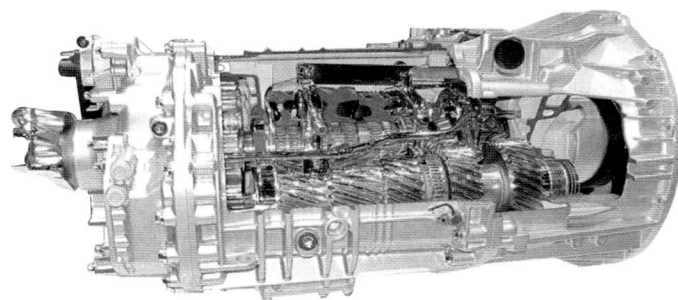

FIGURE 45-55 Detroit's single countershaft DT-12.

FIGURE 45-56 The concentric pneumatic clutch actuator (CPCA) that actuates the clutch.

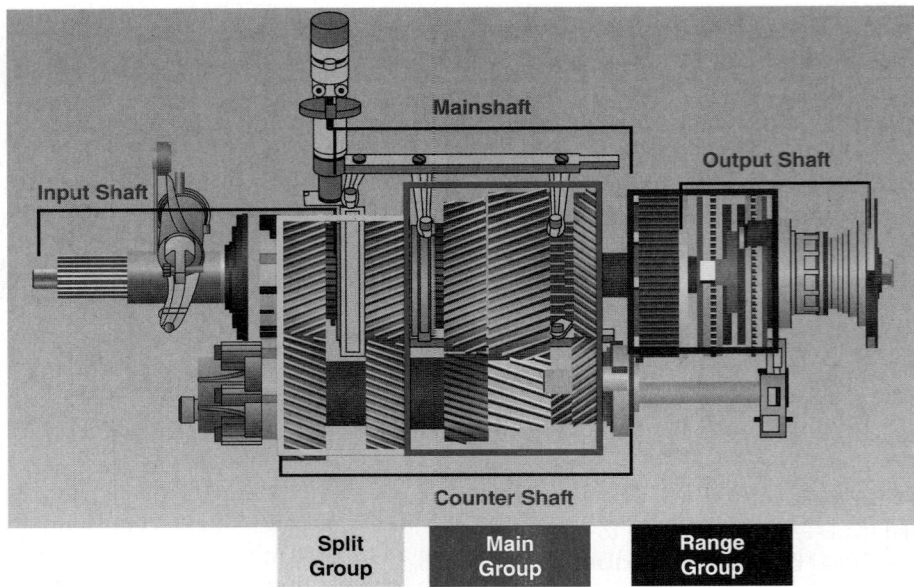

FIGURE 45-57 The DT-12 has three modules or groups.

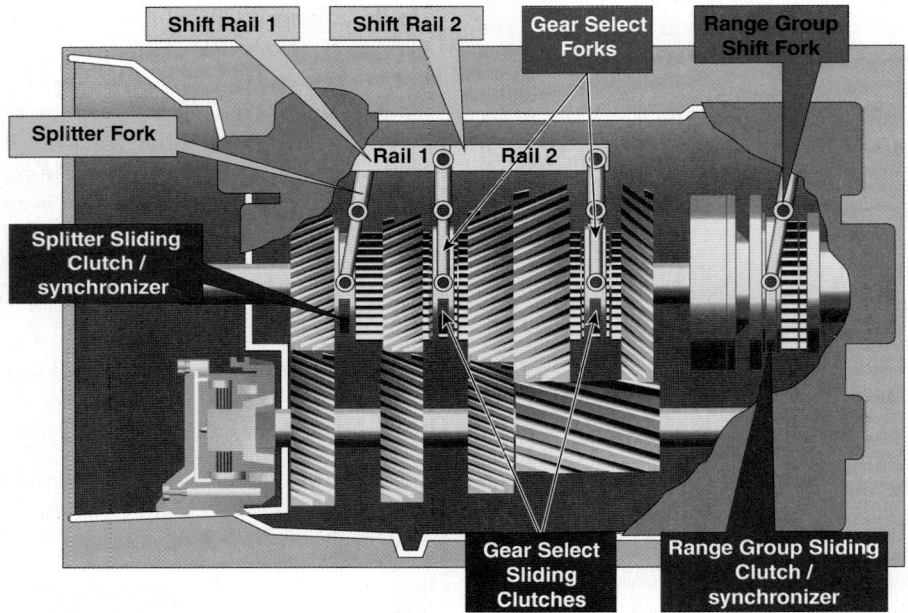

FIGURE 45-58 Each mainshaft gear position is used four times in the DT-12 power flow.

brakes are held on by the transmission controller through the ABS system until the clutch engages when starting on a hill. There are three selectable operating modes for the transmission: (1) Automatic Economy, (2) Automatic Performance, and (3) Manual (the Automatic Economy mode is the default).

DT-12 Operation

Engine power is delivered by the clutch to the input shaft and is channeled through a splitter gear set at the front of the transmission. The shift control determines whether the power flows through the high or the low splitter gear set. In direct drive models, the front splitter gear is low split, and, in overdrive models, the front splitter is the high or overdrive

split. After the splitter gear set, the power is delivered to the countershaft. The mainshaft has only two forward speed gears plus direct for a total of three ranges and one reverse. From the countershaft, the power is delivered to the engaged mainshaft gear. From the mainshaft, the power is delivered to a planetary range gear set in the rear of the transmission. The range planetary gear set provides low range by inputting the sun gear and holding the ring gear, and the carrier of the planetary gear set becomes output. In high range, the power passes through the planetary gear set unchanged. The range is selected by an air cylinder, which is, in turn, controlled by the transmission TCM. The DT-12 transmission depicted in **FIGURE 45-58**, uses each mainshaft gear four times by using the splitter gear set twice in low range and twice in high range, for a total of 12 forward speeds. Power flows in the DT-12 are relatively simple, as mentioned previously, each mainshaft gear is used four times. Use Figure 45-58 to follow the transmission power flows.

First range: In first range, power is delivered to the countershaft through the front, low-split gear set and is delivered to the first mainshaft speed gear. Power than passes through the planetary range gear set in low range.

Second range: To move to second range, the splitter gear set is shifted to the rear high-split gear set. Power flows from the rear splitter gear set to the countershaft and back to the same mainshaft speed gear and through the planetary range set in low range.

Third range: In third range the input once again shifts to the low-split gear set. The power flows to the countershaft and back to the now selected second mainshaft speed gear. Power flows once again through the planetary gear set in low range.

Fourth range: For fourth range, the splitter gear is shifted to high split again. Power flows to the countershaft and back to the second mainshaft speed gear and again through the planetary range set in low range.

Fifth range: For fifth range, again the splitter gear set is shifted to low split. This time, however, the mainshaft is connected to the back of the rear splitter gear set and the countershaft speed gears are not used. Power flows to the countershaft through the low-split gear set and back down to the mainshaft through the rear, high-split gear set, and from there directly to the mainshaft. Once more, the power flows through low range in the planetary range set.

Sixth range: For sixth range, the splitter gear is shifted to the rear, high split. This puts the splitter section and the mainshaft sections of the transmission into direct range. In other words, the input is connected to the front side of the rear splitter gear, and the mainshaft is connected to the rear of the gear. The power, however, is still flowing from the mainshaft through the low range of the planetary section.

Seventh range: For seventh range, the planetary range section is put into high range, or direct. At that point, power passes through the range section unchanged. The front section of the transmission repeats the exact same sequence as above from first to sixth range, ending up with 12 forward ranges in total.

The DT-12 uses an air-operated countershaft brake to control shaft and gear speeds in the transmission to enable it to synchronize speeds for shifting. The countershaft brake is a multidisc clutch attached to the front end of the countershaft inside the clutch housing of the transmission. The countershaft brake can be seen in **FIGURE 45-59**.

The brake is controlled by the transmission ECU and can speed up shift times by being able to slow the countershaft and, therefore, the mainshaft gearing, when necessary.

These transmissions use a two-pedal design, so there is no clutch pedal. The transmission can operate totally automatically or can be switched to manual by the driver, if desired. As with all automated transmissions, though, the transmission has

FIGURE 45-59 The multidisc countershaft brake is used by the transmission controller to synchronize shaft and gear speeds for clash-free shifting.

FIGURE 45-60 Similar in function to the DT-12, the Volvo I-Shift uses only one countershaft.

mechanisms to prevent abusive operation by the driver. The DT-12 transmission works to optimize shifting strategies for all road, load, and driver conditions.

Volvo Trucks' I-Shift/Mack M-Drive

The Volvo I-shift and the Mack M-Drive are essentially the same transmission. The M-Drive can have several different software variations that suit the more common vocational operations of Mack trucks but, other than that, the design is identical. For that reason, only the Volvo I-shift is discussed here. The Volvo I-Shift, shown in **FIGURE 45-60**, automated transmission is a two-pedal dry clutch design.

The transmission uses a 17" (43.2 cm) single organic disc clutch. The clutch is actuated by a self-contained air-actuated release bearing controlled by the transmission TCM. The Volvo I-Shift clutch is shown in **FIGURE 45-61**.

The transmission design is very similar to the DT-12 transmission. Volvo I-Shift uses only one countershaft. Like the DT-12, the Volvo transmission has a two-speed input splitter

FIGURE 45-61 The large organic disc clutch used by Volvo allows smooth engagement.

FIGURE 45-62 Volvo I-Shift driver interface.

section, a three-speed mainshaft section, and a planetary range section. Therefore, the mainshaft gears are utilized four times each in total: twice in low range through the planetary range section, and twice in high range, for a total of 12 forward speeds. Shifting is accomplished by electric solenoids controlling air shifters that are integral to the transmission shift cover. The power flows are identical to the DT-12 and so are not repeated here. The I-Shift transmission is available in four different models, two of which have overdrive and two of which do not:

- AT2512C—Direct Drive for Volvo D11 and D13 Engines
- ATO2512C—Overdrive for Volvo D11 and D13 Engines
- AT2812C—Direct Drive for Volvo D16 Engines
- ATO3112C—Overdrive for Volvo D16 Engines

The transmission has adaptive shift control. Several selectable shift strategies allow the driver to optimize either performance or fuel economy—or combinations of the two. For example, strategies include:

- B = Basic
- EB = Enhanced Basic
- FE = Fuel Economy
- P = Performance
- CO = Comprehensive

As with all automated transmissions, Volvo's transmissions can also be operated in manual mode, if desired. The I-Shift driver interface is shown in **FIGURE 45-62**. Notice the "M" position for manual control.

The latest version of the I-Shift and the Mack M-Drive offer an optional "crawler" or "creeper gear;" this option adds a deep reduction feature to the transmissions. This is accomplished by lengthening the transmission by approximately 4.5" (12 cm) and installing a new input gear cut directly on the input shaft in mesh with a selectable crawler gear on the front of the countershaft. The countershaft crawler gear is engaged by a sliding clutch when desired. **FIGURE 45-63** shows the new crawler gear arrangement.

This crawler or creeper gear allows much lower reductions than the original I-Shift. To operate in crawler mode, the driver first selects it from his shift control by selecting drive or manual and then pressing the downshift button two to three times (depending on the vehicle normal start gear), until he sees C-1

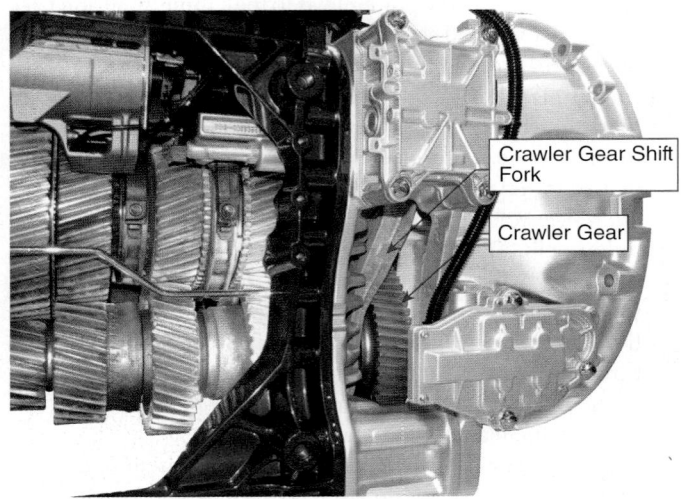

FIGURE 45-63 The new Volvo/Mack Crawler gear.

(Crawler 1) on the dash display. This operation engages the front crawler gears on the input shaft to input the countershaft of the transmission. The driver can select C-1 or C-2. C-1 position engages first gear on the mainshaft to complete the power flow and creates a ratio through the transmission of 32:1, allowing the vehicle to operate as low as 0.6 mph (0.97 kph). In the C-2 position, the second gear on the mainshaft is engaged and the ratio changes to 19:1. If the driver selects C-1 and leaves the transmission in automatic mode, the transmission shifts normally from C-1 to C-2, then to first gear, etc. The driver can also switch the transmission to manual mode, in which case it remains in C-1 until the driver requests a shift with the shift control buttons. If the driver selects the C-1 position in reverse, the ratio is 37:1. According to Volvo Europe, these ratios allow the truck to start a load of 325 tons (635,029 kg) from a standstill, a whopping 650,000 lb (295,835 kg)! In North America, crawler gear-equipped trucks are rated to pull 220,000 lb (99,790 kg).

Dual Clutch I-Shift

Volvo also offers a 12-speed overdrive dual-clutch I-Shift in Europe. Introduced in September 2014, this transmission has two dry-friction input clutches. Each of the transmission's two

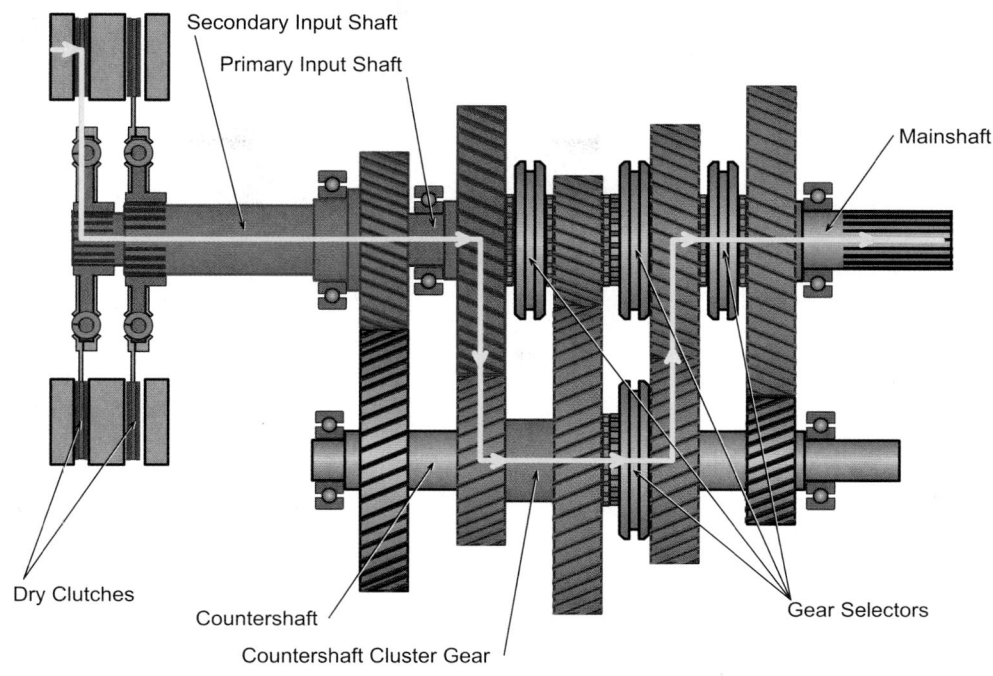

FIGURE 45-64 Dual-clutch transmissions save fuel with no torque brake shifting.

clutches drive a separate input shaft, a solid inner shaft, and a hollow outer shaft. **FIGURE 45-64** is a simplified version of the transmission; note that the planetary range section is not shown in the diagram. Gear selector synchronizers are used alternately on the output shaft and on the countershaft, like the Eaton Procision discussed earlier. The two mainshaft gears are driven by the countershaft either through the primary or the secondary input shafts. That allows for four different ratios. A fifth ratio can be achieved when the mainshaft is driven directly by the primary input shaft when the output shaft is connected to it.

With the primary input shaft connected to the output shaft, the transmission can reach a sixth ratio by switching to the secondary input clutch and driving the primary input shaft through the secondary input shaft and the countershaft. All those ratios pass through a planetary range gear system. That makes for six forward ratios in the low range of the planetary range system. The same six ratios are repeated in high range when the planetary range system allows the power flow to pass through unchanged. That brings the total to twelve forward ratios. All the transmission shifts are full power shifts with no torque break, except for the range shift between sixth and seventh. Compared to its traditional I-Shift, Volvo claims the new I-Shift has increased cycle

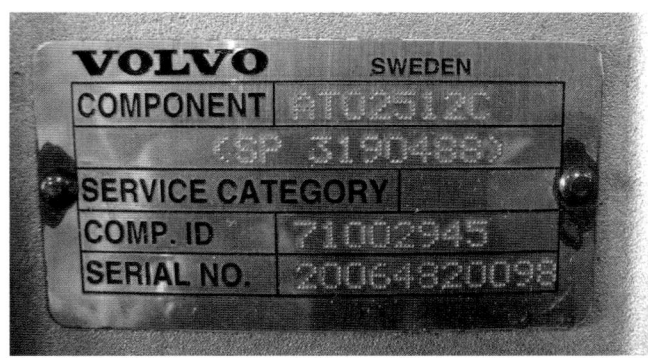

FIGURE 45-65 Volvo I-Shift nameplate.

time from faster shifts and has improved fuel economy. Volvo's dual-clutch model number is the SPO2812. It is capable of handling up to 2065 ft-lb (2800 Nm) of torque.

Volvo Transmission Nomenclature

As expected, Volvo has unique nomenclature for its transmissions. **FIGURE 45-65** shows a Volvo nameplate, and **TABLE 45-10** shows how to decipher the naming convention.

TABLE 45-10 Nomenclature for Volvo ATO2512C

AT	O	XX	12	C
Automated mechanical transmission	Overdrive No letter = Direct	Max input torque Nm (ft-lb) 25= 2500 (1850) 28=2800 (2050) 31=3100 (2300)	12-speed	Design level

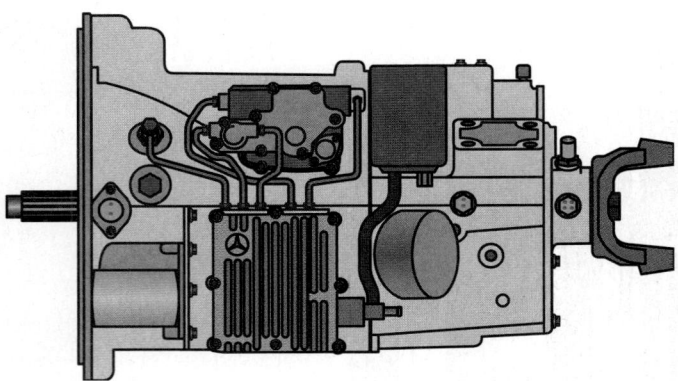

FIGURE 45-66 Daimler Trucks' automatic gear shift (AGS) transmission.

Mercedes Benz/Daimler Trucks Automatic Gear Shift

Mercedes Benz, known in North America as Daimler Trucks, has introduced two transmissions into the AMT market since 2004. Both transmissions are AGS models—the MBT520-6DA and the MBT660-6OA. Both transmissions are six-speed models with a maximum input torque of 520 and 660 ft-lb (705 and 895 Nm), respectively. The MBT520-6DA is a direct-drive model and has a maximum GVW of 40,000 lb (18,144 kg). The MBT660-6OA is an overdrive model capable of a maximum GVW of 60,000 lb (27,216 kg) and a final ratio of 0.73:1. Their overall gear ratio is 9.2:1 and 9.18:1, respectively. An AGS transmission is shown in **FIGURE 45-66**.

Regardless of model, the AGS transmission is a two-pedal design. The self-adjusting, hydraulically actuated clutch is controlled electronically, and the release bearing is of the permanently lubricated-type to reduce maintenance.

AGS transmissions are a completely self-contained package. They come equipped with an on board TCU attached to the central unit that incorporates the following components:

- An attached fluid reservoir to hold the hydraulic actuating fluid for the transmission
- A high-pressure electric fluid pump that pressurizes fluid to 1247 psi (8598 kPa)
- A control valve body that holds the 12-volt electric solenoid valves that direct the flow of hydraulic fluid to operate the transmission
- A fluid accumulator that stores fluid under pressure, even when the vehicle is shut down
- A hydraulically controlled X/Y shifter module that selects shift rail and gear position
- The control solenoid for the hydraulic clutch actuator (the clutch actuator is a release bearing with an integral hydraulic cylinder mounted on the transmission input shaft)

AGS transmissions also have the following sensors:

- Clutch position sensor
- Rail position sensor
- Shift rod position sensor
- Hydraulic fluid level sensor
- Input shaft speed sensor
- Two output shaft speed sensors

The transmission TCM communicates with the engine ECM over the J-1939 data link to request torque break when a shift is required or to accelerate the engine during downshifting. The TCM communicates fault codes when there is a system malfunction. These codes always have several identifiers, including:

- Message identifier (MID); MID 130 identifies the transmission
- Subsystem identifier (SID)
- Parameter identifier (PID)
- Failure mode identifier (FMI) for the detected fault

The AGS series of transmissions are capable of adaptive learning and shift strategy adjustment based on vehicle load, road grade, and driver style. The transmission can provide changing shift schedules to optimize fuel economy and vehicle performance.

In North America, the AGS is available on Detroit Diesel, Freightliner, and Sterling trucks. Nomenclature for the MBT660-6OA is given in **TABLE 45-11**.

> **SAFETY TIP**
>
> The Mercedes Benz AGS series of transmissions operates at extremely high hydraulic pressure—up to 1247 psi (8598 kPa). The accumulator holds this pressure even when the vehicle is not operating. Technicians unfamiliar with this transmission must consult the OEM service manual before attempting any system repairs. Inadvertent release of pressure at this level could cause fluid injection injuries, leading to serious medical problems or death. The OEM manual has procedures to reduce the pressure before working on the transmission. Those procedures should be followed to the letter!

Troubleshooting Automated Manual Transmissions

LO 45-5 Describe the troubleshooting and service procedures for AMTs.

Troubleshooting an AMT fault should be done in a logical sequence. First, find as much information as you can about the

TABLE 45-11 Nomenclature for Daimler Trucks' AGS Model MBT660-6OA

MBT	660	6	O	A
Mercedes Benz Transmission	Input torque	Forward speeds	O = Overdrive D = Direct	Automatic

complaint from the driver. Then, verify the complaint. Overlooking this step has sent many a technician on a wild goose chase to find non-existent complaints!

Once you have established the complaint does exist, rule out any mechanical causes for the complaint, such as air system problems or transmission mechanical problems. Ideally, you should use the proprietary software to diagnose an AMT fault, but most AMTs also have a way to manually display fault codes.

To retrieve fault codes in an Eaton Fuller AMT, start by enabling the system's self-diagnostic mode. Alternatively, use an OEM or aftermarket electronic service tool, such as Eaton's PC-based service tool, ServiceRanger, or MPSI Prolink. Be sure the appropriate cartridge is installed. Note that on Eaton Fuller's Gen 1 and Gen 2 transmissions, electronics do not flash the service transmission light for system codes, only for component codes.

Examples of system codes are the front box control system, the splitter control system, or the engine control system. System codes may or may not be associated with a recognizable symptom when they are set, but the check transmission light does not flash. Component codes are set for component problems, such as the range valve, a speed sensor, and a rail position sensor. Those codes cause the check transmission light to flash. To enable the system's self-diagnostic mode and retrieve codes through the check transmission light, follow the steps in **SKILL DRILL 45-1**.

You can clear inactive fault codes by using an OEM or aftermarket Electronic Service tool, such as Eaton's PC-based service tool, ServiceRanger, or MPSI Prolink with the appropriate cartridge installed. To manually clear all inactive fault codes from the ECU's memory, follow the guidelines in **SKILL DRILL 45-2**.

SKILL DRILL 45-1 Enabling the Self-Diagnostic Mode and Retrieving Codes

1. Place the transmission in neutral.
2. Set the parking brake.
3. To retrieve active codes: Start with the key in the ON position. Turn the key off and on two times within five seconds. End with the key in the ON position. After five seconds, the service lamp should begin flashing two-digit fault codes. If no faults are active, the service light flashes code 25 (no codes). Note: A code 88 may show up in the dash at key ON. That is a normal power-up test of the display.
4. To retrieve inactive codes: Start with the key in the ON position. Turn the key off and on four times within five seconds. End with the key in the ON position. After five seconds, the service lamp should begin flashing two-digit fault codes. If there are no inactive faults, the service light flashes code 25 (no codes).
5. Two-digit fault codes may be read directly from the gear display or by observing the flashing service transmission light, if equipped. Observe the sequence of flashes on the service light and record the codes. The flash codes are displayed as follows: one flash, a short pause, and then three flashes equal code 13. There is a long pause of three to four seconds between codes. Then the next code is flashed. For example, three flashes, a short pause, and then two flashes equal code 32. Another long pause follows and the two codes repeat once more.

SKILL DRILL 45-2 Clearing Inactive Codes

1. Place the shift lever in neutral.
2. Set the parking brake.
3. Turn the ignition key on but do not start the engine.
4. Start with the key in the ON position. Turn the key off and on six times within five seconds. End with the key in the ON position. Note: If the codes have been successfully cleared, the service lamp comes on and stays on for five seconds. The gear display shows code 25 (no codes).
5. Turn the key off and allow the system to power down.

Although Skill Drills 45-1 and 45-2 are specific to Eaton Fuller, most manufacturers of automated transmissions have similar procedures for reading and clearing fault code information. If the transmission is displaying a fault code, consult the manufacturer's fault code listing in the troubleshooting manual. Follow the fault code trouble tree.

The fault code trouble tree is a step-by-step method of diagnosing and repairing the fault. The Eaton Fuller fault code chart lists nearly 100 separate codes, so trying to go through them here would simply take up too much space. Manufacturers have spent millions of dollars setting up trouble trees and fault- and symptom-based diagnosis systems for their products. The best method of troubleshooting complaints is to follow manufacturer recommendations.

▶ TECHNICIAN TIP

Failure to follow the trouble tree to the letter, or skipping steps, is simply a waste of your time and the vehicle owner's time. Do not be temptec to jump ahead when using a trouble tree. If you do, it is more than likely that you will end up having to start all over again.

▶ TECHNICIAN TIP

You can find the OEM manuals, troubleshooting manuals, and fault code guides for Eaton Fuller transmissions on the company website at www.roadranger.com. Meritor information can be found at www.meritor.com. For other automated transmissions, contact the manufacturer. There is no substitute for the OEM manual. If you cannot access one, then you should not take on the repair job.

Using a Diagnostic (Scan) Tool to Diagnose Transmissions

Using electronic diagnostic equipment to troubleshoot components has become a necessity in today's industry. Because you will work with many different diagnostic tools, it is important to locate the correct service manual procedure before attempting to retrieve DTCs. A laptop computer, a hand-held diagnostic tool, or an on board diagnostic component are the most common DTC retrieval systems. The two types of DTCs are active and inactive. These two types of codes tell the technician what has taken place in the system. A digital multimeter is normally used to test the area where the fault code indicates that the malfunction has occurred. As you can see, it is important that a diesel technician in today's high-tech world be proficient at using electronic diagnostic tools to retrieve DTCs and troubleshooting electronic systems.

Every technician's toolkit should contain the basic hand tools for the tasks to be undertaken, such as appropriately sized wrenches and socket sets, screwdrivers, hammers, and pliers. These items let technicians undertake the normal day-to-day activities associated with their position. In addition, special tools are always required to perform particular tasks on specific manufacturer equipment.

These are normally provided by the company the technician works for and may be, in some cases, hired in from tool suppliers because of their specialist nature. Other equipment, such as safety items, is normally provided for as part of the shop equipment. Whatever the case, before attempting a specific task on a vehicle or its components, it is essential to have available as part of the process the following items:

- Technician's common hand tools
- Appropriate service manual
- Job ticket—use appropriate one provided at your facility
- Wheel chocks
- Safety glasses
- Shop towels
- Diagnostic trouble code retrieval tool
- Multimeter
- Diagnostic equipment
- Tachometer
- Temperature gauge
- Other equipment and supplies as required by procedure

▶ TECHNICIAN TIP

Procedures vary with different types of vehicles. Always check the procedure in the service manual before beginning any service or repair.

To use a diagnostic tool and procedure to diagnose automated transmission problems, follow the steps in **SKILL DRILL 45-3**.

Servicing Electronic Shift Controls, Air and Electrical Switches, Displays and Indicators, and Wiring Harnesses

To inspect, adjust, repair, or replace electronic shift controls, air and electrical switches, displays and indicators, and wiring harnesses, follow the steps in **SKILL DRILL 45-4**.

Servicing Automated Transmission ECUs, Sensors, Vehicle Interface, and Related Components

Automated transmissions come in many different types and models, so you must locate the appropriate service manual before beginning any tests or repairs. This procedure does not address any specific transmission, but keeps instructions generic.

To inspect, adjust, repair, or replace electronic shift controls, ECU, wiring harnesses, sensors, control module, vehicle interface module, and related components, follow the steps in **SKILL DRILL 45-5**.

SKILL DRILL 45-3 Using a Scan Tool to Diagnose Transmissions

1. Locate and follow the appropriate procedure in the service manual.
2. Complete the accompanying job sheet or work order with all pertinent information.

3. Move the vehicle into the shop and park it on level ground.
4. Apply parking brakes, chock the vehicle wheels, and observe lockout/tagout procedures.
5. If the vehicle has a manual transmission, place it in neutral; if it has an automatic or automated transmission, place it in park or neutral. Note: Some vehicles with automatic transmissions do not have park.
6. Check for active and inactive DTCs using the appropriate service manual procedure and diagnostic tool.
7. Record any displayed DTCs on the job sheet or work order.
8. Use a multimeter to verify the problem(s) associated with the DTC(s).
9. Record all diagnostic readings.
10. Repair or replace the affected systems or components.
11. Clear all inactive and active DTCs.
12. Road test the vehicle through a complete drive cycle and check for re-occurrence of the codes.
13. List the test results and/or recommendations on the job sheet or work order, clean the work area, and return tools and materials to their proper storage.

SKILL DRILL 45-4 Servicing Electronic Shift Selectors, Switches, Displays, and Wiring Harnesses

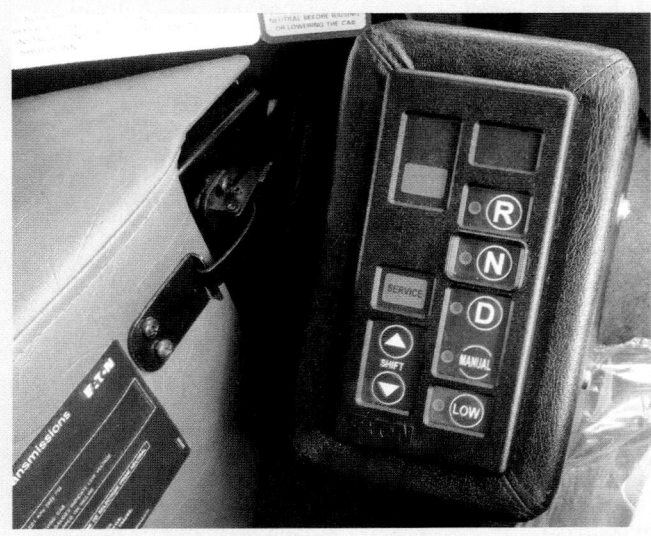

1. Locate and follow the appropriate procedure in the service manual.
2. Complete the accompanying job sheet or work order with all pertinent information.
3. Move the vehicle into the shop, apply parking brakes, and chock the vehicle wheels. Observe lockout/tagout procedures.
4. If the vehicle has a manual or automated transmission, place it in neutral; if it has an automatic transmission, place it in park or neutral. Note: Some vehicles with automatic transmissions do not have park.
5. Use service manual procedures to inspect, repair, or replace the following components:
   a. Electronic shift control
   b. Gear display
   c. Wiring harness
   d. Air and electric switches
6. List the test results and/or recommendations on the job sheet or work order, clean the work area, and return tools and materials to their proper storage.

SKILL DRILL 45-5 Servicing Automated Transmission ECUs, Sensors, Vehicle Interface, and Related Components

1. Locate and follow the appropriate procedure in the service manual.
2. Complete the accompanying job sheet or work order with all pertinent information.
3. Move vehicle into shop, apply parking brakes, and chock the vehicle wheels. Observe lockout/tagout procedures.

4. If the vehicle has a manual or automated transmission, place it in neutral; if it has an automatic transmission, place it in park or neutral. Note: Some vehicles with automatic transmissions do not have park.
5. Test the operation and retrieve DTCs as outlined in the service manual.
6. Use service manual procedures to inspect, repair, or replace external/internal wiring harnesses.
7. Use service manual procedures to test, repair, or replace the following components:
   a. Electronic control unit (ECU)
   b. Vehicle interface module (VIM)
   c. Vehicle interface wiring (VIW)
   d. Engine speed sensor
   e. Transmission temperature sensor
   f. Output speed sensor
   g. Throttle position sensor
   h. Control module
8. Use service manual procedures to test, repair, or replace the electronic shift control(s).
9. List the test results and/or recommendations on the job sheet or work order, clean the work area, and return tools and materials to their proper storage.

Wrap-Up

Ready for Review

▶ Automated manual transmissions (AMTs) are standard mechanical transmissions adapted to computer control.
▶ AMTs were developed to reduce carbon dioxide emissions and to reduce fuel consumption, and their development was driven by EPA-mandated reductions in exhaust emission.
▶ AMTs optimize shift points, leading to increases in fuel economy.
▶ AMTs are also a draw for new drivers because of their ease of operation and reduction in driver fatigue.
▶ AMTs may be a three-pedal design, where the clutch is used by the driver for starting and stopping, or a two-pedal design with no clutch pedal at all.
▶ Some newer AMTs have dual-clutch inputs that even further improve fuel economy.
▶ AMTs reduce driver training requirements, vehicle downtime, and vehicle driveline abuse by the driver.
▶ Most AMTs still require torque to be broken to complete a shift, but the newer dual-clutch models do not. Breaking torque costs fuel.
▶ Dual-clutch AMTs allow very quick, full-power shifting, leading to even greater fuel economy than traditional AMTs.

▶ Eaton Fuller's line-up of AMTs includes the AutoShift, the UltraShift, and the dual-clutch Procision and the Endurant. These are the most popular models of AMT found in North America.
▶ The Eaton Procision is a dual-clutch AMT specifically built for the class 6 and 7 market.
▶ Eaton released the Endurant transmission an AMT built for line-haul trucks.
▶ The brain of the AMT is the computer controller that commands the shift process. Depending on the manufacturer, this computer is called the TCM (transmission control module) or the transmission ECU.
▶ Meritor teamed up with ZF to market ZF's line of AMTs in North America.
▶ ZF now markets its AS-Tronic, TC-Tronic, and Traxon transmissions directly to North American OEMs.
▶ In 2014, Detroit Diesel launched its own version of the Mercedes 12-speed single countershaft AMT popular in Europe and called it the DT-12.
▶ The AS-Tronic has a twin countershaft mainbox with a planetary range section and share very similar power flows with all three module transmissions.
▶ The Volvo I-shift AMT also shares a similar power flow to the AS-Tronic but utilizes only one countershaft in the main box.

▶ AMT shifting is usually accomplished by electric motors and or electric-over-air solenoids.

▶ AMTs software has become increasingly sophisticated and now is capable of adaptive electronic control based on driver, load, terrain, and other operating conditions, thereby optimizing shifting strategies and fuel economy.

▶ To shift without gear clash, AMTs use software to read shaft and gear speeds inside the transmission.

▶ AMT controllers are capable of self-diagnosis and set diagnostic trouble codes (DTCs), alerting the driver to problems.

▶ AMT software is capable of initiating failsafe strategies to protect the transmission while still allowing limited operation.

▶ AMT software is becoming more and more integrated with the rest of the vehicle control systems, allowing safety features, such as hill hold, urge to move, creep mode, and predictive shifting.

▶ Eaton AMTs use air solenoids to shift the range and the splitter sliding clutches in their transmissions equipped with auxiliary sections.

▶ Inertia brakes are used by the AMTs to control transmission shaft speeds for shifting to first or reverse from neutral and to increase shift speed synchronization, when required.

▶ AMTs still require clutches, although there may be no clutch pedal. The clutches can be standard mechanical versions (Eaton AutoShift), a centrifugally operated clutch (some Eaton UltraShifts), an electrically operated clutch (some UltraShift models), air-operated clutch (used on the DT-12 and the AS-Tronic), wet clutch (used by Eaton ASW and the Mercedes AGS), or dual-clutches either dry or wet (the new Volvo I-shift uses a dual dry clutch while the Eaton Procision uses a dual wet clutch for input).

▶ AMT ECUs record active and inactive DTCs that can assist the technician in diagnosing complaints. These codes can usually be retrieved manually and/or by using an electronic service tool.

▶ All manufacturers have detailed troubleshooting strategies and trouble tree sequences listed in their service manuals to assist the technician in his or her diagnosis.

Key Terms

adaptive learning Software than can learn and change strategy based on different operating factors.

air-control solenoid valve An electric-over-air solenoid used to control shifting by controlling the flow of air from the air filter to the range cylinder piston.

automated manual transmission (AMT) A standard manual transmission operated by electronic control.

AS-Tronic ZF's AMT for medium- and heavy-duty trucks and buses.

Automatic Gear Shift (AGS) One of Mercedes' AMTs for lighter-duty trucks.

AutoSelect Eaton's first AMT; very limited electronic control.

AutoShift Eaton's first shift by wire transmission.

carbon dioxide (CO_2) One of the resulting gases produced when burning a hydrocarbon fuel; thought to contribute to global warming.

DT-12 A 12-speed AMT manufactured by Detroit Diesel.

dual-clutch transmission Transmission with two separate input shafts controlled by two separate clutches.

electric shift assembly The shift actuation system for an Eaton AutoShift or UltraShift transmission that contains two shift motors, the shift finger, and the shift finger position sensors.

Engine Synchro Shift (ESS) Meritor's first AMT; limited to synchronizing engine speeds to assist the shifting process.

Freedomline 12- and 16-speed ZF AMTs released in partnership with Meritor.

gear jamming An attempt by the driver to shift without using the clutch; usually causes at least some damage to the transmission sliding clutches. Also called *float shifting*.

I-Shift The Volvo AMT; Mack trucks use the same transmission.

J-1587 An early SAE network communication protocol with a data transmission at 9600 bits per second.

J-1939 A Newer SAE network communication protocol; data transmission at a rate of at least 250,000 bits per second and up to 500,000 bits/second.

momentary engine ignition interrupt relay (MEIIR) A relay controlled by the ECU that cuts the engine ignition or fueling if a DM clutch does not disengage.

Procision Eaton's dual-clutch seven-speed AMT; introduced in 2014.

self-diagnostic The ECU capability to analyze its own functions.

shift by wire Shifting controlled completely by the transmission electronic control.

snapshot A snapshot records all the relevant ECU data before and after a diagnostic code is set to ease diagnoses.

start enable relay The start enable relay is controlled by the ECU and interrupts the circuit to the starter solenoid unless the ECU passes a self-check and verifies the transmission is in neutral.

SureShift Meritor's first line of fully automated transmissions.

system manager A transmission control module used with older Gen 1 and Gen 2 Eaton AutoShift transmissions.

TC-Tronic A ZF AMT that uses a torque converter for input; for heavy applications.

thermal efficiency A measurement of how much of the fuel used is turned into power to drive the vehicle.

transmission control module (TCM)   The unit that controls the shifting in an electronically automated transmission. Also called *transmission electronic control unit (ECU)*

transmission electronic control unit (ECU)   The unit that controls the shifting in an electronically automated transmission. Also called *transmission control module (TCM)*.

Traxon   ZF's latest AMT with five different input modules available.

UltraShift   Eaton's two-pedal AMT; completely shift by wire with no clutch pedal.

Review Questions

1. Which of the following is NOT one of the reasons that automated manual transmissions are becoming more popular?
   a. They have better fuel economy.
   b. They are less expensive than standard transmissions.
   c. They lead to reduced carbon dioxide emissions.
   d. They reduce driver training requirements.

2. The transmission shift tower is replaced by which of the following on an Eaton UltraShift transmission?
   a. A shift motor
   b. A rail select motor
   c. An electric shift fork
   d. An electric shifter assembly

3. Which of the following does not occur before a vehicle with an UltraShift manual transmission can be started?
   a. The transmission ECU must conduct and pass an initiation and self-check.
   b. The transmission ECU must verify a neutral position.
   c. The transmission ECU must turn on the start enable relay.
   d. The MEIIR relay must be turned on.

4. Each time the vehicle is shut down, which of the following does not occur in the Eaton UltraShift transmissions?
   a. The start enable relay is actuated.
   b. The transmission ECU conducts a self-check diagnostic.
   c. The range and splitter air shift cylinders are moved to neutral.
   d. The transmission ECU maps and records the shift rail gates.

5. The Eaton Gen 3 AutoShift transmission has which of the following electronic modules?
   a. A shifter module, a system manager ECU, and a shift control ECU
   b. A shifter module with built-in system manager and a shift control ECU
   c. A single transmission ECU on the transmission
   d. A shifter module with a built-in, single-transmission control ECU

6. How is the auxiliary section high- and low-range shift accomplished on a 10-speed Fuller UltraShift transmission?
   a. By air using two control solenoids
   b. By air using one control solenoid
   c. Electrically using one electric motor
   d. Electrically using two electric motors

7. In a Fuller UltraShift transmission, what must the transmission ECU do in order to make a shift?
   a. It must request the engine ECM to break torque.
   b. It must assume control of the engine.
   c. It must ask the driver to depress the clutch.
   d. It must actuate the MEIIR relay.

8. The rail select sensor on a Fuller UltraShift transmission is a(n):
   a. induction pulse generator.
   b. potentiometer.
   c. rheostat.
   d. Hall effect sensor.

9. The output speed sensor on a Fuller UltraShift transmission is a(n):
   a. induction pulse generator.
   b. potentiometer.
   c. rheostat.
   d. Hall effect sensor.

10. What must the driver do to select high range while driving forward in an UltraShift transmission?
    a. Preselect the range by moving the range lever to high while the transmission is in gear
    b. Preselect the range shift by pushing the up arrows
    c. Select range after the transmission shifts to neutral
    d. The driver cannot select high or low range—only gear numbers.

ASE Technician A/Technician B Style Questions

1. Technician A says that two-pedal AMTs still require a clutch. Technician B says that in three-pedal AMTs, the driver uses the clutch only for starting off and stopping the vehicle. Who is correct?
   a. Technician A
   b. Technician B
   c. Both Technician A and Technician B
   d. Neither Technician A nor Technician B

2. Technician A says that all AMTs use a standard dry disc clutch. Technician B says that the Volvo I-Shift uses a large organic dry disc clutch. Who is correct?
   a. Technician A
   b. Technician B
   c. Both Technician A and Technician B
   d. Neither Technician A nor Technician B

3. Technician A says that the new Eaton Procision uses two multiplate wet clutches as inputs. Technician B says that the Procision transmission has two input shafts. Who is correct?
   a. Technician A
   b. Technician B
   c. Both Technician A and Technician B
   d. Neither Technician A nor Technician B

4. Technician A says that the AS-Tronic transmission from ZF uses a splitter gear at the input to double the ratios in the front box section. Technician B says that the rearward split

in the splitter section of the ZF AS-Tronic is always the high split position. Who is correct?

a. Technician A
b. Technician B
c. Both Technician A and Technician B
d. Neither Technician A nor Technician B

5. Technician A says that the 12-speed Volvo I-Shift transmission has the same basic power flows as the 12-speed AS-Tronic from ZF. Technician B says the 12-speed Volvo I-Shift has only one countershaft. Who is correct?

a. Technician A
b. Technician B
c. Both Technician A and Technician B
d. Neither Technician A nor Technician B

6. Technician A says that the sliding clutches in a Fuller Ultra-Shift transmission have wider tooth spacing than non-automated transmission models. Technician B says that the mainshaft gears in a Fuller UltraShift transmission have wider tooth spacing than non-automated transmission models. Who is correct?

a. Technician A
b. Technician B
c. Both Technician A and Technician B
d. Neither Technician A nor Technician B

7. Technician A says that a Fuller 18-speed UltraShift transmission uses two air solenoids to control the splitter shift in the auxiliary section. Technician B says that a Fuller 18-speed UltraShift transmission uses two air solenoids to control the range shift in the auxiliary section. Who is correct?

a. Technician A
b. Technician B
c. Both Technician A and Technician B
d. Neither Technician A nor Technician B

8. Tech A says the MEIIR relay is controlled by the engine ECM. Technician B says that the MEIIR relay is only actuated when there is catastrophic clutch failure. Who is correct?

a. Technician A
b. Technician B
c. Both Technician A and Technician B
d. Neither Technician A nor Technician B

9. Technician A says that the Eaton Procision seven-speed transmission never needs to break torque while shifting through gears one through seven. Technician B says that the Eaton Procision transmission preselects seventh gear while still in sixth to make the shift quicker. Who is correct?

a. Technician A
b. Technician B
c. Both Technician A and Technician B
d. Neither Technician A nor Technician B

10. Technician A says that the ZF AS-Tronic transmission has an overdrive gear in the range section. Technician B says that the AS-Tronic can have either two or three forward mainshaft gears. Who is correct?

a. Technician A
b. Technician B
c. Both Technician A and Technician B
d. Neither Technician A nor Technician B

CHAPTER 46
Torque Converters

Learning Objectives

After reading this chapter, you will be able to:

- LO 46-1 Explain the basic functions of the torque converter.
- LO 46-2 Describe the components of the torque converter.
- LO 46-3 Explain torque converter operation.
- LO 46-4 Describe the hydraulic circuits associated with torque converters.
- LO 46-5 Troubleshooting torque converter failure.
- LO 46-6 Describe common torque converter service procedures.

You Are the Technician

An international 4200 series truck is brought to your repair shop and the driver complains that his fuel economy has decreased steadily over the last few weeks. The vehicle has an Allison 1000 series automatic transmission. After a preliminary inspection you road test the vehicle, and the engine seems to operate as it should and has plenty of power. The transmission seems to shift gears correctly; however, the check transmission light is illuminated.

1. What could cause this lack of fuel economy?
2. What would you do next to find the problem?
3. Could the transmission cause a low fuel economy complaint?

Introduction

If you have read the chapters on standard transmissions, you know that most of today's truck transmissions have between 10 and 18 gear ratios in order to move the heavy loads expected of them within the narrow engine rpm range available. These ratios range from a low of 15:1, 16:1, or even 17:1, up to overdrive ratios of 0.73:1 and 0.66:1. By contrast, automatic transmissions usually have only four to six gear ratios ranging from a low of usually not more than 6 or 7:1 and ending up with the same overdrive ratios of 0.73 and 0.66:1. Still, automatic transmissions are expected to haul loads that are equal to their 18-speed standard transmission cousins. So, how does an automatic transmission with a low gear ratio of only 4.7:1 haul an 80,000 lb (36,287 kg) load? That is where the **torque converter** comes into play. Torque converters multiply the input torque by as much as three or four to one. In most truck applications, the multiplication is held to around two to one. Let's take the above transmission example with a 4.7:1 first-gear ratio and see what happens when we add a torque converter with a multiplication factor of 2.47:1.

Just as a gear ratio multiplies the output torque in a transmission, the torque converter multiplies the input torque. In our example, that means the overall output available to drive the vehicle amounts to the gear ratio times the torque converter multiplication factor—or 4.7 times 2.47. What results is an equivalent ratio of 11.6:1, which is ample to move the load. A torque converters multiplication factor automatically lessens as the vehicle picks up speed. When the transmission is in first gear, the overall ratio can change from the maximum of 11.6:1 all the way to the actual first-gear ratio of 4.7:1. Rather than having only four or six ratios, the torque converter allows an automatic transmission to have a constantly variable ratio within the limits of the actual gear ratios and the torque converter's multiplication factor. In this chapter, we look at how the torque converter accomplishes this feat.

Functions of Torque Converters

LO 46-1 Explain the basic functions of the torque converter.

All vehicles, whether with standard or automatic transmissions, must have a means of interrupting the engine power from the driveline when the vehicle is stopped. Otherwise, the engine would stall. Standard transmissions have a manual or automatic clutch that performs this function. The clutch physically disconnects the transmission input shaft from the engine when the clutch is disengaged. The automatic transmission uses a torque converter to perform this function. The torque converter is a sophisticated type of **fluid coupling** that allows the vehicle to slow down and stop without any disconnection of components. The torque converter is able to accomplish this because the engine power is transmitted to the driveline through a fluid, rather than a physical, connection. The easiest way to visualize this power transmission is to imagine two electric fans facing each other. Turn one fan on, and observe the other fan. The air being pushed out by the powered fan strikes the blades of the unpowered fan. As illustrated in **FIGURE 46-1**, the blades of the unpowered fan start to turn, even though there is no physical connection between them. The air acts as a fluid transmitting the power from the first fan into the second fan. This is the basic principle of the fluid coupler—power can be transmitted through a fluid to drive another component.

For a functioning fluid coupler to work, however, you need more than just the two fans mentioned above. Because air is easily compressed, the fans could not transmit very much torque. Plus, the fans are open at the sides, so at the first sign of resistance, the fluid (air) would merely deflect to the side. To make a proper fluid coupling, you need first to use a liquid because most liquids are essentially incompressible. In a transmission, hydraulic oil, usually known as transmission fluid, is used to transmit the power. Second, you must stop the fluid from being deflected to the side when the torque increases. To accomplish this, the fans in a fluid coupler are encased in a circular housing. Third, the fans are placed very close to one another and the blades of the fans are slightly angled, as shown in **FIGURE 46-2**, to optimize power transfer. Then, the driving fan is attached to the power source, and the driven fan to the output, to create a functioning fluid coupler.

Using a fluid coupler has many advantages. A fluid coupling allows equipment to start up virtually load-free. When an electric motor starts up, it tends to accelerate very rapidly. A fluid coupling

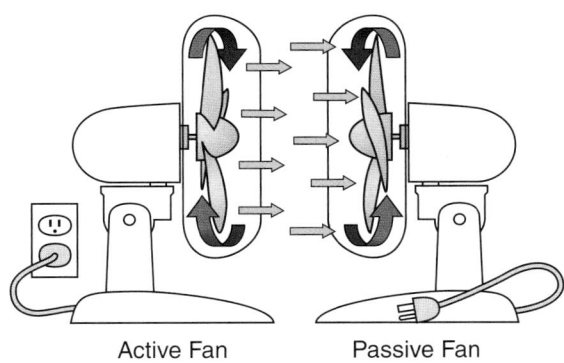

Active Fan   Passive Fan

FIGURE 46-1 Air driven by the powered fan drives the blades of the unplugged fan.

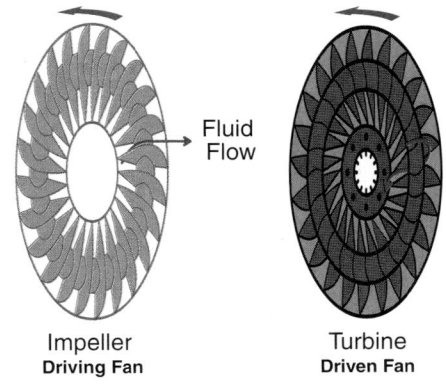

Fluid Flow

Impeller
Driving Fan

Turbine
Driven Fan

FIGURE 46-2 A simple fluid coupling has only two elements: the driving "fan" and the driven "fan" inside a sealed shell.

allows the drive to slip as the motor speed ramps up. That slippage reduces the start-up shock load, the current draw, and the potential for overheating.

A fluid coupler can also cushion the shock from overloads, machinery that jams up, or sudden speed changes by allowing the driven fan to slip. Fluid couplers are used in many applications where low speed start-up torque is not a significant issue, including conveying systems, processing equipment, and assembly-line systems, such as filling and packaging operations. Power can be supplied by electric motors, industrial engines, or power take-off units on mobile equipment, such as tractors in agricultural applications. The fluid coupler is simply designed and it can achieve nearly 100% efficiency at high speeds as long as the load applied is not too great.

The main disadvantage of the fluid coupler is that it is quite inefficient at starting speeds when the input is much faster than the output. The fluid coupler is also incapable of multiplying torque. During start-up operation, the driven element of the coupler is much slower than the speed of the driving element. A lot of the power is wasted and dissipated as heat, caused by the shearing forces and turbulence that is imparted on the fluid by that difference in speed. Because of this, a fluid coupler is not suitable for motive power use where heavy loads must be moved from a standing start. The torque converter uses the advantages of the fluid coupler, allowing the vehicle to be stopped while the engine is still running and being able to transfer power at close to 100% when conditions are correct. The torque converter, however, has a huge advantage over the fluid coupler because the converter can multiply torque. When starting out from a stop, the torque created by the typical internal combustion engine is quite low because the engine speed is quite low also. The torque converter multiplies this torque to allow quicker acceleration and throttle response. Depending on the torque converter design, this multiplication can be two to four times the torque the engine is producing. Most on-highway torque converters multiply torque around 2:1. The simple torque converter, however, never operates at 100% efficiency. The driven element (the **turbine**) can only be accelerated to approximately 95% of the speed of the driving element (the **impeller**). This is due to the turbulence caused by the other element in the converter, the stator, and by the design of the turbine itself.

Today torque converters address this inadequacy by utilizing a **lock-up clutch**. When conditions are correct, the lock-up clutch locks the turbine to the converter shell, and the engine power is transmitted directly to the driveline at a 1:1 ratio, eliminating any loss in efficiency. This chapter discusses how the converter functions, both under load and during lock-up, and explains how these advantages are accomplished.

Components of Torque Converters

LO 46-2 Describe the components of the torque converter.

In the section on the fundamentals of torque converters, we referred to the driving and driven fans in a fluid coupler because they were the simplest way to explain the basic concept.

Of course, the components of a fluid coupling are not actually called fans. Their correct names are the impeller (also known as the pump), which is the driving "fan," and the turbine, which is the driven "fan."

The modern torque converter, shown in **FIGURE 46-3**, includes several components. The shell, or housing, contains all the component parts. The impeller (pump) is the driving member and is part of or attached to the shell. The turbine is the driven member, the stator is the reaction member, and the two halves of the split guide ring are the final components of the torque converter.

The converter also houses the components that make up the lock-up clutch. Components of the lock-up clutch in heavy-duty torque converters include a gear or spline attached to the turbine, a friction disc that fits the spline or gear, the clutch actuation piston, and the backing plate attached to the converter housing that the piston squeezes the friction disc against. We discuss these components individually at first and then explain how they interact with each other.

Converter Shell or Housing

The converter shell is comprised of two halves. The rear half has the shape of a hollowed-out half donut, as shown in **FIGURE 46-4**. The half donut shape is called a **torus**.

FIGURE 46-3 The modern torque converter housing contains all the elements involved in power transfer and lock-up clutch operation.

FIGURE 46-4 The rear half of the converter shell is shaped like a hollowed-out half donut and has the pump drive hub attached (circled).

The rear half of the shell also has a hollow stub attached to its center. This is called the pump drive hub. When installed in the transmission, the pump drive hub drives the transmission oil pump gears. The transmission oil pump is responsible for all the pressures created in the transmission and for supplying the torque converter with fluid. The front part of the torque converter housing usually looks flat on the outside—this is to accommodate the placing of the lock-up clutch components inside the front cover. In some cases, it may have a rounded shape—especially if the converter does not have a lock-up clutch. The front half of the shell normally has a protruding pilot that engages the rear of the crankshaft or the engine flywheel to help support the converter weight, as shown in **FIGURE 46-5**.

In light-duty applications, the two halves of the shell are welded together and the converter is not designed to be overhauled. Rather, it is designed to be replaced. In heavy-duty models, however, the shells are bolted together, and the converter can be disassembled for inspection and repair.

Impeller or Pump

Both impeller and pump are used to name the driving member in the torque converter. We use the term impeller to avoid confusion with the transmission hydraulic pump. The impeller is a series of vanes. The vanes can be cast as part of the rear half of the converter shell or they may be welded to it, as seen in **FIGURE 46-6**. One half of the **split guide ring** is attached to the

FIGURE 46-5 The front half of the shell tends to be flat and has a pilot (circled) that supports the converter in the crankshaft or the flywheel.

FIGURE 46-6 The impeller is responsible for the fluid movement in the converter. **A.** Impeller blades. **B.** Split guide ring.

middle of the impeller's blades to provide strength and create half of a circular passage for fluid flow.

The torque converter shell or housing is physically attached, though not directly, to the engine crankshaft. As a result, the shell and the impeller turn with the engine. During operation, the torque converter is filled with transmission fluid through the pump drive hub. The impeller blades generate centrifugal force that flings the fluid outwards. The curved torus shape of the rear half of the shell then forces the fluid around the split guide ring and forward toward the engine.

Turbine

The turbine sits just in front of the impeller inside the converter housing. The turbine is also shaped like a half-donut (torus) as shown in **FIGURE 46-7**. When the turbine is installed in front of the impeller, the torus shape of the rear converter housing and the turbine combine to form a complete donut shape. The turbine has a series of curved blades that are designed to catch the oil being thrown forward by the rotating impeller. The second half of the split guide ring is attached to the middle of the turbine blades; again, to strengthen the blades and to help form a circular fluid flow between the impeller and the turbine and back again.

The turbine sits very close to the front of the impeller. The turbine does not, however, touch the impeller. Clearances may be as tight as 0.060" to 0.080" (1.5 to 2.0 mm), but the two components do not touch. The turbine is supported by thrust bearings or washers that locate it axially and is not connected to anything in the torque converter. The turbine is, however, splined to the input shaft of the transmission, which enters the torque converter from the rear. The forward end of the input shaft or the front of the turbine is usually supported by a bushing or bearing inside the torque converter housing that serves to radially locate the shaft and the turbine.

Stator or Reaction Member

The outside edges of the turbine and the impeller are very close together inside the torque converter. In contrast, the inner edges are a fair distance apart. The **stator**, a bladed wheel most responsible for torque multiplication, sits

FIGURE 46-7 The turbine's design, along with the impeller, completes the hollow donut shape that the transmission fluid flows through in the torque converter. **A.** Split guide ring. **B.** Turbine blades.

between the turbine and impeller to take up that space. The stator is shaped like a wheel with curved blades for spokes. The outer edge of the "wheel" is positioned very close to the inner edge of the two halves of the split guide ring, as shown in **FIGURE 46-8**.

When the converter is assembled, the two halves of the split guide ring and the outer edge of the stator wheel create an almost complete circular ring. The fluid can flow from the impeller around the ring, through the turbine, and back to the impeller. This ring helps to reduce fluid turbulence inside the converter. The stator itself usually has three components: the inner hub, the **over-running clutch** (or **one-way clutch**), and the actual stator wheel. The inner hub of the stator is splined to the **stator support** or (**ground**) **shaft**, which surrounds and supports the transmission input shaft. Like the input shaft, the stator support shaft, enters the torque converter from the rear. The stator support shaft, (ground shaft) is attached to the transmission hydraulic pump and bolted to the transmission housing. Therefore, the stator support shaft and the inner hub of the stator can never turn. The over-running (one-way) clutch sits on the stator inner hub and supports the stator wheel. That clutch only allows the stator wheel to turn in one direction. The stator wheel's axial position is usually controlled by thrust bearings or washers.

Lock-Up Clutch Assembly

No matter how sophisticated the design, all torque converters allow some inherent slippage between the impeller and the turbine. That is, the impeller can never drive the turbine at engine speed. Speed loss varies but is usually in the neighborhood of 5%. In the past, that level of speed loss was acceptable. The primary focus was on performance, rather than fuel economy and emission control. Today, that level of speed loss cannot be tolerated. All of today's torque converters are equipped with a lock-up clutch designed to lock the turbine to the torque converter shell and thereby eliminate the slippage. Several designs of lock-up clutches have been used in the past, but the most popular in the truck market is the piston-type lock-up clutch.

Lock-up clutches usually have the following components:

- A backing plate that is either part of the front of the torque converter shell or bolted to the shell
- A hydraulic piston that is usually located in the front half of the converter shell
- A friction disc that sits in between the backing plate and the piston, as shown in **FIGURE 46-9**

The friction disc is splined to the turbine. When the piston is actuated hydraulically, it squeezes the friction disc between the piston and the backing plate. That action locks the turbine to the shell, eliminating all slippage.

Operation of Torque Converters

LO 46-3 Explain torque converter operation.

The first thing we must understand about torque converter operation is that the converter must be completely filled with fluid to work properly. Any air inside the converter will cause aeration, excess heat, and very poor torque transmission. Just as in a hydraulic system, the compressibility of the air severely affects efficiency in the torque converter. The automatic transmission oil pressure circuits prioritize fluid delivery to the torque converter to ensure it is always full. The transmission fluid enters and leaves the torque converter at the center hub. We look at the oil pressure circuits involving the torque converter in the Torque Converter Hydraulic Circuits section.

Rotary Flow and Vortex Flow

The torque converter shell is indirectly bolted to the engine crankshaft. Any time the engine is turning, so is the torque converter shell. Remember that the impeller blades are directly connected to the rear half of the shell, so they also turn with the shell. The blades of the impeller are usually straight or very slightly curved as the prime function of the impeller blades is to act on the mass of transmission fluid inside the torque converter and force the fluid toward the outside of the shell. The rotation of the shell causes **centrifugal force**, the apparent force by which a rotating mass tries to move outward away from its

FIGURE 46-8 The outer edge, or wall, of the stator wheel completes the ring formed by the two halves of the split guide ring around which the fluid revolves during circular, 'vortex' flow. **A.** Stator. **B.** Split guide ring. **C.** Outside edge of stator wheel.

FIGURE 46-9 A typical lock-up clutch as is used in a truck torque converter. **A.** Disc splines. **B.** Piston. **C.** Friction disc. **D.** Backing plate.

axis of rotation, which acts on the fluid and the blades of the impeller. **FIGURE 46-10** illustrates this centrifugal effect. The rear half of the split guide ring that is attached to the impeller blades helps to direct and smooth the flow of fluid toward the outside of the housing or shell.

The torus shape of the rear half of the torque converter shell redirects the fluid thrown outward by centrifugal force by sending the fluid forward toward the blades of the turbine. The blades in the torus-shaped turbine are curved significantly, almost cup-shaped, to catch the fluid. The force created by the impeller's rotation is directed against these curved blades, as shown in **FIGURE 46-11**. The curve of the turbine blades, and the front half of the split guide ring attached to them, help to direct the fluid back toward the center of the impeller.

The turbine is not attached to anything inside the torque converter, but the turbine is splined to the transmission input shaft. When an automatic transmission is started in neutral or

park, the input shaft is not physically connected to the driveline by the transmission. On initial start-up, then, there is no load on the input shaft or the turbine. Consequently, the force of the fluid striking the turbine blades quickly spins the turbine up to almost the speed of the impeller. Both of these elements turn at close to the same speed because there is nothing to resist the turbine's motion.

The mass of fluid in the torque converter in this scenario are rotating as a solid circle of fluid traveling in the same direction. The impeller and turbine are rotating with the converter. This type of fluid dynamic in the torque converter is known as **rotary flow** and is illustrated in **FIGURE 46-12A**. As soon as a load is placed on the turbine, however, the situation changes. For example, putting the transmission in drive connects the input shaft and, therefore, the turbine, to the vehicle driveline. Assuming the vehicle is at a standstill and the engine is at idle speed, the turbine immediately comes to a stop because it now has significant load attached to it. That greatly changes the fluid dynamic inside the torque converter. What was a smooth rotary flow instantly changes to a much more turbulent flow, known as **vortex flow**, illustrated in **FIGURE 46-12B**.

In vortex flow, the fluid being thrown outward by the centrifugal force is thrown forward by the torus shape of the rear half of the shell. With the turbine stopped, the fluid must flow through the curves of the turbine blades and return to the impeller. The front half of the split guide ring attached to the turbine blades helps to smooth the semicircular flow through the turbine.

The actual flow is as follows. First, the fluid enters the impeller through the pump drive hub near its center and flows behind the split guide ring to the outside edge due to the impeller's rotation and centrifugal force. The fluid is then forced

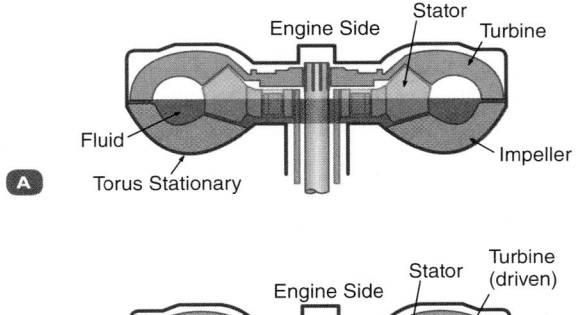

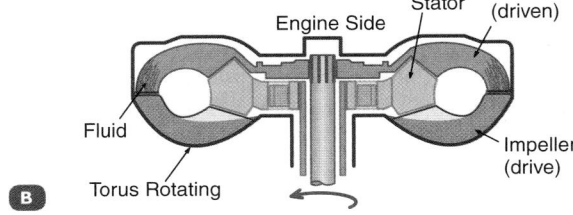

FIGURE 46-10 A. At rest, the converter shell is full of fluid. **B.** As the torque converter shell starts to turn, the centrifugal force throws the oil outward and the torus shape of the impeller forces it forward toward the turbine.

FIGURE 46-11 Unlike the blades of a fluid coupler or the blades in the impeller, the turbine blades are very sharply angled in order to take advantage of as much of the force from the fluid striking them as possible. **A.** Inlet. **B.** Stator. **C.** Input shaft spline. **D.** Inside edge (fluid outlet).

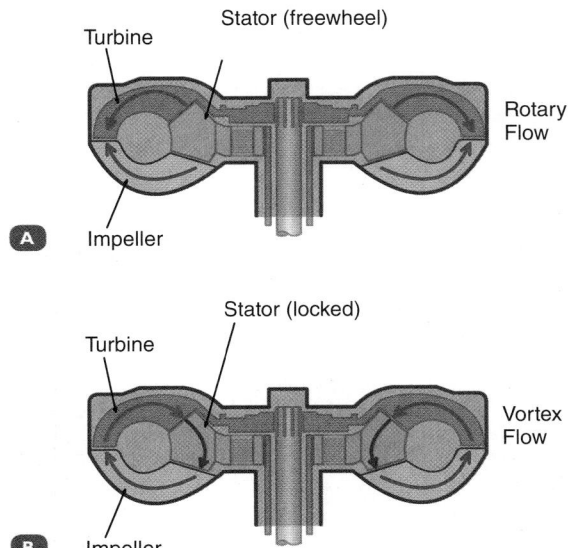

FIGURE 46-12 A. During rotary flow, the fluid travels in a circle following the rotation of the converter shell. **B.** During vortex flow, the fluid flows from the impeller, around the split guide ring, to the turbine, then around the turbine's split guide ring, through the stator, and back to the impeller.

forward by the torus shape of the rear housing of the torque converter and enters the turbine at its outside edge. Fluid continues to flow around the curved blades and behind the front half of the split guide ring. The torus forces the fluid rearward, causing the fluid to exit the turbine near the center of the converter and flow back toward the impeller. Because of the sharp curvature of the turbine blades, the fluid exiting the turbine is now flowing in a direction that opposes the impeller's rotation, as shown in **FIGURE 46-13**. In effect, the fluid exiting the turbine is trying to stop the impeller from rotating.

With the vehicle in gear and at idle speed, the centrifugal force generated by the rotating impeller is very low. Therefore, the force of the fluid exiting the turbine is also very low and has little effect on the impeller's rotation. Still, as the engine accelerates, both the centrifugal force and the turbine exit force increase greatly. Increasing force would cause extreme turbulence, excess heat, and very inefficient power transfer. Why? Because the engine would be trying to drive the impeller at the same time the turbine is trying to stop the impeller. To prevent this, the fluid exiting the turbine needs to be redirected so that it helps the power transfer instead of hindering it. To accomplish this, the center of the torque converter contains the stator placed in between the exit area of the turbine and the inlet area of the impeller as shown in **FIGURE 46-14**.

FIGURE 46-13 Fluid exiting the turbine is flowing opposite to the impeller's rotation.

FIGURE 46-14 The stator redirects fluid flow so it re-enters the impeller in the same direction as impeller rotation. This redirection helps the impeller and increases the force applied to the turbine.

The stator is a wheel with blades instead of spokes. The outer edge of the wheel completes the inner edge of the circular fluid path formed by the two halves of the split guide rings. The fluid flow corkscrews around this circular tube. The **stator inner hub** is splined to the stator support, or (ground) shaft, which is part of the transmission front pump assembly. That means that the inner hub cannot turn. The outer hub or wheel of the stator is mounted on an over-running (one-way) clutch that allows the wheel to turn in only one direction. (Certain heavy-duty and off-road applications use fixed stators that do not turn in either direction, but in highway applications, the stator is always mounted on a one-way clutch.)

The "spokes" of the stator wheel are sharply curved blades. The converter is designed to cause the fluid exiting the turbine during vortex flow to strike the faces of the stator blades. The converter tries to turn the stator with it, but fluid striking the blades in this direction causes the stator wheel to lock on its one-way clutch. The stator remains stationary. The stator blades then sharply redirect the fluid exiting the turbine and cause the fluid to enter the impeller in the same direction that the impeller is turning. The force of the fluid adds to the impeller's rotation and increases the amount of torque that the engine is sending to the transmission and driveline.

It is important to realize that the torque converter does not produce torque out of thin air. The torque increase is based on three things: the angles of the turbine blades, the angle of the stator blades, and the speed differential between the impeller and the turbine. The angle of the blades in the turbine determines the exit angle of the fluid and its speed. The angle of the stator blades determines how much force the fluid imparts on the impeller when it is redirected. The speed difference between the impeller and the turbine also affects the torque multiplication. Of these three, the speed difference between the impeller and the turbine is the most significant factor in torque multiplication. In a standard transmission, when it gears down, speed is sacrificed for increased torque. In an automatic transmission, the torque converter does the same.

Torque Converter Operational Phases

Torque converters have two significant operational phases. As its name suggests, the torque multiplication phase involves increasing torque output when there is significant speed difference between the impeller and the turbine. During this phase, oil flow in the converter is primarily vortex flow. The coupling phase involves an increase in turbine speed and a reduction in the vortex flow, the fluid starts to change more and more to rotary flow. Let's examine these operational phases in more detail.

Torque Multiplication Phase

The **torque multiplication phase** refers to any time the torque converter is increasing the engine's torque output to the transmission's input shaft. Maximum torque multiplication occurs when the engine is accelerated to the maximum speed at which it can turn the impeller while the turbine remains stationary. This is the point where the difference in turbine and impeller speed is greatest. This maximum speed difference is also known as the torque converter's **stall speed**. The engine cannot turn any faster because of the resistance provided by the stationary turbine. Reaching the stall speed rarely occurs in normal driving because the vehicle usually starts to move before maximum torque multiplication is reached.

The torque converter normally only experiences stall speed during a stall test procedure where the vehicle brakes are applied to prevent it from moving, or if the vehicle is severely overloaded. Most on-highway torque converters are set up to have a torque multiplication factor of around 1.75:1 to 2.5:1. Recall that torque multiplication is primarily based on speed difference between the turbine and the impeller. Therefore, torque converters with higher torque multiplication typically have higher stall speeds. Within certain limitations, stall speeds and the torque multiplication factor can be manipulated in the design stage by changing the size of the torque converter elements, the angle of the turbine blades, the angle of the stator blades, and the clearance between the elements. A high-stall or high-torque-multiplication torque converter can be excellent for take-off and picking up heavy loads. A lower-stall torque converter is usually more suitable for highway speed operation.

Over the years, manufacturers have used many torque converter designs to optimize vehicle operation. For example, converters with **variable pitch stators** allow the angle of the stator blades to be changed hydraulically to benefit both starting off and high-speed operation. Converters with twin stators achieve much the same effect and converters with two, or even three, turbines fine-tune vehicle performance. These modifications are not normally seen in on-highway applications today.

In normal operation, starting from a stop with the vehicle in gear (usually "D" or drive range), the impeller is turning at engine speed. At this idle speed, the force of the fluid striking the turbine blades is insufficient to start turning the turbine very much. The force is usually sufficient only to hold an unloaded vehicle stationary on a slight incline. The force may be enough to start turbine creep, causing the vehicle to move forward slightly, and the operator may have to apply the brakes to hold the vehicle stationary. As the operator steps on the throttle, the speed of the impeller increases, as does the fluid force pushing against the turbine blades. The fluid exiting the turbine still has significant energy and this force is redirected by the stator to assist the impeller's and, therefore, the engine's rotation, thus increasing the force leaving the impeller again. This force continues to increase with engine speed. The torque converter multiplies the torque from the engine within its design limitations until the vehicle starts to move. The amount of torque actually necessary to move the vehicle depends on road grade, vehicle load, and other factors. It is important to note that, as soon as the turbine starts to turn and the vehicle begins moving, the torque multiplication factor starts to drop because the speed difference between the impeller and turbine is decreasing. The torque multiplication factor continues to drop as the turbine speed increases and the speed difference between the impeller and turbine diminishes.

Vortex oil flow—the flow of fluid from the impeller through the turbine, through the stator, and back to the impeller—occurs at all times during torque converter operation, but is greatest at peak torque multiplication. That is, vortex flow is greatest at the converter stall speed, as illustrated in **FIGURE 46-15**. As the turbine speed increases, vortex flow—and, therefore, torque multiplication—decreases. In effect, while in operation, the torque converter has an almost unlimited number of torque multiplication ratios—from its design maximum to zero torque multiplication, depending on the speed difference between the impeller and the turbine.

Coupling Phase

During the torque multiplication phase of torque converter operation, vortex fluid flow kept the stator held stationary on its one-way clutch to help multiply torque. As the speed of the turbine approaches the speed of the impeller, the fluid flow changes. Most of the fluid no longer exits the turbine near its center. In fact, the turbine starts to impart centrifugal force on the fluid present in its torus and starts to throw the fluid back the way it came toward the impeller. At this stage, the vortex fluid flow slows down and nearly stops in the converter. Very little fluid is flowing through the turbine blades. Most of the fluid follows the rotation of the torque converter shell. Torque converter operation has now entered the **coupling phase**, illustrated in **FIGURE 46-16**. The fluid inside the converter is basically a solid donut-shaped mass of fluid rotating in the same direction and at nearly the same speed as the converter itself. As mentioned previously, this fluid flow is known as rotary fluid flow. In the coupling phase, however, the stationary stator we used in the torque multiplication phase would now be in the way and would restrict this rotary flow and cause extreme turbulence.

This is the reason that the stator is mounted on an over-running (one-way) clutch. When rotary flow starts to take over inside the converter, the flow of fluid starts to hit the stator blades from the back, and this unlocks the stator one-way clutch and allows the stator to turn freely in the direction of the fluid. The stator is mounted on either a sprag-type one-way clutch,

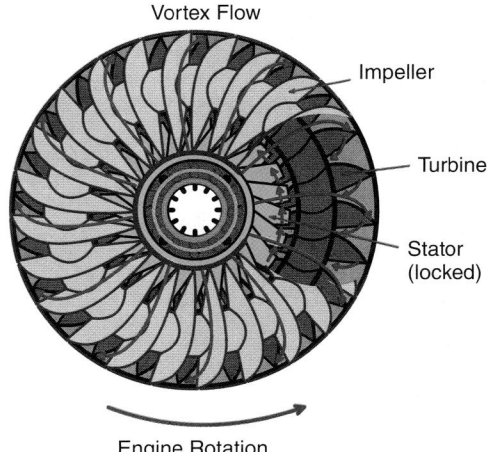

FIGURE 46-15 Vortex flow is greatest at full stall and decreases as the turbine speed catches up to the impeller's speed.

as shown in **FIGURE 46-17A**, or a roller-type one-way clutch, as shown in **FIGURE 46-17B**, so that it locks in one direction and can freewheel in the other. A sprag-type one-way clutch uses a series of peanut-shaped sprags that are specially designed so that they allow rotation in only one direction. A roller-type one-way clutch uses rollers and ramps that cause the rollers to

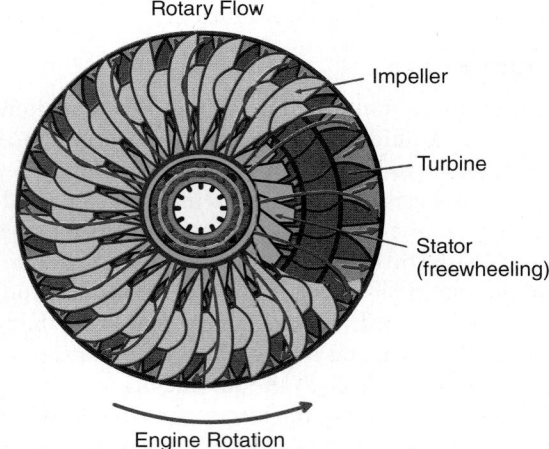

FIGURE 46-16 Rotary flow is greatest during the coupling phase when the fluid and the three converter elements—the turbine, the stator, and the impeller—are all turning in the same direction at nearly the same speeds.

FIGURE 46-17 A. Sprag-type one-way clutch with sprags showing. **B.** Roller-type one-way clutch with rollers and ramps.

jam and lock up if they try to turn in a reverse direction. Most heavy-duty torque converters use a roller-type one-way clutch to hold the stator.

The stator wheel is only unlocked during the coupling phase. During the coupling phase, the impeller, the turbine, the stator, and the fluid are all turning together at essentially the same speed. Also, in this phase, vortex flow in the converter has almost ceased, and rotary flow is at maximum. There is always some fluid flowing around with the converter shell, so some rotary flow is always present, but it is maximum at the coupling phase and minimum at converter stall.

The coupling phase is related to torque demand and not to road speed. That means the coupling phase can happen at any vehicle speed. For example, consider a normal drive cycle in a vehicle with an automatic transmission. You start the vehicle in park and as there is no load on the turbine the converter is in the coupling phase with all three elements turning together, then you put the transmission in drive and the turbine and the stator instantly stop because the turbine now has a load on it. Then you start driving from a standstill, and because you are in a hurry, you stomp on the throttle. What happens? The torque converter impeller speeds up instantly with the engine, and you enter the torque multiplication phase. Vortex flow is high because there is a significant difference between the impeller and the turbine speed. Even though vortex flow and torque multiplication are very high, you are not at maximum torque multiplication because the turbine starts to turn almost right away to drive the vehicle. Remember that you can only achieve maximum torque multiplication at the torque converter stall speed. The stator is locked and redirecting fluid to contribute to the torque multiplication. You are continuing to accelerate when a car pulls out in front of you. Almost instantly, you take your foot off the throttle. The engine speed and the impeller speed decrease until both are close to the turbine speed. The torque converter enters the coupling phase of operation in which the impeller and turbine are turning close to the same speed. Torque multiplication and vortex flow have almost ceased and rotary flow is now predominant in the converter. The stator is freewheeling with the fluid. If you continue to decelerate, the turbine may even over-run (turn faster than) the impeller as the vehicle weight pushes the turbine faster.

Now, imagine the car ahead quickly moves into the other lane. As you step hard on the throttle pedal once again, the impeller speed instantly increases, returning the converter to high vortex flow. The stator once again locks on its one-way clutch and the converter returns to multiplying torque in order to accelerate.

As you can imagine, this scenario changes constantly based on the demand for torque, or acceleration and deceleration. In most drive cycles, the transmissions torque converter is constantly switching from the torque multiplication phase to the coupling phase and back again. The automatic transmission has a clear advantage over standard transmissions in those situations because the automatic transmission has an automatic device that changes the torque multiplication factor within its design limit based on driver demand. The driver is not required to manually shift gears.

Note that converters in some off-road, slow-moving vehicles use a fixed stator that does not freewheel and is always stationary. In these vehicles, high-speed operation is not a concern, so the stator is solidly mounted to the stator support shaft and cannot turn in either direction. The torque converter elements in such vehicles are designed for high torque multiplication and low speed operation only.

Flex Plates

An engine requires a rotating mass to build inertia to keep it running between power pulses. Inertia is also critical for smoothing out the torsional vibrations created by the impact of these pulses. In standard transmission applications, those functions are accomplished by the engine flywheel.

In light- to medium-duty vehicles with automatic transmissions, the mass of the flywheel is replaced by the mass of the torque converter. The mass of the torque converter absorbs these pulsations and provides the inertia to keep the engine running between power strokes. Vehicles with automatic transmissions use a **flex plate** to connect the crankshaft to the torque converter. The flex plate may have the starter ring gear attached to it.

Heavy-duty vehicle engines usually require substantially more mass for this purpose, so heavy-duty vehicles with automatic transmissions often have a flywheel as well as a torque converter. Regardless, the torque converter cannot be coupled directly to the engine crankshaft or to the flywheel. When the torque converter is under heavy loads (while multiplying torque), its shell actually swells and contracts slightly. The fluid exerts a force over the large surface area of the converter shell to create these expansion and contraction cycles. The swelling is very slight, but over time, the constant fatigue or bending forces caused by this swelling would cause the converter shell or the mounting bolts to fracture and break if it were mounted solidly to the flywheel or crankshaft. To avoid that type of failure, the converter is always bolted to an individual flex plate, like the one shown in **FIGURE 46-18** (for a light-duty vehicle), or to a series of flex plates, as shown in **FIGURE 46-19** (for a heavy-duty vehicle), which in turn are bolted to the crankshaft or flywheel.

In light-duty vehicles, the flex plate is usually a single plate of flexible steel bolted directly to the crankshaft. The single flex plate may also have the ring gear for starting the engine welded to it. (If the ring gear is not on the flex plate, it is attached to the converter itself.) The converter is bolted to the outside of the flex plate.

In heavier applications, the engine flywheel is still used and the ring gear is attached to it, usually by the heat-shrink method. That is, the gear is heated to a specific temperature and placed over the flywheel. As the gear cools, it becomes fixed to the flywheel. Heat shrinking is used so that the gear can be replaced, when needed. The torque converter is typically bolted to a stack of several flexible steel plates, which in turn are bolted to the flywheel. Both methods allow the converter to expand and contract, as necessary, during its operation.

Lock-Up Clutch Operation

A torque converter impeller is incapable of driving the turbine at 100% of impeller (engine) speed. There is always some amount of slippage involved. The amount of slippage is determined by many factors. The design of the turbine and impeller blades, the clearance between the torque converter elements, the viscosity of the fluid, and more can affect the amount of slippage. That slippage can cause speed differences from 5% to 10%. This puts the automatic transmission at a disadvantage, in terms of fuel economy and carbon dioxide emissions, when compared to a standard transmission where the mechanical clutch does not allow any slippage. To compensate for that disadvantage, all modern torque converters are equipped with a lock-up clutch to lock the turbine to the converter shell. Such locking eliminates the inherent slippage and provides a 1:1 drive between the engine and the transmission.

The lock-up clutch usually consists of the three basic components, as shown in **FIGURE 46-20**:

- A hydraulic clutch piston, which is secured to the torque converter shell so it cannot rotate.
- A friction disc that is splined to the converter turbine. (Note that in the Allison transmission 1000, 2000, and 2400 series, the lock-up clutch friction disc and piston are combined as one unit.)

FIGURE 46-18 Flex plate for a light-duty vehicle.

FIGURE 46-19 Flex plates bolted to a flywheel for use in heavy-duty vehicles.

■ A backing plate that is also secured, usually by bolts, to the converter shell. (In some models, the backing plate is a machined surface on the inside of the front half of the converter shell.)

When lock-up is desired, hydraulic pressure is directed to the back of the piston to squeeze the friction disc against the backing plate. All slippage is stopped, and the turbine turns at the same speed as the shell (that is, at engine speed). **FIGURE 46-21** contains a cross-sectional view of a lock-up clutch system.

There are two basic control strategies for lock-up. The first is **programmed (systematic) lock-up**. The second is **modulated lock-up**. In the first type of lock-up strategy, the transmission controller engages lock-up every time the transmission reaches a certain gear range. That occurs whether the transmission controller is hydraulic or electronic. The gear range achieved may be as low as second range. Lock-up is then engaged in every range except first. For that reason, the programmed lock-up strategy is usually the best in terms of fuel economy and, therefore, carbon dioxide emissions. The tradeoff is slower acceleration and limited overall performance after first range.

The second strategy, modulated lock-up, is performance-based. With this strategy, the transmission enters lock up at any time—sometimes even in first range—if certain criteria are met. In most transmissions, however, the transmission must usually be in second range or higher. The usual criteria for lock-up to occur are that the driver should not be trying to accelerate rapidly, and the torque converter should be nearing coupling phase. (In other words, the turbine speed is close to the impeller speed.)

When these criteria are met, the hydraulic system or electronic controller may engage the lock-up clutch. If any of these criteria change, for example, if the driver steps on the throttle to accelerate, to pass a vehicle, or climb a hill, the lock-up clutch usually disengages. Torque multiplication is allowed to occur again to build speed rapidly.

With modulated lock-up, there is no specific time when the lock-up clutch is always engaged. In fact, the lock-up clutch may apply and release multiple times during a drive cycle, even though safeguards are installed to make sure that the lock-up is not constantly engaging and disengaging. Older lock-up clutch designs would disengage as soon as the driver applied the brakes to stop. On vehicles equipped with engine brakes, the clutch normally remains engaged to take advantage of engine braking, usually until the transmission down-shifts to first range. Some newer light-duty vehicles without engine brakes utilize this strategy for enhanced engine braking in certain ranges.

One of the functions of lock-up clutches is to reduce waste in the driveline. That reduction is increasingly important as the Environmental Protection Agency has mandated reducing limits for noxious emissions from all vehicles. Limits for oxides of nitrogen and particulates are near zero, and limits for carbon monoxide are also extremely low. The next challenge for engine and vehicle manufacturers is to reduce the emission of carbon dioxide. The only way to reduce the production of carbon dioxide while burning hydrocarbon fuels is to reduce the amount of fuel consumed. Therefore, manufacturers are pulling out all the stops in terms of maximizing engine thermal efficiencies and minimizing any parasitic load on the engine. Lock-up clutches are essential in today's automatic transmissions as one way to minimize wasted energy in the driveline.

FIGURE 46-20 The three components of a lock-up clutch assembly. **A.** Backing plate. **B.** Piston. **C.** Clutch disc.

FIGURE 46-21 A cross-section of a lock-up torque converter. **A.** Backing plate. **B.** Turbine. **C.** Impeller. **D.** Piston. **E.** Friction disc. **F.** Stator.

Torque Converter Hydraulic Circuits

LO 46-4 Describe the hydraulic circuits associated with torque converters.

The torque converter must be completely full of fluid to operate properly. The transmission hydraulic system therefore prioritizes fluid delivery to the converter. The hydraulic pump at the front of the transmission is driven by the pump drive hub that is welded to the back of the torque converter. As soon as the engine turns, the pump starts pressurizing fluid. As pressure builds, one of the first places the fluid is directed to is the torque converter. Remember that the torque converter is turning and the transmission is stationary, so hoses or pipes cannot be used, but there must be a way to send the pressurized fluid to the rotating torque converter.

Directing fluid to the rotating torque converter is accomplished by using a passage that is formed between the pump drive hub attached to the converter shell and the stator support or ground shaft, which enters the converter from the rear. This passage is shown in **FIGURE 46-22**. Fluid is sent through this passage and enters at the center of the torque converter behind the stator. There it fills the impeller blades and flows forward toward the turbine to fill its blades as well. The exit passage for the fluid is formed between the inside of the stator support shaft and the outside of the input or turbine shaft. The space between these two shafts becomes the exit passage.

As the fluid pressure from the transmission pump builds in the torque converter, the fluid is delivered to the point where the input shaft exits the stator support shaft. That point is just behind the splines that fit into the turbine. The fluid exits through the inside of the stator support shaft.

The fluid pathway in the transmission that leads to the torque converter has a pressure relief valve to restrict converter maximum working pressure. The fluid pathway also features **anti-drain-back check valves** that ensure the fluid does not drain back out of the torque converter when the vehicle is shut off. The exit passage from the converter also includes check valves to keep the converter full of fluid, even when the vehicle is not running. These valves can be dedicated valves or they can be spool valves that close when the vehicle is shut off thereby retaining the fluid. Without these valves, no drive would be possible on start up until the pump had refilled the torque converter. Depending on the transmission and vehicle, refilling the torque converter can take considerable time, from 30 seconds to a minute, or even longer in cold weather when the fluid is cold and viscous.

The torque converter places enormous load and shear forces on the transmission fluid that create tremendous amounts of heat. That heat must be dissipated, so the first place the fluid goes on exiting the torque converter is usually the **transmission oil cooler**. In the transmission oil cooler, the fluid flows through oil passages or tubes that are surrounded by recirculating engine coolant. As the fluid flows through the cooler, the heat is absorbed by the coolant. The fluid then exits the cooler and is returned to the transmission sump for recirculation. The converter in and out hydraulic circuits normally supply the transmission lubrication circuits. Typically, the front components of

the transmission are lubricated from a passage intersecting the converter fluid-in circuit. The rear half is typically lubricated by the converter fluid-out circuit when it returns to the transmission from the oil cooler.

Usually, a third passage into the converter is needed to supply the hydraulic pressure or the lock-up clutch piston application. Most heavy-vehicle manufacturers use a drilled hole in the center of the input shaft to create this passage. The input shaft is usually cross-drilled at a point where it passes through the rear of the hydraulic pump. That point is sealed between two nylon or steel sealing rings. The lock-up clutch apply pressure is delivered to this point and then travels up the input shaft center drilling to the hydraulic passageway for clutch application, as indicated in **FIGURE 46-23**. This apply pressure flows to the front of the **lock-up clutch piston,** pushing it rearward so that it squeezes the **lock-up clutch disc** between the piston and the backing plate. That action locks the disc to the converter shell and thereby eliminates turbine slip.

The process just described is the most common method for hydraulic circuits to apply lock-up clutches in heavy-duty applications. The Allison 1000, 2000, and 2400 series transmissions and most light-duty automotive automatic transmissions, however, use a slightly different method of supplying fluid to and from the torque converter. This method also controls lock-up clutch operation. In these transmissions, the lock-up clutch piston and the friction disc are combined, into a **lock-up clutch/piston assembly,** as shown in **FIGURE 46-24**. This saves manufacturing costs associated with forming a cylinder inside the torque converter in which the lock-up clutch apply piston can operate and eliminates the need for a separate backing plate. The fluid circuits used for this type of lock-up system are as follows. Fluid can flow into and out of the torque through either the cross and center drilling of the input or turbine shaft or the passageway formed between the stator support shaft and the pump drive hub. When the converter is in unlock mode, the converter in-circuit is through a cross and center drilling in the input, or turbine shaft. The fluid from the input shaft enters the torque converter in front of the piston/clutch assembly and it exits the converter between the pump drive hub and

FIGURE 46-22 The arrangement of the different shafts that enter the torque converter from the transmission form passageways that can be used to deliver fluid to and from the converter and to the lock-up clutch. **A.** Lock-up clutch apply passage. **B.** Converter out passageway. **C.** Converter in passageway.

FIGURE 46-23 The lock-up clutch components. **A.** Hydraulic passageway for clutch application. **B.** Turbine front support bushing. **C.** Lock-up clutch disc spline that connects to the turbine. **D.** Lock-up clutch piston splined to the converter shell. **E.** Lock-up clutch backing plate bolted to the converter housing.

the outside of the stator support shaft. Specifically, in the Alison 2400 series, the fluid travels up and around the edge of the piston/lock-up disc.

The transmission fluid flowing from the input shaft and around the outside of the lock-up clutch/piston assembly to the rear of the torque converter is sufficient to push and hold the lock-up clutch/piston assembly rearward and away from the front of the converter housing, keeping the lock-up clutch disengaged. The fluid then exits through the pump drive hub of the converter. To engage the lock-up clutch, the transmission control system reverses the converter fluid flow direction. The fluid now enters the converter through the pump drive hub. With the fluid flowing from the back of the torque converter to the front, the fluid catches the formed cup-like edge of the lock-up clutch/piston assembly and pushes it forward. The fluid pressure squeezes the lock-up clutch/piston assembly against the inside of the converter shell. The back of the converter front housing has a smooth machined area that the clutch friction material engages. Pushing the clutch/piston against the back of the converter front cover locks the turbine to the shell. While the torque converter is in lock-up mode, the fluid does not circulate through the converter—it only applies pressure to the lock-up clutch, although the passage through the center and cross-drilling in the input shaft is open to the sump of the transmission, so fluid behind the piston/clutch assembly can exit. Turning off converter fluid flow when it is not required reduces parasitic loss due to pumping the fluid through the torque converter. Remember that, in lock-up mode, the converter is not generating any heat so there is no need to circulate and cool the fluid. To disengage the clutch, the control again reverses the flow and the piston/clutch assembly releases. This is a considerably cheaper way to create a lock-up clutch as there is no backing plate, no separate piston, and, therefore, no need to form a cylinder in the converter housing.

Most of the lock-up clutches in use today incorporate a spring-loaded torsional damper hub to absorb the damaging torsional vibrations created by power pulsations from the engine. These can be very simple spring dampers or more elaborate models that use coaxial springs, as shown in **FIGURE 46-25**. Some dampers even use internal friction dampening similar to those used on mechanical clutches. Without dampers, the power pulsations from the engine are transmitted directly both to the transmission and the rest of the driveline when the torque converter lock-up clutch is applied. The resulting torsional vibrations can cause catastrophic damage to driveline components.

Troubleshooting Torque Converter Failure

LO 46-5 Troubleshooting torque converter failure.

Torque converters are ruggedly constructed and should last the expected service life of the transmission to which they are connected. Torque converters do not, however, stand up to serial abuse, such as high-speed direction changes and vehicle overloading.

The single most common cause of failure of automatic transmissions overall is loss of fluid, and this type of failure normally requires the overhaul or replacement of the torque converter. Both the transmission and the torque converter are hydraulic devices and without fluid they do not function and fail catastrophically. Before trying to diagnose any problem with the converter or the transmission, ensure that fluid level is correct and in good condition.

There are a number of failures that can occur in the torque converter alone, and they usually fall into three categories: noise, lock-up clutch issues, and performance. Noise complaints are usually caused by bearing or thrust washer failures. Lock-up clutch complaints are usually precipitated by either failure to engage or failure to disengage or shudder on engagement. Performance complaints, such as no power on take-off or the vehicle being sluggish at highway speeds, usually indicate stator problems. Regardless of the complaint, confirm that the engine performance is not to blame before condemning a torque converter.

Converter noise complaints are relatively easy to diagnose because they tend to show up only when the vehicle is placed in gear. When the transmission is in neutral or park, the converter elements are typically rotating at near the same speed because there is no load on the turbine. As soon as

FIGURE 46-24 The Alison 2400 series converter. **A.** Lock-up clutch/piston assembly. **B.** Front housing. **C.** Friction material.

FIGURE 46-25 Lock-up clutch disc with torsional dampening.

the vehicle is placed in gear, the turbine comes to a stop. At that point, its supporting bearings start to turn. If the noise begins, the bearings are likely the source of the complaint. During a road test, converter noise normally ceases when the lock-up clutch engages. Whining noises that seem to emanate from the converter, but do not change, usually indicate one or more of the following:

- Wear in the converter pump drive hub bushing (excessive wear here is normally accompanied with a transmission fluid leak from the front pump seal)
- Wear in the front pump gearing
- Aeration problems that can cause cavitation and rapid destruction of the pump

Aeration of the transmission fluid can be caused by one of two extremes. On the one hand, when the fluid level is too low, air is drawn in to the pump. On the other, when the fluid level is too high, the rotating components of the transmission come in contact with the fluid. What happens is like a kitchen mixer—the rotating components churn up the fluid and mix in significant amounts of air. Both of these conditions cause low fluid pressure and can lead to transmission failure. Proper fluid level is always essential.

Lock-up clutch engagement and disengagement can be monitored by careful observation of engine rpm during a road test. As the lock-up clutch engages, engine rpm drops significantly and on disengagement rpm increases. A shudder felt on lock-up clutch engagement typically indicates a failure of the clutch disc itself, a failure of the lock-up clutch piston seals, or clutch-apply hydraulic circuit failure. Failure of the clutch disc normally causes the transmission fluid to discolor from excessive heat and burnt clutch material. Shudder on engagement of the lock-up clutch can also be caused by not using the recommended transmission fluid. Many manufacturers include friction modifiers in their transmission fluid and using the wrong fluid can cause converter clutch issues and can also cause the transmission's hydraulic clutches to not engage properly. Always use the fluid recommended by the OEM or its equivalent. If lock-up clutch disengagement is the problem, it manifests itself as a stall condition or a shudder as the vehicle is brought to stop. In that case, careful examination of the lock-up control circuit must be conducted to determine if the problem is on the control side or is an internal torque converter problem. To diagnose torque converter complaints that may involve stator operation, both a stall test and a road test are required.

► TECHNICIAN TIP

Aeration of the fluid or cavitation of the front pump causes an extremely loud whining that can be mistaken as front pump or bushing failure. The sound is similar to a power steering system that is low on fluid. If you hear whining, always check the fluid level and condition before condemning any components.

Stall Testing

The stall test procedure can be used to determine engine, torque converter, and transmission performance. It is very commonly the first test a technician performs when diagnosing transmission or converter complaints. The stall test procedure is very straight forward, but there are some preparatory steps that must be undertaken. Although the following method for stall testing an automatic transmission is very general, it does follow the usual steps necessary to determine the problem. Before testing, ensure that the engine can be accelerated to its maximum no-load speed. Also prior to conducting a stall test, check the particular manufacturer's specifications for the specific transmission model so that the test is carried out properly. You may find that certain transmission models must not be stall tested in certain gear ranges, such as low or reverse, as these ranges may produce too much torque on the driveline leading to failure of the drive shaft or other components. Some transmissions allow the tester to engage different hydraulic clutches during a stall test either by selecting different ranges manually or electronically so that the stall test can be used to detect specific clutch failures. Selecting a different range for the stall test does not have an effect on the stall speed as long as the transmission clutches are in good shape. To conduct a stall test, follow the steps in **SKILL DRILL 46-1**.

SKILL DRILL 46-1 Performing a Stall Test

1. Bring the transmission up to its normal operating temperature, usually 160°–220°F (70°–104°C). With the vehicle parked on level ground, shift through all range selections and back to neutral. This ensures that the fluid level check is accurate. Leave the engine running at idle and check the transmission oil level.
2. Check that engine coolant and oil levels are correct.
3. Transmission fluid temperature can increase very rapidly (as fast as one degree per second) during the extreme conditions created by a stall test, so install a temperature gauge at the transmission line fitting that goes to the transmission cooler. This is the fluid output from the converter. Converter out

SKILL DRILL 46-1 Performing a Stall Test (Continued)

temperature should not exceed 300°F (149°C) and sump temperatures should not exceed 250°F (121°C). Most new transmissions are equipped with electronic temperature gauges that can be accessed with a ProLink or similar electronic scan tool. If using a scan tool, the temperature reading is sump temperature.

4. Install a pressure gauge at the transmission line or main pressure tap. This ensures that the transmission and the torque converter are receiving sufficient fluid pressure. Install an accurate tachometer so that the correct engine rpm can be read. (Note that steps 2–4 can usually be eliminated with electronically controlled transmissions by using an Electronic Service Tool (EST), such as a Prolink or the OEM diagnostic software, which can track all three of these items.)

5. Caution: Conducting a stall test purposely puts the torque converter into maximum vortex flow and, therefore, maximum torque multiplication. The vehicle must be positively prevented from moving or serious damage to the vehicle or injury to personnel may occur. Use wheel chocks, full brake effort, and chains, if necessary, to prevent movement. Ensure that no one stands in front or behind the vehicle during the stall test.

6. A stall test places the driveline under great stress. Only maintain a full stall condition on for as long as it takes to read a stabilized rpm, the amount of time required should not usually exceed 10 seconds, and holding a stall for longer can lead to transmission or driveline damage. Closely monitor fluid temperature; the temperature can increase as fast as 1°F (17°C)

per second. Maximum transmission fluid temperature to the transmission cooler should not exceed 300°F (149°C) during a stall test and, if monitoring temperature with a scan tool, sump temperature should not exceed 250°F (121°C).

SAFETY TIP

If engine rpm does not stabilize and continues to rise or the temperature rises above the maximum levels, stop the stall test immediately or serious damage to the transmission can occur!

7. With the vehicle's brakes applied, place the transmission in the correct range—usually first, but not always. Check with the manufacturer to be sure. Accelerate to the maximum rpm the engine can achieve with the turbine stalled. After a few seconds, the engine speed should reach its maximum and stabilize. When that occurs, record the rpm on the tachometer. This is the stall speed. Gently decelerate and place the transmission in neutral.

8. To reduce fluid temperature after stall testing, ensure the transmission is in neutral and run the engine at 1200–1500 rpm for a few minutes. Doing so allows the torque converter to enter the coupling phase, so the shear forces stop and the fluid merely circulates through the converter and the cooler and back to the transmission. Watch transmission fluid temperatures carefully during this operation; if the fluid fails to cool down, it could indicate a seized stator.

Performing a Stall Test When an Engine Has Smoke Controls

If the engine is equipped with **smoke controls**, a slightly different stall test procedure is required. Smoke controls are used on older engines with mechanical fuel injection systems, these controls are designed to reduce black smoke emissions. Smoke control systems restrict the engine fueling until turbo boost is high enough. With these engines, it is not possible to obtain maximum fuel and, therefore, maximum engine rpm during a stationary stall test. Any stall test, then, produces incorrect readings. With smoke-controlled engines, a driving stall test is required. To perform a stall test on a vehicle with smoke controls, follow the steps in **SKILL DRILL 46-2**. Note that some modern electronic engines also limit engine torque while the vehicle is not in motion; it may be necessary to use this driving stall test method with these engines as well. Some electronic control systems may have a special mode for stall testing that over-rides the torque limit.

Interpreting the Stall Test Results

Usually the stall speed figure allows a plus or minus of 50 to 100 rpm. If the reading is plus or minus up to 100 rpm, the engine transmission and the torque converter are functioning correctly. If the engine speed is too high or too low, then there is a problem.

A high stall speed is almost always caused by a slipping clutch inside the transmission. Clutches slip due to low oil level or pressure, a burned clutch pack, seized or "lazy" clutch apply pistons, broken piston or transmission hydraulic circuit seals, and/or other problems in the clutch apply circuit. Further road testing of the vehicle or stall testing in other ranges is then required to isolate the slipping clutch. High stall speed can also be caused by a converter that is not full of fluid. If the transmission hydraulic pressure is correct, however, this should not be an issue.

A low stall speed usually indicates an engine not performing to its capabilities. An extremely low stall test speed, one that is 400 to 600 rpm lower, however, could indicate that the stator may be freewheeling (meaning the stator one-way clutch is not holding when it should). In order for the torque converter to obtain maximum torque multiplication, the stator must be held stationary to redirect the fluid leaving the turbine. If the stator one-way clutch does not hold and redirect the fluid leaving the turbine, it interferes with the impeller rotation and causes extreme turbulence. That prevents the impeller from turning as fast as it should and stall speed is much lower than normal. A driver complaint in this situation could be that the vehicle is very sluggish on take-off but seems normal at highway speeds or after the torque converter lock-up applies.

The opposite of this problem is a stuck stator or one that does not freewheel as it should when the coupling phase is

SKILL DRILL 46-2 Performing a Stall Test on Engines with Smoke Controls

1. Install an accurate tachometer and a method to monitor transmission temperature.
2. With the engine and transmission at operating temperature, road test the vehicle in a location where it can be driven at a speed necessary to conduct the test.

3. Drive the vehicle in a low enough gear that the throttle can be held wide open without exceeding the speed limit. (Do not operate the vehicle in low range as the driveline could be placed under excessive stress.)
4. Holding the throttle in the wide-open position, apply the service brakes until the vehicle comes to a complete stop. Immediately record the engine rpm and then release the throttle. This is the stall speed.
5. To reduce fluid temperature after stall testing, place the transmission in neutral and run the engine at 1200–1500 rpm for a few minutes. Doing so allows the torque converter to enter the coupling phase, so the shear forces stop and the fluid merely circulates through the converter and the cooler and back to the transmission. Watch transmission fluid temperatures carefully during this operation, if the fluid fails to cool down, it could indicate a seized stator.

reached. This problem usually shows up during a vehicle road test. The symptom is that the vehicle performs normally on acceleration, but cannot achieve highway speeds, and it feels sluggish during cruising speeds until the converter lock-up applies. The lock-up clutch may never actually apply in this situation because of the speed difference between the turbine and the impeller. This problem is hard to detect during a stall test as the stator is stationary anyway, but may be verifiable when performing the cool-down phase. After normally stall testing the converter, the fluid temperature tends to increase. When the vehicle is switched to neutral and accelerated to 1200–1500 rpm to circulate and cool the fluid down, a stuck or seized stator causes enough turbulence that the fluid usually remains at a high temperature. The fluid temperature may even increase instead of cooling down! Internal converter problems involving the stator require removal of the transmission in order to repair them. Recall that in light-duty transmissions, the converter is not serviceable and must be replaced (although many aftermarket rebuilders cut open and rebuild light-duty torque converters), but in heavy-duty vehicles, the converter can be overhauled, replacing only the failed components.

Testing Lock-Up Clutch Operation

The lock-up torque converter has been used by manufacturers since the late 1970s to help improve fuel economy when the vehicle is cruising at highway speeds. The lock-up torque converter contains a torque converter lock-up clutch, also known as simply a torque converter clutch (or TCC), which forces the turbine and impeller to match speeds. This system has several possible components that can fail, resulting in a loss of the lock-up ability or a converter that does not unlock. The system has a friction clutch disc that is actuated by a hydraulic piston and control circuit. The hydraulic control system uses an electrical solenoid valve to direct fluid away from, or to, the TCC assembly.

On electronically controlled transmissions, the operation of the TCC solenoid is monitored by the Transmissions Electronic

Control System that controls the transmission. Different manufacturers use different terms for this controller, such as Powertrain Control (PCM), Transmission Control Module (TCM), or Transmission Electronic Control Unit, (ECU). As mentioned in the Automated transmission chapter the SAE recommended term for this controller is the TCM so we use that term here. The transmission TCM can, but does not always, set Diagnostic Trouble Codes (DTCs) if a fault is present in the TCC circuit. For testing of a TCC on an electronically controlled transmission, a factory scan tool is invaluable. If the transmission TCM has set any codes related to the TCC circuit, look up the proper diagnostic procedure in the appropriate service information. Follow the procedure step by step.

Usually, on hydraulically controlled transmissions, the TCM does not set a DTC except in the case of an open circuit or a shorted solenoid for the TCC circuit. On a hydraulically controlled transmission, test-drive the vehicle to see whether you can feel the engagement of the lock-up torque converter. The scan tool might give data as to when the solenoid has been energized to apply the TCC solenoid, but many hydraulically controlled transmissions were built before auto manufacturers gave the technician much diagnostic data through the scan tool. If the TCC is not engaging, always check with the service information for a diagnostic procedure. Before beginning any diagnostics, check to make sure the system has power. Next, inspect and test the solenoid's ground circuit. If the power and ground circuits check out, test the solenoid with an ohmmeter. If the solenoid's resistance is within specifications, remove the solenoid from the transmission. Apply power and ground to the solenoid while attempting to blow air through the solenoid. If the solenoid operates properly, the problem is probably in the torque converter itself. If the solenoid does not allow air to flow, place it in a clean container of automatic transmission fluid and electrically cycle the solenoid to see if you can remove any blockage from the solenoid. If this does not work, it is necessary to replace the solenoid. To perform a lock-up converter test, follow the steps in **SKILL DRILL 46-3**.

SKILL DRILL 46-3 Performing a Lock-Up Converter Test

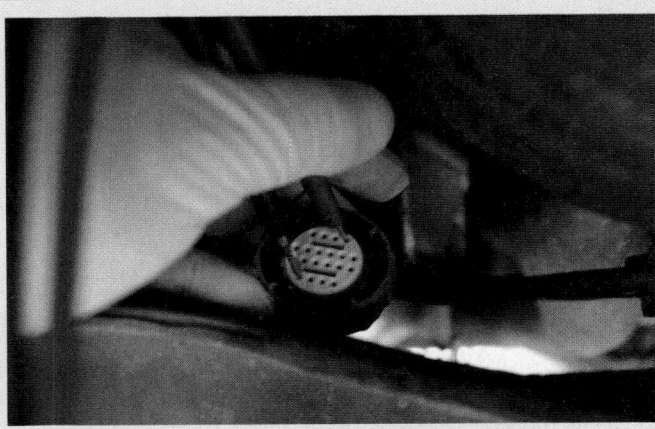

1. Scan the vehicle to identify any DTCs the transmission ECM has identified related to the TCC circuit; record your findings.
2. Look up the diagnostic procedure for the DTC in the service information and follow the step-by-step diagnostic procedure.
3. Test-drive the vehicle and observe the operation of the TCC circuit. When the TCC is applied, the TCC slippage should be less than the maximum slippage specified. (Some manufacturers specify maximum TCC slippage of 70 rpm.) If TCC slippage is greater than specifications, the TCC is not functioning correctly. First suspect an intermittent failure and check for loose wiring or connections.

4. Check the TCC circuit for power at the transmission. The system's fuse may be blown. If it is blown, determine why it blew.
5. If full power and ground are not available at the TCC connector, locate the open or high resistance using a voltmeter to measure voltage drop.
6. If power and ground are available at the TCC connector on the transmission, measure the resistance of the solenoid through the TCC connector. If out of specifications, the transmission needs to be drained and the pan removed to test the wires and solenoid. If the solenoid is not within specifications, replace the solenoid.
7. If power and ground are available to the TCC connector, and the TCC resistance is within specifications, the TCC solenoid needs to be removed and checked to see if the valve is actually opening and closing. Apply power and ground to the solenoid while attempting to blow air through the solenoid. If the solenoid operates properly, the problem is likely in the TCC itself. If the solenoid does not allow air to flow, place the solenoid in a clean container of automatic transmission fluid and electrically cycle the solenoid to see if you can remove any blockage from the solenoid. If this does not work, it is necessary to replace the solenoid.

Pressure Testing an Automatic Transmission

Automatic transmissions, whether they are hydraulically controlled or electronically controlled, use hydraulic devices inside the transmission to apply, drive, or hold mechanical devices. This means that, to perform a proper diagnosis, a technician often must perform a pressure test of the hydraulic system. Most manufacturers supply a test port for testing line pressure on a transmission case. Some manufacturers provide test ports for each of the different gear range circuits in a transmission and possibly for modulator pressure, governor pressure, and/or throttle valve pressure. Use the appropriate service information to determine which test ports the manufacturer has supplied and the specified pressures. It is sometimes useful to install multiple pressure gauges into the different test ports so that the pressure can be monitored in the different circuits of the transmission.

Manufacturer pressure specifications vary greatly, depending on the transmission and its application. Most manufacturers specify a range for the pressure readings in particular gear ranges. Generally, line pressure should be highest in the reverse gear range. Always select a gauge that can read higher than the expected pressure to be read. That said, if you are expecting a reading of 120 psi (827 kPa) and you select a gauge that reads up to 400 psi (2758 kPa), you may not get an accurate reading. A gauge that reads up to 150 psi (1034 kPa) is more accurate.

On electronically controlled transmissions, the procedure might involve using a factory scan tool to actuate the Electronic Pressure Control (EPC) solenoid in order to check the PCM's ability to vary the line pressure to meet the demands of the transmission. Low line pressure can be a sign of a weak or worn front pump, a bad pressure regulation system, or internal leaks in the transmission. Follow the diagnostic procedure found in the service information. High line pressure can be a sign of a stuck pressure regulator valve or failed EPC solenoid. To perform pressure tests, follow the steps in **SKILL DRILL 46-4**.

Leak Testing a Torque Converter

Transmissions have many external seals and gaskets that can be replaced without removing the transmission from the vehicle. Examples include the output seal, the vehicle speed sensor seal, the pan gasket, and the rear housing gasket. A transmission fluid leak can result in failure of the transmission due to a low fluid level. As a technician, it is important that you fix any external leaks on the transmission to prevent this failure.

Most seals on the outside of a transmission require specialized tools to be removed and replaced without removing the transmission from the vehicle. Some of these specialty tools are universal types; others are specific for a particular model of transmission. To inspect for leakage and replace seals, gaskets, and bushings, follow the steps in **SKILL DRILL 46-5**.

Some external leaks require removal of the transmission. A front pump seal leak may also require the replacement of the pump bushing to properly repair the leak. With a worn bushing, the pump drive hub may move up and down excessively, flexing the seal and allowing transmission fluid to flow out of the transmission. Replacement of a front pump bushing requires the

SKILL DRILL 46-4 Performing Pressure Tests

1. Refer to the appropriate service information to find the procedure to test the transmission's hydraulic pressures. Verify the correct transmission fluid level in the transmission.
2. Place a drain pan under the transmission and remove the correct pressure test port plug(s). Place the test port plug(s) off to the side where they will not be lost.
3. Install a transmission pressure tester(s) capable of measuring the maximum pressure into the test port(s) on the transmission.
4. Start the vehicle and place the vehicle in the correct operating conditions to monitor the pressure according to the manufacturer (for example, transmission at operating temperature, in drive, engine idling). Record the pressure(s).
5. Shut off the engine, remove the transmission pressure tester(s), seal the plug threads, and reinstall the test port plug(s).
6. Clean off any transmission fluid that dripped onto the transmission, restart the vehicle to check for leaks, and top off the fluid, if necessary.

SKILL DRILL 46-5 Inspecting for Leakage and Replacing Seals

1. Place the vehicle in a safe condition for the inspection. Carefully inspect the front pump, output shaft, and selector shaft seals for leakage.
2. Inspect the transmission pan gasket, side pan gasket (if equipped), and rear housing gasket and seal.

3. If the output seal is leaking, place a suitable container under the rear housing to catch any fluid that leaks out.
4. Remove the driveshaft and the output flange or yoke—you may need to use a puller for this.
5. Inspect the sealing surface of the output flange or yoke. If the seal has worn a groove in the flange, it may be necessary to replace it.
6. Remove the rear seal using the appropriate tool. Take care not to damage the seal mounting area in the housing.
7. Lubricate the edge of the new seal with clean transmission fluid.
8. Use the correct seal installation tool to install the new seal in the housing. Take note if gasket sealant or locktite is required for the installation.
9. Reinstall the output flange or yoke and the driveshaft.
10. Check and adjust the transmission fluid level.
11. Road test the vehicle and recheck to ensure the repair is successful.

removal of the transmission, the torque converter, and the front pump. The bushing can then be driven out using a driver set.

Servicing Torque Converters

LO 46-6 Describe common torque converter service procedures.

Light-duty torque converters are not designed to be serviceable, as the two halves of the converter shell are welded together. Some aftermarket shops service these converters by cutting them open and then re-welding them after replacing worn components. This procedure is not recommended by the manufacturer, however.

Servicing these torque converters amounts to checking turbine end play and clearances to specification and leak testing. If these converters meet these specifications, they can be reused. Unfortunately, most automatic transmission failures tend to be catastrophic. The converter may be full of debris (metal filings, burnt clutch material, etc.) from the failure. Virtually no amount of flushing completely removes this debris, so converter replacement is recommended at overhaul of most light-duty vehicles.

In contrast, heavy-duty torque converters are designed to be rebuilt and are bolted together to facilitate this process. The overhaul procedures described in this section are general in nature and refer to most—but not all—heavy-duty torque converters. Always consult the manufacturer's manual for the correct procedure. The end play and leakage tests performed on heavy-duty torque converters are the same as those performed on light-duty torque converters.

▶ **TECHNICIAN TIP**

Removing the torque converter is usually a simple matter of pulling it forward out of the front of the removed transmission. The Allison series of torque converters used in their 3000, 4000, and B series transmissions, however, have a bolt located under a plug in the torque converter front cover pilot, as shown in **FIGURE 46-26**. This bolt must be removed in order to remove their torque converters.

The torque converters used in larger vehicles are extremely heavy. Care must be taken when removing them from the transmission. Use a crane and a sling, where possible, to avoid injury. To disassemble a torque converter, follow the steps in **SKILL DRILL 46-6**. To inspect the parts after disassembly, follow the steps in **SKILL DRILL 46-7**.

FIGURE 46-26 The bolt securing the torque converter turbine to the input shaft in the Allison World Transmission; note the hole that allows TCC pressure to pass through.

SKILL DRILL 46-6 Disassembling a Torque Converter

1. Place the torque converter on a bench with a drainage system. When the converter is disassembled, there will be a significant amount of transmission fluid inside, so be prepared.
2. Before removing the bolts, mark the two halves of the shell so that it can be reassembled in the exact same radial location. The converter elements are usually individually balanced, but it always makes sense to reinstall the halves the way they came apart.

3. Check the turbine end play dimension before disassembly. This allows you to correct any deficiencies when you have it apart. This is accomplished by inserting a special tool that grabs the turbine and allows you to lift it. Measure the total movement and calculate the shims required to bring it to specification.
4. Remove the converter bolts (there may be as many as 50). Remove the rear half from the rest of the converter. Although it is the lighter half, it is still quite heavy, so be careful. You may need to tap the shell with a dead blow hammer to separate the halves. When they are apart, discard the sealing O-ring. Remove the stator and the thrust washers/bearings that support it, and then remove the turbine.
5. Next, remove the clutch backing plate. It may be sandwiched between the front and the rear half of the shell, or it may be bolted into the front half of the converter housing. Remove the lock-up clutch disc, noting which side is up in the torque converter, and finally remove the lock-up clutch piston. It also should be marked in terms of its position in the converter shell. To remove the piston, apply a small amount of air pressure to the piston apply side.

SKILL DRILL 46-7 Inspecting Torque Converter Components

1. Inspect both the impeller and the turbine for damaged or loose blades. Inspect the two halves of the split guide ring to ensure they are firmly attached to the impeller and the turbine blades. Any looseness in the blades fails the component. Further inspect the turbine, locating bearing surfaces for any signs of wear or damage. If necessary, replace the turbine.
2. Check the bushing in the front cover of the converter shell that supports the turbine or the end of the input shaft (depending on converter). Replace as necessary. Inspect the turbine thrust washers or bearings and replace as necessary.
3. Inspect the rear half of the converter shell. Look for any impact damage or leaks. Inspect the pump drive hub surface for wear where it is supported in the front pump of the transmission. If

SKILL DRILL 46-7 Inspecting Torque Converter Components (Continued)

wear is present, it usually means replacement of the shell and the front pump bushing. Pay particular attention to the surface of the hub where the front pump seal runs. The seal can cut a groove into the hub, which may cause a leak. Wear here usually requires replacement of the shell.

4. Inspect the bearing surface between the turbine and the front of the converter shell. Damage here requires parts replacement.

5. Inspect the roller bearing or washers behind the turbine that locate it axially, and replace as necessary.

6. Check the stator for movement. It should move free in one direction and not at all in the other. If it moves even slightly in the opposite direction, it must be repaired or replaced.

7. Remove the one-way clutch cover from the stator and inspect the rollers, the springs, and the ramp surfaces. Also inspect the inner hub for scoring and the bearing thrust faces. Replace components as necessary. Carefully inspect the roller ramp area of the one-way clutch for cracks or surface damage caused by high-speed direction changes.

8. Inspect the lock-up clutch piston and backing plate for signs of overheating, bluing, heat checks, etc. Inspect the clutch disc by measuring the remaining friction material and comparing it to manufacturer's specifications. If the disc has a dampened hub, check the dampening springs for looseness.

Reassembling the Torque Converter

After all of the components have been checked and verified to be in working order, clean all components and reassemble the torque converter by reversing the order of disassembly. Replacing the lock-up clutch piston seal and the converter shell O-ring seal, as shown in **FIGURE 46-27**. It is also a good idea to replace the roller bearings that axially locate the turbine, as it is far cheaper than having to redo the job at a later date.

Special care is needed while re-installing the lock-up piston. Most pistons have locating pins or splines that stop the piston from rotating when the clutch applies. Make sure the piston fits over the locating pins properly. Note: Manufacturers recommend reassembly without the use of any grease, as some greases could clog fluid passages or interfere with valve action in transmission control. Only a light coating of the fluid type being used for the transmission should be used.

Turbine End Play and Torque Converter Leak Checks

After reassembly, there are two checks that should be made. The first check is turbine end play. Two methods are commonly used to check this. In the first method, the torque converter is placed face down on a bench and a special tool that expands to grab the splines of the turbine is installed, as shown in **FIGURE 46-28**.

A dial indicator is then used to measure turbine movement as the tool is pulled upwards.

This measurement must be checked against manufacturer's specification. If adjustment is needed, it usually requires a new thrust washer in the converter.

FIGURE 46-27 Take extra care to ensure the O-rings (indicated) are not damaged on installation.

FIGURE 46-28 This special tool locks to the turbine so it can be pulled up against a dial indicator to measure the end play.

The second method is used on Allison World Transmission torque converters. The Allison World 3000, 4000, and B series torque converters have a bolt under a special O-ring sealed cap in the torque converter front cover pilot (in some models this cap is superseded by a threaded plug). The bolt secures the torque converter to the turbine shaft and provides the hydraulic passageway for lock-up clutch operation.

To check end play in these torque converters, the converter is again placed face down on a bench and the distance from the pump drive hub to the turbine thrust face is measured (A). Next, a special tool is placed in the opening of the front cover pilot, and the converter is now placed face down on the tool. The tool forces the turbine upwards to the limit of its movement, and then the distance between the pump drive hub and the turbine is measured again (B). The difference between measurement A and measurement B is compared to a chart in the manufacturer's manual and determines the correct shim thickness to use to provide the correct end play. Overall, turbine end play usually ranges from 0.060" to 0.080" (1.5 to 2.0 mm) in most converters, but some have larger or smaller end play dimensions. Always check the specification. Note that converter end play is manipulated by some manufacturers to change converter stall speed. A larger end play would result in a higher stall speed. Always check OEM literature for the correct dimension.

The second check on the newly reassembled torque converter is a leak check. A special adapter is clamped into the hole formed by the pump drive hub and air pressure is applied to the inside of the converter. Leak checks are then made by either submersing the converter in water or by using a soapy water solution to check the seams of the converter housing. Pay particular attention to the weld joint of the pump drive hub.

Wrap-Up

Ready for Review

- Automatic transmissions have a limited number of gear ratios available when compared to standard transmissions. To provide enough torque multiplication, automatic transmissions need a torque converter to supply the extra degree of torque multiplication.
- Fluid couplings are similar to torque converters in that they transfer power from the source to a driveline through fluid. A fluid coupling, however, cannot multiply torque.
- Torque converters and fluid couplings both have an impeller or pump and a turbine inside a shell that is shaped like a hollowed-out donut. This shape is called a torus.
- Torque converters have an extra element inside, called a stator, which is the primary component that enables a torque converter to multiply torque.
- A torque converter's torque multiplication factor can be controlled by changing the curvature of the elements, the turbine, the stator and the impeller, the sizing of the elements, and the clearance between the elements.
- The impeller is part of the converter housing that is bolted to the engine and so always turns with the engine.
- The turbine is splined to the transmission input shaft to deliver power to the transmission.
- The stator is mounted on a one-way clutch (usually) and can freewheel in one direction, but it locks up if it tries to turn in the opposite direction.
- A torque converter's impeller can only drive the turbine to approximately 90% to 95% of impeller speed. This speed difference is known as slippage, and robs efficiency, so all of today's torque converters are equipped with a lock-up clutch to eliminate the 5% to 10% slippage.

- The torque converter fluid flow can be rotary or vortex. Rotary flow in the torque converter is fluid that follows the rotation of the converter housing. Vortex flow is the flow of fluid from the impeller, through the turbine, through the stationary stator, and back to the impeller.
- Rotary flow is always present in the torque converter but is greatest at the converter's coupling phase, when the turbine speed is within 10% of impeller speed.
- Vortex flow is always present in the torque converter (unless the torque converter is in lock-up), but is greatest at full stall.
- The torque converter has two distinct phases of operation—the torque multiplication phase and the coupling phase.
- The torque multiplication phase occurs anytime the converter is multiplying torque.
- The coupling phase occurs anytime the turbine and the impeller speeds are within 10% of each other.
- During torque multiplication, the stator is held stationary by the one-way clutch; during coupling phase, the stator is freewheeling.
- Variable pitch stators can alter a torque converter's multiplication factor by changing their blade angles.
- Torque converters are connected to the engine crankshaft or flywheel through flex plates, so they can expand and contract while under load.
- Torque converter lock-up can be pre-programmed or modulated. Programmed lock-up is for fuel economy, modulated lock-up is for vehicle performance.
- Transmission fluid is normally delivered to the rotating torque converter through a passage formed between the inside of the converter's pump drive hub and the outside of the stator support shaft.

- ▶ Fluid is returned from the converter to the transmission cooler through a passage formed between the inside of the stator support shaft and the outside of the turbine shaft.
- ▶ Stall testing can help determine whether the engine, the transmission, or the torque converter is the source of a driver complaint.
- ▶ Stall test rpm higher than 100 rpm from specification usually indicates a slipping clutch or a torque converter fluid issue.
- ▶ Stall test rpm lower than 100 rpm from specification typically means an engine that is performing poorly.
- ▶ A stall test rpm that is significantly lower than specification (400 to 600 rpm lower), could indicate a freewheeling stator.
- ▶ Transmission fluid that does not cool down during the cool down phase of a stall test could indicate a stuck or seized stator.
- ▶ Light-duty torque converters should be replaced with a new one when a transmission overhaul is required.
- ▶ Heavy-duty torque converters should be overhauled when the transmission requires an overhaul.
- ▶ The turbine position in relation to the impeller can affect the torque multiplication factor of the torque converter.

Key Terms

anti-drain-back check valves These valves try to keep the torque converter full of fluid when the vehicle is shut off.

centrifugal force Apparent force by which a rotating mass tries to move outward away from its axis of rotation.

coupling phase A torque converter operating phase when the turbine and the impeller are at close to the same speed.

flex plate A flexible plate used to connect the torque converter to the engine.

fluid coupling A power transfer device that uses fluid to transmit power.

ground shaft A stationary shaft that holds the inner hub of the stator one-way clutch. Also called *stator support shaft*.

impeller The bladed element in a torque converter or fluid coupling that is fixed to the housing and, therefore, rotates with it.

lock-up clutch The clutch that locks the turbine to the converter shell when conditions are correct for 100% efficiency.

lock–up clutch disc The friction disc used in a lock-up clutch.

lock-up clutch piston The hydraulically actuated piston that applies the lock-up clutch.

lock-up clutch/piston assembly A combination lock-up clutch disc and piston assembly; used in light-duty vehicles.

modulated lock-up A lock-up clutch application strategy that is designed for maximum vehicle performance.

one-way clutch A roller or sprag-type device that allows rotation in one direction but locks in the opposite direction. Also called *over-running clutch*.

over-running clutch A roller or sprag type device that allows rotation in one direction, but locks in the opposite direction. Also called *one-way clutch*.

programmed lock-up A strategy that applies the lock-up clutch as soon as possible for improved fuel economy. Also called *systematic lock-up*.

rotary flow Fluid flow inside the torque converter that follows the rotation of the housing.

smoke controls A system on mechanically fueled engines to limit smoke emissions.

split guide ring The split guide ring that is attached to the impeller and the turbine blades and creates a circular fluid passage.

stall speed The maximum speed the engine can drive the torque converter impeller with the turbine held stationary.

stator The element inside a torque converter most responsible for torque multiplication.

stator inner hub The inner race of the stator one-way clutch; it splines to the stator ground shaft.

stator support shaft A stationary shaft that holds the inner hub of the stator one-way clutch. Also called *ground shaft*.

systematic lock-up A strategy that applies the lock-up clutch as soon as possible for improved fuel economy. Also called *programmed lock-up*.

transmission oil cooler A series of oil tubes or passages that are cooled by engine coolant.

torque converter A type of fluid coupling that is also capable of multiplying torque.

torque multiplication phase Occurs whenever the impeller is turning significantly faster than the turbine.

torus The hollowed-out donut shape of the rear of the converter housing and the turbine.

turbine The torque converter element that is splined to the transmission input shaft.

variable pitch stator A stator with blades that can change the angle to alter the torque converter multiplication factor.

vortex flow The flow of fluid from the impeller, through the turbine, through the stator, and back to the impeller.

Review Questions

1. What is meant when it is said that a torque converter has a modulated lock-up strategy?
   a. The lock-up clutch will apply as early as possible during the drive cycle.
   b. The lock-up clutch will only apply when the driver requests it.
   c. The lock-up clutch will apply only in high range.
   d. The lock-up clutch will apply based on a number of factors, including throttle request.

2. A stall speed much higher than specified typically indicates which of the following problems?
   a. A slipping clutch
   b. A stuck stator
   c. A freewheeling stator
   d. An engine that needs a tune-up

3. What are the two phases of torque converter operation?
   a. The torque multiplication phase and the lock-up phase
   b. The torque multiplication phase and the coupling phase
   c. The lock-up phase and the coupling phase
   d. The stator phase and the lock-up phase

4. The stall test can be used to determine which of the following?
   a. The condition of the engine only
   b. The condition of the torque converter only
   c. The condition of the transmission only
   d. The condition of the engine, torque converter, and the transmission

5. Which of the following is likely the problem if a stall speed is 600 rpm or more lower than specification?
   a. A stuck stator in the torque converter
   b. A freewheeling stator in the torque converter
   c. A torque converter that is not full of fluid
   d. A transmission that has a seized clutch

6. During a converter stall test, which of the following could indicate a stuck or seized stator?
   a. Extremely low stall speed
   b. Higher than normal stall speed
   c. Low torque during the stall test
   d. No temperature decrease during the cool down phase

7. In a typical torque converter installation, what must be used between the torque converter and the engine flywheel or crankshaft?
   a. A special insulating material
   b. The torque converter front support bushing
   c. A spacer of at least ½-inch thickness
   d. One or more flex-plates

8. A lock-up clutch in the torque converter does which of the following?
   a. Provides 100% efficiency between the impeller and turbine
   b. Increases rotary oil flow in the torque multiplication phase
   c. Allows a higher stall speed
   d. Increases vortex oil flow in the coupling phase

9. Where does the transmission fluid exiting the torque converter usually go after it leaves the converter?
   a. Straight to the transmission sump
   b. To the transmission cooler
   c. To the front lube circuit
   d. To the pump intake

10. When the engine is idling and you are in park or neutral, which of the following is happening in the torque converter?
    a. The impeller is turning; the stator is locked; and the turbine is stopped.
    b. Both the impeller and the turbine are turning, and the stator is locked.
    c. Both the impeller and the turbine are stopped, and the stator is turning.
    d. The impeller, the stator, and the turbine are all turning at close to the same speed.

ASE Technician A/Technician B Style Questions

1. Technician A says that a fluid coupler can be used to transmit torque to a driveline as long as the load is not too great. Technician B says that a fluid coupling can multiply torque up to four to one. Who is correct?
   a. Technician A
   b. Technician B
   c. Both Technician A and Technician B
   d. Neither Technician A nor Technician B

2. Technician A says that the primary key to torque multiplication in a torque converter is the stator. Technician B says that the angle of the blades in the turbine affects the torque multiplication. Who is correct?
   a. Technician A
   b. Technician B
   c. Both Technician A and Technician B
   d. Neither Technician A nor Technician B

3. Technician A says that the stator locks up during the torque converter coupling phase. Technician B says that the stator freewheels during the torque multiplication phase. Who is correct?
   a. Technician A
   b. Technician B
   c. Both Technician A and Technician B
   d. Neither Technician A nor Technician B

4. Technician A says that vortex flow in the torque converter is highest during full stall. Technician B says that vortex flow follows the rotation of the converter housing or shell. Who is correct?
   a. Technician A
   b. Technician B
   c. Both Technician A and Technician B
   d. Neither Technician A nor Technician B

5. Technician A says that the torque multiplication factor of a torque converter is affected by the angle of the stator blades. Technician B says that the turbine end play can affect the torque converter's multiplication factor. Who is correct?
   a. Technician A
   b. Technician B
   c. Both Technician A and Technician B
   d. Neither Technician A nor Technician B

6. Technician A says that selecting drive in an automatic transmission while the rpm is very high can damage the stator one-way clutch. Technician B says that the stator one-way clutch is usually a roller-type clutch in heavy-duty applications. Who is correct?
   a. Technician A
   b. Technician B
   c. Both Technician A and Technician B
   d. Neither Technician A nor Technician B

7. Technician A says that the split guide ring in the torque converter helps to direct the flow of fluid during torque multiplication phase. Technician B says that the split guide

ring in the torque converter helps to direct the flow of fluid during the coupling phase. Who is correct?

a. Technician A
b. Technician B
c. Both Technician A and Technician B
d. Neither Technician A nor Technician B

8. Technician A says that light-duty torque converters should be replaced at transmission overhaul. Technician B says that light-duty torque converters are not designed to be rebuilt. Who is correct?

a. Technician A
b. Technician B
c. Both Technician A and Technician B
d. Neither Technician A nor Technician B

9. Technician A says that turbine end play is an important check when rebuilding a heavy-duty torque converter. Technician B says that stator end play should be checked before disassembly. Who is correct?

a. Technician A
b. Technician B
c. Both Technician A and Technician B
d. Neither Technician A nor Technician B

10. Technician A says that, during the torque multiplication phase in the torque converter, the oil exiting the stator is flowing opposite to impeller rotation. Technician B says that, during the torque multiplication phase in the torque converter, the oil exiting the turbine is flowing opposite to impeller rotation. Who is correct?

a. Technician A
b. Technician B
c. Both Technician A and Technician B
d. Neither Technician A nor Technician B

CHAPTER 47

Planetary Gear Concepts

Learning Objectives

After reading this chapter, you will be able to:

- **LO 47-1** Explain the fundamentals of planetary gearing.
- **LO 47-2** Explain planetary gear power flows.
- **LO 47-3** Explain ratio calculations for planetary gears.
- **LO 47-4** Describe powertrain control devices.
- **LO 47-5** Explain the operation of compound planetary gear set combinations.

You Are the Technician

A truck is brought to your service facility. The vehicle has an Allison AT 545 hydraulically controlled automatic transmission. The driver complains that when his truck is heavily loaded, the engine rpms increase to a very high level when the transmission shifts to second gear. If the driver releases the throttle for a moment, the transmission seems to complete the shift, but it seems that it shifts into third gear—not second. He says the problem does not seem to be as bad when his truck is empty, but he is still not sure if the transmission actually shifts to second. You road test the vehicle and discover that, indeed, the transmission seems to skip second and go directly into third gear.

1. Should you check the transmission fluid level? Why or why not?
2. Should you pressure test the hydraulic circuit for the second-gear hydraulic clutch?
3. Should you replace the transmission? Explain.

Introduction

At the heart of automatic transmission operation is the planetary gear set. Planetary gears are so called because of the way they are designed and how their components interact with each other. Planetary gear operation is quite different than conventional gearing used in standard and automated standard transmissions. All automatic transmissions rely on a combination of **planetary gears** and **powertrain control devices** to create their power flows. Planetary control devices are used to input or hold planetary gear components to affect a power flow. Therefore, before we start discussing automatic transmissions, a solid understanding of planetary gear concepts is required. This chapter explains the rules and laws of simple planetary gears, how they interact with each other, and the devices used to control that interaction.

Fundamentals of Planetary Gearing

LO 47-1 Explain the fundamentals of planetary gearing.

The simple planetary gear set consists of three components. First is the central externally toothed sun gear. Second is the externally toothed planet pinion gears (small gears that connect the sun gear to the ring gear) held in a component called the carrier. The pinions revolve around the sun gear like planets in our solar system. The internally toothed ring gear surrounds the pinion gears, as illustrated in **FIGURE 47-1**. The three different gear components are in constant mesh with one another. Planetary gears are also known as **epicyclical gears**. Epicyclical means that they are arranged so that the three elements revolve around a common centerline.

Planetary gears are extremely versatile. They allow several ratios from one set of gears. One simple planetary gear set can be arranged to produce the following ratios:

- Two different forward reduction ratios to increase output torque while decreasing output speed
- Two different forward overdrive ratios that increase output speed, but decrease output torque
- One reverse reduction ratio
- One reverse overdrive ratio

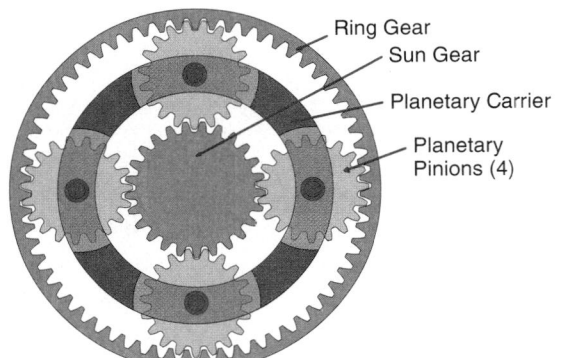

Ring Gear
Sun Gear
Planetary Carrier
Planetary Pinions (4)

FIGURE 47-1 The simple planetary gear set is versatile and strong.

The planetary gear set can also be used to create a direct drive, allowing torque and speed to pass through the gear set unchanged. Planetary gear sets also have excellent torque-carrying capabilities because of the number of teeth involved to transfer the power. When planetary gears are transferring torque, there are usually three or four sets of teeth involved in carrying the load, which makes them very strong for their size. In addition, their epicyclical design allows them to cancel out radial thrust loads.

Planetary gear sets are not without drawbacks, however. Planetary gears are normally helically cut for strength and noise reduction, but that means that they create a serious amount of axial thrust under load. To deal with the thrust forces that are created, needle thrust bearings and/or washers must be used. Planetary powertrain control devices are the devices that allow us to connect to the varying parts of the planetary gear to create power flows. The control devices are operated hydraulically, which is easily accomplished if the control device is a stationary clutch or brake band. When the control device is rotating, however, such as an input clutch, it creates difficulties in supplying application pressure to the clutch. Different methods are used to supply rotating clutches, but most systems use a series of sealing rings to form passages to supply the fluid pressure. (We look at these challenges in the Hydraulically Controlled Automatic Transmissions chapter.)

Rules of Planetary Gears

A planetary gear set can be designed with straight-cut spur-type gears or with stronger and quieter helical cut gears. Spur-cut gears are noisier in operation, but they create no axial thrust. Helical-cut gears are stronger and quieter, but create axial thrust that must be dealt with.

Planetary gears are very strong for their size. Consider a single countershaft transmission geartrain. All the torque is transmitted through one or two teeth in mesh at any given time. In a planetary gear set, there are at least three sets of teeth (the three pinions), transmitting the torque. In heavier applications, the number of pinions is increased, giving even more teeth in contact. Helical planetary gears also have the increased strength benefit that helical gears bring to countershaft transmissions. Because of this, planetary gears can be made very compact and yet still transmit great amounts of torque. In order for planetary gears to transmit torque, the following three criteria must be met. These criteria are known as the rules of planetary gears.

1. One of the three planetary gear components must be inputted from the power source.
2. One of the planetary gear components must be held stationary.
3. One of the planetary gear components must be connected to an output.

The only exception to the rules above occurs when we want a direct drive, or 1:1 ratio, through the gear set. To obtain a 1:1 ratio, two members of the gear set are inputted at the same speed. That causes the third component to turn with them. The third component is connected to the output so the result is direct drive. If these three rules are not met and any of the planetary gear components is free to turn, it does so. The result is neutral and no torque or rotational output can be transmitted.

All simple planetary gears can produce the same seven ratios, regardless of size. The actual reductions and overdrives vary, however, based on the number of teeth on the three components. The key to figuring out which ratio is achieved is the carrier. Recall that the carrier is the component that holds the planetary pinions. The pinions merely connect the carrier to the gear set. The active component is the carrier itself. Knowing which one of the rules of planetary gears applies to the carrier—that is, whether the carrier is the input, the output, or the held member—allows the resulting power flow to be determined.

The Role of the Carrier

The carrier is the key to planetary gear power flows; provided that the rules of planetary gears are met, the following holds true:

1. If the carrier is the **output member** of the gear set, the resulting power flow is always a forward reduction or underdrive ratio.
2. If the carrier is the **input member** of the gear set, the result is always a forward overdrive ratio.
3. If the carrier is the held or **reaction member** of the gear set, then the result is always reverse.

Once it is known what the carrier is doing, figuring out what the other two planetary components are doing becomes easier.

If the carrier is output, which always gives a forward (same direction as input) gear reduction (increased output torque and decreased output speed), the sun gear and the ring gear must be either the input or the held component to satisfy the three rules of planetary gears.

If the carrier is input, the result is always a forward overdrive. That is, the direction is the same as the input and there is decreased torque and increased output speed. In that case, the sun gear and the ring gear must be either the output or the held component to satisfy the three rules of planetary gears.

If the carrier is the held component, the result is always a reverse ratio. That is, the direction is opposite to input. The sun gear and the ring gear must be either input or output to satisfy the rules of planetary gears. If the sun gear is input, the result is a reverse reduction. If the ring gear is input, the result is a reverse overdrive.

Planetary Gear Power Flows

LO 47-2 Explain planetary gear power flows.

The planetary gear set power flows are organized in **TABLE 47-1**. Note that if any two planetary gear set members are input at the same speed, the third becomes the output at the same speed and direction for a 1:1 ratio or direct drive.

Throughout the section on planetary gear power flows, planetary gear motion is described using simplified planetary gear drawings. Each diagram uses the following legend:

- The input component direction is shown with a **red arrow**.
- The output component direction is shown with a **green arrow**.
- The held component is indicated with a black line and ground symbol.
- The reaction direction of the planet pinions is shown with a **brown arrow** (note: only one brown arrow is shown, but of course all of the pinions are rotating in the indicated direction).

Let's examine maximum and minimum forward reduction, maximum and minimum forward overdrive, reverse reduction, and reverse overdrive in greater detail.

Maximum Forward Reduction

During both forward reduction power flows in a planetary gear, the carrier is the output member. The lower of the two ratios or **maximum forward reduction**, shown in **FIGURE 47-2**, is obtained if the sun gear is the input because a smaller input gear always gives a lower output speed. Therefore, the ring gear must be the held component. In Figure 47-2, we see that the input (red arrow) turns the sun gear clockwise, and the ring gear is held. This turns the carrier in a clockwise direction for the output (green arrow). Notice the reaction direction on the carrier pinion gears (brown arrow). The pinions have to walk around the stationary ring gear in a counterclockwise direction. This means that the teeth of the carrier pinion gears are moving away from the sun gear's teeth because of their counterclockwise movement. That movement reduces the effect of the sun gear in trying to move the carrier. To turn the carrier one complete revolution, the sun gear must turn one complete turn plus the number of teeth on the ring gear to drive the carrier one turn because that is the amount that the carrier pinions move

TABLE 47-1 Planetary Gear Power Flows

Sun Gear	Carrier	Ring Gear	Speed	Torque	Direction
Input	Output	Held	Max reduction	Increase	Same as input
Held	Output	Input	Min reduction	Increase	Same as input
Output	Input	Held	Max increase	Decrease	Same as input
Held	Input	Output	Min increase	Decrease	Same as input
Input	Held	Output	Reduction	Increase	Reverse
Output	Held	Input	Increase	Decrease	Reverse

Note: If any two planetary gear set members are input at the same speed, the third member becomes the output at the same speed and direction for a 1:1 ratio or direct drive.

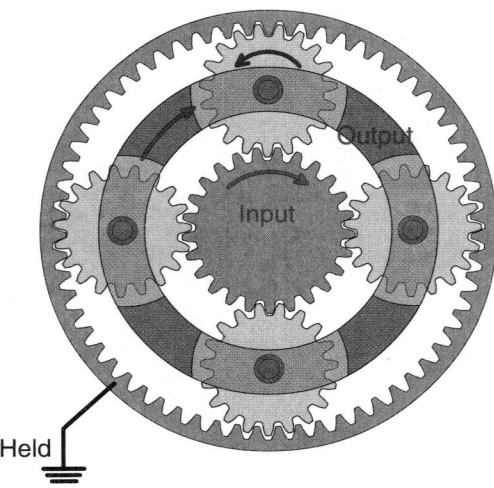

FIGURE 47-2 Maximum forward reduction is obtained with the sun gear as input, the ring gear held, and the carrier as output.

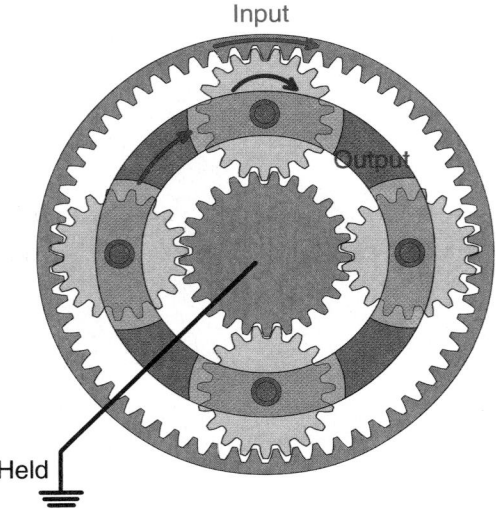

FIGURE 47-3 In the minimum forward reduction power flow, the ring gear is input and the sun gear is held, making the carrier output again.

away from the sun gear's input. Consequently, this power flow gives the maximum forward reduction in speed, but also the maximum increase in torque.

Minimum Forward Reduction

To obtain the higher of the two forward reduction ratios, the carrier is still the output, but the roles of the ring gear and the sun gear are reversed. The ring gear becomes the input component and the sun gear is the held component. This results in the **minimum forward reduction** (or higher ratio of the two) that results in a torque increase and a speed decrease.

In **FIGURE 47-3**, we see clockwise input on the ring gear (red arrow). The ring gear tries to turn the carrier in a clockwise direction, as can be seen by the green arrow. However, notice the reaction direction of the carrier pinion gears (brown arrow). The carrier pinions have to walk around the stationary sun gear, which causes the pinions to rotate clockwise as well. The teeth of the

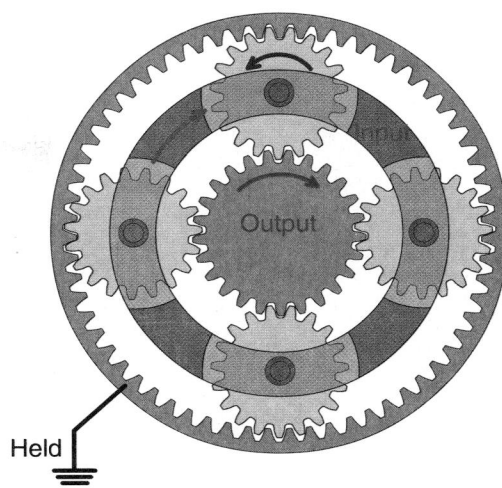

FIGURE 47-4 A maximum forward overdrive power flow. When the carrier is the input member, the result is always an overdrive ratio.

carrier pinion gears then, are moving away from the input of the ring gear, thus reducing its effort to move the carrier. In this power flow, the ring gear must turn one complete revolution plus the number of teeth on the sun gear in order to drive the carrier one full turn. This results in a smaller speed reduction and a smaller torque increase than the maximum forward reduction power flow.

In a typical planetary gear set, the maximum or greater forward reduction (lower ratio) is around 3.4:1, and the minimum or lesser forward reduction (higher ratio) is around 1.4:1. These ratios vary slightly, depending on the actual number of teeth on the ring gear and the sun gear.

Maximum Forward Overdrive

If the carrier is the input component, the result is always a forward overdrive—that is, there is decreased output torque and increased output speed. For forward overdrive to occur, the sun and the ring gear must either be the output component or the held component. Logically, the carrier will drive the sun gear faster than it does the ring gear because the sun gear is smaller and has fewer teeth. When the sun gear is the output component, we achieve the **maximum forward overdrive** (highest output speed) and, to satisfy the rules of planetary gears, the ring gear must become the held component. Following the motion in **FIGURE 47-4**, the carrier is input (red arrow), and the ring gear is held stationary. The carrier rotation forces the sun gear to rotate clockwise with it (green arrow), but notice the reaction direction of the carrier pinion gears (brown arrow). They are forced to rotate counterclockwise by the stationary ring gear teeth. The pinion gear transfers this extra rotation to the sun gear and, therefore, adds to its output speed. In this power flow, one rotation of the carrier drives the sun gear one complete turn plus the number of teeth on the ring gear.

Minimum Forward Overdrive

To achieve the slower overdrive speed, or the **minimum forward overdrive**, the carrier is still the input component. The

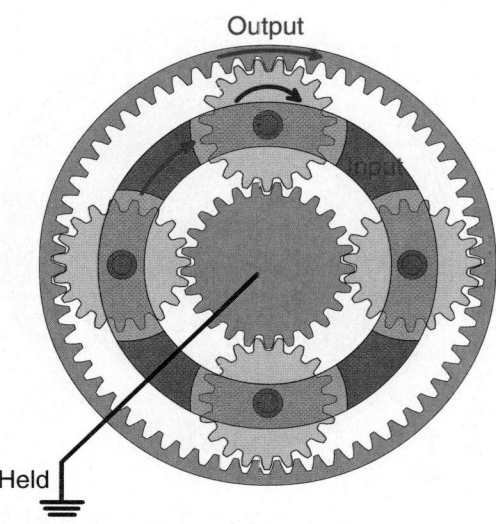

FIGURE 47-5 A minimum forward overdrive power flow. The carrier is still input, but now the sun gear becomes the held member.

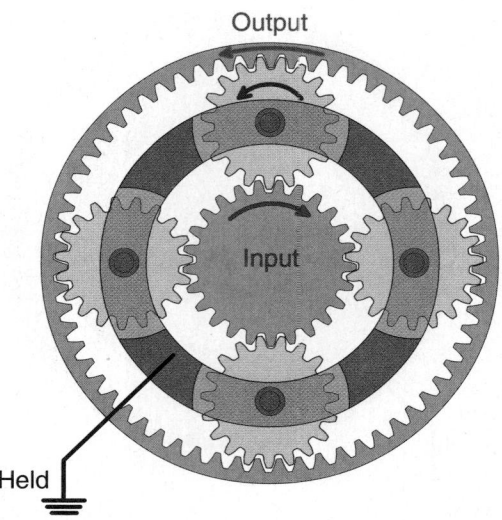

FIGURE 47-6 In reverse, the carrier is the held member of the planetary gear set. If the sun gear is input, the result is a reverse underdrive.

roles of the sun gear and the ring gear, however, are reversed. The ring gear becomes the output component, and the sun gear is the held component.

To follow this power flow, see **FIGURE 47-5**. The carrier is the input, red arrow, the sun gear is held stationary, and the carrier's rotation forces the ring gear to rotate with it in a clockwise direction (green arrow). Again, notice the reaction direction of the carrier pinion gears (brown arrow) as they are forced to rotate around the stationary sun gear. This forces the carrier pinions to turn clockwise. The pinions transfer this clockwise rotation to the ring gear, therefore adding to its output speed. In this power flow, one complete rotation of the carrier drives the ring gear one complete turn plus the number of teeth on the sun gear. The result is still an overdrive, but slower than the previous power flow.

In a typical planetary gear set, the maximum forward overdrive ratio is around 0.29:1 and the minimum forward overdrive is around 0.76:1. Again, these ratios vary slightly, depending on the actual number of teeth on the ring gear and the sun gear.

Reverse Reduction or Underdrive

If the carrier is the held component, the result is always reverse. One combination produces a reverse overdrive and one a reverse reduction. To complete this power flow according to the rules of planetary gears, the ring gear and the sun gear must be either the input or the output component. Logically, a small gear as input always results in a slower output speed. Therefore, when the sun gear is the input component and the ring gear is the output, the result is a **reverse reduction**—that is, there is a torque increase and a speed decrease. The power flow through the planetary gear set when the carrier is held is very straightforward—the carrier pinions merely act as idler gears.

In **FIGURE 47-6**, we see clockwise input on the sun gear (red arrow). This causes the carrier pinion gears to rotate counterclockwise (brown arrow). The pinion gears act as idler gears and transfer this motion to the ring gear, causing it to rotate

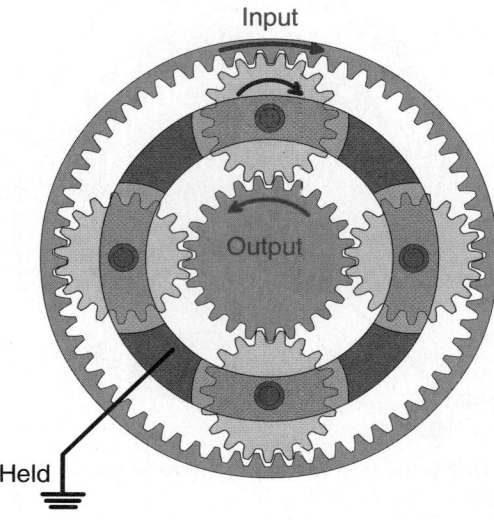

FIGURE 47-7 If the ring gear is the input member and the carrier is held, the sun gear turns in reverse at an overdrive speed.

counterclockwise as well (green arrow). To turn the ring gear one complete turn, the sun gear must turn exactly the same number of teeth that are on the ring gear.

Reverse Overdrive

What happens, then, when the ring gear is the input component and the sun gear is the output component? Switching the sun and ring gear roles with the carrier still the held member results in a **reverse overdrive**.

In **FIGURE 47-7**, we see the ring gear is clockwise input (red arrow) and the carrier is held. This rotation causes the carrier pinion gears to rotate clockwise as well (brown arrow). Again, the pinion gears act merely as idler gears and transfer this motion to the sun gear. The sun gear then turns counterclockwise (green arrow). One rotation of the ring gear drives the sun gear the same number of teeth that are on the ring gear, leading to a reverse overdrive.

In a typical planetary gear set, the reverse reduction ratio is around 2.5:1, and the reverse overdrive ratio is around 0.42:1.

To achieve the seventh possible ratio—that is, direct drive or 1:1—any two of the planetary gear components are inputted at the same speed. The sun gear and ring gear are input, as illustrated in **FIGURE 47-8**. Because two components are turning at the same speed, the carrier pinions cannot rotate and the third component must turn at the same speed as well. In this power flow, the planetary gear set is basically locked together and the third component is connected to the output. What results is a 1:1 or direct ratio that allows torque and speed to travel through the gear set unchanged.

Ratio Calculations for Planetary Gears

LO 47-3 Explain ratio calculations for planetary gears.

Planetary gear ratios depend on the role of the carrier in the power flow, therefore, there are some unique formulas used to calculate them. We still use driven-over-drive as the basic ratio formula. The carrier, however, impacts the ratio if it is the output or the input member. First, we need to know the number of teeth on the ring gear and on the sun gear. Let us assume we have a typical planetary gear set with the following number of teeth on the gears.

Sun gear (S) = 36 teeth
Ring gear (R) = 84 teeth

As they are simply connecting the ring and the sun gear, the pinion gears act as idler gears. The number of teeth on the pinions have no bearing on the ratios.

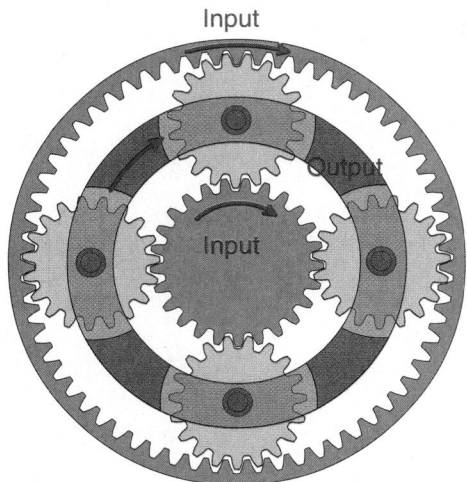

FIGURE 47-8 When any two members of the planetary gear set are input at the same speed and direction, the third member outputs at the same speed.

If the carrier is the output member of the planetary gear set and the sun gear is input, the ring gear is the held member. During this power flow, the carrier reacts against the stationary ring gear, and its pinion teeth have a negative effect on the output. The sun gear must, therefore, rotate once plus rotate the number of teeth on the ring gear to turn the carrier one revolution. The ratio is calculated using the following formula:

$$\begin{aligned}
\text{Ratio} &= \frac{R+S}{S} \\
&= \frac{84+36}{36} \\
&= \frac{120}{36} \\
&= 3.33:1
\end{aligned}$$

This is the maximum forward underdrive or speed reduction.

If the carrier is the output member of the planetary gear set and the ring gear is input, the sun gear is the held member. The formula changes to accommodate the fact that the sun gear with fewer teeth is the reaction member. In that case, the formula looks like this:

$$\begin{aligned}
\text{Ratio} &= \frac{S+R}{R} \\
&= \frac{36+84}{84} \\
&= \frac{120}{84} \\
&= 1.43:1
\end{aligned}$$

This is the minimum forward underdrive or speed reduction.

If the carrier is the input member and the sun gear is the output, the ring gear must be held to satisfy the rules of planetary gears. One turn of the carrier turns the sun gear one revolution plus the number of teeth on the stationary ring gear. That amount of rotation is due to the ring gear being the reaction member and the carrier pinions walking around the ring gear and adding their rotation to the sun gear's output. The formula in this scenario is as follows:

$$\begin{aligned}
\text{Ratio} &= \frac{S}{S+R} \\
&= \frac{36}{36+84} \\
&= \frac{36}{120} \\
&= 0.3:1
\end{aligned}$$

This is the maximum forward overdrive or speed increase.

If the carrier is the input member and the ring gear is the output, the sun gear must be held to satisfy the rules of planetary gears. One turn of the carrier turns the ring gear one revolution plus the number of teeth on the stationary sun gear because it is the reaction member. The pinions are walking around the sun gear and adding their rotation to the ring gear's output. The formula in this scenario is as follows:

$$Ratio = \frac{R}{S+R}$$
$$= \frac{84}{36+84}$$
$$= \frac{84}{120}$$
$$= 0.7:1$$

This is the minimum forward overdrive or speed increase.

When the carrier is the held member, the result is always reverse and the carrier pinions merely act as idler gears. The ratio in that case is simply a matter of driven-over-drive, as described below.

If the sun gear is the input and the ring gear is output:

$$Ratio = \frac{R}{S}$$
$$= \frac{84}{36}$$
$$= 2.33:1$$

This ratio is the reverse underdrive.

If the ring gear is input and the sun gear is output, the formula is as follows:

$$Ratio = \frac{S}{R}$$
$$= \frac{36}{84}$$
$$= 0.43:1$$

This ratio is the reverse overdrive.

The preceding formulas can be used to calculate simple planetary gear ratios only. Most transmissions, however, have power flows that involve more than one planetary gear set, making them compound power flows. In some compound planetary gear sets, rather than components being held stationary, the planetary gears may be acting as the held member, even though they are actually rotating slowly. For this to work, the acting-as-held member must turn slower than the input member. Calculating ratios like these is much more difficult—and is usually unnecessary. We discuss compound planetary gear set arrangements in greater detail in the Compound Planetary Gear Set Power Flows section.

Powertrain Control Devices

LO 47-4 Describe powertrain control devices.

To complete the power flow, planetary gears need an input component, they usually require a held component, and they must have an output component. Powertrain control devices are required to drive (input) or to hold the components of a planetary gear set. There are three basic types of powertrain control devices used in automatic transmissions: the hydraulic clutch, the brake band and servo, and the roller- or sprag-type one-way clutch.

Hydraulic Clutch

The **hydraulic clutch**, shown in **FIGURE 47-9**, can be used either to input rotational power to a planetary gear component or to hold a component stationary. When used to input the gear set, the hydraulic clutch is called a **rotating clutch** and consists of a hub or drum that is splined or attached directly (or indirectly) to the transmission input shaft. The clutch contains a hydraulic piston, return springs to return the piston to its released position, and two sets of clutch plates known as the **friction plates** and **reaction plates**. The friction plates are sandwiched between the reaction plates, and the set of plates is held into the hub by a pressure plate and a retaining snap ring. The friction plates are steel plates with friction material attached to them and the reaction plates are usually plain steel plates.

The friction plates are usually internally splined to a planetary gear component. The reaction plates are normally splined to the clutch hub. When not engaged, the hub and the reaction plates rotate around the stationary friction plates and the gear set component to which they are splined. When pressurized hydraulic fluid is introduced behind the piston, the two sets of plates are squeezed together. That squeezing action causes the rotational force to be delivered to the gear set component splined to the friction plates. When a hydraulic clutch is used to hold components stationary, there is no clutch hub or drum. The clutch reaction plates are splined directly to the inside of the transmission case and the friction plates are splined to the component we want to hold.

This type of clutch is called a **stationary clutch**. **FIGURE 47-10** shows both rotating and stationary clutches. The stationary clutch is actuated by a hydraulic piston installed in the transmission case. When pressure is introduced behind the piston, the two sets of plates are squeezed together, causing the frictions plates to hold a gear set component stationary.

The hydraulic clutch is the strongest planetary geartrain control device. Its capacity can be tailored to the application by changing the clutch apply pressure and/or the number of plates

FIGURE 47-9 The hydraulic clutch is the strongest planetary control device. **A.** Reaction plates. **B.** Clutch hub. **C.** Friction plates. **D.** Piston. **E.** Return springs.

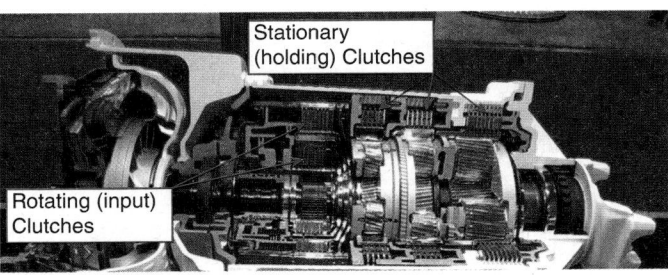

FIGURE 47-10 Stationary clutch reaction plates are splined to the transmission case. **A.** Stationary (holding) clutches. **B.** Rotating (input) clutches.

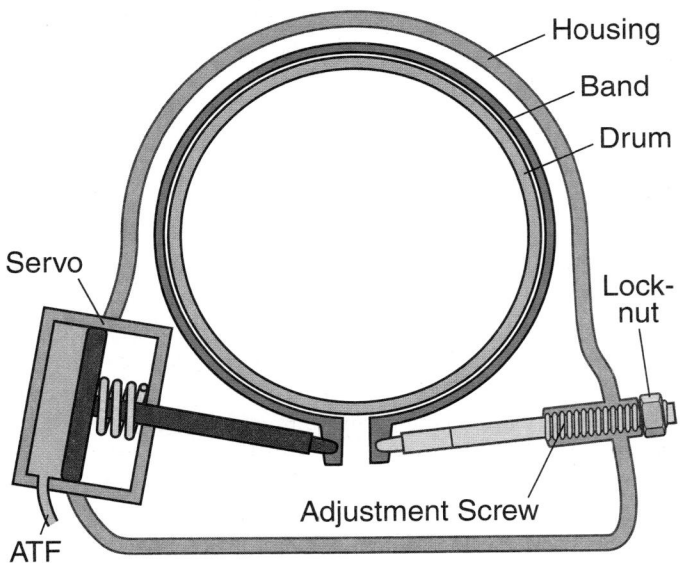

FIGURE 47-11 The brake band can only be used to hold planetary gear components stationary.

FIGURE 47-12 A roller-type one-way clutch. **A.** Inner race. **B.** Springs. **C.** Rollers. **D.** Ramps.

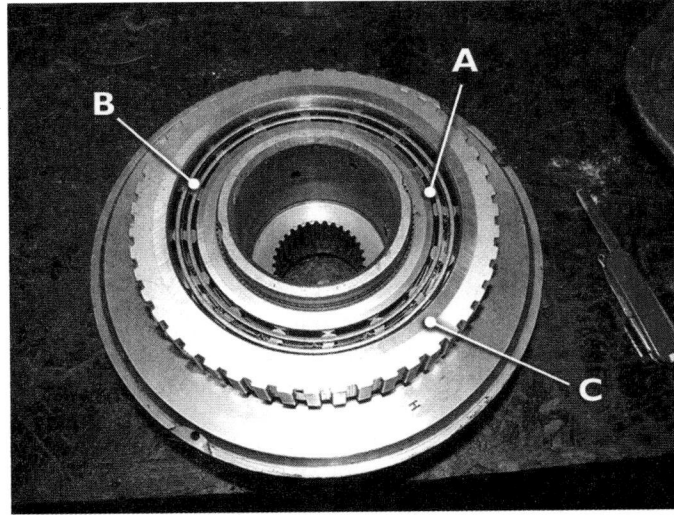

FIGURE 47-13 A sprag-type one-way clutch. **A.** Inner race. **B.** Sprags. **C.** Outer race.

used in the clutch pack. In heavy-duty applications, the hydraulic clutch is usually the only type of powertrain control device used.

Brake Band and Servo

The **brake band** is a metal device, either flexible or rigid, that encircles a powertrain component. Sometimes, the device is simply called a band. The inner surface of the band is coated with a friction material and the band is split so that it has two ends. One end of the band is anchored to the transmission case and the other is attached to a hydraulic piston known as a servo piston, as illustrated in **FIGURE 47-11**.

When the hydraulic piston is actuated, the band is squeezed around the powertrain component, causing it to stop. Bands are only used to hold components stationary and, in some cases, require periodic adjustment as they wear. It is important to note that the friction material on a brake band is extremely thin and wears off very quickly in cases when the band slips. That is, when it cannot hold its components stationary. For that reason, adjustment can rarely be used to repair a transmission in which a band has been slipping.

Roller- or Sprag-Type One-Way Clutches

Roller- and sprag-type one-way clutches were described in detail in the Torque Converter chapter. **FIGURE 47-12** shows a roller-type one-way clutch, and **FIGURE 47-13** shows a sprag-type one-way clutch.

Inside the automatic transmission, these devices may be used to hold something stationary in one direction only, and then freewheel in the other. The advantage of using a one-way clutch in a power flow is that they lock to allow torque to be applied during acceleration, and then unlock and have the connection broken on deceleration. This is desirable in some instances. Consider what happens when a standard transmission vehicle is accelerated in first gear and then the throttle is quickly released. The vehicle goes into severe engine braking mode. The connection from the wheels to the engine is solid, so the vehicle slows very quickly.

Now, consider the same scenario occurring in a vehicle using a one-way clutch as a holding device in the automatic transmission power flow. When the throttle is released and the vehicle weight is pushing, the one-way clutch freewheels to allow the vehicle to coast to a stop very gently. A one-way clutch can be used to the same effect by placing it between a rotating input clutch and the powertrain component that it drives. Instead of driving the component directly, the clutch drives one race of the one-way clutch, and the other race drives the component. Again, when the throttle is released, the solid connection to the driveline is broken and the vehicle gently coasts to a stop.

As far as powertrain control devices are concerned, brake bands and sprag- or roller-type one-way clutches are not as versatile or as strong as hydraulic clutches. Consequently, brake bands and sprag- and roller-type one-way clutches are normally only found in light- to medium-duty automatic transmissions.

Compound Planetary Gear Set Combinations

LO 47-5 Explain the operation of compound planetary gear set combinations.

With seven ratios available from one simple planetary gear set, it might be easy to think that only one gear set would suffice for a typical transmission. And, in theory, it could. There is a snag, however. It would be entirely impossible to have enough control devices to input and hold each of the three gear set components individually or to connect them to the output.

Therefore, most automatic transmissions use more than one set of planetary gears interconnected in such a way that the necessary ratios for the application can be achieved. Planetary gear power flows that utilize more than one gear set to produce the ratios are known as **compound planetary gear sets**.

Several different compound planetary gear arrangements have been designed over the years, including the Simpson, Ravigneaux, Wilson, Lepelletier, ZF gear sets, and others. One of the first popular arrangements was the **Simpson gear set**, which uses two planetary gear sets interconnected by a common sun gear. The Simpson arrangement is capable of producing three forward gear ratios and one reverse. A second very popular arrangement is the **Ravigneaux gear set**. Usually restricted to lighter vehicles, the Ravigneaux gear set uses two interconnected planetary gear sets sharing a common carrier. The Ravigneaux is capable of producing four forward ratios (including one overdrive) and one reverse. Several other arrangements are used to produce various desired ratios. Heavier-duty vehicles commonly use three or more interconnected planetary gear sets to produce six or more forward ratios.

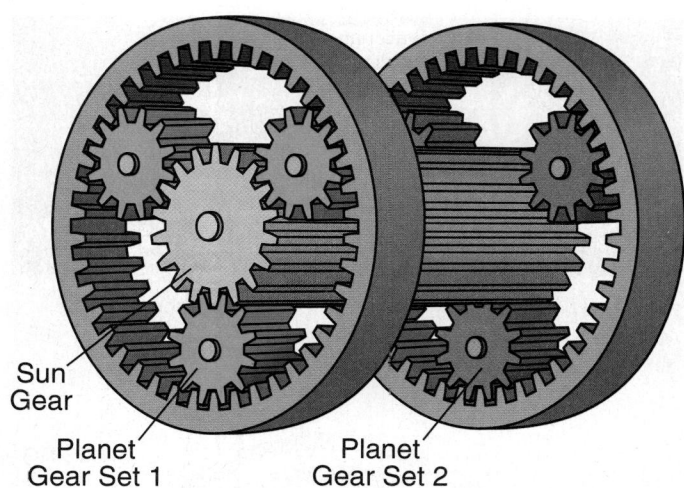

FIGURE 47-14 A Simpson gear set. Note the single sun gear driving two sets of planets.

Simpson Gear Set

One of the simplest and most popular compound gear sets is the Simpson gear set, depicted in **FIGURE 47-14**. It was invented by former Ford Motor Company engineer Howard Simpson. Howard Simpson originally worked for the Ford Motor Company, but left in 1938 and was subsequently hired by Detroit Harvester. In 1945, he decided to become an independent consultant to various companies, including Spicer. In 1947, he was diagnosed with terminal cancer and given six months to live. To his surprise and that of his doctors, he lived until 1963.

Simpson spent much of this time after his cancer diagnosis drawing every planetary gear set arrangement he could think of—and filed patents on them all! In total, 23 patents for gear sets are attributed to him. Although Simpson fleshed out the idea for the gear set that bears his name while working for Ford, he perfected it on his own while working as a consultant. The Simpson gear set was by far the most successful and the most widely known. The Simpson gear set has been used by every North American automobile manufacturer at one time or another and is well-known worldwide. A prolific inventor, Simpson was granted a total of 41 patents in his lifetime, leaving a lifetime of royalty payments to his estate.

By the early 1960s, the Simpson gear set was being used in most North American transmissions and several foreign vehicle manufacturers' transmissions. Elements of the Simpson gear set's basic designs are still seen in many of today's planetary gear set arrangements.

Ravigneaux Gear Set

The second common design of a compound planetary gear set is the Ravigneaux gear set patented by Frenchman Pol Ravigneaux in 1949. The Ravigneaux gear set, like that shown in **FIGURE 47-15**, has been used in several different North American transmissions and in foreign-made transmissions since the 1960s.

The Ravigneaux gear set consists of an interconnected planetary geartrain with two separate sun gears of different

FIGURE 47-15 The Ravigneaux gear set is very popular in light-duty automatic transmissions.

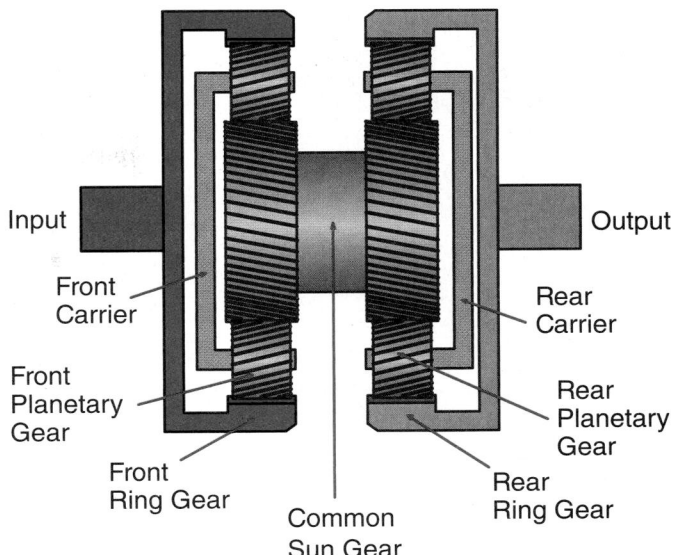

FIGURE 47-16 Simpson planetary gear set.

sizes. One planet carrier holds three long and three short sets of pinion gears; one ring gear meshes with the long planet pinions. The long pinions also mesh with the short pinions and with the large sun gear. The short pinions mesh with the long pinions and the small sun gear.

The Ravigneaux gear set was originally a three-speed gear set able to provide an overdrive with minor modification. Overdrive gearing became very popular in the late 1980s and 1990s to improve fuel economy. Today, this gear set is capable of producing four forward speeds, including an overdrive ratio and one reverse. (Other manufacturers achieved overdrive by modifying the Simpson gear set and adding a separate planetary gear set to provide the overdrive ratio.)

Wilson, Lepelletier, and ZF Gear Sets

The **Wilson gear set** is not as popular as the Simpson or the Ravigneaux, but consists of three interconnected planetary gears that can produce five forward speeds, including one overdrive.

The **Lepelletier gear set**, patented in 1990, uses a separate planetary gear set as the input to a Ravigneaux gear set and it produces six forward speeds, including two overdrives and one reverse.

ZF Friedrichshafen AG has an eight-speed automatic transmission, the 8 HP model, which has been produced for the automotive market since 2009.

Many other combinations of planetary gear arrangements are being used in light- and heavy-vehicle applications today to provide the necessary ratios for modern automatic transmission operation. Transmissions are being manufactured today with nine, and even 10, speeds for gasoline and diesel-powered vehicles. Although gasoline engines do not require this many available speeds to operate, the large number of ratios keep the engine operating close to its optimum rpm range, allowing increases in fuel efficiency.

Compound Planetary Gear Set Power Flows

The Simpson planetary gear set was by far the most recognized and most widely used gear set. Its simplicity makes it a good starting place for understanding simple and compound planetary gear power flows. The only compound power flow in the Simpson planetary gear set is first gear. The other three power flows (second, third, and reverse) are simple power flows using only one of the planetary gears. For illustrative purposes, let's examine the power flow for the Simpson gear set in greater detail.

As illustrated in **FIGURE 47-16**, the Simpson gear set consists of two nearly identical planetary gears sets that share a common sun gear. The forward set's ring gear has a hydraulic clutch splined to it. When the clutch is actuated, the transmission input shaft provides rotational input to the ring gear. This clutch is called the forward clutch because it must be applied in all three forward ranges.

The common sun gear is long enough that it meshes with both the forward and the rear planetary gear sets. The sun gear has a hydraulic clutch attached to it so that, when the clutch is applied, rotational power is supplied to the sun gear. This hydraulic clutch is called the high and reverse clutch. These are the only two inputs in the Simpson gear set: the front planetary ring gear and the common sun gear. All rotational power must enter the transmission through one of these components.

The high and reverse clutch that inputs to the sun gear also has a brake band attached to it. When the brake band is actuated, the sun gear is held stationary. This brake band is called the intermediate- or second-gear band. In some transmissions, instead of a brake band, a stationary hydraulic clutch is used to hold the high and reverse clutch and, therefore, the sun gear, stationary. The carrier of the front planetary gear set is splined to the transmission output shaft and is one of the two components

TABLE 47-2 Application Chart for Simpson Gear Set Powertrain Control Devices

Gear Range	Forward Clutch	High and Reverse Clutch	Rear Carrier One-Way Clutch	Brake Band	Low and Reverse Clutch or Band
Drive low	Applied		Holding		
Manual low	Applied				Applied
Second	Applied			Applied	
Third	Applied	Applied			
Reverse		Applied			Applied

that can provide output power from the Simpson gear set transmission. The rear planetary ring gear is also splined to the transmission output shaft and is the other component that can provide output power from the transmission.

The rear planetary carrier is attached to a roller-type one-way clutch that holds it stationary if it tries to turn in a counterclockwise direction. The rear carrier is also splined to a stationary clutch or a brake band in some transmissions so that the carrier can be held stationary in both directions. This control device is called either the low and reverse clutch or the low and reverse band, the illustrations we use for our Simpson gear set use a brake band to hold the rear carrier.

A powertrain control device **application chart**, such as the one in **TABLE 47-2**, helps us to understand which control devices are in use during which power flow. Knowing which devices are operational during which range is essential to the correct diagnoses of transmission failure. For example, if a transmission with a Simpson gear set does not propel the vehicle when in drive low, but does propel the vehicle when manual low is selected, the problem can be narrowed down to the low and reverse one-way clutch.

Let's examine more closely how compound planetary gear power flows work by following the power flows for a Simpson gear set. Study **FIGURE 47-17** to follow the Simpson gear set power flows.

► TECHNICIAN TIP

With knowledge of the clutch application chart and a pressure tester, a skilled technician can test the transmission and have a good idea as to what the problem is before removing the transmission for overhaul. Without this diagnosis, the technician may overhaul the transmission only to find that the original problem still exists.

Neutral or Park in a Simpson Gear Set

In neutral and park, the transmission input shaft is connected to the torque converter turbine and the forward clutch. As a result, rotational power is available, even though the forward clutch is not hydraulically applied. Power is not transferred beyond the forward clutch hub, so the clutch rotates around the stationary front planetary gear set ring gear.

1   High and Reverse Clutch Hub
2   Front Band
3   Input Shell
4   Forward Clutch Hub
5   Front Ring Gear
6   Planetary Pinions
7   Low and Reverse Band
8   One-Way (overrunning) Clutch
9   Output Shaft
10 Rear Ring Gear
11 Rear Planetary Carrier
12 Shared Sun Gear
13 Front Ring Gear
14 Front Planetary Carrier
15 Forward Clutch
16 High and Reverse Clutch
17 Input Shaft

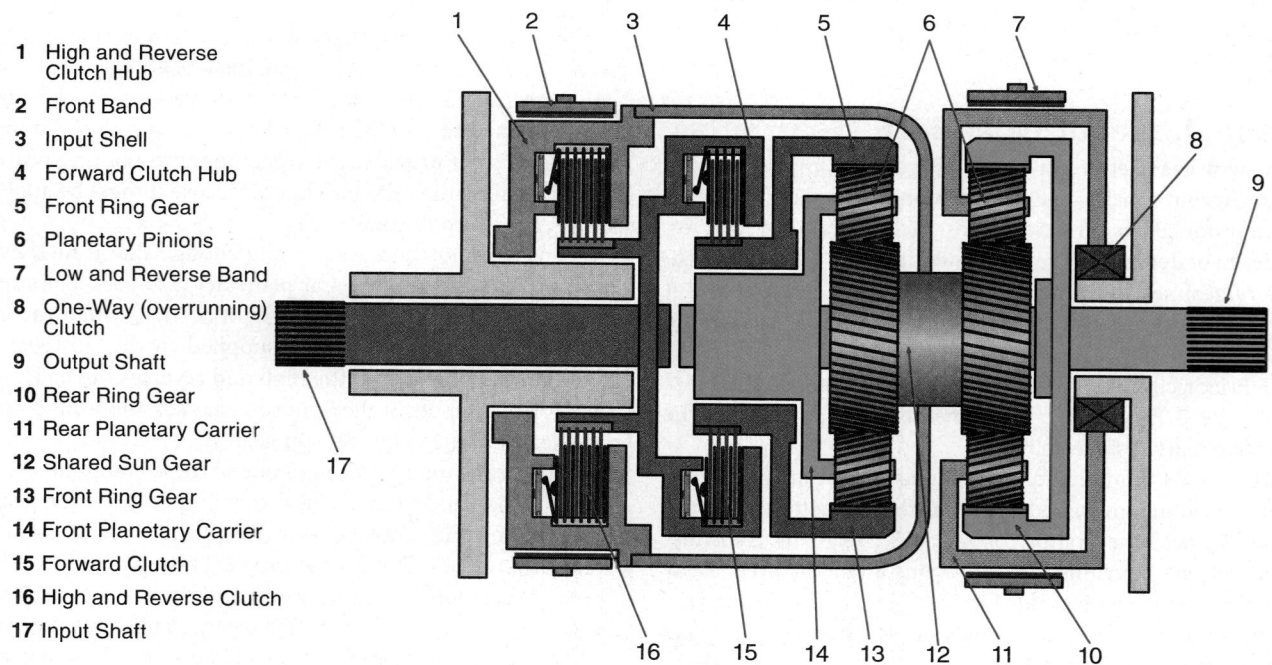

FIGURE 47-17 In neutral, no powertrain control devices are actuated and the power in a Simpson gear set does not go past the forward clutch hub.

First Gear (Low) in a Simpson Gear Set

First gear is the only compound power flow in the Simpson gear set. It is called a compound power flow because it uses both the front and the rear planetary gear sets to achieve the first gear or low ratio. All of the other ratios through the Simpson gear set are simple planetary power flows using only one of the two planetary gear sets.

When drive is selected by the driver, the vehicle starts in drive low, as illustrated in **FIGURE 47-18**. The forward clutch is applied. This brings rotational power to the front planetary ring gear. The front planetary carrier acts as a held member because it is splined to the output shaft. That means the front planetary carrier is being held by the weight of the vehicle connected to it.

It is important to remember that, with planetary gears, even though there is no control device holding a planetary gear component, the component can still act as a held member if it requires torque to cause it to turn. The front planetary sun gear becomes the output of the front gear set. The sun gear turns in reverse direction, counterclockwise, because the carrier is the held member. According to the rules for planetary gear ratios, when the carrier is the held member, the result is always a reverse of direction.

The Simpson geartrain shares a common sun gear, so the sun gear now becomes the input to the rear planetary gear set in reverse, or counterclockwise direction. This input tries to turn the rear carrier in a counterclockwise direction, but the one-way clutch attached to the rear carrier prevents it from turning counterclockwise. Again, the carrier is the held component in the rear planetary set. This reverses the direction again, and the rear gear set ring gear becomes the final output in a forward, clockwise, direction. The rear gear set ring gear

is splined to the output shaft, so power flows to the driveline and wheels.

During drive low operation, the one-way roller clutch is part of the flow. If the driver takes his foot off the accelerator, the power flow is reversed and the wheels try to drive the engine. The one-way clutch freewheels in that direction, however. The connection from the vehicle to the engine is broken, and the vehicle has no engine braking in drive low.

In some circumstances, engine braking is desired and necessary. In those instances, the driver can select manual low. In manual low, with the gear selector in L or 1, the low and reverse band is applied. That holds the rear planetary carrier in both directions, and engine braking occurs.

An interesting aspect to this compound power flow involves the fact that the front planetary carrier is held by the weight of the vehicle because it is splined to the output shaft. Once the vehicle begins to move, so, too, does the output shaft and the attached front carrier. That means that the "held" member or component is now moving!

This works in planetary gears as long as the input to the gear set is turning faster than the moving "held" component. The component still acts as if it is being held, yet the amount it moves contributes to the overall ratio of the compound power flow. To properly understand compound planetary gear power flows, it is essential that the technician realizes that a component can be the held member, even though it is moving. This concept is used extensively in compound planetary flows, the direction that the moving "held" component turns determines if the motion increases or decreases the overall ratio. First gear in the Simpson gear set is the only compound flow. All of the other power flows are simple power flows using only one of the planetary gear sets.

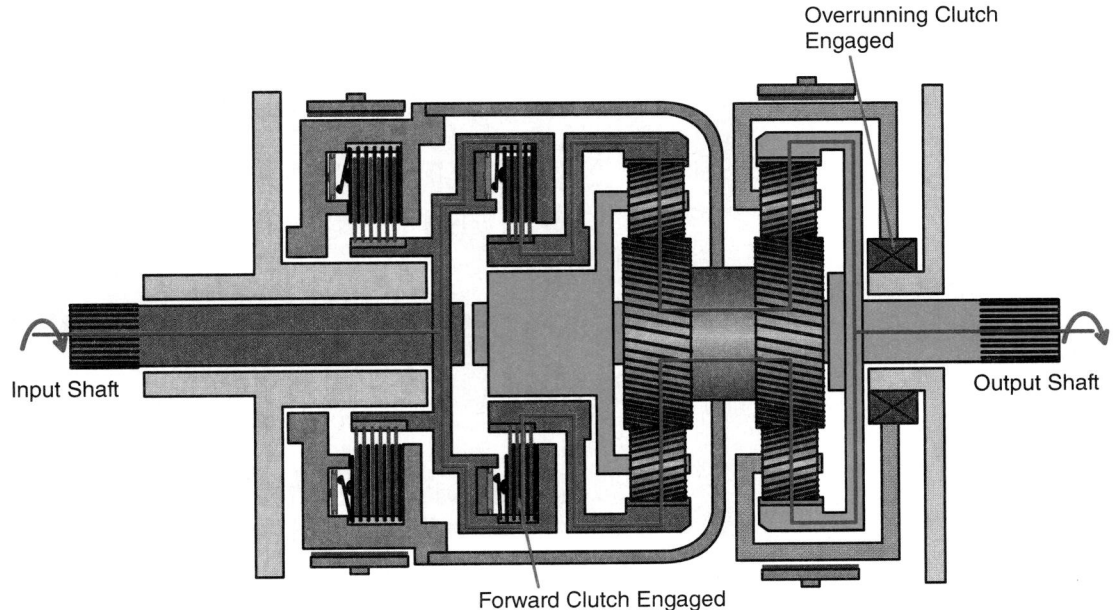

FIGURE 47-18 First gear is the only compound power flow in the Simpson gear set.

In several compound planetary gear set power flows, the held component of a gear set can actually be moving, but it must be at a slower speed than the input component. This movement can either increase or decrease the eventual ratio through the gear set, depending on the direction and speed of the "held" component's movement.

Second Gear in a Simpson Gear Set

As illustrated in **FIGURE 47-19**, second gear in a Simpson gear set is a simple planetary power flow using only the front planetary gear set. The power flow begins again with the forward clutch applied, and that brings rotational power to the forward

ring gear. The band is applied, which holds the high reverse clutch drum stationary—which in turn holds the sun gear stationary through its connected input shell. The forward gear set carrier becomes output and it is splined to the output shaft. This power flow uses the minimum forward reduction of the front planetary gear set.

Third Gear (High or Direct) in a Simpson Gear Set

As **FIGURE 47-20** illustrates, third gear in a Simpson gear set is, again, a simple planetary power flow using only the front planetary gear set. When the transmission shifts to third gear, the brake band used for second gear is released and the high/reverse

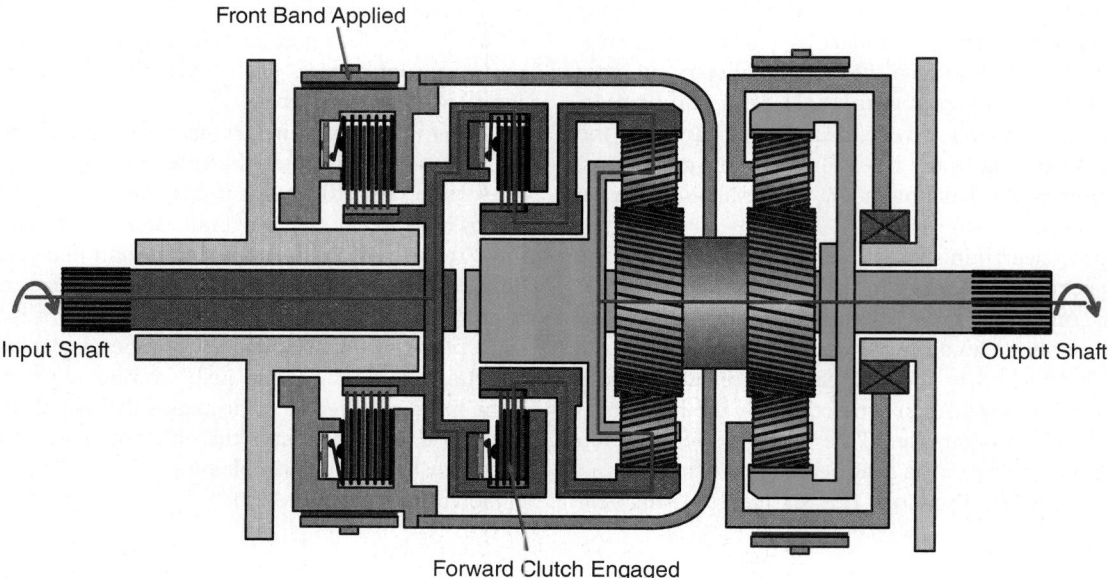

FIGURE 47-19 Second gear in a Simpson gear set.

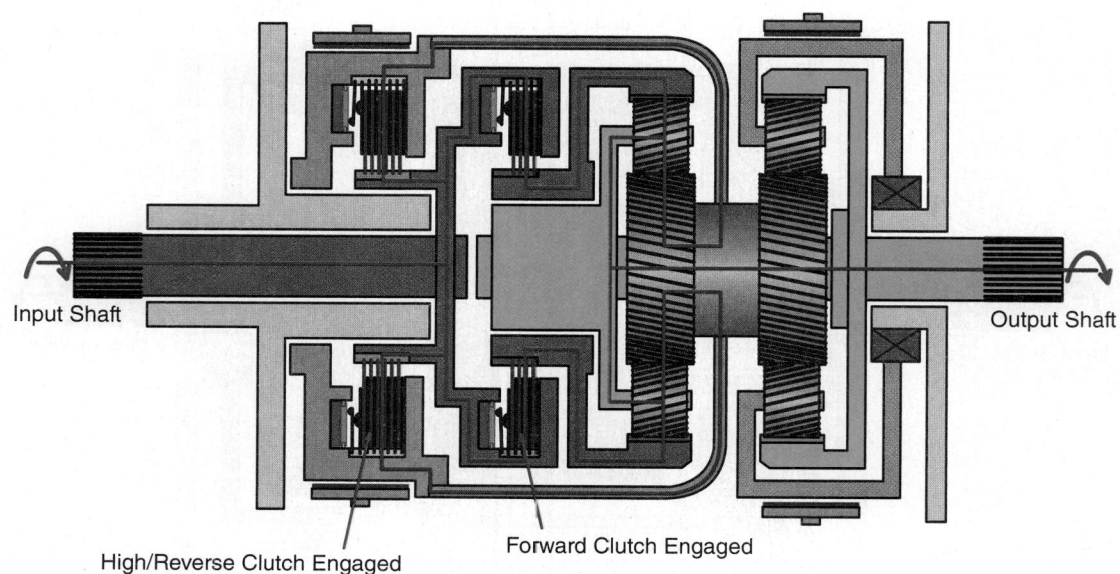

FIGURE 47-20 Third gear in a Simpson gear set is direct drive, or 1:1.

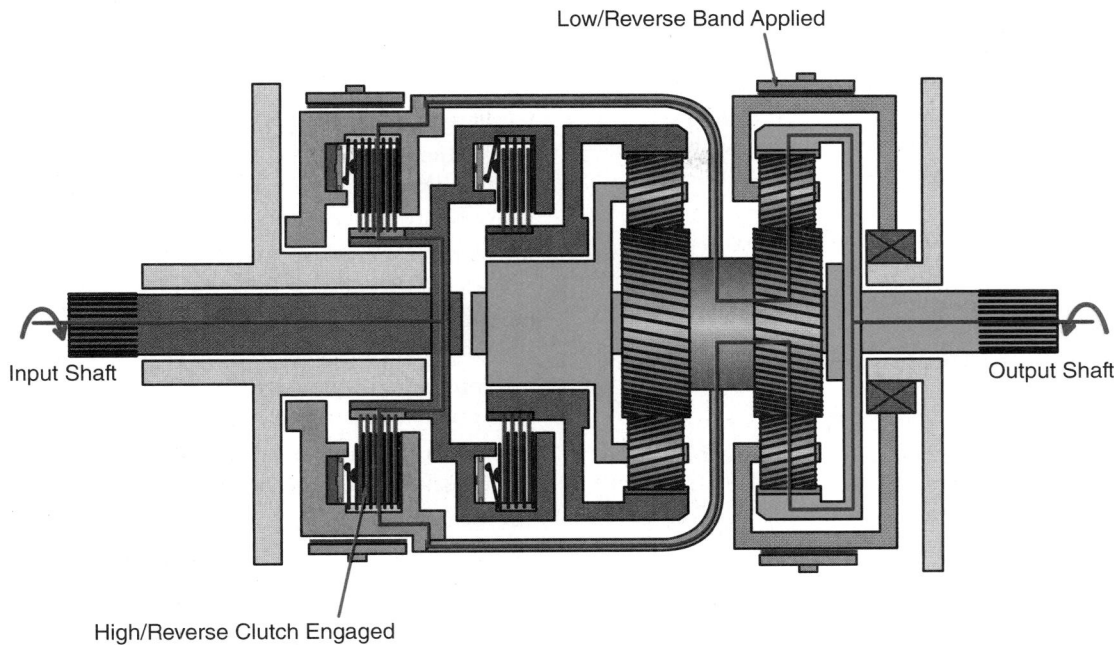

FIGURE 47-21 Reverse is the only gear that does not use the forward clutch.

clutch is applied. This locks the high clutch to the forward clutch and provides an input to the front planetary sun gear through the input shell. The forward clutch is still applied, so there is also an input to the front planetary ring gear at the same speed. These two inputs cause the front planetary gear set to act as one unit. The carrier must turn at the same speed as well. The carrier becomes output and it is splined to the output shaft.

Reverse in Simpson a Gear Set

Reverse in a Simpson gear set is a simple planetary gear power flow using only the rear planetary gear set, as illustrated in **FIGURE 47-21**. Reverse is the only gear in which the forward clutch is not applied, hence its name. The forward clutch hub is, however, splined to the input shaft. When the high/reverse clutch is applied, as it is in reverse, it takes rotational power from the hub of the forward clutch and transfers it to the sun gear through

the input shell. The front planetary ring gear is free to turn, so no power can be transmitted through the front planetary set.

Reverse begins with the clockwise sun gear input to the rear planetary gear set. This input tries to turn the rear planetary carrier clockwise. That makes the one-way clutch ineffective as it freewheels in this direction. In reverse, the low and reverse band is applied to hold the rear carrier stationary. The rear planetary ring gear becomes the output and is splined to the output shaft. Because the rear carrier is the held component, the output direction is reversed.

As mentioned previously, there are many different compound planetary gear set combinations, each with its own specific power flows. We only describe the Simpson gear set power flows as an example. A good understanding of the Simpson power flows will allow you to interpret the power flows of many of the other popular gear sets.

Wrap-Up

Ready for Review

▶ Planetary gears are at the heart of automatic transmission operation.
▶ Planetary gears are very versatile. They provide up to seven possible ratios from one simple planetary gear set—two forward reductions, two forward overdrives, two reverse ratios, and a one-to-one (direct) ratio.
▶ Planetary gears are epicyclical gears. That is, they revolve around a common centerline and thereby cancel out radial thrust.

▶ Helical planetary gears operate very quietly and are very strong for their size as they have multiple sets of teeth involved in their power flows.
▶ According to the rules of planetary gears, in order to have a power flow, one component must be inputted, one component must be held, and one component must be connected to an output.
▶ The carrier is the key to planetary gear power flows. If the carrier is the output, the result is a forward reduction. If the carrier is the input, the result is a forward overdrive. If the carrier is the held component, the result is always reverse.

▶ To produce a one-to-one ratio, two components of the planetary gear set are input at the same speed, and the third component is connected to the output.

▶ When calculating planetary gear ratios, the number of teeth on the stationary or reaction member of the planetary gear set is either added to or subtracted from the output.

▶ Several planetary gear set combinations have been used to provide from three to eight forward speeds. These designs include the Simpson, Ravigneaux, Wilson, Lepelletier, and the ZF gear sets.

▶ Newer automatic transmissions are being produced with up to ten speeds.

▶ Planetary gear sets are controlled by powertrain control devices, such as the hydraulic clutch, the brake band, and one-way (over-running) clutches.

▶ Hydraulic clutches squeeze the friction plates and reaction plates together to either drive a planetary component (rotating clutch) or to hold it stationary (stationary clutch).

▶ Brake bands are applied hydraulically and are used to hold a planetary component stationary.

▶ One-way clutches are used to hold planetary components in one direction to produce a power flow while under load. When the vehicle coasts, the clutch freewheels, preventing engine braking.

▶ Compound power flows are those that use more than one planetary gear set to produce the power flow.

▶ An important aspect of planetary gears is that the held component in a particular power flow does not actually have to be stationary. The component can be moving, as long as it is not moving faster than the input component; this is known as acting as a held component.

▶ The direction and speed of a rotating "held" component determines if the motion increases or decreases the ratio.

Key Terms

application chart A chart showing which powertrain control devices are used for a particular power flow.

brake band A friction faced metal band that surrounds a planetary component; when applied hydraulically, it holds the component stationary.

compound planetary gear set Planetary gear power flow that utilizes more than one gear set to produce the ratios.

epicyclical gear Gears that revolve around a common centerline.

friction plates Steel plates faced with friction material and used in a hydraulic clutch. They are splined to a planetary gear set component.

hydraulic clutch A hydraulically actuated powertrain control device that squeezes friction and reaction plates together

to either drive, (input), or hold a planetary gear component stationary.

input member The element of the planetary gear set that receives input from the power source.

Lepelletier gear set A compound planetary gear set consisting of three interconnected planetary gears capable of producing six forward ratios and one reverse.

maximum forward overdrive The highest (fastest) ratio possible in a planetary gear set.

maximum forward reduction The lowest (slowest) ratio possible in a planetary gear set.

minimum forward overdrive The second highest (fastest) ratio possible in a planetary gear set.

minimum forward reduction The second lowest (slowest) ratio possible in a planetary gear set.

output member The element of the planetary gear set that is connected to the transmission output shaft.

planetary gear A gear arrangement consisting of a ring gear with internal teeth, a carrier with two or more small pinion gears in constant mesh with the ring gear, and an externally toothed sun gear in the center in constant mesh with the planetary pinions.

powertrain control device A device used to input or hold planetary gear components to affect a power flow. These can be hydraulic clutches, brake bands, or one-way sprag or roller clutches.

Ravigneaux gear set A popular compound planetary gear set with two planetary gear sets sharing a common carrier; capable of producing four forward speeds and one reverse.

reaction member The element of the planetary gear set that is held stationary.

reaction plates Metal plates in the hydraulic clutch; usually splined to the clutch hub or the transmission case.

reverse overdrive A reverse direction overdrive ratio through the planetary gear set.

reverse reduction A reverse direction underdrive ratio through the planetary gear set.

rotating clutch A hydraulic clutch used to input a planetary gear component.

Simpson gear set The most common compound planetary gear set; consists of two planetary gears sharing a common sun gear; capable of producing three forward and one reverse ratio.

stationary clutch A hydraulic clutch used to hold a planetary gear component stationary and usually splined to the transmission case.

sun gear The small, externally toothed gear at the center of the planetary gear set.

Wilson gear set A compound planetary gear set consisting of three planetary gears interconnected; capable of producing five forward and one reverse ratio.

Review Questions

1. What is the output on the ring gear of a planetary gear set when the carrier is input and the sun gear is the held component?
   a. Maximum forward reduction
   b. Minimum forward reduction
   c. Maximum forward overdrive
   d. Minimum forward overdrive

2. Which of the following produces a direct ratio from a planetary gear set?
   a. Sun gear input, carrier held, ring gear output
   b. Ring gear input, carrier output, sun gear held
   c. Carrier input, ring gear held, sun gear output
   d. Carrier input, sun gear input, ring gear output

3. How are the planetary gearsets in a Simpson Gear set connected to each other?
   a. By a shared sun gear
   b. By a shared carrier
   c. By a shared ring gear
   d. By shared pinion gears

4. If a simple planetary gear set has 24 teeth on the sun gear and 60 teeth on the ring gear, what is the ratio if the sun gear is input, the ring gear is held, and the carrier is output?
   a. 2.5 to 1
   b. 0.4 to 1
   c. 1.4 to 1
   d. 3.5 to 1

5. What power flow results from a planetary gear set if the carrier is held, the sun gear is input, and the ring gear is output?
   a. Maximum forward reduction
   b. Minimum forward overdrive
   c. Reverse reduction
   d. Reverse overdrive

6. Which of the following planetary geartrain control devices can sometimes be adjusted from the outside of the transmission?
   a. The hydraulic clutch
   b. The roller-type one-way clutch
   c. The servo and band mechanism
   d. The sprag-type one-way clutch

7. Why do we sometimes use a roller-type one-way clutch to hold a member of the planetary gear set?
   a. To prevent engine braking when decelerating
   b. To save money
   c. To provide a much smoother engagement than a hydraulic clutch
   d. Roller-type clutches are easier to install

8. Which of the following is considered the strongest planetary geartrain control device?
   a. Hydraulic clutch
   b. Servo and band mechanism
   c. Sprag-type one-way clutch
   d. Roller-type one-way clutch

9. The power flow through two interconnected planetary gear sets is best described as which kind of power flow?
   a. Double reverse
   b. Versatile
   c. Reverse
   d. Compound

10. The Ravigneaux gearset shares which element?
    a. A common sun gear
    b. A common ring gear
    c. A common carrier
    d. The Ravigneaux gear set has no shared element

ASE Technician A/Technician B Style Questions

1. Technician A says that a simple planetary gear set can produce seven different ratios. Technician B says that planetary gears are epicyclical. Who is correct?
   a. Technician A
   b. Technician B
   c. Both Technician A and Technician B
   d. Neither Technician A nor Technician B

2. Technician A says that if the planetary carrier is the output member, a reverse is the outcome, if the rules of planetary gears are satisfied. Technician B says that if the carrier is input, a forward overdrive is the result, if the rules of planetary gears are satisfied. Who is correct?
   a. Technician A
   b. Technician B
   c. Both Technician A and Technician B
   d. Neither Technician A nor Technician B

3. Technician A says that helical planetary gears do not produce any thrust. Technician B says that planetary gears cancel out radial thrust. Who is correct?
   a. Technician A
   b. Technician B
   c. Both Technician A and Technician B
   d. Neither Technician A nor Technician B

4. Technician A says that holding the sun gear stationary and inputting the ring gear of a planetary gear set produces the maximum forward reduction at the carrier. Technician B says that holding the carrier stationary and inputting the sun gear of a planetary gear set produces a reverse reduction at the ring gear. Who is correct?
   a. Technician A
   b. Technician B
   c. Both Technician A and Technician B
   d. Neither Technician A nor Technician B

5. Technician A says that hydraulic clutches can be used to hold or input planetary gear components. Technician B says that one-way clutches are used to provide engine braking. Who is correct?
   a. Technician A
   b. Technician B
   c. Both Technician A and Technician B
   d. Neither Technician A nor Technician B

6. Technician A says that one-way clutches can be sprag or roller type. Technician B says that a one-way clutch is used in manual low in the Simpson geartrain. Who is correct?
   a. Technician A
   b. Technician B
   c. Both Technician A and Technician B
   d. Neither Technician A nor Technician B

7. Technician A says that brake bands are used to input a planetary gear component. Technician B says that hydraulic clutches can sometimes be adjusted from the outside of the transmission case. Who is correct?
   a. Technician A
   b. Technician B
   c. Both Technician A and Technician B
   d. Neither Technician A nor Technician B

8. Technician A says that two hydraulic clutches are used to input to the Simpson gear set. Technician B says the Simpson gear set shares a common sun gear. Who is correct?
   a. Technician A
   b. Technician B
   c. Both Technician A and Technician B
   d. Neither Technician A nor Technician B

9. Technician A says that to achieve direct in the Simpson gear set, the front ring gear and the front sun gear are inputted and the front carrier is the output. Technician B says that reverse is a compound power flow in the Simpson gear set. Who is correct?
   a. Technician A
   b. Technician B
   c. Both Technician A and Technician B
   d. Neither Technician A nor Technician B

10. Technician A says that second gear in a Simpson gear set is a compound power flow. Technician B says that the Simpson gear set only has one compound power flow. Who is correct?
    a. Technician A
    b. Technician B
    c. Both Technician A and Technician B
    d. Neither Technician A nor Technician B

CHAPTER 48

Hydraulically Controlled Automatic Transmissions

Learning Objectives

After reading this chapter, you will be able to:

- **LO 48-1** Understand the history of transmissions in the North American truck and coach market.
- **LO 48-2** Describe and explain the components of Allison hydraulically controlled automatic transmissions.
- **LO 48-3** Describe and explain Allison transmission power flows.
- **LO 48-4** Describe and explain Allison transmission hydraulic control system components.
- **LO 48-5** Describe and explain the operation of Allison hydraulically controlled automatic transmissions.

You Are the Technician

A vehicle is towed to your repair facility with a complaint that the transmission will not go into gear. You investigate and find that the vehicle is equipped with a four-speed Allison hydraulically controlled automatic transmission. You do a preliminary inspection and discover that the transmission will not go into drive or reverse. The engine runs fine and everything else seems in order.

1. What would you do next to diagnose this vehicle?
2. Could the torque converter cause this problem? Why or why not?
3. Could a failed transmission clutch cause this problem? Explain.

Introduction

Automatic transmissions have been in use in the medium- to heavy-duty truck and bus market in North America for many years. The three major manufacturers of automatic transmissions for this market are ZF Friedrichshafen, Voith, and Allison. In 2006, Caterpillar entered the truck automatic transmission market with its CX28, CX31, and CX35 models to limited success. In 2011, CAT introduced its new CT660 class eight on-highway truck, and the CX-31 is the standard equipment automatic transmission with this vehicle. The market, however, is not evenly divided among manufacturers. The lion's share of the automatic transmission market still belongs to Allison.

Automatic transmissions have several benefits over their manually shifted counterparts. Automatic transmissions add to driver comfort and lessen fatigue. They allow many people to drive a vehicle without having to learn complex shift patterns and schedules. Automatic transmissions can reduce service and down time because drivers are less likely to engage in skip shifting and gear jamming. Finally, because they usually have smoother shifts, automatic transmissions enhance passenger comfort during shifting.

In this chapter, we discover the basics of what makes automatic transmissions work and how they compare with their manual and automated manual transmission counterparts. We focus on hydraulically controlled automatic transmissions and concentrate on Allison automatic transmissions, as they are the most common in North America. The workings of all automatic transmissions are similar, however. Electronically controlled automatic transmissions have dominated the heavy-duty truck market since the 1990s, but their operation and control is based on the purely hydraulic automatics of years past. Understanding the hydraulic controls gives the technician more insight into the logic behind the electronic control strategies, so it makes sense to start there.

The History of Transmissions in the North American Truck and Coach Market

LO 48-1 Understand the history of transmissions in the North American truck and coach market.

Allison transmission is by far the largest supplier of automatic transmissions to the North American truck and coach market. As early as the 1940s, Allison was making transmission models, such as the original CD-850 tank transmission for the American military. The first Allison transmission for commercial vehicles was manufactured in the 1970s. It was called the MT-25 and was followed by the AT series, including the 540, 543, and 545, which were used extensively in school bus applications and other relatively light vehicles. The MT-640/650 was used in mid-range vehicles; the V-730 ("V") drive series was used for inner city transit and coach applications; and the HT-740/750 was used in heavy-duty trucks and bus applications.

By the mid-1970s, Allison had sold over half a million commercial transmissions around the world and, in 1987 alone, sold a staggering 73,976 transmissions! Most of Allison's designs in these years were four-speed models—all of which used the identical gear arrangement with three interconnected planetary gears. Two designs of five-speed models incorporating a lower forward range were also available. The five-speed models used an extra planetary gear set behind the three interconnected sets and were designated deep ratio and close ratio. The deep ratio transmission had a very low ratio for low gear; the close ratio had smaller ratio steps between the five gears. The Allison five-speed models are all but obsolete now and, therefore, are not discussed further.

In the late 1980s, Allison moved into partial electronic control with the Allison Transmission Electronic Control (ATEC), which was eventually renamed Commercial Electronic Control (CEC). Then, in 1991, Allison introduced the World Transmission (WT), the company's first intuitive electronically controlled medium-/heavy-duty transmission. In 1999, Allison added to its line of medium/heavy WT models with the 1000/2000 and 2400 series transmissions for use in lighter-duty and mid-range vehicles. All of Allison's current transmissions are electronically controlled.

Allison is not the only manufacturer with a long history. ZF Friedrichshafen has been manufacturing automatic transmissions since the early 1960s, primarily in Europe. ZF has had several entries into the truck/coach market. ZF launched the Busmatic in 1963, the Ecomat in 1980, and the Ecolife in 2006. Most of ZF's models were available as four-, five-, or six-speed models. All of ZF's current automatic transmission models are completely electronically controlled.

Voith, another European manufacturer, has been making transmissions in Europe since the 1930s. Voith's business was primarily for the locomotive and industrial market, but the company started manufacturing bus transmissions in the 1950s. In 1980, Voith started to supply heavy-duty transmissions to the North American dump truck and bus markets. In 2018, Voith announced that it had more than 300,000 of its DIWA™ bus transmissions in service around the world. The DIWA transmissions use the transmission's torque converter as an integrated retarder to augment the vehicle brakes. Voith's current transmission models are all electronically controlled.

Components of Allison Hydraulically Controlled Automatic Transmissions

LO 48-2 Describe and explain the components of Allison hydraulically controlled automatic transmissions.

Although all automatic transmissions used in the truck and coach market today are fully electronically controlled, the basis for that control has been developed from the hydraulically controlled transmissions used in the past. The lessons we learn in this chapter on hydraulic controls explain the thinking behind the development and utilization of electronic controls in the Electronically Controlled Automatic Transmissions chapter. This section discusses the basic design of a hydraulically controlled automatic transmission, as well as its power flows.

Transmission Design

Early four-speed models of Allison transmissions all had the same planetary gear arrangement, as illustrated in **FIGURE 48-1**. Because this version of the four-speed transmission was the most prevalent design in hydraulically controlled automatic truck transmissions, we look at its power flow in detail. Although power flows for different manufacturers' models vary, they all share the same basic elements. The following section explains the Allison AT, MT, V, and HT series four-speed transmissions power train.

The transmission has three interconnected planetary gear sets named the front, center, and rear planetary sets, as illustrated in **FIGURE 48-2**. The front and the center sets are similar in design to a reversed Simpson gear set, which was discussed in the Planetary Gear Concepts chapter. The front and center sun gears are connected by the sun gear shaft and, therefore, they must turn together.

Referring to Figure 48-2, the three planetary gear sets are interconnected except for the front planetary carrier and the rear planetary ring gear. Those two components are not connected to any other part of the gear train. The front and the center sun gears are splined to the **sun gear shaft** and are connected together. The front planetary ring gear, the center planetary carrier, and the rear planetary carrier are all connected by the **connecting drum**. Because of the connecting drum, all three of these components must always turn together. Finally, the center planetary ring gear and the rear planetary sun gear are part of the **main shaft**, so they must turn together.

There are five multidisc hydraulic clutches in the transmission. From front to back, the first two clutches are the **forward clutch** (so called because it is applied in all forward ranges) and the fourth clutch. The forward and fourth clutches are rotating clutches, and they transmit rotational power to the planetary gearing. Next are the third clutch, the second clutch, and first clutch. These are stationary clutches and, when applied, they hold planetary gear components stationary.

The forward clutch is a rotating clutch and its hub is splined to the input or turbine shaft. When it is applied, it delivers rotational power to the main shaft, so it supplies power to the center ring gear and the rear sun gear. The fourth clutch is a rotating clutch and its hub is splined to the sun gear shaft. The friction discs in the fourth clutch are splined to an extension of the forward clutch hub. When the fourth clutch is applied, it takes rotational input from the input shaft through the forward clutch hub and delivers it to the sun gear shaft and, therefore, to the front and center sun gears. These are the only two ways that rotational input can be delivered to the gear sets.

Third, second, and first clutch are stationary clutches—their steel reaction plates are splined to the transmission case. These three clutches hold components stationary when applied. The friction plates of the third clutch are splined to the outside of the fourth clutch hub. When the third clutch is applied, it holds the fourth clutch hub and, therefore, the front and center sun gears stationary. The friction plates of the second clutch

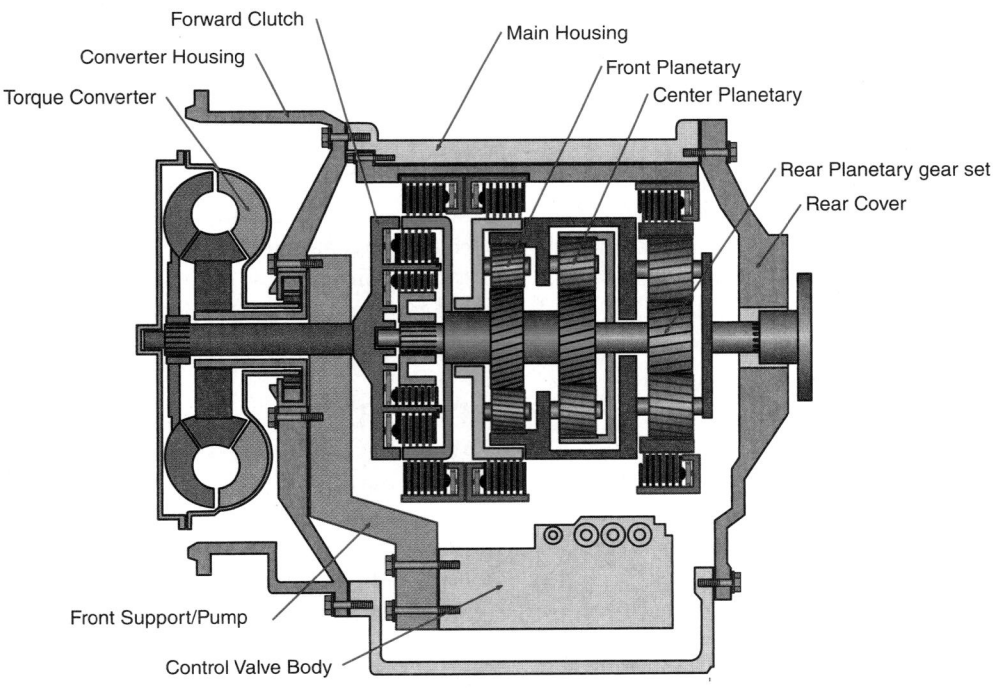

FIGURE 48-1 A cutaway view of the Allison AT 500 series transmission. The gear train, clutches, and power flows for this transmission are the same for all the early four-speed Allison models.

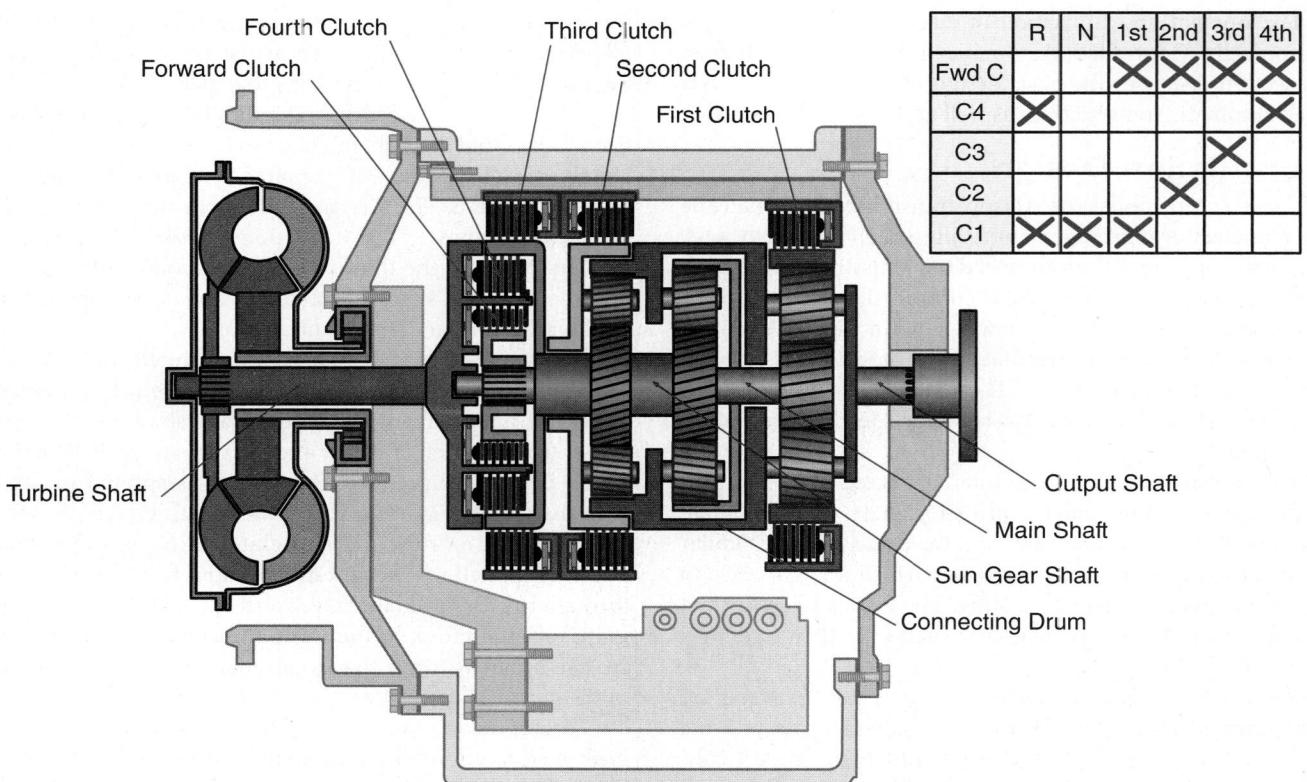

	R	N	1st	2nd	3rd	4th
Fwd C			X	X	X	X
C4	X					X
C3					X	
C2				X		
C1	X	X	X			

FIGURE 48-2 This schematic shows the three planetary gear sets and how they interconnect, as well as the five hydraulic clutches. This design is common to all the four-speed Allison models: the AT, the MT, and the HT series.

are splined to the outside of the front planetary carrier so that, when the second clutch applies, it holds the front carrier stationary. The friction discs from the first clutch are splined to the rear planetary ring gear and, when the first clutch is applied, the ring gear is held stationary.

The only path of power out of the transmission is through the rear planetary carrier. It is the only component that is splined to the output shaft. Remember, though, that the front planetary ring gear, the center planetary carrier, and the rear planetary carrier are all connected by the connecting drum. As a result, all these components are attached to the output shaft.

Allison Transmission Power Flows

LO 48-3 Describe and explain Allison transmission power flows.

It is important for the technician to read and understand the clutch application chart when diagnosing a transmission issue. These charts tell the technician which clutches are applied and, because he knows what each clutch controls, which planetary gear components are involved in the power flow for each range (gear). Knowing which clutches are applied and what they connect to is essential to determine where the cause of the problem might originate. **TABLE 48-1**

is the clutch application chart for the Allison AT, MT, and HT four-speed transmissions.

Neutral

As we see from the clutch application chart and **FIGURE 48-3**, in neutral only the first clutch is applied. Therefore, when either first or reverse is selected, the transmission only needs to engage one of the rotating clutches—either the forward clutch or the fourth clutch—to complete the power flow. Neither of the rotating clutches is applied in neutral, so the power is delivered from the torque converter turbine to the input or turbine shaft and the forward clutch hub—but no further. The transmission is then in neutral.

First Range

When the driver selects any forward range, the transmission always starts in first range and then automatically shifts sequentially to the highest selected range as road speed increases. In the Allison four-speed transmissions, first range is a simple planetary power flow using only one of the planetary gear sets. When the driver selects a forward range, the forward clutch is applied. That action brings rotational input to the transmission main shaft and, therefore, to the center ring gear and the rear sun gear. Because the center sun gear is free to rotate, the first-gear power flow takes place in the rear planetary set. The rear

TABLE 48-1 Clutch Application Chart for the Allison AT, MT, and HT Series Four-Speed Transmissions

Range	Forward Clutch	Fourth Clutch	Third Clutch	Second Clutch	First Clutch
Neutral					Applied
First range	Applied				Applied
Second range	Applied			Applied	
Third range	Applied		Applied		
Fourth Range	Applied	Applied			
Reverse		Applied			Applied

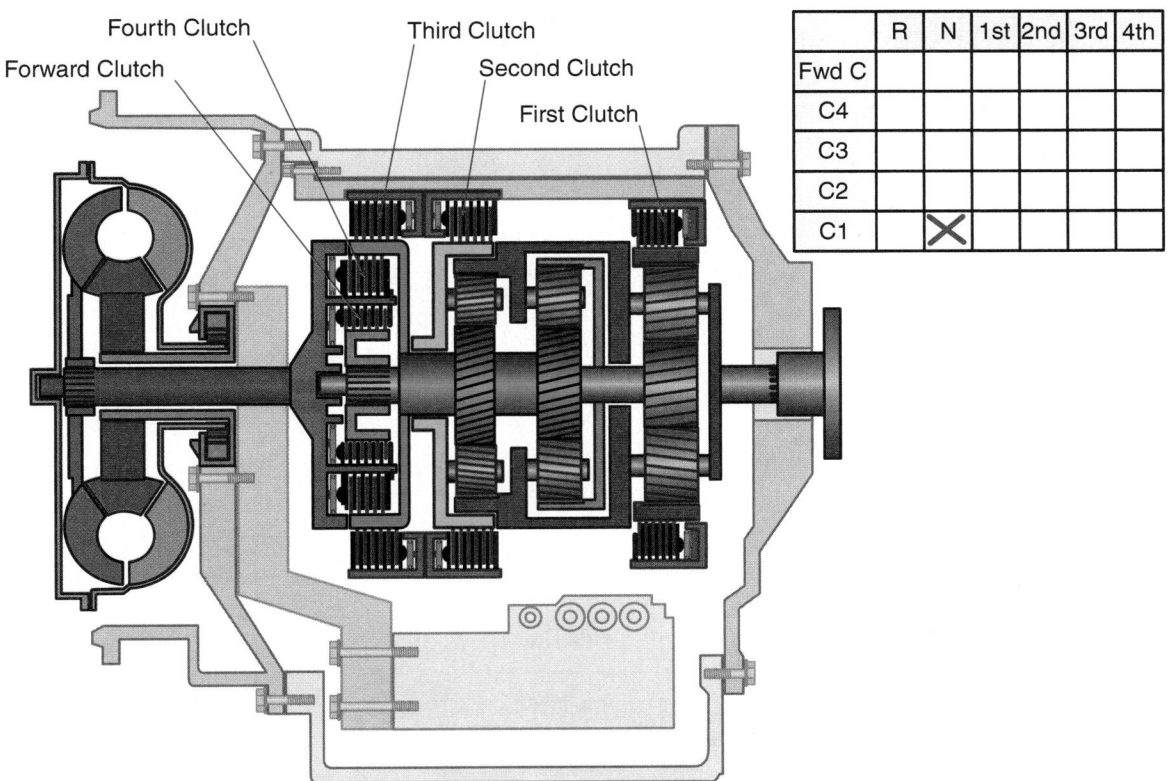

FIGURE 48-3 In neutral, only the first clutch is applied and rotational power does not progress past the input shaft and the forward clutch hub.

sun gear is the input and the rear ring gear is held by the first clutch. The rear carrier becomes the output and it is splined to the output shaft, as illustrated in **FIGURE 48-4**.

Second Range

As the transmission shifts to second range, the forward clutch remains applied, the first clutch is released, and the second clutch applies, as illustrated in **FIGURE 48-5**. This is a compound power flow involving the center and the front planetary gear sets.

Let's start the power flow in the center planetary set. When applied, the forward clutch connects the center ring gear to the input or turbine shaft, so the power flow starts at that point. The center ring gear is input. The center carrier is splined through

the connecting drum to the rear carrier and, therefore, to the output shaft. The weight of the vehicle is preventing the carrier from turning, so the carrier acts as a held component. This causes the center sun gear to become the output and to turn in reverse because the carrier is the "held" component (see Chapter 48 to refresh yourself on the rules on planetary gears, if necessary). The center sun gear is splined to the sun gear shaft, as is the front planetary sun gear. The front sun gear becomes input to the front planetary set in a counterclockwise direction. The second clutch is holding the front planetary carrier stationary, so the front planetary ring gear now becomes clockwise output. The front planetary ring gear is splined through the connecting drum to the rear carrier and the output shaft.

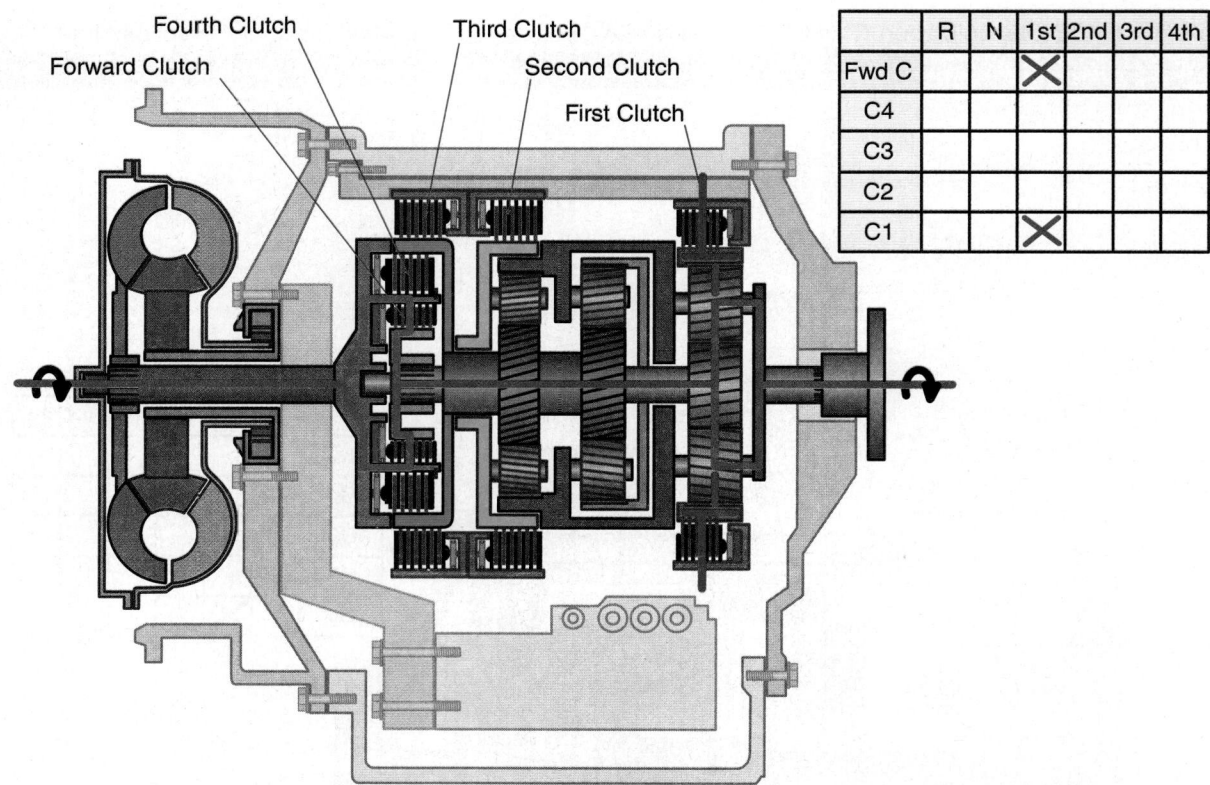

	R	N	1st	2nd	3rd	4th
Fwd C			✕			
C4						
C3						
C2						
C1			✕			

FIGURE 48-4 First range.

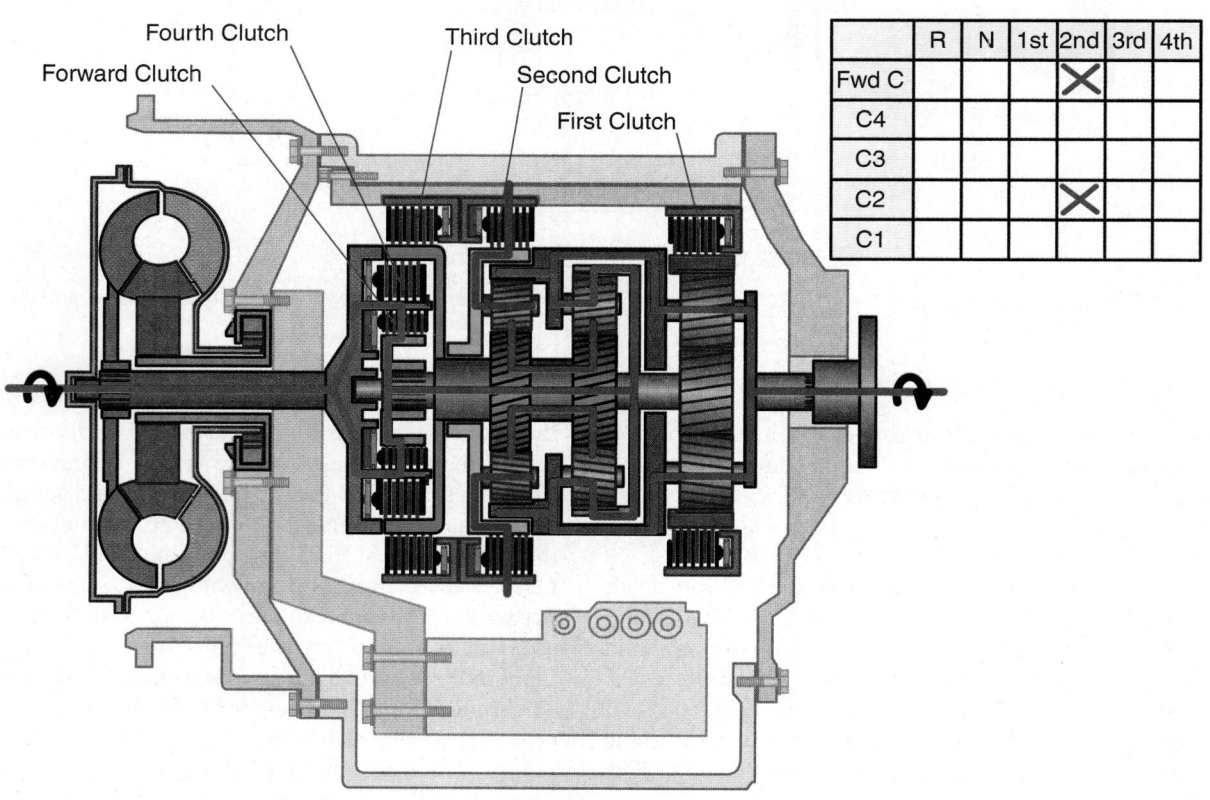

	R	N	1st	2nd	3rd	4th
Fwd C				✕		
C4						
C3						
C2				✕		
C1						

FIGURE 48-5 Second range.

This power flow is very similar to the first gear power flow through a Simpson gear set (that was explained in the Planetary Gear Concepts chapter). As the vehicle begins to move, the center planetary carrier moves with it because it is also splined to the connecting drum and the output shaft. But the center planetary carrier rotates slower than the ring gear input to the center gear set and, therefore, still acts as a "held" component to satisfy the rules of planetary gears that were discussed in the Planetary Gear Concepts chapter.

Third Range

As the transmission shifts to third range, the second clutch is released, and the third clutch is applied. This power flow is illustrated in **FIGURE 48-6**. Third range is a simple planetary flow involving only the center planetary gear set. Forward clutch is applied, bringing rotational input to the center planetary ring gear. Third clutch is applied, and it holds the hub of the fourth clutch stationary. The sun gear shaft, which is splined to the fourth clutch hub, remains stationary as well. So the center ring gear is input, the center sun gear is held, and the center carrier becomes the output. The center carrier is splined through the connecting drum to the rear carrier and, therefore, to the output shaft.

Fourth Range

Fourth range, shown in **FIGURE 48-7**, again is a simple planetary power flow involving only the center planetary gear set. When the transmission shifts into fourth range, the third clutch

is released and the fourth clutch applies. This bring two rotational inputs to the center planetary gear set—one through the forward clutch to the center ring gear and the other from the fourth clutch to the center sun gear. Because the center sun gear and the center ring gear are being turned at the same speed, the center carrier must also turn at the same speed and it is splined through the connecting drum to the rear carrier and the output shaft. This creates a direct-drive ratio through the center gear set. In this power flow, both rotating clutches and, because of their interconnections, the components of the three planetary gear sets all rotate at the same speed.

Even though the power flow is through the center planetary set in fourth range or direct, the front and the rear planetary gear components rotate at the same speed because they both have two inputs. The front planetary gear set has an input from the sun gear and the front ring gear, which is splined to the connecting drum, so the front carrier turns also and goes along for the ride. The rear planetary set has two inputs as well, because the rear sun gear is part of the main shaft and, therefore, is turning at input shaft speed. Because the rear carrier is splined to the connecting drum that is turning at the same speed, the rear ring gear also goes along for the ride.

Reverse

Reverse is a compound power flow, as illustrated in **FIGURE 48-8**. The reverse power flow involves the center and the rear planetary gear sets. The power flow starts from the neutral position. In neutral, the first clutch is applied, holding the rear

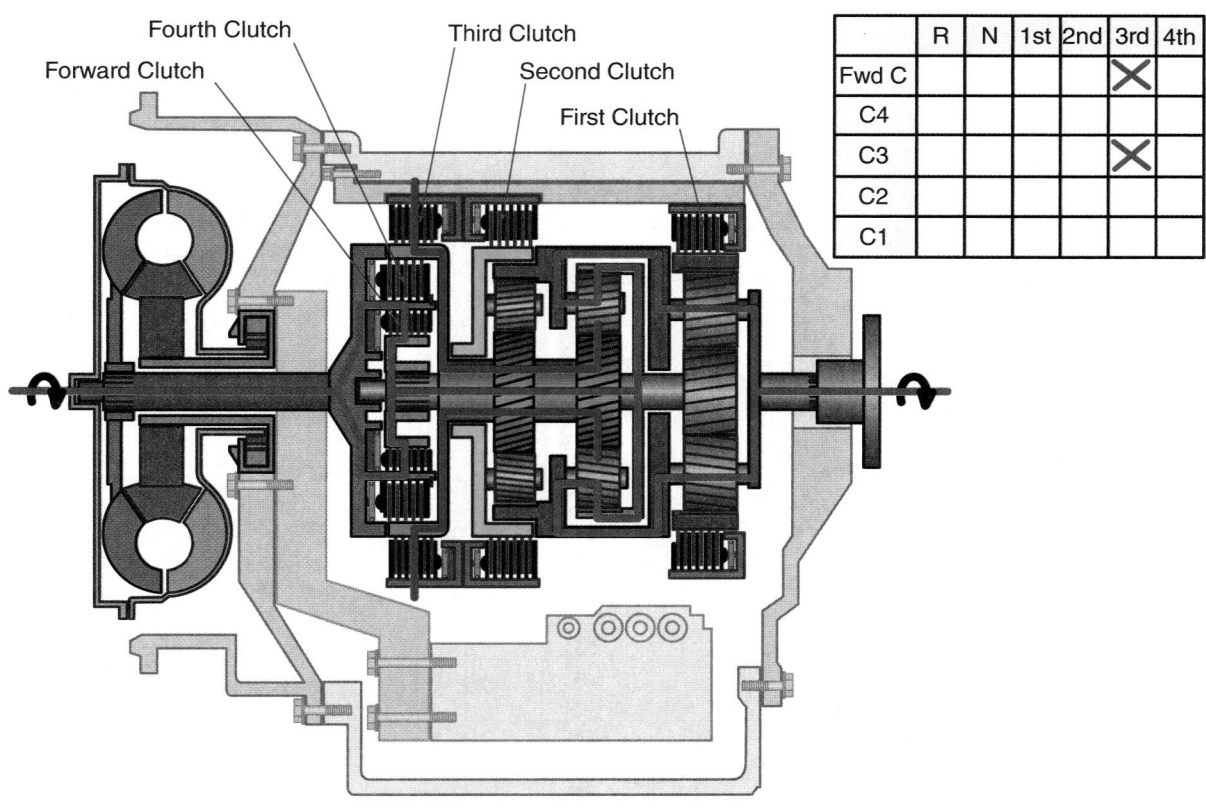

	R	N	1st	2nd	3rd	4th
Fwd C					✕	
C4						
C3					✕	
C2						
C1						

FIGURE 48-6 Third range.

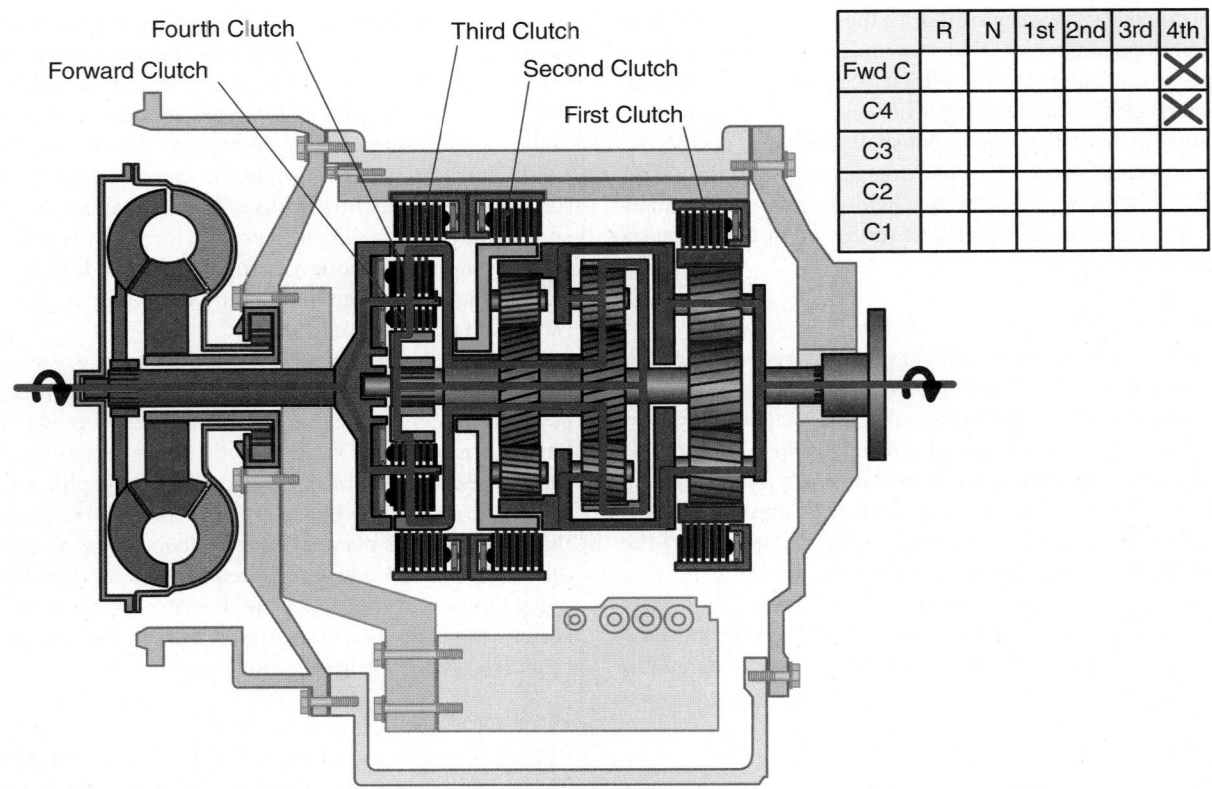

	R	N	1st	2nd	3rd	4th
Fwd C						✕
C4						✕
C3						
C2						
C1						

Fourth Clutch
Forward Clutch
Third Clutch
Second Clutch
First Clutch

FIGURE 48-7 Fourth range.

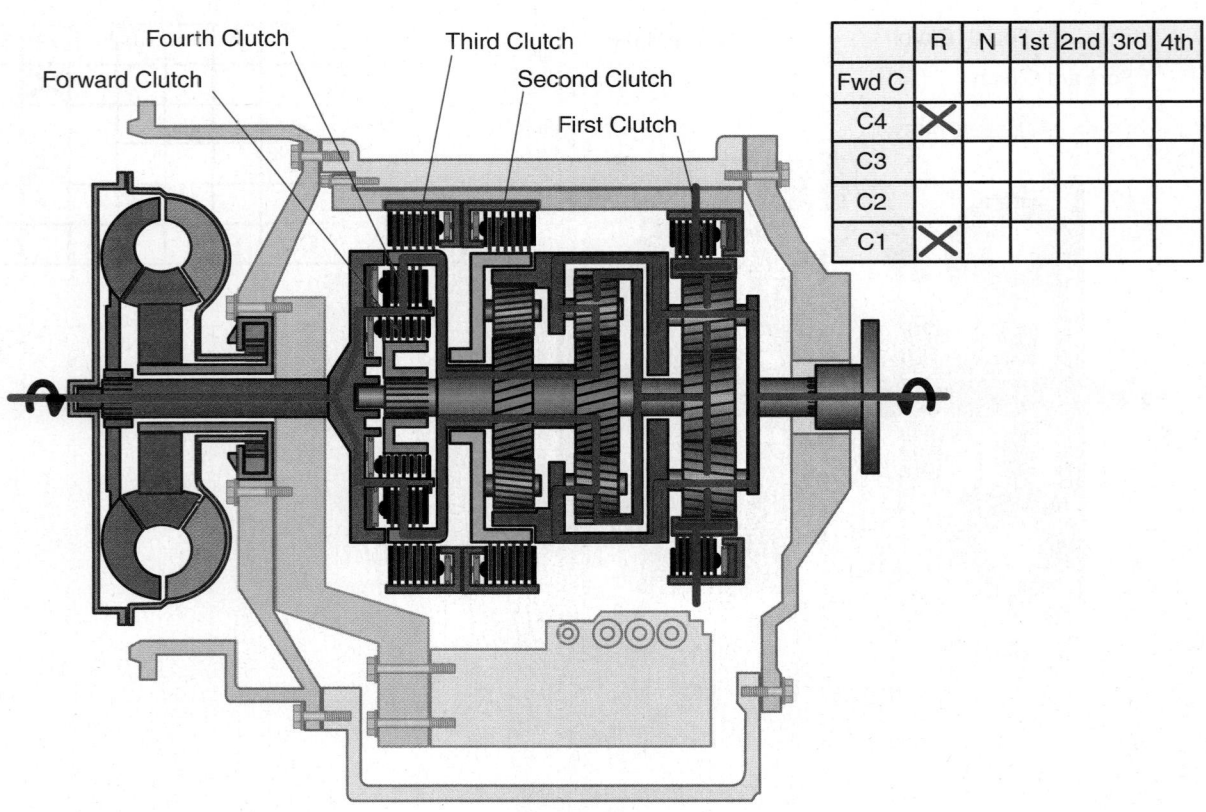

	R	N	1st	2nd	3rd	4th
Fwd C						
C4	✕					
C3						
C2						
C1	✕					

Fourth Clutch
Forward Clutch
Third Clutch
Second Clutch
First Clutch

FIGURE 48-8 Reverse.

ring gear stationary. When the driver selects reverse, the fourth clutch is applied. This brings rotational power from the input or turbine shaft to the center sun gear. The center carrier is splined through the connecting drum to the rear carrier and the output shaft. Consequently, the weight of the vehicle prevents the center carrier from rotating and it becomes the "held" component in the center planetary set. The center sun gear is input. The center carrier is acting as the held component, so the center ring gear becomes the output component in a counterclockwise direction. The center ring gear is part of the main shaft, as is the rear sun gear, so the rear sun gear becomes counterclockwise input to the rear planetary set. The rear planetary ring gear is being held by the first clutch, so the rear planetary carrier becomes output in a counterclockwise direction and it is splined to the output shaft. Again, as the vehicle starts to move in reverse, the center carrier—splined to the connecting drum and therefore the output shaft—turns with it. But the center carrier still acts as the held member as it is turning slower than the center sun gear, satisfying the rules of planetary gears.

Allison Transmission Hydraulic Control System Components

LO 48-4 Describe and explain Allison transmission hydraulic control system components.

All automatic transmissions use hydraulic fluid to control the shifting process, to lubricate and cool the transmission, and to supply fluid to the torque converter. Most heavy-duty transmissions use an internal **gear pump**, consisting of an internal and externally toothed gear, and a crescent. as shown in **FIGURE 48-9**, or a **gerotor pump** (the name comes from generated rotor). A gerotor pump is similar to a gear pump, but it uses a rotor operating inside a matching chamber instead of a gear. The transmission's hydraulic pump is driven by the torque converter pump drive hub to pressurize and circulate fluid throughout the transmission. (If necessary, review the Torque Converters chapter to familiarize yourself with the torque converter pump drive hub.)

Some transmission models use **vane pumps**, a rotating pump with sliding vanes that hold the fluid. Vane pumps can be of fixed or variable displacement to reduce parasitic losses when high flow volume is not required. **Parasitic loss** is an unnecessary load on the engine that decreases fuel economy. Although the use of vane pumps is usually limited to lighter-duty vehicles, the Allison TC-10 class 8 automatic transmission, released in 2012, uses a variable displacement vane pump to enable control of parasitic loss.

There are many hydraulic circuits in the automatic transmission, but all hydraulic flow begins in the sump or transmission oil pan. The sump is designed to hold sufficient fluid for operation when the fluid is fully deployed throughout the transmission's hydraulic circuits. It is important that the level of fluid be checked while the vehicle is running, as some of these hydraulic circuits drain back to the sump when the engine is not running. Checking the transmission fluid level with the engine off and the transmission pump not turning gives a false high reading on the transmission dipstick.

The transmission pump is bolted to the front of the transmission assembly inside the bell housing, as shown in **FIGURE 48-10**. The pump has two shafts coming from it. The first is the stationary stator support shaft for the torque converter stator. The second is the input or turbine shaft, which engages the turbine of the converter. The converter drive hub extends through the front of the pump to engage the pump drive gears so that, when the engine is started, the gears are turning. The gears create a low-pressure area as they separate. Atmospheric pressure acting on the fluid in the sump forces it through a filter and up to the intake side of the pump. (Note: It is essential that the transmission case be vented to allow the atmospheric pressure in. Otherwise, the pump's draw creates a vacuum, leading to starvation of the pump.) The fluid occupies the space created between the gear teeth of the pump and becomes trapped there as the gears pass by the crescent. As the pump gears come back together after the crescent, the teeth are once again forced together and the fluid is pressurized and exits the pressure side of the pump. From there, fluid is directed to many places in the transmission to do its job.

FIGURE 48-9 The Allison transmission uses a gear pump to supply hydraulic flow in the transmission. Note the pump inlet, outlet, the inner and outer gears, and the crescent.

FIGURE 48-10 The hydraulic pump is bolted to the front of the transmission. **A.** Splines of the input shaft. **B.** Stator support shaft.

Depending on the transmission, there can be slight differences in the path the fluid takes from the pump, but almost universally the fluid is first directed to the **main pressure regulator valve (MPRV)**. The MPRV is a spool valve that sets the main or working pressure of the transmission. All of the transmission's hydraulic circuits are fed by the main pressure circuit, as illustrated in **FIGURE 48-11**. From the main pressure regulator, fluid is first directed to the torque converter. Because the converter only works when it is full of fluid, the hydraulic system prioritizes filling the torque converter. All automatic transmissions use a pressure lubrication system and many direct some of the fluid feeding the torque converter to the lubrication passages in the front of the transmission. This lube fluid passes through a restriction or check valve. As a result, the fluid's pressure in the lubrication circuit is substantially lower than the transmission operating pressure.

The fluid is also directed to the manual selector valve in the **control valve body**, like the one pictured in **FIGURE 48-12**. The valve body is a casting that holds the many spool valves needed to operate the transmission. Spool valves are valves with a series of raised lands, or sealing surfaces, and cutaways and are so called because they resemble an empty spool of thread. As spool valves move, the raised lands seal or unseal fluid passageways in the valve body, and the fluid flows through the cutaway portions of the valve to create a fluid circuit. We discuss these valves in more detail in the Hydraulic Circuits section as they come up in the hydraulic flow.

Consult Figure 48-11 to follow the fluid flows through the transmission. The fluid fills the torque converter through the converter in circuit, which was described in some detail in the Torque Converters chapter. The working pressure of the torque converter is maintained by a torque converter pressure regulator valve and is set at a pressure somewhat less than main pressure. In the Allison MT series, the converter working pressure is set at approximately 52 psi (359 kPa). However, during converter operation this pressure can fluctuate.

The fluid exits the converter through the converter out circuit and is directed to the transmission oil cooler. The shear forces in the operating torque converter create tremendous heat, so directing fluid exiting the converter to the cooler makes sense. On the way back from the cooler, the fluid is typically directed into the rear lube circuit. The rear lube circuit lubricates the actual transmission gear sets and shafts. From there, the fluid falls back to the sump to be used again. Lube circuit pressures vary between models, but typical lube pressures range between 10 and 40 psi (69 and 276 kPa).

Transmission Control Valves

The Allison transmission, and all automatic transmissions, whether hydraulically or electronically controlled, use a series of spool-type valves to direct the hydraulic fluid to control the transmission's operation. Spool valves are installed in precisely fitting bores in the control valve body, which is bolted to the bottom of the transmission inside the oil pan. As the valves move, they alternately block and open passages for fluid to flow and, thereby, create hydraulic circuits to control the transmission. Most of these valves are seated by spring force and are moved by fluid pressure pushing against the spring force. The valves contained in the control valve body are responsible for directing fluid to the transmission clutches to control automatic shifting. The following sections describe the valves in an Allison MT series transmission. Consult Figure 48-11 to see the location and connecting passages of the various valves discussed.

Main Pressure Regulator Valve (MPRV)

The first valve in the transmission that we must understand is the main pressure regulator valve, or MPRV. When the vehicle is not running and there is no hydraulic pressure, the MPRV is held in the seated position by a spring at its base. Once the vehicle is started, hydraulic fluid is directed to the MPRV. All MPRVs have similar functions, but we are concentrating on the Allison system. **FIGURE 48-13** shows the MPRV in the Allison series of transmissions and its location in the hydraulic pump body.

As shown in **FIGURE 48-14**, transmission fluid from the pump is delivered to the MPRV between the top and second land of the spool. The fluid flows through cross and center drillings to the top of the valve to push on its top land. As pressure builds, the fluid starts to move the valve down in its bore against spring pressure. That movement first opens the torque converter fluid passage and allows the fluid to flow to the converter in circuit. The fluid is also directed through the valve to the control valve body and to the necessary circuits for transmission operation. As pressure builds on the fluid, the valve moves further down in its bore against spring pressure and a land uncovers a passage, allowing excess fluid flow to return to the transmission sump. At this point, the valve becomes balanced between spring and fluid pressure, and this balance sets the working pressure for the transmission.

The working (main) pressure for each transmission varies, depending on the model and on other factors. Main pressure for the AT series, which can handle input torques of up to 415 ft-lb (563 Nm), ranges between 90 to 125 psi (621 to 862 kPa) at idle and 130 to 150 psi (896 to 1034 kPa) at full stall speed. Because all clutches in the transmission are hydraulically applied, and the clamping force or apply pressure directly affects clutch capacity, higher pressures are required for models that have higher torque inputs, such as the HT 740 series, which is rated up to 1300 ft-lb (1763 Nm). The HT series main pressure can be as high as 235 to 270 psi (1620 to 1861 kPa) at converter stall speed under load. Main pressure is also modified by two other pressures in the transmission—neutral/forward regulator pressure and modulator pressure. Both of these pressures are derived from main pressure and are present in some models, but not all. When present, these pressures act on separate lands of the main pressure regulator valve to keep the main pressure at its lower level.

Manual Selector Valve

When the vehicle is running in neutral, fluid under pressure flows from the MPRV to all the shift signal valves and to the manual selector valve. Pressure continues to flow also through the priority valve, the 1–2 relay valve, and on to the first clutch so that first clutch is applied in neutral. The **manual selector valve**

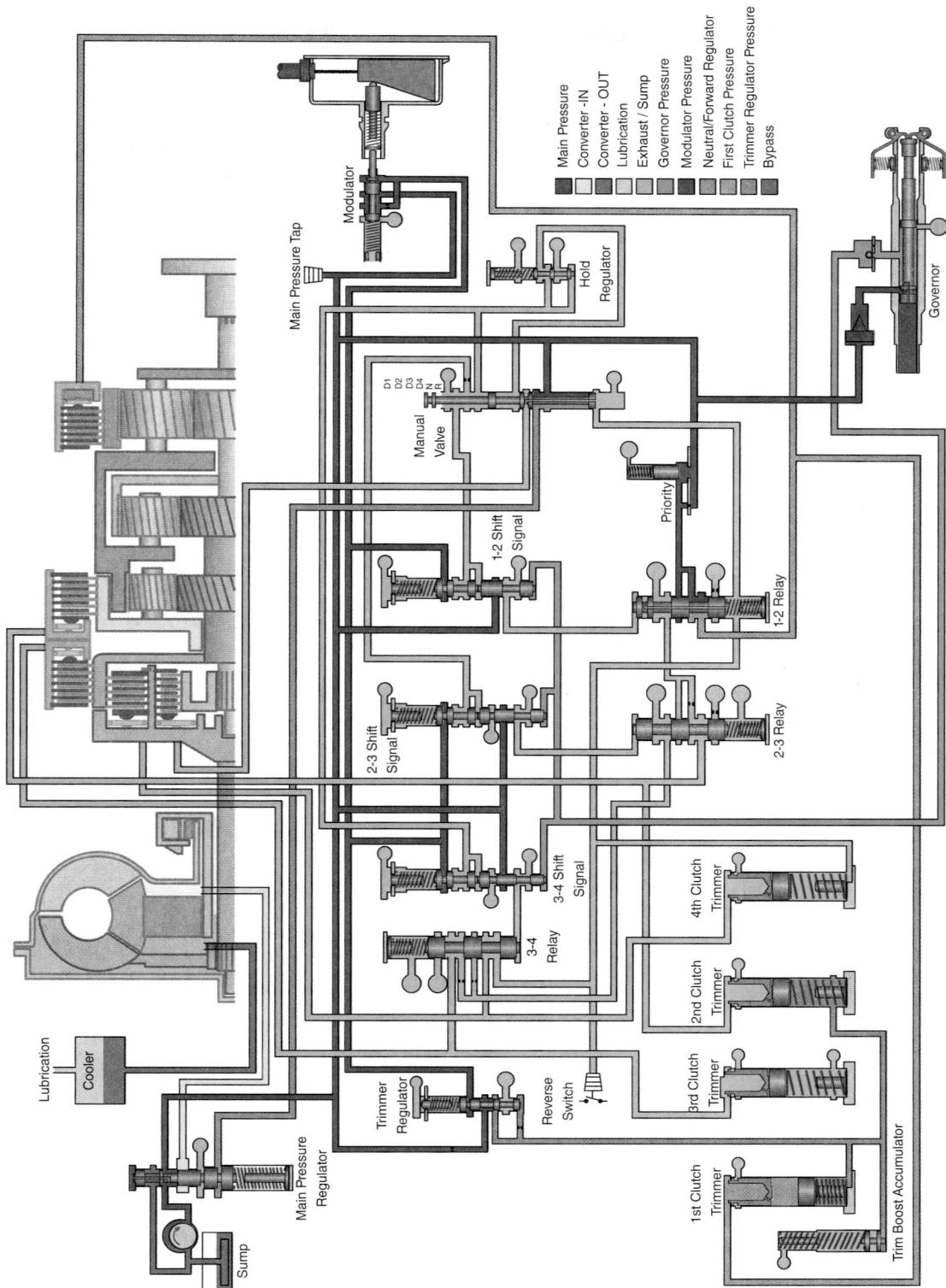

FIGURE 48-11 All of the transmission's hydraulic circuits are supplied by the main pressure circuit from the main pressure regulator valve (MPRV).

FIGURE 48-12 The main valve body holds most of the spool valves necessary for the transmission's shifting and control functions. Most transmissions have the MPRV located in the valve body, but in the Allison transmission, the main pressure regulator valve is located in a bore in the casting of the rear half of the pump housing.

FIGURE 48-13 The MPRV (circled) sets main pressure in the transmission. The Allison MPRV is located in the pump body.

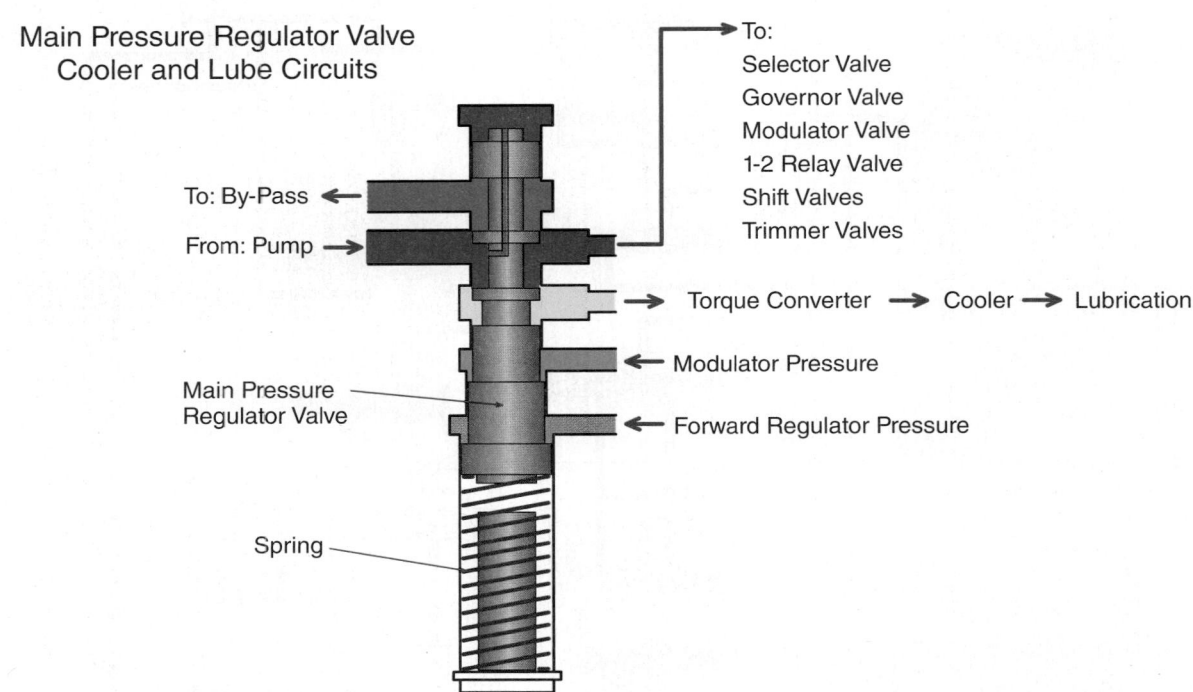

FIGURE 48-14 The MPRV sets the main pressure in the transmission.

is a spool valve in the control valve body and is mechanically positioned when the driver moves the shift selector. The manual valve is responsible for directing fluid pressure to the following circuits in these situations:

- to the forward clutch and to the neutral/forward regulator circuit in neutral or any forward range
- to the fourth clutch circuit when reverse is selected
- to the hold regulator valve, the governor valve, and to the modulator valve in all forward ranges.

To prevent automatic upshifts, the manual valve also redirects hold regulator pressure to the correct shift signal valves when manual first, second, or third is selected.

The positioning of the manual selector valve also controls the operation of the neutral safety switch, which is on the side of the transmission and connected into the starter solenoid circuit of the vehicle. This switch only allows the vehicle to start with the selector valve in neutral. If the selector valve is in any other position, the circuit to the starter solenoid is interrupted.

Modulator Valve

Main pressure from the manual valve flows to the **modulator valve**. The modulator valve is responsible for creating modulator pressure and can be controlled by mechanical throttle cable on diesel engines, by vacuum on gasoline engines, or electrically using an electric solenoid. In light-duty vehicles, the modulator

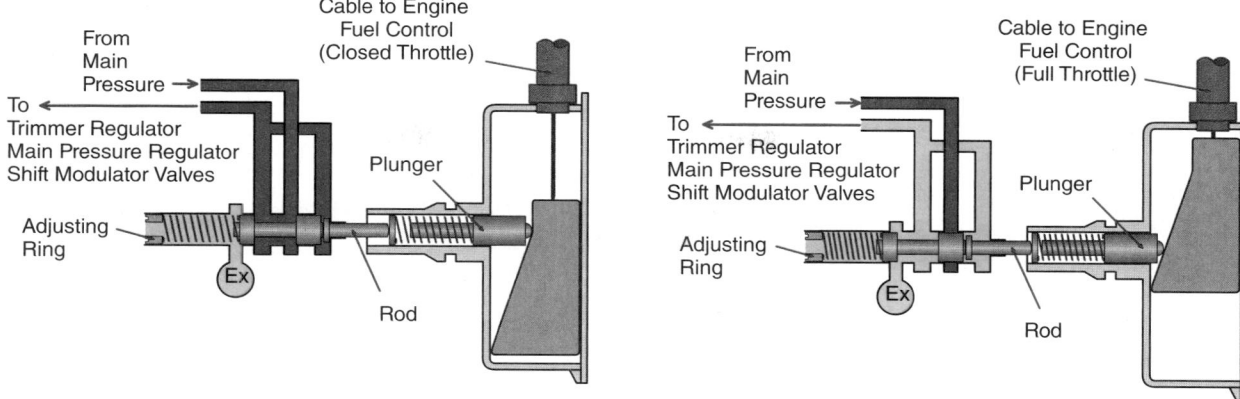

FIGURE 48-15 The mechanical modulator valve is positioned by throttle movement.

valve is sometimes referred to as the **throttle valve**, as its action is dependent on throttle position. As Allison refers to this valve as the modulator valve, we do also from this point on, but remember that throttle valves function in a similar fashion.

The modulator valve modifies main pressure to produce modulator pressure, which in turn is used to influence main pressure in some transmission models. Modulator or throttle pressure is also used to influence shift points and shift harshness or abruptness. The valve itself is a small spool valve with a spring at its base. As illustrated in **FIGURE 48-15**, this spring tries to force the valve to the right. The mechanical throttle mechanism has no influence on the valve with the throttle at idle. This allows main pressure to flow by the valve and into the modulator circuit, creating high modulator pressure.

As the throttle is depressed, however, the mechanical throttle device forces the modulator valve to the left and main pressure is prevented from passing the modulator. As a result, at wide-open throttle, modulator pressure is minimal or non-existent.

The vacuum system works in a similar fashion, but in the vacuum system the mechanical device is replaced by a vacuum diaphragm unit called a vacuum modulator. Inside the vacuum modulator is a spring-loaded diaphragm, which forces the modulator valve to the left when there is no vacuum. When there is high vacuum, the diaphragm is pulled to the right, allowing the modulator valve spring to push the valve to the right. Whether mechanical or vacuum controlled, the result is the same at low idle (no throttle) (high vacuum), modulator pressure is high and at wide-open throttle (low vacuum), modulator pressure is minimal or nonexistent.

The electric modulator system involves a throttle switch that controls an external solenoid that, in turn, positions the modulator valve in one of two positions, depending on throttle position, with a similar effect. At closed throttle, modulator pressure is high, and at 65% throttle or more modulator pressure is minimal. Because the modulator pressure is predicated on throttle position, the pressure becomes a "load" signal to the transmission's hydraulic control. We discuss the modulator circuit and the necessity for this pressure in the Automatic Transmission Shifting section. Note that, in other manufacturer's transmissions, the modulator pressure is low at closed throttle

![photograph of mechanical governor]

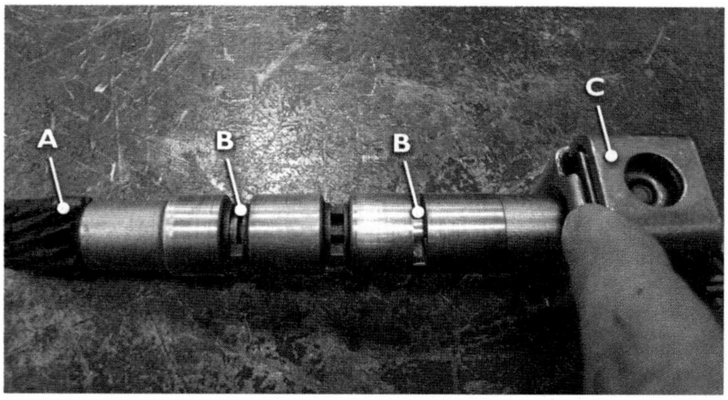

FIGURE 48-16 The mechanical governor containing the governor valve is rotated by a gear on the transmission output shaft so that output speed affects governor pressure. **A.** Drive gear. **B.** Valve lands. **C.** Weights.

and high at wide-open throttle. Regardless, modulator valve pressure influences the transmission in the same way.

Governor Valve

From the manual selector valve, fluid also flows to the **governor valve**, shown in **FIGURE 48-16**. This valve is mounted in a bore in the transmission case.

The governor valve itself is a spool valve mounted in a rotating tube. The tube has a gear on it that meshes with a worm on the transmission output shaft. As the output shaft turns the tube, the governor valve rotates with it. When the vehicle is at a stop, the tube is stationary also. Main pressure delivered to the valve forces the spool outward inside the tube, which opens an exhaust passage from the governor circuit and blocks main pressure from entering the governor circuit. The tube has a pair of centrifugal weights attached to it and, as the vehicle starts to move, the tube and, therefore, the weights, start to turn with the output shaft.

As the weights are thrown outward by centrifugal force, they begin to force the governor spool inward, closing the governor circuit exhaust passage and allowing main pressure to enter the governor circuit, as illustrated in **FIGURE 48-17**.

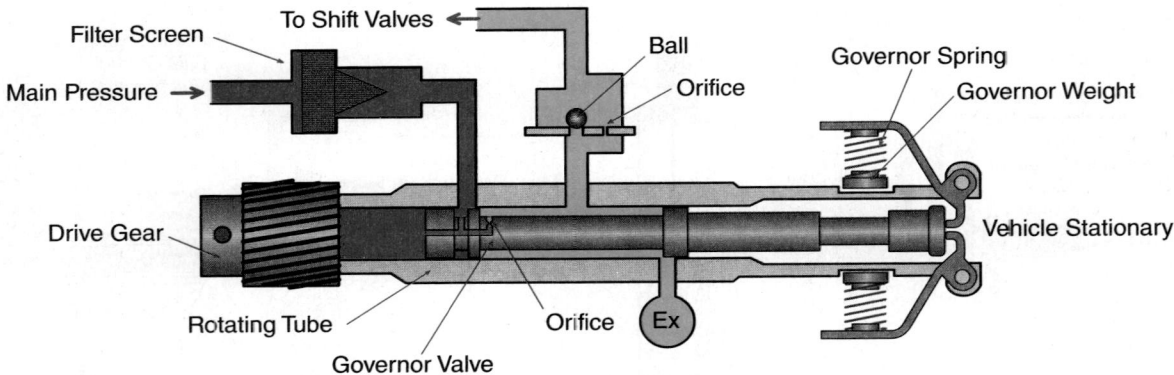

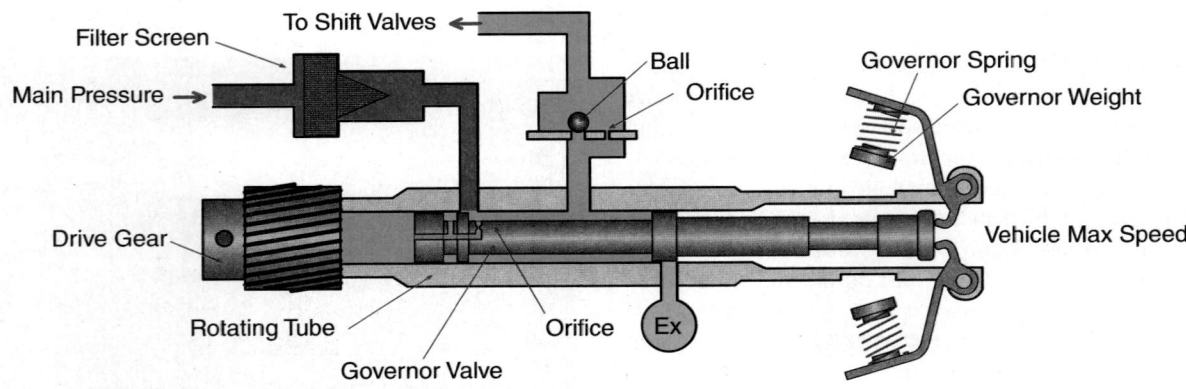

FIGURE 48-17 Governor pressure is directly affected by output shaft speed.

As the output shaft speed increases, so too does governor pressure until maximum vehicle speed and maximum governor pressure is attained. As governor pressure is predicated on road speed, it becomes a "speed" signal to the transmission's hydraulic control. We discuss what we do with this pressure in the Operation of a Hydraulically Controlled Automatic Transmission section.

Shift Signal and Shift Relay Valves

The transmission has three shift signals and three **shift relay valves**. They are essentially the same, so all three sets are discussed at once. The shift relay valve is the simpler of the two valves, so it is looked at first. Recall the hydraulic schematic in Figure 48-11. The 1–2 shift relay valve is a spool valve and it has main pressure flowing through it and on to the first clutch. In the schematic, the valve is in the downshifted position (which appears as up on the schematic) and is held there by a spring at its base. Observing the top of the valve, there is a passage from there to the 1–2 shift signal valve above it. The valve is moved to the upshifted position when main pressure redirected by the 1–2 shift signal valve is sent to that top land and the valve is forced down in its bore. When the relay valve moves down to the upshifted position, it connects the first clutch feed passage to the exhaust passage at the bottom of the valve. The valve movement also redirects the main pressure at the valve into the second clutch apply passage through the 2–3 shift relay valve.

Redirecting pressure in this way applies the second clutch and the transmission attains second range.

Then, as the 2–3 relay valve moves, when pressure is delivered from its shift signal valve, the valve allows the second clutch fed to exhaust and the apply fluid is redirected through the valve to the 3–4 relay valve and the third clutch. And, similarly, as the 3–4 relay valve is moved by its shift signal valve, third clutch is exhausted and the apply fluid flows to the fourth clutch. This means that the same supply of main pressure is responsible for applying all of the clutches in sequence as each shift relay valve moves. This cascading fluid flow allows the clutch apply passage to be isolated by a priority valve, which is covered in detail in the Priority Valve section.

Shift Signal Valves

The **shift signal valves** control the movement of the shift relay valves. The three shift signal valves are all set up the same and consist of two separate spool valves in one bore. The top valve is called the **shift modulator valve** and the lower valve is the actual shift signal valve.

The valves are held in the downshifted position (which is illustrated as down on the hydraulic schematic shown in Figure 48-11) and are held there by a spring at the top. The bottom land for the 2–3 shift signal valve is slightly smaller than the one for the 1–2 and the bottom land for the 3–4 shift signal valve is smaller still.

Typical Automatic Shift

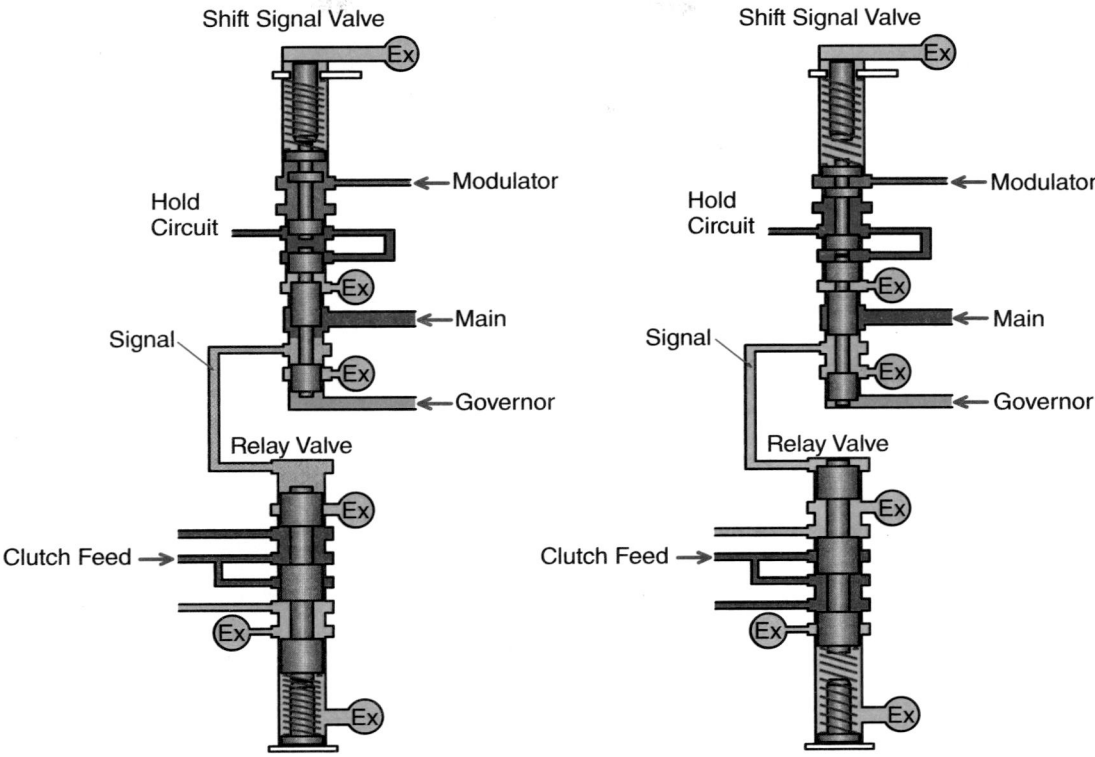

FIGURE 48-18 The shift relay and shift signal valves control the application of clutches.

Governor pressure pushes on the lands of all three of these valves to try to make the shift valves move up to the upshifted position. The governor pressure acting on the three valves is the same but, because of the difference in the bottom land sizes, the valves move in sequence (i.e., first the 1-2, then the 2-3, and then the 3-4) as governor pressure increases with increasing road speed. Main pressure from the MPRV is directed to each of the shift signal valves and deadheads at the large land, as can be seen in **FIGURE 48-18**.

Governor pressure is primarily responsible for moving the signal valves. Governor pressure acts on the bottom land of the valve, trying to move it up against spring pressure. Governor pressure is assisted by modulator pressure. Recall that modulator pressure is high at low throttle and nonexistent when at wide-open throttle. Modulator pressure acts upon the lower area of the shift modulator valves above each shift signal valve. As governor pressure starts to move the shift signal valve up, modulator pressure tries to help the signal valve move up by pushing the shift modulator valve up. At low-to-medium throttle, the relatively high modulator pressure causes the shift signal valve to move up at lower road speeds. At wide-open throttle, modulator pressure disappears and governor pressure must work alone and, therefore, shifts occur at higher road speeds. When the shift signal valve moves, it redirects the deadheaded main pressure to the top of its corresponding shift relay valve, causing it to move. An automatic shift then occurs.

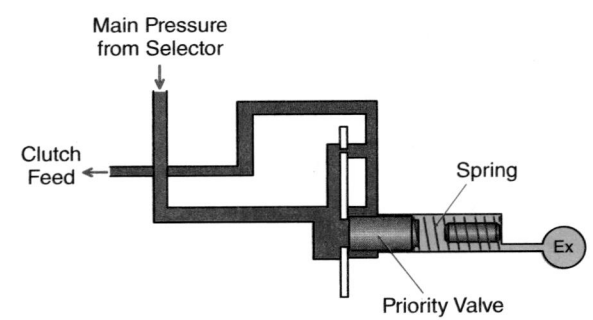

FIGURE 48-19 The priority valve is a kind of check valve that protects control pressure in the transmission.

Priority Valve

All the main pressure used to apply the clutches in the transmission flows through the **priority valve**. This valve is a spool valve that acts as a kind of check valve to protect the transmissions control circuits from a sudden momentary pressure loss. The priority valve circuit is illustrated in **FIGURE 48-19**.

During certain operating modes, there is a chance that the fluid required to apply a clutch piston might momentarily exceed the transmission pump's output. The pressures that control the transmission shift valves (and other valves) may drop off. In that situation, the priority valve closes to maintain control pressure and prevent the transmission from reacting erratically.

Trimmer Valves and Trimmer Regulator Valve

Consulting again the schematic in Figure 48-11, there are four **trimmer valves** and a **trimmer regulator valve**. There is a trimmer valve for every clutch except the forward clutch. The job of the trimmer valve is to soften or smooth out the application of the clutches. (The forward clutch application always starts from a neutral position. The circuit that supplies the forward clutch is fitted with a restricted orifice that slows down the flow of fluid and effectively softens its engagement.) In order for the clutches to have the correct capacity, the fluid pressure must be high enough and the size of the application piston must be large enough to apply the correct clamping force. This might seem like common sense, but the speed at which the piston moves to apply the clutch is also influenced by these factors. Unexpected quickness in the piston movement can lead to harsh, abrupt shifting.

FIGURE 48-20 shows a trimmer valve. Notice that the valve cup has a small orifice, which allows pressure at the top and bottom to equalize. The larger bottom land then forces the trimmer back up, sealing the clutch apply circuit.

Allison transmissions use the trimmer valves to slow down the shift slightly to make the engagement more gradual and, therefore, more comfortable for the driver and the passengers. Other transmission manufacturers accomplish this shift cushioning by using accumulators and/or restricted orifices in the clutch apply passage. Accumulators are spring-loaded pistons that move as the clutch applies. Because these pistons must stop moving before apply pressure can build, they soften the clutch application. Allison's trimmers perform a similar function. The trimmers consist of a bore with a spring-loaded plug at its base, a pin that limits the plug's movement down in the bore, and the trimmer cup that sits on top of the plug.

Each trimmer valve is connected to the application circuit for its clutch. When the clutch is applying, the apply pressure is also delivered to the trimmer cup. The pressure initially forces the cup and the plug down slightly in the trimmer bore. The upper end of the cup exposes an exhaust passage, this allows some of the apply pressure to escape, slowing down and softening the clutch application.

As illustrated in **FIGURE 48-21**, the fluid also passes through the small orifice in the base of the trimmer cup. Fluid pressure forces the trimmer plug down in its bore until the plug contacts the stop pin. When the trimmer plug stops moving, the pressure beneath the trimmer cup builds up until it matches the pressure above the cup. When pressure equalizes, the trimmer cup is forced back upward in its bore as the surface area beneath the cup is larger than the surface area above it. The upward movement of the cup seals off the exhaust passage and clutch pressure builds to maximum. This slowing of the clutch application leads to softer shifts as the applying clutch is allowed to slip a little more as it engages.

Trimmer Regulator Valve

The trimmer regulator valve is a spool valve that is supplied with main pressure, which is directed through the valve to the base of the trimmer valve bores. Fluid pressure here tends to accelerate the trimming action and causes the clutch application to speed up. Faster clutch application leads to harder shifts. In certain operational modes, such as under heavy loads or rapid acceleration, faster clutch application is desirable, as a faster shift means less clutch slippage and clutch disc wear.

As illustrated in **FIGURE 48-22**, the position of the trimmer regulator valve is controlled by modulator pressure. During closed throttle or light operation, modulator pressure is high. High pressure forces the trimmer regulator to the bottom in its bore against spring pressure. In this position, the trimmer regulator does not allow main pressure to flow to the base of the trimmer plugs. Shifting is slower and softer, but with more clutch slippage.

As the throttle is depressed for rapid acceleration or heavy-load operation, modulator pressure drops off. The decrease allows the trimmer regulator spring to move the valve and allows more and more main pressure to flow to the base of the trimmer plugs. (The trimmer regulator valve is in this position in the schematic in Figure 48-11.) Shifts become faster and harsher with less clutch slippage. Less clutch slippage is necessary for heavy-load operations, as the increased load could lead to rapid clutch wear.

Hold Regulator Valve

The shift selector valve supplies main pressure to the **hold regulator valve,** which directs that pressure to the corresponding

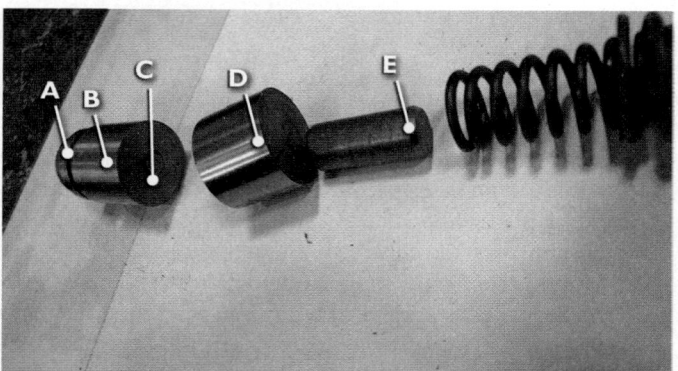

FIGURE 48-20 Trimmer valve. **A.** Small land. **B.** Trimmer cup. **C.** Trimmer orifice. **D.** Trimmer plug. **E.** Pin.

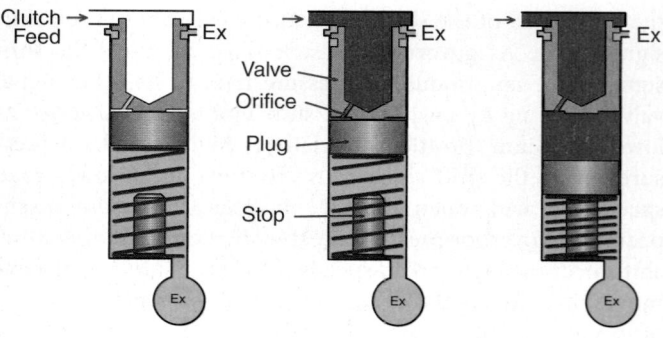

Trimmer Valve Operation

Clutch Feed → | Ex
Valve
Orifice
Plug
Stop
Ex

FIGURE 48-21 Trimmer valve action.

shift signal valve depending on the driver's gear selection. For example, if the driver selects Drive 1, indicating that he does not want the vehicle to shift out of first gear, the hold regulator valve directs fluid to three shift signal valves: the 3–4 shift signal, the 2–3 shift signal, and the 1–2 shift signal valves. Remember that the shift signal valves are actually two separate valves—the shift signal and the shift modulator valve.

The fluid from the hold regulator is directed between the shift modulator and the shift signal valves, preventing governor pressure from pushing the shift signal valve up effectively preventing a shift. In Drive 2, only the 2–3 and the 3–4 shift signal valves are fed from the hold regulator. In Drive 3, only the 3–4 shift signal valve is fed. Under normal operating conditions, hold regulator pressure stops the vehicle from shifting any higher and holds the transmission in the range selected by the driver. Governor pressure may be high enough to overcome hold regulator pressure and force an upshift in some extreme overspeed conditions. Using hold regulator pressure to prevent upshifts, instead of locking out the upshift completely, helps to protect the transmission from abuse.

Torque Converter Lock-Up Clutch Control

Torque converter lock-up clutches were discussed in the Torque Converters chapter. Review that chapter if necessary to refresh your understanding of their operation. Torque converters all have an inherent slippage factor of 5% to 10% between the impeller and the turbine. That is, there is always a loss between the engine output and the transmission input shaft.

To eliminate this loss, all torque converters since the 1980s include lock-up clutches to lock the turbine to the converter shell and thereby eliminate the efficiency loss. The torque converter lock-up clutch is applied hydraulically by the transmission's hydraulic control system. The torque converter lock-up clutch application timing can be either scheduled or it can be modulated.

In **scheduled lock-up**, as soon as the transmission shifts into a certain range or has attained a predetermined road speed, the lock-up clutch is applied. This application may be directly controlled by an electric solenoid-controlled valve or a spool valve that is moved by governor pressure. When these valves are moved, they direct hydraulic pressure to the lock-up clutch circuit. By contrast, **modulated lock-up** allows the lock-up timing to be affected by load and driver input conditions.

Scheduled lock-up increases fuel economy, but modulated lock-up has superior acceleration performance. Most modern commercial vehicles have scheduled lock-up for fuel efficiency. Modulated lock-up is more commonly found in light-duty vehicles where performance—not fuel efficiency—is the key desired attribute.

When a vehicle has modulated torque converter lock-up, the spool valve responsible for lock-up clutch application is acted on by both governor and modulator pressure. Consequently, lock-up occurs at lower speeds under light loads and at higher speeds under heavy loads or rapid acceleration. In some hydraulically controlled transmission models, when the torque converter lock-up spool valve moves to engage the lock-up clutch, the converter also directs fluid to a special land on the MPRV. Fluid pressure on the land causes main pressure to reduce, reducing clutch capacity because there is less torque when the converter is in lock-up. Manufacturers commonly used this design function to reduce parasitic losses caused by the transmission's hydraulic pump.

Trimmer Regulator Valve Circuit

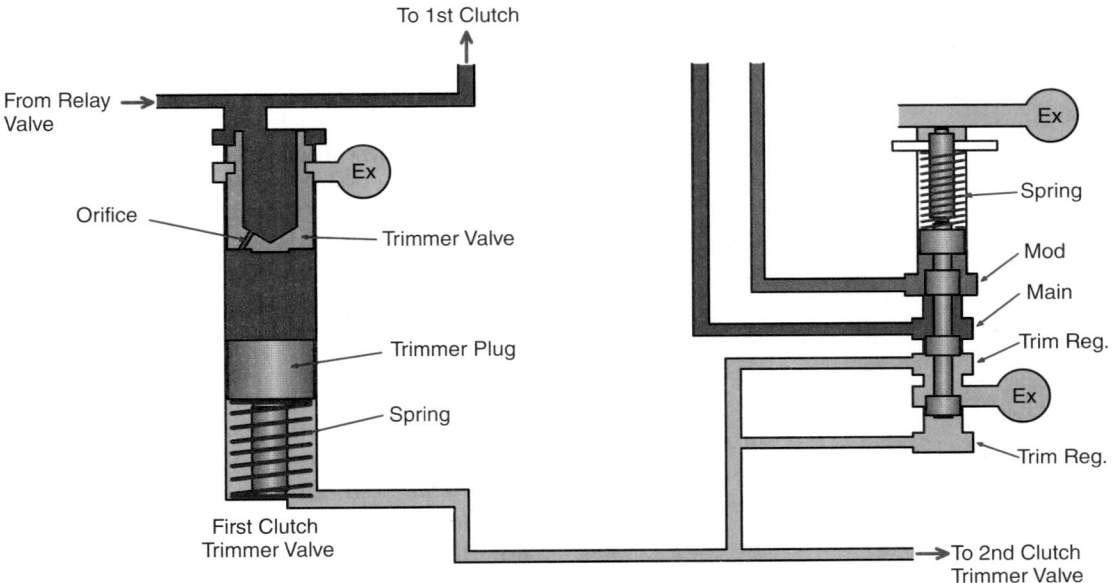

FIGURE 48-22 The trimmer regulator valve controls how quickly the trimmer valves complete their process based on throttle position.

Hydraulic Circuits

A **hydraulic circuit** is simply a pathway connecting one part of the transmission's hydraulic control with another part. There are several circuits in a transmission. Some, such as the forward clutch circuit or the fourth clutch circuit, are strictly connecting circuits. Several other circuits can be called control circuits because they control spool valve movement.

In the Allison AT, MT, and HT, the control circuits are the neutral forward regulator circuit (NFRC), the governor circuit, and the modulator circuit. Most circuits start at the control valve body or at the MPRV. The control valve body has a series of slots that coincide with the different lands of the spool valves. These slots are sealed off from each other by a gasket and a **separator plate**.

The separator plate has precisely sized and positioned orifices and/or openings that then coincide with various openings cast or cut into the transmission case. The openings can be directly drilled passages to a hydraulic clutch or can be "worm track" shaped passages that deliver fluid from one land of a certain valve through the separator plate and then back to a land on another valve. Worm tracks are visible in the case shown in **FIGURE 48-23**. When a valve moves, fluid pressure is redirected by the valve to make the transmission operate.

Operation of Allison Hydraulically Controlled Automatic Transmissions

LO 48-5 Describe and explain the operation of Allison hydraulically controlled automatic transmissions.

Now that we have discussed the valves in the hydraulically controlled automatic transmission and their functions, let's turn to seeing how the transmission operates. Specifically, this section covers automatic upshifting and automatic downshifting. All of the spool valves and the hydraulic circuits must work together to control the transmission shifting process. Although this section describes only the Allison transmission, other hydraulically controlled automatic transmissions operate in a very similar fashion.

FIGURE 48-23 These worm tracks **A.** along with the separator plate **B.** direct fluid from one valve of the control valve body **C.** to another.

Automatic Transmission Shifting

As the discussion moves through an automatic shifting sequence, continue to refer to Figure 48-11 to follow the flow of fluid. As soon as the vehicle is started (in neutral), main pressure is established by the spring-loaded MPRV. The main pressure circuit delivers that pressure to the shift signal valves and the priority valve through the 1–2 relay valve and into the first clutch. This circuit is illustrated in **FIGURE 48-24**. Main pressure is also delivered through the manual selector valve to the NFRC, to the governor valve, and to the modulator valve.

The neutral forward regulator pressure is present in neutral and any forward range, but is not present in reverse. The NFRC's purpose is to lower main pressure in any forward range and neutral but allow a higher main pressure in reverse. The circuit accomplishes this by sending pressure back to a land on the MPRV, which assists main pressure in opening the MPRV. Consequently, the main pressure is lower in forward range when this neutral forward regulator pressure is present. This assist pressure is not present in reverse. Therefore, main pressure climbs higher to increase the clutch clamp load in reverse. This is done because reverse range has the greatest torque multiplication and, therefore, requires increased clutch clamp load.

> ▶ **TECHNICIAN TIP**
>
> In some transmissions, a driver may select either first or second range (and the transmission actually starts off in that gear), but the Allison transmission always start off in first range, regardless of which forward range is selected.

Now, let us assume the driver selects Drive 4th or simply "D." The manual valve is moved, and main pressure is directed to the forward clutch. The forward clutch is the only clutch that does not have a trimmer valve to cushion the clutch application. The forward clutch engagement is softened by placing a restricted orifice in the forward clutch apply circuit, which slows down the clutch application.

Remember that first clutch is applied in neutral and now, with the forward clutch applied, the vehicle attains first range. Next, the driver accelerates and the vehicle begins moving. The governor valve starts to spin and the centrifugal force on the weights begins to move the governor spool valve inboard in its bore. Main pressure starts to leak into the governor circuit and builds more pressure in the circuit as speed increases. The governor pressure circuit delivers governor pressure to the base of the shift signal valves and tries to push them up in their bore.

At the same time, modulator pressure is changing, either because of throttle position (diesel engines) or vacuum drop (gasoline engines). Modulator pressure is initially quite high at idle, but as the throttle is moved, the pressure begins to drop. The modulator circuit delivers modulator pressure to the bottom land of the shift modulator valves sitting on top of the shift signal valves and tries to raise the shift modulator valves. This assists governor pressure in moving the shift signal valves up. The reason for this design is so that, when throttle is light and modulator pressure is high, the governor pressure does not have to climb as high to move the shift signal valve. An earlier shift is achieved, in terms of road speed. As the throttle position is increased, the modulator pressure drops and governor pressure must climb higher to cause the shift signal valve to move, resulting in shifts at higher road speeds.

In some older transmission models, modulator pressure also acts on a land on the MPRV. Pressure on that land reduces main pressure so when throttle is light and modulator pressure is high, main pressure is relatively low, and this reduces parasitic load on the engine when high torque and, therefore, maximum clutch capacity, is not required. The shift is softer as well because the lower pressure causes the shift to occur more slowly. This adds to passenger and driver comfort. However, when the vehicle is heavily loaded or acceleration is very rapid (wide-open throttle), modulator pressure drops to almost zero. Governor pressure alone must move the shift signal and the shift modulator valves up in their bores. To do this, road speed must increase to build governor pressure. With modulator pressure reduced, there is no longer pressure acting on the land of the MPRV. Main pressure then rises, causing faster, harder shifts with less slippage. So, the modulator valve is a type of load sensor that can "modulate" or adjust shift points based on load, while the governor tries to shift based on speed alone. It is important to note that even though modulator pressure can assist in the upshift process if there is no governor pressure, due to a worn governor gear or other issue, upshifts cannot occur.

Recall that the 1–2, the 2–3, and the 3–4 shift signal valve bottom lands are of differing sizes, so they shift in sequence and not simultaneously. When governor pressure, based on road speed, and modulator pressure, based on load, combine with sufficient force to move the 1–2 shift signal valve up in its bore, the valve moves up and redirects the main pressure that was deadheading at the shift signal valve. The main pressure is now sent to the top of the 1–2 shift relay valve, causing it to move down in its bore. The relay valve's movement causes the main pressure applying first clutch to exhaust at the relay valve. The main pressure coming from the priority valve is now redirected through the 1-2 relay valve to the second clutch apply circuit.

Remember that all of the clutches except forward have a trimmer valve in their apply circuit, and the main pressure being sent to apply the clutch activates the trimmer. This slows down and softens the clutch application. The actual speed of the trimmer's operation and, therefore, clutch application speed, is affected by two factors. First is the modulator circuit pressure and its effect on main pressure, if present. Second is the modulator circuit's effect on the trimmer regulator valve and the pressure it sends beneath the trimmers.

Once the trimmer cup has moved back up and sealed off the apply circuit exhaust passage, the clutch application pressure builds to main pressure and the clutch is fully engaged. Although shifts at much lower speeds are possible with light throttle acceleration, the maximum speed at which the 1–2 shift occurs is approximately 18 mph (29 kph).

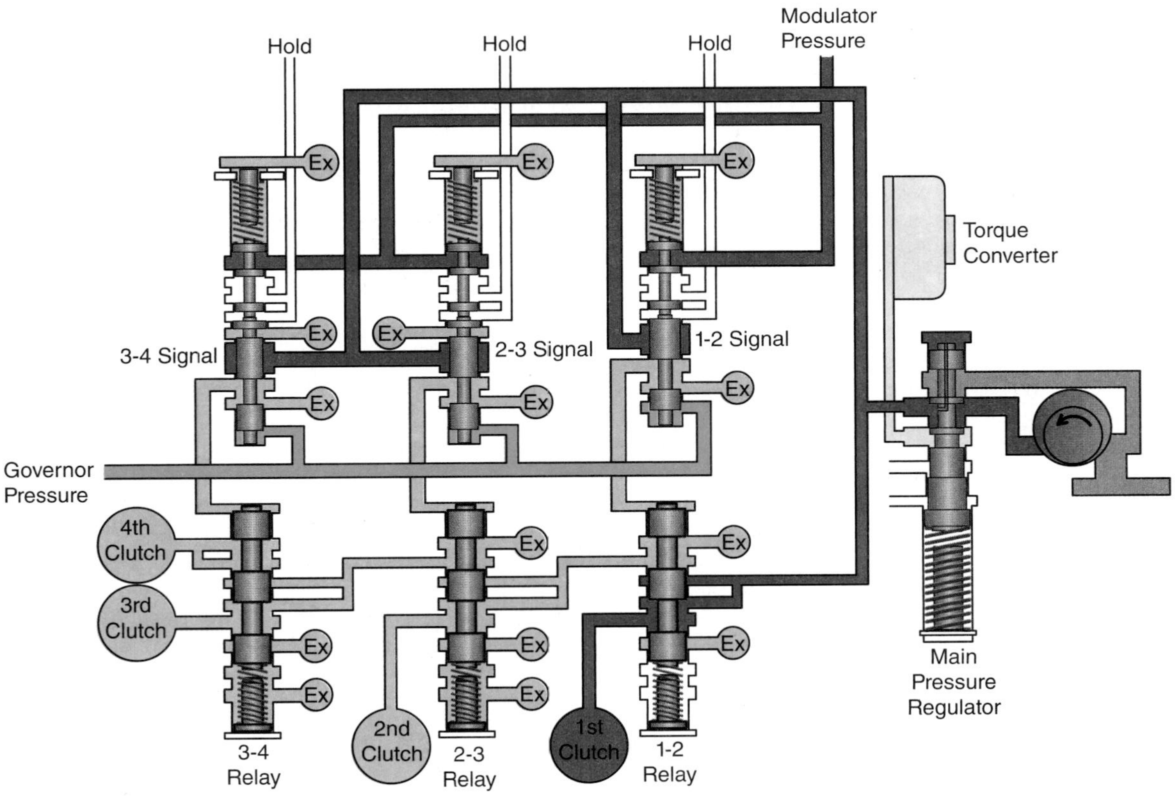

FIGURE 48-24 The cascading flow of hydraulic pressure used to apply the clutches assures that, whether upshifting or downshifting, as one clutch is released, the next required clutch is applied.

The shifting continues in the exact same manner for the 2–3 and 3–4 shifts as the vehicle accelerates. The average maximum speed at which the 2–3 shift occurs is 28 mph (45 kph) and the 3–4 at 45 mph (72 kph). As each shift signal valve moves, it moves its corresponding shift relay valve. The movement of the relay valve exhausts the applied clutch pressure and redirects fluid to the oncoming clutch apply circuit—the third clutch for third range and the fourth clutch for fourth range.

Automatic Downshifting

Automatic downshifting occurs because of spring pressure and the reduction of governor and modulator pressure. Let us assume the upshifting procedure has occurred and the vehicle is cruising in fourth range at highway speeds. Now, assume the driver starts to decelerate.

As the driver allows the vehicle to slow down, two things occur. First, governor pressure decreases with the decrease in vehicle speed. Second, modulator pressure increases with the decrease in throttle position. As governor pressure decreases beyond a certain point, the combination of governor and modulator pressure is no longer able to hold the 3–4 shift signal valve up against its spring. The spring force, therefore, pushes the valve back to the downshifted position. This action exhausts the main pressure, pushing on the 3–4 shift relay valve, and spring force at the relay valves base forces the valve back to the downshifted position. The 3–4 relay valve movement exhausts the main pressure applying the fourth clutch through the relay valve, and main pressure redirects to the third clutch through the still upshifted 2-3 relay valve. This process continues sequentially until the vehicle reaches first range.

Full Throttle Downshift

Anyone who has driven a vehicle with an automatic transmission is familiar with forced **full throttle downshifts** (also called detent downshift or kick down depending on the manufacturer). Forced throttle downshifts allow the driver to make the transmission downshift in order to gain torque multiplication and faster acceleration when needed, such as when trying to overtake a slower moving vehicle. Some transmissions facilitate full throttle downshifts by using a kick-down or throttle valve that is physically attached to the vehicle's throttle lever, similar to the one shown in **FIGURE 48-25**. In the Allison AT, MT, and

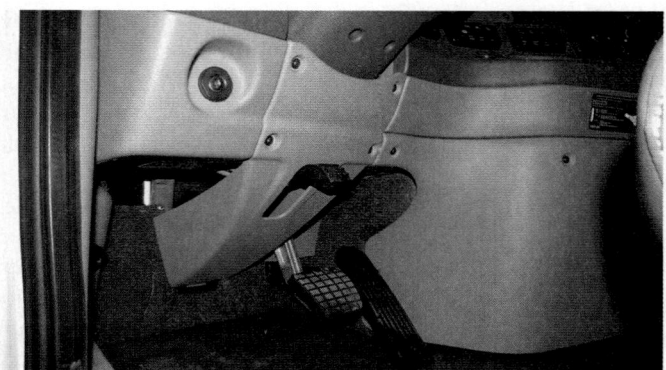

FIGURE 48-25 The throttle valve is attached to a vehicle's throttle lever.

HT transmissions, however, full throttle downshifts are caused by changing pressures inside the transmission. All automatic transmissions, however, provide a throttle downshift or kickdown when conditions are right and the driver steps hard on the throttle.

As the driver presses on the throttle, modulator pressure that had previously been used to assist the governor in causing an upshift, starts to drop off. Recall that modulator pressure in the Allison is high at closed throttle and almost nonexistent at wide-open throttle. As modulator pressure drops, governor pressure alone may not be sufficient to hold the shift signal valves in the upshifted positions. If this is the case, the shift signal valve springs push the valves back to the downshifted position. Depending on road speed and the range the vehicle has attained, the transmission may shift from fourth all the way down to first during a forced throttle downshift. However, a full throttle downshift usually causes a downshift of one or two ranges to give the desired torque multiplication to accelerate the vehicle.

Shift Point Control

The transmission shift points are usually adjustable and several methods are used to adjust the shift points. In lighter-duty vehicles, shift points are adjusted by controlling the spring pressure on the vacuum modulator diaphragm. In turn, that adjustment modifies the movement of the modulator valve and, therefore, adjusts the shift point. The shift point can be achieved by adjusting the throttle cable, which has the same effect.

FIGURE 48-26 Retainer cam blocks on each shift signal valve in an Allison transmission valve body can be rotated, increasing the tension on the valve's return spring.

In the Allison transmission, precise control of shift points is accomplished in one of two ways. The first way involves adjusting the spring tension on the modulator valve itself. Adjusting the modulator spring affects all shifts throughout the transmission's operating range. The second way involves adjusting the spring tension on the individual shift signal valves, which affects that particular shift only.

The springs are held in their bores in the control valve body by a pin and a unique ramped retainer block cam, shown in **FIGURE 48-26**. This block cam can be rotated by using a special tool. The tension on the spring can be increased or decreased, as desired. Each notch of the retainer cam increases or decreases the shift point by approximately 2 mph (3.2 kph).

Adjusting shift points can be accomplished in the field, but Allison recommends that, to properly adjust shift points, a valve body test bench is required. The control valve body and the transmission governor are attached to the bench and road speed is simulated. The modulator pressure and individual shift points can then be set to specification for the particular vocation of the transmission. Hold regulator pressure and modulated lock-up output shaft rpm for most models can also be adjusted on the test bench.

Reverse Hydraulic Operation

The shift to reverse begins in neutral. Remember that, in neutral, the first clutch is already applied. As the driver selects reverse, the manual valve is moved in its bore and main pressure in the neutral forward regulator circuit is exhausted through the valve. This action causes main pressure to increase as neutral forward regulator pressure is no longer pushing on the land on the MPRV to reduce it.

The main pressure is purposefully highest in reverse because reverse gear ratio can be higher than 5:1. The high ratio requires higher pressure to provide extra clamping force and, therefore, capacity in the clutches. The following fluid flow begins at the bottom of the manual selector valve, as shown in Figure 48-11. Main pressure is directed from the manual valve through the base of the 1–2 shift relay valve and into the reverse circuit, which connects to the fourth clutch apply circuit through the bottom of the 3–4 shift relay valve. The fluid is directed through the base of the 1–2 relay valve to prevent it from shifting should road speed be high enough in reverse for the governor to move the 1–2 shift signal valve. If this occurs, the pressure at the top of the valve and the bottom of the valve are equal and the valve spring ensures the valve does not move. The reverse apply circuit also has an electrical pressure switch installed in it. The switch turns on the vehicle's reverse lights when pressure is detected in the circuit.

Wrap-Up

Ready for Review

▶ Automatic transmissions used in today's vehicles are electronically controlled, but their function is based on their hydraulically controlled predecessors.

▶ Automatic transmissions increase driver and passenger comfort and reduce driver training requirements.

▶ Allison first started making transmissions for tanks in the 1940s and now makes a range of transmissions for trucks and buses all over the world.

▶ All automatic transmissions use torque converters and a set of planetary gears to create their power flows.

▶ Truck automatic transmission planetary gear components are controlled by either stationary or rotating multi-plate hydraulic clutches.

▶ Since 2000, all Allison automatics for on highway use in North America are electronically controlled.

▶ Truck and bus automatic transmissions use combinations of three or four planetary gear sets to create their required ratios.

▶ Knowledge of a transmission's clutch application chart is invaluable when trying to diagnose problems.

▶ Power flows in automatic transmissions may be simple (only one planetary gear set is involved) or compound (two or more planetary gear sets are involved).

▶ All automatic transmissions incorporate a hydraulic clutch to supply fluid pressure for transmission operation. This pump can be of fixed or variable displacement to control parasitic loads.

▶ In order for the transmission's pump to operate, atmospheric pressure must enter the transmission sump, so an air vent is essential.

- ▶ Automatic transmissions use a pressurized lubrication system and have a cooler to control fluid temperature.
- ▶ Fluid exiting the hydraulic pump is directed to the main pressure regulator valve—a spool valve that balances pump output against spring pressure and other forces and creates main or control pressure. All other hydraulic circuits in the transmission are supplied by the main or control pressure.
- ▶ The manual selector valve directs main pressure to the appropriate clutches and control circuits to allow the transmission to attain a gear and shift automatically.
- ▶ The control valve body holds the spool valves responsible for shifting and shift quality control.
- ▶ The modulator valve uses main pressure to create modulator pressure. Modulator pressure is varied depending on throttle position and is, therefore, a load signal to the transmission's hydraulic control.
- ▶ Modulator pressure can be used to influence shift quality and shift timing and to increase main pressure to increase clutch capacity when required.
- ▶ The governor valve uses main pressure to create governor pressure based on output shaft speed. This pressure provides a speed signal to the control valve body.
- ▶ Upshifts are made by governor pressure and modified by modulator pressure. Without governor pressure, no upshifts are possible.
- ▶ Shift signal valves are acted upon by governor pressure and modulator pressure to control upshift points. When the shift signal valve moves, it causes the shift relay valve to move.
- ▶ Shift relay valves are moved by pressure directed from the shift signal valve. When shift relay valves move, they exhaust an applied clutch and send pressure to the on-coming clutch.
- ▶ The priority valve acts as a check valve to protect the transmission's hydraulic pressure supply.
- ▶ Trimmer valves cause a "leak" in a clutch apply circuit to soften the clutch application.
- ▶ The trimmer regulator valve allows the action of the trimmer valve to be increased or decreased based on throttle position to make shifts softer or harsher.
- ▶ All automatic transmissions use a lock-up clutch in the torque converter to eliminate the inherent 5% to 10% slippage between the impeller and the turbine and increase fuel economy.
- ▶ Torque converter lock-up in commercial vehicles is primarily scheduled, meaning that the torque converter locks up when a specific range has been achieved to increase fuel efficiency.
- ▶ Modulated lock-up is throttle-based and can increase performance.
- ▶ In the Allison transmission, the neutral forward regulator circuit (NFRC) can be used to lower main pressure in neutral and all forward ranges.
- ▶ NRFC pressure is not present in reverse, so reverse has the highest main pressure.

- ▶ The valves in the control valve body are separated from the worm tracks in the transmission case by a separator plate and gaskets, allowing the valves to take fluid from one passage and direct it to another.
- ▶ During automatic upshifting, governor pressure acts on the shift signal valve to move it up. Modulator pressure helps the valve move up.
- ▶ Modulator pressure in Allison transmissions is high at closed or light throttle and low at wide-open throttle. Shifts occur at lower speed during light-throttle operation and at higher speeds during full-throttle operation.
- ▶ Automatic downshifting is caused by the shift signal valve spring pressure overcoming dropping governor pressure.
- ▶ Full-throttle downshifts are caused by the disappearance of modulator pressure as the throttle is pushed, and governor pressure alone is not able to keep the shift signal valve in the upshifted position.
- ▶ Shift points in Allison hydraulically controlled transmissions can be altered by changing spring tension on the modulator valve or the shift signal valve.

Key Terms

connecting drum A device used by Allison to connect some of the planetary gear components.

control valve body The heart of the hydraulic control; it holds the spool valves responsible for shifting and transmission control.

DIWA™ A dedicated bus transmission from Voith.

full throttle downshift A downshift forced by the driver by pushing on the throttle. Also called *detent downshift* or *kick down*, depending on the manufacturer.

forward clutch A clutch that is applied in all forward gears or ranges; it is not found on overdrive transmissions.

gear pump A pump consisting of an internal and external toothed gear and typically a crescent.

gerotor pump A pump consisting of a rotor turning inside a matching chamber.

governor valve A valve that creates a pressure based on road speed.

hold regulator valve A spool valve that creates a pressure used to prevent upshifts.

hydraulic circuit A pathway connecting one part of the transmission's hydraulic control with another part.

main pressure regulator valve (MPRV) A spool valve that produces main or control pressure.

main shaft The shaft that is driven by the countershaft and provides output for the transmission. Also called *output shaft*.

manual selector valve The spool valve that is moved by the operator's shift linkage to select a gear.

modulated lock-up A lock-up clutch application strategy that is designed for maximum vehicle performance.

modulator valve A valve that produces a pressure based on throttle position. Also called the *throttle valve*.

parasitic loss An unnecessary load on the engine that wastes fuel.

priority valve A check valve that protects the hydraulic controls.

scheduled lock-up Torque converter lock-up that occurs at a preset point; this saves fuel.

separator plate A plate that separates the control valve body and the transmission case.

shift modulator valve A valve that is moved by modulator pressure and governor pressure for shifting.

shift relay valve The spool valve that directs clutch apply pressure to the correct clutch.

shift signal valve A spool valve that is moved by governor pressure for shifting.

sun gear shaft The shaft that connects the front and center sun gears in the Allison transmission.

throttle valve A valve that produces a pressure based on throttle position. Also called the *modulator valve*.

trimmer regulator valve A valve that modulates trimmer valve action.

trimmer valve A valve used to soften a clutch application.

vane pump A hydraulic pump that uses sliding vanes to move the fluid.

Review Questions

1. If the throttle or modulator valve in an automatic transmission were to stick in the closed throttle position, the probable complaint is which of the following?
   a. Soft early upshifts
   b. No upshifts
   c. Delayed upshifts
   d. No complaint
2. Which of the following hydraulic pressures provides a load signal to the control valve body?
   a. Hold regulator pressure
   b. Governor pressure
   c. Modulator pressure
   d. Main pressure
3. Which of the following pressures provides a "speed" sensitive signal to the control valve body?
   a. Hold regulator pressure
   b. Governor pressure
   c. Modulator pressure
   d. Main pressure
4. Which of the following applies the transmission's clutches?
   a. Hold regulator pressure
   b. Governor pressure
   c. Modulator pressure
   d. Main pressure
5. Loss of governor pressure in an automatic transmission causes which of the following symptoms?
   a. No downshifts
   b. No upshifts
   c. High main pressure
   d. Low main pressure

6. Which of the following statements about the lubrication circuit in an automatic transmission is correct?
   a. It is a splash lubricated by the internal rotating components.
   b. It is usually at line pressure.
   c. It is usually supplied by the converter/cooler circuit.
   d. It operates at converter pressure.
7. Which of the following is NOT one of the functions of the main pressure regulator valve?
   a. It indirectly feeds the transmissions lube circuits
   b. It dumps excess pressure to the pump's inlet side or to the sump when operating pressure is reached.
   c. It feeds the converter-in circuit.
   d. It directs oil from the converter out circuit to sump.
8. The _____ circuit can be used to raise or boost main or control pressure in automatic transmissions.
   a. throttle or modulator
   b. governor
   c. converter-out
   d. lubrication
9. In an Allison transmission, the _____ valve has a cam that can be adjusted to change shift points.
   a. governor
   b. shift relay
   c. selector
   d. modulator
10. On Allison transmissions, the _____ valves direct clutch apply pressure to the clutch packs.
    a. shift signal
    b. trimmer
    c. shift relay
    d. modulator

ASE Technician A/Technician B Style Questions

1. Technician A says that most commercial vehicles have scheduled torque converter lock-up. Technician B says that modulated torque converter lock-up saves fuel. Who is correct?
   a. Technician A
   b. Technician B
   c. Both Technician A and Technician B
   d. Neither Technician A nor Technician B
2. Technician A says that the trimmer regulator valve is used to modify shift harshness based on throttle position. Technician B says that trimmer valves are used to let clutches slip a bit before they are fully applied. Who is correct?
   a. Technician A
   b. Technician B
   c. Both Technician A and Technician B
   d. Neither Technician A nor Technician B
3. Technician A says that in the hydraulically controlled Allison transmissions, modulator pressure is high at wide-open throttle. Technician B says that in the hydraulically controlled Allison transmissions, high modulator pressure causes harsh shifting. Who is correct?
   a. Technician A
   b. Technician B

c. Both Technician A and Technician B
d. Neither Technician A nor Technician B

4. Technician A says that downshifting in hydraulically controlled Allison transmissions is caused by spring force. Technician B says that a downshift can be made at higher road speed by pushing the throttle to the floor. Who is correct?
   a. Technician A
   b. Technician B
   c. Both Technician A and Technician B
   d. Neither Technician A nor Technician B

5. Technician A says that all of the pressures found in hydraulically controlled Allison transmissions are derived from main or control pressure. Technician B says that hydraulically controlled Allison transmission lubrication circuits are at main pressure. Who is correct?
   a. Technician A
   b. Technician B
   c. Both Technician A and Technician B
   d. Neither Technician A nor Technician B

6. Technician A says that, in the Allison AT 500 series transmission, the center planetary gear set is involved in four out of the five gear ranges. Technician B says that the center planetary gear set is not involved in first range. Who is correct?
   a. Technician A
   b. Technician B
   c. Both Technician A and Technician B
   d. Neither Technician A nor Technician B

7. Technician A says that the Allison AT 500 series transmission uses five hydraulic clutches. Technician B says the Allison AT 500 series transmission use three interconnected planetary gear sets. Who is correct?
   a. Technician A
   b. Technician B
   c. Both Technician A and Technician B
   d. Neither Technician A nor Technician B

8. Technician A says that, in the Allison AT 500 series transmission, the connecting drum is attached to the front carrier, the center carrier, and the rear carrier. Technician B says that, in the Allison AT 500 series transmission, the front sun gear is part of the main shaft. Who is correct?
   a. Technician A
   b. Technician B
   c. Both Technician A and Technician B
   d. Neither Technician A nor Technician B

9. Technician A says that the center ring gear is attached to the connecting drum in the Allison AT 500 series transmission. Technician B says that the rear carrier is attached to the output shaft in the Allison AT 500 series transmission. Who is correct?
   a. Technician A
   b. Technician B
   c. Both Technician A and Technician B
   d. Neither Technician A nor Technician B

10. Technician A says that, in fourth range in the Allison AT 500 series transmission, the two rotating clutches are turning at the same speed. Technician B says that in fourth range in the Allison AT 500 series transmission all three planetary gear sets are turning at the same speed. Who is correct?
    a. Technician A
    b. Technician B
    c. Both Technician A and Technician B
    d. Neither Technician A nor Technician B

CHAPTER 49

Electronically Controlled Automatic Transmissions

Learning Objectives

After reading this chapter, you will be able to:

- **LO 49-1** Describe the operation of Allison Automatic Transmission Electronic Control (ATEC) and Commercial Electronic Control (CEC).
- **LO 49-2** Describe the operation and power flows of Allison World Transmissions (WT).
- **LO 49-3** Describe the operation of the World Transmission Electronic Control (WTEC) and later models WTEC II and WTEC III.

- **LO 49-4** Describe the operation of the electronic controls in Allison fourth- and fifth-generation transmissions.
- **LO 49-5** Describe the operation and power flows of the Allison TC-10-TS transmission.
- **LO 49-6** Explain the operation and power flows of Voith transmission's DIWA drive transmission.
- **LO 49-7** Describe ZF Friedrichshafen AG (ZF) EcoMat and EcoLife and Caterpillar CX-28, CX-31, and CX-35 transmissions.

You Are the Technician

A vehicle with an Allison ATEC transmission is brought to your shop in northern Minnesota on a particularly icy day when overnight temperatures were well below zero. The driver complains that, when he first started the vehicle, the transmission would not go into gear for over five minutes. Then, the transmission would not shift out of first gear until he had driven for another minute, but now it seems to shift normally. The driver had not driven this vehicle previous to today and is concerned that transmission damage may have occurred. You check the fluid level, and it is correct. The fluid itself is bright red and shows no signs of contamination. You then perform a stall test and a road test and find that the vehicle is performing as it should.

1. What could be the cause of this condition?
2. Should you remove the oil pan and look for clutch damage?
3. Could this be normal operation for this vehicle?

Introduction

Controlling automatic transmissions electrically is not a new concept. As far back as the 1950s and 1960s, it made sense to operate the transmission electrically in certain off-road and industrial applications. Using electric controls eliminated the need for mechanical connections and meant that the controls could be located at virtually any remote location instead of having to be located precisely at the transmission. Allison invented an electrical control known as a shift pattern generator (SPG) that used pitot tube pressure to measure rotational speed. Allison used SPG primarily in its series of transmissions developed for off-highway use.

Allison was not the only early adopter of electrically controlled automatic transmissions. Voith DIWA drive bus transmissions were always controlled electrically, as were the ZF bus and coach transmissions (the EcoLife and the EcoMat). Controlling bus transmissions electrically made a lot of sense as typically the transmission was at the rear of the bus and the shift controls were at the front. Over the years, however, increased competition in the transportation field has caused companies to insist on ever higher fuel efficiency as a way to keep costs under control. As a result, electrical control of automatic transmissions has been replaced by increasingly sophisticated electronic control technology.

This chapter introduces the electronically controlled automatic transmissions commonly used in the North American market. The dominant company in this market is Allison—throughout its history, it has produced over 7,000,000 commercial vehicle transmissions worldwide to date. Because Allison is the primary heavy-duty transmission manufacturer in North America, this chapter concentrates on Allison products. Other transmissions examined include the Voith DIWA series transmissions, the ZF bus transmission models, and, briefly, discusses Caterpillar's CX series of automatic transmissions used in its CT660 on-highway trucks.

Basics of Electronic Control— Allison Transmission Electronic Control (ATEC) and Commercial Electronic Control (CEC)

LO 49-1 Describe the operation of Allison Automatic Transmission Electronic Control (ATEC) and Commercial Electronic Control (CEC).

Allison's initial foray into electronic control began with its original MT-600, HT-700, and V-series (bus) transmissions. The original electronic control was called the **Allison Transmission Electronic Control (ATEC)**. This system is now called the **Commercial Electronic Control (CEC)**, but it is essentially the same system. The mechanical components of these transmissions are identical to their hydraulically controlled counterparts discussed in the chapter on Hydraulically Controlled Automatic Transmissions and so are not discussed again in this chapter. If necessary, take time to review the mechanical transmission operation material in that chapter before continuing on in this chapter.

All automatic transmissions require at least three inputs in order to be able to shift properly:

- The driver's gear selection
- A load-sensitive signal
- A speed-sensitive signal

Without these three inputs, automatic transmissions would not know when to shift. In hydraulically controlled transmissions, those three inputs are provided by the mechanical shift selector, the modulator or throttle valve as the load sense, and the centrifugal governor as the speed sense.

The ATEC/CEC system is completely drive by wire. That is, there is no mechanical connection to the transmission. The only connections in and out of the transmission are electrical. The driver's gear selector consists of either a push button control pad or an optional shift lever. Either way, all the selections are made electronically. The load-sensitive signal, the modulator valve, is replaced by a throttle position sensor (TPS), and the centrifugal governor input, or speed-sensitive signal, is replaced by a vehicle speed sensor (VSS). These inputs and more are sent to the **transmission electronic control unit (ECU)**. As mentioned in the chapter on automated transmissions the accepted SAE term for the transmission controller is TCM; however, Allison called their controller the transmission ECU until the advent of the world transmission fourth generation so the term is used in the following two sections. Remember regardless of the term used they both refer to the same component the electronic module that controls the transmission. The transmission ECU, or TECU, is the brains of the control system. It processes the received data and decides when shifts should occur (**FIGURE 49-1**). The transmission controller then issues commands to solenoids inside the transmission to obtain the desired range.

Transmission Electronic Control Unit or ECU

The transmission electronic control unit provides all the shifting "thought process" for the transmission. The unit receives signals from the driver and the transmission and then decides on the best shift strategy for the operating conditions. There have been three different types of ECUs used by the Allison CEC (**FIGURE 49-2**). The first, and now obsolete, Splashproof model ECU was replaced by the Sealed-standard ECU. The third type, the Sealed-Plus 11, includes an additional connector that allows a remotely mounted operator interface for remote power take-off (PTO) operation and other special features.

Each transmission ECU is fitted with a **programmable read-only memory (PROM) chip** (**FIGURE 49-3**). PROM chips are essential to the proper functioning of the transmission and unique to vocation of the particular vehicle in which they are found, such as a fire truck or garbage truck. PROM chips allow the same ECU to be used in all installations because each ECU contains its own replaceable PROM chip. The PROM chip is the only serviceable part in the ECU. It is accessed through a small cover in the ECU case. Installing the wrong PROM chip can severely affect vehicle performance.

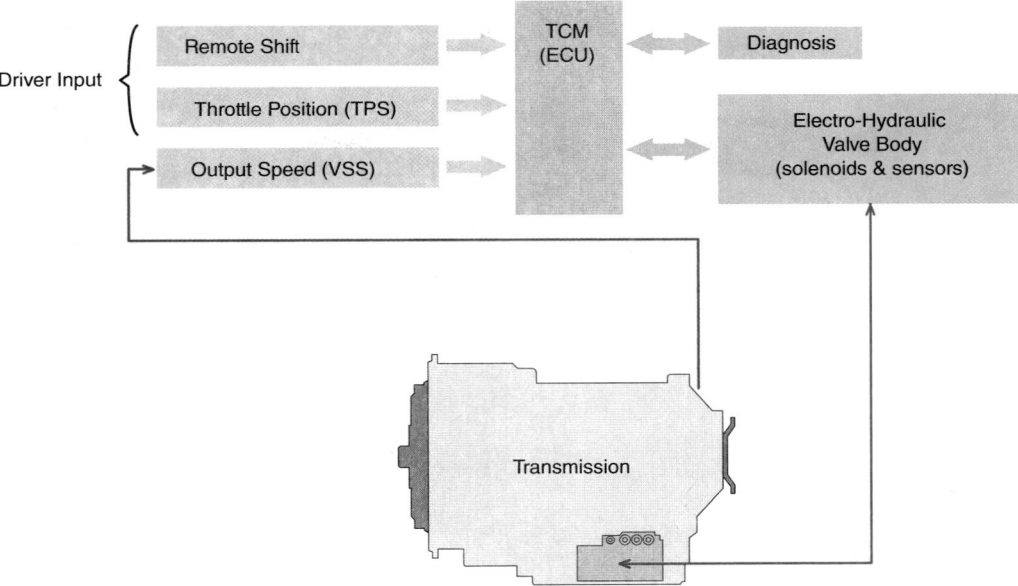

FIGURE 49-1 The transmission controller receives inputs from the shifter, the TPS, and the VSS and then controls solenoids in the electrohydraulic valve body to shift the transmission.

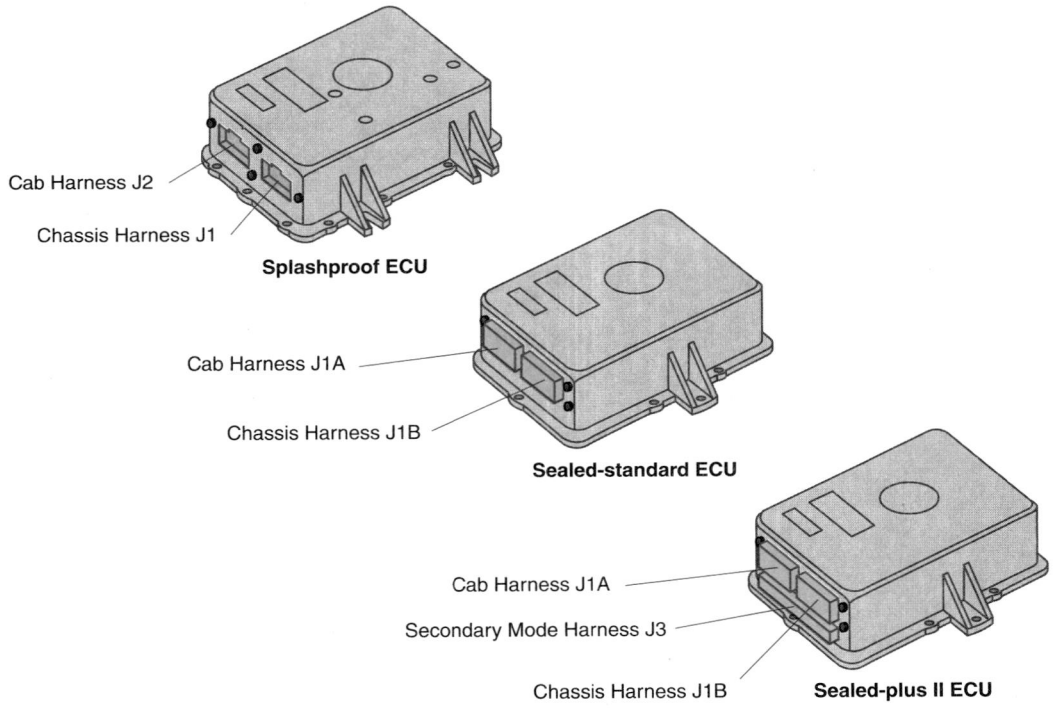

FIGURE 49-2 The ATEC/CEC electronic control unit had three generations.

Transmission Inputs

The Driver's Input or Shift Control

The shift control can be a push button unit used to activate gear changes (**FIGURE 49-4**). The gear range selections are usually R, N, D, 3, 2, and 1. In some applications, however, there may be fewer choices. When the driver selects a range, the information is relayed to the transmission ECU.

Lever-type shift selectors usually have the same six gear positions as shift-button selectors or fewer. When the driver moves the Allison supplied shift lever, it actuates Hall-effect switches. The Hall-effect switches send a corresponding signal to the transmission ECU. If necessary, the vehicle can be also equipped with a remote shift control unit for special applications.

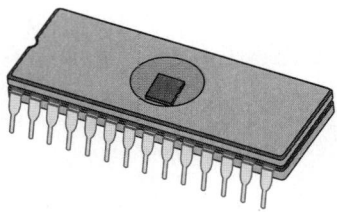

FIGURE 49-3 The PROM chip s replaceable in order to change the shift programming to suit a spec fic vehicle vocation.

FIGURE 49-4 The driver's input can be a push button control as shown or a shift lever type.

FIGURE 49-5 The vehicle interface module allows for communication between the engine and transmission, when necessary.

Throttle Position Sensor

On non-electronic engines, the TPS can be original equipment manufacturers (OEM) or Allison supplied. With an OEM-supplied TPS, the signal may have to pass through a communications adapter, called a vehicle interface module, before the signal can be read by the transmission ECU (**FIGURE 49-5**).

The TPS replaces the modulator throttle valve used on hydraulically controlled transmissions and gives the transmission ECU the load-sensitive signal required for shift timing and strategies. The Allison-supplied TPS is a cable-actuated linear potentiometer. As the throttle is actuated, the potentiometer sends a voltage signal to the transmission ECU, and the ECU converts this voltage into "counts." **Counts** is the term Allison uses to monitor the TPS position (**FIGURE 49-6**).

The sensor's range is from 0 to 255 counts, which equates to the sensor's ability to travel approximately 1.5". The sensor's actual movement in operation, however, equates to only about 100 counts, or the equivalent of 0.75". On installation, the sensor is set up so the throttle movement takes place in the middle of the sensor's range. Setting the sensor up at the midpoint allows the sensor to be self-correcting. As the throttle cable stretches over time, the sensor can reset itself so that idle and wide-open throttle still fall within the acceptable counts range. When the vehicle is shut down, the ECU records the minimum and maximum throttle positions during that drive cycle. Each time the vehicle is started, the ECU sets minimum and maximum travel at 15 counts past the last recorded reading and then adjusts the reading to reflect actual throttle movement. Those adjustments act to recalibrate the TPS on each drive cycle. Another critical adjustment that can be made by the technician is the ability to set error zones in the sensor's range. When counts from 0 to 14 and from 233 to 255 are set as error zones, the ECU can detect a broken cable or other serious problem. If the ECU reads data in the error zones, it generates a code and turns on the check transmission/do-not-shift light.

Vehicle Speed Sensor (VSS)

The **vehicle speed sensor (VSS)** is an inductive pickup sensor that reads the speed of the transmission output shaft (**FIGURE 49-7**). An inductive pickup is simply a coil of wire wrapped around a permanent magnet core. The pickup is placed in close proximity to a tone wheel (a toothed ring) splined to the output shaft. As the shaft rotates and the teeth on the wheel approach the magnet, the magnetic field builds and collapses.

The rising and falling levels of the magnetic field send an alternating current to the transmission ECU, which reads the voltages cross counts (i.e., the number of times the voltage changes from positive to negative) and translates the number of cross counts as output shaft speed. The VSS sensor provides a road-speed signal used with the TPS to determine shift timing. As such, the VSS replaces the centrifugal governor used on hydraulically controlled transmissions.

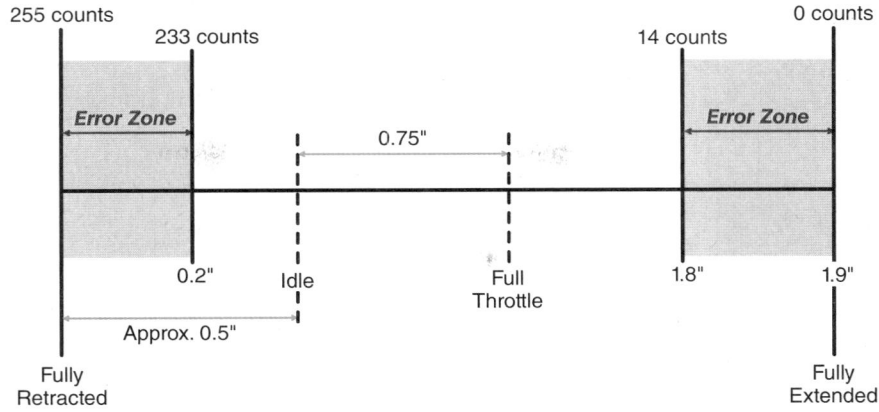

FIGURE 49-6 The transmission ECU converts the voltage signal from the Allison TPS into "counts."

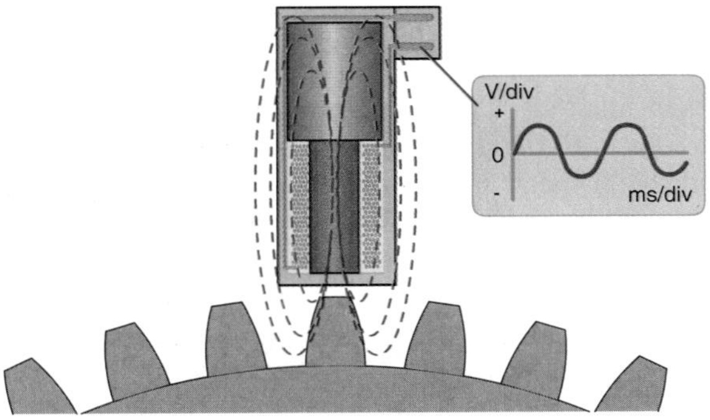

FIGURE 49-7 A vehicle speed sensor (VSS) produces an AC voltage signal that rises in frequency and amplitude as speed increases.

FIGURE 49-8 The plate on the side of the transmission contains important information about the transmission. Never remove the information plate.

Fluid Sensors

Fluid sensors are a critical part of electronically controlled automatic transmissions. The most common sensors monitor pressure and temperature.

Forward and Reverse Pressure Switches The forward and reverse pressure switches are threaded oil-pressure switches plumbed into the forward and reverse hydraulic circuits. The contacts in these switches are normally open and close, respectively, when the forward range or reverse circuit is pressurized. The transmission ECU can determine that a forward or reverse range has been achieved by monitoring these switches.

Fluid Temperature Sensor Severe transmission damage can occur if the transmission fluid is either too hot or too cold. The transmission, therefore, has a temperature sensor that is monitored by the ECU. In on-highway models, the sensor is mounted on the valve body wiring harness inside the transmission oil pan.

The ECU does not allow shifts into any gear range if the fluid temperature is below −25° F (−32° C). As the fluid temperature rises, the controller allows limited shifts to first or reverse only while the temperature is between −25° F and +25° F (−32° C to +4° C). If the fluid temperature increases to 270° F (132° C), the check transmission light on the shift control is illuminated, a code is recorded in the transmission ECU's memory,

and, in on-highway models, a shift to top gear is inhibited. Certain emergency vehicle applications do not inhibit top gear for high temperature, but the check transmission/do not shift light illuminates and a code is set.

Oil Pressure Switch/Sensor The transmission ECU relies on two other inputs—the oil temperature sensor and one of the three additional sensor types:

- The lube oil pressure switch
- The low oil level pressure sensor
- The fluidic oil level sensor

Inputs to those three additional sensors are used more for transmission protection rather than shift strategy, however.

It is important for the technician to know which of the above type of switch/sensor is installed because the electrical circuit for each type reacts differently during testing. The installed switch can be determined by calling Allison Electronic Control Information System (ECIS), available through authorized Allison dealers, with the transmission assembly number from the plate on the side of the transmission case (**FIGURE 49-8**). The PROM chip in the transmission ECU must also be programmed correctly to the type of switch, so care must be taken if either the switch/sensor or the PROM chip needs replacing.

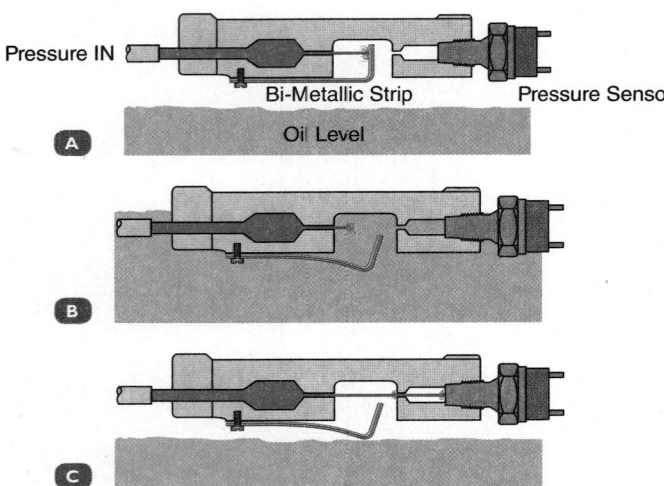

FIGURE 49-9 Low oil level/pressure sensor at: **A.** Cold temperature. **B.** Normal temperature. **C.** Normal temperature, low level.

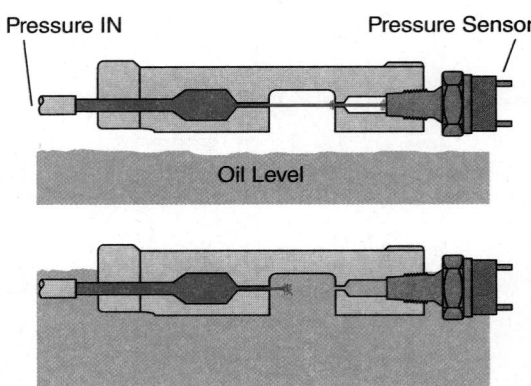

FIGURE 49-10 Fluidic oil level sensor.

The first type of switch/sensor is a simple oil pressure switch (called a lube pressure switch by Allison) that is plumbed into the transmission lube oil circuit. The switch contacts are normally open and close when lube oil pressure is present. If the switch contacts remain open after the vehicle is started, the check transmission/do not shift light is illuminated and a trouble code is set in the transmission ECU's memory.

The second type is the low oil level/pressure sensor. This sensor is bolted to the bottom of the **electrohydraulic valve body**, also known as the **electrohydraulic control** which is the central transmission control consisting of solenoids, spool valves, and pressure switches. The low oil level/pressure sensor bolted to the electrohydraulic control has pressurized lube oil spraying from a small orifice in the body of the sensor. The effect of the lube oil going through the orifice creates a stream of lube oil exiting one side of the sensor. A pressure switch with normally open contacts is plumbed into an opening on the other side of the sensor. The sensor is mounted in such a way that when the oil reaches operating temperature, the higher oil level caused by thermal expansion surrounds the opening on the sensor and dissipates the flow of the stream of oil exiting the sensor (**FIGURE 49-9**).

When the transmission is cold, a bi-metallic strip blocks the flow of oil, so the sensor works a bit differently. When the vehicle is started, a pressurized stream of oil flows from the orifice on one side of the switch. Because the transmission is cold at start-up, the fluid level is below the opening in the sensor, but the bi-metallic strip blocks the stream of pressurized oil from reaching the pressure switch on the other side and closing its contacts. As the transmission warms up, the bi-metal strip flexes out of the way, but, by that time, the warming transmission fluid expands and fills the opening in the sensor. The presence of the fluid in the sensor opening dissipates the oil flow and prevents it from closing the switch contacts. A stream of fluid that reaches the switch after the fluid is warm indicates that the fluid level is low. A code is

then generated and the check transmission/do not shift light is illuminated.

The fluidic oil level sensor is very similar to the low oil level/pressure sensor but without a bi-metallic strip (**FIGURE 49-10**). The transmission ECU is programmed to ignore signals from the sensor until the fluid temperature reaches operational levels, so the bi-metal strip is not required. The pressure switch that the fluidic sensor uses is a normally closed switch. If the fluid level is low, pressurized transmission fluid reaches the switch after the transmission warms up. The contacts open, a code is generated, and the check transmission/do not shift light is illuminated.

Wiring Harnesses

Transmissions are supported by one of two general types of wiring harness. The **chassis wiring harness** is the wiring that connects the transmission, the TPS, and the VSS to the transmission ECU. The **cab harness** connects the shift selector to the ECU and also contains the bi-directional communications connector to allow the transmission ECU to "talk" to Detroit Diesel DDEC systems and the diagnostic data link (DDL) connector. The diagnostic data link (DDL) connector is the place on the vehicle where the technician can plug in diagnostic software. (Technicians using a Pro-Link or other electronic service tool can connect to the DDL and access trouble codes stored in the ECU.) The cab harness also contains various interface wiring for optional transmission strategies, such as brake interlocks and low floor operating/no-shift options.

Solenoids

Inside the ATEC/CEC transmission, the hydraulic circuitry is changed somewhat when compared to its hydraulically controlled predecessor. Whereas hydraulically controlled Allison transmissions use spool valves exclusively to control fluid flow, ATEC/CEC transmissions use solenoids in addition to spool valves. The solenoids direct the flow of main pressure to control the transmission shifting and other functions. The solenoids use a spring-loaded check ball to control fluid flow. Solenoids have three components:

A **Latching Solenoid**

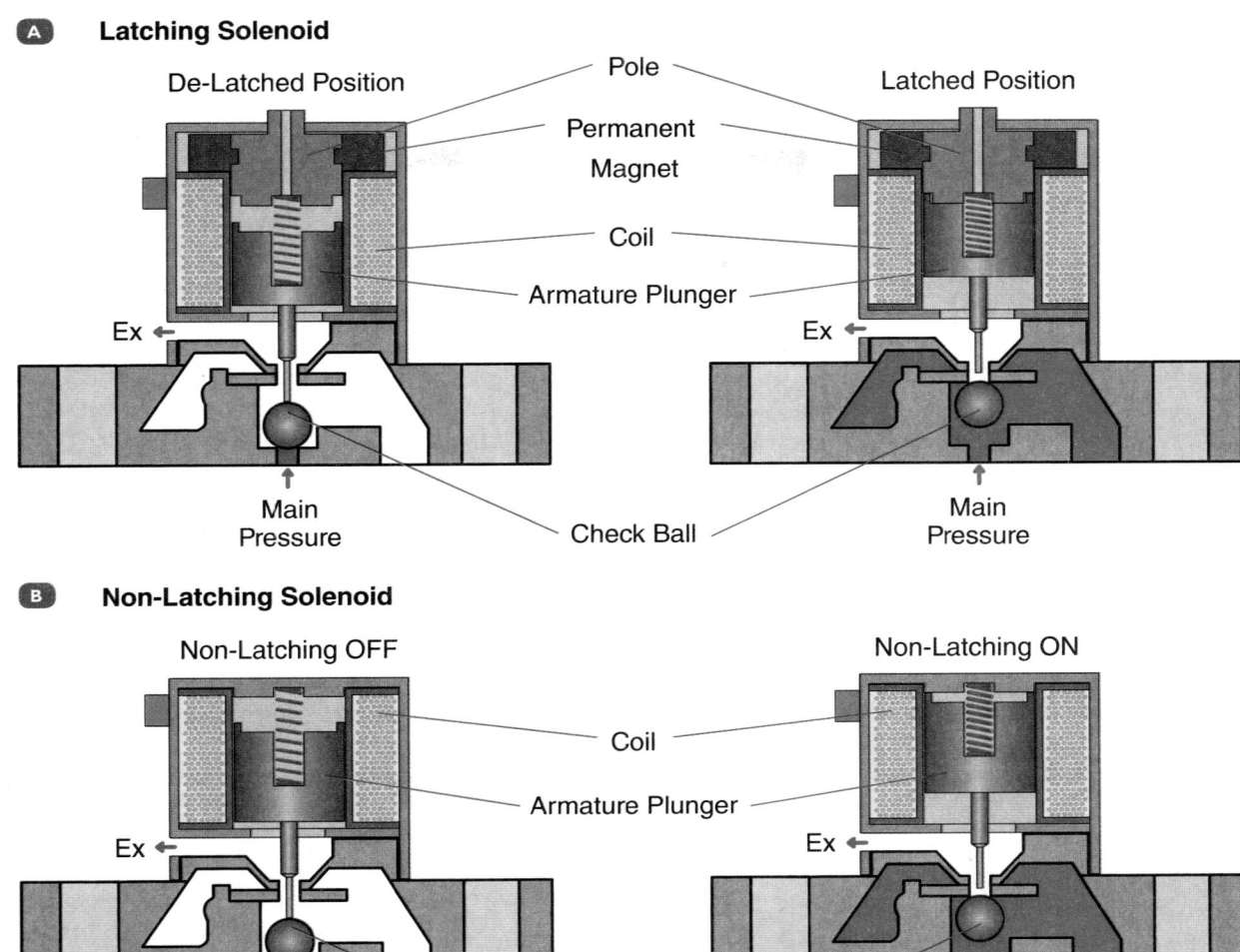

FIGURE 49-11 The ATEC/CEC transmission uses two types of solenoids: latching and non-latching. **A.** Momentary application of power to a latching solenoid moves it to an open position, and it stays there until energized again. **B.** Non-latching solenoid require continuous voltage to remain open.

- An inlet port controlled by the ball
- A circuit port leading to the hydraulic circuit the solenoid controls
- An exhaust port

When the solenoid is closed, the hydraulic circuit that is controlled is open to the exhaust port. When the solenoid is opened, the exhaust port is sealed, and the inlet port is connected to the hydraulic circuit.

The ATEC/CEC system uses two types of solenoids—latching and non-latching solenoids (**FIGURE 49-11**). **Latching solenoids** require only a short burst of electricity to cause them to move. Once they do, they latch, or stay in that position. Another burst of electricity causes the solenoid to unlatch and move back to the starting position. Therefore, these solenoids do not require constant power. That reduces the amount of heat that would build up in the solenoid coil and extends

the life of the solenoids. This latching feature also gives some transmission operability during electrical power failure. Fail-safe operational strategies are discussed later in the chapter. As their name implies, **non-latching solenoids** do not stay in an open position unless they have a constant voltage supply. As soon as the voltage disappears, they return to their starting, or closed, position.

Solenoid Usage

There are up to nine solenoids in the transmission: solenoids A, B, C, D, E, F, G, H, and J. (There is no "I" solenoid.) The solenoids are located in an electrohydraulic valve body and can either be clamped to or bolted to the valve body (**FIGURE 49-12**).

The hydraulic circuits of the transmission are altered so that the solenoids control the flow through the main valve body. The solenoids are mounted such that they have main pressure present

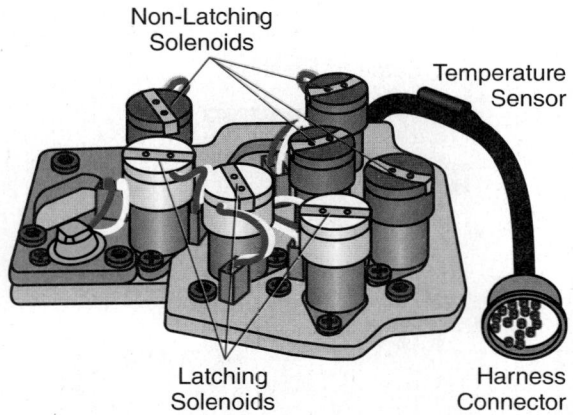

Non-Latching
Solenoids

Temperature
Sensor

Latching
Solenoids

Harness
Connector

FIGURE 49-12 The electrohydraulic valve body holds the solenoids and the forward and reverse pressure switches.

at their base. That pressure is blocked when the solenoid is closed, but when the solenoid is opened electrically, main pressure is redirected to the appropriate valves in the main valve body. In hydraulically controlled transmissions, the shift signal valves control the shift relay valves. In the ATEC/CEC transmissions, however, the shift signal valves are replaced with latching solenoids A, B, C, and D. The shift relay valves in the ATEC/CEC are simply called the shift valves and the solenoids control the following functions:

- Solenoid A controls the low to first shift valve on five-speed models.
- Solenoid B controls the first to second shift valve.
- Solenoid C controls the second to third shift valve.
- Solenoid D controls the third to fourth shift valve.

Based on control functions, five-speed models have all four shift solenoids (A–D). Four-speed models only require three shift solenoids (B–D), and three-speed models used in some buses only require two shift solenoids (B and C).

Likewise in the ATEC/CEC, the manual valve is replaced by two solenoid-controlled valves: the neutral range valve and the forward reverse valve. The neutral range valve position is controlled by solenoid H (non-latching) and solenoid J (latching). The forward reverse valve position is controlled by solenoid F (latching).

Solenoid E (non-latching) controls the flow of main pressure to the bottom of the trimmer regulator valve to control shift quality. Solenoid G (non-latching) controls the flow of main pressure to the torque converter lockup clutch relay valve when lockup is desired.

Shift Logic

The transmission ECU receives range request data from the gear selector, throttle position data or load request from the TPS, and vehicle road speed from the VSS. Based on this input—along with input from the temperature sensor, pressure switches, and the vehicle interface—the transmission controller energizes and de-energizes the solenoids to provide an appropriate range for vehicle operation. These shift timing strategies are known as **shift logic**.

Remember that the ATEC/CEC transmission mechanical systems are relatively identical to the hydraulically controlled models discussed in the chapter Hydraulically Controlled Automatic Transmissions. Review that chapter, if necessary, to understand the power flows. **TABLE 49-1** is the clutch application chart for the ATEC/CEC transmission.

Let's examine the fluid flows in the transmission in more depth using a typical four-speed transmission as our example (**FIGURE 49-13**).

On start-up, the pump directs fluid to the main pressure regulator valve. As the valve moves down in its bore and against spring pressure, a passage to the torque converter opens, allowing the converter to fill. Fluid is simultaneously directed into the main pressure circuit of the electrohydraulic valve body and through the solenoid priority valve to all the solenoids. In addition, fluid flows through three valves—the direction priority valve, the 2-3 shift valve, and the 1-2 shift valve—and into the first clutch causing the first clutch to apply. As the main pressure regulator valve moves further down in its bore, it opens an exhaust passage back to the transmission sump. The valve becomes balanced against the pressure setting main in reverse increases clutch capacity to handle the higher torque load.

Just as in the older hydraulic-controlled models, other pressures can be brought to bear against the main pressure regulator valve as a way to lower its pressure during forward range and converter lockup operation. Main pressure is again highest in reverse range when forward regulator and lockup pressures are not influencing the main pressure regulator valve (MPRV). And in both the hydraulically controlled Allison transmissions, as well as in the ATEC/CEC, increasing main pressure in reverse increases clutch capacity to handle the higher torque load.

As we continue the discussion of shift logic, please note the hydraulic circuits shown in the supporting schematics are simplified for clarity.

ATEC/CEC Neutral

In neutral, solenoid J is the only energized or "open" solenoid. Solenoid J (latching) requires only momentary power to open. When J does open, main pressure is directed to the top of the neutral-range

TABLE 49-1 Clutch Application Chart for the ATEC/CEC Transmission

Range	Forward Clutch	Fourth Clutch	Third Clutch	Second Clutch	First Clutch
Neutral					Applied
First range	Applied				Applied
Second range	Applied			Applied	
Third range	Applied		Applied		
Fourth range	Applied	Applied			
Reverse		Applied			Applied

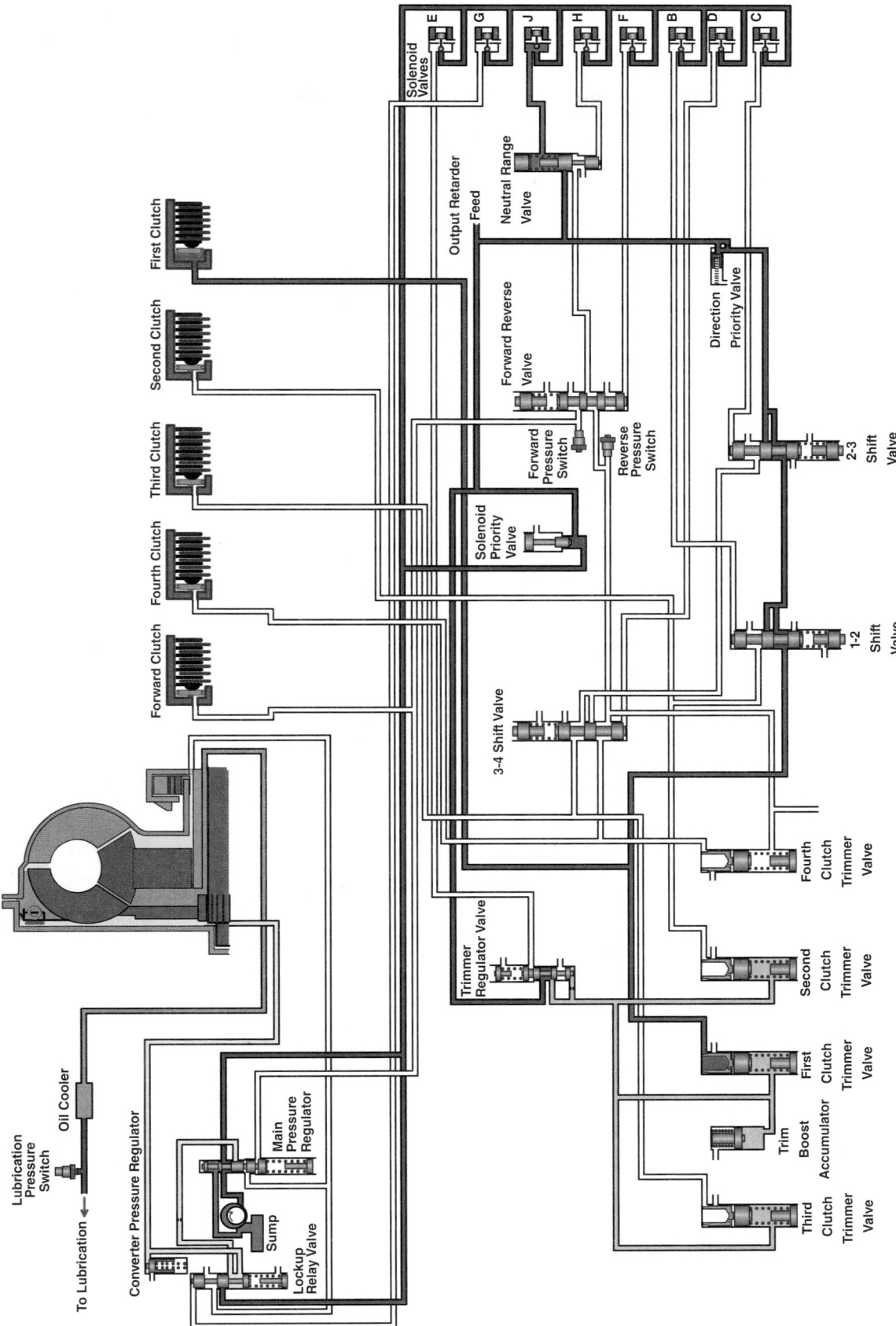

FIGURE 49-13 This complete hydraulic schematic of the ATEC/CEC series of transmissions can be referenced while following the fluid flows.

valve, keeping the valve seated in its bore. This action prevents internal leakage from causing the neutral-range valve to move up and cause an unwanted range selection. With the neutral-range valve in this position, main pressure deadheads at the valve and cannot flow to the forward reverse valve. First clutch is the only clutch applied so the transmission is in neutral (**FIGURE 49-14**).

ATEC/CEC First Range

As the driver selects first range, solenoid H becomes energized and solenoid J is energized momentarily to close its check ball. The pressure above the neutral-range valve is then exhausted through solenoid J. Non-latching solenoid H sends main pressure to the bottom of the neutral-range valve, and the valve moves up in its bore. This allows the main pressure that had been deadheaded at the neutral-range valve now to be directed to the forward reverse valve. Latching solenoid F is also energized momentarily to open. When solenoid F opens, main pressure is sent to the bottom of the forward reverse valve, moving the valve up in its bore. With the valve in this position, the main pressure from the neutral range valve flows through the forward reverse valve and into the forward clutch circuit, applying the forward clutch. The first clutch and forward clutch are now applied; the transmission attains first range (**FIGURE 49-15**). Fluid flowing to the forward clutch is also directed to the main pressure regulator valve to reduce main pressure.

ATEC/CEC Second Range

As the vehicle accelerates, the ECU commands a shift to second range. Solenoid F remains open as it is latching. Solenoid H

remains energized, so the forward clutch remains applied. Latching solenoid B is momentarily energized and opens. This sends main pressure to the top of the 1-2 shift valve and causes the valve to move down in its bore. That movement exhausts first clutch at the valve. At the same time, the movement redirects the main pressure that was going to first clutch to the second clutch circuit, applying the clutch. Forward and second clutches are now applied, and the transmission attains second range (**FIGURE 49-16**).

ATEC/CEC Third Range

As the vehicle continues to accelerate, the transmission ECU commands a shift to third. Solenoid F remains open as it is latching. Solenoid H remains energized, so forward clutch remains applied. Latching solenoid C is momentarily energized and opens. The opening causes the 2-3 shift valve to move in its bore and exhausts the second clutch at the valve. The motion redirects the main pressure to the third clutch. Forward and third clutch are applied, and the transmission attains third range (**FIGURE 49-17**).

ATEC/CEC Fourth Range

After continued acceleration, the ECU commands a shift to fourth range. Solenoid F remains open as it is latching. Solenoid H remains energized, so the forward clutch remains applied. Latching solenoid D is energized momentarily, and this causes the 3-4 shift valve to move in its bore. That movement exhausts third clutch at the valve and also redirects the main pressure to the fourth clutch so forward and fourth clutches are applied, and the transmission attains fourth range (**FIGURE 49-18**).

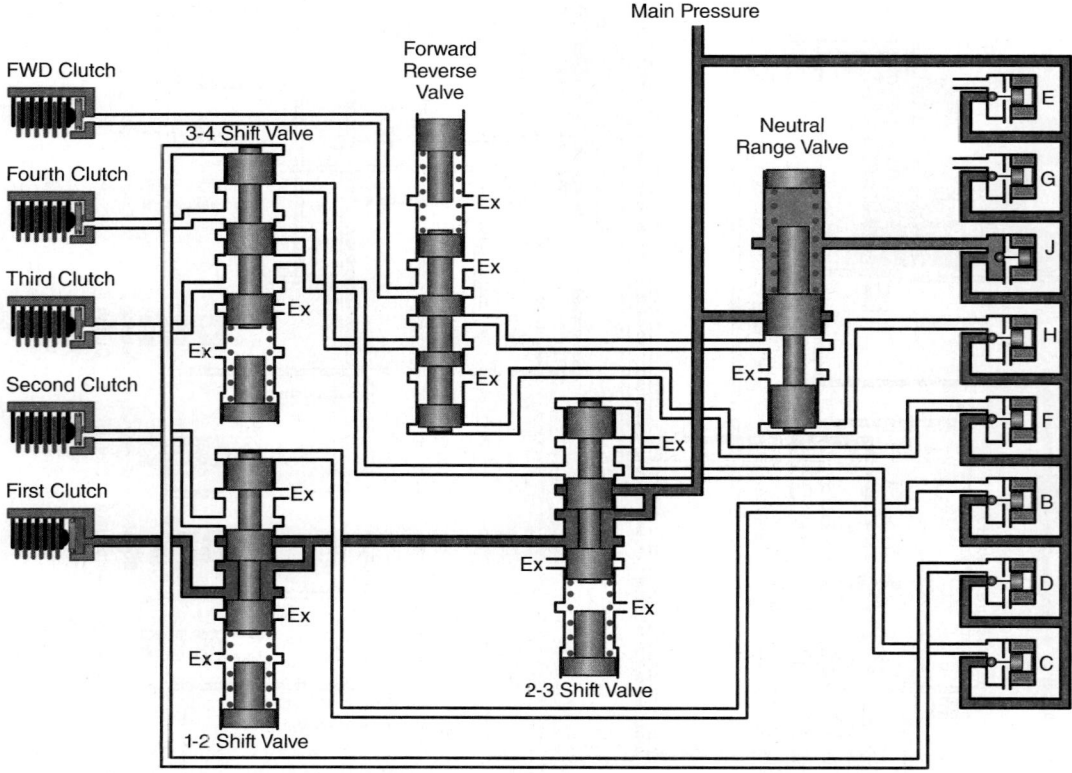

FIGURE 49-14 Neutral fluid flow. In neutral, only solenoid J is open. Solenoid J is latching and only requires momentary energizing to remain open.

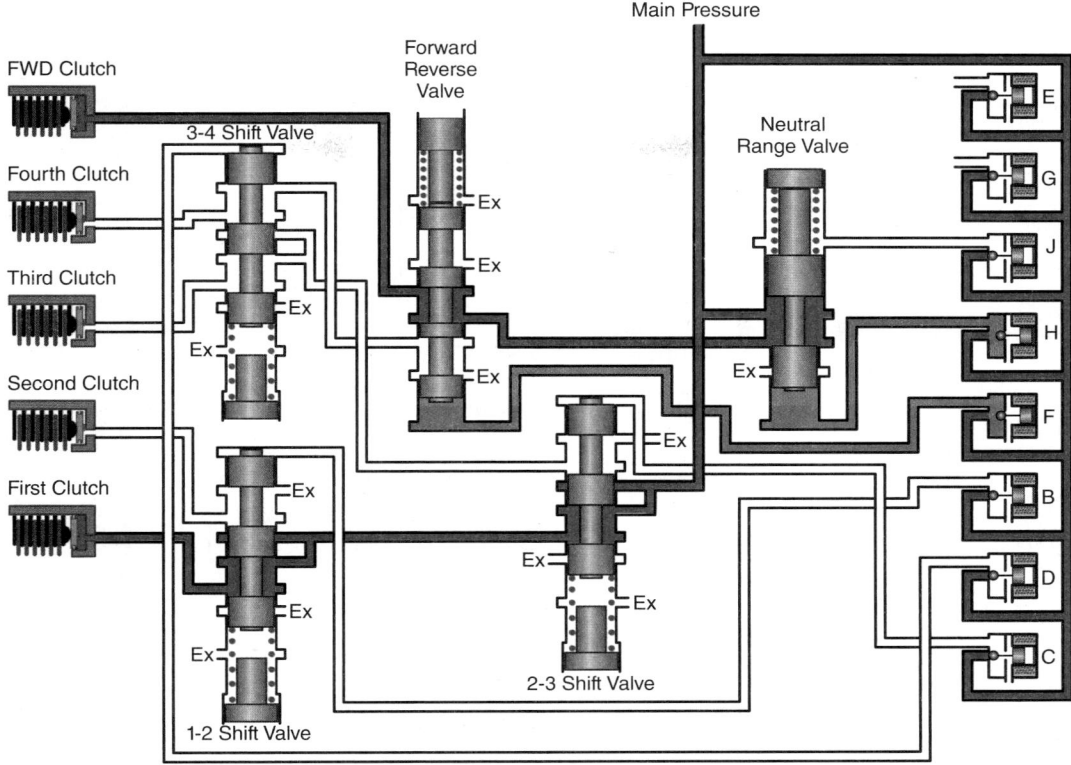

FIGURE 49-15 First range. In first range, latching solenoid F is momentarily energized to open, non-latching solenoid H is energized and holds F open, and latching solenoid J is momentarily energized to close.

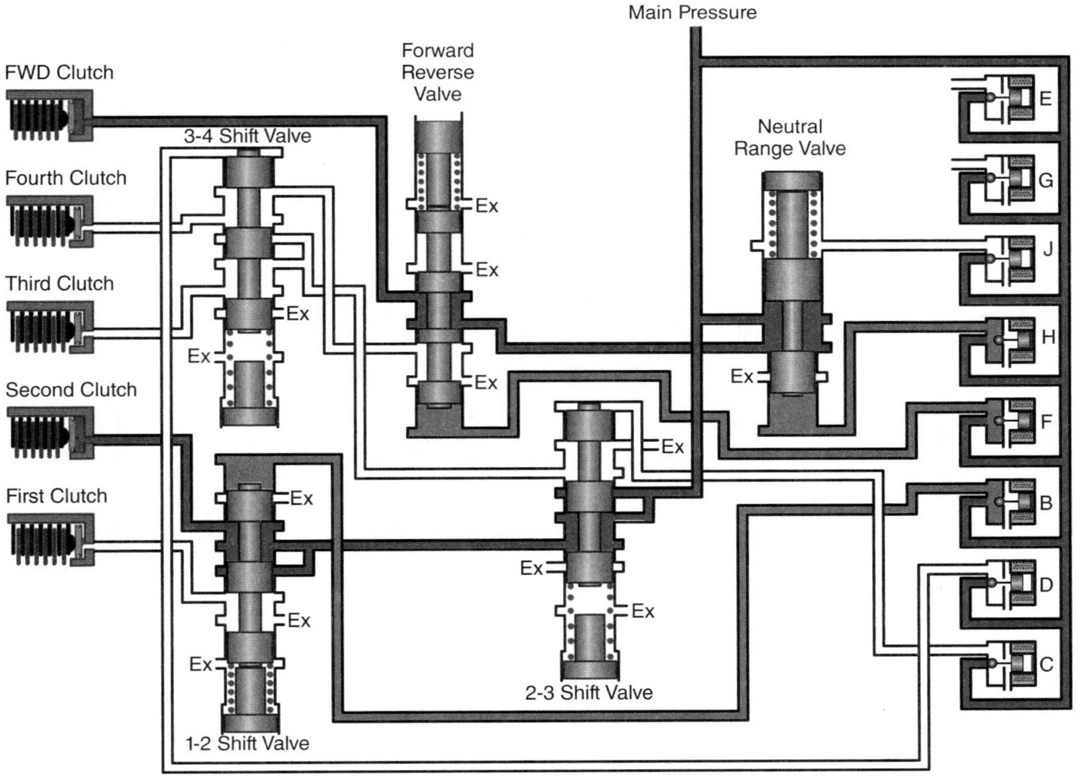

FIGURE 49-16 Second range. To achieve second range, the transmission ECU momentarily energizes latching solenoid B to open sending fluid to the 1-2 shift valve.

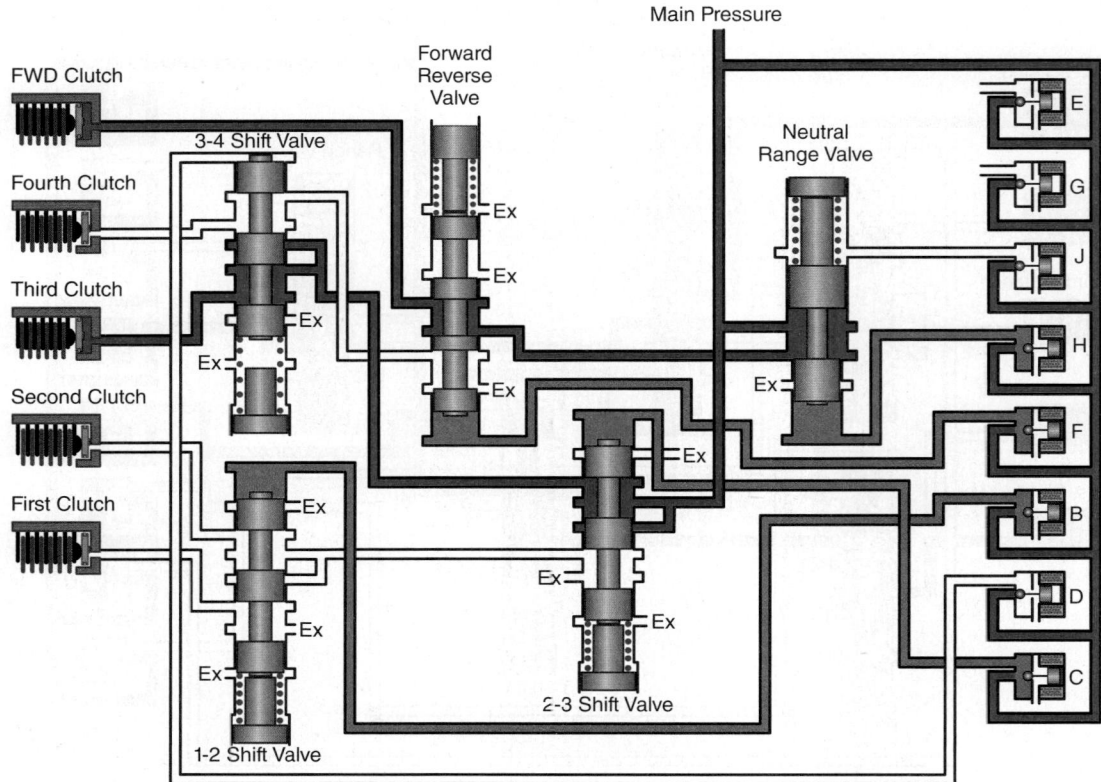

FIGURE 49-17 Third range. To shift to third, the ECU momentarily energizes latching solenoid C to open sending pressure to the 2-3 shift valve.

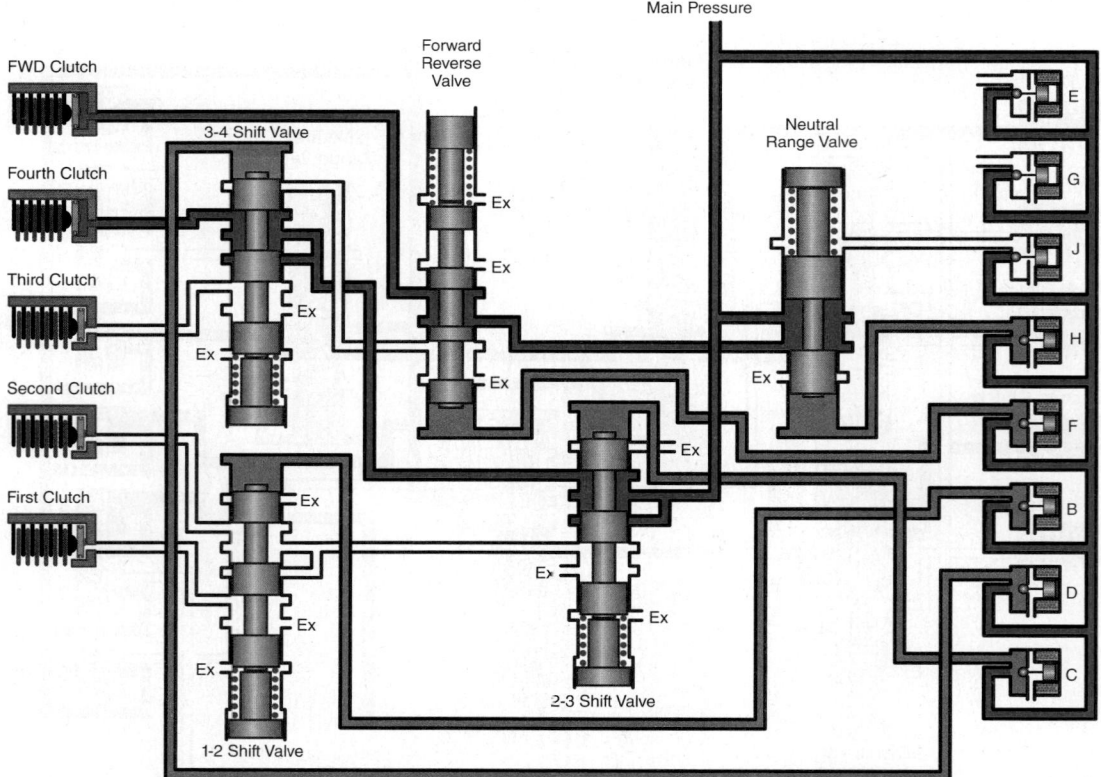

FIGURE 49-18 Fourth range. To achieve fourth range, the ECU momentarily energizes latching solenoid D to open it sending pressure to the 3-4 shift valve.

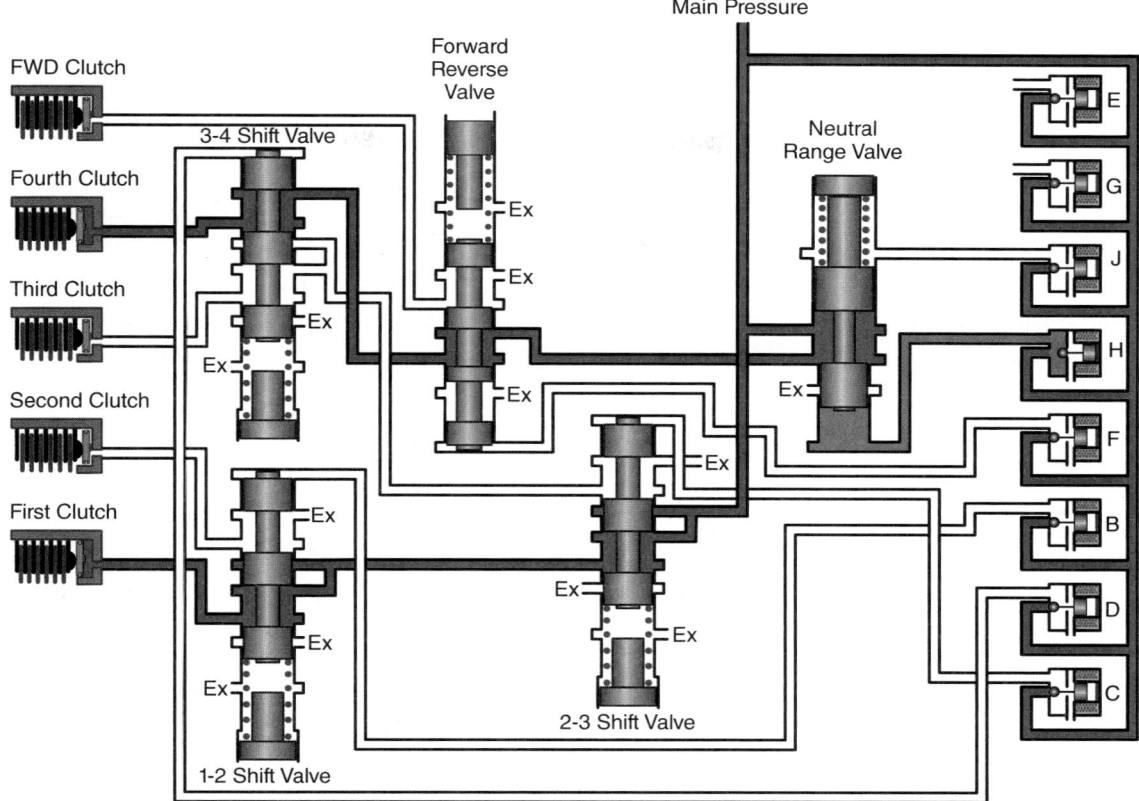

FIGURE 49-19 Reverse. The shift to reverse starts when neutral latching solenoid J is momentarily energized to close and non-latching solenoid H is energized to open.

ATEC/CEC Reverse

Reverse begins with the transmission in neutral. Recall from Figure 49-13 that, in neutral, main pressure flows from the direction priority valve, down through the 2-3 shift valve and the 1-2 shift valve, and into the first clutch, applying it. Latching solenoid J is in the open position holding the neutral-range valve down in its bore, causing main pressure to be blocked at the valve. As the driver shifts the selector to reverse, solenoid J is momentarily energized to close its valve and exhaust the pressure above the neutral-range valve at the solenoid. Non-latching solenoid H becomes energized, and that sends pressure to the bottom of the neutral range valve, moving it up in its bore. This redirects the main pressure deadheaded at the neutral-range valve towards the forward reverse valve. Latching solenoid F is closed, and spring pressure holds the forward reverse valve down in its bore. The main pressure flows through the forward reverse valve to the 3-4 shift valve and on to the fourth clutch applying it. Since first and fourth clutch are applied, the transmission shifts into reverse (**FIGURE 49-19**).

Trimmer Operation

As in the hydraulically controlled Allison transmissions, shift quality is controlled by trimmer valves. A **trimmer** is an accumulator used in the ATEC and CEC systems to smooth out the shift process. Each clutch, with the exception of the forward clutch, has its own trimmer. Recall from the chapter on Hydraulically

Controlled Automatic Transmissions that trimmers work as a kind of accumulator system to slow down clutch application to make the shift softer. In hydraulically controlled transmissions, the speed of the trimmer operation is controlled by the trimmer regulator valve, which in turn is controlled by modulator pressure. As a result, at low speeds, shifts are slower and smoother. At high speed/load conditions, the trimmer works more quickly, resulting in faster and harsher shifts with less slippage.

In the ATEC/CEC system, the trimmer regulator valve is controlled by non-latching solenoid E. During light-load, low-throttle shifts, solenoid E is energized. Solenoid E lifts the trimmer regulator valve in its bore and blocks the flow of trimmer regulator pressure to the bottom of the trimmers. With no fluid pressure beneath the trimmer valves, the trimming action takes a longer time to accomplish, so shifts are softer and slower. Under heavier loads or higher-speed shifting, the ECU de-energizes non-latching solenoid E. When this happens, the trimmer regulator valve spring forces the valve back down in its bore. This allows main pressure to leak through the valve and into the bottom of the trimmer valves. Oil pressure beneath the trimmers causes the trimming action to speed up, so shifts occur faster and harsher with less clutch slippage. The ECU bases the decision on whether to energize solenoid E on several inputs, including TPS, VSS, sump temperature, and other inputs. Typically, however, solenoid E is energized until a throttle level of approximately 60% and de-energized at a throttle level above 60% (**FIGURE 49-20**).

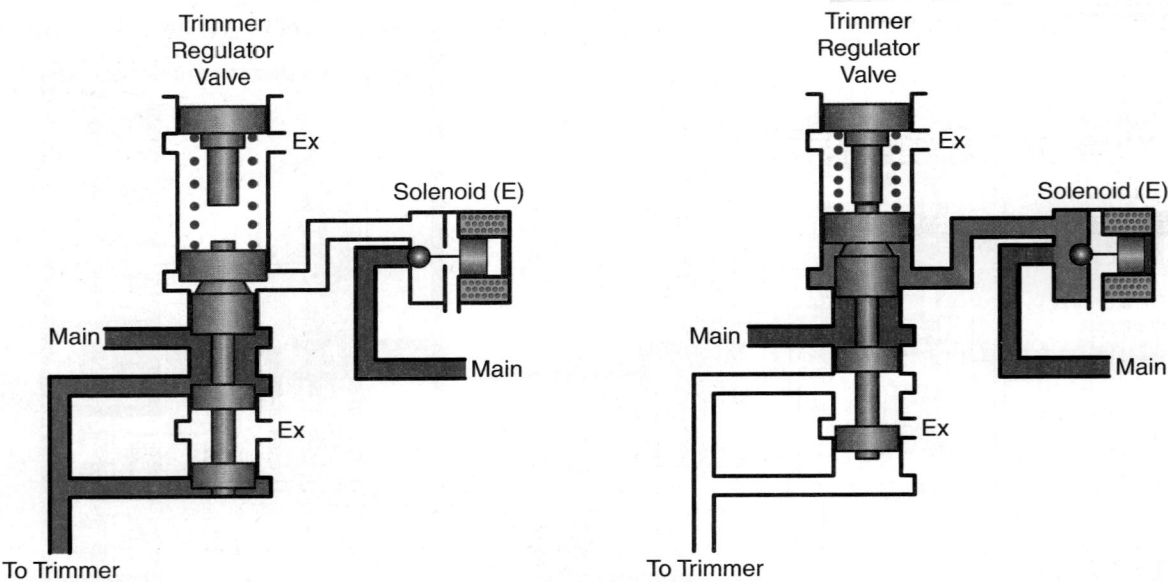

FIGURE 49-20 The trimmer regulator valve has only two positions. Shifts made with 60% throttle or less have full trimming and are softer, while shifts made above 60% throttle are harsher.

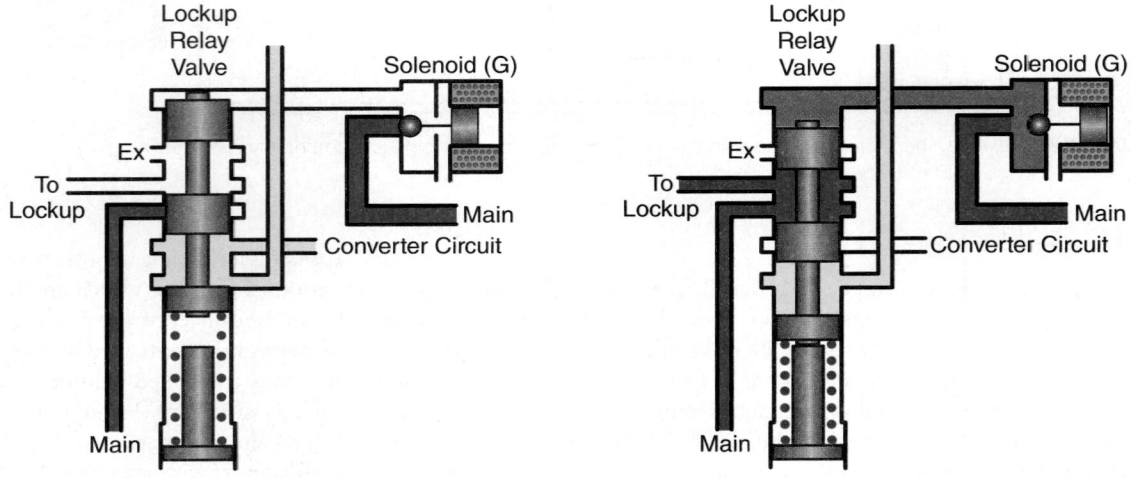

FIGURE 49-21 Torque converter lockup is controlled by non-atching solenoid G.

Torque Converter Lockup Control

Non-latching solenoid G controls the torque lockup relay valve. When the transmission ECU determines the correct conditions have been met, the transmission energizes solenoid G to move the lockup relay valve, thereby redirecting main pressure to the lockup clutch piston in the torque converter (**FIGURE 49-21**).

Transmission Operation during Electrical Failure

If electric power is lost, all of the latching solenoids stay in their current position, meaning that the transmission stays in the range it was in at the time of the power loss. Non-latching solenoid E is de-energized, returning the trimmer regulator valve to its at-rest position. Non-latching solenoid G is de-energized and releases the torque converter clutch.

At the bottom of the neutral range valve, non-latching solenoid H is also de-energized. Fluid flowing through the valve, however, causes the neutral range valve to remain in the open position. (This occurs because of the difference in the size of the lands where the fluid flows through the valve. The top land is larger in area than the bottom land, and so the valve remains open.)

Once the vehicle is shut off, fluid flow stops, and spring force pushes the neutral-range valve to the bottom of its bore. On restart, the latching solenoids continue to remain in position, but there is no flow through the neutral-range valve. The transmission, therefore, stays in neutral. This fail-safe strategy allows the vehicle to be driven to a shop after electrical failure. Once the engine is shut off, the fluid pressure holding up the neutral range valve is lost and the transmission does not go back into gear on restart (**FIGURE 49-22**).

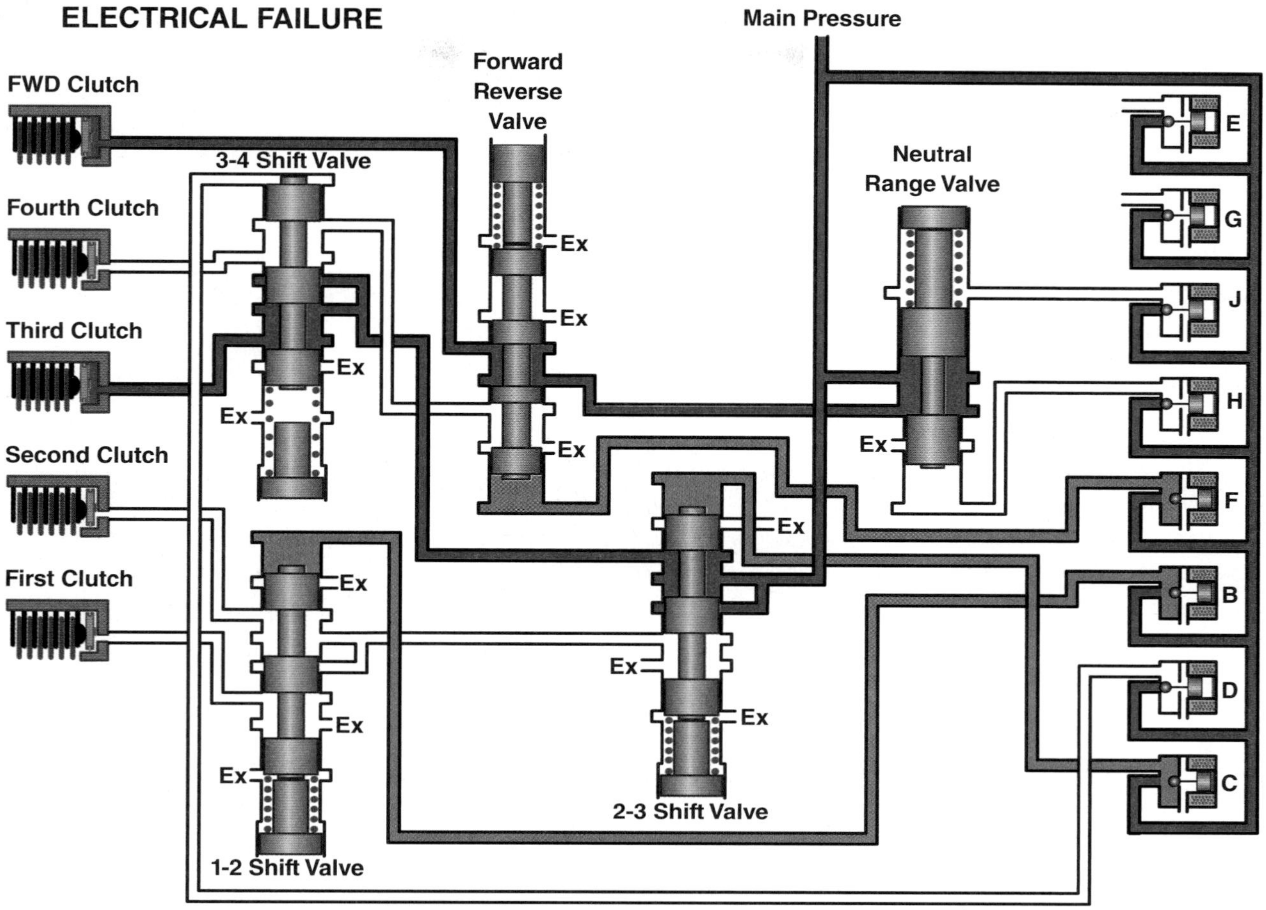

ELECTRICAL FAILURE

FWD Clutch

Fourth Clutch

Third Clutch

Second Clutch

First Clutch

3-4 Shift Valve

Forward Reverse Valve

Main Pressure

Neutral Range Valve

1-2 Shift Valve

2-3 Shift Valve

E
G
J
H
F
B
D
C

Ex

FIGURE 49-22 During electrical failure, all latching solenoids remain in their positions, so the transmission stays in the range it is in until the engine is turned off.

World Transmission

LO 49-2 Describe the operation and power flows of Allison World Transmissions (WT).

In 1991, Allison launched its World Transmission into the marketplace (**FIGURE 49-23**). The World Transmission was a completely new transmission with six forward speeds, including two overdrives. In addition to the six-speed design, Allison offers a seven-speed model that incorporates an extra "low" gear into the six-speed model. The seven-speed transmission has one extra planetary gear set and one extra stationary clutch. The "low" gear is obtained by passing the output of the traditional six-speed model through the fourth planetary set.

All designs of the World Transmission are equipped with what has come to be known as adaptive logic control. That means that the transmission is capable of adapting shift strategies based on drive-cycle experience. The transmission ECU constantly monitors and adjusts shift points and processes to maintain optimum shift quality, fuel economy, and driver comfort. Eventually, Allison dropped the World Transmission moniker and began referring to the model line by its series numbers (e.g., the 3000, 4000, and B series). In the truck and coach market, however, the name World Transmission is still widely used. In an attempt to align model functionality with the needs of particular markets, Allison

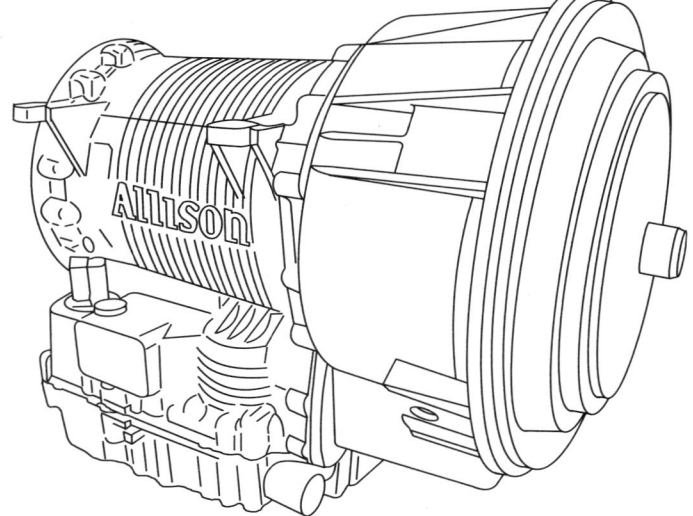

FIGURE 49-23 The World Transmission was introduced by Allison in 1991.

has recently created a long list of market-specific names—the Highway Series, the Rugged-Duty Series, the Motor Home Series, Transport/Shuttle Series, and several others. Despite the name changes, the transmission model numbers remain basically the same.

TABLE 49-2 Specifications for Allison's MD-3060-PR Medium-Duty Transmission

MD	3	0	6	0	P	R
Medium-duty or HD for Heavy-duty	#3 is medium-duty, #4 is heavy-duty	0 is close ratio, 5 is wide ratio	Number of forward speeds 6 or 7	Major revisions	Power take off provision	R is Retarder T is for drop box or transfer case

TABLE 49-3 Specifications for Allison's Bus Model Number B500 PR Transmission

B	5	0	0	P	R
Bus	Series 300, 400, or 500; higher # series can handle more input torque	0 is close ratio, 5 is wide ratio	Major revisions	Power take off provision	Retarder

TABLE 49-4 Allison's Highway Series Transmissions and Their Capacity Ratings

				RATINGS				
Model	Ratio	Park Pawl	Max Input Power[1] hp (kW)	Max input Torque[1] ft-lb (N m)	Max Input Torque w/SEM or Torque Limiting[1,2] ft-lb (N m)	Max Turbine Torque[3] ft-lb (N m)	Max GVW lb (kg)	Max GCW lb (kg)
1000 HS	Close	Yes	340[4,7] (254)[4,7]	575 (780)	660[4,7] (895)[4,7]	950[4] (1288)[4]	19,500 (8845)	26,001 (11,800)
2100 HS	Close	No	340[4,7] (254)[4,7]	575 (780)	660[4,7] (895)[4,7]	950[4] (1288)[4]	26,000 (11,800)	26,000 (11,800)
2200 HS	Close	Yes	340[4,7] (254)[4,7]	575 (780)	660[4,7] (895)[4,7]	950[4] (1288)[4]	26,000 (11,800)	26,001 (11,800)
2300 HS[5]	Close	No	325 (242)	n/a	450 (610)	950[4] (1288)[4]	33,000 (15,000)	33,000 (15,000)
2350 HS[7]	Close	Yes	340[4] (254)[4]	575 (780)	660[4] (895)[4]	950[4] (1288)[4]	30,000 (13,600)	30,000 (13,600)
2500 HS	Wide	No	340[4,7] (254)[4,7]	575 (780)	660[4,7] (895)[4,7]	950[4] (1288)[4]	33,000 (15,000)	33,000 (15,000)
2550 HS[7]	Wide	Yes	340 (254)	575 (780)	660[4] (895)[4]	950[4] (1288)[4]	30,000 (13,600)	30,000 (13,600)
3000 HS	Close	n/a	370 (276)	1100 (1491)	1250[6] (1695)[6]	1600[4] (2169)	80,000 (36,288)	80,000 (36,288)
4000 HS	Close	n/a	565 (421)	1770 (2400)	1850[8] (2508)[8]	2600 (3525)	–	–
4500 HS	Wide	n/a	565 (421)	1650 (2237)	1850[8] (2508)[8]	2600 (3525)	–	–

[1] Gross ratings as defined by ISO 1585 or SAE J1995. [2] SEM = engine controls with Shift Energy Management. [3] Turbine torque limit based on iSCAAN standard deductions. [4] SEM and torque limiting are required to obtain this rating. [5] Only available with VORTEC 8.1L gasoline-powered engine applications. [6] Requires Allison Transmission engine-transmission combination approval. Only available in gears three through six. [7] Check with your OEM to ensure offerings. [8] Only available in gears three through six.

Source: Information from Allison International, Inc. Permission requested.

The World Transmissions came in three general series:

- MD series for medium-duty
- HD series for heavy-duty applications
- B series for Bus and Coach applications

Specifications for model number MD-3060-PR are in **TABLE 49-2** and Allison's specifications for bus model number B490 PR are in **TABLE 49-3**.

In 1999, Allison introduced the 1000, 2000, and 2400 series transmissions. These lighter-duty transmissions shared the same power flow and geartrain design as the World Transmission. A key difference, however, was in the control system. In the lighter series of transmissions, the control system uses a quite different design than the original **World Transmission Electronic Control (WTEC)** systems—WTEC, WTEC II, and WTEC III.

The addition of the 1000, 2000, and 2400 series transmissions enabled Allison to match transmissions to a variety of engines that produce between 165 and 565 hp (121–421 kW) and generate from 420 to 1850 ft-lb of torque (568–2508 Nm). **TABLE 49-4** lists the models in Allison's Highway series and the transmission capacity rating of each.

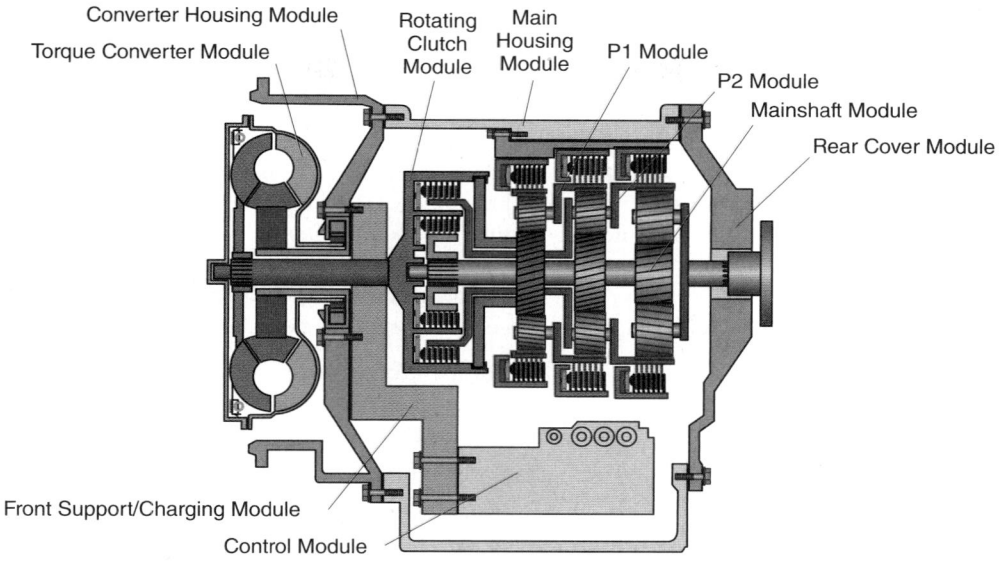

FIGURE 49-24 The World Transmission is modular in design.

World Transmissions—3000, 4000, and B Series

The six-speed World Transmission uses three planetary gear sets. They are named P1, P2, and P3 and are numbered from front to back. The transmission also uses five hydraulic clutches, again numbered from front to back. C-1 and C-2 are rotating clutches contained in the rotating clutch module, which can be used to provide input to the transmission. Clutches C-3, C-4, and C-5 are stationary clutches.

The 4000 series transmission is also available in a seven-speed model, which features an extra planetary gear set and an additional stationary clutch C-6. The seventh speed is an extra low gear for starting out. The 3000 series transmissions are available with a transfer case (drop box) for four-wheel drive operation. These transmissions also feature an extra planetary gear set in the transfer case and two more clutches (C-6 and C-7). The C-6 clutch provides an extra low forward speed through the transfer case when applied. The C-7 clutch locks the front and rear wheel drives together for low-traction situations.

The World Transmission design is divided into modules or major component groups (**FIGURE 49-24**). The modules are as follows:

- Torque converter module
- Torque converter housing module
- Electrohydraulic Control module
- Front support/charging pump module
- Rotating clutch module
- Rear cover module
- Mainshaft module
- P1 planetary module
- P2 planetary module
- Main housing module

Modules

Torque Converter Module The torque converter module is a typical lockup torque converter. The lockup clutch

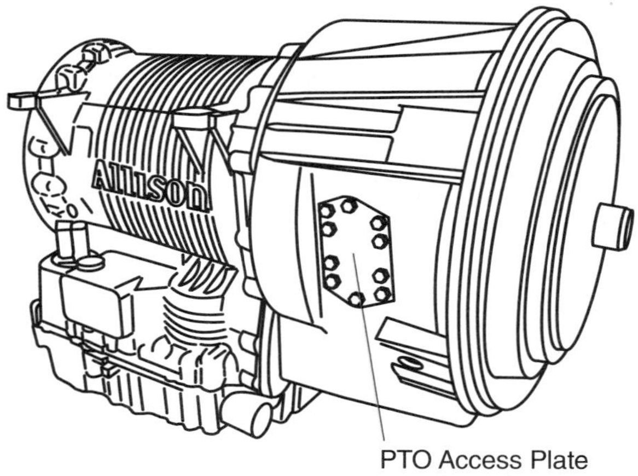

FIGURE 49-25 World Transmission models with power take-off provision have PTO access plates on both sides of the torque converter housing module.

incorporates a torsional damper to reduce shock on lock-up engagement and reduce the impact of engine torsional vibrations on the rest of the driveline. The torque converter hub drives the front charging pump directly on 3000, 4000, and B series without PTO provision. With PTO provision, the input converter drive hub drives the PTO gear which, in turn, drives the charging pump. The input torque converter has raised ribs on it. The engine speed sensor uses those ribs to sense engine rpm.

Torque Converter Housing Module The torque converter housing module bolts the transmission to the rear of the engine flywheel housing. Likewise, the torque converter housing is also bolted to the transmission main housing. A gasket seals the connection between the torque converter housing and the main housing. The torque converter housing module also has access plates for PTOs on the left and right side on models with PTO provision (**FIGURE 49-25**).

Electrohydraulic Control Module The **electrohydraulic control module** is attached to the bottom of the main housing module. The module houses the electric solenoids and the various valves necessary to control the transmission operation. Also contained in the electrohydraulic control module are the lube and main pressure filters and the pressure taps for main pressure, as well as for each of the clutch-apply passages. Finally, the electrohydraulic control module also includes the internal solenoid and switch harness and the pass-through connector that attach the module to the vehicle harness.

A gasket seals the electrohydraulic control module to the bottom of the main housing module. Care must be taken when separating the module. First, remove all of the attaching bolts. Then, break the gasket seal only at the specified pry points.

Front Support/Charging Pump Module The front support/charging pump module includes the gerotor-style charging pump assembly, the front support bushings and bearings, and the stator support shaft. The module bolts to the main housing module and is sealed with a gasket.

Main Housing Module The main housing module contains all of the transmission's internal components. When all other modules are removed from the housing, the C-5 clutch plates, the C-3 and C-4 clutch assemblies, and the P-1 ring gear remain in the housing.

Rotating Clutch Module The rotating clutch module is attached to the turbine shaft and contains the two rotating clutches C-1 and C-2 (**FIGURE 49-26**). When applied, C-1 transfers rotational power from the turbine shaft to the mainshaft module. When C-2 is applied, it transfers rotational power to the P-2 carrier. There is a third piston inside the rotating clutch module called the balance piston; it is located between

the C-1 piston return spring assembly and the C-1 pressure plate. The balance piston traps lubrication pressure between itself and the C1 piston. This trapped lubrication pressure is balanced against exhaust backfill pressure behind the C1 piston. The balance of pressures enhances control of exhausting and applying rotating clutches. The balance piston also provides a base for the C1 spring assembly to work against when returning the C1 piston to its seat.

Another component of the rotation clutch module is the P-1 planetary sun gear. Input torque is available at the P-1 sun gear whenever the module is rotating.

Mainshaft Module The P-2 and P-3 sun gears are splined to the mainshaft module, so rotating power is transferred to the sun gears when C-1 clutch is applied and the turbine shaft is turning.

Planetary Modules The P-1 planetary module consists of the P-1 carrier and the P-2 ring gear. They are splined to each other and held together by a snap ring. The P-2 planetary module consists of the P-2 carrier and the P-3 ring gear. They, too, are splined to each other and held together by a snap ring.

Rear Cover Module The rear cover module is bolted to the rear of the main housing module and sealed with a gasket. The function of the rear cover module is to contain and provide support to the output shaft. The P-3 carrier is splined to the output shaft and is part of the rear cover module. Also included as part of the rear cover module is the C-5 clutch piston. On models with an output retarder, the output cover module is replaced with a retarder module. A **retarder** is any system used to slow a vehicle's momentum and augment the service brake.

Power Flows

The operation of the torque converter and basic planetary gearing concepts were covered in earlier chapters and will not be repeated here. Please review those chapters as necessary.

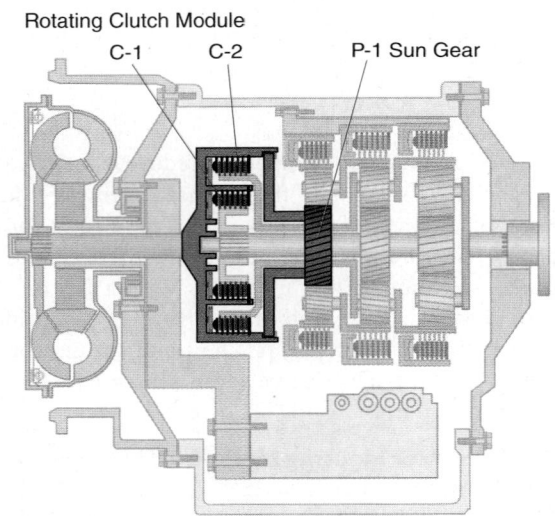

FIGURE 49-26 The rotating clutch module contains clutches C-1 and C-2 (the rotating input clutches), and the P-1 sun gear is splined to the module.

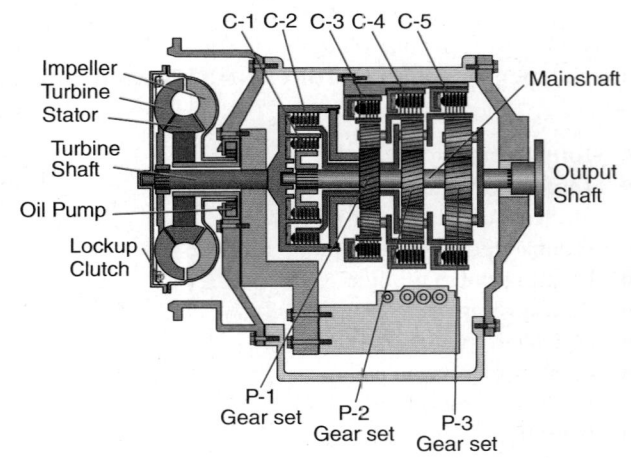

FIGURE 49-27 Cutaway view of a typical six-speed World Transmission.

To anchor our discussion of power flows, we will use **FIGURE 49-27**, which shows a cutaway view of a typical 6-speed World Transmission. As mentioned previously, the World Transmission has three sets of interconnected planetary gears numbered P-1, P-2, and P-3 (in order from front to back). The P-1 sun gear is part of the rotating clutch module and turns whenever the module does. The P-1 ring gear is not attached to any other component. It is, however, splined to the C-3 clutch plates, so when C-3 is applied, the plate holds the P-1 ring gear stationary. The P-1 carrier is splined to the P-2 ring gear and turns with it. The P-2 sun gear is splined to the mainshaft. The P-2 carrier is splined to the P-3 ring gear. The P-3 sun gear is splined to the mainshaft, and the P-3 carrier is splined to the output shaft. All power flows, therefore, must go through the P-3 carrier to reach the output shaft.

As shown in **FIGURE 49-28**, there are five clutches in the transmission numbered, front to back, C-1, C-2, C-3, C-4, and C-5. Three of the clutches are stationary (C-3, C-4, and C-5), are splined to the transmission case, and hold the following components when applied:

- C-3 holds the P-1 ring gear stationary.
- C-4 holds the P-2 ring gear stationary when applied. This also holds the P-1 carrier stationary as it is splined to P-2 ring gear.

- When C-5 is applied, it holds the P-3 ring gear and, therefore, the P-2 carrier stationary.

The two remaining clutches, C-1 and C-2, are rotating clutches. Both are contained in the rotating clutch module, which is splined to the turbine shaft. Both clutches enable rotational power to enter the geartrain. When C-1 is applied, it brings rotational power from the turbine shaft to the mainshaft and, therefore, to the P-2 and P-3 sun gears. When C-2 is applied, it brings rotational power from the turbine shaft to the P-2 carrier and, therefore, to the P-3 ring gear that is splined to it. The P-1 sun gear also enables rotational power to enter the geartrain. Because the P-1 sun gear is splined to the rotating clutch module, there is always rotational power at the P-1 sun gear whenever the turbine shaft turns.

Clutch Application Chart To achieve a powerflow through the world transmission two of the five clutches must be applied and as with previous Allison models one clutch is applied as soon as the engine is running. When the engine is started in neutral C-5 is applied, however if the vehicle is moving while in neutral range, the transmission attains neutral 1, 2, 3, or 4, depending on the speed of the vehicle this corresponds to clutch C-5, C-4, C-3, and C-4. This capability minimizes the rotational speed of the transmission's internal components while moving in neutral and readies the transmission for

SIMPLIFIED GEARTRAIN

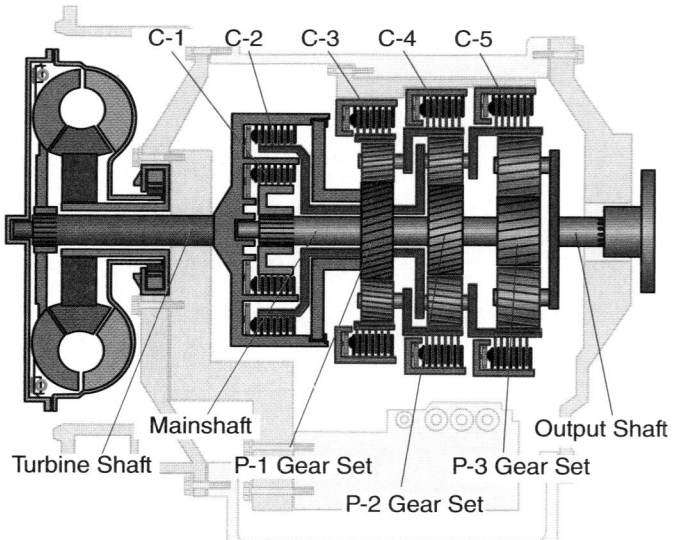

	R	N	1st	2nd	3rd	4th	5th	6th
C1			X	X	X	X		
C2						X	X	X
C3	X				X		X	
C4				X				X
C5	X	X	X					

FIGURE 49-28 Simplified schematic illustrating the geartrain of the World Transmission. All six-speed models share the same power flows.

NEUTRAL

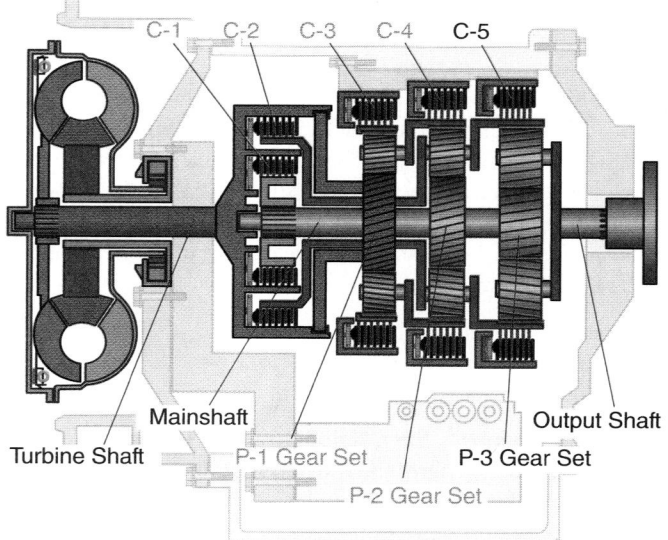

	R	N	1st	2nd	3rd	4th	5th	6th
C1								
C2								
C3								
C4								
C5		X						

FIGURE 49-29 When the vehicle is in neutral, only one clutch is applied—C-5, C-4, or C-3—depending on whether the vehicle is moving.

TABLE 49-5 Clutch Application Chart for Allison World Transmissions

Range	C-1	C-2	C-3	C-4	C-5
Neutral 1					Applied
Neutral 2				Applied	
Neutral 3			Applied		
Neutral 4				Applied	
First	Applied				Applied
Second	Applied			Applied	
Third	Applied		Applied		
Fourth	Applied	Applied			
Fifth		Applied	Applied		
Sixth		Applied		Applied	
Reverse			Applied		Applied

*Note: This chart covers all Allison World Transmissions except the seven-speed models, which have an extra clutch.

shifting into gear at that particular speed. This means that when the transmission is eventually put into a forward range, the transmission ECU only has to control one applying clutch to achieve the correct range for that speed.

TABLE 49-5 illustrates how each clutch in a World Transmission is applied in each gear. As the table shows, only one clutch at a time is applied when the transmission is in neutral. Again which clutch is applied depends on whether the vehicle is moving.

WT Neutral Power Flow The transmission can obtain four different neutral power flows based on vehicle speed.

As shown in **FIGURE 49-29**, in neutral the C-5 clutch is applied holding the P-3 ring gear stationary. No other clutch is applied, so rotational power does not go any further than the rotating clutch module and the P-1 sun gear. Since only one clutch is applied, the transmission is in neutral. If the vehicle is moving, the applied clutch changes based on vehicle speed. As speed increases, the transmission releases and applies clutches in the following sequence:

1. Release C-5 and apply C-4.
2. Release C-4 and apply C-3.
3. Release C-3 and apply C-4 again.

This shifting controls the rotational speed of the transmission components and prepares the transmission to shift into range at that speed. Only one clutch is applied at any one time, however, so the transmission remains in neutral.

WT First Range When any forward range is selected, the transmission shifts into first range. First range is a simple planetary gear power flow involving only the P-3 planetary gear set. In first range, the C-5 clutch is still applied, holding the P-3 ring gear stationary. The C-1 clutch is applied, which brings rotational power to the mainshaft and the P-3 sun gear. The P-3 sun gear is input, the P-3 ring gear is held, and the P-3 carrier becomes output. The P-3 carrier is splined to the output shaft, so first range is obtained (**FIGURE 49-30**).

FIRST GEAR

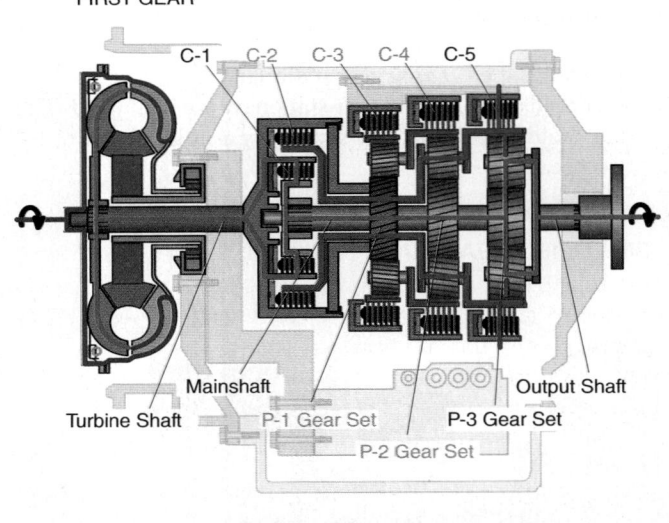

	R	N	1st	2nd	3rd	4th	5th	6th
C1			X					
C2								
C3								
C4								
C5			X					

FIGURE 49-30 In first range, clutches C-1 and C-5 are applied, and only the P-3 planetary gear set is involved in the power flow.

WT Second Range As the vehicle accelerates, it automatically shifts to second range if any range higher than first has been selected. Second range is a compound planetary gear power flow involving P-3 and P-2 planetary gear sets (**FIGURE 49-31**).

As the shift to second is made:

- C-5 clutch is released.
- C-4 clutch is applied.
- C-1 clutch remains applied.
- C-4 clutch holds the P-2 ring gear stationary.

SECOND GEAR

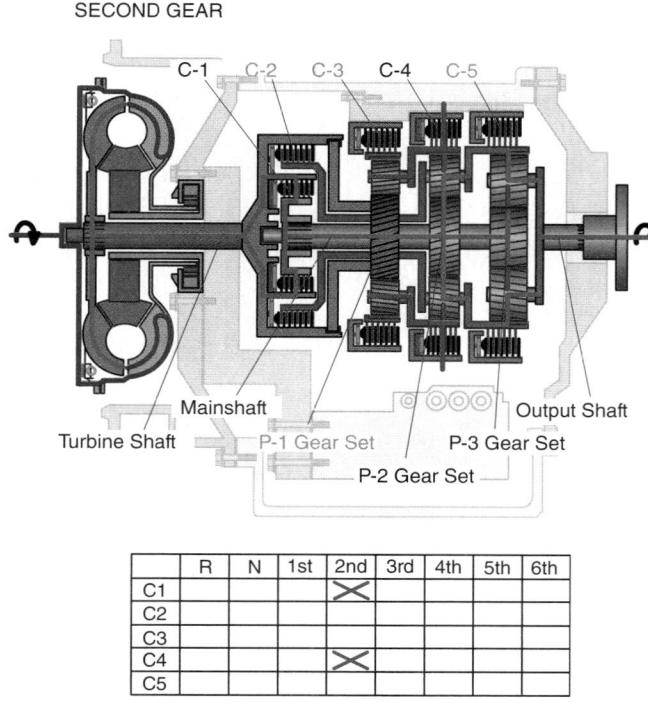

	R	N	1st	2nd	3rd	4th	5th	6th
C1				✕				
C2								
C3								
C4				✕				
C5								

FIGURE 49-31 In second range, clutches C-1 and C-4 are applied, and the P-2 and P-3 planetary work together to produce the power flow.

THIRD GEAR

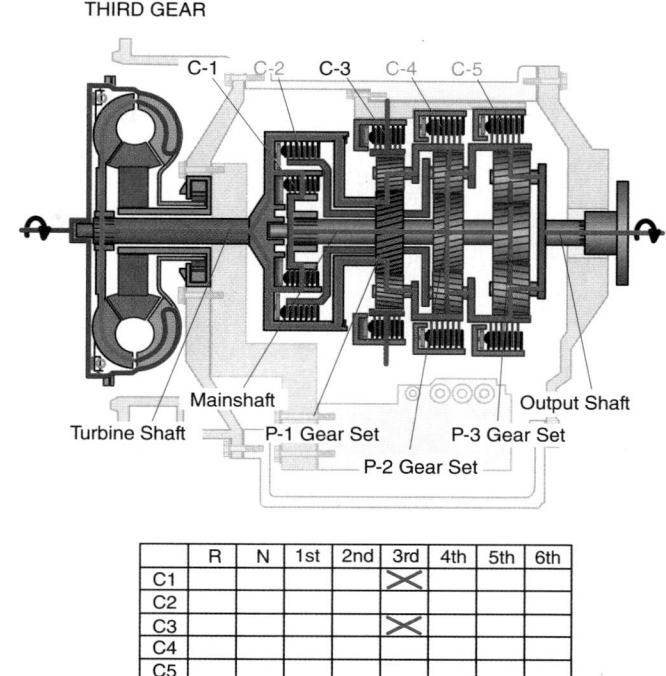

	R	N	1st	2nd	3rd	4th	5th	6th
C1					✕			
C2								
C3					✕			
C4								
C5								

FIGURE 49-32 In third range, clutches C-1 and C-3 are applied, and all three planetary gear sets work together to produce the power flow.

Those transitions bring rotational power to the mainshaft and, therefore, to the P-2 and the P-3 sun gears. The P-2 sun gear becomes input to the P-2 planetary gear set, and C-4 holds the P-2 ring gear stationary. As a result, the P-2 carrier becomes output. The P-2 carrier is splined to the P-3 ring gear, so the P-3 ring gear is turning as well. The P-3 sun gear is splined to the mainshaft and so still acts as an input to the P-3 planetary gear set. This means the P-3 planetary gear set has two inputs: the P-3 sun gear and the P-3 ring gear—which are not turning at the same rate. The P-3 ring gear is turning slower than the P-3 sun gear. This makes the P-3 ring gear act as a held member. In this configuration, the P-3 sun gear is input, the P-3 ring gear acts as a held member, and the P-3 carrier becomes the final output and is splined to the output shaft.

In this power flow, the only change to the output speed over first range comes from the rotation of the P-3 ring gear. Its movement adds to the rotation of the P-3 carrier.

WT Third Range As long as the selected range is higher than second, the transmission automatically shifts to third range when conditions are correct. Third range is a compound power flow that uses all three planetary gear sets (**FIGURE 49-32**).

When the shift to third range is made:

- C-4 clutch is released.
- C-3 clutch is applied.
- C-3 holds the P-1 planetary ring gear stationary.
- C-1 clutch remains applied.

Here's how the power flow occurs in the shift to third range. The P-1 sun gear is part of the rotating clutch module and, therefore, rotates with it. That makes the P-1 sun gear an input to the P-1 planetary gear set. The P-1 ring gear is held by C-3, and the P-1 carrier becomes output. The P-1 carrier is splined to the P-2 ring gear, so both P-1 carrier and P-2 ring gear rotate together. Because the C-1 clutch is still applied, the P-2 planetary gear set now has two inputs: the P-2 sun gear and the P-2 ring gear. The P-2 ring gear, however, is turning slower than the P-2 sun gear, so the P-2 ring gear acts as a held member. The P-2 carrier, then, becomes output of the P-2 planetary gear set, and the P-2 carrier is turning faster than it did in second range because of the rotation of the P-2 ring gear. The P-2 carrier is splined to the P-3 ring gear, so it is turning also.

As in the second range, the P-3 ring gear provides a second input into the P-3 planetary gear set, but now the P-3 ring gear is turning at increased speed. The P-3 sun gear is still being driven by the C-1 clutch and the mainshaft, so the P-3 sun gear still turns faster than the P-3 ring gear. The P-3 carrier becomes the final output, and it is splined to the output shaft. The ratio in third range is created by P-1 adding speed to the output from P-2 and then P-2 adding speed to the output from P-3.

WT Fourth Range As long as the selected range is higher than third, the transmission automatically shifts to fourth range when conditions are correct. Fourth range is a simple

FOURTH GEAR

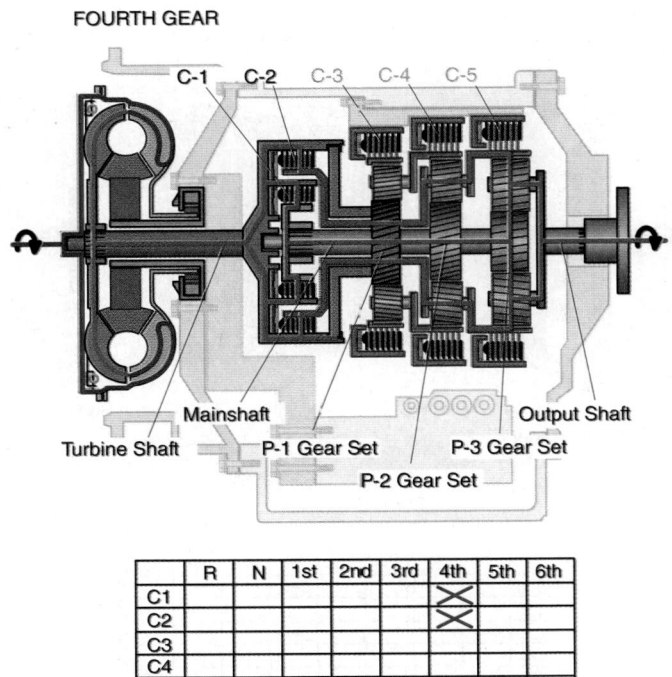

Turbine Shaft
Mainshaft
P-1 Gear Set
P-2 Gear Set
P-3 Gear Set
Output Shaft

	R	N	1st	2nd	3rd	4th	5th	6th
C1						✕		
C2						✕		
C3								
C4								
C5								

FIGURE 49-33 In fourth range, clutches C-1 and C-2 are applied, and all three planetary gear sets rotate together at the same speed, even though the power flow is through the P-3 planetary gear set.

FIFTH GEAR

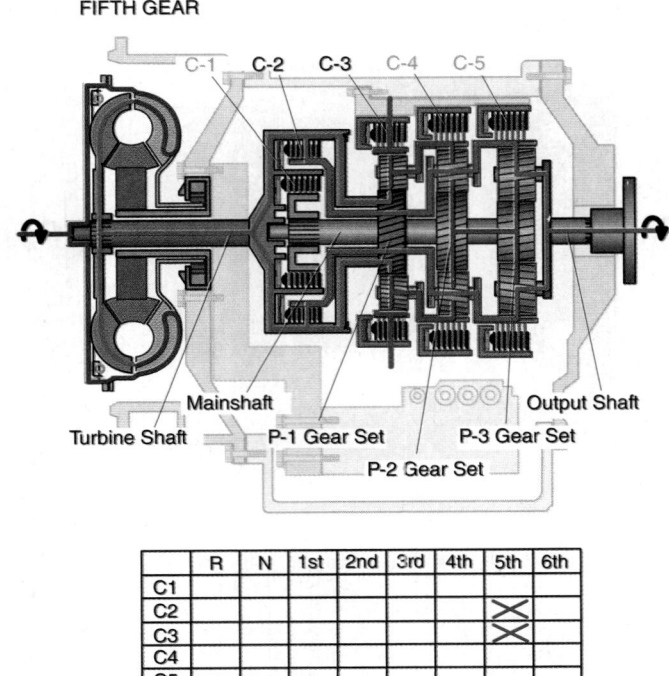

Turbine Shaft
Mainshaft
P-1 Gear Set
P-2 Gear Set
P-3 Gear Set
Output Shaft

	R	N	1st	2nd	3rd	4th	5th	6th
C1								
C2							✕	
C3							✕	
C4								
C5								

FIGURE 49-34 In fifth range, clutches C-2 and C-3 are applied, and all three planetary gear sets work together to produce the power flow.

planetary power flow that involves only the P-3 planetary gear set (**FIGURE 49-33**).

In fourth range, C-3 clutch is released, C-2 clutch applies, and C-1 clutch remains applied. The power flow is achieved in the following sequence: C-1 clutch delivers rotational power to the mainshaft and the P-3 sun gear; and C-2 cutch delivers rotational power through the P-2 carrier to the P-3 ring gear, which is splined to it. This gives the P-3 planetary gear set two inputs rotating at the same speed. The P-3 carrier must then also rotate at the same speed, as it is splined to the output shaft. This provides a direct or a one-to-one ratio.

In fourth range, even though the power flow is through the P-3 planetary gear set, the interconnections of the drivetrain components means that they all turn as one unit at the same speed x. Remember that the P-2 planetary has two inputs as well: the P-2 planetary carrier and the P-2 sun gear (from the mainshaft). That double input makes the P-2 ring gear turn at the same speed x.

The P-2 ring gear is splined to the P-1 carrier, and the P-1 sun gear is part of the rotating clutch module. That means the P-1 planetary gear set also has two inputs and, therefore, its ring gear must also turn at the same speed x. So, in fourth range, the rotating clutch module and all three planetary gear sets are all turning as one unit at the same speed as the turbine shaft.

WT Fifth Range As long the selected range is higher than fourth, the transmission automatically shifts into fifth range when conditions are correct. Fifth range is the first of

two overdrive ranges and is a compound planetary gear flow that uses all three planetary gear sets to achieve the final ratio (**FIGURE 49-34**).

In fifth range, C-2 and C-3 are applied and produce the following power flow. The P-1 sun gear is part of the rotating clutch module and, therefore, always provides rotational input to P-1. C-3 is holding the P-1 ring gear stationary, and so the P-1 carrier becomes output. The P-1 carrier is splined to the P-2 ring gear, and so it becomes one of two inputs to the P-2 planetary gear set. C-2 clutch is applied and supplies rotational input to the P-2 carrier, which is the second input to the P-2 planetary gear set. This causes the P-2 sun gear to become output as it turns clockwise at a higher speed than the P-2 carrier. The P-2 sun gear is splined to the mainshaft as is the P-3 sun gear. The P-3 sun gear becomes an overdrive input to the P-3 planetary gear set. The P-3 planetary gear set also has an input from the P-3 ring gear, which is splined to the P-2 carrier that, in turn, is being driven by the P-2 clutch. Because the P-3 ring gear is turning slower (at turbine shaft speed) than the P-3 sun gear, the P-3 ring gear acts as a held member. The P-3 carrier becomes the final output and is splined to the output shaft. In this powerflow the rotation of the P-2 ring gear actually slows down the output of the P-2 sun gear and therefore the input to the P-3 sun gear

WT Sixth Range As long as the selected range is higher than fifth, the transmission automatically shifts into sixth range when conditions are correct. Sixth range is the highest overdrive range and is a compound ratio that

SIXTH GEAR

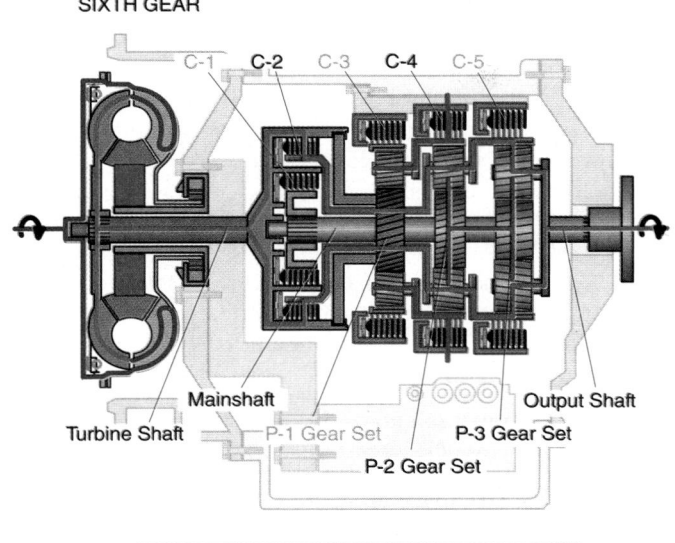

FIGURE 49-35 In sixth range, clutches C-2 and C-4 are applied, and the P-2 and P-3 planetary gear sets work together to produce the power flow.

	R	N	1st	2nd	3rd	4th	5th	6th
C1								
C2								✕
C3								
C4								✕
C5								

REVERSE GEAR

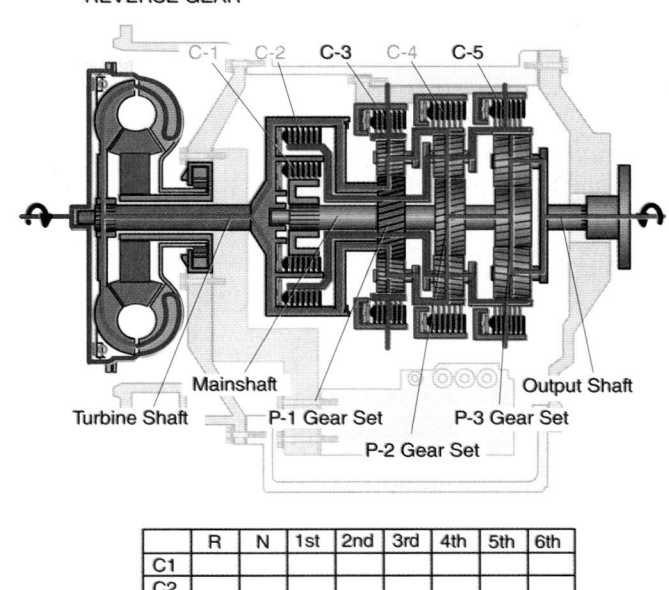

FIGURE 49-36 In reverse, clutches C-3 and C-5 are applied, meaning that rotational input comes from the always rotating P-1 sun gear. All three planetary gear sets are involved in the reverse power flow.

	R	N	1st	2nd	3rd	4th	5th	6th
C1								
C2								
C3	✕							
C4								
C5	✕							

uses the P-2 and P-3 planetary gear sets to achieve the ratio (**FIGURE 49-35**).

In sixth range C-2 and C-4 are applied, C-2 supplies rotational input to the P-2 carrier, and C-4 holds the P-2 ring gear stationary. That flow makes the P-2 sun gear output at an even faster overdrive than it did in fifth range. Why is it faster? Because when (a) the P-2 carrier is the input member and (b) the P-2 sun gear is the output the carrier, the pinion gears use the ring gear as a reaction member to push against in order to drive the sun gear. In fifth range, the reaction member (the P-2 ring gear) is moving away from the input member (the carrier), so the sun gear is not pushed as much. In sixth range, the ring gear is held stationary, and that allows the full reaction, or push, and allows the sun gear to have a higher speed output. The P-2 sun gear is splined to the mainshaft, as is the P-3 sun gear, so the P-3 planetary gear set again has two inputs: the P-3 sun gear and the P-3 ring gear. The P-3 ring gear is splined to the P-2 carrier and, therefore, driven by the C-2 clutch. The P-3 ring gear, however, is rotating slower (at turbine speed) than the P-3 sun gear (overdrive), and so the P-3 ring gear acts as a held member. That causes the P-3 carrier to become final output, as it is splined to the output shaft.

WT Reverse In reverse, all three planetary gear sets work together to create the power flow. Reverse range always starts from neutral gear. Recall that, in neutral, C-5 is the only clutch applied, and it holds the P-3 ring gear stationary. As the operator selects reverse, the C-3 clutch is applied and, in turn, holds the P-1 ring gear stationary. Neither of the rotating

clutches C-1 or C-2 is applied, so the rotational input in reverse must come from the P-1 sun gear. Recall that the P-1 sun gear is attached to the rotating clutch module and turns with it at all times.

So the power flow in reverse is as follows. The P-1 sun gear is input, and the P-1 ring gear is being held by the C-3 clutch. As a result, the P-1 carrier becomes output. The P-1 carrier is splined to the P-2 ring gear, making the P-2 ring gear input to the P-2 planetary set. The P-2 carrier is splined to the P-3 ring gear, which is being held stationary by the C-5 clutch, so the P-2 carrier is the held member in the P-2 gear set. Because the carrier is held, the P-2 sun gear becomes output in reverse. The P-2 sun gear is splined to the mainshaft, as is the P-3 sun gear, so the P-3 sun gear becomes reverse input for the P-3 gear set. The P-3 ring gear is being held by the C-5 clutch and the P-3 carrier becomes the final output and it is splined to the output shaft. The reverse power flow is illustrated in **FIGURE 49-36**.

Electrohydraulic Control— WTEC II and WTEC III

LO 49-3 Describe the operation of the World Transmission Electronic Control (WTEC) and later models WTEC II and WTEC III.

Allison's electronic control system was originally called **World Transmission Electronic Control (WTEC)**. Since the original model was launched, WTEC has gone through four revisions, including WTEC II and WTEC III. Each revision incorporated several improvements over its predecessor. The third revision was simply known as fourth-generation electronic control, and the fourth and current revision is known as fifth-generation electronic control. In the fourth generation, the electrohydraulic valve body and the control strategies were altered in major ways. For that reason, earlier WTEC controls are discussed separately from the fourth and the current fifth-generation electronic controls. Let's start by examining the WTEC II and WTEC III versions in greater detail.

Electronic Control Unit

As with earlier Allison transmissions, in the WTEC controls system, the Allison transmission Electronic Control Unit, or ECU, is completely drive by wire. That is, the driver has no mechanical input to the transmission.

The transmission ECU receives input information from a number of sources. Feedback information comes from the transmission itself in the form of output speed, input speed, engine speed, transmission temperature, transmission oil level, and the solenoids. The ECU also receives input from the driver's interface via the shift selector. Input from various optional input functions come through the vehicle interface wiring (VIW) or through the vehicle interface module (VIM). Finally, the ECU receives input from the electronic engine, namely from the throttle position sensor.

The transmission ECU then uses all of that information to control shifting, diagnose transmission operation, and control output and input functions that control the numerous available features of the transmission, such as shift interlocks, remote shift selectors, and PTO operation.

The transmission control also has various self-preservation strategies to protect the transmission from abuse. The controller inhibits neutral to range shifts if input rpm is too high and also prevents high-speed direction changes. If the driver tries to shift from reverse to forward while the vehicle is

in motion, the controller waits until the vehicle speed is near zero before allowing the change. If the driver selects a lower range than the current road speed requires, the transmission does not downshift until a safe speed has been reached. Transmission oil temperature is also closely monitored, and the controller modifies shift capabilities based on temperature to protect the transmission.

Solenoids and Solenoid Control

The WTEC II and III transmissions ECUs use solenoids in the electrohydraulic control module to control the shifting process. The World Transmission electrohydraulic control uses two general types of solenoids:

- **Normally open solenoids** that close when energized
- **Normally closed solenoids** that open when energized

Normally open solenoids allow fluid flow while de-energized and stop flow when energized; normally closed solenoids allow fluid flow when energized and stop fluid flow when de-energized.

In general, the solenoids redirect solenoid regulator pressure, which is used to control the position of the solenoid regulator valves below them. When solenoid regulator pressure is directed to the top of the solenoid regulator valve, the valve is positioned down in its bore and directs control main pressure to the appropriate clutch applying it. This process is illustrated in **FIGURE 49-37** under solenoid E. Main pressure that was dead-heading at the solenoid regulator valve is thereby able to flow into the clutch apply passage.

Solenoids A and B are normally open (N/O) solenoids. Solenoids C, D, E, and F are normally closed (N/C) solenoids. Solenoid A controls C-1 clutch; solenoid B controls C-2 clutch; solenoid C controls C-3 clutch; solenoid D controls C-4 clutch; solenoid E controls C-5 clutch; and solenoid F

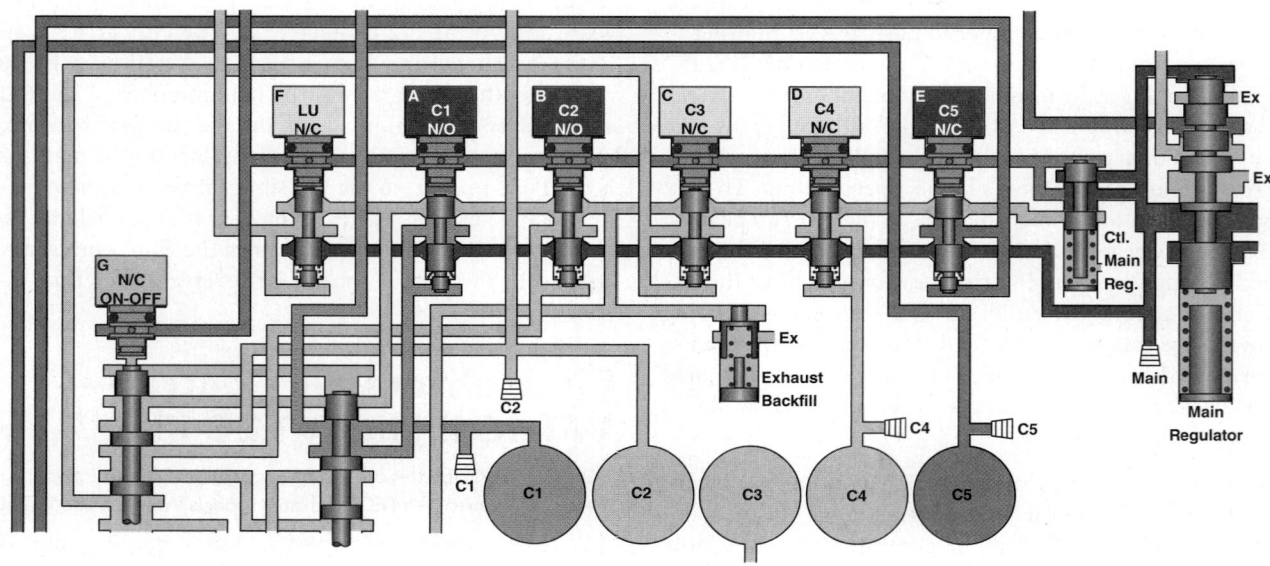

FIGURE 49-37 The WTEC II and III electrohydraulic valve body uses two general types of solenoids: normally open and normally closed. When they are open, they cause the valves they control to move.

controls the torque converter lockup clutch. All models of the Allison WTEC II and III transmissions contain an additional solenoid—solenoid G. Solenoid G is a normally closed solenoid that controls the position of the C-1 and C-2 latch valves. (Latch valves are covered in greater detail later in the chapter.)

The solenoids used with the WTEC controlled transmission are controlled by the transmission ECU using a pulse-width-modulated circuit. **Pulse-width modulation** means that the control command to the solenoid is pulsed on and off at a set frequency. There are two levels of pulse width modulation used—primary modulation and secondary modulation.

Primary modulation is the control used to actually open the solenoid to allow fluid flow to control the clutch application. The primary modulation control is set at 63 Hz, meaning that the control current to the solenoid is turned on and off 63 times a second. The computer alters the duty cycle of the solenoid current to precisely control the speed of the clutch application. The **duty cycle** is the amount of time during each 1/63 of a second that the current is allowed to flow to the solenoid.

Secondary modulation (or **sub-modulation**) means that the control current being modulated at 63 Hz and controlling the solenoids is itself being modulated at 7812 Hz. This sub-modulation allows the transmission ECU to provide a constant average current to the solenoids. The secondary or sub-modulation is too fast to interfere with primary modulation controlling the solenoid opening, but allows the ECU to

increase or decrease the current to the solenoids to account for differences in operating temperature, voltage fluctuations, and solenoid degradation. The secondary modulation leads to more consistent solenoid response.

Shift Control Logic

The WTEC is programmed to adapt to provide optimum shift characteristics, regardless of changes in vehicle load, terrain, and transmission component wear (e.g., solenoid degradation or clutch wear). The control has a flash memory that is programmed with the optimal shift calibrations for a given vocation. The transmission inputs—engine speed, turbine speed, output shaft speed, throttle percentage, engine and transmission temperature, etc.—allow the transmission to compare actual shifts to the pre-programmed optimal shifts (**FIGURE 49-38**).

The controller compares each shift in progress to a set of pre-programmed values. Then the next time a shift of that kind is made, the controller adjusts the control signal of the solenoid to make the actual shift profile match the desired shift profile.

The transmission has two adaptive modes—fast adaptive and slow adaptive. **Fast adaptive** is used when the transmission is new and makes large changes to bring the shift close to the optimal profile quickly. After the shift is close to the profile in memory (this is called convergence), the transmission switches to slow adaptive mode. In **slow adaptive** mode, the transmission makes small changes to the shifts. These small changes are designed to make up for transmission clutch wear and solenoid

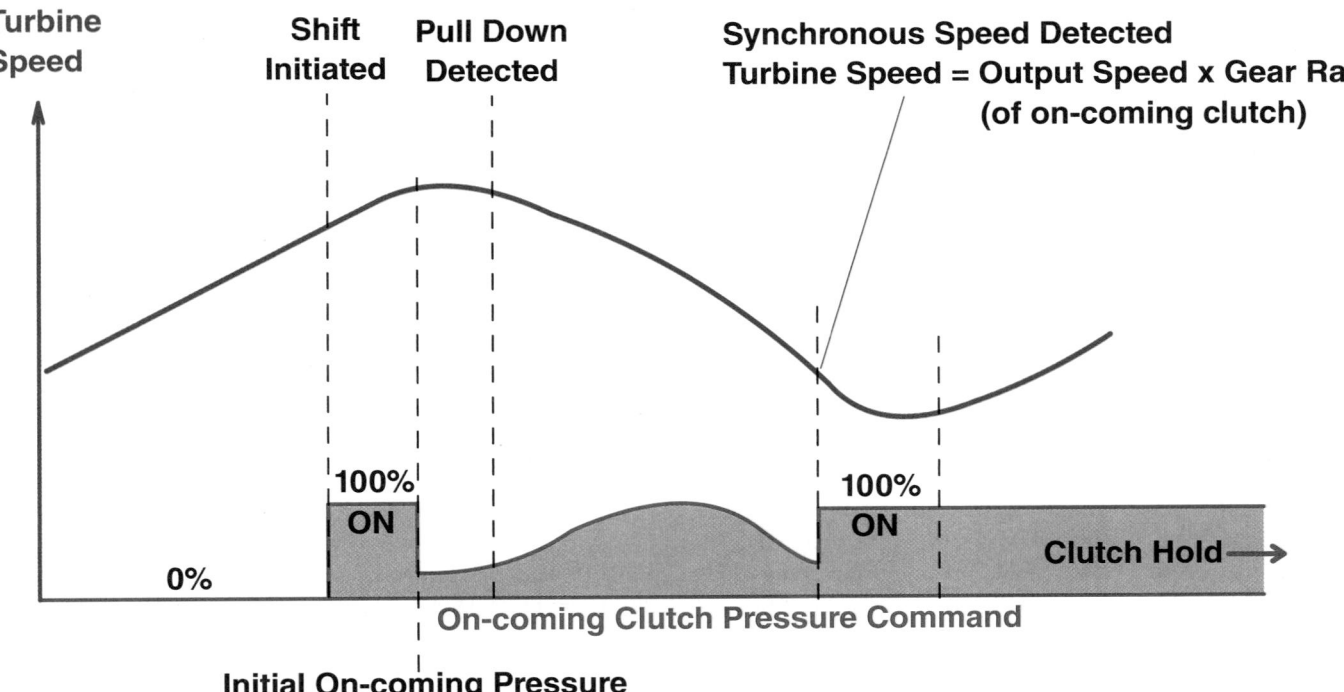

FIGURE 49-38 The transmission ECU monitors shifts in progress and tries to get them to match ideal shift characteristics programmed into the ECU memory by actively controlling clutch application pressures during a shift.

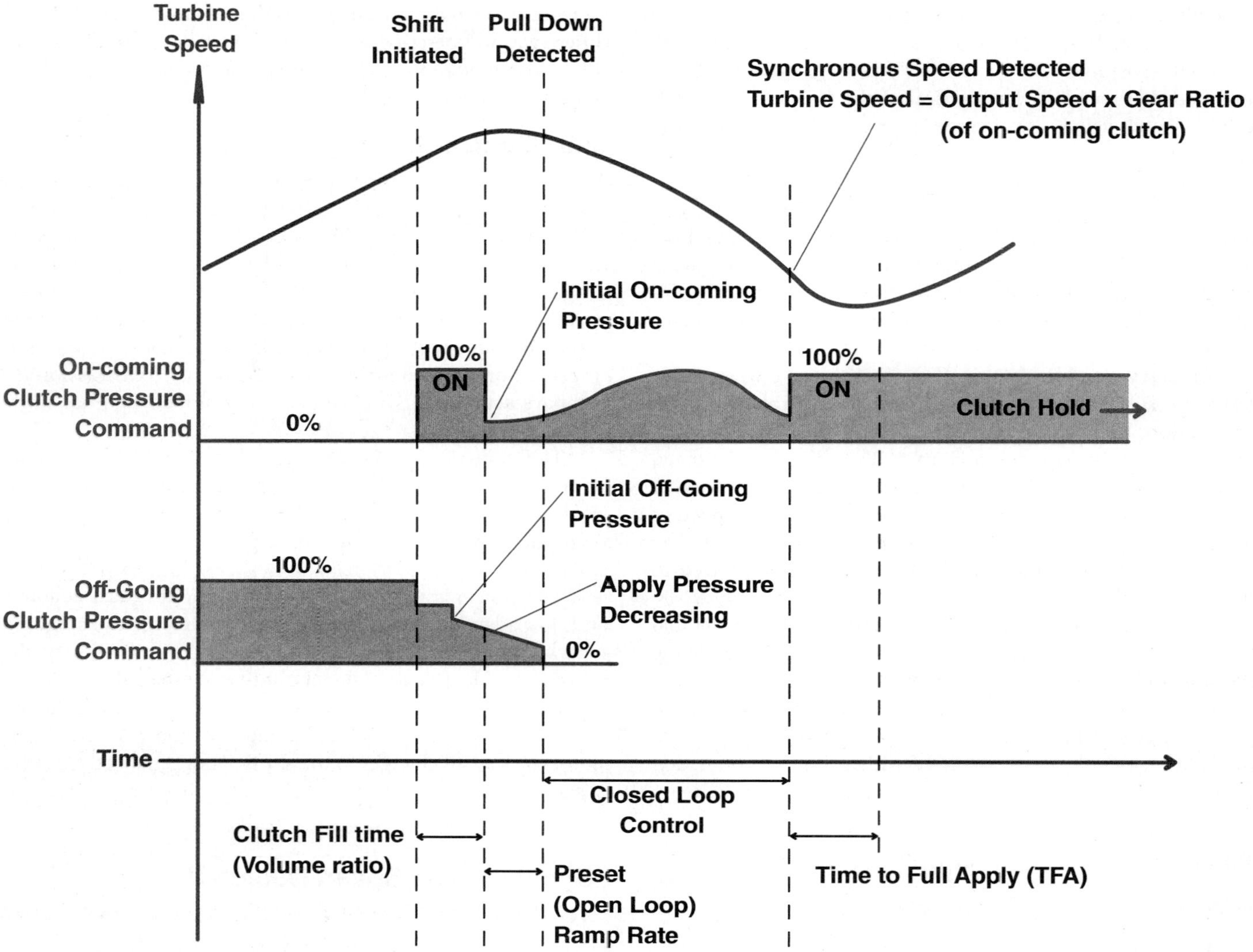

FIGURE 49-39 The transmission ECU sends signals to on-coming and off-going clutch solenoids to control the shift in progress.

drift or degradation. After a transmission has been rebuilt, or if a new transmission is being installed, the controller should be reset to fast adaptive, using the Allison DOC® software electronic service tool or a similar device, so the shifts reach convergence as soon as possible.

Shift Sequence

The transmission monitors turbine speed to determine when a shift should be initiated. **FIGURE 49-39** illustrates the shift sequence. As the turbine speed increases to the shift initiation point, the transmission controller commands the solenoid that controls the on-coming clutch to full pressure for a short time so that the clutch piston starts moving. This process is known as clutch fill or volume ratio. (Volume Ratio is an important diagnostic tool, for delays during this period can signal problems with specific clutches.)

At the same time, the off-going clutch control solenoid is being commanded to reduce the pressure on its clutch piston. After clutch fill, the transmission controller applies pressure

to the on-coming clutch piston at what is known as the fixed ramp rate, or **open-loop ramp rate** (meaning that the clutch pressure is being increased at a fixed rate). The off-going clutch pressure drops at a fixed **ramp-off rate** as well (meaning that the off-going clutch pressure is being reduced at a preset rate). This continues until the transmission controller detects turbine pull down. **Turbine pull down** is the reduction in turbine speed as the on-coming clutch starts to squeeze its clutch plates and the transmission is starting to attain the next range.

At this point, the off-going clutch is commanded to zero pressure, and the controller starts closed-loop control of the shift in progress. During closed loop, the controller is monitoring the decrease in turbine speed and trying to get the rate of decrease to match the ideal shift profile in its calibration. The controller constantly monitors engine speed, input shaft speed, and output shaft speed. The period of this monitoring and adjusting during a shift in progress on a World Transmission is known as **closed-loop control**.

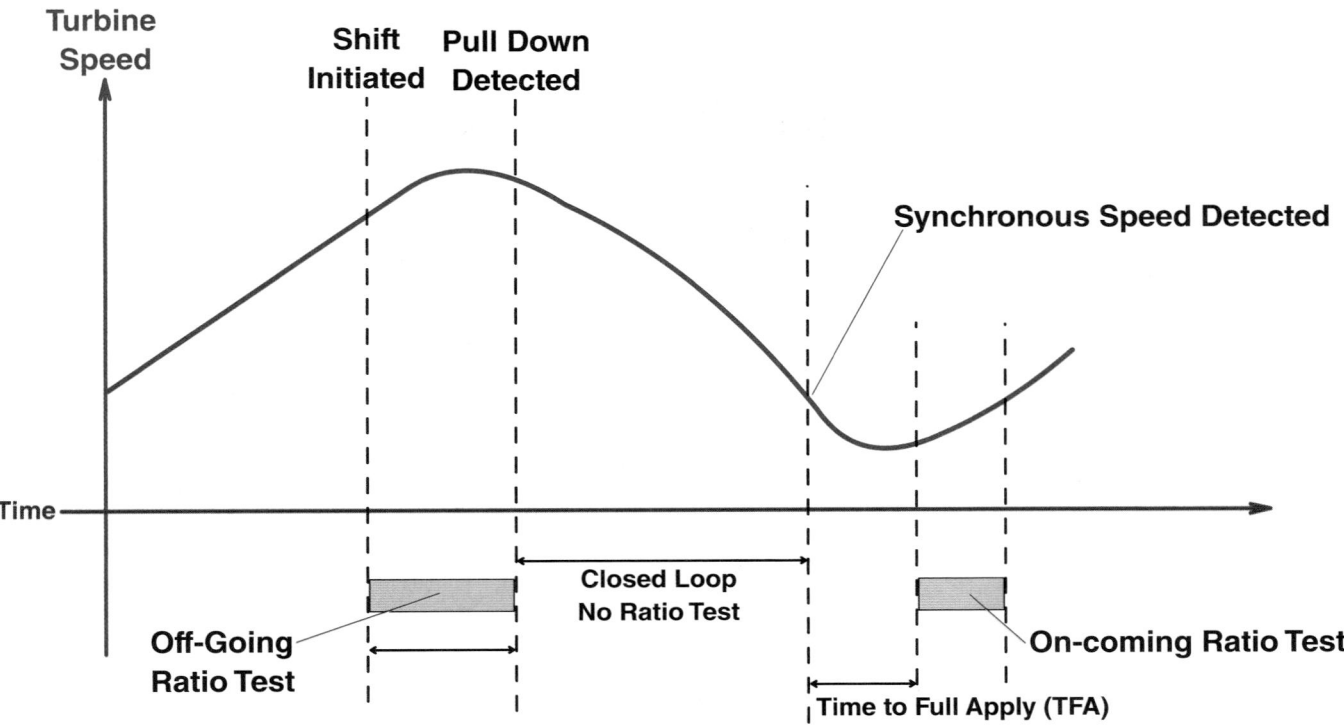

FIGURE 49-40 The controller performs range verification tests to ensure the transmission is in the correct range and not slipping.

The transmission ECU is actively adjusting on-coming clutch application pressure using pulse-width modulation to control shift quality. Closed-loop control continues until **synchronous speed** is detected. Synchronous speed occurs when the output shaft speed times the gear ratio of the on-coming range equals the input shaft speed. Synchronous speed signifies that the transmission has now attained the on-coming ratio and clutch slip is no longer occurring. At this point, the controller commands the on-coming clutch solenoid to 100% duty cycle to fully clamp the piston and the clutch plates with full main pressure. This period is called **time to full apply** (TFA). After TFA, the solenoid duty cycle is reduced to clutch hold. Full main pressure is maintained in the clutch with less current flowing through the solenoid.

Range Verification and Ratio Tests

The transmission controller initiates a series of tests at each stage of a shift in progress—and even when no shifts are in progress. When no shifts are in progress, the transmission controller initiates a **range verification test** to ensure that the transmission is in a selected range (**FIGURE 49-40**). This enables the transmission controller to compare output speed times the gear ratio to the turbine speed and determine if the clutch is slipping. For example, if the output speed is 250 rpm and the gear ratio is 4:1, then the turbine speed should be 1000 rpm. If it is higher, that means the clutch is slipping. If the range verification test fails for any reason, the controller commands the transmission to down shift to the last known attained range.

Ratio tests are performed at the beginning and end of a shift in process. The **off-going ratio test** is performed during the beginning of a shift in progress and assures that the off-going

clutch actually released. If this test fails, the transmission is once again commanded to the previous range. The **on-coming ratio test** is performed at the end of a shift in progress after synchronous speed has been detected and assures that the transmission attained the desired range. As with the range verification and off-going ratio tests, if the on-coming ratio test fails, the transmission is commanded to the last known attained range.

Hydraulic Control

The World Transmission electrohydraulic control module is a complex system including multiple elements. A schematic of the system in neutral gear is depicted in **FIGURE 49-41**.

Recall from the chapter on Hydraulically Controlled Automatics that the electrohydraulic control system starts with the hydraulic charging pump. The gerotor-style charging pump is driven by the torque converter pump drive hub and, therefore, turns at engine speed. The charging pump draws fluid from the sump and delivers it through the main filter and onto the MPRV, which is a normally closed spring-loaded valve. The fluid then flows through the MPRV and onto the solenoid regulator valves. Fluid pressure is also directed to the top of the MPRV, and as pressure increases, fluid forces the valve down in its bore. In moving down, the valve opens a passage to the torque converter. Further movement of the MPRV opens a passage to the exhaust hydraulic circuit (to the oil sump), and then the valve becomes balanced between spring force at the bottom and fluid pressure at the top.

This process sets main pressure for the transmission. In neutral and reverse, main pressure is at its highest—between 275 and 320 psi (19.3 and 22.5 kg/cm^2), depending on transmission model. Main pressure also varies, depending on the

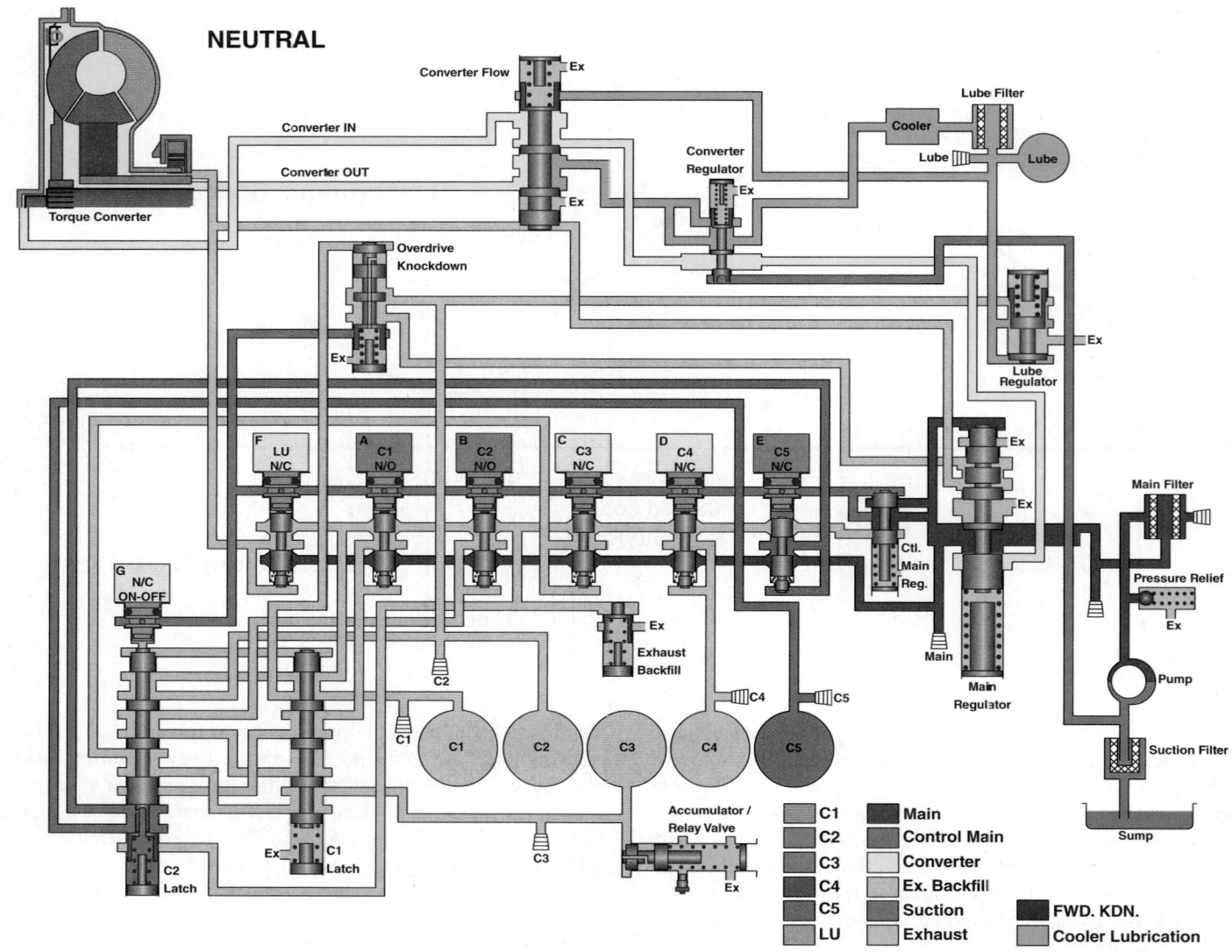

NEUTRAL

FIGURE 49-41 Hydraulic schematic of the World Transmission WTEC III.

TABLE 49-6 Main Pressure and Lube Pressure for Each Gear

MAIN PRESSURE		
Gear	**Lockup**	**Pressure**
Neutral and Reverse	Lockup not applied	275–320 psi (19.3–22.5 kg/cm²)
Forward with converter active	Lockup not applied	239–285 psi (16.8–20.0 kg/cm²)
2, 3, 4	Lockup applied	165–205 psi (11.6–14.4 kg/cm²)
5, 6	Lockup applied	155–175 psi (10.9–12.3 kg/cm²)

LUBE PRESSURE	
Gear	**Pressure**
Neutral, Reverse, 1, 2, 3	22 psi (1.5 kg/cm²)
4, 5, 6	17 psi (1.2 kg/cm²)

transmission range and operating mode. The circuit to the MPRV contains a pressure relief valve; this valve is set to exhaust main pressure at 600 psi (42.2 kg/cm²). **TABLE 49-6** shows the ranges for main and lube pressure for each gear.

Fluid going to the MPRV is also directed to the top of the solenoid regulator valve. As pressure moves this valve down in its bore, the pressure opens a passage to the solenoids. The valve becomes balanced at 100 psi (7.0 kg/cm²). This new pressure is known as control main pressure and is the pressure that transmission solenoids redirect to control the position of the solenoid regulator valves at the bottom of each shift control solenoid (solenoids A, B, C, D, E, and the converter control solenoid F).

► TECHNICIAN TIP

Main pressure varies slightly from model to model up to WTEC III.

The Allison Fourth-Generation Electronic control has more complete control of main pressure due to the modulated main solenoid.

Solenoid Fluid Flows

The solenoids control the flow of pressurized hydraulic fluid to apply the clutches necessary to attain each range. Solenoids are operated both to apply on-coming clutches and release off-going clutches as a shift occurs. Let's examine more closely the solenoid operation and fluid flows for each range.

WTEC Neutral Fluid Flow

As was illustrated in Figure 49-41, solenoids A, B, and E are energized when the transmission is in neutral. Because solenoids A and B are normally open, they stop fluid from flowing to their solenoid regulator valves and thereby prevent their respective clutches from being applied. Solenoid E is normally closed, so, when it is energized, its solenoid regulator valve is positioned down. That downward position acts to direct control main pressure to the C-5 clutch. The result is that the C-5 clutch is applied, and because it is the only applied clutch, neutral is obtained. This is the process for a transmission in neutral when the vehicle is not in motion.

If, however, the transmission is in neutral while the vehicle is moving, the transmission ECU energizes solenoid E, then D, then C, and then D again, depending on the rotational speed of the transmission's components. These solenoids correspond to clutch C-5, C-4, C-3, and C-4 again. By energizing those solenoids in that particular sequence, the ECU can control the rotational speed of the internal transmission components. Because only one of those solenoids is energized at any time, the transmission remains in neutral.

WTEC First Range

Solenoids B and E are energized in first range. As the driver selects first range, solenoid A is de-energized. Recall that solenoid A is normally open, so when it is de-energized, it directs solenoid regulator pressure to the top of its solenoid regulator valve, causing the valve to move down in its bore. This action directs control main pressure to the C-1 clutch applying it. Solenoid B remains energized, so C-2 clutch is not applied. Solenoid E remains energized, so C-5 also remains applied. Since C-1 and C-5 are applied, the transmission attains first range. This process is illustrated in **FIGURE 49-42**.

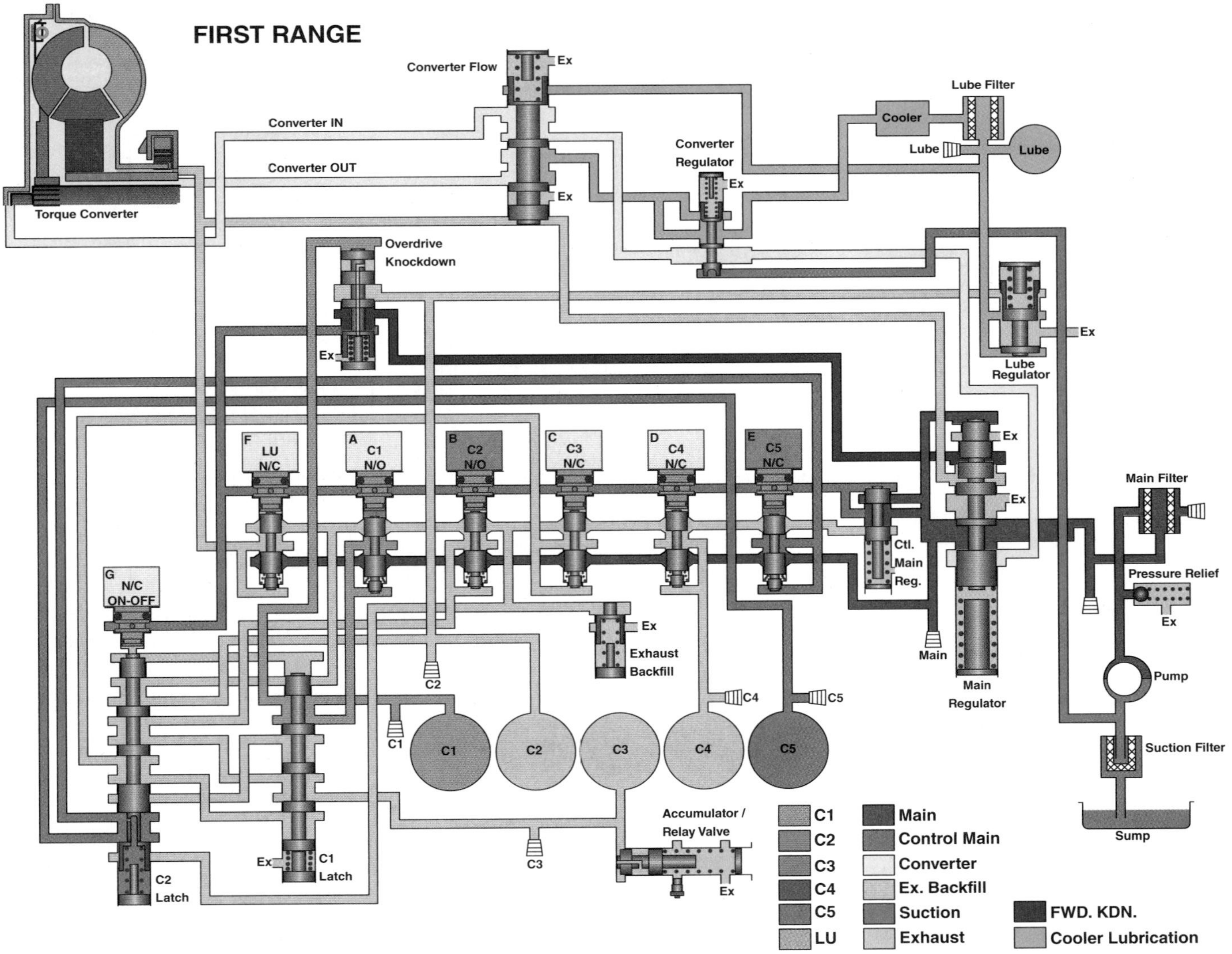

FIGURE 49-42 Hydraulic flow in a WTEC III in first range.

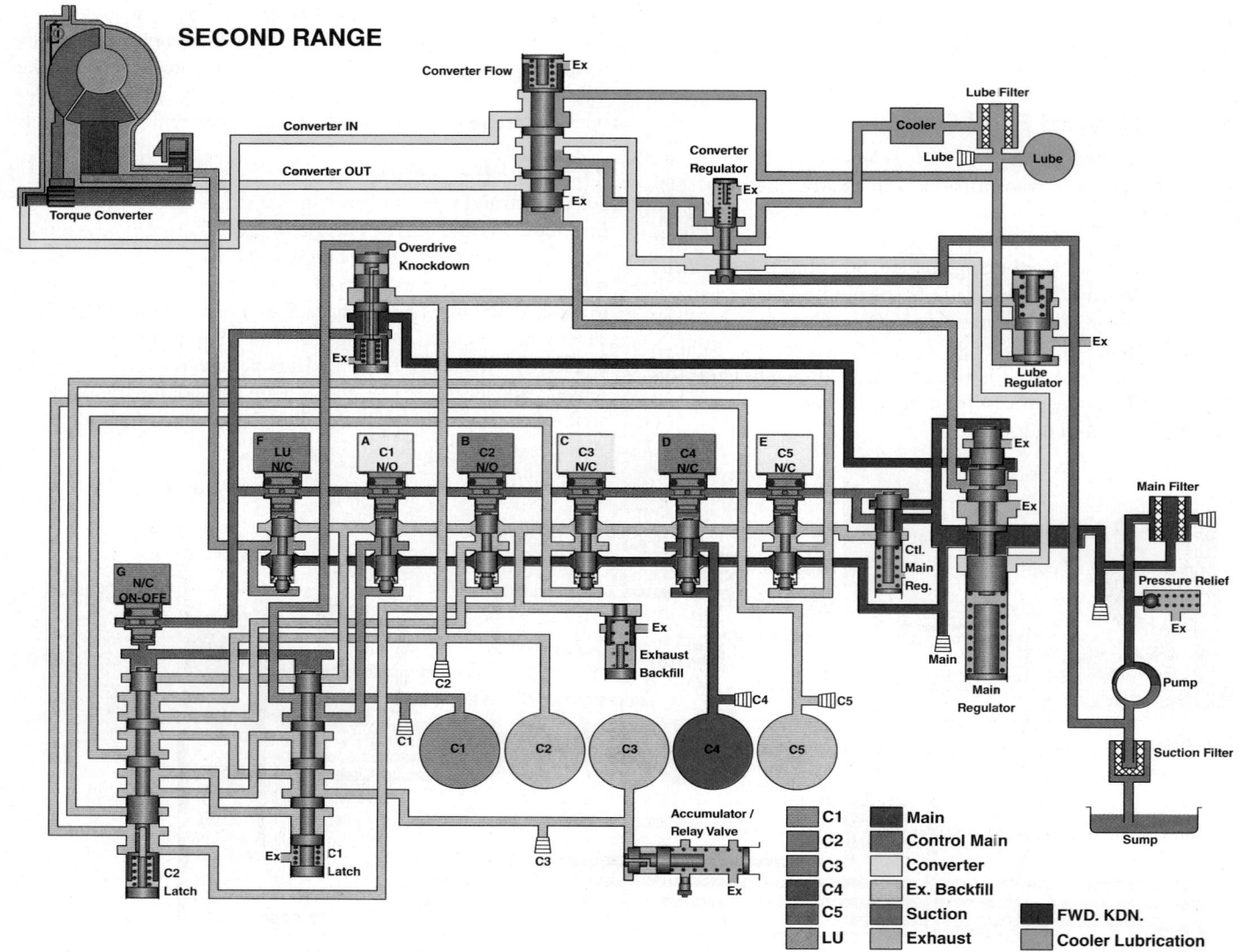

SECOND RANGE

FIGURE 49-43 Hydraulic flow in a WTEC III in second range.

WTEC Second Range

In second range, the solenoids B, D, and F are energized. As the transmission shifts to second range, solenoid E is de-energized, and solenoid D is energized. That action exhausts C-5 clutch and applies C-4 clutch. Solenoid A remains de-energized, so

C-1 remains applied. Solenoid B remains energized, so C-2 clutch is not applied. Because C-1 and C-4 are applied, the transmission attains second range, as is shown in **FIGURE 49-43**. At this point, solenoid F is energized and applies the torque converter lockup clutch.

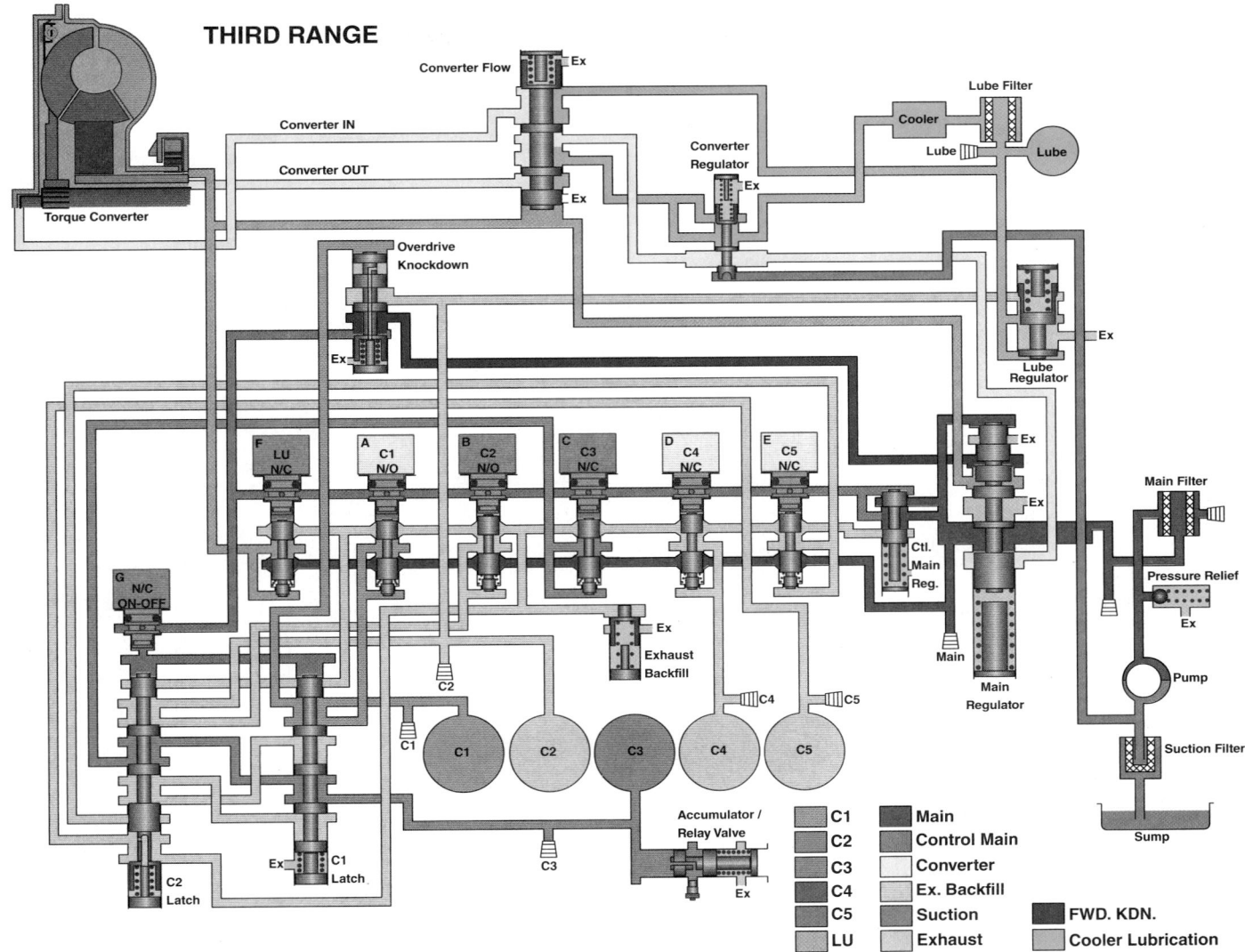

FIGURE 49-44 Hydraulic flow in a WTEC III in third range.

WTEC Third Range

In third range, solenoids B, C, and F are energized. As the transmission shifts to third range, solenoid D is de-energized, and solenoid C is energized. This process exhausts C-4 clutch and applies C-3 clutch. Solenoid A remains de-energized, so C-1 clutch remains applied. Solenoid B remains energized, so C-2 clutch is not applied. Because C-1 and C-3 are applied, the transmission attains third range, as is illustrated in **FIGURE 49-44**. Solenoid F remains energized applying the torque converter lockup clutch.

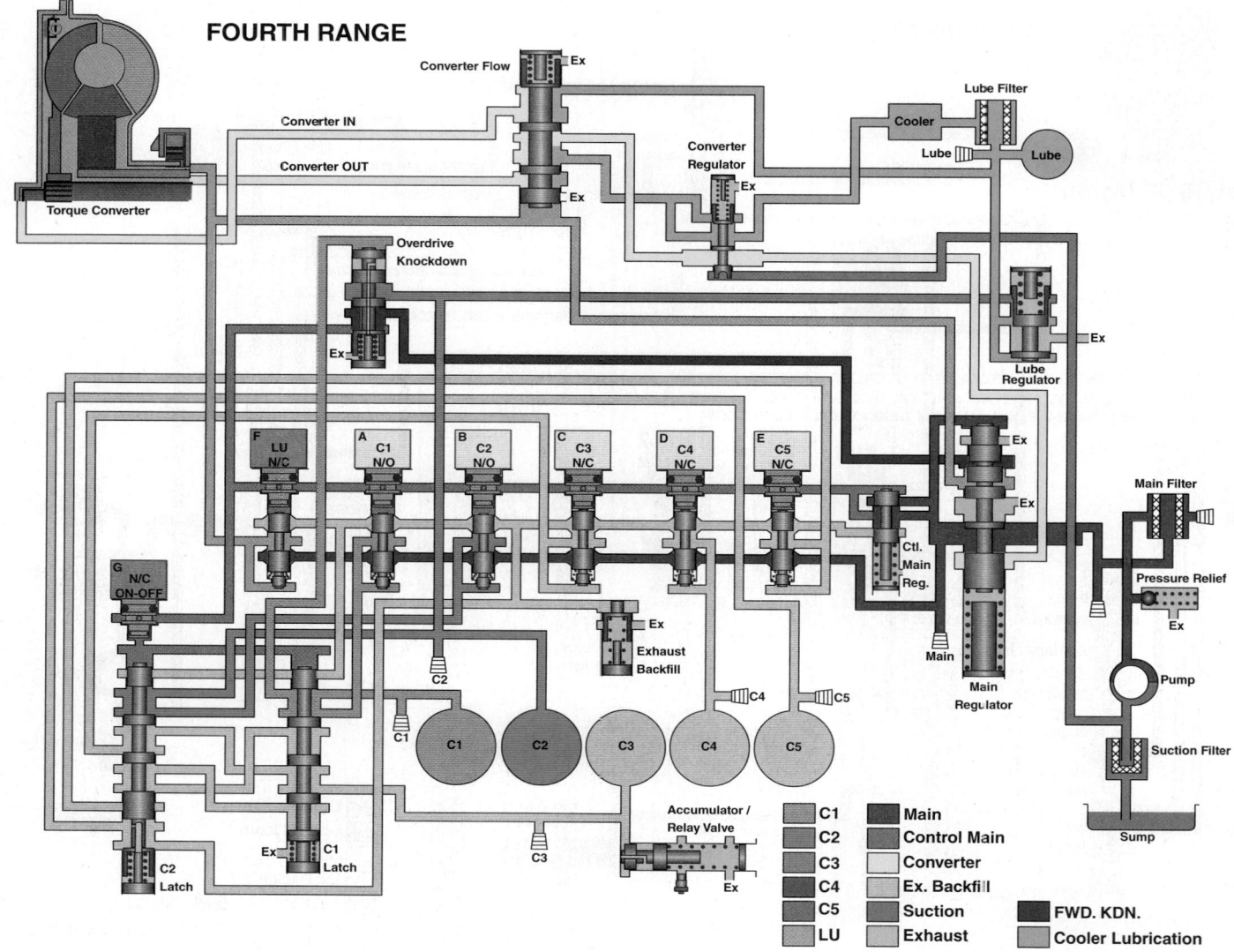

FIGURE 49-45 Hydraulic flow in a WTEC III in fourth range.

WTEC Fourth Range

When the transmission is in fourth range, solenoid F is the only energized solenoid. As the transmission shifts to fourth range, solenoids B and C are de-energized. De-energizing solenoid C exhausts the C-3 clutch. De-energizing normally open solenoid B causes its solenoid regulator valve to move down in its bore. That process sends control main pressure to the C-2 clutch and applies it. Since C-1 and C-2 are both applied, the transmission attains fourth range. **FIGURE 49-45** illustrates the system in fourth range. Notice that solenoid F remains energized applying the torque converter lockup clutch.

WTEC Fifth Range

In fifth range, solenoids A, C, and F are energized. As the transmission shifts to fifth range, solenoid A is energized, which exhausts the C-1 clutch. Solenoid B remains de-energized,

FIFTH RANGE

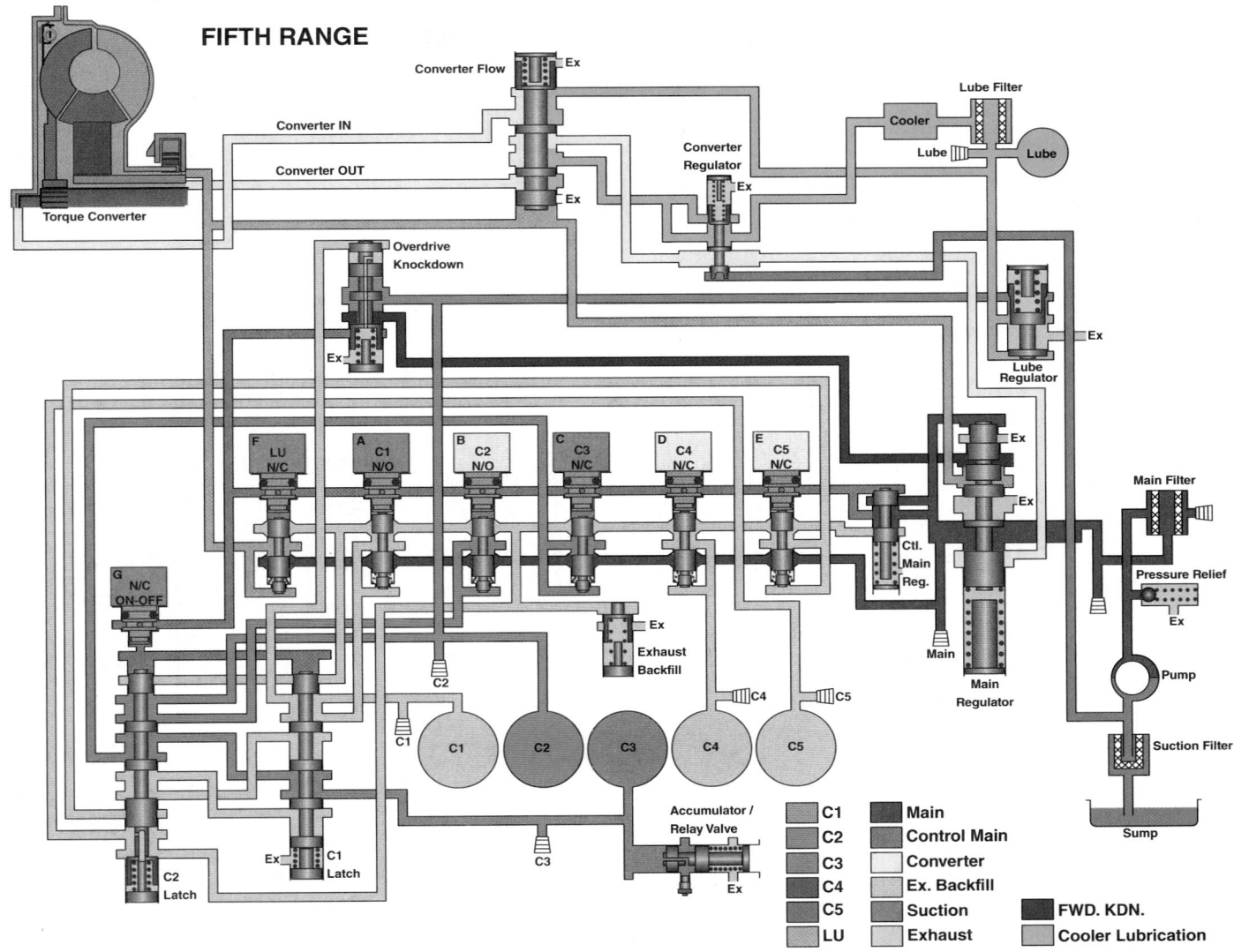

FIGURE 49-46 Hydraulic flow in a WTEC III in fifth range.

keeping the C-2 clutch applied. Solenoid C is energized, and that applies the C-3 clutch. Since C-2 and C-3 are applied, the transmission attains fifth range, as is shown in **FIGURE 49-46**. Solenoid F again remains energized applying the torque converter lockup clutch.

WTEC Sixth Range

In sixth range, solenoids A, D, and F are applied. Solenoid A remains energized keeping C-1 clutch unapplied. Solenoid B is

de-energized, so C-2 remains applied. Solenoid C is de-energized, exhausting C-3 clutch. Solenoid D is energized, applying C-4 clutch. Since C-2 and C-4 are applied, the transmission attains sixth range. This is shown in **FIGURE 49-47**. Solenoid F again remains energized applying the torque converter lockup clutch.

WTEC Reverse

In reverse, solenoids A, B, C, and E are energized. Reverse starts from a neutral position. Recall that in neutral,

SIXTH RANGE

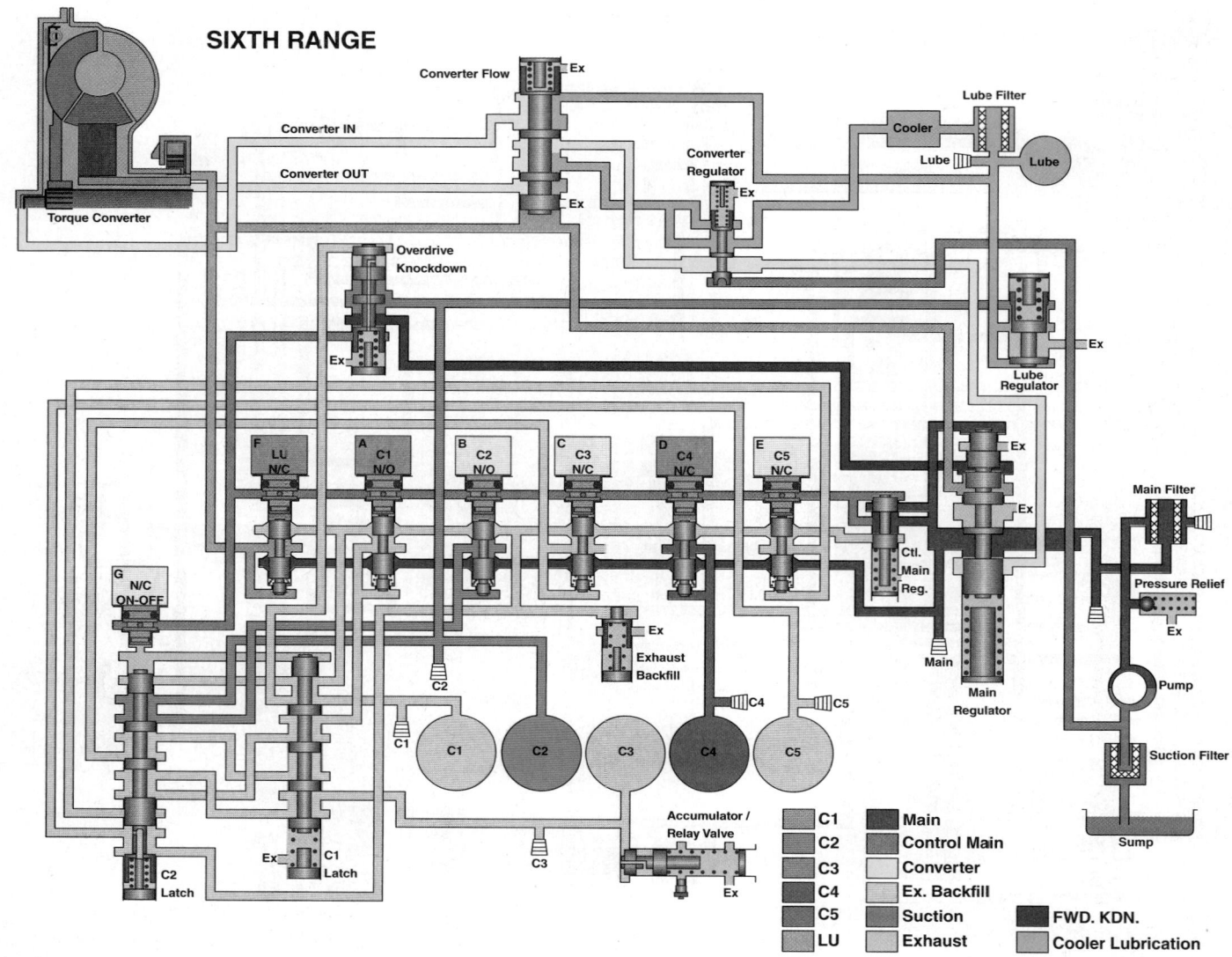

FIGURE 49-47 Hydraulic flow in a WTEC III in sixth range.

solenoids A, B, and E are energized. Energizing normally open solenoid A means that C-1 clutch is not applied. Energizing normally open solenoid B means that C-2 clutch is not applied. Normally closed solenoid E is energized, and that applies C-5 clutch. As the driver selects reverse, normally closed solenoid C is energized, which applies the C-3 clutch.

Since C-5 and C-3 are applied, the transmission attains reverse. **FIGURE 49-48** illustrates the WTEC III transmission in reverse.

As a review for the section on solenoid fluid flows, **TABLE 49-7** shows the position of each solenoid in each range.

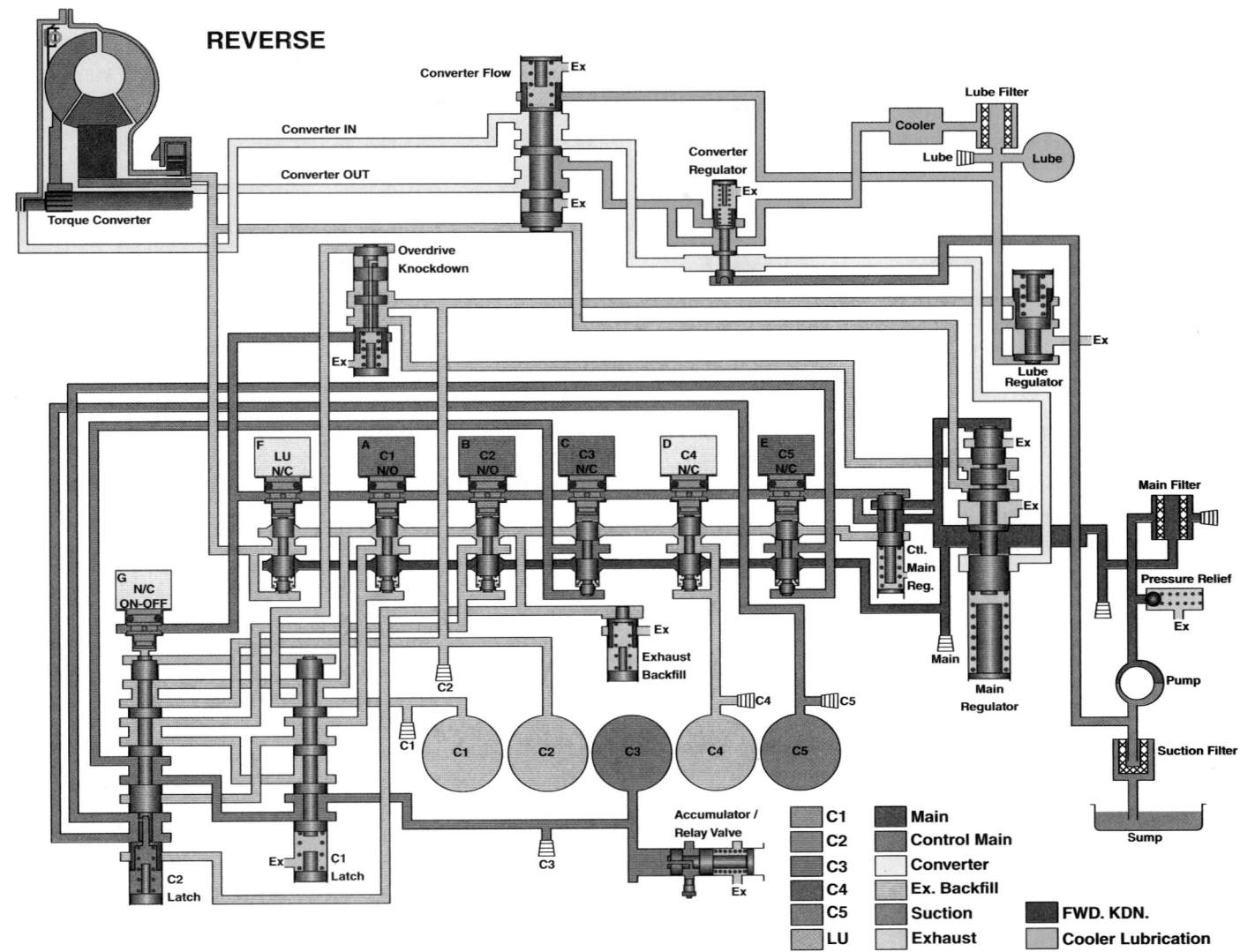

FIGURE 49-48 Hydraulic flow in WTEC III in reverse range.

TABLE 49-7 Solenoid Position in Each Range

Range	A (N/O)	B (N/O)	C (N/C)	D (N/C)	E (N/C)	F (N/C)	G (N/C)	Applied Clutches
Neutral 1	ON	ON			ON			C-5
Neutral 2	ON	ON		ON				C-4
Neutral 3	ON	ON	ON					C-3
Neutral 4	ON	ON		ON				C-4
Reverse	ON	ON	ON		ON			C-3 / C-5
First		ON			ON			C-1 / C-5
Second		ON		ON		ON*	ON	C-1 / C-4
Third		ON	ON			ON*	ON	C-1 / C-3
Fourth						ON*	ON	C-1 / C-2
Fifth	**ON**	**ON**				**ON***	**ON**	**C-2 / C-3**
Sixth	ON			ON		ON*		C-2 / C-4

* Solenoid F controls the lockup and is normally energized in all ranges above first. Under certain operating conditions, however, solenoid F may be de-energized.

Latch Valves

The WTEC transmission utilizes two latch valves, C-1 latch and C-2 latch, to assure fail-safe operation during electrical failure (**FIGURE 49-49**). **Fail-safe operation** occurs when the transmission control system is not operating due to electrical failure. The transmission's hydraulics are designed to allow minimal function so that the vehicle can be moved. The C-1 and C-2 latch valves, along with the normally open and normally closed solenoids, play the main role in fail-safe operation. The two latch valves are spring-loaded spool valves and, during normal operation, their position is controlled by normally closed solenoid G. The fluid is directed in such a way to apply clutches C-1, C-2, C-3, and C-5 from solenoids A, B, C, and E. That fluid must flow through one or both latch valves on the way to the clutches. Solenoids D (C-4) and F (lockup clutch) are the only solenoids that send fluid directly to the clutches they control.

When solenoid G is energized, it directs solenoid regulator pressure to the top of both latch valves. That application of pressure tries to move the valves down in their bore against spring pressure. The valves may or may not move, however, depending on the fluid flow through them. Fluid flow through the valves may keep them in a closed position—even though the G solenoid is energized.

Latch Valve Fluid Flows

The design of the latch valves and their fluid flows allows for the following electrical failure fail-safe operational modes in each gear.

- If the transmission is in neutral or reverse when electrical failure occurs, the transmission fails to neutral with no clutches (NNC) applied.
- First range fails to third range.
- Second, third, fourth, and fifth ranges fail to fourth range.
- Sixth range fails to fifth range.

These fail-safe modes allow limited (limp home) operation of the transmission during electrical failure. Refer to the hydraulic flow schematic in **FIGURE 49-50** as you read the following sections on latch valve fluid flows during electrical failure.

WTEC Neutral Range Fail-safe

When a WTEC transmission is in neutral, solenoids A, B, and E are energized. Fluid flow from solenoid E flows through the C-2 latch valve and into the C-5 clutch. Only C-5 is applied when the transmission is in neutral.

Electrical failure in neutral de-energizes normally open solenoids A and B and normally closed solenoid E. The latch valves are positioned up in their bores. Fluid from solenoid A flows through the C-1 latch valve and deadheads at the C-2 latch valve. Fluid from solenoid B flows through the C-2 latch valve and deadheads at the C-1 latch valve. Fluid flow from solenoid E stops, so C-5 is no longer applied. Because the transmission is in neutral, no clutches are applied. This situation is called **neutral with no clutches (NCC)**.

WTEC First Range Fail-safe

When the transmission is in first range, solenoids B and E are energized. Solenoid E keeps the C-5 clutch applied. Normally closed solenoid G is energized during the N-1 shift, sending solenoid regulator pressure to the top of the latch valves. That pressure causes the C-1 latch valve to move down in its bore against spring pressure. The C-2 latch valve remains up because the C-5 clutch apply pressure flowing through the valve does not let the valve move down. Normally open solenoid A directs control main pressure through the C-1 latch valve and into C-1 clutch. C-1 and C-5 are applied, so the transmission attains first range. After the shift, solenoid G is de-energized, but the fluid

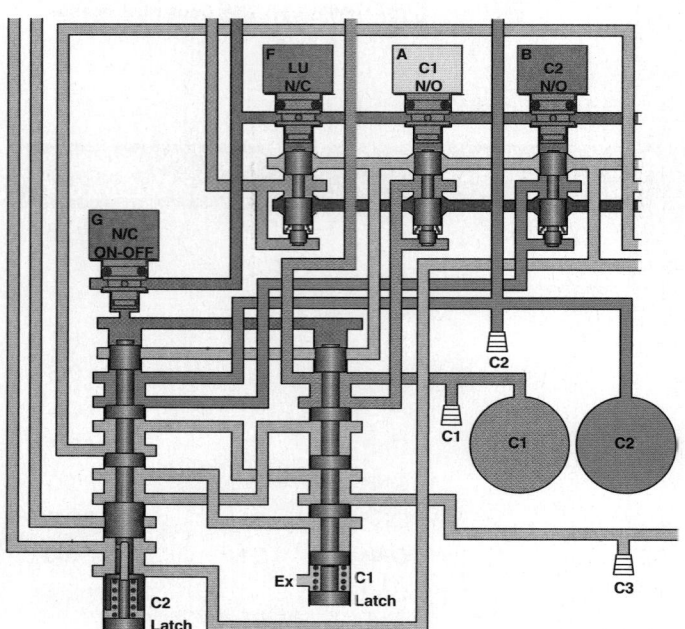

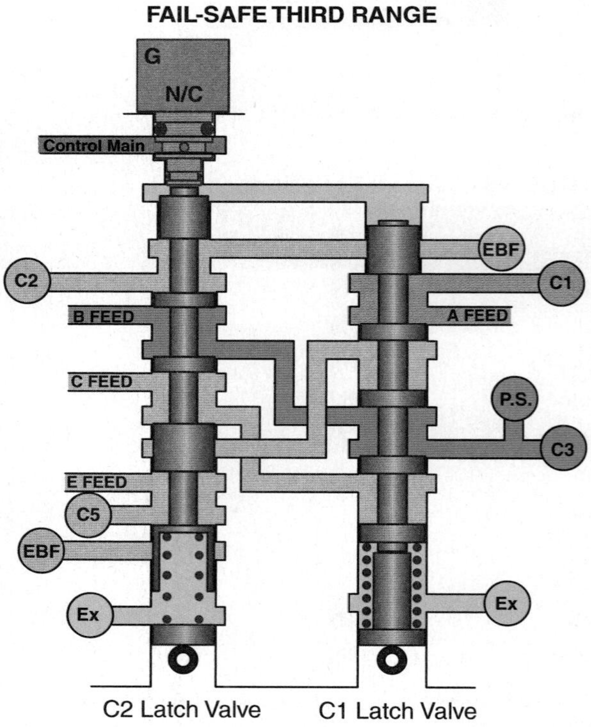

FIGURE 49-49 The C-1 and C-2 latch valves assure fail-safe operation in the event of electrical failure.

FAIL-SAFE THIRD RANGE

FIGURE 49-50 Detail of the C-1 and C-2 latch valves.

flow from solenoid A through the C-1 latch valve to C-1 clutch keeps the valve in a down-stroked position.

During electrical failure in first range, all solenoids are de-energized. Fluid no longer flows from solenoid E, so the C-5 clutch is exhausted. Fluid flow from the normally open solenoid A through the C-1 latch valve keeps the valve positioned down because of differential land sizes in the valve. Fluid flows from normally open solenoid B through the C-2 latch valve, which is positioned up. Fluid continues to flow through the C-1 latch valve and into the C-3 clutch circuit. The C-3 circuit is then applied.

Because C-1 and C-3 are applied, the transmission attains third range. If the vehicle is shut down during electrical failure, on restart the normally open solenoids A and B still allow fluid to flow. The C-1 latch valve will have moved up in its bore, however, causing the fluid to deadhead at the latch valves. The result is neutral no clutches (NCC).

WTEC Second Range Fail-safe

In second range, solenoids B, D, F, and G are energized. As the shift from first to second occurs, normally closed solenoid G is de-energized. Nonetheless, the flow to C-5 through latch valve C-2 holds the latch valve up in its bore. Fluid flowing through normally open solenoid A flows through the C-1 latch valve (holding it down in its bore) and continues on to C-1 clutch. Solenoid D directly applies the C-4 clutch—the only clutch control solenoid that does not flow through the latch valves.

As the shift is being made, normally closed solenoid E is de-energized and cuts off the flow to the C-5 clutch. After the shift has been made, solenoid G is energized, sending fluid to the top of the latch valves. As a result, latch valve C-2 moves down in its bore, and latch valve C-1 remains down in its bore. Solenoid F is energized to apply the lockup clutch. Because C-1 clutch and C-4 clutch are applied, the transmission attains second range.

During electrical failure in second range, all solenoids are de-energized. Normally closed solenoid D closes and stops the flow of fluid to the C-4 clutch. The fluid flow from solenoid A keeps the C-1 latch valve down in its bore and continues to supply the C-1 clutch. Fluid immediately flows from the de-energized normally open solenoid B to the C-2 latch valve, keeping it down in its bore—even though there is no pressure at the top of the valve. This fluid flows through the C-2 latch valve and on to the C-2 clutch. At that point, the C-2 clutch is applied. Normally closed solenoid F exhausts the lockup clutch. Because C-1 and C-2 clutches are applied, the transmission attains fourth range. If the transmission is shut down, both latch valves move back up in their bores. Upon restart, both latch valves block the flow of fluid from normally open solenoid A and B. The result is again NCC.

WTEC Third Range Fail-safe

Solenoids B, C, G, and F are energized in third range. Solenoid G keeps both latch valves down in their bores. Solenoid F applies the lockup clutch. Normally closed solenoid C is energized. This directs fluid through the C-2 and the C-1 latch valves and into the C-3 clutch, applying it. Fluid flows from normally open solenoid A through the C-1 latch valve and into the C-1 clutch, applying it. Because C-1 and C-3 are applied, the transmission attains third range.

During electrical failure in third range, all solenoids are de-energized. Solenoid F exhausts the lockup clutch. Solenoid C exhausts the C-3 clutch. Solenoid G exhausts the pressure from the top of the latch valves. Fluid begins to flow immediately from normally open solenoid B through the C-2 latch valve. The valve is held down in its bore. Continuation of the fluid flow applies the C-2 clutch. Fluid flow through the C-1 latch valve keeps it down in its bore and supplies C-1 clutch. Because C-1 and C-2 are applied, the transmission attains fourth range. If the vehicle is shut down, upon restart the latch valves have moved up in their bores due to spring pressure. Flow through normally open solenoids A and B simply deadheads at the valves. The transmission attains NCC.

WTEC Fourth Range Fail-safe

In fourth range, solenoids G and F are energized. Solenoid G delivers pressure to the top of the latch valves, which holds them down in their bore. Fluid flows from normally open solenoid A through the C-1 latch valve and into C-1 clutch. Fluid from normally open solenoid B flows through the C-2 latch valve and into the C-2 clutch. Because the C-1 and the C-2 clutches are applied, the transmission attains fourth range. Solenoid F applies the lockup clutch.

During electrical failure in fourth range, solenoid F exhausts the lockup clutch. Solenoid G exhausts the pressure from the top of the latch valves, but the fluid flowing through them to C-1 and C-2 clutch keeps the valves down in their bore. Since C-1 and C-2 clutches are applied, the transmission stays in fourth range. If the vehicle is shut down, upon restart the latch valves have moved up in their bores due to spring pressure. Flow through normally open solenoids A and B simply deadheads at the valves, and the transmission attains NCC.

WTEC Fifth Range Fail-safe

In fifth range, solenoids A, C, G, and F are energized. Solenoid G keeps both latch valves down in their bores. Solenoid F applies the lockup clutch. Normally closed solenoid C is energized. The energized solenoid C directs fluid through the C-2 and the C-1 latch valves and into the C-3 clutch, applying it. Fluid flows from normally open solenoid B through the C-2 latch valve and into the C-2 clutch, applying it. Because C-2 and C-3 are applied, the transmission attains fifth range.

During electrical failure in fifth range, all solenoids become de-energized. Solenoid F exhausts the lockup clutch, and solenoid G exhausts the fluid from the top of the latch valves. Fluid flowing from normally open solenoid B through the C-2 latch valve and into the C-2 clutch keeps the valve down in its bore and the C-2 clutch applied. Fluid immediately flows from normally open solenoid A through the C-1 latch valve, keeping the valve down in its bore. Fluid flows onto the C-1 clutch, applying it. Because clutches C-1 and C-2 are applied, the transmission attains fourth range. If the vehicle is shut down, upon restart, the latch valves have moved up in their bores due to spring pressure and flow through normally open solenoid A. Fluid flow through solenoid B simply deadheads at the valves, and the transmission attains NCC.

WTEC Sixth Range Fail-safe

In sixth range, solenoids A, D, and F are energized. Solenoid G is de-energized. This exhausts the fluid from the top of the latch valves, and latch valve C-1 moves up in its bore. Latch valve C-2 stays down, however, because of the fluid from normally open solenoid B flowing through it and into the C-2 clutch. Solenoid F applies the lockup clutch. Solenoid D applies the C-4 clutch. Because C-2 and C-4 are applied, the transmission attains sixth range.

During electrical failure in sixth range, all solenoids are de-energized. Solenoid F exhausts the lockup clutch, and solenoid D exhausts the C-4 clutch. Fluid continues to flow from normally open solenoid B through the C-2 latch valve and into the C-2 clutch. Fluid immediately begins to flow from normally open solenoid A through the C-1 latch valve, which is positioned up. This fluid flows to the C-2 latch valve and through it back to another port on the C-1 latch valve. Fluid flows through this port in the C-1 latch valve and into the C-3 clutch, applying it. Because C-2 and C-3 are applied, the transmission attains fifth range. If the vehicle is shut down, upon restart the latch valves have moved up in their bores due to spring pressure. Fluid flow through normally open solenoid A and B simply deadheads at the valves, and the transmission attains NCC.

Reverse Range Fail-safe

When the transmission is in reverse, solenoids A, B, C, and E are energized. Solenoids A and B are normally open, so energizing them stops fluid flow. Solenoid C sends fluid pressure through the C-2 and the C-1 latch valves and into the C-3 clutch. Solenoid E sends fluid pressure through the C-2 latch valve to the C-5 clutch. Both latch valves are positioned up in their bores. Because C-3 and C-5 clutches are applied, the transmission attains reverse.

▶ TECHNICIAN TIP

These fail-safe strategies activate a limp-home mode to allow the vehicle to be driven to a repair depot during an electrical failure. Note that, although the vehicle can be moved during electrical failure, as soon as the engine is shut off and the transmission oil pressure drops, the transmission then reverts to neutral no clutches and the vehicle can no longer be driven.

During electrical failure in reverse, all solenoids are de-energized. Solenoid C exhausts the C-3 clutch. Solenoid E exhausts the C-5 clutch. Fluid immediately begins to flow from normally open solenoid A through the C-1 latch valve and deadheads at the C-2 latch valve. Fluid also immediately begins to flow from normally open solenoid B through the C-2 latch valve and deadheads at the C-1 latch valve. No clutches are applied, and the transmission attains NCC.

Allison Fourth- and Fifth Generation Electrohydraulic Control Valve Body

LO 49-4 Describe the operation of the electronic controls in Allison fourth- and fifth-generation transmissions.

The next revision of the Allison electronic control is simply called Allison Fourth-Generation Electronic Control. Fourth generation was released in the 2004–2005 model year and introduced several changes to the electrohydraulic valve body and control strategy. For example, the solenoids used in fourth-generation

systems have different functioning and locations compared to the solenoids in the WTEC II and WTEC III transmissions.

The transmission ECU is renamed **transmission control module (TCM)** conforming with the SAE recommended acronym, (**FIGURE 49-51**), and the clutch control solenoids have been renamed **pressure control solenoids (PCS)**. PCS1 replaces solenoid A; PCS2 replaces solenoid B; PCS3 replaces solenoids C and E; and PCS4 replaces solenoid D. Solenoid E as a standalone part has been eliminated altogether. Solenoid F has been renamed **torque converter control (TCC)**, and Solenoid G, which controls the position of the C-1 and C-2 latch valves, has been renamed **shift solenoid 1 (SS1)**. A new solenoid has been introduced called the **modulated main solenoid (Mod Main)**. The TCM uses the Mod Main to reduce main pressure when desired.

The pressure-control solenoids and the Mod Main solenoid are very different internally from their predecessors in the WTEC II and WTEC III controlled transmissions. The WTEC II and WTEC III solenoids had an inlet port, an outlet port, and an exhaust port. The flow of fluid was controlled by the transmission ECU using pulse-width modulation to control the opening and closing of a check ball in the solenoid. That process would direct fluid either to the outlet port or to exhaust.

In contrast, the fourth-generation control system uses variable-bleed solenoids (VBS). **Variable-bleed solenoids** control application by allowing some of the pressure going to a device to bleed off to exhaust. Variable-bleed solenoids have three ports:

- A supply port that is fed control main pressure
- A control port that sends that pressure to the solenoid regulator valve
- An exhaust port

Each pressure-control solenoid is connected to an accumulator, which absorbs pressure pulsations that can be caused by the pulse-width modulation of the solenoid. **FIGURE 49-52** shows a variable-bleed solenoid in high-pressure state and in a controlling pressure state.

The TCM (formerly the transmission ECU) precisely controls the current being applied to the solenoids by changing

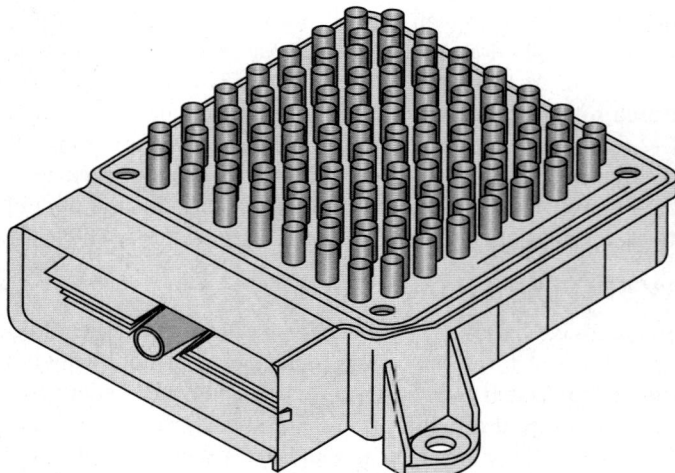

FIGURE 49-51 The fourth-generation transmission control module is common to all 1000, 2000, 3000, and 4000 product families.

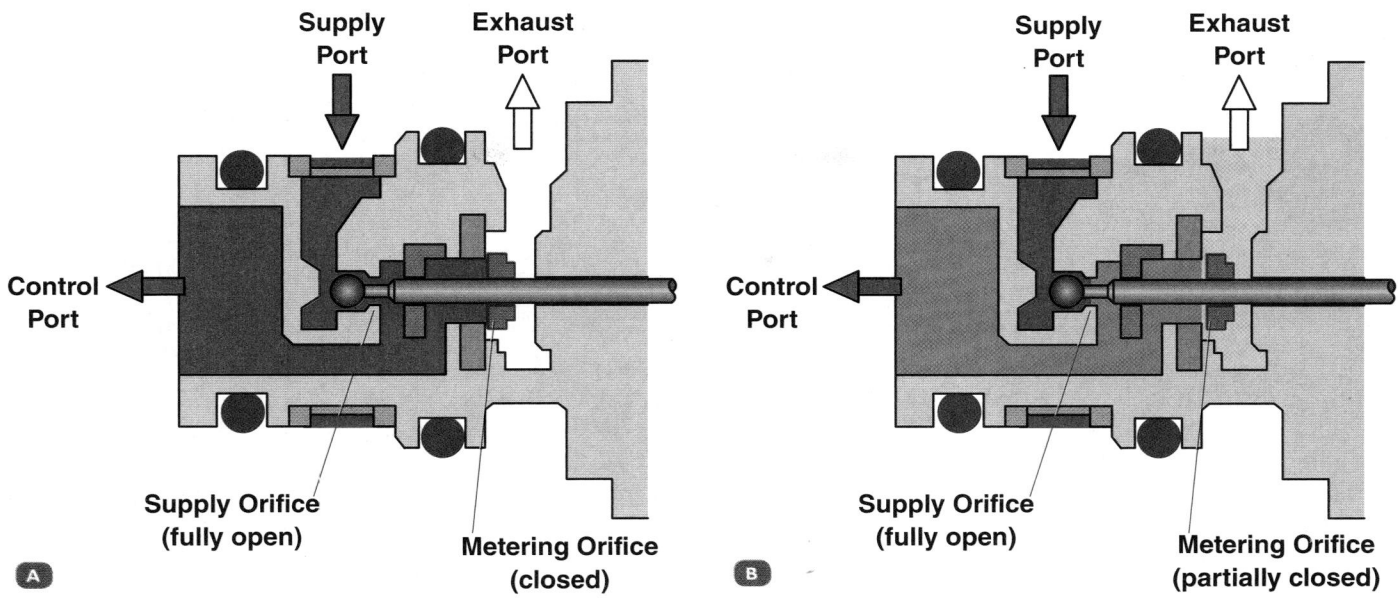

FIGURE 49-52 The variable-bleed solenoids (VBS) used with fourth-generation control allow more accurate control of clutch application. **A.** VBS in high-pressure state. **B.** VBS in controlling pressure state.

TABLE 49-8 Fourth-Generation Solenoid Application Chart

Range	PSC1 N/O	PCS2 N/O	PCS3 N/C	PC4 N/C	SS1 N/C	Mod Main N/C
Neutral **	ON	ON	ON			Optional*
Reverse	ON		ON			Optional*
First		ON	ON			Optional*
Second		ON		ON	ON	Optional*
Third		ON	ON		ON	Optional*
Fourth					ON	Optional*
Fifth	ON		ON		ON	Optional*
Sixth	ON			ON		Optional*

* The modulated main solenoid may be energized by the TCM when lower main pressure is desired in any operating range.

** Four different neutral configurations can be attained if the vehicle is moving in neutral range.

the duty cycle of the pulse-width-modulated control circuit. Changing the duty cycle controls the size of the bleed orifice. The sizing of the bleed orifice is what allows the transmission to control precisely the speed of application of the clutch. VBS are called either normally high (maximum pressure is supplied to the control circuit) or normally low (minimum pressure supplied to the control circuit).

The SS1 solenoid is not a VBS. Rather, it is an on/off solenoid. PCS3 controls clutch C-5 when the C-1 and C-2 latch valves are in the up or un-stroked position. PCS3 also controls clutch C-3 when the C-1 latch valve is in the down or stroked position. TABLE 49-8 is the fourth-generation solenoid application chart for six-speed transmissions without a retarder.

The Mod Main solenoid directs pressure to a land on the main pressure regulator valve, and this reduces main pressure. The Mod Main is used in neutral, first, and second when conditions are correct; it is also used in reverse, but only when throttle is less than

18%. Reducing main pressure when possible lowers the parasitic load the transmission hydraulic pump places on the engine.

As with the WTEC II and WTEC III control systems, the fourth-generation transmission can attain four different neutral configurations if the vehicle is moving while in neutral. The clutch applications depend on component rotational speed. Check the OEM manual for applications. Note that the clutch application chart and power flows for the fourth-generation transmissions are identical to those for the earlier World Transmission models.

Fourth-Generation Fluid Flows

Fourth-Generation Neutral

Normally open solenoids PCS1 and PCS2 and normally closed PCS3 solenoid are energized. Main pressure dead-heads at the PCS1 and PCS2 solenoids. Main pressure flows through the

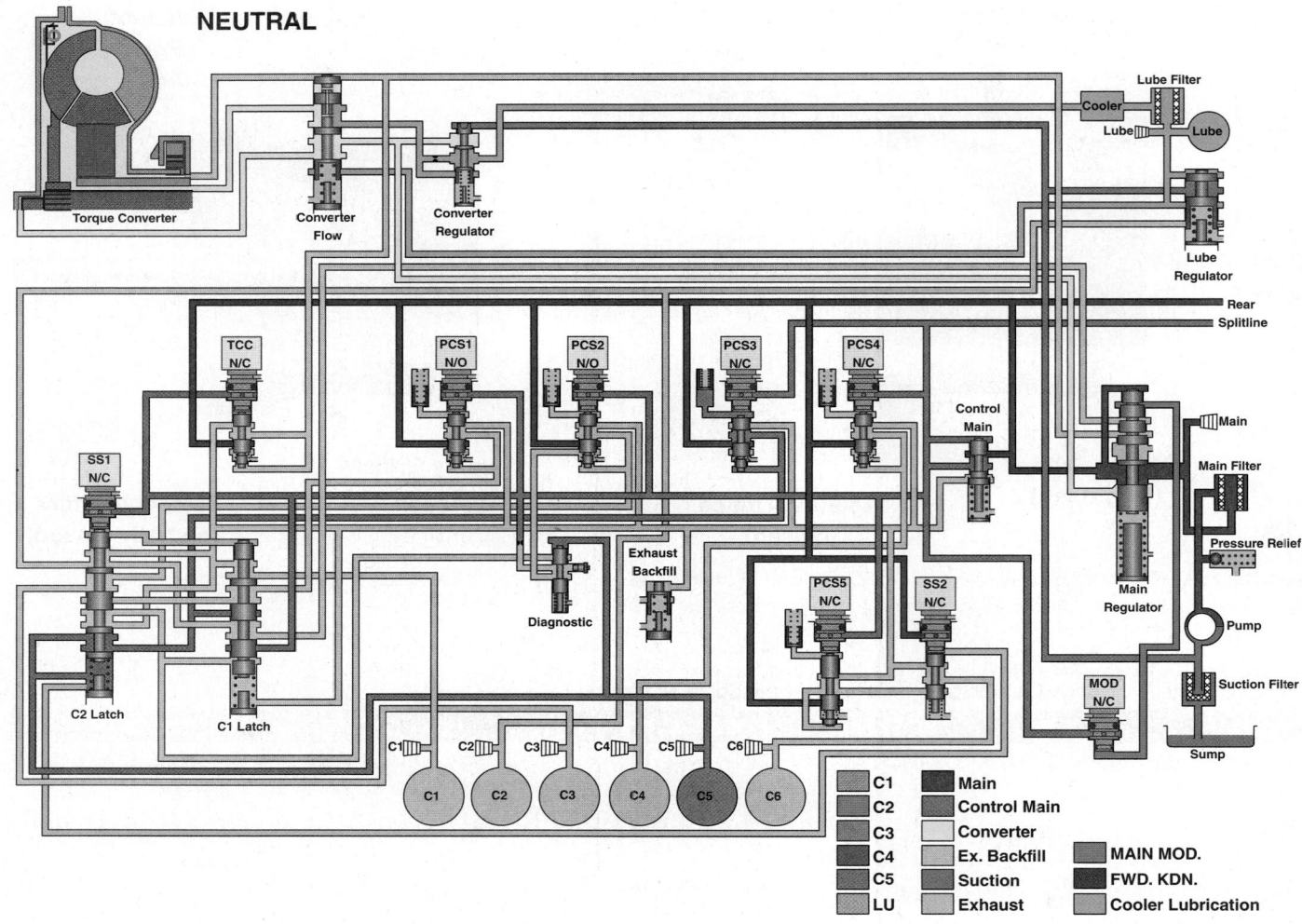

FIGURE 49-53 Neutral hydraulic flow for World Transmission fourth-generation control.

open PCS3 solenoid through the C-2 latch valve and applies the C-5 clutch. Normally closed Mod Main solenoid is energized to lower main pressure (**FIGURE 49-53**).

Fourth-Generation First Range

During the shift to first, normally closed solenoid SS1 is energized briefly to position the C-1 latch valve down. The C-2 latch valve remains up because of the fluid pressure flowing to C-5 clutch. Normally open solenoid PCS2 and normally closed solenoid PCS3 remain energized, but normally open solenoid PCS1 is de-energized. Main pressure flows through PCS1 and the C-1 latch valve and applies the C-1 clutch. The normally closed Mod Main solenoid may be energized to reduce main pressure, if desired, by the TCM (**FIGURE 49-54**).

Fourth-Generation Second Range

During the shift to second range, normally closed solenoid PCS3 is de-energized, thereby exhausting C-5. Normally closed solenoid PCS4 is energized, causing main pressure to flow through its solenoid regulator valve to C-4. The normally

closed Mod Main solenoid is de-energized to increase main pressure if the situation warrants. Normally open solenoid PCS2 remains energized. When second range is attained, normally closed solenoid SS1 is energized, positioning the C-2 latch valve down. The C-1 latch valve remains down. The TCM may again lower main pressure by energizing the normally closed main modulator solenoid. Normally closed solenoid TCC (torque converter clutch) is energized, applying the lockup clutch (**FIGURE 49-55**).

Fourth-Generation Third Range

In third range, normally closed solenoid PCS4 is de-energized to exhaust C-4 clutch, and the Mod Main solenoid is de-energized to increase main pressure. Normally closed solenoid PCS3 is energized, and main pressure flows through its solenoid regulator valve and the C-1 and C-2 latch valves. That flow applies the C-3 clutch. Normally open PCS2 solenoid remains energized. Normally closed solenoid SS-1 remains energized. Normally closed solenoid TCC (torque converter clutch) is energized, thereby applying the lockup clutch (**FIGURE 49-56**).

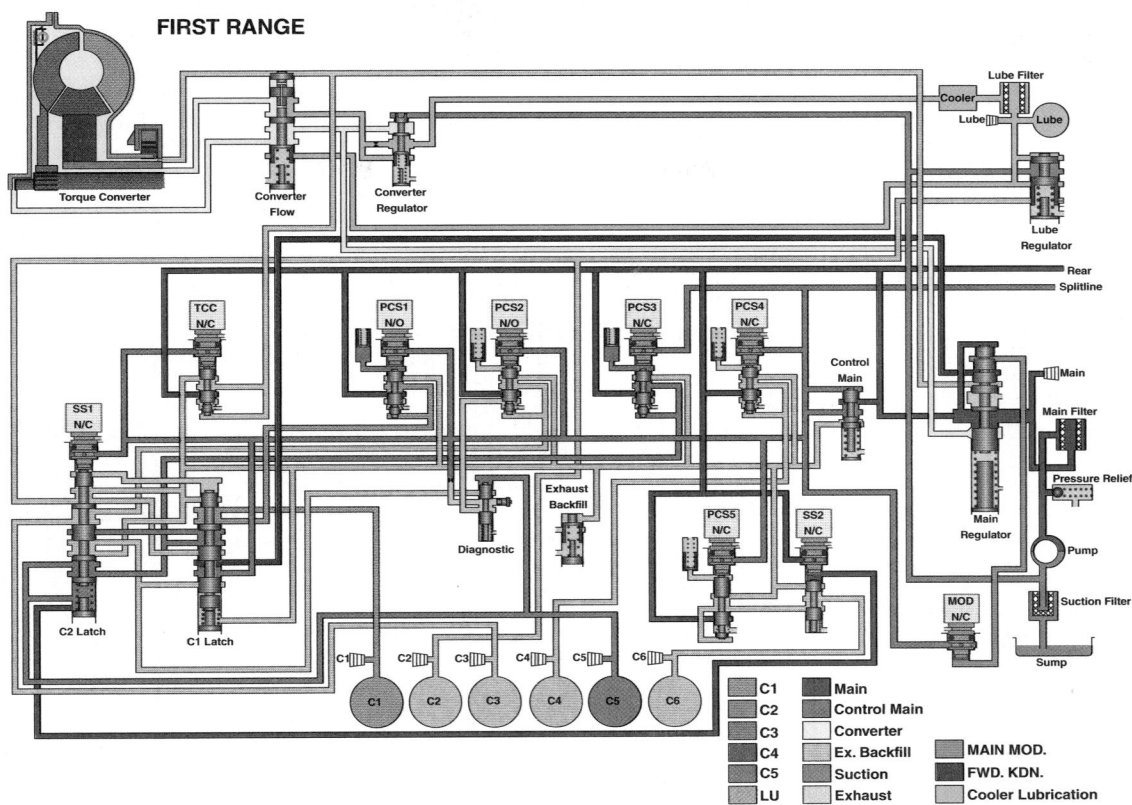

FIGURE 49-54 First range hydraulic flow for World Transmission fourth-generation control.

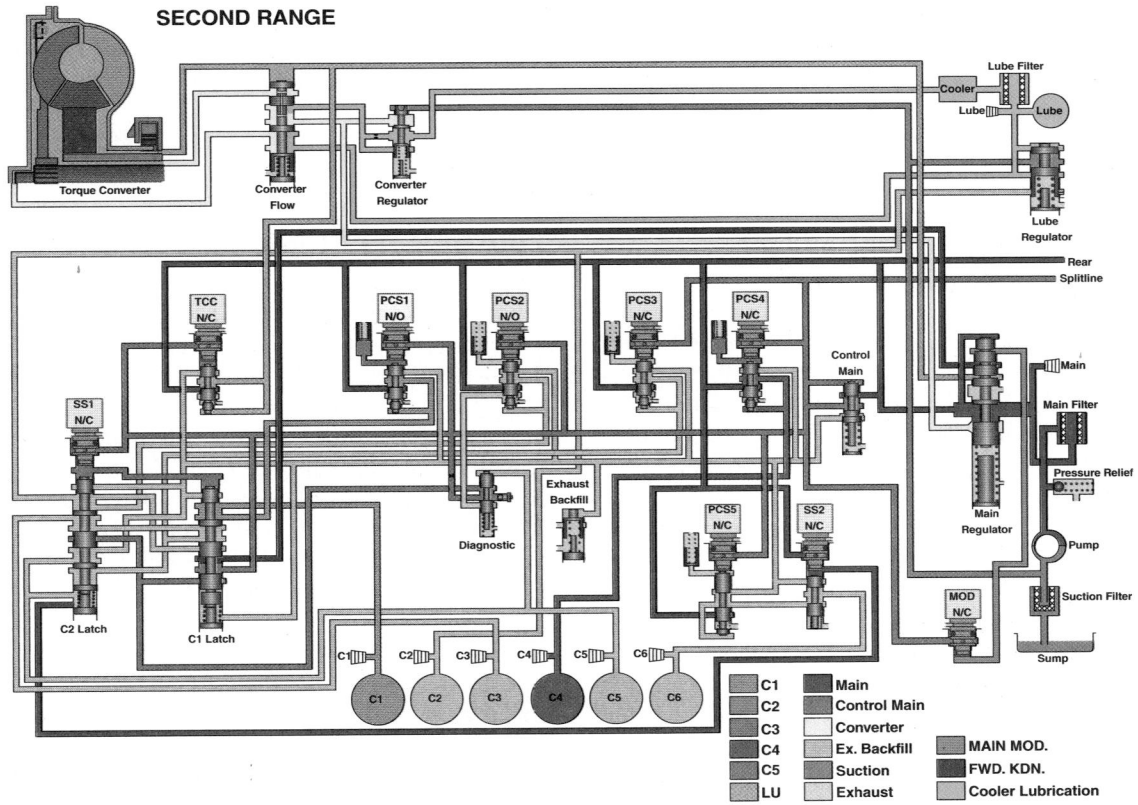

FIGURE 49-55 Second range hydraulic flow for World Transmission fourth-generation control.

THIRD RANGE

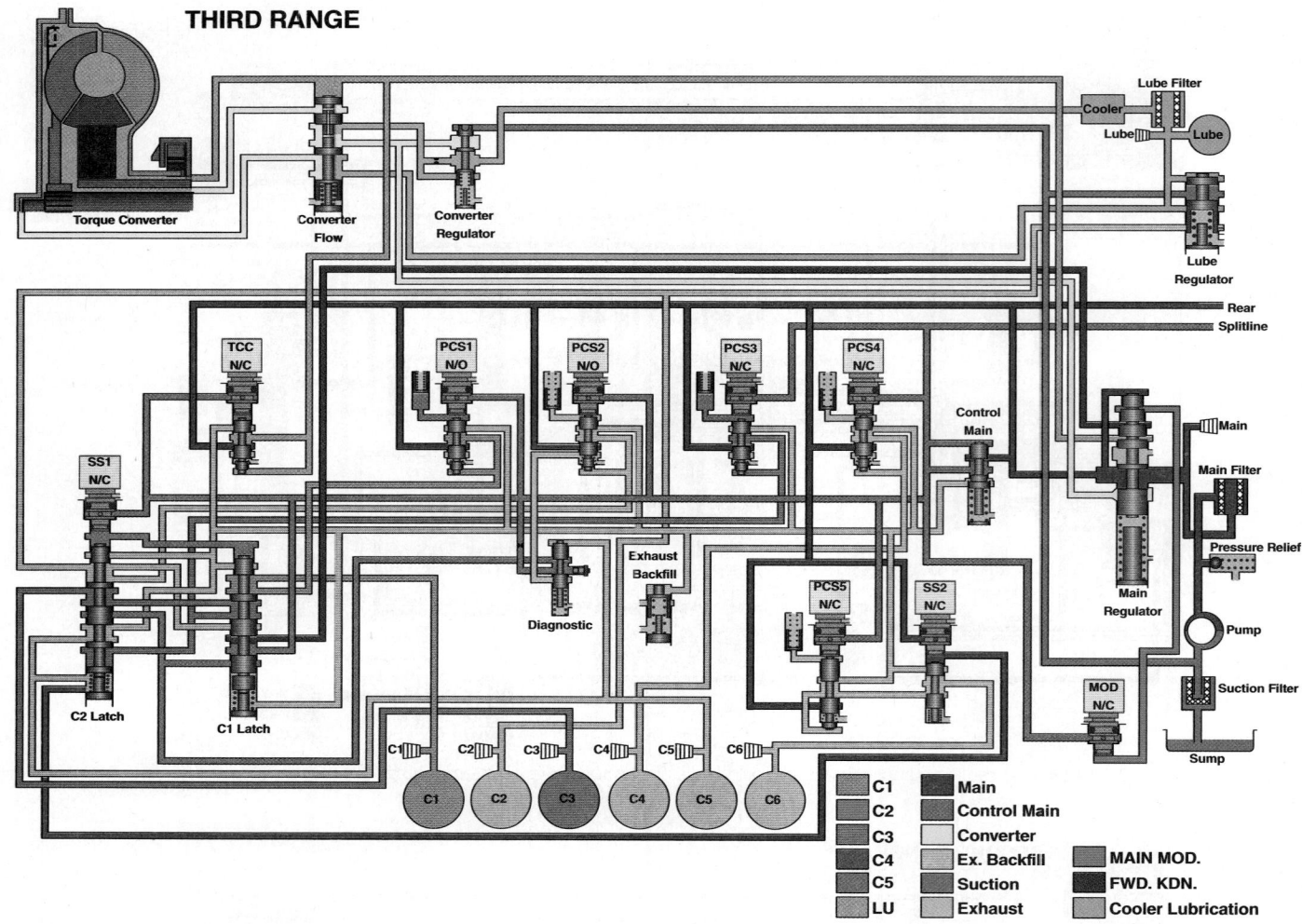

FIGURE 49-56 Third range hydraulic flow for World Transmission fourth-generation control.

Fourth-Generation Fourth Range

In fourth gear, normally closed solenoid PCS3 is de-energized, exhausting C-3 clutch, and normally open solenoid PCS2 is de-energized. That allows main pressure to flow through its solenoid regulator valve and the C-2 latch valve to apply the C-2 clutch. Normally closed solenoid SS-1 remains energized. Normally closed solenoid TCC (torque converter clutch) is energized, applying the lockup clutch (**FIGURE 49-57**).

Fourth-Generation Fifth Range

Normally open PCS1 solenoid is energized, exhausting the C-1 clutch. Normally open solenoid PCS2 remains de-energized, and main pressure still flows through its solenoid regulator valve and the C-2 latch valve to apply C-2 clutch. Normally closed solenoid PCS3 is energized, allowing main pressure to flow through its solenoid regulator valve to apply the C-3 clutch. Normally closed solenoid TCC is energized, applying the lockup clutch. Normally closed solenoid SS-1 remains energized (**FIGURE 49-58**).

Fourth-Generation Sixth Range

Normally open solenoid PCS2 remains de-energized, allowing main pressure to continue to flow through the C-2 latch valve to apply the C-2 clutch. Normally closed solenoid PCS3 is de-energized, exhausting the C-3 clutch. Normally closed solenoid PCS4 is energized, and main pressure now flows through its solenoid regulator valve to apply the C-4 clutch. Normally closed solenoid SS-1 is de-energized, and spring pressure positions the C-1 latch valve up in its bore. The C-2 latch valve remains down, however, because of the pressure flowing to the C-2 clutch. Normally closed solenoid TCC is energized, applying the lockup clutch (**FIGURE 49-59**).

Fourth-Generation Reverse

The shift to reverse starts in the neutral position. Normally open solenoids PCS1 and PCS2 and normally closed PCS3 solenoid are energized. Main pressure deadheads at the PCS1 and PCS2 solenoids. Main pressure flows through the open PCS3 solenoid through the C-2 latch valve and applies the C-5 clutch. Normally closed Mod Main solenoid is energized to lower main pressure.

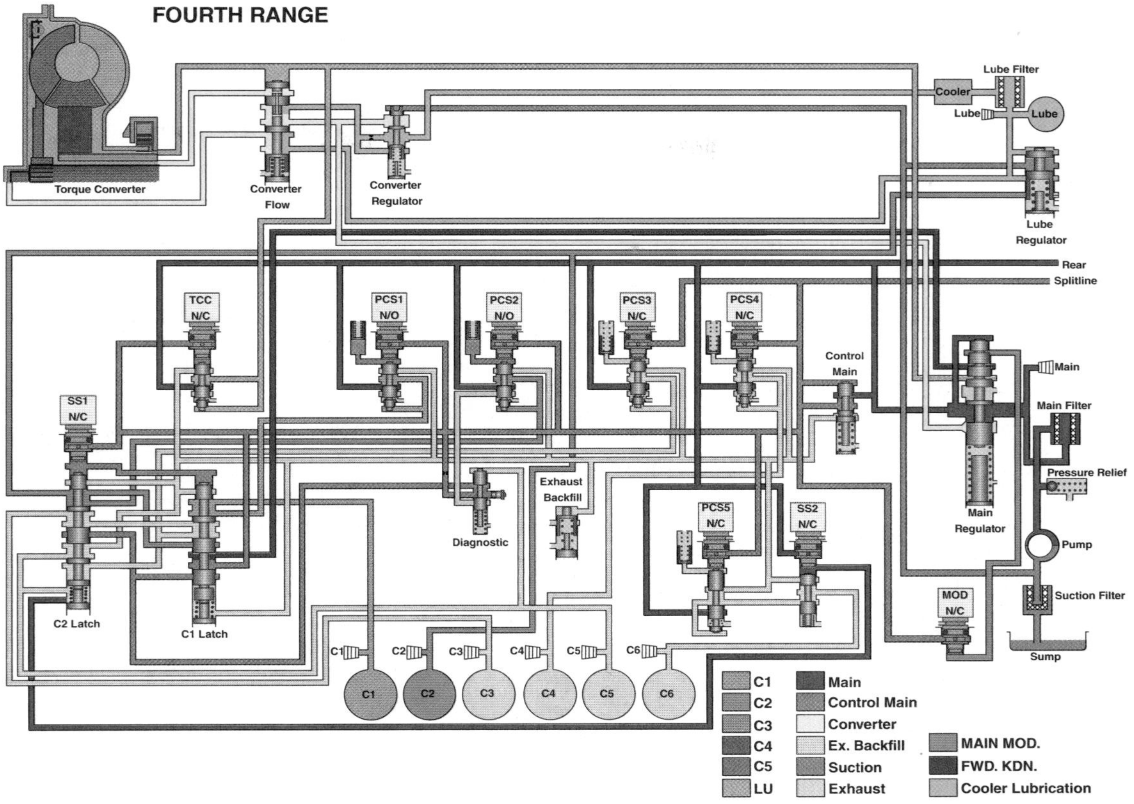

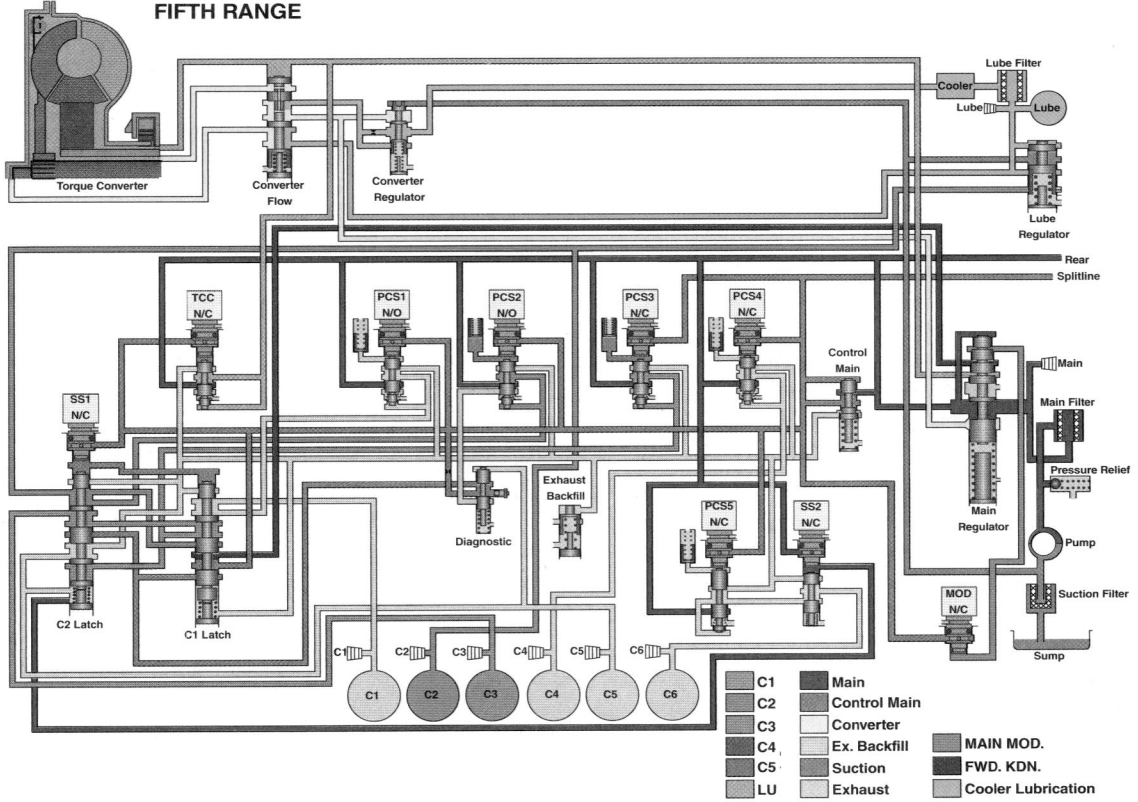

FIGURE 49-57 Fourth range hydraulic flow for World Transmission fourth-generation control.

FIGURE 49-58 Fifth range hydraulic flow for World Transmission fourth-generation control.

SIXTH RANGE

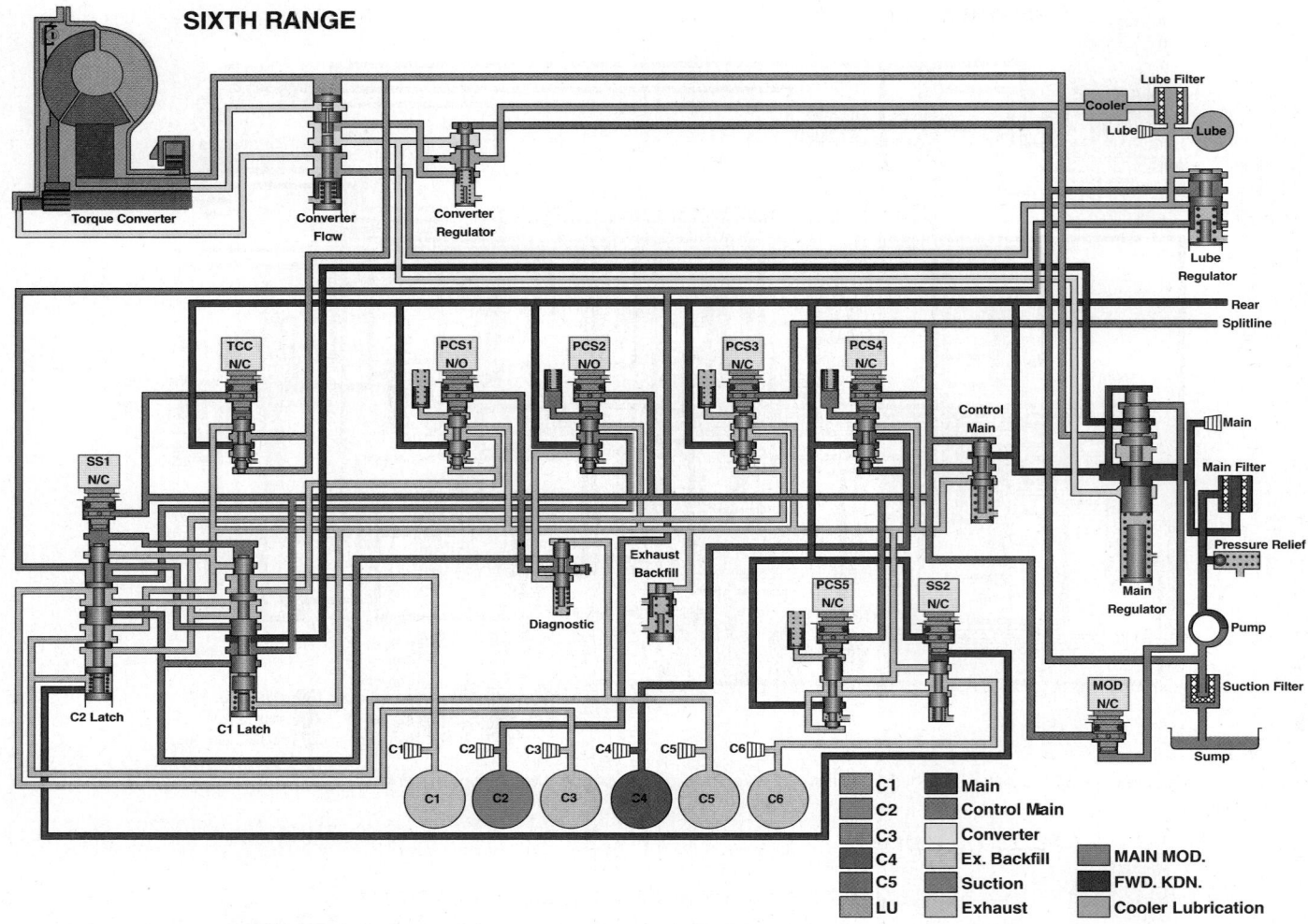

FIGURE 49-59 Sixth range hydraulic flow for World Transmission fourth-generation control.

In shifting into reverse, normally open solenoid PCS2 is de-energized and main pressure flows through both its solenoid regulator valve and the C-2 latch valve. The C-3 clutch is then applied. The normally closed Mod Main solenoid may or may not be energized (**FIGURE 49-60**).

Other Valves Used in the Electrohydraulic Valve Body

There are several other valves in the control valve body of the World Transmission including the converter regulator valve, the converter flow valve, the lube regulator valve, the overdrive knock-down valve, and the exhaust backfill valve. These valves are illustrated in **FIGURE 49-61**.

Converter Regulator Valve

The converter regulator valve controls maximum torque converter working pressure and oil flow by controlling the converter in-circuit. As fluid flows to the torque converter, it passes through the converter regulator valve, then through the converter flow valve into the converter, and back out to the converter flow valve.

From here, the returning fluid can take two separate paths. It can either flow into the lubrication circuit, or it may return to the charging pump intake. One path flows through a restriction and then around the center land area of the converter regulator valve into the lube circuit. The oil in the lube circuit passes through the transmission oil cooler, the lube filter, and the lubrication circuit, and then is directed back to the converter flow valve where it deadheads.

When converter in pressure is lower than desired, the converter regulator valve is in the down position, and there is no restriction to the converter in-flow. The converter out-flow is directed at the valve in two locations. The converter out-flow deadheads at the upper land of the converter regulator valve, and all the flow must enter the lube circuit through the restriction and the lower land of the converter regulator valve. As converter pressure rises to 130 psi (9.14 kg/cm²), the converter regulator moves up in its bore, and some of the return flow that was deadheading at the upper land flows by it and into the lube circuit. This action starts to restrict converter in flow as well.

The second path the returning fluid can take returns it to the charging pump. The converter regulator valve exhausts

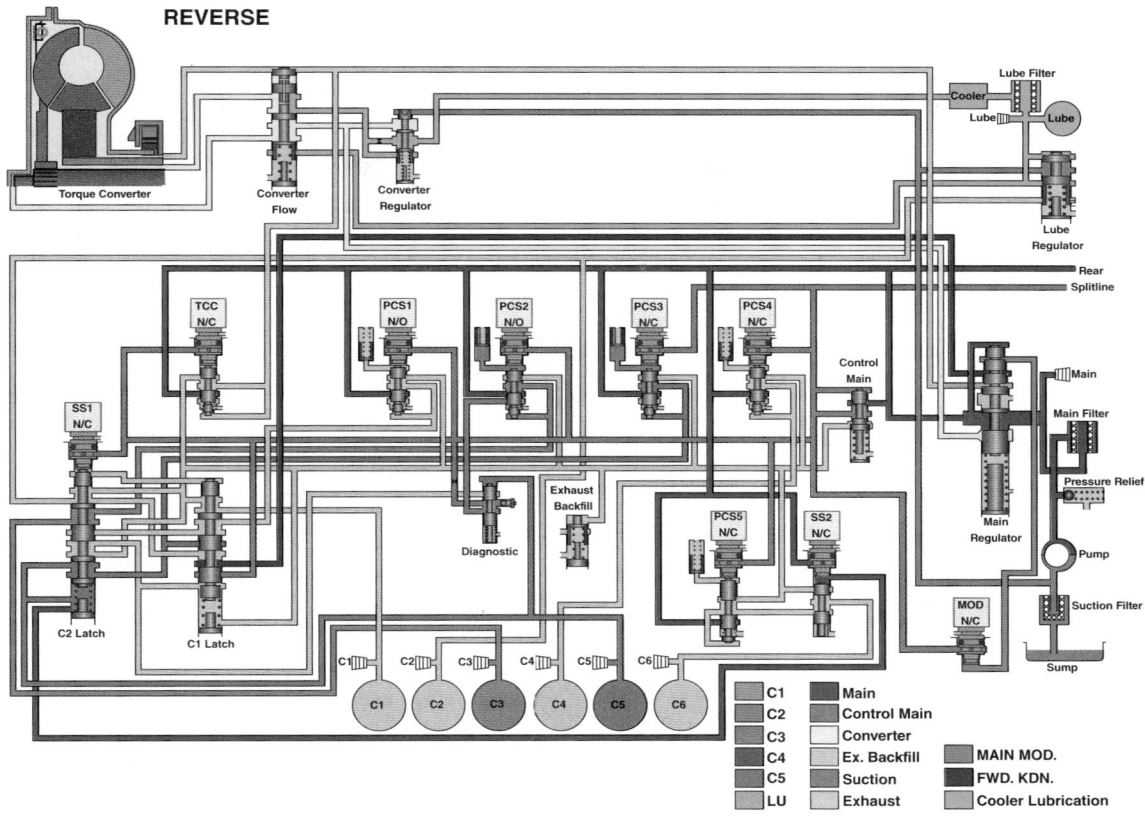

FIGURE 49-60 Reverse range hydraulic flow for World Transmission fourth-generation control.

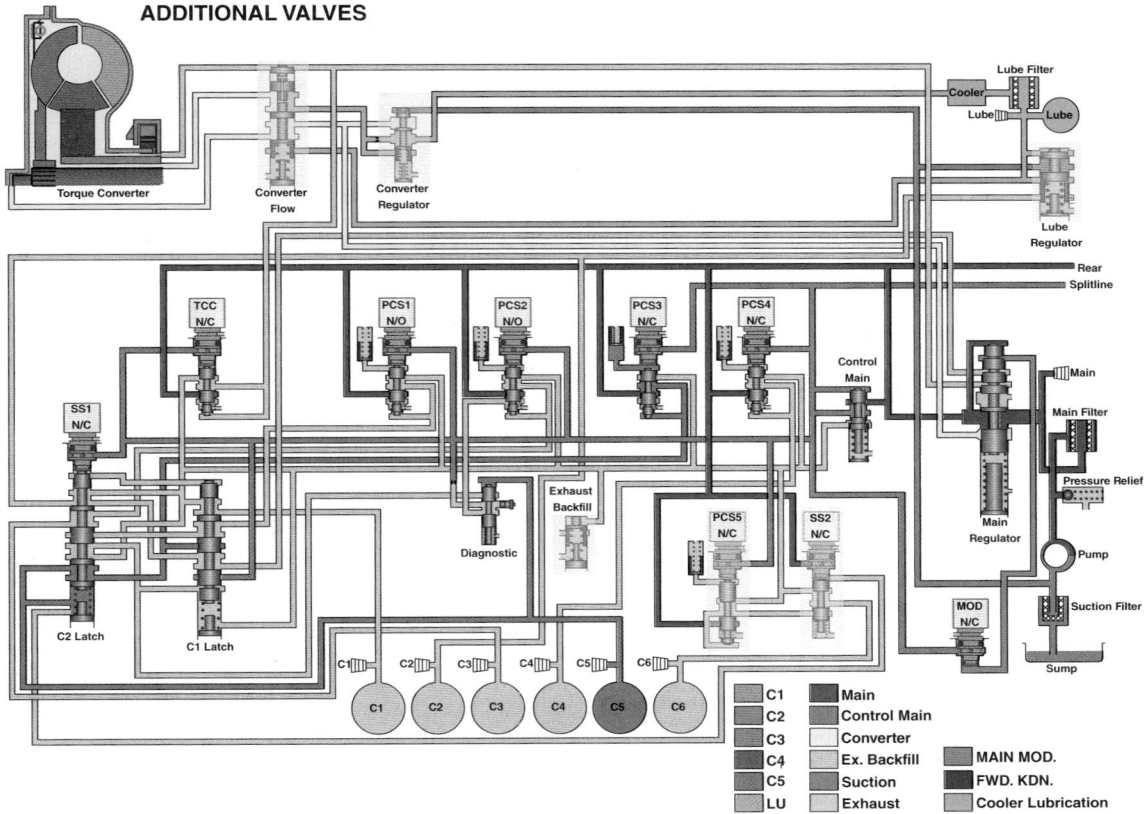

FIGURE 49-61 Additional valves in a fourth-generation World Transmission.

some of the converter in-flow to the pump intake. When converter pressure rises above 130 psi (9.14 kg/cm²), the converter regulator valve moves further up in its bore and allows some of the converter in-circuit to flow directly into the lubrication circuit.

Lubrication Pressure Regulator Valve

The lube pressure regulator is connected to the lubrication circuit and regulates lubrication pressure at either 17 or 22 psi (1.2–1.5 kg/cm²), depending on the gear range. The lube pressure regulator also returns excess fluid to the pump intake directly, rather than to the sump, thereby minimizing oil churning in the sump.

Converter Flow Valve

When the TCC solenoid (the equivalent of WTEC solenoid F) is energized, it applies the lockup clutch. The torque converter clutch apply circuit is also directed to the bottom of the converter flow valve. This moves the valve up in its bore and blocks the flow of fluid from the converter regulator valve to the converter in-circuit. The flow from the converter regulator valve now flows directly to the lube circuit. The fluid returning from the lube circuit that normally deadheads at the converter flow valve is now directed through a central drilling in the flow control valve and into the torque converter. This greatly reduces the flow through the torque converter when the torque converter is in lockup. (Recall that high fluid flow is not needed during lockup, but we must keep the converter full of fluid.) Reducing the flow through the torque converter removes some parasitic load from the engine. Parasitic loss is further reduced because the lockup clutch apply circuit is directed to the main pressure regulator valve to reduce main pressure when in lockup.

Overdrive Knock-Down Valve

The overdrive knock-down valve actually reduces main pressure in all ranges except reverse. The valve has control main pressure directed to it at all times. This valve is not present in the fourth-generation control. Instead, the fourth-generation control uses the main modulator solenoid to lower main pressure when required. When C-1 clutch is engaged, the knock-down valve directs control main pressure (100 psi [7.0 kg/cm²]) to a land on the main pressure regulator valve. The valve moves down, reducing main pressure. When the C-2 clutch is applied, the valve stays up in its bore, and apply pressure from the C-2 clutch circuit is delivered to the main pressure regulator valve. The effect is to further decrease main pressure.

In neutral and reverse ranges, no pressure is delivered to this land on the main pressure regulator. Therefore, main pressure is at its highest in these ranges. C-2 clutch apply pressure from the overdrive knock-down valve is also directed to a land on the lube regulator valve. That application of pressure helps move the valve off its seat. The result is a reduction in lubrication pressure whenever the C-2 clutch is applied. Lube pressure is 22 psi (1.5 kg/cm²) in first, second, and third ranges and 17 psi (1.2 kg/cm²) in fourth, fifth, and sixth ranges.

Since 2010, the fourth-generation electrohydraulic valve body uses a pulse-width-modulated main modulator solenoid designated as open-ended, normally high (OE NH) (**FIGURE 49-62**). That means the solenoid is normally closed and pressure is normally HIGH. This solenoid controls the flow of control main pressure to the bottom of the MPRV to control actual main pressure. Increasing pressure at the bottom of the MPRV causes main pressure to increase. This gives the TCM much greater control over main pressure.

Exhaust Backfill Valve

The exhaust backfill valve maintains a very low pressure in the exhaust passages for the clutch packs. This minimal pressure of 2 to 3 psi (0.14 to 0.21 kg/cm²) is not sufficient to apply or delay release of the clutches. Minimal pressure does, however, keep the cavity behind the clutch piston full of fluid to ensure quick response during shifts.

Accumulator Relay Valve

Recall from Figure 49-47, in the WTEC II- and WTEC III-controlled transmissions, the accumulator relay valve delays activation of the C-3 pressure switch until the clutch apply

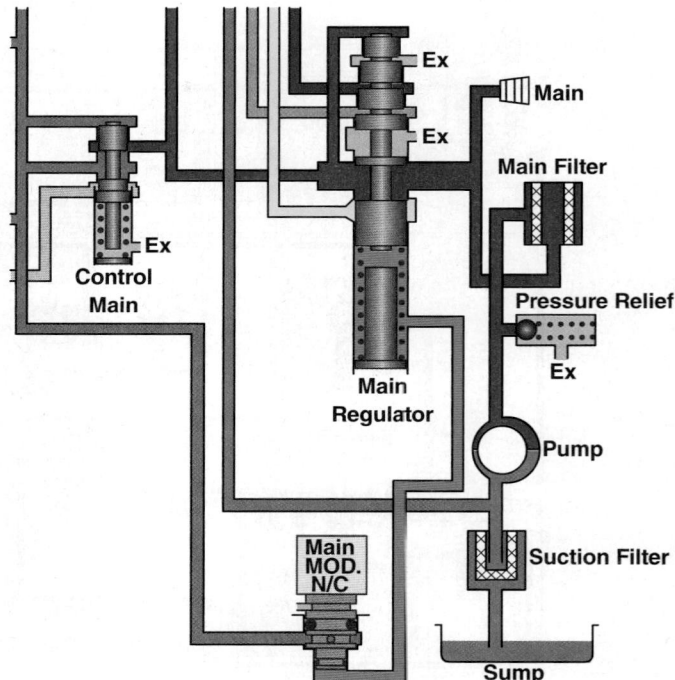

FIGURE 49-62 From 2010 model year orward, a pulse-width-modulated main modulator solenoid is used. This solenoid allows greater control over transmission main pressure by changing the pressure present at the bottom of the MPRV.

pressure is high. Without the accumulator, the pulse-width-modulated apply signal would cause fluctuations in the apply pressure which, in turn, would cause the switch to turn on and off rapidly. As clutch pressure builds, the accumulator is moved in its bore until the center-drilled hole in the valve communicates apply pressure to the C-3 switch. The C-3 pressure switch informs the controller whether the C-3 clutch is engaged. That is, the C-3 pressure switch signals the controller whether the transmission is in reverse, third range, fifth range, or not.

The fourth-generation valve body does not use an accumulator relay valve. Instead, fourth-generation transmissions use a valve called the diagnostic valve to control the PS1 pressure switch. As was illustrated in Figure 49-59, the position of the diagnostic valve is controlled by the latch valve's position. The PS1 switch relays information to the transmission controller regarding the position of the PCS2 solenoid when the vehicle is second, third, fourth, and fifth range. The PS1 switch also relays information the C-5 clutch is applied in reverse.

Prognostics

Since 2009, Allison fourth-generation controlled transmissions have come with an optional feature called **prognostics**, which can be enabled or disabled by the operator. Fifth-generation controllers come standard with prognostics installed in the software. The prognostics feature is software programmed into the TCM that monitors and alerts the operator when the transmission fluid or filter needs changing or when the transmission clutches need servicing. The transmission controller calculates the need for service through drive cycle data and by monitoring shifts in progress.

The prognostics are accessed through the two-digit display on the shift selector and the driver is alerted by a wrench symbol or the service transmission light. If the wrench symbol or the service light illuminates for two minutes after drive is selected, that indicates an issue with the transmission fluid. If the wrench or the light flashes on and off for two minutes after drive is selected, it indicates an issue with the filter. Finally, if the wrench or light comes on and stays on in all ranges, it indicates that there is a problem with the transmission clutches. Understanding the warning lights allows the operator to schedule maintenance when required and before a problem gets worse. Fifth-generation electronics have a more advanced display and report oil life as a percentage remaining in the display window of the controller. Oil life remaining is based on transmission duty cycle. The filter monitor reports the transmission filters as being OK or not OK. Filter life is based on pressure differential across the filter. Transmission clutch life is based on several factors in the transmission operation, but primarily on clutch fill time, and indicates the clutch life as TRANSHEALTH OK or not OK on the display.

Allison Fifth-Generation Electronic Control

In 2013, Allison introduced the fifth-generation electronic control of the World Transmission. There are very few physical differences between the fourth and fifth generations. In the fifth-generation controls, Allison mostly added sophistication and functionality to the transmission-control software. One difference in the prognostic software is that filter life is measured by pressure differential across the filter. As pressure builds in front of the filter, the PS-2, or pressure switch valve, moves to turn off the PS-2 switch. This makes the filter life prognostics much more accurate. Pulse-width modulation of the pressure control solenoids and the open-ended (OE) solenoid is controlled at a frequency between 12,000 and 19,000 Hz in the fifth generation.

Fifth-generation transmission controllers are common across the Allison product line but offer different software versions, depending on the vocation of the vehicle. The fifth-generation controllers include an integral **inclinometer/accelerometer** to allow further refinement of transmission shifting based on topography and operating conditions, such as load and road grade. Fifth-generation controllers also have other software enhancements, such as greater control over programming in/out functions and the ability to integrate and control diverse optional equipment functionality. The fifth-generation electronics allow features, such as intuitive shift scheduling, which uses various inputs to predict the best shift schedule for the particular load, terrain, operating conditions, etc. Neutral stop is a feature that puts the transmission in neutral when the vehicle is stopped; this saves fuel, and the transmission software applies various clutches to hold the vehicle so there is no rollback. Neutral coast is also available to save even more fuel. Integrated with the vehicle's engine, the software can eliminate jack rabbit starts and aggressive accelerations by controlling engine torque rise.

Retarders

Allison World Transmissions can be equipped with an optional hydraulic output retarder. As shown in **FIGURE 49-63**, the output retarder is mounted at the rear of the transmission in place of the rear cover.

FIGURE 49-63 The retarder is part of the transmission output module.

The **hydraulic retarder** is used as a supplement to the vehicle braking system and is completely electronically controlled. The use of a retarder can increase service brake life by more than double. In addition, having a retarder on a transmission can increase braking efficiency, especially on long grades where service-brake fade can be a serious issue. Hydraulic retarders help to minimize service-brake use and keep brake temperatures down. (Lower brake temperatures result in less fade.) In some instances, the retarder can handle 90% or more of the braking effort.

The retarder is an assembly consisting of the following component parts:

- The rotor, which is splined to the output shaft of the transmission
- A stationary housing
- A retarder accumulator, which is maintained full of transmission fluid
- A control valve assembly

The rotor's cast-iron components include cupped vanes formed into each side face (**FIGURE 49-64**). The rotor sits in the middle of the stationary housing, which also has cupped vanes on its inside surfaces. The cupped surfaces of the stationary housing, however, are in the opposite direction of those on the rotor. During normal driving, the space between the rotor and the stationary cupped vanes of the housing is empty.

In order to control retarder operations, the transmission controller receives inputs from a number of sources. The controller usually receives the vehicle speed directly from the VSS, which is mounted on the output module of the transmission. The controller also gathers information about the arrangement of braking from the vehicle CAN BUS. (The CAN BUS is the controller area network connection on the vehicle. All of the vehicle's electronic controllers are connected together through the CAN BUS and communicate with each other.) The braking information or request can be generated from multiple sources:

FIGURE 49-64 The hydraulic retarder consists of a vaned rotor splined to the transmission output shaft and two stationary vaned elements in the housing.

- A lever operated by the driver
- A separate foot pedal not connected to the vehicle brake pedal
- A variable force switch connected to the foot pedal output
- An auto-retard schedule managed by the transmission controller
- A combination of the above

In addition to speed and braking information, the dash switch sends input to the controller retarder enable switch.

When retardation is required, the controller uses pulse-width modulation to control a solenoid, which, in turn, controls the retarder inlet valve. This valve controls transmission fluid under pressure in the accumulator that is directed to the space between the rotor and the stationary vanes. Retarder capacity is directly related to the amount and pressure of the fluid in this space. The rotor drives the fluid against the stationary cupped vanes. The friction of the fluid causes the forward momentum of the vehicle to change into heat energy. The fluid is constantly replenished by the transmissions hydraulic circuit. Fluid continuously flows through the retarder to the outlet and on to the transmission cooler.

By increasing fluid pressure, more energy can be absorbed, but the temperature of the fluid must be closely monitored. The transmission controller monitors brake request, retarder fluid temperature, transmission sump temperature, transmission range, and output shaft speed. If any parameter is out of range, the transmission controller disables the retardation. Specifically, the controller stops retardation when output shaft speed approaches the vehicle's calibrated minimum 165 to 450 rpm to provide a smooth transition to the service brakes only (**FIGURE 49-65**). Hydraulic retarders are capable of retardation equivalent to 600 horsepower (447 kW)—and more.

Most OEM hydraulic retarders function in a similar fashion, but some include extra features. For example, retarders that include a friction braking feature use a multiple-disc hydraulic clutch inside the retarder to provide even more braking effort. Hydraulic retarders generate enormous amounts of heat, so the transmission heat exchanger system (cooler) and the engine cooling system must be in good working order for them to function correctly.

Shift Selectors

World Transmission shift controllers perform a diagnostic function when a transmission diagnostic trouble code (DTC) is set or when maintenance is required.

WTEC II and WTEC III transmissions have self-diagnostic capability only. When a problem is discovered, the transmission ECU sets a DTC. The codes can be accessed using the push button controller (**FIGURE 49-66A**). To enter the diagnostic mode, press the up and down arrow buttons simultaneously with the key on but the engine off (KOEO). The codes are set as a two-digit main code and a two-digit sub-code and are displayed in sequence on the two-digit selector display.

To display the codes for a transmission with a lever shift, press the diagnostic button (the button with the Allison logo) momentarily with KOEO. If the transmission is fitted with

HYDRAULIC RETARDER (ON)

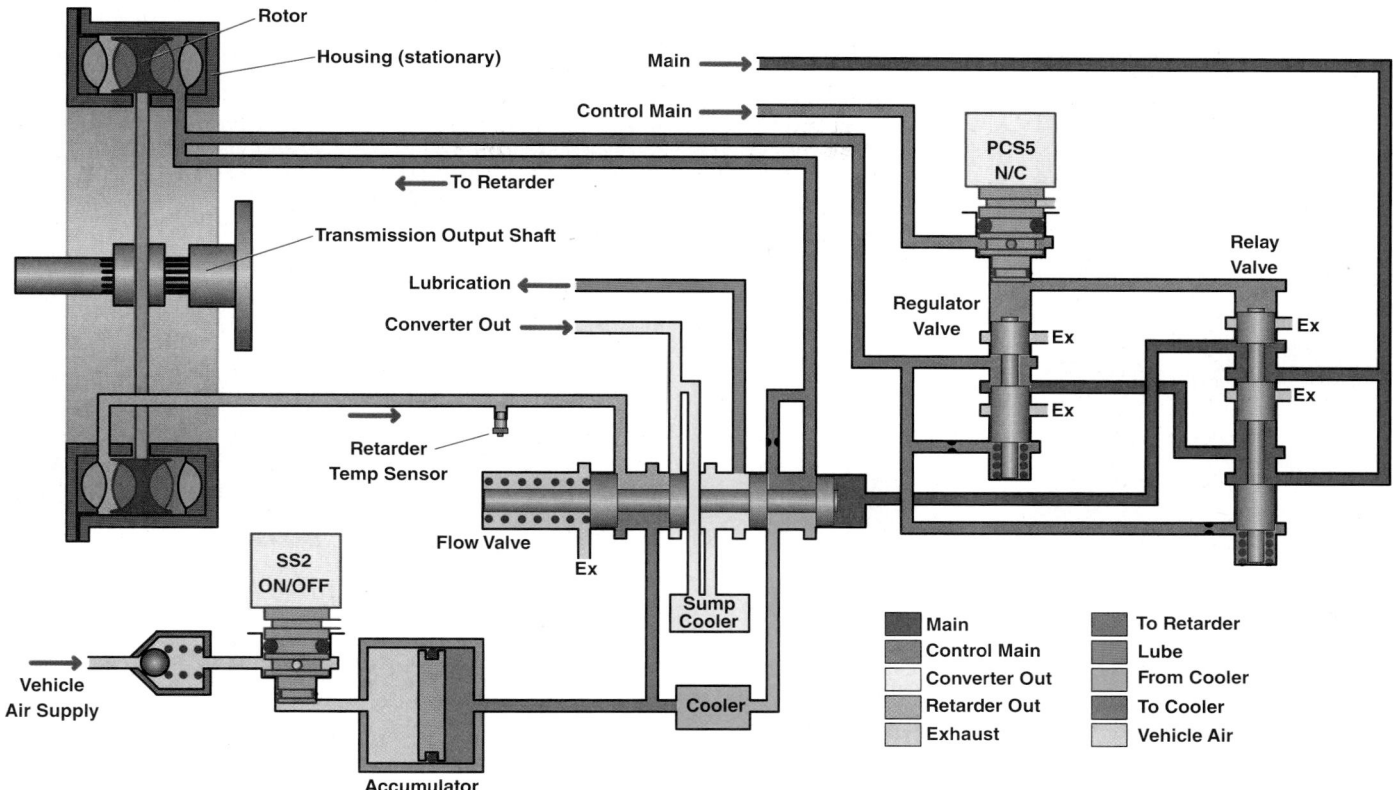

FIGURE 49-65 Retardation is controlled by filling the space the rotor occupies with transmission fluid under pressure.

an oil lever sensor, the oil level is displayed first, as shown in **FIGURE 49-66B**.

After displaying the oL code to indicate "oil level," the display shows an additional code. For example, the display reads oL/ok, if the oil level is good. If oil level is low, oL/Lo is displayed, followed by a number to indicate how low the oil is. For example, oL/Lo/2 means the oil is low by 2 quarts. If the oil level is high, the display shows oL/Hi, followed by a number indicating how much excess oil is in the system. For example, a display reading of the following "oL" then "Hi" then "1" indicates there is one excess quart of oil in the system. If the conditions are not correct to check the oil level, the display flashes oL, followed by a number, for example, 70, as shown in **FIGURE 49-66C**.

Each number indicates a specific issue needs to be addressed:

- X and a number between 1 and 8 indicate that the oil needs to settle for a longer period before the level can be displayed.
- 50 indicates that engine speed is too low.
- 59 indicates engine speed is too high.
- 65 indicates neutral is not selected.
- 70 indicates transmission oil temperature is too low.
- 79 indicates oil temperature is too high.
- 89 indicates that the output shaft is rotating, the vehicle must be stopped.
- 95 indicates a failed sensor.

On vehicles equipped with an oil-level sensor, pushing the up and down button together twice causes the display to enter the diagnostic mode. (On lever selectors, push the diagnostic button twice.) Up to five codes can be stored, and the code for the most recent fault is flashed out in the following format: d1, followed by two digits followed by two more digits. For example, d1,25,11 (**FIGURE 49-66D**).

The system repeats the first code again and again. To switch to the second code, momentarily push the mode button. The second code is flashed out in the same format. During the diagnostic procedure, the LED in the mode button lights if the code is active. Active codes indicate an issue happening with the transmission at that actual moment. If the code is inactive (historic), the LED is not lit. Record all codes. Any of the five code positions that does not have a stored code flashes "—". From the fifth code position, pushing the mode button momentarily returns the display to the first code position again.

The following is an example of two codes after entering the diagnostic mode code "d1," "13," "12," and "d2," "21," "12" are displayed. Code 13 indicates a problem with the TCM and 12 indicates low voltage. Code 21 12, 21 indicates a problem with the TPS and 12 again indicates low voltage. There are well over 100 diagnostic codes and sub-codes that can be displayed, and the troubleshooting manual will guide the technician in the proper diagnostic routine to correct the problem.

FIGURE 49-66 A. Older WTEC II and III controller. **B.** oL indicates oil level is being shown. **C.** Code number (70 indicates that transmission oil temperature is too low to read the oil level). **D.** Display shows first of five code positions: d1, d2, d3, d4, d5.

Clearing Codes on WTEC II and III Disconnecting the ECU power clears all active code indicators and keeps them in the code queue as inactive. Code indicators can be removed manually. While in the diagnostic mode, push and hold the mode button for three seconds until the mode LED flashes. That indicates that all active indicators are removed. Inactive codes can also be removed. While still in the diagnostic mode, press and hold the mode button again for 10 seconds until it flashes again. All inactive indicators are cleared when the TCM is powered down.

To exit the diagnostic mode on a push-button shifter, press any range button. On lever-type selectors, push the diagnostic button once, or move the lever to any other position.

The fourth- and fifth-generation control systems use SAE J-2012 codes that are onboard diagnostics generation II (OBD II) compliant. These codes contain one letter followed by four digits. Codes can be read from the Allison shift selector, with an aftermarket diagnostic reader, or using the Allison DOC software along with a computer.

The letter in a J-2012 code signifies the general component or system.

- B = Body systems
- C = Chassis systems
- P = Powertrain systems
- U = Network systems

The first digit after the letter code indicates DTC groupings.

- 0 = SAE/ISO controlled
- 1 = Manufacturer controlled
- 2 = SAE/ISO controlled in powertrain manufacturer controlled in any other system
- 3 = Reserved for SAE/ISO or manufacturer controlled

The second digit after a powertrain DTC refers to which system is affected. For example, 7, 8, and 9 indicate transmission issues. Some examples include P-07XX, P-08XX, and P-09XX. The XX will be the actual two-digit fault code. P-00XX, P-01XX, and P-02XX pertain to the fuel system. P-03XX is ignition systems.

The fourth-generation Allison shift selectors have a two-digit display similar to the WTEC II and WTEC III, and the codes are accessed in the same way in all three models. To read the fourth-generation diagnostic codes, turn the key on, but keep the engine off. Push the up and down arrows together twice or the diagnostic button twice on lever shifters.

The order in which the codes appear is dictated by the recency of the problem (more recent troubles are indicated first). The first code to be displayed is the position of the code (d1). The last code set is always d1 and is followed by a single letter (c, p, or u) and then by a sequence of two two-digit codes. For example, d1, followed by p, followed by 07, followed by 27 tells us the following information: first code position d1 is code p0727; the "p" indicates an issue with the powertrain. Code p0727 means engine speed sensor input to the transmission no signal.

To determine if a second code is present, push the mode button momentarily. You can toggle through up to five codes before the display returns to the first code. To clear the codes on a fourth-generation system, press and hold the mode button for ten seconds while in diagnostic mode. This clears both active and inactive codes. Before clearing codes, always record them for future reference.

TABLE 49-9 contains a few of the fourth-generation WT control DTCs. It is by no means a comprehensive list, as there are well over a hundred DTCs that can be set. Always consult the OEM manual for troubleshooting.

Post-2009 Fourth-Generation Transmission Controls with Prognostics The process for reading the codes is slightly different when the vehicle is equipped with fourth-

TABLE 49-9 Sample of Fourth-Generation Trouble Codes

Diagnostic Code	Code Indicator
P063F	Auto Configuration Engine Coolant Temp Input Not Present
P0658	Actuator Supply Voltage 1 Low
P0659	Actuator Supply Voltage 1 High
P0701	Transmission Control System Performance
P0702	Transmission Control System Electrical
P0703	Brake Switch Circuit Malfunction
P0708	Transmission Range Sensor Circuit High Input
P070C	Transmission Fluid Level Sensor Circuit—Low Input
P070D	Transmission Fluid Level Sensor Circuit—High Input
P0711	Transmission Fluid Temperature Sensor Circuit Performance
P0712	Transmission Fluid Temperature Sensor Circuit Low Input
P0713	Transmission Fluid Temperature Sensor Circuit High Input
P0716	Turbine Speed Sensor Circuit Performance
P0717	Turbine Speed Sensor Circuit No Signal
P0719	Brake Switch ABS Input Low
P071D	General Purpose Input Fault
P0721	Output Speed Sensor Circuit Performance
P0722	Output Speed Sensor Circuit No Signal
P0726	Engine Speed Sensor Circuit Performance
P0727	Engine Speed Sensor Circuit No Signal

FIGURE 49-67 Fifth-generation shift selectors have a graphical display capable of displaying a message, rather than a simple code.

generation controls and prognostics are enabled. On vehicles equipped with prognostics, a small wrench icon is momentarily displayed between the two digits on the fourth-generation shift selector when the vehicle is started. The wrench icon should then go out. If, however, the icon remains illuminated, it indicates that maintenance is required. When the oil should be changed, the wrench illuminates for two minutes after drive range is selected and then goes out. When the filter is due for a change, the wrench icon flashes on and off for two minutes after drive range is selected and then goes out. When clutch maintenance is required, the wrench icon comes on and remains on for the entire operating time of the vehicle.

The shift controller can access the oil level, prognostic features, and the diagnostic codes by following this procedure. All these actions are done with KOEO with the vehicle stopped. Push the up and down arrows together once on a push-type lever or the Allison diagnostic button once on a lever shifter; the display shows the oil level. Pushing the button twice displays the remaining oil life with the oL code followed by a number from 0 to 99. The number indicates the percentage oil life remaining.

Pushing the buttons three times puts the display into filter life mode. The display then shows FM followed by either "oK" if the filter is good or "Lo" if the filter should be changed.

Pushing the buttons four times puts the system into clutch life, or transmission maintenance, mode. If internal transmission maintenance is required, the display reads TM followed by either "oK" or "Lo."

While the display is in oil-life-monitor mode, pushing the mode button for ten seconds resets that monitor. (The same is true when the display is in filter-life-monitor mode.) The oil life monitor resets to 99 and the filter monitor resets to "oK." Note that, after model year 2010, the oil filter is monitored by pressure differential, so the filter life monitor goes back to "Lo" if the filter is clogged.

To access the diagnostic codes on fourth-generation systems with prognostics, press the up and down buttons together five times on the push button selector. For lever selectors, push the diagnostic button five times. The diagnostic codes are displayed in the same format as for fourth-generation systems without prognostics described previously. To clear codes while in the diagnostic mode, push and hold the mode button for ten seconds. That clears both active and inactive codes. Be sure to record all of the codes before clearing them.

Fifth-Generation Shift Selectors The fifth-generation Allison shift selectors are capable of displaying two digits for gear selection. These selectors also have multi-character graphic-display capabilities. That means that fifth-generation shift selectors can display prognostic information, full codes, and code descriptions, making it easier for technicians to diagnosis problems.

The process for using the shift selector to check transmission function is essentially the same as for the fourth generation with prognostics. Press the up and down arrows together on a push button selector (or push the diagnostic button once on a lever selector) to obtain information about transmission oil level. Push twice for the oil-life monitor, three times for the filter-life monitor, and four times for the transmission-life monitor. Although the basic process is the same, however, what the technician sees on the fifth-generation shift selector is more sophisticated. The fifth-generation selector displays a message, rather than a simple code. For example, TRANS OIL 3 QUARTS HI, or, TRANS OIL LEVEL OK (**FIGURE 49-67**).

To access diagnostic codes, push the buttons once. The display cycles through showing the oil level function, followed by prognostics, followed by the diagnostic codes. The display shows both the code and whether it is active or not, for example, P0730 ACTIVE. To check prognostics only use the same technique as for fourth generation.

SKILL DRILL 49-1 Accessing Prognostics and Resetting Maintenance Flags

1. Locate a vehicle with fourth-generation control and lever-type shifter.
2. Drive the vehicle until it is at operating temperature, then park the vehicle in the shop, set the parking brake, and chock the wheels.
3. With the engine running and the shift control lever in neutral, press the Allison diagnostic button on the shift control once.
4. Record the oil level as it is displayed; i.e., oL oK or oL Lo followed by the number of quarts it is low.
5. Place the shifter in any gear and back into neutral; this exits the oil level mode.

6. Press the diagnostic button twice quickly, record the oil life percentage, if necessary, and reset the oil life percentage by holding down the mode button for 10 seconds.
7. Again, place the shifter in any gear and back into neutral.
8. Press the diagnostic button 3 times quickly and read the filter status; FM and either oK or Lo. Lo means the filter should be changed. To reset the filter status, hold down the mode button for 10 seconds while in the filter status mode.
9. Again, move the shifter to any gear and back to neutral.
10. Press the diagnostics button 4 times quickly and record the transmission health; the display reads TM and either oK or Lo. Lo Means that the transmission clutches require maintenance. The transmission health monitor cannot be reset from the shift control, it can only be reset with the Allison diagnostic software.
11. Again, place the lever in any gear and back to neutral.
12. Press the diagnostic button five times quickly and read any diagnostic codes as they are displayed (there may not be any codes). The codes are displayed two characters at a time, such as d1, P, 07, 22 for diagnostic code 1 P0722, and each code continues to flash until the mode button is pushed once, then the next code is displayed.
13. Record each code for reference, then, to clear active and inactive codes, press and hold the mode button for 10 seconds.
14. Shut off the vehicle and discuss any required service procedure with your supervisor.

Resetting the maintenance flags and the codes is the same procedure as for the fourth generation with prognostics described previously. To access the prognostics and reset the maintenance flags through the lever type shift control, follow the steps in **SKILL DRILL 49-1**.

Allison introduced a comprehensive dedicated diagnostic software package in 2002 called Allison DOC® (**FIGURE 49-68**). The software is capable of diagnosing faults and monitoring transmission operation and adaptations. Allison DOC software version 12.0 is the current package available from authorized Allison dealers. The software enables technicians to diagnose transmission operation and record operational data for all Allison's electronically controlled transmissions—from the ATEC/CEC through all versions of the WT—and is also capable of diagnosing the Allison TC-10-TS. As described in the next section, the Allison TC-10-TS is a ten-speed, twin-countershaft, fully automatic transmission designed for on-highway Class 8 tractors. Allison has offices all over the world and hundreds of qualified dealers in North America.

TC-10-TS

LO 49-5 Describe the operation and power flows of the Allison TC-10-TS transmission.

In late 2012, Allison released a new transmission model called the TC-10-TS, which stands for twin-countershaft (TC), ten-speed (10), tractor series (TS) (**FIGURE 49-69A**). The TC-10-TS employs the blended architecture of a traditional,

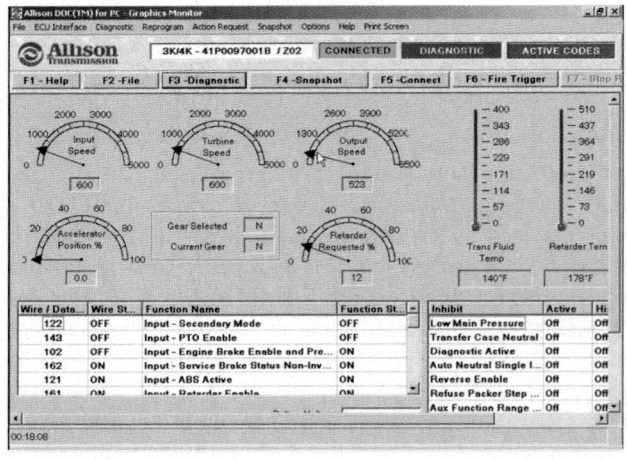

FIGURE 49-68 Screen from Allison DOC diagnostic software.
© Allison Transmission

twin-countershaft main box, a planetary two-speed range section, and electronically controlled hydraulic clutches for shifting. With ten forward speeds and two reverse speeds, plus the comfort and ease of operation of an automatic transmission, this unit was designed to carve out a niche in the Class 8 on-highway tractor market. This transmission is used primarily in the markets using less-than-truck-load and around-town delivery vehicles. At present Navistar, Kenworth and Peterbilt offer the TC-10 as an option in their trucks.

FIGURE 49-69 A. The Allison TC-10 TS is specifically targeted at the Class 8 on-highway tractor market. **B.** The TC-10 has two countershafts, only one of which is used for any particular range.

The TC-10-TS model is a completely unique design that incorporates the following features:

- Torque converter input module with lockup clutch
- Twin-countershaft five-speed main gear box with five multi-disc wet clutches (**FIGURE 49-69B**)

- A two-speed planetary range rear section controlled by two additional wet clutches

As shown in **FIGURE 49-70**, the TC-10-TS has five wet clutches in the main box. With a clutch for every gear, shifting takes place under power with no efficiency losses required when torque is

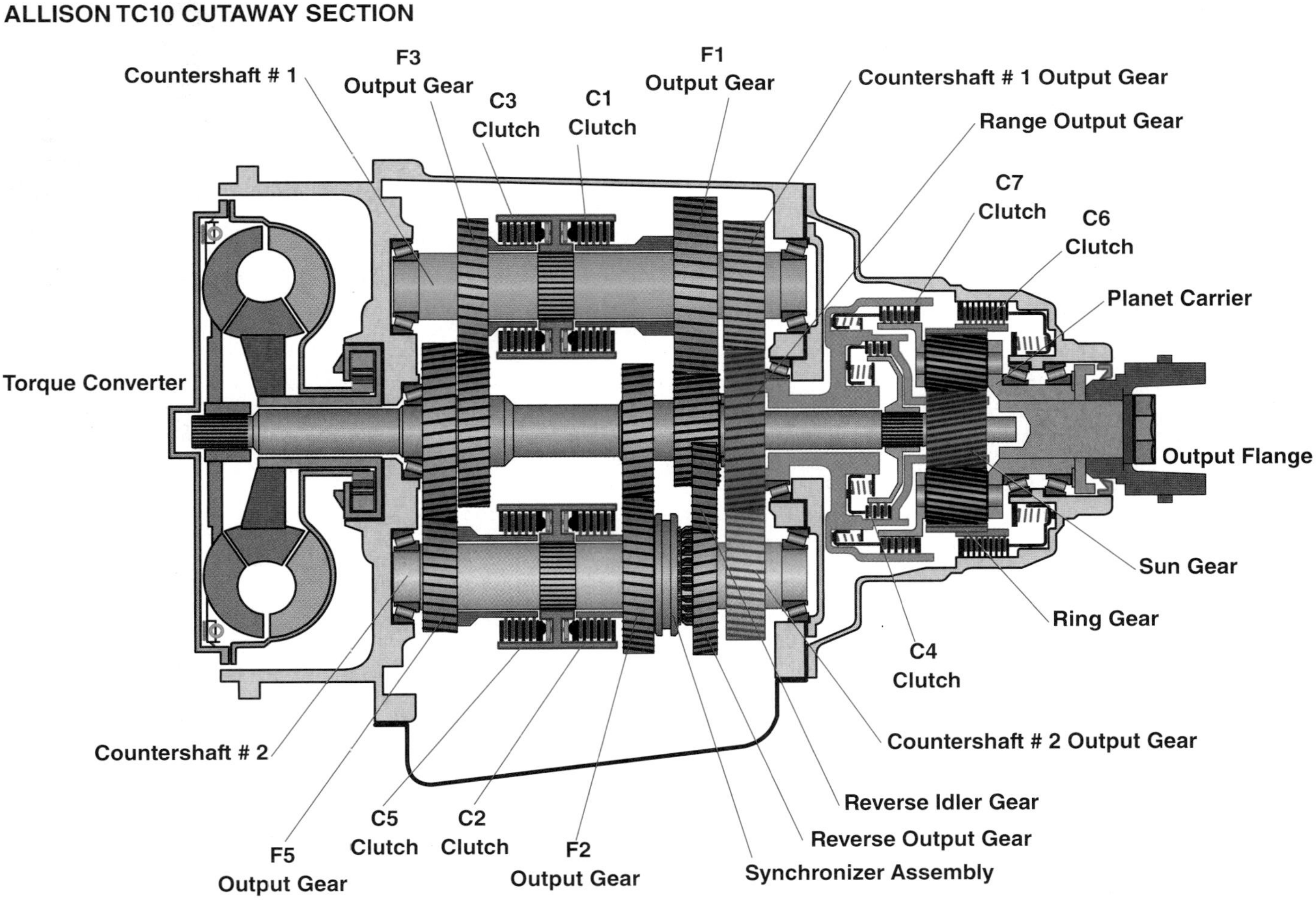

ALLISON TC10 CUTAWAY SECTION

Countershaft # 1
F3 Output Gear
C3 Clutch
C1 Clutch
F1 Output Gear
Countershaft # 1 Output Gear
Range Output Gear
C7 Clutch
C6 Clutch
Planet Carrier
Torque Converter
Output Flange
Sun Gear
Ring Gear
C4 Clutch
Countershaft # 2
Countershaft # 2 Output Gear
F5 Output Gear
C5 Clutch
C2 Clutch
F2 Output Gear
Reverse Idler Gear
Reverse Output Gear
Synchronizer Assembly

FIGURE 49-70 Cutaway schematic of the TC-10 transmission.

broken to make a shift. The power is reduced slightly during shifts to soften the shift and, unlike in automated manual transmissions, it is unnecessary to completely break torque for a shift to occur.

Allison has historically made transmissions for use in Class 8 on-highway tractors, but the TC-10-TS is the first Allison transmission targeted specifically to the on-highway tractor market. After conducting extensive field testing of the TC-10, Allison claims the transmission can produce a 3% to 5% better fuel economy than the automated transmissions available when it was introduced. Acceleration is also improved with the TC-10-TS because the transmission's clutches are basically handing off power from one to another. Under power during fleet testing, this transmission produces 20% faster acceleration. Plus, the transmission controller is adaptive. The shift can be tailored to the load and the terrain without driver input, further improving fuel economy. The TC-10-TS is available for engines with up to 600 hp (447 kW) and 1700 ft-lb (2304 Nm) of torque. (The company states the TC-10-TS transmission is capable of handling 1850 ft-lb (2508 Nm) of torque, but for now it recommends a maximum torque of 1700 ft-lb (2304 Nm). **TABLE 49-10** shows the TC-10-TS clutch application.

TC-10-TS Power Flows

TC-10-TS Neutral

In neutral, the C-6 clutch is applied and holds the ring gear of the planetary gear set stationary and the synchronizer is rearward. The input shaft only rotates with the torque converter turbine (**FIGURE 49-71**).

TC-10-TS First Range

As shown in **FIGURE 49-72**, in first range, the C-1 clutch applies, and the synchronizer moves forward. C-1 clutch locks the F-1 output gear to the right-side counter shaft, and the synchro position unlocks the reverse gear. Power flows from the input shaft to the right-side countershaft through C-1. Then power flows back to the range output gear through the right-side countershaft output gear. The range output gear turns the sun gear of the planetary range section. C-6 is holding the ring gear, so the range carrier is output. That means the range planetary gear set is in low range.

TC-10-TS Second Range

The power flow for second is the same as first with the exception that C-1 is released and C-2 is applied (**FIGURE 49-73**). C-2 locks the F2 output gear to the left-side counter shaft through the synchronizer, which is in the forward position. Note that the C-2 clutch can connect either the reverse output gear or F-2 output gear to the left-side countershaft, depending on the position of the synchronizer. If the synchronizer is forward, the F-2 gear is connected by C-2. If the synchronizer is rearward, then the reverse gear is connected to the countershaft. In the second range, power is delivered to the range output gear through the left countershaft from the F-2 output gear. C-6 is still applied and holding the ring gear of the planetary range gear set. The planetary gear set, therefore, remains the same as for first gear—in low range.

TC-10-TS Third Range

In third range, the power flow switches back to the right-side countershaft (**FIGURE 49-74**). C-2 is released, and C-3 is applied. That brings power from the input shaft to the range output gear through the F-3 output gear at the front of the right countershaft. Again, the planetary range section remains the same.

TC-10-TS Fourth Range

In fourth range, the countershafts are not used (**FIGURE 49-75**). C-3 clutch is released and C-4 clutch is applied. Rotational power is brought directly from the input shaft to the sun gear in the planetary range section. C-6 is still holding the planetary range section ring gear, and the range planetary carrier remains the output.

TABLE 49-10 TC-10 Clutch Application Chart

RANGE	RATIO	STEP	C1	C2	C3	C4	C5	C6	C7	SF*	SR*
N	–	–						×			×
1	7.40	–	×					×		×	
2	5.44	1.36		×				×		×	
3	4.25	1.28			×			×		×	
4	3.43	1.24				×		×		×	
5	2.94	1.17					×	×		×	
6	2.16	1.36	×						×	×	
7	1.59	1.36		×					×	×	
8	1.24	1.28			×				×	×	
9	1.00	1.24				×			×	×	
10	0.86	1.17					×		×	×	
R1	6.71	–		×				×			×
R2	1.96	–		×					×		×

*The SF and SR categories refer to the synchronizer forward or rearward.

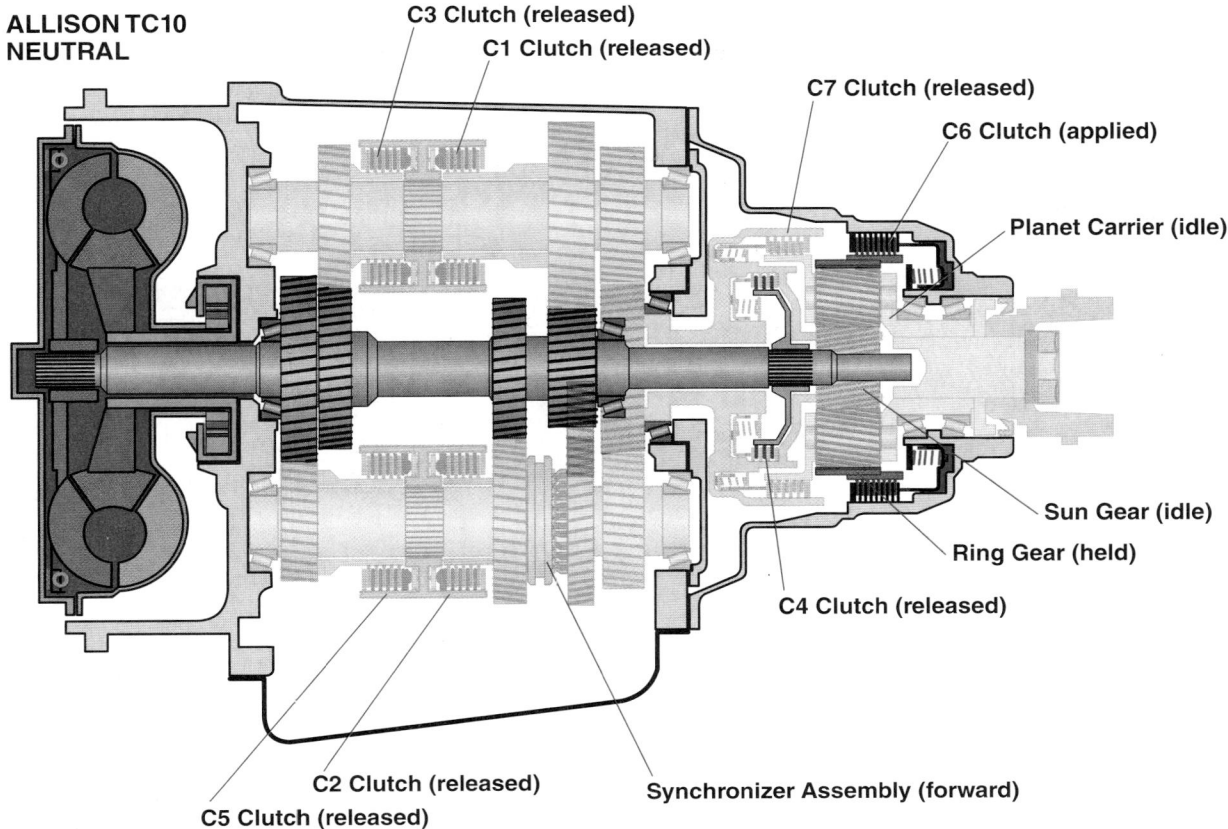

ALLISON TC10
NEUTRAL

C3 Clutch (released)
C1 Clutch (released)
C7 Clutch (released)
C6 Clutch (applied)
Planet Carrier (idle)
Sun Gear (idle)
Ring Gear (held)
C4 Clutch (released)
C2 Clutch (released)
C5 Clutch (released)
Synchronizer Assembly (forward)

FIGURE 49-71 In neutral, no power is transmitted beyond the input shaft.

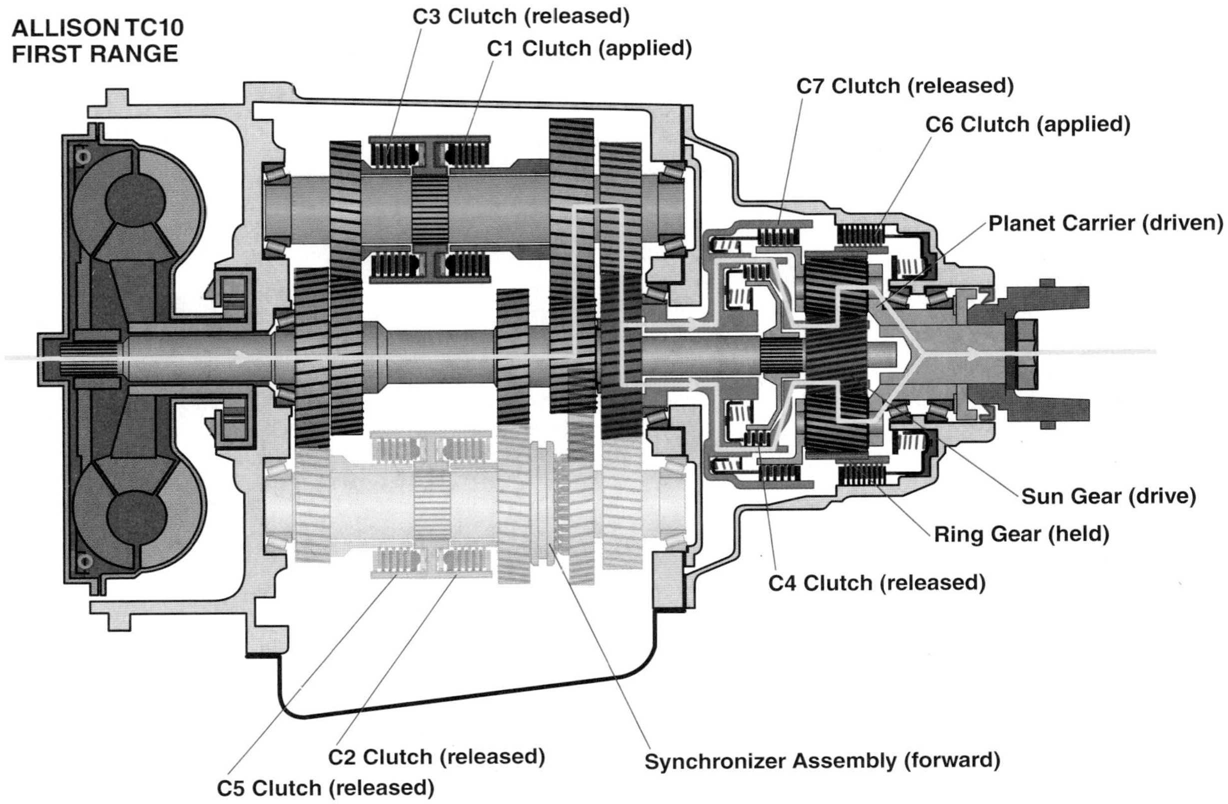

ALLISON TC10
FIRST RANGE

C3 Clutch (released)
C1 Clutch (applied)
C7 Clutch (released)
C6 Clutch (applied)
Planet Carrier (driven)
Sun Gear (drive)
Ring Gear (held)
C4 Clutch (released)
C2 Clutch (released)
C5 Clutch (released)
Synchronizer Assembly (forward)

FIGURE 49-72 First range.

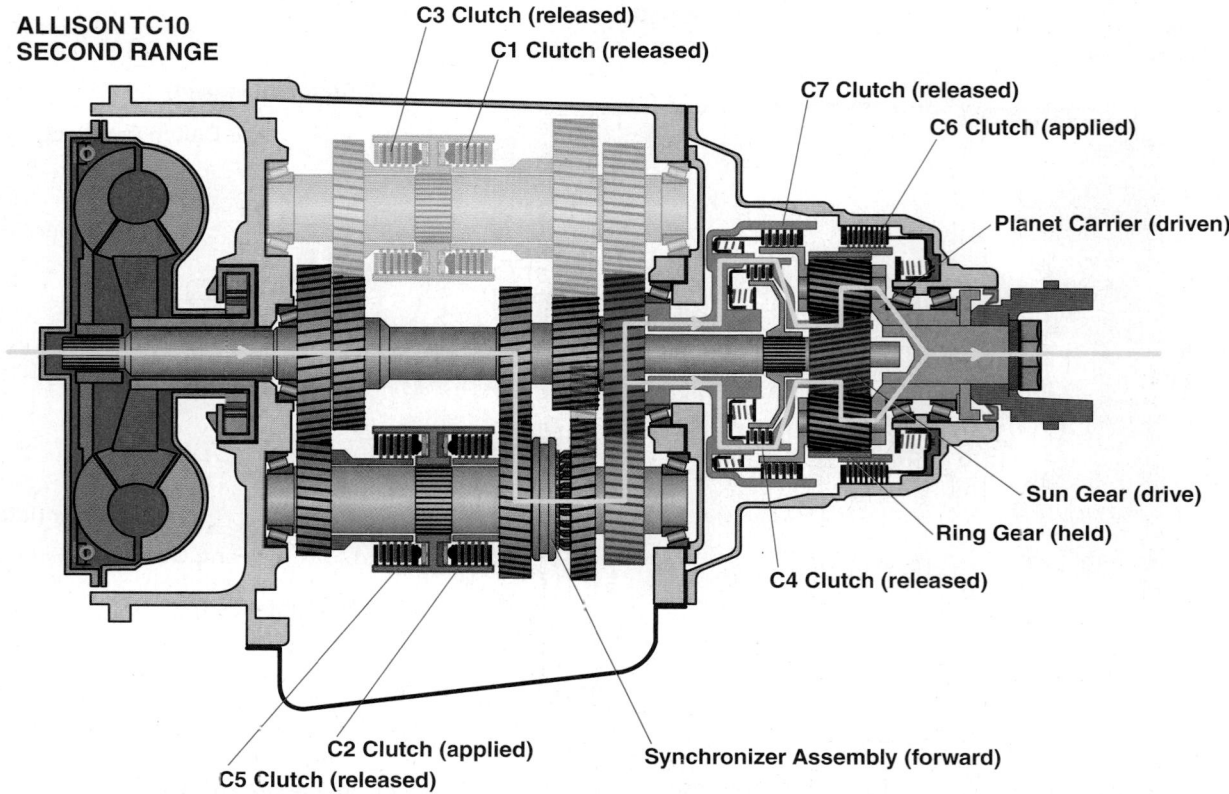

ALLISON TC10 SECOND RANGE

C3 Clutch (released)
C1 Clutch (released)
C7 Clutch (released)
C6 Clutch (applied)
Planet Carrier (driven)
Sun Gear (drive)
Ring Gear (held)
C4 Clutch (released)
C2 Clutch (applied)
C5 Clutch (released)
Synchronizer Assembly (forward)

FIGURE 49-73 Second range.

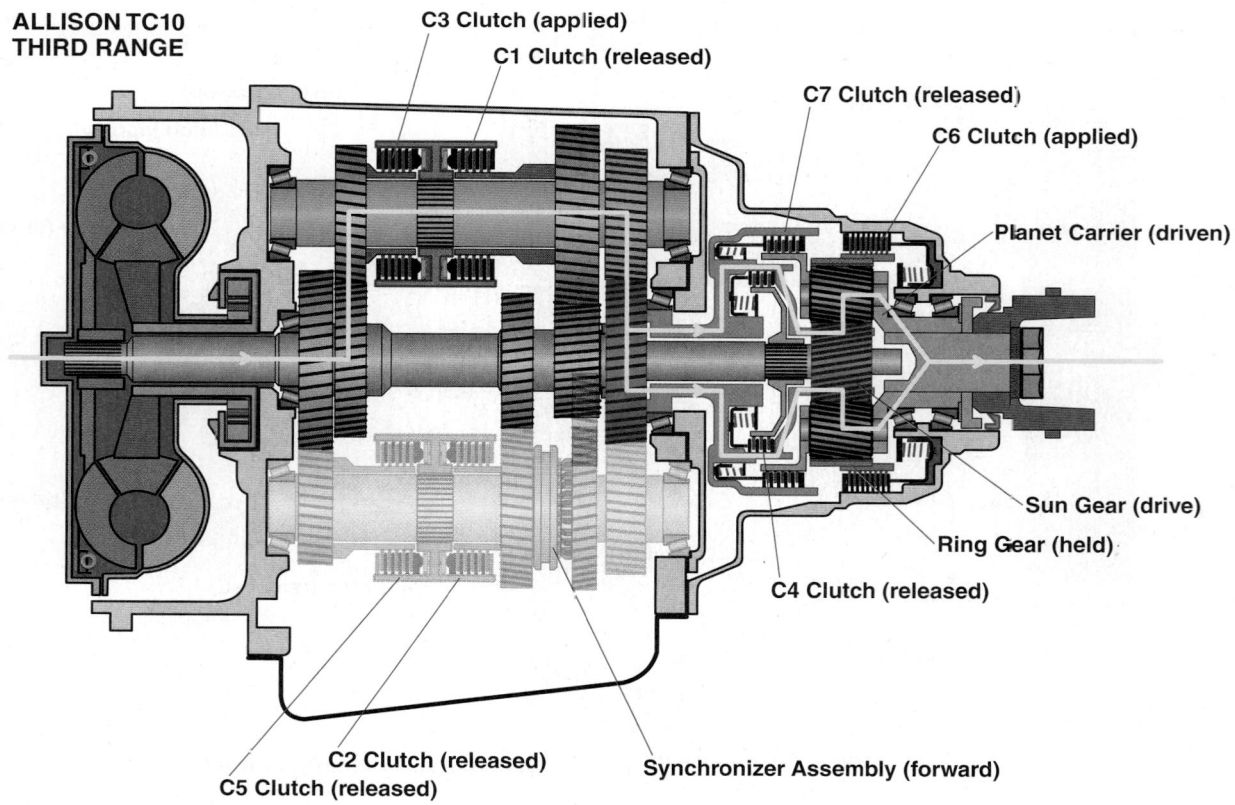

ALLISON TC10 THIRD RANGE

C3 Clutch (applied)
C1 Clutch (released)
C7 Clutch (released)
C6 Clutch (applied)
Planet Carrier (driven)
Sun Gear (drive)
Ring Gear (held)
C4 Clutch (released)
C2 Clutch (released)
C5 Clutch (released)
Synchronizer Assembly (forward)

FIGURE 49-74 Third range.

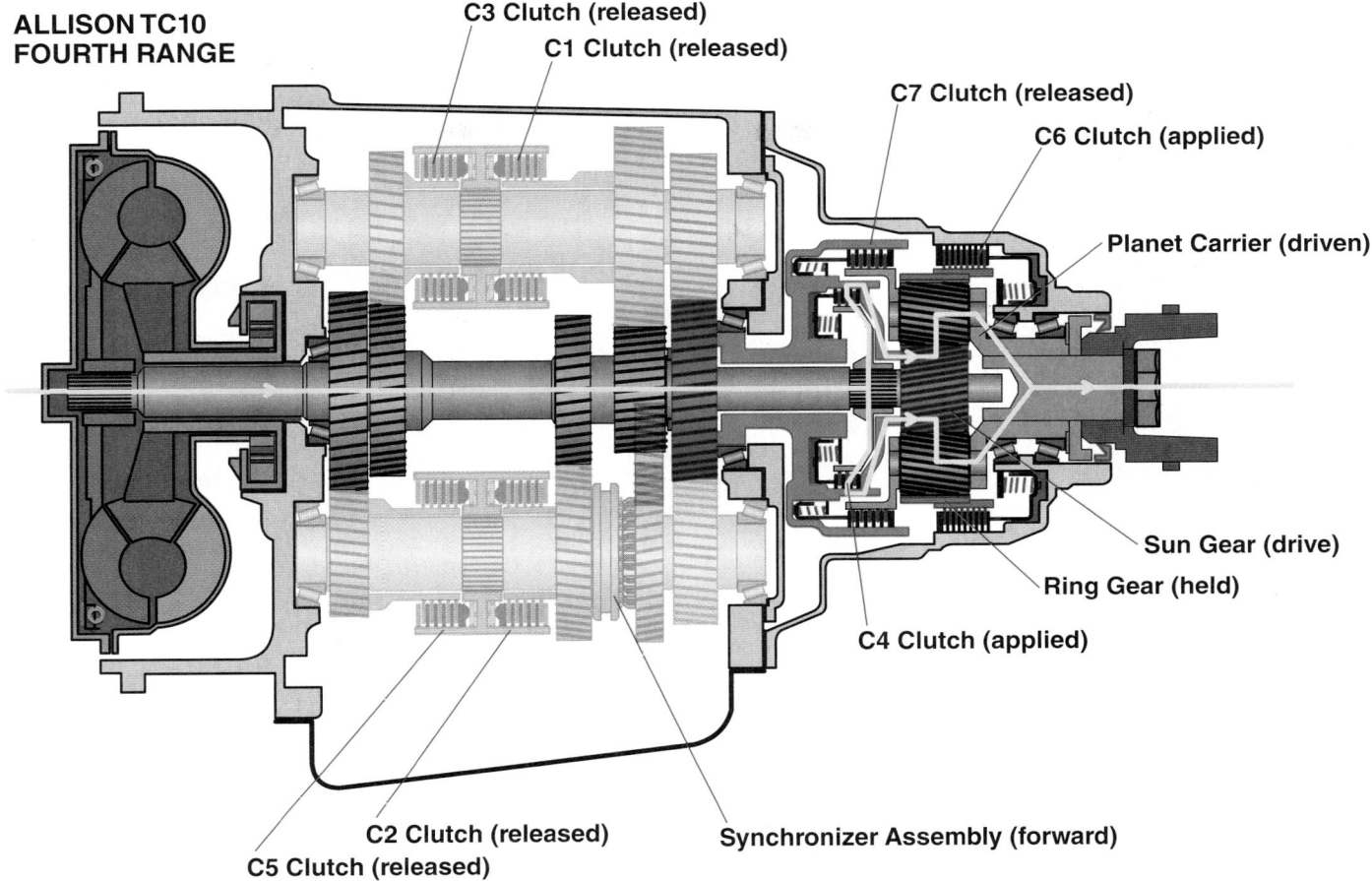

ALLISON TC10 FOURTH RANGE

C3 Clutch (released)
C1 Clutch (released)
C7 Clutch (released)
C6 Clutch (applied)
Planet Carrier (driven)
Sun Gear (drive)
Ring Gear (held)
C4 Clutch (applied)
C2 Clutch (released)
C5 Clutch (released)
Synchronizer Assembly (forward)

FIGURE 49-75 Fourth range.

TC-10-TS Fifth Range

In fifth range, C-4 is released, C-5 is applied, and C-6 remains applied. C-5 locks the F-5 output gear to the left-side countershaft. Power flows from the input shaft to the left-side countershaft through F-5 and then to the range output gear. The planetary range section remains unchanged, and the planetary carrier is still the output (**FIGURE 49-76**).

TC-10-TS Sixth Range

In sixth range, the planetary range section changes to high range or direct (straight through operation). C-6 is released, and C-7 is applied. C-7 remains applied for ranges six through ten. C-6 releases the planetary ring gear, and C-7 locks the planetary carrier to the range output gear and, therefore, to the planetary sun gear. This causes all three members of the range planetary to lock together and turn as one unit (**FIGURE 49-77**).

For ranges six through ten, the first five power flows are repeated with one important exception. Instead of being reduced through the planetary range section, power flows pass straight through it unchanged. In the sixth range, then, C-1 is applied and locks the F-1 output gear to the right-side

countershaft. Power flows from the input shaft through F-1 and back to the range output gear. From there, power flows directly to the output shaft through the locked-together range planetary gear set.

TC-10-TS Seventh Range

In seventh range, C-7 remains applied, C-1 is released, and C-2 is applied. That sequence locks the F-2 output gear to the left-side countershaft through the synchronizer, which is in the forward position. Power flows from the input shaft to the left-side countershaft through F-2 and then to the range output gear. From there, power flows directly to the output shaft through the locked-together range planetary set (**FIGURE 49-78**).

TC-10-TS Eighth Range

In eighth range, C-7 is still applied, C-2 is released, and C-3 applies. C-3 locks the F-3 output gear to the right-side counter shaft. Power flows from the input shaft through F-3 to the range output gear and, from there, directly to the output shaft through the range planetary gear set that is locked together (**FIGURE 49-79**).

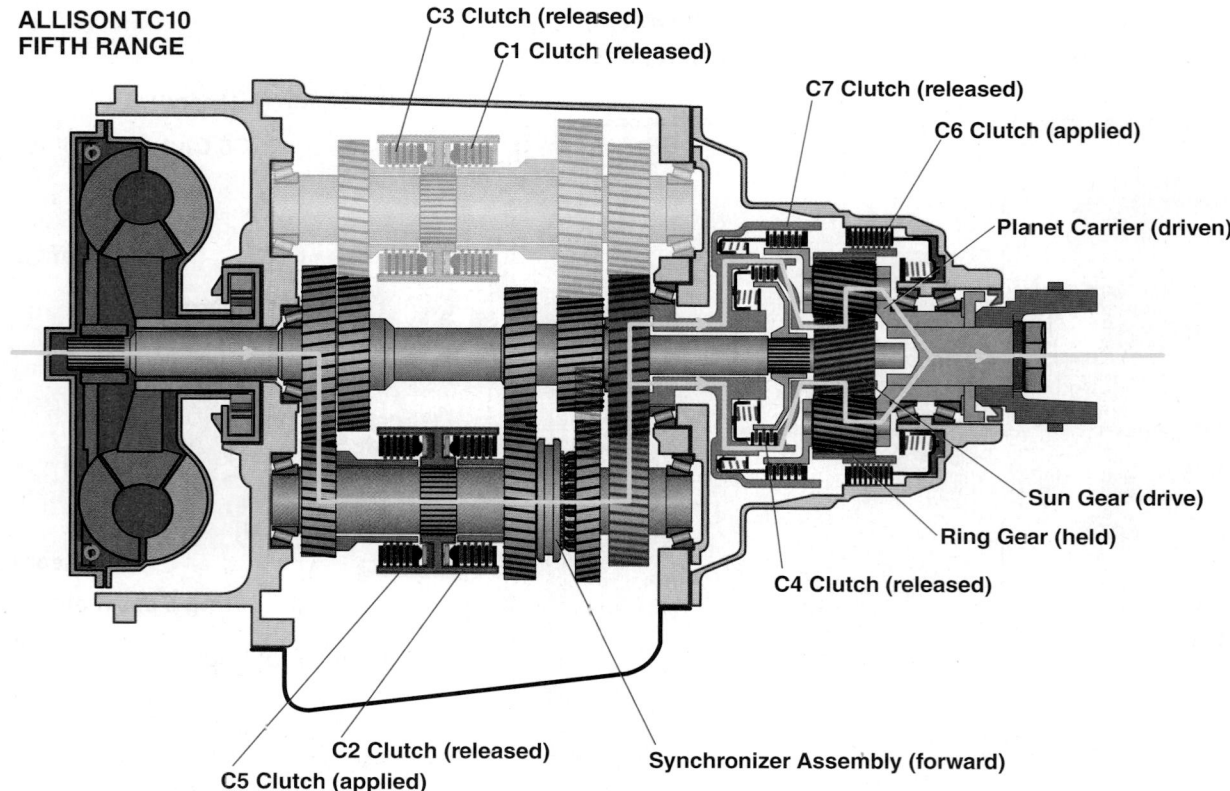

FIGURE 49-76 Fifth range.

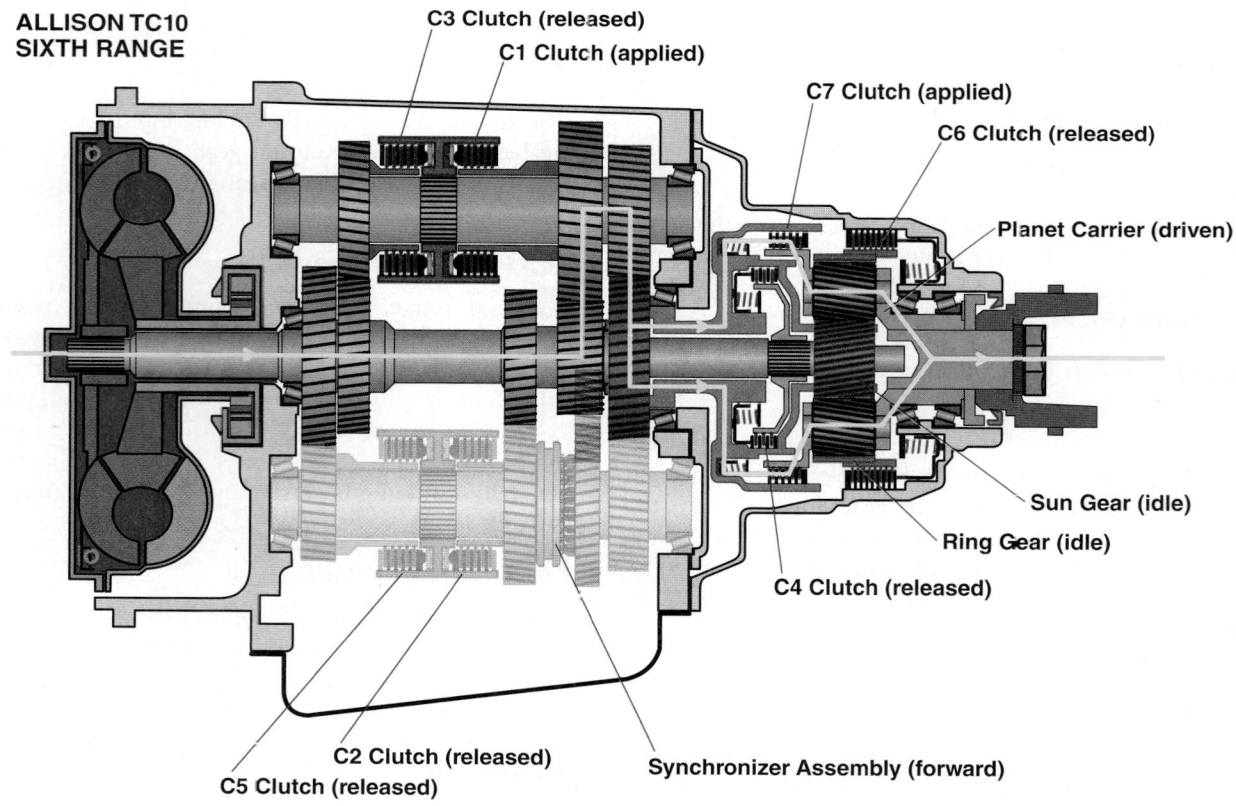

FIGURE 49-77 Sixth range.

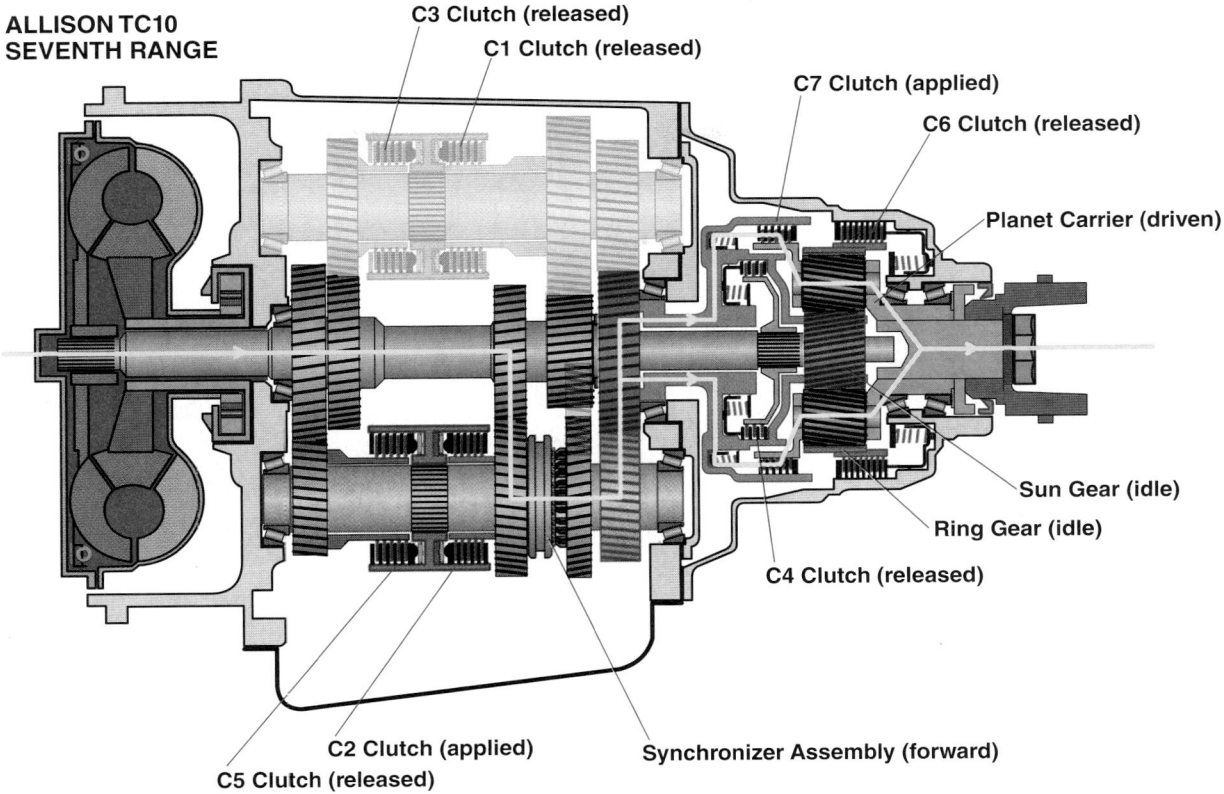

ALLISON TC10 SEVENTH RANGE

C3 Clutch (released)
C1 Clutch (released)
C7 Clutch (applied)
C6 Clutch (released)
Planet Carrier (driven)
Sun Gear (idle)
Ring Gear (idle)
C4 Clutch (released)
C2 Clutch (applied)
C5 Clutch (released)
Synchronizer Assembly (forward)

FIGURE 49-78 Seventh range.

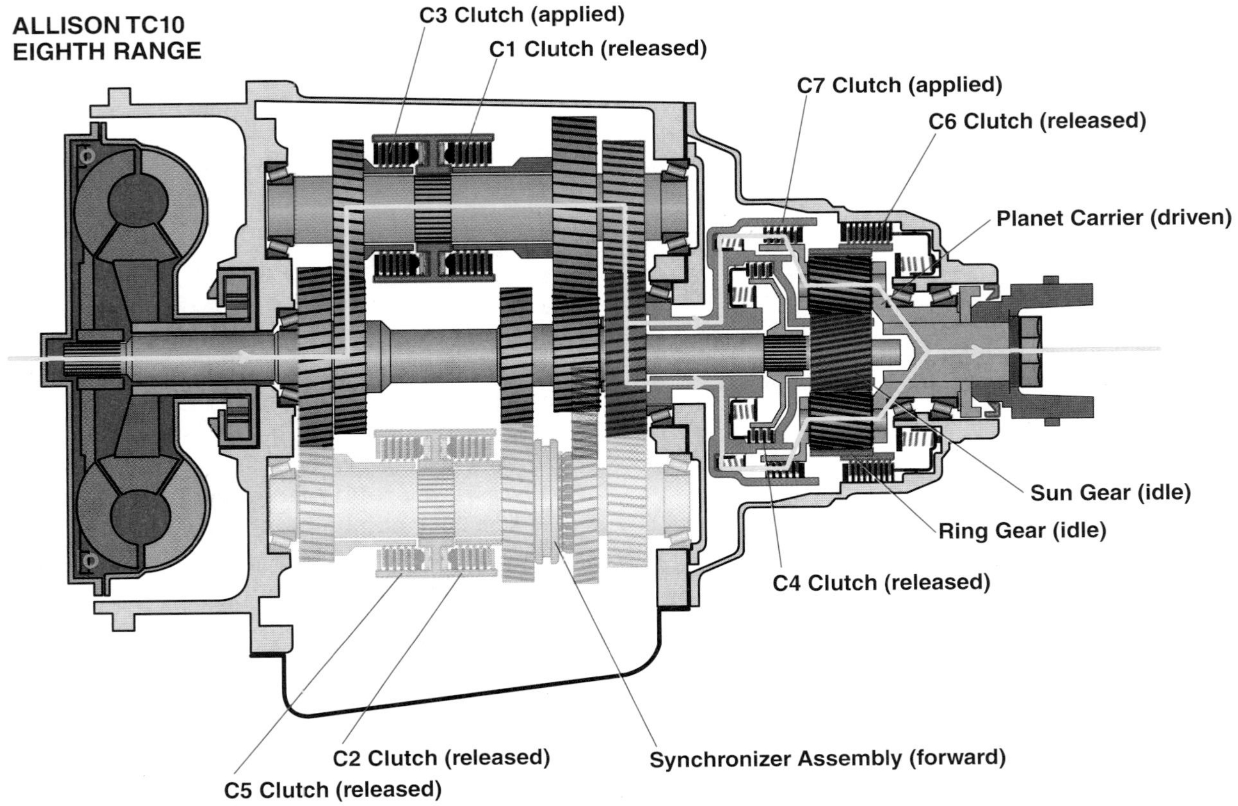

ALLISON TC10 EIGHTH RANGE

C3 Clutch (applied)
C1 Clutch (released)
C7 Clutch (applied)
C6 Clutch (released)
Planet Carrier (driven)
Sun Gear (idle)
Ring Gear (idle)
C4 Clutch (released)
C2 Clutch (released)
C5 Clutch (released)
Synchronizer Assembly (forward)

FIGURE 49-79 Eighth range.

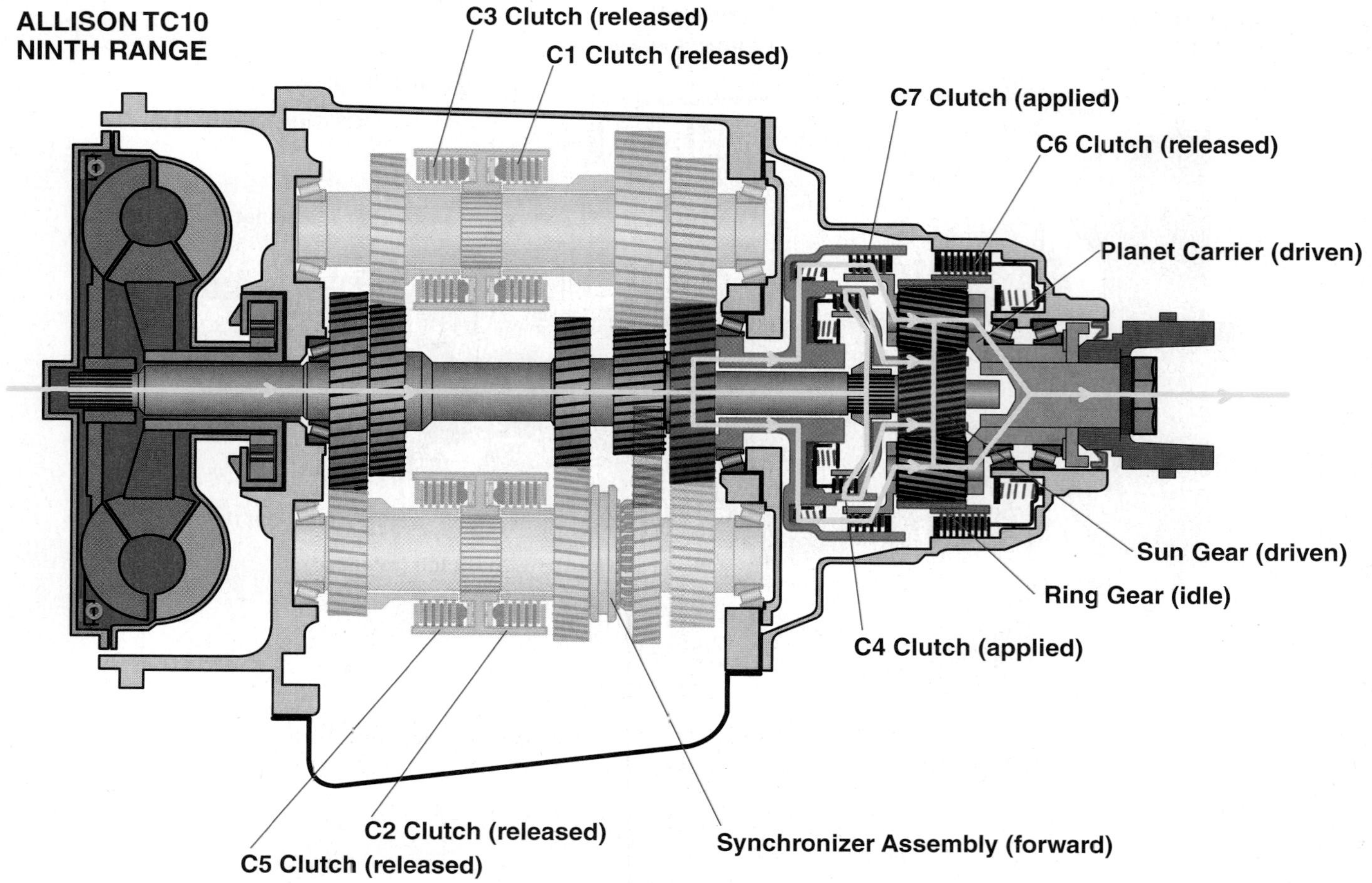

**ALLISON TC10
NINTH RANGE**

C3 Clutch (released)

C1 Clutch (released)

C7 Clutch (applied)

C6 Clutch (released)

Planet Carrier (driven)

Sun Gear (driven)

Ring Gear (idle)

C4 Clutch (applied)

C2 Clutch (released)

C5 Clutch (released)

Synchronizer Assembly (forward)

FIGURE 49-80 Ninth range.

TC-10-TS Ninth Range

In the TC-10-TS, ninth range is direct. That means that power flows straight through from the engine to the output shaft. In ninth range, C-3 is released, and C-4 is applied. The counter shafts are not used as in fourth range. C-4 locks the input shaft to the sun gear of the range planetary. C-7 is still applied, so the carrier of the range planetary is also locked to the sun gear. As a result, the planetary gear set turns as one unit, and power passes straight through from the input shaft to the output shaft (**FIGURE 49-80**).

TC-10-TS Tenth Range

Tenth range is an overdrive range in the TC-10-TS. In tenth, C-4 is released, and C-5 applies. C-7 remains applied. C-5 locks the F-5 output gear to the left-side countershaft. Power flows from the input shaft to the left-side countershaft through F-5 and then to the range output gear. From the range output gear, power flows directly to the output shaft through the locked-together planetary range section (**FIGURE 49-81**).

TC-10-TS Reverse

The TC-10-TS has two reverse ranges: one low range and one high range. In reverse low, C-6 and C-2 are applied, and the

synchronizer is rearward. C-6 holds the ring gear of the planetary range section. Because the synchronizer is in the rearward position, C-2 locks the reverse output gear to the left-side countershaft. Power then flows from the input shaft to the reverse idler gear. Power continues to flow to the reverse output gear and the left-side countershaft. From there, power flows to the range output gear to the sun gear of the planetary range gear set. C-6 is holding the ring gear of the range planetary, so the range planetary carrier is the final output and is connected to the output shaft (**FIGURE 49-82**).

In reverse high range, the power flow is exactly the same as for reverse low range except that C-6 is released and C-7 applies. C-7 locks the range planetary carrier to the range planetary sun gear. The three members of the planetary are locked together, so reverse gear moves into high range (or direct). Power flows straight through the planetary gear set unchanged. C-2 is still applied, and the synchronizer is still in the rearward position. C-2 still locks the reverse output gear to the left-side countershaft. Power flows from the input shaft through the reverse idler to the reverse output gear to the left countershaft. From there, it flows to the planetary range sun gear through the range output gear. Because the range planetary is locked together, however, power flows from there directly to the output shaft (**FIGURE 49-83**).

CHAPTER 49 Electronically Controlled Automatic Transmissions

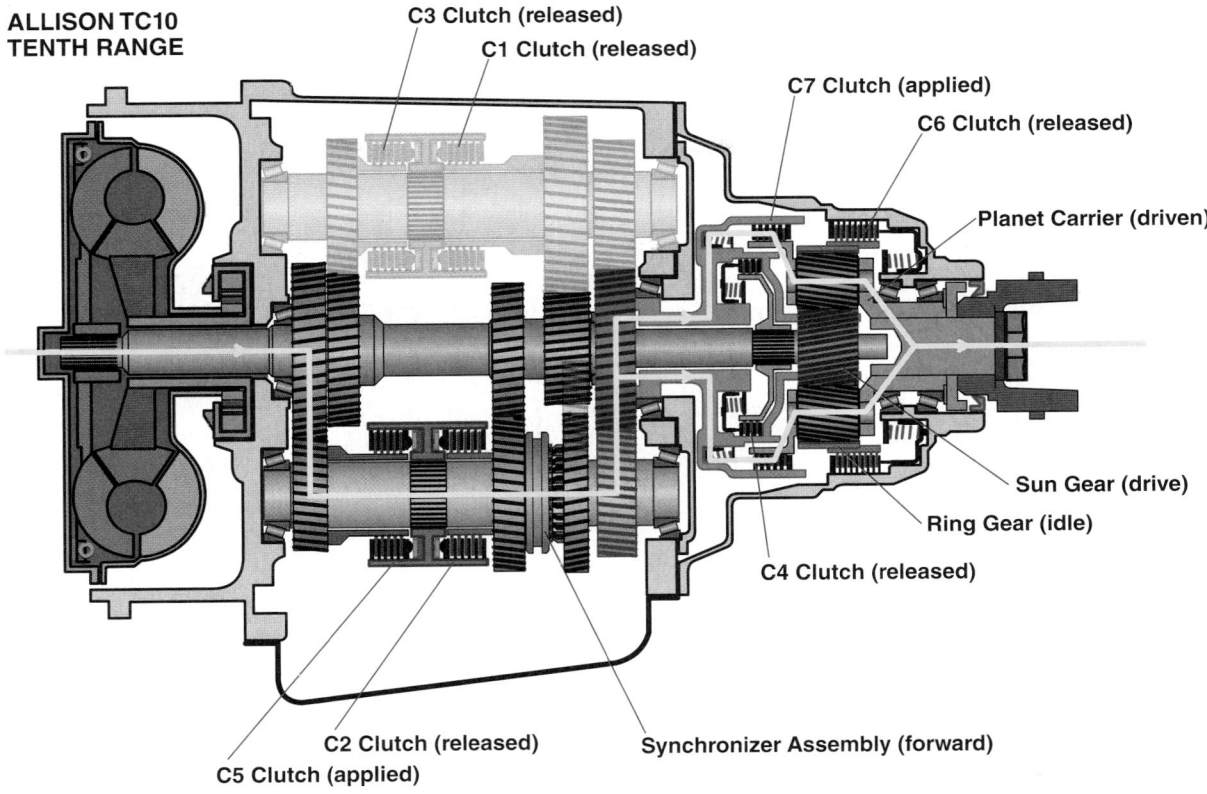

**ALLISON TC10
TENTH RANGE**

C3 Clutch (released)

C1 Clutch (released)

C7 Clutch (applied)

C6 Clutch (released)

Planet Carrier (driven)

Sun Gear (drive)

Ring Gear (idle)

C4 Clutch (released)

Synchronizer Assembly (forward)

C2 Clutch (released)

C5 Clutch (applied)

FIGURE 49-81 Tenth range.

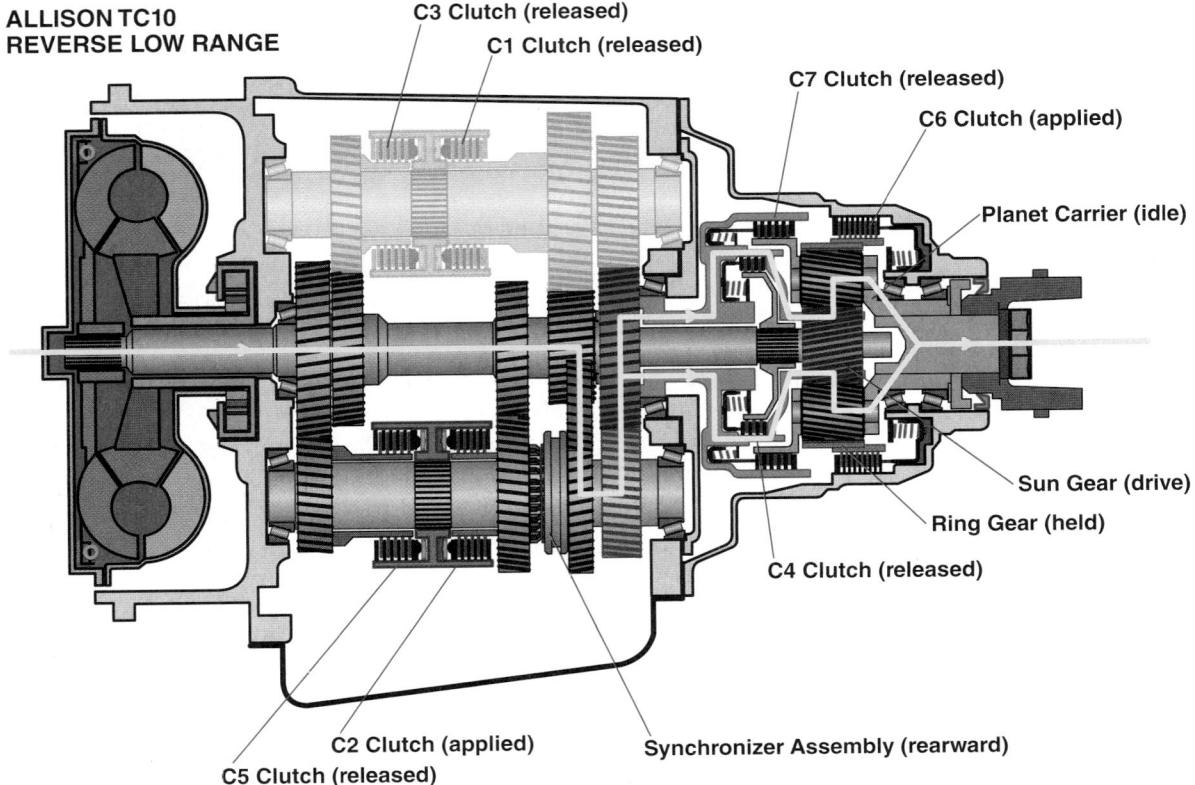

**ALLISON TC10
REVERSE LOW RANGE**

C3 Clutch (released)

C1 Clutch (released)

C7 Clutch (released)

C6 Clutch (applied)

Planet Carrier (idle)

Sun Gear (drive)

Ring Gear (held)

C4 Clutch (released)

C2 Clutch (applied)

C5 Clutch (released)

Synchronizer Assembly (rearward)

FIGURE 49-82 Reverse 1, also called reverse low range.

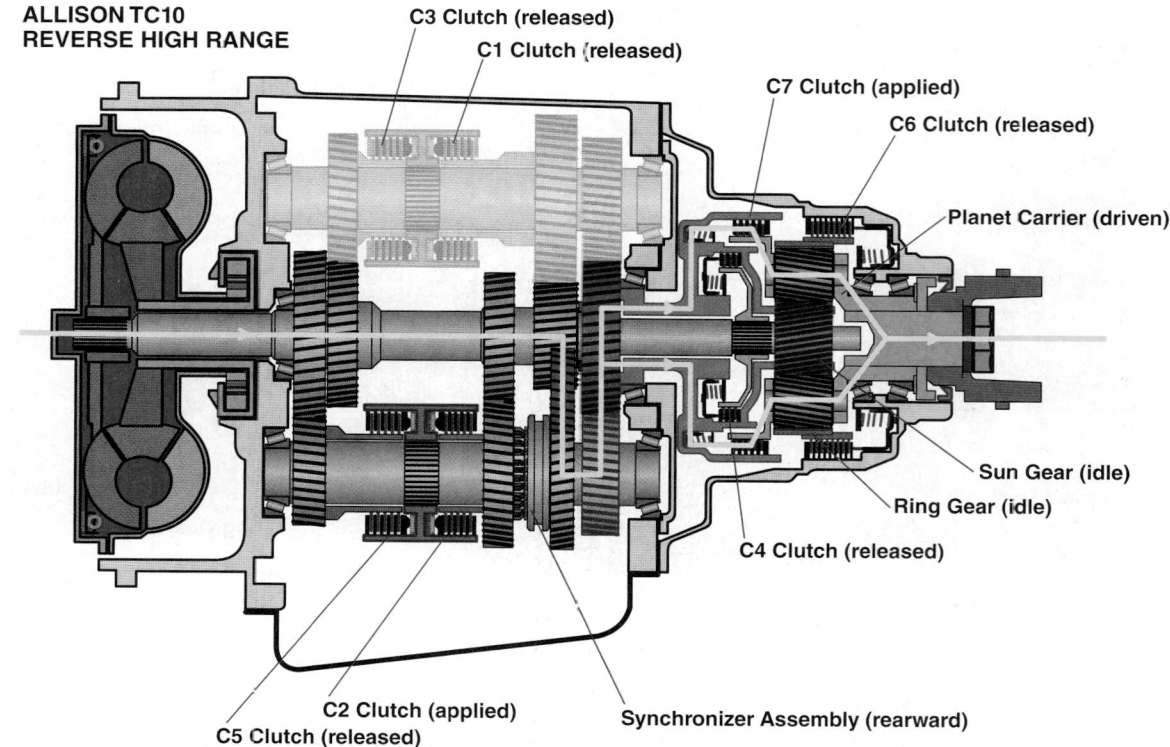

ALLISON TC10 REVERSE HIGH RANGE

C3 Clutch (released)
C1 Clutch (released)
C7 Clutch (applied)
C6 Clutch (released)
Planet Carrier (driven)
Sun Gear (idle)
Ring Gear (idle)
C4 Clutch (released)
Synchronizer Assembly (rearward)
C2 Clutch (applied)
C5 Clutch (released)

FIGURE 49-83 Reverse 2, also called reverse high range.

TC-10 Hydraulics and Electronic Control

The TC-10 uses the Allison fifth-generation electronic control and is capable of all the features of that control system. The hydraulic shift control system also very similar to the 3000, 4000 series Allison models discussed previously and, therefore, it is not discussed here.

Allison Nine Speed

Allison introduced a nine-speed version of their 1000, 2000, 2400 series transmission in September 2018 at the IAA, a large international commercial vehicle show in Hannover, Germany. The nine-speed is based on the proven quality of the successful 1000, 2000, 2400 product line and includes one extra planetary gear set and one extra clutch to achieve the nine speeds. The transmission has a very low start gear and can feature an integral start-stop system to save fuel. Shifting strategies include first gear lockup and acceleration control to maximize fuel economy. This transmission is designed firstly for the class 3 to 7 market primarily in distribution, but also for the construction industry. By increasing to nine speeds the transmission utilizes a much lower rpm range and boasts up to a 10% fuel saving compared to other transmissions with similar vocations. Unfortunately, as of this writing, the internal workings of the nine speed were not available, but this transmission will allow Allison to be competitive in the class 3 to 7 range from as early as 2018 to coincide with the Environmental Protection Agency (EPA) Phase 2 GHG and Fuel Efficiency Standards. The Allison nine-speed is scheduled for release in North America in 2020.

FIGURE 49-84 The Voith DIWA drive transmission is very popular in transit applications.

Voith DIWA Transmissions

LO 49-6 Explain the operation and power flows of Voith transmission's DIWA drive transmission.

The Voith Turbo Company makes transmission systems for a variety of applications worldwide. Its systems are in use in rail, marine, and trucking applications. The transit bus market, however, is the company's largest market for transmissions in terms of numbers. The Voith DIWA transmission is used in over 200,000 buses and coaches worldwide and increasingly in North America. **FIGURE 49-84** shows a Voith DIWA transmission.

This transmission has a unique design with a differential torque converter drive principal called DIfferential-WAndler, giving the DIWA its name. ("Wandler" is the German word for a torque converter.) Differential drive with wandler means that the input torque during DIWA operation is split between mechanical

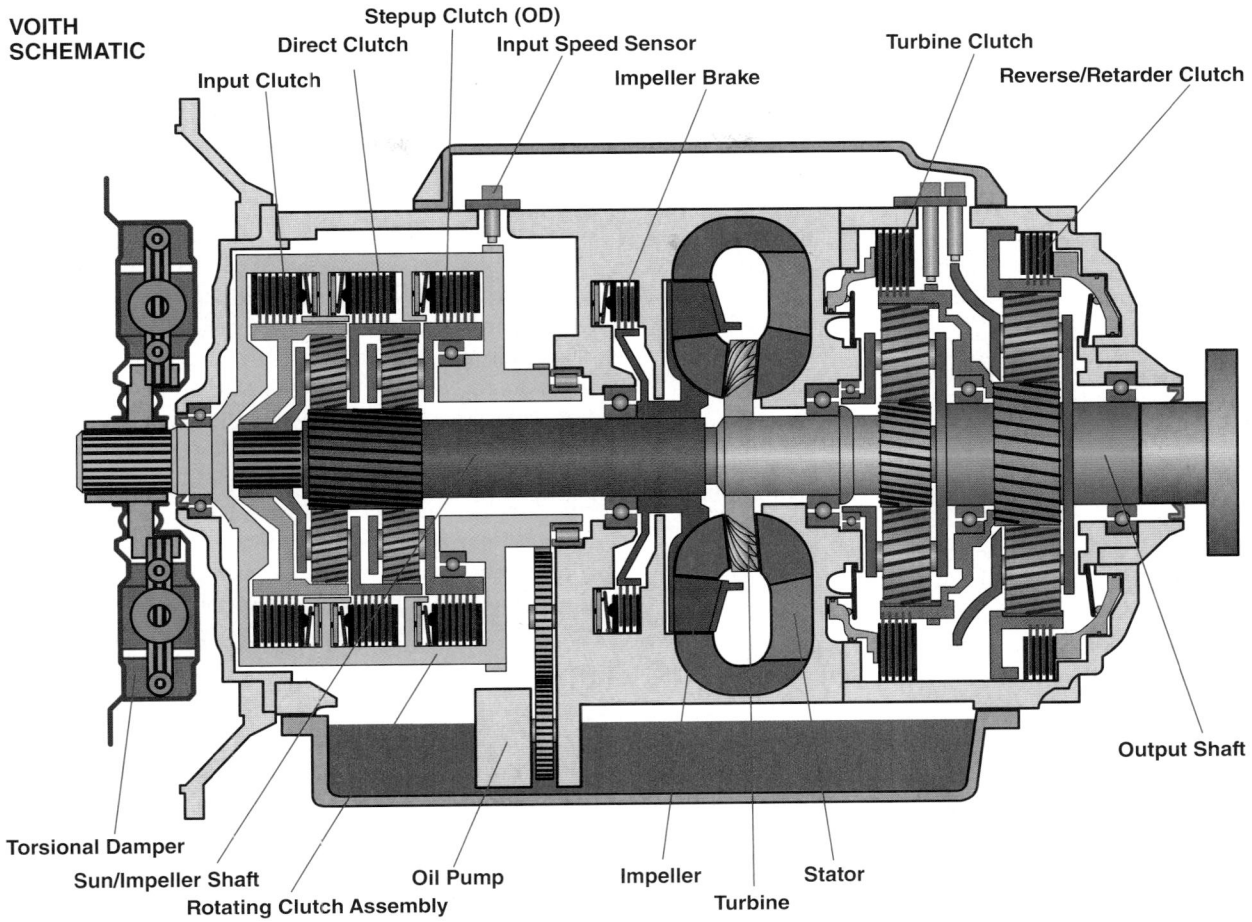

VOITH SCHEMATIC

Input Clutch
Direct Clutch
Stepup Clutch (OD)
Input Speed Sensor
Impeller Brake
Turbine Clutch
Reverse/Retarder Clutch

Torsional Damper
Sun/Impeller Shaft
Rotating Clutch Assembly
Oil Pump
Impeller
Turbine
Stator
Output Shaft

FIGURE 49-85 The Voith DIWA drive transmission.

and torque-converter operation. The DIWA transmission, therefore, has a much greater range of operation in first gear.

The DIWA transmission uses first gear to accelerate to speeds that would normally require a conventional automatic transmission to shift at least once and sometimes twice. That capability is particularly beneficial in bus applications. In stop-and-go traffic, the DIWA usually does not need to shift at all, yet it is just as capable of high-speed operation as a vehicle that does shift in stop-and-go traffic. Reduced shifting increases fuel economy, adds to passenger comfort and means less wear and tear on the transmission itself. Low-speed operation appears seamless. **FIGURE 49-85** shows a cutaway view of the Voith DIWA drive transmission.

DIWA Transmission Operation

The counter-rotating torque converter is the heart of the DIWA transmission's operation. The converter is mounted in the middle of the transmission and doubles as a fully functional hydraulic retarder on deceleration in all gears except first. The DIWA system torque converter is different from the standard converters that we looked at in the chapter on Torque Converters. The DIWA system converter has the same three components as other torque converters, but their arrangement is different. The impeller, or pump, is at the front of the transmission, but it is counter-rotating. In other words, the impeller at the front of the

converter turns in a counterclockwise direction when viewed from the front.

Another difference between DIWA and other transmissions is the position of the stator. Instead of the turbine being opposite the impeller, the stator is positioned at the rear. DIWA operation is the same regardless of whether the transmission is a three-speed or four-speed overdrive model.

DIWA Torque Converter Oil Flow

The DIWA torque converter is responsible for the hydrodynamic input to the transmission gearing. The mechanical portion of the differential input system is covered later in the DIWA Power Flows section. The following is a description of the torque converter fluid flow and operation.

As the counterclockwise-rotating impeller (or pump) throws the transmission fluid outward by centrifugal force and rearward because of the housing shape, the fluid contacts the stator first—not the turbine, as is the case in most torque converters. Recall that in the DIWA system, the stator is at the rear of the torque converter. The stator redirects the fluid flow and sends it back toward the impeller in a direction opposite to the impeller's rotation. The fluid then strikes the smaller, center-mounted turbine. The fluid striking the turbine causes the turbine to turn clockwise. The fluid then exits the turbine and enters the impeller in the same direction that it is turning, multiplying the torque. The rotating turbine provides input to the sun gear of the planetary gear set immediately behind the torque converter.

DIWA Transmission Components

All power enters the transmission through a torsional damper attached to the engine flywheel. In the front section of the overdrive transmission, a single, rotating clutch drum attached to the transmission input shaft contains three clutches:

- The input clutch
- The third gear clutch, also called the lockup clutch, as it provides 1:1 operation
- The step-up clutch (overdrive or fourth gear clutch)

Those three clutches control the operation of two planetary gears. The front planetary carrier is splined to the output shaft, and the second planetary ring gear is splined to the front carrier. The first clutch (the input clutch) in the rotating clutch module drives the front planetary ring gear when applied. The second clutch (the lockup clutch) drives the second planetary ring gear and, by connection, the front carrier when it is applied. The third clutch (the overdrive clutch) drives the second planetary carrier when it is applied. There is also a stationary clutch that, when applied, locks the converter's impeller to the transmission housing for second, third, and fourth gears and retarder operation.

The torque converter of the DIWA transmission is in the middle of the transmission and provides input to the gearing in the rear of the transmission. The rear section of the transmission has two planetary gear sets and two stationary clutches. The planetary gear immediately behind the torque converter receives the hydrodynamic input from the torque converter during first gear and reverse operation. The ring gear of this planetary gear set is splined to the sun gear of the rear (reverse and braking) planetary gear set. The carrier of the first planetary ring gear set in the rear of the transmission is splined to the output shaft. The rear (reverse and braking) planetary gear set sits at the very back of the transmission, and its carrier is also splined to the output shaft. So, three of the four planetary gear sets in this transmission have their carriers splined to the output shaft. Only the second planetary gear in the front section does not.

There are two clutches in the rear section. The first is the turbine clutch, which applies during DIWA operation in first gear (when torque converter operation is necessary). The first clutch holds the first planetary ring gear in this section stationary. The rear planetary gear clutch applies for reverse and for retarder operation and holds the rear planetary ring gear stationary.

DIWA Power Flows

DIWA Neutral

In neutral, no clutches are applied, and torque flows only to the rotating clutch housing. The rest of the transmission is disconnected from the power flow (**FIGURE 49-86**).

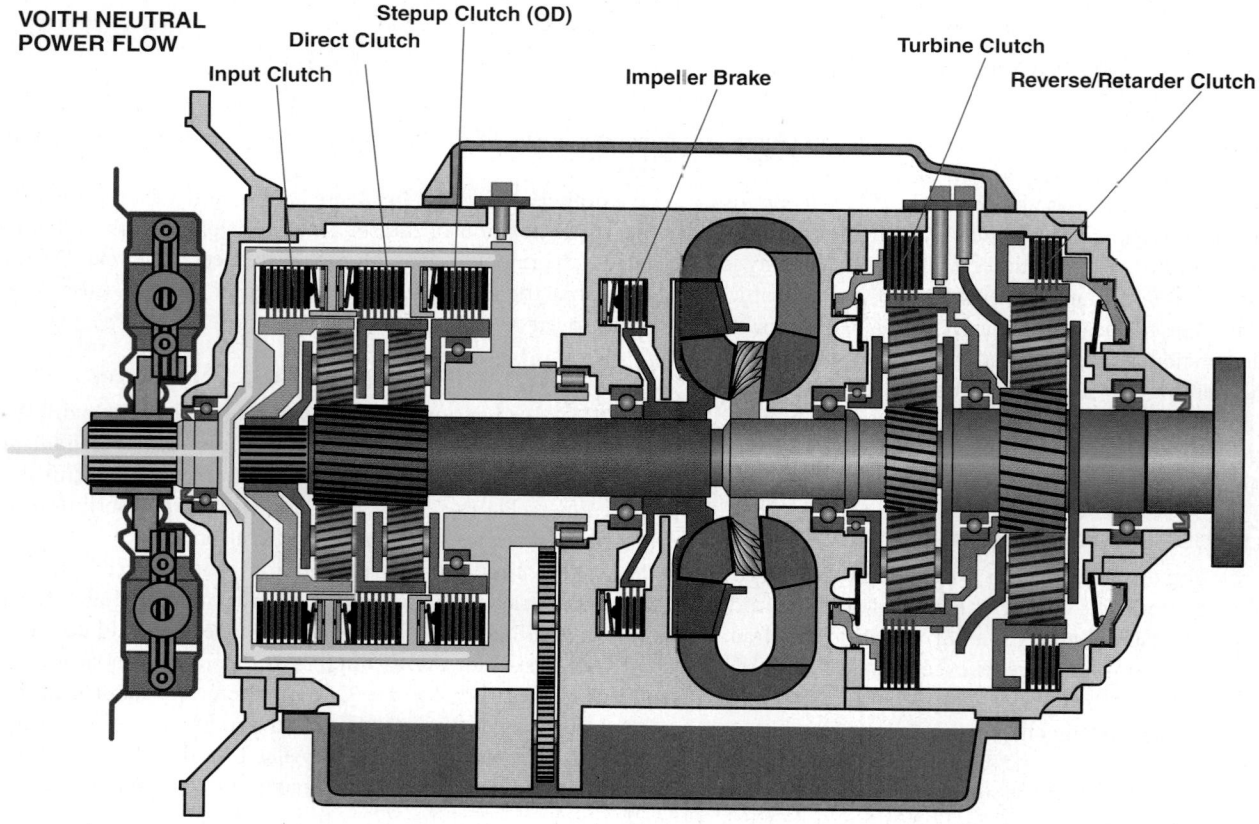

FIGURE 49-86 Voith power flows in neutral.

DIWA Automatic Neutral at Standstill

Automatic neutral at standstill is an optional feature. When the vehicle is at a standstill with the service or parking brake applied, the reverse clutch and the turbine clutch are applied at the same time. This results in the vehicle being held stationary, as two elements of the planetary gear set behind the turbine (the ring gear and the carrier) are held. This system automatically releases the front input clutch at a standstill. Doing so takes the load off the engine and applies the two rear clutches to hold the vehicle stationary. The engine load is automatically reduced, thereby increasing fuel economy in stop-and-go operation.

DIWA First Gear

In first gear, as the vehicle accelerates, the input clutch and the turbine clutch are applied, and engine torque is split between mechanical input and hydrodynamic input (**FIGURE 49-87**). The mechanical input comes from the front planetary gear set. The hydrodynamic input comes from the planetary gear set directly behind the torque converter.

In the front planetary gear set, the ring gear is input by the input clutch, and the front carrier is splined to the output shaft. As such, the front carrier acts as a held member, causing the sun gear to rotate in the opposite direction. The sun gear drives the impeller of the torque converter counterclockwise, and the torque converter turbine drives the sun gear of the planetary gear set behind the turbine in a clockwise direction. The ring gear of this planetary set is held stationary by its clutch, and its carrier becomes output. The carrier is splined to the output shaft, so this is the hydrodynamic drive.

As the vehicle starts to move, the load becomes heavier on the sun gear driving the impeller. As a result, the sun gear starts to act as a held member in the front planetary set. The front carrier becomes output because it is splined directly to the output shaft. The load becomes stronger on the sun gear in the front planetary gear, and it acts more and more as a held member. The output from the front carrier increases as the vehicle's speed increases.

The output is a combination of the drive through the gear set behind the torque converter and the ever-increasing drive through the front planetary carrier. As the vehicle accelerates, more of the power flow is transferred from the hydrodynamic side behind the torque converter to the mechanical side at the front planetary carrier. This combination of powerflows allows the Voith transmission to achieve speeds in first gear that would normally require one or two shifts in other automatic transmissions.

DIWA Second Gear

The shift to second is controlled electronically and is essentially the same as first (**FIGURE 49-88**). A key difference, however, is that the torque converter's operation is completely stopped. The turbine clutch is released, and the impeller clutch (brake) is applied. This holds the front planetary sun gear stationary. The front ring gear is still input, the sun gear is held, and the carrier (splined to the output shaft) is output. The result is a pure mechanical power flow.

DIWA Third Gear

In third gear, the input clutch is released, and the third, or lockup, clutch applies (**FIGURE 49-89**). That combination drives

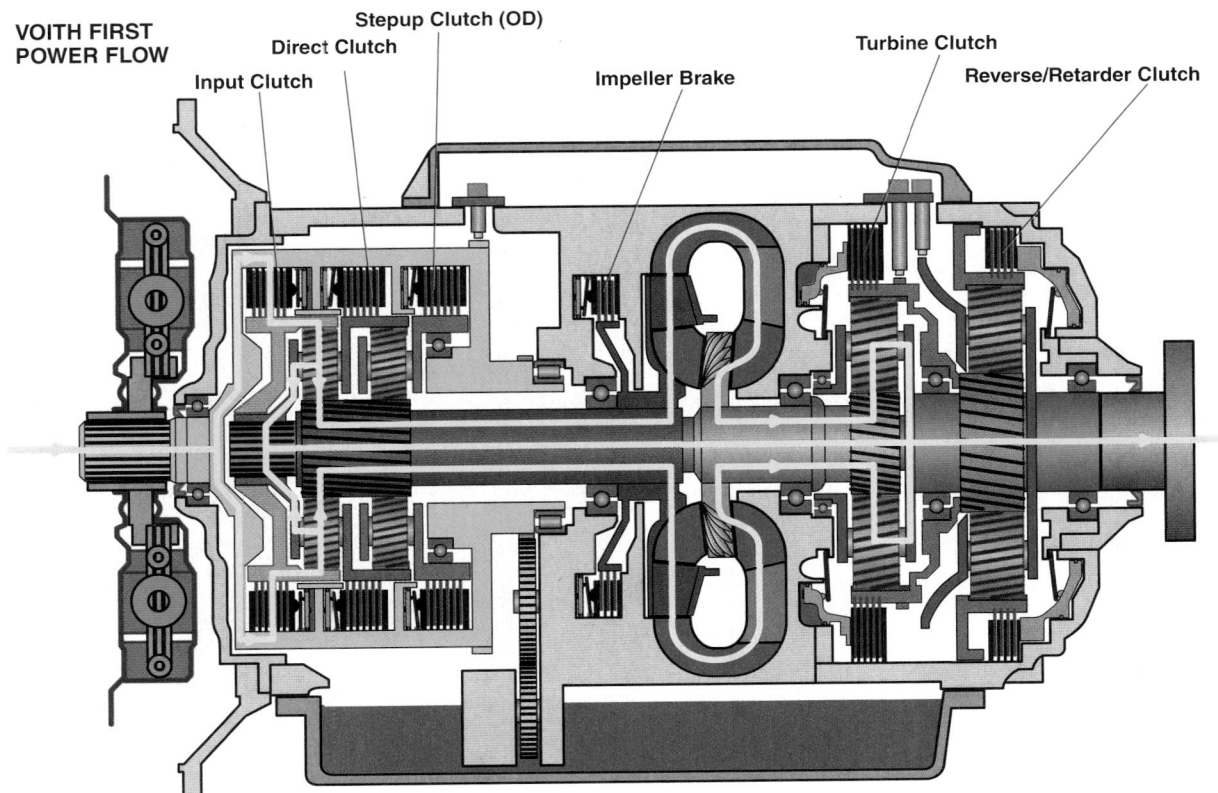

FIGURE 49-87 Voith power flows in first DIWA drive.

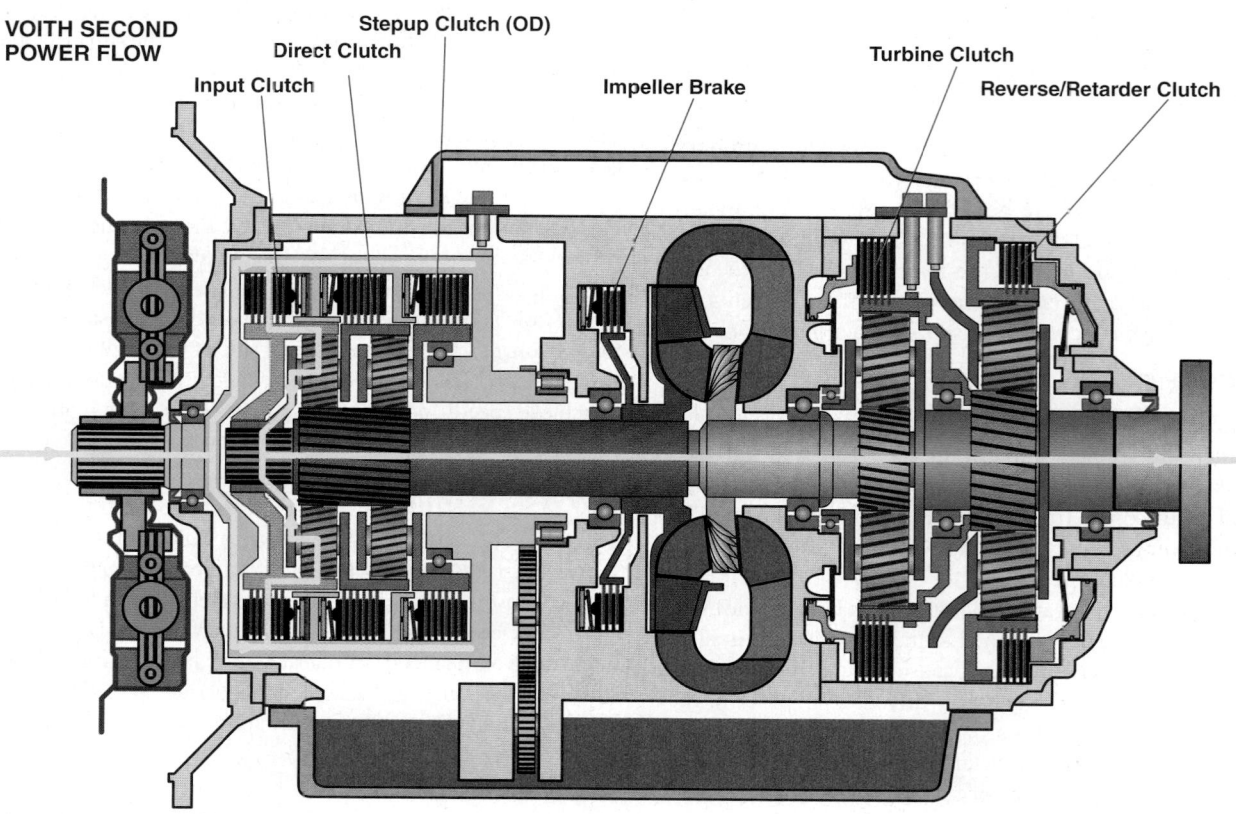

VOITH SECOND POWER FLOW

Input Clutch

Direct Clutch

Stepup Clutch (OD)

Impeller Brake

Turbine Clutch

Reverse/Retarder Clutch

FIGURE 49-88 Voith power flows in second.

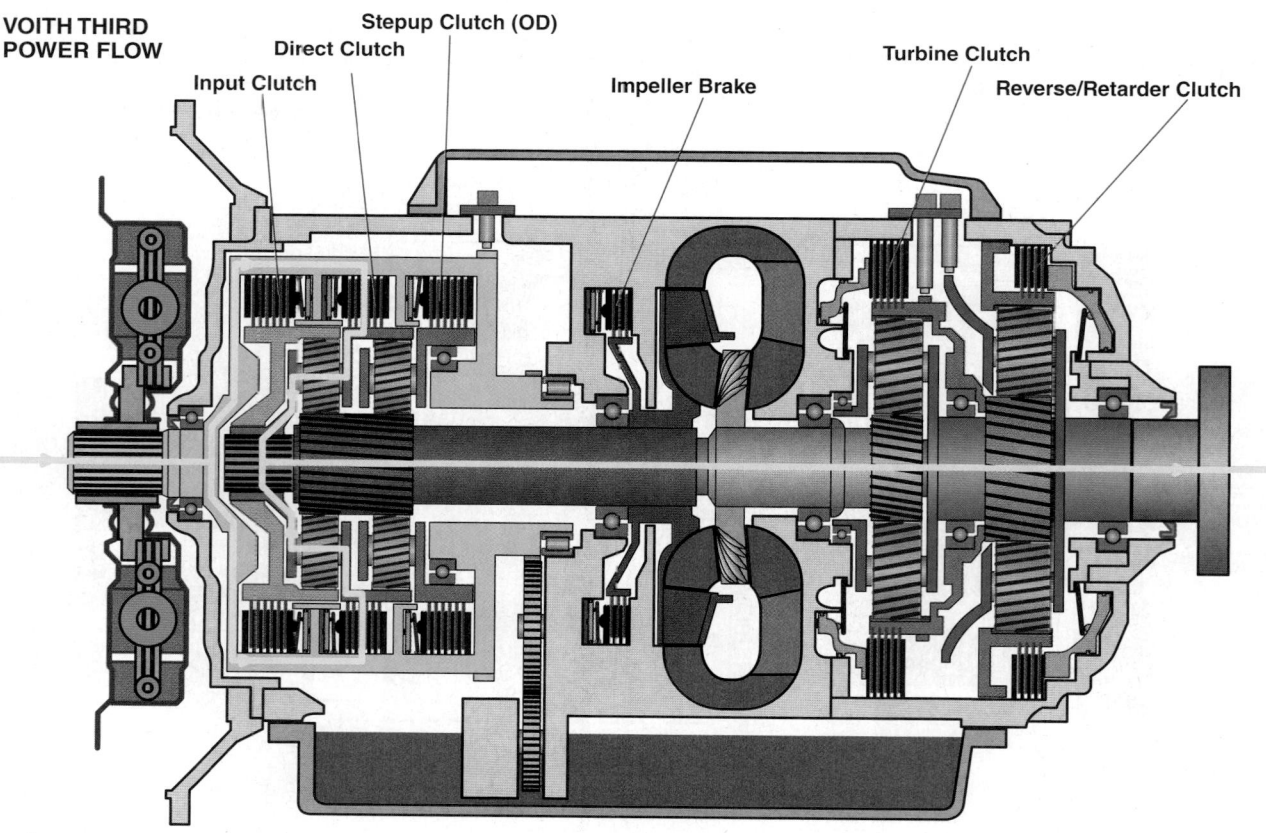

VOITH THIRD POWER FLOW

Input Clutch

Direct Clutch

Stepup Clutch (OD)

Impeller Brake

Turbine Clutch

Reverse/Retarder Clutch

FIGURE 49-89 Voith power flows in third.

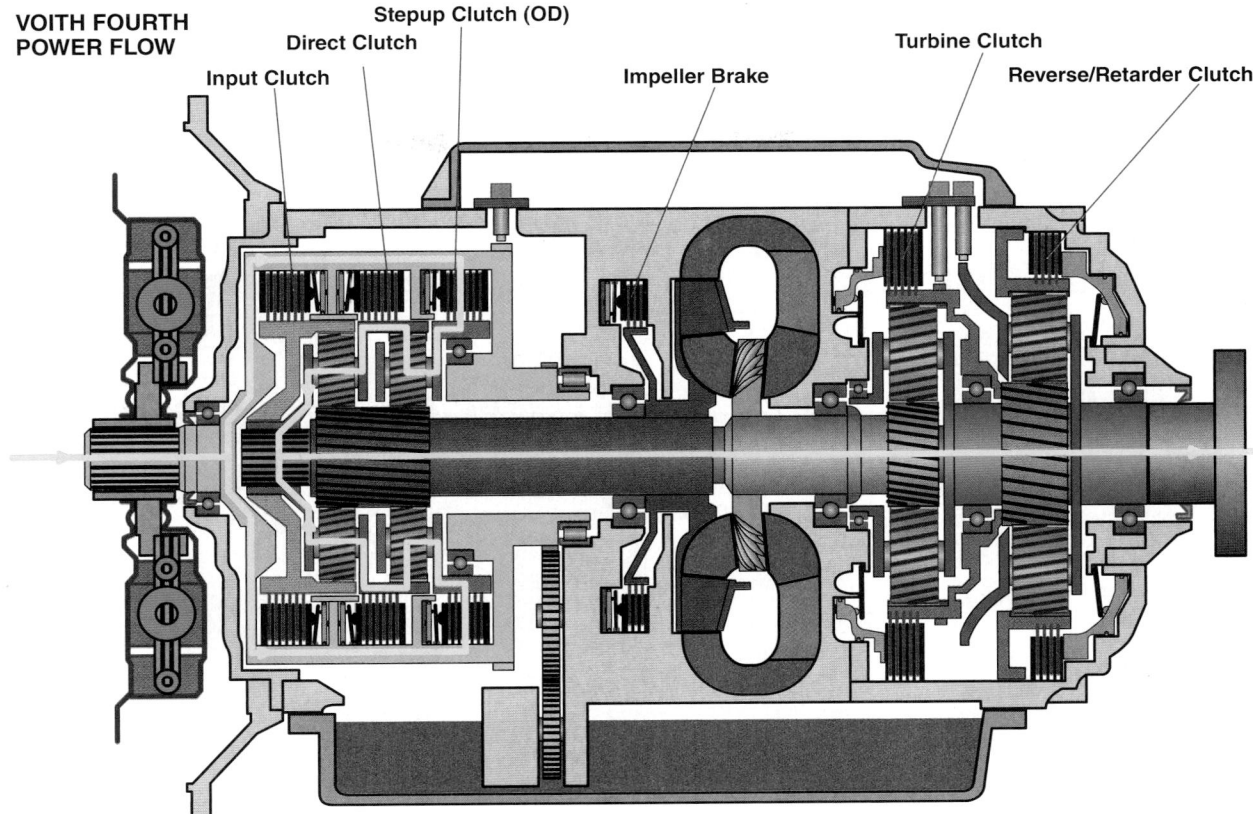

VOITH FOURTH POWER FLOW

Input Clutch — Direct Clutch — Stepup Clutch (OD) — Impeller Brake — Turbine Clutch — Reverse/Retarder Clutch

FIGURE 49-90 Voith operations for fourth gear.

the second planetary ring gear, which is splined to the front carrier. In turn, the front carrier is splined directly to the output shaft, so the output shaft is driven directly by the rotating clutch assembly. A one-to-one ratio results.

DIWA Fourth Gear

In fourth gear, the fourth clutch applies. This inputs the carrier of the second planetary gear set. The sun gear in the second set is held by the impeller brake (clutch). With the carrier input and the sun gear held, the result is overdrive output on the second planetary ring gear. The second planetary ring gear is splined to the front carrier, which is, in turn, splined to the output shaft. The result is fourth range overdrive (**FIGURE 49-90**).

DIWA Reverse

In reverse the input is the same as for first gear (**FIGURE 49-91**). The input clutch is applied, and that drives the forward ring gear. The turbine clutch is not applied, but the reverse/retarder clutch is applied. That combination holds the ring gear of the rear planetary gear stationary.

The power flow proceeds as follows. The front planetary ring gear is input. The front carrier has the load of the output shaft and the vehicle weight holding it stationary. That causes the sun gear to turn in reverse and inputs the impeller of the torque converter counterclockwise. As the vehicle accelerates, the impeller begins to turn faster, driving the turbine and the sun gear of the planetary set behind the torque converter clockwise.

The carrier in this set is loaded by vehicle weight, so its ring gear turns in reverse. The ring gear of this planetary set is connected to the sun gear of the rear planetary set, so its sun gear becomes reverse input to the rear planetary. The rear planetary ring gear is held by the reverse clutch, so its carrier becomes output (still in reverse), and the rear carrier is splined to the output shaft.

Retarder Operation

Retardation in first range is accomplished by lightly applying the reverse clutch with a pressure of approximately 17 to 18 psi (1.2 to 1.3 kg/cm^2) to slow down the output shaft (**FIGURE 49-92**). In second, third, and fourth gears, retarder operation uses the torque converter as a hydraulic retarder. The reverse clutch, the impeller clutch (i.e., brake), and the input clutch associated with the particular range are all applied for retardation. The reverse clutch drives the turbine, which throws oil against the stationary impeller in the torque converter. The resultant retarding force slows the output shaft. The braking effort is controlled by the torque converter fluid pressure. Increased operating pressure provides greater retardation; decreased operating pressure provides less. The heat generated by the retardation is dissipated in the transmission integral heat exchanger.

Control System

The DIWA.5 Transmission with the Intelligent Control Unit E-300 comes equipped with **SensoTop**, an **adaptive control** feature that senses topography and vehicle load and adjusts shift

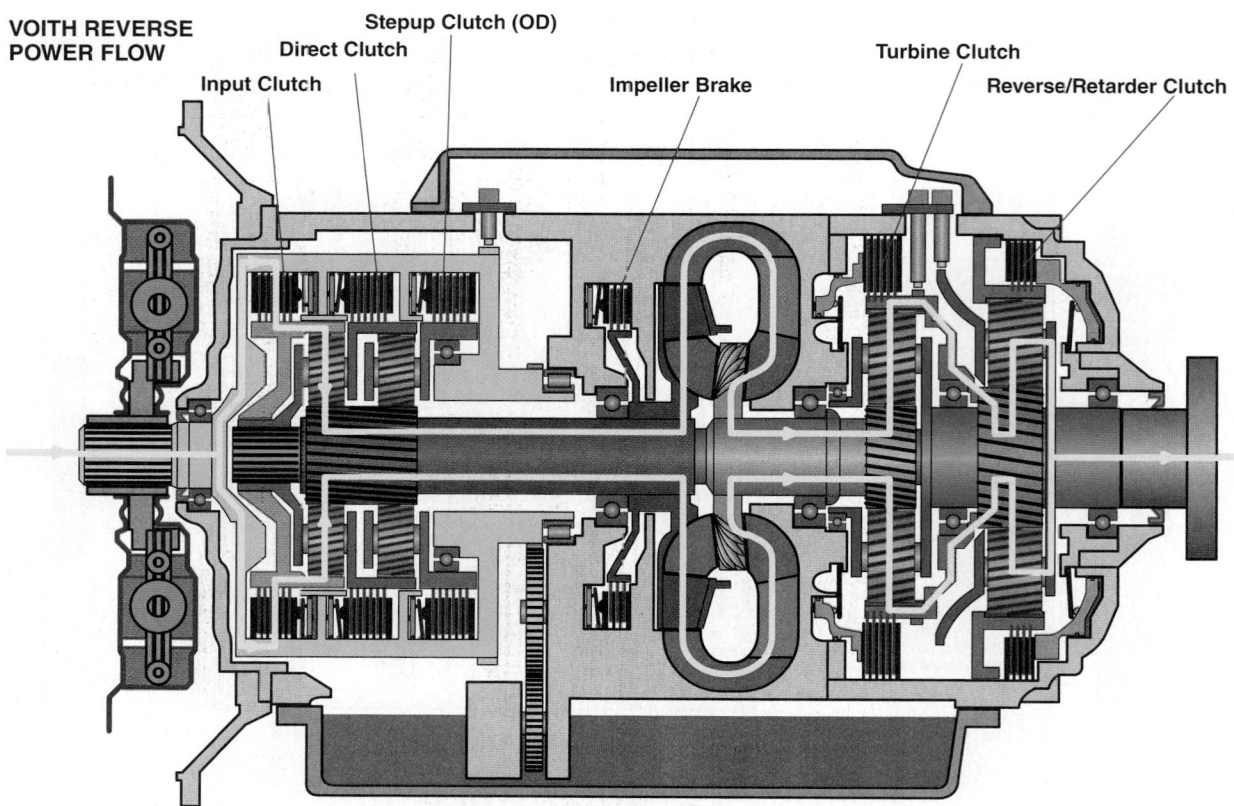

FIGURE 49-91 Voith operations for reverse.

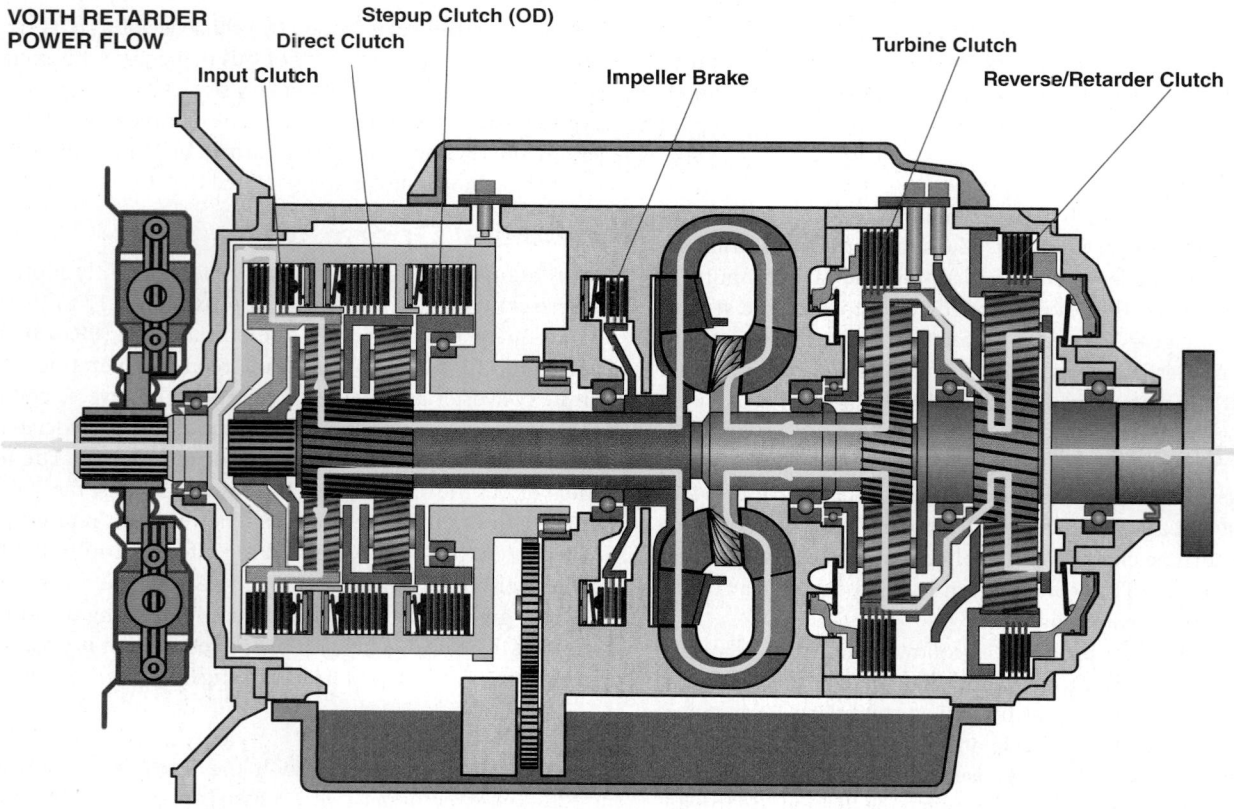

FIGURE 49-92 Voith operations for retarder power flow.

control to obtain maximum economy and comfort. As with other transmission control systems, adaptive control allows the transmission TCM to "learn" and adapt shifts based on any number of input data. Most systems include inclinometers or a similar component to sense road grade and gather information on load factors, fuel, rates, and more. As with most information in the system, the information collected by SensoTop travels through the CAN from the engine ECM.

To diagnose transmission problems and record operating events, the DIWA transmission uses a dedicated software diagnostic program called ALADIN® with a user-friendly interface. Voith also offers a satellite monitoring system than can remotely diagnose problems with the transmission and relay them to the nearest service depot. Voith headquarters are in Hiedenheim, Germany, and the company also has offices in York, Pennsylvania and Sacramento, California.

ZF Friedrichshafen AG EcoMat and EcoLife Transmissions

LO 49-7 Describe ZF Friedrichshafen AG (ZF) EcoMat and EcoLife and Caterpillar CX-28, CX-31, and CX-35 transmissions.

ZF is a leading transmission manufacturer and has been designing and producing transmissions for various world markets for well over 50 years. ZF produces two automatic transmissions for the truck and coach market—the EcoMat and the EcoLife. The EcoMat is available in five- and six-speed models and can accept up to approximately 1300 ft-lb (1762 Nm) of input torque. Eco-Mat is used in both trucks and buses (**FIGURE 49-93**).

The EcoLife is ZF's latest six-speed transmission model that can handle up to 1475 ft-lb (2000 Nm) of input torque. Both Eco-Mat and EcoLife transmissions utilize three planetary gears, six hydraulic clutches, and an integrated retarder for braking assist. ZF's proprietary TopoDyn software allows the transmission controller to learn load and road grade conditions and optimize shift profiles to suit the terrain and drive cycle. That capability leads to more efficient operation and greater driver and passenger comfort. Until 2009, ZF was in partnership with Arvin Meritor in North America, and the company still has a network of U.S. dealers marketing and servicing these transmissions.

Caterpillar Automatic Transmissions

Caterpillar has made electronically controlled transmissions for the off-road market for years. In 2006, the company launched its first line of automatic truck transmissions for the on-highway market. The on-highway line consists of three models:

- CX28 is a medium-duty, six-speed transmission rated for 400 hp (300 kW) with input torque of 1250 ft-lb (1770 Nm) (**FIGURE 49-94**).
- CX31 is a six-speed model for medium-duty applications rated for up to 525 hp (391 kW) and 1770 ft-lb (2400 Nm) of input torque.
- CX35 is a heavy-duty, eight-speed model rated for up to 625 hp (456 kW) and 2150 ft-lb (2915 Nm) of input torque.

The CX28 and CX31 on-highway models have three planetary gear sets and five hydraulic clutches and are capable of six forward speeds.

In all models, the clutches are numbered C-1 to C-5, and the clutch application chart and the power flows are the same as the Allison World Transmission (**FIGURE 49-95**). The heavy-duty CX35 model has four planetary gear sets and six hydraulic clutches and is capable of eight forward speeds. The CX transmissions are completely drive by wire. In other words, they are solely electronically controlled. The transmission ECU has adaptive control built in so that it can optimize shifting for any operating cycle and load configuration.

The CX line of transmissions uses electronic clutch-pressure control (ECPC) units to control clutch application. The ECPC units consist of a pulse-width-modulated solenoid that, in turn, controls a modulating spool valve that directs main pressure of 350 psi (24.6 kg/cm²) to the clutches. When making a shift, the transmission ECU first sends a full-duty cycle signal to the ECPC solenoid. The signal tells the transmission to initiate clutch application and then varies the duty cycle to control the quality of the shift in progress. Each clutch uses its own ECPC unit to control its application, and all the ECPC units are identical (**FIGURE 49-96**).

FIGURE 49-93 ZF transmissions are sold all over the world.

FIGURE 49-94 Caterpillar's CX-28 Transmission.

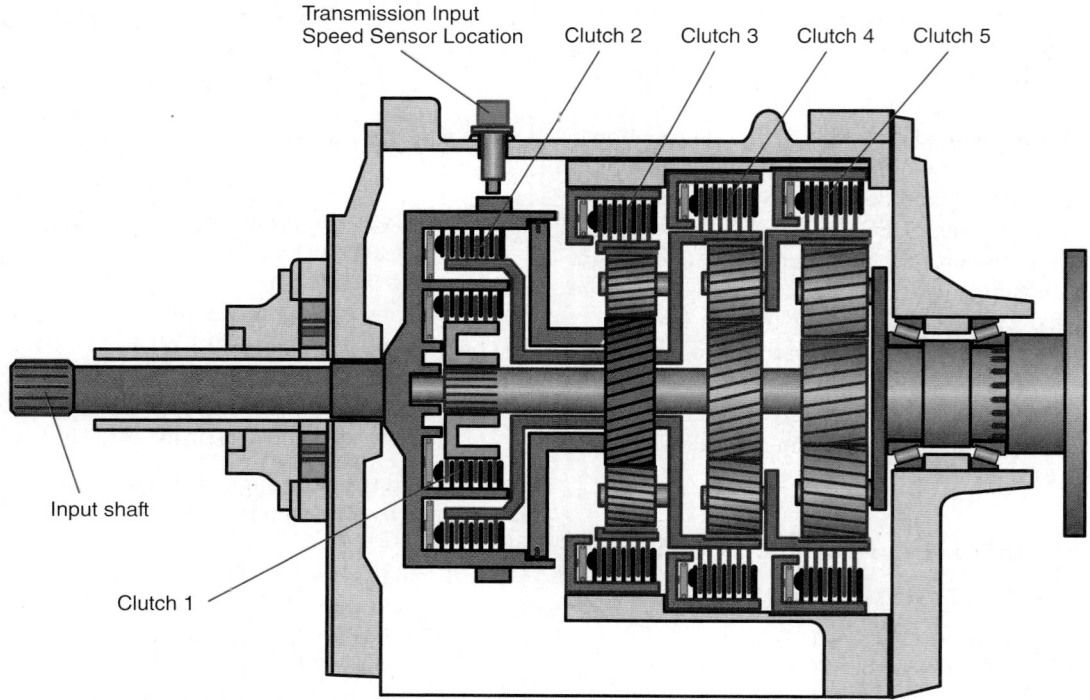

FIGURE 49-95 The clutches and planetary gear arrangement in the Cat CX-28 and CX-31 transmissions are the same as in the Allison World Transmission. The clutches are numbered 1 to 5 in this diagram.

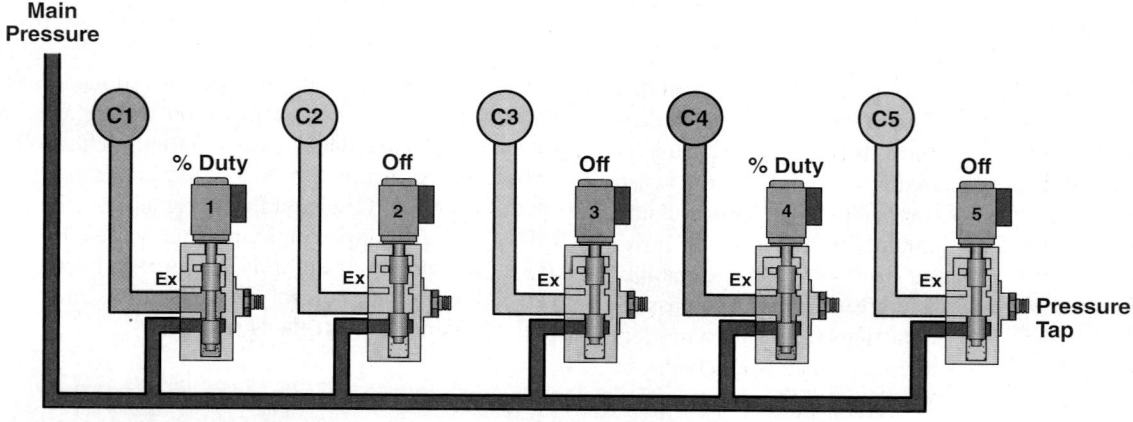

FIGURE 49-96 Each clutch in a CX transmission is controlled by its own individual ECPC unit.

The transmissions are equipped with a lockup converter, which locks up as the vehicle approaches maximum speed in second range. The lockup converter is applied for all forward ranges above second. CX transmissions have two selectable operational modes: economy mode and performance mode. In economy mode, shifting occurs at lower road speeds to save fuel. In performance modes, shifts occur at close to the rated rpm to allow for greater acceleration.

CX transmissions have self-diagnostic capability and set a DTC in the ECU memory and turn on an amber or red warning lamp when a problem exists. Cat Electronic Technician (ET) software is a proprietary diagnostic software program that can be utilized to access DTC information.

The ECU adaptive control on CX transmissions continuously monitors and adjusts the shifting process to make up for transmission wear and system degradation. After transmission overhaul or replacement, the adaptive control must be reset. Caterpillar calls this resetting of adaptive control "the transmission calibration procedure." It basically entails incorporating the learned adjustments to the shift process. Recalibration can only be accomplished with the Cat ET service program.

The CX series transmissions have not yet made a big impact on the North American automatic transmission market due, in part, to Caterpillar's decision to drop out of the on-highway truck engine market back in 2010. Despite reduced activity in the on-highway truck engine market,

Caterpillar now produces its own line of on-highway trucks (the CT 660 and the CT 681) in which the CX31 transmission is standard equipment when an automatic is specified. These trucks currently use Navistar engines and are strictly for vocational applications—mostly dump and cement trucks.

Although Cat does have a visible presence on North American highways with the CT 660 and CT 681trucks, the company has not yet garnered significant market share. As a result, the CX series of transmissions are mostly serviced only at Caterpillar dealerships.

Wrap-Up

Ready for Review

▶ Electronic control of transmissions has been in place in the light-duty market since the early 1980s and the truck market since the late 1980s.

▶ In general, transmissions require at least three inputs to function: input from the driver, a road speed input, and a load factor input.

▶ In electronic transmission control systems, a lever selector or a push button controller provides the drivers input; a vehicle speed sensor (VSS) provides the speed input; and a throttle position sensor (TPS) provides the load factor input.

▶ Most electronically controlled transmissions use inputs from a variety of other sources—such as pressure switches, temperature switches, and oil pressure sensors—to fine tune transmission shift control.

▶ All electronic controlled transmissions are connected to the vehicle by a multiple wiring harnesses and connectors.

▶ Electronically controlled transmissions use a variety of computer-controlled solenoids to control shifting.

▶ Allison is by far the world-leading manufacturer of electronically controlled automatic transmissions.

▶ Allison electronic control systems have undergone several advancements through the years, starting with the Allison ATEC/CEC system, which offered minimal electronic control, through the fifth generation version of the Allison World Transmission series, which offers increasingly sophisticated electronic control.

▶ The driving force behind electronic control advancements is fuel economy.

▶ The careful system monitoring characteristic of electronic control results in better control of the shift timing and process leads to increased fuel economy and greatly increased transmission durability.

▶ Lockup torque converters are computer controlled and lead to even better fuel economy.

▶ The Allison World Transmission is modular in design, so individual modules can be serviced independently if necessary to decrease down time.

▶ The Allison World Transmission has six forward ranges with two overdrives, a design that increases fuel economy.

▶ The Allison World Transmission has three speed sensors, which allow it to compare input speed, turbine speed, and output speed. That comparison tells the transmission

controller if a transmission clutch is slipping, so it can protect the transmission.

▶ The Allison World Transmission has several protection strategies built in, such as range inhibitors when input speeds are too high, high-speed direction-change inhibitors, and temperature-based inhibitors.

▶ The Allison World Transmission has built-in fail-safe operation that provides minimal transmission function should electrical power be lost. Fail-safe operation ensures that the vehicle is not stuck on the side of the road.

▶ Electronically controlled transmissions have varying levels of adaptive control. That is, the transmission controller can adapt shifting to different operating conditions, load levels, and other conditions.

▶ The Allison TC-10-TS transmission is a fully wet-clutch-controlled electronic transmission with ten forward ranges and twin countershafts. The TC-10-TS is specifically designed for the Class 8 on-highway truck market.

▶ The TC-10-TS also has fully electronically controlled shifting and adaptive control.

▶ Allison recently announced the release of a nine-speed version of their popular 1000, 2000, 2400 series of transmission scheduled for North American release in 2020.

▶ Allison DOC software can be used to diagnose and monitor all of Allison's electronically controlled transmissions.

▶ The Voith DIWA drive transmission is primarily used in transit and coach applications, as its differential inputs (mechanical and hydrodynamic) allow it to operate in first range over a wide speed range without shifting.

▶ The Voith DIWA is more popular in the rest of the world but is making significant inroads in North America.

▶ The Voith DIWA has its own dedicated software diagnostic program, known as ALADIN, which can read diagnostic trouble codes and monitor transmission operation.

▶ ZF electronically controlled transmissions are primarily used in transit and coach operations and have yet to make a significant dent in the North American market. ZF is a huge global marketer of transmissions, and its presence in in North America is likely to grow.

▶ Caterpillar's CX series of electronically controlled transmissions has not yet made a significant impact on the North American market, but, with CAT poised to re-enter the on-highway engine market soon, the company may see its sales of these transmissions increase.

Key Terms

adaptive control An advanced control system feature that adjusts output signals to optimize an operating variable such as economy, comfort, noise level or safety.

Allison Transmission Electronic Control (ATEC) The original version of Allison's electronic control systems that evolved into Commercial Electronic Control (CEC).

cab harness The harness that connects the shift selector to the electronic control unit.

chassis wiring harness The wiring that connects the transmission, the throttle position sensor (TPS), and the variable speed sensor to the transmission electronic control unit.

Commercial Electronic Control (CEC) The second iteration of Allison's electronically controlled transmission.

counts The unit for digital signal conversion that Allison uses to describe throttle position based on the variable voltage signal from a TPS.

duty cycle The percentage of time a PWM signal is ON in comparison to OFF time.

electrohydraulic control module (electrohydraulic valve body) The valve body used to control electronically controlled transmissions and consisting of solenoids, spool valves, and, usually, pressure switches.

fail-safe operation The minimal transmission function that occurs when electrical power is lost.

fast adaptive A type of adaptive control used when the transmission is new and makes large changes to bring the shift close to the optimal shift profile quickly.

hydraulic retarder Retarder systems that pump transmission fluid between a turning cupped rotor and stationary cupped housing, thereby creating fluid pressure and fluid friction that slow the vehicle.

inclinometer/accelerometer Sensors included in the transmission control system that allow it to adapt to topography and operating conditions.

latching solenoids Solenoids that need only a short burst of electricity to move to an open or closed position and they remain in that state until they are energized again.

modulated main solenoid A pulse-width-modulated solenoid that controls main pressure in fourth generation and later World Transmissions.

neutral with no clutches (NCC) The status of a vehicle in neutral gear when no clutches are applied and an indication of a possible failure mode for Allison World Transmission.

non-latching solenoid A solenoid that requires constant electric power to remain in the open position.

normally closed solenoid A solenoid that blocks the flow of fluid when it is not electrically energized.

normally open solenoid A solenoid that is open when not electrically energized.

off-going ratio test A test performed at the beginning of a shift in progress in the World Transmission to ensure that the off-going clutch has released.

on-coming ratio test A test performed near the end of a shift in progress in the World Transmission to ensure that the on-coming clutch has applied.

open-loop ramp rate A predictable increase in clutch apply pressure; the open-loop ramp rate is controlled by the transmission ECU.

pressure control solenoid (PCS) The term to denote clutch control solenoids in an Allison Fourth-Generation Electrohydraulic Control transmission.

primary modulation The pulse-modulated signal sent to a solenoid to initiate fluid flow.

prognostics A self-diagnostic maintenance schedule that informs the driver when the oil, filters, or the transmission itself requires service. Prognostics are offered on the Allison World Transmissions since 2009 and can be turned on or off by the vehicle owner, if desired.

programmable read-only memory (PROM) chip A memory chip particular to the application of the vehicle in which it is found.

pulse-width modulation (PWM) An electrical signal that varies in on and off time.

ramp-off rate The specific reduction in clutch apply pressure for the clutch that is being released during a shift in the World Transmission.

range verification tests Tests constantly being performed by the Allison World Transmission control system whenever there is no shift in progress; the test compares turbine times the gear ratio to the output speed to ensure the transmission is not slipping.

ratio test A test performed at the beginning and end of a shift in process.

retarder Any system used to slow a vehicle's momentum and augment the service brake.

secondary modulation (sub-modulation) A very high-frequency pulse-width modulation of the current flowing through the primary modulated circuit of a World Transmission solenoid. The secondary modulation occurs at between 12,000 and 19,000 Hz and is used to fine tune the solenoid function.

SensoTop A system used by Voith that senses topography and adapts the shifting schedule accordingly.

shift logic The logical process created by the transmission controller using data gained from the vehicle to determine when and how shifting should occur.

shift solenoid 1 (SS1) The solenoid used in fourth-generation and later World Transmissions to control the position of the C-1 and C-2 latch valves.

slow adaptive A type of adaptive control that involves making small changes to the shifts as a way to mitigate the effects of clutch wear and solenoid drive and degradation.

synchronous speed The point at which the on-coming clutch has applied and there is no more slippage. Turbine shaft seed times the gear ratio equals output shaft speed.

time to full apply (TFA) The point after synchronous speed has been detected at which the solenoid controlling the on-coming clutch in a World Transmission is commanded to full pressure (that is, to fully apply the clutch).

torque converter control (TCC) A control solenoid used in fourth-generation and later World Transmissions.

transmission control module (TCM) The electronic controller that issues commands to the solenoids inside the transmission to obtain the desired range. Also known as the transmission electronic control unit (ECU).

transmission electronic control unit (ECU) The electronic controller that issues commands to the solenoids inside the transmission to obtain the desired range. Also called the transmission control unit (TCU).

trimmer An accumulator used in the ATEC/CEC systems to smoothen out the shift process.

turbine pull down A decrease in turbine speed as a shift is in progress that results from the on-coming clutch starting to control its geartrain component; the signal for the transmission to enter closed-loop control of the shift in progress.

variable-bleed solenoid (VBS) Hydraulic solenoids used in late-model Allison World Transmissions, which control application by allowing some of the pressure going to a device to bleed off to exhaust.

vehicle speed sensor (VSS) An inductive pickup sensor that reads the speed of the transmission output shaft.

World Transmission Electronic Control (WTEC) Allison's original electronic transmission control system for the World Transmission.

Review Questions

1. In the Allison ATEC/CEC transmission, solenoids are used to do which of the following?
   a. Send fluid directly to clutches
   b. Act as system pressure-modulation devices
   c. Control the flow of transmission fluid to valves
   d. Replace the function of the load- and speed-sensing devices
2. What is the purpose of the transmission temperature and oil level sensors?
   a. They act as system-protection devices.
   b. They act as additional flow-control devices.
   c. They are used only as troubleshooting tools.
   d. They are installed to assist in stall testing.
3. When the fluid in an Allison ATEC/CEC transmission is extremely cold (below $-25°$ F [$-32°$ C]), the transmission controller allows which of the following?
   a. No shifting
   b. Shifts from neutral to first or reverse only
   c. All range shifts to occur
   d. Weather does not affect the transmission shifts.
4. In Allison ATEC/CEC transmissions, what replaces the modulator valve used in hydraulically controlled transmissions?
   a. The vehicle speed sensor
   b. The transmission oil pressure control valve
   c. The throttle position sensor
   d. The transmission temperature sensor
5. What happens if you are driving a vehicle with an ATEC/CEC transmission in fourth range and electrical power to the transmission TCU is lost?
   a. The transmission immediately shifts to neutral.
   b. The transmission downshifts until it reaches first range.
   c. The transmission shifts to the next lower range (third).
   d. The transmission remains in fourth range until the vehicle is shut off.
6. What is meant by synchronous speed as it relates to the Allison World Transmission TCU?
   a. The output shaft speed times the gear ratio equals the engine speed.
   b. The turbine speed equals the output shaft speed.
   c. The engine speed times the gear ratio equals the turbine speed.
   d. Turbine shaft speed equals output shaft speed times the gear ratio of the on-coming clutch.
7. During a shift, the World Transmission enters closed-loop control between which of the following points?
   a. Turbine pull-down detected and synchronous speed
   b. Shift initiation and turbine pull-down
   c. Synchronous speed and shift initiation
   d. The WT has closed loop control during the entire shift
8. During closed-loop control, the TCU is controlling shift quality by doing which of the following?
   a. Using the fixed ramp rate
   b. Applying full-line pressure to the on-coming clutch
   c. Varying the on-coming clutch application pressure using pulse-width modulation
   d. None of the above is correct
9. Which of the following is NOT one of three ways that the engine's rotational power can be transmitted to the geartrain in a World Transmission?
   a. Through the P-2 and P-3 sun gears
   b. Through the P-1 sun gear
   c. Through the P-2 carrier
   d. Through the P-2 ring gear
10. When a World Transmission (WT) is in reverse, the input power from the engine enters the geartrain through which of the following?
    a. P-1 sun gear
    b. P-1 carrier
    c. P-2 carrier
    d. P-2 and P-3 sun gears

ASE Technician A/Technician B Style Questions

1. Technician A says that the Allison transmission's TCU switches to slow adaptive mode after optimum shift quality has been attained. Technician B says that the TCU must be switched to fast adaptive mode after transmission replacement. Who is correct?
   a. Technician A
   b. Technician B
   c. Both Technician A and Technician B
   d. Neither Technician A nor Technician B

2. Technician A says that the Allison World Transmission series is a true "drive by wire" transmission. Technician B says that the World Transmission series still has a mechanical gearshift linkage. Who is correct?
   a. Technician A
   b. Technician B
   c. Both Technician A and Technician B
   d. Neither Technician A nor Technician B

3. Technician A says the Allison World Transmission is capable of inhibiting neutral to range shifts if the engine rpm is too high. Technician B says that the TCU is capable of inhibiting downshifts if the road speed is too high. Who is correct?
   a. Technician A
   b. Technician B
   c. Both Technician A and Technician B
   d. Neither Technician A nor Technician B

4. Technician A says that the Voith DIWA drive transmission has two inputs to the transmission geartrain: mechanical and hydrodynamic. Technician B says in the Voith DIWA drive transmission, the torque converter doubles as a retarder. Who is correct?
   a. Technician A
   b. Technician B
   c. Both Technician A and Technician B
   d. Neither Technician A nor Technician B

5. Technician A says that the Allison TC-10 has two countershafts. Technician B says that the Allison TC-10 uses both countershafts for each power flow like the Eaton Fuller Twin countershaft transmission does. Who is correct?
   a. Technician A
   b. Technician B
   c. Both Technician A and Technician B
   d. Neither Technician A nor Technician B

6. Technician A says that prognostics in an Allison World Transmission can alert the driver when an oil or filter change is required. Technician B says that prognostics in an Allison World Transmission can alert the driver when the transmission clutches are in danger of failing. Who is correct?
   a. Technician A
   b. Technician B
   c. Both Technician A and Technician B
   d. Neither Technician A nor Technician B

7. Technician A says that the Caterpillar CX-28 transmission power flow is identical to the Allison World Transmission. Technician B says that the Caterpillar CX-28 uses two rotating clutches. Who is correct?
   a. Technician A
   b. Technician B
   c. Both Technician A and Technician B
   d. Neither Technician A nor Technician B

8. Technician A says that the four-speed Voith DIWA drive transmission has three hydraulic clutches in its rotating clutch module. Technician B says that the four-speed Voith DIWA has three planetary gear sets in the front section. Who is correct?
   a. Technician A
   b. Technician B
   c. Both Technician A and Technician B
   d. Neither Technician A nor Technician B

9. Technician A says that the four-speed Voith DIWA drive transmission has four hydraulic clutches in total. Technician B says the four-speed Voith DIWA drive transmission has four planetary gear sets in total. Who is correct?
   a. Technician A
   b. Technician B
   c. Both Technician A and Technician B
   d. Neither Technician A nor Technician B

10. Technician A says that the Voith DIWA drive transmission uses a differential input in reverse. Technician B says that the Voith DIWA drive transmission uses a differential input in all forward gears. Who is correct?
   a. Technician A
   b. Technician B
   c. Both Technician A and Technician B
   d. Neither Technician A nor Technician B

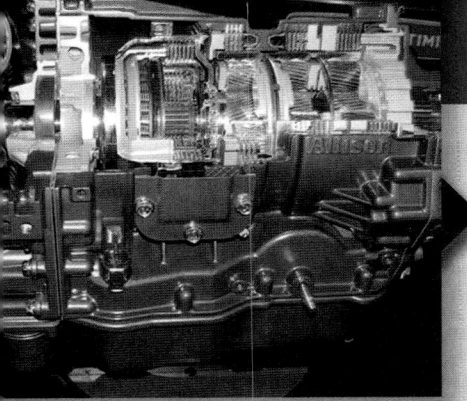

CHAPTER 50

Maintaining Automatic Transmissions

Learning Objectives

After reading this chapter, you will be able to:

- **LO 50-1** Explain the fundamentals of transmission fluids.
- **LO 50-2** Explain the basic troubleshooting process for automatic transmissions.
- **LO 50-3** Describe automatic transmission maintenance procedures.
- **LO 50-4** Explain transmission replacement procedures.

You Are the Technician

A vehicle is brought to your shop and the driver complains that his transmission is noisy. He explains that the noise only occurs after driving for a few miles and then only when he is accelerating. He says it sounds like someone threw a bag of small ball bearings into his transmission and he is very worried about it. You do a preliminary check and discover the transmission is an Allison AT 540 series. The vehicle seems to be involved in construction, as the entire underside of the vehicle and the transmission are caked in mud. You check the fluid and find that it is at the correct level and is a normal pink color. (Note that some newer fluids are not bright pink.) Next, you road test the vehicle. Sure enough, you hear a high-frequency rattling sound as you accelerate. What are your next steps?

1. Would you inspect the transmission flex plate? If so, what would you look for?
2. What would you need to do to determine if there are ball bearings loose in the transmission?
3. Would you check the transmission vent? If so, what would you expect to find?
4. Would you recommend the transmission be replaced?

Introduction

Overhauling of automatic transmissions is a task rarely undertaken by most shops and requires the utmost in cleanliness and several specialized tools. For that reason, we will not attempt to discuss overhaul procedures in this chapter. Nonetheless, truck technicians must have a good understanding of what is involved in maintaining a typical automatic transmission, including the ability to diagnose basic transmission failures and recommend repair strategies. Those topics are the focus of this chapter.

Allison is the most prolific supplier of automatic transmissions to the North American heavy truck market, so this chapter provides a general maintenance guideline based on Allison transmission models. In no way is the information in this chapter meant to supplant Allison's or any other manufacturer's service recommendations, however. Always check the literature for your particular transmission model before proceeding. Also, do not assume that the schedules and recommended fluids are interchangeable between all transmission manufacturers. Always consult the Original Equipment Manufacturers (OEM) manual before servicing any transmission.

Fundamentals of Transmission Fluids

LO 50-1 Explain the fundamentals of transmission fluids.

Transmission fluid, like that shown in **FIGURE 50-1**, is the life blood of all automatic transmissions. If it is not maintained at the correct level and condition, failure of the transmission is inevitable. Therefore, it is essential that the OEM's transmission maintenance schedule is adhered to.

Looking at a transmission fluid, it can be easy to assume that they are all alike. Nothing could be further from the truth. Several types of transmission fluids include **friction modifiers** that change the coefficient of friction of the transmission clutch pack. Friction modifiers also change the clutch pack's engagement and disengagement characteristics. Using fluids with friction modifiers in transmissions that are not designed for them can lead to severe oxidation issues, clutch pack slippage, and outright failure of the transmission. And vice versa, using fluid without friction modifiers in a transmission that requires them can cause transmission failure as well. Transmission seal life can also be affected by using the wrong types of fluid. External leakage and internal leakage leading to clutch failure can result. Always adhere strictly to the transmission manufacturer's recommendation for the correct type of fluid and never mix fluids in a transmission.

Fluid Level

Transmission fluid performs several functions. It lubricates and cools the transmission. Fluid also transmits hydraulic power through the torque converter and acts as the hydraulic force to apply clutches. Therefore, the proper fluid level must be maintained at all times. Fluid level that is too low or too high causes severe problems in the transmission. If the fluid is too low, the hydraulic pump is starved of fluid during operation. Air is drawn

into the pump intake, leading to **aeration** and loss of pressure. Aeration is the direct mixing of air with the fluid, which causes bubbles. Aeration can lead to burned out clutches because of low application pressures and a loss of converter efficiency. Aerated fluid loses viscosity and so becomes less effective as lubrication.

All transmissions have a **transmission vent** that allows atmospheric pressure to enter the transmission. If that vent is not clear, the pump inlet can create very low pressures. Low pressures can cause cavitation, which is the formation of air bubbles in the transmission fluid as a result of the low pressure. Cavitation can damage the pump, as bubbles implode explosively and break down the actual metal. A pump experiencing cavitation is usually extremely noisy and eventually fails.

> ▶ **TECHNICIAN TIP**
>
> If the fluid level is correct and the fluid still becomes aerated, check the transmission vent. If the vent is blocked, it can stop atmospheric pressure from entering the transmission as the fluid is drawn in by the pump. The blockage can lead to the creation of a low-pressure area which, in turn, can lead to cavitation at the pump inlet and aeration of the fluid.

The correct fluid level in an automatic transmission is normally just below the rotating components. If the fluid level

FIGURE 50-1 Transmission fluid requirements can vary by manufacturer, so always follow OEM recommendations.

FIGURE 50-2 Always clean around the dipstick tube before checking oil level.

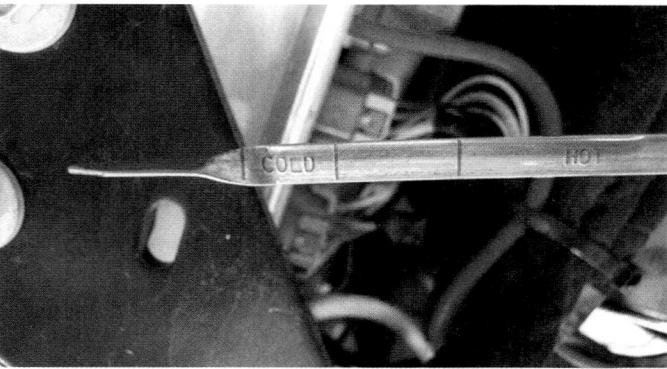

FIGURE 50-3 The temperature of the fluid is critical to getting a correct level reading.

is too high, aeration again becomes a problem—the rotating components in the transmission run in the fluid, churning it up and aerating it. The aeration causes the same problems as occur when the fluid level is too low. Also, if the fluid is aerated because the fluid level is too high, the fluid may continue to foam and expand until it starts to leak from the vent and the dipstick tube. **FIGURE 50-2** shows the dipstick tube for a heavy-duty transmission.

A missing or defective seal ring on the transmission filter(s) can also lead to aeration, allowing large amounts of air to be drawn in by the pump. For these reasons, most manufacturers insist that the fluid be checked and rechecked in a certain manner to ensure the level is correct.

Check the transmission fluid level at least twice to check that the reading is consistent. If it is not, investigate the cause before proceeding. For example, a clogged transmission vent can lead to inconsistency.

Cleanliness is also very important. Before removing the dipstick, clean the area around the stick and the fill tube. If adding fluid, always use only clean fluid from a sealed container and a clean funnel. Any dirt entering the transmission can lead to stuck valves in the valve body and shifting problems. Read the manufacturer's recommendation for the fluid temperature while checking fluid level. There is usually a large difference between the hot and cold levels of the fluid.

Most manufacturers recommend that the engine be running when checking transmission fluid levels. To check the fluid, start the vehicle with the transmission in neutral and the emergency brake applied. Place the transmission in reverse, then forward, and then back to neutral. Moving through the ranges in that manner ensures that the fluid passages are full. Then, remove the dipstick and clean and reinstall it. Make sure it is completely seated before removing it again. Check the fluid level against the dipstick markings, as shown in **FIGURE 50-3**. Repeat the procedure to ensure consistency.

If necessary, transmission fluid level can be checked when the fluid is cold, between 60°F and 120°F (16°C and 49°C), to ensure there is sufficient fluid to run the vehicle. A hot level check should be performed as soon as possible after the transmission reaches normal operating temperature of 160°F to 200°F (71°C to 93°C).

> **▶ TECHNICIAN TIP**
>
> When checking transmission fluid, adhere strictly to the OEM-recommended procedure. Any variation could lead to a false reading. For example, if the engine speed is increased, the reading may be lower than normal due to the fluid being drawn faster by the pump. Temperature is critical as well. The difference between cold and operating temperatures can be as much as three or four liters, depending on the transmission.

Minimum Operating Temperature

If a transmission is to be operated in cold ambient temperatures, the transmission fluid may need preheating before the transmission can be operated safely. Allison **TranSynd fluid** is a synthetic fluid made by Castrol to Allison specifications. If TranSynd is being used, the fluid requires preheating if ambient temperatures are below –22°F (–30°C).

If preheating is necessary because of the ambient temperature, one of these methods can be used:

- A sump heater can be installed to preheat fluid before operating the transmission.
- If no sump heater is available, allow the transmission to warm up in neutral for a minimum of 20 minutes at idle.

Allison electronically controlled transmissions have **cold operation inhibits** in their software to prevent the transmission from shifting when the fluid is below certain temperatures. For example, the Allison Transmission Electronic Control/ Commercial Electronic Control (ATEC/CEC) model of Allison transmissions does not allow any shifting if the fluid temperature is below –25°F (–32°C) and only limited shifting to first or reverse when its temperature is –25°F to 25°F (–32°C to –4°C).

Fluid Change Frequency

The oil change interval for Allison transmissions varies by transmission model and duty cycle or vocation. A typical oil and filter change interval for the MT series non-electronic control transmissions is 25,000 miles (40,000 km) when using non-synthetic TES-389TM fluids. Using TES-295TM-approved synthetic fluid extends the fluid change interval to 100,000 miles (160,000 km), but the filter change interval is set at 50,000 miles (80,000 km).

TABLE 50-1 Fluid and Filter Change Intervals on Allison 4000 Series Transmissions

				4000 SERIES High-Capacity Filters Fluid and Filter Change Interval Recommendations			
				Prognostics Turned Off or Not Calibrated in TCM		Prognostics Turned On	
		Transmission Model	Duty Cycle	Allison Approved TES-295TM Fluid	Allison Approved TES-389TM Fluid	Allison Approved TES-295TM Fluid	Allison Approved TES-389TM Fluid
FLUID		4000 w/2" and 4" Sump	General	300,000 miles (480,000 km) or 6000 hours or 48 months	25,000 miles (40,000 km) or 1000 hours or 12 months	When indicated by controller or 60 months, whichever occurs first	When indicated by controller or 24 months, whichever occurs first
			Severe	150,000 miles (240,000 km) or 6000 hours or 48 months	12,000 miles (20,000 km) or 500 hours or 6 months		
FILTERS	Main Filter	4000 w/ 2" and 4" Sump	General	75,000 miles (120,000 km) or 3,000 hours or 36 months	25,000 miles (40,000 km) or 1,000 hours or 12 months	When indicated by controller or 60 months, whichever occurs first	When indicated by controller or 24 months, whichever occurs first
			Severe	75,000 miles (120,000 km) or 3000 hours or 36 months	12,000 miles (40,000 km) or 500 hours or 6 months		
	Internal Filter	4000 w/ 2" and 4" Sump	All	Overhaul	Overhaul	Overhaul	Overhaul
	Lube/ Auxiliary Filter	4000 w/ 2" and 4" Sump	General	75,000 miles (120,000 km) or 3000 hours or 36 months	25,000 miles (40,000 km) or 1000 hours or 12 months	When indicated by controller or 60 months, whichever occurs first	When indicated by controller or 24 months, whichever occurs first
			Severe	75,000 miles (120,000 km) or 3000 hours or 36 months	12,000 miles (20,000 km) or Or 500 hours or 3 months		

The fluid change frequency changes, however, for the newer computer-controlled transmissions. Since 2009, Allison computer software has been equipped with **prognostic capability**. That is, the computer's programming allows it to closely monitor the transmission's drive cycles and recommend fluid and filter changes based on actual load and driving conditions. This option can be turned on or off by the vehicle operator through the transmission software. When Allison's Prognostics is turned on, the service interval is controlled entirely by the software. The software notifies the operator, through the display panel, when a fluid and/or filter change is required. **TABLE 50-1** is a chart depicting fluid and filter change intervals, with or without the Prognostics feature being activated, for the 4000 series transmissions.

The fluid/filter change frequencies on other Allison series and models can differ from those depicted in Table 50-1, and early initial filter changes are required for certain transmissions. More frequent fluid changes may be required if the vehicle is operated in severe conditions or extended duty cycles. It is essential to check the correct fluid/filter change frequency for the specific model being serviced. The correct change frequency and fluid capacities can be found at the following Allison website:

http://www.allisontransmission.com/docs/default-source/service-documents/st1099s.pdf?sfvrsn=2

Allison also has a fluid filter change interval calculator available at the following web address:

https://www.allisontransmission.com/my-allison/my-allison-basic

Fluid Analysis

When operating conditions vary from the norm, Allison recommends that **fluid analysis** be conducted to determine oil change frequencies. Fluid analysis can optimize transmission longevity and service scheduling. In order for fluid analysis to be successful, testing must be frequent and consistent so that trends can be established. **TABLE 50-2** contains Allison's recommended limit for fluid conditions and contaminants.

Fluid Handling

Transmission fluid must be handled with extreme care to prevent the entry of contaminants. Never use a container that has held **ethylene glycol** or other anti-freeze solutions to transfer transmission fluid. Glycol-based products can quickly destroy some clutch plate friction material, leading to complete failure of the transmission. Failure of, or simply lack of, transmission fluid is the primary cause of automatic transmission failures and it must be carefully monitored, adhering to proper fluid and filter change schedules and promptly repairing any fluid leaks .

Types of Transmission Fluids

As with other vehicle fluids, there are many types of transmission fluids available on the market. Which fluid is used depends on the make and model of transmission being serviced. There is also a selection of additives that can be used that claim to enhance the performance of transmission fluids. As with the fluid itself, follow the manufacturer's recommendations when determining if and which additives to use. Note: Most manufacturers do not recommend using any additives in their transmissions.

Recommended Transmission Fluids

Different manufacturers recommend using different transmission fluids depending on the design and construction of their transmissions. Because there is no universal transmission fluid that works for all models and manufactures of transmission,

always consult the manufacturer's documentation for your transmission model before using a particular transmission fluid. This section concentrates on Allison transmission's fluid recommendations.

TranSynd, shown in **FIGURE 50-4**, is a full synthetic automatic transmission fluid made specifically for Allison transmission by Castrol Ltd. TranSynd is recommended in all Allison on-highway transmissions. TranSynd meets the Allison Transmission Engineering Specification 295, or TES-295TM, fluid specification and qualifies for an extended service schedule and for severe-duty operation. A list of other manufacturer's fluids that meet the TES-295TM fluids can be found at the following website:

http://www.allisontransmission.com/service/autoapp/172/viewpage.jsp?ThisPage=3

In the past, Allison's TES-228TM specification for approved fluids covered non-synthetic on-highway fluids. This specification is no longer recognized. Non-synthetic fluids approved for use in Allison transmissions must now meet the Allison TES-389TM standard. A list of these fluids can be found at the following website:

https://www.allisontransmission.com/parts-service/approved-fluids/on-highway-fluids

Note: Allison highly recommends that only synthetic fluids be used in all of their transmissions.

Previously, off-highway model transmission fluids were classified as C-type fluids. The "C" is for construction, with the classification C-4 being the last of these. C-type fluids were automotive oil-type fluids approved for use in certain applications. Allison has done away with the "C" classification and, since November 2010, recommends that all off-highway fluids used be synthetic. These fluids must now meet the Allison TES-468TM standard to be approved for use in the company's 5000 to 9000 series off-highway units. A current listing of these products can be found at the following website:

http://www.allisontransmission.com/service/autoapp/172/viewpage.jsp?ThisPage=11.

TABLE 50-2 Allison Transmission Fluid Condition and Contamination Limits

Condition Limit	Contaminant Limit
• Viscosity +/− 25% change from new fluid	• Water 0.2% maximum
• Total Acid Number (TAN) +3.0* change from new fluid	• Glycol 0; no trace allowed. If glycol is detected the transmission requires overhaul to repair glycol damage.
• Solids 2% by volume maximum	

* mg of KOH (potassium hydroxide) required to neutralize a gram of fluid

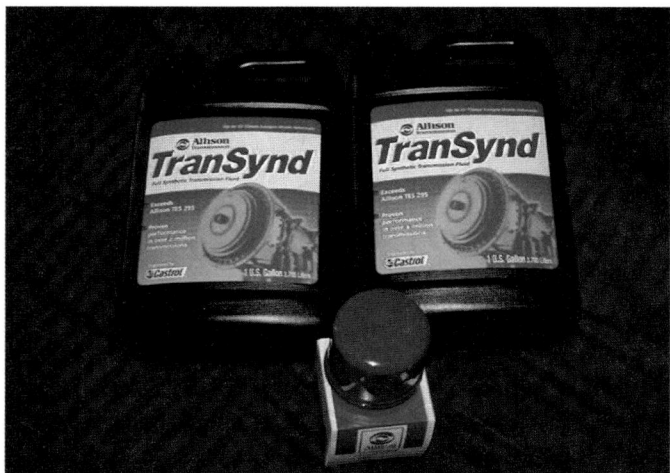

FIGURE 50-4 TranSynd or equivalent is the recommended fluid for all Allison on-highway transmissions.

Supplemental Additives

Most transmission manufacturers do not recommend any **supplemental additives** be used in their transmissions. Additives are products that are manufactured and marketed to increase the efficiency of transmission fluids and may alter the frictional, anti-wear, and/or oxidation properties of the fluid. Use of some supplemental additives, may void the transmission warranty and should not be used.

Basic Troubleshooting Procedures for Automatic Transmissions

LO 50-2 Explain the basic troubleshooting process for automatic transmissions.

Automatic transmissions are somewhat of a mystery to a lot of technicians, especially in the heavy-truck field, as they are not as common as standard transmissions. Nonetheless, automatic transmissions are diagnosed using the same basic step-by-step process used to diagnose any failed or suspect component. As always, a good understanding of the transmission's function and access to the OEM service manual are important before diagnosis is undertaken.

Automatic Transmission Diagnostics

When diagnosing problems with automatic transmissions, always stick to the basics. Check oil level and condition before starting any diagnoses. The next step is to road test the vehicle to verify any complaint. If the transmission has a fluid leak, take the necessary steps to ensure that the level remains sufficient during the road test or more damage could occur. Record the pertinent information, exactly what the problem is, and when it occurs—for example, during shifting or in a certain range. Does the problem occur only when the fluid is hot or cold?

When the problem is verified and recorded, the technician can then start the diagnostic procedure. Older transmissions have symptom-based diagnostic charts for the technician to follow, and these can assist greatly in the process. Automatic transmissions with electronic controls can self-diagnose and inform the operator or the technician with detailed trouble codes. Self-diagnostic trouble codes simplify diagnostic procedures by leading the technician to the manufacturer's step-by-step troubleshooting charts to assist in the process. These charts should always be followed in sequence to eliminate any chance of misdiagnosis. There are three broad areas of failures that can occur: mechanical, hydraulic, or electronic. By following the diagnostic charts, the technician can quickly get to the root cause of the complaint.

Symptom-Based Diagnoses

A good understanding of the transmission's power flow is an invaluable asset when trying to diagnose a complaint. Knowing which clutches are involved in the power flow when a transmission problem presents itself can greatly

FIGURE 50-5 Pressure testing can be a valuable diagnostic tool.

speed up the diagnostic process. The transmission control system, whether electronic or purely hydraulic, can also frequently be the root cause of some complaints. Having a good knowledge of the control systems operation can, again, be of enormous assistance to the technician trying to pinpoint a problem.

Pressure testing can be used to determine if the problem is mechanical or hydraulic. In older transmission models, testing pressure was limited to main or line pressure testing, cooling circuit pressure tests, and flow tests. The Allison World Transmission models include pressure test points, like those shown in **FIGURE 50-5**, for each of the individual clutch apply circuits, as well as the lube and main pressure.

Common transmission complaints include slipping clutches, either in drive or reverse or in a certain transmission range. Slipping clutches can usually be verified by conducting a stall test and/or road testing the vehicle after verifying the fluid level is, and remains, correct throughout the procedure. Refer to the Torque Converters chapter for the stall test procedure.

After confirming the complaint with a stall test or road test, always refer to the transmission manufacturer's troubleshooting recommendations before proceeding further. There are myriad differences between individual manufacturer's transmissions and there is no universal procedure for their diagnoses. Always follow the OEM service manual for your transmission.

Out-of-Service Criteria for Automatic Transmissions

Although the Commercial Vehicle Service Alliance (CVSA) does not specify Out-of-Service (OOS) criteria for automatic transmissions, the National Fire Prevention Association (NFPA) does include OOS criteria for vehicles covered by its standards. The following defects of the transmission shall cause a vehicle to be taken OOS according to NFPA:

- Any automatic transmission that overheats in any range
- Any automatic transmission that has a "do not shift" light illuminated

- Any transmission components that exhibit serious leakage of transmission fluid

Certain state transit organizations also list OOS criteria for automatic transmissions. The following are a selection of their criteria. A vehicle shall be taken out of service if any of the following defects are present:

- Transmission lines or hoses that have persistent leakage or a fluid leak onto any exhaust system component (transmission fluid can ignite when heated sufficiently)
- Any transmission that is loose in its mounting or has transmission mounts that are broken, damaged, or missing
- A defective neutral safety switch
- Any transmission that does not operate in any of the selected gear settings

Maintenance of Automatic Transmissions

LO 50-3 Describe automatic transmission maintenance procedures.

This section covers several maintenance procedures for automatic transmissions. It is by no means meant to replace manufacturers' recommendations for transmission service or inspection. It is merely a guideline. Always follow the relevant manufacturer's procedures for any maintenance or service task you are performing.

General Transmission Inspection

Before beginning the diagnostic procedure, it is important to inspect the transmission visually. The most important check

for any automatic transmission complaint is transmission fluid level. Low or high fluid level or deteriorated/contaminated fluid are at the root of a large percentage of automatic transmission problems.

In addition, it is important to identify visible transmission fluid leaks. If leaks are detected, take steps to ensure the fluid level remains at the full level during all diagnostic procedures. Leaks can be hard to pinpoint as air movement and vehicle vibration can spread the fluid far from the original leak point. A leak detection dye can be helpful in finding the leak. Follow the steps in **SKILL DRILL 50-1** to check fluid level and determine the source of a leak.

▶ **TECHNICIAN TIP**

Broken or corroded connectors and wiring are a frequent cause of problems with electronically controlled transmissions.

▶ **TECHNICIAN TIP**

Transmissions that use vacuum modulator valves (for example, gasoline engines) can develop a pinhole in the modulator's diaphragm. This can lead to transmission fluid being drawn into the engine through the vacuum line. The transmission fluid is then consumed by the engine, leading to low fluid levels without a visible leak.

Performing an Oil and Filter Change

The oil and filter change procedures for automatic transmissions depend on the model that is being serviced. What follows is merely a guideline. Always check the service manual

SKILL DRILL 50-1 Checking Fluid Level and Inspecting Fluid Loss

1. Look up the procedure for checking the transmission fluid level in the appropriate service information.
2. Locate the transmission dipstick (if equipped). Most, but not all, transmissions are checked with the engine at operating temperature, idling, and the transmission in park. If the transmission has a dipstick, wipe it off and reinsert it into the transmission before checking the level of fluid on the dipstick.

Check both sides of the dipstick; the side that is the lowest is the accurate fluid level. On some transmissions, the fluid returning to the transmission pan splashes up on one side of the dipstick, resulting in a high reading on that side.
3. If the transmission fluid level is low, add the recommended type and amount of transmission fluid. Be careful not to overfill the transmission.
4. Inspect the transmission for signs of leakage. Some places to check are the transmission pan, area around the entrance of the filler tube to the transmission, extension housing gasket, output shaft seals, selector shaft seal, area around the electrical connectors that go into the transmission case, front pump seals, fluid cooler lines, and the fittings. Also, if the vehicle has a vacuum modulator, remove the vacuum hose from the modulator and see if there is any transmission fluid in the hose. If there is, the modulator diaphragm is leaking; replace the modulator.
5. If fluid level is low and no external leakage is visible, check coolant overflow tank for contamination with transmission fluid, remove the radiator cap (with vehicle cold), and check for any transmission fluid in the radiator; if fluid is present in either location, it is an indication that the transmission cooler is leaking internally and must be replaced. Note: If there is a cooler leak, the

SKILL DRILL 50-1 Checking Fluid Level and Inspecting Fluid Loss (Continued)

transmission likely has been contaminated with engine coolant and requires overhaul.

6. If the transmission has a large amount of transmission fluid or engine oil covering it, you may need to clean it with a pressure washer, some engine degreaser, or use a leak detection dye in the transmission fluid.

7. Restart the vehicle and allow it to run for a while. The leak detection dye is easy to spot using a black light, or look for fresh transmission fluid leaking.

8. Record the location of the leak and inform the customer to obtain approval for repairs.

   Other important visual checks include:
   - Loose fasteners (transmission and its mounting components)
   - Visible transmission fluid leaks

- Transmission vent is clear (a clogged vent can lead to fluid aeration from pump cavitation)
- Correct movement and positioning of the manual shift linkage, if equipped
- Full and correct movement of mechanical throttle, **modulator cable**, or linkage and valve (if equipped)
- Leaks in air or vacuum modulator connection (if equipped); if a vacuum modulator is used, always check the inside of the vacuum line—it is a common source of an undetected transmission fluid leak
- Damaged or loose hydraulic connections and hoses
- Electrical connections and harnesses for abrasive wear and/or corrosion

---

for the transmission being serviced. Certain transmissions require that the transmission oil pan be removed to replace the filter; with other models, the filter can be accessed from the outside. Also keep in mind that a typical oil and filter change usually does not replace the quantity of fluid in the torque converter. (Some torque converters may have removable plugs to drain this fluid, but this is not conventional.) Aftermarket equipment can be installed in series with the transmission cooler circuit to flush the entire transmission torque converter and cooler with pressurized transmission fluid. These systems, however, are not recommended by manufacturers, and their efficiency is questionable at best. To change the oil and filter in a transmission, follow the steps in **SKILL DRILL 50-2**.

▶ TECHNICIAN TIP

The Allison AT series internal filter has an O-ring on the connecting tube where it fits into the transmission housing. Failure to replace this seal can lead to fluid aeration and, if the seal is doubled up by failing to remove the old O-ring, the filter tube is not seated and can drop out of the housing after service, causing transmission failure.

▶ TECHNICIAN TIP

A normal fluid and filter service typically leaves between five and eight quarts (4.5 and 7.5 liters), of the original fluid in the system that cannot be drained, most of it inside the torque converter, so be very careful of fluid compatibility issues.

SKILL DRILL 50-2 Changing the Transmission Oil and Filter

1. Ensure that the transmission is at operating temperature.
2. Remove the drain plug, if equipped, and allow the fluid to drain completely. Pay particular attention to the consistency and color of the fluid as it drains.
   - Most transmission fluids are red and relatively clear. Note: Some newer transmission fluid may have more of a brownish tinge, so be careful not to condemn the fluid if you are not sure.

- Fluid that has a milky or light pink color can indicate contamination with engine coolant. (Most transmissions use engine coolant to cool the fluid.) Engine coolant destroys transmission bushings and clutch plates. If transmission fluid has been contaminated with coolant, the transmission and torque converter should be overhauled and the cooler replaced.
- If the fluid has a shiny metallic look, it indicates an internal failure of some kind, which should be investigated. Significant metal deposits require that the transmission and torque converter be overhauled and all bearings and bushings replaced. Flushing the cooler may not remove all of the metal, however, so is not recommended in this case. The cooler should be replaced. Some service centers place an auxiliary filter in the return line of the cooler after flushing, but auxiliary filters can become clogged and starve the transmission of fluid. Replacement is the recommended course of action for this type of failure.
- If the fluid is dark or smells burnt, it indicates failure of one or more of the transmissions clutch packs. Overhaul of the transmission and torque converter is required, along with flushing or replacement of the cooler.

SKILL DRILL 50-2 Changing the Transmission Oil and Filter (Continued)

If the cooler is not replaced in any of the above scenarios, the cooler should be checked after reinstallation of the transmission for pressure drop across the total cooler circuit and total flow volume through the cooler circuit. If these are not in specification, replace the cooler.

3. If necessary, remove the oil pan to access the transmission filter. Newer Allison transmissions have two filters—a lube filter and a main filter—that are both accessible from the bottom of the valve body cover.

4. Remove the filter(s) and inspect for any foreign material, such as clutch debris or metal. On an initial filter change, there may be a few small pieces of metal present, but any significant amounts of particles and or metal filings indicate internal failure. If the filter is accessed externally, it is not necessary to remove the oil pan, but the filter(s) should be checked in the same fashion. If the oil pan is removed, inspect it carefully for any metal or clutch debris.

5. On older hydraulically controlled models, it may be necessary to clean or replace the governor screen/filter. This may be accessible from inside the pan (AT series) or externally (MT and HT series). Check the OEM manual for exact locations.

6. After inspection, clean the filter covers and transmission pan carefully and completely before installing the new filter(s). Be careful to install the filter correctly. A missing or incorrectly installed filter seal can cause air to be drawn in by the transmission oil pump and lead to transmission failure.

7. Reinstall the transmission oil pan (if removed). Be careful not to over-torque the pan bolts. They are easily broken. Over-torqueing the bolts also forces the gasket out from between the mating surfaces and can lead to leakage. Pan bolts are rarely torqued to more than 10 to 15 ft-lb (14 to 20 Nm), but always check the service manual for exact levels.

8. Reinstall the drain plug and tighten to specifications.

9. Refill the transmission with the correct fluid to the proper level. Try not to mix fluid types, as some fluids are incompatible with each other. If unsure whether a compatibility issue exists, contact the manufacturer.

10. Start the vehicle with the emergency brake applied. Apply the service brake and select each driving range one at a time. Then place the transmission back in neutral and recheck the fluid level.

11. Road test the vehicle to bring the transmission to operating temperature of between 160°F and 200°F (71°C and 93°C). Recheck the fluid level.

System Pressure Testing

Testing system pressure can be a valuable tool in transmission diagnoses. Hydraulic pressure is used to apply the clutches and make the transmission shift. Low pressure could indicate a failed pump, serious internal leakage, shift valve problems, and/or a failed clutch seal. High pressure could indicate a seized main pressure regulator valve. On some transmissions, it is only possible to test main pressure, whereas on others, such as the Allison World transmission main pressure, each clutch's application pressure and lube pressure can be tested individually. Follow the steps in **SKILL DRILL 50-3** to test system pressure.

Inspecting or Replacing Powertrain Mounts

Powertrain components are supported and aligned in the vehicle by flexible **mounts** usually made of rubber and steel. These mounts allow slight movement of the components as torque and

SKILL DRILL 50-3 Performing Automatic Transmission Pressure Tests

1. Refer to the appropriate service information to find the procedure to test the transmission's hydraulic pressures. Verify the correct transmission fluid level in the transmission.

2. Place a drain pan under the transmission and remove the correct pressure test port plug(s). Place the test port plug(s) off to the side where they will not be lost.

3. Install a transmission pressure tester(s) capable of measuring the maximum pressure into the test port(s) on the transmission.

4. Start the vehicle and place the vehicle in the correct operating conditions to monitor the pressure according to the manufacturer (for example, transmission at operating temperature, in drive, idling). Record the pressure(s).

5. Shut off the engine, remove the transmission pressure tester(s), seal the threads, and reinstall the test port plug(s).

6. Clean off any transmission fluid that dripped onto the transmission, restart the vehicle to check for leaks, and top off the fluid, if necessary.

braking forces are acting upon them. The mounts also absorb vibrations emanating from the engine and transmission and prevent those vibrations from being transferred to the vehicle frame.

These mounts are extremely resilient but can fail due to repeated flexing. Another common cause of failure is fluid contamination. If the rubber in the mount is subjected to contamination by hydrocarbon-based fluid, engine oil, fuel, transmission fluid, etc., it will break down, and the mount will fail. Failed mounts allow excessive movement of the powertrain and can lead to damage and/or erratic vehicle operation. Powertrain mounts should be inspected regularly and replaced if defective. Follow the steps in **SKILL DRILL 50-4** to inspect and replace (if necessary) powertrain mounts.

Allison Shift Point Adjustment

Most of today's automatic transmissions have no provision for shift point adjustment, as shifting is controlled electronically by the transmission control unit. Non-electronic Allison transmission models and certain other hydraulically controlled transmissions do allow for some adjustment of **shift points**.

Most hydraulically controlled transmissions have either a vacuum modulator valve (gasoline engines only) or throttle cable. When a transmission is equipped with a vacuum modulator, sometimes the spring tension inside the modulator can be adjusted by turning an adjusting screw. Increasing spring tension by tightening the screw causes shift point speeds to increase. Loosening the screw decreases shift points. The same type of shift point adjustment can sometimes be accomplished by adjusting the throttle cable or linkage. Refer to the individual transmission manufacturer's instructions for adjusting shift points.

Hydraulically controlled Allison transmissions have an adjustable cam that holds the tension on each of the shift signal valves and on the modulator valve, as shown in **FIGURE 50-6**. These **valve adjusting cams** have notches that allow the cam to be rotated to increase or decrease spring tension on each individual shift signal valve.

A special cam adjusting tool is shown in **FIGURE 50-7**. The J-24314 adjusting tool is from Kent Moore and can be used to adjust the cam's position. Each notch the cam is rotated increases or decreases that shift point by 2 mph (3.2 kph) for the shift that valve controls. Changing the tension on the modulator valve spring changes modulator pressure and changes all of the shift points at once.

These adjustable cams in the Allison transmission control valve body are accessed by removing the transmission oil pan. Allison recommends the use of a **valve body test stand**—either the Kent Moore J-25000-1 or the Aidco Model 250—in order to calibrate the shift points. To accomplish this, the valve body and modulator valve are removed and bolted to the test stand. The transmission governor is also removed and installed in the test stand. (It is very important that the correct governor for the transmission model be used. Check the three-digit code stamped into the head of the governor against the OEM specification.) The test stand supplies pressurized transmission fluid

---

SKILL DRILL 50-4 Inspecting, Replacing, and Aligning Powertrain Support Mounts

1. First, look up the correct procedure for checking and replacing powertrain mounts in the service information, especially if they are hydraulic-style mounts. Place the vehicle on a hoist to inspect the powertrain mounts under the vehicle.

2. Use a pry bar to carefully push up on the engine and transmission while watching the powertrain mounts. Look for cracks in the rubber and metal. Check that the bolts are tight. If the rubber section of the powertrain mount separates from the metal bracket, or if the rubber is torn, the mount needs to be replaced.

3. Lower the vehicle back down and start the engine.

4. Apply the brake and place the vehicle into gear.

5. Apply the throttle slowly and watch for excessive engine movement on the mounts.

6. Repeat step 5 with the vehicle in reverse to check the opposite mounts.

7. To remove a damaged powertrain mount, remove any components that are in the way.

8. Use an engine support fixture, engine hoist, or transmission jack, depending on the mount to be replaced, to raise the engine or transmission just far enough that the weight is off of the powertrain mount. Be VERY careful not to cause the vehicle to shift on the hoist!

9. Remove the bolts securing the mount to the transmission or engine, and then the bolts securing the mount to the frame of the vehicle.

10. Remove the old mount and compare it to the new mount.

11. Place the new mount in the correct position according to the manufacturer's service information and lower the jack slightly. Be careful to keep your fingers away from any pinch points should the powertrain slip or shift.

12. Reinstall the bolts loosely to ensure alignment

13. Lower the engine or transmission back down and torque the bolts to specifications.

14. Reinstall all components that were removed to access the powertrain mount.

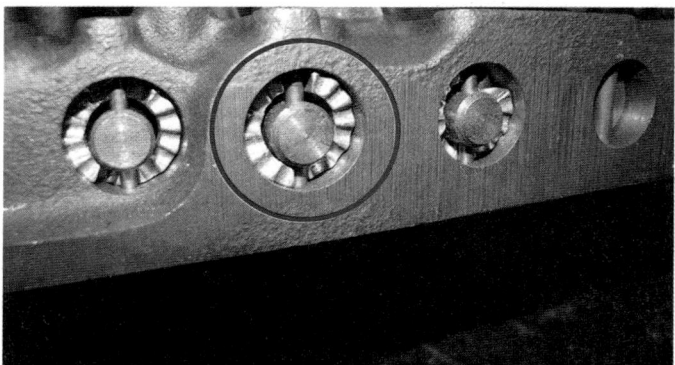

FIGURE 50-6 Allison hydraulically controlled transmissions have adjustable cams (circled) holding the shift signal valve and the modulator valve spring tension, which can be adjusted.

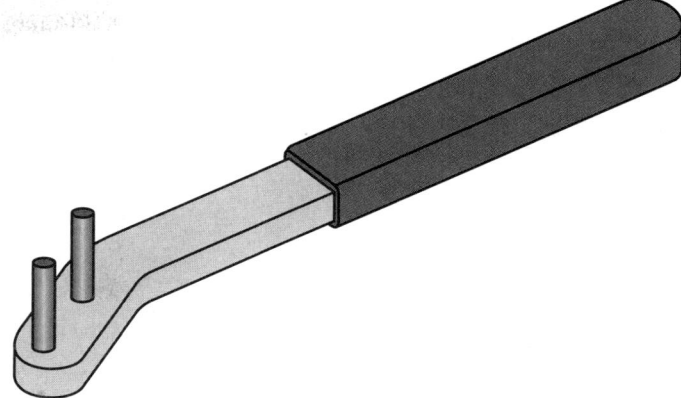

FIGURE 50-7 The Allison shift point adjustment cams are rotated using a Kent Moore special tool (J-24314) or equivalent.

and drives the governor, simulating a vehicle drive cycle. The shift points are then set to specification.

In the absence of a test stand, this procedure can be accomplished in the field by road testing the vehicle and recording the shift points at wide-open throttle. The results are then compared to the specification. If the results are not within specification, the transmission oil pan is removed and the shift signal valve tension is adjusted. Increasing the tension raises the shift point; decreasing the tension lowers it. The cams are then rotated the correct number of notches to achieve the correct shift points. If all of the shift points are low or high, the modulator valve or

throttle cable linkage should be checked for proper fit and adjustment before rechecking the shift points. If all the shift points are high or low, the cam on the modulator valve spring can be used to adjust all the shift points at once. Whether adjusting individual shift valve cams or the modulator cam, one notch changes the shift point/s by approximately 2 mph (3.2 kmh). After the adjustments are made, the vehicle should be road tested again to confirm shift points.

To perform shift point adjustments on Allison hydraulically controlled transmission, follow the guidelines in **SKILL DRILL 50-5**.

SKILL DRILL 50-5 Performing a Shift Point Adjustment on Hydraulically Controlled Allison Transmissions

1. Locate and follow the appropriate procedure in the service manual.
2. Complete the accompanying job sheet or work order with all the pertinent information.
3. Warm the transmission or test stand set-up to normal operating temperature. Note: Check the engine for satisfactory performance before making any adjustments.
4. Check the engine no-load governor setting and adjust, if needed.
5. Check the throttle linkage that controls the modulator valve mechanical actuator and adjust, if needed.
6. Check and adjust the modulator valve for satisfactory performance (see service manual).

7. Check the shift selector linkage for proper range selection.
8. To use the road test method with tachometer readings, follow the steps outlined below. Note: Before beginning the road test, compare the vehicle tachometer reading against the reading of a test tachometer to determine tachometer error.
   a. Drive the vehicle and record the engine rpm at which each full throttle upshift occurs. Note: The 1–2 upshift should occur within 400 rpm of the governed rpm. The 2–3 upshift should be within 300 rpm of the governed rpm. And the 3–4 upshift should be within 200 rpm of the governed rpm.
   b. Adjust as required according to the instructions in the Allison Shift Point Adjustment section.
   c. Perform another road test to determine if the adjustments were correct.
9. To use the road test method with speedometer readings follow these steps:
   a. Record the top speed of the vehicle in each selector hold position (first, second, and third ranges).
   b. Select "D" (drive) and operate the vehicle at full throttle, recording the speed at which each automatic upshift occurs. Note: The 2–3 and 3–4 upshifts should occur at approximately 2 mph (3.2 kph) below the speed recorded in the previous step for the second and third ranges, respectively. The 1–2 upshift is not adjusted relative to the top speed attained in the step above, but the 2–1 downshift at closed throttle should occur at 3 to 5 mph (4.8 to 8 kph).

SKILL DRILL 50-5 Performing a Shift Point Adjustment on Hydraulically Controlled Allison Transmissions (Continued)

c. Adjust as required according to the instructions in the Allison Shift Point Adjustment section.

d. Perform another road test to determine if the adjustments were correct.

10. To use the test stand method, follow the steps outlined below. Note: Follow manufacturer's set-up procedures when using the test stand method:

a. Check shift point specifications as given in the service manual.

b. Make all determinations from output shaft speed instead of engine-governed speed.

c. Check individual output shaft speed ranges for each shift.

d. Retest to ensure that the adjustments made were correct.

11. List the test results and recommendations on the job sheet or work order, clean the work area, and return tools and materials to their proper storage.

Electronically Controlled Automatic Transmission Diagnoses and Service Procedures

All electronically controlled automatic transmissions are capable of self-diagnoses and typically set a code and turn on a check transmission light when a fault is detected. With that said there are times when the problem is strictly mechanical or hydraulic and no codes are set, in these cases the technician must use the same procedures for symptom-based diagnoses used with hydraulically controlled transmissions. For electronic problems, however, a high-quality or factory scan tool can be an invaluable asset while diagnosing electronically controlled transmission problems. A generic scan tool that can read codes helps in diagnoses, but factory diagnostic software is usually the best to view live data from and test the sensors and actuators inside the transmission. Allison transmissions diagnostic software is known as Allison DOC, which, since 2017, is a subscription-based software package that covers Allison's entire range of transmissions. The software can be used to monitor transmission operation, read diagnostic trouble codes (DTCs), follow diagnostic procedures, test and evaluate components, and reset maintenance flags. To scan the transmission control module, follow the steps in **SKILL DRILL 50-6**.

To inspect, adjust, repair or replace electronic shift controls, electronic control unit, wiring harnesses, sensors, control module, vehicle interface module, and related components, follow the guidelines in **SKILL DRILL 50-7**.

Transmission Replacement Procedures

LO 50-4 Explain transmission replacement procedures.

As mentioned previously, overhauling of automatic transmissions is rarely done in most shops as the process requires several specialized tools for each transmission type and an extremely clean environment to complete the procedure. However, technicians likely will be required to remove transmissions and reinstall new or rebuilt units. It is always best to try to pinpoint the problem in an automatic before the transmission is removed. The more information that can be relayed to the transmission repair shop or person the better. Trying to diagnose an issue with the transmission on the bench or disassembled can be much more difficult without first narrowing down the complaint to a specific clutch or component. The transmission should only be removed for repair or overhaul after careful inspection and eliminating all other possibilities. Follow the steps in **SKILL DRILL 50-8** to remove the transmission.

SKILL DRILL 50-6 Scanning the TCM

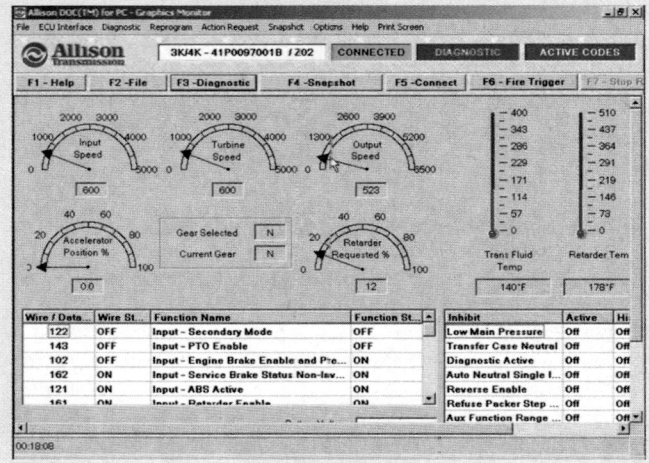

© Allison Transmission

1. Connect the Allison DOC software to the vehicle's Data Link Connector (DLC). For the location of the DLC, consult the service information. Allison's software tool can be run from a tablet, laptop computer, or mobile desktop unit.

2. Retrieve any DTCs from the vehicle. Record the codes.

3. Using the service information, research the diagnostic procedure for any codes found.

4. If there are multiple codes, evaluate the service information to see if codes are related to each other.

5. Follow the diagnostic procedure step-by-step until you have completed the diagnostic procedure and found the cause of the DTC.

6. Consult with the customer before completing any repair.

7. Use the software to erase codes or reset maintenance reminders after the repair, if necessary. Note: The latest TCMs will reset the DTCs themselves as soon as the fault no longer exists.

8. Road test the vehicle to check for reoccurrence of the code/codes.

SKILL DRILL 50-7 Inspecting, Adjusting, Repairing, or Replacing Electronic Shift Controls, Electronic Control Unit, Wiring Harnesses, Sensors, Control Module, Vehicle Interface Module, and Related Components

1. Locate and follow the appropriate procedure in the service manual.
2. Complete a job sheet or work order with all pertinent information.
3. Move vehicle into workshop, apply parking brakes, and chock the vehicle wheels. Observe lockout/tagout procedures.
4. If the vehicle has a manual transmission, place it in "neutral"; if it has an automatic transmission, place it in "park" or "neutral."

Note: Some vehicles with automatic transmissions do not have "park."
5. Test operation and retrieve DTCs as outlined in the service manual.
6. Use service manual procedures to inspect and repair or replace external/internal wiring harnesses.
7. Use service manual procedures to test, repair, or replace the following components:
    a. Electronic Control Unit (ECU)
    b. Vehicle Interface Module (VIM)
    c. Vehicle Interface Wiring (VIW)
    d. Engine speed sensor
    e. Turbine speed sensor
    f. Output speed sensor
    g. Throttle position sensor
    h. Control module
8. Use service manual procedures to test, repair, or replace electronic shift selector(s).
9. List the test results and/or recommendations on the job sheet or work order, clean the work area, and return tools and materials to proper storage.

SKILL DRILL 50-8 Removing the Transmission and Checking the Condition of Transmission Mounts, Insulators, and Mounting Bolts

1. Locate and follow the appropriate procedure in the service manual.
2. Complete the accompanying job sheet or work order with all pertinent information.
3. Move the vehicle into the shop, apply the parking brakes, and chock the vehicle wheels. Observe lockout/tagout procedures.
4. Since this is a procedure for a vehicle with an automatic transmission, place it in "park" or "neutral." Note: Some vehicles with automatic transmissions do not have "park."
5. Drain the oil from the transmission by removing the drain plug from the control module. Note: The transmission fill tube may have to be removed if it interferes with transmission removal.
6. Disconnect any hydraulic hoses from the transmission and plug all openings.
7. Drain coolant from the cooler, if present, and plug all openings.

8. Disconnect the input and output speed sensors, retarder sensors/connectors, the speedometer/ tachometer from the transmission, and the external harness from the feed-through harness.
9. Remove any linkages that may be present.
10. Mark the driveshaft yoke or flange on the transmission's output shaft. The marks ensure that the driveshaft is properly reconnected.
11. Place a transmission jack tightly against the transmission's underside. Secure the transmission to the jack
12. Remove the torque converter flex plate bolts.
13. Remove the transmission support mount/s bolts.
14. Remove the bolts that hold the transmission to the flywheel housing.

SAFETY TIP

Do not work underneath the transmission while disconnecting it from the vehicle. The transmission could fall, causing serious injury or death.

15. Slide the transmission away from the engine approximately 4" to 5" (100 to mm) and remove the adapter ring, if used.
16. Lower the transmission to the floor.
17. Check the transmission mounts, bolts, and insulators for wear. Replace, if required.
18. List the test results and recommendations on the job sheet or work order, clean the work area, and return tools and materials to their proper storage.

Inspecting the Flex Plate and the Torque Converter

While the transmission is operating, the flex plate that connects the torque converter to the engine crankshaft is constantly flexing and, therefore, is subject to fatigue wear and cracking. While the transmission is out of the vehicle carefully examine the flex plate and the torque converter mounting pads, bolts, and studs. Cracks in the flex plate usually form near the torque converter mounting hardware or the bolts securing the flex plate to the crankshaft. Inspect these areas very carefully. To inspect the torque converter and the flex plate, follow the steps in **SKILL DRILL 50-9**.

Checking the Transmission Cooler and Lines

After transmission failure, it is common to find debris in the transmission cooler system. It is essential that this system be flushed clean or replaced when replacing the transmission. Otherwise, this debris will contaminate the new transmission.

Although replacement of the cooler is the manufacturer's recommendation, most shops still opt for flushing. It is, however, essential that all the debris is removed. Follow the steps in **SKILL DRILL 50-10** to flush the cooler system.

SKILL DRILL 50-9 Inspecting the Torque Converter and Flex Plate

1. Remove the bolts securing the flex plate to the crankshaft.
2. Inspect the bolt holes used for mounting the flex plate to the crankshaft and the flex plate to the torque converter for cracks and bolt hole elongation.
3. Inspect the bolts or studs used for connecting the flex plate to the crankshaft and the flex plate to the torque converter for damaged threads.
4. Inspect the torque converter pilot for signs of damage.
5. Inspect the crankshaft pilot bore for signs of damage.
6. Inspect the torque converter mounting pads for damage.
7. Inspect the pump drive tangs for damage.
8. Install the required tool into the turbine to check for torque converter end play. Use a dial indicator to measure the amount of turbine movement.

SKILL DRILL 50-10 Inspecting and Flushing Cooler Lines

1. First, look up the recommended transmission cooler service method in the appropriate service information, and check the instruction manual for the flush equipment you are using or for the aerosol can of transmission cooler flush. Remove the fluid cooler lines from the transmission if the transmission is still in the vehicle.

2. Using compressed air (do not exceed 30 psi [207 kPa]), blow into one cooler line while catching the residue in a container as it comes out of the other line. Switch directions and repeat.
3. Install the cooler flush machine or aerosol can lines onto the transmission cooler lines so that the flow is in the reverse direction. If using the aerosol cooler flush can, place the other cooler line into a catch can.
4. Start the flush machine or aerosol can and allow it to run for the recommended time.
5. If necessary, switch directions on the lines so they can be flushed in the other direction.
6. Remove the flush machine and blow out the lines again so no residue remains inside the lines.
7. Reinstall the lines onto the transmission or cap them if the transmission is removed from the vehicle.
8. After properly filling the transmission with fluid, start the vehicle and inspect the lines and fittings for any signs of leakage.
9. Check inside the radiator for signs of the transmission cooler leaking into the radiator.

Once you are certain that the flex plate and torque converter mountings and the cooler system are functioning correctly, reinstall the overhauled or repaired transmission following the general procedures listed in **SKILL DRILL 50-11**. These are general procedures only; consult the manual for your particular transmission when necessary.

▶ **TECHNICIAN TIP**

When flushing cooler lines, pay particular attention to the maximum pressure recommended by the manufacturer. Exceeding this pressure could destroy the cooler and/or the lines and hoses.

▶ **TECHNICIAN TIP**

Transmission coolers are usually heat-exchangers that are cooled by the engine coolant. If the transmission oil has become cloudy or milky in appearance, an internal leak of the transmission cooler is very likely. If this is the case, the cooler must be replaced.

Adjusting Shift Linkage and Neutral Safety Switch

Most transmissions today are drive-by-wire. That is, the shift selector has no linkage connecting it to the transmission. By contrast, older transmissions and the lighter-duty 1000, 2000, and 2400 series Allison transmissions still have mechanical **shift cables** or linkage that may require adjustment. These transmissions use a **neutral safety switch** that prevents the vehicle from being started if the transmission is in any drive gear. (Some transmission OEMs refer to this switch as the PRNDL switch.) This adjustment ensures that the transmission is in the range selected according to the gear position indicator needle on the dash or the shift lever and that the neutral safety switch only allows the vehicle to be started in neutral or park. **SKILL DRILL 50-12** contains steps for adjusting a general selector cable or linkage and the neutral safety switch.

SKILL DRILL 50-11 Reinstalling an Automatic Transmission

1. Locate and follow the appropriate procedure in the service manual.
2. Complete the accompanying job sheet or work order with all pertinent information.
3. Check transmission housing for wear and damage.
4. Put the transmission on a transmission jack and raise it to a point where the transmission is level with the flywheel housing or adapter ring (if used).

SAFETY TIP

Do not work underneath the transmission while connecting it to the vehicle. The transmission could fall, causing serious injury or death.

5. Move the transmission forward until the transmission mates with the flywheel housing and install the mounting bolts.
6. Install the torque converter flex plate bolts that hold the transmission to the flywheel housing and torque to manufacturer's specifications.
7. Install the transmission support mount bolts.
8. Remove the transmission jack.
9. Reconnect the driveshaft to the transmission's output shaft, ensuring that the marks you made on the driveshaft yoke or flange line up.
10. Reconnect all linkages that were disconnected.
11. Reconnect the input and output speed sensors, retarder sensors/connectors, the speedometer/tachometer to the transmission, and the external harness to the feed-through harness.
12. Reconnect all hydraulic hoses.
13. Reconnect the transmission fill tube, if removed.
14. Fill the transmission with the proper amount and type of automatic transmission fluid and check the level.
15. List the test results and recommendations on the job sheet or work order, clean the work area, and return tools and materials to their proper storage.

SKILL DRILL 50-12 Inspecting, Adjusting, and Replacing the Manual Valve Shift Linkage and the Neutral Safety Switch

1. Look up the proper service procedure in the appropriate service information. Follow the procedure step-by-step to inspect and adjust the manual valve and the neutral safety switch.
2. Place the gear selector in the park position.
3. If necessary, raise the vehicle on a hoist to access the neutral safety switch and manual valve linkage.

4. Disconnect the shift linkage from the transmission.
5. Place the manual valve in the park position. The valve should snap into position.
6. The shift linkage should fit right onto the manual valve with no pulling on the linkage or the manual valve.
7. If the linkage does not line up, loosen the adjustment on the shift linkage and adjust the linkage so that it lines up properly with the manual valve.
8. Tighten the adjustment on the shift linkage.
9. Double-check that the gear position indicator still indicates the vehicle is in park.
10. Use an ohmmeter to check that the neutral safety switch has continuity on the correct terminals. If not, loosen the switch and adjust its position. If continuity is never obtained, or is obtained in every gear, replace the switch. The vehicle should start only in the park and neutral positions. Make sure the brake pedal is firmly applied, then check that the vehicle starts only in the park and neutral positions.
11. Run the shifter through all of the gear ranges, checking for proper operation.

Wrap-Up

Ready for Review

▶ Automatic transmissions are rarely overhauled in the field as most repair facilities do not have the cleanliness or special tooling required.

▶ Fluid is the life blood of automatic transmissions. Low, high, or contaminated fluid are, by far, the most frequent cause of transmission failure. So proper maintenance of fluid is essential.

▶ Not all automatic transmission fluids are the same. Some contain friction modifiers and/or are not compatible with transmission seals. It is essential that the manufacturer's recommended fluid is used.

▶ Fluid levels that are high or low can lead to aeration and rapid failure of the transmission.

▶ When checking fluid, always clean around the dipstick area to prevent contamination.

▶ Always check fluid under the correct conditions—usually with the vehicle running and the fluid at operating temperature.

▶ Some transmissions may have cold operation inhibits and may not function until the fluid warms up.

▶ Fluid change intervals vary widely based on transmission vocation, fluid type, and other factors. Always consult the manufacturer's recommendations to find the correct change interval.

▶ Since 2009, Allison World Transmissions have a feature called Prognostics that tracks drive cycle information and, when turned on, can tell the operator when fluid and filter changes are necessary.

▶ Fluid analysis may be required when fluid change intervals cannot be decided upon based on the manufacturer's information.

▶ TranSynd is a synthetic transmission fluid made by Castrol to Allison transmission engineering specifications and is the fluid recommended by Allison for use in all their transmissions.

▶ Most manufacturers do not recommend the use of any fluid additives in their transmissions.

▶ When diagnosing a transmission issue, always verify the complaint with preliminary checks and a road test.

▶ Follow symptom-based diagnoses charts when available from the manufacturer.

▶ On electronically controlled transmission, use the diagnostic fault code information and follow the manufacturer's trouble tree charts and/or symptom-based charts when necessary. Failure to do so usually leads to wasted efforts.

▶ Stall testing can be used to check clutch function in some instances.

▶ Pressure testing transmissions can help to pinpoint problem areas.

▶ There are no CVSA out-of-service criteria for automatic transmissions; however, the National Fire Prevention Association and some state transit commissions do have out-of-service criteria.

▶ An oil and filter change at the proper interval is the single most important maintenance procedure on automatic transmissions.

▶ During an oil and filter change, it is usually impossible to remove all of the old fluid. Typically, between 5 and 8 quarts (4.5 and 7.5 liters) of fluid remains. Always be sure of fluid compatibility.

▶ Powertrain mount hold, cushion, and alignment should be checked regularly and replaced when necessary.

▶ A shift point adjust could be done on older transmissions, but is rarely possible on today's electronically controlled units.

▶ Electronically controlled transmission manufacturers produce sophisticated diagnostic software programs to evaluate their transmissions

▶ Most failed transmissions are simply exchanged in the field so, after diagnoses, the technician's next task is usually a transmission removal and replacement with an overhauled unit.

▶ The flex plate should be inspected for cracks whenever a transmission is removed.

▶ The transmission cooler can be a source of coolant contamination of the transmission fluid.

▶ When a transmission is replaced, the cooler system, lines, and hose should be flushed to remove any debris from the failed transmission.

▶ The shift linkage and the neutral safety switch should be adjusted when a transmission is replaced to ensure the vehicle only starts in neutral or park.

Key Terms

aeration Air in the fluid.

cold operation inhibit Restriction on transmission operation when the temperature is too cold for the transmission fluid to do its job.

ethylene glycol A chemical that resists freezing but is very toxic to people and animals.

fluid analysis Chemical analysis of the transmission fluid revealing contaminant levels.

friction modifier Additive in transmission fluid designed to enhance the friction characteristics of certain clutch materials.

modulator cable A mechanical cable connected to the throttle that operates the modulator valve.

mount Steel-backed rubber support that holds the powertrain components.

neutral safety switch A switch operated by the transmission shift linkage that prevents the vehicle from being started except when in park or neutral. Also known as the PRNDL switch on some transmissions.

prognostic capability The ability by some transmission ECUs to predict fluid and filter change intervals.

shift cable A mechanical cable connected to the driver's shift lever and the transmission manual valve.

shift point The road speed at which a shift occurs.

supplemental additive Aftermarket additive available for automatic transmissions but not recommended by manufacturers.

transmission vent A vent on the transmission that is open to atmospheric pressure.

TranSynd fluid A full synthetic fluid produced by Castrol, to Allison specification; TranSynd is the recommended fluid for all Allison transmissions.

valve adjusting cam Small cam on the end of the shift signal and modulator valves that, when turned, adjust the shift point.

valve body test stand A special test stand specifically for testing and setting up Allison transmission control valve bodies and shift points.

Review Questions

1. Which of the following is the primary cause of failure of an automatic transmission?
   a. Fluid loss or contamination
   b. Excess fluid pressure
   c. Torque overload
   d. Driver abuse

2. Which of the following could lead to pump cavitation?
   a. Incorrect transmission fluid
   b. High temperature fluid
   c. Elevated fluid temperature
   d. Clogged transmission vent

3. What is meant by friction modifiers when discussing transmission fluids?
   a. Additives that change the friction characteristics of the clutches
   b. Additives that change the characteristics of the clutch seals
   c. Additives that reduce friction on bearing surfaces
   d. Additives that increase friction on bearing surfaces

4. What is meant by pump cavitation?
   a. Cavities in the pump
   b. Bubbles in the fluid caused by low pressure
   c. Bubbles in the fluid caused by component rotation
   d. Cavities in the torque converter pump

5. Approximately how much fluid is not replaced during a typical fluid and filter change on an automatic transmission?
   a. 1 to 2 quarts (0.9 to 1.9 liters)
   b. 3 to 4 quarts (2.8 to 3.8 liters)
   c. 5 to 8 quarts (4.7 to 5.7 liters)
   d. 10 to 15 quarts (9.5 to 14.2 liters)

6. What should you do if you find transmission fluid in the vacuum modulator line?
   a. Replace the rubber part of the line and flush it.
   b. Remove the modulator valve and clean it.
   c. Replace the diaphragm in the modulator valve.
   d. Replace the modulator valve.

7. What Is the current recommended fluid for Allison on-highway automatic transmissions?
   a. C-4 oil
   b. TES 295TM fully synthetic
   c. TES-228TM synthetic
   d. TES-389TM

8. Would high oil level lead to transmission slippage and why or why not?
   a. Yes, because the rotating components would aerate the oil.
   b. No, high oil level would be ok as long as it is not enough to leak.

c. No, high oil level can sometimes keep the oil at a cooler temperature.

d. Yes, high oil level can cause hydraulic lock, stopping the clutches from applying.

9. What is the oil drain interval for an Allison transmission is equipped with Transynd fluid and prognostics?

a. 500,000 miles (800,000 km), or every five years

b. 100,000 miles (160,000 km), or every two years

c. 50,000 miles (80,000 km), or once a year

d. When indicated by the gear shift display or five years

10. When you remove a transmission oil pan, you find black or brown fibrous dust in the oil and accumulated in the oil pan. What would cause these deposits?

a. Thrust washer wear

b. Fluid oxidation

c. Friction clutch deterioration

d. Transmission cooler contamination

ASE Technician A/Technician B Style Questions

1. Technician A says that all automatic transmission fluids are the same. Technician B says that all synthetic automatic transmission fluids are compatible. Who is correct?

a. Technician A

b. Technician B

c. Both Technician A and Technician B

d. Neither Technician A nor Technician B

2. Technician A says using synthetic fluids greatly extends automatic transmission fluid change intervals. Technician B says that transmission vocation can influence fluid change intervals. Who is correct?

a. Technician A

b. Technician B

c. Both Technician A and Technician B

d. Neither Technician A nor Technician B

3. Technician A says that automatic transmission fluid should usually be checked with the vehicle running and the transmission at operating temperature. Technician B says that automatic transmissions using synthetic fluid can be topped up with regular fluid as long as it is not more than two quarts (1.9 liters) low. Who is correct?

a. Technician A

b. Technician B

c. Both Technician A and Technician B

d. Neither Technician A nor Technician B

4. Technician A says that automatic transmission fluid that looks milky or pink can mean a failed transmission cooler. Technician B says that transmission fluid that has a shiny look to it can mean internal failure of transmission components. Who is correct?

a. Technician A

b. Technician B

c. Both Technician A and Technician B

d. Neither Technician A nor Technician B

5. Technician A says that the shift points can be adjusted in most of today's automatic transmissions. Technician B says that most of today's automatic transmissions are drive-by-wire and the only adjustment that may have to be done is the manual shift linkage and the neutral safety switch. Who is correct?

a. Technician A

b. Technician B

c. Both Technician A and Technician B

d. Neither Technician A nor Technician B

6. Technician A says that most hydraulically controlled transmissions require regularly scheduled oil and filter changes. Technician B says that some electronically controlled transmissions can indicate when an oil change is required. Who is correct?

a. Technician A

b. Technician B

c. Both Technician A and Technician B

d. Neither Technician A nor Technician B

7. Technician A says that shift point adjustment can be performed on most hydraulically controlled transmissions. Technician B says that shift point adjustment on hydraulically controlled Allison transmissions involves removal of the transmission oil pan. Who is correct?

a. Technician A

b. Technician B

c. Both Technician A and Technician B

d. Neither Technician A nor Technician B

8. Technician A says that loss of transmission oil is the most common cause of automatic transmission failure. Technician B says that slight loss of transmission fluid over time is normal and just needs topping up from time to time. Who is correct?

a. Technician A

b. Technician B

c. Both Technician A and Technician B

d. Neither Technician A nor Technician B

9. Technician A says that "TranSync" is the fluid that Allison recommends for all its transmissions. Technician B says that, if a transmission has TM-389TM fluid installed, it can be topped up with "TranSynd." Who is correct?

a. Technician A

b. Technician B

c. Both Technician A and Technician B

d. Neither Technician A nor Technician B

10. Technician A says that each notch of the adjustment cam on an Allison transmission shift signal valve changes the shift point by 2 mph (3.2 kph). Technician B says that the cam is turned clockwise to increase the shift point and counterclockwise to decrease the shift point. Who is correct?

a. Technician A

b. Technician B

c. Both Technician A and Technician B

d. Neither Technician A nor Technician B

CHAPTER 51

Heavy-Duty Drive Shaft Systems

Learning Objectives

After reading this chapter, you will be able to:

- **LO 51-1** Describe and explain the fundamentals of driveshaft systems.
- **LO 51-2** Describe and explain the operation of driveshafts.
- **LO 51-3** Describe and explain driveshaft angle cancellation.
- **LO 51-4** Check and adjust driveline angularity.
- **LO 51-5** Troubleshoot driveshaft vibrations and failures.
- **LO 51-6** Inspect and maintain driveshafts.

You Are the Technician

A vehicle is brought to your service facility and the driver complains of a high-pitched squeaking noise while the vehicle is moving. You ask the driver to explain the circumstances of the noise, and he says that it only makes the noise when he is going forward; not when in reverse. You do a preliminary inspection and can see nothing out of the ordinary, so you road test the vehicle and, sure enough, it does have a squeaking noise as you drive forward slowly. The frequency of the noise seems to be too fast for a wheel end. You have a closer look at the vehicle and see small streaks of rust around the front universal joint bearing caps.

1. What might the rust around the U-joint indicate, and what can be done about it?
2. If you find that there is side-to-side play in the U-joint, what would this indicate?
3. Would you recommend the U-joint be replaced?

Introduction

Before the invention of the driveshaft, rotational power from the engine of a vehicle was transmitted to the drive axle using a series of sprockets and a chain. Originally, only one of the wheels received driving power, which led to a lot of vehicles getting stuck when the drive wheel encountered slippery conditions.

FIGURE 51-1 shows a chain drive from an old Cadillac. This drive system drove a differential gear set that sent power to both wheels. The system was inherently noisy and dirty, and notorious for failing.

In 1903, Clarence Spicer was issued a patent for an encased **Cardan joint** for use in vehicle driveshafts. At that time, he was the only manufacturer of these so-called **universal joints (U-joints)** for this purpose. Cardan joint is the original name for a universal joint. As seen in **FIGURE 51-2**, it consists of a cross with four machined end posts called **trunnions**, over which are installed four bearing caps with needle roller bearings. These bearing caps are installed into two yokes attached to two shafts—an input or driving shaft and an output or driven shaft. The universal joint and the yokes connect the two shafts together and the joint allows the driven shaft to operate at an angle to the driving shaft.

Mr. Spicer soon had orders from most of the automotive manufacturers of the day for his universal joint driveline system. The actual Cardan, or universal joint, that Mr. Spicer used in his patented "Casing for a Universal Joint" had been around for a long time before he considered its use in automobiles.

The invention of the universal joint is generally attributed to the Italian mathematician Gerolamo Cardano (hence the name Cardan Joint), who described the operation of the joint in detail in 1545, but did not actually produce it. Cardano died in 1576 before the joint was produced. The concept was studied by Robert Hooke between 1667 and 1675. In some countries, therefore, the Cardan joint is known as a **Hooke joint**. Hooke was the first to document that the joint produced **non-uniform velocity** when operated at an angle. That is, the driven shaft turns at a constantly changing speed. The Non-Uniform Velocity section discusses the concept of this speed change in greater detail.

The scientific community traces the universal joint back to the **gimbals** used by the ancient Greeks as early as 220 B.C., and some suggest the use of gimbals began even farther back in China. Two-axis gimbals have an object suspended on the center axis of a circle that, in turn, is suspended on the center axis of a second circle. That construction allows the object to stay horizontal no matter the angle of the support. For example, gimbals allow a gyroscope or compass on a ship to be kept at the exact same position, even when rough seas toss the ship around. The universal joint operates on the same principle as gimbals, but the pivot points for the circles are on the inside of the joint (the cross), and the circles are the two shafts that the joint connects. Whatever the definitive origin of the joint, its use today in the automotive world is attributed to Clarence Spicer's patent. The universal joint is essential to the operation of most modern vehicles.

This chapter explains the principles of operation, construction, and types of vehicle driveshafts and joints used in the medium- to heavy-duty truck and coach market. Included in the chapter are discussions on the theory of non-uniform velocity, driveline angularity, Cardan joints, constant velocity joints, and hanger bearings. The chapter also covers troubleshooting driveshaft vibration and typical failures, as well as inspection and maintenance of driveshafts.

FIGURE 51-1 Chain drives like this one were notoriously unreliable.

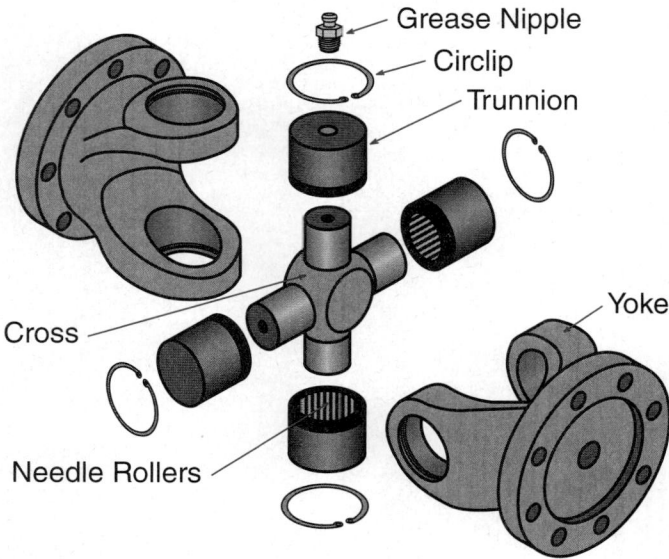

FIGURE 51-2 An exploded view of a typical U-joint.

Fundamentals of Driveshaft Systems

LO 51-1 Describe and explain the fundamentals of driveshaft systems.

Although there are many aspects to the modern driveshaft, such as the one shown in **FIGURE 51-3**, any driveshaft must meet the following criteria in order to perform its function.

1. **Strength**: The shaft must be strong enough to withstand the maximum torque from the engine multiplied through the transmission gearing.

FIGURE 51-3 A typical modern driveshaft.

2. **Variable length**: The shaft must allow the shaft to change length as the suspension oscillates.
3. **Angle of drive**: The shaft must transmit torque through constantly changing drive angles.

Strength

The primary function of a driveshaft is to provide the strength needed to withstand the peak torque delivered from the engine while providing an ample safety margin. It might seem that increasing strength can be achieved simply by increasing the weight of the driveshaft. As the driveshaft is made heavier to carry more load, however, the shaft's maximum speed of rotation is affected. The heavier the shaft is, the lower its maximum speed can be.

As a driveshaft speeds up, centrifugal force acting on its weight tends to move the shaft off its axis of rotation, causing a whipping action. The speed at which the centrifugal force causes the shaft to move off its axis is known as **critical speed**. If a shaft operates at or above this speed, the resultant vibration will destroy the shaft and can damage the entire powertrain. This problem can be alleviated by changing the weight, diameter, or length of the shaft. The shaft can be made lighter by using a thinner-walled tube, but this affects its overall strength. The tube can be made larger in diameter, which makes it less likely to bow off its centerline, but doing so increases the weight. Finally, the shaft length can be reduced, but this then requires that several shafts must be connected together to achieve the necessary length. Therefore, the overall shaft dimensions and weight must be carefully selected to match the vehicle and vocation requirements. In essence, the shaft must be made as light as possible but as strong as necessary for its function.

Variable Length

The second function of a driveshaft is that it must allow the shaft to change in length due to the varying distance between the transmission and the drive axle caused by suspension oscillations (jounce and rebound). As the vehicle encounters a bump in the road, its suspension moves upward (jounce). This movement typically decreases the distance from the transmission output to the rear axle slightly. Conversely, a dip in the road causes the suspension to move down (rebound). Rebound typically increases the distance from the transmission to the rear axle slightly. Torque effects of braking and acceleration cause the rear suspension to wind up (acceleration) or wind down (braking). Both of these reactions tend to slightly increase the distance from the transmission to the axle. For these reasons, it is essential that the operating length of the driveshaft can change.

Angle of Drive

The engine and transmission are rigidly bolted together and so are always on the same plane when the vehicle moves along the road. Not so for the vehicle's suspension. The suspension moves up and down relative to the transmission, so the position of the drive axle relative to the transmission is constantly changing. The torque forces of braking and acceleration add to this change in drive angle. Therefore, a driveshaft must be capable of transmitting torque to the rear axle while operating through constantly changing drive angles. This is the third essential function of the driveshaft.

Driveshaft Series

By far the most common driveshaft used in the heavy-duty truck market in North America is the Spicer 10 series, 1710 and 1810, driveshaft. Driveshaft capacity is the maximum torque that the shaft can handle. This capacity is denoted by the series number. The 10 series driveshafts have recently been replaced by the Spicer Life series SPL-140 through SPL-350HD. Again, the driveshaft capacity is denoted by the series number with the SPL-350HD capable of handling 25,815 ft-lb (35,000 Nm) of torque. The Life series driveshaft feature sealed u-joints and slip yokes and has greatly extended lubrication intervals.

There are several other limitations on the shaft design, such as maximum shaft length, maximum rpm, maximum **torsional excitation**, and maximum **inertial excitation** (discussed further in the Driveline Vibration Diagnostics section). The last two of these are extremely complicated calculations based on the diameter, length, and weight of the shaft. As mentioned earlier, the universal joint operating at an angle causes the driven shaft to experience a constantly variable speed, speeding up and slowing down relative to the drive from the transmission. Torsional and inertial excitation refers to the inherent vibration effects caused by the acceleration and deceleration of the rotating driveshaft's mass. As such, calculating excitation levels is better off left to the engineers. Drive shaft manufacturers list recommended limits for the various shaft sizes and operating angles. **TABLE 51-1** shows some of the limits for the various shaft series numbers. Please note the chart is a guideline only; always consult the manufacturer for accurate and up-to-date recommendations. Note that the safe operating rpm given is for a shaft operating at a three-degree angle; as the operating angle of a shaft increases, the maximum operating rpm of the shaft decreases.

Spicer recently introduced the Spicer Life series designed to supersede the 10 series. A conversion table from the 10 series to the Life series is shown in **TABLE 51-2 and TABLE 51-3**.

TABLE 51-1 Recommended Limits for Driveshafts by Series

Series	Tube Diameter	Maximum Shaft Length	Maximum Shaft Torque	Max Speed at 3.0-degree U-joint Angle
1610	4.00" × 0.134" (101.6 × 3.4 mm)	70" (177.8 cm)	5700 ft-lb (7728 Nm)	4000 rpm
1710	4.00" × 0.134" (101.6 × 3.4 mm)	70" (177.8 cm)	7700 ft-lb (10,440 Nm)	4000 rpm
1710 HD	4.09" × 180" (103.9 × 4.6 mm)	70" (177.8 cm)	10,200 ft-lb (13,829 Nm)	4000 rpm
1760	4.0" × 0.134" (101.6 × 3.4 mm)	70" (177.8 cm)	10,200 ft-lb (13,829 Nm)	4000 rpm
1760 HD	4.09" × 0.180" (103.9 × 4.6 mm)	70" (177.8 cm)	12,200 ft-lb (16,541 Nm)	4000 rpm
1810	4.5" × 0.134" (114.3 × 3.4 mm)	75" (190.5 cm)	12,200 ft-lb (16,541 Nm)	3400 rpm
1860 HD	4.59" × 0.180" (116.6 × 4.6 mm)	75" (190.5 cm)	16,500 ft-lb (22,371 Nm)	3400 rpm

TABLE 51-2 Ten Series Equivalents in Life Series of Spicer Driveshafts

Older Spicer 10 Series Driveshafts	Equivalent Spicer Life Series Driveshaft
1710 is replaced by	SPL-140
1760 is replaced by	SPL-170
1810 is replaced by	SPL-250/SPL 350

TABLE 51-3 The Operating Limits and Sizes for the Life Series Driveshafts

Series	Torque Rating		Tubing OD		Wall Thickness	
	(lbs. ft.)	Nm				
SPL 140	7744	10,500	107 mm	4.21 in	3.5 mm	.138 in
SPL 140HD	10,325	14,000	110 mm	4.33 in	5 mm	.197 in
SPL 170	12,539	17,000	126 mm	4.96 in	3 mm	.118 in
SPL 170 HD	12,539	17,000	128.5 mm	5.06 in	4.25 mm	.167 in
SPL 170 I/A	11,063	15,000	116.7 mm	4.59 in	4.57 mm	.180 in
SPL 250	16,595	22,500	128.5 mm	5.06 in	4.25 mm	.167 in
SPL 250HD	18,439	25,000	130 mm	5.12 in	5 mm	.197 in
SPL 250 lite HT	18,439	25,000	118.6 mm	4.67 in	5.2 mm	.205 in
SPL 250 I/A	15,489	21,000	128.5 mm	5.06 in	4.25 mm	.167 in
SPL 350	22,127	30,000	138.5 mm	5.45 in	4.25 mm	.167 in
SPL 350HD	25,815	35,000	140 mm	5.51 in	5 mm	.197 in
SPL 350 lite	18,439	25,000	118.6 mm	4.67 in	5.2 mm	.205 in
SPL 250 lite HT	22,127	30,000	120.2 mm	4.73 in	6 mm	.236 in

► TECHNICIAN TIP

A vehicle uses a **driveline** to connect the output of the transmission to the input of the drive axle. A driveline may consist of only one driveshaft, but most heavy truck drivelines have multiple driveshafts, hanger bearings, and universal joints making up the driveline.

Components of Driveshafts/Drivelines

Depending on the vehicle and the installation requirements, many components can be used to make up a driveline. Certain manufacturers have a propensity for using different types of yokes, universal joints, and shaft support systems. In heavy-truck installations, several driveshafts are typically used. Some

FIGURE 51-4 Driveshaft tubing may be forged or manufactured using the drawn-over-mandrel method, which produces consistent wall thickness and strength. Then the tube is welded to the yokes.

FIGURE 51-5 Tube yokes are welded to the tube and have two bores to accept the U-joint bearing caps.

straight trucks can have as many as four or even more driveshafts connected together to connect the transmission to the rear axle. The most popular components used in modern truck drivelines include the driveshaft tube, driveshaft yokes, slip joints, coupling shafts, center support bearing (hanger bearings), universal joints, and fastening systems.

Driveshaft Tube

The driveshaft tube can be made from steel, aluminum, or fiberglass. Steel is the material of choice for the heavy-truck market because of its strength.

Steel tubing can be manufactured in several ways. A flat piece of steel can be bent into the shape of a tube and the seam welded. Another method of manufacture is by forging. A forged seamless tube that is extruded and has no welding is shown in **FIGURE 51-4**. A Drawn-Over-Mandrel (DOM) tube is a welded tube drawn over a mandrel (a die the size and shape of the tube). DOM construction provides an extremely consistent wall thickness and smoothness for increased strength and stability. Forged or DOM tubes are often used in heavy-duty applications.

Regardless of construction, driveshaft tubes are hollow. Consequently, they tend to amplify any sounds like a bell. To combat this, sound deadeners made of a variety of materials—even cardboard—are placed into the tube at manufacture to stop the shaft from conducting noise.

Driveshaft Yokes

All driveshafts have yokes—the yoke is the component that allows the driveshaft to be connected to the other components of the driveline. Three types of yoke are prevalent in heavy-duty applications: tube, end, and flange yokes.

Tube Yokes   Tube yokes, such as the one shown in **FIGURE 51-5**, are pressed into the tube at manufacture and welded in place. Tube yokes have full round bores that accept two of the pressed-in U-joint bearing caps. There are several sizes of tube yokes to accommodate different universal joint sizes. Universal joint bearing caps are retained in the tube yoke ears by internal or external snap rings or circlips (also known as C-clips), bolted in bearing caps, or bolted spring clips.

FIGURE 51-6 End yokes are usually splined to a component. This interaxle input yoke is of the half-round design.

End Yokes   End yokes are designed to be installed over the splined output shaft of the transmission, or the splined input shaft of the drive axle, as shown in **FIGURE 51-6**, or a splined shaft that is part of the driveshaft itself. End yokes are usually bolted to their respective shafts. End yokes can come in full-round or half-round designs. The full-round design allows the

Companion Flange

Flange Yoke

FIGURE 51-7 A flange yoke connects to a driveline component with a matching companion flange.

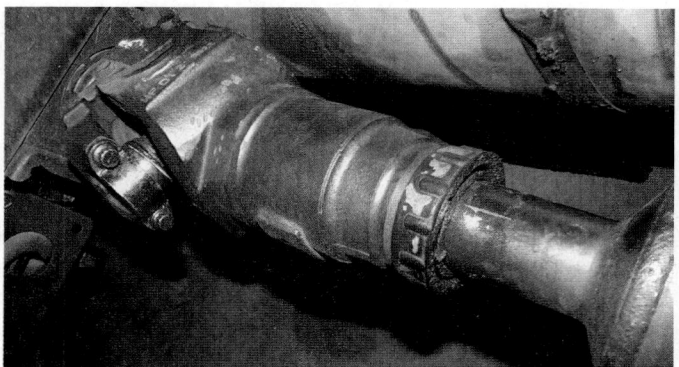

FIGURE 51-8 A slip joint allows the driveshaft to change in length as required due to suspension oscillation.

FIGURE 51-9 Failure to correctly reinstall a separated slip joint leads to vibration. Always mark the joint before removal.

bearing caps to be retained by internal or external snap rings or circlips, bolt-in bearing caps, or bolted spring clips. Half-round designs use attaching hardware, such as U-bolts, wing-shaped bearing caps bolted to the yoke, or bolted half-round straps. Half-round yokes using straps as attaching hardware usually have small metal tangs cast into the yoke to prevent the installed universal joint bearing caps from moving outward.

Flange Yoke A **flange yoke** holds two of the universal joint bearing caps and incorporates a flat flange with a series of mounting holes so that the flange can then be attached to a component. **FIGURE 51-7** shows a flange yoke. Universal joint bearing caps are retained in the flange yoke ears by internal or external snap rings or circlips, bolt-in bearing caps, or bolted spring clips. A flange yoke is designed to be bolted to a matching flange mounted on the component called a companion flange.

Sometimes, a **companion flange** is matched with a flange yoke and used instead of an end yoke. The flange yoke and the companion flange bolt together when the driveshaft is installed, as seen in **FIGURE 51-7**. A companion flange is splined to the output shaft of the transmission or the input shaft of the drive axle. A companion flange does not have bores to accept the universal joint bearing caps and so must be used with a flange yoke. The flange is held in place on the shaft by a large nut or bolt. The companion flange can be round or square in shape, but must match the shape of the flange yoke that bolts to it.

Slip Joint

A **slip joint** is a two-piece splined component consisting of a splined shaft fitted into a splined sleeve. **FIGURE 51-8** shows a slip joint. A slip joint allows the driveshaft to lengthen or shorten while operating and is essential in a driveline to accommodate length changes caused by suspension oscillation (jounce and rebound) and the effects of braking and acceleration. Some, but not all, slip joints have a master spline, so they cannot be re-assembled incorrectly. If they do not have a master spline, it is essential that the technician mark the mating position of the two halves of the slip joint before removal, as shown in **FIGURE 51-9**. Otherwise, a serious driveline vibration could result.

Most slip joints used on newer heavy trucks have a coating called Glidecoat. This blue nylon coating is designed to reduce friction in the slip joint. Care must be taken not to damage the coating while removing or installing the yoke. Some slip joints have a threaded-on seal cap, or gland nut, that must be removed before the joint can be separated. Still others have a pressed-on seal cover that needs to be popped off to separate the joint. Spicer Life series driveshaft slip yokes are permanently lubed and feature a flexible boot that covers the slip joint and typically do not require periodic service.

Coupling Shaft

A **coupling shaft** is usually a short driveshaft without a slip joint that is used in a multiple shaft driveline. A coupling shaft

FIGURE 51-10 A coupling shaft is a short shaft supported by a hanger bearing.

FIGURE 51-11 A hanger bearing is a rubber-encased bearing bolted to the vehicle frame that supports the driveshaft.

may also be known as a **jack shaft**. A coupling shaft is shown in **FIGURE 51-10**.

When a coupling shaft is used, the driveline must also have a hanger (center) bearing to support the non-drive end of the coupling shaft. A **center bearing**, also called a **hanger bearing**, is shown in **FIGURE 51-11**. The center bearing is used to support a multiple piece driveshaft. The center bearing consists of a bearing pressed on to a machined surface after the splined area of a driveshaft's slip yoke spline. The bearing is supported in a molded rubber cushion bracket that is, in turn, bolted to the vehicle framework. The rubber cushion used can be slotted rubber or solid depending on the severity of the expected duty cycle of the driveline. Long shaft systems may have more than one center or hanger bearing. Center bearings are typically permanently lubricated and do not require periodic maintenance.

Universal Joints

The universal (Cardan) joint is essential to the operation of today's motor vehicles. It consists of a cross with four finely machined round trunnions equally spaced at 90 degrees apart. The trunnions hold the four bearing caps, which are fitted with long needle bearings to distribute the load. **FIGURE 51-12** shows a universal joint with one of the bearing caps removed.

The cross is drilled with passages that connect the center of the four trunnions with a grease fitting that is installed in the cross at the center or on the outside of one or two of the bearing caps. The purpose of the passage is to supply lubricating grease to all the trunnions and bearing caps.

The bearing caps fitted over the trunnions contain thrust washers or hardened thrust surfaces to resist axial movement of the cross. A seal keeps grease in and dirt out. The seals are specially designed to allow grease to purge from the seals when the joint is lubricated, but they do not allow water or dirt to enter.

Two of the bearings are fitted into a yoke that is welded to a driveshaft component. The other two bearings are fitted to a second yoke either attached to another shaft or an end yoke fitted to a transmission or drive axle. The joint allows the two connected yokes to rotate at different angles to each other. Note that some U-joints are permanently lubricated and do not have grease fittings.

FIGURE 51-12 Lubrication is essential to U-joint longevity. Grease fittings, or "zerks," are provided, along with a cross-drilled joint to ensure that the lubricant reaches all four trunnions and bearing caps.

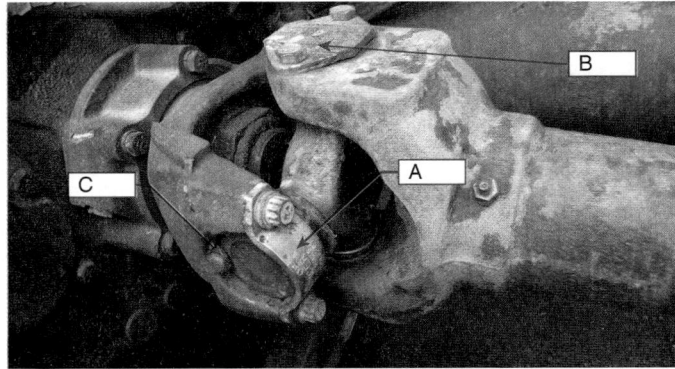

FIGURE 51-13 A U-joint fastening system using bolt-on straps **(A)** in the half-round end yoke and caps bolted directly to the tube yoke **(B)**. The cast lugs in the yoke **(C)** prevent the caps from moving outward.

Fastening Systems

The universal joint can be attached to the driveshaft components in several ways. The caps can be a press fit into the shaft yoke and be retained with snap rings or clips. Alternatively, the caps can be held in place with straps and bolts or U-bolts and nuts. Finally, the bearing caps themselves may have a machined flange that, in turn, bolts directly to the yoke. **FIGURE 51-13** shows two popular types of attaching the joint to the driveshaft components.

FIGURE 51-14 The spring-tab bearing cap retainers on this Spicer Life series driveshaft and the attaching bolts must be replaced any time they are removed.

FIGURE 51-15 These cold-formed semi-circular straps on the Spicer Life series driveshafts may be reused, but the attaching bolts must be replaced.

Bolt-on, semi-circular straps hold the joint to the half-round end yoke. Note the small cast lugs in the yoke used to prevent axial movement of the joint. In addition, the bearing caps on the tube yoke have flanges that are bolted to the yoke directly.

Manufacturers recommend that most fastening devices not be reused when servicing universal joints. Spicer states that reusing the fastening hardware may cause failure of the driveline and lead to catastrophic damage to the vehicle and even personal injury or death. Spicer Life series driveshafts use bolt-on spring-tab retainers for their bearing caps like the ones shown in **FIGURE 51-14**. These spring tabs must be replaced, along with their bolts, every time they are removed. The Life series driveshaft uses cold-formed semi-circular retaining straps, such as those shown in **FIGURE 51-15**. On quick release half-round end yokes, these straps may be reused, but the bolts that attach them must be replaced.

Operation of Driveshafts

LO 51-2 Describe and explain the operation of driveshafts.

When a driveshaft is considered for a certain application, several things must be considered. For example, it is critical to know how much torque the shaft must be capable of transmitting without failure, how fast the shaft must rotate, what angle it must operate at, and how long the shaft must be.

Shaft Mass and Critical Speed

The driveshaft and driveline must obviously be made strong enough to carry the torque load that is transmitted through them. The crudest calculation of the peak torque that the shaft must carry is the product of the engine's peak torque multiplied by the transmission's lowest gear ratio. If the transmission is an automatic, engine peak torque must be multiplied by the torque converter stall ratio or torque multiplication factor and the transmission's lowest gear ratio. Manufacturers, however, choose the strength of a driveshaft based on one of two or both of the following calculations—maximum driveshaft low gear torque or wheel slip.

Maximum driveshaft low gear torque is calculated by multiplying the following figures:

- Net engine torque (or 95% of gross engine torque)
- Transmission lowest gear ratio
- Transmission efficiency (0.8 for automatic transmission, 0.85 for standard)
- Torque converter stall ratio or peak torque multiplication, if applicable.

Mathematically, that looks like this:

Net engine torque × Transmission lowest gear ratio × Transmission efficiency × Torque converter stall ratio

Manufacturers may also have to figure in the torque multiplying effect of a transfer case and its efficiency factor of about 95%.

The second calculation is based on wheel slip. The amount of torque that can be built up by the vehicle system before the drive wheels slip on regular pavement is known as wheel slip torque. It is calculated as follows:

$$\frac{0.71 \times \text{axle weight capacity rating} \times \text{tire rolling radius}}{11.4 \times \text{drive axle ratio}}$$

The lesser of the two calculations can be used in on-highway applications but, in off-highway uses, the low gear torque result only should be used.

The driveline also has a significant amount of extra strength built in as a safety margin. Recall from the Fundamentals of Driveshaft Systems section that critical speed is an issue in trying to increase the strength of a driveshaft by increasing its weight. As the mass of the shaft increases, the centrifugal force acting on it as it rotates increases. As a result, the shaft's critical speed rpm decreases. **FIGURE 51-16** illustrates the bow related to critical speed.

As the shaft approaches critical speed, it starts to vibrate violently. The intensity of the vibration increases until it reaches critical speed. At critical speed, the shaft usually fails catastrophically. To combat critical speed problems, the mass of the driveshaft can be reduced. Doing so, however, decreases its torque-carrying capability.

A second option is to decrease the shaft length. A longer shaft has more of a tendency to sag, while a shorter shaft reduces this tendency. Using a shorter shaft decreases the overall mass

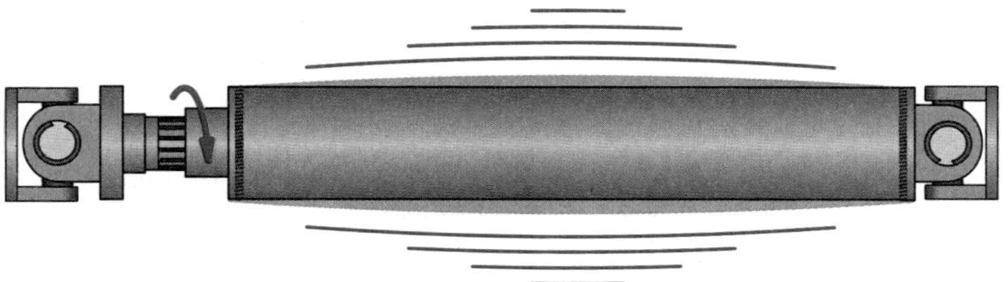

FIGURE 51-16 As the rotating shaft approaches critical speed, its mass causes the shaft to bow off its axis, causing imbalance and vibration.

of the shaft, but requires the use of a multi-piece driveshaft to reach the required length. Multi-piece driveshafts can lead to vibration problems caused by noncanceling universal joint operating angles.

A third way to combat critical speed vibrations is by increasing the diameter of the shaft tube. The larger diameter makes the shaft stronger and less likely to sag, but the larger diameter carries a weight penalty.

In addition to certain failure, another phenomenon, called a harmonic vibration, is associated with operating a driveshaft at or near their critical speed. A **harmonic vibration** is an inherent vibration that occurs at exactly half critical speed rpm and creates a noticeable vibration that causes damage to the universal joints and, indeed, the whole driveline. Although not as severe as critical speed vibration, harmonic vibration must still be avoided for a driveline to provide worry-free service.

So, the careful selection of tubing, length, and driveline components is essential when the truck is being designed or after any modifications to driveline length, shaft speed, or torque capacity are made so that the vehicle does not operate at or near critical speed or half critical speed during normal use. The bottom line is that a driveshaft is constructed as light as possible, but as strong as necessary, to do the job required of it.

Non-Uniform Velocity

All driveshafts that use U-joints have a natural tendency to vibrate because of a phenomenon called non-uniform velocity. Non-uniform velocity happens when any shaft with a universal joint operates at an angle different from the axis of rotation of the drive component. This concept must be understood in order to understand the dynamics of a driveshaft in operation.

The universal joint allows a shaft to deliver torque through an angle. That is, the input or driving component of the shaft is at one angle, and the output component is at a different angle. That relationship causes the output component to turn at a velocity that is not constant. In fact, the driven shaft component accelerates and decelerates twice during each revolution, even though it is physically attached to the input.

It can be difficult to visualize this concept. Consider the input component as turning in a circle. The output component, because of the angle, is then turning, not in a circle, but in an ellipse. To help visualize the difference, imagine looking at a coin straight on. The coin forms a circle. If you were to slightly turn the coin at an angle, the coin seems to be elliptical or oval-shaped.

That is exactly what is happening with the driven component of the shaft. The yoke ears of the drive and driven parts of

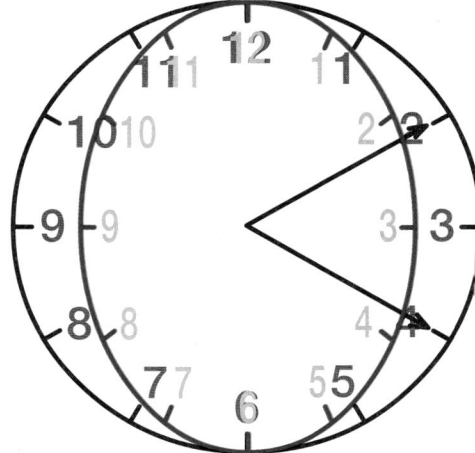

FIGURE 51-17 Notice that the hand of the clock is ahead of the two on the ellipse as it points to the two on the circle. That difference in location indicates that the driven shaft, the ellipse, had to speed up. When the hand points to four on the circle, it is before four on the ellipse, indicating that the driven shaft had to slow down.

the joint are rotating in different planes because of the angle. One of the best ways to explain the non-uniform velocity is to consider the input component of the shaft, which is traveling in a circle, as the face of a clock with the hours marked on it and then take the driven component, which is travelling in an ellipse, and superimpose its motion over the clock face, as illustrated in **FIGURE 51-17**.

The ellipse is inside the circle of the clock face. The two shafts are physically connected, so they revolve around a common center point and meet at the three, six, nine, and twelve o'clock positions. An arrow drawn from the center to the two o'clock position on the outer circle shows that the line intersects the inner ellipse at slightly past two o'clock. That difference indicates that the output member (the ellipse) has accelerated in relation to the input member (the circle).

At the three o'clock position, the timing of the circle and the ellipse coincide. But that changes at the five o'clock position. An arrow pointing to the five o'clock position on the circle (the input member) bisects the ellipse (the output member) at some time before five o'clock. That means that the driven member has now slowed down in relation to the input member.

The process is then repeated as the input component moves toward the nine o'clock and then the twelve o'clock positions. The output component must again speed up and slow down to match it. If we divide the motion into quadrants, as the input component rotates through a complete circle of 360 degrees, the driven component accelerates for the first 90 degrees of rotation (or the first quadrant) and then decelerates for the next 90 degrees of rotation (or the second quadrant), and then accelerates for the third quadrant and decelerates for the fourth quadrant. The rate of acceleration and deceleration is entirely based on the severity of the angle of drive. In other words, the higher the working angle, the greater the speed fluctuations are. **FIGURE 51-18** shows typical yoke speed vibrations.

Consider that a driveshaft has to transmit rotating power to a drive axle. If we were to connect the shaft directly to an output with this non-uniform velocity, the acceleration and deceleration would be transmitted to the drive axle and wheels. That would lead to unacceptable vibrations, as the vehicle would be trying to accelerate and decelerate constantly. In order to connect the shaft to a drive axle, we must first correct the non-uniform velocity by using another universal joint with an equal—or very close to equal—operating angle, which cancels out the changing velocity and delivers a constant rotational speed to the drive axle, as is illustrated in the graph in **FIGURE 51-19**.

There is more to the story, however. This phenomenon of non-uniform velocity can lead to driveshaft vibrations even if we cancel out the speed fluctuations with a second universal joint. The inertial forces caused by the acceleration and deceleration of the driveshaft's mass can, by itself, lead to vibrations as overall shaft speed increases. The intensity of the speed fluctuations is a direct result of the severity of the operating angles and the shaft rotational speed. This means that the safe rotational speed of a shaft decreases as shaft operating angles increase. These inertial forces caused by the shaft accelerating and decelerating are hard to calculate, but they must be taken into consideration when designing a driveline.

Driveshaft Angle Cancellation

LO 51-3 Describe and explain driveshaft angle cancellation.

The non-uniform velocity of a universal joint working through an angle must be canceled out by installing another joint with an equal and opposite working angle at the other end of the shaft. When working with Cardan joint angularity, there are three basic rules to follow.

1. There must be some working angle at the joint—at least one-half to one degree.
2. Operating angles at either end of a driveshaft must be equal to within one degree to obtain acceptable **cancellation** of the non-uniform velocity created by joint working angles.
3. Working angles should be kept as small as possible—three degrees or less according to most OEMs—to minimize vibrations caused by shaft inertial accelerations.

Rule Number One

All Cardan joints use needle roller bearings to carry the torque load exerted on a driveshaft. These needles require lubrication if they are to survive. If a joint works with no angle at all, the needle rollers remain stationary in the caps and eventually squeeze all of the lubricant out of the needle contact points in the caps and the trunnions. Without the lubricant, the needles start to dig into the trunnions. This causes an effect known as **false brinelling,** which is the wearing away of the trunnion in the shape of the needles. False brinelling leads to joint failure. When the joint works at least a slight angle, for example one-half to one degree minimum, the needles roll during operation. The rolling motion distributes the lubricant each time the needles move, so false brinelling does not occur.

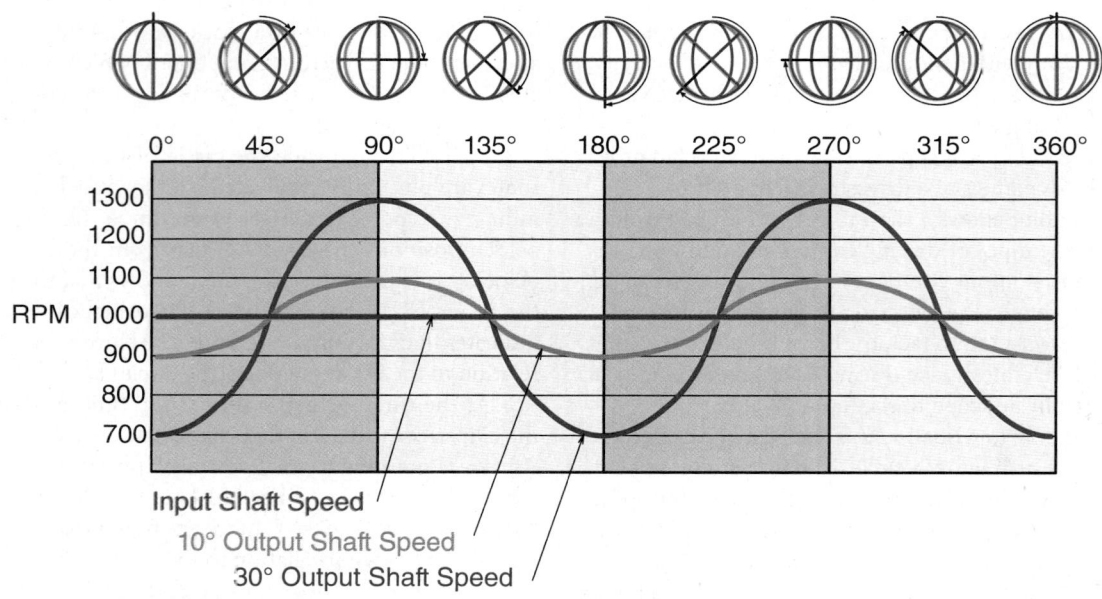

Input Shaft Speed

10° Output Shaft Speed

30° Output Shaft Speed

FIGURE 51-18 The frequency of the accelerations and decelerations are constant, each occurring twice per revolution. The amplitude or intensity of the speed fluctuations is based on the severity of the drive angle.

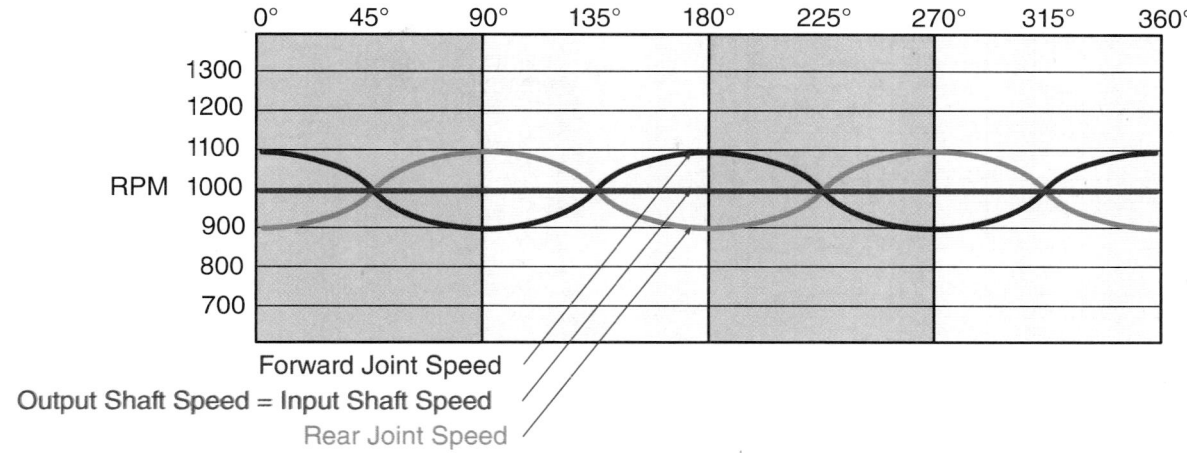

FIGURE 51-19 Installing a second universal joint with an equal and opposite angle at the other end of the driven shaft serves to cancel out the non-uniform velocity.

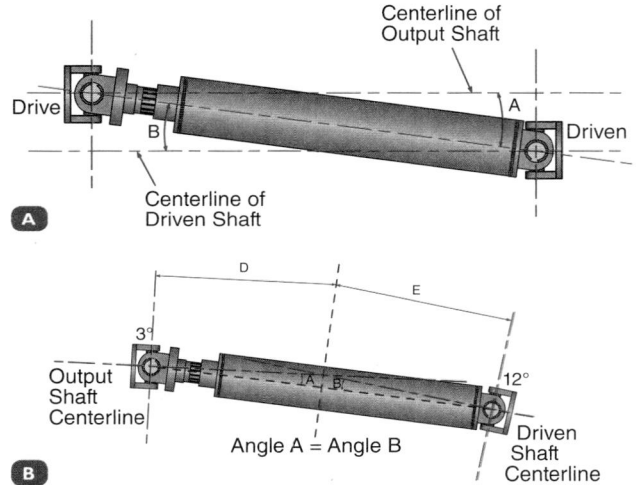

FIGURE 51-20 **A.** The parallel or waterfall joint arrangement is the preferred arrangement. **B.** The intersecting angle or (broken back) arrangement can be used when length changes are not excessive.

Rule Number Two

The operating angles at each end of a driveshaft must be kept equal to within one degree if the non-uniform velocity caused by the joint angle is to be canceled out. There are two ways of achieving this cancellation. The first is called the **waterfall arrangement** or **parallel joint arrangement**. The other is the **broken back arrangement** or **intersecting angle arrangement**.

In the parallel arrangement, shown in **FIGURE 51-20A**, the side view centerline of the transmission output and the drive axle input are parallel. The U-joint angles at either end are equal to within one degree and opposite to each other. This is the preferred method of cancellation, as the two joints remain equal to each other during suspension oscillation and shaft length changes.

The broken back or intersecting angle method, shown in **FIGURE 51-20B**, is used when the proximity of the two components would lead to extreme operating angles if a waterfall or

parallel arrangement were used. In the broken back method of cancellation, the U-joint operating angles must still be equal at each end of the shaft. The output and input components are no longer parallel, however. For this method to provide good non-uniform velocity cancellation, the angles formed by the U-joints must intersect at a line perpendicular to the exact center of the shaft length. Because of this last requirement, the broken back or intersecting angles cancellation method cannot be used where operating length changes can be excessive, as this would cause the angles to no longer intersect at the center of the shaft and lead to vibration. Broken back installations are usually only found between the two axles of a tandem drive because driveshaft length changes are minimal in this location.

Rule Number Three

The operating angles of universal joints should be kept as small as possible—preferably three degrees or less. Because of the phenomenon of non-uniform velocity of a shaft driven at an angle, all driveshafts have an inherent torsional excitation caused by the inertial forces of the shaft as it accelerates and decelerates twice per revolution.

The magnitude of this torsional excitation is directly proportional to the acuteness of the angle of operation, the weight of the shaft, and the speed of the shaft. **FIGURE 51-21** shows how joint operating angle affects the expected life of the joint. Keeping angles small allows for maximum working life.

To minimize vibration, one of three things must occur. The angle must be lessened, the shaft must turn at a lower speed, or the shaft must become lighter. The shaft speed must be consistent with the vehicle for which it is transmitting torque. Therefore, limiting shaft speed is not one of the favored options. The weight of the shaft material can be altered, but that has a direct impact on the shaft's torque-carrying capabilities. The best solution to deal with inertial and torsional excitation is to keep the operating angle small.

Several manufacturers produce charts, such as the one shown in **TABLE 51-4**, specifying maximum rotational speed for a given joint operating angle. The weight of shaft must also be

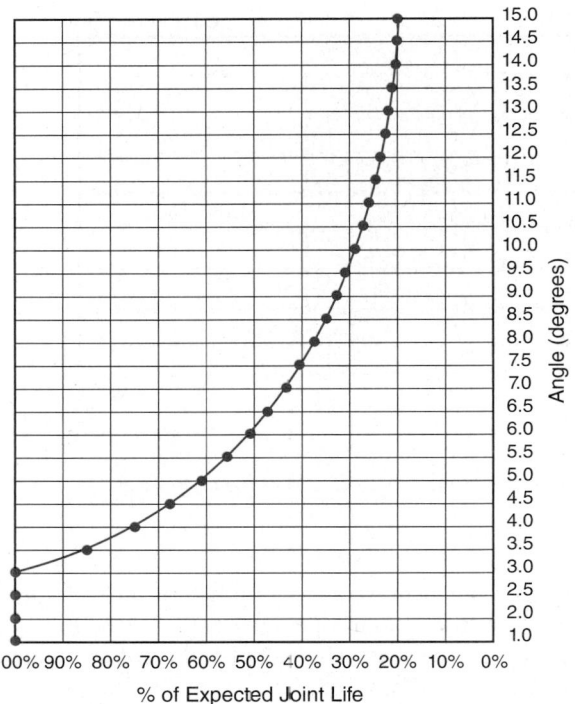

FIGURE 51-21 Relationship of joint life to operating angle.

TABLE 51-4 U-joint Operating Angles and Shaft Speeds

Driveshaft rpm	Maximum Normal Operating Angles
5000	3° 15'
4500	3° 40'
4000	4° 15'
3500	5° 0'
3000	5° 50'
2500	7° 0'
2000	8° 40'
1500	11° 30'

considered, so the maximum operating angle changes, based on the "series" or load-carrying capability of the shaft in question along with its rotational speed. Universal joint longevity is also greatly affected by large joint working angles.

A universal joint operating at an angle of three degrees can be expected to last 90% or more of its normal wear life. As angles increase, this wear life reduces drastically. A joint that has a normal wear life of 100,000 miles (160,000 km) lasts for only 60,000 miles (96,000 km) when operated at an angle of five degrees, and for only 30,000 miles (48,000 km) at a 10-degree working angle. Smaller working angles reduce the chance of vibration and allow the longest wear life for universal joints.

Phasing

The working angles of a driveshaft system must be very carefully selected in order to prevent unacceptable vibration of the rotating shaft. However, there is another element to the story. In order for cancellation to occur and for vibrations to be eliminated, the canceling joint angle must be in the same phase in terms of rotation.

As we discussed in the Non-Uniform Velocity section, if we divide a circle into quadrants of 90 degrees each, the driven shaft accelerates for the first 90 degrees, decelerates for the second 90 degrees, etc. **Phasing** of the universal joint operating angles means that the output yoke of the joint doing the cancellation of the non-uniform velocity has to be doing exactly the opposite of the driven yoke of the input universal joint—meaning that it must decelerate for the first 90 degrees of rotation and accelerate for the second 90 degrees in order to deliver a uniform velocity to the rear axle. To accomplish this, the inboard yoke ears of the driven shaft must line up. This places their respective joints in phase with each other, as in **FIGURE 51-22**. An out-of-phase driveshaft causes the accelerations and decelerations of the joints on either end of the shafts to be out of sync with each other. The result can be seen in **FIGURE 51-23**. Failure to correctly phase the universal joints worsens the vibration, rather than cancels it.

The most common cause of out-of-phase problems is a failure by the technician to mark the slip yoke of a split driveshaft before disassembly. Always mark the slip yoke position before removal so that it can be reinstalled correctly.

Cross-Phasing and Incremental-Phasing Adjustments

Ninety-nine percent of all driveshaft systems are installed with the driveshafts in phase. In other words, the inboard yokes of

Align the arrows.

Yokes in Line

FIGURE 51-22 An in-phase driveshaft has its inboard yoke ears in line.

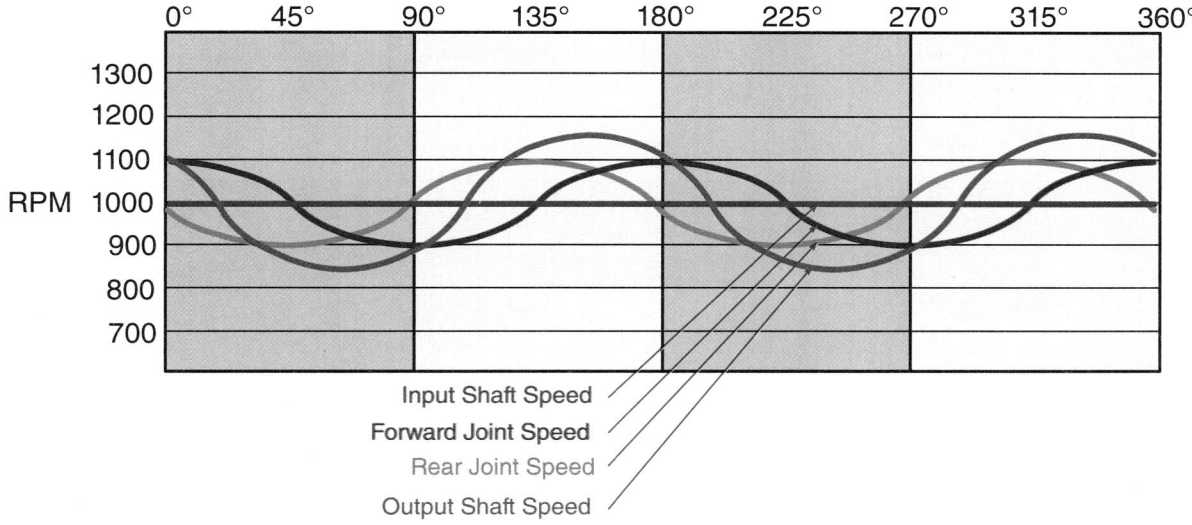

FIGURE 51-23 Failure to phase the driveshaft means the cancellation is occurring at the wrong time, in terms of shaft rotation, and leads to extreme vibration.

any shaft assembly are in line with each other. However, certain systems are set up so that the short coupling shaft of a multi-piece driveshaft may be set at a 90-degree phase angle. This **cross-phasing** is usually done to correct an inherent vibration usually caused by the driveline system of the vehicle. Cross-phased coupling shaft angles are kept very small to prevent driveline vibration.

Sometimes one end of the driveshaft is offset from the centerline of the transmission or drive axle—meaning that the driveshaft is angled to the left or right of the transmission or drive axle centerline. This type of installation is known as a broken-back configuration. It is not to be confused with the broken back method of angle cancellation mentioned in the Driveshaft Angle Cancellation: Rule Number Two section.

A broken-back installation can result in a vibration that can sometimes be dealt with by cross-phasing. These crossed-phase installations are not very common, but a technician should be aware of their existence. Certain late-model vehicles (some Volvo models, for example) are purposely built with a cross-phased driveshaft that is out of phase by a few degrees more than 90. On first observance, shaft arrangements that are not exactly in phase or cross-phased at 90 degrees can seem strange to a technician. These configurations are computer-designed to combat resident system vibrations in the vehicle, however, and should not be altered. For the technician, the important point is to always mark the slip yoke elements before removing the shaft so that it can be re-installed with the correct phase angle.

Checking and Adjusting Driveline Angularity

LO 51-4 Check and adjust driveline angularity.

Driveline angularity simply refers to the angles at the universal joints. For the most part, driveline angles should not need to be reset in the field. If any modification is performed on the vehicle, such as shortening or lengthening the frame or adjusting vehicle ride height, it may be necessary to check and adjust angles to avoid vibrations. This may also be necessary when diagnosing driveline vibration after all other possibilities have been eliminated.

Unless the vehicle or the driveline has been obviously tampered with, problems other than driveline angles are more likely to be the cause of driveline vibrations. One type of tampering that can lead to driveline angle problems is drivers that "soften" the ride by lowering air bag suspension pressure and ride height. Doing so can lead to excessive operating angles, which can cause vibration.

Measuring and Calculating Driveline Angles

Most driveline manufacturers offer computer-based programs to analyze driveline angles. Software, such as the Eaton Driveline Angle Analyzer (DAA), can determine if vibration will occur. These programs take into account driveline weight and length to determine torsional inertials and are much more accurate at predicting vibrations than simple manual calculations.

A manual calculation procedure is an acceptable preliminary check for angle issues that may cause vibration. If, after following the manual procedure, a vibration still exists, it may be due to torsional inertials that should be calculated using the computer-based programs. Driveline angles are best measured with an electronic angle gauge or inclinometer, such as the Spicer Anglemaster, to ensure that readings are accurate. Readings should be accurate to within one-quarter of a degree.

The process is relatively simple when the components of the driveline have angles only in the side view. Some vehicles, however, have angles that occur in more than the side plane. In these drivelines, the shaft may move to the right or left side when viewed from above as it goes from the front to back. Side-to-side angles are called the **plan angle**, or the top-view angle.

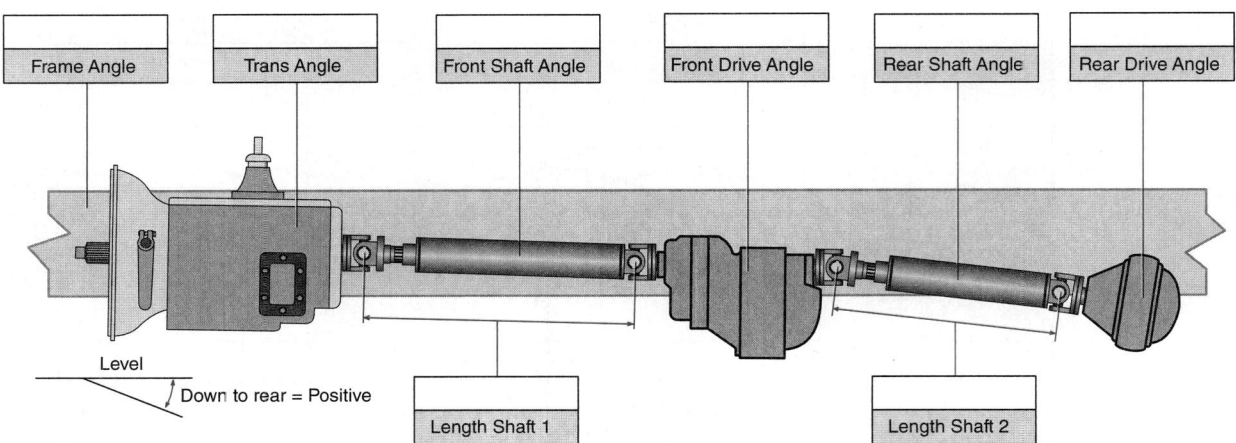

FIGURE 51-24 A worksheet is a helpful aid when recording angles, but it is not absolutely necessary.

Components that have slopes in two planes (side view and top view) create a compound angle and they must be calculated differently.

To calculate side view only angles, the angle of slope of each component in the driveline is measured and the operating angle between any two components is calculated. When a vehicle is observed from the side, any slope that goes lower as it moves toward the rear of the vehicle is a down slope and is expressed as a positive angle. If the component slope goes higher as it moves to the back of the vehicle, it is an upward slope and recorded as a negative angle.

To begin the process, on vehicles sprung with leaf springs or rubber spring systems, make sure that the vehicle is as close to its normal operating condition as possible in terms of loading. Calculating the angles to try and solve a vibration problem will not be successful if the vehicle normally operates with much heavier loads than when tested. On systems with air springs, ensure ride height is within specification before beginning the measurements.

Most manufacturers have worksheets, like the one shown in **FIGURE 51-24**, that can be used to record the angles that correspond to the driveline being worked on. If no worksheet is available, simply write down all the components and record their slopes. We will use a two-piece, single-axle driveline for our example for a total of three operating angles.

The first measurement is the frame slope. This angle, shown in **FIGURE 51-25**, can be eliminated when doing manual calculations but is called for when using computerized drive angle analyzer programs.

The next measurement is the transmission slope. This measurement can usually be taken from any flat surface of the transmission that is parallel to its centerline, as illustrated in **FIGURE 51-26**. Alternatively, the transmission angle can be measured from its end yoke bearing caps using adapters supplied with the Spicer Anglemaster tool. Note that if you are measuring from the end yoke, the yoke ears must be positioned vertically.

Next, measure the slope of the first driveshaft, shown in **FIGURE 51-27**, which is usually a coupling shaft. Shaft slope measurements can be taken on any clean and smooth section

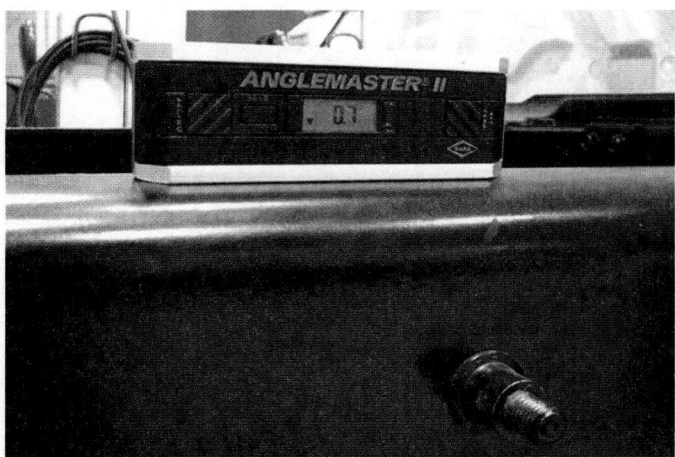

FIGURE 51-25 The frame slope should be measured so that driveline angles can be corrected.

of the driveshaft tube. Then, measure the slope of the next shaft and, finally, measure the slope of the drive axle.

The drive axle slope is usually measured at the flat section near the spring mounts, as shown in **FIGURE 51-28**, but it can be measured from the drive axle end yoke ears using the adapter. Again, the yoke ears should be vertical. If all slopes are down and all readings are positive, to calculate the working angle of each joint, simply subtract the smaller number from the larger number at each joint and that is the U-joint working angle.

Driveline Angle Examples

Consider the following example. The transmission's slope is four degrees down, the coupling shaft is five degrees down, the second driveshaft is six degrees down, and the drive axle is seven degrees down. Given those parameters, the following are true:

- The calculation for the first U-joint angle is: 5 degrees – 4 degrees = 1 degree
- The calculation for the second U-joint is: 6 degrees – 5 degrees = 1 degree
- The third U-joint angle is: 7 degrees – 6 degrees = 1 degree

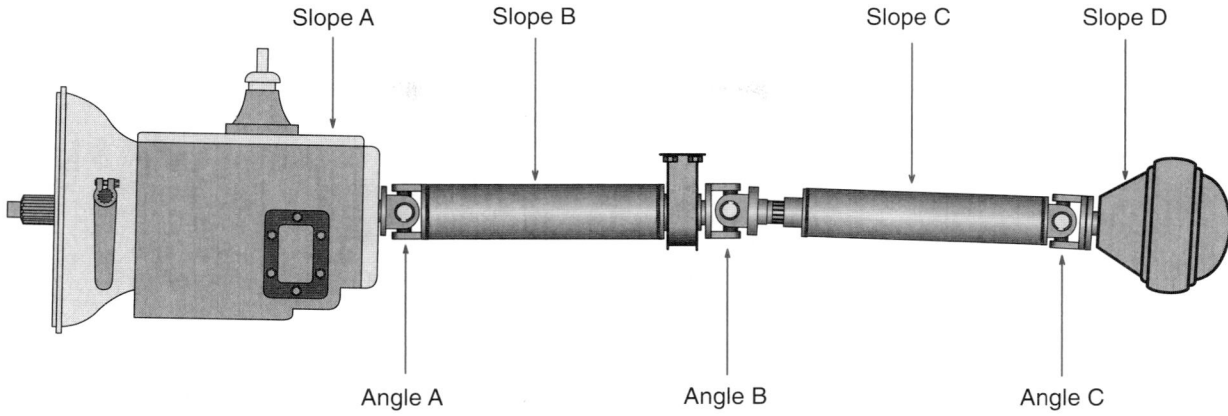

FIGURE 51-26 Measure the transmission slope from any flat surface parallel to its centerline.

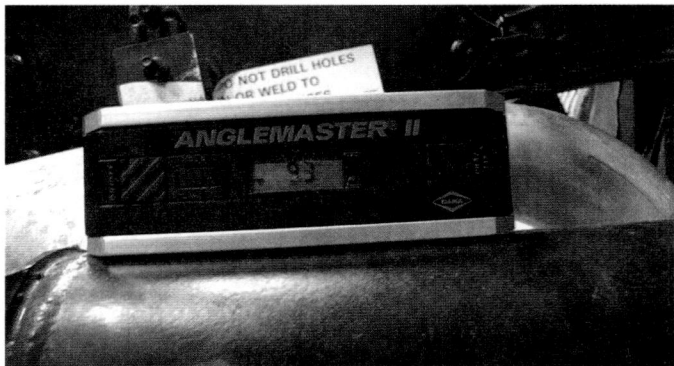

FIGURE 51-27 Measure the slope of the first driveshaft.

FIGURE 51-28 The drive axle slope is measured on a flat surface close to the wheel end.

These angles satisfy the three rules for universal joint angles:

- Rule One states that there must be at least one-half to one degree of operating angle so that the needle bearings rotate.
- Rule Two states that the angles at opposite ends of a shaft must be equal to within one degree.
- Rule Three states that working angles be kept to less than three degrees.

Given the angles and their conformance to the rules, the driveline in this example should not cause a vibration because of driveline angles.

Now, let's consider another example. This time, we use a driveline with a two-piece main driveshaft and tandem drive axles with a one-piece rear driveshaft. That makes a total of five operating angles, as illustrated in **FIGURE 51-29**.

Here are the parameters for this driveshaft:

- The transmission measures one degree down
- The coupling shaft measures one degree up or minus one degree
- The second driveshaft measures two degrees down
- The power-divider measures 0.5 degrees down
- The rear driveshaft measures three degrees down
- The rear-rear drive axle measures three degrees down

Given those conditions, the operating angles are as follows:

- For the first U-joint angle, the transmission and the first shaft slopes are in different directions, so the degrees have

to be added rather than subtracted—one degree down for the transmission and one degree up for the first shaft. The operating angle is two degrees.

- The calculation for the second joint angle is one degree up for the coupling shaft and two degrees down for the second shaft, so the operating angle is three degrees.
- The third operating angle is two degrees down for the second shaft and 0.5 degrees down for the power-divider, so the operating angle is 2.5 degrees.
- The fourth operating angle is 0.5 degrees down for the power-divider and three degrees down for the rear driveshaft, so the operating angle is 2.5 degrees.
- The fifth operating angle is three degrees down for the rear driveshaft and three degrees down for the rear-rear drive axle, so the operating angle is zero degrees.

This second example meets the three rules of driveline angles for all the operating angles except for the fifth one. The fifth operating angle fails Rule Two because it is not within one degree of the fourth operating angle. Therefore, it does not cancel out the non-uniform velocity in the rear driveshaft and will cause vibration. The fifth operating angle also fails Rule One in that the operating angle must be at least one-half to one degree. This angle is zero degrees, so, by itself, it will cause the bearing to wear out prematurely because the needle bearings will not rotate.

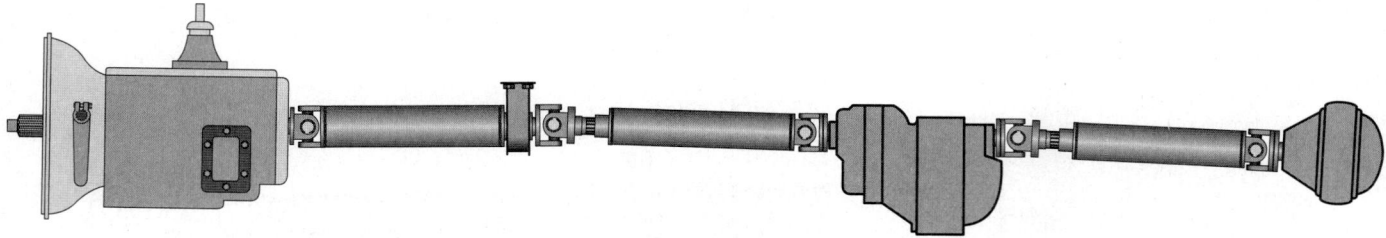

FIGURE 51-29 A five-angle driveshaft—typical of a heavy-duty on-highway truck.

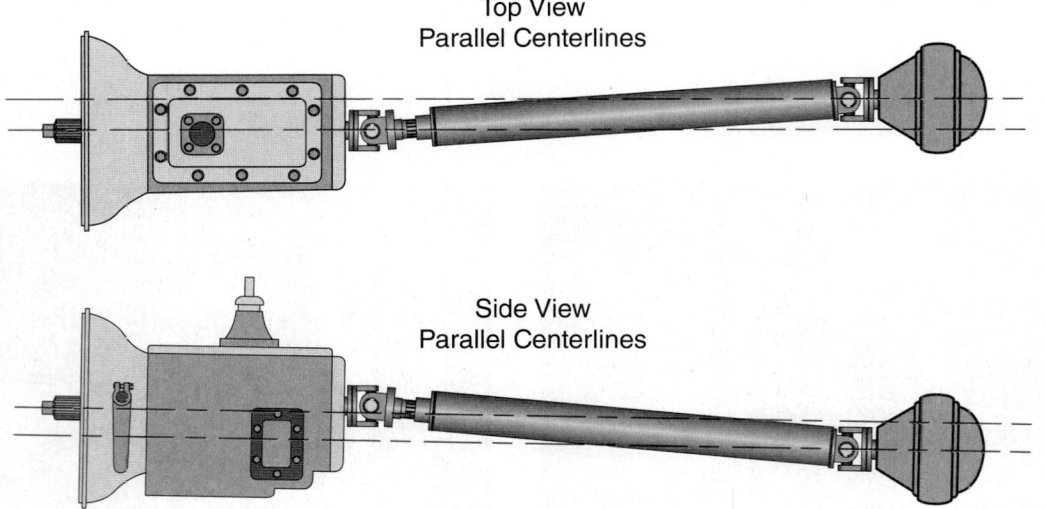

Top View
Parallel Centerlines

Side View
Parallel Centerlines

FIGURE 51-30 Compound angles are angles that exist in two planes, both from the side view and from the top view. These must be calculated differently.

This problem can be corrected by installing shims under the rear-rear axle spring mounts to rotate the axle until it is only 0.5 degrees down. This makes the fifth operating angle 2.5 degrees and satisfies all three rules.

Compound Driveline Angles

Compound driveline angles involve angles in two planes—the side view and the plan or top view, as illustrated in **FIGURE 51-30**. When compound angles are encountered, we must still take the same measurements as in our previous examples. However, with compound angles, we must also calculate the true operating angle by combining the measured side view angle with the plan view angle.

The only way to obtain the plan or top view angle is through careful calculation, or by using a plan view angle chart, such as the one shown in **FIGURE 51-31**. This chart can be found in most manufacturers' driveline manuals. The chart's x-axis is the driveshaft length in inches, and the y-axis is the number of inches the shaft is offset over its length. The point of intersection is marked on the chart and then a line is drawn from the corner, where the x- and y-axes meet, to a circular line on the right-hand side of the chart that is graduated in degrees. This is the plan or top view angle.

Once you have determined the plan view angle, use the following formula to obtain the true U-joint operating angle.

$$C = \sqrt{S^2 + T^2}$$

where

C = true operating compound angle
S = side view angle
T = top view angle

For example, if the side view or measured angle is 2.5 degrees and the top view or calculated angle is 1.5 degrees, then the compound angle is as follows:

$$C = \sqrt{2.5^2 + 1.5^2}$$
$$= \sqrt{8.5}$$
$$= 2.92$$

When calculating the true U-joint operating angles for both ends of the shaft, the resultant angles must meet the same three rules for all driveline angles to avoid vibration and premature wear out:

1. They must be at least one-half to one degree.
2. They must be equal to within one degree.
3. They should be less than three degrees.

Compound angles are not very common in vehicle drivelines, but they can be quite common in Power Take Off (PTO) drivelines.

Calculating driveline angles to solve vibration problems is a limited answer to a sometimes very complex issue. These simple measurements do not take into account inertial excitations and

For Driveshafts That Have a Top View Working Angle

FIGURE 51-31 Plan view angle calculation chart.

FIGURE 51-32 Double Cardan joints give constant velocity to the driven shaft by using the same cancellation principles that we use on shafts with a U-joint at each end.

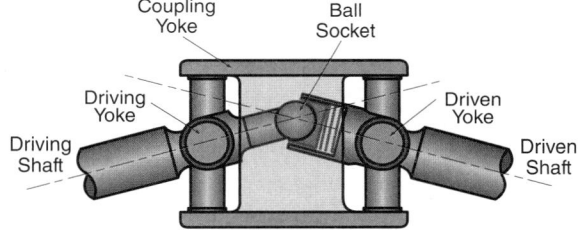

FIGURE 51-33 Because the two shafts are connected by a ball and socket, the two U-joint angles are always equal.

critical speed issues. Drive line angle analyzer computer programs take shaft diameter, shaft length, and weight into consideration—meaning these programs consider these other sources of vibration. When possible, the technician should use these programs to eliminate the need for complex calculations and ensure much greater accuracy in determining the source of a vibration.

Constant Velocity Joints

Constant velocity joints are not commonly found on heavy-duty truck systems and so are only briefly mentioned here. The earliest style of constant velocity joint in automotive use was the double Cardan style. This arrangement had two Cardan joints in the same housing, as can be seen in **FIGURE 51-32**.

In between the two U-joints and inside the housing is a ball-and-socket connector. One half of the shaft is connected to the ball, and the other shaft is connected to the socket. This means that no matter what angle the joint operates at, the angle of each of the U-joints are always equal, as illustrated in **FIGURE 51-33**.

Because of this equalization, the non-uniform velocity is immediately canceled out before it reaches the driven shaft. This joint creates constant velocity by the same cancellation method as regular U-joints except that the two joints are connected together. True constant velocity joints are joints that can operate at angles but do not create the speeding up and slowing down as discussed with Cardan joints. These include the **Rzeppa joint**, shown in **FIGURE 51-34**, which is very

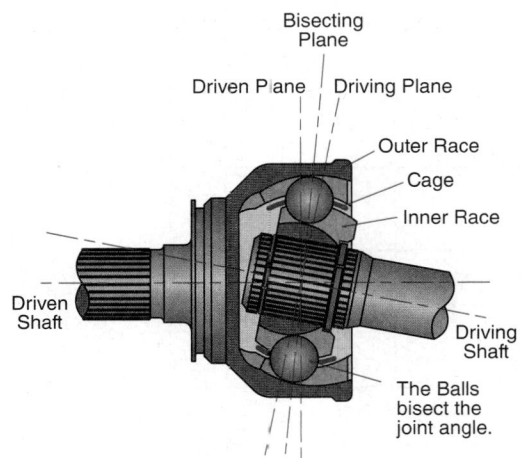

FIGURE 51-34 Rzeppa joints create true constant velocity, as the operating angle of the joint always bisects the drive balls.

FIGURE 51-35 Check shaft for missing balance weights.

commonly found as the outside joint in a front-wheel drive, light-duty vehicle.

Designed in 1926, Rzeppa joints are named for their inventor Alfred Rzeppa, an engineer for Ford Motor Company. These joints have a series of six balls inside. The drive angle always bisects the balls, leading to perfect cancellation of the angles and constant velocity of the driven shaft. These types of joints are capable of operating at much greater angles and higher speeds than traditional Cardan U-joints. These true constant velocity joints have several variations, including a plunge style that allows length changes to occur.

Troubleshooting Driveshaft Vibrations and Failures

LO 51-5 Troubleshoot driveshaft vibrations and failures.

Even though drivelines can be a common source of vibration complaints, it is necessary to eliminate all other possibilities before condemning the driveshaft. Vibrations from other systems, such as the engine, clutch, or wheel ends, can mimic driveshaft problems. The experienced technician is usually capable of discerning driveline vibrations from wheel end vibrations by recognizing the frequency of the vibration. Driveline vibrations occur at driveshaft speed or faster, while wheel end vibrations are at least three times slower. Understanding the vibrations, measuring driveshaft runout, and analyzing driveshaft failure are all critical aspects to troubleshooting this system.

Driveline Vibration Diagnostics

A simple road test can be used to eliminate the engine, clutch, and/or transmission as a source of vibration. Accelerate the vehicle to a speed slightly faster than the one at which the vibration is the worst. Then, depress the clutch and let the vehicle slow down through the speed where the vibration was the worst. By depressing the clutch, the engine and the clutch slow down to idle and the transmission input is removed. No change in the vibration indicates that the engine, clutch, and transmission are not the cause, and the driveshaft could be the cause. If the

driveline is, indeed, the source of the vibration, it could be one of several different kinds of vibrations. Possible driveline system vibrations include transverse vibrations, torsional vibrations, inertial excitation, and secondary couple vibrations.

Transverse vibrations are caused by an out-of-balance driveshaft or system and occur once per shaft revolution. Always check shafts for missing balance weights. These shafts are very heavy and small imbalances can cause large vibrations. Balance weights are shown in **FIGURE 51-35**.

There are two causes of **torsional vibrations** in the driveline. One source originates from the power impulses from the engine caused by the forces on the crankshaft during each power stroke. With today's engines that produce high torque at low speed, these impulses cause a twisting force to be placed on the crankshaft up to 20 times a second at rated speed. If these impulses are not properly muted by the clutch or powertrain system, they can be transmitted throughout the driveline.

The other cause of driveline torsional vibrations is from the U-joint angles or phasing. Remember that a U-joint working at an angle causes the driven yoke to accelerate and decelerate twice per revolution. If proper cancellation is not achieved by correct angles and phasing, the driveshaft is subjected to twisting forces. Just as a coat hanger that is bent back and forth repeatedly snaps in two, enough torsional forces in the driveshaft lead to driveshaft failure. Vibrations from angularity or phasing problems occur at twice driveshaft speed.

Inertial excitation vibrations stem from the operating angles of the U-joint at the drive end of the driveshaft and are caused by the sheer weight of the driveshaft being accelerated and decelerated twice per revolution. These vibrations are hard to pinpoint. There are only two possible solutions for inertial excitation. The first is to decrease the operating angle and thereby reduce the magnitude of the acceleration and decelerations. The second is to reduce the driveshaft weight, which is seldom practical. Even though the driveline angles may be correctly canceling each other out, the larger the angle at the drive end, the more severe the inertial excitation is.

Secondary couple vibrations are vibrations that are passed through or coupled through the hanger bearing in a heavy-duty driveshaft. These vibrations are then passed along the entire length of the driveline. Secondary couple vibrations occur at twice driveshaft speed and can affect the whole driveline. They are most often observed by failure of the hanger bearing rubber support. Secondary couple vibrations can be lessened by making sure the U-joint angle at the front of the coupling shaft is as small as possible.

Critical speed vibrations occur if the driveshaft is operated faster than its critical speed. Recall that critical speed is the speed at which the centrifugal force acting on the rotating shaft becomes stronger than the shaft material and it starts to bow off its centerline. Critical speed vibrations occur at driveshaft speed and always cause shaft failure eventually.

Diagnosing Vibrations

Most original equipment manufacturers produce vibration diagnostic flow charts that can be used to systematically rule out all other possibilities. To begin diagnosing vibrations, gather as much information as possible from the operator about the vibration. Ask when the vibration started, if it is present at all times with the vehicle running, only when moving, or only when the vehicle or its trailer is loaded, at what speed vibration occurs, and so on. This information can help to rule out other causes and pinpoint the problem.

Next, try to recreate the vibration with the driver in the vehicle, if possible. Take note of the frequency, wheel speed, engine speed, or driveshaft speed. After gathering all the information necessary to narrow the problem down, follow a flow chart like the one in **FIGURE 51-36**.

If the driveshaft is isolated as the cause of the vibration, the shafts must be carefully inspected for missing balance weights or any build-up of foreign material, which could be the cause of vibration caused by imbalance. Dents in the driveshaft tubing displace shaft mass towards the center rather than the outside where it was when the shaft was initially balanced. Dents are a common cause of vibration and also weaken the tube's section modulus (strength). Dented tubing should be replaced.

Measuring Driveshaft Runout

Shaft runout is another possible cause of vibration. Driveshaft runout can be caused by a bent driveshaft, damaged yokes, or worn U-joints. A dial indicator is normally used to measure driveshaft runout.

Before measuring runout, first sand and clean around the front, center, and rear of the driveshaft to remove any uneven build-up of paint or rust. This gives the dial indicator a smooth surface for accurate measurements. Mount the dial indicator perpendicular to the shaft. The indicator base must be placed on a rigid surface floor pan, frame, or special post stand. The driveshaft must NOT be at a sharp angle during runout measurement. Make sure that the vehicle axles are in their normally weighted positions.

With the transmission in neutral, turn the driveshaft. Measure runout at the front, center, and rear of the shaft, as shown in **FIGURE 51-37**. Compare your measurements to specs. Generally, driveshaft runout should not exceed 0.010" to 0.015" (0.25 to 0.38 mm), but always check the manufacturer's specification. If driveshaft runout is beyond specs, try removing and rotating the shaft 180 degrees in the rear yoke; sometimes this can bring the runout back into spec. Make sure the universal joints

are in good condition and that the yokes are not damaged. If, after eliminating all other causes of vibration, and runout is okay, the shaft could be out of balance; again try rotating the shaft 180 degrees in the rear yoke to see if it significantly lessens the vibration. If there is still a vibration present, the driveshaft should be sent out for balancing. Alternatively, balance weights can be added to the shaft and held in place by a gear clamp in a trial-and-error fashion, but this is a very time-consuming method and usually not worth the down time.

Driveline angles can be measured, as was discussed in the Measuring and Calculating Driveline Angles section. Measuring the angles in that way does not take inertial excitations into consideration, however. The best way to eliminate a driveline vibration is to use one of the computerized drive line angle analyzer programs offered by manufacturers, such as the Eaton DAA (Drive Line Angle Analyzer). These programs take driveshaft weight, length, and angles into consideration and are much better at eliminating driveshaft inertial excitations, as well as angle vibration problems.

Analyzing Driveshaft Failure

Driveshafts can fail for a number of reasons, including brinelling, spalling, galling, fractured or broken U-joints, accelerated wear, twisted tubing, or failure of the hanger bearings.

Brinelling

Brinelling, as mentioned in the Driveshaft Angle Cancellation: Rule Number One section and shown in **FIGURE 51-38**, occurs when the rollers in the universal joint are hammered into the trunnions, leaving indentations. This can happen for several reasons. If the U-joint operates at a zero angle, the rollers do not rotate and the lubrication is squeezed out between the rollers and trunnions. This leads to brinnelling-like wear on the trunnions, called false brinelling. The operating angle must be adjusted to have a least one-half to one degree or this failure will occur over and over again. Over tightening of retaining straps or distorted or damaged end yokes can cause the same problem by restricting the roller's rotation.

Excess torque can also lead to brinelling, as the trunnion metal is repeatedly overloaded. The perpetual hammering eventually leads to brinelling. Brinelling can also occur if the slip yoke is seized. In that case, brinelling appears on the front and rear of the trunnion, rather than on the torque faces (the sides of the trunnion). As the shaft tries to lengthen or shorten, the seized slip yoke causes the front and back of the trunnions to be hammered. Brinelling can also result after a long service life as the normal wearing of the universal joint.

Spalling or Galling

Spalling and galling are the transfer of metal from one surface to the other caused by excessive friction between them. **FIGURE 51-39** shows an example of extreme spalling.

This is normally caused by either a lack of or contamination of the joint lubricant. Water and dirt are the most likely contaminants. Lack of lubricant indicates poor maintenance practices. Either reason can lead to burned trunnions. End galling of the trunnions is usually caused by excessive joint operating angles.

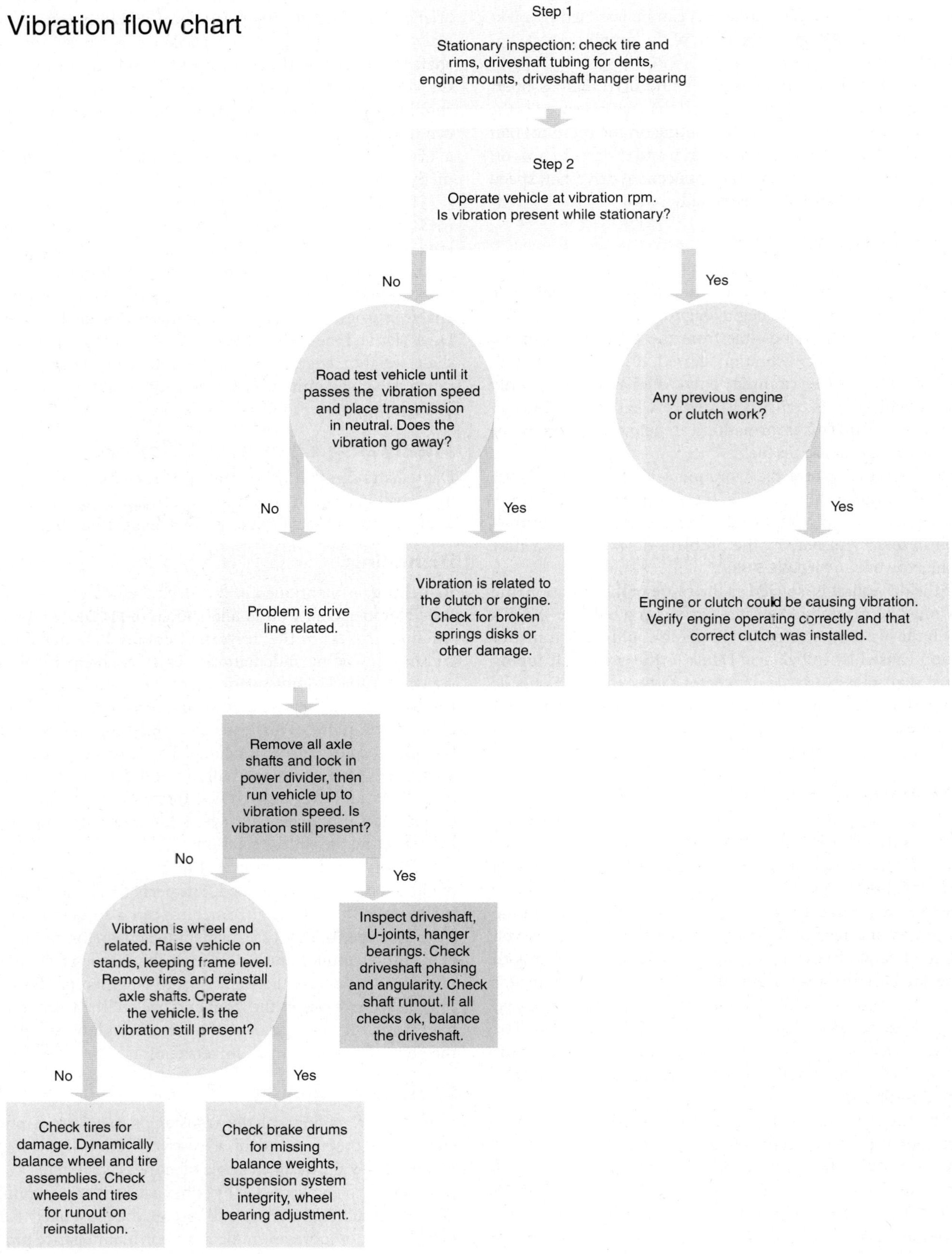

Vibration flow chart

Step 1

Stationary inspection: check tire and rims, driveshaft tubing for dents, engine mounts, driveshaft hanger bearing

Step 2

Operate vehicle at vibration rpm. Is vibration present while stationary?

No

Road test vehicle until it passes the vibration speed and place transmission in neutral. Does the vibration go away?

No

Yes

Yes

Any previous engine or clutch work?

Yes

Vibration is related to the clutch or engine. Check for broken springs disks or other damage.

Engine or clutch could be causing vibration. Verify engine operating correctly and that correct clutch was installed.

Problem is drive line related.

Remove all axle shafts and lock in power divider, then run vehicle up to vibration speed. Is vibration still present?

No

Yes

Vibration is wheel end related. Raise vehicle on stands, keeping frame level. Remove tires and reinstall axle shafts. Operate the vehicle. Is the vibration still present?

Inspect driveshaft, U-joints, hanger bearings. Check driveshaft phasing and angularity. Check shaft runout. If all checks ok, balance the driveshaft.

No

Yes

Check tires for damage. Dynamically balance wheel and tire assemblies. Check wheels and tires for runout on reinstallation.

Check brake drums for missing balance weights, suspension system integrity, wheel bearing adjustment.

FIGURE 51-36 Vibration diagnostic flow chart.

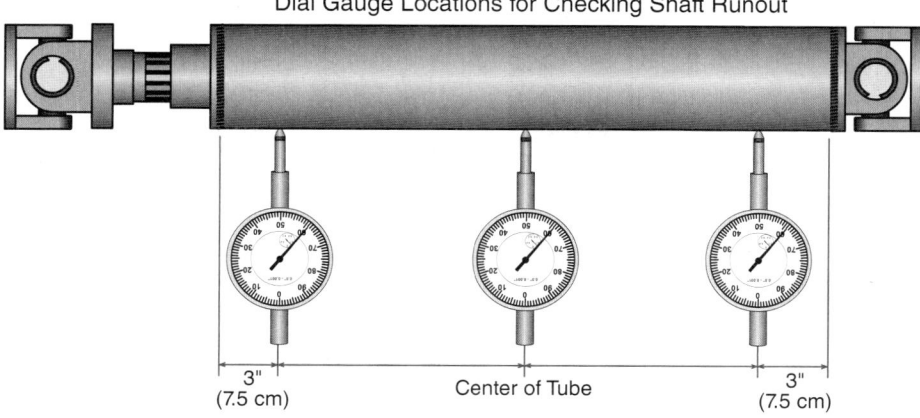

Dial Gauge Locations for Checking Shaft Runout

3" (7.5 cm) Center of Tube 3" (7.5 cm)

FIGURE 51-37 Runout should be checked at least 3" (7.5 cm) from the ends of the shaft and in the center.

FIGURE 51-38 Brinelling causes wear on the trunnions in the shape of the roller bearings.

FIGURE 51-40 U-joint breakage is usually caused by shock loading, as is the case in this image of a broken U-joint cross. Notice the uniform roughness of the break.

FIGURE 51-39 Contaminated lubricant or lack of lubricant leads to spalling. This image is an extreme case of spalling.

U-Joint Fractures and Breakage

Fractures and breakage, as shown in **FIGURE 51-40**, are usually the result of shock loads. Common sources of shock loads are overloading the vehicle, popping the clutch, spinning the tires on a slippery surface and suddenly hitting dry pavement, or sending excessive torque through the joint.

Fractures may also occur at weld seams due to fatigue that may be caused by excessive working angles introducing torsional stresses on components. Welding on the tube near the weld seams can also weaken the metal and lead to weld seam failures. Never weld balance weights in place within one inch of a weld seam.

Accelerated Wear

Any joint that operates at an angle of more than three degrees experiences reduced wear life. (Recall that the life expectancy is directly related to the size of the angle.) Excess torque and overloading contributes to a shortened wear life as well.

Reusing attachment hardware can lead to wear, specifically in the end yoke. Attachment hardware is designed to stretch as it is torqued so that it effectively clamps the U-joint caps in the yoke. Hardware that is reused can be deformed enough to allow the cap to move. The increased motion causes wear. Always replace attaching hardware when reinstalling a U-joint. One exception to this rule is the Spicer Life series cold-formed metal straps.

Twisted Tubing

Twisted tubing, like that shown in **FIGURE 51-41**, is usually caused by excessive torque loading of the driveline. Excessive torque loading is typically due to driver error, such as trying to pull away with the trailer brakes applied, popping the clutch with excessive rpm, or slamming into a loading dock. If twisting occurs, a check should be made to determine if the driveline is capable of transferring the engine/transmission torque available.

Hanger Bearing Failures

Hanger bearing failures are actually quite rare because the bearing is sealed and permanently lubricated. The stamped steel cavity surrounding the hanger bearing does need to be packed with water-proof grease at installation. If this procedure is overlooked, the bearing fails prematurely.

Failure of the hanger or "center" bearing is depicted in **FIGURE 51-42**. This type of failure usually occurs in the rubber support block and is most often caused by excessive angles at the coupling shaft drive end. This angle should be less than one and a half degrees, if possible. Remember that it must also have at least one-half degree so that the rollers turn. This problem usually manifests as black rubber dust surrounding the hanger bearing. On every revolution, the coupling shaft tries to straighten out its angle, and the rubber block must absorb this motion. Some heavy-duty coupling shafts can weigh in excess of 100 lb (45.5 kg). The rubber support must be strong enough for the shaft it is attached to. Hanger bearing failure is usually due to shaft imbalance or excessive torsionals leading to failure of the rubber mount. Because they are permanently lubricated, bearing failure is normally attributed to external damage to the bearing or its seals.

Hanger bearing failures can also occur due to overloading the shaft or excessive driveline vibrations. A lot of hanger bearings have a slotted rubber support. Collapsed slots are an indicator that the shaft is too heavy for the rubber support and that the slotted support should be changed for a solid rubber support.

Inspection and Maintenance of Driveshafts

LO 51-6 Inspect and maintain driveshafts.

Regular driveshaft maintenance is usually limited to inspecting the shaft and components for wear or damage and properly lubricating the driveshaft following the manufacturer's recommended procedures. Any inspection for wear MUST be done prior to lubricating the components. The reason for this is simple: The lubricant itself may mask wear in the universal joints and make it hard to detect.

Begin with a careful visual inspection of the driveshaft. Look for any broken or loose fasteners. Pay particular attention to the universal joint attaching hardware and the center bearing support bracket. Look for broken yoke tabs or missing spring clips or locks. Check the tubes for damage, dents, or missing balance weights, all of which can cause vibration problems. Also make sure that there is no foreign material stuck to the shafts, as this can also result in balance vibrations. **FIGURE 51-43** illustrates how problems with the shaft can produce various vibrations.

Look for any unusual rust streaking or rust patterns at or near the universal joints, the end yoke attaching bolts or nuts, and the center bearing hanger bolts. Rust streaking at any of these components can be a telltale sign of wear or looseness. Carefully check the center bearing rubber support. Rubber dust here is an indicator or excessive movement either from wear or vibration.

Next, check all of the universal joints for wear. Grasp both sides of each joint and try to rotate them in opposite directions to each other, checking for radial play, as depicted in **FIGURE 51-44**. There should be no perceptible movement between the trunnions and the caps. Even slight movement here fails the joint, and it should be replaced. Next, grasp the shaft side of the joint and move it vertically and horizontally, as shown in **FIGURE 51-45**, to check for end play between the joint bearing caps and the ends of the trunnions. For most manufacturers, this end play cannot exceed 0.006" (0.15 mm). Although some manufacturers recommend universal joint replacement if there is any noticeable end play, check the OEM manual to be sure.

Grasp each of the end yokes where they enter the transmission and the drive axle pinion(s) and rotate them back and forth and up and down to check for looseness. There should be no perceptible free play at these components. If play is present, consult the transmission or axle manufacturer's manual for instructions on how to repair the situation. There may be slight perceptible end play at the input shaft of an inter-axle differential. This is allowable, but the play should not be between the

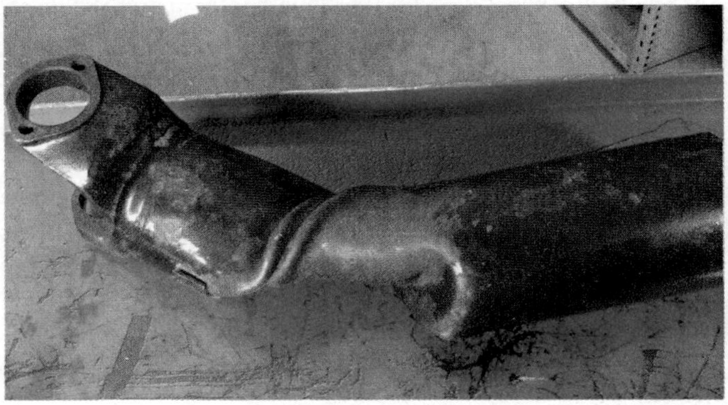

FIGURE 51-41 Extreme torque load caused this driveshaft to twist like a pretzel.

FIGURE 51-42 Failed hanger bearing with collapsed slotted upper support.

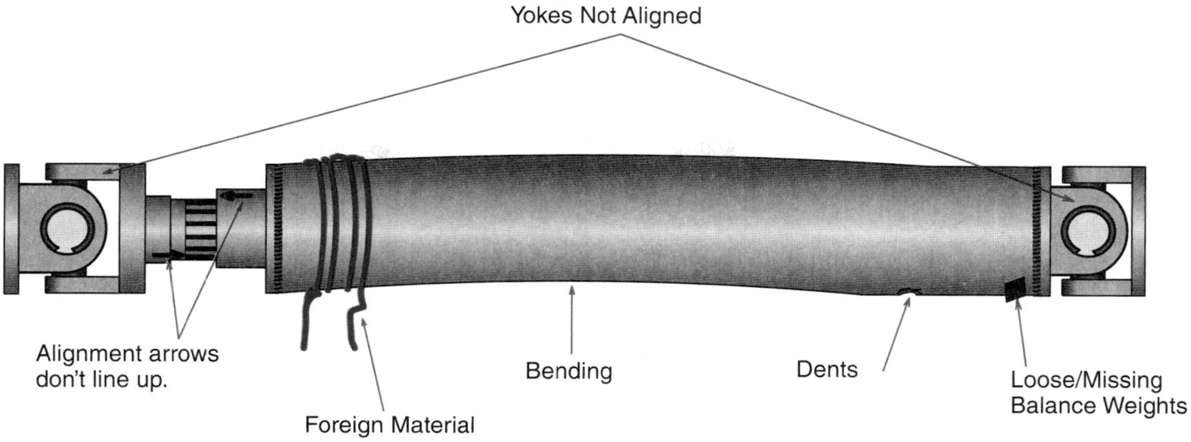

Yokes Not Aligned

Alignment arrows don't line up.

Foreign Material

Bending

Dents

Loose/Missing Balance Weights

FIGURE 51-43 Any of the problems indicated in the diagram can cause driveshaft vibrations.

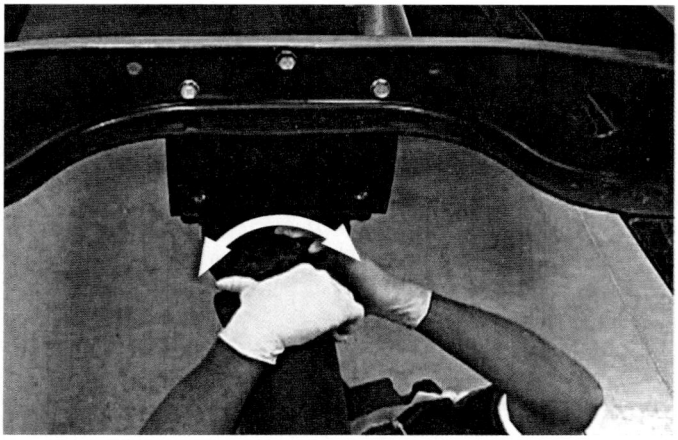

FIGURE 51-44 Any perceptible movement indicates a failed joint.

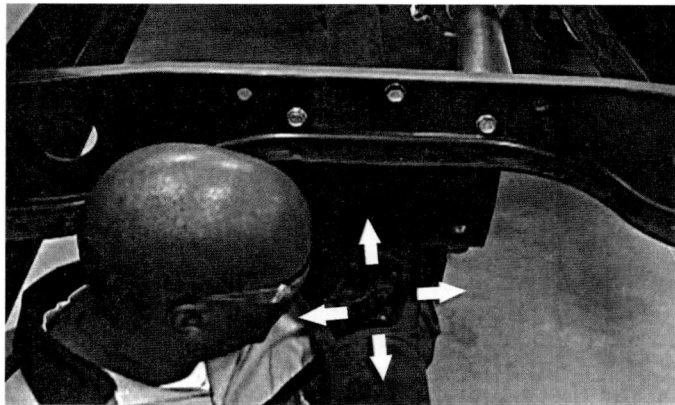

FIGURE 51-45 Endplay between the trunnions and the bearing caps should not exceed 0.006" (0.15 mm).

end yoke and the input shaft. Consult the manufacturer's manual for specifications, if necessary.

Grasp the slip yoke and move it up, down, and radially to check splines for looseness and radial play. Maximum play should be no more than 0.012" (3 mm), but measurable play exceeding 0.004" to 0.006" (0.1 to 0.15 mm) should be investigated and corrected. Play in the slip joint components can cause driveshaft vibration because the play allows the shaft to move away from its centerline while rotating.

Check the hanger bearing for wear, as shown in **FIGURE 51-46**. The rubber supports vary in stiffness, but there should be no play in the actual bearing itself. Also inspect the hanger bearing for any sign of rubber dust. The presence of rubber dust indicates that the hanger bearing may be failing or that the driveshaft is oscillating at the bearing for some reason. The shaft may be overloaded or sustaining excessive vibration. The reason for the rubber support wearing must be corrected or the shaft eventually fails.

Lubrication

Lack of proper lubrication is one of the most common causes of universal joint and driveshaft failures. Regular lubrication with

FIGURE 51-46 Slip yoke play allows the driveshaft to rotate off center, leading to vibration.

high quality grease that meets or exceeds the manufacturer's specifications assists in achieving maximum joint wear life. Although each manufacturer has its own recommendations, the lubricant used should meet the following minimum specifications:

TABLE 51-5 Normal Lubrication Intervals

City	On-Highway	Line Haul	Off-Highway	Industrial
Every 5000 to 8000 miles, or	Every 10,000 to 15,000 miles, or	Every 10,000 to 15,000 miles, or	Every 5000 to 8000 miles, or	Every 500 hours, or
8000 to 12,800 kilometers, or	16,000 to 24,000 kilometers, or	16,000 to 24,000 kilometers, or	8000 to 12,800 kilometers, or	every 250 hours for continuous use, or
3 months, whichever comes first	3 months, whichever comes first	3 months, whichever comes first	3 months, whichever comes first	severe service

TABLE 51-6 Extended Lubrication Intervals for Spicer Life Series Driveshafts

City	On-Highway	Line Haul	Off-Highway	Industrial
Every 25,000 miles, or	Every 100,000 miles, or	Every 100,000 miles or	Every 25,000 miles, or	Every 500 hours, or
40,000 kilometers, or	160,000 kilometers, or	160,000 kilometers, or	40,000 kilometers, or	every 250 hours for continuous use, or
6 months, whichever comes first	6 months, whichever comes first	6 months, whichever comes first	6 months, whichever comes first	severe service

- The grease should be good quality Extreme Pressure (EP) grease.
- The grease should meet National Lubricating Grease Institute (NLGI) Grade 2 specification.
- The grease should have an operating range of at least 325°F to −10°F (163°C to −21°C).
- The grease should be compatible with commonly used multi-purpose greases. When lubricating universal joints, it is essential to purge grease from all four caps until the new grease is visible exiting the cap seals. This eliminates the old grease and lessens compatibility issues.

Knowing the correct lubricant is only one aspect of proper lubrication. In addition, the components must be lubricated at the correct intervals. Lubricating intervals vary by manufacturer and by driveshaft design. **TABLE 51-5** indicates a general lubrication interval. Always check with the vehicle or driveshaft manufacturer to be certain of the correct lubrication frequency.

Spicer Life series drive shafts have initial lubrication specifications of 100,000 miles (160,000 km), or 1 year for city use, and 300,000 miles (560,000 Km), or 3 years for on-highway and line-haul, and after that follow the schedule in **TABLE 51-6**, which provides the relubrication intervals for the Spicer Life series. These drivelines have booted and permanently lubed slip joints that don't require periodic lubrication.

Dana Spicer Life series XS universal joints have an initial lubrication interval of 350,000 miles (560,000 km) and 100,000 miles (160,000 km) after that. The latest U-joints from the Spicer Life series are available as maintenance-free. All Spicer Life series slip joints are permanently lubed at the factory. The Meritor RPL Permalube non-greaseable driveline universal joints are lubricated for the life of the vehicle and so require little or no maintenance. Certain Meritor drivelines with permanently lubed universal joints may still need to have the slip yoke lubricated.

Probably the most important advice for technicians performing lubrication service on a driveshaft is to be sure that the

FIGURE 51-47 New grease should purge from all four bearing caps when lubricating new or in-service U-joints. If a cap fails to purge grease, it is essential to investigate the cause.

universal joints purge grease from all four universal joint caps. If one cap fails to purge after all attempts have been made, the joint must be disassembled to find out the reason.

Using a hand or an air-powered grease gun, fully lubricate each of the universal joints. As the grease is being forced into the joint, watch the bearing caps for any water or rust that purges from them. Sometimes a very small amount of clear water, one or two drops from condensation, may be present. The presence of water droplets is acceptable unless there is any sign of water contamination of the lube or rust-colored material or dirt purging from the caps. In that case, the joint must be replaced. Be sure that grease is pumped into the joint caps until they are completely purged and only new grease is coming out of the caps, as shown in **FIGURE 51-47**. This ensures that there is sufficient grease in each cap and that there are not any compatibility issues with dissimilar greases.

If one or more of the caps do not purge grease immediately, try to lessen the pressure on the cap that does not purge by using a jack with slight pressure to push the opposite cap

FIGURE 51-48 When lubricating a slip yoke, block the bleed hole in the Welch plug until new grease purges from the slip yoke.

against its trunnion while trying to get grease to purge. If this is unsuccessful and the universal joints have bolt-in caps, try loosening the bolts on the problem cap a couple of turns each and again try to purge the cap. If these methods fail, the shaft or the joint must be removed to investigate and remedy the situation. A universal joint bearing cap that does not purge grease while being lubricated will almost certainly fail, so keep at it until it purges, or replace the joint. After all caps have been purged with fresh grease, wipe up the excess grease to protect the environment and keep the vehicle underside clean.

Next, the slip joints need to be lubed. Slip joints have a Welch plug pressed into the end of the sliding tube. Where the tube turns into the yoke, the plug has a small hole in the center for air to escape, as **FIGURE 51-48** shows.

Apply grease until it purges from the Welch plug hole and, again, watch for any signs of contamination. Even though contamination here is not as critical as with universal joint bearing caps, serious contamination should be investigated. When grease purges from the Welch plug hole, cover the hole with a finger and continue to pump the grease into the joint until it purges from the seal end. Again, purge until fresh grease is seen exiting the seal.

After completion, clean up the excess grease. If the vehicle is to be parked outside in colder climates for a significant amount of time, it is a good idea to road test the vehicle so that the slip joint reciprocates a bit and purges any excess grease. In vehicles not road tested in cold weather, the grease can solidify while the vehicle is parked. When the vehicle is finally driven, the solid plug of grease can force the Welch plug out of the joint. After further driving, the grease starts to soften and eventually all the grease is thrown out of the joint by centrifugal force. This leads to premature slip joint failure.

Replacing a Universal Joint

Replacing a universal joint may or may not require that the driveshaft be removed from the vehicle. If so, the shaft must be separated from the end yokes before being taken to a work bench or press to complete the joint replacement.

The following are general steps for truck universal joint replacement procedures. Each driveline system has individual attaching hardware styles (bolts and straps, clips, etc.), and most manufacturers insist that attaching hardware be replaced if it is removed. Therefore, before attempting to remove the shaft or any components, make sure the correct parts are on hand to complete the job. There are several different pulling and pushing tools available to replace universal joints. Regardless of the type of tool used, the same basic instructions apply when working with all driveshafts.

The most important aspects of universal joint replacement are being careful not to damage the shaft and to use as little force as possible when removing the joint. Take extreme care not to damage the shaft itself, as dents in the shaft cause vibrations and lead to premature joint failure. Scratches and gouges can lead to localized stress risers, which weaken the shaft. The yokes can be damaged in several ways as well, so take care when working with them. The ears can be expanded by stretching them apart and be distorted or twisted by hammering and indiscriminate use of excessive force. Remember to use as little force as possible when removing universal joints. It is not recommended to use torches to heat components to ease removal because the heat can change the metallurgy of the shaft or yoke material.

Removing the Driveshaft

Driveshaft manufacturers recommend that none of the attaching hardware should be reused; any bolts, straps, or clips normally should be replaced, as they are torqued to yield when installed correctly and may not secure the driveshaft if they are used again. Therefore, before removing any driveshaft hardware, ensure that replacement hardware is readily available.

The first step in removal of a universal joint is to always attach slings or hangers to support the shaft before removing the attaching hardware. Be sure to use enough supports so that the shaft does not fall when one or the other end is removed. If working on a driveline with more than one shaft, each section of the shaft requires at least two slings or hangers. When removing a multi-piece shaft, start at the drive axle end and work forward.

Before removing the sections of a multi-shaft driveline, always mark the slip joints with paint or a marking pencil so they can be reinstalled correctly. (White correction fluid from the office supplies makes a good marking compound.) It is also a good idea to mark the tube yokes and end yokes so that the shaft is re-installed correctly. Typically, if the shaft is rotated 180 degrees in the end yokes on installation it makes no difference, but better safe than sorry. If the universal joint is bolted to a half-round end yoke, after installing the correct support slings, remove the attaching hardware that holds the joint bearing caps into the end yoke. Remove the shaft to the bench to complete joint removal. As shown in **FIGURE 51-49**, always use a sling to support the driveshaft before removing the attaching bolts.

There are several commercially available pullers that can be used to remove the bearing caps from the shafts with a full-round end yoke. Using pullers, such as the Tiger Tool U-Joint puller shown in **FIGURE 51-50**, is the manufacturers' recommended procedure to prevent damage to the yoke and/or shaft.

The attaching hardware on the full-round end yoke caps should be removed and the puller installed according to the manufacturer's procedure. The puller removes the cap using a steady pulling action that pushes against one yoke ear and pulls against another. No damage to the yoke itself occurs during this process. When the first cap is removed, the tool is re-installed to remove the other cap. The shaft is then taken to the bench to remove the other caps. If a universal joint is to be reused, ensure that the correct bearing caps are re-installed on their original trunnions. In some shops, a popular method of removing the caps is to use a floor jack and a hammer. The joint cap to be removed is placed in the vertical position and a jack is positioned close to the joint under the yoke, the jack is operated, and the weight of the vehicle is used to remove the cap. Sometimes a hammer is used to try and break the cap loose if it is seized.

No matter how common, THIS METHOD IS NOT RECOMMENDED BY ANY MANUFACTURER. We discuss the process here only to try and avoid damage to equipment and/or injury to technicians. It is NOT recommended.

Using the weight of the vehicle to force the cap out can cause several problems. First, the bearing cap can let go suddenly if it is seized. The jack can slip, causing the vehicle to drop, quickly resulting in crush injuries and vehicle damage. The jack itself can cause damage to the shaft by bending it or gouging at the point of contact. The yoke ears can be spread by the uneven forces being applied, and using hammers can cause damage to the shaft or yoke.

Using the proper pulling tools avoids all these dangers and is the only procedure that should be followed. If only one universal joint is being replaced, the entire removal procedure can be accomplished with the shaft still in place on the vehicle and supported. Simply remove one cap at a time with the puller. If more than one joint is to be replaced, the shaft can be taken to the work bench and the work can be completed there, using either the puller or a suitable hydraulic press. Alternatively, if the shaft has a slip joint, the joint may be separated to remove one section of the shaft. When separating a slip joint, make sure to mark the position of the slip joint so that it can be re-installed correctly.

Some slip joints have a threaded seal cap that must be unscrewed before the slip joint can be separated, as depicted in **FIGURE 51-51**. Remember that a heavy-duty driveshaft can weigh well over 100 lb (46 kg), so get assistance when removing the shaft. There are several different pullers available for universal joints, and the method described above can be adapted to use with any one of them. The relatively low cost of these pullers should mean that all shops use them. Unfortunately, however, some do not and resort to the jack method. Remember, the jack method is likely to cause injury and/or shaft damage and should not be used.

FIGURE 51-49 Always use a sling to support the driveshaft before removing the attaching bolts.

FIGURE 51-50 Aftermarket U-joint removal tools from the Tiger Tool Company.

FIGURE 51-51 It may be necessary to unscrew the seal cap on a slip joint to separate it. Be sure to mark both halves so they can be reassembled correctly.

After the joint has been removed, the yoke ears should be checked for wear and removal damage. Slight burrs can be removed with a small rat tail file. Remove heavy rust with an emery cloth to make the re-installation process easier.

Finally, check the yokes for distortion by using a yoke alignment bar. Slide the bar through both yoke ears. If the bar does not go through, it indicates that the yoke has been twisted due to excessive torque or disassembly damage. In that case, the yoke should be replaced.

Inspecting and Installing Universal Joints

According to most manufacturers' procedures, all driveshaft attaching hardware—bolts, nuts, straps, and lock plates—should be replaced after being removed and should never be reused. When hardware is installed properly, straps and bolts are usually torqued to yield and may be distorted. Consequently, re-using hardware may allow bearing caps to move or the attachment may loosen.

Before installing a new universal joint, carefully inspect the new joint by removing all the bearing caps and checking the rollers and the cap seals. Check for any debris or dirt in the joint and make sure that the grease zerk is in good order. Also note the location of the grease zerk. If the grease zerk is mounted on one side (for example, toward the front or back) of the universal joint cross, that side should be installed toward the driveshaft tube. Doing so ensures that the zerk is accessible by a grease gun after installation. In some cases, it may still be possible to grease the joint if the zerk is installed toward the end yoke, but it is always better to be safe than sorry.

Remember that new universal joints are packaged with just enough lubricant to hold the rollers in place and stave off rusting. The joints MUST be fully lubricated after installation. When installing universal joint caps, it is essential that the cap and bearings be on the trunnion before forcing the cap back into the yoke ears. Otherwise, one or more of the rollers can fall between the cap and the trunnion end. Preventing that involves positioning the trunnion through the yoke, installing the cap on the trunnion, and then forcing the cap and trunnion back into the yoke ear. Universal joints should be removed and installed using steady controlled pressure only and using the proper pulling and pushing tools. A dead blow or brass hammer may be used to help seat bearing caps, but be very careful not to damage the shaft, the yokes, and/or the universal joint itself. To disassemble and inspect a U-joint with a bolted end, follow the steps in **SKILL DRILL 51-1**. To install universal joints, follow the guidelines in **SKILL DRILL 51-2**.

▶ TECHNICIAN TIP

It cannot be stressed enough how easy it can be to "drop a roller" (when one of the roller bearings fall into the bearing cap unseen by the technician) while installing universal joints. Take extreme care to avoid this scenario. If it is suspected that a roller has dropped, be sure to re-check the joint carefully. A dropped roller causes a new joint to fail very quickly.

▶ TECHNICIAN TIP

New universal joints only have enough lube to retain the roller bearings and prevent rust. It is essential that they are completely lubricated after installation with new grease purging from all four bearing caps or they will likely fail.

Inspecting and Replacing Center (Hanger) Bearings

The center (hanger) bearing supports the end of a split driveshaft and is a very important part of any driveline. The bearing itself is usually sealed. It usually cannot be lubricated, but if it

SKILL DRILL 51-1 Disassembling and Inspecting a Universal Joint with a Bolted End

1. Locate and follow the appropriate procedure in the service manual.

2. Complete the accompanying job sheet or work order with all pertinent information.

3. Remove the U-joint from driveshaft:
   a. Bend tangs of lock plates away from cap screw heads (if equipped).
   b. Remove cap screws and lock plates.
   c. Remove bearing caps from the yoke. Note: If caps are seized, use the appropriate puller.

4. Inspect U-joint with bolted ends:
   a. Clean all U-joint parts.
   b. Check bearing journals for evidence of wear or heat damage; also, check ends of crosses.
   c. Make sure lubricant passages in cross are clean.
   d. Check for missing, worn, or damaged needle bearings.
   e. Apply the recommended lubricant to rollers in caps.
   f. Turn caps on journals to check for wear. Note: If any parts are worn or damaged, replace the entire U-joint.

5. List the test results and/or recommendations on the job sheet or work order, clean the work area, and return tools and materials to their proper storage.

SKILL DRILL 51-2 Installing Universal Joints

1. With all the caps removed from the cross, position it in the tube yoke with one of the trunnions protruding above the yoke ear.
2. Place the bearing cap over the trunnion, making sure that the rollers remain properly seated in the cap. Then, slide the cap into position while holding the cross so that the rollers remain engaged with the trunnion. If the cap binds in the yoke, tap it lightly with a dead blow hammer until it is flush. Always tap the center of the cap only—not the edges.
3. Install the cap retaining bolts with the lock strap if equipped, but do not fold the lock strap tangs to secure the bolt at this time. (Wait until the joint is properly lubricated.)
4. With one cap installed correctly, turn the yoke over and raise the cross sufficiently to engage the rollers of the second cap with its

trunnion. Do not raise the cross so high that the other trunnion comes out of its cap. Then, push the second cap into position and secure it.
5. Rotate the joint on its bearing to be sure there is no binding. If it binds, tap the yoke ears lightly with a dead blow or brass hammer; if it still binds, the joint should be disassembled to find the cause.
6. If the shaft is being installed into a half-round end yoke, place the two other caps on their trunnions and tie the exposed caps together with electrical tape so they do not fall off when positioning the shaft for installation. Install the shaft and the attaching hardware.
7. If installing the shaft into a full-round yoke, repeat the installation instructions used on the bench by lifting the first trunnion through the end yoke, then installing its cap so the rollers are seated. Push the bearing cap into place. Depending on the type of joint, it may be necessary to use a pushing installation tool to install the caps. Lift the last trunnion through the end yoke just enough so that the rollers of the bearing cap are held in place by the trunnion as the cap is installed. Push it into position.
8. After the shaft is installed, follow the lubricating instructions in the Lubrication section of this chapter. It may be necessary to loosen the attaching bolts during the lubrication procedure. If your U-joint bolts have locking straps, do not fold over the lock strap tabs until you have correctly lubricated the U-joints. Remember that grease must purge from all four caps. After lubricating the joints, correctly fold up the lock strap tangs, if equipped, to secure the attaching bolts.

SKILL DRILL 51-3 Removing and Reinstalling the Driveshaft

1. Locate and follow the appropriate procedure in the service manual.
2. Complete the accompanying job sheet or work order with all pertinent information.
3. Move the vehicle into shop, apply parking brakes, and chock the vehicle wheels. Observe lockout/tagout procedures.
4. If the vehicle has a manual transmission, place it in "neutral." If it has an automatic transmission, place it in "park" or "neutral."
5. Jack up the rear of vehicle and place jack stands under frame.
6. Mark all joints and yokes with a paint marker to retain balance and phasing.

7. Support the drive shaft with a suitable sling and remove the driveshaft attaching bolts. Study the driveshaft to determine how it is fastened.
8. Remove the center support bearing if a two-piece driveshaft is used. Check between center support and frame for shims. If shims are used, they must be replaced when the driveshaft is reinstalled.
9. Remove the driveshaft from vehicle. Tape the U-joint bearing caps to prevent loss of needle bearings. The slip yoke should also be protected to prevent damage during removal. When removing, replacing, or servicing a driveshaft, careless handling can damage the shaft and U-joints.
10. Service the driveshaft according to the service manual.
11. Reinstall driveshaft:
    a. Place in position and check alignment marks. All mounting surfaces should be clean and free of nicks before assembly.
    b. Replace all fasteners with new ones and install correctly and tighten evenly.
    c. Replace fasteners in center support bearing, if used.
    d. Torque all fasteners to manufacturer's specifications.
12. Grease each U-joint. Continue to grease until the air is removed and grease purges from the bearing cap seals. Once new grease is observed from seals, wipe seals of all grease with a shop towel.
13. Jack up the rear of the vehicle and remove jack stands.
14. Lower the vehicle to floor.
15. List the test results and/or recommendations on the job sheet or work order, clean the work area, and return tools and materials to their proper storage.

has a grease zerk, it requires lubrication at the same interval as the rest of the driveline.

The center support bearing is mounted in a rubber support to allow flexibility as the driveline moves up and down. Failure of the center bearing can cause vibration and noise in the driveline. The rubber support can become damaged by being in contact with petroleum products, which swell the rubber. Excessive vibration weakens the rubber. The rubber can also be damaged simply by age and weathering, which eventually causes the rubber to break down and disintegrate. Follow the procedure in **SKILL DRILL 51-3** to inspect and, if necessary, replace the center bearing. Follow the procedure in **SKILL DRILL 51-4** to remove and reinstall the driveshaft and center support bearing and mounts.

SKILL DRILL 51-4 Inspecting and Servicing Center Support Bearings

1. Safely raise the vehicle on an approved lift. Inspect the center bearing components for any major defects, such as looseness or noises.
2. Inspect the center bearing for proper mounting.
3. Inspect the bearing mount rubber insert for dry rotting and cracking.

4. If the bearing must be replaced, follow the manufacturer's specifications and procedures for proper installation of a new bearing. Typical bearing replacement may go as follows:
   a. Mount the driveshaft in an approved vice.
   b. Mark the shafts so they may be properly phased when put back together.
   c. Separate the two driveshafts.
   d. Remove the U-shaped metal mounting bracket.
   e. Remove the rubber mount from around the center bearing.
   f. Remove any snap rings or circlips that may be holding the bearing in place.
   g. Use an appropriate puller or press to remove the bearing from the driveshaft.
   h. Check the splines for the slip yoke for any defects.
   i. Check the slip yoke on the mating shaft for wear and defects.
   j. Press on a new bearing.
   k. Reinstall any necessary snap rings or circlips.
5. Install a new rubber mount around the new bearing. Reinstall the mounting bracket.
6. Put the two shafts back together, paying attention to driveshaft phasing.
7. Remove the driveshaft from the vice, and reinstall it into vehicle.

Wrap-Up

Ready for Review

▶ Most, if not all, heavy-vehicle drivelines consist of one or more driveshafts coupled by universal joints, also known as Cardan joints.

▶ Robert Hooke discovered that a shaft driven at an angle through a universal joint accelerates and decelerates twice per revolution. In some places, universal joints are known as Hooke joints because of this.

▶ Driveshafts must meet three criteria: They must be strong enough to transmit the maximum engine torque without failure. They must allow the shaft length to change due to suspension oscillation and torque wind up. And they must be able to operate at constantly changing operating angles.

▶ Most truck driveshafts are denoted by series, with the 1710 and 1810 series being the most popular in North America.

▶ The Spicer Life series driveshaft is fast becoming the driveshaft system of choice for most new trucks.

▶ Driveshaft tubing can be seamed or seamless and constructed by being welded, forged, or with a welded

tube drawn over mandrel. The drawn-over-mandrel design is very consistent in tube strength and thickness.

▶ Driveshafts are connected to the vehicle components and to each other using various yokes. Yokes have two openings, called ears, to accept two of the universal joint bearing caps. These ears can be full-round (circles) or half-round, which require bolt-on straps.

▶ Tube yokes are welded to the tube ends. End yokes are splined to components, such as drive axles. Both have round or half-round ears.

▶ Flange yokes are splined to components and have a flat flange that, in turn, is bolted to a companion flange with two full-round yoke ears.

▶ Truck drivelines usually have more than one driveshaft—requiring the use of a center (hanger) bearing for support.

▶ Slip yokes allow the driveshaft length to change.

▶ Most manufacturers recommend that driveshaft attaching bolts and most hardware be replaced and not reused.

▶ The critical speed of a driveshaft is the speed at which it bows off its centerline due to centrifugal force. If operated at or beyond its critical speed, a driveshaft fails catastrophically.

▶ Critical speed can be increased by reducing the shaft weight, increasing shaft diameter, or shortening the shaft's length. Therefore, most trucks with long drivelines have numerous short shafts connected together.

▶ The shaft on the driven side of a universal joint operating at an angle accelerates and decelerates twice per revolution. The rate of this non-uniform velocity increases as the operating angle of the universal joint increases.

▶ The intensity of the acceleration and deceleration causes inertial excitation of the shaft, leading to vibration. As the operating angles increase, maximum shaft speed must decrease or the U-joint fails. Therefore, the maximum rpm of the shaft is restricted by its angle of operation.

▶ The non-uniform velocity of the universal joint must be canceled out by a second universal joint with an equal and opposite angle at the other end of the shaft.

▶ This cancellation can be accomplished in two ways: with a parallel joint arrangement (also known as a waterfall arrangement) or with an intersecting angle arrangement (also known as a broken back arrangement).

▶ Driveshafts with universal joints must be phased so the velocity cancellation occurs during the correct quadrant of rotation.

▶ Driveline angles should be at least one-half degree to ensure lubricant distribution in the joint, the angle at each end of a driveshaft should be equal to within one degree, and the angles should be kept as small as possible (three degrees or less) to minimize inertial excitation of the driveshaft.

▶ Constant velocity joint arrangements eliminate the need for angle cancellation and phasing because the driven shaft turns at a steady speed when constant velocity joints are used.

▶ Driveline vibration can be caused by a bent or dented driveshaft, foreign material build-up on the shaft, worn U-joints or slip yokes, driveshaft imbalance, driveline angles out or too steep, or a driveshaft being out of phase.

▶ When lubricating universal joints, it is crucial that grease purges from all four caps. Otherwise, the joint should be replaced.

▶ Universal joints should always be replaced using proper tooling only.

Key Terms

brinelling Damage that occurs when the rollers in the universal joint are hammered into the trunnions, leaving indentations.

broken back arrangement A method of angle cancellation in which the U-joint angles intersect at a point exactly at the middle of the shaft length. Also known as an *intersecting angle arrangement*.

cancellation The act of canceling the non-uniform velocity in a driveshaft.

Cardan joint A joint with four trunnions and four bearing caps. Also known as a *Hooke joint* or a *universal joint*.

center bearing A bearing pressed on to a machined surface after the splined area of a driveshaft's slip yoke spline; used to support a multiple piece driveshaft. Also called a *hanger bearing*.

companion flange A splined flange attached to a vehicle component, such as a drive axle pinion shaft, that bolts to a flange yoke on a driveshaft.

constant velocity joint A joint that delivers a uniform speed to the driven shaft.

coupling shaft A short shaft usually at the front of a driveline. Also known as a *jack shaft*.

critical speed The rotational speed at which a driveshaft starts to bow off its center line due to centrifugal force, leading to vibration and shaft failure.

cross-phasing When a coupling shaft is phased at 90 degrees to the second driveshaft.

driveline A series of driveshafts, yokes, and support bearings used to connect a transmission to the rear axle.

driveline angularity Refers to the angles at the universal joints.

end yoke A splined yoke attached to a component, such as a transmission output shaft.

false brinelling A condition where lubricant is squeezed out from between the needles and the trunnions of a U-joint leading to frettage wear; caused by too small or no angle at the joint so lubricant is not distributed.

flange yoke A yoke with two ears to hold a U-joint and a flat flange to bolt to a companion flange.

gimbals Two or more concentric circles used to support an item; while the circles can move, the supported object remains stationary.

hanger bearing A bearing pressed on to a machined surface after the splined area of a driveshaft's slip yoke spline; used to support a multiple piece driveshaft. Also called a *center bearing*.

harmonic vibration An inherent vibration that occurs at precisely 50% of a shaft's critical speed.

Hooke joint A joint with four trunnions and four bearing caps. Also known as a *Cardan joint* or a *universal joint*.

inertial excitation The force caused by the speeding up and slowing down of the shaft driven through an angle. These stem from the operating angles of the U-joint at the drive end of the driveshaft and are caused by the sheer weight of the driveshaft being accelerated and decelerated twice per revolution.

intersecting angle arrangement A method of angle cancellation in which the U-joint angles intersect at a point exactly at the middle of the shaft length. Also known as a *broken back arrangement*.

jack shaft A short shaft usually at the front of a driveline. Also known as a *coupling shaft*.

non-uniform velocity The phenomenon that a shaft driven through an angle accelerates and decelerates twice per revolution.

parallel joint arrangement Two or more universal joint arrangements where the joint angles form parallel lines; a method of angle cancellation for use with parallel angles. Also known as the *waterfall arrangement*.

phasing Lining up the inboard yoke ears of driveshaft so that the non-uniform velocity cancellation occurs in the proper quadrant of the circle.

plan angle An angle where the driveshaft moves toward the side of a vehicle when viewed from above.

Rzeppa joint A constant velocity joint invented by Alfred Rzeppa in 1926.

secondary couple vibrations A vibration, caused by U-joint angles, that travels the length of the driveshaft.

slip joint A splined shaft and tube assembly that allows driveshaft length changes.

torsional excitation Twisting forces caused by inertial excitation.

torsional vibrations Vibrations caused by twisting forces on the driveshaft; these occur twice per revolution.

transverse vibrations Vibrations caused by shaft imbalance; these occur once per revolution.

trunnion The smooth ends of the U-joint cross that accepts the bearing caps.

tube yoke A yoke with two ears that accept a U-joint and that is welded to the driveshaft tube.

universal joint A cross-shaped joint with bearings on each leg where one set of parallel legs is connected to the end of one shaft and the other set of parallel legs is connected to the end of a second shaft. This arrangement allows the shafts to operate at shallow angles to each other. Also called a *U-joint*, a *Cardan joint*, or a *Hooke joint*.

waterfall arrangement Two or more universal joint arrangements where the joint angles form parallel lines; a method of angle cancellation for use with parallel angles. Also called *parallel joint arrangement*.

Review Questions

1. For optimal performance, most of today's manufacturers recommend that U-joint operating angles should be no more than which of the following?
   a. 1 degree
   b. 3 degrees
   c. 5 degrees
   d. 7 degrees
2. The broken back driveshaft arrangement cannot be used in which of the following situations?
   a. When operating length changes are excessive
   b. Between the two drive axles on a tandem
   c. When operating length changes are minimal
   d. When slip joints are used
3. Double Cardan joints use two joints connected together to provide which of the following?
   a. Constant velocity to the driven shaft
   b. Higher torque capacity
   c. More driveshaft length
   d. None of these answers are correct.

4. The working angle of a U-joint is restricted by which of the following?
   a. The torque it must transmit
   b. The speed at which it must operate
   c. The diameter of the driveshaft
   d. The size of the U-joint
5. U-joint working angles must be equal to within which of the following limits?
   a. 5 degrees
   b. 3 degrees
   c. 2 degrees
   d. 1 degree
6. What is the minimum U-joint operating angle that manufacturers recommend?
   a. 1/4 degree
   b. 1/2 degree
   c. 1 degree
   d. 3 degrees
7. The critical speed of a drive shaft is most affected by which of the following?
   a. The shaft length
   b. The tube diameter
   c. The shaft weight
   d. The wall thickness
8. Why does lowering the air bags sometimes cause driveline vibrations?
   a. U-joint operating angles can be altered.
   b. The drive shaft critical speed increases.
   c. Drive shaft inertial excitations are decreased.
   d. The driveshaft is closer to the ground.
9. If a drive shaft has a plan angle and a side view angle, what must you do to determine the true operating angle?
   a. Add the two angles together and divide by two.
   b. Add the squares of the two angles and get the square root of the total.
   c. Add the two angles, square the result, and then get the square root of the answer.
   d. The true operating angle is the side view angle.
10. How much radial clearance is allowed at the universal joint?
    a. zero clearance
    b. 0.006" (0.15 mm) clearance
    c. 0.012" (3 mm) clearance
    d. 0.010"–0.030" (0.25 to 0.76 mm) clearance

ASE Technician A/Technician B Style Quiz

1. Technician A says that when a driveshaft operates at an angle, the driven shaft accelerates and decelerates once per revolution. Technician B says that using a U-joint at the front and back with equal angles cancels the non-uniform velocity. Who is correct?
   a. Technician A
   b. Technician B
   c. Both Technician A and Technician B
   d. Neither Technician A nor Technician B

2. Technician A says that a driveline is made up of more than one driveshaft. Technician B says that multi-shaft drivelines must have a center or hanger bearing. Who is correct?
   a. Technician A
   b. Technician B
   c. Both Technician A and Technician B
   d. Neither Technician A nor Technician B

3. Technician A says that that driveline attaching bolts should not be reused. Technician B says that Spicer Life series spring clips can be reused as long as they are not bent. Who is correct?
   a. Technician A
   b. Technician B
   c. Both Technician A and Technician B
   d. Neither Technician A nor Technician B

4. Technician A says that some driveshafts are cross phased or phased at 90 degrees. Technician B says that, when a driveshaft slip yoke is removed, you should mark its position so that it is reassembled correctly in phase. Who is correct?
   a. Technician A
   b. Technician B
   c. Both Technician A and Technician B
   d. Neither Technician A nor Technician B

5. Technician A says that critical speed is when a driveshaft starts to bow off its center line due to centrifugal force. Technician B says that a driveshaft operating at or above critical speed vibrates violently. Who is correct?
   a. Technician A
   b. Technician B
   c. Both Technician A and Technician B
   d. Neither Technician A nor Technician B

6. Technician A says that drive shaft angularity is the first thing to check when diagnosing drive shaft vibrations. Technician B says that a driveshaft out of phase usually causes a vibration. Who is correct?
   a. Technician A
   b. Technician B
   c. Both Technician A and Technician B
   d. Neither Technician A nor Technician B

7. Technician A says that, as long as a drive shaft has canceling angles, it does not vibrate. Technician B says that drive shaft operating angles are limited by the speed the shaft must rotate. Who is correct?
   a. Technician A
   b. Technician B
   c. Both Technician A and Technician B
   d. Neither Technician A nor Technician B

8. Technician A says that a dent in a driveshaft may cause the shaft to vibrate. Technician B says that foreign material on the driveshaft may cause vibration. Who is correct?
   a. Technician A
   b. Technician B
   c. Both Technician A and Technician B
   d. Neither Technician A nor Technician B

9. Technician says that small amounts of rust purging from the U-joint while greasing it is expected and that you should keep greasing the joint until all the rust is gone. Technician B says that a couple of drops of clear water escaping the U-joint grease seals while lubricating the joint is normal. Who is correct?
   a. Technician A
   b. Technician B
   c. Both Technician A and Technician B
   d. Neither Technician A nor Technician B

10. Technician A says that, when checking U-joints, end play between the U-joint trunnions and the bearing cap should be no more than 0.006" (0.15 mm). Technician B says that slip yoke radial play should not exceed 0.030" (0.76 mm). Who is correct?
    a. Technician A
    b. Technician B
    c. Both Technician A and Technician B
    d. Neither Technician A nor Technician B

CHAPTER 52

Heavy-Duty Drive Axles

Learning Objectives

After reading this chapter, you will be able to:

- **LO 52-1** Explain fundamentals of axles.
- **LO 52-2** Explain the design and functions of differential gear sets.
- **LO 52-3** Describe the various types of differential gear sets.
- **LO 52-4** Explain the design and operation of double reduction and multi-speed drive axles.

- **LO 52-5** Explain the operation of inter-axle differentials (power dividers).
- **LO 52-6** Explain the role of drive axles and drivelines in greenhouse gas reduction stategies.

You Are the Technician

You are in the office of your Seattle service facility and one of your newer fleet drivers is recounting to his dispatcher a situation that happened to him. He is quite distraught as he tells the dispatcher what occurred. Seemingly, the previous night, the driver was on I-90 heading for Seattle carrying a load through the mountains. There were only light snow flurries, but as he climbed one stretch of mountain road, he seemed to lose traction to the rear axles of his tandem tractor. He was quite frightened by the event and eventually was able to stop the vehicle in a lay-by and engage his inter-axle and main differential locks. He said he had no more problems after locking the differentials and he made it to Seattle without further incident. The driver notices you there and asks for your input.

1. What would you tell the driver about the correct way to use differential locks in a poor traction situation?
2. What would inform the driver about the damage that could happen to the vehicle by using the differential locks in this way?
3. What service, if any, would you recommend to the driver to ensure that significant damage has not occurred in the driveline?

Introduction

This chapter explains the principles, operation, and construction of different types of axles and drive axles used in the medium- to heavy-duty truck and coach market. Included in the chapter are sections on non-drive (dead) axles and drive (live) axles. Steering axles are discussed in the Steering Systems and Integral Steering Gears chapter, so this chapter focuses on drive axles, including single-reduction and double-reduction single-speed drive axles and multi-speed drive axles (including both planetary and double-reduction helical two-speed types). This chapter also discusses differential gears, controlled traction differentials, locking differentials, tandem drive systems, inter-axle differentials, and differential locking systems.

Fundamentals of Axles

LO 52-1 Explain fundamentals of axles.

Three distinct types of axles are used in truck applications. Every on-highway vehicle has a steering axle, such as the one shown in **FIGURE 52-1** (at the front), which allows the vehicle to turn. Some heavy-duty vehicles use dual steering axles. It is very common to see dual steering axles on cement trucks and/ or heavy cranes. The heaviest vehicles may even have multiple (more than 2) steering axles. Very long vehicles, such as articulating fire trucks (tiller trucks), may have steering axles in the rear. In the case of tiller fire trucks, the rear axle of the trailer portion of the truck can be steered to negotiate narrow streets and tight corners.

The second type of axle is called a **dead axle**. Dead axles are designed to carry the vehicle's weight and come in a variety of shapes and sizes. Dead axles can be used on trucks, either in front of or behind the drive axle, when a vehicle needs to carry extra load. Dead axles can be fixed; that is, they are mounted permanently in place, or they can be lift axles that can be raised and lowered so they are only utilized when the vehicle is loaded. Lift axles that are located in front of the drive, or main axles, on trucks and/or trailers are known as **pusher axles**, and lift axles that are located behind the drive

axle are known as **tag axles**. Pusher and tag axles are used to allow the vehicle to carry more payload and are lowered into place pneumatically when the vehicle is heavily loaded. When the vehicle is unloaded, the extra axles are raised either pneumatically or through springs. Self-steering axles, like the one shown in **FIGURE 52-2**, can be used as pusher axles or tag axles. A **self-steering axle** allows the wheels of the axle to automatically follow the curve of a turn; this prevents the tire scrubbing during the turn. Self-steering axles are equipped with a tie rod and tie rod ends, king-pins, steering arms, and, typically, have dampers to prevent the wheels from wobbling. Regardless of whether they are pusher or tag type, steerable dead axles steer in the direction of the turn, and their steering geometry is set so that they remain straight while going forward. See the Front Axle and Vehicle Alignment Factors chapter for an explanation of basic steering geometry. These axles are raised or lowered by the operator using an air or electric control in the cab. Note that some states require these controls to be outside the cab. Most steering axles are dead axles in that they only carry the vehicle weight. A steer axle may also, however, be a drive axle, as is the case with four-wheel or six-wheel drive trucks.

The third type of axle is the **drive axle** (or **live axle**), so called because they contain the gearing necessary to drive the vehicle. Drive axles can be single- or two-speed and single- or double-reduction, meaning that the overall final drive ratio is the result of two separate gear reductions in the axle. They can also be arranged as a **tandem** drive where the driving force is divided between two drive axles, or **tridem** in which three drive axles split the driving force.

Drive axles are usually mounted at the rear but can also be mounted at the front of the vehicle in the case of vehicles with front- and rear-wheel drive axles. These can be four-wheel-drive with one drive axle at the front and one at the back, or six-wheel-drive with one drive axle at the front and a tandem drive at the rear. Front-wheel drive axles must also double as steering axles to turn the vehicle.

Steering Axles

All vehicles must have a way to steer. The most popular type of steer axle in trucks is the one-piece I-beam style. This type of

FIGURE 52-1 Steering axles are usually I-beam type. They support the vehicle weight through the front suspension and allow the vehicle to be turned.

FIGURE 52-2 A self-steering tag or pusher axle can usually be lifted when not needed.

FIGURE 52-3 Steer axles on heavy trucks are usually of the I-beam type.

axle consists of the I-beam with flat pads to accept the spring mounts for the front suspension, as shown in **FIGURE 52-3**.

The wheel spindles, also known as steering knuckles, are attached to the I-beam with kingpins and bushings. The tie rod arms are attached to the bottom of the spindles and are connected together by a tie rod (also called a cross tube). The tie rod arms (also called Ackerman arms) connect to the tie rod with tie rod ends, which are small ball joint connectors that thread into the tie rod. The left-side spindle has a steering arm at the top, which connects to the drag link. The drag link is a rod with two ball joint-style ends, and its length is usually adjustable, so the steering can be set up properly. The drag link is moved by the pitman arm, attached to the steering box, to steer the vehicle. Note that some heavy-duty vehicles have dual steering boxes—one on each side of the vehicle. In those cases, each steering arm connects to one of the steering boxes. **FIGURE 52-4** shows one of the two steering boxes.

The kingpins are retained in the steer axle by one of two methods. Either the pin is tapered and retained by a nut, or the pin is straight and held in place by a wedge-shaped pin installed through an eye in the I-beam. The spindles have bushings at the top and bottom so that they can rotate around the kingpin. A load-supporting thrust bearing allows the spindle to turn, even when heavily loaded. Although the I-beam is the most common used for truck front steer axles, tubular steer axles are sometimes used.

Steering axles are covered in greater detail in the Front Axles and Vehicle Alignment Factors chapter.

Dead Axles

Truck dead axles are usually pusher or tag axles and are typically mounted on a pivoting frame. These dead axles can be raised or lowered by the driver in the cab when needed and allow the vehicle to carry more payload. A pusher axle is shown mounted on the dump truck in **FIGURE 52-5**. The amount of load the axles carry can be adjusted by the driver controlling the air pressure in the axle's air bag suspension.

FIGURE 52-4 The second power steering box is controlled hydraulically by the main power steering box.

FIGURE 52-5 Dead axles, like this pusher axle, can be raised or lowered, when required, by the driver.

Stingers

A stinger is a lift axle that actually extends the outer bridge of a vehicle (the distance between its front axle and the last axle on the vehicle. A stinger mounts to the rear of the vehicle frame and is folded up and out of the way when not in use. When deployed, the stinger folds down and effectively lengthens the vehicle frame and extends the outer bridge by approximately 15′, which allows the vehicle to increase its payload by as much as five tons under the Federal Bridge formula. See Chapter 1 for a complete explanation of the Federal Bridge formula. Stingers are a bolt-on option and can be added to the back of most trucks, but they are most common on cement mixers. A stinger is shown in **FIGURE 52-6**.

Trailer Dead Axles

In addition to carrying the vehicle's weight, trailer dead axles serve as attachment points for the brakes and suspension. Most trailer axles are designed for specific vocations. The

FIGURE 52-6 Stingers effectively lengthen the vehicle's wheel base or outer bridge and can increase payloads by up to five tons.

FIGURE 52-7 Most trailer dead axles are tubular in design because that profile is the strongest.

most common trailer axle consists of a tubular cross shaft attached to two spindles, which in turn support the wheels. Tubular axles have the strongest section modulus, so the axle can carry maximum weight. **FIGURE 52-7** shows a typical tandem trailer axle.

Drop center tubular axles are concave in the middle and are commonly found in situations when product-handling tubes and pipes are required to run under the trailer. With **crank axles**, the main beam is much lower than the wheel ends. Crank axles are used with certain types of trailers with low floors, such as furniture vans. Trailer dead axle configurations can be single, tandem, tridem, or any other configuration necessary to the trailer's vocation. A tandem-trailer axle arrangement can be fixed or movable, in which case the axle set can be moved forward or backward along the trailer frame.

Drive Axles

Internal combustion engines in heavy vehicles usually produce rotating power in a clockwise direction (viewed from the front) and send it through a transmission and a drive line to the rear of the vehicle. Here, the power must turn a corner in order to drive the wheels and propel the vehicle. The primary function

FIGURE 52-8 Drive axles allow the rotational power from the engine to turn 90 degrees so the wheel can drive the vehicle forward.

of a drive (live) axle, therefore, is to allow the rotational power to turn 90 degrees so that we can drive the vehicle. **FIGURE 52-8** shows a typical tandem drive axle.

The drive axle also provides a significant gear reduction—or even two gear reductions—to provide the final torque increase in a powertrain. For that reason, it is sometimes known as the final drive. The drive axle contains the **differential gears**, which allow for speed differences between the two axle shafts of the drive axle when turning. Differential gears are discussed in the Types and Functions of Differential Gear Sets sections.

Types of Drive Axle Gearing and Housings

Drive axle gearing comes in many varieties. In addition to plain and spiral bevel gears, there are durapoid, hypoid, amboid, topoid, and generoid options. All of these types of gearing are protected and contained in the differential housing.

In the past, **worm-and-crown** (or **worm wheel**) gears were used to drive the wheels at 90 degrees to the driveshaft. These older gear arrangements were capable of very high gear reduction in a compact space. Worm-and-crown gear sets consist of a shaft with machined roll threads on the worm, which is in mesh with a crown gear (the worm wheel). The worm can be mounted below or above the crown wheel. A worm mounted below the crown wheel is called underslung. A worm mounted above the crown wheel is called top-mount and is shown in **FIGURE 52-9**.

The ratio between these gears is determined by the number of threads, or leads, on the worm—so these gears are capable of large gear reductions in a small space. Worm and crown gears were used in the early days of automobiles and trucks. Today they are, for the most part, considered obsolete. Some light-duty vehicle manufacturers are experimenting with worm gear variations again, however, in search of possible fuel economy gains.

Generally speaking, all of today's trucks use bevel gears that intersect at a 90-degree angle to take the powerflow from the rotating drive shaft and turn it out toward the wheels. **FIGURE 52-10** shows bevel gears.

Bevel gears consist of a relatively small driving gear known as the **pinion gear** and a large gear known as the **crown gear** or **ring gear**. Bevel gears have their teeth cut at a 45-degree angle from their axis, allowing them to mesh at 90 degrees to each other. The

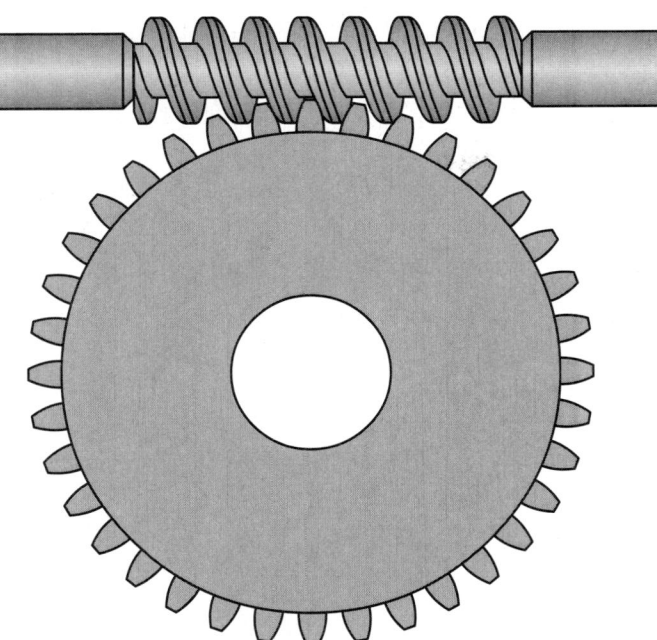

FIGURE 52-9 Top-mount worm gear.

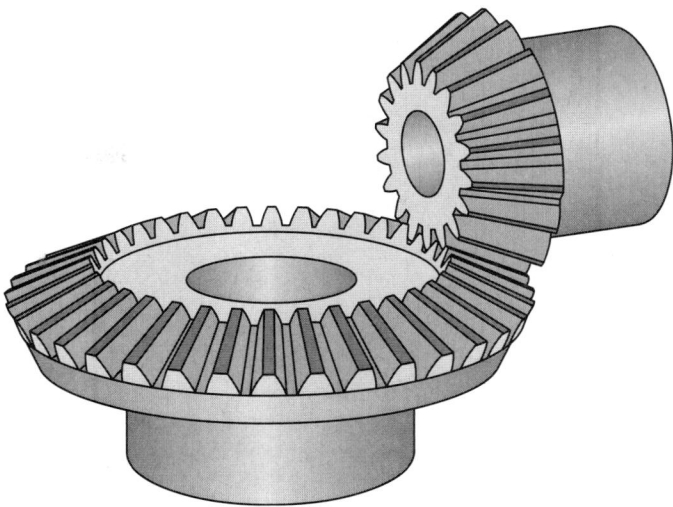

FIGURE 52-10 Plain bevel gears are not often used as they are inherently noisy and weaker than other designs.

FIGURE 52-11 Spiral bevel gears commonly used in Mack drive axles.

FIGURE 52-12 Durapoid spiral bevel gearing used by Mack. Notice the sheer face of the tooth on the drive flank and the more angled face on the coast side. This design adds strength.

pinion gear is rotated by the drive line and drives the crown gear. The crown gear is attached to the **differential case**, which houses the differential gears. The differential gears connect to the axle shafts. Although their basic design is the same, several different types of bevel gears are used on heavy-duty trucks.

Plain Bevel Gears

Plain bevel gears, shown in **FIGURE 52-10**, have straight-cut teeth similar to the spur-type gearing discussed in the Basic Gearing Concepts chapter. Consequently, plain bevel gears are inherently noisy and only have one set of teeth in mesh at any time. That is, one tooth must carry the entire torque load. The plain bevel pinion gear is mounted at the centerline of the crown gear.

Spiral Bevel Gears

The next development in bevel gears was the **spiral bevel gear**. The teeth of a spiral bevel gear are cut in a spiral design. The spiral cuts improved on bevel gear sets much as helical gears improved on spur cut gears. That is, the design of spiral bevel gears increased torque capacity because more than one set of teeth were involved in torque transfer. Spiral bevel gearing can be seen in **FIGURE 52-11**.

Spiral bevel gears also reduce the noise associated with plain bevel gearing because of the wiping or sliding effect of the tooth contact. Spiral bevel gears still have the pinion gear mounted at the centerline of the crown gear.

Durapoid Gearing

Durapoid gearing is a specially designed spiral bevel gear set designed to provide increased strength and load carrying capability. The durapoid tooth design, shown in **FIGURE 52-12**, implements non-symmetrical tooth flanks. While the drive side of the tooth has a relatively sheer face, the coast side of the tooth has a sloped face. The different faces create a buttress effect for the tooth and increase the load-carrying capability of the tooth.

FIGURE 52-13 In a hypoid gear set, the pinion is mounted below the centerline of the crown gear.

FIGURE 52-14 The amboid gear set has the pinion mounted above the crown gear centerline and, unlike the hypcid design, the tooth drive face side of the amboid crown gear is the concave, not the convex.

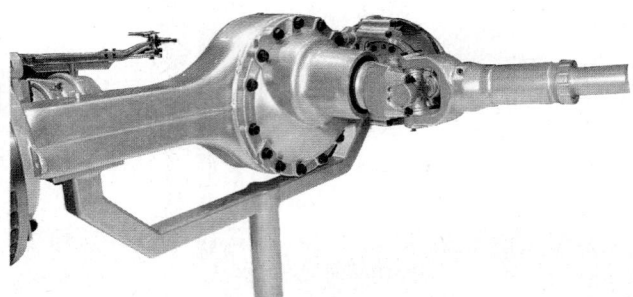

FIGURE 52-15 Detroit Deisel's topoid system places the pinion higher on the ring gear than an amboid system.

Durapoid tooth design also incorporates a centralized tooth contact pattern. Conventional gearing has a tooth contact pattern that spreads from the inside toward the outside of the tooth under load. By contrast, the centralized pattern of durapoid gearing eliminates the end loading of the tooth. As loads increase, the contact spreads out in both directions along the tooth face. The load is then distributed more evenly. In a durapoid gear set, the pinion is mounted on the centerline of the crown wheel. Mack trucks use durapoid gearing extensively.

Hypoid Gearing

Hypoid gearing is another form of bevel gearing. Hypoid gearing was developed to increase the strength of a normal spiral bevel gear and to lower the center of gravity of the vehicle. The hypoid gear set looks very similar to a spiral bevel set with one notable exception—on hypoid gears, the pinion gear is mounted below the centerline of the crown wheel, as can be seen in **FIGURE 52-13**. That difference explains how the teeth of hypoid gears achieve a deeper engagement on the pinion. More teeth are in contact—greatly increasing the strength of the gear set. Having the pinion mounted lower also allows the drive train package to be lowered and that, ultimately, lowers the vehicle's center of gravity.

The hypoid gear set is the most popular design in use today on heavy trucks. The primary drawback to hypoid gear sets is that the deeper mesh of the pinion gear leads to even higher friction between the gear teeth. The point at which the teeth of the crown gear and the pinion mesh is subjected to extreme pressure under load. That pressure necessitates the pinion and the crown gear to be rigidly supported. Even then, they still try to push each other apart.

To counteract this force, sometimes a thrust screw and block are mounted in the carrier at the back of the crown wheel at the point of the gear set contact. The thrust block is adjusted so under normal conditions it has a slight clearance from the back side of the crown gear. As the load is increased and the crown gear starts to flex away from the pinion, the crown gear contacts the thrust block, stopping its flexing so that it remains in mesh with the pinion.

Amboid

At first glance, **amboid gears** resemble hypoid but, on further inspection, it is clear that, on amboid gears, the pinion gear is mounted above the centerline of the crown gear. A second notable difference between amboid and hypoid is that the teeth on the crown gear are spiraled in the opposite directions. An amboid gear set is shown in **FIGURE 52-14**.

Both designs have their pinion gear teeth cut in the same direction. This means that, in the hypoid, the drive side of the crown gear teeth is the convex side. The opposite is true on amboid gears—the drive side of the crown gear teeth is the concave side. Like hypoid gearing, amboid gearing uses more than two teeth in contact to carry the torque load.

Amboid gearing was developed for use in special applications and is typically only found in the rear-rear axle of a tandem drive. Because the pinion is above the centerline of the crown gear, the input to the drive axle is higher, so the operating angles used on the connecting driveshaft universal joints can be smaller.

Topoid

Detroit Deisel introduced a style of drive axle in which the pinion position is even higher than in the amboid type. Detroit calls this system **topoid**. A topoid gear is simply a higher-mounted amboid system. **FIGURE 52-15** shows a topoid system. According to Detroit, the high design of the topoid system reduces driveline angles and vibration.

FIGURE 52-16 A generoid gear set with a sheer tooth face on the drive side and a sloped tooth face on the coast side.

FIGURE 52-17 The integral drive axle housing has the mounts for the drive axle bearings machined into it.

Generoid

The **generoid** gear design, also known as the **hypoid generoid**, is similar to the durapoid in that there is a sheer drive tooth face (the convex face) and a sloped or buttressed coast tooth face (the concave face).

The generoid, shown in **FIGURE 52-16**, uses an asymmetrical tooth with a sheer flank on the drive side and a sloped buttress on the coast side. The generoid gear set also uses a centralized contact pattern, eliminating tooth end loading. That design feature gives the hypoid generoid even more strength than the traditional hypoid design.

Like the durapoid, a distinguishing feature of the generoid gear set is its tooth contact pattern, which is centered on the crown gear tooth face. Recall that the regular hypoid set has a contact pattern that starts near the toe (the inside end) of the tooth face. Drive axle gear contact patterns are fully discussed in the Servicing and Maintaining Drive Axles chapter.

Even though some manufacturers use the generoid design, the hypoid gear set is still the more prevalent of the two. Because the power flow in all bevel gears is turning a 90-degree bend through the gear set, the load and friction created at the intersection of the bevel gear teeth is extreme.

A special lubricant must be used to combat the extreme friction created by bevel gears. Bevel gear lubricant has Extreme Pressure (EP) additives to prevent metal-to-metal contact of the bevel gear teeth.

Drive Axle Housings

Two general housing types are used for drive axles. The housings have one key point of differentiation—whether the carrier is removable. The **carrier** is the component that holds the support bearings for the drive axle gearing. When an axle has an **integral carrier housing**, shown in **FIGURE 52-17**, the carrier is not removable. The integral carrier housing is very popular in lighter-duty vehicles. In the integral carrier-type, the housing has all of the bearings supports machined into it. So the carrier is part of—or integral to—the housing. The drive axle gearing and bearings are accessed through a removable pan bolted to the back of the housing.

FIGURE 52-18 The banjo housing has the removable carrier bolted to it.

The second type of housing is the **removable carrier-type**. The removable carrier housing is also known as a **banjo** housing because the shape of the housing resembles a banjo with two necks. **FIGURE 52-18** shows a removable carrier housing. In this style, the entire carrier, with all of the gears and bearings, is bolted into the front of the housing. To access the gearing or bearing for repair, the entire carrier is removed from the housing.

In vehicles with four- or six-wheel rear drive, all the drive axles are interconnected by power dividers that split the torque between the available drive wheels. Power dividers are discussed in greater detail later in the chapter in the Power Divider Components section. In vehicles with front-wheel drive, the front drive axle is connected by a transfer case that splits the power and torque between the front and rear axles. Transfer cases are covered in the Standard Transmissions chapter.

Functions of Differential Gear Sets

LO 52-2 Explain the design and functions of differential gear sets.

The term *differential* is used mistakenly by some technicians as a synonym for a drive axle because that is where the **differential gear set** is housed inside the axle. The drive axle gearing, as we know, is used to turn the power from the engine 90 degrees so it can be sent to the wheels and to provide a final gear reduction. The differential gears are a set of gears integral to the drive axle that are for a completely different purpose than the drive axle gearing. A differential gear set is shown in **FIGURE 52-19**.

FIGURE 52-19 The differential gear set is held in the differential case inside the drive axle.

FIGURE 52-21 The differential cross is sandwiched between the two case halves and, therefore, must turn with the case.

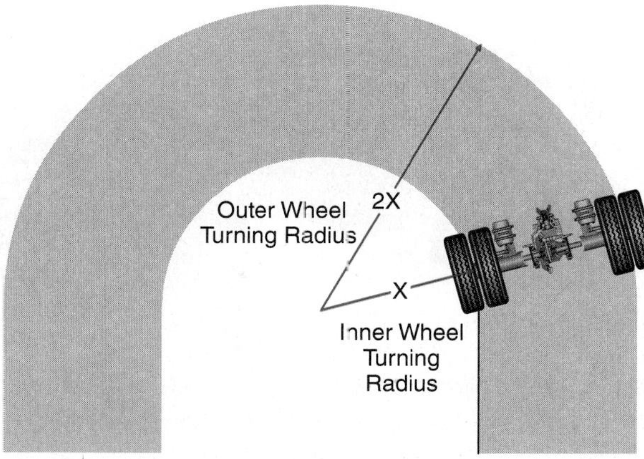

FIGURE 52-20 The wheel on the outside of an axle has to travel further than the wheel on the inside during a turn.

To illustrate the function of a differential gear set, let's consider a rear drive vehicle with four wheels—two steering and two driving. If the vehicle is traveling in a straight line, then all the wheels are turning at the same speed. (For the moment, we are ignoring any discrepancies in the tire sizes or irregularities in the terrain.)

When the vehicle comes to a turn, however, the situation changes. As the vehicle moves through a turn, the wheels on the inside of the turn have to turn slower than the wheels on the outside of the turn. This is because the wheels on the inside are closer to the apex of the turn than the wheels on the outside. This phenomenon is illustrated in **FIGURE 52-20**. The inside wheels follow a smaller curve than the outside and, therefore, travel a shorter distance.

The difference in turning radius presents no problems for the wheels on a non-drive steering axle, as they are not connected to each other and turn freely on their bearings. It is a different story for the rear wheels, however, because they are solidly connected to the vehicle drive line. Provisions must be made for them to turn at unequal speeds. This is where the differential gears come in to play.

Differential gears allow for the wheels to turn at unequal speeds. The differential gear set is a gear arrangement that allows the available power being delivered to the crown gear of the drive axle to be split exactly equally between two drive wheels.

The differential gear set simultaneously allows one wheel to turn faster or slower than the other when required. The need for unequal speeds is caused by vehicle turning, tire size mismatch, and uneven terrain. It is very important for the technician to understand that even though the wheels connected to the differential gear set can turn at different speeds, the torque being delivered to each is equal, even if one of the wheels is stopped, as in a spin-out situation.

The differential gears are contained inside the differential case. The crown or ring gear is bolted or riveted to the differential case. When the crown gear is turned by the drive axle pinion gear, the differential case, therefore, must turn with it. The differential case in heavy vehicles is made up of two halves—the flange half and the plain half—bolted together. The flange half is the side that has the crown gear attached to it. In heavy-duty vehicles, the two halves of the differential case sandwich a four-legged **differential cross** (also known as a **differential spider**) between them. The cross or spider legs are fitted into four holes bored into the differential case, as shown in **FIGURE 52-21**. Therefore, the cross always rotates with the differential case and the crown wheel. It is important to note that the differential case is line-bored for the cross legs when assembled, so before disassembling a case, mark the case halves so they can be reassembled correctly.

Inside the differential case are the actual differential gears. The typical differential gear set consists of four beveled **spider gears** (sometimes referred to as **differential pinion gears**) and two beveled **side gears**. The spider gears are fitted to the four legs of the differential cross, so they must rotate with it. The side gears are splined to the two axle shafts to drive the wheels. The side gears are in constant mesh with the differential spider gears. The differential spider gears and side gears normally have thrust washers between them and the differential case to reduce wear.

As the vehicle moves in a straight direction, the crown gear and the differential case rotate. As the case rotates, the spider gears basically drag the side gears along as the cross tumbles end over end with the case. In straight-line operation, when there is no speed difference between the wheels on either side of the vehicle, the differential gears are stationary in relation to the differential case. The differential gears are not rotating inside

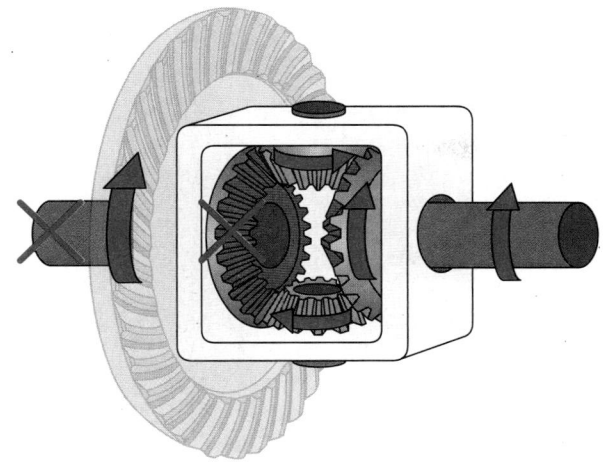

FIGURE 52-22 As the vehicle negotiates a turn, the inside side gear slows down and causes the spider gears to turn. The spider gears then transfer that motion to the other side gear, causing it to speed up.

FIGURE 52-23 Thrust washers absorb the heavy thrust loads caused by bevel gears.

the case. They are merely acting as a solid connection between the differential case and the two side gears and, therefore, the wheels.

The situation changes, though, when the vehicle starts to turn. When negotiating a turn, it helps to think of the vehicle centerline as the arc the vehicle must follow through the turn. Think of the arc in terms of the speed the differential case is turning through the turn. The wheel on the inside of the turn and its axle shaft and side gear are on a smaller arc than the centerline arc and so must turn at a slower speed than the differential case speed. At the same time, the wheel on the outside and its axle shaft and side gear are on a larger arc than the centerline and so must turn at a faster speed than the differential case. **FIGURE 52-22** illustrates these differences. As the vehicle negotiates a turn, the side gear splined to the wheel on the inside of the turn slows down and its teeth cause the spider gears to turn by the number of teeth that the side gear turns slower. The spider gear teeth then transfer that motion to the other side gear, causing it to speed up by the exact same amount so it turns faster.

The differential gear set allows this to happen because the spider gears can turn not only with the cross, but they can turn on the cross as well. As the inner wheel starts to slow down during the curve, its axle shaft and side gear automatically turn slower than the case and the spider gears. The spider gears start to walk around the slower moving inner side gear. As they do so, the walking motion of the spider gears' teeth is transferred to the side gear on the outer side of the curve, automatically causing it to speed up by the exact same amount. This means the outer wheel speeds up by the same amount that the inner wheel slows down. The power being sent to each wheel is still exactly equal, but the wheels can turn at different speeds when needed. There is no lost motion through differential gears—the outer gear always speeds up by the exact amount that the inner gear slows down.

In any driving situation, when we add the speed of each of the two axles together, the total always equals 200% of case speed—no matter how much the difference in speed is. For example, on negotiating a turn, if the inner wheel, axle shaft, and side gear slow down to 96% of the differential case speed, that means that the outer wheel, axle shaft, and side gear must increase in speed to 104% of case speed to compensate. This compensation is automatic and occurs without any driver or vehicle action.

If a vehicle were built without a differential, the wheel speed differences on turns would cause the axle shafts to "wind up" in different directions during turns. The resultant twisting forces would lead to serious fatigue failures of the axle shafts. It is very important to note that the difference in wheel speed encountered in normal vehicle operation is usually very slight. For example, in a drive of 1000 miles (1600 km), with 10% being curves, the total rotation of the differential side gears is very small—probably 100 to 200 revolutions for the whole 1000 mile (1600 km) trip.

The rotation between the differential gears also occurs relatively slowly and, therefore, normally there is little wear between the case and the gears. Consider that at 60 mph (96 kph) an average truck wheel turns approximately 500 times a minute as it travels in a straight line. On most curves at that road speed, the wheel speed difference is in the neighborhood of 4%, meaning that the rotation of each side gear occurs at around 10 rpm. Because of the relatively slow speed and small distance that they turn, side gears and spider gears do not have to be supported by bearings and run steel-on-steel. Certain models may have friction bearings (bushings) to support the spider gears, but in most cases the spider gears are simply made of hardened steel and have no bushings. The differential side and spider (pinion) gears normally have steel thrust washers separating them from the differential case, as shown in **FIGURE 52-23**.

In normal operation, differential gears should have a long and sturdy life expectancy. Driver abuse, however, can cause them to wear prematurely. The prime example of abuse is spinning one wheel wildly while in slippery conditions. Drivers may think that "burning" out a stuck vehicle by spinning the tires is a harmless strategy when needed. Doing so, however, causes the differential gears to spin at extreme speeds inside the case. Because they are not built for that kind of operation, they fail rapidly, and the damage can cost thousands of dollars to fix.

FIGURE 52-24 Spider gear damaged by the heat generated from spinning out.

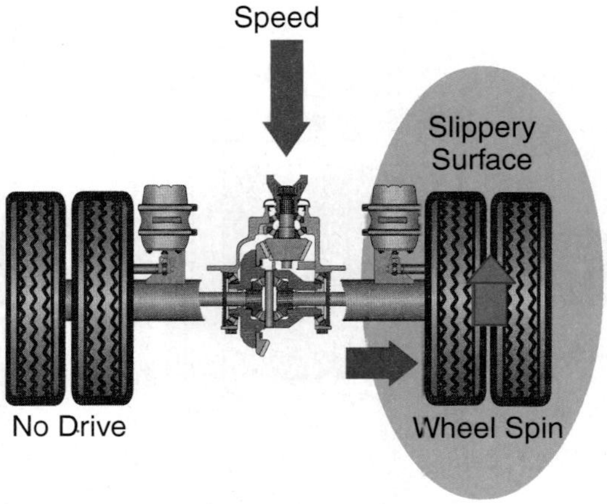

Speed

Slippery Surface

No Drive

Wheel Spin

FIGURE 52-25 A wheel on a slippery surface does not provide much resistance, so little torque is generated. In a spin-out condition, the spinning wheel, its axle shaft, and its side gear are turning twice as fast as the differential case.

Recall that the speed of each wheel and side gear added together equals twice the speed of the differential case. When one wheel is stationary, the other spinning wheel and its axle shaft and side gear are traveling at twice the differential case speed, the spider gears are spinning wildly as well, and the case is revolving around the stationary side gear at case speed. This kind of abuse can cause a lifetime of normal wear in only a few seconds! Never allow one wheel to spin uncontrollably. The damage may not be immediately noticeable, but it is there, and the useful life of the differential gear set is reduced. The spider gear pictured in **FIGURE 52-24** has been damaged by spinning one wheel of a differential. The gear has been alternately welded to and broken away from its cross leg by the heat caused by spin out, as is evidenced by the metal transfer inside its bore. It is hard to imagine the amount of heat that was generated to cause this damage.

Types of Differential Gear Sets

LO 52-3 Describe the various types of differential gear sets.

All differential gear sets perform the same function in the vehicle. Just because they perform the same function does not mean that all differentials are identical, however. There are, in fact, several types. Controlled traction, locking, biased torque (proportional), double reduction, and inter-axle differentials are the main types of differential gear sets. This section describes them all in more detail.

Controlled Traction and Locking Differentials

The major benefit of a differential is that it allows wheels to rotate at different speeds, when necessary. Unfortunately, that benefit is also its major drawback. During low traction conditions, the wheel that has the least traction spins wildly, as mentioned in the previous section. When this spinout condition is observed, it can lead a person to think that the differential is sending all of the power to one wheel only, but this is not the case. Think of it this way: If a bolt is loosely installed and the technician attempts to torque it to specification with a torque wrench, it quickly becomes apparent that it is impossible to

build any torque until the bolt starts to tighten in its bore. Without resistance, the bolt merely turns freely.

The same is true for the powertrain of a vehicle. In order for the engine to build torque, there must be some resistance to motion, such as the load of the vehicle. When a wheel is on a slippery surface, the engine can only build as much torque as is required to make the wheel slip. Once the wheel loses traction, the torque required to keep it spinning is even less, as illustrated in **FIGURE 52-25**.

The differential gear set is still dividing the available torque equally between the two driving wheels, but the small amount of torque needed to keep the wheel spinning is not sufficient for the wheel with good traction to move the vehicle.

In order to overcome this drawback of differential gears, engineers have developed several controlled traction and locking differentials.

Controlled Traction Differentials

A **controlled traction differential** allows the engine to build more torque before the wheels can slip. There is some form of resistance that must be overcome before the side gears can move inside the differential case. Most commonly, this resistance to motion is provided by a spring-loaded clutch pack.

In a controlled traction differential, such as the one shown in **FIGURE 52-26**, a series of friction plates are splined to a movable spline that slides along one axle shaft. The spline has clutching teeth to engage matching teeth on one of the side gears. There is also a series of reaction plates, which are splined or lugged to the differential case. These two sets of plates are interleaved to form a clutch pack similar to the clutch packs found in automatic transmissions. Instead of being hydraulically applied, though, these clutch packs are permanently loaded by springs that pressurize the clutch pack or packs. The spline can be made to engage the side gear by using an air or electric shifter. This allows the controlled traction to be engaged or disengaged as required. Some installations have the controlled traction permanently engaged.

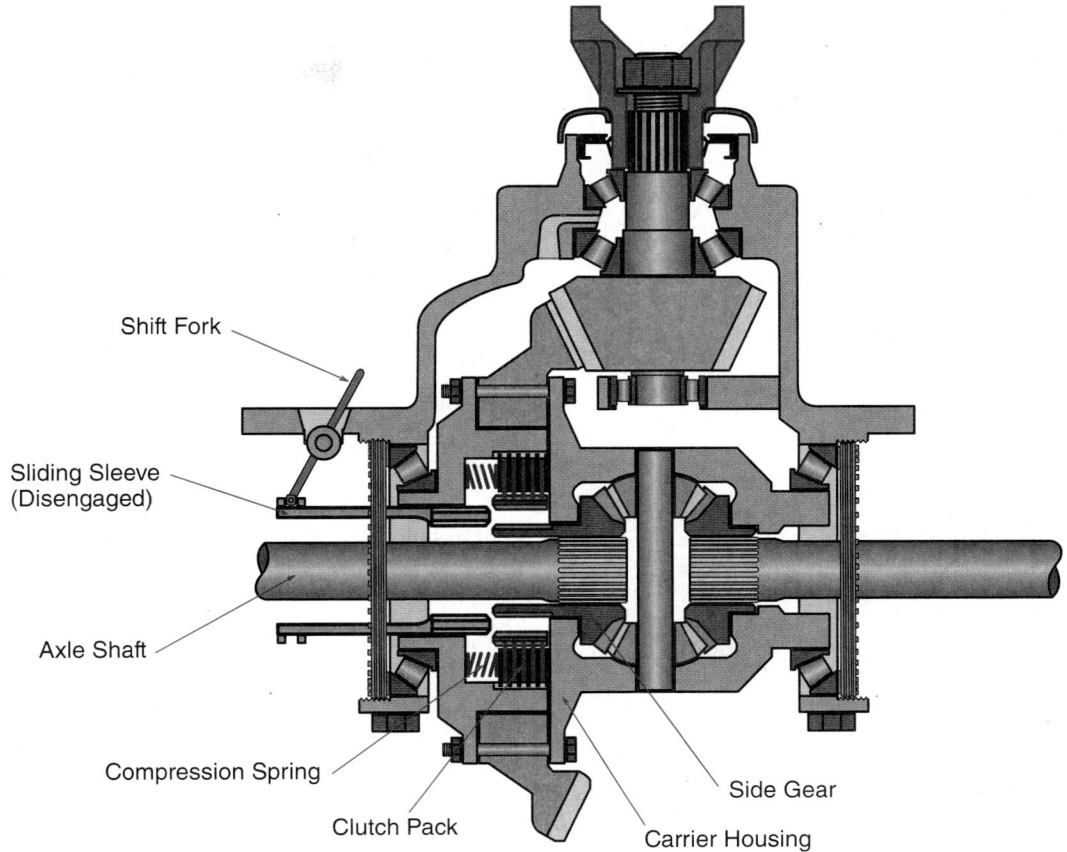

Shift Fork

Sliding Sleeve
(Disengaged)

Axle Shaft

Compression Spring

Clutch Pack

Side Gear

Carrier Housing

FIGURE 52-26 Controlled traction differentials, when used, only allow wheel slip after the engine builds enough torque to cause the clutch plates to slip. This amount of torque is engineered to be enough to move the loaded vehicle, as long as one wheel has sufficient traction. Some controlled traction differentials are driver selectable, like the one illustrated here.

The purpose of this controlled traction arrangement is to provide resistance that must be overcome before the side gear can rotate inside the case. This resistance is easily overcome by the twisting forces on the axle shafts during turns. In slippery conditions, the resistance causes more torque to build before a wheel can start slipping. The controlled traction differential is carefully designed so that the amount of torque necessary to cause the wheels to slip is more than is required for one wheel with good traction to overcome the vehicle load and move the vehicle forward. Other designs of controlled traction differentials use a spring-loaded cone clutch design on the side gears rather than clutch plates, but they are similar in operation.

Locking Differentials

Locking differential systems actively prevent differential action from occurring when engaged. Heavy-duty locking differentials can be engaged or disengaged by the vehicle operator, when required. These locking differentials should only be used when the vehicle encounters a low traction condition that may allow one wheel to spin. When activated, these systems prevent one side gear from turning, which stops any movement of the spider gears in the differential. This means that the second side gear cannot move either.

Most heavy-duty designs of locking differentials incorporate the following features:

- One axle shaft has a second spline after the spline that engages the side gear.
- Mounted on this spline is a sliding clutch or collar.
- The sliding clutch or collar has clutching teeth on the side that faces the differential case.
- The differential case has clutching teeth that match those on the sliding clutch or collar.

The gear is moved by a shift fork that is air or electrically operated. When the lock is disengaged, as shown in **FIGURE 52-27A**, the differential operates normally. When the driver encounters low-traction conditions, he can engage the lock. At that point, the sliding clutch or collar engages the clutching teeth on the differential case, as shown in **FIGURE 52-27B**. This effectively locks the axle shaft to the case. Because the axle shaft is also splined to the side gear, the side gear cannot rotate in the case, and that prevents any differential action from occurring. Remember that for one side gear to rotate, the other must rotate in the opposite direction. Therefore, if one side gear cannot rotate, neither can the other.

FIGURE 52-27 A. Heavy-duty locking differential with the lock disengaged. **B.** Heavy-duty locking differential with the lock engaged.

FIGURE 52-28 Differential locks are usually applied by an air-actuated piston controlled by the driver using a dash-mounted switch.

The control switch for tandem vehicles can simultaneously control all three locks if equipped, both main differential locks and the inter-axle differential lock. Differential locks should in no circumstances be used or engaged when driving on dry pavement. Doing so stops differential action and can damage the drive axle.

Biased Torque (Proportional) Differentials

Several **biased torque differential** (also called **proportional differential**) systems have been developed that are capable of sending more torque to one wheel than the other when a wheel slip condition is encountered. That is, more torque is diverted to the wheel with good traction. Diverting torque in that way is commonly referred to as biasing torque. The most famous biased torque main differential is probably the **Torsen** differential by General Motors, which is illustrated in **FIGURE 52-29**.

The Torsen differential uses a torque biasing principle to send more torque to the wheel with good traction. These differentials have a resistance to rotation caused by gear interference. The resistance creates a bias effect and allows an increased amount of available torque—up to 6:1—to be sent to the wheel with good traction. Some models offer even higher torque biasing. If, however, one wheel is off the ground, no torque can be sent to the wheel with good traction. Logically, no torque can be created because there is no resistance (six times zero is still zero). For these vehicles to drive with a wheel off the ground, some resistance to rotation has to be introduced to the free wheel, otherwise no torque can be created.

Originally resistance was introduced by applying the vehicle's Antilock Brake System (ABS) brakes selectively on the wheel with no traction. Three to six times the torque could then be sent to the wheel with traction. Similar to a controlled traction differential, the Torsen 2R creates friction inside the case by forcing the side gear against the case to create some resistance. The differential then biases that available torque to move the vehicle using the wheel with good traction.

Eaton/Dana introduced a similar design called **TruTrac**, shown in **FIGURE 52-30**, and Auburn gear developed an electronically controlled bias torque differential using clutch packs that are electrically applied.

Provided there is no difference in wheel speed, the lock can be engaged at any time—whether the vehicle is moving or not. Locking the differential allows the vehicle to build enough torque to move the vehicle as long as one wheel has sufficient traction. The driver should only engage the lock during times of poor traction. As soon as possible, the driver should disengage the lock to allow the differential to resume its function of compensating for wheel speeds in turns and uneven tire sizes.

Most **differential locks** are air operated and consist of a differential lock switch on the dashboard, as shown in **FIGURE 52-28**. In most cases, the shifter mechanism for the lockout is spring-loaded to the unlocked position. When the lockout is engaged, air is directed to the shifter piston to engage the lock. Some tandem vehicles have multiple locks; for example, main differential locks and an inter-axle differential lock. The driver can engage the locks while stopped if he is ready to enter a low traction area or situation. Likewise, the driver can engage the locks while the vehicle is moving when conditions warrant, as long as no wheels are actually turning at different speeds or slipping. In order to engage the locks while driving, the driver merely flips the switch to lock while he maintains speed. Next, he releases the throttle momentarily and then resumes normal throttle operation. In a low-traction condition, when the wheels start to slip, the driver cannot engage the locks until the wheel slip stops, or severe damage could result. He has to release the throttle first to stop the wheel slip and then engage the locks before resuming normal throttle operation.

Torsen Gearset

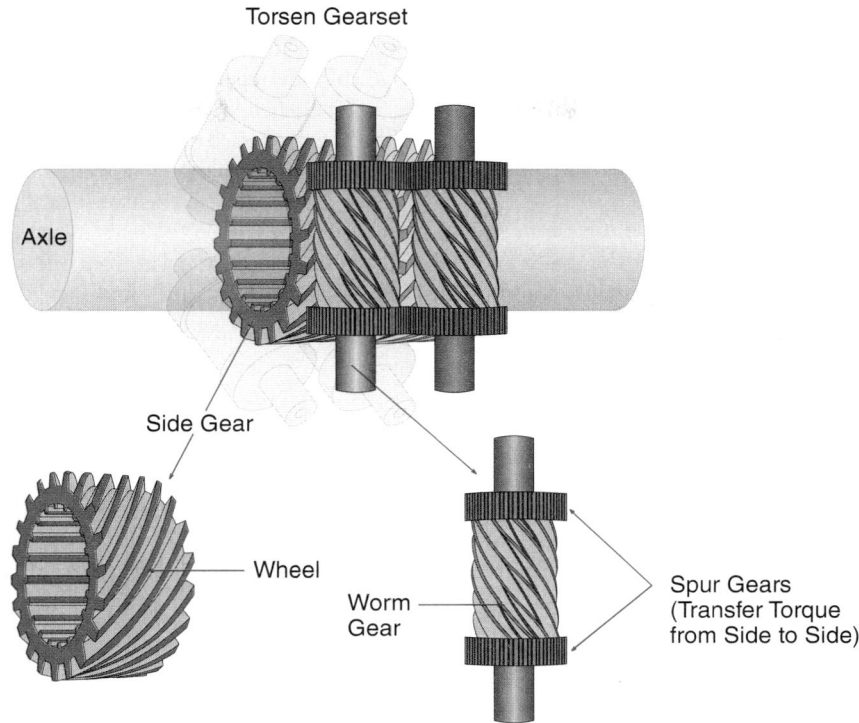

FIGURE 52-29 Biased torque or proportional differentials, like the Torsen differential shown here, sends more of the available torque to the wheel with good traction.

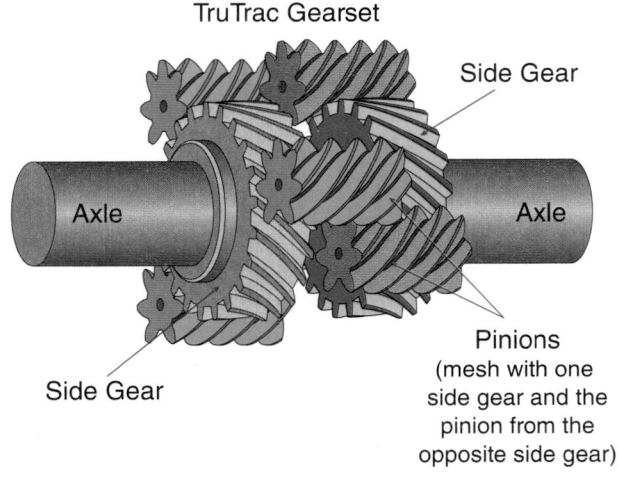

FIGURE 52-30 Eaton/Dana now supplies a differential called TruTrac that is available for medium-duty trucks.

Double Reduction and Multi-Speed Drive Axles

LO 52-4 Explain the design and operation of double reduction and multi-speed drive axles.

Drive axles are available in double reduction designs, double reduction two-speed, planetary double reduction, and planetary two-speed designs for different vehicle applications.

A drive axle that is called a **double reduction drive axle** uses two gear reductions at all times—meaning that the axle has one gear ratio multiplied by another to create the overall reduction through the axle. The first reduction is through the crown and pinion gears and the second is either through a set of helical gears (helical double reduction) or through a set of planetary gears (planetary double reduction).

Helical Double Reduction Drive Axles

A **helical double reduction drive axle** is a double reduction drive axle that uses a helical gear set for the second gear reduction. Although helical double reduction drive axles are not as common today as in the past, they are still used in some vehicles. Helical double reduction axles were developed for two reasons. First was to reduce the size of the crown gear and make it less likely to flex under load. The drive axle could then handle higher torque loads. The second reason was to reduce the overall size of the drive axle housing while still achieving a large overall reduction.

The first reduction in a helical double reduction drive axle consists of a small conventional crown and pinion gear set. The second reduction is accomplished by a set of helical gears. By using the two reductions together, we can achieve a large overall gear ratio with a much smaller drive axle package. Large crown gears tend to flex under heavy load as they try to move away from the pinion gear. A smaller-diameter crown gear helps to prevent this. The pinion is mounted in the drive axle as normal, but the crown gear is not attached to the differential case. Instead, the crown wheel drives a cross shaft mounted on bearings in the drive axle carrier that has a small helical gear (called the helical pinion gear) mounted on it. The helical pinion gear meshes with a much larger helical gear that is bolted to the differential case.

In this arrangement, the power flow goes through two reductions: one through the crown and pinion gear set and the other through the helical gear set. This compounds the overall reduction through the axle. A compound gear ratio is one where two or more reductions are used to increase the overall ratio. The final drive axle ratio is the product of the reductions (the two individual ratios multiplied together).

Double reduction helical drive axles are available in front-mount or top-mount designs, depending on the needs of the application. In a top-mount design, the crown and pinion gear set is mounted above the differential case. A front-mount design has the differential case mounted in line with and directly behind the crown and pinion gears. Front-mount designs allow for the entire drivetrain package to be lowered, thereby lowering the center of gravity of the vehicle.

Mack trucks quite commonly use a top-mount arrangement like the one pictured in **FIGURE 52-31**, to achieve a large double reduction. In these models, the banjo housing seems to have been turned on its back with the round side (usually facing rearward) pointing down.

Helical Double Reduction Two-Speed Drive Axles

Helical double reduction drive axles are also available as two-speed models. **Helical double reduction two-speed drive axles** use two selectable sets of helical gears as the second gear reduction. A helical double reduction two-speed drive axle is illustrated in **FIGURE 52-32**. The overall reduction is selectable

by the driver, effectively extending the operating ranges of the vehicle. This is accomplished by mounting two different-sized helical pinion gears on the cross shaft driven by the crown gear.

These helical pinion gears are in constant mesh with two large helical gears bolted to either side of the differential case. The helical pinions are not splined to the cross shaft and, therefore, are free to rotate on it. Between the two helical pinions is a sliding clutch or collar that is splined to the cross shaft. When the shift fork moves the sliding clutch or collar from one side to the other, it disengages one of the helical gear sets and engages the other. The fork is moved by an electric motor or an air shifter controlled by the driver.

FIGURE 52-31 Mack uses a top-mount design, double reduction drive axle quite extensively.

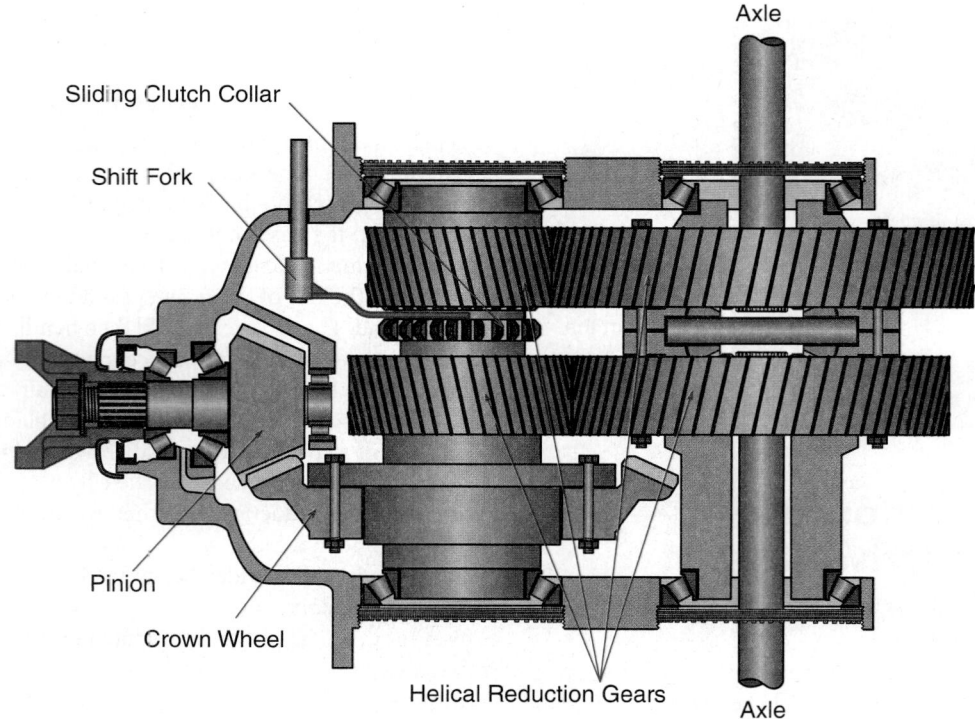

FIGURE 52-32 Helical double reduction two-speed drive axles are seldom seen today, but were quite common in the past.

Adding two-speed capability to a double reduction drive axle effectively doubles the transmission ranges available to the driver for vehicle and road conditions. The driver could use the two-speed drive axle as a split shift between ratios when, and if, necessary. Although the ratios available to the driver are potentially doubled with this arrangement, to take advantage of them the driver may have to perform an axle shift between each gear stick shift. The extra shift increases driver work load. Regardless of whether the double reduction two-speed is in high or low range, it always uses two reductions through the drive axle. The first reduction is through the crown and pinion gears and the second is through whichever helical gear set is engaged at the time.

Planetary Two-Speed and Planetary Double Reduction Axles

A **planetary two-speed drive axle**, as shown in **FIGURE 52-33**, uses a double reduction to achieve a low range ratio through the drive axle, and a single reduction in high range. The first reduction in low range is the normal crown and pinion gear. The second reduction in low range is a planetary gear set built into the crown wheel and the differential case. For high range, only the crown and pinion gears are used to achieve the ratio. As with double reduction helical drive axles, this setup allows transmission ranges to be split and potentially doubles the number of gear ratios available to the operator.

Some planetary two-speed drive axles, called dual-range drive axles, are set up to provide a low range that is typically used only for off-road or high torque operation. The axles shift

to high range for normal highway use. In a planetary drive axle, the crown gear has a set of internal teeth machined on its inner circumference. This becomes the ring gear of the planetary gear set. A housing is bolted to the crown gear instead of the differential case, and the differential case is able to rotate inside this housing.

The planetary two-speed drive axle differential case, shown in **FIGURE 52-34**, has four legs to hold the planetary pinion gears. The differential case, then, actually becomes the carrier of the planetary gear set. The sun gear is a hollow gear mounted in such a way that its teeth are constantly in mesh with the planetary pinions held on the differential case legs. Bolted to the side of the differential case on the outside of the planetary pinions is the high-speed plate. It has teeth cut on its inside surface that match the teeth on the sun gear. The sun gear has another set of clutching teeth machined on its outer edge. These clutching teeth match a set of clutch teeth machined into the inside circumference of the side bearing adjuster on that side of the drive axle. The sun gear also has a groove to accept a shift fork, which can move the sun gear in or out using an electric motor or an air shifter.

The operation of the two-speed planetary drive axle is quite simple. In high range, the shift fork moves the sun gear outward, as shown in **FIGURE 52-35A**, which disengages the clutching teeth from the bearing adjuster and slides the outer end of the sun gear teeth into mesh with the high-speed plate bolted to the planetary carrier (the differential case). The sun gear teeth are still in mesh with the planetary pinions as well.

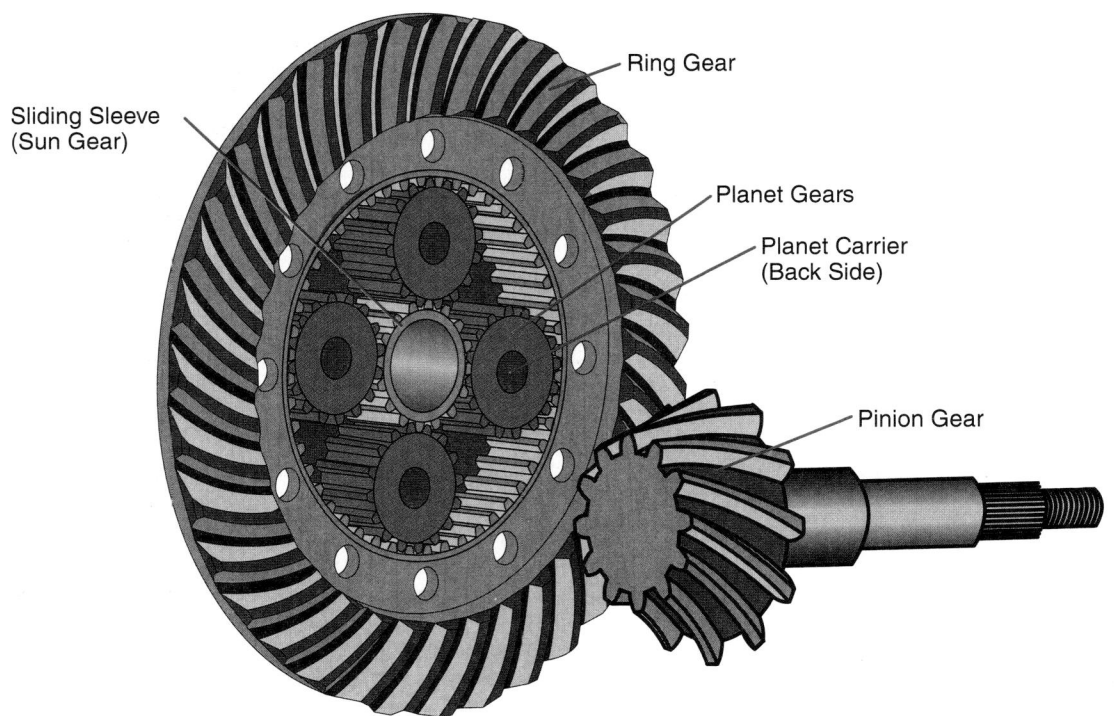

FIGURE 52-33 Planetary drive axles use a planetary gear to create two-speed capability.

FIGURE 52-34 A planetary two-speed drive axle showing the ring gear A, sun gear clutching teeth B, sun gear C, The high speed plate D, carrier pinions E and the differential gear set cross F.

FIGURE 52-35 A. For high speed, the sun gear is moved outward so the sun gear engages the teeth in the high-speed plate. **B.** The sun gear is moved inboard for low range, locking the sun gear's clutching teeth to the bearing retainer so it cannot turn.

The **high range** power flow is as follows:

- The drive axle pinion gear brings rotational power to the crown gear.
- The ring gear machined on its inner circumference transfers that rotation to the planetary pinions mounted to the differential case.
- The sun gear is now splined to the carrier through the high-speed plate.
- The planetary pinions cannot rotate, so the ring gear drives the carrier (the differential case) at the same speed as the crown gear.

When low range is selected by the operator, the shifter fork moves the sun gear to an inboard position, shown in **FIGURE 52-35B**. This causes its clutching teeth to engage with the clutching teeth on the bearing adjuster and hold the sun gear stationary. The power flow is as follows:

- The drive axle pinion gear brings rotational input to the crown gear.
- The ring gear, machined on the inner circumference of the crown gear, transfers the input to the planetary pinion gears attached to the legs of the differential case.
- The planetary pinions are forced to rotate around the stationary sun gear.
- The planet pinions drive the carrier (the differential case) at a speed roughly one-third slower than the crown gear's rotation.

FIGURE 52-36 shows a cutaway view of the sun gear's position for both high range (A) and low range (B). In certain vocations, a vehicle's planetary drive axle may be permanently fixed in low range by replacing the shift motor with a holding plate. This axle then becomes known as a **planetary double reduction drive axle**. The planetary double reduction always uses the two reduction through the drive axle, hence the double reduction part of its name. Planetary double reduction axles are usually only found in off-road vocational trucks. A planetary double reduction drive axle can easily be converted to a planetary two-speed by installing a shift motor and providing the necessary control circuit for the operator to control the sun gear's position.

Axle Shift Control

There are two methods of control for shifting dual range or two-speed drive axles—air and electric. In both systems, the driver has a control switch to select the different speeds. The driver may use the axle speeds as a supplement to the gear shift ratios, when necessary, based on load and terrain factors. In some cases, the driver may not need to use it at all.

Electric Shift Control

An electric shifter, shown in **FIGURE 52-37**, uses an electric motor to move the shift fork to select high and low range. The

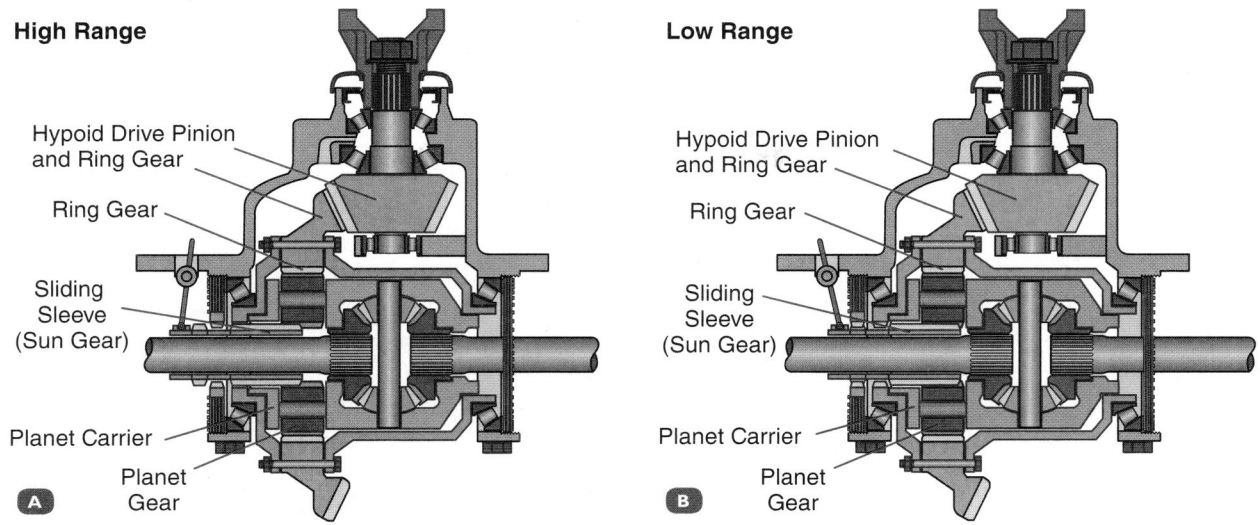

High Range

Hypoid Drive Pinion and Ring Gear

Ring Gear

Sliding Sleeve (Sun Gear)

Planet Carrier

Planet Gear

A

Low Range

Hypoid Drive Pinion and Ring Gear

Ring Gear

Sliding Sleeve (Sun Gear)

Planet Carrier

Planet Gear

B

FIGURE 52-36 A. High range with the sun gear positioned outward and locked to the high-speed plate. In this position, the power from the crown gear is transferred directly to the differential case. **B.** Low range with the sun gear positioned inward and locked stationary to the bearing retainer clutch plate. In this position the sun gear cannot turn and the power flows through the planetary gear set to the differential case.

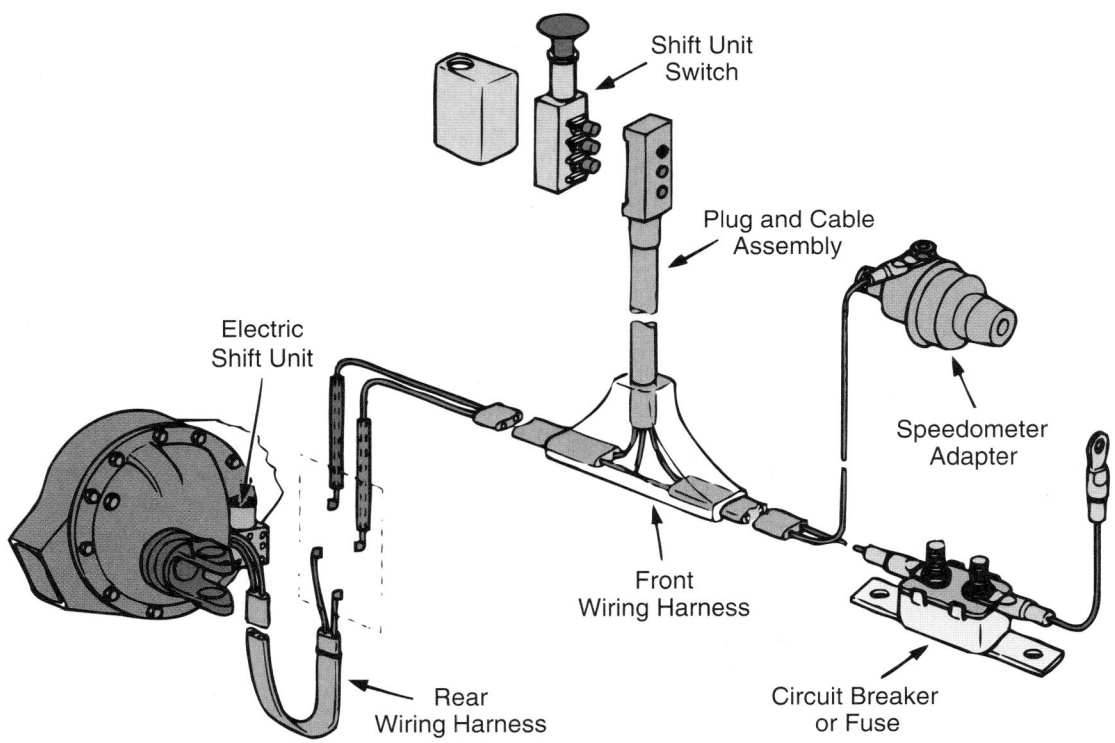

Shift Unit Switch

Plug and Cable Assembly

Electric Shift Unit

Speedometer Adapter

Front Wiring Harness

Rear Wiring Harness

Circuit Breaker or Fuse

FIGURE 52-37 The driver controls the drive axle range shift by using the high–low switch on the gearstick.

electric shift unit is attached to the drive axle housing and contains the following items:

- The motor itself
- A worm gear set
- A slider unit that moves the shift fork
- A control circuit with two switches a resistor and a diode

External to the electric shift unit are the following:

- A wiring harness
- A driver-operated control switch, usually mounted on the gear shift lever
- A speedometer adapter if the vehicle has a transmission-driven speedometer

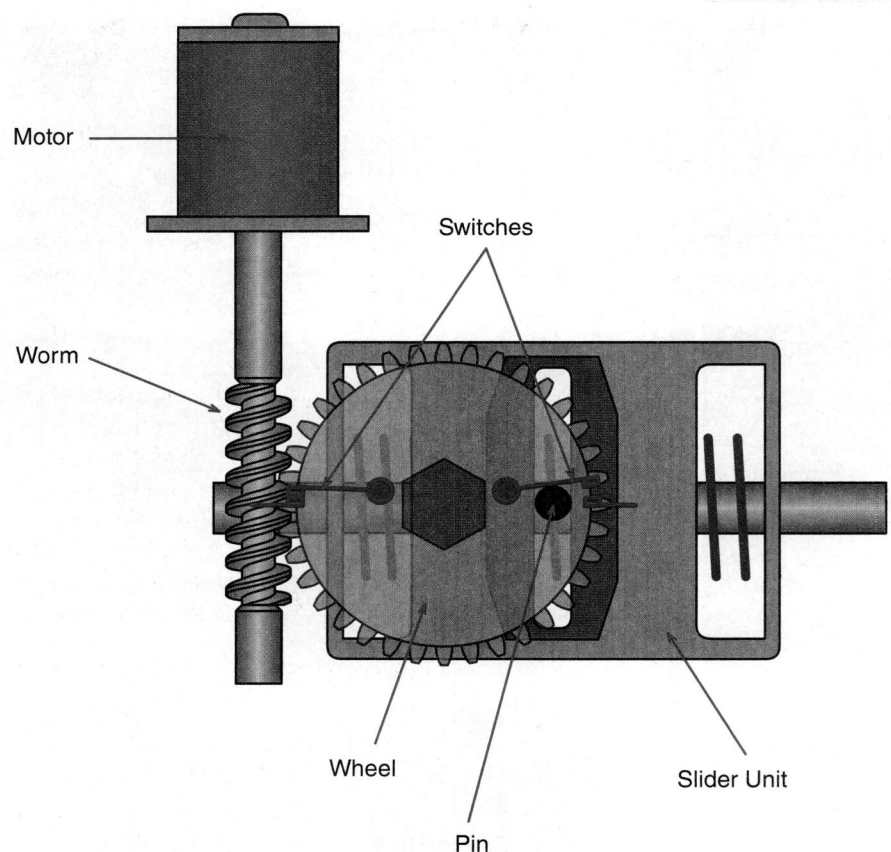

FIGURE 52-38 The pin on the worm wheel opens the circuit when high or low range is achieved.

When the driver requests a shift, the control switch sends power through the high-range switch. That turns the worm drive. The rotating worm wheel moves the slider unit and the shift fork to high range. A pin on the worm wheel, shown in **FIGURE 52-38**, contacts the high-speed switch. The switch opens and the motor stops as high range is achieved.

For low range, the control switch sends power through the low-range switch, again causing the motor to turn the worm drive. The rotating worm wheel now causes the slider unit and the shift fork to move back to the low-range position until a second pin on the worm wheel contacts the low-range switch. When that happens, the switch opens and stops the rotation of the motor.

Regardless of whether the shift unit is moving toward high or low range, the control circuit allows a second path to ground through the resistor. That ground circuit ensures that the motor stops abruptly when the range is reached. A diode in the low-range circuit stops the speedometer adapter from being powered through the resistor circuit when in high range. The speedometer adapter corrects the speed signal to the speedometer when the vehicle is in low range.

Air Shift Control

Air shift systems, like the one shown in **FIGURE 52-39**, are much simpler than electric. Air shift systems consist of a shift motor unit attached to the drive axle. The shift unit contains a piston, a strong return spring, and a mechanism to engage the shift fork in the drive axle.

External to the shift unit are the following components:

- Air lines
- An air control switch (usually attached to the shift lever)
- A control solenoid
- A quick-release valve
- A speedometer adapter if the vehicle has a transmission-driven speedometer; most vehicles with electronic controls do not need a speedometer adapter.

The control solenoid is turned on when the ignition switch is on, allowing air to flow into the control circuit from the vehicle air tanks. Air flows to the control switch on the shift lever. When the driver places the control switch in the low-range position, the air flow is stopped at the control switch. When the driver selects high range, air flows through the switch and the quick-release valve to the shift unit. Air pushes against the piston and the piston then moves the mechanism attached to the shift fork. The drive axle shifts to high range.

When the driver shifts back to low range, the air flowing through the control valve is cut off. The air in the line to the quick-release valve exhausts at the control switch. This causes the quick-release valve to exhaust the air going to the shift control unit such that the return spring forces the piston and the shift mechanism back to the low-range position. The key-on control solenoid assures that the drive axle shifts to low range when the key is turned off. If the vehicle has a speedometer

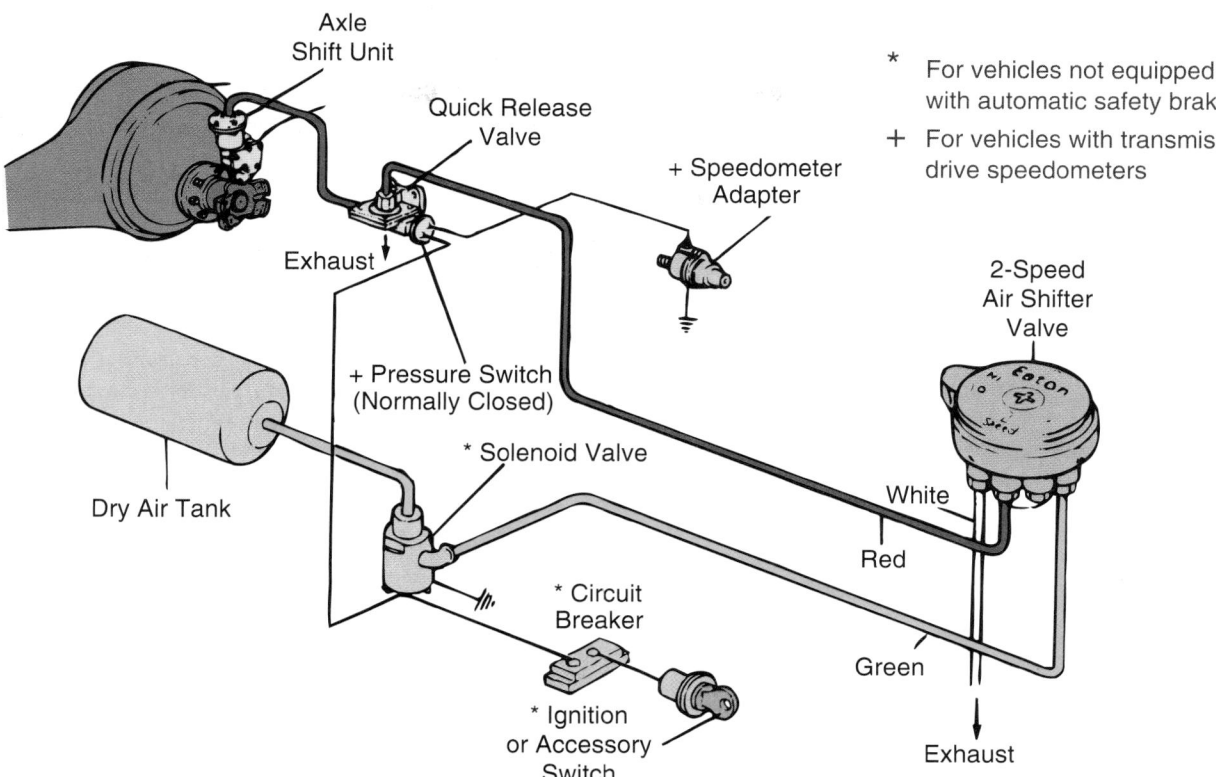

FIGURE 52-39 Air shift systems usually contain a quick release valve so that shifts occur faster.

adapter, it is powered through a normally closed pressure switch that is opened when the drive axle shifts to high range. That means the adapter is used only in low range.

Inter-Axle Differentials (Power Dividers)

LO 52-5 Explain the operation of inter-axle differentials (power dividers).

As engine Horsepower (HP) and torque ratings steadily increased over the years, trucks became capable of carrying heavier payloads. This necessitated the use of more than one drive axle to help spread the vehicle weight. Tandem drives are now the rule, rather than the exception, in Class 8 tractors, such as the one shown in **FIGURE 52-40**. Tandem drives are increasingly popular in straight truck applications as well. Some Class 8 vehicles even have tridem drive axles with three interconnected drive axles all sharing the work of propelling the vehicle.

Tandem and tridem drive arrangements must allow for differences in axle speeds between the drive axles. Speed differences can be caused by mismatched tire sizes or wear conditions, irregular road surfaces, and turning radius differences. An inter-axle differential accommodates these speed differences.

An **inter-axle differential**, also called a **power divider**, works in the same way as a drive axle differential. Instead of equally splitting the available torque to each wheel end, however, it splits the torque between two drive axles. At the same time, the differential allows the axles to turn at different speeds, when required.

FIGURE 52-40 Tandem drives are now the norm for Class 8 vehicles.

The inter-axle differential is contained in the front drive axle of a tandem drive. A power divider, such as the one shown in **FIGURE 52-41**, is commonly used in the trucking industry to accommodate wheel speed differences. A power divider combines an inter-axle differential gear set and a regular crown-and-pinion gear drive axle with its own differential gear set.

As its name suggests, the power divider allows the power from the vehicle drive line to be equally split between the front-rear drive axle and the rear-rear drive axle of a tandem. Even as it splits the power, the power divider allows the axles to rotate at different speeds. A tridem drive consists of three interconnected drive axles, so it requires two power dividers—one in the front and one in the center drive axle positions. The final or rear-rear drive axle of the tandem or tridem has a normal drive axle arrangement with a regular differential for wheel speed differences.

Power Divider Components

The power divider has several components, as illustrated in **FIGURE 52-42**:

- The input shaft
- The helical drop gears
- The front side gear (usually part of the upper helical drop gear)
- The rear side gear (usually part of the output shaft)
- The output shaft
- The inter-axle differential with its case, as well as cross and spider gears
- The crown-and-pinion gear set (driven by the helical drop gears)
- The wheel differential and case with its side and spider gears

In addition, the power divider is also likely equipped with a lube pump and an inter-axle differential locking mechanism.

These components work together. The vehicle drive shaft is connected to the input shaft of the power divider and it is splined to the cross of the inter-axle differential. The cross rotates with the input shaft and delivers power in equal quantities to the front and rear side gears of the inter-axle differential. The front side gear is part of the upper helical drop gear, like the one pictured in **FIGURE 52-43**. The **helical drop gear** drives the pinion gear of the front drive axle of a tandem. The input shaft passes through this gear but is not attached to it. The gear rides on a bushing or bearing on the input shaft. The upper helical drop gear is in mesh with the lower helical drop gear which, in turn, is splined to the pinion gear of the front drive axle of the tandem. When the axle rotates, power is transferred to the crown gear and then to the wheel differential

FIGURE 52-41 Power dividers allow for the drive axles of a tandem to turn at different speeds while splitting the available driving torque equally between them.

FIGURE 52-43 Notice the spline in the inter-axle differential cross. All of the input torque is delivered through the hollow front side gear to the cross.

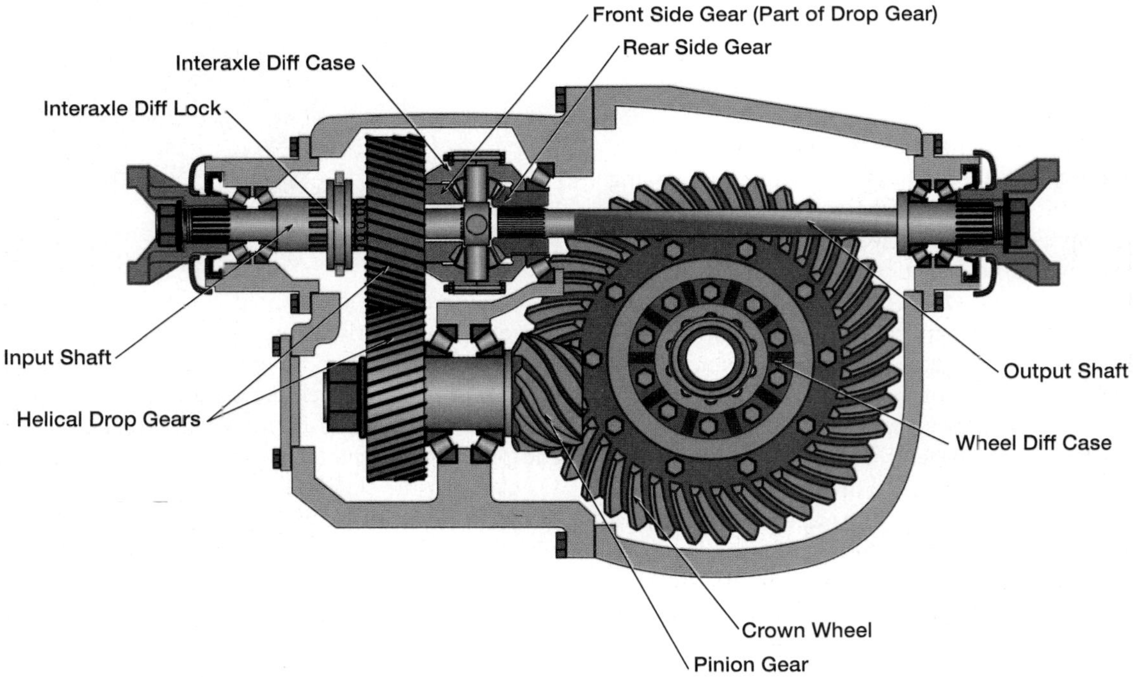

FIGURE 52-42 The major power divider components.

case. At that point, the power is split again, through the differential gears, between the two drive wheels of the axle.

The rear side gear is part of or splined to the **output shaft** (or **through shaft**), like the one pictured in **FIGURE 52-44**. Half of the power from the inter-axle differential cross is transferred to the rear side gear and the output shaft. The output shaft exits the rear of the power divider housing and connects to a short driveshaft which, in turn, connects to the rear-rear drive axle pinion gear.

The power is then split at the rear-rear drive axle differential to the rear two driving wheels. In this way, each of the four driving wheels receives exactly 25% of the available power.

In straight-ahead driving with tires of equal size, that is the extent of the power divider operation. As the vehicle turns or when tire sizes are mismatched, however, the situation changes. The power divider must allow each drive axle to turn at different speeds. The power divider performs two functions. It allows two drive axles to rotate at different speeds, when necessary, while still splitting the available torque and power between them equally.

The inter-axle differential of the power divider is the key to this ability. The input shaft of the power divider is splined to the cross of the inter-axle differential only. The cross contains the four differential spider gears—one on each cross leg. The gears and the cross are assembled into a case. As the cross rotates, the spider gears essentially drag the two side gears along. The spider gears are also capable of rotating on the cross when necessary, allowing the two side gears to rotate at different speeds when required by the driving situation. When one of the two axles of the tandem is turning slower than the other due to mismatched tires, turning, or road surface variations, the side gear driving the slower moving axle slows down slightly, and the spider gears in the inter-axle differential begin to turn. The rotation of the spider gears causes the side gear that drives the other axle of the tandem to speed up. The differential still splits power equally, but the drive axles are

allowed to turn at different speeds when required. Remember that, by design, there should be only a very slight speed difference between the two axles. For that reason, it is important that tires be matched to within 1/8" (3.2 mm) of rolling radius or 3/4" (19.5 mm) rolling circumference between the front and rear drive axles of the tandem. Failure to match the tire sizes can lead to failure of the inter-axle differential due to excessive rotation. Even allowing a tire to become underinflated can lead to serious differences in the rolling radius and cause excessive wear on the differential gears.

Power dividers typically have an inter-axle differential lock similar to the ones found in the main differential. The lock can be engaged by the driver during low traction situations. Proper use of this lock is discussed in the Preventing Inter-Axle Differential Spinout section.

FIGURE 52-45 shows the power flow through a power divider's inter-axle differential with and without the inter-axle differential lock engaged.

FIGURE 52-44 The rear side gear of the inter-axle differential is splined to the through shaft, so half the available torque is sent to the rear drive axle of the tandem.

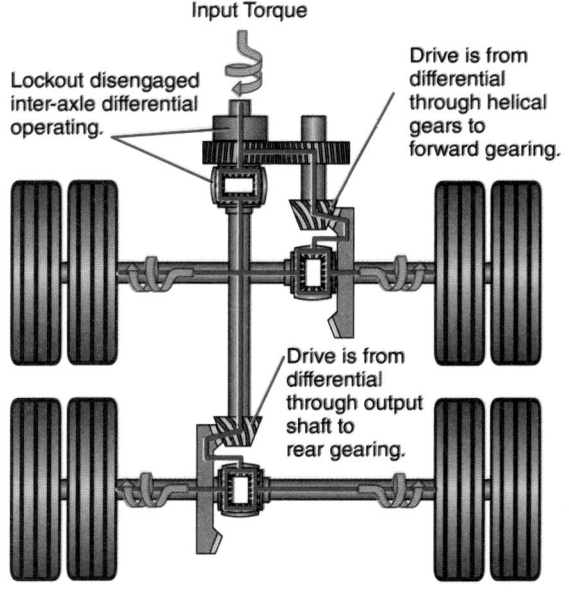

Torque is transmitted to both axles through inter-axle differential action.

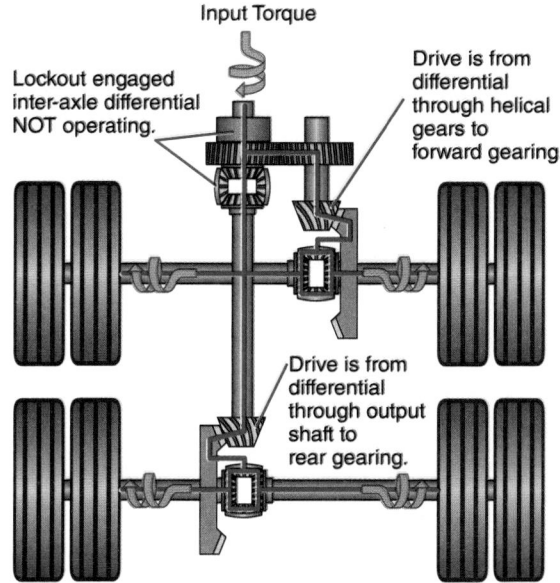

Torque is transmitted to both axles without inter-axle differential action.

FIGURE 52-45 Power flow through the inter-axle differential. Each wheel receives 25% of the available torque.

Proportional Differentials in Mack Trucks

Mack trucks have a uniquely designed proportional differential gear set, which can be used as a wheel differential or an inter-axle differential. When poor traction conditions are encountered, the Mack design, shown in **FIGURE 52-46**, can automatically send 75% of available torque to the drive axle wheels with the best traction.

The Mack differential uses a driving cage with 24 oval-shaped wedges that drive an inner and an outer cam using the cam and wedge principal. The inner cam drives the rear drive axle of the tandem and the outer cam drives the front drive axle of the tandem. In normal operation, the driving cage and the angular position of the wedges drive the two cams at equal speeds and the entire assembly rotates as a unit. When a low traction or an unequal speed situation occurs, one of the cams overruns (turn faster than) the driving cage. For example, if the rear drive axle loses traction, then its cam turns faster than the driving cage. That forces the wedges up and into the outer cam and transfers more torque to the front axle, as illustrated in **FIGURE 52-47**. If the situation is reversed and the front drive axle loses traction, the outer cam overruns the driving cage and forces the wedges down into the inner cam. More torque is transferred to the rear drive axle.

FIGURE 52-46 Mack trucks use a proprietary inter-axle differential capable of sending 75% of the available torque to the drive axle with more traction.

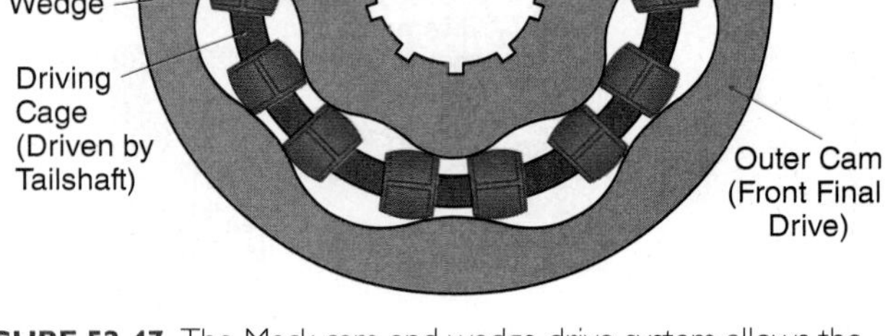

Simplified Cam and Wedge Power Divider

Inner Cam (Rear Final Drive)

Wedge

Driving Cage (Driven by Tailshaft)

Outer Cam (Front Final Drive)

FIGURE 52-47 The Mack cam and wedge drive system allows the cam attached to the drive axle with less traction to overrun. This forces the wedges into the other cam and sends more torque to the drive axle with traction.

Mack's ingenious system allows variable speeds between the two drive axles. At the same time, the system also allows up to 75% of the available torque to be applied to the axle with better traction. The Mack inter-axle differential also comes with a driver-operated differential lock. The lock is splined to the input shaft and has a series of clutching teeth that can engage matching teeth on the inside of the differential's outer cam. When the lock is engaged, the clutching teeth mesh. As that happens, it locks the outer cam to the input shaft so that the shaft and the cam must turn at the same speed. Because the wedges cannot move, they drag the inner cam along. Both drive axles then turn at the same speed and receive the same torque.

As with all differential locks, the Mack lock can be engaged at any time provided there is no axle slip occurring. The lock should only be used in poor traction conditions.

Preventing Inter-Axle Differential Spinout

Spinout, as mentioned previously, is a situation in which one wheel of a drive axle (or one drive axle of a tandem) loses traction and spins out of control while the other remains stationary. Spinout in an inter-axle differential is much more damaging as the differential travels at driveshaft speed, typically more than three times as fast as a main differential. Spinout can occur under three conditions:

- Starting on a slippery surface, such as ice, snow, loose gravel, mud, or wet conditions
- Driving in slippery conditions, such as climbing a hill in a snow storm; spinout in this situation can cause the driver to lose control of the vehicle
- Backing under a trailer

Backing under a trailer is a condition usually unique to tandem drives. As the driver tries to back under a trailer to hook up, the rear-rear axle becomes loaded first. If the conditions are not ideal, the front drive axle of the tandem can lose traction and spin out.

Careful use of the inter-axle differential locks can avoid spinout. Recall that in a single drive axle, spinout happens when a single wheel loses traction and spins wildly at twice normal speed while the other wheel is stationary. In a tandem drive, however, spinout usually occurs when one drive axle's wheels lose traction and spin wildly at twice normal speed while the second drive axle's wheels remain stationary. **FIGURE 52-48** illustrates this concept.

Spinout is very damaging to the inter-axle differential gears. Consider what occurs when a single drive axle spins out. Instead of just turning several revolutions per mile, one side gear is stationary, and the other is spinning at twice the speed of the case.

Spinout in an inter-axle differential is even more detrimental because it turns at a much higher speed. In a single drive axle spinout, the differential case is turning at a greatly reduced speed. That is because its drive comes through the reduction of the crown-and-pinion gears. In a tandem drive axle spinout, the inter-axle differential case rotates at driveshaft speed, or up to three to five times faster. Therefore, one side gear is turning at twice driveshaft speed, and the spider gears are going approximately twice as fast as that again!

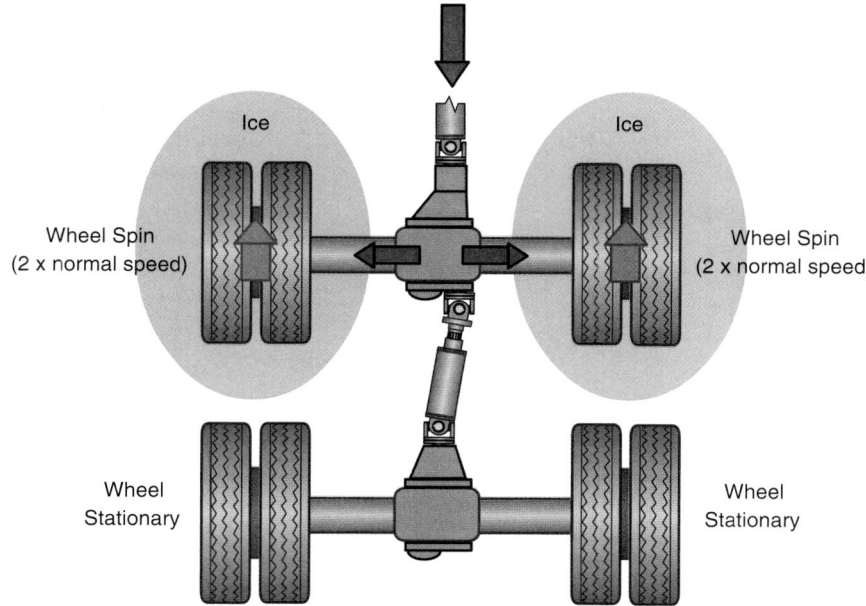

FIGURE 52-48 Tandem axle spinout can occur with one drive axle stationary and the other drive axle spinning at double normal speed.

As a result, most, if not all, inter-axle differentials are equipped with an inter-axle differential lock similar to the one shown in **FIGURE 52-49**, to prevent inter-axle spinout.

The lock is a sliding clutch splined to the input shaft just in front on the upper helical drop gear. The lock has a series of clutching teeth that match another series of clutching teeth on the drop gear. Remember that the helical drop gear is splined to or part of the front side gear of the inter-axle differential. The sliding clutch is moved by an air-operated motor that the driver controls. When the driver engages the lock, the sliding clutch locks the upper helical drop gear (and, therefore, the front inter-axle differential side gear) to the input shaft. The input shaft is splined to the inter-axle differential cross as well, so the cross and the front side gear must now turn at the same speed. Because the spider gears can no longer turn, the rear side gear cannot turn either; it must go along for the ride. All inter-axle differential action, therefore, stops, positively preventing spin-out from occurring.

FIGURE 52-49 The inter-axle differential lock is a sliding clutch that is splined to the input (indicated) shaft of the power divider. When engaged, it locks the front side gear to the input shaft.

As with the single drive axle differential lock, the inter-axle differential lock can be engaged at any speed provided no wheels are turning at different speeds or slipping. To engage the inter-axle differential lock, the driver follows the same procedure as for main differential locks. The lock can be engaged while stopped or while driving. While driving, the driver maintains speed while pushing the switch to engage the lock. The driver then releases the throttle momentarily to allow the lock to engage before resuming normal throttle operation. It is essential that the wheels are not slipping while engaging the lock or severe damage occurs.

Types of Axle Shafts

The axle shafts that actually drive the wheel come in two basic designs: semi-floating, shown in **FIGURE 52-50A**, and full floating, shown in **FIGURE 52-50B**. With **semi-floating axle shafts**, the outer end of the axle shaft supports the entire vehicle weight at the wheel end, as the wheel is bolted directly to the axle shaft flange. The inner end of the semi-floating axle shaft "floats" in the side gear. That is, the inner end of the axle carries none of the vehicle weight, hence the name semi-floating. Semi-floating axle shafts are used on light- and medium-duty vehicles only. Semi-floating axle shafts are unable to carry the weight of a heavy-duty truck and its cargo.

Heavier vehicles, including most on-highway trucks, use full-floating axle shafts exclusively. A **full-floating axle shaft** does not carry any of the vehicle weight on either end of the shaft. The inner end of a full-floating axle shaft floats in the side gear, while the outer end is bolted to the wheel hub. The wheel hub is mounted on two opposing tapered roller bearings. Those bearings are supported by the spindle, which is attached to the drive axle housing. Vehicle weight is transmitted through the frame to the springs to the axle housing and then through the bearing to the wheel hub and through the tire to the ground. Only vehicle torque is transmitted to the wheel hub through the axle shaft. Because the shaft carries none of the vehicle weight, it is known as full floating.

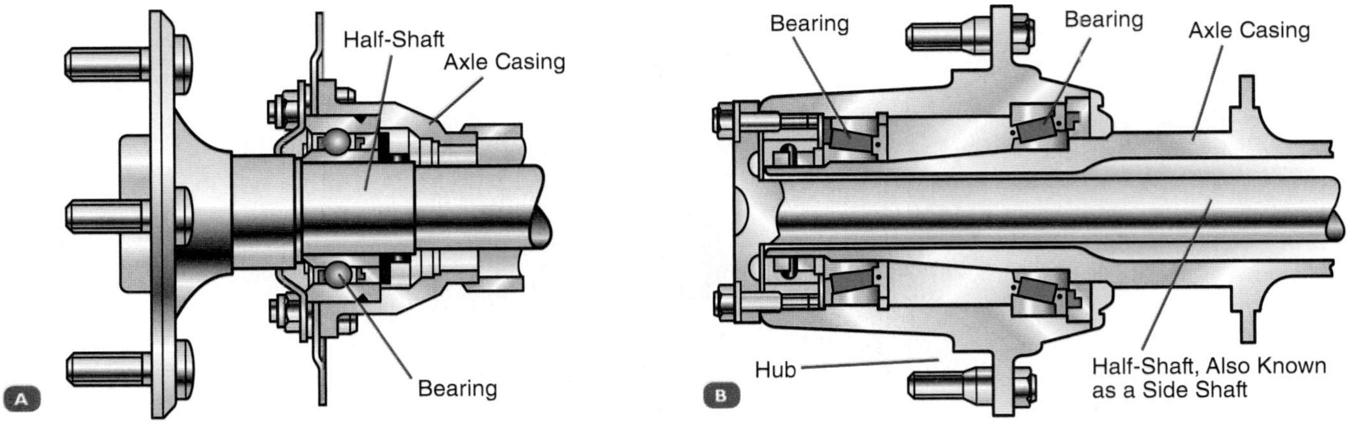

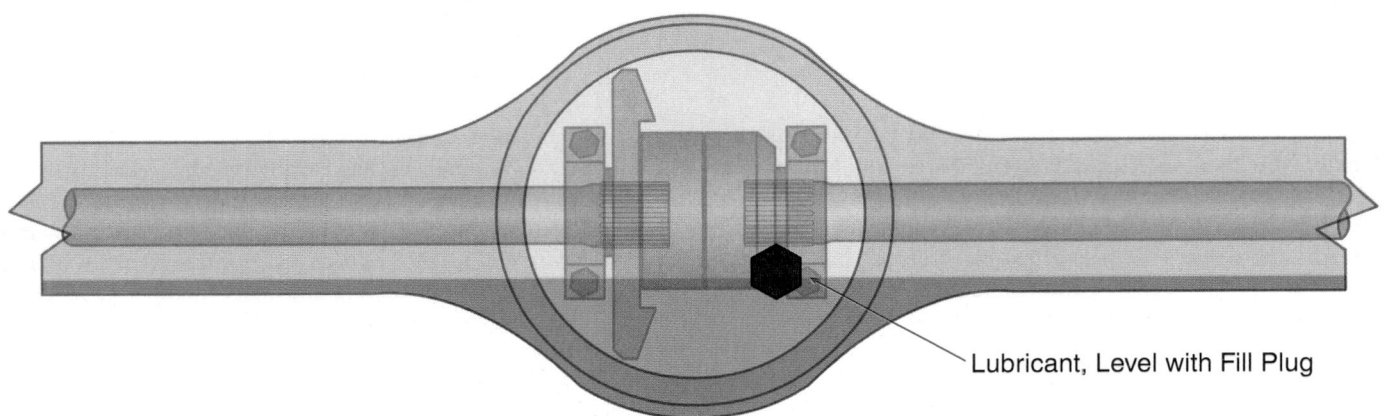

FIGURE 52-50 The two most common types of axle shafts are the full floating and the semi-floating type. **A.** A semi-floating axle shaft carries the vehicle weight on the outside end of the axle shaft, while the inside end carries no weight. **B.** A full-floating axle shaft carries none of the vehicle weight.

FIGURE 52-51 Most drive axles are lubricated by splash caused by the rotation of the crown wheel. It is essential that the correct fluid level is maintained.

Drive Axle Lubrication

In most drive axles, lubrication relies on the movement of the crown wheel. A fluid level plug is threaded into the drive axle housing or on the rear cover (on lighter-duty models) and the fluid is to be filled to the level of the plug, as illustrated in **FIGURE 52-51**. Some drive axles may have more than one level plug. In those instances, both must be filled to the level of the plugs. Always consult the manufacturer's manual to determine the proper filling sequence on these axles.

With fluid at approximately half way up the differential case, the fluid bathes the differential gears and the side bearings. As the crown wheel rotates through this fluid, its teeth throw the fluid upward in the drive axle. The fluid then follows the curvature of the housing and is directed by channels formed in the carrier housing and/or stamped metal slingers and troughs to the pinion bearings. The fluid splashes all around the inside of the housing onto the side bearings as well. The flowing and splashing movement allows the fluid to complete its purpose of lubricating, cooling, and carrying away foreign material from components that are in contact with each other. This type of lubrication is known as splash lubrication and is similar to what occurs in most standard transmissions.

FIGURE 52-52 Most power dividers are equipped with a gear-driven lubrication pump (indicated) to supply vital lubrication to the inter-axle differential components.

Splash lubrication can also be used in the power divider of a tandem drive. The inter-axle differential creates a unique problem for this type of lubrication system, however. The inter-axle differential component can be lubricated in the same fashion with formed channels bringing essential lube to its components. Because of the differential's rotational speed, however, it tends to throw the lubricant away from itself by centrifugal force. To combat this problem, most power dividers are equipped with an internal or external lube pump, similar to the one pictured in **FIGURE 52-52**.

Although there are other designs, the most common type of gear lube pump is one that is driven by the same spline on the input shaft that the inter-axle differential lock is splined to. This gear pump then channels fluid, under pressure, through drilled passages in the input shaft. That is how lube oil is delivered to the essential components in the top part of the power divider, the input shaft front and rear support bearings, the upper drop gear bushing or bearing, and to the center of the inter-axle differential itself. The channeling of fluid ensures positive lube for those components whenever the vehicle is in motion. Nonetheless, the power divider still relies on splash lubrication to lubricate, cool, and clean the crown-and-pinion and the main differential gearing and bearings. Drive axle lubrication is fully discussed in the Servicing and Maintaining Drive Axles chapter.

Role of Drive Axles and Drivelines in Greenhouse Gas Reduction Strategies

LO 52-6 Explain the role of drive axles and drivelines in greenhouse gas reduction stategies.

The systematic reduction of harmful emissions from commercial transportation vehicles has been ongoing for more than 40 years. From 2002 through 2010, the mandated reductions have decreased tailpipe emissions of oxides of nitrogen (NOx), gases, carbon monoxide (CO), and hydrocarbons (HCs) to trace levels. Since then, the mandate has been to reduce carbon dioxide levels because it is a greenhouse gas (GHG) and contributes to global warming.

The only way to reduce carbon dioxide emissions from a diesel engine is to use the fuel more efficiently. Great strides have been made in engine design to accomplish this. Transmissions and drivelines also have a tremendous effect on overall fuel economy and, therefore, GHG emissions from heavy trucks. Drive axle ratios, frictional losses, poor shift timing, and more can all influence GHG emissions. For years the Class 8 truck market has been dominated by manual transmissions, with some automatic, (torque converter transmissions), such as the Allison TC-10. To achieve the required GHG reductions, all systems of the vehicle must work together to optimize fuel economy. This includes strategies to reduce parasitic losses.

FIGURE 52-53 The new Paccar tandem axle does not use drop gears to drive the front axle's pinion, thus reducing frictional parasitic losses.

Direct drive transmissions have less frictional losses and can increase fuel efficiency in line-haul trucks. Paccar has developed a tandem drive axle that does not use drop gears to drive the front axle of the tandem, which reduces frictional losses and increases efficiency. **FIGURE 52-53** shows the new Paccar axle. Paccar engineers say that fuel efficiency can be increased by 0.5% to 1% using this axle.

In the Paccar axle, the input shaft drives the interaxle differential cross as normal, but the rear inter-axle side gear drives a hollow front pinion shaft that drives the front axle's crown gear. The front inter-axle side gear drives the through shaft, which passes through the hollow front pinion gear to drive the rear axle's pinion.

Another strategy being used to adapt the driveline to try and squeeze the absolute maximum usable power from each gallon of fuel is what has become known as **down-speeding**, which refers to running the engine at lower speeds than usual, but still achieving the necessary road speeds. Down-speeding as a fuel-reduction strategy is not new—it began in the 1970s as the "gear fast run slow" system, but it is being increasingly utilized by Original Equipment Manufacturers (OEMs) to meet their required GHG targets. The principle is quite simple; when an engine runs slower, it has fewer firing impulses per hour and, although it uses more fuel per firing impulse, the total fuel usage over a given time is less. The reason for this is simple—turbochargers can be designed to deliver the necessary boost pressure throughout the engine operation range; however, at lower rpm, the time window for the boosted air to be pumped through the intake valves is longer than when the engine is running at higher rpm. This extra air, coupled with the fact that there is more actual time for the fuel to burn, allows the engine to burn more fuel during the power stroke at the lower rpm. This extra fuel allows more pressure to be created in the cylinder to push the piston down, resulting in more torque or pulling power.

As engine speed increases, the actual time available to ingest air and to burn the fuel completely becomes shorter, so the engine management system must start to reduce the fuel load, or the burn is incomplete, leading to CO and HC emissions. So torque (pulling power) is usually highest at lower rpm, whereas HP (the speed at which work is performed) is greatest at higher speeds because, although there is less cylinder pressure per impulse, there are more power impulses per minute.

To explain this in a very simplistic fashion and without using complicated engine power formulas, we can theorize that an imaginary engine produces peak HP at 2000 rpm (rated speed) and peak torque at 1000 rpm. When this imaginary engine is running at 2000 rpm, or rated speed (HP), it has 1000 power strokes per cylinder per minute, whereas the engine running at 1000 rpm, peak torque, has only 500 power strokes per cylinder per minute.

Again, without using complicated formulas, let's say that each cylinder receives 100% fuel at 1000 rpm and 75% fuel at 2000 rpm. As the amount of fuel in the cylinder directly influences the force on the piston, we say that at peak torque, 1000 rpm, 100% fueling creates a force on the piston of 10,000 psi (703 kg/cm^2) and, at rated speed, 2000 rpm, 75% fueling creates a force of 7500 psi (527 kg/cm^2) on the piston. Given that there are six pistons, the total pressure being created to turn the crankshaft per four-stroke cycle is 10,000 psi (703 kg/cm^2) times six, or 60,000 psi (4218 kg/cm^2).

At rated speed 2000 rpm, the force of 7500 psi (703 kg/cm²) per cylinder times six results in 45,000 psi (3164 kg/cm²) per four-stroke cycle. So, we can see that the twisting force on the crankshaft, or pulling power per engine cycle, is much greater at the peak torque rpm than at the rated speed or peak HP rpm, meaning that at peak torque the engine can pull more load. But, if speed is taken into account, HP is greatest at higher rpm.

- At peak torque, we have 60,000 psi (4218 kg/cm²) per cycle and there are 500 cycles at 1000 rpm, so total pressure created is 60,000 times 500 or 30,000,000 psi (2,109,209 kg/cm²) per minute.
- At rated speed, we have 45,000 psi (3164 kg/cm²) per cycle, but we have 1000 cycles per minute; therefore, 45,000 times 1000 or 45,000,000 psi (3,163,813 kg/cm²) per minute.

To relate this to fuel usage, we look at 100% fuel used per cycle at peak torque and 75% fuel used per cycle at peak HP. Let's say for simplicity again that 100% fuel is 200 mm³ (0.012 in³); therefore, 75% fuel is 150 mm³ (0.009 in³).

- At peak torque, we use 200 mm³ (0.012 in³) per cycle times 500 cycles per minute or 100,000 mm³ (6.1 in³) total fuel per minute.
- At rated speed or peak HP, we use 150 mm³ (0.01 in³) per cycle times 1000 cycles per minute or 150,000 mm³ (9.2 in³) of fuel per minute.

This makes it clear that this "gear fast run slow" strategy—now known as down-speeding—decreases fuel usage while being capable of pulling a greater load.

The down-speeding concept has come a long way from its inception. At first, the target engine speeds for a line-haul truck operating at 65 mph (104.6 kph) were in the range of 1400 to 1600 rpm, but lately those target rpm have been coming down even more. Today's range of down-speeded powertrains are hitting 65 mph (104.6 kph) at 1100 to 1200 rpm and there are plans to reduce rpm to as low as 900 at 65 mph (104.6 kph).

This down-speeding is being accomplished by integrating extremely high-speed axles with direct or overdrive transmissions. The target market for this strategy is primarily Class 8 strictly line-haul trucks using direct-drive transmissions and higher speed axles and Class 8 regional delivery/line-haul trucks with over-drive transmissions and slower-geared drive axles. However, there is more to the down-speeding picture than meets the eye; as the engine rpm decreases, the inherent engine friction losses are diminished. Slower-moving pistons and other components reduce the frictional drag on the engine's rotation. Other parasitic loads are also reduced at lower engine speeds.

There are drawbacks to down-speeding, though. As lower engine peak torque rpms were introduced, it created another problem—specifically sharp increases in torsional vibrations. These torsional vibrations are a natural occurrence with all engines. They are caused by the twisting forces on the crankshaft

created with each firing impulse. At peak torque rpm, under full load, we have the maximum force on the piston and, therefore, the crankshaft. These torsionals are transmitted from the crankshaft to the driveline and can wreak havoc on its components if not dealt with correctly. When "gear fast run slow" strategies were initially developed with the onset of electronically controlled engines, these torsionals began to cause catastrophic failures in the driveline.

Broken U-joints, ring and pinion gears, transmission input shaft spline wear, and synchronizer pin breakage became more common. After investigation, it was determined that torsional vibrations were being amplified by the natural resonant frequencies of the driveline systems and were causing these failures. The industry developed soft-dampened or long-travel-damper clutches to deal with this problem. These clutches allowed a lot more movement in the clutch damper hub to absorb these damaging torsionals before they were transmitted to the driveline. Over the years, improvements were made to these clutches (friction dampening and other improvements) to further reduce the effects of torsional vibrations.

Today's down-sped trucks are reducing engine speed even more and torsional vibrations are becoming a greater issue. According to engineering data, the torque impact to the driveline system increases by approximately 8% to 17% for every 100 rpm reduction in engine speed. **FIGURE 52-54** depicts the increase in driveline torque with higher ratio drive axles which corelate to reduction in rpm.

More robust drivelines and axles are necessary to deal with the new range of down-sped trucks. Spicer introduced the SPL 350 line of its Life Series drive shafts to address increased driveline torque associated with down-sped systems. The SPL-350 can handle up to 40% more torque than the SPL-250 series. In contrast to the bad news, however, each 100 rpm reduction increases fuel economy by 1%, so going from 1400 to 1100 rpm can save 3% fuel usage. **FIGURE 52-55** depicts the fuel savings associated with down-speeding.

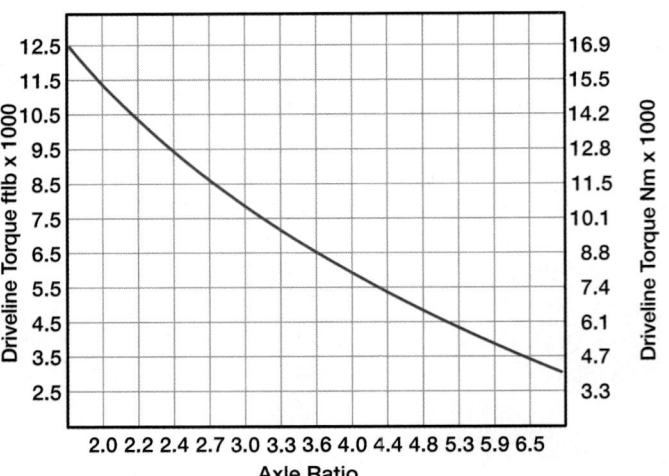

FIGURE 52-54 Higher axle ratios decrease engine rpm at cruising speed leading to increases in driveline torque.

In line-haul operations, today's down-sped truck likely has a direct drive transmission with a very high-speed axle ratio of between 2.47 and 2.64 or an overdrive transmission with an axle ratio of around 3.36:1. However, the torque impact on drivelines is greatest when pulling away loaded using a direct-drive transmission. So, if the vehicle is required to make a significant number of stops, an overdrive transmission is usually a better option, allowing the use of a slightly lower-speed axle and reducing the overall strain on the driveline.

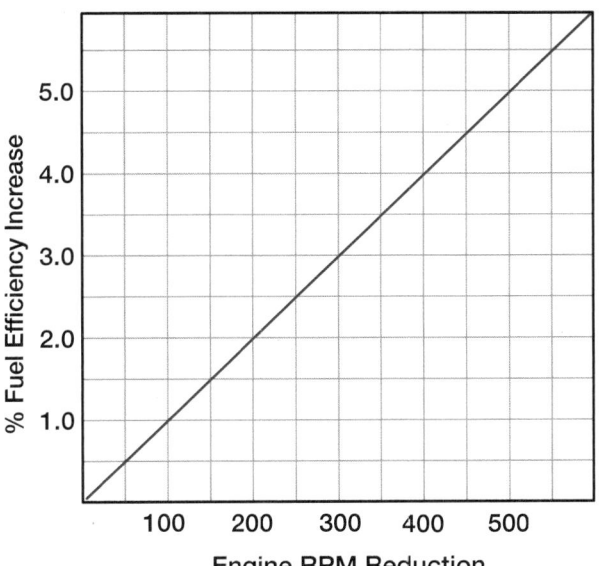

FIGURE 52-55 Decreasing rpm increases fuel economy.

Another strategy being adopted in line-haul applications is a change to 6 × 2 drive. Eliminating the second axle of a tandem can result in significant fuel savings. OEMs are claiming up to a 1.2% fuel economy increase when compared to tandem drive. This savings is a result of decreased friction and increased axle efficiency. Critics of this strategy point to decreased traction and the overwork of the single drive axle, but in most line-haul operations these worries are not serious. Dana is currently testing a new axle based on its Advantek series of axles that belays the fears of poor traction associated with 6 × 2 and low breakaway tractive effort attributed to down-sped drivelines. This axle is called a dual-range disconnect tandem drive, shown in **FIGURE 52-56.**

The system uses a planetary gear set in the front axle to allow a low ratio of approximately 3.5:1 for take-off when both axles are providing tractive effort. As road speed increases, the planetary gear shifts the front axle into high range of approximately 2:1, allowing cruising rpm of around 1100 at 65 mph (104.6 kph). As the shift is being made into high range, the front axle also stops driving the through shaft so the rear-rear axle of the tandem freewheels and turns the truck into a 6 × 2 drive.

Plans are in place to reduce rpm further using axle ratios as low as 2.08:1 and 1.91:1 with engines running as low as 900 rpm at 65 mph (104.6 kph). These ratios need significant driveline protections as the driveline torque and the potential for driveline system failures increase.

Electronically controlled drivelines work in concert with the engine and other system controllers to optimize shifting and driveline torque by constantly relearning. Inclinometers are used in most applications today to sense road grade

FIGURE 52-56 The dual-range disconnect axle from Dana has a low ratio to start and then switches to a high ratio and disconnects the rear axle of the tandem.

and terrain topography. Monitoring torque demand and fuel usage allows the driveline to work with smart torque controls, such as allowing higher torque to be developed in top gear or in the top two gears, so less shifting is required. Road speed limits are used in lower gears to force the driver to upshift early if he or she is manually controlling the transmission. Another strategy is a transmission that does not shift to overdrive when loaded but allows overdrive when unloaded.

These strategies and more are being used by manufacturers. The transmission and driveline are no longer passive members of the powertrain system, but constantly adapt to whatever driving situation arises to maximize fuel economy. As technicians, it is crucial that we know precisely how the driveline system operates and reacts to different driving conditions so that we know what is considered normal for that system.

Wrap-Up

Ready for Review

- Truck axles can be divided into three categories—steer axles, dead axles, and live axles.
- Most truck steer axles are a solid I-beam that is attached to the front suspension and has steering knuckles to allow the vehicle to be turned.
- Dead axles merely support the vehicle weight and have numerous subcategories. Tag axles are mounted behind the drive axles of the vehicle; pusher axles are mounted in front of the drive axle.
- Tag and pusher axles typically have air suspension systems and can be raised or lowered by the operator, when necessary, to support the vehicle load.
- Tag and pusher axles can be self-steering to prevent tire scrub on turns.
- Trailer axles come in many types, depending on the trailer vocation.
- Live axles actually drive the vehicle, so they are also called drive axles.
- Drive axles allow the power from the engine to turn a 90-degree corner to send that power to the wheels.
- Drive axles usually provide the final gear reduction in a drive train and, therefore, are also known as final drives.
- All drive axle gears are bevel gears—meaning that they intersect at an angle (in this case, 90 degrees).
- Bevel gear sets usually consist of a large crown (or ring) gear and a smaller pinion gear.
- Bevel gears are subdivided into several types, including: plain bevel, spiral bevel, durapoid, hypoid, amboid, topoid, and hypoid generoid.
- Plain bevel gears are similar to spur gears and have the same problems with noise and weakness. Plain bevel gear pinons are mounted at the crown gear's centerline.
- Spiral bevel gears are quieter and stronger than plain bevel and their pinion gears are mounted at the centerline of the crown gear.
- Durapoid gears are spiral bevel gears with an asymmetrical tooth design that adds strength.
- Hypoid gears are a type of spiral bevel gear that mounts the pinion below the centerline of the crown gear. Hypoid gearing is by far the most popular gear design used in truck drive axles.

- Amboid gears are a type of spiral bevel gearing in which the pinion gear is mounted above the centerline of the crown gear. Amboid gears are typically found only in the rear-rear axle of a tandem drive vehicle.
- Generoid or hypoid generoid gears have asymmetrical tooth flanks for extra strength.
- The drive axle is commonly misnamed the differential because the differential gear set is inside the drive axle. The drive axle and the differential are, however, different.
- The differential gear arrangement allows the power from the engine to be split equally between two axle shafts, while allowing the axle shafts to turn at different speeds, when required.
- The differential gear set consists of two side gears, four pinion or spider gears, and a differential spider or cross.
- The differential gears are contained in the differential case.
- As a vehicle turns a corner, the inner wheel must slow down and the outer wheel must speed up. The differential gear set allows this to happen.
- The differential always splits the available torque equally between the two wheels. Spinning wheels in a low-traction condition can cause a lifetime of damage in a very short period of time.
- Controlled traction differentials allow the engine to build more torque before a wheel can spin in low traction situations.
- Bias torque differentials can send more torque to the wheel with good traction.
- Differential locks are used during low traction situations only.
- Double reduction drive axles use two gear reductions at all times.
- Planetary two-speed drive axles use a planetary gear set to produce two ratios through the drive axle.
- Tandem or tridem systems use inter-axle differentials to divide the torque between the two or three axles.
- An inter-axle differential splits the available torque between two drive axles, not the wheels.
- Spinout situations are especially damaging for inter-axle differentials because inter-axle differentials turn at driveshaft speed, not at wheel speed.

- Axle shafts on lighter-duty vehicles are called semi-floating.
- Heavier vehicles use full-floating axle shafts.
- Most drive axle lubrication is affected by splash from the rotation of the crown wheel.
- Power dividers typically have a gear pump to ensure adequate lubrication of the inter-axle differential gears.
- Although down-sped axles can help achieve greater fuel economy, they increase driveline torque.

Key Terms

amboid gear A bevel gear arrangement with the pinion gear mounted above the centerline of the crown gear.

banjo A drive axle housing with a removable carrier. Also called a *removable carrier type*.

biased torque differential A differential capable of sending more torque to one wheel than the other when a wheel slip condition is encountered. Also known as a *proportional differential*.

carrier The component that holds the support bearings for the drive axle gearing.

controlled traction differential A differential that allows the engine to build more torque before the wheels can slip.

crank axle A dead axle in which the main beam is lower than the wheel spindles.

crown gear A large bevel gear that is driven by a smaller pinion gear in the bevel gear set. Also known as a *ring gear*.

dead axle An axle that supports vehicle weight only.

differential case The housing that holds the differential gears.

differential cross The mechanism that holds the differential pinion or spider gears. Also known as the *differential spider*.

differential gear A gear arrangement that splits the available torque equally between two wheels, while allowing them to turn at different speeds, when required.

differential gear set Consists of two side gears, four pinion gears, and a cross; allows for speed difference between the two axle shafts of the drive axle when turning.

differential lock A device that prevents differential action by locking one side gear to the differential case.

differential pinion gear A beveled gear that is a component of the differential gear set; it is fitted to the four legs of the differential cross and rotates with it. Also known as a *spider gear*.

differential spider The mechanism that holds the differential pinion or spider gears. Also known as the *differential cross*.

double reduction drive axle A drive axle that always uses two gear reductions.

down-speeding A strategy that reduces rpm while still achieving desired road speed.

drive axle The axle that drives the vehicle by turning the power from the driveshaft 90 degrees to deliver it to the wheels and providing the final gear reduction in the drive train. Also known as a *live axle*.

drop center tubular axle A dead axle used on trailer that drops in the middle.

durapoid gearing A specially designed spiral bevel gear set designed to provide increased strength and load-carrying capability.

full floating axle shaft An axle that carries none of the vehicle weight.

generoid An asymmetrical tooth design similar to the durapoid; it gives added strength to the hypoid and amboid gear sets. Also called *hypoid generoid*.

helical double reduction drive axle A double reduction drive axle that uses a helical gear set for the second gear reduction.

helical double reduction two-speed drive axle A double reduction drive axle that uses two selectable sets of helical gears as the second gear reduction.

helical drop gear The set of gears that drive the pinion gear of the front drive axle of a tandem.

hypoid gearing A type of spiral bevel gear set that mounts the pinion gear below the centerline of the crown gear.

integral carrier housing A drive axle housing that does not have a removable carrier.

inter-axle differential A differential gear set that splits the available torque equally between two drive axles. Also called a *power divider*.

live axle The axle that drives the vehicle by turning the power from the driveshaft 90 degrees to deliver it to the wheels and providing the final gear reduction in the drive train. Also known as a *drive axle*.

locking differential A system that actively prevents differential action from occurring when engaged.

output shaft The output shaft of an inter-axle differential. The rear side gear is part of or splined to the output shaft. Also known as the *through shaft*.

pinion gear A small driving gear.

plain bevel gear A bevel gear set with straight-cut teeth.

planetary double reduction drive axle A planetary drive axle that is permanently fixed in low range.

planetary two-speed drive axle A two-speed drive axle that uses a planetary gear set for the low range.

power divider A differential gear set that splits the available torque equally between two drive axles. Also called an *inter-axle differential*.

proportional differential A differential capable of sending more torque to one wheel than the other when a wheel slip condition is encountered. Also known as a *biased torque differential*.

pusher axle A rear, non-drive rear mounted axle, ahead of the drive axle.

removable carrier type A drive axle housing with a removable carrier. Also called a *banjo*.

ring gear A large bevel gear that is driven by a smaller pinion gear in the bevel gear set. Also known as a *crown gear*.

self-steering axle   An axle with steering linkage that allows its wheels to automatically follows the curve of a turn.

semi-floating axle shaft   An axle shaft that carries the entire weight of the vehicle on its outer end.

side gears   Part of the differential gear set; the side gears are splined to the axles.

spider gear   A beveled gear that is a component of the differential gear set; it is fitted to the four legs of the differential cross and rotates with it. Also known as a *differential pinion gear*.

spinout   A low-traction situation where one drive wheel or one drive axle spins wildly while the other remains stationary.

spiral bevel gear   A bevel gear set with spirally or helically cut gears.

tag axle   A rear non-drive axle mounted behind the drive axle.

tandem   Two drive axles connected by a power divider.

through shaft   The output shaft of an inter-axle differential. The rear side gear is part of or splined to the through shaft. Also known as *output shaft*.

topoid   A type of amboid gear set with the pinion gear mounted even higher than a normal amboid set.

Torsen   A biased torque differential from General Motors.

tridem   Three drive axles connected by power dividers.

TruTrac   A biased torque differential produced by Dana.

worm-and-crown   Older drive axle gear arrangement capable of very high gear reductions in a compact space. Also known as *worm wheel*.

worm wheel   Older drive axle gear arrangement capable of very high gear reductions in a compact space. Also known as *worm-and-crown*.

Review Questions

1. In a single-speed drive axle, the differential case always travels at which of the following speeds?
   a. 50% of crown gear speed
   b. 200% of crown gear speed
   c. 0% of crown gear speed
   d. 100% of crown gear speed
2. In a normal or non-locking differential, if one axle is turning at 96% of case speed, at what speed is the other axle turning?
   a. 96% of case speed
   b. 100% of case speed
   c. 104% of case speed
   d. 92% of case speed
3. The inter-axle differential is more susceptible to spinout damage than a main differential for which of the following reasons?
   a. It is smaller than a main differential.
   b. It turns much faster than a main differential.
   c. Its differential case is smaller.
   d. It has to carry four times the torque of a main differential.

4. Which of the following describes a planetary double reduction drive axle?
   a. The axle has two speeds.
   b. It has a helical gear mounted on either side of the differential case.
   c. It uses a planetary gear set for high speed.
   d. It uses a planetary gear set for a compound ratio.
5. When a vehicle is moving and no differential action is taking place, which of the following is a correct statement about the spider and side gears?
   a. They are stationary inside the differential case.
   b. They are moving opposite to the case direction.
   c. They are each turning opposite directions.
   d. They are free-wheeling in the same direction.
6. Which of the following describes a double reduction helical drive axle?
   a. The axle has two speeds.
   b. It has a two helical gear mounted on either side of the differential case.
   c. It uses two reductions through the axle at all times.
   d. It is a special axle used in low floor buses.
7. A(n) type of housing is used with a removable carrier.
   a. Integral
   b. Unit
   c. Banjo
   d. Final drive
8. Which of the following axle types normally result in wheel loss should the axleshaft break?
   a. Semi-floating
   b. Full floating
   c. 3/4 floating
   d. Non-floating
9. Lubrication in most drive axles is achieved by:
   a. a gear-driven oil pump.
   b. pinion gear pumping action.
   c. differential action.
   d. splash from the ring gears' rotation.
10. Which of the following gears are responsible for differential action?
   a. The ring and pinion gears
   b. The ring and side gears
   c. The spider and pinion gears
   d. The spider and side gears

ASE Technician A/Technician B Style Questions

1. Technician A says that drive axles allow the power from the engine to turn 90 degrees to turn the wheels. Technician B says that a drive axle usually provides the last gear reduction in a drivetrain system. Who is correct?
   a. Technician A
   b. Technician B
   c. Both Technician A and Technician B
   d. Neither Technician A nor Technician B
2. Technician A says that a hypoid gear set has the pinion gear mounted above the centerline of the crown wheel. Techni-

cian B says that a generoid gear set uses a stronger tooth design. Who is correct?
- **a.** Technician A
- **b.** Technician B
- **c.** Both Technician A and Technician B
- **d.** Neither Technician A nor Technician B

3. Technician A says that a differential gear set allows for drive axle wheel speed difference in turns. Technician B says that a differential gear set can allow a single wheel on a drive axle to spin wildly while the other wheel remains stationary. Who is correct?
- **a.** Technician A
- **b.** Technician B
- **c.** Both Technician A and Technician B
- **d.** Neither Technician A nor Technician B

4. Technician A says that a controlled traction differential allows the engine to build more torque in poor traction conditions. Technician B says that controlled traction differentials prevent any differential action from occurring while engaged. Who is correct?
- **a.** Technician A
- **b.** Technician B
- **c.** Both Technician A and Technician B
- **d.** Neither Technician A nor Technician B

5. Technician A says that in a tandem drive vehicle, most of the driving effort is provided by the front-rear axle. Technician B says that the rear-rear drive axle only receives 50% of the available driving torque. Who is correct?
- **a.** Technician A
- **b.** Technician B
- **c.** Both Technician A and Technician B
- **d.** Neither Technician A nor Technician B

6. Technician A says that two-speed drive axles offer more speed ranges to a vehicle operator. Technician B says that two-speed helical axles use a smaller crown gear that is less apt to flex under load. Who is correct?
- **a.** Technician A
- **b.** Technician B
- **c.** Both Technician A and Technician B
- **d.** Neither Technician A nor Technician B

7. Technician A says that an inter-axle differential divides the available power between the front and rear axles of a tandem drive. Technician B says that each wheel of a normal tandem axle receives exactly 25% of the available torque. Who is correct?
- **a.** Technician A
- **b.** Technician B
- **c.** Both Technician A and Technician B
- **d.** Neither Technician A nor Technician B

8. Technician A says that a durapoid bevel gear tooth is stronger than a regular bevel gear tooth. Technician B says that a durapoid bevel gear set is a spiral bevel gear set. Who is correct?
- **a.** Technician A
- **b.** Technician B
- **c.** Both Technician A and Technician B
- **d.** Neither Technician A nor Technician B

9. Technician A says that an amboid gear set has the pinion mounted below the center line of the crown gear. Technician B says that an amboid gear set's crown gear teeth are concave on the drive side. Who is correct?
- **a.** Technician A
- **b.** Technician B
- **c.** Both Technician A and Technician B
- **d.** Neither Technician A nor Technician B

10. Technician A says that most inter-axle differentials today are pressure lubricated. Technician B says that the inter-axle differential lock can be engaged while the vehicle is moving, as long as there is no wheel spin occurring. Who is correct?
- **a.** Technician A
- **b.** Technician B
- **c.** Both Technician A and Technician B
- **d.** Neither Technician A nor Technician B

CHAPTER 53

Servicing and Maintaining Drive Axles

Learning Objectives

After reading this chapter, you will be able to:

- **LO 53-1** Explain the fundamentals of drive axle service.
- **LO 53-2** Describe the process of drive axle overhaul.
- **LO 53-3** Describe the correct conventional and durapoid generoid contact pattern and the adjustment procedures.
- **LO 53-4** Describe the overhaul procedure for the inter-axle differential (power divider).
- **LO 53-5** Describe common component failures in drive axle systems and explain how to determine the root cause.

You Are the Technician

A Class 8 tractor with tandem drive axles is brought to your shop by a tow truck. The complaint is that the engine runs but the vehicle does not move. You do a preliminary investigation with a colleague and discover that the clutch and transmission seem to be okay, as the driveshaft from the transmission to the power divider turns. You can hear a loud grinding noise coming from the general direction of the power divider and recommend its overhaul. During the overhaul you find that the inter-axle differential cross is shattered. You examine the rest of the axle components and find other issues. The front and rear side gears and the spider gears of the inter-axle differential are prematurely worn and the lubricant shows signs of severe metal contamination.

1. What do you conclude from your examination of the components?
2. What do you think might have caused the broken inter-axle differential cross?
3. What replacements and/or services would you recommend for this vehicle?
4. What advice would you give to the truck owner?

Introduction

This chapter explains the procedures involved in the over-hauling and maintenance of drive axles and inter-axle tandem drives. Although most technicians are not required to perform this work, studying this chapter leads to a deeper understanding of the function and maintenance of heavy-duty drive axles. Included in the chapter are the procedures for the four common adjustments required for all drive axles: **pinion depth** (the position that the pinion gear is mounted in relation to the crown gear), pinion bearing **preload** (preload is negative end play), side bearing preload, and gear set backlash.

Fundamentals of Drive Axle Service

LO 53-1 Explain the fundamentals of drive axle service.

Proper maintenance practices are necessary to keep drive axles in service. Always stick to the original equipment manufacturers' (OEMs) recommended maintenance schedules. They have been created to ensure that the axle has a long service life. Failure to perform maintenance in a timely fashion can result in a costly drive axle repair. Fundamental to caring properly for drive axles is knowing how and when to service their lubrication system.

Drive Axle Lubrication

Use of the proper lubricant is the most basic, but also one of the most important, aspects of drive axle maintenance. All manufacturers require drive axle lubricants to meet the API GL-5 and/or the military MIL-L-2105D standard.

SAFETY TIP

There is no greater consideration than personal safety and the safety of others. Always keep this as your first priority when performing maintenance to the vehicle drive train. There are several precautions that must be taken to minimize the risk of injury. Failure to follow these precautions may result in personal injury, vehicle damage, or death. Observing these simple rules creates the safest environment for all.

- Always make sure the vehicle is on a level surface.
- Keep the vehicle transmission in neutral whenever possible.
- Remove the vehicle keys to prevent a person from starting the vehicle with someone underneath it. Avoid going under any running vehicle unless t is absolutely necessary.
- Chock the front and back of wheels on both sides of the vehicle to positively prevent movement.
- Always wear safety glasses, and wear a bump cap/helmet while under the vehicle.

That is true whether the lubricant is mineral-based or synthetic. Most manufacturers now recommend a synthetic formulation for their drive axle lubricant. Use of synthetics allows a much longer drain interval in most applications, and synthetics can handle severe service applications. Eaton/Dana specifications for synthetic drive axle lubricant are SHAES-256 Rev. C for on-highway use and SHAES-429 for off-highway vocational

TABLE 53-1 SAE Grades by Ambient Temperature Range

Grade	Ambient Temperature Range
75W	−40°F to −15°F (−40°C to −26°C)
75W-80	−40°F to 80°F (−40°C to 21°C)
75W-90	−40°F to 100°F (−40°C to 38°C)
75W-140	−40°F and above (−40°C and above)
80W-90	−15°F to 100°F (−26°C to 38°C)
80W-140	−15°F and above (−26°C and above)
85W-140	10°F and above (−12°C and above)

use. The lubricants are available in two weights—75W-90 and 85W-140. This lubricant (also referred to simply as *lube*) meets all the performance requirements of the majority of manufacturer's standards but, as always, check the OEM manual. Lubricant meeting the SHAES-256 Rev. C is available from several manufacturers. **TABLE 53-1** lists the various SAE grades of drive axle lubricants and the associated ambient temperature range for each.

The level of the drive axle lubricant should be checked as often as recommended by the manufacturer. Making sure that the lubricant level is correct is a simple way of avoiding sudden catastrophic failures. It also provides an opportunity to inspect the drive axle for leaks and repair them before they can cause a serious low lube level failure. For on-highway applications, Dana Spicer recommends checking the fluid level and inspecting for leaks every 12,000 miles (16,000 km) for on-highway applications. For off-highway applications, the frequency increases to checking levels and inspecting for leaks every 40 hours the vehicle is in service.

To check the lube level, ensure that the vehicle is on level ground and then remove the filler plug in the axle housing. Lubricant should be level with the bottom of the hole. If the level is below this hole, add the required amount and then re-install the plug. Do not over-torque the plug. The plug should be tightened to not more than 35 ft-lb (47 Nm). Never mix synthetic and mineral lube types as they may not be compatible. If the type of fluid is in doubt, the fluid should be drained and replaced.

A low level of lubricant could be a sign of leakage. In fact, drive axles can be prone to leakage. Common leak points occur at the flange gasket or in the sealant where the differential carrier is bolted to the axle housing, the pinion seal, the wheel end hub seals, and the unit atmospheric vent. To inspect a drive axle for fluid leakage, follow the steps in **SKILL DRILL 53-1**. Other reasons for low fluid levels could be poor service procedures. For example, when the wheel hubs of the axle are removed for brake work it is essential that the axle is properly refilled to the correct level.

Lube Change Intervals and Procedures

Lube change intervals are not universal. They vary depending on the vehicle vocation. **TABLE 53-2** shows typical change

SKILL DRILL 53-1 Inspecting Drive Axles for Leaks and Determining the Cause

1. Put the vehicle on an approved lift and make sure it is secure. Inspect the pinion flange for any fluid leakage.
2. Check the pinion bearing cage flange where it bolts to the carrier. If leaks are present, check the bolts for looseness and retorque, if necessary. Sometimes retorquing the attaching bolts can resolve the leak.
3. Visually inspect the area around the carrier housing flange for any seepage or drips.
4. Check and clean the breather or vent for leakage and/or any blockage that may cause a pressure build-up to occur in the axle.
5. Check for leakage around the brake drums; failed hub seals can cause axle fluid leaks in this location.
6. Check the fluid level for lack of fluid or overfilling of the differential, as either one can indicate that a leak is present.

TABLE 53-2 Typical Change Intervals for Drive Axle Lubricant

HEAVY-DUTY				
Synthetic or Mineral	Lubricant	SAE	Change Interval for Line Haul	Change Interval for Vocational
Synthetic	SHAES-256 Rev C	SAE 75W-90	500,000 miles (800,000 km) or 5 years	N/A
Synthetic	SHAES-429	SAE 75W-90 SAE 80W-140	N/A	180,000 miles (288,000 km) or 3 years
Mineral Base	SAE J2360	75W, 75W-90, 75W-140, 80W-90, 85W-140	120,000 miles (193,000 km) or 1 year	60,000 miles (96,500 km) or 1 year
MEDIUM-DUTY				
Synthetic or Mineral	Lubricant	SAE	Change Interval for Line Haul	Change Interval for Vocational
Synthetic	SHAES-256 Rev C	SAE 75W-90	250,000 miles (400,000 km) or 3 years	N/A
Synthetic	SHAES-429	SAE 75W-90 SAE 80W-140	N/A	180,000 miles (288,000 km) or 3 years
Mineral Base	SAE J2360	75W, 75W-90, 80W-90, 85W-140	100,000 miles (160,000 km) or 1 year	60,000 miles (96,500 km) or 1 year

intervals by vocation. Note, however, that some manufacturers recommend oil sampling as the basis for setting up a change schedule.

Manufacturers also list change intervals for severe duty service. The severe service recommendations should be used when the vehicle consistently operates under any or all the following conditions:

- at or near maximum gross combination weight (GCW) or gross vehicle weight (GVW) ratings
- in dusty or wet environments
- on grades greater than 8%

Historically, manufacturers typically have recommended an initial fluid change at 3000 to 5000 miles (4800 to 8000 km) for their axles when mineral-based lubricant is used. The purpose of this early fluid change (or drop) was to remove metal particles normally produced by the axle gearing during the break-in period. Today, the computerized gear-manufacturing process is much more precise. Consequently, most manufacturers no longer require this initial fluid drop, as these particles are not produced. Always check the OEM manual to be sure, however. All manufacturers have eliminated this early fluid drop when the axle is filled with synthetic lube.

Regardless of the interval, drive axle lubricant does need to be changed regularly. When changing the drive axle lube, the axle should be at normal operating temperature. If working with an axle that is equipped with a lube pump, the screen or strainer should be cleaned, or the filter, if present, should be replaced at the same time as the lube. **SKILL DRILL 53-2** contains guidelines for changing drive axle lubricant. An important part of this

SKILL DRILL 53-2 Changing the Lubricant and Filters on a Drive Axle

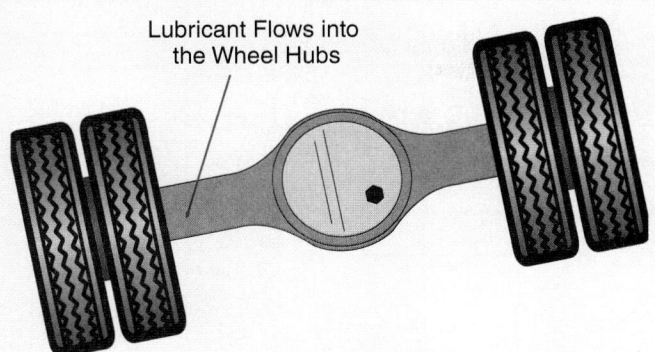

Lubricant Flows into the Wheel Hubs

1. Remove the axle drain plug, and drain the lube into a suitable container. Allow time for the lube to drain completely. *Note:* When working with some axles, there may be more than one drain point. Consult the OEM manual for the particular model being serviced.
2. Remove and discard the filter, if equipped, draining the fluid into a suitable container.
3. Clean the filter mounting flange carefully to avoid contamination.

4. Lubricate the new filter's seal with axle lubricant and install the new filter, paying attention to the correct tightening procedure (usually listed on the filter).
5. Reinstall the drain plug and torque to 35 ft-lb (47 Nm).
6. Remove the fill plug in the rear of the axle, and fill the axle with the recommended lubricant to the level of the bottom of the fill hole. *Note:* If the mounting angle of the drive axle is severe (more than seven or eight degrees), it may be necessary to fill from an alternate location. Check the service manual for the particular axle being serviced.
7. Raise the axle right hand side by six inches or more. Leave it sit like that for one minute before lowering the right-hand side. This ensures that the wheel hubs have the correct level of lubricant.
8. Repeat Step 4 for the left-hand side of the axle. Failure to perform this procedure for both sides of the axle may result in the hub bearings having a lack of lubricant and subsequent failure of the bearings!
9. Allow the axle to rest for one minute. Then check and top up the fluid, as necessary, until it is level with the bottom of the fill hole.
10. Reinstall the fill plug and torque to 35 ft-lb (47 Nm).

procedure is ensuring wheel hubs are filled with oil to the correct level. The correct level is illustrated in **FIGURE 53-1**.

▶ **TECHNICIAN TIP**

Some manufacturers require that the external drive axle filter, if used, be changed every 100,000 miles (160,000 km), regardless of whether synthetic or mineral-based lubrication is used. Always consult OEM documentation for the correct service intervals.

Drive Axle Overhaul, Removal, and Inspection

LO 53-2 Describe the process of drive axle overhaul.

Most technicians never encounter a situation where they are called on to overhaul a drive axle—and this text does not attempt to be a comprehensive instruction guide for doing so. When it comes to overhauling, however, all drive axles share some basic similarities, and those major points are discussed in

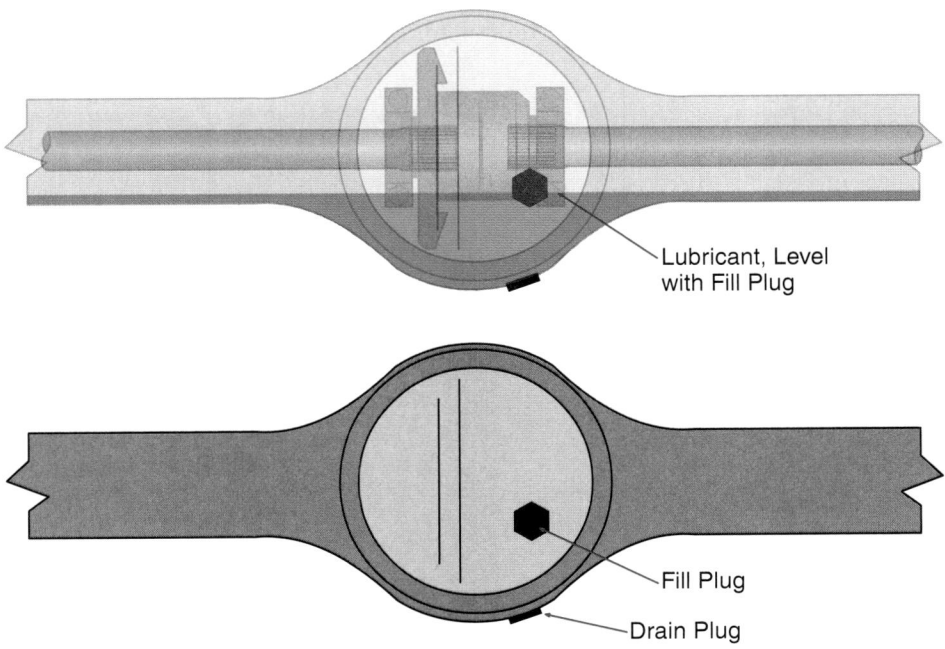

Lubricant, Level with Fill Plug

Fill Plug

Drain Plug

FIGURE 53-1 The correct fluid level is even with the bottom of the fill hole.

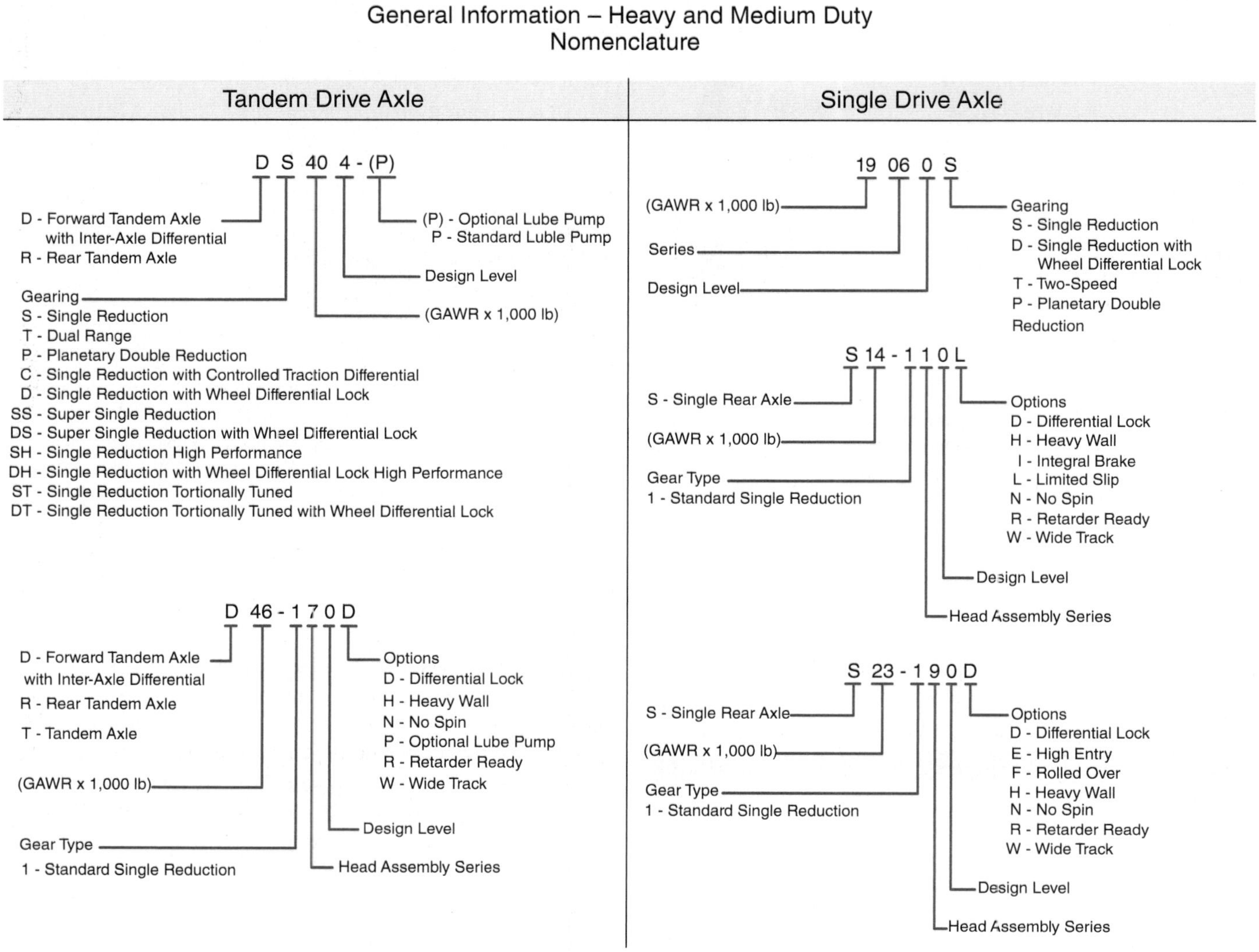

General Information – Heavy and Medium Duty
Nomenclature

Tandem Drive Axle	Single Drive Axle

Tandem Drive Axle

D S 40 4 - (P)

D - Forward Tandem Axle
    with Inter-Axle Differential
R - Rear Tandem Axle

Gearing
S - Single Reduction
T - Dual Range
P - Planetary Double Reduction
C - Single Reduction with Controlled Traction Differential
D - Single Reduction with Wheel Differential Lock
SS - Super Single Reduction
DS - Super Single Reduction with Wheel Differential Lock
SH - Single Reduction High Performance
DH - Single Reduction with Wheel Differential Lock High Performance
ST - Single Reduction Tortionally Tuned
DT - Single Reduction Tortionally Tuned with Wheel Differential Lock

(P) - Optional Lube Pump
P - Standard Luble Pump

Design Level

(GAWR x 1,000 lb)

D 46 - 1 7 0 D

D - Forward Tandem Axle
    with Inter-Axle Differential
R - Rear Tandem Axle
T - Tandem Axle

(GAWR x 1,000 lb)

Gear Type
1 - Standard Single Reduction

Options
D - Differential Lock
H - Heavy Wall
N - No Spin
P - Optional Lube Pump
R - Retarder Ready
W - Wide Track

Design Level

Head Assembly Series

Single Drive Axle

19 06 0 S

(GAWR x 1,000 lb)

Series

Design Level

Gearing
S - Single Reduction
D - Single Reduction with
    Wheel Differential Lock
T - Two-Speed
P - Planetary Double
    Reduction

S 14 - 1 1 0 L

S - Single Rear Axle

(GAWR x 1,000 lb)

Gear Type
1 - Standard Single Reduction

Options
D - Differential Lock
H - Heavy Wall
I - Integral Brake
L - Limited Slip
N - No Spin
R - Retarder Ready
W - Wide Track

Design Level

Head Assembly Series

S 23 - 1 9 0 D

S - Single Rear Axle

(GAWR x 1,000 lb)

Gear Type
1 - Standard Single Reduction

Options
D - Differential Lock
E - High Entry
F - Rolled Over
H - Heavy Wall
N - No Spin
R - Retarder Ready
W - Wide Track

Design Level

Head Assembly Series

FIGURE 53-2 Drive axle nomenclature.

this chapter. It cannot be stressed strongly enough that the correct OEM overhaul manual must be used to successfully overhaul a particular drive axle. Attempting this process without proper documentation can lead to errors and failure of the axle.

The absolute first step in overhauling a drive axle is confirming the manufacturer and model number of the component. **FIGURE 53-2** shows the breakdown of a DANA model DS404-(P) tandem drive axle. Other manufacturers have similar coding for their drive axles. Knowing which axle you are working on allows you to get the right service literature and the right replacement parts.

All axles have the model number stamped on the axle housing or on a plate attached to the drive axle, a Spicer information plate can be seen in **FIGURE 53-3**. Before doing any work, the technician should use the model number to find the correct overhaul information for that particular axle.

Overhauling a heavy-duty drive axle requires removal and disassembly of the differential carrier. Only then can the drive axle components be inspected. The overhaul is a complex

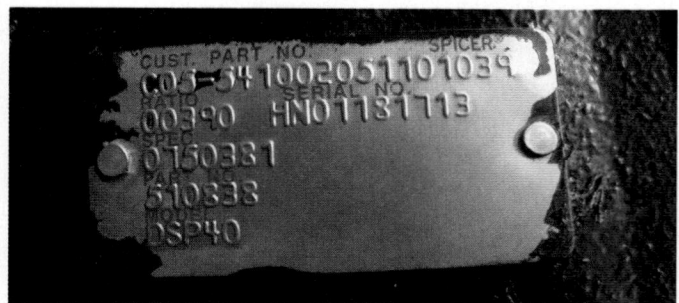

FIGURE 53-3 Use the axle manufacture's model number to find the correct overhaul manual for the drive axle being serviced before work begins.

process. It requires removing and inspecting the crown and pinion gear set, setting bearing preloads, and setting correct gear **contact patterns** (where the drive axle pinion contacts the crown or ring gear). The differential gear set must also be disassembled, inspected, reassembled, and reinstalled. The series of procedures in this section are merely a general overview for overhauling a typical heavy-duty drive axle.

Removing and Disassembling the Differential Carrier and Differential Case

As with most overhaul procedures, overhauling a drive axle begins with the processes of removal and disassembly. Specifically, the differential carrier must be removed and disassembled, and then the differential case must also be disassembled.

Safety is critical when removing the differential carrier as these components can be extremely heavy and must be handled carefully and securely. One of the first steps to removing the differential carrier is to remove the axle shafts. Note: Be particularly careful when removing the axle shafts on a vehicle with a locking differential. If your axle has a differential lock, put the axle in the locked position, as shown in **FIGURE 53-4,** and ensure it stays there before removing the axle shafts. The lock sits on an outboard spline on the left axle. If the axle shaft is removed from the vehicle when the axle lock is in the unlocked position, the lock drops and it is difficult to reinstall the axle shaft. To remove the differential carrier, follow the steps listed in **SKILL DRILL 53-3.**

SAFETY TIP

To remove the drive axle differential carrier, the drive shaft must be removed. Heavy-duty driveshafts can be extremely heavy. Use a sling to support the shaft before removal.

FIGURE 53-4 On drive axles with a differential lock, place the axle **A.** in the locked position to keep the sliding clutch **B.** in place during removal.

SAFETY TIP

Not all axles have tapered locating wedges but, if they do, when the axle flange is loosened, they can fly outward from the studs and strike a person with considerable force. Always leave the stud nuts installed by a couple of threads until the axle flanges are loosened.

Prior to disassembling the differential carrier, determine if the gear set is likely to be reused. If so, it is advisable to check the gear set backlash and contact pattern before differential carrier disassembly so that it can be reinstalled with the same settings. To disassemble the differential carrier, follow the steps in **SKILL DRILL 53-4.**

SKILL DRILL 53-3 Removing the Differential Carrier

1. Support the vehicle on stands at a sufficient level that allows enough room to work beneath it and remove the differential carrier without interference from the frame and/or suspension.
2. Using a sling for support, remove the driveshaft from the drive axle and ensure it is sufficiently out of the way to allow differential carrier removal.
3. Drain the axle fluid into a suitable container. The fluid can be an important indicator of the axle's condition. Watch for evidence of metal contamination, indicating extreme wear, or sludge, usually caused by overheating or lack of lubricant.

4. Loosen the nuts holding the axles in place at the wheel hub until they are holding by one or two threads. Leave them in place to stop the axle stud locating wedges from flying off.
5. Using a large brass drift and a hammer, strike the axle flanges to loosen the tapered locating wedges in the axles. These steel wedges center the axle shaft as it is bolted to the wheel hub.
6. Remove the nuts, wedges, and the axles and mark the axles as either right or left.
7. Support the differential carrier with a suitable floor jack and platform designed for the purpose. Restrain the front of the differential carrier to the jack. The rear side of the carrier is much heavier than the front and will try to roll off as it is removed. Before removing the differential carrier attaching bolts, ensure the carrier is securely supported.
8. Remove the differential carrier retaining cap screws or stud nuts, leaving the top two loose to hold the weight while the carrier mounting flange is loosened.
9. Loosen the differential carrier-to-housing mounting flange by using a pry bar in the pry slots on the flange or by moving the front of the housing back and forth.
10. Remove the top two retainers, pull the differential carrier forward, and lower it to the floor.
11. Mount the differential carrier in a suitable stand for overhaul.

SKILL DRILL 53-4 Disassembling the Differential Carrier

1. Mark with punch marks one of the differential **side bearing bore** legs (the bore in the casting that holds the side bearing races) and the **side bearing retaining caps** (semi-circular caps that clamp the side bearing into the casting). This allows the caps to be reinstalled on the correct side.

2. If the differential carrier has a **thrust screw**, loosen the jamb nut and back out or remove the thrust screw. *Note:* If the thrust screw has a swaged on end block do not completely remove the screw or the swaged block will be forced off the screw. The thrust screw (circled), if present, is located on the ring gear side of the differential carrier housing.

3. Remove the **bearing adjuster locks** (cotter pins, lock plates, etc. that stop the adjusters from turning) and loosen the four (or more) bearing cap retaining cap screws. Back out the **bearing adjusters** (threaded rings that position the side bearings) two to three turns. Remove the bearing cap screws (A), support caps (B), and the adjusters (C). Keep each side together as a set to ensure you are able to reinstall them in the correct location.

4. Using a sling and a hoist, remove the differential case and crown gear as an assembly and place it on a work bench. To remove the taper roller bearings from either the differential case or the pinion gear, use a wedge-type bearing puller. Place the assembly in the press with the puller vertical at first and use the press to force the wedge between the bearing and its seat. This allows the puller to loosen the bearing.

5. After the bearing has been loosened, retighten the wedge-type puller to ensure it has maximum surface contact and install the assembly into the press with the puller horizontal to finish the removal procedure.

▶ TECHNICIAN TIP

It may be easier to remove the side bearings after the differential case is disassembled.

6. Remove the crown gear, if replacing, by removing the retaining cap screws or drilling and punching out the rivets. The crown gear may need to be pressed off or lightly tapped off the differential case with a soft hammer. Always protect the crown gear from falling or damage could occur.

▶ TECHNICIAN TIP

Some differential carrier thrust screws have a thrust block swaged to the end of the screw. During the disassembly, do not remove the thrust screw completely on this type; doing so forces the block off the end of the screw.

The heavy-duty differential case has two halves: the **flange case half** and the **plain case half**. The crown gear is attached to the flange case half. The differential case is cross-drilled for the differential cross legs while it is bolted together, so it is essential that the case halves are reassembled in the same orientation. Therefore, before disassembly, mark the case halves.

SKILL DRILL 53-5 Disassembling the Differential Case

1. Place the differential case on the bench with the flange side down. Mark the differential case halves with a punch so that they can be reassembled in the correct position. Remove the differential case cap screws.

2. Remove the plain half of the differential case. The plain half of the differential case is opposite the crown gear side. It may be necessary to lightly tap the case to separate the two halves.

3. Remove the thrust washer and right-hand side gear. Inspect the running surfaces for wear. Remove the differential cross, spider gears, and their thrust washers together and check the case for wear from the spider gears/washers. Remove each spider gear and thrust washer from the cross. Carefully inspect the spider gear running surfaces inside the gears and on the cross for excessive wear.

4. Remove the left side gear and thrust washer and check the running surfaces of the differential case and the side gear for wear.

To disassemble the differential case, follow the steps in **SKILL DRILL 53-5.**

Removing the Drive Pinion

The drive pinion can be mounted in the differential carrier in several different ways:

- It may be removed from the back of the differential carrier.
- It may have a pinion housing that is removed from the front of the differential carrier.
- It may simply have a pinion bearing cage bolted to the front of the differential carrier.

The last of these is by far the most popular in the heavy-duty vehicle market, and it is the type that we discuss in this section. As always, consult the OEM manual for the particular drive axle being worked on before removing the drive pinion.

The pinion is supported by two opposing tapered roller bearings and, usually, by a small **spigot bearing** (also called a **pinion pilot bearing**) that supports the pinion at the inside end. This type of mounting is called a **straddle mount pinion**. If there is no spigot bearing, the pinion mounting is known as an **overhung mount pinion**. Most heavy-duty pinions are straddle mounted.

To remove the pinion yoke nut, use a yoke holding tool to stop the pinion from rotating. Pinion nuts on heavy-duty axles are installed with upwards of 750 ft-lb (1017 Nm) of torque. A torque multiplier may be necessary to remove the nut, and a yoke puller, such as the one in **FIGURE 53-5**, may be necessary to remove the yoke.

After removing the yoke, remove the cap screws holding the pinion bearing cage to the front of the differential carrier. The **pinion bearing cage** is a plate at the front of the differential

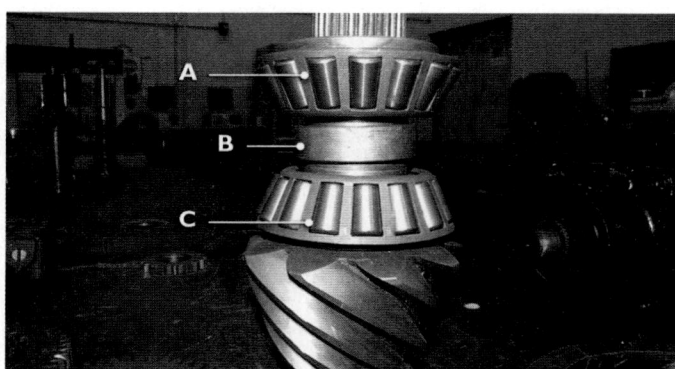

FIGURE 53-5 A yoke puller tool.

carrier that holds the two outer cups of the pinion bearings. Remove the pinion and cage as a unit. As shown in **FIGURE 53-6**, there are a few shims behind the pinion cage. It is essential that these shims are kept together as they are the pinion depth-setting shims. Measure and record the thickness of the shim pack in case they are misplaced and hold the removed shims together with a plastic zip tie.

The pinion gear may be loose in the bearings. Be careful not to drop it. If necessary, use a press to push the pinion out of the bearing cage. The front pinion bearing remains in the cage and the rear bearing comes out with the pinion. Do not lose the hardened steel spacer between the two bearings—it is responsible for setting pinion bearing preload. **FIGURE 53-7** shows a spacer.

Using a suitable pry bar, remove the pinion seal from the bearing cage. Doing so frees the front pinion bearing. Remove and discard the seal. Then, use a press and a suitable bearing removal puller to press the rear tapered bearing off the pinion shaft. Be sure to mount the puller vertically in the press first to start the bearing moving. After the bearing has moved, tighten the puller bolts and mount the puller horizontally to remove the bearing. At this point, use the hydraulic press to remove the pinion spigot or pilot bearing from the rear of the pinion shaft, if necessary. Finally, use a puller or a soft steel drift to remove the bearing cups from the pinion cage, being careful not to damage the cage casting.

Inspecting Drive Axle Components

With the differential carrier, differential case, and drive pinion removed and/or disassembled, a careful inspection of the drive axle components is possible. Clean and carefully examine all the components, looking for any signs of wear or damage. If a proper diagnosis was made before the axle was removed, the technician should have an idea of the kind of problem to look for.

A common problem is noise. A growling noise usually indicates one of three problems: general bearing failure; gear whine, which can be caused by worn gears; or bearing failure that allows the gear set to misalign. Clunking or banging is usually the result of gear damage. Regardless, always inspect the entire drive axle. Do not overlook the other components—even if you find the problem component right away.

FIGURE 53-6 The correct pinion shim pack thickness is essential when reassembling the drive axle. Always measure and record the thickness and keep the shim pack together. **A.** Pinion depth setting shims. **B.** Pinion cage.

FIGURE 53-7 The hardened steel spacer between the pinion bearings has a precise thickness and is responsible for pinion bearing preload. **A.** Front pinion bearing. **B.** Hardened steel spacer. **C.** Rear pinion bearing.

If there is any doubt as to the serviceability of the problem component, replace it. The downtime necessary to redo the job makes it unfeasible to attempt reusing any questionable components. Many shops insist on replacing all bearings in a drive axle when rebuilding, regardless of their condition, as the cost of the bearings is nothing compared to having a repeat failure.

If you are reusing bearings, inspect the bearings and races very carefully. A bearing race may show signs of fatigue even while the bearing rollers still look alright. Do not be fooled! It is also difficult to see wear on the inner race of tapered roller bearings because the rollers are in the way. Make sure you check it nonetheless. Also check the bore in the differential carrier that supports the pinion spigot bearing and check the side bearings and their mounting areas in the differential carrier for unusual wear.

Inspect all parts for steps or grooving caused by wear. Look for any pitting or cracks on gear contact areas. Scuffing, deformation, or discoloration can be signs of excessive heat in the axle, usually caused by lubrication issues—either low lubricant level or the wrong type of lubricant. Likewise, check the teeth of the crown, pinion, and differential gears for excessive wear, pitting, and/or spalling at the contact areas.

Inspect all machined surfaces of the cast iron parts of the differential carrier and pinion cage for cracks and/or scoring or obvious wear. Check for nicks or burrs on mating surfaces, and inspect all cap screws for bends, cracks, or thread damage.

After inspection, all reusable parts should be thoroughly cleaned and then lightly oiled and wrapped in rust preventative paper until reassembly.

SAFETY TIP

To receive the maximum value from an axle overhaul, it is always a good idea to replace all the lower-cost parts, bearings, thrust washers, seals, etc. Changing all these items increases the service life of the overhauled axle.

The Crown and Pinion Gear Set

One component that needs special attention during inspection and throughout the overhaul process is the crown and pinion gear set. As illustrated in **FIGURE 53-8**, the crown and pinion gear set is a matched set and must be serviced as such. There are several numbers stamped into both the crown and the pinion gear for identification purposes. Never use a crown gear from one set with the pinion gear from another—it is a recipe for disaster. Record the information found on the crown and pinion gears, so that the right gear set can be ordered. Heavy-duty axles are available in many different ratios and they will fit in the carrier, but the ratio would be incorrect. Installing the wrong ratio gear set can be easily done if technicians are not careful.

Drive Axle Overhaul—Reassembly

Reassembling the drive axle components begins with installing the pinion bearings. Once the pinion bearings are installed, then the bearing preload is set. After that, the pinion and the cage are reassembled into the carrier.

Regardless of the drive axle type, all drive axle overhauls require the same four adjustments during the process. Two of the adjustments determine the gear set contact pattern and two of the adjustments ensure gear set rigidity.

The first adjustment is pinion depth. This adjustment sets the running position of the pinion gear in relation to the crown gear and affects the gear set contact pattern. Pinion depth is discussed in the Setting Pinion Depth section.

Pinion gear bearing preload is the second adjustment. Pinion bearing preload is critical to hold the pinion gear rigid so it does not move away from the crown gear under load. Too little pinion bearing preload allows the gear to move away from the crown gear. Too much preload, however, causes the pinion bearing to fail rapidly. Pinion bearing preload is precisely set by steel shims.

▶ TECHNICIAN TIP

Bearing life is greatly affected by endplay and/or preload; a bearing with too much of either fails rapidly. Slight bearing preload (negative endplay), meaning that the bearing is installed with no endplay and then tightened slightly past that point, provides the longest bearing life. If preload can be precisely measured, as with pinion bearing preload, it is the best possible setting for the bearing; however, if the preload is slightly high, even by 0.001", (0.025 mm), the bearing fails very quickly. So, in cases where preload cannot be precisely measured, slight endplay is used.

The third adjustment when overhauling a drive axle is side bearing preload. The side bearings support the differential case, which, in turn, supports the crown gear. Side bearing preload ensures that the crown gear is held rigidly and that it does not move away from the pinion gear under load. As with pinion bearing preload, too little side bearing preload allows the crown gear to move, and too much preload causes the side bearings to fail.

The last adjustment common to all drive axle overhauls is setting the gear set backlash. Gear set backlash allows the gears to expand while they are running. Along with the pinion depth setting, gear set backlash also controls the gear set's contact pattern.

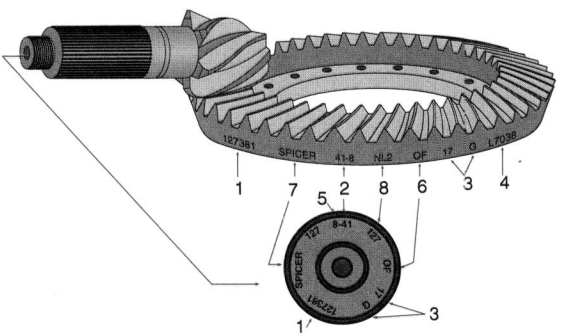

1	Part number
2	Number of ring gear teeth
3	Manufacturing numbers
4	Matching gear set number
5	Number of pinion teeth
6	Date code
7	Indicates genuine Spicer parts
8	Heat code

FIGURE 53-8 Crown and pinion gear set.

Installing the Pinion Bearing

The basic procedure for installing pinion bearings starts by installing the tapered roller pinion bearing cups in the pinion cage. Be sure to use a suitable bearing installer that fits the cups properly. After installation, check that the cup is seated properly by checking the cup-to-seat clearance with a feeler gauge. The clearance should be less than 0.001" (0.025 mm).

Using the press, install the pinion spigot (pilot) bearing. **FIGURE 53-9** shows a pinion spigot bearing. If the bearing is secured with a snap ring, install the snap ring now. If not, after installation the spigot bearing usually must be staked in position on the pinion with a staking tool.

With the spigot bearing in place, press the rear pinion tapered roller bearing onto the pinion and install it into the pinion cage. Be careful to install the correct bearing. The rear pinion may have a larger inside diameter than the front.

Finally, install the pinion bearing spacer and then the front pinion bearing. It may be necessary to press the front bearing into place on newer models with an interference fit. Lubricate the bearings liberally.

Setting Pinion Depth

To set pinion depth, you need the pinion variation number found on the bottom of the pinion gear. (Note that some newer pinion gears do not have a variation number due to the accuracy of the manufacturing process.) The drive pinion of an axle is set up to sit an exact distance from the vertical centerline of the crown gear. This is known as pinion depth. Pinion depth setting has to be accurate to within 0.001" (0.025 mm). This positioning, along with gear set backlash, ensures that the contact pattern of the gear set teeth is correct for optimum longevity, strength, and quietness. That exact distance is called the nominal pinion dimension. The design of the gear set calls for the pinion to run at a set nominal distance from the crown gear's centerline, as illustrated in **FIGURE 53-10**. Some pinions have a variation number, meaning they must run at the nominal dimension plus or minus the variation amount.

Manufacturing process tolerances in the past were such that each gear set was slightly different, and each pinion ran best at a slightly different distance from the crown gear centerline. When the gear set manufacturing was completed, each set was run and lapped together on a special machine. The distance from the crown centerline was then changed until the contact pattern was perfect. So, each pinion ran best either closer to or farther away from the centerline of the crown. The pinion was then engraved with this **pinion variation number**. Positive numbers indicated a distance further away from the centerline; negative numbers indicated that the pinion must be closer to the crown gear centerline. The pinion variation number shown in **FIGURE 53-11** is +2. This is why crown and pinion gears are sold only as a matched set and must never be interchanged from one axle to another.

Modern drive axles, manufactured with computer-controlled machines, may not have a pinion variation number. That is because manufacturing tolerances are much finer. It is still essential, however, that the crown and pinion gear are changed as a set. In a drive axle, pinion depth is controlled in one of

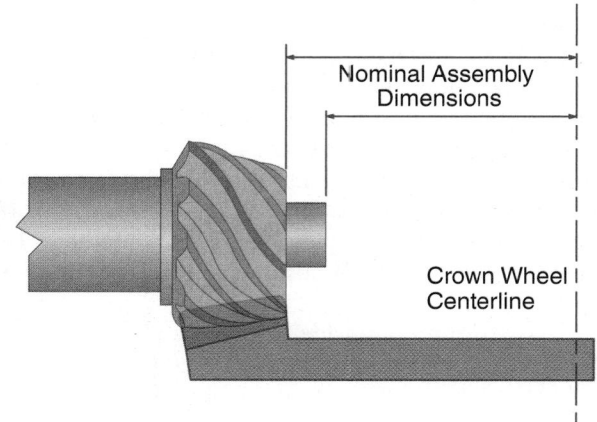

FIGURE 53-10 All pinion gears must run at a specific distance from the crown gear centerline to have the correct contact pattern where the gears mesh.

FIGURE 53-9 Spigot bearing may be retained with a snap ring or may be staked to the pinion.

FIGURE 53-11 If necessary, pinion variation numbers were inscribed on the pinion after the manufacturing process. This pinion's variation number is +0.002.

FIGURE 53-12 Pinion depth setting shims.

two ways, depending on the drive axle design. When the pinion is supported by the actual axle housing, pinion depth can be controlled with shims under the rear pinion bearing cone or cup. When the pinion cage is removable, as is most common on heavy-duty axles, it can be controlled by the pinion cage shim pack, as shown in **FIGURE 53-12**.

Despite being a simple process, quite often errors are made determining the shim pack thickness. If a gear set is to be reused, simply use the shims that were originally installed. After reassembly is complete, perform a contact pattern check and adjustment, if necessary. If the gear set is being replaced, it is necessary to determine the new shim pack thickness. Different procedures should be followed based on whether the drive axle is fitted with a removable pinion cage or has integral pinion support.

Determining the Shim Pack Thickness for a Drive Axle with a Removable Pinion Cage   In all installations, the shim pack should consist of at least three shims. There should be a thin shim on both the outside and inside of the shim pack to promote good sealing of the pinion cage. The pinion cage, shims, and differential carrier housing all have oil return holes. These must be lined up when installing the cage.

Measure and record the thickness of the shim pack installed with the original pinion. Next, examine the old pinion to find its pinion variation number and record this. From these two numbers, we can determine the nominal shim pack thickness. The **nominal shim pack** is one that would be used if the pinion had a zero variation. If the old pinion number is negative, that means the pinion must be run closer to the crown gear centerline. Therefore, the shim pack used should have been thinner than nominal by the pinion variation number. For example, imagine you are working with a shim pack whose original shim pack thickness is 0.067" (1.7 mm) and has a pinion variation number of −5. The nominal shim pack thickness is 0.072" (1.85 mm). That is 0.067" (1.7 mm) plus the 0.005" (0.15 mm) removed when the original pinion was installed.

If the old pinion variation number is positive, the pinion would have had to be run at the nominal distance plus the variation number. In that case, shims would have to be added to the nominal shim pack to make the pinion run correctly. To find the nominal shim pack, we would have to remove the thickness of the variation number from the original shim pack to find the

nominal shim pack thickness. For example, if the original shim pack thickness is 0.067" (1.7 mm) and the old pinion variation number is +9, then the nominal shim pack is 0.058" (1.47 mm). That is 0.067" (1.7 mm) minus the 0.009" (0.23 mm) added to make the pinion run correctly on the original installation.

Once the nominal shim pack thickness is established, check the variation number on the new pinion. If it is positive, shims must be added because the pinion needs to run at the nominal distance plus the variation (further away from the crown gear vertical centerline). If the new pinion variation number is negative, shims must be removed because the pinion must run at nominal distance minus the variation (closer to the crown gear vertical centerline). For example, if the nominal shim pack thickness that we calculated by adding or removing the original pinions variation number is 0.067" (1.7 mm) and the new pinions variation number is −3, then 0.003" (0.076 mm) must be removed from the shim pack to move the pinion closer to the crown gear, so 0.067" − 0.003" = 0.064" (1.7 mm − 0.076 mm = 1.624 mm). If the nominal shim pack is again 0.067" (1.7 mm) and the new pinion's variation number is +7, then 0.007" must be added to the shim pack to move the pinion further away from the crown gear. In that case, 0.067" + 0.007" = 0.074" (1.7 mm + 0.178 mm = 1.88 mm).

Determining the Shim Pack Thickness for a Drive Axle with Integral Pinion Support   If the drive axle does not have a removable pinion cage, the pinion depth setting shims are usually behind the pinion rear bearing cone or the rear bearing cup in the housing. In this case, a thicker shim moves the pinion closer to the crown gear centerline. That means the process for determining shim pack thickness must be reversed.

If the original shim is 0.050" (1.27 mm) and the old pinion variation number is −6, it still means that the pinion must run 0.006" (0.152 mm) closer to the crown gear centerline. Because of the shim's position, however, we would have to have used a shim 0.006" (0.152 mm) thicker than normal to move the pinion closer to the crown gear. To find the nominal shim thickness, we subtract the 0.006" (0.152 mm) variation from the original shim of 0.050" (1.27 mm) to arrive at a nominal shim thickness of 0.044" (1.12 mm).

Conversely, if the original shim is 0.050" (1.27 mm) and the old pinion variation number is +3, that means that the pinion has to run 0.003" (0.076 mm) further away from the crown gear centerline. Consequently, when the axle was originally set up at the factory, a shim pack 0.003" (0.076 mm) thinner than a nominal shim pack must have been used. To find the nominal shim pack in this example, we take the original shim thickness of 0.050" (1.27 mm) and add the 0.003" (0.076 mm) that would have been taken away to move the pinion further away from the crown gear centerline. Doing so gives us a nominal shim thickness of 0.053" (1.35 mm).

Once we have the nominal shim thickness, we check the new pinion variation number. If it is negative, it means that the pinion must run closer to the crown gear centerline, and a thicker shim is needed to push the pinion toward the crown gear. For example, if the nominal shim thickness is 0.064" (1.63 mm) and the pinion variation is −5, the pinion must run 0.005" (0.127 mm) closer to the crown gear centerline. Because of the shim position, we have to add 0.005" (0.127 mm) to the shim to push the pinion gear back toward the crown gear, so the shim must be 0.069" (1.76 mm). If the new pinion variation number is positive, we need to move the pinion away from the crown gear to make it run correctly. Therefore, a thinner shim is required. For example, if nominal shim thickness is again 0.064" (1.27 mm) and the pinion variation is +6, we must move the pinion 0.006" (0.152 mm) further away from the pinion for it to run correctly. Because of the shim position, we must use a shim 0.006" (0.152 mm) thinner, so 0.064" − 0.006" = 0.058" (1.27 mm − 0.152 mm = 1.118 mm).

This all may seem confusing, but remember this simple fact: If a pinion variation number is positive, it must run that number of thousandths of an inch *further away* from the crown gear centerline, and if it is negative, it must run that number of thousandths of an inch *closer* to the crown gear centerline. Finding the correct nominal shim dimension first eliminates errors caused by trying to add or subtract numbers that are positive and negative. Start with nominal shim pack (which is a zero-variation shim thickness) and then move the pinion closer if negative and further away if positive by the variation number marked on the new pinion.

Setting Pinion Bearing Preload

Once the pinion bearing is installed, the next step in reassembling the drive axle is to set the bearing pinion preload. Pinion bearing preload is extremely important, as it ensures that the pinion remains rigid in the axle and does not move away from the crown gear as load is applied. Correct pinion bearing preload also ensures that the bearings are not overtightened. The preload must be set correctly or failure of the axle is likely.

Pinion bearing preload is controlled by the hardened steel spacer between the inner and outer pinion bearings. To increase preload, decrease the thickness of the spacer. A basic procedure for setting pinion bearing preload is given in **SKILL DRILL 53-6**, which is a typical pinion bearing preload setting procedure. Some drive axles use different methods. For example, lighter-duty axles use a collapsible spacer between the bearing and

preload is set by tightening the yoke to crush the spacer until preload is correct. (Never reuse a collapsible spacer!) Still other axles use shims under the inner race of the front pinion bearing. Following the proper documentation for the particular axle you are working on is essential.

To set pinion bearing preload on a typical drive axle with a removable pinion cage, follow the steps in Skill Drill 53-6.

Selecting pinion bearing shim with a new gear set requires another step than those in Skill Drill 53-6. When a new gear set is used, the pinion bearing may experience **bearing growth** (expansion of the bearing cone) as it is pressed onto the pinion, and this can slightly change its dimensions. When replacing the gear set, a trial assembly of the pinion cage and bearings is recommended. Install the two pinion bearing cups into the cage and assemble the cage with the two bearing cones and the spacer, as shown in **FIGURE 53-13**.

Support the inner race of the rear pinion bearing on the press and using the press method described in Skill Drill 53-6, determine the shim thickness required to create the proper rotating torque (**FIGURE 53-14**).

Note: Even though the trial assembly method can be used to determine the approximate shim thickness required, the final rotating torque must be checked by the method in Skill Drill 53-6. Bearing growth as the bearings are pressed onto the pinion can change the required shim thickness by 0.001" (0.025 mm) or more, which can significantly alter the final rotating torque.

Installing the Pinion Gear

Once correct pinion preload has been determined, use the correct installation tool and install a new pinion oil slinger, if required, and a new yoke seal. An **oil slinger** is a metal ring designed to throw oil to assist lubrication or block dirt. It is usually pressed onto the pinion yoke. Install the pinion yoke and torque the pinion nut to the specification. The pinion nut may be reused if the nylon locking material is still in good shape. If not, replace the nut.

SKILL DRILL 53-6 Setting Pinion Bearing Preload

1. Install the rear pinion on the pinion shaft. Install the bearing cage, the hardened steel spacer, and the outer bearing inner cone, and then support the pinion under a press. Both bearings should be lightly coated with oil.

2. Using a correctly sized sleeve, press on the outer bearing inner race. Increase the press load to the amount recommended in the overhaul manual—typically 10 to 20 tons (9072 kg to 18,144 kg). This load accurately represents the load placed on the bearings when the pinion yoke or gear is properly torqued.

3. Tie a length of string to one of the cage mounting holes and wrap the string around the pinion cage several times. Attach a pull scale that reads in pounds or kilograms to the other end of the string. In a steady motion, start rotating the cage by hand and keep it rotating by pulling the scale.

4. Record the force required to keep the cage rotating, NOT the force required to start it rotating.

5. Multiply the pounds or kilograms pulled by the radius of the cage where the string was attached. This indicates the rotating torque of the pinion in inch-pounds or kilograms per centimeter. Typical settings are between 15 and 30 in-lb or 17 and 34 kg/cm. Always check the OEM manual for the correct specification and remember that a bearing with excess preload will fail rapidly.

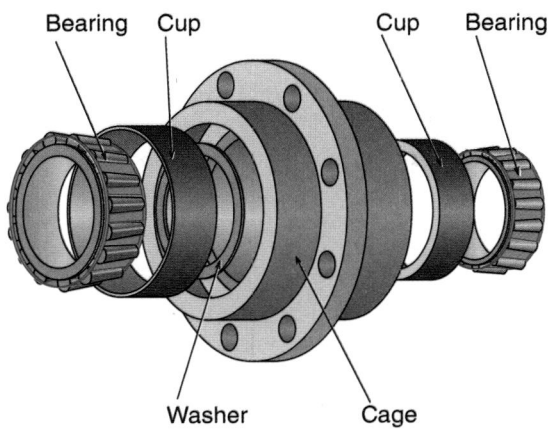

FIGURE 53-13 When installing a new gear set, a trial assembly process is recommended.

The pinion nut torque specifications vary widely, depending upon which axle is being worked on. Pinion nut torque is seldom less than 550 ft-lb (760 Nm) and can be as high as 1500 ft-lb (2033 Nm). The use of a torque multiplier is strongly recommended. After the pinion is reinstalled in the pinion cage, it is time to check and set the pinion depth.

Reassembling the Differential Case and Differential Carrier

After setting the pinion depth, you can begin the process of reassembling the differential case and the differential carrier. Remember that the differential case is a matched assembly and must be reassembled in a specific orientation by lining up the marks made before disassembly. To reassemble the differential case, follow the steps in **SKILL DRILL 53-7**.

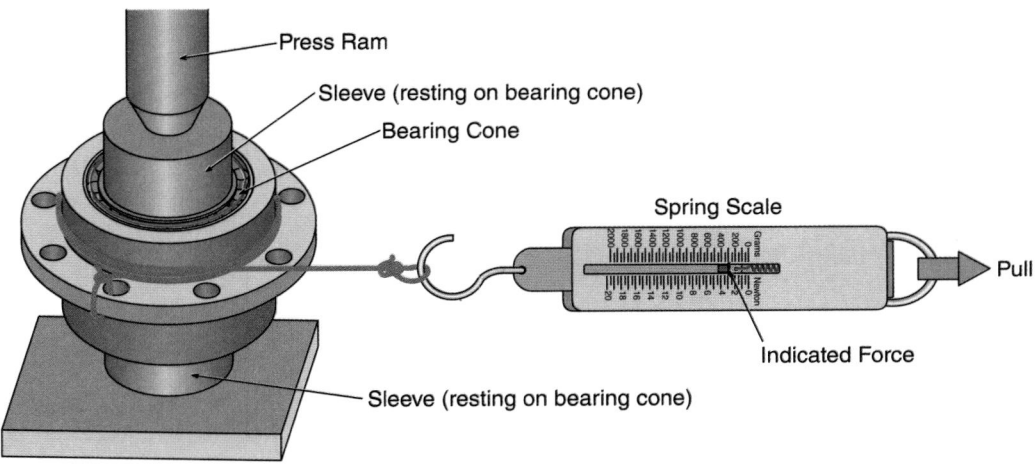

FIGURE 53-14 Using a trial assembly allows the technician to determine approximate shim thickness.

SKILL DRILL 53-7 Reassembling the Differential Case

1. Press the side bearing cones on the differential case halves using a suitable driving sleeve that pushes on the inner race.
2. Assemble the differential gears and the case as follows:
   a. Put one thrust washer and side gear into the flange case half.
   b. Place the spider gears on the spider or cross and the spider gear thrust washers into place, and place the assembled cross into the differential case.
   c. Install the other side gear and its thrust washer.
   d. Lining up the match marks made before disassembly, install the plain case half over the assembled differential gears and torque to specification, typically in the area of 115 to 130 ft-lb (156 to 176 Nm). Check the OEM manual for the correct specifications.
3. Check the rotation of the differential gears. They may require up to 50 ft-lb (68 Nm) torque to rotate. Check the OEM manual for the specification. If the required torque is higher than specified, it indicates a problem. Disassemble and recheck the gears for damage. The gears may turn at slightly lower torque values, but there should be no perceptible play in the gears.
4. Install the crown gear (if removed) onto the flange half of the differential case and tighten the nuts and bolts to specification. Note that some crown gears may need light heating to fit onto the flange. Always heat in an oven to no more than the specified temperature or damage to the gear will occur. NEVER use an oxy-acetylene torch to heat the gear as its manufacturer's heat treating will be destroyed.

Reassembling the Drive Axle Carrier

Reassembling the drive axle carrier involves several key procedures, including setting the side bearing preload, setting gear set backlash, checking the crown gear run out, setting gear contact patterns, and installing the thrust screw (if equipped).

Setting Side Bearing Preload and Gear Set Backlash

Several methods are available for setting side bearing preload. Some manufacturers recommend tightening the bearing adjuster until there is no play in the bearings and then tightening two or more extra notches. Others recommend measuring the distance between the bearing caps and tightening the adjusters until the bearing caps are pushed outwards by a certain amount—indicating preload. Still others recommend using the rotating torque method used in pinion bearing preload setting (the rotating torque method can only be used before the pinion is installed in the carrier). The fourth method, which is by far the simplest as it is used to set preload and backlash using the one procedure, is listed step-by-step in **SKILL DRILL 53-8**. Note that the process is accomplished using bearing adjusting tools. These can be purchased from an aftermarket supplier or they can be fabricated in shop, like the one pictured in **FIGURE 53-15**.

Checking Crown Gear Runout

After the differential case and crown gear are installed, crown gear runout should be checked. Significant runout causes problems with the gear set. Check for crown gear runout by following the steps in **SKILL DRILL 53-9**.

FIGURE 53-15 Bearing adjusting tool fabricated in the shop.

SKILL DRILL 53-8 Setting Side Bearing Preload and Gear Set Backlash

1. Lubricate the differential side bearings and install the differential case with the bearing cups into the differential carrier.
2. Install the adjusters and the bearing caps, aligning the match marks on the caps and differential carrier bearing bores that were made at disassembly. Be very careful to ensure that the adjuster threads are not cross-threaded. Take some time and make sure they are in place correctly. Do not try to thread them in from the outside of the cap. Tighten the cap screws on the bearing cap finger tight then lightly tighten with a wrench until the caps are flush to the differential carrier.
3. Adjust the plain case half, the side opposite the crown gear, bearing adjuster outward until one thread is visible outboard of its bearing cap.

4. Install a magnetic base dial indicator so that the finger rests on the back of one of the crown gear teeth.
5. Tighten the flange side adjuster using a bearing adjusting tool, while checking for gear set backlash with the dial indicator until there is no backlash (i.e., the crown gear is snug up against the pinion gear).
6. Rotate the crown gear through one full rotation, again checking for gear set backlash at ¼ intervals, and retighten the adjuster at the point where the most backlash is measured until again there is no backlash. This seats the side bearings properly.
7. Tighten the plain side bearing adjuster until measured backlash is approximately 0.002" (0.051 mm). This backlash proves that the crown gear has moved outward from the pinion and establishes the correct amount of side bearing preload.
8. Set the gear set backlash to the specification. That is typically between 0.006" and 0.018" (0.152 and 0.457 mm) for new gearing. If using the old crown and pinion, set backlash to the amount measured before disassembly. To set backlash while maintaining the side bearing preload, back off one bearing adjuster and tighten the other one by the exact same amount. This way the crown gear can be moved away from the pinion gear (to increase backlash) or moved toward the pinion gear (to decrease backlash) while maintaining the side bearing preload established in steps 1 through 7.
9. When backlash is correct, torque the cap screws on the **side bearing caps** to the specification, which can be in excess of 350 ft-lb (488 Nm) on heavy-duty drive axles. Do not install the adjuster locks at this time, wait until a pattern check has indicated the correct contact pattern.

SKILL DRILL 53-9 Measuring Crown Gear Runout

1. Locate and follow the appropriate procedure in the service manual.
2. Complete the accompanying job sheet or work order with all pertinent information.
3. Place a dial indicator with magnetic base to the differential carrier's flange.

4. Position the plunger or pointer against the back of the ring gear, and set the dial indicator to zero. Make sure the indicator is stable. If not stable, you may get an inaccurate reading.
5. Rotate the ring gear one complete turn while reading the dial indicator.
6. Record the total indicated runout (TIR) by adding the high and low spots. For example, +0.010" (0.254 mm) + −0.003" (0.0762 mm) is 0.013" (0.330 mm) TIR.
7. Check TIR against manufacturer's specifications. TIR should not normally exceed 0.005" (0.127 mm). If runout exceeds specifications, the differential and ring gear assembly must be removed from the carrier, and Steps 8, 9, and 10 must be completed. If runout is within specifications, the procedure is complete.
8. Check all parts of the crown gear and carrier for the damage that caused the runout to exceed specifications.
9. Repair or replace parts.
10. Reinstall ring gear to the carrier and recheck runout.
11. List the test results and/or recommendations on the job sheet or work order, clean work area, and return tools and materials to proper storage.

Setting Gear Set Contact Patterns

LO 53-3 Describe the correct conventional and durapoid generoid contact pattern and the adjustment procedures.

The **gear set contact pattern** is the indication as to where the gears contact each other during operation. The correct contact pattern is essential to ensuring that the gears are meshed correctly and provide maximum strength and endurance. In order to check the pattern, the technician must know and understand the names of the surfaces of the crown gear teeth. The technician must also know which side of the crown gear tooth is the coast side and which is the drive side. In spiral bevel and hypoid gear sets, the drive side of the crown gear is the convex side of the tooth. In amboid gear sets, the drive side of the crown gear is the concave side of the tooth.

Gear Tooth Nomenclature

After assembly of any drive axle, it is essential that the contact pattern is checked. All conventional drive axles using hypoid gearing have the same desired hand-rolled contact pattern. Study the names of the tooth surfaces shown in **FIGURE 53-16** to ensure the contact pattern check is performed correctly and the results can be properly interpreted. The contact pattern itself consists of a **lengthwise bearing** along the **tooth face** from the toe to the **heel** and a **profile bearing** between the **top land** and the **root**. The correct contact pattern ensures that, as the gear set is loaded, the contact spreads toward the heel of the tooth, along its face width, so the whole tooth can carry the load. If the contact pattern runs off the tooth face at any point, the gear set will make noise. A whining noise will be heard on acceleration or deceleration, depending on where the pattern runs off the tooth. This type of contact also weakens the gear set as less than the entire tooth is involved in carrying the load.

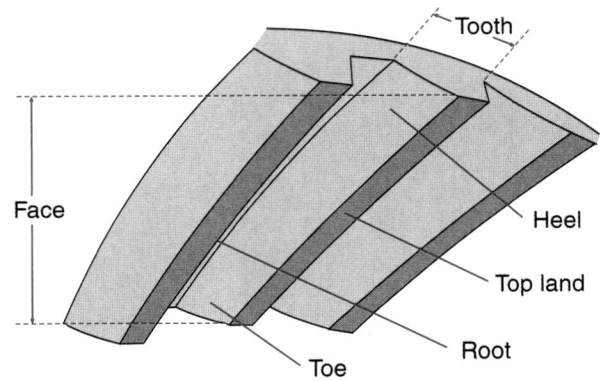

FIGURE 53-16 Proper gear tooth nomenclature is essential to check and correct the contact pattern.

The pattern is normally checked on the drive side of the crown gear teeth. To check contact pattern, six or more teeth of the crown gear are lightly marked on their drive side with a tooth marking compound. The crown gear is then rolled by hand in a reverse direction while a resistance load is applied to the pinion by having an assistant hold the pinion. The load increases the chance of getting a good view of the pattern. Rotate the marked teeth through mesh in one direction a couple of times, then bring the marked teeth to the top to read the pattern.

A good, conventional hypoid pattern has the following three elements:

1. The pattern must start near to, but clear of, the toe of the tooth.
2. The pattern should cover at least 50% of the crown gear tooth face width.
3. The pattern should be centered between the top land and the root of the tooth.

Correct Contact Pattern (for new gears)

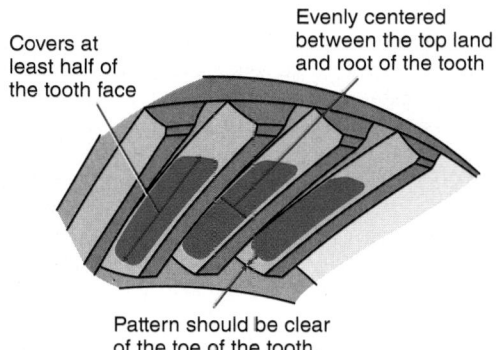

Covers at least half of the tooth face

Evenly centered between the top land and root of the tooth

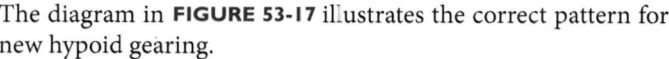

Pattern should be clear of the toe of the tooth.

FIGURE 53-17 A satisfactory hand-rolled contact pattern for conventional hypoid gearing.

FIGURE 53-18 Actual gear contact patterns are slightly different than the theoretical pattern depicted in Figure 53-17. The contact is more oval in shape, as shown here.

The diagram in **FIGURE 53-17** illustrates the correct pattern for new hypoid gearing.

Actual contact patterns, however, are slightly different than the one illustrated. **FIGURE 53-18** shows an actual correct contact pattern for new conventional gearing. Notice that the pattern is more oval but meets the three criteria of being clear of the toe, covering half of the tooth face, and being centered between the top land and the root.

The difference in pattern shape is caused by the slight crowning of new teeth. The pattern flattens out as the gears wear together. As a gear set wears more and more, it creates a pattern with more of a pocket (or V) shape toward the heel end of the tooth. Nonetheless, the gear set still has the same three elements of a good pattern starting near the toe, having 50% or more of the tooth covered, and being centered between the top land and the root.

The two elements of drive axle assembly that affect contact pattern are the gear set backlash and the pinion depth setting. The gear set backlash affects the positioning of the pattern along the face width of the tooth. Increasing backlash moves the pattern along the tooth face toward the heel of the tooth and decreasing backlash moves the pattern along the tooth face toward the toe of the tooth. The pinion depth setting affects the position of the contact pattern between the top land and the root of the tooth. Moving the pinion gear mounting closer to the vertical center of the crown gear moves the pattern down the tooth face toward the root of the tooth, while moving the pinion further away from the vertical center of the crown gear causes the pattern to move up the tooth face toward the top land of the tooth. The adjustments are somewhat interrelated in that, if the pinion gear is moved closer to the crown gear's center, it moves deeper into mesh and, therefore, decreases backlash; conversely, if the pinion is moved further from the center, backlash increases. When a pattern adjustment is necessary, always adjust the pinion position first, if necessary, and then readjust backlash to establish the desired pattern. **TABLE 53-3** shows incorrect patterns and what has to be done to correct them. While using the table though, remember that if you have to move the pinion toward the crown gear's center, this action

decreases backlash, so the crown gear should be moved away from the pinion before the pinion gear is repositioned. If this is not done, there may not be sufficient clearance for the deeper meshed pinion. This could cause damage to the gear faces. Once the gear contact pattern is satisfactory, install the side bearing adjuster locks.

Durapoid Spiral Bevel Gearing and Generoid Gearing Contact Patterns

Most gear sets that a technician will come across will use the conventional pattern described previously. As the conventional gear set is loaded, the contact spreads toward the heel of the tooth, so setting the pattern close to the toe of the tooth makes sense. As load increases, more of the tooth comes into contact. Durapoid and generoid gearing, however, are different. Mack has used durapoid spiral bevel gearing for years in several of their drive axles. This gearing has a different contact pattern. The same is true for hypoid generoid or amboid generoid gearing, which looks very similar to conventional hypoid and amboid gearing, but which also has a different contact pattern.

Generoid gearing has been used by Rockwell in the past and Meritor is using it in some of their drive axles. These gear sets are described in detail in the Heavy-Duty Truck Drive Axles chapter. Both durapoid spiral bevel and hypoid generoid gear sets have a centralized contact pattern, meaning that the hand-rolled pattern is centered along the face of the crown gear tooth and is also centered between the top land and the root. This is because, as these gear sets are loaded, the tooth contact spreads in both directions along the face of the crown gear tooth, rather than toe to heel, as in the conventional hypoid and amboid gears. **FIGURE 53-19** is a depiction of a correct centralized pattern for both durapoid and generoid gear sets. Centralized contact patterns are adjusted in the same way as the conventional patterns above.

Without the proper OEM documentation for the axle being worked on, a technician may be fooled by this type of gearing and try to set a pattern that is unachievable. Always have the correct OEM manual for the drive axle being worked on. Most

TABLE 53-3 Troubleshooting Tooth Patterns

Incorrect Pattern	Problem	Solution
Pattern too close to toe	Pattern too close to edge of tooth toe	Move ring gear away from pinion to increase backlash
Pattern too close to heel	Pattern too far along tooth toward tooth heel	Move ring gear toward pinion to decrease backlash
Pattern too close to tooth root	Pattern too close to tooth root	Move pinion away from ring gear
Pattern too close to top land	Pattern too close to tooth top land	Move pinion toward ring gear

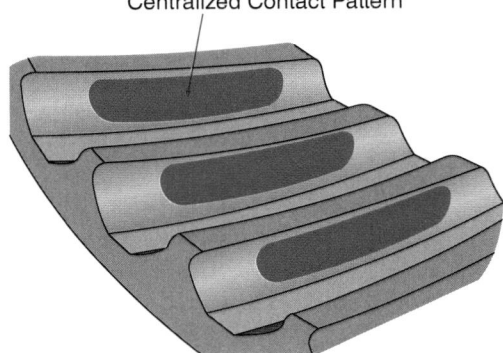

Centralized Contact Pattern

FIGURE 53-19 A centralized contact pattern is used for durapoid and hypoid generoid gear sets. Under load the contact spreads in both directions along the tooth face width.

manuals for heavy-duty drive axles are readily available online as long as you have the axle model number.

Installing the Thrust Screw

If the drive axle has a thrust screw, like that shown in **FIGURE 53-20**, it should be adjusted after the gear set contact pattern is correctly adjusted. The typical adjustment of the thrust screw involves tightening the screw to a set torque or just until it contacts the back of the crown gear. Then, the screw is backed out a certain amount, usually 1/4 to 1/2 turn. Finally, the lock nut is torqued to specification while the screw is held stationary.

The thrust block normally does not contact the crown wheel during operation. Instead, it runs with approximately 0.010" to 0.020" (0.254 to 0.508 mm) running clearance. Contact with the thrust screw is made only when the crown gear flexes under heavy load.

FIGURE 53-20 Tighten the thrust screw until it contacts the back of the crown gear, then back it out ¼ to ½ turn (check OEM documentation for exact specification). This establishes the correct running clearance of between 0.010" and 0.020" (0.254 and 0.508 mm).

FIGURE 53-21 A power divider has a normal wheel differential and an inter-axle differential.

Overhauling the Inter-Axle Differential (Power Divider)

LO 53-4 Describe the overhaul procedure for the inter-axle differential (power divider).

The power divider, shown in **FIGURE 53-21**, has two differential gear sets: the inter-axle differential (the "power divider") and the main (or wheel) differential. The power divider removal procedures are very similar to the differential carrier removal procedure described in the Removing and Disassembling the Differential Carrier and Differential Case section. The overhaul procedures for the power divider's normal drive axle crown and pinion gear set and main differential for wheel speed differences is very similar to the drive axle overhaul procedures discussed in the Drive Axle Overhaul—Removal and Inspection section, with the exception that it has a drop gear attached to the axle drive pinion, rather than a yoke. Therefore, this section discusses the overhaul procedures for the power divider's inter-axle differential components only.

The power divider assembly can be removed with the remainder of the main differential carrier still mounted in the axle housing, by splitting the power divider housing from the main differential carrier, or it can be removed with the entire assembly. Removing the entire assembly is accomplished in a similar fashion to the differential carrier removal discussed in the Removing and Disassembling the Differential Carrier and Differential Case section. The only difference is that the assembled differential carrier and inter-axle differential is much heavier and more awkward to handle. Exercise extreme caution to ensure that the assembly is securely attached to the lifting device used for the safe removal of the unit.

Whether the differential carrier is removed with the inter-axle differential or not, the overhaul procedure is the same. We will proceed assuming the entire unit has been removed and mounted on a suitable stand.

To disassemble the power divider, follow the steps in **SKILL DRILL 53-10**. To reassemble it, follow the steps in **SKILL DRILL 53-11**.

SKILL DRILL 53-10 Disassembling the Power Divider

1. Turn the support stand so that the power divider housing is facing up. Loosen the input yoke attaching nut and use a suitable puller to remove the yoke. Remove the cap screws and lock washers that secure the power divider housing to the differential carrier housing.

2. If the power divider housing is tight to the differential carrier, lightly tap the drive yoke to loosen it or tap the housing near the dowel pins to break it free. There may be recesses where a pry bar can be inserted to help break the housing free. Use a suitable lifting device to lift the housing clear.

3. Using the hoist place the housing on a work bench. Remove the inter-axle differential from the differential carrier housing and set aside. The inter-axle differential may be a welded assembly and non-serviceable. If that is the case, it must be replaced as a unit.

SKILL DRILL 53-10 Disassembling the Power Divider (Continued)

4. Remove the front side gear/drop gear of the inter-axle differential by removing the snap ring holding the front side gear/drop gear to the input shaft. Then remove the side gear/drop gear, the thrust washer, and "D" washer (if equipped). Set everything aside. If not already removed, remove the input yoke. Hold the yoke in a holding fixture to remove the nut. The torque on this nut is usually in excess of 1000 ft-lb (1355 Nm). Use a puller, if necessary, to remove the yoke from the input shaft.

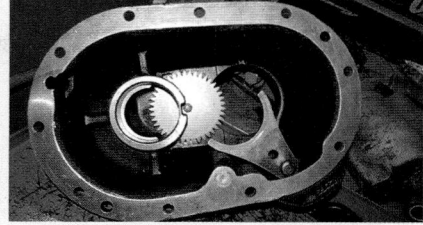

5. Remove the nut that secures the oil pump drive gear and remove the gear. Remove the differential lock cylinder from the front of the housing. Remove the shift bar nut and the shift piston and spring.

6. Remove the shift bar and yoke and the inter-axle differential sliding clutch from the rear of the housing. (This may have to done as the input shaft is removed.)

7. Remove the cap screws and washers securing the input shaft bearing cage to the front of the housing. Remove the input bearing cage and its shim pack. Measure and record the shim pack thickness for use on reassembly. Be careful not to misplace the shims—these shims are responsible for setting input shaft endplay, and you will need them during reassembly.

8. Remove the input shaft from the front of the housing.

9. Most, but not all, inter-axle differentials have a lube pump. Remove the cap screws holding the oil pump cover to the front of the housing and remove the oil pump. Discard the seal. Remove the magnetic lube strainer screen from the power divider front cover. Remove the pipe plug in the front cover to aid in cleaning the housing lube passages. Next, press the input bearing from the input shaft. Install a support to hold the sliding clutch on the input shaft against the back of the bearing and press the bearing off.

10. Remove the output shaft by pulling it up and out of the differential carrier cover. Discard the two O-rings. Remove the output shaft snap ring and remove the side gear and bearing. Replace the bearing by pressing it off the side gear with a suitable bearing puller. Replace the output shaft bearing cup in the housing. Clean all components and inspect carefully, as described previously, to determine suitability for reuse. Clean lube passages in the power divider cover.

▶ **TECHNICIAN TIP**

Late-model drive axles may be equipped with a spring and thrust button mounted between the input shaft and output shaft. Take care not to lose these components.

▶ **TECHNICIAN TIP**

At this point, if overhaul of the power divider drive axle portion is necessary, follow the procedure for drive axle overhaul discussed in the Drive Axle Overhaul—Removal and Inspection section.

SKILL DRILL 53-11 Reassembling the Power Divider

1. Press a new bearing onto the output shaft side gear. Install it on the output shaft, and install the snap ring. Install two new O-rings.
2. Replace the output shaft bearing cup in the housing and install the output shaft. If the output shaft has a spring and button, install them now.
3. Install the inter-axle differential.

4. Reassemble the input shaft by pressing on a new bearing cone and slide the differential lock sliding clutch over the shaft.
5. Install the side gear/drop gear and the snap ring and fit the inter-axle differential lock shift yoke and bar into the groove on the sliding clutch.
6. Reinstall the oil plug, the magnetic strainer, the oil pump gears, and the oil pump cover with a new O-ring seal.
7. Install the oil pump drive gear and retaining nut.
8. Slide the assembled shaft into place in the cover, feeding the shift yoke bar through the hole.
9. Install a new bearing cup and yoke seal in the input shaft bearing retainer cap and install the original shim pack.
10. Use a silicone-based gasket compound and install the assembled cover on the differential carrier. Tighten the cap screws to specification.

▶ TECHNICIAN TIP

Older-model interaxle differentials gear sets could be overhauled, but late-model units are permanently welded and must be replaced if there is any sign of excessive wear.

SKILL DRILL 53-12 Checking Input Shaft End Play

1. With the power divider cover installed, remove the input shaft bearing retainer and the shim pack. Hold the bearing retainer against the power divider cover with finger pressure and measure the clearance between the retainer and the cover with a feeler gauge.
2. Add 0.005" (0.127 mm) to the measurement above if new gearing is installed and 0.015" (0.381 mm) if the old gearing was reused. This results in the proper endplay of 0.003" to 0.007" (0.076 to 0.178 mm) for new gearing and 0.013" to 0.017" (0.330 to 0.432 mm) for used gearing.
3. Install the correct amount of shims, then torque the bearing retainer cap screws to specification and recheck the endplay. If the endplay is in the correct range, install an input yoke washer and torque the retaining nut to specification.

To check the input shaft endplay, follow the steps in **SKILL DRILL 53-12** in conjunction with the torque chart in **TABLE 53-4**. To reinstall the differential carrier or power divider assembly, follow the steps in **SKILL DRILL 53-13**. Note that the procedures for reinstalling a differential carrier and a power divider assembly are almost identical, so the general procedures in Skill Drill 53-13 apply to both.

SAFETY TIP

Disassembling the power divider can be done with the differential carrier still installed in the axle housing. In that case, as the power divider housing cap screws are removed, the housing may suddenly fall free of the differential carrier. Make sure that the power divider housing is securely supported before proceeding. Also, take steps to ensure that the inter-axle differential does not fall from the differential carrier housing when the inter-axle housing is removed.

TABLE 53-4 Torque Chart

Size	Torque in ft-lb	Torque in Nm
Input Shaft Nut		
1-5/8 – 18	780–960	1057–1301
M42 X 1.5	840–1020	1140–1383

Size	Torque in ft-lb	Torque in Nm
Bearing Cover Cap Screw		
1/2 – 13 (Grade 5)	75–85	101–115

SKILL DRILL 53-13 Reinstalling the Differential Carrier or Power Divider Assembly

1. Clean the axle housing interior with rags and a mild solvent to remove any metal particles. Clean flange mounting surface of all old gasket material.

2. Run a new bead of silicone gasket compound or install a new gasket. Install the differential carrier by reversing the removal process.

3. Install both axle shafts with a new gasket—installing the locating wedges and nuts. Torque the nuts to the correct specification.

4. Connect all air lines. Fill the axle with the correct lubricant until it is level with the fill hole. Lift the right side of the vehicle six inches or more for one minute. Then lower the right side and lift the left side for the same amount of time. Lower the left side and let the vehicle sit for one minute. Recheck and top up lubricant, as necessary. This procedure ensures that the wheel hubs have a sufficient level of lubricant and that the level in the drive axle housing is correct.

> ► **TECHNICIAN TIP**

If the vehicle is equipped with a main differential lock, the lock must be manually engaged before the differential carrier is reinstalled. Otherwise, it is difficult to install the axle shaft.

Diagnosing Component Failures in Drive Axle Systems

LO 53-5 Describe common component failures in drive axle systems and explain how to determine the root cause.

Failure analysis is a very important component of a technician's skill set. The ability to determine what, specifically, caused a failure to occur is essential to performing a complete repair and not having a repeat failure. If a power divider is disassembled and a broken inter-axle differential cross is discovered, as shown in **FIGURE 53-22**, it cannot be simply said that the cross itself was the cause of the failure. That is where the failure happened—but what caused it?

All other parts of the axle must be examined and a determination made as to the root cause of the failure. Several things must be considered when deciding the cause of failure—vehicle vocation, load, driver experience, road conditions, maintenance records, and an accurate report as to how and when the failure occurred. If the technician simply replaces the broken components without finding the cause, the vehicle will likely be back with the same or a similar failure in the future.

The true cause of a failure can usually be determined by knowing what to look for. Most manufacturers have guide books available to help the technician decide on a failure's root cause. Drive train systems are frequently the subject of premature failures caused by overloading, driver error or abuse, or poor maintenance practices. This section covers a methodical five-step process for diagnosing failures and then discusses the most common types of drive axle failures.

FIGURE 53-22 Re-assembling a failed component without discovering the cause of failure usually means the failure will re-occur.

Process for Diagnosing Failures

There are five general steps to diagnosing a component failure:

1. Record all the known details of the failure.
2. Investigate the vehicle history and condition.
3. Inspect the failed components carefully.
4. Determine the cause of the failure.
5. Ensure that the cause has been corrected.

Step One—Record Details of the Failure

Step one of diagnosing drive axle failures is to record all the known details of the failure. Start by checking the vehicle service history. Then, talk to the driver and ask the following questions:

- What is the vehicle used for?
- Is this problem a repeat failure or the first occurrence?

- How was the truck operating when the failure occurred?
- Did the driver notice anything unusual at the time of the failure?
- Were there any noises or vibrations?
- Was the vehicle or any of its components overheating?

Step Two—Investigate the Vehicle History and Condition

The second step in the diagnosis process is to investigate the vehicle history and its condition. Start this step by looking for any leaks, cracks, or other damage that may have contributed or caused the failure. Does the vehicle look like it receives regular maintenance or is it in poorly maintained condition? Record anything noteworthy that could be a contributing factor to the failure. Even something seemingly small at this point may help diagnosis once the component is disassembled.

Step Three—Inspect the Failed Components Carefully

Step three of the diagnosis process is to inspect the failed components carefully. While disassembling a unit, try to disturb as little as possible until the exact failed piece is discovered. Do not aggressively clean the parts as vital evidence may be washed away. Wait until disassembly is complete. Examine the lubricant. Is it full of metal shavings? Is the level and quality of the lubricant sufficient? Once the failed component is found, carefully examine it and all the parts it interacts with to determine what type of failure occurred. For example, was it fatigue failure, shock load failure, or was it a defect in the component?

Step Four—Determine the Cause of the Failure

Replacing a failed component without knowing why it failed is a recipe for disaster. It is up to the technician to determine what actually happened to the failed part and decide how to prevent reoccurrence.

When examining gears and shafts, remember the following: gears and shafts are typically made of ductile iron and are usually case- or induction-hardened—typically to a depth of no more than 0.050" (1.27 mm). The hardening allows the components' surface to resist wear, but the ductile core allows them to flex as they are loaded so that they can absorb some shocks. This flexibility allows them to bend before they break—a characteristic that provides insight into the actual cause of a failure.

The different types of failure that can occur are covered in detail in the Types of Drive Axle Failures section.

Step Five—Ensure That the Cause Has Been Corrected

The final step is to ensure that the cause has been corrected. Merely finding out what actually happened to a component may not be sufficient in proper failure analysis. For example, while examining a failed gear tooth, it can be clearly seen that a gas

pocket makes up a large percentage of the break site. It is safe to assume that the failure is a defect in material and replacing the components and rebuilding the unit will solve the problem. However, if a broken tooth is found and there is evidence of a fatigue failure—for example, beach marks—a determination must be made as to the cause of the constant overloading that led to the break.

Is the vehicle being used for a purpose that it is not capable of? If so, repairing the problem just means the vehicle will eventually be back with a repeat failure. When a shock load failure is discovered, it is necessary to investigate why it happened. Was it abuse? Would a driver education program help? If a lubrication failure occurred, does the vehicle maintenance program need to be revamped?

It is essential that the root cause of the problem has been determined and repaired, or at least documented on the work order, before a vehicle is returned to service. This protects the reputation of the technician and the service facility and allows the vehicle owner to consider what steps must be taken to prevent reoccurrence of the failure.

Types of Drive Axle Failures

Drive axle components can fail in several ways. The principal types of drive axle component failure include:

- shock load failures
- fatigue failures
- abuse failures
- lubrication failures

Proper repair of drive axles involves diagnosing and recognizing the characteristics of each type of failure.

Shock Load Failures

Shock load failures occur when a component is momentarily overloaded to a level that surpasses the base strength of the material, causing it to fail immediately. A shock load failure results in a broken component. **FIGURE 53-23** shows an extreme shock load failure.

FIGURE 53-23 A. Shock failures are recognizable by the uniform roughness **B.** of the surface areas where a break has occurred. However, if a component is run after the break, there will be some areas that are smoothed out.

If it is a shaft that breaks, the failure usually occurs at a section break. A **section break** is a point where the shaft changes in shape, thereby changing its section modulus (a measure of its load carrying capability). For example, where a spline or thread begins is a section break. So is the point where the shaft is suddenly thicker or thinner.

Shock failure breakage leaves a relatively flat and uniformly rough surface at the fracture area, as can be seen in Figure 53-23. Notice how the break follows the contour of the groove in the shaft. This groove constitutes a section break. Sometimes a shaft breaks on an angle, but again leaves the fractured surface uniformly rough. If the shaft has turned after the failure, the break surface may have smoothened out somewhat from rubbing against itself.

Shock load failure on a gear usually results in a broken gear tooth. The tooth surface will, again, be uniformly rough and there will typically be a raised area on the compression side of the break. If the gear is operated after breaking, this area may be worn down. Sometimes a defect in the manufacturing process can lead to gear tooth fracture. Small imperfections known as **gas pockets** or **stringers** can occur. Gas pockets (stringers) occur during the casting process when the metal of the entire tooth is not uniformly fused together with the metal of the rest of the gear. This type of imperfection significantly weakens the gear tooth. Gas pockets can be identified by a difference in texture and shape of the fracture surface. Some of the break area will be rough, as in a normal shock load failure, but other parts of the break area will have an unusual texture. For example, it could be smooth or even hollowed out. This change in texture will be quite obvious to the technician.

Fatigue Failures

Fatigue failures are those that occur over a period of time. They occur gradually and progress until the component fails. Fatigue failures can be classed into three separate types of failures—bending stresses, torsional or twisting stresses, and surface fatigue.

In bending fatigue failures, the component is stressed by enough load to crack the component, but insufficient to break it outright. The stress occurs repeatedly until the component finally does break. Bending fatigue usually occurs with gear teeth, and the break area is characterized by what are known as **beach marks**. Beach marks are semi-circular marks that indicate repeated cracking of the component. The crack continues to progress until the part fails, leaving telltale beach marks in the fracture, as can be seen in **FIGURE 53-24**. A fatigue failure indicates repeated overloading of the component, so the technician must take steps to prevent the overloading. Otherwise, the component will fail again.

Twisting or torsional failures usually occur with shafts that are constantly exposed to twisting forces sufficient to crack the material but insufficient to break it outright.

Torsional failures generally result in either a scalloped or star-type fracture. As shown in **FIGURE 53-25**, a scalloped-shaped fracture shows beach marks similar to a bending failure. In a star-type fracture, such as the one shown in **FIGURE 53-26**, some

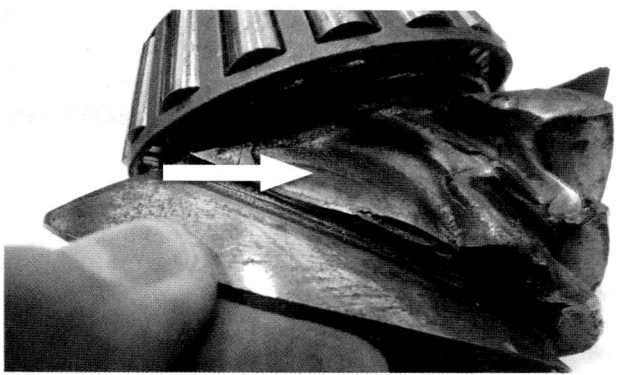

FIGURE 53-24 Gear teeth fatigue fractures are characterized by beach marks (indicated).

FIGURE 53-25 This input shaft shows classic beach marks indicative of a torsional fatigue failure.

FIGURE 53-26 This fuller main shaft shows a star-type fracture caused by repeated fatigue stresses.

of the break area is smoothed out by the shaft spinning after the break occurred.

Surface fatigue is the final type of fatigue failure. Surface fatigue is caused by overloading to such a degree that the hard surface of gear teeth breaks down and starts flaking away. This type of failure leads to pitting and spalling as the flaking progresses, resulting in eventual failure. There are many situations when minor pitting of a gear tooth is not cause for concern. As pitting progresses and the tooth surface breaks down, however, the involute shape of the tooth is lost, leading to noise and vibration. More information on spur gear wear patterns can be found in the Regular Wear or Maintenance Failures section of the Servicing Standard Transmissions chapter.

Abuse Failures

Several failures are the result of poor driver training and/or outright driver abuse. So-called **abuse failures** occur as a result of lack of driver training or caring. Dumping the clutch, backing into a loading dock, spinout, poor gear selection, and even downhill coasting are driver actions that can all lead to abuse failures.

Dumping the clutch is common, and yet preventable, abuse. When the driver dumps the clutch instead of smoothly engaging it, enormous stress load is placed on the entire driveline. Common failures that occur from this abuse are twisted main-shafts in the transmission, as shown in **FIGURE 53-27**; driveshaft torsional failures; broken universal joints; and axle shaft torsional failures.

Backing into a loading dock at speed is a driver abuse that can cause shock failures. Likewise, backing under a trailer too roughly or a trailer that is set too low for the tractor to pick up can also lead to failures.

Spinout—whether in a main differential or an inter-axle differential—is another common source of driver abuse that can cause catastrophic damage. When the driver allows the wheels to spin, the differential side and spider gears are rotating at enormous speeds. That creates a great deal of heat, which thins the gear lube and causes it to be thrown away from the components that need it the most. Differential spider gears can become welded to the cross legs because of the extreme heat. **FIGURE 53-28** shows an inter-axle differential cross that has sustained catastrophic damage due to spinout.

How serious is spinout? Just one instance of uncontrolled spin can cause the side and spider gears to turn more than they would for the lifetime of the vehicle if operated normally. That is a lifetime of wear in just a few seconds! Therefore, spinout should be avoided at all costs by proper driver training and the use of differential lockouts, if available.

In addition to failure caused by wear, spinout can also lead to severe shock loads if the wildly spinning wheels suddenly gain traction. **FIGURE 53-29** shows a side gear shattered by a sudden shock load caused by a spinning wheel suddenly gaining traction.

Poor gear selection by the driver can also lead to severe shock loads as the driver tries to re-engage the clutch. If the gear selection does not match the vehicle road speed, the driveline must absorb the shock, possibly leading to failure. Related to poor gear selection is choosing to coast downhill with the clutch disengaged. Doing so is another common driver abuse that contributes to shock load failure. This commonly happens when the vehicle is going too fast. The driver panics and tries to re-engage the clutch so that he can make use of the engine brakes. The result of the sudden shock load is typically a driveline failure.

The preceding is by no means a comprehensive list of failures that can occur due to abuse. It is merely a sampling of common driver-caused failures that are totally preventable with proper training.

Lubrication Failure

Lubrication failures are normally due to poor maintenance, incorrect lubrication, lack of lubrication, and/or contaminated lube. Driveline lubricants are the life blood of components, so

FIGURE 53-28 Spinout can cause catastrophic failures, such as in this inter-axle differential.

FIGURE 53-27 A twisted main shaft—typically caused by a sudden overload, like dumping the clutch.

FIGURE 53-29 Sudden shock when a spinning wheel hits dry pavement can lead to shock failures, such as this broken differential side gear.

any lubricant failure can lead directly to component failure. **FIGURE 53-30** shows an input gear from a standard transmission that basically melted during operation due to lack of lubricant. Think of the heat required to do that to a component.

Contaminated lubricant is a serious problem. Lubricant can become contaminated in several ways. One way is by mixing the wrong type of lubricants. Contamination also occurs when dirt is ingested through improperly filtered vents during normal component breathing. (All drive train components are vented to the atmosphere to allow components to breathe as the lubricant heats up and cools down.) Lubricant can also be contaminated by the introduction of foreign material during poor maintenance practices or because of component breakdown. Water can also contaminate lubricant. If the vehicle is operated in a wet area in which water rises above the component vent level, water ingestion could occur.

FIGURE 53-30 It is hard to imagine the amount of heat that can be generated when components have insufficient lubricant, but results like this burned input gear from a Fuller transmission are commonplace when lubrication is absent.

Wrap-Up

Ready for Review

- Proper maintenance, as with all other components, is essential to the service life of a drive axle. Timely fluid checks and changes can go a long way to protecting the equipment.
- Most drive axles today are shipped with synthetic lubricant instead of a mineral oil-based lubricant.
- It was common in the past for drive axles to require an initial fluid change at 3000 to 5000 miles (4828 to 8047 km); however, with the manufacturing accuracy of today, this is usually no longer necessary.
- Always check for metal particles in the drive axle lubricant during service. This can be a good indicator of a failing drive axle.
- When filling or topping up drive axle lubricant, always use the correct fluid and be aware that some drive axles require fluid to be added in more than one location.
- Most technicians will never overhaul a drive axle but, if it is attempted, it is essential that the correct service manual for the particular drive axle be available and consulted.
- All drive axles require the same four adjustments during overhaul: pinion bearing preload, pinion depth setting, side bearing preload, and the gear set backlash adjustment. Some axles also require other adjustments.
- Always mark the components, such as the side bearing retaining caps and the differential case halves, during disassembly so they can be reassembled correctly.
- The differential case in heavy-duty drive axles has two halves, the plain half and the flange half that the crown gear is attached to.
- The differential gears, the spider gears, and the side gears run on thrust washers. These and the surfaces they contact should be carefully inspected for wear.
- Pinion gears can be overhung (only two bearings) or straddle mounted, in which case they have a third spigot bearing supporting the end of the shaft.

- Note the position of all shims or shim packs and keep them separate while disassembling the drive axle. These are critical for setting pinion depth, pinion bearing preload, and power divider input shaft end play.
- All components in the axle should be checked for wear and damage—not just the obviously failed pieces.
- While rebuilding a drive axle, remember that the cost of replacement parts is small compared to having to redo the job. Replace all questionable parts.
- Crown and pinion gears are replaced as a set only. Most manufacturers sell replacement differential gears as a set also.
- Pinion depth may need to be adjusted to account for a pinion variation number.
- When reassembling the differential case, check the torque required to rotate the differential gears.
- Contact pattern is controlled by pinon depth and gear set backlash.
- Pinion and side bearing preload ensure rigidity in the gear set.
- After reassembling a drive axle, it is essential to check and, if necessary, correct the contact pattern.
- A conventional contact pattern should have three elements: close to but clear of the toe of the tooth, centered between the top land and the root, and extended across at least 50% of the tooth face.
- Durapoid and generoid gear sets have a centralized tooth contact pattern.
- After the contact pattern is correct, the thrust screw, if present, should be adjusted.
- Inter-axle differentials can be serviced without removing the entire power divider/differential carrier assembly.
- Power divider input shafts have end play, not preload.
- Component failures occur because of four basic issues: shock load failures, fatigue failures, lubrication failures, and abuse failures.
- When a component fails, it is essential to determine the correct cause to prevent re-occurrence.

Key Terms

abuse failure Failure directly attributed to driver or other person's actions operating a component, system or vehicle outside normal operating range.

beach mark Semi-circular mark in a fracture indicating repeated overload.

bearing adjuster Threaded wheel used to tighten the side bearing races.

bearing adjuster lock A Locking device used to secure the bearing adjusters.

bearing growth The increase in bearing size as it is pressed on to a shaft.

contact pattern The contact area between two gear teeth in contact.

fatigue failure Failure of components due to repeated overload.

flange case half The half of the differential case that the crown gear attaches to.

gas pocket Imperfection in the adhesion of molten metal during the casting or forming process, also known as a *stringer*.

gear set contact pattern The indication as to where the gears will contact each other during operation.

heel The end of a crown gear tooth furthest from the center of its axis.

lengthwise bearing The contact pattern along the tooth face from the toe toward the heel.

lubrication failure Failure caused by incorrect lubricant, contaminated lubricant, or lack of lubricant.

nominal shim pack A shim pack that is used if the pinion has a zero variation.

oil slinger A stamped steel ring used to throw lubricant in a certain direction.

overhung mount pinion A pinion mounted with only two opposed tapered roller bearings.

pinion bearing cage A removable casting that holds the two bearing races that support the pinion gear.

pinion depth The mounting position of the pinion in relation to the crown gear center of axis.

pinion pilot bearing A small bearing that supports the inboard end of the pinion gear when the pinion is straddle mounted. Also called *spigot bearing*.

pinion variation number A dimension to add or remove from the nominal pinion depth dimension.

plain case half The half of the differential case that does not bolt to the crown gear.

preload Negative endplay, or less than zero clearance.

profile bearing Contact pattern between the root and the top land of the tooth.

root The radius shape between the bottoms of two teeth. Also called *fillet radius*.

section break A point where the diameter of a shaft or thickness of a component changes.

shock load failure Fracture caused by one sudden shock.

side bearing bore The opening machined into the differential carrier that holds the side bearing races.

side bearing cap The cap that bolts the side bearing races to the side bearing bores.

spigot bearing A small bearing that supports the inboard end of the pinion gear when the pinion is straddle mounted. Also called *pinion pilot bearing*.

straddle mount pinion A pinion supported by two opposed tapered roller bearings and a small spigot bearing.

stringer Small inclusion in a cast or formed metal that weakens it, also known as a *gas pocket*.

thrust screw A screw that stops the crown gear from flexing under load.

tooth face The area that actually comes in contact with a mating gear and is parallel to the gear's axis of rotation.

top land The apex of a tooth.

Review Questions

1. Which of the following are two critical adjustments of a rear drive axle assembly not related to tooth contact pattern?
   a. Pinion depth and gear set backlash
   b. Crown gear depth and pinion depth
   c. Side bearing and pinion bearing preload
   d. Crown gear and pinion torque

2. If a drive axle's contact pattern is too close to the toe, which of the following must be done to correct it?
   a. Increase backlash
   b. Decrease backlash
   c. Move the pinion toward the crown gear
   d. Move the pinion away from the crown gear

3. If a drive axle tooth contact pattern is too low on the tooth (at the root), which of the following must be done to correct it?
   a. Increase backlash
   b. Decrease backlash
   c. Move the pinion toward the ring gear
   d. Move the pinion away from the ring gear

4. You examine a pinion gear that has broken and you see beach marks clearly present at the break point. Which of the following likely caused the break?
   a. A sudden shock to the drive train
   b. A repeated overloading of the drive train over a period of time
   c. A failure of the axle lubrication system
   d. Spinout

5. You examine a failed inter-axle differential and find the inter-axle differential cross has broken in several places at once. Each of the breaks has the same uniformly rough-looking surface. Which of the following could have caused this failure?
   a. A sudden shock to the drive train
   b. A repeated overloading of the drive train over a period of time
   c. A failure of the axle lubrication system
   d. Gas pockets or stringers

6. When setting pinion bearing preload on a heavy-duty drive axle, which of the following is a true statement?
   a. More shims between the bearings gives more preload.
   b. More shims between the bearings gives less preload.
   c. Preload should be adjusted by changing the torque on the pinion nut.
   d. Preload is adjusted by changing the bearings.

7. Which of the following is the main disadvantage of a non-locking rear drive axle differential assembly?
   a. It may not provide equal speed to both drive wheels.
   b. It does not allow for torque division.
   c. It does not redirect torque.
   d. It allows vehicle speed to increase.

8. Which of the following are two critical adjustments of a rear drive axle assembly that control tooth contact pattern?
   a. Pinion depth and gear set backlash
   b. Crown gear depth and pinion depth
   c. Side bearing and pinion bearing preload
   d. Crown gear and pinion torque

9. Which of the following describes a good hand-rolled, conventional tooth contact pattern in a hypoid drive axle?
   a. Close to the heel, centered between the top land and the root, and halfway along the tooth face
   b. Centered between the top land and the root, and centered between the toe and the heel
   c. Close to the toe, centered between the top land and the root, and halfway along the tooth face
   d. Close to the toe, close to the heel, and full contact along the tooth face

10. Which of the following describes a good hand-rolled generoid tooth contact pattern in a durapoid spiral bevel drive axle?
    a. Close to the heel, centered between the top land and the root, and halfway along the tooth face
    b. Centered between the top land and the root, and centered between the toe and the heel
    c. Close to the toe, centered between the top land and the root, and halfway along the tooth face
    d. Close to the toe, close to the heel, and full contact along the tooth face

ASE Technician A/Technician B Style Questions

1. Technician A says that drive axles do not usually require any regular maintenance as they are sealed units. Technician B says that some drive axles with synthetic lube do not need any maintenance for 500,000 miles. Who is correct?
   a. Technician A
   b. Technician B
   c. Both Technician A and Technician B
   d. Neither Technician A nor Technician B

2. Technician A says that a drive axle must always be filled from the plug at the rear of the housing to the correct level. Technician B says that some drive axles have more than one fill plug. Who is correct?
   a. Technician A
   b. Technician B
   c. Both Technician A and Technician B
   d. Neither Technician A nor Technician B

3. Technician A says that the pinion depth adjustment influences the drive axle's contact pattern. Technician B says that the gear set back lash influences the drive axle's contact pattern. Who is correct?
   a. Technician A
   b. Technician B
   c. Both Technician A and Technician B
   d. Neither Technician A nor Technician B

4. Technician A says that most power dividers today have lubrication pumps to lubricate the inter-axle differential. Technician B says that single axle drive axles rely on splash from the crown gears rotation to provide lubrication. Who is correct?
   a. Technician A
   b. Technician B
   c. Both Technician A and Technician B
   d. Neither Technician A nor Technician B

5. Technician A says that bearing growth refers to the increase in a bearing's size as it is pressed onto a shaft. Technician B says that bearing growth has no effect on pinion bearing preload as long as the original pinion bearing shim is used while installing a new pinion gear. Who is correct?
   a. Technician A
   b. Technician B
   c. Both Technician A and Technician B
   d. Neither Technician A nor Technician B

6. Technician A says that a main differential lock should be engaged before attempting to remove and reinstall the axle shafts. Technician B says that the inter-axle differential can be removed without removing the main differential carrier of the power divider. Who is correct?
   a. Technician A
   b. Technician B
   c. Both Technician A and Technician B
   d. Neither Technician A nor Technician B

7. Technician A says that pinion bearing preload can be measured with a string and a fish scale. Technician B says that pinion bearing preload in heavy-duty axles is controlled by the torque on the pinion nut. Who is correct?
   a. Technician A
   b. Technician B
   c. Both Technician A and Technician B
   d. Neither Technician A nor Technician B

8. Technician A says that side bearing preload holds the differential carrier rigid. Technician B says that gear set backlash is set after side bearing preload. Who is correct?
   a. Technician A
   b. Technician B
   c. Both Technician A and Technician B
   d. Neither Technician A nor Technician B

9. Technician A says that side gear support bearings should always be changed when overhauling a drive axle. Technician B says that spinout damage is usually visible as excess heat stress on the differential components. Who is correct?
   a. Technician A
   b. Technician B
   c. Both Technician A and Technician B
   d. Neither Technician A nor Technician B

10. Technician A says that, after replacing the pinion seal, installing the pinion yoke nut with a one-inch air gun is sufficient. Technician B says that some pinion nuts require as much as 1500 foot-pounds (2034 Nm) of torque. Who is correct?
    a. Technician A
    b. Technician B
    c. Both Technician A and Technician B
    d. Neither Technician A nor Technician B

CHAPTER 54

Electric Drive Vehicles and AC Traction Motors

Learning Objectives

After reading this chapter, you will be able to:

- **LO 54-1** Identify factors influencing the adoption of commercial battery electric vehicles (CBEVs) and Advanced Driver Assistance Systems (ADAS).
- **LO 54-2** Identify, describe, and classify types of commercial electric vehicles.
- **LO 54-3** Identify and describe features of CBEVs.
- **LO 54-4** Identify and describe CBEV architecture.
- **LO 54-5** Identify and describe the types, construction, and operation of traction motor propulsion systems.
- **LO 54-6** Identify and describe the types of induction-type traction motors.
- **LO 54-7** Identify and describe the types, construction, and operation of permanent magnet motors.

- **LO 54-8** Identify and describe the types, construction, and operation of switched reluctance motors (SRMs).
- **LO 54-9** Outline the methods used to switch traction motors from propulsion mode to generator mode.
- **LO 54-10** Explain the purpose of CBEV transmissions and identify the types of gear reduction systems they use.
- **LO 54-11** Identify and describe the categories, construction, and operation of energy storage systems (ESS).
- **LO 54-12** Describe and explain the design and operation of CBEV charging systems and electrical connectors.
- **LO 54-13** Identify and describe the hazards of high-voltage CBEV systems and common safety precautions.

You Are the Technician

To comply with occupational health and safety legislation, your workplace, a full-service commercial vehicle dealership, has a joint management-worker committee that is required to identify workplace health and safety hazards and ensure deficiencies and hazards are remediated. The committee has invited your expertise as a technician to help identify potential hazards for servicing hundreds of new battery electric vehicles. This hazard identification exercise is done with the purpose of developing safe working practices and procedures related to servicing CBEVs. As you prepare to meet with the committee and outline your observations, include answers to the following questions:

1. Identify and describe safety hazards CBEVs pose to technicians, customers, and other dealership employees encountering CBEVs in and around the service bays.
2. Identify and explain where the best reference and training material is located to use to properly educate employees and incorporate into workplace practices and procedures
3. Identify and explain what resources a technician requires to competently and safely service CBEVs.

Introduction

Two new major technologies are expected to fundamentally change the way current chassis systems are designed, operated, and serviced. One is automated, or autonomous driving systems, more accurately called Advanced Driver Assistance Systems (ADAS). The commercial vehicle ADAS concept includes elements of advanced driver assistance adopted from automobile manufacturers to enhance vehicle and passenger safety (**FIGURE 54-1**). The second disruptive technology is commercial battery electric vehicles (CBEVs), which are expected to replace diesel engine-based powertrains. CBEVs do not use an engine, but are propelled exclusively by electric traction motors supplied with electric current from onboard batteries. In most applications, the batteries are recharged at a charging station connected to the power grid. One exception is commercial vehicles using hydrogen fill-ups to operate fuel cells. Fuel cells produce electric current used to both operate traction motors and charge batteries.

This chapter examines CBEV technology from a technician's perspective to help provide the foundational information about their construction and operation necessary to develop service skills and practices.

Factors Influencing Adoption of CBEV and ADAS

LO 54-1 Identify factors influencing the adoption of commercial battery electric vehicles (CBEVs) and Advanced Driver Assistance Systems (ADAS).

Many of the components and systems used for CBEV and ADAS are well known. But several factors have pushed both technologies off the shelf into marketable product. For ADAS, it is primarily efficiency and safety. Limiting the driver's involvement to more complex tasks, or even dispensing with the driver, would allow longer service hours, eliminate the expense of driver wages, and result in potentially fewer accidents caused by driver error. For CBEVs, electrification makes sense to original equipment manufacturers (OEMs) looking for solutions to reduce greenhouse gas (GHG) emissions as much as 40% by 2027 compared to 2010 levels. An even greater

interest in promoting the uptake of CBEVs is in Europe and China where environmental policy to discourage or even ban the use of diesels is more widely supported (**FIGURE 54-2**). Initial purchase costs for CBEVs are higher than conventional diesel-powered equipment, but the industry points to cost per mile reductions of around 60% for maintenance and 70% fuel cost. Zero local emissions and the potential for improved public safety are important reasons for favorable taxation and other legislative policy supporting adoption of both ADAS and CBEV technology.

Classification of Medium and Heavy Duty (MHD) Electric Vehicles

LO 54-2 Identify, describe, and classify types of commercial electric vehicles.

Dedicated electric vehicles without batteries are common in public transportation systems where electric current is supplied through overhead conductors (**FIGURE 54-3**). Street cars, electric buses, and locomotives use the alternating current (AC) power source to supply electric traction motors. Brushes maintain a sliding contact with the overhead electrical conductors. To remain mobile when overhead electrical power is unavailable, a few vehicles use a small engine to move the vehicle short distances. In Europe, the use of what are called electric highways is expanding. These roads also provide overhead power lines to supply Class 8 vehicles (**FIGURE 54-4**). In contrast to these single power source electric vehicles, the term hybrid-electric vehicle (HEV) refers to a vehicle propulsion system having at least two

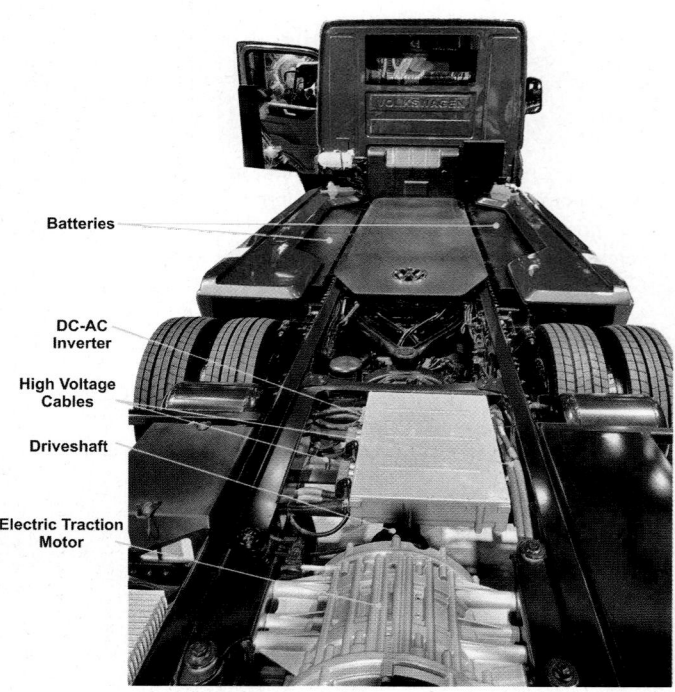

FIGURE 54-2 A single axle battery electric drive chassis from Volkswagen.

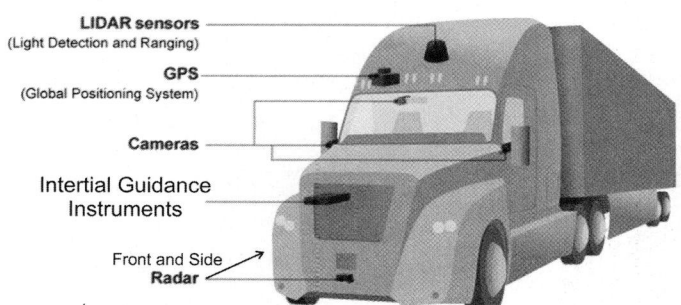

FIGURE 54-1 Elements of Advanced Driver Assistance Systems (ADAS) or autonomous-drive truck.

FIGURE 54-3 Electric buses receive electric power from overhead conductors.

FIGURE 54-4 An electrified Class 8 tractor used on an electric highway.

sources of power. One is an electric motor and the other is an internal combustion engine. Electrical energy powering the motor can originate from batteries, fuel cells, or even capacitors.

Plug-In HEV and Range Extended Electric Vehicles (REEV)

Another variation of HEV is a plug-in hybrid-electric vehicle (PHEV) (**FIGURE 54-5**). These vehicles can operate as battery-electric vehicles (BEVs) by recharging at a charging station, which enables them to run on only battery power alone and indefinitely, as long as they are recharged within the vehicles normally short driving time or distance (**FIGURE 54-6**). An engine is still needed to propel the vehicle once the batteries are depleted or the charge falls below a threshold required to operate on battery power alone. Once started, the engine does one or a combination of things. If the vehicle is a series-parallel hybrid, power from the motor and engine is blended to propel the vehicle. If the engine does not assist propulsion, such as in a series hybrid configuration, the engine drives a generator that recharges the batteries. Battery recharging takes place in both hybrid configurations using an engine-driven generator.

HEV	PHEV	BEV
Hybrid Electric Vehicle	Plug-in Hybrid Electric Vehicle	Battery Electric Vehicle
ICE	ICE	
Regenerative Braking	Regenerative Braking	Regenerative Braking
Electric Motor	Electric Motor	Electric Motor
Batteries	Batteries	Batteries
Gasoline / Diesel	Gasoline / Diesel	

FIGURE 54-5 Comparing internal combustion engines (ICEs), hybrids, plug-in hybrids, and battery-electric vehicles.

A variation of the PHEV is a range extended electric vehicle (REEV). This powertrain configuration recharges batteries while it is operating to extend the driving range. Examples in this category are the Class 8 Nikola One and Two battery electric trucks that use fuel cells to recharge the batteries, as does the WrightSpeed truck chassis (**FIGURES 54-7** and **54-8**). WrightSpeed Class 7–8 trucks use a compact turbine engine to

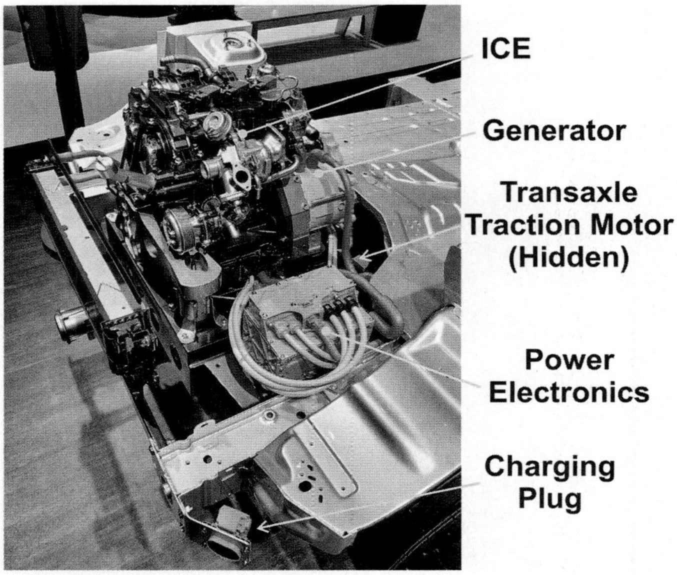

FIGURE 54-6 A plug-in hybrid electric powertrain for a Class 3 delivery truck. The vehicle combines the use of an engine-mounted electric generator and an ICE engine to propel the vehicle.

drive a generator to slow the rate of charge depletion in the batteries. Like automotive equivalents of the Chevy Bolt and Volt, this configuration helps lower the number and weight of batteries needed to give it a range of between 300 and 500 miles when loaded. However, the smaller range extending generator cannot maintain the batteries' state of charge when operating under load and the charge eventually depletes.

Fuel Cell Electric Vehicles

An example of a current vehicle producing electricity from fuel cells is the Nikola Motor Company trucks, the Nikola One and Two. The Nikola's use 800-volt electric drive motors supplied

FIGURE 54-7 A turbine-driven generator can extend the driving range of a CBEV by charging the batteries.

energy by fuel cells. Fuel cells operate on an electrochemical principle that reverses the more familiar process of electrolysis. In electrolysis, electric current passed through electrodes in water breaks the molecule into hydrogen and oxygen. In fuel cells, compressed hydrogen and atmospheric oxygen combine to generate electric current to charge the battery packs. The Nikola's have a driving range of 500 to 1200 miles before needing 20 minutes to fill up with hydrogen. The on-board hydrogen storage tanks can be filled at special filling stations. The fueling procedure is almost identical to refueling with compressed natural gas. Hydrogen is pumped into pressurized tanks at pressures up to 700 bar (10,153 psi). Gaseous hydrogen is reduced to a pressure of 45 psi (3 bar) through pressure regulators before reaching the fuel cells. Each tank can hold 80 liters of hydrogen weighing about 6.44 kg or 14 lb, to supply a voltage of 250 V to 450V (**FIGURE 54-9**).

At start-up, the vehicle depends completely on the batteries to power the motors and auxiliary systems. Only after 5–30 seconds of warm-up operation can the fuel cells begin to generate

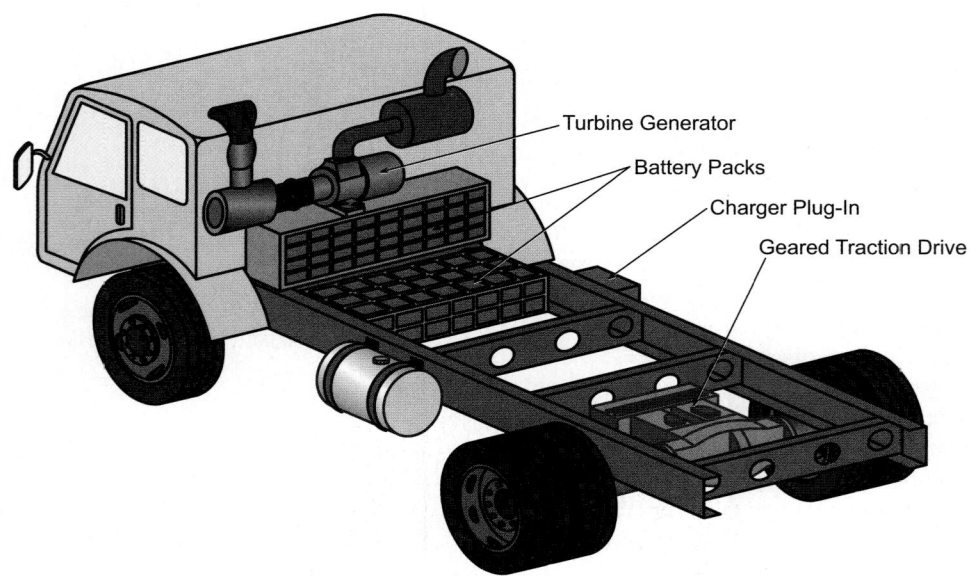

FIGURE 54-8 WrightSpeed uses a microturbine generator to extend the driving range of refuse haulers in stop-and-go urban traffic.

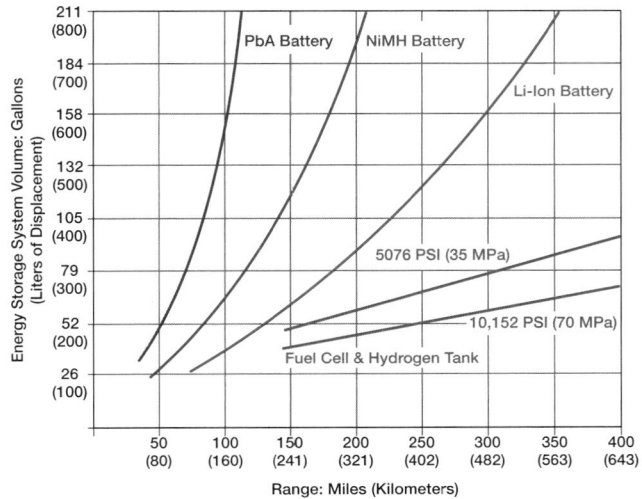

FIGURE 54-9 The chassis of a delivery vehicle using fuel cells. This vehicle has a 300 mile or 500 km range.

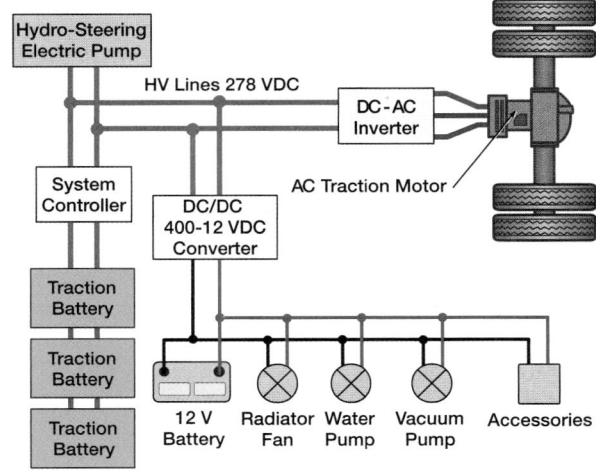

FIGURE 54-10 Fuel cells use hydrogen costing twice as much as diesel fuel, but extend the driving range without adding significant weight compared to other energy storage systems.

FIGURE 54-11 A common system layout for a CBEV chassis.

current. Once warm, the fuel cell provides adequate current flow for cruising speed. However, during acceleration, and under heavy load, the batteries must supplement the fuel cell output current. Fuel cells have an advantage over batteries because a fuel cell-powered truck requires less energy storage by weight and volume compared to a battery-only vehicle (**FIGURE 54-10**).

Evolution to CBEVs

LO 54-3 Identify and describe features of CBEVs.

Medium-Heavy Duty chassis hybrid drive (MHD)-HEVs have not been well-accepted, despite their ability to reduce fuel consumption by as much as 30%. Higher initial purchase cost is the result of adding an electric powertrain, batteries, and supporting electronic control and power systems to a chassis already equipped with an internal combustion engine. The advantages of having higher torque output accompanied by reduced emissions and fuel consumption are offset by the complexity of hybrid powertrain designs. Substantially higher initial costs mean HEVs cannot produce a return on investment within the industry metric of two years. Because HEVs are also impractical

for on-highway applications, such as line haul, many of those MHD hybrid programs are now displaced by battery-only electric vehicle initiatives.

In comparison to HEVs and internal combustion engine vehicles (ICEVs), CBEVs are much simpler and more flexible in the configuration of their propulsion systems (**FIGURE 54-11**). In some cases, the reduced complexity can translate into purchase costs that are comparable with traditional diesel engine powertrains. Routine maintenance costs involved in replacing drive belts, fuel, oil, and air filters are nonexistent. No separate exhaust or starting system is required either. Electric motors are much simpler in design than internal combustion engines, having a rotor as the only major moving part. Motor rotation is selectable, allowing it to turn clockwise to move the vehicle forward and counterclockwise to reverse its direction. Because the design of electric motors selected for propulsion systems produce maximum torque output at low rpm, such as when starting with a heavy load, few or no other powertrain components are needed. This means a clutch or multi-step standard or automatic transmission with torque converters are eliminated. Motors can directly drive the wheels or may have only a single step gear reduction system. Shorter driving ranges and the need for a powerful charging station for CBEVs means medium-duty trucks and transit buses that return to a base every day are currently the best application for CBEVs.

CBEV Flexibility and Efficiency

CBEVs have tremendous design flexibility provided by motors at wheel ends or attached to the input of a drive axle. Rather than transmit torque through rigid shafts, energy flow in CBEVs is easily routed through electrical cables. A single electric traction motor may be bolted to the input of a rear axle. Alternatively, heavy complex transmission power dividers and differentials are replaced by connecting a motor at two or more wheel ends and using a single step gear reduction mechanism providing anywhere between 2:1 and 6:1 motor speed reduction (**FIGURE 54-12**). Eliminating the engine as a prime mover, or the device supplying the traction force, means accessories, such as the air conditioning compressor, air compressors, coolant, and power steering pumps, are electrified as well. High and low-voltage electric motors drive these devices on demand. Operating only as they are needed reduces parasitic power losses common to engine-driven accessories.

Regenerative Braking

A feature carried over from HEVs to CBEVs is regenerative braking. Regenerative braking recaptures some of the energy that would normally be lost as heat from mechanical brakes. By switching a CBEV electric drive motor(s) into generator mode, the mechanical resistance generating electricity can also brake the vehicle while producing electricity to charge batteries. High mechanical resistance to wheel rotation is achieved by supplying the motor stator windings with a small amount of direct current (DC) rather than high-voltage AC to drive the motor. The mechanical rotation of the motor, in turn, generates a much higher AC output compared to the DC input. AC output in generator mode is converted to DC used to recharge the batteries. If the batteries are already charged or near a fully charged state, the current produced by the motors turned generators must be used somewhere else. Large power resistors can convert the current into heat. A unique electrical circuit called a **chopper circuit** redirects the generator output current into DC dissipated through resistive heating (**FIGURE 54-13**). This enables the regenerative braking to remain effective even when the batteries cannot absorb a charge. Regenerative braking not only improves vehicle efficiency, but can dramatically reduce brake wear since braking force is supplied by the motors switched into generator mode. As more electric power is generated by wheel rotation, increased braking force supplied by electric generation means less wear takes place in brake friction materials. Blended braking takes place when regenerative braking and mechanical friction braking work together. Algorithms controlling generator fields are used to provide effective braking combined with feedback to the operator that simulates mechanical-only braking (**FIGURE 54-14**).

CBEV Design Changes

Two different approaches to CBEV design depend on whether the vehicle is made by established OEMs or start-up companies, such as Tesla, Thor Trucks, and Nikola Motor Company. For OEMs, such as Daimler's E-Mobility group, Volvo, Mercedes,

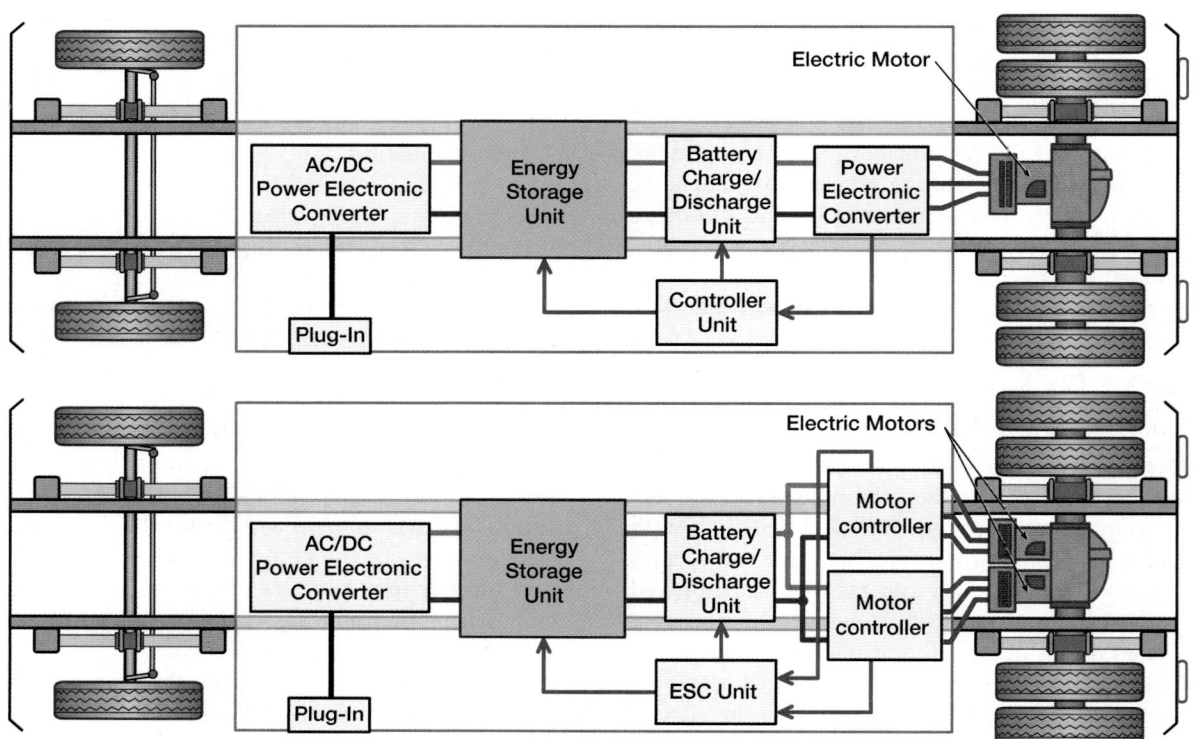

FIGURE 54-12 Two common configurations for CBEVs eliminating the transmission or transmission and differential.

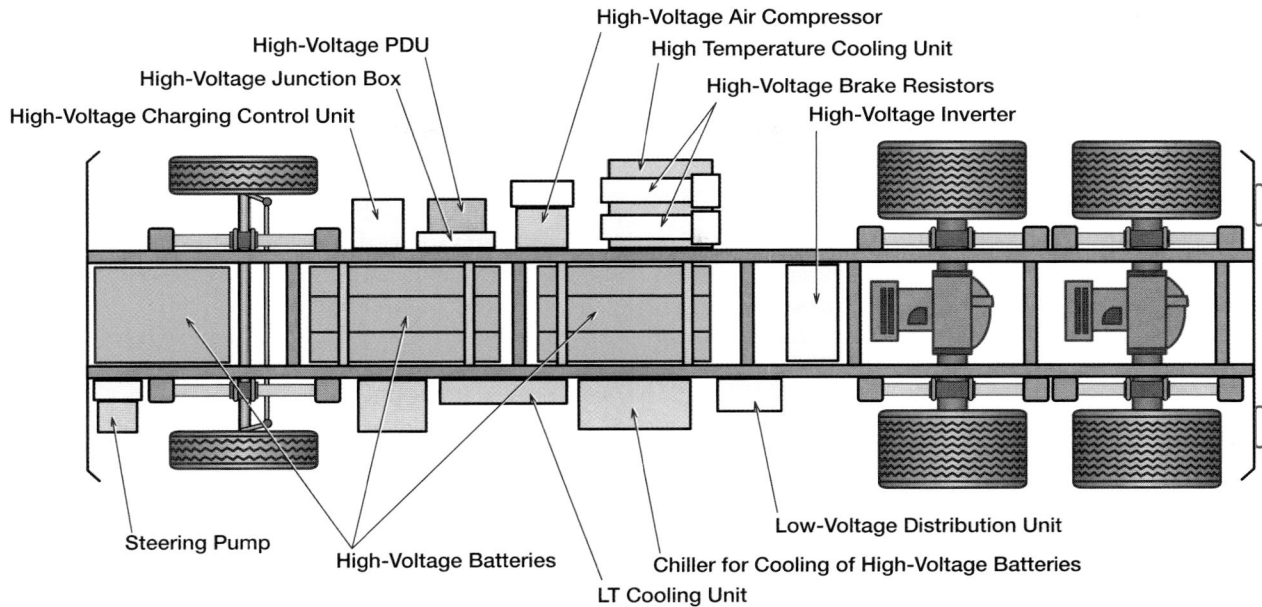

High-Voltage Air Compressor
High Temperature Cooling Unit
High-Voltage PDU
High-Voltage Brake Resistors
High-Voltage Junction Box
High-Voltage Inverter
High-Voltage Charging Control Unit

Steering Pump
High-Voltage Batteries
Low-Voltage Distribution Unit
Chiller for Cooling of High-Voltage Batteries
LT Cooling Unit

FIGURE 54-13 The high-voltage brake resistors of this Mercedes truck are used to absorb electric current during regenerative braking if the batteries are full or the supply of current is excessive.

FIGURE 54-14 Blended regenerative braking combines the action of mechanical friction brakes with regenerative braking to slow the vehicle.

Energy Storage
Single Electric Traction Motor
Power Electronics
Conventional Drivetrain
Electrically Driven Air Compressor

FIGURE 54-15 One approach to building CBEV is to retrofit a chassis with an electric drive motor that replaces the engine and transmission.

Navistar, and DAF, the most cost-effective path to CBEV production is to retrofit the diesel engine powertrain with a single electric motor (**FIGURE 54-15**). Further refinement of the chassis takes place progressively as more components are replaced to create a vehicle reflecting development as a dedicated electric-only powertrain. This means the chassis for Freightliner's e-Cascadia Class 8 tractor or the electric drive eM2 medium-duty trucks remains essentially unchanged except for the replacement of engines and transmissions with electric drive axles supporting the load on a standard "H" or ladder frame. Legacy components, such as cabs and hoods once enclosing

the engine, remain in place. To remain compatible with the remaining chassis systems, other systems, such as suspensions, braking, and the 12- or 24-volt electrical system undergo little alteration.

In contrast to legacy vehicles converted to CBEV from traditional OEMs, a look at prototype vehicles from start-up CBEV companies shows a radical departure from conventional vehicle design (**FIGURE 54-16**). Clean sheet models, where engines and large radiators are not used, allow for major alternations to hoods and cabs. Cabs are built lower, are more spacious, and are more aerodynamic. Electric motors are placed at the wheel ends and batteries are between box-type frames after the driveline is removed. The use of regenerative braking can change the brake system type, operation, and design of other wheel end components (**FIGURE 54-17**). Friction braking systems are more compact because they do not require as much brake torque

(**FIGURE 54-18**). Electrically operated brakes and hydraulic brakes frequently replace conventional air brake systems in current CBEVs in Europe.

Commercial Battery Electric Vehicle Architecture

LO 54-4 Identify and describe CBEV architecture.

Basic building blocks for CBEVs use a combination of electric motors, power electronics, and energy storage devices, which are typically lithium batteries. To understand the architecture of a contemporary CBEV, it is helpful to understand that any CBEV is comprised of three major divisions or systems (**FIGURE 54-19**). These are:

1. Electric propulsion system consisting of one or more electric motors and associated electronic control units to manage electric current. An inverter converting DC stored in batteries to AC used by the motor is included in this system.
2. An energy source that is at least a battery, or more commonly a combination of batteries, ultra-capacitors, or fuel cells. The energy source also requires power control electronics to convert AC and DC to different voltages when charging and discharging batteries, as well as controlling the charging rate to battery cells.
3. Auxiliary systems are electrically driven vehicle support devices. These can include electrical components used by the temperature control systems for the cab, cooling for batteries, motors and power electronics, and air and power steering pumps. The auxiliary power supply provides electric current at different voltages required by CBEV auxiliary components. **DC to DC converters,** which increase or decrease DC battery voltage supplied to auxiliary electrical devices, are needed for this job.

Electronic Control Units

Within each of the major systems are subsystems. For example, one subsystem is the electronic system controller (ESC), which is a general term for a major electronic control unit common to all three major systems. This device takes driver inputs from the chassis and brake and accelerator pedals, and produces electrical control signals to regulate the current flow between the

FIGURE 54-16 Ford's prototype Class 8 electric truck the F-Vision uses unconventional design without the limitations of accommodating an engine and radiator.

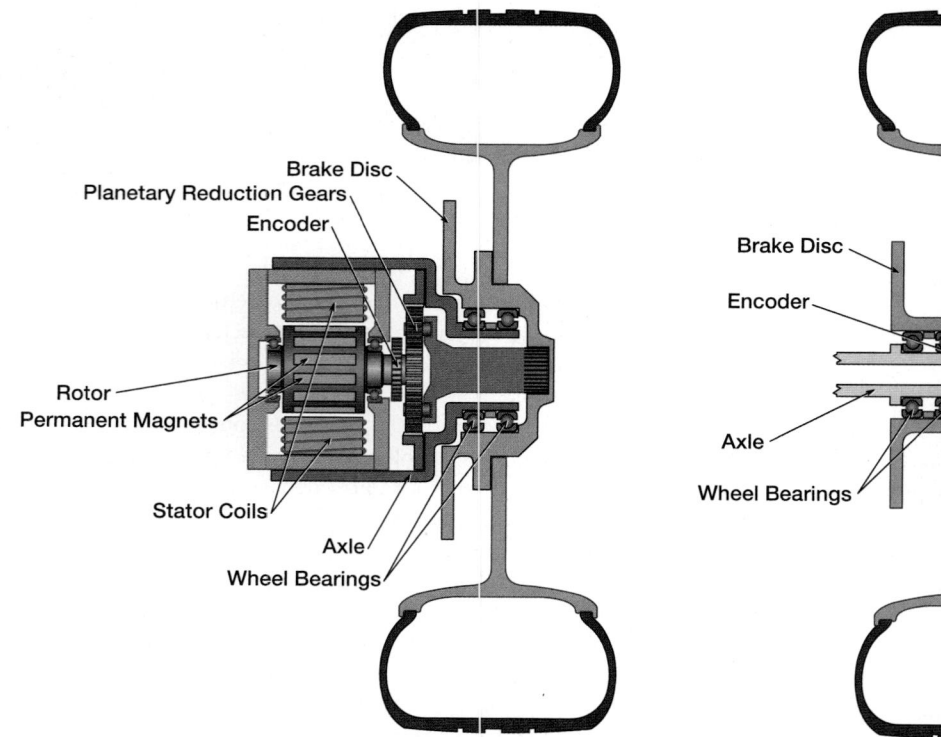
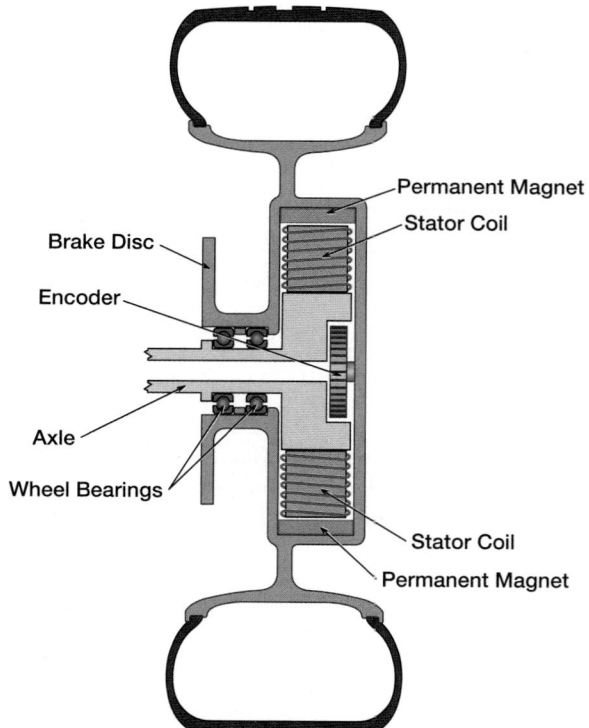

FIGURE 54-17 Brake rotor's size is reduced when hub motors are combined with regenerative braking capability.

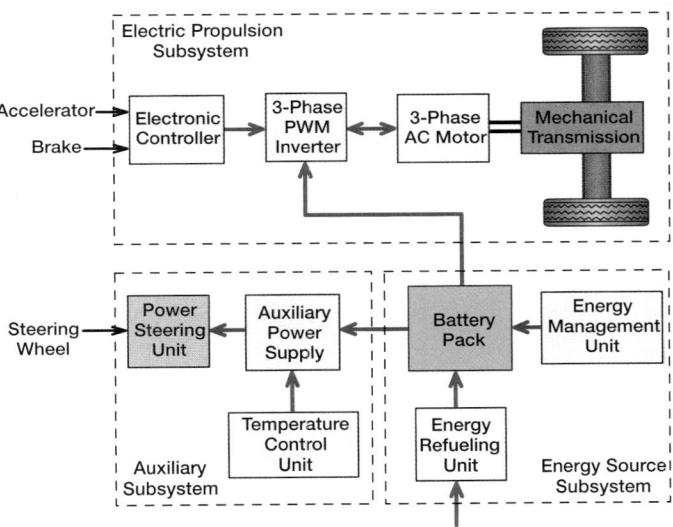

FIGURE 54-18 An air disc brake rotor integrated into a wheel hub motor.

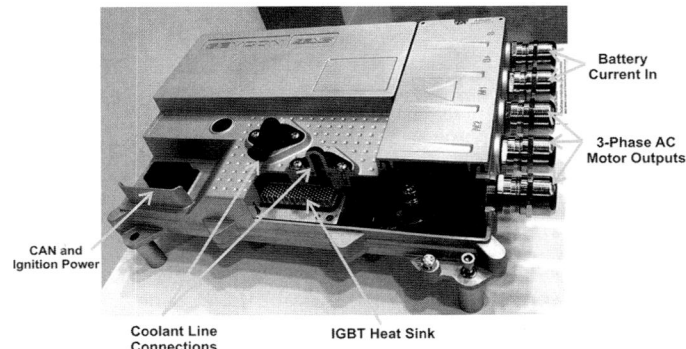

FIGURE 54-20 The traction motor operation is regulated by an electronic control module that converts DC to AC while varying the voltage and frequency of AC output.

FIGURE 54-19 A block diagram showing the layout of a basic system division in a CBEV.

electric motor and the energy source. Regenerative braking is also controlled by this module to switch the direction of current flow and type of current supplied to the stator. Using network communication, the ESC coordinates the actions of the energy management electronic control unit regulating the charge rate of the battery cells. It also works with the energy-refueling control unit or charging controller converting high-voltage AC to DC used to charge the batteries when the vehicle is plugged into the power grid.

Motor Control Modules

An electronic control device is needed to regulate the speed and torque output of the electric motor. These devices are often called inverters because CBEV propulsion systems must convert

DC battery voltage to AC. DC waveform is inverted or switched to an AC sine wave shape. Motor speed is also controlled by the frequency of AC voltage change, which is varied by the motor controller. This capability lends the controller other terms such as AC drive, variable speed drive (VSD), or **variable frequency drive (VFD)**. Most traction motors use AC because it conducts with less resistance than DC. The switching of AC polarity back and forth in a conductor, alternating between pushing and pulling electrons, translates into less voltage drop through long motor windings compared to DC. Motors run cooler and more efficiently on AC. Increasing AC switching frequency further lowers a motor windings resistance to AC. If the motor uses AC, the correct term for the motor control module's primary function is frequency converter (**FIGURE 54-20**).

Motor control modules are positioned between the DC battery supply and the motor. Battery current is carried directly into the motor control module using heavily insulated orange-colored conductors designating the cables as having dangerously high voltage levels. DC in the control module is then directed into capacitors to smoothen voltage fluctuations, thus providing a clean power supply signal for the next step of inversion. Inverter circuits containing **insulated gate bipolar transistors (IGBT)** convert DC to AC power output supplied to motor windings. During inversion, the AC signal frequency and voltage are adjusted to match motor speed and torque demands. Increasing or decreasing voltage changes motor torque, while changing the AC frequency changes speed.

To rapidly switch current flow on and off, blocking hundreds of volts, while conducting hundreds of amps, requires the use of IGBTs. These devices combine a field effect transistor (FET) and conventional bipolar transistors. They consist of four alternating semiconductor layers (P-N-P-N) that conduct or block current flow, which are in turn biased by an insulated metal-oxide-semiconductor (MOS) gate. To handle high amounts of current with little voltage drop, many IGBT are connected in parallel and invert low amperage current at high voltage to reduce heat generated by low-voltage, high-amperage current. These devices, while very efficient, still generate some heat. To increase module longevity, a cooling circuit is placed beneath the IGBT to increase the modules reliability.

Traction Motor Propulsion System

LO 54-5 Identify and describe the types, construction, and operation of traction motor propulsion systems.

When adapted to propel a vehicle, electric motors are called traction motors. The primary qualification for a motor is the ability to efficiently deliver high propulsion torque over a wide speed range. Power consumption and torque output at various speeds, heat, noise, durability, and cost are various factors traded off for optimal motor choice for a particular application. CBEV motors are capable of operating over a much wider speed and load range than common industrial motors. Traction motors must also have the capability of producing high intermittent torque output, twice that of industrial motors when heavily loaded or accelerating, without burning out. Continuous torque output performance levels are higher as well. These requirements translate into the necessity of using new materials, sophisticated electronic controls, and clever design variations. Factors considered for motor selection include:

- Frequency of starting/stopping
- Expected rates of acceleration and deceleration
- Torque requirement for low-speed hill climbing and cruise speed
- Range of vehicle speed operation

A motor that is ideal for urban stop-and-go driving conditions is not often the best motor for high speed operation on a highway where little brake regeneration takes place. For line-haul tractors operating under high loads at steady speed, high-torque, low-speed motors rotating at approximately 1000 rpm are mounted inside the wheel hub and are known as in-wheel motors or hub motors. These motors use a planetary gear reduction system to drive the wheel at a realistic speed. Placing traction motors there eliminates the need for transmissions and differentials. When these major components are removed, the vehicle is lightened, and more room is available to place batteries in between the frame rails. The disadvantages are the motors larger size, weight, and cost because of the low-speed design and the use of multiple motors. Advanced algorithms to control wheel speed when cornering and for antilock brake system (ABS) and traction control are also needed.

For urban driving with low speed, frequent stop-start conditions, a single motor is used to reduce cost. Because the urban vocational chassis driving torque demands are not as high as a line-haul tractor, using only one or two motors provides acceptable power output. A single motor consumes less power and requires few supporting electronic control systems. The disadvantage is a differential is required when only one motor is used (**FIGURE 54-21**). A gear reduction system may be used to multiply torque from a high-speed motor and a transfer case is used for four-wheel drive. To prevent motor burn-out, many motors use water-cooled cases to absorb excess heat. A separate cooling system for motors, batteries, and electronic control modules is necessary on CBEV chassis.

Dual-Traction Motors

Two motors can be connected through a single drive mechanism and the power output regulated to balance the work done by each motor (**FIGURE 54-22**). The two-motor design offers these advantages:

- Lower, safer voltage requirements for each motor, rather than a single motor requiring higher input voltage
- Improved power density, which means more torque is delivered by two motors than a single motor
- Higher power efficiency than a single motor design with the same power output due to lower motor amperage
- Reduced space and weight compared to using two separate motors
- A back up motor to keep the vehicle mobile if one motor fails
- 1.5 times more surface area for improved liquid cooling

Other configurations for dual-traction motors place the motors in the same axis as the drive axle.

Types of Traction Motors

LO 54-6 Identify and describe the types of induction-type traction motors.

Electric motors have been around a long time. DC motors using brushes, a commutator, armature, and series-wound field coils are used for starting motors. These motors have

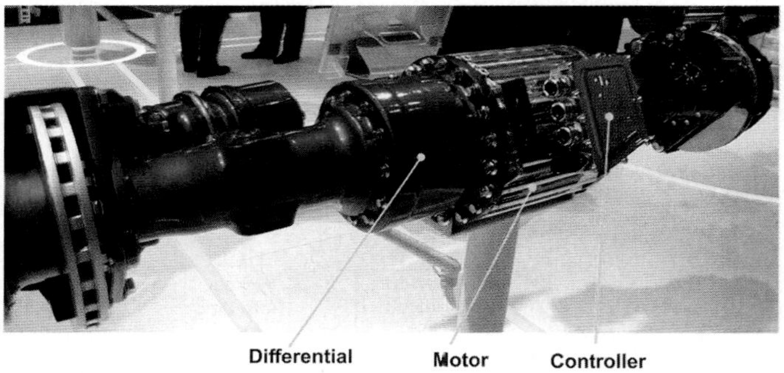

FIGURE 54-21 This single electric motor integrated into a drive axle for an urban truck requires a differential.

FIGURE 54-22 Dual-traction motors can operate at lower amperage providing greater efficiency, less weight, and more power output than two separate motors or a single high-amperage motor.

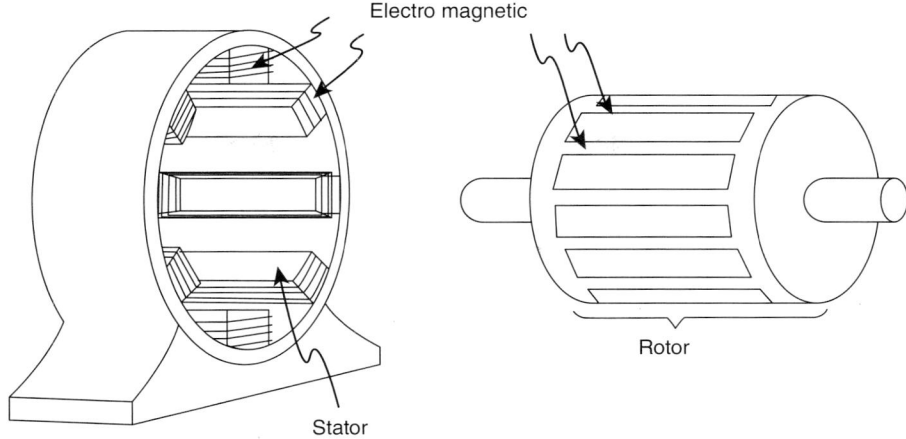

FIGURE 54-23 The magnetic field of the stator switches polarity and moves in and out from the motor centerline. The moving magnetic field induces current flow in the rotor bars.

the highest torque output at stall speed but are very inefficient and wear out quickly when under load. Eliminating the brushes would be a first major step to improving a DC motor. Improving motor efficiency while removing the problem of rapidly wearing brushes was solved coincidently by Nikola Tesla—the namesake for two new but different CBEV startup companies. Tesla invented the AC **induction motor (IM)**, which is the type used by close to 90% of all industrial motors used in the world today. IMs are not always the best choice for traction motors. The induction of current producing motor rotation is inefficient at times. To improve motor efficiency so it consumes less battery power and drives at a high torque, permanent magnets are used. Magnets do not require current to produce a magnetic field and, therefore, can naturally reduce power consumption while exerting force. Three major categories of motors are used in today's CBEVs, including:

1. AC induction motors (IMs)
2. Permanent magnet (AC and DC type)
3. Switched reluctance motors (SRM)

AC Induction Motor Operating Principles

Like DC motors covered in the chapter on starting systems, AC induction motors also use principles of magnetic repulsion to produce motor rotation. What is different in the AC motor is the commutator is eliminated and the job of switching magnetic field polarity is performed instead by the changing direction of AC.

Traditional AC induction motors are simple, relatively inexpensive devices consisting of a rotor and stator (**FIGURE 54-23**). Interaction of magnetic poles created in the rotor and stator produce motor rotation. The rotor is made of several solid metal conductor bars attached to the motor shaft and enclosed by the stator. Stationary wire windings arranged in slots on inside circumference of the motor housing make up the stator (**FIGURE 54-24**).

FIGURE 54-24 A three-phase motor stator.

Induction motors derive their name from the use of AC passing through the stator that induces current flow in the rotor conductor bars. Basic principles of magnetic induction explain how current is induced in the rotor by the frequent and rapidly switching magnetic poles in the stator. Remembering that current flow in a conductor not only produces a magnetic field, but the direction of flow establishes magnetic polarity. This means a winding in the stator, next to the rotor can have a north or south orientation, depending on the direction of current flow (**FIGURE 54-25**). Continuous cycling of AC in the stator windings switches its magnetic poles from north to south and back again many times per second. Electromagnetic poles briefly formed in the stator influence the area directly below it in the rotor. Consequently, current flow is induced in conductor bars of the rotor. These bars, which are commonly made of copper

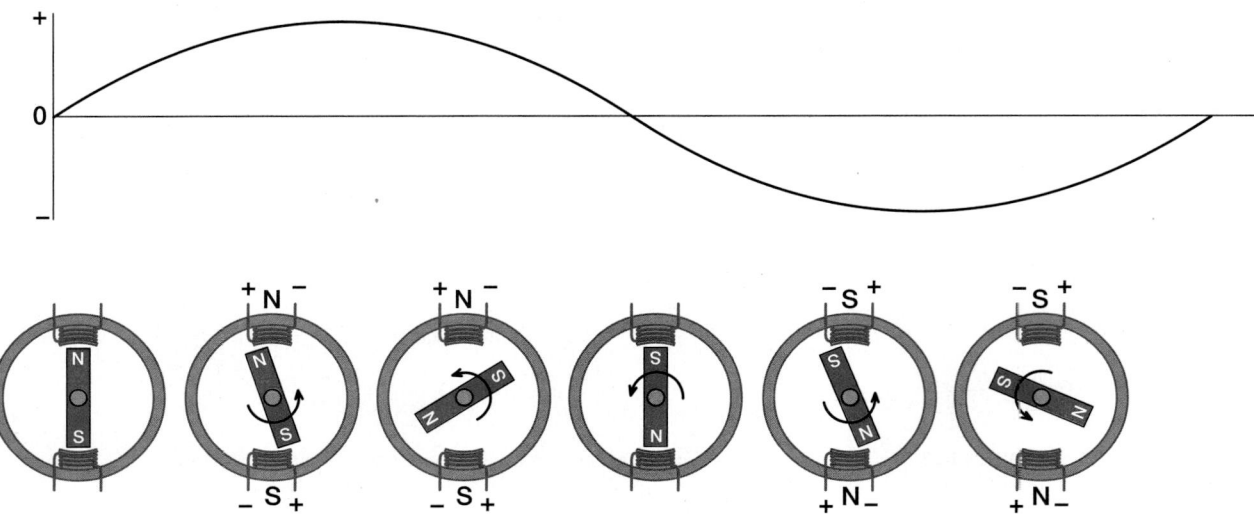

FIGURE 54-25 Principles of AC induction motor operation through 360 degrees of rotation. Current flow in the rotor is induced by switching the stator's magnetic field. The cyclic change of AC direction in the stator switches its magnetic field from north to south and back again many times per second.

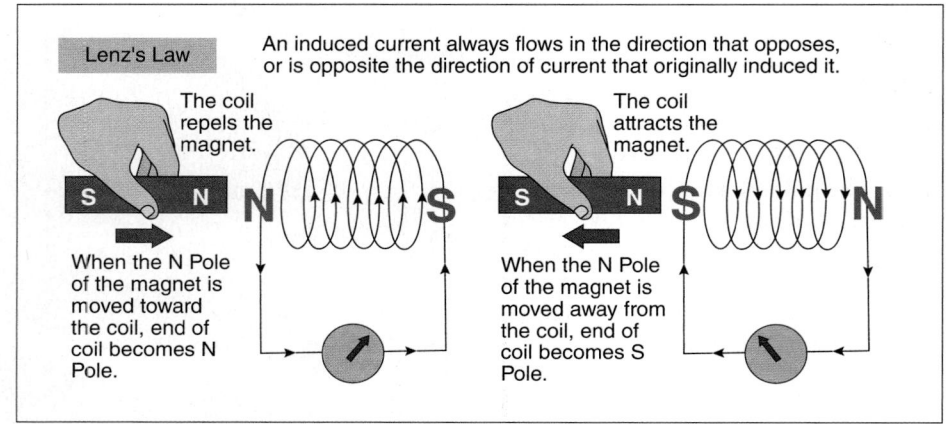

FIGURE 54-26 Lenz's Law.

or aluminum, conduct induced current around the rotor, which in turn creates its own magnetic field in the rotor.

When the motor is energized, the magnetic pole created in an area on the rotor is formed from current induced by the expanding magnetic field in the stator. Initially, the stator and area directly opposite it on the rotor are the same. That means a north pole is arranged opposite a north pole and a south pole opposite a south pole. Magnetic induction like this is predicted by Lenz's Law (**FIGURE 54-26**). This situation would cause the areas of magnetic influence on both the rotor and stator to oppose one another and cause the rotor to move. Because of the way the three stator coil wires are wound, magnetic fields having opposite polarity are slightly offset and next to one another on the rotor and stator (**FIGURE 54-27**). Magnetic forces of repulsion are stronger, especially if the air gap between the rotor and stator is very small. But opposite magnetic poles attracting one another assist forces of repulsion causing rotor rotation. So,

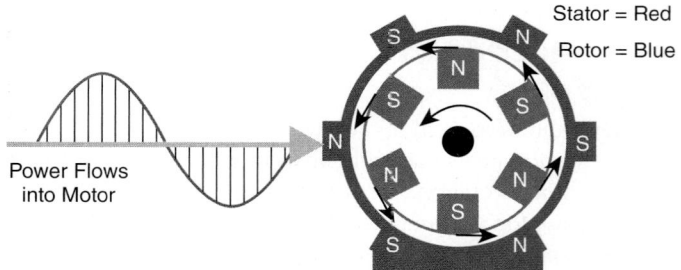

FIGURE 54-27 Magnetic poles in the rotor and stator simultaneously pull and push the rotor to produce rotation.

simultaneously, magnetic repulsion between the stationary stator coils pushes against the rotor bars while magnetic attraction pulls the rotor bars in the same direction. What would normally happen next after the rotor moves is the magnetic poles on the

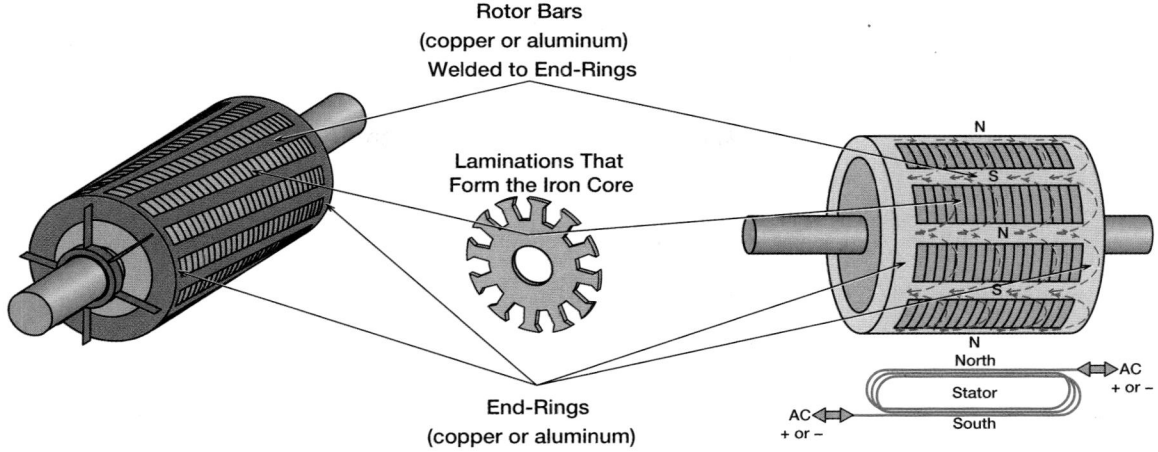

FIGURE 54-28 The squirrel-cage rotor of an induction-type AC motor has conducting bars that become magnetized under the influence of the stator's frequently cycling magnetic field.

rotor and stator would align as north–south, effectively ending rotor movement. However, the direction of current flow in the stator suddenly reverses due to cycling frequency of AC and switches the stator's magnetic field polarity.

The effect of current induction caused by a changing magnetic field is to, once again momentary, creating like magnetic poles on the rotor and stator opposite one another. At this point, the rotor moves incrementally once more due to the force of magnetic repulsion between like poles in alignment. It is important to observe that as the rotor turns, the frequently changing direction of AC flow through the stator operates to maintain an alignment of like poles on the rotor that strongly repel one another. This cycle is repeated each time the direction of AC flow through the stator windings changes.

Rotor Construction

Close to 90% of induction motors use a squirrel-cage-type rotor. The physical appearance of the rotor lends the squirrel-cage name because it resembles an exercise wheel in a rodent cage. These motor rotors have the simplest and most rugged type of construction. It typically consists of a cylinder with a laminated iron core having parallel slots along its axis for holding the rotors conductors (**FIGURE 54-28**). The conductors are not wires but heavy bars of copper or aluminum or iron alloys. Bars are placed in the slots and welded or bolted to two thick short-circuiting end-rings. The end-rings electrically connect the rotor conductors to each other to complete a circuit with other conductor bars in order to establish a magnetic field. No insulation is required between the laminated iron core and the conductor bars. This is because only low-voltage current is induced in the rotor bars and current flow takes the path of least resistance through the bars.

The rotor slots are usually cut at an angle to the shaft axis for two reasons. One is to help the motor run more quietly since the magnetic fields are slightly skewed to offset alignment with the rotor field coils. This feature tends to reduce a vibration or magnetic hum as the rotor speed changes slightly every time the

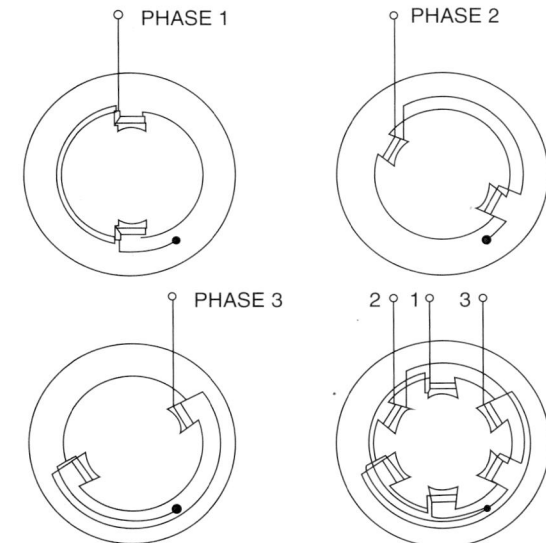

FIGURE 54-29 A three-phase stator has three separate circuits forming magnetic fields.

conductor bars align with the rotor magnetic field. A second similar reason is the skew of the conductor bars helps to prevent locking up of the rotor bars with stator coils due to the potential for a synchronization of magnetic attraction forces that can take place when the motor initially starts or under heavy motor loads.

Three-Phase Motor Stator Construction

Induction-type traction motors use three-phase AC. This refers to the motor's use of three separate stator windings arranged 120 degrees offset from one another (**FIGURE 54-29**). Each of the windings is laid over the other and has a main power lead for each phase of AC power supply connected to it. The other ends of the conductors are connected in series to one another if the motor is a Delta wound stator. Alternatively, the three conductor ends can be joined to form a wye-wound stator (**FIGURE 54-30**). Three-phase induction motors are used as traction motors because they can form an angle between the magnetic field of the stator and rotor, allowing the direction of motor rotation to be electrically changed. By simply reversing the power connections, the three-phase motor can provide forward or reverse direction. Some motors may use a Hall-effect sensor, called the **resolver**, that measures the rotor position and speed to provide a feedback signal to a motor controller to properly manage the motor operation. Since overspeed conditions will damage the motor if it is being driven during retarding mode operation, the resolver is a critical sensor for the motor controller to reduce current flow and shut down the system.

Three-Phase AC Versus Single Current

Three-phase AC power is not like single-phase household current supplying AC using two wires and a ground (**FIGURE 54-31**). Single-phase only uses one conductor to supply power and the other is a neutral. Three-phase current uses three separate wires to supply power, and two others that are either a neutral and a ground wire. When graphed over a 360-degree cycle time, three power wires, each winding is 120 degrees out of phase with the others (**FIGURE 54-32**). When a cycle of 360 degrees has completed, three phases of power have each peaked in voltage twice—once negative and once positive. That means there are six power peaks in a three-phase current compared to just two in a single-phase

current. With a three-phase current supply, a steadier flow of power is delivered at a more regular rate, which contains more energy. Practically, this means three-phase current can supply more power or energy per unit of time than single-phase current. When comparing motors, a single-phase 5 hp motor draws significantly more amperage than an equivalent 5 hp motor operating using three-phase motor, making three-phase power a more efficient choice for industrial applications.

Another important observation to make about three-phase stators is the appearance that the magnetic field rotates around the stator (**FIGURE 54-33**). In one moment, a single phase of the stator may establish a dominant north polarity on the rotor, then diminish in strength before forming a dominant south polarity. This alternating, back-and-forth switching of the stator's magnetic field polarity makes it appear to rotate around the stator. Enhancing the effect of the appearance of a revolving magnetic field is that the second and third stator phases do this sequentially too, switching magnetic poles 120 degrees apart. Understanding how the magnetic field appears to rotate makes it easier to explain how the frequency of AC and the number of poles formed in the stator by winding coils in each phase determines the motor's speed. The formula to calculate this is:

$$\text{rpm} = (120 \times \text{AC frequency})/\text{Number of poles in the motor}$$

For a common four-pole, 1800 rpm motor operating on household current:

$$1800 \text{ rpm} = (120 \times 60)/4$$

Increasing the number of poles reduces the motor speed but, since the number of poles cannot be physically altered, when operating the frequency of AC is changed to vary motor speed. Torque is increased or decreased proportionally to voltage in the stator winding. Also important to remember is that to change the direction of motor rotation, any two of the three phase power connections to the stator windings can be switched to rotate the magnetic field in the opposite direction.

To identify the correct connections for each phase of a motor-generator, motor leads are color-coded and labeled. In the US, the previous standard was L1/L2/L3 for phase rotation of incoming current and T1/T2/T3 for outgoing current leads. That means the L1 wave leads L2, which leads L3, where the phase rises to a positive voltage. Other designations for generators

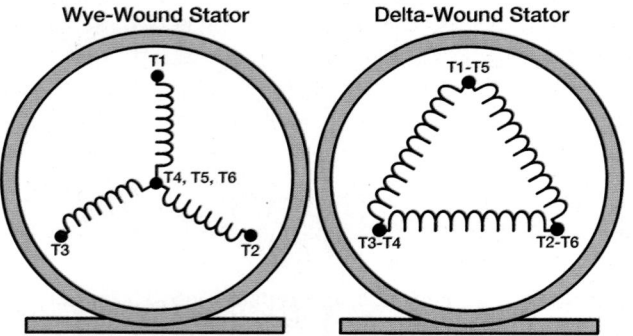

FIGURE 54-30 The wire ends of a stator's windings are connected in either a delta- or Wye-shaped pattern.

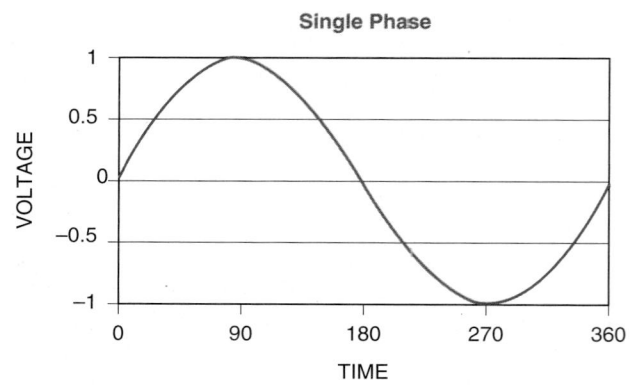

FIGURE 54-31 Single-phase versus three-phase current.

include A-B-C, R-S-T. The International Electrotechnical Commission (IEC) has created a standard IEC 60034-8 for "Terminal Markings and Direction of Rotation" that ensures that clockwise rotation of the drive shaft occurs for a positive voltage rise of the electrical phase in sequence designated U-V-W (**FIGURE 54-34**). Switching A with phase B reorders the direction of the rotating magnetic field so that the field appears to turn in the opposite direction, thus changing motor direction. Switching B with C does the same thing, as does switching A with C.

Induction Motor Slip

It is impossible for the rotor of an induction motor to turn at the same speed as the apparent speed of the rotating magnetic field in the stator. If rotor speed and the apparent movement

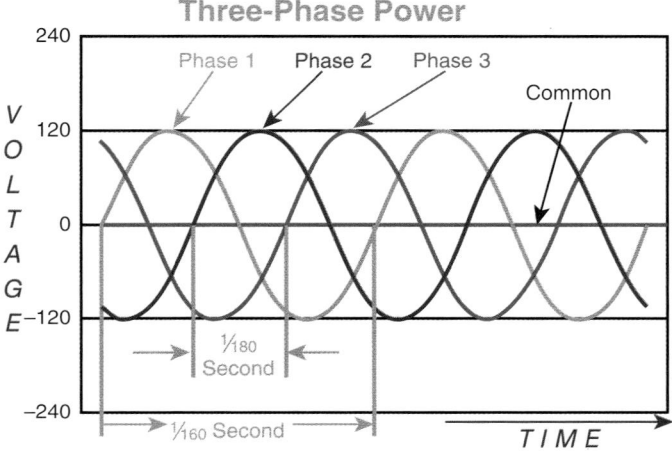

FIGURE 54-32 Three-phase current peaks more often per cycle than single phase.

of the stators magnetic field were the same, the magnetic fields in both would be aligned, directly opposite one another, so no movement of the rotor could take place. The time delay between the induction of the magnetic fields in the rotor and stator help create a lag between the appearance and North-South switch of magnetic fields in each. To rotate, a small angle must exist between the rotor and the stators magnetic poles for two reasons. First, the difference in the angle is necessary to impart a push or repulsion force between the two opposing magnetic fields. The second, more important reason is an angle must exist between the rotor's conductor bars and stator field to induce a magnetic field in the rotor. If the magnetic field and the conductor bar are on the same plane or exactly parallel to one another, no induction can take place—there must be an angle (**FIGURE 54-35**).

As the angle between a conductor and magnetic field increase, more current flow is induced in a conductor. The greatest amount of current is induced at an angle of 90 degrees between the conductor and magnet. To maintain an angle enabling the induction motor to run, the rotor must rotate at a speed at least slightly slower than that of the stator's rotating magnetic field. The difference between the speed of the rotating stator field and the rotor speed is called **slip angle** (**FIGURE 54-36**). The smaller the slip angle, the narrower the angle between the magnetic field and rotor conductor bars. Slip angle decreases the closer the rotor speed approaches the stator field speed. When slip angle is small, there is little or no load on the motor. Increasing the load on an AC induction motor simultaneously increases the slip angle along with torque output due to the larger angle between the magnetic fields.

The speed difference, or slip, between actual and synchronized rotor-stator magnetic field speed movement varies from about 0.5% to 5.0%. Even with no load, some slip is present in an

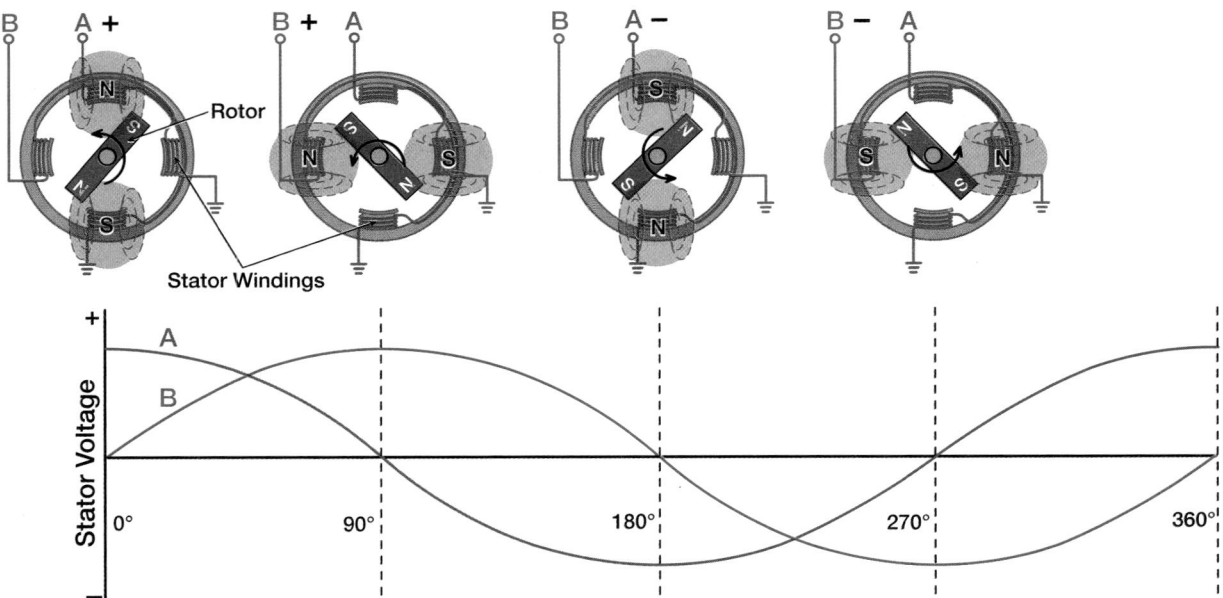

FIGURE 54-33 This two-phase motor demonstrates how the magnetic field appears to rotate around the stator by switching the polarity using AC.

FIGURE 54-34 Note the motor leads for each phase are marked. Here it is L1, L2, and L3, plus a neutral wire.

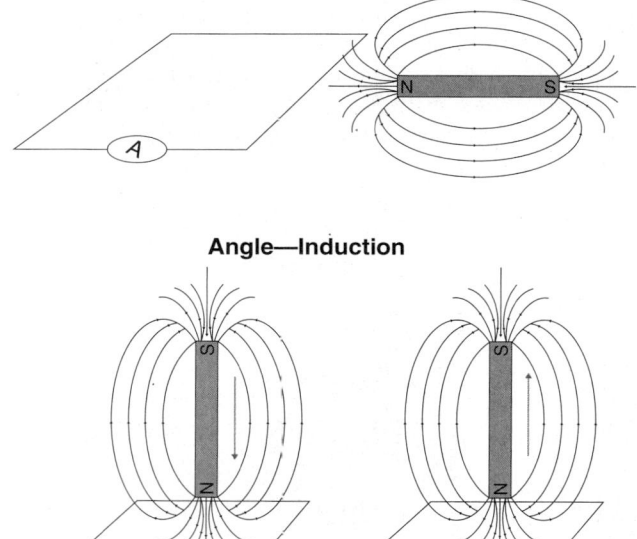

No Angle—No Induction

Angle—Induction

FIGURE 54-35 When the magnet is in the same plane or parallel to the conductor loop, (Top) no current is induced, even if the magnet is moved closer and further away.

induction motor. The fact that induction motors do not allow the rotor and stator magnetic fields to synchronize speed lends induction motors the name **asynchronous motors**, meaning not synchronized.

Understanding the relationship between slip angle and induced current in the rotor explains why current flow to a motor increases when shaft rotation is slowed under load. As

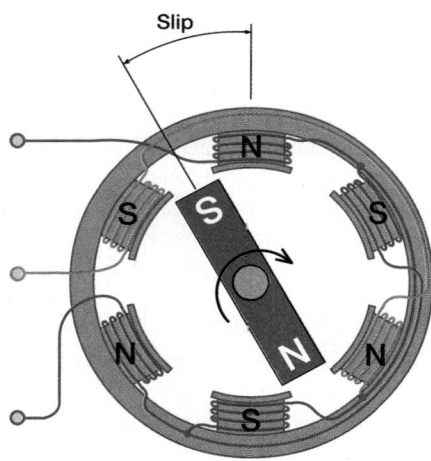

FIGURE 54-36 AC induction motor slip is the difference in speed between the rotating magnetic field in the stator and induced magnetic field in the rotor. Slip is measured in percentage difference.

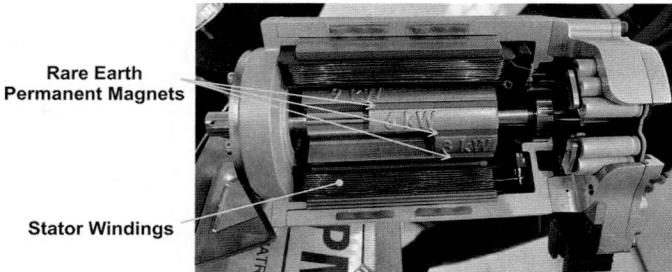

Rare Earth Permanent Magnets

Stator Windings

FIGURE 54-37 This cutaway of a permanent magnet motor demonstrates the idea that longer or bigger magnets increase motor torque output.

slip approaches near zero, and the rotor catches up to stator field speed, little current flow is induced in the rotor. Increasing slip increases torque output because the angle between the stator and rotor magnetic field increases. This in turn induces more current flow in the rotor as more electrical energy converts to an increase of magnetic field strength. Only a slight change in rotor speed is necessary to produce the usual current changes required to increase or decrease motor torque. As a result, induction motors are also called constant-speed motors.

Permanent-Magnet Motors

LO 54-7 Identify and describe the types, construction, and operation of permanent magnet motors.

To increase the energy efficiency of an electric motor, the conductor bars in the rotor are replaced with permanent magnets (PMs) (**FIGURE 54-37**). Rather than use electrical current to produce a magnetic field, the magnets embedded in the rotor supply the necessary energy for magnetic repulsion, which reduces power consumption and motor size. Not only is energy consumption reduced, but output torque and the capacity

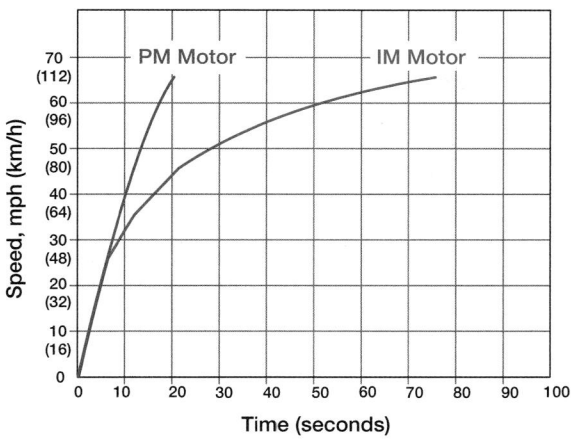

FIGURE 54-38 Comparing a similar size of IM and PM motor acceleration rates.

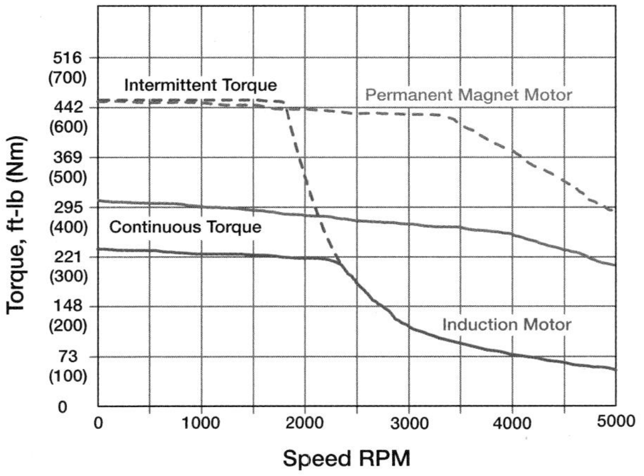

FIGURE 54-39 Comparing the power output of a permanent magnet motor with an induction motor.

for intermittent motor overload during acceleration power is increased (**FIGURE 54-38**). PM motors also generate less rotor heat than inductive types, which further improves efficiency (**FIGURE 54-39**). In fact, PM motors typically use 27% less energy than a comparable IM in stop-and-go, low-speed operation since electrical energy is not used to induce magnetic fields in the rotor. But as the PM motor's size increases to increase torque output, magnetic losses increase proportionately, reducing its efficiency. During steady-state on-highway operation, the IM and PM motors are closer in terms of energy needed to drive the same distance. IMs are also much less expensive to produce, costing 25% less than a PM motor.

To create efficient PM motors, powerful rare-earth magnets contain what are called rare-earth metals, such as neodymium, cobalt, or yttrium. Magnet alloys made using these metals are not actually rare, but only unevenly distributed in the world, amplifies the magnetic field strength. In fact, these magnets are powerful enough to be a health and safety hazard. Even a small magnet, if swallowed, can pinch and damage human tissue if it is trapped between a steel or iron surface.

▶ TECHNICIAN TIP

The greater forces exerted by rare-earth magnets create hazards that may not occur with other types of magnet. Neodymium magnets larger than a few cubic centimeters are strong enough to cause injuries to body parts pinched between two magnets, or a magnet and a ferrous metal surface, even causing broken bones. Never allow fingers or any body parts to get between a rotor and stator using permanent magnets.

Types of Permanent Magnet Motors

Two categories of PM motors are used in CBEVs. One uses three-phase AC in the stator to produce motor rotation, the other uses electronically commutated DC supplied to stator windings that operate similarly to a stepper motor. AC-powered PM motors can also be called sinusoidal commuted (PMSC) too Figure 54-45. The motor controller for an electronically commutated PM motor selectively switches stator coils on and off to produce a rotating magnetic field that optimizes torque and speed output from the rotor (**FIGURES 54-40** and **54-41**). These motors are also referred to as brushless DC motors like those

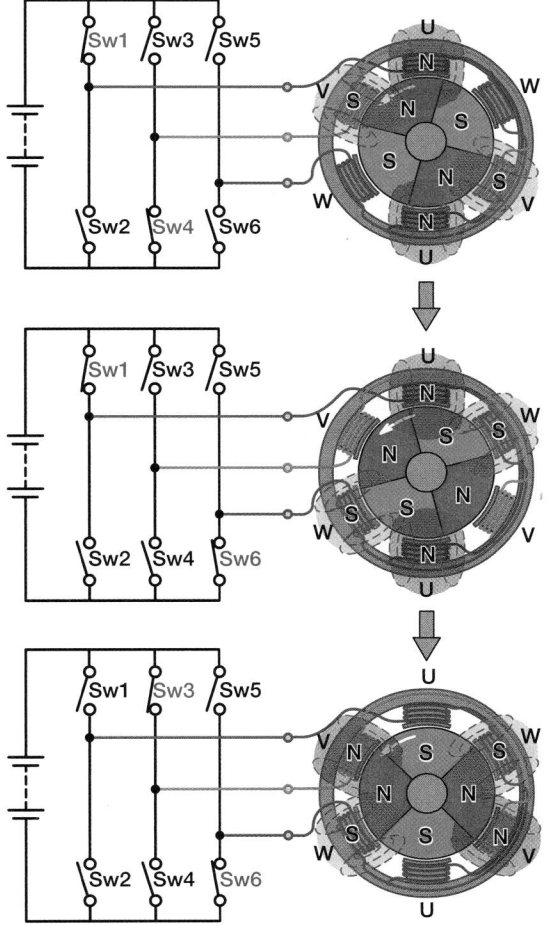

FIGURE 54-40 Switching the stator coils on and off in the correct sequence creates magnetic fields capable of turning the permanent magnet rotor. A Hall-effect sensor is used to sense rotor position for precise field current switching logic.

Electronically Commutated Motor

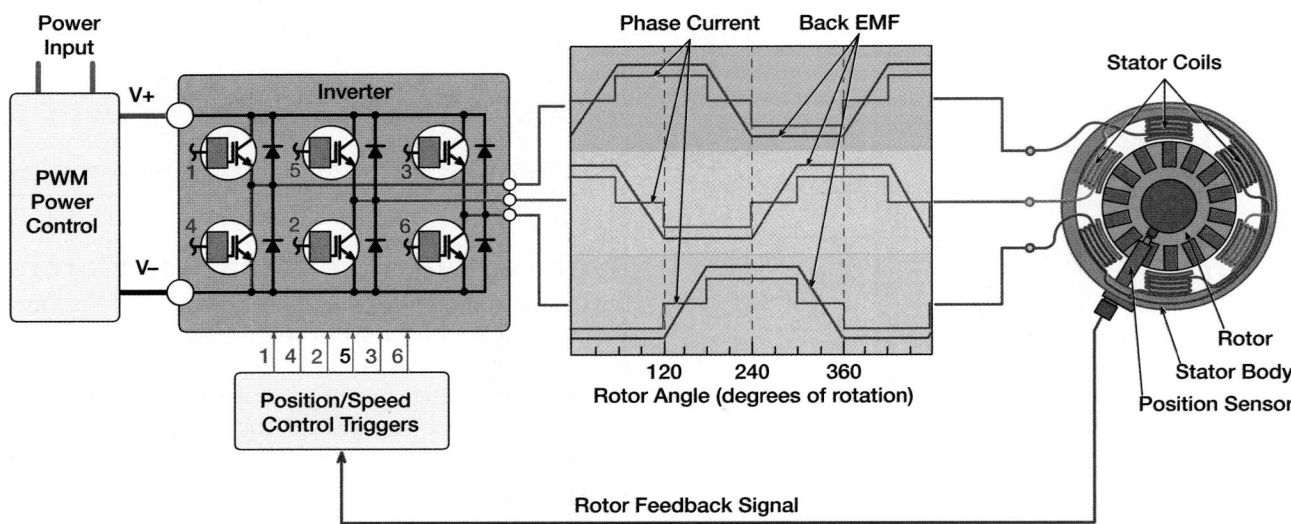

FIGURE 54-41 A Hall-effect sensor commonly provides feedback about motor position. Rotor position data is used by switching logic to energize the appropriate stator coil to turn the motor forward or backward.

FIGURE 54-42 Multiple coils of an electronically commutated permanent magnet motor.

current because energizing of the stator poles must be precisely timed to ensure that it takes place as the rotor's magnetic pole is approaching alignment with the energized stator pole.

This explains why another term given to these AC motors is permanent magnet synchronous motors (PMSM)—because there is no slip angle between the stator and rotor. Unlike DC stepper motors, which often can operate in open-loop mode, electronically commutated PM motors require rotor position feedback from a position sensor or encoder, such as a Hall-effect sensor (**FIGURE 54-43**). A circuit board with the sensor may even be integrated into the motor to enable precise control commutation of stator current using rotor position. Motor direction, speed, and torque output are regulated according to the current level supplied to the stator and switching logic in the motor controller for energizing stator coils. Stator coils can also be energized in a way to hold the vehicle in position on a steep incline.

▶ TECHNICIAN TIP

Motors with permanent magnets produce large amounts of electric current when towed. Magnets inside the motor induce current flow in the stator, which can severely damage motor control electronic drivers. Carefully follow manufacturer recommendations for towing CBEVs with PM motors.

used in cordless power tools, but there are differences. Both AC and DC can be used to power the PM motor but a different ratio exists between the number of stator poles and rotor magnets.

Electronically commutated PM motors are recognized by their individually wound stator coils that do not overlap one another (**FIGURE 54-42**). Several coils in a large motor are connected in parallel but are grouped into poles like IMs. Each set or group of coils, called a pole, is controlled by separate power feeds from the motor controller. Organizing the stator like this allows for more precise control of stator field energization to synchronize the rotation of the magnetic field in the stator with the rotor. It's necessary to precisely control the stator coil

External Rotors

One innovation to further increase motor efficiency is to create a motor with what is termed an external rotor (**FIGURE 54-44**). TM4, a Dana-owned company, uses an external rotor that switches position with the stator. The rotor moves but the stator has a fixed position inside the rotor. Both parts are enclosed in a motor housing. A large-diameter PM rotor is used, which has the advantage of providing more torque output due to the distance of the motor shaft to the outside rotor dimension (**FIGURE 54-45**). With a longer radius from the motor shaft to the rotor surface acted on by magnetic forces of repulsion, the increased torque

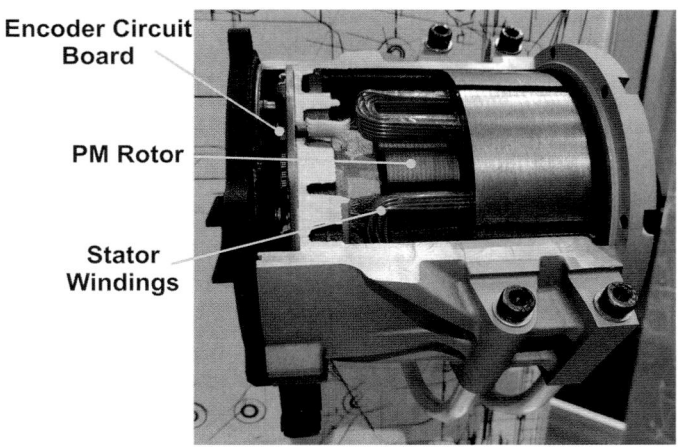

FIGURE 54-43 An encoder or position sensor is used in this PM motor for a mild-hybrid drive motor that operates as both a starter and alternator.

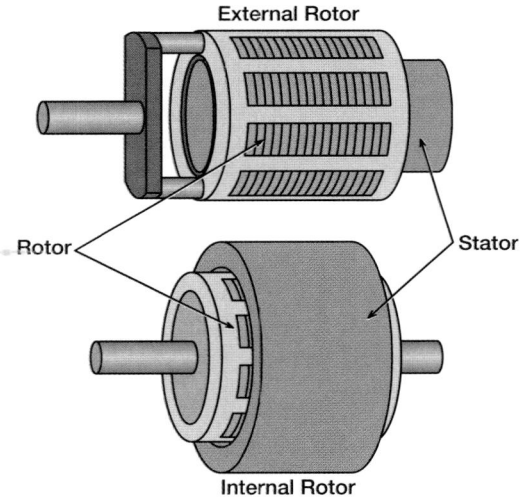

FIGURE 54-44 An external motor rotor is capable of providing more torque from the same motor energy consumption.

FIGURE 54-45 A permanent magnet motor contains rare earth type magnets embedded in the rotor.

FIGURE 54-46 Multiple electrical conductors entering the external rotor motor indicate an electrically commutated motor control strategy.

is calculated by multiplying magnetic force X radius. Increasing the rotor radius mathematically increases torque supplied from the same magnetic force. Stator windings are electrically commutated in this motor, which is evidenced by the multiple motor current conductors used for this motor (**FIGURE 54-46**).

Switched Reluctance Motors (SRMs)

LO 54-8 Identify and describe the types, construction, and operation of switched reluctance motors (SRMs).

One other type of DC motor that is used as a traction motor operating similarly to the electronically commutated motor is the **switched reluctance motor (SRM)**. Unlike the AC IM or PM motors, the rotor in a DC-SRM is simply a machined piece of steel with protrusions called poles. Rather than using principles of magnetic repulsion, the SRM uses the principle of magnetic attraction to drive the motor. Electromagnetic fields in the stator attempt to pull the steel rotors pole pieces into alignment using magnetic attraction. As the stator pole pairs are energized, the rotor turns to align its steel poles with the energized stator poles. High magnetic reluctance or magnetic field resistance exists when the poles are misaligned, but reluctance decreases as the rotor more closely aligns with stator poles. **Reluctance torque** is the name given to this movement from high to low magnetic reluctance, which is another way of describing torque generated due to magnetic attraction.

To prevent the motor rotation from stopping when stator and rotor poles align, SRMs have fewer poles on the rotor than on the stator. Current to a stator coil is shut off as the rotor pole piece moves into alignment while another pole is energized (**FIGURE 54-47**). Energizing of the stator poles must be precisely timed to ensure that it occurs as the rotor pole is approaching alignment with the energized stator pole. This explains why Hall-effect position sensors are required.

A disadvantage of SRMs is they have fewer poles, which means a larger angle is needed to complete each step of rotor movement. This supplies high torque output, but also creates a condition referred to as cogging, which is observed as a buzzy torsional vibration along the rotor shaft. Newer designs have minimized the rotational vibration by placing a few permanent magnets in the rotor to create smoother power output.

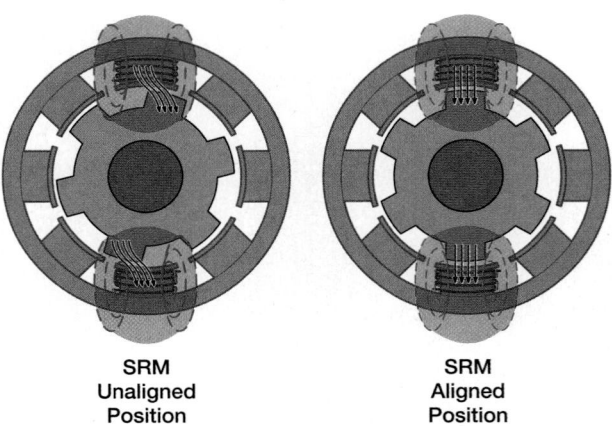

SRM
Unaligned
Position

SRM
Aligned
Position

FIGURE 54-47 High magnetic reluctance condition exists in the left motor, low reluctance in the right motor.

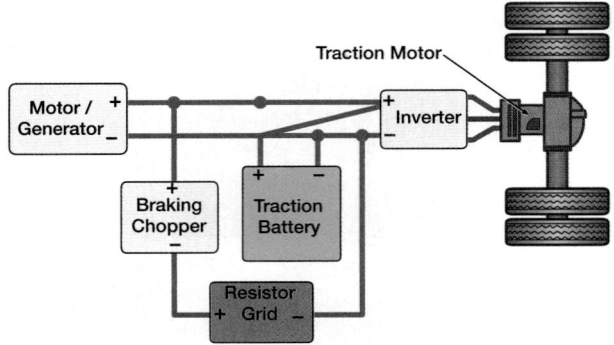

FIGURE 54-48 The chopper circuit redirects current to resisters to dissipate current from regenerative braking that cannot be absorbed by the batteries.

An advantage of switched reluctance motors without rotor magnets or conductor bars is they have lower inertia, enabling them to turn faster and accelerate more quickly than motors with permanent magnets and rotor bars. Without magnets in the rotor, the simpler motor is less expensive and can withstand higher temperatures without requiring cooling.

Generator Mode

LO 54-9 Outline the methods used to switch traction motors from propulsion mode to generator mode.

Regenerative braking involves switching electric motor operation to electric generator mode. Energy used to drive the motor, now turned generator, is used to supplement braking force from the friction brakes with the added benefit of charging the batteries. In both PM and IM drive systems, the magnetic fields of the rotor generate mechanical rotational resistance by inducing current in the stator or cutting magnetic lines of force produced by current flow through the stator. Essentially, rotor magnetic field rotation is resisted by stator magnetic fields. IM-turned generators automatically produce current under at least three conditions:

1. Automatically when their rotors turn faster than synchronous speed (creating negative slip)
2. Some residual magnetism is present in the rotor and negative slip is present
3. Some DC current is sent through one or more phases of the stator to induce magnetic fields in the rotor.

To absorb electrical energy produced during braking, a battery requires some space or discharged capacity to store current. If the battery is fully charged, it cannot take advantage of regenerative charging and more work must be done by the mechanical brake friction material unless regenerative current is dissipated elsewhere. Resistors are commonly used to convert regenerative braking energy into heat. A chopper circuit diverts current from a generator into the resistors (**FIGURE 54-48**). Operating closer to 80% or less gives the battery enough capacity to absorb a regenerative charge from the generator.

It's important to note that a contribution from the mechanical braking system is needed because regenerative braking from a generator drops off when rotor speed is slower. This means regenerative braking cannot bring a vehicle to a complete stop. A second problem is CBEVs do not have drive motors on all wheels to supply regenerative braking. For safe, balanced braking, all wheels are required to have braking capability, but regenerative braking is only available to wheels with motors. Regenerative braking can also cause wheels to lock-up if road surfaces are slippery, so the braking system must be integrated with traction control strategies.

To meet the complex objectives of the mechanical and regenerative braking system, the vehicle control unit (VCU) calculates demand conditions and determines appropriate electrical signals for commanded brake and drive torque. Brake torque distribution is divided into three areas: generator or regenerative brake torque, front and rear axle(s) brake torque, and mechanical brake torque. The calculations for the distribution of brake torque vary according to system inputs and braking strategies for ABS and traction control.

Electric Motor (EM) Mechanical Transmission

LO 54-10 Explain the purpose of CBEV transmissions and identify the types of gear reduction systems they use.

Two methods are used to achieve high power to weight density and high-efficiency electric drives. The first method is to use high-speed motors and multiply torque through gear reduction drives. While motor volume and weight are substantially reduced, mechanical losses take place through gear reduction and the use of differential gears for torque transmission. Another strategy is to use high-torque, low-speed motors turning at a maximum speed of 1000 rpm. Dual motors can blend torque through gear mechanism and torque multiplied through two-speed electrically shifted transmissions (**FIGURE 54-49**).

When mounted inside the wheel, this configuration is known as in-wheel motors or hub motors. Tesla motors combine high-speed wheel motors with a two-stage gear reduction, torque multiplication set-up. A 4:1 gear reduction at the motor combined with a 6:1 gear reduction in the wheel allows the motor to turn closer to its maximum speed while using smaller diameter driveshafts because torque handled in the last gear step (**FIGURE 54-50**).

In a CBEV, the transmission is typically of single-speed spur, helical, or planetary gear type, which multiplies torque for high-speed motor output. Consider a motor rotating at 1000 rpm would need to rotate a 235/80R 22.5 tire 556 times over the course of 1 mile (1.6 km). At 60 mph or close to 100 kph, this motor would require a 1.8 gear reduction (**FIGURE 54-51**). Faster turning motors would require even higher gear reduction ratios.

FIGURE 54-49 Two low-speed electric motors transmit torque to the rear drive axle through a two-speed transmission.

Energy Storage System (ESS)

LO 54-11 Identify and describe the categories, construction, and operation of energy storage systems (ESS).

The energy storage system (ESS) primarily holds electrical energy used by the electric traction motor and auxiliary systems. The system also provides important features for electrical safety and system protection. Five major components make up the ESS:

1. High-voltage battery modules comprised of hundreds or thousands of smaller battery cells.
2. A high-voltage contactor control unit that connects and disconnects the battery modules from the rest of the vehicle using normally open relays (**FIGURE 54-52**).
3. A high-voltage service disconnect switch that is used to manually disconnect the battery pack from the rest of the vehicle, such as when servicing the high-voltage system (**FIGURE 54-53**).
4. A fuse for the high-voltage cables that is designed to open when excess current is drawn through the high-voltage battery cables.
5. The battery management system (BMS), which is primarily responsible for charge equalization of battery cells and modules. The charging and discharge rate of modules and cells is controlled by the BMS.

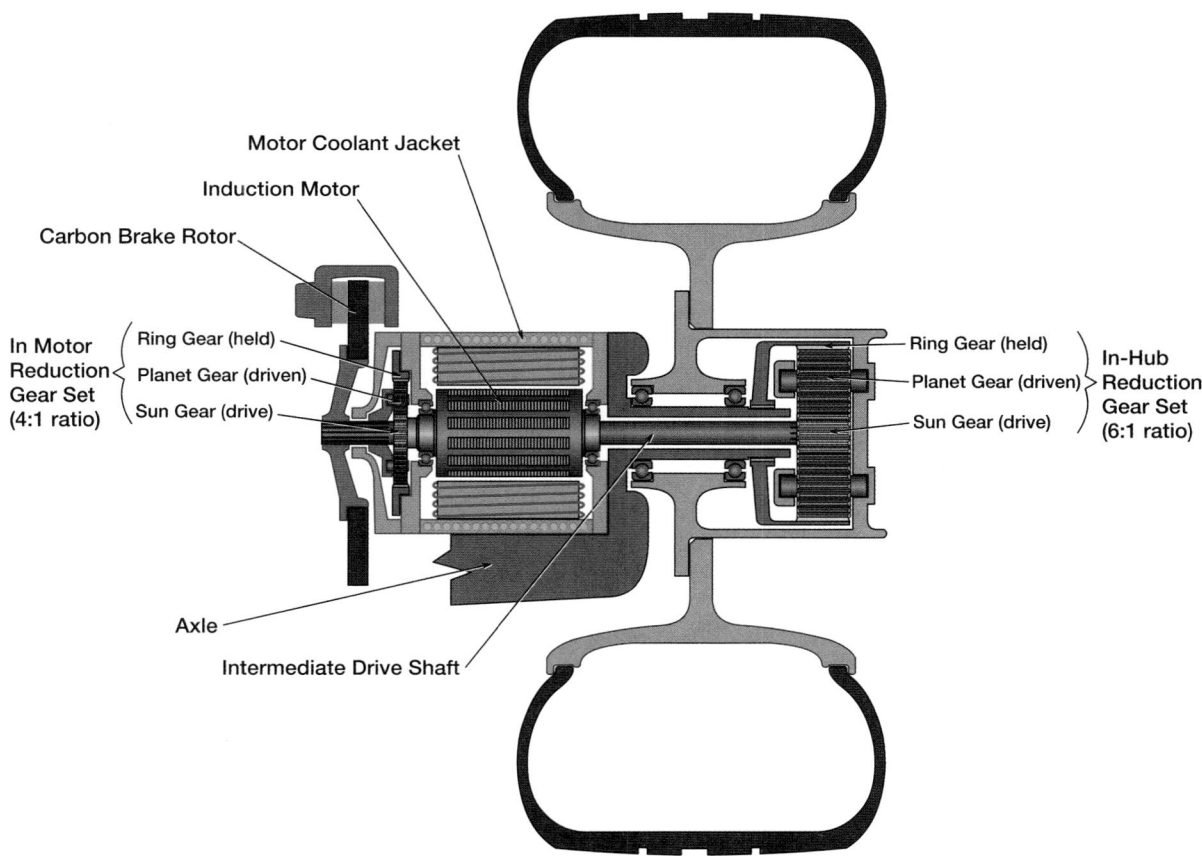

FIGURE 54-50 Tesla's wheel motors turn at 18,000 rpm at 87 mph and are rated at 271 hp, so four motors would have a total potential output of 1084 hp. A 4:1 and 6:1 gear reduction system is used.

FIGURE 54-51 A 2:1 gear ratio and differential for an CBEV drive. The dotted line represents the axis for an axle shaft.

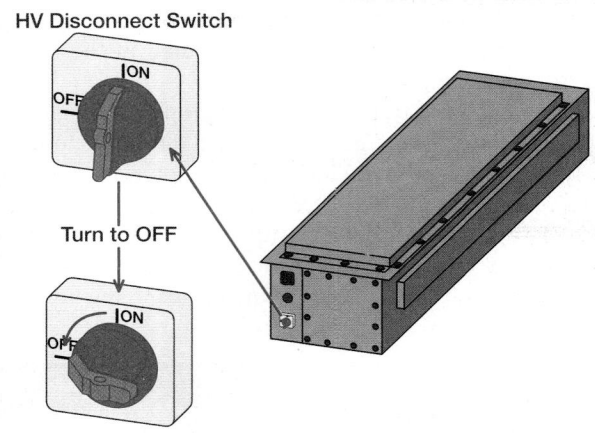

FIGURE 54-53 A manual high-voltage disconnect switch for disconnecting battery pack voltage to the vehicle when servicing the high-voltage system.

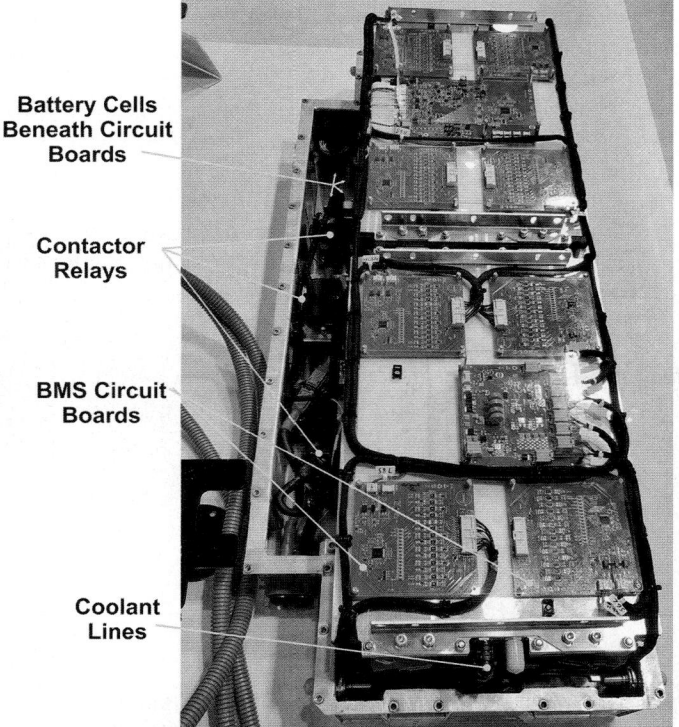

Battery Cells
Beneath Circuit
Boards

Contactor
Relays

BMS Circuit
Boards

Coolant
Lines

FIGURE 54-52 A typical lithium battery pack enclosure with contactors used to disconnect the batteries.

FIGURE 54-54 A CHAdeMO electrical charging connector allows for up to 400 kW by charging at 1000 V with 400 amps DC. CHAdeMO is a Japanese manufacturer association.

The ESS is also tasked with storing energy produced by regenerative braking, and controlling the charge rate through a BMS. An optional chopper circuit may be included and used to divert regenerative current to large resistors if the batteries are full or unable to accept a charge. A battery charger with rectifiers converting AC from the power grid to DC is only found on light-duty vehicles. Additional costs and current heating of power the rectifiers limit the maximum conversion capacity of onboard battery chargers. Batteries requiring more than 240 V AC and 75 amps use an external charging station to supply DC to charge batteries (**FIGURE 54-54**).

Three major types of energy storage or energy production technologies are:

- Lithium batteries
- Fuel cells
- Ultra-capacitors

Storage capacity in CBEVs is very high; as much electrical energy is used driving a single mile as an average household uses per day. It's estimated that an average heavy-duty Class 7–8 CBEV has a consumption of 2–3 kilowatts per mile (1.6 km). The estimated consumption used per mile requires adequate energy storage to meet the goal of recharging only after a typical driver shift of 8 hours or 400 miles (640 km). Tesla semi's battery pack is expected to have a capacity of 800 to 1000 kWh, giving it a range between as little as 250 miles to over 500 miles. When regenerative braking is included, or a range-extending microturbine generator is added, the driving range lengthens even farther. Fuel cells, which are used in extended range BEVs, have much farther driving ranges. Fuel cell trucks, like the Nikola One and Two, have the benefit of lighter weight, a farther driving range, and the shortest refueling period of 20 minutes with hydrogen, giving fuel cells a competitive advantage (TABLE 54-1).

Ultra-capacitors physically store electrical energy on capacitor plates with very high surface areas. Their advantage is they can be charged and discharged more quickly than batteries. This feature makes ultra-capacitors ideal for energy storing from regenerative braking and supplying energy during sudden acceleration. However, ultra-capacitors have low energy storage density, meaning they cannot hold large amounts of energy in reserve relative to their weight. This means impossibly large ultra-capacitors are needed to supply travel range, so they can only be used to complement a battery storage system as voltage stabilizers, providing current for brief rapid discharge and charge absorption.

▶ TECHNICIAN TIP

One method to compare the energy storage density of electric and diesel-powered vehicles is to compare storage capacity to **diesel gallon equivalent (DGE)**. In North America, the Department of Energy has assigned 1 gallon (0.83 imperial gallons; 3.8 liters) of diesel fuel the equivalent of 38.1 kilowatt hours of electricity. This means 300 gallons of fuel would equal a battery storage capacity of 11,430 kilowatts. Given that diesel engines use three times as much energy compared to an electric truck, due to mechanical energy losses and lower efficiency compared to electric vehicles, a realistic energy storage capacity comparison is 3800-kilowatts of DGE onboard a typical Class 8 tractor.

Lithium-Ion Batteries

The costliest and heaviest component of a CBEV are the batteries. Lithium-ion batteries are the dominant energy storage and battery technology in CBEVs for several reasons. First, lithium has what is called high standard specific energy potential (expressed in watts/kg). This means the lithium battery can produce more electrical energy when compared to almost any other battery on a weight basis if it is used in transportation applications (TABLE 54-2). In other words, not only do lithium

TABLE 54-1 Fuel Cell versus Diesel Performance: Comparing Nikola One and Two Specifications with Conventional Diesel-Powered Class 8 Tractor

Performance Criteria	Diesel Engine	Nikola 2
Horsepower	500 hp	up to 1000 hp
Torque	1650 ft-lb (2237 Nm)	up to 2000 ft-lb (2712 Nm)
Range	500–750 miles (805–1207 km)	up to 500–1000 miles (805–1609 km)
Top Speed Up Hills (6%)	20–40 mph (32–64 km/h)	65 mph (105 kph)
Braking on Descent	Exhaust & Friction Brakes	Recharging & Saving Brakes
Braking	Air Disc with Air Parking	Air Disc with Air Parking
Acceleration 0–60 mph Under Load	60 seconds	30 seconds
MPG	7.5 mpg (3.2 km/L)	13–15 mpg (5.5–6.4 km/L)
Weight	19,000–23,000 lb (8618–10,433 kg)	18,000–21,000 lb (8165–9525 kg)
Traction Motor	NA	6 wheel motors operating at 800-V AC Motors
Battery Capacity		240 kWh–320 kWh
Energy System	Compression Ignition	Hydrogen Fuel Cell

TABLE 54-2 Comparing the Storage Density of Various Energy Storage Systems

Energy Type	Energy Density Relative to Gasoline*
Gasoline	1.00/1.00
Diesel	0.75/1
Battery—Lead-acid	23–43/1
Battery—Nickel Metal Hydride (NiMH)	15–18/1
Lithium Battery—Lithium Iron (LiFePO$_4$)	10–14/1
Lithium Battery—Lithium cobalt (LiCoO$_2$)	8–11/1

*Mass/Energy Storage Volume Relative to Gasoline

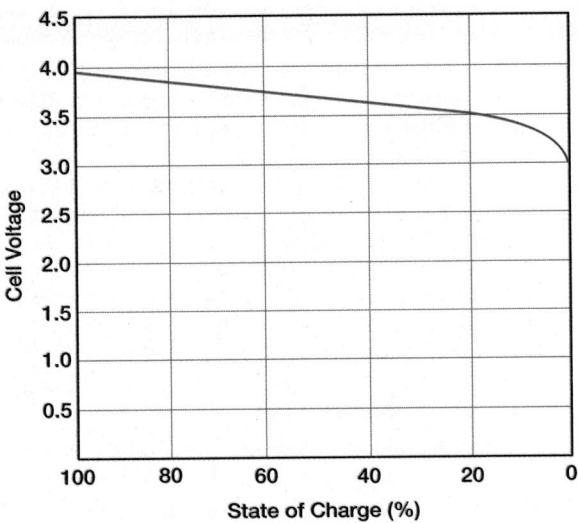

FIGURE 54-55 Lithium batteries maintain a high cell voltage until they are almost completely discharged.

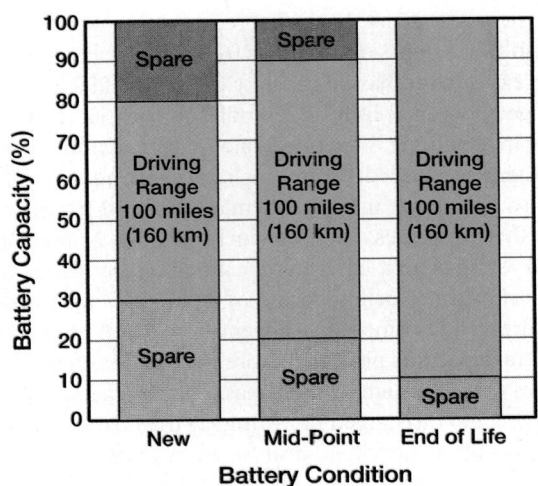

FIGURE 54-56 To extend battery life, a battery charges to only about 80% and discharges to 30%. More capacity is used as a battery ages.

cells produce higher fully charged voltage of between 3.3 and 4.3 volts, but they have more amperage from each pound, kilogram, or volume measurement compared with any other battery such as lead (2.1 volts in lead acid) or nickel (1.2 volts in NiMh). The battery voltage discharge curve from a lithium battery is flat until the battery reaches a discharged state of less than 20%, where its voltage drops quickly (**FIGURE 54-55**). Lithium is also very light, the lightest of all metallic battery materials, so storage systems using lithium have the highest energy density capacity.

As mentioned in an earlier chapter, lithium batteries are available with several different chemistries. Classification and specifications of the lithium batteries vary according to the materials used to alloy with lithium in the negative battery pole. Popular commercially available batteries use lithium and carbon or graphite-lithium alloys in the positive terminal, which gives the battery the name lithium-ion. These batteries are different from disposable lithium metal batteries. But at the negative terminal, either lithium cobalt oxide (LiCoO), lithium manganese dioxide ($LiMn_2O_4$), or lithium iron phosphate ($LiFePO_4$) are used to form the material that holds the high negative charge. Tesla trucks batteries are expected to use lithium-nickel-cobalt-aluminum oxide alloys in the negative terminal.

Batteries used in CBEVs are different from those used in consumer electronic products, such as cell phones and laptop computers. For example, safety concerns with LiCoO, commonly used in consumer electronics, make this chemistry less suitable for transportation applications because of potentially explosive thermal runaway events, caused by overcharging or puncturing the battery. Puncturing or overheating these batteries allows cell electrodes to short together. The electrolyte paste is also combustible and can violently react with oxygen. Transportation batteries are heavier because thicker cell separators are needed to prevent shorting or puncturing during an accident. Cooling and heating systems are required to improve battery efficiency from cold and damaging heat when heavily

charging or discharging. Lithium-ion chemistry is a choice in trade-offs between power density and high energy output, balanced against fire resistance, environmental friendliness, longevity, and very rapid charge rates.

Lithium iron phosphate batteries are demonstrated to last for as long as 10 years and more than 7000 partial charge cycles, while lithium-manganese batteries are expected to last up to 40 years. To achieve this, lithium-ion batteries are typically charged no more than 80% to 90% of their maximum state-of-charge (SoC) and are not allowed to discharge below a minimum SoC threshold of typically 15% or 2.5 volts. This essentially provides an 80% depth of discharge–charge cycle. Battery management control units electrically disconnect the battery to prevent any further discharge. Battery life can be extended three times further if a 40% charge-discharge cycle is maintained. Operating at extremes of high or low SoCs can shorten battery life, so a charged battery is maintained close to only 4.2 volts and considered discharged at 3.0 volts. Battery resistance and heating increases at high SoC and batteries deteriorate quickly when left fully charged for a prolonged time. When discharged, physical changes at the battery terminals can form what are called dendrites or thin conductive filaments that can short out the battery cell. Batteries are expected to last a minimum of eight years, enduring several thousand partial charge and discharge cycles, yet retain 80% capacity of a new battery before they are considered defective (**FIGURE 54-56**).

Lithium Battery Construction

To produce the high-voltage and amperage output battery packs, individual low-voltage lithium-ion battery cells are connected in series, forming battery groups or modules. Ninety-six batteries connected in series and charged to 4.2 volts supplies over 400 volts DC (**FIGURE 54-57**). Several modules connect to form a battery pack. Cells are constructed in a variety of shapes, but for transportation use, cylindrical and more expensive rectangular-shaped **prismatic cells** are built (**FIGURE 54-58**). Of these types, the "18650" cylindrical cell, which is about the same size

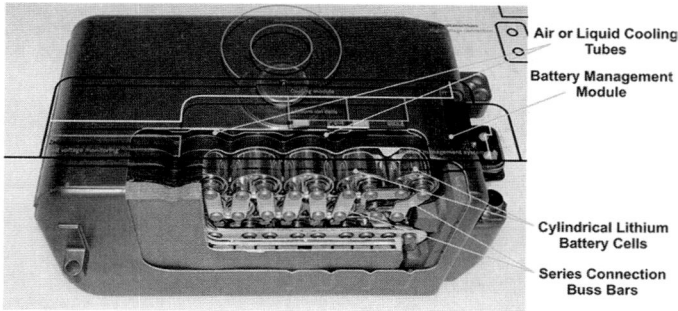

FIGURE 54-57 A liquid-cooled 96-cell battery module with a BMS module.

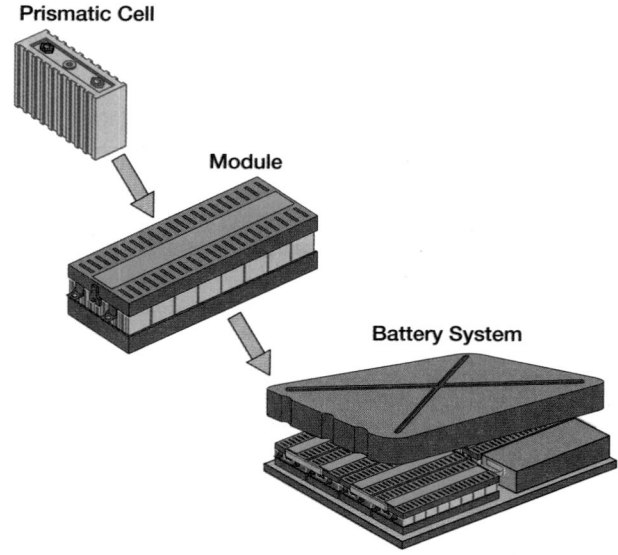

FIGURE 54-58 Rectangular-shaped lithium-ion cells, called prismatic cells, are grouped together to form modules. Several modules with BMS systems are connected to form battery packs.

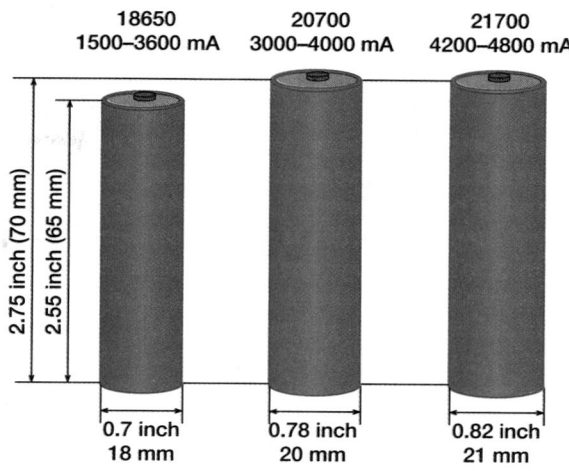

FIGURE 54-59 Three common cylindrical cell dimensions are the most common batteries used in lithium-ion battery packs.

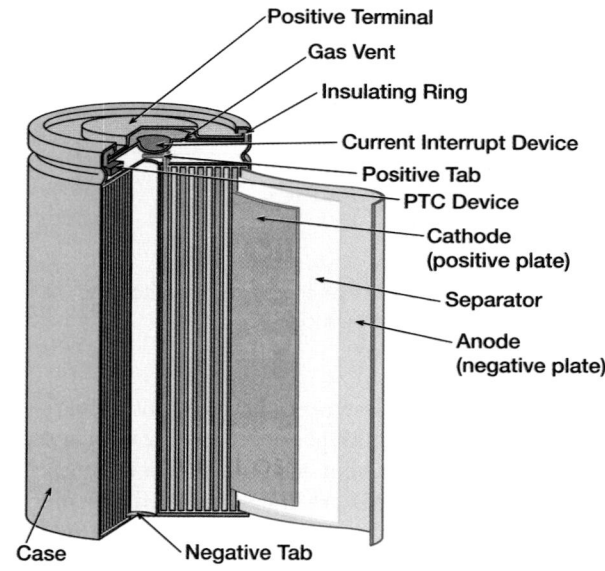

FIGURE 54-60 Construction of a cylindrical-shaped battery cell.

as an AA-type battery, was popularized by its use in the first Tesla car. Several thousand of these batteries were connected to build the first relatively low-cost battery pack in the Tesla roadster that launched enormous renewed interest in BEVs. The designation 18650 cell refers to the cell's dimension of 18 mm (0.71") diameter and 65 mm (2.56") length. It has a 2600 milliamp hours (mAh) capacity. Later batteries use a 20700 and a 21700 cell (20 and 21 mm [0.79" and 0.83"] diameter and 70 mm [2.76"] length) (**FIGURE 54-59**). The 21700 or 2170 has a 4200 mAh capacity, providing much more output with a minimal increase in weight.

These cylindrical cells are made from layers of thin metal electrodes wound together with a separator and electrolyte between the layers. Vents and safety devices to prevent overcharging or gas explosions are connected and the cells are integrated into a module. The lithium-nickel-cobalt-aluminum oxide strip in the 2170 battery at 32" (81 cm) long is a third longer compared to 24" (61 cm) for the earlier 18650 (**FIGURE 54-60**). Tesla's SD100D box beam battery for the truck holds 76,800 2170-type cells with 360 cells per module for eight modules

and is air-cooled. A high-capacity, longer-range, liquid-cooled battery pack consists of 2070 batteries arranged into 240 cells per module connected to form 12 modules in a battery pack (**FIGURE 54-61**).

Battery Management System Modules

The CBEV's vehicle control module operates using battery power as a single, high-voltage battery unit; however, a smaller, separate battery control system exerting control over individual modules and cells is needed to extend battery longevity and consistent power output. In battery packs using thousands of individual cells, small changes in an individual battery resistance changes its ability to charge and discharge, which ultimately affects the battery pack capacity. A single battery in a module having less capacity than the other batteries eventually loses its ability to have a 100% SoC.

FIGURE 54-61 Eight battery packs made of numerous modules are used by the Mercedes CBEV eTruck.

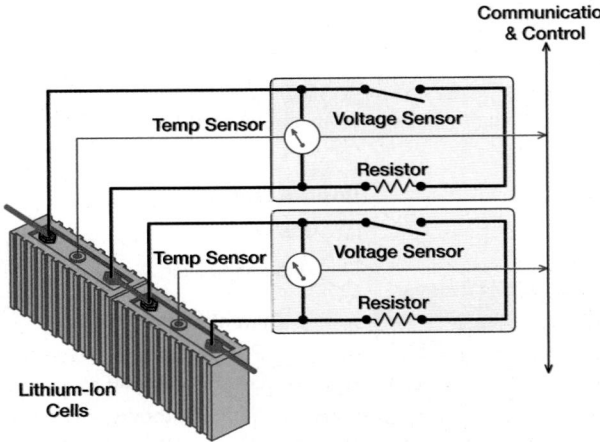

FIGURE 54-62 A battery management system monitors individual cell voltages and temperatures to balance SoCs.

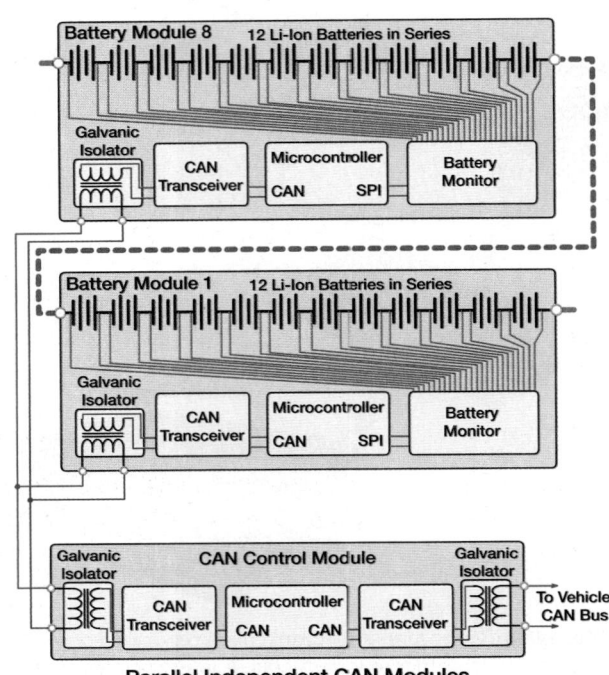

Parallel Independent CAN Modules

FIGURE 54-63 A BMS with charge control for 12 cells and capable of transmitting detailed cell SoC condition.

A dead battery could allow other batteries to discharge into it, draining the battery module or even overheating and damaging the battery. To prevent a failure in the expensive battery pack, individual cells are then packaged together, and their temperature and voltage are monitored (**FIGURE 54-62**). A battery control module measures battery temperature and voltage to equalize the battery charge rate. Lower-voltage batteries receive more charging voltage, and less-resistive batteries capable of faster charging receive slightly lower current. A common configuration for battery management is to connect a battery-monitoring module to 12 batteries connected in series having approximately 50 volts (**FIGURE 54-63**). A microcontroller uses monitoring data to individually charge or discharge batteries to balance their SoCs. Battery data is communicated through a controller area network (CAN) transceiver with other modules to coordinate module charge and discharge rates. The modules can be connected in series or parallel and a variety of configurations with the same elements—a temperature and voltage monitor along with a CAN transceiver—are used (**FIGURE 54-64**). A **galvanic isolator** circuit is used in situations where two circuits, with different ground potentials, could potentially share a common chassis ground. The isolator prevents current from one battery module unintentionally traveling to another through a common ground. Digital isolators can accomplish the same purpose.

Battery Cooling

While lithium-ion cells have low resistance to charging and discharging current, heat is till generated during both processes. To prevent catastrophic battery pack failure and extend battery life, battery packs are either air- or liquid-cooled (**FIGURE 54-65**). Corrugated metal passageways in contact with the cells use circulating air or liquid coolant to cool heated batteries (**FIGURE 54-66**). Because lithium batteries are temperature sensitive, in cold weather they lose efficiency, so the system regulates battery temperature to warm up cold batteries.

Battery Charging

LO 54-12 Describe and explain the design and operation of CBEV charging systems and electrical connectors.

Comparing battery capacity of 1 to 2 megawatts/hour on Tesla's trucks and 240 kilowatts/hour on trucks like the Mercedes

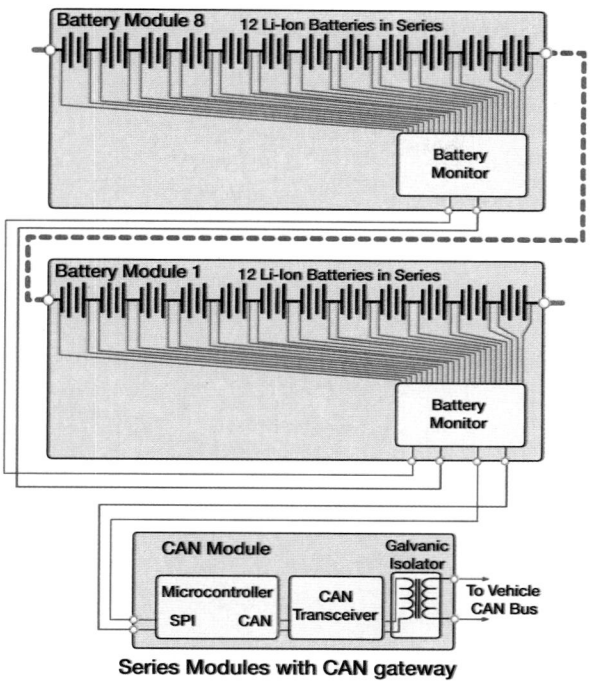

Series Modules with CAN gateway

FIGURE 54-64 A BMS for eight battery modules communicating data to the CANbus to coordinate charging and discharging of battery modules.

Actros eTruck; these batteries are 8 to more than 30 times larger than BEV automobiles. Charging with an extension cord using single phase household current is impractical because of the time it would require to recharge (100+ hours). Unlike light-duty BEVs, which commonly have an AC to DC rectifier or battery charger built into the vehicle to charge batteries using household current, heavy-duty CBEV trucks and buses use DC charging with a minimum DC voltage of 700 V or higher, but below 1000 V peak. DC chargers for fast battery charging in North American light-duty vehicles use a

480 VAC input (**FIGURE 54-67**). Charge time can be calculated using the formula: Charging Time (H) = Battery Capacity (kWh)/ Charging Power (kW)

To recharge to 400 miles of battery range in 30 minutes, a charge rate for Tesla trucks would likely require as much as 1.6 MW current. To do this, four 500-amp delivery circuits are needed, each supplying a voltage between 200 to 1000 volts. A rapid battery exchange feature where charged batteries are rotated with discharged batteries is also expected to reduce vehicle downtime due to battery depletion. Incentives to reduce battery charging time to under 15 minutes, adding 200 miles to its range, or by exchanging batteries are provided emission credits.

Charging Plug Standards

Unlike light-duty vehicles, no industry-wide or global standards currently exist that are used by all CBEVs or other heavy-duty charging plugs capable of providing safe and durable connectors. Connector styles vary between countries and organizations establishing electrical connector standards. Efforts are underway to define a common electric vehicle charging system configuration outlining operational, functional, and dimensional requirements for the vehicle electrical charging connector. CHARIN (Charging Interface Initiative) is one organization that is working quickly with the Society of Automotive Engineers (SAE) to standardize fast chargers for CBEVs. For a heavy plug to be easy to insert and remove, it is likely to need a motorized system to assist the connection process. Tesla trucks, however, have an eight-pin charging plug (**FIGURE 54-68**). Eight pins are needed for its four 500-amp current supply circuits.

Charging connectors also require several safety features to prevent any electrical shock to users in wet conditions. Some of the other features include:

- Prevents movement of the vehicle when connected to the electric vehicle supply equipment.
- Polarized and keyed connector plug allowing it to connect to the vehicle in only one way.

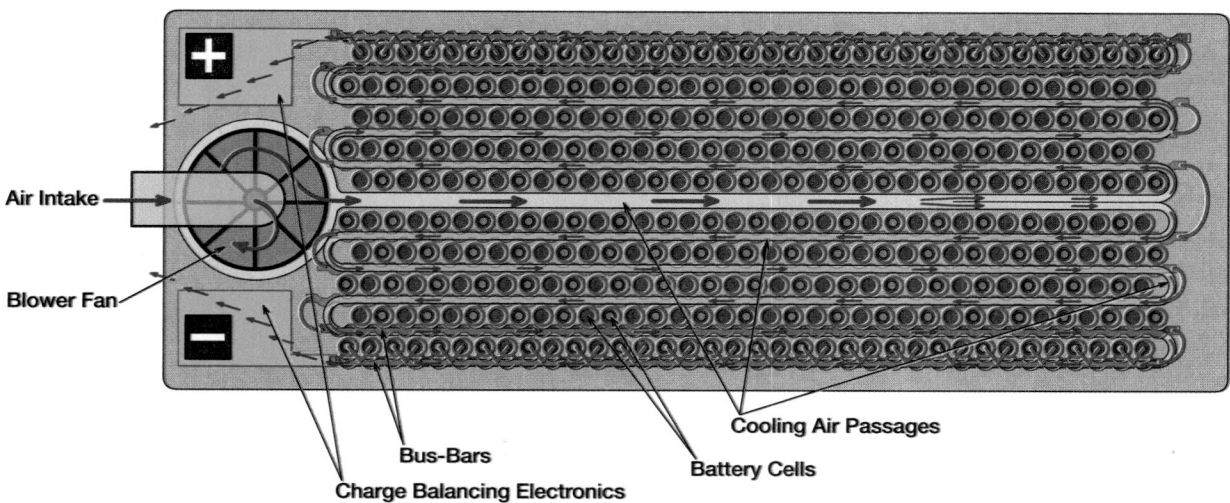

FIGURE 54-65 An air-cooled module configuration for the smaller of two battery packs used by the Tesla truck.

FIGURE 54-66 Coolant lines connected to the battery packs of a transit bus.

- Not interchangeable with other wiring devices or plugs.
- Physically isolating pins inside the connector after they are mated so there is no access to the pins from the outside of the connector.
- When not mated, no power is present on the pins.
- Electrical current does not flow unless it is commanded by the vehicle.
- Proximity detection of the plug. This uses a first break last make connection strategy, preventing power from connecting to the batteries until the plug is completely seated and mated. Current is interrupted when the proximity detection pin first breaks contact between the vehicle and charging side of the connection. This proximity strategy also prevents arcing of pins when electrical current is flowing.
- Communication signaling between the charging station plug and vehicle.
- Fault detection of electrical insulation failure or low resistance in high-voltage cables. When electrical resistance of cable insulation is low, power is interrupted.
- Ground Fault Interruption (GFI) Circuit Protection: Current flow in and to the ground circuit are compared and contactors are opened if a short circuit to ground is present.

SAE J-Plug (2001 Version)

The SAE has developed a couple of standards for electrical connectors used in North America. The SAE J1772-2001 plug standard is for single phase charging with 120–240VAC current at less than 80 amps (**FIGURE 54-69**). This plug is also called

FIGURE 54-67 A charging station with 400 VAC at 63 amps, 500 VAC at 120 amps, and a DC 500-volt 120-amp current supply. Charging plugs are different on each charging cord.

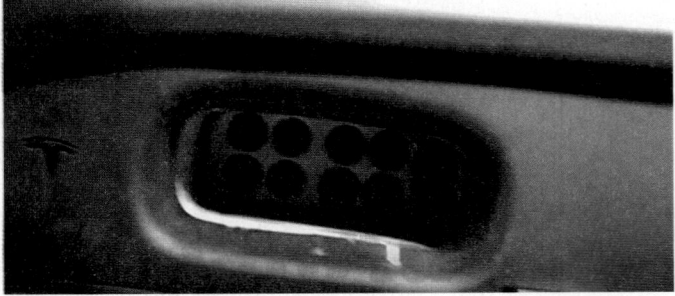

FIGURE 54-68 Tesla's eight-pin charging plug.

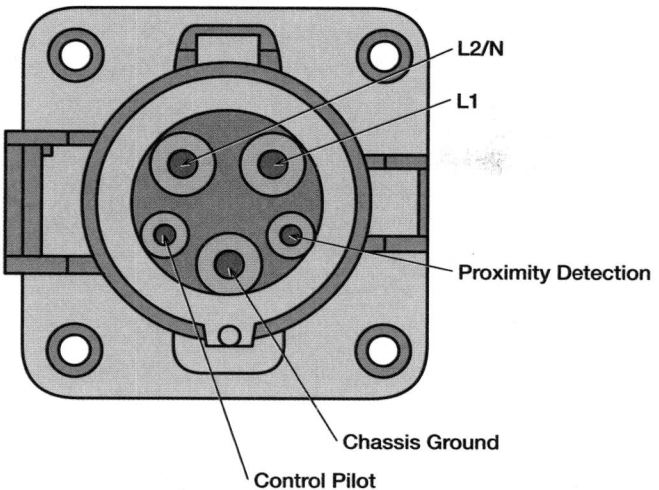

FIGURE 54-69 Pin callouts for an SAE "J" plug.

TABLE 54-3 Proximity

Proximity Switch Position	Voltage on Proximity Pin
Not Connected	4.5
Button Pressed	3.0
Connected	1.5

an IEC Type 1 (International Electrotechnical Commission), also known as a "J" plug. It incorporates safety standards for proximity detection and uses a control pilot circuit. A proximity detection pin on the charging station plug is connected to a switch that changes the resistance of low-voltage current passing through the switch when a physical connect/disconnect button on the plug is pressed. The button must be pressed when connecting and removing the connector from the vehicle. The change in resistance on the proximity pin is sensed by the charging station (**TABLE 54-3**). Any time the switch is pressed, the charging station contactor relays immediately stop current flow. When charging current is interrupted, this change is also detected by the control pilot circuit causing the contactor-power relays in the ESS battery box to open, interrupting all current flow to batteries (**FIGURE 54-70**).

Positioning the pilot pin in the connector at a shallow depth means it will break connection first before the power pins. Because the deeply recessed power pins are a last-make, first-break type, no arcing of electrical current across the pins takes place, which could eventually cause high resistance and erosion of the power pins. Note too that a loss of pilot current takes place if the electrical supply plug is in the charging port of the vehicle and it is removed. Once the pilot circuit disconnects, the contactor relays in the battery pack open too, isolating the batteries and prevent any arcing on the power pins.

Type 2 Connector

Another popular and more powerful connector, used more commonly in Europe, but also found in North America, is the

FIGURE 54-70 Location of the seven-pin IEC Type 2 connector charging an airport shuttle bus.

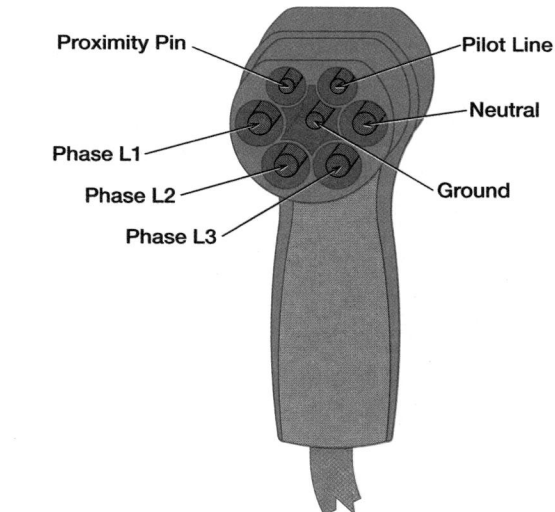

FIGURE 54-71 A seven-pin IEC Type 2 connector, also known as the Mennekes or VDA connector.

IEC Type 2 connector, also known as the Mennekes, and VDA connector. The connector is circular in shape, with a flattened top edge. Its seven-pin interface, using five large and two smaller ones, can charge a vehicle's batteries using three-phase AC and low-voltage DC (**FIGURE 54-71**) also include:

- Proximity pilot (PP) for pre-insertion signal communication
- Control pilot (CP) for post-insertion signal communication
- Line (L1): single-phase AC
- L1, L2, and L3 for three-phase AC
- Combination of pins for low- and mid-level DC and AC charging

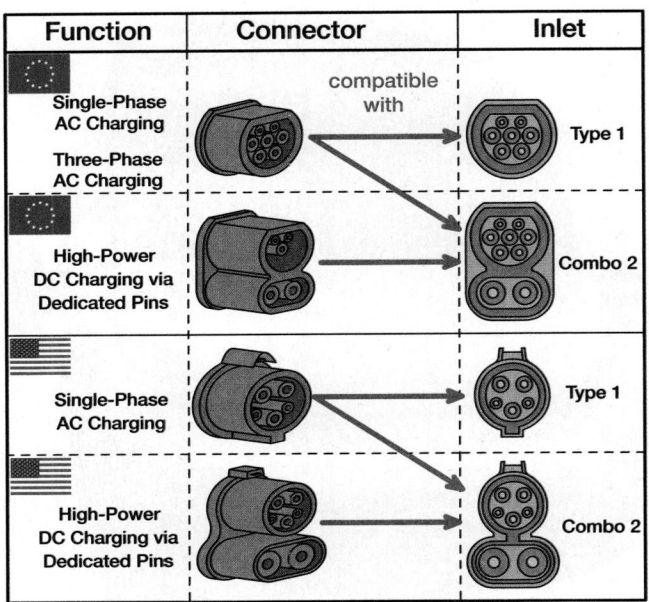

Function	Connector	Inlet
🇪🇺 Single-Phase AC Charging / Three-Phase AC Charging	compatible with	Type 1
🇪🇺 High-Power DC Charging via Dedicated Pins		Combo 2
🇺🇸 Single-Phase AC Charging		Type 1
🇺🇸 High-Power DC Charging via Dedicated Pins		Combo 2

FIGURE 54-72 Two styles of combo connectors are used in North America and Europe.

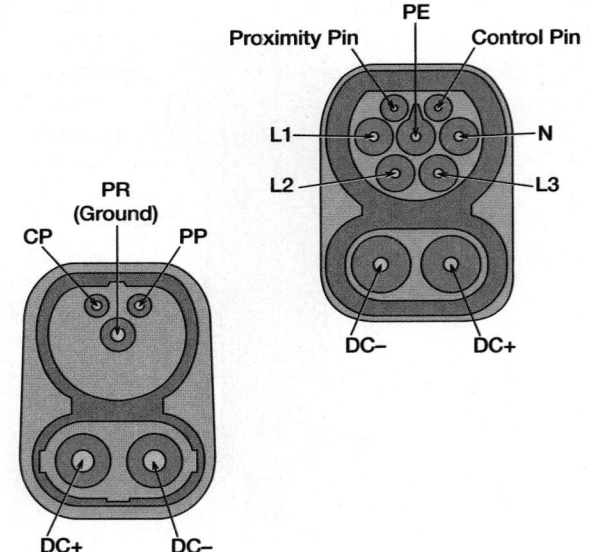

FIGURE 54-73 Pin-outs for the CCS 1 and CCS 2 connectors.

Combined Charging System (CCS) Technology

Combined Charging System 2 (CSS2) couplers combine a version of the J1772-2009 connector with two additional large pins to enable fast DC charging at 200–450 volts DC (**FIGURE 54-72**). It uses power-line communication (PLC) technology to communicate between the vehicle, off board charger, and electrical grid networks. A CCS 1 is used in Europe, combining the Type 2 connector with additional DC charging pins, and the CCS 2 connector is used in North America (**FIGURE 54-73**).

FIGURE 54-74 A new proposed electrical connector standard for CBEVs can handle up to two megawatts of charging current.

Chargepoint CBEV Connector

A high-power connector capable of supply up to 2 megawatts of power is expected to be adopted for use by CBEVs. It can supply power through four separate circuits with 500 amp delivery at 200–1000 VDC, and connect to four BMS interfaces if battery packs are divided into two, three, or four parts. The plug also can upload and download high-speed communication for autonomous vehicles. To assist insertion, a motorized mechanism is used in its rugged design to allow robotic connection. It can also be operated manually and is designed to withstand rough handling. Optional auxiliary cooling can be supplied through the plug (**FIGURE 54-74**).

High-Voltage Hazards and Safety

LO 54-13 Identify and describe the hazards of high-voltage CBEV systems and common safety precautions.

In the automotive industry, high-voltage refers to current levels above 60 VDC and 30 VAC. These are considered minimum thresholds when risk exists for significant personal injury or even death from electrical energy. In addition to other hazards associated with servicing and repair of commercial vehicles, CBEVs introduce stored energy, high-voltage hazards capable of delivering a fatal electric shock. These include:

- Components and cables with stored high voltage that contain dangerous voltages even after a vehicle is switched off.
- Storage of electrical energy with the potential to arc and short to ground causing explosions or fires due to electrical short circuits.
- The potential for fires and explosion from the release of gases and harmful liquids from damaged or overcharged batteries.
- Permanent magnet electric motors that may allow the vehicle to move unexpectedly due to magnetic forces within the motors.
- Handling risks associated with battery replacement.

Given that battery voltages of up to 400 volts are encountered in light-duty BEV and at least 850–1000 volts are expected for commercial vehicles, technicians must develop a wider knowledge base and skill sets related to electrical vehicle repair. Access to specialized tools, equipment, and service information is mandatory in order to be able to work safely.

Because of the increased risk associated with higher voltage, most jurisdictions have established health and safety or occupational safety standards mandating that technicians working directly on high-voltage systems have documented qualifications associated with performing electrical work. This means that before working on high-voltage systems and components, technicians must complete related service training in an approved manner, which is usually done by a manufacturer. The length and content of electrical service training depends on brand, model, and type of electric vehicle, as well as the technician's responsibilities. Depending on whether the technician is repairing, servicing, salvaging, or repairing accident damage can affect the type of training qualifications. In the US, OSHA requires work places performing service and repairs to have an effective Lockout/Tagout (LOTO) program in place to protect workers from unexpected startup or release of stored electrical energy that can lead to serious injury or even death.

▶ TECHNICIAN TIP

High-voltage circuits are not always connected with large cables. The safest way to identify high-voltage equipment or circuits is to first identify high-voltage components and circuits using OEM service literature. Look for high-voltage warning labels and orange insulation of electrical conduit. Inspect the vehicle for any equipment or circuits that may have been added after the truck was built, which could potentially interference with high-voltage circuit isolation.

High-Voltage Cables

To help technicians recognize the increased risk of high-voltage injury, high-voltage cables and distribution components are color-coded orange. High voltage and amperage flowing through electrical cables are different than 12- or 24-volt system wiring because they require significantly larger cross-section. Double layers of heat, chemical, and abrasion-resistant insulation is used on conductors with a braided metal shielding layer to trap and drain electromagnetic interference with other circuits

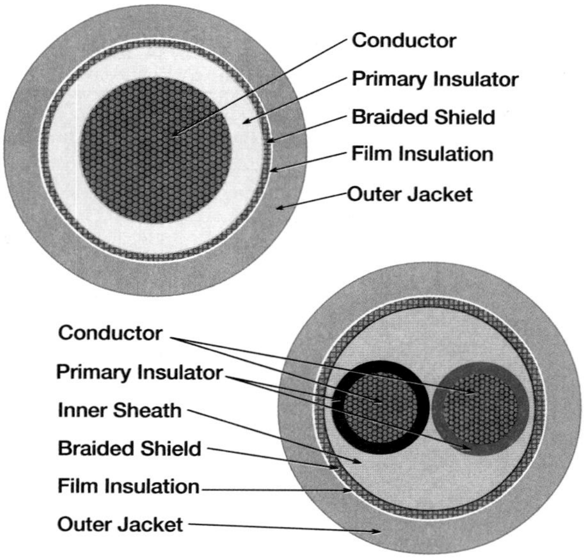

FIGURE 54-75 High-voltage cables are color-coded and use double layers of insulation and a braided metal electromagnetic shielding layer.

(**FIGURE 54-75**). This shielding layer prevents transmission of electromagnetic fields from the wire when the sheilding wire is connected to a ground circuit. Any current induced from changing magnetic field strength is drained to ground.

High-voltage circuits and components do not share a chassis ground with the 12- or 24-volt electrical system. All high-voltage conductors for DC voltage are two-wire, carrying positive and negative current, which means the ground circuits are isolated.

Pilot Control Circuit

Another important cable feature is the use of what is often called a safety line or pilot control circuit. This optional cable feature is a low-voltage wire conductor used to test insulation resistance and detect whether all high-voltage components are correctly connected (**FIGURE 54-76**). The pilot control circuit

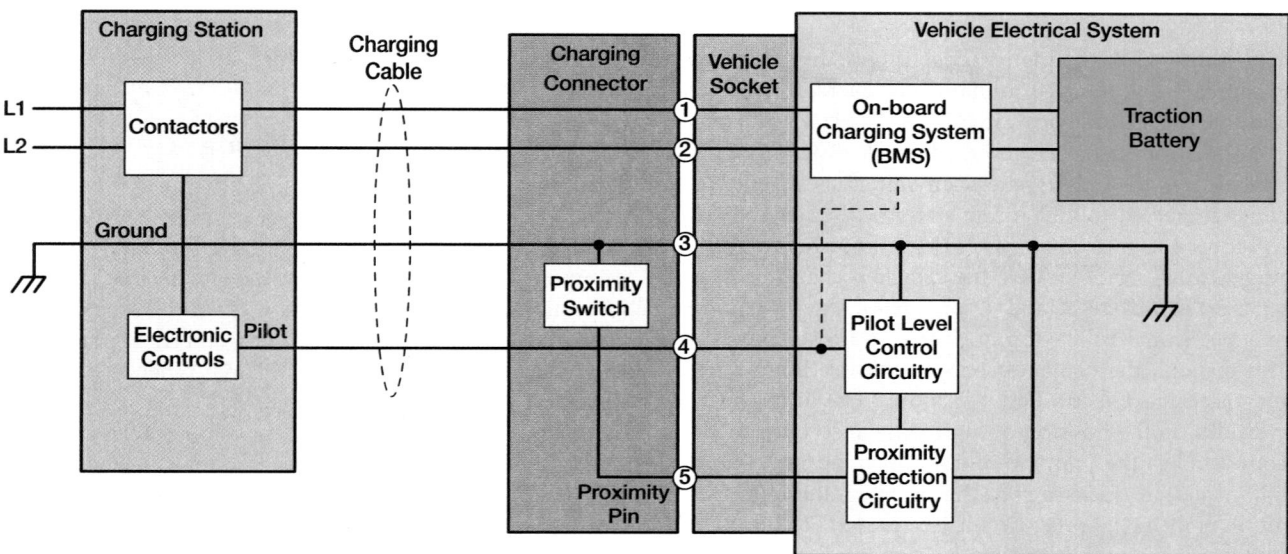

FIGURE 54-76 A block diagram showing the connections between the pilot control circuit and proximity circuit.

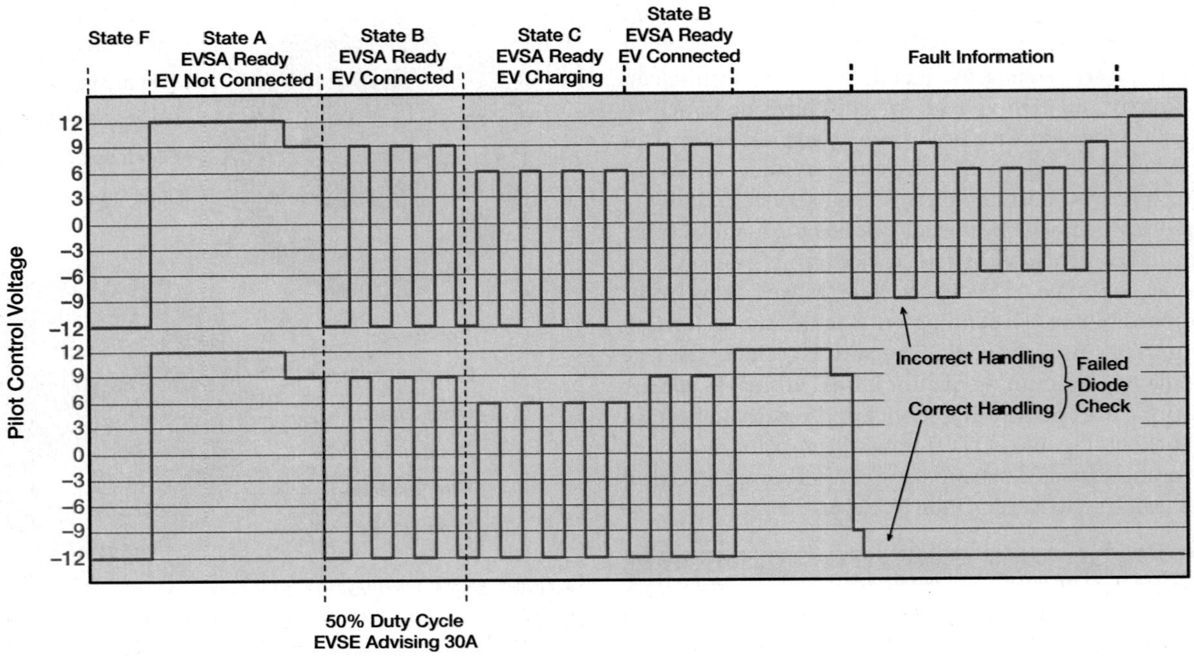

FIGURE 54-77 The waveform of the pilot control circuit transmits high-voltage system status and fault information.

TABLE 54-4 Control Pilot States: Voltage Level on Control Pilot Circuit Indicating Vehicle System Status

Control Pilot Designation	Control Pilot Positive Voltage	Control Pilot Negative Voltage	Frequency	Resistance	System Status
State A	+12 V	N/A	DC	N/A	Not Connected
State B	+9 V	−12 V	1000 Hz	2.74k	EV Connected (Ready)
State C	+6 V	−12 V	1000 Hz	882	EV Charging
State D	+3 V	−12 V	1000 Hz	246	EV Charge Ventilation Required
State E	0 V	0 V	N/A	N/A	Error
State F	N/A	−12 V	N/A		Unknown/Error

wire runs through all the high-voltage cables and connectors and is supplied less than 10 milliamps of current at 12 volts by a module associated with the ESS. A 1-kHz 12-volt pulse width modulation signal represented at six different voltage states labeled A to F, designate such things as whether the vehicle is connected to a charging station, whether the vehicle can accept energy from a charging station, whether indoor charging ventilation is required, the vehicle is charging, a fault exists, etc. (**FIGURE 54-77** and **TABLE 54-4**). The circuit also has an input from the proximity circuit and disconnects the batteries through the contactor relays until the charging station plug is connected or when it is about to be disconnected. Zener diodes on the housing of high-voltage components are also connected to the pilot circuit and inject current into the signal if insulation is leaking or other short circuit failures are present. A fault in the pilot circuit is reported in the driver's information display if the vehicle is connected to a charging station and displays the message "not ready," or the vehicle

does not operate with charged batteries and it is not connected to a charging station.

Insulation Resistance Testing

The high-voltage systems are continuously monitored for faults by one or more of the high-voltage systems control modules. During operation, all high-voltage circuits and components are monitored, and are disabled when abnormal operation is detected. When a fault occurs in the high-voltage system, Diagnostic Trouble Codes (DTC) are stored in the High Voltage Control Module (HCM). When the high-voltage system is active, an insulation stress test is regularly performed with a 60-second interval by the battery management control module. The resistance between the high-voltage conductors and the housing of the battery pack is measured. The control module calculates and compares new measurements with the previously measured resistances of the high-voltage system. If the insulation of a cable is externally damaged, for example, by abrasion, or a rodent has chewed a cable, the insulation resistance changes and the discrepancy sets a fault code. If insulation faults are detected by low resistance measurements between the high-voltage components and high-voltage lines, the contactor opens.

> ▶ TECHNICIAN TIP
>
> Because of the critical safety-related construction of high-voltage cables, they should not be repaired. The insulation resistance monitoring system also prevents cable repair because slight changes in resistance will set faults. In fact, small changes in cable resistance, such as takes place in wet weather or road spray containing road salt, can cause an insulation resistance fault.

Isolating High-Voltage System

Before working on a vehicle, the high-voltage circuits must be isolated, and electrical current should not have a pathway to leave the batteries. Using procedures to ensure high-voltage current remains inside the batteries is known as **high-voltage isolation**. Each high-voltage circuit connected to the battery has its own protective connecting relay, called contactors, that can interrupt the current flow from the batteries (**FIGURE 54-78**). When DC is used and separate positive and negative cables conduct current on an isolated ground chassis, the input and output terminals of the contactors have two poles and throws, each dedicated to positive and negative current flow. The contactor relays are only switched by the high-voltage system control module. When deenergized, they are open, and the high-voltage battery supply is disconnected from the high-voltage system. Various conditions are sensed by the control logic for opening the relays. The easiest way to isolate the high battery voltage is to turn off the vehicle and remove the ignition key, to open the contactors. A safe work practice is to relocate remote start key FOBs. Remote FOBs should be moved as far away from the vehicle as necessary to prevent accidental closing of the high-voltage system contactors that could send lethal current outside the ESS.

Most high-voltage systems have a maintenance connector or manual disconnect switch near to the high-voltage battery as an additional safety feature for de-energizing the high-voltage system (**FIGURE 54-79**). If the maintenance connector is unlocked and switched off, the pilot line is disconnected. This opens the contactors, causing the high-voltage battery to be disconnected from the high-voltage system.

Personal Protective Equipment

When working with high-voltage, protective insulating linesperson gloves are recommended. Gloves should be rated for a minimum of 1000 volts. The American National Standards Institute (ANSI) Class "0" is the accepted standard when working on electric vehicles. Leather "over gloves" can be used to protect the rubber gloves. Gloves need to be inspected before using and tested in according to a manufacturer's procedure each time they are used.

All electrical meters and test equipment used must be rated to a minimum of CAT III. This standard is set by the International Electrotechnical Commission (IEC). Meter operation should be validated before using. An acceptable procedure is to measure a known low voltage with an auto ranging meter and then use it to test for high voltage without changing the settings. Testing for high voltage is primarily used to confirm that the system is not live before beginning any work. OEM software or scan tools should be used to monitor live high-voltage readings. This ensures that there is no connection between the high-voltage circuits and the vehicle technician. Insulated tools to prevent conduction of high voltage should be used when working on circuits with any potential for high-voltage electrical current.

> ▶ TECHNICIAN TIP
>
> Beware that when A VOLTMETER IS SET TO DC, IT WILL ALWAYS INDICATE A READING OF ZERO VOLTS WHEN CONNECTED TO AN AC CIRCUIT!

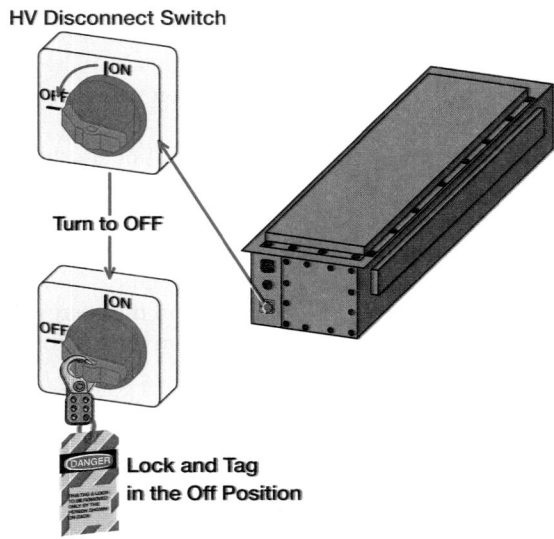

FIGURE 54-79 A manual shut-off switch near the battery can be switched off and locked out to prevent high-voltage system energization during service.

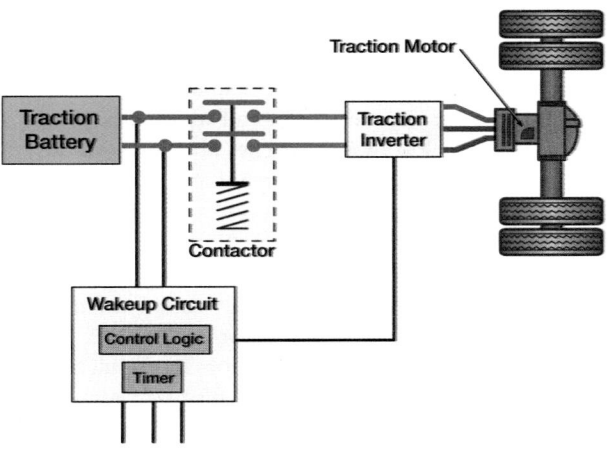

FIGURE 54-78 A module associated with the high-voltage system opens and closes the contactor relay.

Wrap-Up

Ready for Review

▶ Commercial battery electric vehicles (CBEVs) do not use an engine but are propelled exclusively by electric traction motors supplied with current from on board batteries.

▶ Electric propulsion system consisting of one or more electric motors and associated electronic control units to regulate electric current. An inverter that takes DC power stored in batteries and changes it to AC used by the motor is included in this system.

▶ Hybrid-electric vehicles (HEVs) refer to a vehicle propulsion system having at least two sources of power. One is an electric motor and the other is an internal combustion engine. Electrical energy powering the motor can originate from batteries, fuel cells, or even capacitors.

▶ Plug-in hybrid-electric vehicles (PHEVs) can operate on only battery power alone and indefinitely if they are recharged after normally short driving time or distances.

▶ A range extended electric vehicle (REEV) recharges batteries while it is operating to extend the driving range.

▶ Nikola Motor Company trucks, the Nikola One and Two, are REEVs. The Nikola's use 800-volt electric drive motors supplied energy by fuel cells.

▶ Fuel cells operate on an electrochemical principle that reverses the more familiar process of electrolysis. In fuel cells, compressed hydrogen and atmospheric oxygen combine in the fuel cell to generate electrical current to charge the battery packs.

▶ WrightSpeed Class 7–8 trucks use a compact turbine engine to drive a generator that charges batteries; this slows the rate of charge depletion. Range-extending generators cannot maintain the battery's state of charge when operating under load.

▶ Electric motors' design chosen for propulsion systems have their maximum torque output at low rpm, such as when starting with a heavy load. A clutch, multi-step standard, or automatic transmission with torque converters are not necessary.

▶ CBEVs use traction motors at wheel ends or attached to the input of drive axle.

▶ Accessories such as the air conditioning compressor, air compressors, and coolant and power steering pumps are driven by electric motors and not the engine.

▶ Regenerative braking recaptures some of the energy that would normally be lost as heat from the frictional materials in mechanical brakes.

▶ Regenerative braking not only improves vehicle efficiency but can dramatically reduce brake wear, since braking force is supplied by the motors switching into generator mode.

▶ Auxiliary systems are electrically driven vehicle support devices. These can include electrical components used by the temperature control systems for the cab; cooling for batteries, motors, and power electronics; and air and power steering pumps.

▶ The auxiliary power supply provides electric current at different voltages required by CBEV auxiliary components. DC-to-DC converters increase or decrease storage system battery voltage supplied to auxiliary electrical devices.

▶ An electronic control module is needed to regulate the speed and torque output of the electric motor. These devices change the frequency of AC and are often called inverters because some CBEV propulsion systems convert DC battery voltage to AC.

▶ Motor speed is also controlled by the frequency of AC voltage, which is varied by the motor controller. Controllers are also called AC drives, variable speed drives (VSDs), or variable frequency drives (VFDs).

▶ Most traction motors use AC because it conducts with less resistance than DC. AC motors run cooler and more efficiently on AC. Increasing AC frequency further lowers a motor windings resistance to AC.

▶ AC induction motors are simple, relatively inexpensive devices consisting of a rotor and stator. Interaction of magnetic poles created in the rotor and stator produces motor rotation.

▶ A Hall-effect sensor called the resolver measures the rotor position and speed to provide a feedback signal to a motor controller to properly regulate traction motor operation.

▶ Slip angle decreases the closer the rotor speed approaches the stator field speed. When slip angle is small, there is little or no load on the motor. Increasing the load on an AC induction motor simultaneously increases the slip angle along with torque output due to the larger angle between the magnetic fields.

▶ Switching the connection of any two phases of a three-phase AC in the stator can produce forward and reverse motor operation.

▶ In permanent magnet (PM) motors, the conductor bars in the rotor are replaced with PMs to increase the energy efficiency of an electric motor.

▶ PM motors are either electrically commutated using DC supplied to the stator coils or use AC and are called sinusoidal commuted (PMSC) too.

▶ PM motors require rotor position feedback from a position sensor or encoder, such as a Hall-effect sensor.

▶ An external rotor PM motor switches position with the stator. The rotor moves but the stator has a fixed position inside the rotor to provide more torque output.

▶ Switched reluctance motor (SRM) uses a rotor made from a machined piece of steel with protrusions called poles. SRM uses the principle of magnetic attraction and not magnetic repulsion to drive the motor.

▶ Electromagnetic fields in the SRM motors stator pull the steel rotors pole pieces into alignment using magnetic attraction.

▶ SRMs without rotor magnets or conductor bars have lower inertia, enabling them to turn faster and accelerate more quickly.

▶ To absorb electrical energy produced during braking, a battery requires some space or discharged capacity to store current. This mean they are charged no more than 80% to 90% of their maximum state-of-charge.

▶ The battery management system (BMS) is primarily responsible for charge equalization of battery cells and modules. The charging and discharge rate of modules and cells is controlled by the BMS.

▶ CBEV trucks and buses use DC charging with a minimum DC voltage of 700 V or higher, but below 1000 V peak.

▶ Charging electrical connectors require several safety features to prevent any electrical shock to users in wet conditions.

▶ A high-power connector capable of supplying up to 2 megawatts of power is expected to be adopted for use by CBEVs. The chargepoint CBEV connector can supply power through four separate circuits with 500-amp delivery at 200–1000 VDC.

▶ High voltage refers to current levels above 60-volts DC and 30-volts AC. These are considered minimum thresholds when risk exists for significant personal injury or even death from electrical energy.

▶ High-voltage cables and distribution components are color-coded orange. They do not share a chassis ground with the 12- or 24-volt electrical system.

▶ The pilot control circuit is used to test insulation resistance and detect whether all high-voltage components are correctly connected.

▶ A proximity detection pin on the charging station plug detects when the charging station electrical connector is about to be plugged in or disconnected. This event disconnects power before the plug is removed to prevent arcing at electrical contact.

Key Terms

DC to DC converters Electrical devices which increase or decrease DC battery voltage supplied to auxiliary electrical devices.

chopper circuit A type of circuit used by motor control units to divert excess current from a generator into the absorption resistors.

diesel gallon equivalent (DGE) The equivalent amount of electrical energy found in a gallon of diesel fuel.

galvanic isolator A device used to prevent high and low voltage sources on a vehicle from sharing a ground circuit.

high-voltage isolation A service procedure used to verify high-voltage current remains inside the battery pack during vehicle service.

induction motor An asynchronous-type AC electric motor where alternating current in the stator induces magnetic fields in the rotor.

prismatic cells The rectangular-shaped type of lithium-ion cells.

reluctance torque The term given to the movement from high to low magnetic field resistance or reluctance, which is another

way of describing torque generated due to principles of magnetic attraction in an SRM.

resolver A Hall-effect sensor type used to sense rotor position and provide electrical feedback to electronic control units controlling motor operation.

slip angle The difference between the apparent speed of the rotating magnetic field in the stator winding and the rotor speed.

switched reluctance motor (SRM) An electronically commutated traction motor using a rotor constructed from a machined piece of steel with protrusions called poles. SRM motors use principles of magnetic attraction to drive the motor.

synchronous motors A category of AC motor design where the rotational speed of the rotor and stator magnetic fields are identical synchronized in rotational speed.

variable frequency drives (VFD) Electronic control units that change the switching frequency of AC, which is used to regulate the speed of an AC induction motor.

Review Questions

1. What technology is used by range-extended electric vehicles (REEVs) to increase the distance a vehicle can travel?
   a. A series or series-parallel engine arrangement in the powertrain
   b. The use of a compact turbine engine to drive a generator
   c. An onboard plug-in battery charger
   d. A fuel cell

2. Which reason best explains why a multi-step transmission is not required for a BEV?
   a. They use a gear reduction system in the differential.
   b. Electric motors produce high horsepower at low speeds.
   c. Electric motors produce highest torque at low-speed.
   d. Multiple electric motors are used at each wheel end.

3. What is the purpose of power resistors and a chopper circuit?
   a. Reduce current flow to stator windings
   b. Used to help start the AC motor by creating an unbalanced magnetic field in the stator
   c. To prevent damage to sensitive electronic circuits caused by generator voltage spikes
   d. To absorb and dissipate heat from electric current generated during regenerative braking

4. Which of the following methods is used to regulate the speed of an AC traction motor?
   a. Vary the current's voltage
   b. Vary the current's amperage
   c. Vary the current's frequency
   d. Invert DC to AC

5. Which of the following methods is used to regulate the torque output of an AC traction motor?
   a. Vary the current's voltage
   b. Vary the current's reluctance
   c. Vary the current's frequency
   d. Invert DC to AC

6. Which method is used to cause magnetic poles in the stator and rotor of an AC induction motor to remain opposed to one another?
   a. The use of brushes and a commutator directing current flow through the rotor
   b. Current flow in each of the three stator windings that is out of phase with each other
   c. Cyclic switching of the direction of AC flow
   d. Using a Hall-effect sensor to measure motor position and switch current flow

7. How is the direction of motor rotation changed in a three-phase AC induction motor?
   a. By switching any two of the line current connections to the motor's stator
   b. By reversing the polarity of current flow into the motor
   c. By changing the frequency of AC
   d. By switching all three-line current connections to the motor stator

8. Which of the following is the major advantage of permanent magnet-type traction motors?
   a. They are less expensive to manufacture.
   b. They do not require complex electronic controls.
   c. They do not require commutation.
   d. They use less electrical energy to produce high torque output.

9. What does the number "21" in a 21700 series lithium-ion battery represent?
   a. Its output measured in milliwatts
   b. The series of battery
   c. It's a prismatic rectangular cell
   d. Its diameter is 21 mm

10. What is the minimum charging voltage for a DC fast charger used by CBEVs?
    a. 480 volts
    b. 700 volts
    c. 1000 volts
    d. 1400 volts

ASE Technician A/Technician B Style Questions

1. Technician A says that commercial battery electric vehicles generally use high-voltage DC to charge batteries and operate electric traction motors. Technician B says that CBEV traction motors use AC, and DC is used to charge batteries. Who is correct?
   a. Technician A
   b. Technician B
   c. Both Technician A and Technician B
   d. Neither Technician A nor Technician B

2. Technician A says that batteries for lithium-ion power packs use cylindrical-shaped cells. Technician B says lithium battery cells are rectangular-shaped. Who is correct?
   a. Technician A
   b. Technician B
   c. Both Technician A and Technician B
   d. Neither Technician A nor Technician B

3. Technician A says that the rotor of an AC induction-type traction motor contains permanent magnets. Technician B says that switched reluctance-type motors use permanent magnets in the rotor. Who is correct?
   a. Technician A
   b. Technician B
   c. Both Technician A and Technician B
   d. Neither Technician A nor Technician B

4. Technician A says that the rotor is the only moving part in a traction motor. Technician B says that the rotor is stationary in a traction motor using an external rotor. Who is correct?
   a. Technician A
   b. Technician B
   c. Both Technician A and Technician B
   d. Neither Technician A nor Technician B

5. Technician A says that a slip angle refers to the difference in the apparent rotational speed of the magnetic field in stator compared with the rotating speed of the rotor. Technician B says that a small slip angle must always be present in an AC induction motor to enable the motor to rotate. Who is correct?
   a. Technician A
   b. Technician B
   c. Both Technician A and Technician B
   d. Neither Technician A nor Technician B

6. Technician A says that current drawn by an AC induction motor increases as slip angle increases. Technician B says that current drawn by an AC motor decreases as slip angle increases. Who is correct?
   a. Technician A
   b. Technician B
   c. Both Technician A and Technician B
   d. Neither Technician A nor Technician B

7. Technician A says electronically commutated permanent magnet motors have a power line supplied to each of its multiple sets of stator coils and that current to each set of coils is switched on and off by a motor controller. Technician B says that electronically commutated motors require a Hall-effect sensor to identify motor position to energize the correct stator winding in the proper sequence. Who is correct?
   a. Technician A
   b. Technician B
   c. Both Technician A and Technician B
   d. Neither Technician A nor Technician B

8. Technician A says an AC induction motor can generate electrical current when the vehicle wheels drive a rotor with some residual magnetism. Technician B says that an AC induction motor cannot generate electrical current. Who is correct?
   a. Technician A
   b. Technician B
   c. Both Technician A and Technician B
   d. Neither Technician A nor Technician B

9. Technician A says that to extend the life cycle of lithium-ion batteries, they should be deeply discharged to less than 20% state of charge and then charged fully to a 100% charge condition. Technician B says that the longest battery life is obtained by recharging discharged batteries to no more than 80% state of charge. Who is correct?
   a. Technician A
   b. Technician B
   c. Both Technician A and Technician B
   d. Neither Technician A nor Technician B

10. Technician A says that whenever a high-voltage electrical connector is disconnected anywhere on a vehicle, a pilot or safety line closes the circuit through electrical contactors in the battery pack and alerts the driver through a message "NOT READY." Technician B says that the voltage level of the pilot signal indicates whether the vehicle is ready to operate or is charging. Who is correct?
   a. Technician A
   b. Technician B
   c. Both Technician A and Technician B
   d. Neither Technician A nor Technician B

CHAPTER 55

Autonomous Driving and Advanced Driver Assistance Systems for Commercial Vehicles

Learning Objectives

After reading this chapter, you will be able to:

- **LO 55-1** Identify and describe the current state of implementation of automated driving systems in commercial vehicles.
- **LO 55-2** Identify and describe autonomous control-enabling technologies.
- **LO 55-3** Describe the purpose and operation of GPS and applications to automated driving systems and commercial vehicles.
- **LO 55-4** Identify and explain the purpose of autonomous vehicle communication technology.

You Are the Technician

A late-model tractor has arrived at your shop with the complaint that the cruise control has stopped operating. When verifying the fault, you notice fault lamps for the Advanced Driver Assistance System (ADAS) are illuminated in the instrument cluster. While further inspecting the vehicle, you also notice the windshield is cracked near the center location of a camera for the lane-departure system and bugs are smeared over the windshield swept by the wipers. You also notice the front bumper is slightly bent from physical contact with a hard object. As you prepare to make service recommendations, consider the following questions.

1. Would the high-definition (HD) camera for the lane-departure and lane-centering system likely cause the cruise control with distance warning to fail?
2. What service procedure or inspection steps would you undertake after noticing the bent bumper?
3. What effect would a bent tie rod have on the ADAS?

Introduction

The year 2019 marks the break-out year for production models of heavy-duty commercial vehicles capable of driving over public roadways without driver input by combining automated steering, acceleration, deceleration, and braking functions. Daimler's flagship class 8 tractor Cascadia is the first commercial vehicle produced in North America equipped with a set of technologies that sense and automatically respond to road and traffic conditions enabling it to perform dynamic driving tasks. Electric class 8 trucks arriving from Tesla and Nicola in 2019 have similar autonomous driving system capabilities. Trucks and buses with autonomous driving capabilities are not new to anyone following the rapid evolution of automobiles using automated driving systems. But there are features unique to commercial vehicles. One important feature to trucks is described by Tesla as an Enhanced Autopilot feature, which enables a driver of a single lead tractor unit to connect to the controller area networks (CANs) of follower trucks to control multiple vehicles in convoys without the need for human input in the follower vehicles. This concept, called **platooning**, allows trucks to travel much closer together in a more efficient operating mode while synchronizing functions of braking, steering, and acceleration. Platooning allows a single human driver in a column of trucks to lead other trucks, where the driver may be available but only in a standby role (**FIGURE 55-1**). For now, follower trucks must have a driver available to take over from the automated driving system if a problem occurs that requires the driving system to relinquish control.

At 2019's year-end, Daimler plans to introduce even more advanced vehicles capable of performing all aspects of the dynamic driving task under most normal and some adverse driving traffic and road conditions. No default to a human driver intervention is expected to be necessary with the later versions of Daimler's self-driving systems. In more advanced autonomous systems, the vehicle monitors the roadway, tracking objects and reading road signage to allow it to safely accelerate, brake, turn, and steer while strategically responding to driving events, such as determining when to change lanes, use signals, merge, or operate in low-speed traffic jams (**FIGURE 55-2**). The dynamic driving system is filled with many additional safety features to avoid collisions with other vehicles, prevent contact with pedestrians, and use driving strategies to increase vehicle visibility during adverse weather and nighttime driving conditions.

Sophisticated autonomous capabilities aren't exclusive to a few models of trucks and buses. Many of the features used by autonomous driving vehicles are already found in lighter vehicles manufactured today, but are categorized as Advanced Driver Assistance Systems (ADAS) or, more simply, Advanced Driving Systems (ADS) (**FIGURE 55-3**). Collision avoidance, adaptive cruise control, and stability control systems are three examples among more than a dozen basic elements of safety systems that combine to form various levels of autonomous, self-driving capabilities (**FIGURE 55-4**). TuSimple is a one example of a global autonomous trucking solutions company that is working with original equipment manufacturer (OEM) truck makers to develop a commercial-ready Level 4 (Society

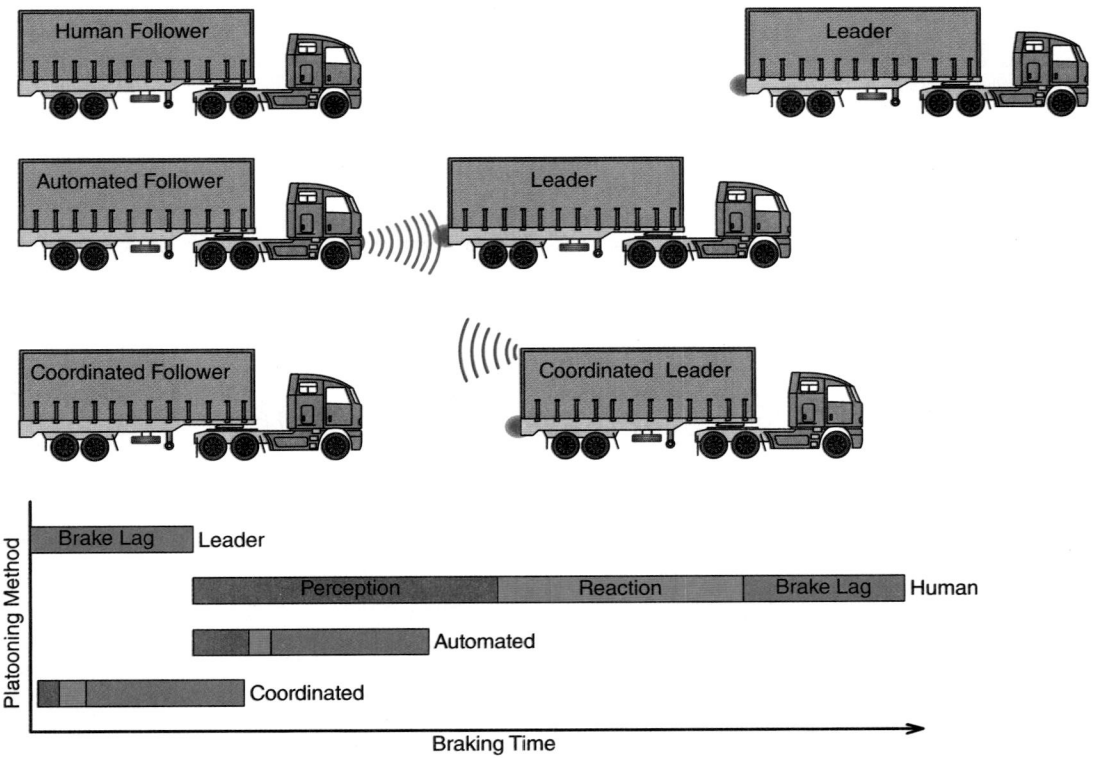

FIGURE 55-1 Platooning saves fuel by allowing trucks to travel together more closely. Three types of methods are used to form a platoon.

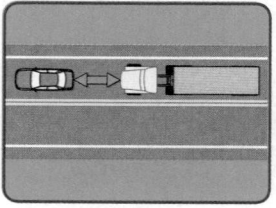

FIGURE 55-2 This Ford tractor prototype does not use mirrors, but cameras, to monitor surrounding traffic, signage, road conditions, and the presence of pedestrians.

of Automotive Engineers [SAE]) fully autonomous driving system. Currently, TuSimple is demonstrating its system installed on Navistar trucks operating in autonomous mode on several routes daily moving from inventory depot-to-depot.

There is a fear that the point of introducing driverless vehicle technology is to eliminate the driver. Manufacturers, industry groups, and legislators point out that this isn't the case. The primary reason for using an autonomous driving control system is not to reduce or eliminate human input, or even make the driver more comfortable. Instead, increased road safety is the primary reason for adopting ADAS. Given the National Highway Traffic Safety Administration (NHTSA) statistic that 94% of motor vehicle collisions are caused by human error, ADAS offers the possibility to make commercial vehicles almost accident-free. Pursuing the goal of reducing collisions and fatalities involving class 7 and 8 trucks is increasingly important because the number of collisions and fatalities involving these vehicles is increasing at a disproportionate rate to their numbers on the road. While comprising only 4% of all on-road vehicles, this class of vehicles is involved in 7% of pedestrian fatalities, 11% of bicyclist fatalities, and 12% of car and light-truck occupant fatalities.

AVAILABLE NOW

| Adaptive Cruise Control | Lane Departure Warnings | Collision Mitigation | Electronic Stability Control |

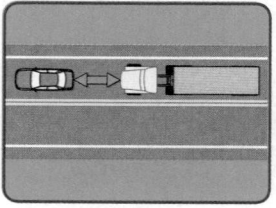

THE NEXT EVOLUTION

Driver Assisted Platooning   Lane Keeping Assist   Traffic Jam Assist   Auto Docking

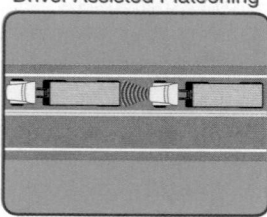

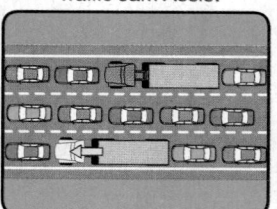

INCREASING LEVELS OF AUTOMATION

Highway Autopilot   Vehicle to Vehicle Connectivity   Unmanned Vehicles on Private Sites   Unmanned Vehicles on Public Roads

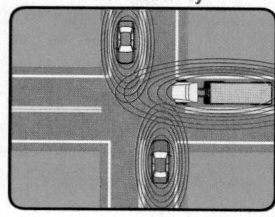

FIGURE 55-3 The current state of ADAS and future direction of autonomous driving technology.

FIGURE 55-4 This Mercedes Sprinter with ADAS uses switches on the steering wheel to engage either an advanced automated driving system or conventional cruise control.

FIGURE 55-5 A review operators' manual message. Before servicing ADAS, its normal operation needs to be understood to verify a complaint or determine whether the system is functioning normally.

Understanding and servicing rapidly evolving autonomous and semi-autonomous driving technology now making its way into the commercial field may appear overwhelming. However, this chapter's purpose is to break down the purpose and construction of automated driving systems into its more easily understandable parts, and by identifying and explaining the operation of the system elements in order to effectively diagnose and service these systems (**FIGURE 55-5**). Technology enabling autonomous driving capabilities is examined from a technician's perspective, pointing out service and maintenance practices associated with each building block of advanced or automated driving systems. To help technicians understand

FIGURE 55-6 This WABCO brake relay valve has electrical actuators to provide ADAS control or electronic control of the braking system by the autonomous driving system with mechanical control redundancy.

these systems, this chapter identifies and examines technologies essential for enabling, semi-autonomous, and fully autonomous driving systems.

What Is Autonomous Driving Capability?

LO 55-1 Identify and describe the current state of implementation of automated driving systems in commercial vehicles.

Automation is a term referring to the use of control systems that reduce or eliminate human intervention needed to operate machinery. When the concept of automation is applied to a vehicle, it broadly describes a driving control system operating autonomously—that is, with no human intervention or operating with varying, but limited, degrees of human involvement. Automated driving systems and autonomous driving are terms used interchangeably to describe the vehicles capabilities. A completely **autonomous vehicle** is controlled by a machine rather than a human. Fully automated vehicles use advanced software combined with environmental sensors tracking objects, signage, people, bicycles, road obstacles, and other traffic to operate dynamic driving outputs, such as braking, steering, engine speed, powertrain, and safety system accessories (**FIGURE 55-6**). Sophisticated sensor inputs combined with software essentially automates the driving task (**FIGURE 55-7**). If any defensive or collision-avoiding maneuvers are necessary, the machine senses and responds to these events and has a built-in response to adapt to a driving emergency situation or a driving system failure. Control isn't limited to braking, engines, and steering since many other electronically controlled devices are involved to improve safety and efficiency, such as the transmission, lighting, wipers, and horn. Technically, current vehicle with autonomous driving systems are not driverless. Legislation requires a qualified driver with a valid commercial driver's license to remain at the controls and be ultimately responsible for properly operating the vehicle. Drivers are essential to control the vehicle when driving situations or fault conditions

FIGURE 55-7 A screen from an ADAS camera illustrating the idea of object detection of road markings, guard rails, and other objects while traveling along the road using advanced software.

prevent safe automated system operation. Drivers are also indispensable due to shortcomings in current technology. An example is collision-avoidance systems that prevent trucks and buses from accurately identifying pedestrians and groups of people. Lane-centering systems can also fail to recognize road markings or pedestrians and bicyclists, which can result in fatal contact (**FIGURE 55-8**). Trip pre-inspection procedures and customer service while preparing and finishing a delivery still require drivers.

Semi-automated driving systems do not rely entirely on the machine but require human involvement or intervention when the machine cannot perform the driving task demanded for a driving condition. The driver engages the driving system whenever the driving environment allows the use of automation. In current truck systems, the most advanced vehicles pull over to the shoulder of the road if the driving system cannot safely respond to the operating environment or the driver fails to take control, if requested. If any faults are present in the components or systems needed for ADAS or autonomous capabilities, the systems do not operate rather than adapt a strategy to accommodate the fault. For example, when a fault is present, such as in the ABS system, cruise controls do not work in autonomous mode and require a specific procedure to engage a conventional cruise control. This safety interlock in the driving system is necessary because ABS-related faults prevent the side and frontal collision-avoidance systems from operating and may indicate faults in the collision-avoidance system, rather than the ABS.

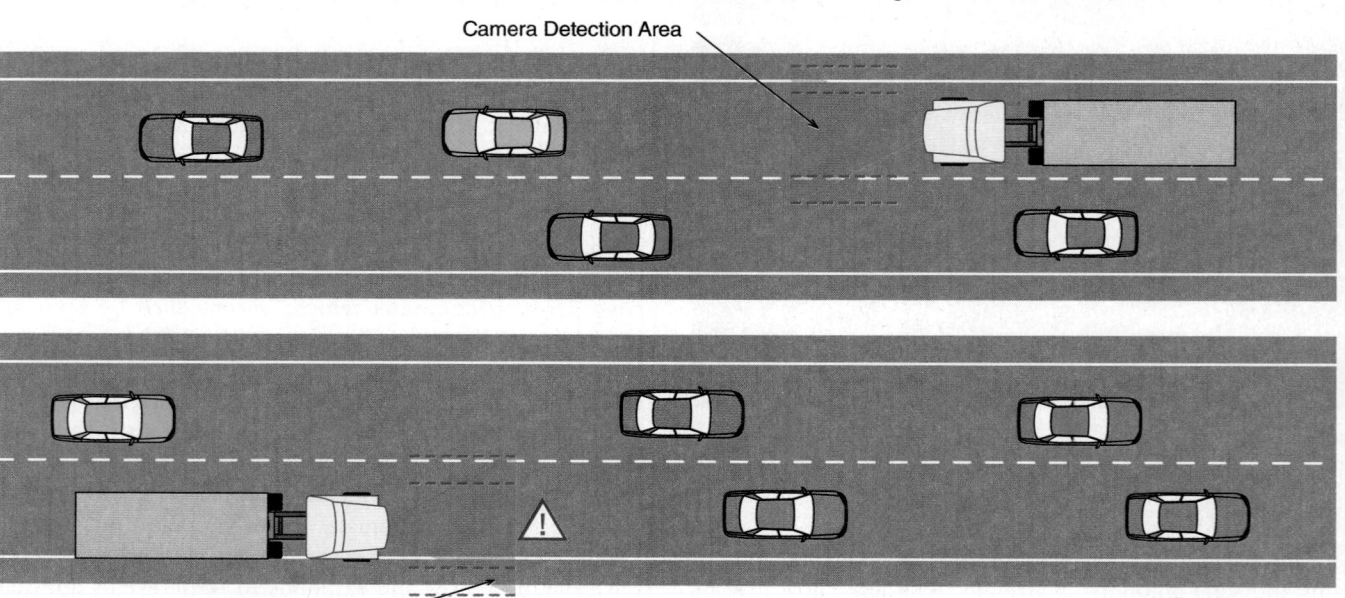

A front mounted camera monitors the road ahead of the vehicle and the lane markings on each side of the vehicle.

Camera Detection Area

Lane Departure Detection
- Vehicle speed is >35 mph (60 km/h).
- Camera detects lane markings.
- If lane departure detected without the turn indicator activated
    - Driver is alerted to the lane departure by a combination of the following methods:
        - visual indicator
        - audible indicator
        - vibration of drivers wheel

FIGURE 55-8 Lane-centering and departure-warning systems rely on a camera to identify lane markings. which are used to center the vehicle steering.

SAE Classification of Autonomous Technologies

Autonomous control encompasses a wide range of capabilities, including the machine ability to control the vehicle's acceleration, braking, and steering functions. System capabilities also vary according to the ability to sense and process the environmental conditions, such as whether it is dark, snowing, or raining, to whether it can read road signage, detect pedestrians, and predict the operation of other vehicles nearby. To help make clear what is only implied by the broad term "autonomous vehicle control," the SAE has developed a standard to categorize and describe various degrees of autonomous system control. The SAE J3016 standard classifies autonomous vehicle control into six categories according to degree of sophistication and type of driver assistance system, and whether the driver assistance systems are combined and function as automated driving control (**TABLE 55-1**).

The NHTSA recognizes and supports the SAE classification categories, which have increasing sophistication and functionality beginning with no assistance system in Level 0 to full autonomous Level 6 systems. Level 6 is a vehicle without a steering wheel or pedals for a driver to operate or even intervene if the driving system failed. Descriptions for each level indicate the minimum capabilities for each driving system, outlining the jobs performed by the human and the machine. Current commercial vehicles have Level 2 capabilities, but 2020 model vehicles are expected to arrive with Level 3 and higher classifications.

The most significant capability difference between Level 2, where the human driver performs part of the dynamic driving task, and Level 3 is that the automated driving system performs the entire dynamic driving task under almost all driving situations (**TABLE 55-2**). Level 3 automation also provides the capability to platoon trucks by bridging the CAN of the lead truck with follower trucks. **Network bridging** means the actions of

TABLE 55-1 SAE J3016 Classification of Autonomous Vehicle Control Systems

SAE level	Name	Narrative Definition	Execution of Steering and Acceleration/ Deceleration	Monitoring of Driving Environment	Fallback Performance of Dynamic Driving Task	System Capability (driving modes)
Human driver monitors the driving environment.						
0	No Automation	The full-time performance by the *human driver* of all aspects of the *dynamic driving task*, even when enhanced by warning or intervention systems	Human driver	Human driver	Human driver	n/a
1	Driver Assistance	The *driving mode*-specific execution by a driver assistance system of either steering or acceleration/deceleration using information about the driving environment and with the expectation that the *human driver* perform all remaining aspects of the *dynamic driving task*	Human driver and system	Human driver	Human driver	Some driving modes
2	Partial Automation	The *driving mode*-specific execution by one or more driver assistance systems of both steering and acceleration/ deceleration using information about the driving environment and with the expectation that the *human driver* perform all remaining aspects of the *dynamic driving task*	**System**	Human driver	Human driver	Some driving modes
Automated driving system ("system") monitors the driving environment.						
3	Conditional Automation	The *driving mode*-specific performance by an *automated driving system* of all aspects of the dynamic driving task with the expectation that the *human driver* will respond appropriately to a *request to intervene*	System	**System**	Human driver	Some driving modes
4	High Automation	The *driving* mode-specific performance by an automated driving system of all aspects of the *dynamic driving task*, even if a *human driver* does not respond appropriately to a *request to intervene*	System	system	**System**	Some driving modes
5	Full Automation	The full-time performance by an *automated driving system* of all aspects of the *dynamic driving task* under all roadway and environmental conditions that can be managed by a *human driver*	System	System	System	**All driving modes**

Source: © 2014 SAE International. The summary table may be freely copied and distributed provided SAE International and J3016 are acknowledged as the source and must be reproduced AS-IS.

TABLE 55-2 Automated Driving Capabilities

SAE – NHTSA Level	Driving Functions				
	Steering-Braking Deceleration Turning	Sensing Environment (nearby traffic, signage, objects, pedestrians)	Default Mode During System Failure	Driving Modes (cruising, traffic jams, urban, night, low-visibility weather)	Platooning (1 or more vehicles following)
0 – Human	Human	Human	Human	All Human	NA
1 – Driver Assisted	Human/Machine	Human	Human	Some Machine	NA
2 – Partial Automation	Machine	Human/Machine	Human	Some machine	Yes
Automated Driving					
3 – Conditional Automation	Machine	Machine	Human	Most Machine	Yes
4 – High Automation	Machine	Machine	Machine	Most Machine	Yes
5 – Full Automation	Machine	Machine	Machine	All Machine	Yes

Source: Information adapted from SAE J3016

the lead vehicle are duplicated by the follower vehicles through wireless communication. Stop-and-go traffic jams and urban driving conditions are the most challenging to automate; however, traffic jams are now machine navigable, but many urban driving conditions still require a driver. To provide support for the broad SAE J3016 standards, dozens of supporting documents and technical standards are currently under development. Examples of supporting work are the test procedures to evaluate automated systems on commercial vehicles. The SAE J-3045 Truck & Bus Lane Departure Warning Systems Test Procedure and Automatic Emergency Braking Performance Assessment Test Methods is one current standard that measures the effectiveness of automatic braking systems and lane-centering systems (**FIGURE 55-9**). Several types of radar-based automatic braking systems measure the distances and speeds of objects in the vehicles path to warn the driver of an impending collision and automatically applies the brakes to avoid or mitigate (reduce) damage caused by a collision.

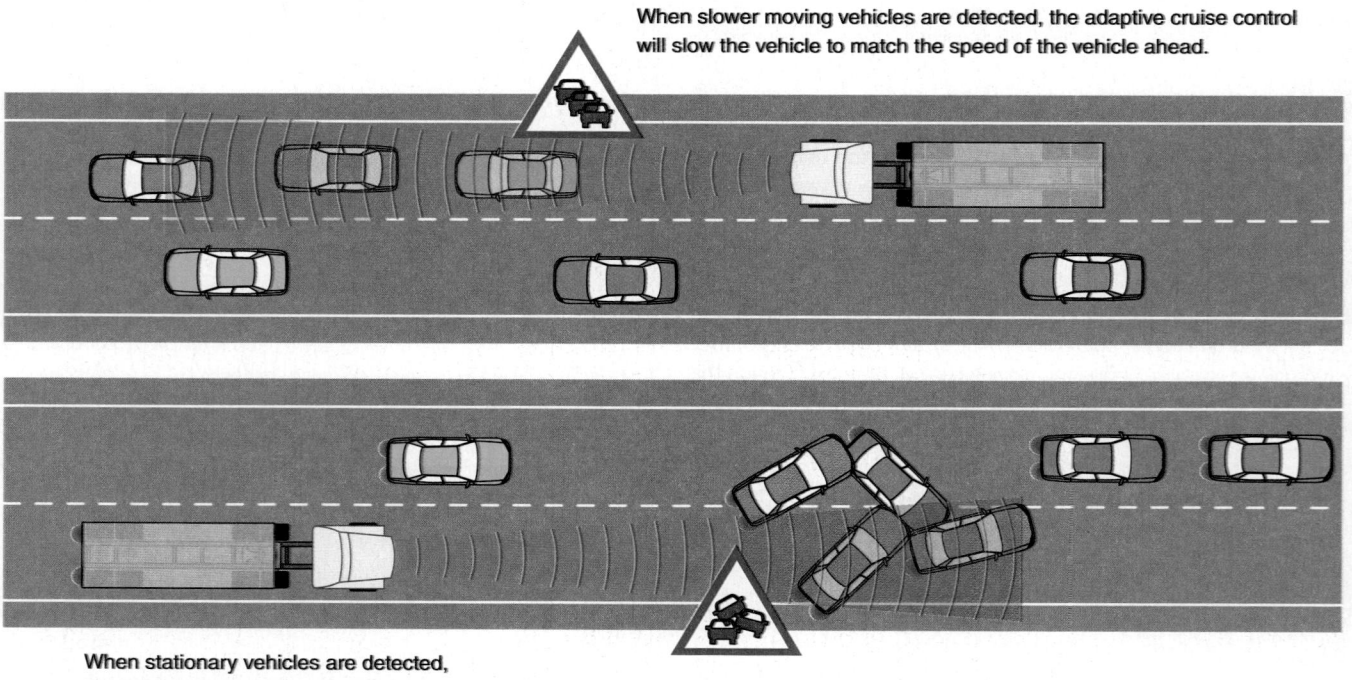

When slower moving vehicles are detected, the adaptive cruise control will slow the vehicle to match the speed of the vehicle ahead.

When stationary vehicles are detected, full emergency braking will be applied.

FIGURE 55-9 The automatic emergency braking system applies the brakes when a collision is imminent. Several versions of this system are used with different marketing names.

If a vehicle is equipped with an advanced driver assistance feature, it does not necessarily qualify it as having any level of automation. Momentary intervention systems, such as ABS, roll-over protection, and collision-avoidance systems, are elements of automated driving systems. However, these systems are only automated safety features. Because they do not continuously automate any part of the human driver's dynamic driving tasks, they are, therefore, not included in the SAE J3016 classification.

Telematics and Automated Driving

Even without the use of sophisticated semi- and fully autonomous control, fleet operations are rapidly incorporating advanced electronic communications into trucks and buses. Connectivity is the term given to communication technology between vehicles and between a vehicle and the infrastructure, such as with traffic lights or traffic control systems. One type of connectivity is the integration of **telematics**, which is the transmission and receiving of information from remote objects over cell phone or satellite communication networks (**FIGURE 55-10**). Telematics is widely recognized as delivering a tremendous number of benefits for technicians, drivers, and fleet managers. Using telematics, CAN communication data, combined with global positioning system (GPS) signals capable of tracking and navigating equipment anywhere, is typically viewed through web portals after it's analyzed with special software applications (**FIGURE 55-11**). The analysis supplies subscribers with an enormous amount of decision-making information to enable more productive vehicle operations maintained by superior management, service, and maintenance practices (**FIGURE 55-12**). Map data provided by GPS satellites provides drivers with improved situational awareness of the road ahead to help understand the type of driving conditions that can be expected, the presence of resources, such as fueling stations and rest stops, or whether to take an alternative route.

Advanced Driver Assistance Systems

Semi-autonomous driving technology has been available in commercial trucks for some time, but is better known as ADAS. In fact, the technology that is moving vehicles toward more autonomous

control simply incorporates or fuses these capabilities together to function better as a whole, rather than independent systems. ADAS are themselves not autonomous driving systems but are a variety of vehicle safety technologies that use onboard radar, GPS, cameras, and other sensors to surveil the vehicle's environment with the purpose to either alert the driver of a potential hazard or automatically intervene to prevent a collision.

Heavy-duty vehicle manufacturers have produced a variety of advanced driver assistance and safety systems having similar purposes that are integrated or fused to create a level

FIGURE 55-11 A CAN module that receives GPS signals and broadcasts them over the CAN.

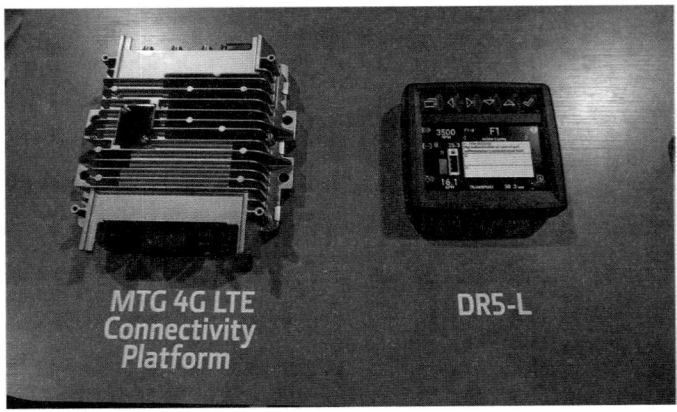

FIGURE 55-10 A cell phone module that connects the CAN to a mobile telematics network.

FIGURE 55-12 GPS data supplies the vehicle map. Location is tracked by a telematics service provider.

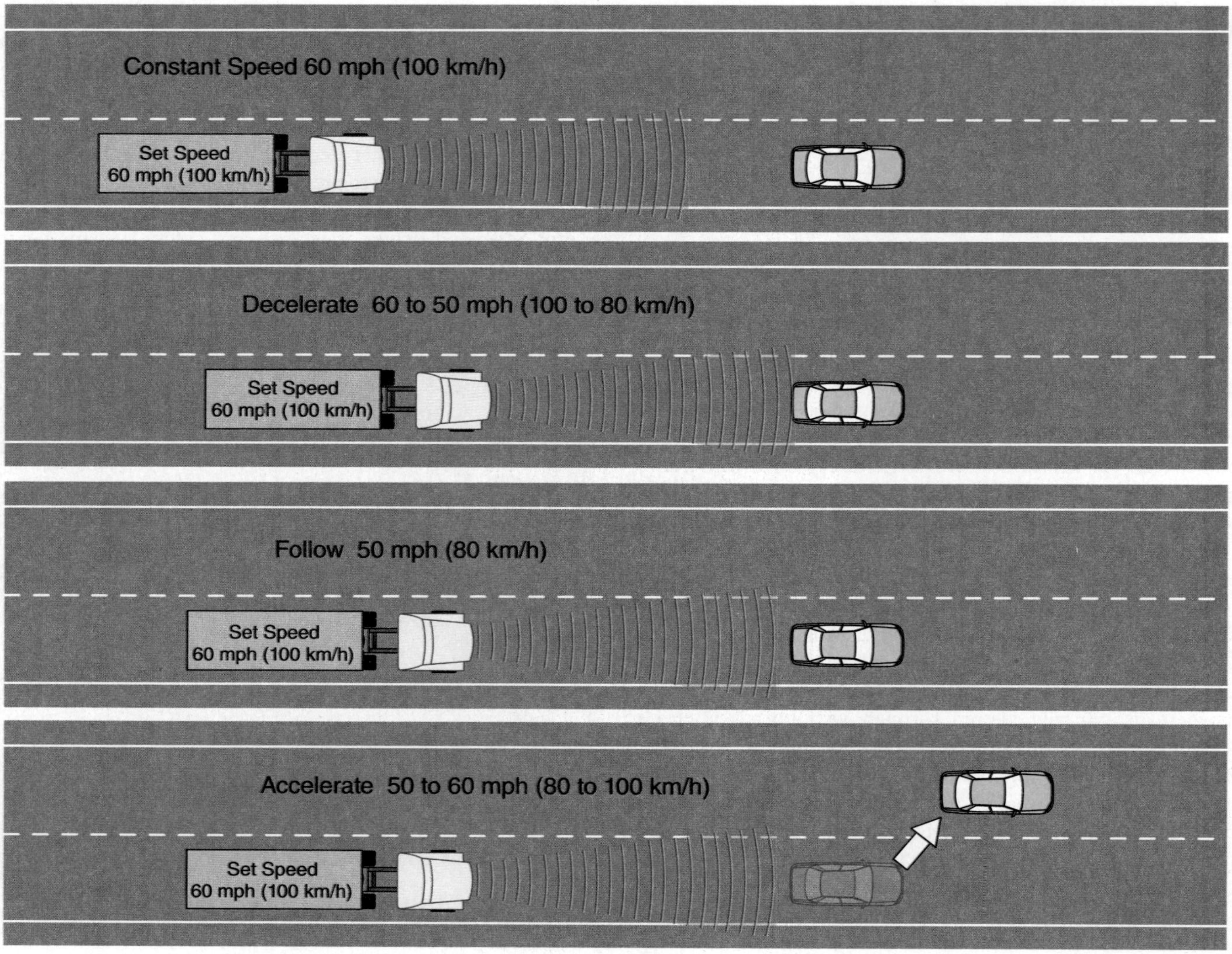

FIGURE 55-13 Operating modes of an adaptive cruise control as an ADAS feature.

of autonomous driving capabilities. While features and purposes of dozens of available systems have common capabilities, the marketing names are different, which helps OEM brand their distinctive system. Common ADAS and driving safety systems integrated to form autonomous driving systems include:

- Adaptive Cruise Control (ACC)—Uses front radar and cameras to help maintain road speed and safe driving distances. Traveling distance behind a lead vehicle is automatically adjusted to obtain a safe following distance. ACC can currently help achieve SAE Level 3 automated driving (**FIGURE 55-13**).
- Blind-Spot Monitoring (BSM)—Uses side radar and cameras to prevent collisions with objects in a blind spot or adjacent lane when changing lanes. BSM may operate with the automatic emergency brake system.
- Forward Collision Warning (FCW)—Uses front radar and cameras to alert the driver of an impending collision. May operate with the automatic emergency braking system.

- Lane Departure or Centering System—Uses cameras to identify road markings and center the vehicle in the road lane (**FIGURE 55-14**).
- Lane Change Assistance—Uses cameras and radar to warn the driver and prevent collisions if other traffic or objects interfere with the predicted pathway while changing lanes.
- Pedestrian Detection System (PDS)—Uses cameras and radar to identify pedestrians and crowds.
- Road Sign Recognition (RSR)—Uses cameras to read road signs, such as speed limits, and integrates the information into the driving system decisions.
- Turning Assistance—Uses LIDAR and radar to monitor both the blind spot and predicted turning pathway while turning a corner. It alerts the driver if pedestrians, bicyclists, and other vehicles can potentially collide and then applies the brakes.
- Autonomous Emergency Braking (AEB)—Uses radar and cameras as a collision mitigation or avoidance system to apply the vehicle brakes. Usually used with forward collision avoidance system. The service brakes or the park brake circuit may be activated by AEB (**FIGURE 55-15**).

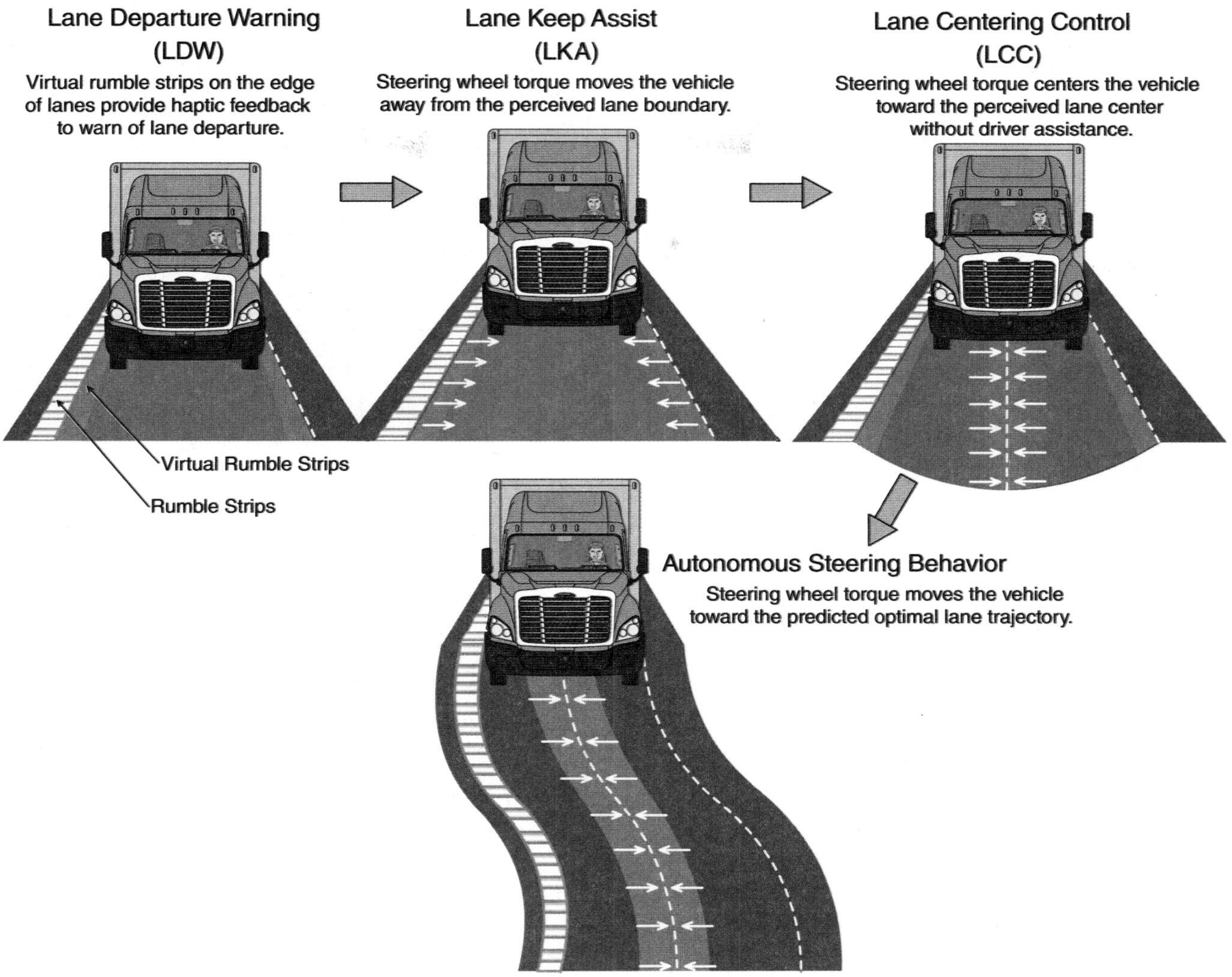

Lane Departure Warning (LDW)

Virtual rumble strips on the edge of lanes provide haptic feedback to warn of lane departure.

Virtual Rumble Strips

Rumble Strips

Lane Keep Assist (LKA)

Steering wheel torque moves the vehicle away from the perceived lane boundary.

Lane Centering Control (LCC)

Steering wheel torque centers the vehicle toward the perceived lane center without driver assistance.

Autonomous Steering Behavior

Steering wheel torque moves the vehicle toward the predicted optimal lane trajectory.

FIGURE 55-14 Various names are given to lane-control systems that steer the truck to the lane center and warn the driver the truck is drifting from the lane.

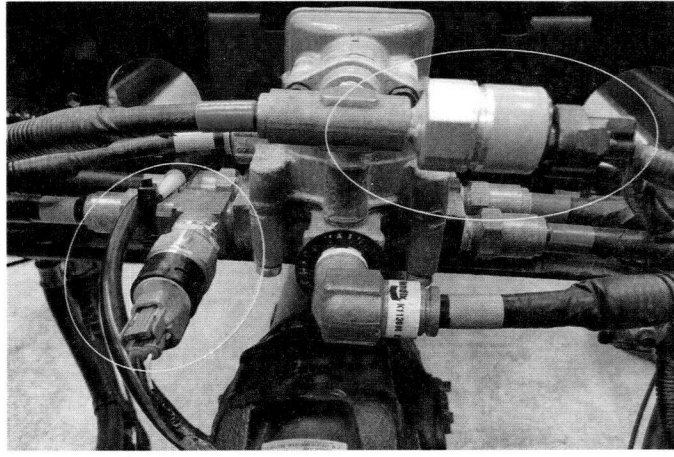

FIGURE 55-15 This SR-7 spring brake valve is configured to allow the AEB control system to electrically apply the spring or emergency brakes. Electric-over-air solenoids are on the Park and control port of the valve.

- Vehicle-to-Vehicle or Vehicle-to-X Communication System—Uses short-range radio signals to receive communication from other vehicles, infrastructure, or objects in the environment, such as pedestrians, to avoid collisions. Two short-range radio antennas and a radio transceiver are used.
- Trailer Sweep Assist—Uses cameras and side radar to alert the driver that the trailer is not tracking correctly and may collide with a stationary object, like a sign or pole.

ADAS Development

ABS brakes are considered the technological beginning of all ADAS technology. Until a legislated requirement for ABS was established in 1998, no other electronic intervention system assisted driving tasks, such as braking. Later, in 2004, adding steering angle, YAW, and lateral acceleration sensors to the ABS system, along with more sophisticated control modules processing advanced algorithms, enabled the use of vehicle electronic stability control (ESC) systems (**FIGURE 55-16**). ESC is

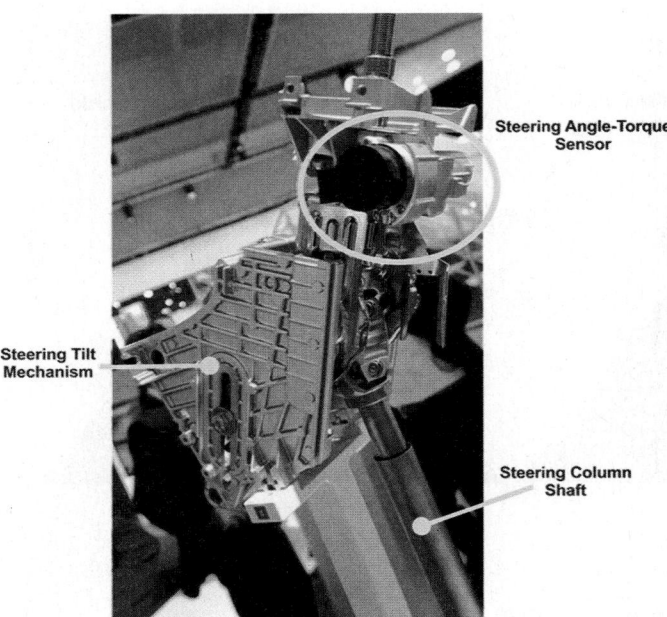

FIGURE 55-16 Adding a steering angle sensor enables new stability control capabilities when combined with ABS.

FIGURE 55-17 An advanced electronic brake system control module and valving on a European HD chassis. Also called ABS in North America.

required for all class 7 and 8 commercial vehicles since August 2017. An ESC system that prevents loss of stability control, jackknifing, and roll-over accidents is an automatic intervention system that applies brakes on a straight truck, tractor, or trailer (**FIGURE 55-17**). Even more features and capabilities are integrated into the base ABS when a front and side radar is connected. ACC uses the radar to enable the driver to set the cruise control yet maintain a safe following distance behind a forward vehicle. As the gap between the truck or bus and forward vehicle starts to close, the system can choose to warn the driver, reduce the throttle, engage the engine brake, and even apply the brakes, to prevent a collision. Radar-based automatic or active braking system, which is available as a separate stand-alone feature without ACC, calculates distances and relative speeds of objects ahead in the truck or bus pathway to either warn or, if necessary, apply brakes to avoid a collision or mitigate damage during a collision. Active braking systems do not require the cruise control to engage to operate. When ACC is used on Level 2 vehicles, it can follow a predetermined route or another vehicle down to speeds of 0 mph.

> ▶ TECHNICIAN TIP
>
> The steering angle sensor is a critical input to the ACC and ADAS features. Whenever steering linkage parts are replaced, such as tie rod ends or drag links, the steering wheel may not return to its original position and steering sensor must be recalibrated. Service software, such as Bendix's ACOM or Meritor Toolbox, is available to guide a technician through the service procedure.

Predictive Cruise Control

Adaptive cruise control is different from predictive cruise control in that it helps minimize fuel consumption by taking over the braking, coasting, and accelerating decisions from the driver using GPS and map data. Using data from GPS maps, engine load, and tractor trailer weight, the control system calculates transmission shift schedules and new vehicle speed. Vehicle cruise speed is changed to allow acceleration before climbing hills to avoid downshifts (**FIGURE 55-18**). Because the maps tell the predictive cruise control which side of the hill the vehicle is on, it can decelerate before descending a hill to minimize engine brake use. The vehicle arrives at its destination in the same amount of time after using less fuel.

Autonomous Control Enabling Technologies

LO 55-2 Identify and describe autonomous control-enabling technologies.

Today's systems use data from a wide variety of vehicle sensors to support ADAS and autonomous driving systems (**FIGURE 55-19**). Important technology to enable ADAS, automated driving functions, and autonomous driving systems include:

1. **High-Definition Cameras**—High-definition cameras with one to two megapixels sensors capable of low-light level image detection are necessary (**FIGURE 55-20**). One or two forward facing cameras are needed to read road signs, identify lane markings for lane detection systems, and combine their images with a radar system to identify objects, such as bikes, pedestrians, crowds, obstacles, and other road traffic. Distance estimates require the use of two cameras. Combined with radar data, cameras provide even more precise measurements of speed and distance, as well as recognize outlines of obstacles and moving objects. Rear-facing side cameras can identify objects beside the vehicle, such as other traffic, pedestrians, and bicycles.

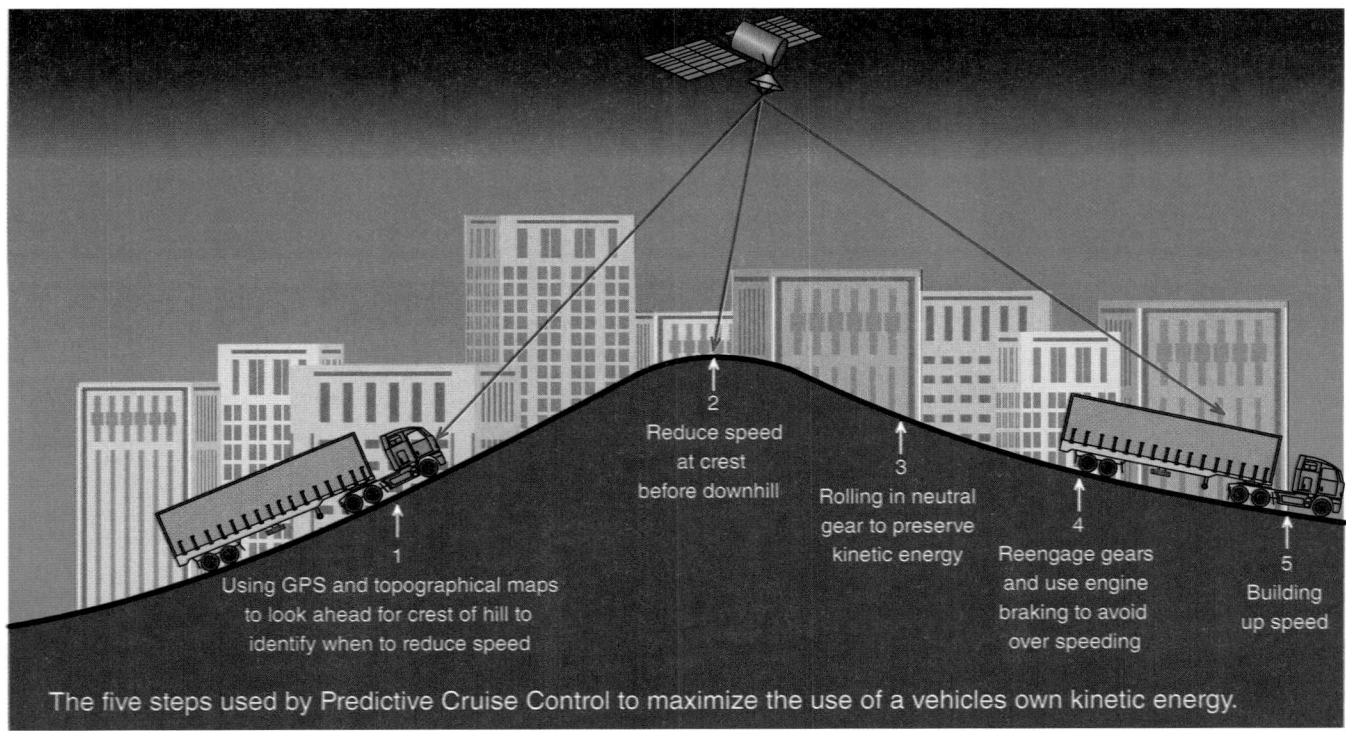

FIGURE 55-18 Using GPS data to provide topographical information, the vehicle control systems can adjust vehicle speed and transmission shift schedules to improve fuel economy with no loss of travel time.

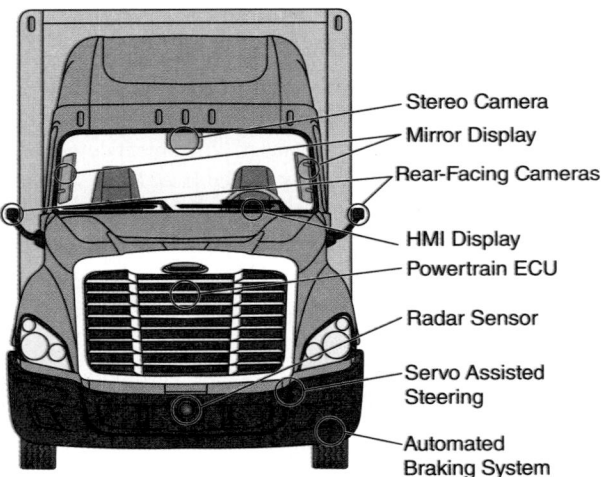

FIGURE 55-19 Locations of critical ADAS and automated driving system sensors.

FIGURE 55-20 A dual-lens camera in an image processing unit. In this image, one lens monitors the road, the other monitors the driver.

2. RADAR—Radar is an acronym for Radio Detection And Ranging Radar. Radar is an object detection system that uses radio waves to determine the range, angle, or velocity of objects (**FIGURE 55-21**). Radar transmitters and receivers, which are combined in a single unit, are located in the front and side of the vehicle to monitor traffic (**FIGURE 55-22**). Two radar sensors are used for either short-range object detection (24 GHz with better image resolution) or long-range detection (77 GHz). Long-range radar typically has a current range of 820 feet (250 meters) with a narrow

window to view the pathway directly ahead of the vehicle (**FIGURE 55-23**). TuSimple trucks claim the ability to "see" and respond to situations 3281 feet (1000 meters) ahead of the vehicle. Short-range radar uses a wider field of view to check for vehicles that may cut in front of a truck or bus, but has a useful working range of only 230 feet (70 meters). The short-range radar at the front of the vehicle is the primary input for ACC. A side-mounted radar monitoring the blind spot is also short-range, sweeping an area 20" in front and behind the transceiver plus extending 10' feet to the right

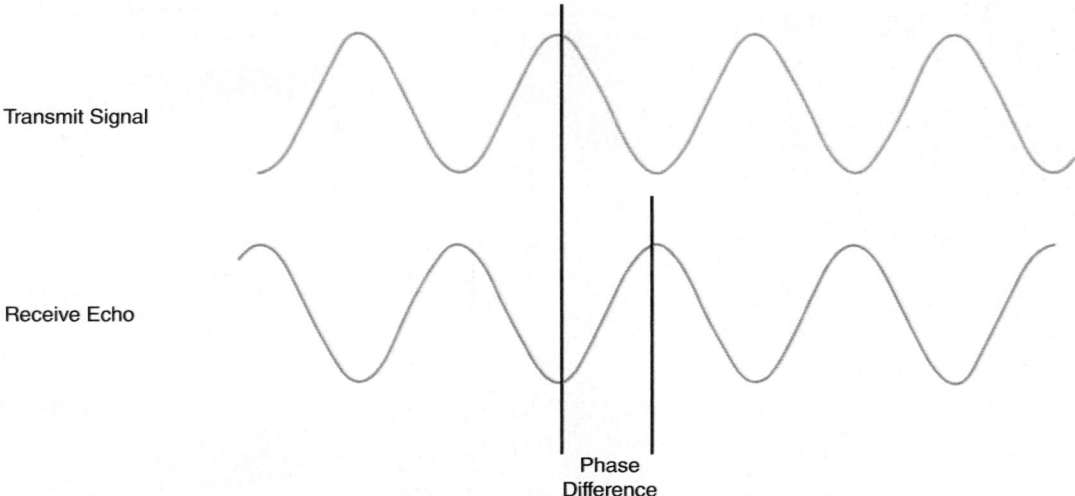

FIGURE 55-21 Radar bounces radio waves off objects and measures how much time it takes before they return to estimate object distance, size, and speed.

FIGURE 55-22 Front radar transceivers for a variety of heavy-duty trucks and buses.

side where the radar is positioned (**FIGURE 55-24**). Radar is also used for:

- Blind spot monitoring
- Lane centering and the lane-change assistant
- Collision warning or collision avoidance
- Cross-traffic monitoring
- Automatic emergency braking
- Automatic distance control in cruise mode

3. **LIDAR** is an acronym for Light Detection and Ranging, which operates like radar but uses narrow laser light beams rather than radio waves. The laser-type object detection and imaging system, which emits pulsed laser light, is reflected off objects and returned to a detector to measure the time it traveled. Rapidly sweeping around a vehicle enables LIDAR

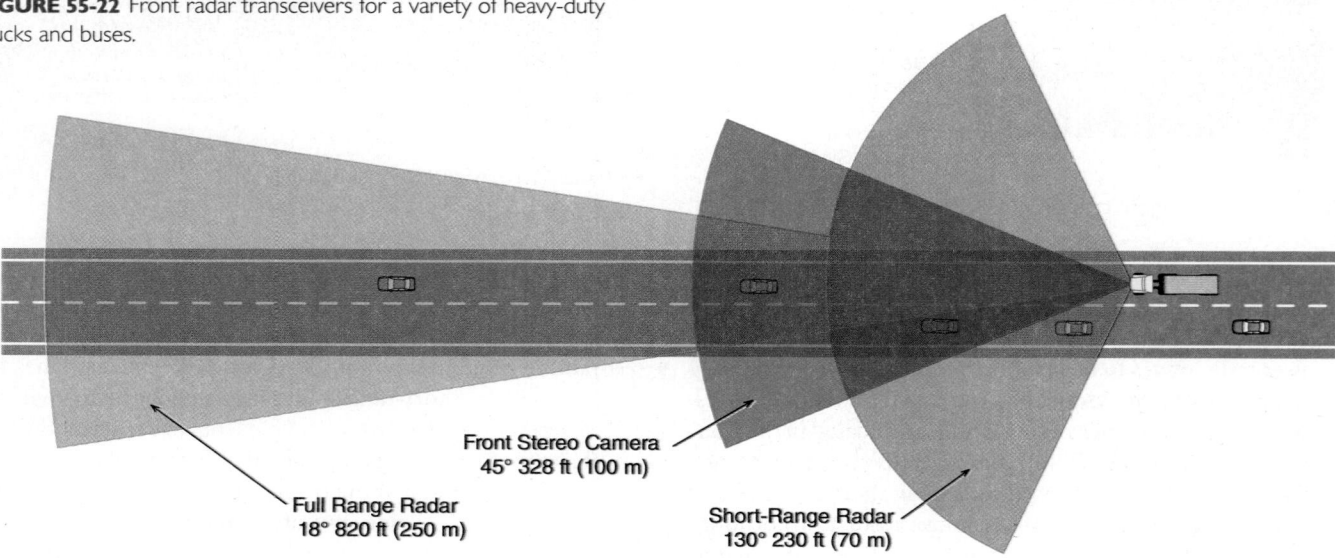

Front Stereo Camera
45° 328 ft (100 m)

Full Range Radar
18° 820 ft (250 m)

Short-Range Radar
130° 230 ft (70 m)

FIGURE 55-23 The range and type of forward-looking radars and cameras.

FIGURE 55-24 A side-mounted radar transceiver for a Bendix Wingman.

FIGURE 55-26 A LIDAR sensor provides better images in adverse weather conditions and can more accurately estimate distances.

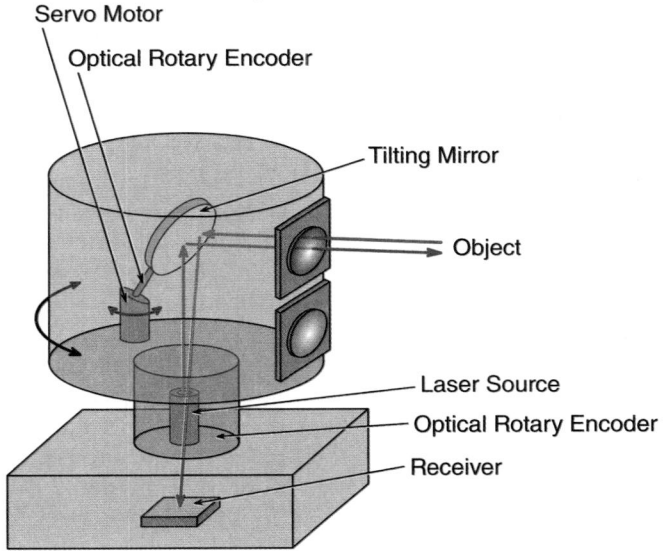

FIGURE 55-25 A cross-sectional view of a LIDAR with an older rotating beam and mirror.

and locate a vehicle on a map. Inertial guidance systems are vehicle-based navigation systems used when satellite GPS or communication with a base station is unavailable to track vehicle position or its orientation relative to a known starting point. Traveling through a tunnel or an area, such as a street canyon surrounded by tall buildings where radio signals are unavailable, is a place where position is tracked using inertial guidance. Inertial guidance systems use what is called dead reckoning navigation, a method that tracks movement from a starting point using vehicle sensors measuring speed, direction, and rate of acceleration. A simple compass would be an example of an instrument used by an inertial guidance system. The distance and direction traveled from the last know position are used to update the vehicle position when GPS signals are not available.

▶ **TECHNICIAN TIP**

Sometimes heavy rain, mud, snow or slush, dust, or bugs may block the radar sensor. The ACC disengages in this situation. If the fault is caused by rain, the system can re-engage when the rainfall slows. However, the ignition switch needs cycling off and then on again to reset. Snow and slush need to be cleaned off the radar before cycling the ignition switch. With the OnGuard system the cruise control switch can be cycled on and off three times to set the cruise speed without the radar. However, other ADAS do not operate, such as the collision avoidance and the driver warning, such as the beeping noise, do not activate. Remember too that misalignment of the radar can cause errors, which should be detected when the key is initially cycled on. New sensors can self-align but a sensor with loose screws, or mounted on a severely bent bumper or bracket, cannot self-correct.

to render a three-dimensional (3D) representation of objects around the vehicle (**FIGURE 55-25**). Currently, the cost of the rotating mirror systems makes it less popular than camera and radar-based systems, but it has advantages over a camera and radar object detection. One is its unaffected by light level and has better poor weather performance, such as in fog, rain, and snow. LIDAR is better at estimating distances, is accurate over a longer distance range, and requires less intensive signal processing than a video camera (**FIGURE 55-26**). Rotating-mirror LIDAR designs have given way to newer low-cost solid-state LIDAR using semiconductor technology.

4. **Satellite Global Positioning Systems (GPS)**, and inertial guidance systems—These systems sense vehicle position

Autonomous Drive Processing Systems

These four technologies just briefly described supply the main inputs to a processing system consisting of sophisticated microcontrollers running application-specific software responsible for interpreting sensor data. The decision-making system provides an appropriate dynamic driving system output signal. Software algorithms (algorithms are mathematical formulas used to solve a problem) take sensor data and process the information through a specific set of logic steps, procedures, or rules. A system response determines whether the truck or bus should steer around an object, stop, or change the speed if it is not traveling at an ideal speed or a collision is imminent. Tesla's Enhanced Autopilot and Daimler's Detroit Assurance™ safety system are examples of a suite of software applications used by the dynamic driving system to autonomously operate a vehicle. The latest microcontroller chips used by several autonomous driving systems, such as Tesla's, are made by Nvidia with the graphics processing unit (GPU) from its Titan series containing 21 billion transistors. These chips are used by artificial intelligence (AI) systems capable of having human-like learning. Another term for AI with human-like learning capabilities is deep learning, where the driving system quickly learns from new inputs or new driving experiences to choose the optimal control path and avoid repeating mistakes.

ACC in Detroit's Assurance driving systems is used by Daimler in Freightliner trucks to control acceleration and deceleration, while Active Lane Assist handles automated steering input (**FIGURE 55-27**). ACC allows the driver to remain

in cruise control mode even in congested traffic as the truck slowly moves at the speed of traffic. The ACC fully stops the vehicle, if necessary, but if the truck stops for more than two seconds, the ACC must be reactivated by toggling the set/resume button.

Steering wheel torque sensors are used to verify the driver has hands on the steering wheel. Resistance to steering wheel movement by the servo-operated steering gear is sensed to keep the ACC enabled. The use of steering wheel torque sensors also allows the driver to override any action of the driving system. For example, if the vehicle is operating too close to a bicycle or a road construction crew, the driver can move the wheel and re-center the vehicle to another lane position without resistance from the steering gear.

Another autonomous driving system used in Freightliner Inspiration Truck series is called Highway Pilot. Highway Pilot integrates a set of cameras, radar systems with lane stability, collision avoidance, speed control, braking, steering, and other safety monitoring systems to create a Level 3 autonomous driving system.

GPS Navigation

LO 55-3 Describe the purpose and operation of GPS and applications to automated driving systems and commercial vehicles.

Because GPS is integrated into a variety of telematic and navigation functions, it is important to briefly examine the technology to understand its capabilities and limitations. The GPS, also called the **global navigation satellite system (GNSS)**, is a worldwide radio-navigation system that significantly accelerates the advancement of autonomous driving and navigation. To pinpoint a vehicle's location, use navigation maps, and manage the movement of freight, accurate positioning and the ability to track movement is provided by low-power radio waves transmitted by satellites in the GPS. GPS has provided this capability since the mid-1990s, when the navigation system built originally in the 1970s for the American military was opened up to civilian use. Several other GPS' are operated by other nations and used in North America and around the world. For example, Russia has a system called GLONASS; Europe has the Galileo System; Japan has the Quasi-Zenith Satellite System (QZSS); and China has the Compass System. Each system's fundamental operational concepts are the same but have slightly different position-sensing advantages for navigation purposes depending on where the navigated object is located. However, almost all GPS use dual-frequency receivers receiving two different GPS signals—satellite position and orbiting information. When integrated together, the accuracy of the signal to locate a position is significantly enhanced.

Identifying Global Positions

Inexpensive GPS receivers, which are often integrated into the onboard network, are essential for any application requiring navigation or position-sensing capabilities. In North

FIGURE 55-27 This snow plow truck has a set of switches to allow it to re-center the lane-assist system.

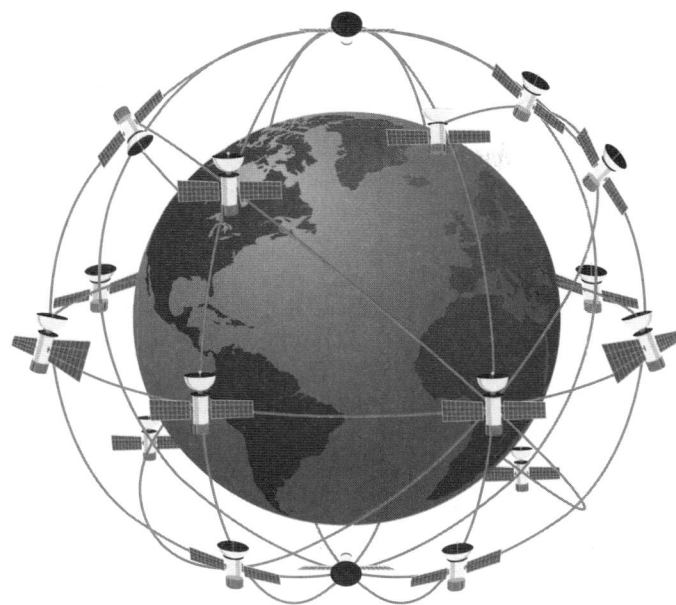

FIGURE 55-28 GPS signals are received from orbiting satellites.

America, the GPS used consists of a constellation of 30 satellites orbiting the earth with 24 or more satellites visible to receivers on earth (**FIGURE 55-28**). To identify any position on earth, a GPS receiver needs to receive signals from three or more of these satellites. After the signals are received by a GPS receiver, a mathematical concept called triangulation is applied to find the receiver's position. Triangulation works when a receiver connects with signals transmitted from each satellite at precisely the same time. Since the orbiting satellites are located at different distances from the receiver, the signals arrive at slightly different times (**FIGURE 55-29**). A time stamp on each signal allows the receiver to calculate how far it is from each satellite. By subtracting the time a signal was transmitted from the time it was received, the GPS receiver can measure the distance between it and each satellite. If the GPS receiver also knows the exact position of the satellites when the signals are transmitted, the intersection point of signals form a 3D position with calculated coordinates indicating how far east or west (longitude) and north or south (latitude) the receiver is from the satellite. Additionally, the altitude or height above sea level of the receiver is calculated.

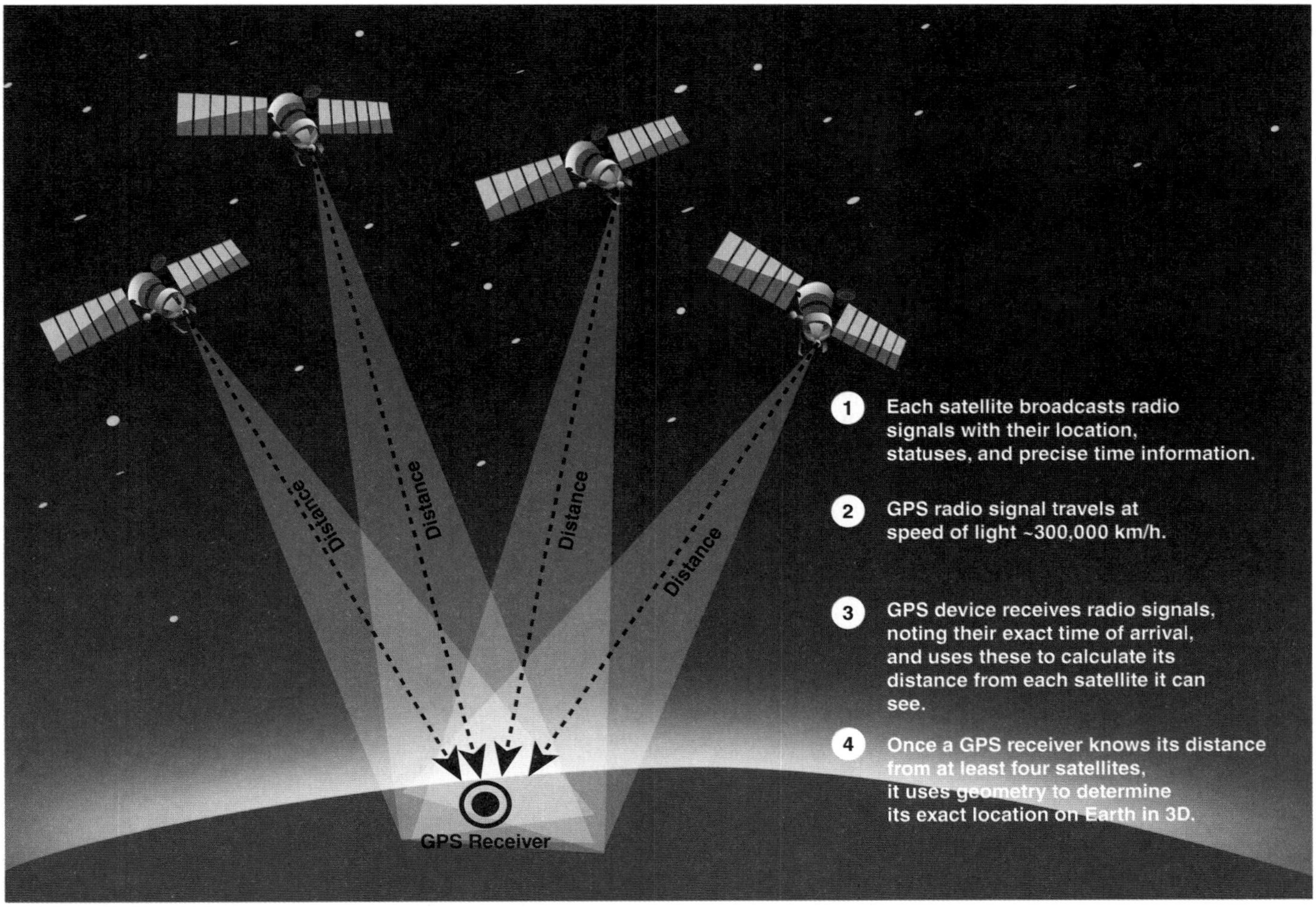

Distance   Distance   Distance   Distance

1 Each satellite broadcasts radio signals with their location, statuses, and precise time information.

2 GPS radio signal travels at speed of light ~300,000 km/h.

3 GPS device receives radio signals, noting their exact time of arrival, and uses these to calculate its distance from each satellite it can see.

4 Once a GPS receiver knows its distance from at least four satellites, it uses geometry to determine its exact location on Earth in 3D.

GPS Receiver

FIGURE 55-29 GPS receivers receive satellite position data to calculate the distance and the altitude to each satellite.

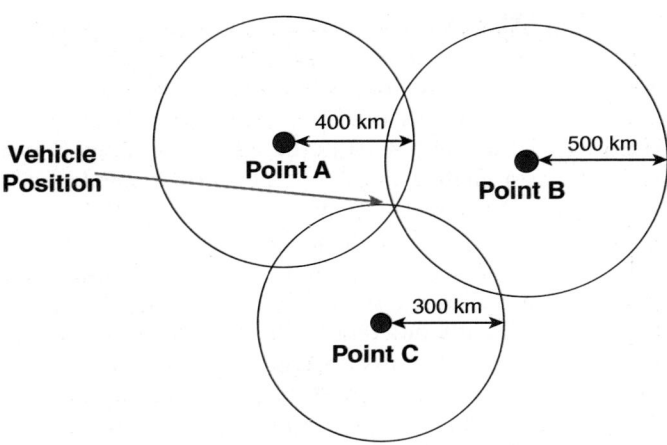

FIGURE 55-30 When at least three GPS signals are received, the GPS unit can triangulate the vehicle position and altitude by measuring the distance and angle to each satellite.

Without signals from at least three different satellites, significant error has to be factored into the receiver's location (**FIGURE 55-30**). For example, if the receiver is located at a high altitude and three signals are not received, the receiver may use sea level as a reference point for location and locate the receiver a distance at least equal to the altitude away from the actual location.

GPS Signal Information

Note that the receiver needs to determine the location of the GPS satellites to calculate a position relative to the satellites. Two types of satellite data are required by the GPS receiver: the almanac and the ephemeris. The almanac and ephemeris contain information about the orbital information and location of the satellites. Both sets of data are transmitted intermittently by the GPS satellites, which are collected and stored by the GPS receiver. Unfortunately, this information is not continuously updated, and the receiver may need as long as 15 minutes to update almanac data and two hours for ephemeris information. When started, the conventional GPS must rely on data sent before the vehicle was shut down. Without the latest satellite information, the receiver cannot accurately locate a position, which explains why sometimes it takes a long time to initially start up some types of GPS receivers or why the location position has significant error. Street canyons surrounded by tall buildings, underground tunnels, and parking areas, as well as routes with a sight line to satellites blocked by hills or mountains, cannot receive satellite signals and the signals cannot be used to provide steering or route guidance. In that case, inertial guidance systems supplement GPS data. Unless the signal data is corrected, error in a conventional GPS unit also prevents a GPS from precisely centering a truck or bus in lane or identifying where a stop sign may be located.

Corrected and Assisted GPS

Conventional GPS signals can only provide positional accuracy to within 33" (10 m). Disturbances in the atmosphere, accuracy of GPS clocks, and satellite data can skew accurate positioning. To correct the problem encountered by a conventional GPS and provide precise location, GPS CAN units data-supplement satellite information with what is called **Assisted GPS or A-GPS** provided by cell phone networks. Cell phone service providers collect the almanac and ephemeris data more quickly from satellite-linked computer servers connected to the Internet rather than from satellite data transmissions. This data is transmitted to cell phone users or vehicles connected to the same mobile communication networks.

GPS signals can also be corrected using at least one of several supplemental ground-based reference stations. When the precise position of a ground station is known, data from ground reference stations are transmitted to the GPS receiver in order to apply a correction factor. These supplemental correction systems can obtain positional accuracy to less than ½" or 1.27 cm for computer-aided construction equipment or autonomous machinery operating in farm fields navigating between rows requiring high positional accuracy (**FIGURE 55-31**). Differential global positioning system (DGPS), wide-area augmentation system (WAAS), real-time kinematic (RTK), and dual-frequency receivers are terms used to categorize these third-party suppliers of supplemental GPS information needed to correct satellite GPS error. These systems are privately owned but provide satellite differential correction subscription services used to improved positional accuracy to the decimeter or less than ½". Peterbilt uses this type of GPS signal correction method for their semi-autonomous trucks and claim a positional accuracy down to +5 cm (2") Applying this same technology to platooning, corrected GPS allows one truck to drive a route (with a human driver) and "map" it, then transfer that data map to other trucks driving the route. Additional trucks follow a mapped route with little to no driver intervention required.

Autonomous Communication Technology

LO 55-4 Identify and explain the purpose of autonomous vehicle communication technology.

Communication between autonomous vehicles and other vehicles is the next evolutionary stage of automated driving technology. When equipped with receivers and transmitters, these connected vehicles wirelessly exchange information between the vehicle and its operating environment. The types of communication can be categorized according to the types of transmitters and receivers.

The first level is vehicle-to-vehicle or V2V. V2V communication enables vehicles within a 328 yd (300 m) radius to exchange information about their speed, location, and travel direction up to 10 times per second. V2V is a safety feature that

Machine Control to Control Absolute Position

3D Machine Control System (GNSS)

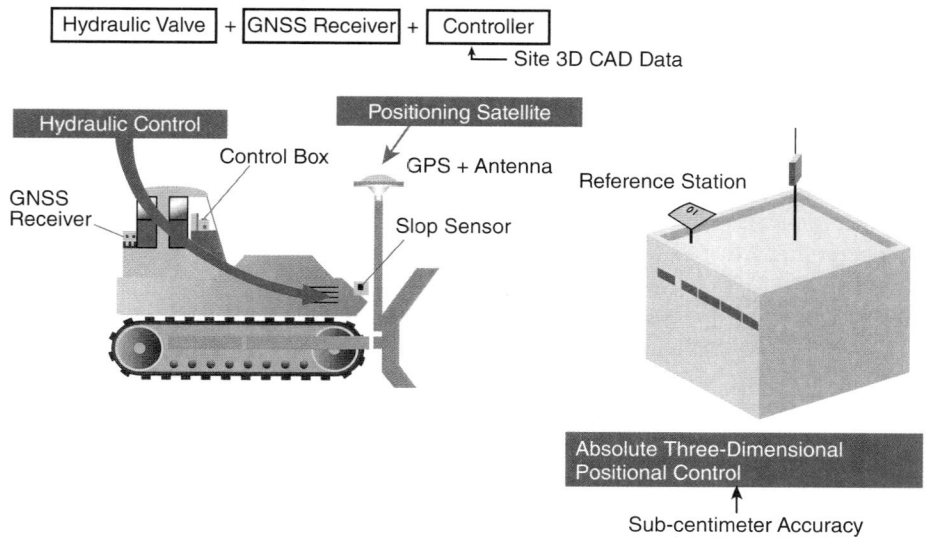

FIGURE 55-31 Computer-aided construction equipment is a current example of the use of corrected GPS signals necessary for precise positional accuracy to within less than 2" or 5 cm.

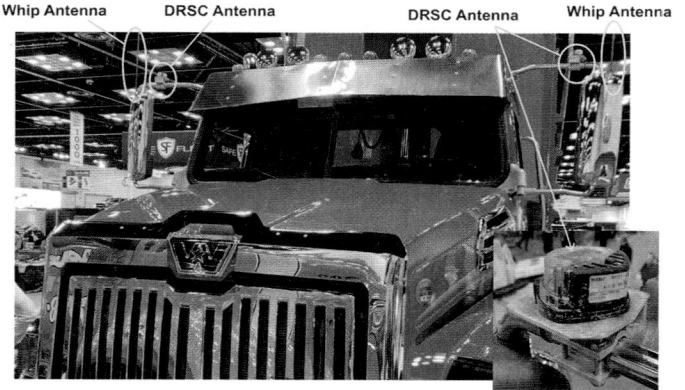

FIGURE 55-32 Dedicated Short-Range Communications, or DSRC, radio antennas are used for a vehicle-to-vehicle communication system. DRSC antennas are critical to the ability of trucks to platoon.

can warn drivers of potential collisions that can't be anticipated by the dynamic driving system. For example, a radar or camera can't see around corners or whether a vehicle is entering an intersection if the line of site is blocked. A connected vehicle can receive a message from another connected vehicle crossing in front of a truck or bus pathway, applying the brakes automatically on vehicles. This communication standard, defined by the IEEE as 802.11p wireless communication, and the SAE-J2735 standard are likely to become regulation for all new vehicles. The standards outline the elements of what is called a Basic Safety Message (BSM). BSMs are likely required to include vehicle size, position, speed, direction, acceleration rate, and

brake system status. Messages are transmitted over a Dedicated Short-Range Communications (DSRC) radio channel, which is a bidirectional short-to-medium range wireless communication that operates on the radiofrequency of 5.725 MHz to 5.875 MHz and is capable of transmitting 10–20 gigabytes/second (Gbps) of information per second. DRSC is similar to WiFi signals, but its frequency is not as likely to encounter interference from other radio signals (**FIGURE 55-32**).

In the United States, the Federal Communication Commission (FCC) has currently allocated 75 MHz radiofrequency spectrum in the 5.9 GHz band (5.850–5.925 GHz) for use by Intelligent Transportation Systems (ITS) to provide very high data rate transmission for safety-critical V2V communications. V2V is expected to operate like a mesh network, which means every node, whether it is a truck, bus, car, or signal light can transmit, receive, and retransmit signals. To compensate for the short transmission distance, the signals can pass along several nodes and, after passing from five to 10 vehicles, traffic conditions and messages are collected from over a mile (1.6 km) ahead.

Setting aside the radio band is an important part of legislated plans for connected vehicles. DSRC radio antennas are critical for V2V communication systems. To communicate wirelessly between trucks, antennas are necessary to enable trucks to platoon.

Other message types are planned, including:

- Pedestrians-to-vehicle (V2P or P2V)
- Vehicle-to-infrastructure (V2I)—Communication from traffic lights or alerts from road hazards.

Wrap-Up

Ready for Review

▶ Automation is the use of control systems that reduce or eliminate human intervention to operate machinery. Autonomous driving systems are a rapidly evolving technology sector that has made its way into the commercial vehicles.

▶ Dynamic driving system automation doesn't always imply fully autonomous operation. Instead, it refers to varying degrees of machine operation performed without human intervention.

▶ The SAE has established standards that define and describe five different levels of automated driving systems.

▶ ADAS or advanced driver assistance systems are the building blocks for autonomous and semi-autonomous driving vehicles.

▶ Automating vehicle steering, braking, and engine speed to navigate while avoiding objects, and performing other driving function, can also increase road safety and provide a wealth of features and data to equipment managers. Any degree of automation can allow the operator to pay more attention to complex driving tasks.

▶ Platooning is an advanced driver-assistance feature in automated vehicles that allows trucks to travel much closer together to improve fuel economy.

▶ When platooning, trucks can communicate wirelessly or use frontal radar to prevent collisions when the adaptive cruise control system is engaged.

▶ Adaptive cruise control is one of several ADAS technologies that allows the vehicle to maintain a safe distance from a lead vehicle.

▶ Several ADAS technologies are used by manufacturers that have similar functions but use different marketing names. Automatic Emergency Braking (AEB) is a common function that is part of the collision avoidance system. It brakes the vehicle to prevent frontal collisions.

▶ Radar, LIDAR, stereo cameras, and GPS are critical technologies to ADAS and autonomous driving systems.

▶ Telematically connected vehicles can transmit machine data collected from the onboard CAN, where it can be collected, analyzed, and viewed through an Internet portal. Data is typically transmitted via the Internet or cell phone signals and includes any measurable information on the vehicle, such as GPS data, fault information, and data from engines, powertrains, and trailers.

▶ Onboard networks are important enabling technology for autonomous machine operation.

▶ GPS units use satellites to accurately identify the position of a vehicle. A land-based fixed-location signal is used to correct error in GPS signals that are derived only from satellites. The signal correction generally requires a subscription from a signal or telematics service provider.

▶ GPS units must have unobstructed site lines through the sky to satellites for signals to reach the antenna. This means that GPS does not work underground or in street canyons where buildings obstruct signals.

▶ Vehicle-to-vehicle communication carries basic safety messages and is currently used to enable the platooning of trucks.

Key Terms

assisted GPS or A-GPS A GPS location signal correction method provided by cell phone networks. Supplemental satellite data is supplied more quickly to cell phone users or vehicles connected to the same mobile communication networks.

automation A term referring to the use of control systems that reduce or eliminate human intervention needed to operate machinery. When the concept of automation is applied to a vehicle, it broadly describes a driving control system operating autonomously—that is, with no human intervention, or operating with varying, but limited, degrees of human involvement.

autonomous vehicle A vehicle controlled by a machine rather than a human. Fully automated vehicles use advanced software combined with environmental sensors tracking objects, signage, people, bicycles, road obstacles, and other traffic to operate dynamic driving outputs, such as braking, steering, engine speed, powertrain, and safety system accessories.

global navigation satellite system (GNSS) A worldwide radio-navigation system using signals from orbiting satellites to precisely locate the position of receivers on the earth surface.

platooning A feature of Level 3 and higher autonomous vehicles that allows a single human driver in a column of trucks to lead other driverless trucks to travel much closer together in a more efficient operating mode while synchronizing functions of braking, steering, and acceleration.

semi-automated driving systems A driving control system that relies partly on a human driver and partly machine control. Some human involvement or intervention is required when the machine cannot perform the driving task demanded for a driving condition.

Review Questions

1. What is the role of a driver in a follower truck that is in a platoon with several other trucks?
   a. To only steer the vehicle
   b. To communicate with the lead truck's driver
   c. To only brake
   d. To take control of the vehicle if the driving system relinquishes control

2. Which of the following is the primary reason for the use of autonomous vehicle control in commercial vehicles?
   a. To replace the driver
   b. To save fuel and lower maintenance costs
   c. To avoid frontal collisions
   d. To increase vehicle safety and reduce or eliminate collisions

3. What is the most likely response of a truck with ADAS using multiple radar and camera input if there is a fault in the ABS?
   a. The truck will automatically pull over to the side of the road when the fault is detected.
   b. The collision avoidance system will not operate.
   c. The cruise control will not operate.
   d. The system will adapt to the fault and operate normally.

4. What is the minimum SAE level of automation that enables the use of truck platooning?
   a. Level 2
   b. Level 3
   c. Level 4
   d. Level 5

5. Which level of SAE classification does a vehicle have with automated driving capabilities?
   a. Level 1
   b. Level 2
   c. Level 3
   d. Level 4

6. Which of the following sensors provides enhanced stability control when added to the ABS control system?
   a. Steering angle sensor
   b. Magnetoresistive compass
   c. Vehicle inclination sensor
   d. Radar

7. Which input is most critical to the operation of the predictive cruise control?
   a. Forward radar
   b. LIDAR
   c. Side radar
   d. GPS signal

8. Which sensor has the best ability to locate and identify objects in adverse driving conditions, such as when it is snowing?
   a. 77 GHz radar
   b. LIDAR
   c. Stereo cameras
   d. 24 GHz radar

9. Which sensor is the most critical to the operation of the turning assistant ADAS?
   a. A side-mounted radar
   b. LIDAR
   c. Stereo cameras
   d. GPS

10. Which of the following technologies is necessary to enable network bridging of trucks to platoon?
    a. Short- and long-distance radar
    b. LIDAR
    c. Stereo cameras
    d. DRSC radios and antennas

ASE Technician A/Technician B Style Questions

1. Technician A says that SAE Level 3 autonomous trucks can operate without a driver. Technician B says only follower trucks in a platoon can operate without a driver. Who is correct?
   a. Technician A
   b. Technician B
   c. Both Technician A and Technician B
   d. Neither Technician A nor Technician B

2. Technician A says that autonomous driving trucks classified as SAE Level 3 have ADAS features. Technician B says a vehicle with ADAS features does not qualify as fully autonomous vehicle. Who is correct?
   a. Technician A
   b. Technician B
   c. Both Technician A and Technician B
   d. Neither Technician A nor Technician B

3. Technician A says that a truck manufactured in 2019 will have electronic stability control (ESC), which is an ADAS feature. Technician B says there is no mandatory requirement anywhere for ESC. Who is correct?
   a. Technician A
   b. Technician B
   c. Both Technician A and Technician B
   d. Neither Technician A nor Technician B

4. Technician A says that a frontal radar system for adaptive cruise control has a wide angle of detection but cannot detect objects more distant than the length of a football field. Technician B says frontal radar can detect objects further than a kilometer (3281'). Who is correct?
   a. Technician A
   b. Technician B
   c. Both Technician A and Technician B
   d. Neither Technician A nor Technician B

5. Technician A says that a LIDAR is a better object detection system when operating in fog, snow, or rain, and at night. Technician B says frontal radar can detect and identify objects better in poor weather conditions and at night. Who is correct?
   a. Technician A
   b. Technician B
   c. Both Technician A and Technician B
   d. Neither Technician A nor Technician B

6. Technician A says that without a GPS signal while driving inside a long tunnel or when traveling through a mountain pass, a truck's or bus's position cannot be determined. Technician B says that a corrected or assisted GPS signal can accurately pinpoint a vehicle's location in these circumstances. Who is correct?
   a. Technician A
   b. Technician B
   c. Both Technician A and Technician B
   d. Neither Technician A nor Technician B

7. Technicians A and B were discussing a driver's complaint that the cruise control does not maintain a consistent road speed. The driver reported the cruise control unpredictably slows down and speeds up when used. Technician A says that the adaptive cruise control system is operating normally and no repair is needed. Technician B says that the inconsistent cruise speed is normal operation of predictive cruise control. Who is correct?
   a. Technician A
   b. Technician B
   c. Both Technician A and Technician B
   d. Neither Technician A nor Technician B

8. Technician A says that the GPS receiver can provide a positional accuracy of less than 5 cm (2"). Technician B says a GPS signal from a satellite can provide a signal accuracy of only 10 m (33"). Who is correct?
   a. Technician A
   b. Technician B
   c. Both Technician A and Technician B
   d. Neither Technician A nor Technician B

9. Technician A says that if the front radar sensor is badly misaligned, the adaptive cruise control will not work. Technician B says that a fault in the ABS may prevent the adaptive cruise control from working. Who is correct?
   a. Technician A
   b. Technician B
   c. Both Technician A and Technician B
   d. Neither Technician A nor Technician B

10. Technician A says that one of several methods to platoon a series of trucks is to equip them with a DRSC radio to bridge the CAN. Technician B says that a fault in the ABS may prevent the adaptive cruise control from working. Who is correct?
   a. Technician A
   b. Technician B
   c. Both Technician A and Technician B
   d. Neither Technician A nor Technician B

CHAPTER 56

Hybrid Drive Systems and Series-Type Hybrid Drives

Learning Objectives

After reading this chapter, you will be able to:

- **LO 56-1** Define and explain the fundamentals of hybrid drives.
- **LO 56-2** Identify and differentiate between the types of hybrid drives.
- **LO 56-3** Outline hybrid drive electrical safety.
- **LO 56-4** Define and describe series-type hybrid drive systems.
- **LO 56-5** Outline maintenance and service for hybrid drive systems.

You Are the Technician

As a transit bus technician, you are skilled and qualified to work on diesel-powered bus chassis. Recently, a few of the hybrid drive buses in the fleet, which are now out of the manufacturer's warranty period, have begun to require more frequent replacement of service brakes. Brake drums are showing evidence of hard heavy braking, and brake shoes are wearing away almost as fast as the conventional bus chassis in the fleet. One hybrid bus in particular has arrived for yet another inspection of the braking system due to a driver's complaint about poor braking. Because the bus has a series type hybrid powertrain, you realize that a significant amount of braking is supposed to be performed by the electric traction motor generator. As you consider what elements of the hybrid system to inspect, and search original equipment manufacturers (OEM) literature for the correct diagnostic and inspection procedures, consider the following:

1. Is there some method to adjust the amount of braking performed by the regenerative braking feature of the series hybrid?
2. List some potential problems with the hybrid powertrain that may contribute to more work being performed by the regular service brakes and not the regenerative braking system.
3. During a road test of the braking system, is there some feature that you or the driver could easily observe that will verify the regenerative braking is taking place?

Introduction

Understanding the word "hybrid" as meaning mixed or combined in nature helps explain the concept of a **hybrid-electric vehicle (HEV)**—a type of vehicle that combines an internal combustion engine with an electric propulsion system into a new or hybrid powertrain configuration. Hybrids are fundamentally different from **battery-electric vehicles (BEV)**, which use only batteries to power electric traction motors to move a vehicle. A variety of hybrid drive vehicle configurations are used in commercial vehicles and are classified by the way propulsion is supplied to the wheels. Hybrid propulsion systems can use any type of engine—gasoline, natural gas, diesel, or even turbine engines—to assist an electric motor to propel the vehicle (**FIGURE 56-1**). A hybrid vehicle's purpose is primarily to reduce fuel consumption and have varying capabilities to travel using electric-only operation. But in commercial vehicles, particularly buses, hybrids also have the added advantage of reducing noxious emissions in dense city cores, and quieter operation in residential or noise sensitive areas. In most applications, the engine drives an electric generator used to charge batteries and powering the electric motors. And, in all hybrids, the use of regenerative braking to recharge batteries helps recover energy normally wasted during braking.

Fundamentals of Hybrid Drives

LO 56-1 Define and explain the fundamentals of hybrid drives.

HEVs are now employed in many commercial vehicle applications due to their capability to reduce both fuel consumption and noxious emissions produced from burning fuel. Estimates suggest that hybrids improve fuel consumption by between 20% and 60%. However, real-world observed fuel consumption in a number of applications is substantially less than those estimates suggest. Urban transit buses, refuse haulers, intercity pick-up, delivery, and utility vehicles are the most common applications in which hybrid drive systems have the potential to excel. Even the military has seized on the hybrid advantage for situations where fuel economy is mission critical—for example, when supply lines are stretched, or when stealth is required.

Vehicles operating in urban driving conditions are best suited to hybrid use, as much of the energy derived from burning fuel is lost through idling and braking. Studies have shown that approximately 65% of energy used to accelerate a city bus is quickly dissipated into heat by frequent braking (**FIGURE 56-2**). Garbage trucks lose 59%, while delivery vehicles picking up and moving small parcels lose half the energy produced by the engine the same way. Because hybrid drive systems are designed to produce electricity when braking, by switching traction motors to power absorbing generators, the motor generators connected to the wheels assist mechanical braking systems and store this energy in onboard batteries. In turn, the batteries supply electric current to the traction motors for acceleration. (A **traction motor** is an electric motor that provides propulsion to a vehicle.) This feature, by which generators recover energy normally lost during braking, is called **regenerative braking**.

The inefficiencies of conventional powertrain systems are not limited to losses from braking. Another inefficiency stems from the amount of engine idle time. Engine idle time is in the range of 50% for many vehicles operating in urban driving conditions. The stop-start feature used by some mild hybrid drives shuts off the engine when not in use can help reduce this loss. Electric motors can also assist engines to accelerate over a wider engine rpm operating range and during stop-and-go operation where they do not use fuel efficiently. Because some hybrid drive configurations can limit the rate of engine rpm

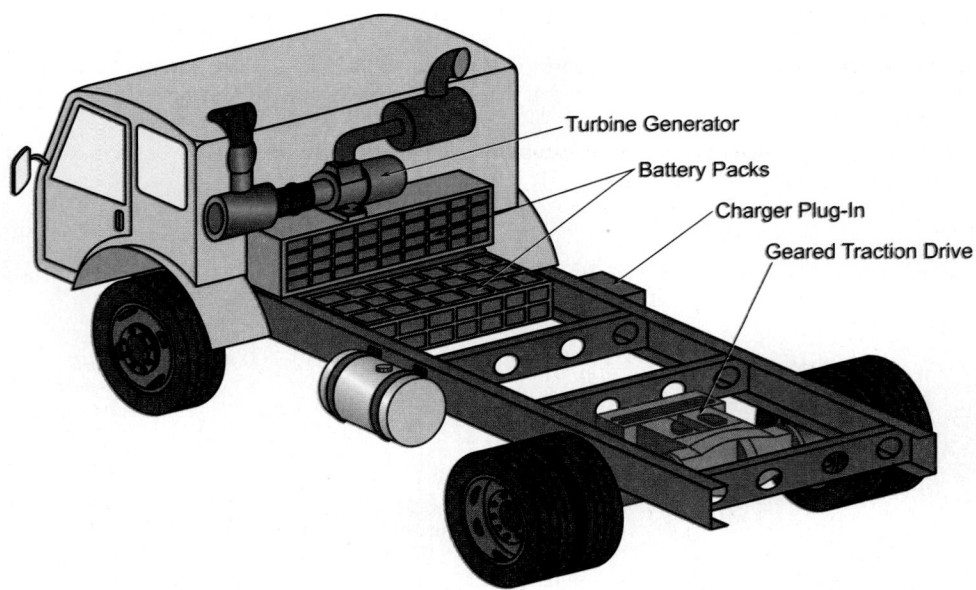

FIGURE 56-1 A turbine engine driving a generator that charges battery packs enables the hybrid turbine to extend travel range. Retrofitted garbage trucks achieve 44 mpg (18.7 km/L). The same electric vehicle architecture is predicted to operate some models of the heavy-duty Tesla electric truck.

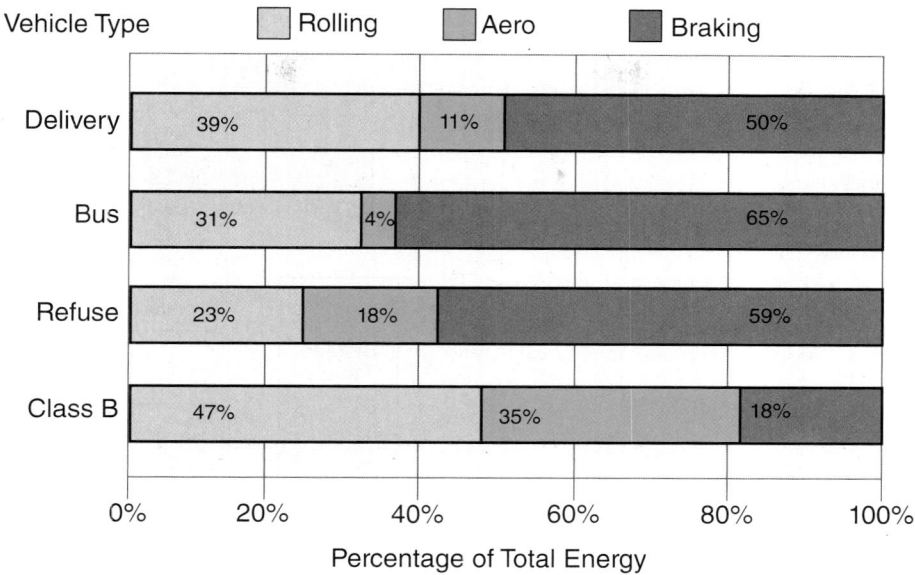

FIGURE 56-2 Substantial energy is lost to vehicle braking. During braking, all electric hybrid drive vehicles generate electricity that is later used to propel the vehicle.

change, they enable the engine to operate in a narrower, more fuel-efficient operating range, producing the fewest emissions and high torque-speed range, while using less fuel.

Other hybrid drivetrain advantages include:

- Increased foundation brake service life and reduced need for brake service using regenerative braking
- Extended engine life due to more favorable operating conditions
- Electric drive motors provide more torque for faster acceleration and added pulling power
- Smoother acceleration
- Quieter vehicle operation
- Compatible with all fuels and engine designs, so no requirement to change fueling infrastructure
- All engine emissions are reduced and less-frequent exhaust aftertreatment system service is required
- Minimum driver training required

Types of Hybrid Drives

LO 56-2 Identify and differentiate between the different types of hybrid drives.

Even though all electric hybrid systems are configured with engines, electric motors, and batteries to propel the vehicle, not all hybrid systems are alike. Different configurations offer unique advantages. The following are the most common configurations of hybrid drive systems in use:

1. **Series drive**—Only an electric traction motor supplies torque to propel the vehicle (**FIGURE 56-3**). The engine drives a generator used to charge a bank of batteries and supply current to the electric motor (e.g., BAE HybriDrive® System).
2. **Parallel drive**—Both the engine and electric motor work together, blending motor and engine torque to propel the vehicle (**FIGURE 56-4**).

3. **Series-parallel drive**—A more complex system enabling an engine only, an electric motor only, and a combined engine-motor operating mode (**FIGURE 56-5**). Also called a power-split configuration, the engine and motor operation is optimized for driving conditions (e.g., Arvin Meritor, Allison EV).
4. **Plug-in hybrid electric vehicle (PHEV)**—Refers to any type of hybrid-electric vehicle containing a battery storage system that uses an external source to recharge the battery when the vehicle is not in operation. These vehicles also have an ability to drive or operate for an extended period in all-electric mode.
5. **Mild hybrid systems**—Also referred to as start-stop systems, used primarily for urban pick-up and delivery vehicles. The vehicle uses a small electric motor to power engine-mounted accessories with the engine off when stopped at intersections or when coasting. The same motor restarts the engine and provides torque assistance to accelerate the engine when the vehicle resumes operation.
6. **Range extenders**—Similar to a series-type hybrid, but uses a much smaller engine to drive an electric generator to charge batteries. This less costly system uses a larger set of batteries to supply the electric traction motors with electricity. What is different from other series hybrid drives is the size of the engine and generator are smaller and cannot fully supply electric power to the motors but are intended only to extend the duration of a battery charge.

One popular type of PHEV is the municipal utility truck. These trucks typically travel shorter distances than others but are operated in residential neighborhoods continuously for extended periods, running the lift boom, powering lights, tools, and other accessories (**FIGURE 56-6**). Ordinarily, the engine is required to operate hydraulic pumps or generators. Using stored battery energy allows the vehicle to operate at a job site without engine idling, which reduces emissions from idling and

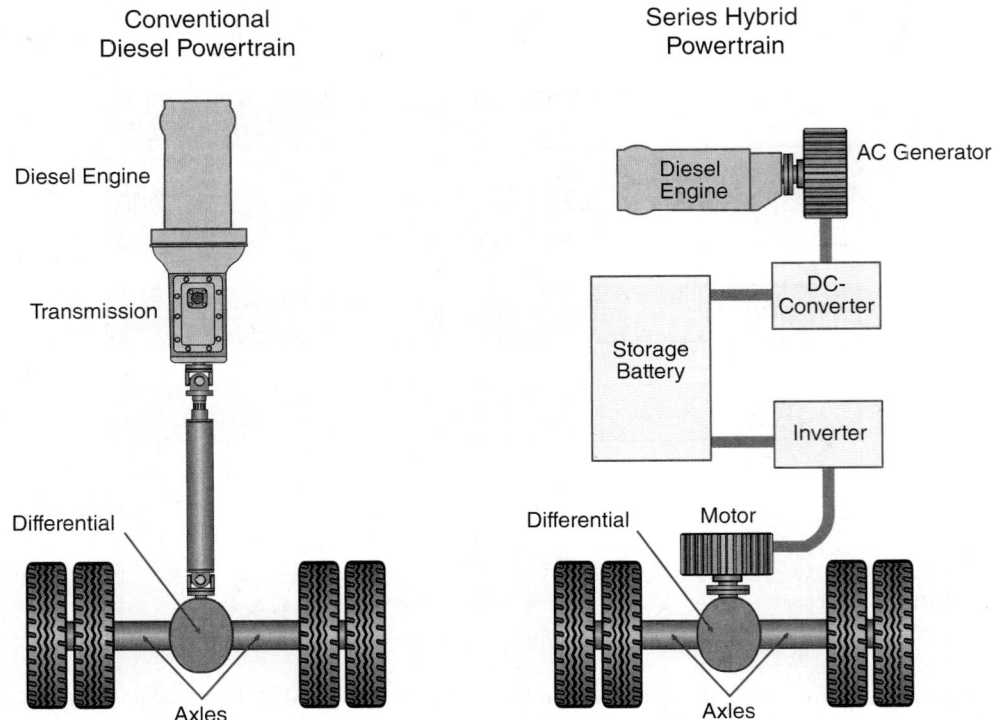

Conventional
Diesel Powertrain

Series Hybrid
Powertrain

FIGURE 56-3 Series drive—Only an electric traction motor supplies torque to propel the vehicle. The engine drives a generator used to charge a bank of batteries and supply current to the electric motor.

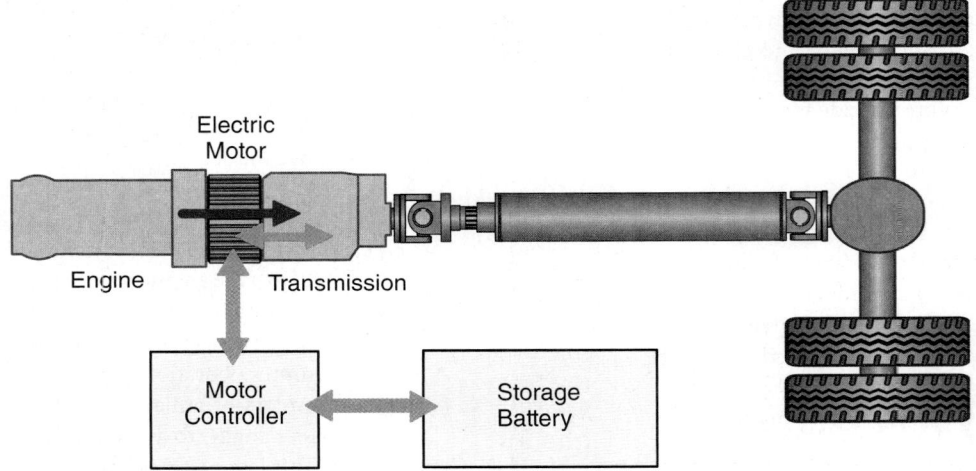

FIGURE 56-4 A parallel-drive hybrid configuration allows a combination of engine and electric motor torque to propel the vehicle.

exposure to diesel exhaust. Vehicle operating costs are lowered by reducing fuel consumption and engine wear. When in drive mode, low-speed driving conditions are ideally suited to using only the electric traction motors.

Comparing Parallel and Series Systems

Compared to a parallel system, a series system requires a larger electric motor and battery pack, but a smaller internal combustion engine. A series hybrid does not require a transmission because the electric motor is capable of a wide range of speeds and high torque output. The series drive system works best in frequent stop-and-go service because the electrically driven propulsion system has highest torque at low speeds, providing smooth, fast acceleration regardless of the grade. The efficiency differences between a series hybrid and conventional bus decline as average vehicle speed increases and the number of stops decreases. Parallel-drive systems are better suited to higher speeds with less stop-and-go operation. (Parallel-drive systems are covered in the Allison EV Drive Hybrid Systems

Hybrid Dual-Mode Drivetrain Below 48 MPH—Zero Emissions/Battery Electric

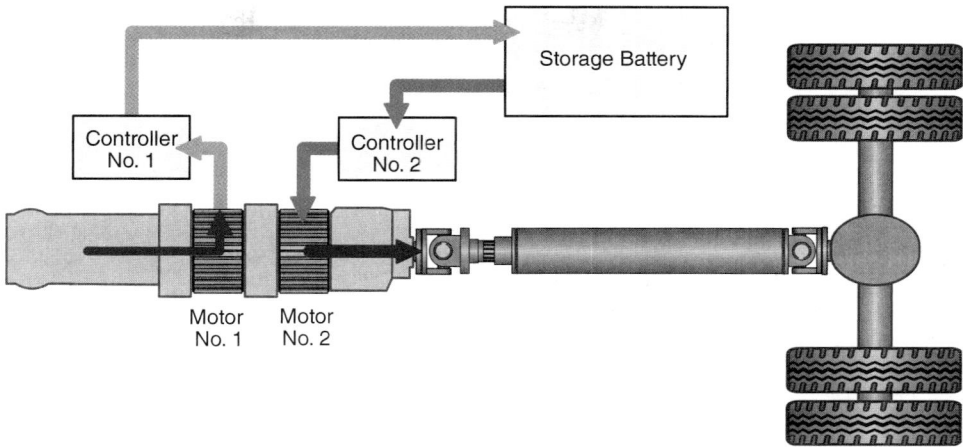

Hybrid Dual-Mode Drivetrain Above 48 MPH

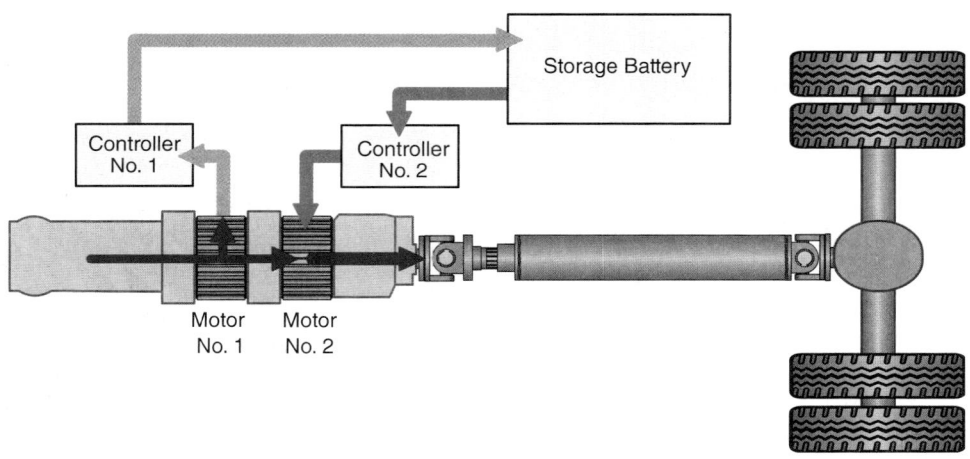

FIGURE 56-5 Series-parallel drive is a more complex system enabling an engine only, electric motor only, and a blended or combined engine-motor operation. Also called a power split configuration, the engine-and-motor operation is optimized for driving conditions.

FIGURE 56-6 Plug-in hybrid vehicles, such as this utility truck, can operate hydraulic power equipment using battery power only.

chapter.) One disadvantage of both systems is a 50% to 70% higher initial purchase cost. **TABLE 56-1** compares series, parallel, and series-parallel hybrid drives.

Non-Electric Hydraulic Launch Assist

An alternative to HEVs is the **hydraulic launch assist (HLA)** system. The concept of HLA uses hydraulic regenerative braking to capture braking energy and recycles the energy to help launch the vehicle during acceleration. In an HLA system, application of standard friction service brakes is prevented until just before a complete vehicle stop. During braking, friction components normally used to slow the vehicle, such as drums and shoes, are replaced by a hydraulic pump. Braking power is, instead, absorbed by the force used to pump hydraulic fluid from a low-pressure reservoir into a hydraulic-gas accumulator. Nitrogen gas inside the accumulator is compressed by the fluid to 5000 psi (34,470 kPa), which effectively absorbs the vehicle's kinetic

TABLE 56-1 Comparison of Series, Parallel, and Series-Parallel Hybrid Drives

	Driving Performance			Fuel Economy Improvement		
	Acceleration	Continuous High Output	Idling Stop	Energy Recovery	High-Efficiency Operation Control	Total Efficiency
Series	●	○	●	●	◖	◖
Parallel	●	●	◖	●	●	◖
Series-parallel	○	○	○	○	●	●

● Best ◖ Good ○ Poor

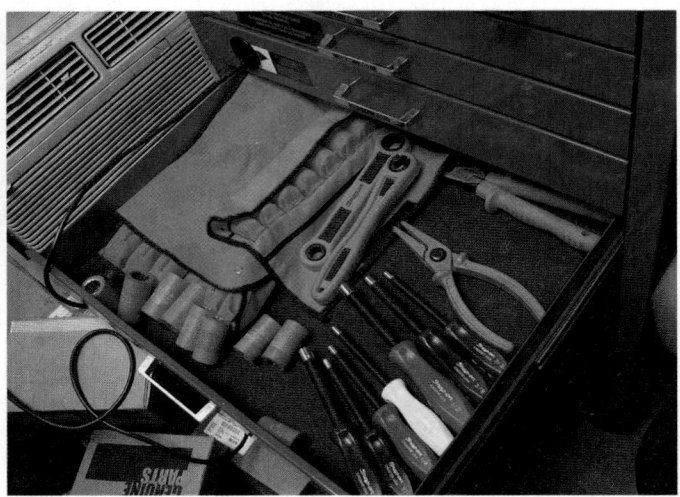

FIGURE 56-7 Eaton's hydraulic launch assist (HLA) pressurizes hydraulic fluid to capture braking energy. Pressurized fluid is used to power a hydraulic motor and launch the vehicle. The primary benefits of HLA are faster acceleration and reduced emissions and fuel consumption.

TABLE 56-2 Specifications of a Typical HLA System

Weight of HLA system	1250 lb (568 kg)
Max pressure	5000 psi (351.5 kg/cm^2)
Total system oil volume	21 gallons (80 L)
Torque	2550 ft-lb (3457 Nm)
Active speed range	Up to 25 mph (40 kph)
Minimum wheelbase, single	191" (485 cm)
Minimum wheelbase, tandem	215" (546 cm)

FIGURE 56-8 Insulated service tools are required when working on high-voltage hybrid systems.

energy and turns it into stored potential energy (**FIGURE 56-7**). This hydraulic-over-gas capture performed by the HLA system is reported to convert close to 70% of normally lost braking energy and, at the same time, cut brake wear 50%. When it is time to accelerate the vehicle again, fluid in the high-pressure accumulator is metered to the combined driveline pump and motor where the device operates as a motor. The HLA motor accelerates the vehicle by transmitting torque to the driveshaft.

HLA systems are a parallel hybrid system, allowing the engine to drive the vehicle when the HLA is off-line. Improvements to fuel economy are estimated between 15% to 30% with corresponding reductions in emissions. HLA has two modes of operation: economy and performance. In economy mode, energy stored in the accumulator during braking is used only to initially accelerate the vehicle. Once emptied, the engine begins to propel the vehicle. In performance mode, both the engine and accumulator provide driveline torque until the accumulator empties. Performance mode provides more torque for 2% quicker acceleration but does not provide the same reduction to fuel consumption as economy mode. **TABLE 56-2** lists some common specifications of an HLA system.

Hybrid Drive Electrical Safety

LO 56-3 Outline hybrid drive electrical safety.

Electric hybrid drive system components use lethal high-voltage power devices operating up to 900 volts and contain energy storage systems over 700 volts direct current (DC). Although systems are designed to provide safe propulsion energy under normal conditions, during accidents or servicing personal injury, death, and expensive equipment damage can occur. Unique service procedures are outlined in mandatory training courses provided by the original equipment manufacturers (OEM) and electrical safety code is enforced by local electrical authorities. Special tools must be used in addition to personal protective equipment (PPE) to ensure that the technician is kept as safe as possible during service procedures (**FIGURE 56-8**).

Effects of Electric Shock

Shock hazard to the human body is a function of the type of current (alternating current [AC] or DC), voltage, amperage, and skin resistance. Generally, 10 times the amount of DC has the same effect as AC. Under the right conditions, 5 milliamps of AC can be dangerous, and 500 milliamps lethal, as electricity can affect the contraction of heart muscles and muscles controlling breathing. A level of 60 Hz AC is especially lethal because it closely corresponds to heart rate and can cause the heart to beat irregularly. Higher-frequency AC conducts with less resistance than low-frequency current. At high levels, electricity generates enough heat to destroy nerve muscle and blood tissue. The effects of electricity can be experienced as:

- Tingling sensation (AC)
- Burning sensation
- Muscle contractions
- Ventricular fibrillation (irregular heart rhythm)
- Cardiac arrest (heart stoppage)
- Pulmonary arrest (stopped breathing)

Reactions to electricity can have serious consequences, as a person may jump or fall in response to even a light shock. High-amperage shorts can produce blinding light, fires, and explosions. **TABLE 56-3** describes effects of different levels of electric current. **TABLE 56-4** shows the effects of electricity on different skin conditions.

High-Voltage Disconnect

Disconnecting and discharging any residual current in electric vehicle (EV) components is imperative before performing any service work. Always assume the electrical system is live, even after disconnecting the battery power supply and testing for the presence of current with an approved electrical meter. Appropriate PPE safety is necessary; glasses, footwear, and gloves should always be worn, and all jewelry removed. A long-sleeved, heavy denim shirt offers protection from inadvertent upper body electrical contact. When the ignition key is switched off, most hybrid systems use a set of relays called contactors to disconnect power from the rest of the system components. A master disconnect switch is used in bus applications and should also be switched off, effectively disconnecting and isolating the vehicle batteries from the rest of the electrical system. Specialized electrical connectors in the battery storage system and power cables are provided to add another level of redundancy to power disconnect procedures. Inverters and propulsion control modules should usually be disconnected, and a waiting period of several minutes is needed to allow capacitors to discharge. Additional power disconnect verification procedures are recommended by OE system manufacturers, which should be followed. For example, a lock-out device clamped on the master disconnect switch can prevent accidental energizing of high-voltage circuits when the vehicle is being serviced (**FIGURE 56-9**).

When working on the battery storage system, two persons are required in case one person is harmed or becomes incapable of removing themselves from a live electrical circuit. Scaffolding, as shown in **FIGURE 56-10**, is a must when working around or servicing overhead battery systems. In addition, non conductive body hooks and Class D fire extinguishers are required at scaffolding level.

> ▶ **TECHNICIAN TIP**
>
> *Floating ground* refers to the electrical ground separation between the chassis and the high-voltage electrical system. Dedicated circuits are used for the high-voltage system current, which does not share a ground path with the low-voltage system. An electrical system has a galvanic isolation monitor that continuously checks to ensure that a high value of electrical resistance insulates the high-voltage from the low-voltage electrical system. Any time the potential for stray currents is detected, fault codes are logged, warning lights may be illuminated, and the vehicle may even shut down.

TABLE 56-3 Effects of Various Levels of Alternating and Direct Current

Effect	AC	DC
Sensation	1 milliamp at 60 Hz	5 milliamps
Muscle contraction	60 milliamps at 60 Hz	300–500 milliamps
Let-go limit	10.5 milliamps	15–88 milliamps
Minimal hazard with worst case	60 V peak AC (not RMS)	42 V
Non-lethal under most conditions	60–150 V	60–150 V

TABLE 56-4 Electrical Resistance of Skin Under Various Conditions

Skin Condition	Resistance
Open skin (wound)	500–1000 ohms
Wet skin	10,000–20,000 ohms
High ionic content wet skin (i.e., sweating)	5000–10,000 ohms
Under high-voltage conditions	500 ohms

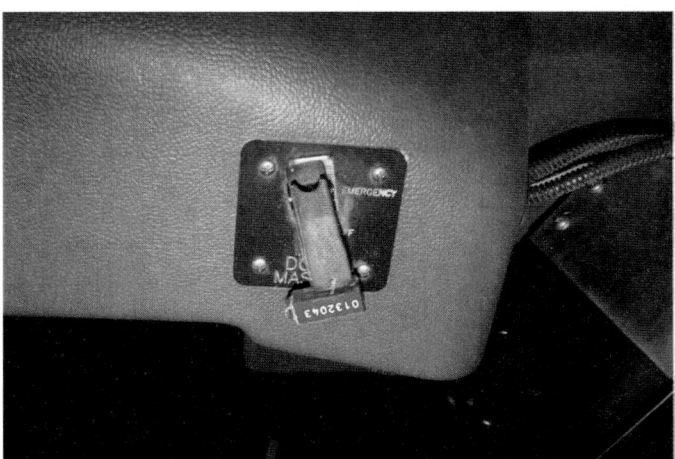

FIGURE 56-9 A lock-out device clamped on the master disconnect switch can prevent accidental energizing of high-voltage circuits when the vehicle is being serviced.

FIGURE 56-10 The use of purpose-built stairs and a buddy system is critical to safety when serving roof-mounted equipment tubs and batteries.

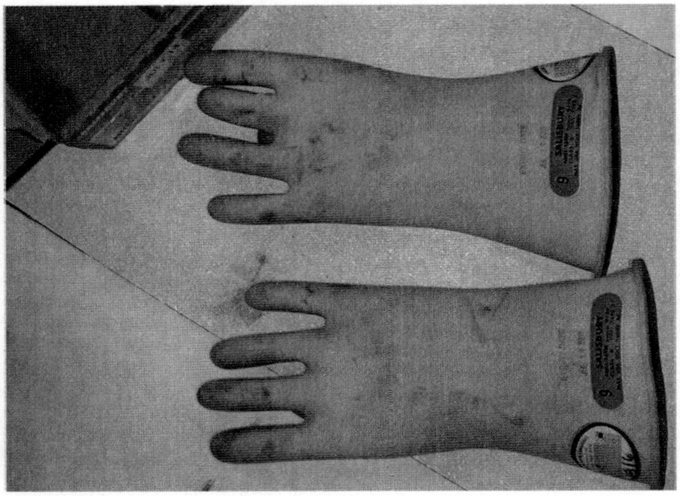

FIGURE 56-11 When working on hybrid drive electrical systems, technicians must wear Class 0 insulating gloves.

Insulated Gloves

One of the first lines of defense when it comes to preventing contact with energized electrical components and/or electrical power cables are insulating gloves, commonly known as lineman gloves (**FIGURE 56-11**). The Occupational Safety and Health Administration (OSHA) requires the use of rubber-insulated gloves for those persons working on or near energized circuits and/or other electrical sources that are considered either high- or low-voltage applications. Lineman gloves are categorized by the amount of AC and DC voltage they have been proof-tested to block in addition to the designated maximum-use voltage. The voltage protection is referenced as a Class rating, which is broken down starting with Class 00 having the lowest voltage protection up to Class 4 with highest protection. Class 0 lineman gloves recommended for use on high-voltage hybrid circuits offer protection from 1500 to 5000 volts.

Routine Inspection

Routine periodic inspection of a hybrid drive system typically involves checking for the following:

- Loose bolts, mounting components, and grounding straps
- Loose, worn, or frayed electrical components
- Improperly routed or frayed vehicle electrical harnesses
- Damaged or loose hoses
- Fluid leaks
- Damaged, dented, or out-of-phase drive shafts
- Checking for fault codes or warning light illumination

Technicians must know the correct jacking and hoisting procedures prior to servicing the vehicle found in the OEM service manual.

Collisions

In the event of a collision:

- Turn off ignition switch, master, and battery isolator switches
- Inspect all EV propulsion system components for external damage

- Inspect all cooling lines and connections for leaks
- Place the vehicle in the service facility for a full inspection
- Emergency responders are recommended to use a Class 0, 1000-volt cable cutter with a 2" opening size to cut power from the battery storage to the vehicle system.
- Type D, smothering-type fire extinguisher is recommended for fires

Lithium-ion and lead-acid batteries, if ruptured, both produce flammable hydrogen gas. Corrosive battery acid leaks from lead-acid batteries. The chemical composition of the nickel-metal hydride battery electrolyte can cause severe burns to skin if it comes into contact with the body. It is essential that precautions are always followed if the hybrid vehicle has been in a collision because of the dangers associated with leaking batteries.

Series-Type Hybrid Drive Systems

LO 56-4 Define and describe series-type hybrid drive systems.

Series-type hybrid drive configurations use an electric generator to charge batteries that supply the vehicle's electric traction motor with electricity. The generator is driven by an engine. Transit buses typically use these systems. Two types are now common. The conventional configuration for a series-hybrid propulsion system uses an engine that is powerful enough to maintain the batteries in a good state of charge. The engine is smaller in comparison to one used to power a non-hybrid chassis with regenerative braking and low load periods, allowing the engine-generator to top up the battery charge.

Another category of series hybrid is called range extenders. These configurations use even smaller engines and generators but have a larger battery bank, which is expected to receive an initial charge through the power grid. The engine-generator operates to extend the battery state of charge to provide extended travel range on the battery's initial charge (**FIGURE 56-12**). The use of a turbine engine to power a generator enables the system to achieve much greater fuel efficiency since the turbine operates at an optimal speed range. The capstone-type microturbine engine originally proposed to drive an AC generator uses no oil to lubricate its bearings, instead turbine bearings are supported with only high-pressure air (**FIGURE 56-13**). Since diesel or natural gas fuels are used, and very high combustion temperatures and pressures inside the turbine completely consume any type of fuel, the capstone turbine requires no exhaust aftertreatment. When the extended-range hybrid engines are retrofitted to garbage trucks by Wrightspeed, the trucks are reported to achieve 44 mpg (18.7 kg/L).

BAE HybriDrive Propulsion Systems

BAE is an aerospace and defense technology company and is also one of the leading developers and manufacturers of hybrid drive propulsion systems for the military and heavy-duty commercial vehicles. Since 1996, BAE Systems has collaborated with Daimler in hybrid-electric propulsion systems for transit buses. The company's **HybriDrive® propulsion system** is currently the best-selling heavy hybrid drive and is in service in more than 4000 transit buses in cities around the world.

HybriDrive systems are also available in series-parallel-type drive configurations. In 2012, BAE and Caterpillar collaborated to integrate the Caterpillar CX model transmissions into its HybriDrive parallel propulsion system. The series-parallel

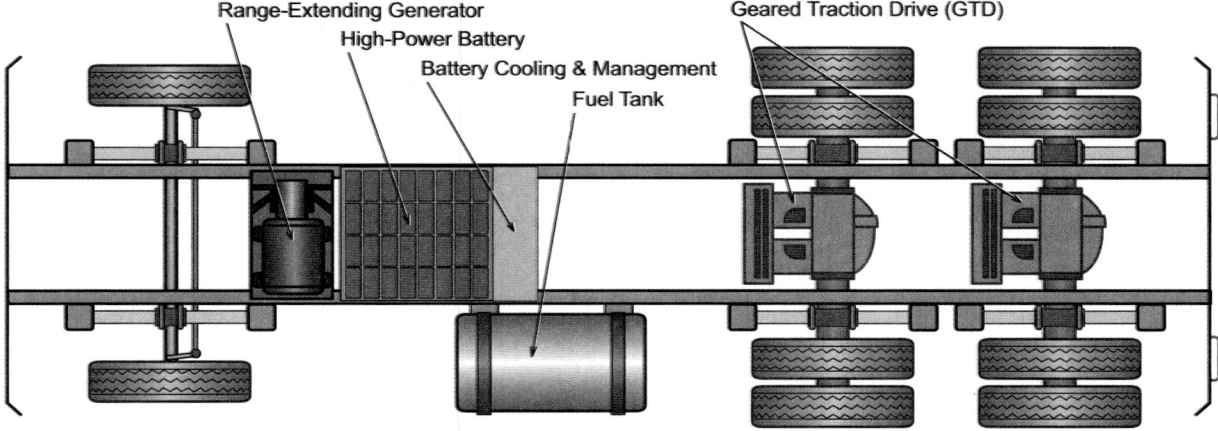

FIGURE 56-12 Wrightspeed's HD chassis model called Route is a series-type extended-range electric vehicle. This configuration is expected to resemble some models of Tesla's battery electric series of trucks.

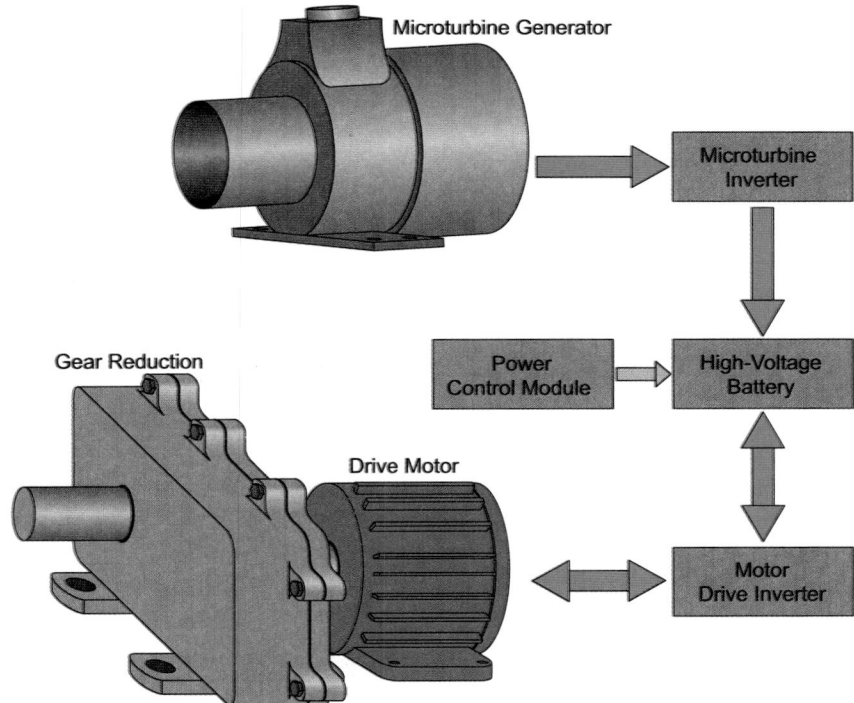

FIGURE 56-13 The microturbine engine for extended-range series-hybrid vehicles burns fuel so cleanly and efficiently that no exhaust aftertreatment system is necessary.

system normally uses a transmission, and the HybriDrive parallel system is based on a single, electric, motor-generator interfacing between the truck's engine and the CX Series transmission.

This chapter primarily focuses on the HybriDrive series system shown in **FIGURE 56-14**, as it represents one of the most common hybrid propulsion systems and also the first system, introduced back in 1998. **TABLE 56-5** compares different models of hybrid drive systems.

HybriDrive series-type is available as different levels or "Generations" of hybrid systems. The differences between the

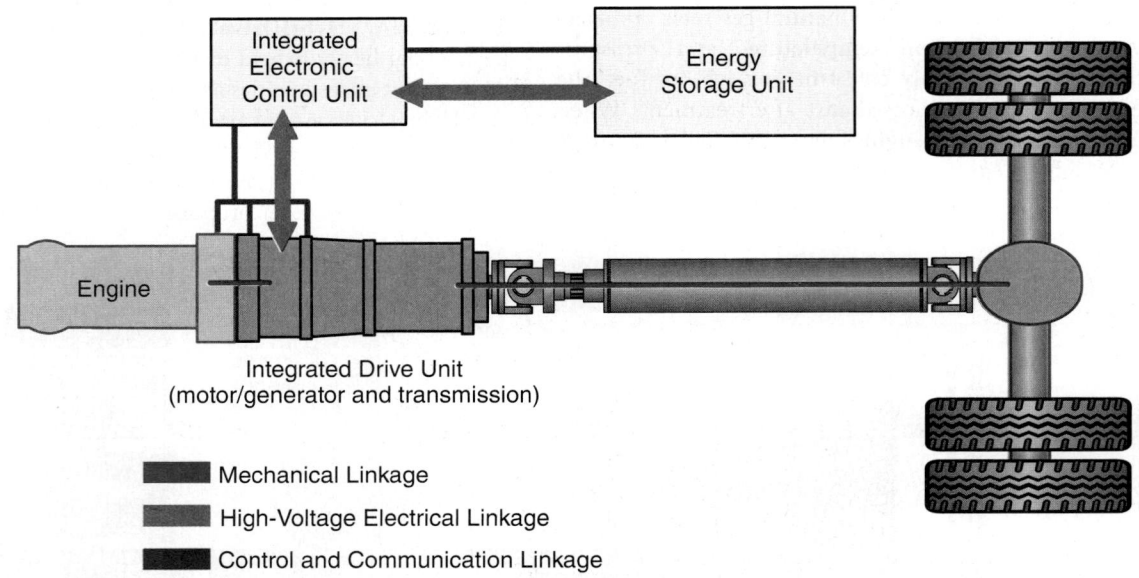

Mechanical Linkage

High-Voltage Electrical Linkage

Control and Communication Linkage

FIGURE 56-14 BAE's HybriDrive is an example of a popular heavy-duty series-type hybrid powertrain.

TABLE 56-5 Comparison of Different Types of Hybrid Drive Systems

	BAE Systems (HybriDrive propulsion system)	Allison EP 40	Allison EP 50
Power	• 250 hp (186 kW) continuous (320 hp [239 kW] peak) • Torque 2700 ft-lb (3660 Nm) at 0 rpm	• Continuous: 280 hp (209 kW) • Rated input torque: 910 ft-lb (1235 Nm) • Rated input speed: 2300 rpm • Acceleration power: 350 hp (261 kW)	• Continuous: 330 hp (298 kW) peak • Torque 1050 ft-lb (1423 Nm) • Rated input speed: 2300 rpm • Acceleration power: 400 hp (298 kW)
Engine	• Orion VI Transit Bus • Gen 1 Cummins B Series • Gen 2 Cummins C Series		
Electric Drive Motor	• Three-phase alternating current (AC) induction-type	• Three-phase asynchronous induction motor/generator	• Three-phase asynchronous induction motor/generator
Motor Horsepower	• 160 hp (119 kW) continuous using 436 VAC at 2300 rpm • 450 ft-lb (610 Nm) of torque at 0 rpm • 4.69:1 gear reduction produces 2100 ft-lb (2847 Nm) of torque at 0 rpm at the output shaft yoke	• Input continuous: 280 hp (209 kW) • Rated input torque: 910 ft-lb (1235 Nm) • Rated input speed: 2300 rpm • Acceleration power: 350 hp (261 kW)	• Input continuous: 330 hp (246 kW) • Rated input torque: 1050 ft-lb (1420 Nm) • Rated input speed: 2300 rpm • Acceleration power: 400 hp (298 kW)
Generator Type	• Permanent magnet	• Three-phase asynchronous induction motor/generator	• Three-phase asynchronous induction motor/generator
Energy Storage Type	• Sealed lead-acid (Gen 1) • Lithium-ion (Gen 2)	• Nickel-metal hydride (NiMH)	• NiMH
Voltage	• 520–700 VDC • 436 VAC continuous	• 600 VAC • ESS Voltage Range: 432–780 VDC • DPIM Voltage Range: 350 VDC	• 600 VAC • ESS Voltage Range: 432–780 VDC • DPIM Voltage Range: 350 VDC

VAC = Volts of AC current; **VDC** = Volts of DC current

First Generation

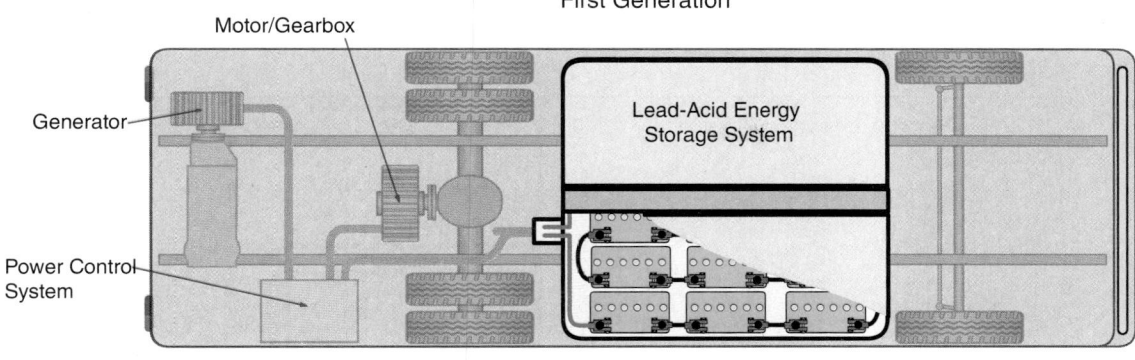

Motor/Gearbox

Generator

Lead-Acid Energy
Storage System

Power Control
System

Second Generation

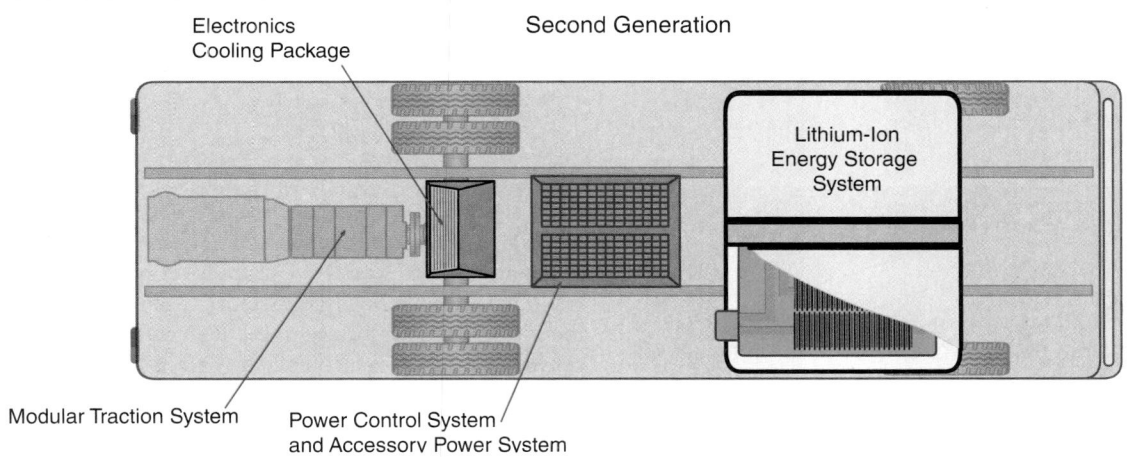

Electronics
Cooling Package

Lithium-Ion
Energy Storage
System

Modular Traction System   Power Control System
and Accessory Power System

FIGURE 56-15 The HybriDrive system Gen 1 and Gen 2.

systems are not obvious but, according to the manufacturer, a number of subsystems on the higher level versions have been improved, including the engine, generator, propulsion control, and cooling and packaging (**FIGURE 56-15**). The most significant difference in the systems is the energy storage components; lead-acid batteries were used in the original release of the systems, but now lithium-ion batteries are used on later systems.

The BAE HybriDrive series system is designed for applications requiring low average vehicle speeds and frequent stop-and-start operation. The HybriDrive parallel system is designed for use on vehicles with operating cycles having faster operating speeds and fewer frequent stops, such as medium duty trucks.

HybriDrive Series Propulsion System Overview

Many buses using the BAE HybriDrive systems are coupled to a Cummins diesel engine to obtain the highest fuel efficiency with the lowest emissions. In such installations, the engine operates at a fixed speed.

Connected directly to the engine is an electrical generator used to produce electrical power for the drive motor and to charge the batteries. A single electric drive motor coupled to the driveline has two functions. As with any series hybrid drive system, the first function is to provide all the power necessary to propel the vehicle. The second function is to create regenerative

braking, which enables the generator to convert braking force into electrical current rather than to lose energy to heat through traditional friction brakes.

Onboard battery banks supply electrical current needed during acceleration and store current recovered from regenerative braking. Specialized computer software operates the propulsion control system module, which electronically controls the complete system by processing input data and sending electrical output signals to all system actuators.

The batteries compose the largest part of the electrical storage subsystem. A battery monitoring subsystem maintains the charge of each individual battery and performs battery diagnostic checks.

Hybrid vehicles produce significantly lower emissions than conventional diesel-powered buses, as the energy storage system supplies power during start-up and acceleration. At these times, the diesel engine is idling.

Major System Components of Series HybriDrive

HybriDrive includes the following major system components (**FIGURE 56-16**):

- Propulsion control system (PCS)
- AC traction generator (ACTG)

Orion VII Hybrid Transit Bus

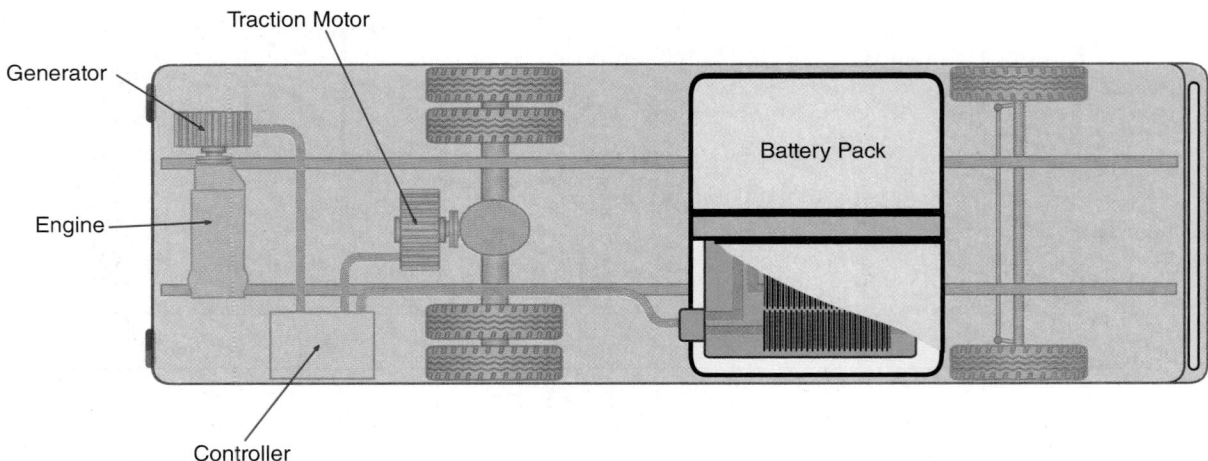

FIGURE 56-16 Location of major HybriDrive system components.

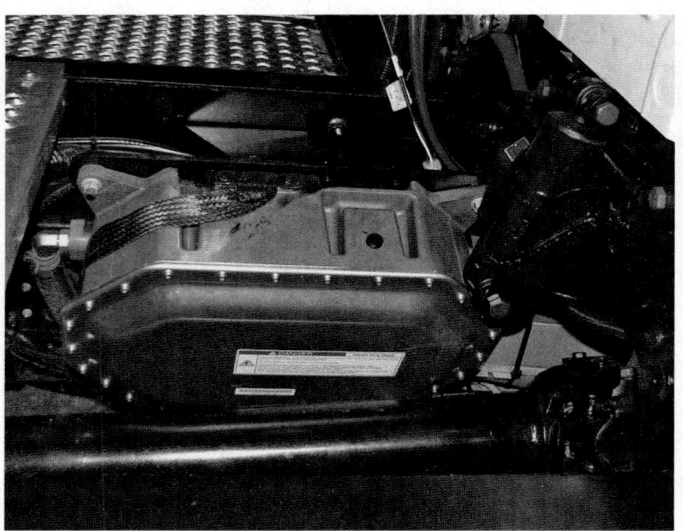

FIGURE 56-17 The PCS is the central control module for the entire HybriDrive system. Three 40-pin electrical connectors and two oil-cooling lines connect to the PCS.

- AC traction motor (ACTM)
- Energy storage system (ESS) and fresh air cooling system for the ESS required for operation above 100°F (38°C)

The systems also include battery monitoring systems and current inverters, as well as diagnostic service software supplied by the manufacturer (BAE) called the Intuitive Diagnostic System (IDS). Also available is an optional data logging module that is used to record all system information available on the network data bus.

Propulsion Control System Module

The **propulsion control system (PCS) module** is the system element controlling the operation of the entire HybriDrive System (**FIGURE 56-17**). It is a microcontroller-based device that supplies electrical output signals based on input data collected

from a vehicle's sensors, such as the accelerator position sensor, brake switch, and gear range selector. **FIGURE 56-18** shows a schematic of the HybriDrive propulsion system.

Three low-voltage connectors, each with 40-pins, form the input-output interface of the PCS with the system. Critical sensor input data is also collected from the electrical generator (ACTG), the transmission (ACTM), and the energy storage system (ESS) modules and enters the PCS through the connectors.

The ignition switch is also a critical input signal that initiates system operation by "waking-up" the PCS, which, in turn, activates other system components. Software inside the PCS containing control algorithms using sensor data to regulate engine speed and the supply of alternating electrical current from the inverters, which determines the output torque of the traction motor.

Even the batteries' state of charge is monitored and controlled by the PCS module. Diagnostic software continuously checks the complete system operation and sends fault information, as well as system status, to the diagnostic connector, where it can interface with the **Intuitive Diagnostic System (IDS)** software used by service technicians.

Fault codes are retained in the PCS non-volatile memory (NVM), which means that they can only be erased using the IDS service tool. System warning lights are also outputs of the PCS. To maintain module reliability and durability, the PCS, which weighs roughly 185 lb (84 kg), is cooled using the transmission fluid.

The system uses the following inputs and outputs to operate the system at maximum efficiency:

- PCS inputs
  - Throttle pedal
  - Brake pedal
  - Emergency override switch
  - Gear selector switch
  - Master switch

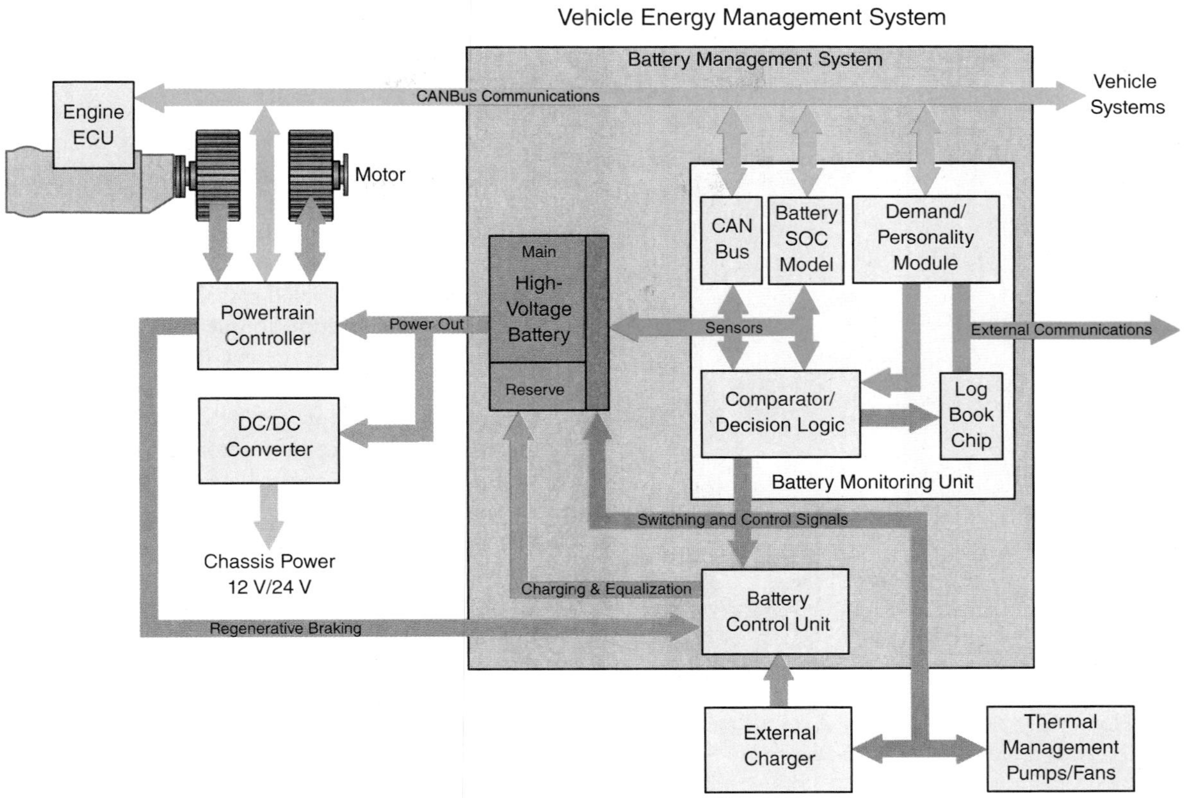

Vehicle Energy Management System

FIGURE 56-18 Diagram of the operation of a battery management system in a hybrid vehicle chassis.

- Master disconnect switch
- Engine test switch
- Brake regeneration disable switch (optional)
- High idle switch (optional)

- PCS outputs
  - Stop HEV indicator
  - Check HEV indicator
  - REGEN applied indicator
  - Motor over-speed warning indicator
  - HEV maintenance required indicator
  - Electric current to inverters
  - Battery state of charge control
  - Serial data via DINEX and SAE J1939 data link

AC Traction Generator (ACTG)

Connected directly to the flywheel of the engine is the **alternating current traction generator (ACTG)**, which converts mechanical energy produced by the engine into electrical current for the propulsion system (**FIGURE 56-19**). This component is a permanent magnet-brushless design generator, producing three-wave AC voltage at approximately 436 volts and 600 amps maximum with 160 hp (119 kW) input. Generator output is partly controlled by the speed of the engine, which is regulated by the PCS to between 800 and 2300 rpm. Even though the generator is air-cooled, heat produced during current production may require supplemental cooling using a fresh air plenum for vehicles operating in

FIGURE 56-19 Rear view of a typical transit bus using the HybriDrive Traction Generator (ACTG) that is located directly behind the engine. No physical connection is made between the engine and drive axle. **A.** ACTG. **B.** Diesel engine.

temperatures greater than 100° F (38° C). In addition to the 280 lb (127 kg) weight of the generator is an oil scavenging pump used to pump synthetic automatic transmission fluid for lubricating and cooling the traction motor. **FIGURE 56-20** shows a PCS with high-voltage connection points to the ACTM and ACTG.

FIGURE 56-20 High-voltage connection points **A.** to the ACTM-ACTG from the PCS central control module for the entire HybriDrive system. Note the electrical connectors for sensors **B.** that also connect to the PCS.

SAFETY TIP

When power-washing engines, dirt washed from the engine can easily enter the ACTG. After start-up, damage occurs quickly inside the generator due to abrasive wear from the dirt. To prevent this, always use a protective apron when cleaning the engine to prevent the entry of dirt into the air-cooled generator.

SAFETY TIP

The traction motor of most hybrid drive systems is not field serviceable. One of the reasons is the safety hazard created when disassembling these motors. The permanent magnets making up the motor stator windings draw the rotor tightly against it with tremendous force. Fingers caught between the rotor or other metal parts and field are instantly amputated and crushed. Never disassemble a permanent magnet motor of this size without the proper training and service tools.

AC Traction Motor (ACTM)

The **alternating current traction motor (ACTM)** has two functions. One is to resist driveline rotation when commanded by the PCS during braking. This effectively turns the traction motor into an electrical generator, which then sends current to charge the onboard batteries. The other function is as a high-speed, three-phase, induction-type traction motor (**FIGURE 56-21**). Induction motors work well in hybrid drive systems, because they produce the greatest amount of torque at low rpm, when the opposing magnetic

fields in the stator and rotor are strongest. In the HybriDrive system, maximum torque is 2100 ft-lb (2847 Nm) of torque at 0 rpm.

The highest torque at starting is useful to accelerate the vehicle when it is necessary to overcome vehicle inertia. Induction motors also have no brushes, which eliminates reoccurring maintenance caused by wear and extends component reliability.

The motor is connected directly to the vehicle's differential through a standard driveshaft and yoke arrangement Maximum speed of the motor is 15,000 rpm; however, a 4.69:1 gear reduction box is used to multiply torque output while reducing motor speed. With maximum current flow from both the batteries and the generator, the motor can momentarily produce up to 250 hp (186 kW) at approximately 600 VAC operating between 0 and 3200 rpm. Since the motor has three phases, or windings, in the stator, the angles between the magnetic field of the stator and rotor can be electrically altered by switching power inputs among the three phases to reverse the direction of motor rotation.

A special rotor position sensor called the resolver measures the rotor position and speed for the PCS to optimally manage the motor operation by choosing which phase of field winding to best use in forward and reverse range, reduce current flow, and shut down the system, as needed. Because overspeed conditions will damage the motor, the resolver is a critical sensor for the PCS.

During regenerative braking, reverse braking torque drives the motor to produce current to charge the batteries, which is later recycled to propel the vehicle. This arrangement helps the HybriDrive to reduce fuel consumption and friction brake wear. Regenerative braking energy recovered from the ACTM is automatically reduced when the batteries are fully charged to prevent overcharging of the batteries. Over-charging can potentially overheat the batteries and cause them to explode. As part of the fault protection system, two temperature sensors inside the motor are used to protect the motor against overheating (**FIGURE 56-22**). The motor, which weighs 450 lb (205 kg), is also oil cooled and lubricated with synthetic transmission fluid. **FIGURE 56-23** illustrates fluid lines to the ACTM.

SAFETY TIP

If a HybriDrive propulsion system needs towing, both rear axles must be removed before towing. If not removed, the lack of pressurized lubrication, supplied by a rotating engine will allow damage to rotating parts driven by the shafts, which will damage internal components.

Energy Storage System (ESS)

To maximize acceleration energy, the energy storage system supplies current to the ACTM when current demand exceeds availability from the ACTG. The ESS also stores electrical current produced during regenerative braking to maximize reductions to fuel consumption. The DC Power Link Contactor is a switch that connects the ESS to the PCS. When closed, it completes the path between the ESS and PCS through the battery cables.

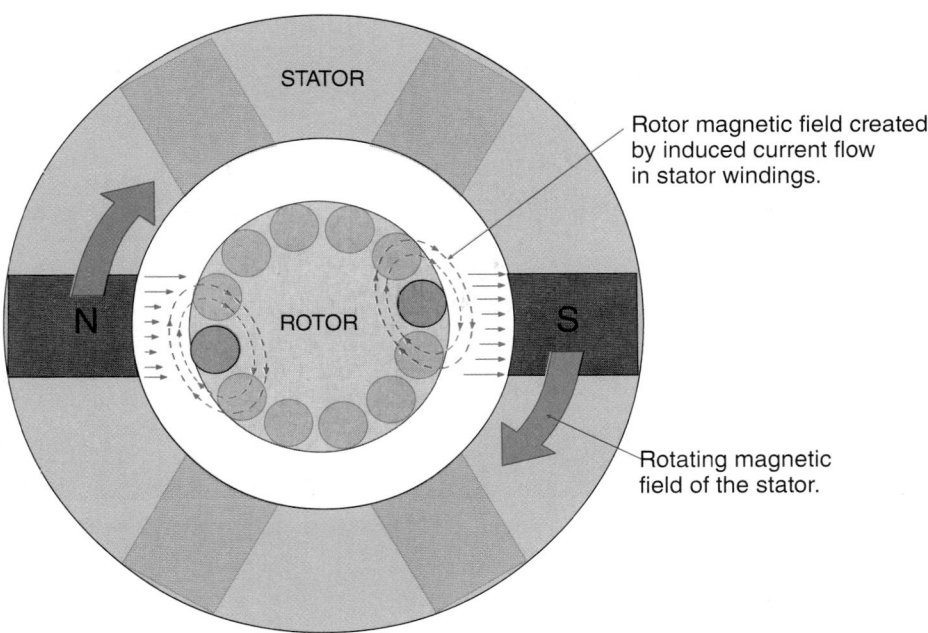

End view showing the magnetic interaction between the stator and two rotor segments.

FIGURE 56-21 The ACTM is a three-phase induction motor, which means it uses three stator windings that can have power inputs switched among the three phases to enable the direction of the motor to change. The PCS controls the phasing of stator energization, which in turn causes the motor to change direction.

Elements of the ESS include battery modules; a battery management system (BMS; the BMS manages the charging and discharging of the batteries to ensure long battery life and safe operation); an **electronic cooling package (ECP)** (an electronically managed cooling system for the battery modules); and system safety protection devices, such as fuses and contactor switches. The original Gen 1 systems used lead-acid storage batteries, while the Gen 2 system uses lithium-phosphate ion batteries stored in tubs on the vehicle roof to keep them cooler and cleaner. Harm to passengers is reduced in the event of a severe gassing or battery fire (**FIGURE 56-24**).

FIGURE 56-22 The traction motor is a three-phase design, which enables precision control of speed and direction of rotation. The resolver, a type of position sensor, measures motor rotor angle and speed.

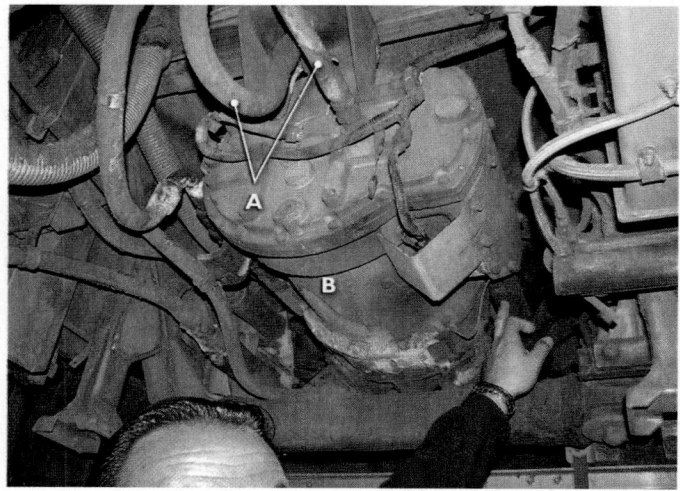

FIGURE 56-23 **A.** Transmission fluid line connections to the **B.** HybriDrive AC traction motor (ACTM).

FIGURE 56-24 **A.** Lithium-ion batteries for the energy storage system (ESS) are located in the "roof tubs." Batteries are stored on the roof to keep them cooler and cleaner. Fires and battery gassing are less likely to endanger passengers. **B.** Lithium-ion battery cells are packaged in interconnected modules of 80 volts each.

Unlike hybrid drive systems used in light-duty vehicles, in heavy-duty commercial vehicles, nickel-metal hydride (NiMH) batteries are not used because they are regarded as having reached their maximum potential. Further technological advancements and cost reductions are not expected for NiMH batteries. Lithium-ion batteries are now commonplace because they offer higher energy density than NiMH batteries and do not experience adverse memory effects due to inconsistent charging. Lithium batteries also have the lowest self-discharge rate compared to other battery technologies. That is, lithium batteries maintain a charge for a very long time when idled.

Compared with lead-acid batteries, a lithium battery pack is less than one-quarter of the weight and charges faster. Upgrading to lithium batteries reduces battery pack weight from 4100 to 1000 lb (1818 to 455 kg), which means roof structures in buses do not need as much reinforcement and fuel consumption can decrease. Frequent charge and discharge cycles shorten battery life. Service life of lead-acid batteries is between two and three years compared to six years for lithium batteries.

The lithium-ion ESS contains a total of 16 lithium-ion modules producing 39.6 VDC per module connected to total approximately 633 VDC. During **charge-depleting (CD) operating mode**, the vehicle is powered only—or almost only—by the energy stored in the batteries and not the engine-driven generator. If an ESS under-voltage condition is detected, generator current is diverted from driving the AC traction motor and into the energy storage modules instead.

State of ESS Charge

In **charge-sustaining (CS) mode**, the batteries' state of charge (SOC) may rise and fall slightly. The SOC, on the average, remains at its initial level and can be recharged through

FIGURE 56-25 The master disconnect and other lock-out type switches are critical safety items. **A.** Master disconnect switch. **B.** HEV fault lamp.

TABLE 56-6 Condition of Good Versus Defective Battery Modules

Condition	Good Battery Modules	Defective Battery Modules
Discharge voltage at high amperage draw	Higher voltage	Lower voltage
Charging voltage at high amperage	Lower voltage	Higher voltage
Charge time	Faster	Slower
Capacity	High discharge amperage	Low discharge amperage

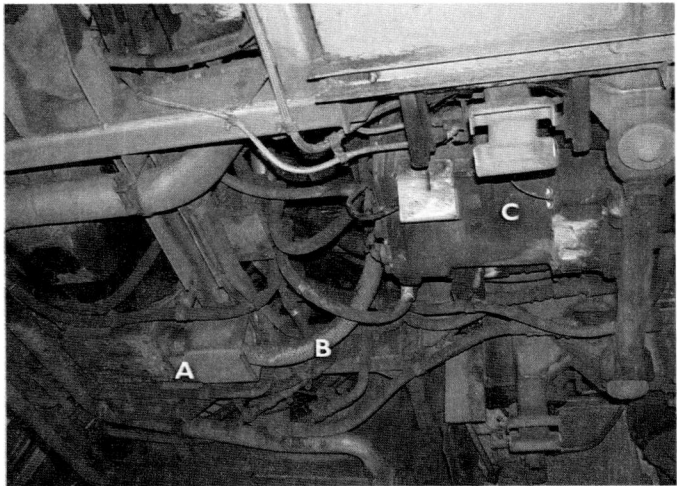

FIGURE 56-26 Three-phase voltage waveforms originating from the PCS are used to operate the ACTM. Three-phase voltage operates the motor four times more efficiently than a high-voltage, single-phase source. Line-to-line voltage is 346 volts AC; peak-to-peak voltage is 580 volts AC. **A.** PCS module. **B.** High-voltage cables. **C.** Traction motor.

regenerative braking. Energy storage modules are kept at as low as 40% SOC. This may seem low, but the batteries are required to have capacity to store current produced by regenerative braking energy extracted from the AC traction motor.

Without battery storage capacity, regenerative braking is automatically reduced when the ESS modules are fully charged, which causes the friction-type service brakes to work harder, dissipate more heat, and waste fuel.

A **master disconnect switch** located in the battery compartments enables technicians to disconnect the power circuit for maintenance or emergencies. This switch has a lock-out feature that prevents anyone other than the technician from reconnecting vehicle power.

The ESS master disconnect switch is different from the 12/24-volt chassis electrical master switch (**FIGURE 56-25**). This switch controls the vehicle chassis electrical system allowing the lights, engine, and HybriDrive propulsion system to operate when it is switched to the on position.

Battery Monitoring System

The battery monitoring system operates to equalize charges evenly across all the battery modules. Because batteries often have slightly different resistances to charging and discharging, the battery monitor controls the charge and discharge rate to each module.

Voltage to each module changes when discharging, such as under acceleration or during regenerative braking, when batteries are charged at high amperage. Defective battery modules are identified by their inability to accept a charge. The IDS service tool does not monitor individual module amperage, so module voltage is used for comparison.

For example, operative modules in good condition (**TABLE 56-6**) have less internal resistance and charge at a lower voltage compared with weak or defective modules. Modules in poor condition have the largest charging voltage differences with good modules when charge amperage is highest, such as

during regenerative braking. Voltage during acceleration when high current is drawn from the batteries drops much more compared with good modules. Diagnostic software flags bad battery modules under these conditions.

Current Inverters

Wave inverters are devices that change the shape of electrical current waves. A **DC-to-AC inverter** takes the straight, unchanging wave of DC and flips, or inverts, the current's polarity to resemble an AC wave signal. Similarly, an **AC-to-DC inverter** switches the polarity of an AC signal to resemble the straight wave polarity of DC (**FIGURE 56-26**).

Both types of current inverters are used in the HybriDrive system. AC produced by the ACTG is rectified to 580 VDC to charge the batteries. To operate the ACTM 633 VDC, battery voltage is converted to three-phase 346 V—phase-to-phase or line-to-line volts. The frequency of the AC voltage is varied to change the traction motor speed. At 250 hp (186 kW) maximum, 346 VAC has a maximum frequency of 500 Hz.

Intuitive Diagnostic System (IDS)

The IDS is BAE's service software. It is PC-based and enables technicians to connect through the J-1939 connector to:

- Monitor system parameters
- View programmable parameters and make adjustments to customer programmable parameters
- View and erase fault codes
- View fault history
- Perform diagnostic tests

The IDS is able to read data and fault codes generated by the onboard diagnostic system.

- Above normal component temperature
- Under- and over-voltage conditions
- Battery under- and over-charging
- Motor over-speed

The PCS monitors the system for failure conditions. Under extreme conditions the system de-rates or shuts down. If failures occur and the system shuts down, a PCS (Emergency) Override Switch can be pushed and held to override most shutdown conditions for up to ten seconds continuously and thirty seconds total. The PCS emergency override switch is used only to move a vehicle to a safe location if stalled on a roadway. Two dash lights indicate problems with the propulsion system.

The Stop HEV indicator is illuminated when an active severe fault is detected. In these circumstances, the vehicle will not move unless the emergency override switch is pushed and a warning buzzer sounds. A Check HEV Indicator lights when a less serious but active fault is detected and the vehicle is operable in a de-rated condition. When inactive faults are logged by the onboard diagnostic system, the HEV Maintenance Required Indicator illuminates. This light is located in the engine compartment.

▶ TECHNICIAN TIP

Corrosion caused by water intrusion in the wiring harness is a common cause of HEV problems and fault codes. Contributing to the problem is the position of protective split loom around vehicle cables, which can form "drip loops." These occur when water from road spray easily enters the split loom and collects. To minimize the likelihood of this problem, always orientate split in the cable loom away from the curbside and engine grates and down to allow water to drain.

Unique System Inputs

To calculate the amount of torque to apply to the rear axles, a throttle pedal position sensor provides a varying voltage signal to the PCS. Based on signal values and a throttle torque map containing look-up table values, the PCS determines the frequency and voltage supplied to the ACTM.

Brake Pressure Sensor

A brake pressure signal is needed to calculate the amount of regenerative braking performed by the ACTM (**FIGURE 56-27**). Although the braking performed by ACTG is designed to simulate the action of conventional friction brakes, the brake "feel"

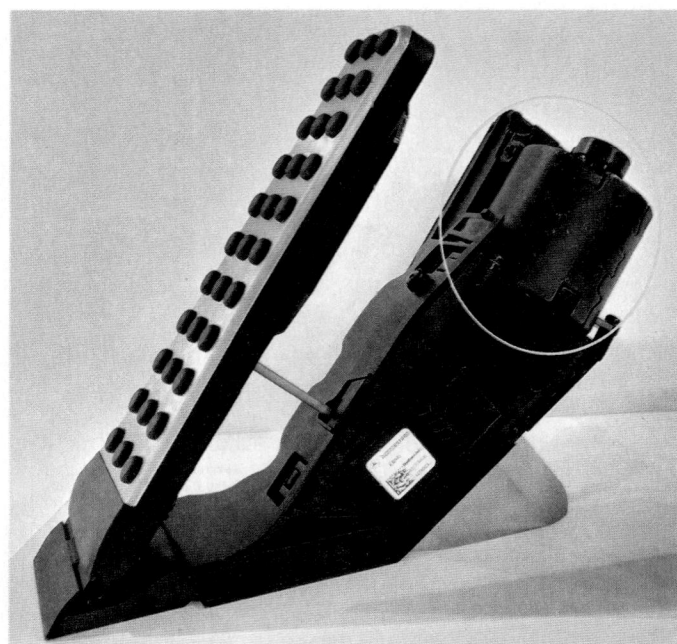

FIGURE 56-27 An electric motor on the underside of the pedal pushes the pedal back against the driver's foot to supply force feedback.

of regenerative brakes may be too aggressive under some situations, such as on a bus with standing passengers. For safety reasons, an adjustment to the degree of regenerative braking is possible on the HybriDrive. A scale of 1 to 10 is used for the adjustment, with 10 being the most aggressive, but recovery of braking energy is best for greatest efficiency. In transit applications, the setting may be set as low as between 3 and 5.

Regeneration Disable Switch

An optional switch located near the driver is available to turn regenerative braking off for one key cycle. Slippery road conditions may be one situation for which it would be desirable to turn off the regenerative braking for better vehicle dynamic control. Wheel lock-up conditions are sensed by the antilock brake system (ABS), which sends a message along the CAN data bus to disengage the ACTM regeneration.

When the regeneration system is on, current is produced by the ACTM and ACTG to charge the batteries to a 40% state of charge. When regeneration is off, the ACTG charges battery modules ONLY when vehicle is parked in neutral. A dash light informs the driver whenever any brake regeneration is taking place.

Engine Test Switch

To service the engine separately from the hybrid drive system, it is preferable to disconnect all high-voltage supply and operate the engine using the throttle pedal. To accomplish this, an engine test switch is used. As a two-position toggle switch, the normal position integrates engine operation into the HybriDrive system and the vehicle responds as intended. With the switch in the engine test position, only the engine responds to the throttle pedal, and all high-voltage contacts are open.

Maintenance and Service

LO 56-5 Outline maintenance and service for hybrid drive systems.

Preventative maintenance on the HybriDrive propulsion systems consists of inspections prescribed in the service manual and scheduled changes of coolant and traction motor oil. An air filter in the battery compartment is changed at two-year intervals. None of the major system components are rebuilt in the field but simply replaced after diagnostic tests have identified a replaceable unit.

Whenever the PCS is removed for replacement, it is a good practice to record all programmable parameters to adjust the replacement module efficiently. In addition to the electrical safety precautions outlined in the section, special tools like the ones shown in Figure 56-8 should be used when working on hybrid vehicles. Other electrical safety general procedures for component replacement include:

1. Switching off the master disconnect switch and locking out the switch until repairs are completed. Locking out the switch prevents accidental reconnection of power during maintenance. The master disconnect switch disables the master switch and ignition signal, preventing the engine from starting or the PCS to energize. The master disconnect also disables the contactors in PCS and ESS.

2. Disconnect and remove all ESS high-voltage connectors while wearing high-voltage type 00 lineman's gloves. Connections inside the battery storage enclosure are never to be performed without specialized OEM training.

3. Disconnect and tag external harnesses, lines, and cooling connections to replacement components.

4. Validate the repair after service is completed by a proper road test or by operating the component under the appropriate condition to evaluate its performance. Fault codes should be erased before testing begins to determine whether they reoccur. Before returning the vehicle to service, any fault codes should be erased once more.

> **SAFETY TIP**
>
> Even after the master disconnect switch is opened and locked-out, the battery system has the potential to deliver a severe shock hazard since the battery modules are not de-energized by this switch. Extreme caution must always be used when working around the ESS. Before touching any electrical conductor during HybriDrive service, always verify that an electrical circuit is de-energized by using a digital multimeter (DMM).

Wrap-Up

Ready for Review

- A variety of hybrid drive vehicle configurations are used in commercial vehicles. In essence, hybrid propulsion systems can use any type of engine—gasoline, natural gas, diesel, turbine, or reciprocating—assisted by an electric motor to accelerate the vehicle.

- Hybrid electric vehicles simultaneously reduce both fuel consumption and emissions produced from burning fuel.

- Vehicles operating in urban driving conditions are best suited to hybrid use, as much of the energy derived from burning fuel is lost through idling and braking.

- The main configurations of hybrid vehicles are series, parallel, series-parallel, and plug-in hybrid vehicles.

- A series system requires a larger electric motor and battery pack, but a smaller internal combustion engine, and works best in stop-and-go situations. Parallel systems are better suited to higher speeds with less stop-and-go operation.

- An alternative to electric hybrid drives is the hydraulic launch assist (HLA) system. The concept of HLA uses hydraulic regenerative braking to capture braking energy and help launch the vehicle during acceleration.

- Hybrid drive system components use lethal high-voltage power devices operating up to 900 volts and contain energy storage systems over 700 volts DC, so special tools and personal protective equipment must be used during servicing to ensure technician safety.

- BAE is an aerospace and defense technology company and is also one of the leading developers and manufacturers of hybrid drive propulsion systems for the military and heavy-duty commercial vehicles. It manufactures series-type and parallel-type hybrids.

- HybriDrive includes the following major system components: propulsion control system (PCS); AC traction generator (ACTG); AC traction motor (ACTM); energy storage system (ESS)—and fresh air cooling system for the ESS required for operation above 100° F (38° C).

- The entire HybriDrive system is controlled by a microprocessor-controlled propulsion control system. Multiple inputs and outputs enable the PCS to operate the system at maximum efficiency.

- The alternating current system generator (ACTG) is a permanent magnet-brushless design generator that is air cooled.

- The alternating current traction motor (ACTM) resists driveline rotation when commanded by the PCS during braking. It also functions as a high-speed, three-phase, induction-type motor.

- Without battery capacity, regenerative braking is automatically reduced when the ESS modules are fully charged, which causes the friction-type service brakes to work harder, dissipate more heat, and waste fuel.

- The battery monitoring system operates to equalize charges evenly across all the battery modules. Defective battery modules are identified by their inability to accept a charge.

- ▶ HybriDrive systems use DC-to-AC and AC-to-DC inverters.
- ▶ A brake pressure signal is needed to calculate the amount of regenerative braking performed by the ACTM because the braking feel of regenerative brakes can be too aggressive in some situations, such as mass transit.
- ▶ Regenerative braking can be turned on or off by the driver.
- ▶ To service the engine separately from the hybrid drive system, it is preferable to disconnect all high-voltage supply and operate the engine using the throttle pedal.

Key Terms

AC-to-DC inverter A device that switches the polarity of an AC signal to resemble the straight wave polarity of DC.

alternating current traction generator (ACTG) A device that converts mechanical energy produced by the engine into electrical current for the propulsion system.

alternating current traction motor (ACTM) A motor that supplies propulsion force and functions as an electrical generator in a hybrid drive system.

charge-depleting (CD) operating mode A mode of operation in which the vehicle is powered only—or almost only—by the energy stored in the battery.

charge-sustaining (CS) mode A mode of operation in which the batteries' state of charge (SOC) may rise and fall slightly and energy storage modules are kept at a 40% state of charge.

DC-to-AC inverter A device that takes the straight, unchanging wave of DC and flips, or inverts, the current's polarity to resemble an AC wave signal.

electronic cooling package (ECP) A system of fans and electronic controls that maintains a hybrid ESS within a set temperature range.

hybrid electric vehicle (HEV) A type of vehicle that combines an internal combustion engine with an electric propulsion system into a new or hybrid powertrain configuration.

HybriDrive propulsion system A series-type hybrid propulsion system developed by BAE, an aerospace and defense technology company.

hydraulic launch assist (HLA) An alternative to electric hybrid drive's regenerative braking. A hydraulic pump pressurizes fluid and stores it in a hydraulic-gas accumulator during a brake application. The use of standard friction service brakes is prevented until just before a complete vehicle stop.

Intuitive Diagnostic System (IDS) Proprietary software system available on BAE propulsion systems to aid technicians in diagnosing service issues.

master disconnect switch A switch located in the battery compartments that enables technicians to disconnect the power circuit for maintenance or emergencies.

parallel drive A vehicle in which both the engine and electric motor work together, blending motor and engine torque, to propel the vehicle.

plug-in hybrid electric vehicle (PHEV) Any type of hybrid electric vehicle containing a battery storage system that uses an external source to recharge the battery when the vehicle is not in operation.

propulsion control system (PCS) module A microcontroller-based device that supplies electrical output signals based on input data collected from a vehicle's sensors.

regenerative braking A type of braking in which the kinetic energy of the vehicle's motion is captured rather than being lost to heat as it is in a conventional braking system. This is accomplished by using the drive motors as generators, which recharge the traction batteries.

series drive A propulsion system where an engine-driven electric generator supplies current to an electric traction motor to propel the vehicle.

series-parallel drive A more complex system enabling an engine only, an electric motor only, and a combined engine-motor operation. Also called *power-split configuration*.

traction motor An electric motor that provides propulsion to a vehicle.

wave inverter A device that changes the shape of electrical current waves.

Review Questions

1. The most popular HybriDrive series electric hybrid drive system propels the vehicle with which of the following?
   a. One electric motor only
   b. Two electric motors
   c. An electric motor and an internal combustion engine working together at all times
   d. An internal combustion engine at some times and an electric motor at others, or a combination of the two

2. What is a PHEV?
   a. A series electric hybrid drive
   b. A parallel electric hybrid drive
   c. A series-parallel electric hybrid drive
   d. An electric hybrid vehicle that plugs into grid current to charge the batteries

3. A series-parallel electric hybrid drive system uses which of the following to propel the vehicle?
   a. An electric motor only
   b. Two electric motors
   c. An electric motor and an internal combustion engine working together at all times
   d. An internal combustion engine at some times and an electric motor at others, or a combination of the two

4. Which type of battery is used as storage in the Gen 2 BAE HybriDrive series system?
   a. Lead acid
   b. Nickel-metal hydride
   c. Glass mat
   d. Lithium-ion

5. Which type of current is used to power the BAE HybriDrive series system electric motor?
   a. AC
   b. DC
   c. AC and DC together
   d. AC is used during certain operations, and DC is used during others.

6. What type of hybrid drive configuration does an extended range hybrid vehicle use?
   a. Series
   b. Parallel
   c. Series parallel
   d. Plug-in battery

7. What component is directly attached to the engine flywheel in the BAE series HybriDrive system?
   a. The electric motor/generator
   b. The transmission
   c. The AC traction generator
   d. The AC traction motor

8. How many battery modules are used in the Gen 2 BAE Series HybriDrive system?
   a. 8
   b. 16
   c. 24
   d. 32

9. Much of the energy required to accelerate a city transit bus is lost to heat caused by frequent braking. What is the estimated percentage of that energy loss?
   a. 35%
   b. 45%
   c. 55%
   d. 65%

10. What cools the AC traction motor in the BAE HybriDrive system?
    a. Transmission fluid
    b. Air
    c. Engine coolant
    d. Engine oil

ASE Technician A/Technician B Style Questions

1. Technician A says that a hybrid electrical vehicle only uses an electric motor to propel the vehicle and an engine to charge the vehicle batteries when necessary. Technician B says that the type of a hybrid that Technician A is describing is known as a series hybrid. Who is correct?
   a. Technician A
   b. Technician B
   c. Both Technician A and Technician B
   d. Neither Technician A nor Technician B

2. Technician A says that a parallel-drive hybrid is one in which both the engine and the electric motor combine to drive the vehicle at all times. Technician B says that series-parallel drive hybrid can use the engine, the electric motor, or both together to drive the vehicle. Who is correct?
   a. Technician A
   b. Technician B
   c. Both Technician A and Technician B
   d. Neither Technician A nor Technician B

3. Technician A says that not all hybrid drive vehicles are electric. Technician B says that hybrid drive electrical systems can be serviced in the same way as regular vehicle electrical systems. Who is correct?
   a. Technician A
   b. Technician B
   c. Both Technician A and Technician B
   d. Neither Technician A nor Technician B

4. Technician A says that electrical hybrid drive systems require an electrical storage system. Technician B says that most electrical hybrid drive systems use regenerative braking. Who is correct?
   a. Technician A
   b. Technician B
   c. Both Technician A and Technician B
   d. Neither Technician A nor Technician B

5. Technician A says that regenerative braking means that the foundation brakes can regenerate themselves after they wear. Technician B says that foundation brakes last longer when regenerative braking is used. Who is correct?
   a. Technician A
   b. Technician B
   c. Both Technician A and Technician B
   d. Neither Technician A nor Technician B

6. Technician A says that the original BAE HybriDrive system is a series hybrid. Technician B says that the original BAE HybriDrive system has two electric traction motors. Who is correct?
   a. Technician A
   b. Technician B
   c. Both Technician A and Technician B
   d. Neither Technician A nor Technician B

7. Technician A says that lead-acid batteries are used to store electricity on the latest hybrid drive systems. Technician B says that the BAE Gen 2 HybriDrive system uses nickel-metal hydride batteries as a power storage system. Who is correct?
   a. Technician A
   b. Technician B
   c. Both Technician A and Technician B
   d. Neither Technician A nor Technician B

8. Technician A says that electrical hybrid drive systems use a high-voltage traction motor to propel the vehicle. Technician B says that electrical hybrid drive systems require high-voltage disconnect systems to shut off the high voltage for service. Who is correct?
   a. Technician A
   b. Technician B
   c. Both Technician A and Technician B
   d. Neither Technician A nor Technician B

9. Technician A says that AC is used to power the traction motor in BAE HybriDrive systems. Technician B says the nickel-metal hydride batteries in the BAE Gen 2 HybriDrive systems are AC batteries. Who is correct?
   a. Technician A
   b. Technician B
   c. Both Technician A and Technician B
   d. Neither Technician A nor Technician B

10. Technician A says that when a hybrid drive vehicle is brought into the shop for service, the high-voltage system should be locked out. Technician B says that when a hybrid vehicle must be towed, both axles should be removed so that the driveshaft does not rotate or damage the hybrid drive components. Who is correct?
   a. Technician A
   b. Technician B
   c. Both Technician A and Technician B
   d. Neither Technician A nor Technician B

CHAPTER 57

Allison EV Drive and Series-Parallel Hybrid Systems

Learning Objectives

After reading this chapter, you will be able to:

- **LO 57-1** Describe the construction and operation of Allison EV drive hybrid system.
- **LO 57-2** Identify and explain the function of the Allison EV drive system components.
- **LO 57-3** Explain the function of the energy storage system (ESS).
- **LO 57-4** Describe the operating modes of parallel hybrids.
- **LO 57-5** Outline basic service and maintenance procedures for Allison EP drive systems.

You Are the Technician

As a transit bus technician, you are skilled and qualified to work on diesel-powered bus chassis. Recently, a few of the hybrid-drive buses in the fleet, which are now out of the manufacturer's warranty period, have begun to receive more complaints about braking. Passengers are falling during braking, and there are even a few reports of injuries due to overly aggressive braking. Examining the service records, you notice the buses all have far less frequent brake service and foundation replacement than what is expected from a hybrid chassis. After inspecting all the brake foundation components on one chassis, you find them all to be in proper working condition. Inspection and test procedures performed on the air brake circuits and values all are within normal expected limits. While road testing the bus, you do find that even under very light brake pedal application force, the bus does brake very aggressively. Because it is a series-parallel-type hybrid powertrain, you realize that a significant amount of braking is supposed to be performed by the electric traction motor generator. As you consider which elements of the hybrid system to inspect, and search original equipment manufacturers (OEM) literature for the correct inspection and diagnostic procedures, consider the following:

1. List the safety procedures that should be followed before beginning any inspection of diagnostic work on an Allison EV hybrid powertrain.
2. Identify potential problems with the hybrid powertrain that may contribute to more work being performed by the regenerative braking system and not the service braking system.
3. What strategy does the Allison EV system uses to ensure there is an adequate buffer or storage capacity in the batteries for regenerative braking if the batteries become excessively charged?

Introduction

In addition to series-type hybrids, series-parallel drive is the next most common configurations of hybrid drive system with the Allison EV Drive Hybrid Systems the most representative model used in heavy-duty commercial vehicles. In parallel drive hybrids, both the engine and electric motor work together, blending motor and engine torque to propel the vehicle. Series-parallel drive is a more complex system enabling operating modes of an engine only, an electric motor only, and a combined engine-motor operation. Also called a power-split configuration, the engine and motor operation is optimized for a variety of driving conditions.

Arvin Meritor markets a dual-mode hybrid system specifically designed for line-haul application, but as the Allison system is the most common series-parallel hybrids, this chapter discusses that system in greater detail.

Overview of Allison EV Drive Hybrid System

LO 57-1 Describe the construction and operation of Allison EV drive hybrid system.

EP40 system and EP50 system are model names derived for Allison's Electric Propulsion (EP) system, or alternatively Allison's Electrically Variable (EV) Drive. Although the two models are almost identical in construction and operation, the EP40 is capable of continuously delivering 280 hp (209 kW), while the EP50's output is higher at 330 hp (246 kW).

The Allison EP Drive system is a series parallel-type hybrid drive. Unlike series hybrid systems, such as the BAE Hybri-Drive, which use only an electric motor for propulsion torque, series parallel systems use a transmission, which blends a combination of output torque from both the electric traction motor and engine.

A dedicated engine-mechanical pathway and an electrical motor pathway for traction torque, along with a combination of both, are possible through the powertrain. Allison describes the hybrid architecture as a two-mode compound-split system. That is because the system's capabilities allow for (1) an electric only or (2) diesel only operation for traction power and (3) an infinitely variable combination of both (**FIGURE 57-1**).

Torque from both sources is blended to optimally match vehicle operating conditions and the electric propulsion-drive operating state. Its automatic transmission does not used fixed gear ratios. Instead, the power continuously varies from the engine and two electric motors when the vehicle is driving in a forward direction. When decelerating, the EP system uses regenerative braking to recover braking energy. Like other hybrids, the electric **traction motors** turn into generators, producing electric current used to charge an on board bank of nickel-metal hydride (NiMH) batteries. Regenerative braking used to recharge batteries also slows the vehicle, like a retarder does in a conventional automatic transmission, which in turn reduces brake wear and fuel consumption.

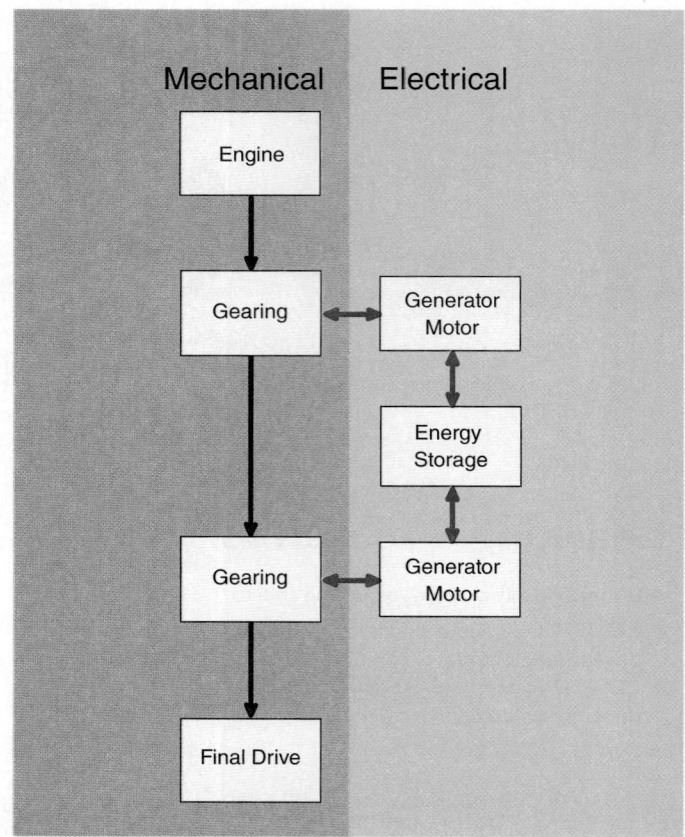

FIGURE 57-1 Unlike series hybrids, where only the engine generates electricity, series-parallel hybrids can use both the engine and electric motor to propel the vehicle.

Series-Parallel Drive Advantages and Disadvantages

Real-world comparisons of the EP system to the series Hybri-Drive system show that EP offers slightly greater reduction in fuel consumption compared to the HybriDrive system operated on an identical route. The EP is capable of faster acceleration, too, if its adjustable HyGain accelerating setting feature is set-up for performance mode. Late-model Allison H-EP40/50s also have a unique feature referred to as **smart electrification**. This feature enables the system's engine and electric motors to switch over to generating mode to produce as much as 300 amps at 24 volts at idle. Idle electrical generation at this magnitude is an ideal feature for buses replacing traditional hydraulically driven motors for accessory systems with electric drive motors operating the radiator cooling fan, coolant pumps, power steering pumps, charge air cooler fans, and hybrid drive cooling fans. Introduced in 2011, electrically driven accessories are supplied current using a highly efficient solid-state direct current (DC)-to-DC converter (**FIGURE 57-2**), eliminating the need for a traditional belt-driven alternator and associated maintenance requirements. On board battery current is not used. Consequently, hybrid- and starting-battery life increase due to less frequent and deep charge and discharge cycles (**FIGURE 57-3**).

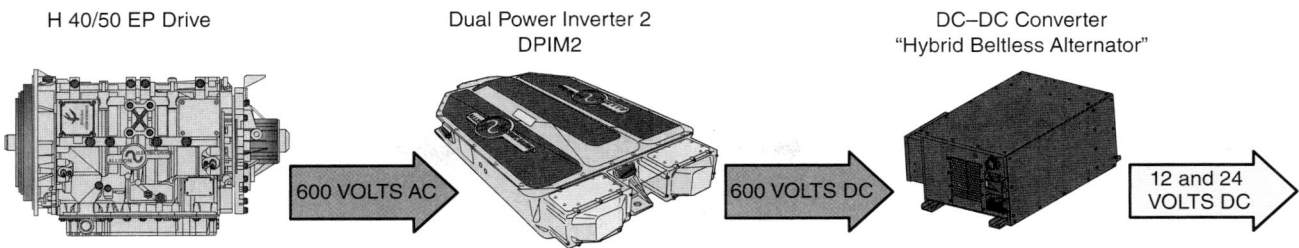

H 40/50 EP Drive   Dual Power Inverter 2   DC–DC Converter
                              DPIM2   "Hybrid Beltless Alternator"

600 VOLTS AC →   600 VOLTS DC →   12 and 24 VOLTS DC →

FIGURE 57-2 The use of an optional DC-DC converter, which takes power from the engine-driven generator and converts it to 12/24-volts DC, eliminates the need for an alternator.

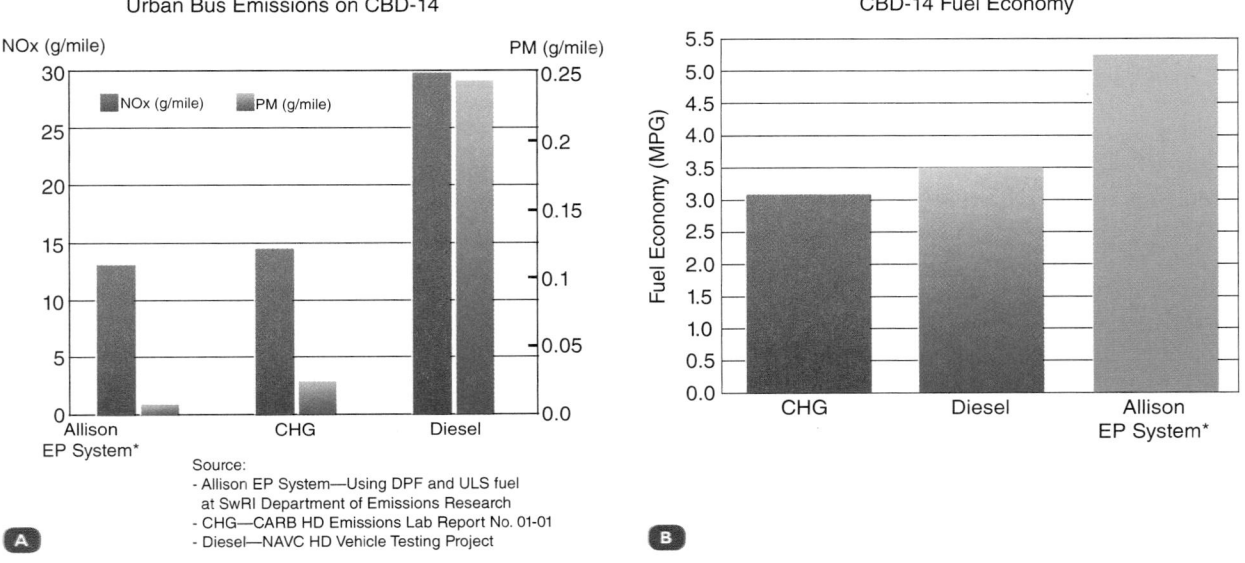

Urban Bus Emissions on CBD-14

CBD-14 Fuel Economy

Source:
- Allison EP System—Using DPF and ULS fuel at SwRI Department of Emissions Research
- CHG—CARB HD Emissions Lab Report No. 01-01
- Diesel—NAVC HD Vehicle Testing Project

A   **B**

FIGURE 57-3 A. Dual-mode hybrids deliver improved fuel economy with lower emissions. Combining torque from the engine and electric traction motor supplies superior torque. **B.** The Allison EP system has adjustable acceleration rates to balance fuel economy with performance.

Despite the EP system advantages, currently less than a third of Allison EV Drive Hybrid Systems sold are Allison EP drives. The addition of the transmission and associated components adds approximately 1500 lb (682 kg) to vehicle weight. Additional capital purchase costs are also associated with the system. **FIGURE 57-4** shows the layout of a transit bus using a series parallel-dual mode Allison EP system.

System Components

LO 57-2 Identify and explain the function of the Allison EV drive system components.

The Allison EV drive system consists of the following major components:

- EV drive transmission unit
- Transmission control module (TCM)
- Vehicle control module (VCM)
- Traction motors
- Energy storage system (ESS)
- Dual power inverter module (DPIM)

EV Drive Transmission Unit

The EV drive transmission unit provides a pathway for transmitting electric motor or engine torque (or a blend of both) using three planetary gear sets. Inside the unit, there are three planetary gear sets, two wet-type hydraulic clutches, and two motor/generators. The EV drive transmission itself consists of several standard modules illustrated in **FIGURES 57-5** and **57-6**:

- Input housing module
- Main (stator) housing module
- Control valve assembly/oil pan module
- Clutch housing module
- Rear cover module

Transmission Control Module (TCM)

The transmission control module (TCM) is one of the most important of twelve microcontroller-based ECUs the EP system uses. Most of the EP system operation is directly controlled by this processing module, which collects input signals to determine electrical outputs controlling the EV transmission operation.

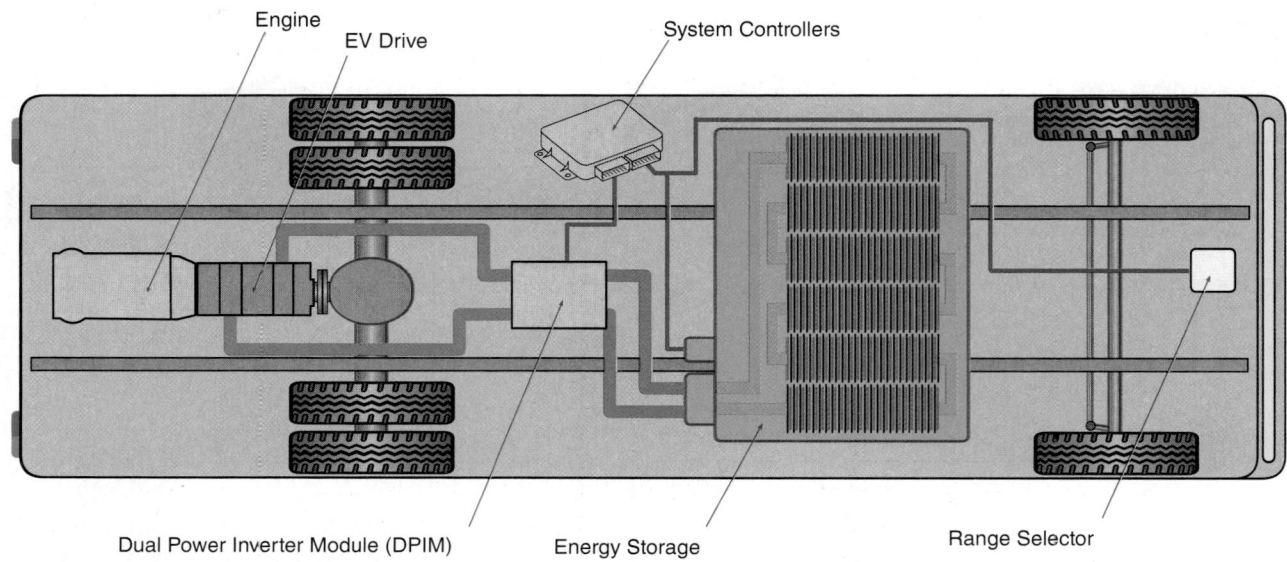

FIGURE 57-4 Configuration of a transit bus series-parallel, dual-mode Allison EP system.

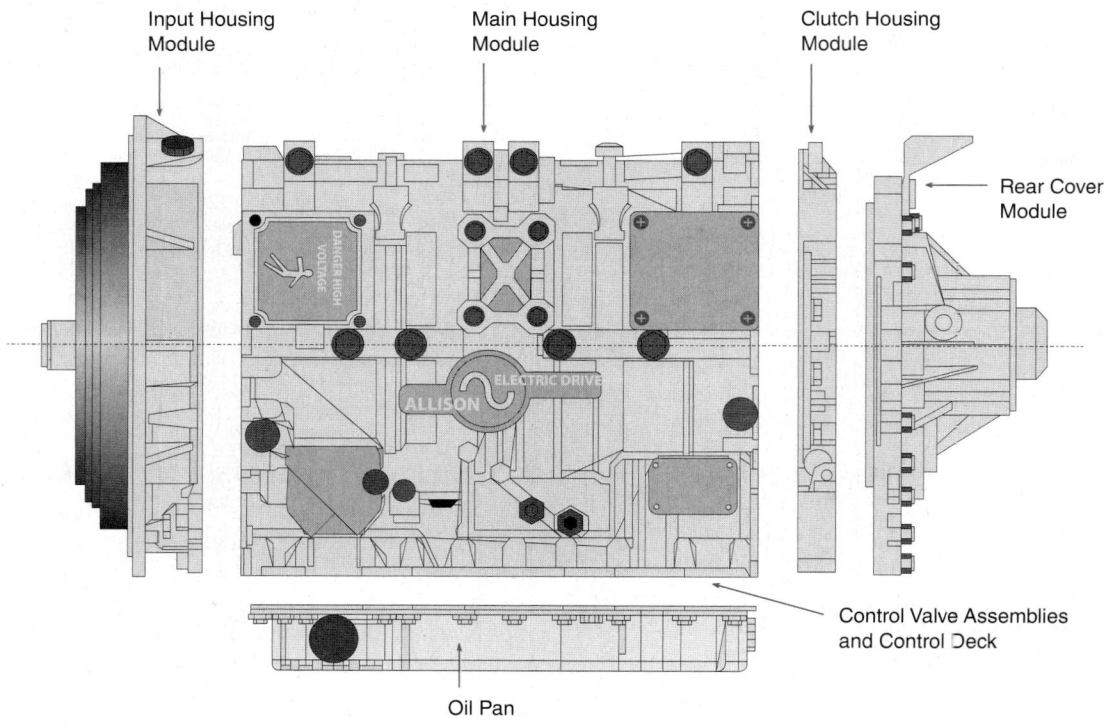

FIGURE 57-5 Standard modules of an Allison EV transmission.

Image Courtesy of Allison Transmission.

Torque blending, adaptive hydraulic clutch control, diagnostic system management, hydraulic oil level monitoring, and start-up and shut down routines are some of the basic important functions. In addition to J1939 controller area network (CAN) messages used as inputs for the TCM, several input circuits are connected to the TCM, such as:

- Ignition sense—Detects the ignition key switch state
- Hydraulic transmission control pressure sensors

- Transmission oil sump temperature
- Oil level sensor
- Transmission output speed
- ESS relay status
- Accelerator interlock—Disables the engine throttle, keeping it at neutral when passenger doors are open
- Fast idle switch—Increases idle speed in steps when activated
- Engine brake enable—Status of the engine brake on/off

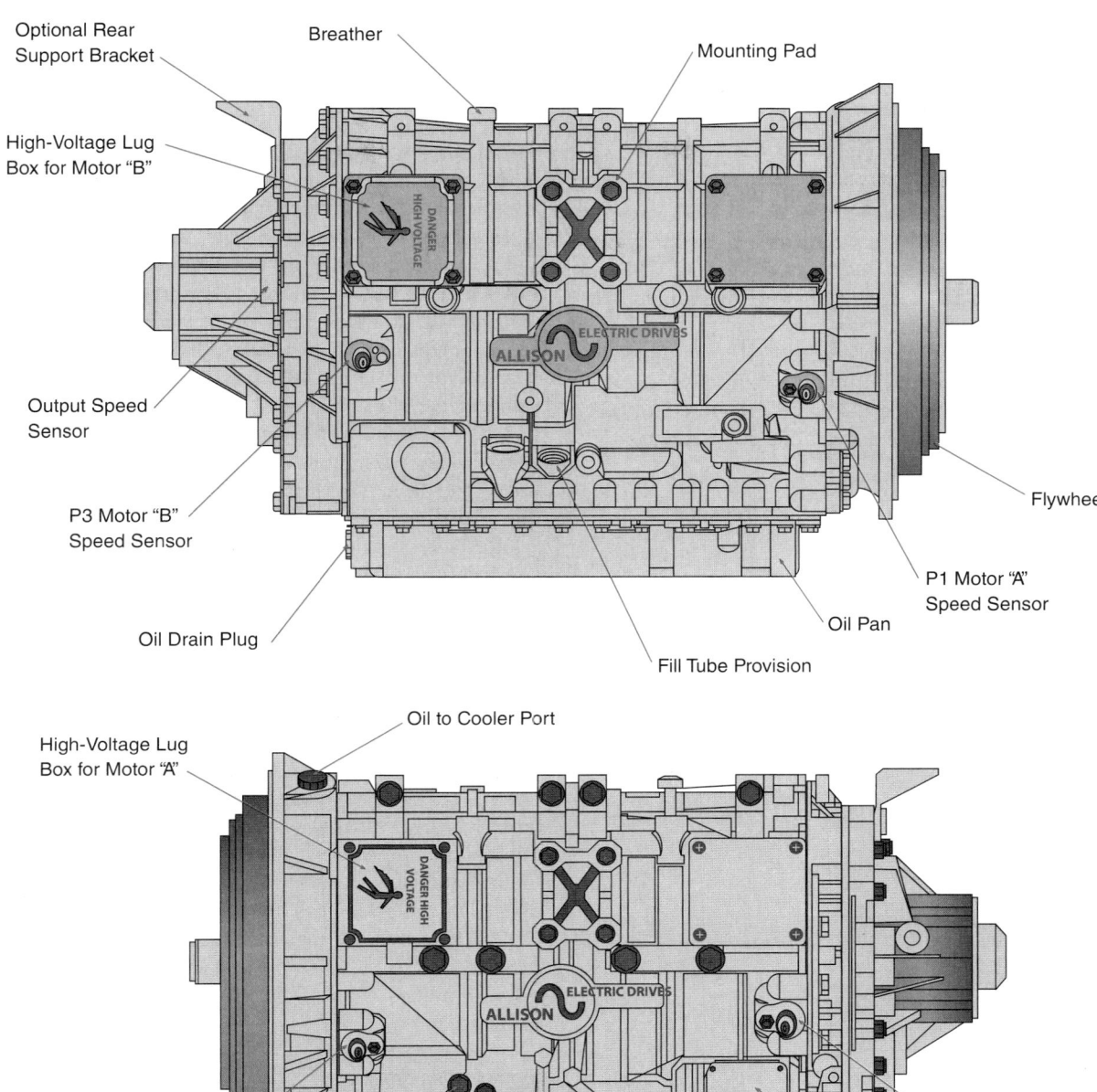

FIGURE 57-6 Side views of the Allison EV transmission.

Likewise, the TCM outputs include:

- Auxiliary function range inhibit—Prevents selection to forward or reverse range when auxiliary equipment is enabled
- Front operation—Enables vehicle start-up and operation from the driver's compartment

- Remote shutdown—Requests system shutdown
- Hydraulic clutch trim solenoids (two)
- Hydraulic clutch-blocking solenoid drivers
- DPIM wake-up signal
- ESS wake-up signal
- Engine controller wake-up signal
- Speedometer signal

- Engine brake enable
- Auxiliary brake enable indicator lamp
- Power take off (PTO) enable

Vehicle Control Module (VCM)

The vehicle control module (VCM) is the other microprocessor-based controller that operates with the TCM to process data and determine electric signal outputs for the EP system and other vehicle features (**FIGURE 57-7**). Both the TCM and VCM are identical-looking modules, sharing identical components. However, the VCM function concerns the vehicle-to-powertrain interface, such as limiting operation of auxiliary systems—such as rear door opening when vehicle is moving—relay control, solenoids, and warning lamp operation. The TCM and VCM both communicate over the SAE J1939 CAN network with other control modules.

VCM system inputs include:

- Vehicle switches
- Shift selector input
- Brake pressure sensor
- System override requests

Outputs include:

- Accelerator pedal sensor supply
- Shift selector serial data link
- Dash indicator lamp control
- Main pressure boost solenoid commands
- Reverse warning
- Propulsion system inhibits
- Transmission boost solenoid

▶ TECHNICIAN TIP

Allison's EP pushbutton shift selector features transmission fluid level reading. High fluid levels cause transmission fluid to contact rotating parts, aerating the fluid. Aerated fluid is compressible, resulting in low hydraulic clutch application force, slipping, and overheating. The power inverters (DPIMs) also use transmission fluid for cooling and can easily be damaged by aerated or contaminated fluid and or low fluid levels.

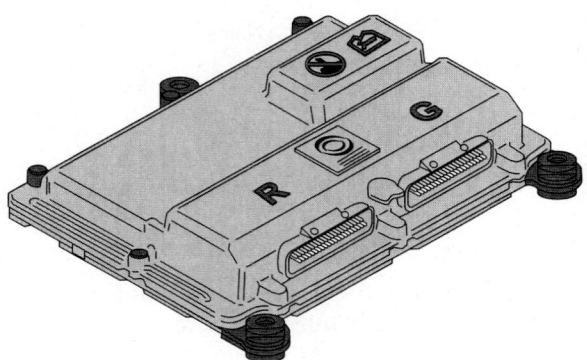

FIGURE 57-7 The transmission control module and vehicle control module are identical-looking modules. It functions exclusively to control and monitor transmission operation.

Image Courtesy of Allison Transmission.

Traction Motors

EP systems use two electric asynchronous induction motors operating on high-voltage, variable-frequency alternating current (AC). Both motors A and B are capable of continuously producing up to 100 hp (75 kw) and can rotate in either direction from 0 to 5000 rpm. Both motors are arranged concentrically around the transmission mainshaft, with the motor nearest the engine flywheel called Motor A, and the rear motor near the output yoke called Motor B (**FIGURE 57-8**).

The motor stator windings are pressed into the EV stator housing and the motor has two temperature-sensing thermistors embedded in the winding, which supply motor temperature data to the DPIM. For service reasons, only one sensor is connected to the DPIM. In the event one fails, the sensor wiring can be connected to the spare thermistor. A Hall-effect speed sensor is in each motor's housing. These sensors provide motor speed and direction data to the TCM. Motor A's role is to crank the engine during start-up and to supply torque to blend with Motor B. Two of the EV's three planetary gear sets (P1 and P2) are in Motor A's housing to enable these functions. Motor B supplies the initial traction force when accelerating from a stop. While in reverse, Motor B is the only source of torque. The third planetary gear set is located in Motor B's housing.

When the engine start button is depressed, motor speed and direction tests are performed before the engine cranks by applying a low power input to both motors.

In an **asynchronous AC motor**, the magnetic field in the rotor is induced by induction of the magnetic field in the stationary stator (**FIGURE 57-9**). This explains why asynchronous motors are sometimes called induction motors. In asynchronous motors, no brushes are used to supply current to the rotor like a DC motor. Instead, the continuously switching direction of AC-type current flow and corresponding magnetic field polarity in the stationary stator induces current flow in the rotor windings. Flow of current induced in the rotor, in turn,

FIGURE 57-8 Inside the Allison EV transmission there are two electric motors that are used in either of two driving modes; low-speed or high-speed operation. The rear motor, low speed, is shown here.

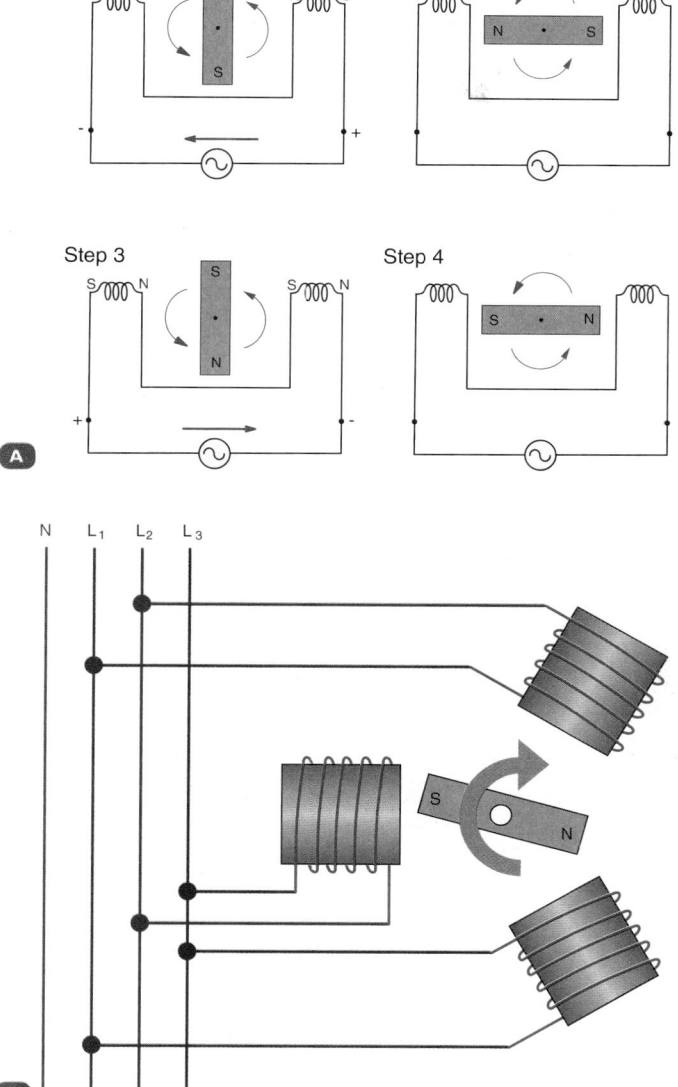

Step 1   Step 2

Step 3   Step 4

A

N   L₁   L₂   L₃

B

FIGURE 57-9 A. The change in the direction of AC flow through the stator windings switches its magnetic field poles. **B.** Constant change in the direction of AC flow in the stator also induces current flow in the rotor bars. Current passing through the rotor creates magnetic fields having the same polarity of the stators magnetic poles, according to laws of electromagnetic induction. Motor rotation is maintained by frequent switching of the stator and rotors magnetic poles. The strength of magnetic repulsion between the rotor and stator fields spins the motor at a speed proportional to the switching frequency of the AC polarity.

produces magnetic fields used for repulsion forces to rotate the motor rotor. Induction in both the rotor and stator takes place as the direction of AC flow moves from zero volts to peak volts in the stator winding. The sudden change and movement of the stator's magnetic field induces current flow in the rotor winding. Because AC continuously switches direction, the stator current moves from peak volts in a positive direction to zero and then to peak volts in the negative direction. The effect of the change in direction of current flow produces a magnetic field of

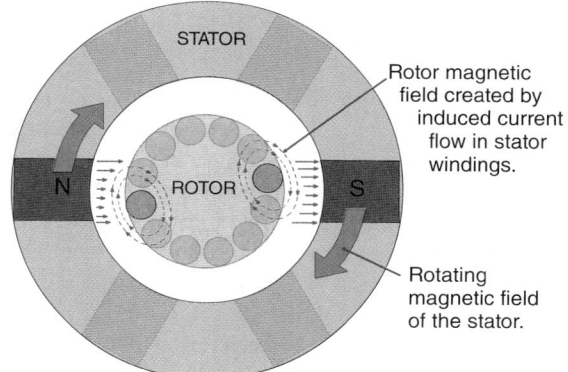

A End view showing the magnetic interaction between the stator and two rotor segments.

FIGURE 57-10 A. Three-phase motors can rotate in either direction, depending on the electrical connection to the stator. **B.** By changing which phase of three, first receives the zero-to-peak-positive wave, the position of the magnetic poles established control over the direction of rotor movement.

the opposite polarity in the rotor. Asynchronous AC motors can use wire-wound or solid conductor bars in the rotor, but solid bar conductors, which are commonly laminated soft iron, are most commonly used (**FIGURE 57-10**).

► TECHNICIAN TIP

To control vehicle movement when the vehicle is stopped on an uphill grade in forward range, the EP limits rotation of the output shaft to a near zero vehicle speed. It accomplishes this by applying reverse torque through the drive motors when the throttle is at idle stop and no service brakes are applied.

► TECHNICIAN TIP

To simulate feedback of a conventional automatic transmission using a torque converter, creep torque is applied at closed throttle, with the service brake unapplied. Creep torque is limited to 5 mph (8 kph) and creates the impression of using a conventional powertrain system.

Energy Storage System

LO 57-3 Explain the function of the energy storage system (ESS).

The **energy storage system (ESS)** function is to store and supply direct current energy for the electric drive system (**FIGURE 57-11**). Electrical energy to charge the ESS is generated by both drive motors during regenerative braking and from Motor A in mode one when not in use for propulsion. Only 40% of the electrical energy to accelerate the bus originates from regenerative braking—the remaining energy originates from the engine.

The state of charge (SOC) of the ESS is carefully controlled to maintain energy levels for accelerating but, more importantly, to maintain a buffer to allow adequate battery capacity to absorb energy during regenerative braking. This means that, under most conditions, ESS batteries are never fully charged, so battery capacity is available to store energy. Without the charge buffer to absorb energy, regenerative braking cannot be used, as it would damage the batteries through overcharging. Extra friction brake wear would take place, too. One advantage of using NiMH batteries instead of other batteries is the ability of the NiMH battery to be charged and discharged repeatedly without significantly shortening its service life cycle (**FIGURE 57-12**).

If the ESS SOC is reported to be too high, Motor A is run in the opposite direction of the engine's rotation at idle to dissipate excess stored energy. Under these conditions, the TCM requests the engines ECM to command the exhaust brake to close, creating high engine exhaust back pressure, which converts more electric motor energy into heat and rotational force.

ESS Construction

The ESS battery tub contains 240 NiMH modules weighing under 1000 lb (455 kg) operating at a voltage range of 432–780 VDC. To achieve this voltage from a 1.2-volt NiMH cell, 40 cells are arranged to form a module. Two modules are connected to form a subpack. Two parallel connected subpacks form a substring having approximately 312 VDC. Six battery substrings form the battery group of approximately 624 VDC enclosed in separate enclosed housing called a tub. A battery control

FIGURE 57-11 The energy storage system (ESS) consists of nickel-metal hydride (NiMH) batteries connected in series and parallel used to supply electric current to the motor and absorb electrical energy produced during regenerative braking.

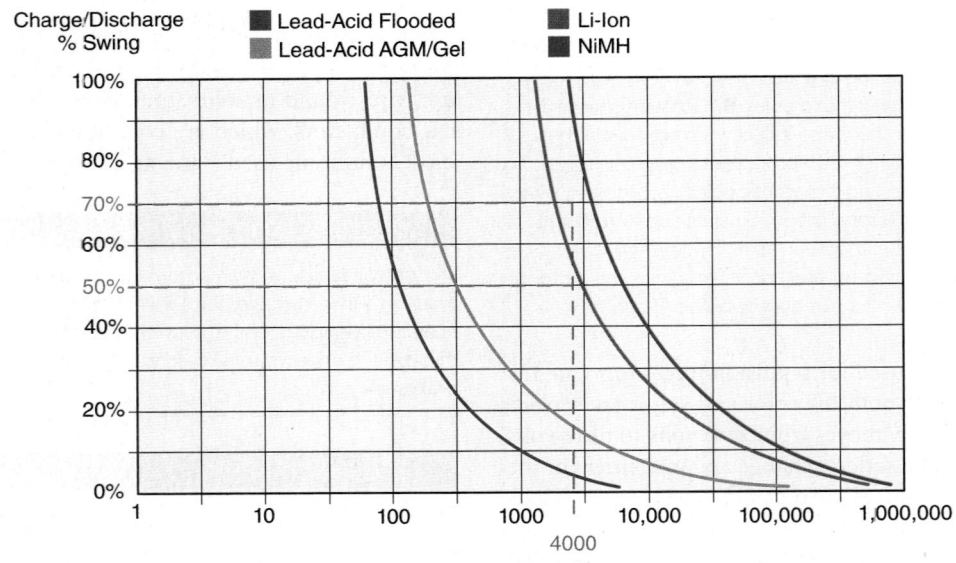

FIGURE 57-12 Note one advantage of NiMH batteries is the ability to be charged and discharged repeatedly without a shortened life cycle.

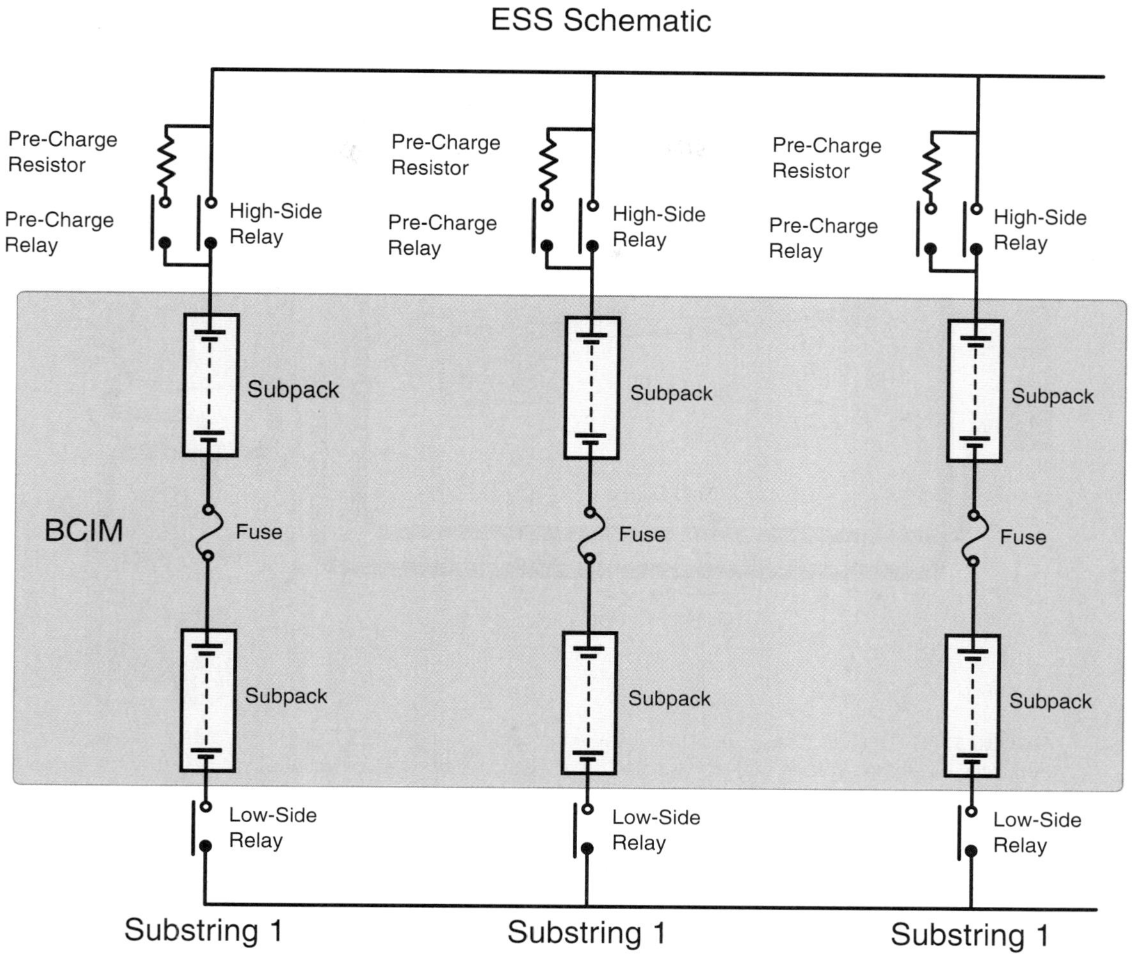

ESS Schematic

Pre-Charge Resistor   Pre-Charge Resistor   Pre-Charge Resistor

Pre-Charge Relay   High-Side Relay   Pre-Charge Relay   High-Side Relay   Pre-Charge Relay   High-Side Relay

BCIM

Subpack   Subpack   Subpack

Fuse   Fuse   Fuse

Subpack   Subpack   Subpack

Low-Side Relay   Low-Side Relay   Low-Side Relay

Substring 1   Substring 1   Substring 1

FIGURE 57-13 Schematic overview of the ESS and pre-charge relays used to gradually increase current into the DPIM.

interface module (BCIM) monitors each subpack operation and condition by measuring voltage and temperature. Data from the BCIM is reported over the CAN to the TCM module, which processes data regarding SOC, temperature, cooling fan status, and diagnostic information, such as fault codes.

The TCM provides to the ESS overall system control and battery protection strategies. Since charge and discharge cycles produce heat, each subpack is fan cooled. Under excessive heat conditions, a refrigerant line to an auxiliary AC cooler can be opened to reduce inlet air temperature to the batteries. To service individual subpacks, three plastic blocks connecting cables to the batteries are used to break the current path to battery substrings. High-voltage DC energy passes through the ESS tubs through two high-voltage connections, one positive polarity and one negative polarity. **FIGURE 57-13** shows a schematic representation of the substrings.

Dual Power Inverter Module (DPIM)

DPIM Function and Construction

The main function of the **dual power inverter module (DPIM)** (**FIGURE 57-14**) is to convert energy from the ESS into ACs used to power the variable frequency drive motors and AC produced during regenerative braking into DC current to charge the

FIGURE 57-14 The Dual Power Inverter Module (DPIM) is a DC-AC and AC-DC electronic wave inverter used to power the EP drive propulsion system and charge the batteries in the Energy Storage System (ESS).

batteries. To vary motor torque and speed, the DPIM also functions to vary the frequency and voltage of the AC. As current in and out of both motors is controlled by the DPIM, two identical wave inverters are found in the DPIM housing, each dedicated to a motor (**FIGURE 57-15**).

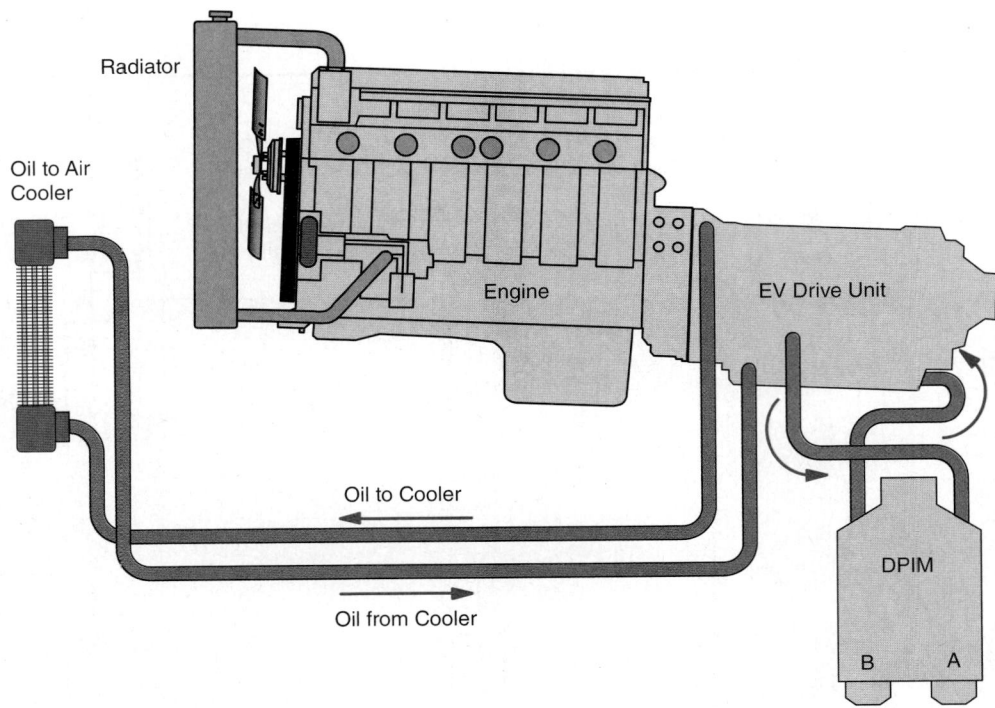

Radiator

Oil to Air Cooler

Engine

EV Drive Unit

Oil to Cooler

Oil from Cooler

DPIM

B   A

FIGURE 57-15 The DPIM has two identical wave inverters to convert ESS DC to high-voltage, varying-frequency AC. A high-voltage cable for each phase of AC connects to each motor carrying varying voltage and frequency AC to independently operate motors. Note the oil cooling of the DPIM.

A specialized field effect transistor (FET), called an **insulated gate bipolar transistor (IGBT)**, inverts DC to three-phase, variable-frequency, and variable-voltage AC. IGBTs are commonly used in many home appliances and sound amplifiers, which are fast-switching, voltage-controlled power transistors capable of handling current in the order of hundreds of amperes while blocking voltages up to 6000 volts. Heat generated by the IGBT is absorbed by heat sinks on each transistor and then removed by transmission fluid circulating around the heat sink.

The DPIM receives signals from the TCM over the CAN commanding motor torque and ESS current flow. Two microcontrollers for each inverter contain the necessary logic to control DPIM operation, run self-diagnostics, and communicate with the TCM. Three low-voltage connectors power and communicate with the DPIM, and three high-voltage connections for each phase of AC are made to the DPIM.

A high-voltage DC positive and negative cable for the DPIM is connected to the ESS. These high-voltage circuits are isolated for use by the ESS and DPIM only and are not connected to any other positive, negative, or ground circuit. For safety reasons, DPIM self-diagnostics capabilities continuously monitor the high-voltage DC circuits to ensure they remain isolated from the vehicle chassis.

DPIM Operation

A sudden in-rush of DC into the DPIM from the ESS can damage the DPIM. To enable a gradual build-up of current in the DPIM, a pair of relays located on each battery substring and a current-limiting resistor regulates current build-up and charging of a large voltage smoothing capacitor inside the DPIM. A fuse is also used in the DPIM to prevent catastrophic damage from over-current situations. During the one-half-second start-up period, the DPIM passes through three operating conditions:

1. Initial state—All battery relays are open, and no current flows into or out of the ESS (**FIGURE 57-16**).
2. Pre-charge state—The battery pre-charge relay and the low-side relays are closed, allowing current to flow through the pre-charge resistor, which slowly increases voltage to charge the DPIM capacitor (**FIGURE 57-17**).
3. Operational state—Voltage to the DPIM reaches 400 volts in 200 milliseconds, achieving 85% of ESS voltage. The high-side relays close and pre-charge relays open to allow full voltage to the DPIM (**FIGURE 57-18**).

If a significant voltage difference is measured between the ESS and the DPIM, fault is logged. This indicates that the pre-charge sequence failed, and the engine will not crank. Voltage in the DPIM must fall to zero during shut down, eliminating safety hazards in the system.

To dissipate any residual charge in the DPIM or on the DC bus after the unit is switched off, DPIM current passes through a 10-KΩ resistor bank inside the DPIM, which is also connected to the motor stator windings that turn current to heat.

During shut down, the EV drive shift selector remains illuminated for several seconds while the TCM saves the system-adaptive and diagnostic information from the last key-on event.

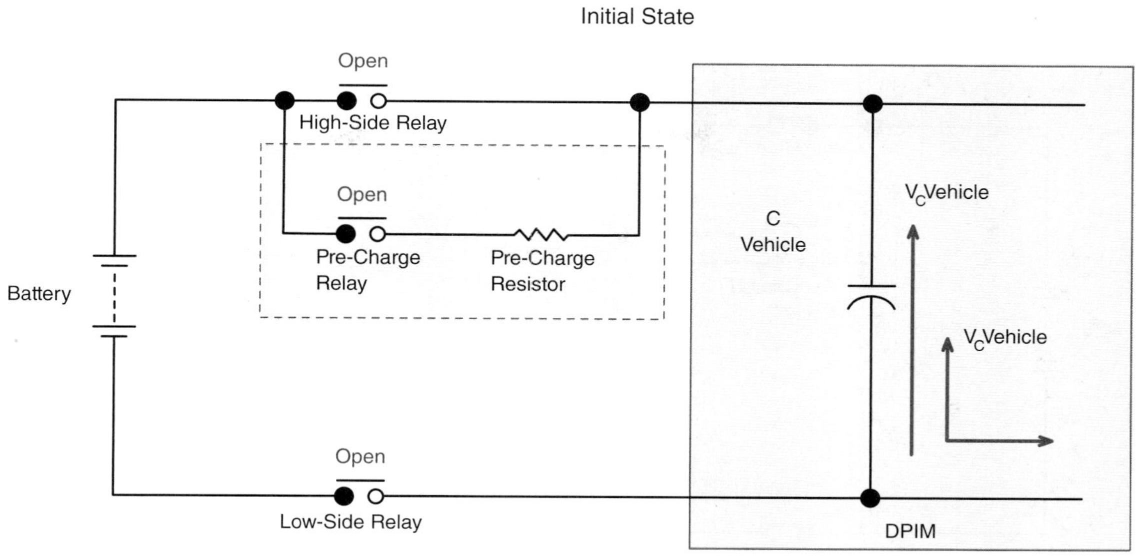

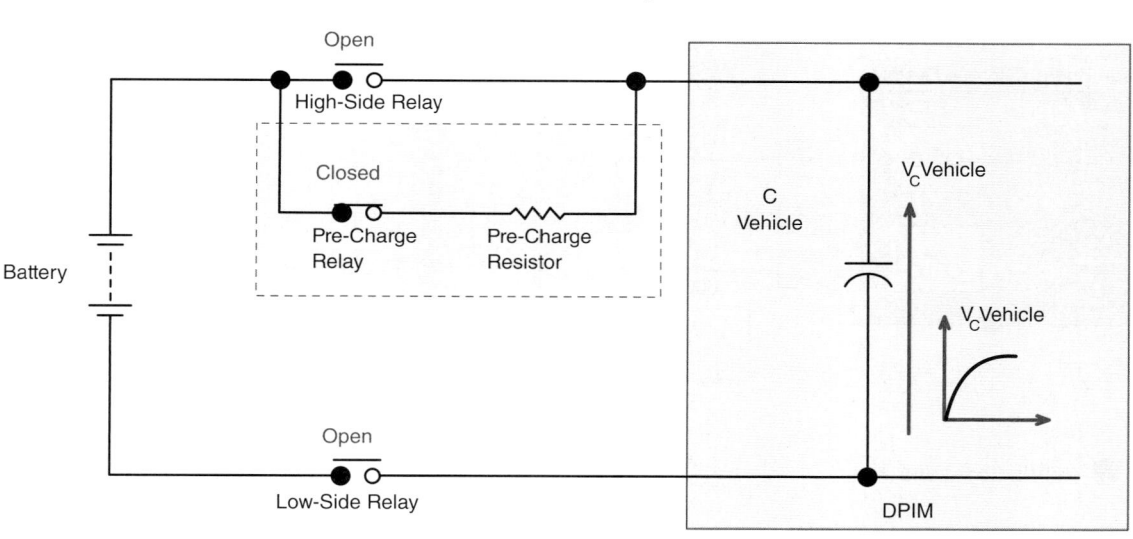

FIGURE 57-16 All relays are open during initial state, and no current flows to the DPIM to charge an internal capacitor.

FIGURE 57-17 In the pre-charge state, the pre-charge relay and low-side relays close, allowing current to flow through resistors and slowly charge the DPIM.

Once information is stored and the charge depleted, the shift selector display goes out, indicating the system shut-down sequence is complete.

High-Voltage Interlock Loop (HVIL)

The Allison EP uses a **high-voltage interlock loop (HVIL)** to prevent access to potentially hazardous energized electrical circuits (**FIGURE 57-19**). The HVIL consists of a 12-volt relay control circuit connected in series to switches on cover plates located on all hybrid components where potential electrical hazards exist. When any switch in a HVIL circuit is detected as open during ignition key-on, the pre-charge sequence does not take place. The engine does not crank, and the STOP SYSTEM lamp remains illuminated.

An open HVIL circuit detected during forward or reverse operation logs fault codes, but does not result in an active system shutdown. However, while passing through neutral position between forward and reverse, the fault results in system shut down.

SAFETY TIP

The HVIL disconnects power from the ESS to the DPIM, but it is not to be relied on to disable the high-voltage system. Turning the ignition key off powers down the system. Specific procedures to disconnect high-voltage connections are described in OEM training programs and are to be followed before any system work is performed. Always treat the high-voltage electrical system as if it is powered on. Make sure vehicle ignition is switched off, and always follow the electrical disconnect or isolation verification procedure before performing any service work where a potentially hazardous electrical current may exist.

Operational State

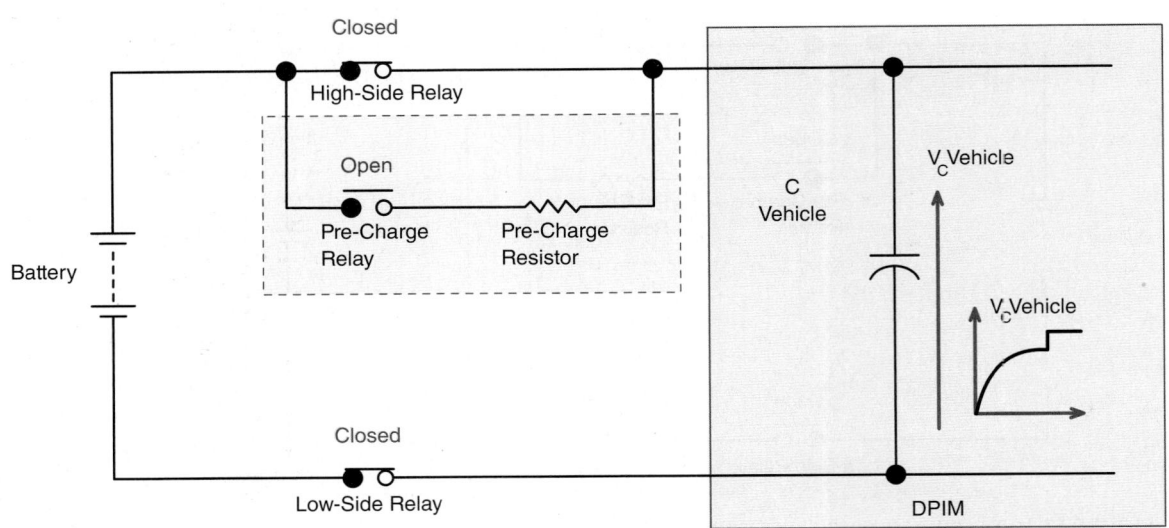

FIGURE 57-18 In the operational state, both high-side and low-side relays are closed, allowing 85% of total ESS voltage to reach the DPIM.

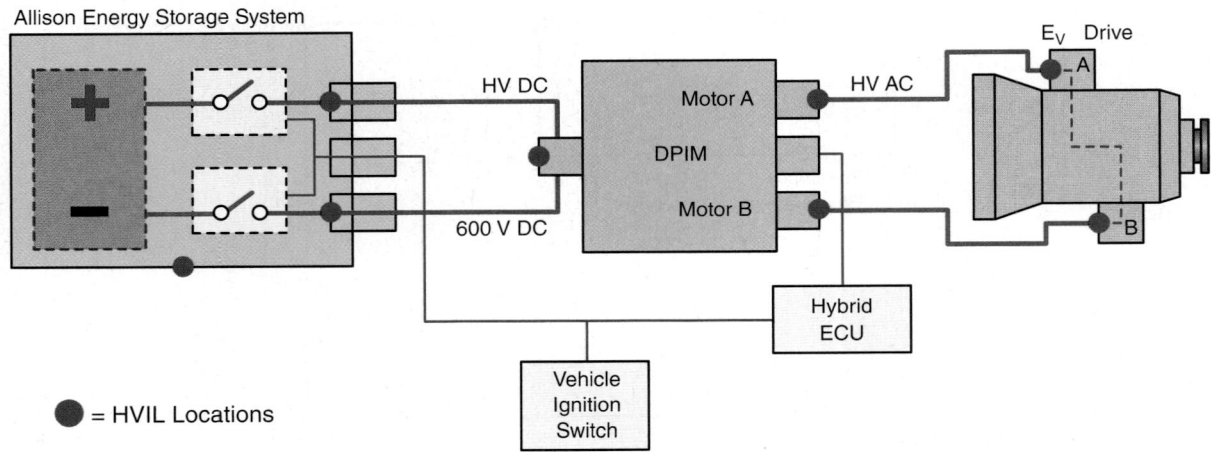

FIGURE 57-19 High-voltage interlock loops are switches that prevent the pre-charging of the DPIM if any access cover is open to potentially energized circuits.

Operating Modes

LO 57-4 Describe the operating modes of parallel hybrids.

Parallel hybrids can operate in various modes; for example, the capability to operate in "hush" mode. This electric-only operation minimizes noise when operating in sound-sensitive areas and eliminates emissions when operating in places like long tunnels.

Split-Mode Operation

The EP system has two forward modes of operation. **Mode 1** is for low-speed operation and **Mode 2** for high-speed operation. Generally, the EP control maintains Mode 2 operation until vehicle speed is under 20 or 25 mph (32 to 40 kph), at

which point it switches to Mode 1. Initially, only Motor B is used to accelerate the vehicle from rest. However, torque from the engine and Motor A is blended to supplement torque from Motor B in Mode 2. Blending torque from the motors and engine together is referred to as **compound split operation**. Exactly when the EV shifts between modes, or which torque inputs it uses, varies based upon specific measured conditions, such as the throttle position, programmed acceleration rate, available battery current, and vehicle speed. Three planetary gear sets and two hydraulic clutches operating under electronic control of the TCM and VCM function to obtain engine-motor torque blending and forward and reverse operating modes. The split between mechanical and electric torque, EV gear ratios, and torque ratios are continuously adjusted by the TCM until maximum power output is reached. Torque blending algorithms programmed into the TCM calculate the most efficient combination to obtain best performance and lowest fuel consumption by adjusting engine speed and torque, motor speed and torque, and current consumption from power stored in the ESS batteries. **FIGURE 57-20** illustrates the differences in acceleration between the Allison hybrid and a conventional diesel engine.

Dual-Mode Hybrid Drive

Although most hybrid systems today are designed for start-stop applications, Meritor produces a **dual-mode hybrid drivetrain** specifically designed for line haul trucks. The Meritor dual-mode hybrid drivetrain uses a relatively simple operating principle, combining both mechanical and electrical propulsion systems.

At speeds under 48 mph (77 kph), torque for vehicle propulsion is produced entirely by an electric motor supplied with current from lithium-ion batteries. At speeds in excess of 48 mph (77 kph), the drivetrain transitions to a diesel-engine power system, supplemented occasionally with the electric motor providing torque during hill climbs or passing—situations similar to a parallel hybrid system. Like other newer hybrid systems, the Meritor uses Li-ion batteries that are recharged through regenerative braking because the motor, located in series with the driveline, can switch to generation mode.

The advantages of this dual-mode system include the following:

- Fuel efficiency—Savings through regenerative braking.
- Stop-start fuel savings—Eliminates fuel consumption and emissions when vehicle is not in motion.
- Full electric, zero-emission mode in emission restricted areas.
- The electrification of accessories (e.g., air or air conditioning compressors)—Provides further efficiency benefits, as batteries can supply continuous power during overnight rest periods, thereby eliminating the need for engine idling or other additional anti-idling systems.
- Smaller engines—Motors can supply additional acceleration boost on grades and start-up.
- Silent-mode operation.

EP System Maintenance

LO 57-5 Outline basic service and maintenance procedures for Allison EP drive systems.

Transmission service is the primary area for maintenance in EP system. To protect passengers and technicians from shock hazards, the EP systems use an isolation fault detection monitor to identify high-voltage circuit shorts to the vehicle chassis. Various DTCs are logged when the isolation resistance between the high-voltage circuit and the chassis ground is measured at less than 50 million ohms. These fault codes are displayed on the push button shift selector (PBSS) display and illuminate the hybrid-electric vehicle (HEV) fault lamp.

Warning Lights

A check system warning light alerts the operator that an EP system fault has occurred, but does not lead to a system de-rate or shut down (**FIGURE 57-21**). However, a stop system warning light indicates the propulsion system shut down with a 30-second warning period.

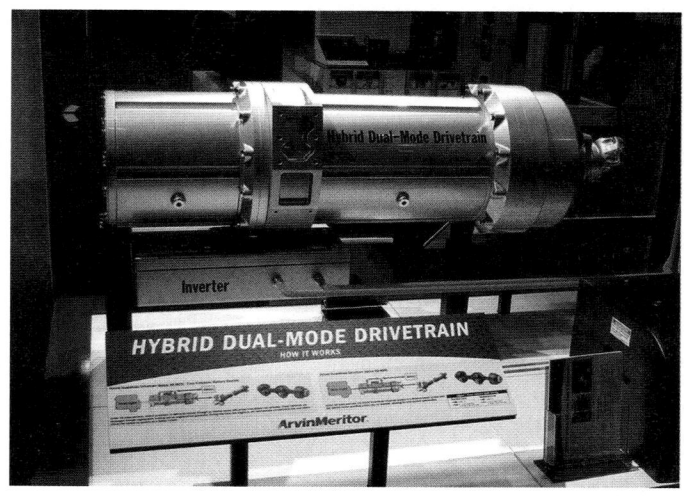

FIGURE 57-20 The ArvinMeritor dual-mode hybrid system acts as a series hybrid below 48 mph (77 kph) and as a parallel hybrid at speeds above 48 mph (77 kph).

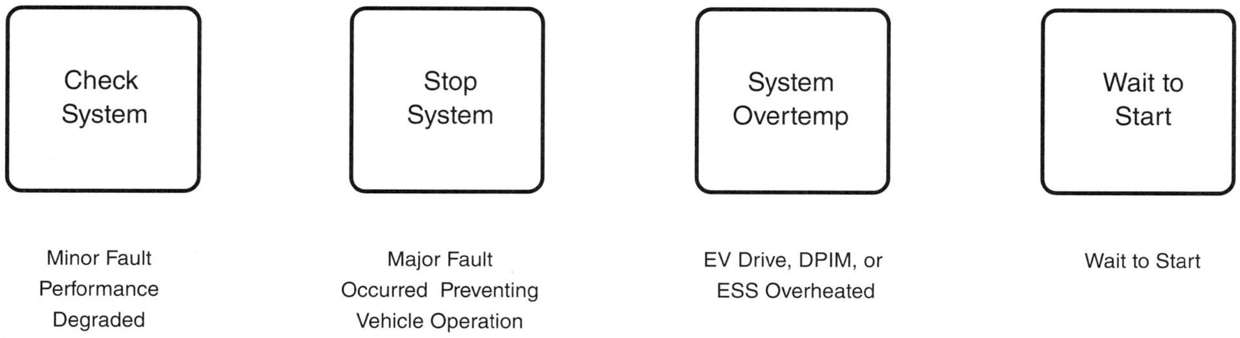

Check System	Stop System	System Overtemp	Wait to Start
Minor Fault Performance Degraded	Major Fault Occurred Preventing Vehicle Operation	EV Drive, DPIM, or ESS Overheated	Wait to Start

FIGURE 57-21 Diagnostic warning lights for the EP system.

A system over-temperature warning light alerts the operator when any of the EP system components are outside normal heat ranges. Over-heat conditions result in reduced performance or system shut down.

Allison DOC Service Tool

The personal computer (PC)-based service software for the EP system is called **Allison DOC**. (DOC is an abbreviation for diagnostic optimized connection.) Allison DOC can display logged fault codes, record snap shot data of operating conditions for later playback, and display system operating conditions in real time. The TCM contains a number of self-diagnostic routines that monitor the EP system sensors, solenoids, and speed ratios to validate that these devices are operating correctly.

Allison DOC can access and run these diagnostic routines as well. Similarly, the DPIM and ESS controllers perform diagnostic tests not conducted by the TCM, which are initiated by Allison DOC too.

Diagnostic Code Display

DTCs can be viewed and cleared using the PBSS display. DTCs are displayed in the sequence in which they were logged into the TCM. All codes consist of OEM-unique four-digit codes displayed as a two-digit main code followed by a two-digit subcode with more specific information about the system area where the fault has occurred. For example, the first two digits may indicate an electrical short to ground while the last two digits indicate a hydraulic pressure sensor wire.

Oil Filtration

Four separate hydraulic filters are in the EP drive transmission in the system. The filters include the:

- Suction filter screen
- Control main filter
- Trim solenoid filters
- Transmission fluid filter

Wrap-Up

Ready for Review

- Parallel drive and series-parallel drive are two common configurations of Allison EV/EP Drive Hybrid Systems used in heavy-duty commercial vehicles.
- Allison makes one of the most common series-parallel hybrids.
- Allison describes the hybrid architecture as a two-mode compound-split system that allows for only electric or only a diesel engine for traction power and an infinitely variable combination of both.
- Its automatic transmission does not used fixed gear ratios. Instead, the power continuously varies from the engine and two electric motors when the vehicle is driving in a forward direction.
- Real-world comparisons of the EP system to the series HybriDrive system show that EP offers slightly greater reduction in fuel consumption compared to the series only HybriDrive system operated on an identical route.
- Allison EV drive systems consists of an EV drive transmission unit, transmission control module (TCM), vehicle control module (VCM), traction motors, energy storage system (ESS), and a dual power inverter module (DPIM).
- The EV drive transmission unit provides a pathway for transmitting electric motor or engine torque (or a blend of both) using three planetary gear sets.
- The EV drive transmission unit includes several modules: an input housing module, main (stator) housing module, control valve assembly/oil pan module, clutch housing module, and rear cover module.

- Most of the EP system operation is directly controlled by the transmission control module, which collects input signals to determine electrical outputs controlling the EV transmission operation.
- The TCM and VCM both communicate over the SAE J1939 CAN network with other control modules.
- EP systems use two electric asynchronous motors operating on high-voltage, variable-frequency AC.
- In an asynchronous AC motor (also called an induction motor), the magnetic field in the rotor is induced by induction of the magnetic field in the stationary stator.
- The state of charge of the ESS is carefully controlled to maintain energy levels for accelerating. Therefore, under most conditions, ESS batteries are never fully charged, so battery capacity is available to store energy.
- The ESS battery tub contains multiple battery modules arranged in groups of 40 cells to create a module. Two modules are connected to form a subpack; two subpacks connected in parallel form a substring; and six substrings form the battery group.
- A battery control interface module (BCIM) monitors each subpack operation and condition by measuring voltage and temperature.
- The main function of the DPIM is to convert energy from the ESS into ACs used to power the variable frequency drive motors. To vary motor torque and speed, the DPIM also functions to modify the frequency and voltage of the AC.
- During the one-half second start-up period, the DPIM passes through three operating conditions: initial state, pre-charge state, and operational state.

- ▶ The Allison EP uses a high-voltage interlock loop (HVIL) to prevent access to potentially hazardous energized electrical circuits.
- ▶ Parallel hybrids can operate in various modes; for example, hush mode, split mode, or dual mode.
- ▶ Hush mode minimizes noise and eliminates emissions.
- ▶ Split mode involves two forward modes of operation—one for low-speed operation and one for high-speed operation.
- ▶ The Meritor dual-mode hybrid drivetrain uses a relatively simple operating principle, combining both mechanical and electrical propulsion systems.
- ▶ Allison EP systems use an isolation fault detection monitor to identify high-voltage circuit shorts to the vehicle chassis.
- ▶ Diagnostic trouble codes (DTCs) are displayed in the sequence in which they were logged into the TCM.
- ▶ Warning lights include a check system light, a stop system light, and an over-temperature light.
- ▶ The PC-based service software for the EP system is called Allison DOC. It can display logged fault codes, record snap shot data of operating conditions for later playback, and display system operating conditions in real time.

Key Terms

Allison DOC PC-based service software for Allison's EP system.

asynchronous AC motor A motor in which the magnetic field in the rotor are induced by frequently switching current polarity in the stator windings.

compound split operation Blending torque from the motors and engine together.

dual-mode hybrid drivetrain A hybrid system that combines both mechanical and electrical propulsion systems.

dual power inverter module (DPIM) Allison's control module responsible for converting energy from the ESS into alternating current used to power the electric traction motors.

energy storage system (ESS) A battery system that stores and distributes electrical current to the various components of a hybrid drive system.

EP40 system and EP50 system Models of Allison's Electric Propulsion system. Also known as *Allison's Electrically Variable (EV) Drive.*

high-voltage interlock loop (HVIL) A device that prevents access to potentially hazardous energized electrical circuits.

insulated gate bipolar transistor (IGBT) A three-terminal power semiconductor device primarily used as an electronic switch.

Mode 1 In split-mode operation, the mode that is for low-speed operation.

Mode 2 In split-mode operation, the mode that is for high-speed operation.

smart electrification A feature that enables the EP 40/50 system's motors to switch over to generating mode to produce as much as 300 amps at 24 volts at idle.

traction motor An electric motor that provides propulsion to a vehicle.

Review Questions

1. How many gear ratios does the Allison EP hybrid transmission have?
   a. 3
   b. 5
   c. 6
   d. It has infinite ratios.
2. How many hydraulic clutch packs does the Allison EV drive transmission have?
   a. 2
   b. 3
   c. 4
   d. 5
3. How many planetary gear sets does the Allison EV drive transmission have?
   a. 1
   b. 2
   c. 3
   d. 4
4. The Allison EP 40 and EP 50 Hybrid systems propel the vehicle with which of the following?
   a. An electric motor only
   b. Two electric motors
   c. An electric motor and an internal combustion engine working together at all times
   d. An internal combustion engine at some times, and an electric motor at others, or a combination of the two
5. What is used to cool the Allison EP HybriDrive DPIM?
   a. Air
   b. Transmission fluid
   c. Engine oil
   d. Engine coolant
6. How many traction motors are used by the Allison EP 40 and 50 HybriDrive system?
   a. 1
   b. 2
   c. 3
   d. 4
7. Which of the following describes an asynchronous AC induction motor?
   a. The magnetic field in the rotor is induced by the stator.
   b. The magnetic field in the rotor is produced by electrical current supplied through brushes.
   c. The magnetic field in the stator is induced by the rotor.
   d. The magnetic field in the stator is produced by electrical current supplied through brushes.

8. How much horsepower is produced by the Allison EP 50 HybriDrive system?
   a. 180 hp
   b. 230 hp
   c. 280 hp
   d. 330 hp

9. What is meant by smart electrification when discussing the Allison EP HybriDrive systems?
   a. The traction motors can generate electricity at idle.
   b. The traction motors produce electricity during braking.
   c. The alternator is shut off when it is not needed.
   d. The starter is powered by the hybrid batteries.

10. How many battery modules are in the Allison EP drive Energy Storage System?
    a. 40
    b. 140
    c. 240
    d. 340

ASE Technician A/Technician B Style Questions

1. Technician A says that the Allison EP drive hybrid systems are series-parallel systems. Technician B says that the Allison EP drive can operate as a parallel system if required. Who is correct?
   a. Technician A
   b. Technician B
   c. Both Technician A and Technician B
   d. Neither Technician A nor Technician B

2. Technician A says that the Allison EV drive transmission has one electric traction motor. Technician B says that the Allison EV drive has three planetary gear sets. Who is correct?
   a. Technician A
   b. Technician B
   c. Both Technician A and Technician B
   d. Neither Technician A nor Technician B

3. Technician A says that the battery modules used in the Allison EP system contain 40 cells of 1.2 volts each. Technician B says that the energy storage system has 40 battery modules. Who is correct?
   a. Technician A
   b. Technician B
   c. Both Technician A and Technician B
   d. Neither Technician A nor Technician B

4. Technician A says that traction motors used in the Allison EP hybrid system use DC voltage. Technician B says that the Allison EP hybrid energy storage system operates at a voltage range of 432 to 780 VDC. Who is correct?
   a. Technician A
   b. Technician B
   c. Both Technician A and Technician B
   d. Neither Technician A nor Technician B

5. Technician A says that the DPIM converts AC to DC. Technician B says that the DPIM converts DC to AC. Who is correct?
   a. Technician A
   b. Technician B
   c. Both Technician A and Technician B
   d. Neither Technician A nor Technician B

6. Technician A says that the Allison EP hybrid system has two modes of operation—Mode 1 and Mode 2. Technician B says that, in the Allison EP system, Mode 2 is for low-speed operation. Who is correct?
   a. Technician A
   b. Technician B
   c. Both Technician A and Technician B
   d. Neither Technician A nor Technician B

7. Technician A says that the Allison EV drive transmission has six forward ratios. Technician B says that the Allison EV drive transmission has five hydraulic clutches. Who is correct?
   a. Technician A
   b. Technician B
   c. Both Technician A and Technician B
   d. Neither Technician A nor Technician B

8. Technician A says that Allison EP hybrid systems are capable of logging fault codes when a problem occurs. Technician B says that Allison EP hybrid system fault codes are two-digit main codes followed by a second two-digit subcode. Who is correct?
   a. Technician A
   b. Technician B

   c. Both Technician A and Technician B
   d. Neither Technician A nor Technician B

9. Technician A says that the Allison EP 40 and 50 save more fuel when compared to the BAE Hybri Drive system. Technician B says that the late-model Allison transmission EV drive can generate electricity at idle. Who is correct?
   a. Technician A
   b. Technician B
   c. Both Technician A and Technician B
   d. Neither Technician A nor Technician B

10. Technician A says that the Allison EP hybrid system uses information from up to 12 microcontroller-based ECUs to function. Technician B system the TCM is the most important microcontroller-based ECUs for the EV drive operation. Who is correct?
    a. Technician A
    b. Technician B
    c. Both Technician A and Technician B
    d. Neither Technician A nor Technician B

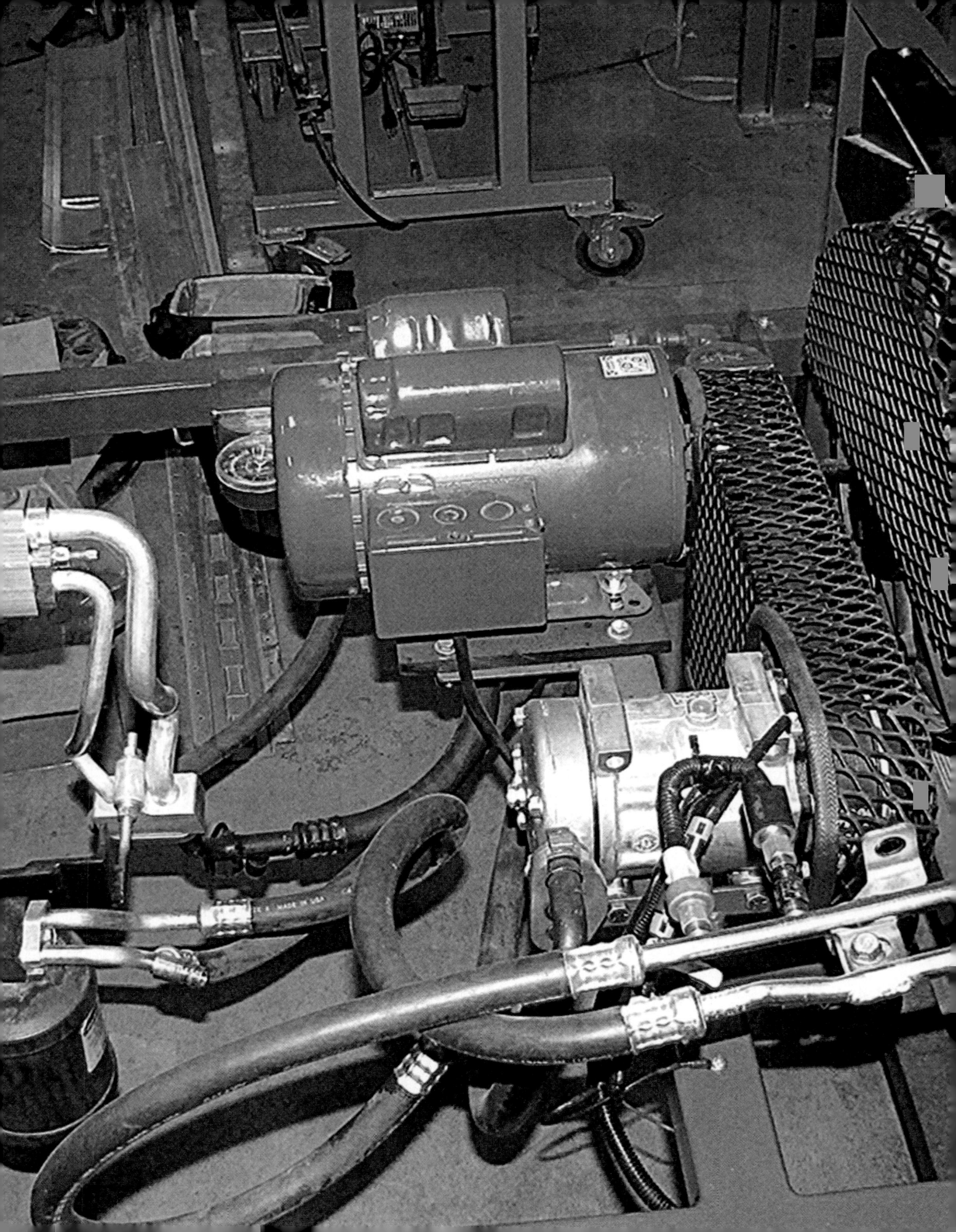

SECTION 5
Heating, Ventilation, and Air Conditioning

CHAPTER 58   Principles of Heating and Air Conditioning
Systems

CHAPTER 59   Servicing Heating and Air Conditioning
Systems

CHAPTER 60   Trailer Refrigeration

CHAPTER 58

Principles of Heating and Air Conditioning Systems

Learning Objectives

After reading this chapter, you will be able to:

- **LO 58-1** Describe the development of air conditioning systems.
- **LO 58-2** Identify and describe the benefits of air conditioning systems.
- **LO 58-3** Identify and describe air conditioning components and explain their operating principles.
- **LO 58-4** Describe the basic refrigeration cycle.
- **LO 58-5** Describe the purpose and operation of refrigeration system components.
- **LO 58-6** Explain the operating principles of a thermal expansion valve (TXV) air conditioning system.

- **LO 58-7** Identify and explain the function of the evaporator.
- **LO 58-8** Identify and explain the function of the receiver-dryer.
- **LO 58-9** Identify its purpose and explain the function of refrigerant oil.
- **LO 58-10** Identify and explain the purpose of air conditioning controls.
- **LO 58-11** Describe the function of the air conditioning protection and diagnostic system (APADS).
- **LO 58-12** Describe the function of the air distribution system.

You Are the Technician

The driver of a late-model highway tractor is complaining that the truck's air conditioning system blows warm air with increasing frequency. Some days it works well, and other days it begins to blow warm air after an hour or so of good operation. After verifying that the driver understands how to properly operate the air conditioning system, you attempt to verify the complaint and find that the air conditioning system is operating correctly. Air conditioning system pressures are within normal limits, and all fan and vent controls work properly. After checking the service manual for the air conditioning system to identify more detailed diagnostic strategies, you learn the vehicle uses an air conditioning protection and diagnostic system (APADS) common to many heavy-duty (HD) vehicles. Using the driver's information display located in the instrument panel, you access fault codes from the climate control system module and find there is a low-voltage code for the air conditioning compressor clutch. Before you undertake further diagnostic steps, consider the following:

1. Why would the low-voltage fault code cause intermittent operation of the air conditioning system?
2. How does APADS identifies low voltage to the air conditioning clutch compressor?
3. How is the function of an APADS-equipped air conditioning system restored after a fault is detected or a repair is made?

Introduction

Although air conditioning systems are now used almost universally in vehicles of all types, there was a time when mobile air conditioning installed in off-road equipment, trucks, coaches, and other heavy-duty (HD) commercial vehicles was considered by some to be strictly a luxury accessory to provide a more comfortable interior for a vehicle's operator and passengers. Furthermore, the relatively short hot-weather seasons in the extreme northern and southern hemispheres made it difficult to justify the expense and maintenance of an air conditioning system. Nonetheless, air conditioning systems offer important benefits that were finally realized.

This chapter introduces the basics of air conditioning systems, including how the refrigeration system works, the components of the system, the fluids used throughout the system, and system controls and diagnostics.

Development of Air Conditioning Systems

LO 58-1 Describe the development of air conditioning systems.

Air conditioning systems absorb heat from a cab or vehicle interior through an **evaporator** and transfers that heat to the atmosphere using a heat exchanger called a **condenser**. A refrigerant gas circulated through the air conditioning system by a pump, known as the compressor, absorbs cab heat and releases it to the atmosphere (**FIGURES 58-1** and **58-2**).

The challenge of creating an air conditioning system similar to the type used by modern commercial vehicles was solved in the 1920s with the development of efficient refrigerant compressors and safe refrigerants. Until then, earlier crude refrigeration systems pumped toxic, flammable gases, such as ammonia (NH_3), methyl chloride (CH_3Cl), and sulfur dioxide (SO_2), throughout the air conditioning system as refrigerants. Several fatal accidents occurred in the 1920s when methyl chloride leaked out of refrigerators. As a result, refrigerator owners began leaving their refrigerators in their backyards. A collaborative effort between three American corporations—Frigidaire, General Motors (GM), and DuPont—to search for a less dangerous method of refrigeration produced today's refrigeration systems. In 1928, Thomas Midgley, Jr., aided by Charles Kettering (Detroit Diesel engine developer, founder of Delco Electric, and president of GM) invented a "miracle compound" called **Freon**. Freon was produced by reacting carbon tetrachloride, commonly used as "carb-cleaner," with fluorine gas.

Development of Modern Refrigerants

Freon, a brand trademark name of DuPont Chemicals, is a colorless, odorless, nonflammable, and noncorrosive gas or liquid. Different types of Freon refrigerants were developed and were classified by DuPont as R-11, R-12, R-22, R-502, etc., based on various physical properties, such as their boiling point. Other names given to the same refrigerant made by other companies include Aircon 12, Genetron 12, Prestone 12, and Freeze 12. Because Freon was nontoxic, it eliminated the danger from refrigerator leaks. In just a few years, refrigerators using Freon became the standard for almost all home kitchens and, later, mobile air conditioning. However, decades later, it was discovered that the refrigerant's chlorine-based composition of a fluorine hydrocarbon compound, commonly called **chlorofluorocarbons (CFCs)**, damaged Earth's ozone layer.

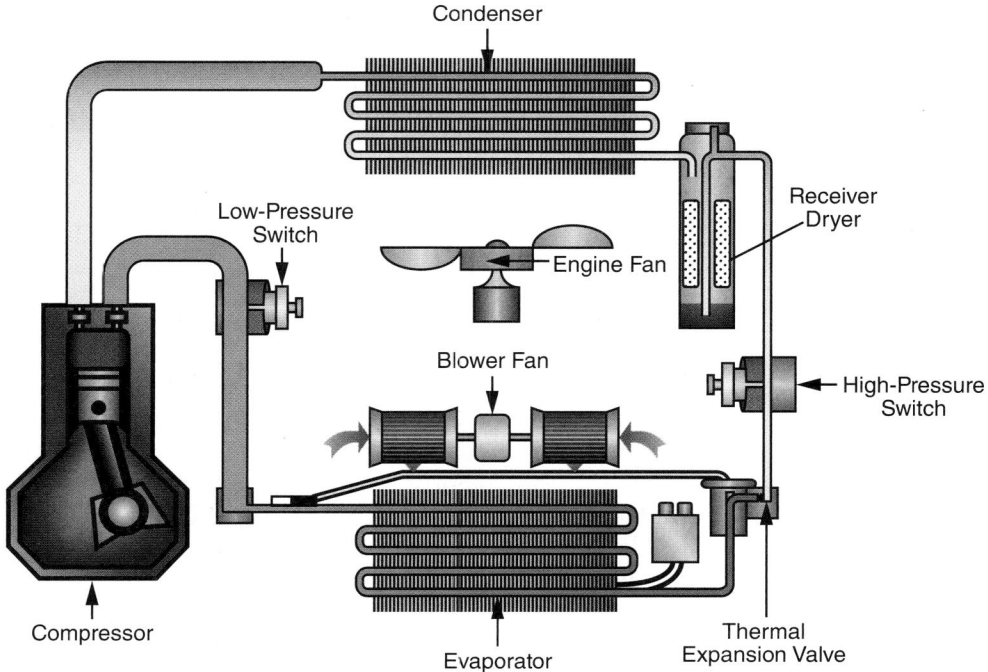

FIGURE 58-1 Typical layout of common HD mobile air conditioning system. The configuration results in safer and more efficient climate control.

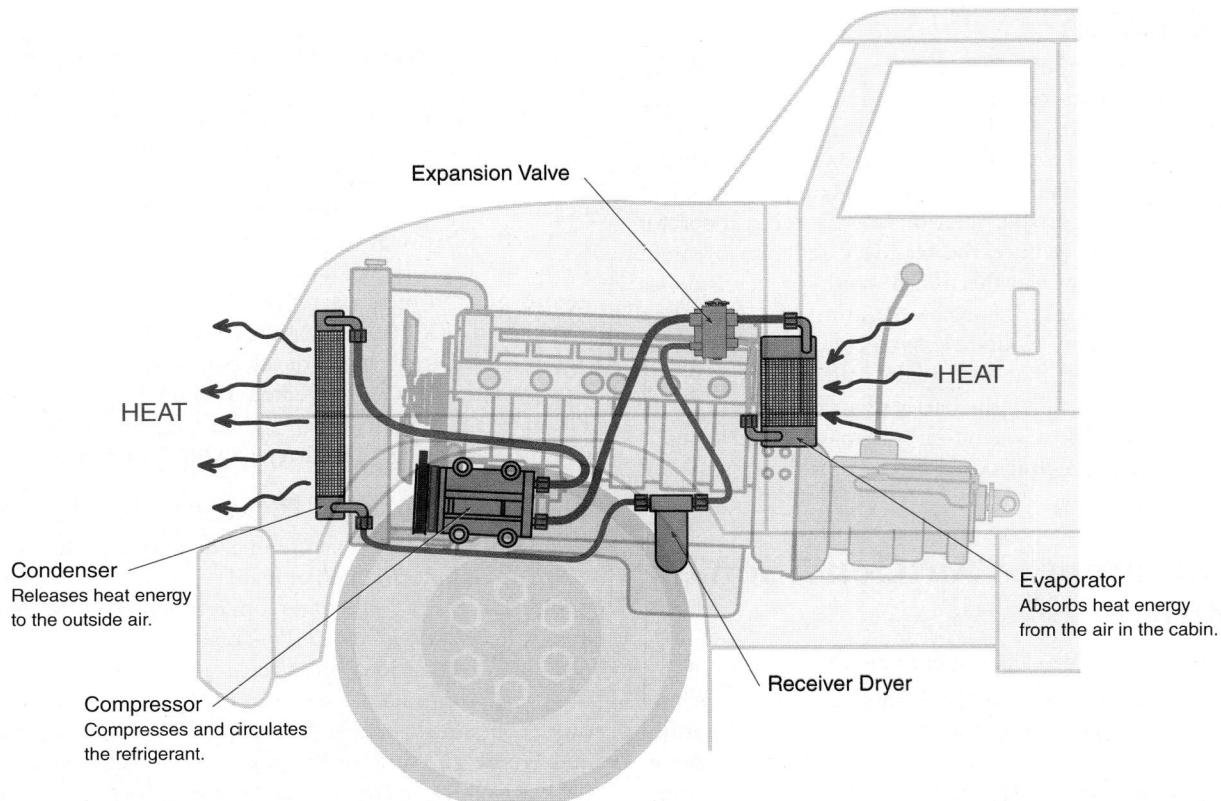

FIGURE 58-2 Basic components of an air conditioning system.

A replacement for Freon is R-134a, a hydrofluorocarbon (HFC), but even this refrigerant has ozone-depleting (ODP) and Global Warming Potential (GWP) properties. Most recently developed is HFO1234yf, a near drop-in replacement for the R134a refrigerant is a **hydrofluoro-olefin (HFO)**-based refrigerant. It has a GWP that is 99.7% lower than R134a. When released into the atmosphere, it quickly decomposes, giving it a lifetime of only 11 days, compared to 13 years for R134a and more than 500 years for CO_2 (carbon dioxide), another gas considered for replacing R-134a. Although refrigerants are relatively safe, they are suffocants, meaning they can displace oxygen in the air if an evaporator suddenly ruptured inside a vehicle.

Air Conditioning Benefits

LO 58-2 Identify and describe the benefits of air conditioning systems.

Heating, ventilation, and air conditioning (HVAC) systems as a feature in mobile applications came as an afterthought to manufacturers years after the first vehicles were invented. The expense of optional air conditioning was difficult to justify in the northern and southern hemispheres where it didn't operate year around. Today, however, almost 100% of all commercial vehicles are equipped with air conditioning systems.

Air Conditioning and Driver Fatigue

As a matter of safety, mobile air conditioning has tremendous benefits. A comfortable vehicle environment reduces driver fatigue and distraction, as high humidity and low airflow can increase the level of driver discomfort—even when the temperature level is held constant. The more comfortable the cab and the operator, the more safely and productively a vehicle can be operated. Consider that the temperature in an operator's cab can be as high as 149° F (65° C). Heat sources include solar heat that enters the cab through windows and body panels but cannot leave easily. Transmissions, engines, road surfaces, and exhaust heat can also enter the operator's compartment, driving up temperatures. Even the body heat of the operator and passengers can add to an already high temperature in the cab. Heat load, also called sun load, sensors are used in some air conditioning systems to measure the amount of heat from the sun potentially entering the cab.

Air Conditioning and Vehicle Safety

A second benefit of air conditioning in a commercial vehicle is found when weather and vehicle environmental conditions converge to increase cab moisture condensation on colder interior window surfaces. In these circumstances, the air conditioning system can operate to clear the windows with greater efficiency than a heated **defroster** alone. The evaporator, which is the cold surface of the air conditioning system that normally cools the cab, is positioned in parallel with the heater core airflow. Before moisture-laden outside or interior cab air reaches the heater core, the air conditioning system dehumidifies the air by causing moisture to condense on the cold surfaces of the evaporator (**FIGURE 58-3**). Warm, drier air is blown over the

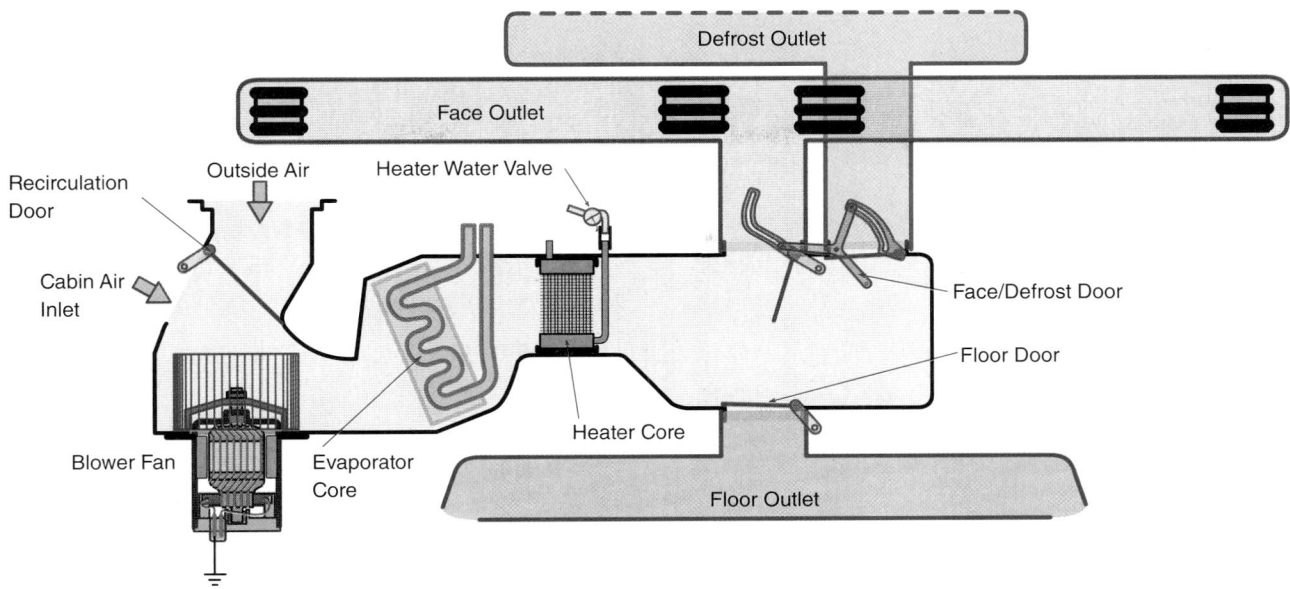

FIGURE 58-3 The evaporator is located before the heater core, in series with the core, which allows the air to be dehumidified before passing onto the windows in defrost mode.

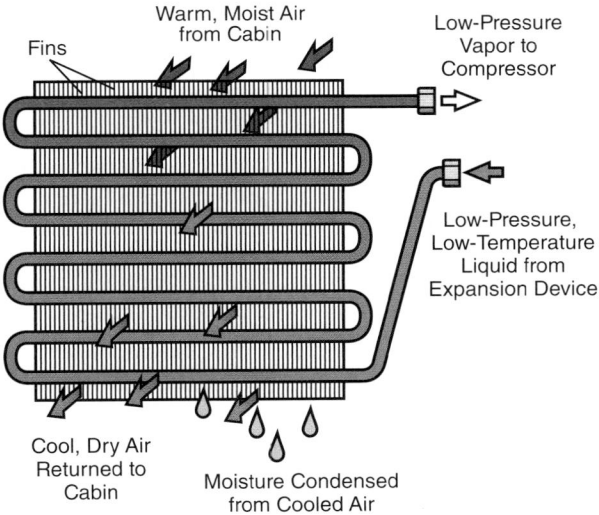

FIGURE 58-4 Moisture condensed on a cold evaporator helps remove dirt and other air particulates, which improves the quality of cabin air.

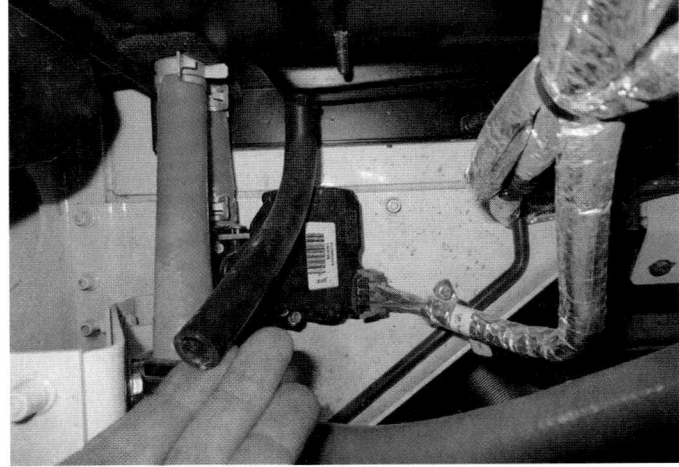

FIGURE 58-5 A drain tube in the bottom of the evaporator housing removes condensed water and dirt from the air system.

windows to improve visibility more quickly than airflow without prior dehumidification. A defroster and/or a dehumidification function to de-fog the windshield and interior windows in all motor vehicles is required by Federal Motor Vehicle Safety Standard (FMVSS) 103 (Canadian Motor Vehicle Safety Standard (CMVSS 103) motor vehicle safety standard legislation.

Air Conditioning and Respiratory Illness

A third safety benefit of air conditioning is its ability to clean and filter air entering the operator/passenger compartment. When operating equipment in a dusty environment—such as in underground mining, agriculture, and construction—operators

benefit from cleaner air in cabs equipped with air conditioning. For people with respiratory problems, an air conditioned cab environment can also reduce symptoms caused by dust, allergens, and air pollution. The air conditioning system removes dust, pollen, and particulate matter from the air by passing the incoming air over the damp evaporator. The dampness is produced by condensation of moisture in the air on the cold surfaces of the evaporator (**FIGURE 58-4**). Dirt and condensed moisture are purged from the evaporator through a drain in the bottom of the evaporator plenum (**FIGURE 58-5**). Today, most late-model vehicles are also equipped with an air filter located at the cab air inlet to help maintain a cleaner, dust-free cab interior (**FIGURE 58-6**).

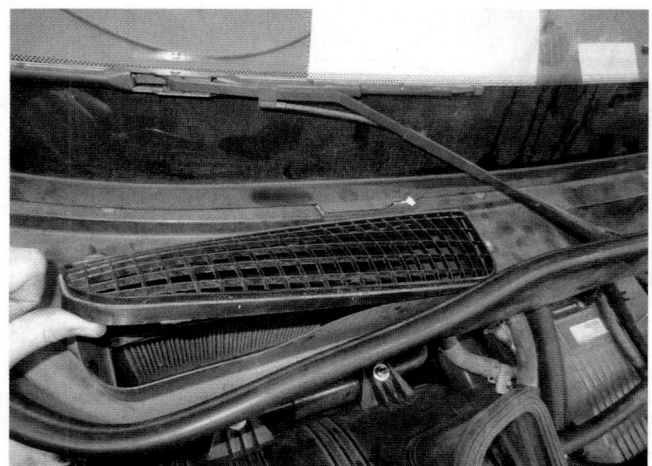

FIGURE 58-6 Many HD vehicles now use additional filter elements to clean air entering the vehicle cabin.

Air Conditioning Operating Principles

LO 58-3 Identify and describe air conditioning components and explain their operating principles.

Cabs in trucks and off-road machinery are hard to heat and cool. They have large glass areas and are not always well-insulated. Hot and cold weather directly affect the temperature inside the cab. This means that any air conditioning system must have the capacity to do a lot of heating and cooling. The ideal cab environment has a moderate humidity level and should reach a temperature of 70° F to 80° F (20° C to 27° C) within several minutes of operation. To maintain this comfortable temperature range for the driver and any passengers, most air conditioning compressors cycle on and off using thermostatic or pressure control switches. Heating is regulated by circulating engine coolant through an in-cab heat exchanger called a **heater core**. Both devices operate to maintain optimal temperature and humidity for a vehicle operator and any passengers.

Terms and Concepts Related to the Refrigeration Cycle

Like all forms of energy, heat can be transferred from one place to another. For example, the air conditioning system's evaporator removes heat from the cab and transfers it to the atmosphere via the condenser. The heater core uses engine coolant to transfer heat to the cab. In both of those situations, transfer cannot take place unless there is a difference in temperature between two objects. Furthermore, heat can only move from warmer to cooler objects. Therefore, when thinking about heat transfer, it's important to remember that there is technically no such concept as cold, only difference in heat energy between objects. Stated another way, cold is simply an absence of heat.

The amount of heat an object has can be observed in how much its molecules move or vibrate. More heat energy in a substance directly translates into increased movement or molecular vibration (Heat = Speed). Hotter molecules also move, or

vibrate, faster than cooler molecules. Heat transfer takes place from hot to cold because fast, hot molecules collide with cooler, slower molecules, transferring energy into the cooler molecule, thereby speeding up its movement. A slow molecule cannot make a fast molecule move faster any more than a slow truck can collide with a fast bus to make it go faster.

Terminology of Heat Movement

Heat transfer takes place in three ways in a vehicle's **heating ventilation and air conditioning (HVAC) system**:

1. **Conduction** takes place when heat is transferred through a solid, such as a body panel, the metal fins of a condenser, or an evaporator.
2. **Convection** refers to the transfer of heat through a gas. For example, convection takes place when a denser, heavier, colder gas, such as air, displaces a lighter, less dense, warmer air, causing the air to move and circulate.
3. **Radiant heat transfer** takes place through a medium, such as a gas or vacuum, but the medium itself does not heat up. For example, sunlight penetrates a windshield and heats surfaces inside the vehicle, but does not heat the air; warm surfaces do that. Heat from the sun is transferred to Earth through space by radiant heat.

Terminology of Heat Measurement

Heat is measured in a number of different ways. Probably the most familiar measurement of heat uses a thermometer. Heat measured using a thermometer is referred to as **sensible heat** because it is heat that can be sensed or felt. Ambient air temperature is an example of a measurement of sensible heat.

Another common measurement of heat is **latent heat**, which describes the quantity of heat required to produce a change of state from a solid to a liquid or a liquid to a gas. Latent heat cannot be measured with a thermometer, so it is often described as hidden heat. For example, to change water into ice (change its state), it is necessary to remove heat energy. The process of changing water to ice is called **latent heat of fusion**. There is also **latent heat of vaporization** and **condensation** (**FIGURE 58-7**). The processes of removing and adding heat energy form the basis of refrigeration.

Finally, a third common heat measurement is the calorie, which is the basic unit for measuring the quantity of heat energy. A **calorie** is an International System of Units (SI) or metric term for the amount of energy required to raise the temperature of 1 gram of water by 1° C. **Specific heat** is the amount of heat a substance must absorb to undergo a temperature change of 1° F. A more familiar term for heating and air conditioning is the measuring unit of **British thermal unit (BTU)**. One BTU (252 calories) is the amount of energy required to heat or cool 1 pound of water 1° F (**FIGURE 58-8**), and 144 BTU are required to change 1 pound of water to 1 pound of ice or vice versa. 12,000 BTU/h equals 1 ton of refrigeration (TR), which is the amount of heat required to change one ton of ice to water in 24 hours. **TABLE 58-1** compares different heating and cooling capacities.

Most truck air conditioning units commonly transfer between 20,000 and 40,000 BTU/h from the cab to

Latent Heat
of Vaporization →

212° F

Latent Heat
of Condensation ←

32° F

0° F

+16 BTU | +144 BTU | +180 BTU | +970 BTU

Ice   Water   Steam

FIGURE 58-7 When a substance changes state, much more heat is required than changing its temperature a few degrees.

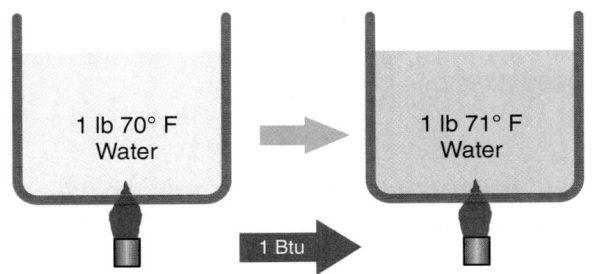

1 lb 70° F
Water → 1 lb 71° F
Water

1 Btu →

FIGURE 58-8 One BTU is the amount of energy required to heat or cool 1 pound of water 1° F.

TABLE 58-1 Order of Magnitude for Different Amounts of Heating

Unit	Equivalent
1 BTU	252 calories Amount of energy required to heat 1 lb of water 1° F
144 BTU	Amount of energy required to change 1 lb of water into 1 lb of ice (or melt 1 lb of ice completely)
12,000 BTU/h	1 ton of refrigeration (TR) Amount of energy needed to change 1 ton of ice to water in 24 hours
20,000–40,000 BTU/h	1.6–3.3 TR Common refrigeration capacity of air conditioning systems on medium-sized house and heavy-duty trucks
110,000–126,000 BTU/h	9.2 TR Common refrigeration capacity of air conditioning systems on school and transit buses
50,000–80,000 BTU/h	Common heating capacity of heating systems on heavy-duty trucks
126,000 BTU/h	Common heating capacity of heating systems on transit buses and medium-sized homes

the atmosphere. This is equal to 1.6–3.3 TR. For comparative purposes, an air conditioner for a medium-sized home likely has between 1.5 and 2.5 TR capacity. Those systems may require several hours to reduce the temperature inside a home by 10 to 20 degrees, whereas the truck lowers the same interior temperatures in just a few minutes. Air conditioning units for highway coaches and transit buses have a cooling capacity in excess of 110,000 BTU/h using multiple evaporators. Much higher capacity is needed, as each passenger emits approximately 580 BTU of heat per hour. In addition to the body heat from passengers, heat enters through open doors as passengers enter and exit a transit bus. Added to that heat load is radiant heat from the sun entering through the large areas of glass and engine heat that's conducted through the coach body.

The heating capacity of a truck's heating system is between 50,000 and 80,000 BTU/h, with buses exceeding 126,000 BTU/h, which is approximately the same as an average heating furnace of a medium-sized home (**FIGURE 58-9**). Smaller electric auxiliary air conditioning units used by on-highway tractors supply between 6000 and 15,000 BTU/h (**FIGURE 58-10**). These units enable major reductions in engine idle time needed to keep a cab and bunk heated or cooled. The units also help drivers comply with anti-idle laws during rest breaks when cab heating and cooling are still needed (**FIGURE 58-11**).

Temperature and Pressure Relationships

The concept of temperature is related to pressure. The force with which molecules strike the sides of a container is directly proportional to the container's temperature, as the speed of molecular moment or vibration is related to temperature. Higher temperature produces greater molecular speed.

FIGURE 58-9 Buses typically do not produce enough engine heat at idle or low loads to supply enough heat for passengers. Auxiliary coolant heaters burn fuel to heat passenger compartment coolant.

FIGURE 58-10 An auxiliary air conditioning unit can reduce idle time by using an electrically operated compressor like the one shown here.

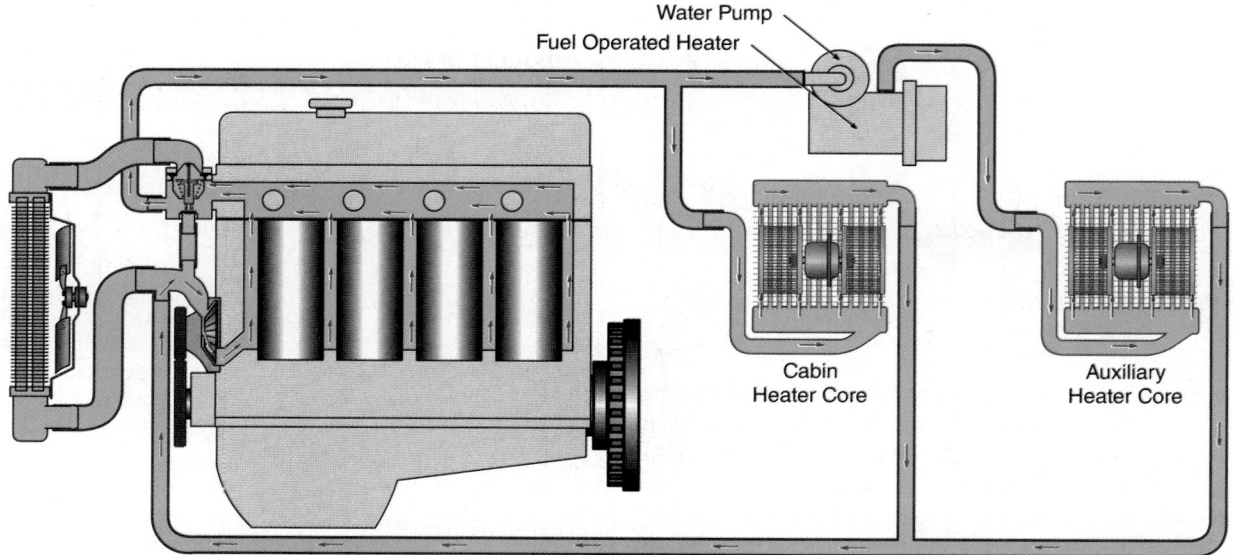

FIGURE 58-11 Auxiliary heaters and air conditioning units allow the engine to remain off and maintain cab temperature.

This concept is observed in the combustion cycle of a diesel engine where compressing air produces higher cylinder temperatures (**FIGURE 58-12**). In a similar way, lowering the pressure of a fixed volume of gas reduces its temperature. Technicians commonly experience this effect using air tools. Cold air exhausts from an air tool if the compressed air driving the tool is at room temperature when it is pressurized.

Pressure is measured using a variety of units, but common units used in HVAC are pounds per square inch (psi) or kilopascals (kPa). Pressure gauges report pressure measurement using two different reference points—atmospheric pressure called gauge pressure (psig) and a complete vacuum called absolute pressure (psia). When a gauge is calibrated to atmospheric pressure for a reference point, it reads 0 psi (0 kPa) in a room when not connected to a source of pressure. This means a gauge

pressure of 0 at a room pressure is actually 14.7 psi (97 kPa) when room pressure is compared using an absolute vacuum for a reference point, and the units for pressure for this type of gauge are **psig** indicating psi, gauge (kPaG, kPa gauge). A gauge that uses an absolute vacuum as a reference point is calibrated to read 14.7 psi (97 kPa) at sea level. This gauge reference is called absolute and the units are **psia** for psi absolute (kPaA, kPa absolute). Typically, pressure measurements above atmospheric pressure are considered to be gauge pressures, and pressures below atmospheric pressure are considered absolute pressures.

Temperature, Pressure, and State

Boiling points of liquids are affected by the pressure exerted upon them (**FIGURE 58-13**). (That is why cooling systems use radiator caps to increase cooling system pressure and boiling point.)

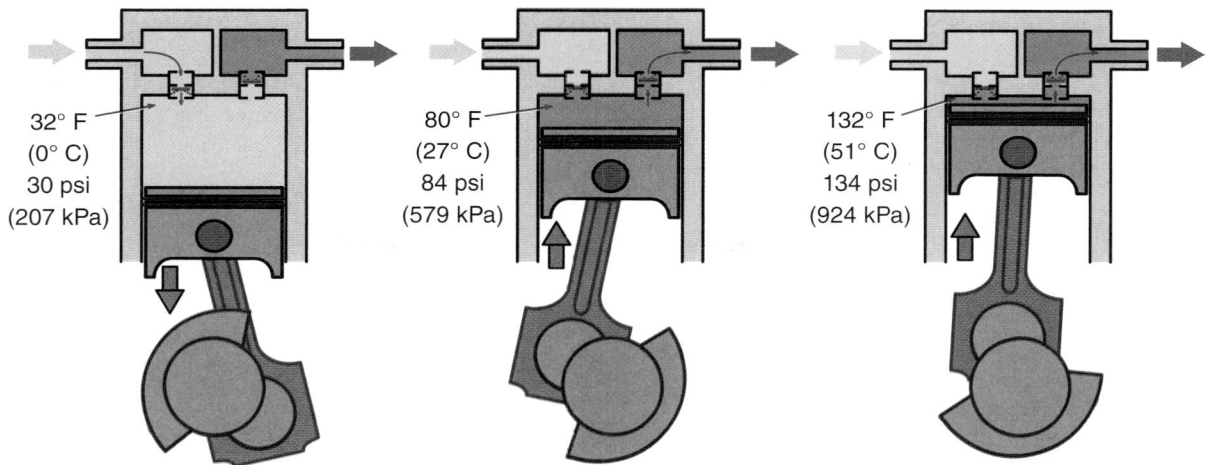

FIGURE 58-12 Compressing a gas increases its temperature.

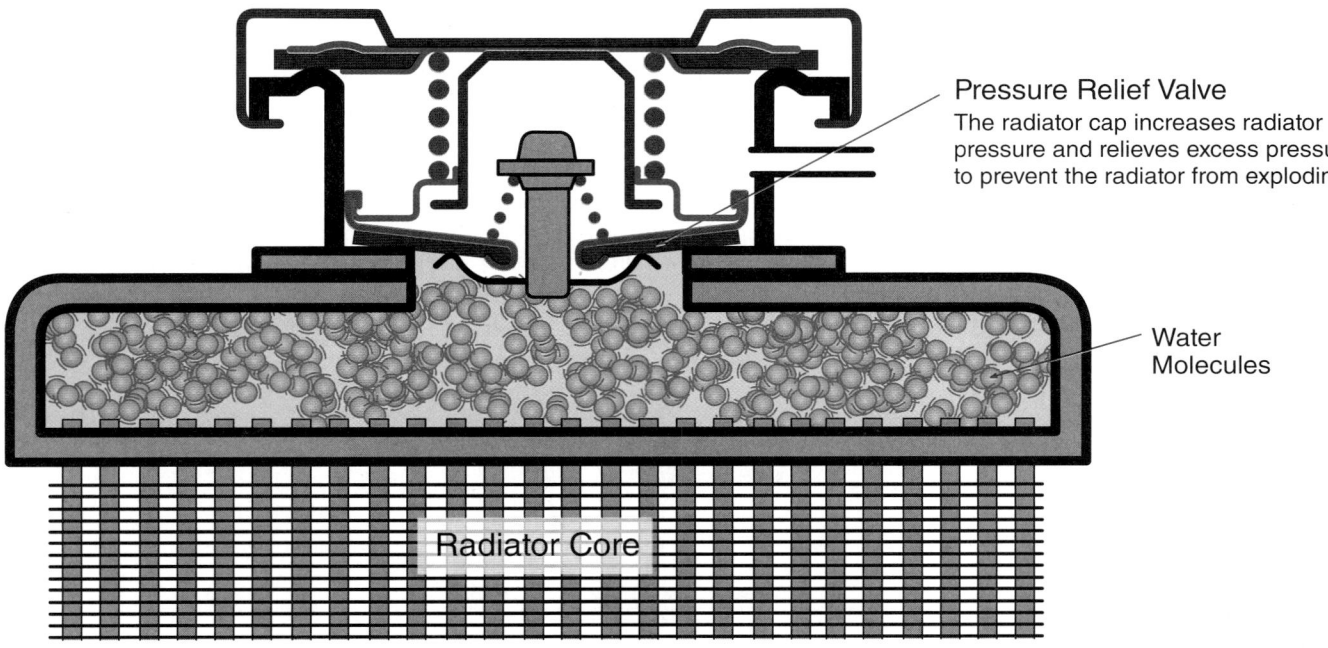

Pressure Relief Valve
The radiator cap increases radiator pressure and relieves excess pressure to prevent the radiator from exploding.

Water Molecules

Radiator Core

Pressure in the radiator prevents the water vapor from expanding.

FIGURE 58-13 Increasing the pressure in the cooling system also increases the boiling point of the coolant.

There is also a direct relationship between the boiling point of a liquid and the pressure exerted on the liquid's surface. For example, water at sea level boils at 212° F or 100° C. At higher altitudes, however, the boiling point drops because lower pressure allows the molecules to move more vigorously. Denver, Colorado, sits at an altitude of 1 mile (1.6 km) above sea level, and water there has a boiling point of 203° F (95° C). The cooling system of an engine takes advantage of this principle by pressurizing the radiator to increase the boiling point of coolant. For every 1-psi increase in cooling system pressure, there is a 3° F increase in the boiling point. A 10-psi radiator cap does not allow coolant to boil over until it reaches 242° F (10 psi × 3° F = 30° F; 30° F + 212° F = 242° F). Increasing the boiling point of engine coolant keeps the coolant as a liquid, which can cool more effectively than water vapor.

Simply changing the pressure of a liquid allows a change of state to take place. This principle is used to remove water from air conditioning systems after they have been opened to the atmosphere. Evacuating air from the system, which reduces the pressure applied to water, causes any moisture in the system to boil at room temperature. Therefore, changing refrigerants back and forth between a gas and liquid state is accomplished simply by compressing a gas refrigerant or lowering the pressure of a liquid refrigerant.

Latent Heat of Evaporation and Condensation

One more important point to understand about the relationship between pressure, temperature, and state of matter is that to obtain a change in state—solid to liquid or liquid to gas, and vice versa—requires much more heat than is required simply to increase the temperature by a single degree. For example, it only requires 140 BTU of heat to increase the temperature of 1 lb (450 g) of water from room temperature to 212° F (100° C). To change the same amount of water into a vapor or steam having a temperature of 212° F (100° C) requires 970 BTU. Conversely, changing steam to water or water to ice requires removal of the same amount of heat (**FIGURE 58-14**). When a liquid or vapor changes state and requires removal or addition of heat, even though a tremendous amount of heat transfer takes place, there is no change in sensible heat. Ice and water can exist at the same temperature, likewise water and steam. Remember that heat removed or added without a change in temperature is called latent heat.

The following four rules help summarize the basic principles of refrigeration:

- **Rule 1**—To refrigerate is to remove heat. The absence of heat is cold.
- **Rule 2**—Heat can pass into anything that has less heat. Nothing can stop the movement of heat; the transfer of heat can only be slowed down.

- **Rule 3**—If a change of state is to take place, there must be a transfer of heat. For a liquid to change to a gas, the liquid must absorb heat. Heat is removed from a liquid through vapor. For a vapor to change into a liquid, the vapor must give up heat. Heat is always transferred to a cooler surface or medium.
- **Rule 4**—All refrigeration systems use two principles to move heat from one place to another. Latent heat of vaporization is used to absorb large amounts of heat inside the cab or passenger compartment. Latent heat of condensation is used to release large amounts of heat outside in the condenser. The evaporator absorbs heat; the condenser releases heat.

Basic Refrigeration Cycle

LO 58-4 Describe the basic refrigeration cycle.

Removing heat from an object or substance is simple. Because heat always moves toward a colder object, all that is necessary for cooling is to provide an even colder substance for heat to flow into. Consider adding ice cubes to a warm drink. The warmer liquid becomes cooler as heat from the beverage flows into the colder ice. As the ice cubes absorb the liquid's heat and melt, the liquid's temperature drops. Getting sprayed with water on a warm day removes heat in a similar way. Water sprayed against the skin absorbs heat and converts to a vapor, which takes heat with it. As water gets warmer while in contact with the skin,

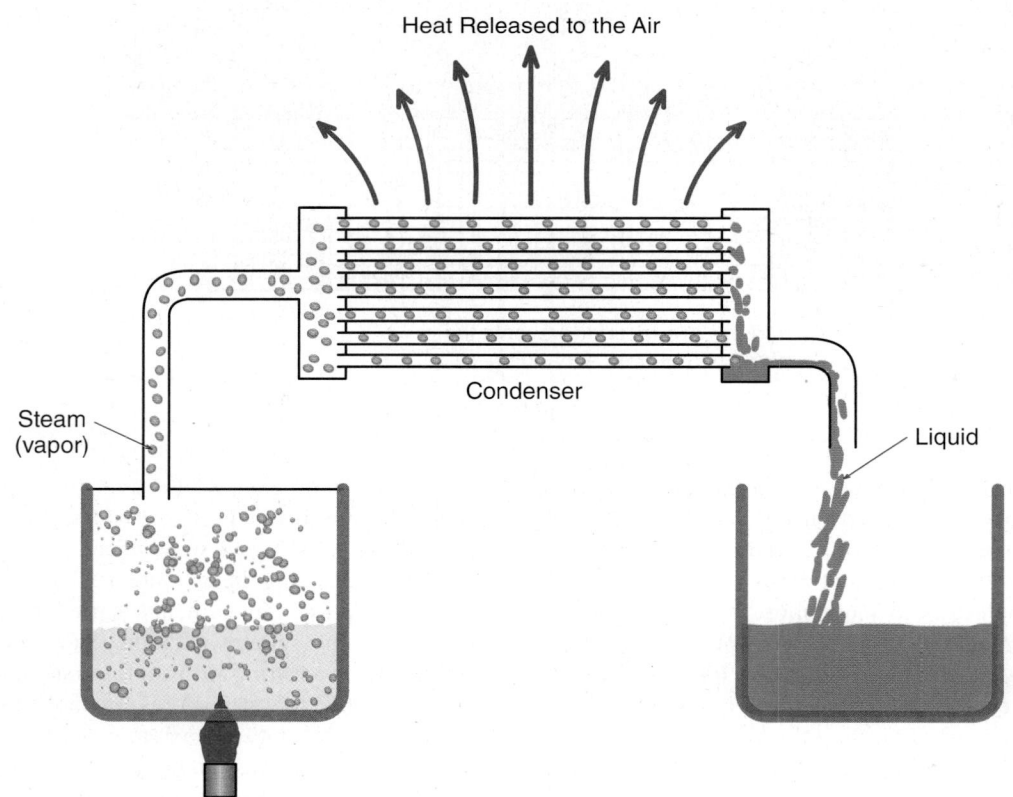

FIGURE 58-14 Changing state requires the addition or removal of heat.

evaporation takes place, and the skin becomes cooler. The process of removing heat through evaporation is called latent heat of evaporation.

Latent Heat of Evaporation

The same principles of heat transfer apply to cooling the interior of a vehicle. A liquid refrigerant is placed in a metal-finned evaporator inside the vehicle. Reducing the pressure of the refrigerant causes the refrigerant to want to boil, or convert to a vapor. However, heat is required for the refrigerant to change into a vapor. Cabin air is the best source of heat, and so the physical properties of the refrigerant liquid enable it to absorb heat and boil. Evaporating the refrigerant is no different than evaporating water from skin—instead of removing heat from the skin, the refrigerant removes heat from the air surrounding the evaporator. Cooler cabin air results from the heat transfer into the evaporating refrigerant. The process of evaporating refrigerant using the latent heat properties of refrigerant to absorb heat from the air removes an enormous amount of heat. Since the liquid does not simply change temperature but changes state, much more heat is absorbed by the refrigerant.

To build an efficient air conditioning system, though, a process of continually evaporating the refrigerant is required, as is another separate process to remove heat from the refrigerant.

Latent Heat of Condensation

Once again, using a process where the refrigerant can change state transfers much more heat than only changing the refrigerant's temperature a few degrees. Using a refrigerant compressor and a condenser, which is a type of heat exchanger, enables the process of latent heat removal from the refrigerant through condensation. The compressor pulls vaporized refrigerant from the evaporator and compresses it once again to increase its temperature. Compressing the gas and sharply increasing its pressure causes the refrigerant to physically convert into a liquid (**FIGURE 58-15**). If the compressed gas is circulated through a condenser, large amounts of latent heat are transferred from the gas to the atmosphere as the gas changes to a liquid.

Refrigeration System Components

LO 58-5 Describe the purpose and operation of refrigeration system components.

Air conditioning and refrigeration systems transfer heat from the cab and passenger compartment to the air stream outside the vehicle. They also remove moisture from the air passing through the evaporator and channel it to a drain leading outside the vehicle.

The refrigeration system operates in a closed loop. This means the refrigerant is used over and over again as it circulates through the system. A typical mechanical refrigeration system consists of the six principle parts shown in **FIGURE 58-16**:

- Compressor with an electric on/off clutch
- Condenser
- Expansion device
- Evaporator
- Receiver-dryer or accumulator
- Refrigerant and oil

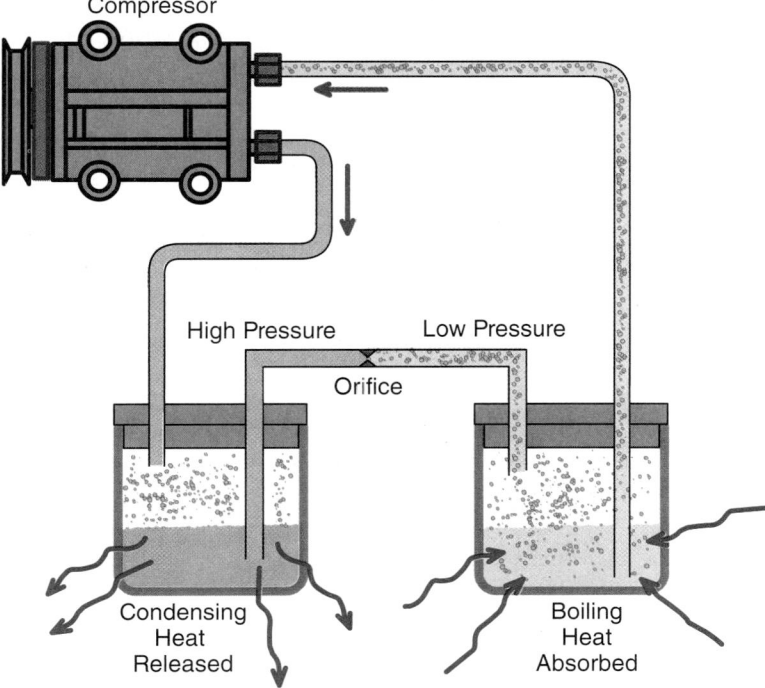

FIGURE 58-15 Removing pressure from refrigerant causes it to absorb heat and boil. Compressing refrigerant increases its temperature and causes it to convert into a liquid.

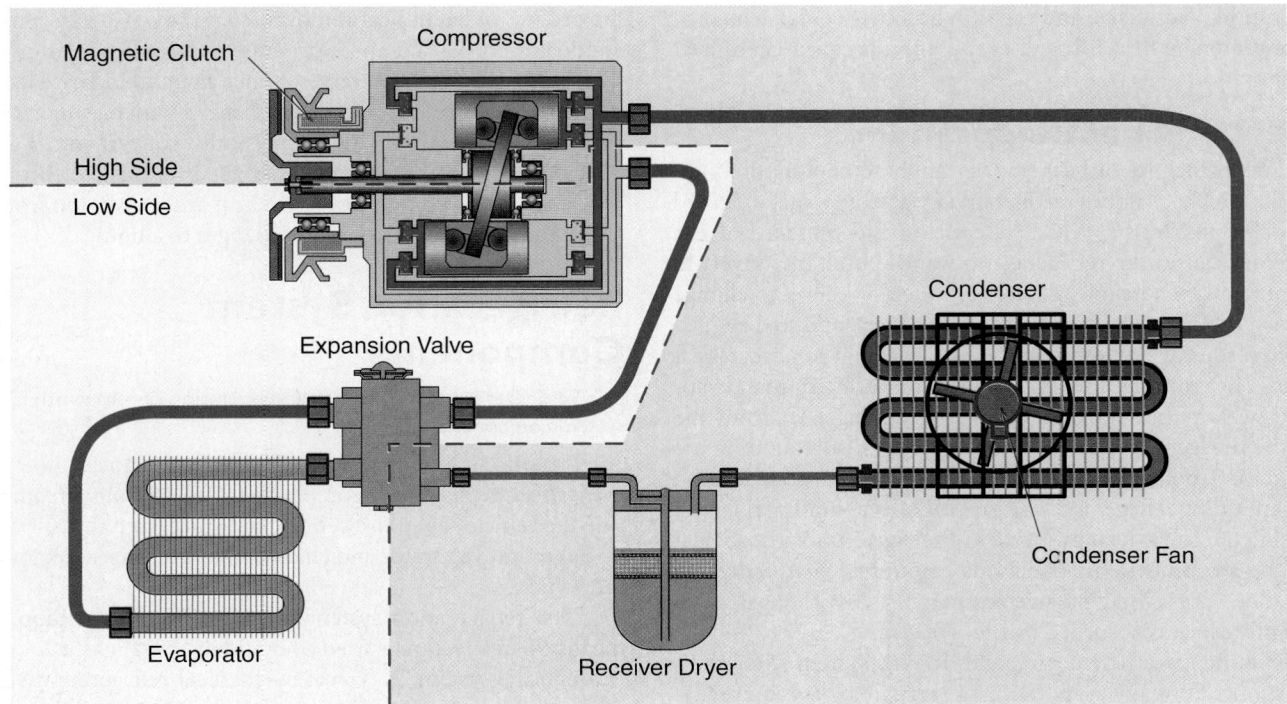

FIGURE 58-16 The components of the air conditioning system. The compressor and expansion valve divide the system between high and low pressure sides.

Air Conditioning Compressor and Clutch

The compressor is an engine-driven pump that increases refrigerant pressure and circulates refrigerant through the system. As the refrigerant is compressed, its temperature rises. As the boiling point of the refrigerant increases under pressure, the refrigerant returns to a liquid state. Cool, low-pressure gas from the evaporator enters the compressor, where it is converted to high-pressure, high-temperature refrigerant gas leaving the compressor.

Three basic types of air conditioning compressors can be used to build pressure exceeding 350 psi (2413 kPa): piston, rotary vane, and scroll. Piston-type compressors are almost universally used in commercial vehicles (**FIGURE 58-17**). Depending upon manufacturer and design, these compressors may have from 1 to 10 cylinders and may or may not have provisions to hold lubricating oil in a sump.

Compressors may have their pistons arranged in an in-line, axial, radial, or V design inside the compressor housing. A V type is shown in **FIGURE 58-18**. Generally, the compressor's capacity to move refrigerant is a primary determinant of the system's ability to remove heat. Increasing compressor displacement is proportional to the BTU capacity of the system in conjunction with other components. Highly refined mineral or synthetic oils lubricate the compressor's moving parts. These oils are specially formulated to dissolve in refrigerant and circulate through the system.

Piston compressors are designed to have an intake stroke and a compression stroke for each cylinder. On the intake stroke,

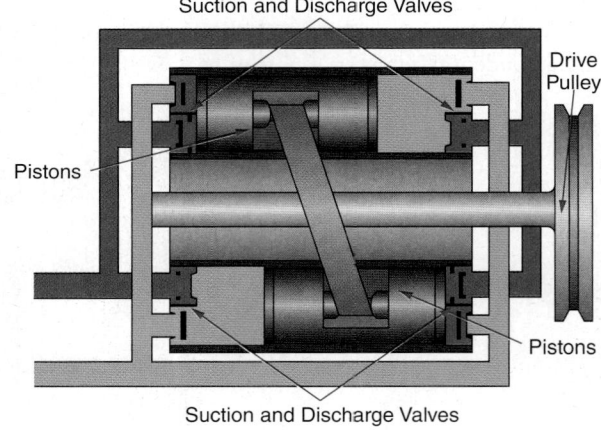

FIGURE 58-17 The operation of an axial piston compressor.

the refrigerant from the low-pressure side of the system leaves the evaporator and is drawn into the compressor. The intake of refrigerant typically occurs through thin, flexible, plate-type reed valves. Another of these one-way valves controls the flow of refrigerant vapors out of the cylinder during compression stroke. During the compression stroke, the refrigerant vapor is compressed, increasing both the pressure and the temperature of the heat-carrying refrigerant.

Because compressors cannot compress liquids, they are designed to operate on refrigerant vapor only. Liquid refrigerant in the compressor will cause damage to the compressor reed valves and may also damage the compressor pistons and connecting rods through hydrostatic lock-up.

Rotary Piston Compressors

Rotary piston compressors have cylindrical-shaped housings and enclose multiple pistons. In addition to being compact in design, the primary advantage of rotary piston compressors is their minimization of noise, vibration, and harshness (NVH). Consider that a two-cylinder compressor produces two large pumping pulses per rotation, whereas a 10-cylinder swash plate creates 10 smaller pulses.

Common manufacturers of rotary piston compressors found on mobile HD equipment include Sanden, Sankyo, Zexel, Calsonic, and Seltec. These compressors use a variable angle swash plate that drives pistons via a connecting rod. As the swash plate rotates through 360 degrees of motion, each piston moves through two strokes—one in, and one out. Check valves in the head of the compressor convert these pulses into suction and discharge strokes (**FIGURE 58-19**).

Most of these compressors have variable displacement capabilities and use the pressure sensed in the low, or suction, side of the system to change the angle of the swash plate (**FIGURE 58-20**). When little cooling loads are sensed by the compressor, such as when evaporator pressures are very low and little refrigerant is evaporating, the swash plate angle is smaller, and less refrigerant is moved by shorter piston strokes. Conversely, when a higher heat load or more refrigeration is required, the swash plate angle increases, lengthening the piston stroke. So, at low heat loads, the compressor may have an energy-efficient two-cubic-inch displacement, while at high heat loads it may have 10 or 12 cubic inches of displacement. Considering truck compressors under maximum heat loads may draw as much as 8 hp (6 kW)

and buses more than 12 hp (9 kW), reducing compressor energy consumption is important for meeting greenhouse gas emission targets. Rotary compressors in trucks have between 5 and 10 cylinders and a displacement of 7 to 15 cubic inches.

Electric Compressors

Anti-idling laws are requiring manufacturers to add air conditioning capabilities to cool the bunk area of a truck when the engine is off. An example is the ParkSmart system used by Freightliner, which is designed to deliver heating and cooling to maintain a cab temperature when the engine is off. As a stand-alone heating or cooling system, it does not have enough capacity to raise or lower the cabin temperature without the engine-assisted HVAC system. The ParkSmart air conditioning

FIGURE 58-19 Rotary piston compressors pull refrigerant from the evaporator and increase its pressure in the condenser.

![compressor cross-section]

FIGURE 58-18 A cross-sectional view of an air conditioning compressor used for a bus or trailer refrigeration unit.

FIGURE 58-20 A rotary piston compressor using a variable angle swash plate changes the stroke length of its pistons.

unit contains a direct current (DC) electric motor-driven refrigerant compressor. There is no connection to the engine-driven air conditioning system (**FIGURE 58-21**).

Compressor Clutches

Mobile HD air conditioning compressors are usually belt-driven from the engine's crankshaft. They have an electromagnetic clutch that enables the compressor to shut off when compressor operation is not required. Engagement and disengagement of the compressor is electrically controlled by system electronic control units, air conditioning control panel settings, or system demands. Most systems use the clutch to cycle compressor operation on and off, depending on heat loads.

When the evaporator requires refrigerant, the compressor engages and circulates refrigerant. When sufficient refrigerant pressures and quantity are available to the evaporator, the compressor disengages to conserve energy. On current air conditioning systems, three basic parts make up the clutch: a drive plate, which is attached to the compressor shaft; a belt pulley,

which is mounted on bearings attached to an extension of the compressor housing; and a magnetic coil (**FIGURE 58-22**).

The magnetic coil engages and disengages the compressor. The coil is mounted behind the belt pulley, is attached to the compressor housing, and does not rotate with the pulley or drive shaft. Electrical connections for the clutch operation are made directly through wires, which are part of the field coil assembly (**FIGURE 58-23**). When a magnetic field is created by applying electrical current into the coil, the drive plate is pulled against a friction surface of the pulley, causing the pulley to rotate with the compressor shaft. When not energized, the clutch allows the pulley to freewheel, minimizing parasitic energy losses, as well as wear and tear on the compressor.

Refrigerant Condensers

The hot, gaseous refrigerant pressurized by the compressor is sent to the condenser (**FIGURE 58-24**). Outside air flows over the

FIGURE 58-21 Freightliners ParkSmart system uses an electrically driven air conditioning compressor that operates separately from the main air conditioning system.

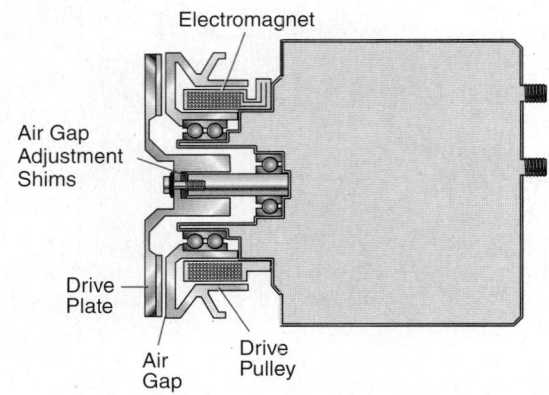

FIGURE 58-22 Construction of a typical HD electromagnetic compressor clutch.

FIGURE 58-23 The compressor clutch and electromagnet are separate pieces of the clutch unit.

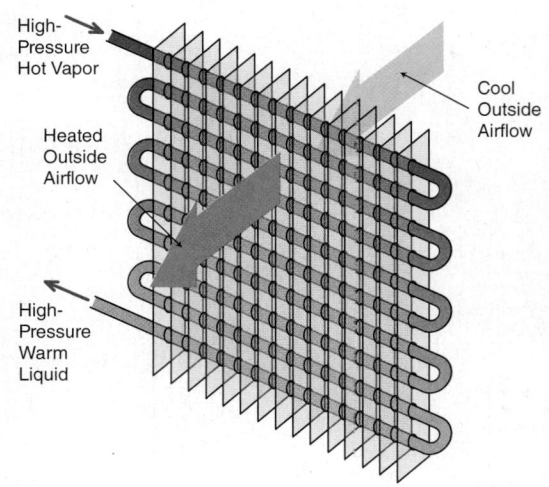

FIGURE 58-24 Pressurizing refrigerant increases it temperature. Heat absorbed by the refrigerant is released to the atmosphere through the condenser.

fins of the condenser and absorbs heat from the refrigerant as it converts from a liquid to a gas. Enough heat is removed from refrigerant to lower the temperature below its boiling point, and the refrigerant condenses to a liquid inside the condenser. As the gas condenses, its latent heat is removed during condensation. High-pressure, warm liquid leaves the condenser.

The condenser typically consists of coiled tubing mounted in a series of thin cooling fins. This arrangement provides maximum surface area for heat transfer using a minimum amount of engine compartment space. Some condensers consist of a tube merely bent into a serpentine shape (**FIGURE 58-25A**). Refrigerant moves from top to bottom with a single pass. Newer parallel-style condensers use a manifold on each side of the condenser, creating multiple paths for refrigerant flow (**FIGURE 58-25B**).

The condenser is mounted directly in front of the radiator, where it can receive full airflow created by forward vehicle motion and the engine fan. The condenser receives the heat-laden, high-pressure refrigerant vapor from the compressor's discharge hose. Refrigerant vapor enters at the top of the condenser and flows through its coils. Heat follows its natural tendency to move from hot to cold and radiates from the hot refrigerant vapors to the cooler atmosphere.

Condensers and the Refrigeration Cycle

As the refrigerant vapors are cooled and flow down through the condenser, condensation eventually occurs, at which point the gas becomes liquid refrigerant. The largest amount of heat is given off by the refrigerant at the point of condensation. The refrigerant in the lower portion of the condenser is a warm, high-pressure liquid. In an air conditioning system operating under an average heat load, the condenser has a combination of hot refrigerant vapor in the upper two-thirds of its coils, with the lower third of the coils containing the warm liquid refrigerant, which has condensed. This high-pressure, liquid refrigerant flows from the condenser and on toward the evaporator. It's important to

remember that whenever air is introduced into the refrigeration system, it accumulates in the upper portion of the condenser, minimizing its effective capacity. Airflow across the condenser is critical for optimal cooling and component durability. Engines using on/off cooling fans incorporate air conditioning switches that open or close at preset high-pressure, side-system pressures. These controls activate the cooling fan, increase the speed of variable speed fans, and open shutters (if equipped) whenever system pressures exceed maximum thresholds.

Refrigerant Expansion Devices

An expansion device restricts the high-pressure, warm liquid refrigerant line and is designed to lower the pressure of refrigerant entering the evaporator. The device may be a thermostatically controlled valve or a restricted orifice that meters the release of the refrigerant into the evaporator and regulates the rate at which refrigerant expands inside the evaporator. Regulating refrigerant flow into the evaporator is necessary to obtain maximum cooling while ensuring complete evaporation of the liquid refrigerant within the evaporator. There are two major types of expansion devices used in commercial vehicle air conditioning systems. One is the **thermostatic expansion valve (TXV)**, and the other is a fixed-orifice tube with pressure control obtained by cycling the compressor clutch on and off. The more energy-efficient system, the **cycling clutch orifice tube (CCOT)**, is used in some models made by Navistar, Peterbilt, Freightliner, and Volvo. Typically the TXV system is more commonly used due to the larger capacity and physical size of commercial vehicle evaporators.

Thermostatic Expansion Valve (TXV)

LO 58-6 Explain the operating principles of a thermal expansion valve (TXV) air conditioning system.

The TXV expansion device lowers the pressure of the warm, high-pressure liquid refrigerant entering the evaporator and allows the refrigerant to expand to greater volume. Refrigerant from the receiver-dryer enters the expansion valve as a liquid under high pressure. A variable size orifice in the TXV creates a pressure differential between the evaporator and refrigerant line, forming what are called the "high" and "low" side of the air conditioning system. The terms high side and low side simply refer to the two different pressures found in the air conditioning system. The compressor forms the other dividing point in the air conditioning between high and low systems. As warm liquid refrigerant passes through the metering orifice in the TXV, the refrigerant forced through the small variable size orifice is sprayed out into the evaporator (**FIGURE 58-26**). Atomized refrigerant flows into the evaporator after the TXV and easily converts to a vapor under these conditions. More significantly, the orifice causes the refrigerant's pressure to drop, which lowers its boiling point, setting up conditions for a change of state. Heat on the evaporator surface is latent heat that more easily enters the refrigerant now because the refrigerant has a lower boiling point and can absorb lots of additional heat allowing the refrigerant to boil. Movement of heat from the cab air and into

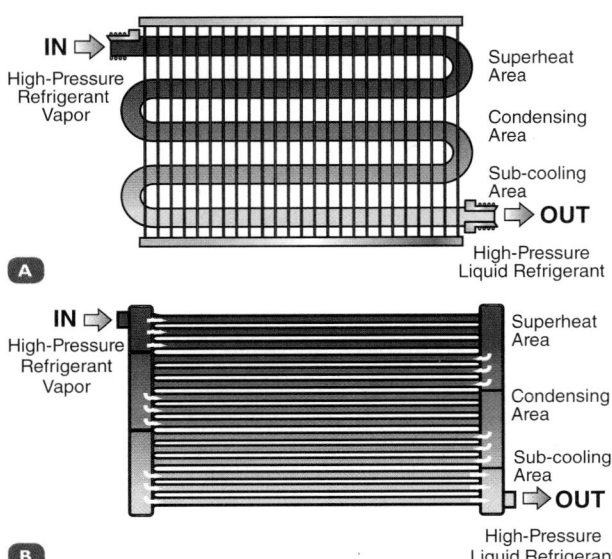

FIGURE 58-25 Comparing the construction of **A.** serpentine- versus **B.** manifold-style condensers.

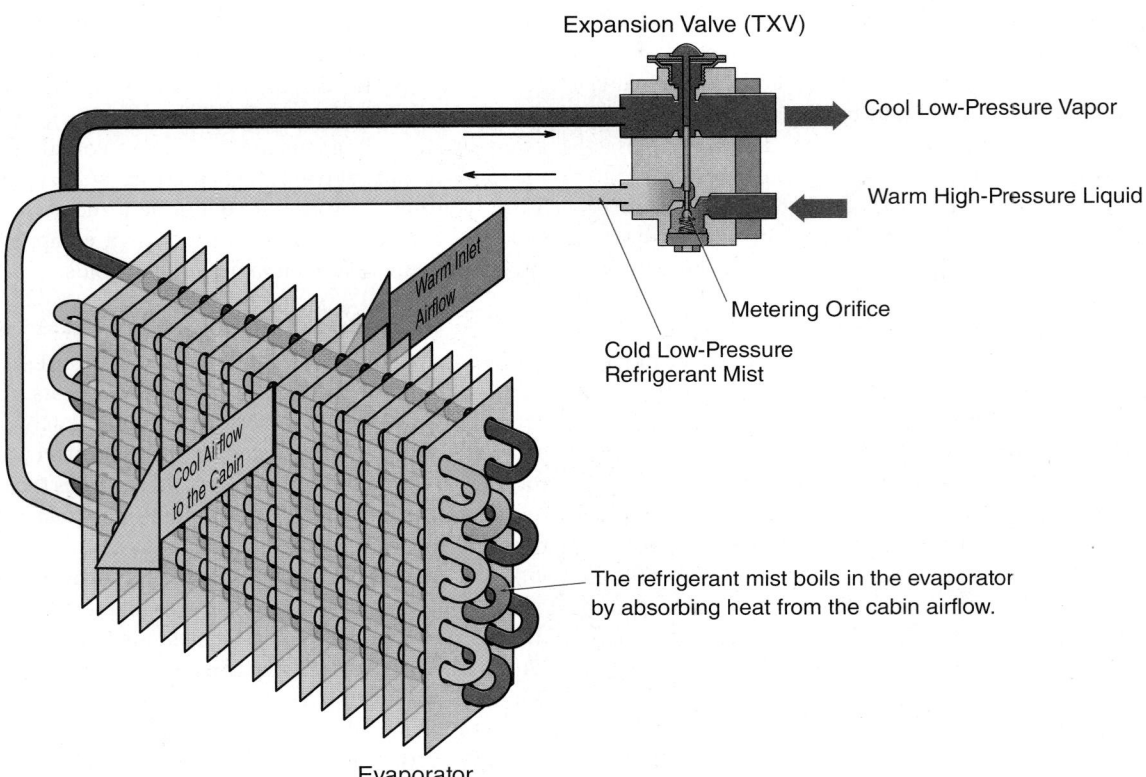

FIGURE 58-26 The TXV system meters refrigerant into the evaporator at a much lower pressure. Lowering pressure lowers the refrigerant's boiling point.

the refrigerant lowers the temperature of circulating cab air. The TXV takes advantage of the properties of latent heat of evaporation by enabling the refrigerant to absorb tremendous amounts of heat relative to the pressure change.

Two types of TXVs are H-block and externally balanced TXV. An externally balanced TXV is easily recognized by a long capillary tube carrying refrigerant pressure and a temperature-sensing bulb, both attached to the evaporator outlet.

H-Block TXV

This TXV valve gets its name from its H-shaped design. There are two refrigerant passages through the valve, which form the legs of the H. One passage is connected to the refrigerant line from the condenser to the evaporator; it contains the ball and spring valve that meters the flow of refrigerant to the evaporator (**FIGURE 58-27**). The other passage is in the refrigerant line from the evaporator to the compressor is called the equalizer; it contains the valve's temperature-sensing diaphragm element. The temperature-sensing element contains a small amount of refrigerant. The expansion and contraction of the sensing element, along with spring tension and refrigerant pressure, varies the amount of refrigerant flow through the system.

Early H-valves used with fixed displacement compressors had a low-pressure cut out switch installed in the valve to sense dangerously low-side pressure at the evaporator outlet. These H-valves also used a low-pressure cycling switch to disconnect the compressor clutch and prevent evaporator freeze-up caused

by excessive refrigerant flow. More recent H-valve designs used with variable displacement compressors do not use a low-pressure cycling switch.

H-Valve TXV Operation

Unlike a CCOT system, which meters refrigerant at a fixed rate, the TXV meters refrigerant into the evaporator at a variable rate. To maintain the evaporator at the correct temperature and pressure needed to produce the most efficient cooling, the TXV contains an orifice that changes the diameter of the evaporator inlet based on evaporator outlet pressure and temperature. A state of balance between evaporator outlet temperatures and pressures and spring tension acting on the inlet orifice ball-valve regulates the quantity of refrigerant flowing into the evaporator to maintain optimal evaporator pressures and temperatures. Linkage attached to a spring-loaded ball valve at the high-pressure inlet of the TXV is kept in a state of balance between spring tension below the ball valve, which closes the orifice, and low-side refrigerant pressure, which either closes or opens the orifice. Evaporator outlet temperature also can change the position of the linkage or state of balance between high-side spring tension and the diaphragm, which ensures all the refrigerant has properly vaporized inside the evaporator.

TXV Orifice State of Balance

Liquid refrigerant under pressure entering the TXV is automatically lowered after initially passing through the

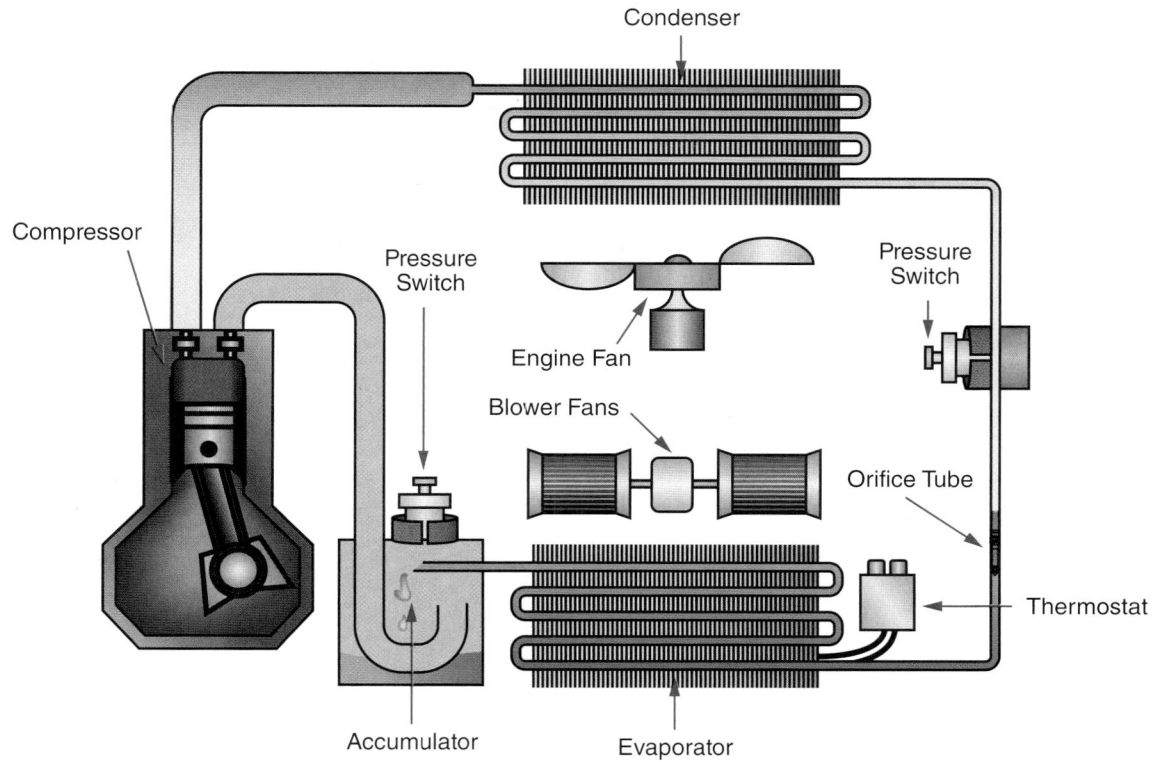

FIGURE 58-27 CCOT systems use an accumulator located after the evaporator. The accumulator prevents liquid refrigerant from entering the compressor.

orifice restriction. Refrigerant flows through the normally open spring-tensioned ball valve because the pressure at the evaporator outlet and inlet are initially the same, which leaves the orifice open at its widest diameter. But two factors cause a change in the orifice size: outlet temperature and pressure. Lower evaporator outlet than inlet pressure opens the orifice, while very cold, evaporator outlet temperatures close the orifice. Regulating this action is a diaphragm at the low-pressure outlet of the TXV that is connected to the linkage influencing the spring tension acting on the ball-valve opening. The diaphragm is acted upon two sides; by refrigerant pressure at the evaporator outlet, and on another side, above the diaphragm by the temperature of refrigerant. Refrigerant trapped in the cavity above the diaphragm drops its pressure if it is cooled too much by the temperature of refrigerant leaving the evaporator. This condition where refrigerant trapped above the diaphragm gets cold, causes a reduction in the diaphragm's refrigerant volume and pressure, which **pulls** the diaphragm linkage closed. Reducing the size of the TXV orifice allows less refrigerant into the evaporator and the evaporator gradually warms up. If increasing evaporator temperatures begin to warm the refrigerant above the diaphragm, refrigerant pressure above the diaphragm **pushes** the linkage to open the orifice ball valve. This temperature-compensating feature prevents the evaporator from flooding with too much refrigerant and freezing when the orifice is open too far. Construction of the temperature-compensating feature also opens the orifice if the evaporator becomes too warm from insufficient refrigerant flow.

Evaporator outlet pressure acting below the diaphragm also causes the orifice to open if the evaporator outlet pressure is too far below inlet pressure. Low outlet pressure is caused by too little refrigerant flow. Low outlet pressure **below** the diaphragm **pulls** the linkage to open the orifice, thus permitting more refrigerant to flow. Increasing evaporator outlet pressure below the diaphragm pushes the linkage to close the orifice. This pressure regulating action ensures enough refrigerant completely boils in the evaporator. It also maintains the correct volume of refrigerant flow through large commercial vehicle evaporators by opening the orifice if insufficient evaporator outlet pressure is caused by a lack of refrigerant flow. Excessive refrigerant flow through the evaporator is prevented because that condition increases outlet pressure and closes the orifice (**FIGURE 58-28**).

The orifice opening fluctuates toward the open or closed position to create the low pressure needed for the liquid refrigerant to effectively vaporize as it passes through the evaporator. It's important that a TXV quickly respond to changes in heat load conditions. When the evaporator pressure changes in response to varying heat loads, the valve orifice changes size to regulate refrigerant flow. For example, if high cabin temperatures evaporate more refrigerant, the evaporator temperature increases. This requires more refrigerant to absorb and transfer more heat. In these circumstances, the thermostatic bulb pressure above the diaphragm forces the TXV valve to open. The opposite happens if evaporator temperature drops and less refrigerant is required.

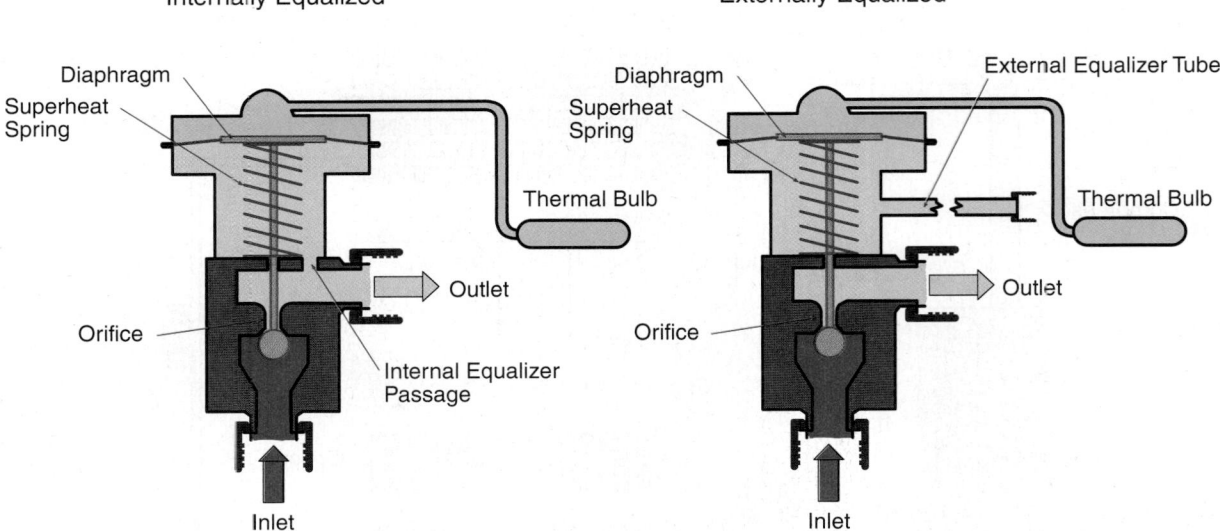

FIGURE 58-28 Two methods of thermostatic expansion valve equalization.

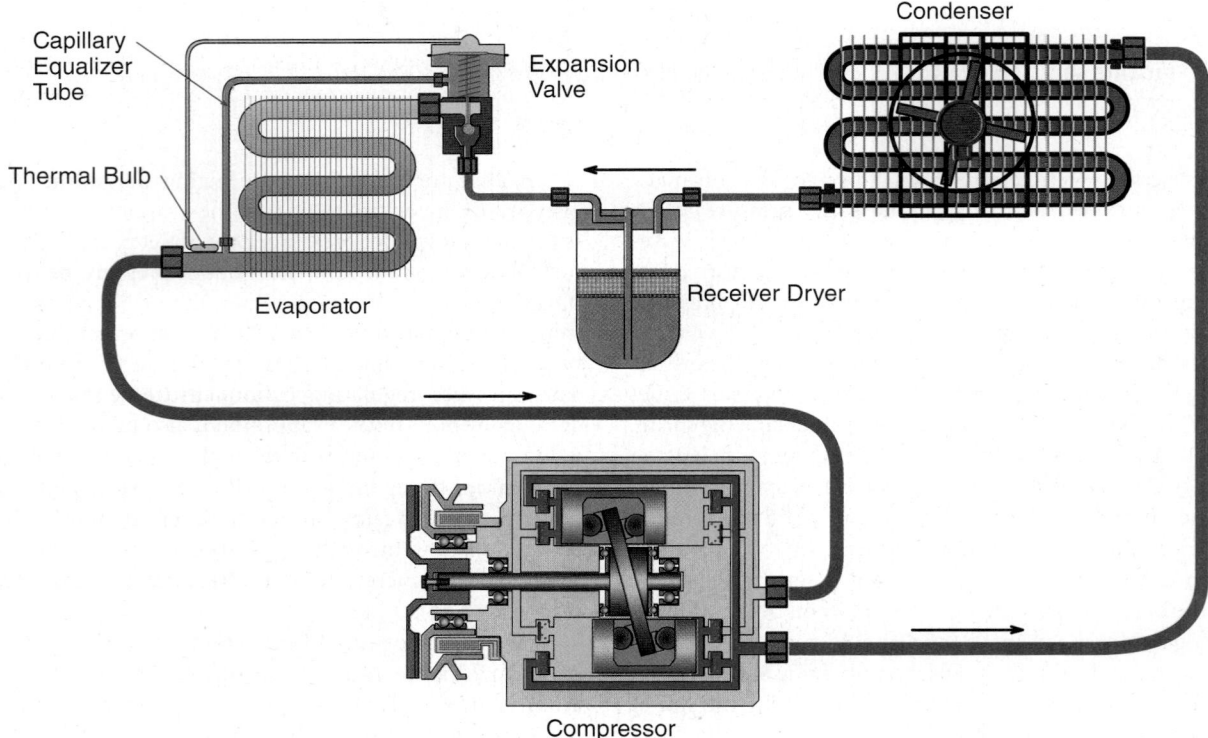

FIGURE 58-29 An externally balanced TXV uses a capillary tube connected to the evaporator outlet.

Externally Balanced TXVs

In TXVs that are not H-valve type, equalizing or balancing pressure below the control diaphragm can also be supplied by a capillary tube connected to the low-pressure outlet side of the evaporator (**FIGURE 58-29**). The refrigerant pressure on the lower side of the diaphragm is proportional to temperature as well. A remote temperature-sensing bulb attached securely to the low-pressure outlet line is filled with a temperature-sensitive gas, which is usually the same as the system's refrigerant. Gas pressure above the diaphragm must be higher than evaporator outlet pressure below the diaphragm to open the restriction orifice. Usually about a 5° F (15° C) or more temperature difference between evaporator inlet and outlet is required to open the valve. Anything less than that means too much refrigerant is entering the evaporator. And if the evaporator is too cold, moisture will freeze on the fins and plates, preventing effective cooling. This condition where excess refrigerant floods the evaporator is called **evaporator freezing**.

Gas temperature in the temperature-sensing bulb changes the pressure above the diaphragm. If more refrigerant enters the evaporator, the outlet temperature becomes colder and the restriction orifice is narrowed as the diaphragm pressure decreases. Warmer evaporator outlet temperatures apply more pressure above the diaphragm and cause the orifice to open wider.

TXV Valve Spring

The TXV spring tension can be externally adjusted on some valves to control the "superheat" function. Superheat is simply the change in temperature from the inlet to outlet side of the evaporator. Ideally, there should be only a small temperature increase across the evaporator if the correct amount of refrigerant is metered by the TXV. However, the spring is generally adjusted to provide for a temperature differential of 4° F to 16° F (−15.5° C to −8.8° C) between the evaporator inlet and outlet temperatures. Allowing the outlet temperature to rise higher in comparison to inlet temperature or pressure ensures refrigerant vapor at the evaporator outlet does not contain any droplets of liquid refrigerant, which could cause the evaporator to freeze up due to excess refrigerant flow or potentially damage the compressor. On very large evaporators in commercial vehicles,

where the refrigerant travels a long way, an externally balanced TXV is used. In these valves, a capillary tube connects the outlet pressure of the evaporator to the underside of the diaphragm instead of having an internal passage supplying evaporator inlet pressure (**FIGURE 58-30**). The lower diaphragm chamber pressure reflects the evaporator outlet temperature on externally balanced TXV to improve the superheat function of the TXV.

▶ **TECHNICIAN TIP**

The temperature-sensing bulb for the TXV is clamped on the evaporator outlet pipe. It is insulated from the outside air with special insulating tape, allowing it to only measure outlet temperature of the refrigerant as it leaves the evaporator. Only air conditioning insulating tape designed for insulating the bulb should be used. Using electrical tape or other substitutes causes the evaporator to flood with refrigerant and freeze.

Orifice Tube Pressure Regulation

A simple, plastic tube with a calibrated brass orifice is used on current CCOT systems to produce refrigerant pressure drop in the evaporator (**FIGURE 58-31**). Orifice tubes also serve the same basic function as the expansion valve, but have a different construction. And, like the expansion valve, orifice tubes are mounted on the inlet side of the evaporator (**FIGURE 58-32**). The tubes are enclosed with filter screens to remove contaminants that could plug the narrow orifice tube and prevent refrigerant flow (**FIGURE 58-33**).

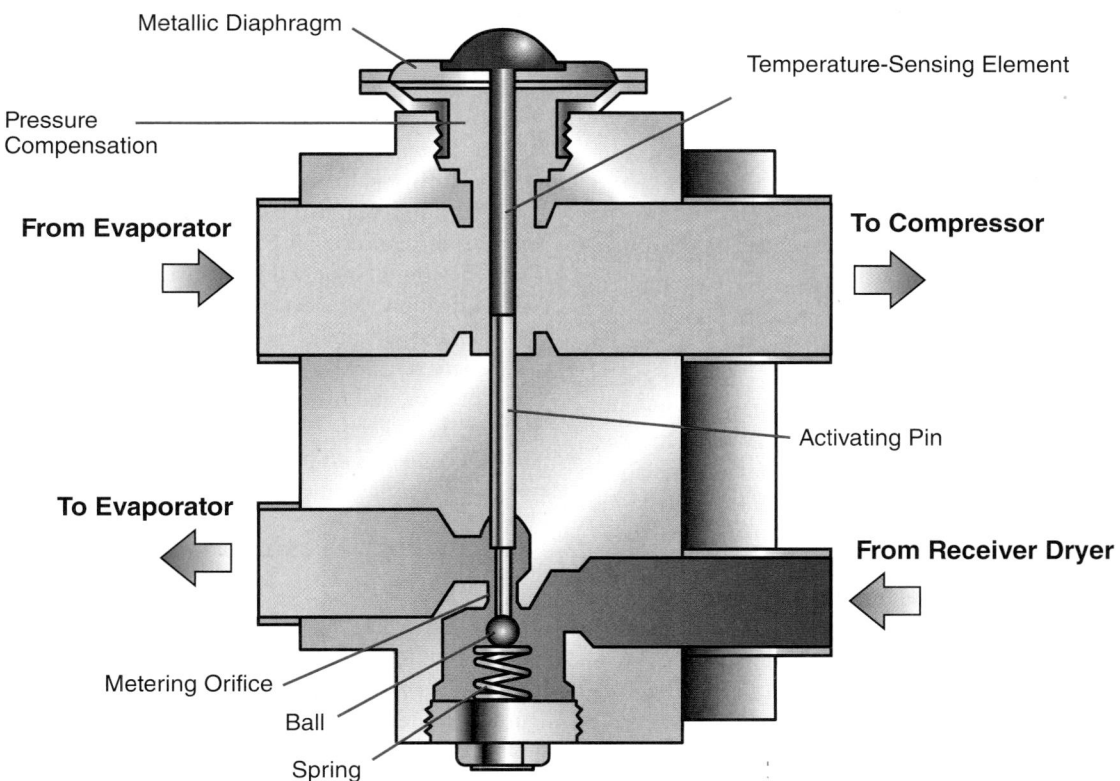

FIGURE 58-30 This H-type TXV is internally balanced. It senses evaporator outlet pressure at the surface below the temperature-sensing diaphragm.

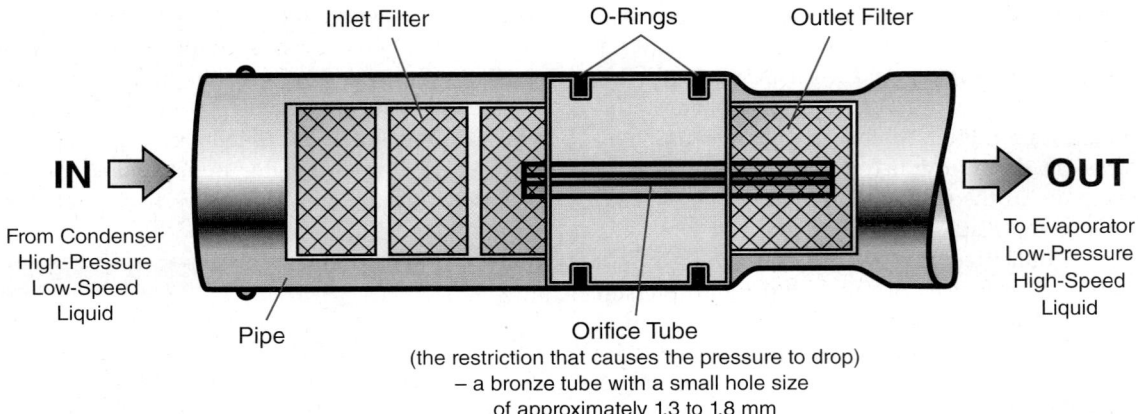

FIGURE 58-31 A fixed-orifice tube is located at the evaporator inlet.

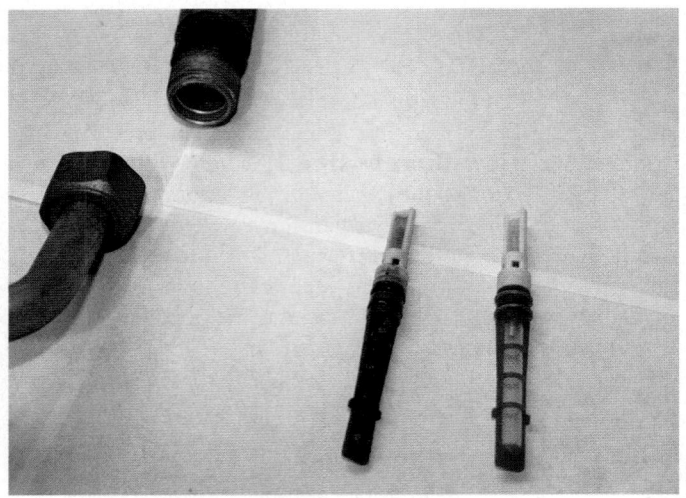

FIGURE 58-32 A CCOT system uses an orifice restriction enclosed in a filter screen to reduce refrigerant pressure entering the evaporator.

Because the orifice tube does not vary in size, pressure control in the evaporator is accomplished by switching the compressor clutch on and off using a pressure signal from a pressure switch located near the evaporator outlet or suction side (**FIGURE 58-34**). The switch, called the pressure cycling switch, is connected in series with a thermostatic temperature switch in the cab to switch the refrigerant flow from the compressor on and off (**FIGURE 58-35**). Orifice tubes are available in diameters ranging from 0.0047" to 0.078" (0.1194 mm to 1.98 mm). A retrofit orifice tube called a variable orifice valve (VOV) is also available. These tubes have bimetallic-controlled orifice diameters and offer lower evaporator discharge temperatures at low engine speed, such as when the vehicle is stuck in traffic and little refrigerant is pumped, even though high heat loads are present. Other benefits are improved fuel economy, lower emissions, and less compressor wear.

The pressure cycling switch has two set points—one for low-pressure cut out and one for higher cut-in pressure. Depending on the type of refrigerant, the switch opens when evaporator outlet pressure typically reaches approximately 25 psi and closes

when outlet pressure reaches 35 psi. Unlike TXV systems, low evaporator pressures in this system indicate excessive refrigerant flow and less refrigerant is required. Very low evaporator outlet pressure causes the compressor to stop pumping refrigerant and the refrigerant inside the evaporator boils. Increasing evaporator pressure closes the pressure cycling switch to increase the supply of refrigerant to the evaporator. Increased refrigerant flow, in turn, lowers evaporator outlet pressure.

Pressure Cycling Switch Function

The purpose of the pressure cycling switch is to maintain an evaporator pressure of approximately 29 psi to have optimal evaporator temperature for cooling. When refrigerant has evaporated in the evaporator core, its pressure rises. The pressure cycling switch closes, causing the compressor to pump more refrigerant and re-flood the evaporator. Cycling the compressor on and off prevents evaporator freeze-up due to excessive refrigerant flow. The switch also prevents the compressor from operating during cold weather. In subzero conditions, refrigerant gas is a liquid and incapable of flowing or dissolving and carrying oil through the air conditioning system. If the compressor switches on with only liquid refrigerant, it seizes due to a lack of lubrication. Low levels of refrigerant detected by the pressure switch also do not allow the compressor to operate. Without adequate refrigerant gas, no oil can circulate and lubricate the compressor, and the compressor can burn out.

This switch is usually threaded on a standard Schrader valve fitting. It is often possible to remove and replace the switch without having to discharge the system.

Evaporator Pressure Control Using Thermistors

Navistar used a CCOT system on many of its vehicles between 2001 and 2007. Rather than using a pressure cycling and thermostatic switch, the Navistar system uses three thermistors as input to the electrical system control module (**FIGURE 58-36**). One thermistor measures the evaporator core temperature, and the other two measure the evaporator inlet and outlet temperatures. By measuring the temperature difference of refrigerant entering and leaving the evaporator, the amount of

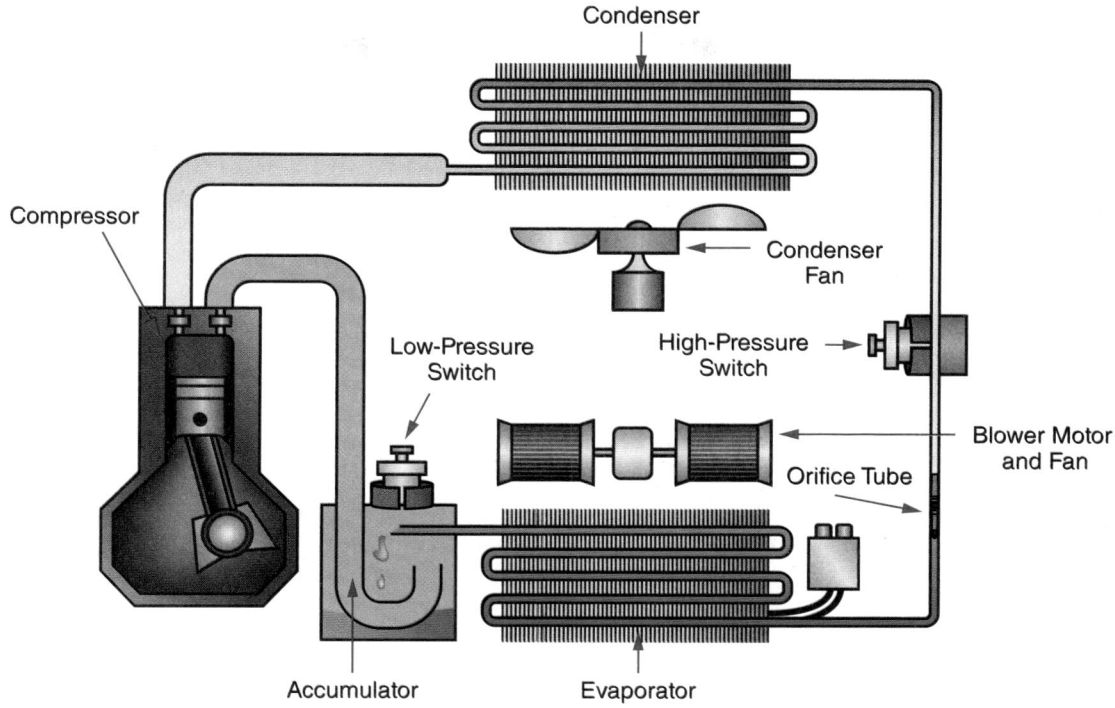

FIGURE 58-33 The pressure cycling switch is located on the accumulator of a CCOT system.

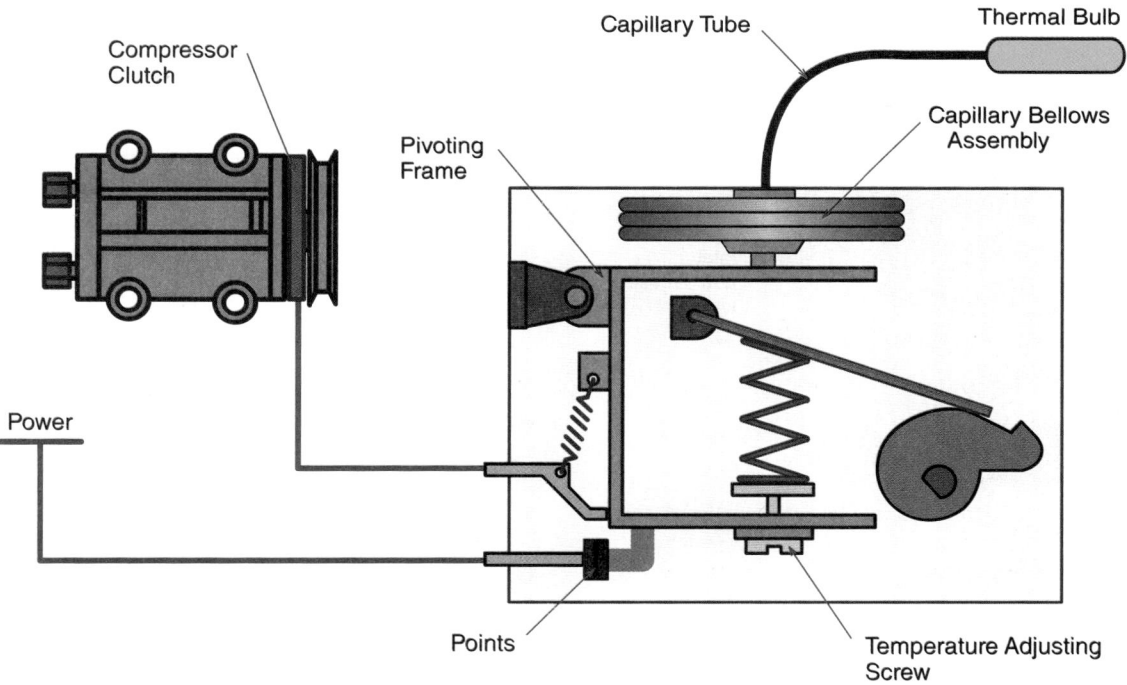

FIGURE 58-34 A mechanical thermostatic switch cycles the compressor on and off and is in series with the pressure cycling switch.

refrigerant entering the evaporator or its average temperature can be accurately controlled by cycling the compressor clutch on and off. To prevent evaporator freeze-up, sensor input from the third thermistor can provide data to the control unit to cycle the compressor clutch. Algorithms stored in the control module determine when and how long to energize the compressor clutch (**FIGURE 58-37**). A pressure transducer at the condenser outlet provides further pressure protection and control of items, such as the engine fan, and high and low system pressure protection.

FIGURE 58-35 A thermistor on the accumulator of a CCOT system. The CCOT system used by Navistar regulates evaporator temperature and pressure using inputs from three thermistors.

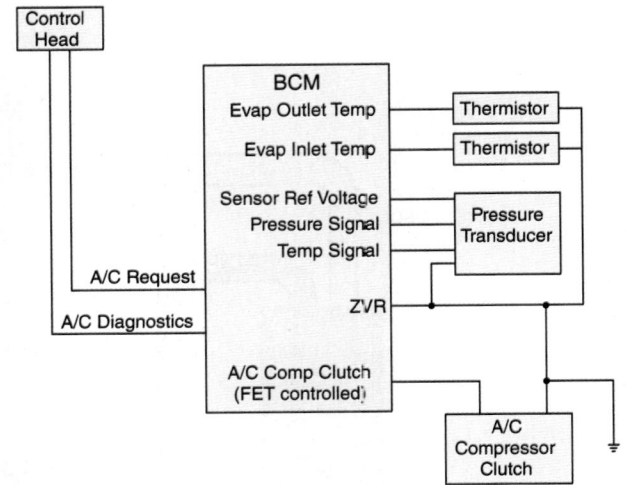

FIGURE 58-37 Inputs from two thermistors and a pressure transducer control the air conditioning clutch operation of 2007 and earlier Navistar air conditioning systems.

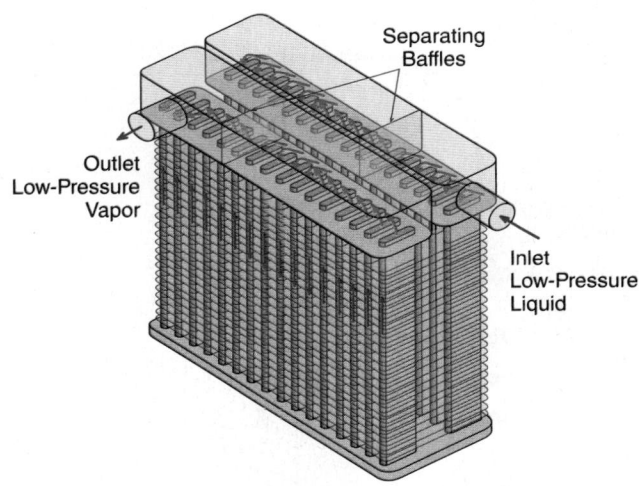

FIGURE 58-36 A plate-and-fin evaporator construction uses manifolds on both sides of the evaporator and has multiple pathways for refrigerant to cross the evaporator.

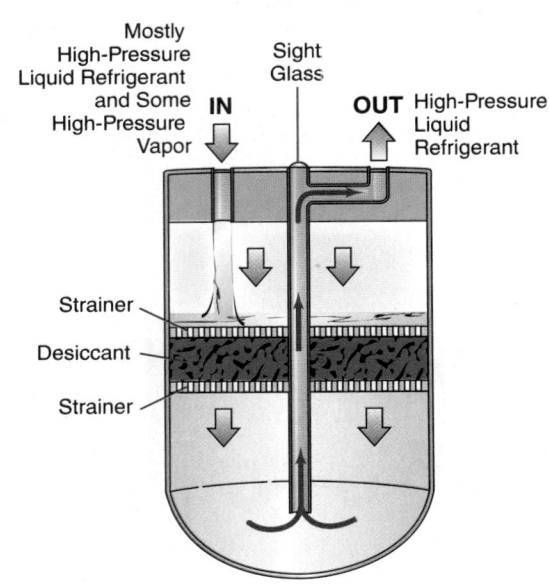

FIGURE 58-38 Cross section of a receiver-dryer.

Evaporators

LO 58-7 Identify and explain the function of the evaporator.

The evaporator is a heat exchanger located inside the cab or passenger compartment containing the chamber where refrigerant boils and converts to a vapor. When a liquid evaporates, it must absorb a tremendous amount of heat to change state. The source of heat is warm cabin air blowing across the surface of the evaporator. The evaporator also removes moisture from the cabin air. As moist recirculated or outside air passes over the cold evaporator fins, water vapor condenses and drips to the bottom of the evaporator housing. From there it flows through a drain out of the housing.

Like the condenser, the evaporator has a couple of common constructions. The serpentine coil evaporator is constructed from a metal coil mounted in a series of thin cooling fins. The design provides a maximum amount of heat transfer in a minimum amount of space. A plate-and-fin construction uses manifolds on both sides of the evaporator and has multiple pathways for refrigerant to cross the evaporator (**FIGURE 58-38**). Under normal operation, warm air from the passenger compartment is blown across the coils and fins.

Evaporator Pressure Regulation

The thermostatic expansion valve, or orifice tube, continually meters the proper amount of refrigerant required to maintain optimal heat transfer efficiency. This action also ensures that all the liquid refrigerant has changed to a vapor by the time it reaches the evaporator outlet. The refrigerant vapor then continues on to the inlet (suction) side of the compressor.

If too much refrigerant is allowed to enter, the evaporator floods. This results in poor cooling, because the refrigerant can neither boil away rapidly nor vaporize. It may even freeze moisture in the fins, preventing airflow and causing cooling loss. On the other hand, if too little refrigerant is metered, the evaporator starves. Poor cooling again results because insufficient amount of refrigerant boils away or vaporizes too quickly before passing through the evaporator.

The temperature of the refrigerant vapor at the evaporator outlet is approximately 4° F to 16° F (−16° C to −9° C) higher than the temperature of the liquid refrigerant at the evaporator inlet. This temperature differential is the **superheat** mentioned earlier, which provides for optimal cooling efficiency and ensures that the vapor does not contain any droplets of liquid refrigerant that would be harmful to the compressor. The warm air blown across the evaporator usually contains some moisture (humidity). The moisture in the air normally condenses on the evaporator coils and drains off as water. Dehumidification of the air is an added feature of the air conditioning system that adds to passenger comfort. It can also be used as a means of controlling fogging of the vehicle windows. Under certain conditions, however, too much moisture may accumulate on the evaporator coils and freeze before it can drain off. An example is when humidity is extremely high and maximum cooling mode is selected. A thermostatic control sensor or thermistor, a part of what is called the superheat switch, is located in the evaporator and can help prevent this condition by shutting off the compressor.

Blower Motor Circulation and Evaporator Pressure

An important component in the cooling action of the evaporator is the blower motor/fan, also located in the evaporator housing. The blower draws warm air from the passenger compartment, over the evaporator, and blows the cooled air into the passenger area. A fan switch controls the blower motor with settings from low to high. High blower speed provides the greatest volume of circulated air. A reduction in blower speed decreases the air volume. However, the slower speed of the circulated air allows the air to remain in contact with the fins and coils of the evaporator for a longer period of time. This results in more heat transfer to the cooler refrigerant. Therefore, the coldest air temperature from the evaporator is when the blower is operated at its slowest speed.

In large buses, one or more evaporators are used to cool the passenger compartment. Each evaporator is connected in parallel to the high-pressure refrigerant circuit and each uses a dedicated TXV valve. Zone cooling or the ability to switch off the air in areas is done using a temperature sensitive electrically controlled valve to switch refrigerant flow on or off through each evaporator (**FIGURE 58-39**).

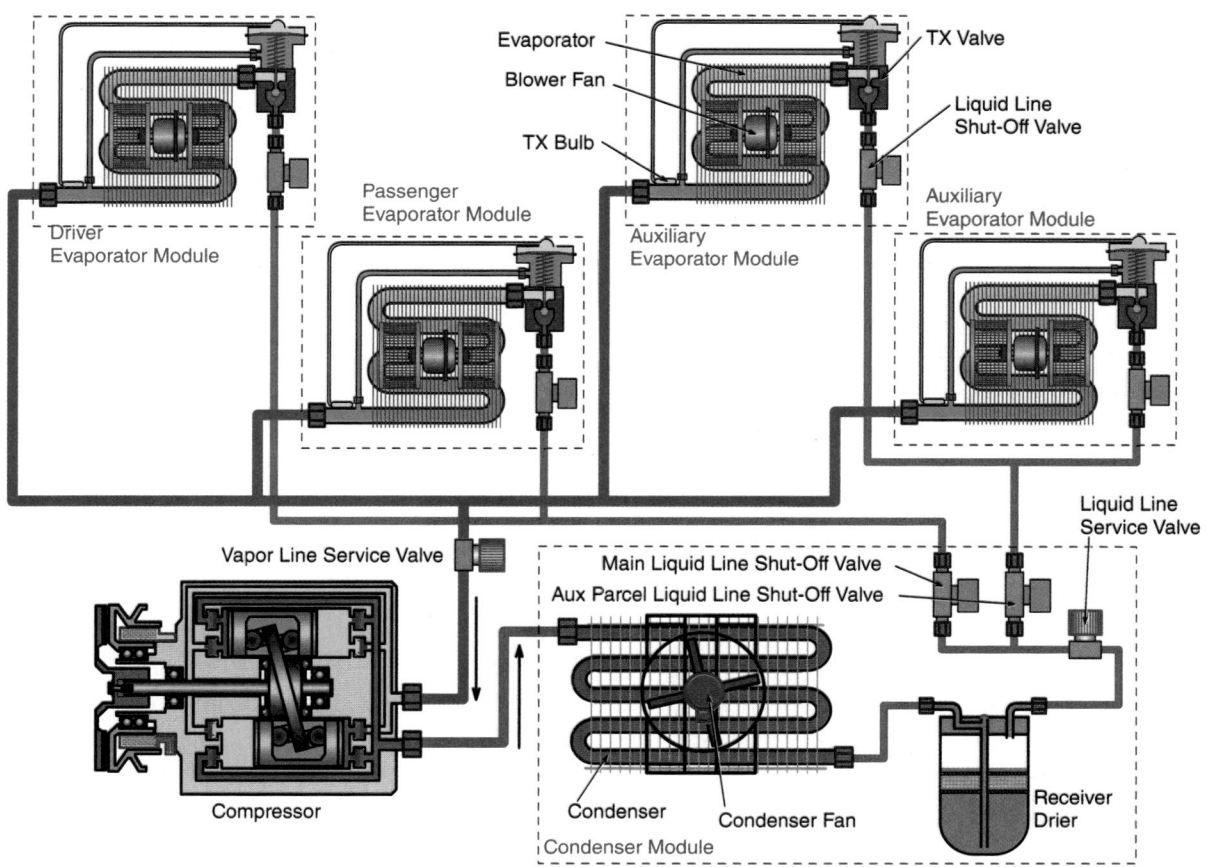

FIGURE 58-39 Multiple evaporators are connected in parallel to the air conditioning high-pressure refrigerant circuit for zone cooling.

Receiver-Dryers

LO 58-8 Identify and explain the function of the receiver-dryer.

The primary function of the **receiver-dryer** is to serve as a storage reservoir for refrigerant. A second function is to absorb any moisture in the air conditioning system. Receiver-dryers are used primarily on TXV air conditioning systems and receive liquid refrigerant from the condenser, storing the liquid until it is needed by the evaporator. Capacity of the receiver-dryer varies according to operating conditions. Typically, in truck systems, the dryer holds about half a pound (226 g) of extra refrigerant, which is used as a buffer against slight leaks and high refrigerant operating demands. Because the receiver-dryer receives liquid refrigerant from the condenser, it is mounted either adjacent to the condenser or somewhere downstream before the expansion valve. It consists of a tank, a filter, a drying agent (desiccant), a pick-up tube, and a sight glass (on some applications) (**FIGURE 58-40**).

As a dryer, the receiver-dryer also acts as a moisture protection element for the system. The portion of the receiver-dryer that contains the drying agent absorbs any potential moisture from the refrigerant. If moisture does enter the air conditioning system, it produces ice crystals that block refrigerant flow, damaging compressors. If water overloads and contaminates the desiccant, the material disintegrates and contaminates the system with abrasive grit that restricts system passageways.

Moisture can also contribute to the breakdown of lubricating oils. In older R-12 systems, moisture would combine with refrigerant chlorine to form hydrochloric acid that would internally corrode lines and other components. The removal of chlorine from new refrigerants prevents acids from forming, so line corrosion is reduced, and it is no longer necessary to check oil acidity.

Desiccant drying agents inside the receiver-dryer are compatible with refrigerant oils that can be absorbed by the desiccant. Receiver-dryers have a moisture-indicator sight glass for determining the amount of moisture absorbed by the desiccant. This moisture sight glass should not be confused with the sight glass for examining the condition of refrigerant. A good desiccant is light blue; a moisture-laden desiccant is pinkish or green.

Receiver Dryer Site Glass

Receiver-dryers often incorporate an important diagnostic aid—the refrigerant sight glass. In order to inspect the condition of the refrigerant, a glass insert at the receiver-dryer outlet allows the technician to detect contaminated or undercharged refrigerant (**FIGURE 58-41**). If the system is undercharged, refrigerant vapor (gas bubbles in liquid flowing into the evaporator) is present in the glass after the system has been run and stabilized. Degraded desiccant and discolored contaminated refrigerant are also detected by examining the refrigerant flow through the sight glass.

Cycling Clutch Orifice Tube Accumulators

Accumulators are used in CCOT or fixed-orifice tube (FOT) systems. The accumulator has functions similar to the receiver dryer, but is located in the low-pressure side of the system. In these systems, the restriction orifice is placed in the inlet of the evaporator that has a fixed diameter. At higher engine speeds and low heat loads, the evaporator floods with liquid. If liquid is allowed to reach the compressor, damage results. The accumulators in these systems collect liquid refrigerant leaving the evaporator and separate vapor from liquid before the refrigerant enters the compressor. Desiccant is placed in the accumulator to absorb moisture. A receiver-dryer may also be used in CCOT systems, but an accumulator located after the evaporator is mandatory (**FIGURE 58-42**).

Refrigerant and Oil

LO 58-9 Identify its purpose and explain the function of refrigerant oil.

Two fluids are used in automotive air conditioning systems—refrigerant and refrigeration oil. Refrigerant itself is the central element of the entire air conditioning process because it absorbs heat from the cab/passenger compartment air and transfers it to the atmosphere. Refrigerant also behaves like a solvent of refrigerant oil in order to dissolve and carry the oil

FIGURE 58-40 Elements of a receiver-dryer. **A.** High-pressure cut out switch. **B.** Sight glass. **C.** Moisture indicator. **D.** Fan switch.

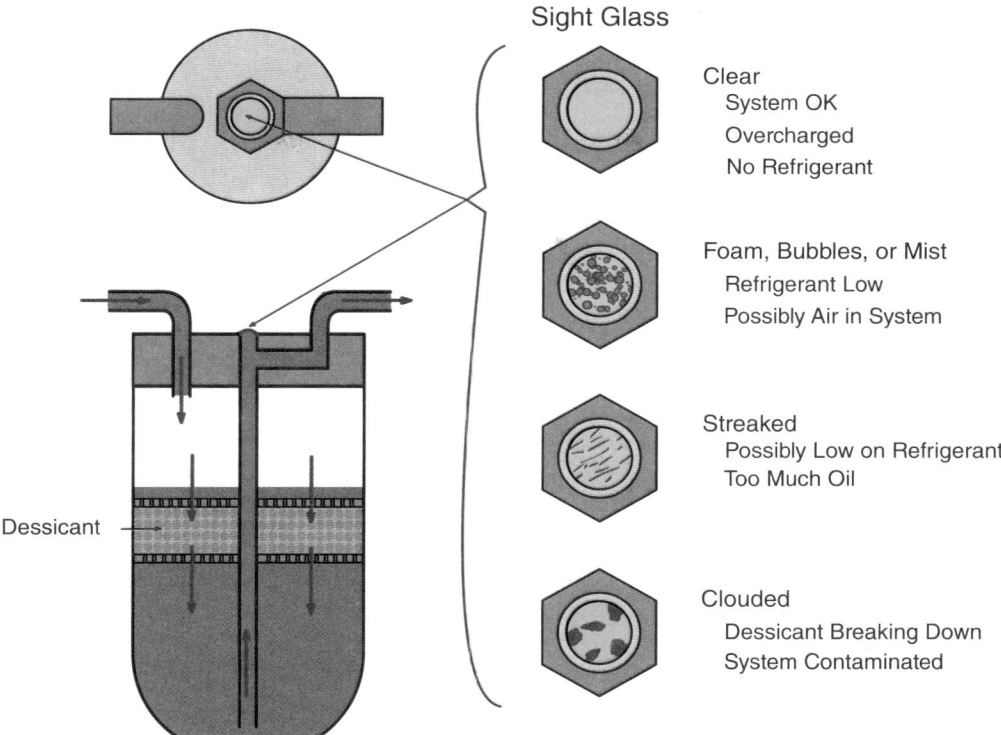

Sight Glass

Clear
  System OK
  Overcharged
  No Refrigerant

Foam, Bubbles, or Mist
  Refrigerant Low
  Possibly Air in System

Streaked
  Possibly Low on Refrigerant
  Too Much Oil

Clouded
  Dessicant Breaking Down
  System Contaminated

FIGURE 58-41 The color and consistency of the refrigerant is an indicator of the degree to which it is degraded.

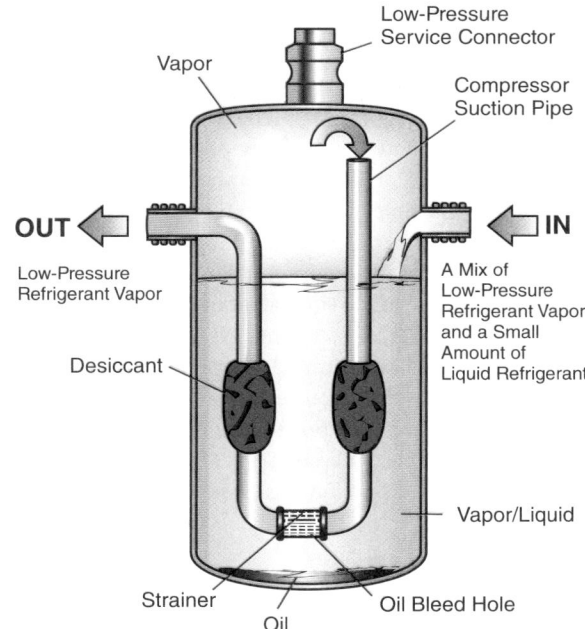

FIGURE 58-42 An accumulator located after the evaporator is mandatory on a CCOT system.

FIGURE 58-43 Labels like this one, indicating the type and amount of refrigerant and oil a system uses, are located beneath the hood or in the engine compartment.

through the air conditioning system. Refrigeration oil lubricates the compressor and expansion valve. Without oil and refrigerant, the air conditioning compressor is quickly damaged if operated. The amount of oil and refrigerant a system uses is identified on a label beneath the hood or engine compartment (**FIGURE 58-43**).

▶ **TECHNICIAN TIP**

Never attempt to hot-wire the operation of an air conditioning compressor in a system low on refrigerant. Pressure switches within the air conditioning system disable the compressor to protect it from a loss of lubricant, which is carried through the air conditioning system by the refrigerant.

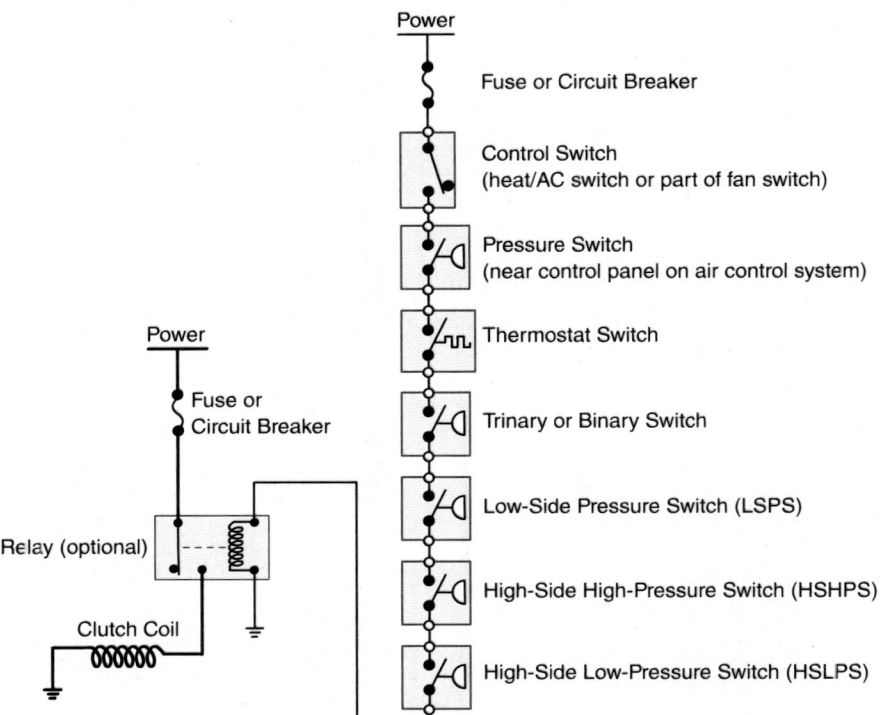

FIGURE 58-44 The switches to control the air conditioning compressor clutch are connected in series. Opening any switch disables the air conditioning compressor.

Properties of Refrigerants

A variety of available refrigerants are suited to specific applications. Refrigerant used in the air conditioning system of a truck, bus, or automobile is different from refrigerant used to freeze food products, make ice, or cool an office building. Different chemical formulations of refrigerants are used, as are blends and refrigerants having specialized additive packages to meet specific service requirements. Ideal refrigerant properties and characteristics include:

- *A low boiling point and freezing point.* Refrigerants vary according to boiling point, which ultimately determines where the refrigerant is used. The lower the boiling point, the colder the evaporator temperature is. R-134a refrigerant, which is commonly used in passenger compartment systems, boils at –14.9° F (–26.1° C). R-402a for trailer refrigeration boils at –56° F (–49° C).
- *A low specific heat and high latent heat.* Specific heat refers to the amount of heat that refrigerant must absorb to change its temperature by 1° F (17° C). Low specific heat means the refrigerant easily absorbs heat and changes state. A refrigerant with a high specific heat loses its ability to refrigerate on a weight basis. Similarly, a refrigerant having a high latent heat capacity absorbs more heat per unit of weight. Combining a refrigerant with high latent heat and low specific heat increases the effectiveness of a refrigerant on a per-lb (per-kg) basis. If refrigerants did not have low specific heat capabilities and high latent heat properties, condensers and evaporators would need to be much larger.

Saturated Temperature

The pressure-temperature relationship of R-134a is important for the HVAC technician in diagnosing and testing air conditioning operation. After the system has been operated, the temperature and pressure of the refrigerant follow a fixed relationship. This means that if you know the pressure of the gas, you can determine its temperature or the temperature inside a condenser or evaporator. For example, the temperature of the evaporator can be measured to determine if it is cold enough to properly cool the vehicle. For technicians using imperial measurement, the evaporator pressure is close to the equivalent of its temperature of 20° F to 80° F (–6.7° C to 27° C). A name given to this pressure temperature-relationship is saturated temperature. Saturated temperature refers to the temperature at which a refrigerant changes from a liquid to vapor or vapor to liquid at a given pressure. If the R-134a refrigerant in a system has a stable pressure of 30° F (–1° C), for example, its pressure is close to 30 psi (207 kPa).

Refrigerant Types

Traditionally, refrigerants are manufactured from hydrogen, fluorine, chlorine, and carbon molecules. Three categories of refrigerant compositions are used today—hydrofluorocarbons (HFCs), hydrochlorofluorocarbons (HCFCs), and hydrofluoroolefin (HFO). These designations refer to the chemical composition of each type of refrigerant. **TABLE 58-2** lists current HFC and HFO refrigerants. A fourth category of refrigerants is made from only chlorine, fluorine, and carbon (CFC) and is no longer produced due to its destructive effect on the ozone layer. Freon, or R-12, is an example of this banned refrigerant.

TABLE 58-2 Current HFC, HFO, and HCFC Refrigerants

DuPont Number	Refrigerant Name	Application	Cylinder Color
R-23	Trifluoromethane	Low temperatures	Light gray
R-134a	Tetrafluoroethane	Automotive and residential refrigeration systems	Light sky blue
R-404a	R-125 + R-143a + R-134a	Medium and low temperature	Orange
R-407c	R-32 + R-125 + R-134a	R-22 CFC replacement	Chocolate brown
R-410a	R-32 + R-125	CFC replacement for R-12 residential air conditioning	Rose
R-507	R-125/143a	CFC replacement for low-temperature commercial refrigeration	Light brown
HFO-1234YF	Solstice YF or Opteon YF	Automotive and residential refrigeration systems	NA

Because the chemical names of typical refrigerants are long and complex, an industry standard method of designating refrigerants by number was developed by DuPont in 1956. Refrigerant names, such as R-12, R-134a, R-402, R-404a, R-22, and R503, are familiar to anyone working with air conditioning in the past decade. The method essentially counts the number of chlorine, fluorine, carbon, and other atoms in the composition. R-143a used in air conditioning and R-404a used in trailer refrigeration are both HFCs.

R-134a Replacement

HFO-1234yf, is a hydrofluoroolefin (HFO) with the formula $CH_2=CFCF_3$ is the first replacement for R-134a. As mentioned earlier, R-134a had some ODP and GWP, in contrast to the HFO near drop-in replacement. Other properties include:

- Low toxicity
- Low GWP; GWP = 4
- Zero ozone-depletion potential
- Low total contribution to climate change
- Almost identical operating pressures as current HFC-134a system

When released into the atmosphere, HFO-1234yf decomposes, giving it a lifetime of only 11 days, compared to 13 years for R134a and more than 500 years for CO_2 (carbon dioxide), another gas considered for replacing R-134a. The refrigerant was first used in a production car in 2012 and by 2018, 50% of automobiles used it. The refrigerant has one major concern—it will burn but requires over 400° C (752° F) to ignite it, and it burns slowly. Almost every other fluid under the hood lights more easily and burns hotter than R1234yf, so the industry has determined that, with proper air conditioning system design, it does not increase the likelihood of vehicle fires.

▶ TECHNICIAN TIP

CFCs are no longer used as refrigerants. Extensive scientific studies have proven that refrigerant made from these compounds destroys the ozone layer. The United States and Canada were among the many countries that ratified the Montreal Protocol, an agreement introduced in the 1980s to limit the production and use of chemicals known to deplete the ozone layer. As a result, environmental regulations in both countries govern the tasks of servicing the air conditioning system. Refrigerants, such as R12, commonly referred to as Freon, have been banned since 1995. Most original equipment manufacturers (OEMs) now use R-134a or R-1234yf, an HFO. A number of refrigerants other than R-134a have been listed by the Environmental Protection Agency (EPA) as acceptable under its Significant New Alternatives Policy (SNAP) program, or are under SNAP review.

Ozone Depletion and Global Warming Potential

Ozone is an important component of Earth's upper atmosphere. A variation of an oxygen molecule, ozone filters out harmful ultraviolet radiation from the sun's rays and helps maintain stable Earth temperature. Stratospheric ozone is found in a layer between 10 and 30 miles above Earth's surface. Tropospheric ozone, or ground-level ozone, is harmful and a primary constituent of photochemical smog.

Research has demonstrated that CFC refrigerant molecules destroy stratospheric ozone by connecting the oxygen with chlorine. Any release or venting of CFC-based refrigerants to the air has a powerfully destructive effect on ozone, which led to the banning of CFC refrigerants. Therefore, any new refrigerants are categorized by the effect they have on the ozone.

Different from its effect on the ozone layer is a refrigerant's **global warming potential (GWP)**. GWP is a measure of a refrigerant's contribution to global warming over 100 years for a given mass compared to the same mass of carbon dioxide. Carbon dioxide's GWP is defined as 1.0. The most common refrigerant used in automotive air conditioning systems, R-134a, has a high GWP of 1200, but because it contains no chlorine, it has no impact on the ozone layer. TABLE 58-3 lists the properties of R-134a.

TABLE 58-3 R-134a Properties

Boiling Point	−14.9° F (−26.1° C)
Auto-Ignition Temperature	1418° F (770° C)
Ozone Depletion Level	0
Solubility in Water	0.11% by weight at 77° F (25° C)
Cylinder Color Code	Light blue
Global Warming Potential (GWP)	1200

Special-Purpose Refrigerant

Some brands of refrigerants contain special additives or blends of refrigerants. For example, some refrigerants are bottled with a specific amount of refrigeration oil to allow the addition of oil to the system when replacing refrigerant. Other refrigerants use an additive with specialized lubricants to prolong the life of compressor seals and moving parts. Some aftermarket additives even contain aerobic chemical hardeners, which are intended to plug very small pinhole leaks when in contact with air.

Leak-tracing dye is the most common refrigerant additive and is often added during manufacturing. Refrigerant leaks cannot be detected directly since refrigerant instantly vaporizes. While some oil residue accompanies refrigerant leaks, smaller leaks are not visually detectable. The dyes can be seen at the location of a refrigerant leak using an ultraviolet light. Note, however, if a leak is large enough, pressure testing with nitrogen is recommended instead of leak detection with dyes. Refrigerants containing dyes should be added to a system only if it is at least 40% full.

Refrigeration Oil

Air conditioning systems need lubricant for several reasons. First is to reduce friction between moving surfaces and bearings inside the compressor to ensure a long service life. Additionally, thermostatic expansion valves must be lubricated to operate freely. Lubricant also coats the inside of the air conditioning system to prevent any corrosive substances from attacking the internal system components. Oil is helpful in keeping the system's seals soft and pliant, which reduces seepage from the system and increases compressor efficiency. In reciprocating piston compressors, the 90–120w viscosity lubricant helps the piston rings seal tightly against their cylinder walls to prevent leakage and apply maximum pressure to the refrigerant.

Refrigerant oil used in early systems was made from mineral oil specially formulated for air conditioning systems. That refrigeration oil was free of sulfur, so it would not form corrosive substances. It was also non-foaming and wax-free to allow free flow through the system. Any water was removed from the oil to prevent contamination. But, as oil is hygroscopic, it absorbs moisture from the air if the system is open or the storage container is not sealed. Because refrigerenat must dissolve oil and moves it through the system, better synthetic oils are needed. Two types are **polyalkylene glycol (PAG)** and **polyalphaolefin (PAO)**. PAG is used in all R-134a systems, while PAO is used in systems converted from R-12 refrigerant or special blends of refrigerant.

Air Conditioning Controls

LO 58-10 Identify and explain the purpose of air conditioning controls.

A variety of controls are used to regulate the operation of the air conditioning system (**FIGURE 58-44**). These controls are necessary to:

- Adjust operator/passenger comfort levels in the cab of the vehicle
- Improve cooling efficiency of the system
- Protect major components from damage

Many of these controls are used to operate a compressor by switching the compressor clutch on and off, as needed. Controls protect the compressor and other air conditioning system components from excessive system pressures, low system pressures, and low ambient temperatures that can damage the compressor in a variety of ways.

First, if the refrigerant level is too low and the system is undercharged, oil will not be circulated through the compressor. This happens when oil is dissolved in the refrigerant and the compressor can be damaged, eventually seizing after it pushes oil out into the system. Second, during low-temperature operation, refrigerant pressure will be low, causing the same problems of oil miscibility, which is the ability of oil to dissolve into the refrigerant gas. Similarly, at low temperatures, refrigerant oil that is in the vicinity of 90–120w viscosity will also thicken to the point where it is not easily moved. Finally, compressor controls are required to protect the system from damage due to excessive system pressures. For instance, if there is little or no airflow through the condenser, heat will not be removed, and system refrigerant pressures will increase dramatically. If refrigerant pressure is high enough, hoses can burst and O-rings can begin to leak. Before that point, the high pressures can easily prompt slippage of the compressor clutch, causing damage or clutch burnout.

Compressor Controls

Common compressor controls include:

- Thermostatic switch
- Low-pressure cutout switch
- Pressure-cycling switch
- Trinary switch
- High-pressure cutout switch
- High-pressure fan switch
- Ambient temperature switch

The air conditioning system does not use all these switches. The evaporator expansion device may not need these controls for system protection or to regulate system pressures and temperatures. The presence of an on/off engine cooling fan also changes the control configuration.

Thermostatic Switch

The thermostatic switch, also called the cold switch, is an evaporator temperature-sensing switch. It is used with either the CCOT or TXV metering systems. Using a temperature-sensitive capillary tube located where it can sense changes in the evaporator outlet temperature, the switch either opens or closes the contacts inside the switch. In turn, this action causes the compressor clutch to be engaged or disengaged.

Two types of thermostatic switch are possible. One is built to work within a preset temperature range. It has two temperature presets—one for off, and one for on. When temperature in the evaporator coils approaches freezing, the switch contacts open, disengage the compressor clutch, and allow the refrigerant in the evaporator to absorb more heat. The temperature then rises in the evaporator due to the lack of refrigerant flow. At a preset high temperature, the switch closes, engages the clutch, and compressor operation resumes.

The second type is adjustable, so the on and off points can be varied according to system and operator requirements. Newer systems use a thermistor in the evaporator that is monitored by the body control, climate control, or electrical system control module.

Low-Pressure Cutout Switch

The low-pressure cutout switch is connected in the compressor clutch electrical circuit. When a predetermined low charge is sensed, the switch stops compressor operation. This protects the compressor from damage due to insufficient refrigerant oil. It is usually mounted somewhere in the low-pressure or suction side of the system. Low-pressure cutout switches prevent cold weather operation of the compressor because system pressure and temperatures closely match. (Trinary switches often incorporate this same switch.)

Pressure-Cycling Switch

Located on the accumulator, the pressure-cycling switch is used on CCOT (orifice-tube) systems. This switch controls the cycling of the compressor by sensing pressure in the evaporator and accumulator. Low pressure is an indicator of low evaporator temperature, just as high pressure is of higher temperature. When the evaporator pressure is low, it is an indication that the evaporator is full of liquid and no more refrigerant should be pumped into it. At around 25 psi (172 kPa), the switch opens the compressor circuit. As the refrigerant absorbs heat and the pressure rises, the cycling switch may close again at around 35 psi (241 kPa), operating the compressor and causing refrigerant to flood the evaporator once more. This switch is usually located on a standard Schrader valve fitting. It is possible to remove and replace the switch without having to discharge the system.

Trinary Switch

The **trinary switch** is mounted in the high-pressure refrigerant line. It is known as a trinary switch because of its three sets of internal contacts. Typically, the switch serves three functions:

1. Low-pressure protection
2. High-pressure cutout
3. Engine fan on/off

It may also have an input from the thermostatic switch to cycle the compressor on and off.

One set of switch contacts is used to signal when system pressure drops too low, about 10–15 psi (69–103 kPa). Another set of contacts is used to signal high system pressure, about 385 psi (2654 kPa). The air conditioning compressor clutch is disengaged during either of these conditions.

The final set of switch contacts is used to cycle the engine fan during normal air conditioning operation. The on/off engine fan is engaged above pressures of 230 psi (1586 kPa) to create airflow across the condenser and lower high-side system pressure.

A similar binary switch has only two sets of contacts: one to shut off the clutch when system pressures are excessive, and another to cycle the engine fan on and off when system pressures are high. The binary switch is used along with a low-pressure switch to shut the compressor off if refrigerant pressures are too low.

High-Pressure Cutout Switch

If system pressures become too great, the likelihood of compressor damage and burst lines increases. Venting of refrigerant to the atmosphere is prohibited by law, so it is necessary to use a high-pressure cutout switch.

High-Pressure Fan Switch

High-pressure fan switches can also control the operation of the engine fan. When system pressures in the high side are great, more airflow across the condenser is required to lower condenser pressures. The switches are connected to an electric-over-air control valve that cycles the air-operated fans on and off. On newer electronically controlled engines, an electronic control unit (ECU) controls engine fan operation. In these cases, the ECU uses a high-side pressure switch for input to control the fan speed.

Fan Timers

Too-frequent cycling of the engine fan can cause premature wear of the fan's clutch friction discs. Many systems use a fan timer to lengthen the time a fan stays engaged after it has been signaled to cycle on. The engine fan typically stays engaged for between 45 and 120 seconds after the request for fan engagement by the high-pressure fan switch.

Ambient Temperature Switch

The ambient temperature switch is an outside air temperature-sensing switch. It is designed to delay compressor operation when it senses a very low outside air temperature. When temperatures are low, oil can become too viscous to lubricate the compressor properly. Operating the compressor when outside air temperature is very low could damage compressor seals, gaskets, or reed valves due to cold components and lack of proper oil circulation.

At cold ambient temperatures, this sensing switch opens its electrical contacts. Current to the compressor clutch cannot pass, and compressor operation cannot occur. Compressor internal components are, therefore, protected. The ambient temperature switch contacts close when a preset temperature is reached, normally 32° F to 50° F (0° C to 10° C), depending on application. At this point, the electrical circuit to the compressor clutch is restored and compressor operation can occur. The ambient temperature switch is usually located near the outside of the hood or engine compartment or other suitable location where it can easily sense outside air temperature.

HVAC ECU—Network Control

Contemporary vehicles all use controlled area networks with typically an air conditioning electronic control unit (ECU) with an output to the electrical system. The air conditioning module has several air conditioning system inputs hardwired to it and a J-1939 controller area network (CAN) or J-1708 data bus connection (**FIGURE 58-45**). Control logic rules are stored in the ECU that determine when it is optimal or safe for the air conditioning system clutch to engage (**TABLE 58-4**). Damage to air conditioning system components is avoided that is caused by either low or excessive refrigerant pressure, low voltage burnout of the clutch coil, or damaged condenser fan clutches.

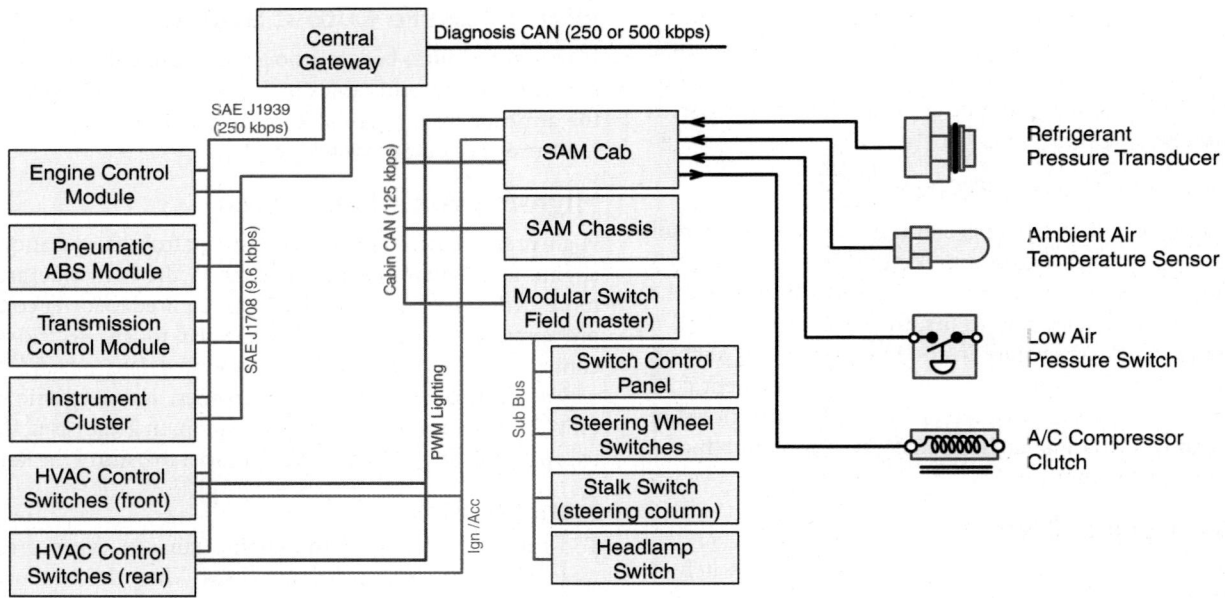

FIGURE 58-45 Network control of the air conditioning system provides optimal system operation, reliability, and durability since the system will not operate in potentially unsafe conditions.

TABLE 58-4 ECU Logic Rules for Air Conditioning Clutch Engagement

Common A/C Clutch Engagement Conditions		
ECU Logic to Send A/C Clutch Engagement Command		
Input	**Input Type**	**Condition**
Blower switch position	Input to A/C ECU	Any speed except off
A/C switch pressed	Input to A/C ECU	A/C switch light-emitting diode (LED) is on
Defrost Mode Switch - ON	Input to A/C ECU	Driver demand
No more than 4 A/C clutch engagements per minute	A/C ECU	Timer logic requires a minimum cycle time of 18 seconds
Vehicle air pressure status	J-1939 CAN	Air pressure greater than 60 psi (415 kPa)
Engine rpm	J-1939 CAN	rpm = 450 or higher for at least 5 seconds
Ambient temperature	J-1939 CAN	Ambient = 40° F to 200° F (4.5° C to 93° C)
Refrigerant pressure (high side)	Input to ECU	Refrigerant pressure = above 34 psi (234 kPa)
Battery voltage	J-1939 CAN	12.5 V or higher
Evaporator temperature	Input to ECU	38.5° F (3.5° C) or higher

Inputs from the air pressure are needed if the vehicle has an air operated fan clutch. Minimum air pressure is needed to prevent the clutch from dragging and burning out. To read fault codes on a Navistar chassis, follow the steps in **SKILL DRILL 58-1**.

Air Conditioning Protection and Diagnostic System (APADS)

LO 58-11 Describe the function of the air conditioning protection and diagnostic system (APADS).

In order to extend the lifespan of the air conditioning system on medium- and HD trucks, a supplier to the HD OEM industry, called Index Sensors, has developed systems that operate to prevent conditions that can damage the air conditioning system and to enhance system reliability. The **APADS/air conditioning protection unit (ACPU)** is an electronic microcontroller-based device that operates both air conditioning controls and diagnostic systems (**FIGURE 58-46**). Several variations of APADS are manufactured with LEDs, data bus fault code diagnostics, and various numbers of input or output connectors. Typically, the unit receives input from two pressure switches and a thermostat, and may also read vehicle parameters from the vehicle SAE J1708/J-1939 data bus. The input signals are interpreted by control logic, which process outputs to the clutch coil and fan actuator circuit and generate diagnostic codes. In the APADS-equipped air conditioning system, the controller becomes the only device through which power is switched to the clutch coil.

SKILL DRILL 58-1 Obtaining Navistar Air Conditioning Fault Codes

ECG Display

Reset Button

To obtain air conditioning-related fault codes, an electronic service tool is not required. Codes are retrievable from the driver's instrument cluster. To obtain fault codes, use the following steps as a general guideline:

1. Switch the ignition On.
2. Set the park brake and place the transmission in neutral.
3. Confirm the Park Brake Indicator.
4. Observe the electronic gauge cluster. It should display a version code for the electronic gauge control (EGC) software version after the key is switched on.
5. Press the cruise and RESUME switches on at the same time.
6. Check the ECG display. If no DTCs are set, the liquid-crystal display (LCD) displays NO FAULTS.
7. If DTCs are set, the LCD displays the total number of active codes (A), and the previously active faults, (P).
8. Wait. After 10 seconds, the fault codes display automatically and scroll through the DTCs with approximately 10 seconds separating each code.
9. To manually scroll through fault codes, press the Select/Reset button in the instrument cluster to advance to the next code.

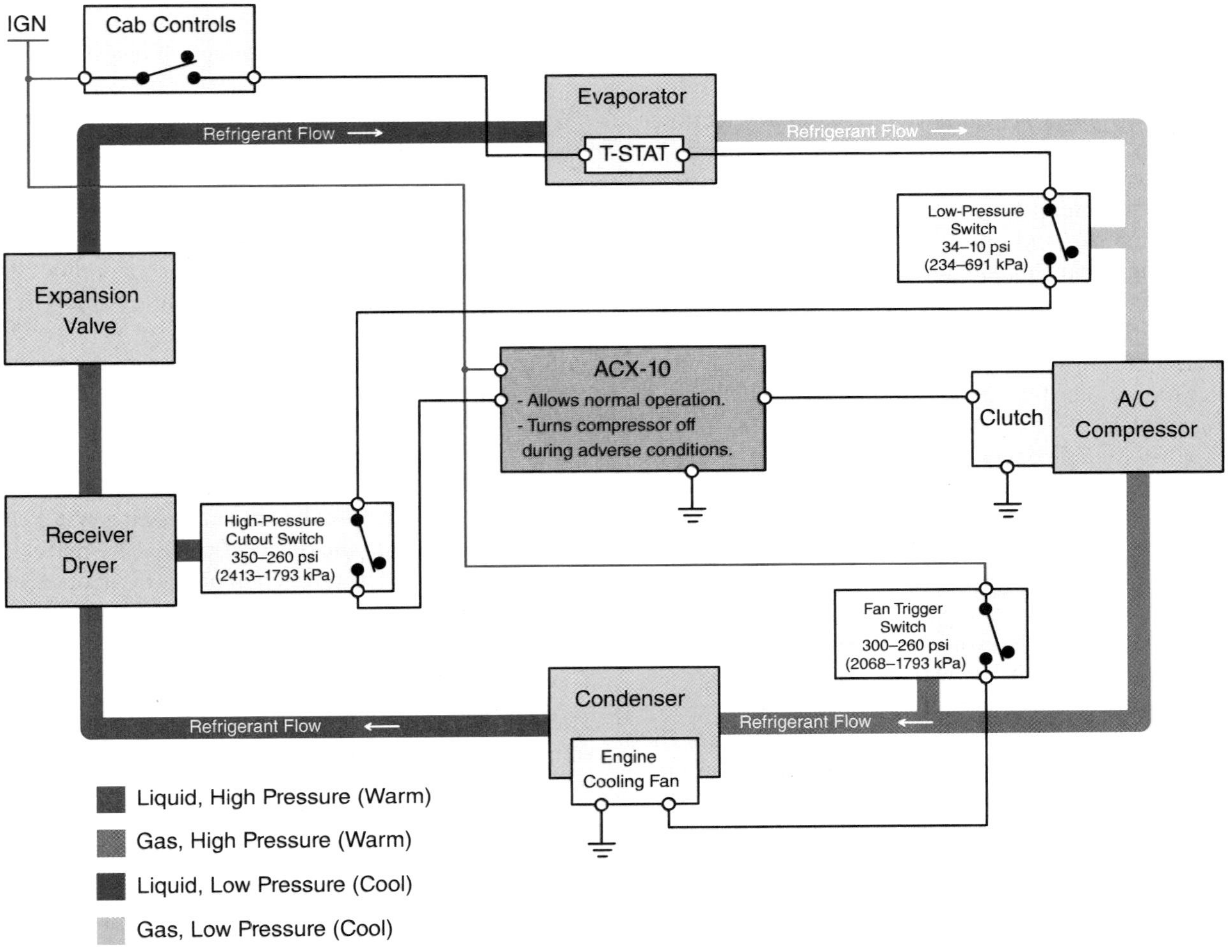

IGN

Cab Controls

Refrigerant Flow →

Evaporator

T-STAT

Refrigerant Flow →

Low-Pressure
Switch
34–10 psi
(234–691 kPa)

Expansion
Valve

ACX-10

- Allows normal operation.
- Turns compressor off
  during adverse conditions.

Clutch

A/C
Compressor

Receiver
Dryer

High-Pressure
Cutout Switch
350–260 psi
(2413–1793 kPa)

Fan Trigger
Switch
300–260 psi
(2068–1793 kPa)

Condenser

Engine
Cooling Fan

Refrigerant Flow ←

Refrigerant Flow ←

■ Liquid, High Pressure (Warm)

■ Gas, High Pressure (Warm)

■ Liquid, Low Pressure (Cool)

■ Gas, Low Pressure (Cool)

FIGURE 58-46 The functional schematic of an APADS control system.

APADS is claimed to eliminate the problems that make the air conditioning system one of the highest maintenance expense items for most HD commercial vehicles. A study by Index Sensors that used 55 pairs of trucks operating for 9 million miles found that those equipped with APADS spent 65% less on air conditioning system maintenance than identical trucks without APADS. Yearly air conditioning system maintenance costs averaged $86 per truck with APADS and $244 for non-equipped control vehicles.

Current late-model vehicles incorporate similar operation logic rules to operate the air conditioning system using network inputs.

Air Conditioning System Failures

The durability of the compressor and refrigerant hoses is adversely affected by operation of the air conditioning system with reduced or excessive refrigerant charge. Operation with a partial charge of refrigerant can cause compressor lubricant starvation, compressor overheating due to rapid cycling, and seal failure, and can lead to damaged hoses and fittings due to exposure to excessive temperatures. Operation with excessive refrigerant charges can severely stress the entire air conditioning system, causing hose and fitting leaks. Low system voltages can cause the compressor clutch to slip and overheat and loosen electrical connections, which in turn can cause erratic compressor cycling and compressor clutch failures. Traditional electrical control systems based upon a series of simple pressure switches are unable to prevent or detect these harmful modes of operation.

The APADS control system is composed of an electronic control module, two smart pressure switches, and a conventional evaporator thermostat. Because the APADS actively monitors the air conditioning system conditions and controls the refrigerant compressor and on/off fan, reliability is improved. Air conditioning system maintenance is reduced because the control algorithms of APADS do not allow operation in unstable and self-destructive modes. Additionally, diagnostic capabilities aid technicians in servicing the air conditioning system by communicating specific fault codes that warn of existing or impending problems.

The control module operates as the main air conditioning system control. The module provides an on/off output to the compressor clutch coil and the fan actuator circuit trigger. Both of these outputs are a function of the APADS control logic. Since the module controls the compressor clutch coil, it incorporates its own high-current drivers that eliminate external relays usually used to engage the compressor clutch. The APADS receives inputs from two smart switches with self-diagnostic capabilities and the evaporator thermostat. Fault diagnostic communication is established through the JJ-1708/J-1939 data bus. The module is designed to interface with electronically controlled diesel engines.

Air Conditioning Compressor Control Rules

The APADS control module enforces several rules for proper operation of the air conditioning compressor:

1. *Compressor hold-off period*—The compressor remains off for the first 15 seconds after ignition switch engagement while battery voltage is low. This prevents low-voltage compressor clutch burnout.
2. *Compressor lubrication period*—The evaporator thermostat input is ignored, and the compressor is turned on for 15 seconds directly after the hold-off period times out. This lubricates the compressor and air conditioning system. If the high- or low-pressure switches indicate out-of-bound or fault conditions, the compressor is turned off.
3. *Compressor cycle limit*—All three inputs (thermostat, high-pressure switch, and low-pressure switch) that can control the compressor are governed by control logic that limits the maximum cycle rate to once every 15 seconds.
4. *Evaporator thermostat primary control*—The compressor cycles at the frequency governed by the thermostat but is limited to a maximum of one cycle per 15 seconds (Rule 3).
5. *High-pressure reset*—When the high-pressure switch indicates an excessively high-pressure condition, the compressor is allowed to stay on for a mathematically calculated variable period, limited to 10 seconds. The compressor is allowed to turn on after the high-pressure switch resets and Rule 3 is satisfied.

Other rules include:

- *Freeze-up protection*—The thermostatic sensor prevents the compressor from operating if it detects an evaporator condition.
- *High-pressure cutout*—The compressor is not allowed to run for an extended period of time if the high-pressure switch indicates a high-pressure condition. This prevents leaks, line bursts, and excessive heat and pressure loads in the system.
- *Low-pressure cutout*—The compressor is not allowed to run if the low-pressure switch indicates low refrigerant pressure.
- *Low-voltage cutout*—The compressor is not allowed to engage if ignition voltage is less than 11 volts plus the expected clutch voltage drop.
- *High-voltage cutout*—The compressor is not allowed to run if ignition voltage is greater than 16 volts.
- *Diagnostic cutout*—The air conditioning system is turned off when any of the diagnostic faults are detected. These faults include low refrigerant pressure, an open clutch circuit, or a shorted clutch circuit.

Engine Fan Operation

The APADS module incorporates an adaptive fan-on timing control to limit fan hub wear from excessive cycling and slipping. If the high-pressure switch indicates a high-pressure condition and road speed is less than 5 mph (8 kph), the fan is turned on for 180 seconds. A high-pressure condition and road speed of 5 mph (8 kph) or greater, but less than 30 mph (48 kph), switches the fan on for 90 seconds. If the high-pressure switch indicates a high-pressure condition and road speed is 30 mph (48 kph) or greater, the fan is turned on for 45 seconds.

When the parking brake is set, there is no road speed, and if the high-pressure switch detects a high-pressure condition, the fan is requested until the parking brake is released or road speed is detected. During that time, if a driver shuts the air conditioning system off, the fan remains on for two minutes to reduce system pressure.

APADS Inputs

The APADS module receives inputs from the vehicle data link, the evaporator thermostatic switch, a high-pressure system switch, and a low-pressure system switch (**FIGURE 58-47**). Both switches have resistors connected in parallel with the electrical contacts to allow diagnosing of sensor wiring and connector faults. This switch circuit is configured to provide a low-resistance current path when it closes.

The low-pressure switch contacts are open when the pressure is sufficiently high, above 34 psi (234 kPa). Contacts close when the pressure falls below approximately 10 psi (69 kPa) and reopen after the pressure climbs back above 34 psi (234 kPa). Low-pressure switch activity is the primary indicator of a loss of charge and is also used to prevent compressor operation in extremely cold temperatures.

The high-pressure switch contacts are closed when the pressure is sufficiently low, below 260 psi (1793 kPa). Contacts open when the pressure climbs above approximately 300 psi (2068 kPa) and re-close after the pressure falls back below 260 psi (1793 kPa). The high-pressure switch is the primary control for the fan and is used to prevent compressor operation when excessive discharge pressures are present.

Evaporator Thermostat

The main air conditioning system on/off switch and the evaporator thermostatic switch are in series and are connected to the module. The series switches are configured to switch to battery voltage to command compressor operation. The thermostat contacts close when the temperature is greater than 38° F (3° C). The contacts open when the evaporator temperature drops below approximately 32° F (0° C). The thermostat is used to turn off the compressor whenever frost begins to form on the evaporator.

Diagnostic LEDs

Red and green LEDs are used on some APADS. Whenever a system fault is detected, the APADS broadcasts diagnostic information over the data bus. Diagnostic blink codes are supplied by combinations of blinking lights and colors of the LEDs (**FIGURE 58-48**).

Air Distribution System

LO 58-12 Describe the function of the air distribution system.

The air distribution system directs the flow of heated and conditioned air throughout the cab. The HVAC system is commonly built as a single module assembly mounted on

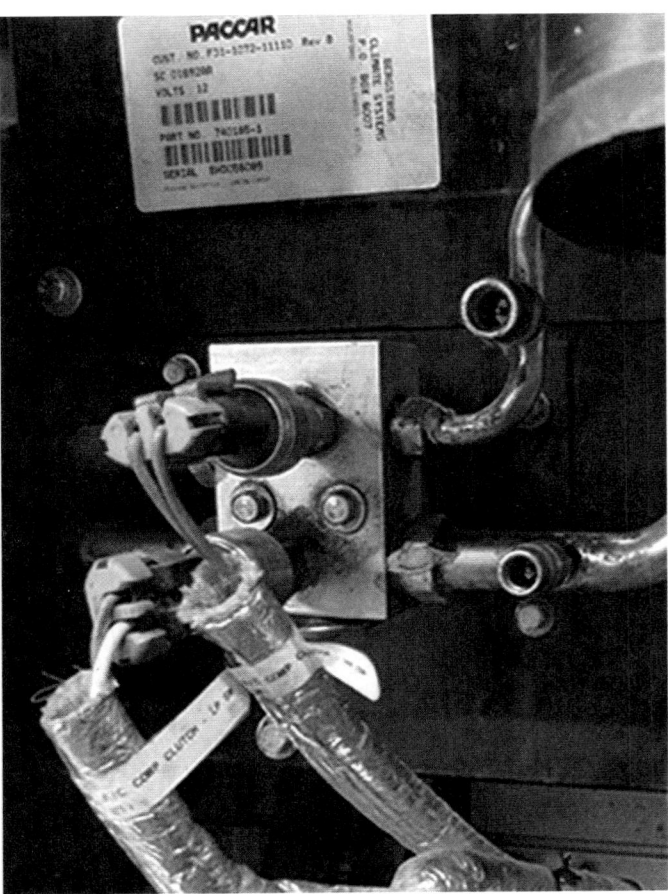

FIGURE 58-47 Location of the high- and low-pressure switches on the H-type TXV for an APADS system.

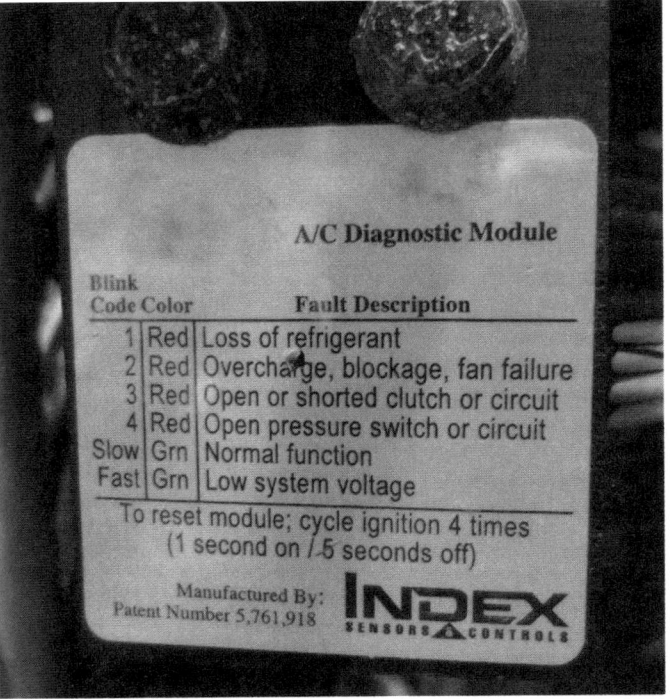

FIGURE 58-48 Diagnostic blink codes are obtained from the APADS module from two LEDs.

FIGURE 58-49 The HVAC components are located in a module mounted to the firewall of the cab.

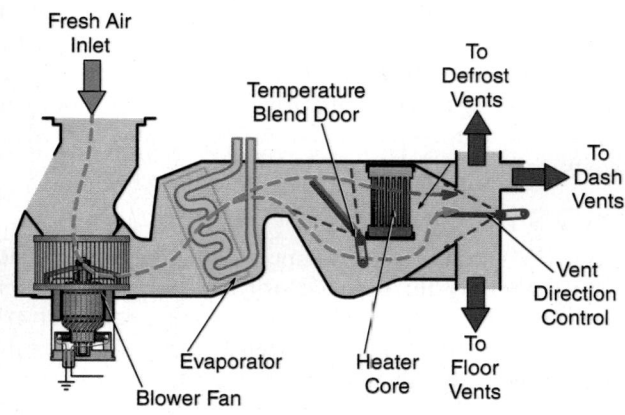

FIGURE 58-51 Air doors regulate the distribution of conditioned air into the cab.

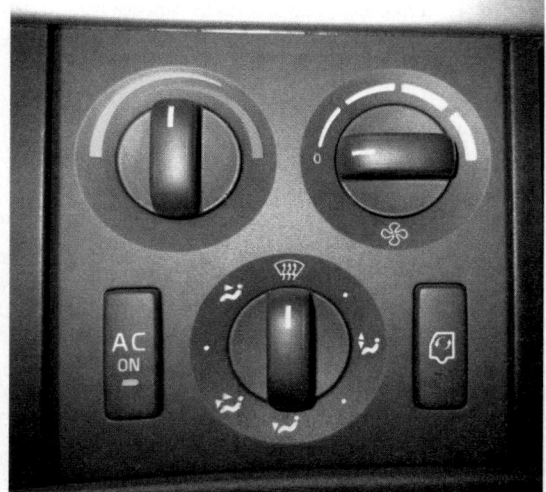

FIGURE 58-50 A set of switches controls the HVAC system operation.

the firewall with half of the module extending into the cab (**FIGURE 58-49**). A set of controls in the dash regulates blower motor speed, outlet of cab temperature, and HVAC mode (**FIGURE 58-50**). A separate air conditioning request switch is used to enable dehumidification of air when humidity levels in the cab are high, causing window fogging. Switching the air conditioning on and recirculating air quickly dehumidifies the cab and clears up window fogging. As a safety feature, when placed in defrost mode, most systems automatically switch on the air conditioning system to dehumidify airflow to the windshield. Mode refers to the various options for airflow through the HVAC module. Ducts through the cab direct airflow to the windshield, dash vents, or floor. Standard modes of air distribution include:

- Defrost mode, which directs warm dehumidified air to the windshield
- Floor mode, which directs air to the footwells

- Vent mode, which directs airflow midlevel through the dash vents
- Bilevel mode, which is a combination of two or three other modes
- MAX air conditioning mode directs all airflow to the midlevel vent air outlets and the air is recirculated inside the vehicle. This mode is used to block out any outside odors, smoke, or dust, or to rapidly cool the cab during hot weather start-up.
- Fresh air or recirculate mode, which brings in fresh outside air or recirculates cab air. Recirculate mode is only used when outside temperatures are very hot or cold and the load on the HVAC system is too high to change or maintain cab temperature.

Air Door Actuators

The default operation of the HVAC module during any failure is to direct heated air to the windshield since a clear, condensate-free windshield is critical for safety. The air conditioning evaporator and heater core air ducts are connected in series, but a blend-air door can regulate varying proportions of heat or cooled air into the air ducts (**FIGURE 58-51**). Electric motor actuators are used to control the operation of four air doors.

- Floor defrost door directs air to the floor or defrost ducts.
- Vent defrost door directs air to vent or defrost ducts.
- Recirculation mixes the proportion of inside and outside air drawn into the blower motor.
- Blend-air door blends air conditioning and heater core air flow and regulates temperature.

On late-model vehicles, these actuators, as well as the blower motor, use brushless DC stepper motors (**FIGURE 58-52**). Brushless stepper motors use permanent magnets in the rotor and electromagnetic coils for the motor field windings. Because they do not use current to produce magnetic fields in the rotor, depending instead on permanent magnets, the

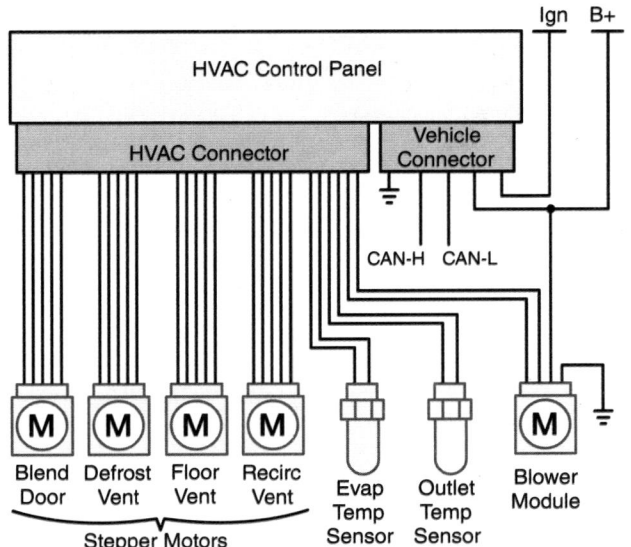

FIGURE 58-52 Brushless DC stepper motors control the operation of air doors in the air distribution system.

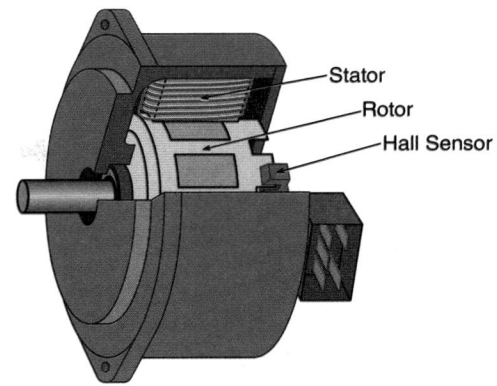

FIGURE 58-53 Actuators for the cab air door controls are operated by brushless stepper motors providing low power consumption, high speed, and positional control.

power consumption is lower. No commutator is needed since a microcontroller switches current on and off in two, three, or four field windings. Speed stability and position are very accurately controlled using microcontroller-regulated operation (**FIGURE 58-53**). When used for actuators the motors can have slim body profiles, yet provide high torque output, due to the use of permanent magnets. A Hall-effect sensor is built into many motors to provide position feedback to the microcontroller. To verify the actuators are correctly positioning the doors, a calibration process takes place where the actuators learn the doors' maximum and minimum rotation for open and closed doors.

Hall-effect switches inside actuator motors are used to teach the air conditioning ECU door maximum and minimum positions (open and closed positions). After an actuator replacement, the ECU must learn new air door positions to properly activate the stepper motors with the correct electrical signals. To recalibrate actuator doors on a Navistar and several other trucks, follow the steps in **SKILL DRILL 58-2**.

Never force an actuator using a stepper motor into a position because the motors do not turn easily and can break actuator parts, plus movement of permanent magnets inside the motors generates a voltage that could damage an ECU. To properly align a stepper motor used for an air door actuator, follow the steps in **SKILL DRILL 58-3**.

SKILL DRILL 58-2 Air Door Actuator Recalibration

1. Cycle the ignition key Off and then On.
2. Switch the blower motor on to any speed but off.
3. Place the mode selector to defrost mode.
4. Remove the 5-amp fuse for the HVAC control head.
5. Reinstall the fuse after waiting for 30 seconds.
6. Listen for actuator door movement, but do not operate control head.
7. After the actuator door movement has stopped, start the engine and check for proper operation of all HVAC modes and settings.

SKILL DRILL 58-3 Installing an Actuator Motor

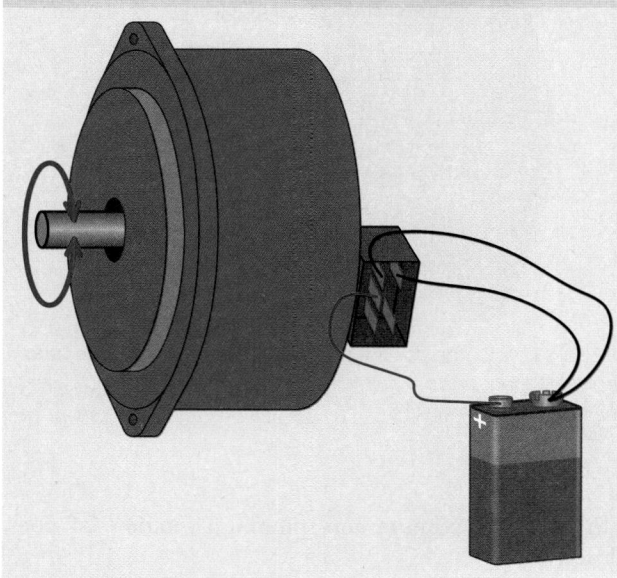

1. Place the door actuator in the approximate position as the collar of a stepper motor actuator.
2. With the harness plug disconnected, use a pair of jumper wires to connect a 9-volt battery to the correct pins on the stepper motor. Depending on the type of motor, two pins are for a negative ground and two for a positive voltage.
3. Switch the battery leads to turn the motor in the opposite direction.
4. Rotate the motor under battery power until the actuator lever collar is aligned with the door shaft.
5. Torque the actuator mounting screws to specification.
6. Calibrate the motor position using **SKILL DRILL 58-2**.

Wrap-Up

Ready for Review

- Freon, a brand trademark name of DuPont Chemicals, is a colorless, odorless, nonflammable, and noncorrosive gas or liquid chlorofluorocarbon (CFC).
- Modern mobile air conditioning has tremendous safety benefits. A comfortable vehicle environment reduces driver fatigue and distractions and can increase driver productivity.
- The greater the heat energy in a substance, the faster its molecules vibrate (heat = speed).
- Conduction, convection, and radiation are three types of heat transfer.
- Heat is measured in a number of different ways; most commonly sensible heat is measured with a thermometer.
- A calorie is the basic unit for measuring the quantity of heat energy.
- The concepts of gas temperature and pressure are related.
- Boiling points of liquids are affected by the pressure exerted upon them.
- Air conditioning and refrigeration systems operate in a closed loop in which the refrigerant is used over and over as it circulates through the system.
- The air conditioning compressor is an engine-driven pump that increases refrigerant pressure and circulates refrigerant through the system.
- Three basic types of air conditioning compressors can be used to build pressure exceeding 350 psi (2413 kPa): piston, rotary vane, and scroll. Piston compressors are almost universally used in commercial vehicles.

- Rotary piston compressors have cylindrical-shaped housings and enclose multiple pistons. The primary advantage of rotary compressors is their minimization of NVH (noise, vibration, and harshness).
- Mobile HD air conditioning compressors are usually belt-driven from the engine's crankshaft and have an electromagnetic on/off clutch.
- The condenser typically consists of coiled tubing mounted in a series of thin cooling fins and is mounted directly in front of the radiator, where it can receive full airflow created by forward vehicle motion and the engine fan.
- An expansion device restricts the flow of high-pressure, warm liquid refrigerant line and is designed to lower the pressure of refrigerant entering the evaporator.
- The TXV expansion device lowers the pressure of the warm, high-pressure liquid refrigerant entering the evaporator and allows the refrigerant to expand to greater volume.
- Unlike a CCOT system, which meters refrigerant at a fixed rate, the TXV meters refrigerant into the evaporator at a variable rate.
- The thermostatic expansion valve controls refrigerant flow by the action of a spring-loaded control valve. Evaporator temperature and pressure are two factors that change the size of the restriction opening.
- The orifice tube is a simple, plastic tube with a calibrated brass orifice used on current CCOT systems to produce refrigerant pressure drop in the evaporator.
- The evaporator is a heat exchanger located inside the cab or passenger compartment containing the chamber where refrigerant boils and converts to a vapor.

- The primary function of the receiver-dryer is to serve as a storage reservoir for refrigerant. A second function is to absorb any moisture in the air conditioning system.

- Accumulators are used in CCOT or fixed-orifice tube (FOT) systems.

- Automotive air conditioning systems use two fluids: refrigerant (to absorb heat) and refrigeration oil (to lubricate the compressor and expansion valves).

- The lower the boiling point of a refrigerant, the colder the evaporator temperature is.

- A refrigerant with a high specific heat loses its ability to refrigerate on a weight basis. Similarly, a refrigerant with a high latent heat capacity absorbs more heat per unit of weight. Combining a refrigerant with high latent heat and low specific heat increases effectiveness of a refrigerant on a per-lb (per-kg) basis.

- Saturated temperature refers to the temperature at which a refrigerant changes from a liquid to vapor or vapor to liquid at a given pressure.

- Refrigerants are manufactured from hydrogen, fluorine, chlorine, and carbon molecules. Two categories of refrigerant compositions are used today: hydrofluorocarbons (HFCs) and hydrochlorofluorocarbons (HCFCs).

- The most common refrigerant used in automotive air conditioning systems, R-134a, has a GWP of 1200, as it contains no chlorine and has no impact on the ozone layer. Most recently developed is HFO1234yf, an HFO class of refrigerant a near drop-in replacement for the R134a refrigerant with almost no negative environmental impacts.

- Air conditioning systems need lubricant to reduce friction between moving surfaces and bearings inside the compressor and thermostatic expansion valves, and to prevent any corrosive substances from attacking the internal system components.

- Common compressor controls include the thermostatic switch, low-pressure cutout switch, pressure-cycling switch, trinary switch, high-pressure cutout switch, high-pressure fan switch, and ambient temperature switch.

- Venting of refrigerant to the atmosphere is prohibited by law.

- Too-frequent cycling of the engine fan can cause premature wear of the fan's clutch friction discs.

- The APADS/air conditioning protection unit (ACPU) is an electronic, microcontroller-based device that operates both air conditioning controls and the diagnostic system.

- The APADS control system is composed of an electronic control module, two smart pressure switches, and a conventional evaporator thermostat.

- The APADS module receives inputs from the vehicle data link, the evaporator thermostatic switch, and high- and low-pressure system switches.

Key Terms

APADS/air conditioning protection unit (ACPU) An electronic microcontroller-based device that operates both air conditioning controls and diagnostic systems.

British thermal unit (BTU) The amount of energy required to heat or cool 1 pound of water 1° F.

calorie The unit of energy that reflects the amount of energy required to raise the temperature of 1 gram of water by 1° C.

chlorofluorocarbons (CFCs) A chlorine-based composition of a fluorine hydrocarbon compound.

condensation Moisture that collects on cooler surfaces as a result of hot vapors coming into contact with the cooler surface.

condenser A component of the HVAC system that transfers heat from the refrigerant to the atmosphere.

conduction The transfer of heat through a solid item, such as a body panel or evaporator.

convection The transfer of heat through a gas.

cycling clutch orifice tube (CCOT) A fixed-orifice tube for evaporator pressure control obtained by cycling the compressor clutch on and off.

defroster A HVAC air circuit that operates to clear the windows by blowing dehumidified air into the cab.

evaporator The cold surface of the air conditioning system heat exchanger that absorbs heat from a cab or vehicle interior and transfers that heat to the atmosphere through a condenser.

evaporator freezing A condition in which excess refrigerant floods the evaporator reducing its temperature to below the freezing point of water.

Freon A refrigerant produced by reacting carbon tetrachloride, commonly used as "carb-cleaner," with fluorine gas.

global warming potential (GWP) A measure of a refrigerant's contribution to global warming over 100 years for a given mass compared to the same mass of carbon dioxide.

hydrofluoro-olefin (HFO) Is the most recently developed, near drop-in replacement for the R134a refrigerant. It's chemical name is HFO1234yf.

heater core An in-cab heat exchanger that regulates heating by circulating engine coolant.

heating ventilation and air conditioning (HVAC) system The system in the vehicle responsible for heating and cooling the air.

latent heat The quantity of heat required to produce a change of state from a solid to a liquid or a liquid to a gas.

latent heat of fusion The process of removing heat energy to matter to effect a change of state.

latent heat of vaporization The process of adding heat energy to matter to produce a change of state.

polyalkylene glycol (PAG) Synthetic oil used in all R-134a systems.

polyalphaolefin (PAO) Synthetic refrigerant oil used in air conditioning systems.

psia The units of pressure, in pounds per square inch, using sea level as a reference. Atmospheric pressure at sea level = 0 psia.

psig The units of pressure, in pounds per square inch, expressed relative to atmospheric pressure. Atmospheric pressure at sea level = 14.7 psig.

radiant heat transfer The transfer of heat through a medium, such as a gas or vacuum, which does not cause the medium itself to heat.

receiver-dryer A storage reservoir for refrigerant that also absorbs moisture from the air conditioning system.

rotary piston compressors HVAC compressors that use cylindrical-shaped housings and enclose multiple pistons to minimize of noise, vibration, and harshness.

sensible heat Heat that can be sensed or felt.

specific heat The amount of heat a substance must absorb to undergo a temperature change of 1° F.

superheat The temperature differential between the refrigerant vapor at the evaporator outlet and the refrigerant vapor at the evaporator inlet.

thermostatic expansion valve (TXV) An expansion device used in commercial vehicle air conditioning systems.

trinary switch An air conditioning system switch with three sets of internal contacts to protect against low pressure, cutout in case of high pressure, and turn the engine fan on and off.

Review Questions

1. Which of the following is the most recent category or type of air conditioning refrigerant?
   a. Freon
   b. R-134a
   c. HFO
   d. HCHC

2. Which of the following functions of an air conditioning system is directly related to safe vehicle operation?
   a. It reduces driver fatigue.
   b. It cleans and filters air.
   c. It keeps the operator and passengers comfortable.
   d. It is automatically activated in defrost mode.

3. Which measurement of heat best describes the amount required to produce a change of state?
   a. Latent
   b. Sensible
   c. Radiant
   d. Convection

4. What would be the equivalent pressure in "psig" units be for a 3-psia measured at sea level?
   a. 0 psig
   b. 3 psig
   c. -3 psig
   d. 17.7 psig

5. How many cylinders does a rotary compressor typically have that is used in a highway tractor?
   a. 2–4
   b. 4–8
   c. 5–10
   d. 6–12

6. Consider a truck with 36,000 BTU cooling capacity. How many tons of air conditioning does this system have?
   a. 1 ton
   b. 2.2 tons
   c. 3 tons
   d. 4 tons

7. Which of the following statements is correct concerning the TXV expansion device?
   a. The TXV expansion device lowers the pressure of the warm, high-pressure liquid refrigerant entering the evaporator and allows the refrigerant to expand to greater volume.
   b. An orifice in the TXV creates a pressure differential, forming the dividing point in the low side of the air conditioning system.
   c. The high-side pressure and low-side temperature regulate the valve operation.
   d. It must be combined with a high-side pressure switch to regulate evaporator temperature.

8. What is the advantage of a rotary type variable displacement air conditioning compressor?
   a. It regulates evaporator pressure.
   b. It has fewer moving parts.
   c. It uses less energy.
   d. It can pump more refrigerant than other types of compressors.

9. How is lubricating oil circulated in an air conditioning system?
   a. Refrigerant dissolves oil like a solvent and circulates oil.
   b. The compressor pumps oil.
   c. It is stored in each component needing oil for lubrication.
   d. The velocity of refrigerant gas carries oil.

10. Which of the following devices senses evaporator pressure to control the cycling of the air conditioning clutch in a Navistar CCOT system?
    a. Thermistors
    b. Pressure transducer and high-pressure switch
    c. Cab thermostatic switch
    d. CAN controls

ASE Technician A/Technician B Style Questions

1. Technician A says that heat energy in an air conditioning system travels from cold to hot. Technician B says that the air conditioning system's condenser removes heat from the cab and transfers it to the atmosphere via the evaporator. Who is correct?
   a. Technician A
   b. Technician B
   c. Both Technician A and Technician B
   d. Neither Technician A nor Technician B

2. Technician A says that reducing refrigerant pressure causes the refrigerant to absorb heat. Technician B says reducing refrigerant pressure causes it to evaporate. Who is correct?
   a. Technician A
   b. Technician B
   c. Both Technician A and Technician B
   d. Neither Technician A nor Technician B

3. Technician A says that increasing refrigerant pressure causes its temperature to increase. Technician B says increasing refrigerant pressure causes it to vaporize. Who is correct?
   a. Technician A
   b. Technician B
   c. Both Technician A and Technician B
   d. Neither Technician A nor Technician B

4. Technician A says that air conditioning systems trasnfers cold from the atmosphere and into the passenger compartment. Technician B says that air conditioning systems dehumidify and clean air passing through the evaporator. Who is correct?
   a. Technician A
   b. Technician B
   c. Both Technician A and Technician B
   d. Neither Technician A nor Technician B

5. Technician A says that outside air flows over the fins of the condenser transferring heat from the refrigerant, causing it to convert from a gas to a liquid. Technician B says that the condenser compressor pressure helps convert hot gas to a liquid in the condenser. Who is correct?
   a. Technician A
   b. Technician B
   c. Both Technician A and Technician B
   d. Neither Technician A nor Technician B

6. Technician A says that the thermostatic expansion valve controls refrigerant flow through the action of a variable orifice control valve. Technician B says that approximately a 5° F (15° C) temperature difference between evaporator inlet and outlet is required to open the valve. Who is correct?
   a. Technician A
   b. Technician B
   c. Both Technician A and Technician B
   d. Neither Technician A nor Technician B

7. Technician A says that the refrigerant HFO-1234YF is currently used in vehicle air conditioning systems. Technician B says that the refrigerant R-143a is used in vehicle air conditioning systems. Who is correct?
   a. Technician A
   b. Technician B
   c. Both Technician A and Technician B
   d. Neither Technician A nor Technician B

8. Technician A says that the low-pressure cut out switch is connected in series with the compressor clutch electrical circuit. Technician B says that when a low refrigerant charge is sensed, the switch opens and prevents compressor operation. Who is correct?
   a. Technician A
   b. Technician B
   c. Both Technician A and Technician B
   d. Neither Technician A nor Technician B

9. Technician A says that a pressure-cycling switch is used in CCOT (orifice-tube) systems and is located on the accumulator. Technician B says that it is not possible to remove and replace the switch without having to discharge the system. Who is correct?
   a. Technician A
   b. Technician B
   c. Both Technician A and Technician B
   d. Neither Technician A nor Technician B

10. Technician A says that the air conditioning control module receives information from the vehicle data link for chassis air pressure in the air reservoirs to protect the air conditioning system components. Technician B says that the battery voltage is critical to protect air conditioning system components. Who is correct?
    a. Technician A
    b. Technician B
    c. Both Technician A and Technician B
    d. Neither Technician A nor Technician B

CHAPTER 59

Servicing Heating and Air Conditioning Systems

Learning Objectives

- **LO 59-1** Outline the steps and procedures to performance test an air conditioning (A/C) system.
- **LO 59-2** Describe and explain the purpose and procedures used to perform refrigerant leak testing.
- **LO 59-3** Identify and outline procedures used to recover, recycle, and charge an A/C system with refrigerant.
- **LO 59-4** Outline the procedure to inspect a condenser for air flow restrictions.
- **LO 59-5** Outline the procedures used to inspect and service the evaporator housing.
- **LO 59-6** Identify and explain major service and repair operations related to A/C system service.

You Are the Technician

A three-year-old refuse-hauling truck has had its air conditioning (A/C) system repaired multiple times in the past eight months. On its fourth visit to your shop, the driver complains once again that the system is blowing only warm air. After verifying the complaint, you connect a manifold gauge set to the A/C system and attempt to complete an A/C-system performance test. The test could not be completed, however, because after about 30 seconds of operation, the A/C compressor clutch disengaged the compressor. You noticed during that time that the compressor operation was also very noisy. Examining the manifold gauge pressures during the system's brief operation, you discover that the pressures were abnormally low and likely caused by an undercharge of refrigerant. A leak somewhere in the A/C system is the most likely cause for the low pressures. Before you begin any further diagnostic work, or repairs, consider the following questions:

1. What qualifications would be required of the technician to perform this A/C repair?
2. Outline three techniques that are used to identify and locate a refrigerant leak.
3. Explain the reasons that would best account for noisy compressor operation.

Introduction

Servicing and maintaining the proper operation of a HVAC (Heating, Ventilation, and Air Conditioning) or climate control system on a commercial vehicle has greater importance than in many other modes of transportation. One reason is because cabin temperature and humidity are very important for comfort and safety reasons. Keeping windows defrosted and a driver undistracted by high heat and humidity levels not only contributes to safer operation, but also improves productivity. The cab of a commercial vehicle is, after all, a workplace for drivers. Likewise, passengers on commercial buses can spend long periods of time on board the vehicle, and a positive travel experience is beneficial to commercial success.

Heating and air conditioning (A/C) systems on commercial vehicles work even harder than those in automobiles, as commercial vehicles often have large glass areas that expose the interior to more radiant heat. Cabin climate is more difficult to maintain when it is hot or cold outside, because commercial vehicles have large exterior surface areas and are not well-insulated. The system must be capable of reaching an ideal temperature of 70° F to 80° F (20° C to 26° C) after a few minutes, as well as exchanging the air in the cabin with fresh air every few minutes to remove odors, smoke, and exhalation. Transit buses have high-demand HVAC requirements, including an air flow of between 2500 and 3500 cfm (71 and 99 cubic meter/minute) and the cooling capacity of 20 to 30 times that of a medium-sized home A/C unit. These A/C systems operate between 1000 and 3000 hours a year in the climate extremes of the United States. As much as 25% of fuel cost in these applications is for producing the power required to operate A/C compressors and generating electricity to drive electric blower motors for evaporators and condensers. Addtionally, cost of A/C system maintenance is also one of the highest vehicle servicing expenses, according to a study by Index Sensors, which identified maintenance costs averaging as much as $244 a year on heavy trucks.

Servicing A/C systems has become more complex due to legislated requirements to minimize release of refrigerants into the atmosphere. The Montreal protocol, with which most countries in the world have agreed to comply, aims to reduce global warming and damage caused by refrigerants to the atmosphere's upper ozone layer. In North America, legislation in Canada and the United States demands that anyone handling refrigerants or working on A/C systems must receive special training and have qualifications for working with refrigerants before undertaking any repairs. In the United States, Section 609 of the Clean Air Act outlines standards and requirements for servicing motor vehicle air conditioning (MVAC) and MVAC-like appliances. Both US law and the Canadian code outlined in technician certification for Canadian Ozone Depletion Prevention prohibit the intentional release of refrigerant.

Even though servicing and maintaining A/C systems requires specialized certification and training, this chapter focuses on the fundamentals of A/C service on basic mobile systems required by certified technicians.

The Air Conditioning Service Process

LO 59-1 Outline the steps and procedures to performance test an air conditioning (A/C) system.

There are many variations in the design and construction of A/C and refrigeration systems used in commercial vehicles. But whether it is a medium-duty truck with a day cab, or a highway coach having the cooling capacity of a commercial office building, the following basic tasks are involved in servicing and repairing most A/C systems:

- Performance testing
- System analysis: Determining whether faults are related to the refrigerant **charge** or the electrical system
- Electrical and onboard network diagnostics
- Leak testing
- Reclaiming refrigerant
- Repairing faults
- System evacuation
- Charging with refrigerant
- System performance retesting

The integration of CAN communication with the electronic control of cab climate systems adds another major element to A/C system analysis and service. One advantage is most current model vehicles have diagnostic software available to assist pinpoint testing of A/C systems for quick identification of system faults and can provide guided diagnostic procedures. Electronic pressure transducers measuring refrigerant system pressures and other system sensors provide instant visualization of system operation on a computer screen (**FIGURE 59-1**) However, system sophistication is accompanied by an increased number of service procedures. Mechatronic devices, which are mechanical components with embedded microcontrollers, require specialized calibration procedures. A/C system protection features that extend system durability and increase reliability add complexity to diagnostic steps and components that may need pinpoint testing.

Performance Testing

After collecting as much information from a customer as possible, any proper diagnostic strategy has two essential steps:

1. Verify complaint
2. Visual inspection

Carrying out a *performance test* of the A/C system is the first step in the diagnostic process. **Performance testing** is the term used to describe the standard A/C test procedure that can verify a complaint and involves a visual inspection. During standard performance testing procedures, A/C system components are identified and visually inspected and their condition noted. The system is operated until temperatures and pressures stabilize before measuring the center vent's outlet temperature and refrigerant pressures. Actual measured values are recorded and compared with original equipment manufacturers (OEM) specifications to determine whether the A/C system is operating

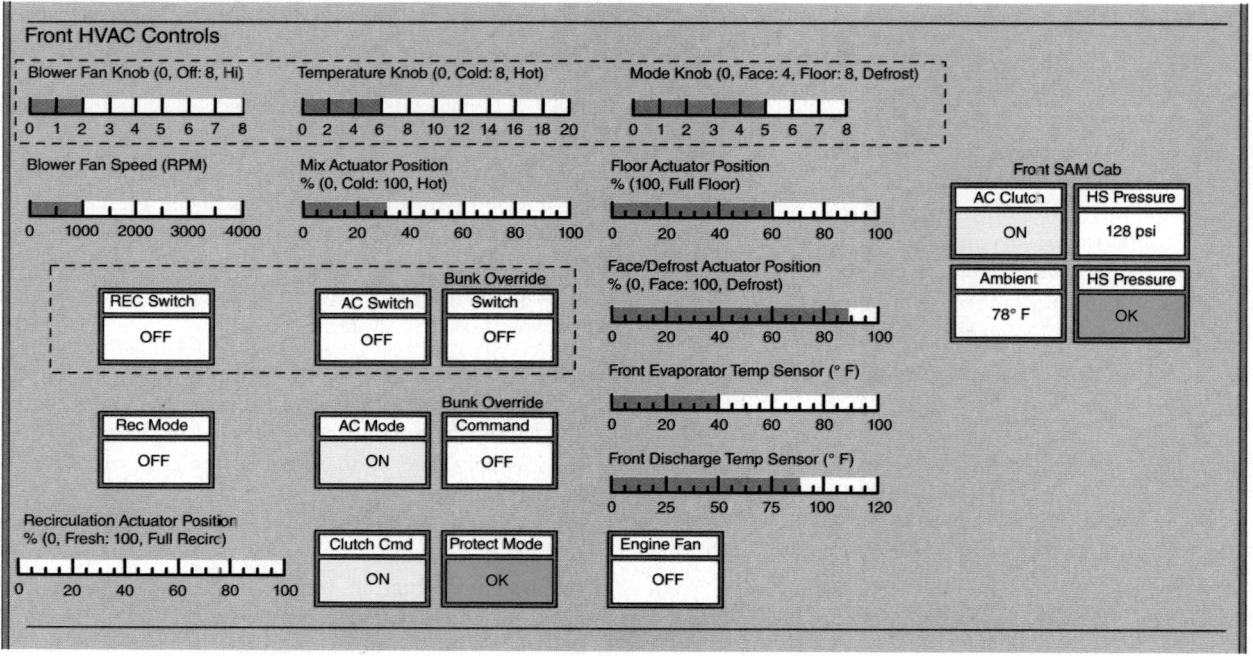

FIGURE 59-1 A representative display for service and diagnostic software for a commercial vehicle A/C system.

within expected range of values. Details of procedures for performance testing vary slightly between manufacturers but involves these steps:

1. Switching on the A/C to its maximum cooling setting with the windows closed and raising the engine speed to 1100–1500 rpm.
2. After about five minutes of operation with the blower fan speed on high, the center vent outlet temperature in the cabin is measured with a thermometer.
3. Outside air temperatures and relative humidity are observed and recorded as well, then compared to the temperature and humidity specifications in a manufacturer's service literature.
4. A manifold pressure gauge set is connected before the test begins to measure refrigerant pressures. Running and resting pressures with the engine off are observed and recorded in a chart like **TABLE 59-1**.

A general rule is the difference between outside ambient and vent temp should be 25° F to 30° F (14° C to 16° C) lower. If air humidity is high, only over 70%, added warm moisture adds extra heat load to an A/C system, resulting in increased system outlet temperatures and high-side refrigerant pressures. Using the table of collected information, a technician can analyze the data to determine whether the system likely has the correct charge of refrigerant, whether the refrigerant contains air, or an incorrect type of refrigerant was used. Temperatures at the vent outlet can not only validate a complaint of "low cooling," a condition when the cab is too warm with the A/C operating, but also indicate whether the blower controls are working correctly, and if heater shut-off valves for coolant are opened or closed. Most importantly, this first diagnostic step helps determine if an A/C complaint is the result of a problem with the refrigerant system or the electrical control system. Results from the performance test—whether the A/C

TABLE 59-1 A/C System Performance Testing Parameters

AC Performance Test Parameters	Observed Measurement	Service Manual
Current ambient air temperature		
Current relative humidity (RH%)		
Center vent outlet temperature		
Sleeper lower vent outlet temperature		
High-side pressure (Resting)		
Low-side pressure (Resting)		
High-side pressure (Running)		
Low-side pressure (Running)		

A/C Electrical System Troubleshooting

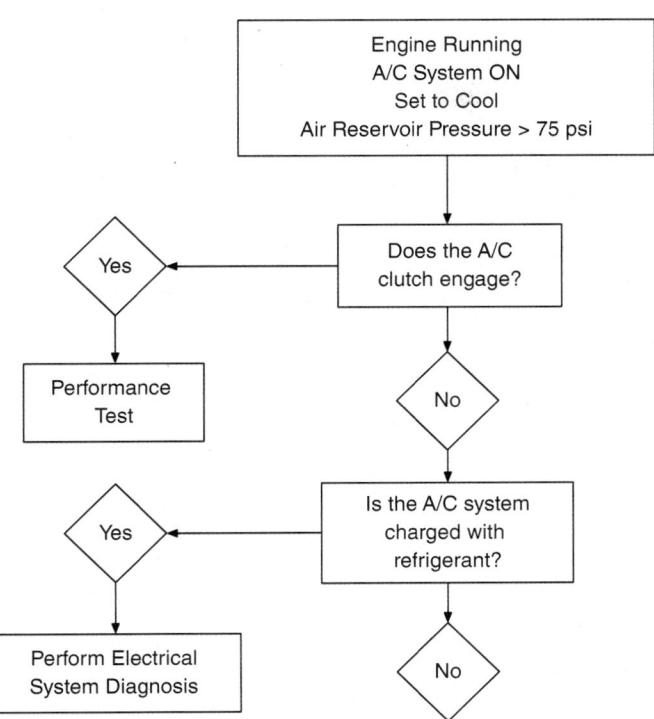

FIGURE 59-2 Performance testing determines whether a complaint is valid, and what subsequent procedures should be followed if a problem is found.

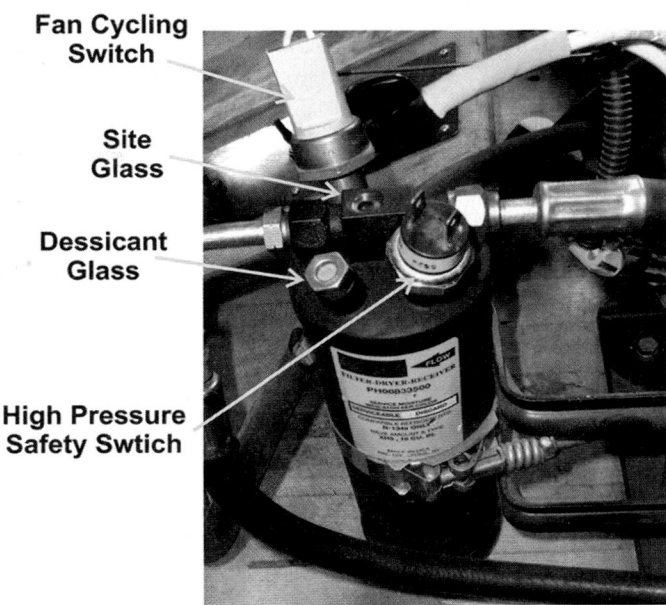

FIGURE 59-3 A receiver dryer with a site glass to indicate the refrigerant state of charge and a site glass for the moisture-detecting desiccant.

compressor switches on or not, and whether there was adequate cooling, leads to the next set of diagnostic procedures (**FIGURE 59-2**).

Refrigerant State of Charge

The correct refrigerant **charge** (the weight of refrigerant) in the A/C system is critical for proper cooling. An inadequate charge means not enough refrigerant can circulate to absorb and release heat. Too much refrigerant can result in low cooling as well because the system's pressures remain too high for the refrigeration cycle to operate effectively. In either situation, an incorrect refrigerant charge pressure changes the boiling point of the refrigerant, making it unable to effectively remove heat in the evaporator. While performance testing, a system with a site glass installed in the receiver dryer enables a technician to monitor the refrigerant condition and charge (**FIGURE 59-3**). A steady stream of bubbles or foam in the site glass indicates an undercharged system. No bubbles or very few should be observed. The desiccant site glass also indicates whether the system has moisture contamination. If it does, the normally light blue moisture indicator turns green or white.

High- and Low-Pressure Safety Switches

The A/C system incorporates safety features to prevent system damage and prolong component life. For example, the

Performance Testing Diagnosis

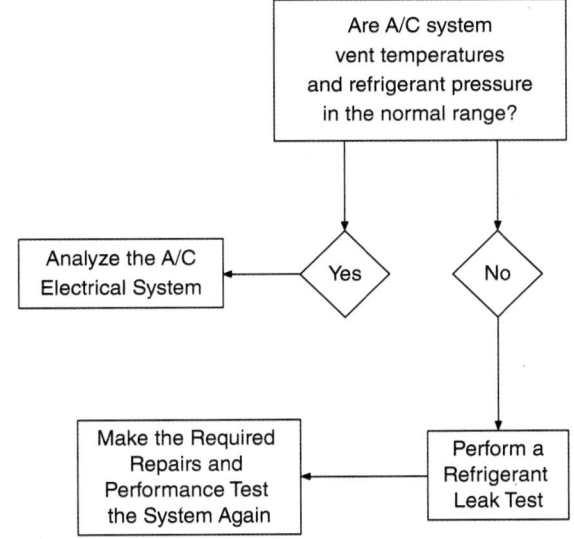

FIGURE 59-4 If the A/C system does not operate, the problem may be electrical or the result of a low refrigerant charge.

low-pressure refrigerant switch prevents the compressor from operating if a leak results in low refrigerant charge accompanied by low operating pressures (**FIGURE 59-4**). Without an adequate refrigerant charge, lubricating oil that is dissolved and carried through the system by the refrigerant cannot circulate. The result is a noisy compressor or a premature compressor failure without adequate lubrication. A high-pressure safety switch also

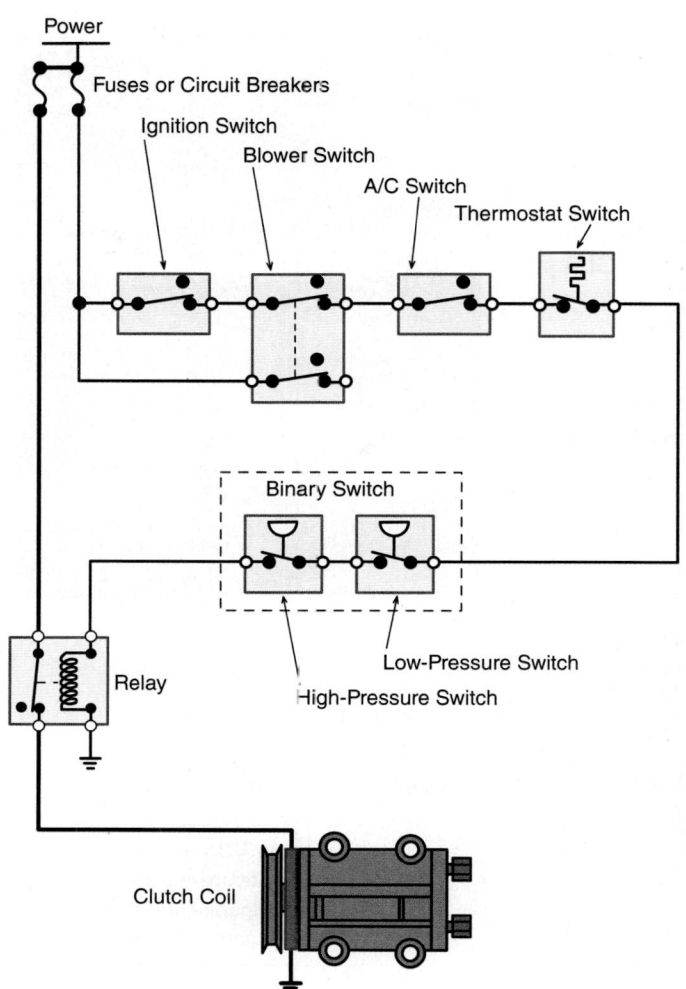

FIGURE 59-5 A/C electrical system switches are commonly connected in series through either a ground or chassis positive circuit. All switches must be closed for power to reach the compressor or for control module logic operations to energize the compressor relay.

FIGURE 59-6 An air conditioning identification sticker.

opens the circuit to power the compressor clutch (**FIGURE 59-5**). Excessive refrigerant pressure can cause refrigerant lines to burst and damage a compressor due to high discharge pressure. Since the system pressures vary greatly during operation, the switches are designed to allow operation within a wide operating range before the electrical current to the compressor is interrupted. Because the safety switches are all connected in series, any abnormal operating condition opens a switch and shuts down the system.

The correct weight for a system charge for the air conditioner is located on the OEM A/C decal in or around the engine compartment or on the driver's door jamb (**FIGURE 59-6**). The sticker should include information about the oil capacity, charge amount, and type of refrigerant.

Manifold Gauge Pressure Measurements

During a performance test, a set of manifold gauges is connected to the A/C high- and low-pressure side refrigerant ports

(**FIGURES 59-7** and **59-8**). Quick connector couplings of two different sizes ensure the high side is connected to the smaller fitting and the low side gauge to the larger low-pressure port fitting (**FIGURE 59-9**).

When the manifold gauge set is initially connected to the refrigerant system, the engine should be off. The manifold gauge set valves should be both closed to prevent refrigerant from flowing to the center port of the gauge set. Both gauges should read identical pressures at rest and correspond to a standard pressure temperature relationship for R-134a gas (**TABLE 59-2**).

A minimum of 50 psi (6.6 kPa) refrigerant pressure at room temperature 70° F (21° C) is needed before testing can begin. If refrigerant pressure is too low, an undercharged condition exists and the system should be leak-tested first. After repairing any leak and recharging the system, the performance testing procedure can begin.

Manifold gauge readings are also recorded when the system is operating with the engine running. When operating, the air flow from the vents should be checked for normal flow. Restricted evaporators or plugged cabin filters block air flow.

Proper air flow through the condenser should be checked by inspecting for obstructions. Bent cooling fins, closed winter fronts, and oil-contaminated condenser tubes cause abnormal pressure readings and low-cooling. The engine fan should

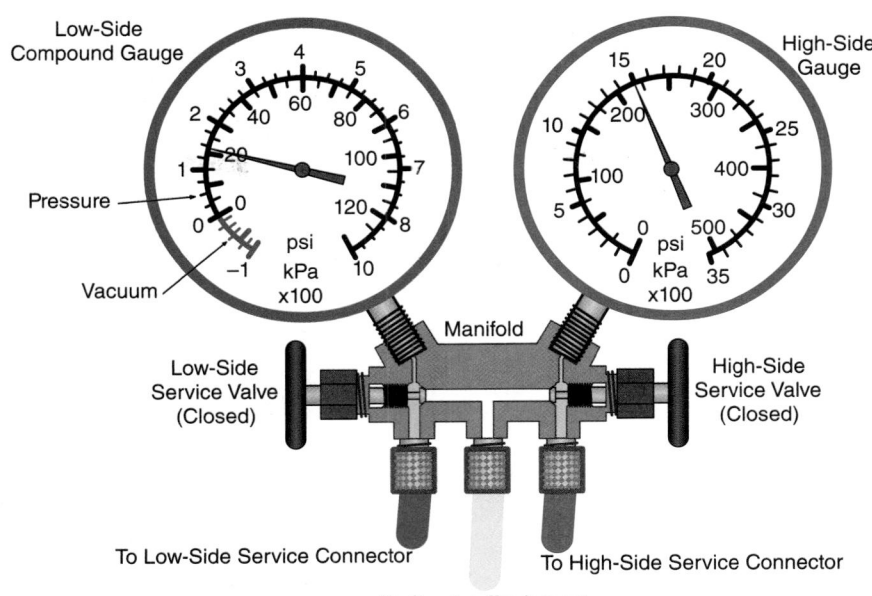

FIGURE 59-7 Features of a manifold gauge set used to measure refrigerant pressure and perform AC service procedures.

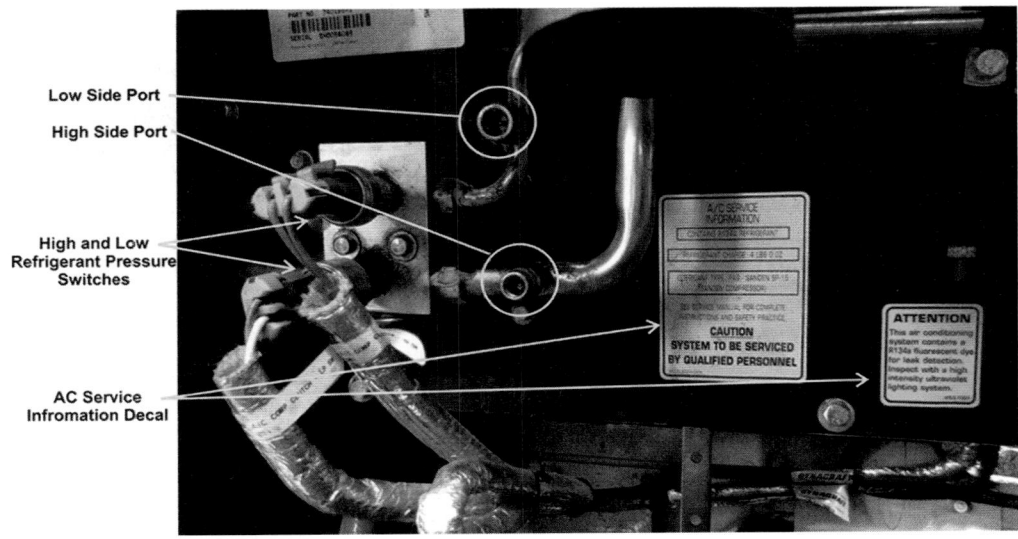

FIGURE 59-8 High- and low-pressure switches located on the expansion valve. The normally covered service ports for the high and low side have protective caps removed.

switch on and off at the correct pressure and should stay on for a minimum cycle time of between 45 and 90 seconds. Fans normally engage when system pressures exceed 275 psi ± 10 psi (1896 kPa ± 69 kPa) and disengage when pressures fall below 230 ± 10 psi (1586 kPa ± 69 kPa). Too-frequent fan cycling caused by short cycle times prematurely wear on-off fan clutch material. A control module with a timer ensures the fan stays on a minimum amount of time to remove heat from the refrigerant and limit fan on/off cycle frequency.

Interpreting Manifold Gauge Results

Resting pressure observations are made with the engine off after the system pressures have stabilized for 15–20 minutes. Any refrigerant in the evaporator has boiled by then and pressures

FIGURE 59-9 Features of a quick connector coupler. The rapid on-off action during connection and disconnection minimizes refrigerant loss.

TABLE 59-2 System Resting Pressures

Ambient Temperature (° F)	System Pressure (psi)	Ambient Temperature (° C)	System Pressure (kPa)
45	40.0	7.2	5.8
50	45.4	10.0	6.6
55	51.2	12.7	7.4
60	57.4	15.5	8.3
65	64.0	18.3	9.3
70	71.1	21.1	10.3
75	78.6	23.9	11.4
80	86.7	26.7	12.6
85	95.2	29.4	13.8
90	104.3	32.2	15.1
95	113.9	35.0	16.5
100	124.1	37.8	18.0
105	134.9	40.6	19.6
110	146.3	43.3	21.2

Kenworth service manual

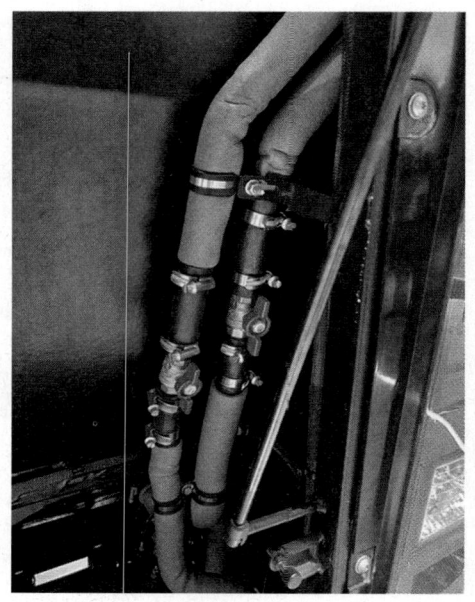

FIGURE 59-10 Quarter-turn valves should be open when the heating system is used and closed when the A/C system is operating to prevent convection flow of coolant through the heater core.

TABLE 59-3 Expected Range of Vent Outlet Temperatures and Manifold Gauge Pressure Readings

Outside Temperature	Center Vent	High-Side Gauge Pressure psi (kPa)	Low-Side Gauge Pressure psi (kPa)
70° F (21° C)	43–49° F (6.1–9.4° C)	95–130 (655–896)	7–14 (48–97)
80° F (27° C)	47–51° F (8.3–10.5° C)	100–135 (689–931)	10–17 (69–117)
90° F (32° C)	53–57° F (11.7–15° C)	120–155 (827–1069)	14–21 (97–145)
100° F (38° C)	59–63° F (15–17.2° C)	155–185 (1069–1276)	19–26 (131–179)
110° F (43° C)	65–69° F (18.3–20.5° C)	185–205 (1276–1413)	24–31 (165–214)
High humidity	Slight increase	No change	Slight increase

in the high and low side should equalize. If pressure readings between both gauges are significantly different, unequal pressures are likely due to a system restriction. The restriction is preventing the high-side refrigerant pressure from flowing into the low side when the A/C clutch is disengaged. Abnormally high resting pressures indicate the refrigerant is likely contaminated with another gas—usually air.

Abnormally low resting pressure indicates a system leak and a loss of some or all the refrigerant charge. In this situation, any remaining refrigerant is removed, the system leak tested, repaired, and recharged with the correct weight of refrigerant. If the system is overcharged, the resting state pressures do not indicate this condition (**TABLE 59-3**).

If an overcharge condition is suspected, due to under-cooling and abnormally high low side pressures, all the refrigerant should be removed and the correct charge weight of refrigerant reinstalled. Normal refrigerant pressures for R-134a follow a standard pressure temperature curve with a system refrigerant pressure corresponding to a narrow range of evaporator temperature. Normal system pressures to observe during a performance test are in **TABLE 59-3**.

A/C Clutch Cycle Time and System Performance

During A/C system operation, there should be a temperature difference between the larger diameter low-pressure lines and the narrower high-pressure lines. Normal cycling of the compressor clutch is no more than four times per minute when refrigerant low-side pressure is above 7 psi (48 kPa). Water should drain out of the evaporator housing drain tube to verify it is clear and the system is working normally. Heater hoses with shut-off valve should be closed to prevent any unnecessary heating of the cab outlet air (**FIGURE 59-10**). Even if the heater control valve is switched off, the external coolant line valve should be closed to prevent circulation of hot engine coolant through convection current flow (**FIGURE 59-11**). Medium-duty vehicles often use electrically controlled coolant bypass valves (**FIGURE 59-12**). These devices, often called three-way valves, not only prevent any coolant flow to the heater core when the A/C is on, but speed-up engine warm-up by automatically opening and closing when commanded by a

FIGURE 59-11 Quarter-turn coolant shut-off valves on this bus are located above a supplemental coolant heater. These valves are closed during seasonal A/C system operation.

control module (**FIGURE 59-13**). These devices should not be confused with heater core pressure protection valves. These mechanically operated, pressure-sensitive valves are installed in the heater core or in coolant lines to enable coolant to bypass the core when excessive cooling system pressure is sensed. This valve prevents damage and leaks from the heater core.

Faster than normal A/C compressor cycling times are caused by excessively low pressure at the low-pressure cut-out switch. Low ambient temperature can have the same effect due to lower refrigerant pressures in cold weather. However, most systems latch the A/C system off if a switch opens and this condition requires an ignition off/on cycle to reset. Fast compressor cycling can also be caused by:

- Overcharged system
- Contamination of refrigerant with another gas or unapproved refrigerant system
- Undercharge system
- Defective low-pressure protection switch

Orifice Tube System

In a typical orifice tube system, an undercharge of refrigerant causes a rapid clutch cycle time (rapid turning on and off) of the A/C clutch. The excessive cycling frequency is caused by inadequate flow of refrigerant into the evaporator or excessive refrigerant charge. What little liquid refrigerant enters the evaporator quickly turns to vapor, causing evaporator pressures to increase. The pressure cycling switch used to regulate evaporator pressure responds to the higher pressure, also casued by excess refrigerant by frequently cycling the compressor clutch

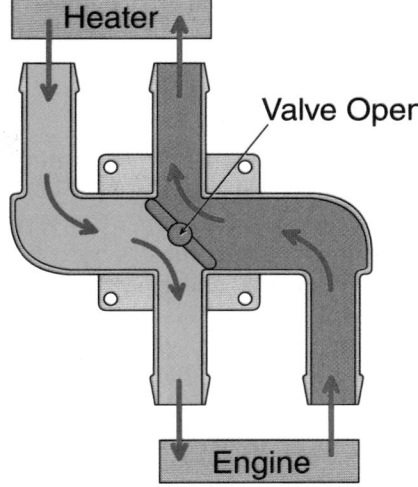

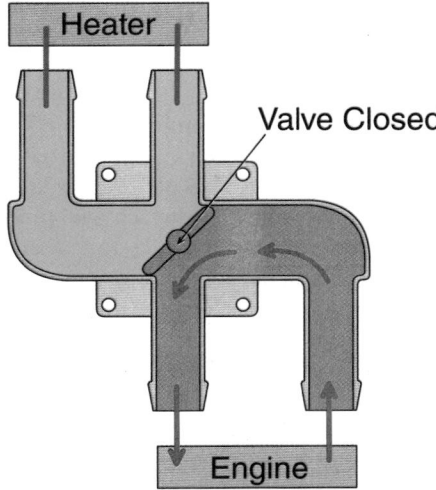

FIGURE 59-12 An electrically operated coolant bypass valve automatically closes the heater coolant circuit when commanded by a control module.

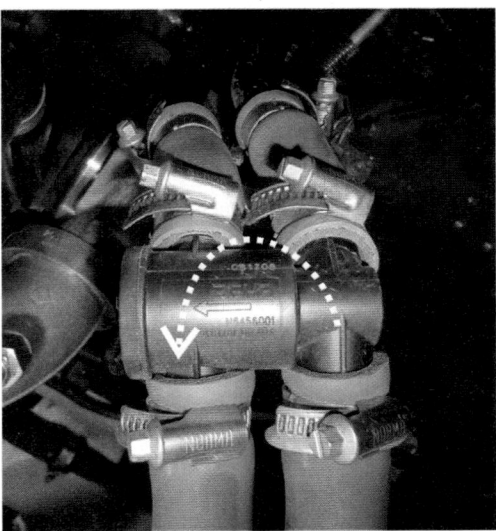

FIGURE 59-13 This bypass valve is a pressure-sensitive protection valve that redirects excessively pressurized coolant away from the heater core.

on and off. The air from the ducts feels warm to the hand instead of cold, and the A/C gauge readings are lower than normal.

Thermal Expansion Valve System

An undercharged system with a thermal expansion valve (TXV) operates with below-normal high and low system pressures. A low-pressure switch located in the trinary or binary switch, or at the evaporator inlet, disables the A/C system. The low-pressure switch typically disables the A/C system if pressures fall below 10 psi (69 kPa). In an undercharged TXV system, the A/C undercools as well.

Overcharging the A/C system affects the orifice tube and TXV systems in the same manner. Both the low- and the high-side gauges read higher than normal pressures. The air in the ducts feels only slightly cool, and the **air conditioning compressor clutch** runs for a few seconds, then quickly turns off. This behavior is caused by flooding of the evaporator with excessive refrigerant or the operation of the high-pressure switches disabling the A/C system.

Abnormal Noises

The compressor is the most common source of abnormal noises arising from the A/C. If the compressor fails internally, it may make a knocking noise. Low oil levels or low refrigerant levels starve the compressor of oil, which also produces compressor noise. While performance-testing the system, abnormal noises can occur while the A/C system is operating. Listen for noises that may occur when the compressor clutch is engaged. If the noise disappears when the compressor clutch disengages, then the noise is from the A/C system. Be sure to listen for noises in the engine compartment, as well as in the vehicle's passenger compartment. Turn off and on the compressor clutch and move the controls on the dash, listening to determine whether the noises appear and disappear.

Evaporator Odors

In addition to low cooling, another common driver complaint is unusual smells when running the A/C. This is caused by a warm evaporator or an evaporator not operating at the correct pressure. Water build up in the evaporator tubes or housing allows bacteria to breed, which emits an unpleasant odor until the evaporator becomes cold. Also, the evaporator housing has a drain tube for water condensed from the moist air on the cold evaporator surfaces. If the drain is plugged, then the water provides a breeding ground for bacteria and the smell is distributed throughout the cabin. This problem is corrected by cleaning the drain and spraying the housing with a strong disinfectant. After allowing the disinfectant to soak the evaporator, the system is operated at high speed to clean the housing. To eliminate A/C system odors in the case of a clogged drain, follow the steps in **SKILL DRILL 59-1**.

Leak Testing

LO 59-2 Describe and explain the purpose and procedures used to perform refrigerant leak testing.

After the performance testing and analysis of system operation is completed, one of two repair pathways is used to either correct electrical system malfunctions or identity refrigerant leaks. Three acceptable and commonly used methods to identify leaks include:

1. Pressurizing the A/C system with nitrogen
2. Fluorescent dye and an ultraviolet lamp
3. Electronic leak detectors

Electronic leak detectors and fluorescent dye are used with a system that is almost fully charged but the location of small slow leaks must be pinpointed. Nitrogen pressure testing is used on empty or nearly empty systems. Any refrigerant that is in the system is first recovered and nitrogen gas is introduced. Soapy water solution is applied at potential leak points to identify leaks with bubbles.

Electronic Leak Detection Testing

The use of a Society of Automotive Engineers (SAE)-compliant electronic leak detector is considered the safest and most accurate method for locating a refrigerant leak. The latest SAE standard, the J-2791 electronic refrigerant leak detector, accurately detects refrigerant leaks down to 0.1 oz (3 g) per year. Three sensitivity levels are typically available on the detector to identify large and small leaks. The detector "beeps," activates a light, or both when a leak is found.

To obtain the most accurate results, leak detection must be performed with the system under pressure with no less than 50% refrigerant charge in the system. Finding smaller leaks, however, may require that the system refrigerant pressure be increased above normal before the leaks can be located.

The detector needs to be moved slowly and evenly beneath the components and lines. Heavier-than-air refrigerant falls downward so a leak detector used above a leak will not locate escaping refrigerant. Starting with the sensitivity on a high setting and turning down the sensitivity as the alarms and lights get louder and brighter helps pinpoint the problem. Moving slowly with a steady hand is critical to effectively using this device.

When using the detector, be sure there is no wind or draft on the vehicle. A draft or air movement over the vehicle could cause the refrigerant to not enter the detector. To test for leaks using an electronic leak tester, follow the steps in **SKILL DRILL 59-2**.

Refrigerant Dye with Ultraviolet Light

Using ultraviolet (UV) light and refrigerant dye is a common way to test for leaks in an A/C system. Some vehicle manufacturers add dye during the manufacturing process. When using dye for the first time on an A/C system, the dye needs to be injected as a concentrate into the system. Most machines have a special port for injecting the dye along with some refrigerant. Injecting concentrated dye into the low side of the A/C system should be done with the vehicle off. When installing dye for the first time, the A/C system needs to be operated for at least 20 minutes so that the dye is distributed throughout all parts of the A/C system.

If the vehicle already has dye installed, or after the vehicle has been test-driven after a new dye injection, locating the leak requires using a UV light. When using a UV light, make sure

SKILL DRILL 59-1 Eliminating Air Conditioning System Odors

1. Verify that the drain is not plugged.
2. Turn the blower fan on medium speed.
3. Operate the system in all zones and determine if the smell is stronger in one position than the others. If so, inspect that portion of the system. If the smell is equally strong in all positions, inspect the heater/evaporator housing. If the odor is caused by mold or bacteria buildup, use an anti-odor kit to clean and kill any buildup.

SKILL DRILL 59-2 Testing for Leaks Using an Electronic Leak Detector

1. Verify the A/C system has refrigerant by connecting a manifold pressure gauge set and comparing the readings against the pressure-temperature (PT) chart.
2. Select a sensitive setting for the detector. Slowly move the wand around and under all the A/C lines and components. If a leak is detected, turn the sensitivity down and pinpoint the exact location of the leak. Once the leak is located, move the wand tip from the leak to outside the vehicle. This allows the detector to "breathe" clean air, cleaning out its sensors and stopping the alarm.
3. **Reclaim** the refrigerant and repair the leak.
4. Always recheck for a leak after the system has been properly recharged.

all safety precautions are followed, including wearing UV safety glasses. Finding leaks with a UV light is easier in the dark and when using special UV filter glasses. To perform a dye test to find a leak, follow the steps in **SKILL DRILL 59-3**.

Nitrogen Leak Testing

Nitrogen testing has been used in the home and transport refrigeration repair industry for a long time. Nitrogen works very well for leak-testing discharged systems or after repairs have been made and before recharging the system. Nitrogen testing requires a nitrogen supply tank, pressure regulator, and A/C

port adapters. The nitrogen is used to simulate working conditions of the A/C system and provides enough force to make high-pressure gas leaks visible with soapy water (**FIGURE 59-14**). To perform nitrogen testing to find a leak, follow the steps in **SKILL DRILL 59-4**.

SAFETY TIP

When nitrogen testing, safety glasses, gloves, and a face shield are required. Weak components or hoses may burst under nitrogen testing conditions.

SKILL DRILL 59-3 Testing for Leaks Using Dye

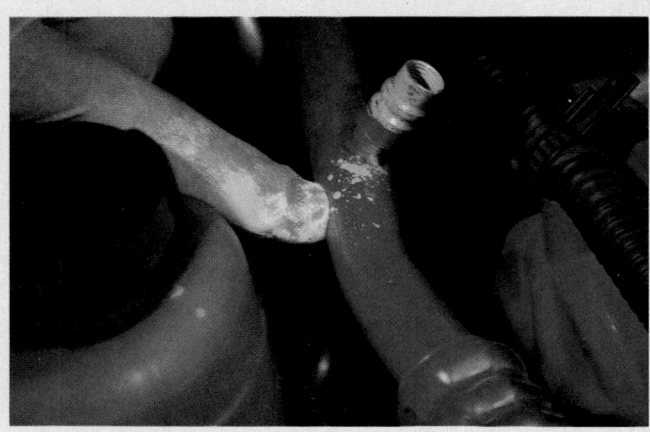

1. Check system pressure to be sure there is enough refrigerant to turn on the compressor. Turn on the compressor. If the compressor does not come on, add refrigerant in small increments until the compressor runs.
2. Add the dye through the low-pressure port using a dye injection system. Run the A/C system to circulate the dye. The system may have to run for several minutes or even several days to expose a leak, depending on the size of the leak. If the leak cannot be located, allow the customer to drive the vehicle for a few days to a week and return the vehicle for inspection.
3. Using a black light, follow the lines, hoses, components, and compressor seal, looking for the orange or green glow of the dye, which indicates a leak. If a leak is not found in the lines or hoses, it may be in the evaporator; the blower motor resistor may need to be removed to access the evaporator housing.
4. Recover the refrigerant in the system, repair the leak, evacuate and recharge the refrigerant, and recheck for leaks.

SKILL DRILL 59-4 Performing Nitrogen Testing to Find a Leak

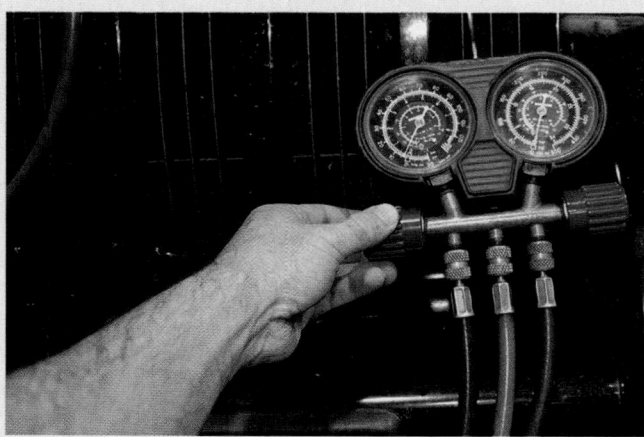

1. The A/C system needs to be emptied and all refrigerant reclaimed. See **SKILL DRILL 59-6** to perform this procedure.
2. Attach the nitrogen hose of the nitrogen bottle pressure regulator to the low- or high-side service port on the vehicle.

Once the quick coupler on the nitrogen hose has been connected and the Schrader valve depressed, start the nitrogen leak test procedure.

3. Adjust the regulator on the nitrogen tank to 100 psi (689 kPa). As the pressure in the system rises, look and listen for any leaks. If a leak is located, stop the process and repair the problem.
4. Adjust the regulator on the nitrogen tank to 200 psi (1379 kPa). When 200 psi (1379 kPa) is reached, look for bulging hoses and listen for noises from leaks.
5. Adjust the regulator on the nitrogen tank to 300 psi (2068 kPa). Once 300 psi (2068 kPa) is reached, allow the system to maintain that pressure for one minute. Do not exceed 350 psi (2413 kPa); doing so could cause the high-pressure relief valve to vent.
6. After one minute, start to spray the soapy water leak solution on all the fittings, hoses, and A/C system components. After spraying the leak solution on the A/C system, it may take upwards of 20 minutes for a leak to present itself.
7. After the nitrogen test is finished, release the nitrogen to the atmosphere. Repair the leak.

SAFETY TIP

Dry nitrogen is the only gas to be used in the A/C system for leak detecting and removing traces of flushing chemicals from the system. Using any other gas may cause harm and damage to the system. Dry nitrogen is an inert gas and does not explode or ignite when in contact with other gases, such as compressed air and oxygen.

Nitrogen Flushing and Purging

Nitrogen has another use other than for leak testing. As a dry inert gas, nitrogen can effectively purge damp air, traces of refrigerant, debris, and loose particles from refrigerant parts. By purging nitrogen gas through dirty contaminated lines and components, such as evaporators, condensers, and valves, the parts are cleaned and potential damage from system contamination is prevented (**FIGURE 59-15**). Compressors and parallel flow-type condensers are never flushed, but most other components are. Receiver driers are always replaced and never flushed. The direction of purging and flushing must be made in the direction of reverse flow to prevent dirt and contaminants from becoming stuck in the system (**FIGURE 59-16**). In contrast to purging with nitrogen, flushing with refrigerant gas may also be necessary for some components, particularly after a failure of a compressor or receiver dryer. Flushing removes moisture-laden oil and some contaminated oil that cannot be removed by purging with gas. When a part is flushed, liquid refrigerant is forced through it. Refrigerant is a solvent and liquid refrigerant dissolves contaminant to effectively flush them from a system.

Reclaiming and Recharging Refrigerant

LO 59-3 Identify and outline procedures used to recover, recycle, and charge an A/C system with refrigerant.

The A/C system refrigerant must be removed and reclaimed before performing any repair or nitrogen testing. None is allowed to be vented to the atmosphere, according to regulations

FIGURE 59-14 A nitrogen tank and assorted chemicals, including UV dye, for servicing A/C systems.

established by the Environmental Protection Agency (EPA), section 609 of the Clean Air Act. Reclaiming refrigerant involves first checking the system to see if there has been any sealant added to it. Sealant is an aftermarket substance sold to close minor refrigerant leaks. If sealant has contaminated refrigerant, it cannot be mixed with good refrigerant and must be recovered in a separate container designated for contaminated refrigerant. To identify the refrigerant type, follow the steps in **SKILL DRILL 59-5**. This refrigerant is processed separately and cannot be recycled by a shop recovery-recycler unit. Next, the refrigerant should be identified to verify it is good quality and not something other than R-134a or newer refrigerant used in commercial vehicle A/C systems. A refrigerant recovery-recycling unit vacuums the refrigerant from the system through lines connected to the high and low side ports (**FIGURE 59-17**). After all refrigerant is removed, its weight is measured and the amount of refrigerant and oil that were removed from the system is recorded in a log book (**FIGURE 59-18**). If a significant amount of oil is removed, then the A/C system should be flushed, and the correct original amount of oil added through the high-side line only. (The low-side valve is closed to prevent oil hydrostatically locking the compressor.) The amount of reclaimed refrigerant should be compared to the OEM decal in or around the engine compartment to determine whether the A/C system may have been under- or overcharged. If undercharged, suspect a leak and leak check with nitrogen.

To perform the reclaim process, follow the steps in **SKILL DRILL 59-6**.

Refrigerant Identification

To prevent cross-contamination of refrigerants during recovery, the type of refrigerant in a system should be first identified using a refrigerant identifier (**FIGURE 59-19**). This easy-to-use device connects to the low-side A/C fitting and

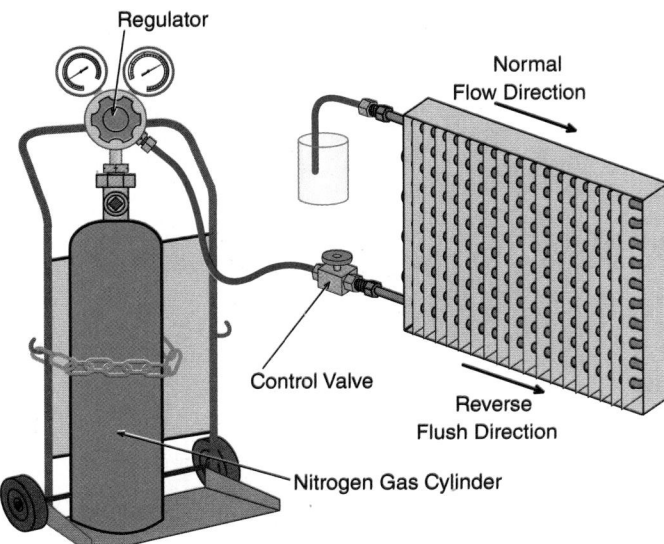

FIGURE 59-15 Purging and flushing of contaminants from an A/C system is done with refrigerant and nitrogen gas.

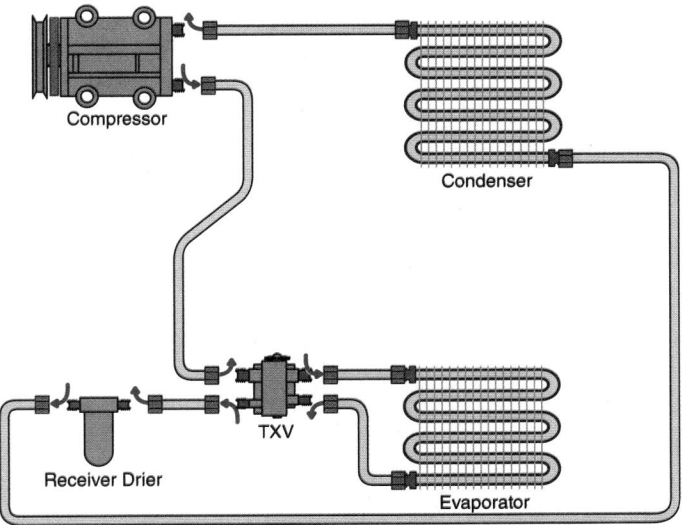

FIGURE 59-16 The direction of purging gas flow through components must be opposite of normal flow to prevent driving dirt and contaminates further into a system.

SKILL DRILL 59-5 Identifying the Refrigerant Type

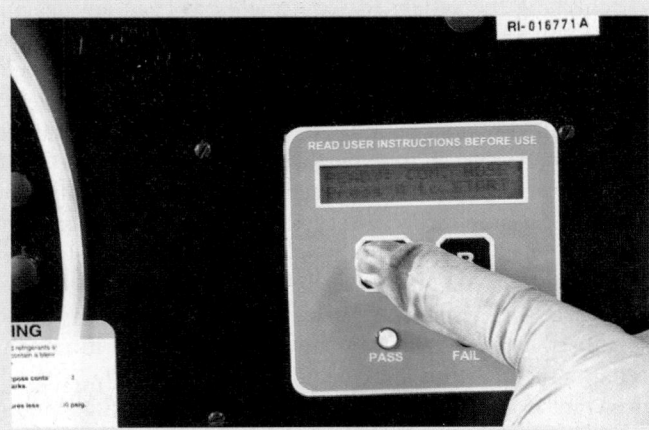

1. Use a sealant identifier to check whether there is any sealant in the system. If there is, follow the recycling equipment instructions and recover refrigerant in a specially designated refrigerant cylinder.
2. Turn on the refrigerant identifier and allow the machine to warm up.
3. Locate the high- and low-side pressure service ports. Connect the refrigerant identifier to the low side of the A/C system and open the service valve. Follow the prompts on the refrigerant identifier, and record the refrigerant type and amount of air, if any.
4. Ensure that the refrigerant decal matches the refrigerant types on the refrigerant identifier. Close the service valve and disconnect the refrigerant identifier.

5. If the refrigerant does not match the refrigerant decal, reclaim the contaminated refrigerant into a designated contamination tank and label the refrigerant for disposal. If the refrigerant is 100% pure and matches the vehicle decal, continue to the next step.
6. Select the proper pressure gauge set for the refrigerant type in the vehicle. After selecting the pressure gauge set, make sure the service valves on the gauges are in the closed position.
7. Connect the service chuck of each of the pressure gauge lines to the A/C system.
8. Open the gauge valves and observe the high- and low-pressure gauges. Record the pressure. If the high- and low-side gauges are the same pressure and do not match pressures expected for the refrigerant, then use the PT chart to determine whether there are non-condensable gases (air) in the A/C system.
9. Measure the ambient temperature 6" to 8" (15 to 20 cm) in front of the condenser and the pressure on the pressure gauge set.
10. Compare the A/C gas pressure to the PT chart for that type of refrigerant. If the pressure on the gauge is higher than the PT chart, the A/C system has non-condensable gases. If the pressure on the gauge is lower than the PT chart, the A/C system is low on refrigerant and a leak should be suspected. If the reading matches another refrigerant on the chart, then the refrigerant needs to be identified before recycling. An acceptable reading (one in the normal ranges) on the gauges corresponding to the temperature reading, as compared to the PT chart, indicates that there are no non-condensable gases in the system. The A/C system could still be below the charge amount recommended, but it is not completely out of refrigerant.

FIGURE 59-17 A refrigerant recovery, recycler, and charging station.

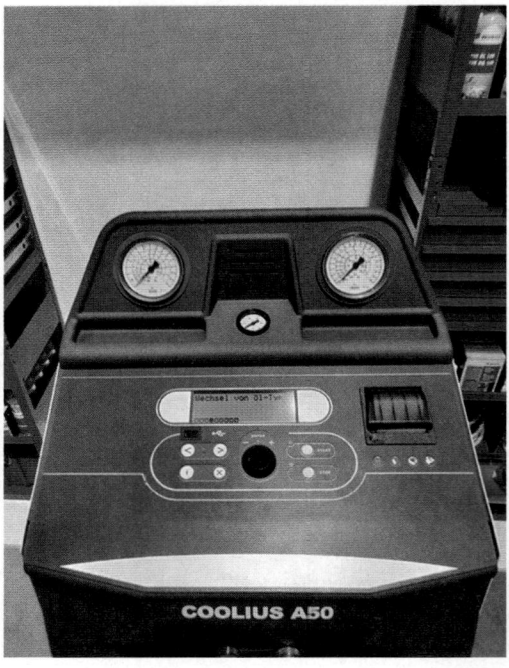

FIGURE 59-18 The charging station panel contains information about recovered quantities of refrigerant and oil.

SKILL DRILL 59-6 Reclaiming and Recovering the Air Conditioning System Refrigerant

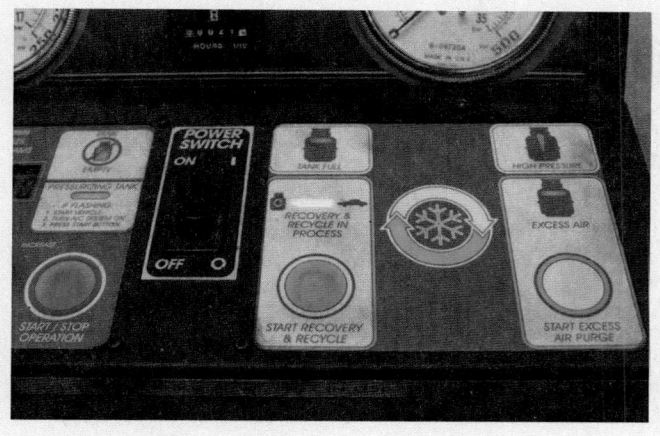

1. Identify the refrigerant using the refrigerant identifier, and verify that there is no sealer in the system.
2. The reclaiming or **recovering** of refrigerant refers to a process of an A/C machine removing and storing used refrigerant in a designated container. Start the reclaim process by connecting the A/C recovery machine to the low- and high-side service ports.
3. Open the gauge valves and turn on the A/C machine. Select the reclaim mode and follow the prompts on the screen.
4. When the refrigerant has been removed, record the amount and compare it to the decal on the vehicle.
5. The A/C machine drains any excess oil that might have been reclaimed. The refrigerant oil that is drained should be minimal or nonexistent. Record the amount of oil that is discharged and install the same amount if the total oil removed is less than 1 oz (30 mL). If the oil drain discharges more than 1 oz (30 mL), the A/C system needs to be flushed using a flushing machine to remove all the oil from the system.
6. After the old oil is flushed and purged, reinstall the specified amount of new oil into the system.

takes a sample of the refrigerant. A readout, such as 100% R-134a, indicates pure R-134a; anything less means the system is contaminated. For example, the display may indicate 60% R-134a and 40% R-12. As long as the refrigerant is pure or undiluted, it can be recycled using a reclaiming machine and reused. If it is cross-contaminated by the wrong refrigerant or the wrong oil, then it is considered a hazardous waste and must be recovered in a separate designated gas cylinder and disposed of according to local regulations. The A/C decal on the vehicle lists the type of refrigerant and how much should be in the system.

System Evacuation

After repairs are completed, the A/C system can be flushed and purged. Evacuation of the A/C system following flushing and purging is the next step after all repairs are made. Evacuation is the process of removing water and moisture from the A/C system, which can interfere with expansion valve operation. Water is removed by boiling it out using very low pressure. To create a low pressure or vacuum in the A/C system a vacuum pump is used. This process usually requires a strong negative pressure of −28 to −29 in Hg (−711 to −737 mm Hg) for a minimum of 15 minutes at room temperature for removal of all the moisture. If shop temperatures are cooler, more time is needed to evacuate the system to remove water from items like desiccant in the receiver dryer and water trapped in polyalkylene glycol (PAG) oil, which is hydroscopic, meaning it absorbs water. A vacuum pump can be connected to the center port of a manifold gauge set and both hand valves opened to pull a vacuum in the system. The vacuum gauge on the manifold gauge set can be used to measure the negative pressure or a more accurate micron gauge can be used. After the system has been evacuated, the hand valves of the high- and low-side service gauges are closed. The

FIGURE 59-19 Refrigerant identifier.

gauge reading should be carefully monitored for 10 minutes to see whether the pressure remains steady. If the pressure rises, there is likely a leak and the system needs reinspecting for leaks. To use a vacuum gauge to evacuate an A/C system, follow the steps in **SKILL DRILL 59-7**.

Adding Oil

After the evacuation is complete, the oil for the A/C system can be added. Oil level in the compressor is measured with a dipstick inserted through a port plug. Larger compressors on buses may use a sight glass. After the oil is added to the A/C system, the vehicle is ready for the charging process. Oil is added to a port in a small cartridge in the high-side refrigerant line of the recycling-recovery machine. The amount of oil added is according to an OEM recommendation for component replacement. Each component has a specific quantity of

SKILL DRILL 59-7 Using a Vacuum Gauge to Evacuate an Air Conditioning System

1. Connect the high and the low side to the A/C manifold gauges.
2. Open the high- and low-side valves on the gauges.
3. Connect the vacuum pump to the center hose (normally a yellow hose), and turn on the pump.
4. After 20 minutes, turn off the pump and close the gauge valves.
5. Note the vacuum readings. The vacuum should reach a minimum of 28" Hg or 29" Hg (95 or 98 kPa). Watch the gauges for 5 minutes to be sure the vacuum holds. If the vacuum drops off, there is a leak in the A/C system.

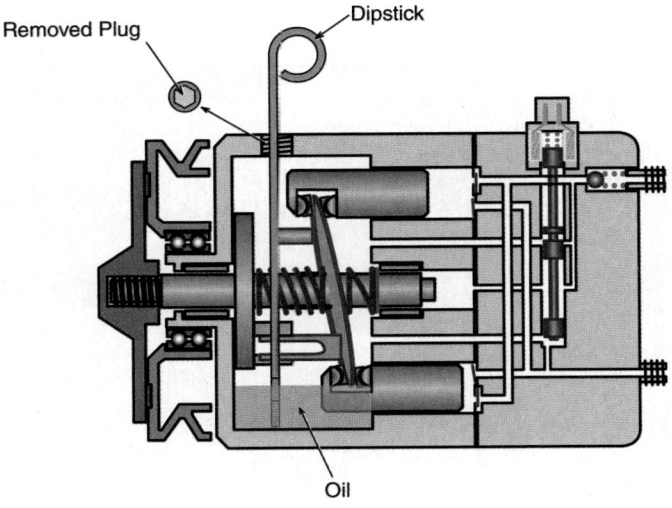

FIGURE 59-20 The oil level of a rotary compressor is checked using a dip stick before the system is evacuated.

oil that should be installed that was likely removed when the component was replaced. If no components are replaced 1 oz (30 mL) or less of refrigerant oil should be added to the system. Adding oil is done after evacuation but before charging the system (**FIGURE 59-20**).

Charging with Refrigerant

Charging the system with the correct weight of refrigerant is a critical process. Most shops use a recovery machine that operates as an automatic charging station. Each has different operating procedures, but all have high- and low-side service gauges, service lines, and a vacuum pump integrated with the refrigerant recovery module. After the correct amount is added while the engine is stopped, a good practice is to rotate the compressor shaft by hand to push out any liquid

that may have entered the compressor during the charging process. The engine may need to be started with the A/C system operating to draw the final quantity of refrigerant to enter the system.

Post-Repair Performance Testing

Performance testing after repairs are completed is recommended to verify no other preexisting failures or system faults appear. All temperature and pressure readings are recorded and, if software is available, faults should be cleared before performance testing begins. If no further faults are identified by the onboard diagnostic system, the vehicle can be returned to service.

▶ TECHNICIAN TIP

If the duct temperature is warmer than the ambient temperature, then the heater control valve may be stuck open, or the blend door is not positioned properly. Use hose pinch pliers to shut off the flow to the heater core and then retest the A/C system. To performance test an A/C system, follow the steps in **SKILL DRILL 59-8**.

▶ TECHNICIAN TIP

Performance testing of the A/C system must be done before and after the repair. Doing so helps ensure that you identify any faults before starting the repairs, as well as verify that the faults are completely repaired.

▶ TECHNICIAN TIP

Generally, the duct temperature should be no greater than 17° F (8.3° C) above the evaporator temperature. The optimum vent temperature is from 38° F to 48° F (3.3° C to 8.9° C). The A/C clutch cycle should not allow the duct temperature to have greater than a 5° shift from high to low while staying within the range of 33° F to 48° F (3.3° C to 8.9° C). If the shift is out of the 5° range, the thermal switch or the pressure cycle switch may need to be replaced, if equipped.

SKILL DRILL 59-8 Performance Testing an Air Conditioning System

1. Start and run the engine. Place a fan in front of the vehicle to simulate the airflow that occurs when driving.
2. Close all windows. Set the A/C to its maximum setting.
3. Raise the engine rpm to 1200–1500.
4. Check the vent temperature in the cabin using a thermometer. Compare the temperature recorded to the diagnostic chart in the manufacturer's service manual.

SKILL DRILL 59-9 Inspecting the Evaporator Housing Water Drain

1. Determine that the drain tube is clogged by allowing the A/C system to run while observing the drain tube for water drops. In the case of a plugged drain, no water or very few drops are found.
2. Carefully use low-pressure shop air and an air nozzle to blow air into the drain tube. Note that water will come out of the drain tube when the clog is removed and can result in a large discharge of smelly water.

3. When the water has completely drained, the task has been performed. Advise the customer to periodically check for a water puddle under the vehicle; if one is not present, the clog may have reoccurred, and removal of the evaporator may be necessary to open the evaporator housing and clean out any remaining debris.

Inspecting the Condenser for Airflow Restrictions

LO 59-4 Outline the procedure to inspect a condenser for air flow restrictions.

The condenser is normally inspected when high-side pressures are too high and the system is not cooling well. Road debris, leaves, and animal fur and feathers are common culprits, but anything that blocks the front of the condenser can cause this issue. Shine a flashlight through the back of the condenser. Look in from the outside of the vehicle for the light coming through the condenser. Move the light across the entire condenser. If the light is not showing, the condenser needs to be externally cleaned.

When cleaning the condenser for debris, shop air or a water hose may be used to remove the debris, but be careful to not fold over the fins. If the shop air and a water hose do not remove the restriction, the condenser must be removed and cleaned.

▶ TECHNICIAN TIP

There are factory adjustments on both the thermal cycle switch and the pressure cycle switch. The adjustments are for achieving optimum performance at the factory. Trying to adjust either of the switches

because of an incorrect temperature shift may mask the faulty switch for a short time. If these switches are incorrectly functioning, replacement is the recommended procedure for the repair.

Inspecting the Evaporator Housing

LO 59-5 Outline the procedures used to inspect and service the evaporator housing.

As the A/C system is running, the evaporator sweats water throughout the day. The water collected needs to be drained from the evaporator housing. A drain hose is connected to the evaporator housing and exits through the vehicle's firewall. Checking that the drain is not plugged is a common diagnostic procedure. To inspect the evaporator housing water drain, follow the steps in SKILL DRILL 59-9.

Cabin Air Filter

Many vehicles now include a cabin air filter in the HVAC system to filter the air before it enters the system. The filter is housed in the fresh air intake and can be accessed from one of a variety of positions, depending on the vehicle. The access may be from under the hood near the firewall, under the windshield, or behind the glove box (FIGURE 59-21). It is usually fairly easy

FIGURE 59-21 Location of a cabin air filter on an International 4200.

FIGURE 59-23 Refrigerant identifiers.

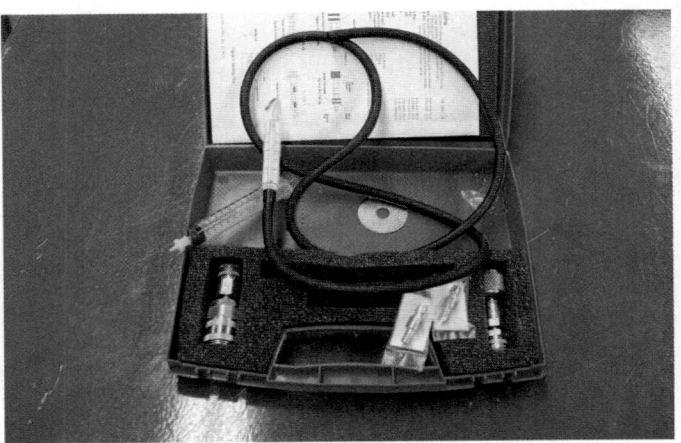

FIGURE 59-22 Sealant detector.

FIGURE 59-24 Reclaim/recycle machine.

to remove and replace once the access cover is found. This filter should be inspected during every service and replaced according to the manufacturer's specified interval, typically once a year. Inspect the filter and check it for any cracks, tears, or deformities that would cause it to be ineffective.

Maintenance and Repair

LO 59-6 Identify and explain major service and repair operations related to A/C system service.

To maintain and repair A/C systems, the following tools are required:

- *Sealant detector*: Sealant detectors detect the presence of sealant in the A/C system. Allowing sealant to be drawn into a refrigerant identifier or **air conditioning machine** can ruin them (**FIGURE 59-22**).
- **Refrigerant identifiers**: Refrigerant identifiers connect to the low-side fitting of the A/C system to determine whether the refrigerant is pure or whether it is contaminated with another refrigerant or air. Identifying refrigerant can save the costly procedure of flushing out a reclaim/

recycle machine and prevent unnecessary disposal of contaminated refrigerant (**FIGURE 59-23**).

- **Reclaim/recycle machine**: If the A/C machine is used for any A/C work on a customer's vehicle, it must meet the EPA requirements. This machine connects to the A/C service ports on the vehicle and can measure pressures, but also has a storage tank to hold refrigerant (**FIGURE 59-24**). It also has a vacuum pump to evacuate A/C systems. Refrigerant must be recovered or pulled into the machine by a pump before repairs are completed. Once the repairs are done, the A/C system must be evacuated or vacuumed out to create a low pressure to remove moisture and the machine normally can refill the vehicle's A/C system either from the recycled refrigerant tank, which contains refrigerant that was removed from other vehicles, sent through a filter, then stored in the tank, or from a second virgin refrigerant tank, which contains new refrigerant. Most shops draw from the recycle tank until it is too low to charge a vehicle, and then use the virgin tank.
- **Manifold gauge set**: A reliable pressure gauge set is one of the most important A/C tools to obtain. Manifold gauge sets are available in both mechanical and digital styles and

are used to diagnose and service A/C systems. Both types of gauge sets have a low-side and a high-side pressure gauge connected to a common manifold that can be used for servicing of the A/C system. The hoses can access a common gauge manifold through hand-operated valves that open or close the manifold passageway to the center port of the manifold (**FIGURE 59-25**). The two hand valves are at each end of the common manifold. The high- and low-side hoses supply pressure directly to the manifold gauges whether the valves are open or closed. However, when using the gauge set, make sure both service knobs are in the closed position before connecting them to a system. Opening the service valves only connects the passageways from the hoses to the center service port. On a digital gauge set, it is necessary to calibrate each gauge to zero so the pressures read accurately. Follow the instructions in the operator's manual for the procedure on calibrating the gauge to zero.

Both the high-pressure and the low-pressure gauges are non-liquid-filled if they are mechanical gauges. Oil-filled gauges do not allow the needle to move fast enough to see **pressure transients**, which are fluctuations observed as the gauges respond to pressure changes rather than holding at one position or moving smoothly up and down the gauge. Being able to see the needle oscillations provides valuable information when performing certain diagnostic tests. For example, a compressor with one bad piston causes the high-side pressure to bounce when that piston is trying to push refrigerant. Another example is when water is in the system and freezes a line. When it starts to thaw, the affected side's gauge bounces as the pressure changes from the temporary blockage. Gauge sets are also built into most R/R/R machines (Recover, Recycle, evacuate, leak test, and Recharge).

- **PT chart**: A PT chart, which stands for pressure-temperature chart, is used to determine what the high- and low-side pressures should be at a given outside temperature and humidity in a properly functioning system (**FIGURE 59-26**).

- **Vacuum pump**: Vacuum pumps are rated in the total volume of air that can be removed every minute. They are used to create low pressure or vacuum in the system. The volume is measured in cubic feet per minute (CFM). The most common pumps are the 52-CFM and 6-CFM models, although some new A/C machines have a 7-CFM pump.
- *Electronic leak detector*: Sometimes called a "sniffer," this device is used to locate small refrigerant leaks by electronically detecting refrigerant gas (**FIGURE 59-27**).
- *Dye leak detector*: This solution is used to detect refrigeration leaks (**FIGURE 59-28**).
- **Oiler**: This device is used to add oil to the A/C system.
- **Vacuum gauge**: This gauge is designed to read negative pressure or vacuum (**FIGURE 59-29**).
- **Micron gauge**: This electronic device is designed to precisely measure negative pressure or vacuum (**FIGURE 59-30**).
- *Line wrenches*: Line wrenches are like box-end wrenches or wrenches designed to more completely enclose system fittings. A slot is cut out of the box-end part of a wrench to allow the technician to slide the wrench over the tube or hose.

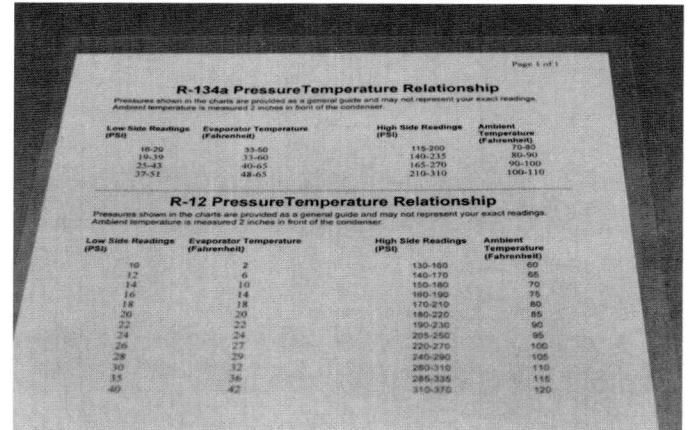

FIGURE 59-26 PT chart.

FIGURE 59-25 Internal passageways of the manifold and gauge set.

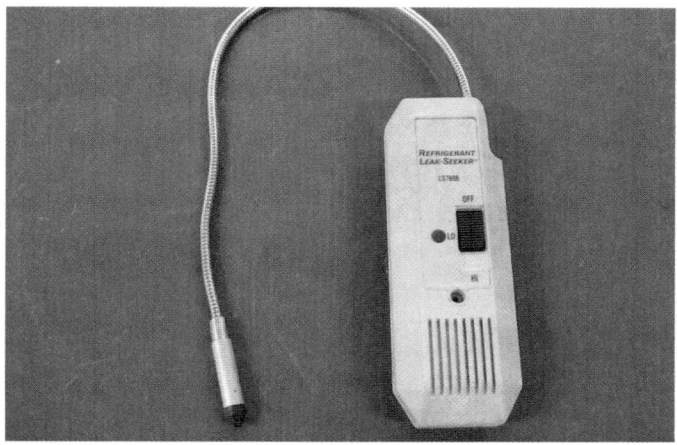

FIGURE 59-27 Electronic leak detector.

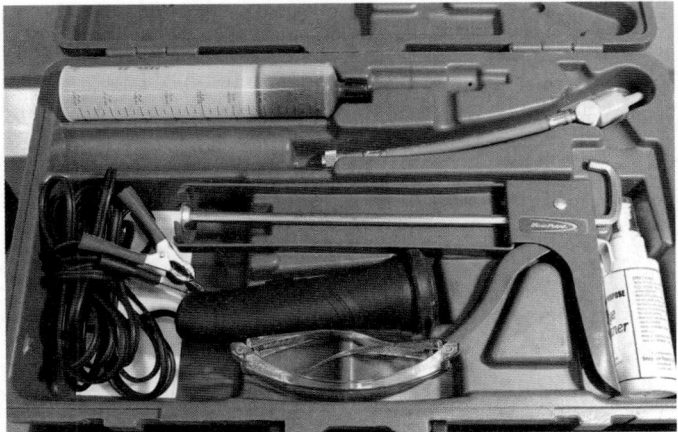

FIGURE 59-28 Dye leak detector.

FIGURE 59-29 Vacuum gauge.

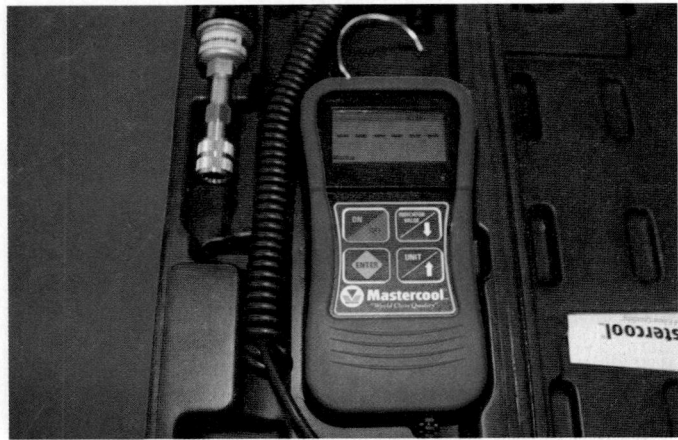

FIGURE 59-30 Micron gauge.

The low-pressure gauge is unique in that it displays both pressure and vacuum. It has a maximum pressure of about 120 psi (827 kPa) and a low pressure of 30" Hg (vacuum measured in inches of mercury, or 102 kPa). The low-pressure gauge needs to display vacuum readings

for diagnostic purposes and to ensure that the proper vacuum levels are achieved when evacuating the system. The high-side pressure gauge usually has a maximum pressure of about 500 psi (3,447 kPa). Most systems run with the high-side pressure around 120 psi (827 kPa); but if the condenser fan is not functioning, the pressure could rise as high as 400 psi (2,758 kPa). This is why such a large pressure range is used on the high-side gauge. Otherwise, if the system pressure exceeds the maximum gauge reading, the gauge could be damaged, or it could even explode.

▶ TECHNICIAN TIP

The amount of refrigerant removed provides insight into the condition of the vehicle's A/C system. Compare the weight removed to the A/C decal-specified capacity. If the amount recovered is less than the decal indicates, there is likely a leak in the system. If there is more refrigerant in the system than specified, then the system is overcharged. If it had the correct amount of refrigerant, then the system most likely has no leaks.

Recycling, Labeling, and Storing Refrigerant

In certain situations, the A/C machines recycle tank may become full of refrigerant. This prevents further recovery of any more A/C refrigerant. Installing another empty container for recycled refrigerant allows the A/C machine to continue to be used. Note that the refrigerant tank cannot be a virgin disposable tank containing only new refrigerant. The new virgin refrigerant tanks are a one-use-only tank and have a one-way check valve in the valve stem to prevent refilling of the tank. To recycle refrigerant, follow the steps in **SKILL DRILL 59-10**.

▶ TECHNICIAN TIP

Recycling refrigerant is one of the processes the A/C machine can perform. After reclaiming the refrigerant, most A/C machines automatically recycle the refrigerant. The filter system in the machine returns the refrigerant to an acceptable level of cleanliness.

Inspecting the Condition of Removed Refrigerant Oil

After the reclaim process, the A/C machine deposits any oil removed during the reclaim into a graduated container on the machine. By measuring the amount of oil removed, the technician knows exactly how much oil needs to be put back into the system. Only new oil should be installed.

After the A/C system has been diagnosed and tested, the system fault can be repaired. Take the appropriate action and precautions that the repair requires. Finish the repair and continue to the evacuation.

▶ TECHNICIAN TIP

It is the responsibility of the repair technician to read the O-ring package label and verify the O-rings selected are compatible with the type of refrigerant in the system.

SKILL DRILL 59-10 Recycling Refrigerant

1. Obtain a DOT-approved refrigerant container. The recommended size for most repair shops is a 60 lb (27 kg) container.
2. Connect the A/C machine's hoses to the tank with the appropriate adapters in an A/C retrofit kit. Use either the high- or low-side adapters from to connect the quick-connect hose fittings to the ¼" SAE fittings on the tank.
3. Open the refrigerant tank valves. Open the quick-connect valves on the quick connectors. At this point, the recycled refrigerant tank can recover enough refrigerant for one initial refrigerant charge using the same method as recovering refrigerant from a vehicle.
4. Use the keypad on the A/C machine and select the "charge" mode. Determine the amount of refrigerant you want to transfer from the virgin tank and enter that weight into the display.
5. Begin to charge the recycled refrigerant tank. Do not fill the tank to more than 60% of the total gross capacity of the tank. The total gross capacity is written on the tank, and the technician must mathematically determine what 60% of it is.
6. After the recycled tank is filled with refrigerant, label the tank with the type and the weight of refrigerant. By labeling the tank with the type and weight, the next technician can determine the type and whether there is enough free space to charge any more refrigerant into the tank.
7. Close the recycled refrigerant tank valves and disconnect the hoses from the tank.
8. Store the refrigerant in a cool, dry place where the sunlight cannot directly hit the tank.

Air Conditioning System Flush

The A/C system should be flushed if the compressor breaks apart or if the dryer desiccant bag breaks open. In both situations, the loose parts or desiccant pellets start to move through the system, causing blockages. Another reason to flush the A/C system is contaminated oil. A special flushing machine is used to purge the A/C system. However, not all of the components are designed to be flushed, such as the compressor, orifice tube or TXV, accumulator, and receiver filter dryer. Be sure to check the manufacturer's service information to verify which components can safely be flushed. After the system has been reclaimed, remove the hoses from the A/C machine and connect the flushing machine. Several different types of machines are available, but normally a cleaning agent is poured into the machine, then an air hose is plugged into the machine. A valve on the machine releases the cleaning agent through the system, pushed by the shop's air pressure. Another valve is used to push air through the system to remove the cleaning agent. Some shops prefer to use nitrogen to blow any residual cleaning agent from the system because it contains no moisture, unlike air. The system is now ready to have oil added and the system recharged. Follow the instructions provided with the flushing machine carefully.

Inspecting and Replacing a Drive Belt

Inspecting the drive belt of the compressor is an important part of A/C maintenance and repair. If the belt is worn, the engine cannot drive the compressor properly. On hot days, the refrigerant pressures are high and the compressor needs an effective drive belt to prevent slipping and causing excessive heat buildup around the clutch. The A/C system requires that the compressor move the refrigerant at the correct velocity for the cooling of the passenger compartment to be at its peak efficiency. The drive belt is the first link in the system and needs to be in good condition and properly tensioned to ensure efficient A/C operation.

Inspecting, Testing, and Replacing the Compressor Clutch

Testing of the clutch assembly should occur when the A/C pressure is high enough to switch on the clutch, but the clutch is not switching on or is not staying engaged. Typically, this component is checked using a digital volt-ohmmeter (DVOM). The technician needs to determine whether the clutch coil is receiving full power and ground. If it is powered, but still does not engage, then the clutch coil should be checked for high resistance. If the resistance is too high when compared with specifications, it needs to be replaced. Clutch coil resistance is usually three to five ohms. If full power and ground are not present, then wiring and circuit devices need to be inspected and tested according to recommended procedures.

The air gap is the space between the clutch assembly and the A/C pulley. This gap needs to be measured to verify it is correct according to specifications in the service information. If the gap is too small, the clutch drags on the pulley, creating excess heat and eventually wearing or burning out the clutch. If the gap is too large, the coil is not able to create a strong-enough magnetic pull to engage the clutch and hold it against the pulley, or it engages it but is not able to hold it in place when the engine's rpm are raised and the A/C is operating. A voltage drop in the electrical circuit that energizes the clutch coil may also prevent the compressor clutch from engaging. If it does engage, it is not able to grip tightly enough and begins to slip, creating heat and scoring the clutch surface.

> **▶ TECHNICIAN TIP**
>
> A brown dust around the A/C compressor clutch indicates that there is slippage that could be caused by low voltage and current to the compressor clutch circuit. Slippage could also be caused by the clutch air gap being set too wide.

An A/C compressor pulley or bearing may need service when noise is detected from the bearing when the engine is running. If the bearing has failed, then the pulley must be removed. When replacing the compressor clutch and bearing, the pulley needs to be removed as well.

> **▶ TECHNICIAN TIP**
>
> Removing the A/C compressor clutch requires special tools. Each type of compressor clutch has its own unique mechanism and tools necessary for removal. Before attempting to remove the A/C compressor clutch on the A/C compressor, make sure you follow the manufacturer's safety procedures and use the proper tools for the job.

To inspect, test, and replace the compressor clutch, follow the steps in **SKILL DRILL 59-11**.

Removing, Inspecting, and Reinstalling the Compressor

The compressor needs to be inspected any time there is a compressor failure or leaks are suspected.

To remove, inspect, and reinstall the compressor, follow the steps in **SKILL DRILL 59-12**.

Removing and Inspecting Air Conditioning Mufflers, Hoses, Lines, and Fittings

The removal of hoses and lines is done for replacement purposes or to access another component. Some lines have male and female threaded ends that connect, while others use spring-lock-type retainers to push and lock fittings together. If the hoses are threaded together, line wrenches are used, and both hex-head fittings must be held when loosening and tightening together to prevent twisting of thin-walled metal lines. If the lines use a spring lock, there is a spring lock release tool sized specifically to fit the line. The spring lock tool is inserted

---

SKILL DRILL 59-11 Inspecting, Testing, and Replacing the Compressor Clutch

1. Inspect the air gap of the clutch. With the clutch disengaged, use feeler gauges to measure the air gap between the **drive pulley** and the clutch drive plate. If the air gap is too small, follow the manufacturer's procedure to adjust the air gap.

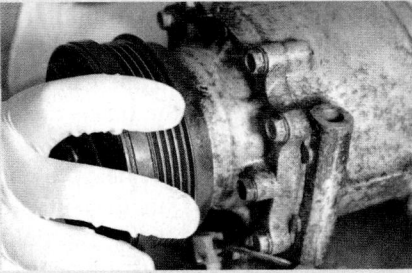

2. If the air gap is too large, check to see whether the pulley bearing is worn or warped, causing the pulley to wobble and make contact with the clutch. The clutch should also be checked electrically using a DVOM to ensure that the clutch coil is not being energized or partially energized when it should not be. (Typically, this situation is caused by a rewiring of the system following an improper diagnosis.) Too large of an air gap is most likely caused by excessive wear of the clutch and usually requires replacement.

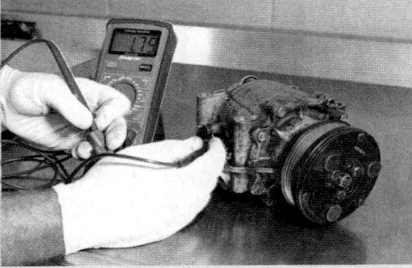

3. To check the condition of the electrical circuit, perform an amperage test to the compressor clutch. Measure the vehicle's voltage and clutch resistance (12-volt clutch resistance typically should be three to five ohms). If the measurements are within specification, adjust the clutch air gap. If the amperage is out of specification, diagnose the electrical system and replace the clutch.

SKILL DRILL 59-11 Inspecting, Testing, and Replacing the Compressor Clutch (Continued)

4. Remove the clutch plate center bolt or nut. If the compressor uses selective shims to adjust the air gap, be careful to remove these for later use.

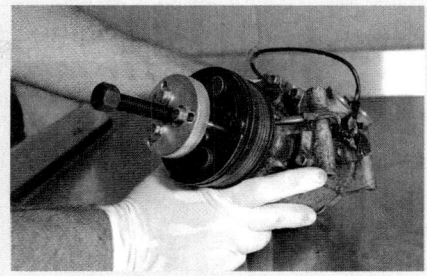

5. Using the appropriate puller, remove the clutch plate.

6. Remove the pulley snap ring, and slide the pulley and bearing off the compressor input shaft.

7. Remove the snap ring from the compressor clutch coil, and pull from compressor.

8. Reinstall the components in reverse order. When reinstalling the clutch plate, be sure to adjust the air gap (typical air gap is 0.012" to 0.025" [0.03 to 0.06 mm]). Check specifications in your service information for the correct air gap. Adjust the air gap as required using selective shims.

9. Torque the center bolt or nut to specifications.

SKILL DRILL 59-12 Removing, Inspecting, and Reinstalling the Compressor

1. Reclaim the refrigerant, making note of the amount removed. Compare this amount to the factory specifications. Remove the belt using a serpentine belt tool or the proper wrench. Remove tension from the tensioner and slide the belt off, noting routing for reinstallation.

2. Disconnect the refrigerant hoses from the compressor. Cap the lines to prevent moisture from entering the system and absorbing into the receiver dryer and refrigerant oil.

3. Disconnect the compressor clutch.

SKILL DRILL 59-12 Removing, Inspecting, and Reinstalling the Compressor (Continued)

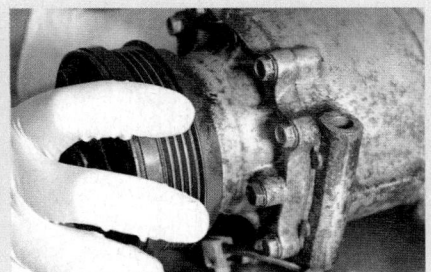

4. Remove the mounting bolts following the manufacturer's specifications. Pour oil from the compressor into a graduated cylinder, and check the oil for acid using acid-test strips.

5. Measure the resistance of the clutch coil, and check the pulley for wobble that may be caused by a faulty bearing. Inspect the compressor fittings and plugs for corrosion. Look up specifications for the oil fill capacity for the new compressor.

6. Install the new compressor; tighten the mounting hardware to specifications.

SKILL DRILL 59-13 Removing and Inspecting Air Conditioning Mufflers, Hoses, Lines, and Fittings

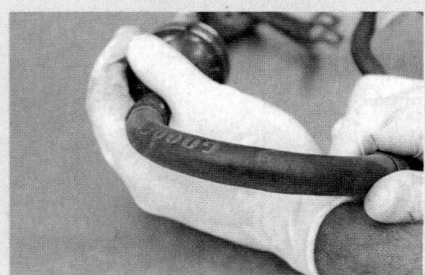

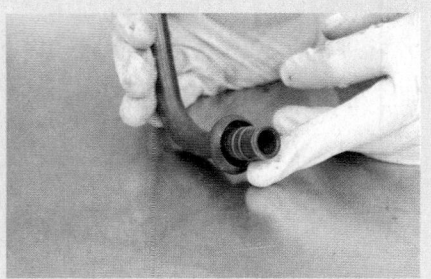

1. After performing a refrigerant reclaim process, disconnect, remove and inspect the muffler, hoses, lines, and fittings. Shake the muffler and listen for noise. If the muffler sounds like it contains loose debris, it is faulty and needs to be replaced.

2. Inspect each hose to ensure that it is flexible, not stiff, cracked and brittle. The A/C fittings need to be positioned so that there is no rubbing against other components. The hoses and lines must be kept away from heat sources in the engine compartment, which could burn them, and from moving parts, which could wear a hole in them.

3. Replace, lubricate, and install O-rings to prevent refrigerant leaks at fitting points.

between the fittings and stretches a locking spring, allowing the lines to pull apart.

Any time lines are loosened, the sealing **O-rings** in the fittings must be replaced or there is potential for leaks.

To remove and inspect A/C **mufflers**, hoses, lines, and fittings, follow the steps in **SKILL DRILL 59-13**.

Removing, Inspecting, and Reinstalling the Condenser

The condenser may be removed to access the radiator or if replacing the condenser because it is plugged, damaged, or leaks. Since the condenser sits in the front of the vehicle, it is damaged quite often in collisions or by debris flying off the road. Some

basic hand tools are necessary, as well as wrenches or spring clip removal tools. The process for removing the condenser varies by vehicle type, make, and model. Refer to the service information for specific steps. Also refer to the service information to determine how much oil is needed for the replacement condenser. To remove, inspect, and reinstall a condenser, follow the steps in **SKILL DRILL 59-14**.

Removing, Inspecting, and Installing the Receiver/Dryer or Accumulator

The receiver/dryer or **accumulator** needs to be removed and inspected whenever there are leaks or the desiccant is failing to dry the refrigerant. Desiccant failures arise when the system is

SKILL DRILL 59-14 Removing, Inspecting, and Reinstalling the Condenser

1. After reclaiming the A/C system, remove all necessary components to access the condenser. This may include removing other coolers and coverings. Refer to the manufacturer's specific procedures on component removal.
2. Remove the inlet and outlet lines on the condenser.
3. Remove the hold-down bolts for the condenser.
4. Install the new condenser. Fasten the condenser with the mounting hardware.
5. Install new O-rings on the A/C lines.
6. Install the inlet and outlet lines.
7. Replace all of the components in reverse order from removal. Evacuate the A/C system if all other A/C repairs are complete.

SKILL DRILL 59-15 Removing, Inspecting, and Installing the Receiver/Dryer or Accumulator

1. After reclaiming the A/C system, remove the inlet and outlet lines from the receiver/dryer or the accumulator.
2. Remove the mounting clamps from the receiver/dryer or accumulator; remove the receiver/dryer or accumulator.
3. Lubricate and install new O-rings on both the inlet and the outlet lines.
4. Install the new receiver/dryer or accumulator and tighten the clamps. Install the inlet and outlet lines.
5. Proceed to the evacuation if all other repairs were made.

left open for long periods of time and the desiccant absorbs too much moisture. It can also occur if the desiccant bag ruptures and desiccant has entered the rest of the system or if the compressor has come apart internally. Refer to the service information of the vehicle for the specific procedure. Also refer to the service information to determine the amount of oil needed. To remove, inspect, and install the receiver/dryer or accumulator/dryer, follow the steps in **SKILL DRILL 59-15**.

Removing, Inspecting, and Installing a TXV

A TXV is removed for inspection if the diagnostic process determined the TXV was stuck open or closed, during performance testing, and when measuring system pressures. If stuck open, the high-side pressures are low, and the low-side pressures are high. If stuck closed, the high-side pressures are high, and the low-side pressures are abnormally low and could even go into a vacuum.

When working with the expansion valve, caution must be used in all aspects of the removal and installation of the valve. Typically, the TXV is mounted on the front of the evaporator. When removing and installing the inlet and outlet lines to the evaporator, a line wrench must be used so the fittings are not damaged or rounded off. A second wrench is used to hold the other fitting on the line, so it doesn't twist and break off. One nut is on the line; the other nut is on the TXV. Twist the nut on the line and hold the nut on the TXV to prevent deforming or breaking the TXV. The lines from the evaporator are brass or aluminum, and the fittings are steel alloy, so the use of an only open-ended wrench will easily slip, plus the lines at the evaporator can bend if not held at two points. The exact procedure for removing, inspecting, and installing a TXV varies widely from vehicle to vehicle and by TXV manufacturer. Refer to the service information for the precise process. To remove, inspect, and install a TXV, follow the steps in **SKILL DRILL 59-16**.

Removing, Inspecting, and Installing an Orifice Tube

The orifice tube needs to be replaced when the same gauge readings as a blocked TXV are observed. The filter screen of an orifice tube can plug up with debris and restrict refrigerant flow. The tube should also be replaced if the compressor internally disintegrates because it can trap debris from the compressor and become clogged. The process for removing, inspecting, and installing an orifice tube varies from model to model and vehicle to vehicle. Refer to the service information for the precise procedure.

To remove, inspect, and install an orifice tube, follow the steps in **SKILL DRILL 59-17**.

Removing, Inspecting, and Reinstalling the Evaporator

Removal of the evaporator is typically done only if it is being replaced. Often, the entire HVAC module can be removed from outside the cab. Once the HVAC module is removed, the A/C evaporator is disconnected and removed. The lines in and out of the evaporator must be disconnected before the HVAC can be removed. However, the specific procedure for removing the evaporator varies greatly, because it is located differently in each type of vehicle make and model. Refer to the service information for the particular vehicle for specific instructions. To remove, inspect, and reinstall the evaporator, follow the manufacturer's service information.

Evacuating the Air Conditioning System Using a Micron Gauge

The micron gauge is used in conjunction with the mechanical pressure-vacuum gauge on the A/C machine. The micron gauge can measure vacuum very precisely. Where a vacuum gauge has markings at 29", then 30" of vacuum, the micron gauge can measure accurately between 29" and 30" to determine exactly how well the system is being evacuated. The efficiency of many vacuum pumps is measured in microns; the fewer microns it can reduce system pressure to, the better the pump. For example, if there are two pumps and one can draw down to 500 microns and the other down to 25 microns, the second pump will do a better job of removing moisture while evacuating the A/C system. Some A/C machines have a micron gauge built in. With the micron gauge, the height of a column

---

SKILL DRILL 59-16 Removing, Inspecting, and Installing a TXV

1. After reclaiming the A/C system, use a wrench to loosen the bolt holding the liquid and suction line block to the expansion valve.

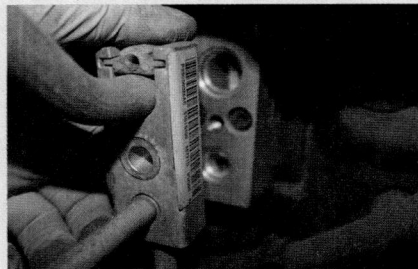

2. Remove the center stud going through the expansion valve. Gently remove the lines from the expansion valve.

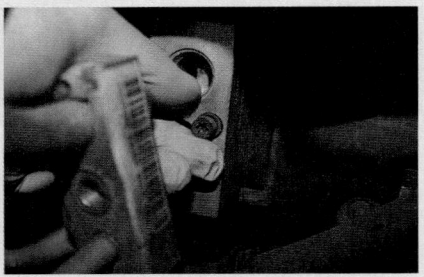

3. Remove the bolts holding the expansion valve to the evaporator inlet.

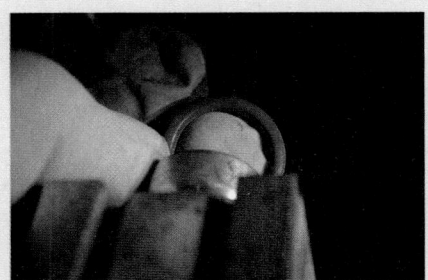

4. Install new gaskets or O-rings onto the new expansion valve and the suction and liquid lines.

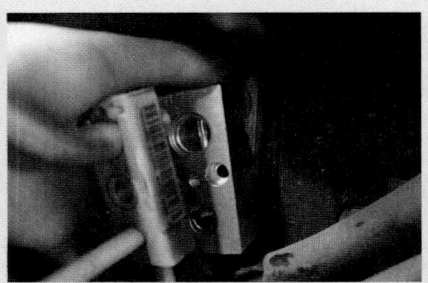

5. Install the new expansion valve and torque the bolts to specification.

6. Install a new mounting stud. Reinstall the lines to the expansion valve and tighten retaining nut. Evacuate the system if all other repairs were made.

SKILL DRILL 59-17 Removing, Inspecting, and Installing an Orifice Tube

1. Locate the orifice tube and determine whether it is serviceable. After locating the serviceable orifice tube, remove the line where the orifice tube is housed.

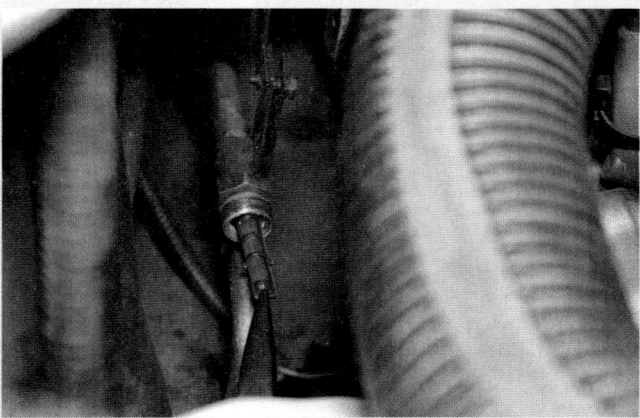

2. Using small needle-nose pliers or the orifice tube removal tool, pull out the old orifice tube from the housing. Note the color of the old orifice tube that designates orifice size in some tubes.

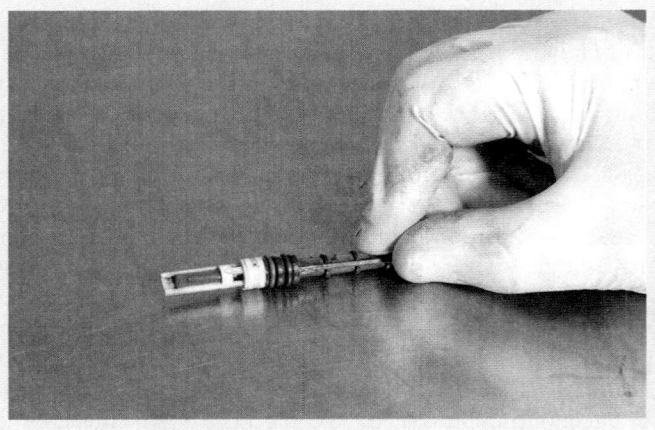

3. Select the new orifice tube, making sure to replace with the properly colored tube. Lubricate the orifice tube O-rings, and install the new one with the direction arrow pointing in the direction of refrigerant flow.

4. Lubricate and install new O-rings on the line, and reinstall the line. Proceed to the evacuation if all other repairs were made.

of mercury is measured with a perfect vacuum applied to one side and acted upon by atmospheric pressure on another. The column height is measured in microns, or one-thousandths of one millimeter. To put it in perspective, in 1", there are 25,400 microns. So, a mercury column height of 0 microns equals a perfect vacuum (roughly 30" Hg), and 25,400 microns equals approximately 29" Hg. This ultra-fine measurement of vacuum allows accurate measurement of vacuum readings to ensure that all the moisture has been removed from the A/C system.

When the micron gauge reaches 29" Hg, there are remaining to be removed to reach a perfect vacuum. 25,400 microns of mercury column height of pressure. A mechanical gauge is not accurate enough to observe such a small pressure change. If using a micron gauge, watch until it hits 1000 microns or less. A

reading of 1000 microns indicates that likely all the moisture in a system has boiled away under very low pressure. The micron gauge should indicate the system pressure has reached the boiling point of water at room temperature pressure within five minutes after switching on the pump. If it does not, then there is likely a leak in the system. To use a micron gauge to evacuate an A/C system, follow the steps in **SKILL DRILL 59-18**.

▶ TECHNICIAN TIP

If the micron gauge pressure does not hit 1000 microns within the total vacuum time, then spin the clutch of the compressor and watch the pressure gauge. If the pressure rises, the clutch seal is faulty.

SKILL DRILL 59-18 Using a Micron Gauge to Evacuate an Air Conditioning System

1. Refer to the boiling point chart for the boiling point pressure in microns. Connect the vacuum pump to the center port of the manifold gauge set and open both hand valves after connecting the gauges to the A/C system.
2. Switch-on the vacuum pump on to begin the air evacuation process. Evacuate the system of air for a minimum of 15 minutes. Time the pressure drop of the gauge reading.
3. The pressure gauge should reach the boiling point pressure from the boiling point chart within five minutes.
4. If the pressure gauge reaches the boiling point pressure within five minutes, continue to allow the machine to evacuate the A/C system until the micron gauge reaches 1000 microns. When the micron gauge reaches 1000 microns, the A/C system should be moisture-free.

Determining Recommended Oil and Capacity

The refrigerant R-134a uses a polyalkylene glycol (PAG) oil. Each individual A/C system has a capacity of a specific oil. If just one component is replaced, an OEM capacity chart lists how much oil should be replaced for that particular component. Unless the entire system is replaced, some oil will remain in the system. Read the manufacturer's service information for specific instructions to calculate how much oil should be added for each service procedure.

▶ TECHNICIAN TIP

When using a micron gauge, observe the gauge readings as the pressure drops. The micron gauge may hover around 1300. When the numbers hover at 1300 microns, the A/C system is boiling off moisture. Pay close attention at this point. If the numbers drop from 1300 to 1200 to 1100 to 1000, the A/C system is likely moisture-free. If the numbers fall from 1300 directly to 1000 and below, the moisture in the A/C system likely instantly froze due to low temperatures. The freezing of moisture is due to the lack of heat inside the A/C system due to the pressure drop. If the pressure gauge falls from 1300 to 1000 instantly, the vehicle needs to be moved to a warmer environment. The freezing point of water in a vacuum cycle becomes a problem around an ambient temperature of 60° F (16° C) and below.

Adding the Proper Oil Amount

Oil should be put back into the A/C system after the evacuation cycle and while pressure is lower than atmospheric pressure in the A/C system. The oiler uses atmospheric pressure to push oil into the A/C system. When the A/C system is still at a vacuum state. Since system pressure is close to a vacuum, the oil is easily pulled into the system by the low pressure or vacuum. However, a higher gas pressure is required behind the oil to push all the oil into the system. Most A/C machines have a port that a special graduated oil-filled cylinder screws

into. A pressure relief port on one side of the sealed oil-filled cylinder is opened where the cylinder attached. Gas pressure in the relief port combines to force the oil into the A/C system. To add oil to the A/C system, follow the steps in **SKILL DRILL 59-19**.

Vacuum pump oil is one of the regular maintenance items that technicians are prompted to change after approximately each 10 hours of vacuum use. Vacuum pump oil can be changed by the shop technician. Failure to change the oil results in increased pump wear, as well as preventing the pump drawing a deep vacuum. Changing the pump oil regularly extends the life of the pump and enables it to reach maximum vacuum quicker. A drain pan to catch the old oil drained from the pump and new vacuum pump oil is needed for the pump. To change the vacuum pump oil in an A/C machine, follow the steps in **SKILL DRILL 59-20**.

▶ TECHNICIAN TIP

Before charging the A/C system, be sure to have a minimum of 5 lb (2.3 kg) of refrigerant plus the charge amount for a complete system fill in the stored in the A/C machine. Any less refrigerant than 5 lb causes an insufficient refrigerant prompt on the A/C machine. If this occurs, reclaim the A/C system and add refrigerant to the A/C machine.

Inspecting and Testing the Heater Control Valves

The heater control valves should be tested if the customer complains of no heat or poor A/C. The heater control valve regulates coolant flow to the heater core for heat and limits flow during A/C system operation. Some valves are air-controlled, very few are cable-controlled, and most are manual or electrically controlled actuators. Cable-controlled models must be checked to ensure that the cable is moving freely and completely opening and closing the valve. Air-controlled models should be checked to verify that the air is supplied to the valve at the right time

SKILL DRILL 59-19 Adding Oil to the Air Conditioning System

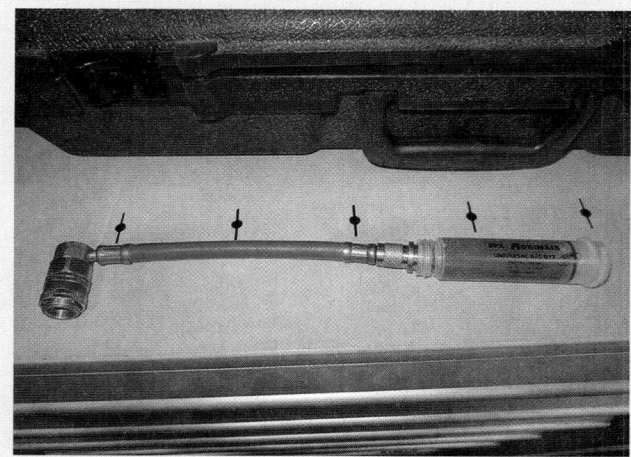

1. Evacuate the A/C system and watch the vacuum gauge to ensure that there are no leaks in the system causing the failure to achieve a good vacuum reading or causing the loss of vacuum after the gauge valves are closed. If no leaks appear after five minutes, install the oil. Open the oiling valve as recommended by the A/C machine information to meter the correct amount of oil into the graduated cylinder.

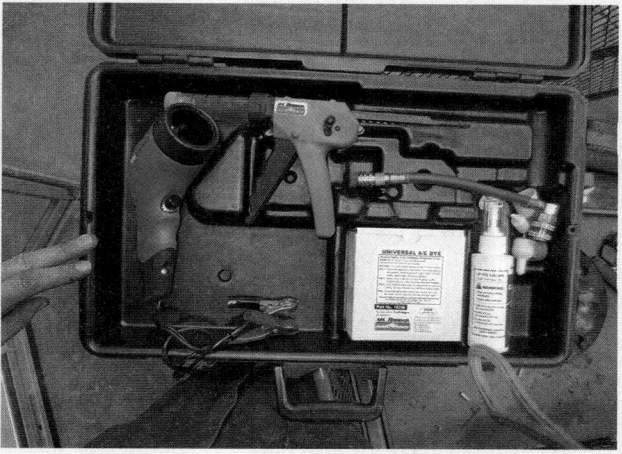

2. Shut off the oiling valve when the proper amount of oil has been added. Recharge the A/C system with the amount of refrigerant noted on the under-the-hood A/C decal or in the service information.

SKILL DRILL 59-20 Changing Vacuum Pump Oil

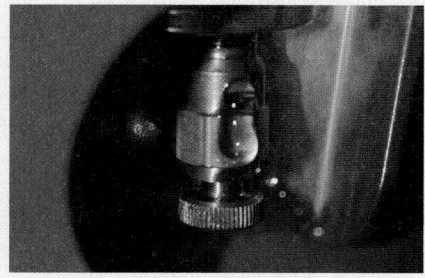

1. When it is time to change the vacuum pump oil, the machine warms up the oil so it is easier to drain. In most machines, the vacuum pump is behind a cover inside of the A/C machine, which must be removed to access the pump. Remove the pump drain plug and drain the oil.

2. Refer to the A/C machine user manual to find out what type and how much oil to install. Remove the fill plug, install the drain plug, and tighten. The fill plug is near the top, but not normally all the way on the top. Use a funnel to add the new oil.

3. Turn on the pump and check for leaks. Check that the oil level is halfway up the oil level sight glass indicator. If under the halfway mark, add oil. If over, drain some oil, Recheck. Reinstall the fill plug and check for leaks.

and that the valve holds pressure (no leaks). If there is a problem with cable or air operation, then the control head in the dash must be removed, inspected, and repaired or replaced. If the cable or air controls are working, then the operation of the valve should be inspected. Have someone move the temperature lever from hot to cold while watching the valve. If the cable vacuum or electric actuator servo is moving the control arm on the valve, then the valve is probably okay and the problem is elsewhere in the system, although the valve could be plugged or

slipping on the rotator shaft. Therefore, it may require removal from the heater hose and visually inspected to confirm the valve opens and closes correctly.

Removing, Inspecting, and Reinstalling the Heater Core

Heater cores are usually removed only because leaks are present. Leaks from the heater core can result in coolant misting out of the vents or coolant dripping from the same drain hole used by the

A/C evaporator. Because this process is different for every model of vehicle follow the steps outlined in the vehicle manufacturer's service information. One thing to remember is that the heater core inlet and outlet tubes are made of thin metal and older ones are soldered into thin metal tanks. Twisting the heater hoses to disconnect them almost always results in damage to the heater core tubes. Instead, carefully use a knife to slit the hose lengthwise over the heater core tubes, and then peel the hoses off the tubes.

Wrap-Up

Ready for Review

▶ Technicians must be EPA 609-certified to handle refrigerants.
▶ Performance testing of the A/C system is one of the first steps in diagnosis.
▶ A performance test involves external cooling for the condenser, running the engine between 1100 and 1500 rpm, placing the A/C on max cold, the fan on high, and measuring the duct temperature, and then comparing the duct temperature to a system performance chart from the manufacturer.
▶ Servicing the A/C system involves performance testing the system, diagnosing any issues, leak testing, identifying the refrigerant, reclaiming the refrigerant, performing any repairs, evacuating the system, recharging, retesting for leaks, and performance testing.
▶ Identifying refrigerant helps avoid mixing refrigerants, which cannot be reused and must be stored separately.
▶ An undercharged A/C system contains less refrigerant than the system calls for.
▶ The one rule for diagnosis of poor quality refrigerant is: "when in doubt, remove it out."
▶ The compressor is the most common source of abnormal noises arising from the air conditioner.
▶ If the high-side pressures are too high and the system is not cooling well, check the air flow through the condenser.
▶ Clearing the drain hose can clear up odors. If this does not work, an anti-odor kit may be required.
▶ Confirm the quality and type of refrigerant in the system by using a refrigerant identifier.
▶ The air distribution system is designed to circulate air through the heating and cooling system, then into the passenger cabin.
▶ Charge refers to the amount of refrigerant in the A/C system.
▶ Steps to the diagnosis and repair of A/C systems are pretest and inspection, leak test, reclaiming refrigerant, problem repair, evacuation, charging, and post-testing.
▶ Problems with A/C system performance may be due to system leaks, compressor failure, or system blockages.
▶ A/C performance testing should be done before and after a repair.
▶ A/C system inspection should include possible condenser airflow restrictions, evaporator housing water drain, air filter, hoses and belts, cooling fan, fan clutch, fan shroud, and heater control valves.
▶ A/C systems are equipped with protective devices designed to shut down the system if refrigerant pressures are too high or low.

▶ Tools needed to maintain and repair A/C systems include: sealant detector, reclaim/recycle machine, refrigerant identifiers, pressure gauge sets, A/C machine, anemometer, retrofit kit, pressure-temperature chart, vacuum pump, electronic leak detector, dye leak detector, oiler, vacuum gauge, micron gauge, and line wrench.
▶ Methods of leak testing are electronic detector testing, dye testing, and nitrogen testing.
▶ Any time the A/C system is opened, the refrigerant must be recovered (reclaimed).
▶ The A/C system should be flushed if the compressor internally disintegrates, the desiccant bag breaks open, or the oil is contaminated.
▶ Following a repair, the A/C system should be evacuated via an A/C machine or A/C manifold gauges and a vacuum pump.

Key Terms

accumulator A device placed between the evaporator and the compressor to collect liquid refrigerant and prevent it from entering the compressor. See also hydraulic accumulator.

air conditioning compressor clutch An engagement device connected to the compressor crankshaft to lock the crankshaft with a belt-driven pulley.

air conditioning machine A machine designed to recover, recycle, evacuate, leak test, and recharge (R/R/R) the A/C system.

charge The amount of refrigerant present in the system or the process of installing refrigerant in the system.

drive pulley Any belt-driven pulley used to power an accessory, such as power steering or the A/C compressor.

manifold gauge set A set of calibrated gauges for measuring high and low pressure A/C gases that can show pressure and vacuum readings for use with A/C systems.

micron gauge A device designed to measure the amount of vacuum very precisely.

muffler A device to quiet the pipes of the A/C system with baffles placed inside to deaden the sound of refrigerant moving.

oiler A device used to add oil to the A/C system.

overcharging Overfilling of the A/C system; may result in poor cooling or mechanical failure of the system.

performance testing The process of recreating a driving situation to inspect A/C performance and vent temperature.

pressure transients Minor fluctuations on the gauges that may indicate a problem.

PT chart   A pressure-temperature chart that shows the relationship between A/C pressures and evaporator temperature.

reclaim/recycle machine   An A/C machine designed to remove and recycle refrigerant for reuse.

reclaiming   The process of removing refrigerant from the A/C system by using an A/C machine; also called refrigerant *recovering machine*.

recovering   See *reclaiming*.

refrigerant identifiers   Devices used to check for impurities in the A/C gas.

state of charge   The amount of refrigerant in a system compared to how much should be in it.

vacuum gauge   A gauge designed to read negative pressure or vacuum.

vacuum pump   A pump used to evacuate the A/C system of air and put the system into a deep vacuum or low pressure to remove moisture.

Review Questions

1. Compared to a medium-sized home, what capacity will a typical transit bus A/C system have?
   a. Four to six times more than a house
   b. 20 to 30 times more than a house
   c. One-third less than a house
   d. The same capacity as a house
2. Which of the following is the first step in the A/C system inspection and diagnostic process?
   a. System pressure test
   b. Diagnosis of faults
   c. Performance testing
   d. Check for codes in computer
3. Which of the following is correct regarding refrigerant identification?
   a. The identifier connects to the low-side center-port of the manifold gauge set and samples the refrigerant.
   b. The only way to determine the type of refrigerant in a system is with the use of a sealant detector.
   c. The identifier reports the concentration of R-134a in a percentage.
   d. Concentration of refrigerant gas is performed before checking for the presence of A/C system sealant.
4. Which of the following is found on the A/C information decal?
   a. The volume of refrigerant
   b. The weight of a full refrigerant charge
   c. The viscosity of system oil
   d. Maximum safe operating pressure
5. Which of the following is correct concerning the state of refrigerant charge?
   a. State of charge in the A/C system refers to the amount of refrigerant in the system compared to how much should be in the system.
   b. State of charge is best measured by removing all of the refrigerant and recharging the system with the proper amount of refrigerant, as specified by the service information.

   c. An overcharged A/C system will cool better but use more energy.
   d. An undercharged A/C system will operate more quietly than a properly charged system.
6. Which of the following is correct concerning a refrigerant undercharge of the A/C system?
   a. Undercharging the A/C system increases high-side pressure but has lower low-side pressure readings.
   b. Both the low- and the high-side gauge pressure indicate higher than normal operating pressures.
   c. Both the low- and high-side pressure readings are below normal.
   d. An undercharge condition can only be determined by measuring air vent temperatures.
7. Which of the following are factors negatively affecting A/C system performance?
   a. Low humidity
   b. A white or reflective vehicle color
   c. High outside temperatures
   d. High airflow across the condenser
8. Which of the following is a step in A/C system performance testing?
   a. The engine's rpm should be at idle, which is the speed where most cooling is needed.
   b. An engine fan should push air out from under the hood to simulate real-world driving conditions.
   c. Set the blower motor speed to low to measure the coldest vent temperatures.
   d. The measurement of outlet temperature is made at the center dash vents.
9. Which of the following is correct concerning the evaporator housing water drain?
   a. As the A/C system is running, the evaporator drain should not leak water throughout the day.
   b. A drain hose is connected to the top of the evaporator housing and exits through the vehicle's firewall.
   c. The evaporator drain is connected to the bottom of the evaporator housing.
   d. Warm air should be felt leaving the evaporator drain when the A/C system is operating.
10. Which of the following conditions is caused by an excessive air gap in the A/C compressor clutch?
    a. A noisy clutch
    b. A pulley that continuously turns when the engine is running
    c. A burned clutch
    d. A clutch that fails to disengage

ASE Technician A/Technician B Style Questions

1. Technician A states that the wider the gap on an A/C clutch, the greater the electrical resistance measurement is observed when checking the windings. Technician B states that a wide clutch gap causes the compressor to remain engaged. Who is correct?
   a. Technician A
   b. Technician B

c. Both Technician A and Technician B
d. Neither Technician A nor Technician B

2. Technician A states that an A/C performance test usually requires that an auxiliary condenser fan be used during the test. Technician B states that a performance test shows if the A/C system is contaminated with sealer. Who is correct?
a. Technician A
b. Technician B
c. Both Technician A and Technician B
d. Neither Technician A nor Technician B

3. Technician A states that refrigerant in a vehicle should be identified before recovering the refrigerant. Technician B states that a sealant detector should be used to check refrigerant before it is recovered. Who is correct?
a. Technician A
b. Technician B
c. Both Technician A and Technician B
d. Neither Technician A nor Technician B

4. Technician A states that when evacuating an A/C system, the vacuum should be maintained for approximately 10 minutes after the system reaches the boiling point pressure of water. Technician B states that the primary purpose of evacuating an A/C system is to remove any air from the system. Who is correct?
a. Technician A
b. Technician B
c. Both Technician A and Technician B
d. Neither Technician A nor Technician B

5. Technician A states that the A/C system should be flushed if the compressor came apart. Technician B states that the system should be flushed if the oil is contaminated. Who is correct?
a. Technician A
b. Technician B
c. Both Technician A and Technician B
d. Neither Technician A nor Technician B

6. Technician A states that when using pressurized nitrogen to locate a leak, an electronic detector should be used. Technician B states that electronic detectors are used when the system has at least a minimal refrigerant charge. Who is correct?
a. Technician A
b. Technician B
c. Both Technician A and Technician B
d. Neither Technician A nor Technician B

7. Technician A states that micron measurement units are a much more accurate unit of measuring vacuum than inches of mercury (Hg). Technician B states that micron measurement units are provided on most manifold gauge sets low-side gauge. Who is correct?
a. Technician A
b. Technician B
c. Both Technician A and Technician B
d. Neither Technician A nor Technician B

8. Technician A states that to determine how much refrigerant is needed in a system, you must refer to identifying labels on the vehicle or the service manual. Technician B states that to determine the amount of refrigerant is needed, you just charge the system until the pressures reach normal values. Who is correct?
a. Technician A
b. Technician B
c. Both Technician A and Technician B
d. Neither Technician A nor Technician B

9. Technician A states that when removing any part of an A/C system, the oil should be drained from it and measured so that the same amount can be reinstalled. Technician B states that oil should only be in the compressor, and if any oil is found in any other components, it means that the receiver dryer is faulty. Who is correct?
a. Technician A
b. Technician B
c. Both Technician A and Technician B
d. Neither Technician A nor Technician B

10. Technician A states that if moisture enters the A/C system, acid is created. Technician B states that evacuating an A/C system boils away moisture, which is removed from the system as a gas. Who is correct?
a. Technician A
b. Technician B
c. Both Technician A and Technician B
d. Neither Technician A nor Technician B

CHAPTER 60

Trailer Refrigeration

Learning Objectives

- **LO 60-1** Identify and explain the fundamentals of transport refrigeration.
- **LO 60-2** Identify and calculate heating and cooling requirements for transportation temperature control.
- **LO 60-3** Identify and describe types of transport refrigeration systems.
- **LO 60-4** Explain the operation of heating, cooling, and defrost cycles used in truck-transport temperature control systems.
- **LO 60-5** Explain the operation of major components used in trailer refrigeration systems.
- **LO 60-6** Identify and explain the differences between the severity of reefer alarm codes.
- **LO 60-7** Identify and explain minimal requirements for truck-trailer refrigeration system maintenance.

You Are the Technician

A refrigerated trailer has arrived at your shop with the complaint that the product in the trailer is taking a very long time to cool. The driver is concerned there is a problem with the trailer reefer. When asked about water draining from the reefer container, the driver reported they thought an excessive amount of water was draining from the trailer. To investigate the complaint, you performed a visual inspection of the reefer and checked for any fault code displayed on the control unit, but everything appeared to be in proper working order. The trailer was cooling, and the interior temperature was approaching the temperature set point. (The temperature was only 2° above the set point when inspected.) However, you did confirm that, based on your experience, the reefer was frequently defrosting and it was draining quite a bit more water than usual compared to other loads. When asked about the type of product that was being transported, the driver replied that it was a fresh load of strawberries. Remembering information from a refrigeration course about the differences between the heat loads of various products, you informed the driver that the refrigeration system was functioning correctly and the observations were normal. You explained to them that the strawberries had a high moisture content or what is simply termed a "wet load." In preparing your report for the work order, consider answering the following questions:

1. How does the type and condition of product refrigerated by a trailer affect the heat load a trailer refrigeration unit must remove? (Include the concept of specific heat in your answer.)
2. How does a load with a high moisture content affect the time it takes to cool a product?
3. List at least three other factors that would affect the time it takes for the refrigeration unit of the trailer to cool the product.

Introduction

Transporting temperature-sensitive goods—such as fresh produce, flowers, meat, or dairy products—requires temperature-regulated containers. In hot weather, cooling is needed to prevent products from spoiling or melting. Even though refrigeration is what immediately comes to mind when thinking about transportation of temperature-sensitive perishable goods, in the winter or in cold climates, heating is also needed to prevent damage to perishable products due to freezing. A more descriptive term than "transport refrigeration" is **transport temperature control**, which refers to heating or cooling over a wide range of outside temperatures and product storage temperatures.

This chapter introduces the types of transport refrigeration, the different heating and cooling cycles, system components, and basic maintenance practices for truck-trailer temperature control system.

Fundamentals of Transport Refrigeration

LO 60-1 Identify and explain the fundamentals of transport refrigeration.

Several manufacturers produce temperature-control systems, which are installed in trailers, shipping containers, and truck boxes. The name for the major component regulating truck-trailer temperature-control systems is commonly called a reefer, which is a contraction of the term refrigeration unit. A distinction should, however, be made between these types of temperature-control units that can both heat and cool products and air-conditioning (A/C) systems, which also use principles of refrigeration (**FIGURE 60-1**). Background for this chapter information builds on information presented in the previous chapters on air conditioning systems.

Refrigeration is a process of transferring heat away from a product storage container to achieve a temperature of 65° F (18° C) or colder (**FIGURE 60-2**). In contrast, A/C is designed to maintain clean, fresh, comfortable air temperatures between 65° F (18° C) and 75° F (24° C) for people. Blower fan speeds are high in A/C-only systems for the following functions: rapidly cooling hot cabin air temperatures, dehumidification, and refreshing the passenger compartment with clean air. Blower fan speeds are not as important in refrigeration systems as they are in A/C systems. In terms of product temperature control, some trailers and truck boxes have only heating systems to protect temperature-sensitive products from freeze damage when transporting in very cold climates and winter weather. But most truck and trailer refrigeration systems are capable of both heating and cooling product.

The major components and the operation of a refrigeration system are like those outlined in the Principles of Heating and Air-Conditioning Systems chapter. One major difference between the A/C system and a truck-trailer refrigeration system is that a heating cycle is added to the cooling-refrigeration system cycles. Heating cycles have two purposes.

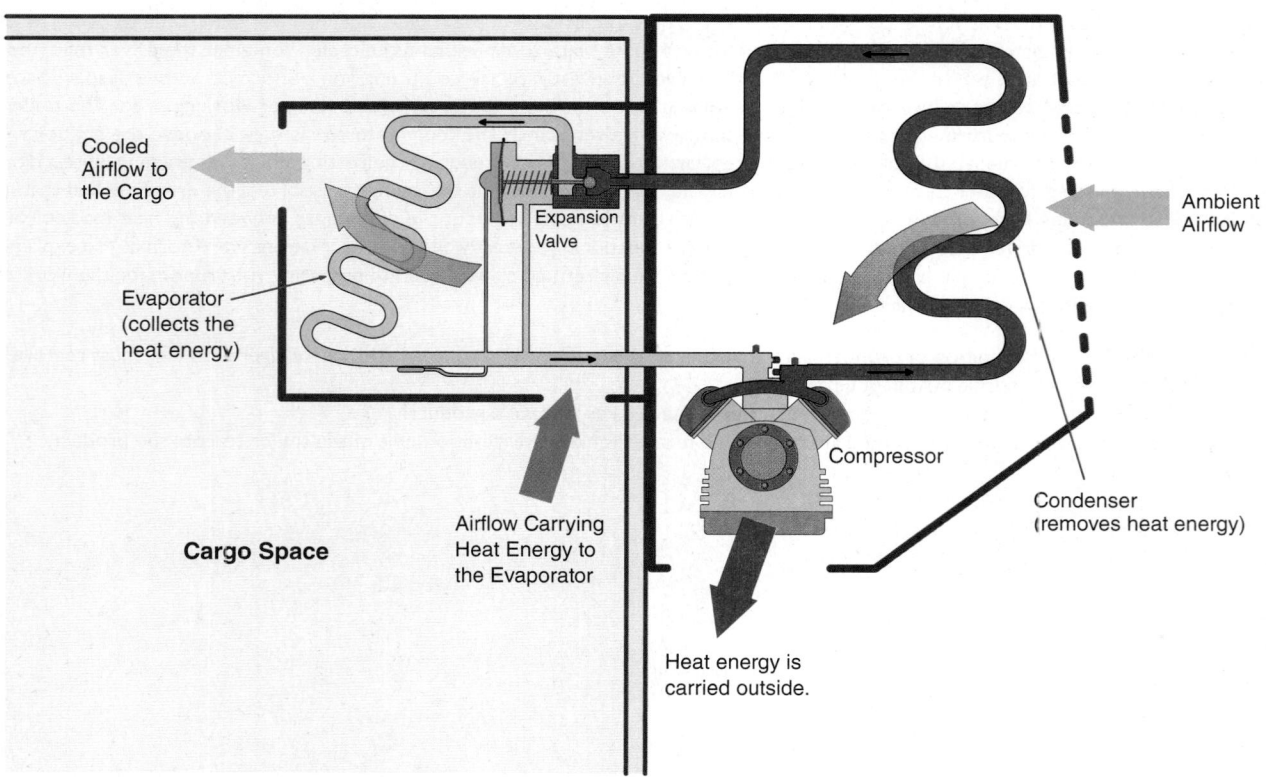

FIGURE 60-1 Refrigeration removes heat from the truck box or trailer body.

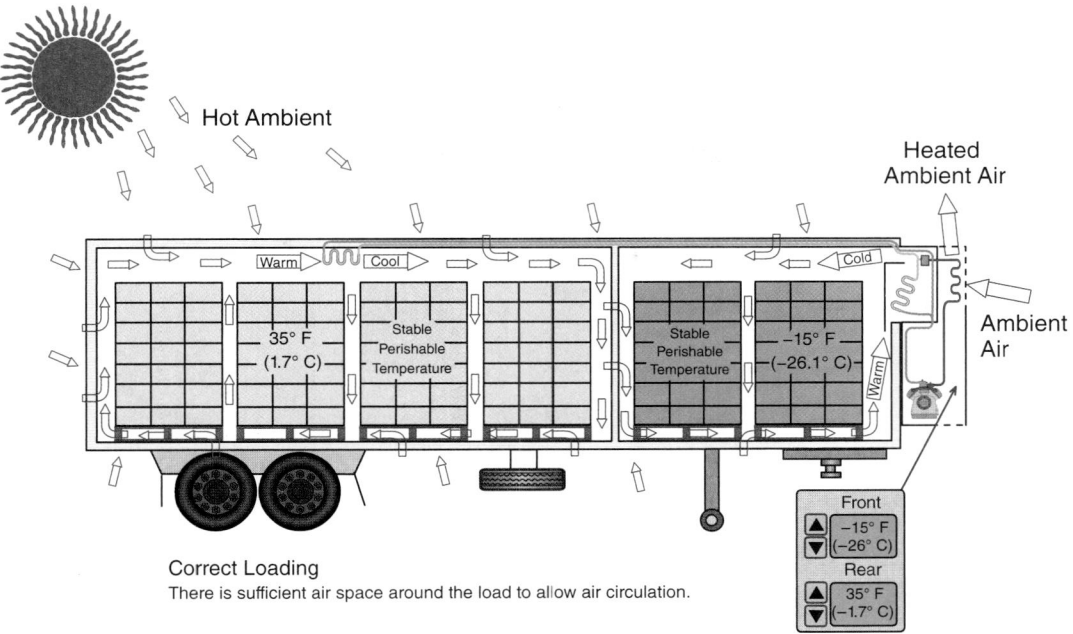

FIGURE 60-2 Refrigeration is different from air conditioning in that refrigeration produces much colder product temperatures.

The first is to warm product when transporting it through cold temperatures. The second purpose for a short heating cycle is an essential feature of the subzero temperature refrigeration system necessary to defrost evaporators, which are designed to freeze product. Regular defrosting of the evaporator is important because moisture easily freezes on contact with a cold evaporator (**FIGURE 60-3**). Ice quickly builds up over condensed moisture on the evaporator, which blocks airflow. If air cannot pass over the evaporator plates, fins, or tubes, the evaporator becomes almost completely ineffective for freezing product or maintaining temperatures below the freezing point of water. To remove the ice, the evaporator is temporarily heated

with hot refrigerant gases to melt the ice before resuming another longer cooling cycle (**FIGURE 60-4**). This heat cycle is not unlike the automatic **defrost cycle** of a refrigerator in the home. More frequent defrosting of a frozen evaporator takes place and is particularly important when very damp products are refrigerated (commonly termed a **wet load**).

To defrost the reefer's evaporator, the major components involved in heating and cooling refrigerant reverse refrigerant flow and operation of the cooling cycle where the evaporator refrigerant, which normally absorbs heat, instead releases heat. The condenser, which during a cooling cycle transfers heat from the refrigerant to the atmosphere, is not included in this cycle

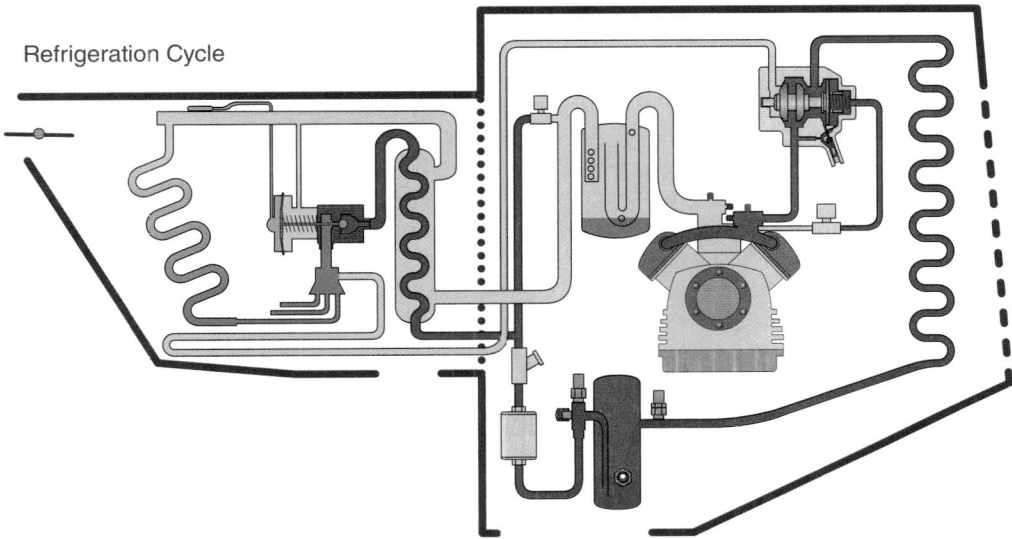

FIGURE 60-3 The self-powered refrigeration system can cool the truck body containing temperature-sensitive product.

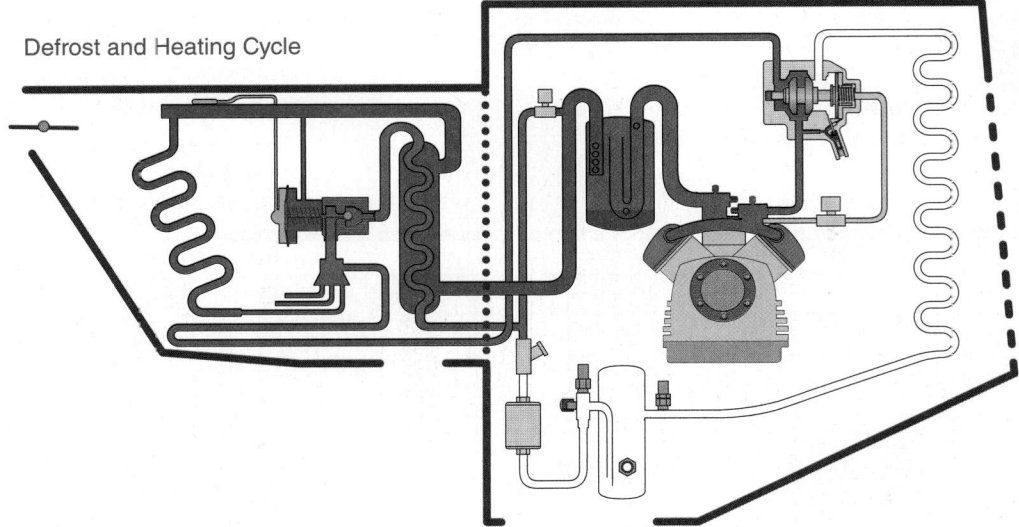

FIGURE 60-4 Self-powered refrigeration systems can also heat the truck box to prevent product from freezing.

and refrigerant flow through it is blocked. Heat for the defrost and heating cycle is generated by compressing refrigerant in the compressor. Heated refrigerant leaves the discharge port or compressor outlet and travels to the evaporator to thaw a frozen evaporator or heat the cargo compartment containing product.

Heating Principles

LO 60-2 Identify and calculate heating and cooling requirements for transportation temperature control.

Like A/C systems, a reefer unit removes heat from a temperature-controlled box or trailer body faster than it enters in order to cool the product. Heat enters the refrigerated area from different sources compared to a passenger cabin. Other heat-producing sources include:

- Product that is loaded when warm
- Direct transfer of the sun's energy into the cargo box and high outside temperatures
- Doors opening during loading and unloading
- Cargo respiration (ripening), which releases heat

While a person may emit close to 580 BTU (146 kcal) of heat per hour, ripening product can also produce heat. For example, Thermo King, a major reefer manufacturer, notes that 2000 lb (909 kg) of strawberries at 32° F (0° C) produces 113–158 BTU (28–40 kcal) per hour of heat. At 40° F (4° C), the strawberries ripen faster to produce 150–283 BTU (38–71 kcal) per hour. At 60° F (16° C), the same strawberries produce up to 846 BTU (213 kcal) per hour while ripening.

To reduce heat loads from radiant solar heat and prevent heat absorption, steel trailers are often painted white or aluminum-cladded trailers are polished to reflect bright sunlight and heat. Solid foam insulation in the ceilings and walls of a refrigerated truck or trailer minimizes heat transfer through conduction but it can become waterlogged and transfer heat, particularly from road surfaces and outside air. If needed to

TABLE 60-1 Specific Heat Values of Water and Air

Substance	Density	Specific Heat
Water	64 lb/cubic foot	1 BTU
Air	0.0807 lb/cubic foot	0.240 BTU 0.07 watts

Source: catalog.conveyorspneumatic.com

improve cooling in warmer spots in the trailer, powerful evaporator fans can blow more than 3000 cubic feet (85 cubic meters) of air per minute to increase convection heat movement inside a cooled container. Duct work and curtain-like barriers can improve spot cooling areas within the cargo box. Door seals are carefully designed and must be properly maintained to keep warm, moist air out of the box.

Effect of Water Vapor on Cooling Efficiency

The cooling or heating capacity of a reefer is measured in BTU (British Thermal Unit) per hour. A BTU is the amount of heat required to change the temperature of one pound of water by 1° Fahrenheit. This definition is based on the idea of specific heat, a concept discussed in the chapter on Principles of Air Conditioning, which refers to the amount of heat required to change the temperature of a substance by 1° F for a given weight (**TABLE 60-1**). Applying these concepts to refrigeration, a reefer with 20,000 BTU/h (5040 kcal/h) refrigeration capacity cooling a load containing 5000 lb (2273 kg) containing only water could theoretically lower the temperature of water 4° F every hour (20,000 BTU/5000 lb = 4 hours). In contrast to water, dry air, that is air without any water content, needs only about a quarter of the energy required by water to change its temperature. This means that air, with its unique specific heat value, needs only 0.24 BTU to change one pound of air 1° F. Because air has a lower specific heat value compared to water, to lower just the air temperature of an empty cargo box without any consideration for water content from 70° F to 32° F (20° C to 0° C) requires much less energy and take place much faster with the same reefer cooling 5000 lb of water. Expressed another way using numerical values, a 1600 cubic ft box contains air weighing 0.0807 lb/cu ft or 12,929 kg/cubic meter contains only 129.12 lb of air. This would require close to 31 BTU per 1° F to lower the air's temperature. Only 1178 BTU is needed to take it from 70° F to 32° F (20° C to 0° C). A 20,000 BTU reefer could theoretically accomplish this change in just over ten minutes compared to approximately 9.5 hours for water only. Naturally, these approximate calculations do not account for a number of other variables. For example, in real-world terms, air always contains some water content. Because the water content of the load has a major influence on how quickly a reefer can reach optimal temperatures, a product load with higher moisture content requires much more energy to heat or cool than dry air because its specific heat value is greater.

Energy Required for Cooling Product Versus Freezing

Latent heat, which is a term related to specific heat, is also described in the chapter on Principles of Air Conditioning. It refers to the hidden heat or energy required to change the state of a substance from a liquid to gas or liquid to a solid and vice versa. When only the latent heat of a substance is added or removed, its temperature does not change, just its physical state. Since the latent heat value for water temperature is very high in comparison to other substances, much more energy is required to lower a product's temperature across the freezing point of water than is required to simply cool a product or bring it near water's freezing point. This is significant for technicians because the efficiency and capacity of different refrigeration systems across various temperature changes are not the same. Some systems can do a better job of freezing and maintaining a cold temperature than they can just cooling product to near its freezing point. The opposite situation can take place too. To illustrate this point, TABLE 60-2 shows the cooling capacity of various models of transport refrigeration units at different outside temperatures. Note that some models do a better job cooling product having a higher cooling capacity above water's freeze point, while others have more cooling capacity at temperatures below water's freezing point. The significance of this observation for technicians is important when investigating a common complaint that the reefer is not cooling properly or that a specific reefer cannot maintain a particular temperature compared to other refrigeration units.

Types of Transport Refrigeration Systems

LO 60-3 Identify and describe types of transport refrigeration systems.

Two major classifications of truck–trailer or transport refrigeration systems are distinguished by the method used to power or drive the refrigeration compressor. Compressors can be powered by the vehicle's engine, self-powered with an engine integrated into the refrigeration unit and driven by an electric motor or a combination of engine and electric power. **Vehicle-powered refrigeration units** are used in smaller delivery vans and trucks. In these systems, the compressor is located on the engine of the vehicle. Refrigerant is used both to cool and defrost the evaporator, as needed. Whenever the load requires just heating, such as in the winter, the system usually does not have the capacity to supply enough heat, so engine coolant is used to transfer heat to the temperature-controlled product compartment.

Self-powered refrigeration units use a small horsepower diesel engine to power the refrigeration system. The fuel economy, durability, and low maintenance requirement, as well as the availability of high torque output at low engine speeds, make the capabilities of diesel engines an ideal choice for this type of application (**FIGURE 60-5**). Note, however, that in most reefer systems, the engine does not always drive the compressor. In **stand-by mode**, such as when a vehicle is parked at a yard, the reefer can also use an electric motor to drive the compressor

TABLE 60-2 Cooling Capacity of Various Models of Transport Refrigeration Units

Model	BTU/h at 35° F (2° C)	BTU/h at 0° F (−18° C)	BTU/h at −20° F (−29° C)
Trailer Unit – A	46,000 (11,592 kcal/h)	38,500 (9702 kcal/h)	30,000 (7560 kcal/h)
Trailer Unit – B	46,000 (11,592 kcal/h)	32,000 (8064 kcal/h)	21,000 (5292 kcal/h)
Trailer Unit – C	43,500 (10,962 kcal/h)	27,000 (6804 kcal/h)	16,000 (4031 kcal/h)
Self-Powered Truck Unit – A	25,000 (6300 kcal/h)	18,000 (4536 kcal/h)	12,000 (3024 kcal/h)
Self-Powered Truck Unit – B	22,600 (5695 kcal/h)	12,500 (3150 kcal/h)	7500 (1890 kcal/h)
Self-Powered Truck Unit – C	15,750 (3969 kcal/h)	11,000 (2520 kcal/h)	6750 (1701 kcal/h)

FIGURE 60-5 Diesel engines efficiently power refrigeration units.

FIGURE 60-6 A self-powered refrigeration unit for a straight truck.

when supplied with electric current from a connection to a power grid or a shore power source. The use of electric motors in standby mode typically allows refrigeration to take place for weeks and longer without the need to fill the fuel tank or perform engine-related maintenance.

SAFETY TIP

Three-phase, 60-cycle current powers the electric compressor drive motor using either 220 or 460 volts alternating current (AC). This means potentially lethal three-phase AC electric power is present whenever the reefer unit is operating in either diesel or stand-by electric mode and whenever it is connected to a source of external power. Extreme caution must be exercised when servicing these units. Typically, but not always, high-voltage wiring is identified by orange-colored heavy nylon covering or conduit. Only certified and properly trained technicians should service the electrical components of a reefer.

These self-powered units are further classified by application, depending on whether they are mounted onto smaller truck boxes, as in **FIGURE 60-6**, or larger trailer applications, as in **FIGURE 60-7**. Self-powered reefers are self-contained units integrating the compressor, evaporator, blower fans, and electric motor, control valves, engine, etc. into a single module that can be suspended from a truck box or trailer body. In smaller units, the compressor is a two-cylinder reciprocating-type, while larger units use compressors that have four cylinders arranged in a V bank. The more recent trend is to use quieter-operating scroll-type compressors that, compared to reciprocating-type compressors, can use 70% fewer parts and weigh up to 200 lb less. Smaller reefers use a quieter, more efficient scroll-type compressor. In addition to the compressor design, other differences exist among the components used by various manufacturers

FIGURE 60-7 A self-powered refrigeration unit for a semi-trailer.

Multi-Temperature Systems

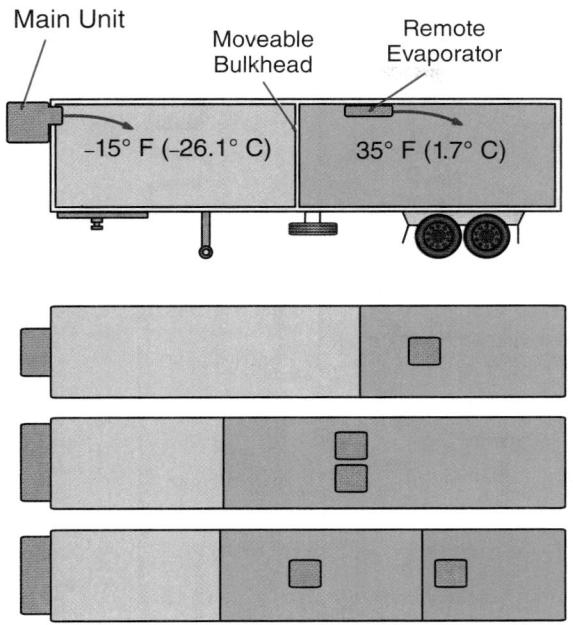

FIGURE 60-8 A multi-temp reefer has more than one evaporator. A single-temp reefer has only one.

of truck and trailer reefers. Software controls and telematic solutions, which provide two-way communication between the reefer and a dispatch center, is an area of tremendous development. Nonetheless, all self-powered refrigeration systems operate in basically an identical manner.

One of the latest advancements in powering larger truck refrigeration units is the use of a truck engine-driven, hydraulically operated electric power generator. Because the engine in a truck is likely more environmentally cleaner and fuel efficient than a trailer's reefer engine, the reefer's compressor can be driven using an electric motor powered by the truck engine. In one common configuration, a power take off (PTO)-type hydraulic pump driven by the engine supplies the pressurized hydraulic fluid to a hydraulically driven generator. The generator, in turn, supplies the high-voltage, three-phase current used to operate the electric motor. These E-drive or hybrid reefers can also operate more cleanly and quieter while substantially reducing fuel consumption.

Self-powered refrigeration systems can also be configured to control a single temperature or multiple temperatures in different areas or zones of the trailer. On the outside, a **multi-temp unit** looks like a single temperature system **FIGURE 60-8**. However, multi-temp units can regulate temperature using additional evaporators mounted in the ceiling. Each compartment outfitted with its own dedicated evaporator can heat or cool product as necessary using a separate thermostatic control. The front compartment is usually reserved for frozen product and is generally cooler than the rear, which has fresh produce and a higher temperature setting.

Overview of Heating, Cooling, and Defrost Cycles

LO 60-4 Explain the operation of heating, cooling, and defrost cycles used in truck-transport temperature control systems.

Truck-trailer refrigeration systems use the same principles of refrigeration—and many of the same components—as A/C systems. Compressors, evaporators, condensers, accumulators, and thermostatic expansion valves are found in both systems. What is different is that the reefer has several modes, or cycles, of operation that involve cooling, heating, and defrosting the evaporator, plus a unique valve to control the heating/defrost-cooling operating mode (**FIGURE 60-9**).

Three-Way (3-Way) Valve

Controlling the direction of refrigerant flow determines whether the reefer is in cooling or heating mode (**FIGURE 60-10**). Either an electrically controlled set of solenoids or a refrigerant control valve called a **three-way valve** directs hot refrigerant gas to the condenser (when in cool mode) or directly to the evaporator (when in the heat or defrost mode) (**FIGURES 60-11, 60-12**, and **60-13**). The position of the three-way valve spool is electrically controlled using a combination of spring and gas pressure. When the valve is de energized, spring pressure moves the valve to a cool-mode position. When the valve is energized, gas pressure forces the valve into the heat mode.

Heating Cycle

If a product requires heating, such as transporting bananas in cold climates and during the winter, the function of the refrigeration components can be changed. This means that the evaporator is needed to release heat into the product compartment. Refrigerant flow though the condenser is blocked during heating and defrost mode because hot refrigerant gas discharged from the compressor is rerouted through the three-way valve to the evaporator. Mechanical energy from the compressor is converted into heat transferred into the refrigerant through compression. Even when it is very cold, heat can still be added to the refrigerant using the compressors energy.

During heating mode, the evaporator is pressurized with hot refrigerant gases, and the condenser is used to absorb heat by evaporating refrigerant. But heating capabilities are not as great as cooling capacity. For example, at $-0.4°$ F ($-18°$ C), container temperatures may be heated to reach $40°$ F ($5°$ C), but the evaporator temperature does not exceed $60°$ F ($15.5°$ C). Electric heaters and heat from an engine's cooling system can supplement or entirely used without the refrigeration cycle to provide the heating capacity of the refrigeration system in heat mode.

Cooling Cycle

During cooling cycle, the refrigeration cycle is identical to one found in a conventional A/C system. Refrigerant absorbs heat from the product in the trailer or box. The compressor pulls the refrigerant into its cylinders to compress the gas and raise its temperature. Hot refrigerant gases are pushed into the

1. Compressor
2. Discharge Service Valve
3. Discharge Vibrasorber
4. Discharge Line
5. Thre-Way Valve
6. Condenser Pressure Bypass
   Check Valve
7. Condenser Coil
8. Condenser Check Valve
9. High-Pressure Relief Valve
10. Receiver Tank
11. Receiver Tank Sight Glass
12. Receiver Tank Outlet Valve (RTOV)
13. Liquid Line
14. Liquid Line Dryer
15. Heat Exchanger
16. Expansion Valve
17. Expansion Valve Feeler Bulb
18. Equalizer Line
19. Distributor
20. Evaporator Coil
21. Suction Line
22. Accumulator
23. Suction Vibrasorber
24. Suction Service Valve
25. Throttling Valve
26. Pilot Solenoid
27. Hot Gas Line
28. Defrost Check Valve
29. Bypass Check Valve
30. Bypass Service Valve
31. Modulator Valve
32. Hot Gas Bypass Valve

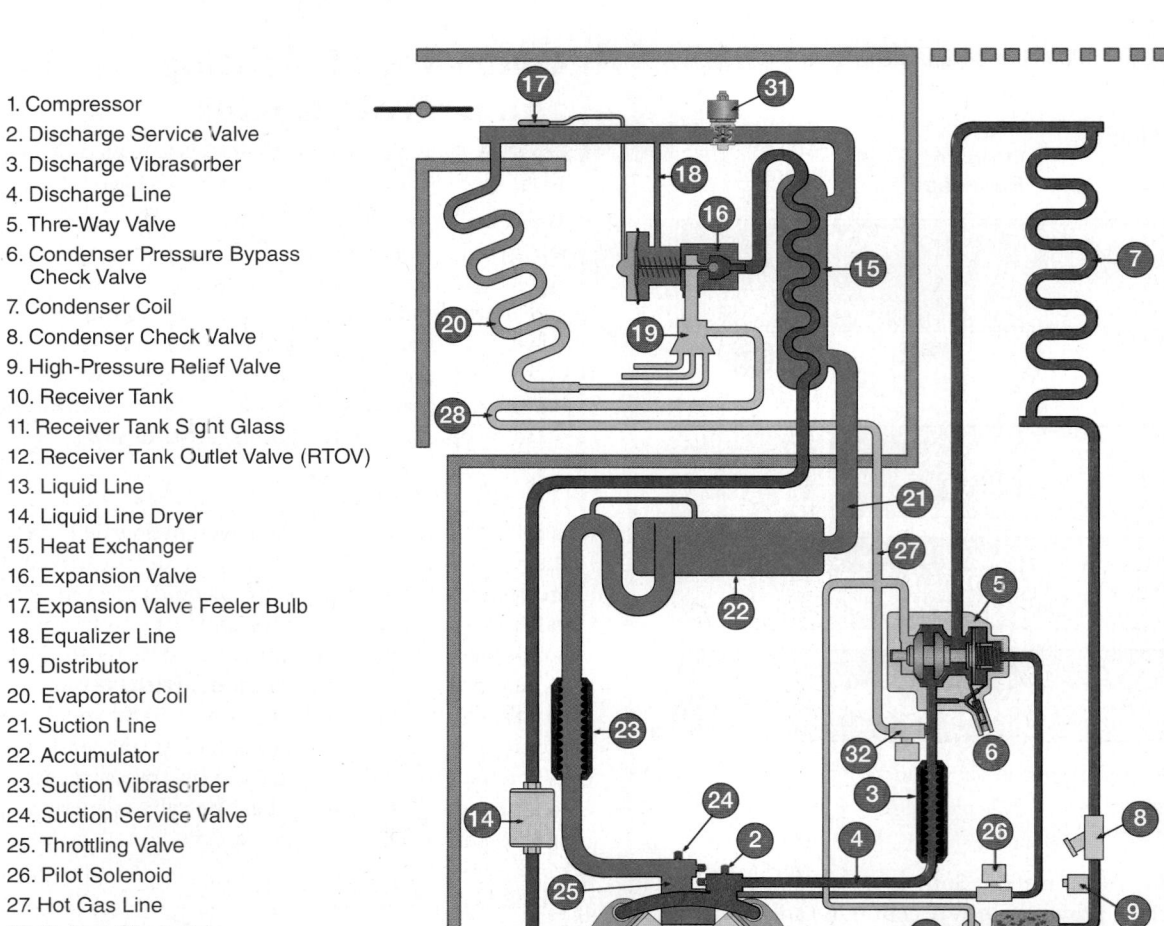

FIGURE 60-9 Refrigerant circuits and components of a trailer refrigeration unit for heating and cooling.

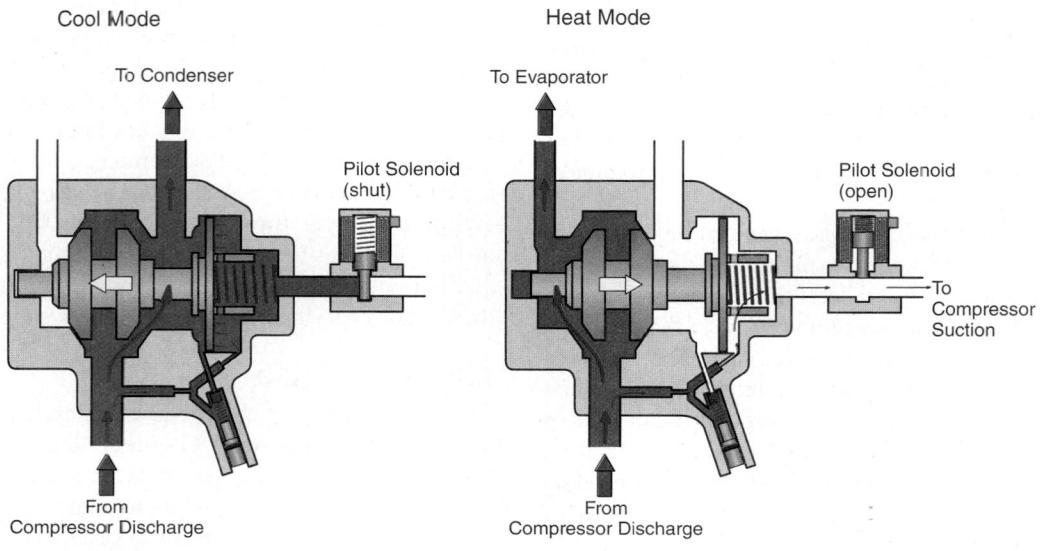

FIGURE 60-10 A three-way valve directs the flow of hot refrigerant gases to the condenser during cooling or the evaporator during heat and defrost cycles.

condenser, where they release heat to the atmosphere and condense into a warm liquid. That warm liquid refrigerant travels back to the evaporator and passes through an expansion valve before re-entering the evaporator. Because of the restriction in the expansion valve, refrigerant pressure is reduced, enabling the refrigerant to absorb tremendous amounts of heat as it evaporates. Powerful evaporator blower motors push the air inside the product compartment across the evaporator, where the chemical and physical properties of expanding refrigerant absorbs heat from the air.

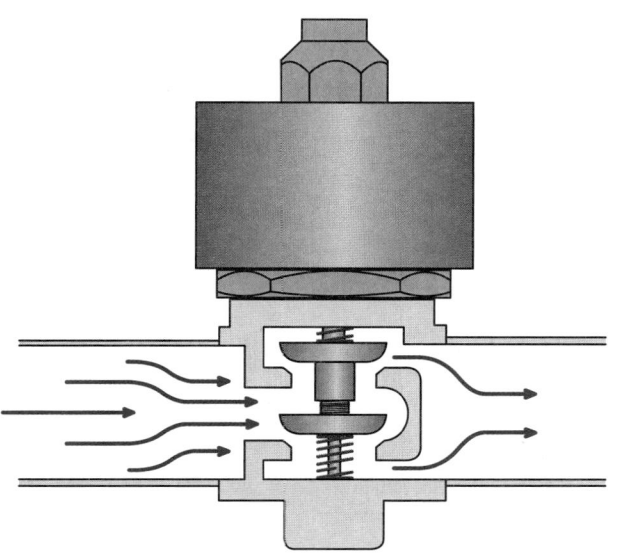

FIGURE 60-11 Electrically operated solenoids are used to redirect the flow of hot refrigerant.

Defrost Cycle and Damper Door Operation

The purpose of the defrost cycle is to remove ice from the evaporator built up when the evaporator operates at temperatures below the freezing point of water. In defrost mode, the reefer operates almost identically as in the heating cycle except that, during the defrost mode, a damper door, unique to a reefer, is closed to prevent air flow from crossing the warm evaporator and into the container with perishable or frozen product (**FIGURE 60-14**). Closing the damper door during defrost, but not during a heating cycle, enables warm air to recirculate around the evaporator but not flow into the refrigerated container area. Without the dampener door or a door that is stuck open, the container temperature would potentially increase and thaw frozen product. When the reefer is defrosting, melting ice drips into a heated defroster pan and drains through a pipe to the ground outside of the reefer. Hot refrigerant gases pass through a section of line below the pan and prevent the cold container temperatures from re-freezing the water to enable the defroster pan to completely drain during a defrost cycle.

Enabling Conditions for the Defrost Cycle

Defrost mode can be configured to take place under a large number of circumstances. In automatic mode or continuous run when transporting a perishable product, the temperature difference across the evaporator is continuously measured. Evaporator return and supply air temperature are monitored too. Large differences in the evaporator temperature indicate it's frozen and initiates a defrost cycle. Pressure differences can be monitored by the system controls the same way

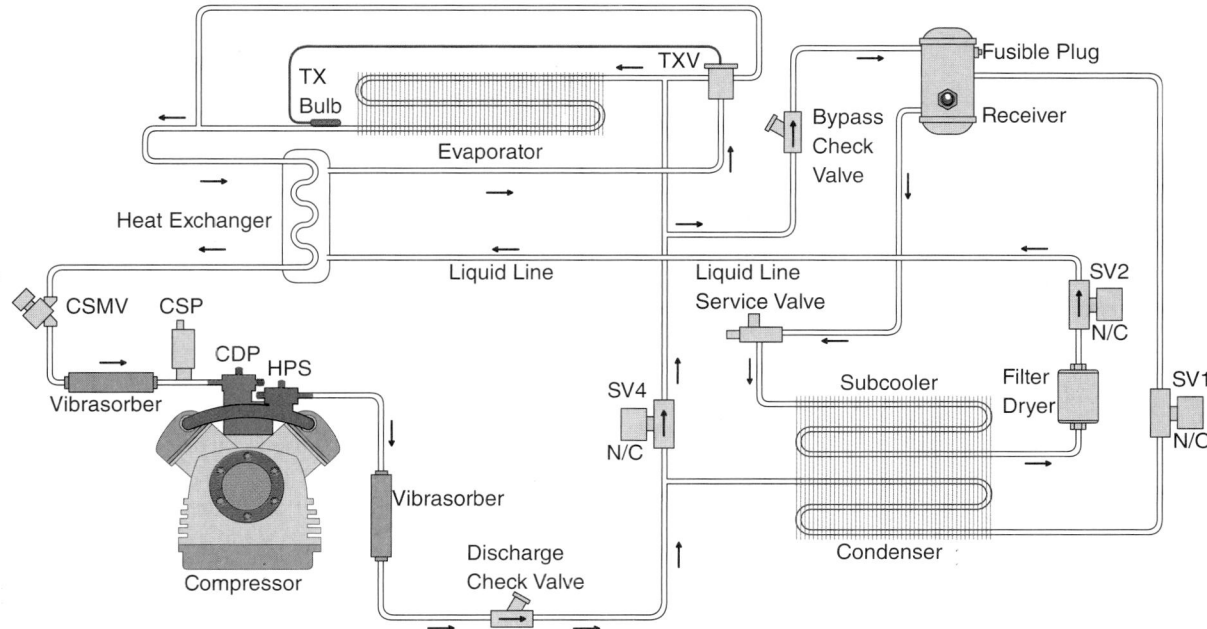

Refrigerant Circuit During Heating and Defrost

FIGURE 60-12 The operation of refrigerant solenoids in a Carrier reefer used to place the reefer in heating mode.

Refrigerant Circuit During Cooling

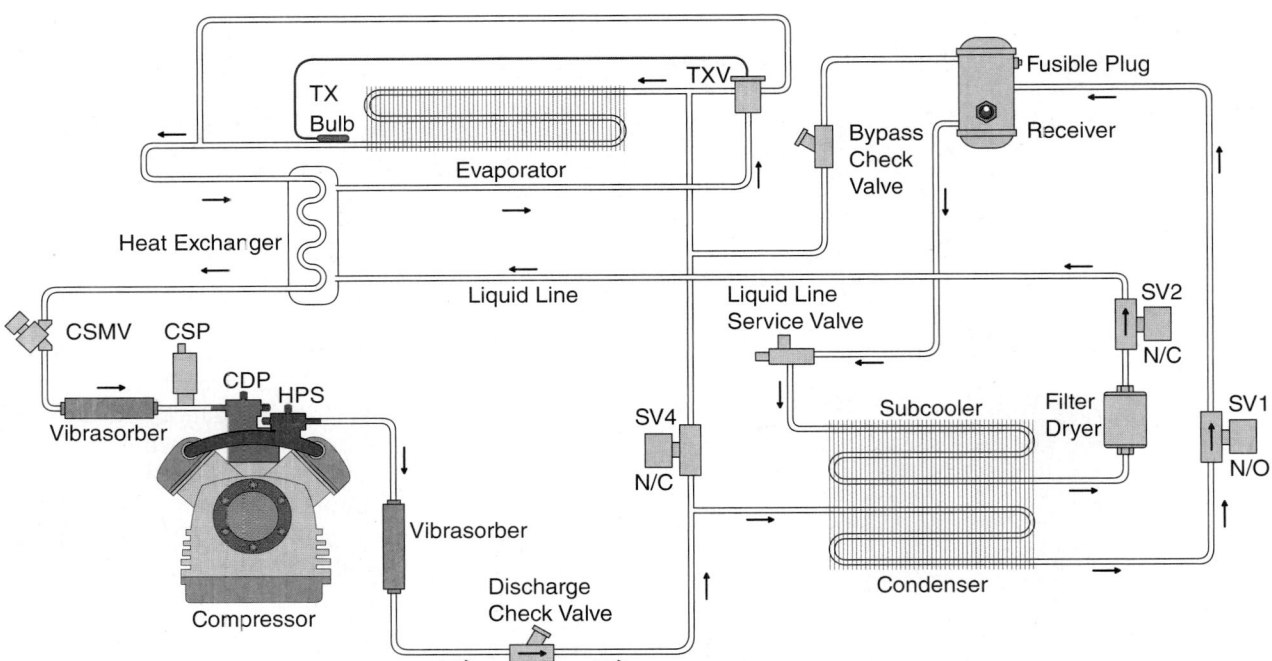

FIGURE 60-13 The operation of refrigerant solenoids in a Carrier reefer used to place the reefer in cooling mode.

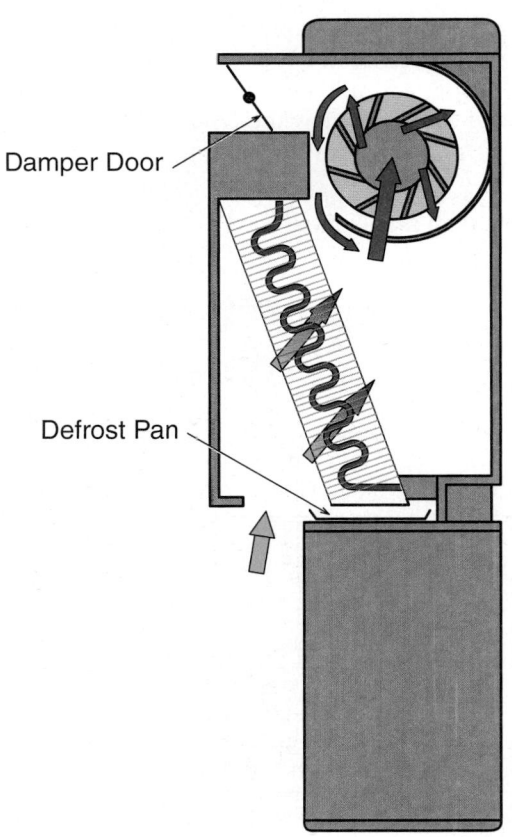

FIGURE 60-14 Damper doors allow for better control of the evaporator air flow, which makes for more efficient defrosting.

to switch the reefer from cooling into a defrost mode. An increasing refrigerant pressure differential across the evaporator indicates that frost or ice has formed on the evaporator and the controls should initiate a defrost cycle. This automatic defrost cycle can start if the temperature difference begins to increase too, indicating the evaporator is too cold and the likelihood that frost or ice has begun to build-up over the evaporator.

Most reefer units do not enter the automatic defrost mode unless the evaporator coil temperature is below approximately 45° F (7.2° C). The defrost mode is terminated when coil temperature rises to 55° F (12.8° C).

If an evaporator temperature sensor indicates that the evaporator is within an expected range but the technician or operator suspects the evaporator may not be defrosted, or to check the operation of the dampener door and other system operation features during diagnostic and maintenance procedures, a manual defrost event can be initiated using a manual defrost switch or the touch panel on the reefer controls. The evaporator can also be scheduled to defrost automatically every three, four, six, or eight hours of operation, which takes place in addition to any automatically commanded defrost event. Software logic used by the electronic control systems can also establish new defrost cycles independent of any automatic defrost. Manual defrosting and the scheduled defrost cycles are performed outside of any automatic event to ensure the reefer is not inadvertently operated for extended time with a frozen evaporator. To perform a manual defrost, follow the steps in **SKILL DRILL 60-1.**

SKILL DRILL 60-1 Performing a Manual Defrost

1. Determine whether a manual defrost cycle is recommended. Performing a manual defrost cycle can take place to:
   - Address customer concerns the unit is not cooling properly (possibly caused by a frozen evaporator)
   - Inspect the operation of the damper door, heating tray, and drains
   - Whenever there is a wet product or cargo, doors have been frequently opened
2. Inspect door seals and switches for correct operation to identify any unusual cause for excessive moisture build-up in the cargo container.
3. Verify enabling conditions are met by first observing the evaporator temperature displayed on the control unit screen.

Evaporator outlet temperatures must be below 45° F (7° C). Product doors must also be closed if equipped with door switches.

4. Check the control panel to verify that no critical alerts or alarms that could impair reefer operation or shut it down are present. Record any alerts or alarm codes and clear codes.
5. To initiate the defrost, press the control panel key for manual defrost for typically five seconds. Alternatively toggle the defrost switch for the time recommended by the user manual. Note that manual defrost cycles are normally time-initiated and temperature-terminated. A fail-safe backup time can be programmed into some reefers to end the defrost to prevent a prolonged defrost cycle, which could potentially warm product.
6. If required, inspect system operation after the defrost cycle begins. A manual defrost cycle is used to melt ice and frost from the evaporator coil surfaces, and warm the drain pan to allow water dripping from the evaporator to exit down the drain line without refreezing in the pan. Check that the drains are clear by verifying water run-off. Inspect the damper door to see that it closes during the defrost.
7. Verify the defrost cycle terminates automatically when the coil temperature is typically greater than or equal to 58° F (14.5° C) or the manual defrost timer expires. A manual defrost cycle can also be ended by turning the unit off and back on.
8. If the control unit has a data logger, obtain a report of system operation and store it on a USB flash drive. Verify no fault codes or alarms were triggered during the defrost cycle.

Components of Trailer Refrigeration Systems

LO 60-5 Explain the operation of major components used in trailer refrigeration systems.

Trailer refrigeration systems contain the same basic components as an A/C system. These include:

- Refrigerant compressors
- Condensers
- Receiver tanks
- Liquid line dryers
- Evaporators
- Expansion valves
- Refrigerant

Refrigerant Compressors

To provide the cooling and freezing capabilities for the large cargo areas of truck-trailer refrigeration systems, compressors need a much greater capacity to move refrigerant. While smaller rotary-piston compressors may be found on vehicle-powered systems, reciprocating-piston compressors are the traditional type used in self-powered refrigeration systems. The Thermo King compressor shown in **FIGURE 60-15** has a compression ratio of 50:1 and operates up to 350 psi (2413 kPa).

FIGURE 60-15 Plate-type one-way check valves are located in the cylinder head of this four-cylinder refrigerant compressor by Thermo King.

When the piston is at the bottom of its stroke, refrigerant travels from the crankcase sump and enters the cylinder through a port machined into the cylinder wall. Downward movement of the piston decreases the volume of the crankcase, forcing vapor from the crankcase through cylinder

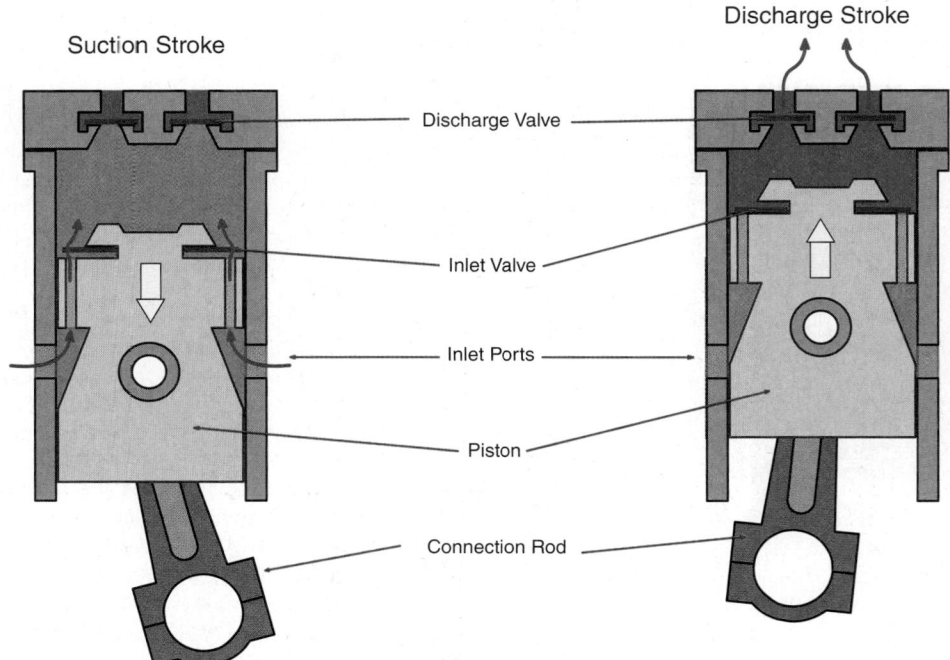

FIGURE 60-16 Operation of a reciprocating design refrigerant compressor.

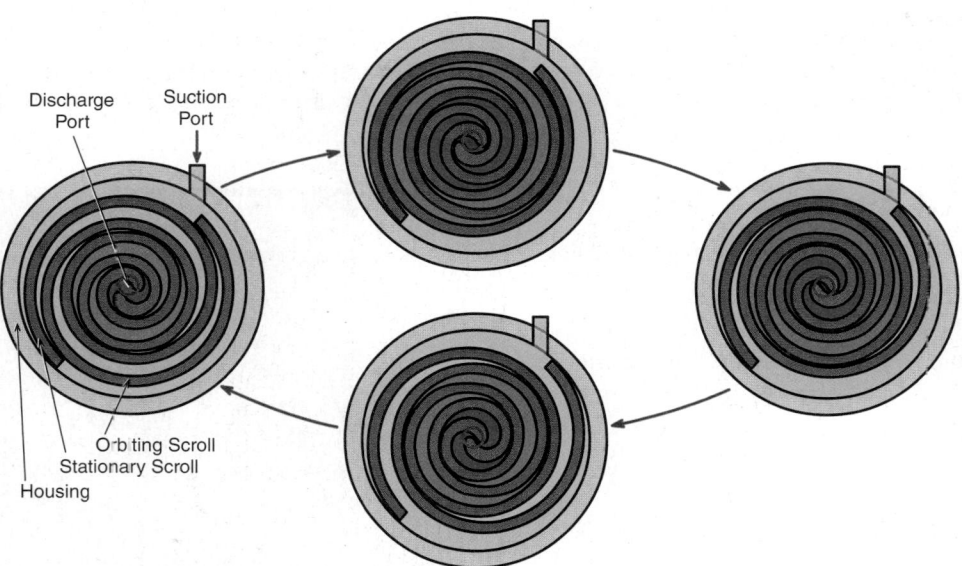

FIGURE 60-17 Scroll compressors compress refrigerate by squeezing the gas between the raised spiral channels moving in opposite direction to one another.

wall ports and into the area above the piston (**FIGURE 60-16**). When the piston begins to move upwards, refrigerant vapor is compressed and passes through the one-way discharge valve plate before it enters into the discharge manifold. Piston position seals the cylinder wall ports to prevent the return of vapor back to the crankcase. Upward piston movement also increases the volume of the crankcase, creating a negative pressure. Refrigerant from the suction or return line to the compressor is pulled through one-way check valves, also located in the cylinder head, and into the crankcase area.

Scroll-Type Refrigerant Compressors

Manufacturers have turned to using scroll-type compressors for the latest refrigeration reefer systems. Advances in metal machining techniques plus industry pressure have produced greater use of scroll compressors that are more reliable, use less fuel, have quieter operation, and lighter weight compared to reciprocating compressors. Scroll-type compressors use two plates with thin metal spiral channels whose raised grooves are wound in opposite directions and placed together opposing one another (**FIGURE 60-17**). One plate can be fixed while the other rotates or both can rotate with one having a different center of rotation (**FIGURE 60-18**). Fluids and gases enter the scroll from the outside edge of the metal spirals, between the open space at the two ends of the spirals. Turning one or both spirals in the opposite direction traps gases or liquids between the spiral channels, trapping and then pushing gases and fluids between the spirals toward the center point. Gases or liquids can exit the spirals at this center point through a one-way check valve. Two to 2½ rotations of the scrolls are required to compress the gases and liquids. Because there is no reciprocating action, they operate more quietly. The two-plate spiral design enables the compressor to be built much more compactly having less weight and with fewer parts operating with greater reliability. Tests demonstrate the scroll compressor operates more efficiently since it discharges gases and liquids during a full rotation versus less than half a rotation for a reciprocating compressor. To inspect compressor oil level, follow the steps in **SKILL DRILL 60-2**.

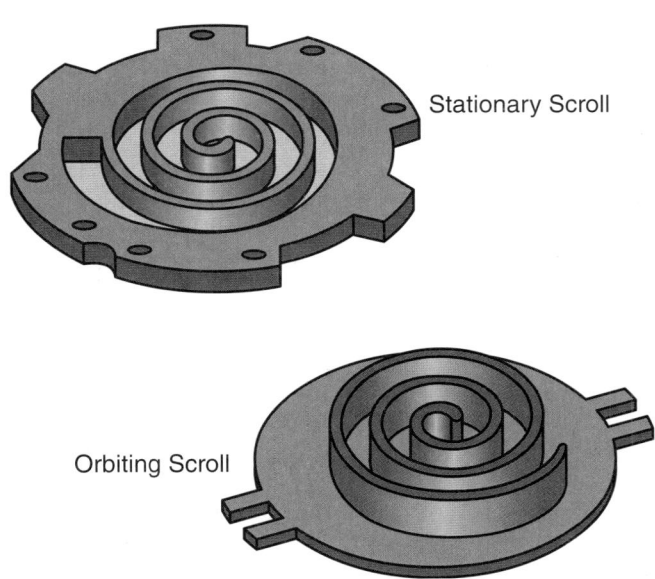

Stationary Scroll

Orbiting Scroll

FIGURE 60-18 The stationary and orbiting or moving section of a scroll-type compressor.

Refrigerant Throttling Valve Operation

Scroll type compressors never use a one-way check valve at the inlet, but reciprocating compressors must use an intake throttling valve designed to limit the maximum amount of refrigerant entering the compressor. Excessive inlet refrigerant flow produces excessive discharge pressures and overloads the compressor. That excessive load can increase engine fuel consumption and overload the electric motors of units with optional electric stand-by systems. Four-cylinder reciprocating compressors have the throttling valve mounted on top of the compressor. The throttling valve has little impact on compressor operation when cargo temperatures are low, because refrigerant pressures are correspondingly low. However, during heating and defrosting, when system pressures are higher, flow increases proportionately and can flood the compressor with hot liquid refrigerant that can severely damage and destroy a compressor without the ability to compress liquids. A properly adjusted and functioning throttle valve begins to limit the flow of refrigerant into the compressor as system pressures increase. Shims are used to adjust the operation of the valve. A deteriorated or improperly adjusted throttle valve can cause inadequate refrigerant flow, which starves the compressor and causes the whole system to lose effectiveness, reducing cooling and heating performance.

Discharge and Suction Service Valves

The discharge and suction service valves are located on top of the compressor. These valves are points where system pressures are measured and the system can be isolated from the compressor if the compressor requires removal (**FIGURE 60-19**). Because the valve stems used in the service valves can leak a small amount of refrigerant around the seals, a tightly sealed protective cap is required when the system is operating. Back seating the service valves is required to enable flow of refrigerant. This means the valves are turned completely backwards to the end of their travel limits to close a seal around the valve stem. Forward seating valves, which means turning them all the way closed, isolate the compressor from the remaining system refrigerant (**FIGURE 60-20**). When the compressor is replaced, forward seating the service valve allows the compressor to be

SKILL DRILL 60-2 Inspecting Compressor Oil Level

Sight Glass

1. Operate the reefer unit in cooling mode for at least 20 minutes.
2. Inspect the front oil sight glass on the compressor crankcase to ensure that no foaming of the oil is present after 20 minutes of operation. Report condition for correction if oil is foaming.
3. Switch unit off to check the oil level in the crankcase. The correct oil level range should be between the bottom to one-eighth level of the sight glass. If the level is above one-eighth, oil must be removed from the compressor. Insufficient oil level must be reported and corrected.

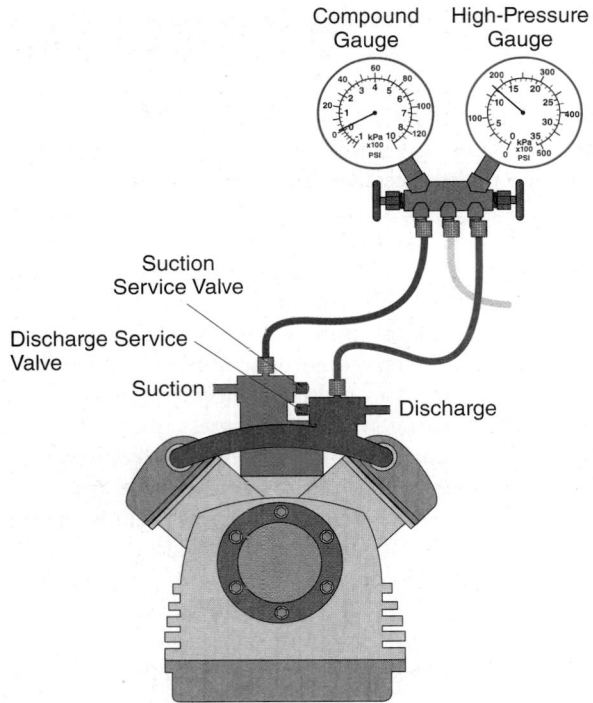

FIGURE 60-19 Connection of manifold gauge set to service ports on compressor.

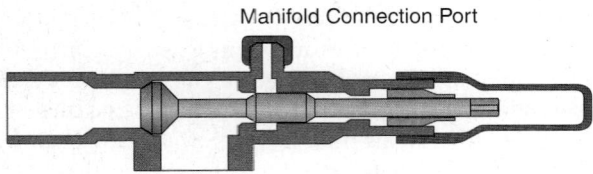

Compressor or Receiver Isolated from the Refrigerant Circuit

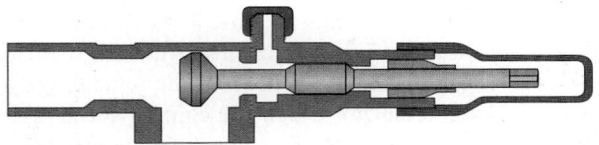

Manifold Connection Port Open to the Refrigerant Circuit

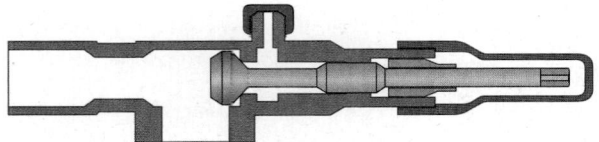

Manifold Connection Port Isolated from the Refrigerant Circuit (normal operation)

FIGURE 60-20 Operation of service valve used to isolate the refrigerant compressor.

simply reconnected and evacuated before the valves are opened again. The entire system is not opened and exposed to air and does not require evacuating for hours to remove moisture or potentially waste refrigerant.

Vibrasorbers

Flexible braided stainless-steel lines connect the compressor inlet and outlet to the system. The lines are called **vibrasorbers** and, as the name suggests, they absorb compressor movement, vibrations, and refrigerant pressure pulsations that would otherwise be transmitted to the more fragile copper refrigerant lines. Continuous line vibration work-hardens copper, leading to cracking and refrigerant leakage.

The Condenser

During cooling mode, the refrigerant leaves the compressor, passes through the three-way valve, and enters the condenser. Because the boiling point of refrigerant vapor increases when the liquid is pressurized, the vapor physically wants to condense. In doing so, tremendous amounts of latent heat are released into the atmosphere, as the refrigerant passes through the condenser, changing state from a vapor to a liquid. When the refrigerant changes from a vapor to a liquid, latent heat energy contained in the refrigerant is removed and released into the atmosphere. Typically, the vapor passing through the condenser is about 30° F higher than ambient temperature.

Condenser Check Valves

Unlike a conventional A/C system, a one-way check valve is used at the compressor outlet to permit refrigerant flow in only one direction. A refrigerant check valve at the condenser outlet allows refrigerant to flow through the condenser only during the cool mode and blocks refrigerant flow during the heat mode.

Receiver Tank

Because the amount of refrigerant needed during reefer operation depends on a variety of factors, such as ambient and container temperature, storage of extra refrigerant by the receiver tank is needed for efficient reefer operation. Often the tank has a sight glass on the top and/or bottom to provide a means of checking the system refrigerant level. Warm liquid refrigerant from the condenser pours into the receiver tank and pools at the bottom, so the lower sight glass should always be filled during operation. High-pressure liquid is pushed through the receiver tank outlet valve (RTOV) to the liquid line that connects it to the evaporator. A bypass check valve in the receiver is closed during cooling mode and opens during heating mode to connect the receiver inlet directly with the evaporator, which enables refrigerant to bypass the expansion valve (**FIGURE 60-21**).

The Liquid Line Dryer

The liquid line dryer located after the receiver tank operates like a filter and a device to remove moisture and other contaminants from the refrigerant during unit operation. These dryers have a service interval and require regular replacement—or mandatory replacement whenever the system is opened to the atmosphere. A heat exchanger encloses the suction line between the dryer and the expansion valve. Cooler refrigerant leaving the

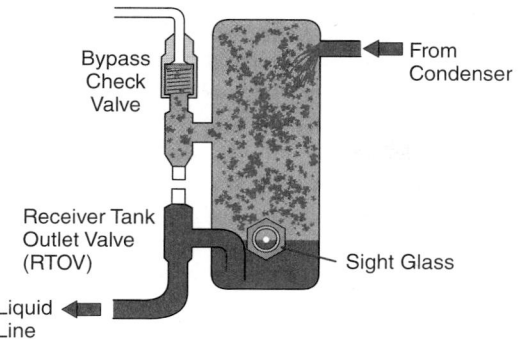

FIGURE 60-21 The receiver tank stores refrigerant and has check valves to direct the flow of refrigerant.

evaporator absorbs heat energy from the warm liquid suction line. By pre-cooling the refrigerant in the liquid line before it reaches the expansion valve, evaporator temperatures can be colder, increasing cooling capacity.

The Evaporator

The evaporator absorbs heat from the temperature-controlled product compartment. Reefer evaporators are very large and extend into the product compartment. High-velocity blower fans push air through the evaporator coils, keeping the air typically 10° F to 15° F warmer than the evaporator and minimizes the build-up of ice and frost. A powerful evaporator fan draws cargo air through the evaporator coil. When using R-404a refrigerant, an evaporator pressure of about 15 psi (103 kPa) provides a temperature of 0° F (–18° C) on the surface of the evaporator.

The Expansion Valve

The thermostatic expansion valve (TXV) regulates the flow of liquid refrigerant into the evaporator to produce the low evaporator temperatures. It is called an expansion valve because it causes liquid refrigerant to expand into a gas state. The valve

uses a variable size orifice that restricts the flow of liquid refrigerant, which in turn causes the refrigerant pressure to drop. Dropping the pressure forces the liquid refrigerant to expand into a gas state. Expansion takes place because lowering refrigerant pressure reduces the refrigerant's boiling temperature. As the boiling temperature of refrigerant drops, tremendous amounts of latent heat are absorbed by evaporator plates that passes into the refrigerant to enable it to change state from a liquid to a gas. This heat is removed from the cargo compartment during the cooling cycle by the refrigerant circulating through the evaporator.

A mechanically operated expansion valve for a reefer is usually an externally equalized type due to the large size of evaporator using multiple refrigerant circuits. Refrigerant flow through this type of TXV is a function of orifice diameter inside the expansion valve. The orifice size is in turn a function of spring pressure acting on a valve, plus refrigerant pressure and temperature acting to achieve a state of balance across a diaphragm controlling the size of the TXV orifice. The valve is normally closed by spring pressure and opened by a diaphragm that can lift linkage to increase or decrease the size of the restricting orifice. A pressure-sensing line connected to the outlet of the evaporator acts on one side of a diaphragm and a temperature-sensing thermostatic bulb acts against the opposite side of the diaphragm. This pressure-sensing line, called the equalizer line, connects the outlet pressure to the TXV to regulate refrigerant flow according to evaporator outlet pressure (**FIGURE 60-22**). Flow through the TXV is balanced according to outlet pressure against an adjustable spring in the valve. Increasing outlet pressure opens the valve against spring tension, which increases refrigerant flow through the valve to make the evaporator colder. Lower evaporator outlet pressure restricts refrigerant flow, resulting in a warmer evaporator.

The TXV's temperature-sensing bulb filled with refrigerant is also tightly attached to the outside of the evaporator outlet line. The refrigerant pressure inside the bulb acts against the

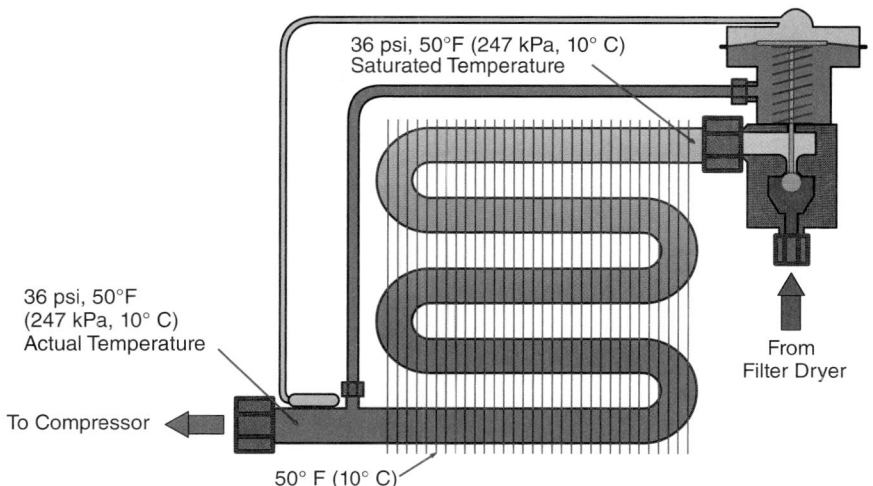

36 psi, 50°F (247 kPa, 10° C)
Saturated Temperature

36 psi, 50°F (247 kPa, 10° C) Actual Temperature

To Compressor

50° F (10° C)

From Filter Dryer

FIGURE 60-22 Opening and closing of the thermostatic expansion valve is a function of spring tension, evaporator outlet pressure, and temperature.

pressurized side of the diaphragm and is also used to control the opening diameter of the TXV to change and adjust the flow of refrigerant into the evaporator. A cold evaporator outlet reduces refrigerant pressure in the bulb and, in turn, reduces refrigerant flow. A warm evaporator outlet increases the diameter of the valve's variable orifice size, which increases refrigerant flow. This arrangement of a pressure- and temperature-sensing function within the TXV adjusts refrigerant flow through the TXV to ensure that as little liquid as possible leaves the evaporator and that most of the refrigerant converts to a vapor.

Located between the expansion valve and the evaporator coils is a distributor. This part of the evaporator supplies refrigerant to several routes to improve the evaporator's efficiency.

Electronic Expansion Valves

Electronic expansion valves are used on many of the latest reefers to control refrigerant flow through the evaporator. Unlike mechanical expansion valves, electronic valves are operated by an electronic control module, which determines the valve position regulating refrigerant flow in response to a variety of temperature and pressure sensors. Faster, more precise control of refrigerant flow is enabled through the use of electronic expansion valves. The position of a pin inside the valve controlling the size of a refrigerant orifice opening is performed by a stepper motor (**FIGURE 60-23**). The motor can be positioned and held in as many as 2000 possible steps and move 200 steps per second. The use of an electronic valve that can be instantly commanded closed can introduce a safety feature called compressor flooding protection. If a condition is sensed where too much liquid leaves the evaporator, it can enter and hydraulically lock a compressor, causing severe damage. The electronic valve can also correct for forces, such as the pressure of refrigerant striking the valve to open or close the variable orifice.

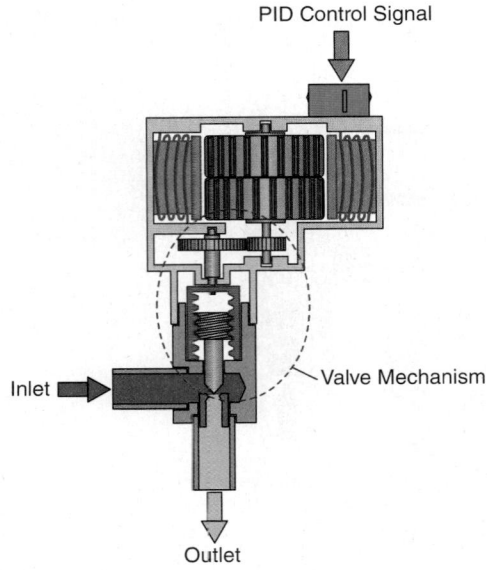

FIGURE 60-23 An electrically controlled stepper motor regulates the opening of the expansion valve orifice in an electronically controlled expansion valve.

Refrigerant and Refrigerant Oils

Colder temperatures used in refrigeration unit requires different refrigerants than used by only passenger compartment A/C systems. To be compatible with the refrigerant, oil, which is dissolved by refrigerant and carried through the system to lubricate parts, such as the compressor, has different properties than other refrigerant oils.

The boiling point of refrigerant primarily determines whether it is used for A/C or refrigeration. Most current truck-trailer refrigeration systems use environmentally friendly R-404a refrigerant having low ozone-depletion potential. But R-404A is soon scheduled to be phased out of production. Refrigerants like R-404A with very low boiling points are capable of refrigerating temperatures well below 0° F (−18° C). **TABLE 60-3** compares R404a, which boils at −50° F (−45.5° C), to R134a, which boils at −15° F (−26.5° C) and is commonly used in A/C systems. Each refrigerant is assigned a unique color code for its container to prevent cross contamination and allow easier identification.

After chlorofluorocarbon (CFC) refrigerants were banned in the mid-1990s, no suitable alternative refrigerant was available. In the interim period, refrigerant R502, a hydrochlorofluorocarbon (HCFC), was chosen as a transitional refrigerant until reliable chlorine-free refrigerants were available. Today, truck-trailer refrigeration units use a chlorine-free refrigerant known as R404a, which is a hydrofluorocarbon (HFC). R-404a is currently recommended for temperature control to −20° F (−29° C), and R134a is recommended for applications no lower than 0° F (−18° C). In Europe, a new refrigerant named R-452A is currently in use since 2004 but pending approval in the United States. The refrigerant is intended to replace R-404a after its scheduled phase out due to its moderate ability to deplete atmospheric ozone. R-452A blends three different chlorine gases including hydrofluoroolefin (HFO) and has a much lower potential for depleting ozone than R-404A.

Carbon dioxide and nitrogen gases, which have no ozone-depletion potential, have also been demonstrated to work as effective refrigerants and are now commercially available. Like other gases, these two can be used to move heat either in and out from the cargo box but have even less detrimental effect on the environment environmental. The gases require very high pressure to operate as a refrigerant and compressor discharge temperatures are very high. The apparent disadvantage is actually an advantage since the high discharge temperatures can defrost and heat very well. The higher temperatures and pressures create even greater gas density that improve system efficiency.

TABLE 60-3 Boiling Points of Common Refrigerants at Sea Level

Type	Boiling Point	Container Color
R134a	−15.7° F (−26.5° C)	Light blue
R12	−21° F (−29.4° C)	White
R502	−49° F (−45° C)	Purple
R404a	−50° F (−45.5° C)	Orange

A large amount of refrigerant that is heavier than air is contained in a truck trailer refrigeration system. If it is suddenly released, it can displace air at ground level and suffocate a technician. Always work in well-ventilated areas when servicing refrigeration systems.

Compressor Oils

Refrigeration compressors are much like engines, with moving parts that require constant lubrication. Without oil, a compressor quickly overheats and destroys itself. Using transitional R-502 required alkylbenzene-type compressor lubricant. With the production of chlorine-free refrigerants, a polyolester (POE) oil base, which is compatible with R134a and R404a, is now used.

Alarm Codes

LO 60-6 Identify and explain the differences between the severity of reefer alarm codes.

The potential economic loss of high-value cargo caused by a failure of the reefer to regulate temperature demands comprehensive diagnostic capabilities and warnings are built into the control system. Alarm codes, which is another name for diagnostic fault codes, are set and stored in memory by the control unit whenever the microcontroller detects an abnormal or unexpected condition (**FIGURE 60-24**). An alarm code can guide the service technician to pinpointing the cause of a problem with the help of original equipment manufacturers (OEM) service literature with diagnostic troubleshooting trees. Multiple alarms or faults can be present simultaneously and the correct priority for diagnosing which fault should be identified first is established by the OEM service literature. Alarms are displayed on the control unit screen and some alarms, such as a load exceeding a set point, can emit an audible warning (**FIGURE 60-25**). When telematic communication with reefers is subscribed to from a service provider, real-time monitoring of the reefer can be performed. Remote control of the reefer is also possible.

Alarms can be classified into four categories according to severity.

1. Log Alarms—the lowest level of severity, this alarm notes a corrective action may soon be required to prevent a more serious problem. An example is a scheduled service is soon due according to hour meter time.
2. Check Alarms—this level of alarm indicates a more serious fault is present but the reefer will still run. Some reefer functions or optimal operation may not be possible. Water in fuel or a defective air temperature sensor are examples of a check alarm.
3. Prevent Alarms—this alarm level indicates faults requiring the reefer shut down but typically restarts after some time interval. When the unit restarts, it may run with reduced performance. The loss of a critical pressure sensor or malfunction of a damper door during a heating or cooling cycle may set a prevent alarm code.
4. Shut down Alarms—are the most serious type of fault that shuts down the reefer unit due to the likelihood of potential damage to the reefer or product. Excessive engine coolant temperature or low oil pressure are examples of faults that may temporarily shut down and allow a restart but may also prevent the engine or refrigeration system to restart if severe enough. Serious abnormalities in a cooling or heating cycle also shut down the reefer.

FIGURE 60-24 The control panel of a reefer contains a service information screen for retrieving alarm faults.

FIGURE 60-25 A list of alarm faults located on the inside of a door panel for an older Thermo King trailer reefer.

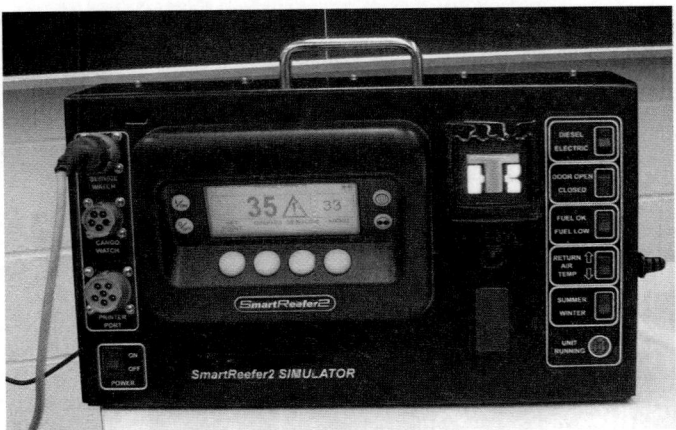

FIGURE 60-26 Alarm codes can be retrieved from the control panel of a reefer using specialized service software.

All instances of alarms should be documented and reported. **FIGURE 60-26** shows that faults and alarms can also be retrieved from diagnostic service ports.

Pre-trip inspection procedures is a diagnostic strategy that forces the reefer to perform a functional test of all the reefers systems and circuits. If equipped, the reefer can be enabled to enter a pre-trip functional test initiated using software or the control panel menu item to verify that there are no malfunctions in the reefer operation and no alarms are set.

Refrigeration System Maintenance

LO 60-7 Identify and explain minimal requirements for truck-trailer refrigeration system maintenance.

Although reefers use diesel engines requiring special maintenance, most other maintenance of trailer refrigeration systems is relatively simple. On board electronic self-diagnostic systems are used extensively for pre-trip inspections functional tests, but the engine should be checked regularly for oil leakage at both the engine and compressor. Belts and hoses should be inspected regularly, too. Most engines require oil and filter changes at 1500 hours, or about once every three to six months. The use of synthetic oil lengthens the interval between oil drains to between 3000 and 4000 hours.

When making inspections to investigate cooling complaints, ensure that all air passages, including the channels in the floor, are clean and free of any debris that could block return airflow. Inspect the evaporator for any paper or plastic scraps that may block air passages.

Wrap-Up

Ready for Review

▶ Although they operate on the same principles as other air-conditioning (A/C) systems, refrigerated trailers utilize a far more sophisticated A/C system than a regular vehicle.

▶ One major difference between an A/C system and a truck-trailer refrigeration system is that heating is a critical function of a transport refrigeration system.

▶ Modern fresh air exchange systems primarily operate through the use of a heat exchanger where older "refrigerated air" is used to cool incoming fresh air as it is vented from the reefer.

▶ Many reefers can be divided into different compartments or zones through the use of specially constructed movable bulkheads. This enables the simultaneous transportation of different types of perishable goods within the same reefer.

▶ The cooling capacity of a particular reefer is dependent on a number of factors, including its construction, the size of the reefer, the products it is designed to carry, whether it will carry varied product in different cooling zones, and whether the cargo must remain frozen or merely cooled.

▶ Poor circulation is a major contributor to cargo deterioration during transportation.

▶ Most reefer cooling units are driven by a small diesel engine. Modern units are required to have modern emissions systems for auxiliary power units (APUs),

common rail (CR) fuel systems, exhaust gas recirculation (EGR), and diesel particulate filters (DPFs).

▶ The compressor performs two functions: it creates the required pressures to facilitate the "change of state" required for operation of the system, and it moves refrigerant through the system to carry heat absorbed from the evaporator to the condenser.

▶ Along with the vehicle's A/C system, the refrigerant is the "lifeblood" of trailer refrigeration. It is responsible for absorbing heat from the inside of the insulated compartment and releasing it to the air outside the compartment from the condenser.

▶ The system is effectively divided into two sides by the compressor and the expansion valve. The high-pressure side is the part of the system between the compressor outlet and the expansion valve inlet, and the low-pressure side is the part of the system between the expansion valve outlet and the compressor inlet.

Key Terms

defrost cycle A situation in which the evaporator releases heat instead of absorbing it, and the condenser absorbs heat instead of transferring it to the atmosphere.

multi-temp unit A reefer configured to control multiple temperatures in different areas of the trailer.

reefer A truck-trailer refrigeration temperature-control system.

self-powered refrigeration units A transport refrigeration system powered by a small horsepower diesel engine.

stand-by mode A reefer operating mode during which the engine is not driving the compressor.

three-way valve A valve that directs hot refrigerant gas to either the condenser (in cool mode) or directly to the evaporator (in heat or defrost modes).

transport temperature control Heating or cooling over a wide range of outside temperatures and product storage temperatures.

vehicle-powered refrigeration units A transport refrigeration system that is powered by a compressor located in the vehicle's engine.

vibrasorbers Flexible stainless-steel lines that connect the compressor inlet and outlet to the trailer refrigeration system and absorb compressor movement and vibration.

wet load Refers to very damp products that are refrigerated.

Review Questions

1. Refrigeration is a process of transferring heat away from a product storage container to achieve a temperature of:
   a. 60° F (16° C) or colder.
   b. 62° F (17° C) or colder.
   c. 65° F (18° C) or colder.
   d. 68° F (20° C) or colder.
2. During which of the following cycles is the damper door closed?
   a. During cooling
   b. During heating
   c. During defrost
   d. During refrigeration
3. Which of the following components is unique to reefer refrigeration operation?
   a. Compressor
   b. Expansion valve
   c. Condenser
   d. Three-way valve
4. During the heating cycle, to which of the following major components does the refrigerant flow to first after leaving the high-pressure discharge side of the compressor?
   a. The condenser
   b. The evaporator
   c. The expansion valve
   d. The pan heater
5. If a trailer reefer is not equipped with a three-way valve, which of the following devices controls the direction of refrigerant flow to switch from cooling to heating mode?
   a. Electronic expansion valves
   b. A receiver reservoir using two sight glasses
   c. Electrically operated pilot or check valves
   d. A reversible compressor clutch drive gear
6. Which of the following statements is most correct concerning the defrost cycle?
   a. The purpose of the defrost cycle is to remove ice and frost from the evaporator.
   b. When defrosting, ice is melted in a heated defroster pan.

c. The damper door is in the same position during defrost mode and heat mode.
d. The cargo doors must be open to initiate a defrost cycle.
7. What type of compressor is the most lightweight and enables the most efficient reefer operation?
   a. Vane-type
   b. Reciprocating piston
   c. Scroll-type
   d. One equipped with a throttling valve
8. In transportation refrigeration, the V-type compressor typically:
   a. Has a throttling valve.
   b. Is *not* lubricated with refrigerant oil.
   c. Weighs less than an equivalent scroll-type compressor.
   d. *Does not* use outlet check valves to control refrigerant flow.
9. Which alarm code would most likely be set if no oil pressure was sensed in the diesel engine?
   a. A log alarm
   b. A check alarm
   c. A shut down alarm
   d. A pre-trip alarm
10. What type of refrigerant is used in modern truck-trailer refrigeration units?
    a. R143a
    b. R404a
    c. R22
    d. R162

ASE Technician A/Technician B Style Questions

1. Technician A says that most engines require oil and filter changes at 1500 hours, or about once every three to six months. Technician B says that the use of synthetic oil lengthens the interval between oil drains. Who is correct?
   a. Technician A
   b. Technician B
   c. Both Technician A and Technician B
   d. Neither Technician A nor Technician B
2. Technician A says that a number of manufacturers distribute refrigeration temperature-control systems that are installed in trailers, shipping containers, or truck boxes. Technician B says that these systems are more familiarly called reefers, a common term for truck-trailer refrigeration temperature-control systems. Who is correct?
   a. Technician A
   b. Technician B
   c. Both Technician A and Technician B
   d. Neither Technician A nor Technician B
3. Technician A says that the cooling or heating capacity is measured in BTU per hour. Technician B says that BTU per minute is the amount of heat required to change the temperature of one pound of water by 1° F. Who is correct?
   a. Technician A
   b. Technician B

c. Both Technician A and Technician B
d. Neither Technician A nor Technician B

4. Technician A says that the position of a three-way valve controls whether the refer is in a cooling or heating cycle. Technician B says that a three-way valve controls the flow of air through the reefer. Who is correct?
a. Technician A
b. Technician B
c. Both Technician A and Technician B
d. Neither Technician A nor Technician B

5. Technician A says that only a set of electrically operated solenoids or pilot valves controls the direction of refrigerant flow, essentially determining whether the reefer is in cooling or heating mode. Technician B says that the three-way valve directs hot refrigerant gas to either the evaporator (when in heating or defrost mode) or directly to the condenser (when in the cooling mode). Who is correct?
a. Technician A
b. Technician B

c. Both Technician A and Technician B
d. Neither Technician A nor Technician B

6. Technician A says that a trailer reefer's heating capabilities are not as high as cooling capacity. Technician B says that heat from the reefer's engine coolant can supplement heating capacity of the refrigeration system in heat mode. Who is correct?
a. Technician A
b. Technician B
c. Both Technician A and Technician B
d. Neither Technician A nor Technician B

7. Technician A says that most units will not enter the defrost mode unless the evaporator coil temperature is below approximately 45° F (7.2° C). Technician B says that defrost cycle can be scheduled to automatically take place. Who is correct?
a. Technician A
b. Technician B
c. Both Technician A and Technician B
d. Neither Technician A nor Technician B

8. Technician A says that a reefer that does not seem to be cooling efficiently can be manually defrosted to make sure the evaporator is not frozen. Technician B says that an excessive wet load of ripening produce can slow the cooling performance of a reefer. Who is correct?
   a. Technician A
   b. Technician B
   c. Both Technician A and Technician B
   d. Neither Technician A nor Technician B

9. Technician A says that a pre-trip inspection, which performs a functional test of the reefer's operation, is a good way to verify there are no faults with the reefer before it enters service. Technician B says that the presence of an alarm can be checked using service software or a display screen on the control panel. Who is correct?
   a. Technician A
   b. Technician B
   c. Both Technician A and Technician B
   d. Neither Technician A nor Technician B

10. Technician A says that R-404A refrigerant is banned and is now replaced by a better gas developed in Europe called R-502. Technician B says that carbon dioxide and nitrogen gas cannot be used as refrigerants because they both cause global warming. Who is correct?
   a. Technician A
   b. Technician B
   c. Both Technician A and Technician B
   d. Neither Technician A nor Technician B

CHAPTER 61   **Principles of Hydraulic Systems**

CHAPTER 61

Principles of Hydraulic Systems

Learning Objectives

After reading this chapter, you will be able to:

- **LO 61-1** Explain the fundamental concepts of a hydraulic system.
- **LO 61-2** Explain principles of hydraulic work and power and perform related calculations.
- **LO 61-3** Identify basic components and their purpose in a hydraulic system.
- **LO 61-4** Identify and describe the types, operation, and construction of hydraulic pumps.
- **LO 61-5** Identify the purpose, classification, and properties of hydraulic fluids and additives.
- **LO 61-6** Describe the construction and operation of hydraulic fluid reservoirs, filters, and coolers.

- **LO 61-7** Identify and describe the purpose, types, and construction of hydraulic conductors, lines, hoses, and tubes.
- **LO 61-8** Identify and describe the types, operation, and construction of hydraulic actuators.
- **LO 61-9** Identify and describe the types of hydraulic directional control valves.
- **LO 61-10** Identify and describe the types of pressure-relief valves.
- **LO 61-11** Identify and describe the types, operation, and construction of hydraulic accumulators.
- **LO 61-12** Outline common preventative maintenance and inspection practices for hydraulic systems.

You Are the Technician

You are assigned to diagnose and repair a hydraulic system-related complaint for a late-model utility truck with several hydraulic actuators, including a lifting boom, outrigger stabilizers, and a hydraulic lift platform at the rear of the vehicle. The complaint is that the hydraulic equipment is working slower than normal and the oil temperature is hotter than usual. On initial inspection, you discover that the boom is operated with a closed-center directional control valve and the system has an engine-driven axial piston pump As you consider next steps, answer the following questions:

1. What would you check for at the hydraulic system reservoir that could contribute to this problem?
2. How would you confirm whether system performance is at or below normal level?
3. If the system is in fact operating at a lower performance level than normal, what system components could be the root cause of this issue?

Introduction

Hydraulic systems and components are used everywhere in commercial vehicles. Fluids under pressure are used to transmit power in systems as varied as hydraulic braking, power steering, fan drives for transit buses, automatic transmissions, air conditioning, engine cooling, lubrication, and fuel systems. Fluid power is particularly important in vocational applications where hydraulic equipment is used, including booms, winches, and buckets on utility vehicles; tailgate hoists for pick-up and delivery trucks; cylinders on refuse trucks to load, pack, and unload waste; dump hoists; and plow trucks. Hydraulic motors drive mixing drums on concrete trucks, and various types of hydraulic equipment is used by hydrovac excavating equipment on trucks. Many more applications of hydraulics are used by specialized vocational vehicles (**FIGURES 61-1** and **61-2**). The extensive use of hydraulics makes understanding hydraulic principles and the construction of hydraulic circuits and components essential for technicians who are expected to diagnose and service these systems. The study and practice of hydraulic system service is wide, encompassing diverse fields, such as in off-road equipment used by the agricultural or construction industry, aircraft, and factories using hydraulic equipment to produce products. Rather than describe and explain hydraulic applications for an entire industry, this chapter focuses on basic hydraulic concepts and foundational information associated with the construction and operation of hydraulic systems used on commercial vehicles. Operating concepts of hydraulic circuits, fluid properties and characteristics, pump design and operation, hoses, common control valves, and repair techniques are just a few of the topics presented in the chapter. This information provides background needed by commercial vehicle technicians to develop the skillsets required to service hydraulic systems.

Fundamentals of Hydraulic Systems

LO 61-1 Explain the fundamental concepts of a hydraulic system.

Hydraulic system operating principles encompass two different types of fluid actions. One is **hydrodynamics**, involving fluids in motion, and the other is **hydrostatics**, which deals with actions of fluids under pressure. A simple but broad definition of hydraulics is the action of pressurized liquids in motion in pipes and **cylinders**. Narrowing hydraulics to a concept dealing with pipes and pressurized liquids is origins of the term itself. The word hydraulics is derived from the Greek word—hydro, meaning water and aulos, meaning pipe.

Hydraulic pressure and flow are used extensively for a number of reasons. One of the main advantages is hydraulic systems can lift, move, or push very heavy objects more simply and efficiently by transferring force through fluids and actuators which are output devices. Hydraulic systems can do this because they are capable of force multiplication. Cumbersome mechanical linkage, gear drives, cables, and chains are eliminated by simpler hydraulic systems. Energy is instead transferred by pressurized hydraulic fluids flowing through flexible pipes or lines. Hydraulic devices, such as pumps, motors, and cylinders, are powerful devices for their size, and a single hydraulic pump can operate many hydraulic circuits with extraordinary power. Many of the advantages offered by hydraulic systems are obtained through a hydraulic system's ability to exploit simple physics of force and pressure using fluid energy. Pressurized fluid exerted against the surface area inside a cylinder or vanes can multiply hydraulic force to produce powerful mechanical outputs used to do work or create some action. Mechanical advantages needed to rapidly lift, pull, or turn heavy loads with high force are extracted from the long rotational distance traveled by **prime movers**, such as diesel engines and electric motors that drive hydraulic pumps.

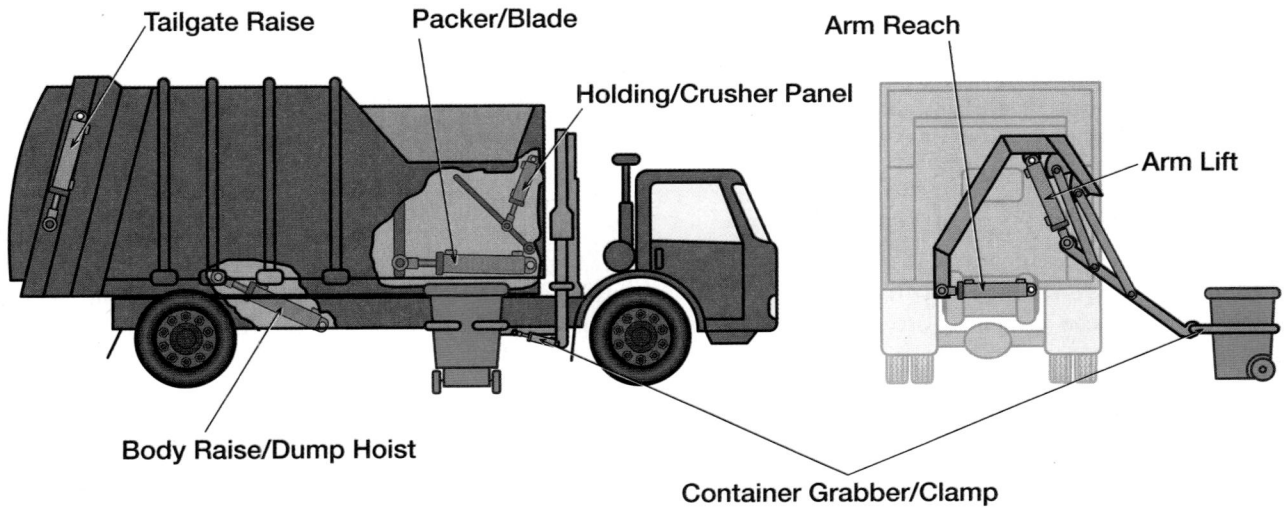

FIGURE 61-1 Refuse trucks use a large number of hydraulic cylinders to lift, pack, and unload waste.

FIGURE 61-2 A hydrovac truck has an extensive hydraulic system with numerous hydraulic components and circuits used to excavate with high-pressure water.

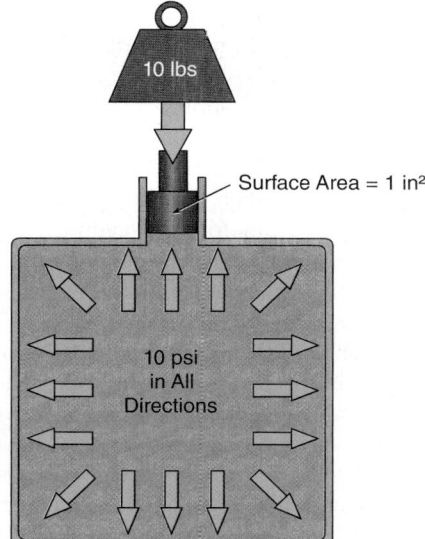

FIGURE 61-3 A force of 10 lb (4.5 kg) acting against an area of 1" (2.54 cm) produces 10 lb (4.5 kg) of pressure for every square inch (cm²) against the bottle's interior walls.

Fluid pressure is converted into mechanical force by hydraulic actuators, a term given to system output devices, such as cylinders and motors.

Before moving further into hydraulic system features, construction, operation, and other advantages, it is important to first understand some simple physics underlying hydraulic principles.

Explaining Force Pressure and Area

One of the most basic rules of physics to understand and apply to all hydraulic systems is called **Pascal's Law**. This law explains the relationship between a liquid's force, pressure, and surface area acted on, using the language of math. Pascal's Law is based on the observation that when force is applied to a fluid in a closed system, pressure created by the force is transmitted without loss to all other areas of the system. This means that pressure exerted by a fluid acting against the container walls is the same pressure anywhere else in the container (**FIGURE 61-3**).

Pascal's Law is possible because fluids are not compressible. Fluids behave like a column of solid, such as steel or concrete,

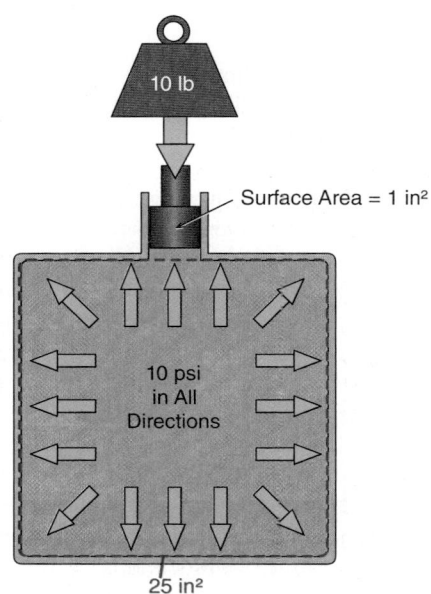

Pascal's Law: Force = Pressure x Area
10 psi x 25 in² = 250 pounds of force

FIGURE 61-4 Pascal's Law predicts the force acting against the bottles walls equals 250 lb (113 kg).

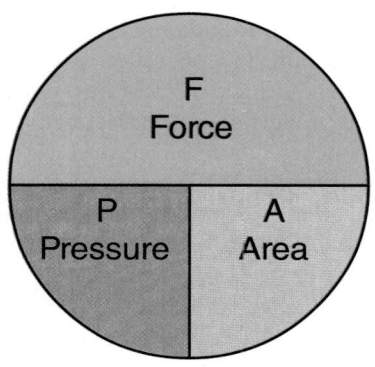

Force = Pressure x Area
Pressure = Force ÷ Area
Area = Force ÷ Pressure

FIGURE 61-5 The technician's triangle for Pascal's law. The triangle is used to solve for one variable if two are already known.

when compressed, except fluids do not bend or break. Note in **FIGURE 61-4** that with 10 lb (4.5 kg) of force acting on the bottle stopper, 10 psi (69 kPa) of force acts on the bottle walls. Pascal's Law extends further to explain that the total force acting against the bottle walls is determined using a simple formula (**FIGURE 61-5**):

$$\text{Force} = \text{Pressure} \times \text{Area}$$
$$\text{Area} = \text{Force/Pressure}$$
$$\text{Pressure} = \text{Force/Area}$$

In the case of a bottle with 25 square inches (161 cm²) of total wall surface area, and with a pressure of 10 psi (69 kPa) inside the bottle, the total force exerted against the wall is 250 lb (113 kg).

Imperial measurements of pressure are often reported in units of pounds per square inch (psi). Another unit, a Bar, which is equal to 14.50 psi, is a metric unit of pressure, but is not approved as part of the International System of Units (SI). Metric units of pressure or SI units are called the pascal. 1 Pascal of pressure unit equivalent is Newton/square meter (N/m^2). However, a pascal unit is equal to only 0.000145 psi. This explains why kilopascals (kPa) or megapascals (mPa) are often used to measure pressure. To help convert pressure measurements, remember that 1 bar, a common unit to measure fluid pressure, equals 100 kPa. Atmospheric pressure is equal to 101.325 kPa or very close to 1 bar.

Pascal's Law can further explain force how hydraulic force is multiplied and mechanical advantages are achieved in hydraulic systems. In **FIGURE 61-6**, two different surface areas of pistons in a hydraulic circuit are used. The force applied to the piston on the left is 10 lb (4.5 kg) acting against 1 square inch (6.5 cm²) of area. This force generates 10 psi (69 kPa) of pressure in the container, which is predicted using Pascal's Law where Pressure = Force × Area. Transmitting this force through a column of fluid to another area on the right that is 10 times the size of the area on the left produces 10 times the force from the left-side piston. Again, this result is calculated using Pascal's Law where Force = 10 psi × 10 square inches = 100 pounds (69 kPa × 65 cm² = 45 kg).

Applying Pascal's Law

Pascal's law can also predict how much area or hydraulic pressure is needed to lift a specific weight. In **FIGURE 61-7**, the weight of 8000 lb (3629 kg) equals the force required by the hydraulic system to lift a weight. Using Force = Pressure × Area equation and knowing the cylinder area is 10 square inches (65 cm²), Pressure = 8000 lb/10 square inches = 800 psi (3629 kg/65 cm² = 5516 kPa). Considered another way, knowing only system **working pressure** and the area of a cylinder could be used to calculate the maximum weight the cylinder is capable of lifting.

Explaining Mechanical Advantage

Mechanical advantage is a ratio obtained by comparing a system's mechanical input force with a mechanical output force. Hydraulic systems can multiply force but energy inputs naturally must equal energy outputs after subtracting

for some efficiency losses. In other words, energy to produce higher output force from a smaller input force must come from somewhere. To multiply an output force, energy must be derived from some source, so a long distance traveled by a smaller input force is traded off or exchanged for a higher output force with less travel distance (**FIGURE 61-8**). A name given to the energy exchanged in the trade-off between distance and force to gain a mechanical advantage is sometimes

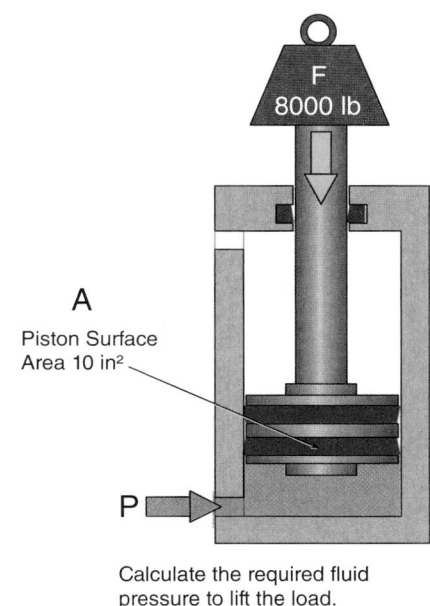

Calculate the required fluid pressure to lift the load.
P = F ÷ A
P = 8000 ÷ 10
P = 800 psi

FIGURE 61-7 Pascal's Law is used to calculate the minimum size of a hydraulic cylinder, the maximum force of a system, or system pressure needed to lift a weight.

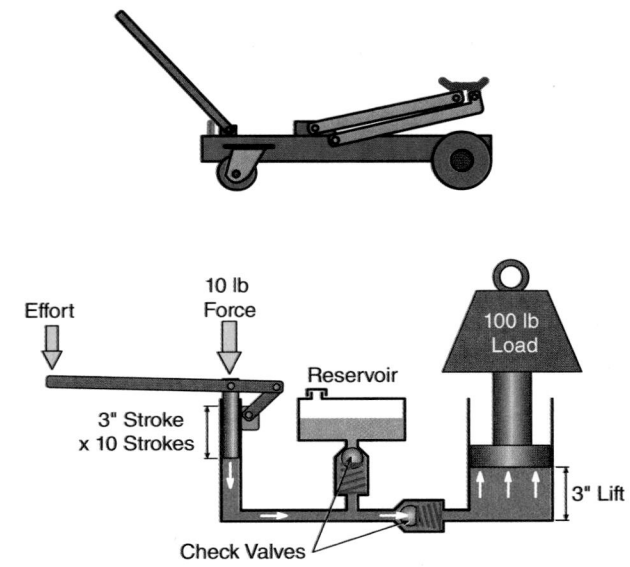

FIGURE 61-8 10 lb can't lift 100 lb unless there is a tradeoff between the distance traveled by the pump lever and the height the 100 lb weight is lifted.

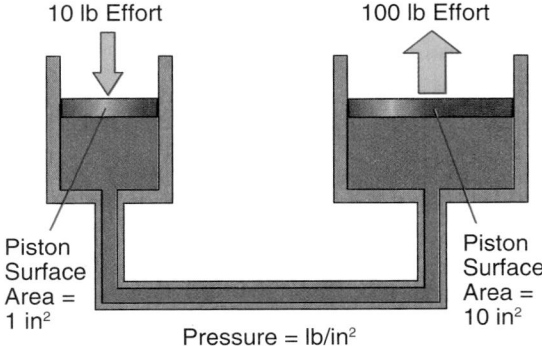

FIGURE 61-6 Force is multiplied ten to one in this hydraulic system, which is predicted by Pascal's Law. This system can also be understood to have a 10:1 mechanical advantage.

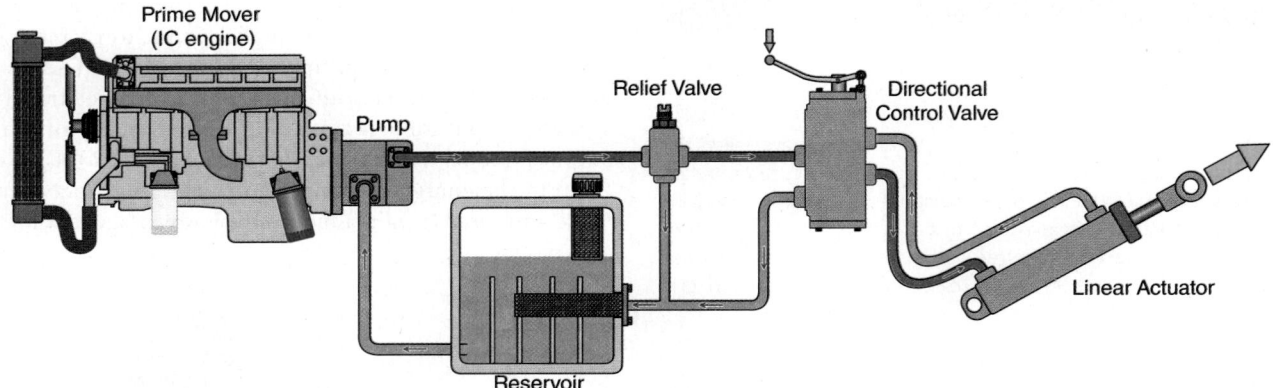

FIGURE 61-9 A prime mover provides the energy input to a hydraulic system. The amount of power produced by a prime mover is proportional to the hydraulic systems output minus efficiency losses.

FIGURE 61-10 This 12-volt electric motor attached to a hydraulic pump with a fluid reservoir is an example of a hydraulic systems prime mover.

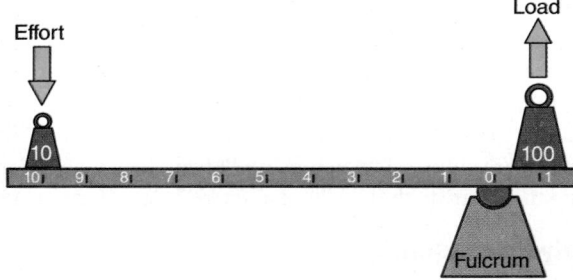

FIGURE 61-11 A hydraulic mechanical acvantage multiplies an input force to move a heavier output force by trading off the longer distance traveled by a prime mover.

called the principle of energy conservation in a hydraulic system. Energy cannot be created or destroyed, only changed from one type to another.

Understanding this concept helps explain the effects on hydraulic system output caused by changing hydraulic pump sizes, system pressure, cylinder dimensions and other elements of the system configuration. Energy in hydraulic systems is transferred into the hydraulic system by a prime mover – typically the rotational force and speed of an engine or electric motor (**FIGURES 61-9** and **61-10**).

Area, force, and pressure ratios between system input and outputs predicted by Pascal's Law are used to calculate the hydraulic systems mechanical advantage. An analogy to help explain the idea of a mechanical advantage in hydraulics is illustrated by a lever in **FIGURE 61-11**. A 10 lb (4.5 kg) weight can be used to lift 100 lb (45 kg) by moving the fulcrum point closer to the heavier weight. In hydraulics, this is like using a 10 lb (4.5 kg) input force to move 100 lb (45 kg) through a 1:10 area ratio. Note that the 10 lb (4.5 kg) weight always travels 10 times farther than the heavier weight to move the 100 lb (45 kg) of weight one tenth that distance. Stated another way, the 1:10 mechanical advantage requires the input force to travel 10 times farther than the output force. Distance is traded to obtain force multiplication so the 100 lb (45 kg) weight moves only one tenth the distance of the lighter weight.

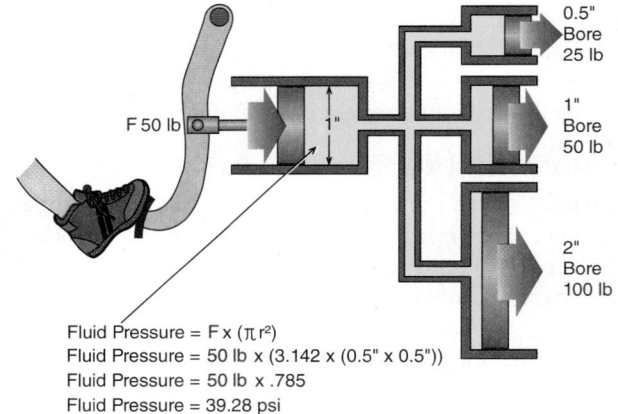

Fluid Pressure = F x (π r²)
Fluid Pressure = 50 lb x (3.142 x (0.5" x 0.5"))
Fluid Pressure = 50 lb x .785
Fluid Pressure = 39.28 psi

FIGURE 61-12 The ratio of input force tc output force depends on the relative differences in surface areas of a hydraulic circuit.

Pascal's Law can predict what the mechanical advantage ratio is in hydraulic circuits based on area ratios. In **FIGURE 61-12,** the input force of 50 lb (23 kg) generates 39.28 psi (270.8 kPa) with a one-inch master cylinder bore. Acting on various surface areas, wheel cylinders having half, the same or, twice the surface area of the master cylinder bore each produces a different output force. Force is either multiplied or reduced 1:0.5, 1:1, or 1:2. demonstrating the mechanical advantage ratio corresponds to each cylinder area ratio.

Area, Pressure, and Force Multiplication

To further understand how the force-distance tradeoff operates to multiply output force, it's helpful to examine the stroke length of an input force compared to the length of the output stroke. **FIGURE 61-13** shows how far two-wheel cylinders travel given a 10" stroke in the master cylinder. As already seen, a 10" stroke from a 1" diameter bore and an area ratio of 1:2 with an output piston multiplies force two times, increasing a 50 lb input to 100 lb. The 1:2 area ratio, while doubling output force, cuts the output stroke length by the same factor, or half in this case. This means the 1:2 mechanical advantage input stroke normally moves a *single* output device half its input stroke travel or one output length unit compared to two lengths of the same unit for the input stroke travel. However, if there are *two* identical-diameter output cylinders, the area increases by a factor of two. Using the area ratio to calculate the new output stroke travel shows the distance is cut in half again with two cylinders compared to a single cylinder. This means a 10" input stroke travel produces an output travel of only 2.5" with two identical cylinders that are twice the area of the input cylinder. Adding a third cylinder with the same area increases the total area to three times the input area or reduces output stroke length to a third, which is 1.67" output stroke travel.

To summarize how mechanical advantage is achieved, the displacement of the hydraulic pump equals the displacement of a cylinder or other actuator. The pump compensates for its relatively weaker output force by rotating many more times, travelling more distance rotationally to provide the force necessary to increase the actuators output force (**FIGURE 61-14**).

Work and Power in a Hydraulic Circuit

LO 61-2 Explain principles of hydraulic work and power and perform related calculations.

The point of looking at these relationships between actuator distance travel, pressure, area, and force is to understand the concept of hydraulic power—the amount of work performed for a given amount of time. Recall that work is a function of force multiplied by distance (Work = Force × Distance). Imperial units for work are foot-pounds (ft-lb) or kilogram-meter (kg-m) units for measurements. An actuator moving 3' while applying a force of 1000 lb produces 3000 ft-lb of work. Calculating power adds a time factor to the equation for work to determine how much work is done over a specific amount of time. Expressed another way: how fast the actuator moves to perform work is a measure of its power. If an actuator does that same work of lifting 3000 ft-lb, but completes the task in two seconds, power is calculated using the formula (**FIGURE 61-15**):

Power = Work/Time where time is measured in seconds. In this case power = 3000 ft-lb/2 seconds = 1500 ft-lb/second. SI units are kg-m/second using metric equivalents to measure the power.

What this calculation demonstrates is actuator speed and force from a hydraulic system relies on the input force and speed of a prime mover. Faster rotational speed and or greater input force from prime movers and hydraulic pumps can potentially produce faster, more forceful actuator output.

Calculating Hydraulic Horsepower

The speed and force accompanying the extension of a hydraulic cylinder or power from a fluid-powered motor depends on the hydraulic supply of fluid volume and pressure. Flow, expressed

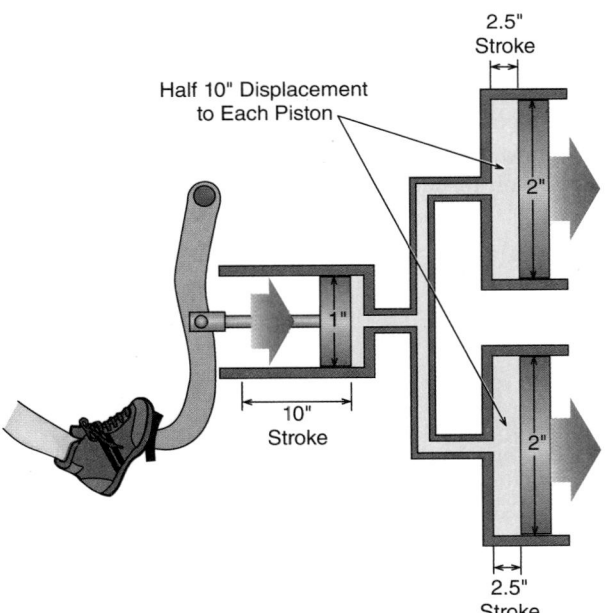

If only one 2" piston Stroke = 5"
for two 2" pistons Stroke = 2.5" each

FIGURE 61-13 Increasing the surface area of the output cylinders multiplies force but shortens distance traveled.

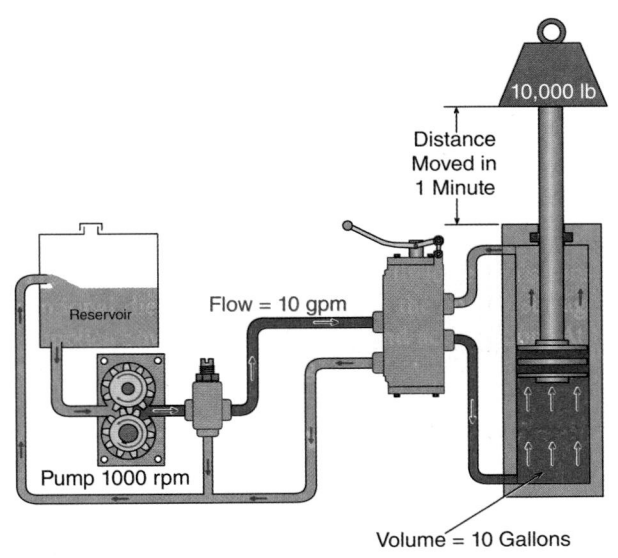

FIGURE 61-14 The long rotational distance (1000 rpm) traveled by a prime mover is traded off to increase the cylinders output force that extends a shorter distance than the prime mover travels in one minute.

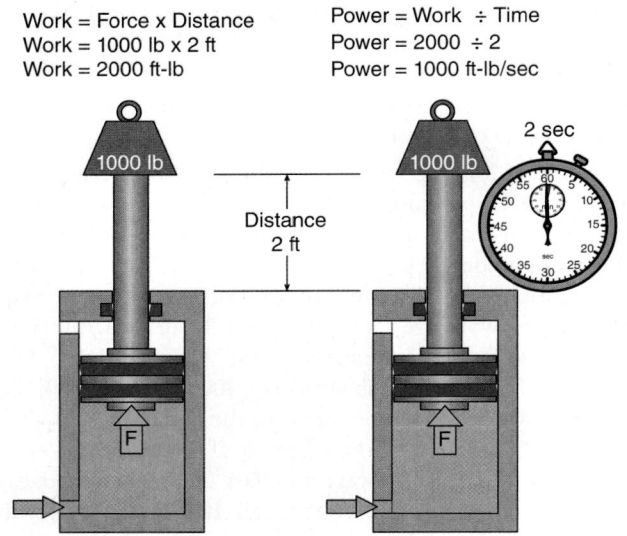

Work = Force x Distance
Work = 1000 lb x 2 ft
Work = 2000 ft-lb

Power = Work ÷ Time
Power = 2000 ÷ 2
Power = 1000 ft-lb/sec

FIGURE 61-15 Comparing work and power. Power is the amount of work performed over time.

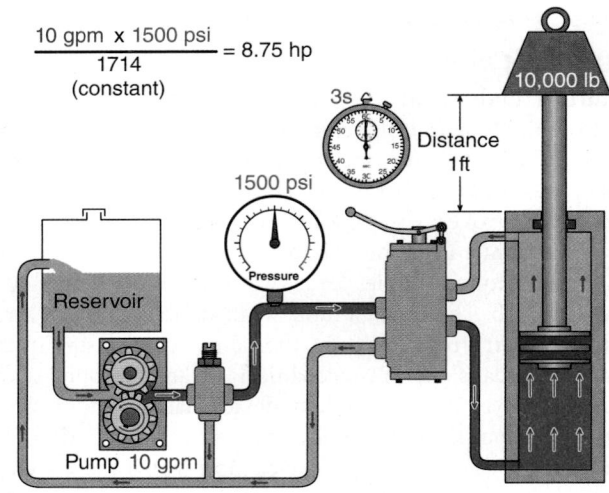

$$\frac{10 \text{ gpm} \times 1500 \text{ psi}}{1714 \text{ (constant)}} = 8.75 \text{ hp}$$

FIGURE 61-16 Data points in a simple hydraulic system used to calculate hydraulic horsepower.

$$10 \times 1000 \div 1714 = 5.8 \text{ hp}$$
$$5.8 \text{ hp} \times 231 \text{ in}^3/\text{min} = 1340 \text{ in}^3/\text{min}$$

as the volume or quantity of fluid measured per minute (gallons or liters per minute), determines the speed at which an unloaded hydraulic cylinder extends or a hydraulic motor turns. Flow in a system is produced by a fluid pump driven by a prime mover. Pressure, expressed in pounds per square inch (psi), determines the amount of force exerted (**FIGURE 61-16**).

Horsepower is a common unit for measuring power from a hydraulic system. The formula used to calculate horsepower is hp = Flow × Pressure/1714. The number 1714 is one the industry uses to define one horsepower. It equals the energy required to pump 1714 gallons per minute (gpm) at 1 psi (1 hp = 1714 gpm × 1 psi). A hydraulic horsepower is also equal to 231 in³/min at 1 psi. Because hydraulic pump displacement is commonly measured in cubic inches of displacement per rotation, the number 231 is used to calculate the necessary pump speed to produce adequate flow for a system. Example: A hydraulic system requires a flow rate of 10 gpm at an operating pressure of 1000 psi. The hydraulic horsepower requirement is:

What is the minimum speed the pump must rotate to supply 5.8 hp if it has 3 in³ of displacement per rotation?

$$1340 \text{ in}^3/\text{min}/3 \text{ in}^3 = 447 \text{ rpm}$$

Hydraulic System Components

LO 61-3 Identify basic components and their purpose in a hydraulic system.

When installed in a commercial vehicle, regardless of their application, a hydraulic system all have a minimum set of components and operating principles common to any hydraulic system (**FIGURE 61-17**). These include:

- A power take-off (Optional)
- A power source or prime mover
- A hydraulic pump
- Hydraulic fluid
- A reservoir to store fluid

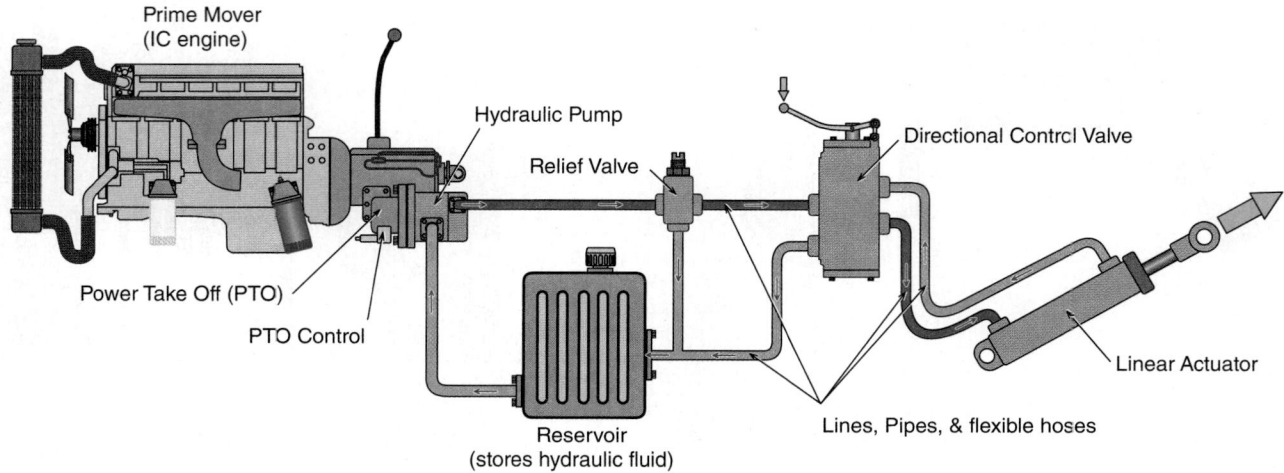

FIGURE 61-17 Elements common to all hydraulic systems used in a commercial vehicle.

- Lines, pipes, and flexible hoses
- A directional control valve to change the direction of fluid flow
- A system pressure protection valve, called a relief valve
- Linear or rotary actuators to perform work

Power Take-Off Devices

Hydraulic systems on trucks and buses take mechanical rotary power from a prime mover and convert it to a hydraulic pressure inside a hydraulic pump. A **power take off (PTO)** is a gear-driven device that is frequently used on commercial vehicles to engage and disengage a pump drive mechanism from the engine or transmission supplying mechanical power (**FIGURE 61-18**). Both excessive and insufficient gear lash or clearances between PTO drive gears cause excessive noise and potential gear damage. Establishing correct gear backlash is an adjustment required when installing the PTO. When installing a transmission-mounted PTO, follow the steps in **SKILL DRILL 61-1**. If system demands are high and it is not practical to take power from a transmission, engine-mounted PTOs today are often driven from the rear of the engine. Rear engine PTOs (REPTO) are more reliable because torsional vibrations from the rear of an engine are lower compared

to a front mounted take-off (**FIGURE 61-19**). PTOs are generally activated using a cable or air cylinder controlled electrically or mechanically by the driver from inside the cab. A sliding clutch locked to the PTO drive shaft is moved in and out of a drive gear. The latest PTOs used on buses, trucks, and emergency vehicles use a wet disc clutch, like the ones used in automatic transmissions, to engage the PTO shaft. An air or hydraulic line engages and disengages this clutch. Cab switches and engine software can be programmed to not only activate, drive, and disengage the PTO when specific operating conditions are met to improve safety and efficiency, but also operate at a predetermined engine speed. For a safety related example, the PTO safety interlocks may require extended outriggers to retract before the vehicle is moved or the park brakes applied before the PTO is engaged. Safety interlocks is a term used to describe safety-related operating conditions that must be met before the system will operate (**FIGURE 61-20**). After the PTO has engaged, the hydraulic pump's fluid flow is transferred through a system of pipes, lines, and control valves, and is then converted back into mechanical power—either as linear motion, with linear actuators, or as rotary motion, with a hydraulic motor.

FIGURE 61-18 This power take off device is bolted to the transmission and is driven by a countershaft. An integral air cylinder on top of the PTO moves a sliding yoke to engage or disengage the pump from the countershaft.

FIGURE 61-19 A Rear Engine Power Take Off is an optional feature used for high-demand hydraulic systems. The hydraulic pump is bolted to the rear cover.

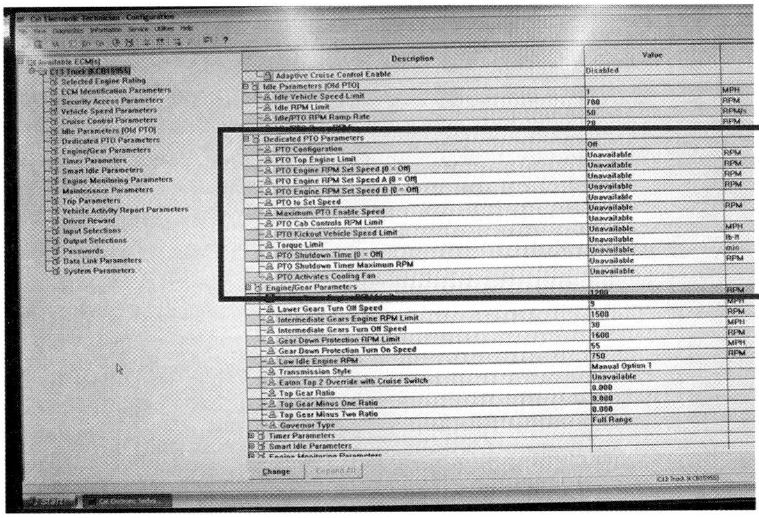

FIGURE 61-20 A menu's screen showing some possible programmable engine parameters to control the PTO operation.

SKILL DRILL 61-1 Adjusting PTO Gear Backlash

Wet-Type Clutch

Drive Gear

Air or Hydraulic Signal Port

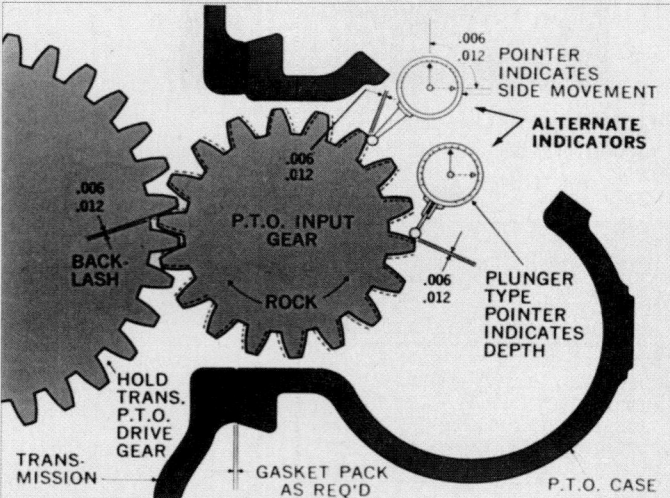

.006 .012 POINTER INDICATES SIDE MOVEMENT

ALTERNATE INDICATORS

.006 .012

P.T.O. INPUT GEAR

ROCK

.006 .012

.006 .012 BACK-LASH

PLUNGER TYPE POINTER INDICATES DEPTH

HOLD TRANS. P.T.O. DRIVE GEAR

TRANS-MISSION

GASKET PACK AS REQ'D

P.T.O. CASE

PTOs are often removed during clutch replacement or when transmission service is required. Occasionally, PTOs require replacement or are installed with hydraulic accessories. During installation, the gear backlash between the PTO drive gear and transmission drive gear must be adjusted with precision selective shims. To adjust PTO drive gear backlash during installation:

1. Verify that if the hydraulic pump attached to the PTO weighs 40 lb (18.1 kg) or more, including the weight of fittings and hoses that the pump attached to, the PTO is properly supported with brackets, having at least two attachment points on the pump and transmission

2. For PTOs having either six or eight molting bolts (two standard configurations), drain the transmission fluid in manual transmissions and remove the PTO opening cover plate, if installed. Automatic transmissions do not require draining, but some fluid will drain when the PTO cover is removed.

3. Clean the gasket mounting surface.

4. Rock the PTO drive gear in the transmission by hand to verify the presence of backlash in the transmission and to provide a reference to compare PTO backlash.

5. Install PTO mounting studs with Loctite thread sealer and tighten to specification.

6. Place a sealing gasket over the PTO opening on the transmission, and a metal selective shim of typically either 0.010" or 0.020" thickness. Install a second sealing gasket between the shim and PTO case.

7. Install and tighten the PTO case to the transmission opening. Move the rotatable drive flange for the hydraulic pump mounting, if necessary. Loosen and retighten the flange as necessary.

8. Remove the PTO inspection cover plate on the PTO or inspection plug to access the PTO drive gear.

9. Mount a dial indicator outside the PTO case and set the set the plunger on the tip of a PTO drive gear to measure its movement.

10. Hold the transmission drive gear with a long screwdriver or bar and rock the PTO drive gear back and forth by hand to measure its backlash with the dial indicator. Observe the total indicated movement of the drive gear. Move the plunger around to several points on the drive gears to measure the backlash movement. The drive gear must move a minimum of 0.006" but no more than 0.012".

11. If backlash is incorrect, remove or add metal shims to obtain the correct backlash. Generally, a 0.010" shim will change backlash approximately 0.006", while a 0.020" shim changes backlash approximately 0.012".

12. Start the vehicle engine for a few seconds with transmission and PTO in neutral. Listen for abnormal noises. Note: Do not work beneath a vehicle with a running engine. An operator must always remain in the cab to stop the vehicle from moving or to quickly shut off an engine.

SKILL DRILL 61-1 Adjusting PTO Gear Backlash (Continued)

13. Verify there is no abnormal whining noise from the PTO, which indicates the PTO is mounted with the drive gears too tightly with inadequate backlash. A clattering-like noise indicates a PTO backlash that is excessive. Reinspect and re-shim, as required.

14. Install self-locking nuts on the PTO studs and tighten to specification after correct back lash is set and refill the transmission with oil.

15. Coat the splines of the hydraulic pump at the PTO coupler with specialized high-pressure, high-temperature, anti-fretting grease. Also, PTOs for automatic transmissions use a hydraulic line with pressurized transmission fluid to supply the PTO drive gear during operation. Manual transmissions do not use this line. Verify the line is connected.

16. Top up the transmission fluid level and operate the PTO for 5 to 10 minutes and check for oil leaks and unusual noises.

17. While running the PTO, verify correct shift engagement operation. On automatic transmissions, the drive gear in the transmission turns when the transmission is in neutral. Shift the transmission into drive to stop gear rotation and gear clash when engaging the PTO. Manual transmissions PTOs are shifted when the clutch is disengaged.

18. Wet-type clutch shifted-type PTOs, commonly found on newer automatic transmissions in refuse trucks, can be activated when the vehicle is in motion and the engine speed is below 1000 rpm. Activation pressure in the clutch pack during engagement allows the clutch to slip slightly while engaging gears and then gradually increase to full pressure.

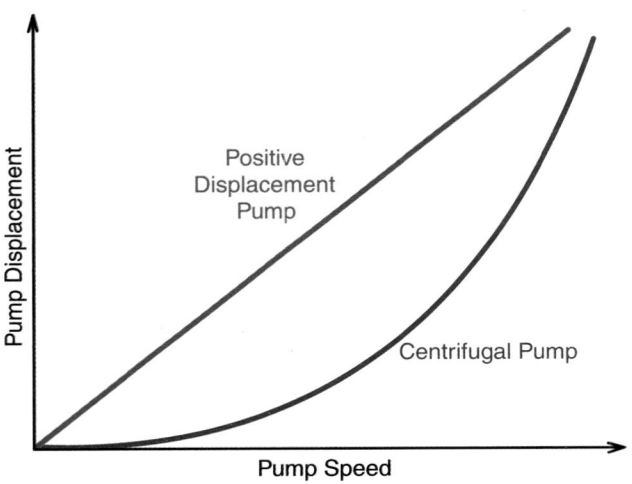

FIGURE 61-21 A positive displacement's pump output is linear with pump speed.

Rarely are hydraulic pumps belt-driven due to the limitations of a belt-drive system to transmit torque. An example is a double V-belt drive can only transmit up to 15 hp. One exception is hydraulic pumps used on automotive tow trucks using a medium-duty chassis. These vehicles can use an underhood belt-drive hydraulic pump engaged with an electric, on-off clutch. The maximum output capabilities of these pumps should be no more than 15 gallons per hour (gph) displacing 2.5 in³/rotation.

Hydraulic Pumps

LO 61-4 Identify and describe the types, operation, and construction of hydraulic pumps.

As mentioned, hydraulic pumps extract the mechanical energy from the prime mover, converting it to hydraulic energy present in fluid flow. Pumps only produce liquid flow or volume but do not produce pressure. Pressure is created only when flow is restricted or stopped. This explains why pumps are rated according to flow or pump volume output measured in gallons or liters of flow per minute. Three common types of hydraulic pump are:

1. Gear
2. Piston
3. Vane

Each pump type has unique construction features and operating characteristics that are optimally matched with different configurations of hydraulic systems. Hydraulic symbols represent a variety of pump designs. These pumps can be further categorized as fixed or variable displacement. Flow from a positive displacement pump, also called a fixed displacement pump, varies according to rotational speed. Positive displacement pumps used by almost all truck and bus hydraulic systems not only have a fixed output that varies only with speed, but each rotation of the pump produces a specific volume of fluid, that changes linearly with speed (**FIGURE 61-21**). For example, if a positive displacement pump produces 5 in³ of fluid each time it rotates, the flow rate from the pump is easily calculated by multiplying rpm times the pump's rated displacement. This pump displaces 500 in³ of fluid at 100 rpm and 5000 in³/min at 1000 rpm. When graphed, output volume is linear compared to speed.

In contrast, a centrifugal pump has low efficiency at low speeds but increases its efficiency with speed (**FIGURE 61-22**). Fluid enters the center of an impeller wheel and is pressurized by the accelerating liquids over the curved vane surface where it leaves the vane tips. These pumps typically cannot pressurize fluids to more than 61–80 psi (414–552 kPa) and are not used for high-pressure hydraulic systems.

More efficient, but more complex and expensive, **variable displacement pumps** have a mechanism to change the pump flow independently of rotation speed. An external lever or internally controlled mechanism mechanically reduces or varies

FIGURE 61-22 The curved-shaped impellers of this centrifugal pump spins fluid of the impeller tips at high speed. Fluid enters at the center of the impellers.

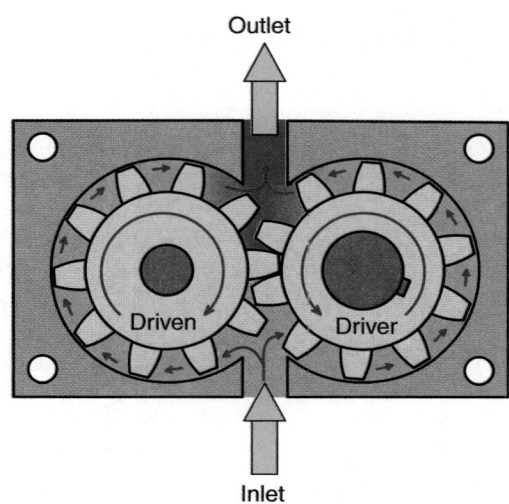

FIGURE 61-23 A gear pump uses a driven and idler gear to sweep liquids around the outer circumference of the gears.

pump displacement to conserve energy when high flow rates are not required but can instantly increase volume when demand changes.

Pumps are selected according to the manufacturer's specification for flow rate and pressure required by the hydraulic system. Systems specifications are stated as gpm or liters per minute (lpm) for flow and pressure in psi or bar. It is these details that determine how fast the pump should operate. A smaller displacement pump needs to turn faster than a larger displacement pump. However, a larger displacement pump is not always as efficient. Calculations for horsepower, pump speed, and displacement are covered in the previous section for determining hydraulic power requirements.

All pumps have an inlet or suction side and an outlet or pressure side. The suction or inlet connects to the reservoir return hose through a filter. Placing the filter in series with the suction side rather than the pressure side prevents dirt and contaminants from entering and damaging the pump or hydraulic system. The inlet or outlet port location may change, depending on the direction of pump rotation. A **unidirectional pump** shaft is designed to rotate in only one direction—either clockwise (CW; right hand) or counterclockwise (CCW; left hand), not both. These pumps are identified by a larger low-pressure inlet port compared to a smaller high-pressure outlet port. Bidirectional pumps can rotate in either direction and have identically sized inlet and outlet ports. However, they still must be connected correctly to pull fluid in the correct port when rotating CCW or CW. To identify the direction of pump rotation, the pump is

placed on its sump or belly side. CW or CCW direction of rotation of the pump shaft is made when viewed from the pump drive end.

Gear Pumps

Gear pumps are the most common design in use for truck-mounted hydraulic systems. These use two gears meshed together in a common housing (**FIGURE 61-23**). One gear has a shaft connected to it—the drive gear—and is offset from the pump center. The other gear, called the idler gear, is driven and turns on a shaft in the housing. Liquids at the pump inlet are trapped between the gear teeth and swept to the outlet inside the cavity formed between a pair of teeth and the pump walls. Gear teeth tips form a seal with the pump walls to prevent back leakage of liquids through the pump when it is stopped (**FIGURE 61-24**). The explanation for this pump's popularity is because gear pumps are simple with only two moving parts, which makes them rugged and relatively inexpensive. These pumps can build enormous pressure, typically up to 2500 psi (17,237 kPa), without damage and are tolerant of dirt and other contaminants.

Gear pumps are categorized as fixed- or positive-displacement-type pumps. They are rated according to

FIGURE 61-24 The tips of gear pump teeth form a seal between the walls of the pump housing and teeth to prevent back leakage through the pump.

FIGURE 61-25 A variable displacement piston pump. The external compensator valve that varies swashplate angle is circled.

FIGURE 61-26 A two-cylinder radial piston pump for a common rail engine.

displacement per revolution, maximum working pressure, and speed limitation. Without special controls, this pump is best matched with what is called an open-center hydraulic system. Open-center systems use a fluid direction control valve that allows all the output of a pump to flow through its open center and back to the reservoir at low pressure. Only when the control valve is repositioned does pump build pressure and its output is directed to perform work. Gear pumps are rated in terms of their cubic inch displacement, maximum pressure rating, and maximum input speed limitation.

Reciprocating Piston Pumps

Reciprocating piston pumps are constructed from a cylinder block containing cylinders with pistons that move in and out of the cylinders to pump fluids using a pressure differential (**FIGURE 61-25**). The piston's movement also pushes fluid out from the pump through an outlet check valve. Fluid drawn from the reservoir generally passes through a one-way check valve to prevent liquids from returning to the reservoir when the piston pushes fluid out the outlet check valve. The pump's displacement is measured according to the total volume of the pump's cylinders. Piston pumps can produce even higher pressure than gear pumps, typically 5000 psi (34,474 kPa), and are useful operating hydraulic booms and cranes

demanding high flow and pressure. Like the gear pump, piston pumps are best suited for use in open center hydraulic systems.

However, these pumps are more complex and costly, and have lower tolerance to contamination before they are damaged. Pistons are arranged in several ways to form different classifications of pumps.

- Axially—Pistons extending parallel to one another along the pump axis.
- Radially—Several pistons extending in opposite directions from the axis of the pump drive shaft (**FIGURE 61-26**).
- Inline—Pistons arrange in a line, one after another.

Piston pumps designs are also fixed- or variable-displacement type. A fixed displacement piston pump has a non-adjustable component called a **swashplate** that is tilted at an angle and connects to the backside of each piston with a connecting rod and articulating joint. The pump driveshaft turns the cylinder block and the swashplate, but the swashplate angle remains stationary or fixed. This arrangement causes the pistons to move back and forth in the block's cylinder bores to move fluid in and out of the pump (**FIGURE 61-27**). Pump output flow is directly proportional to input shaft speed. The variable-displacement version of this pump uses a mechanism to tilt or change the angle of the swashplate (**FIGURE 61-28**). When vertical, no reciprocating piston action takes place in the cylinders. Without a swashplate angle, both the block and swashplate turn using little energy. By tilting or changing the angle of the swashplate, reciprocating action takes place. The farther the plate tilts, the longer the piston stroke (**FIGURE 61-29**). The displacement of the pump increases as the swashplate angle moves from vertical to an angle of a maximum of 30 or 40 degrees.

An internal valve called the compensator adjusts the swashplate angle using an internal or external pressure signal that is sensitive to either flow, pressure, or both pressure and flow. A signal from the directional control valve can provide a load-sensitive adjustment to the swashplate angle.

Vane Pumps

To pump liquids, vane pumps use spring-loaded plates that are held in a slotted rotor to sweep fluids around an eccentric-shaped cavity (**FIGURE 61-30**). The eccentric housing shape causes the cavity formed by the vanes at the pump inlet to progressively become smaller while sweeping fluid around to its outlet. Vane pumps are less frequently used than gear or piston pumps, but spring-loaded plates operate quietly and self-adjust to compensate for wear. Vane pumps are available as either fixed- or variable-displacement pumps. A mechanism changing the position of the rotor within the housing or the kidney-shaped dimensions of the housing varies the pump's displacement. Vane pumps can operate typically up to 2000 psi (13,790 kPa). However, vane pumps are more commonly used in lubrication and both low- and high-pressure fuel systems (**FIGURE 61-31**).

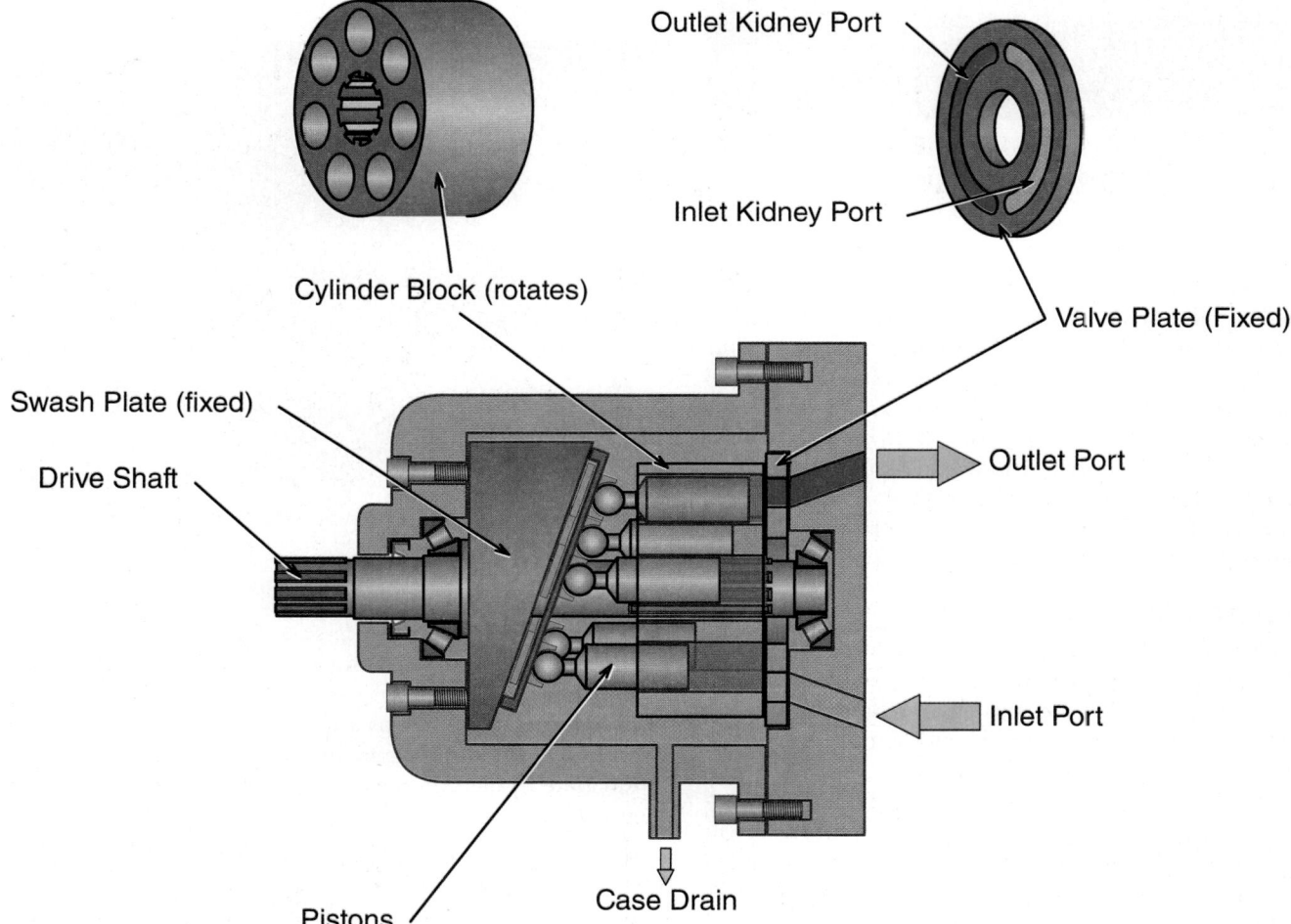

FIGURE 61-27 An internal view of a fixed piston pump.

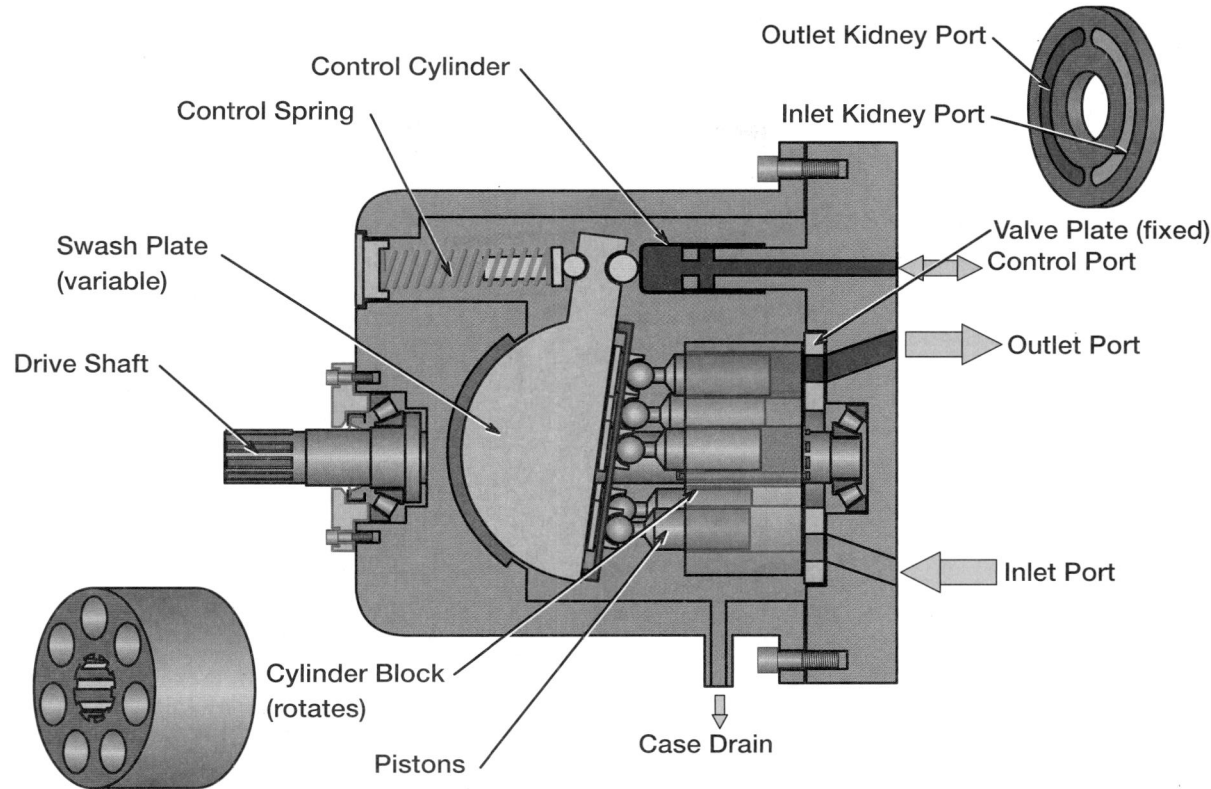

FIGURE 61-28 An internal view of a variable-displacement pump.

FIGURE 61-29 An axial piston pump with a swashplate.

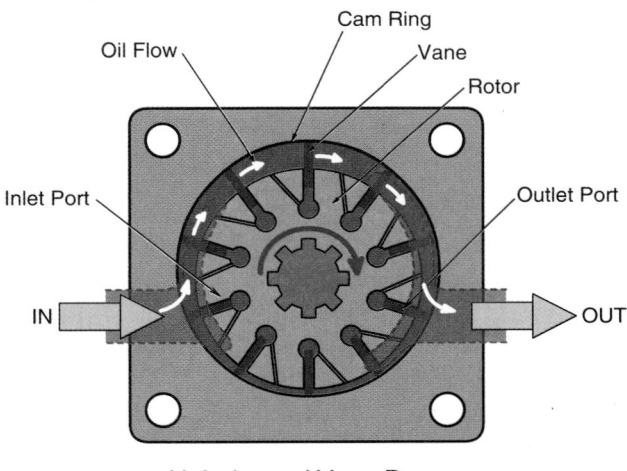

FIGURE 61-30 Internal construction of a vane-type pump.

The Dump Pump

As the name suggests, a dump pump is a pump and control system designed specifically for one application—operating the hoist on a dump truck. The unique design and features of these pumps means they generally cannot be used for any other hydraulic application. Dump pumps integrate three components:

1. A rugged gear pump having approximately 6 in³ displacement

2. A two- or three-position, directional control valve

3. A pressure relief valve

Two variations of the pump are used: a two-line and three-line system using one or two return lines plus a pressure line (**FIGURE 61-32**). A two-line system uses only a pressure and single return line to the hydraulic dump box hoisting cylinder. This installation is used if the box is only used to

FIGURE 61-31 A variable-displacement vane pump has a mechanism to change the offset between the eccentric-shaped housing and the rotor.

Two-Line Installation

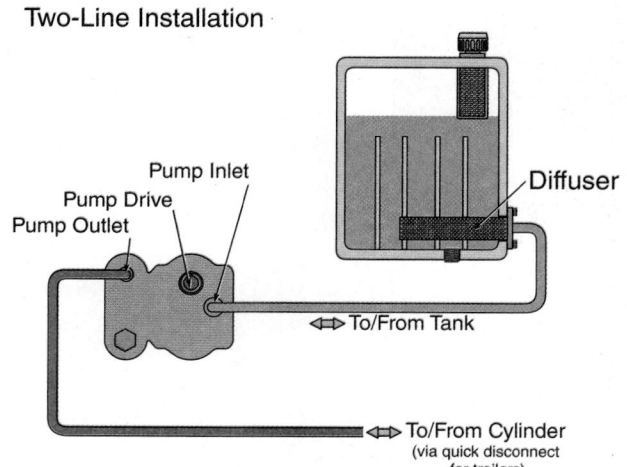

FIGURE 61-32 One return hose and one pressure line connect the dump pump to the system reservoir and dump hoist cylinder.

dump loads and does not require holding in a neutral position to spread loads or dispense asphalt where the box is held at many angles. A three-line system allows the pump to be held in a neutral position longer (**FIGURE 61-33**). Return-circuit oil in a three-line system is recirculated back to the reservoir tank when the spool-type directional control valve that lifts, lowers, and holds the box is held in neutral. A two-valve system recirculates oil only inside the pump in neutral and can overheat the oil (**FIGURE 61-34**). The box lowers more slowly in two-line systems and, if the PTO remains accidently engaged when driving, much more resistance to return oil flow around the spool valve creates very high loading of the PTO, potentially resulting in catastrophic damage.

Dump trailers can connect to dump pump outlet lines using quick-connect connectors. When a dump trailer is used, the tractor has a reservoir, pump, a hydraulic cooler, control valve, and quick-coupled connectors installed in a package called a "wet line" (**FIGURE 61-35**).

Three-Line Installation

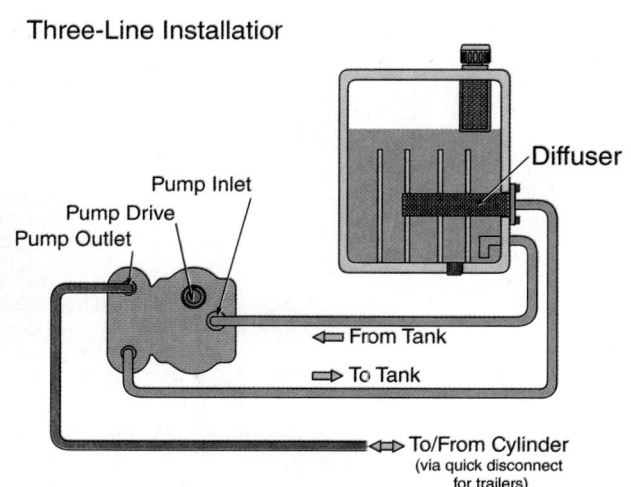

FIGURE 61-33 Two return hoses and one pressure line connect the dump pump to the system reservoir and dump hoist cylinder.

▶ **TECHNICIAN TIP**

A three-line dump pump system that produces excessive oil misting around the tank vent may have the return lines crossed. Verify the return lines are correctly connected at both the pump and reservoir.

Pump Symbols

FIGURE 61-36 shows some common pump symbols used in hydraulic circuit diagrams. Note that the symbols for pumps do not distinguish between piston, vane, and gear pumps.

Hydraulic Fluids

LO 61-5 Identify the purpose, classification, and properties of hydraulic fluids and additives.

Almost any liquid can function as a hydraulic fluid. But common hydraulic fluids are refined from a petroleum oil base to lubricate hydraulic components. Additives blended into the fluids provide additional properties and characteristic to fluids to increase the system efficiency, protect the system from corrosion, and prolong system service life. Hydraulic fluid is an essential element of any hydraulic system due to the vital functions it performs. Its job includes:

- Transmitting energy
- Lubricating components
- Preventing rust and corrosion
- Sealing clearances
- Transferring heat from components to the reservoir or heat exchanger
- Cleaning and carrying solid contaminants to filters

Hydraulic fluid's incompressibility enables it to transmit force yet conform to any shape of housing or line. It is important to note that any liquid compresses slightly under pressure. One percent is the amount hydraulic fluid

Two-Line Installation

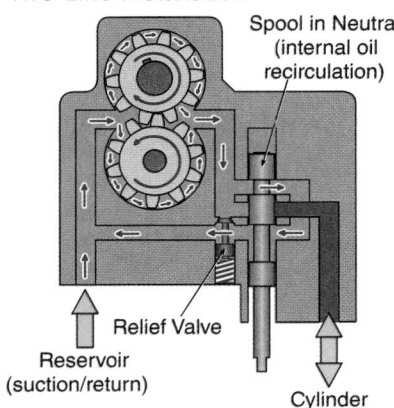
Spool in Neutral (internal oil recirculation)
Relief Valve
Reservoir (suction/return)
Cylinder

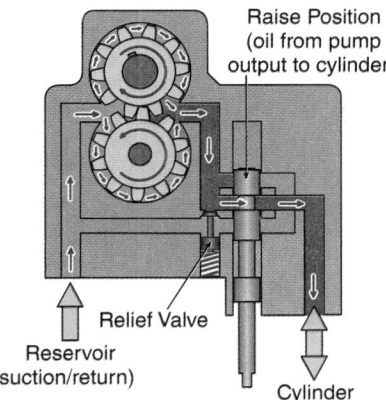
Raise Position (oil from pump output to cylinder)
Relief Valve
Reservoir (suction/return)
Cylinder

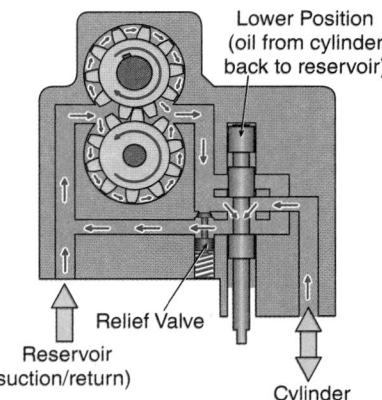
Lower Position (oil from cylinder back to reservoir)
Relief Valve
Reservoir (suction/return)
Cylinder

Three-Line Installation

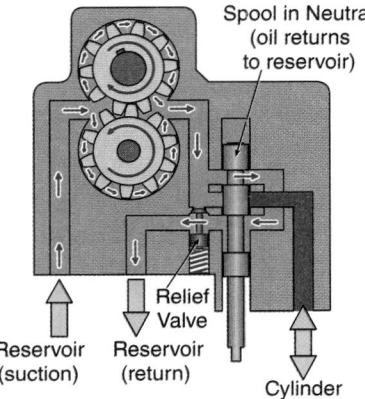
Spool in Neutral (oil returns to reservoir)
Relief Valve
Reservoir (suction)
Reservoir (return)
Cylinder

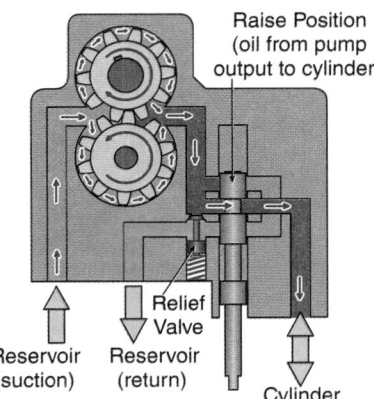
Raise Position (oil from pump output to cylinder)
Relief Valve
Reservoir (suction)
Reservoir (return)
Cylinder

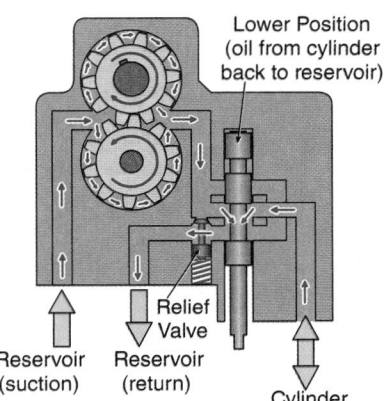
Lower Position (oil from cylinder back to reservoir)
Relief Valve
Reservoir (suction)
Reservoir (return)
Cylinder

FIGURE 61-34 Recirculating the hydraulic oil only internally around the spool valve when in neutral is inefficient and can overheat the oil.

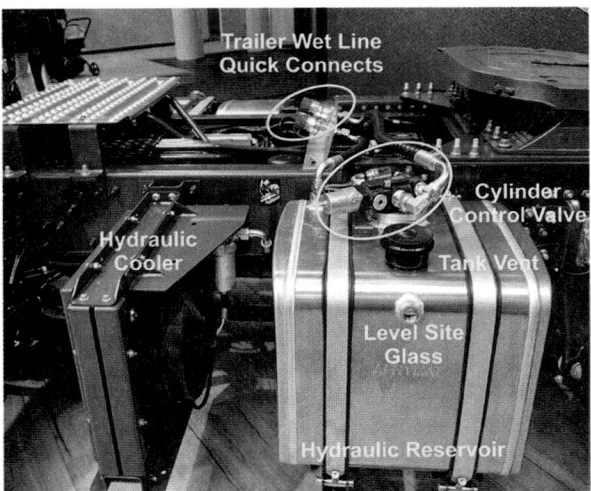
Trailer Wet Line Quick Connects
Cylinder Control Valve
Hydraulic Cooler
Tank Vent
Level Site Glass
Hydraulic Reservoir

FIGURE 61-35 A wet line package for a tractor, allowing it to operate dump trailers.

is expected to compress under a 3000 psi (20,684 kPa) load. The significance is there is some springiness to hydraulic systems and stored energy can release with powerful, destructive consequences.

Fluid Viscosity

Viscosity is defined as a fluid's resistance to flow at a given temperature. Low-viscosity liquids like water flow very easily, while high-viscosity fluids like molasses do not. Viscosity of hydraulic fluid is a critical property because a fluid must flow easily throughout the system. But thin fluids cannot lubricate well, more easily leak past seals, and create potentially damaging pressure drops flowing at high velocity. If a fluid is too thick, it cannot properly lubricate components or reach sensitive areas, such as valve spools in control valves or cylinder walls in piston pumps. Correct viscosity helps improve system efficiency because power isn't consumed forcing fluid to circulate through small clearances.

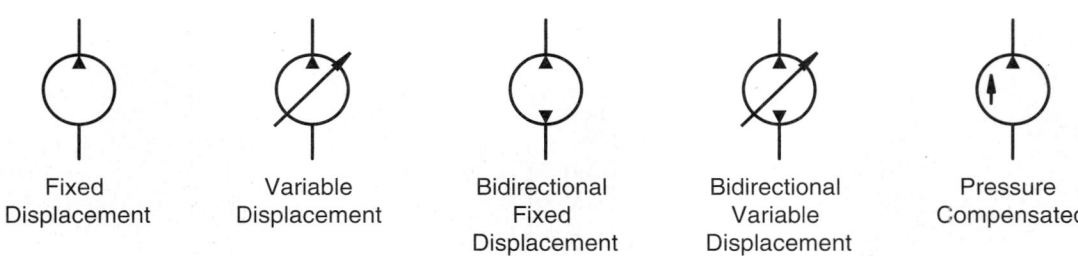

FIGURE 61-36 Examples of pump symbols.

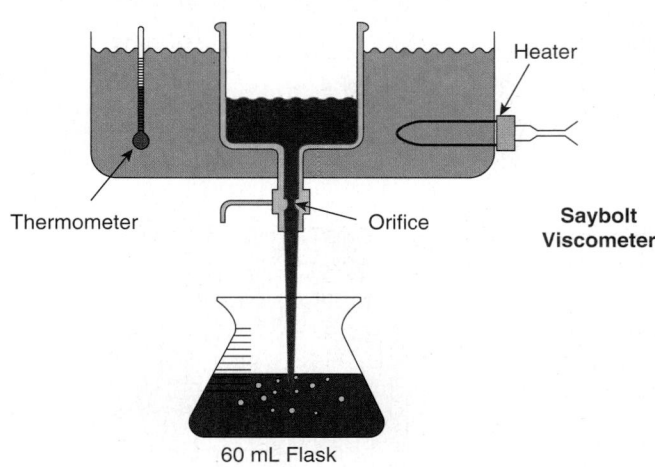

FIGURE 61-37 Kinematic viscosity, which is another measurement of fluid's resistance to flow under the weight of gravity, can be measured by how much fluid flows through a calibrated orifice over a specified time.

Temperature has a major influence on oil viscosity. A fluid's viscosity index (VI) measures how much change takes place in a fluid's viscosity according to temperature. A high VI means little change in viscosity takes place, while a low VI means the opposite. Viscosity of a hydraulic fluid is affected by pressure, causing its density to change and thicken. Viscosity typically doubles for every 5000 psi (34,474 kPa) of fluid pressure.

Units for testing fluid viscosity, which is measured as its resistance to flow at a specific temperature, are centistokes. 1 centistoke = 0.6 cm²/min under the influence of gravity. The concept is illustrated in **FIGURE 61-37** where the fluid is heated and how far the fluid travels is measured.

SAE and ISO Viscosity Measurement

Apart from the test method, two measurement systems are used to classify the viscosity of hydraulic fluids. One standard is established by the Society of Automotive Engineers (SAE) and the other the International Organization for Standardization (ISO). SAE viscosity ratings use two test standards—a hot and cold test temperature (**FIGURE 61-38**). Hot viscosity is measured at 212° F (100° C) and cold ratings are tested at 0° F (–18° C). Common hot SAE viscosity ratings are SAE20, SAE30, and SAE50. Cold ratings are designated by a W suffix such as 5W, 10W, 15W, and 20W. A SAE 20 oil does not have the same viscosity as a 20W fluid. Multi-viscosity fluids, where two numbers appear together, blend oils and additives to produce an oil with

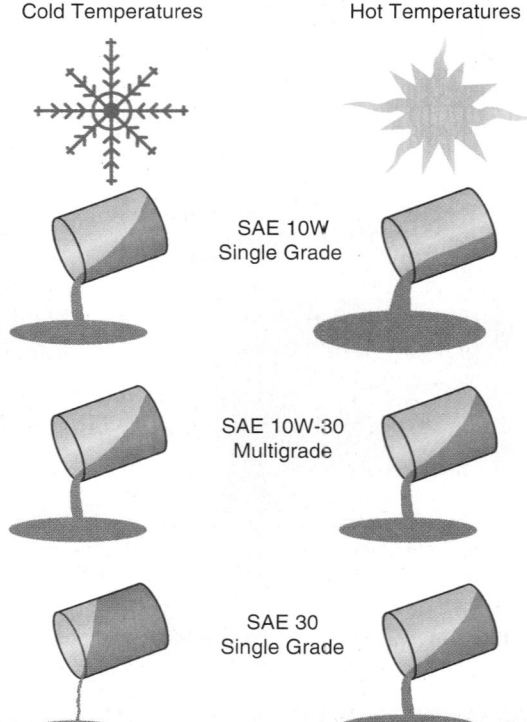

FIGURE 61-38 Temperature changes an oil's viscosity. Multi-grade oils have a lower viscosity index than single-weight oils. That means multi-grade oil viscosity does not change as dramatically with temperature.

a lower VI index. Multi-viscosity oils, such as 10w-30 and 15w-40 do not change viscosity as much as a single viscosity 10w or 15w, or SAE 30 or SAE 40 when used alone. A multi-viscosity oil pours and circulates easier when cold and does not thin out as much when hot as a single-viscosity grade.

Like SAE oils, ISO viscosity ratings are measured at two temperatures using centistokes. However, the cold test temperature is 104° F (40° C), which falls between the SAE test temperatures of summer and winter (212° F and 0° F [100° C and 18° C], respectively). A single number is assigned to ISO hydraulic fluid viscosity ratings which corresponds to its centistoke measurement and there is no separate system to rate multi-viscosity fluids. A lower ISO viscosity number is less viscous than a higher number since ISO viscosity rating numbers increase with higher oil viscosity (**TABLE 61-1**). Common hydraulic fluid viscosities selected for hydraulic equipment are between ISO 22 and 68 with 32 the most common viscosity rating.

TABLE 61-1 ISO and SAE Fluid Viscosity Comparisons

ISO Grade	SAE Grade Equivalent	Viscosity Centistokes	
		40° C	100° C
32	10W	32	5.4
46	20	46	6.8
68	20W	68	8.7
100	30	100	11.4
150	40	150	15
220	50	220	19.4

Source: Chart derived from data downloaded from engineering toolbox https://www.engineeringtoolbox.com/iso-grade-oil-d_1207.html, accessed February 9, 2019.

FIGURE 61-40 A pail of biodegradable hydraulic oil, which is vegetable oil-based.

FIGURE 61-39 A pail of petroleum hydraulic fluid with SAE and ISO specifications.

Types of Hydraulic Fluids

There are four basic types of hydraulic fluids:

- **Petroleum-based fluids:** Petroleum-based hydraulic fluids are refined mineral oils with additives to improve fluid properties and characteristics. Petroleum oils offer advantages, such as low cost, wide availability, good lubricity, and low toxicity (**FIGURE 61-39**).
- **Fire-resistant fluids:** There are several types of fire-resistant fluids useful in operating conditions, such as metal foundries or underground mining applications, where a burst hose could ignite a fire on a hot engine. Water-based fluids are available as oil-in-water emulsions, which are at least 80% water and have the ISO designation

HFA. Water-in oil emulsions, which are typically about 40% water, are designated HFB. Water–glycol fluids consist of up to 60% water, a glycol and a water-soluble thickener; there are designated HFC.

- **Synthetic fluids:** Synthetic fluids are made from a base stock oil molecule called polyalphaolefin (PAO), or alkylated naphthalene (AN). Synthetic fluids are used in extreme operating temperature or pressure conditions where petroleum-based stock oils quickly break down or have performance problems. Synthetic fluids are chemically stabile and have a low VI. This means the fluid viscosity does not change very much over a wide range of temperatures. Disadvantages of synthetics include a high purchase cost and potential material incompatibility with certain types of seals.
- **Biodegradable fluids:** Biodegradable hydraulic fluid or oil are growing in popularity because leaks do not cause harm to the environment or when operating in an environment where major leaks of petroleum-based oils require reporting. These fluids are usually made of vegetable-oil-base stocks, such as rapeseed oil or canola oil. Disadvantages include a high VI, meaning they thicken up too much when cold and thin too much when hot. These oils are generally more expensive to purchase (**FIGURE 61-40**).

Hydraulic Oil Additives

Additives and VI improvers may also be added to the hydraulic fluid. Common additive categories include:

- Anti-wear additives that improve lubrication of components subject to high contact pressure.
- Anti-foaming agents that improve the separation of air from the fluid and reduce foaming inside a reservoir.

- De-emulsifiers are used to separate water from fluid to enable its removal from a system and prevent corrosion.
- Corrosion inhibitors that reduce rust formation on exposed steel and iron surfaces,
- Automatic transmission fluid (ATF), which has low viscosity and a low VI index, is blended with hydraulic oil. ATF also contains additional anti-foaming agents, making it suitable for power steering circuits and compact hydrostatic drive systems. However, ATF can break down and burn at high temperatures.

Hydraulic Fluid Reservoirs

LO 61-6 Describe the construction and operation of hydraulic fluid reservoirs, filters, and coolers.

Hydraulic systems need a continuous supply of fluid that changes depending on the position of actuators, such as cylinders that may or may not be extended. Small leaks around seals and fitting can allow oil to escape the system depleting the oil volume available to a pump. To maintain system operation, an excess fluid reserve stored in a reservoir is used to supply the hydraulic pump inlet.

Reservoirs have additional functions, such as helping to cool oil that's heated as it is worked under pressure. The sides of the tank can radiate excess heat to prevent oil from thinning. Dirt and particles picked up from oil introduced by retracting cylinders or pieces of seals and wearing metal settles in the reservoir, to help remove contaminants (**FIGURE 61-41**).

Air and gas bubbles are another system contaminant the reservoir removes. Air entering through seals, turbulent fluid velocities, or gases from vaporizing liquids have time to separate from fluid in the tank. The rising and falling level of fluid in the tank caused by system actions requires atmospheric air to enter and leave with each level change. A tank vent with a filter is used to minimize any fluid contamination caused by dust carried by the air. Moisture is another contaminant that enters with air. Cool fluid surfaces cause moisture to condense in hydraulic fluid. The tank bottom provides a location where water and fluids can separate in the presence of de-emulsifier additives. A tank reservoir generally has a sight glass or external tube to visually indicate the level of fluid.

A reservoir has features, such as a pump inlet and return ports, located at opposite ends of the reservoir to enable returning oil to lose heat, release gas bubbles, and provide time for contaminants to settle out. Locating the inlet of suction port too close to fluid entry will draw contaminants and hot oil into the system. To direct oil against the tank walls where heat can escape, prevent oil from sloshing, and lengthen the flow pathway through the reservoir, baffle plates may be used. Baffles are positioned to direct the return oil toward the walls of the reservoir to improve heat transfer oil absorbs when sheared and pressurized (**FIGURE 61-42**).

Fluid Filtering

Hydraulic filters are necessary to prevent small abrasive particles from damaging sensitive precision-machined components. Filters can be categorized according to their location, construction type, pressure rating, flow rating, and particle filtration size. Filter materials range from the use of paper to synthetic fibers or microglass, which is a type of glass fiber (**FIGURE 61-43**). Because of the variety of pressures in a hydraulic system, it is important to note hydraulic filters are categized according the maximum working pressure. Low-pressure filters can tolerate up to 350 psi, or 24 bar; medium-pressure—up to 2000 psi, or 138 bar; and high-pressure—up to 6500 psi, or 450 bar. Filter media is reinforced with steel mesh in hydraulic filters to prevent media damage from

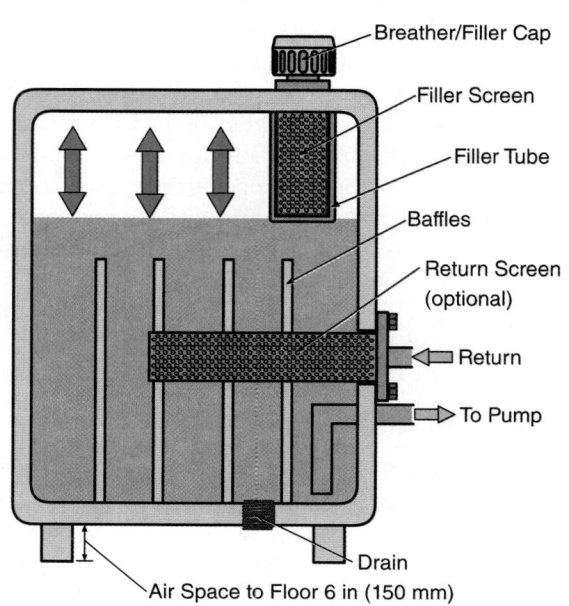

Breather/Filler Cap
Filler Screen
Filler Tube
Baffles
Return Screen (optional)
Return
To Pump
Drain
Air Space to Floor 6 in (150 mm)

FIGURE 61-41 Typical construction features of a hydraulic reservoir.

Dump Box Hoist Cylinder
Oil Reservoir
Safety Support Prop

FIGURE 61-42 Location of a hydraulic reservoir on a dump truck.

FIGURE 61-43 The light-yellow filter **A.** media is cellulose while the white media **B.** is microglass.

FIGURE 61-44 A high-pressure hydraulic filter in a thick steel case. Media is reinforced with fine steel mesh.

high-pressure fluid flow (**FIGURE 61-44**). Paper cellulose filters have resin coatings to prevent pores from closing caused by water absorption by paper media.

Filter efficiency is based on the size and percentage of particles a filter can trap. Particle sizes are measured in microns (μm). One micron is one-millionth of one meter, or 39 millionths of an inch (0.0000394"). The limit of human visibility is approximately 40 μm and a grain of salt is 70 μm. The size of the most damage-causing particles is not sand or small rocks but fine particles dissolved in hydraulic fluid smaller than 14 μm. The greatest wear takes place when particle size is between 5 and 8 μm. Contaminants can be removed from a hydraulic system using filters located at six possible points within the system:

- **Air breather cap filter**: Large volumes of air can move in and out of a hydraulic tank as the level rises and falls. The air must be filtered to remove water and dust particles before they contaminate the fluid. In addition, fine oil droplets from the hydraulic oil potentially released into the atmosphere are separated by the filter.
- **Hydraulic tank**: The tank acts as a sediment filter whereby large particles and water can settle at the bottom of the tank and be collected during an oil change. A bung plug located at the bottom of the tank can be momentarily removed to drain free water collected in the tank.
- **Suction side filter**: Suction filters are a coarse filter removing particles between 25 to 250 μm in size. By removing larger particles, the suction filter extends the service life of filters on the pressure side of the system. These filters are located in series with the return line filters bringing fluid back to the tank. Suction side filters clean the oil before it enters the pump, but they can potentially restrict flow, and deprive the pump of oil.
- **Pressure filter**: A pressure filter is installed between the pump and any directional control valves to remove fine particles, down to 3 μm in some systems.
- **Return filter**: A return filter cleans oil returning from the valves and actuators before the fluid enters the reservoir tank.
- **Bypass filter**: The filtration system filters only part of the system's oil flow, so a dedicated pump and bypass filtration system is often installed to add additional filtering capacity. Bypass filters can be smaller, and the finest, most-efficient filters are used without restricting flow through the system.

Hydraulic Coolers

Hydraulic oil cooler circuits operate with the reservoir like an engine cooling system. When hydraulic fluid in the reservoir is cold, a thermostatic or pressure-based bypass valve directs warm returning fluid directly to the reservoir. As fluid temperature rises and viscosity decreases, a greater volume of fluid is passed through the cooler. Large hydraulic systems use hydraulic coolers to help limit the fluid's maximum temperature. Most coolers are airflow type and very similar to engine coolant radiators.

Hydraulic Lines and Hoses

LO 61-7 Identify and describe the purpose, types, and construction of hydraulic conductors, lines, hoses, and tubes.

Hydraulic fluid is distributed between components through a combination of rigid steel pipe or tubing and flexible hose assemblies. The selection of lines used in hydraulic circuits must take into consideration a couple of physical laws describing the properties of a fluid, gas, or liquid flowing through a hydraulic line. For example, Pascal's Law also applies to the working and burst pressure of hoses and pipe. Working pressure is the maximum pressure a hydraulic conductor can safely hold. Burst pressure is working pressure plus a safety factor for unintended pressure changes. The **burst pressure** for a hydraulic hose is the manufacturer rating for the maximum pressure a particular hose can contain before it explodes or ruptures. The safety factor chosen depends on conditions, such as the tensile or yield strength of materials. However, a typical burst factor for hydraulic hose is 4:1, which means the hose should not leak or burst if momentarily operated four times above the highest anticipated pressure. Pascal's Law explains how the internal diameter (ID) of a line sets pressure limits because the ID has surface area acted upon by hydraulic pressure. A smaller ID means less total pressure is exerted against the walls of the line or hose. Increasing a line or hoses ID doesn't make it stronger. Instead, an increasing ID allows more total force to be exerted against the conductor walls. This means a smaller ID line can have a higher working pressure and burst pressure than a larger line if the wall thickness is the same (**FIGURE 61-45**).

Another physical principle explains the interaction of fluid velocity and pressure. Applied to hydraulic lines, it is important to understand that when fluid velocity increases, fluid pressure

must drop if the volume is to remain constant. In other words, fluid pressure and speed vary as the line narrows or widens. As the line narrows, fluid velocity increases and the pressure decreases. As the line widens, the fluid velocity decreases and the pressure increases (**FIGURE 61-46**). These relationships are explained by another fluid law called the Bernoulli principle. The Bernoulli principle explains why line diameter and pressure must be taken into account when selecting the size and type of line for conducting hydraulic fluid to avoid several unwanted characteristics created by pressure drops and high fluid velocities.

Both rigid and flexible lines are used as hydraulic conductors, and each have unique advantages. Flexible hose assemblies are necessary to allow movement of actuators. They can also dampen hydraulic vibration caused by pressure pulsations in fluid and dampen pressure spikes better than comparable rigid steel pipe or tubes. Rigid steel tubes, however, are better at conducting heat away from hot fluid, are more economical, more durable, and take up less space than comparable flexible hoses.

Safety and Hydraulic Line Service

Before proceeding any further on the topic of hydraulic lines and hoses, it is critical for technicians to understand that a task as simple as disconnecting and removing a hydraulic line or hose can have lethal, life-changing, and catastrophic consequences. These hazards are avoidable if important safety procedures are correctly followed. There are at least four types of dangers technicians are exposed to when working on hydraulic systems. These include:

1. Burns from high-temperature fluid. Hydraulic systems create hot, high-pressure fluids as they are pressurized while transferring large amounts of energy. Shearing of fluid between gear teeth, vanes, and valves, plus friction inside lines created by high-velocity fluid flow produces heat that is absorbed by fluid. Fluid temperatures can reach as high as 140° F (60° C) that can burn and scald a technician.

2. Trapped potential energy: Lines under pressure can disconnect, burst, or break and fluid can hit technicians when pressure is relieved from a system. Bruises, cuts, and abrasions from whipping hydraulic lines can result. Occupational Safety and Health Administration (OSHA) regulations require this energy is released before servicing a system. The pressure may originate from stored high-pressure fluid

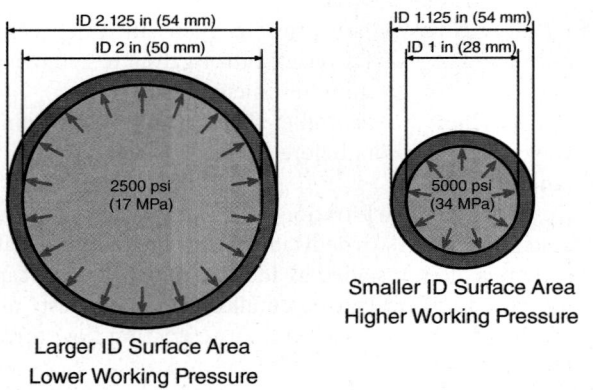

FIGURE 61-45 Increasing the inside diameter (ID) of a hose reduces its working and burst pressure because the conductor has a larger ID surface area acted on by fluid pressure.

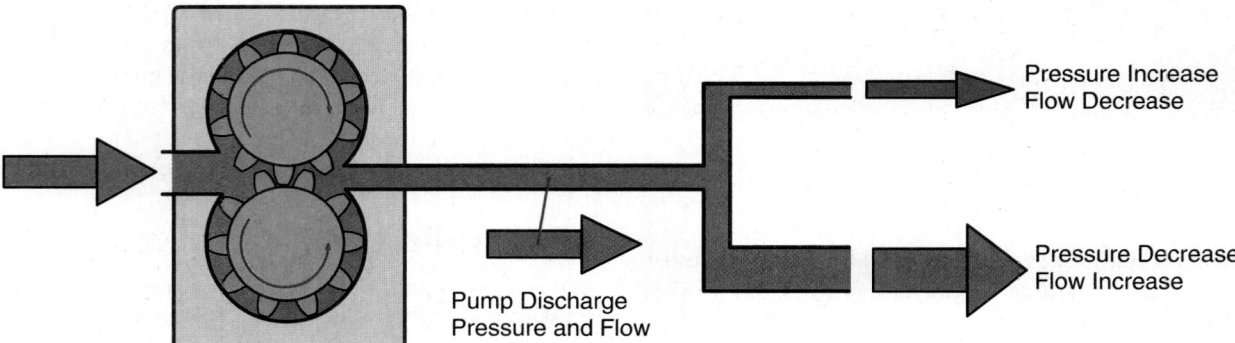

FIGURE 61-46 Fluid pressure and velocity vary as the line narrows or widens. The Bernoulli principle applies to all three types of hydraulic lines: pipes, tubes, and hoses.

FIGURE 61-47 A small dump box is supported by a prop rod to prevent the box from falling while working on the chassis.

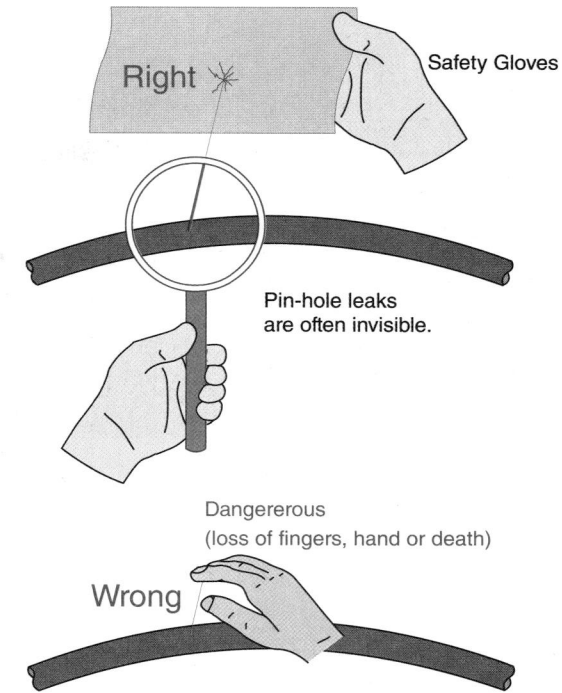

FIGURE 61-48 Never check for hidden leaks with a hand. Always use a piece of cardboard or paper to avoid hydraulic injection of fluid through skin.

FIGURE 61-49 This scale model shows the use of dump box props used to prevent crush injuries when working on the chassis with the box raised.

in a gas or spring accumulator used by many hydraulic systems. One of the most common and overlooked causes of trapped potential energy is a hydraulic actuator, such as an extended actuator cylinder, that has a load. If a bucket, blade, box, or boom is not relaxed and supported, pressure in the cylinder is released when a hydraulic line is disconnected. A control valve can move or be accidentally bumped to cause fluid to suddenly return through a line from the cylinder as well (**FIGURE 61-47**).

3. Hydraulic injection of fluid into the skin: Just 40 psi (276 kPa) of fluid pressure is necessary to penetrate skin and cause fluid to enter tissue or even the blood stream. The consequences are too often fatal or lead to losses of limbs and fingers. When high-pressure fluid is injected, only a slight stinging sensation is experienced that is easy to ignore. Injuries like this cause severe pain after several hours or a day. A diagnosis can be too late if the technicians is unaware of the reason for the injury or pain. Inspecting for pinhole leaks in hoses or cracking a pressurized line open can easily produce a narrow, dangerous stream of hydraulic fluid that cannot be easily observed (**FIGURE 61-48**).

4. Crushing hazards from heavy hydraulic components or hydraulically operated components, such as blades, buckets, or booms when a line is unintentionally disconnected or burst (**FIGURE 61-49**).

Hydraulic System Safety Practices

To address these safety concerns, technicians should follow several important safety practices when working around hydraulic systems and be aware of when servicing hydraulic lines.

- Ensure all hydraulic pressure is bled or released before disconnecting oil lines or opening the system. Cycle closed center control valves back and forth. Verify open center control valves are in fact centered.
- In hydraulic systems using accumulators, consult manufacturer service literature to identify and follow the procedure to depressurize accumulators.

FIGURE 61-50 Always lower the cylinder locks and pin in place when working below a bucket, boom, blade, or box. Use the control valve to lower the cylinder to a relaxed position against the lock.

FIGURE 61-51 Wipe hydraulic quick connectors clean before coupling. Verify the return and pressure lines are correctly connected to the correct coupler.

- Block, chain, or securely tie hydraulic equipment and the vehicle to prevent any uncontrolled movement when working on hydraulic components.
- Always lower the hydraulic actuators to the ground or move to a resting position before working on the system.
- Block working units and actuators on safety stands when working on them.
- Use original equipment manufacturers (OEM) equipment cylinder or lift locks when working on equipment (**FIGURE 61-50**).
- When lifting cab-over trucks with hydraulic rams, lock the ram in an extended position with the accompanying ram lock.
- Never service the hydraulic system while the engine or machine is operating except to bleed a system.
- Do not remove cylinders until the working units, such as buckets, blades, booms, and boxes, are resting securely on safety stands, prop rods, or blocks.
- Be sure all line and connections are tight, not damaged or leaking, to prevent pressurized oil from becoming a fire hazard.
- Hydraulic pumps, PTOs, and cylinders are heavy. Use a lifting crane or other purpose-made lift to support them while removing them.
- Do not operate a hydraulic system if oil temperatures are above a safe limit of 140° F/60° C.
- Wipe all quick-connect couplers clean before connecting to prevent damage to the coupler mechanism and leaks (**FIGURE 61-51**).
- When connecting quick couplers to other hydraulic equipment, good practice is to connect the return line hose first and disconnect it last to avoid trapping any pressure in the high-pressure supply line from the pump.
- Verify a quick-coupler pressure and return hose are connected correctly. Reversing flow through this circuit will likely damage seals of equipment-supplied pressure.

Rigid Lines (Pipe and Tubing)

There are two types of rigid fluid conductors, defined by two terms that are often confused: pipe and tubing. The main differences between pipe and tubing are their construction materials and applications. **Pipe** is typically constructed from cold-drawn seamless or welded steel but may also be made from stainless steel for special applications. The diameter of the pipe follows a standard for pressure rating called pipe schedule. The schedule number on pipe products indicates the thickness of the pipe wall. As the schedule number increases, the thicker the wall thickness becomes (**FIGURE 61-52**). Also, while the schedule number can be the same on different-diameter pipes, the actual wall thickness is different (**TABLE 61-2**).

The use of pipe as opposed to tubing is intended for industrial applications requiring long, straight runs where pipe is not normally bent or shaped other than in smooth turns (not tight angles). It is treated by heating and is then slowly cooled, to anneal or soften the material to enable bending and flaring.

Metric-size pipe dimensions are specified by Diameter Nominal (DN) standard, and for imperial measure, nominal pipe size (NPS) standard specified in inches. Note that the size given for the pipe refers to its inside diameter and not its actual outside diameter (OD) (see Table 61-2). Schedule specifications refer to a table of standards that define the wall thickness and inside diameter (ID) for a specific size of pipe.

> ▶ **TECHNICIAN TIP**
>
> Never use galvanized pipe or fittings for hydraulic system applications. The zinc coating can react with the hydraulic fluid and flake off the pipe walls and fittings, resulting in fluid contamination and potentially damaging components.

Tubing is normally made from **seamless** steel, but may be made from stainless steel for special applications. Normally used for on-machine plumbing, annealed and thinner-walled tubing is designed to be bent and shaped to accommodate its installation on the vehicle or machine. Its dimensions are specified by the OD and wall thickness.

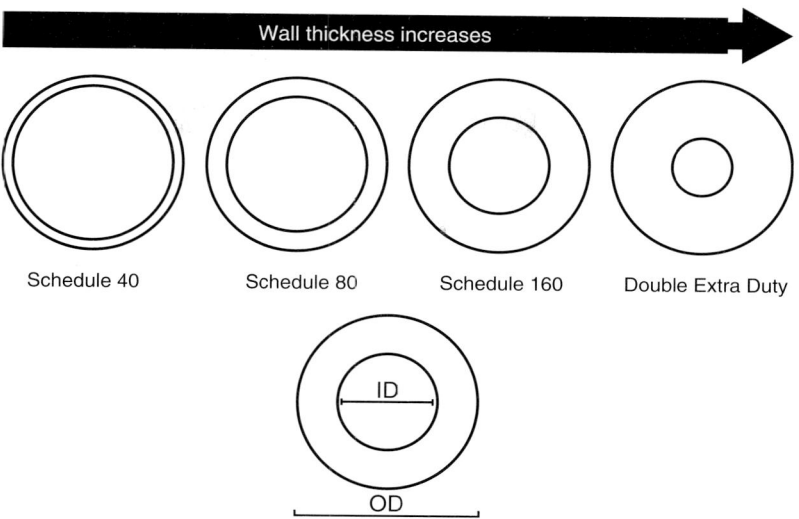

FIGURE 61-52 Schedule specifications for wall thickness and pipe sizes.

TABLE 61-2 Nominal Pipe Size (Metric and Imperial), Showing Outside Diameter (OD) and Schedule Specification/Inside Diameter (ID)

Diameter Nominal (DN)	Nominal Pipe Size (NPS)	Pipe OD		Schedule 40 Standard ID		Schedule 80 ID		Schedule 160 ID		Double Extra-Duty ID	
		(mm)	(")	(mm)	(")	(mm)	(")	(mm)	(")	(mm)	(")
3 mm	1/8"	10.287	0.405	7.341	0.289	5.461	0.215	—	—	—	—
6 mm	1/4"	13.716	0.540	9.246	0.364	7.671	0.302	—	—	—	—
10 mm	3/8"	17.145	0.675	12.522	0.493	10.744	0.423	—	—	—	—
13 mm	1/2"	21.336	0.840	15.799	0.622	13.868	0.546	11.836	0.466	6.401	0.252
19 mm	3/4"	26.670	1.050	20.930	0.824	18.847	0.742	15.596	0.614	11.024	0.434
25 mm	1"	33.401	1.315	26.645	1.049	24.308	0.957	20.701	0.815	15.215	0.599
32 mm	1 1/4"	42.164	1.660	35.052	1.380	32.461	1.278	29.464	1.160	22.758	0.896
38 mm	1 1/2"	48.260	1.900	40.894	1.610	38.100	1.500	33.985	1.338	27.940	1.100
51 mm	2"	60.325	2.375	52.502	2.067	49.251	1.939	42.901	1.689	38.176	1.503

Metric sizes and imperial dimensions for tubing do not have direct equivalents to one another in either size or capacity, but there is little difference between the maximum working pressure of the metric size and its closest equivalent imperial size. For example, a 12 mm OD by 2 mm wall tube is expressed as a 12 × 2 tube, which has a working pressure of 3697 psi (25,489 kPa). Its closest inch equivalent is a ½" by 0.0854" tube, which has the same working pressure. TABLE 61-3 provides an outline of the range of operating pressures that can be used with tubing. Notice that the thickness of the wall of the tube has a direct influence on the possible working pressures.

▶ TECHNICIAN TIP

Never use copper tubing for hydraulic system applications. Copper does not have adequate tensile or burst strength to tolerate high hydraulic pressure. Hydraulic pressure pulsations and vibration also cause the copper to become progressively brittle with time and will crack.

TABLE 61-3 Metric Tubing Sizes: Outside Diameter × Wall Thickness and Working Pressure (Metric and Imperial)

Tubing OD × Wall Thickness	Working Pressure (bar)	Working Pressure (psi)
8 mm × 1 mm	333.91	4843
8 mm × 2 mm	539.86	7830
8 mm × 2.5 mm	649.83	9425
12 mm × 1.5 mm	189.95	2755
12 mm × 2 mm	254.89	3697
12 mm × 2.5 mm	319.92	4640
15 mm × 1 mm	184.92	2682
15 mm × 1.5 mm	279.93	4060
15 mm × 2 mm	335.91	4872
15 mm × 2.5 mm	408.86	5930
22 mm × 1 mm	124.93	1812

For conversions from bar to MPa/kPa, see front of this text.

Flexible Line Hoses

Flexible hydraulic hoses typically consist of three layers: an inner tube (usually a synthetic rubber or thermoplastic); a reinforcement layer, which is one or more layers of a steel mesh or textile braid; and an outer cover of synthetic rubber or thermoplastic. Hoses may have additional layers of various materials to anchor the three primary layers and prevent **chafing**—including an external, braided wire cover (**FIGURE 61-53**).

Flexible hoses are intended for use where there is vibration or relative movement between components on equipment. Hydraulic hose must be selected for the proper diameter and type for oil flow at the specified rate for system flow and pressure. If the hose is undersized it creates unnecessary flow restriction, which adds extra heat to the system and increases neutral system operating pressure. Using an oversized hose for the application can result in leakage or bursting under pressure or, erosion of metal on the inlet side of the pump, caused by low-pressure—a condition called **cavitation erosion**.

The SAE has established construction standards and code designations for hose application and the type of fluid conducted by hose (**FIGURE 61-54**). The SAE J-517 hydraulic hose standards designations for truck and bus hydraulic systems are SAE: 100R4, 100R1, 100R2, and 100R9. The differences between these hoses depends on materials and their construction (**TABLE 61-4**). These designations can be found printed at regular intervals on the outside of the hose. Hose dimensions are based on a "dash" number size system where each dash equals $\frac{1}{16}$". This means a 100R1-16 hose number is dash 16 (-16)

is equal to one inch. A dash 24 (-24) has an ID of 1½". The prefix 100R2 for an SAE 100R2-12 indicates it is a high-pressure hose with an inside diameter of ¾".

It's important to note that the SAE hoses have a maximum recommended oil velocity rating according to their usage in a system. High-velocity oil can erode the inside of pipes, tubes, and hoses, so a hose that is too small and has very high pressure could quickly fail. Oil velocity is expressed in feet per second (fps) and the SAE recommends hoses maximum fluid velocity for use in the following places should not exceed:

- Inlet or suction side hose—4 fps
- Return hose—8 fps
- Pressure hose—15 fps

Fluid velocity can be calculated using the formula Velocity = GPM × 0.3208 ÷ ID Area. GPM refers to the flow rate and "A" is the inside area of the hose. The hose selection must comply with SAE J-517 hydraulic hose standards.

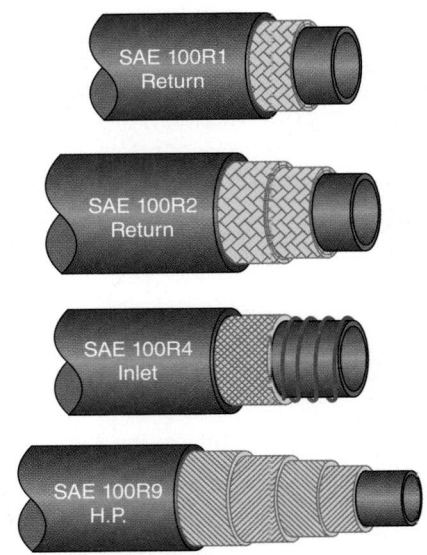

FIGURE 61-54 Construction of SAE J-5 7 hydraulic hoses used in commercial vehicle applications.

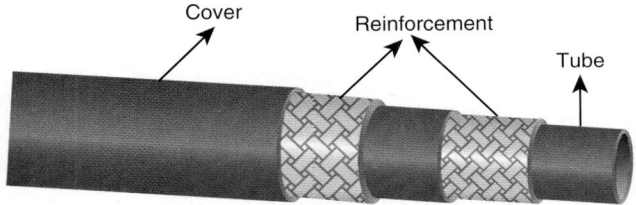

FIGURE 61-53 How a hydraulic hose is constructed.

TABLE 61-4 SAE-Rated Hoses

SAE Number	Inner Tube	Reinforcement	Cover
SAE 100R1	Synthetic rubber	I High-tensile steel coating	Synthetic rubber
SAE 100R2	Synthetic rubber	2 Wire braids 2 Spiral plies I Wire braid	Synthetic
SAE 100R3	Synthetic rubber	2 Textile braids	Synthetic
SAE 100R4	Synthetic rubber	Braided textile fibers or spiral-body wire	Synthetic
SAE 100R5	Synthetic rubber	I Textile braid I High-tensile steel wire braid	Cotton braid
SAE 100R6	Synthetic rubber	I Textile braid	Synthetic rubber
SAE 100R7	Thermoplastic	Synthetic fiber	Thermoplastic
SAE 100R8	Thermoplastic	Synthetic fiber	Thermoplastic
SAE 100R9	Synthetic rubber	4 Spiral plies wrapped in alternating directions	Synthetic rubber
SAE 100R10	Synthetic rubber	4 Spiral plies of heavy wire wrapped in alternating directions	Synthetic rubber
SAE 100R11	Synthetic rubber	6 Spiral plies of heavy wire wrapped in alternating directions	Synthetic rubber

A will-fit replacement hose that does not meet the requirements for usage, pressure, or flow rates can be enormously disruptive to a hydraulic system. To avoid potential problems, use hose manufacturer's data about their products to verify the correct hose selection is made for the specific application.

Table 61-4 lists various hoses according to their rating by the SAE and describes their construction.

Line and Hose Diameter

As mentioned already, the ID of the line or hose is critical to the efficient flow of the hydraulic fluid. If the ID is too small, then the flow is restricted, which causes higher fluid **velocity** and fluid **turbulence** (**FIGURE 61-55**). Fluid turbulence inside lines results in pressure drops, fluid heating, and wasted energy. The correct ID ideally creates a smooth, non-turbulent flow, better described as laminar flow. Hose dimensions are indicated by a dash number that indicates the ID of the hose in sixteenths of an inch (multiples of 1.58 mm). For example, a -8 (dash 8) hose has an ⁸⁄₁₆" (½") ID, which in metric is 12.64 mm (8 × 1.58).

Although desirable, laminar flow is difficult to achieve in hydraulic systems; a tradeoff is often necessary between minimizing the space occupied by lines and hoses and the dimensions required for ideal performance of the hose or lines. To achieve the same fluid flow rate within a circuit, three different usage of line diameters are used to balance flow rates. These include:

1. The supply or suction line from the tank or reservoir to the pump has very low or even negative pressure that requires a large ID to provide adequate flow of fluid to the pump inlet (**FIGURE 61-56**).
2. Lines operating with high pressure are the smallest in diameter but can still maintain laminar flow.

3. Fluid returning from the directional valves to the tank or reservoir is at an intermediate pressure and requires an intermediate-diameter conductor.

Proper Routing of Hydraulic Lines

General guidelines to consider when routing hydraulic lines include the following:

- Support long runs of pipe or tubing at regular intervals.
- Avoid contact of edges with sharp corners where chafing can occur.
- Keep lines away from hot components, such as exhaust systems and coolant heaters.
- Route lines to protect them from impact damage.

Line and Hose Fittings

Fittings are used to connect rigid and flexible hydraulic lines to other hydraulic components. A variety of fittings are used and are categorized several ways. For hydraulic systems, three major types of fitting are:

- National pipe thread
- Flare type fittings
- O-ring seal fittings

The most widely used fitting for hydraulic lines and hoses is the national pipe tapered (NPT) thread (**FIGURE 61-57**). As the name suggests, it is easily identified by the tapered shape of the fitting. The design provides a self-sealing action by forcing or wedging the internal and external thread flanks against one another as it is tightened. Because the fitting thread shape is tapered, an interference fit, which wedges metal-to-metal threads together, is formed threading a male end into a female thread. NPT type of thread is thin, has a different thread pitch than other fasteners, and unfortunately does not seal at the thread root of the fitting. This explains why NPT threads require pipe sealant tape or liquid Teflon to prevent leakage past the threads (**FIGURE 61-58**). A variation of the tapered NPT is National Pipe Thread Straight thread fitting for fuel (NPTF). The straight thread shape allows the fitting

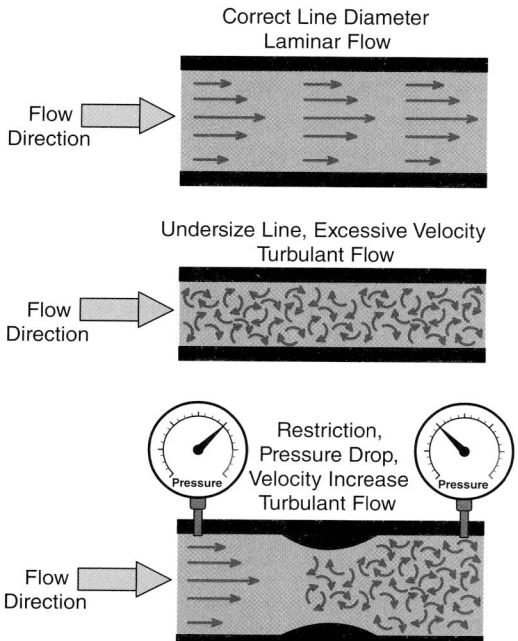

Correct Line Diameter
Laminar Flow

Flow Direction

Undersize Line, Excessive Velocity
Turbulant Flow

Flow Direction

Restriction,
Pressure Drop,
Velocity Increase
Turbulant Flow

Flow Direction

FIGURE 61-55 Excessive fluid velocity in a line creates fluid turbulence. Restrictions also create pressure drops.

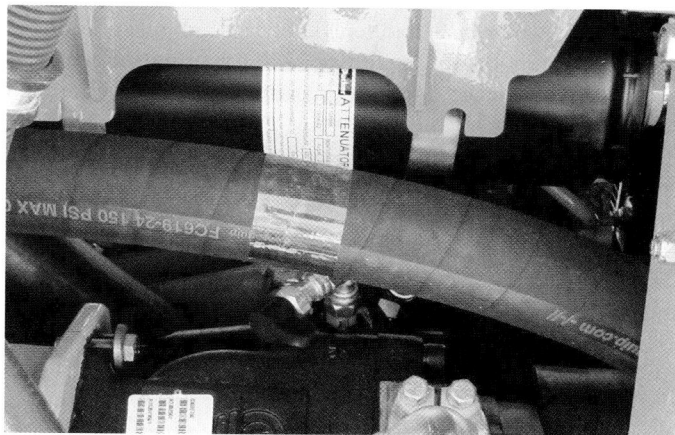

FIGURE 61-56 The supply from the reservoir to the pump requires a large internal diameter to allow free flow of fluid to the pump inlet.

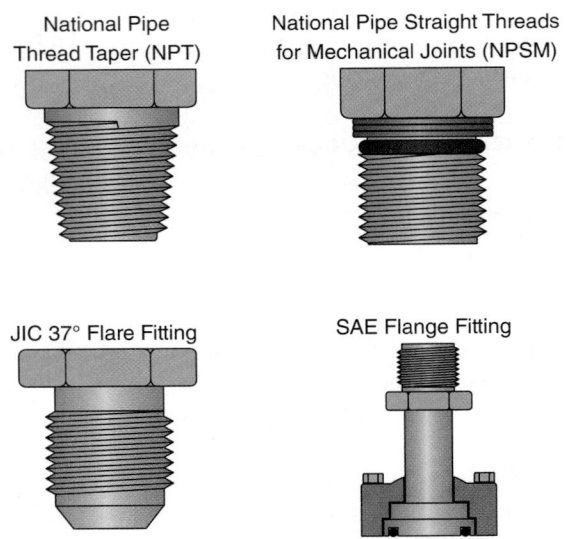

National Pipe Thread Taper (NPT)

National Pipe Straight Threads for Mechanical Joints (NPSM)

JIC 37° Flare Fitting

SAE Flange Fitting

FIGURE 61-57 Four of the most common types of hydraulic fittings with high-pressure sealing features.

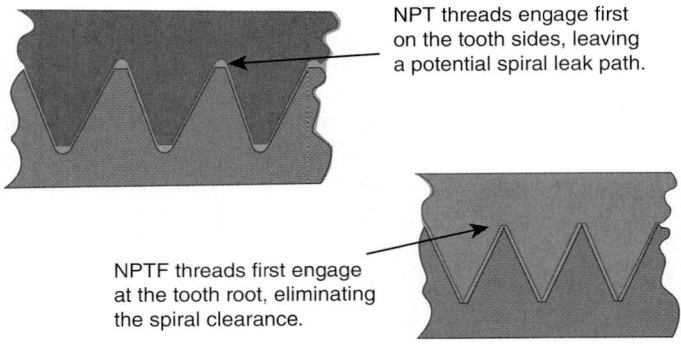

NPT threads engage first on the tooth sides, leaving a potential spiral leak path.

NPTF threads first engage at the tooth root, eliminating the spiral clearance.

FIGURE 61-58 NPT and NPTF.

to seal at the thread root to prevent leakage. Both fitting types are theoretically not re-useable and should be replaced when removed or disconnected.

NPT and NPTF fittings are used on lower-pressure hydraulic fittings. A better high-pressure seal is obtained using what are called flare fittings. Another name given to this fitting is Mated Angle Seals. A sealing surface is formed between angled mating surfaces when male and female fittings are joined. Either a 45-degree or 37-degree angle flare at the mating surface ends prevent fluid leakage. When the angle at the mating surface is 45 degrees, it is classified as a SAE 45° Fitting, which is different from the Joint Industry Council (JIC) 37° mating angle (**FIGURE 61-59**). SAE fittings are considered to operate in lower-pressure applications, such as for fuel, oil, and refrigerant line fittings. JIC 37° angle seats are used on medium-pressure and high-pressure lines on hydraulic systems. The fittings are not interchangeable.

O-ring seal fittings use the threaded part of the connector to attach fittings but an O-ring to seal the joint. Threads pull the O-ring against the sealing surface, which sits in a machined groove. The O-ring is flattened against a washer or a part of the opposite side fitting, making a seal that is excellent for high-pressure applications (**FIGURE 61-60**).

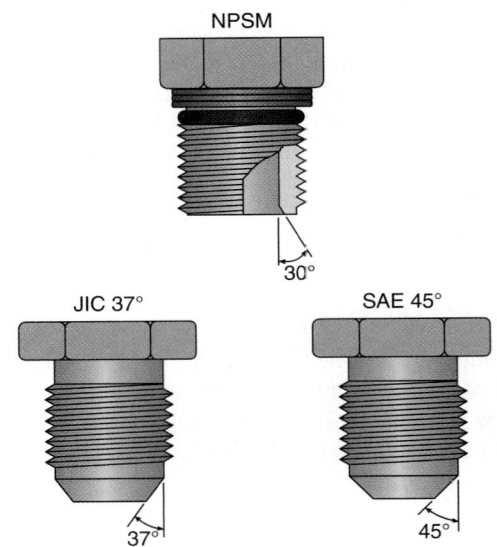

NPSM

30°

JIC 37°

37°

SAE 45°

45°

FIGURE 61-59 Comparing the shape and angle of flare-type sealing surfaces used by three different hydraulic fitting standards.

FIGURE 61-60 This hydraulic relay valve for a PTO uses O-rings to seal the fitting threads.

SAE O-Ring Flanges make high-pressure, large-diameter connections. A passage is drilled through a flange with a center outlet, surrounded by a smooth flat face that has four mounting bolt holes that clamps an O-ring beneath the flange. There are no threads on this coupling. The flange has a machined groove for the O-ring.

▶ **TECHNICIAN TIP**

When selecting fittings according to hose and line size, remember that hose dimensions are measured on the inside diameter, tubing and pipe on the outside.

Hose End Fittings

Permanent hose fitting ends are either **swaged** or **crimped** onto the rubber hose end and they cannot be removed and used on another hose assembly (**FIGURE 61-61**). However, reusable hose ends can be field-installed. These swiveling fittings have three-part ends, one of which is a nut with a left-hand thread that is first tightened over a rubber hose end. Next, a narrow pipe, with a right-hand thread is installed with a JIC or other hydraulic-style fitting, is tightened into the end of the hose to provide a surface for a wrench to help turn the fitting into the hose (**FIGURE 61-62**). These types of fittings can be field-assembled with a couple of wrenches and a vice. The third type of hose end is the quick-disconnect hose end. Quick connect fittings are used to connect a hydraulic system on a truck with a wet-line to a dump trailer or a skid steer load to a hydraulically powered accessory, such as a broom or jack hammer.

Flex Hose Installation Guidelines

Specific guidelines for routing flexible hose include the following:

- Leave extra length to accommodate length changes when hose is pressurized (**FIGURE 61-63**).

FIGURE 61-61 A permanent hose end is crimped onto the hose.

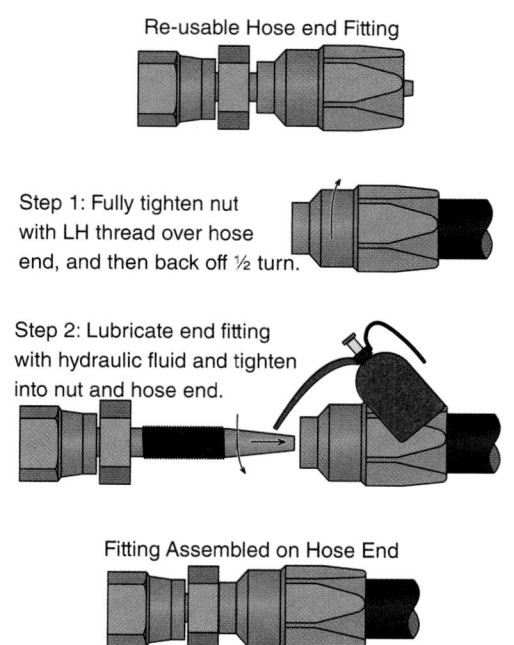

FIGURE 61-62 Steps involved to assemble a re-usable hydraulic hose end fitting.

- Make hose sufficiently long to distribute movement in flexing situations and to avoid abrasion (**FIGURE 61-64**).
- Avoid twisting of hose bent in two planes by clamping the hose at the change of plane (**FIGURE 61-65**).
- Avoid tight bends through use of appropriate fittings (**FIGURE 61-66**).

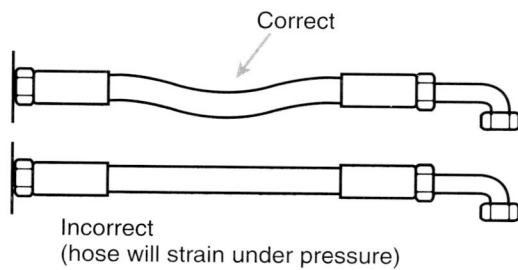

FIGURE 61-63 Example of correct and incorrect hose length for pressure.

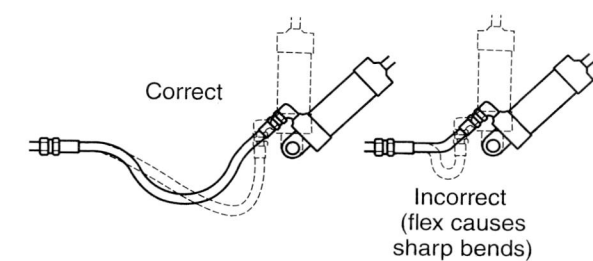

FIGURE 61-64 Example of correct and incorrect length for flexing.

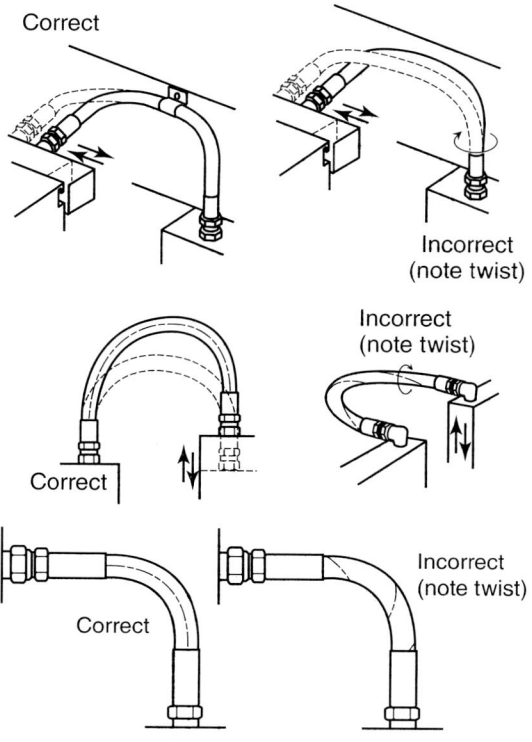

FIGURE 61-65 Examples of correct and incorrect clamping to avoid twists.

- Avoid abrasion with use of proper bracketing (**FIGURE 61-67**).
- Avoid hose collapse through use of enough slack (**FIGURE 61-68**).
- Protect hoses from hot surfaces in the system (**FIGURE 61-69**).
- Simplify hose routing where possible (**FIGURE 61-70**).
- Simplify connections where possible (**FIGURE 61-71**).

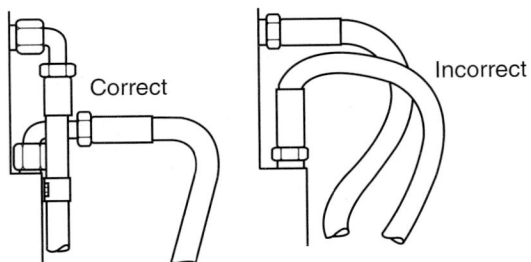

FIGURE 61-66 Example of avoiding tight bends with appropriate fittings.

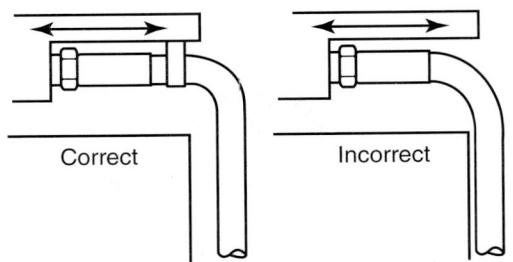

FIGURE 61-67 Example of avoiding abrasion with proper bracketing.

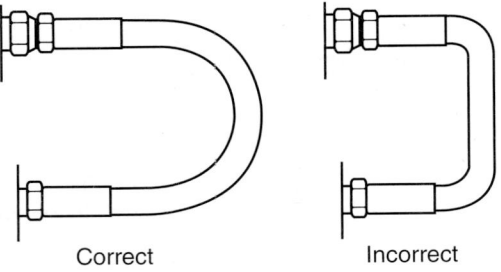

FIGURE 61-68 Example of correct and incorrect slack.

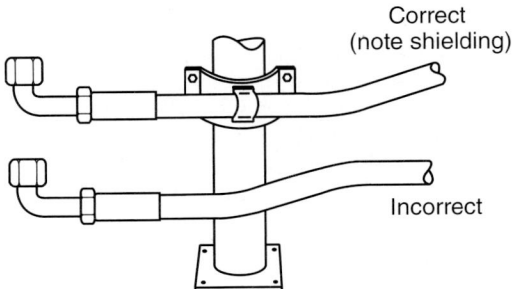

FIGURE 61-69 Example of use of shielding to protect hoses from hot surfaces.

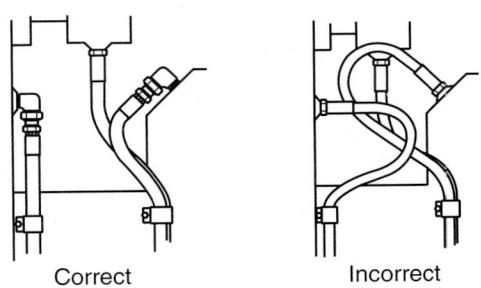

FIGURE 61-70 Example of simplified hose routing.

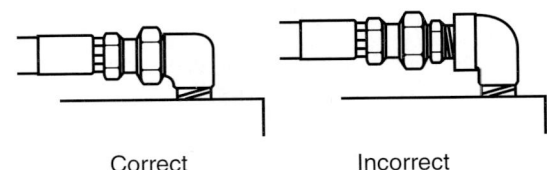

FIGURE 61-71 Example of use of simplified connections.

Hydraulic Actuators

LO 61-8 Identify and describe the types, operation, and construction of hydraulic actuators.

Hydraulic actuators convert the fluid energy back into mechanical energy to perform work. There are two basic types: linear actuators, such as hydraulic cylinders, or rams; and rotary actuators or hydraulic motors. Schematic symbols can represent various types of hydraulic actuators. This section describes the two basic types, their common identifying symbols, their functions and applications, and identifies the parts of each type of actuator. **FIGURE 61-72** shows the actuator symbols used in hydraulic circuit diagrams. Note that the symbols for hydraulic motors do not distinguish between piston, vane, and gear motors.

Linear Actuators (Hydraulic Cylinders)

Hydraulic cylinders are used in steering systems, plow blade lift and angle mechanism, and hoist cylinders for dump trucks. Cylinders can be used to provide either angular or linear motion. When cylinders are used for angular motion, they are **trunnion-mounted**, which is an articulating or swivel joint that allows a cylinder to move at one or two anchor points. Being arranged like this enables the cylinder to move in an arc. An example of an application of trunnion connected angular motion is a cylinder that extends the tailgate of a refuse truck (**FIGURE 61-73**).

Cylinders used for linear motion are mounted rigidly so that they cannot move from their original alignment. All motion resulting from their extension or retraction is linear and along the centerline of the cylinder. Hydraulic rams are **linear** actuators. They supply force to produce either linear or angular motion (**FIGURE 61-74**). They come in various types: single-acting and telescoping cylinders, and double-acting cylinders.

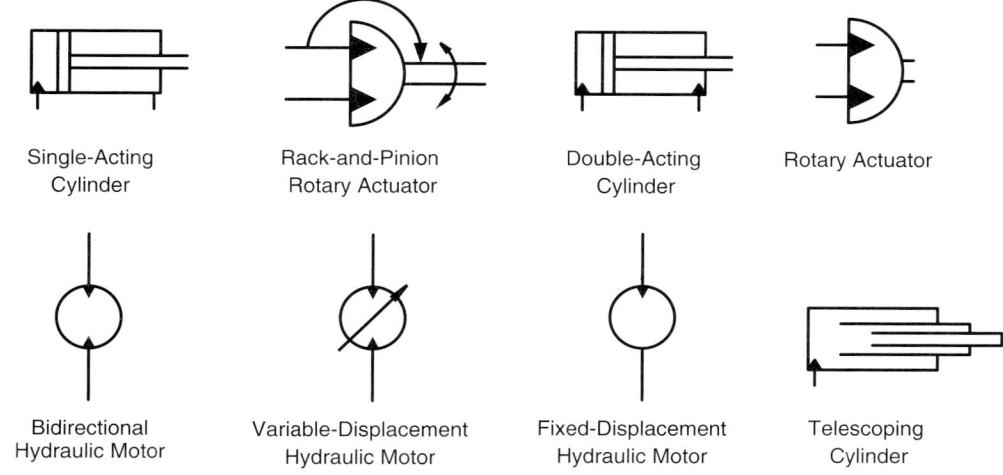

Single-Acting
Cylinder

Rack-and-Pinion
Rotary Actuator

Double-Acting
Cylinder

Rotary Actuator

Bidirectional
Hydraulic Motor

Variable-Displacement
Hydraulic Motor

Fixed-Displacement
Hydraulic Motor

Telescoping
Cylinder

FIGURE 61-72 Symbols for common types of hydraulic actuators.

FIGURE 61-73 The lift cylinder on this dump box has two trunnion joints.

FIGURE 61-74 The two outriggers on each side of this mobile crane are designed to stabilize a truck chassis and are a type of double-acting linear actuator.

Construction of Hydraulic Actuators

The construction of single- and double-acting cylinders is similar, but they operate differently. In the single-acting cylinder, fluid power applies in only one direction and relies on the weight of the load to return it to the original position. In the double-acting cylinder, fluid power is provided in both directions and retraction is not load-dependent.

Both types of cylinder are constructed in a similar way. That is, each has a housing that enables mounting to a secure location, fixing it at one end. The **housing** has a **bore** inside it within which a piston can move. Connected to the piston is a **rod** that moves with the piston, thereby providing linear movement to anything that is attached.

Single-acting cylinders have a **vent** at one end to allow the cylinder to remain at atmospheric pressure on that side of the cylinder, whereas the double-acting cylinder has hydraulic fluid

at each side of the piston. The parts of a single-acting cylinder are shown in **FIGURE 61-75** and the parts of a double-acting cylinder in **FIGURE 61-76**.

Single-Acting and Telescoping Cylinders

In a single-acting cylinder, the oil flows into only one side of the cylinder, normally to extend the cylinder, and can be retracted by oil flow. Cylinders are returned to their original positions by either the load or a spring (**FIGURE 61-77**).

Telescoping cylinders are most frequently single-acting cylinders that have two or more sections that are extended sequentially from largest to smallest diameter (**FIGURE 61-78**). The most familiar applications using single-acting telescoping cylinders is the dump box hoist (**FIGURE 61-79**).

Double-Acting Cylinders

Double-acting cylinders have two oil **ports**. Oil flows into one port to extend the cylinder, and oil flows into the other port to retract the cylinder (**FIGURE 61-80**). An example of an application of a double-acting cylinder is the packer-ejector in a garbage truck.

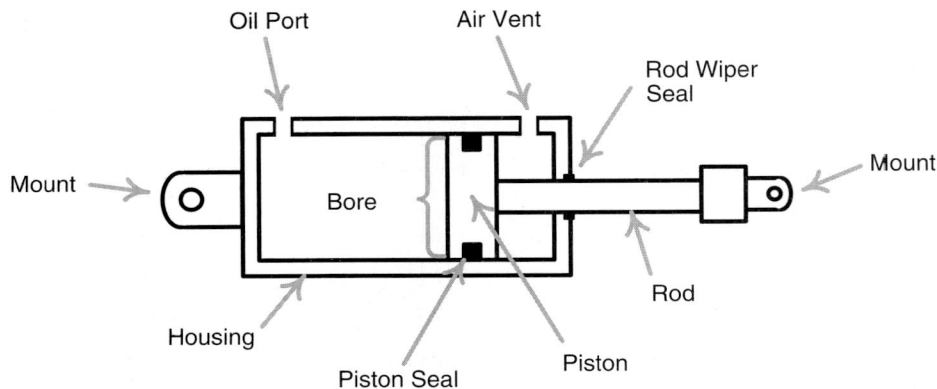

FIGURE 61-75 Single-acting cylinder construction.

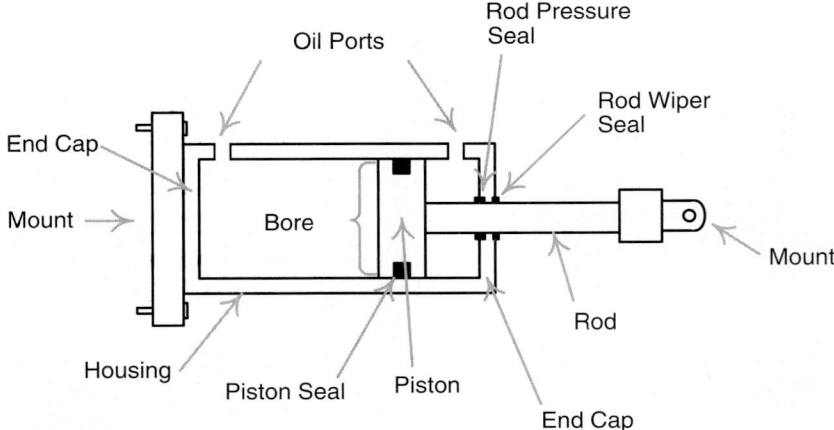

FIGURE 61-76 Double-acting cylinder construction.

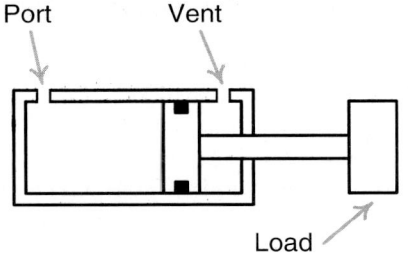

FIGURE 61-77 Example of a single-acting hydraulic cylinder.

FIGURE 61-78 Example of a telescoping cylinder for a dump truck.

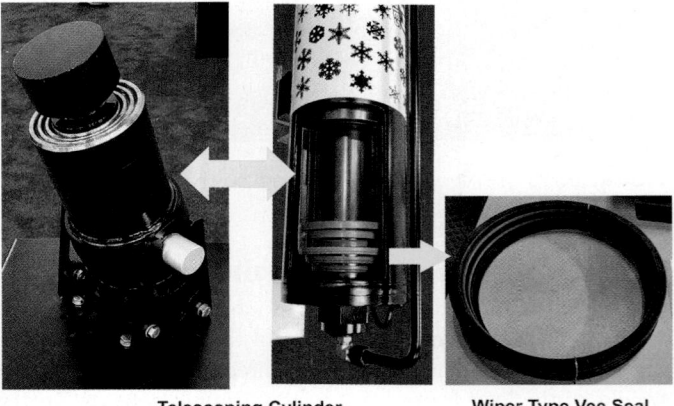

Telescoping Cylinder   Wiper Type Vee Seal

FIGURE 61-79 A cross-sectional view of a compact telescoping cylinder and cylinder seals.

Rotary Actuators

Typically, hydraulic motors provide continuous rotary motion, whereas rotary actuators may only provide a limited rotation, usually up to a maximum of 360 degrees. Rotary motion provides speed and torque as the force output to perform work (**FIGURE 61-81**). An example of an application of a rotary motor actuator is a winch that draws a metal cable.

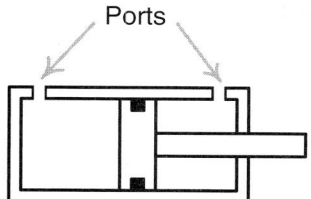

FIGURE 61-80 Example of a double-acting cylinder.

FIGURE 61-81 An auger at the rear of this sand and salt spread uses a rotary motor to turn the auger.

Rack-and-Pinion Actuators

Rack-and-pinion actuators convert linear motion to circular motion. They utilize a linear **piston (rack)** with gear **teeth** on its shaft. The rack is driven by oil entering one of the ports at each end of the piston. The **pinion** is a gear attached to the output shaft that is rotated by the movement of the rack. The shaft can be rotated from a few degrees to more than 360 degrees, depending on the stroke of the piston and the number of gear teeth. To increase the output torque capability, two racks may be used to rotate the pinion.

Hydraulic Motors

Hydraulic motors are almost identical to hydraulic pumps in their construction and components (**FIGURE 61-82**). They provide continuous rotation (in excess of 360 degrees), using a fluid power input to provide a mechanical power output. (In contrast, a hydraulic pump uses a mechanical power input to produce a fluid power output.) As with hydraulic pumps, there are many different designs of hydraulic motor in order to best match specific applications. Hydraulic motors are available in fixed- and variable-displacement arrangements and in the following types:

- Gear
- Vane
- Piston

Vane-type rotary actuators (**FIGURE 61-83**) have a construction similar to vane-type pumps. The vane motor is an alternative solution to the external gear actuator when used for high-speed,

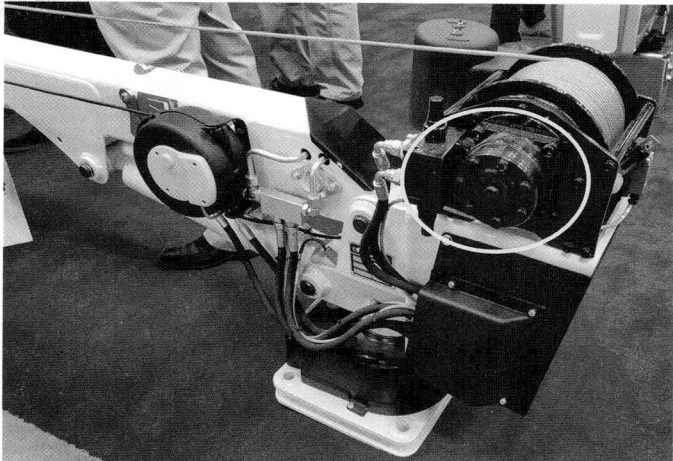

FIGURE 61-82 This hydraulic motor on a service truck operates a cable-type winch.

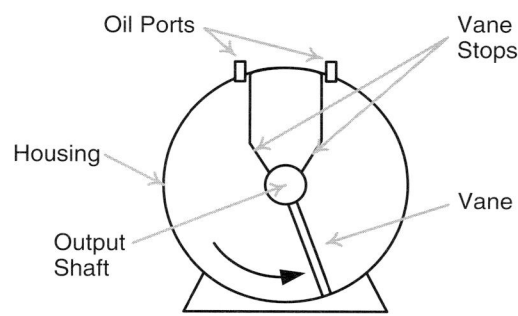

FIGURE 61-83 Vane-type rotary actuator construction.

low-torque applications. Just like a vane pump, it is constructed of vanes that rotate inside a housing, and the center of the motor is connected to an output shaft that turns. Fluid enters the oil port on one side of the motor and leaves from the oil port on the other side.

The rack-and-pinion rotary actuator (**FIGURE 61-84**) has two opposing single-acting linear actuators attached to a common piston rod, or rack. The rack piston has teeth machined into it, which rotate a pinion gear when the pistons move back and forth, according to which end of the piston hydraulic fluid is applied. Rotation can be less or more than 360 degrees.

In a hydraulic motor (**FIGURE 61-85**), the hydraulic fluid enters the inlet port and passes around the gears in the chamber, forcing the gears to turn. It then leaves through the outlet port. The driving gear drives the output shaft via a keyway to drive the item being rotated. The driven gear acts as an idler in this example.

Control Valves

LO 61-9 Identify and describe the types of hydraulic directional control valves.

Directional pressure control valves direct the flow of hydraulic fluid. Operation of directional control valves is observed

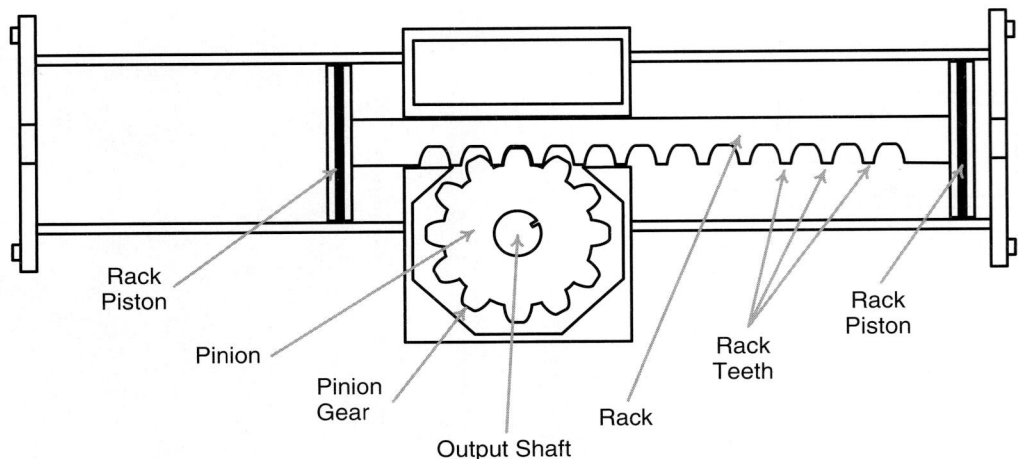

FIGURE 61-84 Rack-and-pinion rotary actuator construction.

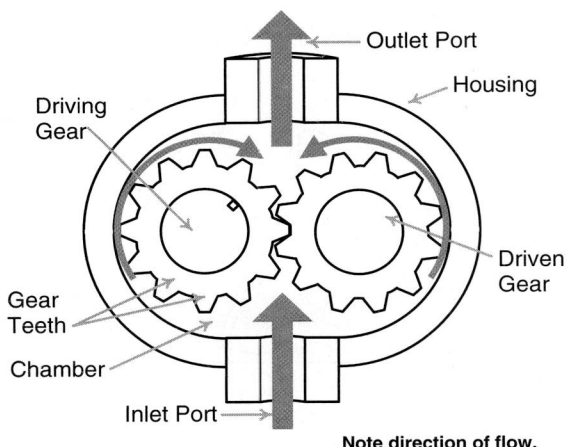

Note direction of flow.

FIGURE 61-85 The parts of a hydraulic motor.

when an operator pulls a valve lever to extend a linear actuator (hydraulic cylinder). It is a directional control valve that is connected to the operator's lever that redirects fluid flow. This valve controls the oil flow to and away from the actuator. Additional valves can also support the function of control valves to regulate hydraulic pressure, volume, and fluid direction. This support category of valves includes check valves, flow control valves, and pressure relief valves.

Types of Directional Control Valves and Circuits

Before examining the types of direction control valves, it is important to understand two of the most common types of directional control circuits—open and closed center control circuits. These circuits not only describe a type of circuit, but also the construction and operation of directional control valves.

Open Center Control Valves and Circuits

The term open center control describes a type of hydraulic circuit operation and a construction category for a directional

control valve. In an open center system, pump flow is continuous through the control valve, but pressure supplied to output actuators is intermittent. In the valve's neutral or centered position, pump flow has an unrestricted pathway through a center passage in the directional control valve (**FIGURE 61-86**). After flowing through the directional control valve, fluid simply returns to the reservoir tank. If the pump is operating and the valve remains in neutral centered position, the loop of hydraulic flow is continuous. If the shape of the control valve is constructed using a spool valve, whenever the valve is moved from its neutral center, flow is redirected toward an actuator (**FIGURE 61-87**). Hydraulic flow-pressure redirected by the valve creates force, which in turn moves a load. Moving the valve back to its neutral position reestablishes the pump to control valve to return circuit flow. Open center valves are often used on dump trucks, refuse vehicles, tow trucks, and most other commercial vehicle applications.

Closed Center Control Valves and Circuits

The term closed center control describes a type of hydraulic circuit and a construction category for a directional control valve. In a closed center system, flow is intermittent, but pressure is continuous. If the hydraulic pump is operating, very little flow is allowed, and the pump operates to maintain only a small stand-by pressure at the directional control valve center port (**FIGURE 61-88**). Unlike the open center valve, the center is closed or blocks fluid flow through the closed center valve. The standby pressure is necessary to maintain some internal pump lubrication. If the control valve is moved from its center neutral position, a fluid pathway opens, and pump flow is directed to an output actuator (**FIGURE 61-89**). These systems commonly use a variable displacement-type pump that senses the change in pressure or flow or both pressure and flow to increase pump output. Closed center valves are typically used in on-demand-only hydraulic systems for plow and utility trucks with buckets and boom using electrically driven hydraulic motors or with variable displacement engine-driven piston pumps.

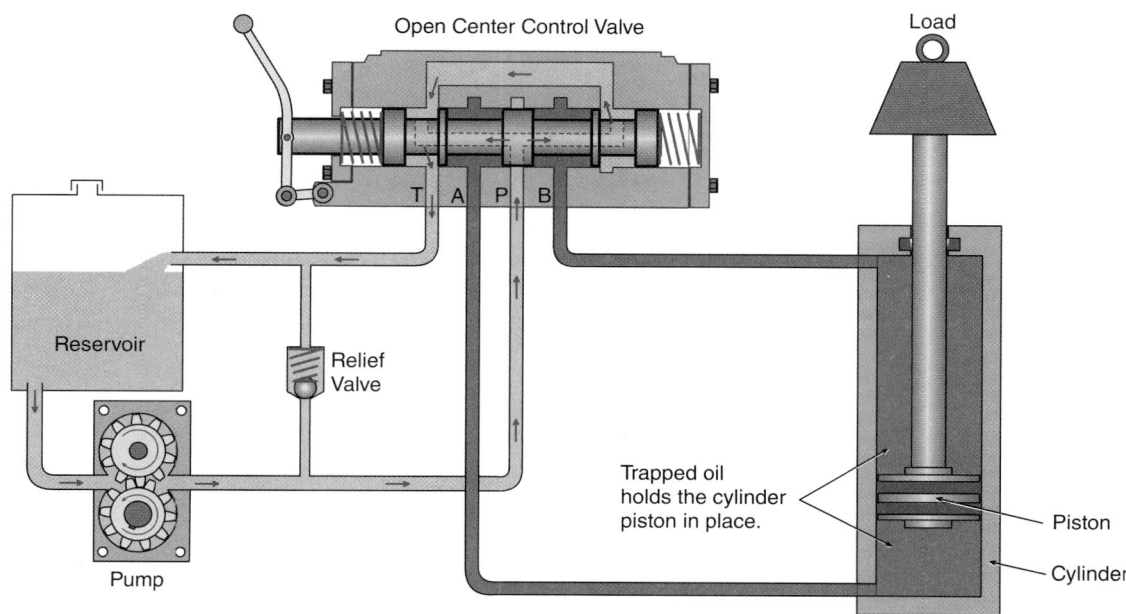

FIGURE 61-86 A 4/2 open-center directional-control valve in the centered position. Oil circulates from the pump (P-port) through the valve and back to the reservoir tank (T-port). It has four connections to it and two valve positions. A and B ports are switching positions or utilization ports.

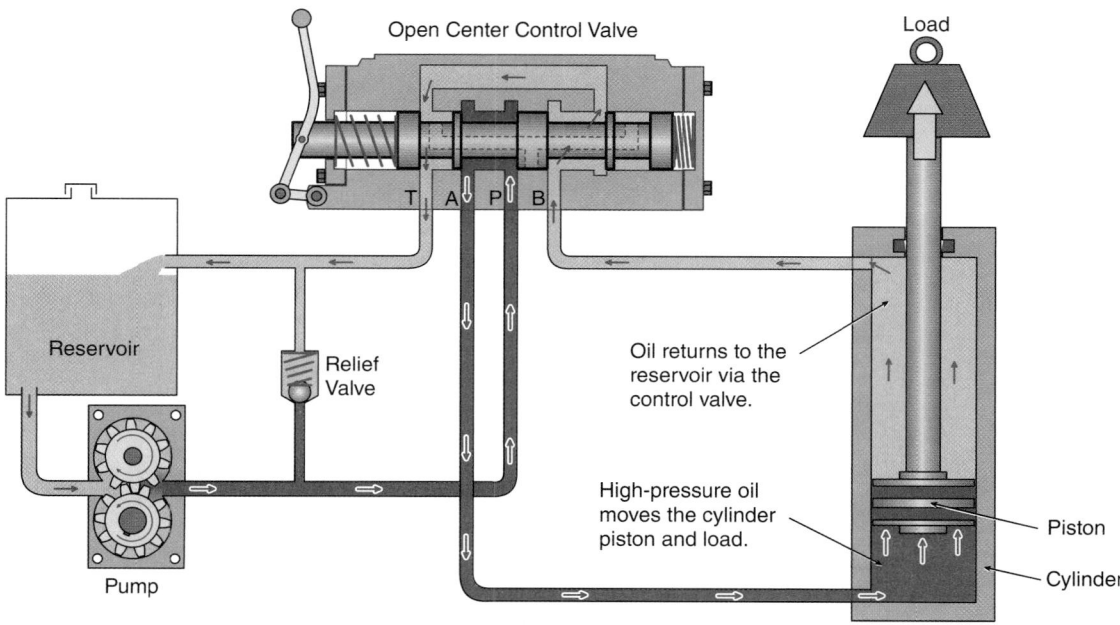

FIGURE 61-87 A 4/2 open-center directional-control valve switched to the A position to raise a double-acting cylinder.

Construction of Directional Control Valves

A directional control valve function is to direct hydraulic oil flow within the circuit. There are four directional control valve mechanism types:

1. **Spool-type**: Spools are by far the most common directional control valve mechanism for hydraulic applications.
2. **Sliding plate**: The sliding-plate mechanism opens and closes ports using a sliding plate that allows or prevents flow. They are normally designed to provide for multiple directional

operation of hydraulic equipment. For example, in a fork lift truck operation, it may be desirable to lift, tilt, and otherwise control the load all at the same time.
3. **Rotating plate**: The rotating-plate mechanism varies hydraulic fluid flow by rotating a plate to change the size of an open or closed port.
4. **Cartridge**: The cartridge mechanism is like an electric-over-hydraulic relay that normally consists of a solenoid-operated valve that allows or blocks flow, depending on the valve's activation or non-activation by an electric current.

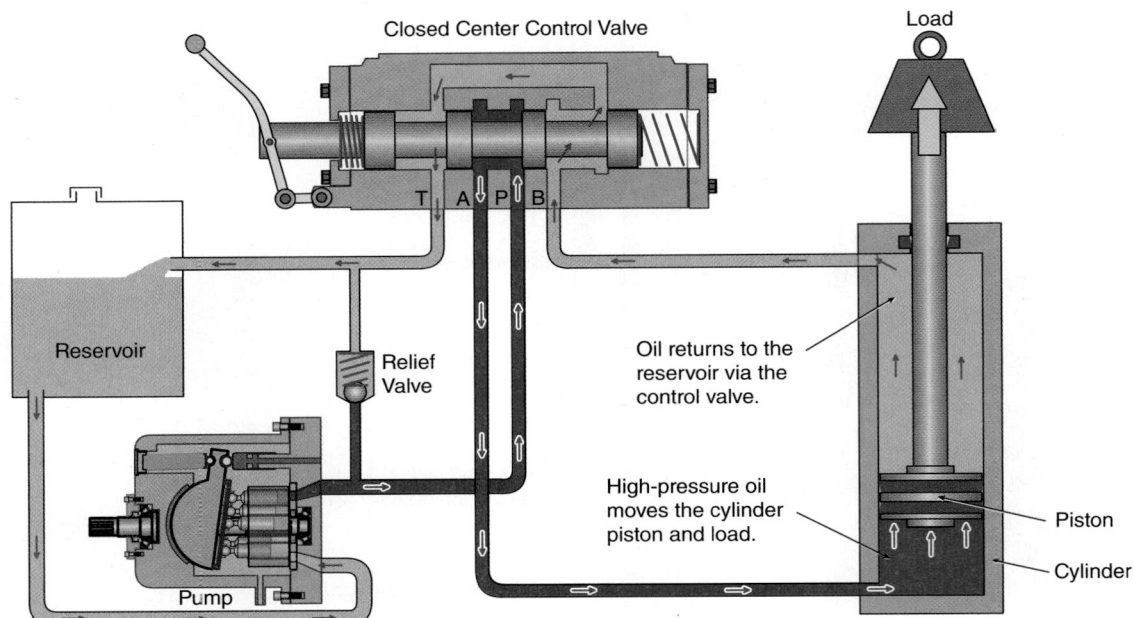

FIGURE 61-88 A four port two position (4/2) closed-center directional-control valve switched to the A position to raise a double-acting cylinder T port is for tank. P is for pressure. Utility ports are A an B.

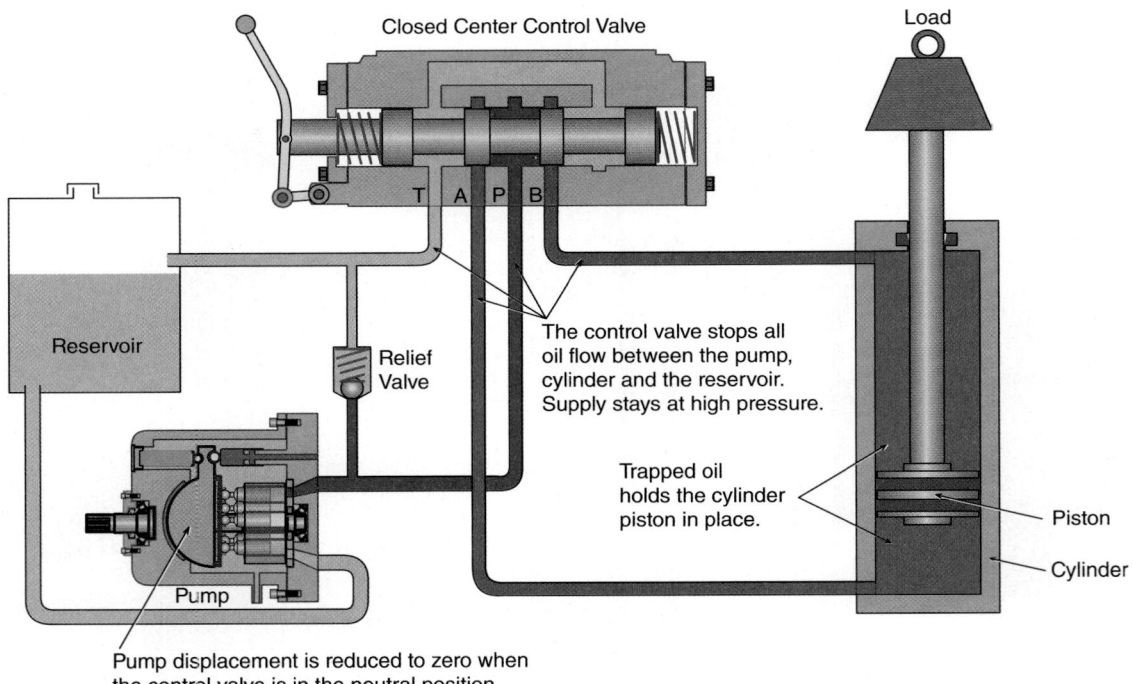

FIGURE 61-89 A 4/2 closed-center directional-control valve in a neutral or unswitched position blocking the pressure or P-port.

It is not always necessary for an operator to manipulate a control valve to change the direction of fluid flow. The most common actuators are (**FIGURE 61-90**):

- **Manual**: A hand-operated lever is used to mechanically move a spool into position.
- **Solenoid**: The **plunger** in an electrical **solenoid** is used to push the valve spool into position (**FIGURE 61-91**).

- **Proportional Solenoid**: The plunger in an electronically positioned solenoid is used to push the spool to a position determined by the level of current supplied to the solenoid.
- **Servo**: The valve spool is positioned electronically through a microcontroller-operated **servo** mechanism using external position sensors to provide **feedback** circuits to accurately position actuators.

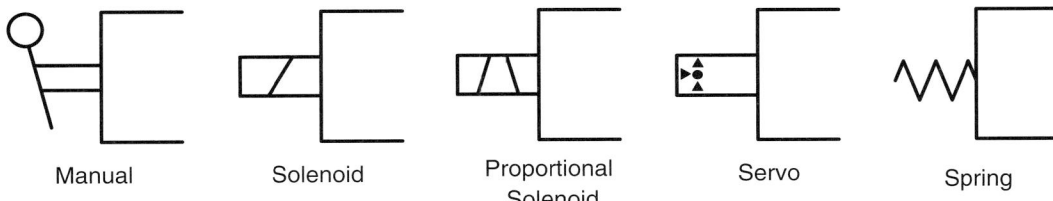

FIGURE 61-90 Symbols used for common directional valve actuators.

FIGURE 61-91 The control valve body for a semi-automated snowplow truck with platooning capabilities.

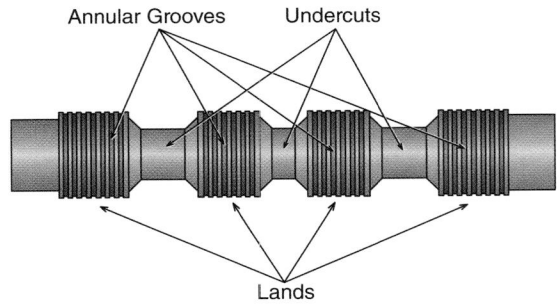

FIGURE 61-92 Annular grooves, lands, and undercuts on a spool.

Spool-Type Directional Control Valves

The spool-type directional control valve normally consists of a cylindrical steel shaft with two or more cutouts machined into it. This can make the shaft resemble a bobbin or spool used for storing yarn—hence the origin of the term "spool" for this type of valve. A spool-type directional control valve has a sliding spool that moves within a bore in the valve to cover and uncover flow paths in the valve. The raised parts of the spool (the parts with the larger diameters) are called **lands**. The lands block internal flow paths. The lands have annular grooves cut into them; fluid collects in these grooves to create viscous seals to prevent leakage across the land. The narrower parts of the spool (the sections with smaller diameters) are called **undercuts**. These provide the flow paths between the valve ports (**FIGURE 61-92**).

One way that valves are classified is according to the number and function of ports. A P port indicates pressure, T port is return to tank, and two, three, and four output or switched

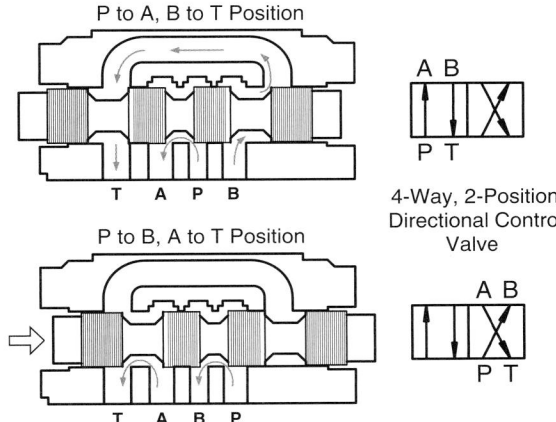

FIGURE 61-93 Example of a four port two-position valve (4/2). T port is for tank. P is for pressure. Utility ports are A an B.

utility ports designated A, B ,C or D are typically connected to actuators and are most common on commercial vehicles.

Depending on the spool design, a directional control valve may have two or three functional positions, which are discussed in the following sections.

Two-Position Directional Control Valves

A two-position valve has two functional positions that control the direction of operation of an actuator. The two positions are extend and retract for a cylinder; and forward and reverse for a hydraulic motor (**FIGURE 61-93**).

With a two-position valve, the actuator cannot be stopped and held except at the ends of its **stroke**.

Three-Position Directional Control Valves

A three-position valve spool incorporates a third functional position that allows for additional functional operations when the spool is placed in its center position. Three-position valves normally have a spring on each end of the spool to return it to its center neutral position when the valve is not actuated. There are four common center positions:

1. **Closed center**: In the closed-center position, all four ports are blocked in a neutral centered position (**FIGURE 61-94**).
2. **Open center**: In the open-center position, all four ports are connected (**FIGURE 61-95**).
3. **Tandem center**: In the tandem-center position, the two actuator ports are blocked, and the pressure and tank ports are connected (**FIGURE 61-96**).
4. **Float (or motor) center**: In the float-center position, the pressure port is blocked, and the rest of the ports are connected (**FIGURE 61-97**).

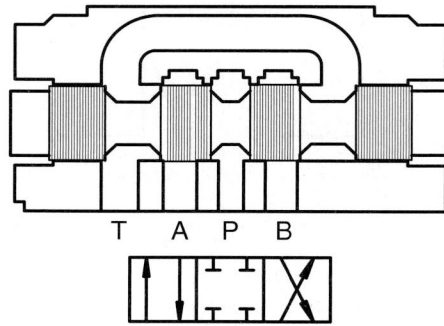

FIGURE 61-94 Example of a four port three-position valve (4/3) in the closed-center position.

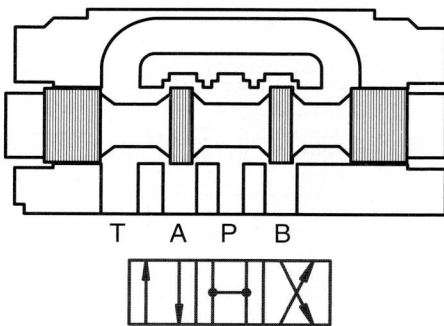

FIGURE 61-95 Example of a four port three-position valve (4/3) in the open-center position.

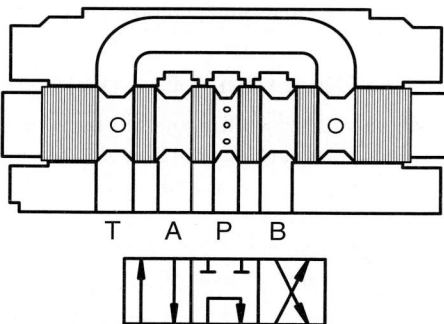

FIGURE 61-96 Example of a four port three-position valve (4/3) in the tandem-center position.

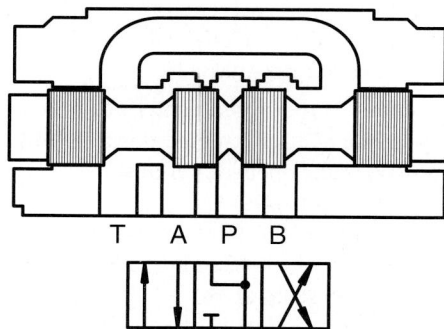

FIGURE 61-97 Example of a four port three-position valve (4/3) in the float-center position.

▶ **TECHNICIAN TIP**

Servo valves are extremely sensitive to contaminated fluid. Valve problems in these systems are often associated with contaminated fluid.

Pressure-Relief Valves

LO 61-10 Identify and describe the types of pressure-relief valves.

Relief valves are pressure-limiting devices used to protect hydraulic systems and their components from over pressurization. A relief valve is calibrated to remain closed until a designed or adjusted pressure setting is reached. If the pressure applied to the valve exceeds this threshold, the valve opens and typically redirects fluid back to the reservoir. If there is no place for fluid to travel from a pump output, the excessive hydraulic pressure and the heat it creates could damage the pump or other components, such as hoses. Excessive input torque from a prime mover against a dead-headed pump (a pump with no outlet flow) could also tear a pump apart. Pressure relief is available in several configurations to meet the hydraulic circuit's requirements. For example, a relief valve that regulates the whole system pressure operates at a higher maximum relief pressure than one that is intended to protect a hydraulic cylinder from intermittent shock loads or over pressurization from excessive loads. There are two types of pressure-relief valves: direct-acting and pilot-operated.

Pressure Control Valves

The main types of pressure control valves are:

- **Pressure-relief valves**: Pressure-relief valves determine or limit the maximum operating pressure in the system and provide a safety valve to prevent system over-pressurization.
- **Unloading valves**: Unloading valves are remotely piloted (signaled by another hydraulic circuit) valves that unload the pump so that it operates at only low flow-pressure when specific pressure conditions are met in the system.
- **Sequencing valves**: Sequencing valves are remotely piloted valves that are used to control the sequence, or order, of operation of actuators in the system.
- **Pressure-reducing valves**: Pressure-reducing valves limit the maximum pressure that can occur in a portion or branch of a system (unlike the pressure-relief valve, which controls the entire system).
- **Brake valves**: Brake valves provide back pressure to limit speed on a hydraulic motor operating an over-running load (such as a piece of earth-moving equipment going downhill).
- **Counterbalance valves**: Counterbalance valves provide a back pressure to hold a vertical load in place until certain pressure requirements are met.

Check Valves

Check valves are used to block fluid flow in one direction but allow flow in the opposite direction (**FIGURE 61-98**). They typically consist of a spring-loaded ball that sits on a seat in the valve and is retained by a spring retainer. Flow that hits from the

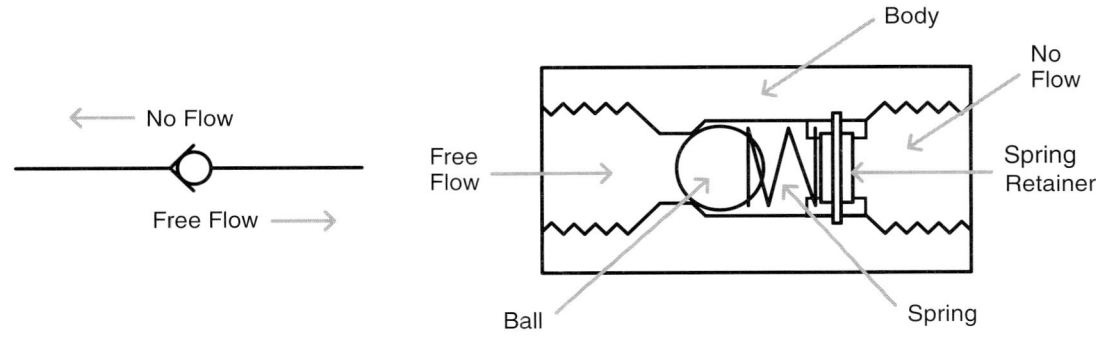

FIGURE 61-98 Example of a check valve.

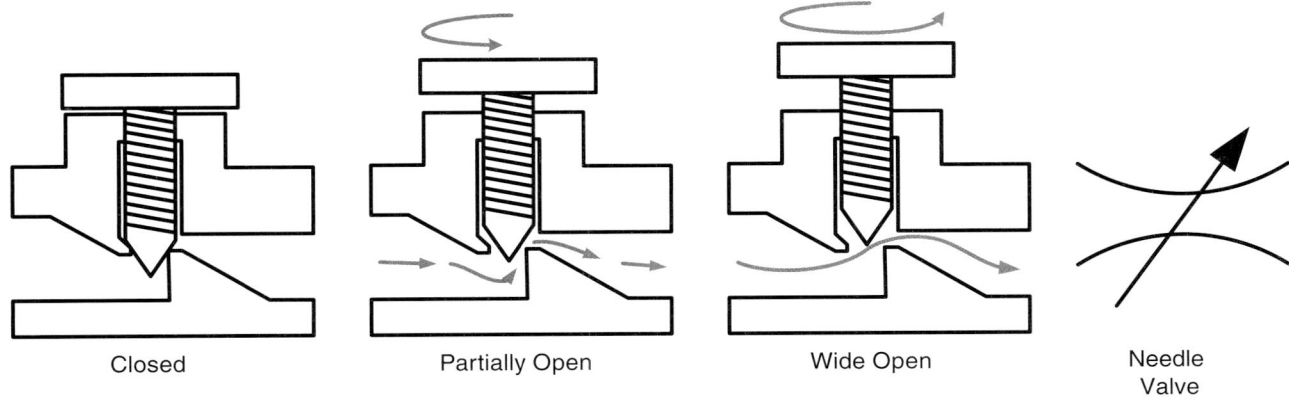

FIGURE 61-99 Example of needle valve positions.

upper, or ball, end forces the ball against the spring and allows flow. Flow coming from the opposite end forces the ball onto the seat and, therefore, prevents flow.

Flow Control Valves

Needle valves are the most common type of flow control valve. They are used to control and maintain the hydraulic fluid at a set and required pressure inside the hydraulic system. Pressure-compensated flow control valves are used when a constant flow needs to be maintained.

Needle Flow Control Valves

Needle valves use a **tapered** screw, which moves within the valve throat to adjust the size of the flow opening and, consequently, the flow rate through the valve. The head of the valve is normally designed with an adjusting knob or screw. The flow through the valve is dependent on the pressure drop across the valve (inlet pressure minus the outlet pressure) (**FIGURE 61-99**).

> ▶ **TECHNICIAN TIP**
>
> Most flow control valves are needle valves.

Hydraulic Accumulators

LO 61-11 Identify and describe the types, operation, and construction of hydraulic accumulators.

A **hydraulic accumulator** stores hydraulic energy. It performs several functions, which often involve supplementing

pump flow whenever the pump cannot meet system demands (**FIGURE 61-100**). Accumulator functions include the following:

- Acting as an emergency power source in the event of pump or engine failure
- Providing a pressure source to hold loads in place if the pump is shut down
- Providing additional energy during peak load demand and recharging during low-demand periods, just like a battery and alternator in a car
- Dampening pressure and flow pulsations created by actuators or pumps
- Providing fluid flow to supplement the pump output in order to increase actuator speed
- Acting as a shock absorber for an actuator (an accumulator can operate faster than a relief valve)

Two common types of accumulators include:

- Gas charged
- Spring charged

Gas-Charged Accumulators

In the case of a gas-charged accumulator, hydraulic fluid enters an accumulator housing cavity surrounding a gas-filled bladder. As fluid enters the cavity, gas is compressed by pressurized fluid. If the system pressure falls due to a system failure, then the pressure in the bladder that's charged at higher pressure

FIGURE 61-100 Examples of hydraulic accumulators.

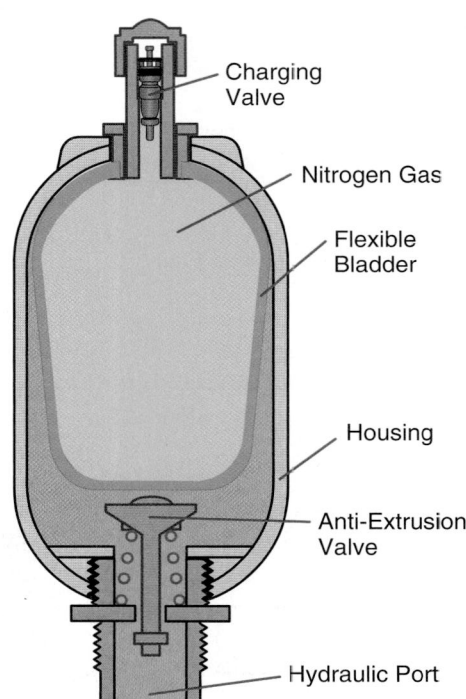

FIGURE 61-101 Example of a bladder-type gas-charged accumulator.

Charging Valve

Nitrogen Gas

Flexible Bladder

Housing

Anti-Extrusion Valve

Hydraulic Port

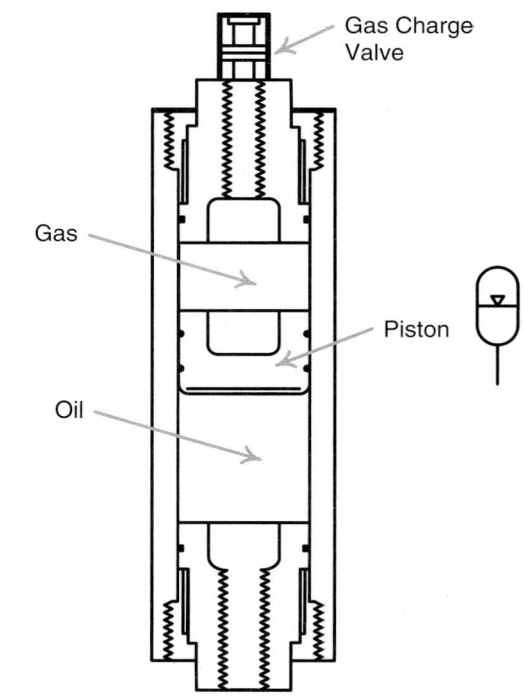

FIGURE 61-102 Example of a piston-type gas-charged accumulator.

Gas Charge Valve

Gas

Piston

Oil

than the failed system pushes fluid into the main hydraulic system (**FIGURE 61-101**). The accumulator can only store a small amount of fluid, which means it cannot operate for more than a few seconds at most.

Oxygen, or air, is not suitable for use in gas-charged accumulators, since these gases will ignite and explode when contacting pressurized petroleum based hydraulic fluids. Nitrogen which is almost inert is commonly used instead. Gas-charged accumulators are used in a variety of applications, including chassis hydraulic braking systems.

Another common type of gas accumulator is a piston-type. This operates in the same way as a gas bladder except a gas is stored and pressurized behind a piston rather than a bladder. A piston-type gas-charged accumulator is recognized by its cylindrical-shaped body with a piston separating the fluid and the gas (**FIGURE 61-102**).

SAFETY TIP

Never use oxygen or air to charge accumulators! Nitrogen is the most common gas used to charge an accumulator. Using oxygen or air could result in an explosion if it comes into contact with the petroleum-based hydraulic fluid.

Spring-Loaded Accumulators

A spring-loaded accumulator has a cylindrical body with a piston to separate the fluid and the mechanical energy force. A strong spring provides the force on the piston to expel the fluid from the accumulator (**FIGURES 61-103** and **61-104**). Using a spring reduces the physical size of the accumulator assembly. This kind of accumulator cannot supply a constant pressure,

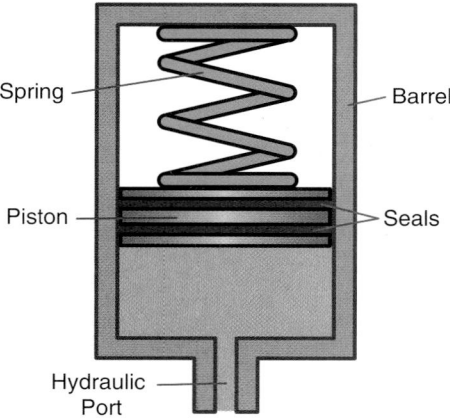

FIGURE 61-103 Example of a spring-loaded accumulator.

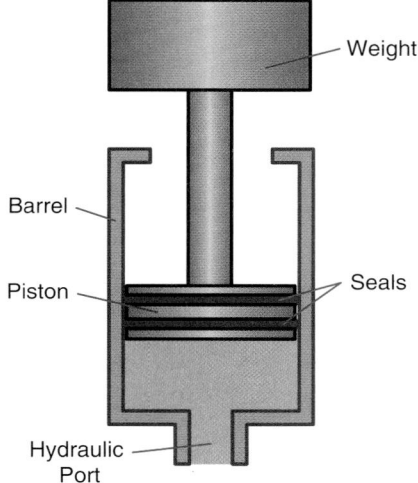

FIGURE 61-104 Example of a weight-loaded accumulator.

nor can it use all the fluid from the accumulator because there needs to be some fluid in the accumulator to enable it to provide pressure to the system.

Hydraulic System Preventative Maintenance

LO 61-12 Outline common preventative maintenance and inspection practices for hydraulic systems.

As with every heavy-duty vehicle system, preventative maintenance is critical for the hydraulic systems and accessories on a vehicle. There are important benefits to regular preventative maintenance of hydraulics systems, including:

- It prolongs the life of the system.
- It reduces system down-time.
- It reduces or eliminates preventable failures.
- It reduces operational costs.
- It reduces repair costs.
- It reduces lost productivity.

Although regular preventative maintenance may initially increase down-time, it prevents longer, more expensive repairs in the future. Ideally, preventative maintenance should be performed when equipment is not scheduled to be in use.

Common Failure Modes

There are several common factors that can damage a hydraulic system. These include:

- Excessive speed
- Excessive heat
- Excessive pressure
- Contamination
- Cavitation

Excessive speed, heat, and pressure can result from operator error. Often, however, they are the result of initial damage caused by contamination. Contaminated fluid is the most common source of hydraulic system damage. In most environments, it is readily preventable with regular maintenance.

Pump Cavitation

Pump cavitation is a unique failure in hydraulic systems. **Cavitation** is the formation of gas bubbles at the inlet of the pump due to low inlet pressure. The fluid can boil and create gas bubbles, which forcefully implode with high energy. The result is metal erosion at the pump inlet. Restricted filters, poor quality fluids, or system designs contribute to cavitation failures (**FIGURE 61-105**). Cavitation describes the collapse bubbles in the pump, which creates a distinctive loud popping noise.

Causes of Pump Cavitation

Cavitation erosion results from a restriction in the pump suction line, allowing a negative pressure to form in the line. A clogged suction filter, a kinked or collapsed suction line, or a suction line that is too small or too long, and even a clogged reservoir breather can contribute to a negative pressure at the pump inlet.

Fluid **aeration** is different from cavitation because it is caused by outside air entering the fluid. Aeration is commonly caused by a low fluid level, leaking fittings in the suction line,

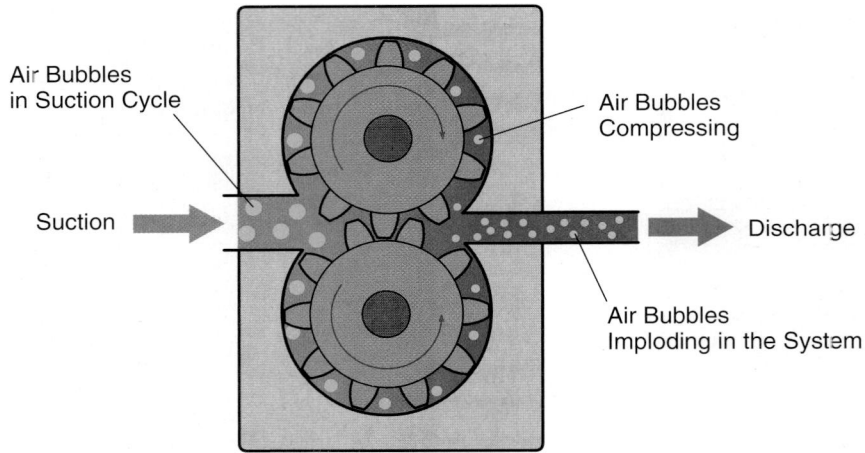

FIGURE 61-105 Example of pump cavitation.

or leaking seals somewhere in the system, allowing air to enter. When new components are installed, air can also enter the system if large cavities are not filled with oil during installation. Fluid aeration is evidenced by excessive foam present in the fluid reservoir.

Effects of Pump Cavitation

It is important to inspect hydraulic pumps for cavitation because the effects can damage the entire hydraulic system. Some of the effects of pump cavitation include:

- Excessive pump noise
- Excessive pump wear due to bubbles and cavities imploding and damaging the pump components
- System contamination due to debris from pump component damage

Common Causes of Pump Failure

Pump inspections and installation and maintenance procedures should be followed carefully to avoid some of the common causes of pump failure. These include:

- Contaminated fluid (the most common cause of pump failure)
- Cavitation
- Incorrect fluid
- Running dry
- Shearing shafts due to excessive system pressure causing pump mechanism to stall
- Clogged or kinked case drain lines
- Abuse and incorrect operating procedures (examples: excessive pressures or speeds)

▶ TECHNICIAN TIP

Contaminated fluid is the most common cause of pump failure.

These problems can all be avoided by regular inspection and maintenance following OEM recommendations and operating within the system's designed capacity.

Common Problems Encountered During Inspections

Typical problems that may be identified when carrying out a preventative maintenance inspection include:

- Not enough hydraulic fluid in the reservoir, which can cause the system to run erratically
- Clogged or dirty oil filters, which can reduce system life
- A loose suction-inlet line, which can aerate fluid and result in a loss of system pressure
- Contaminated or incorrect fluid in the system
- Leaks in components, hoses, or lines, which can be caused by loose lines

To identify these and other problems, it is helpful to create and use an inspection checklist and record inspection observations in a log.

Scheduling Preventative Maintenance

Manufacturers provide inspection and maintenance schedules as part of the customer support. There are several items that form the basis for scheduling preventative maintenance:

- The age of the equipment
- The frequency of use
- The intensity of use

There are also several predictable conditions affecting maintenance scheduling, such as entering or leaving storage and seasonal peak-use patterns.

▶ TECHNICIAN TIP

The more frequently equipment is used, the more often it should be inspected. Also adjust system maintenance schedules to account for environmental conditions in which the equipment operates. Exceed or reduce the manufacturer's recommendations for inspection schedules only if the operating conditions justify changing the schedule.

Unusual conditions that can affect maintenance scheduling include:

- Weather fluctuations, such as an unseasonably late snowstorm
- Temperature extremes, such as 115° F (46° C) heat in a normally temperate zone
- Unusual working environments, such as desert (high heat and dust) or rain forest (prolonged heat and excessive humidity)

Preventative Maintenance Best Practices

A number of best practices should be followed when undertaking preventative maintenance procedures. Best practices vary, depending on the type of equipment. The following is not an exhaustive list but provides some general guidelines:

- Conduct daily visual and operational inspections.
- Maintain a daily inspection log.
- Conduct routine fluid analyses.

Know and follow the manufacturer's maintenance recommendations, including:

- Fluid and filter types
- Fluid cleanliness recommendations
- Fluid and filter replacement indicators (housing pressure gauges) or schedules
- Normal system operating conditions
- Schedule routine maintenance before it becomes urgent.
- Schedule routine maintenance when equipment is normally off-line, whenever possible.
- Anticipate replacement of system components based on their expected life and use patterns.

▶ TECHNICIAN TIP

Replacement of aging and worn parts before they fail minimizes the possibility of consequential damage to other system components.

Performing Preventative Maintenance

At a minimum, the following steps should be accomplished during a routine preventative maintenance inspection:

- Clean the exteriors of system components, hoses, and lines before beginning a preventative maintenance inspection in order to detect leaks and to check for wear.
- Check the fluid level before starting the system. Note: A low fluid level may indicate system leaks. Inspect for leaks by checking the equipment and the floor around it for leaked fluid. Note: Leak inspection should be done both with the system operating, and with the system shut down.
- Inspect hoses, lines, and system components for visible wear.
- Check outputs for proper system operation, including pressure and temperature gauges.
- Check for normal actuator functionality.
- Listen for unusual sounds.
- Look and feel for unusual vibrations.
- Replace fluid and filters according to the manufacturer's recommendations.

▶ TECHNICIAN TIP

Replacing fluid can be a very costly and time-consuming procedure. Fluid should be changed only if it has had its chemical structure damaged to the point that it cannot be returned to its original condition. Fluid that is simply dirty can usually be filtered to return it to a usable state. Moisture can be removed by evacuating the reservoir with a vacuum pump, which causes moisture to boil out of fluid. Fluid samples taken before scheduled preventative maintenance provide the information needed to make this decision.

Changing Hydraulic Fluid and Filters

To change hydraulic fluid, follow the guidelines in **SKILL DRILL 61-2**. To change a hydraulic filter, follow the guidelines in **SKILL DRILL 61-3**.

SKILL DRILL 61-2 Changing Hydraulic Fluid

1. Assemble the following tools and materials:
   - Appropriate tool to fit hydraulic reservoir drain plug
   - Clean, lint-free shop towels
   - Hydraulic fluid specified by the manufacturer
   - Safety glasses or goggles
   - Gloves
2. Put on safety glasses or goggles, and gloves.
3. Operate the directional control valve levers to release system pressure and retract all cylinders.
4. Slowly open the reservoir filler cap to relieve pressure on the reservoir.
5. Drain the hydraulic fluid by removing the drain plug in the reservoir.
6. Open the inspection plate on the reservoir.
7. Remove any dirt and foreign material that has settled to the bottom of the reservoir.
8. Replace the inspection plate and drain plug.

SKILL DRILL 61-2 Changing Hydraulic Fluid (Continued)

9. Remove, clean, and replace the inlet screen, if present.
Note: If the filter needs changing, change it after this step (see Skill Drill 54-2).

10. Fill the reservoir to the fill line with clean hydraulic fluid.

11. Bleed the system, if necessary.

12. Operate the system and check for leaks.

13. Check the fluid level to ensure it is still within specifications.

14. Clean the work area and return tools and materials to their proper storage.

SKILL DRILL 61-3 Changing a Hydraulic Filter

1. Assemble the following tools and materials:
- Wrench for removing filter
- Clean, lint-free shop towels
- Appropriate new filter
- Safety glasses or goggles
- Gloves

2. Put on safety glasses or goggles, and gloves.

3. With the system shut down, operate the directional control valve levers and place all actuators in a resting position to relieve system pressure.

4. Clean the area around the filter.

5. Remove the old filter.

6. Clean the filter housing (if it is a cartridge-type filter).

7. Install a new filter and tighten to the manufacturer's specifications.

8. Operate the system and check for leaks.

9. Clean the work area, and return tools and materials to their proper storage

▶ TECHNICIAN TIP

Filters should be changed only when they have reached the terminal pressure drop recommended by the manufacturer. Pressure drop indicators, restriction guages or other devices on the filter housing, should be used to make this decision.

▶ TECHNICIAN TIP

Follow shop guidelines and of environmental regulation directions about proper disposition of filter media and used hydraulic fluid. In some regions, filters are considered hazardous waste and cannot be disposed of in landfills.

Wrap-Up

Ready for Review

▶ The fundamental operating concept of all hydraulic applications is the use of fluid to transmit power. One of the main advantages of hydraulic systems is that they can be designed to lift very heavy objects through the use of mechanical advantage and by using the fluid as the transfer medium.

▶ Hydraulic systems fall into two basic types: open loop and closed loop. In an open-loop system, fluid flows from a reservoir to the pump, through the system, and back to the reservoir, where it is directed to the pump again. In a closed-loop hydraulic system, no reservoir is used. Fluid circulates from the pump, through the system, and directly back to the pump.

- Vital functions of hydraulic fluid include: transmitting energy, lubricating components, preventing rust and corrosion, sealing clearances, carrying solid contaminants to filters, and providing electrical insulation for certain applications. These capabilities make hydraulic fluid one of the most important components of any hydraulic system.
- Pascal's law states that "pressure applied to a fluid in one part of a closed system will be transmitted without loss to all other areas of the system." This means that pressure applied to a fluid in one part of a closed system is transmitted equally to all other areas of the system.
- The main differences between pipe and tubing are their construction materials and applications. Piping is intended for industrial applications requiring long, straight runs, and is not normally bent or shaped, other than in smooth turns. Tubing is designed to be bent and shaped to accommodate the installation on the machine.
- Never use galvanized pipe or fittings for hydraulic system applications. The coating can react with the hydraulic fluid and come off the pipe walls and fittings, causing contamination and damaging components.
- The Bernoulli principle describes the behavior of a fluid, gas, or liquid as it flows through a pipe, tube, or hose. Bernoulli stated that if the flow of a fluid remains constant, the pressure or speed of fluid must change for flow volume to remain constant changing one of the two measures (up or down) affects the other oppositely.
- The two measures used for fluid flow are velocity and pressure. When velocity increases, the pressure must drop if the flow is to remain constant. Fluid pressure and speed vary as a hydraulic line narrows or widens.
- The purpose of a hydraulic pump is to provide the system with a constant supply of hydraulic fluid. It does this by producing flow in the system. The fluid flow is used by actuators in the system to perform work.
- Gear pumps consist of a housing, a drive gear (driven by the shaft), a driven gear, and other mechanisms, such as pressure plates.
- A vane pump consists of a rotor containing sliding vanes in slots. The rotor is offset from the centerline of the housing.
- Piston pumps are high-pressure pumps that maintain a constant, regular oil flow. They can operate more efficiently with high and low shaft speeds, can tolerate higher pressures over longer periods, and are generally less noisy than gear pumps.
- Vane pumps and piston pumps (but not gear pumps) can have a variable displacement capability. Variable displacement pumps have a mechanism that allows the displacement to be changed.
- Cavitation is the formation of air or gas bubbles at the inlet of the pump under low pressure when the pump does not completely fill with fluid. The term is also used to describe the collapse of air and gas bubbles in the pump, which erodes metal and creates a distinctive noise.

- Hydraulic actuators convert the fluid energy back into mechanical energy to move the load. They can come in two forms: linear actuators, such as hydraulic cylinders or rams, and rotary actuators or hydraulic motors.
- The main types of pressure control valves are pressure-relief valves, unloading valves, sequencing valves, pressure-reducing valves, brake valves, and counterbalance valves.
- Check valves are used to prevent flow in one direction but allow free flow in the opposite direction.
- Needle valves are the most common type of flow control valve. They are used to control and maintain the hydraulic fluid at a set and required pressure inside the hydraulic system.
- A directional control valve is an important component within a hydraulic system. Its function is to direct hydraulic oil flow within the circuit.
- An accumulator is an energy-storage device. Since hydraulic fluid cannot be compressed, the hydraulic energy must be changed into mechanical or pneumatic energy.
- Oxygen, or air, is not suitable for use in gas-charged accumulators, because it may cause an explosion if they come into contact with the hydraulic fluid. Nitrogen, which is almost inert in its natural state, is commonly used.
- A spring-loaded accumulator has a cylindrical body with a piston to separate the fluid and the mechanical energy force. A strong spring provides the force on the piston to expel the fluid from the accumulator.
- A weight-loaded accumulator has a cylindrical body with a piston separating the fluid from the mechanical energy force. A weight on top of the piston (or a very heavy piston) provides the force on the piston to expel the fluid from the accumulator.
- Accumulators are used to store energy and, therefore, can pose significant safety hazards. Understand the safety hazards and always use appropriate safety precautions.
- Regular preventative maintenance prolongs the life of the system, reduces system down-time, operational and repair costs, and potentially eliminates preventable failures. Ideally, preventative maintenance should be performed when a machine is not scheduled to be in use.
- Excessive speed, excessive heat, excessive pressure, and contamination can all damage a hydraulic system.

Key Terms

aeration Air in the fluid.

burst pressure The maximum pressure a manufacturer designates a hose to withstand before a particular hose explodes or ruptures.

cavitation The formation of air bubbles in fluid caused by lower boiling point produced by reduced pressure.

chafing   Wear or abrasion due to prolonged or constant friction.

cylinder   An actuator that converts hydraulic power into linear mechanical force. Also known as *ram*.

hydraulic accumulator   A device that stores hydraulic energy and acts as an emergency power source in the event of system pump failure.

hydraulic cylinder   A device that uses hydraulic fluid pressure and converts it to linear mechanical movement. Also referred to as a *ram*.

land   The largest diameter in a spool; used to block flow paths.

linear   Extending or moving in a straight-line direction.

Pascal's law   The law of physics that states that pressure applied to a fluid in one part of a closed system will be transmitted equally to all other areas of the system.

pipe   A rigid tube of metal, plastic, or other substance, used to conduct gas or fluid flow.

seamless pipe   Formed in one piece; lacking seams, thus smooth and regular.

swashplate   A plate in a variable displacement pump the tilts and changes the stroke length of axial pistons.

telescoping cylinder   A linear single acting cylinder extending from a series of nested cylinder sections.

trunnion-mounted   Articulating connection points on the ends of a hydraulic cylinder.

tubing   Metal pipe that is intended to be bent and shaped to fit an application.

undercuts   The smallest diameter in a spool; used to create a flow path when the valve is open.

variable displacement pump   A type of pump with the ability to change output volume, as in a pump with a mechanism that allows the output to vary.

viscosity   The measurement of the resistance to flow of a liquid

working pressure   The normal range of pressure within a hydraulic system while the system is being operated.

Review Questions

1. Which of the following devices converts fluid pressure into mechanical force?
   a. Hydraulic pump
   b. Prime mover
   c. Directional control valve
   d. Linear actuator
2. Which of the following components in a hydraulic system stores hydraulic energy?
   a. Actuator
   b. Reservoir
   c. Pump
   d. Accumulator
3. Which of the following is responsible for producing pressure in a hydraulic circuit?
   a. Circuit resistance
   b. Hydraulic pumps

c. Prime movers
d. Linear actuators

4. Which of the following types of positive-displacement pumps operates at the highest pressure?
   a. Gear pump
   b. Vane pump
   c. Piston pump
   d. Variable displacement pump
5. Which of the following calculations is used to correctly predict the output force of a single acting cylinder?
   a. Pressure × Volume
   b. Pressure × Piston surface area
   c. Work/Time
   d. rpm × Pump displacement/rotation
6. Which type of pump is best adapted for a hydraulic system using a closed-center directional-control valve?
   a. Gear pump
   b. Variable displacement pump
   c. Vane pump
   d. Belt-driven pump
7. What is the inside diameter of a hose 100R4-18?
   a. 1"
   b. 18 mm
   c. 18 Gauge
   d. 1⅛"
8. Which hose is most likely to have the largest internal diameter?
   a. A return circuit hose
   b. A medium-pressure hose
   c. A high-pressure hose
   d. A suction side hose
9. Which fluid has the most viscosity when cold?
   a. ISO 32
   b. SAE 15w
   c. ISO 150
   d. SAE 50
10. The flow characteristics of lines and hoses used in a hydraulic circuit is best predicted by:
    a. the Bernoulli principle.
    b. Pascal's law.
    c. line length and outside diameter.
    d. Law of Energy Conservation.

ASE Technician A/Technician B Style Questions

1. Technician A says that a single-acting cylinder relies on the weight of the load to return it to the original position. Technician B says that a double-acting cylinder is also load dependent. Who is correct?
   a. Technician A
   b. Technician B
   c. Both Technician A and Technician B
   d. Neither Technician A nor Technician B
2. Technician A says that check valves allow fluid flow in both directions. Technician B says that check valves prevent

flow in one direction and allow free flow in the opposition direction. Who is correct?
   a. Technician A
   b. Technician B
   c. Both Technician A and Technician B
   d. Neither Technician A nor Technician B

3. Technician A says that oxygen should be used to charge an accumulator. Technician B says that the accumulator should be fully charged before it is removed from the system. Who is correct?
   a. Technician A
   b. Technician B
   c. Both Technician A and Technician B
   d. Neither Technician A nor Technician B

4. Technician A says that to detect hydraulic pinhole leaks, a piece of cardboard should be used. Technician B says that pinhole leaks can be identified by wearing gloves and checking for fluid "wetting" of the gloves while moving one's hand around potential leak points. Who is correct?
   a. Technician A
   b. Technician B
   c. Both Technician A and Technician B
   d. Neither Technician A nor Technician B

5. Technician A says that before servicing a hydraulic system, the directional control valves should be cycled through all positions and centered. Technician B says that booms and buckets should be placed in a resting position and any pressurized hydraulic components relieved of pressure. Who is correct?
   a. Technician A
   b. Technician B
   c. Both Technician A and Technician B
   d. Neither Technician A nor Technician B

6. Technicians A and B were examining some milky-colored hydraulic fluid. Technician A says that the fluid is likely water-contaminated. Technician B says that a vacuum pump should be used to evacuate the pressure in the fluid reservoir to correct the problem. Who is correct?
   a. Technician A
   b. Technician B
   c. Both Technician A and Technician B
   d. Neither Technician A nor Technician B

7. Technician A says that a defective relief valve could cause the hydraulic cylinders to move slowly and lack normal force. Technician B says that a variable displacement pump with a high swashplate angle could produce those symptoms. Who is correct?
   a. Technician A
   b. Technician B
   c. Both Technician A and Technician B
   d. Neither Technician A nor Technician B

8. Technician A says that the same pressure applied over different-sized surface areas produces the same level of force. Technician B says that the same pressure applied over different-sized surface areas produces different levels of force. Who is correct?
   a. Technician A
   b. Technician B
   c. Both Technician A and Technician B
   d. Neither Technician A nor Technician B

9. Technician A says that a corroded steel line conducting high-pressure hydraulic fluid can be replaced by a thicker walled, non-corroding copper line. Technician B says that a galvanized line is a better choice for replacing the steel line. Who is correct?
   a. Technician A
   b. Technician B
   c. Both Technician A and Technician B
   d. Neither Technician A nor Technician B

10. Technician A says that petroleum-based hydraulic fluids need additives to work well. Technician B says that because synthetic hydraulic fluids have a high VI index, they thin out at high temperature and require additives. Who is correct?
   a. Technician A
   b. Technician B
   c. Both Technician A and Technician B
   d. Neither Technician A nor Technician B

SECTION 7

Preventative Maintenance and Inspection

CHAPTER 62   Developing a PM Inspection System

Developing a PM Inspection System

Learning Objectives

After reading this chapter, you will be able to:

- **LO 62-1** Identify and describe the categories of preventative maintenance (PM).
- **LO 62-2** Explain the reasons for implementing a PM program.
- **LO 62-3** Explain who performs PM.
- **LO 62-4** Explain the reasons for using different PM service intervals.
- **LO 62-5** Outline and describe requirements for the Commercial Vehicle Safety Alliance Inspections PM program standards.
- **LO 62-6** Explain how safety inspection programs are administered.
- **LO 62-7** Identify the types and classifications of PM lubricants.
- **LO 62-8** Explain the purpose of safety recalls and identify sources for recall information.

- **LO 62-9** Describe practices for preparing and handling vehicles for PM inspections.
- **LO 62-10** Outline general inspection procedures and inspection criteria for major vehicle areas.
- **LO 62-11** Identify and describe out-of-service criterial and inspection procedures for the braking system.
- **LO 62-12** Outline procedures for inspecting tires and wheels.
- **LO 62-13** Outline inspection procedures for verifying correct wheel alignment.
- **LO 62-14** Outline general inspection procedures for performing under-vehicle inspections.
- **LO 62-15** Outline general inspection procedures inspecting cargo-handling devices.

You Are the Technician

A large number of transportation-related businesses depend on your shop to provide running repairs, as well as to perform regularly scheduled maintenance and safety inspections for a variety of types of trucks and buses. One of the difficulties you have when making service recommendations to customers is providing the best advice to clients with different expectations for the level of maintenance support you can provide. Some customers want to keep repair and vehicle maintenance costs as low as possible and want only the minimum amount of work performed in order to keep the equipment operating on the road. Other customers want the security of knowing their vehicles are in the best condition to avoid unexpected break-downs and disruptions to their business operations. Some customers prefer to do most of their own repairs and need only annual safety inspections, which you can provide. As you prepare your recommendations for each of these categories of customers, consider the following:

1. List in point form the reasons for performing proactive maintenance inspections.
2. For each of the categories of customers above, which type of PM schedule (PM- A, B, or C inspection, if any at all) is likely to be used by the customer? Explain your answer.
3. List in point form the requirements for facilities and technicians to perform safety inspections and meet the standards for issuing a Commercial Vehicle Safety Alliance (CVSA) safety inspection decal.

Introduction

Preventative maintenance and inspection (PMI) and PM programs have two dimensions. The first is PM inspection programs are a necessity for compliance with safety legislation for commercial vehicles to ensure they maintain minimum operating standards related to vehicle and road safety. A second dimension is the benefit of PMI to business operations. Commercial vehicles generate revenue and uptime is as critical to an owner or operator as keeping the doors open for any other business. Well-designed and executed PM programs contribute to a better business return on investment. PM for commercial vehicles is necessary in spite of their rugged construction, designed to withstand continuous daily operation in extreme operating environments. Time and other wear factors eventually cause deterioration to the point where a vehicle cannot operate efficiently, safely, or reliably. Common points of wear and deterioration include the various points in the braking system, steering, and suspension components that wear with constant maneuvering while carrying heavy loads; engine oils that absorb combustion contaminants; and driveline and hitching devices rotating, pulling, and undergoing frequent shock loading. To minimize the disruption of unscheduled repairs, PM is a set of service operations that involve scheduled inspections, adjustment, cleaning, testing, parts replacement, and vehicle repair to prevent unexpected breakdowns, extend service life, and minimize vehicle downtime. From a business perspective, PM has the added benefit of increasing resale value and **return on investment (ROI)**, lowering overall lifetime cost of operation, plus increasing productivity since the vehicle will provide more efficient service with improved reliability (**FIGURE 62-1**). PM adds resale value to a vehicle because a vehicle in good condition with extended service life provided by PM will get the maximum value when traded in for a new replacement.

Legislative Requirement for PM

Safety legislation requires all commercial motor vehicles (CMVs) to undergo PM. The legislation defines a CMV as a vehicle that is used in an interstate commerce business and meets one or more of the following specifications:

- Weight of in excess of 10,001 pounds
- Designed for transportation of 16 passengers or more, including a unpaid driver
- Designed for transportation of nine passengers, including a paid driver
- Involved in transporting hazardous materials within state or interstate in a quantity requiring placards

As an example, companies that operate commercial vehicles within the United States to move freight, passengers, or transport any cargo interstate, must be registered with the **Federal Motor Carrier Safety Administration (FMCSA)**. Any hazardous materials carriers who move enough materials requiring a safety permit must also register for a **United States Department of Transportation (USDOT) number**. The USDOT number functions as a unique identifier for the carrier company, which is used to collect and monitor a company's safety information (**FIGURE 62-2**). Individual states may require additional identifiers and in other counties, unique identifying numbers are used to track vehicle safety at a national and regional level.

Categories of Preventative Maintenance and Inspection (PMI)

LO 62-1 Identify and describe the categories of preventative maintenance (PM).

There are three primary bases for the establishment of a PMI schedule.

1. Time (number of months or hours)
   a. Engine hours are used for long-haul vehicles.
   b. Months are used for shorter-haul vehicles.
2. Mileage
   a. Recommended by manufacturer for normal use (shorter-haul and long-haul mixture use).
3. Amount of fuel consumed
   a. Easily monitored by the cost of fuel and mileage traveled.

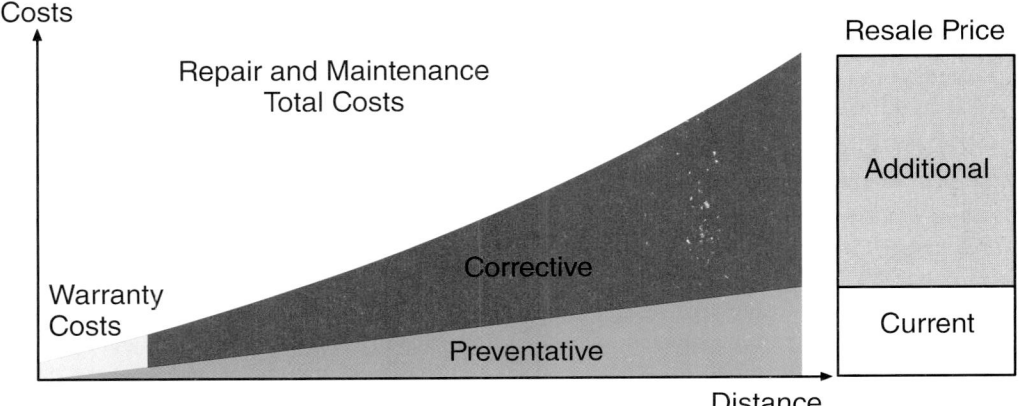

FIGURE 62-1 The relationship between PM costs and resale price.

FIGURE 62-2 A federal and regional identifying number. The US Department of Transportation requires commercial vehicles to have a unique identifying number to track safety records.

PMI falls into three basic categories, and each category has a scheduled interval with its own checklist. Typical PMI programs include:

- **PM-A**—This inspection generally is a visual check of all safety-related items, such as brakes, tires, horn, wipers, steering components, suspension components, and lighting. The chassis is lubricated and fluid levels are checked. Minor adjustments are also performed. The normal interval for a PM-A is approximately halfway between normal oil change intervals. So, a PM-A takes place every 10,000 miles or 16,000 km.
- **PM-B**—This inspection is more comprehensive than a PM-A. It includes all checks and adjustments performed in a PM-A as well as an oil change and oil and fuel filter change. The inspection items include the engine and driveline plus greater detail checks of the braking, steering, and other chassis systems. A PM-B is performed at every oil change, while a PM-A is performed between PM-B inspections and only the chassis is greased—no oil is changed.
- **PM-C**—This is typically an annual inspection that includes all the items in PM-A and B plus a comprehensive inspection of all chassis components. Scheduled fluid changes and component adjustment, repair, or replacement are performed at this time (**FIGURE 62-3**). This inspection is often referred to as an annual safety inspection or DOT inspection required to maintain operational certification.

Industry Approaches to PM

PM is generally proactive, which means maintenance work is scheduled to prevent unexpected breakdowns from occurring. Proactive PM is typically based on distance traveled, engine hours, time, or fuel used. **Proactive maintenance** reflects the understanding that the cost of repairing an unexpected breakdown is usually much greater than PM. Small problems are corrected before they turn into bigger, more expensive problems and cause unanticipated downtime or become a liability

due to unsafe service conditions. Experience has demonstrated that not following a proactive maintenance strategy, and instead pursuing a cost-minimization maintenance strategy or a **reactive maintenance** strategy, meaning service is performed only after equipment is broken, may keep vehicle and fleet operating costs low only temporarily (**TABLE 62-1**). But as time passes and distance traveled increases, the cost of repairs eclipses what proactive PM would have cost, and vehicle uptime falls (**FIGURE 62-4**). Unexpected failures, faster component wear out, consequential damage from failures, and downtime due to unexpected repairs, drive up the maintenance costs on a vehicle that does not have PM performed.

Predictive PM is based on a statistical analysis of when equipment and component failures are likely to occur and replacing parts or equipment before that point. For example, large truck leasing and rental companies sell used vehicles at an optimal point in vehicle lifecycle before repair costs sharply increase and before resale value falls. Some equipment or parts may be prone to high-frequency failures because of operating conditions. Engine overhauls or vehicle rebuild procedures are also performed based on anticipated service life rather than at the point of failure. The results of a study by a major engine manufacturer compared the operational costs of engine run to failure and one overhauled using predictive maintenance. Running to failure increased repair costs as much as 60% (**FIGURE 62-5**).

To maximize equipment's service availability, regular PM service is performed on a scheduled basis. However, when PM is performed is also dependent on whether a vehicle is available for service or operating near a service facility. Trucks, trailers, and buses traveling long distances every week or on the road for a month or more may not fit neatly into scheduled maintenance intervals. However, PM is a highly managed aspect of commercial vehicle fleet operation, and to efficiently allocate shop time, manage expenses, maintain warranty requirements, follow recommendations by manufacturers, and ensure compliance with a variety of legislative safety standards, most PM is scheduled.

Why Perform PM?

LO 62-2 Explain the reasons for implementing a PM program.

The most obvious reason for implementing a maintenance program is that it reduces costs. Regardless of whether it makes good business sense, legislation in most developed countries forbids the operation of a CMV in a condition likely to cause an accident or breakdown. Any motor vehicle discovered to be in an unsafe condition while being operated on the highway may be allowed to continue its operation only to the nearest place where repairs can safely be completed. Most countries mandate regular inspections. In the United States, FMCSA legislation (FMCSA 49 CFR Section 396.3: Inspection, Repair, and Maintenance) demands that every motor carrier and equipment provider must systematically inspect, repair, and maintain, or cause to be systematically inspected, repaired, and maintained, all motor vehicles and intermodal

B & C PM PREVENTIVE MAINTENANCE CHECKSHEET FOR SERVICE TRUCKS

FHWA ANNUAL INSPECTION - INITIAL BOX IF PERFORMED

COMPANY NAME:

INSPECTION DATE:	UNIT#:	MILES:	HOURS:

EMPLOYEE NAME:		BRANCH:	

☐ DENOTES MANDATORY FHWA ITEMS, WHICH MUST BE FREE OF DEFECTS TO CERTIFY!

	AT EVERY B-PM SERVICE DO THE FOLLOWING ITEMS: 1 THROUGH 64	INITIALS
01	FHWA INSPECTION DUE: ☐ YES ☐ NO	
02	☐ CHECK SAFETY EQUIPMENT - REFLECTOR KIT, CONES, WHEEL CHOCKS & FIRE EXTINGUISHER	
03	☐ WARNING DEVICES: ☐ WATER ☐ AIR ☐ OIL	
04	☐ HORNS: ☐ AIR ☐ ELECTRIC	
05	☐ WIPERS & BLADES	
06	FLOOR MAT SHIFT BOOT	
07	☐ SEATS SEAT BELTS	
08	☐ GLASS & WINDOW OPERATION ☐ MIRRORS	
09	CLUTCH FREE PLAY & CLUTCH BRAKE OPERATION (IF EQUIPPED)	
10	BACKUP ALARMS	
11	FOOT BRAKE PARKING BRAKE	
12	☐ VERIFY CHECK VALVE OPERATION ☐ INTERLOCK OPERATION (IF EQUIPPED)	
13	☐ 4-WAY WHEEL LOCK OPERATION (IF EQUIPPED) ☐ AIR SHIFT OPERATION (IF EQUIPPED)	
14	☐ CHECK GEAR SHIFT ☐ CHECK FOR CURRENT & PROPER REGISTRATION AND PERMITS	
15	ALTERNATOR OUTPUT & RECORD	
16	☐ NOISE IN ENGINE ☐ EXCESSIVE SM0KE	
17	ENGINE OIL PRESSURE: @IDLE @MAX RPM	
18	ACCELERATOR PEDAL	
19	☐ EASE OF STEERING & NOISE • EXHAUST MUFFLER & PIPING	
20	AIR DRYER OPERATION IF EQUIPPED)	
21	☐ LIGHTS ☐ SIGNAL LAMPS ☐ STOP LAMPS	
22	☐ MUD FLAPS ☐ AIR TANK DRAINS ☐ BATTERY BOX	
23	CAB MOUNTS: FRONT REAR	
24	☐ SHEET METAL ☐ IDLER PULLEY	
25	COOLANT - RECORD ANTFIREEZE PROTECTION _____ ☐ DCA ☐ FULL	
26	RADIATOR MOUNTING DEV CES0 RADIATOR HOSES	
27	WATER PUMP (CLEAN OUT WEEP HOLE) ☐ INSPECT BELTS, AND FAN HUB	
28	☐ ENGINE AIR COMPRESSOR & LINES OR MASTER CYLINDER AND LINES AS EQUIPPED	
29	STARTER, MOUNTING & WIRING	
30	CHANGE ENGINE OIL AND FILTER	
31	☐ CHECK FUEL SYSTEM / FILTER CHANGED (BY MANUFACTURERS SCHEDULE) ☐ YES ☐ NO	
32	AIR FILTER CHANGED (BY RESTRICTION GUAGE OR MANUFACTURERS SCHEDULE) ☐ YES ☐ NO	
33	INSPECT AIR INTAKE PIPING, CHARGE AIR COOLER, AND HOSES	
34	☐ POWER STEERING & STEERING SYSTEM COMPONENTS	
35	CHECK BATTERIES - HOLD DOWNS, CLEAN TERMINALS	
36	MOTOR SUPPORTS	
37	CHECK TRANSMISSION FLUID LEVEL, INSPECT FOR LEAKS, MOUNTING BOLTS AND BRACKETS	
38	CHECK DIFFERENTIAL, INSPECT FOR LEAKS, MOUNTING BOLTS AND BRACKETS	
39	DRIVE SHAFT & U-JOINTS	
40	☐ BRAKE ADJUSTMENT & OVERALL SYSTEM OPERATION	
41	☐ BRAKE SHOES	
42	CHECK WHEEL SEALS AND HUBS	
43	☐ CHECK SUSPENSION AND FRAME	
44	INSPECT PTO SYSTEM HOSES AND MOUNTING BRACKETS	
45	☐ CHECK TREAD DEPTH & AIR TIRES TO SPECIFICATIONS	

FIGURE 62-3 A PM inspection sheet used for both PM-B and PM-C inspections. During a PM-B inspection, the items under the PM-C section are not performed.

		INITIALS
46	LUBRICATE ALL FITTINGS	
47	OVERALL BODY CONDITION, CHECK FOR DAMAGE, DENTS, HOLES, DECALS & MARKINGS	
48	INSPECT LIFT GATE AND ALL DOORS,AND LATCHES	
49	INSPECT FLOOR,LOAD SECUREMENT DEVICES,	
50	VERIFY ALL WARNING DECALS IN PLACE	
	PTO DRIVEN COMPRESSOR SECTION (If gasoline powered use the Compressor PM form)	
51	CHECK FOR HYDRAULIC OIL LEAKS	
52	CHECK HYDRAULIC OIL & FILTER AND CHANGE ACCORDING TO MANUFACTURERS GUIDELINES	
53	INSPECT OIL SEPERATOR & CHANGE ELEMENT ACCORDING TO MANUFACTURERS GUIDELINES	
54	INSPECT GAUGES AND INSTRUMENTS	
55	INSPECT ALL PIPING AND CONNECTIONS (HYDRAULIC AND AIR)	
56	TEST AUTOMATIC SHUTDOWN (IF EQUIPPED)	
57	INSPECT ALL MOUNTINGS & BRACKETS (TIGHTEN AS NEEDED)	
58	INSPECT ALL ELECTRICAL CONNECTIONS	
59	CHANGE COMPRESSOR CRANKCASE OIL (CHANGE FILTER IF EQUIPPED)	
60	INSPECT COMPRESSOR AIR FILTER AND CHANGE IF NECESSARY	
61	INSPECT ALL GUARDS AND BRAKETS,REPAIR OR REPLACE AS NECESSARY	
62	INSPECT DRIVE COUPLER AND OR BELTS (AS EQUIPPED)	
63	CHECK AND CLEAN SCAVENGER ORIFICE & RELATED PARTS PER MAINTENANCE SCHEDULE	
64	INSPECT PTO MOUNTING AND BE SURE PUMP SPLINES/ COUPLING ARE PROPERLY LUBRICATED	
	AT EVERY C-PM SERVICE ADD THE FOLLOWING ITEMS: 65 & 66	
65	CHANGE TRANSMISSION FLUID AND FILTERS	
66	CHANGE FUEL FILTER	

COMMENTS:

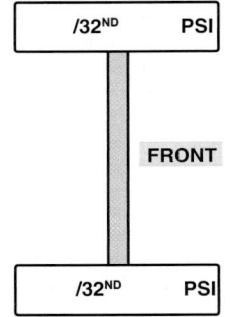

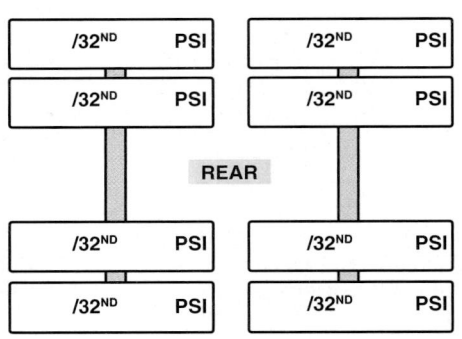

FHWA ANNUAL INSPECTION COMPLETE THE FOLLOWING:

VIN# _____

INSPECTOR'S NAME (PRINT)	SIGNATURE:

I CERTIFY THIS VEHICLE TO BE FREE OF ANY DEFECTS AS DESCRIBED IN 49 C.F.R. PART 396.17

THIS INSPECTOR MEETS THE QUALIFICATION REQUIREMENTS IN SECTION 396.19.   ☐ YES

FIGURE 62-3 A PM inspection sheet used for both PM-B and PM-C inspections. During a PM-B inspection, the items under the PM-C section are not performed. (*Continued*).

TABLE 62-1 Reactive Maintenance Versus Proactive Maintenance

Reactive Maintenance	Proactive Maintenance
Late detection of problem by operator	Early detection by skilled technician or advanced monitoring techniques
Immediately out of service with indefinite downtime	Planned service with scheduled return to service
Expediting parts at high cost and waiting for parts	Parts on hand and best value obtained by preordering parts
Dispatching a technician for possible road call; disrupting employee work schedules	Scheduling labor and planned allocating of resources
Idle driver and/or passengers; disruption to freight delivery schedule	No disruption to driver passengers or freight delivery
High costs and safety risks	Low costs and safety risks
Consequential damage from failure	Corrective action limiting consequential damage

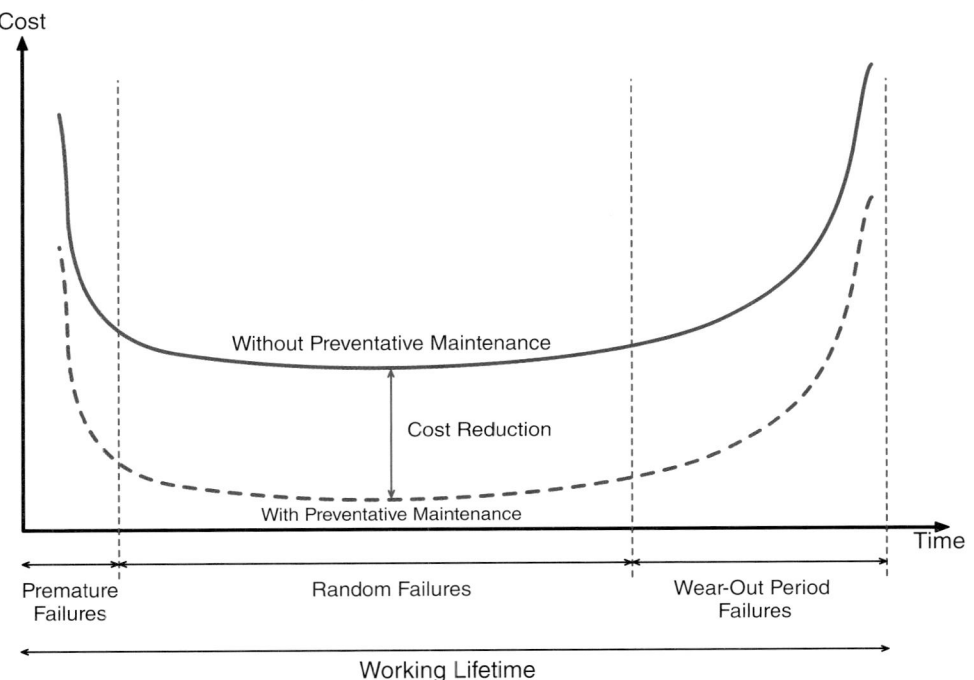

FIGURE 62-4 The cost of maintaining a vehicle with and without preventative maintenance.

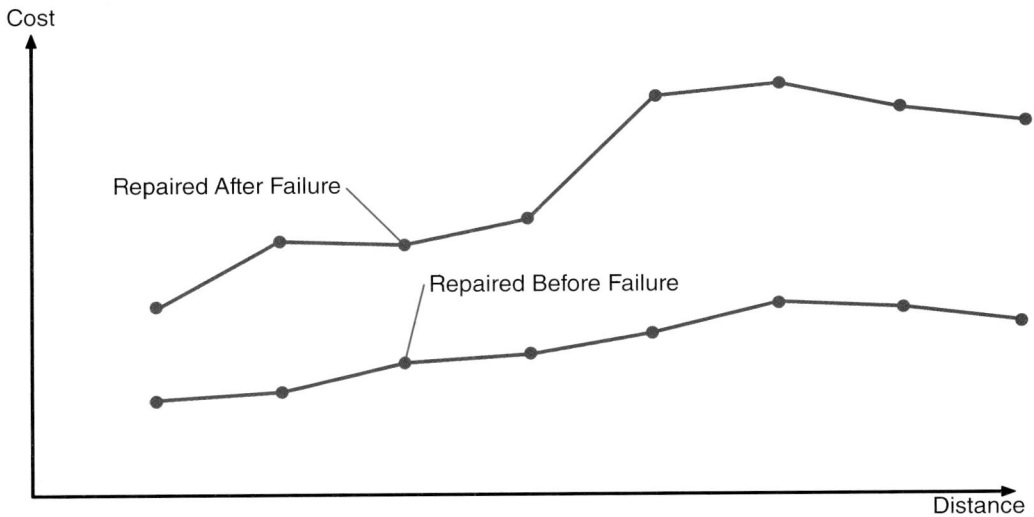

FIGURE 62-5 The difference in maintenance costs before and after a failure.

equipment subject to its control. Note it is the carrier or company registering the vehicle with USDOT that is responsible for compliance. The object of the legislation is public safety for operators and other road users. Other parts of the legislation outline in detail the scope of the maintenance programs, including requirements for:

- Identification of vehicles according to year, make, model, serial number, and name of owner or company owning the equipment.
- Systematic safety inspections and procedures to remove unsafe vehicles from service.
- Vehicle components and systems to be inspected during safety inspections.
- Inspection and lubrication of chassis.
- Record keeping for inspections identifying the nature and due date of the various inspection and maintenance operations to be performed.
- Record keeping of inspection, repairs, and maintenance indicating their date and nature; and a record of tests conducted on push-out windows, emergency doors, and emergency door marking lights on buses.

▶ TECHNICIAN TIP

CSA 2010 basic scores are calculated ratings on compliance, safety, and accountability initiated by the FMCSA. The system uses the Safety Measurement System (SMS), which is used to identify carrier companies for safety audits. Scores are calculated based on Behavior Analysis and Safety Improvement Categories (BASICs), which includes measures involving driver fitness, collisions, traffic violations, etc. It is good practice to perform regular FM inspections to avoid an increase in BASIC scores since any safety defects related to maintenance triggers audits. The Canadian equivalent to BASIC scores is the Commercial Vehicle Operator Registration (CVOR) record. It measures the safety performance of carriers also to improve its commercial vehicle safety performance.

Legal liability for vehicle safety extends beyond most legislation and regulation requirements. For instance, requiring an employee to operate a dangerous vehicle while knowing, or having reason to know, that use of the vehicle creates unreasonable risk or harm makes the organization's manager liable for negligent entrustment. Having a proper PM program with good record keeping enables a company and its managers to avoid prosecution in the event of a collision or fatality. If the steering or brakes failed and resulted in a serious accident or fatality and the vehicle were impounded for investigation, vehicle maintenance records would be examined to determine whether the vehicle was properly inspected and maintained in a safe operating condition.

Who Performs PM?

LO 62-3 Explain who performs PM.

Carriers registering a vehicle with the USDOT are ultimately responsible for the vehicle safety, but drivers are the first persons responsible for identifying potential safety issues and the possibility of imminent breakdowns. When the driver communicates vehicle problems, proactive maintenance can

take place. In the United States, FMCSA legislation requires drivers to prepare a report in writing at the completion of each day's work for each commercial vehicle the driver has operated that day. Specifics of the legislation are contained in FMCSA 49.396.11: **Driver Post-Operation Vehicle Inspection Report (DVIR)** (**FIGURE 62-6**). Inspection reports supply useful data for PM work and alert management to any unsafe operating condition.

The driver is required to monitor and report on the following vehicle parts and systems:

- Vehicle safety items, such as the tires, rims, wipers, horn, brakes, steering, trailer brake connections, coupler condition, and parking brake.
- Vehicle glass, body condition, lighting, mirrors, and emergency equipment (i.e., flares and a first-aid kit).

It's helpful to a fleet operation for drivers to also report **drivability items**, such as engine misfires, rough idle, excessive exhaust smoke, and malfunction indicator lights (MIL) and other system warning lights.

PM is normally performed by certified technicians attached to a fleet operation or by service repair centers with the capability to properly complete PMIs and repairs. PM work is detail-orientated and requires technicians to develop good powers of observation gained through training and experience.

PM Service Intervals

LO 62-4 Explain the reasons for using different PM service intervals.

Legislation governing commercial vehicle maintenance and safety only requires a carrier, that is, the company registering the vehicle for a USDOT number, to "systematically inspect, repair, and maintain, or cause to be systematically inspected, repaired, and maintained, all motor vehicles and intermodal equipment subject to its control." Parts and accessories required in the regulations "shall be in safe and proper operating condition at all times." It is, therefore, the responsibility of a carrier to develop a PM program to meet those performance standards and have records documenting that vehicles are being maintained and repaired as needed (**FIGURE 62-7**).

Several factors are used to determine the frequency of a PM schedule. One is the operating condition of the vehicle. Dusty conditions, extreme cold or heat, stop-and-go driving, off- or on-road operation, and traveling at continuous on-highway speeds are just a few operating conditions that influence **PM service intervals**. Most commercial vehicles operate under severe conditions rather than normal conditions. **Severe service operating conditions** include:

- Towing or hauling heavy loads
- Extensive idling and/or stop-and-go, low-speed driving encountered in inner-city traffic
- Delivery
- Off-road dusty conditions
- Multiple drivers

DRIVER'S INSPECTION REPORT

Date:_____

TRACTOR/TRUCK NO.:_____ TRAILER(S) NO.(S):_____

TRACTOR/TRUCK	Defective?	Remarks	TRACTOR/TRUCK	Defective?	Remarks
Air compressor			Brake connections		
Air lines			Brakes		
Battery			Coupling chains		
Brake accessories			Coupling (kingpin)		
Brakes			Doors		
Carburetor			Hitch		
Clutch			Landing gear		
Defroster			Lights—all		
Drive line			Roof		
Engine			Springs		
Fifth wheel			Tarpaulin		
Front axle			Tires		
Fuel tank			Wheels		
Heater			OTHER		
Horn			Condition of vehicle is satisfactory? ○ Yes ○ No		
Lights					
Mirrors			Defects corrected? ○ Yes ○ No		
Muffler					
Oil pressure			Defects need not be corrected for vehicle safety. ○ Yes ○ No		
On board recorder					
Radiator			DRIVER'S Signature:		
Reflectors					
Safety equipment			MECHANIC Signature:		
Springs					
Starter					
Steering					
Tachograph					
Tires					
Transmission					
Wheels					
Windows					
Windshield wipers					
OTHER					

FIGURE 62-6 A Driver Vehicle Inspection Report (DVIR).

Manufacturer recommendations for PM schedules found in service literature and owner's manuals differentiate between **normal service operating conditions** and severe service operating conditions, and the recommendations should be followed. Experience with a particular piece of equipment may require a modified PM schedule. For example, hydraulic brake calipers may require lubrication of sliders twice a year rather than once a year to minimize brake pad wear caused by sticking caliper sliding surfaces.

Effective Maintenance Program

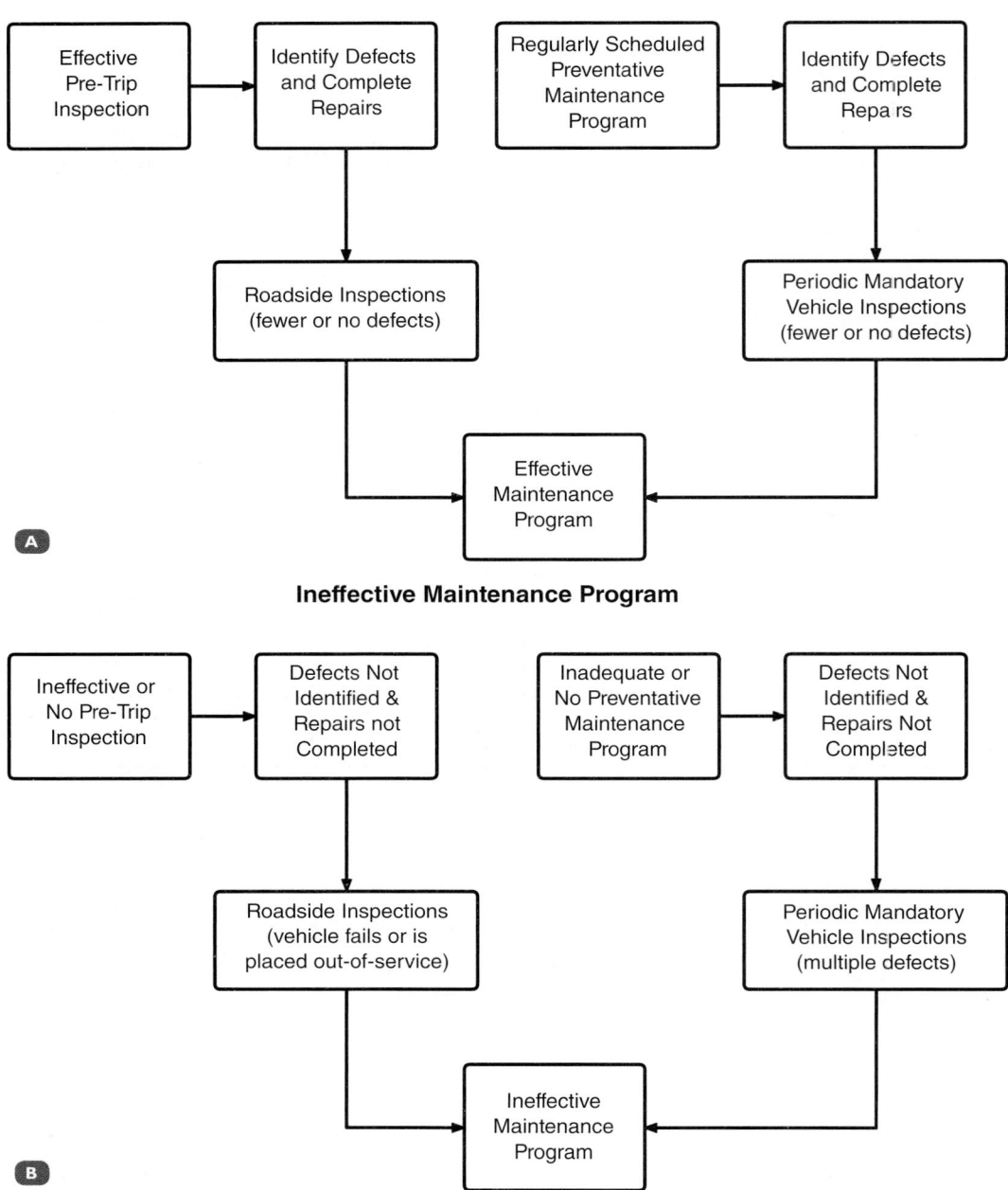

FIGURE 62-7 Contrasting the outcomes of **A.** an effective and **B.** an ineffective PM program.

Developing a PM Service Checklist

At a minimum, a **PM service checklist** should include an itemized task list of procedures that includes mechanical safety items related to braking, steering, suspension, lighting, mirrors, wipers, horns, tires, wheels, etc. The task list should also include items related to maintenance on engines, drivelines, electrical system, body/cab, fluids, filters, and other items regularly requiring periodic adjustment, lubrication, or replacement. Inspection of fire protection, emergency exit,

and evacuation equipment is critical for buses and motor coaches. The type of checklist, as well as the inspection schedule, varies with vehicle type and operating service. A procedure should be in place ensuring that safety-related vehicle defects discovered during inspections are reported, repaired, and validated before the vehicle is released for operation. DVIRs and other driver communications should outline a procedure to ensure equipment managers are promptly notified about vehicle defects.

Commercial Vehicle Safety Alliance Inspections

LO 62-5 Outline and describe requirements for the Commercial Vehicle Safety Alliance Inspections PM program standards.

The **Commercial Vehicle Safety Alliance (CVSA)** is a non-profit organization dedicated to improving the safe operation of commercial vehicles in North America by establishing a uniform, reciprocal enforcement of commercial vehicle safety standards. The driving force behind the organization was the recognition that commercial vehicle highway safety was nearly the same in most US, Canadian, and Mexican jurisdictions. Even though common criteria for regulation and inspection were used in most states and provinces, there was no mechanism to recognize enforcement standards in each region. A significant duplication of work and record keeping by government agencies and the motor carrier industry was taking place until a North American standard for commercial vehicle safety was in place.

The CVSA establishes transportation safety standards for motor carriers, drivers, vehicles, and inspectors through compliance, education, training, and enforcement programs. The organization has also developed policies and procedures requiring drivers to immediately notify management of any roadside vehicle out-of-service order (OOSO) and has recommended various minimum inspection standards and criteria that its members agree to follow. Not only are the standards uniform, but each enforcement jurisdiction recognizes each other's work in inspecting commercial vehicles, their drivers, and their cargo.

CVSA's core functions are to support the North American Standard Inspection Program and all its components, which include:

1. North American Standard Inspection Procedures
2. Training curriculum
3. Inspector certification
4. North American Standard Out-of-Service Criteria
5. CVSA decal program

Out-of-Service Criteria (OOSC)

Of particular interest to technicians are the **North American Standard Out-of-Service Criteria (OOSC)**. This standard is used by all law enforcement agencies throughout North America. Two of its four parts outline out-of-service safety standards. Part two of the standard describes the critical vehicle inspection items and provides direction to each commercial vehicle inspector in North America to identify at what point a CMV can no longer be safely operated because of mechanical conditions that could potentially cause an accident or breakdown. Part four of the standard establishes criteria for placing a motor carrier out of service. The standards are minimum requirements, and the CVSA encourages the use of higher safety standards. Other parts deal with drivers out of service and transportation of hazardous waste. The only difference between the US and Canadian editions of the North American Standard OOSC is

FIGURE 62-8 A CVSA decal.

that the US edition references the **Federal Motor Carrier Safety Regulation (FMCSR)** violation codes. Inspection items and failure conditions are the same.

A commercial vehicle may qualify for a CVSA decal if it passes a Level I or V inspection and no defects are found in critical inspection items listed in the CVSA OOSC. This means the vehicle is free of any mechanical-, cargo-, and driver-related safety violations. The decal is valid for three months (**FIGURE 62-8**). Defects that are noted during inspection that are not critical inspection items do not affect decal qualification.

Record Keeping

The use of software-based record keeping is almost universal in fleet operations. Software can customize maintenance schedules, create and track work orders, track fuel consumption, record maintenance histories, track tire service, record accidents, monitor labor, and produce invoices. Managers can accurately monitor the cost of PM and associated vehicle costs to make decisions and have insight into business operations. Navistar's "On Command" system is an example of the latest sophisticated service reporting software. The software not only tracks all service work and electronically stores inspection reports plus work orders, it also has a global positioning system (GPS) feature (**FIGURE 62-9**). Service software like Navistar's GPS tracks a vehicle and, in the event of a problem, it can perform a customized search and direct the operator to the nearest repair facility.

Additionally, engine software from many manufacturers typically has a programmable engine parameter that can alert the driver when a PM is due (**FIGURE 62-10**). Normally a maintenance light in the dash lights up to alert the driver when the programmable preset value for time or distance is reached. For example, as vehicles are required to reduce noxious emissions, they are equipped with features like exhaust aftertreatment

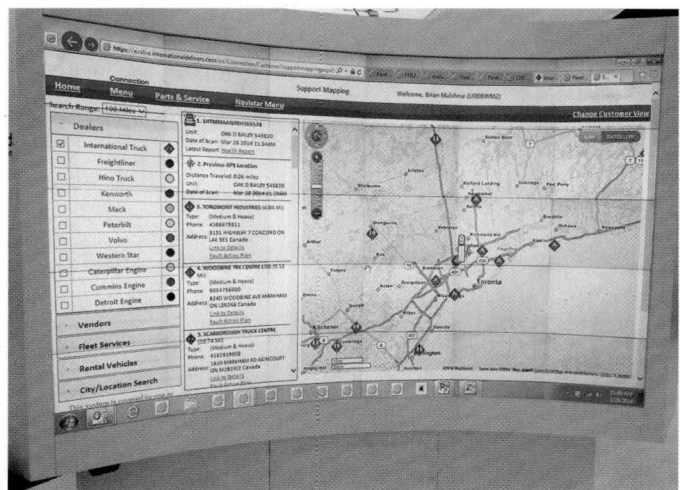

FIGURE 62-9 Navistar's "On Command" system.

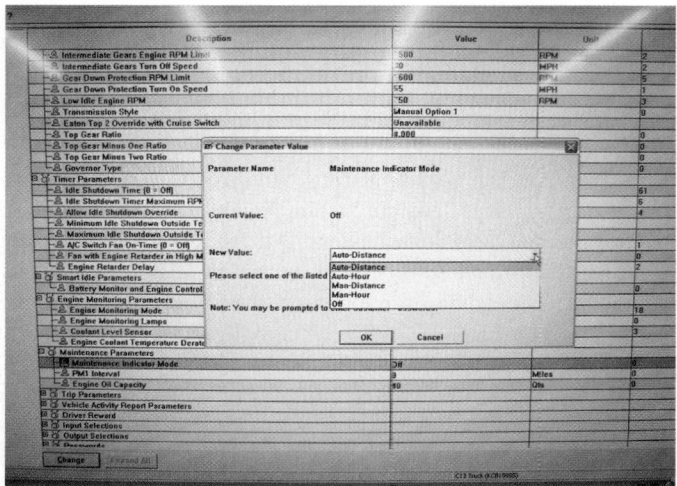

FIGURE 62-10 Many computerized vehicle systems have programmable PM notifications and alert the operator when a PM is due.

systems, which add new maintenance considerations. Diesel particulate filters typically require service between 250,000 and 450,000 miles. Ash accumulations in the filters need purging. Selective catalyst reduction (SCR) systems also use a catalyst for the diesel exhaust fluid (DEF), which needs refilling. This is a good example of where good record keeping is particularly pertinent.

PMI Record-Keeping Requirements

Record keeping is an essential component of the PMI process. Inspections have to be carried out by authorized inspectors who have both training and experience. Normally, evidence of the inspector's qualifications is required to be held on the operator's premises. In the United States, record-keeping requirements fall under the regulation 49 CFR, part 396.21. The qualified inspector performing the inspection must prepare a report that identifies:

- The individual performing the inspection and the date the vehicle was inspected
- The motor carrier operating the vehicle
- The vehicle components inspected and the results of the inspection, including those components not meeting the minimum standards

The original or a copy of the inspection report must be retained by the entity responsible for the inspection for a period of 14 months. The inspection report must be available for review on demand of an authorized federal, state, or local official. A decal or sticker may be placed on the vehicle instead of carrying the report. If a decal is used, it must contain the name and address of the motor carrier or other entity where the inspection report is maintained and certain other information as outlined in 49 CFR, part 396.17.

Inspector Qualifications

In most countries, an inspector carrying out this work is required to be registered and appropriately qualified. In the United States, the requirements are as follows:

- **Criteria:** He or she must understand the inspection criteria set forth in 49 CFR, part 393 and appendix G, and must be capable of identifying defective components.
- **Master:** He or she must have mastered the methods, procedures, tools, and equipment used when performing an inspection.
- **Capability:** He or she must be capable of performing an inspection by reason of experience, training, or both, through the successful completion of a state- or federally sponsored training program, and have a combination of training and/or experience totaling at least one year. The training and/or experience may consist of the following:

  - Participation in a manufacturer-sponsored training program or similar commercial training program designed to train students in truck operation and maintenance.
  - Experience as a mechanic or inspector of another commercial vehicle.
  - Experience as a commercial vehicle inspector for a state, provincial, or federal government.

Evidence of an individual's qualifications must be retained by the motor carrier while the individual is performing annual inspection and for one year thereafter. Brake inspectors are expected to have similar, but separate, qualifications to inspect brakes.

Administration of Safety Inspection Programs

LO 62-6 Explain how safety inspection programs are administered.

To implement minimum CVSA standards and the requirement that all commercial motor vehicles must pass at least an annual safety inspection, the most efficient method is to have enforcement authorities in the local state, province, or territory administer periodic inspection programs. CVSA members are represented by various Departments of Transportation, Public Utility and Service Commissions, State Police, Highway Patrols, and Ministries of Transport. Inspections are conducted by authorities where the vehicle is garaged to ensure inspection programs performed by commercial carriers are comparable to, or as effective as, the federal periodic inspection requirements of the FMCSA. jurisdictions

California Basic Inspection of Terminal Program

An example of a commercial vehicle safety inspection program administered at a State level is California's Basic Inspection of Terminal (BIT) program. Formerly called the Biennial Inspection of Terminal, the BIT program is implemented by the California Highway Patrol (CHP) and requires any motor vehicle over 10,000 lb gross vehicle weight (GVW) undergoes a safety inspection within 90-day or less intervals. The main difference between a BIT inspection and any other terminal inspection conducted by the CHP is that by law, BIT inspections are user-funded. That means a fee is paid by the motor carrier directly to the CHP for each inspection. This program ensures that the mandatory safety inspections are being performed correctly and records are properly kept. BIT inspectors visit terminal facilities, such as a warehouse, bus barn, or truck yard, where the CMV and towed vehicles are normally parked when not in use. A terminal can also be considered to include the private residence of an owner-operator or other small business utilizing CMVs, if that is where the firm conducts business.

Changes began in January 2016 that allow CHP to more closely coordinate inspectors to focus on unsafe motor carriers. On-highway and other safety-related behavior determines when inspections take place, moving the inspection to a performance-based program. Performance is measured using safety data uploaded into an FMCSA database that prioritizes carriers with poor safety records for inspection. Roadside inspections revealing no defects or crash history means the CHP has discretion not to inspect a terminal more often than once every six years. Changes in 2016 expanded the BIT program to all vehicles in the state that operate as CMVs. Every carrier in California that did not have a USDOT number is assigned one. Carriers must display either a California or DOT number or both.

The CHP program requires that documentations for carrier inspections be retained for at least two years. At a minimum, the following items need to be inspected:

- Brake adjustment
- Brake system component and leaks
- Steering and suspension systems
- Tires and wheels
- Vehicle hitching devices, such as fifth wheels, king pins, pintle hooks, drawbars, chains, and associated components (**FIGURE 62-11**).

Inspection documentation must include identification of the vehicle, including make, model, license number, serial number, company vehicle number, or other means to accurately identify the vehicles.

FIGURE 62-11 The operation of emergency door, exits, and push-out windows is part of a regular inspection procedure on all types of buses.

The date and nature of each inspection, and a description of any repairs performed, must be included. All inspections must bear the signature of an authorized representative attesting to the qualifications of the inspector, that a proper inspection was performed, and to the completion of all required repairs.

▶ **TECHNICIAN TIP**

CVSA 2010 Basic Scores Safety Measurement System is a safety rating system for commercial vehicles that includes a category for vehicle maintenance. Carrier scores are calculated using the FMCSA SMS, which is used to identify carrier companies for safety audits. Scores are calculated based on Behavior Analysis and Safety Improvement Categories (BASICs), which includes measures involving driver fitness, collisions, traffic violations, etc. It is good practice to perform regular PM inspections to avoid an increase in BASIC scores since any safety-related defects related to maintenance triggers audits. The Canadian equivalent to BASIC score is the Commercial Vehicle Operator Registration (CVOR) record. It measures the safety performance of carriers, as well, to improve its CMV safety performance.

Lubricants Used in PMI

LO 62-7 Identify the types and classifications of PM lubricants.

The lubricants used in PMI include oils, transmission and axle lubricants, chassis lubricants, and even trailer chassis lubricants.

Oil

It was once normal practice for engines to need one grade of oil for summer and another for winter. Now, oils are graded or classified by the American Society of Automotive Engineers (SAE) through the viscosity index. Engine oil with an SAE number of 50 has a higher viscosity, or thickness, than SAE 20 oil. Oils with low viscosity ratings (such as SAE 5W, 10W, and 20W) with the suffix W for winter, are tested at a low temperature, around 0° F (–18° C), and refer to their viscosity at that temperature. Oils without a W suffix, such as SAE 20, 30, 40, and 50, are tested at a high temperature, around 210° F (99° C), and refer to their viscosity at that temperature. Modern oils are blends of oils that combine cold and hot viscosity properties. These oils are blended with additives, called viscosity index improvers, to form multi-grade, or multi-viscosity, oils. They provide better lubrication in both cold and hot engine operating conditions.

API Oil Certification Mark

Oil is also classified by the American Petroleum Institute (API) service classification. Oils for spark-ignition engines use the prefix S, and diesel or compression-ignition engines use C. Manufacturers recommend the SAE and API classifications for a particular engine, which must be followed.

Vehicles with the aftertreatment systems must use oils that are compatible with those devices to prevent catalyst poisoning or deactivation and plugging. API certification marks for diesel engine oils meeting the CK-4 and the new FA-4 standards are the latest standards for diesel oil introduced in 2016 (**FIGURE 62-12**). CK-4 is designed for compatibility with biofuels and the latest exhaust aftertreatment systems. It is backward compatible with CJ-4 and CI-4 oil.

FA-4 oils are a new category for use in high-speed four-stroke cycle diesel engines designed to provide better engine protection and help meet the 2017 model year on-highway greenhouse gas (GHG) and Tier 4 non-road exhaust emission standards. The "F" in FA-4 designates the oil as a fuel-efficient oil, which is expected to reduce fuel consumption by up to 1.6%.

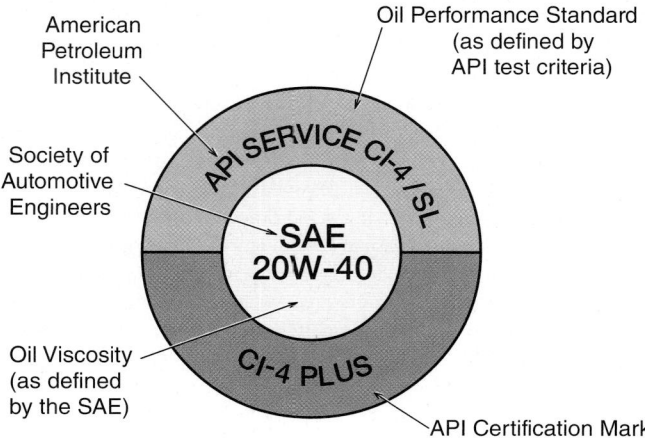

FIGURE 62-12 1. The top half designates the oil's performance standard set by the API test criteria. 2. The center identifies the oil's viscosity, which is a standard defined by the SAE. 3. The bottom half is the API certification mark.

Chassis Lubricants

Chassis lubricants are greases classified in terms of their penetrating ability. There are two popular types of on board automatic chassis lubrication systems:

1. *Automatic chassis lubrication system (ACLS):* Uses air- or electric-driven grease pumps with piston distributors, or metering valves at the ends of the dispensing lines connected to a manifold with grease lines to lubrication points (**FIGURE 62-13**).
2. *Manual-manifold or distribution block:* A non-automatic grease distributor manifold that technicians supply with pressurized grease at prescribed service intervals. A manifold is connected to 12 to 24 grease lines attached to critical lubrication points.

Most manufacturers recommend the use of synthetic lubricants for transmissions, differentials, and power dividers.

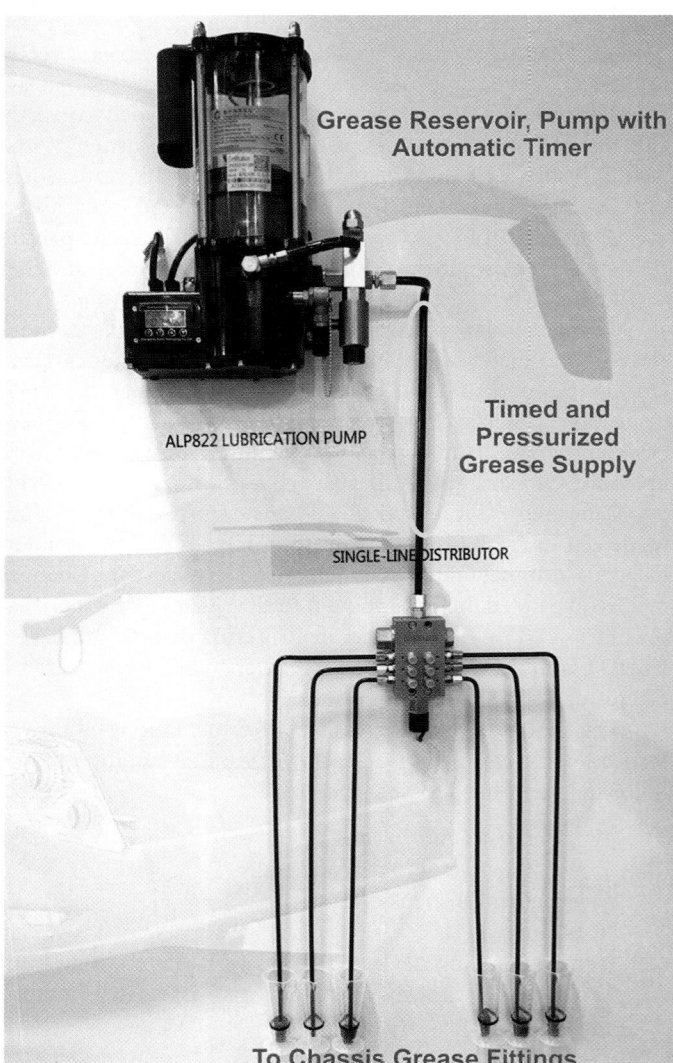

FIGURE 62-13 The reservoir and lines for an automatic-type chassis grease lubrication system. A pump dispenses pressurized grease at timed intervals to supply lubrication at certain points.

Finding Information on Recalls

LO 62-8 Explain the purpose of safety recalls and identify sources for recall information.

Given that there are thousands of vehicles built every day, it is to be expected that something will go wrong in the assembly process. In the medium- and heavy-duty truck industry, errors occur due to a particular component failure that is often discovered at the time of a system failure or at a scheduled service interval.

Manufacturers are required to provide information about component failures to their clients (normally through the dealer network) and to the government department that deals with such matters. Normally, the clients are informed and asked to have the vehicle made available for repairs to be made at the manufacturer's cost.

When carrying out an inspection, it is good practice to identify whether the vehicle you are inspecting has been subject to a recall and whether the repair has been completed. Depending on the issue, information can be sought through the appropriate manufacturer or regulatory body. There are several ways of finding out this information online; some of the methods include the following:

- Check the particular vehicle service history.
- Check the manufacturer service bulletins at OEM web sites
- In the United States, the National Highway Traffic Safety Administration (NHTSA) of the USDOT provides recall information, including vehicle and equipment campaigns from 1966 to present. The campaigns include motor vehicle products that experienced a safety-related defect or did not comply with FMVSS.

The Environmental Protection Agency's (EPA) Office of Transportation and Air Quality is responsible for ensuring that motor vehicles comply with the federal emission standards throughout the useful life of those vehicles. The EPA can require manufacturers to recall vehicles when a substantial number of a model or engine family used by a set of vehicles fails to meet emission standards. Vehicle manufacturers can also voluntarily issue recalls for emission-related problems.

Preparation for PM and PMI

LO 62-9 Describe practices for preparing and handling vehicles for PM inspections.

It is very important to use the right tool or piece of equipment and to not substitute the wrong tool for the right one. Failure to use the correct tool or piece of equipment could result in personal injury and damage to equipment.

If customers observe that service personnel take care of vehicles by driving carefully and installing protective floor mats and seat covers, and if the shop is well-maintained, the service department's image can be positively enhanced in the customer's eyes.

Follow established shop service practices and sound maintenance principles, be aware of how the shop is organized, and become familiar with specialty tools used to perform efficient and safe service.

Shop Housekeeping Practices

- Keep the shop floor and workbenches clean.
- Store flammable liquids and oily rags in an approved container.
- Properly tag malfunctioning equipment and report it to a supervisor.
- Maintain shop equipment in good working order.
- Never use a tool unless trained to correctly use it.
- Use the right tool for the right job.

Vehicle Care Practices

- Where appropriate, install seat covers and protective floor mats before beginning any service work, and install seat covers before entering the cab for any reason.
- Check that the garage door is open enough to allow vehicle entry and exit.
- Check brake operation before operating any vehicle.
- Check around the vehicle for objects or personnel before attempting to start or move a vehicle.
- Respectfully care for a customer's vehicle.

Shop and Inspection Standards

It is very important that the shop be set up for functionality (**FIGURE 62-14**). Proper PM and PMI functionality requires that there are lights, air hoses, tools, equipment, refuse and oil containers, safety stands, and other equipment present and in proper position to complete the inspection. Since there are many types of vehicles built by a variety of manufacturers and equipped with different components, it is impossible to compile a single list of specific procedures for every PMI. However, the generic guidelines are suitable when completing a PMI. Note that all manufacturers and the CVSA specify maximum wear specification before a vehicle out of service criteria (OOSC) is reached. Note these are not acceptable limits but excessive OOS limits and components should be replaced

FIGURE 62-14 A shop is set up to perform PMIs.

TABLE 62-2 Specialty Tools and Their Uses

Tool	Usage
Brake lining measurement tool	Used to measure the thickness of a brake lining to see whether it is within specifications
Belt tension gauge	Used to measure tension on a belt
Headlight adjustment tool or screen	Used to adjust headlights to specifications
Portable light tester	Used to test trailer lights and antilock brakes when there is no trailer supplying power
Tire Square	A large carpenter square used to ensure that the tires on an axle are square to each other
Battery load or conductance tester	Used to measure battery capacity
Coolant hydrometer or refractometer	Used to test the ethylene glycol (antifreeze) mixture in the cooling system or DEF concentrations. A standard hydrometer can also be used, but the Technology Maintenance Council (TMC) recommends the use of a refractometer for testing antifreeze strength.
Cooling system pressure tester	Used to test for cooling system leaks when there is coolant loss or overheating problems
Scan tools and service software	Used to retrieve diagnostic codes from the vehicle's ECU's and reset maintenance monitors
Dial indicator gauge	Used to measure runout, roundness, and wear on various components, such as bushings, tie rods, and king pins
Tire tread depth gauge	Used to measure tire wear to determine tire replacement requirement
Alignment equipment (i.e., tram bars and electronic alignment racks)	Used to align a tractor and trailer axles
Digital volt-ohmmeter (DVOM)	Used to measure amperage, voltage, resistance, and frequency signals of electrical and electronic components
Test strips and coolant	Used to measure nitrate concentration and pH of vehicle coolant
Infrared thermometer	Used to measure the temperature of various liquids and components
Fifth-wheel test pin and king pin gauge	Used to test the fifth-wheel latching, adjustment, and wear on trailer king pin
Torque wrenches	Used to verify or adjust wheel nut torque

before they reach these points. As a general rule, if something is disassembled or part of a system under repair, replacement is recommended when wear exceeds a 40% threshold of a maximum limit. Otherwise, an allowance factor should be made for further wear that is expected to occur before the next inspection.

Specialty Tools

When conducting inspections, there are a number of tools that not only make the job easier, but also prevent potential damage to the vehicle itself. The tools listed in **TABLE 62-2** are the essential tools that should be available to technicians. The list is not exhaustive, and some manufacturers specify particular tools for their vehicles.

PMI Process

LO 62-10 Outline general inspection procedures and inspection criteria for major vehicle areas.

The PMI process can be carried out in a variety of ways, but a methodical approach is best to ensure task efficiency and to avoid missing items due for inspection. The process should begin with a walk-around inspection.

Performing a Walk-Around Inspection

A walk-around inspection should be undertaken prior to beginning a PMI to assess the general condition of the vehicle. Use an inspection sheet to document all examined items and note any

deficiency requiring follow-up repair, replacement, or adjustment. To perform a walk-around inspection, follow the steps in **SKILL DRILL 62-1**.

Performing Internal Cab Inspections

Double checking the itemized inspection list ensures that every item is thoroughly inspected after an initial walk-around inspection. After the initial walk-around inspection, the technician should continue in a sequential manner commencing with an internal cab inspection. There are three components to an internal cab inspection:

- Key-off inspection; see **SKILL DRILL 62-2**
- Key-on inspection; see **SKILL DRILL 62-3**
- Engine-on inspection; see **SKILL DRILL 62-4**

After completing the key-off inspection tasks, continue the inspection in the key-on engine off state. To complete the steps in this part of the inspection, the key must remain on after the first step or task.

After the initial key-on inspection, complete the engine-running inspection. With the engine running, and when measuring charging system voltage, the starter operation should be checked again to identify any unusual noises, starter drag, or starter difficulty. Once started, listen to the engine and note any unusual operating conditions. Check for excessive exhaust smoke when the throttle is depressed. Verify the charging system is operating by observing the voltmeter.

SKILL DRILL 62-1 Performing a Walk-Around Inspection

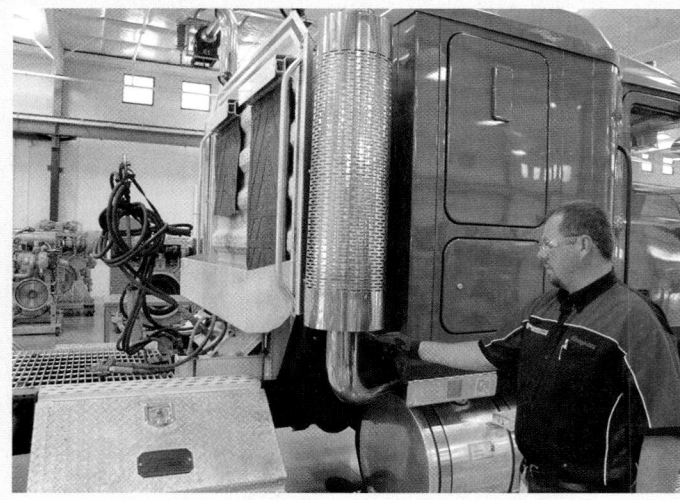

1. Identify leaks. Inspect for leaks from the various vehicle systems, including:
    - Fuel
    - Air system
    - Coolant
    - Engine oil

- Wheel hub and axle leaks
- Transmission fluid
- Power steering fluid
- Brake fluid
- Hydraulic fluid
- DEF

2. Measure and record the depth of tire tread, inflation pressure, general tire condition, and unusual wear conditions.
3. Inspect condition of suspension system, including springs, airbags, leveling system, shock absorbers, U-bolts, brackets, pins, fasteners, center bolts, and missing components. Record any observed deficiencies.
4. Inspect condition of the frame, crossmembers, mounting systems for axles, engine, transmission, and cab for bending, cracks, or missing parts. Inspect for missing or loose fasteners. such as cracked or bent frames or rims.
5. Inspect condition of body sheet metal, glazing materials, such as windshields, and mirrors, window glass, weather stripping, hood and door latches, and door hinges.
6. Inspect condition of seatbelts, presence of flares and other safety equipment stored in the cab, current inspection decals, and up-to-date vehicle documents.
7. Inspect condition of all lighting, headlights, four-way hazard flashers, marker lights, reflectors, and conspicuity markings.
8. Inspect condition of hitching devices, fifth wheels, pintle hooks, air lines, gladhands, and trailer cable.

SKILL DRILL 62-2 Performing an Internal Cab Key-Off Inspection

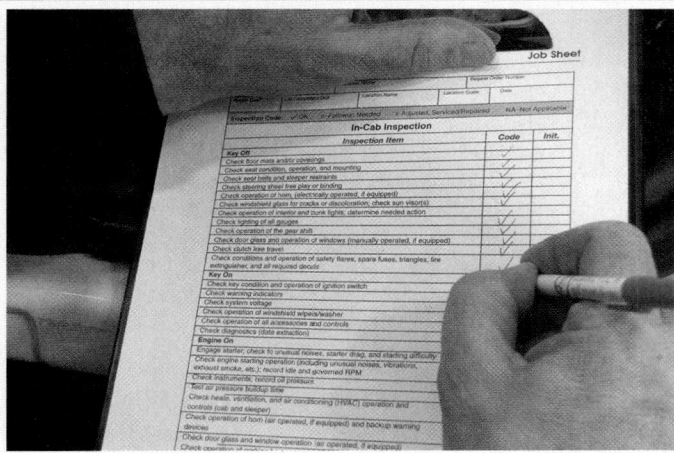

1. Begin the inspection process with the key off.
    - Inspect the floor mats and coverings to ensure that they are in good condition.
    - Inspect and verify that the gear shift boot and floor has no holes or splits in it.
2. Next, check both the driver and passenger seats.
    - Inspect the front and back of both seats for major tears that could hinder entry and exit.
    - Inspect the seats for smooth operation and secure mounting.
    - Inspect any seat adjustment controls to ensure that they are functioning correctly and that any locking mechanisms work correctly.
    - Inspect the operation of seatbelts and sleeper restraints, if equipped.

3. While seated in the driver's seat, inspect gauges and controls near the steering wheel.
    - Inspect and record any excessive free play or binding of the steering wheel as it is turned from lock to lock, left and right.
    - Verify the operation of the electric and air horn.
    - Inspect the windshield glass for chips, cracks, or discoloration and the sun visors for condition and operation.
    - Operate the lighting controls and check that all the gauges illuminate.
    - Check the operation of any cab interior and bunk lights.
4. With the clutch depressed, check the operation of the gear shift by shifting it through the gears.
    - Note if there are any obstructions, binding, looseness, or any other condition that may seem abnormal or may prevent safe operation.
5. Check the clutch free travel by applying light pressure to the pedal. Measure how far the clutch pedal must be depressed before disengaging the clutch, and ensure that the free travel is within recommended specifications.
6. Examine the operation of windows and vents plus the operation of any other movable windows, their channel guides, and their locking devices.
7. Inspect the condition and document the presence of safety flares, spare fuses, triangles, fire extinguisher, and all required decals.
    - Depending on location and operation of the vehicle, regulations determine the type of equipment to be carried. For instance, in the United States it is normal to carry three bidirectional reflective triangles, an approved fire extinguisher (properly charged and mounted), and three emergency flares.

SKILL DRILL 62-3 Performing an Internal Cab Key-On Inspection

1. First, check the ignition key condition and operation of the ignition switch, making sure it operates in all positions.
2. Switch the key in the ignition in the on position.
3. Inspect all the instrument warning indicators:
   - The low oil pressure light and the air pressure warning system should have a visible and audible alert.
   - Verify the illumination of any electronic engine, aftertreatment system, or antilock brake system (ABS) warning lights. It is important to remember that these lights normally cycle on, then off, and then on again if there are faults. Record whether any faults are active or if historical faults are present. Use the driver's information center to retrieve fault codes.
   - Observe and record the DEF fluid level.
   - Check the system voltage. Note the reading on the voltage gauge and record it on the checklist. Then crank the engine, which should show a gauge reading decrease. When the engine starts, check the system voltage again. When increasing the engine speed, record maximum voltage.
   - Verify the operation of windshield wipers and washers by moving the switch through its positions; check that the wipers park correctly when turned off. Ensure that the washer spray nozzles function and are adjusted properly.
   - Check the operation of all other accessories and controls, such as remote mirrors, heated mirrors, cruise control (the on and off function only), powered windows, and any other installed accessories.
4. Retrieve and save any diagnostic or maintenance information from the diagnostic data link using an appropriate electronic service tool. Review the information to determine whether maintenance reminders need resetting or further diagnostic follow-up is required for any active or historical faults.

SKILL DRILL 62-4 Performing an Engine-Running Inspection

1. With the engine running, check all the vehicle instruments:
   - Tachometer
   - Fuel gauge
   - Coolant temperature gauge
   - Oil pressure gauge
   - Voltmeter gauge
   - All other engine system gauges
   Record the oil pressure and voltage on the checklist.
2. Test the air pressure build-up time by depressing the brake pedal and any other air system operating controls to reduce all air pressures to less than 80 psi (553 kPa).
   - Run the engine at a minimum of 1200 rpm and record the time it takes to increase from 85 psi (586 kPa) to 100 psi (689 kPa). The time should not exceed 25 seconds. If it does, note the deficiency as an out-of-service condition for further follow-up before releasing the vehicle.
3. Check the heater, ventilation, and air-conditioning (HVAC) controls in the cab and the sleeper.
   - Verify operating controls respond smoothly, place the control in each of the HVAC modes.
   - Verify that all air vents are opening and closing properly and that the fan motor operates at every available speed selection position.
   - Verify that the air conditioner is operating by listening for the noise of the air-conditioner compressor clutch engaging when the air conditioner is turned on.
   - Verify conditioned air is flowing from the HVAC vents.
   - Verify air-horn operation (if equipped), and any backup warning devices by operating them.
   - Check that any backup warning devices (lights and beepers) work properly when the transmission is placed in reverse.
4. Inspect door glass and window operation for binding, cracked or broken glass, or missing channels.
5. Verify the operation of the parking brake holding power by trying to move the vehicle after the brake is applied.
   - If the vehicle moves, it may simply mean that the parking brake is out of adjustment, and further inspection is required.
   - Verify that the parking brake releases properly by moving the vehicle after releasing the brake.
6. Inspect the operation of the clutch and clutch brake (if equipped) by placing the vehicle in gear and slowly releasing the clutch until the vehicle moves. Verify the clutch brake slows the transmission input shaft when the clutch pedal is ½" from the floor.
7. Verify the correct operation of the following shut-down systems if equipped:
   - Mechanical
   - Electronic
   - Emergency
   At a minimum, turning the key to the off position should shut down the engine.

Performing Exterior Inspections

This inspection covers the cab doors, body and component mountings, batteries and mountings, lines, fifth-wheel coupling mountings, frame and suspension, suspension ride height, electrical components, exhaust, and lubrication. To inspect the cab door, follow the steps in **SKILL DRILL 62-5**.

After the inspection of the cab door and the deck plate, move on to inspecting the mirrors, cab, and fuel systems. To inspect the body and component mountings, follow the guidelines in **SKILL DRILL 62-6**.

The next exterior inspection involves battery inspection and load testing. Inspect the battery boxes, their covers, battery cleanliness, and their hold-downs to ensure that they are securely attached and have no missing hardware. Check for any damage, holes, and tears to the cover and box, which should be securely attached to the vehicle. Look for any cracked or missing mounting components. Verify there is no major corrosion on the bottom inside of the box. To inspect the batteries and their mountings, follow the procedure in **SKILL DRILL 62-7**.

SKILL DRILL 62-8 has guidelines for inspections that involve air lines and the fifth-wheel coupling mountings. The next step

in exterior inspections is to check the frame and suspension of the vehicle, as described in **SKILL DRILL 62-9**.

Inspections of the electrical components, exhaust, and lubrication system are performed next. Prior to beginning these inspections, it is important to:

- Turn on all the vehicle lights and turn signals. It may be helpful to have someone in the cab for these checks.
- Check all exterior lights, lenses, covers, and reflectors for secure mounting and correct location. Verify lenses are not clouded and the correct color. There are legislated standards that determine the lighting and reflector requirements for all vehicles, including tractors and trailers. All lights installed at the date of manufacture must be present and working.
- Verify that any additional lighting or accessories do not interfere with legislated lighting standards. All lights and lenses must have white or amber color to the front, red to rear. No forward-facing light or reflector should produce or reflect light other than white, yellow, or amber. No rear-facing light or reflector, except the reverse lights and license plate light, should reflect or produce white light. If any optional lights

---

SKILL DRILL 62-5 Performing a Cab Door Inspection

- Check for any missing or flat rollers.
- Check the window tracks to verify that they are not loose or bent.

4. Examine the panels and hinges for damage and determine whether the seals are in good condition. Also check any stops in the end of the window tracks to verify they are in place and are tight.

5. Examine the condition of any grab handles, steps, and deck plates. Note any missing grab handles, and make sure the handles on the vehicle are securely attached.

6. Inspect for seal leaks by inserting a piece of paper between the door and seal. Attempt to slide the paper from side to side or in and out of the cab after the door is closed. If the paper does not encounter significant resistance, the area is likely leaking. Recommend seal replacement or a door adjustment.

1. Begin by inspecting the cab door operation. Ensure that the locks, latches, and hinges do not bind when the door is opened or closed. Ensure that they are securely attached.

2. Verify that the doors lock and unlock from the outside when using the key and from the inside. Check the locks for ease of operation.

3. Check all components on the cab door.
- Pull the straps and test the handles to make sure they are in good condition.

SKILL DRILL 62-6 Performing a Body and Component Mountings Inspection

1. Inspect the vehicle mirrors for secure mountings and brackets.
   - Mirror glass should be free of cracks or chips and should be securely fastened in its frame.
   - If mirrors are heated and remotely adjustable, verify the heating and remote adjustment controls are working properly.

2. Inspect and record all physical body damage in the cab and sleeper area.
   - Note any dents, breaks, or cracks in fiberglass or broken/missing rivets or bolts.
   - Inspect for holes in the sleeper or cab.

3. Check the fuel tanks, lines, caps, and vents for any seepage or leakage in the fuel system. Verify prescribed components are installed.
   - Verify that fuel lines are not within 6" (150 mm) of any exhaust component unless they are shielded.
   - Verify that the lines are tight at the fittings and that the tank fill caps do not have any missing gaskets or seals.

4. Inspect the fuel tank mountings to ensure they are not loose, broken, or missing any mounting bolts or brackets. Remember that some fuel tanks use springs or rubber bushings to permit movement.
   - Make sure that tank straps and strap insulators are in the proper position. Look for any cracks in the mounts themselves and check that vents are not blocked.
   - The vent tubes should not have kinks in them. Check for dirt accumulation around the vent to prevent potential blockages from occurring in the future.

SKILL DRILL 62-7 Inspecting Batteries and Mountings

1. Inspect the battery hold-downs, connections, cables, and cable routing for security and make sure they are attached to the battery box frame.

- Verify that the hold-downs fit properly and that they do not crush or distort the battery box or contact any of the terminals.
- Inspect any fasteners for rust or other corrosion, and inspect connections, cables, and cable routing for corrosion. Ensure that there are no holes or tears in the cable insulation and that the battery connections are tight.
- Inspect the cleanliness of batteries and clean any grime from the batteries to prevent surface discharge. Verify there are no leaks or cracks.
- Inspect the condition of the ground connection, and check that any other cables do not rub on any other components.
- Verify the battery cables are tight and posts are clean and tight.

2. Verify the batteries are all the same size and brand. Record the battery's state of charge by measuring the open circuit voltage of each battery. The results should be 12.4 volts or higher on a 12-volt battery.
   - Conduct a battery load test or a conductance test and compare with specifications on the battery case.

are installed, they must be acceptable according to published standards for the region the vehicle operates in.

- All lights should have the correct wattage for its application and have a DOT, SAE, Economic Commission for Europe (ECE), or other regulated standard marked on the bulb and lamp.

- Inspect for cracked or clouded lenses and internal moisture and for proper operation.
- Inspect any visible wiring for general condition.

To inspect low-beam headlight aim, perform the steps outlined in **SKILL DRILL 62-10**.

SKILL DRILL 62-8 Inspecting Lines and Fifth-Wheel Coupling Mountings

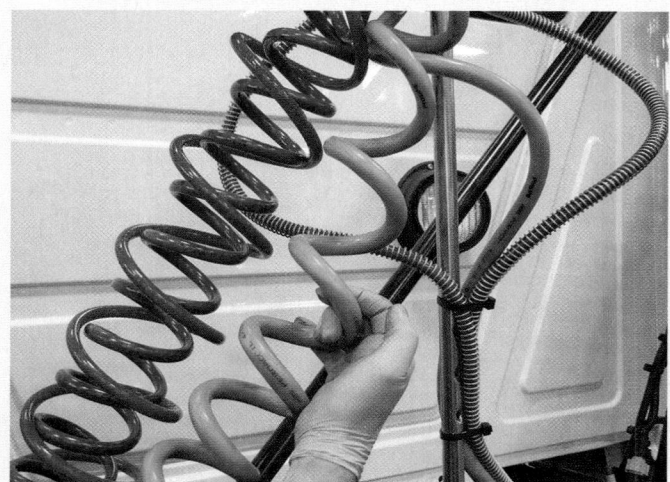
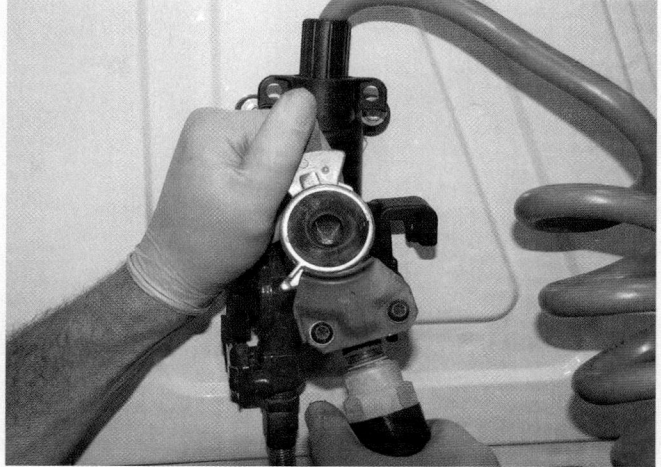

1. Inspect coupling air lines, their holders, gladhands, and the multi-wire connectors.
   - Inspect the air lines for chafing or rubbing on the deck plate, kinks, knots, or twisting in the lines. Make sure they are securely mounted.
   - Inspect for any broken or missing fasteners, and check that the holders keep the lines and cords from dragging on the deck plate or other components.
   - Inspect that the seals on the gladhands are not damaged and inspect for cracks or looseness of the flange. Ensure that the fittings are not loose.
2. Inspect the trailer cable connection by checking each circuit for power using a test light or by turning on the appropriate light switch and determining whether the system is working. Inspect any trailer cords for chafing, and ensure that the cord ends are not worn or broken.
3. Inspect the air drier purge valve operation, mounting, fittings, and connections for leaking air. Check that any associated electrical connections are secure.
4. Inspect the components for loose, broken, or missing mounting bolts, and check the brackets for cracks.

5. Check the fifth-wheel coupling for cracked mounting plates or feet, loose bolts, broken or damaged side rails, or worn bushings.
6. Inspect for missing or damaged slide locking pins. If equipped, the system should also be inspected for a damaged air hose or cylinder. Inspect the operation of the release mechanism and secondary locking mechanism.
7. Using a fifth-wheel test pin, or test gauge to verify that the locking jaws fully close into the locked position. Inspect for any excessive play between the test device and jaws. Some free play is acceptable but varies between plate models; refer to the OEM service manual for acceptable limits.
8. If the vehicle has a pintle hook, the assembly and mounting should be inspected for excess wear and loose or missing fasteners. A fastener is not considered missing if there is an empty hole in the device but no corresponding hole in the frame, or vice versa.
9. Inspect for cracks in the frame or mounts, cracks in the hook assembly, or any welded repair. It is not acceptable for there to be any welding repairs on the pintle hook or hitching device. Ensure that the latch locks the pintle hook in the closed position, and check for the presence of a safety pin. Check for excessive play in the pintle hook latch.

To inspect electrical components, exhaust, and lubrication, follow the steps in **SKILL DRILL 62-11**.

Inspecting the Braking System

LO 62-11 Identify and describe out-of-service criterial and inspection procedures for the braking system.

Brakes are a special area of extreme importance in terms of operational efficiency and safety. As such, brakes are one of the highest priorities in PMI, and if they are found defective the vehicle must be designated out of service until deficiencies are corrected.

A vehicle or combination vehicle is designated OOSC if 20% or more of its service brakes have one of the following defects:

- Any steering-axle brake defect listed in next section
- Won't actuate effectively or friction material won't contact drum/rotor
- Audible air leak
- Missing brake on any axle required to have brakes

CVSA Defective Brakes Criteria

A vehicle or combination vehicle is OOS if 20% or more of its service brakes have one of the following defects:

- Any steering-axle brake defect listed in next section
- Won't apply effectively or friction material won't contact drum/rotor
- Audible air leak at chamber
- Missing brake on any axle required to have brakes

SKILL DRILL 62-9 Inspecting Frame and Suspension and Suspension Ride Height

1. Inspect the vehicle frame and the frame members for bending or other types of deformities and for any cracks and excessive rust or scale.
  - Inspect the frame members for cracks, breaks, bending, looseness, or twisting. In addition, they should be inspected for any loose or missing fasteners, including fasteners attaching functional components, such as the engine, transmission, steering gear, suspension, body parts, and fifth-wheel coupling.

2. Inspect for any condition that causes the body or frame to be in contact with a tire or any part of the wheel assemblies and for missing or unengaged locking pins in adjustable axle assemblies.

3. Measure and record the vehicle's suspension ride height. Inspecting the vehicle's suspension ride height is an important aspect of exterior inspections. Every manufacturer has a procedure for this. Some of the most common methods are:
  - Measuring from level ground to the bottom of both frame rails.
  - Measuring from level ground to the bottom of the rear-most airbag.
  - Measuring from level ground to the top of the fifth-wheel plate.
  - Measuring from the bottom of the airbag to the bottom of the frame rail.
  - Measuring from the top of the axle housing to the bottom of the frame rail.

When inspecting, check for missing, non-functioning, loose, contaminated, or cracked parts on the brake system (**FIGURE 62-15**). Inspect for "S" cam cam-over. Listen for audible air leaks around brake components and lines. Check that the slack adjusters are the same length (from center of "S" cam to center of clevis pin), and that the air chambers on each axle are the same size. Inspect the required brake system warning devices, such as ABS malfunction lamps and low air pressure warning devices. Inspect tractor protection system, including the bleed-back through valves and seals on the trailer.

SKILL DRILL 62-10 Inspecting and Adjusting Low-Beam Headlight Aim

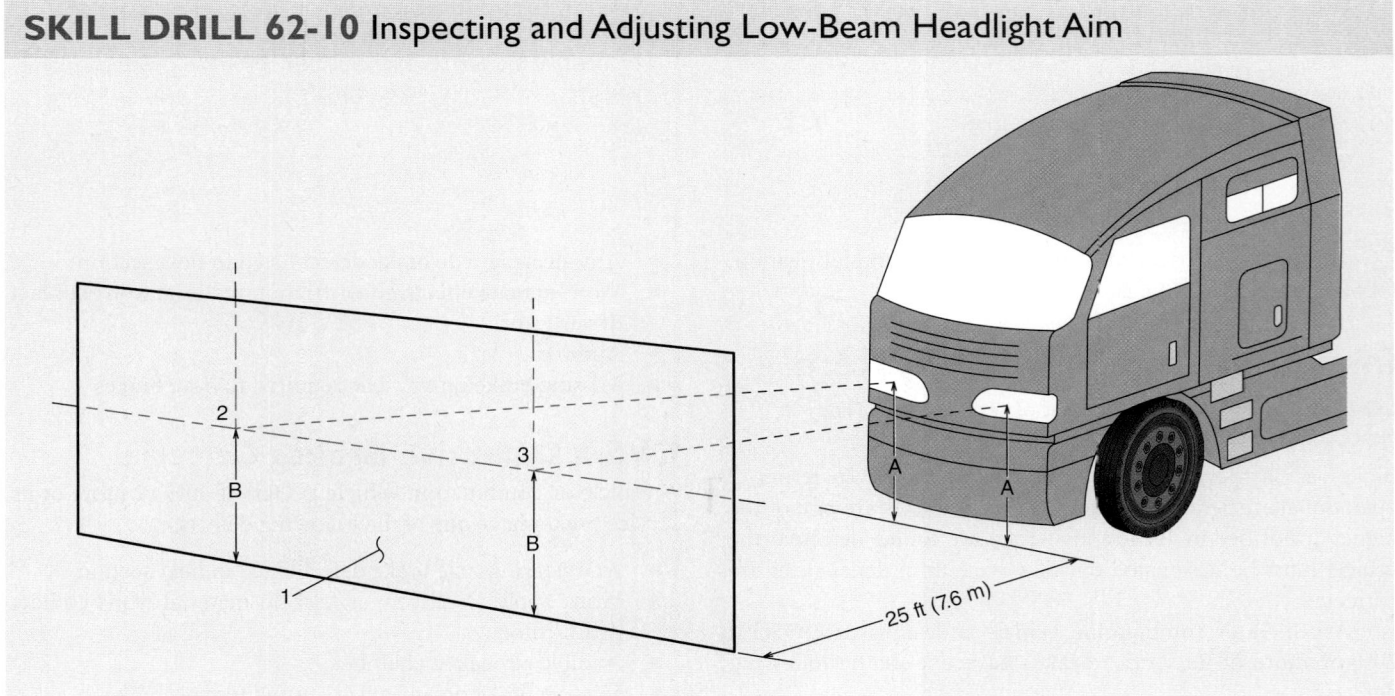

25 ft (7.6 m)

SKILL DRILL 62-10 Inspecting and Adjusting Low-Beam Headlight Aim (Continued)

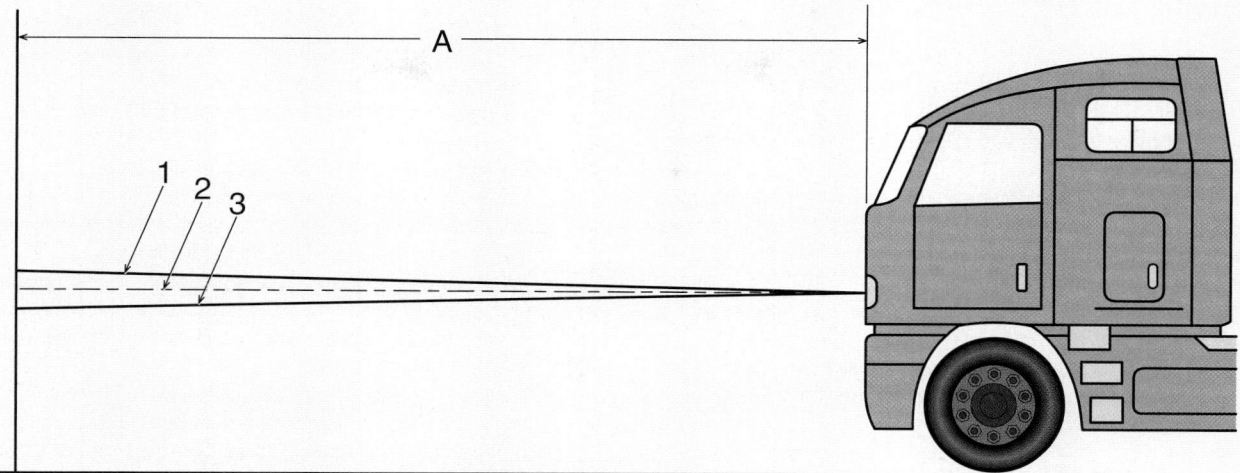

1. To verify correct headlight low-beam aim, use the following as a general guideline. Park the vehicle on a level floor approximately 25" (7.6 m) away from a screen or wall. Ideally the vehicle should be loaded as it would be in normal use.
2. Locate in the headlight center on each side of the vehicle. A small dot or indentation is present in all headlights at approximately center of the light.
3. Measure the distance from the ground to the headlight center point mark.
4. Transfer the distance of the headlight height from the floor to the screen or wall directly in front of the vehicle.
5. Switch on the low-beam headlights and find the center of the projected beam where it strikes the wall. An intense point of light usually identifies this spot. Verify the same headlight height from the floor matches the beam height projected onto the wall.
6. Variations of no more than plus or minus 6" are acceptable at 25'. The center height of the low-beam projection should vary no more than +6" from the height on the vehicle.
7. If necessary, adjust the headlight vertical aim using the adjustment screws at the rear of the headlight.

SKILL DRILL 62-11 Inspecting Electrical Components, Exhaust, and Lubrication (Including Fifth Wheel)

1. Inspect license plates and brackets to verify that the license has not expired and that the brackets are securely mounted. Verify that license plate lights are working.
2. Inspect the exhaust system for leaks, proper routing, and damaged or missing components.
   - It is especially important that the exhaust system not be leaking at a point forward of, or directly below, the driver/sleeper compartment. Ensure that the exhaust outlet is behind or above any part of the vehicle designed to be occupied.
   - Verify that the exhaust system does not rub or contact any other objects and that no part of the exhaust system is positioned in a location that could result in burning, charring, or damaging the electrical wiring, fuel supply, or any combustible part of the vehicle.
   - Verify that aftertreatment system components, electrical harness, and air and fuel lines are connected and present.
   - Record the level of the diesel exhaust fluid—use a refractometer to verify DEF quality.
3. Inspect hangers and clamps for looseness and damage, and verify that components are securely suspended and attached to the vehicle.
   - Inspect for any missing fasteners on the exhaust pipes and mufflers, and inspect any supports for excessive rust or cracks.
   - Verify the muffler has no holes, large dents, or other damage that could restrict exhaust gas flow.
4. Inspect the front and rear cab mounts for wear and secure attachment to the frame and cab structure, and ensure that all fasteners are present and tight.

SKILL DRILL 62-11 Inspecting Electrical Components, Exhaust, and Lubrication (Including Fifth Wheel) (Continued)

- Verify the cab rear air ride height is correct, if equipped. The cab should be positioned approximately in the center of its limits of travel.
- Inspect the cab latches and cables for secure attachment, wear, or damage and for bincing.

5. Check wiper blades for deterioration, cracks/tears, hardening, missing pivot parts, and secure attachment to the arm assembly. Operate wipers/washers to make sure the wipers cover the whole window with no streaks.
- Wiper arms should be inspected for damage, looseness, or wear in linkage and for bends and spring tension.
- Windshield washer nozzles should be examined for build-up of foreign material and their hoses for attachment, wear, and proper routing.

6. Verify the headlight alignment using a marked screen wall, mechanical headlight aimer, or photoelectric aimer.

7. Lubricate all cab and hood grease fittings and wipe grease fittings. Replace any fittings that are damaged.
- All grease fittings should take grease; if they do not, they should be replaced.
- Lubricate door and hood hinges, atches, strikers, lock cylinders, safety latches, linkages, and cables.

8. Lubricate all fifth-wheel grease fittings and plate. Wipe grease fittings and replace any fittings that are damaged.
- All grease fittings should accept grease; if they do not, they should be replaced. This process should be undertaken while rocking the fifth wheel front to back to disperse the lubricant evenly on the pivots.
- Lubricate the fifth-wheel plate (unless it is Teflon coated) by applying a liberal amount of lubricant to the throat and back half of the plate. Smooth the lubricant over the back half of the plate, from about the front edge of the throat to the back of the plate.

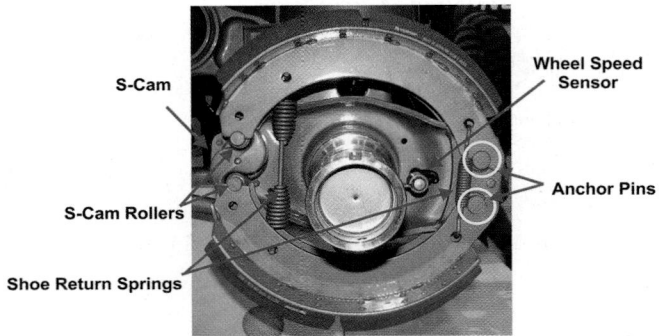

FIGURE 62-15 Typical components of an air brake assembly.

FIGURE 62-16 With the backing plate removed, brake block and lining can be inspected for thickness and condition.

Drum Brakes OOSC

OOS criteria for inspecting drum brakes include:
- Broken or missing
  - brake shoe(s) or lining,
  - return springs (shoe or brake chamber),
  - anchor pin or spider,
  - cam roller, camshaft,
  - chamber pushrod, yoke, clevis pin, slack or automatic adjuster,
  - parking brake power spring or air chamber mounting bolt (**FIGURE 62-16**).
- Loose air chamber, spider or camshaft support bracket
- Lining has crack/void, observable on edge, wider than $\frac{1}{16}$"
- Portion of lining is missing, to the extent that rivet/bolt is exposed
- Lining has crack, observable on edge, longer than $1\frac{1}{2}$"
- Loose lining segment, permitting about $\frac{1}{16}$" movement
- An entire segment of lining is missing
- Evidence of oil, grease, or brake fluid contamination of the friction surface of the brake drum and the brake friction material

- Lining thickness less than $\frac{1}{4}$" or to wear indicator, if so marked, at shoe center

Air Disc Brakes OOSC

When inspecting air disc brakes, the following are OOSC criteria:

- Broken or missing caliper, brake pad, pad retaining component, pushrod, yoke, clevis pin, brake adjuster, parking brake power spring, or chamber return spring air chamber mounting bolt
- Loose or missing brake chamber or caliper mounting bolt
- Rotor has evidence of severe rusting or metal-to-metal contact over the rotor friction surface or on either side (**FIGURE 62-17**).
- Evidence of oil or grease contamination of the friction surface of the brake rotor and the brake friction material
- Brake pad thickness is less than $\frac{1}{16}$" or to wear indicator, if pad is so marked.

FIGURE 62-17 Components of a disc brake system. Hold down retainer for air disc brake pads must be in place to be considered safe.

90-degrees

Stroke Indicator

FIGURE 62-18 Stroke indicators provide a quick visual check of brake adjustment. The indicator on the chamber pushrod should stay between the two limits markers of brake stroke.

Brake Pushrod Adjustment Limits

The following are OOSC criteria when inspecting brake stroke travel:

- With engine off, air reservoir at no more than 90 to 100 psi (621 to 689 kPa) (dump excess pressure)
- Brakes fully applied, push rod stroke is ¼" or more beyond adjustment limit (**FIGURE 62-18**).

Front Steering Axle Brakes

The following are OOSC criteria when inspecting front steer axle brakes:

- Any inoperative or missing brake on either wheel of any steering axle of any vehicle equipped or required to be equipped with steering axle brakes, including the dolly and front axle of a full trailer and tractors required to have steering axle brakes
- Defects of drum air brakes, air disc brakes, and hydraulic brakes apply to front steering axle brakes
- Mismatched air chamber sizes for drum air brakes and air disc brakes. A mismatch on an air disc brake exists only when there is measurable difference in air chamber clamp sizes
- Mismatched slack adjuster length for drum and air disc brakes

FIGURE 62-19 A brake drum and air brake rotor in new condition.

- Any bolt-type brake chamber with any other type of brake chamber
- The use of spring brake chambers
- Non-manufactured hole/crack in spring brake housing

Parking Brake and Emergency Braking

The following are OOSC criteria when inspecting parking brake and emergency braking functions:

- Inoperable emergency braking system on 25% or more of the brakes on a trailer
- No brakes are applied when parking brake control is actuated
- A brake malfunction causing smoke or fire to emit from wheel end, not including overheating, due to severe brake use
- Missing or inoperative components, including tractor-protection valve and/or trailer supply valve

Drum and Rotors

The following are OOSC criteria when inspecting brake drums and rotors:

- External crack that is visible or opens upon brake application
- Rotor with a crack in length of more than 75% of the friction surface that passes completely through the rotor (**FIGURE 62-19**)
- Portion of drum/rotor missing or in danger of falling off

Hoses and Tubing

The following are OOSC criteria when inspecting brake hoses and tubing:

- Damage through outer reinforcing ply
- Rubber-impregnated fabric cover is not reinforcement ply

- Thermoplastic nylon may have braid reinforcement or color difference between cover and inner tube
- Bulge/swelling when air applied
- Audible leak at other than proper connection
- Cracked, broken, or crimped and restricting air flow
- Improper splice (such as hose ends forced over piece of tubing and secured with hose clamps)

Air Pressure Gauge and Low-Pressure Warning System

The following are OOSC criteria when inspecting the air pressure gauges:

- Inoperative or defective primary or secondary pressure gauge
- Air loss rate is excessive if an 80 to 90 psi (552 to 621 kPa) reservoir pressure is not maintained with governor cut in, engine idling, and service brakes fully applied.
- Both the audible and visual warning devices fail to operate as required.

Air Compressor

The following are OOSC criteria when inspecting the air compressor:

- Loose mounting bolts
- Cracked/broken/loose pulley

- Cracked/broken mounting bracket/brace/adapter
- Separated from original attachment points

Inspecting Air Brake Circuits

With air brakes, the truck's air supply and air circuits must operate correctly. There is a series of tests to perform to validate correct air brake system operation. These tests may require two people. To perform a full inspection of the air brake system, follow the procedures outlined in the Skill Drills in the chapter on Air Brake Circuits and Valves.

Inspecting Tires and Wheels

LO 62-12 Outline procedures for inspecting tires and wheels.

Inspecting wheels and tires is critical to the safe operation of any road transport vehicle. Underinflated tires, tires with poor tread, mismatched tires, and poorly mounted tires can contribute to poor handling in bad road conditions at the very least, and can lead to blowouts, wheel separations, and collisions.

The following Skill Drills may seem routine, but finding potential trouble spots requires a careful observation. Inspecting the condition of the wheel bearings is also part of this inspection process. To inspect tires and wheels, follow the steps in SKILL DRILL 62-12.

SKILL DRILL 62-12 Inspecting Tires and Wheels

1. First, check tires for irregular wear patterns.
   - Run your hand over the tread and feel for areas of uneven wear and confirm with a visual inspection.
   - Take note of any flat spots on the tread.
   - Irregular tire wear patterns may indicate other problems, such as uneven loading from a mispositioned fifth wheel, loose front-end linkage, worn wheel bearings, over- or underinflated

tires, bad shock absorbers, out-of-balance wheels, poor alignment, or ABS system faults.
2. Verify the tires are correctly matched and properly installed. This involves noting any missing balance weights and making sure the tires are a matched set. Note any deficiencies.
   - Verify the tire diameter and tread are the same on all tires at each wheel end. This is particularly important on dual tire installations.
   - Ideally, all tires across the same axle should be matched in tread design and by manufacturer. A vehicle may still be allowed to operate if two tires on one side of the axle have different tread from a matching set on the other side of the axle.
   - NOTE: Bias and radial tires should NOT be mixed on any vehicle, regardless of tread design.
3. Check the overall condition of the tire, tread, and sidewalls. Note any of the following:
   - Cuts
   - Tears
   - Cracks
   - Bulges
   - Feathered edges
   - Spotty or excessive wear on the outside ribs
   - Excessive heel and toe wear on lug-type tire
   - Broken wheel studs and missing wheel nuts
4. Check the valve caps and stems.
   - Note any loose or leaking caps, oxidized or rotted valve stems, or missing caps.
   - Verify valve stems are properly aligned (180 degrees apart on dual wheels).

SKILL DRILL 62-12 Inspecting Tires and Wheels (Continued)

5. Measure and record tread depth.
   Measure the tread depth in three places with a tread depth gauge at equal intervals around the center of the tire.
   - Record the tread depth on a checklist sheet. The minimum depth allowed by the FMCSA is ⅟₃₂" (3.175 mm) on the steering axle and ²⁄₃₂" (1.588 mm) on drive trailer axles.
6. Measure and record tire air pressure. Adjust tire pressure, if necessary. Use an appropriate tire pressure gauge to measure the pressure on each tire, recording the pressure on the PMI checklist.
   - A vehicle should not be driven if the tire pressure is less than 80% of the maximum recommended pressure.
7. Next, inspect wheel nuts, studs, rims, spacers, and mounting hardware.
   - Look and feel for cracks, corrosion, missing wheel nuts, broken studs, and rust streaks between mating surfaces and the wheels around the studs. Rust streaks indicate loose parts.

- Note any oil or grease leaks from the hubs, slipped wheels, and any other obvious damage.
- It is important that the wheel nuts are tightened to the manufacturer's specifications, so use a torque wrench to verify the correct tightness on the wheel nuts.
8. On vehicles with tandem wheels, check dual mating with a square. Measure the difference in tread between the two tires on each dual set using the mating square.
   - The difference in tread should not be more than a ¼" (6.35 mm), and the smaller tire must be on the inside.
   - Mismatched dual tires overload the larger diameter tire, causing it to overdeflect and overheat. The smaller diameter tire, lacking proper road contact, wears faster and unevenly. Tread or ply separation, tire body breaks, and blowouts may result from mismatched tires.

Wheel End OOS Criteria

The following are disqualifying OOSC criteria when inspecting wheel ends and hubs:

- Lock/side ring is bent, broken, or cracked, or improperly seated/sprung/mismatched
- Cracked rim (any circumferential crack except one intentionally made at the valve stem hole)
- Disc wheel cracked between any two holes (hand hole, stud hole, center hole)
- Disc wheel with two cracks
- Disc wheel with one crack extending 3" or more
- Disc wheel with 50% or more of stud holes elongated
- Spoke wheel with two or more cracks (of 1" or greater length) across spoke or hub section
- Spoke wheel with two or more web areas cracked
- Tubeless demountable adapter crack (cracks at three or more spokes)
- Fasteners loose/missing/broken/cracked or stripped on disc/spoke wheel. For a 10-hole wheel assembly: Three missing or defective wheel fasteners in any location, or two missing/defective adjacent fasteners
- For eight-hole-or-less wheel assembly: Any two missing or defective wheel fasteners
- Crack in any weld attaching the disc wheel to rim.
- Crack in weld attaching tubeless demountable rim to adapter
- Welded repair on any aluminum wheel on steering axle
- Welded repair, other than disc-to-rim attachment, on steel disc wheel on steering axle
- Any bearing (hub) cap, plug, or filler plug is missing or broken, affording view of hub assembly
- Visible smoke from wheel hub assembly due to bearing failure (**FIGURE 62-20**)
- Any wheel seal is leaking, producing evidence of wet contamination of the brake friction material and accompanied by evidence that further leaking will occur

FIGURE 62-20 This area should be carefully inspected to check for wheel seal leaks.

- Lubricant is leaking from the hub and is present on the wheel surface and is accompanied by evidence that further leakage will occur
- No visible or measurable amount of lubricant is showing in hub

Inspecting Wheel Alignment

LO 62-13 Outline inspection procedures for verifying correct wheel alignment.

Performing a wheel alignment inspection is good practice for the safe operation of any road transport vehicle. Incorrect wheel alignment can contribute to the unnecessary rapid wear of tires and affect handling of the vehicle itself.

The guidelines for performing a wheel alignment inspection in **SKILL DRILL 62-13** may seem routine, but following the procedures outlined helps to significantly reduce unnecessary tire wear and steering-related complaints.

Performing Under-Vehicle Inspections

LO 62-14 Outline general inspection procedures for performing under-vehicle inspections.

The under-vehicle inspection should focus mainly on the suspension, transmission and drivetrain of the vehicle. Drivelines in most medium- and heavy-duty vehicles are long, so it is necessary to inspect it using either a creeper or raised on a hoist or accessed from a pit.

In general, inspect for:

- Indication of leaks
- Air and electrical lines for correctly clipping and abrasion damage
- Wheel seal leaks
- Thickness of brake friction material and brake adjustment
- Condition of brake chambers, slack adjusters, and camshafts
- Correct phasing of the driveline
- Exhaust system leaks and aftertreatment components are intact and correctly connected

- Any missing bolts or fasteners
- The steering linkages are correctly attached and not excessively worn
- U-bolt and spring saddles—any rust around bolts and spring saddles indicate movement

Frame, Mountings, Electrical, and Exhaust

The vehicle frame resists twisting, bending, and buckling while supporting heavy loads at high speeds so it is prone to cracks. Inspect all the frame areas, especially frame cross members, for bending or other types of deformities. Note any cracks or excessive rust or scale, which indicate a potential weak point. **SKILL DRILL 62-14** contains guidelines for performing inspections on the under-vehicle frame, mountings, electrical, and exhaust.

Transmission and Drivetrain

The next area to inspect is the transmission and drive area. To perform this inspection, verify the bolts attaching the transmission to the engine flywheel-housing are present and tight. Check the mounting area for any cracks and the rubber isolators for wear, oil contamination, and damage. Also look for gaps between the transmission case and flywheel housing. To perform an under-vehicle transmission and drivetrain inspection, follow the steps in **SKILL DRILL 62-15**.

Inspecting the Engine Compartment

The engine compartment inspection focuses on pumps, pulleys, belts, the air-conditioning (A/C) unit, and fluids. This inspection involves steps with the engine off and with the engine on. To perform an engine-off engine compartment inspection, follow the steps in **SKILL DRILL 62-16**. The following Skill Drills cover the various aspects of each.

SKILL DRILL 62-13 Inspecting Wheel Alignment

1. Inspect the front axle king pin wear by checking for excessive play between the king pin and the axle spindle.
   - With the vehicle raised just off the ground, insert a pry bar under the tire and move the bar vertically to inspect the thrust bearings and shims.

- Rock the tire at a 45-degree angle to inspect wheel bearings and king pins for wear. Apply the brakes to differentiate wear in the king pins and wheel bearings. When the brakes are applied, movement is caused by wear in the king pins and bushings.

2. Check tandem axle alignment and spacing by verifying that the axles are perpendicular to the vehicle centerline. A tram gauge is used to verify the distance from axle shaft centers to center are identical. Axles out of alignment can cause misalignment in the steering wheel to compensate for a misaligned thrust angle. An incorrect thrust angle will cause the front tires to scrub sideways and wear quickly. Misalignment can also cause the vehicle to oversteer when turning in one direction and understeer when turning in the other direction.

3. Measure toe-in, caster, and camber angles using the appropriate alignment equipment. This may involve mounting alignment sensors on wheels and checking alignment angles on each wheel end.

SKILL DRILL 62-14 Inspecting Under-Vehicle Frame, Mountings, Electrical, and Exhaust

1. Check for any loose or missing fasteners, especially those attaching critical components, such as the:
   • Engine
   • Transmission

• Steering gear
• Suspension
• Body parts
• Fifth wheel

2. Check for any condition that causes the body or frame to be in contact with a tire or any part of the wheel assemblies. This is a potentially dangerous condition that could result in a blowout.

3. Check for missing or unengaged locking pins in the sliding axle assemblies.

4. Inspect engine mounts for looseness and deterioration.
   • Look for missing or loose fasteners.
   • Check the rubber mounts for cracks, deterioration, and splitting.
   • Check that any mounting pads have not shifted.

5. Check the vehicle wiring, routing, and hold-down clamps and ensure the wire insulators are not cracked, chafed, or charred.
   • Verify that the wiring is clear of moving parts and heat-producing sources, such as exhaust. Verify wiring and air lines are properly clipped and routed.

SKILL DRILL 62-15 Inspecting the Under-Vehicle Transmission and Drivetrain

1. Inspect the transmission case, seals, lines, cooler, and fittings for leaks and cracks.
   • Check the fittings for tightness.
   • Check the case plugs and fittings for seepage.
   • Check the cooler lines for chafing, leaks, or seepage.
   • If the vehicle is equipped with air lines, check the lines for signs of leakage and wear, and make sure the lines are not routed near moving parts.
   • With transmission breathers, make sure the vent is open and is not clogged with any debris to restrict flow, and make sure the cap is present.

2. Inspect the transmission oil.
   • Verify the oil level, type, and condition.
   • Check the oil for the presence of water metallic particles or other contamination.

• Smell the oil to confirm it is not burned.
• Add only lubricants recommended by the manufacturer. For transmission and differentials, most manufacturers require synthetic lubricants.
• To add oil to an automatic transmission, the method recommended by the manufacturer should be followed. In such cases, normally the transmission oil level is checked with the transmission in neutral or park and with the engine running.

3. Inspect U-joints, yokes, drivelines, and center support bearings. With the vehicle parked level, wheels chocked, and the transmission in neutral:
   • Inspect universal joints for looseness, damage, and proper phasing.
   • They are considered in phase when the driveline yokes are in the same position along the drive shaft.
   • If vibration complaints are reported, measure the driveline angles with a driveline protractor and record results on a worksheet for measuring angles.
   • Inspect each U-joint for wear in the trunnion or cross. Push up and down on the joints after rotating the joint 90 degrees each time. No movement should be detected. Verify grease is purging from each cap when lubricated.
   • Inspect pinion shafts and yokes to verify they are tight, and seals are not leaking.

4. Inspect the drive shaft for damage and missing counterweights, the welds on the drive shaft for cracks, and the input and output yokes for looseness.
   • Check each slip yoke by twisting it in opposite directions and pushing up and down while looking for excessive play.
   • Check for loose hanger support bearings and insulating rubbers are intact.
   • Check that all fasteners are present and tight.

SKILL DRILL 62-15 Inspecting the Under-Vehicle Transmission and Drivetrain (Continued)

5. Inspect the axle housings for cracks and leaks, and check the axle breather.
   - Inspect for leaks at the mounting gaskets, bolts, pinion seal, rear cover flanges, and axle housing.
   - Verify all fasteners are present and secure.
   - Turn the protective cap on the breather vent to confirm it is venting.
6. Inspect the drive axle(s) oil level, type, and condition.
   - Using a finger or a piece of bent wire, check the oil level and confirm it is flush with the bottom of the fill hole.
   - Inspect the oil for the presence of water (milky color) or metallic particles (silver sheen).
   - Use the recommended type of oil when adding oil to the axle.
7. Check the oil level and condition in all non-drive hubs.
   - Check that the oil level is flush with the bottom of the fill hole.
   - Check for the presence of water or metallic particles.
   - Top off any fluid with the manufacturer-recommended oil.
   - Check for leaks around the fill plug and mating surface.
8. Verify the power divider shifts and locks. This is done by lifting the two rear axles and rotating the tires. See the chapter Servicing Heavy-Duty Axles for this procedure.

SKILL DRILL 62-16 Inspecting Engine-Off Engine Compartments

1. Check the belts, pulleys, and tensioners.
   - Check the belts for cracks, glazing, jagged or streaked sidewalls, tensile breaks in the cord body, and uneven ribs on serpentine belts. Use a belt gauge to check for wear on serpentine belts. (See the chapter on Charging Systems for a more comprehensive inspection procedure on accessory drive belts.)
   - Verify that the drive belts ride correctly in the pulley grooves. Listen for a chirping or squealing sound that indicates belt and pulley misalignment or belt slippage.
   - Check that the tensioners and idler pulleys are correctly positioned beneath the belt.
   - Check that the pulleys do not have excessive play or wobble and that they are aligned.
   - Verify that the pulleys do not have embedded foreign objects.
2. Check the engine oil.
   - Always clean around the dipstick with a clean rag before removing the dipstick to check the oil.
   - Check that the oil is at the proper level and check the dipstick for signs of coolant and fuel contamination (e.g., dirt, milky color, burnt, or unusual fuel smells).

- Check the entire engine compartment for any visible signs of leaks, focusing on seals, gaskets, hoses, filters, and drain plugs. NOTE: It can be hard to determine where leaking fluids are coming from, so pressure washing the engine may be necessary to identify a leak location.
3. If the servicing mileage/km specifications have been reached, take an oil sample. To take an oil sample:
   1. Start and warm the vehicle to operating temperature.
   2. Drain the oil and check the magnetic drain plug for contamination.
   3. Take an oil sample following recommended Test Monitoring Center (TMC) procedures using the oil sample syringe.
   NOTE: Samples should be taken from oil midway through the draining. Evidence of metal shavings or other contamination on the magnetic drain plug could indicate problems within the engine.
4. If the servicing mileage/km specifications have been reached, change the engine oil in accordance with the manufacturer's specifications.
   - Inspect and clean the magnetic drain plugs.
   - Replace the oil filter and refill with oil to the correct specification.
5. Check electrical wiring, routing, and hold-down clamps, including the engine control module (ECM). Check that the wiring is clear of moving parts and heat-producing sources, such as the engine, and that it is not pinched.
   - Wire insulators should be free of cracks and should not show chafing or charring.
   - Wires should also not rub together.
   - Hold-down clamps should be secure and should not pinch the wiring.
   - For ECUs, check that all sensor wires are no closer than 6" (15.24 cm) to any hot surfaces. NOTE: If any wires are closer than 6" (15.24 cm) and cannot be rerouted, add heat shields.
   - Also check all wiring and connectors on microcontroller units.
6. Check the throttle linkages and return springs, making sure that the linkages do not bind when applied and that return springs are not broken and have retained their tension.

899999999999999999999999999999999999

SKILL DRILL 62-16 Inspecting Engine-Off Engine Compartments (Continued)

- Check the starter mounting and connections to verify they are securely mounted.
- All electrical connections should be tight, and wiring should not be rubbing or chafing.
- Check the alternator mounting, wiring, and wire routing to make sure all the electrical connections are tight and not corroded and that there is no rubbing or chafing.
- Check that the windshield washer fluid container is filled to the proper level.

7. Check the hydraulic clutch slave and master cylinders' fluid levels and look for any indication of leaks (if equipped). Also look for any leaks on lines, hoses, and fittings, and make sure the lines are properly routed.

8. Inspect power brake booster(s), hoses, and check/control valves for secure mounting. Inspect all lines and hoses for leaks or kinks.

Steering and Air-Conditioning Components

This engine compartment inspection focuses on the power steering pump and A/C components. All inspections revolve around the principles of secure mounting, verifying proper working condition, and leak detection. To perform an engine-off engine compartment inspection specifically on the steering and A/C components, follow the steps in **SKILL DRILL 62-17**. To perform an engine-off engine compartment inspection specifically on the fuel, intake, cooling, and cab tilt systems, follow the procedures in **SKILL DRILL 62-18**.

SKILL DRILL 62-17 Conducting an Engine-Off Engine Compartment Inspection: Steering and Air-Conditioning Components

1. Visually inspect the power steering fluid and filter.
- Locate the power steering reservoir and clean around the dipstick before removing it to check the fluid level.
- Add the recommended fluid, if necessary. Never mix fluid types.
- Check for leaks if the fluid is low.
- Inspect the filter located in the reservoir and clean or replace it, if necessary according to OE recommendations.

2. Inspect the power steering pump.
- Check the power steering pump, mounting, and hoses for leaks, condition, and routing.
- carefully observe the conditions of the seals and fitting around the pump and make sure the pump is securely mounted.
- Confirm no engine oil has entered the reservoir.

3. Inspect the steering gear for leaks and secure mounting.
- Check all fittings and seams for seepage or leakage.
- Check input and output shafts for any leakage.

- Check that mounting hardware is present and secure.
- Check for bent steering linkage, cracks, or other damage to the gear mounting areas.

4. Inspect the Pitman arm-to-steering sector shaft.
- Check the mounting of the Pitman arm-to-steering gear output shaft for looseness.
- Check that the splines on the Pitman arm-to-steering output shaft align and are tight.
- Check for excessive play in the steering gear output shaft.

5. Inspect the steering shaft U-joints.
- Inspect all steering shaft U-joints for excessive side shift, correct alignment of joints, and rotational play.
- Inspect the pinch bolts at the steering shaft and verify the secure attachment to steering gear.

6. Check the tie rod ends and drag links by slightly shaking the steering wheel back and forth.
- Check tie rod ends for excessive axial and radial play (up and down, side to side of joint).
- Check drag link joints for excessive axial and radial play (up and down, side to side).
- Check that the threaded portion of the tie-rod end assembly is inserted far enough into the cross-tube and securely clamped.

7. Inspect the linkage-assist power steering cylinders.
- Check for secure attachment.
- Check for leaks at fittings, hoses, and piston seals.

8. Locate the A/C condenser/compressor and check the front side of the condenser for debris that might cause an airflow restriction.
- Verify the condenser is mounted tightly and the condenser lines are not showing signs of leakage.

Check the compressor for:
- Broken brackets
- Loose or missing bolts
- Alignment of belt and pulleys
- The condition of the refrigerant hoses

NOTE: All service ports must have dust caps.

SKILL DRILL 62-18 Conducting an Engine-Off Engine Compartment Inspection: Fuel, Intake, Cooling, and Cab Tilt Systems

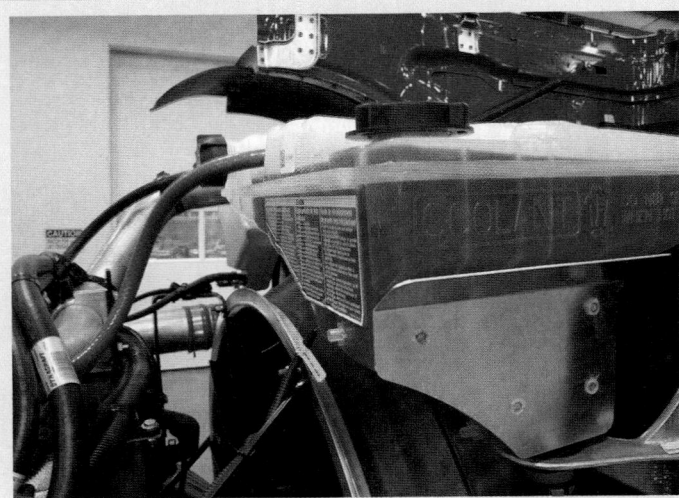

1. Check the fuel pump and fuel line mountings. Road and engine vibrations may damage the pump if it is not secure.
   • Check the water separator/fuel heater.
   • Check the water separator, drain off excess water, and check that the fuel heater functions properly.
   • Replace the fuel filter(s) according to the prescribed schedule.
   • Prime and bleed the fuel system using prescribed procedures.
2. Inspect the intake system.
   • Inspect the air filter housing for damage and properly connected hoses.
   • Record the reading on the filter monitoring device, and reset the air filter restriction indicator to zero.
   • Visually inspect the turbocharger for leaks; check mountings and connections.
   • Inspect the charge air hoses and pipes.
3. Inspect the radiator for leaks, damage, and air flow restrictions caused by debris.
   • Make sure the radiator is securely mounted.

• Service the coolant filter according to the manufacturer recommendations
• Inspect the coolant recovery system for holes and proper mounting.
• Verify the coolant recovery system cap is secure.
• Inspect the radiator hoses for leaks and cracks, and check the clamps for tightness.
4. Inspect the coolant for contamination, additive concentration, and freeze protection levels.
   • Contaminants may be oil, rust, or precipitate drop-out.
   • Inspect the coolant for correct additive concentrations either by the test strip or titration method, and record the results on the checklist.
   • Measure and record the protection or freeze point level using a refractometer.
   • The protection level should be between $-25°$ F and $-35°$ F ($-32°$ C to $-37°$ C).
   • If the system has the correct protection level but additional coolant is needed, fill with the manufacturer's recommended coolant.
5. Pressure test the cooling system and radiator cap (according to the manufacturer's recommendations) to ensure correct pressure in the coolant system.
   • Check the fan assembly and shroud mounting.
   • Check that the blade assembly is free of cracks.
   • Grasp the fan blades and check for excessive play in the shaft.
   • Check for adequate clearance between all moving parts.
6. If equipped, inspect the tilt cab system's hydraulic pump.
   • Verify there is adequate clearance in front of the cab before using the tilt system.
   • Verify there is nothing loose in the passenger compartment that could fall through the windshield when the cab is raised.
   • Inspect the tilt cab system hydraulic lines and cylinders for leaks and damage.
   • Inspect the oil level and service, as required.
   NOTE: If the vehicle does not have a hydraulic tilt cab system, verify the safety locking devices are working properly.

During the engine-on inspection, start the vehicle and let it idle for a few minutes. To perform an engine-on engine compartment inspection to check for leaks, levels, and operation of systems, follow the steps in **SKILL DRILL 62-19**.

Inspecting Cargo-Handling Devices

LO 62-15 Outline general inspection procedures inspecting cargo-handling devices.

When inspecting cargo handling equipment, there are two types of operating lift gate systems that use hydraulic power: the single-acting hydraulic cylinder and the double-acting hydraulic cylinder. When checking the hydraulic fluid, identify which type of system you are inspecting.

The single-acting hydraulic cylinder uses hydraulic power in one direction of the lift only. Fluid level should always be checked with the cylinder in the retracted position (cylinder all the way in).

The double-acting cylinder uses hydraulic power in both directions. Fluid level should always be checked with the cylinder(s) in either a retracted or extended position. Check the condition of the hydraulic fluid to ensure efficient operation of the equipment, and change any dirty fluid. To inspect cargo-handling devices, follow the guidelines in **SKILL DRILL 62-20**.

SKILL DRILL 62-19 Conducting an Engine-On Engine Compartment Inspection: Leaks, Levels, and Operation of Systems

1. After the engine has been running, inspect all oil, coolant, air, and fuel lines for leaks.
   - Inspect the air induction system by inspecting the charge air cooler and piping for leaks.
   - All hoses should be free from cracks and any blockages, and they should be mounted securely.
2. If the vehicle is equipped with an automatic transmission, the oil level should be checked to make sure it is at the full mark on the dipstick.
   NOTE: On vehicles equipped with automatic transmissions, the fluid level is checked with the engine running. Always consult the appropriate service manual for the correct procedure.
   - The oil should be checked for the presence of water or metallic particles, which may indicate unusual wear conditions in the transmission.

- Verify the oil does not smell burned, which indicates slipping clutches and bands. If it is changed or transmission oil is added, verify it is the recommended fluid.
3. Measure the alternator amperage and voltage output and record the results.
   - Performance test the A/C to verify that the entire system is functioning properly.
4. While in the cab, verify the operation of the engine/exhaust brake.
   - To test the engine brake, consult the appropriate service manual.
   - For the exhaust brake, build the air pressure to at least 85 psi (586 kPa).
   - With the engine idling, activate the exhaust brake with the switch on the dash. The brake should exhaust, releasing the brake's air supply system. Decelerating the engine should engage the brake. Accelerating the engine should release the brake.
5. Inspect the operation of the fan clutch following the manufacturer's procedures.
   - The clutch should engage at the correct engine temperature.
   - All fan clutches engage when the engine reaches a predetermined temperature above the thermostat opening temperature.
   - The clutch may also engage when the A/C system is switched on. Next, verify that the HVAC inlet filters are clean and that the inlet ducts are clear of debris.
6. Inspect the engine compartment exhaust system for leaks, proper routing, and damaged or missing components; and check the mountings for looseness and damage.
   NOTE: No part of the exhaust system should be positioned in a location that could result in burning, charring, or damaging the electrical wiring, fuel supply, or any combustible part of the vehicle.

SKILL DRILL 62-20 Inspecting Cargo-Handling Devices

1. Inspect all hydraulic components for leaks, also check hoses for any cracking, chafing, or incorrect routing.
2. Inspect all electrical components.
   - Identify any frayed wiring.
   - Check the condition and operation of switches.
   - Check the condition of connections.
   - Check the electric motor that drives the hydraulic pump for any loose mounting.
   - Check for the presence of a protective cover over the components.
3. Check lift gate components and operation by ensuring that the lift gate operates both up and down and does not drift down or lower too fast.
   - It should operate smoothly (no binding) and not rise too slowly.
   - Make sure there are not any unusual noises during operation.

SKILL DRILL 62-20 Inspecting Cargo-Handling Devices (Continued)

4. Check for broken welds, and ensure that there is no binding at pivot points and no frayed lift cables. Also check the presence of warning/operation decals, and check that any safety catches operate correctly.

5. Check that all stops, safety mechanisms, and chains work properly.

- Tracks should be clear of debris, and the lift gate should not bind during operation.

6. Finally, lubricate the ramp according to the procedures in the service manual.

Wrap-Up

Ready for Review

▶ Preventative maintenance and inspection (PMI) is critical to making sure heavy-duty vehicles are roadworthy and conform to federal, state, and local laws for safe operation.

▶ Preventative maintenance (PM) has the added benefit of increasing resale value and return on investment (ROI), lowering overall lifetime cost of operation, and increasing a vehicle's reliability.

▶ In the United States, commercial vehicles moving freight or passengers, or transporting any cargo interstate, must be registered with the Federal Motor Carriers Safety Administration (FMCSA) and have a United States Department of Transportation (USDOT) number.

▶ Time, mileage, and amount of fuel consumed are the three bases for the establishing a PMI schedule.

▶ PM-A is a visual check of all safety-related items, such as brakes, tires, horn, wipers, steering components, suspension components, and lighting.

▶ PM-B is a comprehensive inspection that includes all the items found in a PM-A, but adds an oil and fuel filter change.

▶ PM-C is typically an annual inspection that includes all the items in PM-A and PM-B, with additional inspection of all chassis components. Scheduled fluid changes, component adjustment, and repair or replacement are performed at this time.

▶ PM is generally proactive, which means maintenance work is scheduled to prevent unexpected breakdowns from occurring.

▶ Proactive maintenance reflects the understanding that the cost of repairing an unexpected breakdown is usually much greater than PM.

▶ Drivers are the first persons responsible for identifying potential safety issues and the possibility of imminent breakdowns.

▶ In the United States, FMCSA legislation requires drivers to prepare a report in writing at the completion of each day's work for every commercial vehicle that driver has operated that day.

▶ It is the responsibility of a carrier to develop a PM program to meet performance standards and have records documenting that vehicles are maintained and repaired as needed.

▶ At a minimum, a PM service checklist should include an itemized task list of procedures that include mechanical safety items related to braking, steering, suspension, lighting, mirrors, wipers, horns, tires, and wheels.

▶ The use of software-based record keeping is almost universal for fleet operations. Software can customize maintenance schedules, create and track work orders, track fuel consumption, record maintenance histories, track tire service and accidents, monitor labor, and produce invoices.

▶ The nonprofit organization Commercial Vehicle Safety Alliance (CVSA) enforces uniform standards for commercial vehicle safety across the United States, Canada, and Mexico.

▶ A commercial vehicle may qualify for a CVSA decal if it passes inspection, meaning that no defects are found during a Level I through V inspection.

▶ Record keeping is an essential component of the PMI process. Inspections have to be carried out by duly authorized inspectors who can demonstrate both training and experience.

▶ Oils are graded or classified by the American Society of Automotive Engineers (SAE) through the viscosity index.

▶ Given that there are thousands of vehicles built every day, it is it is to be expected that something can go wrong in the assembly process. When carrying out an inspection, it is good practice to try to identify whether the vehicle that is inspected has been subject to a recall and whether the repair has been completed.

▶ In the United States, the National Highway Traffic Safety Administration (NHTSA) of the USDOT provides recall information, including vehicle and equipment campaigns from 1966 to present.

▶ It is very important to use the right tool or piece of equipment. Do not substitute the wrong tool for the right one.

▶ It is essential that a shop be set up for functionality. This means that there are lights, air hoses, tools, equipment, refuse and oil containers, jack stands, and other equipment present and in proper position to perform preventative maintenance inspections.

▶ Brakes and steering are of extreme importance in terms of operational efficiency and safety. Of all the PMI areas, brakes are one of the highest in priority, and if they are found defective, the vehicle must be designated out of service.

- With air brakes, the truck's air pressure system has to be operating properly. There is a series of tests to perform on the air brake system. These tests may require two people.
- Inspecting wheels and tires is absolutely critical to the safe operation of any road transport vehicle. Underinflated tires, tires with poor tread, mismatched tires, and poorly mounted tires can contribute to poor handling in bad road conditions at the very least, and can lead to blowouts and accidents in worst-case scenarios.
- Performing a wheel alignment inspection is good practice for the safe operation of any road transport vehicle. Incorrect wheel alignment can contribute to the unnecessary rapid detrition of tires and affect handling of the vehicle itself.
- The under-vehicle inspection should focus mainly on the transmission and drivetrain of the vehicle. Drivelines in most medium- and heavy-duty vehicles are long, so you often need to use a creeper, unless it can be raised on a hoist or accessed from a pit.
- To perform an inspection of the drive area, check that the bolts attaching the transmission to the flywheel are present and tight.
- When inspecting cargo-handling equipment, there are two types of operating lift gate systems that use hydraulic power: single-acting hydraulic cylinder and double-acting hydraulic cylinder.

Key Terms

Commercial Vehicle Safety Alliance (CVSA) A nonprofit organization dedicated to improving the safe operation of commercial vehicles in North America by establishing a uniform, reciprocal enforcement of commercial vehicle safety standards.

CSA 2010 basic score Calculated ratings on compliance, safety, and accountability initiated by the Federal Motor Carrier Safety Administration (FMCSA).

drivability items Inspection items including instrument warning lights, engine misfires, and rough idle.

Driver Post-Operation Vehicle Inspection Report (DVIR) In the United States, FMCSA legislation requires drivers to prepare a report in writing at the completion of each day's work for each commercial vehicle the driver has operated that day. Specifics of the legislation are contained in FMCVS 49.396.11.

Federal Motor Carrier Safety Administration (FMCSA) All companies that operate commercial vehicles within the United States to move freight, passengers, or transport any cargo interstate, must be registered with the FMCSA.

Federal Motor Carrier Safety Regulation (FMCSR) Regulations issued by the Federal Motor Carrier Safety Administration (FMCSA), published in the US Federal Register, and compiled in the US Code of Federal Regulations (CFR).

North American Standard Out-of-Service Criteria (OOSC) Defects that require a vehicle to be taken out of service until repaired.

PM-A PM-A inspections are visual assessments of all safety-related items, such as brakes, tires, horn, wipers, steering components, suspension components, and lighting.

PM-B PM-B inspections include all of the checks and adjustments performed in PM-A, as well as an oil change, and oil filter and fuel filter changes. The inspection items include the engine and driveline, as well as greater detail checks of the braking, steering, and other chassis systems.

PM-C PM-C inspections are annual and include all the items in PM-A and B, as well as comprehensive checks of all chassis components. Scheduled fluid changes and component adjustment, repair, or replacement are performed at this time.

PM service checklist An itemized task list of mechanical safety procedures.

PM service intervals The frequency of a PM schedule.

predictive PM A statistical analysis of when equipment and component failures are likely to occur, including replacing parts or equipment before malfunctions happen.

proactive maintenance Reflects the understanding that the cost of repairing an unexpected breakdown is usually much greater than preventative maintenance.

reactive maintenance Service is only performed after equipment is broken, temporarily keeping vehicle and fleet operating costs low.

return on investment (ROI) The ratio of dollars spent on a vehicle for its purchase and maintenance compared to how much the vehicle earns.

severe service operating conditions Conditions consist of towing or hauling heavy loads, extensive idling and/or stop-and-go, low-speed driving encountered in inner-city traffic, delivery, off-road dusty conditions, and multiple drivers.

United States Department of Transportation (USDOT) number Any hazardous materials carriers who move enough materials requiring a safety permit must also register for a USDOT number.

Review Questions

1. An oil and filter and fuel filter change takes place at:
   a. PM-A.
   b. PM-B.
   c. PM-C.
   d. PM-D.
2. Which of the following is a mandatory requirement for every commercial vehicle?
   a. Bi-annual inspections
   b. A unique identifying number to track safety records
   c. A PM inspection check list
   d. Spare fuses
3. Who is the first person responsible for identifying potential vehicle safety issues?
   a. Vehicle technician
   b. Commercial vehicle carrier
   c. Vehicle driver
   d. Vehicle owner

4. Commercial Vehicle Safety Alliance (CVSA) membership includes:
   a. Only the United States.
   b. North American countries.
   c. Only Mexico.
   d. Only Canada.

5. Who is responsible for ensuring a vehicle is systematically inspected, repaired, and maintained?
   a. Vehicle technician
   b. Vehicle driver
   c. Vehicle owner
   d. Commercial vehicle carrier

6. What technical standard is used to determine if a vehicle cannot be safely operated?
   a. OOS criteria established by CVSA
   b. A technician's judgment
   c. Judgment of the driver
   d. Information on a vehicle inspector's inspection checklist

7. What service classification of oils are used by all diesel engines?
   a. S series
   b. C series
   c. Multigrade
   d. FE Fuel economy

8. Where are CVSA inspection standards enforced?
   a. Only the United States
   b. North American-wide
   c. They are voluntary and not enforceable
   d. Only Canada

9. What is the correct service recommendation if 80 to 90 psi (552 to 621 kPa) of vehicle air pressure cannot be maintained when the engine is running and the brakes are applied?
   a. Repair the air leak
   b. Replace the air compressor
   c. Replace the governor
   d. Remove the vehicle from service

10. How far can a vehicle be driven if its operation is found have a safety defect?
   a. Nowhere, it must be repaired on-site.
   b. It must be towed to a repair facility.
   c. It can be driven to the closest repair facility.
   d. Less than 3 miles (5 km)

ASE Technician A/Technician B Style Questions

1. Technician A says that the type of checklist, as well as the inspection schedule, varies with vehicle type and operating service. Technician B says that inspection of fire protection, emergency exit, and evacuation equipment is critical for buses and motor coaches. Who is correct?
   a. Technician A
   b. Technician B
   c. Both Technician A and Technician B
   d. Neither Technician A nor Technician B

2. Technician A says that a DVIR is a driver vehicle inspection report. Technician B says that a DVIR covers vehicle safety items, such as the tires, rims wipers, horn, brakes, steering, trailer brake connections, coupler condition, and parking brake. Who is correct?
   a. Technician A
   b. Technician B
   c. Both Technician A and Technician B
   d. Neither Technician A nor Technician B

3. Technician A says that proactive maintenance is costly and, in the long run, reactive maintenance costs less money. Technician B says reactive maintenance is more convenient. Who is correct?
   a. Technician A
   b. Technician B
   c. Both Technician A and Technician B
   d. Neither Technician A nor Technician B

4. Technician A says that adding a few additional lights is acceptable as long as the other lights on the vehicle meet safety standards. Technician B says that installing aftermarket headlight bulbs that are much brighter than the original bulbs is acceptable practice. Who is correct?
   a. Technician A
   b. Technician B
   c. Both Technician A and Technician B
   d. Neither Technician A nor Technician B

5. Technician A says that ¼" or more brake pushrod travel beyond the brake stroke indicator is acceptable. Technician B says that ¼" more brake stroke travel needs to be found on more than 20% of the vehicle brakes to meet OOS criteria. Who is correct?
   a. Technician A
   b. Technician B
   c. Both Technician A and Technician B
   d. Neither Technician A nor Technician B

6. Technician A says that, in most countries, an inspector carrying out this work is required to be registered and appropriately qualified. Technician B says that, in the United States, the requirements include, in part, at least five years of experience as a commercial vehicle mechanic. Who is correct?
   a. Technician A
   b. Technician B
   c. Both Technician A and Technician B
   d. Neither Technician A nor Technician B

7. Technician A and B were discussing whether a trailer should be removed from service because one of its four spring brake chambers was not working. Technician A says that the trailer should be taken out of service. Technician B says more than one brake needs to be defective. Who is correct?
   a. Technician A
   b. Technician B
   c. Both Technician A and Technician B
   d. Neither Technician A nor Technician B

8. Technician A says that the center of the low-beam head-lights should be at the same height from the ground as the headlight center when a truck is 25' away from a screen. Technician B says the low beams must be 8" lower. Who is correct?
   a. Technician A
   b. Technician B
   c. Both Technician A and Technician B
   d. Neither Technician A nor Technician B

9. While discussing the inspection recommendations for a truck, Technician A said that an amber-colored lighted license plate frame was not acceptable. Technician B says that the driver can choose any color for a lighted frame they want. Who is correct?
   a. Technician A
   b. Technician B
   c. Both Technician A and Technician B
   d. Neither Technician A nor Technician B

10. Technician A says that all exterior lights and lens covers should have an SAE or DOT code. Technician B says that only bulbs should have an ECE, SAE, or DOT marking. Who is correct?
   a. Technician A
   b. Technician B
   c. Both Technician A and Technician B
   d. Neither Technician A nor Technician B

APPENDIX A

2018 ASE MEDIUM/HEAVY TRUCK MASTER SERVICE TECHNOLOGY (MTST) TASK LIST CORRELATION GUIDE

ASE Task List	ASE Priority Number	Chapter
Required Supplemental Tasks		
1. Identify general shop safety rules and procedures.	N/A	3
2. Utilize safe procedures for handling of tools and equipment.	N/A	4
3. Identify and use proper placement of floor jacks and jack stands.	N/A	6
4. Identify and use proper procedures for safe lift operation.	N/A	6
5. Utilize proper ventilation procedures for working within the lab/shop area.	N/A	3
6. Identify marked safety areas.	N/A	3
7. Identify the location and the types of fire extinguishers and other fire safety equipment; demonstrate knowledge of the procedures for using fire extinguishers and other fire safety equipment.	N/A	3
8. Identify the location and use of eye wash stations.	N/A	3
9. Identify the location of the posted evacuation routes.	N/A	3
10. Comply with the required use of safety glasses, ear protection, gloves, and shoes during lab/shop activities.	N/A	3
11. Identify and wear appropriate clothing for lab/shop activities.	N/A	3
12. Secure hair and jewelry for lab/shop activities.	N/A	3
13. Demonstrate awareness of the safety aspects of supplemental restraint systems (SRS), electronic brake control systems, and hybrid vehicle high-voltage circuits.	N/A	32, 38, 54, 56, 57
14. Demonstrate awareness of the safety aspects of high-voltage circuits (such as high-intensity discharge (HID) lamps, ignition systems, injection systems).	N/A	20, 54, 56, 57
15. Locate and demonstrate knowledge of material safety data sheets (MSDS).	N/A	3
Tools and Equipment		
1. Identify tools and their usage in automotive applications.	N/A	5
2. Identify standard and metric designation.	N/A	5
3. Demonstrate safe handling and use of appropriate tools.	N/A	5
4. Demonstrate proper cleaning, storage, and maintenance of tools and equipment.	N/A	5
5. Demonstrate proper use of precision measuring tools (i.e., micrometer, dial-indicator, dial-caliper).	N/A	5
Preparing Vehicle for Service		
1. Identify information needed and the service requested on a repair order.	N/A	2
2. Identify purpose and demonstrate proper use of fender covers, mats.	N/A	2
3. Demonstrate use of the three Cs (concern, cause, and correction).	N/A	2
4. Review vehicle service history.	N/A	2
5. Complete work order to include customer information, vehicle identifying information, customer concern, related service history, cause, and correction.	N/A	2
Preparing Vehicle for Customer		
1. Ensure vehicle is prepared to return to customer per school/company policy (floor mats, steering wheel cover, etc.).	N/A.	2

ASE Task List	ASE Priority Number	Chapter
Workplace Employability Skills		
Personal Standards		
1. Reports to work daily on time; able to take directions and motivated to accomplish the task at hand.	N/A	2
2. Dresses appropriately and uses language and manners suitable for the workplace.	N/A	2
3. Maintains appropriate personal hygiene.	N/A	2
4. Meets and maintains employment eligibility criteria, such as drug/alcohol-free status, clean driving record.	N/A	2
5. Demonstrates honesty, integrity, and reliability.	N/A	2
Work Habits/Ethic		
1. Complies with workplace policies/laws.	N/A	2
2. Contributes to the success of the team, assists others, and requests help when needed.	N/A	2
3. Works well with all customers and coworkers.	N/A	2
4. Negotiates solutions to interpersonal and workplace conflicts.	N/A	2
5. Contributes ideas and initiative.	N/A	2
6. Follows directions.	N/A	2
7. Communicates (written and verbal) effectively with customers and coworkers.	N/A	2
8. Reads and interprets workplace documents; writes clearly and concisely.	N/A	2
9. Analyzes and resolves problems that arise in completing assigned tasks.	N/A	2
10. Organizes and implements a productive plan of work.	N/A	2
11. Uses scientific, technical, engineering, and mathematics principles and reasoning to accomplish assigned tasks.	N/A	2
12. Identifies and addresses the needs of all customers, providing helpful, courteous, and knowledgeable service and advice as needed.	N/A	2
I. DIESEL ENGINES		
All ASE tasks for this standard can be found in *Fundamentals of Medium/Heavy Duty Diesel Engines* (ISBN 9781284150919)		
II. DRIVETRAIN		
A. General		
1. Research vehicle service information, including fluid type, vehicle service history, service precautions, and technical service bulletins.	P-1	2
2. Identify drivetrain components, transmission type, and configuration.	P-1	43
3. Use appropriate electronic service tool(s) and procedures to diagnose problems; check, record, and clear diagnostic codes; interpret digital multimeter (DMM) readings.	P-1	45
B. Clutch		
1. Inspect and adjust clutch, clutch brake, linkage, cables, levers, brackets, bushings, pivots, springs, and clutch safety switch (includes push-type and pull-type); check pedal height and travel; determine needed action.	P-1	40, 41
2. Inspect clutch master cylinder fluid level; check clutch master cylinder, slave cylinder, lines, and hoses for leaks and damage; determine needed action.	P-1	40, 41
3. Inspect, adjust, repair, and/or replace hydraulic clutch slave and master cylinders, lines, and hoses; bleed system.	P-2	40, 41
4. Inspect, adjust, lubricate, or replace release (throw-out) bearing, sleeve, bushings, springs, housing, levers, release fork, fork pads, rollers, shafts, and seals.	P-1	40, 41
5. Inspect, adjust, and/or replace single-disc clutch pressure plate and clutch disc.	P-1	40, 41
6. Inspect, adjust, and/or replace two-plate clutch pressure plate, clutch discs, intermediate plate, and drive pins/lugs.	P-1	40, 41

(continued)

ASE Task List	ASE Priority Number	Chapter
7. Inspect and/or replace clutch brake assembly; inspect input shaft and bearing retainer; determine needed action.	P-1	40, 41
8. Inspect, adjust, and/or replace self-adjusting/continuous-adjusting clutch mechanisms.	P-1	41
9. Inspect and/or replace pilot bearing.	P-1	41
10. Identify causes of clutch noise, binding, slippage, pulsation, vibration, grabbing, dragging, and chatter problems; determine needed action.	P-1	41
11. Remove and install flywheel; inspect mounting area on crankshaft; inspect rear main oil seal; measure crankshaft end play; determine needed action.	P-1	41
12. Inspect flywheel and starter ring gear; measure flywheel face; measure pilot bore runout; determine needed action.	P-1	41
13. Inspect flywheel housing-to-transmission housing/engine mating surface(s); measure flywheel housing face and bore runout; determine needed action.	P-2	41
C. Transmission		
1. Inspect transmission shifter and linkage; inspect and/or replace transmission mounts, insulators, and mounting bolts.	P-1	44
2. Inspect transmission for leakage; determine needed action.	P-1	44
3. Replace transmission cover plates, gaskets, seals, and cap bolts; inspect seal surfaces and vents; determine needed action.	P-1	44
4. Check transmission fluid level and condition; determine needed action.	P-1	44
5. Inspect transmission breather; inspect transmission oil filters, coolers, and related components; determine needed action.	P-2	44
6. Inspect speedometer components; determine needed action.	P-2	44
7. Inspect and test function of REVERSE light, NEUTRAL start, and warning device circuits; determine needed action.	P-1	44
8. Inspect, adjust, and replace transmission covers, rails, forks, levers, bushings, sleeves, detents, interlocks, springs, and lock bolts/safety wires.	P-2	44
9. Identify causes of transmission noise, shifting concerns, lockup, jumping out-of-gear, overheating, and vibration problems; determine needed repairs.	P-1	44
10. Inspect, test, repair, and/or replace air shift controls, lines, hoses, valves, regulators, filters, and cylinder assemblies.	P-2	44
11. Remove and reinstall transmission.	P-2	44
12. Inspect input shaft, gear, spacers, bearings, retainers, and slingers; determine needed action.	P-3	44
13. Inspect and adjust power take-off (PTO) assemblies, controls, and shafts; determine needed action.	P-3	43
14. Inspect and test transmission temperature gauge, wiring harnesses, and sensor/sending unit; determine needed action.	P-2	50
15. Inspect and test operation of automatic transmission, components, and controls; diagnose automatic transmission system problems; determine needed action.	P-2	50
16. Inspect and test operation of automated mechanical transmission, components, and controls; diagnose automated mechanical transmission system problems; determine needed action.	P-2	45
D. Driveshaft and Universal Joints		
1. Inspect, service, and/or replace driveshafts, slip joints, yokes, drive flanges, support bearings, universal joints, boots, seals, and retaining/mounting hardware; check phasing of all shafts.	P-1	51
2. Identify causes of driveshaft and universal joint noise and vibration problems; determine needed action.	P-1	51
3. Inspect driveshaft center support bearings and mounts; determine needed action.	P-1	51
4. Measure driveline angles; determine needed action.	P-2	51

ASE Task List	ASE Priority Number	Chapter
E. Drive Axles		
1. Check and repair fluid leaks; inspect drive axle housing assembly, cover plates, gaskets, seals, vent/breather, and magnetic plugs.	P-1	53
2. Check drive axle fluid level and condition; check drive axle filter; determine needed action.	P-1	53
3. Inspect, adjust, repair, and/or replace air-operated power divider (inter-axle differential) assembly including: diaphragms, seals, springs, yokes, pins, lines, hoses, fittings, and controls.	P-2	53
4. Inspect drive axle shafts; determine needed action.	P-2	53
5. Remove and replace wheel assembly; check rear wheel seal and axle flange for leaks; determine needed action.	P-1	53
6. Inspect, repair, or replace drive axle lubrication system pump, troughs, collectors, slingers, tubes, and filters.	P-3	53
7. Identify causes of drive axle(s) drive unit noise and overheating problems; determine needed action.	P-2	53
8. Inspect and test drive axle temperature gauge, wiring harnesses, and sending unit/sensor; determine needed action.	P-2	53
9. Remove and replace differential carrier assembly.	P-2	53
10. Identify causes of drive axle wheel bearing noise and check for damage; determine needed action.	P-1	53
11. Inspect and/or replace components of differential case assembly including spider gears, cross shaft, side gears, thrust washers, case halves, and bearings.	P-3	53
12. Inspect and replace components of locking differential case assembly.	P-3	53
13. Inspect differential carrier housing and caps, side bearing bores, and pilot (spigot, pocket) bearing bore; determine needed action.	P-3	53
14. Inspect and replace ring and drive pinion gears, spacers, sleeves, bearing cages, and bearings.	P-3	53
15. Measure ring gear runout; determine needed action.	P-2	53
16. Measure and adjust drive pinion bearing preload.	P-3	53
17. Measure and adjust drive pinion depth.	P-3	53
18. Measure and adjust side bearing preload and ring gear backlash.	P-2	53
19. Check and interpret ring gear and pinion tooth contact pattern; determine needed action.	P-2	53
20. Inspect, adjust, or replace ring gear thrust block/screw.	P-3	53
III. BRAKES		
A. General		
1. Research vehicle service information, including fluid type, vehicle service history, service precautions, and technical service bulletins.	P-1	33, 34, 35, 36, 37
2. Identify brake system components and configurations (including air and hydraulic systems, parking brake, power assist, and vehicle dynamic brake systems).	P-1	33, 34, 35, 36, 37, 38, 55
3. Identify brake performance problems caused by the mechanical/foundation brake system (air and hydraulic).	P-1	33, 34, 35, 36, 37, 38
4. Use appropriate electronic service tool(s) and procedures to diagnose problems; check, record, and clear diagnostic codes; interpret digital multimeter (DMM) readings.	P-1	33, 34, 35, 36, 37, 38
B. Air Brakes: Air Supply and Service Systems		
1. Inspect, test, repair, and/or replace air supply system components such as compressor, governor, air drier, tanks, and lines; inspect service system components such as lines, fittings, mountings, and valves (hand brake/trailer control, brake relay, quick release, tractor protection, emergency/spring brake control/modulator, pressure relief/safety); determine needed action.	P-1	34, 35, 36
2. Test gauge operation and readings; test low pressure warning alarm operation; perform air supply system tests such as pressure build-up, governor settings, and leakage; drain air tanks and check for contamination; determine needed action.	P-1	34, 35
3. Demonstrate knowledge and understanding of air supply and service system components and operations.	P-1	33, 34

(continued)

ASE Task List	ASE Priority Number	Chapter
4. Inspect air compressor drive gear components (gears, belts, tensioners, and/or couplings); determine needed action.	P-3	34, 35
5. Inspect air compressor inlet; inspect oil supply and coolant lines, fittings, and mounting brackets; repair or replace as needed.	P-1	34, 35
6. Inspect and test air tank relief (safety) valves, one-way (single) check valves, two-way (double) check valves, manual and automatic drain valves; determine needed action.	P-1	34, 35
7. Inspect and clean air drier systems, filters, valves, heaters, wiring, and connectors; determine needed action.	P-1	34, 35
8. Inspect and test brake application (foot/treadle) valve, fittings, and mounts; check pedal operation; determine needed action.	P-1	34, 35
C. Air Brakes: Mechanical/Foundation Brake System		
1. Inspect, test, repair, and/or replace service brake chambers, diaphragms, clamps, springs, pushrods, clevises, and mounting brackets; determine needed action.	P-1	33, 36
2. Identify slack adjuster type; inspect slack adjusters; perform needed action.	P-1	33, 36
3. Check camshafts (S-cam), tubes, rollers, bushings, seals, spacers, retainers, brake spiders, shields, anchor pins, and springs; perform needed action.	P-1	33, 36
4. Inspect rotor and mounting surface; measure rotor thickness, thickness variation, and lateral runout; determine needed action.	P-1	33, 36
5. Inspect, clean, and adjust air disc brake caliper assemblies; inspect and measure disc brake pads; inspect mounting hardware; perform needed action.	P-1	33, 36
6. Remove brake drum; clean and inspect brake drum and mounting surface; measure brake drum diameter; measure brake lining thickness; inspect brake lining condition; determine needed action.	P-1	33, 36
7. Diagnose concerns related to the mechanical/foundation brake system including poor stopping, brake noise, premature wear, pulling, grabbing, or dragging; determine needed action.	P-1	33, 36
D. Air Brakes: Parking Brake System		
1. Inspect, test, and/or replace parking (spring) brake chamber.	P-1	36
2. Inspect, test, and/or replace parking (spring) brake check valves, lines, hoses, and fittings.	P-1	34, 35, 36
3. Inspect, test, and/or replace parking (spring) brake application and release valve.	P-1	34, 35, 36
4. Manually release (cage) and reset (uncage) parking (spring) brakes.	P-1	36
5. Identify and test anti-compounding brake function; determine needed action.	P-2	34, 35
E. Hydraulic Brakes: Hydraulic System		
1. Check master cylinder fluid level and condition; determine proper fluid type for application.	P-1	38
2. Inspect hydraulic brake system for leaks and damage; test, repair, and/or replace hydraulic brake system components.	P-1	38
3. Check hydraulic brake system operation including pedal travel, pedal effort, and pedal feel; determine needed action.	P-1	38
4. Diagnose poor stopping, premature wear, pulling, dragging, imbalance, or poor pedal feel caused by problems in the hydraulic system; determine needed action.	P-2	38
5. Test master cylinder for internal/external leaks and damage; replace as needed.	P-2	38
6. Test metering (hold-off), load sensing/proportioning, proportioning, and combination valves; determine needed action.	P-3	38
7. Test brake pressure differential valve; test warning light circuit switch, bulbs/LEDs, wiring, and connectors; determine needed action.	P-2	38
8. Bleed and/or flush hydraulic brake system.	P-2	38
F. Hydraulic Brakes: Mechanical/Foundation Brake System		
1. Clean and inspect rotor and mounting surface; measure rotor thickness, thickness variation, and lateral runout; determine necessary action.	P-1	33, 36
2. Inspect and clean disc brake caliper assemblies; inspect and measure disc brake pads; inspect mounting hardware; perform needed action.	P-1	33, 36

ASE Task List	ASE Priority Number	Chapter
3. Remove, clean, and inspect brake drums; measure brake drum diameter; measure brake lining thickness; inspect brake lining condition; inspect wheel cylinders; determine serviceability.	P-1	33, 36
4. Check disc brake caliper assembly mountings and slides; replace as needed.	P-2	38
G. Hydraulic Brakes: Parking Brake System		
1. Check parking brake operation; inspect parking brake application and holding devices; adjust, repair, and/or replace as needed.	P-1	38
H. Power Assist Systems		
1. Check brake assist/booster system (vacuum or hydraulic) hoses and control valves; check fluid level and condition (if applicable).	P-1	38
2. Check operation of emergency (back-up/reserve) brake assist system.	P-1	38
3. Identify concerns related to the power assist system (vacuum or hydraulic), including stopping problems caused by the brake assist (booster) system; determine needed action.	P-2	38
4. Inspect, test, repair, and/or replace hydraulic brake assist/booster systems, hoses, and control valves.	P-1	38
I. Vehicle Dynamic Brake Systems (Air and Hydraulic): Antilock Brake System (ABS), Automatic Traction Control (ATC) System, and Electronic Stability Control (ESC) System		
1. Observe antilock brake system (ABS) warning light operation including trailer and dash-mounted trailer ABS warning light; determine needed action.	P-1	37
2. Observe automatic traction control (ATC) and electronic stability control (ETC) warning light operation; determine needed action.	P-2	37
3. Identify stopping concerns related to the vehicle dynamic brake systems: ABS, ATC, and ESC; determine needed action.	P-2	37, 55
4. Diagnose problems in the vehicle dynamic brake control systems; determine needed action.	P-2	37, 55
5. Check and test operation of vehicle dynamic brake system (air and hydraulic) mechanical and electrical components; determine needed action.	P-1	37, 38, 55
6. Test vehicle/wheel speed sensors and circuits; adjust, repair, and/or replace as needed.	P-1	37, 38
7. Bleed ABS hydraulic circuits.	P-2	38
8. Verify power line carrier (PLC) operation.	P-3	26, 37
J. Wheel Bearings		
1. Clean, inspect, lubricate, and/or replace wheel bearings and races/cups; replace seals and wear rings; inspect spindle/tube; inspect and replace retaining hardware; adjust wheel bearings; check hub assembly fluid level and condition; verify end play with dial indicator method.	P-1	7, 28
2. Identify, inspect, and/or replace unitized/preset hub bearing assemblies.	P-2	28
IV. SUSPENSION AND STEERING SYSTEMS		
A. General		
1. Research vehicle service information, including fluid type, vehicle service history, service precautions, and technical service bulletins.	P-1	31, 32
2. Disable and enable supplemental restraint system (SRS); verify indicator lamp operation.	P-1	32
3. Identify suspension and steering system components and configurations.	P-1	29, 31, 32
4. Use appropriate electronic service tool(s) and procedures to diagnose problems; check, record, and clear diagnostic codes; interpret digital multimeter (DMM) readings.	P-1	32, 37, 55
B. Steering Column		
1. Check steering wheel for free play, binding, and proper centering; inspect and service steering shaft U-joint(s), slip joint(s), bearings, bushings, and seals; phase steering shaft.	P-1	32
2. Diagnose causes of fixed and driver adjustable steering column and shaft noise, looseness, and binding problems.	P-1	32
3. Check cab mounting and adjust cab ride height.	P-2	32

(continued)

ASE Task List	ASE Priority Number	Chapter
4. Remove the steering wheel (includes steering wheels equipped with electrical/electronic controls and components); install and center the steering wheel.	P-1	29, 32
5. Inspect, test, replace, and calibrate steering angle sensor.	P-2	32, 37, 55
C. Steering Pump and Gear Units		
1. Check power steering pump and gear operation, mountings, lines, and hoses; check fluid level and condition; service filter; inspect system for leaks.	P-1	32
2. Flush and refill power steering system; purge air from system.	P-1	32
3. Diagnose causes of power steering system noise, binding, darting/oversteer, reduced wheel cut, steering wheel kick, pulling, non-recovery, turning effort, looseness, hard steering, overheating, fluid leakage, and fluid aeration problems.	P-1	29, 32
4. Inspect, service, and/or replace power steering reservoir, seals, and gaskets.	P-2	32
5. Inspect and/or replace power steering system cooler, lines, hoses, clamps, mountings, and fittings.	P-2	32
6. Inspect and/or replace power steering gear(s) (single and/or dual) and mountings.	P-2	32
D. Steering Linkage		
1. Inspect, service, repair, and/or replace tie rod ends, ball joints, king pins, pitman arms, idler arms, and other steering linkage components.	P-1	28, 29, 32
E. Suspension Systems		
1. Inspect, service, repair, and/or replace shock absorbers, bushings, brackets, and mounts.	P-1	31
2. Inspect, repair, and/or replace leaf springs, center bolts, clips, pins, bushings, shackles, U-bolts, insulators, brackets, and mounts.	P-1	31
3. Inspect, repair, and/or replace axle and axle aligning devices such as: radius rods, track bars, stabilizer bars, and torque arms; inspect related bushings, mounts, shims and attaching hardware; determine needed action.	P-1	31
4. Inspect, repair, and/or replace tandem suspension equalizer components; determine needed action.	P-3	31
5. Inspect, repair, and/or replace air springs, mounting plates, springs, suspension arms, and bushings.	P-1	31
6. Inspect, test, repair, and/or replace air suspension pressure regulator and height control valves, lines, hoses, dump valves, and fittings; check and record ride height.	P-1	31
7. Inspect and service king pins, steering knuckle bushings, locks, bearings, seals, and covers.	P-1	31
8. Measure, record, and adjust ride height; determine needed action.	P-1	31
9. Diagnose rough ride problems; determine needed action.	P-3	31
F. Wheel Alignment Diagnosis and Repair		
1. Demonstrate understanding of alignment angles.	P-1	29, 31, 32
2. Diagnose causes of vehicle wandering, pulling, shimmy, hard steering, and off-center steering wheel problems.	P-1	29, 31, 32
3. Check, record, and adjust camber.	P-2	29
4. Check, record, and adjust caster.	P-2	29
5. Check, record, and adjust toe settings.	P-1	29, 32
6. Check rear axle(s) alignment (thrustline/centerline) and tracking.	P-2	29, 31
7. Identify turning/Ackerman angle (toe-out-on-turns) problems.	P-3	29, 32
8. Check front axle alignment (centerline).	P-2	29
G. Wheels and Tires		
1. Inspect tire condition; identify tire wear patterns; measure tread depth; verify tire matching (diameter and tread); inspect valve stem and cap; set tire pressure; determine needed action.	P-1	27
2. Diagnose wheel/tire vibration, shimmy, pounding, and hop (tramp) problems; determine needed action.	P-2	27

ASE Task List	ASE Priority Number	Chapter
3. Check wheel mounting hardware; check wheel condition; remove and install wheel/tire assemblies (steering and drive axle); torque fasteners to manufacturer's specification using torque wrench.	P-1	27, 28
4. Inspect tire and wheel for proper application (size, load range, position, and tread design); determine needed action.	P-2	27

H. Frame and Coupling Devices

1. Inspect, service, and/or adjust fifth wheel, pivot pins, bushings, locking mechanisms, mounting hardware, air lines, and fittings.	P-1	39
2. Inspect frame and frame members for cracks, breaks, corrosion, distortion, elongated holes, looseness, and damage; determine needed action.	P-1	30
3. Inspect, install, and/or replace frame hangers, brackets, and cross members; determine needed action.	P-3	30
4. Inspect, repair, or replace pintle hooks and draw bars (if applicable).	P-2	
5. Inspect, service, and/or adjust sliding fifth wheel, tracks, stops, locking systems, air cylinders, springs, lines, hoses, and controls.	P-2	39

V. ELECTRICAL/ELECTRONIC SYSTEMS

A. General

1. Research vehicle service information, including vehicle service history, service precautions, and technical service bulletins.	P-1	14, 15, 16
2. Demonstrate knowledge of electrical/electronic series, parallel, and series-parallel circuits using principles of electricity (Ohm's Law).	P-1	10
3. Demonstrate proper use of test equipment when measuring source voltage, voltage drop (including grounds), current flow, continuity, and resistance.	P-1	13
4. Demonstrate knowledge of the causes and effects of shorts, grounds, opens, and resistance problems in electrical/electronic circuits; identify and locate faults in electrical/electronic circuits.	P-1	10, 11
5. Use wiring diagrams during the diagnosis (troubleshooting) of electrical/electronic circuit problems.	P-1	19
6. Measure parasitic (key-off) battery drain; determine needed action.	P-1	16, 18
7. Demonstrate knowledge of the function, operation, and testing of fusible links, circuit breakers, relays, solenoids, diodes, and fuses; perform inspection and testing; determine needed action.	P-1	10, 11
8. Inspect, test, repair (including solder repair), and/or replace components, connectors, seals, terminal ends, harnesses, and wiring; verify proper routing and securement; determine needed action.	P-1	19
9. Use appropriate electronic service tool(s) and procedures to diagnose problems; check, record, and clear diagnostic codes; interpret digital multimeter (DMM) readings.	P-1	13, 26
10. Diagnose faults in the data bus communications network; determine needed action.	P-2	26
11. Identify electrical/electronic system components and configuration.	P-1	8, 25
12. Check frequency, pulse width, and waveforms of electrical/electronic signals using appropriate test equipment; interpret readings; determine needed repairs.	P-2	13, 24, 25
13. Understand the process for software transfer, software updates, and/or reprogramming of electronic modules.	P-3	22, 25, 26

B. Battery System

1. Identify battery type and system configuration.	P-1	14, 15, 16
2. Confirm proper battery capacity for application; perform battery state-of-charge test; perform battery capacity test, determine needed action.	P-1	16
3. Inspect battery, battery cables, connectors, battery boxes, mounts, and hold-downs; determine needed action.	P-1	16
4. Charge battery using appropriate method for battery type.	P-1	16
5. Jump-start vehicle using a booster battery and jumper cables or using an appropriate auxiliary power supply.	P-1	16
6. Check low voltage disconnect (LVD) systems; determine needed action.	P-1	15
7. Inspect, clean, and service battery; replace as needed.	P-1	16

(continued)

ASE Task List	ASE Priority Number	Chapter
8. Inspect and clean battery boxes, mounts, and hold-downs; repair or replace as needed.	P-1	16
9. Test, and clean battery cables and connectors; repair or replace as needed.	P-1	16
10. Identify electrical/electronic modules, radios, and other accessories that require reinitialization or code entry after reconnecting vehicle battery.	P-2	22, 15
C. Starting System		
1. Demonstrate understanding of starter system operation.	P-1	17
2. Perform starter circuit cranking voltage and voltage drop tests; determine needed action.	P-1	17
3. Inspect and test starter control circuit switches (key switch, push button, and/or magnetic switch), relays, connectors, terminals, wires, and harnesses (including over-crank protection); determine needed action.	P-1	17
4. Diagnose causes of no-crank or slow crank condition; differentiate between electrical and engine mechanical problems; determine needed action.	P-1	17
5. Perform starter current draw tests; determine needed action.	P-2	17
6. Remove and replace starter; inspect flywheel ring gear or flex plate.	P-1	17
D. Charging System		
1. Identify and understand operation of the generator (alternator).	P-1	18
2. Test instrument panel mounted voltmeters and/or indicator lamps; determine needed action.	P-1	18
3. Inspect, adjust, and/or replace generator (alternator) drive belt; check pulleys and tensioners for wear; check fans and mounting brackets; verify proper belt alignment; determine needed action.	P-1	18
4. Inspect cables, wires, and connectors in the charging circuit.	P-1	18
5. Perform charging system voltage and amperage output tests; perform AC ripple test; determine needed action.	P-1	18
6. Perform charging circuit voltage drop tests; determine needed action.	P-1	18
7. Remove, inspect, and/or replace generator (alternator).	P-1	18
E. Lighting Systems		
1. Diagnose causes of brighter-than-normal, intermittent, dim, or no-light operation; determine needed action.	P-1	18, 20
2. Test, replace, and aim headlights.	P-1	20, 62
3. Inspect cables, wires, and connectors in the lighting systems.	P-1	20
4. Diagnose faults in tractor-to-trailer multi-wire connector(s), cables, and holders; determine needed action.	P-2	20, 26, 37
5. Diagnose faults in switches, relays, bulbs/LEDs, wires, terminals, connectors, sockets, and control components/modules of exterior lighting systems; determine needed action.	P-2	10, 11, 20
6. Diagnose faults in switches, relays, bulbs/LEDs, wires, terminals, connectors, sockets, and control components/modules of interior lighting systems; determine needed action.	P-2	10, 11, 20
7. Diagnose faults in switches, relays, bulbs/LEDs, wires, terminals, connectors, sockets, and control components/modules of auxiliary lighting circuits; determine needed action.	P-2	10, 11, 20
F. Instrument Cluster and Driver Information Systems		
1. Check gauge and warning indicator operation.	P-1	21
2. Diagnose faults in the sensor/sending units, gauges, switches, relays, bulbs/LEDs, wires, terminals, connectors, sockets, printed circuits, and control components/modules of the instrument cluster, driver information systems, and warning systems; determine needed action.	P-2	21, 24
3. Inspect, test, replace, and calibrate (if applicable) electronic speedometer, odometer, and tachometer systems.	P-3	21
G. Cab and Chassis Electrical Systems		
1. Diagnose operation of horn(s), wiper/washer, and occupant restraint systems.	P-1	22
2. Understand operation of safety systems and related circuits (such as speed control, collision avoidance, lane departure, and camera systems).	P-3	37, 55

ASE Task List	ASE Priority Number	Chapter
3. Understand operation of comfort and convenience systems and related circuits (such as: power windows, power seats, power locks, remote keyless entry, steering wheel controls, and cruise control).	P-3	22
4. Understand operation of entertainment systems and related circuits (such as radio, DVD, navigation, speakers, antennas, and voice-activated accessories).	P-3	22
5. Understand the operation of power inverter, protection devices, connectors, terminals, wiring, and control components/modules of auxiliary power systems.	P-3	11, 12, 22
6. Understand operation of telematics systems.	P-3	25, 26, 55

VI. HEATING, VENTILATION, AND AIR CONDITIONING (HVAC)

A. General

ASE Task List	ASE Priority Number	Chapter
1. Research vehicle service information, including refrigerant/oil type, vehicle service history, service precautions, and technical service bulletins.	P-1	58, 59, 60
2. Identify heating, ventilation, and air conditioning (HVAC) components and configuration.	P-1	58, 59
3. Use appropriate electronic service tool(s) and procedures to diagnose problems; check, record, and clear diagnostic codes; interpret digital multimeter (DMM) readings.	P-1	58, 59
4. Diagnose heating and air conditioning problems; determine needed action.	P-1	58, 59
5. Identify refrigerant type; test for contamination; select and connect proper gauge set/test equipment; record temperature and pressure readings.	P-1	59
6. Perform A/C system performance test; determine needed action.	P-1	59
7. Perform A/C system leak test; determine needed action.	P-1	59
8. Inspect condition of refrigerant oil removed from A/C system; determine needed action.	P-1	59
9. Determine oil and oil capacity for system application and/or component replacement.	P-1	59

B. Refrigeration System Components

ASE Task List	ASE Priority Number	Chapter
1. Inspect, remove, and replace A/C compressor drive belts, pulleys, and tensioners; verify proper belt alignment.	P-1	18
2. Check A/C system operation including system pressures; visually inspect A/C components for signs of leaks; check A/C monitoring system (if applicable).	P-1	58, 59
3. Inspect A/C condenser for airflow restrictions; determine needed action.	P-1	59
4. Inspect, test, service, and/or replace A/C compressor and clutch assembly; check compressor clutch air gap; determine needed action.	P-2	59
5. Inspect, service, and/or replace A/C system hoses, lines, fittings, O-rings, seals, and service valves.	P-2	59
6. Inspect, remove, and/or replace receiver/drier or accumulator/drier.	P-1	59
7. Inspect, remove, and/or replace expansion valve or orifice (expansion) tube.	P-2	59
8. Inspect evaporator housing water drain; perform needed action.	P-1	59
9. Diagnose A/C system conditions that cause the protection devices (pressure, thermal, and/or control module) to interrupt system operation; determine needed action.	P-2	58, 59
10. Determine procedure to remove and reinstall evaporator.	P-3	59
11. Determine procedure to inspect and/or replace condenser.	P-2	59

C. Heating, Ventilation, and Engine Cooling Systems

ASE Task List	ASE Priority Number	Chapter
1. Inspect engine cooling system and heater system hoses and pipes; determine needed action.	P-1	58, 59
2. Inspect HVAC system heater ducts, doors, hoses, cabin filters, and outlets; determine needed action.	P-1	58, 59
3. Identify the source of A/C system odors; determine needed action.	P-1	58, 59
4. Diagnose temperature control problems in the HVAC system; determine needed action.	P-2	58, 59
5. Determine procedure to remove, inspect, reinstall, and/or replace engine coolant and heater system components.	P-2	58, 59

(continued)

ASE Task List	ASE Priority Number	Chapter
D. Operating Systems and Related Controls		
1. Verify HVAC system blower motor operation; confirm proper air distribution; confirm proper temperature control; determine needed action.	P-1	22
2. Inspect and test HVAC system blower motors, resistors, switches, relays, wiring, and protection devices; determine needed action.	P-1	22, 58, 59
3. Diagnose A/C compressor clutch control systems; determine needed action.	P-2	58, 59
4. Diagnose malfunctions in the vacuum, mechanical, and electrical components and controls of the HVAC system; determine needed action.	P-3	58, 59
E. Refrigerant Recovery, Recycling, and Handling		
1. Understand correct use and maintenance of refrigerant handling equipment.	P-1	59
2. Understand how to identify A/C system refrigerant; test for sealants; recover, evacuate, and charge A/C system; add refrigerant oil as required.	P-1	59
3. Understand how to recycle, label, and store refrigerant.	P-1	58, 59
VII. CAB		
A. General		
1. Research vehicle service information, including vehicle service history, service precautions, and technical service bulletins.	P-1	2
2. Use appropriate electronic service tool(s) and procedures to diagnose problems; check, record, and clear diagnostic codes; check and record trip/operational data; reset maintenance monitor (if applicable); interpret digital multimeter (DMM) readings.	P-1	45, 49
B. Instruments and Controls		
1. Inspect mechanical key condition; check operation of ignition switch; check operation of indicator lights, warning lights and/or alarms; check instruments; record oil pressure and system voltage; check operation of electronic power take-off (PTO) and engine idle speed controls (if applicable).	P-1	21, 22, 61
2. Check operation of all accessories.	P-1	22
3. Understand operation of auxiliary power unit (APU)/electric power unit (EPU).	P-3	18
C. Safety Equipment		
1. Test operation of horns (electric and air); test warning device operation (reverse, air pressure, etc.); check condition of spare fuses, safety triangles, fire extinguisher, and all required decals; inspect seat belts and sleeper restraints; inspect condition of wiper blades, arms, and linkage; determine needed action.	P-1	22, 62
D. Hardware		
1. Test operation of wipers and washer; inspect windshield glass for cracks or discoloration; check sun visor; check seat condition, operation, and mounting; check door glass and window operation; verify operation of door and cab locks; inspect steps and grab handles; inspect mirrors, mountings, brackets, and glass; determine needed action.	P-1	22, 62
2. Record all physical damage.	P-2	62
3. Lubricate all cab grease fittings; inspect and lubricate door and hood hinges, latches, strikers, lock cylinders, safety latches, linkages, and cables.	P-2	62
4. Inspect cab mountings, hinges, latches, linkages, and ride height; determine needed action.	P-1	62
5. Inspect quarter fender, mud flaps, and brackets; determine needed action.	P-1	62
VIII. HYDRAULICS		
A. General		
1. Research vehicle service information, including vehicle service history, service precautions, fluid type, and technical service bulletins.	P-3	61
2. Verify placement of equipment/component safety labels and placards; determine needed action.	P-3	61
3. Identify hydraulic system components; locate filtration system components; service filters and breathers.	P-3	61

ASE Task List	ASE Priority Number	Chapter
4. Check fluid level and condition; purge and/or bleed system; take a hydraulic fluid sample for analysis; determine needed action.	P-3	61
5. Inspect hoses and connections for leaks, proper routing, and proper protection; determine needed action.	P-3	61
6. Use appropriate electronic service tool(s) and procedures to diagnose problems; check, record, and clear diagnostic codes; interpret digital multimeter (DMM) readings.	P-3	26, 61
7. Read and interpret system diagrams and schematics.	P-3	61
8. Perform system temperature, pressure, flow, and cycle time tests; determine needed action.	P-3	61
9. Perform system operational tests; determine needed action.	P-3	61
B. Pumps		
1. Identify causes of pump failure, unusual pump noises, temperature, flow and leakage problems; determine needed action.	P-3	61
2. Determine pump type, rotation, and drive system.	P-3	61
3. Remove and install pump; prime and/or bleed system.	P-3	61
4. Inspect pump inlet and outlet for restrictions and leaks; determine needed action.	P-3	61
C. Filtration/Reservoirs (Tanks)		
1. Identify type of filtration system; verify filter application and flow direction.	P-3	61
2. Service filters and breathers.	P-3	61
3. Identify causes of system contamination; determine needed action.	P-3	61
4. Inspect, repair, and/or replace reservoir, sight glass, vents, caps, mounts, valves, screens, supply, and return lines.	P-3	61
D. Hoses, Fittings, and Connections		
1. Diagnose causes of component leakage, damage, and restriction; determine needed action.	P-3	61
2. Inspect hoses and connections for leaks, proper routing, and proper protection; determine needed action.	P-3	61
3. Assemble hoses, tubes, connectors, and fittings.	P-3	61
E. Control Valves		
1. Pressure test system safety relief valve; determine needed action.	P-3	61
2. Perform control valve operation pressure and flow tests; determine needed action.	P-3	61
3. Inspect, test, and adjust valve controls (electrical/electronic, mechanical, and pneumatic).	P-3	61
4. Identify causes of control valve leakage problems (internal and external); determine needed action.	P-3	61
5. Inspect pilot control valve linkages, cables, and PTO controls; adjust, repair, or replace as needed.	P-3	61
F. Actuators		
1. Identify actuator type (single-acting, double-acting, multi-stage, telescopic, and motor).	P-3	61
2. Identify the cause of seal failure; determine needed action.	P-3	61
3. Identify the cause of incorrect actuator movement and/or leakage (internal and external); determine needed action.	P-3	61
4. Inspect actuator mounting, frame components, and hardware for looseness, cracks, and damage; determine needed action.	P-3	61
5. Remove, repair, and/or replace actuators.	P-3	61
6. Inspect actuators for dents, cracks, damage, and leakage; determine needed action.	P-3	61

GLOSSARY

A-, B-, or C-train A three-unit combination of tractor plus two trailers.

absorbed glass mat (AGM) battery A battery in which electrolyte is absorbed in a fine glass mat that prevents the solution from sloshing or separating into layers of heavier acid and water.

abuse failure Failure directly attributed to driver or other person's actions operating a component, system or vehicle outside normal operating range.

AC ripple A pattern produced by DC voltage fluctuations from the alternator created by differences between the peak voltage and the minimum voltages of overlapping AC sine waves.

alternating current traction generator (ACTG) A device that converts mechanical energy produced by the engine into electrical current for the propulsion system.

alternating current traction motor (ACTM) A motor that supplies propulsion force and functions as an electrical generator in a hybrid drive system.

accumulator A device placed between the evaporator and the compressor to collect liquid refrigerant and prevent it from entering the compressor. See also hydraulic accumulator.

Ackermann angle The angle the steering arms make with the vehicle center line. The angle should project towards the center of the rear axle. Also called *toe-out on turns*.

Ackermann principle The geometric alignment of a vehicle's steering arms that enables the wheels to toe out on turns with the inside wheels of a turn rotating in a smaller circle radius than the wheels on the outside.

active sensor A sensor that uses a current supplied by the ECU to operate. An internal microcontroller conditions the sensor's electrical signal.

AC-to-DC inverter A device that switches the polarity of an AC signal to resemble the straight wave polarity of DC.

adaptive control An advanced control system feature that adjusts output signals to optimize an operating variable such as economy, comfort, noise level or safety.

adaptive cruise control (ACC) A specialized cruise mode that enables the vehicle to recognize potential collisions with vehicles or objects it is following and reduce the vehicle speed.

adaptive learning Software than can learn and change strategy based on different operating factors.

addendum The top, thinner part of an involute tooth contact area.

adjusting ring A large threaded ring in the clutch cover of a pull-type clutch used to adjust the clutch internally.

adsorption A process in which material collects on the surface and the air dryer adsorbs moisture from the air and then discharges it in the purge cycle.

aeration Air in the fluid.

airbag The spring component of an air-spring suspension; a tough rubber bag filled with air. Also called *air spring* and *bellows*.

Air Dryer Integrated System (AD-IS) An air supply system component that contains an air dryer and several pressure protection valves to regulate charging of the air reservoirs.

air filter/pressure regulator The Fuller air filter/pressure regulator cleans the pressurized air supply going to the transmission and regulates it to 58 to 63 psi (400 to 434 kPa).

air spring The spring component of an air-spring suspension; a tough rubber bag filled with air. Also called *bellows* or *air bag*.

air conditioning compressor clutch An engagement device connected to the compressor crankshaft to lock the crankshaft with a belt-driven pulley.

air conditioning machine A machine designed to recover, recycle, evacuate, leak test, and recharge (R/R/R) the A/C system.

air-control solenoid valve An electric-over-air solenoid used to control shifting by controlling the flow of air from the air filter to the range cylinder piston.

air-over-hydraulic braking system A braking system that uses compressed air to provide power assistance to the hydraulic components in the braking system.

AL factor The size or surface area of a brake chamber multiplied by the length of the slack adjuster in inches.

Allison DOC PC-based service software for Allison's EP system.

Allison Transmission Electronic Control (ATEC) The original version of Allison's electronic control systems that evolved into Commercial Electronic Control (CEC).

alternating current (AC) A type of current flow that continuously changes direction and polarity.

aluminum alloy Aluminum mixed with other metals to increase its strength.

amboid gear A bevel gear arrangement with the pinion gear mounted above the centerline of the crown gear.

ammonia sensor A sensor used by selective catalyst reduction (SCR) that provides data to the ECU used to determine if ammonia values exceed anticipated range.

amperage A unit of measurement for the quantity of electrons in electric current movement.

ampere (amp) The unit for measuring the quantity of electrons flowing past one point in a circuit per unit of time.

amp-hour A measure of how much amperage a battery can continually supply over a 20-hour period before the battery voltage falling below 10.5 volts.

anaerobic sealers A category of sealant that cures or hardens in the absence of oxygen or air.

analog meter A meter that uses a sweeping needle that continuously measures electrical values.

analog signal An electric current that is proportional to a continuously changing variable.

analog to digital conversion The process when an analog waveform is sampled and measured many times a second to generate a digital representation of the waveform.

angle spring clutch A clutch manufactured by Eaton/Spicer Corporation that uses three pairs of angled springs pushing against levers to supply the clamp load.

annealing A metal working process to where the outer surface of hardened metal parts is made softer and more pliable. Metal is heated and cooled slowly, often with oil, to anneal a metal surface.

anti-compounding valve An air control system design feature that prevents simultaneous application of the service and spring brakes.

anti-drain-back check valves These valves try to keep the torque converter full of fluid when the vehicle is shut off.

anti-fade An opposite condition of heat fade where the coefficient of friction increases as the brakes get hotter.

antilock braking system (ABS) An electronic control system that works with the service brake system to monitor and automatically limit wheel lockup events during vehicle braking.

anti-rattle springs Flat springs used to stop the intermediate plate from rattling on a 14" (35.6 cm) double-disc clutch with a pot-style flywheel.

APADS/air conditioning protection unit (ACPU) An electronic microcontroller-based device that operates both air conditioning controls and diagnostic systems.

application chart A chart showing which power train control devices are used for a particular power flow.

applied stroke measurement The pushrod stroke length with a 90 psi (621 kPa) service brake application.

arbitration The process of deciding which messages have priority to transmit over the network to prevent data collision between positive and negative signals canceling one another.

armature The only rotating component of the starter; has three main components: the shaft, windings, and the commutator.

articulation The movement of the suspension system in reaction to road bumps or terrain.

aspect ratio The ratio of sidewall height to section width of a tire.

assisted GPS or A-GPS A GPS location signal correction method provided by cell phone networks. Supplemental satellite data is supplied more quickly to cell phone users or vehicles connected to the same mobile communication networks.

AS-Tronic ZF's AMT for medium- and heavy-duty trucks and buses.

asynchronous AC motor A motor in which the magnetic field in the rotor are induced by frequently switching current polarity in the stator windings.

synchronous motors A category of AC motor design where the rotational speed of the rotor and stator magnetic fields are identical or synchronized in rotational speed.

A-train A combination vehicle in which the second trailer is a full trailer unit connected by a draw bar to a single hitch point on the lead (first) trailer.

A-type lock A single swinging lock jaw and plunger for simple operation.

automated manual transmission (AMT) A standard manual transmission operated by electronic control.

automatic disengagement lockout (ADLO) A device that prevents the starter motor from operating if the engine is running.

automatic drain valve A drain valve located on the bottom of the air system reservoirs that automatically drains any accumulations of water or oil whenever the air reservoir cycles.

Automatic Gear Shift (AGS) One of Mercedes' AMTs for lighter-duty trucks.

automatic slack adjusters (ASAs) Automatically adjust brake stroke to maintain the correct shoe-to-drum clearance.

automatic slip regulation (ASR) A traction control system that minimizes wheel spin.

automatic traction control (ATC) A traction control system that minimizes wheel slip or spin due to excessive drive torque. Also called *electronic stability regulation (ESR)*.

automation A term referring to the use of control systems that reduce or eliminate human intervention needed to operate machinery. When the concept of automation is applied to a vehicle, it broadly describes a driving control system operating autonomously – that is, with no human intervention, or operating with varying, but limited, degrees of human involvement.

autonomous vehicle A vehicle controlled by a machine rather than a human. Fully automated vehicles use advanced software combined with environmental sensors tracking objects, signage, people, bicycles, road obstacles, and other traffic to operate dynamic driving outputs, such as braking, steering, engine speed, powertrain, and safety system accessories.

auto-ranging multimeter A multimeter that has fewer positions on its range selection knob and automatically selects the correct range when meter test leads are connected to a circuit.

AutoSelect Eaton's first AMT; very limited electronic control.

AutoShift Eaton's first shift by wire transmission.

auxiliary section A section bolted to the main transmission with two, three, or four ratios to multiply the ratios available to the driver.

auxiliary spring A second leaf spring in a leaf-spring suspension that does not take any of the weight until the vehicle is close to fully loaded.

axial thrust Thrust that tries to move the gears apart along their axis.

axis The centerline that a gear or wheel revolves around.

axle parallelism When the rear wheels of a vehicle follow the front wheels in a parallel manner.

axle perpendicularity When the axles are square with the vehicle frame.

axle setback The difference in distance between any axle end and the perpendicular centerline. Also called *setback* or *skew*.

axle spread The distance between the centerline of two axles.

axle stop A rubber (usually) bumper that stops the axle from contacting the vehicle frame during severe suspension articulation. Also called *jounce block*.

axle The shaft of the suspension system to which the hubs and wheels are attached; used to transmit driving torque to the wheels.

backing plate A metal plate covering the inboard side of brake foundation components in the wheel end.

backlash The clearance between teeth in mesh with each other.

back-taper The tapered profile of the teeth on a sliding clutch such that the outer edge is thicker than the inner; the profile helps keep the clutch engaged under load.

balancers A device designed to adjust battery voltage to compensate for unequal charges in multiple batteries. Also called *battery equalizers*.

ball hitch A single-point connection configuration for a hitch that uses a tongue-shaped draw bar, which loops over a ball connected to the tow vehicle.

ball-nut rack A metal block with a threaded hole that is part of the recirculating-ball steering system.

banjo A drive axle housing with a removable carrier. Also called a *removable carrier type*.

battery equalizers A device designed to adjust battery voltage to compensate for unequal charges in multiple batteries. Also called *balancers*.

battery-isolator systems A system designed to separate the main starting battery and the auxiliary battery. Also called a *split-charge relay*.

battery-management system (BMS) A system of electrical devices used to manage battery performance.

baud rate The rate at which serial data is transmitted.

BCE Before Common Era or before year 1.

beach mark Semi-circular mark in a fracture indicating repeated overload.

bead breaker A tool used to break the tire bead seal from the rim.

bead seat The edge of the rim that creates a seal between the tire bead and the wheel.

bearing adjuster Threaded wheel used to tighten the side bearing races.

bearing adjuster lock A Locking device used to secure the bearing adjusters.

bearing growth The increase in bearing size as it is pressed on to a shaft.

bearing preload The load applied to a bearing before any vehicle weight or rolling loads are applied.

bellcrank A shaft used in a mechanical linkage with a pivot in the center that reverses the normal direction of motion.

bellows The spring component of an air-spring suspension; a tough rubber bag filled with air. Also called *air spring* and *air bag*.

belt routing label A label that shows the correct position and routing of the drive belts.

bevel gear Gear cut on an angle allowing a power flow to turn a corner.

biased torque differential A differential capable of sending more torque to one wheel than the other when a wheel slip condition is encountered. Also known as a *proportional differential*.

bias-ply tire A type of tire ply construction where plies are arranged in a latticed, crisscrossing structure, with alternate plies crossing over each other and laid with the cord angles in opposite directions.

bidirectional communication Two-way multiplex communication. A communication channel between an electronic service tool and vehicle network where commands are sent and data received by the service tool.

bimetallic gauge A gauge in which two dissimilar pieces of metal are bonded together and expand at different rates when heated, thereby converting the heating effect of electricity into mechanical movement.

bipolar semiconductor A semiconductor having a junction between P and N material that conducts current through both the semiconductor materials and junction.

bipolar transistor A transistor that combines either two P or N materials with a single P or N-type material forming PNP or NPN transistors.

bit The smallest piece of digital information that is either a 1 or 0.

bit arbitration The process of deciding which messages have priority to transmit over the network to prevent data collision between positive and negative signals canceling one another.

bitter end The dead end of the wire rope.

blink code A method of providing fault code data for a specific system that involves counting the number of flashes from a warning lamp and observing longer pauses between the light blinks. Also called *flash code*.

blocking ring A synchronizer part that uses friction to increase or decrease a gear's speed to match shaft speed, so that the synchronizer sleeve or collar can lock the gear to the shaft.

Bluetooth A short-range wireless technology that can automatically connect a device into a network.

bobtailing proportioning relay (BPR) valve A specialized relay valve used to reduce delivery pressure to the rear brakes of a tractor when no trailer is towed.

bobtailing A tractor traveling without a trailer.

bolt circle pattern The number and spacing of the wheel nuts or wheel studs on the wheel hub on the wheel rim.

bolts An externally threaded fastener used in combination with a nut to clamp a joint.

boot loader A small but secure set of instructions stored in a separate area of microcontroller memory that decides if there is a set of valid program and data files stored in the microcontroller. The boot loader determines whether the ECU begins to operate or not.

bottle jacks Portable jacks that usually have a hydraulic ram mechanism to raise a component.

bow A type of frame damage characterized by the upward bending of the frame rails that can be caused by uneven loading of the frame. The opposite of sag.

Bowden cable A flexible metal cable with an inner and outer cable that is used to transmit mechanical force through the inner cable passing through the stationary hollow outer cable.

brake band A friction faced metal band that surrounds a planetary component; when applied hydraulically, it holds the component stationary.

brake block Brake friction material that is 0.75" (19 mm) thick.

brake drum A short, wide, hollow cylinder that is capped on one end and bolted to a vehicle's wheel; it has an inner friction surface that the brake shoe is forced against.

brake fade The inability of the brake to maintain its effectiveness. Brake fade causes a need for increased pedal application force to maintain the same braking effectiveness.

brake fluid Hydraulic fluid that transfers forces under pressure through the hydraulic lines to the wheel braking units.

brake foundations The braking components found at the wheel ends.

brake lag The time delay between driver brake pedal application and brake actuation due to the slower speed of air pressure transmission through air lines and valves.

brake lines Made of seamless, double-walled steel, and able to transmit more than 1000 psi (6895 kPa) of hydraulic pressure through the hydraulic brake system.

brake lining Brake friction material that is 1/2" (13 mm) thick.

brake shoes A steel shoe and brake lining friction material that apply force to the brake drum during braking.

brake stroke length The distance travelled by the brake chamber pushrod.

brake torque The force applied to the foundation brakes during braking.

break torque The unloading of the driveline to allow a shift to occur.

Bridge Formula B *See* Federal Bridge Gross Weight Formula.

brinelling damage that occurs when the rollers in the universal joint are hammered into the trunnions, leaving indentations.

British thermal unit (BTU) The amount of energy required to heat or cool one pound of water 1°F.

broken back arrangement A method of angle cancellation in which the U-joint angles intersect at a point exactly at the middle of the shaft length. Also known as an *intersecting angle arrangement.*

B-train A combination vehicle in which the tractor pulls a semi-trailer and a third, full trailer behind the semi-trailer.

B-type lock A fifth wheel locking mechanism that uses two swinging jaws and a yoke to lock the jaws securely around the king pin.

bump steer The undesired condition produced after hitting a bump which pushes or pulls steering linkage. The steering wheel may also be violently forced from the driver's grip during severe bump steer.

burst pressure The maximum pressure a manufacturer designates a hose to withstand before a particular hose explodes or ruptures.

byte A unit of eight bits.

cab forward (CF) A tractor with the engine located ahead of the cab.

cab harness The harness that connects the shift selector to the electronic control unit.

cab-over-engine (COE) A tractor with the engine located beneath the cab.

calibration A process of refining data used by a control system to optimize system performance.

caliper A hydraulic device that uses pressure from the master cylinder to apply the brake pads against the rotor.

calorie The unit of energy that reflects the amount of energy required to raise the temperature of 1 gram of water by 1°C.

cam brakes An "S"-shaped shaft head that twists between two rollers to expand a set of brake shoes.

camber The side-to-side vertical tilt of the wheel. It is viewed from the front of the vehicle and measured in degrees. See also *negative camber* and *positive camber.*

cam-opposite A situation when the cam rotates opposite the drum's rotation to energize the brakes.

cam-over conditions When the linings and or brake components are worn enough to allow the cam to rotate past the rollers.

cam-same An arrangement where the cam rotates the same direction the drum's rotation to energize the brakes.

cancellation The act of cancelling the non-uniform velocity in a driveshaft.

cap screw An externally threaded fastener that turns into a threaded hole.

capacitance touchscreen A display screen that uses two transparent plates, one of which is electrically charged.

capacitive coupling A category of EMI interference transmitted into wiring harnesses and circuits by strong electrostatic charges on body panels and other large surfaces.

capacitor A circuit-control device made up of two plates separated by an insulating material.

carbon dioxide (CO_2) One of the resulting gases produced when burning a hydrocarbon fuel; thought to contribute to global warming.

Cardan joint A joint with four trunnions and four bearing caps. Also known as a *Hooke joint* or a *universal joint.*

carrier The component that holds the support bearings for the drive axle gearing.

cast drums Brake drums made from cast iron.

cast ductile iron Cast iron that is ductile (bendable), not brittle.

cast spoke wheel A type of heavy-duty commercial wheel that uses three, five, or six cast iron spokes integrated with a bearing hub.

caster adjusting shim An angular shim used at the front leaf-spring mount to roll the I-beam axle forward or back to set the caster angle.

caster shimmy The rapid, side-to-side movement of the steering wheel resulting from excess positive caster.

caster The angle formed through the wheel pivot points when viewed from the side in comparison to a vertical line through the wheel.

cavitation The formation of air bubbles in fluid caused by lower boiling point produced by reduced pressure.

C-channel C-shaped steel beam that is the most common frame rail in heavy trucks.

center bearing A bearing pressed on to a machined surface after the splined area of a driveshaft's slip yoke spline; used to support a multiple piece driveshaft. Also called a *hanger bearing*.

center of gravity (CG) Also called the center of balance. The center of gravity, or CG, of an object is the point, or position, at which the item's weight is evenly dispersed, and all sides are in balance. If the item were to be supported in a direct vertical axis from the center of gravity, it would balance perfectly.

centrifugal force Apparent force by which a rotating mass tries to move outward away from its axis of rotation.

centrifuge drums Brake drums made with a cast-iron core surrounded by a steel band.

ceramic friction facings Friction facings made mostly of man-made materials specifically designed to produce desirable characteristics.

chafing Wear or abrasion due to prolonged or constant friction.

chain blocks A chain block is a piece of equipment used to lift heavy items. The typical block, also known as chain falls, consists of two grooved wheels with a chain wound around them in the same fashion as a block and tackle. The chain wound around the two wheels creates a simple machine that uses the leverage and the increased lifting ability created by the two wheels to lift heavy weights.

charge The amount of refrigerant present in the system or the process of installing refrigerant in the system.

charge-depleting (CD) operating mode A mode of operation in which the vehicle is powered only—or almost only—by the energy stored in the battery.

charge-sustaining (CS) mode A mode of operation in which the batteries' state of charge (SOC) may rise and fall slightly and energy storage modules are kept at a 40% state of charge.

chassis wiring harness The wiring that connects the transmission, the throttle position sensor (TPS), and the variable speed sensor to the transmission electronic control unit.

chemical fade A type of brake fade that takes place when steam or gases from vaporized lining materials form between hot lining and the drum, reducing the coefficient of friction.

chlorofluorocarbons (CFCs) A chlorine-based composition of a fluorine hydrocarbon compound.

chocks Blocks of material placed against a wheel to prevent undesired rolling movement.

chopper circuit A type of circuit used by motor control units to divert excess current from a generator into the absorption resisters.

chuff test A test performed on the antilock braking systems that results in air pressure being exhausted from the modulator and making a short chuffing sound.

circuit (wire) tracer An electronic service tool used to trace a single wire over a distance where multiple wires are bundled, shorted, or open.

circuit breaker A device that trips and opens a circuit, preventing excessive current flow in a circuit. It is resettable to allow for reuse.

clamp force The force squeezing the clutch disc between the pressure plate and the flywheel. Also called *clamp load*.

clamp load The force squeezing the clutch disc/s between the pressure plate and the flywheel. Also called *clamping force*.

clearance-sensing ASA A type of automatic slack adjuster that reduces pushrod travel based on torque input to the ASA.

clock spring A special rotary electrical connector located between the steering wheel and the steering column that maintains a constant electrical connection with the wiring system while the vehicle's steering wheel is being turned.

clockwise The clockwise direction of rotation of a gear as you look at it corresponding to the motion of the clock; also known as *forward*.

closed-loop systems A control strategy to correct for system error by using feedback from the system output to adjust a process generating the output.

clutch alignment tool A tool that holds the clutch discs in alignment as the clutch is installed and without which it is impossible to slide the transmission input shaft through the new clutch discs.

clutch bell housing The housing surrounding the clutch that bolts to the flywheel housing.

clutch bell housing pilot A small protrusion on the front of the clutch bell housing that fits into a mating recess in the flywheel housing.

clutch brake A small frictional brake usually mounted on the transmission input shaft; designed to slow down or stop the inertia of the transmission gearing so shifts into first or reverse can be made without clashing.

clutch-brake actuation The point of clutch-pedal actuation on a pull-type clutch when the clutch brake is being actuated or squeezed. Also called *squeeze*.

clutch capacity The amount of torque the clutch can safely handle without slipping.

clutch chatter The condition of the clutch alternately engaging and slipping quite rapidly when the driver engages the clutch.

clutch cover The outside part of the clutch that is bolted to the flywheel and that holds all the clutch components, except the clutch disc. Mistakenly, but commonly, called the pressure plate.

clutch disc or friction disc A plate or disc that has friction material on both sides and is splined to the transmission input shaft.

clutch free travel The free play between the clutch fork and the release bearing.

clutch jacks A clutch jack is a hydraulic jack equipped with exchangeable transmission input shafts that are used to align a clutch assembly and then raise it into place while it is being installed or removed.

clutch linkage The mechanical connection between the driver's clutch pedal and the clutch-cross shaft.

coefficient of friction (CoF) The amount of force required to move an object while in contact with another, divided by its weight.

coil spring A helical metal spring.

coil spring-style clutch A clutch that uses coils springs mounted perpendicular to the pressure plate to provide the clamp load.

cold curing A retreading process that uses a molded, pre-cured tread strip or tread ring, which is glued to the casing.

cold operation inhibit Restriction on transmission operation when the temperature is too cold for the transmission fluid to do its job.

cold-cranking amps (CCA) A measurement of the load, in amps, that a battery can deliver for 30 seconds while maintaining a voltage of 1.2 volts per cell (7.2 volts for a 12-volt battery) or higher at 0°F (−18°C).

collar shift transmission A transmission that uses sliding clutches or sliding collars to select gear ratios.

collision avoidance system (CAS) A vehicle stability control system that detects objects beside and in front of a vehicle that have the potential to collide with the vehicle.

combination (series-parallel) circuit A circuit that uses elements both of series and parallel circuits.

combination valve A valve that combines either all or some of the following into one housing—the proportioning valve, the metering valve, and the pressure differential valve.

combination vehicles Two or more combined or coupled vehicle units.

combined Watts and Ohm's laws Mathematical equations predicting the relationship between power, amperage, resistance, and voltage.

combo stud A mounting stud attached to an air spring that also receives the fitting to fill the spring with air.

comeback A colloquial term for repair work that returns with the original complaint.

Commercial Electronic Control (CEC) The second iteration of Allison's electronically controlled transmission.

Commercial Vehicle Safety Alliance (CVSA) A nonprofit organization dedicated to improving the safe operation of commercial vehicles in North America by establishing a uniform, reciprocal enforcement of commercial vehicle safety standards.

comminuted fracture A fracture where the bone is broken into three or more pieces.

companion flange A splined flange attached to a vehicle component, such as a drive axle pinion shaft, that bolts to a flange yoke on a driveshaft.

compatibility A friction-reducing property obtained when dissimilar metals are used to slide across one another rather than using the same materials, which increases friction.

compound or open fracture is a fracture where the bone pierces the skin, causing bleeding and damage to the surrounding tissue.

compound planetary gear set Planetary gear power flow that utilizes more than one gear set to produce the ratios.

compound ratio Any gear ratio that involves more than one pair of gears.

compound shift A shift where two parts of the transmission are being shifted at once.

compound split operation Blending torque from the motors and engine together.

compression A force that pushes down on the top flange of a frame rail between two support points, which tends to squeeze the flange of the frame rail together.

condensation Moisture that collects on cooler surfaces as a result of hot vapors coming into contact with the cooler surface.

condenser A component of the HVAC system that transfers heat from the system to the atmosphere.

conductance test A type of battery test that measures a battery's capacity using alternating current (AC) voltage.

conduction The transfer of heat through a solid item, such as a body panel or evaporator.

Conductive-coupling A category of EMI transmitted into a circuit by wiring connected to a source of interference.

conductor A material that easily allows electricity to flow through it. It is made up of atoms with very few outer shell electrons, which are loosely held by the nucleus.

conformity coating A protective chemical coating or polymer film barrier sprayed onto the circuit board and components to insulate them from chemical contaminants and moisture and also to dampen some vibration.

connecting drum A device used by Allison to connect some of the planetary gear components.

constant mesh transmission A transmission in which the main and countershaft gears are always in mesh.

constant velocity joint A joint that delivers a uniform speed to the driven shaft.

constant-current charger A battery charger that automatically varies the voltage applied to the battery to maintain a constant amperage flow into the battery.

constant-ratio steering gears Steering gears that use sector shafts with teeth of equal lengths.

constant-voltage charger A direct current (DC) power that is a step-down transformer with a rectifier to provide the DC voltage to charge.

contact patch The area of the tire that is in actual contact with the road.

contact pattern The contact area between two gear teeth in contact.

control valve body The heart of the hydraulic control; it holds the spool valves responsible for shifting and transmission control.

controlled area network (CAN) A distributed network control system in which several control modules exert varying degrees of control over common chassis electrical components.

controlled traction differential A differential that allows the engine to build more torque before the wheels can slip.

convection The transfer of heat through a gas.

conventional current theory The theory that the direction of current flow is positive to negative.

conventional steering system A steering system with a solid axle and a single steering gear.

converter dolly A single or set of dual axles that supports a fifth wheel. Converter dollies convert semi-trailers into full trailers.

convoluted air spring An air spring with a top and bottom mounting plate and one, two, or three girdle hoops. The girdle hoops add lateral stability to the spring.

coolant label A label that lists the type of coolant installed in the cooling system.

counterclockwise The counterclockwise direction of rotation of a gear as you look at it corresponding to the motion of the clock; also known as *backward*.

counter-electromotive force (CEMF) An electromagnetic force produced by the spinning magnetic field of the armature, or rotor which induces current in the opposite direction of battery current through the motor or alternator.

countershaft The shaft inside a transmission driven by the input gear.

counts The unit for digital signal conversion that Allison uses to describe throttle position based on the variable voltage signal from a TPS.

coupler Trailer hitching device, similar to pintle hooks, but in which the towing horn pivots and is not fixed.

coupling phase A torque converter operating phase when the turbine and the impeller are at close to the same speed.

coupling shaft A short shaft usually at the front of a driveline. Also known as *jack shaft*.

crack pressure The air signal pressure required to begin delivery of air pressure from a relay valve.

crank axle A dead axle in which the main beam is lower than the wheel spindles.

cranking amps (CA) A measurement of the load, in amps, that a battery can deliver for 30 seconds while maintaining a voltage of 1.2 volts per cell (7.2 volts for a 12-volt battery) or higher at 32°F (0°C).

creep The type of movement of components across another component caused by thermal expansion and contraction. Creep takes place when a cylinder head expands and contracts across the engine block.

critical speed The rotational speed at which a driveshaft starts to bow off its center line due to centrifugal force, leading to vibration and shaft failure.

cross members Cross beams that join the two frame rails together to form a ladder-type frame.

cross-phasing When a coupling shaft is phased at 90 degrees to the second driveshaft.

cross-shaft A rotating shaft that holds the clutch-release fork.

crown gear A large bevel gear that is driven by a smaller pinion gear in the bevel gear set. Also known as a *ring gear*.

CSA 2010 basic score Calculated ratings on compliance, safety, and accountability initiated by the Federal Motor Carrier Safety Administration (FMCSA).

C-train A combination vehicle similar to an A-train but using a convertor dolly that has two parallel drawbars.

current clamp A device that clamps around a conductor to measure current flow. It is often used in conjunction with a digital volt-ohmmeter (DVOM).

current track Another name for a DIN diagram.

cycling clutch orifice tube (CCOT) A fixed-orifice tube for evaporator pressure control obtained by cycling the compressor clutch on and off.

cylinder An actuator that converts hydraulic power into linear mechanical force. Also known as *ram*.

"D" capacity The maximum horizontal pulling force that can be safely applied to the fifth wheel. Also called *draw bar capacity*.

D'Arsonval gauge A type of electromagnetic gauge that moves a pointing needle directly proportional to current flow through an electromagnet attached to the pointer.

dampening disc A disc with a ring of torsional dampening springs around its hub designed to absorb engine torsional vibrations.

data bus The typology forming the communication pathway of electronic control modules in a network.

data link adapter A device used to translate serial data from the DLC into a format readable by a desktop or laptop computer.

Data Mechanical (DM) centrifugal clutch A centrifugally actuated clutch, used with an Ultra-Shift automated transmission.

daytime running lights (DRL) Forward running lights designed to improve vehicle visibility in the daytime.

DC to DC converters Electrical devices which increase or decrease DC battery voltage supplied to auxiliary electrical devices.

DC-to-AC inverter A device that takes the straight, unchanging wave of DC and flips, or inverts, the current's polarity to resemble an AC wave signal.

dead axle An axle that supports vehicle weight only.

dedendum The lower, thicker, part of an involute tooth contact area.

deep-cycle battery A battery used to deliver a lower, steady level of power for a much longer time.

defrost cycle A situation in which the evaporator releases heat instead of absorbing it, and the condenser absorbs heat instead of transferring it to the atmosphere.

defroster A HVAC air circuit that operates to clear the windows by blowing dehumidified air into the cab.

degree of freedom The extent an engine control system is capable of accommodating faults by adjusting control variables. A high degree of operational freedom means the model is able to select from a wide range of forward control paths to compensate for faults.

delta windings Stator windings in which the windings are connected in the shape of a triangle or the Greek letter Delta.

demountable rim A type of wheel rim that can be removed from the cast iron spoke hub attached to the axle. Also called an *open-center rim*.

depletion mode A condition in a unipolar-type semiconductor when either a P or N channel current carrying pathway is disrupted by the polarity of voltage applied to the gate.

derivative feedback control An error correction method that calculates the trajectory of current error to correct future error.

desiccant Silica beads used in the air dryer to trap and hold moisture and oil until the dryer is purged.

detent balls Spring-loaded steel balls that hold the shift rails in position.

Deutsch connector A compact, environmentally sealed electrical connector that uses solid, round, metal pins and hollow female sockets.

Deutsches Institut für Normung (DIN) diagram A schematic wiring diagram on which symbols, terminal connection numbers, line symbols, and operational status of items, such as switches and relays, are defined by a DIN standard. Also called *current track*.

D-flash (data flash) A category of reprogramming or memory update of only the data or calibration information in an ECU or microcontroller.

diagnostic data link (DDL) A special five- or nine-pin connector to connect the vehicle to a computer.

Diamond Logic Navistar's proprietary software used to service and perform service programming of the vehicle electrical system.

diamond A type of frame damage characterized by one frame rail moving forward or backward in relation to the other.

diaphragm spring clutch A clutch that uses a single diaphragm spring, also known as a Belleville spring, to provide the clamping force.

die A metal machining tool used to cut external threads.

diesel gallon equivalent (DGE) The equivalent amount of electrical energy to found in a gallon of diesel fuel.

diesel particulate filter (DPF) A component of the diesel exhaust aftertreatment system that filters soot from diesel exhaust.

differential braking Applying the brakes on an individual slipping wheel to transfer torque to a stationary or slowly turning wheel with traction.

differential case The housing that holds the differential gears.

differential cross The mechanism that holds the differential pinion or spider gears. Also known as the *differential spider*.

differential gear A gear arrangement that splits the available torque equally between two wheels, while allowing them to turn at different speeds, when required.

differential gear set Consists of two side gears, four pinion gears, and a cross; allows for speed difference between the two axle shafts of the drive axle when turning.

differential lock A device that prevents differential action by locking one side gear to the differential case.

differential mode transmission A digital signal transmission technology in which network modules detect the voltage difference between two wires to determine if a signal is a 1 or a 0.

differential pinion gear A beveled gear that is a component of the differential gear set; it is fitted to the four legs of the differential cross and rotates with it. Also known as a *spider gear*.

differential spider The mechanism that holds the differential pinion or spider gears. Also known as the *differential cross*.

differential voltage Refers to the voltage difference on a wire pair when one wire's voltage is the mirror-opposite voltage. A wide separation between the voltage pulses represents a 1 and a narrow separation represents a 0.

digital multimeter A type of multimeter that provides numerical displays of electrical data.

digital signals Electrical signals that represent data in discrete, finite values. Digital signals are considered as binary, meaning it is either on or off, yes or no, high or low, 0 or 1.

DIP switches A small slide switch located at the rear of the speedometer head placed in either an on or off (1 or 0) position.

direct current (DC) Movement of current that flows in one direction only.

direct drive A starter motor drive system in which the motor armature directly engages the flywheel through a pinion gear.

direct TPMS A type of automated tire pressure monitoring system that measures tire pressure, and possibly temperature, via a sensor installed inside each wheel.

directional slip angle The difference between the vehicle's steered (intended) direction and the actual direction of travel. The difference between these two directions is called the directional slip angle.

directional stability control (DSC) systems A stability control system that assists the driver in maintaining a vehicle's intended driving path by controlling yaw.

disc wheel A closed center steel or aluminum wheel that supports a tire and attaches to the hub using wheel studs and nuts.

dislocation The displacement of a joint from its normal position; it is caused by overextending the ligaments beyond their elastic limit.

disturbances Uncontrolled outside factors influencing a process that interferes with a control system task.

DIWA™ A dedicated bus transmission from Voith.

domain controllers ECUs used in major control systems, such as the engine or electrical system, that regulate the operation of multiple components or other subsystem ECUs.

double check valves A brake valve with two air inlets and one air outlet. Only the higher inlet pressure leaves the single valve outlet.

double reduction drive axle A drive axle that always uses two gear reductions.

double-clutch A technique drivers use to synchronize gear and shaft speed.

down-speeding A strategy that reduces rpm while still achieving desired road speed.

drag link A connecting linkage that transfers movement of the pitman arm to the upper steering arm.

draw bar capacity The maximum horizontal pulling force that can be safely applied to the fifth wheel. Also called *"D" capacity*.

draw bars Bars used to connect tow vehicles to a tractor or lead towing unit.

drivability items Inspection items including instrument warning lights, engine misfires, and rough idle.

drive axle The axle that drives the vehicle by turning the power from the driveshaft 90 degrees to deliver it to the wheels and providing the final gear reduction in the drive train. Also known as *live axle*.

drive pin Pin used in a pot-type flywheel to drive the intermediate plate.

drive pulley Any belt-driven pulley used to power an accessory, such as power steering or the A/C compressor.

driveline angularity Refers to the angles at the universal joints.

driveline A series of driveshafts, yokes, and support bearings used to connect a transmission to the rear axle.

Driver Post-Operation Vehicle Inspection Report (DVIR) In the United States, FMCSA legislation requires drivers to prepare a report in writing at the completion of each day's work for each commercial vehicle the driver has operated that day. Specifics of the legislation are contained in FMCVS 49.396.11.

Drivers Vehicle Inspection Report (DVIR) A daily report the driver of a commercial vehicle must complete.

drop arm An arm that transfers the steering box output shaft motion to the steering linkage by converting rotational movement into liner motion. Also called the *pitman arm*.

drop center tubular axle A dead axle used on trailer that drops in the middle.

dropbox A component that is bolted to the back of the transmission and connects the front and rear axles via the drive shaft; allows the output of a transmission to flow to both the rear and the front axles. Also called *transfer case*.

drop-center wheel rim A type of wheel rim design used by tubeless tires to ease installation of a tire over a rim. The center section of the rim between the two bead seats has a smaller radius area.

dryer integrated module (DRM) An AD-IS-type dryer with the addition of an air reservoir used to assist purging of the spin-on dryer desiccant cartridge.

DT-12 A 12-speed AMT manufactured by Detroit Diesel.

dual-circuit integrity test A test performed to verify the functioning of the automatic emergency brake system.

dual-circuit system A split between the primary and secondary air brake circuits on commercial vehicles done for safety purposes. A failure in one circuit does not affect the operation of the second air or hydraulic brake circuit.

dual-clutch transmission Transmission with two separate input shafts controlled by two separate clutches.

dual-mass flywheel A flywheel with two sections separated by torsional springs; one section attaches to the engine crankshaft and the clutch cover is bolted to the other section.

dual-mode hybrid drivetrain A hybrid system that combines both mechanical and electrical propulsion systems.

dual power inverter module (DPIM) Allison's control module responsible for converting energy from the ESS into alternating currents used to power the electric traction motors.

dump valve A driver-operated air valve to release the air from an air suspension system while at the loading dock.

duplex gauge Two air gauges in a single housing.

durapoid gearing A specially designed spiral bevel gear set designed to provide increased strength and load-carrying capability.

duty cycle The percentage of time a PWM signal is ON in comparison to OFF time.

dynamic imbalance A condition of a rotating assembly, such as a tire, wheel, or flywheel, where its weight is not symmetrically balanced around the center line of rotation and is offset from the vertical axis center.

ear protection Protective gear worn when the sound levels exceed 85 decibels, when working around operating machinery for any period of time, or when the equipment you are using produces loud noise.

edge code A code representing the CoF of a brake lining and its composition.

e-fuse A software-controlled fuse that uses field effect transistors for the circuit control device. Also called *virtual fuses*.

elastic limit The amount of force required to permanently deform a material.

elastomer A rubber-like material that stretches and has elastic properties. Elastomer materials are often used to make seals and gaskets.

electric shift assembly The shift actuation system for an Eaton AutoShift or UltraShift transmission that contains two shift motors, the shift finger, and the shift finger position sensors.

electrical capacity The amount of electrical current a lead-acid battery can supply.

electrical resistance A material's property that reduces voltage and amperage in an electrical current.

electrical system template A vehicle-specific software file that contains all the electrical system control logic and operating parameters.

electrohydraulic control module (electrohydraulic valve body) The valve body used to control electronically controlled transmissions and consisting of solenoids, spool valves, and, usually, pressure switches.

electrolysis The use of electricity to break down water into hydrogen and oxygen gases.

electrolyte An electrically conductive solution.

electromagnet A conductor wound into a coil that produces a magnetic field when current flows through it.

electromagnetic induction The production of an electrical current in a conductor when it moves through a magnetic field or a magnetic field moves past it.

electromagnetic interference (EMI) An electrical system problem caused by the transmission of unwanted electrical signals into current-sensitive vehicle circuits.

electron theory of current movement The movement of negatively charged electrons to a positive charge pole.

Electronic Air Control (EAC) A controller area network (CAN)-operated air supply system that regulates the air compressor load and unload cycle, plus additional optional air supply system components.

electronic commutation A method to produce motor rotation using switching transistors to control current flow through a DC motor armature rather than brushes.

electronic control system An arrangement of electronic and electrical devices designed to automatically regulate the operation of a component or system output and maintain it within a desired operating range.

electronic cooling package (ECP) A system of fans and electronic controls that maintains a hybrid ESS within a set temperature range.

Electronic Service Analyst (ESA) Paccar's proprietary software used to service and perform service programing of the vehicle electrical system.

electronic stability control (ESC) A general term for vehicle control systems that optimize braking and steering in emergency situations and minimizes the likelihood of a rollover, loss of vehicle direction, and wheel slip.

electronic pad wear indicators Devices that measure brake pad wear electronically and send signals directly to the driver.

electrostatic theory The idea that like charges repel one another and unlike electrical charges attract.

emergency brake circuit The air circuit responsible for the application and release of power springs in the brake chambers. Also referred to as the spring brake circuit or *park brake circuit*.

end termination The way the end of a wire rope is treated, usually by forming an eye that becomes the attachment for the wire rope.

end yoke A splined yoke attached to a component, such as a transmission output shaft.

energy storage system (ESS) A battery system that stores and distributes electrical current to the various components of a hybrid drive system.

engine dynamometer A machine that measures engine or brake system output. Horsepower, torque and speed are measured by an engine dynamometer.

engine hoist A crane used to lift engines.

engine identification label or information plate A label that contains the engine, serial number, date of manufacture, engine family, model number, size, horsepower rating, rated RPM, idle RPM, fuel rate, timing, and valve lash settings.

Engine Synchro Shift (ESS) Meritor's first AMT; limited to synchronizing engine speeds to assist the shifting process.

engine-driven hydraulic pump A power steering pump driven by a belt or gear driven by the engine.

enhancement mode A condition in a unipolar-type semiconductor when either a P- or N-channel current-carrying pathway is made conductive by the polarity of voltage applied to the gate.

Environmental Protection Agency (EPA) A US Federal government agency that deals with issues related to environmental safety.

EP40 system and EP50 system Models of Allison's Electric Propulsion system. Also known as *Allison's Electrically Variable (EV) Drive*.

EPDM belts A drive-belt material that is resistant to damage from heat and stretching.

epicyclical gear Gears that revolve around a common centerline.

equalizer bracket A bracket connecting the rear of the front leaf spring to the front of the rear leaf spring on a tandem-axle suspension; used to equalize the loading of each axle during suspension articulation.

equalizer The support for a tandem-drive axle, using a standard leaf-spring suspension system; it supports the rear of the front spring and the front of the rear spring.

equalizing beam suspensions Used on tandem-suspension systems; two large equalizing beams between the two axles equalize the load between the four wheels.

equalizing beam A beam with each end attached to the axles of a tandem-axle arrangement and its center attached to the frame directly or through a spring system. The beam reduces the impact of road bumps to the frame by 50% and equalizes the load carried by each of the axles. Also called a *walking beam*.

error signal A term describing the modified input signal to a controller with a correction factor based on the output error. Error signal is calculated by adding or subtracting from the controller's set-point input signal.

error A term describing the difference between a system output or process variable and its desired or set-point value.

ethylene glycol A chemical that resists freezing but is very toxic to people and animals.

evaporator freezing A condition in which excess refrigerant floods the evaporator reducing its temperature to below the freezing point of water.

evaporator The cold surface of the air conditioning system that absorbs heat from a cab or vehicle interior and transfers that heat to the atmosphere through a condenser.

exclusion seal A part of a seal or type of seal that functions as a barrier to dirt and contaminants.

exhaust gas recirculation (EGR) A system that recycles exhaust gas to reduce combustion temperatures.

external bleeding The loss of blood from an external wound; blood can be seen escaping.

extreme pressure (EP) additive Additives usually found in hypoid gear lube and which should not be used in Fuller Roadranger transmissions and most heavy-duty transmissions because it tends to oxidize at relatively low temperatures.

fail-safe operation The minimal transmission function that occurs when electrical power is lost.

false brinelling A condition where lubricant is squeezed out from between the needles and the trunnions of a U-joint leading to frettage wear; caused by too small or no angle at the joint so lubricant is not distributed.

fast adaptive A type of adaptive control used when the transmission is new and makes large changes to bring the shift close to the optimal shift profile quickly.

fatigue failure Failure of components due to repeated overload.

fault code state change A diagnostic technique where the opposite fault code is introduced than the reported one to differentiate problems in sensors, harnesses, and ECUs.

fault healing The specific strategy used by an MPC systems to compensate for a fault in a fault tolerant system.

fault-tolerant systems A feature of a control system enabling it to accommodate a fault without significantly affecting its operation.

Federal Bridge Formula *See* Federal Bridge Gross Weight Formula.

Federal Bridge Gross Weight Formula Laws that limit the weight-to-length ratio of heavy trucks with the goal of protecting roads and bridges from the damage caused by the concentrated weight of shorter trucks. Also known as *Bridge Formula B* or *Federal Bridge Formula*.

Federal Motor Carrier Safety Administration (FMCSA) All companies that operate commercial vehicles within the United States to move freight, passengers, or transport any cargo interstate, must be registered with the FMCSA.

Federal Motor Carrier Safety Regulation (FMCSR) Regulations issued by the Federal Motor Carrier Safety Administration (FMCSA), published in the US Federal Register, and compiled in the US Code of Federal Regulations (CFR).

Federal Motor Vehicle Safety Standard 121 (FMVSS 121) The legislated performance standard for air brake systems on commercial vehicles.

field effect transistor (FET) A unipolar transistor that uses an electric field to control the conductivity of a semiconductor material.

fifth wheel A plate-type coupling device designed to support the weight of a semi-trailer.

fillet radius The radius shape between the bottoms of two teeth. Also called *root*.

firmware Program files stored in the microcontroller that contain machine code instructions to operate the circuits of a microcontroller.

first aid The care given by the first person to come to the aid of an injured party at the scene of the injury before formal medical care can be given.

first-degree burns Burns that show reddening of the skin and damage to the outer layer of skin only.

fishplate Flat plate used to re-enforce the frame rail, or a plate bolted to the frame rail web to attach components to the frame.

fishtailing A condition when the drive axles of a vehicle laterally push the rear of a vehicles and steering control is lost. Also called *power jackknifing*.

flange The flat surface at the top and bottom of a frame rail.

flange case half The half of the differential case that the crown gear attaches to.

flange yoke A yoke with two ears to hold a U-joint and a flat flange to bolt to a companion flange.

flash code A strategy used by ECUs to report fault codes by flashing or blinking fault lamps, using long and short pauses between the light flashes to represent numerical fault codes. Also called *blink code*.

flashing The process of installing new or reprogramming calibration or firmware data in an ECU's flash memory storage area.

flat-type flywheel A flywheel that is predominately flat, the clutch cover bolts to it.

flex plate A flexible plate used to connect the torque converter to the engine.

flitch plates Angle iron that is attached to the fifth wheel on one side and is bolted to the frame on another side.

floating caliper A disc brake caliper that is both supported and slides along on two pins.

flooded lead-acid battery A lead-acid battery in which the plates are immersed in a water–acid electrolyte solution.

floor jack A type of hydraulic jack mounted on four wheels that can be rolled into position.

flotation tire Large tires used on the front axle with a low aspect ratio. Also called *wide-base tire*.

flow-control valve A valve used in power steering pumps to regulate the volume of fluid flow out of the power steering pump.

fluid analysis Chemical analysis of the transmission fluid revealing contaminant levels.

fluid coupling A power transfer device that uses fluid to transmit power.

fluorescent bulb A light bulb that uses electrically heated filaments located at each end of a tube filled with a small amount of mercury or a noble gas, such as neon, argon, or xenon.

flywheel A heavy round metal disc attached to the end of the crankshaft to smooth out vibrations from the crankshaft assembly and provide one of the friction surfaces for a clutch disc used on manual transmission/transaxle applications.

flywheel housing The round housing bolted to the rear of the engine to which the clutch bell housing is bolted.

flywheel housing face The part of the flywheel housing that mates to the clutch bell housing.

flywheel housing pilot A small recess in the flywheel housing that receives the clutch bell housing pilot.

flywheel friction surface The flat friction surface of the flywheel face.

foot valve The foot-operated valve that controls the application and release of brakes. The foot valve is the center of the brake delivery system and is also called the *treadle valve*.

forging A metal stamping process where metal parts softened by heat are repeatedly struck with a forging die to shape a metal part.

forward bias A condition in which a diode or transistor conducts current.

forward clutch A clutch that is applied in all forward gears or ranges; it is not found on overdrive transmissions.

frame angle The angle the vehicle's frame makes with regard to horizontal measurement to the ground. See also *positive frame angle* and *negative frame angle*.

frame centerline alignment An alignment method that uses the vehicle frame and not its axles as the reference point for making alignment adjustments.

frame rail web The upright section of the frame rail. Also called *web*.

free play Clearance between two components.

free stroke measurement The brake pushrod stroke length using a lever to move the slack adjuster.

Freedomline 12- and 16-speed ZF AMTs released in partnership with Meritor.

Freon A refrigerant produced by reacting carbon tetrachloride, commonly used as "carb-cleaner," with fluorine gas.

frequency The number of events or cycles that occur in a period, usually 1 second.

frequency-operated button (FOB) The user element of the RKE system carried by the driver that transmits radio signals with coded digital information to a network radio receiver to operate the door locks or other electrical accessories.

frequency-sensing relay A relay connected to the alternator that detects alternating current only when the alternator is charging.

friction The relative resistance to motion between any two bodies in contact with one another.

friction dampening Controlling torsional vibration by using friction material in between the various plates in a clutch friction disc.

friction modifier Additive in transmission fluid designed to enhance the friction characteristics of certain clutch materials.

friction plates Steel plates faced with friction material and used in a hydraulic clutch. They are splined to a planetary gear set component.

front/rear split A brake system in which the front brakes operate on one hydraulic circuit and the rear brakes from the other.

fuel cell An electrochemical device that combines hydrogen and oxygen to produce electricity, heat, and water.

full fielding A test procedure that bypasses the internal voltage regulator to determine whether the alternator can produce output current.

full floating axle shaft An axle that carries none of the vehicle weight.

full throttle downshift A downshift forced by the driver by pushing on the throttle. Also called *detent downshift* or *kick down*, depending on the manufacturer.

full trailer A trailer that is supported at both ends with an axle and does not rest on a fifth wheel.

full-box rail A box-shaped frame rail.

fully oscillating fifth wheel A type of fifth wheel designed to provide front-to-rear and side-to-side movement between the tractor and semi-trailer.

galvanic corrosion Corrosion of the material caused by the electrolytic effect that can occur when two dissimilar metals are in contact.

galvanic isolator A device used to prevent high and low voltage sources on a vehicle from sharing a ground circuit.

galvanic reaction A chemical reaction that produces electricity when two dissimilar metals are placed in an electrolyte.

gas pocket Imperfection in the adhesion of molten metal during the casting or forming process, also known as a *stringer*.

gas welding goggles Close-fitting safety goggles with a dark tinted lens.

gassing A situation that occurs when overcharging or rapid charging causes some gas to escape from the battery.

gateway module A module that translates communication protocols to enable inter-network communication between different networks operating on-board a vehicle.

gear jamming An attempt by the driver to shift without using the clutch; usually causes at least some damage to the transmission sliding clutches. Also called *float shifting*.

gear pump A pump consisting of an internal and external toothed gear and typically a crescent.

gear ratio The relationship between two gears in mesh as a comparison to input versus output.

gear reduction Any gear set that reduces output speed while at the same time increases output torque. Also known as *underdrive ratio*.

gear set contact pattern The indication as to where the gears will contact each other during operation.

gear slip out The condition in which a transmission jumps out of gear and to neutral when under load, caused by worn components, such as sliding clutches and shift forks. Also called *jump out*.

gel-cell battery A type of battery to which silica has been added to the electrolyte solution to turn the solution to a gel-like consistency.

generoid An asymmetrical tooth design similar to the durapoid; it gives added strength to the hypoid and amboid gear sets. Also called *hypoid generoid*.

geometric centerline alignment An alignment method that establishes a vehicle's centerline by placing a line from the midpoint of the front axle and the midpoint of the rear-most axle.

gerotor pump A pump consisting of a rotor turning inside a matching chamber.

gimbals Two or more concentric circles used to support an item; while the circles can move, the supported object remains stationary.

gladhands The air couplers attached to the trailer hoses connecting the tractor and trailer air systems.

glazing A cause of brake fade characterized by a hard, glassy, burnt appearance to the lining surface, diminishing its CoF.

global navigation satellite system (GNSS) A worldwide radio-navigation system using signals from orbiting satellites to precisely locate the position of receivers on the earth surface.

global warming potential (GWP) A measure of a refrigerant's contribution to global warming over 100 years for a given mass compared to the same mass of carbon dioxide.

governor cut-in pressure The pressure at which the governor loads or starts the compressor.

governor cut-out pressure The pressure at which the governor unloads or ends the compressor operation.

governor valve A valve that creates a pressure based on road speed.

governor An air control valve that regulates the air compressor cut-in and cut-out pressure. The governor also controls the purging of the air dryer.

gradability The capability of a vehicle to maintain forward motion on a specified grade while sustaining a minimum speed.

graphing meter An electrical test instrument used to analyze waveforms and graphically plot an electrical value of a signal over time.

greenstick fracture A bone broken on one side only.

gross combined weight rating (GCWR) A specific maximum weight limit determined by the vehicle manufacturer that takes into account two individual (yet attached) vehicles—the tow vehicle or tractor, and the trailer.

gross trailer weight (GTW) The maximum carrying capacity of a trailer calculated by measuring the trailer weight and load.

gross vehicle weight (GVW) The maximum design weight of a vehicle including a full tank of fuel, fully loaded to its capacity, and with all passengers.

gross vehicle weight rating (GVWR) The design rating specified by a manufacturer as the recommended maximum weight of a vehicle when fully loaded to capacity, including all passengers and a full tank of fuel.

gross weight limit The maximum legal weight of a vehicle that can travel on roads and bridges.

ground The name given to their negative current pathway through a vehicle chassis.

ground shaft A stationary shaft that holds the inner hub of the stator one-way clutch. Also called *stator support shaft*.

grounded circuit A circuit characterized by an unwanted low resistance connection between battery positive power and chassis ground.

guide studs Long threaded studs that stop a component from falling while the attaching bolts are removed.

hairline fracture A cracked bone that has not separated.

Hall-effect sensor A sensor commonly used to measure the rotational speed of a shaft; it has the advantage of producing a digital signal square waveform and has strong signal strength at low shaft rotational speeds.

halogen bulb A light bulb produced by adding small quantities of gases from the halogen family, such as iodine or bromine.

halogen infrared discharge (HID) bulb A light bulb that has a special coating on an inside portion of the bulb wall that reflects infrared heat back onto the filament, causing it to burn hotter.

hanger bearing A bearing pressed on to a machined surface after the splined area of a driveshaft's slip yoke spline; used to support a multiple piece driveshaft. Also called a *center bearing*.

hardening A manufacturing process that makes the surface of a gear much harder than its core: typically, the surface is hardened to a depth of not more than 0.050" (1.2 mm).

harmonic vibration An inherent vibration that occurs at precisely 50% of a shaft's critical speed.

hazard Something that can cause an accident, a sickness, or an injury.

hazardous environment A place where hazards exist.

hazardous material A material that can cause damage or injury to a person.

H-Bridge A control circuit taking its name from the shape of four transistors arranged to switch the polarity of current applied to a load. It is often used to change the direction of DC electric motors or rapidly open and close injector solenoids.

headgear Protective gear that includes items like soft caps, bump caps, or hard hats.

heat fade The loss or reduction in the CoF as the brake temperature increases.

heater core An in-cab heat exchanger that regulates heating by circulating engine coolant.

heating ventilation and air conditioning (HVAC) system The system in the vehicle responsible for heating and cooling the air.

heat-treated alloy steel Highly engineered steel with a yield strength of at least 110,000 psi (758 MPa).

heel The end of a crown gear tooth furthest from the center of its axis.

height-control valve An air valve that maintains air-spring suspension ride height.

helical double reduction drive axle A double reduction drive axle that uses a helical gear set for the second gear reduction.

helical double reduction two-speed drive axle A double reduction drive axle that uses two selectable sets of helical gears as the second gear reduction.

helical drop gear The set of gears that drive the pinion gear of the front drive axle of a tandem.

helical gear A gear with teeth cut on an angle or spirally to its axis of rotation.

herringbone gear A gear cut with opposite helices on each side of the face.

hertz (Hz) The unit for electrical frequency measurement, in cycles per second.

hexadecimal code A numbering system using a combination of 0s, 1s, and letters to represent data. It shortens the length of binary words and numbers to make them more readable.

high-carbon steel Steel alloyed with carbon at levels of 0.9% to 2.5%.

high-impedance multimeter A meter that samples very little of a circuit's own current to take a measurement.

high-intensity discharge (HID) lamps Lamps that use an electric arc to produce higher light outputs of between 2800 and 3800 lumens.

high-voltage interlock loop (HVIL) A device that prevents access to potentially hazardous energized electrical circuits.

high-voltage isolation A service procedure used to verify high-voltage current remains inside the battery pack during vehicle service.

hoisting The action of lifting a load using cables or ropes.

hold regulator valve A spool valve that creates a pressure used to prevent upshifts.

Hooke joint A joint with four trunnions and four bearing caps. Also known as a *Cardan joint* or a *universal joint.*

Hooke's law A law of physics that states that force delivered by a spring to an object is directly related to its compression or extension; the greater the spring is compressed, the more force the spring delivers.

horsepower A unit of measure of power that conveys how fast the engine can turn while producing torque.

hot curing A retreading process in which the casing is covered with uncured rubber and then placed in a mold and heated. Also called *mold curing.*

hub piloted disc wheel A type of disc wheel that uses a series of machined pads on the hub to help center the wheel.

Huck® fastener A riveted connection with ridges instead of threads and with the nut swaged onto the bolt, preventing the collar from being tightened after the fastener is installed.

hybrid electric vehicle (HEV) A type of vehicle that combines an internal combustion engine with an electric propulsion system into a new or hybrid powertrain configuration.

HybriDrive Propulsion System A series-type hybrid propulsion system developed by BAE, an aerospace and defense technology company.

hydraulic accumulator A device that stores hydraulic energy and acts as an emergency power source in the event of system pump failure.

hydraulic circuit A pathway connecting one part of the transmission's hydraulic control with another part.

hydraulic clutch A hydraulically actuated power train control device that squeezes friction and reaction plates together to either drive, (input), or hold a planetary gear component stationary.

hydraulic cylinder A device that uses hydraulic fluid pressure and converts it to linear mechanical movement. Also referred to as a *ram.*

hydraulic jack A type of vehicle jack that uses oil under pressure to lift vehicles.

hydraulic launch assist (HLA) An alternative to electric hybrid drive's regenerative braking. A hydraulic pump pressurizes fluid and stores it in a hydraulic-gas accumulator during a brake application. The use of standard friction service brakes is prevented until just before a complete vehicle stop.

hydraulic retarder Retarder systems that pump transmission fluid between a turning cupped rotor and stationary cupped housing, thereby creating fluid pressure and fluid friction that slow the vehicle.

hydrofluoro-olefin (HFO) Is the most recently developed, near drop-in replacement for the R134a refrigerant. It's chemical name is HFO1234yf.

hydrometer An instrument used to measure the specific gravity of liquids.

hydrophilic A material property indicating it resists absorbing water.

hydroscopic A material property indicating it absorbs water.

hypoid gearing A type of spiral bevel gear set that mounts the pinion gear below the centerline of the crown gear.

hysteresis This occurs when something is deflected, but does not rebound with the same force, usually due to the internal friction inherent in the material as it deflects.

I-beam I-shaped beam used for frame rails on heavier vehicles; can be aluminum or steel.

idle validation switch (IVS) A throttle input circuit used for safety reasons to verify throttle position.

idler gear Gear used in transmissions to drive a vehicle backward.

impeller The bladed element in a torque converter or fluid coupling that is fixed to the housing and, therefore, rotates with it.

incandescent bulb A conventional bulb that electrically heats a filament of metal to the temperature at which it produces light.

inclinometer/accelerometer Sensors included in the transmission control system that allow it to adapt to topography and operating conditions.

included angle The angle of camber added or subtracted to the king pin inclination angle.

indirect TPMS A type of automated tire pressure monitoring system that uses the anti-lock braking system of a vehicle to measure the difference in the rotational speed of the four wheels to determine tire pressure.

induction motor An asynchronous type AC electric motor where alternating current in the stator induces magnetic fields in the rotor.

inductive amp clamp A device that measures amperage by measuring a conductor's magnetic field strength, which is proportional to amperage.

inductive coupling A category of EMI transmitted by changing magnetic field strength in a conductor or device inducing current flow in a nearby conductor through mutual induction.

inertia brake A type of transmission shaft brake geared to one countershaft, which controls gearing rotational speed while shifting.

inertia shift Weight that moves from the rear of the vehicle to the front during braking.

inertial excitation The force caused by the speeding up and slowing down of the shaft driven through an angle. These stem from the operating angles of the U-joint at the drive end of the driveshaft and are caused by the sheer weight of the driveshaft being accelerated and decelerated twice per revolution.

inlet pressure regulating valve Regulates the maximum air intake pressure supplied to the air compressor from a turbocharged engine's intake manifold.

input member The element of the planetary gear set that receives input from the power source.

input shaft The component to which the clutch discs are splined.

insulated gate bipolar transistor (IGBT) A three-terminal power semiconductor device primarily used as an electronic switch.

insulator A material that holds electrons tightly and prevents electron movement.

integral carrier housing A drive axle housing that does not have a removable carrier.

integral feedback control An error-correction algorithm that analyzes the time that error deviations are present above or below the set-point, and increases controller gain if error is not quickly corrected.

intelligent charger A battery charger that varies its output according to the sensed condition of the battery it is charging.

inter-axle differential A differential gear set that splits the available torque equally between two drive axles. Also called a *power divider*.

interleaf friction Friction caused by the leaves in a multi-leaf spring pack rubbing together during suspension articulation; can be effective in stopping unwanted oscillation.

interlock system A system that prevents the transmission from engaging two mainshaft gears at once.

intermediate plate A cast iron plate that is connected to the flywheel or the clutch cover, also known as a separator plate.

intermittent circuit A circuit characterized by uneven current flow.

internal bleeding Bleeding that cannot be seen externally.

intersecting angle arrangement A method of angle cancellation in which the U-joint angles intersect at a point exactly at the middle of the shaft length. Also known as a *broken back arrangement*.

Intuitive Diagnostic System (IDS) Proprietary software system available on BAE propulsion systems to aid technicians in diagnosing service issues.

inversion valve A normally open valve that requires air pressure to close. Another name often given to a *spring brake relay valve*.

inverter A device that changes direct current into alternating current. Also called a *wave inverter*.

involute A gear design shape that compensates for the changing point of contact between gears as they rotate through mesh.

I-Shift The Volvo AMT; Mack trucks use the same transmission.

ISO 11446 connector A type of connector commonly used in Europe that uses dedicated pins to transmit ABS information between the tractor and trailer.

ISO 3731 connector A type of connector commonly used in Europe that uses dedicated pins to transmit ABS information between the tractor and trailer.

isometric diagram A wiring diagram used to locate a component within a system that shows the outline of a vehicle or piece of equipment where the component can be found.

J-1587 An early SAE network communication protocol with a data transmission at 9600 bits per second.

J-1939 A Newer SAE network communication protocol; data transmission at a rate of at least 250,000 bits per second and up to 500,000 bits/second.

J-560 trailer connector A trailer cord plug and receptacle located at the rear of the tractor.

jack bolt A bolt that forces the pressure plate forward and secures the clutch discs in a DM clutch.

jack shaft A short shaft usually at the front of a driveline. Also known as a *coupling shaft*.

jack stands Metal stands with adjustable height to hold a vehicle once it has been jacked up.

jackknife A condition when the drive axles of a vehicle push the rear of a vehicle around its center point and steering control is lost. Generally caused by aggressive over braking or lockup of the trailer wheels, which folds the orientation of the combination vehicle into a shape of a pocket-knife. Also called *fishtailing*.

jounce The upward motion of the wheels and axles in reaction to road bumps or terrain.

jounce block A rubber (usually) bumper that stops the axle from contacting the vehicle frame during severe suspension articulation. Also called *axle stop*.

jump out The condition in which a transmission jumps out of gear and to neutral when under load, caused by worn components, such as sliding clutches and shift forks. Also called *gear slip out*.

key-off electrical loads Unwanted drain on the vehicle battery when the vehicle is off. Also called *parasitic draw*.

kinetic energy The energy of a body in motion.

kinetic friction The friction between two surfaces that are sliding against each other.

king pin The main pivot in the steering mechanism of a vehicle.

king pin inclination angle (KPI) The angle formed between true vertical and the angle of the king pin. Also called *steering axis inclination angle*.

Kirchhoff's law A law that states that the sum of the voltage drops in a series circuit equals source voltage.

labor guide A guide that provides information to make estimates for repairs.

ladder logic The designed-in logic sequence of a circuit control devices that determines what steps activates a specific output.

ladder-type frame A frame consisting of two rails joined together by a series of cross members.

land The largest diameter in a spool; used to block flow paths.

landing gear Retractable legs attached to the trailer, which support a semi-trailer when it is not resting on a fifth wheel.

latching solenoids Solenoids that need only a short burst of electricity to move to an open or closed position and they remain in that state until they are energized again.

latent heat The quantity of heat required to produce a change of state from a solid to a liquid or a liquid to a gas.

latent heat of fusion The process of removing heat energy to matter to effect a change of state.

latent heat of vaporization The process of adding heat energy to matter to effect a change of state.

lateral stability The vehicle's ability to be stable from side to side.

lay The distance it takes for one strand to complete one revolution of the wire rope.

leading shoes An arrangement for brake shoes where they are self energize in the forward direction of brake drum rotation.

leading/trailing shoe drum brake arrangement A type of brake shoe arrangement where one shoe is positioned to self energize and the opposite shoe does not.

leaf spring A spring formed by elliptical steel leaves; can be single leaf or multi-leaf.

left-hand camshafts S-cams that rotate in a counterclockwise direction to apply the brakes.

lengthwise bearing The contact pattern along the tooth face from the toe toward the heel.

Lepelletier gear set A compound planetary gear set consisting of three interconnected planetary gears capable of producing six forward ratios and one reverse.

lever A simple machine that can allow a large object to be moved with less force.

lift axle A non-drive (dead) axle that can be mechanically raised and lowered to meet requirements regulated for maximum axle weight loads.

lifting Raising the vehicle from underneath.

lifting equipment Also known as lifting gear, any equipment or devices used to lift a load vertically. This can include jacks, a block and tackle, hydraulic lift, hoist, gantries, cranes, slings or rigging, wire rope/cables, and any other items used to lift a load vertically.

light-emitting diode (LED) A diode that produces light in different colors, depending on the doping material used in its manufacture.

limiter valve An air pressure proportioning valve used to increase brake application pressure to the front brakes when a trailer is not towed by a tractor. Also known as a *ratio valve*.

linear Extending or moving in a straight-line direction.

line-haul A truck that spends most of its time in on-highway operations transporting medium to heavy load.

lithium-ion (Li-ion) battery A type of battery that uses lithium in the battery electrodes.

live (drive) axle The axle that drives the vehicle by turning the power from the driveshaft 90 degrees to deliver it to the wheels and providing the final gear reduction in the drive train. Also known as a *drive axle*.

load leveler A bar with moveable attachment points also known as a spreader bar.

load test A battery capacity test that electrically loads the battery to a high rate of discharge, while measuring final voltage after 15 seconds of electrical load.

load-dumping A feature that allows temporary suppression of high-voltage spikes when electrical loads are suddenly removed from the alternator.

loading The state of the air compressor when it is building system air pressure. The unloader valves are not active.

lock out tag out (LOTO) A system used to make sure that defective equipment is not used until it has been properly repaired.

lock–up clutch disc The friction disc used in a lock-up clutch.

locking differential A system that actively prevents differential action from occurring when engaged.

locking tang A small flat piece of metal that stops the large internal adjusting ring from moving when the clutch is operating.

lock-up clutch piston The hydraulically actuated piston that applies the lock-up clutch.

lock-up clutch/piston assembly A combination lock-up clutch disc and piston assembly; used in light-duty vehicles.

lock-up clutch The clutch that locks the turbine to the converter shell when conditions are correct for 100% efficiency.

long stroke chambers Brake chambers manufactured with a 3" (76 mm) maximum stroke travel.

look-up tables Groups of set-point values arranged in a table used by a control system as a reference point to adjust system output signals. Look-up tables are also used by the ECU as mathematical short cuts to provide answers to complex problems.

low-inertia A new design auxiliary section that momentarily disengages the auxiliary from the main box during compound shifts, making it easier to move the shift lever.

low profile (LP) tire A type of tire that has a shorter sidewall height than conventional tires.

low-voltage burn-out A damaging condition for starter motors in which excess current flows through the starter, causing the motor to burn out prematurely.

low-voltage disconnect (LVD) A device that monitors battery voltage and disconnects non-critical electrical loads when battery voltage level falls below a preset threshold value.

L-plate L-shaped beams that can be bolted to the outside of the C-channel to increase the rails' RBM.

lubrication failure Failure caused by incorrect lubricant, contaminated lubricant, or lack of lubricant.

lumen The units used to measure light intensity.

magnetic reed switch Automatic-type switch with contacts opened or closed by magnetic fields.

magnetic switch A magnetic relay-type switch designed to handle higher current flow than smaller ISO relays.

magnetism A fundamental force that can be used push or pull electrons.

main pressure regulator valve (MPRV) A spool valve that produces main or control pressure.

main shaft The shaft that is driven by the countershaft and provides output for the transmission. Also called *output shaft*.

manifold gauge set A set of calibrated gauges for measuring high and low pressure A/C gases that can show pressure and vacuum readings for use with A/C systems.

manual selector valve The spool valve that is moved by the operator's shift linkage to select a gear.

manual slack adjusters A manually adjusted lever between the brake chamber and the S-cam to maintain brake shoe to drum clearance.

manual-ranging multimeter A multimeter that must be set to the correct range first based on anticipated values measured.

map (pictorial) diagram A wiring diagram that shows the entire vehicle wiring circuit using pictorial symbols.

Mapless MPC An advanced type of Model Predictive Control system control system that does not use look-up tables and has a model-optimizing mechanism to correct model errors in real-time.

Mapped MPC A type of Model Predictive Control system that generates the optimal set of control signals using virtually generated set-points or predicts which set of look-up tables to use as set-points.

master disconnect switch A switch located in the battery compartments that enables technicians to disconnect the power circuit for maintenance or emergencies.

maximum bending moment The point on the frame at which the load force is concentrated.

maximum forward overdrive The highest (fastest) ratio possible in a planetary gear set.

maximum forward reduction The lowest (slowest) ratio possible in a planetary gear set.

mechanical advantage Occurs when we give up either speed or torque to increase either torque or speed through a machine.

mechanical fade Loss of brake effectiveness that occurs when drums expand due to heat.

mechanical jack A type of jack that utilizes mechanical power to provide lifting. A screw jack is a type of mechanical jack.

mechanics lien A mechanics lien allows the repair facility to withhold a vehicle until the bill is paid.

mechatronics The integration of mechanical systems, electronic devices, and microcontroller-based systems.

medium-carbon steel Steel alloyed with carbon at levels of 0.25% to 0.6%.

metering valve A valve that delays brake application pressure to the front disk brakes until a certain level of pressure builds in the system.

Metri-Pack connector A pull-to-seat electrical connector with flat terminals instead of round.

microcontroller A special-purpose integrated circuit processor with limited capabilities, designed to perform a set of specific tasks.

micron gauge A device designed to measure the amount of vacuum very precisely.

minimum forward overdrive The second highest (fastest) ratio possible in a planetary gear set.

maximum forward reduction The lowest (slowest) ratio possible in a planetary gear set.

miter boxes A gear arrangement that allows sharp angle changes in the steering column.

mobile gantry crane An A-frame on wheels that can be moved around the shop to provide an attachment point for a chain block.

Mode 1 In split-mode operation, the mode that is for low-speed operation.

Mode 2 In split-mode operation, the mode that is for high-speed operation.

Model Predictive Control (MPC) A category of control system method that relies on a data model of expected system behavior to generate control system signals.

Modified Individual Regulation (MIR) A method to prevent brake pull of the steering caused by unequal ABS acting on the front steer axle.

Modular Switch Field (MSF) A control unit used by Freightliner to process all cab switch signals and broadcast them to the SAM-cab module through a star point connector.

modulated lock-up A lock-up clutch application strategy that is designed for maximum vehicle performance.

modulated main solenoid A pulse-width-modulated solenoid that controls main pressure in fourth generation and later World Transmissions.

modulator cable A mechanical cable connected to the throttle that operates the modulator valve.

modulator valve A valve that produces a pressure based on throttle position. Also called the *throttle valve*.

momentary contact switches Manual-type switch that may be toggled or pushed, but does not latch into position. Horn contact or starter button are examples of momentary contact switches.

momentary engine ignition interrupt relay (MEIIR) A relay controlled by the TCU that cuts the engine ignition or fueling if a DM clutch does not disengage.

mono-leaf spring A leaf spring with a single leaf; usually found in front spring applications only.

mount Steel backed rubber support that holds the powertrain components.

movable cam rings Rings used in self-adjusting clutches that take up the space of the threaded adjusting ring in the clutch cover.

muffler A device to quiet the pipes of the A/C system with baffles placed inside to deaden the sound of refrigerant moving.

multi-leaf spring A leaf spring with more than one steel plate or leaf stacked together and used for a spring. Also called a *spring pack*.

multi-mesh gearing Mainshaft and countershaft gears that have finer cut teeth—meaning more teeth are in mesh for increased strength.

multiple-countershaft transmission A transmission with more than one countershaft; used to distribute the torque between more teeth on the mainshaft and countershaft speed gears to increase torque capacity of the transmission.

multiplex switch A switch arrangement using two or more switches that can share a single wire for a switch pole and throw circuit, but transmit unique circuit control information from each switch.

multiplexing (MUX) Transmission of more than one electrical signal or message that takes place over a single wire or pair of wires.

multi-temp unit A reefer configured to control multiple temperatures in different areas of the trailer.

N material A material with a movable negative charge.

N-95 mask A face mask that filters out 95% of all airborne particles.

negative camber When the top of the tire is closer to the center of the vehicle than the bottom of the tire.

negative frame angle The condition where the vehicle's rear is lower than the front.

negative offset When the hub mounting surface is towards the brake side or back of the wheel's centerline.

negative scrub radius A condition in which the projected KPI intersects with the road surface outboard from the tire's vertical centerline.

Nernst cells A technology used by exhaust gas sensors that measures the unknown gas concentration by comparing it to a known gas concentration.

network node A point on a network.

neutral axis The area in the middle of a frame rail web where the tension and compression forces cancel each other out. Also called *neutral fiber*.

neutral fiber The area in the middle of a frame rail web where the tension and compression forces cancel each other out. Also called *neutral axis*.

neutral safety switch A switch operated by the transmission shift linkage that prevents the vehicle from being started except when in park or neutral. Also known as the PRNDL switch on some transmissions.

neutral with no clutches (NCC) The status of a vehicle in neutral gear when no clutches are applied and an indication of a possible failure mode for Allison World Transmission.

nickel–metal hydride (NiMH) battery A battery in which metal hydroxide forms the negative electrode and nickel oxide forms the positive electrode.

NOx sensor A sensor that detects oxygen ions originating from nitric oxide (NOx) from among the other oxygen molecules present in the exhaust gas.

nomenclature The meaning of the letters and digits in truck transmission's model numbers.

nominal crack pressure (NCP) The minimum air signal pressure required to begin delivery of air pressure from a relay valve.

nominal diameter A size-code figure, for reference purposes only, as indicated in the tire and rim size designation.

nominal shim pack A shim pack that is used if the pinion has a zero variation.

non-asbestos organic (NAO) lining Brake friction material commonly used in line-haul tractors where far less braking takes place.

non-drive (dead) axle An axle that does not supply power to the wheels.

non-latching solenoid A solenoid that requires constant electric power to remain in the open position.

non-uniform velocity The phenomenon that a shaft driven through an angle accelerates and decelerates twice per revolution.

normally closed solenoid A solenoid that blocks the flow of fluid when it is not electrically energized.

normally open solenoid A solenoid that is open when not electrically energized.

North American Standard Out-of-Service Criteria (OOSC) Defects that require a vehicle to be taken out of service until repaired.

no-slack coupler A type of fifth wheel lock mechanism that uses serrated edges between the locking bar and wedge to ensure no play in the coupling.

NPN transistor A type of bipolar transistor with two blocks of N material and one block of P material.

nuts An internally threaded fastener used in combination with a bolt to clamp a joint.

Occupational Safety and Health Administration (OSHA) The agency that ensures safe and healthy working conditions by setting and enforcing standards and by providing training, outreach, education, and assistance.

off-going ratio test A test performed at the beginning of a shift in progress in the World Transmission to ensure that the off-going clutch has released.

Ohm's law An electrical law that defines the relationship between amperage, resistance, and voltage.

ohm The unit for measuring electrical resistance.

oil slinger A stamped steel ring used to throw lubricant in a certain direction.

oil weep Very minor oil seepage usually caused by a wicking effect and not usually a reason for a repair.

oiler A device used to add oil to the A/C system.

onboard diagnostics (OBD) Self-diagnostic capabilities of electronic control modules that allow them to evaluate voltage and current levels of circuits to which they are connected and determine if data is in the correct operational range.

on-coming ratio test A test performed near the end of a shift in progress in the World Transmission to ensure that the on-coming clutch has applied.

one-way check valve A valve with the purpose to protect the air reservoirs and other air system storage units from completely draining if a leak occurs downstream of one reservoir.

one-way clutch A roller or sprag-type device that allows rotation in one direction but locks in the opposite direction. Also called over-running clutch.

open center rim A type of wheel rim that can be removed from the cast iron spoke hub attached to the axle. Also called a *demountable rim*.

open-loop ramp rate A predictable increase in clutch apply pressure; the open-loop ramp rate is controlled by the transmission ECU.

operator's manual A document that contains the correct operating procedures for the vehicle and systems and how the systems should function.

organic facings Friction facings made of various natural materials, such as cotton fibers, rubber, aluminum, glass, copper or brass fibers, and carbon material.

organic light-emitting diode (OLED) A light-emitting diode that uses carbon-based semiconductor material.

O-ring Rubber-type rings available in different sizes used to seal pipe fittings.

oscillation The rhythmic up and down motion of the suspension caused by road shock. It must be stopped by dampening or vehicle stability could be lost.

output member The element of the planetary gear set that is connected to the transmission output shaft.

output shaft The output shaft of an inter-axle differential. The rear side gear is part of or splined to the output shaft. Also known as the *through shaft*.

outrigger brackets A frame-body attachment consisting of brackets welded to the vehicle and then bolted to the frame web.

overall diameter The diameter of an inflated tire at the outermost surface of the tread.

overcharging Overfilling of the A/C system; may result in poor cooling or mechanical failure of the system.

overcrank protection (OCP) thermostat A thermostat that monitors the temperature of the motor and opens a relay circuit to interrupt the current to the solenoid if prolonged cranking causes the motor temperature to exceed a safe threshold.

overdrive ratio A ratio that provides a speed increase and output torque decrease.

overhead gantry crane A moveable frame work with a chain block or other hoisting mechanism attached.

overhung mount pinion A pinion mounted with only two opposed tapered roller bearings.

overrunning alternator decoupler (OAD) A pulley that uses an internal spring and clutch system that allows it to rotate freely in one direction and provide limited, spring-like movement in the other direction.

over-running clutch A roller or sprag type device that allows rotation in one direction, but locks in the opposite direction. Also called one-way clutch.

overslung A suspension where the leaf spring sits on top of the axle.

P material A material with a movable positive charge.

parallel alternators The practice of connecting alternators in parallel to provide higher charging voltage at idle with more available amperage.

parallel circuit A circuit in which all branch components are connected directly to the voltage supply.

parallel drive A vehicle in which both the engine and electric motor work together, blending motor and engine torque, to propel the vehicle.

parallel joint arrangement Two or more universal joint arrangements where the joint angles form parallel lines; a method of angle cancellation for use with parallel angles. Also known as the *waterfall arrangement*.

parallel wiring A type of custom-made wiring harness that encloses multiple conductors into a single vinyl insulator covering.

parallelogram A design element in suspension systems to keep the wheels or the axles in alignment throughout suspension articulation.

parasitic draw Unwanted drain on the vehicle battery when the vehicle is off. Also called *key-off electrical load*.

parasitic loss An unnecessary load on the engine that wastes fuel.

park brake circuit The air circuit responsible for the application and release of power springs in the brake chambers. Also referred to as the spring brake circuit or *emergency brake circuit*.

park/emergency braking system The air circuit responsible for the application of the spring brakes for parking. It also has the capability to enable several controlled brake applications if a major air leak occurs in either the primary or secondary air brake circuits.

parts manual A written or electronic manual for identifying and finding needed vehicle parts.

Pascal's law The law of physics that states that pressure applied to a fluid in one part of a closed system will be transmitted equally to all other areas of the system.

passive sensor A sensor that does not use a current supplied by the ECU to operate.

pass-thru programmers A vehicle communication device compliant with the SAE standard J-2534 to flash or reprogram ECUs.

peak torque The maximum torque an engine can produce.

performance testing The process of recreating a driving situation to inspect A/C performance and vent temperature.

P-flash (program flash) A category of reprogramming or memory update of only the program information in an ECU or microcontroller.

phasing Lining up the inboard yoke ears of driveshaft so that the non-uniform velocity cancellation occurs in the proper quadrant of the circle.

phenolic A lightweight synthetic high-temperature-resistant material.

photodiode A diode that forwards bias only when light strikes it.

photometric certification A certification based on testing lamps to evaluate factors, such as light color, brightness, and the angle at which the light is effectively observed.

photon A particle of energy and the basic unit of light.

phototransistor A transistor that is forward biased when light strikes its base, which is made from a photo-sensitive semiconductor.

photovoltaic (PV) effect The conversion of light into electricity.

PID tuning A process performed on instrumented systems during calibration where the control algorithms are adjusted under experimental conditions to achieve optimal system outputs.

piezoelectric effect A type of electricity produced by bending or squeezing a unique type of quartz crystal.

piezoresistive sensor A sensor that uses a piezoresistive crystal arranged with a Wheatstone bridge to measure the change in resistance of the piezo crystal; these sensors are adapted to measuring vibration and dynamic or continuous pressure changes.

pilot bearing A bearing that supports the front of the transmission input shaft; mounted in the flywheel or the rear of the crankshaft.

pilot bearing bore The hole in the center of the flywheel that holds the pilot bearing.

pilot pad The lugs attached to the bearing hub to center the wheel assembly correctly during assembly.

pinion bearing cage A removable casting that holds the two bearing races that support the pinion gear.

pinion depth The mounting position of the pinion in relation to the crown gear center of axis.

pinion gear A small driving gear.

pinion pilot bearing A small bearing that supports the inboard end of the pinion gear when the pinion is straddle mounted. Also called *spigot bearing*.

pinion variation number A dimension to add or remove from the nominal pinion depth dimension.

pintle hook Trailer hitching device that uses a fixed towing horn that connects with a drawbar eye attached to the towed vehicle.

pipe A rigid tube of metal, plastic, or other substance, used to conduct gas or fluid flow.

pitch The number of teeth per unit of pitch diameter on a gear.

pitch circle The theoretical point on the tooth face halfway between the root and the top land where only rolling motion exists. Also called the *pitch diameter*.

pitch diameter The theoretical point on the tooth face halfway between the root and the top land where only rolling motion exists. Also called the *pitch circle*.

pitman arm A pitman arm connects the steering sector shaft to the steering linkage. It converts the sector shaft movement to a sweeping arc resembling linear movement. Also called a *drop arm*.

plain bevel gear A bevel gear set with straight-cut teeth.

plain case half The half of the differential case that does not bolt to the crown gear.

plan angle An angle where the driveshaft moves toward the side of a vehicle when viewed from above.

planetary double reduction drive axle A planetary drive axle that is permanently fixed in low range.

planetary gear A gear arrangement consisting of a ring gear with internal teeth, a carrier with two or more small pinion gears in constant mesh with the ring gear, and an externally toothed sun gear in the center in constant mesh with the planetary pinions.

planetary gear reduction drive A type of gear reduction system in which a planetary gear set reduces the starter profile to multiply motor torque to the pinion gear.

planetary two-speed drive axle A two-speed drive axle that uses a planetary gear set for the low range.

platooning A feature of level 3 and higher autonomous vehicles that allows a single human driver in a column of trucks to lead other driverless trucks to travel much closer together in a more efficient operating mode while synchronizing functions of braking, steering, and acceleration.

plug-in hybrid electric vehicle (PHEV) Any type of hybrid electric vehicle containing a battery storage system that uses an external source to recharge the battery when the vehicle is not in operation.

PM service checklist An itemized task list of mechanical safety procedures.

PM service intervals The frequency of a PM schedule.

PM-A PM-A inspections are visual assessments of all safety-related items, such as brakes, tires, horn, wipers, steering components, suspension components, and lighting.

PM-B PM-B inspections include all of the checks and adjustments performed in PM-A, as well as an oil change, and oil filter and fuel filter changes. The inspection items include the engine and driveline, as well as greater detail checks of the braking, steering, and other chassis systems.

PM-C PM-C inspections are annual and include all the items in PM-A and B, as well as comprehensive checks of all chassis components. Scheduled fluid changes and component adjustment, repair, or replacement are performed at this time.

pneumatic balance The correct timing of brake application air pressure to each vehicle axle at the correct pressure.

Pneumatic Booster System (PBS) Injection Booster An option for the Bendix EAC system, which injects a blast of compressed air into the engine intake manifold to reduce turbocharger lag.

pneumatic imbalance The incorrect timing of brake application air pressure to vehicle axles or brake application at the wrong pressure. Pneumatic imbalance leads to tractor jackknifing or trailer swing-out.

pneumatic or air jacks A type of vehicle jack that uses compressed gas or air to lift a vehicle.

PNP transistor A type of bipolar transistor with two blocks of P material and one block of N material.

polarity The state of charge, positive or negative.

policy An overriding way of acting or behaving.

polyalkylene glycol (PAG) Synthetic oil used in all R-134a systems.

polyalphaolefin (PAO) Synthetic refrigerant oil used in air conditioning systems.

polymeric positive temperature coefficient (PPTC) device (resettable fuse) A thermistor-like electronic device used to protect against circuit overloads. Also called *resettable fuse*.

portable lifting hoists A type of vehicle hoist that is portable and can be moved from one location to another.

positive camber When the tires are closer together at the bottom and farther apart at the top when viewed from the front of a vehicle.

positive frame angle The condition where the vehicle's rear is higher than the front.

positive offset When the plane of the hub mounting surface is shifted from the centerline towards the outside or front side of the wheel.

positive scrub radius A condition in which the projected KPI point of contact intersects with the road surface inboard of the tire's vertical centerline.

positive temperature coefficient (PTC) thermistor A thermistor in which resistance increases as the temperature increases.

potentiometer A variable resistor with three connections—one at each end of a resistive path, and a third sliding contact that moves along the resistive pathway.

pot-type flywheel A flywheel shaped like a deep pot inside which all the components of the clutch are housed, except for the clutch cover.

power divider A differential gear set that splits the available torque equally between two drive axles. Also called an *inter-axle differential*.

power flow The path that power takes from the beginning of an assembly to the end. In a transmission, power flow changes as different gears are selected by the driver.

power line carrier (PLC) technology A data transmission technology enabling data exchange between the tractor and trailer ABS.

power springs Springs in brake actuators used to apply park brakes or internal pushrod lock mechanisms.

power steering pump A hydraulic pump that provides hydraulic pressure to the steering gear, which reduces the force required by the driver to turn the steering wheel.

Power Steering System Analyzer (PSSA) A combination flow meter, shut-off valve, and pressure gauge used to diagnose hydraulic problems in power steering systems.

power take off (PTO) device A device attached to the transmission that is gear-driven and can be used to run accessories.

powertrain control device A device used to input or hold planetary gear components to affect a power flow. These can be hydraulic clutches, brake bands, or one-way sprag or roller clutches.

power unit The hydraulic assist portion of the power steering gear.

PPE (personal protective equipment) Safety equipment designed to protect the wearer; boots, gloves, eye protection, and hearing protection, when required.

pre-dampening A series of small torsional dampening springs designed to prevent gear rattle at idle.

predictive PM A statistical analysis of when equipment and component failures are likely to occur, including replacing parts or equipment before malfunctions happen.

preload Negative endplay, or less than zero clearance.

preset hub A wheel hub that uses a precision spacer and close-tolerance bearings to eliminate the need for manual adjustment.

pressure plate The friction surface of the clutch cover; the plate that squeezes the clutch disc against the flywheel.

pressure bleeder A device that bleeds a hydraulic system by pressurizing the fluid.

pressure control solenoid (PCS) The term to denote clutch control solenoids in an Allison Fourth Generation Electrohydraulic Control transmission.

pressure protection valve A normally closed valve that opens after a preset pressure is reached. Pressure protection valves are used to limit maximum charging pressure of air system reservoirs or circuits draining out of the reservoir.

pressure transients Minor fluctuations on the gauges that may indicate a problem.

pressure-balanced A feature of air control system valves that ensures air application pressure is consistently maintained to the brake chambers, even when small leaks drain air from delivery components, such as lines and chambers.

pressure-compensating balance valve A term identical to the pressure-balanced valves feature of air brake valves that ensures a consistent delivery of air pressure is maintained despite leaks in the delivery system lines or air chambers.

pressure-compensating relay valve A relay valve having a pressure-balanced inlet and exhaust valve to ensure consistent air delivery pressure to the brakes.

pressure-sensitive switches Automatic-type switches that are activated by gas or liquid pressure.

prevailing torque The amount of frictional torque possessed by a fastener that is used to resist loosening.

primary battery A battery in which chemical reactions are not reversible and the battery cannot be recharged.

primary circuit Refers to the split brake circuit system used on commercial vehicles. The primary circuit generally operates the rear brakes, while the *secondary circuit* operates the front brakes.

primary modulation The pulse-modulated signal sent to a solenoid to initiate fluid flow.

primary piston A brake piston in the master cylinder moved directly by the pushrod or the power booster; it generates hydraulic pressure to move the secondary piston.

primary reservoir One of two air reservoirs responsible for holding pressurized air for the dual-circuit air brake system.

primary winding The electromagnetic coil of wire in it, which creates the magnetic field in a step-up or step-down transformer.

priority valve A check valve that protects the hydraulic controls.

prismatic cells The rectangular-shaped type of lithium ion cells.

proactive maintenance Reflects the understanding that the cost of repairing an unexpected breakdown is usually much greater than preventative maintenance.

procedure A step-by-step process to complete a task.

Procision Eaton's dual-clutch seven-speed AMT; introduced in 2014.

profile bearing Contact pattern between the root and the top land of the tooth.

prognostic capability The ability by some transmission ECUs to predict fluid and filter change intervals.

prognostics A self-diagnostic maintenance schedule that informs the driver when the oil, filters, or the transmission itself requires service. Prognostics are offered on the Allison World Transmissions since 2009 and can be turned on or off by the vehicle owner, if desired.

Programmable Logic Controllers (PLC) Electronic control modules that use inputs from switches and sensors, and evaluate the signals according to a stored logic program.

programmable read-only memory (PROM) chip A memory chip particular to the application of the vehicle in which it is found and cannot be easily written over.

programmed lock-up A strategy that applies the lock-up clutch as soon as possible for improved fuel economy. Also called *systematic lock-up*.

proof load A factor representing the maximum useable load limit of a fastener before deforming or its threads stripping.

proportional differential A differential capable of sending more torque to one wheel than the other when a wheel slip condition is encountered. Also known as a *biased torque differential*.

proportional feedback control An error-correction algorithm that adjusts controller gain up or down in proportion to the size of error.

Proportional-Integral-Derivative (PID) controls Error-correction algorithms comprised of proportional-, integral-, and derivative-type calculations.

proportioning valve Valves used mostly on older vehicles equipped with rear drum brakes to reduce rear wheel hydraulic brake pressure under hard braking or light loads. Located in line with the rear brakes.

propulsion control system (PCS) module A microcontroller-based device that supplies electrical output signals based on input data collected from a vehicle's sensors.

prove-out sequence A sequence in which the warning lights for several brief seconds with the key on and engine off or during key-on engine cranking.

proximity switches Switches designed to sense the approach of metal components.

psia The units of pressure, in pounds per square inch, using sea level as a reference. Atmospheric pressure at sea level = 0 psia.

psig The units of pressure, in pounds per square inch, expressed relative to atmospheric pressure. Atmospheric pressure at sea level = 14.7 psig.

PT chart A pressure-temperature chart that shows the relationship between A/C pressures and evaporator temperature.

pull-down switch A switch connected between the ECU and a negative ground current potential.

pull-to-seat terminal A terminal installed by inserting the wire through the connector cavity, crimping on a terminal, and then pulling the terminal back into the connector cavity to seat it.

pull-type clutch A clutch with an integral release bearing, which is pulled toward the transmission to disengage the clutch.

pull-up switch A switch connected between the ECU and a battery positive.

pulse charger A battery charger that sends current into the battery in pulses of one-second cycles; used to recover sulfated batteries.

pulse width modulation (PWM) An electrical signal that varies in on and off time.

purge cycle The time between the closing and opening of the dryer purge valve, or the loading and unloading of the air compressor. Oil and moisture trapped in the dryer desiccant are purged when the air compressor unloads.

pusher axle A rear, non-drive rear mounted axle, ahead of the drive axle.

push-pull park/emergency control valve Hand-operated dash valve used to control the operation of the spring brakes for a straight truck, tractor, and/or trailer.

push-to-seat terminal A terminal inserted into the back of the connector cavity to seat after the terminal is crimped to the wire.

push-type clutch A clutch in which the release bearing is pushed towards the engine to release the clutch.

quick-adjust A small mechanism used to turn the large adjusting ring in the clutch cover when adjustment is required.

quick-release (QR) valve An air valve that is used to speed up the release of air pressure from air lines. The valve exhaust closes when supplied air and then opens when air pressure drops.

rack-and-pinion gear A gear consisting of a flat rack with either spur or helically cut teeth on one side and a meshing circular pinion gear.

rack-and-pinion steering system A type of steering gear arrangement that uses two gears. A smaller round pinion gear located at the end of the steering shaft connects to a linear gear, called the rack. The pinion gear moves the rack from side-to-side as the pinion rotates. The side-to-side motion of the rack controls the direction of the steer tires.

radial thrust Thrust that tries to push gears in aluminum alloy mesh apart perpendicular to their axis.

radial-belted tire A tire construction with belts placed at 90 degrees to the tire centerline, wrapped from side to side around the tire beads.

radial-ply tire A tire with two or more layers of casing plies and cord loops running radially from bead to bead.

radiant heat transfer The transfer of heat through a medium, such as a gas or vacuum, which does not cause the medium itself to heat.

ramp-off rate The specific reduction in clutch apply pressure for the clutch that is being released during a shift in the World Transmission.

range gear Any speed gear; in Eaton transmissions, it refers to the low-range gear in the auxiliary section.

range shift cylinder The shift cylinder to control range shifts in the auxiliary.

range verification tests Tests constantly being performed by the Allison World Transmission control system whenever there is no shift in progress; the test compares turbine times the gear ratio to the output speed to ensure the transmission is not slipping.

ratio step The difference between one ratio and the next available.

ratio test A test performed at the beginning and end of a shift in process.

ratio valve An air pressure proportioning valve used to increase brake application pressure to the front brakes when a trailer is not towed by a tractor. Also known as a *limiter valve*.

ratiometric This sensor has an output signal that changes in proportion to the supply voltage.

Ravigneaux gear set A popular compound planetary gear set with two planetary gear sets sharing a common carrier; capable of producing four forward speeds and one reverse.

reaction member The element of the planetary gear set that is held stationary.

reaction plates Metal plates in the hydraulic clutch; usually splined to the clutch hub or the transmission case.

reactive maintenance Service is only performed after equipment is broken, temporarily keeping vehicle and fleet operating costs low.

rebound The downward motion of the wheel and axle after a road bump or shock has occurred.

recall or service campaign A corrective measure conducted by manufacturers when a safety issue or recurring problem is found with a vehicle.

receiver-dryer A storage reservoir for refrigerant that also absorbs moisture from the air conditioning system.

recirculating-ball steering gear A steering gear that uses a worm gear inside a metal ball-nut having a threaded hole for the worm. Gear teeth are cut into one outside edge of the ball-nut, which engages the sector shaft.

reclaim/recycle machine An A/C machine designed to remove and recycle refrigerant for reuse.

reclaiming The process of removing refrigerant from the A/C system by using an A/C machine; also called refrigerant *recovering machine*.

recovering See *reclaiming*.

rectification A process of converting alternating current (AC) into direct current (DC).

reductant quality (RDQ) sensor A sensor that measures the quality of diesel exhaust fluid (DEF).

reduction gear drive A starter motor drive system in which the motor multiplies torque to the starter pinion gear by using an extra gear between the armature and the starter drive mechanism.

reefer A truck-trailer refrigeration temperature-control system.

Reference Datum Line (RDL) The arbitrary reference point from where the center of gravity is measured. Determined by the equipment manufacturer.

reference voltage (Vref) A precisely regulated voltage supplied by the ECU to sensors; the value is typically 5V DC, but some manufacturers use 8 or 12 volts.

refrigerant identifiers Devices used to check for impurities in the A/C gas.

refrigerant label A label that lists the type and total capacity of refrigerant that is installed in the A/C system.

regenerative braking A type of braking in which the kinetic energy of the vehicle's motion is captured rather than being lost to heat as it is in a conventional braking system. This is accomplished by using the drive motors as generators, which recharge the traction batteries.

regrooving A process that uses a heated cutting tool to carve new tread or add stripes to a tire.

relay valve Critical air control valve s used to speed up the flow of air during brake application and release. It uses a small signal pressure to control a larger volume of reservoir pressure.

release bearing A hollow bearing through which the input shaft passes, which allows for the push or pull against rotating clutch release levers to release the clutch.

release bolt A bolt that compresses the power spring of spring brakes and releases the park brake.

release fork (yoke) The actuator that moves the release bearing.

release-bearing travel The distance the release bearing moves while releasing the clutch in a pull-type clutch.

reluctance torque The term given to the movement from high to low magnetic field resistance or reluctance, which is another way of describing torque generated due to principles of magnetic attraction in a SRM.

reluctor A toothed wheel used with magnetic sensors, usually to measure shaft speed.

reluctor wheel The toothed wheel mounted on the wheel hub, which is used by the wheel speed sensor to generate wheel speed data. Also called the *exciter ring*.

remote sensing An alternator voltage regulator that has an input circuit with a direct connection to the battery positive terminal. It is used to provide an optimal level for charging voltage.

remote shift linkage A transmission shift linkage that is not mounted directly above the shift cover and that must be properly maintained and lubricated to prevent hard shifting.

removable carrier type A drive axle housing with a removable carrier. Also called a *banjo*.

repair order A form used by shops to collect information regarding a vehicle coming in for repair, also referred to as a work order or job sheet.

reserve capacity The time, in minutes, that a new, fully charged battery at 80°F (26.6°C) supplies a constant load of 25 amps without its voltage dropping below 10.5 volts for a 12-volt battery.

residual magnetism The small amount of magnetism left on the rotor after it is initially magnetized by the coil windings' magnetic field.

resilient mounts Attachments that are spring-loaded or made with rubber or polyurethane elements that accommodate movement.

resist bending moment (RBM) The frame strength calculated using the section modulus of the frame rail and its yield strength.

resistive circuit A circuit in which current has excessive unwanted resistance and cannot properly function due to excessive resistance.

resistive touchscreen A display screen composed of two flexible, transparent sheets lightly coated with an electrically conductive, yet slightly resistive, material.

resistor A component designed to produce electrical resistance.

resolver A Hall-effect sensor type used to sense rotor position and provide electrical feedback to electronic control units controlling motor operation.

resonance The frequency at which the driveline's vibrations are the most damaging.

resonant frequency The frequency at which the driveline enters a resonant condition, where all the components start to oscillate in unison.

respirator PPE used to protect the wearer from inhaling harmful dusts or gases.

retarder Any system used to slow a vehicle's momentum and augment the service brake.

retreading The process of applying new tread to an existing tire casing to extend the service life of the tire.

return on investment (ROI) The ratio of dollars spent on a vehicle for its purchase and maintenance compared to how much the vehicle earns.

reversible sleeve piston A type of air spring with a piston that pushes into the air-spring bag or bellows as the suspension articulates. Also known as a *rolling lobe piston*.

reverse bias A situation in which a diode blocks current flow.

reverse idler shaft Shaft that supports the reverse idler gear.

reverse overdrive A reverse direction overdrive ratio through the planetary gear set.

reverse reduction A reverse direction underdrive ratio through the planetary gear set.

RFI A category of EMI caused by radio waves inducing current in wiring or electrical components that acts as a receiving antenna.

rheostat A variable resistor constructed of a fixed input terminal and a variable output terminal, which vary current flow by passing current through a long resistive tightly coiled wire.

rigger A person who specializes in lifting and moving heavy objects.

rigging/rigging gear All the components used to attach the mechanical hoisting equipment to the load being lifted. This can include rope, wire rope/cables, slings, shackles, eyebolts, eye nuts, links, rings, turnbuckles, rigging hooks, and rigging.

right-hand camshafts Camshafts that rotate in a clockwise direction to apply the brakes.

rigid fifth wheel A type of fifth wheel that does not oscillate about either axis of the vehicle. It does not articulate from side-to-side or front-to-back. It is fixed in location.

rim diameter The distance across the center of the rim, from bead seat to bead seat. Also known as *wheel diameter*.

rim flange The exterior lip that holds the tire in place.

rim width The distance across the rim flanges at the bead seat.

ring gear A large bevel gear that is driven by a smaller pinion gear in the bevel gear set. Also known as a *crown gear*.

RKE An acronym for a remote keyless entry system. It uses a short-range radio transceiver to remotely operate door locks and other electrical accessories.

road feel The force transmitted from the tires back through the steering system to the driver.

Roadranger valve The driver's shift knob that controls range and splitter shifting.

roll stability control (RSC) A vehicle control system that measures lateral acceleration of a vehicle to minimize the likelihood of a vehicle rollover.

rolling circumference The distance covered by one revolution of the tire.

rolling lobe piston A type of air spring with a piston that pushes into the air-spring bag or bellows as the suspension articulates. Also known as a *reversable sleeve piston*.

rolling resistance The tendency of a tire to resist rolling along naturally when under load.

root The radius shape between the bottoms of two teeth. Also called *fillet radius*.

root diameter The smallest circle of the gear measured at the fillet radius (root) of the teeth.

rotary flow Fluid flow inside the torque converter that follows the rotation of the housing.

rotary piston compressors HVAC compressors that use cylindrical-shaped housings and enclose multiple pistons to minimize of noise, vibration, and harshness.

rotary switches Manual-type switch rotated to select an output. Wiper speed and blower motor speed are common examples.

rotary valve A valve connected to the input shaft of the steering gear that controls the direction of pressurized fluid through the steering gear. Along with the torsion bar, changes in torque applied to the steering wheel and the direction of torque alters the direction of fluid flow through the valve. Also called a *spool valve*.

rotating clutch A hydraulic clutch used to input a planetary gear component.

roto-chambers Actuators with a unique diaphragm and piston construction that delivers consistent output force, regardless of the pushrod position.

rotor The main rotating component of a disc brake system that is attached to the wheel hub.

RTV Silicone (Room-Temperature-Vulcanizing) A sealer that begins to harden or chemically cure when exposed to air at room temperature. The curing process is called vulcanization, and causes the rubber to stiffen to various degrees of hardness required for specific applications.

rubber spring A suspension system utilizing rubber as the spring medium; commonly found on heavier vehicles.

Rzeppa joint A constant velocity joint invented by Alfred Rzeppa in 1926.

SAE J1128 standard A standard that specifies the dimensions, test methods, and requirements for single-core primary wire intended for use in road vehicle applications.

SAE J-560 standard The SAE standards for the configuration of trailer electrical cables and plugs.

safe working load (SWL) The maximum safe lifting load for lifting equipment.

safety interlock A safety feature commonly used by electrically operated devices that prevents unsafe operation by locking out its operation unless a set of safe operating conditions are met.

safety relief valve A pressure relief valve located in the service-supply or wet tank; used to prevent tank rupture from over-pressurization. The valve typically opens at pressures above 150 psi (1,034 kPa).

sag A type of frame damage characterized by the downward bending of the frame rail between two support points. The opposite of *bow*.

S-cam A cam shaft used to force brake shoes against the brake drum.

scheduled lock-up Torque converter lock-up that occurs at a preset point; this saves fuel.

schematic diagram A line drawing that explains how a system works by using symbols and connecting lines.

screw An externally threaded fastener that turns into a hole that may or may not be threaded.

scrub angle The distance between two imaginary points on the road surface—the point of centerline contact between the road surface and the tire, and the point where the king pin inclination angle projects its contact with the road surface. The difference between the two points is either positive or negative, depending on whether the KPI line is inside or outside of the tire centerline. See also *positive scrub radius* and *negative scrub radius*.

SDS (safety data sheet) A sheet standardized by the GHS that provides information about handling, use, and storage of a material that is hazardous.

sealed lead-acid (SLA) battery A battery that does not have a liquid electrolyte nor requires the addition of water. Also called a *valve-regulated lead-acid battery (VRLA)* or *recombinant battery*.

sealed release bearing A release bearing with no grease nipple or zerk.

seamless pipe Formed in one piece; lacking seams, thus smooth and regular.

secondary battery A rechargeable battery.

secondary circuit Refers to the split brake circuit system used on commercial vehicles. The *primary circuit* generally operates the rear brakes, while the secondary circuit operates the front brakes.

secondary couple vibrations A vibration, caused by U-joint angles, that travels the length of the driveshaft.

secondary modulation (sub-modulation) A very high-frequency pulse-width modulation of the current flowing through the primary modulated circuit of a World Transmission solenoid. The secondary modulation occurs at between 12,000 and 19,000 Hz and is used to fine tune the solenoid function.

secondary piston A piston that is moved by hydraulic pressure generated by the primary piston in the master cylinder.

secondary reservoir One of two air reservoirs responsible for holding pressurized air for the dual-circuit air brake system.

secondary safety latch An additional mechanism used as an added step to unlatch or release a fifth wheel locking jaw.

secondary winding The coil of wire in which voltage is induced through mutual induction in a step-up or step-down transformer.

second-degree burns Burns that involve blistering and damage to more than the outer layer of skin.

section break A point where the diameter of a shaft or thickness of a component changes.

section change A point where a component becomes thicker or thinner or rigid, forming a weak point where breakage can begin.

section height The height of the sidewalls.

section modulus An engineering calculation used to determine the strength of a frame rail based only on its shape, height, width, and thickness.

section width The distance between the outside of the sidewalls on an inflated tire without any load on it.

self-adjusting clutches Clutches with an automatically adjusting system that relies on pressure plate movement to cause an adjustment.

self-dampening The interleaf friction in a leaf-spring pack that helps to stop spring oscillation.

self-diagnostic The TCU capability to analyze its own functions.

self-energization A braking effect that causes the shoe-drum friction to rotate the brake shoe into the drum with more force.

self-exciting alternator An alternator that relies on the residual magnetism found in the rotor to produce current and switch on the voltage regulator to supply additional current to the rotor.

self-powered refrigeration units A transport refrigeration system powered by a small horsepower diesel engine.

self-steering axle An axle with steering linkage that allows its wheels to automatically follows the curve of a turn.

semi-automated driving systems A driving control system that relies partly on a human driver and partly machine control. Some human involvement or intervention is required when the machine cannot perform the driving task demanded for a driving condition.

semiconductor A material that can have properties of both conductors and insulators and that can switch back and forth between either state using small electrostatic charges.

semi-floating axle shaft An axle shaft that carries the entire weight of the vehicle on its outer end.

semi-metallic lining Brake friction material comprising heat-resistant semi-metallic blends that are used for higher temperatures and severe service ratings.

semi-oscillating fifth wheel Fifth wheels that pivot slightly in both horizontal and vertical directions; the standard type of fifth wheel used in on-highway applications.

semi-trailer A trailer that has some of its load carried by the tractor through a hitching device.

sensible heat Heat that can be sensed or felt.

sensing The voltage reference point the alternator uses for regulation of the output.

sensor count A unit for sensors digital output that is proportional to an analog signal output.

SensoTop A system used by Voith that senses topography and adapts the shifting schedule accordingly.

separator plate A plate that separates the control valve body and the transmission case.

serial communication Communication using zeroes and ones to transmit data in a series, one bit after another in sequence.

serial data Pieces of data sent by the master module.

series circuit A common type of electrical circuit with multiple loads and circuit devices, but has only one path for current to flow.

series drive A propulsion system where an engine driven electric generator supplies current to an electric traction motor to propel the vehicle.

series-parallel drive A more complex system enabling an engine only, an electric motor only, and a combined engine-motor operation. Also called *power-split configuration*.

service brake priority A trailer spring brake relay valve that does not allow the park-spring brakes to release until the trailer air reservoir is filled.

service history A complete list of all the servicing and repairs that have been performed on a vehicle.

service information system (SIS) An online version of the printed service manual that usually includes access to all the other manuals produced for the vehicle.

service manual An indexed book produced by the manufacturer or by the after-market to describe the service and repair procedures required on a vehicle.

service reservoir The first air reservoir to receive air from the air compressor or dryer. Water and oil condense in this tank, which supplies the primary and secondary air reservoirs. Also called the *supply reservoir*.

ServiceLink Freightliner's proprietary software used to service and perform service programming of the vehicle electrical system.

servo action A drum brake design where one brake shoe, when self energized, applies an increased energizing force to the other brake shoe, in proportion to the initial energizing force; further enhances the self-energizing feature of some drum brakes.

setback The distance one wheel end is set back from the axles perpendicular angle with the frame.

set-point A term for the targeted or desired operating range of a controlled system.

severe service operating conditions Conditions consist of towing or hauling heavy loads, extensive idling and/or stop-and-go, low-speed driving encountered in inner-city traffic, delivery, off-road dusty conditions, and multiple drivers.

severe-duty service A vehicle that is operated under extreme (maximum) loading most of the time, or one that is operated on heavy grades.

shear stress The force applied against a material along two different planes that acts on the material at a 90-degree angle.

shedding A process that reduces the plate surface area and, therefore, reduces capacity. Shedding may also produce short circuits between the bottom of positive and negative plates.

shift by wire Shifting controlled completely by the transmission electronic control.

shift cable A mechanical cable connected to the driver's shift lever and the transmission manual valve.

shift cover The cover on the transmission that holds the shift rails and forks.

shift finger A flat-sided piece that sits into the shift gates.

shift forks The forks that move the sliding clutches or collars in the transmission.

shift gate Rectangular notches either formed in or attached to the shift rails.

shift lever The shift control the driver uses to change the main box gear position.

shift lever and tower The shift lever and the tower that connects it to the transmission.

shift logic The logical process created by the transmission controller using data gained from the vehicle to determine when and how shifting should occur.

shift modulator valve A valve that is moved by modulator pressure and governor pressure for shifting.

shift point The road speed at which a shift occurs.

shift relay valve The spool valve that directs clutch apply pressure to the correct clutch.

shift signal valve A spool valve that is moved by governor pressure for shifting.

shift solenoid 1 (SS1) The solenoid used in fourth-generation and later World Transmissions to control the position of the C-1 and C-2 latch valves.

shift tower A raised section with a pivot into which the shift lever fits.

shipping blocks Wooden blocks that support the release bearing and cage the pressure plate on pull-type clutches.

shipping bolts Bolts used to cage the pressure plate of self-adjusting clutches, such as the Eaton Solo and the SACH's Twin Xtend.

shock A condition where the rate of blood flow to a person's extremities is diminished.

shock absorber A (usually) hydraulic piston and cylinder arrangement designed to minimize spring oscillation.

shock bracket A bracket, usually part of the spring mount, that the shock absorber bolts to.

shock load failure Fracture caused by one sudden shock.

short circuit An electrical circuit that is formed between two points, allowing current to flow through an unintended pathway.

shot-peened A metal surface treatment to prevent stress fractures. Steel shot is blasted at a metals surface to close any microscopic pores.

shunt truck A tractor designed to move semi-trailers around a warehouse yard or intermodal facility. Also known as a *terminal tractor*.

shunts Internal conductors with small calibrated resistance that direct current flow into the meter while measuring amperage.

shunt-type motors Another name for a parallel-wound motor where the armature and field windings are connected in parallel.

side bearing bore The opening machined into the differential carrier that holds the side bearing races.

side bearing cap The cap that bolts the side bearing races to the side bearing bores.

side gears Part of the differential gear set; the side gears are splined to the axles.

sidesway A type of frame damage characterized by a sideways bending or deformation of the frame.

simple machine The simplest mechanism that allows us to gain mechanical advantage.

Simpson gear set The most common compound planetary gear set; consists of two planetary gears sharing a common sun gear; capable of producing three forward and one reverse ratio.

sine wave A mathematical function that describes a repetitive waveform, such as an alternating current signal.

single-countershaft transmissions A transmission with only one countershaft.

skew The difference in distance between any axle end and the perpendicular centerline. Also called *axle setback* or *setback*.

slack adjuster A mechanical lever between the brake chamber and the foundation brake assembly.

slave air valve The valve on the side of a Fuller transmission that controls air flow to the range shift cylinder.

slave cylinder The hydraulic cylinder used to release the clutch in hydraulically actuated clutch systems.

sleep mode A state of a microcontroller or ECU when power consumption is lowest.

slider mechanism A plate the fifth wheel is attached to that has a ratchet-like set of plungers that enable the fifth wheel to be repositioned forward or backward along the tractor frame.

sliding clutch A device with splines on the inside and outside used as a gear-selection method for manual transmissions.

sliding collar A device with splines on the inside only, used as a gear-selection method in manual transmissions.

sliding-bridge jacks Jacks that are typically found on hoist mechanisms that can be slid into position to raise a portion of a vehicle.

sliding-gear transmission A transmission with gears that are splined to a transmission mainshaft and are slid into and out of mesh with a corresponding countershaft gear.

slip angle The difference between the apparent speed of the rotating magnetic field in the stator winding and the rotor speed.

slip joint A splined shaft and tube assembly that allows drive-shaft length changes.

slip yoke A splined tube that allows for driveshaft length changes.

slow adaptive A type of adaptive control that involves making small changes to the shifts as a way to mitigate the effects of clutch wear and solenoid drive and degradation.

smart charger A battery charger with a microcontroller regulating charging rates.

smart electrification A feature that enables the EP 40/50 system's motors to switch over to generating mode to produce as much as 300 amps at 24 volts at idle.

smart switches Automatic-type switches with self-diagnostic capabilities. These switches usually have a resister connected in parallel with switch contacts.

smoke controls A system on mechanically fueled engines to limit smoke emissions.

snapshot A snapshot records all the relevant TCU data before and after a diagnostic code is set to ease diagnoses.

snub braking A braking technique that should be used when downhill braking. It requires the truck brakes to be applied hard to slow the truck down to about 5 mph (2 kph), then continued repeatedly until the bottom of the hill is reached.

snubber A shock-absorbing insulator used to absorb shock loads transmitted by the trailer when the tow vehicle is accelerating or decelerating.

soft skills Communication and other skills that are very important to employers.

soft-dampened clutch A clutch with extra-long travel windows for its dampening springs; used to combat resonance in a driveline.

solid I-beam A type of solid steering axle named for its forged I-beam design.

specific gravity (SpGr) A measurement of the density of a substance.

specific heat The amount of heat a substance must absorb to undergo a temperature change of 1°F.

speed gears The gears on the countershaft and mainshaft that create the transmission ratios, also known as *range gears*.

spider gear A beveled gear that is a component of the differential gear set; it is fitted to the four legs of the differential cross and rotates with it. Also known as a *differential pinion gear*.

spigot bearing A small bearing that supports the inboard end of the pinion gear when the pinion is straddle mounted. Also called *pinion pilot bearing*.

spinout A low-traction situation where one drive wheel or one drive axle spins wildly while the other remains stationary.

spiral bevel gear A bevel gear set with spirally or helically cut gears.

spiral-wound cell battery A type of AGM battery in which the positive and negative electrodes are coiled into a tight spiral cell with an absorbent micro-glass mat placed between the plates.

split guide ring The split guide ring that is attached to the impeller and the turbine blades and creates a circular fluid passage.

split-charge relay A system designed to separate the main starting battery and the auxiliary battery. Also called a *battery-isolator system*.

splitter shift cylinder The shift cylinder that controls the splitter sliding clutch.

splitter valve A small valve in the splitter cylinder cover on a Fuller transmission that controls air flow to the front or rear of the splitter cylinder piston.

spool valve A valve that has a series of lands and cutaways in a precise fitting bore connected to the input shaft of the steering gear that controls the direction of pressurized fluid through the steering gear. Along with the torsion bar, changes in torque applied to the steering wheel and the direction of torque alters the direction of fluid flow through the valve. Also called a *rotary valve*.

sprain An injury in which a joint is overextended beyond its natural movement limit.

spreader bar This is a bar with moveable attachment points, also known as a *load leveler*.

spring brake Brakes commonly used on rear drive axles that contain power springs that are used to apply park brakes. They are also referred to as "maxi-brakes."

spring brake priority A trailer spring brake relay valve that allows the park-spring brakes to release with only air supplied by the trailer supply valve.

spring brake relay valve A specialized relay valve that is used to supply air to hold off the spring brakes or release air and apply the spring brakes. Also called an *inversion valve*.

spring pack A leaf spring with more than one steel plate or leaves stacked together and used for a spring. Also called a *multi-leaf spring*.

spring rate The amount of force required to deflect the spring; a low spring rate means a softer spring and, therefore, ride; a higher spring rate adds more lateral stability, but gives a harsher ride.

sprung weight The portion of the vehicle supported by the springs; includes the frame, the body, the load, and any accessories.

spur gear A gear with teeth cut parallel to its axis of rotation.

squeeze The point of clutch-pedal actuation on a pull-type clutch when the clutch brake is being actuated or squeezed. Also called *clutch-brake actuation*.

stabilizer bars Transversely mounted bars that control axle alignment and add lateral stability while the vehicle is turning by transferring some of the load from the side of the vehicle on the outside of a turn to the side on the inside of the turn.

stable or simple fracture A complete break, but the bone has not moved out of place.

stall speed The maximum speed the engine can drive the torque converter impeller with the turbine held stationary.

standard hub A wheel hub that uses manually adjusted wheel bearing end play.

stand-by mode A reefer operating mode during which the engine is not driving the compressor.

start enable relay The start enable relay is controlled by the TCU and interrupts the circuit to the starter solenoid unless the TCU passes a self-check and verifies the transmission is in neutral.

startability The capability of a vehicle to commence moving forward on a specified grade.

starting, lighting, and ignition (SLI) battery A battery designed for one, short-duration, deep discharge of up to 50% depth of discharge (DOD) during engine cranking.

state observers A limited number of sensors that are used by MPC systems to predict operating state or conditions.

state of charge The amount of refrigerant in a system compared to how much should be in it.

state of charge test A test that indicates how charged or discharged a battery is, not how much capacity it has.

static imbalance A condition of a rotating assembly, such as a tire, wheel, or flywheel, where the weight is not symmetrically balanced around the center line of rotation and the offset is at the vertical axis center.

static radius The distance from the tire center to ground level.

stationary clutch A hydraulic clutch used to hold a planetary gear component stationary and usually splined to the transmission case.

stator inner hub The inner race of the stator one-way clutch; it splines to the stator ground shaft.

stator support shaft A stationary shaft that holds the inner hub of the stator one-way clutch. Also called *ground shaft*.

stator The element inside a torque converter most responsible for torque multiplication.

steering arm An arm that extends from the steering knuckle. The tie-rods connect to these arms in order to steer the wheels.

steering axis inclination angle (SAI) The angle formed by an imaginary line running through the upper and lower steering pivots relative to vertical as viewed from the front. The angle is measured between true vertical and the angle of the king pin. Also called *king pin inclination angle (KPI)*.

steering axle An axle that has articulating steering knuckles that allows the vehicle to turn.

steering column A column affixed between the steering wheel and the steering box, usually made to collapse during a crash.

steering gear A device that converts the rotary motion of the steering wheel to the linear motion needed to steer the vehicle.

steering geometry A geometric arrangement of linkages in the steering of a vehicle designed to solve the problem of keeping the wheels properly oriented through various positions of the steering and suspension systems.

steering knuckle A device that connects the front wheel to the suspension; it pivots on the top and bottom, thus allowing the front wheels to turn.

steering linkage Steel rods that connect the steering box to the steering arms on the steering knuckle.

steering ratio The mechanical advantage produced by the steering gear, which converts large turns of the steering wheel into smaller turns of the tire to ease steering for the driver.

steering shafts The shaft that connects the steering wheel to the steering gear assembly of a vehicle.

steering stops Bolts used to limit the turning angle of the steering knuckle.

steering system A term used to describe all the components and parts involved in steering a vehicle.

steering-angle sensor A sensor that measures the rotational angle of the steering wheel.

step-down transformer A transformer used to reduce voltage in the secondary coil. A battery charger would use a step-down transformer to change 120 volts (AC) into 12 volts (AC) used to charge a 12-volt battery.

step-up transformer A transformer used to increase the voltage from a lower input voltage to a higher output, such as an ignition coil.

stiction A term for static friction caused by binding actuators.

straddle mount pinion A pinion supported by two opposed tapered roller bearings and a small spigot bearing.

strain An injury caused by the overextension of muscles and tendons.

strand A part of a wire rope consisting of several wires twisted together.

stress concentration Anything that reduces or changes the integrity or strength of the material. Also called *stress riser*.

stress riser Anything that reduces or changes the integrity or strength of the material. Also called *stress concentration*.

stringer Small inclusion in a cast or formed metal that weakens it, also known as a *gas pocket*.

stroke-sensing ASA A slack adjuster that adjusts slack based on the slack adjuster stroke length.

stud piloted disc wheel A type of disc wheel that retains the disc using studs attached to the hub and a tapered, or ball-type, wheel nut to center the disc onto the hub.

stud An externally threaded fastener that does not have a head.

sulfation A chemical reaction that results in the soft sulfate turning to a hardened crystalline form that cannot be driven from the plates in the battery.

sun gear The small, externally toothed gear at the center of the planetary gear set.

sun gear shaft The shaft that connects the front and center sun gears in the Allison transmission.

super single tire Wide-base, low-profile tire used to replace two conventional single tires on an axle to save weight and reduce wheel end parts.

superheat The temperature differential between the refrigerant vapor at the evaporator outlet and the refrigerant vapor at the evaporator inlet.

supplemental additive Aftermarket additive available for automatic transmissions but not recommended by manufacturers.

supply reservoir The first air reservoir to receive air from the air compressor or dryer. Water and oil condense in this tank, which supplies the primary and secondary air reservoirs. Also called the *service reservoir*.

SureShift Meritor's first line of fully automated transmissions.

swaged When two metal components are fitted together by deforming the metal of one to fit the other precisely.

swashplate A plate in a variable displacement pump the tilts and changes the stroke length of axial pistons.

swing clearance The clearance remaining between a trailer and tractor when the combination vehicle is cornering.

swing shackle A spring mounting system consisting of two upright flat bars side-by-side. The top of the bars is pinned to the frame spring bracket and the bottom of the bars are pinned to the rear leaf-spring eye. Shackles allow the leaf-spring length to change as the suspension oscillates.

switched reluctance motor (SRM) An electronically commutated traction motor using a rotor constructed from a machined piece of steel with protrusions called poles. SRM motors use principles of magnetic attraction to drive the motor.

synchronized transmission A transmission that uses sliding clutches or collars fitted over synchronizer hubs that are splined to the mainshaft to select gear ratios.

synchronizer A device to match shaft and gear speeds for clash-free engagement.

synchronous speed The point at which the on-coming clutch has applied and there is no more slippage. Turbine shaft speed times the gear ratio equals output shaft speed.

Synflex A reinforced nylon material used to make flexible air lines.

synthetic-based lubricant A lubricant that is manufactured, rather than refined, and so has much longer service life; it can be a blend of natural and synthetic materials.

system error A term describing the difference between a system output or process variable and its desired or set-point value.

system manager A transmission control module used with older Gen 1 and Gen 2 Eaton AutoShift transmissions.

systematic lock-up A strategy that applies the lock-up clutch as soon as possible for improved fuel economy. Also called *programmed lock-up*.

tachograph A logging device fitted to a vehicle to record various pieces of information, such as time, speed, rest periods, and distance travelled by each of the vehicle's drivers.

tag axle A rear non-drive axle mounted behind the drive axle.

tandem Two drive axles connected by a power divider.

tandem axle A two-axle tractor or trailer configuration.

tap A metal machining tool used to cut internal threads.

taper-current charger A battery charger that applies either constant voltage or constant amperage to the battery through a manually adjusted current-selection switch.

TC-Tronic A ZF AMT that uses a torque converter for input; for heavy applications.

technical service bulletin (TSB) Information issued by manufacturers to alert technicians of unexpected problems or changes to repair procedures.

telematics A branch of information technology that uses specialized applications for long-distance transmission of information to and from a vehicle.

telescoping cylinder A linear single acting cylinder extending from a series of nested cylinder sections.

tensile strength The amount of force required before a material deforms or breaks.

tension A force that tries to pull apart the bottom flange of a frame rail supported between two points.

terminal tractor A tractor designed to move semi-trailers around a warehouse yard or intermodal facility. Also known as a *shunt truck*.

test light The simplest piece of electrical test equipment, which consists of either a 12- or 24-volt incandescent light bulb connected to an insulated lead and a sharpened metal probe.

thermal efficiency A measurement of how much of the fuel used is turned into power to drive the vehicle.

thermal fuse A type of fuse opened by heat produced from resistance caused by high amperage flow.

thermistor A temperature-sensitive variable resistor commonly used to measure coolant, oil, fuel, and air temperatures.

thermocouple A thermoelectric device consisting of two dissimilar metals that produce voltage when heated.

thermostatic expansion valve (TXV) An expansion device used in commercial vehicle air conditioning systems.

third-degree burns Burns that involve white or blackened areas and damage to all skin layers and underlying structures and tissues.

thread chaser Metal working tool used to clean dirty, corroded, or damaged threads.

three Cs Concern (the concern, or problem, with the vehicle); cause (the cause of the concern); and correction (fixing the problem).

three-coil gauge A gauge in which three field coils are wound in series, with a coil at minimum reading, one at maximum reading, and one between the two.

three-way valve A valve that directs hot refrigerant gas to either the condenser (in cool mode) or directly to the evaporator (in heat or defrost modes).

throttle valve A valve that produces a pressure based on throttle position. Also called the *modulator valve*.

through shaft The output shaft of an inter-axle differential. The rear side gear is part of or splined to the through shaft. Also known as *output shaft*.

thrust angle The relationship between the centerline of the vehicle and the angle of the rear tires.

thrust line The direction in which the rear axle wheels are pointing.

thrust screw A screw that stops the crown gear from flexing under load.

tie-rod end Articulating ball-and-socket joints attached to each end of the tie-rod.

tie-rod A steering component that transfers linear motion from the steering box to the steering arms at the front wheels.

time division multiplexing A type of multiplexing used in onboard networks and that works by dividing the time communication available to each network module or device.

time to full apply (TFA) The point after synchronous speed has been detected at which the solenoid controlling the on-coming clutch in a World Transmission is commanded to full pressure (that is, to fully apply the clutch).

tire bead A rubber section of the tire that contacts the wheel rim. The rubber bead contains steel wire wound together to form a cable; when bundled together, they sit at the wheel rim to form an airtight seal between the tire and the rim.

tire casing The foundational body of the tire, consisting of several layers of fabric cord, called plies, encased with a rubber compound; a network of cords that give the tire shape and strength; also known as casing cords.

tire flap A piece of rubber that wraps around the rim to protect the inner tube from chafing, pinching, and cracking caused by friction between the valve stem slot in the rim and the edges of the tire bead.

tire inflation pressure The level of air in the tire that provides it with load-carrying capacity and that affects overall vehicle performance.

tire pressure gauge A gauge used to measure the air pressure within a tire.

tire pressure monitoring system (TPMS) A system within wheel sensors that monitors tire inflation pressure and temperature.

tire tread separation The separation of the tread from the tire casing.

TMC RP 618 A procedure established by The Maintenance Council for obtaining acceptable wheel bearing end play of 0.001" and 0.005" (0.025 mm and 0.127 mm).

toe A measurement of how much the front wheels are turned in or out from a straight-ahead position. The angle is referenced from a position directly above the tires and facing forward.

toe-in A condition that exists when, as seen from above, the wheels are closer together at the front and farther apart at the rear.

toe-out on turns A geometric steering concept that the inner wheel should have a greater turning angle than the outside wheel. Also called *Ackermann angle*.

toe-out A condition that exists when, as seen from above, the wheels are closer together in the rear and farther apart at the front.

toggle switches Manual-type switch featuring the use an angled lever having an internal spring-loaded mechanism to rapidly switch into its latched or closed position.

tongue weight (TW) The weight supported by the ball (tongue) in a ball hitch.

tooth face The area that actually comes in contact with a mating gear and is parallel to the gear's axis of rotation.

top land The apex of a tooth.

topoid A type of amboid gear set with the pinion gear mounted even higher than a normal amboid set.

torque The twisting force applied to a shaft that may or may not result in motion.

torque converter A type of fluid coupling that is also capable of multiplying torque.

torque converter control (TCC) A control solenoid used in fourth-generation and later World Transmissions.

torque limiting A reduction in engine power out; used as strategy to reduce wheel slip or loss of directional control.

torque multiplication phase Occurs whenever the impeller is turning significantly faster than the turbine.

torque rise The difference between engine torque produced at rated speed (maximum engine rpm under load) and peak torque. Torque rise is expressed as a percentage of torque at the rated speed.

torque rod A rod that transfers acceleration, braking, and lateral forces from the axle to the frame and maintains axle alignment. Torque rods can usually be adjusted by one method or another to realign the axles, when required.

torque sticks A steel rod used as an extension on an impact gun used to limit maximum torque applied to a fastener.

Torsen A biased torque differential from General Motors.

torsion bar Bars in a vehicle's suspension system that twist in response to the movement of the wheels and absorb their vertical movement.

torsion rod A thin, spring-like metal rod that connects to one end of the rotary valve to change its position.

torsional excitation Twisting forces caused by inertial excitation.

torsional vibrations Vibrations caused by twisting forces on the driveshaft; these occur twice per revolution.

torus The hollowed-out donut shape of the rear of the converter housing and the turbine.

total indicated runout (TIR) The difference between the high and low measurement of a flat surface, such as the flywheel friction surface.

total mesh adjustment A setting of the appropriate depth for the sector shaft and nut so as not to bind or have excess free play.

toxic dust Any dust that can cause physical harm.

track rod Typically, transversely mounted torque rods that counteract lateral forces acting on the vehicle.

tracking The directional pathway taken by the axles and wheel.

traction battery A rechargeable battery used for propulsion in hybrid electric vehicles.

traction control An enhancement to the ABS that is used to improve vehicle stability when accelerating.

traction motor An electric motor that provides propulsion to a vehicle.

tractor protection (TP) valves A valve that controls the supply of air to the trailer from the tractor. The valve automatically isolates the tractor air reservoirs from being completely drained if a trailer breaks away from a tractor.

trailer The cargo-carrying portion of a combination vehicle.

trailer axle A non-drive axle used by trailers that generally has no steering linkage unless it is a self-steering axle.

trailer brake control (TC) valve A hand-operated, cab-mounted control valve used to manually apply the trailer service brakes.

trailer supply valve A push-pull valve in the cab used to supply air pressure to the trailer air brake reservoirs.

trailer swing-out A condition caused by incorrect pneumatic balance between a tractor and trailer. Typically, trailer brakes are applied at too high a pressure, locking the trailer brakes. The trailer tires slide and cause the trailer to swing out into an adjacent lane.

trailing arms Refers to large strong beams attached to the vehicle frame and to the axle, they support the spring medium.

trailing shoes Brake shoes installed so that they are applied in the opposite direction to the forward rotation of the brake drum; not self-energizing and less efficient at developing braking force.

transfer case A component that is bolted to the back of the transmission or connected to it by a short drive shaft; allows the output of a transmission to flow to both the rear and the front axles. Also called *dropbox*.

transient voltage suppression (TVS) diodes Specialized diodes in the rectifier bridge that become resistive, rather than conductive, at a specific voltage level.

transmission control module (TCM) The electronic controller that issues commands to the solenoids inside the transmission to obtain the desired range. Also known as the *transmission electronic control unit (ECU)*.

transmission electronic control unit (ECU) The electronic controller that issues commands to the solenoids inside the transmission to obtain the desired range. Also called the *transmission control unit (TCU)*.

transmission jacks Are specialized jacks that are fitted with several sets of mounting brackets, allowing them to fit to the shape of many different transmissions.

transmission oil cooler A series of oil tubes or passages that are cooled by engine coolant.

transmission vent A vent on the transmission that is open to atmospheric pressure.

transport temperature control Heating or cooling over a wide range of outside temperatures and product storage temperatures.

transverse vibrations Vibrations caused by shaft imbalance; these occur once per revolution.

TranSynd fluid A full synthetic fluid produced by Castrol, to Allison specification; TranSynd is the recommended fluid for all Allison transmissions.

Traxon ZF's latest AMT with five different input modules available.

tread A cap of molded rubber compound attached to the top of a tire's belt system.

treadle valve The center of the brake delivery system. Also called the *foot valve*.

trickle charger A battery charger that charges at a low amperage rate.

tridem Three drive axles connected by power dividers.

trimmer regulator valve A valve that modulates trimmer valve action.

trimmer valve A valve used to soften a clutch application.

trimmer An accumulator used in the ATEC/CEC systems to smoothen out the shift process.

trinary switch An air conditioning system switch with three sets of internal contacts to protect against low pressure, cutout in case of high pressure, and turn the engine fan on and off.

trunnion The smooth ends of the U-joint cross that accepts the bearing caps.

trunnion-mounted Articulating connection points on the ends of a hydraulic cylinder.

TruTrac A biased torque differential produced by Dana.

tube yoke A yoke with two ears that accept a U-joint and that is welded to the driveshaft tube.

tubeless tire A tire in which the air is not sealed in an inner tube.

tube-type tire A tire in which an inner tube containing the air is separate from the casing.

tubing Metal pipe that is intended to be bent and shaped to fit an application.

turbine The torque converter element that is splined to the transmission input shaft.

turbine pull down A decrease in turbine speed as a shift is in progress that results from the on-coming clutch starting to control its gear train component; the signal for the transmission to enter closed-loop control of the shift in progress.

turbocharger cut-off valves An air-operated valve that closes the air inlet to the air dryer to prevent engine intake boost pressure from leaking out the dryer's purge port.

turning radius The diameter of a circle the vehicle can turn in when the steering wheel is turned to the limit.

twin-leading-shoe drum brake Brake shoe arrangement in which both brake shoes are self-energizing in the forward direction.

twist A type of frame damage that occurs when one rail bends up and the other rail bends down.

two-height fifth wheel A specialty stationary fifth wheel that can be either air or hydraulically raised or lowered.

Type 1 circuit breaker A cycling circuit breaker that automatically resets.

Type 2 circuit breaker A non-cycling circuit breaker.

Type 3 circuit breaker A circuit breaker that requires manual reset.

Type K thermocouple A low-cost, general-purpose, temperature-sensing element connected to the same meter terminals for measuring DC millivolts.

typology Refers to the arrangement of communication pathways between electrical control units.

U-bolt A frame-body attachment that goes over a sub-frame attached to the vehicle body and down both sides of the frame rail before being clamped at the bottom flange of the rail.

U-joint A cross-shaped joint with bearings on each leg where one set of parallel legs is connected to the end of one shaft and the other set of parallel legs is connected to the end of a second shaft. This arrangement allows the shafts to operate at shallow angles to each other. Also called a *universal joint*.

ultra-capacitor A type of high-capacity and high-energy density capacitors.

UltraShift Eaton's two-pedal AMT; completely shift by wire with no clutch pedal.

unconscious bias Means that you are predisposed to think a certain way about a subject or a person.

undercuts The smallest diameter in a spool; used to create a flow path when the valve is open.

underdrive ratio Any ratio that decreases output speed while increasing output torque. Also known as a *gear reduction*.

underslung A suspension system where the leaf spring is mounted under the axle.

undertread The depth of the area between the bottom of the original tread grooves and the top of the uppermost breaker.

Unified Diagnostic Service (UDS) A global electronic service and communication protocol for mechatronic devices that has encrypted security features to prevent malicious network hacking.

Unified Thread Standard (UTS) A standard outlining the properties and characteristics of fasteners using imperial units of measurement.

unipolar semiconductor A semiconductor device made of either P or N material that conducts current through only one channel.

United States Department of Transportation (USDOT) number Any hazardous materials carriers who move enough materials requiring a safety permit must also register for a USDOT number.

universal joint A cross-shaped joint with bearings on each leg where one set of parallel legs is connected to the end of one shaft and the other set of parallel legs is connected to the end of a second shaft. This arrangement allows the shafts to operate at shallow angles to each other. Also called a *U-joint*, a *Cardan joint*, or a *Hooke joint*.

unloader valves Air-operated piston-like valves used to physically hold open the air compressor's air intake check valves.

unloading The state of the air compressor when it is not building air pressure. Unloader valves hold the check valves open.

unsprung weight The vehicle weight not supported by the suspension system; includes the axles, the tires, wheels, and the brakes.

untripped rollovers A vehicle rollover condition produced when an unavoidable outside disturbance causes the rollover.

upper coupler A steel plate and a king pin fastened to the underside of the forward portion of a semi-trailer frame and designed to tow and support the weight of the trailer.

vacuum booster A vacuum-operated power assist system for hydraulic brakes.

vacuum gauge A gauge designed to read negative pressure or vacuum.

vacuum pump A pump used to evacuate the A/C system of air and put the system into a deep vacuum or low pressure to remove moisture.

Valley Forge (VF) diagram A schematic wiring diagram that uses SAE-type symbols.

valve adjusting cam Small cam on the end of the shift signal and modulator valves that, when turned, adjust the shift point.

valve body test stand A special test stand specifically for testing and setting up Allison transmission control valve bodies and shift points.

valve-regulated lead–acid (VRLA) battery A type of sealed lead-acid battery used in heavy-duty equipment. It does not require the addition of water. Also called a *sealed lead-acid battery (SLA) or recombinant battery.*

vane pump A hydraulic pump that uses sliding vanes to move the fluid.

variable capacitance pressure sensor A type of active sensor that measures both dynamic and static pressure.

variable displacement pump A type of pump with the ability to change output volume, as in a pump with a mechanism that allows the output to vary.

variable frequency drives (VFD) Electronic control units that change the switching frequency of AC, which is used to regulate the speed of an AC induction motor.

variable pitch stator A stator with blades that can change the angle to alter the torque converter multiplication factor.

variable reluctance (VR) sensor A sensor used to measure rotational speed, including wheel speed, vehicle speed, engine speed, and camshaft and crankshaft position.

variable-bleed solenoid (VBS) Hydraulic solenoids used in late-model Allison World Transmissions, which control application by allowing some of the pressure going to a device to bleed off to exhaust.

variable-ratio steering gears Steering gears that use sector shafts with long and short lengths of teeth.

variable spring rate A spring or suspension system where more force is required to deflect the spring as load is added; allows a soft rate when unloaded and a much stiffer suspension when loaded.

vehicle emission control information (VECI) label Indicates that the vehicle conforms to the emission control regulations for the year it was built.

vehicle hoist A type of vehicle lifting tool designed to lift the entire vehicle.

vehicle identification number (VIN) A number that identifies the vehicle make, model, year, configuration, and the individual serial number of a vehicle.

vehicle safety certification (VSC) label A label certifying that the vehicle meets the Federal Motor Vehicle Safety standards at date of manufacturer.

vehicle speed sensor (VSS) An inductive pick-up sensor that reads the speed of the transmission output shaft.

vehicle-powered refrigeration units A transport refrigeration system that is powered by a compressor located in the vehicle's engine.

vertical load The weight supported by a hitching device, which is applied downwards by the weight of the trailer.

vibrasorbers Flexible stainless-steel lines that connect the compressor inlet and outlet to the trailer refrigeration system and absorb compressor movement and vibration.

vibration analyzer A device used to identify the root cause of vehicle vibration.

virtual fuse A software-controlled fuse that monitors circuit amperage and shuts off the circuit when amperage exceeds a predetermined threshold. Also called *e-fuses.*

virtual sensor Virtual sensors do not physically exist but data from the sensor are made to appear real using software. A virtual sensor uses predictive algorithms to report data, meaning it calculates an estimated value for a physical variable that usually cannot be directly measured.

viscosity The measurement of the resistance to flow of a liquid.

vocation The type of service a vehicle is involved in.

vocational A truck that is dedicated to a specific type of service job, or function.

volt The electrical unit used to measure potential difference or electrical pressure.

voltage The speed at which electrons travel from atom to atom.

vortex flow The flow of fluid from the impeller, through the turbine, through the stator, and back to the impeller.

walking beam A beam with each end attached to the axles of a tandem-axle arrangement and its center attached to the frame directly or through a spring system. The beam reduces the impact of road bumps to the frame by 50% and equalizes the load carried by each of the axles. Also called an *equalizing beam*.

water fade A type of brake fade that occurs when water gets between the friction surfaces and the drum that acts as a lubricant and reduces braking efficiency.

water wicking The movement of water through wiring due to its adhesive and cohesive properties.

waterfall arrangement Two or more universal joint arrangement where the joint angles form parallel lines; a method of angle cancellation for use with parallel angles. Also called *parallel joint arrangement*.

Watt's law An electrical law that defines the relationship between power, amperage, and voltage.

wave inverter A device that changes the shape of electrical current waves.

Weather-Pack connector An environmentally sealed push-to-seat electrical connection system supplied in one- to six-pin configurations.

web The upright portion of the frame rail. Also called *frame rail web*.

wedge brakes Brakes that use a wedge pushed between two rollers as a lever to apply the brakes.

welding helmet A helmet that protects your eyes and your face from the UV radiation and flying sparks or particles during arc welding operations.

wet load Refers to very damp products that are refrigerated.

wet tank Another name for the service or supply air reservoir. It is called a wet tank since moisture and vaporized oil condense in this tank.

wheel alignment The positioning of the tires relative to the vehicle. Also called *tracking*.

wheel cylinders A hydraulic cylinder with one or two pistons, seals, dust boots, and a bleeder screw that pushes the brake shoes into contact with the brake drum to slow or stop the vehicle.

wheel end The assembly at the end of the axle.

wheel end play The free movement of the wheel hub assembly along the axle spindle axis.

wheel hop A situation where the wheels literally hop off the ground and lose their contact with the road, usually caused by excessive suspension wind-up due to extreme braking, but can also occur on acceleration.

wheel lockup A condition where the drive or steer tires have stopped rotating when braking.

wheel offset The distance from the hub mounting surface to the centerline of the wheel.

wheel rim The outer circular lip of the metal on which the inside edge of the tire is mounted.

wheel slip A condition in which excess torque from the drivetrain causes the tire to break free from the road surface. Also called *wheel spin*.

wheel spin A condition in which excess torque from the drivetrain causes the tire to break free from the road surface. Also called *wheel slip*.

wheel studs The threaded fasteners that attach the wheel to the vehicle.

wide-base tire Large tire with a low aspect ratio. Also called *flotation tire*.

wide-range planar sensor A type of sensor technology that uses a current pump to calculate relative concentrations of oxygen, nitric oxide, and ammonia in exhaust gases.

Wilson gear set A compound planetary gear set consisting of three planetary gears interconnected; capable of producing five forward and one reverse ratio.

working pressure The normal range of pressure within a hydraulic system while the system is being operated.

World Transmission Electronic Control (WTEC) Allison's original electronic transmission control system for the World Transmission.

worm gear A gear with a helical, threaded shaft used in a steering gear and meshes with a ball nut that transfers motion from the steering wheel to the steering linkage. Also called the *worm shaft*.

worm-and-crown Older drive axle gear arrangement capable of very high gear reductions in a compact space. Also known as *worm wheel*.

worm wheel Older drive axle gear arrangement capable of very high gear reductions in a compact space. Also known as *worm-and-crown*.

wye windings Stator windings of an induction motor or alternator in which one end of each phase winding is connected together at a single central point.

yaw The rotation of a vehicle around its vertical axis; the difference between the vehicle's intended direction and the actual direction of travel.

yaw control Minimizing the slip or difference between the desired or steered direction of a vehicle and actual direction a vehicle is moving.

yield strength An engineering term used to describe the amount of force required to permanently deform a material. Yield strength occurs at the material's elastic limit—the maximum force a material can withstand and still return to its original configuration.

Zener diode A type of diode that behaves like a typical silicon diode up to a precise voltage threshold, called the Zener point. After it reaches the Zener point voltage, the diode conducts in both directions.

Zener point The voltage at which a diode conducts current in both directions instead of just one.

zero offset When the plane of the hub mounting surface is even with the centerline of the wheel.

INDEX

A

absorbed glass mat (AGM) batteries, 333, 333*f*, 344–346, 412
  advantages, 344
  gel cell, 346
  precautions of, 344–345
  spiral cell optima, 345–346
abuse failure, axle, 1556
accelerated wear, 1491
accelerator position sensor (APS), 567
accumulator, 1722
Ackermann angle, 751
Ackermann principle, 759
active sensor, 557, 558*f*
AC-to-DC inverter, 1637
actual frame strength, 775, 775*f*
actuator adaptation adjustments and MPC, 620–622, 621*f*
adaptive control, 1445
adaptive cruise control (ACC), 1014, 1039, 1608
adaptive learning, 1281
addendum, 1190
adjusting ring, 1167
adsorption, 921
Advanced Driver Assistance Systems (ADAS), 1564, 1601
aeration, 1454, 1794
air bags, 811
air brake systems, 908–909, 908*f*, 909*f*
  foundation, subcomponents of, 880*f*
  pressure balance, 957*t*–960*t*, 966–967
    service, 969–974
    and valves inspection, 967–969
  principles of, 908
  subsystems and control circuits, 909–910, 910*f*, 911*f*, 911*t*, 912*f*
air build-up time, 970–971
air compressor, 912, 913*f*, 969
  capacity, 913*f*
  discharge line, 912–913
  governor
    compressor unloader valves, 915–917, 916*f*, 917*f*, 918*f*
    inlet regulating valve, 917
    loading and unloading operation, 914–915, 915*f*
    turbocharger cut-off valve, 918–919, 918*f*
  operation, 912, 914*f*
air conditioning protection and diagnostic system (APADS)
  engine fan operation, 1692–1693
  failures of, 1692
  inputs of, 1693
  rules of, compressor, 1692

air conditioning protection unit (ACPU), 1690
air conditioning system, 1663, 1663*f*, 1664*f*
  benefits of, 1664–1665
  controls of, 1688–1690
  development of, 1663–1664
  distribution system, 1693–1695
  evaporators, 1682–1683
  operating principles of, 1666–1670
  receiver-dryers, 1684, 1684*f*
  refrigerant and oil, 1684–1688
    properties of, 1686
    types, 1687–1688, 1687*t*
  refrigeration cycle, 1670–1671
  refrigeration system, components, 1671–1675
  TXV, 1675–1682, 1676*f*
air delivery and control systems, 926, 927*f*
  foot valves, 927, 927*f*
    construction, 928, 928*f*
    operation, 928, 929*f*, 930*f*, 931*f*
    troubleshooting problems with, 929–930, 931*f*
  inversion valve, 941–942, 941*f*
  park/emergency brake circuit, 939, 940*f*
  pneumatic brake balance, 934–935
    anti-compounding relay valves, 935–937, 936*f*
    brake proportioning relay valves, 938, 938*f*
    crack pressure, 935
    front axle limiter valves, 938–939, 939*f*
    pneumatic brake imbalance, 935
    QR valves, 939, 939*f*
    relay valve crack pressures, 935
  push-pull control valves, 939–941, 940*f*
  relay valves, 930–933, 933*f*, 934*f*
    operation-applying brakes, 934
    operation-releasing brakes, 934, 934*f*
    pressure compensating balance, 934
  trailer air circuits, 943, 943*f*
  trailer spring brake valves, 945–947, 946*f*
  trailer system valves, 944–945, 945*f*
air disc brakes (ADB), 876, 900, 900*t*, 901*f*
  actuation, 900
  auto-adjustment of, 901, 902*f*, 903*f*
  OOSC, 1824
  released, 900–901
  servicing, 1000–1004
    brake lathe, 1003*f*
    brake pad inspection, 1001–1002, 1001*f*, 1002*f*, 1003*f*
    inspecting caliper sliders, 1004
    rotor replacement, 1003–1004
    rotor surface inspection, 1003, 1004*f*

Air Dryer Integrated System (AD-IS) dryer, 923
air dryers, 921–922, 922*f*, 972
  advanced technologies, 923–925, 923*f*, 924*f*
  charging cycle, 922–923, 922*f*
  with oil separator, 921–922, 922*f*
  purging cycle, 922–923, 922*f*
air filter/pressure regulator, 1231, 1256
air jack, 140
air lines and hoses, 973–974
air management unit, 665, 665*f*
air pressure, 908, 909*f*, 917*f*
air reservoirs, 919, 919*f*, 972
air shift system problems, 1255–1258, 1255*f*, 1256*f*
  air filter/pressure regulator, 1256
  air leaks, 1256–1257, 1256*f*
  crossed air lines, 1256
  Roadranger valve, 1257–1258, 1257*f*
air spring, 799
  control, 814–815, 814*f*, 815*f*
  equalizing beam suspensions, 814
  oscillations, 813
  suspension systems, 811–812, 812*f*, 823
    air-spring construction, 812–813, 812*f*, 813*f*
    combination leaf/air-spring, 813–814, 813*f*
    inspecting, 823, 825
    maintaining, 823
    testing, 825
air supply system, components of, 910*f*, 911–912
  air compressor, 912, 913*f*
    discharge line, 912–913
    operation, 912, 914*f*
  air compressor governor, 913–914, 914*f*
    compressor unloader valves, 915–917, 916*f*, 918*f*
    governor loading and unloading operation, 914–915, 915*f*
    inlet regulating valve, 917
    turbocharger cut-off valve, 918–919, 918*f*
  air dryers, 921–922, 922*f*
    advanced technologies, 923–925, 923*f*, 924*f*
    charge and purge cycle, 922–923, 922*f*
  air reservoirs, 919, 919*f*
  diagnosing problems in, 925–926, 925*f*
  reservoir air control valves, 920, 920*f*
    drain valves, 920–921, 920*f*, 921*f*
    pressure protection valves, 920, 920*f*
air systems
  advantages of, 908–909, 909*f*
  disadvantages of, 909

air conditioning (A/C) systems, 1701
  compressor clutch, 1708
  maintenance and repair, 1716–1719, 1716f, 1717f, 1718f
    compressor clutch inspection, 1719–1722
    compressor inspection, 1720–1722
    condenser inspection, 1722–1723
    drive belt inspection, 1719
    evaporator inspection, 1724
    heater control valves, 1726–1727
    heater core inspection, 1727–1728
    micron gauge, 1724–1726
    oil and capacity, 1726–1727
    orifice tube inspection, 1724–1725
    receiver/dryer or accumulator, 1722–1723
    removal of hoses and lines, 1720, 1722
    system flush, 1719
    TXV inspection, 1723–1724
  performance testing, 1715
  reclaiming/recovering of refrigerant, 1713
  service process, 1702f
    abnormal noises, 1708
    clutch cycle time, 1706–1707, 1706f, 1707f
    evaporator odors, 1708
    high-/low-pressure safety switches, 1703–1704, 1703f, 1704f
    interpreting manifold gauge results, 1705–1706, 1706t
    manifold gauge pressure measurements, 1704–1705, 1705f, 1706t
    orifice tube system, 1707–1708
    performance testing, 1701–1703, 1702t, 1703f
    refrigerant state of charge, 1703, 1703f
    thermal expansion valve system, 1708
  using vacuum gauge to evacuate, 1714
air conditioning machine, 1716
air-control solenoid valve, 1283
airflow restrictions, inspecting condenser for, 1715
air-over-hydraulic braking systems, 1049
alcohol evaporator systems, 972–973
alcohol injector systems, 972–973
alkylated naphthalene (AN), 1772
Allison DOC, 1656
Allison electrohydraulic control valve body
  fifth-generation
    retarders, 1425–1426, 1425f, 1426f, 1427f
    shift selectors, 1426–1430, 1428f, 1429f, 1430f
  fourth-generation fluid flows, 1417–1422, 1418f, 1419f, 1420f, 1421f, 1422f, 1423f
  other valves
    accumulator relay valve, 1424–1425
    converter flow valve, 1424
    converter regulator valve, 1422, 1424

    exhaust backfill valve, 1424
    lubrication pressure regulator valve, 1424
    overdrive knock-down valve, 1424, 1424f
    prognostics, 1425
Allison EV Drive Hybrid Systems, 1644
Allison hydraulically controlled automatic transmissions, 1356–1358, 1357f, 1358f, 1372–1375
  automatic downshifting
    full throttle downshift, 1374, 1374f
    reverse hydraulic operation, 1375
    shift point control, 1374–1375, 1375f
  automatic transmission shifting, 1372–1374, 1373f
Allison transmission. See also Allison hydraulically controlled automatic transmissions
  hydraulic control system components, 1363, 1363f
    control valves, 1364–1372, 1365f, 1366f, 1367f, 1369f, 1370f, 1372f
    hydraulic circuits, 1372, 1372f
  power flows
    first range, 1358, 1360f
    fourth range, 1361, 1362f
    neutral, 1358, 1359f
    reverse, 1361–1363, 1362f
    second range, 1359, 1360f, 1361
    third range, 1361, 1361f
  TC-10-TS transmission, 1430–1432, 1431f, 1432t
    Allison nine speed, 1440
    power flows, 1432–1440, 1433f, 1434f, 1435f, 1436f, 1437f, 1438f, 1439f, 1440f
Allison Transmission Electronic Control (ATEC), 1380. See also Commercial Electronic Control (CEC)
  shift logic
    first range, 1388, 1389f
    fourth range, 1388, 1390
    neutral, 1386, 1386t, 1388f
    reverse, 1391, 1391f
    second range, 1388, 1389f
    third range, 1388, 1390f
  solenoids, 1384–1386, 1385f, 1386f
  trimmer operation
  torque converter lock-up control, 1392, 1392f
  transmission operation during electrical failure, 1392, 1393f
  wiring harnesses, 1384
Allison World Transmissions, 1393–1394, 1393f, 1394t. See also World Transmission (WT)
alternating current (AC), 206, 206f, 279, 534
alternating current traction generator (ACTG), 1631, 1633

alternating current traction motor (ACTM), 1632, 1634
alternator, 416f
  advantages, 414–415
  removing, inspecting and replacing of, 442–445
  ripple, 426
aluminum alloy, 776
amboid gear, 1508
American Petroleum Institute (API) Oil Certification Mark, 1814, 1814f
ammonia sensors, 578–560
amperage, 199
ampere (amp), 199
amp-hour, 329
amps-volts and resistance (AVR) test instrument, 205f
anaerobic sealers, 184
analog meters, 302, 303f
analog signals, 539, 539f
analog to digital conversion, 543, 543f, 544f
AND gate, 548
angle spring clutch, 1143
angular motion, 1783
annealing, 129
anti-compounding relay valves, 935–937, 936f
anti-drain-back check valves, 1325
anti-fade, 884
antifriction bearings, 163–166, 164f
  construction of, 164–165, 165f
    roller, 166
    shape and operation of, 165–166, 166f
    tapered roller, 166
  troubleshooting failures, 172–173
antilock braking system (ABS), 194, 910, 963–964, 1013–1014
  applying trailer/engine brakes, 1013f
  collision avoidance, 1037–1040
    ACC, 1039
    aligning front radar sensor, 1039
    lateral and vertical adjustment of radar sensor, 1040
    operation of yaw sensor, 1038f
    radar adjustments, 1038–1039
    sensors, 1038f
    version of ACom is used to recalibrate ECU, 1038f
  components, 1018
  configurations, 1029–1030
  developments, 1013
  DSC, 1036–1037
    additional sensors, 1037
    components, 1037f
    ECU in individual brakes, 1036f
    yaw control, 1036
  ECU configuration, 1018–1019
  emergency braking systems, 1015f
  engine retarders, 1019–1021
  ESC at wheel ends, 1014f
  front axle modulator valves, 1025f

fundamentals, 1014–1016
  features and benefits, 1015, 1016*t*
  vehicle steering control, 1016*f*
inlet valve, 1025*f*
maintenance and service procedures,
    1040–1042
  ACC CAS, 1040*f*
  ATC, and ESC systems, 1041*f*
  Blink Codes, 1042
  diagnostic modes, 1042
  fault location, 1041*t*
  front sensor, 1042*f*
modulator valve, 1024, 1024*f*
operation of modulator valves, 1025–1029
  ABS trailer cords, 1027
  brake control, 1026*f*
  Chuff test, 1027*f*
  European trailers, 1028*f*
  indicator lights and switches, 1028–
    1029
  inlet and exhaust solenoid valve, 1025*f*
  ISO pin numbers, 1029*t*
  J-560 Standards for trailer plugs, 1027*t*
  modulator function, 1026*f*
  pin function, 1027*f*
  steer axle control, 1026
overview, 1013–1014
requirements, 1016–1018
  brake release, 1017*f*
  cab ABS warning lights, 1017*f*
  trailers, 1017*f*
RSC, 1034–1035
  braking strategies, 1034–1035
  lateral acceleration sensors, 1034*f*
  sophisticated systems, 1035*f*
  steering angle sensor calibration,
    1035
  tripped *vs.* untripped rollovers, 1034
testing wheel speed sensor codes, 1022*f*
vehicle dynamic control systems,
    1031–1034
  advanced ATC, 1033
  differential braking, 1032–1033
  ECU, conventional relay valve, 1033*f*
  torque distribution, 1032*f*
  torque limiting, 1031–1032
  traction control, 1031
  uneven wheel speeds, 1032*f*
  valve connection, signal port, 1033*f*
wheel rotational speed, 1022*f*
wheel sensor assembly, 1023*f*
wheel speed sensors, 1021, 1023–1024
  acceptable air gap, 1023*f*
  location, 1021*f*
  modulator valves, 1023–1024
  rotational velocity data, 1021*f*
yaw rotation, 1014*f*
anti-rattle springs, 1180
application chart, 1348
applied stroke measurement method,
    981–983, 984*f*

armature, 385, 386*f*
  shaft and windings, 385–386
articulated bus, 11*f*
articulation, 16, 800
ArvinMeritor dual-mode hybrid system,
    1655*f*
aspect ratio, 683
  low profile tires, 685
  super single tires, 685–686, 686*f*
  wide-base, 685–686, 686*f*
assisted GPS, 1616
AS-Tronic, 1278
asynchronous AC motor, 1648
asynchronous motors, 1578
A-train, 20, 20*f*, 1103–1104
A-type lock, 1115
automated manual transmission (AMT),
    1275
  Eaton Fuller autoshift and ultrashift
      operations
    clutches used with autoshift and
        ultrashift, 1286, 1286*f*
    driver interface, 1281–1282, 1282*f*
    electric shift assembly, 1282–1283,
        1282*f*, 1283*f*
    electronically controlled range valve,
        1283–1284, 1284*f*
    electronically controlled splitter valve,
        1284–1285
    inertia brake, 1285–1286, 1285*f*
    momentary engine ignition interrupt
        relay, 1282
    position sensors, 1283, 1283*f*, 1284*f*
    shaft speed sensors, 1281, 1281*f*
    start enable relay, 1282
    transmission controller, 1280–1281,
        1280*f*, 1281*f*
  Eaton Fuller transmission nomenclature,
      1287–1288, 1287*t*
  electronically, types of
    Detroit Diesel's DT-12, 1279, 1279*f*
    Eaton Fuller's automated
        transmissions, 1276–1278, 1276*f*,
        1277*f*, 1278*f*
    Mercedes Benz's AGS, 1279, 1279*f*
    Meritor/ZF's automated transmissions,
        1278–1279, 1278*f*
    Volvo Trucks' I-shift, 1279, 1279*f*
  role of torque break in shifting, 1276
  troubleshooting, 1308
automated transmission
  Eaton Procision dual-clutch. *See* Eaton
      Procision dual-clutch automated
      transmission
  ECUs, sensors, vehicle interface, and related
      components, 1308
  manual. *See* automated manual
      transmission (AMT)
  Meritor and ZF, 1278–1279, 1278*f*
automatic chassis lubrication system (ACLS),
    1814, 1814*f*

automatic disengagement lockout (ADLO),
    392
automatic drain valves, 920–921, 921*f*
Automatic Gear Shift (AGS), 1279
automatic slack adjusters (ASAs), 894–896,
    898*f*, 899, 978*f*, 980, 980*f*
  adjusting, 997–998
  adjustment locking pin, 983*f*
  drum brake stroke measurement, 981*t*
  functional testing of, 998–1000
  maintenance, 899–900
  manual, 1000
  replacing, 896–897, 999–1000
automatic slip regulation (ASR), 1031
automatic traction control (ATC), 1013
automatic transmission fluid (ATF), 1773
automation, 1603
Automotive Service Excellence (ASE), 32
autonomous communication technology,
    1616–1617
autonomous control enabling technologies
  high-definition cameras, 1610
  LIDAR, 1612–1613, 1613*f*
  RADAR, 1611–1612
  satellite Global Positioning System, 1613
autonomous drive processing systems,
    1614
autonomous driving capability, 1603, 1606*t*
  ADAS development, 1609–1610
  driver assistance systems, 1607–1609
  telematics and, 1607
Autonomous Emergency Braking (AEB),
    1608, 1609*f*
autonomous technologies, SAE classification
    of, 1605–1607, 1605*t*
autonomous vehicle, 1603
auto-ranging multimeter, 303
AUTOSAR (Automotive Open System
    Architecture), 292
AutoSelect, 1276
AutoShift, 1277
auxiliary sections, 1220–1221
auxiliary springs, 804–805, 805*f*
auxiliary/exclusion lip, 177
axial thrust, 1196
axis, 1189
axle(s), 745, 745*f*
  parallelism, 764
  perpendicularity, 762
  setback, 759
  spread, 1106
  stops/jounce blocks, 800, 800*f*

B

backing plate, 1064
backlash, 1191
back-taper, 1255
ball hitch, 22, 1109
ball-nut rack, 839
banjo, 1509

barrier voltage (threshold voltage), 278–279, 279f
Basic Safety Message (BSM), 1608, 1617
battery
　balancers, 348
　equalizers, 348, 351f
　failure. *See* battery failure, causes of
　inspection, testing, and maintenance
　　capacity of, 364
　　conductance, 364–366
　　state of charge, 361–363
　operation, 320–322
　　classification, 320–323
　　functions, 321–322
　ratings, 328–332, 329f
　　internal resistance of, 330–332
　　multiple-battery configurations, 329–330
　service precautions, 357
battery charging, 1588–1592
　CCS, 1592
　Chargepoint CBEV Connector, 1592
　charging plug, standards, 1589–1590
　IEC Type 2 connector, 1591
　SAE J-plug, 1590–1591
battery failure, causes of, 357–359
　internal resistance, 358
　sulfation, 358–359
　　electrolyte level and condition, 359
　　grid corrosion, 359, 359f
　　test, performance, 359
　　vibration, 359
Battery Management System Modules, 1587–1588
battery-isolator systems, 348
Battery-management systems (BMS), 347–350, 352f
　balancers and equalizers, 348–350
　isolators, 348
　low-voltage disconnect, 348
battery-powered electric vehicles (BEVs), 12, 13f
baud rate, 542
baulk rings. *See* blocking ring/blocker rings
beach marks, 1557
bead breaker, 706
bead seat, 719
beam-type torque wrenches, 123
bearing
　adjuster, 1540, 1548
　adjuster locks, 1540, 1550
　classification, 162–163, 162f, 163f
　configurations, 163f
　fit, 166–169
　friction and, 160–162, 161f, 162f
　functions, 160–162, 160f, 161f
　growth, 1546
　inspection, 172
　installation, 170
　ISO numbering system, 164f
　maintenance, 169–171, 171f

packing with grease, 171–172
preload, 731–732, 732f, 733f
removal, 167–168, 168f, 169f
sleeve, 162
types of failures, 173–174, 173t
bellcrank, 1212
bellows, 811
belt routing label, 45
bench *vs.* on-vehicle programming, 632–633, 632f
Bendix AD-IS air dryer, 923, 923f, 924f
Bendix air disc brake system, 903f
Bendix Air System Inspection Cup (BASIC), 963
Bendix caliper assembly, components of, 1004f
Bendix D2 governor circuit, 916f
Bendix Electronic Air Control (EAC) air supply system, 925f
Bernoulli principle, 1775
bevel gears, 1197–1198, 1506
bias-belted tires, 687
biased torque differential, 1514
bias-ply tire, 686
bidirectional communication, 645
bimetal temperature coefficient devices, 257
bimetallic gauges, 496–497, 497f
binary code, 540–541
biodegradable hydraulic fluids, 1772, 1772f
bipolar diode, 279
bipolar junction transistors (BJTs), 284, 284f, 284t, 285
bipolar semiconductor, 276, 276f, 277f
bipolar transistor, 284
　testing, 286
bit arbitration, 659
bitter end, 154
blink codes/flash codes, 494, 1019
blocking ring/blocker rings, 1210
Bluetooth, 668, 668f
bobtailing, 938
bobtailing proportioning relay (BPR) valve, 938, 938f
body effect/body-gate, 291
body electrical system
　accessory electrical circuits and systems, 512–529
　fundamentals of, 475–476, 475f
　instrumentation, 493–508
　　driver information screens, 505–507
　　gauge operating system, 495–500
　　gauge problems, troubleshooting, 507–508
　　sending units, 500–504
　　speedometer, 504–505, 504f
　　warning lights, 494–495, 494f
　introduction, 475
　lighting system, 474–489
bolt circle, 719, 719f
　pattern, 720
bolt-mounted rotors, 1005f

bolts, 94
boot loader, 631, 631f
bore, 1784
Bosch connectors, 457
Bosch's recirculating-ball steering gear, 853, 853f
bottle jacks, 140
bow, 784
Bowden cable, 521
box-end wrenches, 117–118, 117f
brake drum, 886–887, 887t, 986–989, 987f, 1055
　broken, 988f
　cracked, 988f
　inspection replacement guide, 989t
　mounting, 887
　with pilot pads, 988f
　service guidelines, 989t
　terminology, 887f
brake shoe service, 879–881, 880f, 881f, 989–994, 1055
　disassembling brakes, 990–992
　inspecting and removing, 881, 989–990, 990f, 991
　installing, 991–993
brake/braking system, 868f, 869f, 873–874, 873f, 874f, 953–955, 1821–1826
　ADB, 900, 900t, 901f
　　actuation, 900
　　auto-adjustment of, 901, 902f, 903f
　　released, 900–901
　air brake foundation systems, 875, 875f
　air *vs.* hydraulic, 874–875, 874f, 875f
　application pressure, 938f
　automatic emergency, 963
　balance, 953
　band, 1345
　block, 879
　　material, 882, 883f
　brake chambers and actuators, 888, 888f
　　dual-brake chambers, 889–891, 889f, 890f, 891f
　　long stroke chambers, 888–889, 889f
　　release (caging) bolts, 891, 893, 893f
　　roto-chambers, 893–894, 894f
　brake fade, 883, 884f
　cam brake system operation, 876–877, 877f
　chambers, 890f
　chemical fade, 886
　coefficient of friction (CoF), 882, 882f, 883t
　common complaints, 955–956
　CVSA defective brakes criteria, 1821, 1824–1826
　　air brake circuits, 1826
　　air compressor, 1826
　　air disc brakes OOSC, 1824
　　air pressure gauge and low-pressure warning system, 1826
　　brake pushrod adjustment limits, 1825

drum and rotors, 1825
  drum brakes OOSC, 1824
  front steering axle brakes, 1825
  hoses and tubing, 1825–1826
  parking brake and emergency braking,
    1825
drum. *See* brake drum
dust hazards, 953
edge codes, 882–883, 883*f*, 883*t*
fade, 883, 884*f*
fluid, 1055
fluid, dry and wet boiling points of,
    884*t*
force multiplication, 873*f*
foundation technologies, 872*f*, 875
heat fade, 884, 884*t*, 885*t*
influence of vehicle weight and speed, 870,
    871*f*
inspecting and adjusting air, 979–984,
    980*f*
  actuator stroke table, 982*t*
  brake adjustment indicators, 983–984
  inch, 980–981
  measuring brake stroke, 981–984
  pushrod, 985, 985*f*, 986*f*
lag, 909
lines, 1059
lining, 879
malfunctions, 955
mechanical fade, 885
noises, 955–956
pedal, releasing, 931*f*
physical concepts, 868, 870, 870*f*
preliminary inspection, 956–963,
    978–979
proportioning relay valves, 938, 938*f*
pull, 956
self-energization, 877–878, 878*f*
  left-/right-hand camshafts, 878, 878*f*
  S-cam brackets, 878–879, 879*f*
slack adjusters, 894, 895*f*
  automatic, 895–896, 898*f*, 899
  manual, 895
steer, 956
stroke length, 956, 981–982, 985, 1000
subsystems, 875
timing imbalance, 966
torque
  and balance, 872*f*, 886
  and inertia shift, 870, 872, 872*f*
troubleshooting problems, 956
truck and bus, 869*f*
valves, 1791
vehicle preparation and safety, 978
water fade, 884–885
wedge brakes, 903, 903*f*
break torque, 1276
Bridge Formula B, 17, 1106
brinelling, 1480
British thermal unit (BTU), 1666
broken back arrangement, 1481

B-train, 20, 20*f*, 1104
buffer memory, 625
bulkhead module (BHM), 664
bump steer, 844
burst pressure, 1775

C

cab forward (CF), 1101
cab-over-engine (COE), 1101
  configuration, 17*f*
  front axle set-forward/-back in, 17*f*
  tandem-axle tractor, 7*f*, 16, 16*f*
cabs, 16*f*
  aerodynamic features, 17*f*
  door inspection, 1819
  harness, 1384
calibration, 614
  coding numbers, 633
  files, 613–614
  memory, 630–632, 630*f*, 631*f*
California Basic Inspection of Terminal
    Program, 1813
caliper pistons, 1047
calorie, 1666
cam brakes, 876
  system operation, 876–877, 877*f*
camber, 751–752, 752*f*
  handling characteristics, 752–753, 752*f*,
    753*t*
camera monitor system (CMS), 528, 528*f*
cam-over condition, 979
camshafts, 994–996
  cam-opposite, 878
  cam-same, 878
  inspecting spider plate, 995–996
  installing, 995–996
  lip-type grease seals, 996
  removing, 995
  wear points on, 994*f*
CAN 2.0, 654–655, 654*f*
CAN DBC files, 670
Canadian Center for Occupational Safety
    and Health (CCOSH), 57
cancellation, 1480
CAN-FD, 654–655, 654*f*, 655*f*
cap screw, 94, 98*f*, 100*t*, 101*f*
capacitance touchscreens, 506–507, 508*f*
capacitive coupling, 551, 551*f*
capacitors, 293–294, 293*f*, 294*f*
  applications, 294–295, 294*f*, 295*f*
  testing, 295, 295*f*
carbon dioxide (CO_2), 1275
carbon monoxide (CO), 61
Cardan joint, 1472
cargo-handling devices inspection, 1832–1834
carrier, 1339, 1509
cartridge mechanism, 1788
casings belt system, 686–687, 687*f*
cast drums, 886
cast ductile iron, 1189

cast spoke hubs, 737–738, 737*f*, 738*f*
caster, 753–756
  adjusting shim, 805
  shimmy, 755. 755*f*
cast-spoke drums, 887
Caterpillar automatic transmissions,
    1447–1449, 1447*f*, 1448*f*
cavitation, 1454
  erosion, 1779, 1794–1795
C-channel, 772
  frame rail, 776, 776*f*
center bearing, 1477
center of gravity (CG), 146–147
centralized/distributed network control,
    649–651, 651*f*
centrifugal force, 1318
centrifuge drums, 886
ceramic friction facings, 1145
chain and filter wrenches, 119–120, 120*f*
chain blocks, 147, 147*f*
Chalmers suspension, 810
charge, 1701, 1703
charge-depleting (CD) operating mode, 1636
charge-sustaining (CS) mode, 1636
charging batteries, 366–369
  jump-starting vehicles, 369
  series/parallel, 368–369
  types of, 367–368
charging systems and services, 409–445
  alternating current generation, principles,
    415–417
  alternator components, 417–427
  introduction, 410–412
  mild-hybrid alternators, 412
  voltage regulation, 427–434
chassis control module (CHM), 664
chassis equipment, 16–17
chassis lubricants, 1814
chassis wiring harness, 1384
check valves, 1791–1792, 1792*f*
chemical fade, 886
chisels, 128–129, 128*f*
  pry bars, 129, 129*f*
  punches, 128–129, 129*f*
chlorofluorocarbons (CFCs), 1663
chocks, 141
chuff test, 963
circuit breakers, 245
  classification of, 245*t*
circuit control devices, servicing
  ISO relay testing, 269–271
  mag switches and relays, 268–269
  solenoids, 267–268, 267*f*
  switches, 267
circuit (wire) tracer, 312, 312*f*
circuits, 231*f*
  arrangement
    combination, 235
    parallel, 233–235, 234*f*, 235*f*, 236*f*
    series, 232–233, 233*f*, 234*f*
  classification, 232

circuits (*Continued*)
current flow in, 231–235, 231*f*
malfunctions
grounded circuits, 240, 241*f*
high-resistance circuits, 240–241, 241*f*, 242*f*
intermittent circuits, 241–242, 242*f*
open circuit faults, 239, 239*f*, 240*f*
short circuits, 240, 240*f*, 241*f*
operational state, 232, 232*f*
protection devices
circuit breakers, 245
harness protection, 244, 245*f*
inspecting and testing, 246–247
PPT coefficient fuses, 246
thermal fuses, 243, 243*f*, 243*t*, 244*f*, 244*t*
virtual fuses, 246
city transit bus, 11*f*
clamp circuit, 283
clamp force (clamp load), 1138
clearance-sensing ASAs, 895
climate control system, 1701
clock spring, 833
clocking, 724–726, 724*f*, 725*f*
clockwise rotation, 1191
closed center control valves and circuits, 1787–1788
closed loop systems, 606, 607*f*
closed-center position, 1790, 1791*f*
closed-loop control, 1404
clutch alignment tool, 1173
clutch application chart, 1397–1398, 1398*t*
clutch bell housing, 1176
clutch brake, 1152
clutch capacity, 1138
clutch chatter, 1172
clutch cover, 1137
clutch disc/friction disc, 1136
clutch jacks, 141, 141*f*, 1174
clutch linkage, 1164
clutch-brake actuation, 1166
coefficient of friction (CoF), 162, 882, 882*f*, 883*t*, 1137
coil spring, 799, 874*f*
coil spring-style clutch, 1140
cold curing, 691
cold operation inhibit, 1455
cold-cranking amps (CCA), 328
collar shift transmission, 1204, 1208
collision avoidance systems (CAS), 1014, 1038
color-coded hoses, 943*f*
combination leaf/air-spring, 813–814, 813*f*
combination (series-parallel) circuits, 235
combination valve, 1068
combination vehicles, 20, 1101
converter dollies, 1102–1103
tractors, 1101–1102
trailers, 1102
trailer-train, 1103
combination wrenches, 117*f*, 118, 118*f*

combined Watts and Ohm's laws, 239
combo stud, 813
comeback, 46
commercial battery electric vehicles (CBEV), 1564
architecture, 1570–1571
electronic control units, 1570–1571
motor control modules, 1571
design, 1568–1570
evolution, 1567–1570
flexibility and efficiency, 1568
regenerative braking, 1568
Commercial Electronic Control (CEC), 1380, 1381*f*. *See also* Allison Transmission Electronic Control (ATEC)
shift logic
first range, 1388, 1389*f*
fourth range, 1388, 1390
neutral, 1386, 1386*t*, 1388*f*
reverse, 1391, 1391*f*
second range, 1388, 1389*f*
third range, 1388, 1390*f*
solenoids, 1384–1386, 1385*f*, 1386*f*
trimmer operation
torque converter lock-up control, 1392, 1392*f*
transmission operation during electrical failure, 1392, 1393*f*
wiring harnesses, 1384
commercial motor vehicles (CMVs), 1803
identifying number, 1804*f*
commercial vehicle industry, careers in, 30–33
ASE certification, 32
educational requirements, 32
hands-on training for students, 31*f*
job classifications, 31
master technicians
S- and H-Series certification, 32–33
specialty technicians, 32
parts department in, 30*f*
service technicians, 31
technician duties, 30
working conditions, 33
Commercial Vehicle Safety Alliance (CVSA), 782, 1811–1812
decal, 1811*f*
defective brakes criteria, 1821, 1824–1826
OOSC, 1811
record keeping, 1811–1812
Commercial Vehicle Service Alliance, 1458
commercial vehicles
classifications, 5*f*
terms and conventions, 22–25
vocational applications of, 6–11
construction, 7
fire service, 7–8
heavy haul, 8–9, 8*f*
intercity coach, 9
line-haul, 9

logging, 9–10, 9*f*
mining operation trucks, 10
pick-up and delivery, 7
refuse collection, 10
rescue vehicles, 10
school buses, 10, 11*f*
urban transit coach, 10–11
comminuted fracture, 88
companion flange, 1476
compass, 505
compatibility, 162
composite leaf springs, 803, 803*f*
compound planetary gear set, 1346
power flows, 1347–1351, 1347*f*, 1348*t*, 1349*f*, 1350*f*, 1351*f*
Ravigneaux gear set, 1346–1347, 1347*f*
Simpson gear set, 1346, 1346*f*
Wilson, Lepelletier, and ZF gear sets, 1347
compound ratios, 1193
compound shift, 1220
compound split operation, 1654
compound/open fracture, 88
comprehensive component monitor (CCM), 581–582, 581*f*, 582*t*
compressed air, 908, 908*f*
compression, 772, 773*f*
compressor discharge line, 912–913
compressor operation, 912, 914*f*
compressor unloader valves, 915–917, 916*f*, 918*f*
condensation, 1666
condenser, 1663
conductance test, 364
conduction, 1666
conductive coupling, 551, 551*f*
conductors, 198
conformity coating, 626–627, 629*f*
connecting drum, 1357
constant mesh transmission, 1204, 1208–1209
constant velocity joints, 1487–1488, 1487*f*, 1488*f*
constant-current chargers, 368
constant-rate leaf-spring assemblies, 803–804, 803*f*
constant-ratio steering gear, 838, 839*f*
constant-voltage chargers, 367
construction and operation, battery, 323–328
contact patch, 677, 797
contact patterns, gear, 1538
control axle torque, 797
control valves, 1786–1787
body, 1364
controlled area networks (CANs), 513, 536, 605, 606*f*, 653–660, 1601, 1607*f*
CAN 2.0, 654–655, 654*f*
FD (flexible data rate), 654–655, 654*f*, 655*f*
J-1939 *vs.* J-1708/1587, 654
multiplexing data bus signals, 658, 658*f*
data bus arbitration, 659, 660*f*
ethernet principles of, 659

priority bits, 659
    time division, 658–659
overview, 653–654
    serial communication, 655–656, 655f, 656f
    terminating resisters, 657–658, 657f
    twisted wire pair data buses, 656–657, 656f
controlled traction differential, 1512
controller gain, 610, 610f
convection, 1666
conventional current theory, 204
conventional steering system, 833, 834f
converter dolly, 1102
convoluted air spring, 812
coolant label, 45
corrosion damage, 784, 784f
coulomb, 200
counterbalance valves, 1791
counterclockwise direction, 1191
counter-electromotive force (CEMF), 382, 416
countershaft, 1203
counts, 1382, 1383f
coupler, 21, 22f, 1101
coupling phase, 1321
coupling shaft, 1476–1477
crack
    in frame between bolt holes, 790
    pressure, 935
    repair, 788–790, 789f, 789t
    in web/flange, 791
crank axles, 1506
cranking amps (CA), 328
crash-and-rescue truck, 10f
creep, 182
critical speed, 1473
cross members, 773, 776–777, 776f, 777f
cross-phasing, 1483
cross-shaft, 1164
crowfoot wrenches, 118, 119f
crown gear, 1506
cruise control, 1610
C-train, 20, 21f, 1105
CU domains, 604–606, 605f, 606f
cube relays, 262
cubic feet per minute (CFM), 1717
current clamp, 371
current flow, direction of, 203–205, 203f
current inverters, 1637–1638
cycling clutch orifice tube (CCOT), 1675

D

"D" capacity, 1112
dampening discs, 1147
Darlington pair configuration, 602, 602f
D'Arsonval gauges, 497, 497f
dash gauges, 925f, 972
data bus, 643, 649
    arbitration, 659, 660f
data link adapters, 315, 315f
data link connector (DLC), 642, 642t

data mechanical (DM) clutch, 1173
daytime running lights (DRL), 485
DC motor, principles of, 379–381, 381f
DC-to-AC inverter, 1637
dead axle, 1504–1506
dead blow hammer, 129
dead short, 240
dedendum, 1190
deep-cycle batteries, 323
defrost cycle, 1733
defroster, 1664
degree of freedom, 623
delta windings, 421–422, 422f
demountable rim, 717–718, 717f
depletion mode, 288
depletion zone, 276
derivative feedback control, 611
desiccant, 921, 922f
detent balls, 1207
Detroit Diesel's DT-12, 1279, 1279f, 1301–1302, 1301f, 1302f
Deutsch connectors, 457
Deutsches Institut für Normung (DIN) diagrams, 462
D-flash (data flash), 629
diagnostic data link (DDL), 48, 48f, 1384
diagonal side cutters, 126–127, 126f, 127f
dial-type torque wrenches, 123
diamond, 783f, 784
diamond logic, 513
diaphragm spring clutch, 1141
die, 95, 96f
diesel exhaust fluid (DEF), 254, 256
    sensors, 580, 580f
diesel particulate filter (DPF), 36
differential braking, 1032
differential case, 1507
differential cross, 1510
differential gear, 1506, 1509
differential lock, 1514
differential mode transmission, 656
differential pinion gear, 1510
differential spider, 1510
differential voltage, 542
digital logic gates, 547–549
digital multimeters, 204, 302, 302f
digital signal processors (DSPs), 293
digital signals, 540
digital volt-ohmmeter (DVOM), 1719
diodes, 276–277, 277f
    clamping test, 280
    forward and reverse bias, 277–278, 278f
    types of, 280f
        LEDs, 281–282, 281f
        OLEDs, 282, 282f
        photodiodes, 283, 283f
        suppression of voltage spikes with, 283, 283f
        Zener, 280–281, 281f
direct current (DC), 205, 205f, 279, 534
direct drive, 378, 379f

direct tire pressure monitoring system (direct TPMS), 696, 712
directional control valves and circuits
    construction of, 1788–1790
    spool-type directional, 1790–1791
    types, 1787–1788
directional slip angle, 1036
directional stability control (DSC) systems, 1014, 1036
disc brake pads, replacement of, 1007–1008, 1008f
disc brakes, 876f, 885f
disc wheel, 718–719, 718f
    inspection, 730, 730f
    separator plates, 725–726
dislocation, 89
distribution block, 1814
disturbances, 609
DIWA™ transmissions, 1356
    components, 1442
    control system, 1445, 1447
    operation, 1441
    power flows
        automatic neutral at standstill, 1443
        first gear, 1443, 1443f
        fourth gear, 1445, 1445f
        neutral, 1442–1443, 1442f
        reverse, 1445, 1446f
        second gear, 1443, 1444f
        third gear, 1443, 1444f
    retarder operation, 1445, 1446f
    torque converter oil flow, 1441–1442
domain controllers, 604
doping, 276
double check valve, 936, 940–941
double decker bus, 11f
double pole double throw (DPDT) switch, 252
double reduction drive axle, 1515
double-acting cylinders, 1784–1785, 1785f
double-clutch, 1207
down-speeding, 1527
drag links, 479f, 749, 750f, 833, 845–846
draw bars, 21, 1107
    capacity, 1112
drivability items, 1808
drive axles, 1504
    leaf-spring suspensions, 805–807
    overhaul, removal, and inspection, 1537–1549
        axle manufacturer's model number, 1538f
        bearing adjusting tool, 1548f
        carrier, reassembly, 1548
        checking crown gear, 1548
        components inspection, 1542–1543
        crown and pinion gear set, 1543, 1543f
        differential carrier, 1539f, 1540f
        differential case, 1541f
        drive pinion, 1541–1542
        fluid level, 1537f

drive axles (*Continued*)
  gear set installation, 1547*f*
  nomenclature, 1538*f*
  overhaul-reassembly, 1543
  pinion bearing, 1544
  pinion bearing preload, 1546, 1546*f*
  pinion depth, 1544
  pinion gears, 1544*f*, 1546–1547
  shim pack thickness, 1542*f*, 1545
  shims, 1545*f*
  side bearing preload and gear set
    backlash, 1548, 1548*f*
  spigot bearing, 1544*f*
  trial assembly, 1547*f*
  yoke puller tool, 1542*f*
  power divider, overhauling
    checking input shaft end play, 1554
    differential carrier, 1555
    disassembling power divider,
      1552–1553
    reassembling, 1554
    torque chart, 1554*t*
  servicing and maintaining, 1534–1559
    actual gear contact patterns, 1550*f*
    change intervals for lubricant, 1536*t*
    changing lubricant and filters, 1537*f*
    component failures, 1555–1559
      abuse, 1558
      causes, 1555–1556
      diagnosing process, 1555
      extreme shock load, 1556*f*
      fatigue, 1557
      gear teeth fatigue, 1557*f*
      lubrication, 1558–1559
      overload, 1558*f*
      shock load failures, 1556–1157
      spinning wheel, 1558*f*
      spinout, 1558*f*
      standard transmission, 1559*f*
      star-type fracture, 1557*f*
      torsional fatigue, 1557*f*
    introduction, 1535
    leaks and determining cause, 1536*f*
    lube change intervals and procedures,
      1535–1537
    lubrication, 1535
    overhauling inter-axle differential
      (power divider), 1552
    SAE grades by ambient temperature
      range, 1535*t*
  setting gear set contact patterns,
    1549–1552
    conventional hypoid gearing, 1550*f*
    durapoid spiral bevel, 1550*f*
    gear tooth nomenclature, 1549, 1549*f*
    generoid gearing contact patterns,
      1550–1551
    thrust screw, 1551, 1552*f*
    troubleshooting, 1551*t*
    wheel/inter-axle differential, 1552*f*
drive pins, 810, 1149

drive pulley, 1720
driveline angularity, 1483
drivelines, 1474. *See also* driveshaft
    systems
Driver Post-Operation Vehicle Inspection
    Report, 1808, 1809*f*
Driver Vehicle Inspection Reports (DVIR),
    39, 39*f*
driveshaft systems
  analyzing failures
    brinelling, 1489, 1491*f*
    hanger bearing, 1492, 1492*f*
    spalling/galling, 1489, 1491*f*
    twisted tubing, 1491–1492, 1492*f*
    U-joint fractures and breakage, 1491,
      1491*f*
  angle cancellation, 1480
    cross-phasing, 1482–1483
    phasing, 1482, 1482*f*
    rule number one, 1480
    rule number three, 1481–1482, 1482*f*,
      1482*t*
    rule number two, 1481, 1481*f*
  companion flange, 1476
  components of, 1474–1475
    coupling shaft, 1476–1477, 1477*f*
    fastening systems, 1477–1478, 1477*f*,
      1478*f*
    slip joint, 1476, 1476*f*
    tubes, 1475, 1475*f*
    universal joints, 1477, 1477*f*
    yokes, 1475–1476, 1475*f*, 1476*f*
  driveline angles, 1483
    compound, 1486–1487, 1486*f*, 1487*f*
    constant velocity joints, 1487–1488,
      1487*f*, 1488*f*
    examples, 1484–1486, 1486*f*
    measuring and calculating, 1483–1484,
      1484*f*, 1485*f*
  end yoke, 1475, 1475*f*
  flange yoke, 1476, 1476*f*
  fundamentals of, 1472–1473
    angle of drive, 1473
    strength, 1472–1473
    variable length, 1473
  inspection and maintenance of,
    1492–1493, 1493*f*
    center (hanger) bearing, 1497–1499
    inspecting and installing, 1497
    lubrication, 1493–1495, 1494*f*, 1494*t*,
      1495*f*
    removing process, 1495–1497, 1496*f*
    replacing, 1495
  operation of
    critical speed, 1478–1479, 1479*f*
    non-uniform velocity, 1479–1480,
      1479*f*, 1480*f*
    shaft mass, 1478–1479
  series, 1473, 1474*t*
  tube yoke, 1475, 1475*f*
  vibrations, 1488

    diagnosis, 1488–1489, 1488*f*
    measuring runout, 1489
drop arm, 749
drop center tubular axle, 1506
drop-bed auto hauler, 7*f*
dropbox, 1238
drop-center wheel rim, 680
drop-front frame, 777*f*
drum brakes OOSC, 1824
Dryer Integrated Module (DRM), 923, 924*f*
DT-12, Detroit Diesel's, 1279
  operation, 1301*f*, 1302–1303, 1302*f*, 1303*f*
dual power inverter module (DPIM),
    1651–1653, 1651*f*
  function and construction, 1651–1652
  operation, 1652–1653
dual spring brake, 889*f*
dual-brake chambers, 889–891, 889*f*, 891*f*
dual-brake circuits, 875
dual-circuit air brake system, 911*f*
dual-circuit system, 910
dual-clutch transmission, 1276
dual-mass flywheel, 1148
dual-mode hybrid drive train, 1655
dump truck, 8*f*
dump valve, 814
duplex gauge, 967, 967*f*, 968*f*
durapoid gearing, 1507
dust lip, 176
dust masks, 66, 67*f*
duty cycle, 546, 546*f*, 1403
dynamic imbalance, 708
dynamometer test cell, engine, 32*f*

E

EAC air supply system. *See* Bendix
    Electronic Air Control (EAC) air
    supply system
ear protection, 67–68, 68*f*
Eaton Fuller transmission nomenclature,
    1287, 1287*t*
Eaton Fuller's automated transmission,
    1276–1278, 1276*f*, 1277*f*, 1278*f*
Eaton Procision dual-clutch automated
    transmission
  Eaton Procision operation, 1288–1290,
    1289*f*, 1290*f*
  Procision transmission power flows
    fifth gear, 1295, 1295*f*
    first gear, 1293, 1293*f*
    fourth gear, 1294, 1294*f*
    second gear, 1293, 1293*f*
    seventh gear, 1295–1296, 1296*f*
    sixth gear, 1295, 1295*f*
    third gear, 1294, 1294*f*
  shift control, 1290–1291, 1291*f*
ECU programming, 1020
ECU tampering, 631–632
edge codes, 882–883, 883*f*, 883*t*
e-fuses, 246

elastomer, 174
electric brakes systems (EBSs), 1013
electric current, 200
    heating effect of, 207–208, 207f
electric motor (EM), mechanical
        transmission, 1582–1583
electric powered vehicles, 13
electric shift assembly, 1282
electrical accessories
    connecting and programming, 513–515,
        513f
    introduction, 513
    mirrors, 526–529, 526f
    power door locks, 524–526, 524f, 525f
    power windows, 521–524, 521f
        Bowden cable-type, 522, 522f
        motors and switches, 522, 522f, 523f
        scissor-type regulator, 521–522, 522f
        sensors, 522–523, 524f
    windshield wiper and cleaning systems,
        515–521
electrical capacity, 328
electrical conductivity, 198–199, 198f, 199t
electrical current
    calculating electric power, 200–201
    movement of, 199–205, 199f, 200f, 201f
    resistance, 201, 202f
electrical equipment safety, 62–63
    electrical panels, 62, 62f
    overloaded circuits, 62
    tools and portable equipment, 63
    trouble lights and extension cords, 62–63,
        63f
electrical measurement, multimeter
    ammeters, 309–311, 310f
    diode scale, 311–312
    ohmmeters, 304–308, 306f
    temperature, 311
    voltmeters, 307f, 308–309
electrical resistance, 201
electrical signals, classification, 538–542
electrical system wiring
    color coding, 451
    connectors
        body types, 455–459, 456f, 458f
        terminal designs, 454–455, 455f
    diagrams, 460–461
        DIN, 462–469, 466f
        isometric, 462
        map (pictorial), 461, 462f, 463f
        schematic, 462
        Valley Forge, 469–471, 470f
    failure and repair, 459–460
    number coding, 453
    requirements, 450
    sizing and voltage drops, 451
    wire insulation, 451
electrical units of measurement, 304t
electrical vs. electronic devices, 275, 275f
electrical wiring and circuit diagrams,
        449–471

electrically erasable programmable read-only
        memory (EEPROM), 625
electricity/electrical system, 197
    behavior of, 194–197
    from chemistry, 225–226
    distributed control of, 193–194, 194f
    electrical vs. electronic circuits, 208
    hydraulic and particle models of, 195–197,
        195f, 196f
    from magnetism, 216–225, 217f, 218f
    movement of, 197–199, 197f, 198f
    polarity, 203–205, 204f, 205f
    principles of, 191–208
    sources of, 213–216
        from friction, 213–214, 213f, 214f, 215f
        from heat, 215, 215f
        from light, 215, 215f
        from pressure, 216, 217f
    template, 515, 515f
    trends and market forces, 192–194, 193f
electrochemistry, 225–226
electrohydraulic control, 1384, 1396. See also
        World Transmission Electronic
        Control (WTEC)
electrohydraulic valve body. See
        electrohydraulic control
electrolysis, 332
electrolyte, 320, 326–327
electromagnet, 218
electromagnetic induction, 221, 221f, 222f
electromagnetic interference (EMI), 550–552
electromagnetism, 218–220, 219f, 220f
electromechanical relays, 262–264, 262f,
        263f, 264f
electron theory of current movement, 204
Electronic Air Control (EAC), 923
electronic control, basic. See Allison
        Transmission Electronic Control
        (ATEC); Commercial Electronic
        Control (CEC)
electronic control loops, principles of,
        606–607, 607f
    closed-loop feedback, problems, 609–610,
        609f, 610f
    open- and closed-loop error, 607–608,
        608f, 609f
    PI feedback control, 610–611, 611f
    PID control, 611–612, 611f, 612f
    proportional feedback control, 610
electronic control module (ECM), 241, 535,
        541, 543f
electronic control system, 597–604, 597f
    areas of, 604
        ECU domains, 604–606, 605f, 606f
        mechanical, 596, 596f
        MIMO, 612–613, 613f
            calibration files, 613–614
            look-up tables, 613–614, 613f, 614f,
                615f, 615t
        organization of, 597–598, 599f
        output functions, 601–604, 601f, 604f

    processing functions, 598–600, 600f,
        601f
    sensing functions, 598
    overview, 596–597
electronic control units (ECUs), 192, 258,
        632, 632f, 1275
    replacement of, 632–634
    reprogramming, 632–634, 632f
        bench vs. on-vehicle, 632–633, 632f
        service programming, types, 633–634
    transmission, 1380, 1381f
electronic cooling package (ECP), 1635
electronic pad wear indicators, 1001, 1002f
electronic service analyst (ESA), 513
electronic service tools, 646, 646f
    CAN DBC files, 670
    network communication node, 668, 668f
    operating principles of, 669
    RP-1210 API, 669–670, 670f
electronic shock absorbers, 802
electronic signal processing, 534
    elements of, 537–538
    information processing capabilities, 535
    power and efficiency, 535
electronic stability control (ESC), 1013
electronically commutated motors, 499
electronically controlled accessories,
        647–648, 647f
electronically controlled air-suspension
        systems, 815–816, 816f
    independent front suspension, 816–817,
        817f
    Kenworth air spring systems, 816, 817f
electronically controlled leveling system,
        815, 816f
electrostatic discharge (ESD), 214, 290
electrostatic force, 195–197, 197f
electrostatic law, 196–197, 196f
electrostatic theory, 196
embedded devices, 626
emergency brake circuit, 910
emergency braking system, 1014
emitter-collector circuit, 284
end terminations, 153–155
end yoke, 1475, 1475f
Energy Storage System (ESS), 1583–1588
    fuel cells, 1584
    Lithium Ion Batteries
        construction, 1586–1587
    ultracapacitors, 1585
energy storage system (ESS), 1632,
        1634–1637, 1650–1651, 1650f
    battery monitoring system, 1637
    construction of, 1650–1651
engine dynamometer, 31
engine hoists, 150–151, 151f
    and stands, 152
engine identification label, 45, 45f
Engine Synchro Shift (ESS), 1278
engine-driven hydraulic pump, 848
engine-running inspection, 1818

enhancement mode, 287
Environmental Protection Agency (EPA), 58, 1711
EP40 systems, 1644
EP50 systems, 1644
EPDM belt, 423
epicyclical gear, 1339
equal brake pressure, 935
equalizer, 807
equalizer bracket, 807
equalizing beam, suspensions, 808–809, 808f, 809f
    Chalmers rubber-spring, 810–811, 810f, 811f
    leaf-spring, 809, 809f
    rubber-spring, 809–810, 810f
    solid-mount, 809
error, 608
error signal, 608
ethylene glycol, 1457
EV drive transmission unit, 1645
evaporator, 1663
evaporator housing inspection, 1715
    cabin air filter, 1715–1716, 1716f
    water drain, 1715
excessive corrosion, 784, 784f
exciter ring, 1021
exclusion seal, 176
exhaust extraction system, 61f
exhaust gas recirculation (EGR), 36
exhaust gas sensors, 576–580, 576f
    NOx, 578–580, 579f
    oxygen, 577–578, 578f
exterior inspections, 1819
external bleeding, 87
extreme pressure (EP)
    additive, 1245
    system maintenance, 1655–1656
        Allison DOC service tool, 1656
        diagnostic code display, 1656
        oil filtration, 1656
        warning lights, 1655–1656

F

failsafe operation, 1414
fall protection system, 63f
false brinelling, 1489
fast adaptive, 1403
fasteners, 776–778, 776f, 777f
    frame reinforcement, 778, 779f
    reinforced frame rails, 778, 778f
fastening systems, 1477–1478, 1477f, 1478f
fatigue failures, 1557–1558
fault code state change, 589, 589f, 590f
fault healing, 623
fault-tolerant systems, 622–623, 623f
Federal Bridge Formula, 17, 1106
Federal Bridge Gross Weight Formula, 17, 1106
Federal Motor Carrier Safety Administration (FMCSA), 1803–1804

Federal Motor Carrier Safety Regulation (FMCSR), 1811
Federal Motor Vehicle Safety Standard (FMVSS), 515, 956, 969, 1665
    FMVSS, 121, 874, 909, 911f, 912–913, 930, 943
feedback circuits, 1789
field effect devices, 287
field effect semiconductors, 287–290, 287f
    biasing, 289–290
    enhancement and depletion mode, 287–289, 288f, 289f
    FETs and electrostatic discharge, 290
    principles, 287, 288f
field effect transistor (FET), 246, 276, 287, 648
fifth wheels, 21, 22f, 1100–1126
    combination vehicles, 1101–1106
        A-train, 1104f
        A-type trailer, 1103–1104
        B-train, 1105f
        B-type trailer, 1104
        C train, 1105f
        cab-over-engine tractors, 1102f
        conventional cab-forward tractors, 1102f
        converter Dollies, 1102
        C-type trailer, 1105
        full trailer, 1103f
        landing gear, 1103f
        pup trailer, 1104f
        shunt truck/yard tractor, 1102f
        single point hitch, rear coupler, 1103f
        tractors, 1101–1102
        trailers, 1102
        trailer-train, 1103
    construction, 1114–1116
        A-type lock jaw mechanism, 1115, 1116f
        B-type lock, 1115, 1116f
        cast steel, 1114f
        jaw release lever, 1115f
        layout, 1114f
        locking mechanisms and coupling jaws, 1115
        no-slack coupling, 1115–1116
        proper and improper loading, 1115f
        top plates, 1114
    coupling devices, 1107–1109
        2" receiver tube is in hitch plate, 1109f
        air-cushioned pintle hook, 1108f
        anticipated load, 1109f
        ball hitches, 1107–1109
        chain length, 1109f
        coupler, 1107f
        draw bar, 1108f
        European vehicles, 1107f
        pick-up and gooseneck trailers, 1109f
        pintle hooks, 1107, 1107f
        snubber, 1108
        tongue weight, 1109
    landing gear, 1126, 1126f
    maintenance and service, 1119–1125
        adjustments, 1124

        A-type lock adjustment, 1124
        B-type lock, 1124, 1124f, 1125f
        disengaged hook, 1123f
        engaged hook, 1123f
        king pin, 1120–1123, 1121f, 1122f, 1123f
        lock gauge, 1124f
        lubrication, 1120, 1121f
        no-slack locks, 1124
        SAE standards, 1122f
        slider mechanism, 1125f
        upper coupler checks, 1120
    mounting, 1116–1119, 1117f
        flitch plates, 1117f
        location, 1118–1119
        manual slide release, 1118f
        no-slack wedge-type lock mechanism, 1117f
        sliders, 1117–1118
        swing clearance, trailer and tractor, 1118f
        wedge-type, 1117f
    plate-type coupling devices, 1110–1112, 1110f
        anti-friction plate, 1110f
        clearance angles, 1111f
        frameless dump trailer, 1112f
        fully (double oscillating), 1111
        height adjustable, 1112f
        horizontal axis, 1110f
        pivot points, 1112f
        rigid-type fifth wheel, 1112f
        rigid-type/no-tilt, 1111
        semi-oscillating type, 1111, 1111f
        tankers, 1112f
        two-height, 1111–1112
    ratings and capacity, 1112–1114
        flat deck trailer, 1113f
        king pin, 1113f, 1114f
        lower couplers, 1113f
        upper couplers, 1113
    semi-trailer, 1101f
    specialized hitching, 1101f
    troubleshooting and locking complaints, 1119, 1119t, 1120t
    vehicle weight ratings and capacity, 1106–1107, 1106t
fillet radius, 1190
fire extinguisher
    fire blankets, 72
    locations of, 70
    operation of, 71–72
    types of, 70–71, 71f
    usage of, 72
fire suppression systems, 69–72
fire truck, 7–8, 8f
fire-resistant hydraulic fluids, 1772
fires, classification of, 70
firmware, 629
first aid, principles of, 86–90
    basics, 86–87
    bleeding, 87–88

broken bones, 88–89
burns, 89–90, 89*f*
eye injuries, 88
overextensions and dislocations, 89
steps, 87
fishplate, 778
fishtailing, 1031
flange case half, 1540
flange yoke, 1476, 1476*f*
flanges, 772
flash loader, 631
flash memory, 625
flashing, 632
flat nose pliers, 127, 128*f*
flatbed truck, 9*f*
flat-type flywheels, 1148
flex hose installation, 1782–1783, 1782*f*
flex plate, 1323
    inspection, 1466
flexible hydraulic hoses, 1779, 1779*f*
    and line diameter, 1780
    routing lines, 1780
flitch plates, 1116
float-center position, 1790
floating caliper system, 902*f*
flooded lead-acid batteries, 324–328
    amperage and voltage, 324
    cases, 327
    deep-cycle *vs.* SLI battery, 325–326, 325*f*
    separator plates, 324–325
    sizing and terminal configuration,
        327–328
floor jacks, 140, 142
flotation tire, 685
flow control valves, 850, 1792
flow volume, 859
fluid analysis, 1457, 1457*t*
fluid change frequency, 1455–1457, 1456*t*
fluid coupling, 1315
fluid flows
    fourth-generation
        fifth range, 1420, 1421*f*
        first range, 1418, 1419*f*
        fourth range, 1420, 1421*f*
        neutral, 1417–1418, 1418*f*
        reverse, 1420, 1422, 1423*f*
        second range, 1418, 1419*f*
        sixth range, 1420, 1422*f*
        third range, 1418, 1420*f*
    latch valve, WTEC
        fifth range failsafe, 1415
        first range failsafe, 1414–1415
        fourth range failsafe, 1415
        neutral range failsafe, 1414
        reverse range failsafe, 1416
        second range failsafe, 1415
        sixth range failsafe, 1415–1416
        third range failsafe, 1415
    solenoid, WTEC
        fifth range, 1410–1411, 1411*f*
        first range, 1407, 1407*f*

fourth range, 1410, 1410*f*
neutral, 1407
reverse, 1411–1412, 1413*f*, 1413*t*
second range, 1408, 1408*f*
sixth range, 1411, 1412*f*
third range, 1409, 1409*f*
fluids, transmission
    analysis, 1457, 1457*t*
    automatic, maintenance of
        inspection, 1459–1460
        oil and filter change, 1459–1461
        powertrain mounts, replacing, 1462
        shift point adjustment, 1462–1463
        system pressure testing, 1461
    cleanliness, 1455
    electronically controlled automatic, 1464
    fundamentals of, 1454
    handling, 1457
    interval, 1455–1457, 1456*t*
    level, 1454–1455, 1454*f*, 1455*f*
    operating temperature, 1455
    replacement procedure, 1464–1465
        cooler and lines, checking, 1466–1467
        flex plate, inspecting, 1466
        neutral safety switch, adjusting,
            1467–1468
        shift linkage, adjusting, 1467–1468
    troubleshooting procedures, 1458
        diagnosing problems, automatic, 1458
        out-of-service criteria, 1458–1459, 1458*f*
        symptom-based diagnoses, 1458, 1458*f*
    types of, 1457–1458, 1457*f*, 1458*f*
fluorescent bulb, 479
fluorescent lights, 62*f*
flux, 218
flux density, 218
flywheel, 1136
    friction surface, 1177
    housing, 1177
    housing face, 1177
    housing pilot, 1176
foot valves, 927, 927*f*
    in balanced position, 930*f*
    construction, 928, 928*f*
    operation, 928, 929*f*, 930*f*, 931*f*
    troubleshooting problems with, 929–930,
        931*f*
forging, 129
forward bias, 278–279
forward clutch, 1357
Forward Collision Warning (FCW), 1608
foundation brakes, 987*f*
    components, 875*f*
fourth-generation fluid flows
    fifth range, 1420, 1421*f*
    first range, 1418, 1419*f*
    fourth range, 1420, 1421*f*
    neutral, 1417–1418, 1418*f*
    reverse, 1420, 1422, 1423*f*
    second range, 1418, 1419*f*
    sixth range, 1420, 1422*f*

third range, 1418, 1420*f*
frame
    angle, 755–756, 756*f*
    centerline alignment, 760–761, 761*f*
    exterior inspections of, 783
    hangers, 822–823
    manual alignment, 785–786
    material, 776
    rail design, 772, 773*f*
    rail web, 773
    strength
        RBM, 774
        section modulus, 774
        yield strength, 774–775
    stresses, 773–774
    template for splicing, 788*f*
frame-supported attachments, 779, 779*f*
    fishplate mounts, 780–781, 781*f*
    outrigger mounts, 780, 780*f*
    resilient mounting systems, 781–782, 781*f*
    stresses caused, 782, 782*f*
    U-bolt mounts, 779–780, 779*f*, 780*f*
free play, 1164
free stroke measurement method, 981
freedomline, 1278
freightliner smartplex network
    air management unit, 665, 665*f*
    elements, 662, 664–665, 664*f*, 665*f*
    overview, 662
    power distribution module, 665
    power net distribution box, 665
freon, 1663
frequency, 540
frequency-operated button (FOB), 525
frequency-sensing relay, 393
fresh-air-supply respirator, 67
friction, 1137
    dampening, 1148
    modifier, 1454
    plates, 1344
front axle inspection, 765, 765*f*
    tie-rods and tie-rod ends, 766
front axle limiter valves, 938–939, 939*f*
front spring, components, 820–821
front steering axle brakes, 1825
front support/charging pump module, 1396
front/rear split, 1057
fuel cell, 225–226, 226*f*
fuel tank repair, 70
full fielding, 432
full floating axle shaft, 1525
full throttle downshift, 1374
full trailer, 20, 1102
full-box rails, 772
fully oscillating fifth wheel, 1111

G

gallium arsenide phosphide (GaAsP), 282
gallium phosphide (GaP), 282
galvanic batteries, 320

galvanic corrosion, 784
galvanic isolator, 1588
galvanic reaction, 225, 225f
garbage trucks, 10, 10f
gas pocket, 1557. *See also* stringers
gas shock absorbers, 802
gas welding goggles, 65, 66f
gaskets, 181, 181f
    clamping force, 182, 182f
    installation guidelines, 183, 183f
    scrapers, 125, 125f
    surface finish, 182–183, 182f, 183f
gassing, 332
gateway module, 651
gear(s), 1188–1198
    autonomous drive steering, 838, 838f
    countershaft transmission, 1189f
    fundamentals, 1189–1192
        anatomy, 1190f
        backlash clearance, 1191f
        design, 1189
        direction of rotation, 1191
        external, 1191f
        external and internal tooth, 1191f
        face contact during mesh, 1190
        interaction, 1191
        involute tooth, 1190, 1190f
        levers, 1192f
        nomenclature, 1189–1190
    irregular speed, 1189f
    jamming, 1276
    manual recirculating-ball steering,
        839–840, 840f
    overview, 1189
    power recirculating-ball steering,
        840–841, 841f
    pump, 1363
    rack-and-pinion steering, 844–845, 844f
    ratio calculations, 1192–1196
        1:1 and 2:1 ratio, 1193
        compound, 1193–1194, 1195f
        idler, 1194–1196, 1195f
        simple, 1192–1193
    rattle at idle, 1252, 1252f
    reduction, 1193
    rotary valve, 841–843, 842f, 843f
    set contact pattern, 1549
    slip out, 1254
    steering ratio, 838–839, 839f
    torsion rod, 844, 844f
    types, 1196–1198
        bevel, 1197f
        helical, 1196–1197, 1196f, 1197f
        herringbone, 1197, 1197f
        rack-and-pinion, 1198, 1198f
        spiral bevel, 1197f
        spur, 1196, 1196f
        worm, 1198, 1198f
gel-cell batteries, 346
general freight truck, 9f
generator mode, 1582

generoid, 1509
geometric centerline alignment, 760
gerotor pump, 1363
gimbals, 1472
gladhands, 943, 944f
glazing, 955
    of brake lining, 886
Global Harmonized System (GHS), 73–75,
    74f
global navigation satellite system (GNSS),
    1614
global warming potential (GWP), 1687
governor, 913
    compressor unloader valves, 916f
    cut-in/cut-out pressure, 971
    exhaust, 914
    movement of piston, 915, 915f
    reservoir, 914
    unloader, 914
    valve, 1367–1368, 1367f
GPS navigation, 1614–1616
    global positions, identifying, 1615–1616
    signal information, 1616
gradability, 14
graphing meters, 312–313
gravel hauler, 10f
greenhouse gas (GHG), 192, 411
greenstick fracture, 88
gross combined weight rating (GCWR), 19,
    1107
gross trailer weight (GTW), 22, 23t
gross vehicle weight (GVW), 19, 19t, 1106
gross vehicle weight rating (GVWR), 19, 19f,
    1106
gross weight limits, 17, 1106
ground, 206
ground shaft, 1318
grounded circuit, 240
growling, transmission noise, 1252
guide studs, 1173

H

H bridge, 601
hacksaws, 128, 128f
hairline fracture, 88
hall-effect sensor, 573–574, 574f, 575f
    pinpoint testing of, 590–591, 590f
halogen bulb, 480
halogen infrared discharge (HID) bulb,
    480
hammers, 129–130, 129f, 130f
hand-operated lever, 1789
hanger bearing, 1477
    failures, 1492, 1492f
hardening, 1189
harmonic vibration, 1479
hat-style cross member, 777f
hazards, 55, 58
    classification of, 73
    hazardous environments, 58–59

hazardous materials, 63
    educational component of, 75
    legal responsibilities of, 73–75
    safety data sheet, 76–86
    identifying workplace, 59–60
    symbols and labels, 75, 75f
headgear, 64–65
heat fade, 884, 884t, 885t
heater core, 1666
heating, ventilation, and air conditioning
    (HVAC), 1664, 1666
heat-treated alloy-steel frame, 776
heavy duty automated transmissions, 1248
heavy duty manual transmissions, 1248
heavy truck stopping rules, 900t
heavy vehicles, classification of
    by combination, 20
    by weight and length, 17–19
        Federal Bridge Gross Weight Formula,
        17–18
        vehicle weight ratings, 19–20
heavy-duty clutches, 1135–1159
    actuation systems, 1154–1157
        air-assisted types, 1156–1157
        automatic, 1157
        cable linkage, 1156f
        electrically operated inertia brake, 1154f
        hydraulic, 1155, 1156f
        low-capacity inertia brake, 1154f
        mechanical Linkage, 1154–1155, 1155f
    brakes, 1152–1154
        conventional type, 1153
        squeezed, 1153f
        three two-piece and one torque
            limiting, 1153f
        torque design, 1153–1154, 1153f, 1154f
    components, 1144–1145
        cushion segments (marcel springs), 1145f
        friction discs, 1144
        organic facings, 1144–1145
        organic friction discs, 1144f
    fundamentals, 1136–1139
        basic functions, 1137–1138
        capacity, 1138
        coefficient of friction, 1137f
        dual-assembly with Eaton transmission,
            1137f
        early cone-type, 1136f
        flywheel function, 1137f
        modern types, 1136–1137
        overview, 1136
        role of friction, 1137
        torsional vibrations, 1138f
        two friction discs, 1138f
        types and design, 1139–1144
    organic facings, 1145–1152
        catapult clutch release fork, 1151f
        ceramic, 1145–1146, 1145f
        cutout, 1147f
        dampened/dampening disc, 1146f,
            1147f

dual-mass flywheel, 1148*f*
flat-type flywheel, 1148*f*
flywheels, 1148–1149
fork fits over non-rotating, 1150*f*
housings, 1152
hydraulic actuation systems, 1151*f*
intermediate plates, 1149
long travel damper, 1147*f*
mesothelioma, 1145*f*
normal travel damper, 1147*f*
pilot bearings, 1149–1152, 1149*f*
pot-type flywheel, 1149*f*
pre-dampening springs, 1148*f*
pull-type, 1150*f*
push-type, 1149*f*
release bearings, 1149–1152
rigid and dampened disc styles, 1146,
    1146*f*
SAE flywheel housing bore size chart,
    1152*t*
torsional vibrations, 1146*f*
traditional clutch fork, 1151*f*
typical clutch housing bolted to
    transmission, 1152*f*
vibration control, 1146–1148
preventative maintenance, 1164–1171
actuation components, 1164*f*
adjustment systems for angle-spring
    clutch, 1168*f*
angle-spring, 1167*f*, 1168
bleeding, hydraulic type, 1170, 1171*f*
clutch adjustment, 1164
flushing, hydraulic type, 1170*f*, 1171*f*
hydraulically actuated pull-type, 1171
linkage adjustment, 1166–1167
Lipe/Haldex adjustment, 1169
lutch-brake, 1167*f*
manual bleeding, 1170
pressure/vacuum bleeding, 1170
properly adjusted threaded release
    sleeve-type of clutch, 1169*f*
pull-type, 1166, 1168*f*, 1169*f*
push-type, 1164–1167, 1165*f*, 1166*f*
quick-adjustment device, 1168*f*
release-bearing travel, 1167–1168
release-fork free travel/play, 1170
servicing, 1163–1184
    bolt circle area, 1178*f*
    common wear areas, bell housing, 1176*f*
    component inspection, 1176–1178
    cross shaft inspection and repair, 1176
    dial indicator checks, 1177, 1177*f*
    drive pin clearance on 14" (35.6 cm)
        clutch, 1178*f*
    flywheel, 1178
    fork, cross shaft, and bushings, 1176*f*
    input shaft spline for wear, 1176*f*
    installation procedures, 1179–1183,
        1180*f*, 1181*f*
    14" (35.6 cm) dual-disc pull-type,
        1180

15.5" (39.4 cm) dual-disc pull-type,
    1181*f*
friction discs, 1179*f*
intermediate plate, 1180*f*, 1181*f*
new pilot bearing, 1179*f*
positive separator pins, 1182*f*
push-type clutch, 1179
rem, 80*f*
shipping blocks, removal, 1182
transmission, 1182
overview, 1164
repair and replacement procedures,
    1173–1175
    manual transmission, 1174–1175
replacing intermediate-plate drive pins,
    1178
SAE specification for dimension A,
    1176*f*
self-adjusting clutch repair and
    replacement, 1183–1184
solo clutch, 1183*f*, 1184*f*
troubleshooting problems, 1171–1173
    cast iron temperature 2100°F
        (1150°C), 1172*f*
    ceramic friction material becomes
        burned, 1172*f*
    common complaints, causes and
        corrections, 1173*f*
    operator error, 1172*f*
two-pedal centrifugal clutch actuation,
    1157
DM autoclutch, 1157*f*
ECA, mechatronic device, 1158*f*
electric, 1157–1158
electronic clutch actuator, 1157*f*
types and design
angle spring, 1143
clamp release by pedal, 1142*f*
clutch cover, 1141*f*
coil spring-style push-type, 1140–1141
diaphragm spring clutch, 1141–1143
dual-disc pull-type, 1140*f*
Eaton easy pedal advantage angle spring
    clutch, 1143*f*
Eaton self-adjusting clutch, 1144*f*
finger-like segments of diaphragm,
    1141*f*
normal flexing, 1142*f*
pull-type clutch, 1139*f*
ramped cam rings, 1144*f*
Rockwell pull-type diaphragm spring
    clutch, 1143*f*
self-adjusting clutches, 1143–1144
spring force, 1141*f*
standard push-type vehicle clutch,
    1139*f*
Volvo I-shift clutch, 1139*f*, 1142*f*
wet, 1158–1159
Eaton FO-8406-ASW models, 1158*f*
heavy-duty drive axles, 1503–1531
differential gear sets, 1509–1515

air-actuated piston, 1514*f*
biased torque (proportional)
    differentials, 1514–1515
controlled traction differentials,
    1512–1513
differential case, 1510*f*
locking differentials, 1513
locking with lock, 1514*f*
outside and inside wheel, 1510*f*
series of friction plates, 1512*f*
spider gear, 1512*f*
thrust washers, 1511*f*
TruTrac, 1515
two case halves, 1510*f*
vehicle negotiates turn, 1511*f*
wheel on slippery surface, 1512*f*
double reduction and multi-speed,
    1515–1521
air shift control, 1520–1521, 1521*f*
axle shift control, 1518*f*
electric shift control, 1518–1520
helical double reduction, 1515–1516
helical two-speed drive axles, 1516*f*
high speed, 1518*f*
high-low switch, 1519*f*
high-speed plate, 1519*f*
low range, 1519*f*
planetary gear, 1517*f*
planetary two-speed and double
    reduction, 1517
ring gear, 1518*f*
sun gear, 1518*f*
top-mount design, 1516*f*
two-speed drive, 1516–1517
worm wheel, 1520*f*
fundamentals, 1504–1509
GHG reduction strategies, 1527–1530
Dana, dual-range disconnect, 1529*f*
decreasing RPM, 1529*f*
engine RPM, 1528*f*
Paccar tandem axle, 1527*f*
I-beam type, 1504*f*
inter-axle differentials (power dividers),
    1521–1527
axle shafts, 1525, 1526*f*
components, 1522, 1522*f*
crown wheel, 1526*f*
drive axle lubrication, 1525–1527
lubrication pump, 1526*f*
Mack cam, 1524*f*
Mack trucks, 1524, 1524*f*
rear side gear, 1523*f*
sliding clutch, 1525*f*
spinout, 1524–1525
spline, 1522*f*
tandem, 1522*f*, 1525*f*
torque, 1523*f*
wedge drive system, 1524*f*
overview, 1504
steering axles, 1504–1505
amboid, 1508, 1508*f*

heavy-duty drive axles (*Continued*)
banjo, 1509*f*
dead axles, 1505, 1505*f*, 1506*f*
Detroit Diesel's, 1508*f*
drive, 1506, 1506*f*, 1509
durapoid, 1507–1508
gearing and housings, 1506–1507
generoid, 1509, 1509*f*
hypoid, 1508
I-beam type, 1505*f*
integral, 1509*f*
plain bevel gears, 1507
second power steering box, 1505*f*
self-steering tag/pusher axle, 1504*f*
spiral bevel gears, 1507
stingers, 1505, 1506*f*
top-mount worm gear, 1507
topoid, 1508
trailer dead axles, 1505–1506
heavy-duty onboard diagnostics (HD-OBD),
646
heel, 1549
height-control valve, 814, 816*f*
helical double reduction drive axle,
1515–1516
helical double reduction two-speed drive
axle, 1516–1517
helical drop gear, 1522
helical gears, 1196–1197
herringbone gears, 1197
hertz (Hz), 206, 540
Hex Head/Allen sockets, 122, 123*f*
hexadecimal code, 541, 541*f*
high voltage interlock loop (HVIL),
1653–1654, 1654*f*
high-carbon steel, 774
high-efficiency particulate assistance
(HEPA), 953
high-impedance multimeters, 302
high-intensity discharge (HID) lamp, 480
high-/low-bias sensors, 588
highly saturated nitrile (HSN), 174
high-torque-rise engines, 12–13
high-voltage, hazards and safety, 1592–1595
high-voltage cables, 1593–1595
insulation resistance testing, 1593–1595
pilot control circuit, 1593–1595
isolating high-voltage system, 1595
protective equipment, 1595
Highway Pilot, 1614
hitching devices, 21–22
hoisting, 139
equipment certification, 145
safe use of equipment, 145
hold regulator valve, 1370–1371
Hooke joint, 1472
Hooke's law, 1141
of elasticity, 804
horsepower, 12
hose end fittings, 1781–1783
hot curing, 691

hub(s)
cast spoke, 737–738, 737*f*, 738*f*
classification, 731
fundamentals, 731, 731*f*
lubricants, 738–740, 738*f*, 740*f*
overview, 716, 716*f*
piloted disc wheel, 721–723, 722*f*, 723*f*
piloted wheel retention, 723–724, 724*f*
preset, 735–736, 735*f*, 736*f*
seals, 738–739, 738*f*
failures, 739–740, 740*f*
types of, 739, 739*f*
standard, 733–735, 733*f*
adjusting wheel bearings, 734, 734*f*
measuring wheel end play, 735
and stud piloted disc wheels, 721, 721*f*,
722*f*
clocking, 724–726, 724*f*, 725*f*
mounting, 722–723, 722*f*, 723*f*
retention, 723–724, 724*f*
wheel bearing preload, 731–732, 732*f*, 733*f*
and hydrodynamic wedge lubrication,
732–733, 733*f*
Huck® fasteners, 777–778, 777*f*
HVAC (heating, ventilation, and air
conditioning), 1701
hybrid battery-management systems,
350–352
hybrid drive electrical safety, 1626–1628
electric shock, effects of
collisions, 1628
high voltage disconnect, 1627–1628
insulated gloves, 1628
routine inspection, 1628
hybrid drives
electrical safety. *See* hybrid drive electrical
safety
maintenance and service, 1639
non-electric hydraulic launch assist,
1625–1626
parallel and series systems, 1624–1625
types of, 1623–1624
hybrid-electric vehicle (HEV), 1622
hydraulic accumulators, 1792
failure modes, 1794
gas-charged, 1792–1793
maintenance practices, 1796–1797
pump cavitation, 1794–1796
spring-loaded, 1793–1794, 1794*f*
hydraulic actuators
construction of, 1784–1785
linear, 1783
rotary, 1785–1786
hydraulic brake antilock braking system
(HABS), 1082
hydraulic braking systems, 874–875, 874*f*,
875*f*, 1046–1096
45-degree SAE flare in steel brake line, 1061*f*
ABS configurations, 1082
Bendix A2L, 1066–1068
brake drums, 1065

brake shoe configurations, 1062, 1063*f*
combination valve, 1068*f*
configurations, 1048–1053
5 truck chassis, 1049*f*
air-operated foot valve, 1051*f*
air-over types, 1049–1051, 1050*f*
brake fluid reservoir attachment, 1050*f*
CAN data input, 1053*f*
disc brakes, 1048*f*
electric trailer brakes, 1052
electromagnet brake drum, 1052*f*
full brake power systems, 1052
hydraulically assisted braking systems,
1049
layout, 1052*f*
surge brakes, 1051–1052, 1051*f*
vacuum boosters, 1049
contemporary 4-channel, 4-sensor HABS,
1083*f*
control components, 1082
conventional type, 1055–1058
brake fluid leakage, 1057
components, 1056*f*
diagonal split system, 1057*f*
example, 1056*f*
front to rear split brake circuits, 1057*f*
low fluid warning, 1058
master cylinder operation, 1055–1057
pressure differential switch, 1057, 1058*f*
disc brakes, 1069–1076
ABS relocator ring, 1073*f*
beam caliper designed by Meritor, 1071*f*
bonded ceramic pad, 1075*f*
brake pad features, 1073–1075, 1075*f*
caliper pistons, 1072
fixed calipers, 1070–1071, 1075*f*
fixed rotor assembly, 1071*f*
floating calipers, 1069–1070
hat, 1073*f*
heavy-duty vehicle, 1069*f*
measurement operations, 1075*f*
measuring rotor thickness with Vernier,
1074*f*
reaction-beam calipers, 1070, 1071*f*
rotors, 1072–1074
square-cut O-ring, 1072*f*
sticking/binding, 1070*f*
visual inspection criteria, 1073*f*
wheel-end components, 1069
drum brakes, 1061–1064
external star wheel, 1064*f*
features, 1047–1048
flaring procedures, 1060
flex line construction uses Teflon inner
seal layer, 1059*f*
fluid properties, 1059*t*
fluids, 1058–1061
four-channel assembly, 1085*f*
full power type, 1087–1092
ABS braking mode (brakes applied),
1091

air removal, 1087*f*
ATC mode (no brakes applied), 1091
electric motors, 1088*f*
gas accumulator, 1088*f*
HCU Memory Log, 1092
HPB components, 1089
HPB inspection, 1091
mechanically operated hydraulic relay
　　valves, 1089*f*
modulator valves, 1090*f*
Navistar full power braking control
　　system, 1087*f*
normal braking mode, 1089
park brake cylinder, 1091*f*
pilot signals to HCU, 1088*f*
pressure bleed with air over fluid, 1092*f*
relay valve, 1089*f*
spring applied air released park, 1091
HABS assemblies, 1084–1087, 1085*f*
isolation mode, 1086*f*
lines and hoses, 1059
location of low brake fluid level switch,
　　1058*f*
Lucas Girling, 1066–1068, 1068*f*
metering, 1068
modulator valves, 1082*f*, 1083*f*, 1084*f*
normal mode, 1085*f*
off position, 1067*f*
overview, 1047, 1047*f*
parking and emergency systems,
　　1092–1094
　　cable-operated caliper, 1094*f*
　　complaints and remedies, 1095*t*–1096*t*
　　inspection, 1094–1096
　　manually operated hand brake, 1093*f*
　　park brake, applied position, 1095*f*
　　park brake in off position, 1094*f*
　　propeller shaft, 1093*f*
　　spring brake and adjusting nut, 1094*f*
　　toolbox tracking activity, 1093*f*
power-assist type, 1076–1081
　　air powered booster inspection, 1081
　　air-hydraulic booster, 1080–1081
　　booster chamber, 1078*f*
　　checking booster system, 1077
　　direct-type booster, 1081*f*
　　electric motor, 1079*f*
　　fluid flow, 1080*f*
　　hydraulic, 1077–1078, 1077*f*
　　hydroboost system with ABS, 1078*f*
　　hydroboost unit, 1079*f*
　　indirect air booster assembly, 1081
　　inspection, 1080
　　leaks on hydraulic brake booster, 1080*f*
　　operating modes, 1078–1079
　　vacuum brake booster, 1076–1077,
　　　1076*f*
　　vacuum brakes servo integrity test, 1077
primary shoe lining grips drum, 1062*f*
proportioning valves, 1068, 1068*f*
reapply mode, 1086*f*

SAE and ISO standards use differently
　　shaped flares, 1060*f*
secondary shoe, 1062*f*
service brake, 1067*f*
servo brake arrangement, 1064*f*
single-leading/trailing-shoe configuration,
　　1062–1063
spring-applied pedestal action, 1066*f*
springs, 1065
star wheel-type adjuster, 1064, 1064*f*
Steel Brake Lines, 1060
two-leading brake shoes, 1063, 1063*f*
two-wheel cylinder, 1061*f*
WABCO HPB HCU, 1087*f*
wedge-type adjuster, 1065, 1065*f*
wheel cylinders, 1065–1068
　　with automatic star-wheel, 1065*f*
　　with piston, 1066*f*
wire braking systems, 1053–1055
　　brake-by-wire caliper uses high-speed
　　　actuators, 1055*f*
　　brake-by-wire system construction,
　　　1054
　　electrically operated hand brake, 1054*f*
　　electromechanical braking, 1054
　　fixed piston-type caliper, 1055*f*
hydraulic circuit, 1372
　　horsepower, 1760–1761
　　work and power, 1760
hydraulic clutch, 1344
hydraulic coolers, 1774
hydraulic cylinders, 1758*f*, 1783–1784
hydraulic filter, 1774, 1774*f*
hydraulic fluids, 1768–1769, 1796–1797
　　fluid viscosity, 1770–1771, 1771*f*
　　reservoirs, 1773–1774, 1773*f*
　　types, 1772–1773
hydraulic jack, 140
hydraulic launch assist (HLA), 1625
hydraulic lines and hoses, 1774–1775
　　fittings, 1780–1783
　　flexibility, 1779–1780
　　rigid lines, 1777–1778
　　safety and service, 1775–1777
hydraulic motors, 1786
hydraulic multiplication of driver input
　　force, 873*f*
hydraulic oil additives, categories, 1772–1773
hydraulic pumps, 1763–1764
　　dump, 1767–1768
　　gear, 1764–1765
　　reciprocating piston, 1765–1766
　　types of, 850–852, 850*f*, 852*f*
　　vane, 1766–1767, 1786*f*
hydraulic retarder, 1426
hydraulic shock absorbers, 800–802, 800*f*,
　　801*f*
hydraulic systems
　　area, pressure, and force multiplication,
　　　1760
　　components, 1760–1763

filters, 1774
force pressure and area, 1757–1758
fundamentals of, 1756–1757
mechanical advantage, 1758–1759
preventative maintenance, 1794–1795
working pressure, 1758
Hydraulically Actuated Electronically con-
　　trolled, Unit Injector (HEUI) fuel
　　system, 224*f*
hydraulically assisted power steering, 848,
　　848*f*
　　coolers, 850
　　electronically controlled variable
　　　displacement pump, 853, 853*f*
　　fluid and hoses, 848–850, 849*f*
　　pumps, 850
hydrodynamics, 1756
hydrogenated nitrile, 174
hydrometer, 326, 326*f*, 362*f*
hydrophilic, 1058
hydroscopic, 1058
hydrostatics, 1756
hypoid gearing, 1508
hysteresis, 802

I

I-beams, 772
idle validation switch (IVS), 567
idler gears, 1194–1196
impact wrenches, 132
impeller, 1316
incandescent bulb, 478
inclinometer/accelerometer, 1425
included angle, 758, 758*f*
independent front suspension, 816–817, 817*f*
indirect tire pressure monitoring system
　　(indirect TPMS), 697
inductive amp clamps, 311
inductive coupling, 551, 551*f*
inertia brake, 1154, 1285
inertia shift, 870, 872, 872*f*
inertial excitation, 1473
information plate, 45
information processing capabilities
　　programmable vehicle, 537
　　safety, 536
　　　self-diagnostic capabilities, 537
　　　telematics, 535, 536*f*
inlet regulating valve, 917
input member, 1340
input shaft, 1136, 1203
inspection pits, 144, 144*f*
insulated gate bipolar transistor (IGBT), 290,
　　1571, 1652
insulators, 198
integral carrier housing, 1509
integral feedback control, 611, 611*f*
integrated circuits (IC), 291–292, 292*f*
intelligent charger, 368
inter-axle differentials, 1521

intercity coach, 9
interference fit, 167
interleaf friction, 798
interlock system, 1206
intermediate plate, 1139
intermittent circuits, 241
internal bleeding, 88
internal cab inspections, 1816–1818
internal diameter (ID), 1775
internal leakage, testing for, 860
International Organization for
      Standardization (ISO), 262, 1771
    relays, 262–263, 262f, 263f
      micro, 262, 263t
      mini, 262, 263t
intersecting angle arrangement, 1481
interstate, 6
Intuitive Diagnostic System (IDS), 1632,
    1638
inversion valve, 941–942, 941f
inverter, 207
involute tooth, 1190
ion, 197
I-Shift, 1279
ISO 3731 connector, 1028
isometric diagrams, 462

J

J-560 trailer connector, 485, 1017
J-1587 SAE communication protocol, 1286
J-1939 SAE communication protocol, 1280
    vs. J-1708/1587, 654
jack bolt, 1173
jack shaft, 1477
jackknife/jackknifing, 935, 1015
Joint Industry Council (JIC), 1781
jounce, 798
jump out, 1254
junction field effect transistor (JFET), 289

K

keep-alive memory (KAM), 624f, 625
Kenworth air spring systems, 816, 817f
key-off electrical loads, 322
kinetic energy, 868
kinetic friction, 1137
king pin, 746, 847, 847f, 1112–1113
King pin inclination (KPI) angle, 757
Kirchhoff's law, 233
knocking, transmission noise, 1252, 1252f
knuckle, 848

L

labor guide, 37
ladder logic, 476, 546–549, 652
ladder-type frame/chassis, 12f, 772, 773f
lands, 1790
latch valve, 1414, 1414f
    fluid flows, WTEC
      fifth range failsafe, 1415

first range failsafe, 1414–1415
fourth range failsafe, 1415
neutral range failsafe, 1414
reverse range failsafe, 1416
second range failsafe, 1415
sixth range failsafe, 1415–1416
third range failsafe, 1415
latching solenoids, 1385
latent heat, 1666
latent heat of fusion, 1666
latent heat of vaporization, 1666
lateral stability, 797
lead-acid battery classification, 323
leading/trailing shoe drum brake
    arrangement, 1062–1063
leaf spring mounting systems
    drive axle leaf-spring suspensions
      single-drive axle, 806–807, 807f
      tandem-drive axle, 807–808, 807f
    front steering-axle, 805–806, 805f, 806f
leaf spring systems, 799, 818
    auxiliary springs, 804–805, 805f
    composite leaf springs, 803, 803f
    constant-rate leaf-spring assemblies,
      803–804, 803f
    multi-leaf spring packs, 802–803, 802f,
      803f
    parabolic leaf springs, 804, 804f
    taper leaf springs, 804
    variable-rate/progressive-rate leaf springs,
      804, 804f
leak testing, refrigerant, 1708–1711
    electronic leak detector, 1708–1709
    nitrogen flushing and purging, 1710, 1711f
    nitrogen testing, 1709–1710, 1711f
    refrigerant dye with UV, 1708–1709
left-hand camshafts, 878, 879f
lengthwise bearing, 1549
Lepelletier gear set, 1347
lever, 1191
lift, 750, 750f
lift axles, 750
lifting
    ancient Roman lifting device, 137f
    equipment, 137
    history of, 137
    manual, 137–139
    prevent back injuries, 137f
    in shop, 139–142
      chocking, 141, 141f
      jack stands, 140f, 141, 141f
      jacks, 139–141, 139f
      mechanical lifting devices, 139
light, 477, 478f
light-emitting diodes (LEDs), 281, 301–302,
    481
    vs. incandescent bulb power consumption,
      282t
    lights, 62f, 69f
lighting system, 476
lighting technologies

DRL, 485
fluorescent bulb, 479–480, 480f
halogen bulb, 480, 481f
headlamp, 483–485, 484f
HID, 480–482, 481f
incandescent bulbs, 478, 478f
LEDs, 482–483, 482f, 483f
limiter (ratio) valve, 938, 939
line wrenches, 118, 118f
linear actuators, 1783
line-haul, 1246
    trucks, 9
liquid-crystal display (LCD), 505–506
lithium-ion (Li-ion) batteries, 339–343, 339f,
    341t
    advantages, 339–340
    construction and operation, 340–341
    iron phosphate, 342–343
    safety, 343
live (drive) axle, 745, 745f, 1504
load/loading, 917
    leveler, 146, 146f
    range, 798–799, 798f
    test, 364
local interconnect network (LIN), 525, 649,
    650f
    centralized network, 649–651, 650f, 651f
locked-out control panel, 40f
locking differentials, 1513–1514
locking jaw pliers, 127, 127f
locking tang, 1168
Lock-Out Tag-Out (LOTO) system, 39
lock-up clutch, 1316
    disc, 1325
    piston, 1325
logging trucks, 9–10
logic gates, 547
long stroke chambers, 888–889, 889f
look-up tables, 613–615, 613f, 614f, 615f,
    615t
low profile (LP) tires, 685
low-inertia, 1226
low-/no-maintenance batteries, 332–333
low-torque-rise engines, 13
low-voltage burn-out, 383
low-voltage disconnects (LVD), 348
L-plate, 778
lubricants used in PMI, 1813–1814
lubrication failures, 1558–1559
lumen, 481

M

magnetic fields, creation of electron flow
    induction and twisted pair wires, 224–225,
      225f
    magnetic induction/electromagnetic
      induction, 221
    mutual induction, 224
    self-induction, 222–223
magnetic induction, 216

magnetic reed switch, 255–256
magnetic (mag) switch, 264–265
magnetism, 216
main housing module, 1396
main pressure regulator valve (MPRV), 1364,
    1366f
mainshaft, 1204, 1357, 1396
make/break relays, 263
manifold gauge set, 1716
manual front wheel limiter valve, 938f
manual lifting, 137–139
    OSHA guidelines for, 138–139
manual selector valve, 1364–1366
manual slack adjusters, 894–895
manual-manifold, 1814
manual-ranging multimeters, 303, 304f
mapless MPC, 619
mapped MPC, 619
Martensite spotting, 986, 987f
mass airflow (MAF) sensor, 574–576, 576f
master disconnect switch, 1637
match mounting, 682
maximum bending moment, 775, 775f
maximum forward overdrive, 1341
maximum forward reduction, 1340
measuring parasitic draw, 369–372
    identify and test LVD systems, 371
    recycling, 371–372
measuring tools, 131
mechanical advantage, 1189
mechanical control system, 596, 596f
mechanical fade, 885
mechanical gauges, 495–496
mechanical jack, 140
mechanical lifting devices, 139
mechanic's lien, 43
mechatronics, 275, 596
medium- and heavy-duty (MHD) electric
    vehicles, classification
    fuel cell electric vehicles, 1566–1567
    PHEV, 1565–1566
    REEV, 1565–1566
medium-carbon steels, 775
memory reflash, 625
Mercedes Benz's Automatic Gear Shift
    (AGS), 1279, 1279f
Meritor and ZF
    automated transmissions, 1278–1279,
        1278f
    nomenclature, 1300, 1301t
    three module transmissions
        Detroit Diesel's DT-12, 1301–1302,
            1301f, 1302f
        DT-12 operation, 1301f, 1302–1303,
            1302f, 1303f
        nomenclature, 1300, 1301t
Meritor compressor, 918f
Meritor's air disc brake system, 902f
metal oxide semiconductor field effect
    transistors (MOSFETs), 290–291,
    290f, 291f, 602

metering valve, 1068
metri-pack connector, 456–457
microcontrollers, 292–293
    construction and operation of, 623–624,
        624f
    elements, 626f
    functions, 625–627, 626f, 627f, 628f
    memory addresses, 629–630, 630f
    memory types, 624–625, 624f
        EEPROM, 625
        flash memory, 625
        NVM, 624, 624f
        RAM, 625, 625f
        ROM, 624–625, 624f
    vs. microprocessor architecture, 628, 628f
        calibration data, 629
        calibration memory, 630–632, 630f,
            631f
        ECU tampering, 631–632
        firmware, 629
        memory data buses and addresses, 629
        program, 630–632, 630f, 631f
            vs. data files, 631, 631f
    reprogramming, 629f
micrometers, 131, 131f
micron gauge, 1717
microprocessor, 292
    vs. microcontroller, 292f
minimum dual spacing, 720, 721f
minimum forward overdrive, 1341
minimum forward reduction, 1341
mining operation trucks, 10
miter boxes, 837
mobile floor cranes, 150–151
mobile gantry crane, 147
mobile service techs, 33f
Mode 1 operation, 1648, 1654
Mode 2 operation, 1648, 1654
model optimizer, 619
model predictive control (MPC), 615–616,
    616f
    actuator adaptation adjustments and,
        620–622, 621f
    learning, 619
    mapless, 619, 619f
    mapped, 619
    model optimization, 619, 620f
    model-based diagnostics, 622, 622f
        fault-tolerant systems, 622–623, 623f
    operation, 616–619, 616f, 617f, 618f, 619f
    role of state observers, 617–618, 617f, 618f
    virtual objects, 619–620, 620f
        adaptation adjustments, 620
Modified Individual Regulation (MIR), 1026
modulated lock-up, 1324, 1371
modulated main solenoid (Mod Main), 1416
modulator cable, 1460
modulator valve, 1017, 1366–1367
momentary contact switches, 254
momentary engine ignition interrupt relay
    (MEIIR), 1282

mono-leaf springs, 805
motor generator units (MGUs), 412
motor vehicle air conditioning (MVAC),
    1701
mountainous highway, 6
mounts, 1462
movable cam rings, 1183
mufflers, 1722
multi-leaf spring, 799, 802f
    packs, 802–803, 802f, 803f
multi-mesh gearing, 1218
multimeters, 302–304
    electrical measurements, 302–312
    manual and auto-ranging meters, 303–304
    shunts, 304
multi-piece rim inspection, 730, 730f
multiple network capabilities, 651–653, 653f
multiple-countershaft transmission,
    1217–1218
multiple-input multiple-output (MIMO)
    control systems, 612–613, 613f
    calibration files, 613–614
    look-up tables, 613–614, 613f, 614f, 615f,
        615t
multiplex switch, 259–260
multiplexing (MUX), 658
multi-pole multi-throw (MPMT), 252
multi-temp unit, 1737
mutual induction, 224, 224f

N

N material, 276
N-95 mask, 953, 954f
NAND gate, 548, 549f
National Fire Prevention Association
    (NFPA), 1458
National Highway Traffic Safety Administra-
    tion (NHTSA), 192, 1602, 1605
National Institute of Occupational Safety and
    Health (NIOSH), 953
National Pipe Tapered (NPT), 1789
National Pipe Thread Straight thread fitting
    for fuel (NPTF), 1780
Navistar's Diamond logic electrical system,
    666, 666f, 667f
Navistar's "On Command" system, 1812f
needle flow control valves, 1792
needle-nose pliers, 127
negative camber, 751
negative frame angle, 755, 756f
negative ion, 197
negative offset, 720
negative scrub radius, 758
Nernst cells, 576
network bridging, 1605
network data bus problems, 661–662, 662f
network domains and gateway modules, 651,
    652f
network messages, 659–660, 661f
network node, 649

network typology, 649, 649f
neutral fiber, 773
neutral safety switch, adjusting, 1467–1468
neutral with no clutches (NCC), 1414
nickel-metal hydride (NiMH) batteries, 338–339, 339f, 1650f
nomenclature, 1246
nominal crack pressure (NCP), 935
nominal diameter, 682
nominal shim pack, 1545
non-asbestos organic (NAO) lining, 882
non-drive (dead) axle, 745–746, 745f
    drag link, 749, 749f, 750f
    pitman arm, 749
    steering axles, 746–748, 746f, 747f, 748f
    steering stops, 748, 749f
non-latching solenoids, 1385
non-uniform velocity, 1472
non-volatile memory (NVM), 624, 624f
NOR gate, 548, 549f
normal service operating conditions, 1809
normally closed (NC), 252
normally closed solenoids, 1402
normally open (NO), 252
normally open solenoids, 1402
North American Standard Out-of-Service Criteria (OOSC), 1811
North American truck and coach market, 1356
no-slack coupler, 1115
NOT gate, 548
NOx sensor, 578–580, 579f
NPN transistors, 284
nuts, 94
    grades and classes of, 102
    lock, 105–107
    splitter, operation of, 111f

O

Occupational Safety and Health Administration (OSHA), 57, 138–139, 953, 1775
    rules for lifting equipment, 148
odors brakage, 956
off-going ratio test, 1405
off-highway, 6
ohms, 202
Ohm's law, 201–203, 203f, 235
    and power, 235–239, 236f, 237f, 237t
        advantages of, 237–238, 238f
        calculations, 238–239
oil consumption, 962
oil droplets, 922
oil, PMI, 1814
oil slinger, 1546
oil weep, 1250
oiler, 1717
on-board diagnostic (OBD)
    and network communication, 645–646, 645f, 646f
    system circuits, 239

on-coming ratio test, 1405
one-way check valves, 914, 920
one-way clutch, 1318
on-highway, 6
open center control valves and circuits, 1787
open center rim, 717–718, 717f, 718f
open-center position, 1790, 1791f
opened inlet valves, 916f
open-end wrenches, 117, 117f
open-loop ramp rate, 1404
operating environment, 5–6
operating modes, 1654–1655
operator's manual, 46
OR gate, 548
organic facings, 1144
organic light-emitting diodes (OLEDs), 282
Original Equipment Manufacturers (OEM), 24, 799, 1701
    recommendation clutch servicing, 1182
O-rings, 1722
oscillation, 797
oscilloscopes, 312–313
out-of-service criteria (OOSC), 1811
    air disc brakes, 1824
    drum brakes, 1824
    wheel end, 1827
out-of-service (OOS) criteria, 1458
output member, 1340
output shaft, 1204, 1523. See also mainshaft
outrigger brackets, 780
outside limit (OL), 271
overall diameter, 682
overcharging, 1708
overcrank protection (OCP) thermostat, 392
overdrive ratio, 1193
overhead gantry crane, 147, 148f
overhung mount pinion, 1541
overrunning alternator decoupler (OAD), 423
over-running clutch, 1318
overslung, 798
oxygen sensors, 577–578, 578f

P

P material, 276
pap (pictorial) diagrams, 461
parabolic leaf springs, 804, 804f
parallel alternators, 431
parallel circuit, 233
parallel drive, 1623, 1624f
parallel joint arrangement, 1481
parallel wiring, 452
parallelogram, 799, 799f
parasitic draw, 322
parasitic loss, 1363
park/emergency brake circuit, 939, 940f
parking brakes, 875
    function, 984–986
parts manuals, 48–49
Pascal's Law, 1757, 1757f, 1758

passive sensor, 557, 558f
pass-thru programmers, 633, 633f
peak torque, 12
performance testing, 1701
    post-repair, 1714
permanent magnet synchronous motors (PMSM), 1580
permissible exposure limit (PEL), 61
personal protective equipment (PPE), 55, 55f, 63–72, 953
    breathing protection, 66–67
        dust masks, 66, 67f
        fresh-air-supply respirator, 67
        respirator, 66–67, 67f
    eye protection, 65–66
        arc welding, 66
        full-face shields, 65
        safety glasses, 65, 65f, 66f
        safety goggles, 65, 65f
        welding and cutting, 65–66
    eyewash stations, 69, 69f
    hearing protection, 67–68, 68f
    jewelry, 68
    long hair/loose clothing, 68–69
    protective clothing, 63–65
        gloves, 63–64, 64f
        headgear, 64–65
        work boots/shoes, 64, 64f
petroleum-based hydraulic fluid, 1772, 1772f
P-flash (program flash), 629
phasing, 1482, 1482f
phenolic, 1072
photodiodes, 283
photolithography, 291
photometric certification, 476
photons, 476
phototransistor, 283
photovoltaic (PV) effect, 215
PID tuning, 612
Piezoelectric effect, 216
piezoresistive sensor, 569–570, 570f
pilot bearings, 1149, 1177
pilot pad, 721, 722f
pinion bearing cage, 1541
pinion depth, 1535
pinion gears, 1197, 1339, 1506
pinion pilot bearing, 1541
pinion variation number, 1544
pintle hooks, 21, 22f
pipe, 1777
pipe wrenches, 119, 119f
piston pumps, 1765
pitch, 1190
pitch circle, 1190
pitch diameter, 1190
pitman arm, 749, 845, 845f
plain bevel gear, 1507
plain case half, 1540
plan angle, 1483
planetary gear, 1339
    fundamentals
        role of the carrier, 1340

rules of planetary gears, 1339–1340
power flows. *See also* power train control device
  maximum forward overdrive, 1341, 1341*f*
  maximum forward reduction, 1340–1341
  minimum forward overdrive, 1341–1342, 1342*f*
  minimum forward reduction, 1341, 1341*f*
  organized, 1340*t*
  reverse overdrive, 1342–1343, 1342*f*, 1343*f*
  ratio calculations for, 1343–1344
  reduction drive, 378, 380*f*
planetary modules, 1396
planetary two-speed drive axle, 1517
platooning, 193, 193*f*, 1601, 1601*f*
PLC smart mode operation, 669
pliers, types of, 125–128
  diagonal side cutters, 126–127, 126*f*, 127*f*
  flat nose, 127, 128*f*
  locking jaw, 127, 127*f*
  long-nosed, 128*f*
  needle-nose, 127
  slip joint, 126, 126*f*
  snap ring, 126*f*
  specialty, 125–126, 126*f*
  wire strippers combined crimping tool, 127, 127*f*
plug-in hybrid electric vehicle (PHEV), 1623
plunger, 1789
PM service checklist, 1810
PM service intervals, 1808
Pneumatic Booster System (PBS) Injection Booster, 925
pneumatic brake balance, 934–935, 965–966, 968*f*
  anti-compounding relay valves, 935–937, 936*f*
  brake proportioning relay valves, 938, 938*f*
  crack pressure, 935
  front axle limiter valves, 938–939, 939*f*
  pneumatic brake imbalance, 935
  QR valves, 939, 939*f*
  relay valve crack pressures, 935
pneumatic brake imbalance, 935
pneumatic jack, 140
PNP transistors, 284
point-to-point wiring problems, 643
polarity, 203
  and chassis ground, 206–207, 207*f*
policy, 58
polyalkylene glycol (PAG), 1688, 1726
polyalphaolefin (PAO), 1688, 1772
polymeric positive temperature coefficient (PPTC) device, 246
poor lifting techniques, 56*f*
portable lifting hoists, 143, 143*f*
positive camber, 751
positive frame angle, 755

positive ion, 197
positive offset, 720
positive scrub radius, 758
positive temperature coefficient (PTC) devices, 257
positive temperature coefficient (PTC) thermistor, 246
potentiometers, 261, 566–569
pot-type flywheel, 1148
power distribution module (PDM), 665
power dividers, 1521–1523
power flow, 1206
power jackknifing, 1031
power line carrier (PLC) communication SAE J2497, 669
  smart mode operation, 669
power line carrier (PLC) technology, 669, 1019
power net distribution box (PNDB), 665
power spring, 912*f*
power steering pump, 848
power steering system analyzer, 858
power take-off (PTO), 194, 1238, 1761, 1761*f*
power train control device, 1339
  brake band and servo, 1345, 1345*f*
  hydraulic clutch, 1344–1345, 1345*f*
  roller-/sprag-type one-way clutches, 1345–1346, 1345*f*
power unit, 848
powertrain mounts, replacing, 1462
powertrains, 13–15, 14*f*
pre-dampening, 1148, 1252
predictive PM, 1804
preload, 1535
preset hubs, 735–736, 735*f*, 736*f*
  locking nut, maintenance, 736, 736*f*, 737*f*
pressure bleeding/bleeder, 1170
pressure control solenoids (PCS), 1416
pressure differential sensors, 571, 571*f*
pressure plate, 1136
pressure protection valve, 814
pressure sensors, 569–571
  piezoresistive, 569–570, 570*f*
  pinpoint testing of, 588–589, 589*t*
  strain gauge, 569–570, 569*f*, 570*f*
  variable capacitance, 570–571, 571*f*
pressure transients, 1717
pressure-compensating, 929
pressure-reducing valves, 1791
pressure-relief valves, 1791–1792
pressure-sensitive electrical switch, 930, 931*f*
pressure-sensitive switches, 256–257
prevailing torque, 105
preventative maintenance and inspection (PMI), 1803–1804
  lubricants used in, 1813–1814
  preparation for, 1815–1816
  process, 1816–1821
    batteries and mountings, 1820–1821
    body and component mountings inspection, 1820
    cab door inspection, 1819

engine-running inspection, 1818
exterior inspections, 1819
internal cab inspections, 1816–1818
walk-around inspection, 1816–1818
preventative maintenance (PM)
  costs and resale price, 1803*f*
  implementing, 1804, 1808
  industry approaches to, 1804
  inspection sheet, 1805*f*–1806*f*
  legislative requirement for, 1803
  maintenance program, 1810*f*
  preparation for, 1815–1816
    shop and inspection standards, 1815
    shop housekeeping practices, 1815
    specialty tools, 1816, 1816*t*
    vehicle care practices, 1815
  service checklist, 1810
  service intervals, 1808–1810
  USDOT, 1808
primary batteries, 320
primary circuit, 910, 911*f*
primary modulation, 1403
primary piston, 1055
primary reservoir, 919
primary winding, 224
prime movers, 1756, 1756*f*
priority bits, 659
priority valve, 1369, 1369*f*
proactive maintenance, 1806
proactive PM, 1804
procedure, 58
Procision, 1288
profile bearing, 1549
prognostic capability, 1456
prognostics, 1425, 1456
programmable logic controllers (PLCs), 546
programmable read-only memory (PROM) chip, 1380, 1382*f*
programmed (systematic) lock-up, 1324
proof load, 101
proper manual lifting techniques, 137–139
  OSHA standards for, 138
proportional differentials, 1514
proportional feedback control, 610
proportional solenoid, 1789
proportional-integral (PI) feedback control, 610–611, 611*f*
Proportional-Integral-Derivative (PID) controls, 611–612, 611*f*, 612*f*
proportioning valves, 938, 1068
propulsion control system (PCS) module, 1631, 1632
prove-out sequence, 494
proximity switches, 254
pry bars, 129, 129*f*
psia unit, 1668
psig unit, 1668
PT chart, 1717
pull-down circuit, 262
pull-down switch, 559, 559*f*
pullers, 130, 130*f*, 131*f*
pull-to-seat terminals, 455

pull-type clutch, 1139
pull-up resistors, diagnosis, 582, 583f
pull-up switch, 558–559, 559f
pulse width modulation, 543–546, 544f
pulsed chargers, 368
pulse-width modulation (PWM), 428, 1403
    sensor, 568–569, 568f, 569f
pump maximum-relief pressure, 859
pump symbols, 1768
pumping oil, 969–970
punches, 128–129, 129f
purge cycle, 922
purge valve, 922
pusher axle, 750, 1504
pusher axles, 750, 750f
push-pull control valves, 939–941, 940f
push-pull park/emergency, 940f
push-to-seat terminals, 455
push-type clutch, 1139

Q

quick-adjust device, 1168
quick-connect air fittings, 920, 920f
quick-release (QR) valves, 939, 939f

R

rack-and-pinion actuators, 1786
rack-and-pinion gears, 1198
rack-and-pinion steering, 844–845, 844f
radial lip seals, 175–176, 176f
    construction
        composite PTFE, 178–179, 179f
        dual seals, 180
        seal cases, 177–178, 178f, 179f
        unitized seals, 179–180, 180f
radial thrust, 1196
radial-belted tire, 687
radial-ply tires, 686–687
radiant heat transfer, 1666
radio frequency interference (RFI), 550, 552, 552f
radio signals, 549–550, 549f
radiofrequency identification (RFID), 525
rails, 776–777, 776f, 777f
rain and dirt sensors, 521, 521f
ramp-off rate, 1404
random-access memory (RAM), 625, 625f
range extenders, 1628
range gears, 1203
range shift cylinder, 1231
range verification test, 1405
ratchets, 120–123
    size of, 121f
ratio control valve, 939
ratio steps, 1203
ratio tests, 1405
ratiometric, 566, 566f
Ravigneaux gear set, 1346–1347, 1347f
reaction beam, 1070
reaction member, 1340

reaction plates, 1344
reactive maintenance strategy, 1804
    vs. proactive maintenance, 1807f
read-only memory (ROM), 624–625, 624f
rear axle alignment, 826–827
rear beam suspension components, 822
rear cover module, 1396
rear spring suspension components, 820, 821, 822
rebound, 798
recall information, 1815
receiver-dryer, 1684
recirculating-ball steering gear systems, 839, 840f
reclaiming/recovering, 1713
reclaim/recycle machine, 1716
rectification, 424
reductant quality (RDQ) sensor, 580
reduction gear drive, 378, 379f
reefer, 1732
reference datum line (RDL), 146
reference voltage (Vref), 560–562, 561f, 562f
refrigerant
    identifying type of, 1712
    reclaiming and recharging, 1711–1713, 1712f
        charging with, 1714
        identification, 1711, 1713f
        system evacuation, 1713–1714, 1714f
refrigerant identifiers, 1716
refrigerant label, 43
refuse collection vehicles, 10
regenerative braking, 1622
regrooving, 693
reinforced frame rails, 778, 778f
relay valves, 930–933, 933f, 934f, 936f
    air circuit with, 933f
    air line connections to, 934f
    application and release of, 934f
    crack pressures, 935
    operation-applying brakes, 934
    operation-releasing brakes, 934, 934f
    pressure compensating balance, 934
release bearing, 1140
release (caging) bolts, 891, 893, 893f
release fork (yoke), 1149
release-bearing travel, 1166–1167
reluctance, 217
reluctance torque, 1581
reluctor, 1261
remote power module (RPM), 666
remote sensing, 432
remote shift linkage, 1253
removable carrier type, 1509
repair order/job card, 37–38, 37f
rescue vehicles, 10
reserve capacity (RC), 329
reservoir air control valves, 920, 920f
    drain valves, 920–921, 921f
    pressure protection valves, 920, 920f

reservoir drain valve, 921, 921f
reservoir safety valve, 919, 919f
resettable fuse, 246
residual magnetism, 419
resilient mounts, 781
resist bending moment (RBM), 774
resistance, 232
resistive circuits, 241
resistive sensors, 561–569
    potentiometers, 566–569
    rheostat, 564, 565f
    thermistor, 562–564, 563f, 564f
    three-wire, 564–566, 565f, 566f
resistive touchscreens, 506, 507f
resistors, 201
    fixed, 260, 260f
    stepped, 260–261, 261f
    variable
        potentiometers, 261–262, 261f
        rheostats, 261, 261f
resolver, 1576, 1634
resonance, 1147
resonant frequency, 1147
respirator, 66–67, 67f
retarder, 1396
retreading, 690
return on investment (ROI), 1803
reversable sleeve pistons, 812
reverse bias, 278, 279
reverse overdrive, 1342
reverse reduction, 1342
rheostats, 261, 564, 565f
rigging/rigging gear, 139, 145f
right-hand camshafts, 878, 879f
rigid fifth wheel, 1111
rigid fluid, 1777
rim diameter, 719
rim flange, 719
ring gear, 1339, 1506. See also crown gear
road feel, 833
road grade, 6f
road train, 21f
Roadranger valve, 1228, 1257–1258, 1257f
roll stability control (RSC), 1034
roller power steering pump, 851f
rolling circumference, 683
rolling lobe pistons, 812
rolling resistance, 679
rollover stability control (RSC), 1013
room temperature vulcanizing (RTV) silicone, 178, 184
root, 1190, 1549. See also fillet radius
root diameter, 1190
rotary flow, 1319
rotary piston compressors, 1673, 1673f
rotary switches, 254
rotary valve, 841–843, 842f, 843f
    alignments on, 843f
    cross-section of, 842f
    drilled passageways, 850f

rotating clutch, 1344, 1396
rotating-plate mechanism, 1788
roto-chambers, 893–894, 894f
rotor, 418–420, 1055
rotor running clearance inspection, 1005–1007, 1006f, 1007f
RP-1210 API, 669–670, 670f
rubber center bushings, 823
rubber springs, 799
Rutherford model, 197
Rzeppa joint, 1487

S

SAE and ISO viscosity measurement, 1771
SAE J-560 standard, 1027
SAE J1128 standard, 451
safe working load (SWL), 145
safety
    accidents, 55–56
    electrical equipment, 62–63
        electrical panels, 62, 62f
        overloaded circuits, 62
        tools and portable equipment, 63
        trouble lights and extension cords, 62–63, 63f
    evacuation plans, 56, 57f
    general, 55
    work area, 56–57
safety data sheets (SDS), 73, 76–86, 79f, 81f, 83f, 85f
safety interlock, 513
safety locks, 143
safety relief valve, 919
sag, 783, 783f
S-cam, 876f
    brackets, 878, 879f, 880f
    brake foundation system, 877f
    foundation brake, 875
scanners, 314–315
    code readers, 314–315
    functions, 314
    vehicle communication interface adapters, 315
scheduled lock-up, 1371
school buses, 10, 11f
    students diagnosing electrical system of, 31f
screw, 94
screwdrivers, 124–125
    gasket scrapers, 125, 125f
    parts of, 124f
    Robertson screwdriver tips, 125f
    technique for using, 125f
scrub angle, 758
sealants, 181, 182f
    classification and application of, 184, 184f
sealed release bearing, 1164
seals
    composite, 178
    functions of, 174–176, 174f
    installing wheel, 180–181

mechanical wedge, 175, 176f
O-rings
    back-up, 175, 175f
    lathe cut, 175
    materials and property, 174t
    square cut, 175f
    service and maintenance, 184–185
secondary batteries, 320, 320f
secondary circuit, 910, 911f
secondary couple vibrations, 1488
secondary modulation, 1403
secondary piston, 1055
secondary reservoir, 919
secondary safety latch, 1115
secondary winding, 224
section break, 1557
section change, 788
section height, 682
section modulus, 774
section width, 682
self-adjusting clutches, 1143
self-dampening friction, 798
self-diagnostic, 1276
self-energization, 877–878, 878f
    left- and right-hand camshafts, 878, 878f
    S-cam brackets, 878, 879f
self-exciting alternators, 420
self-induction, 222–223, 222f, 223f
self-locking hardware, 105–107
    lock nuts, 105–107
    locking washers, 105
self-powered refrigeration units, 1735
self-steering axle, 1504
semi-automated driving systems, 1604
semiconductors, 195, 275–276
semi-floating axle shaft, 1525
semi-metallic linings, 882
semi-oscillating fifth wheel, 1111
semi-trailer, 20, 21f
sensible heat, 1666
sensor count, 560
sensor fault detection principles
    comprehensive component monitor (CCM), 581–582, 581f, 582t
    high- and low-bias, 588
    onboard diagnostics, 580–581, 581f
    pull-up resistors, diagnosis, 582, 583f
    smart-diagnosable switches, 582–583, 584f
    three-wire sensor circuit monitoring, 586–588, 587f, 587t, 588f
    two-wire pull-up circuit monitoring, 584–586, 585f, 586t
    voltage drop measurement, 582, 583f
sensors
    active vs. passive, 557
    ammonia, 578–579
    applications of, 557
    diesel exhaust fluid, 580, 580f
    faults and onboard diagnostics, 580–581, 581f

overview, 557
piezoresistive, 569–570, 570f
pinpoint testing of, 588–591
    hall-effect, 590–591, 590f
    mass airflow sensors, 591
    pressure, 588–589, 589t
    thermistors, 589–590, 590t
    variable reluctance, 590
PWM throttle position, 568–569, 568f, 569f
soot, 564, 564f
switches as, 558–561
    digital signals, 558
    pull-up and pull-down, 558–560
    reference voltage, 560
    zero volt return, 560–561
technology, 557
three-wire resistive, 564–566, 565f, 566f
throttle position. See accelerator position sensor (APS)
variable reluctance, 572–573, 572f, 573f
virtual, 557
voltage generating, 571–574
wide-range planar, 577–578, 578f
SensoTop, 1445
separator plate, 1372
sequencing valves, 1791
serial communication, 655–657, 655f, 656f
serial data, 542–543, 643
series circuit, 232
series drive, 1623, 1624f
series motors, 381–384
    current flow, 382–383
    low-voltage burn-out, 383–384
    operational characteristics, 382–383
series-parallel drive, 1623, 1625f
    advantages/disadvantages, 1644–1645
series-type hybrid drive systems, 1628–1638
    BAE systems, 1629–1631, 1630f
    components of, 1631–1632
    current inverters, 1637–1638
    energy storage system (ESS), 1634–1637
    propulsion control system module, 1632–1634
    series propulsion, 1631
    unique system inputs, 1638
service brake air leakage, 960–962, 961f
service brake priority, 946
Service Campaigns, 49
service chamber, 891f
service history, 46, 47f
service information resources, 45–49
    component manuals, 48
    online service resources, 47–49
    operator's manual, 46
    parts manuals, 48–49
    service history, 46, 47f
    service manual, 47
    TSB, 47
    vehicle recalls/service campaigns, 49
service information system (SIS), 47

service manual, 47
service reservoir, 919
serviceLink, 513
servo mechanism, 1789
setback, 759
set-point, 597, 598f
severe service operating conditions, 1808
severe-duty service, 1246
shaft manufacturers, 782
shear stress, 101
shedding, 359
shift by wire, 1275
shift cable, 1467
shift cover, 1236
shift finger, 1205
shift forks, 1206
shift gates, 1205
shift lever, 1173, 1205
shift linkage, adjusting, 1467–1468
shift logic, 1386
shift modulator valve, 1368
shift point, 1462
shift relay valve, 1368
shift signal valves, 1368–1369, 1369f
shift solenoid 1 (SS1), 1416
shift tower, 1173, 1205
shims, 880f
shipping blocks, 1173
shipping bolts, 1173
shock, 88
shock absorbers, 798, 800, 824
    inspecting and maintaining, 824
    valves, 801f
shock bracket, 805
shock load failures, 1556–1557
shop safety equipment, 60–61
short circuits, 240
shot-peened, 802
shunt truck, 1102
shunts, 304
shunt-type motors, 516
side bearing bore, 1540
side bearing caps, 1540, 1548
side gears, 1510
sidesway, 783f, 784
signal detection and actuation module (SAM), 664
signal line pressure, 929
signaling-type torque wrenches, 123–124, 124f
simple machine, 1191–1192
Simpson gear set, 1346, 1346f
    first gear (low) in, 1349, 1349f
    neutral/park in, 1348
    reverse in, 1351, 1351f
    second gear in, 1350
    third gear (high/direct) in, 1350–1351, 1350f
sine wave, 206
single pole single throw (SPST), 252

single-acting cylinder, 1784, 1785f
single-axle straight truck, 940f
single-countershaft transmissions, 1211–1212
single-cylinder compressor, 913f
single-service brake chamber, 890f
skew, 759
slack adjusters, 894, 895f, 936f
    automatic, 895–896, 898f, 899
        inspection and maintenance, 996–1000
            adjusting ASA, 997–998, 997f
            clearance sensing, 998, 999f
            functional testing of ASAs, 998–1000
            stroke-sensing slacks, 998
    manual, 895
slave air valve, 1231
slave cylinder, 1155
sleep mode, 627
sliding clutch, 1204. See also sliding collar
sliding collar, 1204
sliding-bridge jacks, 140
sliding-gear transmission, 1204
sliding-plate mechanism, 1788
slip angle, 1577
slip joint, 1476, 1476f
    pliers, 126, 126f
slip yoke, 1173
slow adaptive, 1403
smart charger, 344
smart electrification, 1644
smart switches, 258–260
smart-diagnosable switches, 582–583, 584f
smoke controls, 1328
snap ring pliers, 126f
snapshot, 1281
sniffer, 1717
snub braking, 935
Society of Automotive Engineers (SAE), 36, 1708, 1771
sockets, 120–123
    features of, 121f
    flat black, 122f
    Hex Head/Allen, 122, 123f
    stamped steel, 121f
    Torx, 122, 122f, 123f
soft brake complaints, 955
soft skills, 33
soft-dampened clutches, 1147
software-based record keeping, 1811
software-controlled fuses, 246
solar cells, 215
solenoids, 265–266, 266f, 1789
    operation, 266
solid I-beam, 746
soot sensors, 564, 564f
specific gravity (SpGr), 326
specific heat, 1666
speed gears, 1204
speedometers, 504–505

speltered socket end, 153–154
spider gear, 1510
spigot bearing, 1541
spinout, 1524–1525
spiral bevel gear/gearing, 1197–1198, 1507
spiral-wound cell batteries, 345, 346f
splicing frames, 787–788, 787f, 788f, 789f
split guide ring, 1317
splitter shift cylinder, 1233
splitter valve, 1233
spool valve, 841, 1364
spool-type, 1788
sprain, 89
spreader bar, 146, 146f
spring brake, 942
    actuator, 892
    chamber, 891f
    priority, 946
    relay valve, 941
    servicing, 985–986
spring pack, 799
spring rate, 798–799, 798f
springs, 799
sprung weight, 796–798, 797f
spur gears, 1196
squeeze, 1166. See also clutch-brake actuation
stabilizer bars, 812
stable/simple fracture, 88
stall speed, 1321
standard hub, 733–735, 733f
standard transmission, 1202–1240
    air control, 1231–1236
        air control systems, 1232f
        high range high split, 1236f
        high range low split, 1235f
        low range high split, 1235f
        low range low split, 1234f
        range shift control, 1231–1233
        Roadranger, 1233f
        slave air valve in high range, 1233f
        slave air valve in low range, 1232f
        splitter operation, 1233–1234, 1234f
    air shift system problems
        air filter/pressure regulator, 1256
        air leaks, 1256–1257, 1256f
        crossed air lines, 1256
        Roadranger valve, 1257–1258, 1257f
    auxiliary sections, 1220–1231
        15-speed deep-reduction transmission, 1224f
        18-speed transmission with a four-speed, 1229–1231
        first gear, 1226f
        first-gear, low-range power flow, with first gear, 1222f
        first-gear main box, and high range, 1223f
        high range high split, 1231f
        high range low split, 1231f
        low-inertia, 1226–1229, 1228f, 1229f

low-range high-split power flow, 1230f
low-range low-split power flow, 1230f
power flows, 1221f, 1227f
range preselect lockout system, 1223f
Roadranger valve, 1228f
sixth-gear power flow, 1227f
three-speed, 1220f, 1222–1226
two-piece deep-reduction, 1225f
two-speed, 1220–1221, 1221f
two-speed, power flow, 1221–1222
failure, analysis of
    abuse failures, 1270–1271
    regular wear/maintenance failures,
        1270
floating mainshaft system, 1217–1218
FR Model Transmission Shift Controls,
    1236–1238, 1237f
    air module, 1236f
    SynchroSaver, 1237–1238
fundamentals, 1203–1207
    four shafts, requirements, 1204f
    mainshaft, 1204
    reverse idler shaft, 1204
    shift controls, 1205–1206
    shift finger, 1205f
    shift patterns, 1205f, 1206f
    shift rail interlock, 1206–1207, 1206f
    sliding clutch, 1205f
    sliding collar, 1205f
    spring-loaded detent balls, 1207f
    transmission shafts, 1203
    trucks, 1203f
    vehicle efficiency, 1203f
inspection procedures
    air system inspection, 1259
    general precautions and procedures,
        1258
    power take-off inspection, 1259
    transmission oil cooler and filter,
        1258–1259
lubrication
    service interval, 1246–1248, 1246t,
        1247t, 1248f
    transmission operating angle,
        1245–1246, 1246f
main box power flows, 1218–1220
multiple countershaft transmissions,
    1217–1220
    power flows, 1218
overview, 1203
power take offs, 1238–1240, 1239f, 1240f
preventative maintenance, 1248–1249,
    1249f
properly timed drive gear set, 1218f
PTO driven by countershaft, 1240f
repair procedures
    input shaft replacement, 1259–1261
    range synchronizer, overhauling, 1263
    rear seals replacement, 1261–1263
    reassembling and timing auxiliary
        section, 1263–1264

reinstalling auxiliary section, 1264
removing and disassembling auxiliary
    section, 1263, 1263f
shift bar cover removal, 1238f
single-countershaft transmission operation
    and power flows, 1213–1217
    overdrive shifting, 1212
sliding-gear and constant-mesh
    transmissions, 1207–1211
    block- or insert-type synchronizer,
        1209–1210, 1210f
    constant-mesh synchronized
        transmissions, 1209
    disc-and-plate-type synchronizer, 1211,
        1211f
    pin-type synchronizer, 1210–1211,
        1210f
    plain-type synchronizer, 1209, 1209f
    sliding clutches, 1208f
transfer case, 1238–1240, 1239f
triple-countershaft transmission, 1217f
troubleshooting
    gear slip out, 1254–1255, 1254f
    hard shifting, 1253–1254, 1254f
    oil leaks, 1249–1251
    transmission noise diagnoses, 1251–1252
    vibration, 1252–1253, 1253f
two diametrically opposed countershafts
    split, 1217f
stand-by mode, 1735
start enable relay, 1282
startability, 13
starter control circuits
    inspecting and testing, 401
    solenoid control relay, 390–394
        ADLO lockout, 392–393
        OCP, 392
        series-parallel electrical systems,
            393–394
        voltage-sensing relay, 393
starter motor, repairing, 404–405
    engine and starter rotation, 405
    starter no-load test, 404–405
starters, components of
    armature, 385–386
    commutator and commutation, 386
    drive mechanism, 389–390
    housing and field coils, 385
    solenoid and shift mechanism, 386–389
Starting, Lighting, and Ignition (SLI)
    batteries, 321, 323
starting systems, 394–403
    and circuits, 377–379
        classifications, 378–379
        demands on, 377–379
    diagnosis chart, 396t–397t
    electrical and mechanical problems, 395
    starter motor testing, 396–403
        circuit current draw, 399–401
        current draw, 397–398
        draw test, analysis of, 398–399

voltage measurement, 396–397
state observers, 616, 616f
state of charge (SOC), 1703–1704
    testing, 327t, 361, 361t
static imbalance, 702, 708
static radius, 683
stationary clutch, 1344
stator, 420–422, 420f, 1317
    inner hub, 1320
    support shaft, 1318
steer axle control, 1026
steering axis inclination angle (SAI), 757
steering system, 833
    arms, 746, 847, 847f
    axles, 746–748, 746f, 747f, 748f, 1504
        king pin profiles, 747–748, 747f, 748f
    classifications, 833–835, 834f, 835f
    components of, 836
        columns and shafts, 836–838, 837f
        wheels, 836, 836f
    conventional, 834f
    fundamentals of, 833, 833f
    gears, 833
        autonomous drive steering, 838, 838f
        hydraulic assist to, 841
        integral, 843f
        manual recirculating-ball steering,
            839–840, 840f
        power recirculating-ball steering,
            840–841, 841f
        rack-and-pinion steering, 844–845, 844f
        rotary valve, 841–843, 842f, 843f
        steering ratio, 838–839, 839f
        torsion rod, 844, 844f
    geometry, 758
        Ackermann angle/principle, 758–759,
            759f
        axle setback, 759, 759f
        axle tracking, 759–760
        trailer axles, 759–760
    hydraulically assisted power steering, 848,
        848f
        coolers, 850
        electronically controlled variable
            displacement pump, 853, 853f
        fluid and hoses, 848–850, 849f
        pumps, 850
        types of hydraulic pumps, 850–852,
            850f, 851f, 852f
    knuckle, 746, 836, 848
    linkage, 845
        drag link, 845–846
        king pin, 847, 847f
        pitman arm, 845, 845f
        steering arms, 847, 847f
        tie-rod ends, 846, 846f
    maintenance and service of, 854
        bleeding air from steering system, 860
        centering steering gear, 856
        checking oil aeration, 860
        complaints, 855t

steering system (*Continued*)
  internal leakage test, 859–860
  over-center adjustment, 857, 857*f*
  PSSA, 857–859, 857*f*
  steer-axle steering-stop adjustment, 854, 856, 856*f*
  worm gear preload adjustment, 856
ratio, 838–839, 839*f*
removing and replacing
  supplemental restraint system, 860–862
  wheel, 861–862
rotary valve, 842*f*
semi-automated steering gears, 853, 853*f*
shafts, 836
steering-angle sensors, 833
steering-related problems, 855*t*
stops, 748, 748*f*, 749*f*, 848
step-down transformers, 224
stepper motor gauges, 498–499, 499*f*
  bipolar, 500, 502*f*
  unipolar, 500, 501*f*
step-up transformers, 224
stiction, 612, 612*f*
stopping distance requirements, 877*t*
straddle mount pinion, 1541
straight truck, 7*f*
  with tandem axle, 15*f*
strain, 89
strain gauge pressure sensors, 569–570, 569*f*, 570*f*
strand, 152
stress
  concentration, 773
  riser, 773
stringers, 1557
stroke-sensing ASAs, 895
stroke-sensing slacks, 998
stud, 95
stud piloted disc wheels, 721, 721*f*, 722*f*
  clocking, 724–726, 724*f*, 725*f*
  mounting, 722–723, 722*f*, 723*f*
  retention, 723–724, 724*f*
stud piloted wheel mounting, 722–723, 722*f*
stud-mounted rotors, 1005*f*
sub-modulation. *See* secondary modulation
sulfation, 331
sun gear, 1339
  shaft, 1357
super single tire. *See* wide-base tire
superheat, 1683
supplemental additive, 1458
supply reservoir, 919
SureShift, 1278
suspension systems, 16–17, 796*f*
  air-spring, 811–812, 812*f*
    combination leaf/air-spring, 813–814, 813*f*
    construction, 812–813, 812*f*, 813*f*
    axle stops/jounce blocks, 800, 800*f*
    components of, 799
    electronic shock absorbers, 802

electronically controlled air-suspension systems, 815–816, 816*f*
  independent front suspension, 816–817, 817*f*
  Kenworth air spring systems, 816, 817*f*
equalizing beam suspensions, 808–809, 808*f*, 809*f*
  air-spring, 814–815, 814*f*, 815*f*
  Chalmers rubber-spring, 810–811, 810*f*, 811*f*
  leaf-spring, 809, 809*f*
  rubber-spring, 809–810, 810*f*
  solid-mount, 809
functions of
  connect axles to frame, 796
  control axle torque, 797
  ensure contact with road, 797, 797*f*
  lateral stability, 797
  support sprung weight, 796
fundamentals of, 796
gas shock absorbers, 802
hydraulic shock absorbers, 800–802, 800*f*, 801*f*
in-service inspection of, 819–820
inspection and maintenance, 817
  air-spring systems, 823
  conducting, 818–819
  equalizer beam suspension systems, 820–822
  frame hangers, 822–823
  leaf-spring systems, 818
  out-of-service criteria for, 817–818, 818*f*
  rear beam suspension components, 822
  rear spring suspension components, 820
  removing and replacing front spring components, 820
  rubber center bushings, 823
  shock absorbers, 824
  unloading suspension for measuring play, 819–820
jounce, 798
leaf-spring systems
  auxiliary springs, 804–805, 805*f*
  composite leaf springs, 803, 803*f*
  constant-rate leaf-spring assemblies, 803–804, 803*f*
  drive axle leaf-spring, 805–807
  multi-leaf spring packs, 802–803, 802*f*, 803*f*
  parabolic leaf springs, 804, 804*f*
  taper leaf springs, 804
  variable-rate/progressive-rate leaf springs, 804, 804*f*
overslung and underslung, 798
parallelogram, 799, 799*f*
rebound, 798, 798*f*
servicing, 824–825
  adjusting and aligning axles, 826–827
  adjusting ride height, 825–826

shock absorbers, 800
spring rate and load range, 798–799, 798*f*
sprung weight and unsprung weight, 797–798, 797*f*
torque rods, 799–800, 800*f*
swaged, 778
swaged end, 154
swashplate, 1766
swing clearance, 1117
swing shackle, 806
switch reluctance motor (SRM), 1581–1582
switches, 252, 252*f*, 253*t*
  assorted, 254*t*
  automatic
    magnetic reed, 255–256, 255*f*, 256*f*
    pressure-sensitive, 256–257, 256*f*, 257*f*
    temperature-sensitive, 257, 257*f*, 258*f*
  current ratings, 255
  as digital signals, 558
  magnetic (mag), 264, 265*f*
  as sensors. *See* sensors, switches as
  smart
    multiplex, 259–260, 260*f*
    pull-up and pull-down, 258–259, 258*f*, 259*f*
  smart-diagnosable, 559–560
  types of, 252–254, 253*f*, 254*f*, 255*f*
synchronized transmission, 1204
synchronizer, 1204
synchronous speed, 1405
Synflex, 910
synthetic hydraulic fluids, 1772
synthetic-based lubricant, 1245
system components
  DPIM, 1651–1653, 1651*f*
  ESS, 1650–1651
  EV drive transmission unit, 1645
  TCM, 1645–1648
  traction motors, 1648–1649
  VCM, 1648
system pressure testing, 1461
systematic lock-up, 1324

T

tachographs, 505
tachometers, 505
tag, 750, 750*f*
tag axle, 750, 1504
tandem drive, 1504
tandem-axle tractor, 927*f*
tandem-center position, 1790, 1791*f*
tanker, 8*f*
tap, 95
taper leaf springs, 804
taper-current chargers, 368
tapered screw, 1792
TC-10-TS power flows
  eighth range, 1435, 1437*f*
  fifth range, 1435, 1436*f*
  first range, 1432, 1433*f*

fourth range, 1432, 1435f
hydraulics and electronic control, 1440
ninth range, 1438, 1438f
reverse, 1438, 1439f, 1440f
second range, 1432, 1433f
seventh range, 1337f, 1435
sixth range, 1435, 1436f
tenth range, 1438, 1439f
third range, 1432, 1434f
TC-Tronic, 1279
Technical Service Bulletin (TSB), 47
Teflon, 162, 179f
telematics technology, 667, 667f, 1607
telescoping cylinders, 1784, 1785f
tensile strength, 99, 775
tension, 772, 773f
terminating resisters, 657–658, 657f
test lights, 300–302, 300f
    self-powered, 300–301
    self-powered LED, 301–302, 302f
thermal efficiency, 1275
thermal expansion valve (TXV), 1708
thermistor, 562–564, 562f, 563f, 564f
    pinpoint testing of, 589–590, 590t
thermocouple, 215, 215f
thermoelectric device (TED), 216, 216f
thermoelectricity, 215
thermometer in reservoir, 858f
thermostatic expansion valve, 1675
    defined, 1675–1676, 1676f
    orifice tube pressure regulation,
        1679–1681
    types, 1676–1679
thread chasers, 108
threaded fasteners, 94–97
    mechanical strength, 99–102
    nuts, 102
    specifications, 97–99
        M-series fasteners, 99
        UNC, 97–98, 98f, 99f
        UNEF, 98–99
        UNF, 98, 98f, 99f
        UTS, 97, 99f, 99t, 100t
    thread repair, 107–111, 110f
        chasers, 108–109
        drilling and tapping, 107
        epoxy, 109
        extracting broken fasteners, 110–111
        threaded inserts, 109–110
        using taps, 108
        welding, 109
    tightening fasteners, 103–104
    types of, 94–95, 95f
        left-/right-handed threads, 97, 97f
        machining threads, 95–96
        preload, 96–97, 97f
the three Cs, 37
three module transmissions
    Eaton Endurant, 1296–1297, 1296f, 1297f
    Mercedes Benz/Daimler trucks automatic
        gear shift, 1306, 1306f, 1306t

Volvo Trucks' I-Shift/Mack M-Drive,
    1303–1305, 1303f, 1304f
    dual clutch I-Shift, 1304–1305, 1305f
    Volvo transmission nomenclature,
        1305, 1305f, 1305t
    ZF/Meritor, 1297–1300, 1298f, 1299f,
        1300f
    Detroit Diesel's DT-12, 1301–1302,
        1301f, 1302f
    DT-12 operation, 1301f, 1302–1303,
        1302f, 1303f
three-coil gauge, 498
three-position directional control valves,
    1790, 1791f
three-way valve, 1737
three-wire resistive sensors, 564–566, 565f,
    566f
three-wire sensor circuit monitoring,
    586–588, 587f, 587t, 588f
throttle position sensors. See accelerator
    position sensor (APS)
throttle valve, 1367
through shaft, 1523
thrust
    angle, 760–761
    line, 760
    screw, 1540, 1548
tie-rod, 746
    ends, 757, 846, 846f
time division multiplexing, 658–659
time to full apply (TFA), 1405
tipper truck, 8f
tire pressure monitoring system (TPMS),
    696–701, 698f
    sensor testing and learning, 700
    SmarTire®, 697–700, 699f, 701f
tire(s)
    arrangements, 680, 681f
    balancing, 706–709, 708f
    beads, 687–688, 688f
    casings, 686–687, 687f
        belt system, 686–687, 687f
        bias-ply tires, 687
    classifications of, 680
    construction, 686, 686f, 688–690, 690f
    flap, 680
    fuel economy, 688–690, 690f
    functions, 678–679, 678f, 679f
    fundamentals of, 677–679
    identification and sizing, 682–683, 683f,
        684f, 685t
    inflation factors, 693, 693f
        automatic system, 695–697, 695f
        pressure, 693–695, 693t, 694f, 694t, 695f
        safety, 697
    inflation pressure, 693
    inspecting for air loss, 710–711
    maintenance and service, 701
        adjusting pressure and gauges, 702–703,
            703f
        dismounting, 704–705

fitting, wheel rim, 707
issues, 702
repairs, 703–709
Schrader valve, replacing, 706–707
screw-in valve stem, replacing, 707
tire balance, 707–708, 708f
tools, 701–702
wear patterns inspection, 703, 704t
overview, 677
patching, 709–710
pressure gauge, 701
principles, 677–679, 678f
radial
    beads, 687–688, 688f
    bias-belted, 687
    inner liner, 688
    sidewalls, 688
regrooving, 693
retreading, 690–691, 690f, 691t
    depth, 692–693, 692f, 693f
    tread separation, 692, 692f, 692t
rolling circumference adaptation, 1021
run-out, measuring, 711
service calls, reason for, 677, 677t
service safety, 679–680, 679f, 680f
tread, 688, 689t
tread separation, 692, 692f, 692t
tubeless vs. tube-type tires, 680–682, 681f,
    682f
vehicle wheel end, 677, 677f
and wheels, inspecting, 1826–1828
TMC bearing RP, 618, 734
toe, 756, 1549
toe-in, 756
toe-out, 756
    on turns, 751, 759, 759f
toggle switches, 254
tongue weight (TW), 22, 1108
tool storage, 116–117
tooth face, 1190, 1549
top land, 1190, 1549
topoid, 1508
torque, 146, 1189
    balance, 965
    converter. See torque converter
    converter module, WT, 1395
    coupling phase, 1321–1323, 1322f
    limiting, 1031
    multiplication phase, 1320–1321, 1321f
    rise, 12
    rods, 799–800, 800f
    sticks, 104, 104f
    wrenches, 123–124
torque converter, 1315
    components
        converter shell/housing, 1316–1317
        impeller/pump, 1317, 1317f
        lock-up clutch assembly, 1318, 1318f
        stator/reaction member, 1317–1318,
            1318f
        turbine, 1317, 1317f

torque converter (*Continued*)
  functions of, 1315–1316, 1315*f*
  housing module, WT, 1395, 1395*f*
  hydraulic circuits, 1324–1326, 1325*f*
  lock-up clutch control, 1371
  operation
    flex plates, 1323, 1323*f*
    lock-up clutch operation, 1323–1324,
      1324*f*
    operational phases, 1320–1323, 1321*f*,
      1322*f*
    rotary flow and vortex flow, 1318–1320,
      1319*f*, 1320*f*
  servicing
    reassembling, torque converter, 1333,
      1333*f*
    turbine end play and torque converter
      leak checks, 1333–1334, 1333*f*
  troubleshooting, failure
    leak testing torque converter, 1330–1331
    lock-up clutch operation, 1329
    pressure testing automatic transmission,
      1330
    stall testing and result, 1327–1329
torque converter control (TCC), 1416
torsen, 1514
torsion bars, 799
torsion rod, 844, 844*f*
torsional excitation, 1473
torsional vibrations, 1138, 1488
torus, 1316
torx sockets, 122, 122*f*, 123*f*
total indicated runout (TIR), 1177
total mesh adjustment, 857
toxic dust, 67
  safely cleaning, 68
tracking, 750
traction batteries, 323
traction control, 1031
traction motors, 1622, 1644, 1648–1649
  AC induction motors, 1576–1578
    induction motor slip, 1577
    operating principles, 1572–1575
    rotor construction, 1575
    three-phase AC *vs.* single current,
      1576–1577
    three-phase motor, stator construction,
      1575–1577
  dual-traction motors, 1572
  permanent-magnet motors, 1578–1581
    commutated DC to stator, 1579
    external rotors, 1580
    PMSM, 1580
    three-phase AC to stator, 1579
  SRM, 1581–1582
tractor
  protection valves, 944–945, 945*f*
  with tandem drive axle, 15*f*
  and trailer braking systems, 874*f*
trailer brake control (TC) valve, 944
trailer refrigeration

alarm codes, 1747–1748, 1747*f*, 1748*f*
components of
  condenser, 1744–1745
  evaporator, 1745–1746
  refrigerant and compressor oils,
    1746–1747
  refrigerant compressors, 1741–1744
heating principles, 1734–1735
maintenance, 1748
trailer(s), 1102
  air circuits, 943, 943*f*, 944*f*
  cords and plugs, 485–489
  refrigeration. *See* trailer refrigeration
  spring brake valves, 945
    priority of, 945–947, 946*f*
  supply valve, 944
  swing-out, 935, 1015
  system valves
    TC valve, 944
    tractor protection valves, 944–945, 945*f*
    trailer air supply valve, 944
  trailer-supply control valves, 940*f*
trailing arms, 799, 813
trailing shoe, 1063
transfer case, 1238
transistor bias, 284–285, 285*f*
transistor gain, 602
transit bus, well-equipped, 31*f*
transmission control module (TCM), 1275,
    1416, 1645–1648
transmission control valves, Allison
  governor valve, 1367–1368, 1367*f*
  hold regulator valve, 1370–1371
  manual selector valve, 1364–1366
  modulator valve, 1366–1367
  MPRV, 1364, 1366*f*
  priority valve, 1369, 1369*f*
  shift signal valves, 1368–1369, 1369*f*
  torque converter lock-up clutch control,
    1371
  trimmer valve, 1370, 1370*f*, 1372*f*
transmission ECU, inputs, 1380, 1381*f*
  driver's input/shift control, 1381, 1382*f*
  fluid sensors, 1383–1384, 1383*f*, 1384*f*
  throttle position sensor, 1382, 1382*f*
  VSS, 1382, 1383*f*
transmission jacks, 140, 140*f*
transmission oil cooler, 1325
transmission system. *See* standard
    transmission
transmission vent, 1454
transport refrigeration
  fundamentals of, 1732–1734
  types of, 1735–1737
  units, cooling capacity, 1735*t*
transport temperature control, 1732
transverse vibrations, 1488
TranSynd fluid, 1455
Traxon, 1279
tread, 688, 689*t*
  depth, 692–693, 692*f*, 693*f*

treadle and brake application valve, 927*f*
triangulation, 1615
triboelectric series, 213, 214*t*
triboelectricity, 213
trickle chargers, 368
tridem, 1504
trimmer, 1391
  regulator valve, 1370, 1372*f*
  valve, 1370, 1370*f*
trinary switch, 1689
truck
  crash-and-rescue, 10*f*
  drive wheels, 14*t*
  dump, 8*f*
  fire, 7–8, 8*f*
  flatbed, 9*f*
  frames. *See* truck frames
  garbage, 10, 10*f*
  general freight, 9*f*
  line-haul, 9
  logging, 9–10, 9*f*
  mining operation, 10
  straight, 7*f*
  terms and abbreviations, 23*t*
  tipper, 8*f*
truck equipment manufacturer (TEM), 664
truck frames
  alignment, 785–786
    repair, 786–787, 787*f*
  construction of
    fasteners, 777–778, 778*f*, 779*f*
    frame material, 776
    rails, cross members, and fasteners,
      776–777, 776*f*, 777*f*
  damage, types of
    bow, 784
    corrosion damage, 784, 784*f*
    diamond, 783*f*, 784
    sag, 783, 783*f*
    sidesway, 783*f*, 784
    twist, 783*f*, 784
  frame-supported attachments, 779, 779*f*
    fishplate mounts, 780–781, 781*f*
    outrigger mounts, 780, 780*f*
    resilient mounting systems, 781–782,
      781*f*
    stresses caused, 782, 782*f*
    U-bolt mounts, 779–780, 779*f*, 780*f*
  fundamentals of, 772–773, 773*f*
    actual frame strength, 775, 775*f*
    frame stresses, 773–774
    tension and compression, 772, 773*f*
  inspection, service, and maintenance of
    out-of-service criteria, 782–783
  strength
    RBM, 774
    section modulus, 774
    yield strength, 774–775
  welding frames
    crack repair, 788–790, 789*f*, 789*t*
    splicing frames, 787–788, 787*f*, 788*f*, 789*f*

trunnion, 1472
trunnion-mounted, cylinders, 1783
TruTrac design, 1514
tub, 1650
tube yoke, 1475, 1475f
tubeless tire, 680
tube-type tire, 680
turbine, 1316
    pull down, 1404
turbocharger cut-off valve, 918–919, 918f
turbulence, 1780
turning radius, 758
turnpike, 6
twin-leading-shoe drum brake, 1063
twist, 783f, 784
    twisted tubing, 1491–1492, 1492f
    twisted wire pair data buses, 656–657, 656f
two-cylinder compressor, 913f
two-height fifth wheel, 1111–1112
two-position directional control valves,
        1790, 1790f
two-wire pull-up circuit monitoring,
        584–586, 585f, 586t
Type 1 circuit breakers, 245
Type 2 circuit breakers, 245
Type 3 circuit breakers, 245
Type K thermocouples, 311
typology, 649, 649f

U

U-bolts, 805
U-joint fractures and breakage, 1491, 1491f
U-joints, 837
ultra-capacitors, 346–347, 348f
UltraShift, 1280
ultraviolet (UV) light, 1708
unconscious bias, 34
undercuts, 1790
underdrive ratio, 1193
underslung, 798
undertread, 693
under-vehicle inspections, 1828–1832
    engine compartment, 1828, 1830–1832
    frame, mountings, electrical, and exhaust,
        1828–1829
    steering and air conditioning
        components, 1831–1832
    transmission and drive train, 1828–1830
unidirectional pump, 1764
unified diagnostic service (UDS), 520,
        660–661
Unified National Coarse (UNC)
    rod, 1173
    thread, 97–98, 98f, 99f
Unified National Extra-Fine (UNEF) series,
        98–99
Unified National Fine (UNF) thread, 98,
        98f, 99f
Unified Thread Standard (UTS), 97, 99f, 99t,
        100t

unipolar semiconductor, 287–290, 287f
unique system inputs, 1638
United States Department of Transportation
        (USDOT) number, 1803, 1808
universal joints, 837, 1472, 1477, 1477f
unloader (unloading) valves, 916–917, 1791
unloading, 916
unsprung weight, 797–798, 797f
untripped rollovers, 1034
upper couplers, 21, 1110
urban environment, 6
urban transit coach, 10–11

V

vacuum gauge, 1717
vacuum pump, 1717
vacuum-boosted hydraulic braking system,
        1049
Valley Forge (VF) diagram, 469–471
valve adjusting cam, 1462
valve body test stand, 1462
valve-regulated lead-acid (VRLA) battery,
        323, 333, 343–346
vane pump, 1363
variable capacitance pressure sensor,
        570–571, 571f
variable displacement pumps, 1763
    electronically controlled, 853, 853f
Variable Frequency Drive (VFD), 1571
variable pitch stator, 1321
variable reluctance (VR) sensors, 207f,
        572–573, 572f, 573f, 1021
    pinpoint testing of, 590
variable spring rate, 810
variable-bleed solenoids, 1416
variable-rate/progressive-rate leaf springs,
        804, 804f
variable-ratio steering gear, 838, 839f
vehicle alignment
    angles, 751
    camber, 751–752, 752f
        handling characteristics, 752–753, 752f
    caster, 753, 754f
        adjusting, 755
        frame angle, 755–756, 756f
        shimmy, 755, 755f
        and stability, 753–754, 754f
    fundamentals of, 750–751, 751f
    king pin-inclination angle, 757–758, 757f
        included angle, 758, 758f
        scrub radius, 758
    lubricating king pins, 766
    measuring toe-out, 763
    toe, 756, 756f
        and tire wear, 756–757, 757f, 757t
vehicle control module (VCM), 1648
vehicle emission control information (VECI)
        label, 45
vehicle hoists, 142–144
    CG, 146–147

engine hoists/cranes, 150–151
    equipment, 144–152
    inspection pits, 144, 144f
    OSHA rules for lifting equipment, 148
    safety on lifting equipment, 151–152
    stability on hoist, 142–143
    types of lifting equipment, 147–150
        chain blocks, 147
        mobile gantry crane, 147
        overhead gantry crane, 147–148, 148f
        sling and chain capacity, 149–150, 149f,
            150f
        slings and shackles, 149, 150f
vehicle identification number (VIN), 24–25,
        44, 45f, 647
    decoding, 24–25
    ISO standard 3779, 24f
    North American system, 24f
    numbers indications of, 25t
    production date code and locating, 24
vehicle information labels, 43–45
vehicle networks, 640f, 641f, 642t
    advantages, 643, 645
        electronically controlled accessories,
            647–648, 647f
        OBD, 645–646, 645f, 646f
        sensor, reducing, 648
        software control of electrical system,
            645
    CAN data bus, 640, 640f
    construction, 648
        centralized/distributed, 649–651, 651f
        domains and gateway, 651, 652f
        LIN, 649, 650f
        multiple capabilities, 651–653, 653f
        physical layers, 649, 650f
        typology, 649, 649f
    data bus problems, 661–663, 662f
    ECUs communication, 640, 640f
    freightliner smartplex, 661–665
    messages, 659–660, 661f
    overview, 640–642, 640f
    point-to-point wiring system, 641f, 642,
        642f
        failure, solution to, 643, 643f
    serial data, 643
    social network, 640
    unified diagnostic service, 660–661
vehicle recalls, 49
Vehicle Safety Certification (VSC) label, 45,
        45f
vehicle speed sensor (VSS), 1382, 1383f
vehicle weight and speed, 870, 871f
vehicle-powered refrigeration units, 1735
Vernier gauge, 131f
vertical load, 1112
vibrasorbers, 1744
vibration analyzers, 313–314
virtual fuse/fusing, 246, 291
virtual sensor, 557
viscosity, 1770, 1771f

viscosity index (VI), 1771
visual stroke indicator, 983*f*
vocational applications, 1246
  of commercial vehicles, 6–11
    construction, 7
    fire service, 7–8
    heavy haul, 8–9, 8*f*
    intercity coach, 9
    line-haul, 9
    logging, 9–10, 9*f*
    mining operation trucks, 10
    pick-up and delivery, 7
    refuse collection, 10
    rescue vehicles, 10
    school buses, 10, 11*f*
    urban transit coach, 10–11
  design factors for, 11–13
    chassis frames, 11–12, 12*f*, 15*f*
    engines, 12–13, 16*f*
Voith DIWA transmissions. *See* DIWA™
    transmissions
voltage, 199
  generating sensors, 571–574
    hall-effect, 573–574, 574*f*, 575*f*
    variable reluctance, 572–573, 572*f*, 573*f*
  measurement test, 396–397
volts, 200
Volvo transmission nomenclature, 1305,
    1305*f*, 1305*t*
Volvo Trucks' I-shift, 1279, 1279*f*
vortex flow, 1329

W

wafer, 291
walk-around inspection, 1816–1817
walking beam, 808
wall organizer, 37*f*
water fade, 884–885
water wicking, 459
waterfall arrangement, 1481
Watt's law, 237, 237*f*
wave inverters, 207, 1637
Weather-Pack connectors, 456–457
wedge brakes, 875, 876*f*, 903, 903*f*
welding
  frames
    amperage and voltage recommenda-
        tions for, 789*t*
    crack repair, 788–790, 789*f*, 789*t*
    splicing frames, 787–788, 787*f*, 788*f*,
        789*f*
  helmet, 66, 66*f*
wet tank, 919
wheel, 728, 728*f*
  alignment. *See* wheel alignment
  bearing preload, 731–732, 732*f*, 733*f*
  cylinders, 1055
  diameter, 719
  dimensions, 719
    center bore, 720

diameter, 719, 719*f*
offset, 720, 720*f*, 721*f*
terminology, 719–720, 719*f*
end, 717, 717*f*
  OOSC, 1827
  play, 735
fastener tightening sequence, 727–728,
    727*f*
hop, 797
hub quick inspection, 728–729, 729*f*
  disc, 730, 730*f*
  lateral runout, 729, 729*t*
  multi-piece rim, 730, 730*f*
  radial runout, 729–730, 729*f*
installation, 727–728
lockup, 1014
nut torque *vs.* clamping force, 726–727,
    726*f*, 727*f*
  fastener tightening sequence, 727–728,
    727*f*
offset, 719–720, 720*f*, 721*f*
  minimum dual spacing, 720, 721*f*
  terminology, 719–720, 719*f*
rims, 718
  fundamentals of, 717
  overview, 716, 716*f*
run-out, measuring, 711
slip, 1031
spin, 1031
studs, 723, 724*f*
types, 717–719
wheel alignment, 750
  in-service, 761–763, 762*t*
    axle parallelism, 764
    axle tracking, 764
    KPI, checking, 764
    measuring toe-in and toe-out, 763
    prealignment inspection, 763
  loaded *vs.* unloaded, 761
  types of, 760, 760*f*
    frame centerline alignment, 760–761,
        761*f*
    geometric centerline alignment, 760,
        761*f*
    thrust angle, 760, 761*f*
whining, transmission noise, 1252
wide-base tire, 685
wide-range planar sensor, 577–578, 578*f*
Wilson gear set, 1347
wire rope, 152
  advantages of, 152–153
  clips, 154*f*
  designs of, 153*f*
  end terminations, 153–155, 154*f*
  inspection, 155
wire strippers combined crimping tool, 127,
    127*f*
wireless network communication
  bluetooth technology, 668, 668*f*
  overview, 667–668
  telematics technology, 667*f*

work order, preparing, 38
workplace
  habits and employability skills, 33–42
    customer service, 41–42
    customer's vehicle protection, 42
    defective equipment reports, 39–40
    empathy, 34
    ethics, 41
    interpersonal communications, 36
    listening, 33–34, 34*f*
    professional appearance, 40*f*
    questioning, 35
    reading, 36
    shop forms, 38–39
    speaking, 34–35
    telephone communication, 35–36, 36*f*
    time management, 40–41
    verbal/non-verbal feedback, 34–35
    writing, 36–37
  legal requirements in, 57–58
    environmental protection, 58
    OSHA, 57–58
    policies and procedures, 58
  safety and emergency procedures in,
      58–63
    hazardous environments, 58–59
    safety measures, 59
    shop safety equipment, 60–61
    shop safety inspections, 62
    workplace signs, 60, 61*f*
    workshop organization, 60
workshop, well-organized/-lit, 33*f*
World Harmonized OBD (WH-OBD), 646
World Transmission Electronic Control
      (WTEC), 1394. *See also* World
      Transmission (WT)
  definition, 1401
  ECU, 1402
  hydraulic control, 1405–1406, 1406*f*,
      1406*t*
  latch valve fluid flows, 1414, 1414*f*
    fifth range failsafe, 1415
    first range failsafe, 1414–1415
    fourth range failsafe, 1415
    neutral range failsafe, 1414
    reverse range failsafe, 1416
    second range failsafe, 1415
    sixth range failsafe, 1415–1416
    third range failsafe, 1415
  solenoid control
    range verification and ratio tests, 1405,
        1405*f*
    shift control logic, 1403–1404, 1403*f*
    shift sequence, 1404–1405, 1404*f*
  solenoid fluid flows
    fifth range, 1410–1411, 1411*f*
    first range, 1407, 1407*f*
    fourth range, 1410, 1410*f*
    neutral fluid flow, 1407
    reverse, 1411–1412, 1413*f*, 1413*t*
    second range, 1408, 1408*f*

sixth range, 1411, 1412f
third range, 1409, 1409f
solenoids, 1402–1403, 1402f
WTEC II and WTEC III, 1401–1416
World Transmission (WT)
clutch application chart, 1397–1398, 1398t
fifth range, 1400, 1400f
first range, 1398
fourth range, 1399–1400, 1400f
modules, 1395–1396, 1395f
neutral power flow, 1397f, 1398
power flows, 1396–1401, 1396f, 1397f, 1398f, 1399f, 1400f
reverse, 1401, 1401f
second range, 1398–1399, 1399f
sixth range, 1400–1401, 1401f
third range, 1399, 1399f
WT-3000, 4000, and B Series, 1395, 1395f
worm gears, 839, 840, 1198

worm shaft, 841
worm wheel, 1506
worm-and-crown gears, 1506
wrenches, 117–120
adjustable, 119, 119f
box-end, 117–118, 117f
chain and filter, 119–120, 120f
combination, 117f, 118, 118f
crowfoot, 118, 119f
impact, 132
line, 118, 118f
open-end, 117, 117f
pipe, 119, 119f
torque, 123–124
WTEC II. *See* World Transmission Electronic Control (WTEC)
WTEC III. *See* World Transmission Electronic Control (WTEC)
Wye windings, 421, 421f

X
XOR gate, 549, 549f

Y
yaw control, 1036
yield strength, 101, 101f, 774–775

Z
Zahnradfabrik Friedrichshafen (ZF), 1297–1300
gear sets, 1347
Zener diodes, 280
Zener point voltage, 279
zero offset, 720
zero-volt return (ZVR), 560–562
ZF Friedrichshafen AG EcoMat and EcoLife transmissions, 1447–1449, 1447f